D1090984

WHO'S WHO 2009

AN ANNUAL
BIOGRAPHICAL DICTIONARY

ONE HUNDRED AND SIXTY-FIRST
YEAR OF ISSUE

A & C BLACK
LONDON

PUBLISHED BY A&C BLACK PUBLISHERS LIMITED, 36 SOHO SQUARE, LONDON W1D 3QY

www.acblack.com

COPYRIGHT © 2008 A&C BLACK PUBLISHERS LTD

"WHO'S WHO" IS A REGISTERED TRADE MARK IN THE UNITED KINGDOM

ISBN 978-1-408-10248-0
Online edition ISBN 978-0-199-54465-3
www.ukwhoswho.com

PRINTED IN THE UNITED KINGDOM BY
CPI WILLIAM CLOWES LTD, BECCLES NR34 7TL

This book is produced using paper that is made from wood grown in managed, sustainable forests.
It is natural, renewable and recyclable. The logging and manufacturing processes conform
to the environmental regulations of the country of origin.

CONTENTS

HISTORICAL NOTE

The first edition of *Who's Who* was published in 1849. It consisted of an almanac followed by thirty-nine lists of ranks and appointments and the names of those holding them. As might be expected, there were lists of peers, members of the House of Commons, judges, archbishops and bishops. Additionally, however, there were the names of the Governor and board of directors of the Bank of England, of British envoys abroad, of the directors of the East India Company and of the officers (including the actuaries) of the life and fire assurance companies in London.

The range of lists was expanded over the next half century to more than two hundred and fifty, to include, amongst others, the Police Commissioners, the officers of the principal railways, the members of the London School Board and the Crown Agents – together with the editors of significant newspapers and magazines whose names, the editor noted, were "given here, not for contributors, but that the public may know who lead public opinion".

In 1897 substantial changes were made to the nature and content of the book. The major change was the addition of a section of biographies in which details were given of the lives of some five and a half thousand leading figures of the day.

Now, as then, the book aims to list people who, through their careers, affect the political, economic, scientific and artistic life of the country. *Who's Who* places its emphasis on careers whilst giving opportunity for the inclusion of family and other individual details, such as the recreations which have become a distinctive feature of the book.

An invitation to appear in *Who's Who* has, on occasion, been thought of as conferring distinction; that is the last thing it can do. It recognises distinction and influence. The attitude of the present editorial board remains that of the editor of the 1897 edition, who stated in his preface that the book seeks to recognise people whose "prominence is inherited, or depending upon office, or the result of ability which singles them out from their fellows in occupations open to every educated man or woman".

PREFACE

Who's Who is the recognised source book of information on people of influence and interest in all fields.

This, the 2009 edition, contains more than 33,000 biographies, approximately one thousand of these making their first appearance in *Who's Who*. They are of all kinds of people from all parts of the world and from all walks of life: the arts, business and finance, the church, the civil service, education, entertainment and sport, government, the law, local government, the media, medicine, professional institutions, science and the trade unions.

Each entry is in a standard form, full name and present post being followed by date of birth and family details, education, career in date order, publications, recreations and address.

The entries are carefully updated both from information supplied by biographees on their annual proofs and from many independent sources of reference. As a result, tens of thousands of amendments are made, more than half the entries requiring change. The book includes an obituary and a comprehensive list of abbreviations used in the entries.

OBITUARY

Deaths notified from mid-September 2007 to mid-September 2008

Abbott, James Alan, 24 May 2008.
Abse, Leo, 19 Aug. 2008.
Ackers, Sir James George, 31 March 2008.
Ackrill, Prof. John Lloyd, FBA, 30 Nov. 2007.
Alexander, Richard Thain, 20 April 2008.
Allen of Abbeydale, Baron (Life Peer); Philip Allen, GCB, 27 Nov. 2007.
Allen, Prof. Percival, FRS, 3 April 2008.
Alun-Jones, Sir (John) Derek, 19 Jan. 2008.
Anderson, Prof. Dennis, OBE, 20 April 2008.
Anderson, Maj.-Gen. Sir John Evelyn, KBE, 9 Sept. 2007.
Andreski, Prof. Stanislav Leonard, 26 Sept. 2007.
Archer, Prof. John Stuart, CBE, 9 Dec. 2007.
Armstrong, Anne Legendre, (Mrs Tobin Armstrong), 30 July 2008.
Ash, Rear-Adm. William Noel, CB, LVO, 4 June 2008.
Ashton of Hyde, 3rd Baron; Thomas John Ashton, TD, 2 Aug. 2008.
Ashton, Roy, 30 April 2007.
Audley, Sir (George) Bernard, 4 Jan. 2008.
Avonside, Lady; Janet Sutherland Shearer, OBE, 15 Feb. 2008.
Aylesford, 11th Earl of; Charles Ian Finch-Knightley, 19 Feb. 2008.

Backhouse, Sir Jonathan Roger, 4th Bt, 15 Nov. 2007.
Bailey, Sir Stanley Ernest, CBE, QPM, 10 Aug. 2008.
Baker, Anthony Castelli, LVO, MBE, 8 Feb. 2008.
Baker, Arthur John, CBE, 3 March 2007.
Baker, Douglas Robert Pelham, 21 Jan. 2008.
Balcon, Dr Raphael, 15 Jan. 2008.
Baldwin, John, OBE, 28 Nov. 2007.
Balfour-Paul, (Hugh) Glencairn, CMG, 2 July 2008.
Bamfield, Clifford, CB, 2 Nov. 2007.
Banbury, (Frederick Harold) Frith, MBE, 14 May 2008.
Bangor, Bishop of; Rt Rev. (Phillip) Anthony Crockett, 30 June 2008.
Barnes, Rev. Cyril Arthur, 11 Jan. 2008.
Barr, His Honour Reginald Alfred, 13 Sept. 2007.
Barr, William Greig, 23 April 2008.
Barraclough, Air Chief Marshal Sir John, KCB, CBE, DFC, AFC, 10 May 2008.
Barron, Prof. John Penrose, 16 Aug. 2008.
Bartlett, Prof. Neil, FRS, 5 Aug. 2008.
Bartosik, Rear-Adm. Josef C., CB, DSC, 14 Jan. 2008.
Basing, 5th Baron; Neil Lutley Sclater-Booth, 24 Nov. 2007.
Bate, Maj.-Gen. William, CB, OBE, 13 Jan. 2008.
Baxandall, Prof. Michael David Kighley, FBA, 12 Aug. 2008.
Baynes, Pauline Diana, (Mrs F. O. Gasch), 1 Aug. 2008.
Beare, Robin Lyell Blin, 26 Nov. 2007.
Beaumont of Whitley, Baron (Life Peer); Rev. Timothy Wentworth Beaumont, 8 April 2008.
Beddington, Charles Richard, 6 May 2008.
Béjart, Maurice Jean, 22 Nov. 2007.
Bell, James Steven, CMG, CBE, DFC, QPM, CPM, 20 Nov. 2000.
Benney, (Adrian) Gerald (Sallis), CBE, RDI, 26 June 2008.
Berkson, David Mayer, 10 Dec. 2007.
Bethell, 4th Baron; Nicholas William Bethell, 8 Sept. 2007.
Bevan, Rear-Adm. Christopher Martin, CB, 13 April 2008.
Bhutto, Benazir, 27 Dec. 2007.
Bickerton, Frank Donald, CBE, 12 April 2008.
Bide, Sir Austin Ernest, 11 May 2008.
Birdsall, Doris, CBE, 11 June 2008.
Birks, His Honour Michael, 11 Aug. 2008.
Black, Sheila Psyche, OBE, Sept. 2007.
Blackwell, John Charles, CBE, 30 Jan. 2008.
Blake, Sir (Thomas) Richard (Valentine), 17th Bt, 29 May 2008.
Blamire-Brown, John, 4 May 2008.
Blease, Baron (Life Peer); William John Blease, 16 May 2008.
Bleehen, Prof. Norman Montague, CBE, 1 Feb. 2008.
Bock, Prof. Claus Victor, 5 Jan. 2008.
Bonelli, Pierre Sauveur Ernest, 1 April 2004.
Bourne, Sir Clive John, 10 Jan. 2007.
Bowater, Sir J(ohn) Vansittart, 4th Bt, 24 April 2008.
Bowie, Stanley Hay Umphray, FRS, 3 Sept. 2008.
Bradley, William Ewart, 5 March 2008.
Bradshaw, Sir Kenneth Anthony, KCB, 31 Oct. 2007.
Braithwaite, (Arthur) Bevan (Midgley), OBE, 25 April 2008.
Braithwaite, His Honour Bernard Richard, 4 Aug. 2008.
Brand, Alexander George, 14 April 2008.
Brash, Robert, CMG, 22 Oct. 2007.
Bratt, Guy Maurice, CMG, MBE, 15 May 2006.
Breach, Gerald Ernest John, 3 March 2008.
Brennan, Edward A., 27 Dec. 2007.
Bridge of Harwich, Baron (Life Peer); Nigel Cyprian Bridge, PC, 20 Nov. 2007.

Bridges, Sir Phillip Rodney, CMG, 26 Dec. 2007.
Brien, Alan, 23 May 2008.
Brigden, Wallace, 11 March 2008.
Broadbent, Edward Granville, FRS, 9 March 2008.
Broinowski, John Herbert, CMG, 16 April 2005.
Brown, Arthur Ivor Parry, 15 Nov. 2007.
Brown, Sir George Noel, 26 July 2007.
Brown, Harold James, AM, 3 Nov. 2006.
Brown, Hugh Dunbar, 10 March 2008.
Brown, Roy Dudley, 8 April 2008.
Bruce-Lockhart, Baron (Life Peer); Alexander, (Sandy), John Bruce-Lockhart, OBE, 14 Aug. 2008.
Brunton, Sir (Edward Francis) Lauder, 3rd Bt, 1 Jan. 2007.
Brus, Prof. Wlodzimierz, 31 Aug. 2007.
Bryant, Richard Charles, CB, 22 May 2008.
Buckland, Maj.-Gen. Ronald John Denys Eden, CB, MBE, 22 Jan. 2008.
Bull, Dr John Prince, CBE, 7 Aug. 2008.
Bullen, Air Vice-Marshal Reginald, CB, GM, 27 Jan. 2008.
Bunch, Sir Austin Wyeth, CBE, 30 June 2008.
Burlison, Baron (Life Peer); Thomas Henry Burlison, 20 May 2008.
Burrell, Sir (John) Raymond, 9th Bt, 29 May 2008.
Burrows, (Lionel) John, CBE, 28 Aug. 2008.
Butler, Rt Hon. Sir Adam Courtauld, PC, 9 Jan. 2008.
Butler, Prof. Michael Gregory, 25 Nov. 2007.
Butterfield, Charles Harris, QC (Singapore), 15 April 2008.
Button, Henry George, 11 March 2008.

Cachelin, Commissioner Francy, 16 Aug. 2007.
Cadogan, Peter William, 18 Nov. 2007.
Campbell, Sir Alan Hugh, GCMG, 7 Oct. 2007.
Campbell, Ian, 9 Sept. 2007.
Campbell, Ken, 31 Aug. 2008.
Campbell, Ross, OC, DSC, 15 Aug. 2007.
Carden, Sir John Craven, 7th Bt, 4 April 2008.
Carey, Group Captain Alban Majendie, CBE, 11 March 2008.
Cartland, Sir George Barrington, CMG, 31 July 2008.
Catford, Sir (John) Robin, KCVO, CBE, 27 May 2008.
Chadwick, Rt Rev. Graham Charles, 28 Oct. 2007.
Chadwick, Prof. Henry, KBE, FBA, 17 June 2008.
Chapman, Prof. Norman Bellamy, 6 March 2008.
Charles, Jack, 19 Jan. 2006.
Chatfield, 2nd Baron; Ernle David Lewis Chatfield, 30 Sept. 2007 (*ext*).
Chesterton, Sir Oliver Sidney, MC, 14 Oct. 2007.
Chew, (Victor) Kenneth, TD, 7 May 2008.
Child, Christopher Thomas, 12 May 2008.
Chilton, Brig. Sir Frederick Oliver, CBE, DSO, 1 Oct. 2007.
Chipp, David Allan, 9 Sept. 2008.
Cholmondeley Clarke, Marshal Butler, 21 Nov. 2007.
Church, James Anthony, (Tony), 25 March 2008.
Clare, Prof. Anthony Ward, 28 Oct. 2007.
Clarke, Sir Arthur Charles, CBE, 19 March 2008.
Clay, His Honour John Lionel, TD, 29 March 2008.
Coady, Aubrey William Burleton, CMG, Sept. 2006.
Cochrane, Christopher Duncan, QC, 23 May 2008.
Cocke, Thomas Hugh, 23 April 2008.
Codrington, Sir William Alexander, 8th Bt, 1 Dec. 2006.
Cohen, Hon. Leonard Harold Lionel, OBE, 25 Dec. 2007.
Coldstream, Prof. John Nicolas, FBA, 21 March 2008.
Colgrain, 3rd Baron; David Colin Campbell, 7 Feb. 2008.
Collard, Douglas Reginald, OBE, 22 Oct. 2007.
Colquhoun of Luss, Captain Sir Ivar Iain, 8th Bt, 31 Jan. 2008.
Colvin, Sir Howard Montagu, CVO, CBE, FBA, 27 Dec. 2007.
Compton, Rt Hon. Sir John George Melvin, KCMG, OCC, PC, 7 Sept. 2007.
Cook, Beryl Frances, OBE, 28 May 2008.
Cooke of Islandreagh, Baron (Life Peer); Victor Alexander Cooke, OBE, 13 Nov. 2007.
Cooke, Prof. Brian Ernest Dudley, 28 Sept. 2007.
Cooke, Jean Esme Oregon, RA, 6 Aug. 2008.
Coombe, His Honour Michael Ambrose Rew, 20 Oct. 2007.
Corbett, Hon. Michael McGregor, 16 Sept. 2007.
Coren, Alan, 18 Oct. 2007.
Cornish, Jack Bertram, 24 Dec. 2007.
Costello, Gordon John, 27 June 2007.
Cotton, Hon. Sir Robert Carrington, KCMG, AO, 25 Dec. 2006.
Cotton, Sir William Frederick, (Sir Bill Cotton), CBE, 11 Aug. 2008.
Coupland, Prof. Rex Ernest, 22 June 2008.
Court, Hon. Sir Charles Walter Michael, AK, KCMG, OBE, 22 Dec. 2007.
Couve de Murville, Most Rev. Maurice Noël Léon, 3 Nov. 2007.

Cowgill, Bryan, 14 July 2008.
Cox, Prof. (Charles) Brian, CBE, 24 April 2008.
Cox, Dennis George, 31 Oct. 2007.
Cox, Sir Geoffrey Sandford, CNZM, CBE, 2 April 2008.
Cox, Norman Ernest, CMG, 6 April 2008.
Croan, Thomas Malcolm, 8 June 2008.
Crofton, 7th Baron; Guy Patrick Gilbert Crofton, 25 Nov. 2007.
Croll, Prof. Elisabeth Joan, CMG, 3 Oct. 2007.
Crook, Prof. John Anthony, 7 Sept. 2007.
Croome, (John) Lewis, CMG, 7 March 2008.
Cross, Hannah Margaret, (Mrs E. G. Wright), 19 Jan. 2008.
Crow, (Hilary) Stephen, CB, 5 Dec. 2007.
Crowe, William James, Jr, 18 Oct. 2007.
Crowfoot, Maj.-Gen. Anthony Bernard, CB, CBE, 13 Sept. 2008.
Cruft, John Herbert, 17 May 2008.
Curie, Eve, (Mrs Henry R. Labouisse), 22 Oct. 2007.
Curry, Alan Stewart, 20 Aug. 2007.
Cushing, David Henry, FRS, 14 March 2008.

D'Aeth, Prof. (Hugh) Richard (Xenophon), 19 Feb. 2008.
Dalton, Sir Howard, FRS, 12 Jan. 2008.
Daniell, Ralph Allen, CBE, 12 Nov. 2007.
Darby, Sir Peter Howard, CBE, QFSM, 21 May 2008.
D'Arcy, Most Rev. (Joseph) Eric, 12 Dec. 2005.
Darcy de Knayth, Baroness (18th in line); Davina Marcia Ingrams, DBE, 24 Feb. 2008.
Davey, Keith Alfred Thomas, CB, 8 Nov. 2007.
Davidson, Ivor Macaulay, 22 Jan. 2008.
Davidson, Dr (William) Keith, CBE, 21 May 2007.
Davies, Dr Arthur Gordon, 19 Jan. 2008.
Davies, Caleb William, CMG, 1 Nov. 2007.
Davies, David Levric, CB, OBE, 7 Feb. 2008.
Davis, Michael McFarland, 11 Nov. 2007.
Davis, Hon. Sir Thomas Robert Alexander Harries, KBE, 23 July 2007.
Daws, Dame Joyce Margaretta, DBE, 13 June 2007.
DeBakey, Dr Michael Ellis, 11 July 2008.
Dehqani-Tafti, Rt Rev. Hassan Barnaba, 29 April 2008.
Dell, Ven. Robert Sydney, 19 Jan. 2008.
Dewar, His Honour Thomas, 31 Dec. 2007.
Dick, Air Vice-Marshal Ronald, CB, 25 March 2008.
Dole, John Anthony, 19 March 2008.
Donovan, Charles Edward, 25 Nov. 2007.
Douglas, Gavin Stuart, RD, QC (Scot.), 6 March 2008.
Douglas, Margaret Elizabeth, (Mrs T. Lancaster), OBE, 20 Aug. 2008.
Downes, George Robert, CB, 7 Jan. 2008.
Draycott, Gerald Arthur, 15 March 2008.
Drnovšek, Janez, 23 Feb. 2008.
Dronfield, Ronald, 17 Dec. 2007.
Du Boulay, Prof. (Francis) Robin (Houssemayne), FBA, 2 Jan. 2008.
Ducat-Amos, Air Comdt Barbara Mary, CB, RRC, 7 Jan. 2008.
Dunn, Air Marshal Sir Eric Clive, KBE, CB, BEM, 16 July 2008.
Dunwoody, Gwyneth Patricia, MP, 17 April 2008.

Edwards, Prof. John Hilton, FRS, 11 Oct. 2007.
Elles, Neil Patrick Moncrieff, 29 June 2008.
Elliott, Hon. Lord; Walter Archibald Elliott, MC, 9 Aug. 2008.
Elliott, Katharine Barbara, 17 May 2008.
Elliott, Michael, CBE, FRS, 17 Oct. 2007.
Elsmore, Sir Lloyd, OBE, 12 Nov. 2007.
Elton, (Peter) John, MC, 21 May 2008.
Emanuel, Aaron, CMG, 13 March 2008.
Emmerson, Rt Rev. Ralph, 31 Dec. 2007.
Erickson, Prof. Charlotte Joanne, 9 July 2008.
Esplin, Air Vice-Marshal Ian George, CB, OBE, DFC, 15 April 2008.

Faber, Sir Richard Stanley, KCVO, CMG, 18 Oct. 2007.
Fairtlough, Gerard Howard, CBE, 15 Dec. 2007.
Falconer, Hon. Sir Douglas William, MBE, 18 Dec. 2007.
Farley, Prof. Martyn Graham, 3 Nov. 2007.
Fee, John Fitzgerald, 11 Nov. 2007.
Fields, Terence, 28 June 2008.
Fifoot, Paul Ronald Ninnes, CMG, 22 Feb. 2008.
Fischer, Prof. Ernst Otto, 23 July 2007.
Fitzalan-Howard, Maj.-Gen. Lord Michael, GCVO, CB, CBE, MC, 2 Nov. 2007.
Forrester, Prof. Peter Garnett, CBE, 23 March 2008.
Fossett, Steve   *[Deceased.*
Foster, Sir John Gregory, 3rd Bt, 24 Nov. 2006.
Frankel, William, CBE, 18 April 2008.
Fraser, George MacDonald, OBE, 2 Jan. 2008.
Fraser, Lt-Comdr Ian Edward, VC, DSC, RD, RN, 1 Sept. 2008.
Fraser, Peter Marshall, MC, FBA, 15 Sept. 2008.
Frede, Prof. Michael, FBA, 11 Aug. 2007.
Frodsham, Anthony Freer, CBE, 3 Nov. 2007.

Frood, Alan Campbell, CBE, 5 Nov. 2007.
Furmston, Bentley Edwin, 7 Oct. 2007.

Gadsby, (Gordon) Neville, CB, 29 Dec. 2007.
Gaius, Rev. Sir Saimon, KBE, 14 July 2006.
Gall, Thomas Mitchell; Hon. Mr Justice Gall, 20 Jan. 2006.
Galway and Kilmacduagh, Bishop of, (RC); Most Rev. James McLoughlin, 25 Nov. 2005.
Gardiner, Dame Helen Louisa, DBE, MVO, 21 July 2001.
Garrett, John Laurence, 11 Sept. 2007.
Garrioch, Sir (William) Henry, 18 Feb. 2008.
Genders, Rt Rev. Roger Alban Marson, (Bishop Anselm), CR, 19 June 2008.
George, Llewellyn Norman Havard, 24 March 2006.
George, Peter John, OBE, 20 Feb. 2008.
Gething, Air Commodore Richard Templeton, CB, OBE, AFC, 15 May 2004.
Gibbs, Rt Rev. John, 20 Dec. 2007.
Gibson, John Sibbald, 15 May 2008.
Gibson-Barboza, Mario, Hon. GCMG, 26 Nov. 2007.
Gilbert, Stuart William, CB, 23 Nov. 2007.
Gill, Air Vice-Marshal Harry, CB, OBE, 20 Jan. 2008.
Gilmour of Craigmillar, Baron (Life Peer); Ian Hedworth John Little Gilmour, PC, 21 Sept. 2007.
Glendyne, 3rd Baron; Robert Nivison, 27 June 2008.
Glossop, Peter, 7 Sept. 2008.
Glover, Trevor David, 12 Sept. 2007.
Godfrey, Gerald Michael, CBE, 29 Oct. 2007.
Godfrey, Louise Sarah, (Mrs Stanley Bland), QC, 12 June 2002.
Goldsmith, John Stuart, CB, 19 July 2007.
Gooch, Major Sir Timothy Robert Sherlock, 13th Bt, MBE, 9 April 2008.
Goodall, Ralph William, 16 March 2008.
Goodfellow, Rosalind Erica, 25 Aug. 2008.
Goodridge, Rt Rev. Sehon Sylvester, 28 Dec. 2007.
Gorell, 4th Baron; Timothy John Radcliffe Barnes, 25 Sept. 2007.
Gould, Prof. Frank William, 3 June 2008.
Govan, Sir Lawrence Herbert, 6 Nov. 2007.
Gowing, Prof. Noel Frank Collett, 17 Sept. 2007.
Graham, Euan Douglas, CB, 14 Dec. 2007.
Grant, His Honour (Hubert) Brian, 22 March 2008.
Gray, Robert, CBE, 10 Sept. 2008.
Gray, Simon James Holliday, CBE, 6 Aug. 2008.
Gray, Prof. (Thomas) Cecil, CBE, 5 Jan. 2008.
Green, Terence Arthur, 19 Jan. 2008.
Green, Thomas Charles, CB, 20 Oct. 2007.
Grey Egerton, Sir (Philip) John (Caledon), 15th Bt, 19 Feb. 2008.
Grierson, Sir Michael John Bewes, 12th Bt, 24 March 2008 (*ext*).
Grima, Andrew Peter, 26 Dec. 2007.
Grimshaw, Maj.-Gen. Ewing Henry Wrigley, CB, CBE, DSO, 1 Nov. 2007.
Grobler, Richard Victor, CBE, 21 July 2008.
Groves, John Dudley, CB, OBE, 26 Dec. 2007.
Gruenberg, Prof. Karl Walter, 10 Oct. 2007.
Gunnell, (William) John, 28 Jan. 2008.
Gutteridge, Prof. William Frank, MBE, 22 May 2008.
Guyatt, Richard Gerald Talbot, CBE, 17 Oct. 2007.

Halliday, Vice-Adm. Sir Roy William, KBE, DSC, 23 Nov. 2007.
Hampden, 6th Viscount; Anthony David Brand, 4 Jan. 2008.
Hamylton Jones, Keith, CMG, 23 Nov. 2007.
Handley, Vernon George, CBE, 10 Sept. 2008.
Hardwick, Christopher, 16 Aug. 2008.
Hardy, Rev. Prof. Daniel Wayne, 15 Nov. 2007.
Hargroves, Brig. Sir (Robert) Louis, CBE, 22 Feb. 2008.
Harman, Very Rev. (Robert) Desmond, 18 Dec. 2007.
Harnden, Arthur Baker, CB, TD, 23 Feb. 2008.
Harper, John Mansfield, 3 March 2008.
Harris, David, 2006.
Harris, John Robert, 15 Feb. 2008.
Harris, Philip, 2 June 2008.
Harrison, Maj.-Gen. Ian Stewart, CB, 2 April 2008.
Harrowby, 7th Earl of; Dudley Danvers Granville Coutts Ryder, TD, 9 Oct. 2007.
Hart, His Honour Donald, QC, 24 April 2007.
Hartog, Harold Samuel Arnold, Hon. KBE, 23 Sept. 2007.
Harvey, John Edgar, CBE, 13 Jan. 2008.
Harvey-Jones, Sir John Henry, MBE, 9 Jan. 2008.
Hassett, Gen. Sir Francis George, AC, KBE, CB, DSO, LVO, 11 June 2008.
Hauser, Frank Ivor, CBE, 14 Oct. 2007.
Hawkes, Prof. John Gregory, OBE, 6 Sept. 2007.
Hawley, Sir John Frederick, KCMG, MBE, 31 Jan. 2008.
Heanley, Charles Laurence, TD, 9 Feb. 2008.
Henao, Rev. Sir Ravu, OBE, 18 Oct. 2007.
Henderson, Douglas Mackay, CBE, 10 Nov. 2007.
Herbison, Dame Jean Marjory, DBE, CMG, 20 May 2007.
Hester, Rev. Canon John Frear, 9 Feb. 2008.
Heston, Charlton, 5 April 2008.

Hexham and Newcastle, Bishop of, (RC); Rt Rev. Kevin John
    Dunn, 1 March 2008.
Hezlet, Vice-Adm. Sir Arthur Richard, KBE, CB, DSO, DSC, 7 Nov. 2007.
Hickling, Rev. Canon Colin John Anderson, 19 Nov. 2007.
Higgs, Sir Derek Alan, 28 April 2008.
Higman, Prof. Graham, FRS, 8 April 2008.
Hill, George Raymond, 22 March 2008.
Hill, Ian Macdonald, 22 Sept. 2007.
Hill, John Edward Bernard, 6 Dec. 2007.
Hill, Sir John McGregor, FRS, 14 Jan. 2008.
Hillary, Sir Edmund Percival, KG, ONZ, KBE, 11 Jan. 2008.
Hillery, Dr Patrick John, 12 April 2008.
Hoare, Sir Timothy Edward Charles, 8th Bt, OBE, 18 Jan. 2008.
Hobden, Reginald Herbert, DFC, 12 Aug. 2008.
Hocking, Philip Norman, 17 Aug. 2008.
Hoddinott, Prof. Alun, CBE, 12 March 2008.
Hodgson, Ven. (John) Derek, 22 Nov. 2007.
Hodgson, William Donald John, 14 Feb. 2008.
Hogg, Prof. Richard Milne, FBA, 6 Sept. 2007.
Holland, David Cuthbert Lyall, CB, 21 Sept. 2007.
Holme of Cheltenham, Baron (Life Peer); Richard Gordon Holme, CBE,
    PC, 4 May 2008.
Homan, Rear-Adm. Thomas Buckhurst, CB, 1 March 2008.
Honeycombe, Sir Robert William Kerr, FRS, 14 Sept. 2007.
Hope, Sir John Carl Alexander, 18th Bt, 30 Oct. 2007.
Hornby, Richard Phipps, 22 Sept. 2007.
Horsford, Maj.-Gen. Derek Gordon Thomond, CBE, DSO, 5 Oct. 2007.
Howard, Air Vice-Marshal Peter, CB, OBE, 21 Oct. 2007.
Howell, Air Vice-Marshal (Evelyn Michael) Thomas, CBE, 5 May 2008.
Howell, Sir Ralph Frederic, 14 Feb. 2008.
Hudson, Prof. John Pilkington, CBE, GM, 6 Dec. 2007.
Hunt of Tanworth, Baron (Life Peer); John Joseph Benedict Hunt,
    GCB, 17 July 2008.
Hutchinson, Prof. George William, 22 Oct. 2004.
Hutchison, Prof. Terence Wilmot, FBA, 5 Oct. 2007.
Hutton, (Hubert) Robin, OBE, 25 Jan. 2008.
Huydecoper, Jonkheer (Jan Louis) Reinier, Hon. GCVO, 19 Oct. 2005.

Innes, Lt-Col William Alexander Disney, 20 March 2008.
Irvine, His Honour James Eccles Malise, 29 Dec. 2007.
Israel, Rev. Dr Martin Spencer, 23 Oct. 2007.

Jack, Prof. Ian Robert James, FBA, 3 Sept. 2008.
Jaffré, Philippe Serge Yves, 5 Sept. 2007.
James, Richard Austin, CB, MC, 10 Sept. 2008.
Jardine of Applegirth, Sir Alexander Maule, (Sir Alec), 12th Bt, 6 April 2008.
Jayawardena, Lal, 8 April 2004.
Jenkins, John Owen, MBE, 19 April 2008.
Jenkyns, Henry Leigh, 28 Sept. 2007.
Jennett, Prof. (William) Bryan, CBE, 26 Jan. 2008.
Jennings, Anthony Francis, QC, 21 Jan. 2008.
Jennings, Very Rev. Kenneth Neal, 14 Dec. 2007.
Johnson, Prof. Francis Rea, 6 July 2007.
Johnston, Rt Hon. Lord; Alan Charles Macpherson Johnston, PC, 14 June 2008.
Joyce, William R., Jr, 17 April 2007.

Kane, Col John Mark, CMG, OBE, 8 Sept. 2008.
Kausimae, Sir David, KBE, 14 Sept. 2007.
Kaye, Michael, OBE, 3 May 2008.
Keatinge, Prof. William Richard, 11 April 2008.
Kemp, Sir (Edward) Peter, KCB, 24 June 2008.
Kendall, Prof. David George, FRS, 23 Oct. 2007.
Kennedy-Good, Sir John, KBE, QSO, 11 July 2005.
Kenyon, Sir George Henry, 2 June 2008.
Kernohan, Thomas Hugh, CBE, 3 Dec. 2007.
Kerr, Deborah Jane, (Deborah Kerr Viertel), CBE, 16 Oct. 2007.
Kershaw, Sir (John) Anthony, MC, 29 April 2008.
Kidd, Prof. Frank Forrest, 15 March 2008.
Kidwell, Raymond Incledon, QC, 3 Oct. 2007.
Kilby, Michael Leopold, 9 Sept. 2008.
Kimber, Sir Charles Dixon, 3rd Bt, 10 April 2008.
Kingsley, Roger James, OBE, 2 Jan. 2008.
Kington, Miles Beresford, 30 Jan. 2008.
Kirby, David Donald, CBE, 12 April 2008.
Kitaj, R. B., RA, 21 Oct. 2007.
Kneale, George Victor Harris, CBE, 8 April 2007.
Knowles, Prof. Jeremy Randall, CBE, FRS, 3 April 2008.
Knowles, Sir Richard Marchant, 18 Feb. 2008.
Kornberg, Prof. Arthur, 26 Oct. 2007.
Kyrle Pope, Rear-Adm. Michael Donald, CB, MBE, 14 Sept. 2008.

Laing, Sir (John) Maurice, 22 Feb. 2008.
Laking, Sir George Robert, KCMG, 10 Jan. 2008.

Lamb, Prof. Willis E(ugene), Jr, 15 May 2008.
Lambert, Patricia, OBE, 6 July 2008.
Lambert, Verity Ann, OBE, 22 Nov. 2007.
Lambton, Prof. Ann Katharine Swynford, OBE, FBA, 19 July 2008.
Lamer, Rt Hon. Antonio, CC, PC (Can.), 24 Nov. 2007.
Lamond, James Alexander, 20 Nov. 2007.
Lang, Prof. Andrew Richard, FRS, 30 June 2008.
Langley, Maj.-Gen. Sir (Henry) Desmond (Allen), KCVO, MBE, 14 Feb. 2008.
Lathe, Prof. Grant Henry, 2 July 2007.
Laurence, Dan Hyman, 5 Feb. 2008.
Laurence, Sir Peter Harold, KCMG, MC, 26 Nov. 2007.
Lawther, Prof. Patrick Joseph, CBE, 6 June 2008.
Leasor, (Thomas) James, 10 Sept. 2007.
Lederberg, Prof. Joshua, 2 Feb. 2008.
Lees, Prof. Dennis Samuel, CBE, 11 Feb. 2008.
Lemkin, James Anthony, CBE, 12 May 2008.
Leslie, Sir Peter Evelyn, 27 Sept. 2007.
Lewen, John Henry, CMG, 10 March 2008.
Lewis, Prof. Geoffrey Lewis, CMG, FBA, 12 Feb. 2008.
Lewitter, Prof. Lucjan Ryszard, 19 Sept. 2007.
Lipton, Prof. Peter, 25 Nov. 2007.
Little, Most Rev. Thomas Francis, KBE, 7 April 2008.
Long, Ven. John Sanderson, 4 June 2008.
Long, Captain Rt Hon. William Joseph, OBE, PC, 10 Feb. 2008.
Lord, William Burton Housley, CB, 28 July 2008.
Lovegrove, His Honour Geoffrey David, QC, 21 Jan. 2008.
Loveridge, Sir John Warren, 13 Nov. 2007.
Lownie of Largo, His Honour Ralph Hamilton, 28 Nov. 2007.
Lusty, Prof. James Richard, 4 Feb. 2008.
Lynton, Norbert Casper, OBE, 30 Oct. 2007.
Lyons, Bernard, CBE, 12 April 2008.
Lyons, Charles Albert, 1 Jan. 2008.
Lyons, (Isidore) Jack, 18 Feb. 2008.
Lyttelton, Humphrey Richard Adeane, 25 April 2008.

Mabon, Rt Hon. (Jesse) Dickson, PC, 10 April 2008.
McAlpine, (Robert Douglas) Christopher, CMG, 1 Sept. 2008.
Macara, Sir Hugh Kenneth, 4th Bt, April 1986 (*ext*).
McArdle, Rear-Adm. Stanley Lawrence, CB, LVO, GM, 4 Dec. 2007.
Macarthur, Rev. Arthur Leitch, OBE, 1 Sept. 2008.
MacArthur, Ian, OBE, 30 Nov. 2007.
McConville, Michael Anthony, MBE, 30 May 2008.
MacDougall, John William, MP, 13 Aug. 2008.
McEachern, Allan, 11 Jan. 2008.
MacEwen, Ann Maitland, 20 Aug. 2008.
Macfadyen, Rt Hon. Lord; Donald James Dobbie Macfadyen, PC, 11 April 2008.
McGrigor, Captain Sir Charles Edward, 5th Bt, 1 Oct. 2007.
McIlwain, Alexander Edward, CBE, 18 July 2008.
Macintosh, Farquhar, CBE, 18 Nov. 2007.
McIntyre, Prof. Donald Ian, 16 Oct. 2007.
McIntyre, William Ian Mackay, CBE, 20 March 2008.
McKay, Prof. Alexander Gordon, OC, 31 Aug. 2007.
Mackenzie, James, 29 Oct. 2007.
McWatters, George Edward, 19 Dec. 2007.
Maddocks, Rt Rev. Morris Henry St John, 19 Jan. 2008.
Mailer, Norman Kingsley, 10 Nov. 2007.
Main, Sir Peter Tester, ERD, 17 May 2008.
Mair, Prof. William Austyn, CBE, 17 Jan. 2008.
Mallon, Rt Rev. Mgr Joseph Laurence, 31 Oct. 2007.
Mallon, Most Rev. Peter Joseph, 3 Feb. 2007.
Mamo, Sir Anthony Joseph, OBE, 1 May 2008.
Manners, 5th Baron; John Robert Cecil Manners, 28 May 2008.
Mansfield, Rear-Adm. David Parks, CB, 2 Jan. 2008.
Marceau, Marcel, 22 Sept. 2007.
Marland, Michael, CBE, 3 July 2008.
Marsden, John Christopher, MBE, 19 Aug. 2008.
Marshall, Noël Hedley, CMG, 16 Aug. 2008.
Marshall, Peter Izod, 24 Oct. 2007.
Marten, Francis William, CMG, MC, 9 Dec. 2007.
Martin, Prof. Geoffrey Haward, CBE, 20 Dec. 2007.
Mason, Sir Frederick Cecil, KCVO, CMG, 18 Jan. 2008.
Mason, Sir John Charles Moir, KCMG, 16 March 2007.
Mason, Prof. Stephen Finney, FRS, 11 Dec. 2007.
Matheson, Very Rev. James Gunn, 28 Oct. 2007.
Mawson, Stuart Radcliffe, 20 Feb. 2008.
May, Prof. Brian Albert, 17 Nov. 2007.
Mayfield, Lt-Col Richard, DSO, LVO, 30 Nov. 2007.
Meade-King, Charles Martin, 27 April 2008.
Mellers, Prof. Wilfrid Howard, OBE, 16 May 2008.
Mendl, His Honour James Henry Embleton, 13 July 2008.
Merrivale, 3rd Baron; Jack Henry Edmond Duke, 1 Nov. 2007.
Michie of Gallanach, Baroness (Life Peer); Janet Ray Michie, 6 May 2008.
Middleton, Francis, 15 Nov. 2002.
Miles, Prof. Albert Edward William, 7 March 2008.

Miller, Alan John McCulloch, DSC, VRD, 2 Feb. 2008.
Miller, Michael, RD, QC, 20 Feb. 2008.
Minghella, Anthony, CBE, 18 March 2008.
Mitchell, John Wesley, FRS, 12 July 2007.
Mitra, Ashesh Prosad, FRS, 3 Sept. 2007.
Montgomery, Col John Rupert Patrick, OBE, MC, 27 June 2008.
Moody, Leslie Howard, 28 April 2008.
Moore, Maj.-Gen. Sir (John) Jeremy, KCB, OBE, MC, 15 Sept. 2007.
Moore, Noel Ernest Ackroyd, 30 May 2008.
Mordue, Richard Eric, 19 June 2008.
Morgan-Owen, John Gethin, CB, MBE, QC, 17 Jan. 2008.
Morison, Air Vice-Marshal Richard Trevor, CBE, 23 April 2008.
Morrice, Norman, 11 Jan. 2008.
Morris, Sir (James) Richard (Samuel), CBE, 1 July 2008.
Morris, Max, 27 Aug. 2008.
Morris, Prof. Norman Frederick, 29 Feb. 2008.
Mortimer, Katharine Mary Hope, (Mrs Robert Dean), 15 July 2008.
Moses, Eric George Rufus, CB, 7 Aug. 2008.
Moss, Martin Grenville, CBE, 19 Nov. 2007.
Moule, Rev. Prof. Charles Francis Digby, CBE, FBA, 30 Sept. 2007.
Muller, Ralph Louis Junius, 11 Oct. 2007.
Mullett, Leslie Baden, 13 March 2008.
Munro, Dame Alison, DBE, 2 Sept. 2008.
Murphy, Rear-Adm. Anthony Albert, CBE, 9 Aug. 2008.
Murphy, Sir Leslie Frederick, 29 Sept. 2007.
Murray, Charles Henry, 31 Jan. 2008.
Murray, Sir James, KCMG, 28 Nov. 2007.
Mursell, Sir Peter, MBE, 23 Aug. 2008.
Musson, Gen. Sir Geoffrey Randolph Dixon, GCB, CBE, DSO, 10 Jan. 2008.

Naylor, Prof. Malcolm Neville, RD, 15 April 2008.
Neal, Sir Leonard Francis, CBE, 4 May 2008.
Nelson, Bertram James, OBE, 24 Feb. 2008.
Newman, Barry Hilton, 12 July 2008.
Newton, Sir (Harry) Michael (Rex), 3rd Bt, 29 Feb. 2008.
Newton, Sir Kenneth (Garnar), 3rd Bt, OBE, TD, 12 Aug. 2008.
Nicolle, Anthony William, OBE, 8 June 2008.
Nind, Philip Frederick, OBE, TD, 27 May 2008.
Nixon, Sir Edwin Ronald, CBE, 17 Aug. 2008.
Noakes, Rt Rev. George, 14 July 2008.
Norman, Andrew John, 24 Sept. 2007.
Norman, Geoffrey, OBE, 10 Feb. 2008.
Norman, Sir Robert Henry, OBE, 3 April 2007.

Obasi, Godwin Olu Patrick, OFR, 3 March 2007.
Odgers, Paul Randell, CB, MBE, TD, 24 Dec. 2007.
O'Higgins, Prof. Paul, 13 March 2008.
Oliver of Aylmerton, Baron (Life Peer); Peter Raymond Oliver, PC, 17 Oct. 2007.
Orgel, Prof. Leslie Eleazer, FRS, 27 Oct. 2007.
Orr, Sir David Alexander, MC, 2 Feb. 2008.
Orr, James Bernard Vivian, CVO, 14 June 2008.
Ortoli, François-Xavier, 30 Nov. 2007.
Orton, Peter Charles, CVO, 5 Dec. 2007.
Ottewill, Prof. Ronald Harry, OBE, FRS, 4 June 2008.
Ounsted, John, 2 Dec. 2007.
Owen, Gerald Victor, QC, 24 July 2007.
Owen, Prof. Walter Shepherd, 10 Oct. 2007.

Parker, Hugh, 16 June 2008.
Parkinson, James Christopher, MBE, TD, 6 Sept. 2007.
Parmoor, 4th Baron; Milo Cripps, 12 Aug. 2008.
Parry, Margaret Joan, 30 Jan. 2008.
Parton, Prof. John Edwin, 31 Oct. 2002.
Pathak, Raghunandan Swarup, 17 Nov. 2007.
Payne-Gallwey, Sir Philip Frankland, 6th Bt, 3 Feb. 2008 (*ext*).
Peck, His Honour David Edward, 22 Dec. 2007.
Pennington, Prof. Robert Roland, 12 Feb. 2008.
Perryman, (Francis) Douglas, 21 Sept. 2007.
Peterkiewicz, Prof. Jerzy, 26 Oct. 2007.
Peters, Theophilus, CMG, 9 Feb. 2008.
Peterson, Oscar Emmanuel, CC, OOnt, 23 Dec. 2007.
Peto, Sir Michael Henry Basil, 4th Bt, 2 Aug. 2008.
Phelps, Richard Wintour, CBE, 17 April 2008.
Pickard, Hon. Neil Edward William, 13 April 2007.
Pinner, Hayim, OBE, 5 Nov. 2007.
Pocock, Air Vice-Marshal Donald Arthur, CBE, 30 July 2008.
Podro, Prof. Michael Isaac, CBE, FBA, 28 March 2008.
Poston, James, CBE, 13 Oct. 2007.
Potter, Donald Charles, QC, 8 March 2008.
Pout, Harry Wilfrid, CB, OBE, 15 July 2006.
Prentice, Thomas, MC, 17 Nov. 2007.
Prescott, Brig. Peter George Addington, MC, 31 Oct. 2007.

Prichard-Jones, Sir John, 2nd Bt, 2 July 2007.
Pumfrey, Rt Hon. Sir Nicholas Richard, PC; Rt Hon. Lord Justice Pumfrey, 24 Dec. 2007.
Puxon, (Christine) Margaret, (Mrs Margaret Williams), QC, 1 April 2008.
Pym, Baron (Life Peer); Francis Leslie Pym, MC, PC, 7 March 2008.

Quinn, James Charles Frederick, 11 Feb. 2008.

Radnor, 8th Earl of; Jacob Pleydell-Bouverie, 11 Aug. 2008.
Ramsay, Donald Allan, CM, FRS, 25 Oct. 2007.
Rayner, Edward John, 12 July 2008.
Reeves, Christopher Reginald, 20 Nov. 2007.
Reid, Sir Norman Robert, 17 Dec. 2007.
Richards, Denis Edward, CMG, 27 April 2008.
Richardson, Joanna Leah, 7 March 2008.
Richmond, Prof. John, CBE, 27 March 2008.
Ricketts, Sir (Robert) Tristram, 8th Bt, 7 Nov. 2007.
Ritchie of Dundee, 5th Baron; Harold Malcolm Ritchie, 11 Jan. 2008.
Ritchie, Prof. J(oseph) Murdoch, FRS, 9 July 2008.
Rix, Sir John, MBE, 13 Oct. 2007.
Robbe-Grillet, Alain, 18 Feb. 2008.
Roberts, Bertie, 28 Feb. 2007.
Roberts, Eirlys Rhiwen Cadwaladr, CBE, 18 March 2008.
Roberts, John Lewis, CMG, 2 July 2007.
Robertson, (Richard) Ross, 3 May 2007.
Robertson, Prof. William Bruce, 20 April 2008.
Robinson, Peter, 3 Oct. 2007.
Roddick, Dame Anita Lucia, DBE, 10 Sept. 2007.
Rooke, Sir Denis Eric, OM, CBE, FRS, 2 Sept. 2008.
Root, Rev. Canon Howard Eugene, 19 Nov. 2007.
Rose, Mark Wilson, 8 March 2008.
Ross, Rev. Andrew Christian, 26 July 2008.
Ross Goobey, Alastair, CBE, 2 Feb. 2008.
Rougier, Hon. Sir Richard George, 25 Oct. 2007.
Routledge, Alan, CBE, 25 July 2008.
Rowley, Sir Charles Robert, 7th and 8th Bt, 11 May 2008.
Roxburgh, Rt Rev. James William, 10 Dec. 2007.
Rudduck, Prof. Jean, 28 March 2007.
Russell, John, CBE, 23 Aug. 2008.
Russell-Johnston, Baron (Life Peer); (David) Russell Russell-Johnston, 27 July 2008.
Ryan, Thomas Anthony, (Tony), 3 Oct. 2007.
Ryder, Eric Charles, 5 July 2008.

Saffman, Prof. Philip Geoffrey, FRS, 17 Aug. 2008.
Saint Laurent, Yves Henri Donat, 1 June 2008.
Samuels, Hon. Gordon Jacob, AC, CVO, 10 Dec. 2007.
Sanders, Cyril Woods, CB, 3 March 2008.
Sanders, Raymond Adrian, 2 March 2002.
Sanderson, Very Rev. (William) Roy, 19 June 2008.
Saunders, Prof. Derek William, CBE, 12 June 2008.
Savile, 3rd Baron; George Halifax Lumley-Savile, 2 June 2008.
Savill, Colonel Kenneth Edward, CVO, DSO, 29 Dec. 2007.
Sayce, Roy Beavan, 11 March 2008.
Sayeed, Dr (Abulfatah) Akram, OBE, 18 Jan. 2008.
Sayers, Prof. Bruce McArthur, 12 May 2008.
Scannell, Vernon, 16 Nov. 2007.
Scarascia-Mugnozza, Carlo, 13 May 2004.
Schermers, Prof. Henry Gerhard, 31 Aug. 2006.
Scofield, (David) Paul, CH, CBE, 19 March 2008.
Scothorne, Prof. Raymond John, 11 Sept. 2007.
Scott, Kenneth Farish, MC, 25 Dec. 2007.
Scott, Michael John, 30 May 2008.
Scott Wright, Prof. Margaret, 11 March 2008.
Serpell, Sir David Radford, KCB, CMG, OBE, 28 July 2008.
Seward, William Richard, 12 April 2008.
Shaughnessy, 4th Baron; Michael James Shaughnessy, 9 Dec. 2007.
Shaw, Dr Gavin Brown, CBE, 11 Nov. 2007.
Shearer, Magnus MacDonald, 22 July 2007.
Sheffield, John Vincent, CBE, 9 May 2008.
Sheldon, Bernard, CB, 19 Feb. 2008.
Shepperd, Sir Alfred Joseph, 15 Oct. 2007.
Sherrin, Edward George, (Ned), CBE, 1 Oct. 2007.
Shield, Leslie, TD, 16 June 2008.
Shipton, Sidney Lawrence, OBE, 12 Jan. 2008.
Sidey, Thomas Kay Stuart, CMG, 28 Oct. 2007.
Siegert, Air Vice-Marshal Cyril Laurence, CB, CBE, MVO, DFC, AFC, 17 Sept. 2007.
Simmons, Marion Adèle, QC, 2 May 2008.
Simpson, His Honour Keith Taylor, 5 May 2008.
Sinclair, Hon. Ian David, OC, QC, 7 April 2006.
Singhvi, Laxmi Mall, 6 Oct. 2007.
Sizer, Prof. John, CBE, 22 March 2008.

Slater, John Christopher Nash, QC, 11 Nov. 2007.
Small, (Charles) John, 24 May 2006.
Smallwood, John Frank Monton, CBE, 14 Dec. 2007.
Smith, Prof. Frederick Viggers, 6 July 2006.
Smith, Hedworth Cunningham, CBE, 15 March 2007.
Smith, Ian Douglas, 20 Nov. 2007.
Smith, James Ian, CB, 1 Dec. 2007.
Smith, Peter Graham, CB, 17 June 2008.
Smith, Roger Bonham, 29 Nov. 2007.
Snodgrass, John Michael Owen, CMG, 4 Feb. 2008.
Soeharto, General Mohamed, Hon. GCB, 27 Jan. 2008.
Solzhenitsyn, Alexander Isayevitch, 3 Aug. 2008.
Soulbury, 2nd Viscount; James Herwald Ramsbotham, 12 Dec. 2004.
Southerton, Thomas Henry, 27 June 2008.
Spanton, (Harry) Merrik, OBE, 11 Nov. 2007.
Spear, Prof. Walter Eric, FRS, 21 Feb. 2008.
Spearing, George David, 9 Feb. 2007.
Spencer, Prof. Anthony James Merrill, FRS, 26 Jan. 2008.
Spinney, Ronald Richard, CBE, 13 July 2008.
Spriggs, Elizabeth, 2 July 2008.
Stallard, Baron (Life Peer); Albert William Stallard, 29 March 2008.
Stanbury, Richard Vivian Macaulay, 29 June 2008.
Stanier, Field Marshal Sir John Wilfred, GCB, MBE, 10 Nov. 2007.
Staple, Rev. David, OBE, 26 Sept. 2007.
Stead, Rev. Canon (George) Christopher, FBA, 28 May 2008.
Steele, Kenneth Walter Lawrence, CBE, KPM, 14 April 2008.
Stevenson, WIlliam Trevor, CBE, 22 April 2008.
Stewart, James Cecil Campbell, CBE, 22 May 2008.
Stewart, Hon. Kevin James, AO, 22 Aug. 2006.
Stewart, Sir Robertson Huntly, CBE, 13 Aug. 2007.
Stockhausen, Karlheinz, 5 Dec. 2007.
Stokes, Baron (Life Peer); Donald Gresham Stokes, TD, 21 July 2008.
Straker, Rear-Adm. Bryan John, CB, OBE, 25 Dec. 2007.
Stuart, Michael Francis Harvey, 29 June 2008.
Suddaby, Arthur, CBE, 23 Jan. 2008.
Sumption, Anthony James Chadwick, DSC, 8 Jan. 2008.
Sumray, Monty, CBE, 2 June 2008.
Sutton, Sir Frederick Walter, OBE, 7 Dec. 2004.
Swartz, Col Hon. Sir Reginald William Colin, KBE, ED, 2 Feb. 2006.
Symington, Prof. Sir Thomas, 30 April 2007.

Tatlow, John Colin, 9 April 2008.
Taylor, David George Pendleton, CBE, 8 Nov. 2007.
Taylor, Sir Robert Richard, KCVO, OBE, 7 June 2008.
Telford, Sir Robert, CBE, 10 March 2008.
Tempany, Myles McDermott, OBE, 14 March 2008.
Temple, Sir Richard Anthony Purbeck, 4th Bt, MC, 5 Dec. 2007.
Templeton, Sir John Marks, 8 July 2008.
Thickett, Michael Godfrey, CMG, 20 June 2008.
Thoday, Prof. John Marion, FRS, 25 Aug. 2008.
Thomas of Gwydir, Baron (Life Peer); Peter John Mitchell Thomas, PC, QC, 4 Feb. 2008.
Thomas, Cedric Marshall, CBE, 26 Feb. 2008.
Thomas, Colin Agnew, 24 June 2008.
Thomas, David Hamilton Pryce, CBE, 1 Sept. 2008.
Thomas, Kenneth Rowland, OBE, 12 Aug. 2008.
Thompson, Maj.-Gen. Christopher Noel, CB, 9 Dec. 2007.
Thompson, Colin Edward, CBE, 5 Oct. 2007.
Thompson, Hon. Lindsay Hamilton Simpson, AO, CMG, 16 July 2008.
Thomson, Sir John Sutherland, (Sir Ian), KBE, CMG, 13 March 2008.
Thorne, Stanley George, 26 Nov. 2007.
Thurnham, Peter Giles, 10 May 2008.
Tickle, Brian Percival, CB, 18 May 2008.
Toganivalu, Ratu Josua Brown, CBE, Aug. 2002.
Tomkins, Sir Edward Emile, GCMG, CVO, 20 Sept. 2007.
Torrance, Very Rev. Prof. Thomas Forsyth, MBE, FBA, 2 Dec. 2007.
Toy, Sam, OBE, 24 March 2008.
Trant, Gen. Sir Richard Brooking, KCB, 3 Oct. 2007.
Trasenster, Michael Augustus Tulk, CVO, 17 July 2008.
Troup, Vice-Adm. Sir (John) Anthony (Rose), KCB, DSC, 8 July 2008.
Tsuji, Yoshifumi, 11 Feb. 2007.

Tuohy, Thomas, CBE, 12 March 2008.
Turner, Norman Henry, CBE, 8 Dec. 2007.
Tuti, Rt Rev. Dudley, KBE, 31 Jan. 2006.
Tweedsmuir, 3rd Baron; William de l'Aigle Buchan, 29 June 2008.

Valentine, (Christopher) Robert, 20 Dec. 2007.
Vallat, Prof. Sir Francis Aimé, GBE, KCMG, QC, 6 April 2008.
Vallings, Vice-Adm. Sir George Montague Francis, KCB, 25 Dec. 2007.
Vanderfelt, Sir Robin Victor, KBE, 29 Oct. 2007.
Varah, Rev. (Edward) Chad, CH, CBE, 8 Nov. 2007.
Varley, Baron (Life Peer); Eric Graham Varley, PC, 29 July 2008.
Vercoe, Rt Rev. Whakahuihui, PCNZM, MBE, 13 Sept. 2007.
Vernon, Sir Nigel John Douglas, 4th Bt, 4 Sept. 2007.
Vestey, Edmund Hoyle, 23 Nov. 2007.
Vickers, James Oswald Noel, OBE, 1 June 2008.
Vickers, Prof. Michael Douglas Allen, OBE, 16 Nov. 2007.
von Wechmar, Baron Rüdiger, Hon. GCVO, 17 Oct. 2007.

Walford, John Howard, 3 Feb. 2008.
Walker, James Findlay, QPM, 2 Oct. 2007.
Walker, Sir James Graham, MBE, 9 July 2004.
Walls, Prof. Eldred Wright, 24 March 2008.
Walters, Rear-Adm. John William Townshend, CB, 7 May 2008.
Ward, Prof. Alan Gordon, CBE, 3 Oct. 2007.
Wardlaw, Sir Henry John, 21st Bt, 8 Aug. 2005.
Warren, Jack Hamilton, OC, 2 April 2008.
Waterton, Sqdn Leader William Arthur, AFC, GM, 17 April 2006.
Watkins, Rt Hon. Sir Tasker, VC, GBE, PC, 9 Sept. 2007.
Watson, Rear-Adm. Alan George, CB, 25 Feb. 2008.
Watson, Henry, CBE, QPM, 22 Jan. 2004.
Watson, (John Hugh) Adam, CMG, 21 Aug. 2007.
Watts, Sir Arthur Desmond, KCMG, QC, 16 Nov. 2007.
Watts, John Francis, 14 May 2007.
Weatherstone, Sir Dennis, KBE, 13 June 2008.
Weaver, Oliver, QC, 18 April 2008.
Webb, George Hannam, CMG, OBE, 9 Dec. 2007.
Weissmüller, Alberto Augusto, 12 Oct. 2007.
Weller, Dr Thomas Huckle, 23 Aug. 2008.
Wesil, Dennis, 7 April 2008.
Whale, John Hilary, 17 June 2008.
Wheeler, Sir Charles (Cornelius-), CMG, 4 July 2008.
Wheler, Sir Edward Woodford, 14th Bt, 22 June 2008.
Wheway, Albert James, 17 Dec. 2007.
White, (Edward) Martin (Everatt), 26 Jan. 2008.
Whiteside, Prof. Derek Thomas, FBA, 22 April 2008.
Wigmore, His Honour James Arthur Joseph, 4 Dec. 2007.
Williams, Albert, 28 Nov. 2007.
Williams, Kevin Raymond, 20 Feb. 2008.
Williams, Paul Glyn, 10 Sept. 2008.
Willis, Air Chief Marshal Sir John Frederick, GBE, KCB, 9 Jan. 2008.
Willoughby, Kenneth James, 24 Dec. 2007.
Wilson, Ven. (John) Hewitt, CB, 29 June 2008.
Wilson, John Murray, MBE, 28 Dec. 2007.
Wilson, Leslie William, 7 Dec. 2007.
Wilson, Lynn Anthony, 9 July 2008.
Wiltshaw, Eve, OBE, 13 May 2008.
Winstanley, John, MC, TD, 4 Jan. 2008.
Wolf, Prof. Peter Otto, 6 Oct. 2007.
Woolhouse, Prof. John George, CBE, 1 Feb. 2008.
Woollcombe, Rt Rev. Kenneth John, 3 March 2008.
Woozley, Prof. Anthony Douglas, 6 April 2008.
Worthington, Prof. Brian Stewart, FRS, 9 Dec. 2007.
Wright, Stanley Harris, 23 July 2008.

Yates, Rt Rev. John, 26 Feb. 2008.
Young, Rt Rev. David Nigel de Lorentz, CBE, 10 Aug. 2008.
Young, Sir Richard Dilworth, 16 May 2008.

Zarnecki, Prof. Jerzy, (George), CBE, FBA, 8 Sept. 2008.

ABBREVIATIONS USED IN THIS BOOK

Some of the designatory letters in this list are used merely for economy of
space and do not necessarily imply any professional or other qualification.

A

AA	Anti-aircraft; Automobile Association; Architectural Association; Augustinians of the Assumption; Associate in Arts
AAA	Amateur Athletic Association; American Accounting Association
AAAL	American Academy of Arts and Letters
AA&QMG	Assistant Adjutant and Quartermaster-General
AAArb	Member, Association of Arbitrators (South Africa)
AAAS	American Association for the Advancement of Science
AABC	(Register of) Architects Accredited in Building Conservation
AAC	Army Air Corps; Amateur Athletic Club
AACE	Association for Adult and Continuing Education
AAF	Auxiliary Air Force (now see RAuxAF)
AAFCE	Allied Air Forces in Central Europe
AAG	Assistant Adjutant-General
AAI	Associate, Chartered Auctioneers' and Estate Agents' Institute (later, after amalgamation, ARICS)
AAIL	American Academy and Institute of Arts and Letters (now see AAAL)
AAM	Association of Assistant Mistresses in Secondary Schools
AAMC	Australian Army Medical Corps (now see RAAMC)
A&AEE	Aeroplane and Armament Experimental Establishment
A&E	Accident and Emergency
A&R	Artists and Repertoire
A and SH	Argyll and Sutherland Highlanders
AAPS	Aquatic and Atmospheric Physical Sciences
AAS	American Astronomical Society
AASA	Associate, Australian Society of Accountants (now see FCPA)
AASC	Australian Army Service Corps
AATSE	Australian Academy of Technological Sciences and Engineering
AAUQ	Associate in Accountancy, University of Queensland
AB	Bachelor of Arts (US); able-bodied seaman; airborne; Alberta (postal)
ABA	Amateur Boxing Association; Antiquarian Booksellers' Association; American Bar Association
ABBSI	Associate Member, British Boot and Shoe Institute
ABC	Australian Broadcasting Commission; American Broadcasting Companies; Amateur Boxing Club; Associate, Birmingham Conservatoire
ABCC	Association of British Chambers of Commerce
ABF	Army Benevolent Fund
ABI	Association of British Insurers
ABIA	Associate, Bankers' Institute of Australasia
ABINZ	Associate, Bankers' Institute of New Zealand
ABIPP	Associate, British Institute of Professional Photography
ABIS	Association of Burglary Insurance Surveyors
ABM	Advisory Board of Ministry
ABNM	American Board of Nuclear Medicine
ABP	Associated British Ports
Abp	Archbishop
ABPI	Association of British Pharmaceutical Industry
ABPsS	Associate, British Psychological Society (now see AFBPsS)
ABRC	Advisory Board for the Research Councils
ABSA	Association for Business Sponsorship of the Arts
ABSM	Associate, Birmingham and Midland Institute School of Music
ABTA	Association of British Travel Agents
ABTAPL	Association of British Theological and Philosophical Libraries
AC	Companion, Order of Australia; Ante Christum (before Christ)
ACA	Associate, Institute of Chartered Accountants
Acad.	Academy
ACARD	Advisory Council for Applied Research and Development
ACAS	Advisory, Conciliation and Arbitration Service; Assistant Chief of the Air Staff
ACC	Association of County Councils; Anglican Consultative Council
ACCA	Associate, Association of Chartered Certified Accountants (formerly Chartered Association of Certified Accountants)
ACCE	Association of County Chief Executives
ACCEL	American College of Cardiology Extended Learning
ACCM	Advisory Council for the Church's Ministry (now see ABM)
AcDip	Academic Diploma in the History of Art
ACDP	Australian Committee of Directors and Principals
ACDS	Assistant Chief of Defence Staff
ACE	Association of Consulting Engineers; Member, Association of Conference Executives; Allied Command Europe

ACENVO	Association of Chief Executives of National Voluntary Organisations (now see ACEVO)
ACEO	Association of Chief Education Officers
ACertCM	Archbishops' Certificate in Church Music
ACEVO	Association of Chief Executives of Voluntary Organisations
ACF	Army Cadet Force
ACFA	Army Cadet Force Association
ACFAS	Association Canadienne-Française pour l'avancement des sciences
ACFHE	Association of Colleges for Further and Higher Education
ACG	Assistant Chaplain-General
ACGI	Associate, City and Guilds of London Institute
ACGS	Assistant Chief of the General Staff
ACI	Airports Council International (Europe)
ACIArb	Associate, Chartered Institute of Arbitrators
ACIB	Associate, Chartered Institute of Bankers
ACIBS	Associate, Chartered Institute of Bankers in Scotland
ACII	Associate, Chartered Insurance Institute
ACIM	Associate, Chartered Institute of Marketing
ACIS	Associate, Institute of Chartered Secretaries and Administrators (formerly Chartered Institute of Secretaries)
ACLS	American Council of Learned Societies
ACM	Association of Computing Machinery
ACMA	Associate, Chartered Institute of Management Accountants (formerly Institute of Cost and Management Accountants)
ACMI	Associate, Chartered Management Institute
ACNS	Assistant Chief of Naval Staff
ACommA	Associate, Society of Commercial Accountants (now see ASCA)
ACORD	Advisory Committee on Research and Development
ACOS	Assistant Chief of Staff
ACOST	Advisory Council on Science and Technology
ACP	Association of Clinical Pathologists; Associate, College of Preceptors; African/Caribbean/Pacific
ACPO	Association of Chief Police Officers
ACR	Accredited Conservator-Restorer
ACRE	Action with Rural Communities in England
ACS	American Chemical Society; Additional Curates Society
acsc	passed Advanced Command and Staff Course
ACSEA	Allied Command South East Asia
ACSM	Associate, Camborne School of Mines
AcSS	Member, Academy of Learned Societies for the Social Sciences
ACT	Australian Capital Territory; Australian College of Theology; Associate, College of Technology; Association of Corporate Treasurers
ACTSS	Association of Clerical, Technical and Supervisory Staff
ACTT	Association of Cinematograph, Television and Allied Technicians
ACTU	Australian Council of Trade Unions
ACU	Association of Commonwealth Universities
ACWA	Associate, Institute of Cost and Works Accountants (now see ACMA)
AD	Dame of the Order of Australia; Anno Domini (in the year of the Lord); Air Defence
aD	ausser Dienst
ADAS	Agricultural Development and Advisory Service
ADB	Asian Development Bank; Associate of the Drama Board (Education)
ADB/F	African Development Bank/Fund
ADC	Aide-de-camp; Association of District Councils
ADCM	Archbishop of Canterbury's Diploma in Church Music
AD Corps	Army Dental Corps (now RADC)
ADC(P)	Personal Aide-de-camp to HM The Queen
ADEME	Assistant Director Electrical and Mechanical Engineering
Ad eund	Ad eundem gradum ; and see under aeg
ADFManc	Art and Design Fellow, Manchester
ADGMS	Assistant Director-General of Medical Services
ADipC	Advanced Postgraduate Diploma in Management Consulting
Adjt	Adjutant
ADJAG	Assistant Deputy Judge Advocate General
ADK	Order of Ahli Darjah Kinabalu
ADM	Advanced Diploma in Midwifery
Adm.	Admiral
ADMS	Assistant Director of Medical Services
ADOS	Assistant Director of Ordnance Services
ADP	Automatic Data Processing
ADPA	Associate Diploma of Public Administration

ADS&T	Assistant Director of Supplies and Transport
ADSS	Association of Directors of Social Services
Adv.	Advisory; Advocate
AdvDip	Advanced Diploma
ADVS	Assistant Director of Veterinary Services
ADWE&M	Assistant Director of Works, Electrical and Mechanical
AE	Air Efficiency Award
AEA	Atomic Energy Authority; Air Efficiency Award (*now see* AE); American Economic Association
AEAF	Allied Expeditionary Air Force
AEC	Agriculture Executive Council; Army Educational Corps (*now see* RAEC); Atomic Energy Commission
AECMA	Association Européenne des Constructeurs de Matériel Aérospatial
AEE	Atomic Energy Establishment
AEEU	Amalgamated Engineering and Electrical Union
AEF	Amalgamated Union of Engineering and Foundry Workers (later AEU, then AEEU); American Expeditionary Forces
aeg	*ad eundem gradum* (to the same degree-of the admission of a graduate of one university to the same degree at another without examination)
AEI	Associated Electrical Industries
AELTC	All England Lawn Tennis Club
AEM	Air Efficiency Medal
AER	Army Emergency Reserve
AERE	Atomic Energy Research Establishment (Harwell)
Æt., Ætat.	*Ætatis* (aged)
AEU	Amalgamated Engineering Union (later AEEU)
AEWVH	Association for the Education and Welfare of the Visually Handicapped
AF	Admiral of the Fleet
AFA	Amateur Football Alliance; Associate, Institute of Financial Accountants
AFAIAA	Associate Fellow, American Institute of Aeronautics and Astronautics
AFASIC	Association for All Speech Impaired Children
AFB	Air Force Base
AFBPsS	Associate Fellow, British Psychological Society
AFC	Air Force Cross; Association Football Club
AFCAI	Associate Fellow, Canadian Aeronautical Institute
AFCEA	Armed Forces Communications and Electronics Association
AFCENT	Allied Forces in Central Europe
AFD	Doctor of Fine Arts (US)
AFDS	Air Fighting Development Squadron
AFGE	Associate Fellow, Guild of Glass Engravers
AFHQ	Allied Force Headquarters
AFI	American Film Institute
AFIA	Associate, Federal Institute of Accountants (Australia)
AFIAP	Artiste, Fédération Internationale de l'Art Photographique
AFIAS	Associate Fellow, Institute of Aeronautical Sciences (US) (*now see* AFAIAA)
AFIMA	Associate Fellow, Institute of Mathematics and its Applications
AFM	Air Force Medal
AFNORTH	Allied Forces in Northern Europe
AFOM	Associate, Faculty of Occupational Medicine
AFRAeS	Associate Fellow, Royal Aeronautical Society (*now see* MRAeS)
AFRC	Agricultural and Food Research Council (*now see* BBSRC)
AFRSPSoc	Associate Fellow, Remote Sensing and Photogrammetry Society
AFSOUTH	Allied Forces in Southern Europe
AFV	Armoured Fighting Vehicles
AG	Attorney-General
AGAC	American Guild of Authors and Composers
AGARD	Advisory Group for Aerospace Research and Development
AGAvA	Associate, Guild of Aviation Artists
AGC	Adjutant General's Corps
AGH	Australian General Hospital
AGI	Alliance Graphique Internationale; Associate, Institute of Certificated Grocers
AGR	Advanced Gas-cooled Reactor
AGRA	Army Group Royal Artillery; Association of Genealogists and Record Agents
AGRI	Animal Genetic Resources Information
AGSM	Associate, Guildhall School of Music and Drama; Australian Graduate School of Management
AHA	Area Health Authority; American Hospitals Association; Associate, Institute of Health Service Administrators (later AHSM)
AHA(T)	Area Health Authority (Teaching)
AHI	Association of Heritage Interpretation
AHQ	Army Headquarters
AHRB	Arts and Humanities Research Board (*now see* AHRC)
AHRC	Arts and Humanities Research Council
AHSM	Associate, Institute of Health Services Management
AH-WC	Associate, Heriot-Watt College, Edinburgh
ai	*ad interim*
AIA	Associate, Institute of Actuaries; American Institute of Architects; Association of International Artists
AIAA	American Institute of Aeronautics and Astronautics
AIACE	Association Internationale des Anciens des Communautés Européennes
AIAgrE	Associate, Institution of Agricultural Engineers
AIAL	Associate Member, International Institute of Arts and Letters
AIAS	Associate Surveyor Member, Incorporated Association of Architects and Surveyors
AIB	Associate, Institute of Bankers (*now see* ACIB)
AIBD	Associate, Institute of British Decorators
AIBP	Associate, Institute of British Photographers
AIC	Agricultural Improvement Council; Associate of the Institute of Chemistry (later ARIC, MRIC; *now see* MRSC)
aic	armour infantry course
AICA	Associate Member, Commonwealth Institute of Accountants; Association Internationale des Critiques d'Art
AICE	Associate, Institution of Civil Engineers
AIChE	American Institute of Chemical Engineers
AICPA	American Institute of Certified Public Accountants
AICS	Associate, Institute of Chartered Shipbrokers
AICTA	Associate, Imperial College of Tropical Agriculture
AID	Artificial Insemination by Donor
AIDB	Accountancy Investigation Discipline Board
AIDS	Acquired Immunity Deficiency Syndrome
AIE	Associate, Institute of Education
AIEE	Associate, Institute of Electrical Engineers
AIF	Australian Imperial Forces
AIFireE	Associate, Institution of Fire Engineers
AIG	Adjutant-Inspector-General
AIH	Associate, Institute of Housing
AIHort	Associate, Institute of Horticulture
AIIA	Associate, Insurance Institute of America; Associate, Indian Institute of Architects
AIIMR	Associate, Institute of Investment Management and Research
AIIRA	Associate, International Industrial Relations Association
AIL	Associate, Institute of Linguists
AILA	Associate, Institute of Landscape Architects (later ALI)
AIM	Associate, Institution of Metallurgists (later MIM); Australian Institute of Management; Alternative Investment Market; Advanced Institute of Management Research
AIMarE	Associate, Institute of Marine Engineers
AIMBE	American Institute for Medical and Biological Engineering
AIMC	Associate, Institute of Management Consultants
AIME	American Institute of Mechanical Engineers
AIMgt	Associate, Institute of Management (*now see* ACMI)
AIMSW	Associate, Institute of Medical Social Work
AInstM	Associate Member, Institute of Marketing
AInstP	Associate, Institute of Physics
AInstPI	Associate, Institute of Patentees and Inventors
AIP	Association of Independent Producers
AIPR	Associate, Institute of Public Relations
AIProdE	Associate, Institution of Production Engineers
AIQS	Associate Member, Institute of Quantity Surveyors
AIRCENT	Allied Air Forces Central Europe
AIRTE	Associate, Institute of Road Transport Engineers
AIRTO	Association of Independent Research and Technology Organizations
AIS	Associate, Institute of Statisticians (later MIS)
AISA	Associate, Incorporated Secretaries' Association
AIStructE	Associate, Institution of Structural Engineers
AITI	Associate, Institute of Translators and Interpreters
AITP	Associate, Institute of Town Planners, India
AJAG	Assistant Judge Advocate General
AJEX	Association of Jewish Ex-Service Men and Women
AK	Knight, Order of Australia; Alaska (postal)
AKC	Associate, King's College London
AL	Alabama (postal)
ALA	Associate, Library Association (*now see* MCLIP); Association of London Authorities
Ala	Alabama
ALAA	Associate, Library Association of Australia
ALAI	Associate, Library Association of Ireland
ALAM	Associate, London Academy of Music and Dramatic Art
ALCD	Associate, London College of Divinity
ALCM	Associate, London College of Music
ALCM (TD)	Associate, London College of Music (Teaching Diploma)
ALCS	Authors Lending and Copyright Society
ALFSEA	Allied Land Forces South-East Asia
ALI	Argyll Light Infantry; Associate, Landscape Institute (*now see* MLI)
ALICE	Autistic and Language Impaired Children's Education
ALLC	Association for Literary and Linguistic Computing
ALP	Australian Labor Party
ALPSP	Association of Learned and Professional Society Publishers
ALS	Associate, Linnean Society; Amyotrophic Lateral Sclerosis
Alta	Alberta
ALVA	Association of Leading Visitor Attractions
AM	Albert Medal; Member, Order of Australia; Master of Arts (US); Alpes Maritimes

AMA	Association of Metropolitan Authorities; Assistant Masters Association (later AMMA, *now see* ATL); Associate, Museums Association; Australian Medical Association
AMARC	Associated Marine and Related Charities
Amb.	Ambulance; Ambassador
AMBIM	Associate Member, British Institute of Management (later AIMgt)
AMC	Association of Municipal Corporations
AMCST	Associate, Manchester College of Science and Technology
AMCT	Associate, Manchester College of Technology
AMDEA	Association of Manufacturers of Domestic Electrical Appliances
AME	Association of Municipal Engineers
AMEME	Association of Mining Electrical and Mechanical Engineers
AMet	Associate of Metallurgy
AMF	Australian Military Forces
AMFL	Allied Command Europe Mobile Force Land
AMICE	Associate Member, Institution of Civil Engineers (*now see* MICE)
AMIChemE	Associate Member, Institution of Chemical Engineers
AMIEE	Associate Member, Institution of Electrical Engineers (later MIEE)
AMIERE	Associate Member, Institution of Electronic and Radio Engineers
AMIMechE	Associate Member, Institution of Mechanical Engineers (*now see* MIMechE)
AMInstCE	Associate Member, Institution of Civil Engineers (*now see* MICE)
AmInstEE	American Institute of Electrical Engineers
AMINucE	Associate Member, Institution of Nuclear Engineers
AMIRSE	Associate Member, Institute of Railway Signalling Engineers
AMIStructE	Associate Member, Institution of Structural Engineers
AMMA	Assistant Masters & Mistresses Association (*now see* ATL)
AMN	Ahli Mangku Negara (Malaysia)
AMP	Advanced Management Program; Air Member for Personnel
AMRC	Association of Medical Research Charities
AMREF	African Medical and Research Foundation
AMRI	Associate Member, Royal Institution
AMRINA	Associate Member, Royal Institution of Naval Architects
AMRSH	Associate Member, Royal Society of Health
AMS	Assistant Military Secretary; Army Medical Services
AMSI	Associate Member, Securities Institute
AMSO	Air Member for Supply and Organisation
AMTE	Admiralty Marine Technology Establishment
AMTRI	Advanced Manufacturing Technology Research Institute
ANAF	Arab Non-Arab Friendship
Anat.	Anatomy; Anatomical
ANC	African National Congress
ANECInst	Associate, NE Coast Institution of Engineers and Shipbuilders
Anon.	Anonymously
ANU	Australian National University
ANZAAS	Australian and New Zealand Association for the Advancement of Science
Anzac	Australian and New Zealand Army Corps
AO	Officer, Order of Australia; Air Officer
AOA	Air Officer in charge of Administration
AOC	Air Officer Commanding
AOC-in-C	Air Officer Commanding-in-Chief
AOD	Army Ordnance Department
AOE	Alberta Order of Excellence
AOER	Army Officers Emergency Reserve
APA	American Psychiatric Association
APACS	Association of Payment and Clearing Systems
APD	Army Pay Department
APEX	Association of Professional, Executive, Clerical and Computer Staff
APHA	American Public Health Association
APIS	Army Photographic Intelligence Service
APM	Assistant Provost Marshal
APMI	Associate, Pensions Management Institute
APNI	Alliance Party of Northern Ireland
APR	Accredited Public Relations Practitioner
APS	Aborigines Protection Society; American Physical Society
APsSI	Associate, Psychological Society of Ireland
APSW	Association of Psychiatric Social Workers
APT&C	Administrative, Professional, Technical and Clerical
APTC	Army Physical Training Corps
AQ	Administration and Quartering
AQMG	Assistant Quartermaster-General
AR	Associated Rediffusion (Television); Arkansas (postal)
ARA	Associate, Royal Academy; Armada de la República Argentina
ARACI	Associate, Royal Australian Chemical Institute
ARAD	Associate, Royal Academy of Dancing
ARAeS	Associate, Royal Aeronautical Society
ARAgS	Associate, Royal Agricultural Societies (*ie* of England, Scotland and Wales)
ARAIA	Associate, Royal Australian Institute of Architects
ARAM	Associate, Royal Academy of Music
ARAS	Associate, Royal Astronomical Society

ARB	Architects' Registration Board
ARBA	Associate, Royal Society of British Artists
ARBS	Associate, Royal Society of British Sculptors
ARC	Architects' Registration Council (*now see* ARB); Agricultural Research Council (later AFRC); Aeronautical Research Council; Arthritis and Rheumatism Council
ARCA	Associate, Royal College of Art; Associate, Royal Canadian Academy
ARCamA	Associate, Royal Cambrian Academy of Art
ARCIC	Anglican-Roman Catholic International Commission
ARCM	Associate, Royal College of Music
ARCO	Associate, Royal College of Organists
ARCO(CHM)	Associate, Royal College of Organists with Diploma in Choir Training
ARCP	Affiliate, Royal College of Physicians
ARCPsych	Associate Member, Royal College of Psychiatrists
ARCS	Associate, Royal College of Science; Accreditation Review and Consulting Service (*now see* ISI)
ARCST	Associate, Royal College of Science and Technology (Glasgow)
ARCUK	Architects' Registration Council of the United Kingdom (*now see* ARB)
ARCVS	Associate, Royal College of Veterinary Surgeons
ARE	Associate, Royal Society of Painter-Printmakers (*formerly* of Painter-Etchers and Engravers); Arab Republic of Egypt; Admiralty Research Establishment
AREINZ	Associate, Real Estate Institute, New Zealand
ARELS	Association of Recognised English Language Schools
ARHistS	Associate, Royal Historical Society
ARIAS	Associate, Royal Incorporation of Architects in Scotland
ARIBA	Associate, Royal Institute of British Architects (*now see* RIBA)
ARIC	Associate, Royal Institute of Chemistry (later MRIC; *now see* MRSC)
ARICS	Professional Associate, Royal Institution of Chartered Surveyors (*now see* MRICS)
ARINA	Associate, Royal Institution of Naval Architects
ARLIS	Art Libraries Association
ARLT	Association for the Reform of Latin Teaching
ARMS	Associate, Royal Society of Miniature Painters
ARP	Air Raid Precautions
ARPS	Associate, Royal Photographic Society
ARR	Association of Radiation Research
ARRC	Associate, Royal Red Cross; Allied Command Europe Rapid Reaction Corps
ARSA	Associate, Royal Scottish Academy
ARSC	Association of Recorded Sound Collections
ARSCM	Associate, Royal School of Church Music
ARSM	Associate, Royal School of Mines
ARTC	Associate, Royal Technical College (Glasgow) (*now see* ARCST)
ARWA	Associate, Royal West of England Academy
ARWS	Associate, Royal Society of Painters in Water-Colours
AS	Anglo-Saxon
ASA	Associate Member, Society of Actuaries; Associate of Society of Actuaries (US); Australian Society of Accountants; Army Sailing Association; Advertising Standards Authority; Alment Aksjeselskap
ASAA	Associate, Society of Incorporated Accountants and Auditors
ASAI	Associate, Society of Architectural Illustrators
AS&TS of SA	Associated Scientific and Technical Societies of South Africa
ASAQS	Association of South African Quantity Surveyors
ASBAH	Association for Spina Bifida and Hydrocephalus
ASC	Administrative Staff College, Henley
ASCA	Associate, Society of Company and Commercial Accountants
ASCAB	Armed Services Consultant Approval Board
ASCAP	American Society of Composers, Authors and Publishers
ASCE	American Society of Civil Engineers
ASCHB	Association for Study of Conservation of Historic Buildings
ASCL	Association of School and College Leaders
AScW	Association of Scientific Workers (later ASTMS)
ASD	Armament Supply Department
ASE	Amalgamated Society of Engineers (later AUEW, then AEU, subsequently AEEU); Association for Science Education
ASEAN	Association of South East Asian Nations
ASH	Action on Smoking and Health
ASIAD	Associate, Society of Industrial Artists and Designers
ASIP	Associate, UK Society of Investment Professionals
ASLE	American Society of Lubrication Engineers
ASLEF	Associated Society of Locomotive Engineers and Firemen
ASLIB or Aslib	Association for Information Management (*formerly* Association of Special Libraries and Information Bureaux)
ASM	Association of Senior Members; Australian Service Medal
ASME	American Society of Mechanical Engineers; Association for the Study of Medical Education
ASO	Air Staff Officer
ASSC	Accounting Standards Steering Committee
ASSET	Association of Supervisory Staffs, Executives and Technicians (later ASTMS)
AssocEng	Associate of Engineering

AssocISI	Associate, Iron and Steel Institute
AssocMCT	Associateship of Manchester College of Technology
AssocMIAeE	Associate Member, Institution of Aeronautical Engineers
AssocRINA	Associate, Royal Institution of Naval Architects
AssocSc	Associate in Science
Asst	Assistant
ASTA	Association of Short Circuit Testing Authorities
ASTC	Administrative Service Training Course
ASTMS	Association of Scientific, Technical and Managerial Staffs (subsequently part of MSF)
ASTS	Army School of Training Support
ASVU	Army Security Vetting Unit
ASWE	Admiralty Surface Weapons Establishment
ATA	Air Transport Auxiliary
ATAE	Association of Tutors in Adult Education
ATAF	Allied Tactical Air Force
ATC	Air Training Corps; Art Teacher's Certificate
ATCDE	Association of Teachers in Colleges and Departments of Education (*now see* NATFHE)
ATCL	Associate, Trinity College of Music, London
ATD	Art Teacher's Diploma
ATI	Associate, Textile Institute
ATII	Associate Member, Chartered Institute (*formerly* Incorporated Institute, then Institute) of Taxation
ATL	Association of Teachers and Lecturers
ato	Ammunition Technical Officer
ATP	Association of Tennis Players
ATPL (A) or **(H)**	Airline Transport Pilot's Licence (Aeroplanes), or (Helicopters)
ATR (BC)	Art Therapist Registered (Board Certified)
ATS	Auxiliary Territorial Service (later WRAC)
ATTI	Association of Teachers in Technical Institutions (*now see* NATFHE)
ATV	Associated Television (*formerly* Association TeleVision)
AUA	American Urological Association; Association of University Administrators
AUCAS	Association of University Clinical Academic Staff
AUEW	Amalgamated Union of Engineering Workers (later AEU, then AEEU)
AUS	Army of the United States
AUT	Association of University Teachers
AVCC	Australian Vice-Chancellors' Committee
AVCM	Associate, Victoria College of Music
AVD	Army Veterinary Department
AVLA	Audio Visual Language Association
AVMA	Association for Victims of Medical Accidents
AVR	Army Volunteer Reserve
AWA	Anglian Water Authority
AWHCT	Associate, West Ham College of Technology
AWO	Association of Water Officers (*now see* IWO)
AWRE	Atomic Weapons Research Establishment
aws	Graduate of Air Warfare Course
AZ	Arizona (postal)

B

b	born; brother
BA	Bachelor of Arts
BAA	British Airports Authority; British Accounting Association
BAAB	British Amateur Athletic Board
BAAL	British Association for Applied Linguistics
BAAS	British Association for the Advancement of Science
BAB	British Airways Board
BAC	British Aircraft Corporation
BAcc	Bachelor of Accountancy
BaccPhil	Baccalaureate in Philosophy
BACM	British Association of Colliery Management
BACS	British Academy of Composers & Songwriters
BACSA	British Association for Cemeteries in South Asia
BACUP	British Association of Cancer United Patients
BADA	British American Drama Academy
BAe	British Aerospace
BAED	Bachelor of Arts in Environmental Design
B&FBS	British and Foreign Bible Society
BAFO	British Air Forces of Occupation
BAFPA	British Association of Fitness Promotion Agencies
BAFTA	British Academy of Film and Television Arts
BAG	Business Art Galleries
BAgrSc	Bachelor of Agricultural Science
BAI	*Baccalarius in Arte Ingeniaria* (Bachelor of Engineering)
BAIE	British Association of Industrial Editors
BALPA	British Air Line Pilots' Association
BAO	Bachelor of Art of Obstetrics
BAOMS	British Association of Oral and Maxillo-Facial Surgeons
BAOR	British Army of the Rhine (*formerly* on the Rhine)

BAOS	British Association of Oral Surgeons (*now see* BAOMS)
BAppSc(MT)	Bachelor of Applied Science (Medical Technology)
BAPS	British Association of Plastic Surgeons
BARB	Broadcasters' Audience Research Board
BARC	British Automobile Racing Club
BArch	Bachelor of Architecture
Bart	Baronet
BAS	Bachelor in Agricultural Science
BASc	Bachelor of Applied Science
BASCA	British Academy of Songwriters, Composers and Authors (*now see* BACS)
BASE	British Association for Service to the Elderly
BASEEFA	British Approvals Service for Electrical Equipment in Flammable Atmospheres
BASES	British Association of Sport and Exercise Sciences
BASHH	British Association for Sexual Health and HIV
BASW	British Association of Social Workers
Batt.	Battery
BBA	British Bankers' Association; Bachelor of Business Administration
BBB of C	British Boxing Board of Control
BBC	British Broadcasting Corporation
BBFC	British Board of Film Classification
BBS	Bachelor of Business Studies
BBSRC	Biotechnology and Biological Sciences Research Council
BC	Before Christ; British Columbia; Borough Council
BCA	Bachelor of Commerce and Administration
BCAR	British Civil Airworthiness Requirements
BCC	British Council of Churches (later CCBI)
BCE	Bachelor of Civil Engineering; Before the Christian Era
BCh or **BChir**	Bachelor of Surgery
BChD	Bachelor of Dental Surgery
BCIA	British Clothing Industries Association
BCL	Bachelor of Civil Law
BCMF	British Ceramic Manufacturers' Federation
BCMS	Bible Churchmen's Missionary Society
BCOF	British Commonwealth Occupation Force
BCom or **BComm**	Bachelor of Commerce
BComSc	Bachelor of Commercial Science
BCPC	British Crop Protection Council
BCS	Bengal Civil Service; British Computer Society; Bachelor of Combined Studies
BCSA	British Constructional Steelwork Association
BCSC	British Council of Shopping Centres
BCTS	Bristol Certificate in Theological Studies
BCURA	British Coal Utilization Research Association
BCYC	British Corinthian Yacht Club
BD	Bachelor of Divinity
Bd	Board
BDA	British Dental Association; British Deaf Association; British Dyslexia Association
Bde	Brigade
BDQ	Bachelor of Divinity Qualifying
BDS	Bachelor of Dental Surgery
BDSc	Bachelor of Dental Science
BE	Bachelor of Engineering; British Element
BEA	British East Africa; British European Airways; British Epilepsy Association
BEAMA	Federation of British Electrotechnical and Allied Manufacturers' Associations (*formerly* British Electrical and Allied Manufacturers' Association)
BE&A	Bachelor of Engineering and Architecture (Malta)
BEARR	British Emergency Aid for Russia and the Republics
BEC	Business Education Council (*now see* BTEC)
BEc	Bachelor of Economics
BECTU	Broadcasting, Entertainment, Cinematograph and Theatre Union
BEd	Bachelor of Education
Beds	Bedfordshire
BEE	Bachelor of Electrical Engineering
BEF	British Expeditionary Force; British Equestrian Federation
BEM	British Empire Medal
BEMAS	British Educational Management and Administration Society
BEME	Brigade Electrical and Mechanical Engineer
BEng	Bachelor of Engineering
BEO	Base Engineer Officer
Berks	Berkshire
BERR	Department for Business, Enterprise and Regulatory Reform
BES	Bachelor of Environmental Studies
BESO	British Executive Service Overseas
BEVA	British Equine Veterinary Association
BFA	Bachelor of Fine Arts
BFI	British Film Institute
BFMIRA	British Food Manufacturing Industries Research Association
BFPO	British Forces Post Office
BFSS	British Field Sports Society
BFUW	British Federation of University Women (*now see* BFWG)
BFWG	British Federation of Women Graduates

BGCStJ	Bailiff Grand Cross, Most Venerable Order of the Hospital of St John of Jerusalem
BGS	Brigadier General Staff
BHA	British Hospitality Association
Bhd	Berhad
BHF	British Heart Foundation
BHL	Bachelor of Hebrew Letters
BHRA	British Hydromechanics Research Association
BHRCA	British Hotels, Restaurants and Caterers' Association (*now see* BHA)
BHS	British Horse Society
BI	British Invisibles
BIBA	British Insurance Brokers' Association
BIBRA	British Industrial Biological Research Association
BICC	British Insulated Callender's Cables
BICERA	British Internal Combustion Engine Research Association (*now see* BICERI)
BICERI	British Internal Combustion Engine Research Institute
BICSc	British Institute of Cleaning Science
BIDA	British Interior Design Association
BIEC	British Invisible Exports Council (*now see* BI)
BIEE	British Institute of Energy Economics
BIFA	British Independent Film Awards
BIFU	Banking Insurance and Finance Union
BII	British Institute of Innkeeping
BIIBA	British Insurance & Investment Brokers' Association (*now see* BIBA)
BIM	British Institute of Management
BIR	British Institute of Radiology
BIS	Bank for International Settlements; British Interplanetary Society
BISF	British Iron and Steel Federation
BISFA	British Industrial and Scientific Film Association
BISPA	British Independent Steel Producers Association
BISRA	British Iron and Steel Research Association
BITC	Business in the Community
BJ	Bachelor of Journalism
BJOG	British Journal of Obstetrics and Gynaecology
BJP	Bharatiya Janata Party
BJSM	British Joint Services Mission
BJur	Bachelor of Law
BKSTS	British Kinematograph, Sound and Television Society
BL	Bachelor of Law; British Library
BLA	British Liberation Army
BLDSA	British Long Distance Swimming Association
BLE	Bachelor of Land Economy
BLegS	Bachelor of Legal Studies
BLESMA	British Limbless Ex-Servicemen's Association
BLitt	Bachelor of Letters
BM	British Museum; Bachelor of Medicine; Brigade Major; British Monomark
BMA	British Medical Association
BMedSci	Bachelor of Medical Science
BMEO	British Middle East Office
BMet	Bachelor of Metallurgy
BMEWS	Ballistic Missile Early Warning System
BMG	British Military Government
BMH	British Military Hospital
BMilSc	Bachelor of Military Science
BMJ	British Medical Journal
BMM	British Military Mission
BMR	Bureau of Mineral Resources
BMRA	Brigade Major Royal Artillery
Bn	Battalion
BNA	British Nursing Association
BNAF	British North Africa Force
BNC	Brasenose College
BNEC	British National Export Council
BNF	British National Formulary
BNFL	British Nuclear Fuels Ltd
BNOC	British National Oil Corporation; British National Opera Company
BNP	Banque Nationale de Paris
BNSC	British National Space Centre
BNSc	Bachelor of Nursing Science
BOAC	British Overseas Airways Corporation
BoT	Board of Trade
Bot.	Botany; Botanical
BOTB	British Overseas Trade Board
BOU	British Ornithologists' Union
Bp	Bishop
BPA	British Paediatric Association (later CPCH; *now see* RCPCH); Bachelor of Performing Arts
BPG	Broadcasting Press Guild
BPharm	Bachelor of Pharmacy
BPIF	British Printing Industries Federation
BPMF	British Postgraduate Medical Federation

BProc	Bachelor of Procurationis
BPsS	British Psychological Society
BR	British Rail
Br.	Branch
BRA	Brigadier Royal Artillery; British Rheumatism & Arthritis Association
BRB	British Railways Board
BRCS	British Red Cross Society
BRE	Building Research Establishment
Brig.	Brigadier
BRIT	British Recording Industry Trust
BritIRE	British Institution of Radio Engineers (*now see* IERE)
BRNC	Britannia Royal Naval College
BRS	British Road Services
BRTP	Bachelor of Regional and Town Planning
BRurSc	Bachelor of Rural Science
BS	Bachelor of Surgery; Bachelor of Science; British Standard
BSA	Bachelor of Scientific Agriculture; Birmingham Small Arms; Building Societies' Association
BSAA	British South American Airways
BSAP	British South Africa Police
BSAS	British Society of Animal Science
BSBI	Botanical Society of the British Isles
BSC	British Steel Corporation; Bengal Staff Corps
BSc	Bachelor of Science
BScA, BScAgr	Bachelor of Science in Agriculture
BSc(Dent)	Bachelor of Science in Dentistry
BScEcon	Bachelor of Science in Economics
BScEng	Bachelor of Science in Engineering
BSc (Est. Man.)	Bachelor of Science in Estate Management
BScN	Bachelor of Science in Nursing
BScSoc	Bachelor of Social Sciences
BSE	Bachelor of Science in Engineering (US); Bovine Spongiform Encephalopathy
BSEE	Bachelor of Science in Electrical Engineering
BSES	British Schools Exploring Society
BSF	British Salonica Force
BSFA	British Science Fiction Association
BSFS	Bachelor of Science in Foreign Service
BSI	British Standards Institution
BSIA	British Security Industry Association
BSJA	British Show Jumping Association
BSME	Bachelor of Science in Mechanical Engineering; British Society of Magazine Editors
BSN	Bachelor of Science in Nursing
BSNS	Bachelor of Naval Science
BSocSc	Bachelor of Social Science
BSocStud	Bachelor of Social Studies
BSRA	British Ship Research Association
BSRIA	Building Services Research and Information Association
BSS	Bachelor of Science (Social Science)
BSSc	Bachelor of Social Science
BST	Bachelor of Sacred Theology
BSurv	Bachelor of Surveying
BSW	Bachelor of Social Work
BT	Bachelor of Teaching; British Telecommunications
Bt	Baronet; Brevet
BTA	British Tourist Authority (*formerly* British Travel Association)
BTC	British Transport Commission
BTCV	British Trust for Conservation Volunteers
BTDB	British Transport Docks Board (*now see* ABP)
BTEC	Business and Technology (*formerly* Technician) Education Council
BTh	Bachelor of Theology
BTP	Bachelor of Town Planning
BTS	Bachelor of Theological Studies
Btss	Baroness
BUAS	British Universities Association of Slavists
Bucks	Buckinghamshire
BUGB	Baptist Union of Great Britain
BUNAC	British Universities North America Club
BUPA	British United Provident Association
BURA	British Urban Regeneration Association
BV	Besloten Vennootschap
BVA	British Veterinary Association; British Video Association
BVC	Bar Vocational Course
BVetMed	Bachelor of Veterinary Medicine
BVI	British Virgin Islands
BVM	Blessed Virgin Mary
BVMS	Bachelor of Veterinary Medicine and Surgery
BVPA	British Veterinary Poultry Association
BVSc	Bachelor of Veterinary Science
BWI	British West Indies
BWM	British War Medal

C

C	Conservative; 100
c	child; cousin; *circa* (about)
CA	Central America; County Alderman; Chartered Accountant (Scotland and Canada); California (postal)
CAA	Civil Aviation Authority
CAABU	Council for the Advancement of Arab and British Understanding
CAAV	(Member of) Central Association of Agricultural Valuers
CAB	Citizens' Advice Bureau; Centre for Agricultural and Biosciences (*formerly* Commonwealth Agricultural Bureau)
CABE	Commission for Architecture and the Built Environment
CACTM	Central Advisory Council of Training for the Ministry (later ACCM; *now see* ABM)
CAER	Conservative Action for Electoral Reform
CAF	Charities Aid Foundation
CAFCASS	Child and Family Court Advisory and Support Service
CAFOD	Catholic Agency for Overseas Development
CAJ	Committee on the Administration of Justice
CALE	Canadian Army Liaison Executive
Calif	California
CAM	Communications, Advertising and Marketing
Cambs	Cambridgeshire
CAMC	Canadian Army Medical Corps
CAMRA	Campaign for Real Ale
CAMS	Certificate of Advanced Musical Study
CAMW	Central Association for Mental Welfare
C&G	City and Guilds of London Institute
Cantab	*Cantabrigiensis* (of Cambridge)
Cantuar	*Cantuariensis* (of Canterbury)
CAP	Common Agricultural Policy
Capt.	Captain
CARD	Campaign against Racial Discrimination
CARDS	Community Assistance for Reconstruction, Development and Stabilisation
CARE	Cottage and Rural Enterprises
CARICOM	Caribbean Community
CARIFTA	Caribbean Free Trade Area (*now see* CARICOM)
Carms	Carmarthenshire
CAS	Chief of the Air Staff
CASE	Council for the Advancement and Suppport of Education
CASI	Canadian Aeronautics and Space Institute
CAT	College of Advanced Technology; Countryside Around Towns
CATE	Council for the Accreditation of Teacher Education
Cav.	Cavalry
CAWU	Clerical and Administrative Workers' Union (later APEX)
CB	Companion, Order of the Bath; County Borough
CBC	County Borough Council
CBCO	Central Board for Conscientious Objectors
CBE	Commander, Order of the British Empire
CBI	Confederation of British Industry
CBII	Companion, British Institute of Innkeeping
CBIM	Companion, British Institute of Management (later CIMgt)
CBiol	Chartered Biologist
CBNS	Commander British Navy Staff
CBS	Columbia Broadcasting System
CBSI	Chartered Building Societies Institute (*now see* CIB)
CBSO	City of Birmingham Symphony Orchestra
CC	Companion, Order of Canada; City Council; County Council; Cricket Club; Cycling Club; County Court
CCAB	Consultative Committee of Accountancy Bodies
CCAHC	Central Council for Agricultural and Horticultural Co-operation
CCBE	Commission Consultative des Barreaux de la Communauté Européenne
CCBI	Council of Churches for Britain and Ireland (*now see* CTBI)
CCC	Corpus Christi College; Central Criminal Court; County Cricket Club
CCE	Chartered Civil Engineer
CCETSW	Central Council for Education and Training in Social Work
CCF	Combined Cadet Force
CCFM	Combined Cadet Forces Medal
CCG	Control Commission Germany
CCH	Cacique's Crown of Honour, Order of Service of Guyana
CChem	Chartered Chemist
CCHMS	Central Committee for Hospital Medical Services
CCIA	Commission of Churches on International Affairs
CCIPD	Companion, Chartered Institute of Personnel and Development
CCIS	Command Control Information System
CCJ	Council of Christians and Jews
CCLRC	Council for the Central Laboratory of the Research Councils
CCMI	Companion, Chartered Management Institute
CCMS	Committee on the Challenges of Modern Society
CCPR	Central Council of Physical Recreation
CCQI	Companion, Chartered Quality Institute
CCRA	Commander Corps of Royal Artillery
CCRE	Commander Corps of Royal Engineers

CCREME	Commander Corps of Royal Electrical and Mechanical Engineers
CCRSigs	Commander Corps of Royal Signals
CCS	Casualty Clearing Station; Ceylon Civil Service; Countryside Commission for Scotland
CCSU	Council of Civil Service Unions
CCTA	Commission de Coöpération Technique pour l'Afrique; Central Computer and Telecommunications Authority
CCTS	Combat Crew Training Squadron
CD	Canadian Forces Decoration; Commander, Order of Distinction (Jamaica); Civil Defence; Compact Disc
CDA	Co-operative Development Agency; Christian Democratic Alliance
CDC	Centers for Disease Control and Prevention
CDEE	Chemical Defence Experimental Establishment
CDipAF	Certified Diploma in Accounting and Finance
CDir	Chartered Director
CDISS	Centre for Defence and International Security Studies
Cdo	Commando
CDRA	Committee of Directors of Research Associations
Cdre	Commodore
CDS	Chief of the Defence Staff
CDU	Christlich-Demokratische Union
CE	Civil Engineer
CEA	Central Electricity Authority
CEC	Commission of the European Communities
CECD	Confédération Européenne du Commerce de Détail
CECG	Consumers in European Community Group
CEDA	Committee for Economic Development of Australia
CEDEP	Centre Européen d'Education Permanente
CEDR	Centre for Effective Dispute Resolution
CEE	Communauté Economique Européenne
CEED	Centre for Economic and Environmental Development
CEF	Canadian Expeditionary Force
CeFA	Certificate for Financial Advisers
CEFAS	Centre for Environment, Fisheries and Aquaculture Science
CEFIC	Conseil Européen des Fédérations de l'Industrie Chimique
CEGB	Central Electricity Generating Board
CEH	Centre for Ecology & Hydrology
CEI	Council of Engineering Institutions
CEIR	Corporation for Economic and Industrial Research
CEM	Council of European Municipalities (*now see* CEMR); College of Emergency Medicine
CEMA	Council for the Encouragement of Music and Arts
CeMAP	Certificate in Mortgage Advice and Practice
CeMGA	Centre for the Measurement of Government Activity
CEMR	Council of European Municipalities and Regions
CEMS	Church of England Men's Society
CEN	Comité Européen de Normalisation
CENELEC	European Committee for Electrotechnical Standardization
CEng	Chartered Engineer
Cento	Central Treaty Organisation
CEnv	Chartered Environmentalist
CEO	Chief Executive Officer
CEPES	Comité européen pour le progrès économique et social
CEPS	Center for Economic Policy Studies
CEPT	Conférence Européenne des Postes et des Télécommunications
CeRGI	Certificate of Regulated General Insurance
CERL	Central Electricity Research Laboratories
CERN	Organisation (*formerly* Centre) Européenne pour la Recherche Nucléaire
CERT	Charities Effectiveness Review Trust
CertCPE	Certificate in Clinical Pastoral Education
CertDS	Certificate in Dramatic Studies
Cert Ed	Certificate of Education
CertHE	Certificate in Higher Education
CertITP	Certificate of International Teachers' Program (Harvard)
CertTP	Certificate in Town Planning
CEST	Centre for Exploitation of Science and Technology
CET	Council for Educational Technology
CETSW	Council for Education and Training in Social Work
CF	Chaplain to the Forces; Companion, Order of Fiji
CFA	Canadian Field Artillery
CFE	Central Fighter Establishment
CFM	Cadet Forces Medal
CFPS	Certificate of Further Professional Studies
CFR	Commander, Order of the Federal Republic of Nigeria
CFS	Central Flying School; Chronic Fatigue Syndrome
CGA	Community of the Glorious Ascension; Country Gentlemen's Association
CGeog	Chartered Geographer
CGeol	Chartered Geologist
CGIA	Insignia Award of City and Guilds of London Institute (*now see* FCGI)
CGLI	City and Guilds of London Institute (*now see* C&G)
CGM	Conspicuous Gallantry Medal
CGRM	Commandant-General Royal Marines

CGS	Chief of the General Staff
CH	Companion of Honour
Chanc.	Chancellor; Chancery
Chap.	Chaplain
ChapStJ	Chaplain, Order of St John of Jerusalem (*now see* ChStJ)
CHAR	Campaign for the Homeless and Rootless
CHB	Companion of Honour of Barbados
ChB	Bachelor of Surgery
CHC	Community Health Council
Ch.Ch.	Christ Church
CHE	Campaign for Homosexual Equality
CHIU	Committee for Heads of Irish Universities
ChLJ	Chaplain, Order of St Lazarus of Jerusalem
(CHM)	*see under* ARCO(CHM), FRCO(CHM)
ChM	Master of Surgery
Chm.	Chairman or Chairwoman
CHN	Community of the Holy Name
CHSC	Central Health Services Council
ChStJ	Chaplain, Most Venerable Order of the Hospital of St John of Jerusalem
CI	Imperial Order of the Crown of India; Channel Islands
CIA	Chemical Industries Association; Central Intelligence Agency
CIAD	Central Institute of Art and Design
CIAgrE	Companion, Institution of Agricultural Engineers
CIAL	Corresponding Member of the International Institute of Arts and Letters
CIArb	Chartered Institute of Arbitrators
CIB	Chartered Institute of Bankers
CIBS	Chartered Institution of Building Services (*now see* CIBSE)
CIBSE	Chartered Institution of Building Services Engineers
CIC	Chemical Institute of Canada
CICAP	Criminal Injuries Compensation Appeal Panel
CICB	Criminal Injuries Compensation Board
CICHE	Committee for International Co-operation in Higher Education
CICI	Confederation of Information Communication Industries
CID	Criminal Investigation Department
CIE	Companion, Order of the Indian Empire; Confédération Internationale des Etudiants
CIEx	Companion, Institute of Export
CIFE	Council (*formerly* Conference) for Independent Further Education
CIGasE	Companion, Institution of Gas Engineers (*now see* CIGEM)
CIGEM	Companion, Institution of Gas Engineers and Managers
CIGRE	Conférence Internationale des Grands Réseaux Electriques
CIGS	Chief of the Imperial General Staff (*now see* CGS)
CIHM	Companion, Institute of Healthcare Management
CIHR	Canadian Institutes of Health Research
CIIA	Canadian Institute of International Affairs
CIL	*Corpus inscriptionum latinarum*
CILT	Chartered Institute of Logistics and Transport
CIM	China Inland Mission; Chartered Institute of Marketing
CIMA	Chartered Institute of Management Accountants
CIMarE	Companion, Institute of Marine Engineers
CIMEMME	Companion, Institution of Mining Electrical and Mining Mechanical Engineers
CIMgt	Companion, Institute of Management (*now see* CCMI)
CIMGTechE	Companion, Institution of Mechanical and General Technician Engineers
CIMO	Commission for Instruments and Methods of Observation
CIMR	Cambridge Institute for Medical Research
C-in-C	Commander-in-Chief
CINCHAN	Allied Commander-in-Chief Channel
CInstLM	Companion, Institute of Leadership and Management
CINOA	Confédération Internationale des Négotiants en Œuvres d'Art
CIOB	Chartered Institute of Building
CIPA	Chartered Institute of Patent Agents
CIPD	Companion, Institute of Personnel and Development (*now see* CCIPD); Chartered Institute of Personnel and Development
CIPFA	Chartered Institute of Public Finance and Accountancy
CIPL	Comité International Permanent des Linguistes
CIPM	Companion, Institute of Personnel Management (later CIPD)
CIPR	Chartered Institute of Public Relations
CIQA	Companion, Institute of Quality Assurance (*now see* CCQI)
CIR	Commission on Industrial Relations
CIRES	Co-operative Institute for Research in Environmental Sciences
CIRIA	Construction Industry Research and Information Association
CIRP	Collège Internationale pour Recherche et Production
CIS	Institute of Chartered Secretaries and Administrators (*formerly* Chartered Institute of Secretaries); Command Control Communications and Information Systems; Commonwealth of Independent States
CISAC	Confédération Internationale des Sociétés d'Auteurs et Compositeurs; Centre for International Security and Arms Control
CIT	Chartered Institute of Transport; California Institute of Technology
CITB	Construction Industry Training Board
CITD	Certificate of Institute of Training and Development
CITP	Chartered Information Technology Professional
CIU	Club and Institute Union
CIV	City Imperial Volunteers
CIWEM	Chartered Institution of Water and Environmental Management
CJ	Chief Justice
CJM	Congregation of Jesus and Mary (Eudist Fathers)
CL	Commander, Order of Leopold
cl	*cum laude*
Cl.	Class
CLA	Country Land & Business Association (*formerly* Country Landowners' Association)
CLIC	Cancer and Leukemia in Childhood
CLIP	Chartered Institute of Library and Information Professionals
CLit	Companion of Literature (Royal Society of Literature Award)
CLJ	Commander, Order of St Lazarus of Jerusalem
CLP	Constituency Labour Party
CLRAE	Congress (*formerly* Conference) of Local and Regional Authorities of Europe
CLY	City of London Yeomanry
CM	Member, Order of Canada; Congregation of the Mission (Vincentians); Master in Surgery; Certificated Master; Canadian Militia
CMA	Canadian Medical Association; Cost and Management Accountant (NZ)
CMAC	Catholic Marriage Advisory Council
CMarSci	Chartered Marine Scientist
CMath	Chartered Mathematician
CMB	Central Midwives' Board
CMC	Certified Management Consultant
CME	Continuing Ministerial Education
CMet	Chartered Meteorologist
CMF	Commonwealth Military Forces; Central Mediterranean Force
CMG	Companion, Order of St Michael and St George
CMILT	Chartered Member, Chartered Institute of Logistics and Transport
CMIWSc	Certified Member, Institute of Wood Science
CMJ	Commander, Supreme Military Order of the Temple of Jerusalem
CMLJ	Commander of Merit, Order of St Lazarus of Jerusalem
CMM	Commander, Order of Military Merit (Canada)
CMO	Chief Medical Officer
CMP	Corps of Military Police (*now see* CRMP)
CMS	Church Mission (*formerly* Church Missionary) Society; Certificate in Management Studies
CMT	Chaconia Medal of Trinidad
CNAA	Council for National Academic Awards
CND	Campaign for Nuclear Disarmament
CNI	Companion, Nautical Institute
CNO	Chief of Naval Operations
CNOCS	Captain Naval Operational Command Systems
CNR	Canadian National Railways
CNRS	Centre National de la Recherche Scientifique
CNZM	Companion, New Zealand Order of Merit
CO	Commanding Officer; Commonwealth Office (after Aug. 1966) (*now see* FCO); Colonial Office (before Aug. 1966); Conscientious Objector; Colorado (postal)
Co.	County; Company
Coal.L or Co.L	Coalition Liberal
Coal.U or Co.U	Coalition Unionist
COBSEO	Confederation of British Service and Ex-Service Organisations
CODEST	Committee for the Development of European Science and Technology
C of E	Church of England
C of I	Church of Ireland
C of S	Chief of Staff; Church of Scotland
COHSE	Confederation of Health Service Employees
COI	Central Office of Information
CoID	Council of Industrial Design (*now* Design Council)
Col	Colonel
Coll.	College; Collegiate
Colo	Colorado
Col.-Sergt	Colour-Sergeant
Com	Communist
Comd	Command
Comdg	Commanding
Comdr	Commander
Comdt	Commandant
COMEC	Council of the Military Education Committees of the Universities of the UK
COMET	Committee for Middle East Trade
Commn	Commission
Commnd	Commissioned
CompAMEME	Companion, Association of Mining Electrical and Mechanical Engineers
CompICE	Companion, Institution of Civil Engineers
CompIEE	Companion, Institution of Electrical Engineers (later FIEE)

CompIERE	Companion, Institution of Electronic and Radio Engineers
CompIGasE	Companion, Institution of Gas Engineers
CompILE	Companion, Institution of Lighting Engineers
CompIMechE	Companion, Institution of Mechanical Engineers
CompInstE	Companion, Institute of Energy
CompInstMC	Companion, Institute of Measurement and Control
CompIWES	Companion, Institution of Water Engineers and Scientists
CompOR	Companion, Operational Research Society
CompTI	Companion of the Textile Institute
Comr	Commissioner
Comy-Gen.	Commissary-General
CON	Commander, Order of the Niger
ConfEd	Confederation of Education Service Managers
Conn	Connecticut
Const.	Constitutional
CONUL	Council of National and University Librarians
Co-op.	Co-operative
COPA	Comité des Organisations Professionels Agricoles de la CEE
COPEC	Conference of Politics, Economics and Christianity
COPUS	Committee on the Public Understanding of Science
Corp.	Corporation; Corporal
Corresp. Mem.	Corresponding Member
COS	Chief of Staff; Charity Organization Society
COSA	Colliery Officials and Staffs Association
CoSIRA	Council for Small Industries in Rural Areas
COSLA	Convention of Scottish Local Authorities
COSPAR	Committee on Space Research
COSSAC	Chief of Staff to Supreme Allied Commander
COTC	Canadian Officers' Training Corps
CP	Central Provinces; Cape Province; Congregation of the Passion
CPA	Commonwealth Parliamentary Association; Chartered Patent Agent; Certified Public Accountant (USA)
CPAG	Child Poverty Action Group
CPAS	Church Pastoral Aid Society
CPC	Conservative Political Centre
CPCH	College of Paediatrics and Child Health (*now see* RCPCH)
CPE	Common Professional Examination
CPEng	Chartered Professional Engineer (of Institution of Engineers of Australia)
CPFA	Member or Associate, Chartered Institute of Public Finance and Accountancy
CPHVA	Community Practitioners & Health Visitors' Association
CPhys	Chartered Physicist
CPL	Chief Personnel and Logistics
CPLS	Certificate of Professional Legal Studies
CPM	Colonial Police Medal
CPR	Canadian Pacific Railway
CPRE	Campaign to Protect Rural England (*formerly* Council for the Protection of Rural England)
CPRW	Campaign for the Protection of Rural Wales
CPS	Crown Prosecution Service; Certificate in Pastoral Studies
CPSA	Civil and Public Services Association (*now see* PCS); Church of the Province of South Africa
CPSM	Council for Professions Supplementary to Medicine
CPSU	Communist Party of the Soviet Union
CPsychol	Chartered Psychologist
CPU	Commonwealth Press Union
CQ	Chevalier, National Order of Quebec
CQI	Chartered Quality Institute
CQSW	Certificate of Qualification in Social Work
CR	Community of the Resurrection
cr	created or creation
CRA	Commander, Royal Artillery
CRAC	Careers Research and Advisory Centre
CRadP	Chartered Radiation Protection Professional
CRAeS	Companion, Royal Aeronautical Society
CRAG	Clinical Resources and Audit Group
CRASC	Commander, Royal Army Service Corps
CRC	Cancer Research Campaign (*now see* CRUK); Community Relations Council
CRCP(C)	Certificant, Royal College of Physicians of Canada
CRE	Commander, Royal Engineers; Commission for Racial Equality; Commercial Relations and Exports; Conference of Rectors of European Universities (*formerly* Association of European Universities)
Cres.	Crescent
CRMP	Corps of Royal Military Police
CRNCM	Companion, Royal Northern College of Music
CRO	Commonwealth Relations Office (*now see* FCO)
CRSNZ	Companion, Royal Society of New Zealand
CRUK	Cancer Research United Kingdom
CS	Civil Service; Clerk to the Signet; Companion, Order of Samoa
CSA	Confederate States of America; Child Support Agency
CSAB	Civil Service Appeal Board
CSB	Bachelor of Christian Science
CSC	Conspicuous Service Cross; Congregation of the Holy Cross
CSCA	Civil Service Clerical Association (later CPSA)

CSCE	Conference on Security and Co-operation in Europe
CSci	Chartered Scientist
CSD	Civil Service Department; Co-operative Secretaries Diploma; Chartered Society of Designers
CSDE	Central Servicing Development Establishment
CSEU	Confederation of Shipbuilding and Engineering Unions
CSFI	Centre for Study of Financial Innovation
CSG	Companion, Order of the Star of Ghana; Company of the Servants of God
CSI	Companion, Order of the Star of India
CSIR	Commonwealth Council for Scientific and Industrial Research (*now see* CSIRO); Council of Scientific and Industrial Research, India
CSIRO	Commonwealth Scientific and Industrial Research Organization (Australia)
CSM	Civil Service Medal (Fiji)
CSO	Chief Scientific Officer; Chief Signal Officer; Chief Staff Officer; Central Statistical Office (*now see* ONS)
CSP	Chartered Society of Physiotherapists; Civil Service of Pakistan
CSS	Companion, Star of Sarawak; Council for Science and Society; Certificate in Social Studies
CSSB	Civil Service Selection Board
CSSD	Czech Social Democratic Party
CSSp	Holy Ghost Father
CSSR	Congregation of the Most Holy Redeemer (Redemptorist Order)
CStat	Chartered Statistician
CSTI	Council of Science and Technology Institutes
CStJ	Commander, Most Venerable Order of the Hospital of St John of Jerusalem
CSU	Christlich-Soziale Union in Bayern
CSV	Community Service Volunteers
CSW	Certificate in Social Work
CT	Connecticut (postal)
CTA	Chaplain Territorial Army; Chartered Tax Adviser
CTB	College of Teachers of the Blind
CTBI	Churches Together in Britain and Ireland
CTC	Cyclists' Touring Club; Commando Training Centre; City Technology College
CText	Chartered Textile Technologist
CTh	Certificate in Theology
CU	Cambridge University
CUAC	Cambridge University Athletic Club; Colleges and Universities of the Anglican Communion
CUAFC	Cambridge University Association Football Club
CUBC	Cambridge University Boat Club
CUCC	Cambridge University Cricket Club
CUF	Common University Fund
CUHC	Cambridge University Hockey Club
CUMS	Cambridge University Musical Society
CUNY	City University of New York
CUP	Cambridge University Press
CUPGRA	Cambridge University Postgraduate Research Association
CURUFC	Cambridge University Rugby Union Football Club
CV	Cross of Valour (Canada)
CVCP	Committee of Vice-Chancellors and Principals of the Universities of the United Kingdom (*now see* UUK)
CVO	Commander, Royal Victorian Order
CVS	Council for Voluntary Service
CVSNA	Council of Voluntary Service National Association
CWA	Crime Writers Association
CWGC	Commonwealth War Graves Commission
CWS	Co-operative Wholesale Society
CWU	Communication Workers Union

D

D	Duke
d	died; daughter
DA	Dame of St Andrew, Order of Barbados; Diploma in Anaesthesia; Diploma in Art; Doctor of Arts
DAA	Diploma in Archive Administration
DAA&QMG	Deputy Assistant Adjutant and Quartermaster-General
DAAD	Designers and Art Directors Association
DAAG	Deputy Assistant Adjutant-General
DA&QMG	Deputy Adjutant and Quartermaster-General
DAC	Development Assistance Committee; Diocesan Advisory Committee
DAcad	Doctor of the Academy
DACG	Deputy Assistant Chaplain-General
DACLAM	Diplomate, American College of Laboratory Animal Medicine
DACOS	Deputy Assistant Chief of Staff
DAD	Deputy Assistant Director
DAdmin	Doctor of Administration
DADMS	Deputy Assistant Director of Medical Services
DADOS	Deputy Assistant Director of Ordnance Services
DADQ	Deputy Assistant Director of Quartering

DADST	Deputy Assistant Director of Supplies and Transport
DAEd	Diploma in Art Education
DAG	Deputy Adjutant-General
DAgr	Doctor of Agriculture
DAgrFor	Doctor of Agriculture and Forestry
DAMS	Deputy Assistant Military Secretary
D&AD	Design and Art Direction (*formerly* Designers and Art Directors Association)
DAppSc	Doctor of Applied Science
DAQMG	Deputy Assistant Quartermaster-General
DArch	Doctor of Architecture
DArt	Doctor of Art
DArts	Doctor of Arts
DASc	Doctor in Agricultural Sciences
DASS	Diploma in Applied Social Studies
DATA	Draughtsmen's and Allied Technicians' Association (later AUEW(TASS))
DATEC	Art and Design Committee, Technician Education Council
DAvMed	Diploma in Aviation Medicine, Royal College of Physicians
DBA	Doctor of Business Administration
DBE	Dame Commander, Order of the British Empire
DBTS	Diploma in Biblical and Theological Studies
DC	District Council; District of Columbia
DCA	Doctor of Creative Arts; Department for Constitutional Affairs
DCAe	Diploma of College of Aeronautics
DCAS	Deputy Chief of the Air Staff
DCB	Dame Commander, Order of the Bath
DCC	Diploma of Chelsea College
DCCH	Diploma in Community Child Health
DCDS	Deputy Chief of Defence Staff
DCE	Diploma of a College of Education
DCG	Deputy Chaplain-General
DCGS	Deputy Chief of the General Staff
DCh	Doctor of Surgery
DCH	Diploma in Child Health
DCHS	Dame Commander, Order of the Holy Sepulchre
DCL	Doctor of Civil Law; Dr of Canon Law
DCLG	Department for Communities and Local Government
DCLI	Duke of Cornwall's Light Infantry
DCLJ	Dame Commander, Order of St Lazarus of Jerusalem
DCM	Distinguished Conduct Medal
DCMG	Dame Commander, Order of St Michael and St George
DCMS	Department for Culture, Media and Sport
DCnL	Doctor of Canon Law
DCNZM	Distinguished Companion, New Zealand Order of Merit
DCO	Duke of Cambridge's Own
DCom or DComm	Doctor of Commerce
DCP	Diploma in Clinical Pathology; Diploma in Conservation of Paintings
DCS	Deputy Chief of Staff; Doctor of Commercial Sciences
DCSF	Department for Children, Schools and Families
DCSG	Dame Commander, Order of St Gregory the Great
DCSO	Deputy Chief Scientific Officer
DCT	Doctor of Christian Theology
DCVO	Dame Commander, Royal Victorian Order
DD	Doctor of Divinity
DDAM	Diploma in Disability Assessment Medicine
DDes	Doctor of Design
DDGAMS	Deputy Director General, Army Medical Services
DDH	Diploma in Dental Health
DDL	Deputy Director of Labour
DDME	Deputy Director of Mechanical Engineering
DDMI	Deputy Director of Military Intelligence
DDMO	Deputy Director of Military Operations
DDMS	Deputy Director of Medical Services
DDMT	Deputy Director of Military Training
DDNI	Deputy Director of Naval Intelligence
DDO	Diploma in Dental Orthopaedics
DDPH	Diploma in Dental Public Health
DDPR	Deputy Director of Public Relations
DDPS	Deputy Director of Personal Services
DDR	Deutsche Demokratische Republik
DDRA	Deputy Director Royal Artillery
DDra	Doctor of Drama
DDS	Doctor of Dental Surgery; Director of Dental Services
DDSc	Doctor of Dental Science
DDSD	Deputy Director Staff Duties
DDSM	Defense Distinguished Service Medal
DDST	Deputy Director of Supplies and Transport
DDWE&M	Deputy Director of Works, Electrical and Mechanical
DE	Doctor of Engineering; Delaware (postal)
DEA	Department of Economic Affairs
DEc	Doctor of Economics
DECC	Department of Energy and Climate Change
decd	deceased
DEconSc	Doctor of Economic Science

DEd	Doctor of Education
DEFRA	Department for Environment, Food and Rural Affairs
Deleg.	Delegate
DEME	Directorate of Electrical and Mechanical Engineering
DEMS	Defensively Equipped Merchant Ships
(DemU)	Democratic Unionist
DenD	Docteur en Droit
DEng	Doctor of Engineering
DenM	Docteur en Médecine
DEOVR	Duke of Edinburgh's Own Volunteer Rifles
DEP	Department of Employment and Productivity; European Progressive Democrats
Dep.	Deputy
DERA	Defence Evaluation and Research Agency
DES	Department of Education and Science (later DFE); Dr in Environmental Studies
DèsL	Docteur ès lettres
DèS or DèsSc	Docteur ès sciences
DesRCA	Designer of the Royal College of Art
DESU	Diplôme d'Etudes Supérieures d'Université
DETR	Department of the Environment, Transport and the Regions
DFA	Doctor of Fine Arts
DFAS	Decorative and Fine Art Society
DFC	Distinguished Flying Cross
DFE	Department for Education (later DFEE)
DFEE or DfEE	Department for Education and Employment (later DFES)
DFES or DfES	Department for Education and Skills
DFFP	Diploma in Fertility and Family Planning
DFH	Diploma of Faraday House
DFID	Department for International Development
DFil	Doctor en Filosofía
DFLS	Day Fighter Leaders' School
DFM	Distinguished Flying Medal
DFPHM	Diplomate Member, Faculty of Public Health Medicine
DfT	Department for Transport
DG	Director General; Directorate General; Dragoon Guards
DGAA	Distressed Gentlefolks Aid Association
DGAMS	Director-General Army Medical Services
DGCHS	Dame Grand Cross, Order of the Holy Sepulchre
DGDP	Diploma in General Dental Practice, Royal College of Physicians
DGEME	Director General Electrical and Mechanical Engineering
DGLP(A)	Director General Logistic Policy (Army)
DGMS	Director-General of Medical Services
DGMT	Director-General of Military Training
DGMW	Director-General of Military Works
DGNPS	Director-General of Naval Personal Services
DGP	Director-General of Personnel
DGPS	Director-General of Personal Services
DGS	Diploma in Graduate Studies
DGStJ	Dame of Grace, Order of St John of Jerusalem (*now see* DStJ)
DGU	Doctor of Griffith University
DH	Doctor of Humanities
DHA	District Health Authority
Dhc	Doctor *honoris causa*
DHE	Defence Housing Executive
DHEW	Department of Health Education and Welfare (US)
DHL	Doctor of Humane Letters; Doctor of Hebrew Literature
DHLitt	Doctor of Humane Letters
DHM	Dean Hole Medal
DHMSA	Diploma in the History of Medicine (Society of Apothecaries)
DHQ	District Headquarters
DHS	Dame, Order of the Holy Sepulchre
DHSS	Department of Health and Social Security
DHum	Doctor of Humanities
DHumLit	Doctor of Humane Letters
DIA	Diploma in Industrial Administration
DIAS	Dublin Institute of Advanced Sciences
DIB	Doctor of International Business
DIC	Diploma of the Imperial College
DICTA	Diploma of Imperial College of Tropical Agriculture
DIG	Deputy Inspector-General
DIH	Diploma in Industrial Health
DIMP	Darjah Indera Mahkota Pahang (Malaysia)
DIntLaw	Diploma in International Law
Dio.	Diocese
DipA	Diploma of Arts in Theology
DipAA	Diploma in Applied Art
DipAD	Diploma in Art and Design
DipAE	Diploma in Adult Education
DipAe	Diploma in Aeronautics
DipAgr	Diploma in Agriculture
DipArch	Diploma in Architecture
DipASE	Diploma in Advanced Study of Education, College of Preceptors
DipASS	Diploma in Applied Social Studies
DipBA	Diploma in Business Administration
DipBS	Diploma in Fine Art, Byam Shaw School

DipCAM	Diploma in Communications, Advertising and Marketing of CAM Foundation	**DLittS**	Doctor of Sacred Letters
DipCC	Diploma of the Central College	**DLJ**	Dame of Grace, Order of St Lazarus of Jerusalem
DipCD	Diploma in Civic Design	**DLO**	Diploma in Laryngology and Otology
DipCE	Diploma in Civil Engineering; Diploma of a College of Education (Scotland)	**DLP**	Diploma in Legal Practice
		DLR	Docklands Light Railway
DipCons	Diploma in Conservation	**DM**	Doctor of Medicine
DipECLAM	Diplomate, European College of Laboratory Animal Medicine	**DMA**	Diploma in Municipal Administration
DipEcon	Diploma in Economics	**DMan**	Doctor of Management
DipECVO	Diploma in Veterinary Ophthalmology, European College of Veterinary Ophthalmologists	**DMCC**	Diploma in the Medical Care of Catastrophe, Society of Apothecaries
DipEd	Diploma in Education	**DMD**	Doctor of Medical Dentistry (Australia)
DipEE	Diploma in Electrical Engineering	**DME**	Director of Mechanical Engineering
DipEl	Diploma in Electronics	**DMet**	Doctor of Metallurgy
DipESL	Diploma in English as a Second Language	**DMI**	Director of Military Intelligence
DipEth	Diploma in Ethnology	**DMin**	Doctor of Ministry
DipEurHum	Diploma in European Humanities	**DMiss**	Doctor of Missiology
DipEVPC	Diplomate, European Veterinary Parasitology College	**DMJ**	Diploma in Medical Jurisprudence
DipFBOM	Diploma in Farm Business Organisation and Management	**DMJ(Path)**	Diploma in Medical Jurisprudence (Pathology)
DipFD	Diploma in Funeral Directing	**DMLJ**	Dame of Merit, Order of St Lazarus of Jerusalem
DipFE	Diploma in Further Education	**DMO**	Director of Military Operations
DipFM	Diploma in Forensic Medicine; Diploma in Financial Management	**DMR**	Diploma in Medical Radiology
		DMRD	Diploma in Medical Radiological Diagnosis
DipFMS	Diploma in Forensic Medicine and Science	**DMRE**	Diploma in Medical Radiology and Electrology
DipGSM	Diploma in Music, Guildhall School of Music and Drama	**DMRT**	Diploma in Medical Radio-Therapy
DipHA	Diploma in Hospital Administration	**DMS**	Director of Medical Services; Decoration for Meritorious Service (South Africa); Diploma in Management Studies
DipHE	Diploma in Higher Education		
DipHSM	Diploma in Health Services Management	**DMSc**	Doctor of Medical Science
DipHIC	Diploma in Hospital Infection Control	**DMSSB**	Direct Mail Services Standards Board
DipHum	Diploma in Humanities	**DMT**	Director of Military Training
DipHV	Diploma in Health Visiting	**DMus**	Doctor of Music
DipICArb	Diploma in International Commercial Arbitration	**DN**	Diploma in Nursing
DipIT	Diploma in Information Technology	**DNB**	Dictionary of National Biography
DipLA	Diploma in Landscape Architecture	**DNE**	Director of Naval Equipment
DipLaw	Diploma in Law	**DNH**	Department of National Heritage
DipLib	Diploma of Librarianship	**DNI**	Director of Naval Intelligence
DipLLP	Diploma in Law and Legal Practice	**DNZM**	Dame Companion, New Zealand Order of Merit
DipLP	Diploma in Legal Practice	**DO**	Diploma in Ophthalmology
DipLS	Diploma of Legal Studies	**DOAE**	Defence Operational Analysis Establishment
DipM	Diploma in Marketing	**DObstRCOG**	Diploma of Royal College of Obstetricians and Gynaecologists (*now see* DRCOG)
DipMed	Diploma in Medicine		
DipMin	Diploma in Ministry	**DOC**	District Officer Commanding
DipN	Diploma in Nursing	**DocArts**	Doctor of Arts
DipNEC	Diploma of Northampton Engineering College (*now* City University)	**DocEng**	Doctor of Engineering
		DoE	Department of the Environment
DIPP	Diploma of Interventional Pain Practice	**DoH**	Department of Health
DipPA	Diploma of Practitioners in Advertising (*now see* DipCAM)	**DoI**	Department of Industry
DipPE	Diploma in Physical Education	**DOL**	Doctor of Oriental Learning
DipPSA	Diploma in Public Service Administration	**Dom.**	*Dominus* (Lord)
DipPSW	Diploma in Psychiatric Social Work	**DOMS**	Diploma in Ophthalmic Medicine and Surgery
DipRE	Diploma in Religious Education	**DOR**	Director of Operational Requirements
DipREM	Diploma in Rural Estate Management	**DOrthRCS**	Diploma in Orthodontics, Royal College of Surgeons
DipSMS	Diploma in School Management Studies	**DOS**	Director of Ordnance Services; Doctor of Ocular Science
DipSoc	Diploma in Sociology	**DP**	Data Processing
DipSocSc	Diploma in Social Science	**DPA**	Diploma in Public Administration; Discharged Prisoners' Aid; Doctor of Public Administration
DipSRAA	Diploma in the Study of Records and Administration of Archives		
DipStat	Diploma in Statistics	**DPD**	Diploma in Public Dentistry
DipSW	Diploma in Social Work	**DPEc**	Doctor of Political Economy
DipTA	Diploma in Tropical Agriculture	**DPed**	Doctor of Pedagogy
DipT&CP	Diploma in Town and Country Planning	**DPH**	Diploma in Public Health
DipTh	Diploma in Theology	**DPh or DPhil**	Doctor of Philosophy
DipTMHA	Diploma in Training and Further Education of Mentally Handicapped Adults	**DPharm**	Doctor of Pharmacy
		DPhilMed	Diploma in Philosophy of Medicine
DipTP	Diploma in Town Planning	**DPhysMed**	Diploma in Physical Medicine
DipTPT	Diploma in Theory and Practice of Teaching	**DPLG**	Diplômé par le Gouvernement
DipTRP	Diploma in Town and Regional Planning	**DPM**	Diploma in Psychological Medicine; Diploma in Personnel Management
DipYCS	Diploma in Youth and Community Studies		
DIS	Diploma in Industrial Studies	**DPMS**	Dato Paduka Mahkota Selangor (Malaysia)
DistTP	Distinction in Town Planning	**DPMSA**	Diploma in Philosophy and Ethics of Medicine, Society of Apothecaries
DIur	Doctor of Law		
DIUS	Department for Innovation, Universities and Skills	**DPP**	Director of Public Prosecutions
Div.	Division; Divorced	**DPR**	Director of Public Relations
Div.Test	Divinity Testimonium (of Trinity College, Dublin)	**DPS**	Director of Postal Services; Director of Personal Services; Doctor of Public Service; Diploma in Pastoral Studies
DJAG	Deputy Judge Advocate General		
DJPD	Dato Jasa Purba Di-Raja Negeri Sembilan (Malaysia)	**DPSA**	Diploma in Public and Social Administration
DJStJ	Dame of Justice, Order of St John of Jerusalem (*now see* DStJ)	**DPSE**	Diploma in Professional Studies in Education
		DPSM	Diploma in Public Sector Management
DJur	*Doctor Juris* (Doctor of Law)	**DPsych**	Doctor of Psychology
DK	Most Esteemed Family Order (Brunei)	**DQMG**	Deputy Quartermaster-General
DL	Deputy Lieutenant; Democratie Libérale	**Dr**	Doctor
DLAS	Diploma in Laboratory Animal Science, Royal College of Veterinary Surgeons	**DRA**	Defence Research Agency (later DERA)
		DRAC	Director Royal Armoured Corps
DLaws	Doctor of Laws	**DRC**	Diploma of Royal College of Science and Technology, Glasgow
DLC	Diploma of Loughborough College	**DRCOG**	Diploma of Royal College of Obstetricians and Gynaecologists
DLES	Doctor of Letters in Economic Studies	**DRD**	Diploma in Restorative Dentistry
DLI	Durham Light Infantry	**Dr ing**	Doctor of Engineering
DLIS	Diploma in Library and Information Studies	**Dr jur**	Doctor of Laws
DLit or DLitt	Doctor of Literature; Doctor of Letters	**DrŒcPol**	*Doctor Œconomiæ Politicæ* (Doctor of Political Economy)

Dr phil	Doctor of Philosophy
Dr rer. nat.	Doctor of Natural Science
Dr rer. pol.	Doctor of Political Science
Dr rer. soc. oec.	Doctor of Social and Economic Sciences
DRS	Diploma in Religious Studies
Drs	Doctorandus
DRSAMD	Diploma of the Royal Scottish Academy of Music and Drama
DS	Directing Staff; Doctor of Science
DSA	Diploma in Social Administration
DSAC	Defence Scientific Advisory Council
DSAO	Diplomatic Service Administration Office
DSC	Distinguished Service Cross
DSc	Doctor of Science
DScA	Docteur en sciences agricoles
DSc(Eng)	Doctor of Engineering Science
DSCHE	Diploma of the Scottish Council for Health Education
DSCM	Diploma of the Sydney Conservatorium of Music
DScMil	Doctor of Military Science
DSc (SocSci)	Doctor of Science in Social Science
DSD	Director Staff Duties; Diploma in Speech and Drama
DSF	Director Special Forces
DSG	Dame, Order of St Gregory the Great
DSIR	Department of Scientific and Industrial Research (later SRC; then SERC)
DSL	Doctor of Sacred Letters
DSLJ	Dato Seri Laila Jasa (Brunei)
DSM	Distinguished Service Medal
DSNB	Dato Setia Negara Brunei
DSNS	Dato Setia Negeri Sembilan (Malaysia)
DSO	Companion of the Distinguished Service Order
DSocSc	Doctor of Social Science
DSP	Director of Selection of Personnel; Docteur en sciences politiques (Montreal)
dsp	*decessit sine prole* (died without issue)
DSport	Doctor of Sport
DSS	Department of Social Security; Doctor of Sacred Scripture
Dss	Deaconess
DSSc	Doctor of Social Science
DST	Director of Supplies and Transport
DStJ	Dame of Grace, Most Venerable Order of the Hospital of St John of Jerusalem; Dame of Justice, Most Venerable Order of the Hospital of St John of Jerusalem
DSTL	Defence Science and Technology Laboratory
DTA	Diploma in Tropical Agriculture
DTech	Doctor of Technology
DTH	Diploma in Tropical Hygiene
DTh or **DTheol**	Doctor of Theology
DThPT	Diploma in Theory and Practice of Teaching
DTI	Department of Trade and Industry
DTLR	Department for Transport, Local Government and the Regions
DTM&H	Diploma in Tropical Medicine and Hygiene
DU or **DUniv**	Honorary Doctor of the University
Dunelm	*Dunelmensis* (of Durham)
DUP	Democratic Unionist Party; Docteur de l'Université de Paris
DVA	Diploma of Veterinary Anaesthesia
DVH	Diploma in Veterinary Hygiene
DVLA	Driver and Vehicle Licensing Authority
DVLC	Driver and Vehicle Licensing Centre
DVM or **DVetMed**	Doctor of Veterinary Medicine
DVMS or **DVM&S**	Doctor of Veterinary Medicine and Surgery
DVO	Driver, Vehicle and Operator
DVOphthal	Diploma in Veterinary Ophthalmology
DVR	Diploma in Veterinary Radiology
DVSc	Doctor of Veterinary Science
DVSM	Diploma in Veterinary State Medicine
DWP	Department for Work and Pensions

E

E	East; Earl; England
e	eldest
EA	Environment Agency
EAA	Edinburgh Architectural Association
EACR	European Association for Cancer Research
EADS	European Aeronautics Defence and Space Company
EAF	East African Forces
EAGA	Energy Action Grants Agency
EAHY	European Architectural Heritage Year
EAP	East Africa Protectorate
EASD	European Association of Securities Dealers
EAW	Electrical Association for Women
EBC	English Benedictine Congregation
Ebor	*Eboracensis* (of York)
EBRD	European Bank for Reconstruction and Development
EBSQ-Vasc	European Board of Surgery Qualification in Vascular Surgery

EBU	European Broadcasting Union
EC	Etoile du Courage (Canada); European Community; European Commission; Emergency Commission
ECA	Economic Co-operation Administration; Economic Commission for Africa
ECAFE	Economic Commission for Asia and the Far East (*now see* ESCAP)
ECB	England and Wales Cricket Board
ECCTIS	Education Courses and Credit Transfer Information Systems
ECE	Economic Commission for Europe
ECGD	Export Credits Guarantee Department
ECHR	European Court of Human Rights
ECLA	Economic Commission for Latin America
ECLAC	United Nations Economic Commission for Latin America and the Caribbean
ECOSOC	Economic and Social Committee of the United Nations
ECSC	European Coal and Steel Community
ED	Efficiency Decoration; Doctor of Engineering (US); European Democrat
ed	edited
EdB	Bachelor of Education
EDC	Economic Development Committee
EdD	Doctor of Education
EDF	European Development Fund
EDG	European Democratic Group; Employment Department Group
Edin.	Edinburgh
Edn	Edition
EDP	Executive Development Programme
EdS	Specialist in Education
Educ	Educated
Educn	Education
EEA	European Environment Agency
EEC	European Economic Community (*now see* EC); Commission of the European Communities
EEF	Engineering Employers' Federation; Egyptian Expeditionary Force
EEIBA	Electrical and Electronic Industries Benevolent Association
EETPU	Electrical Electronic Telecommunication & Plumbing Union (later AEEU)
EETS	Early English Text Society
EFCE	European Federation of Chemical Engineering
EFIAP	Excellence, Fédération Internationale de l'Art Photographique
EFTA	European Free Trade Association
eh	ehrenhalber (honorary)
EI	East Indian; East Indies
EIA	Engineering Industries Association
EIB	European Investment Bank
EIEMA	Electrical Installation Equipment Manufacturers' Association
E-in-C	Engineer-in-Chief
EIS	Educational Institute of Scotland
EISCAT	European Incoherent Scatter Association
EIU	Economist Intelligence Unit
ELBS	English Language Book Society
ELDR	European Liberal, Democrat and Reform Party
ELSE	European Life Science Editors
ELT	English Language Teaching
EM	Edward Medal; Earl Marshal
EMBL	European Molecular Biology Laboratory
EMBO	European Molecular Biology Organisation
EMEA	European Medicines Agency (formerly European Agency for the Evaluation of Medical Products); Europe, Middle East and Africa
EMI	European Monetary Institute
EMP	Electro Magnetic Pulse; Executive Management Program Diploma
EMS	Emergency Medical Service
EMU	European Monetary Union
Eng.	England
Engr	Engineer
ENO	English National Opera
ENSA	Entertainments National Service Association
ENT	Ear Nose and Throat
ENTO	Employment National Training Organisation
EO	Executive Officer
EOC	Equal Opportunities Commission
EOPH	Examined Officer of Public Health
EORTC	European Organisation for Research on Treatment of Cancer
EP	European Parliament
EPICC	European Process Industries Competitiveness Centre
EPOS	Electronic Point of Sale
EPP	European People's Party
EPSRC	Engineering and Physical Sciences Research Council
EPsS	Experimental Psychology Society
er	elder
ER	Eastern Region (BR); East Riding
ERA	Electrical Research Association
ERC	Electronics Research Council

ERD	Emergency Reserve Decoration (Army)
ESA	European Space Agency
ESART	Environmental Services Association Research Trust
ESCAP	Economic and Social Commission for Asia and the Pacific
ESCP-EAP	Ecole Supérieure de Commerce de Paris-Ecole des Affaires de Paris
ESF	European Science Foundation
ESL	English as a Second Language
ESNS	Educational Sub-Normal Serious
ESOL	English for Speakers of Other Languages
ESP	English for Special Purposes
ESPID	European Society for Paediatric Infectious Diseases
ESRC	Economic and Social Research Council; Electricity Supply Research Council
ESRO	European Space Research Organization (now see ESA)
ESSKA	European Society for Surgery of the Knee and Arthroscopy
ESTA	European Science and Technology Assembly
ESU	English-Speaking Union
ETA	Engineering Training Authority
ETH	Eidgenössische Technische Hochschule
ETS	Educational and Training Services
ETS(A)	Educational and Training Services (Army)
ETU	Electrical Trades Union
ETUC	European Trade Union Confederation
ETUCE	European Trade Union Committee for Education
EU	European Union
EUDISED	European Documentation and Information Service for Education
Euratom	European Atomic Energy Community
EurBiol	European Biologist (now see EurProBiol)
EurChem	European Chemist
EurGeol	European Geologist
Eur Ing	European Engineer
EUROM	European Federation for Optics and Precision Mechanics
EurProBiol	European Professional Biologist
EUW	European Union of Women
eV	eingetragener Verein
EVPC	European Veterinary Parasitology College
Ext	Extinct; external

F

FA	Football Association
FAA	Fellow, Australian Academy of Science; Fleet Air Arm
FAAAI	Fellow, American Association for Artificial Intelligence
FAAAS	Fellow, American Association for the Advancement of Science
FAAO	Fellow, American Academy of Optometry
FAAP	Fellow, American Academy of Pediatrics
FAARM	Fellow, American Academy of Reproductive Medicine
FAAV	Fellow, Central Association of Agricultural Valuers
FAAVCT	Fellow, American Academy of Veterinary and Comparative Toxicology
FABE	Fellow, Association of Building Engineers
FACC	Fellow, American College of Cardiology
FACCA	Fellow, Association of Certified and Corporate Accountants (now see FCCA)
FACCP	Fellow, American College of Chest Physicians
FACD	Fellow, American College of Dentistry
FACDS	Fellow, Australian College of Dental Surgeons (now see FRACDS)
FACE	Fellow, Australian College of Educators (formerly of Education)
FACerS	Fellow, American Ceramic Society
FAChAM	Fellow, Australasian Chapter of Addiction Medicine, Royal Australian College of Physicians
FAChPM	Fellow, Australasian Chapter of Palliative Medicine, Royal Australian College of Physicians
FACHSE	Fellow, Australian College of Health Service Executives
FACI	Fellow, Australian Chemical Institute (now see FRACI)
FACM	Fellow, Associaton of Computing Machinery
FACMA	Fellow, Australian College of Medical Administrators (now see FRACMA)
FACMG	Fellow, American College of Medicinal Genetics
FACOG	Fellow, American College of Obstetricians and Gynæcologists
FACOM	Fellow, Australian College of Occupational Medicine
FACP	Fellow, American College of Physicians
FACPM	Fellow, American College of Preventive Medicine
FACR	Fellow, American College of Radiology
FACRM	Fellow, American College of Rehabilitation Medicine
FACS	Fellow, American College of Surgeons
FACVSc	Fellow, Australian College of Veterinary Scientists
FACVT	Fellow, American College of Veterinary Toxicology (now see FAAVCT)
FADM	Fellow, Academy of Dental Materials
FADO	Fellow, Association of Dispensing Opticians
FAEM	Faculty of Accident and Emergency Medicine (now see CEM)
FAeSI	Fellow, Aeronautical Society of India
FAFPHM	Fellow, Australian Faculty of Public Health Medicine

FAGS	Fellow, American Geographical Society
FAHA	Fellow, Australian Academy of the Humanities; Fellow, American Heart Association
FAI	Fellow, Chartered Auctioneers' and Estate Agents' Institute (now (after amalgamation) see FRICS); Fédération Aéronautique Internationale
FAIA	Fellow, American Institute of Architects; Fellow, Association of International Accountants
FAIAA	Fellow, American Institute of Aeronautics and Astronautics
FAIAS	Fellow, Australian Institute of Agricultural Science (now see FAIAST)
FAIAST	Fellow, Australian Institute of Agricultural Science and Technology
FAIB	Fellow, Australian Institute of Bankers
FAIBF	Fellow, Australasian Institute of Bankers + Finance
FAIBiol	Fellow, Australian Institute of Biology
FAICD	Fellow, Australian Institute of Company Directors
FAIE	Fellow, Australian Institute of Energy
FAIEx	Fellow, Australian Institute of Export
FAIFST	Fellow, Australian Institute of Food Science and Technology
FAII	Fellow, Australian Insurance Institute
FAIM	Fellow, Australian Institute of Management
FAIMBE	Fellow, American Institute for Medical and Biological Engineering
FAIP	Fellow, Australian Institute of Physics
FAISB	Fellow, Society for the Study of Artificial Intelligence and the Simulation of Behaviour
FAM	Fellow, Academy of Marketing
FAMA	Fellow, Australian Medical Association
FAMI	Fellow, Australian Marketing Institute
FAMINZ(Arb)	Fellow, Arbitrators and Mediators Institute of New Zealand
FAMM	Fellow, Academy of Medicine, Malaysia
FAmNucSoc	Fellow, American Nuclear Society
FAMS	Fellow, Ancient Monuments Society; Fellow, Academy of Medicine, Singapore
F and GP	Finance and General Purposes
FANY	First Aid Nursing Yeomanry
FANZCA	Fellow, Australian and New Zealand College of Anaesthetists
FANZCP	Fellow, Australian and New Zealand College of Psychiatrists (now see FRANZCP)
FAO	Food and Agriculture Organization of the United Nations
FAOrthA	Fellow, Australian Orthopaedic Association
FAPA	Fellow, American Psychiatric Association
FAPHA	Fellow, American Public Health Association
FAPI	Fellow, Association of Physicians of India
FAPM	Fellow, Association for Project Management (formerly of Project Managers)
FAPS	Fellow, American Phytopathological Society
FAPT	Fellow, Association for Preservation Technology (US)
FArborA	Fellow, Aboricultural Association
FARE	Federation of Alcoholic Rehabilitation Establishments
FARELF	Far East Land Forces
FAS	Fellow, Antiquarian Society; Fellow, Nigerian Academy of Science; Funding Agency for Schools
FASA	Fellow, Australian Society of Accountants (now see FCPA)
FASc	Fellow, Indian Academy of Sciences
fasc.	fascicule
FASCE	Fellow, American Society of Civil Engineers
FASI	Fellow, Architects' and Surveyors' Institute
FASME	Fellow, American Society of Mechanical Engineers
FASPOG	Fellow, Australian Society for Psychosomatic Obstetrics and Gynæcology
FASSA	Fellow, Academy of the Social Sciences in Australia
FAusIMM	Fellow, Australasian Institute of Mining and Metallurgy
FAustCOG	Fellow, Australian College of Obstetricians and Gynæcologists (later FRACOG; now see FRANZCOG)
FAWT	Farm Animal Welfare Trust
FBA	Fellow, British Academy; Federation of British Artists
FBAHA	Fellow, British Association of Hotel Accountants
FBAM	Fellow, British Academy of Management
FBC	Fellow, Birmingham Conservatoire
FBCartS	Fellow, British Cartographic Society
FBCO	Fellow, British College of Optometrists (formerly of Ophthalmic Opticians (Optometrists)) (now see FCOptom)
FBCS	Fellow, British Computer Society
FBCS CITP	Fellow, British Computer Society, with Chartered Professional Status
FBEC(S)	Fellow, Business Education Council (Scotland)
FBEng	Fellow, Association of Building Engineers
FBES	Fellow, Biological Engineering Society (now see FIPEM)
FBHA	Fellow, British Hospitality Association
FBHI	Fellow, British Horological Institute
FBHS	Fellow, British Horse Society
FBI	Federation of British Industries (now see CBI); Federal Bureau of Investigation
FBIA	Fellow, Bankers' Institute of Australasia
FBIAT	Fellow, British Institute of Architectural Technicians

FBIBA	Fellow, British Insurance Brokers' Association (*now see* FBIIBA)
FBID	Fellow, British Institute of Interior Design
FBIDA	Fellow, British Interior Design Association
FBIDST	Fellow, British Institute of Dental and Surgical Technologists
FBII	Fellow, British Institute of Innkeeping
FBIIBA	Fellow, British Insurance and Investment Brokers' Association
FBIM	Fellow, British Institute of Management (later FIMgt)
FBINZ	Fellow, Bankers' Institute of New Zealand
FBIPM	Fellow, British Institute of Payroll Management (*now see* FIPPM)
FBIPP	Fellow, British Institute of Professional Photography
FBIR	Fellow, British Institute of Radiology
FBIRA	Fellow, British Institute of Regulatory Affairs
FBIS	Fellow, British Interplanetary Society
FBKS	Fellow, British Kinematograph Society (*now see* FBKSTS)
FBKSTS	Fellow, British Kinematograph, Sound and Television Society
FBNA	Fellow, British Naturalists' Association
FBOA	Fellow, British Optical Association
FBOU	Fellow, British Ornithologists' Union
FBPharmacolS	Fellow, British Pharmacological Society
FBPICS	Fellow, British Production and Inventory Control Society
FBPsS	Fellow, British Psychological Society
FBritIRE	Fellow, British Institution of Radio Engineers (later FIERE)
FBS	Fellow, Building Societies Institute (later FCBSI; *now see* FCIB)
FBSE	Fellow, Biomaterials Science and Engineering
FBSI	Fellow, Boot and Shoe Institution (*now see* FCFI)
FBSM	Fellow, Birmingham School of Music (*now see* FBC)
FBTS	Fellow, British Toxicology Society
FC	Football Club
FCA	Fellow, Institute of Chartered Accountants; Fellow, Institute of Chartered Accountants in Australia; Fellow, New Zealand Society of Accountants; Federation of Canadian Artists
FCAI	Fellow, New Zealand Institute of Cost Accountants; Fellow, Canadian Aeronautical Institute (*now see* FCASI)
FCAM	Fellow, CAM Foundation
FCAnaes	Fellow, College of Anaesthetists (*now see* FRCA)
FCARCSI	Fellow, College of Anaesthetists, Royal College of Surgeons of Ireland
FCA(SA)	Fellow, College of Anaesthetists (South Africa)
FCASI	Fellow, Canadian Aeronautics and Space Institute
FCBSI	Fellow, Chartered Building Societies Institute (merged with Chartered Institute of Bankers; *now see* FCIB)
FCCA	Fellow, Chartered Association of Certified Accountants
FCCEA	Fellow, Commonwealth Council for Educational Administration
FCCS	Fellow, Corporation of Secretaries (*formerly* of Certified Secretaries)
FCCT	Fellow, Canadian College of Teachers
FCEC	Federation of Civil Engineering Contractors
FCEM	Fellow, College of Emergency Medicine
FCFI	Fellow, Clothing and Footwear Institute
FCGA	Fellow, Certified General Accountants of Canada
FCGC	Fellow, Council of Geriatric Cardiology
FCGI	Fellow, City and Guilds of London Institute
FCGP	Fellow, College of General Practitioners (*now see* FRCGP)
FChS	Fellow, Society of Chiropodists
FCI	Fellow, Institute of Commerce
FCIA	Fellow, Corporation of Insurance Agents
FCIArb	Fellow, Chartered Institute of Arbitrators
FCIB	Fellow, Corporation of Insurance Brokers; Fellow, Chartered Institute of Bankers
FCIBS	Fellow, Chartered Institution of Building Services (*now see* FCIBSE); Fellow, Chartered Institute of Bankers in Scotland
FCIBSE	Fellow, Chartered Institution of Building Services Engineers
FCIC	Fellow, Chemical Institute of Canada (*formerly* Canadian Institute of Chemistry)
FCIEH	Fellow, Chartered Institute of Environmental Health
FCIH	Fellow, Chartered Institute of Housing
FCII	Fellow, Chartered Insurance Institute
FCIJ	Fellow, Chartered Institute of Journalists
FCIL	Fellow, Chartered Institute of Linguists
FCILA	Fellow, Chartered Institute of Loss Adjusters
FCILT	Chartered Fellow, Chartered Institute of Logistics and Transport
FCIM	Fellow, Chartered Institute of Marketing; Fellow, Institute of Corporate Managers (Australia)
FCIOB	Fellow, Chartered Institute of Building
FCIPA	Fellow, Chartered Institute of Patent Agents (*now see* CPA)
FCIPD	Fellow, Chartered Institute of Personnel and Development
FCIPR	Fellow, Chartered Institute of Public Relations
FCIPS	Fellow, Chartered Institute of Purchasing and Supply
FCIS	Fellow, Institute of Chartered Secretaries and Administrators (*formerly* Chartered Institute of Secretaries)
FCISA	Fellow, Chartered Institute of Secretaries and Administrators (Australia)
FCIT	Fellow, Chartered Institute of Transport (*now see* FCILT)
FCIWEM	Fellow, Chartered Institution of Water and Environmental Management
FCIWM	Fellow, Chartered Institution of Wastes Management
FCLIP	Fellow, Chartered Institute of Library and Information Professionals
FCM	Faculty of Community Medicine
FCMA	Fellow, Chartered Institute of Management Accountants (*formerly* Institute of Cost and Management Accountants); Fellow, Communications Management Association
FCMC	Fellow grade, Certified Management Consultant
FCMI	Fellow, Chartered Management Institute
FCMSA	Fellow, College of Medicine of South Africa
FCNA	Fellow, College of Nursing, Australia
FCO	Foreign and Commonwealth Office
FCOG(SA)	Fellow, South African College of Obstetrics and Gynæcology
FCollH	Fellow, College of Handicraft
FCollP	Fellow, College of Preceptors
FCollT	Fellow, College of Teachers
FCommA	Fellow, Society of Commercial Accountants (*now see* FSCA)
FCOphth	Fellow, College of Ophthalmologists (*now see* FRCOphth)
FCOptom	Fellow, College of Optometrists
FCP	Fellow, College of Preceptors
FCPA	Fellow, Australian Society of Certified Practising Accountants
FCPath	Fellow, College of Pathologists (*now see* FRCPath)
FCPCH	Fellow, College of Paediatrics and Child Health (*now see* FRCPCH)
FCPS	Fellow, College of Physicians and Surgeons
FCP(SoAf)	Fellow, College of Physicians, South Africa
FCPSO(SoAf)	Fellow, College of Physicians and Surgeons and Obstetricians, South Africa
FCPS (Pak)	Fellow, College of Physicians and Surgeons of Pakistan
FCQI	Fellow, Chartered Quality Institute
FCRA	Fellow, College of Radiologists of Australia (*now see* FRACR)
FCS	Federation of Conservative Students
FCS or FChemSoc	Fellow, Chemical Society (now absorbed into Royal Society of Chemistry)
FCSD	Fellow, Chartered Society of Designers
FCSHK	Fellow, College of Surgeons of Hong Kong
FCSLT	Fellow, College of Speech and Language Therapists (*now see* FRCSLT)
FCSM	Fellow, Cambridge School of Music
FCSP	Fellow, Chartered Society of Physiotherapy
FCSSA or FCS(SoAf)	Fellow, College of Surgeons, South Africa
FCSSL	Fellow, College of Surgeons of Sri Lanka
FCST	Fellow, College of Speech Therapists (later FCSLT; *now see* FRCSLT)
FCT	Federal Capital Territory (*now see* ACT); Fellow, Association of Corporate Treasurers; Fellow, College of Teachers
FCTB	Fellow, College of Teachers of the Blind
FCU	Fighter Control Unit
FCWA	Fellow, Institute of Costs and Works Accountants (*now see* FCMA)
FD	Doctor of Philosophy
FDA	Association of First Division Civil Servants
FDF	Food and Drink Federation
FDI	Fédération Dentaire Internationale
FDP	Freie Demokratische Partei
FDS	Fellow in Dental Surgery
FDSRCPSGlas	Fellow in Dental Surgery, Royal College of Physicians and Surgeons of Glasgow
FDSRCS or FDS RCS	Fellow in Dental Surgery, Royal College of Surgeons of England
FDSRCSE	Fellow in Dental Surgery, Royal College of Surgeons of Edinburgh
FE	Far East
FEA	Fellow, English Association
FEAF	Far East Air Force
FEANI	Fédération Européenne d'Associations Nationales d'Ingénieurs
FEBS	Federation of European Biochemical Societies
FECI	Fellow, Institute of Employment Consultants
FECTS	Fellow, European Association for Cardiothoracic Surgery
FEE	Fédération des Expertes Comptables Européens
FEF	Far East Fleet
FEFC or FEFCE	Further Education Funding Council for England
FEFCW	Further Education Funding Council for Wales
FEI	Fédération Equestre Internationale; Fellow, Energy Institute
FEIDCT	Fellow, Educational Institute of Design Craft and Technology
FEIS	Fellow, Educational Institute of Scotland
FELCO	Federation of English Language Course Opportunities
FEng	Fellow, Royal Academy (*formerly* Fellowship) of Engineering (*now see* FREng)
FEPS	Federation of European Physiological Societies
FES	Fellow, Entomological Society; Fellow, Ethnological Society
FESC	Fellow, European Society of Cardiology
FETCS	Fellow, European Board of Thoracic and Cardiovascular Surgeons
FF	Fianna Fáil; Field Force
FFA	Fellow, Faculty of Actuaries (in Scotland); Fellow, Institute of Financial Accountants
FFAEM	Fellow, Faculty of Accident and Emergency Medicine (*now see* FCEM)

FFARACS   Fellow, Faculty of Anaesthetists, Royal Australasian College of Surgeons (*now see* FANZCA)
FFARCS   Fellow, Faculty of Anaesthetists, Royal College of Surgeons of England (*now see* FRCA)
FFARCSI   Fellow, Faculty of Anaesthetists, Royal College of Surgeons in Ireland
FFAS   Fellow, Faculty of Architects and Surveyors, London (*now see* FASI)
FFA(SA)   Fellow, Faculty of Anaesthetists (South Africa) (*now see* FCA(SA))
FFB   Fellow, Faculty of Building
FFCM   Fellow, Faculty of Community Medicine (*now see* FFPH); Fellow, Faculty of Church Music
FFCMI   Fellow, Faculty of Community Medicine of Ireland
FFCS   Founding Fellow, Contemporary Scotland
FFDRCSI   Fellow, Faculty of Dentistry, Royal College of Surgeons in Ireland
FFFLM   Fellow, Faculty of Forensic and Legal Medicine, Royal College of Physicians
FFFP   Fellow, Faculty of Family Planning & Reproductive Health Care of the Royal College of Obstetricians and Gynaecologists (*now see* FFSRH)
FFGDP(UK) Fellow, Faculty of General Dental Practitioners of the Royal College of Surgeons
FFHC   Freedom from Hunger Campaign
FFHom   Fellow, Faculty of Homoeopathy
FFI   Finance for Industry; Fauna & Flora International
FFOM   Fellow, Faculty of Occupational Medicine
FFOMI   Fellow, Faculty of Occupational Medicine of Ireland
FFOP (RCPA) Fellow, Faculty of Oral Pathology, Royal College of Pathologists of Australasia
FFPath, RCPI Fellow, Faculty of Pathologists of the Royal College of Physicians of Ireland
FFPH   Fellow, Faculty of Public Health
FFPHM   Fellow, Faculty of Public Health Medicine (*now see* FFPH)
FFPHMI   Fellow, Faculty of Public Health Medicine of Ireland
FFPM   Fellow, Faculty of Pharmaceutical Medicine
FFPRHC   Faculty of Family Planning & Reproductive Health Care, Royal College of Obstetricians and Gynaecologists
FFPS   Fauna and Flora Preservation Society (*now see* FFI)
FFR   Fellow, Faculty of Radiologists (*now see* FRCR)
FFSEM   Fellow, Faculty of Sports and Exercise Medicine, Royal College of Physicians of Ireland and Royal College of Surgeons in Ireland
FFSRH   Fellow, Faculty of Sexual and Reproductive Healthcare of the Royal College of Obstetricians and Gynaecologists
FFSSoc   Fellow, Forensic Science Society
FFTM(Glas) Fellow, Faculty of Travel Medicine, Royal College of Physicians and Surgeons of Glasgow
FG   Fine Gael
FGA   Fellow, Gemmological Association
FGCL   Fellow, Goldsmiths' College, London
FGCM   Fellow, Guild of Church Musicians
FGDS   Fédération de la Gauche Démocratique et Socialiste
FGE   Fellow, Guild of Glass Engravers
FGGE   Fellow, Guild of Glass Engravers (*now see* FGE)
FGI   Fellow, Institute of Certificated Grocers
FGMS   Fellow, Guild of Musicians and Singers
FGS   Fellow, Geological Society
FGSM   Fellow, Guildhall School of Music and Drama
FGSM(MT) Fellow, Guildhall School of Music and Drama (Music Therapy)
FHA   Fellow, Institute of Health Service Administrators (*formerly* Hospital Administrators) (later FHSM); Fellow, Historical Association
FHAS   Fellow, Highland and Agricultural Society of Scotland
FHCIMA   Fellow, Hotel Catering and International (formerly Institutional) Management Association (*now see* FIH)
FHEA   Fellow, Higher Education Academy
FHKAES   Fellow, Hong Kong Academy of Engineering Sciences
FHKAM   Fellow, Hong Kong Academy of Medicine
FHKCP   Fellow, Hong Kong College of Physicians
FHKCS   Fellow, Hong Kong College of Surgeons
FHKIE   Fellow, Hong Kong Institution of Engineers
FHMAAS   Foreign Honorary Member, American Academy of Arts and Sciences
FHRS   Fellow, Heart Rhythm Society
FHS   Fellow, Heraldry Society; Forces Help Society and Lord Roberts Workshops (*now see* SSAFA)
FHSA   Family Health Services Authority
FHSM   Fellow, Institute of Health Services Management (later FIHM)
FH-WC   Fellow, Heriot-Watt College (*now* University), Edinburgh
FIA   Fellow, Institute of Actuaries
FIAA   Fellow, Institute of Actuaries of Australia
FIAAS   Fellow, Institute of Australian Agricultural Science
FIAA&S   Fellow, Incorporated Association of Architects and Surveyors
FIACM   Fellow, International Association of Computational Mechanics
FIAE   Fellow, Irish Academy of Engineering
FIAgrE   Fellow, Institution of Agricultural Engineers
FIAgrM   Fellow, Institute of Agricultural Management

FIAI   Fellow, Institute of Industrial and Commercial Accountants
FIAL   Fellow, International Institute of Arts and Letters
FIAM   Fellow, International Academy of Management
FIAMBE   Fellow, International Academy for Medical and Biological Engineering
FIAP   Fellow, Institution of Analysts and Programmers; Fellow, Indian Academy of Paediatrics
FIArb   Fellow, Institute of Arbitrators (*now see* FCIArb)
FIArbA   Fellow, Institute of Arbitrators of Australia
FIAS   Fellow, Institute of Aeronautical Sciences (US) (*now see* FAIAA)
FIASc   Fellow, Indian Academy of Sciences
FIASSID   Fellow, International Association for the Scientific Study of Intellectual Disability
FIAWS   Fellow, International Academy of Wood Sciences
FIB   Fellow, Institute of Bankers (*now see* FCIB)
FIBA   Fellow, Institute of Business Administration, Australia (*now see* FCIM)
FIBC   Fellow, Institute of Business Consulting
FIBI   Fellow, Institute of Bankers of Ireland
FIBiol   Fellow, Institute of Biology
FIBiotech Fellow, Institute for Biotechnical Studies
FIBMS   Fellow, Institute of Biomedical Sciences
FIBP   Fellow, Institute of British Photographers
FIBScot   Fellow, Institute of Bankers in Scotland (*now see* FCIBS)
FIC   Fellow, Institute of Chemistry (then FRIC; *now see* FRSC); Fellow, Imperial College, London
FICA   Fellow, Commonwealth Institute of Accountants; Fellow, Institute of Chartered Accountants in England and Wales (*now see* FCA)
FICAI   Fellow, Institute of Chartered Accountants in Ireland
FICB   Fellow, Institute of Canadian Bankers
FICD   Fellow, Institute of Civil Defence (*now see* FICDDS); Fellow, Indian College of Dentists; Fellow, International College of Dentists
FICDDS   Fellow, Institute of Civil Defence and Disaster Studies
FICE   Fellow, Institution of Civil Engineers
FICeram   Fellow, Institute of Ceramics (later FIM)
FICES   Fellow, Institute of Chartered Engineering Surveyors
FICFM   Fellow, Institute of Charity Fundraising Managers (*now see* FInstF)
FICFor   Fellow, Institute of Chartered Foresters
FIChemE   Fellow, Institution of Chemical Engineers
FICM   Fellow, Institute of Credit Management
FICMA   Fellow, Institute of Cost and Management Accountants
FICOG   Fellow, Indian College of Obstetricians and Gynaecologists
FICorr   Fellow, Institute of Corrosion
FICorrST Fellow, Institution of Corrosion Science and Technology (*now see* FICorr)
FICPD   Fellow, Institute of Continuing Professional Development
FICS   Fellow, Institute of Chartered Shipbrokers; Fellow, International College of Surgeons
FICT   Fellow, Institute of Concrete Technologists
FICW   Fellow, Institute of Clerks of Works of Great Britain
FIDA   Fellow, Institute of Directors, Australia (*now see* FAICD)
FIDCA   Fellow, Industrial Design Council of Australia
FIDDA   Fellow, Interior Decorators and Designers Association (*now see* FBIDA)
FIDE   Fédération Internationale des Echecs; Fellow, Institute of Design Engineers; Fédération Internationale pour le Droit Européen
FIDEM   Fédération Internationale de la Médaille
FIDM   Fellow, Institute of Direct Marketing
FIDPM   Fellow, Institute of Data Processing Management
FIEAust   Fellow, Institution of Engineers, Australia
FIEC   Fellow, Institute of Employment Consultants
FIED   Fellow, Institution of Engineering Designers
FIEE   Fellow, Institution of Electrical Engineers (*now see* FIET)
FIEEE   Fellow, Institute of Electrical and Electronics Engineers (NY)
FIEEIE   Fellow, Institution of Electronics and Electrical Incorporated Engineers (later FIIE)
FIEEM   Fellow, Institute of Ecology and Environmental Management
FIEHK   Fellow, Institution of Engineering, Hong Kong
FIEI   Fellow, Institution of Engineering Inspection (later FIQA); Fellow, Institution of Engineers of Ireland
FIEIE   Fellow, Institution of Electronic Incorporated Engineers (later FIEEIE)
FIEJ   Fédération Internationale des Editeurs de Journaux et Publications
FIEMA   Fellow, Institute of Environmental Management and Assessment
FIEnvSci Fellow, Institution of Environmental Sciences
FIERE   Fellow, Institution of Electronic and Radio Engineers (later FIEE)
FIES   Fellow, Illuminating Engineering Society (later FIllumES; *now see* FCIBSE); Fellow, Institution of Engineers and Shipbuilders, Scotland
FIET   Fédération Internationale des Employés, Techniciens et Cadres; Fellow, Institution of Engineering and Technology
FIEx   Fellow, Institute of Export
FIExpE   Fellow, Institute of Explosives Engineers

FIFA	Fédération Internationale de Football Association
FIFEM	Fellow, International Federation of Emergency Medicine
FIFF	Fellow, Institute of Freight Forwarders (*now see* FIFP)
FIFireE	Fellow, Institution of Fire Engineers
FIFM	Fellow, Institute of Fisheries Management
FIFor	Fellow, Institute of Foresters (*now see* FICFor)
FIFP	Fellow, Institute of Freight Professionals
FIFST	Fellow, Institute of Food Science and Technology
FIGasE	Fellow, Institute of Gas Engineers (*now see* FIGEM)
FIGCM	Fellow, Incorporated Guild of Church Musicians
FIGD	Fellow, Institute of Grocery Distribution
FIGEM	Fellow, Institution of Gas Engineers and Managers
FIGO	International Federation of Gynaecology and Obstetrics
FIH	Fellow, Institute of Housing (*now see* FCIH); Fellow, Institute of the Horse; Fellow, Institute of Hospitality
FIHE	Fellow, Institute of Health Education
FIHEEM	Fellow, Institute of Healthcare Engineering and Estate Management
FIHM	Fellow, Institute of Housing Managers (later FIH; *now see* FCIH); Fellow, Institute of Healthcare Management
FIHort	Fellow, Institute of Horticulture
FIHospE	Fellow, Institute of Hospital Engineering
FIHT	Fellow, Institution of Highways & Transportation
FIHVE	Fellow, Institution of Heating & Ventilating Engineers (later FCIBS and MCIBS)
FIIA	Fellow, Institute of Industrial Administration (later CBIM and FBIM); Fellow, Institute of Internal Auditors
FIIB	Fellow, International Institute of Biotechnology
FIIC	Fellow, International Institute for Conservation of Historic and Artistic Works
FIIDA	Fellow, International Interior Design Association (*now see* FBIDA)
FIIE	Fellow, Institution of Incorporated Engineers in Electronic, Electrical and Mechanical Engineering (*now see* FIET)
FIIM	Fellow, Institution of Industrial Managers
FIInfSc	Fellow, Institute of Information Scientists (*now see* FCLIP)
FIIP	Fellow, Institute of Incorporated Photographers (*now see* FBIPP)
FIIPC	Fellow, India International Photographic Council
FIIPE	Fellow, Indian Institution of Production Engineers
FIL	Fellow, Institute of Linguists (*now see* FCIL)
FILA	Fellow, Institute of Landscape Architects (*now see* FLI)
FILAM	Fellow, Institute of Leisure and Amenity Management
FILDM	Fellow, Institute of Logistics and Distribution Management (later FILog)
FilDr	Doctor of Philosophy
Fil.Hed.	Filosofie Hedersdoktor
FILLM	Fédération Internationale des Langues et Littératures Modernes
FIllumES	Fellow, Illuminating Engineering Society (*now see* FCIBSE)
FILog	Fellow, Institute of Logistics (later FILT)
FILT	Fellow, Institute of Logistics and Transport (*now see* FCILT)
FIM	Fellow, Institute of Materials (*formerly* Institution of Metallurgists, then Institute of Metals) (*now see* FIMMM)
FIMA	Fellow, Institute of Mathematics and its Applications
FIMarE	Fellow, Institute of Marine Engineers (*now see* FIMarEST)
FIMarEST	Fellow, Institute of Marine Engineering, Science and Technology
FIMatM	Fellow, Institute of Materials Management (later FILog)
FIMBRA	Financial Intermediaries, Managers and Brokers Regulatory Association
FIMC	Fellow, Institute of Management Consultants (*now see* FCMC)
FIMCB	Fellow, International Management Centre from Buckingham
FIMCRCSE	Fellow in Immediate Medical Care, Royal College of Surgeons of Edinburgh
FIMechE	Fellow, Institution of Mechanical Engineers
FIMfgE	Fellow, Institution of Manufacturing Engineers (later FIEE)
FIMFT	Fellow, Institute of Maxillo-facial Technology
FIMgt	Fellow, Institute of Management (*now see* FCMI)
FIMGTechE	Fellow, Institution of Mechanical and General Technician Engineers
FIMH	Fellow, Institute of Materials Handling (later FIMatM); Fellow, Institute of Military History
FIMI	Fellow, Institute of the Motor Industry
FIMinE	Fellow, Institution of Mining Engineers (later FIMM)
FIMIT	Fellow, Institute of Musical Instrument Technology
FIMLS	Fellow, Institute of Medical Laboratory Sciences (*now see* FIBMS)
FIMLT	Fellow, Institute of Medical Laboratory Technology (later FIMLS)
FIMM	Fellow, Institution of Mining and Metallurgy (*now see* FIMMM)
FIMMA	Fellow, Institute of Metals and Materials Australasia
FIMMM	Fellow, Institute of Materials, Minerals and Mining
FIMS	Fellow, Institute of Mathematical Statistics
FIMT	Fellow, Institute of the Motor Trade (*now see* FIMI)
FIMTA	Fellow, Institute of Municipal Treasurers and Accountants (*now see* IPFA)
FIMunE	Fellow, Institution of Municipal Engineers (now amalgamated with Institution of Civil Engineers)
FIN	Fellow, Institute of Navigation (*now see* FRIN)
FINA	Fédération Internationale de Natation Amateur
FINRA	Financial Industry Regulatory Authority
FInstAM	Fellow, Institute of Administrative Management
FInstArb(NZ)	Fellow, Institute of Arbitrators of New Zealand
FInstB	Fellow, Institution of Buyers
FInstBiol	Fellow, Institute of Biology (*now see* FIBiol)
FInstCES	Fellow, Institution of Civil Engineering Surveyors
FInstD	Fellow, Institute of Directors
FInstE	Fellow, Institute of Energy (*now see* FEI)
FInstEnvSci	Fellow, Institute of Environmental Sciences
FInstF	Fellow, Institute of Fuel (later FInstE); Fellow, Institute of Fundraising
FInstFF	Fellow, Institute of Freight Forwarders Ltd (later FIFF)
FInstHE	Fellow, Institution of Highways Engineers (*now see* FIHT)
FInstLEx	Fellow, Institute of Legal Executives
FInstLM	Fellow, Institute of Leadership and Management
FInstM	Fellow, Institute of Meat; Fellow, Institute of Marketing (*now see* FCIM)
FInstMC	Fellow, Institute of Measurement and Control
FInstMSM	Fellow, Institute of Marketing and Sales Management (later FInstM; *now see* FCIM)
FInstMet	Fellow, Institute of Metals (later part of Metals Society; then FIM)
FInstNDT	Fellow, Institute of Non-Destructive Testing
FInstP	Fellow, Institute of Physics
FInstPet	Fellow, Institute of Petroleum (*now see* FEI)
FInstPI	Fellow, Institute of Patentees and Inventors
FInstPkg	Fellow, Institute of Packaging
FInstPS	Fellow, Institute of Purchasing and Supply (*now see* FCIPS)
FInstSM	Fellow, Institute of Sales Management (*now see* FInstSMM)
FInstSMM	Fellow, Institute of Sales and Marketing Management
FInstTT	Fellow, Institute of Travel & Tourism
FInstW	Fellow, Institute of Welding (*now see* FWeldI)
FINucE	Fellow, Institution of Nuclear Engineers
FIOA	Fellow, Institute of Acoustics
FIOB	Fellow, Institute of Building (*now see* FCIOB)
FIOH	Fellow, Institute of Occupational Hygiene
FIOM	Fellow, Institute of Office Management (*now see* FIAM)
FIOP	Fellow, Institute of Printing (*now see* FIP3)
FIOSH	Fellow, Institution of Occupational Safety and Health
FIP	Fellow, Australian Institute of Petroleum
FIPA	Fellow, Institute of Practitioners in Advertising
FIPAA	Fellow, Institute of Public Administration Australia
FIPD	Fellow, Institute of Personnel and Development (*now see* FCIPD)
FIPDM	Fellow, Institute of Physical Distribution Management (later FILDM)
FIPEM	Fellow, Institute of Physics and Engineering in Medicine
FIPENZ	Fellow, Institution of Professional Engineers, New Zealand
FIPG	Fellow, Institute of Professional Goldsmiths
FIPharmM	Fellow, Institute of Pharmacy Management
FIPHE	Fellow, Institution of Public Health Engineers (later FIWEM)
FIPlantE	Fellow, Institution of Plant Engineers
FIPM	Fellow, Institute of Personnel Management (later FIPD)
FIPPM	Fellow, Institute of Payroll and Pensions Management
FIPR	Fellow, Institute of Public Relations (*now see* FCIPR)
FIProdE	Fellow, Institution of Production Engineers (later FIMfgE)
FIPSM	Fellow, Institute of Physical Sciences in Medicine (*now see* FIPEM)
FIP3	Fellow, Institute of Paper, Printing and Publishing
FIQ	Fellow, Institute of Quarrying
FIQA	Fellow, Institute of Quality Assurance (*now see* FCQI)
FIQS	Fellow, Institute of Quantity Surveyors
FIRA	Furniture Industry Research Association
FIRI	Fellow, Institution of the Rubber Industry (later FPRI)
FIRM	Fellow, Institute of Risk Management
FIRSE	Fellow, Institute of Railway Signalling Engineers
FIRTE	Fellow, Institute of Road Transport Engineers
FIS	Fellow, Institute of Statisticians
FISA	Fellow, Incorporated Secretaries' Association; Fédération Internationale des Sociétés d'Aviron
FISE	Fellow, Institution of Sales Engineers; Fellow, Institution of Sanitary Engineers
FISITA	Fédération Internationale des Sociétés d'Ingénieurs des Techniques de l'Automobile
FISM	Fellow, Institute of Supervisory Managers (*now see* FInstLM); Fellow, Institute of Sports Medicine
FISOB	Fellow, Incorporated Society of Organ Builders
FISPAL	Fellow, Institute for Sport, Parks and Leisure
FIST	Fellow, Institute of Science Technology
FISTC	Fellow, Institute of Scientific and Technical Communicators
FISTD	Fellow, Imperial Society of Teachers of Dancing
FIStructE	Fellow, Institution of Structural Engineers
FISW	Fellow, Institute of Social Work
FITD	Fellow, Institute of Training and Development (later FIPD)
FITE	Fellow, Institution of Electrical and Electronics Technician Engineers

FITSA	Fellow, Institute of Trading Standards Administration
FIW	Fellow, Welding Institute (now see FWeldI)
FIWE	Fellow, Institution of Water Engineers (later FIWES)
FIWEM	Fellow, Institution of Water and Environmental Management (now see FCIWEM)
FIWES	Fellow, Institution of Water Engineers and Scientists (later FIWEM)
FIWM	Fellow, Institution of Works Managers (now see FIIM); Fellow, Institute of Wastes Management (now see FCIWM)
FIWO	Fellow, Institute of Water Officers
FIWPC	Fellow, Institute of Water Pollution Control (later FIWEM)
FIWSc	Fellow, Institute of Wood Science
FIWSP	Fellow, Institute of Work Study Practitioners (now see FMS)
FJI	Fellow, Institute of Journalists (now see FCIJ)
FJIE	Fellow, Junior Institution of Engineers (now see CIMGTechE)
FKC	Fellow, King's College London
FKCHMS	Fellow, King's College Hospital Medical School
FL	Florida (postal)
FLA	Fellow, Library Association (now see FCLIP)
Fla	Florida
FLAI	Fellow, Library Association of Ireland
FLAS	Fellow, Chartered Land Agents' Society (now (after amalgamation) see FRICS)
FLCM	Fellow, London College of Music
FLHS	Fellow, London Historical Society
FLI	Fellow, Landscape Institute
FLIA	Fellow, Life Insurance Association
FLLA	Fellow, Association of Lawyers and Legal Advisers
FLS	Fellow, Linnean Society
Flt	Flight
FM	Field-Marshal
FMA	Fellow, Museums Association
FMAAT	Fellow Member, Association of Accounting Technicians
FMedSci	Fellow, Academy of Medical Sciences
FMES	Fellow, Minerals Engineering Society
FMI	Foundation for Manufacturing and Industry
FMinSoc	Fellow, Mineralogical Society of Great Britain and Ireland
FMS	Federated Malay States; Fellow, Medical Society; Fellow, Institute of Management Services
FMSA	Fellow, Mineralogical Society of America
FNA	Fellow, Indian National Science Academy
FNAEA	Fellow, National Association of Estate Agents
FNCO	Fleet Naval Constructor Officer
FNECInst	Fellow, North East Coast Institution of Engineers and Shipbuilders
FNI	Fellow, Nautical Institute; Fellow, National Institute of Sciences in India (now see FNA)
FNIA	Fellow, Nigerian Institute of Architects
FNM	Free National Movement
FNMCP	Fellow, Nigerian Medical College of Physicians
FNMSM	Fellow, North and Midlands School of Music
FNZEI	Fellow, New Zealand Educational Institute
FNZIA	Fellow, New Zealand Institute of Architects
FNZIAS	Fellow, New Zealand Institute of Agricultural Science
FNZIC	Fellow, New Zealand Institute of Chemistry
FNZIE	Fellow, New Zealand Institution of Engineers (now see FIPENZ)
FNZIM	Fellow, New Zealand Institute of Management
FNZPsS	Fellow, New Zealand Psychological Society
FO	Foreign Office (now see FCO); Field Officer; Flag Officer; Flying Officer
FODA	Fellow, Overseas Doctors' Association
FODC	Franciscan Order of the Divine Compassion
FOIC	Flag Officer in charge
FOMA	Flag Officer, Maritime Aviation
FOMI	Faculty of Occupational Medicine of Ireland
FONA	Flag Officer, Naval Aviation
FONAC	Flag Officer, Naval Air Command
FOR	Fellowship of Operational Research
For.	Foreign
FOREST	Freedom Organisation for the Right to Enjoy Smoking Tobacco
FOST	Flag Officer Sea Training
FOX	Futures and Options Exchange
FPA	Family Planning Association
FPC	Family Practitioner Committee (later FHSA); Financial Planning Certificate
FPEA	Fellow, Physical Education Association
FPH	Faculty of Public Health
FPHM	Faculty of Public Health Medicine (see now FPH)
FPhS	Fellow, Philosophical Society of England
FPhysS	Fellow, Physical Society
FPI	Fellow, Plastics Institute (later FPRI)
FPIA	Fellow, Plastics Institute of Australia; Fellow, Planning Institute of Australia
FPM	Faculty of Pharmaceutical Medicine
FPMI	Fellow, Pensions Management Institute
FPRI	Fellow, Plastics and Rubber Institute (later FIM)

FPS	Fellow, Pharmaceutical Society (now also FRPharmS); Fauna Preservation Society (later FFPS)
FPWI	Fellow, Permanent Way Institution
FQNI	Fellow, Queen's Nursing Institute
f r	fuori ruole
FRA	Fellow, Royal Academy
FRAC	Fellow, Royal Agricultural College
FRACDS	Fellow, Royal Australian College of Dental Surgeons
FRACGP	Fellow, Royal Australian College of General Practitioners
FRACI	Fellow, Royal Australian Chemical Institute
FRACMA	Fellow, Royal Australian College of Medical Administrators
FRACO	Fellow, Royal Australian College of Ophthalmologists
FRACOG	Fellow, Royal Australian College of Obstetricians and Gynaecologists (now see FRANZCOG)
FRACP	Fellow, Royal Australasian College of Physicians
FRACR	Fellow, Royal Australasian College of Radiologists
FRACS	Fellow, Royal Australasian College of Surgeons
FRAD	Fellow, Royal Academy of Dancing
FRAeS	Fellow, Royal Aeronautical Society
FRAgS	Fellow, Royal Agricultural Societies (ie of England, Scotland and Wales)
FRAHS	Fellow, Royal Australian Historical Society
FRAI	Fellow, Royal Anthropological Institute of Great Britain & Ireland
FRAIA	Fellow, Royal Australian Institute of Architects
FRAIB	Fellow, Royal Australian Institute of Building
FRAIC	Fellow, Royal Architectural Institute of Canada
FRAIPA	Fellow, Royal Australian Institute of Public Administration
FRAM	Fellow, Royal Academy of Music
FRAME	Fund for the Replacement of Animals in Medical Experiments
FRANZCOG	Fellow, Royal Australian and New Zealand College of Obstetricians and Gynaecologists
FRANZCP	Fellow, Royal Australian and New Zealand College of Psychiatrists
FRANZCR	Fellow, Royal Australian and New Zealand College of Radiologists
FRAPI	Fellow, Royal Australian Planning Institute (now see FPIA)
FRAS	Fellow, Royal Astronomical Society; Fellow, Royal Asiatic Society
FRASE	Fellow, Royal Agricultural Society of England
FRBS	Fellow, Royal Society of British Sculptors; Fellow, Royal Botanic Society
FRCA	Fellow, Royal College of Art; Fellow, Royal College of Anaesthetists
FRCCO	Fellow, Royal Canadian College of Organists
FRCD(Can.)	Fellow, Royal College of Dentists of Canada
FRCGP	Fellow, Royal College of General Practitioners
FRCM	Fellow, Royal College of Music
FRCN	Fellow, Royal College of Nursing
FRCO	Fellow, Royal College of Organists
FRCO(CHM)	Fellow, Royal College of Organists with Diploma in Choir Training
FRCOG	Fellow, Royal College of Obstetricians and Gynaecologists
FRCOphth	Fellow, Royal College of Ophthalmologists
FRCP	Fellow, Royal College of Physicians, London
FRCPA	Fellow, Royal College of Pathologists of Australasia
FRCP&S (Canada)	Fellow, Royal College of Physicians and Surgeons of Canada
FRCPath	Fellow, Royal College of Pathologists
FRCPC	Fellow, Royal College of Physicians of Canada
FRCPCH	Fellow, Royal College of Paediatrics and Child Health
FRCPE or FRCPEd	Fellow, Royal College of Physicians, Edinburgh
FRCPGlas	Fellow, Royal College of Physicians and Surgeons of Glasgow
FRCPI	Fellow, Royal College of Physicians of Ireland
FRCPSGlas	Hon. Fellow, Royal College of Physicians and Surgeons of Glasgow
FRCPsych	Fellow, Royal College of Psychiatrists
FRCR	Fellow, Royal College of Radiologists
FRCS	Fellow, Royal College of Surgeons of England
FRCSCan	Fellow, Royal College of Surgeons of Canada
FRCSE or FRCSEd	Fellow, Royal College of Surgeons of Edinburgh
FRCSGlas	Fellow, Royal College of Physicians and Surgeons of Glasgow
FRCSI	Fellow, Royal College of Surgeons in Ireland
FRCSLT	Fellow, Royal College of Speech and Language Therapists
FRCSoc	Fellow, Royal Commonwealth Society
FRCST	Fellow, Royal College of Surgeons of Thailand
FRCUS	Fellow, Royal College of University Surgeons (Denmark)
FRCVS	Fellow, Royal College of Veterinary Surgeons
FREconS	Fellow, Royal Economic Society
FREng	Fellow, Royal Academy of Engineering
FRES	Fellow, Royal Entomological Society of London
FRFPSG	Fellow, Royal Faculty of Physicians and Surgeons, Glasgow (now see FRCPGlas)
FRG	Federal Republic of Germany
FRGS	Fellow, Royal Geographical Society
FRGSA	Fellow, Royal Geographical Society of Australasia
FRHistS	Fellow, Royal Historical Society

FRHS	Fellow, Royal Horticultural Society (*now see* MRHS)
FRI	Fellow, Royal Institution
FRIAI	Fellow, Royal Institute of the Architects of Ireland
FRIAS	Fellow, Royal Incorporation of Architects of Scotland; Royal Institute for the Advancement of Science
FRIBA	Fellow, Royal Institute of British Architects (*and see* RIBA)
FRIC	Fellow, Royal Institute of Chemistry (*now see* FRSC)
FRICS	Fellow, Royal Institution of Chartered Surveyors
FRIH	Fellow, Royal Institute of Horticulture (NZ)
FRIN	Fellow, Royal Institute of Navigation
FRINA	Fellow, Royal Institution of Naval Architects
FRIPA	Fellow, Royal Institute of Public Administration (the Institute no longer has Fellows)
FRIPH	Fellow, Royal Institute of Public Health
FRIPHH	Fellow, Royal Institute of Public Health and Hygiene (*now see* FRIPH)
FRMCM	Fellow, Royal Manchester College of Music
FRMedSoc	Fellow, Royal Medical Society
FRMetS	Fellow, Royal Meteorological Society
FRMIA	Fellow, Retail Management Institute of Australia
FRMS	Fellow, Royal Microscopical Society
FRNCM	Fellow, Royal Northern College of Music
FRNS	Fellow, Royal Numismatic Society
FRPharmS	Fellow, Royal Pharmaceutical Society
FRPS	Fellow, Royal Photographic Society
FRPSL	Fellow, Royal Philatelic Society, London
FRS	Fellow, Royal Society
FRSA	Fellow, Royal Society of Arts
FRSAI	Fellow, Royal Society of Antiquaries of Ireland
FRSAMD	Fellow, Royal Scottish Academy of Music and Drama
FRSanI	Fellow, Royal Sanitary Institute (*now see* FRSH)
FRSC	Fellow, Royal Society of Canada; Fellow, Royal Society of Chemistry
FRS(Can)	Fellow, Royal Society of Canada (used when a person is also a Fellow of the Royal Society of Chemistry)
FRSCM	Hon. Fellow, Royal School of Church Music
FRSC(UK)	Fellow, Royal Society of Chemistry (used when a person is also a Fellow of the Royal Society of Canada)
FRSE	Fellow, Royal Society of Edinburgh
FRSGS	Fellow, Royal Scottish Geographical Society
FRSH	Fellow, Royal Society for the Promotion of Health
FRSL	Fellow, Royal Society of Literature
FRSocMed	Fellow, Royal Society of Medicine
FRSNZ	Fellow, Royal Society of New Zealand
FRSPS	Fellow, Remote Sensing and Photogrammetry Society
FRSSA	Fellow, Royal Scottish Society for the Arts
FRSSAf	Fellow, Royal Society of South Africa
FRSTM&H	Fellow, Royal Society of Tropical Medicine and Hygiene
FRSV	Fellow, Royal Society of Victoria
FRTPI	Fellow, Royal Town Planning Institute
FRTS	Fellow, Royal Television Society
FRUSI	Fellow, Royal United Services Institute
FRVA	Fellow, Rating and Valuation Association (*now see* IRRV)
FRVC	Fellow, Royal Veterinary College
FRWCMD	Fellow, Royal Welsh College of Music and Drama
FRZSScot	Fellow, Royal Zoological Society of Scotland
FS	Field Security
fs	Graduate, Royal Air Force Staff College
FSA	Fellow, Society of Antiquaries; Financial Services Authority
FSAA	Fellow, Society of Incorporated Accountants and Auditors
FSAC	Fast Stream Assessment Centre
FSACOG	Fellow, South African College of Obstetricians and Gynaecologists
FSAE	Fellow, Society of Automotive Engineers; Fellow, Society of Art Education
FSAI	Fellow, Society of Architectural Illustrators
FSAIEE	Fellow, South African Institute of Electrical Engineers
FSArc	Fellow, Society of Architects (merged with the RIBA 1952)
FSaRS	Fellow, Safety and Reliability Society
FSAScot	Fellow, Society of Antiquaries of Scotland
FSASM	Fellow, South Australian School of Mines
fsc	Foreign Staff College
FSCA	Fellow, Society of Company and Commercial Accountants
FScotvec	Fellow, Scottish Vocational Education Council
FSCRE	Fellow, Scottish Council for Research in Education
FSDC	Fellow, Society of Dyers and Colourists
FSE	Fellow, Society of Engineers; Fellow, Society for the Environment
FSG	Fellow, Society of Genealogists
FSGD	Fellow, Society of Garden Designers
FSGT	Fellow, Society of Glass Technology
FSI	Fellow, Chartered Surveyors' Institution (*now see* FRICS); Fellow, Securities Institute
FSIA	Fellow, Securities Institute of Australia
FSIAD	Fellow, Society of Industrial Artists and Designers (*now see* FCSD)

FSIP	Fellow, Society of Investment Professionals
FSLAET	Fellow, Society of Licensed Aircraft Engineers and Technologists
FSLCOG	Fellow, Sri Lankan College of Obstetrics and Gynaecology
FSLCPaed	Fellow, Sri Lanka College of Paediatricians
FSLTC	Fellow, Society of Leather Technologists and Chemists
FSMA	Fellow, Incorporated Sales Managers' Association (later FInstMSM, then FInstM)
FSMC	Freeman of the Spectacle-Makers' Company
FSME	Fellow, Society of Manufacturing Engineers
FSMPTE	Fellow, Society of Motion Picture and Television Engineers (US)
FSNAD	Fellow, Society of Numismatic Artists and Designers
FSNAME	Fellow, American Society of Naval Architects and Marine Engineers
FSOE	Fellow, Society of Operations Engineers
FSOGC	Fellow, Society of Obstetricians and Gynaecologists of Canada
FSPI	Fellow, Society of Practitioners of Insolvency
FSQA	Fellow, Scottish Qualifications Authority
FSRHE	Fellow, Society for Research into Higher Education
FSRP	Fellow, Society for Radiological Protection
FSS	Fellow, Royal Statistical Society
FSSI	Fellow, Society of Scribes and Illuminators
FSTD	Fellow, Society of Typographic Designers
FSVA	Fellow, Incorporated Society of Valuers and Auctioneers (*now see* RICS)
FT	Financial Times
FTAT	Furniture, Timber and Allied Trades Union
FTC	Flying Training Command; Full Technological Certificate, City and Guilds of London Institute
FTCD	Fellow, Trinity College, Dublin
FTCL	Fellow, Trinity College of Music, London
FTI	Fellow, Textile Institute
FTII	Fellow, Chartered Institute (*formerly* Incorporated Institute, then Institute) of Taxation
FTMA	Fellow, Telecommunications Managers Association (*now see* FCMA)
FTP	Fellow, Thames Polytechnic
FTS	Fellow, Australian Academy of Technological Sciences and Engineering (*now see* FTSE); Flying Training School; Fellow, Tourism Society
FTSC	Fellow, Tonic Sol-fa College
FTSE	Fellow, Australian Academy of Technological Sciences and Engineering
FUCEB	Fellow, University of Central England in Birmingham
FUCUA	Federation of University Conservative and Unionist Associations (*now see* FCS)
FUMDS	Fellow, United Medical and Dental Schools
FUMIST	Fellow, University of Manchester Institute of Science and Technology
FVCM	Fellow, Victoria College of Music
FVRDE	Fighting Vehicles Research and Development Establishment
FWAAS	Fellow, World Academy of Arts and Sciences
FWACP	Fellow, West African College of Physicians
FWAG	Farming and Wildlife Advisory Group
FWCB	Fellow, Worshipful Company of Blacksmiths
FWCMD	Fellow, Welsh College of Music and Drama (*now see* FRWCMD)
FWeldI	Fellow, Welding Institute
FWSOM	Fellow, Institute of Practitioners in Work Study, Organisation and Method (*now see* FMS)
FZS	Fellow, Zoological Society
FZSScot	Fellow, Zoological Society of Scotland (*now see* FRZSScot)

G

GA	Geologists' Association; Gaelic Athletic (Club); Georgia (postal)
Ga	Georgia
GAI	Guild of Architectural Ironmongers
GAP	Gap Activity Projects
GAPAN	Guild of Air Pilots and Air Navigators
GATT	General Agreement on Tariffs and Trade (*now* World Trade Organisation)
GB	Great Britain
GBA	Governing Bodies Association
GBE	Knight or Dame Grand Cross, Order of the British Empire
GBGSA	Governing Bodies of Girls' Schools Association (*formerly* Association of Governing Bodies of Girls' Public Schools)
GBM	Grand Bauhinia Medal (Hong Kong)
GBS	Gold Bauhinia Star (Hong Kong)
GBSM	Graduate of Birmingham and Midland Institute School of Music
GC	George Cross
GCB	Knight or Dame Grand Cross, Order of the Bath
GCBS	General Council of British Shipping
GCC	General Chiropractic Council
GCCC	Gonville and Caius College, Cambridge

GCCF	Grand Commander, Companion Order of Freedom (Zambia)
GCCS	Government Code and Cipher School
GCFR	Grand Commander, Order of the Federal Republic of Nigeria
GCH	Knight Grand Cross, Hanoverian Order
GCHQ	Government Communications Headquarters
GCIE	Knight Grand Commander, Order of the Indian Empire
GCL	Grand Chief, Order of Logohu (Papua New Guinea)
GCLJ	Grand Cross, Order of St Lazarus of Jerusalem
GCLM	Grand Commander, Order of the Legion of Merit of Rhodesia
GCM	Gold Crown of Merit (Barbados)
GCMG	Knight or Dame Grand Cross, Order of St Michael and St George
GCON	Grand Cross, Order of the Niger
GCSE	General Certificate of Secondary Education
GCSG	Knight Grand Cross, Order of St Gregory the Great
GCSI	Knight Grand Commander, Order of the Star of India
GCSJ	Knight Grand Cross of Justice, Sovereign Order of St John of Jerusalem (Knights Hospitaller)
GCSK	Grand Commander, Order of the Star and Key of the Indian Ocean (Mauritius)
GCSL	Grand Cross, Order of St Lucia
GCStJ	Bailiff or Dame Grand Cross, Most Venerable Order of the Hospital of St John of Jerusalem
GCVO	Knight or Dame Grand Cross, Royal Victorian Order
gd	grand-daughter
GDBA	Guide Dogs for the Blind Association
GDC	General Dental Council
Gdns	Gardens
GDR	German Democratic Republic
GDST	Girls' Day School Trust
Gen.	General
Ges.	Gesellschaft
GFD	Geophysical Fluid Dynamics
GFS	Girls' Friendly Society
ggd	great-grand-daughter
ggs	great-grandson
GGSM	Graduate in Music, Guildhall School of Music and Drama
GHQ	General Headquarters
Gib.	Gibraltar
GIMechE	Graduate, Institution of Mechanical Engineers
GKT	Guy's, King's and St Thomas' (Medical and Dental School of King's College London)
GL	Grand Lodge
GLA	Greater London Authority
GLAA	Greater London Arts Association (*now see* GLAB)
GLAB	Greater London Arts Board
GLC	Greater London Council
Glos	Gloucestershire
GM	George Medal; Grand Medal (Ghana); genetically modified
GMB	(Union for) General, Municipal, Boilermakers
GMBATU	General, Municipal, Boilermakers and Allied Trades Union (*now see* GMB)
GmbH	Gesellschaft mit beschränkter Haftung
GMBPS	Graduate Member, British Psychological Society
GMC	General Medical Council; Guild of Memorial Craftsmen; General Management Course (Henley)
GMWU	General and Municipal Workers' Union (later GMBATU; *now see* GMB)
GNC	General Nursing Council
GNVQ	General National Vocational Qualification
GNZM	Knight or Dame Grand Companion, New Zealand Order of Merit
GOC	General Officer Commanding
GOC-in-C	General Officer Commanding-in-Chief
GOE	General Ordination Examination
GOMLJ	Grand Officer of Merit, Order of St Lazarus of Jerusalem
GOQ	Grand Officer, National Order of Quebec
GOSK	Grand Officer, Order of the Star and Key of the Indian Ocean (Mauritius)
Gov.	Governor
Govt	Government
GP	General Practitioner; Grand Prix
Gp	Group
GPDST	Girls' Public Day School Trust (*now see* GDST)
GPMU	Graphical, Paper and Media Union
GPO	General Post Office
GR	General Reconaissance
Gr.	Greek
GRNCM	Graduate of the Royal Northern College of Music
GRSM	Graduate of the Royal Schools of Music
GS	General Staff; Grammar School
g s	grandson
GSA	Girls' Schools Association
GSD	Gibraltar Social Democrats
GSM	General Service Medal; (Member of) Guildhall School of Music and Drama
GSMD	Guildhall School of Music and Drama
GSO	General Staff Officer
GTCL	Graduate, Trinity College of Music

GTS	General Theological Seminary (New York)
GUI	Golfing Union of Ireland
GWR	Great Western Railway

H

HA	Historical Association; Health Authority
HAA	Heavy Anti-Aircraft
HAC	Honourable Artillery Company
HACAS	Housing Association Consultancy and Advisory Service
Hants	Hampshire
HARCVS	Honorary Associate, Royal College of Veterinary Surgeons
Harv.	Harvard
HAT	Housing Action Trust
HBM	His (or Her) Britannic Majesty (Majesty's); Humming Bird Gold Medal (Trinidad)
hc	*honoris causa* (honorary)
HCA	Hospital Corporation of America
HCEG	Honourable Company of Edinburgh Golfers
HCF	Honorary Chaplain to the Forces
HCIMA	Hotel, Catering and International (*formerly* Institutional) Management Association
HCO	Higher Clerical Officer
HCSC	Higher Command and Staff Course
HDA	Hawkesbury Diploma in Agriculture (Australia); Health Development Agency
HDD	Higher Dental Diploma
HDE	Higher Diploma in Education
HDFA	Higher Diploma in Fine Art
HDipEd	Higher Diploma in Education
HE	His (or Her) Excellency; His Eminence
HEA	Health Education Authority (later HDA)
HEC	Ecole des Hautes Etudes Commerciales; Higher Education Corporation
HEFCE	Higher Education Funding Council for England
HEFCW	Higher Education Funding Council for Wales
HEH	His (or Her) Exalted Highness
Heir-pres.	Heir-presumptive
HEO	Higher Executive Officer
HEQC	Higher Education Quality Council (*now see* QAA)
HERDA-SW	Higher Education Regional Development Association - South West
HERO	Higher Education Research Opportunities
Herts	Hertfordshire
HFEA	Human Fertilisation and Embryology Authority
HG	Home Guard
HGTAC	Home Grown Timber Advisory Committee
HH	His (or Her) Highness; His Holiness; Member, Hesketh Hubbard Art Society
HHA	Historic Houses Association
HHD	Doctor of Humanities (US)
HI	Hawaii (postal)
HIH	His (or Her) Imperial Highness
HIM	His (or Her) Imperial Majesty
HIV	Human Immunodeficiency Virus
HJ	Hilal-e-Jurat (Pakistan)
HKIA	Hong Kong Institute of Architects
HKIPM	Hong Kong Institute of Personnel Management
HKSAR	Hong Kong Special Administrative Region
HLD	Doctor of Humane Letters
HLF	Heritage Lottery Fund
HLI	Highland Light Infantry
HM	His (or Her) Majesty, or Majesty's
HMA	Head Masters' Association
HMAS	His (or Her) Majesty's Australian Ship
HMC	Headmasters' and Headmistresses' (*formerly* Headmasters') Conference; Hospital Management Committee
HMCIC	His (or Her) Majesty's Chief Inspector of Constabulary
HMCS	His (or Her) Majesty's Canadian Ship
HMHS	His (or Her) Majesty's Hospital Ship
HMI	His (or Her) Majesty's Inspector
HMMTB	His (or Her) Majesty's Motor Torpedo Boat
HMNZS	His (or Her) Majesty's New Zealand Ship
HMOCS	His (or Her) Majesty's Overseas Civil Service
HMRC	His (or Her) Majesty's Revenue and Customs
HMS	His (or Her) Majesty's Ship
HMSO	His (or Her) Majesty's Stationery Office
HNC	Higher National Certificate
HND	Higher National Diploma
H of C	House of Commons
H of L	House of Lords
Hon.	Honourable; Honorary
HPA	Health Protection Agency
HPk	Hilal-e-Pakistan
HQ	Headquarters

HQA	Hilali-Quaid-i-Azam (Pakistan)
HR	Human Resources
HRA	Horseracing Regulatory Authority
HRGI	Honorary Member, The Royal Glasgow Institute of the Fine Arts
HRH	His (or Her) Royal Highness
HRHA	Honorary Member, Royal Hibernian Academy
HRI	Honorary Member, Royal Institute of Painters in Water Colours
HROI	Honorary Member, Royal Institute of Oil Painters
HRSA	Honorary Member, Royal Scottish Academy
HRSW	Honorary Member, Royal Scottish Water Colour Society
HRUA	Hon. Member, Royal Ulster Academy
HSC	Health and Safety Commission
HSE	Health and Safety Executive
HSH	His (or Her) Serene Highness
HSS	Health and Social Services
Hum.	Humanity, Humanities (Classics)
Hunts	Huntingdonshire
HVCert	Health Visitor's Certificate

I

I	Island; Ireland
IA	Indian Army; Iowa (postal)
IAA	International Academy of Architecture
IAAF	International Association of Athletics Federations (formerly International Amateur Athletic Federation)
IABSE	International Association of Bridge and Structural Engineers
IAC	Indian Armoured Corps; Institute of Amateur Cinematographers
IACP	International Association of Chiefs of Police
IACR	Institute of Arable Crops Research
IADB	Inter American Development Bank
IADR	International Association for Dental Research
IAEA	International Atomic Energy Agency
IAF	Indian Air Force; Indian Auxiliary Force
IAHM	Incorporated Association of Headmasters
IAHS	International Association of Hydrological Sciences
IAM	Institute of Advanced Motorists; Institute of Aviation Medicine
IAMAS	International Association of Meteorology and Atmospheric Sciences
IAMC	Indian Army Medical Corps
IAML	International Association of Music Libraries
IAMTACT	Institute of Advanced Machine Tool and Control Technology
IAO	Incorporated Association of Organists
IAOC	Indian Army Ordnance Corps
IAPS	Incorporated Association of Preparatory Schools
IAPSO	International Association for the Physical Sciences of the Oceans
IARO	Indian Army Reserve of Officers
IAS	Indian Administrative Service; Institute for Advanced Studies; International Academy of Science
IASC	International Arctic Science Committee
IASE	Institute of Advanced Studies in Education
IASPEI	International Association of Seismology and Physics of the Earth's Interior
IASS	International Association for Scandinavian Studies
IATA	International Air Transport Association
IATUL	International Association of Technological University Libraries
IAU	International Astronomical Union
IAVCEI	International Assembly of Volcanology and Chemistry of the Earth's Interior
IAWPRC	International Association on Water Pollution Research and Control
ib. or ibid.	*ibidem* (in the same place)
IBA	Independent Broadcasting Authority; International Bar Association
IBBY	International Board for Books for Young People
IBCA	International Braille Chess Association
IBG	Institute of British Geographers (now part of RGS)
IBRD	International Bank for Reconstruction and Development (World Bank)
IBRO	International Bank Research Organisation; International Brain Research Organisation
IBTE	Institution of British Telecommunications Engineers
IBVM	Institute of the Blessed Virgin Mary
i/c	in charge; in command
ICA	Institute of Contemporary Arts; Institute of Chartered Accountants in England and Wales (*now see* ICAEW)
ICAA	Invalid Children's Aid Association
ICAC	Independent Commission Against Corruption, Hong Kong
ICAEW	Institute of Chartered Accountants in England and Wales
ICAI	Institute of Chartered Accountants in Ireland
ICAO	International Civil Aviation Organization
ICAS	Institute of Chartered Accountants of Scotland
ICBP	International Council for Bird Preservation
ICBS	Irish Christian Brothers' School
ICC	International Chamber of Commerce; International Cricket Council (*formerly* International Cricket Conference)

ICCA	International Council for Commercial Arbitration
ICCROM	International Centre for Conservation at Rome
ICD	*Iuris Canonici Doctor* (Doctor of Canon Law); Independence Commemorative Decoration (Rhodesia)
ICD.D	Institute of Corporate Directors Director (Canada)
ICE	Institution of Civil Engineers
ICED	International Council for Educational Development
ICEF	International Federation of Chemical, Energy and General Workers' Unions
Icel.	Icelandic
ICES	International Council for the Exploration of the Sea
ICF	International Federation of Chemical and General Workers' Unions (*now see* ICEF)
ICFC	Industrial and Commercial Finance Corporation (later part of Investors in Industry)
ICFR	International Centre for Financial Regulation
ICFTU	International Confederation of Free Trade Unions
ICH	International Conference on Harmonisation
ICHCA	International Cargo Handling Co-ordination Association
IChemE	Institution of Chemical Engineers
ICI	Imperial Chemical Industries
ICJ	International Commission of Jurists
ICL	International Computers Ltd
ICM	International Confederation of Midwives
ICMA	Institute of Cost and Management Accountants (*now see* CIMA)
ICME	International Commission for Mathematical Education
ICNL	International Center for Not for Profit Law
ICOM	International Council of Museums
ICOMOS	International Council on Monuments and Sites
ICorr	Institute of Corrosion
ICorrST	Institution of Corrosion Science and Technology (*now see* ICorr)
ICPO	International Criminal Police Organization (Interpol)
ICRC	International Committee of the Red Cross
ICRF	Imperial Cancer Research Fund (*now see* CRUK)
ICS	Indian Civil Service
ICSA	Institute of Chartered Secretaries and Administrators
ICSC	International Council of Shopping Centres
ICSD	International Council for Scientific Development
ICSID	International Council of Societies of Industrial Design; International Centre for Settlement of Investment Disputes
ICSM	Imperial College School of Medicine
ICSS	International Committee for the Sociology of Sport
ICSTIS	Independent Committee for Supervision of Telephone Information Services
ICSTM	Imperial College of Science, Technology and Medicine, London
ICSU	International Council for Science (*formerly* International Council of Scientific Unions)
ICT	International Computers and Tabulators Ltd (later ICL); Information and Communications Technology
ID	Independence Decoration (Rhodesia); Idaho (postal)
IDA	International Development Association
IDB	Internal Drainage Board; Industrial Development Board
IDC	Imperial Defence College (*now see* RCDS); Inter-Diocesan Certificate
idc	completed a course at, or served for a year on the Staff of, the Imperial Defence College (*now see* rcds)
IDDA	Interior Decorators and Designers Association (*now see* BIDA)
IDeA	Improvement and Development Agency for Local Government
IDRC	International Development Research Centre
IDS	Institute of Development Studies; Industry Department for Scotland
IEA	Institute of Economic Affairs
IEC	International Electrotechnical Commission
IED	Institution of Engineering Designers
IEE	Institution of Electrical Engineers (*now see* IET)
IEEE	Institute of Electrical and Electronics Engineers (NY)
IEEIE	Institution of Electrical and Electronics Incorporated Engineers (later IIE)
IEETE	Institution of Electrical and Electronics Technician Engineers (later IIE)
IEI	Institution of Engineers of Ireland
IEIE	Institution of Electronics and Electrical Incorporated Engineers (later IIE)
IEMA	Institute of Environmental Management Assessment
IEME	Inspectorate of Electrical and Mechanical Engineering
IEng	Incorporated Engineer
IERE	Institution of Electronic and Radio Engineers
IES	Indian Educational Service; Institution of Engineers and Shipbuilders in Scotland; International Electron Paramagnetic Resonance Society
IET	Institution of Engineering and Technology
IExpE	Institute of Explosives Engineers
IFAC	International Federation of Automatic Control; International Federation of Accountants
IFAD	International Fund for Agricultural Development (UNO)
IFAW	International Fund for Animal Welfare
IFBWW	International Federation of Building Woodworkers
IFC	International Finance Corporation

IFIAS	International Federation of Institutes of Advanced Study
IFIP	International Federation for Information Processing
IFLA	International Federation of Library Associations
IFMGA	(Member of) International Federation of Mountain Guides Associations
IFOR	Implementation Force
IFORS	International Federation of Operational Research Societies
IFPI	International Federation of the Phonographic Industry
IFRA	World Press Research Association
IFS	Irish Free State; Indian Forest Service; Institute for Fiscal Studies
IG	Instructor in Gunnery
IGasE	Institution of Gas Engineers
IGPP	Institute of Geophysics and Planetary Physics
IGS	Independent Grammar School
IGU	International Geographical Union; International Gas Union
IHA	Institute of Health Service Administrators (later IHSM)
IHBC	(Member of) Institute of Historic Building Conservation
IHM	Institute of Healthcare Management
IHospE	Institute of Hospital Engineering
IHSM	Institute of Health Services Management (*now see* IHM)
IHVE	Institution of Heating and Ventilating Engineers (later CIBS)
IIE	Institution of Incorporated Engineers (*now see* IET)
IIEB	Institut International d'Etudes Bancaires
IIExE	Institution of Incorporated Executive Engineers
IILS	International Institute for Labour Studies
IIM	Institution of Industrial Managers
IIMR	Institute of Investment Management and Research
IIMT	International Institute for the Management of Technology
IInfSc	Institute of Information Scientists
IIRSM	International Institute of Risk and Safety Management
IIS	International Institute of Sociology
IISI	International Iron and Steel Institute
IISS	International Institute of Strategic Studies
IIT	Indian Institute of Technology
IL	Illinois (postal)
ILA	International Law Association
ILAC	International Laboratory Accreditation Co-operation
ILAM	Institute of Leisure and Amenity Management
ILEA	Inner London Education Authority
ILEC	Inner London Education Committee
Ill	Illinois
ILM	Institute of Leadership and Management
ILO	International Labour Office; International Labour Organisation
ILP	Independent Labour Party
ILR	Independent Local Radio; International Labour Review
ILT	Institute for Learning and Teaching in Higher Education
ILTM	Member, Institute for Learning and Teaching in Higher Education (*now see* FHEA)
IM	Individual Merit
IMA	International Music Association; Institute of Mathematics and its Applications
IMC	Instrument Meteorological Conditions
IMCB	International Management Centre from Buckingham
IMCO	Inter-Governmental Maritime Consultative Organization (*now see* IMO)
IME	Institute of Medical Ethics
IMEA	Incorporated Municipal Electrical Association
IMechE	Institution of Mechanical Engineers
IMechIE	Institution of Mechanical Incorporated Engineers (later IIE)
IMEDE	Institut pour l'Etude des Méthodes de Direction de l'Entreprise
IMF	International Monetary Fund
IMGTechE	Institution of Mechanical and General Technician Engineers
IMinE	Institution of Mining Engineers
IMM	Institution of Mining and Metallurgy (*now see* IMMM)
IMMLEP	Immunology of Leprosy
IMMM	Institute of Materials, Minerals and Mining
IMO	International Maritime Organization
Imp.	Imperial
IMRO	Investment Management Regulatory Organisation
IMS	Indian Medical Service; Institute of Management Services; International Military Staff
IMTA	Institute of Municipal Treasurers and Accountants (*now see* CIPFA)
IMU	International Mathematical Union
IMunE	Institution of Municipal Engineers (now amalgamated with Institution of Civil Engineers)
IN	Indian Navy; Indiana (postal)
INASFMH	International Sports Association for People with Mental Handicap
Inc.	Incorporated
INCA	International Newspaper Colour Association
Incog.	Incognito
Ind.	Independent
Inf.	Infantry
INFORM	Information Network Focus on New Religious Movements
INSA	Indian National Science Academy
INSEA	International Society for Education through Art

INSEAD *or* Insead	Institut Européen d'Administration des Affaires
Insp.	Inspector
INSS	Institute of Nuclear Systems Safety
Inst.	Institute
InstBE	Institution of British Engineers
Instn	Institution
InstSMM	Institute of Sales and Marketing Management
INTELSAT	International Telecommunications Satellite Organisation
IOC	International Olympic Committee; Intergovernmental Oceanographic Commission
IOCD	International Organisation for Chemical Science in Development
IoD	Institute of Directors
IODE	Imperial Order of the Daughters of the Empire
I of M	Isle of Man
IOM	Isle of Man; Indian Order of Merit
IOP	Institute of Painters in Oil Colours
IOSCO	International Organisation of Securities Committees
IOSH	Institution of Occupational Safety and Health
IOTA	(Fellow of) Institute of Transport Administration
IoW	Isle of Wight
IP	Intellectual Property
IPA	International Publishers' Association
IPC	International Property Corporation
IPCIS	International Institute for Practitioners in Credit Insurance and Surety
IPCS	Institution of Professional Civil Servants
IPE	International Petroleum Exchange
IPFA	Member or Associate, Chartered Institute of Public Finance and Accountancy (*now see* CPFA)
IPHE	Institution of Public Health Engineers (later IWEM)
IPI	International Press Institute; Institute of Patentees and Inventors
IPlantE	Institution of Plant Engineers
IPM	Institute of Personnel Management (later CIPD)
IPPA	Independent Programme Producers' Association
IPPF	International Planned Parenthood Federation
IPPR	Institute for Public Policy Research
IPPS	Institute of Physics and The Physical Society
IPR	Institute of Public Relations (*now see* CIPR)
IPRA	International Public Relations Association
IProdE	Institution of Production Engineers (later Institution of Manufacturing Engineering)
IPS	Indian Police Service; Indian Political Service; Institute of Purchasing and Supply
IPSM	Institute of Public Sector Managers
IPU	Inter-Parliamentary Union
IRA	Irish Republican Army
IRAD	Institute for Research on Animal Diseases
IRC	Industrial Reorganization Corporation; Interdisciplinary Research Centre
IRCAM	Institute for Research and Co-ordination in Acoustics and Music
IRCert	Industrial Relations Certificate
IREE(Aust)	Institution of Radio and Electronics Engineers (Australia)
IRI	Institution of the Rubber Industry (*now see* PRI)
IRO	International Refugee Organization
IRPA	International Radiation Protection Association
IRRV	(Fellow/Member of) Institute of Revenues, Rating and Valuation
IRTE	Institute of Road Transport Engineers
IS	International Society of Sculptors, Painters and Gravers
Is	Island(s)
ISAA	International Spill Response Accreditation Association
ISABE	International Society for Air Breathing Engines
ISAF	International Sailing Federation; International Security Assistance Force
ISAKOS	International Society for Arthroscopy and Knee Surgery
ISBA	Incorporated Society of British Advertisers
ISC	Imperial Service College, Haileybury; Indian Staff Corps; Independent Schools Council
ISCis	Independent Schools Council Information Service
ISCM	International Society for Contemporary Music
ISCO	Independent Schools Careers Organisation
ISE	Indian Service of Engineers
ISI	International Statistical Institute; Independent Schools Inspectorate
ISIS	Independent Schools Information Service (*see now* ISCis)
ISJC	Independent Schools Joint Council (*now see* ISC)
ISM	Incorporated Society of Musicians
ISMAR	International Society of Magnetic Resonance
ISME	International Society for Musical Education
ISMP	International Senior Management Program
ISMRC	Inter-Services Metallurgical Research Council
ISO	Imperial Service Order; International Organization for Standardization
ISPRS	International Society for Photogrammetry and Remote Sensing
ISSA	International Social Security Association
ISSTIP	International Society for Study of Tension in Performance
ISTC	Iron and Steel Trades Confederation; Institute of Scientific and Technical Communicators

ISTD	Imperial Society of Teachers of Dancing; Institute for the Study and Treatment of Delinquency
IStructE	Institution of Structural Engineers
ISVA	Incorporated Society of Valuers and Auctioneers
IT	Information Technology; Indian Territory (US)
It. or Ital.	Italian
ITA	Independent Television Authority (later IBA)
ITAB	Information Technology Advisory Board
ITB	Industry Training Board
ITC	International Trade Centre; Independent Television Commission
ITCA	Independent Television Association (*formerly* Independent Television Companies Association Ltd)
ITDG	Intermediate Technology Development Group
ITEME	Institution of Technician Engineers in Mechanical Engineering
ITF	International Transport Workers' Federation; International Tennis Federation
ITN	Independent Television News
ITO	International Trade Organization
ITSA	Information Technology Services Agency
ITU	International Telecommunication Union
ITUC	International Trade Union Confederation
ITV	Independent Television
ITVA	International Television Association
IUA	International Union of Architects
IUB	International Union of Biochemistry (*now see* IUBMB)
IUBMB	International Union of Biochemistry and Molecular Biology
IUC	Inter-University Council for Higher Education Overseas (*now see* IUPC)
IUCN	World Conservation Union (*formerly* International Union for the Conservation of Nature and Natural Resources)
IUCW	International Union for Child Welfare
IUGG	International Union of Geodesy & Geophysics
IUGS	International Union of Geological Sciences
IUHPS	International Union of the History and Philosophy of Science
IULA	International Union of Local Authorities
IUPAB	International Union of Pure and Applied Biophysics
IUPAC	International Union of Pure and Applied Chemistry
IUPAP	International Union of Pure and Applied Physics
IUPC	Inter-University and Polytechnic Council for Higher Education Overseas
IUPS	International Union of Physiological Sciences
IUSSP	International Union for the Scientific Study of Population
IUTAM	International Union of Theoretical and Applied Mechanics
IVF	In-vitro Fertilisation
IVS	International Voluntary Service
IWA	Inland Waterways Association
IWEM	Institution of Water and Environmental Management (*now see* CIWEM)
IWES	Institution of Water Engineers and Scientists (later IWEM)
IWGC	Imperial War Graves Commission (*now see* CWGC)
IWM	Institution of Works Managers (*now see* IIM)
IWO	Institution of Water Officers
IWPC	Institute of Water Pollution Control (later IWEM)
IWS	International Wool Secretariat
IWSA	International Water Supply Association
IWSOM	Institute of Practitioners in Work Study Organisation and Methods (*now see* IMS)
IWSP	Institute of Work Study Practitioners (*now see* IMS)
IYRU	International Yacht Racing Union (*now see* ISAF)
IZ	I Zingari

J

JA	Judge Advocate
JACT	Joint Association of Classical Teachers
JAG	Judge Advocate General
Jas	James
JCB	*Juris Canonici* (or *Civilis*) *Baccalaureus* (Bachelor of Canon (or Civil) Law)
JCR	Junior Common Room
JCS	Journal of the Chemical Society
JCD	*Juris Canonici* (or *Civilis*) *Doctor* (Doctor of Canon (or Civil) Law)
JCHMT	Joint Committee on Higher Medical Training, Royal Medical Colleges (*now see* JRCPTB)
JCI	Junior Chamber International
JCL	*Juris Canonici* (or *Civilis*) *Licentiatus* (Licentiate in Canon (or Civil) Law)
JCO	Joint Consultative Organisation (of AFRC, MAFF, and Department of Agriculture and Fisheries for Scotland)
JD	Doctor of Jurisprudence
jd	*jure dignitatis* (by virtue of status)
JDipMA	Joint Diploma in Management Accounting Services
JG	Junior Grade
JILA	Joint Institute for Laboratory Astrophysics
JInstE	Junior Institution of Engineers (*now see* IMGTechE)

JISC	Joint Information Systems Committee, Higher Education Funding Council
jl(s)	journal(s)
JMB	Joint Matriculation Board
JMN	Johan Mangku Negara (Malaysia)
JMOTS	Joint Maritime Operational Training Staff
JNCC	Joint Nature Conservation Committee
Jno. or Joh.	John
JP	Justice of the Peace
Jr	Junior
JRCPTB	Joint Royal Colleges of Physicians Training Board
jsc	qualified at a Junior Staff Course, or the equivalent, 1942-46
JSCSC	Joint Services Command and Staff College
JSD	Doctor of Juristic Science
JSDC	Joint Service Defence College
jsdc	completed a course at Joint Service Defence College
JSLO	Joint Service Liaison Officer
JSLS	Joint Services Liaison Staff
JSM	Johan Setia Mahkota (Malaysia); Master of the Science of Jurisprudence
JSPS	Japan Society for the Promotion of Science
JSSC	Joint Services Staff College
jssc	completed a course at Joint Services Staff College
JSU	Joint Support Unit
jt, jtly	joint, jointly
JUD	*Juris Utriusque Doctor* (Doctor of Both Laws (Canon and Civil))
Jun.	Junior
Jun.Opt.	Junior Optime
JWS or jws	Joint Warfare Staff

K

KA	Knight of St Andrew, Order of Barbados
Kans	Kansas
KAR	King's African Rifles
KBE	Knight Commander, Order of the British Empire
KC	King's Counsel
KCB	Knight Commander, Order of the Bath
KCC	Commander, Order of the Crown, Belgium and Congo Free State
KCGSJ	Knight Commander of Magisterial Grace, Order of St John of Jerusalem (Knights Hospitaller)
KCH	King's College Hospital; Knight Commander, Hanoverian Order
KCHS	Knight Commander, Order of the Holy Sepulchre
KCIE	Knight Commander, Order of the Indian Empire
KCJSJ	Knight Commander of Justice, Sovereign Order of St John of Jerusalem (Knights Hospitaller)
KCL	King's College London
KCLJ	Knight Commander, Order of St Lazarus of Jerusalem
KCMG	Knight Commander, Order of St Michael and St George
KCN	Knight Commander, Most Distinguished Order of the Nation (Antigua and Barbuda)
KCSA	Knight Commander, Military Order of the Collar of St Agatha of Paternò
KCSG	Knight Commander, Order of St Gregory the Great
KCSHS	Knight Commander with Star, Order of the Holy Sepulchre
KCSI	Knight Commander, Order of the Star of India
KCSJ	Knight Commander, Sovereign Order of St John of Jerusalem (Knights Hospitaller)
KCSS	Knight Commander, Order of St Silvester
KCVO	Knight Commander, Royal Victorian Order
KDG	King's Dragoon Guards
KEO	King Edward's Own
KFOR	Kosovo Force
KG	Knight, Order of the Garter
KGB	Komitet Gosudarstvennoi Bezopanosti (Committee of State Security, USSR)
KGCHS	Knight Grand Cross, Order of the Holy Sepulchre
KGCSS	Knight Grand Cross, Order of St Silvester
KGN	Knight Grand Collar, Most Distinguished Order of the Nation (Antigua and Barbuda)
KGSJ	Knight of Grace, Sovereign Order of St John of Jerusalem (Knights Hospitaller)
KGStJ	Knight of Grace, Order of St John of Jerusalem (*now see* KStJ)
KH	Knight, Hanoverian Order
KHC	Hon. Chaplain to the King
KHDS	Hon. Dental Surgeon to the King
KHNS	Hon. Nursing Sister to the King
KHP	Hon. Physician to the King
KHS	Hon. Surgeon to the King; Knight, Order of the Holy Sepulchre
K-i-H	Kaisar-i-Hind
KJSJ	Knight of Justice, Sovereign Order of St John of Jerusalem (Knights Hospitaller)
KJStJ	Knight of Justice, Order of St John of Jerusalem (*now see* KStJ)
KLJ	Knight, Order of St Lazarus of Jerusalem
KM	Knight of Malta
KMJ	Knight, Supreme Military Order of the Temple of Jerusalem

KMLJ	Knight of Merit, Order of St Lazarus of Jerusalem
KNH	Knight Companion, Most Exalted Order of National Hero (Antigua and Barbuda)
KNZM	Knight Companion, New Zealand Order of Merit
KOM	Companion, National Order of Merit (Malta)
KORR	King's Own Royal Regiment
KOSB	King's Own Scottish Borderers
KOYLI	King's Own Yorkshire Light Infantry
KP	Knight, Order of St Patrick
KPM	King's Police Medal
KrF	Kristelig Folkeparti
KRRC	King's Royal Rifle Corps
KS	King's Scholar; Kansas (postal)
KSC	Knight of St Columba
KSG	Knight, Order of St Gregory the Great
KSJ	Knight, Sovereign Order of St John of Jerusalem (Knights Hospitaller)
KSLI	King's Shropshire Light Infantry
KSS	Knight, Order of St Silvester
KStJ	Knight, Most Venerable Order of the Hospital of St John of Jerusalem
KStJ(A)	Associate Knight of Justice, Most Venerable Order of the Hospital of St John of Jerusalem
KT	Knight, Order of the Thistle
Kt	Knight
KUOM	Companion of Honour, National Order of Merit (Malta)
KY	Kentucky (postal)
Ky	Kentucky

L

L	Liberal
LA	Los Angeles; Library Association; Liverpool Academy; Louisiana (postal)
La	Louisiana
LAA	Light Anti-Aircraft
Lab	Labour
LAC	London Athletic Club; Los Angeles County
LACSAB	Local Authorities Conditions of Service Advisory Board
LAE	London Association of Engineers
LAMDA	London Academy of Music and Dramatic Art
LAMSAC	Local Authorities' Management Services and Computer Committee
LAMTPI	Legal Associate Member, Town Planning Institute (*now see* LMRTPI)
Lance-Corp.	Lance-Corporal
Lancs	Lancashire
LAPADA	London & Provincial Antique Dealers' Association
LARSP	Language Assessment, Remediation and Screening Procedure
Lautro	Life Assurance and Unit Trust Regulatory Organisation
LBC	London Broadcasting Company; London Borough Council
LBHI	Licentiate, British Horological Institute
LBIPP	Licentiate, British Institute of Professional Photography
LC	Cross of Leo
LCA	Licensed Companies Auditor
LCAD	London Certificate in Art and Design (University of London)
LCC	London County Council (later GLC)
LCCI	London Chamber of Commerce and Industry
LCD	Lord Chancellor's Department
LCh	Licentiate in Surgery
LCJ	Lord Chief Justice
LCL	Licentiate of Canon Law
LCM	(Member of) London College of Music and Media
LCP	Licentiate, College of Preceptors
LCSP	London and Counties Society of Physiologists
LCST	Licentiate, College of Speech Therapists
LD	Liberal and Democratic; Licentiate in Divinity
LDC	Limited Duration Company (US)
LDDC	London Docklands Development Corporation
LDiv	Licentiate in Divinity
LDP	Liberal Democratic Party (Japan)
Ldr	Leader
LDS	Licentiate in Dental Surgery
LDV	Local Defence Volunteers
LEA	Local Education Authority
LEAD	Leadership in Environment and Development
LEADR	Lawyers Engaged in Alternative Dispute Resolution
LEDU	Local Enterprise Development Unit
LEP	Local Ecumenical Project
LEPRA	British Leprosy Relief Association
LèsL	Licencié ès lettres
LèsSc	Licencié ès Sciences
LG	Lady Companion, Order of the Garter
LGA	Local Government Association
LGSM	Licentiate, Guildhall School of Music and Drama

LGTB	Local Government Training Board
LH	Light Horse
LHD	*Literarum Humaniorum Doctor* (Doctor of Literature)
LHSM	Licentiate, Institute of Health Services Management
LI	Light Infantry; Long Island
LIBA	Lloyd's Insurance Brokers' Association
Lib Dem	Liberal Democrat
LIBER	Ligue des Bibliothèques Européennes de Recherche
LicMed	Licentiate in Medicine
Lieut	Lieutenant
LIFFE	London International Financial Futures and Options Exchange
LIFT	Local Improvement Finance Trust
LIMA	Licentiate, Institute of Mathematics and its Applications; International Licensing Industry Merchandisers' Association
Lincs	Lincolnshire
LIOB	Licentiate, Institute of Building
Lit.	Literature; Literary
LitD	Doctor of Literature; Doctor of Letters
Lit.Hum.	*Literae Humaniores* (Classics)
LittD	Doctor of Literature; Doctor of Letters
LJ	Lord Justice
LLAM	Licentiate, London Academy of Music and Dramatic Art
LLB	Bachelor of Laws
LLC	Limited Liability Company
LLCM	Licentiate, London College of Music
LLD	Doctor of Laws
LLL	Licentiate in Laws
LLM	Master of Laws
LLP	Limited Liability Partnership
LLSC	Local Learning and Skills Council
LM	Licentiate in Midwifery
LMBC	Lady Margaret Boat Club
LMC	Local Medical Committee
LMCC	Licentiate, Medical Council of Canada
LMed	Licentiate in Medicine
LMH	Lady Margaret Hall, Oxford
LMR	London Midland Region (BR)
LMS	London, Midland and Scottish Railway; London Missionary Society; London Mathematical Society
LMSSA	Licentiate in Medicine and Surgery, Society of Apothecaries
LMRTPI	Legal Member, Royal Town Planning Institute
LNat	Liberal National
LNER	London and North Eastern Railway
LOB	Location of Offices Bureau
LOCOG	London Organising Committee, 2012 Olympic Games
L of C	Library of Congress; Lines of Communication
LP	Limited Partnership
LPh	Licentiate in Philosophy
LPO	London Philharmonic Orchestra
LPTB	London Passenger Transport Board (later LTE)
LRAD	Licentiate, Royal Academy of Dancing
LRAM	Licentiate, Royal Academy of Music
LRCP	Licentiate, Royal College of Physicians, London
LRCPE	Licentiate, Royal College of Physicians, Edinburgh
LRCPI	Licentiate, Royal College of Physicians of Ireland
LRCPSGlas	Licentiate, Royal College of Physicians and Surgeons of Glasgow
LRCS	Licentiate, Royal College of Surgeons of England
LRCSE	Licentiate, Royal College of Surgeons, Edinburgh
LRCSI	Licentiate, Royal College of Surgeons in Ireland
LRelSc	Licentiate in Religious Sciences
LRFPS(G)	Licentiate, Royal Faculty of Physicians and Surgeons, Glasgow (*now see* LRCPSGlas)
LRIBA	Licentiate, Royal Institute of British Architects (*now see* RIBA)
LRPS	Licentiate, Royal Photographic Society
LRSM	Licentiate, Royal Schools of Music
LRT	London Regional Transport
LSA	Licentiate, Society of Apothecaries; Licence in Agricultural Sciences
LSC	Learning and Skills Council
LSE	London School of Economics and Political Science
LSHTM	London School of Hygiene and Tropical Medicine
LSO	London Symphony Orchestra
LSS	Licentiate in Sacred Scripture
Lt	Lieutenant; Light
LT	Lady, Order of the Thistle; London Transport (later LRT); Licentiate in Teaching
LTA	Lawn Tennis Association
LTB	London Transport Board (later LTE)
LTCL	Licentiate of Trinity College of Music, London
Lt Col	Lieutenant Colonel
LTE	London Transport Executive (later LRT)
Lt Gen.	Lieutenant General
LTh	Licentiate in Theology
LTS	London Topographical Society
LU	Liberal Unionist

LUOTC	London University Officers' Training Corps
LVO	Lieutenant, Royal Victorian Order (*formerly* MVO (Fourth Class))
LWT	London Weekend Television
LXX	Septuagint

M

M	Marquess; Member; Monsieur
m	married
MA	Master of Arts; Military Assistant; Massachusetts (postal)
MAA	Manufacturers' Agents Association of Great Britain
MAAF	Mediterranean Allied Air Forces
MAAT	Member, Association of Accounting Technicians
MACE	Member, Australian College of Education; Member, Association of Conference Executives
MACI	Member, American Concrete Institute
MACM	Member, Association of Computing Machines
MACS	Member, American Chemical Society
MADO	Member, Association of Dispensing Opticians
MAE	Member, Academia Europaea
MAEE	Marine Aircraft Experimental Establishment
MAF	Ministry of Agriculture and Fisheries
MAFF	Ministry of Agriculture, Fisheries and Food
MAHL	Master of Arts in Hebrew Letters
MAI	*Magister in Arte Ingeniaria* (Master of Engineering)
MAIAA	Member, American Institute of Aeronautics and Astronautics
MAIBC	Member, Architectural Institute of British Columbia
MAICD	Member, Australian Institute of Company Directors
MAICE	Member, American Institute of Consulting Engineers
MAIChE	Member, American Institute of Chemical Engineers
Maj. Gen.	Major General
MALD	Master of Arts in Law and Diplomacy
Man	Manitoba
M&A	Mergers and Acquisitions
MAO	Master of Obstetric Art
MAOT	Member, Association of Occupational Therapists
MAOU	Member, American Ornithologists' Union
MAP	Ministry of Aircraft Production
MAPM	Member, Association for Project Management
MAppSc	Master of Applied Science
MAPsS	Member, Australian Psychological Society
MARAC	Member, Australasian Register of Agricultural Consultants
MArch	Master of Architecture
MARIS	Multi-State Aquatic Resources Information System
Marq.	Marquess
MAS	Minimal Access Surgery
MASAE	Member, American Society of Agricultural Engineers
MASC	Member, Australian Society of Calligraphers
MASc	Master of Applied Science
MASCE	Member, American Society of Civil Engineers
MASME	Member, American Society of Mechanical Engineers
Mass	Massachusetts
MAT	Master of Arts and Teaching (US)
MATh	Master of Arts in Theology
Math.	Mathematics; Mathematical
MATSA	Managerial Administrative Technical Staff Association
MAusIMM	Member, Australasian Institute of Mining and Metallurgy
MB	Medal of Bravery (Canada); Bachelor of Medicine; Manitoba (postal)
MBA	Master of Business Administration
MBASW	Member, British Association of Social Workers
MBC	Metropolitan/Municipal Borough Council
MBCS	Member, British Computer Society
MBE	Member, Order of the British Empire
MBES	Member, Biological Engineering Society
MBFR	Mutual and Balanced Force Reductions (negotiations)
MBHI	Member, British Horological Institute
MBIFD	Member, British Institute of Funeral Directors
MBII	Member, British Institute of Innkeeping
MBIM	Member, British Institute of Management (later MIMgt)
MBKS	Member, British Kinematograph Society (*now see* MBKSTS)
MBKSTS	Member, British Kinematograph, Sound and Television Society
MBL	Master of Business Leadership
MBOU	Member, British Ornithologists' Union
MBPICS	Member, British Production and Inventory Control Society
MBritIRE	Member, British Institution of Radio Engineers (later MIERE)
MBS	Member, Building Societies Institute (*now see* MCBSI)
MBSc	Master of Business Science
MC	Military Cross; Missionaries of Charity
MCAM	Member, CAM Foundation
MCB	Master in Clinical Biochemistry; Muslim Council of Britain
MCBSI	Member, Chartered Building Societies Institute
MCC	Marylebone Cricket Club; Metropolitan County Council

MCCDRCS	Member in Clinical Community Dentistry, Royal College of Surgeons
MCD	Master of Civic Design
MCE	Master of Civil Engineering
MCFP	Member, College of Family Physicians (Canada)
MCGI	Member, City and Guilds of London Institute
MCh or MChir	Master in Surgery
MChD	Master of Dental Surgery
MChE	Master of Chemical Engineering
MChemA	Master in Chemical Analysis
MChOrth	Master of Orthopaedic Surgery
MCIArb	Member, Chartered Institute of Arbitrators
MCIBS	Member, Chartered Institution of Building Services (*now see* MCIBSE)
MCIBSE	Member, Chartered Institution of Building Services Engineers
MCIH	Member, Chartered Institute of Housing
MCIJ	Member, Chartered Institute of Journalists
MCIL	Member, Chartered Institute of Linguists
MCIM	Member, Chartered Institute of Marketing
MCIMarE	Member, Canadian Institute of Marine Engineers
MCIOB	Member, Chartered Institute of Building
MCIPD	Member, Charted Institute of Personnel and Development
MCIPR	Member, Chartered Institute of Public Relations
MCIPS	Member, Chartered Institute of Purchasing and Supply
M.CIRP	Member, International Institution for Production Engineering Research
MCIS	Member, Institute of Chartered Secretaries and Administrators
MCIT	Member, Chartered Institute of Transport (*now see* CMILT)
MCIWEM	Member, Chartered Institution of Water and Environmental Management
MCIWM	Member, Chartered Institution of Wastes Management
MCL	Master in Civil Law
MCLIP	Member, Chartered Institute of Library and Information Professionals
MCMI	Member, Chartered Management Institute
MCollP	Member, College of Preceptors
MCom	Master of Commerce
MConsE	Member, Association of Consulting Engineers
MConsEI	Member, Association of Consulting Engineers of Ireland
MCOphth	Member, College of Ophthalmologists (*now see* MRCOphth)
MCP	Member of Colonial Parliament; Master of City Planning (US)
MCPA	Member, College of Pathologists of Australia (*now see* MRCPA)
MCPP	Member, College of Pharmacy Practice
MCPS	Member, College of Physicians and Surgeons
MCS	Malayan Civil Service
MCSD	Member, Chartered Society of Designers
MCSEE	Member, Canadian Society of Electrical Engineers
MCSP	Member, Chartered Society of Physiotherapy
MCST	Member, College of Speech Therapists
MCT	Member, Association of Corporate Treasurers
MD	Doctor of Medicine; Military District; Maryland (postal)
Md	Maryland
MDC	Metropolitan District Council
MDes	Master of Design
MDiv	Master of Divinity
MDS	Master of Dental Surgery
MDSc	Master of Dental Science
ME	Mining Engineer; Middle East; Master of Engineering; Maine (postal); Myalgic Encephalomyelitis
MEAF	Middle East Air Force
MEC	Member of Executive Council; Middle East Command
MEc	Master of Economics
MECAS	Middle East Centre for Arab Studies
Mech.	Mechanics; Mechanical
MECI	Member, Institute of Employment Consultants
Med.	Medical
MEd	Master of Education
MED	Master of Environmental Design
MEdSt	Master of Educational Studies
MEF	Middle East Force
MEI	Member, Energy Institute
MEIC	Member, Engineering Institute of Canada
MELF	Middle East Land Forces
Mencap	Royal Society for Mentally Handicapped Children and Adults
MEng	Master of Engineering
MEnvS	Master of Environmental Studies
MEO	Marine Engineering Officer
MEP	Member of the European Parliament
MESc	Master of Engineering Science
MetR	Metropolitan Railway
MetSoc	Metals Society (formed by amalgamation of Institute of Metals and Iron and Steel Institute; now merged with Institution of Metallurgists to form Institute of Metals)
MEWI	Member, Expert Witness Institute
MEXE	Military Engineering Experimental Establishment
MF	Master of Forestry
MFA	Master of Fine Arts

MFC	Mastership in Food Control
MFCM	Member, Faculty of Community Medicine (later MFPHM)
MFFP	Member, Faculty of Family Planning, Royal College of Obstetricians and Gynaecologists
MFGB	Miners' Federation of Great Britain (now see NUM)
MFH	Master of Foxhounds
MFHom	Member, Faculty of Homoeopathy
MFOM	Member, Faculty of Occupational Medicine
MFPaed	Member, Faculty of Paediatrics, Royal College of Physicians of Ireland
MFPH	Member, Faculty of Public Health
MFPHM	Member, Faculty of Public Health Medicine (now see MFPH)
MFPHMI	Member, Faculty of Public Health Medicine of Ireland
MGA	Major General in charge of Administration
MGC	Machine Gun Corps
MGDSRCS	Member in General Dental Surgery, Royal College of Surgeons
MGGS	Major General, General Staff
MGI	Member, Institute of Certificated Grocers
MGO	Master General of the Ordnance; Master of Gynaecology and Obstetrics
Mgr	Monsignor
MHA	Member of House of Assembly
MHCIMA	Member, Hotel Catering and International (formerly Institutional) Management Association (now see MIH)
MHK	Member of the House of Keys
MHort (RHS)	Master of Horticulture, Royal Horticultural Society
MHR	Member of the House of Representatives
MHRA	Modern Humanities Research Association
MHRF	Mental Health Research Fund
MHSM	Member, Institute of Health Services Management (now see MIHM)
MI	Military Intelligence; Michigan (postal)
MIAeE	Member, Institution of Aeronautical Engineers
MIAgrE	Member, Institution of Agricultural Engineers
MIAM	Member, Institute of Administrative Management
MIAS	Member, Institute of Aeronautical Science (US) (now see MAIAA); Member, Institute of Architects and Surveyors
MIBC	Member, Institute of Business Counsellors; Member, Institute of Building Control
MIBF	Member, Institute of British Foundrymen
MIBiol	Member, Institute of Biology
MIBritE	Member, Institution of British Engineers
MICE	Member, Institution of Civil Engineers
MICEI	Member, Institution of Civil Engineers of Ireland
MICeram	Member, Institute of Ceramics (later MIM)
MICFor	Member, Institute of Chartered Foresters
Mich	Michigan
MIChemE	Member, Institution of Chemical Engineers
MICM	Member, Institute of Credit Management
MICorr	Member, Institute of Corrosion
MICorrST	Member, Institution of Corrosion Science and Technology (now see MICorr)
MICS	Member, Institute of Chartered Shipbrokers
MIDPM	Member, Institute of Data Processing Management
MIE(Aust)	Member, Institution of Engineers, Australia
MIED	Member, Institution of Engineering Designers
MIEE	Member, Institution of Electrical Engineers (now see MIET)
MIEEE	Member, Institute of Electrical and Electronics Engineers (NY)
MIEEM	Member, Institute of Ecology and Environmental Management
MIEI	Member, Institution of Engineering Inspection
MIEMA	Member, Institute of Environmental Management and Assessment
MIEMgt	Member, Institute of Environmental Management (now see MIEMA)
MIEnvSc	Member, Institute of Environmental Science
MIERE	Member, Institution of Electronic and Radio Engineers (later MIEE)
MIES	Member, Institution of Engineers and Shipbuilders, Scotland
MIET	Member, Institution of Engineering and Technology (formerly Member, Institute of Engineers and Technicians)
MIEx	Member, Institute of Export
MIExpE	Member, Institute of Explosives Engineers
MIFA	Member, Institute of Field Archaeologists
MIFF	Member, Institute of Freight Forwarders (now see MIFP)
MIFireE	Member, Institution of Fire Engineers
MIFM	Member, Institute of Fisheries Management
MIFor	Member, Institute of Foresters (now see MICFor)
MIFP	Member, Institute of Freight Professionals
MIGasE	Member, Institution of Gas Engineers (now see MIGEM)
MIGEM	Member, Institution of Gas Engineers and Managers
MIGeol	Member, Institution of Geologists
MIH	Member, Institute of Housing (now see MCIH); Member, Institute of Hospitality
MIHM	Member, Institute of Housing Managers (later MIH); Member, Institute of Healthcare Management
MIHort	Member, Institute of Horticulture
MIHT	Member, Institution of Highways and Transportation

MIHVE	Member, Institution of Heating and Ventilating Engineers (later MCIBS)
MIIA	Member, Institute of Industrial Administration (later FBIM)
MIIE	Member, Institution of Incorporated Engineers in Electronic, Electrical and Mechanical Engineering (now see MIET)
MIIM	Member, Institution of Industrial Managers
MIInfSc	Member, Institute of Information Sciences (now see MCLIP)
MIL	Member, Institute of Linguists (now see MCIL)
Mil.	Military
MILGA	Member, Institute of Local Government Administrators
MILocoE	Member, Institution of Locomotive Engineers
MILog	Member, Institute of Logistics (now see MILT)
MILT	Member, Chartered Institute of Logistics and Transport
MIM	Member, Institute of Materials (formerly Institution of Metallurgists, then Institute of Metals) (now see MIMMM)
MIMA	Member, Institute of Mathematics and its Applications
MIMarE	Member, Institute of Marine Engineers (now see MIMarEST)
MIMarEST	Member, Institute of Marine Engineering, Science and Technology
MIMC	Member, Institute of Management Consultants
MIMechE	Member, Institution of Mechanical Engineers
MIMEMME	Member, Institution of Mining Electrical & Mining Mechanical Engineers (later MIMinE)
MIMgt	Member, Institute of Management (see now MCMI)
MIMGTechE	Member, Institution of Mechanical and General Technician Engineers
MIMI	Member, Institute of the Motor Industry
MIMinE	Member, Institution of Mining Engineers (later MIMM)
MIMM	Member, Institution of Mining and Metallurgy (now see MIMMM)
MIMMM	Member, Institute of Materials, Minerals and Mining
MIMunE	Member, Institution of Municipal Engineers (now amalgamated with Institution of Civil Engineers)
MIN	Member, Institute of Navigation (now see MRIN)
Min.	Ministry
Minn	Minnesota
MInstAM	Member, Institute of Administrative Management
MInstBE	Member, Institution of British Engineers
MInstCE	Member, Institute of Civil Engineers (now see FICE)
MInstD	Member, Institute of Directors
MInstE	Member, Institute of Energy (now see MEI)
MInstEnvSci	Member, Institute of Environmental Sciences
MInstF	Member, Institute of Fuel (later MInstE)
MInstHE	Member, Institution of Highway Engineers (now see MIHT)
MInstKT	Member, Institute of Knowledge Transfer
MInstM	Member, Institute of Marketing (now see MCIM)
MInstMC	Member, Institute of Measurement and Control
MInstME	Member, Institution of Mining Engineers
MInstMet	Member, Institute of Metals (later part of Metals Society; then MIM)
MInstP	Member, Institute of Physics
MInstPet	Member, Institute of Petroleum (now see MEI)
MInstPI	Member, Institute of Patentees and Inventors
MInstPkg	Member, Institute of Packaging
MInstPS	Member, Institute of Purchasing and Supply
MInstRA	Member, Institute of Registered Architects
MInstRE	Member, Institute of Royal Engineers
MInstT	Member, Institute of Transport (later MCIT)
MInstTA	Member, Institute of Transport Administration
MInstTM	Member, Institute of Travel Managers in Industry and Commerce
MInstW	Member, Institute of Welding (now see MWeldI)
MInstWM	Member, Institute of Wastes Management (now see MCIWM)
MINucE	Member, Institution of Nuclear Engineers
MIOA	Member, Institute of Acoustics
MIOB	Member, Institute of Building (now see MCIOB)
MIOM	Member, Institute of Office Management (now see MIAM)
MIOSH	Member, Institution of Occupational Safety and Health
MIPA	Member, Institute of Practitioners in Advertising
MIPD	Member, Institute of Personnel and Development (now see MCIPD)
MIPlantE	Member, Institution of Plant Engineers
MIPM	Member, Institute of Personnel Management (later MIPD)
MIPR	Member, Institute of Public Relations (now see MCIPR)
MIProdE	Member, Institution of Production Engineers (later MIEE)
MIQ	Member, Institute of Quarrying
MIQA	Member, Institute of Quality Assurance
MIRE	Member, Institution of Radio Engineers (later MIERE)
MIREE(Aust)	Member, Institution of Radio and Electronics Engineers (Australia)
MIRM	Member, Institute of Risk Management
MIRO	Mineral Industry Research Organisation
MIRT	Member, Institute of Reprographic Technicians
MIRTE	Member, Institute of Road Transport Engineers
MIS	Member, Institute of Statisticians
MISI	Member, Iron and Steel Institute (later part of Metals Society)
Miss	Mississippi
MIStructE	Member, Institution of Structural Engineers

MIT	Massachusetts Institute of Technology
MITA	Member, Industrial Transport Association
MITD	Member, Institute of Training and Development (later MIPD)
MITE	Member, Institution of Electrical and Electronics Technician Engineers
MITI	Member, Institute of Translation & Interpreting
MITSA	Member, Institute of Trading Standards Administration
MITT	Member, Institute of Travel and Tourism
MIWE	Member, Institution of Water Engineers (later MIWES)
MIWEM	Member, Institution of Water and Environmental Management (*now see* MCIWEM)
MIWES	Member, Institution of Water Engineers and Scientists (later MIWEM)
MIWM	Member, Institution of Works Managers (*now see* MIIM)
MIWPC	Member, Institute of Water Pollution Control (later MIWEM)
MIWSP	Member, Institute of Work Study Practitioners (*now see* MMS)
MJA	Medical Journalists Association
MJI	Member, Institute of Journalists (*now see* MCIJ)
MJIE	Member, Junior Institution of Engineers (*now see* MIGTechE)
MJS	Member, Japan Society
MJur	*Magister Juris* (Master of Law)
ML	Licentiate in Medicine; Master of Laws
MLA	Member of Legislative Assembly; Modern Language Association; Master in Landscape Architecture; Museums, Libraries and Archives Council
MLC	Member of Legislative Council; Meat and Livestock Commission
MLCOM	Member, London College of Osteopathic Medicine
MLI	Member, Landscape Institute
MLib	Master of Librarianship
MLitt	Master of Letters
Mlle	Mademoiselle
MLO	Military Liaison Officer
MLR	Modern Language Review
MLS	Master of Library Science
MM	Military Medal; Merchant Marine
MMA	Metropolitan Museum of Art
MMan	Master of Management
MMB	Milk Marketing Board
MMD	Movement for Multi-Party Democracy
MME	Master of Mining Engineering
Mme	Madame
MMechE	Master of Mechanical Engineering
MMet	Master of Metallurgy
MMGI	Member, Mining, Geological and Metallurgical Institute of India
MMin	Master of Ministry
MMM	Member, Order of Military Merit (Canada)
MMRS	Member, Market Research Society
MMS	Member, Institute of Management Services
MMSA	Master of Midwifery, Society of Apothecaries
MMus	Master of Music
MN	Merchant Navy; Minnesota (postal)
MNAS	Member, National Academy of Sciences (US)
MND	Motor Neurone Disease
MNECInst	Member, North East Coast Institution of Engineers and Shipbuilders
MNI	Member, Nautical Institute
MNIMH	Member, National Institute of Medical Herbalists
MNSE	Member, Nigerian Society of Engineers
MNZIS	Member, New Zealand Institute of Surveyors
MNZPI	Member, New Zealand Planning Institute
MO	Medical Officer; Military Operations; Missouri (postal)
Mo	Missouri
MoD	Ministry of Defence
Mods	Moderations (Oxford)
MOF	Ministry of Food
MOH	Medical Officer(s) of Health
MOI	Ministry of Information
MoJ	Ministry of Justice
MOM	Member, Order of Merit (Malta)
MOMA	Museum of Modern Art
MOMI	Museum of the Moving Image
Mon	Monmouthshire
Mont	Montgomeryshire
MOP	Ministry of Power
MOrthRCS	Member in Orthodontics, Royal College of Surgeons
MoS	Ministry of Supply
Most Rev.	Most Reverend
MoT	Ministry of Transport
MOV	Member, Order of Volta (Ghana)
MP	Member of Parliament
MPA	Master of Public Administration; Member, Parliamentary Assembly, Northern Ireland
MPAGB	Member, Photographic Alliance of Great Britain
MPBW	Ministry of Public Building and Works
MPH	Master of Public Health
MPhil	Master of Philosophy

MPIA	Master of Public and International Affairs
MPMI	Member, Property Management Institute
MPO	Management and Personnel Office
MPP	Member, Provincial Parliament; Master in Public Policy (Harvard)
MPRISA	Member, Public Relations Institute of South Africa
MPS	Member, Pharmaceutical Society (*now see* MRPharmS)
MR	Master of the Rolls; Municipal Reform
MRAC	Member, Royal Agricultural College
MRACP	Member, Royal Australasian College of Physicians
MRACS	Member, Royal Australasian College of Surgeons
MRad	Master of Radiology
MRAeS	Member, Royal Aeronautical Society
MRAIC	Member, Royal Architectural Institute of Canada
MRAS	Member, Royal Asiatic Society
MRC	Medical Research Council
MRCA	Multi-Role Combat Aircraft
MRCGP	Member, Royal College of General Practitioners
MRC-LMB	Medical Research Council Laboratory of Molecular Biology
MRCOG	Member, Royal College of Obstetricians and Gynaecologists
MRCOphth	Member, Royal College of Ophthalmologists
MRCP	Member, Royal College of Physicians, London
MRCPA	Member, Royal College of Pathologists of Australia
MRCPath	Member, Royal College of Pathologists
MRCPCH	Member, Royal College of Paediatrics and Child Health
MRCPE	Member, Royal College of Physicians, Edinburgh
MRCPGlas	Member, Royal College of Physicians and Surgeons of Glasgow
MRCPI	Member, Royal College of Physicians of Ireland
MRCPsych	Member, Royal College of Psychiatrists
MRCS	Member, Royal College of Surgeons of England
MRCSE	Member, Royal College of Surgeons of Edinburgh
MRCSI	Member, Royal College of Surgeons in Ireland
MRCVS	Member, Royal College of Veterinary Surgeons
MRD RCS	Member in Restorative Dentistry, Royal College of Surgeons
MRE	Master of Religious Education
MRes	Master of Research
MRHS	Member, Royal Horticultural Society
MRI	Magnetic Resonance Imaging; Member, Royal Institution
MRIA	Member, Royal Irish Academy
MRIAI	Member, Royal Institute of the Architects of Ireland
MRIC	Member, Royal Institute of Chemistry (*now see* MRSC)
MRICS	Member, Royal Institution of Chartered Surveyors
MRIN	Member, Royal Institute of Navigation
MRINA	Member, Royal Institution of Naval Architects
MRNZCGP	Member, Royal New Zealand College of General Practitioners
MRPharmS	Member, Royal Pharmaceutical Society
MRSanI	Member, Royal Sanitary Institute (*now see* MRSH)
MRSC	Member, Royal Society of Chemistry
MRSH	Member, Royal Society for the Promotion of Health
MRSL	Member, Order of the Republic of Sierra Leone
MRSocMed	Member, Royal Society of Medicine
MRTPI	Member, Royal Town Planning Institute
MRurSc	Master of Rural Science
MRUSI	Member, Royal United Service Institution
MRVA	Member, Rating and Valuation Association
MS	Master of Surgery; Master of Science (US); Mississippi (postal); Multiple Sclerosis; Motor Ship
MS, MSS	Manuscript, Manuscripts
MSA	Master of Science, Agriculture (US); Mineralogical Society of America; Motor Sports Association
MSAAIE	Member, Southern African Association of Industrial Editors
MSAE	Member, Society of Automotive Engineers (US)
MSAICE	Member, South African Institution of Civil Engineers
MSAInstMM	Member, South African Institute of Mining and Metallurgy
MS&R	Merchant Shipbuilding and Repairs
MSC	Manpower Services Commission; Missionaries of the Sacred Heart
MSc	Master of Science
MScD	Master of Dental Science
MScSoc	Master of Social Sciences
MScSocMed	Master of Science in Social Medicine
MSD	Meritorious Service Decoration (Fiji)
MSE	Master of Science in Engineering (US)
MSF	(Union for) Manufacturing, Science, Finance
MSFA	Member, Society of Financial Advisers
MSHyg	Master of Science in Hygiene
MSI	Member, Securities Institute
MSIA	Member, Society of Industrial Artists
MSIAD	Member, Society of Industrial Artists and Designers (*now see* MCSD)
MSIT	Member, Society of Instrument Technology (*now see* MInstMC)
MSLS	Master of Science in Library Science
MSM	Meritorious Service Medal; Madras Sappers and Miners; Master in Science Management
MSN	Master of Science in Nursing
MSocAdmin	Master of Social Administration

MSocIS	Member, Société des Ingénieurs et Scientifiques de France
MSocSc	Master of Social Sciences
MSocWork	Master of Social Work
MSoFHT	Member, Society of Food Hygiene Technology
MSP	Member, Scottish Parliament; Managing Successful Programmes
MSR	Member, Society of Radiographers
MSRP	Member, Society for Radiological Protection
MSSc	Master of Social Sciences
MSSC	Marine Society & Sea Cadets
MSt	Master of Studies
MSTD	Member, Society of Typographic Designers
MStJ	Member, Most Venerable Order of the Hospital of St John of Jerusalem
MSW	Master of Social Work
MSzP	Magyar Szocialista Párt
MT	Mechanical Transport; Montana (postal)
Mt	Mount, Mountain
MTA	Music Trades Association
MTAI	Member, Institute of Travel Agents
MTB	Motor Torpedo Boat
MTCA	Ministry of Transport and Civil Aviation
MTD	Midwife Teachers' Diploma
MTech	Master of Technology
MTEFL	Master in the Teaching of English as a Foreign or Second Language
MTh	Master of Theology
MTIA	Metal Trades Industry Association
MTIRA	Machine Tool Industry Research Association (*now see* AMTRI)
MTPI	Member, Town Planning Institute (*now see* MRTPI)
MTS	Master of Theological Studies; Ministerial Training Scheme
MUniv	Honorary Master of the University
MusB	Bachelor of Music
MusD	Doctor of Music
MusM	Master of Music
MV	Merchant Vessel, Motor Vessel (naval)
MVB	Bachelor of Veterinary Medicine
MVEE	Military Vehicles and Engineering Establishment
MVO	Member, Royal Victorian Order
MVSc	Master of Veterinary Science
MW	Master of Wine
MWA	Mystery Writers of America
MWeldI	Member, Welding Institute
MWSOM	Member, Institute of Practitioners in Work Study Organisation and Methods (*now see* MMS)

N

N	Nationalist; Navigating Duties; North
n	nephew
NA	National Academician (America)
NAACP	National Association for the Advancement of Colored People
NAAFI	Navy, Army and Air Force Institutes
NAAS	National Agricultural Advisory Service
NAB	National Advisory Body for Public Sector Higher Education
NABC	National Association of Boys' Clubs (later NABC-CYP)
NABC-CYP	National Association of Boys' Clubs - Clubs for Young People
NAC	National Agriculture Centre
NACAB	National Association of Citizens' Advice Bureaux
NACCB	National Accreditation Council for Certification Bodies
NACETT	National Advisory Council for Education and Training Targets
NACF	National Art-Collections Fund
NACRO	National Association for the Care and Resettlement of Offenders
NADFAS	National Association of Decorative and Fine Arts Societies
NAE	National Academy of Engineering
NAEW	Nato Airborn Early Warning
NAHA	National Association of Health Authorities (*now see* NAHAT)
NAHAT	National Association of Health Authorities and Trusts
NAHT	National Association of Head Teachers
NALGO or Nalgo	National and Local Government Officers' Association
NAMAS	National Measurement and Accreditation Service
NAMCW	National Association for Maternal and Child Welfare
NAMH	MIND (National Association for Mental Health)
NAMMA	NATO MRCA Management Agency
NAPAG	National Academies Policy Advisory Group
NARM	National Association of Recording Merchandisers (US)
NAS	National Academy of Sciences
NASA	National Aeronautics and Space Administration (US)
NASD	National Association of Securities Dealers
NASDAQ	National Association of Securities Dealers Automated Quotation System
NASDIM	National Association of Security Dealers and Investment Managers (later FIMBRA)
NAS/UWT	National Association of Schoolmasters/Union of Women Teachers

NATCS	National Air Traffic Control Services (*now see* NATS)
NATFHE	National Association of Teachers in Further and Higher Education (combining ATCDE and ATTI)
NATLAS	National Testing Laboratory Accreditation Scheme
NATO	North Atlantic Treaty Organisation
NATS	National Air Traffic Services
Nat. Sci.	Natural Sciences
NATSOPA	National Society of Operative Printers, Graphical and Media Personnel (*formerly* of Operative Printers and Assistants)
NAYC	Youth Clubs UK (*formerly* National Association of Youth Clubs)
NB	New Brunswick; Nebraska (postal)
NBA	North British Academy
NBC	National Book Council (later NBL); National Broadcasting Company (US)
NBL	National Book League
NBPI	National Board for Prices and Incomes
NC	National Certificate; North Carolina
NCA	National Certificate of Agriculture
NCARB	National Council of Architectural Registration Boards
NCAS	Natural Environment Research Council Centres for Atmospheric Science
NCB	National Coal Board
NCC	National Computing Centre; Nature Conservancy Council (later NCCE); National Consumer Council
NCCE	Nature Conservancy Council for England (English Nature)
NCCI	National Committee for Commonwealth Immigrants
NCCL	National Council for Civil Liberties
NCD	National Capital District, Papua New Guinea
NCDAD	National Council for Diplomas in Art and Design
NCEA	National Council for Educational Awards
NCET	National Council for Educational Technology
NCH	National Children's Homes
NCLC	National Council of Labour Colleges
NCOP	National Council of Provinces (South Africa)
NCOPF	National Council for One Parent Families
NCRI	National Cancer Research Institute
NCSE	National Council for Special Education
NCSS	National Council of Social Service
NCTA	National Community Television Association (US)
NCTJ	National Council for the Training of Journalists
NCU	National Cyclists' Union
NCVCCO	National Council of Voluntary Child Care Organisations
NCVO	National Council for Voluntary Organisations
NCVQ	National Council for Vocational Qualifications
NCYPE	National Centre for Young People with Epilepsy
ND	North Dakota
NDA	National Diploma in Agriculture
NDC	National Defence College; NATO Defence College
NDD	National Diploma in Dairying; National Diploma in Design
NDEA	National Defense Education Act
NDH	National Diploma in Horticulture
NDIC	National Defence Industries Council
NDP	New Democratic Party
NDTA	National Defense Transportation Association (US)
NE	North-east
NEAB	Northern Examinations and Assessment Board
NEAC	New English Art Club
NEAF	Near East Air Force
NEARELF	Near East Land Forces
NEB	National Enterprise Board
NEBSS	National Examinations Board for Supervisory Studies
NEC	National Executive Committee
NECCTA	National Education Closed Circuit Television Association
NECInst	North East Coast Institution of Engineers and Shipbuilders
NEDC	National Economic Development Council; North East Development Council
NEDO	National Economic Development Office
NEH	National Endowment for the Humanities
NEL	National Engineering Laboratory
NERC	Natural Environment Research Council
NESTA	National Endowment for Science, Technology and the Arts
NF	Newfoundland and Labrador (postal)
NFC	National Freight Consortium (*formerly* Corporation, then Company)
NFCG	National Federation of Consumer Groups
NFER	National Foundation for Educational Research
NFHA	National Federation of Housing Associations
NFMS	National Federation of Music Societies
NFS	National Fire Service
NFSH	National Federation of Spiritual Healers
NFT	National Film Theatre
NFU	National Farmers' Union
NFWI	National Federation of Women's Institutes
NGO	Non-Governmental Organisation(s)
NGTE	National Gas Turbine Establishment
NH	New Hampshire
NH&MRC	National Health and Medical Research Council (Australia)

NHBC	National House-Building Council
NHMF	National Heritage Memorial Fund
NHS	National Health Service
NHSU	National Health Service University
NI	Northern Ireland; Native Infantry
NIAB	National Institute of Agricultural Botany
NIACE	National Institute of Adult Continuing Education
NIACRO	Northern Ireland Association for the Care and Resettlement of Offenders
NIAE	National Institute of Agricultural Engineering
NIAID	National Institute of Allergy and Infectious Diseases
NICE	National Institute for Health and Clinical Excellence (formerly National Institute of Clinical Excellence)
NICEC	National Institute for Careers Education and Counselling
NICEIC	National Inspection Council for Electrical Installation Contracting
NICG	Nationalised Industries Chairmen's Group
NICRO	National Institute for Crime Prevention and Re-integration of Offenders
NICS	Northern Ireland Civil Service
NID	Naval Intelligence Division; National Institute for the Deaf; Northern Ireland District; National Institute of Design (India)
NIESR	National Institute of Economic and Social Research
NIH	National Institutes of Health (US)
NIHCA	Northern Ireland Hotels and Caterers Association
NIHEC	Northern Ireland Higher Education Council
NIHR	National Institute of Health Research
NII	Nuclear Installations Inspectorate
NILP	Northern Ireland Labour Party
NIMR	National Institute for Medical Research
NISA	National Ice Skating Association of UK
NISTRO	Northern Ireland Science and Technology Regional Organisation
NISW	National Institute of Social Work
NIU	Northern Ireland Unionist
NJ	New Jersey
NL	National Liberal; No Liability
NLCS	North London Collegiate School
NLF	National Liberal Federation
NLYL	National League of Young Liberals
NM	New Mexico (postal)
NMR	Nuclear Magnetic Resonance
NMRS	National Monuments Record of Scotland
NMSI	National Museum of Science and Industry
NNMA	Nigerian National Merit Award
NNOM	Nigerian National Order of Merit
NO	Navigating Officer
NODA	National Operatic and Dramatic Association
Northants	Northamptonshire
NOTB	National Ophthalmic Treatment Board
Notts	Nottinghamshire
NP	Notary Public
NPA	Newspaper Publishers' Association
NPFA	National Playing Fields Association
NPG	National Portrait Gallery
NPk	Nishan-e-Pakistan
NPL	National Physical Laboratory
NPQH	National Professional Qualification for Headship
NRA	National Rifle Association; National Recovery Administration (US); National Rivers Authority
NRAO	National Radio Astronomy Observatory
NRCC	National Research Council of Canada
NRD	National Registered Designer
NRDC	National Research Development Corporation
NRMA	National Roads and Motorists' Association
NRPB	National Radiological Protection Board
NRR	Northern Rhodesia Regiment
NRSA	National Research Service Award (US)
NS	Nova Scotia; New Style in the Calendar (in Great Britain since 1752); National Society; National Service
ns	Graduate of Royal Naval Staff College, Greenwich
NSA	National Skating Association (now see NISA)
NSAIV	Distinguished Order of Shaheed Ali (Maldives)
NSERC	Natural Sciences and Engineering Research Council, Canada
NSF	National Science Foundation (US)
NSM	Non-Stipendiary Minister
NSMHC	National Society for Mentally Handicapped Children (now see Mencap)
NSPCC	National Society for Prevention of Cruelty to Children
NSQT	National Society for Quality through Teamwork
NSRA	National Small-bore Rifle Association
N/SSF	Novice, Society of St Francis
NSTC	Nova Scotia Technical College
NSW	New South Wales
NT	New Testament; Northern Territory (Australia); Northwest Territories (Canada); National Theatre; National Trust
NT&SA	National Trust & Savings Association
NTDA	National Trade Development Association

NTO	National Training Organisation
NTUC	National Trades Union Congress
NUAAW	National Union of Agricultural and Allied Workers
NUBE	National Union of Bank Employees (later BIFU)
NUFLAT	National Union of Footwear Leather and Allied Trades (now see NUKFAT)
NUGMW	National Union of General and Municipal Workers (later GMBATU)
NUHKW	National Union of Hosiery and Knitwear Workers (now see NUKFAT)
NUI	National University of Ireland
NUJ	National Union of Journalists
NUJMB	Northern Universities Joint Matriculation Board
NUKFAT	National Union of Knitwear, Footwear and Apparel Trades
NUM	National Union of Mineworkers
NUMAST	National Union of Marine, Aviation and Shipping Transport Officers
NUPE	National Union of Public Employees
NUR	National Union of Railwaymen (now see RMT)
NUS	National Union of Students; National University of Singapore
NUT	National Union of Teachers
NUTG	National Union of Townswomen's Guilds
NUTGW	National Union of Tailors and Garment Workers
NUTN	National Union of Trained Nurses
NUU	New University of Ulster
NV	Nevada (postal)
NVQ	National Vocational Qualification
NW	North-west
NWC	National Water Council
NWFP	North-West Frontier Province
NWP	North-Western Province
NWT	North-Western Territories
NY	New York
NYC	New York City
NYO	National Youth Orchestra
NYT	National Youth Theatre
NZ	New Zealand
NZEF	New Zealand Expeditionary Force
NZIA	New Zealand Institute of Architects
NZRSA	New Zealand Retired Services Association
NZTF	New Zealand Territorial Force

O

o	only
OAM	Medal of the Order of Australia
O&E	Operations and Engineers (US)
O&M	organisation and method
O&O	Oriental and Occidental Steamship Co.
OAS	Organisation of American States; On Active Service
OASC	Officer Aircrew Selection Centre
OAU	Organisation for African Unity
OB	Order of Barbados
OBC	Order of British Columbia
OBE	Officer, Order of the British Empire
OC	Officer, Order of Canada (equivalent to former award SM)
OC or o/c	Officer Commanding
oc	only child
OCC	Order of the Caribbean Community
OCDS or ocds Can	Overseas College of Defence Studies (Canada)
OCF	Officiating Chaplain to the Forces
OCPA	Office of the Commissioner for Public Appointments
OCS	Officer Candidates School
OCSS	Oxford and Cambridge Shakespeare Society
OCTU	Officer Cadet Training Unit
OCU	Operational Conversion Unit
OD	Officer, Order of Distinction (Jamaica); Order of Distinction (Antigua)
ODA	Overseas Development Administration
ODI	Overseas Development Institute
ODM	Ministry of Overseas Development
ODPM	Office of the Deputy Prime Minister
ODSM	Order of Diplomatic Service Merit (Lesotho)
OE	Order of Excellence (Guyana)
OEA	Overseas Education Association
OECD	Organization for Economic Co-operation and Development
OED	Oxford English Dictionary
OEEC	Organization for European Economic Co-operation (now see OECD)
OF	Order of the Founder, Salvation Army
OFCOM or Ofcom	Office of Communications
OFEMA	Office Française d'Exportation de Matériel Aéronautique
OFFER	Office of Electricity Regulation
Ofgem	Office of Gas and Electricity Markets
OFM	Order of Friars Minor (Franciscans)

OFMCap	Order of Friars Minor Capuchin (Franciscans)
OFMConv	Order of Friars Minor Conventual (Franciscans)
OFR	Order of the Federal Republic of Nigeria
OFS	Orange Free State
OFSTED	Office for Standards in Education
OFT	Office of Fair Trading
Oftel	Office of Telecommunications
Ofwat	Office of Water Services
OGC	Office of Government Commerce
OGS	Oratory of the Good Shepherd
OH	Ohio (postal)
OHMS	On His (or Her) Majesty's Service
O i/c	Officer in charge
OJ	Order of Jamaica
OK	Oklahoma (postal)
OL	Officer, Order of Leopold; Order of the Leopard (Lesotho)
OLJ	Officer, Order of St Lazarus of Jerusalem
OLM	Officer, Legion of Merit (Rhodesia); Ordained Local Minister
OM	Order of Merit; Order of Manitoba
OMCS	Office of the Minister for the Civil Service
OMI	Oblate of Mary Immaculate
OMLJ	Officer, Order of Merit, Order of St Lazarus of Jerusalem
OMM	Officer, Order of Military Merit (Canada)
ON	Order of the Nation (Jamaica); Ontario (postal)
OND	Ordinary National Diploma
ONDA	Ordinary National Diploma in Agriculture
ONS	Office for National Statistics
Ont	Ontario
ONZ	Order of New Zealand
ONZM	Officer, New Zealand Order of Merit
OON	Officer, Order of the Niger
OOnt	Order of Ontario
OP	*Ordinis Praedicatorum* (of the Order of Preachers (Dominican)); Observation Post
OPCON	Operational Control
OPCS	Office of Population Censuses and Surveys (*now see* ONS)
OPCW	Organisation for the Prohibition of Chemical Weapons
OPEC	Organisation of Petroleum Exporting Countries
OPM	Owner President Management program
OPRA	Occupational Pensions Regulatory Authority
OPS	Office of Public Service
OPSS	Office of Public Service and Science (later OPS)
OQ	Officer, National Order of Quebec
OR	Order of Rorima (Guyana); Operational Research; Oregon (postal)
ORC	Orange River Colony
ORGALIME	Organisme de Liaison des Industries Métalliques Européennes
ORHA/CPA	Office of Reconstruction and Humanitarian Assistance/Coalition Provisional Authority
ORL	Otorhinolaryngology
ORS	Operational Research Society
ORSA	Operations Research Society of America
ORSL	Order of the Republic of Sierra Leone
ORT	Organization for Rehabilitation through Training
ORTF	Office de la Radiodiffusion et Télévision Française
o s	only son
OSA	Order of St Augustine (Augustinian); Ontario Society of Artists
OSB	Order of St Benedict (Benedictine)
osc	Graduate of Overseas Staff College
OSCE	Organisation for Security and Co-operation in Europe
OSCHR	Office for Strategic Co-ordination of Health Research
OSFC	Franciscan (Capuchin) Order
O/Sig	Ordinary Signalman
OSMTH	Ordo Supremus Militaris Templi Hierosolymitani (Supreme Military Order of the Temple of Jerusalem)
OSNC	Orient Steam Navigation Co.
osp	*obiit sine prole* (died without issue)
OSRD	Office of Scientific Research and Development
OSS	Office of Strategic Services
OST	Office of Science and Technology
OStJ	Officer, Most Venerable Order of the Hospital of St John of Jerusalem
OSUK	Ophthalmological Society of the United Kingdom
OT	Old Testament
OTC	Officers' Training Corps
OTL	Officer, Order of Toussaint L'Ouverture (Haiti)
OTS	Office of the Third Sector
OTU	Operational Training Unit
OTWSA	Ou-Testamentiese Werkgemeenskap in Suider-Afrika
OU	Oxford University; Open University
OUAC	Oxford University Athletic Club
OUAFC	Oxford University Association Football Club
OUBC	Oxford University Boat Club
OUCC	Oxford University Cricket Club
OUDS	Oxford University Dramatic Society
OUP	Oxford University Press; Official Unionist Party

OURC	Oxford University Rifle Club
OURFC	Oxford University Rugby Football Club
OURT	Order of the United Republic of Tanzania
Oxon	Oxfordshire; *Oxoniensis* (of Oxford)

P

PA	Pakistan Army; Personal Assistant; Pennsylvania (postal)
PAA	President, Australian Academy of Science
pac	passed the final examination of the Advanced Class, The Military College of Science
PACE	Protestant and Catholic Encounter; Property Advisers to the Civil Estate
PACTA	Professional Associate, Clinical Theology Association
PALS	Partnership for Active Leisure Scheme for Disabled Children
P&O	Peninsular and Oriental Steamship Co.
P&OSNCo.	Peninsular and Oriental Steam Navigation Co.
PAO	Prince Albert's Own
PASOK	Panhellenic Socialist Movement
PBS	Public Broadcasting Service
PC	Privy Counsellor; Police Constable; Perpetual Curate; Peace Commissioner (Ireland); Progressive Conservative (Canada)
pc	*per centum* (in the hundred)
PCC	Parochial Church Council; Protected Cell Company (Guernsey); Private Cell Company
PCE	Postgraduate Certificate of Education
pce	passed command examinations
PCEF	Polytechnic and Colleges Employers' Forum
PCFC	Polytechnics and Colleges Funding Council
PCG	Primary Care Group
PCL	Polytechnic of Central London
PCMO	Principal Colonial Medical Officer
PCNZM	Principal Companion, New Zealand Order of Merit
PCS	Parti Chrétien-Social; Public and Commercial Services Union
PCT	Primary Care Trust
PdD	Doctor of Pedagogy (US)
PDG	Président Directeur Général
PDipHEd	Postgraduate Diploma in Health Education
PDR	People's Democratic Republic
PDRA	post doctoral research assistant
PDSA	People's Dispensary for Sick Animals
PDTC	Professional Dancer's Training Course Diploma
PDTDip	Professional Dancer's Teaching Diploma
PE	Procurement Executive; Prince Edward Island (postal)
PEI	Prince Edward Island
PEN	Poets, Playwrights, Editors, Essayists, Novelists (Club)
PEng	Registered Professional Engineer (Canada); Member, Society of Professional Engineers
Penn	Pennsylvania
PEP	Political and Economic Planning (*now see* PSI)
PER	Professional and Executive Recruitment
PES	Party of European Socialists
PEST	Pressure for Economic and Social Toryism
PETRAS	Polytechnic Educational Technology Resources Advisory Service
PF	Procurator-Fiscal
PFA	Professional Footballers' Association
pfc	Graduate of RAF Flying College
PFE	Program for Executives
PFI	Private Finance Initiative
PGA	Professional Golfers' Association
PGCA	Post Graduate Certificate of Adjudication
PGCE	Post Graduate Certificate of Education
PGCTh	Postgraduate Certificate in Theology
PGDCCI	Postgraduate Diploma in Computing for Commerce and Industry
PGDPT	Postgraduate Diploma in Pastoral Theology
PGTC	Postgraduate Teaching Certificate
PH	Presidential Order of Honour (Botswana)
PHAB	Physically Handicapped & Able-bodied
PhB	Bachelor of Philosophy
PhC	Pharmaceutical Chemist
PhD	Doctor of Philosophy
Phil.	Philology, Philological; Philosophy, Philosophical
PhL	Licentiate in Philosophy
PHLS	Public Health Laboratory Service
PhM	Master of Philosophy (USA)
PhmB	Bachelor of Pharmacy
Phys.	Physical
PIA	Personal Investment Authority
PIARC	Permanent International Association of Road Congresses
PIB	Prices and Incomes Board (later NBPI)
PICAO	Provisional International Civil Aviation Organization (*now* ICAO)
pinx.	*pinxit* (he painted it)
PIRA	Paper Industries Research Association

PITCOM	Parliamentary Information Technology Committee
PJG	Pingat Jasa Gemilang (Singapore)
PJHQ	Permanent Joint Headquarters
PJK	Pingkat Jasa Kebaktian (Malaysia)
Pl.	Place; Plural
PLA	Port of London Authority
PLAB	Professional and Linguistic Assessments Board
PLC or plc	public limited company
Plen.	Plenipotentiary
PLI	President, Landscape Institute
PLP	Parliamentary Labour Party; Progressive Liberal Party (Bahamas)
PLR	Public Lending Right
PMA	Personal Military Assistant
PMC	Personnel Management Centre
PMD	Program for Management Development
PMedSci	President, Academy of Medical Sciences
PMETB	Postgraduate Medical Education and Training Board
PMG	Postmaster-General
PMN	Panglima Mangku Negara (Malaysia)
PMO	Principal Medical Officer; Princess Mary's Own
PMRAFNS	Princess Mary's Royal Air Force Nursing Service
PMS	Presidential Order of Meritorious Service (Botswana); President, Miniature Society
PNBS	Panglima Negara Bintang Sarawak
PNEU	Parents' National Educational Union
PNG	Papua New Guinea
PNP	People's National Party
PO	Post Office
POB	Presidential Order of Botswana
POMEF	Political Office Middle East Force
Pop.	Population
POST	Parliamentary Office of Science and Technology
POUNC	Post Office Users' National Council
POW	Prisoner of War; Prince of Wales's
PP	Parish Priest; Past President
pp	pages
PPA	Periodical Publishers Association
PPARC	Particle Physics and Astronomy Research Council
PPCLI	Princess Patricia's Canadian Light Infantry
PPCSD	Past President, Chartered Society of Designers
PPDF	Parti Populaire pour la Démocratie Française
PPE	Philosophy, Politics and Economics
PPInstHE	Past President, Institution of Highway Engineers
PPIStructE	Past President, Institution of Structural Engineers
PPITB	Printing and Publishing Industry Training Board
PPP	Private Patients Plan
PPRA	Past President, Royal Academy
PPRBA	Past President, Royal Society of British Artists
PPRBS	Past President, Royal Society of British Sculptors
PPRE	Past President, Royal Society of Painter-Printmakers (formerly of Painter-Etchers and Engravers)
PPRIBA	Past President, Royal Institute of British Architects
PPRNCM	Diploma in Professional Performance, Royal Northern College of Music
PPROI	Past President, Royal Institute of Oil Painters
PPRP	Past President, Royal Society of Portrait Painters
PPRSA	Past President, Royal Scottish Academy
PPRSW	Past President, Royal Scottish Society of Painters in Water Colours
PPRTPI	Past President, Royal Town Planning Institute
PPRWA	Past President, Royal Watercolour Association
PPRWS	Past President, Royal Society of Painters in Water Colours
PPS	Parliamentary Private Secretary
PPSIAD	Past President, Society of Industrial Artists and Designers
PQ	Province of Quebec
PQCCC	Post Qualification Certificate in Child Care
PQE	Professional Qualifying Examination
PR	Public Relations; Parti républicain
PRA	President, Royal Academy
PRASEG	Associate Parliamentary Renewable and Sustainable Energy Group
PRBS	President, Royal Society of British Sculptors
PRCA	Public Relations Consultants Association
PRCS	President, Royal College of Surgeons
PrD	Doctor of Professional Practice
PRE	President, Royal Society of Painter-Printmakers (formerly of Painter-Etchers and Engravers)
Preb.	Prebendary
Prep.	Preparatory
Pres.	President
PRHA	President, Royal Hibernian Academy
PRI	President, Royal Institute of Painters in Water Colours; Plastics and Rubber Institute
PRIA	President, Royal Irish Academy
PRIAS	President, Royal Incorporation of Architects in Scotland
Prin.	Principal

PRISA	Public Relations Institute of South Africa
PRL	Liberal Reform Party (Belgium)
PRO	Public Relations Officer; Public Records Office
Proc.	Proctor; Proceedings
Prof.	Professor; Professional
PROI	President, Royal Institute of Oil Painters
PRO NED	Promotion of Non-Executive Directors
PRORM	Pay and Records Office, Royal Marines
Pro tem.	Pro tempore (for the time being)
Prov.	Provost; Provincial
Prox.	Proximo (next)
Prox.acc.	Proxime accessit (next in order of merit to the winner)
PRS	President, Royal Society; Performing Right Society Ltd
PRSA	President, Royal Scottish Academy
PRSE	President, Royal Society of Edinburgh
PRSH	President, Royal Society for the Promotion of Health
PRSW	President, Royal Scottish Water Colour Society
PRUAA	President, Royal Ulster Academy of Arts
PRWA	President, Royal West of England Academy
PRWS	President, Royal Society of Painters in Water Colours
PS	Pastel Society; Paddle Steamer
ps	passed School of Instruction (of Officers)
PSA	Property Services Agency; Petty Sessions Area
psa	Graduate of RAF Staff College
psc	Graduate of Staff College († indicates Graduate of Senior Wing Staff College)
PSD	Petty Sessional Division; Social Democratic Party (Portugal)
PSE	Party of European Socialists
PSGB	Pharmaceutical Society of Great Britain (now see RPSGB)
PSI	Policy Studies Institute
PSIAD	President, Society of Industrial Artists and Designers
PSM	Panglima Setia Mahkota (Malaysia)
psm	Certificate of Royal Military School of Music
PSMA	President, Society of Marine Artists
PSNC	Pacific Steam Navigation Co.
PSO	Principal Scientific Officer; Personal Staff Officer
PSOE	Partido Socialista Obrero Español
PSS	Society of Priests of St Sulpice
PSSC	Personal Social Services Council
PsyD	Doctor of Psychology
PTA	Passenger Transport Authority; Parent-Teacher Association
PTC	Personnel and Training Command
PTE	Passenger Transport Executive
Pte	Private
ptsc	passed Technical Staff College
Pty	Proprietary
PUP	People's United Party; Progressive Unionist Party
PVSM	Param Vishishc Seva Medal (India)
PWD	Public Works Department
PWE	Political Welfare Executive
PWO	Prince of Wales's Own
PWO(U)	Principal Warfare Officer (Underwater Warfare)
PWR	Pressurized Water Reactor
PYBT	Prince's Youth Business Trust

Q

Q	Queen
QAA	Quality Assurance Agency for Higher Education
QAIMNS	Queen Alexandra's Imperial Military Nursing Service
QARANC	Queen Alexandra's Royal Army Nursing Corps
QARNNS	Queen Alexandra's Royal Naval Nursing Service
QBD	Queen's Bench Division
QC	Queen's Counsel; Quebec (postal)
QCA	Qualifications and Curriculum Authority
QCB	Queen's Commendation for Bravery
QCVS	Queen's Commendation for Valuable Service
QCVSA	Queen's Commendation for Valuable Service in the Air
QDR	Qualified in Dispute Resolution
QEH	Queen Elizabeth Hall
QEO	Queen Elizabeth's Own
QFSM	Queen's Fire Service Medal for Distinguished Service
QGM	Queen's Gallantry Medal
QHC	Honorary Chaplain to the Queen
QHDS	Honorary Dental Surgeon to the Queen
QHNS	Honorary Nursing Sister to the Queen
QHP	Honorary Physician to the Queen
QHS	Honorary Surgeon to the Queen
Qld	Queensland
Qly	Quarterly
QMAAC	Queen Mary's Army Auxiliary Corps
QMC	Queen Mary College, London
QMG	Quartermaster-General
QMIPRI	Queen Mary Intellectual Property Research Institute
QMO	Queen Mary's Own

QMUL	Queen Mary, University of London
QMW	Queen Mary and Westfield College, London (*now see* QMUL)
QO	Qualified Officer
QOOH	Queen's Own Oxfordshire Hussars
Q(ops)	Quartering (operations)
QOY	Queen's Own Yeomanry
QPM	Queen's Police Medal
QPSM	Queen's Public Service Medal (New Zealand)
Qr	Quarter
QRIH	Queen's Royal Irish Hussars
QS	Quarter Sessions; Quantity Surveying
qs	RAF graduates of the Military or Naval Staff College
QSM	Queen's Service Medal (NZ)
QSO	Queen's Service Order (NZ)
QTS	Qualified Teacher Status
QUB	Queen's University, Belfast
qv	*quod vide* (which see)
QVRM	Queen's Volunteer Reserve Medal
qwi	Qualified Weapons Instructor

R

(R)	Reserve
RA	Royal Academician; Royal Academy; Royal (Regiment of) Artillery
RAA	Regional Arts Association; Royal Australian Artillery
RAAF	Royal Australian Air Force
RAAMC	Royal Australian Army Medical Corps
RABI	Royal Agricultural Benevolent Institution
RAC	Royal Automobile Club; Royal Agricultural College; Royal Armoured Corps
RACDS	Royal Australian College of Dental Surgeons
RACGP	Royal Australian College of General Practitioners
RAChD	Royal Army Chaplains' Department
RACI	Royal Australian Chemical Institute
RACO	Royal Australian College of Ophthalmologists
RACOG	Royal Australian College of Obstetricians and Gynaecologists
RACP	Royal Australasian College of Physicians
RACS	Royal Australasian College of Surgeons; Royal Arsenal Co-operative Society
RAD	Royal Academy of Dance
RADA	Royal Academy of Dramatic Art
RADAR	Royal Association for Disability and Rehabilitation
RADC	Royal Army Dental Corps
RADIUS	Religious Drama Society of Great Britain
RAE	Royal Australian Engineers; Royal Aerospace Establishment (*formerly* Royal Aircraft Establishment); Research Assessment Exercise
RAEC	Royal Army Educational Corps
RAEng	Royal Academy of Engineering
RAeS	Royal Aeronautical Society
RAF	Royal Air Force
RAFA	Royal Air Forces Association
RAFO	Reserve of Air Force Officers (*now see* RAFRO)
RAFR	Royal Air Force Reserve
RAFRO	Royal Air Force Reserve of Officers
RAFVR	Royal Air Force Volunteer Reserve
RAI	Royal Anthropological Institute of Great Britain & Ireland; Radio Audizioni Italiane
RAIA	Royal Australian Institute of Architects
RAIC	Royal Architectural Institute of Canada
RAM	(Member of) Royal Academy of Music
RAMC	Royal Army Medical Corps
RAN	Royal Australian Navy
R&D	Research and Development
RANR	Royal Australian Naval Reserve
RANVR	Royal Australian Naval Volunteer Reserve
RAOC	Royal Army Ordnance Corps
RAPC	Royal Army Pay Corps
RARDE	Royal Armament Research and Development Establishment
RARO	Regular Army Reserve of Officers
RAS	Royal Astronomical Society; Royal Asiatic Society; Recruitment and Assessment Services
RASC	Royal Army Service Corps (*now see* RCT)
RASE	Royal Agricultural Society of England
RAuxAF	Royal Auxiliary Air Force
RAVC	Royal Army Veterinary Corps
RB	Rifle Brigade
RBA	Member, Royal Society of British Artists
RBK&C	Royal Borough of Kensington and Chelsea
RBL	Royal British Legion
RBS	Royal Society of British Sculptors
RBSA	(Member of) Royal Birmingham Society of Artists
RBY	Royal Bucks Yeomanry
RC	Roman Catholic

RCA	Member, Royal Canadian Academy of Arts; Royal College of Art; (Member of) Royal Cambrian Academy
RCAC	Royal Canadian Armoured Corps
RCAF	Royal Canadian Air Force
RCamA	Member, Royal Cambrian Academy
RCAnaes	Royal College of Anaesthetists
RCAS	Royal Central Asian Society (*now see* RSAA)
RCCM	Research Council for Complementary Medicine
RCDS	Royal College of Defence Studies
rcds	completed a course at, or served for a year on the Staff of, the Royal College of Defence Studies
RCGP	Royal College of General Practitioners
RCHA	Royal Canadian Horse Artillery
RCHME	Royal Commission on Historical Monuments of England
RCM	(Member of) Royal College of Music
RCN	Royal Canadian Navy; Royal College of Nursing
RCNC	Royal Corps of Naval Constructors
RCNR	Royal Canadian Naval Reserve
RCNVR	Royal Canadian Naval Volunteer Reserve
RCO	Royal College of Organists
RCOG	Royal College of Obstetricians and Gynaecologists
RCP	Royal College of Physicians, London
RCPA	Royal College of Pathologists of Australia
RCPath	Royal College of Pathologists
RCPCH	Royal College of Paediatrics and Child Health
RCPE or RCPEd	Royal College of Physicians, Edinburgh
RCPI	Royal College of Physicians of Ireland
RCPSG	Royal College of Physicians and Surgeons of Glasgow
RCPsych	Royal College of Psychiatrists
RCR	Royal College of Radiologists
RCS	Royal College of Surgeons of England; Royal Corps of Signals; Royal College of Science
RCSE or RCSEd	Royal College of Surgeons of Edinburgh
RCSI	Royal College of Surgeons in Ireland
RCT	Royal Corps of Transport
RCVS	Royal College of Veterinary Surgeons
RD	Rural Dean; Royal Naval and Royal Marine Forces Reserve Decoration
Rd	Road
RDA	Diploma of Roseworthy Agricultural College, South Australia; Regional Development Agency
RDC	Rural District Council
RDF	Royal Dublin Fusiliers
RDI	Royal Designer for Industry (Royal Society of Arts)
RDS	Royal Dublin Society
RE	Royal Engineers; Fellow, Royal Society of Painter-Printmakers (*formerly* of Painter-Etchers and Engravers); Religious Education
REACH	Retired Executives Action Clearing House
react	Research Education and Aid for Children with potentially Terminal illness
Rear Adm.	Rear Admiral
REconS	Royal Economic Society
Regt	Regiment
REME	Royal Electrical and Mechanical Engineers
REngDes	Registered Engineering Designer
REOWS	Royal Engineers Officers' Widows' Society
REPAC	Regional Environmental Protection Advisory Committee
REPC	Regional Economic Planning Council
RERO	Royal Engineers Reserve of Officers
Res.	Resigned; Reserve; Resident; Research
RETI	Association of Traditional Industrial Regions
Rev.	Reverend; Review
RFA	Royal Field Artillery
RFC	Royal Flying Corps (*now* RAF); Rugby Football Club
RFCA	Reserve Forces and Cadets Association
RFD	Reserve Force Decoration
RFH	Royal Festival Hall
RFN	Registered Fever Nurse
RFP	Registered Forensic Practitioner
RFPS(G)	Royal Faculty of Physicians and Surgeons, Glasgow (*now see* RCPSG)
RFR	Rassemblement des Français pour la République
RFU	Rugby Football Union
RGA	Royal Garrison Artillery
RGI	Royal Glasgow Institute of the Fine Arts
RGJ	Royal Green Jackets
RGN	Registered General Nurse
RGS	Royal Geographical Society
RGSA	Royal Geographical Society of Australasia
RHA	Royal Hibernian Academy; Royal Horse Artillery; Regional Health Authority
RHASS	Royal Highland and Agricultural Society of Scotland
RHB	Regional Hospital Board
RHBNC	Royal Holloway and Bedford New College, London
RHC	Royal Holloway College, London (later RHBNC)
RHF	Royal Highland Fusiliers

RHG	Royal Horse Guards
RHistS	Royal Historical Society
RHQ	Regional Headquarters
RHR	Royal Highland Regiment
RHS	Royal Horticultural Society; Royal Humane Society
RHUL	Royal Holloway, University of London
RHV	Royal Health Visitor
RI	(Member of) Royal Institute of Painters in Water Colours; Rhode Island
RIA	Royal Irish Academy
RIAI	Royal Institute of the Architects of Ireland
RIAM	Royal Irish Academy of Music
RIAS	Royal Incorporation of Architects in Scotland
RIASC	Royal Indian Army Service Corps
RIBA	(Member of) Royal Institute of British Architects
RIBI	Rotary International in Great Britain and Ireland
RIC	Royal Irish Constabulary; Royal Institute of Chemistry (now see RSC)
RICS	(Member of) Royal Institution of Chartered Surveyors
RIE	Royal Indian Engineering (College)
RIF	Royal Inniskilling Fusiliers
RIIA	Royal Institute of International Affairs
RILEM	Réunion internationale des laboratoires d'essais et de recherches sur les matériaux et les constructions
RIM	Royal Indian Marines
RIN	Royal Indian Navy
RINA	Royal Institution of Naval Architects
RINVR	Royal Indian Naval Volunteer Reserve
RIPA	Royal Institute of Public Administration
RIPH	Royal Institute of Public Health
RIPH&H	Royal Institute of Public Health and Hygiene (now see RIPH)
RIrF	Royal Irish Fusiliers
RLC	Royal Logistic Corps
RLSS	Royal Life Saving Society
RM	Royal Marines; Resident Magistrate; Registered Midwife
RMA	Royal Marine Artillery; Royal Military Academy Sandhurst (now incorporating Royal Military Academy, Woolwich)
RMB	Rural Mail Base
RMC	Royal Military College Sandhurst (now see RMA)
RMCM	(Member of) Royal Manchester College of Music
RMCS	Royal Military College of Science
RMedSoc	Royal Medical Society, Edinburgh
RMetS	Royal Meteorological Society
RMFVR	Royal Marine Forces Volunteer Reserve
RMIT	Royal Melbourne Institute of Technology
RMLI	Royal Marine Light Infantry
RMN	Registered Mental Nurse
RMO	Resident Medical Officer(s)
RMP	Royal Military Police
RMPA	Royal Medico-Psychological Association
RMS	Royal Microscopical Society; Royal Mail Steamer; Royal Society of Miniature Painters; Royal Mail Ship
RMT	National Union of Rail, Maritime and Transport Workers; Registered Massage Therapist
RN	Royal Navy; Royal Naval; Registered Nurse
RNAS	Royal Naval Air Service
RNAY	Royal Naval Aircraft Yard
RNC	Royal Naval College
RNCM	(Member of) Royal Northern College of Music
RNEC	Royal Naval Engineering College
RNIB	Royal National Institute of Blind People (formerly Royal National Institute for the Blind, then Royal National Institute of the Blind)
RNID	Royal National Institute for Deaf People (formerly Royal National Institute for the Deaf)
RNLI	Royal National Life-boat Institution
RNLO	Royal Naval Liaison Officer
RNLTA	Royal Naval Lawn Tennis Association
RNR	Royal Naval Reserve
RNRU	Royal Navy Rugby Union
RNS	Royal Numismatic Society
RNSA	Royal Naval Sailing Association
RNSC	Royal Naval Staff College
RNT	Registered Nurse Tutor; Royal National Theatre
RNTNEH	Royal National Throat, Nose and Ear Hospital
RNUR	Régie Nationale des Usines Renault
RNVR	Royal Naval Volunteer Reserve
RNVSR	Royal Naval Volunteer Supplementary Reserve
RNXS	Royal Naval Auxiliary Service
RNZA	Royal New Zealand Artillery
RNZAC	Royal New Zealand Armoured Corps
RNZAF	Royal New Zealand Air Force
RNZIR	Royal New Zealand Infantry Regiment
RNZN	Royal New Zealand Navy
RNZNVR	Royal New Zealand Naval Volunteer Reserve
ROC	Royal Observer Corps
ROF	Royal Ordnance Factories

R of O	Reserve of Officers
ROI	Member, Royal Institute of Oil Painters
RoSPA	Royal Society for the Prevention of Accidents
(Rot.)	Rotunda Hospital, Dublin (after degree)
RP	(Member of) Royal Society of Portrait Painters
RPC	Royal Pioneer Corps
RPE	Rocket Propulsion Establishment
RPF	Rassemblement pour la France
RPMS	Royal Postgraduate Medical School
RPO	Royal Philharmonic Orchestra
RPR	Rassemblement pour la République
RPS	Royal Photographic Society
RPSGB	Royal Pharmaceutical Society of Great Britain
RRC	Royal Red Cross; Rapid Reaction Corps
RRE	Royal Radar Establishment (later RSRE)
RRF	Royal Regiment of Fusiliers
RRS	Royal Research Ship
RSA	Royal Scottish Academician; Royal Society of Arts; Republic of South Africa
RSAA	Royal Society for Asian Affairs
RSAF	Royal Small Arms Factory
RSAI	Royal Society of Antiquaries of Ireland
RSAMD	Royal Scottish Academy of Music and Drama
RSanI	Royal Sanitary Institute (now see RSH)
RSAS	Royal Surgical Aid Society
RSC	Royal Society of Canada; Royal Society of Chemistry; Royal Shakespeare Company
RSCM	(Member of) Royal School of Church Music
RSCN	Registered Sick Children's Nurse
RSE	Royal Society of Edinburgh
RSF	Royal Scots Fusiliers
RSFSR	Russian Soviet Federated Socialist Republic
RSGS	Royal Scottish Geographical Society
RSH	Royal Society for the Promotion of Health
RSL	Royal Society of Literature; Returned Services League of Australia
RSM	Royal School of Mines
RSM or RSocMed	Royal Society of Medicine
RSMA	(Member of) Royal Society of Marine Artists
RSME	Royal School of Military Engineering
RSMHCA	Royal Society for Mentally Handicapped Children and Adults (see Mencap)
RSNC	Royal Society for Nature Conservation
RSO	Rural Sub-Office; Railway Sub-Office; Resident Surgical Officer
RSPB	Royal Society for Protection of Birds
RSPCA	Royal Society for Prevention of Cruelty to Animals
RSRE	Royal Signals and Radar Establishment
RSSAf	Royal Society of South Africa
RSSAILA	Returned Sailors, Soldiers and Airmen's Imperial League of Australia (now see RSL)
RSSPCC	Royal Scottish Society for Prevention of Cruelty to Children
RSTM&H	Royal Society of Tropical Medicine and Hygiene
RSUA	Royal Society of Ulster Architects
RSV	Revised Standard Version
RSW	Member, Royal Scottish Society of Painters in Water Colours
RTE	Radio Telefis Eireann
Rt Hon.	Right Honourable
RTL	Radio-Télévision Luxembourg
RTO	Railway Transport Officer
RTPI	Royal Town Planning Institute
RTR	Royal Tank Regiment
Rt Rev.	Right Reverend
RTS	Religious Tract Society; Royal Toxophilite Society; Royal Television Society
RTYC	Royal Thames Yacht Club
RU	Rugby Union
RUA	Royal Ulster Academy
RUC	Royal Ulster Constabulary
RUI	Royal University of Ireland
RUKBA	Royal United Kingdom Beneficent Association
RUR	Royal Ulster Regiment
RURAL	Society for the Responsible Use of Resources in Agriculture & on the Land
RUSI	Royal United Services Institute for Defence and Security Studies (formerly Royal United Service Institution)
RVC	Royal Veterinary College
RWA	(Member of) Royal West of England Academy
RWAFF	Royal West African Frontier Force
RWCMD	Royal Welsh College of Music and Drama
RWF	Royal Welch Fusiliers
RWS	(Member of) Royal Society of Painters in Water Colours
RYA	Royal Yachting Association
RYS	Royal Yacht Squadron
RZSScot	Royal Zoological Society of Scotland

S

(S)	(in Navy) Paymaster; Scotland
S	Succeeded; South; Saint
s	son
SA	South Australia; South Africa; Société Anonyme; Society of the Atonement
SAAF	South African Air Force
SABC	South African Broadcasting Corporation
SAC	Scientific Advisory Committee
sac	qualified at small arms technical long course
SACC	South African Council of Churches
SACEUR	Supreme Allied Commander Europe
SACIF	sociedad anónima commercial industrial financiera
SACLANT	Supreme Allied Commander Atlantic
SACRO	Scottish Association for the Care and Resettlement of Offenders
SACSEA	Supreme Allied Command, SE Asia
SA de CV	sociedad anónima de capital variable
SADF	Sudanese Auxiliary Defence Force
SADG	Société des Architectes Diplômés par le Gouvernement
SAE	Society of Automobile Engineers (US)
SAHFOS	Sir Alister Hardy Foundation for Ocean Science
SAMC	South African Medical Corps
SAN	Senior Advocate of Nigeria
SARL	Société à Responsabilité Limitée
Sarum	Salisbury
SAS	Special Air Service
Sask	Saskatchewan
SASO	Senior Air Staff Officer
SAT	Senior Member, Association of Accounting Technicians
SATB	Soprano, Alto, Tenor, Bass
SATRO	Science and Technology Regional Organisation
SB	Bachelor of Science (US)
SBAA	Sovereign Base Areas Administration
SBAC	Society of British Aerospace Companies (formerly Society of British Aircraft Constructors)
SBS	Special Boat Service; Silver Bauhinia Star (Hong Kong)
SBStJ	Serving Brother, Most Venerable Order of the Hospital of St John of Jerusalem
SC	Star of Courage (Canada); Senior Counsel; South Carolina
sc	student at the Staff College
SCA	Society of Catholic Apostolate (Pallottine Fathers); Société en Commandité par Actions
SCAA	School Curriculum and Assessment Authority
SCAO	Senior Civil Affairs Officer
SCAR	Scientific Committee for Antarctic Research
ScD	Doctor of Science
SCDC	Schools Curriculum Development Committee
SCDI	Scottish Council for Development and Industry
SCF	Senior Chaplain to the Forces; Save the Children Fund
Sch.	School
SCI	Society of Chemical Industry
SCIE	Social Care Institute of Excellence
SCIS	Scottish Council of Independent Schools
SCL	Student in Civil Law
SCLC	Short Service Limited Commission
SCLI	Somerset and Cornwall Light Infantry
SCM	State Certified Midwife; Student Christian Movement
SCOB	Supreme Counsellor of Baobab (South Africa)
SCONUL	Standing Conference of National and University Libraries
SCOP	Standing Conference of Principals
Scot.	Scotland
ScotBIC	Scottish Business in the Community
SCOTMEG	Scottish Management Efficiency Group
SCOTVEC	Scottish Vocational Education Council
SCVO	Scottish Council for Voluntary Organisations
SD	Staff Duties; South Dakota (postal)
SDA	Social Democratic Alliance; Scottish Diploma in Agriculture; Scottish Development Agency
SDF	Sudan Defence Force; Social Democratic Federation
SDI	Strategic Defence Initiative
SDLP	Social Democratic and Labour Party
SDP	Social Democratic Party
SE	South-east
SEAC	South-East Asia Command
SEALF	South-East Asia Land Forces
SEATO	South-East Asia Treaty Organization
SEC	Security Exchange Commission
Sec.	Secretary
SED	Scottish Education Department
SEE	Society of Environmental Engineers
SEEDA	South East England Development Agency
SEFI	European Society for Engineering Education
SEN	State Enrolled Nurse; Special Educational Needs
SEP	Stanford Executive Program
SEPA	Scottish Environmental Protection Agency
SEPM	Society of Economic Palaeontologists and Mineralogists
SERC	Science and Engineering Research Council
SERT	Society of Electronic and Radio Technicians (later IEIE)
SESO	Senior Equipment Staff Officer
SF	Sinn Féin
SFA	Securities and Futures Authority
SFC	Scottish Further and Higher Education Funding Council
SFOR	Stabilisation Force
SFTA	Society of Film and Television Arts (now see BAFTA)
SFTCD	Senior Fellow, Trinity College Dublin
SG	Solicitor-General
SGA	Member, Society of Graphic Art
Sgt	Sergeant
SHA	Secondary Heads Association (now see ASCL); Special Health Authority
SHAC	London Housing Aid Centre
SHAEF	Supreme Headquarters, Allied Expeditionary Force
SHAPE	Supreme Headquarters, Allied Powers, Europe
SHEFC	Scottish Higher Education Funding Council (now see SFC)
SHHD	Scottish Home and Health Department
SHND	Scottish Higher National Diploma
SHO	Senior House Officer
SIAD	Society of Industrial Artists and Designers (now see CSD)
SIAM	Society of Industrial and Applied Mathematics (US)
SIB	Shipbuilding Industry Board; Securities and Investments Board (now see FSA)
SICA-FICA	Foundation for International Commercial Arbitration
SICAV	Société d'Investissement à Capital Variable
SICOT	Société Internationale de Chirurgie Orthopédique et de Traumatologie
SID	Society for International Development
SIESO	Society of Industrial and Emergency Services Officers
SIMA	Scientific Instrument Manufacturers' Association of Great Britain
SIME	Security Intelligence Middle East
SIMG	Societas Internationalis Medicinae Generalis
SinDrs	Doctor of Chinese
SIROT	Société Internationale pour Recherche en Orthopédie et Traumatologie
SIS	Secret Intelligence Service
SITA	Société Internationale de Télécommunications Aéronautiques
SITPRO	Simpler Trade Procedures Board (formerly Simplification of International Trade Procedures)
SJ	Society of Jesus (Jesuits)
SJAB	St John Ambulance Brigade
SJD	Doctor of Juristic Science
SK	Saskatchewan (postal)
SL	Serjeant-at-Law; Sociedad Limitada
SLA	Special Libraries Association
SLAC	Stanford Linear Accelerator Centre
SLAET	Society of Licensed Aircraft Engineers and Technologists
SLAS	Society for Latin-American Studies
SLD	Social and Liberal Democrats
SLJ	Seri Laila Jasa (Brunei)
SLP	Scottish Labour Party
SLS	Society of Legal Scholars
SM	Medal of Service (Canada) (now see OC); Master of Science; Officer qualified for Submarine Duties
SMA	Society of Marine Artists (now see RSMA)
SMB	Setia Mahkota Brunei
SMCC	Submarine Commanding Officers' Command Course
SME	School of Military Engineering (now see RSME)
SMEO	Squadron Marine Engineer Officer
SMHO	Sovereign Military Hospitaller Order (Malta)
SMIEE	Senior Member, Institute of Electrical and Electronics Engineers (New York)
SMIRE	Senior Member, Institute of Radio Engineers (New York)
SMMT	Society of Motor Manufacturers and Traders Ltd
SMN	Seri Maharaja Mangku Negara (Malaysia)
SMO	Senior Medical Officer; Sovereign Military Order
SMP	Senior Managers' Program
SMPTE	Society of Motion Picture and Television Engineers (US)
SMRTB	Ship and Marine Requirements Technology Board
SNAME	Society of Naval Architects and Marine Engineers (US)
SNCF	Société Nationale des Chemins de Fer Français
SND	Sisters of Notre Dame
SNH	Scottish Natural Heritage
SNP	Scottish National Party
SNTS	Society for New Testament Studies
SO	Staff Officer; Scientific Officer; Symphony Orchestra
SOAF	Sultan of Oman's Air Force
SOAS	School of Oriental and African Studies
Soc.	Society; Socialist (France)
SOCA	Serious and Organised Crime Agency
Soc & Lib Dem	Social and Liberal Democrats (now see Lib Dem)
SocCE(France)	Société des Ingénieurs Civils de France
SODEPAX	Committee on Society, Development and Peace

SOE	Special Operations Executive; Society of Operations Engineers
SOGAT	Society of Graphical and Allied Trades (*now see* GPMU)
SOLACE or **Solace**	Society of Local Authority Chief Executives
SOLT	Society of London Theatre
SOM	Society of Occupational Medicine
SOSc	Society of Ordained Scientists
SOTS	Society for Old Testament Study
sowc	Senior Officers' War Course
SP	Self-Propelled (Anti-Tank Regiment)
sp	*sine prole* (without issue)
SpA	Società per Azioni
SPAB	Society for the Protection of Ancient Buildings
SPARKS	Sport Aiding Medical Research for Children
SPCA	Society for the Prevention of Cruelty to Animals
SPCK	Society for Promoting Christian Knowledge
SPCM	Darjah Seri Paduka Cura Si Manja Kini (Malaysia)
SPD	Salisbury Plain District; Sozialdemokratische Partei Deutschlands
SPDK	Seri Panglima Darjal Kinabalu
SPG	Society for the Propagation of the Gospel (*now see* USPG)
SPk	Sitara-e-Pakistan
SPMB	Seri Paduka Makhota Brunei
SPMK	Darjah Kebasaran Seri Paduka Mahkota Kelantan (Malaysia)
SPMO	Senior Principal Medical Officer
SPNC	Society for the Promotion of Nature Conservation (*now see* RSNC)
SPNM	Society for the Promotion of New Music
SPR	Society for Psychical Research
SPRC	Society for Prevention and Relief of Cancer
sprl	société de personnes à responsabilité limitée
SPSO	Senior Principal Scientific Officer
SPTL	Society of Public Teachers of Law (*now see* SLS)
SPUC	Society for the Protection of the Unborn Child
Sq.	Square
sq	staff qualified
SQA	Sitara-i-Quaid-i-Azam (Pakistan)
Sqdn or **Sqn**	Squadron
SR	Special Reserve; Southern Railway; Southern Region (BR)
SRA	Solicitors Regulation Authority
SRC	Science Research Council (later SERC); Students' Representative Council
SRCh	State Registered Chiropodist
SRHE	Society for Research into Higher Education
SRIS	Science Reference Information Service
SRN	State Registered Nurse
SRNA	Shipbuilders and Repairers National Association
SRO	Supplementary Reserve of Officers; Self-Regulatory Organisation
SRP	State Registered Physiotherapist
SRY	Sherwood Rangers Yeomanry
SS	Saints; Straits Settlements; Steamship
SSA	Society of Scottish Artists; Side Saddle Association
SSAC	Social Security Advisory Committee
SSAFA	Soldiers, Sailors, Airmens and Families Association-Forces Help (formerly Soldiers', Sailors', and Airmen's Families Association)
SSBN	Nuclear Submarine, Ballistic
SSC	Solicitor before Supreme Court (Scotland); Sculptors Society of Canada; *Societas Sanctae Crucis* (Society of the Holy Cross); Short Service Commission
SSEB	South of Scotland Electricity Board
SSEES	School of Slavonic and East European Studies
SSF	Society of St Francis
SSJE	Society of St John the Evangelist
SSLC	Short Service Limited Commission
SSM	Society of the Sacred Mission; Seri Setia Mahkota (Malaysia)
SSO	Senior Supply Officer; Senior Scientific Officer
SSR	Soviet Socialist Republic
SSRC	Social Science Research Council (*now see* ESRC)
SSSI	Sites of Special Scientific Interest
SSSR	Society for the Scientific Study of Religion
SSStJ	Serving Sister, Most Venerable Order of the Hospital of St John of Jerusalem
St	Street; Saint
STA	Sail Training Association
STB	*Sacrae Theologiae Baccalaureus* (Bachelor of Sacred Theology)
STC	Senior Training Corps
STD	*Sacrae Theologiae Doctor* (Doctor of Sacred Theology)
STEP	Skills To Empower Programme
STETS	Southern Theological Education and Training Scheme
STFC	Science and Technology Facilities Council
STh	Scholar in Theology
Stip.	Stipend; Stipendiary
STL	*Sacrae Theologiae Lector* (Reader or a Professor of Sacred Theology)
STM	*Sacrae Theologiae Magister* (Master of Sacred Theology)

STP	*Sacrae Theologiae Professor* (Professor of Divinity, old form of DD)
STSO	Senior Technical Staff Officer
STV	Scottish Television
SUNY	State University of New York
Supp. Res.	Supplementary Reserve (of Officers)
Supt	Superintendent
Surg.	Surgeon
Surv.	Surviving
SW	South-west
SWET	Society of West End Theatre (*now see* SOLT)
SWIA	Society of Wildlife Artists
SWO	Staff Warfare Officer
SWPA	South West Pacific Area
SWRB	Sadler's Wells Royal Ballet
Syd.	Sydney

T

T	Telephone; Territorial
TA	Telegraphic Address; Territorial Army
TAA	Territorial Army Association
TAF	Tactical Air Force
T&AFA	Territorial and Auxiliary Forces Association
T&AVR	Territorial and Army Volunteer Reserve
TANS	Territorial Army Nursing Service
TANU	Tanganyika African National Union
TARO	Territorial Army Reserve of Officers
TAS	Torpedo and Anti Submarine Course
TASS	Technical, Administrative and Supervisory Section of AUEW (now part of MSF)
TAVRA or **TA&VRA**	Territorial Auxiliary and Volunteer Reserve Association (*now see* RFCA)
TC	Order of the Trinity Cross (Trinidad and Tobago)
TCCB	Test and County Cricket Board (*now see* ECB)
TCD	Trinity College, Dublin (University of Dublin, Trinity College)
TCF	Temporary Chaplain to the Forces
TCPA	Town and Country Planning Association
TD	Territorial Efficiency Decoration; Efficiency Decoration (T&AVR) (since April 1967); Teachta Dala (Member of the Dáil, Eire)
TDA	Training and Development Agency for Schools
TDD	Tubercular Diseases Diploma
TE	Technical Engineer
TEAC	Technical Educational Advisory Council
TEC	Technician Education Council (later BTEC); Training and Enterprise Council
Tech(CEI)	Technician
TechRICS	Technical Member, Royal Institution of Chartered Surveyors
TEFL	Teaching English as a Foreign Language
TEFLA	Teaching English as a Foreign Language to Adults
TEM	Territorial Efficiency Medal
TEMA	Telecommunication Engineering and Manufacturing Association
Temp.	Temperature; Temporary
TEng(CEI)	Technician Engineer (*now see* IEng)
Tenn	Tennessee
TEO	Teaching English Overseas
TeolD	Doctor of Theology
TES	Times Educational Supplement
TESL	Teaching English as a Second Language
TESOL	Teaching English to Speakers of other Languages
TET	Teacher of Electrotherapy
Tex	Texas
TF	Territorial Force
TFR	Territorial Force Reserve
TFTS	Tactical Fighter Training Squadron
TGEW	Timber Growers England and Wales Ltd
TGO	Timber Growers' Organisation (*now see* TGEW)
TGWU	Transport and General Workers' Union
ThD	Doctor of Theology
THED	Transvaal Higher Education Diploma
THELEP	Therapy of Leprosy
THES	Times Higher Education Supplement
ThL	Theological Licentiate
ThM	Master of Theology
ThSchol	Scholar in Theology
TIMS	The Institute of Management Sciences
TISCA	The Independent Schools Christian Alliance
TLS	Times Literary Supplement
TMA	Theatrical Management Association
TMMG	Teacher of Massage and Medical Gymnastics
TN	Tennessee (postal)
TNC	Theatres National Committee
TOPSS	Training Organisation for the Personal Social Services
TPI	Town Planning Institute (*now see* RTPI)

TPsych	Trainer in Psychiatry
TRA	Tenants' and Residents' Association
Trans.	Translation; Translated
Transf.	Transferred
TRC	Thames Rowing Club
TRE	Telecommunications Research Establishment (later RRE)
TRH	Their Royal Highnesses
TRIC	Television and Radio Industries Club
Trin.	Trinity
TRL	Transport Research Laboratory
TRRL	Transport and Road Research Laboratory (*now see* TRL)
TS	Training Ship
TSB	Trustee Savings Bank
tsc	passed a Territorial Army Course in Staff Duties
TSE	Transmissible Spongiform Encephalopathies
TSSA	Transport Salaried Staffs' Association
TSSF	Tertiary, Society of St Francis
TSWA	Television South West Arts
TTA	Teacher Training Agency (*now see* TDA)
TUC	Trades Union Congress
TUS	Trade Union Side
TV	Television
TVEI	Technical and Vocational Education Initiative
TWA	Thames Water Authority
TX	Texas (postal)

U

U	Unionist
u	uncle
UA	Unitary Authority
UACE	Universities Association for Continuing Education
UAE	United Arab Emirates
UAR	United Arab Republic
UAU	Universities Athletic Union
UBC	University of British Columbia
UBI	Understanding British Industry
UC	University College
UCAS	Universities and Colleges Admissions Service
UCCA	Universities Central Council on Admissions
UCCF	Universities and Colleges Christian Fellowship of Evangelical Unions
UCE	University of Central England
UCEA	Universities and Colleges Employers Association
UCET	Universities Council for Education of Teachers
UCH	University College Hospital (London)
UCL	University College London
UCLA	University of California at Los Angeles
UCLES	University of Cambridge Local Examinations Syndicate
UCLH	University College London Hospital
UCMSM	University College and Middlesex School of Medicine
UCNS	Universities' Council for Non-academic Staff
UCNW	University College of North Wales
UCRN	University College of Rhodesia and Nyasaland
UCS	University College School
UCSB	University of California at Santa Barbara
UCSD	University of California at San Diego
UCSF	University of California at San Francisco
UCW	University College of Wales; Union of Communication Workers (*now see* CWU)
UDC	Urban District Council; Urban Development Corporation
UDF	Union Defence Force; Union pour la démocratie française
UDM	United Democratic Movement (South Africa)
UDR	Ulster Defence Regiment; Union des Démocrates pour la Vème République (later RPR)
UDSR	Union Démocratique et Socialiste de la Résistance
UEA	University of East Anglia
UED	University Education Diploma
UEFA	Union of European Football Associations
UEL	University of East London
UEMS	Union Européenne des Médecins Spécialistes
UF	United Free Church
UFAW	Universities Federation for Animal Welfare
UFC	Universities' Funding Council
UGC	University Grants Committee (later UFC)
UHI	University of Highlands & Islands Millennium Institute
UIAA	Union Internationale des Associations d'Alpinisme
UICC	Union Internationale contre le Cancer
UIE	Union Internationale des Etudiants
UISPP	Union Internationale des Sciences Préhistoriques et Protohistoriques
UITP	International Union of Public Transport
UJD	*Utriusque Juris Doctor* (Doctor of both Laws, Doctor of Canon and Civil Law)
UK	United Kingdom

UKAC	United Kingdom Automation Council
UKAEA	United Kingdom Atomic Energy Authority
UKCC	United Kingdom Central Council for Nursing, Midwifery and Health Visiting
UKCCCR	United Kingdom Co-ordinating Committee on Cancer Research
UKCICC	United Kingdom Commanders-in-Chief Committees
UKCIS	United Kingdom Chemical Information Service
UKCOSA	United Kingdom Council for Overseas Student Affairs
UKCP	United Kingdom Council for Psychotherapy
UKERNA	United Kingdom Education and Research Networking Association
UKIAS	United Kingdom Immigrants' Advisory Service
UKIC	United Kingdom Institute for Conservation
UKIP	United Kingdom Independence Party
UKISC	United Kingdom Industrial Space Committee
UKLF	United Kingdom Land Forces
UKMF(L)	United Kingdom Military Forces (Land)
UKMIS	United Kingdom Mission
UKOLN	United Kingdom Office of Library Networking
UKOOA	United Kingdom Offshore Operators Association
UKPIA	United Kingdom Petroleum Industry Association Ltd
UKSC	United Kingdom Support Command
UKSLS	United Kingdom Services Liaison Staff
UKU	United Kingdom Unionist
ULPS	Union of Liberal and Progressive Synagogues
UMDS	United Medical and Dental Schools
UMIST	University of Manchester Institute of Science and Technology
UMP	Union pour un Mouvement Populaire (*formerly* Union pour la Majorité Présidentielle)
UN	United Nations
UNA	United Nations Association
UNCAST	United Nations Conference on the Applications of Science and Technology
UNCIO	United Nations Conference on International Organisation
UNCITRAL	United Nations Commission on International Trade Law
UNCSTD	United Nations Conference on Science and Technology for Development
UNCTAD or Unctad	United Nations Commission for Trade and Development
UNDP	United Nations Development Programme
UNDRO	United Nations Disaster Relief Organisation
UNECA	United Nations Economic Commission for Asia
UNECE	United Nations Economic Commission for Europe
UNED	United Nations Environment and Development
UNEP	United Nations Environment Programme
UNESCO or Unesco	United Nations Educational, Scientific and Cultural Organisation
UNFAO	United Nations Food and Agriculture Organisation
UNFICYP	United Nations Force in Cyprus
UNHCR	United Nations High Commissioner for Refugees
UNICE	Union des Industries de la Communauté Européenne
UNICEF or Unicef	United Nations Children's Fund (*formerly* United Nations International Children's Emergency Fund)
UNIDO	United Nations Industrial Development Organisation
UNIDROIT	Institut International pour l'Unification du Droit Privé
UNIFEM	United Nations Development Fund for Women
UNIFIL	United Nations Interim Force in Lebanon
UNIPEDE	Union Internationale des Producteurs et Distributeurs d'Energie Electrique
UNISIST	Universal System for Information in Science and Technology
UNITAR	United Nations Institute of Training and Research
Univ.	University
UNO	United Nations Organization
UNODC	United Nations Office on Drugs and Crime
UNRRA	United Nations Relief and Rehabilitation Administration
UNRWA	United Nations Relief and Works Agency
UNSCOB	United Nations Special Commission on the Balkans
UP	United Provinces; Uttar Pradesh; United Presbyterian
UPGC	University and Polytechnic Grants Committee
UPNI	Unionist Party of Northern Ireland
UPU	Universal Postal Union
UPUP	Ulster Popular Unionist Party
URC	United Reformed Church; Urban Regeneration Company
URSI	Union Radio-Scientifique Internationale
US	United States
USA	United States of America
USAAF	United States Army Air Force
USAF	United States Air Force
USAID	United States Agency for International Development
USAR	United States Army Reserve
USC	University of Southern California
USDAW	Union of Shop Distributive and Allied Workers
USM	Unlisted Securities Market
USMA	United States Military Academy
USMC	United States Marine Corps
USN	United States Navy
USNR	United States Naval Reserve
USPG	United Society for the Propagation of the Gospel

USPHS	United States Public Health Service
USPS	United States Postal Service
USS	United States Ship
USSR	Union of Soviet Socialist Republics
USVI	United States Virgin Islands
UT	Utah (postal)
UTC	University Training Corps
U3A	University of the Third Age
UTS	University of Technology, Sydney
UU	Ulster Unionist
UUK	Universities UK
UUUC	United Ulster Unionist Coalition
UUUP	United Ulster Unionist Party
UWCC	University of Wales College of Cardiff
UWCM	University of Wales College of Medicine
UWE	University of the West of England
UWIC	University of Wales Institute, Cardiff
UWIST	University of Wales Institute of Science and Technology
UWP	United Workers' Party (Dominica)
UWS	University of the West of Scotland
UWT	Union of Women Teachers

V

V	Five (Roman numerals); Version; Vicar; Viscount; Vice
v	*versus* (against)
v or **vid.**	*vide* (see)
VA	Virginia (postal)
Va	Virginia
VAD	Voluntary Aid Detachment
V&A	Victoria and Albert
VAT	Value Added Tax
VC	Victoria Cross; Voluntary Controlled
VCAS	Vice Chief of the Air Staff
VCDS	Vice Chief of the Defence Staff
VCGS	Vice Chief of the General Staff
VCNS	Vice Chief of the Naval Staff
VCT	Venture Capital Trust
VD	Royal Naval Volunteer Reserve Officers' Decoration (*now* VRD); Volunteer Officers' Decoration; Victorian Decoration
VDC	Volunteer Defence Corps
Ven.	Venerable
Vet.	Veterinary
VetMB	Bachelor of Veterinary Medicine
VG	Vicar-General
Vic	Victoria
Vice Adm.	Vice Admiral
Visc.	Viscount
VLSI	Very Large Scale Integration
VLV	Voice of the Listener and Viewer
VM	Victory Medal
VMA	Fixed Wing Marine Attack
VMGO	Vice Master General of the Ordnance
VMH	Victoria Medal of Honour (Royal Horticultural Society)
VMI	Virginia Military Institute
VMSM	Voluntary Medical Services Medal
Vol.	Volume; Voluntary; Volunteers
VP	Vice-President
VPP	Volunteer Political Party
VPRP	Vice-President, Royal Society of Portrait Painters
VQMG	Vice-Quartermaster-General
VR	*Victoria Regina* (Queen Victoria); Volunteer Reserve
VRD	Royal Naval Volunteer Reserve Officers' Decoration
VRSM	Volunteer Reserves Service Medal
VSO	Voluntary Service Overseas
VT	Vermont (postal)
Vt	Vermont
VUP	Vanguard Unionist Party
VVD	Volkspartij voor Vrijheiden Democratie

W

W	West
WA	Western Australia; Washington (postal)
WAAF	Women's Auxiliary Air Force (later WRAF)
WACL	Women in Advertising and Communications, London
WAOS	Welsh Agricultural Organisations Society

Wash	Washington State
WCC	World Council of Churches
W/Cdr	Wing Commander
WCMD	Welsh College of Music and Drama (*now see* RWCMD)
WDA	Welsh Development Agency
WEA	Workers' Educational Association; Royal West of England Academy
WEU	Western European Union
WFEO	World Federation of Engineering Organisations
WFSW	World Federation of Scientific Workers
WFTU	World Federation of Trade Unions
WhF	Whitworth Fellow
WHO	World Health Organization
WhSch	Whitworth Scholar
WI	West Indies; Women's Institute; Wisconsin (postal)
Wilts	Wiltshire
WIPO	World Intellectual Property Organization
Wis	Wisconsin
Wits	Witwatersrand
WJEC	Welsh Joint Education Committee
WLA	Women's Land Army
WLD	Women Liberal Democrats
WLF	Women's Liberal Federation
Wm	William
WMA	World Medical Association
WMO	World Meteorological Organization
WNO	Welsh National Opera
WO	War Office; Warrant Officer
Worcs	Worcestershire
WOSB	War Office Selection Board
WR	West Riding; Western Region (BR)
WRAC	Women's Royal Army Corps
WRAF	Women's Royal Air Force
WRNS	Women's Royal Naval Service
WRVS	Women's Royal Voluntary Service
WS	Writer to the Signet
WSAVA	World Small Animal Veterinary Association
WSET	Wine and Spirits Educational Trust
WSPA	World Society for the Protection of Animals
WSPU	Women's Social and Political Union
WTO	World Trade Organisation
WUS	World University Service
WV	West Virginia (postal)
WVS	Women's Voluntary Services (*now see* WRVS)
WWF	World Wide Fund for Nature (*formerly* World Wildlife Fund)
WY	Wyoming (postal)

X

X	Ten (Roman numerals)
XO	Executive Officer

Y

y	youngest
YC	Young Conservative
YCNAC	Young Conservatives National Advisory Committee
Yeo.	Yeomanry
YES	Youth Enterprise Scheme
YHA	Youth Hostels Association
YMCA	Young Men's Christian Association
YOI	Young Offenders Institute
Yorks	Yorkshire
YPTES	Young People's Trust for Endangered Species
yr	younger
yrs	years
YT	Yukon Territory (postal)
YTS	Youth Training Scheme
YVFF	Young Volunteer Force Foundation
YWCA	Young Women's Christian Association

Z

ZANU PF	Zimbabwe African National Union Patriotic Front
ZAPU	Zimbabwe African People's Union
ZIPRA	Zimbabwe People's Revolutionary Army

THE ROYAL FAMILY

THE SOVEREIGN

Her Majesty Queen Elizabeth II, (Elizabeth Alexandra Mary) .   .   .   .   .   .   21 April 1926

  Succeeded her father, King George VI, 6 February 1952

  Married 20 Nov. 1947, HRH The Duke of Edinburgh, *now* HRH The Prince Philip, Duke of Edinburgh, KG, KT, OM, GBE, AC, QSO (*b* 10 June 1921, *s* of HRH Prince Andrew of Greece (*d* 1944) and of HRH Princess Andrew of Greece (*d* 1969), *gg-d* of Queen Victoria; *cr* 1947, Baron Greenwich, Earl of Merioneth and Duke of Edinburgh)

  Residences: Buckingham Palace, SW1A 1AA; Windsor Castle, Berkshire SL4 1NJ; Sandringham House, Norfolk PE35 6EN; Balmoral Castle, Aberdeenshire AB35 5TB.

SONS AND DAUGHTER OF HER MAJESTY

HRH The Prince of Wales, (Prince Charles Philip Arthur George), ...   14 Nov. 1948

KG, KT, GCB, OM, AK, QSO, ADC; *cr* 1958, Prince of Wales and Earl of Chester; Duke of Cornwall; Duke of Rothesay, Earl of Carrick and Baron of Renfrew; Lord of the Isles and Great Steward of Scotland

  Married 1st, 29 July 1981, Lady Diana Frances Spencer (*b* 1 July 1961, *y d* of 8th Earl Spencer, LVO, she *d* 31 Aug. 1997), (marriage dissolved, 1996), and has issue –

    HRH PRINCE WILLIAM OF WALES, (PRINCE WILLIAM ARTHUR PHILIP LOUIS), KG .   .   .   21 June 1982

    HRH PRINCE HENRY OF WALES, (PRINCE HENRY CHARLES ALBERT DAVID) .   .   .   15 Sept. 1984

  Married 2nd, 9 April 2005, Mrs Camilla Rosemary Parker Bowles (*now* HRH The Duchess of Cornwall), *d* of late Major Bruce Shand, MC

  Office: Clarence House, SW1A 1BA; *residences:* Highgrove, Doughton, Tetbury, Gloucestershire GL8 8TN; Birkhall, Ballater, Aberdeenshire.

HRH The Duke of York, (Prince Andrew Albert Christian Edward), KG, KCVO, ADC; .   19 Feb. 1960

cr 1986, Baron Killyleagh, Earl of Inverness and Duke of York

  Married 23 July 1986, Sarah Margaret Ferguson, *now* Sarah, Duchess of York (*b* 15 Oct. 1959, 2nd *d* of late Major Ronald Ivor Ferguson, Life Guards), (marriage dissolved, 1996) and has issue –

    HRH PRINCESS BEATRICE OF YORK, (PRINCESS BEATRICE ELIZABETH MARY)   .   .   8 Aug. 1988

    HRH PRINCESS EUGENIE OF YORK, (PRINCESS EUGENIE VICTORIA HELENA) .   .   .   23 March 1990

  Office: Buckingham Palace, SW1A 1AA; *residence:* Royal Lodge, Windsor Great Park, Windsor, Berkshire SL4 2HW.

HRH The Earl of Wessex, (Prince Edward Antony Richard Louis), KG, KCVO, ADC; .   10 March 1964

cr 1999, Viscount Severn and Earl of Wessex

  Married 19 June 1999, Sophie Helen Rhys-Jones (*b* 20 Jan. 1965, *d* of Christopher and late Mary Rhys-Jones), and has issue –

    JAMES ALEXANDER PHILIP THEO MOUNTBATTEN-WINDSOR, (VISCOUNT SEVERN, *qv*)   .   17 Dec. 2007

    LOUISE ALICE ELIZABETH MARY MOUNTBATTEN-WINDSOR, (LADY LOUISE WINDSOR) .   8 Nov. 2003

  Office: Buckingham Palace, SW1A 1AA; *residence:* Bagshot Park, Bagshot, Surrey GU19 5PL.

HRH The Princess Royal, (Princess Anne Elizabeth Alice Louise), KG, KT, GCVO, QSO .   15 Aug. 1950

  Married 1st, 14 Nov. 1973, Captain Mark Anthony Peter Phillips, *qv* (marriage dissolved, 1992), and has issue –

    PETER MARK ANDREW PHILLIPS .   .   .   .   15 Nov. 1977

      Married 17 May 2008, Autumn Patricia, *d* of Brian Kelly

    ZARA ANNE ELIZABETH PHILLIPS, MBE .   .   .   .   .   .   15 May 1981

  Married 2nd, 12 Dec. 1992, Vice Admiral Timothy James Hamilton Laurence, *qv*

  Office: Buckingham Palace, SW1A 1AA; *residence:* Gatcombe Park, Minchinhampton, Stroud, Gloucestershire GL6 9AT.

NEPHEW AND NIECE OF HER MAJESTY

Children of HRH The Princess Margaret (Rose), (Countess of Snowdon, CI, GCVO, *b* 21 Aug. 1930, *d* 9 Feb. 2002) and 1st Earl of Snowdon, *qv*

Viscount Linley, (David Albert Charles Armstrong-Jones), *qv* .   .   .   .   .   3 Nov. 1961

  Married 8 Oct. 1993, Hon. Serena Alleyne Stanhope, *o d* of Viscount Petersham, *qv* and has issue –

    HON. CHARLES PATRICK INIGO ARMSTRONG-JONES   .   .   .   .   .   1 July 1999

    HON. MARGARITA ELIZABETH ALLEYNE ARMSTRONG-JONES   .   .   .   .   14 May 2002

Lady Sarah Chatto, (Sarah Frances Elizabeth Chatto) . . . . . . 1 May 1964
 Married 14 July 1994, Daniel Chatto, *s* of late Thomas Chatto and of Rosalind Chatto, and has
  issue –
  SAMUEL DAVID BENEDICT CHATTO . . . . 28 July 1996
  ARTHUR ROBERT NATHANIEL CHATTO . . . . 5 Feb. 1999

COUSINS OF HER MAJESTY

Child of HRH The Duke of Gloucester (Prince Henry William Frederick Albert, *b* 31 March 1900, *d*
 10 June 1974) and HRH Princess Alice Christabel, Duchess of Gloucester, GCB, CI, GCVO,
 GBE (*b* 25 Dec. 1901, *d* 29 Oct. 2004), 3rd *d* of 7th Duke of Buccleuch

HRH The Duke of Gloucester, (Prince Richard Alexander Walter George), KG, GCVO . . 26 Aug. 1944
 Married 8 July 1972, Birgitte Eva van Deurs, GCVO (*b* 20 June 1946, *d* of Asger Preben Wissing
  Henriksen), and has issue –
  ALEXANDER PATRICK GREGERS RICHARD, (EARL OF ULSTER, *qv*) . . . . 24 Oct. 1974
  DAVINA ELIZABETH ALICE BENEDIKTE, (LADY DAVINA LEWIS) . . . . 19 Nov. 1977
   Married 31 July 2004, Gary Lewis
  ROSE VICTORIA BIRGITTE LOUISE, (LADY ROSE GILMAN) . . . . . 1 March 1980
   Married 19 July 2008, George Edward Gilman
 Residence: Kensington Palace, W8 4PU.

Children of HRH The Duke of Kent (Prince George Edward Alexander Edmund, *b* 20 Dec. 1902,
 d 25 Aug. 1942) and HRH Princess Marina, Duchess of Kent (*b* 13 Dec. 1906, *d* 27 Aug. 1968),
 y d of late Prince Nicholas of Greece

HRH The Duke of Kent, (Prince Edward George Nicholas Paul Patrick), KG, GCMG, GCVO . 9 Oct. 1935
 Married 8 June 1961, Katharine Lucy Mary Worsley, GCVO (*b* 22 Feb. 1933, *o d* of Sir William
  Worsley, 4th Bt) and has issue –
  GEORGE PHILIP NICHOLAS, (EARL OF ST ANDREWS, *qv*) . . . . . 26 June 1962
   Married 9 Jan. 1988, Sylvana Tomaselli, and has issue –
    EDWARD EDMUND MAXIMILIAN GEORGE, (BARON DOWNPATRICK, *qv*) . . . 2 Dec. 1988
    MARINA-CHARLOTTE ALEXANDRA KATHARINE HELEN, (LADY MARINA-CHARLOTTE
     WINDSOR) . . . . 30 Sept. 1992
    AMELIA SOPHIA THEODORA MARY MARGARET, (LADY AMELIA WINDSOR) . . 24 Aug. 1995
  NICHOLAS CHARLES EDWARD JONATHAN, (LORD NICHOLAS WINDSOR). . . . 25 July 1970
   Married 19 Oct. 2006, Princess Paola Doimi de Lupis Frankopan Šubic Zrinski, and has issue –
    ALBERT LOUIS PHILIP EDWARD WINDSOR . . . . . . 22 Sept. 2007
  HELEN MARINA LUCY, (LADY HELEN TAYLOR) . . . . . . 28 April 1964
   Married 18 July 1992, Timothy Verner Taylor, *e s* of Commander Michael Taylor, RN and
    Mrs Colin Walkinshaw, and has issue –
    COLUMBUS GEORGE DONALD TAYLOR . . . . 6 Aug. 1994
    CASSIUS EDWARD TAYLOR . . . . 26 Dec. 1996
    ELOISE OLIVIA KATHARINE TAYLOR . . . . 2 March 2003
    ESTELLA OLGA ELIZABETH TAYLOR . . . . 21 Dec. 2004
 Office: St James's Palace, SW1A 1BQ; *residence:* Wren House, Palace Green, W8 4PY.

HRH Prince Michael of Kent, (Prince Michael George Charles Franklin), GCVO . . 4 July 1942
 Married 30 June 1978, Baroness Marie-Christine Agnes Hedwig Ida von Reibnitz (*b* 15 Jan. 1945,
  d of Baron Günther Hubertus von Reibnitz), and has issue –
  FREDERICK MICHAEL GEORGE DAVID LOUIS, (LORD FREDERICK WINDSOR) . . . 6 April 1979
  GABRIELLA MARINA ALEXANDRA OPHELIA, (LADY GABRIELLA WINDSOR) . . . 23 April 1981
 Residence: Kensington Palace, W8 4PU.

HRH Princess Alexandra (Helen Elizabeth Olga Christabel), The Hon. Lady Ogilvy, . . 25 Dec. 1936
 KG, GCVO
 Married 24 April 1963, Rt Hon. Sir Angus (James Bruce) Ogilvy, KCVO, PC (*b* 14 Sept. 1928,
  d 26 Dec. 2004), *s* of 12th Earl of Airlie, KT, GCVO, MC and has issue –
  JAMES ROBERT BRUCE OGILVY . . . . 29 Feb. 1964
   Married 30 July 1988, Julia, *d* of Charles Frederick Melville Rawlinson, *qv*, and has issue –
    ALEXANDER CHARLES OGILVY . . . . 12 Nov. 1996
    FLORA ALEXANDRA OGILVY . . . . 15 Dec. 1994
  MARINA VICTORIA ALEXANDRA OGILVY . . . . 31 July 1966
   Married 2 Feb. 1990, Paul Julian Mowatt (marriage dissolved, 1997), and has issue –
    CHRISTIAN ALEXANDER MOWATT. . . . . 4 June 1993
    ZENOUSKA MAY MOWATT . . . . 26 May 1990
 Office: Buckingham Palace, SW1A 1AA; *residence:* Thatched House Lodge, Richmond, Surrey
  TW10 5HP.

EDITORS' NOTE

A proof of each entry is posted to its subject every year for personal revision. Any editorial queries concerning content and accuracy are raised with the biographee at this stage, for amendment in the next edition.

Addresses printed in *Who's Who* are those which the subjects of the entries have submitted for publication. Addresses in London, and the names of London clubs, are unaccompanied by the word 'London'.

Entries are listed alphabetically by surname; forenames follow, those which are not customarily used by the subject being placed within brackets. Where a diminutive or alternative name is preferred, this is shown in brackets after all the given names.

Inclusion in *Who's Who* has never, at any time, been a matter for payment or of obligation to purchase.

Can you put a price on a baby's life?

For the Foundation for the Study of Infant Deaths (**FSID**), this is literally a life and death question.

FSID is the UK's leading baby charity fighting sudden and unexpected death in infancy. More than **500** babies die suddenly and unexpectedly every year – more than are claimed by meningitis, leukaemia and other forms of cancer combined.

FSID works to prevent this by:

- Funding research
- Supporting families whose babies have died
- Promoting infant health information to parents, carers and health professionals
- Campaigning to improve investigations when a baby dies

In doing so, it has already saved over **21,000** babies' lives.

FSID needs £1.3 million every year to maintain its research, education and bereavement programmes. Even more, it needs your support.

To make a gift now or include FSID in your Will, please call the Fundraising Department on **020 7222 8003**, or write to:

FSID, Artillery House, 11-19 Artillery Row, London SW1P 1RT

Fax: 020 7222 8002

Email: fundraising@fsid.org.uk

Website: www.fsid.org.uk

FSID

Giving babies the chance of a lifetime

Registered Charity Number 262191

WW09.WWB/e

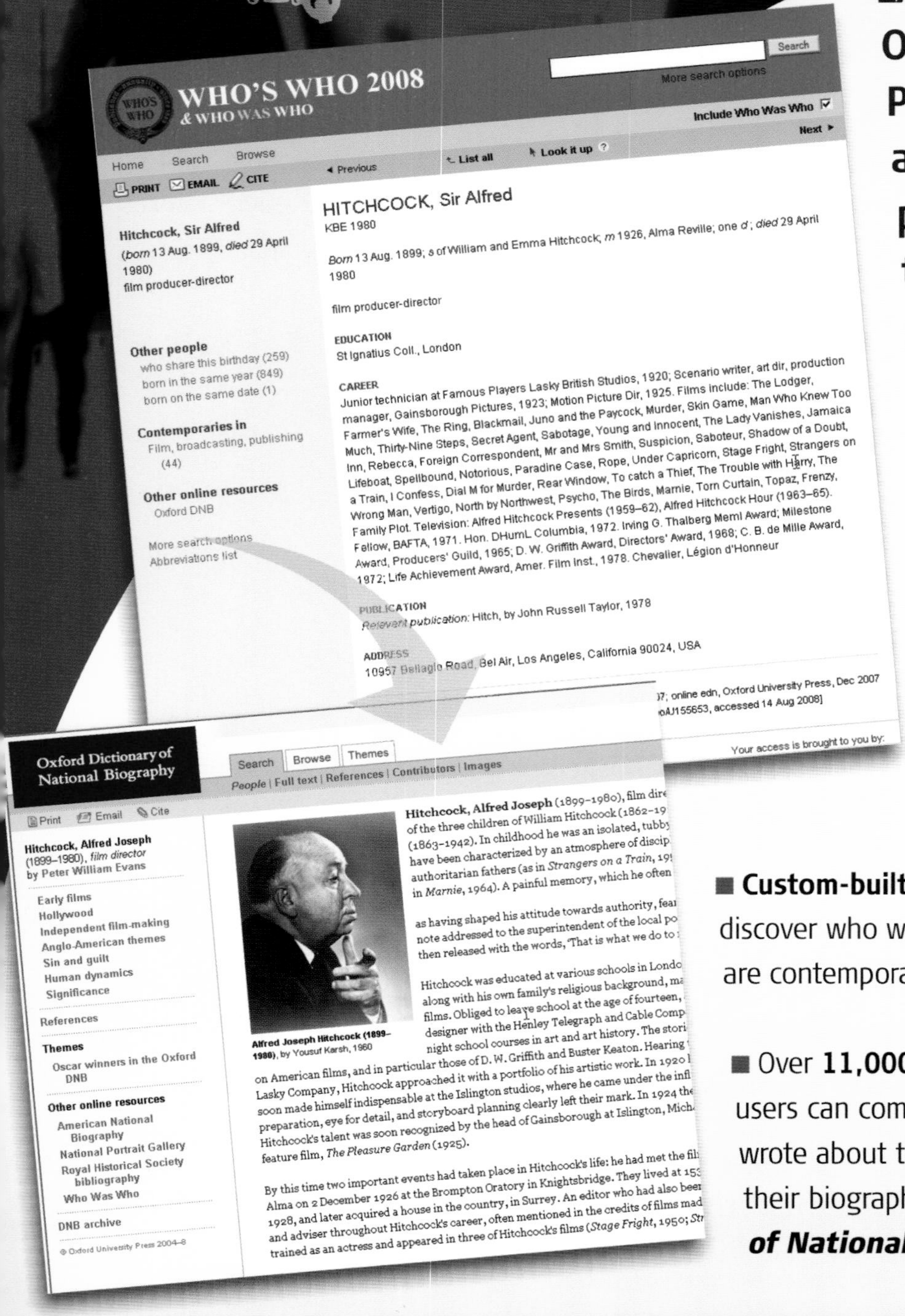

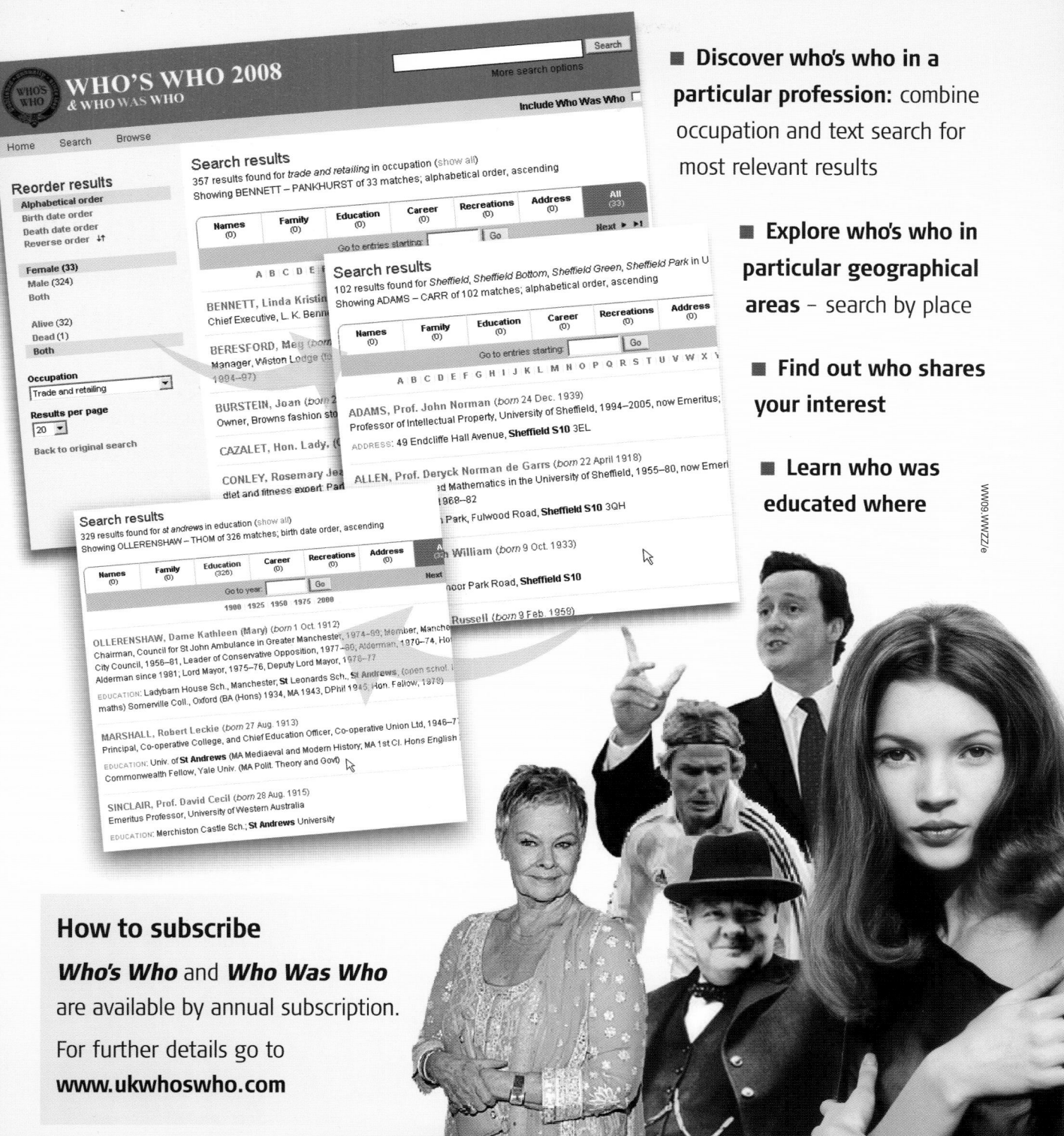

Westie to Weimaraner.

If you're considering giving a home to a dog, why not visit one of our centres at Battersea, Old Windsor or Brands Hatch? You'll find dogs of all shapes and sizes, including many pedigrees. **Please visit www.dogshome.org for a selection of dogs looking for a new home or call 020 7622 3626.**

WW09.WWA/v

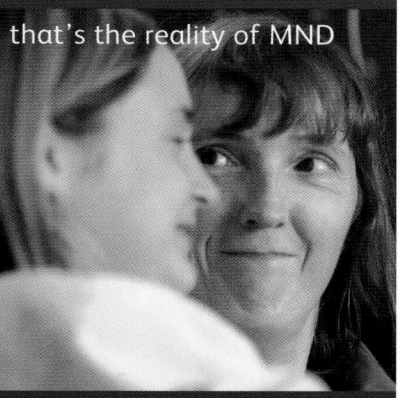

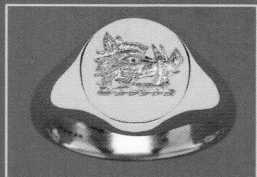

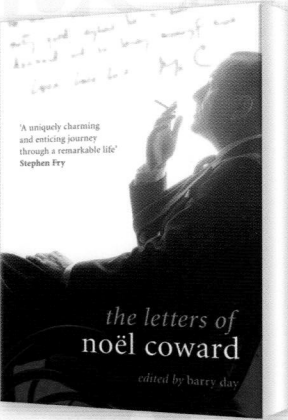
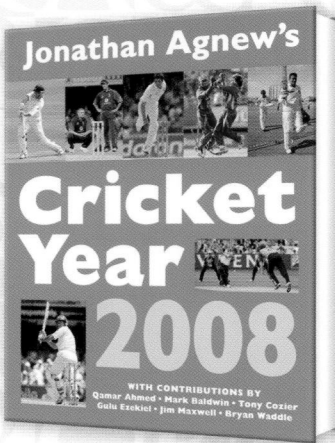

Coram ♥ Family

Transforming young people's lives since 1739

Coram Family is thought to be England's oldest children's charity and remains forefront of childcare in the UK. We have been caring for children since 1739: ever since Captain Thomas Coram decided that he could no longer stand by whilst young children lived and died on the streets of London.

Today we run over 50 different projects for disadvantaged children and their families, helping to give those who have suffered so much in their short lives a second chance to enjoy a happy, healthy and fulfilling life.

Coram Family's services help vulnerable children and young people who have experienced trauma and family breakdown, or whose families are at risk. We provide practical care and support for thousands of children, young people and families every year through a wide range of ground-breaking projects.

"Thank God Coram Family made sure I was alright. When it came time for me to take my first scary steps in the outside world, they really stuck by me. "
Alison, a young person leaving care

Coram Family has a wealth of experience working with children who have been severely damaged by their childhoods. We pioneer new ways of working with children. We listen to and respect them, promoting their rights and challenging discrimination. The work we do enables children who are at risk or who have been separated from their parents, to develop a sense of self-esteem, to find stability and lead fulfilling lives.

"Coram Family changed my outlook completely. Knowing people were really concerned about me and my future made a massive difference, because for the first time I felt safe knowing that they would never give up on me."
Mike

Coram Family relies on donations and legacies to continue providing services for some of the most emotionally and physically deprived children and young people in Britain.

If you would like to make a donation or would like more information about our work please contact us on:

T   020 7520 0330
F   020 7520 0301
E   fundraising@coram.org.uk
W   www.coram.org.uk

Incorporated by Royal Charter in 1739
Registered charity number 312278

WW09/WWC/e

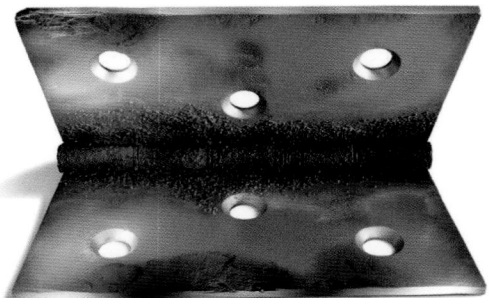

Arthritis may not kill, but it can take lives.

Over 7 million people in the UK alone suffer from this painful, often crippling disease - everyone knows someone whose life has been adversely affected by arthritis. The Arthritis Research Campaign (arc) is the only major charity in the country dedicated to funding research into the different causes, treatments and possible cures. We receive no government funding, so if you should choose to remember us in your will you'll be making a vital contribution towards our important work – work that could make a real difference to millions of lives.

arc 0870 850 5000
www.arc.org.uk
Committed to curing arthritis

Arthritis Research Campaign - Formerly the Arthritis and Rheumatism Council for Research, Copeman House, St Mary's Court, St Mary's Gate, Chesterfield, Derbyshire S41 7TD. *Registered Charity No. 207711*

WW09-WW10a/e

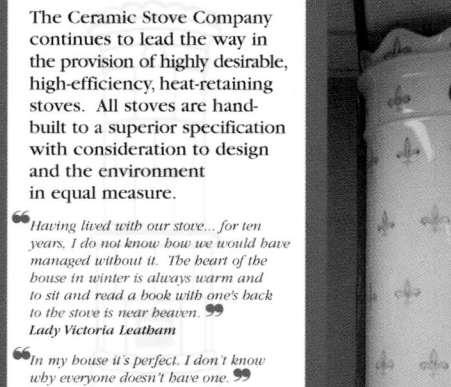

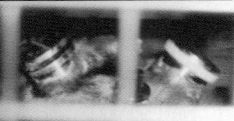

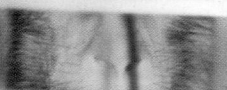
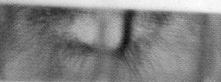

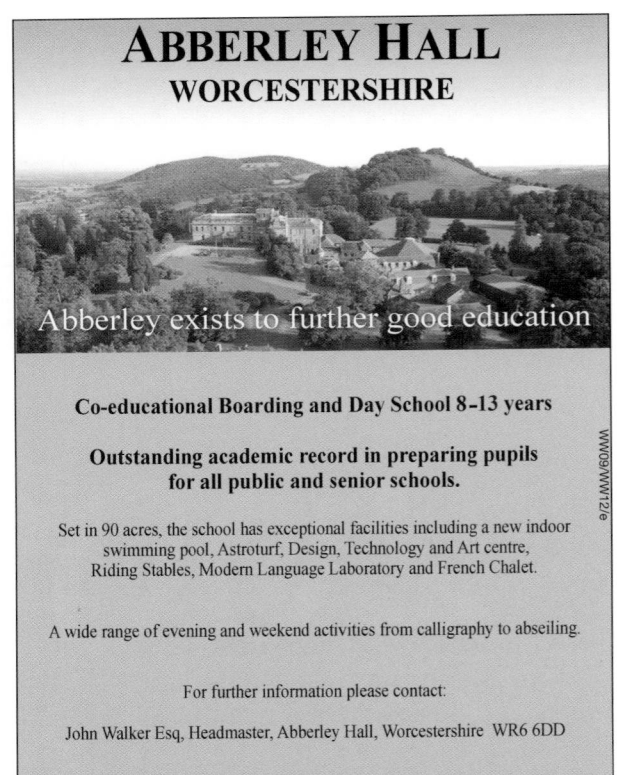

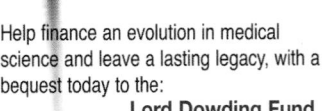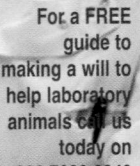

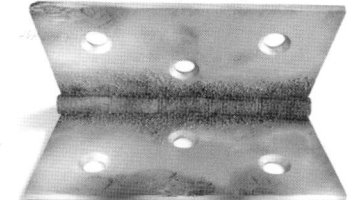

The new Artikulat Loudspeaker System. Gorgeous.

LINN

WW09.WWD/e

A

AARONOVITCH, David Morris; columnist, The Times, since 2005; *b* 8 July 1954; *s* of Dr Sam Aaronovitch and Lavender Aaronovitch; *m* 2005, Sarah Powell; three *d*. *Educ:* William Ellis Sch., Highgate; Manchester Univ. (BA Hons Hist.). Pres., NUS, 1980–82. Researcher and producer, Weekend World, LWT, 1982–87; BBC: Ed., On the Record, 1988–90; Hd, Political News, 1990–93; Managing Ed., Current Affairs, 1993–94; Chief Leader Writer, Independent, 1995–97; columnist: Independent, 1997–2003; Guardian and Observer, 2003–05. *Publication:* Paddling to Jerusalem, 2000. *Recreations:* running, theatre, film, watching football. *Address:* The Times, 1 Pennington Street, E98 1TT; *e-mail:* David.Aaronovitch@btinternet.com.

AARONSON, Graham Raphael; QC 1982; *b* 31 Dec. 1944; *s* of late John and Dora Aaronson; *m*; two *s* one *d*; *m* 1993, Pearl Isobel Buchler; two step *s* one step *d*. *Educ:* City of London Sch.; Trinity Hall, Cambridge (Thomas Waraker Law Schol.; MA). Called to the Bar, Middle Temple, 1966 (Bencher 1991); practised Revenue law, 1968–73 and 1978–. Chairman: Tax Law Review Cttee, 1994–97; Revenue Bar Assoc., 1995–98. Advr on tax reform to Treasury, Israel, 1986–90. Chm., Dietary Res. Foundn, 1989–93. Founder, Standford Grange residential rehabilitation centre for ex-offenders, 1974; Man. Dir, Worldwide Plastics Development, 1973–77; Dir, Bridgend Group PLC, 1973–92. *Address:* Pump Court Tax Chambers, 16 Bedford Row, WC1R 4EB.

AARONSON, Sir Michael John, (Sir Mike), Kt 2006; CBE 2000; Chairman, Frimley Park Hospital NHS Foundation Trust, since 2006; a Civil Service Commissioner, since 2007; *b* 8 Sept. 1947; *s* of Edward John Aaronson and Marian Aaronson (*née* Davies); *m* 1988, Andrene Margaret Sutherland; two *s* one *d*. *Educ:* Merchant Taylors' Sch.; St John's Coll., Oxford (Sir Thomas White Scholar, Trevelyan Scholar; MA). Field Co-ordinator, SCF, Nigeria, 1969–71; HM Diplomatic Service, 1972–88, served Paris, Lagos, Rangoon; Save the Children Fund: Overseas Dir, 1988–95; Dir-Gen., 1995–2005. Dir, Oxford Policy Management Ltd, 2006–. Chm. Bd, Centre for Humanitarian Dialogue (Geneva), 2001–; Gov., Westminster Foundn for Democracy, 2001– (Vice-Chm., 2005–). Mem. Council, RSA, 2004–. Vis. Fellow, Nuffield Coll., Oxford, 2004–; Sen. Res. Associate, KCL, 2005–. Freeman: City of London, 1989; Merchant Taylors' Co., 1989. *Recreations:* sports, the performing arts. *Address:* Dingley Dell, Glaziers Lane, Normandy, Surrey GU3 2EB. *T:* (01483) 811655. *Club:* MCC.

ABBADO, Claudio; Artistic Director, Berlin Philharmonic Orchestra, 1989–2002; Generalmusikdirektor of Vienna, since 1987; *b* Milan, 26 June 1933. Music Dir, La Scala, Milan, 1968–86; Principal Conductor, LSO, 1979–88; Music Director, Vienna State Opera, 1986–91. Founder, European Community Youth Orch., 1978; Artistic Advr, Chamber Orchestra of Europe, 1981–; Founder and Artistic Director: Gustav Mahler Jugend Orchester, 1988; Festival, Wien Modern, 1988; Artistic Dir, Salzburg Easter Fest., 1994. Dr *hc* Aberdeen, 1986; Ferrara, 1990; Cambridge, 1994. Mozart-Medaille, Mozart-Gemeinde, Vienna, 1973; Goldmedaille der Internat. Gustav Mahler Gesellschaft, Vienna, 1985; winner of major international prizes for recordings. Ehrenring, City of Vienna, 1994. Gran Croce d'Italia, 1984; Cross, Légion d'Honneur; Bundesverdienstkreuz (Germany), 1992. *Address:* c/o Askonas Holt Ltd, Lincoln House, 300 High Holborn, WC1V 7JH.

ABBERLEY, Robert; Assistant General Secretary, UNISON, since 2002; *b* 29 Oct. 1952; *s* of late Fred Abberley and of Lillian Abberley. *Educ:* Kingsland Co. Primary Sch., Hereford; Wigmore Co. Secondary Sch., Hereford. C&G Operating Dept Practitioner. Labourer, 1969; apprentice toolmaker, Halls Engrg, Shrewsbury, 1969–70; driver, builders merchants, 1971–72; operating dept asst, Hereford Hosps, 1972–79. Trade Union officer, COHSE, 1979–93; Hd of Health, UNISON, 1993–2002. Member: Adv. Bd, TUC Partnership Inst.; TUC Gen. Council, 2005. Member: NHS Task Force on Staff Involvement in decision making, 1998–99; NHS Modernisation Bd, 1999–; NHS shifting the balance of power task force, 2001; Community Cohesion Rev. Team, 2001–02; Ministerial Adv. Panel on Social Cohesion, 2002; NHSUniv. SHA, 2003–05; NHS Nat. Leadership Network, 2005–; NHS Ministerial Sounding Bd, 2006; Chair, NHS widening participation in learning steering gp, 2005–. Board Member: Care Connect Learning; Coll. of Operating Dept Practitioners, 2007. Pres., Health and Social Services Cttee, Eur. Fedn of Trade Unions, 1983–2002. Member: IAM (Middx); TR Register; Shuttleworth Trust Veterans Assoc. *Recreations:* classic car restoration, motorcycling, music, going to the gym, Manchester United, watching movies, reading biographies. *Address:* UNISON, 1 Mabledon Place, WC1H 9AJ. *Fax:* (020) 7387 4914; *e-mail:* b.abberley@unison.co.uk.

ABBOTT, Anthony John, CMG 2001; OBE 1997 (MBE 1986); HM Diplomatic Service, retired; Head, Pitcairn Logistics Team, New Zealand, 2001–04; *b* Ashton-under-Lyne, 9 Sept. 1941; *s* of Walter Abbott and Mary Abbott (*née* Delaney); *m* 1962, Margaret Stuart Green; three *s* one *d*. *Educ:* All Souls' Sch., Salford; De La Salle Coll., Pendleton. Joined HM Diplomatic Service, 1959: Vice-Consul, Khorramshahr, 1963–65; Helsinki, 1965–68; Press Officer, FCO, 1969–72; Passport Officer, Lusaka, 1972–75; Consul, Santiago, 1976–80; UK Presidency Secretariat to EC, 1981; on secondment to BOTB, 1981–82; Consul, Lisbon, 1983–87; First Sec., Calcutta, 1987–91; EC Monitor, Croatia and Bosnia Herzogovina, 1991; Dep. Head, Trng Dept, FCO, 1992–93; Consul-Gen., Perth, 1993–97; Governor, Montserrat, 1997–2001. EC Monitoring Medal, 1994. Officer, Order of Enfante Dom Henrique (Portugal), 1985. *Recreations:* travel, driving, golf, spectator (all sports). *Address:* Parkhill, 3B/158 Mill Point Road, South Perth, WA 6151, Australia. *Club:* Royal Over-Seas League.

ABBOTT, Diane Julie; MP (Lab) Hackney North and Stoke Newington, since 1987; *b* 27 Sept. 1953; *d* of late Reginald and Julia Abbott; *m* 1991, David Thompson (marr. diss. 1993); one *s*. *Educ:* Harrow County Girls' Grammar Sch.; Newnham Coll., Cambridge. Formerly: Admin. Trainee, Home Office; Race Relations Officer, NCCL; Researcher, Thames Television; Reporter, TV-am; Equality Officer, ACTT; Press and PR Officer, GLC; Principal Press Officer, Lambeth Borough Council. Joined Labour Party, 1971; Mem., NEC, 1994–97. Mem., Westminster City Council, 1982–86. Mem. resp. for equality and women's issues, Mayor of London's Cabinet, 2000–. *Address:* House of Commons, SW1A 0AA.

ABBOTT, John Martin, CBE 2000; QPM 1996; Director General, National Criminal Intelligence Service, 1997–2003; Vice President, Interpol, 1999–2002; *b* 22 March 1949; *s* of late Geoffrey Lowick Abbott and of Gladys Lilian Abbott; *m* 1972, Christine Sowter; two *d*. *Educ:* Univ. of Sussex (BA Hons History 1982). Joined Sussex Police, 1968: served in various ranks throughout Sussex, 1968–86; Supt, seconded to Royal Hong Kong Police, 1986–88; Chief Supt, seconded to Police Staff Coll., Bramshill, 1989–91; Asst Chief Constable, 1991–94; Asst Insp. of Constabulary, 1994–96. Mem. Bd, Sussex CCC, 2006–. *Recreations:* reading, history, golf, keeping fit. *Club:* St Michaels (Lewes).

ABBOTT, Paul; film and television writer; *b* 22 Feb. 1960; *s* of Alan Abbott and late Doreen Abbott; *m* 1993, Saskia; one *s* one *d*. *Educ:* Barden High Sch., Burnley. Writer: television series: Coronation Street, 1985–89; Cracker (episodes), 1993 (Best Drama Series, BAFTA award, 1995); Reckless, 1997; Touching Evil, 1997; Butterfly Collectors, 1999; Secret Life of Michael Fry, 2000; Clocking Off, 2000–03 (Best Drama Series, BAFTA award, 2001); Linda Green, 2001; State of Play, 2003; Shameless, 2004, 2005 (Best Drama Series, BAFTA award, 2005), 2007; TV film, Reckless: The Movie, 1999. *Recreations:* film, theatre, novels, rumours. *Address:* c/o The Agency, 24 Pottery Lane, Holland Park, W11 4LZ. *Clubs:* Century; Writers' Guild of Great Britain.

ABBOTT, Adm. Sir Peter (Charles), GBE 1999; KCB 1994; Vice Chief of the Defence Staff, 1997–2001; Commissioner, Commonwealth War Graves Commission, 2001–06; *b* 12 Feb. 1942; *s* of late Lieut-Col Dennis Abbott, Royal Garwhal Rifles and Delphine McConaghey; *m* 1965, Susan Phillippa Grey; three *d*. *Educ:* St Edward's Sch., Oxford; Queens' College, Cambridge (MA 1966). Articled Clerk, Blackburn, Robson Coates, 1963; 2nd Lieut, RMFVR 1963; Sub Lieut, RN 1964; Commanding Officer, HM Ships Chawton, 1972, Ambuscade, 1976, Ajax, 1983 (and First Frigate Sqdn); RCDS 1985; Flag Officer, Flotilla Two, 1989; ACNS, 1991–93; Dep. SACLANT, 1993–95; C-in-C Fleet, C-in-C Eastern Atlantic Area and Comdr Naval Forces N Western Europe, 1995–97. Chm. Trustees, Royal Naval Mus., 2003–. Officer, US Legion of Merit, 1995.

ABBOTT, Roderick Evelyn; consultant, international trade; *b* 16 April 1938; *e s* of late Stuart Abbott, OBE; *m* 1963, Elizabeth Isobel McLean; three *d*. *Educ:* Rugby Sch.; Merton Coll., Oxford. Board of Trade, 1962–68 (Private Sec. to Pres. of BoT, 1965–66; seconded to DEA, 1966–68); UK Mission to UN, Geneva, 1968–71; Foreign Office, London, 1971–73; EEC, Brussels, 1973–75; EEC Delegation, Geneva, 1975–79; EEC, Brussels, 1979–82; Dir, D-G of External Relns, then External Econ. Relns, EC, Brussels, 1982–96; Ambassador and Perm. Rep. of EC to UN and other internat. orgns, Geneva, 1996–2000; Dep. Dir Gen., Trade, EC, Brussels, 2000–02; Dep. Dir-Gen., WTO, 2002–05. Visiting Fellow: LSE, 2006–; European Univ. Inst., Florence, 2008–. Mem. Adv. Bd, Eur. Centre for Internat. Pol Economy. *Recreation:* travel. *Address:* Avenue Grandchamp 98A, 1150 Brussels, Belgium. *Club:* Royal Commonwealth Society.

ABBOTT-WATT, Thorhilda Mary Vivia, (Thorda); HM Diplomatic Service; Ambassador to Armenia, 2003–06; *b* 11 Feb. 1955; *d* of Samuel Abbott-Watt and Elva Mary Abbott-Watt (*née* Clare Gibson); partner, Reef Talbot Hogg. *Educ:* Stonar Sch., Atworth, Wilts. Joined HM Diplomatic Service, 1974; Third Sec., FCO, 1974–79; temp. duty tours in Latin America, Middle and Far East, 1979–80; Vice Consul, Paris, 1981–84; Third Sec. (Chancery), UK Repn to EU, 1984–86; Second Secretary: FCO, 1986–88; Bonn, 1988–91; First Sec., EU Dept and Western Eur. Dept, FCO, 1991–95; Hd, Commercial Section, Kiev, 1995–98; First Sec. (Political), Belgrade, 1998–99; Hd, Visa Policy Section, Jt Entry Clearance Unit, FCO, 1999–2001; Chargé d'Affaires, Tajikistan, 2001–02. Member: ICA; RA; Life Mem., NACF. *Recreations:* riding, theatre, the arts, sitting in a comfortable chair with a good book. *Address:* c/o Foreign and Commonwealth Office, King Charles Street, SW1A 2AH; *e-mail:* Thorda.Abbott-Watt@fco.gov.uk.

ABDELA, Lesley Julia, MBE 1990; journalist and broadcaster, since 1986; Chief Executive: Project Parity, since 1996; Project Parity Partnerships for Peace, since 2005; Senior Partner: Eyecatcher Associates, since 1986; Shevolution, since 1998; specialist in post-conflict reconstruction, since 1999; *b* London, 17 Nov. 1945; *d* of late Frederick Abdela and Henrietta (*née* Hardy); *m* 1972 (marr. diss.); one *s*; partner, Tim Symonds. *Educ:* Queen Anne's Sch., Caversham; Châtelard Sch., Les Avants, Switzerland; Queen's Coll., Harley Street; Hammersmith Coll. of Art and Building; London Coll. of Printing. Advertising Exec., Royds of London, 1968–72; Derek Forsyth Design Partnership, 1972–73; researcher for Liberal Party, H of C, 1977–79; Founder, 1980, Chair, 1980–85, Trustee, 1980–95, 300 Group (for women in politics). UK Consultant, Project Liberty, Kennedy Sch. of Govt, Harvard Univ., 1992–98. OSCE Dep. Dir for Democracy, UN Interim Admin in Kosovo, 1999; Sen. Civil Soc. Expert in governance, democratisation, gender and human rights, Kosovo, Sierra Leone, Iraq, Afghanistan and Aceh (Indonesia). Political Editor: Cosmopolitan, 1993–96 (first Pol Ed. of a women's mag.); Radio Viva!, 1995; regular contributor to Exec. Woman mag., Mail on Sunday, Sunday Times, Guardian, Times, Independent, Glasgow Herald, etc; writer, researcher and presenter of radio and TV documentaries, incl. Women with X Appeal, 1993, Breaking Glass, 1994. Board Member: Internat. Inst. for Envmt and Develt, 1992–96; British Council, 1995–2000; Mem. Exec. Bd, Women in Mgt, 1985–88. Vice Pres., Electoral Reform Soc., 1995–. Contested (L) E Herts, 1979. Gov., Nottingham Trent Univ., 1997–2000. FRGS; FRSA; MCIJ. Hon. DLitt Nottingham Trent, 1996. *Publications:* Women with X Appeal, 1989; Breaking Through the Glass Ceilings, 1991; What Women Want, 1994; Do

It! – Walk the Talk, 1995. *Recreations:* painting, ski-ing, scuba, reading, looking forward to true equality between women and men in politics and society. *Address:* Park Farm Oast, Bateman's Lane, Burwash, Etchingham, East Sussex TN19 7DR; Harper's Marsh, King's Saltern Road, Lymington, Hants SO41 9QG; *e-mail:* lesley.abdela@shevolution.com.

ABDIN, Dr Hasan; Ambassador of Sudan to the Court of St James's, 2000–06; *b* 1 Jan. 1939; *m* 1966, Manahil A. Abu Kashwa; two *s* three *d*. *Educ:* Univ. of Khartoum (BA 1965); Univ. of Wisconsin (MA 1967; PhD 1970). Lectr in African Hist., Univ. of Khartoum, 1970–77; State Minister, Sudan, 1977–78; Mem., Nat. Assembly, 1978–80; Asst Prof. of Hist., Univ. of King Saud, Riyyadh, Saudi Arabia, 1983–88; Inst. of Asian and African Studies, Univ. of Khartoum, 1988–90; Ambassador to: Algeria, 1990–92; Iraq, 1993–97; Under Sec., Min. of Foreign Affairs, Khartoum, 1998–2000. *Publications:* Introduction to African History (in Arabic), 1974; Early Sudanese Nationalism, 1986. *Recreations:* reading, walking. *Address:* c/o Embassy of the Republic of the Sudan, 3 Cleveland Row, St James's, SW1A 1DD.

ABDULAH, Frank Owen; Deputy Secretary-General, Caribbean Community Secretariat, Guyana, 1989–93; *b* 8 Nov. 1928; *m*; four *d*. *Educ:* Queen's Royal Coll., Trinidad; Oxford (MA, DipEd Oxon). Held several govt posts, 1953–62, before entering Diplomatic Service at Trinidad and Tobago's Independence, 1962; Dep. Perm. Rep. (Minister Counsellor), 1970–73, Perm. Rep. (Ambassador), 1975–83, Trinidad and Tobago Perm. Mission to UN, NY; Perm. Sec. (Acting), Ministry of External Affairs, Port of Spain, 1973–75; High Comr for Trinidad and Tobago in London with concurrent accreditations as Ambassador to Denmark, Finland, France, FRG, Norway and Sweden, 1983–85; Permanent Sec., Min. of External Affairs and Internat. Trade, Trinidad and Tobago, 1985–88. Pres., UNA Trinidad and Tobago, 1987–88. *Recreations:* music, sports. *Address:* 8 Nock Road, Maraval, Trinidad.

ABDY, Sir Valentine (Robert Duff), 6th Bt *cr* 1850; European Representative, Smithsonian Institution, Washington, 1983–95 and 1998 (Member, National Board, 1995–98); *b* 11 Sept. 1937; *s* of Sir Robert Henry Edward Abdy, 5th Bt, and Lady Diana Bridgeman (*d* 1967), *e d* of 5th Earl of Bradford; *S* father, 1976; *m* 1971, Mathilde Coche de la Ferté (marr. diss. 1982); one *s*. *Educ:* Eton. Formerly: Administrator, Musée des Arts Décoratifs, Paris; Dir, Sotheby's. Mem., Scientific Committee, Conservatoire Nationale des Arts et Métiers, 1992; Special Advr, Internat. Fund for Promotion of Culture, UNESCO, 1991–97. Mem., Organising Cttee, Cité de l'Espace, Toulouse, 1999–. FRSA 1998. Chevalier des Arts et des Lettres (France), 1995. *Heir: s* Robert Etienne Eric Abdy, *b* 22 Feb. 1978. *Address:* 2 New Square, Lincoln's Inn, WC2A 3RZ.

ABED, Ringo F.; Ambassador of the Republic of Namibia to the Democratic Republic of the Congo, since 2006; *b* 6 June 1956; *s* of late Benjamin Abed and Albertina Matheus; *m* 1979, Johanna; three *d* (two *s* decd). *Educ:* UN Inst. for Namibia (Dip. Public Admin 1980); Makerere Univ., Kampala (BA Hons 1986). Mem., SW African People's Orgn; in exile in Zambia, then Angola, 1974–89; Dep. Dir, reception and food distribn centres for returning veterans, 1989–92; Mem., OAU Observer Mission to SA, 1992–94; First Sec. (Pol) and Dep. Hd of Mission, Botswana, 1995, SA, 1999; Hd, Privileges and Immunities, Protocol Dept, Min. of Foreign Affairs, until 2000; Counsellor and Dep. Hd of Mission, Congo, 2000–03; Dir, Protocol, Office of the Prime Minister, 2004, Actg Chief of Protocol, 2005, Min. of Foreign Affairs; High Comr to the Court of St James's, 2005–06. *Recreations:* reading, music, travelling. *Address:* Embassy of Namibia, 138 Boulevard du 30 Juin, PO Box 8934, Kinshasa 1, Gombe, Democratic Republic of the Congo; *e-mail:* namembassy_drc@ic.cd.

ABEL, Prof. Edward William, CBE 1997; PhD, DSc; FRSC; Professor of Inorganic Chemistry, University of Exeter, 1972–97, now Emeritus (Head of Department of Chemistry, 1977–88; Deputy Vice-Chancellor, 1991–94); *b* 3 Dec. 1931; *s* of Sydney and Donna Abel; *m* 1960, Margaret R. Edwards; one *s* one *d*. *Educ:* Bridgend Grammar Sch.; University Coll., Cardiff (BSc 1952); Northern Polytechnic, London (PhD 1957). Served Army, 1953–55. Research Fellow, Imperial Coll., 1957–59; Lectr, later Reader, Univ. of Bristol, 1957–71. Vis. Professor: Univ. of British Columbia, 1970; Japanese Soc. for Promotion of Science, 1971; Tech. Univ. of Braunschweig, 1973; ANU, Canberra, 1990; Robert E. Welch Lectures, Texas, 1994. Royal Society of Chemistry: Mem. Council, 1977–82, 1983–87 and 1989–2002; Pres., 1996–98; Chairman: Local Affairs Bd, 1983–87; Divl Affairs Bd, 1989–92; Scientific Affairs Bd, 1992–95; Parly Cttee, 1995–2003; Laboratory of the Govt Chemist Adv. Cttee, 1998–2003; Mem., Dalton Div. Council, 1977–83, 1987–91 (Sec./Treasurer, 1977–82; Vice-Pres., 1983, 1989–91; Pres., 1987–89); Main Group Chem. Medal, 1976; Tilden Medal and Lectr, 1981; Service Medal, 2007. Perm. Sec., Internat. Confs on Organometallic Chem., 1972–89; Mem., UGC, 1986–89 (Chm., Phys. Scis Sub-Cttee, 1986–89); Nat. Advr for Chem., UFC, 1989–92; CNAA: Mem., 1991–93; Chm., Phys. Scis Cttee, 1987–91; Mem., Cttee for Academic Affairs, 1989–91. DUniv North London, 1998; Hon. DSc: Exeter, 2000; Glamorgan, 2004. *Publications:* (ed jtly) Organometallic Chemistry, vols 1–25, 1970–95; (exec. editor) Comprehensive Organometallic Chemistry, 9 vols, 1984; (exec. editor) Comprehensive Organometallic Chemistry II, 14 vols, 1995; papers to learned jls. *Address:* 1A Rosebarn Avenue, Exeter EX4 6DY. *T:* (01392) 270272; *e-mail:* EWAbel@ex.ac.uk.

ABEL, Keith Russell; Founding Director, Abel & Cole, organic food business, since 1988; *b* London, 13 Nov. 1963; *s* of Keith Paterson Abel and Sally Anne Neame; *m* 1992, Catherine Ciapparelli; one *s* one *d*. *Educ:* Rugby Sch.; Leeds Univ. (BA Hons); City Univ. (CPE Law); Inns of Court Sch. of Law. Called to the Bar, 1992. Queen's Award for Industry (Sustainable Develt), 2005. *Publication:* Cooking Outside the Box, 2005. *Recreations:* ski-ing, tennis, shooting, sleeping on Sunday afternoons! *Address:* Abel & Cole Ltd, 16 Waterside Way, Plough Lane, Wimbledon, SW17 0HB. *T:* (01264) 387540; *e-mail:* keith.abel@abel-cole.co.uk.

ABEL, Kenneth Arthur, CBE 1984; Clerk and Chief Executive, Dorset County Council, 1967–91 (Clerk of the Peace, 1967–73); *b* 4 April 1926; *s* of late Arthur Abel, CBE and Frances Ethel Abel; *m* 1955, Sarah Matilda, *d* of late Capt. M. P. Poynor, TD and Norah Elizabeth Poynor; three *s*. *Educ:* Durham Sch.; Glasgow Univ.; Durham Univ. (LLB). Served RA, 1944–48. Admitted Solicitor, 1953; Assistant Solicitor: Warwicks CC, 1953–54; Leics CC, 1954–59; Sen. Asst Solicitor, Northants CC, 1959–63; Dep. Clerk and Dep. Clerk of the Peace, NR Yorks CC, 1963–67. Chm., Assoc. of County Chief Execs, 1982–83. Past Pres., Dorset County Golf Union. DL Dorset, 1977. *Recreations:* golf, gardening. *Address:* Herne's Oak, Bradford Road, Sherborne, Dorset DT9 6BP. *T:* (01935) 813200. *Club:* Sherborne Golf (Sherborne) (Vice Pres.).

ABEL, Roger Lee; Chairman and Chief Executive Officer, Cygnus Oil and Gas Corporation (formerly Touchstone Resources USA Inc.), 2005; *b* Nebraska, 12 Aug. 1943. *Educ:* Colorado Sch. of Mines (BSc Petroleum Engrg 1965); MIT (MSc 1979). FInstPet. Served US Army, 1966–68 (Capt.). Joined Conoco Inc., 1968: prodn engr, 1968–72; Supervising Reservoir Engr, Lake Charles, Louisiana, 1972–73; Staff Engr, N America, 1973–74; Co-ordinator for W Hemisphere Planning Dept, 1974–75; Manager, Planning and Budgets, 1975–77; Exec. Asst to Conoco's Dep. Chm., 1977–78; Sloan Fellow, MIT, 1978–79; Asst Div. Manager, Offshore Div., 1979–80; Vice Pres. and Gen. Manager of Ops for Dubai Petroleum Co., 1980–82; Manager: of Ops, UK and Europe, 1982–84; of Planning, Admin and Engrg, N American Prodn, 1984–86; General Manager: Offshore and Frontier, N American Prodn, 1986–88; Prodn Engrg and Res. Dept, 1988–90; Vice-Pres. and Gen. Manager, Prodn Engrg and Res., 1990–91; Vice Pres., Exploration Prodn-Russia, 1991–93; Chm., Conoco Exploration Prodn Europe Ltd, 1993–97; Pres. and Chief Operating Officer, Occidental Oil & Gas Corp., 1997–99; Exec. Vice Pres., Occidental Petroleum Corp., 1999–2000; Pres., Austex Production Co. LLC, 2002–05. Distinguished Mem., Soc. of Petroleum Engrs (Pres., 1992).

ABELL, (John) David; Chairman, Jourdan (formerly Thomas Jourdan) plc, since 1997; Director, Leicester Football Club plc, since 1999; *b* 15 Dec. 1942; *s* of Leonard Abell and Irene (*née* Anderson); *m* 1st, 1967, Anne Janette Priestley (marr. diss. 1977); three *s*; 2nd, 1981, Sandra Dawn Atkinson (marr. diss. 1986); one *s* one *d*; 3rd, 1988, Juliana, *d* of late Prof. J. L. I. Fennell, PhD, FRSL and of Marina Lopukhin. *Educ:* Univ. of Leeds (BAEcon); London School of Economics (Dip. Business Admin). Assistant to Cash and Investment Manager, Ford Motor Co., 1962–65; Asst, Treasurer's Office, AEI, 1965–67; British Leyland: Central Staffs, 1968–69; Manager, Investments and Banking, 1969–70; Chm. and Chief Exec., Prestcold Div., 1970–72; Corporate Treasurer, 1972; First Nat. Finance Corp., Nov. 1972–Aug. 1973; re-joined British Leyland as Man. Dir, Leyland Australia, 1974–75; Group Man. Dir, Leyland Special Products, 1975; Man. Dir, BL Commercial Vehicles, Chm. and Chief Exec., Leyland Vehicles Ltd, 1978–81; Chm. and Chief Exec., Suter Electrical, subseq. Suter plc, 1981–96. *Recreations:* horse racing and breeding, wine, tennis, music, Rugby, soccer. *Address:* Jourdan plc, Elm House, Elmer Street North, Grantham, Lincs NG31 6RE.

ABELSON, Michael Andrew; a District Judge (Magistrates' Courts), Merseyside, since 2001; a Recorder, since 2000; *b* 22 March 1952; *s* of Harvey Abelson and Eva Abelson (*née* Newman); *m* 1994, Angela Bernadette Therese Walsh, BEd, DipEFL, *d* of Joseph Walsh and Frances Walsh (*née* Begley); one *s*. *Educ:* Leyton County High Sch.; University Coll., London (LLB Hons 1975). Called to the Bar, Middle Temple, 1976; in practice at the Bar, Northern, and Wales and Chester Circuits, 1977–98; Asst Recorder, 1997–2000; acting Stipendiary Magistrate: S Yorks, 1993–98; Gtr Manchester, 1995–98; Stipendiary Magistrate, later a Dist Judge (Magistrates' Courts), Gtr Manchester, 1998–2001. *Recreations:* travel, ski-ing, tennis, badminton. *Address:* Liverpool City Magistrates' Court, Dale Street, Liverpool L2 2JQ. *T:* (0151) 243 5596.

ABENSUR, Eric; Deputy Managing Director, Venda Ltd, since 2007; *b* 7 Jan. 1964. *Educ:* Univ. Paris IX Dauphine (DESS Finance d'Entreprise). Sen. Manager, Ernst & Young, Paris and Los Angeles, 1994–98; Finance Dir, Multimedia Div., France Telecom, 1998–2001; Chief Finance Officer, 2001–02, CEO, 2002–06, Freeserve, then Wanadoo UK, plc; Vice Pres., Orange Home UK plc, 2006–07. *Recreations:* cinema, history of 20th century, golf, squash. *Address:* Venda Ltd, 101 St Martin's Lane, WC2N 4AZ. *T:* (020) 7070 7227, *Fax:* (020) 7070 7111; *e-mail:* eabensur@venda.com.

ABER, Prof. Geoffrey Michael, FRCP; Professor of Renal Medicine, University of Keele, 1982–93; *b* 19 Feb. 1928; *s* of David and Hilda Aber; *m* 1964, Eleanor Maureen; one *s* one *d*. *Educ:* Leeds Grammar School; University of Leeds (MB, ChB, MD with distinction); PhD Birmingham. Leeds Gen. Infirmary, 1952–54; RAMC, 1954–56; Queen Elizabeth Hosp., Birmingham (Univ. of Birmingham), 1956–57, 1958–65; Brompton Hosp., London, 1957–58; Research Fellow: Univ. of Birmingham (Depts of Exptl Path. and Medicine), 1958–59 and 1960–64; McGill Univ., 1959–60; Wellcome Sen. Res. Fellow in Clinical Sci., 1964–65; Keele University: Prof. and Adviser in Clinical Res., 1979–82; Head of Dept. of Postgrad. Medicine, 1982–89; Dean of Postgrad. Medicine, 1989–91. *Publications:* contribs to: Recent Advances in Renal Medicine, 1983; Postgraduate Nephrology, 1985; Textbook of Genitourinary Surgery, 1985; scientific papers in learned jls. *Recreations:* music, sport, motor cars. *Address:* Mill Green House, Stone Rings Grange, Harrogate HG2 9HU. *T:* (01423) 871737; *e-mail:* g.aber@btopenworld.com.

ABERCONWAY, 4th Baron *cr* 1911, of Bodnant; **Henry Charles McLaren;** Bt 1902; *b* 26 May 1948; *s* of 3rd Baron Aberconway and his 1st wife, Deirdre Knewstub; *S* father, 2003; *m* 1981, Sally, *yr d* of Captain C. N. Lentaigne, RN; one *s* one *d*. *Educ:* Eton; Sussex Univ. (BA). *Heir: s* Hon. Charles Stephen McLaren, *b* 27 Dec. 1984. *Address:* 10 Rose Farm Cottages, Shotley, Ipswich, Suffolk IP9 1PH.

ABERCORN, 5th Duke of, *cr* 1868; **James Hamilton,** KG 1999; Lord of Paisley, 1587; Lord of Abercorn, 1603; Earl of Abercorn and Lord of Hamilton, Mountcastle and Kilpatrick, 1606; Baron of Strabane, 1617; Viscount of Strabane, 1701; Viscount Hamilton, 1786; Marquess of Abercorn, 1790; Marquess of Hamilton, 1868; Bt 1660; Lord Lieutenant of Co. Tyrone, since 1987; Lord Steward of HM Household, since 2001; company director; *b* 4 July 1934; *er s* of 4th Duke of Abercorn, and Lady Mary Kathleen Crichton (Dowager Duchess of Abercorn, GCVO) (*d* 1990); *S* father, 1979; *m* 1966, Anastasia Alexandra (OBE 2008), *e d* of late Lt-Col Harold Phillips, Checkendon Court, Reading; two *s* one *d*. *Educ:* Eton Coll.; Royal Agricultural Coll., Cirencester, Glos. Joined HM Army, Oct. 1952; Lieut, Grenadier Guards. MP (UU) Fermanagh and South Tyrone, 1964–70. Dir, Northern Bank Ltd, 1970–97. Chm., Laganside Develt Corp., 1989–96 (Laganside Ltd, 1986–89); Dir, NI Industrial Develt Bd, 1982–87. Member: Council of Europe, 1968–70; European Economic and Social Cttee, 1973–78. President: Royal UK Beneficent Assoc., 1979–; Building Socs Assoc., 1986–92; Patron, Royal Ulster Agricl Soc., 1990–96. Trustee, Winston Churchill Meml Trust, 1991–2001. Col, Irish Guards, 2000–08. High Sheriff of Co. Tyrone, 1970. Hon. Mem., RICS, 1995. Hon. LLB QUB, 1997. *Recreations:* shooting, ski-ing. *Heir: s* Marquess of Hamilton, *qv*. *Address:* Barons Court, Omagh, Northern Ireland BT78 4EZ. *T:* (028) 8166 1470, *Fax:* (028) 8166 2231; 10 Little Chester Street, SW1X 7AL. *T:* (020) 7235 5518; *e-mail:* duke.baronscourt@talk21.com. *Club:* Brooks's.

ABERCROMBIE, Ian Ralph; QC (Scot.) 1994; *b* 7 July 1955; *s* of late Ralph Abercrombie and Jean Abercrombie (*née* Lithgow). *Educ:* Edinburgh Univ. (LLB Hons 1978). Called to the Bar: Scotland, 1981; Lincoln's Inn, 1992. *Address:* Advocates' Library, Parliament House, Edinburgh EH1 1RF; Tippermallo House, Moss-side, Methven, Perthshire PH1 3RH.

ABERDARE, 5th Baron *cr* 1873, of Duffryn, co. Glamorgan; **Alastair John Lyndhurst Bruce;** Director, ProbusBNW Ltd (corporate reputation consultants), since 1999; *b* 2 May 1947; *s* of 4th Baron Aberdare, KBE, PC and Lady Aberdare (*née* (Maud Helen) Sarah Dashwood); *S* father, 2005; *m* 1971, Elizabeth Mary Culbert Foulkes; one *s* one *d*. *Educ:* Eton; Christ Church, Oxford (MA Hons Lit.Hum.). IBM, 1969–91; Partner, Bruce Naughton Wade, 1991–99. Trustee, Nat. Botanic Gdn of Wales, 1994–2006. FRSA. *Publication:* (trans. and ed.) Hector Berlioz: the musical madhouse, 2003. *Recreations:* music (esp. Berlioz), Wales, corporate responsibility, crosswords. *Heir: s* Hon. Hector Morys Napier Bruce, *b* 25 July 1974. *Address:* 16 Beverley Road, SW13 0LX.

ABERDEEN, Bishop of, (RC), since 2003; **Rt Rev. Peter Antony Moran;** *b* 13 April 1935; *s* of Joseph Moran and Gertrude Moran (*née* O'Callaghan). *Educ:* St Aloysius' Coll., Glasgow; Pontifical Gregorian Univ., Rome (PhL 1955; STL 1959); Univ. of Glasgow (MA Hons (Classics) 1963); Univ. of Aberdeen (MEd 1968). Ordained priest, 1959; schoolmaster, Blairs Coll., Aberdeen, 1964–86; Parish Priest: Blairs, 1979–93; Inverurie, 1993–2003; Diocesan Administrator, Aberdeen, 2002–03. *Recreations:* modern languages, dinghy sailing, walking, music, sketching. *Address:* 3 Queen's Cross, Aberdeen AB15 4XU. *T:* (01224) 319154, *Fax:* (01224) 325570; *e-mail:* bishop.rcdioceseofaberdeen@dsl.pipex.com.

ABERDEEN, (St Andrew's Cathedral), Provost of; *see* Kilgour, Very Rev. R. E.

ABERDEEN AND ORKNEY, Bishop of, since 2007; **Rt Rev. Robert Arthur Gillies;** *b* 21 Oct. 1951; *s* of Duncan and Vera Gillies; *m* 1976, Katherine Elizabeth Greening Tucker; three *s* (and one *s* decd). *Educ:* Univ. of Edinburgh (BD Hons 1978); Univ. of St Andrews (PhD 1991). Medical Lab. Technician, 1968–72; ordained deacon, 1977, priest, 1978; Curate, Christ Church, Falkirk, 1977–80; Curate, Christ Church, Edinburgh and Chaplain, Napier Coll., 1980–84; Chaplain, Univ. of Dundee, 1984–90; Rector, St Andrews Episcopal Church, St Andrews, 1991–2007; Synod Clerk, 2005–07, Dean, 2007, Dio. of St Andrews, Dunkeld and Dunblane. Hon. Lectr in Philosophy, Univ. of Dundee, 1985–94. *Publications:* A Way for Healing, 1995; Informing Faith, 1996; Healing Broader and Deeper, 1998; New Language of Faith, 2001; Where Earth and Heaven Meet, 2005; Sounds Before the Cross, 2007. *Recreations:* climbing Scotland's mountains, travelling England's canals, watching ice hockey. *Address:* Diocesan Office, 39 King's Crescent, Aberdeen AB24 3HP. *T:* (01224) 636653; *e-mail:* bishop@aberdeen.anglican.org.

ABERDEEN AND ORKNEY, Dean of; *see* Nimmo, Very Rev. Dr A. E.

ABERDEEN AND TEMAIR, 7th Marquess of, *cr* 1916; **Alexander George Gordon;** DL; Bt (NS) 1642; Earl of Aberdeen, Viscount Formartine, Lord Haddo, Methlic, Tarves, and Kellie, 1682 (Scot.); Viscount Gordon 1814, Earl of Haddo 1916 (UK); *b* 31 March 1955; *s* of 6th Marquess of Aberdeen and Temair and Anne, *d* of Lt-Col Gerald Barry, MC; *S* father, 2002; *m* 1981, Joanna Clodagh Houldsworth; three *s* one *d*. *Educ:* Cothill House, Abingdon; Harrow School; Polytechnic of Central London (DipBE). ARICS 1979–95. With Gardiner and Theobald, Chartered Quantity Surveyors, 1976–82; Speyhawk plc, Property Developers, 1982–86; London & Edinburgh Trust plc, Property Developers, 1986–94; Managing Director: Letinvest, 1989–94; Kellie Estates Ltd, 1995–; Gordon Land Ltd, 2000–; Braiklay Estates Ltd, 2007–; non-executive Director: Mobile Cardiovascular Science plc, 1992–99; Gordon Enterprise Trust, 1998–2002. DL Aberdeenshire, 1998. *Recreations:* golf, music, theatre. *Heir: s* Earl of Haddo, *qv*. *Address:* House of Formartine, Methlick, Ellon, Aberdeenshire AB41 7EQ. *T:* (01651) 851664. *Clubs:* MCC; Royal Aberdeen Golf; Meldrum House Golf.

ABERDEEN AND TEMAIR, June Marchioness of; (Beatrice Mary) June Gordon, CBE 1989 (MBE 1971); DL; Musical Director and Conductor, Haddo House Choral and Operatic Society (formerly Haddo House Choral Society), since 1945; *d* of Arthur Paul Boissier, MA, and Dorothy Christina Leslie Smith; *m* 1939, David George Ian Alexander Gordon (later 4th Marquess of Aberdeen and Temair, CBE, TD) (*d* 1974); two adopted *s* two adopted *d*. *Educ:* Southlands School, Harrow; Royal Coll. of Music. GRSM, ARCM. Teacher of Music, Bromley High School for Girls, 1936–39. Director of Haddo House Choral and Operatic Soc. and Arts Centre, 1945–. Chairman: Scottish Children's League, 1969–94; NE Scotland Music School, 1975–; Adv. Council, Scottish Opera, 1979–92; Chm. (local), Adv. Cttee, Aberdeen Internat. Festival of Music and the Performing Arts, 1980–96. Governor: Gordonstoun Sch., 1971–86; Royal Scottish Acad. of Music and Drama, 1979–82. FRCM 1967; FRSE 1983; FRSAMD 1985. DStJ 1977; GCStJ 1995. DL Aberdeenshire, 1971. Hon. LLD Aberdeen, 1968; Hon. DMus CNAA, 1991. *Publications:* contribs to Aberdeen Univ. Jl, RCM magazine. *Address:* Haddo House, Aberdeen AB41 7EQ. *T:* (01651) 851216. *Club:* New (Edinburgh).

ABERDOUR, Lord; John Stewart Sholto Douglas; *b* 17 Jan. 1952; *s* and *heir* of 22nd Earl of Morton, *qv*; *m* 1985, Amanda, *yr d* of David Mitchell, Kirkcudbright; one *s* two *d*. *Educ:* Dunrobin Castle School. Studied Agriculture, Aberdeen Univ. *Heir: s* Master of Aberdour, *qv*. *Address:* Haggs Farm, Kirknewton, Midlothian EH27 8EE.

ABERDOUR, Master of; Hon. John David Sholto Douglas; *b* 28 May 1986; *s* and *heir* of Lord Aberdour, *qv*.

ABERGAVENNY, 6th Marquess of, *cr* 1876; **Christopher George Charles Nevill;** Baron Abergavenny 1450; Earl of Abergavenny and Viscount Nevill 1784; Earl of Lewes 1876; *b* 23 April 1955; *yr s* of Lord Rupert Charles Montacute Nevill, CVO, *yr s* of 4th Marquess of Abergavenny and of Lady Anne Camilla Eveline Wallop, *d* of 9th Earl of Portsmouth; *S* uncle, 2000; *m* 1985, Venetia Jane, *er d* of late Frederick Gerard Maynard; one *d* (one *s* decd). *Educ:* Harrow. Dir, Nevill Estate Co. Ltd, 1985–. Mem. (C), Wealden DC, 1999. *Heir:* (to Earldom and Barony of Abergavenny and Viscountcy of Nevill only) *kinsman* David Michael Ralph Nevill [*b* 20 June 1941; *m* 1972, Katherine Mary, *d* of Rossmore Derrick Westenra; one *s* two *d*]. *Address:* Eridge Park, Eridge Green, Tunbridge Wells, Kent TN3 9JT. *T:* (01892) 750766. *Club:* White's.

ABERNETHY, Rt Hon. Lord; John Alastair Cameron; PC 2005; a Senator of the College of Justice in Scotland, 1992–2007; *b* 1 Feb. 1938; *s* of William Philip Legerwood Cameron and Kathleen Milthorpe (*née* Parker); *m* 1968, Elspeth Mary Dunlop Miller; three *s*. *Educ:* Clergy Sch., Khartoum; St Mary's Sch., Melrose; Trinity Coll., Glenalmond; Pembroke Coll., Oxford (MA 1961; Hon. Fellow, 1993). Nat. Service, 1956–58 (2nd Lieut, RASC). Called to the Bar, Inner Temple, 1963; admitted Mem., Faculty of Advocates, 1966, Vice-Dean, 1983–92; QC (Scotland) 1979. Advocate-Depute, 1972–75; Standing Jun. Counsel; to Dept of Energy, 1976–79; to Scottish Develt Dept, 1978–79. Legal Chm., Pensions Appeal Tribunals for Scotland, 1979–92 (Pres., 1985–92). Dir, Faculty Services Ltd, 1979–89 (Chm., 1983–89). International Bar Association: Chm., Judges' Forum, 1994–98 (Vice-Chm., 1993–94); Mem. Council, Section on Legal Practice, 1998–2002; Mem. Council, Human Rights Inst., 1998–2000, 2002–05. Pres., Scottish Medico-Legal Soc., 1996–2000. Mem. Exec. Cttee, Soc. for Welfare and Teaching of the Blind (Edinburgh and SE Scotland), 1979–92. Trustee: Arthur Smith Meml Trust, 1975–2001 (Chm., 1990–2001); Faculty of Advocates 1985 Charitable Trust, 1985–. Gov., St Mary's Sch. (Melrose) Ltd, 1998– (Dep. Chm., 2004–). *Publications:* Medical Negligence: an introduction, 1983; (contrib.) Reproductive Medicine and the Law, 1990. *Recreations:* travel, sport, nature conservation, Africana. *Address:* 4 Garscube Terrace, Edinburgh EH12 6BQ. *T:* (0131) 337 3460, *Fax:* (0131) 240 6711.

ABERNETHY, Rt Rev. Alan Francis; *see* Connor, Bishop of.

ABINERI, Claudia; *see* Rosencrantz, C.

ABINGDON, Earl of; *see* Lindsey and Abingdon, Earl of.

ABINGER, 9th Baron *cr* 1835; **James Harry Scarlett;** *b* 28 May 1959; *er s* of 8th Baron Abinger and Isla Carolyn, *o d* of Vice-Adm. J. W. Rivett-Carnac, CB, CBE, DSC; *S* father, 2002; *m* 1995, Tracy Lee, *d* of N. Cloutier, Ottawa; one *s* one *d* (adopted twins). *Educ:* Eton; Univ. of Aberdeen (BSc 1982); Magdalene Coll., Cambridge (MPhil 1994). FRGS, FLS. *Recreations:* diving for treasure, playing the cello. *Heir: b* Hon. Peter Richard Scarlett [*b* 21 March 1961; *m* 1992, Sharon Elizabeth Turl; one *s* one *d*]. *Address:* Le Petit Chafosse, 5 chemin de Montecouvé, 02600 St Pierre Aigle, France. *Club:* MCC.

ABLE, Graham George; Master, Dulwich College, 1997–Aug. 2009; *b* 28 July 1947; *s* of George Jasper Able and Irene Helen Able (*née* Gaff); *m* 1969, Mary Susan Munro; one *s* one *d*. *Educ:* Worksop Coll.; Trinity Coll., Cambridge (MA Nat. Scis 1968, PGCE 1969); MA Social Scis Dunelm 1983. Teacher, Sutton Valence Sch., 1969–83 (Boarding Housemaster, 1976–83); Second Master, Barnard Castle Sch., 1983–88; Headmaster, Hampton Sch., 1988–96. Co-Chm., HMC and GSA Educn and Academic Policy Cttee, 1998–2001; Chm., HMC, 2003. Member: Council and Court, ICSTM, 1999–2006; Council, Roedean Sch., 2000–. Pres., Internat. Boys' Schs' Coalition, 2006–. FRSA 1994. MInstD 1995. *Publications:* (jtly) Head to Head, 1992; (jtly) Head to HoD, 1998. *Recreations:* cricket, golf, sailing, contract bridge. *Address:* Elm Lawn, Dulwich Common, Dulwich, SE21 7EW. *T:* (020) 8693 3601. *Clubs:* MCC, East India (Hon. Mem.).

ABNEY-HASTINGS, family name of **Earl of Loudoun**.

ABOUSEIF, Doris B.; *see* Behrens-Abouseif.

ABOYNE, Earl of; Alistair Granville Gordon; *b* 26 July 1973; *s* and *heir* of Marquess of Huntly, *qv*; *m* 2004, Sophia, *d* of Michael Cunningham; two *d*. *Educ:* Harrow. *Address:* c/o Aboyne Castle, Aberdeenshire AB34 5JP.

ABRAHAM, Ann; UK Parliamentary Commissioner for Administration and Health Service Commissioner for England, since 2002; *b* 25 Aug. 1952; *d* of John Kenneth and Kathleen Mary Marsden. *Educ:* Bedford Coll., Univ. of London (BA Hons German); Postgrad. DMS. MCIH. Housing Manager, Local Govt, 1975–80; Ops Manager, Regional Dir and Ops Dir, Housing Corp., 1980–90; Chief Exec., NACAB, 1991–97; Legal Services Ombudsman for England and Wales, 1997–2002; Health Service Comr for Wales, 2002–03; Welsh Admin Ombudsman, 2002–04. Non-exec. Dir, Benefits Agency, 1997–2001. Mem., Cttee on Standards in Public Life, 2000–02; ex officio Member: Commn for Local Admin in England, 2002–; Administrative Justice and Tribunals Council (formerly Council on Tribunals), 2002– (Mem., Scottish Cttee, 2002–, Welsh Cttee, 2008–). Mem. Exec. Cttee, British and Irish Ombudsman Assoc., 2001– (Chm., 2004–06; Mem. Validation Cttee, 2006–). *Recreations:* walking, family, friends, football. *Address:* Office of the Parliamentary Commissioner for Administration and Health Service Commissioner for England, Millbank Tower, Millbank, SW1P 4QP.

ABRAHAM, Neville Victor, CBE 2001; Chairman: Liberty Wines Ltd, since 2003; Groupe Chez Gérard plc, 1994–2003 (Joint Founder, 1986; Chief Executive, 1994–99); *b* 22 Jan. 1937; *s* of late Solomon Abraham and of Sarah (*née* Raphael); *m* 2005, Nicola (*née* Leach). *Educ:* Brighton Coll.; London Sch. of Econs (BSc Hons). Marketing Asst, Young & Rubicam, 1961–63; Sen. Principal, DTI, 1963–71; Corporate Policy Advr, Harold Whitehead & Partners, 1971–74; Founder, Les Amis du Vin, 1974 (Man. Dir, 1974–86); Chm., Amis du Vin Gp, 1980–84; Dir, Kennedy Brookes plc, 1984–86. Non-executive Director: Brakeley Ltd, 2007–; Le Café Anglais Ltd, 2007–. Vis. Lectr, several business schools, 1972–81. Chairman: Exec. Cttee, Covent Garden Fest., 1993–99; London String Quartet Foundn, 2000–06. Gov., Brighton Coll., 2006–. *Publication:* Big Business and Government: the new disorder, 1974. *Recreations:* music, opera, walking, good food and wine, cricket. *Clubs:* Royal Automobile, Home House, MCC.

ABRAHAM, Sigrid Maria Elisabeth; *see* Rausing, Dr S. M. E.

ABRAHAM-WILLIAMS, Rev. Gethin; ecumenist; Religions and Beliefs Consultant, University of Glamorgan Chaplaincy, 2007–08; General Secretary, CYTÛN: Churches Together in Wales, 1998–2006; *s* of late Lt Col Emlyn Abraham-Williams, TD, DL, and of Anne Elizabeth Abraham-Williams; *m* 1977, Denise Frances Harding; one *s* one *d*. *Educ:* Ysgol yr Urdd, Aberystwyth; Ardwyn Grammar Sch., Aberystwyth; UC of Wales, Aberystwyth; Regent's Park Coll., Oxford (BA Hons Theol. 1964; MA 1967; Chm., Oxford Theol Colls' Union, 1963). Ordained 1965; Asst Minister, Queen's Road Baptist Ch (with Lenton's Lane, Hawkesbury), Coventry, 1964–68; Minister: Chester Rd Baptist Ch, Sutton Coldfield, 1968–73; Sutton Baptist Ch, Surrey, 1973–80; Ecumenical Officer and Exec. Sec., Milton Keynes Christian Council, 1981–90; Bp of Oxford's Ecumenical Officer, Milton Keynes, 1981–90; Gen. Sec., ENFYS: Covenanted Churches in Wales, with Provincial Officer for Ecumenism, Ch in Wales, 1990–98. Ed., Baptist Ministers' Fellowship Jl, 1998–2002. Baptist Union of GB: Member: Council, 1971–73 and 1993–95; Wkg Gp on LEPs, 1982–90; Worship and Doctrine Cttee, 1993–95. Mem., 1981–90, Moderator, 1988–90, Consultative Cttee for LEPs in England; British Council of Churches: Mem., Bd for Ecumenical Affairs, 1987–90; Observer: Nat. (RC) Conf. of Priests, 1983 and 1984; English ARC, 1988–90; Delegated Rep., WCC, 1991–2006; Mem., Steering Cttee, CCBI, 1992–96, 1998–; Mem., Free Church Fed. Council, 1991–96; Mem. Council, CYTÛN, 1995–98; Mem., Ecumenical Adv. Gp, ACC, 1997. Member: Warwicks Probationary and After Care Service, 1970–73; Marjory Fry and St Leonard's Trust Housing Cttee, 1970–73; Westlake Pastoral Lectr, Regent's Pk Coll., Oxford, 1973. Mem., Order of St Luke, 1961; ChStJ, Priory for Wales, 2002. Radio presenter, BBC World Service, Radio 4, Radio Wales, etc. Cross of St Augustine, 2006. *Publications:* (ed) Christian Baptism and Church Membership, Vol. II, 1994; (ed jtly) Letters to Friends, 1996; (ed) Towards the Making of an Ecumenical Bishop in Wales, 1997; (ed) Women, Church and Society in Wales, 2004; (ed) No, please, I don't want to die!, 2006; Spirituality or Religion? Do we have to choose?, 2008; contrib. to Birmingham Post, Expository Times, Epworth Rev., Baptist Times, Cristion, etc. *Recreations:* radio, travel, theatre, books, eating out. *Address:* 13 Millbrook Road, Dinas Powys, Vale of Glamorgan CF64 4BZ. *T:* (029) 2051 5884; *e-mail:* gethin@theaws.com.

ABRAHAMS, Anthony Claud Walter; advocate and solicitor, Brunei Darussalam, 1987–2000; *b* 16 June 1923; *s* of late Rt Hon. Sir Sidney Abrahams, QC, and of Ruth Bowman; *m* 1st, 1950, Laila Myking; two *s* one *d*; 2nd, 1982, Elizabeth, *d* of late Comdr A. E. Bryant, RN. *Educ:* Bedford Sch.; Emmanuel Coll., Cambridge (MA). Barrister-at-law. Served War: Wavell Cadet, Bangalore, 1942–43; commnd 3/12 Royal Bn, Frontier Force Regt, 1943–45; India, N Africa, Italy, Greece (despatches). Called to the Bar, Middle Temple, 1951; practised Midland Circuit, 1951–64. Gov., 1966–88, Chm., 1978–88, Harpur Trust (the Bedford Charity). Centre for British Teachers: Founder, 1964; Dir, 1973–82; Life Pres., 1982. Mem., Educn Cttee, British-Malaysian Soc., 1986–96. Liveryman, Worshipful Co. of Glaziers, 1976. Kt, Order of Uggla (Norway), 1962. *Recreations:* golf, watching cricket and Rugby, wine, travel. *Address:* Berry Cottage, Southey Green, Sible Hedingham, Halstead, Essex CO9 3RN. *Club:* Garrick.

ABRAHAMS, Prof. (Ian) David, PhD; Beyer Professor of Applied Mathematics, University of Manchester, since 1998; President, Institute of Mathematics and its Applications, since 2008; *b* Manchester, 15 Jan. 1958; *s* of late Harry Abrahams and of Leila Abrahams; *m* 2004, Penelope Lawrence Warwick; one *d* and two step *s*. *Educ:* Imperial Coll. London (BSc Eng. Hons 1979; PhD Applied Maths 1982; DIC 1982). Temp. Lectr, Dept of Maths, Univ. of Manchester, 1982–83; Lectr, Sch. of Maths, Univ. of Newcastle upon Tyne, 1983–90; Reader, 1990–93, Prof., 1994–98, Dept of Maths, Keele Univ.; Hd, Applied Maths, Sch. of Maths, Univ. of Manchester, 1998–2007. Nuffield Foundn Sci. Res. Fellow, 1990–91; Royal Soc. Leverhulme Trust Sen. Res. Fellow, 2002–03. Member: Council: IMA, 1998–; Eur. Mechanics Soc., 2000–06; LMS, 2002–06; Bd, Internat. Council for Industrial and Applied Maths, 2003–. *Publications:* contrib. scientific papers on propagation, refraction and diffraction of waves in solids, fluids and electromagnetics. *Recreations:* distance running, motorcycling, fiddling with ALL things mechanical and electrical, watching (almost) all sports. *Address:* School of Mathematics, University of Manchester, Oxford Road, Manchester M13 9PL. *T:* (0161) 275 5901, *Fax:* (0161) 275 5819.

ABRAHAMS, Ivor, RA 1991 (ARA 1989); FRBS 1996; sculptor; *b* 10 Jan. 1935; *s* of Harry Abrahams and Rachel Kalisky; *m* 1st, 1966, Victoria Taylor; (one *s* decd); 2nd, 1974, Evelyne Horvais; one *s*. *Educ:* Wigan Grammar Sch.; St Martin's and Camberwell Schools of Art. NDD(ScSp). Visiting Lecturer: Birmingham College of Art, 1960–63; Coventry College of Art, 1963–66; RCA, Slade Sch., 1980–82. *Major Exhibitions:* Kölnischer Kunstverein, Cologne, 1973; Ikon Gall., Birmingham, 1976; Yorkshire Sculpture Park, Wakefield, 1984. *Public Collections:* Arts Council of GB; Bibliotheque Nat., Paris; Brit. Council; Denver Mus., Colorado; Metropolitan Mus., NY; Nat. Gall. of Australia, Canberra; Tate Gall.; Mus. of Modern Art, NY; V&A Mus.; Wilhelm Lembruck Mus., Duisburg, W Germany; Boymans Mus., Rotterdam, etc. Winston Churchill Fellow, 1990. *Publications:* E. A. Poe: poems and tales (foreword Norbert Lynton), 1976; Oxford Garden Sketchbook (foreword Robert Melville), 1977. *Recreations:* golf, photography. *Address:* c/o Royal Academy, Burlington House, W1V 0DS. *Clubs:* Chelsea Arts, Colony Rooms.

ABRAHAMS, Michael David, CBE 1994 (MBE 1988); DL; Chairman: The London Clinic, since 1996; Kingston Communications plc, since 1999; Amteus plc, since 2006; Ferrexpo plc, since 2007; *b* 23 Nov. 1937; *s* of Alexander Abrahams and Anne Abrahams (*née* Sokoloff); *m* 1968, Amanda Atha; one *s* two *d*. *Educ:* Shrewsbury; Worcester Coll., Oxford. Nat. Service, RM (commnd). Man. Dir, AW (Securities) Ltd, 1968–73; Chairman: Champion Associated Weavers Ltd, 1974–80; Associated Weavers Europe NV, 1974–83; Weavercraft Carpets Ltd, 1980–85; Dep. Chm., John Crowther PLC, 1985–88; Director: Prudential Corp. plc, 1984–2000 (Dep. Chm., 1991–2000); John Waddington plc, 1984–2000; Cavaghan & Gray plc, 1987–98 (Chm., 1992–98); Drummond Gp plc, 1989–2001. Chm., Minorplanet Systems plc, 1997–2004. Pres., British Carpet Mfrs Assoc., 1979–80. Dep. Chm. Council, Prince of Wales's Inst. of Architecture, 1991–96; Dir, Rank Foundn, 1992–2007; Regl Chm., NT for Yorks, 1996–2003; Chm., Ripon City Partnership, 2005–. Jt Chm., Yorks Children's Hosp. Fund (Co-founder), 1989–; Trustee, Hackfall Trust, 1987–. Master, Woolmen's Co., 1996–97. High Sheriff, 1993–94, DL, 1994, N Yorks. Hon. Freeman, City of Ripon, 2002. *Recreations:* hunting, shooting, sailing, art, architecture. *Address:* Newfield, Mickley, Ripon, N Yorks HG4 3JH. *T:* (01765) 635348. *Clubs:* Garrick, Pratt's.

ABRAHAMSEN, Egil; Comdr, Order of St Olav, 1987 (Kt Comdr 1979); Chairman, Norwegian Telecommunications, 1980–95; *b* 7 Feb. 1923; *s* of Anker Christian Abrahamsen and Aagot (*née* Kjølberg); *m* 1950, Randi Wiborg; one *s* two *d*. *Educ:* Technical Univ. of Norway (Naval Architect, 1949); Durham Univ., King's Coll., Newcastle upon Tyne (post-grad. studies and res.); Univ. of Calif, Berkeley (post-grad. studies). Sales Engr, Maschienen-Fabrik Augsburg-Nürnberg, and Karlstads Mekaniska Verkstad AB, Sweden, 1949–50; projects and planning, A/S Rosenberg Mekanisk Verksted, Stavanger, 1951–52; Det Norske Veritas, 1952–85: Surveyor, 1952; Sen. Surveyor, 1954 (resp. for building up Res. Dept); Principal Surveyor, 1957; Dep. Pres., 1966; Vice Pres., 1966; Pres., 1967. Chairman: Norsk Hydro, 1985–92; OPAK, 1985–; Royal Caribbean Cruise-Line, 1987–88; Kosmos, 1988–99; IKO Group, 1988–; Eikland, 1990–99; IM Skaugen ASA, 1990–99. Editor, European Shipbuilding, 1952–60. Fellow, Nat. Acad. of Engrg, USA, 1978; Member: Norwegian Acad. of Technical Scis, 1968; Royal Swedish Acad. of Engrg Scis, 1979; Hon. Mem., Soc. of Naval Architects and Marine Engrs, USA, 1987. DTech *hc* Royal Inst. of Technol., Sweden, 1977. Owes Hon. Prize, for contribn to res. and educn, 1971. Grand Officer, Order of Infante Dom Henrique (Portugal), 1977; Comdr, Order of the Lion (Finland), 1982; Kt, Nat. Order of Merit (France), 1982. *Address:* Maaltrostveien 35, 0786 Oslo, Norway.

ABRAM, Henry Charles, VRD 1958 (bar 1968); Chairman: Henry Abram Ltd, since 1955; Henry Abram & Sons, since 1989; Vice Lord-Lieutenant of Renfrewshire, 1995–2002; *b* 3 March 1924; *s* of Henry Kerr Abram and Madge Ballantyne, Glasgow; *m* 1950, Marie Kathleen Janet Paterson, *d* of Andrew Paterson, Glasgow; four *s*. *Educ:* Kelvinside Acad. Joined family shipping firm, Henry Abram Ltd, 1941; Dir, 1948–; Man. Dir, 1953. Joined RNVR, 1942; served in HMSs Ganges, Porcupine (torpedoed) and Meadowsweet; Lieut, 1946; Lieut-Comdr, 1954; Comdr, 1963; assumed comd and commnd HMS Dalriada, RNR Trg Estabt, Greenock, 1965; retd 1972. Dir, Glasgow Aged Seamen Relief Fund, 1974–2002; Pres., Glasgow Shipowners' and Shipbrokers' Benevolent Assoc., 1976–77; Hon. Vice-Pres., Clyde Maritime Trust, 1990; Mem., Scottish Council, King George's Fund for Sailors, 1988–2001. Deacon Convenor, Trades House of Glasgow, 1978–79; Chm., Trades Hall of Glasgow Trust, 1987–2004; Dir, Merchants House of Glasgow, 1988–2005. Dir, Glasgow Sch. of Art, 1977– (Vice-Chm., 1985; Chm., 1989–92). MRIN 1957; FRSA 1987. DL Strathclyde, 1987. OStJ 1978. *Recreations:* sailing, shooting, stalking, golf, gardening. *Address:* Enterkin, Kilmacolm, Renfrewshire PA13 4NR. *T:* (01505) 872018. *Clubs:* Caledonian, Royal Thames Yacht; Kilmacolm Golf, Prestwick Golf.

ABRAM, Rev. Paul Robert Carrington, MVO 2007; a Deputy Priest in Ordinary to the Queen, 1996–2007; Chaplain of the Chapel Royal of St Peter ad Vincula, Tower of London, 1996–2007; *b* 21 July 1936; *s* of Norman and Madge Alice Abram; *m* 1961, Joanna Rose (*née* Headley); four *d*. *Educ:* The English Sch., Cairo; King Alfred Sch., Plon; Hymers Coll., Hull; Keble Coll., Oxford (BA 1962; MA 1965); Chichester Theol Coll. Ordained deacon, 1962, priest, 1963; Asst Curate, Redcar, 1962–65; Chaplain to the Forces, 1965–89; Vicar of Salcombe and Chaplain, Missions to Seamen, 1989–96; Chaplain for the Pool of London, Mission to Seafarers (formerly Missions to Seamen), 1996–2007. Chaplain: HMS President, 1996–2007; Solicitors' Co., 1996–2007; Builders' Merchants' Co., 1996–2007 (Life Liveryman, 2007); Aldermanic Sheriff, 1999–2000; Security Professionals, 2001–07; NEAC, 2001–07; Lord Mayor of London, 2003–04. FRGS 1960. Medal, Order of St Mellitus, 2007. *Recreations:* sailing, pre-nineteenth century maps, travel, people. *Address:* Paddock End, Kimpton, Andover, Hants SP11 8PG. *Club:* Special Forces.

ABRAMS, Dr Michael Ellis, CB 1992; FRCP, FFPH; public health consultant, since 1992; Chairman, Whittington Hospital NHS Trust, 1998–2003; Deputy Chief Medical Officer, Department of Health (formerly of Health and Social Security), 1985–92; *b* 17 Sept. 1932; *s* of late Sam Philip and Ruhamah Emmie Abrams; *m* 1962, Rosalind J. Beckman; four *c*. *Educ:* King Edward's Sch., Birmingham; Univ. of Birmingham (BSc 1st Cl. Anat. and Physiol. 1953; MB ChB Distinction in Medicine 1956). FRCP 1972; MFCM (Founder Mem.) 1972, FFCM 1983. Ho. Officer posts in United Birmingham Hosps, 1957–58; Univ. Research Fellow, Dept of Exp. Pathology, Univ. of Birmingham, and Medical Registrar, Queen Elizabeth Hosp., Birmingham, 1959; Medical Registrar and MRC Clinical Res. Fellow, Queen Elizabeth Hosp., Birmingham, 1959–62; MRC Clin. Res. Fellow, Dept of Medicine, Guy's Hosp., London, 1962–63; Rockefeller Travelling Fellow, Cardiovascular Res. Inst., Univ. of California Med. Centre, San Francisco, 1963–64; Lectr/Sen. Lectr and Hon. Cons. Phys., Guy's Hosp., 1964–75; Chief Med. Adviser, Guy's Hosp./Essex Gen. Practice Computing Unit, 1968–73; Dir, Inter-Deptl Laboratory, Guy's Hosp., 1971–75; DHSS: SMO, 1975–78; PMO, 1978–79; SPMO, 1979–85. Vice-Chm., Haringey Healthcare NHS Trust, 1993–98; Chm., N Thames Reg., Metropolitan Housing Trust, 1999–2004 (Vice-Chm., 1998–99). Mem. Bd, Dalco Homes Ltd, 1997–98. UK Deleg., Council of Europe Steering Cttee on Bioethics, 1990–97; Mem., WHO Council on Earth Summit Action Prog. for Health and Envmt, 1993–. Hon. Cons. Phys. Emeritus, Guy's Hosp. and Hon. Lectr in Medicine, Guy's Hosp. Med. Sch.; Examr in Human Communication, London Univ., 1972–84. President, Section of Measurement in Medicine, RSM, 1981–83; Chm., Computer Cttee, RCP, 1981–89. Gov., Moselle Sch., 2000–04. Chm. Editl Bd, Health Trends, 1988–99. *Publications:* (ed) Medical Computing Progress and Problems, 1970; (ed) Spectrum 71, 1971; (ed) The Computer in the Doctor's Office, 1980; articles on medical manpower planning, biomedical computing, pulmonary surfactant and glucose tolerance in diabetes. *Recreations:* reading, gardening, beachcombing. *Address:* 97 Wood Vale, N10 3DL.

ABRAMSKY, Jennifer, (Mrs Alasdair Liddell), CBE 2001; Chair, National Heritage Memorial Fund and Heritage Lottery Fund, since 2008; *b* 7 Oct. 1946; *d* of Chimen Abramsky and late Miriam (*née* Nirenstein); *m* 1976, Alasdair D. MacDuff Liddell, *qv*; one *s* one *d*. *Educ:* Holland Park Sch.; Univ. of East Anglia (BA Hons English) (Dep Chm., New Univs Fest., 1968). BBC: joined as Prog. Operations Asst, 1969; Producer, World at One, 1973; Jt Producer and Compiler of Special Prog. on 'Nixon', 1974; Editor: PM Prog., 1978–81; Radio Four Budget Prog., 1979–86; World at One, 1981–86; Today, 1986–87; News and Current Affairs, BBC Radio, 1987–93; set up Radio 4 News FM for duration of Gulf War, 1991; Controller, BBC Radio Five Live, 1993–96; Dir, Continuous News Services, BBC, incl. Radio 5 Live, BBC World, 24 Hour UK TV News, Ceefax and Multimedia News, 1996–98; Dir, BBC Radio, 1999–2000; Dir, BBC Radio and Music, subseq. Audio and Music, 2000–08. Member: ESRC, 1992–96; Editl Bd, British Journalism Rev., 1993–98. Dir Hampstead Th., 2003– (Chm., 2005–). A Governor, BFI, 2000–06; Vice Chm., Digital Radio Develt Bureau, 2002–08. News Internat. Vis. Prof. of Broadcast Media, Oxford Univ., 2001–02. Chm., Bd of Trustees, Univ. of London, 2008–; Gov., Royal Ballet, 2008–; Trustee, Central Sch. of Ballet, 2007–. Fellow, Radio Acad., 1998. Hon. RAM 2002. Hon. MA Salford, 1997; Hon. LittD UAE, 2003; Hon. DLitt Westminster, 2005. Woman of Distinction, Jewish Care, 1990; Sony Radio Acad. Award, 1995. *Recreations:* theatre, music. *Address:* National Heritage Memorial Fund, 7 Holbein Place, SW1W 8NR.

ABRAMSKY, Prof. Samson, PhD; FRS 2004; FRSE; Christopher Strachey Professor of Computing, University of Oxford, since 2000; Fellow, Wolfson College, Oxford, since 2000; *b* 12 March 1953; *s* of Moshe and Chaya-Sarah Abramsky; *m* 1976, Rosalind Susan Herman; two *s*. *Educ:* King's Coll., Cambridge (BA 1975; MA Philosophy 1979; Dip. Computer Sci.); Queen Mary Coll., London (PhD Computer Sci. 1988). FRSE 2000. Programmer, GEC Computers Ltd, 1976–78; Lectr, Dept of Computer Sci. and Stats, QMC, 1980–83; Lectr, 1983–88, Reader, 1988–90, Prof., 1990–95, Dept of Computing, Imperial Coll., London; Prof. of Theoretical Computer Sci., Univ. of Edinburgh, 1996–2000. MAE 1993. *Publications:* (ed jtly) Handbook of Logic in Computer Science, 5 vols, 1992–2000; contrib. numerous articles to computer sci. jls and confs. *Recreations:* reading, music, walking. *Address:* Computing Laboratory, Wolfson Building, Parks Road, Oxford OX1 3QD. *T:* (01865) 283558; Wolfson College, Linton Road, Oxford OX2 6UD.

ABRIKOSOV, Alexei Alexeyevich, DS; Distinguished Scientist, Argonne National Laboratory, since 1991; *b* Moscow, 25 June 1928; *s* of Alexei Ivanovich Abrikosov and Fanny Davidovna (Vulf) Abrikosov; *m* 1977, Svetlana Yuriyevna Bun-kova; two *s* one *d*. *Educ:* Univ. of Moscow (MS 1948); Inst. of Physical Problems, Moscow (DS Physics and Maths 1955). Postgrad. res. associate, then sen. res. worker, Inst. of Physical Problems, USSR Acad. of Scis, 1948–65; Asst Prof., 1951–66, Full Prof., 1966–68, Univ. of Moscow; Hd of Dept, L. D. Landau Inst. of Theoretical Physics, 1965–88; Professor: Gorky Univ., 1971–72; Moscow Physical Engrg Inst., 1974–75; Hd Chair of Theoretical Physics, Moscow Inst. of Steel and Alloys, 1976–92; Dir, Inst. of High Pressure Physics, Moscow, 1988–91. Member: Russian (formerly USSR) Acad. of Scis, 1987; NAS, 2000. Fellow, Amer. Physics Soc., 1992. Foreign Hon. Mem., AAAS, 1991; Foreign Mem., Royal Soc., 2001. Hon. DS: Lausanne, 1975; Bordeaux, 2003; Loughborough, 2004; Tsukuba, 2005; Hong Kong, 2005; Orléans, 2006. Lenin Prize, Govt of USSR, 1966; Fritz London Award, 1972; State Prize, USSR, 1982; Landau Prize, Acad. of Scis, USSR, 1989; Internat. John Barden Award, 1991; (jtly) Nobel Prize for Physics, 2003. *Publications:* Quantum Field Theory Methods in Statistical Physics, 1962; Introduction to the Theory of Normal Metals, 1972; Fundamentals of the Theory of Metals, 1987; contrib. articles to professional jls. *Address:* Argonne National Laboratory, 9700 South Cass Avenue, Argonne, IL 60439–4803, USA. *T:* (630) 2525482.

ABSE, Dr Dannie, FRSL; Specialist in charge of chest clinic, Central Medical Establishment, London, 1954–89; writer; *b* 22 Sept. 1923; *s* of Rudolph Abse and Kate (*née* Shepherd); *m* 1951, Joan Mercer (*d* 2005), art historian; one *s* two *d*. *Educ:* St Illtyd's Coll., Cardiff; University Coll., Cardiff; King's Coll., London; Westminster Hosp., London. MRCS, LRCP. First book of poems accepted for publication, 1946. Qualified at Westminster Hosp., 1950; RAF, 1951–54, Sqdn Ldr; Sen. Fellow of the Humanities, Princeton Univ., 1973–74. Pres., Poetry Soc., 1978–92. FRSL 1983; Fellow, Welsh Acad. of Letters, 1992 (Pres., 1995). Hon. Fellow, Univ. of Wales Coll. of Med., 1999. Hon. DLitt: Wales, 1989; Glamorgan, 1997. *Publications: poetry:* After Every Green Thing, 1948; Walking Under Water, 1952; Tenants of the House, 1957; Poems, Golders Green, 1962; A Small Desperation, 1968; Funland and other Poems, 1973; Collected Poems, 1977; Way Out in the Centre, 1981; Ask the Bloody Horse, 1986; White Coat, Purple Coat, 1989; Remembrance of Crimes Past, 1990; Selected Poems, 1994; On the Evening Road, 1994; Welsh Retrospective, 1997; Arcadia, One Mile, 1998; New and Collected Poems, 2003; Running Late, 2006; *prose:* A Strong Dose of Myself, 1983; Journals from the Ant Heap, 1986; Intermittent Journals, 1994; The Two Roads Taken, 2003; The Presence, 2007; *novels:* Ash on a Young Man's Sleeve, 1954; Some Corner of an English Field, 1957; O. Jones, O. Jones, 1970; There Was a Young Man from Cardiff, 1991; The Strange Case of Dr Simmonds and Dr Glas, 2002; *autobiography:* A Poet in the Family, 1974; Goodbye,

Twentieth Century, 2001; *plays:* House of Cowards, (first prod.) Questors Theatre, Ealing, 1960; The Dogs of Pavlov, (first prod.) Questors, 1969; Pythagoras, (first prod.) Birmingham Rep. Th., 1976; Gone in January, (first prod.) Young Vic, 1978; *anthologies edited:* (with Howard Sergeant) Mavericks, 1957; Modern European Verse, 1964; (with Joan Abse) Voices in the Gallery, 1986; (with Joan Abse) The Music Lover's Literary Companion, 1988; The Hutchinson Book of Post-War British Poets, 1989; Twentieth Century Anglo-Welsh Poetry, 1997; Homage to Eros, 2003. *Recreations:* chess, watching Cardiff City FC. *Address:* 85 Hodford Road, NW11 8NH.

ABTS, Tomma; artist; *b* Kiel, 26 Dec. 1967; *d* of Hermann Abts and Jmke Tammena. *Educ:* Hochschule der Künste, Berlin (Dip. 1993, MA 1995). *Solo exhibitions* include: greengrassi, London, 1999, 2002, 2005; Galerie Giti Nourbakhsch, Berlin, 2001, 2004; Wrong Gall., NY, 2003; Galerie Daniel Buchholz, Cologne, 2003, 2006; Douglas Hyde Gall., Dublin, Kunsthalle Basel, 2005; Kunsthalle Kiel, 2006; David Zwirner, NY, New Mus. of Contemporary Art, NY, travelling to Hammer Mus., LA, 2008; *group exhibitions* include: Egofugal, 7th Internat. Istanbul Biennial, 2001; deutschemalereizweitausenddrei, Frankfurter Kunstverein, 2003; 54th Carnegie Internat., Carnegie Mus. of Art, Pittsburgh, 2004; British Art Show 6, Gateshead, Manchester, Nottingham and Bristol, 2005; Of Mice and Men, 4th Berlin Biennale, Shanghai Biennale - Hyper Design, 2006; Turner Prize: a retrospective 1986–2007, London, transf. Mori Art Mus., Tokyo, 2007; Art Sheffield 08, 2008. Stipendium for London, DAAD, 1995; Paul Hamlyn Foundn Award, 2004; Turner Prize, 2006. *Publications:* exhibition catalogues; *relevant publication*: Vitamin P: Terry Myers on Tomma Abts, ed Valerie Breuvart, 2003.

ABUBAKAR, Prof. Iya; Galadima of Mubi; Senator, Federal Republic of Nigeria; Pro-Chancellor and Chairman of Council, University of Ibadan, 1993; *b* 14 Dec. 1934; *s* of Buba Abubakar, Wali of Mubi, and Fatima Abubakar; *m* 1963, Ummu; one *s* three *d. Educ:* Univ. of Ibadan (BSc London (External)); Cambridge Univ. (PhD). FRAS, FIMA. Ahmadu Bello Univ., Zaria, Nigeria: Prof. of Maths, 1967–75, 1978; Dean, Faculty of Science, 1968–69, 1973–75; Vice-Chancellor, 1975–78. Former Dir, Nat. Mathematical Centre, Abuja. Minister of Defence, Nigeria, 1979–82. Chm., Senate Cttee on Finance and Appropriation. Visiting Professor: Univ. of Michigan, 1965–66; City Univ. of New York, 1971–72. Chairman: Natural Sciences Reg. Council of Nigeria, 1972–75; Nat. Manpower Commn of Nigeria, 1992–. Mem., Nigerian Univs Commn, 1968–73. Dir, Central Bank of Nigeria, 1972–75. Hon. DSc Ife, 1977; Ahmadu Bello, 1980. *Publications:* Entebbe Modern Mathematics, 1970; several research papers on mathematics in internat. jls. *Recreations:* chess, golf, horse riding. *Address:* The Senate, National Assembly, PMB 141, Abuja, Nigeria.

ABULAFIA, Prof. David Samuel Harvard, PhD, LittD; FRHistS; Professor of Mediterranean History, History Faculty, University of Cambridge, since 2000; Fellow, Gonville and Caius College, Cambridge, since 1974; *b* Twickenham, 12 Dec. 1949; *s* of Leon and Rachel Abulafia; *m* 1979, Anna Sapir; two *d. Educ:* St Paul's Sch.; King's Coll., Cambridge (BA 1971; MA); PhD 1975, LittD 1994, Cantab. FRHistS 1981. Rome Schol., British Sch. at Rome, 1972–74; Cambridge University: Asst Lectr, 1978–83; Lectr, 1983–91; Reader, 1991–2000; Chm., History Faculty, 2003–05; Tutor for Grad. Students, Gonville and Caius Coll., 1984–91. Dorfler Meml Lectr, Leo Baeck Coll., 1992; Guest Lectr, project on Objective Cultural Resources, Tokyo Univ., 2000; Crayenborgh Lectr, Leiden Univ., 2002. Project co-ordinator, EU Culture 2000, 2000–03. Mem., Rev. Cttee, Ben Gurion Univ. of the Negev, 1999–2000. Mem. Council, Mediterranean Studies Assoc., 1998–2003. Gov., Perse Sch., 2002–. Gen. Ed., Jl of Medieval Hist., 1989–95. MAE 2002. Commendatore dell'Ordine della Stella della Solidarietà Italiana (Italy), 2003. *Publications:* The Two Italies, 1977 (trans. Italian 1991); Italy, Sicily and the Mediterranean, 1987; Frederick II, 1988, 3rd edn 2002 (trans. Italian 1990, German 1991, Spanish 2006); Spain and 1492, 1992; (ed jtly) Church and City, 1992; Commerce and Conquest in the Mediterranean, 1993; A Mediterranean Emporium, 1994 (trans. Spanish 1996); (ed) The French Descent into Renaissance Italy, 1995 (trans. Italian 2005); The Western Mediterranean Kingdoms, 1997 (trans. Italian 1999); (ed jtly) En las costas del Mediterráneo occidental, 1997; (ed) New Cambridge Medieval History, vol. 5, 1999; Mediterranean Encounters, 2000; (ed jtly) Medieval Frontiers, 2002; (ed) The Mediterranean in History, 2003 (trans. Spanish and German, 2003, French and Greek, 2004, Turkish, 2005); (ed) Italy in the Central Middle Ages, 2004; The Discovery of Mankind, 2008. *Recreation:* travel in reality and in imagination. *Address:* Gonville and Caius College, Cambridge CB2 1TA. *T:* (01223) 332473.

ACHEBE, Prof. Chinua, FRSL 1983; author; Professor Emeritus, University of Nigeria, since 1984; Pro-Chancellor and Chairman of Council, Anambra State University of Technology, Enugu, 1986–88; *b* 16 Nov. 1930; *s* of Isaiah and Janet Achebe; *m* 1961, Christiana Okoli; two *s* two *d. Educ:* Univ. of Ibadan. Nigerian Broadcasting Corp.: Talks Producer, 1954; Controller, 1959; Dir, 1961–66. Rockefeller Fellowship, 1960; Unesco Fellowship, 1963; Professor of English: Univ. of Massachusetts, 1972–75; Univ. of Connecticut, Storrs, 1975–76; Univ. of Nigeria, Nsukka, 1973–81. Fulbright Prof., Univ. of Massachusetts, 1987–88; Vis. Distinguished Prof. of English, City Coll., City Univ. of NY, 1989; Vis. Fellow and Ashby Lectr, Clare Hall, Cambridge, 1993. Chairman: Soc. of Nigerian Authors, 1966; Assoc. of Nigerian Authors, 1982–86. Hon. Vice-Pres., Royal Africa Soc., 1999. Member: Council, Univ. of Lagos, 1966; Exec. Cttee, Commonwealth Arts Orgn, London, 1981. Neil Gunn Internat. Fellowship, Scottish Arts Council, 1975; Hon. Fellow: Modern Language Assoc. of America, 1975; Amer. Acad. of Arts and Letters, 1982; Amer. Acad. of Arts and Scis, 2002. Editor, Okike, 1971–84. Patron, Writers and Scholars Educnl Trust, London, and Writers and Scholars Internat., 1972–90; Governor, Newsconcern Internat. Foundn, London, 1983–90. Goodwill Ambassador, UN Population Fund, 1999–2006. Hon. DLitt: Dartmouth Coll., 1972; Southampton, 1975; Ife, 1978; Nigeria, 1981; Kent, 1982; Guelph and Mount Allison, 1984; Franklin Pierce Coll., 1985; Ibadan, 1989; Skidmore Coll., 1990; Harvard, 1996; Syracuse, 1998; Brown, 1998; Witwatersrand, Cape Town, 2000; Toronto, 2006; DUniv: Open, 1989; Stirling, 1975; Hon. LLD Prince Edward Island, 1976; Hon. DHL: Massachusetts, 1977; Westfield Coll., 1989; Georgetown Univ., 1990. Jock Campbell New Statesman Award, 1965; Commonwealth Poetry Prize, 1972; Commonwealth Foundn Sen. Vis. Practitioner Award, 1983. Nigerian Nat. Order of Merit, 1979; Order of the Fed. Repub. (Nigeria), 1979. *Publications: fiction:* Things Fall Apart, 1958; No Longer at Ease, 1960; Arrow of God, 1964; A Man of the People, 1966; Girls at War (short stories), 1972; Anthills of the Savannah, 1987; *essays:* Morning Yet on Creation Day, 1975; The Trouble with Nigeria, 1983; Hopes and Impediments, 1987; Beware Soul-brother (poems), 1971; (with Robert Lyons) Another Africa (poetry, prose and photographs), 1998; Home and Exile, 2000; Collected Poems, 2004; *for children:* Chike and the River, 1966; (jtly) How the Leopard Got its Claws, 1971; The Flute, 1978; The Drum, 1978. *Recreation:* music. *Address:* Bard College, PO Box 41, Annandale-on-Hudson, NY 12504, USA.

ACHER, Gerald, CBE 1999; LVO 2002; Trustee, KPMG UK Foundation and Senior Adviser, KPMG; *b* 30 April 1945; *s* of David Acher and late Andrée Diana Acher (*née* Laredo); *m* 1970, Joyce Kathleen White; two *s. Educ:* King's Coll. Sch., Wimbledon. Articled clerk, Bird Potter & Co., 1961–66; Peat, Marwick, Mitchell & Co., subseq. KPMG: Asst Manager, 1967–73; Manager, 1973–75; Sen. Manager, 1975–80; Partner, 1980–2001; Mem., UK Bd, 1987–2001; Hd, Corporate Finance, 1990–93; UK Hd of Audit and Accounting, 1993–98; Sen. Partner, London Office, 1998–2001; Chairman: Worldwide Audit and Accounting Cttee, 1995–98; UK Client Service Bd, 1998–2001. Non-executive Director: BPB Industries plc, 2002–; Camelot Gp plc, 2002– (interim Chm., 2004). Member: Adv. Cttee on Business and the Envmt, 1999–2004; DTI Foresight Panel on Crime and Business, 2001–02. Dep. Chm., London First, 2000–; Dir, London First Centre, 1998–2001; Chm., London Mayoral Commn investigating feasibility of an internat. convention centre in London, 2004–. Institute of Chartered Accountants in England and Wales: Mem., 1967–; Mem. Council, 1995–2001; Chm., Audit and Assce Faculty, 1995–2001. MSI 1992. Hon. Treas., Queen's Golden Jubilee Weekend Trust, 2001–02. Gov., 1990–, and Vice Chm., 1995–, Motability; Trustee, Motability Tenth Anniversary Trust, 1991–. Trustee, Aston Martin Heritage Trust, 2001–; Chm., Awards for Young Musicians, 1998–2004. Royal Society of Arts: Fellow, 1998; Treas., 1999; Trustee, 2000–; Chm., 2006–; Mem. Council, 2000–04. Liveryman, Chartered Accountants' Co. (Mem., Ct of Assistants; Master, 2003–04). Chm. Govs, Milbourne Lodge Jun. Sch., 1986–. *Recreations:* classic and vintage car rallying, restoring old houses, mountain walking, opera, classical music, travel, watching sport (especially Rugby), gardening. *Address:* KPMG, 8 Salisbury Square, EC4Y 8BB. *T:* (020) 7311 8640. *Club:* Travellers.

ACHESON, family name of **Earl of Gosford**.

ACHESON, Sir (Ernest) Donald, KBE 1986; Chief Medical Officer, Departments of Health and of Social Security (formerly Department of Health and Social Security), Department of Education and Science and Home Office, 1983–91; *b* 17 Sept. 1926; *s* of Malcolm King Acheson, MC, MD, and Dorothy Josephine Rennoldson; *m* 1st, Barbara Mary Castle (marr. diss. 2002); one *s* four *d* (and one *d* decd); 2nd, 2002, Angela Judith Roberts; one *d. Educ:* Merchiston Castle Sch., Edinburgh; Brasenose Coll., Oxford (Theodore Williams Schol. in pathology, 1946; MA, DM; Hon. Fellow, 1989); Middlesex Hospital (Sen. Broderip Schol. in Med., Surg. and Pathol., 1950). FRCP 1967; FFPH (FFPHM 1972); FFOM 1985; FRCS 1988; FRCOG 1992. Acting Sqdn Leader, RAF Med. Br., 1953–55. Medical Practitioner, 1951; various clinical posts at Middlesex Hosp.; Radcliffe Trav. Fellow of University Coll., Oxford, 1957–59; Medical Tutor, Nuffield Dept of Medicine, Radcliffe Infirmary, Oxford, 1960; Dir, Oxford Record Linkage Study and Unit of Clin. Epidemiology, 1962; May Reader in Medicine, 1965; Fellow, Brasenose Coll., Oxford, 1968; Prof. of Clinical Epidemiology, Univ. of Southampton, and Hon. Consultant Physician, Royal South Hants Hosp., 1968–83; Foundation Dean, Faculty of Med., Southampton Univ., 1968–78; Dir, MRC Unit in Environmental Epidemiology, 1979–83. Member: Wessex Regional Hosp. Bd, 1968–74; Hampshire AHA (Teaching) 1974–78; Chm., SW Hants and Southampton DHA, 1981–83; Member: Adv. Cttee on Asbestos, Health and Safety Exec., 1978; Royal Commn on Environmental Pollution, 1979–83; UGC, 1982–83; GMC, 1984–91; MRC, 1984–91; Chairman: Slow Virus Group, DHSS, 1979–80; Primary Health Care Inner London Gp, DHSS, 1980–81; Enquiry into Public Health in England, 1988; Home Office Adv. Cttee on Health of Prisoners, 1992–94; Internat. Centre for Health and Society, UCL, 1996–2003; Ind. Inquiry into Inequalities in Health, DoH, 1997–98. UK Rep., Exec. Bd, WHO, 1988–90; Special Rep. of WHO in former Yugoslavia, 1992–93. Trustee, SCF, 1991–93. R. Samuel McLaughlin Vis. Prof., McMaster Univ., 1977; King's Fund Travelling Fellow, NZ Postgrad. Med. Fedn, 1979; Vis. Prof. of Internat. Health, Dept of Public Health and Policy, LSHTM, 1991–98. Lectures include: inaugural Adolf Streicher Meml, Stoke-on-Trent, 1978; Walter Hubert, British Assoc. for Cancer Res., 1981; Christie Gordon, Univ. of Birmingham, 1982; Edwin Chadwick Centennial, LSHTM, 1990; Harveian Orator, RCP, 1998. Examiner in Community Medicine: Univ. of Aberdeen, 1971–74; Univ. of Leicester, 1981–82; Examiner in Medicine, Univ. of Newcastle upon Tyne, 1975. Mem., Assoc. of Physicians of GB and Ire, 1965– (Pres. 1979); Pres., RIPH&H, 1999–2004. Founder FMedSci 1998. Hon. Fellow: LSHTM 1985; UCL, 1994. Hon. FRSocMed 1994. Hon. DM Southampton, 1984; Hon. DSc: Newcastle, 1984; Salford, 1991; Ulster, 1998; Hon. MD: QUB, 1987; Nottingham, 1989; Birmingham, 1991; Hon. LLD Aberdeen, 1988. Leon Bernard Foundn Prize, WHO, 1994. *Publications:* Medical Record Linkage, 1967; Multiple Sclerosis, a reappraisal, 1966; Medicine, an outline for the intending student, 1970; One Doctor's Odyssey: the social lesion (memoir), 2007; scientific papers on epidemiology of cancer, multiple sclerosis and other chronic diseases, medical education and organisation and inequalities of medical care. *Recreations:* family, gardening, music. *Club:* Athenæum.

ACHONRY, Bishop of, (RC), since 1977; **Most Rev. Thomas Flynn,** DD; *b* 8 July 1931; *s* of Robert and Margaret Flynn. *Educ:* St Nathy's, Ballaghaderreen; Maynooth College. BD, LPh, MA. Diocesan Religious Inspector of Schools, 1957–64; teaching in St Nathy's College, Ballaghaderreen, 1964–73; President and Headmaster of St Nathy's Coll., 1973–77. DD 1977. *Recreations:* gardening, fishing, golf. *Address:* St Nathy's, Ballaghaderreen, Co. Roscommon, Eire. *T:* (907) 60021.

ACKERMAN, Roy, CBE 2004 (OBE 1991); Chairman, Tadema Studios, since 1980; *b* 22 Feb. 1944; *m* Sally Simpson; one *s* three *d.* Trained as apprentice chef; restaurateur and owner, Quincys Bistro, Oxford, 1975–79; Dep. Chm. and Develt Dir, Kennedy Brooks plc, 1979–88; Chairman: 190 Queensgate plc, 1989–1994; Restaurant Partnership plc, 1989–99; Simpsons of Cornhill plc, 1994–97; Parallel Hotel Outsourcing Co., 2002–. Chairman: Hotel and Catering Trng Bd/Hospitality Trng Foundn, 1988–99; Catering Review Bd, Millennium Dome, 1999–2001. Chm., then Pres., Restaurant Assoc., 1985–95, now Hon. Vice-Pres. Chm., Acad. of Culinary Arts (Hon. Mem.); Pres., Acad. of Food and Wine Service, 2008 (Hon. Fellow); Mem. Council, Wine Guild of UK. Hon. Pres., Henley Fest. of Music and the Arts, 1983 (former Chm.). Presenter, TV series: The Chef's Apprentice; Chef for a Night; Best of British; Cookery Clinic; Cafés of Europe. FRSA. Hon. FCGI; Hon. Fellow: Hotel Catering Inst.; Acad. Culinère Française; British Hospitality Assoc.; Acad. of Culinary Arts. Hon. DBA De Montfort. Personnalité de l'année distinction internat., Paris, 1991. *Publications:* Ackerman Guide, 1987; Roy Ackerman's Recipe Collection, 1988; The Chef's Apprentice, 1992; The Ackerman Martell Guide to Europe, annually, 1992–96; The Chef's Compendium, 1993; The Ackerman Charles Heidsieck Guide, annually, 1993–96; Café Crème Guide to Cafés of Europe, annually, 1998–2003. *Recreations:* Chelsea Arts Club/Garrick Members Table, Mornington Crescent (non league). *Address:* Tadema Studios, PO Box 57132, SW6 4TG; *e-mail:* tadema.studios@btconnect.com. *Clubs:* Garrick, Chelsea Arts.

ACKERMANN, Georg K.; *see* Kahn-Ackermann.

ACKLAND, Joss, (Sidney Edmond Jocelyn), CBE 2001; actor; *b* 29 Feb. 1928; *s* of Norman Ackland and Ruth Izod; *m* 1951, Rosemary Jean Kirkcaldy (*d* 2002); one *s* five *d* (and one *s* decd). *Educ:* Dame Alice Owen's Sch.; Central Sch. of Speech Training and Dramatic Art. Has worked in theatre, 1945–; repertory includes Stratford-upon-Avon, Arts Th., Buxton, Croydon, Embassy, Coventry, Oxford, Chesterfield, Windsor, Pitlochry; tea planter, Central Africa, 1954–55; disc jockey, Cape Town, 1955–57; Mem.,

Old Vic Theatre Co., 1958–61: parts include Toby Belch, in Twelfth Night, Caliban, in The Tempest, Pistol, in Henry IV, Lord Froth, in The Double Dealer, Aegisthus, in The Oresteia, Falstaff, in Henry IV Pt I and the Merry Wives of Windsor; Associate Dir, Mermaid Theatre, 1961–63: dir, The Plough and the Stars; parts include title rôle, Galileo, Bluntschli, in Arms and the Man, Scrofulovsky, in The Bedbug, Kirilov, in The Possessed. *West End theatre* rôles include: title rôle, The Professor, 1966; Gus, in Hotel in Amsterdam, 1968–69; Come As You Are, 1969–70; Brassbound, in Captain Brassbound's Conversion, 1971; Sam, in The Collaborators, 1973; Mitch, in A Streetcar Named Desire, 1974; Stewart, in A Pack of Lies, 1984; Clarence Darrow, in Never the Sinner, 1990; Weller Martin, in The Gin Game, 1999; *West End musicals:* Justice Squeezum, in Lock up your Daughters, 1962; title rôle, Jorrocks, 1967; Frederik, in a Little Night Music, 1975–76; Juan Perón, in Evita, 1978; Captain Hook and Mr Darling, in Peter Pan—the musical, 1985–86; *other musical rôles:* Honoré Lachailles, in Gigi; The King, in The King and I; *National Theatre:* Eustace Perry State, in The Madras House, 1977; Romain Gary, in Jean Seburg (musical), 1983; *Barbican Theatre:* Falstaff, in Henry IV pts I and II (opening prodn), 1982; Captain Hook and Mr Darling, in Peter Pan, 1982; *Chichester Theatre:* Gaev, in The Cherry Orchard, 1981; Ill, in The Visit, 1995; John Tarleton in Misalliance, 1997; Captain Shotover, in Heartbreak House, 2000; *tours:* Petruchio, in The Taming of the Shrew, 1977; Sir, in The Dresser, 1981. *Films* include: Seven Days to Noon, 1949; Crescendo, 1969; The House that Dripped Blood, Villain, 1970; The Happiness Cage, England Made Me, 1971; The Little Prince, The Black Windmill, S-P-Y-S, The Three Musketeers, 1973; Great Expectations, One of our Dinosaurs is Missing, 1974; Operation Daybreak, Royal Flash, 1975; The Silver Bears, 1976; The End of Civilisation as we know it, The Greek Tycoon, Who is Killing the Great Chefs of Europe, 1977; Saint Jack, The Apple, Rough Cut, 1978; Lady Jane, 1984; A Zed and Two Noughts, 1985; Don Masino, in The Sicilian, 1987; Sir Jock Broughton, in White Mischief, The Colonel, in To Kill a Priest, 1988; Lethal Weapon II, The Hunt for Red October, The Palermo Connection, 1989; The Object of Beauty, The Sheltering Desert, 1991; The Bridge, Nowhere to Run, Pin for the Butterfly, The Mighty Ducks, 1992; Occhio Pinocchio (Italy), 1993; Miracle on 34th Street, Mad Dogs and Englishmen, A Kid in King Arthur's Court, Citizen X, 1994; Daisies in December, 'Til the End of Time, Mighty Ducks 3, Surviving Picasso, Deadly Voyage, Giorgino (France), 1995; Firelight, Swept from the Sea, 1996; Son of Sandokan, Game of Mirrors, Milk, 1999; Mumbo Jumbo, 2000; K-19: The Widowmaker, No Good Deed, I'll Be There, 2002; A Different Loyalty, Asylum, 2003; These Foolish Things, 2004; Tolstoy, in Moscow Zero, 2005; Flawless, How About You, 2007; Prisoners of the Sun, 2008. Numerous TV plays and serials, incl. title rôle in Kipling, Alan Holly in First and Last, C. S. Lewis in Shadowlands, Barrett in The Barretts of Wimpole Street, Archie in Voices in the Garden, Terence Fielding in A Murder of Quality, Isaac in The Bible, Onassis in A Woman Named Jackie, Goering in The Man who lived at the Ritz, Heat of the Sun, Henry VII in Henry VIII, title rôle in Icon, 2004; Sir Winston Churchill in Above and Beyond, 2005; John Narbutowiz in Kingdom, Ridcully in The Hogfather, 2006. *Radio* includes: title rôle in Macbeth; Falstaff in Henry IV, parts 1 and 2; Victor Hugo in Les Misérables; The Dog in Investigations of a Dog; God in The Little World of Don Camillo; 1966 And All That; Flashman in Flashman at the Charge; Big Daddy in Cat on a Hot Tin Roof; Socrates in The Life and Death of Socrates. Member: Drug Helpline; Amnesty Internat. *Publication:* I Must Be in There Somewhere (autobiog), 1989. *Recreations:* writing, painting, thirty-two grandchildren, six great-grandchildren.

ACKNER, Hon. Claudia Madeleine, (Hon. Mrs Hughes); Her Honour Judge Ackner; a Circuit Judge, since 2007; *b* 13 Dec. 1954; *d* of Baron Ackner, PC and of Joan May Evans; *m* 1978, Iain Hughes, *qv*; one *s* one *d* (and one *s* decd). *Educ:* Roedean Sch.; Girton Coll., Cambridge (BA 1976). Called to the Bar, Middle Temple, 1977; District Judge, 2000–07; Recorder, 2002–07. Mem., Franco British Irish Judicial Co-operation Cttee, 2006–. *Recreations:* opera, theatre, all things French. *Address:* c/o Chichester Combined Court Centre, Southgate, Chichester, W Sussex PO19 1SX.

ACKROYD, Keith, CBE 1994; FRPharmS; Chairman, Silentnight Holdings plc, 1995–2002 (Director, 1993–2002); *b* 6 July 1934; *s* of Edward Ackroyd and Ethel (*née* Bate); *m* 1958, Ellen Gwenda Thomas; two *s* one *d*. *Educ:* Heath Grammar Sch.; Bradford Sch. of Pharmacy; London Business Sch. FRPharmS 1981. Boots The Chemists Ltd: Apprentice Pharmacist, 1952; Dir, 1975–94; Midlands Area Dir, 1976–77; Man. Dir, 1983–89; Pres., Boots Drug Stores (Canada) Ltd, 1977–79; Boots Company plc: Dir, 1979–94; Man. Dir, Retail Div., 1984–94; Chairman: Halfords Ltd, 1989–94; A. G. Stanley, 1989–94; Do It All Ltd, 1992–94; Director: Carefirst (formerly Takare) plc, 1994–98 (Dep. Chm., 1996–98); Navara (formerly Nottingham Gp) plc, 1994–2001; Cowie plc, 1994–96; Victoria plc, 1998–2008. Chairman: Company Chemists Assoc., 1983–89; British Retailers Assoc., 1988–92; British Retail Consortium, 1992–94; Regl Chm., Trent RHA, later NHS Exec., Trent, 1994–97; Mem., NHS Policy Bd, 1994–97. Member: Passport Agency Bd, 1991–2000; Nat. Bd for Crime Prevention, 1993–95. CCMI (CIMgt 1981); FInstD 1979. Liveryman, Soc. of Apothecaries, 1990–. *Recreations:* drinking wine, country sport. *Address:* Millfield, Bradmore, Nottingham NG11 6PF. *T:* (0115) 921 6052. *Club:* Royal Automobile.

ACKROYD, Norman, CBE 2007; RA 1991 (ARA 1988); RE 1985; artist (painter and etcher); *b* 26 March 1938; *s* of late Albert Ackroyd, master butcher, and Clara Briggs, weaver; *m* 1st, 1963, Sylvia Buckland (marr. diss. 1975); two *d*; 2nd, 1978, Penelope Hughes-Stanton; one *s* one *d*. *Educ:* Cockburn High Sch., Leeds; Leeds Coll. of Art; Royal Coll. of Art (ARCA 1964; Sen. FRCA 2000). Teaches occasionally at RA, Slade, RCA and in N America; Tutor in Etching, Central Sch. of Arts, London, 1965–93; Prof. of Etching, London Inst., 1992. Over 50 one-man exhibns, 1970–, mainly in UK and USA; work in public collections includes: Tate Gall.; BM; V&A; Arts Council; British Council; Mus. of Modern Art, NY; Nat. Galls of Scotland, Norway, Canada, S Africa; Albertina, Vienna; Rijksmus. and Stedelijk, Amsterdam; Musée d'Art Histoire, Geneva; Nat. Gall. of Art, Washington. Mural commissions include: Albany, Glasgow, 1975; Haringey Cultural Centre, 1985; Lloyds Bank Technol. Centre, London, 1990; British Airways, 1991; Freshfields, London, 1992; Tetrapak, London, 1993; British Embassy, Moscow, 2000; Lazards Bank, London, 2003. TV work includes: Artists in Print (etching), 1981; A Prospect of Rivers, 1988; Painting with Acid, 2000. Awards: Bradford Internat. Biennale, 1972, 1982; Royal Soc. of Etchers and Engravers, 1984, 1985; Bronze Medal, Frechen, Germany, 1986. *Publications:* A Cumberland Journey, 1981; Travels with Copper and Zinc, 1983; (with Douglas Dunn) The Pictish Coast, 1988; St Kilda: the furthest land, 1989; Windrush, 1990; A Song for Ireland, 1999; Aran Islands, 2001; Skellig to Skibbereen, 2002; High Islands, 2003; Brancaster Roads, 2004; The Furthest Lands, 2005; numerous collections of etchings from travels in the British Isles, occasionally with poets. *Recreations:* cricket, archæology. *Address:* Royal Academy of Arts, Piccadilly, W1V 0DS. *T:* (020) 7378 6001. *Clubs:* Chelsea Arts, Arts.

ACKROYD, Peter, CBE 2003; writer; Chief Book Reviewer, The Times, since 1986; *b* 5 Oct. 1949; *s* of Graham Ackroyd and Audrey Whiteside. *Educ:* St Benedict's Sch., Ealing; Clare Coll., Cambridge (MA; Hon. Fellow, 2006); Yale Univ. (Mellon Fellow). Literary Editor, 1973–77, Jt Managing Editor, 1978–82, The Spectator. Writer and presenter, TV series: Dickens, 2003; Peter Ackroyd's London, 2004; The Romantics, 2006. Freeman, City of London, 2006. FRSL 1984. Hon. Fellow, Amer. Acad. of Arts and Scis, 2006. Hon. DLitt: Exeter, 1992; London Guildhall, 1999; City, 2000; London, 2001; Brunel, 2006. *Publications: poetry:* London Lickpenny, 1973; Country Life, 1978; The Diversions of Purley, 1987; *novels:* The Great Fire of London, 1982; The Last Testament of Oscar Wilde, 1983 (Somerset Maugham Prize, 1984); Hawksmoor, 1985 (Whitbread Award; Guardian Fiction Prize); Chatterton, 1987; First Light, 1989; English Music, 1992; The House of Doctor Dee, 1993; Dan Leno and the Limehouse Golem, 1994; Milton in America, 1996; The Plato Papers, 1999; The Clerkenwell Tales, 2003; The Lambs of London, 2004; The Fall of Troy, 2006; The Casebook of Victor Frankenstein, 2008; *non-fiction:* Notes for a New Culture, 1976; Dressing Up, 1979; Ezra Pound and his World, 1980; T. S. Eliot, 1984 (Whitbread Award; Heinemann Award); Dickens, 1990; Introduction to Dickens, 1991; Blake, 1995; The Life of Thomas More, 1998; London: the biography, 2000; The Collection, 2001; Albion, 2002; Dickens: public life and private passion, 2002; Chaucer, 2004; Turner, 2005; Shakespeare: the biography, 2005; Newton, 2006; Thames: sacred river, 2007; Poe: a life cut short, 2008. *Address:* c/o Anthony Sheil Associates Ltd, 43 Doughty Street, WC1N 2LF. *T:* (020) 7405 9351.

ACKROYD, Sir Timothy Robert Whyte, 3rd Bt *cr* 1956, of Dewsbury, West Riding of Yorkshire; actor; *b* 7 Oct. 1958; *er s* of Sir John Robert Whyte Ackroyd, 2nd Bt and Jennifer Eileen McLeod (*d* 1997), *d* of H. G. S. Bishop; *S* father, 1995. *Educ:* Bradfield; LAMDA. *Theatre* includes: Agamemnon, 1976; On Approval, 1979; Much Ado About Nothing, 1980; Macbeth, Old Vic. Co., 1980; Man and Superman, 1982; A Sleep of Prisoners, 1983; Pygmalion, 1984; Another Country, 1986; No Sex Please - We're British, 1987; Black Coffee, 1988; Jeffrey Bernard is Unwell, 1989, 1999 (televised); Journey's End, 1993; Bad Soldier Smith, 1995; Saki, 1997; The Rivals, Iphigenia at Aulis, 2000; A Step Out of Time, 2000; A Village Wooing, 2002; Red Lanterns, 2002; Falstaff, in Henry IV, Part I, 2003; Les Parents Terribles, 2004; Hogarth: the compassionate satirist, 2005–07; *television:* Jack Be Nimble, 1979; Luther, 1983; Man and Superman, 1985; Pied Piper, 1989; A Royal Scandal, 1996; The New Professionals, 1998; *films:* Creator, 1984; Bullseye, 1990; Tembo Kali, 1992; *radio* includes: Fugitive Pieces, 1999; Life Story, 2004. Director: Martingale Productions, 1985–86; Archview Films, 1991–95; Ackroyd Pullan, 1995–98; Zuma Productions, 2000–; Messiah Pictures, 2001; Ackroyd & Company, 2004–. Hon. Mem., Theatre of Comedy, 1984. Chm., Ackroyd Trust; Trustee and Patron, Tusk Trust; Trustee, Marjorie and Dorothy Whyte Meml Fund; Patron, London & Internat. Sch. of Acting. Freeman and Liveryman, Carpenters' Co., 1982. *Publication:* Ackroyd's Ark, 2004. *Recreations:* Rugby, cricket, literature, Sumo wrestling. *Heir: b* Andrew John Armitage Ackroyd, *b* 17 Sept. 1961. *Clubs:* Garrick, MCC; Lazarusians.

ACLAND, Sir Antony (Arthur), KG 2001; GCMG 1986 (KCMG 1982; CMG 1976); GCVO 1991 (KCVO 1976); HM Diplomatic Service, retired; Provost of Eton, 1991–2000; *b* 12 March 1930; *s* of late Brig. P. B. E. Acland, OBE, MC, TD and Bridget Susan (*née* Barnett); *m* 1956, Clare Anne Verdon (*d* 1984); two *s* one *d*; *m* 1987, Jennifer McGougan (*née* Dyke). *Educ:* Eton; Christ Church, Oxford (MA 1956). Joined Diplomatic Service, 1953; ME Centre for Arab Studies, 1954; Dubai, 1955; Kuwait, 1956; FO, 1958–62; Asst Private Sec. to Sec. of State, 1959–62; UK Mission to UN, 1962–66; Head of Chancery, UK Mission, Geneva, 1966–68; FCO, 1968, Hd of Arabian Dept, 1970–72; Principal Private Sec. to Foreign and Commonwealth Sec., 1972–75; Ambassador to Luxembourg, 1975–77, to Spain, 1977–79; Deputy Under-Sec. of State, FCO, 1980–82, Perm. Under-Sec. of State, FCO, and Head of Diplomatic Service, 1982–86; Ambassador to Washington, 1986–91. Director: Shell Transport and Trading, 1991–2000; Booker plc, 1992–99. Chairman: Council, Ditchley Foundn, 1991–96; Tidy Britain Gp, 1992–96 (Pres., 1996–2002). Trustee: Nat. Portrait Gall., 1991–98; Esmée Fairbairn Foundn, 1991–2005. Chancellor, Order of St Michael and St George, 1994–2005. Pres., Exmoor Soc., 2007–. Hon. DCL: Exeter, 1988; William and Mary Coll., USA, 1990; Reading, 1992. *Address:* Staddon Farm, near Winsford, Minehead, Som TA24 7HY. *T:* (01643) 831489. *Club:* Brooks's.

ACLAND, Lt-Col Sir (Christopher) Guy (Dyke), 6th Bt *cr* 1890; LVO 1999 (MVO 1990); an Extra Equerry to the Queen, since 1999; Vice Lord-Lieutenant, Isle of Wight, since 2006; *b* 24 March 1946; *s* of Major Sir Antony Guy Acland, 5th Bt, and of Margaret Joan, *e d* of late Major Nelson Rooke; *S* father, 1983; *m* 1971, Christine Mary Carden, *y d* of late Dr John Waring, Totland Bay, Isle of Wight; two *s*. *Educ:* Allhallows School; RMA Sandhurst. Commissioned RA, 1966; served BAOR (26 Field Regt), 1967–70; UK and Hong Kong (3 RHA), 1970–73; BAOR and UK (22 AD Regt), 1974–77; Staff Coll., Camberley, 1978 (psc); served on Staff of HQ Eastern District, 1979–80; commanded Q (Sanna's Post) Bty in BAOR (5 Regt), 1981–83; SO2, Army Staff Duties Directorate, MoD, 1983–85; 2 i/c 1 RHA BAOR, 1986–88; Equerry to HRH The Duke of Edinburgh, 1988–90; SO1, Management Services Orgn 3, MoD, 1990–92; CO, Southampton Univ. OTC, 1992–94; retired 1994. Dep. Master of the Household and Equerry to the Queen, 1994–99. Administrator, HSA Charitable Trust, 2000–06. DL Isle of Wight, 2002. *Recreations:* sailing, gardening. *Heir: s* Alexander John Dyke Acland, *b* 29 May 1973. *Clubs:* Royal Yacht Squadron, Royal Artillery Yacht.

ACLAND, Sir John (Dyke), 16th Bt *cr* 1644, of Columb John, Devon; *b* 13 May 1939; *s* of Sir Richard Thomas Dyke Acland, 15th Bt and Anne Stella (*née* Alford) (*d* 1992); *S* father, 1990; *m* 1st, 1961, Virginia (marr. diss. 2001), *yr d* of Roland Forge; two *s* one *d*; 2nd, 2001, Susan, *d* of Herbert Hooper. *Educ:* Clifton; Magdalene Coll., Cambridge; Univ. of West Indies (MSc). *Heir: s* Dominic Dyke Acland [*b* 19 Nov. 1962; *m* 1990, Sarah Anne, 3rd *d* of Ven. Kenneth Unwin, *qv*; two *s* two *d* (of whom one *s* one *d* are twins)]. *Address:* 26A Cambridge Place, Cambridge CB2 1NS.

ACRES, Paul, QPM 1997; Chief Constable of Hertfordshire, 2000–04; *b* 15 April 1948; *s* of Albert George Acres and Kathleen Acres (*née* Jones); *m* 1971, Jean Parsons; three *s*. *Educ:* City of Bath Boys' Sch. Liverpool and Bootle Constabulary, 1968–74; joined Merseyside Police, 1974: Asst Chief Constable, 1992–94; rcds, 1994; Dep. Chief Constable, 1995–2000. Police Long Service and Good Conduct Medal, 1991. *Recreations:* walking, motor cycling, golf, cycling. *Club:* West Lancashire Golf.

ACTON, 4th Baron *cr* 1869, of Aldenham, Salop; **Richard Gerald Lyon-Dalberg-Acton;** Baron Acton of Bridgnorth (Life Peer) 2000; Bt 1644; Patrician of Naples, 1802; *b* 30 July 1941; *s* of 3rd Baron Acton, CMG, MBE, TD and Daphne, *o d* of 4th Baron Rayleigh, FRS and Mary Hilda, 2nd *d* of 4th Earl of Leitrim; *S* father, 1989; *m* 1st, 1965, Hilary Juliet Sarah (*d* 1973), *d* of Dr Osmond Laurence Charles Cookson, Perth, WA; one *s*; 2nd, 1974, Judith (writer) (marr. diss. 1987), *d* of Hon. Sir (Reginald Stephen) Garfield Todd; 3rd, 1988, Patricia (Law Professor and writer), *o d* of late M. Morey Nassif and of Mrs Nassif, Iowa, USA. *Educ:* St George's Coll., Salisbury, Rhodesia; Trinity Coll., Oxford (BA History 1963, MA 1988). Mgt trainee, Amalgamated Packaging Industries Ltd, Britain, Rhodesia, USA and S Africa, 1963–66; Trainee Dir, 1967–70, Dir, 1970–74, Coutts & Co. Called to the Bar, Inner Temple, 1976; practising barrister, 1977–81; a Senior Law Officer, Min. of Justice, Legal and Parly Affairs, Zimbabwe, 1981–85. A cross-bencher, H of L, 1989–97; joined Lab. Party, 1997; Member: H of L Refreshment Cttee, 1998–99; H of L Constitution Cttee, 2001–05; Jt Cttee on Consolidation Bills, 2002–05,

2006–; H of L Select Cttee on Delegated Powers and Regulatory Reform, 2006–07. Patron: Jubilee Appeal, MIND, 1996–; The Mulberry Bush Sch., 1998–; APEX Trust, 2002–; Frank Longford Trust, 2002–; Hansard Soc., 2003–; Trustee, Old Creamery Th. Co., Iowa, 1995–. Hon. Pres., Assoc. of Amer. Study Abroad Progs in the UK, 2006–. Throne/Aldrich Award, State Historical Soc. of Iowa, 1995. Hon. Citizen of Iowa, 2003. *Publications:* (contrib.) The Spectator Annual, 1993; (with Prof. P. Acton) To Go Free: a treasury of Iowa's legal heritage, 1995 (Benjamin F. Shambaugh award, 1996); A Brit Among the Hawkeyes, 1998; (contrib.) Outside In: African-American history in Iowa 1838–2000, 2001; contribs anthologies and periodicals. *Heir: s* Hon. John Charles Ferdinand Harold Lyon-Dalberg-Acton [*b* 19 Aug. 1966; *m* 1998, Lucinda, *d* of Brig. James Percival]. *Address:* 152 Whitehall Court, SW1A 2EL. *T:* (020) 7839 3077; 100 Red Oak Lane SE, Cedar Rapids, IA 52403, USA. *T:* (319) 3626181.

ACTON DAVIS, Jonathan James; QC 1996; a Recorder, since 2000; *b* 15 Jan. 1953; *s* of Michael James and Elizabeth Acton Davis; *m* 1987, Lindsay Alice Boswell, *qv*; one *s*. *Educ:* Harrow Sch.; Poly. of Central London (LLB London). Called to the Bar, Inner Temple, 1977 (Bencher, 1995, Master of the House, 1999–2005); an Asst Recorder, 1997–2000. General Council of the Bar: Mem., 1993–98; Chm., Professional Conduct and Complaints Cttee, 2001–02 (Vice-Chm., 1999–2000); Mem., Legal Services Consultative Panel, 2004–. *Recreations:* cricket, walking, South West France. *Address:* 1 Atkin Building, Gray's Inn, WC1R 5AT. *T:* (020) 7404 0102; *e-mail:* clerks@atkinchambers.law.co.uk. *Clubs:* Garrick, MCC.

ACTON DAVIS, Lindsay Alice; *see* Boswell, L. A.

ACTON SMITH, Michael; Chief Executive Officer and Founder, Mind Candy, since 2004; *b* London, 3 Sept. 1974; *s* of Charles and Colette Smith. *Educ:* Danesfield Primary Sch.; Sir William Borlase Grammar Sch.; Birmingham Univ. (BSc Geog.). Co-founder and Chm., Firebox.com, 1998; Co-founder, Second Chance Tuesday, 2006. Inventor, Shot Glass Chess Set, 1998; creator of games: Perplex City, 2005; Moshi Monsters, 2008. *Recreations:* games, memes, monsters, poker, puzzles, parties and prime numbers. *Address:* Mind Candy, Battersea Studios, 80 Silverthorne Road, SW8 3HE. *T:* (020) 7501 1901; *e-mail:* michael@mindcandy.com. *Clubs:* Soho House, Adam Street, Paramount.

ACWORTH, Ven. Richard Foote; Archdeacon of Wells, 1993–2003; *b* 19 Oct. 1936; *s* of late Rev. Oswald Roney Acworth and Jean Margaret Acworth; *m* 1966, Margaret Caroline Marie Jennings; two *s* one *d*. *Educ:* St John's Sch., Leatherhead; Sidney Sussex Coll., Cambridge (BA Hist. and Theol. 1962; MA 1965); Cuddesdon Theol Coll. Nat. service, RNVR, 1956–58. Ordained deacon, 1963, priest, 1964; Assistant Curate: St Etheldreda's, Fulham, 1963; All Saints and Martyrs, Langley, Mancs, 1964–66; St Mary's, Bridgwater, 1966–69; Vicar, Yatton, 1969–81; Priest-in-charge, St John's and St Mary's, Taunton, 1981–85; Vicar of St Mary Magdalene, Taunton, 1985–93. *Recreations:* walking, gardening, DIY, ornithology. *Address:* Corvedale Cottage, Croscombe, Wells, Som BA5 3QJ. *T:* (01749) 342242.

See also Brig. R. W. Acworth.

ACWORTH, Brig. Robert William, CBE 1986; Registrar of St Paul's Cathedral, 1991–2001; *b* 11 Dec. 1938; *s* of late Rev. Oswald Roney Acworth and Jean Margaret (*née* Coupland); *m* 1967, Elizabeth Mary, *e d* of late J. N. S. Ridgers; two *s* one *d*. *Educ:* St John's Sch., Leatherhead; RMA, Sandhurst. Commnd, Queen's Royal Regt, 1958; served in Germany, Holland, Norway, Gibraltar, Aden, Oman, Hong Kong, UK and NI; sc 1970; staff and regtl duty, 1971–81; Comdr, 10 UDR, 1981–83; Asst COS, HQ NI, 1983–85; Coll. Comdr, RMA, Sandhurst, 1985–87; Asst COS (Intelligence), HQ AFCENT, 1987–90; Dep. Comdr and COS, SE Dist, 1990–91, retd. Deputy Colonel: Queen's Regt, 1986–92; Princess of Wales's Royal Regt, 1992–94. Pres., Queen's Royal Surrey Regt Assoc., 1995–2005. *Recreations:* gardening, shooting, fishing, golf. *Address:* The Old Rectory, Great Wishford, Salisbury, Wilts SP2 0NN. *T:* (01722) 790583. *Club:* Army and Navy.

See also Ven. R. F. Acworth.

ADAIR, Brian Campbell, TD 1979; NP 1975; Senior Partner, 1973–2005, Consultant, 2005–08, Adairs, Solicitors, Dumbarton; President, Law Society of Scotland, 1992–93; *b* 28 Aug. 1945; *s* of Alan William Adair and Helen Mary Scott or Adair; *m* 1969, Elaine Jean Morrison; one *s* two *d*. *Educ:* Milngavie Primary Sch.; High Sch., Glasgow; Glasgow Univ. (LLB 1967). Commnd TA 1965, 1st Bn Glasgow Highlanders; served Glasgow & Strathclyde Univs OTC, 1967–73, 2nd Bn Lowland Volunteers, 1973–79; retired rank Major. Apprentice Solicitor, McGrigor Donald, Glasgow, 1967–70; Solicitor, Dumbarton CC, 1970–73; constituted own firm, 1973. Temp. Sheriff, 1995–99; part-time Sheriff, 2000–. Mem., Scottish Legal Aid Bd, 1998–2002. Mem. Council, Law Soc. of Scotland, 1980–94 (Vice Pres., 1991–92). Elder, St Paul's Church, Milngavie. Chm. of Govs, High Sch. of Glasgow, 2006– (Gov., 1992–). *Recreations:* holidaying in Arran, entertaining, golf. *Address:* 21 James Watt Road, Milngavie, Glasgow G62 7JX. *T:* (0141) 956 3070. *Club:* Milngavie Golf (Captain, Centenary Year, 1995).

ADAIR, John Eric, PhD; author and teacher of leadership; *b* Luton, 18 May 1934; *s* of Robin and Dorothy Adair; *m* 1977, Thea Talbot; two *s* one *d*. *Educ:* St Paul's Sch.; Hull Nautical Coll. (qualified Arctic trawler deckhand 1955); Trinity Hall, Cambridge (BA 1959); Univ. of London (PhD 1966); Jesus Coll., Oxford (BLitt 1971). FRHistS 1966. National Service: 2nd Lt Scots Guards and Adjutant 9 Regt Arab Legion, 1953–55. Arctic trawler deckhand, 1955. Sen. Lectr, RMA Sandhurst, 1961–67; Hon. Dir of Studies, St George's House, Windsor Castle, 1968; Asst Dir and Hd, Leadership Dept, 1969–71, Associate Dir, 1972–75, Industrial Soc.; Prof. of Leadership Studies, Univ. of Surrey, 1979–84. Vis. Prof., Univ. of Exeter, 1990–2000; Hon. Prof. of Leadership, China Exec. Leadership Acad., Pudong, 2006–. Pres., John Hampden Soc., 1992–. Fellow, Windsor Leadership Trust, 2001–. *Publications:* Hastings to Culloden: battles of Britain (with Peter Young), 1964, 3rd edn 1998; Training for Leadership, 1968; Training for Decisions, 1969; Roundhead General: the life of Sir William Waller, 1969, 2nd edn 1997; Cheriton 1644: the campaign and the battle, 1973; Training for Communication, 1973; Action Centred Leadership, 1973; Management and Morality: the problems and opportunities of social capitalism, 1974; A Life of John Hampden The Patriot 1594–1643, 1976; The Becoming Church, 1976; The Pilgrims' Way: shrines and saints in Britain and Ireland, 1978; The Royal Palaces of Britain, 1981; Founding Fathers: the Puritans in England and America, 1982, 2nd edn 1998; By the Sword Divided: eyewitness accounts of the English Civil War, 1983, 2nd edn 1998; Effective Leadership, 1983, 3rd edn 2008; Effective Decision-Making, 1985; Effective Teambuilding, 1986; How to Manage Your Time, 1987, 2nd edn as Effective Time Management, 1998; No Bosses But Leaders, 1987, 3rd edn 2003; Developing Leaders, 1988; Great Leaders, 1989, 2nd edn as Inspiring Leadership, 2002; Understanding Motivation, 1990, 2nd edn as Leadership and Motivation, 2006; The Challenge of Innovation, 1990, 2nd edn as Leadership for Innovation, 1990; The Art of Creative Thinking, 1990, 2nd edn 2007; Effective Innovation, 1994; Effective Motivation, 1996; Leadership Skills, 1996, 2nd edn as Develop Your Leadership Skills, 2007; Effective Communication, 1997; Decision Making and Problem Solving, 1997, 2nd edn as Decision Making and Problem Solving Strategies; How to Find Your Vocation, 2000; The Leadership of Jesus, 2001; Effective Strategic Leadership, 2002; The Inspirational Leader, 2003; How to Grow Leaders, 2005; Effective Leadership Development, 2006. *Recreations:* English countryside, sketching, reading. *Address:* Westbury Manor, Compton, Guildford GU3 1EE. *T:* (01483) 810241; *e-mail:* ja@johnadair.co.uk.

ADAM, Prof. Andreas Ntinou, FRCR, FRCP, FRCS; Professor of Interventional Radiology, Guy's, King's and St Thomas' School of Medicine (formerly United Medical and Dental Schools of Guy's and St Thomas' Hospital and King's College Medical School), since 1992; President, Royal College of Radiologists, since 2007; *b* 4 May 1951; *s* of Constantinos Adam and Hera Adam (*née* Spanou); *m* 1977, Dr Jane Williams; two *d*. *Educ:* Middlesex Hosp. Med. Sch. (MB BS Hons 1977). MRCP 1979, FRCP 1994; FRCR 1985; FRCS 1998. Hse physician, Middx Hosp., 1977–78; hse surgeon, Kettering Gen. Hosp., 1978; Senior House Officer: Hammersmith Hosp., 1978–79; Middx Hosp., 1979; National Hosp., 1979–80; Registrar: Whittington Hosp., 1980–81; UCH, 1981; Hammersmith Hosp., 1981–83; Senior Registrar: Hammersmith and Hillingdon Hosps, 1983–84; Hammersmith Hosp., 1984–86; Sen. Lectr, 1987–91, Reader, 1991–92, RPMS; Hon. Consultant Radiologist, Guy's and St Thomas' NHS Foundn Trust, 1992–. Jt Ed.-in-Chief, Jl Interventional Radiol., 1992–95; Ed.-in-Chief, Cardiovascular and Interventional Radiol., 1995–2003; Asst Ed., Jl Haepato-Pancreato-Biliary Assoc., 1998–2001; mem., editl bds of numerous jls. Advr to EU on digital imaging, 1991–92; Consultant in Radiol. to WHO, 1999; Specialist Advr on Interventional Radiol., NICE, 2000–; Mem., Adv. Gp on Ionising Radiation, Subgp on High Dose Radiation Effects and Tissue Injury, HPA, 2005–. Rep. of Eur. Assoc. of Radiol., Eur. Agency for Evaluation of Medicinal Products, 2000–04. Lectures include: Alan Goldin Oration, Royal Australasian Coll. of Radiologists, 1993; John Wickham, Internat. Soc. Minimally Invasive Therapy, 1998; Hounsfield, BIR, 2006; Haughton, RCSI, 2007; Holmes, New England Roentgen Ray Soc., 2008. President: Soc. for Minimal Invasive Therapy, 1996–97; British Soc. Interventional Radiologists, 1997–99; BIR, 1998–99; Internat. Soc. Hepatobiliary Radiol., 1998–99; Cardiovascular and Interventional Radiol Soc. of Europe, 2005–07; Eur. Congress of Radiol., 2006; Soc. of Gastrointestinal Intervention, 2007–Oct. 2009; Eur. Soc. Radiol., 2007–08. Fellow: Soc. of Cardiovascular and Interventional Radiol., USA, 1993; Eur. Soc. Gastrointestinal and Abdominal Radiol., 1998; FBIR 2007; Academician, Russian Acad. Med. Scis, 2005. Hon. FRANZCR 2007; Hon. Fellow: Faculty of Radiologists, RCSI, 2007; Greek Soc. Interventional Radiol., 2007. Medal, Russian Acad. Med. Scis, 2004; Gold Medal, British Soc. Interventional Radiologists, 2005; President's Medal, RCR, 2006; Gold Medal, Cardiovascular and Interventional Radiol Soc. Europe, 2007. *Publications:* Clinical Gastroenterology: interventional radiology of the abdomen, 1993; Practical Interventional Radiology of the Hepatobiliary System and Gastrointestinal Tract, 1994; Interventional Radiology: a practical guide, 1995; A Textbook of Metallic Stents, 1996; Interventional Radiology: a multimedia virtual textbook, 1997; Practical Management of Oesophageal Disease, 2000; Diagnostic Radiology, 4th edn 2001, 5th edn 2008; Interventional Radiology in Cancer, 2003; Interventional Radiological Treatment of Liver Tumours, 2008; contrib. numerous scientific papers on aspects of interventional radiol., esp. focusing on use of metallic stents in various organs. *Recreation:* reading history. *Address:* Department of Radiology, 1st Floor Lambeth Wing, St Thomas' Hospital, SE1 7EH. *T:* (020) 7188 5550, *Fax:* (020) 7188 5454; *e-mail:* andy.adam@kcl.ac.uk. *Club:* Athenæum.

ADAM, Brian James; Member (SNP) Aberdeen North, Scottish Parliament, since 2003 (North East Scotland, 1999–2003); *b* 10 June 1948; *s* of James Pirie Adam and Isabel Adam (*née* Geddes); *m* 1975, Dorothy McKillip Mann; four *s* one *d*. *Educ:* Keith Grammar Sch.; Aberdeen Univ. (BSc, MSc). Principal Biochemist: City Hosp., Aberdeen, 1973–88; Aberdeen Royal Infirmary, 1988–99. Mem. (SNP) Aberdeen CC, 1988–99. Joined SNP, 1974. Contested (SNP): Gordon, 1992; Aberdeen N, 1997. *Address:* 8 Newburgh Drive, Aberdeen AB22 8SR. *T:* (01224) 704917.

ADAM, Sir Christopher Eric Forbes, 3rd Bt *cr* 1917; *b* 12 Feb. 1920; *s* of Eric Graham Forbes Adam, CMG (*d* 1925) (2nd *s* of 1st Bt) and of Agatha Perrin, *d* of Reginald Walter Macan; *S* uncle, 1982; *m* 1957, Patricia Anne Wreford (*d* 2008), *y d* of late John Neville Wreford Brown; one adopted *d*. *Heir: cousin* Rev. (Stephen) Timothy Beilby Forbes Adam [*b* 19 Nov. 1923; *m* 1954, Penelope, *d* of George Campbell Munday, MC; four *d*]. *Address:* 46 Rawlings Street, SW3 2LS.

ADAM, Gordon Johnston, PhD; Member (Lab) North East Region, England, European Parliament, Feb. 2000–2004; *b* 28 March 1934; *s* of John Craig Adam and Deborah Armstrong Johnston; *m* 1973, Sarah Jane Seely; one *s*. *Educ:* Leeds Univ. (BSc Hons, PhD). CEng, MIMMM; FEI. NCB, 1959–79. Mem., Whitley Bay Bor. Council, 1971–74; Mem. 1973–80, and Dep. Leader 1975–80, North Tyneside Metrop. Bor. Council (Chm., 1973–74; Mayor, 1974–75). Mem., Whitley Bay Playhouse Theatre Trust, 1975– (Chm., 1975–80). MEP (Lab) Northumbria, 1979–99; contested (Lab) NE Region, 1999; Vice-Chm., Energy, Res. and Technol. Cttee, EP, 1984–99. Chairman: Northumbria Energy Advice Centre, 1994–; Northern Energy Initiative, 1996–2000; NE Reg. Energy Forum, 2004–06; Member: Northern Econ. Planning Council, 1974–79; Northern Arts Gen. Council, 1975–78; Northern Sinfonia Management Cttee, 1978–80; Bd, Northern Stage Co., 1989–2001; Bd, S Tyneside Groundwork Trust, 2004–. Sen. Advr, Energy Policy Consulting, 2006–. Contested (Lab): Tynemouth, 1966; Berwick-upon-Tweed, Nov. 1973 (by-election), Feb. 1974 and 1992. *Recreation:* gardening. *Address:* The Old Farm House, East House Farm, Killingworth Village, Newcastle upon Tyne NE12 6BQ. *T:* (0191) 216 0154.

ADAM, Ian Clark; Chairman, Britannia Building Society, 2004–08 (Director, 1998–2008); *b* 2 Sept. 1943; *s* of George Adam and Natalie Jane Gibson Adam; *m* 1967, Betty Anne Crosbie; one *s* one *d*. *Educ:* Harris Acad., Dundee. CA 1967. Partner, 1976, Sen. Partner, Scotland, 1985–95, Price Waterhouse; Finance Dir, Christian Salvesen plc, 1995–98. Mem., SHEFC, 2003–05, SFC, 2005–. *Recreations:* gardening, golf, reading. *Address:* Gowanfield, 2 Cammo Road, Edinburgh EH4 8EB. *T:* (0131) 339 6401; *e-mail:* ian@clarkadam.freeserve.co.uk. *Clubs:* Royal and Ancient Golf (St Andrews); Royal Burgess Golfing Society (Edinburgh).

ADAM, Sir Kenneth (Klaus Hugo), Kt 2003; OBE 1995; freelance film production designer; *b* 5 Feb. 1921; *s* of Fritz Adam and Lilli Adam (*née* Saalfeld); *m* 1952, Maria-Letizia Moauro. *Educ:* Collège Français, Berlin; St Paul's Sch., London; Bartlett Sch. of Architecture, London (Ext.). Film art dir/prodn designer, 1947–; collaborated on approx. 70 films, including: seven early Bond films; Chitty Chitty Bang Bang, 1967; Sleuth, 1972; Pennies from Heaven, 1981; Addams Family Values, 1993. Exhibitions of designs: Meisterwerke der Film Architektur, touring, Germany and Austria, 1994; Serpentine Gall., 1999–2000; Ken Adam Visionäre Film Welten, Frankfurt, 2002, Berlin, 2002–03; Moonraker, Strangelove and Other Celluloid Dreams: the visionary art of Ken Adam, Hollywood, 2003. Dr *hc* RCA, 1995; Hon. DArts Greenwich, 2000. Academy Awards for Production Design: Barry Lyndon, 1975; The Madness of King George, 1995; BAFTA Awards: Dr Strangelove, 1964; The Ipcress File, 1965; Lifetime Achievement Award,

Hollywood Art Directors, 2002. *Relevant publication:* Moonraker, Strangelove and Other Celluloid Dreams: the visionary art of Ken Adam, by David Sylvester, 1999. *Recreation:* swimming. *Address:* 34 Montpelier Street, SW7 1HD. *T:* (020) 7589 9372, *Fax:* (020) 7584 7090. *Club:* Royal Automobile.

ADAM, Robert, RIBA; Director, Robert Adam Architects, since 1995; *b* 10 April 1948; *s* of Dr Robert Wilson Adam and Jessie Margaret Adam; *m* 1970, Sarah Jane Chalcraft; one *s* one *d*. *Educ:* Canford Sch., Dorset; Regent Street Poly. (DipArch 1973). RIBA 1977. Partner, 1977–, Dir, 1987–, Evan Roberts & Partners, subseq. Winchester Design (Architects) Ltd. Principal buildings include: Sackler Liby, Oxford; Solar House, Wakeham; Dogmersfield Park, Odiham; Millennium Pavilion, Preston Candover, Hants; 198–202 Piccadilly; new country houses in Hants, Dorset and Wilts; Coed Darcy masterplan, Llandarcy, nr Swansea; New district, Leith masterplans. Trustee, 1989–98, Chm., Faculty of Fine Arts, 1993–97, British Sch. at Rome; Chm., Popular Housing Gp, 1995–2003; Mem. Council, RIBA, 1999– (Hon. Sec., 2000–03); Design Advr, CABE, 1999–2003; Founder and Chair, Coll. of Chapters, Internat. Network for Traditional Building, Architecture and Urbanism, 2000–; Acad. of Urbanism, 2006–. Trustee: RIBA Trust, 2003–; Maria Nobrega Charitable Trust, 2003–. *Publications:* Classical Architecture: a complete handbook, 1990; (contrib.) Building Classical, 1993; (contrib.) Companion to Contemporary Architectural Thought, 1993; Buildings by Design, 1994; papers in Architectl Review, Architects Jl, RIBA Jl, Architectl Design, Context 79, City Jl (USA), Archis (Holland). *Recreations:* medieval history, ceramics. *Address:* 9 Upper High Street, Winchester, Hants SO23 8UT. *T:* (01962) 843843. *Clubs:* Athenæum, Home House.

ADAM, Sheila Anne, MD; FRCP, FFPH, FRCGP; Interim Director of Public Health, NHS London (Strategic Health Authority for London), 2006–07; *b* 24 Nov. 1949. *Educ:* Nottingham High Sch. for Girls; Edinburgh Univ. (MB ChB 1972; MD 1983); DCH 1974. MRCP 1976, FRCP 1993; MFPHM 1981, FFPHM 1986; FRCGP 2002. Public Health Registrar, 1975–77, Sen. Registrar and MRC Trng Fellow in Public Health, 1977–81, Oxford RHA; Public Health Consultant, Brent HA, 1981–83; Public Health Consultant, 1983–89, Dir of Public Health, 1989–95, NW Thames RHA; NHS Executive, Department of Health: Hd of Mental Health and NHS Community Care, 1995–97; Dep. Dir of Health Services, 1997–99; Dir of Health Services, 1999–2001; Dep. CMO, 1999–2002, and Dir of Policy, 2001–02, DoH; Dir of Public Health, NE London Strategic HA, 2002–06. QHP 1996–99.

ADAM, Thomas Noble; QC 2008; *b* London, 6 Jan. 1965; *s* of Bruce and Sheila Adam; *m* 1991, Helen Gooch; three *s*. *Educ:* Norwich Sch.; Trinity Coll., Cambridge (BA 1987). Solicitor, Macfarlanes, 1988–91; called to the Bar, Inner Temple, 1991; in practice at the Bar, specialising in commercial law, 1991–. *Publications:* (with C. Hollander) Documentary Evidence, 7th edn, 2000; (contrib.) Professional Negligence and Liability Encyclopedia. *Recreations:* family time, fishing, shooting, Munro-walking, light verse, wine and whisky, boxing. *Address:* c/o Brick Court Chambers, 7–8 Essex Street, WC2R 3LD. *Club:* Hawks.

ADAMI, Edward F.; *see* Fenech-Adami.

ADAMISHIN, Dr Anatoly; Consultant, Sistema Joint-Stock Financial Corporation, Russia, since 2003 (Vice President, International Affairs, 1998); *b* 11 Oct. 1934; *s* of Leonid Adamishin and Vera Gusovskaya; *m* 2000, Svetlana Kharlamova; one *d* by previous marriage. *Educ:* Lomonosov Moscow State Univ.; Diplomatic Acad. of USSR (Dr in Historic Sci. 1979). Joined USSR Diplomatic Service, 1957; First European Dept, Min. of Foreign Affairs, 1957–59; served embassy in Italy, 1959–65; First European Dept, 1965–71; Foreign Policy Planning Dept, 1971–73; Head, Gen. Internat. Issues Dept, 1973–78; Head, First European Dept and Mem., Min. of Foreign Affairs Collegium, 1978–86; Dep. Minister for Foreign Affairs, 1986–90; also Head, USSR Commn for UNESCO Affairs, 1987–90; Ambassador to Italy, 1990–92; First Dep. Minister for Foreign Affairs of Russia, 1992–94; Ambassador to UK, 1994–97; Minister for relations with CIS, Min. of Foreign Affairs, 1997–98. Sen. Fellow, US Inst. of Peace, Washington, 2005–06. *Publications:* Tramonto e rinascita di una grande potenza, 1995; The White Sun of Angola, 2001. *Recreation:* lawn tennis. *Address:* (office) Leontyevski per. 10, 125009 Moscow, Russia.

ADAMKUS, Valdas; President, Republic of Lithuania, 1998–2003 and since 2004; *b* Kaunas, 3 Nov. 1926; *s* of Ignas Adamkavičius and Genovaite Bacevičiūte; *m* 1951, Alma Adamkiene. *Educ:* Munich Univ.; Illinois Inst. of Technology, Chicago. Qualified civil engr, 1960; Chicago Car Plant, 1949–50; Draftsman, Meissner Consulting Engrs, 1950–59; owner and operator, summer resort, Sodus, Michigan, 1960–69; Dir, Envmt Res. Centre, US Envmt Protection Agency, 1969–71; Dep. Adminr, 1971–81, Adminr, 1981–97, Reg. 5 (Great Lakes), US Envmt Protection Agency. Mem., US Delegn in Co-operation with USSR under bilateral envmtl agreement, 1972–91; Chm., US Delegn, Internat. Jt Commn for Great Lakes (US-Canada), 1980–97. Vice Chm., 1958–65, Chm., 1967–97, Santara-Sviesa Cultural-political Fedn; Vice-Chm., Exec. Cttee, American-Lithuanian Community; Mem., American-Lithuanian Council. Hon. Dr: Vilnius, 1989; Indiana St Joseph Coll., 1991; Northwestern, 1994; Kaunas Technology Univ., 1998. *Publication:* Lithuania: the name of my destiny, 1997. *Recreations:* sport activities (golf, swimming), classical music. *Address:* 3 Simono Daukanto Square, 2008 Vilnius, Lithuania.

ADAMS, family name of **Baroness Adams of Craigielea**.

ADAMS OF CRAIGIELEA, Baroness *cr* 2005 (Life Peer), of Craigielea in Renfrewshire; **(Katherine Patricia) Irene Adams;** JP; *b* 27 Dec. 1947; *m* 1968, Allen S. Adams (*d* 1990), MP Paisley North; one *s* two *d*. *Educ:* Stanley Green High Sch., Paisley. Councillor, Paisley Town, 1970; Member: Renfrew DC, 1974–78; Strathclyde Regl Council, 1979–84. MP (Lab) Paisley North, Nov. 1990–2005. *Address:* House of Lords, SW1A 0PW.

ADAMS, Dr Aileen Kirkpatrick, CBE 1988; FRCS; FRCA; Emerita Consultant Anaesthetist, Addenbrooke's Hospital, Cambridge, since 1983; *b* 5 Sept. 1923; *d* of F. Joseph Adams and M. Agnes Adams (*née* Munro). *Educ:* Farringtons School, Chislehurst; Sheffield Univ. MB ChB Sheffield, 1945; MA Cantab 1977; FFARCS 1954; FFA(SA) 1987; FRCS 1988; FDSRCS 1989. Fellow in anaesthesia, Harvard Univ. and Mass. Gen. Hosp., Boston, 1955–57; Consultant Anaesthetist, Addenbrooke's Hosp., Cambridge, 1960–83; Associate Lectr, Univ. of Cambridge, 1977–85; Dean, Faculty of Anaesthetists, RCS, 1985–88. Sen. Lectr, Lagos Univ. Med. Sch., Nigeria, 1963–64. Mem., Cambridge Health Authy, 1978–82. Royal College of Surgeons of England: Mem. Council, 1982–88; Hunterian Prof., 1993; Trustee, Hunterian Collection, 1996–; Royal Society of Medicine: Hon. Treas., 1995–99; Hon. Mem., Anaesthesia Section, 1998– (Pres., 1985–86); Pres., History of Medicine Section, 1994–95; Vice-Pres., Comparative Medicine Section, 2003–04. Hon. Mem., History of Anaesthesia Soc., 1994– (Pres., 1990–92); Pres., British Soc. for the History of Medicine, 2003–05. Hon. Archivist, Royal Coll. of Anaesthetists, 1989–98. Former Examr, Cambridge Univ. and FFARCS. Hon. Mem., Assoc. of Anaesthetists, GB and Ire. Lectures: Monckton Copeman, Soc. of Apothecaries, 2002; Arthur Thompson, Univ. of Birmingham, 2004. Mem., Editl Bd, Anaesthesia, 1972–85. *Publications:* book chapters and papers in med. jls on anaesthetic and related topics, and on history of medicine. *Recreations:* choral singing, outdoor activities, including walking, skiing, history of medicine and music. *Address:* 12 Redwood Lodge, Grange Road, Cambridge CB3 9AR. *T:* and *Fax:* (01223) 356460.

ADAMS, Alan Edgar; Director, A. A. Leadership Ltd, since 2005; Executive Director for Adults and Community Care, Surrey County Council, 2002–05; *s* of Anthony Adams and Olive Adams; one *d*. *Educ:* Nottingham Univ. (BA (Sociol.) 1976; MA (Social Work), Cert. Social Work 1978); Paddington Coll. of Further Educn, London (Further Educn Teachers' Cert.); Hendon Business Sch., Middlesex Poly. (MBA 1991). Dir, Housing and Social Services, Wokingham UA, 1997–2002. Mem., Improvement and Develt Agency Performance Support Team, 2001–. *Recreations:* family, watching sport, flying light aircraft, drums, writing, optimism. *Address:* 9 Edgcumbe Park Drive, Crowthorne, Berks RG45 6HB. *T:* (01344) 773955; *e-mail:* alan32b@hotmail.co.uk. *Club:* Cabair Flying School (Blackbushe).

ADAMS, Prof. Alfred Rodney, FRS 1996; Professor of Physics, University of Surrey, 1987–2008, now Emeritus; *b* 11 Nov. 1939; *s* of Alfred Walter Adams and Lucie Elisabeth Adams; *m* 1966, Helga Fehringer; two *d*. *Educ:* Rayleigh Technical Sch.; Westcliff High Sch.; Univ. of Leicester (BSc, PhD, DSc). FInstP, FIET, FIEEE. Research Fellow: Univ. of Leicester, 1964; Univ. of Karlsruhe, 1965; Lectr, 1967, Reader, 1984, Univ. of Surrey. Royal Soc./Japanese Soc. for Promotion of Science Fellow, 1980, Hitachi Prof., 1992, Tokyo Inst. Tech; CNRS Vis. Researcher, Univ. of Montpellier, 1993. Duddell Medal and Prize, Inst. of Physics, 1995. *Publications:* (ed with Y. Suematsu) Semiconductor Lasers and Photonic Integrated Circuits, 1994; numerous papers in jls on physics and on quantum electronics. *Recreations:* walking, travel, sailing. *Address:* Advanced Technology Institute, School of Electronics and Physical Sciences, University of Surrey, Guildford, Surrey GU2 7XH. *T:* (01483) 689310.

ADAMS, Prof. Anthony Peter, FRCA, FANZCA; Professor of Anaesthetics in the University of London, 1979–2001, now Emeritus, and Joint Vice-Chairman, Division of Surgery and Anaesthesia, 1998–2001, at Guy's, King's and St Thomas' Medical and Dental School of King's College, London; *b* 17 Oct. 1936; *s* of late H. W. J. Adams and W. L. Adams; *m* 1973, Veronica Rosemary John; three *s* one *d*. *Educ:* Epsom College; London Univ. MB BS 1960, PhD 1970; DA 1962; MRCS 1960, LRCP 1960, FRCA (FFARCS 1964); FANZCA (FFARACS 1987). Wellcome Res. Fellow, RPMS, 1964–66; Consultant Anaesthetist and Clinical Lectr, Nuffield Dept of Anaesthetics, Univ. of Oxford, 1968–79; Guy's Hosp. Med. Sch., subseq. UMDS of Guy's and St Thomas' Hospitals, 1979–98: Chm., Div. of Anaesthetics, 1984–89, 1996–97; Vice-Chm., Div. of Surgery and Anaesthesia, 1997–98; Mem., Council of Govs, 1997–98. Civilian Consultant in Anaesthesia to Army, 1988–2001, Consultant Emeritus, 2001–. Member: Standing Cttee, Bd of Studies in Surgery, London Univ., 1979–92; Academic Bd of Medicine, London Univ., 1980–83; Jt Cttee for Higher Trng of Anaesthetists, 1985–90; Specialist Adv. Cttee on Accident and Emergency Medicine, Jt Cttee for Higher Trng in Medicine, 1986–90; Exec. Cttee, Fedn of Assocs of Clin. Profs, 1979–87; Exec. Cttee, Anaesthetic Res. Soc., 1983–94 (Chm., 1991–94; Hon. Mem., 2002–); Council, Assoc. of Anaesthetists of GB and Ireland, 1984–89 (Chm., Safety Cttee, 1987–89); Council, Royal Coll. of Anaesthetists, 1989–97; Chm., Assoc. of Profs of Anaesthesia, 1984–88; Senator, Eur. Acad. of Anaesthesiology, 1985–95, 2000–03 (Mem. Exec. Cttee, 1997–2003). Regional Educnl Adviser (SE Thames RHA) to Faculty of Anaesthetists of RCS, 1980–87; Examiner: FFARCS, 1974–86; DVA, 1986–93; DA and DM, Univ. of WI, 1986–88, 1995, 1997, 1998; MSc, Univ. of Wales Coll. of Medicine, 1988–93; PhD: Univ. of London, 1989, 1997, 1999, 2001, 2004; Univ. of Manchester, 1993; Univ. of Liverpool, 1995; NUI, Galway, 2000; MB ChB Chinese Univ. of Hong Kong, 1990; Professional and Linguistic Assessment Bd Pt 2, GMC, UK, 2001–06. Mem., Bd of Govs, Sutton High Sch. for Girls, 1988–95 (Chm., 1991–95). Pres., Sutton & Dist Med. Soc., 2006–08. Hon. Life Mem., Assoc. Dental Anaesthetists, 2006. Asst Editor, Anaesthesia, 1976–82; Associate Editor: Survey of Anesthesiology, 1984–2001; European Jl of Anaesthesiology, 1987–94; Jl of Anesthesia (Japan), 1995–2002; Mem. Editl Bd, British Jl of Anaesthesia, 1984–97; Chm. Editl Bd, 1997–2000, Editor-in-Chief, 2000–03, European Jl of Anaesthesiology. *Publications:* Principles and Practice of Blood-Gas Analysis, 1979, 2nd edn 1982; Intensive Care, 1984; (ed jtly) Recent Advances in Anaesthesia and Analgesia, vol. 15, 1985, vol. 16, 1989, vol. 17, 1992, vol. 18, 1994, vol. 19, 1995, vol. 20, 1998, vol. 21, 2000, vol. 22, 2002; (ed jtly) Emergency Anaesthesia, 1986 and 1988, Japanese edn 1998; (ed jtly) Anaesthesia, Analgesia and Intensive Care, 1991; contribs to medical jls. *Recreations:* badger watching, English castles, history, tennis, croquet, cinema, theatre, ballet. *Clubs:* Royal Society of Medicine; Halifax House (Oxford).

ADAMS, Rev. David; *see* Adams, Rev. J. D. A.

ADAMS, David H.; *see* Hempleman-Adams.

ADAMS, David Robert Hutchinson, (Robin); Librarian and College Archivist, Trinity College Dublin, since 2002; *b* 9 June 1951; *s* of Cecil David and Ann Gilmore Adams; *m* 1984, Linda Jean Carter; one *s* one *d*. *Educ:* Royal Belfast Academical Instn; Univ. of Ulster (BA); Queen's Univ. of Belfast (Dip. Liby Studies); Univ. of Dublin (MA). Asst Librarian, QUB, 1975–78; Asst Under-Librarian, Cambridge Univ., 1978–86; Principal Asst Librarian, Glasgow Univ., 1986–90; Dep. Librarian, TCD, 1991–2002. Member: Bd, Nat. Preservation Office, 2002–; An Chomhairle Leabharlanna (Liby Council), 2002–; Consortium of Nat. and Univ. Libraries, 2002–; Legal Deposit Adv. Panel, 2005–; Dir, Consortium of Univ. Res. Libraries, 2002–. Dir, Iris Document Delivery Services Ltd, 2002–. Trustee, Worth Liby, 2002–. *Publications:* contrib. articles to professional jls. *Recreations:* fishing, theatre, walking, gardening. *Address:* Trinity College Library, College Street, Dublin 2, Ireland. *T:* (1) 6081661, *Fax:* (1) 6083774; *e-mail:* radams@tcd.ie. *Club:* Bective Angling (Co. Meath).

ADAMS, Ernest Victor, CB 1978; Deputy Secretary and Commissioner, Inland Revenue, 1975–81; *b* 17 Jan. 1920; *s* of Ernest and Amelia Adams; *m* 1st, 1943, Joan Bastin, Halesworth, Suffolk (*d* 1985); one *s* one *d*; 2nd, 1987, Mavisse Evelyn Surtees, Henley-on-Thames. *Educ:* Manchester Grammar Sch.; Keble Coll., Oxford (MA). HM Forces, RA, 1940–45. Inland Revenue Dept, 1947; Sen. Inspector of Taxes, 1956; Principal Inspector of Taxes, 1961; Sen. Principal Inspector of Taxes, 1966; Dep. Chief Inspector of Taxes, 1969. *Address:* 5 Northfield Court, Henley-on-Thames RG9 2LH. *T:* (01491) 572586. *Club:* Phyllis Court (Henley).

ADAMS, Sir Geoffrey Doyne, KCMG 2008 (CMG 2003); HM Diplomatic Service; Ambassador to Iran, since 2006; *b* 11 June 1957; *s* of late Sir Philip George Doyne Adams, KCMG, and of Hon. (Mary) Elizabeth, *e d* of Baron Trevethin and Oaksey (3rd and 1st Baron respectively); *m* 1999, Mary Emma Baxter; two *s* one *d*. *Educ:* Eton; Magdalen Coll., Oxford (BA). Joined HM Diplomatic Service, 1979; Third, later Second, Sec., Jedda, 1982–85; Ecole Nat. d'Admin, Paris, 1985–87; Private Sec. to Perm. Under-Sec. of State, FCO, 1987–91; First Sec., Pretoria and Cape Town, 1991–94; European Secretariat, Cabinet Office, 1995–98; Counsellor and Dep. Hd of Mission, Cairo,

1998–2001; Consul-Gen., Jerusalem, 2001–03; Principal Private Sec. to Sec. of State for Foreign and Commonwealth Affairs, 2003–05. *Address:* c/o Foreign and Commonwealth Office, King Charles Street, SW1A 2AH.

ADAMS, Gerard, (Gerry); MP (SF) Belfast West, since 1997; Member (SF) Belfast West, Northern Ireland Assembly, since 1998; President, Sinn Féin, since 1983 (Vice-President, 1978–83); *b* 6 Oct. 1948; *s* of late Gerard Adams and Annie (*née* Hannaway); *m* 1971, Colette McArdle; one *s*. *Educ:* St Mary's Christian Brothers' Sch., Belfast. Interned for suspected terrorist activity, 1971, 1973; subseq. imprisoned; released, 1976. Mem., NI Assembly, 1982; MP (Provisional Sinn Féin) Belfast W, 1983–92. Thorr Award, Switzerland, 1995. *Publications:* Falls Memories (autobiog.), 1982; Politics of Irish Freedom; Pathway to Peace, 1988; Cage Eleven (autobiog.), 1990; The Street and Other Stories, 1992; Selected Writings, 1994; Before the Dawn (autobiog.), 1996; An Irish Voice: the quest for peace, 1997; An Irish Journal, 2001; Hope and History (memoirs), 2003; An Irish Eye, 2007. *Address:* Sinn Féin, 55 Falls Road, Belfast, N Ireland BT12 4PD.

ADAMS, Sir James; *see* Adams, Sir W. J.

ADAMS, James Noel, DPhil; FBA 1992; FAHA; Senior Research Fellow, All Souls College, Oxford, since 1998; *b* 24 Sept. 1943. *Educ:* North Sydney Boys' High Sch.; Univ. of Sydney (BA); Brasenose Coll., Oxford (MA; DPhil); MA Cantab. Teaching Fellow, Dept of Latin, Univ. of Sydney, 1965–66; Commonwealth Schol., Brasenose Coll., Oxford, 1967–70; Rouse Res. Fellow in Classics, Christ's Coll., Cambridge, 1970–72; University of Manchester: Lectr and Sen. Lectr in Greek and Latin, 1972–82; Reader in Latin, 1982–93; Prof. of Latin, 1993–95; Prof. of Latin, Univ. of Reading, 1995–97. Vis. Sen. Res. Fellow, St John's Coll., Oxford, 1994–95. FAHA 2002. *Publications:* The Text and Language of a Vulgar Latin Chronicle (Anonymus Valesianus), 1976; The Vulgar Latin of the Letters of Claudius Terentianus, 1977; The Latin Sexual Vocabulary, 1982; Wackernagel's Law and the Placement of the Copula *Esse* in Classical Latin, 1994; Pelagonius and Latin Veterinary Terminology in the Roman Empire, 1995; Bilingualism and the Latin Language, 2003; The Regional Diversification of Latin 200 BC–AD 600, 2007; articles in learned jls. *Recreation:* cricket. *Address:* All Souls College, Oxford OX1 4AL.

ADAMS, Jennifer, LVO 1993; OBE 2008; Director of Open Spaces, City of London Corporation (formerly Corporation of London), 2001–08; *b* 1 Feb. 1948; *d* of Arthur Roy Thomas Crisp and Joyce Muriel Crisp (*née* Davey); *m* 1968, Terence William Adams. *Educ:* City of London School for Girls. Final Diploma, Inst. of Leisure and Amenity (FILAM DipPRA); FIHort. Various positions in Parks Dept, London Borough of Wandsworth, 1971–83; Superintendent, Central Royal Parks, later Manager, Inner Royal Parks, 1983–97; Hd of Inner Parks and Commerce, Royal Parks, 1997–2001. Pres., Inst. of Horticulture, 1996–98. Liveryman, Gardeners' Co., 1985. Associate of Honour, RHS, 1999. *Recreations:* walking, gardening, nature conservation.

ADAMS, John; composer; *b* 15 Feb. 1947. *Educ:* Harvard Univ. (scholar). Teacher, San Francisco Conservatory of Music, 1972–82; Music Advr, 1978–82, Composer-in-Residence, 1982–85, San Francisco Symphony. *Compositions include: opera:* Nixon in China, 1987; The Death of Klinghoffer, 1990; I Was Looking at the Ceiling and Then I Saw the Sky, 1995; El Niño, 2000; Doctor Atomic, 2005; A Flowering Tree, 2007; *orchestral works:* Shaker Loops, 1978; Common Tones in Simple Time, 1979; Harmonium, 1980–81; Grand Pianola Music, 1981–82; Harmonielehre, 1984–85; The Chairman Dances, 1985; Short Ride in a Fast Machine, 1986; Tromba Lontana, 1986; Fearful Symmetries, 1988; The Wound-Dresser, 1988–89; Eros Piano, 1989; El Dorado, 1991; Violin Concerto, 1993 (Grawemeyer Award for Music Composition, 1995); Gnarly Buttons, 1996; Century Rolls, piano concerto, 1998; Guide to Strange Places, 2002; My Father Knew Charles Ives, 2003; The Dharma at Big Sur, 2004; *chorus and orchestra:* On the Transmigration of Souls, 2002 (Pulitzer Prize, 2003); *chamber and ensemble works:* Christian Zeal and Activity, 1973; China Gates, 1977; Phrygian Gates, 1977; Chamber Symphony, 1992; John's Book of Alleged Dances, 1994; Road Movies, 1995; numerous recordings. *Address:* c/o Boosey & Hawkes Music Publishers Ltd, Aldwych House, 71–91 Aldwych, WC2B 4HN.

ADAMS, John Crawford, OBE 1977; MD, MS, FRCS; orthopædic practice, retired; Hon. Consulting Orthopædic Surgeon, St Mary's Hospital, London, 1979; Hon. Civil Consultant in Orthopædic Surgery, Royal Air Force, 1984 (Civil Consultant, 1964–84); *b* 25 Sept. 1913; *s* of Archibald Crawford Adams, W Hallam, Derbys; *m* 1940, Joan Bower Elphinstone (*d* 1981); *m* 1990, Marguerite Kyle. *Educ:* MB, BS 1937; MRCS 1937; LRCP 1937; FRCS 1941; MD (London) 1943; MS (London) 1965. Formerly: Chief Asst, Orthopædic and Accident Dept, London Hosp.; Orthopædic Specialist, RAFVR; Resident Surgical Officer, Wingfield-Morris Orthopædic Hosp., Oxford; Consultant Orthopædic Surgeon: St Mary's Hosp., London and Paddington Green Children's Hosp., 1948–79; Brighton Gen. Hosp., 1948–58; St Vincent's Orthopædic Hosp., Pinner, 1952–65. FRSocMed 1948 (Hon. Mem., Sect. of Orthopædics, 1986); Hon. Fellow: British Orthopædic Assoc., 1994 (Hon. Sec., 1959–62; Vice-Pres., 1974–75; Robert Jones Gold Medal and Prize, 1961); Amer. Acad. of Orthopædic Surgeons, 1975. Mem., Council, Jl of Bone and Joint Surgery, 1974–84 (formerly Production Editor). *Publications:* (contrib.) Techniques in British Surgery, ed Maingot, 1950; Outline of Orthopædics, 1956, 14th edn 2007; Outline of Fractures, 1957, 11th edn 1999; Ischio-femoral Arthrodesis, 1966; Arthritis and Back Pain, 1972; Standard Orthopædic Operations, 1976, 4th edn 1992; Shakespeare's Physic, Lore and Love, 1989, new edn as Shakespeare's Physic, 2000; Francis, Forgiven Fraud, 1991; Associate Editor and contributor, Operative Surgery (ed Rob and Smith); contributions to the Journal of Bone and Joint Surgery, etc. *Recreations:* history, writing, silversmithing. *Address:* The Old H H Inn, Cheriton, Alresford, Hampshire SO24 0PY.

ADAMS, Rev. (John) David (Andrew); Headmaster, Weydon School, 1982–98; Chaplain to the Queen, 1994–2007; Secondary School consultant, since 1998; *b* 27 Nov. 1937; *s* of John McCullough McConnell Adams and Sylvia Pansy (*née* Pinner); *m* 1970, Maria Carmen de Azpiazu-Cruz; one *s* one *d*. *Educ:* Trinity Coll., Dublin (BA 1960; Div. Test. 1961; MA 1964; BD 1965); Univ. of Reading (MEd 1974). Curate, St Stephen's, Belfast, 1962–65; part-time teaching and vol. chaplaincy in Europe, 1965–67; Hd, Religious Educn, Tower Ramparts, Ipswich, 1967–70; Counsellor, later Sen. Teacher, Robert Haining Sch., Surrey, 1970–74; Headmaster, St Paul's, Addlestone, 1974–82. Non-stipendiary Curate, St Thomas-on-the-Bourne, Farnham, 1976–2007. *Recreations:* gardening, household chores, birding; the life of George Morley, Bishop of Winchester, 1597–1684. *Address:* Brookside Farm, Oast House Crescent, Farnham, Surrey GU9 0NP. *T:* (01252) 652737.

ADAMS, His Honour John Douglas Richard; a Circuit Judge, 1998–2002; *b* 19 March 1940; *o s* of late Gordon Arthur Richard Adams and Marjorie Ethel Adams (*née* Ongley); *m* 1966, Anne Easton Todd, *o d* of late Robert Easton Todd and Mary Ann Margaret Todd; two *d*. *Educ:* Watford Grammar School; Durham Univ. (LLB 1963). Called to Bar, Lincoln's Inn, 1967; Bencher, Inner Temple, 1997. Lecturer: Newcastle Univ., 1963–71; University College London, 1971–78; also practised at Revenue Bar until 1978; Special Comr of Income Tax, 1978–82; Registrar of Civil Appeals, 1982–98; a Recorder, 1992–98. Hon. Lecturer, St Edmund Hall, Oxford, 1978–2008; Vis. Lectr, Oxford Univ., 1995–2008. Mem. Bd of Trustees, Hospice of St Francis, Berkhamsted, 2004–. *Publications:* (with J. Whalley) The International Taxation of Multinational Enterprises, 1977; (contrib.) Atkin's Court Forms, 1984, 1992; (ed jtly) Supreme Court Practice, 1985, 1991, 1993, 1995, 1997, 1999; (ed jtly) Chitty and Jacob's Queen's Bench Forms, 21st edn, 1986; (ed jtly) Sweet & Maxwell's County Court Litigation, 1993; (ed jtly) Emergency Remedies in the Family Courts, 3rd edn, 1997; (ed jtly) Jordan's Civil Court Service, 2002; (ed jtly) Halsbury's Laws of England, 4th edn, vol. 10. *Recreations:* music, walking, dining. *Address: e-mail:* johndradams@btinternet.com.

ADAMS, Rear-Adm. John Harold, CB 1967; LVO 1957; Senior Partner, John Adams Interviews, 1993–99; *b* Newcastle-on-Tyne, 19 Dec. 1918; *m* 1st, 1943, Mary Parker (marr. diss. 1961); one *s* decd; 2nd, 1961, Ione Eadie, MVO, JP (*d* 1998); two *s* two *d*. *Educ:* Glenalmond. Joined Navy, 1936; Home Fleet, 1937–39; Western Approaches, Channel and N Africa, 1939–42 (despatches); Staff Capt. (D), Liverpool, 1943–45; Staff Course, Greenwich, 1945; HMS Solebay, 1945–47; HMS Vernon, 1947–49; jssc 1949; comd HMS Creole, 1950; Staff Flag Officer Submarines, 1951–52; TAS, Warfare Div., Admty, 1953; Comdr, HM Yacht Britannia, 1954–57; Asst Dir, Underwater Weapons Matériel Dept, 1957–58; Capt. (SM) 3rd Submarine Sqdn, HMS Adamant, 1958–60; Captain Supt, Underwater Detection Estab., Portland, subseq. Admty Underwater Weapons Estab., 1960–62; idc 1963; comd HMS Albion, 1964–66; Asst Chief of Naval Staff (Policy), 1966–68; retd 1968. Lieut 1941; Lieut-Comdr 1949; Comdr 1951; Capt. 1957; Rear-Adm. 1966. Dir, Paper and Paper Products Industry Training Bd, 1968–71; Dir, Employers' Federation of Papermakers and Boardmakers, 1972–73; Dir Gen., British Paper and Board Industry Fedn, 1974–83. Dir, DUO (UK) Ltd, 1983–93. Chm. Governors, Cheam Sch., 1975–87. Paper Industry Gold Medal, 1984. *Recreations:* fishing, photography. *Address:* Yew Tree Cottage, Ibworth, Tadley, Hants RG26 5TJ. *Club:* Army and Navy.

ADAMS, Prof. John Norman; Professor of Intellectual Property, University of Sheffield, 1994–2005, now Emeritus; barrister; *b* 24 Dec. 1939; *s* of Vincent Smith Adams and Elsie Adams (*née* Davison), Gateshead. *Educ:* Newcastle upon Tyne Royal GS; Univ. of Durham. Called to the Bar, Inner Temple, 1984. Solicitor in private practice, 1965–71; Lectr in Law, Univ. of Sheffield, 1971–79; Sen. Lectr, 1979–87, Prof. of Commercial Law, 1987–94, Univ. of Kent. Dir, Intellectual Property Inst., 1991–99. Adjunct Prof. of Law, Notre Dame Law Sch., 2005–. *Publications include:* (with K. V. Prichard-Jones) Franchising, 1981, 5th edn (with K. V. Prichard-Jones and J. Hickey) 2005; (with G. Averley) A Bibliography of Eighteenth Century Legal Literature, 1982; Character Merchandising, 1987, 3rd edn (with J. Hickey and G. Tritton) 2007; (with R. Brownsword) Understanding Contract Law, 1987, 5th edn 2007; Commercial Hiring and Leasing, 1989; (with R. Brownsword) Understanding Law, 1992, 4th edn 2005; (with R. Brownsword) Key Issues in Contract, 1995; (ed) Atiyah's Sale of Goods, 11th edn 2005. *Recreations:* music, walking. *Address:* 26 Priory Terrace, NW6 4DM. *T:* (020) 7328 8676; 49 Endcliffe Hall Avenue, Sheffield S10 3EL. *T:* (0114) 268 7311; Hogarth Chambers, 5 New Square, Lincoln's Inn, WC2A 3RJ. *Clubs:* Savage, Lansdowne.

ADAMS, His Honour (John) Roderick (Seton); a Circuit Judge, 1990–2003; *b* 29 Feb. 1936; *s* of George Adams and Winifred (*née* Wilson); *m* 1965, Pamela Bridget, *e d* of Rev. D. E. Rice, MC; three *s*. *Educ:* Whitgift Sch.; Trinity Coll., Cambridge. BA, 1959, MA 1963. Commnd, Seaforth Highlanders, 1955–56; Parachute Regt, TA, 1959–66. Legal Adviser in industry, 1960–66. Called to the Bar, Inner Temple, 1962; began practice at the Bar, 1967; Dep. Circuit Judge, 1978–80; a Recorder, 1980–90. *Recreations:* hill-walking, fishing, growing old roses. *Address:* 8 Melville Road, Eskbank, Midlothian EH22 3BY. *T:* (0131) 654 9274; Melness House, Sutherland IV27 4YR. *T:* (01847) 601255.

ADAMS, Major Kenneth Galt, CVO 1979; CBE 1989; Hon. Industry Fellow, Comino Foundation, since 1997; *b* 6 Jan. 1920; *s* of late William Adams, OBE, and Christina Elisabeth (*née* Hall); *m* 1988, Sally, *d* of late Col John Middleton and *widow* of Douglas Long. *Educ:* Doncaster Grammar Sch.; Staff Coll., Camberley (psc 1953). Served RASC, 1940–59: War Service, ME and N Africa; DADST WO, 1946–48; DAA&QMG, Aldershot, 1952; DAQMG HQ Northern Comd, 1954–56; Sen. Instr, RASC Officers Sch., 1956–59. Sec., S London Indust. Mission, 1959–61; Proprietors of Hay's Wharf Ltd, 1960–70, Exec. Dir, 1966–70; non-exec. dir and consultant, other cos, until 1985. St George's House, Windsor Castle: Dir of Studies, 1969–76; Fellow, 1976–82; Hon. Fellow, 1990–. Comino Fellow, RSA, 1979–89; Industry Fellow, Comino Foundn, 1989–96. Chairman: S London Indust. Mission, 1971–74; Indust. Christian Fellowship, 1977–86; Vice Chairman: Archbishops' Council on Evangelism, 1965–77; Southwark Cathedral Council, 1967–70; Member: Indust. Cttee, Bd for Social Responsibility of C of E, 1973–81; Bldg EDC, NEDC, 1977–81; Prof. Standards Cttee, BIM, 1976–81; Dept of Employment's Services Resettlement Cttee for SE England, 1967–77; Adv. Cttee, Christian Assoc. of Business Execs, 1975–96 (Pres., 2004–); Adv. Cttee, Inst. of Business Ethics, 1986–96; Hon. Mem., Foundn for Manufg and Industry (Chm., 1993); Trustee, Industrial Trng Foundn, 1980–91. Lay Steward, St George's Chapel, Windsor, 1969–. Freeman: City of London, 1967; Cooks' Co., 1967; Liveryman, Pattenmakers' Co., 1976–96. CCMI (CBIM 1972); FRSA 1979. MA Lambeth, 1979; Hon. DPhil Internat. Management Centres, 1991. Templeton Award, 1996. *Publications:* lectures and papers on developing an affirmative cultural attitude to industry in Britain, and on Christianity and wealth creation. *Recreations:* 19th century novels, pilgrimages. *Address:* 8 Datchet Road, Windsor, Berks SL4 1QE. *T:* (01753) 869708.

ADAMS, Lewis Drummond, OBE 1999; General Secretary, Associated Society of Locomotive Engineers and Firemen, 1994–99; *b* London, 16 Aug. 1939; *s* of Lewis John Adams and Margaret (*née* Drummond); *m* 1958, Jean Marion Bass; one *s* one *d*. *Educ:* Impington Coll., Cambridge; NCLC; Tavistock Inst., London. British Railways: engine cleaner, 1954–55; engine fireman and driver asst, 1955–67; engine driver, 1967–80. Associated Society of Locomotive Engineers and Firemen: Sec., London Dist Council No 1, 1970–80; Executive Committee: Mem., 1981–90; Vice-Pres., 1985–90; Asst Gen. Sec., 1990–93. British Railways: Mem., later Chm., Pension Fund, 1982–93; Member: Wages Grade Pension Fund, 1982–93; Superannuation Fund, 1982–93. Dir, Millennium Drivers Ltd, 1998–. Bd Mem., SRA, 1999–2004. Member: TUC Pension Cttee, 1987–90; Railway Industries Adv. Cttee, 1985–90; British Transport Police Authy, 2004– (Mem. Mgt Cttee, Superannuation Pension Fund, 2006–). *Recreations:* travel, gardening.

ADAMS, Rev. Prof. Marilyn McCord, PhD; Regius Professor of Divinity, University of Oxford, since 2004; Canon Residentiary of Christ Church, Oxford, since 2003; *b* 12 Oct. 1943; *d* of William Clark McCord and Wilmah Brown McCord; *m* 1966, Prof. Robert Merrihew Adams, *qv*. *Educ:* Univ. of Illinois (AB); Cornell Univ. (PhD 1967); Princeton Theol. Seminary (ThM 1984, 1985). University of California, Los Angeles: Associate Prof. of Philosophy, 1972–78; Prof., 1978–93; Chair of Philosophy, 1985–87; Prof. of Histl Theology, 1993–2003, Horace Tracy Pitkin Prof. of Histl Theology,

1998–2003, Yale Univ. Divinity Sch. Ordained deacon and priest, Episcopal Church, USA, 1987; served in parishes in LA and New Haven, Conn. *Publications:* (with Norman Kretzmann) Ockham's Treatise on Predestination, God's Foreknowledge, and Future Contingents, 1969, 2nd edn 1983; (trans.) Paul of Venice, On the Truth and Falsity of Propositions and On the Significatum of a Proposition, 1977; William Ockham, 2 vols, 1987; (ed with Robert Merrihew Adams) The Problem of Evil, 1990; Horrendous Evils and the Goodness of God, 1999; Wrestling for Blessing, 2005; Christ and Horrors: the coherence of Christology, 2006; articles in learned jls. *Address:* Christ Church, Oxford OX1 1DP.

ADAMS, Air Vice-Marshal Michael Keith, CB 1986; AFC 1970; FRAeS; *b* 23 Jan. 1934; *s* of late William Frederick Adams and Jean Mary Adams; *m* 1966, Susan (*née* Trudgian); two *s* one *d. Educ:* Bedford Sch.; City of London Sch. FRAeS 1978. Joined RAF, 1952; qualified Pilot, 1954; Flying Instr, 1960; Test Pilot, 1963 (QCVSA 1967); Staff Coll., Toronto, 1969; CO Empire Test Pilots' Sch., 1975; Dir of Operational Requirements, 1978–81; RCDS, 1982; AOC Training Units, 1983; ACAS (Op. Requirements), MoD, 1984; ACDS (Op. Requirements) Air, MoD, 1985–86; Sen. Directing Staff (Air), RCDS, 1987–88; retd. Dir, Thomson-CSF (UK) Ltd, 1988–94; Dir, International Aerospace, 1989–96 (Chm., 1996). Vice-Pres., RAeS, 1992–95. Chm. Govs, Duke of Kent Sch., Cranleigh, Surrey, 1997–2003. *Recreations:* walking, silversmithing.

ADAMS, Paul Nicholas; Chief Executive, British American Tobacco plc, since 2004; *b* 12 March 1953; *s* of Peter Adams and Joan Adams (*née* Smith); *m* 1978, Gail Edwina McCann; one *s* two *d. Educ:* Culford Sch.; Ealing Coll., London (BA Hons 1977). Mktg Dir, Beecham Products Internat., 1983–86; Vice Pres. Mktg Europe, Pepsi-Cola Internat., 1986–91; British American Tobacco plc: Regl Dir, Asia Pacific, 1991–98, Europe, 1999–2001; Dep. Man. Dir, 2001; Man. Dir, 2002–03. Non-exec. Dir, Allied Domecq plc, 2003–05. *Recreations:* shooting, theatre, Rugby. *Address:* British American Tobacco plc, Globe House, 4 Temple Place, WC2R 2PG. *T:* (020) 7845 1000.

ADAMS, Piers Dermot Meredith; musician; professional virtuoso recorder player, since 1985; *b* 21 Dec. 1963; *s* of late John Adams and of Susan Adams; partner, Julia Bishop; one *d. Educ:* Reading Bluecoat Sch.; Univ. of Bristol (BSc Physics 1984); Guildhall Sch. of Music & Drama (Cert. Perf. in Early Music 1985). Winner (jtly), Moeck Recorder Competition, 1985; début recital, Wigmore Hall, London, 1985; performed, 1986–, in all Europ. countries, most US states, Canada, Mexico, Cuba, Russia, China, Japan, Singapore, Thailand and Australia; soloist: in all South Bank concert halls, London; with many orchs incl. BBC Symphony, Philharmonia, Acad. of Ancient Music and Singapore Symphony; commnd over 25 works by mod. composers, 1986–; Founder and Dir, Red Priest (cult baroque ensemble), 1997–; performed private concerts for the Prince of Wales and the Duke of Edinburgh, 2001, 2002; frequent radio broadcasts; many TV appearances. Ten CD recordings (début CD, 1988). *Recreation:* conspiracy research (9/11, moon landings, JFK, etc). *Address:* c/o Maureen Phillips, Upbeat Classical Management, PO Box 479, Uxbridge UB8 2ZH. *T:* (01895) 259441, *Fax:* (01895) 259341; *e-mail:* admin@upbeatclassical.co.uk.

ADAMS, Richard Borlase, CBE 1983; Managing Director, Peninsular & Oriental Steam Navigation Co., 1979–84 (Director, 1970, Deputy Managing Director, 1974); *b* 9 Sept. 1921; *s* of James Elwin Cokayne Adams and Susan Mercer Porter; *m* 1951, Susan Elizabeth Lambert; two *s* one *d. Educ:* Winchester Coll.; Trinity Coll., Oxford, 1940. War service, Rifle Bde, 1940–46 (Major). Mackinnon Mackenzie Gp of Cos, Calcutta, New Delhi and Hongkong, 1947–63; Chm., Islay Kerr & Co. Ltd, Singapore, 1963–66; British India Steam Navigation Co. Ltd: Dir, 1966; Man. Dir, 1969; Chm., 1970. Dir, Clerical, Medical & General Life Assurance Soc., 1975–88.

ADAMS, Richard Clive; Chairman, Crosswater Solutions Ltd, since 2000; *b* 22 June 1945; *s* of William Henry Adams and Alberta Sarah Adams (*née* Steed); *m* 1971, Elizabeth Anne Coleman; two *s. Educ:* Cotham Grammar Sch., Bristol; Exeter Univ. (BA). Post Office: Asst Postal Controller, 1966–78; Dir of Studies, PO Mgt Coll., 1978–82; Head Postmaster, Northampton, 1982–85; Asst Dir, Corporate Planning, 1985–92; Gp Planning Dir, 1992–97; Sec., 1997–99. Chm., Postal and Logistics Consulting Worldwide Ltd, 2003–06. Mem. Council, CBI, 1998–99. Sec., Postal Heritage Trust, 2004–. *Recreations:* applied arts, railways, wine. *Address:* 48 Overton Drive, Wanstead, E11 2NJ. *T:* (020) 8989 0021.

ADAMS, Richard George; author; *b* 9 May 1920; *s* of Evelyn George Beadon Adams, FRCS, and Lilian Rosa Adams (*née* Button); *m* 1949, Barbara Elizabeth Acland; two *d. Educ:* Bradfield Coll., Berks; Worcester Coll., Oxford (MA, Mod. Hist.). Entered Home Civil Service, 1948; retd as Asst Sec., DoE, 1974. Wrter-in-residence: Univ. of Florida, 1975; Hollins Univ., Virginia, 1976. Pres., RSPCA, 1980–82. Carnegie Medal, 1972; Guardian Award for Children's Literature, 1972. FRSL 1975. *Publications:* Watership Down, 1972 (numerous subseq. edns in various languages; filmed 1978); Shardik, 1974; (with Max Hooper) Nature through the Seasons, 1975; The Tyger Voyage, 1976; The Ship's Cat, 1977; The Plague Dogs, 1977 (filmed 1982); (with Max Hooper) Nature Day and Night, 1978; The Girl in a Swing, 1980 (filmed 1988); The Iron Wolf, 1980; (with Ronald Lockley) Voyage through the Antarctic, 1982; Maia, 1984; The Bureaucats, 1985; A Nature Diary, 1985; (ed and contrib.) Occasional Poets (anthology), 1986; The Legend of Te Tuna, 1986; Traveller, 1988; The Day Gone By (autobiog.), 1990; Tales from Watership Down, 1996; The Outlandish Knight, 2000; Daniel, 2006. *Recreations:* folk-song, chess, fly-fishing. *Address:* 26 Church Street, Whitchurch, Hants RG28 7AR.

ADAMS, Prof. Robert Merrihew, PhD; FBA 2006; Senior Research Fellow, Mansfield College, Oxford, and Visiting Professor, University of Oxford, since 2004; *b* 8 Sept. 1937; *s* of Rev. Arthur Merrihew Adams and Margaret Baker Adams; *m* 1966, Marilyn McCord (*see* Rev. Prof. M. McC. Adams). *Educ:* Princeton Univ. (AB 1959); Mansfield Coll., Oxford (BA 1961, MA 1965); Princeton Theological Seminary (BD 1962); Cornell Univ. (MA 1967; PhD 1969). Pastor, Montauk Community Ch (Presbyterian), Montauk, NY, 1962–65; Lectr, 1968, Asst Prof., 1969–72, Univ. of Michigan, Ann Arbor; University of California, Los Angeles: Assoc. Prof., 1972–76; Prof., 1976–93; Chm., Philos. Dept, 1975–79; Yale University: Prof., 1993–2003; Clark Prof. of Philos., 1995–2003, Emeritus, 2004–; Chm., Philos. Dept, 1993–2001. Wilde Lectr in Natural Religion, Univ. of Oxford, 1989; Gifford Lectr, Univ. of St Andrews, 1999. Fellow, Amer. Acad. of Arts and Scis, 1991. *Publications:* The Virtue of Faith and Other Essays in Philosophical Theology, 1987; (ed with Marilyn McCord Adams) The Problems of Evil, 1990; Leibniz: determinist, theist, idealist, 1994; Finite and Infinite Goods: a framework for ethics, 1999; A Theory of Virtue, 2006; jl articles on topics in ethics, metaphysics, philos. of religion and hist. of mod. philos. *Recreations:* travel, museum visits, birdwatching. *Address:* Mansfield College, Oxford OX1 3TF.

ADAMS, Robin; *see* Adams, D. R. H.

ADAMS, Roderick; *see* Adams, J. R. S.

ADAMS, Suzanne; *see* Cory, S.

ADAMS, Terence David, CMG 1997; FGS; Managing Director, Monument Oil and Gas, 1998–2000; *b* 22 Feb. 1938; *s* of F. E. Adams and E. S. Adams; *m* 1990, Caroline Mary (*née* Hartley); two *s* four *d* by previous marriage. *Educ:* UCW, Aberystwyth (BSc Hons; PhD 1963; Fellow, 2002); Univ. of Dundee (LLM 2004). FGS 1963. International service in petroleum industry with Shell and BP, 1959–98; served in N America, Europe, ME and SE Asia. Pres., Azerbaijan Internat. Operating Co., Baku, 1994–98. Sen. Associate, Cambridge Energy Associates, Cambridge, Mass, 2001–. British Oil Advr, Coalition Provisional Authy, Iraq, 2003–04. Mem. Council, RSAA, 1999–2002. Fellow, East-West Inst., NY, 1999–2002. Medal of Honour, Republic of Azerbaijan, 1998; Hon. Citizen, Republic of Georgia, 1999. *Publications:* numerous scientific articles on micropalaeontology, geomorphology and world energy predictions. *Recreations:* archaeology, palaeontology, music, literature. *Address:* 2 Pearsons Road, Holt, Norfolk NR25 6EJ. *T:* (01263) 711443. *Clubs:* Royal Commonwealth Society; Tanglin (Singapore).

ADAMS, Sir (William) James, KCMG 1991 (CMG 1976); HM Diplomatic Service, retired; Consultant, Control Risks Group, 1992–2001; *b* 30 April 1932; *s* of late William Adams and late Norah (*née* Walker); *m* 1961, Donatella, *d* of late Andrea Pais-Tarsilia; two *s* one *d. Educ:* Wolverhampton Grammar Sch.; Shrewsbury Sch.; Queen's Coll., Oxford. 2nd Lieut RA, MELF, 1950–51. Foreign Office, 1954; MECAS, 1955; 3rd Sec., Bahrain, 1956; Asst Political Agent, Trucial States, 1957; FO, 1958; 2nd Sec., 1959; Manila, 1960; 1st Sec. and Private Sec. to Minister of State, FO, 1963; 1st Sec. (Information), Paris, 1965–69; FCO, 1969; Counsellor, 1971; Head of European Integration Dept (2), FCO, 1971–72; seconded to Economic Commn for Africa, Addis Ababa, 1972–73; Counsellor (Developing Countries), UK Permanent Representation to EEC, 1973–77; Head of Chancery and Counsellor (Economic), Rome, 1977–80; Asst Under-Sec. of State (Public Depts, then Energy), FCO, 1980–84; Ambassador and Consul-Gen. to Tunisia, 1984–87; Ambassador to Egypt, 1987–92. Chm., Egyptian-British Chamber of Commerce, 1992–99. Mem., RC Cttee for Other Faiths, 1995–2002. Chm., Egyptian Growth Investment Co. Ltd, 1997–. Order of the Star of Honour (Hon.), Ethiopia, 1965; Order of the Two Niles (Hon.), Sudan, 1965. *Address:* 13 Kensington Court Place, W8 5BJ. *Club:* Reform.

ADAMS, Prof. William Mark, PhD; Moran Professor of Conservation and Development, University of Cambridge, since 2006; Fellow, Downing College, Cambridge, since 2006; *b* 4 July 1955; *s* of Jimmie and Margaret Adams; *m* 1983, Dr Francine Hughes; one *s* one *d. Educ:* Downing Coll., Cambridge (BA 1976; PhD 1984); University Coll. London (MSc). Asst Lectr, 1984–89, Lectr, 1989–99, Reader, 1999–2004, and Prof. of Conservation and Develt, 2005–06, Dept of Geog., Univ. of Cambridge. *Publications:* Nature's Place, 1986; Green Development, 1990, 2nd edn 2002; Wasting the Rain, 1992; Future Nature, 1995; (with M. Mortimore) Working the Sahel, 1999; (with M. Mulligan) Decolonising Nature, 2003; Against Extinction, 2004. *Recreations:* natural history, running, cycling, mountains, beaches, contemporary and folk music. *Address:* Downing College, Cambridge CB2 1DQ.

ADAMS-CAIRNS, (Andrew) Ruaraidh; Head of Litigation Support, since 1995, and Head of Training and Talent Development, since 2004, Savills; *b* 12 Oct. 1953; *s* of late Alastair Adams-Cairns and Fiona Lauder (*née* Paton of Grandhome); *m* 1983, Susan Ann Foll; two *s. Educ:* Gordonstoun Sch.; Reading Univ. (BSc Est. Man.); RMA Sandhurst. FRICS; MCIArb. Commissioned Queen's Own Highlanders, 1971; Platoon Comdr, Germany, UK, Belize, Gibraltar; Royal Guard, Balmoral (Capt.); Intell. Officer, NI, 1978–79. Joined Savills, 1980; Partner in charge, Salisbury office, 1985–87; Dir, Mixed Develt, 1987–91; Man. Dir, Savills Propriedades, Portugal, 1989–96; Dir, Land and Property, 1987–; Dir and Hd, Residential Valuations, 1998–2004. FRGS. *Publications:* occasional contribs to Estates Gazette, Family Law and Liability Today. *Recreations:* field sports, carpentry, tennis. *Address:* Savills, 20 Grosvenor Hill, Berkeley Square, W1X 0HQ. *T:* (020) 7535 2972. *Club:* Army and Navy.

ADAMSON, Hamish Christopher, OBE 1996; Director (International), The Law Society, 1987–95; *b* 17 Sept. 1935; *s* of John Adamson, Perth, Scotland, and Denise Adamson (*née* Colman-Sadd). *Educ:* Stonyhurst Coll.; Lincoln Coll., Oxford (Schol.; MA Hons Jurisprudence). Solicitor (Hons). Law Society: Asst Sec., then Sen. Asst Sec. (Law Reform), 1966–81; Sec., Law Reform and Internat. Relations, 1981–87. Sec., UK Delegn, Council of the Bars and Law Socs of EC, 1981–95; Exec. Sec., Commonwealth Lawyers' Assoc., 1983–95. Chm., Trustee Cttee, Commonwealth Human Rights Initiative, 1993–95; Mem. Bd Trustees, Acad. of European Law, 1995–2003. Dir, Franco-British Lawyers' Soc., 1991–. *Publications:* The Solicitors Act 1974, 1975; Free Movement of Lawyers, 1992, 2nd edn 1998. *Recreations:* plants, books, travel. *Address:* 133 Hartington Road, SW8 2EY.

ADAMSON, Ian; *see* Adamson, S. I. G.

ADAMSON, Martin Gardiner, CA; Chairman, Associated British Foods, since 2002 (non-executive Director, since 1999); *b* Shanghai, 14 Sept. 1939; *s* of Alan S. Adamson and Janet J. Adamson (*née* Gardiner); *m* 1964, Kathleen Jane Darby; two *s* one *d. Educ:* St Mary's Sch., Melrose; Sedbergh Sch. CA (with Dist.) 1962. Trained with Graham, Smart & Annan, Edinburgh, 1957–62; joined Thomson McLintock & Co., London, 1963; Partner, 1967; Staff Partner, i/c audit practice, 1970–83; Man. Partner, London Office, 1983–86, until merger with Peat Marwick Mitchell to form KPMG; mgt roles with KPMG, 1986–96, including: Partner i/c risk mgt; Mem. Bd. *Recreations:* gardening, golf, reading, theatre. *Address:* Associated British Foods plc, Weston Centre, 10 Grosvenor Street, W1K 4QY. *T:* (020) 7399 6500. *Clubs:* Caledonian, MCC; Royal Cinque Ports Golf; Wilderness Golf (Sevenoaks).

ADAMSON, Nicolas Clark, CVO 2008 (LVO 2002); OBE 1982; Private Secretary to the Duke and Duchess of Kent, since 1993; *b* 5 Sept. 1938; *s* of Joseph Clark Adamson and Prudence Mary (*née* Gleeson); *m* 1971, Hilary Jane Edwards; two *d. Educ:* St Edward's Sch., Oxford; RAF Coll., Cranwell. Commnd RAF, 1959; served various fighter Sqdns, UK and ME, 1960–65; Flt Lieut 1962; Flying Instructor, 1965–67; ADC to Chief of Defence Staff, MoD, 1967–69; transferred to FCO, 1969 as First Sec.; served: Brussels (EC), 1972–75; Islamabad, 1979–82; Paris, 1985–90; Counsellor, FCO, 1990–92; attached CBI, 1992–93; retd from FCO, 1993. *Address:* York House, St James's Palace, SW1A 1BQ. *T:* (020) 7930 4872. *Clubs:* Athenæum, Royal Air Force.

ADAMSON, (Samuel) Ian (Gamble), OBE 1998; medical practitioner; Member (UU), Belfast City Council, since 1989 (Lord Mayor of Belfast, 1996–97); *b* 28 June 1944; *s* of John Gamble Sloan Adamson and Jane (*née* Kerr); *m* 1998, Kerry Christian Carson. *Educ:* Bangor GS; Queen's Univ., Belfast (MB, BCh; BAO 1969). DCH RCSI 1974; DCH RCPSG 1974; MFCH 1988; FRIPH (FRIPHH 1998). Registrar in Paediatrics: Royal Belfast Hosp. for Sick Children, 1975–76; Ulster Hosp., Dundonald, 1976–77; specialist in community child health and travel medicine, N and W Belfast HSS Trust (formerly

Community Unit of Mgt), 1981–2004. Mem. (UU) Belfast East, NI Assembly, 1998–2003. Chm., Farset Youth and Community Devclt, 1988–90. Exec. Bd Mem., Assoc. of Port Health Authies, 2005– (Chairman: Border Inspection Post Cttee, 2005–06; Imported Food Cttee, 2006–). First Pres., Ullans Acad., 1992; Founder Rector, 1994, Chm., 1994–2004, Mem., Implementation Gp, 2005–, Ulster-Scots Acad.; Mem., Ulster-Scots Agency, 2003–; Founder Chairman: Somme Assoc., 1989–; Ulster-Scots Lang. Soc., 1992–2002 (Vice-Pres., 2002–); Founder Member: Cultural Traditions Gp, NI CRC, 1988; Ultach Trust, 1990; Pres., Belfast Civic Trust, 2001–. Historical Advr to Rev. Dr Ian R. K. Paisley, MP, 2007–. SBStJ 1998. Fluent in ten langs, incl. Lakota; holds Wisdom-Keeper status among Lakota (Sioux) nation. *Publications:* The Cruthin, 1974, 5th edn 1995; Bangor: light of the world, 1979, 2nd edn 1987; The Battle of Moira, 1980; The Identity of Ulster, 1982, 4th edn 1995; The Ulster People, 1991; 1690, William and the Boyne, 1995; Dalaradia: kingdom of the Cruthin, 1998. *Recreations:* oil painting, theatre, travel. *Address:* Marino Villa, 5 Marino Park, Holywood, Co. Down, N Ireland BT18 0AN. *T:* (028) 9042 1005. *Clubs:* Ulster Reform (Belfast); Clandeboye Golf.

ADCOCK, Christopher John; Chief Financial Officer, since 2003, and Member of Council, since 2007, Duchy of Lancaster; *b* Berlin, 7 Aug. 1962; *s* of Col Alfred John Adcock, OBE and Eileen Joan Adcock (*née* Linton); *m* 1990, Joanna Sarah Mackinder; one *s* one *d*. *Educ:* Wellington Coll., Berks; Exeter Coll., Oxford (BA 1984). ACA 1988. With Ernst & Whinney, 1984–89. *Recreations:* golf, running, tennis, ski-ing. *Address:* Duchy of Lancaster Office, 1 Lancaster Place, WC2E 7ED. *T:* (020) 7269 1700. *Club:* East Berkshire Golf.

ADCOCK, Fleur, CNZM 2008; OBE 1996; FRSL; poet; *b* 10 Feb. 1934; *d* of Cyril John Adcock and Irene Adcock (*née* Robinson); *m* 1952, Alistair Teariki Campbell (marr. diss. 1958); two *s*. *Educ:* numerous schs in England and NZ; Victoria Univ., Wellington, NZ (MA 1st cl. Hons (Classics) 1956). Worked in libraries, NZ, 1959–62; settled in England, 1963; asst librarian, FCO, 1963–79. Arts Council Writing Fellow, Charlotte Mason Coll. of Educn, Ambleside, 1977–78; Northern Arts Fellow in Lit., Univs of Newcastle upon Tyne and Durham, 1979–81; Eastern Arts Fellow, UEA, 1984. FRSL 1984. Awards include: Cholmondeley, Soc. of Authors, 1976; NZ Nat. Book Award, 1984; Queen's Gold Medal for Poetry, 2006. *Publications:* The Eye of the Hurricane, 1964; Tigers, 1967; High Tide in the Garden, 1971; The Scenic Route, 1974; The Inner Harbour, 1979; (ed) The Oxford Book of Contemporary NZ Poetry, 1982; Selected Poems, 1983; (trans.) The Virgin and the Nightingale: medieval Latin poems, 1983; The Incident Book, 1986; (ed) The Faber Book of 20th Century Women's Poetry, 1987; (trans.) Orient Express: poems by Grete Tartler, 1989; Time Zones, 1991; (trans.) Letters from Darkness: poems by Daniela Crasnaru, 1991; (ed and trans.) Hugh Primas and the Archpoet, 1994; (ed jtly) The Oxford Book of Creatures, 1995; Looking Back, 1997; Poems 1960–2000, 2000. *Recreation:* genealogy. *Address:* 14 Lincoln Road, N2 9DL. *T:* (020) 8444 7881.

ADCOCK, Robert Wadsworth, CBE 1992; DL; Chief Executive and Clerk, Essex County Council, 1976–95; *b* 29 Dec. 1932; *s* of Sir Robert Adcock, CBE; *m* 1957, Valerie Colston Robins; one *d* (one *s* decd). *Educ:* Rugby Sch. Solicitor. Asst Solicitor, Lancs CC, 1955–56; Asst Solicitor, Manchester City Council, 1956–59; Sen. Solicitor, Berks CC, 1959–63; Asst Clerk, later Dep. Clerk, Northumberland CC, 1963–70; Dep. Chief Exec., Essex CC, 1970–76; Clerk of Essex Lieutenancy, 1976–95. Assoc. of County Councils: Advisor, Police Cttee, 1976–83; Advisor, Policy Cttee, 1983–95; Chm., Officers Adv. Gp, 1987–95. Hon. Sec., Assoc. of County Chief Executives, 1983–90 (Chm., 1991–92); Chm., Officers Adv. Panel, SE Regional Planning Conference, 1984–88. DL Essex, 1978. *Recreations:* gardening, ornithology. *Address:* The Christmas Cottage, Great Sampford, Saffron Walden, Essex CB10 2RQ. *T:* (01799) 586363. *Club:* Royal Over-Seas League.

ADDERLEY, family name of **Baron Norton**.

ADDERLEY, Mark David; Chief Executive, National Trust for Scotland, since 2007; *b* 15 Jan. 1965; *s* of David Adderley and Gill Adderley (now Boden); *m* 1989, Miranda Jones; four *d*. *Educ:* King Edward's Sch., Birmingham; Emmanuel Coll., Cambridge (BA 1987; MEng 1992); London Business Sch. (MBA). Analyst, then Sen. Analyst, Associate, then Sen. Associate, Gemini Consulting, 1988–94; Head of Ops, then Sen. Manager Group Integration, Royal Bank of Scotland, 1994–2002; Dir, Scottish Water, 2002–07. Dir, Quality Scotland, 2003–07. *Recreations:* family, outdoor activity, sport, keeping track of 5 girls. *Address:* c/o National Trust for Scotland, Wemyss House, 28 Charlotte Square, Edinburgh EH2 4ET. *T:* (0131) 243 9524, *Fax:* (0131) 243 9592; *e-mail:* madderley@nts.org.uk.

ADDINGTON, family name of **Viscount Sidmouth**.

ADDINGTON, 6th Baron *cr* 1887; **Dominic Bryce Hubbard;** *b* 24 Aug. 1963; *s* of 5th Baron Addington and of Alexandra Patricia, *yr d* of late Norman Ford Millar; *S* father, 1982; *m* 1999, (Elizabeth) Ann Morris; one *d*. *Educ:* Aberdeen Univ. (MA Hons). Lib Dem spokesman on disability and on sport, H of L; elected Mem., H of L, 1999. Vice President: British Dyslexia Assoc.; Adult Dyslexia Orgn; UK Sport Assoc. for People with Learning Disability; Lonsdale Sporting Club; Lakenham Hewett RFC. *Recreation:* Rugby football. *Heir:* *b* Hon. Michael Walter Leslie Hubbard [*b* 6 July 1965; *m* 1999, Emmanuella Ononye]. *Address:* House of Lords, SW1A 0PW.

ADDIS, Richard James; Founder and Editor, The Day; *b* 23 Aug. 1956; *s* of Richard Thomas Addis and Jane Addis; *m* 1983, Eunice Minogue (marr. diss. 2000); one *s* two *d*; partner, Helen Slater; two *s*. *Educ:* West Downs Prep. Sch.; Rugby; Downing Coll., Cambridge (MA). Evening Standard, 1985–89; Dep. Editor, Sunday Telegraph, 1989–91; Exec. Editor, Daily Mail, 1991–95; Editor, The Express, 1995–98; Consultant Editor, Mail on Sunday, 1998–99; Editor, The Globe and Mail, Toronto, 1999–2002; Asst Editor, Financial Times, 2002–06. *Recreations:* flute, skipping, mountains, tennis. *Clubs:* Boodle's, Garrick.

ADDISON, family name of **Viscount Addison**.

ADDISON, 4th Viscount *cr* 1945, of Stallingborough; **William Matthew Wand Addison;** Baron Addison 1937; consultant, environmental impact assessment, since 2002; *b* 13 June 1945; *s* of 3rd Viscount Addison and Kathleen Amy, *d* of Rt Rev. and Rt Hon. J. W. C. Wand, PC, KCVO; *S* father, 1992; *m* 1st, 1970, Joanna Mary (marr. diss. 1990), *e d* of late J. I. C. Dickinson; one *s* two *d*; 2nd, 1991, Lesley Ann, *d* of George Colin Mawer. *Educ:* Westminster; King's Sch., Bruton; Essex Inst. of Agriculture. Chm., DCL Telecommunications, 1997–99; Dir, Commensus, 1999–2002. Mem., Cttee on Jt Statutory Instruments, 1993–99. Vice President: Council for Nat. Parks, 1994–; British Trust for Conservation Volunteers, 1996–2006. Pres., Motor Activities Trng Council, 1996–. *Heir:* *s* Hon. Paul Wand Addison, *b* 18 March 1973.

ADDISON, Kenneth George, OBE 1978; company director; Director, 1971–89, and Deputy Chief General Manager, 1976–84, Sun Alliance & London Insurance Group; *b* 1 Jan. 1923; *s* of Herbert George Addison and Ruby (*née* Leathers); *m* 1945, Maureen Newman; one *s* one *d*. *Educ:* Felixstowe Grammar Sch. LLB Hons London. Served RAF, 1942–46. Joined Alliance Assurance Co. Ltd, 1939; various subsequent appts; Asst Sec., Law Fire Insurance Office, 1960–64; Gen. Manager, Sun Alliance & London Insurance Group, 1971. Chm., Bourne Home Devels Ltd, 1989–93; Dir, Sabre Insurance Co. Ltd, 1990–96. Chairman: Fire Insurers' Res. & Testing Orgn, 1977–84; Management Cttee, Associated Insurers (British Electricity), 1977–84; Internat. Oil Insurers, 1979–82; Dir, Insurance Technical Bureau, 1977–84; Advr, Med. Defence Union, 1986–94 (Dir, 1991–94). Chm., Hearing Aid Council, 1971–78. Dir, Croydon Community Trust, 1990–94. FCIS; FCII (Pres., 1980); FCIArb (Pres., 1968–69). *Publications:* papers on insurance and allied subjects. *Recreations:* swimming, carpentry, gardening. *Address:* Ockley, 13 Hillcroft Avenue, Purley, Surrey CR8 3DJ. *T:* (020) 8660 2793.

ADDISON, Mark Eric, CB 2005; Director General, Department for Environment, Food and Rural Affairs, 2001–06; *b* 22 Jan. 1951; *s* of Sydney Robert James Addison and Prudence Margaret Addison (*née* Russell); *m* 1987, Lucinda Clare Booth. *Educ:* Marlborough Coll.; St John's Coll., Cambridge (BA, MA); City Univ. (MBA); Imperial Coll. (DIC, PhD). Department of Employment, 1978–95: Private Sec. to Parly Under-Sec. of State, 1982; Private Sec. to Prime Minister (Home Affairs, then Parly Affairs), 1985–88; Regl Dir for London, Training Agency, 1988–91; Dir, Finance and Resource Management, 1991–94; DoE, 1995–97; Dir, Safety Policy, HSE, 1994–97; Dir, Better Regulation Unit, OPS, 1997–98; Chief Exec., Crown Prosecution Service, 1998–2001. A Civil Service Comr, 2007–. Non-executive Director: Salix Finance Ltd, 2006–; National Archives, 2007–. *Recreations:* classic motorbikes, gardening, photography. *Address:* *e-mail:* mark@addisonbooth.com.

ADDISON, Michael Francis; His Honour Judge Addison; a Circuit Judge, since 1987; *b* 14 Sept. 1942; *s* of late Joseph Addison and Wendy Blyth Addison; *m* 1979, Rosemary Hardy (*d* 1994); one *s*; *m* 1998, Lucy Carter; one *s* one *d*. *Educ:* Eton; Trinity College, Cambridge (BA). Called to the Bar, Inner Temple, 1965. *Recreation:* gardening. *Address:* 2 Harcourt Buildings, Temple, EC4Y 9DB. *T:* (020) 7353 2112.

ADDYMAN, Peter Vincent, CBE 2000; FSA; Director, York Archaeological Trust, 1972–2002; *b* 12 July 1939; *y s* of Erik Thomas Waterhouse Addyman and Evelyn Mary (*née* Fisher); *m* 1965, Shelton (*née* Oliver), Atlanta, Ga; one *s* one *d*. *Educ:* Sedbergh Sch.; Peterhouse, Cambridge (MA). MIFA 1982; FSA 1967. Asst Lectr in Archaeology, 1962–64, Lectr, 1964–67, QUB; Lectr in Archaeol., Univ. of Southampton, 1967–72. Hon. Fellow, Univ. of York, 1972; Hon. Reader, Univ. of Bradford, 1974–81. Directed excavations: Maxey, 1960; Lydford, 1964–67; Ludgershall Castle, 1964–72; Chalton, 1970–72. Vice-President: Council for British Archaeol., 1981–85 (Pres., 1992–95); Royal Archaeol. Inst., 1979–83; Chairman: Standing Conf. of Archaeol Unit Managers, 1975–78; Inst. of Field Archaeologists, 1983–85; Standing Conf. on Portable Antiquities, 1995–2005; Standing Conf. on London Archaeology, 2005–07; Member: RCHM of England, 1997–99; Ancient Monuments Adv. Cttee, 1998–2001, Places of Worship Panel, 2001–04, English Heritage. Chm., Cultural Resource Management Ltd, 1989–95 (Dir, 1979–95); Academic Dir, Heritage Projects Ltd, 1984–2007; Jt Instigator, Jorvik Viking Centre, York. President: Yorks Archaeol Soc., 1999–2005; Yorks Philosophical Soc., 1999–. Trustee, Nat. Coal Mining Mus., 1995–2002. Gov., Co. of Merchant Adventurers of York, 2006–07. Hon. Freeman, City of York, 2008. Honorary Professor: Univ. of Bradford, 1998; Univ. of York, 1998. Hon. DSc Bradford, 1984; DUniv York, 1985. Comdr, Royal Norwegian Order of Merit, 2004. *Publications:* (gen. editor) The Archaeology of York, vols 1–20, 1976–2002; (ed with V. E. Black) Archaeological Papers from York, 1984; papers in archaeol jls. *Recreations:* gardening, watercolours, travel. *Address:* 15 St Mary's, York YO30 7DD. *T:* (01904) 624311. *Club:* Athenæum.

ADEANE, Hon. (George) Edward, CVO 1985; an Extra Equerry to HRH the Prince of Wales, since 1985; *b* 4 Oct. 1939; *s* of Baron Adeane, GCB, GCVO, PC and Lady Adeane. *Educ:* Eton; Magdalene College, Cambridge (MA). Called to Bar, Middle Temple, July 1962. Page of Honour to HM the Queen, 1954–55; Private Sec. and Treas. to HRH the Prince of Wales, 1979–85; Treas. to TRH the Prince and Princess of Wales, 1981–85; Private Sec. to HRH the Princess of Wales, 1984–85. Director: Guardian Royal Exchange plc, 1985–99; Hambros plc, 1992–98; Hambros Bank Ltd, 1986–98 (Exec. Dir, 1991–98); BNP Paribas UK Holdings Ltd, 1998–2005. Mem., British Library Bd, 1993–99. Trustee: Leeds Castle Foundn, 1991–2004; Lambeth Palace Liby, 1991–2002. *Address:* B4 Albany, Piccadilly, W1J 0AN. *T:* (020) 7734 9410.

ADEBOWALE, Baron *cr* 2001 (Life Peer), of Thornes in the County of West Yorkshire; **Victor Olufemi Adebowale,** CBE 2000; Chief Executive Officer, Turning Point, since 2001; *b* 21 July 1962; *s* of Ezekiel Adebowale and Grace Adebowale. *Educ:* Thornes House Sch., Wakefield; Poly of E London. London Borough of Newham: Private Sector Repairs Administrator and Estate Officer, 1983–84; Sen. Estate Manager, 1984–86; Perm. Property Manager, Patchwork Community Housing Assoc., 1986–88; Regl Dir, Ujima Housing Assoc., 1988–90; Dir, Alcohol Recovery Project, 1990–95; Chief Exec., Centrepoint, 1995–2001. Member: Nat. Council, NFHA, 1991; Adv. Gp, New Deal Task Force, 1997–; Nat. Employment Panel, 2000–; Mental Health Task Force. Mem. Council, Inst. for Fiscal Studies. Mem. Bd Trustees, New Economics Foundn. Patron: British Nursing Council on Alcohol; Rich Mix Centre; Azuka. Hon. Vis. Prof., Lincoln Univ. DUniv UCE, 2001; Hon. Dr UEL. *Recreations:* poetry writing, kite flying, music, playing the saxophone. *Address:* Turning Point, Standon House, 21 Mansell Street, E1 8AA. *T:* (020) 7481 7600.

See also M. Adebowale.

ADEBOWALE, Maria; Director, Capacity Global, since 2001; *b* 6 March 1968; *d* of Ezekiel Adebowale and Grace Olurin Adebowale; *m* 2002, Christoph Schwarte; one *d*. *Educ:* Lancaster Univ. (BA Hons Orgn Studies and Business Law); Huddersfield Poly. (Postgrad. Dip. Law); SOAS, London Univ. (LLM Public Internat. Law). Prog. Asst, Climate Change and Trade, Foundn for Internat. Envmtl Law and Develt, 1994–98; Public Law Tutor, SOAS, 1996–97; Dir, Envmtl Law Foundn, 1998–2001. Mem., UK Sustainable Develt Commn, 2000–03 (Chair, World Summit for Sustainable Develt Wkg Gp, 2002); Comr, English Heritage, 2003–. Chair, Waterwise, 2005–. Trustee, Allavida, 2006–; Matron, Women's Envmtl Network, 2006–. FRSA 2001. *Publications:* contribs to acad. and non-acad. pubns on envmt, human rights and envmtl justice. *Recreations:* arguing about politics with my husband, collecting knackered old Penguin paperback books, watching my daughter play. *Address:* Capacity Global, Menier Gallery, 51–53 Southwark Street, SE1 1RU. *T:* (020) 3117 0102; *e-mail:* info@capacity.org.uk.

See also Baron Adebowale.

ADELAIDE, Archbishop of, since 2005; **Most Rev. Jeffrey William Driver;** Metropolitan of South Australia, since 2005; *b* 6 Oct. 1951; *s* of Ernest Leslie Driver and Joyce Mary Driver; *m* 1978, Lindy Mary Muffet; one *s* one *d*. *Educ:* Aust. Coll. of Theol. (ThL 1977, ThSchol 1983); Sydney Coll. of Divinity (MTh 1991). Newspaper journalist, 1970–74. Ordained deacon, 1977, priest, 1978; Asst Curate, dio. Bathurst, 1977–80; Rector: Mid-Richmond, 1980–84; Jamison, ACT, 1984–89; Archdeacon, Young, NSW, 1989–95; Exec. Dir, St Mark's Nat. Theol Centre, 1995–97; Head, Sch. of Theol., Charles Sturt Univ., 1996–97; Diocesan Archdeacon, Canberra, and Rector of Manuka,

1997–2001; Bishop of Gippsland, 2001–05. *Publications:* various articles and reviews in St Mark's Review. *Recreations:* fly-fishing, gardening. *Address:* Bishop's Court, 45 Palmer Place, North Adelaide, SA 5006, Australia.

ADELAIDE, Archbishop of, (RC), since 2001; **Most Rev. Philip Edward Wilson,** DD; *b* 2 Oct. 1950; *s* of John and Joan Wilson. *Educ:* St Joseph's Coll., Hunters Hill, NSW; St Columba's Coll., Springwood; St Patrick's Coll., Manly; Catholic Inst. of Sydney (BTh 1974); JCL 1992, DD 1996, Catholic Univ. of America, Washington. Ordained priest, 1975; Asst Priest, E Maitland, 1975–77; studied RE, NY, 1977–78; Maitland Diocese: Dir of RE, 1978–80; Bishop's Sec. and Master of Ceremonies, 1980–83; Parish Priest, 1983–87; VG, Diocesan Management and Admin, 1987–90; Dir of Tribunal, 1993–94; Bp of Wollongong, 1996–2000; Coadjutor Archbp of Adelaide, 2000–01. Pres., Australian Catholic Bishops' Conf., 2006–. Co-Chm., Nat. Professional Standards Cttee, 2003–. Prelate of Honour, 1995. *Address:* GPO Box 1364, Adelaide, SA 5001, Australia. *T:* (8) 82108108, *Fax:* (8) 82232307; *e-mail:* phwilson@adelaide.catholic.org.au.

ADELAIDE, Dean of; *see* Renfrey, Rt Rev. L. E. W.

ADER, Peter Charles; His Honour Judge Ader; a Circuit Judge, since 1999; *b* 14 May 1950; *s* of late Max Ader and Inge Ader (*née* Nord); *m* 1979, Margaret Taylor (marr. diss. 2005); one *s* two *d*. *Educ:* Highgate Sch.; Southampton Univ. (LLB). Called to the Bar, Middle Temple, 1973; a Recorder, 1995–99. Freeman, Clockmakers' Co., 1998. *Recreations:* squash, tennis, golf, ski-ing, travel. *Address:* 3 Temple Gardens, Temple, EC4Y 9AU. *T:* (020) 7353 3102.

ADÈS, Prof. (Josephine) Dawn, OBE 2002; FBA 1996; Professor of Art History and Theory, University of Essex, since 1989; *b* 6 May 1943; *d* of A. E. Tylden-Pattenson, CSI; *m* 1966, Timothy Raymond Adès; three *s*. *Educ:* St Hilda's Coll., Oxford (BA 1965); MA London 1968. Essex University: Lectr, 1971–85; Sen. Lectr, 1985–88; Reader, 1988–89; Head of Dept of Art History and Theory, 1989–92. Trustee: Tate Gall., 1995–2005; Nat. Gall., 1998–2005; Henry Moore Foundn, 2003–. *Publications:* Dada and Surrealism Reviewed, 1978; Salvador Dali, 1982, 2nd edn 1995; (jtly) The Twentieth Century Poster: design of the avant garde, 1984; (jtly) Francis Bacon, 1985; Photomontage, 1986; Art in Latin America: the modern era 1820–1980, 1989; Andre Masson, 1994; Figures and Likenesses: the paintings of Siron Franco, 1995; Surrealist Art: the Bergman Collection in the Art Institute of Chicago, 1997; (jtly) Marcel Duchamp, 1999; Salvador Dali's Optical Illusions, 2000; Dali: centenary retrospective, 2004; Undercover Surrealism: Georges Bataille and Documents, 2006. *Address:* Department of Art History and Theory, Essex University, Wivenhoe Park, Colchester, Essex CO4 3SQ.
See also T. J. E. Adès.

ADÈS, Thomas Joseph Edmund; composer, pianist and conductor; Artistic Director, Aldeburgh Festival, since 1999; *b* 1 March 1971; *s* of Timothy Adès and Prof. Dawn Adès, *qv*. *Educ:* University Coll. Sch.; Guildhall Sch. of Music and Drama; King's Coll., Cambridge (MA); St John's Coll., Cambridge (MPhil). Composer in Association, Hallé Orch., 1993–95; Lectr, Univ. of Manchester, 1993–94; Fellow Commoner in Creative Arts, Trinity Coll., Cambridge, 1995–97; Benjamin Britten Prof. of Music, RAM, 1997–2000; Musical Dir, Birmingham Contemporary Music Gp, 1998–2000. *Principal compositions:* Five Eliot Landscapes, 1990; Chamber Symphony, 1990; Catch, 1991; Darknesse Visible, 1992; Still Sorrowing, 1993; Life Story, 1993; Living Toys, 1993; … but all shall be well, 1993; Sonata da Caccia, 1993; Arcadiana (for string quartet), 1994; Powder Her Face (Chamber opera), 1995; Traced Overhead, 1996; These Premises are Alarmed, 1996; Asyla, 1997; Concerto Conciso, 1997–98; America (A Prophecy), 1999; Piano Quintet, 2000; Brahms, 2001; The Tempest (opera), 2003; Violin Concerto, 2005; Tevót, 2007. *Address:* c/o Faber Music, 3 Queen Square, WC1N 3AU. *T:* (020) 7833 7911, *Fax:* (020) 7833 7939. *Club:* Black's.

ADETILOYE, Most Rev. Joseph Abiodun; Metropolitan Archbishop and Primate of Nigeria, 1988–99; Bishop of Lagos, 1985–99; *b* 1929. *Educ:* Melville Hall, Ibadan; King's Coll., London (BD); Wycliffe Hall, Oxford. Ordained, dio. of Lagos, 1954; Bossey Ecumenical Inst., 1961–62; Lectr, 1962, Vice Principal, 1963–66, Immanuel Coll., Ibadan; Provost, Ibadan Cathedral, 1966–70; Bishop of Ekiti, 1970–85. Mem., Eames Commn; Chm., Anglican Encounter in the South, 1994–. DD Gen. Theol. Seminary, NY, 1993. *Address:* c/o PO Box 13 (Bishopscourt, 29 Marina), Lagos, Nigeria. *Fax:* (1) 2636026, 2635681.

ADEY, John Fuller; company director; Chief Executive, National Blood Authority, 1993–98; *b* 12 May 1941; *s* of Frank Douglas Adey and Doreen Adey (*née* Fuller); *m* 1965, Marianne Alyce Banning; two *s* two *d*. *Educ:* Glyn GS, Epsom; St Edmund Hall, Oxford (MA); Harvard Univ. (MBA). CEng 1970; MIMechE 1970; MIEE 1976. Graduate Trainee, AEI Ltd, 1963–65; Design Engineer: Montreal Engrg, 1965–67; Nat. Steel & Shipbuilding, San Diego, 1967–70; various positions, Raychem Ltd, 1972–83; Chief Exec., Chemicals and Plastics, Courtaulds, 1983–86; Man. Dir, Baxter Healthcare, 1986–93. Director: API, 1987–97; Seton Healthcare Gp, 1996–98; non-executive Chairman: Adams Healthcare, 1999–2000; Medical Engineering Investments, 2003–05; non-executive Director: Swindon and Marlborough NHS Trust, 2002–06; New Horizons Ltd, 2005–. Chm., Aldbourne Nursing Home, 2000–. A Gen. Comr of Income Tax, 1985–. Trustee, Royal Merchant Navy Sch. Foundn, 1999– (Chm., 2002–); Gov., John o'Gaunt Sch., Hungerford, 2000 (Chm. Govs, 2001–). *Recreations:* tennis, tinkering with old cars, village life. *Address:* The Old Malt House, Aldbourne, Marlborough, Wilts SN8 2DW.

ADIE, Kathryn, (Kate), OBE 1993; author and freelance broadcaster; Presenter, From Our Own Correspondent, BBC Radio 4, since 1998; *b* 19 Sept. 1945; *d* of Babe Dunnet (*née* Issitt), and adopted *d* of late John Wilfrid Adie and Maud Adie (*née* Fambely). *Educ:* Sunderland Church High Sch.; Newcastle Univ. (BA Hons Scandinavian Studies). FJI 1990. Technician and Producer, BBC Radio, 1969–76; Reporter, BBC TV South, 1977–78; Reporter, TV News, 1979–81, Correspondent, 1982; Chief News Correspondent, BBC TV, 1989–2003. Trustee: Imperial War Mus., 1998–2007; Services Sound and Vision Corp., 2004–. Hon. Prof., Broadcasting and Journalism, Univ. of Sunderland, 1995. Freeman, City of London, 1995; Liveryman, Glaziers' Co., 1996. Hon. Freeman, Borough of Sunderland, 1989. Hon. Fellow: Royal Holloway, London Univ., 1996; Univ. of Central Lancs, 2002; Cardiff Univ., 2004; York St John UC, 2006. Hon. MA: Bath, 1987; Newcastle upon Tyne, 1990; MUniv Open, 1996; Hon. DLitt: City, 1989; Loughborough, 1991; Sunderland, 1993; Robert Gordon, 1996; Nottingham, 1998; Nottingham Trent, 1998; DUniv: Anglia Polytechnic Univ., 1999; Oxford Brookes, 2002. RTS News Award, 1981 and 1987, Judges' Award, 1989; Monte Carlo Internat. TV News Award, 1981 and 1990; BAFTA Richard Dimbleby Award, 1989. *Publications:* The Kindness of Strangers (memoirs), 2002; Corsets to Camouflage: women and war, 2003; Nobody's Child: the lives of abandoned children, 2005; Into Danger, 2008. *Address:* c/o PO Box 317, Brentford TW8 8WX. *T:* and *Fax:* (020) 8838 2871.

ADIE, Rt Rev. Michael Edgar, CBE 1994; Bishop of Guildford, 1983–94; *b* 22 Nov. 1929; *s* of Walter Granville Adie and Kate Emily Adie (*née* Parrish); *m* 1957, Anne Devonald Roynon; one *s* three *d*. *Educ:* Westminster School; St John's Coll., Oxford (MA). Assistant Curate, St Luke, Pallion, Sunderland, 1954–57; Resident Chaplain to the Archbishop of Canterbury, 1957–60; Vicar of St Mark, Sheffield, 1960–69; Rural Dean of Hallam, 1966–69; Rector of Louth, 1969–76; Vicar of Morton with Hacconby, 1976–83; Archdeacon of Lincoln, 1977–83. Chm., Gen. Synod Bd of Education and of National Soc., 1989–94. DUniv Surrey, 1995. *Publication:* Held Together: an exploration of coherence, 1997. *Recreations:* gardening, walking. *Address:* Greenslade, Froxfield, Petersfield, Hants GU32 1EB.

ADIE, Susan Myraid; *see* Sinclair, S. M.

ADJAYE, David, OBE 2007; Founder, and Principal Architect, Adjaye Associates, since 2000; *b* 22 Sept. 1966; *s* of Affram Adjaye and Cecilia Affram-Adjaye. *Educ:* South Bank Univ. (BA Hons Arch. 1990; RIBA Pt 1); Royal Coll. of Art, London (MA Arch. 1993; Sen. Fellow 2007). RIBA 1998. *Building projects* include: Nobel Peace Center, Oslo, 2005; Idea Store Whitechapel, London, 2005 (Inclusive Design Award, RIBA, 2006); Bernie Grant Centre, Stephen Lawrence Centre and Rivington Place, London, 2007; Mus. of Contemporary Art, Denver, 2007. Advr, Thames Gateway Design Panel, 2004. Mem. Bd, Greenwich Dance Agency, 2004–; Trustee: Architl Educn Trust; South London Gall., 2003–. Hon. Dr Arts UEL, 2007. First Prize Bronze Medal, RIBA, 1993. *Publications:* (ed Peter Allison) David Adjaye Houses: recycling, reconfiguring, rebuilding, 2005; (ed Peter Allison) David Adjaye: making public buildings, 2006; contribs to jls incl. Frame, Domus, RIBA Jl, Architects Jl, Archithese, Architectural Record, A+U, El Croquis. *Address:* Adjaye Associates, 23–28 Penn Street, N1 5DL. *T:* (020) 7739 4969, *Fax:* (020) 7739 3484; *e-mail:* info@adjaye.com. *Club:* Shoreditch House.

ADKINS, Richard David; QC 1995; *b* 21 Oct. 1954; *s* of Walter David Adkins and Patricia (*née* Chimes); *m* 1977, Jane Margaret, *d* of Derek and Ella Sparrow; two *s* one *d*. *Educ:* Leamington Coll. for Boys; Hertford Coll., Oxford (MA). Admitted as solicitor, 1978; called to the Bar, Middle Temple, 1982. Cttee Mem., Chancery Bar Assoc., 1991–93. *Publications:* Encyclopaedia of Forms and Precedents, Vol. 3: Arrangements with Creditors, 1985; Company Receivers: a new status?, 1988; contrib. Gore Browne on Companies, 50th edn, 1992–. *Recreations:* opera, ski-ing, tennis. *Address:* 3–4 South Square, Gray's Inn, WC1R 5HP. *T:* (020) 7696 9900. *Club:* Bromley Cricket.

ADLER, Prof. Jeremy David, PhD; Professor of German, 1994–2003, Visiting Professor, 2003–05, Emeritus Professor and Senior Research Fellow, Department of German, since 2005, King's College London; *b* 1 Oct. 1947; *s* of H. G. and Bettina Adler; *m* 1983, Eva Mikulašová. *Educ:* St Marylebone GS; Queen Mary Coll., Univ. of London (BA 1st cl. Hons 1969); Westfield Coll., Univ. of London (PhD 1977). Lectr in German, Westfield Coll., 1970–89; Queen Mary and Westfield College, London: Reader, 1989–91; Prof. of German, 1991–94; Founding Chm., Centre for Modern European Studies, 1990–94. Mem., Council, 1997–99, Senate, 2000–01, London Univ. Mem. Council, Poetry Soc., 1973–77; Jt Hon. Sec., English Goethe Soc., 1987–2004; Member: Bielefeld Colloquium für Neue Poesie, 1979–2002; Council, Goethe Ges., Weimar, 1995–2003; Res. Cttee, Freies Deutsches Hochstift, 2003–; Editl Bd, Central Europe, 2003–; Res. Gp on Prague and Dublin Lit., Osaka, 2006–. Chm., M. L. v. Motesiczky Trust, 1997–2006. Schol., Herzog August Bibliothek, Wolfenbüttel, 1979; Fellow, Inst. of Advanced Study, Berlin, 1985–86. Corresp. Mem., German Acad. of Lang. and Lit., 2005. Goethe Prize, English Goethe Soc., 1977. *Publications:* (ed with J. J. White) August Stramm: Kritische Essays und unveröffentliches Quellenmaterial aus dem Nachlass des Dichters, 1979; (ed) Allegorie und Eros: Texte von und über Albert Paris Gütersloh, 1986; Eine fast magische Anziehungskraft: Goethes Wahlverwandtschaften und die Chemie seiner Zeit, 1987; (with Ulrich Ernst) Text als Figur: Visuelle Poesie von der Antike bis zur Moderne, 1987, 3rd edn 1990; (ed) August Stramm: Die Dichtungen, Sämtliche Gedichte, Dramen, Prosa, 1990; (ed) August Stramm: Alles ist Gedicht: Briefe, Gedichte, Bilder, Dokumente, 1990; (ed) Friedrich Hölderlin: Poems and Fragments, 1998; (ed) H. G. Adler: Der Wahrheit verpflichtet, 1998; (ed) E. T. A. Hoffmann: The Life and Opinions of the Tomcat Murr, 1999; (ed) H. G. Adler: Eine Reise, 1999; (ed jtly) F. B. Steiner: Selected Writings, 2 vols, 1999; (ed jtly) Goethe at 250, 2000; (ed) F. B. Steiner: Am Stürzenden Pfad, Gesammelte Gedichte, 2000; Franz Kafka, 2001; (ed jtly) Models of Wholeness, 2002; (ed jtly) From Prague poet to Oxford anthropologist: Franz Buermann Steiner celebrated, 2003; (ed) H. G. Adler: Die Dichtung der Prager Schule, 2003; (ed) H. G. Adler: Theresienstadt 1941–1945, 2005; (ed) E. Canetti: Aufzeichnungen für Marie-Louise, 2005; (ed jtly) Marie-Louise von Motesiczky 1906–1996: the paintings, 2006; (ed jtly) H. G. Adler: über Franz Baermann Steiner, 2006; (ed jtly) F. B. Steiner: Zivilization und Gefahr, 2008; *poetry:* Alphabox, 1973; Alphabet Music, 1974; Fragments Towards the City, 1977; Even in April, Ferrara and Liberty, 1978; A Short History of London, 1979; The Wedding and Other Marriages, 1980; Triplets, 1980; Homage to Theocritus, 1985; Notes from the Correspondence, 1983; The Electric Alphabet, 1986, 3rd edn 2001; To Cythera!, 1993; At the Edge of the World, 1994; Big Skies and Little Stones, 1997; pamphlets; articles in learned jls, daily press, New York Times, TLS, London Rev. of Books. *Recreations:* mountaineering, painting and drawing, music. *Address:* Department of German, King's College London, WC2R 2LS. *T:* (020) 7848 2124.

ADLER, Prof. Michael William, CBE 1999; MD; FRCP, FFPH; Professor of Genito Urinary Medicine and Consultant Physician, University College London (formerly Middlesex Hospital) Medical School, 1979–2004, now Emeritus Professor; *b* 12 June 1939; *s* of late Gerhard and of Hella Adler; *m* 1st, 1966, Susan Jean (marr. diss. 1978); 2nd, 1979, Karen Hope Dunnell, *qv* (marr. diss. 1994); two *d*; 3rd, 1994, Margaret Jay (*see* Baroness Jay of Paddington). *Educ:* Bryanston Sch.; Middlesex Hosp. Med. Sch. MB BS 1965, MD 1977; MRCP 1970, FRCP 1984; FFPH (MFCM 1977, FFCM 1983). House Officer and Registrar in Medicine, Middlesex, Central Middlesex and Whittington Hosps, 1965–69; Lectr, St Thomas' Hosp. Med. Sch., 1970–75; Sen. Lectr, Middlesex Hosp. Med. Sch., 1975–79. Consultant Physician: Middlesex Hosp., 1979–; Camden and Islington Community Health Services NHS Trust, 1992– (non-exec. Dir, 1992–94); non-exec. Dir, Health Develt Agency, 1999–. Advr in Venereology, WHO, 1983–; Department of Health (formerly DHSS): Mem., Expert Adv. Gp on AIDS, 1984–92; Mem., Sub-Gps on Monitoring and Surveillance, 1987–88 and Health Care Workers, 1987–92; Mem., AIDS Action Gp, 1991–92; Mem., Stocktake Gp, 1997–99; Chief Scientist's Advr, Res. Liaison Gp (Child Health), 1985–90; Mem., and Chm. Steering Gp, Develt of Sexual Health and HIV Strategy, 1999–2001. Medical Research Council: Member: Res. Adv. Gp on Epidemiol Studies of Sexually Transmitted Diseases, 1975–80; Working Party to co-ordinate Lab. Studies on the Gonococcus, 1979–83; Working Party on AIDS, 1981–87; Sub-Cttee on Therapeutic Studies, 1985–87; Cttee on Epidemiol Studies on AIDS, 1985–94; Cttee on Clinical Studies of Prototype Vaccines against AIDS, 1987–89; RCS Cttee on HIV infection/AIDS, 1991–96. Member: Med. Adv. Cttee, Brook Adv. Centres, 1984–94; Working Gp on AIDS, European Commn, 1985–; AIDS Working Party, BMA, 1986–92; Exec. Cttee, Internat. Union Against Sexually Transmitted Infections (formerly Against the Venereal Diseases and Treponematoses),

1986–; DFID (formerly ODA) Health and Population Adv. Cttee on R&D, 1995–99; Steering Cttee, Assoc. of NHS Providers of AIDS Care and Treatment, 1996–2003; Exec. Cttee, Assoc. of Genito Urinary Medicine, 1997–99. Mem., Specialist Adv. Cttee on Genito Urinary Medicine, Jt Cttee of Higher Med. Trng, 1981–86 (Sec., 1981–82; Chm., 1983–86). Royal College of Physicians: Member: Cttee on Genito Urinary Medicine, 1984–91 (Sec., 1984–87; Chm., 1987–91); Working Gp on AIDS, FCM (now FPH), 1985–; Lumleian Lectr, 1996; Member Council: Med. Soc. for the Study of Venereal Diseases, 1999–2002 (Pres., 1997–99); RIPH&H, 1993–94; RCP, 1999–2002. Dir, Terrence Higgins Trust, 1982–88; Mem. Governing Council, Internat. AIDS Soc., 1993–98; Trustee, 1987–2000, Chm., 1991–2000, Nat. AIDS Trust (Chm., Grants and Gen. Purposes Cttee, 1988–91); Adviser: AIDS Crisis Trust, 1986–98; Parly All Party Cttee on AIDS, 1987–. Patron, Albany Soc., 1987–91. Evian Health Award, 1990. Member, Editorial Panel: Sexually Transmitted Infections; Current Opinion on Infectious Diseases; Enfermedades de Transmission Sexual; Venereology; also Ed., AIDS, 1986–94; Consultant Editor, AIDS Letter, RSM, 1987–89. *Publications:* ABC of Sexually Transmitted Diseases, 1984, 5th edn 2004; (ed) ABC of AIDS, 1987, 6th edn 2008; (ed) Diseases in the Homosexual Male, 1988; (jtly) Sexual Health and Care Guidelines for Prevention and Treatment, 1998; articles on sexually transmitted diseases and AIDS in med. jls. *Recreations:* yoga, walking, theatre. *Address:* Department of Sexually Transmitted Diseases, Mortimer Market Centre, Capper Street, WC1E 6AU. *T:* (020) 7380 9946.

ADONIS, family name of **Baron Adonis**.

ADONIS, Baron *cr* 2005 (Life Peer), of Camden Town in the London Borough of Camden; **Andrew Adonis;** Minister of State, Department for Transport, since 2008; *b* 22 Feb. 1963; *m* 1994, Kathryn Davies; one *s* one *d. Educ:* Kingham Hill Sch., Oxon; Keble Coll., Oxford; Christ Church, Oxford (DPhil 1988). Mem., HQ Secretariat, British Gas Corp., 1984–85; Nuffield College, University of Oxford: Res. student, 1985–86; Fellow in Politics, 1988–91; Financial Times: Public Policy corresp., 1991–93; Industry corresp., 1993–94; Public Policy Editor, 1994–96; political columnist and contributing editor, The Observer, 1996–98; Mem., Prime Minister's Policy Unit, 1998–2001; Head of Policy, 2001–03, Sen. Advr on Educn and Public Services, 2003–05, Prime Minister's Office. Parly Under-Sec. of State, DFES, later DCSF, 2005–08. Mem., Oxford City Council, 1987–91. *Publications:* Parliament Today, 1990; Making Aristocracy Work: the peerage and the political system in Britain 1884–1914, 1993; (with T. Hames) A Conservative Revolution?: the Thatcher-Reagan decade in perspective, 1994; (with D. Butler and T. Travers) Failure in British Government: the politics of the poll tax, 1994; (with S. Pollard) A Class Act: the myth of Britain's classless society, 1997; (ed with Keith Thomas) Roy Jenkins: a retrospective, 2004. *Address:* House of Lords, SW1A 0PW.

ADRIANO, Dino, FCCA; Director, 1990–2000, Group Chief Executive, 1998–2000, J. Sainsbury plc (Joint Group Chief Executive, 1997–98); Chairman and Chief Executive, Sainsbury's Supermarkets Ltd, 1997–2000; *b* 24 April 1943; *s* of Dante Adriano and Yole Adriano; *m* 1966, Susan Rivett; two *d. Educ:* Highgate Coll.; Strand Grammar Sch. ACCA 1965, FCCA 1980. Articled clerk, George W. Spencer & Co., Chartered Accountants, 1959–64; joined J. Sainsbury plc, 1964: trainee, Accounting Dept, 1964–65; Financial Accounts Dept, 1965–73; Br. Financial Control Manager, 1973–80; Gen. Manager, Homebase, 1981–86; Area Dir, Sainsbury's Central and Western Area, 1986–89; Homebase: Man. Dir, 1989–95; Chm., 1991–96; Shaw's Supermarkets Inc.: Dep. Chm., 1994; Chm., 1994–96; Dir, Giant Food Inc., 1994–96; J. Sainsbury plc: Asst Man. Dir, 1995–96; Dep. Chief Exec., 1996–97. Dir, Laura Ashley plc, 1996–98. Oxfam: Trustee, 1990–96, 1998–2004; Advr on Retail Matters, 1996–98, 2004–06; Vice-Chm., 2001–04; Trustee: WRVS, 2001–07; Sainsbury Archive, 2007–. Chm. Bd Govs, Thames Valley Univ., 2004–. *Recreations:* opera, music, soccer, culinary arts. *Address:* e-mail: dino_adriano@tiscali.co.uk.

ADRIEN, Hon. Sir Maurice L.; *see* Latour-Adrien.

ADSETTS, Sir (William) Norman, Kt 1999; OBE 1988; President, Sheffield Theatres Trust, since 2006 (Chairman, 1996–2006); *b* 6 April 1931; *s* of Ernest Norman Adsetts and Hilda Rachel Adsetts (*née* Wheeler); *m* 1956, Eve Stefanuti; one *s* one *d. Educ:* King Edward VII Sch., Sheffield; Queen's Coll., Oxford (BA 1955; MA). Commissioned RAF, 1950–52; Marketing Manager, Fibreglass Ltd, 1955–66; Sheffield Insulating Co.: Dir, 1966–89; Man. Dir, 1970–85; Chm., 1985–89; Chm., 1989–96, Pres., 1996–, Sheffield Insulations Gp, subseq. SIG plc. Dir, 1988–91, Dep. Chm., 1991–97, Sheffield Develt Corp.; Chairman: Kelham Riverside Develt Agency, 1998–2002; Sheffield Supertram Trust, 1993–98; Sheffield Partnerships, 1988–93; Sheffield First for Investment, 1999–2002. Chairman: Assoc. for Conservation of Energy, 1985–90, 1993–95; Yorkshire Humberside CBI, 1989–91; Pres., Sheffield Chamber of Commerce, 1988–89. Mem., Arts Council England, 2002–05 (Chm., Yorks Arts Regl Council, 2002–05). Trustee, Research Autism, 2006–. Chairman of Governors: Sheffield Hallam Univ., 1993–99; Mount St Mary's Coll., 1999–. Patron of local charities. *Recreations:* reading, family and local history, grandchildren. *Address:* Churchfield House, Rotherham Road, Eckington, Sheffield S21 4FH. *T:* (01246) 431008, *Fax:* (01246) 431009.

ADSHEAD, Fiona Jane, FRCP, FFPH; Deputy Chief Medical Officer, Department of Health, since 2004; *b* 31 July 1962; *d* of late Lt Comdr and Mrs J. R. Adshead. *Educ:* University Coll. London (BSc 1983; MB BS 1986; MSc 1994). MRCP 1989, FRCP 2005; MFPHM 1999, FFPH 2003. Sen. hse officer posts, Nat. Hosp. for Nervous Diseases, Royal Marsden Hosp., Brompton Hosp. and RPMS, 1987–89; Med. Registrar, St George's Hosp., 1989–90; Clinical Res. Fellow, Inst. of Cancer Res. and Royal Marsden Hosp., 1990–92; Registrar, then Sen. Registrar, Croydon HA, 1993–96; Clinical Lectr, St George's Hosp. Med. Sch., 1996–2000; Consultant in Public Health Medicine, Camden and Islington HA, 2000–02; Dir of Public Health, Camden PCT, 2002–04. *Publications:* contrib. numerous articles to scientific jls. *Recreations:* art, travel, gardening, film, theatre. *Address:* Department of Health, Richmond House, 79 Whitehall, SW1A 2NS. *T:* (020) 7210 5640, *Fax:* (020) 7210 5438; *e-mail:* fiona.adshead@dh.gsi.gov.uk.

ADYE, Sir John (Anthony), KCMG 1993; Director, Government Communications Headquarters, 1989–96; *b* 24 Oct. 1939; *s* of Arthur Francis Capel Adye and Hilda Marjorie Adye (*née* Elkes); *m* 1961, Anne Barbara, *d* of Dr John Aeschlimann, Montclair, NJ; two *s* one *d. Educ:* Leighton Park Sch.; Lincoln Coll., Oxford (MA). Joined GCHQ, 1962; Principal, 1968; British Embassy, Washington, 1973–75; Nat. Defence Coll., Latimer, 1975–76; Asst Sec., 1977–83; Under Sec., 1983–89; Dep. Sec., 1989–92; 2nd Perm. Sec., 1992–96. Chairman: Country Houses Assoc., 1999–2002; CPRE Glos, 2005–. Dir, Nat. Biometric Security Project, Washington, 2003–. Gov., Dean Close Sch., Cheltenham. *Address:* c/o Campaign to Protect Rural England, Community House, Gloucester GL1 2LZ. *Club:* Naval and Military.

AFRIYIE, Adam; MP (C) Windsor, since 2005; *b* 4 Aug. 1965. *Educ:* Addey and Stanhope Sch., New Cross; Imperial Coll., London (BSc 1987). Man. Dir, then non-exec. Chm., Connect Support Services, 1993–; Chairman: DeHavilland Inf. Services, 1998–2005; Adfero, 2005–. Opposition frontbench spokesman on innovation, univs and skills, 2007–. Mem. Bd, Policy Exchange, 2003–05. Gov., Mus. of London, 1999–2005. *Address:* (office) 87 St Leonards Road, Windsor SL4 3BZ; House of Commons, SW1A 0AA.

AFSHAR, Baroness *cr* 2007 (Life Peer), of Heslington in the County of North Yorkshire; **Haleh Afshar,** OBE 2005; PhD; Professor of Politics and Women's Studies, University of York, since 1999; *b* 1944; *d* of Hassan Afshar and Pouran Afshar (*née* Khabir); *m* 1974, Maurice Dodson; one *s* one *d. Educ:* Ecole Jean d'Arc, Tehran; St Martin's Sch., Solihull; Davis's Coll., Brighton; Univ. of York (BA Hons Soc. Scis 1967); Univ. of Strasbourg (Diplôme de Droit Comparée Communauté Européen 1972); PhD Land Economy Cantab 1974. Sen. Res. Officer, Ministry of Co-operatives and Rural Develt, Rural Res. Centre, Tehran; Econ. and Envmt Corresp. and Feature Writer, Kayhan International, English lang. daily newspaper, Tehran, 1971–74; Lectr in Develt, Univ. of Bradford, 1976–85; University of York: Dep. Dir and Lectr in Health Econs, Inst. for Res. in Social Scis, 1985–87; Dept of Politics and Centre for Women's Studies, 1987–. Founder and Co-Chm., Muslim Women's Network, 2002–, Chm. and Facilitator, Listening to Women exercise, conducted by Muslim Women's Network and Nat. Commn for Women, 2005–06. Advr to various pts of Govt on public policy on Muslim women and Islamic law; speaker on various media on Muslim community. Member: Wkg Gp on Ethics and Pharmacogenetics, Nuffield Council on Bioethics, 2002–; UK Drug Policy Commn, 2006–; Educn Honours Cttee, 2007–. Launched Democracy Series, Hansard Soc., with Democracy and Islam (pamphlet), 2006. Mem. editl bds of 10 learned jls. *Publications:* Islam and the Post-revolutionary State in Iran (as Homa Omid), 1994; Islam and Feminisms, 1998; edited: Iran: a revolution in turmoil, 1985; Women, Work and Ideology in the Third World, 1985; Women, State and Ideology, 1987; (jtly) Women, Poverty and Ideology, 1989; Women, Development and Survival in the Third World, 1991; (jtly) Women and Adjustment Policies in the Third World, 1992; Women in the Middle East, 1993; (jtly) The Dynamics of Race and Gender, 1994; Women and Politics in the Third World, 1996; (jtly) Empowering Women for Development, 1997; Women and Empowerment: illustrations from the Third World, 1998; (jtly) Women and Globalization and Fragmentation in the Developing World, 1999; (jtly) Development, Women, and War, 2004; (jtly) Women in Later Life, 2008. *Recreations:* music, opera, ballet, movies, books, cooking, entertaining, Paris, the Pennines. *Address:* Department of Politics, University of York, York YO10 5DD.

AGA KHAN (IV), His Highness Prince Karim, granted title His Highness by the Queen, 1957, granted title His Royal Highness by the Shah of Iran, 1959; KBE 2004; *b* Genthod, Geneva, 13 Dec. 1936; *s* of late Prince Aly Salomon Khan and Princess Joan Aly Khan, later Viscountess Camrose (*née* Joan Barbara Yarde-Buller, *e d* of 3rd Baron Churston, MVO, OBE); became Aga Khan, spiritual leader and hereditary Imam of Ismaili Muslims all over the world on the death of his grandfather, Sir Sultan Mahomed Shah, Aga Khan III, GCSI, GCIE, GCVO, 11 July 1957; *m* 1969, Sarah Frances Croker-Poole (marr. diss. 1995); two *s* one *d*; *m* 1998, Princess Gabriele zu Leiningen (Begum Inaara Aga Khan); one *s*, and one step *d. Educ:* Le Rosey, Switzerland; Harvard University (BA Hons 1959). Founder and Chairman: Aga Khan Foundn, Geneva, 1967 (also branches/affiliates in Afghanistan, Bangladesh, Canada, India, Kenya, Kyrgyzstan, Mozambique, Pakistan, Portugal, Syria, Tajikistan, Tanzania, Uganda, UK and US); Aga Khan Award for Architecture, 1977–; Inst. of Ismaili Studies, 1977–; Aga Khan Fund for Econ. Develt, Geneva, 1984–; Aga Khan Trust for Culture, Geneva, 1988; Aga Khan Agency for Microfinance, 2005. Founder and Chancellor: Aga Khan Univ., Pakistan, 1983; Univ. of Central Asia, 2001. Leading owner and breeder of race horses in France, Ireland and UK; won: Derby, 1981 (Shergar), 1986 (Shahrastani), 1988 (Kahyasi), 2000 (Sinndar); Irish Derby, 1981 (Shergar), 1986 (Shahrastani), 1988 (Kahyasi), 2000 (Sinndar), 2003 (Alamshar); King George VI and Queen Elizabeth Diamond Stakes, 2003 (Alamshar), 2005 (Azamour); St James's Palace Stakes, 2004 (Azamour); Prix de L'Arc de Triomphe, 1982 (Akiyda), 2000 (Sinndar), 2003 (Dalakhani); Prix du Jockey Club, 1960 (Charlottesville), 1979 (Top Ville), 1984 (Darshaan), 1985 (Mouktar), 1987 (Natroun), 2003 (Dalakhani); Prix de Diane, 1993 (Shemaka), 1997 (Vereva), 1998 (Zainta), 1999 (Daryaba). Hon. FRIBA 1991; Hon. Mem., AIA, 1992; Hon. Foreign Mem., Amer. Acad. of Arts and Scis. Hon. Prof., Univ. of Osh, Kyrgyzstan, 2002. Doctor of Laws (*hc*): Peshawar, Pakistan, 1967; Sind, Pakistan, 1970; McGill, 1983; McMaster, 1987; Wales, 1993; Brown, 1996; Hon. DLitt London, 1989; DLitt (*hc*) Toronto, 2004; Dr (*hc*) Evora, Portugal, 2006; DHLitt (*hc*) Amer. Univ. Beirut, 2005. Thomas Jefferson Meml Foundn Medal in Architecture, 1984; Amer. Inst. of Architects' Inst. Honor, 1984; Medalla de Oro, Consejo Superior de Colegios de Arquitectos, Spain, 1987; Médaille d'argent, Académie d'Architecture, Paris 1991; Huésped de Honor de Granada, Spain, 1991; Hadrian Award, World Monuments Fund, 1996; Gold Medal, City of Granada, 1998; State Award of Peace and Progress, Kazakhstan, 2002; Vincent Scully Prize, USA, 2005; Die Quadriga, Germany, 2005; Carnegie Medal of Philanthropy, Scotland, 2005. Commandeur, Ordre du Mérite Mauritanien, 1960; Grand Croix: Order of Prince Henry the Navigator, Portugal, 1960; Ordre National de la Côte d'Ivoire, 1965; Ordre National de la Haute-Volta, 1965; Ordre Malgache, 1966; Ordre du Croissant Vert des Comores, 1966; Ordem Militar de Cristo, Portugal, 2005; Order of Merit, Portugal, 1998; Grand Cordon, Order of the Taj, Iran, 1967; Nishan-i-Imtiaz, Pakistan, 1970; Cavaliere, Gran Croce, Ordine al Merito della Republica Italiana, 1977; Grand Officier, Ordre National du Lion, Sénégal, 1982; Nishan-e-Pakistan, Pakistan, 1983; Grand Cordon, Ouissam-al Arch, Morocco, 1986; Cavaliere del Lavoro, Italy, 1988; Commandeur, Légion d'Honneur, France, 1990; Gran Cruz, Orden del Mérito Civil, Spain, 1991; Order of Friendship, Tajikistan, 1998; Order of Bahrain (1st cl.), 2003; Hon. CC, 2004. *Address:* Aiglemont, 60270 Gouvieux, France. *Clubs:* Royal Yacht Squadron; Yacht Club Costa Smeralda (Founder Pres.) (Sardinia).

AGAR, family name of **Earl of Normanton**.

AGARWAL, Prof. Girish Saran, PhD; FRS 2008; Noble Foundation Chair and Regents' Professor, Department of Physics, Oklahoma State University, since 2004; *b* Bareilly, Uttar Pradesh, 7 July 1946; *s* of late Keladevi and Bhagwat Saran; *m* 1970, Sneh (*d* 2006); two *d. Educ:* Banares Hindu Univ., India (MSc 1966); Univ. of Rochester, USA (PhD 1969). Res. Associate, 1969–71, and Asst Prof., 1970–71, Dept of Physics and Astronomy, Univ. of Rochester, NY; Asst Prof., Inst. für Theoretische Physik, Univ. of Stuttgart, 1971–73; Prof. and Hd, Dept of Physics, Inst. of Sci., Bombay, 1975–77; University of Hyderabad: Prof., Sch. of Physics, 1977–95; Dean, Sch. of Physics, 1977–80; Dir and Dist. Scientist, Physical Res. Lab., Ahmedabad, 1995–2005. Albert Einstein Centenary Res. Prof., Indian Nat. Sci. Acad., 2001–05; Hon. Prof., Jawaharlal Nehru Centre for Advanced Scientific Res., Jakkur, Bangalore, 1995–2000; Visiting Professor: Univ. of Ulm, Germany; Univ. of Essen, Germany; Max-Planck-Inst. für Quantenoptik, Garching; Technische Univ., Vienna; Visiting Fellow: Tata Inst. of Fundamental Res., Bombay, 1973–; Jt Inst. for Lab. Astrophysics, Univ. of Colo, Boulder, 1981–82; SERC Sen. Vis. Fellow, UMIST, 1985–86. Dr *hc* Liege, 2007. Fellow: Amer. Physical Soc., 1981; Indian Acad. of Scis, 1981; Indian Nat. Sci. Acad., 1985; Optical Soc. of America, 1988; Third World Acad. of Scis, 1997. Eastman Kodak Prize, Univ. of Rochester, 1969; Shanti Swaroop Bhatnagar Award in Physical Scis, Govt of India, 1982; Max-Born Award, Optical Soc. of America, 1988; Einstein Medal, Optical and Quantum Electronics Soc.,

USA, 1994; G. D. Birla Prize for Scientific Res., K. K. Birla Foundn, 1994; Third World Acad. of Scis Prize in Physics, 1994; R. D. Birla Prize, Indian Physics Assoc., 1997; Humboldt Res. Award, Germany, 1997. *Publications:* monographs; papers on stochastic processes and quantum optics; contrib. res. articles to jls of Amer. Physical Soc., Inst. of Physics, Optical Soc. of America. *Recreations:* reading magazines and newspapers, watching comedy and movies with message. *Address:* Department of Physics, Oklahoma State University, Stillwater, OK 74078, USA. *T:* (405) 7443862, *Fax:* (405) 7446811; *e-mail:* agirish@okstate.edu.

AGASSI, André; tennis player; *b* Las Vegas, 29 April 1970; *s* of Emmanuel (Mike) and Betty Agassi; *m* 1997, Brooke Shields (marr. diss.); *m* 2001, Stefanie Graf, *qv*; one *s* one *d*. Trained at Nick Bollettieri Tennis Acad., Fla. Professional tennis player, 1986–2006; winner: (inaugural) ATP World Championship, Frankfurt, 1991; Wimbledon, 1992; US Open, 1994, 1999; Australian Open, 1995, 2000, 2001, 2003; French Open, 1999 (one of only five players ever to win all four men's grand-slam titles); Gold Medallist, Olympic Games, 1996. Founder, André Agassi Charitable Foundn, 1996. *Address:* c/o IMG, Suite 1300, 1 Brieview Plaza, Cleveland, OH 44114, USA.

AGG, Stephen James, FCILT; Chief Executive, Chartered Institute of Logistics and Transport, since 2006; *b* 25 Sept. 1952; *s* of Douglas and Ivy Agg; *m* 2007, Maggie Tompsett; one *s* one *d* by a previous marriage. *Educ:* Incorporated Engr. Lowfield Distbn, 1981–86; Jacob's Bakery, 1986–96; Distribn Dir, Danone UK, 1996–99; Logistics Dir, Danone Waters UK, 1999–2002; Man. Dir, Business Services, Freight Transport Assoc., 2002–06. MIRTE 1992; Mem., Soc. of Ops Engrs, 2000; FCILT 2006. *Recreations:* classic cars, walking, rural life, English Setters. *Address:* Chartered Institute of Logistics and Transport, Earlstrees Court, Earlstrees Road, Corby, Northants NN17 4AX. *T:* (01536) 740109; *e-mail:* steve.agg@ciltuk.org.uk.

AGGLETON, Prof. Peter Jeremy, PhD; CPsychol, FBPsS; AcSS; Professor, since 1994, and Director, 1996–2006, Thomas Coram Research Unit, Institute of Education, University of London; *b* 16 Oct. 1952; *s* of David Charles and Pauline Betty Aggleton; partner, Preecha Anurakpongpee. *Educ:* Worcester Coll., Oxford (BA 1974); Aberdeen Univ. (MEd 1977); PhD London 1984. CPsychol 1989; FBPsS 1996; FRIPH (FRIPHH 2001); AcSS 2004. Lecturer: Psychol. and Sociol., Worthing Coll. of Technol., 1975–76; Teacher Educn, City of Bath Tech. Coll., 1977–84; Sen. Lectr, Sociol., Bath Coll. of Higher Educn, 1984–85; Sen. Lectr, 1985–89, Hd, 1989–90, Educn Policy Studies, Bristol Poly.; Dir, Health and Educn Res. Unit, Goldsmiths' Coll., Univ. of London, 1991–92; Chief, Social and Behavioural Studies and Support Unit, Global Prog. on AIDS, WHO, Geneva, 1992–94. Visiting Professor: Univ. of NSW, 2003–; Univ. of Oslo, 2006–. Ed., Culture, Health and Sexuality, 1999–. FRSA 1996. *Publications:* (with H. A. Chalmers) Nursing Models and the Nursing Process, 1986; Deviance, 1987; Health, 1990; Health Promotion and Young People, 1996; (with H. A. Chalmers) Nursing Models and Nursing Practice, 2000; (ed jtly) Young People and Mental Health, 2000; (ed jtly) Sex, Drugs and Young People, 2006; contribs to learned jls incl. Science, Lancet, AIDS Care, AIDS Educn and Prevention, Health Educn Res. *Recreations:* walking, writing, travel, learning foreign languages. *Address:* Thomas Coram Research Unit, Institute of Education, University of London, 27–28 Woburn Square, WC1H 0AA. *T:* (020) 7612 6957, *Fax:* (020) 7612 6927; *e-mail:* p.aggleton@ioe.ac.uk.

AGIUS, Marcus Ambrose Paul; Chairman, Barclays PLC, since 2007; *b* 22 July 1946; *s* of late Lt-Col Alfred Victor Louis Benedict Agius, MC, TD and Ena Eleanora Alberta Agius (*née* Hueffer); *m* 1971, Kate Juliette de Rothschild; two *d*. *Educ:* Trinity Hall, Cambridge (MA); Harvard Business Sch. (MBA). With Vickers plc, 1968–70; joined Lazard Brothers & Co. Ltd, subseq. Lazard London, 1972; Chm., 2001–06; a Dep. Chm., Lazard LLC, 2002–06. Non-executive Director: Exbury Gardens Ltd, 1977–; BAA plc, 1995–2006 (Dep. Chm., 1998–2002; Chm., 2002–06); Sen. Ind. Dir, BBC, 2006–. Trustee, Royal Botanic Gdns, Kew, 2006– (Chm., Foundn and Friends of Royal Botanic Gdns, Kew, 2004–). *Recreations:* gardening, shooting, ski-ing, fine art, sailing. *Address:* Barclays PLC, One Churchill Place, Canary Wharf, E14 5HP. *T:* (020) 7116 1000. *Clubs:* White's; Swinley Forest Golf; Beaulieu River Sailing.

AGNEW OF LOCHNAW, Sir Crispin Hamlyn, 11th Bt *cr* 1629; QC (Scot.) 1995; Rothesay Herald of Arms, since 1986; Chief of the Name and Arms of Agnew; *b* 13 May 1944; *s* of (Sir) Fulque Melville Gerald Noel Agnew of Lochnaw, 10th Bt and Swanzie, *d* of late Major Esmé Nourse Erskine, CMG, MC; *S* father, 1975; *m* 1980, Susan (formerly journalist, broadcaster, Advertising Exec.), *yr d* of late J. W. Strang Steel, Logie, Kirriemuir, Angus; one *s* three *d*. *Educ:* Uppingham; RMA, Sandhurst. Major (retd 1981), late RHF. Admitted to Faculty of Advocates, 1982. Dep. Social Security and Child Support Comr, 2000–; Part-time Chm., Pension Appeal Tribunal, 2002–. Slains Pursuivant of Arms to Lord High Constable of Scotland, 1978–81; Unicorn Pursuivant of Arms, 1981–86. Trustee, John Muir Trust, 1989–2005. Leader: Army Expedn to E Greenland, 1968; Jt Services Expedn to Chilean Patagonia, 1972–73; Army Expedn to Api, NW Nepal, 1980; Member: RN Expedn to E Greenland, 1966; Jt Services to Elephant Island (Antarctica), 1970–71; Army Nuptse Expedn, 1975; Jt British and Royal Nepalese Army Everest Expedn, 1976 (reached the South Col). *Publications:* (jtly) Allan and Chapman, Licensing (Scotland) Act 1976, 2nd edn 1989, 5th edn 2002; (jtly) Connell on the Agricultural Holdings Acts, 7th edn 1996; Agricultural Law in Scotland, 1996; Land Obligations, 1999; Crofting Law, 2000; articles in newspapers and magazines, and in legal and heraldic jls. *Recreations:* mountaineering, sailing (Yacht Pippa's Song), heraldry. *Heir: s* Mark Douglas Noel Agnew of Lochnaw, yr, *b* 24 April 1991. *Address:* 6 Palmerston Road, Edinburgh EH9 1TN.

AGNEW, Fraser; *see* Agnew, W. A. F.

AGNEW, Sir John (Keith), 6th Bt *cr* 1895, of Great Stanhope Street, London; *b* 19 Dec. 1950; *er s* of Major Sir (George) Keith Agnew, 5th Bt, TD, and Anne Merete Louise, *yr d* of Baron Johann Schaffalitzky de Muckadell, Fyn, Denmark; *S* father, 1994. *Educ:* Gresham's Sch., Holt. *Heir: b* George Anthony Agnew, *b* 18 Aug. 1953. *Address:* Rougham Estate Office, Rougham, Bury St Edmunds, Suffolk IP30 9LZ.

AGNEW, Jonathan Geoffrey William; Chairman: Beazley Group, since 2003 (non-executive Director, since 2002); The Cayenne Trust, since 2006; Leo Capital, since 2006; Ashmore Global Opportunities, since 2007; *b* 30 July 1941; *er s* of Sir Geoffrey Agnew and Hon. Doreen Maud, *y d* of 1st Baron Jessel, CB, CMG; *m* 1st, 1966, Hon. Joanna Campbell (marr. diss. 1985); one *s* two *d*; 2nd, 1990, Marie-Claire Dreesmann; one *s* one *d*. *Educ:* Eton College; Trinity College, Cambridge (MA). The Economist, 1964–65; World Bank, 1965–67; Hill Samuel & Co., 1967–73, Dir, 1971–73; Morgan Stanley & Co., 1973–82, Man. Dir, 1977–82; J. G. W. Agnew & Co., 1983–86; Kleinwort Benson Gp, 1987–93 (Gp Chief Exec., 1989–93); Chairman: Limit, 1993–2000; Gerrard Gp, 1998–2000; Nationwide Bldg Soc., 2002–07 (Dep. Chm., 1999–2002; non-exec. Dir, 1997–2007); non-executive Director: Thos Agnew & Sons Ltd, 1969–2007; Rightmove, 2006–; Thos Agnew and Sons Hldgs Ltd, 2007–. Mem. Council, Lloyd's, 1995–99. *Address:* Flat E, 51 Eaton Square, SW1W 9BE. *Clubs:* White's; Automobile (Paris).

AGNEW, Jonathan Philip; cricket correspondent, BBC, since 1991; *b* 4 April 1960; *s* of Philip Agnew and Margaret Agnew; *m* 1996, Emma Norris; two *d* by former marriage. *Educ:* Uppingham Sch. Professional cricketer: début, Leics CCC, 1978; played for England, 1984–85; retd from first class cricket, 1990; cricket corresp., Today, 1990–91. Sports Reporter of Year, Sony, 1992. *Publications:* 8 Days a Week, 1988; Over to You, Aggers (autobiog.), 1997; (ed) Cheltenham & Gloucester Cricket Year (annually), 1999–. *Address:* BBC Radio, Broadcasting House, W1A 1AA.

AGNEW, Sir Rudolph (Ion Joseph), Kt 2002; Chairman, Stena International BV, 1990–2007; Director, Peter Hambro Mining PLC, since 2004; *b* 12 March 1934; *s* of Rudolph John Agnew and Pamela Geraldine (*née* Campbell); *m* 1980, Whitney Warren. *Educ:* Downside School. Commissioned officer, 8th King's Royal Irish Hussars, 1953–57. Joined Consolidated Gold Fields, 1957; Dep. Chm., 1978–82; Gp Chief Exec., 1978–89; Chm., 1983–89; Mem., Cttee of Man. Dirs, 1986–89. Chairman: TVS Entertainment, 1990–93; Federated Aggregates PLC, 1991–95; Bona Shipholding Ltd, Bermuda, 1993–98; LASMO PLC, 1994–2000; Redland plc, 1995–97; Star Mining Corp., 1995–98; Jt Chm., Global Stone Corp. (Canada), 1993–94; non-executive Director: Internat. Tool and Supply (formerly New London) PLC, 1985–96; Standard Chartered PLC, 1988–97; Newmont Mining Corp., USA, 1989–98; Newmont Gold Co., USA, 1989–98; Stena (UK) Ltd, 1990–99; Director: Gold Fields of South Africa Ltd, 1978–89; Renison Goldfields Consolidated, 1978–90; Anglo American Corp. of South Africa, 1980–88; Hanson PLC, 1989–91. Vice President: Nat. Assoc. of Boys' Clubs; Game Conservancy (Fellow); Hawk Trust; Chm., World Conservation Monitoring Centre, 1989–; Fellow, WWF (UK), 2006 (Trustee, 1983–89). CCMI (FBIM 1980); FRSA. *Recreations:* shooting, racing. *Address:* 2nd Floor, 11 Grosvenor Place, SW1X 7HH. *Clubs:* White's, Cavalry and Guards.

AGNEW, Stanley Clarke, CB 1985; FREng; FICE; Chief Engineer, Scottish Development Department, 1976–87, retired; *b* 18 May 1926; *s* of Christopher Gerald Agnew and Margaret Eleanor Agnew (*née* Clarke); *m* 1950, Isbell Evelyn Parker (*née* Davidson); two *d*. *Educ:* Royal Belfast Academical Instn; Queen's Univ., Belfast (BSc Civil Eng., 1947). FIWEM. Service with contractors, consulting engineers and local authorities, 1947–62; Eng. Inspector, Scottish Develt Dept, 1962–68, Dep. Chief Engr, 1968–75. FREng (FEng 1985). *Recreations:* golf, photography, motoring, gardening. *Club:* Murrayfield Golf (Edinburgh).

AGNEW, (William Alexander) Fraser; Cultural Co-ordinator, Newtownabbey Borough Council, since 1981; *b* 16 Aug. 1942; *s* of late James Agnew and Maureen Barbara Agnew (*née* Fraser); *m* 1972, Lila McCausland; one *s*. *Educ:* Ballyclare High Sch.; Univ. of Ulster at Jordanstown; Belfast Tech. Coll.; Coll. of Business Studies. MCIOB (MIOB 1968). Architectural draughtsman and company dir, until 1990; part-time sports journalist; presenter, history programmes on community radio; lecturer. Mem., NI Assembly, 1982–86; Mem. (UU) Belfast North, NI Assembly, 1998–2003. Mem. (UU, 1980–90, Ind., 1990–) Newtownabbey BC (Chairman: Corporate Services Cttee, 1993–94, 1995–96; Culture and Tourism Cttee, 1995–); Mayor, Newtownabbey, 1990–91. Formerly Chm., Ulster Tourist Develt Assoc. Chm., Ulster Young Unionist Council, 1970. Associate Mem., Inst. of Engrg Technol., 1969. Freeman, Newtownabbey, 2007. *Publications:* numerous pamphlets on aspects of Ireland's history. *Recreations:* soccer coaching for children (qualified coach), 5-a-side football, golf. *Address:* 1 Knockview Crescent, Newtownabbey BT36 6UD. *T:* (028) 9050 6147; (office) Mossley Mill, Newtonabbey, Co. Antrim BT36 5QA.

AGNEW-SOMERVILLE, Sir Quentin (Charles Somerville), 2nd Bt *cr* 1957, of Clendry, Co. Wigtown; insurance consultant; *b* 8 March 1929; *s* of Comdr Sir Peter Agnew, 1st Bt and Enid Frances (*d* 1982), *d* of late Henry Boan; assumed additional name of Somerville by Royal licence, 1950; *S* father, 1990; *m* 1963, Hon. April, *y d* and a *co-heiress* of 15th Baron Strange; one *s* two *d*. *Educ:* RNC Dartmouth. *Heir: s* James Lockett Charles Agnew-Somerville, *b* 26 May 1970.

AGRAN, Linda Valerie; Founder, Linda Agran Clothes Storage, 2004; *b* 9 May 1947; *d* of Albert and Gertrude Agran; *m* 1991, Alexander Gordon Scott. *Educ:* Queen Elizabeth's Girls' Grammar Sch., Barnet. William Morris Agency, Columbia Pictures, Paramount Pictures, Warner Bros, 1973–76; Head of Development, 1976, Director, 1982, Euston Films; Writer in Residence, Aust. Film & TV Sch.; Dep. Controller of Drama and Arts, LWT, 1986; Chief Exec., Paravision (UK) Ltd, 1989; completed management buyout to form Agran Barton TV, 1993, Jt Chief Exec., 1993–2000. FRSA. *Television* (as producer or executive producer): series include: Minder; Widows; Paradise Postponed; London's Burning; Hercule Poirot; Moving Story. *Recreations:* cooking good food, drinking fine wines, horse racing, reading, all in the company of close friends.

AGRE, Prof. Peter Courtland, MD; Vice Chancellor for Science and Technology, Duke University Medical Center, since 2005; *b* 30 Jan. 1949; *s* of late Courtland Leverne Agre and of Ellen Violet Agre (*née* Swedberg); *m* 1975, Mary Macgill; one *s* three *d* (and one *d* decd). *Educ:* Theodore Roosevelt High Sch., Minneapolis; Augsburg Coll., Minneapolis (BA 1970); Johns Hopkins Univ. (MD 1974). Fellow, 1978–80, Asst Prof. of Medicine, 1980–81, Univ. of N Carolina; Sen. Clin. Res. Scientist, Wellcome Labs, Research Triangle Park, NC, 1980–81; Johns Hopkins University: Res. Associate, 1981–83, Asst Prof., 1984–88, Associate Prof., 1988–93, Sch. of Medicine; Prof. of Biol Chemistry and of Medicine, 1993–2005. (Jtly) Nobel Prize for Chemistry, 2003. *Publications:* articles in learned jls. *Address:* Duke University Medical Center, Erwin Road, Durham, NC 27710, USA.

AGUIRRE, Marcelino O.; *see* Oreja Aguirre.

ÁGÚSTSSON, Helgi, Hon. GCVO 1990; Icelandic Grand Order of the Falcon, 1990 (Order of the Falcon, 1979); Ambassador of Iceland to the United States of America, also accredited to Argentina, Brazil, Chile, El Salvador, Guatemala, Mexico and Uruguay, since 2002; *b* 16 Oct. 1941; *s* of Ágúst Pétursson and Helga Jóhannesdóttir; *m* 1963, Hervör Jónasdóttir; three *s* one *d*. *Educ:* Univ. of Iceland (Law degree 1970). Joined Foreign Ministry, 1970; served London, 1973–77; Counsellor, 1977; Dir, Defence Div., Foreign Min., 1979 and Chm., US-Icelandic Defence Council; Minister-Counsellor, 1980; served Washington, 1983–87; Dep. Perm. Under-Sec., Foreign Min., 1987, in rank of Ambassador; Ambassador to UK, 1989–94, and to Ireland, Holland and Nigeria, 1990–94; Perm. Under-Sec., Min. for Foreign Affairs, Iceland, 1995–99; Ambassador to Denmark, also accredited to Lithuania, Turkey, Israel and Romania, 1999–2002. Former Pres., Icelandic Basketball Fedn. Decorations from Finland, Denmark, Sweden, Norway, Italy, Spain, Netherlands. *Recreations:* theatre, music, reading, salmon fishing. *Address:* Embassy of Iceland, 1156 15th Street NW, Suite 1200, Washington, DC 20005–1704, USA.

AGUTTER, Jennifer Ann; actress; *b* 20 Dec. 1952; *d* of Derek and Catherine Agutter; *m* 1990, Johan Tham; one *s*. *Educ:* Elmhurst Ballet School, Camberley. *Films:* East of Sudan, 1964; Ballerina, 1964; Gates of Paradise, 1967; Star, 1968; Walkabout, I Start Counting,

The Railway Children, 1969 (Royal Variety Club Most Promising Artist, 1971); Logan's Run, 1975; The Eagle Has Landed, Equus (BAFTA Best Supporting Actress, 1977), The Man In The Iron Mask, 1976; Dominique, Clayton and Catherine, 1977; The Riddle of the Sands, Sweet William, 1978; The Survivor, 1980; An American Werewolf in London, 1981; Secret Places, 1983; Dark Tower, 1987; King of the Wind, 1989; Child's Play 2, 1991; Freddie as Fro7, 1992; Blue Juice, 1995; *stage:* School for Scandal, 1972; Rooted, Arms and the Man, The Ride Across Lake Constance, 1973; National Theatre: The Tempest, Spring Awakening, 1974; Hedda, Betrayal, 1980; Peter Pan, 1997; Royal Shakespeare Co.: Arden of Faversham, Lear, King Lear, The Body, 1982–83; Breaking the Silence, 1985; Shrew, The Unified Field, LA, 1987; Breaking the Code, NY, 1987; Love's Labour's Lost, Barbican, 1995; Mothers and Daughters, Chichester, 1996; Equus, Gielgud, 2007; *television includes:* Long After Summer, 1967; The Wild Duck, The Cherry Orchard, The Snow Goose (Emmy Best Supporting Actress), 1971; A War of Children, 1972; School Play, 1979; Amy, 1980; Love's Labour's Lost, This Office Life, 1984; Silas Marner, 1985; Murder She Wrote, 1986; The Equaliser, Magnum, 1988; Dear John, 1989; Not a Penny More, Not a Penny Less, Tecx, 1990; The Good Guys, Puss in Boots, 1991; The Buccaneers, 1995; And the Beat Goes On, 1996; Bramwell, A Respectable Trade, 1998; The Railway Children, 2000; Spooks, 2002, 2003; The Alan Clark Diaries, 2004. Hon. DLitt Bradford, 2004. *Publication:* Snap, 1983. *Address:* c/o Ken McReddie Associates, 36–40 Glasshouse Street, W1B 5DL. *T:* (020) 7439 1456.

AGUTTER, Richard Devenish; Senior Adviser, KPMG, 1998–2005; *b* 17 Sept. 1941; *s* of late Anthony Tom Devenish Agutter and Joan Hildegare Sabina (*née* Machen); *m* 1968, Lesley Anne Ballard; three *s*. *Educ:* Marlborough Coll. CA 1964. With W. T. Walton, 1960–64; joined Peat Marwick Mitchell, subsequently KPMG, 1964: Partner, 1977–98; Chm., KPMG Internat. Corporate Finance, 1990–96. City of London: Alderman, Ward of Castle Baynard, 1995–2005; Sheriff, 2000–01. Liveryman, Goldsmiths' Co., 1979– (Mem., Ct of Assts, 1999–); Mem., Ct of Assts, Co. of Marketors, 1999–; Hon. Liveryman, Co. of Tax Advisers, 2005 (Mem., Ct of Assts, 2005–; Master, 2008–Sept. 2009); Master, Guild of Freemen, 2004. *Recreations:* wine, gardening, sailing. *Address:* Leabridge Farmhouse, West Burton, near Pulborough, West Sussex RH20 1HD. *T:* (01798) 839169.

AHEARNE, Stephen James, FCA; Chief Financial Officer, 1990–96, and Managing Director, 1992–96, British Petroleum Company PLC; *b* 7 Sept. 1939; *s* of James Joseph Ahearne and Phyllis Eva (*née* Grigsby); *m* 1965, Janet Elizabeth Edwards; two *s*. Qualified as Chartered Accountant, 1962; joined British Petroleum, 1964: Man. Dir, BP Denmark, 1978–81; Exec. Dir, BP Chems, 1981–86; Gp Controller, 1986–88; Gp Planner, 1988–90. Mem., Restrictive Practices Court, 1993–99. Gov., Felsted Sch., 1996–. *Recreations:* tennis, gardening, walking, reading, learning languages.

AHERN, Bertie; Member of the Dáil (TD) (FF), since 1977; Taoiseach (Prime Minister of Ireland), 1997–2008; President, Fianna Fáil, 1994–2008; *b* 12 Sept. 1951; *s* of Cornelius and Julia Ahern; *m* 1975 (separated); two *d*. *Educ:* Rathmines Coll. of Commerce; University Coll., Dublin. Accountant. Asst Chief Whip, 1980–81; spokesman on youth affairs, 1981; Govt Chief Whip and Minister of State at Depts of Taoiseach and Defence, 1982; Minister for Labour, 1987–91; Minister for Finance, 1991–94; Leader of the Opposition, 1994–97. Lord Mayor of Dublin, 1986–87. Member, Board of Governors, 1991–94: IMF; World Bank; EIB (Chm., 1991–92). Grand Cross, Order of Merit with Star and Sash (Germany), 1991. *Recreations:* sports, reading. *Address:* St Luke's, 161 Lower Drumcondra Road, Dublin 9, Ireland.

AHERN, Dermot; Member of the Dáil (TD) (FF) for Louth, since 1987; Minister for Justice, Equality and Law Reform, Republic of Ireland, since 2008; *b* 2 Feb. 1955; *s* of Jerry Ahern; *m* 1980, Maeve Coleman; two *d*. *Educ:* St Mary's Coll. Secondary Sch., Dundalk; University Coll., Dublin (BCL); Law Soc. of Ireland. Mem. (FF) Louth CC, 1979–91. Asst Govt Whip, 1988–91; Minister of State, Dept of Defence and Dept of Taoiseach, and Govt Chief Whip, 1991–92; Minister: for Social, Community and Family Affairs, 1997–2000; for Communications, Marine and Natural Resources, 2002–04; for Foreign Affairs, 2004–08. Mem., British-Irish Parly Body, 1991–97 (Co-Chm., 1993–95). *Recreations:* windsurfing, ski-ing, golf. *Address:* Department of Justice, Equality and Law Reform, 94 St Stephen's Green, Dublin 2, Ireland; *e-mail:* dahern@iol.ie.

AHMAD, Khurshid; Chairman: Institute of Policy Studies, Islamabad, Pakistan, since 1979; Board of Trustees, Islamic Foundation, Leicester, since 1985; Member, Senate of Pakistan, 1985–97, and since 2003; *b* 23 March 1932; three *s* three *d*. *Educ:* Karachi Univ. (LLB; MA Economics; MA Islamic Studies). Dir-Gen., Islamic Foundn, Leicester, 1973–78; Federal Minister for Planning and Develt and Dep. Chm., Planning Commn, Govt of Pakistan, 1978–79. Chm., Internat. Inst. of Islamic Econs, Islamic Univ., Islamabad, 1983–87. Hon. PhD Educn, Nat. Univ. of Malaya; Hon. DLitt Loughborough, 2003. Islamic Develt Bank Laureate for dist. contribn to Islamic econs, 1988; King Faisal, Internat. Prize for service to Islam, 1990. *Publications:* Essays on Pakistan Economy (Karachi), 1958; An Analysis of Munir Report (Lahore), 1958; (ed) Studies in the Family Law of Islam (Karachi), 1960; (ed) The Quran: an Introduction (Karachi), 1966; The Prophet of Islam (Karachi), 1967; Principles of Islamic Education (Lahore), 1970; Fanaticism, Intolerance and Islam (Lahore), 1970; Islam and the West (Lahore), 1972; The Religion of Islam (Lahore), 1973; (ed) Islam: its meaning and message (London, Islamic Council of Europe), 1976; Development Strategy for the Sixth Plan (Islamabad), 1983; Islamic Approach to Development: some policy implications (Islamabad), 1994; Islamic Resurgence: challenges, directions and future perspectives, ed I. M. Abu-Rabi, 1995; The Crisis of the Political System in Pakistan and the Jamaat-e-Islami, 1996; *for Islamic Foundation, Leicester:* Islam: Basic Principles and Characteristics, 1974; Family Life in Islam, 1974; Islamic Perspectives: Studies in honour of Maulana Mawdudi, 1979; The Quran: Basic Teachings, 1979; Studies in Islamic Economics, 1980; contrib. The Third World's Dilemma of Development, Non-Aligned Third World Annual, (USA) 1970. *Recreations:* travelling, reading. *Address:* Islamic Foundation, Markfield Conference Centre, Ratby Lane, Markfield, Leics LE67 9SY. *T:* (01530) 244944; Institute of Policy Studies, Block 19, Markaz F-7, Islamabad, Pakistan. *T:* (51) 2650971; *e-mail:* khurshid@ips.net.pk.

AHMADI, Hon. Aziz Mushabber; Chief Justice of India, 1994–97; *b* 25 March 1932; *s* of M. I. Ahmadi and Shirin I. Ahmadi; *m* 1960, Amena A. Muchhala; one *s* one *d*. *Educ:* Ahmedabad and Surat (LLB). Called to the Bar, Ahmedabad, 1954; Judge, City Civil and Sessions Court, Ahmedabad, 1964–74; Sec., Legal Dept, Govt of Gujarat, 1974–76; Judge, High Court of Gujarat, 1976–88; Judge, Supreme Court of India, 1988–94. Pres., Supreme Court Legal Aid Cttee, 1989; Exec. Chm., Cttee for Implementing Legal Aid Schemes in India, 1994. Chairman: Adv. Bd, Conservation of Foreign Exchange and Prevention of Smuggling Activities Act, 1974; Adv. Bd, Prevention of Black Marketing, Maintenance of Supplies of Essential Commodities Act, 1982–83; Gujarat Third Pay Commn, 1982–85. Member: UN Commn of Inquiry, East Timor, 1999; Internat. Bar Assoc. Mission to Zimbabwe, 2001. Chancellor, Aligarh Muslim Univ., 2003–06. Hon. Bencher, Middle Temple, 1996. Hon. LLD: Kurukshetra, 1994; Maharishi Dayanand, 1995; Kanpur, 1995; Sardar Patel, 1996; Cochin, 1997; Leicester, 1998. *Recreations:* reading, music. *Address:* C-3 Kant Enclave, near Dr Karni Singh Shooting Ranges, Anangpur, Haryana 121003, India. *T:* (129) 2511291, (129) 2511293, *Fax:* (129) 2511285, (11) 26966389; *e-mail:* amahmadi@bol.net.in. *Clubs:* Delhi Gymkhana, India International Centre (New Delhi).

AHMED, Baron *cr* 1998 (Life Peer), of Rotherham in the co. of South Yorkshire; **Nazir Ahmed;** JP; business development manager; *b* 24 April 1957; *s* of Haji Sain Mohammed and Rashim Bibi; *m* 1974, Sakina Bibi; two *s* one *d*. *Educ:* Thomas Rotherham Coll.; Sheffield Hallam Univ. Business development manager: mini-markets, 1979–82; fish and chip shops, 1979–2003; petrol station, 1982–84; marble mining, Azad, Kashmir, 1985–87; business park and property develt, 1990–. Advisor to Nestlé, Nesco Foods and DLV UK, 2003–06. Mem. (Lab) Rotherham MBC, 1990–. Founder, British Muslim Councillors Forum; founder Chm., Muslims for Labour. Chm., S Yorks Lab. Party, 1993–. Chairman: All-Pty Parly Libya Gp, 1999–2001; All-Pty Parly Interfaith Inter-religious Gp; All-Pty Parly Financial Exploitation Gp; founder and Vice-Chm., All-Pty Parly Entrepreneurship Gp. Co-Chm., Govt's Forced Marriage Wkg Gp, 1999–; Chm., Preventing Extremism Together Working Gp on Imams trng and role of mosques, 2005. Mem., Channel 4 Hate Commn (on hate crime), 1999–. Mem. Council, BHF. Pres., S Yorks Victim Support. Led first Hajj delegn on behalf of British govt, 2000. Advr to many internat. orgns on dialogue, tolerance and co-operation. JP Rotherham, 1992. *Recreation:* volleyball. *Address:* 152 East Bawtry Road, Rotherham S60 4LG. *T:* (01709) 730140; House of Lords, SW1A 0PW.

AHMED, Prof. Haroon, ScD; FREng; Professor of Microelectronics, University of Cambridge, 1992–2003, now Emeritus; Fellow, 1967–2007, now Honorary Fellow, Master, 2000–06, Corpus Christi College, Cambridge (Warden of Leckhampton, 1993–98); *b* 2 March 1936; *s* of Mohammad Nizam Ahmed and Bilquis Jehan Ahmed; *m* 1969, Evelyn Anne Travers Goodrich; one *s* two *d*. *Educ:* St Patrick's Sch., Karachi; Imperial College London; King's College, Cambridge (PhD 1963); ScD Cantab 1996. GEC and Hirst Research Centre, 1958–59; Turner and Newall Res. Fellow, 1962–63; University of Cambridge: Univ. Demonstrator, Engineering Dept, 1963–66; Lectr, Engineering Dept, 1966–84; Reader in Microelectronics, 1984–92. Non-exec. Dir, Addenbrooke's NHS Trust, 2001–04. Pres., Cambridge Philosophical Soc., 2004–06. Syndic, CUP, 1996–2002. Higher Educn Advr, Govt of Pakistan, 2006. FREng (FEng 1990). *Publications:* (with A. H. W. Beck) Introduction to Physical Electronics, 1968; (with P. J. Spreadbury) Electronics for Engineers, 1973, 2nd edn 1984. *Recreation:* golf. *Address:* Corpus Christi College, Cambridge CB2 1RH.

AHMED, Masood; Director, External Relations, International Monetary Fund, since 2006; *b* 13 Jan. 1953; *s* of late Aziz Ahmed and Phool Aziz Ahmed; *m* 1979, Priscilla Macleod; one *d*. *Educ:* St Joseph's Sch., Dhaka; Karachi Grammar Sch., Karachi; LSE (BSc Econ. 1974, MSc Econ. with dist. 1975). Res. Asst, then Lectr, LSE, 1975–78; joined World Bank, 1979: Economist, then Dep. Div. Chief, Energy Dept, 1980–86; Div. Chief, N Africa Country Dept, 1987–91; Div. Chief, Internat. Debt and Finance, 1991–93; Dir, Internat. Econs Dept, 1993–97; Vice Pres., Poverty Reduction and Econ. Mgt, 1997–2000; Dep. Dir, Policy Develt and Review, IMF, 2000–03; Dir Gen., Policy and Internat., DFID, 2003–06. *Recreations:* Urdu poetry, biographies, walking. *Address:* External Relations Department, International Monetary Fund, Washington, DC 20431, USA. *Clubs:* Reform, Pall Mall.

AHMED, Samira; Presenter/Reporter, Channel 4 News, ITN, since 2000; *b* 15 June 1968; *d* of Athar Ahmad and Lalita Ahmed (*née* Chatterjee); *m* 1996, Brian Michael Millar; one *s* one *d*. *Educ:* Holy Cross Prep. Sch.; Wimbledon High Sch.; St Edmund Hall, Oxford (BA Hons English 1989); City Univ., London (Postgrad. Dip. Newspaper Journalism 1990). BBC: news trainee, 1990–92; network radio news reporter, 1992; Presenter, World Service TV, 1993; Reporter, Newsnight, 1993–94; News Corresp., 1994–97; LA Corresp., 1996–97; Presenter: Deutsche Welle TV, Berlin, 1998; BBC News 24/BBC World, 1998–99; Islam Unveiled, documentary series, Channel 4, 2004. *Recreations:* cinema, theatre, Berlin, collecting Amar Chitra Katha comics. *Address:* c/o Channel 4 News, ITN, 200 Gray's Inn Road, WC1X 8XZ; *e-mail:* samira.ahmed@itn.co.uk.

AHMED, Shami; Chief Executive, Joe Bloggs Inc. Co., since 1997; *b* Pakistan, 7 July 1962; *s* of Nizam Ahmed and Saeeda Ahmed; *m* 1997, Samina. *Educ:* Barden High Sch., Burnley. Set up wholesale clothing business, Pennywise, with father, 1977; founded: Legendary Joe Bloggs Inc. Co., 1986; Legendary Property Co., 1993. Hon. Fellow, Lancashire Poly., 1991. *Recreation:* swimming. *Address:* (office) 18–24 Bury New Road, Manchester M8 8FR. *T:* (0161) 831 7550.

AHO, Esko Tapani; President, Finnish National Fund for Research and Development, (Sitra), since 2004; Prime Minister of Finland, 1991–95; *b* Veteli, 20 May 1954; *s* of Kauko Kaleva Aho and Laura Kyllikki Aho (*née* Harjupatana); *m* 1980, Kirsti Hannele Söderkultalahti; two *s* one *d*. *Educ:* Master of Pol Scis. Political Sec. to Minister for Foreign Affairs, Finland, 1979–80; MP (Centre Party), Helsinki, 1983–2000; Chm., Finnish Parlt, April 1991; Member: Traffic Commn, 1983–86; Finances Commn, 1987–90. Member: CSCE Cttee, 1984–90; Finnish Delegn, Nordic Council, 1983–89; Finnish Delegn, Council of Europe, 1989–91. Chairman: League, Centre Party Youth, 1974–80; Finnish Centre Party, 1990–2002. Member, Advisory Board: Outokumpu Oy (Metal Ind.), 1985–91; OKO (Bank), 1991; SOK (Diversified Co-op.), 1990–91. Chm., Verbatum Oy, corporate consulting co., 2002–04. Grand Cross, Order of White Rose (Finland), 1992; Cavaliere di Gran Croce, Order of Merit (Italy), 1993. *Recreations:* tennis, literature. *Address:* Sitra, Itämerentori 2, POB 160, 00181 Helsinki, Finland.

AHRENDS, Peter; Founding Partner and Director, Ahrends Burton & Koralek, Architects, since 1961; *b* 30 April 1933; *s* of Steffen Bruno Ahrends and Margarete Marie Sophie Visino; *m* 1954, Elizabeth Robertson (*d* 2007); two *d*. *Educ:* King Edward VII Sch., Johannesburg; Architectural Assoc. Sch. of Architecture (Dipl., Hons). RIBA 1959. Steffen Ahrends & Partners, Johannesburg, 1957–58; Denys Lasdun & Partners, 1959–60; Julian Keable & Partners; major-projects, 1961–, include: *public buildings:* Hampton Site, Nat. Gall. Extn, 1982–85 (comp. winning entry); St Mary's Hosp., Newport, IoW (nucleus low energy hosp.), 1990; White Cliffs Heritage Centre, Dover, 1991; Techniquest Science Centre, 1995 (RIBA Arch. Award); Dublin Dental Hosp., 1994–; Sculpture Court, Whitworth Art Gall., Manchester, 1995 (RIBA Arch. Award); Waterford Visitor Centre, 1998; N Tipperary Council civic offices, Nenagh, 2000–; Offaly Council offices, Tullamore, 2002 (RIBA Award, 2003); Galway Council office extension, library and HQ, 2002; *educational buildings:* New Liby, TCD, 1961 (internat. comp.); Templeton Coll., Oxford, phased completion over 25 years from 1969; residential bldg, Keble Coll., Oxford, 1976 (RIBA Arch. Award, 1978); Arts Faculty Bldg, TCD, 1979; Loughborough Univ. Business Sch., 1997; IT bldg and catering bldg, Inst. of Technology, Tralee, 1998; tourism and leisure bldg, Waterford Inst. of Technology, 1999; first phase bldgs, Inst. of Technology, Blanchardstown, 1999; *residential buildings:* Nebenzahl House, Jerusalem, 1972; Whitmore Court Housing, 1975 (RIBA Good Design in Housing Award, 1977); housing, Newcastle West, Limerick, 2004; *commercial/*

industrial buildings: warehouse, showroom and offices, Habitat, 1974 (Structural Steel Design Award, FT Industrial Arch. Award, 1976); factory, Cummins Engines (Struct. Steel Design Award, 1980); Sainsbury supermarket, Canterbury, 1984 (Struct. Steel Design Award, 1985); W. H. Smith offices, Swindon, 1985; British Embassy, Moscow, 1988–99; John Lewis dept store, Kingston-upon-Thames, 1990; office develt for Stanhope Trafalgar, 1990–; office building, Tel Aviv, 1998; *sports buildings:* Carrickmines Croquet and Lawn Tennis Club, Dublin, 1998; *transport:* Docklands Light Railway Beckton Extension stations, 1987–93; *development plans:* MBA Sch., Templeton Coll., Univ. of Oxford, 1992; Falmer Develt Plan, Univ. of Brighton, 1992; Cardiff Inner Harbour, 1993; Inst. of Technology, Tralee, 1998; Waterford Inst. of Technology, 1998; City Block, Dublin, 2000; Dublin Corp. NEIC Civic Centre, Dublin, 2000; TCD Dublin Docklands Innovation Centre, 2001; Inst. of Technol., Blanchardstown, 2002; Arts Faculty Extension Bldg, TCD, 2002; Bexhill Town Centre Develt Plan, 2004; *competition wins:* Campus Develt Plan, Univ. of Grenoble, 1990–93; Designs on Democracy, Stockport, 2003. Chair: UK Architects Against Apartheid, 1988–93; Newham Design Review Panel; Member: Design Council, 1988–93; Council, AA, 1965–67. Vis. Prof. of Architecture, Kingston Poly., 1983–84; Bartlett Prof. of Arch., Bartlett Sch. of Arch. and Planning, UCL, 1986–89; part-time teaching posts and workshops at AA Sch. of Arch., Canterbury Sch. of Art, Edinburgh Univ., Winter Sch. Edinburgh, Plymouth Poly., Kingston Poly., and Plymouth Sch. of Art; vis. critic and/or ext. examr at Kumasi Univ., AA Sch. of Arch., Nova Scotia Tech. Univ., Strathclyde Univ. Exhibitions of drawings and works: RIBA Heinz Gall., 1980; RIAI, 1981; Douglas Hyde Gall., Dublin, 1981; Braunschweig Tech. Univ., Tech. Univ. of Hanover, Museum of Finnish Arch., 1982; Univ. of Oulu, Alvar Aalto Museum, Finland, 1982; AA HQ, Oslo, 1983. *Publications:* (contrib.) Ahrends Burton & Koralek, Architects (monograph), 1991; (contrib.) Collaborations: the work of ABK, 2002; papers and articles in RIBA Jl and other prof. jls. *Recreations:* architecture, France. *Address:* (office) Studio 1, 7 Chalcot Road, NW1 8LH. *T:* (020) 7586 3311, *Fax:* (020) 7722 5445; *e-mail:* abk@abklondon.com.

AHTISAARI, Martti Oiva Kalevi; President, Republic of Finland, 1994–2000; Founder and Chairman of Board, Crisis Management Initiative, since 2000; *b* 23 June 1937; *s of* Oiva and Tyyne Ahtisaari; *m* 1968, Eeva Irmeli Hyvärinen; one *s.* Finnish diplomat; joined Ministry for Foreign Affairs, 1965; Ambassador to Tanzania, 1973–76; Under-Sec. of State, Internat. Develt Co-operation, 1984–86; Under-Sec. Gen., Admin and Mgt, 1987–91; Sec. of State for Foreign Affairs, 1991–94; UN envoy; UN Comr for Namibia, 1977–81; head, operation monitoring Namibia's transition to independence, 1989–90; senior envoy in Yugoslavia, 1992–93; EU Special envoy in Kosovo, 1999; Mem., observer gp on Austrian govt human rights record, 2000; co-inspector, IRA arms dumps, 2000; Chm., panel on security and safety of UN personnel in Iraq, 2003; special envoy of UN Secretary-General: for the Horn of Africa, 2003–06; for future status process for Kosovo, 2005–08. Chairman: Balkan Children and Youth Foundn, 2000–; Governing Council, Interpeace, 2000–. Mem., Prize Cttee, Mo Ibrahim Foundn, 2007–. Chm. Supervisory Bd, Finnish Nat. Opera, 2004–. Hon. AO 2002. *Address:* (office) Pieni Roobertinkatu 13B 24–26, 00130 Helsinki, Finland.

AIKENS, Rt Hon. Sir Richard (John Pearson), Kt 1999; PC 2008; **Rt Hon. Lord Justice Aikens;** a Lord Justice of Appeal, since 2008; *b* 28 Aug. 1948; *s of* late Basil Aikens and of Jean Eleanor Aikens; *m* 1979, Penelope Anne Hartley Rockley (*née* Baker); two *s* two step *d. Educ:* Norwich Sch.; St John's Coll., Cambridge (BA 1970, MA; Hon. Fellow, 2005). Called to Bar, Middle Temple, 1973 (Harmsworth scholar, 1974; Bencher, 1994); in practice, 1974–99; a Junior Counsel to the Crown, Common Law, 1981–86; QC 1986; a Recorder, 1993–99; a Judge of the High Court of Justice, QBD, 1999–2008; Presiding Judge, SE Circuit, 2001–04; Judge in charge of Commercial Ct, 2005–06. Mem., Supreme Court Rules Cttee, 1984–88. Dir, Bar Mutual Indemnity Fund Ltd, 1988–2000 (Chm., 1998–99). Dir, ENO, 1995–2004. Chm., Temple Music Foundn, 2002–. Governor, Sedbergh Sch., 1988–97. *Publications:* (contributing editor) Bullen and Leake and Jacob, Precedents of Pleading, 13th edn 1990; (jtly) Bills of Lading, 2006. *Recreations:* music, wine, le pays basque. *Address:* Royal Courts of Justice, Strand, WC2A 2LL. *Clubs:* Groucho; Leander.

AIKIN, Olga Lindholm, (Mrs J. M. Driver), CBE 1997; Partner, Aikin Driver Partnership, since 1988; Visiting Lecturer, London Business School, since 1985; Council Member, Advisory Conciliation and Arbitration Service, 1982–95; *b* 10 Sept. 1934; *d of* Sidney Richard Daly and Lilian May Daly (*née* Lindholm); *m* 1st, 1959, Ronald Sidney Aikin (marr. diss. 1979); one *d;* 2nd, 1982, John Michael Driver; one step *d. Educ:* London School of Economics (LLB); King's Coll., London. Called to Bar, Gray's Inn, 1956. Assistant Lecturer, King's Coll., London, 1956–59; Lecturer, London School of Economics, 1959–70; London Business School: Sloan Fellowship Programme, 1970–71; Vis. Lectr, 1971–79; Lectr in Law, 1979–85. Dir, Gen. Law Div., Lion Internat. (Keiser Enterprises Inc.), 1985–90; Chm. Bd of Mgt, Nat. Conciliation Service of Qualitas Furnishing Standards Ltd, 1992–94. *Publications:* (with Judith Reid) Employment, Welfare and Safety at Work, 1971; (with Sonia Pearson) Legal Problems of Employment Contracts, 1990; (ed) IPM Law and Employment series (Discipline; Industrial Tribunals; Redundancy), 1992; articles in Personnel Management. *Recreation:* collecting cookery books and pressed glass. *Address:* 22 St Luke's Road, W11 1DP. *T:* (office) (020) 7727 9791.

See also Hon. F. L. Daly.

AILESBURY, 8th Marquess of, *cr* 1821; **Michael Sydney Cedric Brudenell-Bruce;** Bt 1611; Baron Brudenell 1628; Earl of Cardigan 1661; Baron Bruce 1746; Earl of Ailesbury 1776; Earl Bruce 1821; Viscount Savernake 1821; 30th Hereditary Warden of Savernake Forest; *b* 31 March 1926; *e s of* 7th Marquess of Ailesbury and Joan (*d* 1937), *d of* Stephen Salter, Ryde, Isle of Wight; *S* father, 1974; *m* 1st, 1952, Edwina Sylvia de Winton (from whom he obtained a divorce, 1961), *yr d of* Lt–Col Sir (Ernest) Edward de Winton Wills, 4th Bt; one *s* two *d;* 2nd, 1963, Juliet Adrienne (marr. diss. 1974), *d of* late Hilary Lethbridge Kingsford and Mrs Latham Hobrow, Marlborough; two *d;* 3rd, 1974, Mrs Caroline Elizabeth Romilly (marr. diss. 1990), *d of* late Commander O. F. M. Wethered, RN, DL, JP. *Educ:* Eton. Lt RHG, 1946. Mem., London Stock Exchange, 1954. Heir: *s* Earl of Cardigan, *qv. Address:* Luton Lye House, Savernake Forest, near Marlborough, Wilts SN8 3HP.

AILSA, 8th Marquess of, *cr* 1831; **Archibald Angus Charles Kennedy;** Baron Kennedy 1452; Earl of Cassillis 1509; Baron Ailsa (UK) 1806; *b* 13 Sept. 1956; *er s of* 7th Marquess of Ailsa, OBE and Mary, 7th *c of* John Burn; *S* father, 1994; *m* 1979, Dawn Leslie Anne Keen (marr. diss. 1989); two *d. Recreations:* shooting, ski-ing, cadets and youth-work. Heir: *b* Lord David Thomas Kennedy [*b* 3 July 1958; *m* 1991, Anne Kelly; one *s* one *d*]. *Address:* Cassillis House, Maybole, Ayrshire KA19 7JN. *T:* (01292) 560310. *Club:* New (Edinburgh).

AINGER, Nicholas Richard, (Nick); MP (Lab) Carmarthen West and Pembrokeshire South, since 1997 (Pembroke, 1992–97); *b* Sheffield, 24 Oct. 1949; *m* 1976, Sally Robinson; one *d. Educ:* Netherthorpe Grammar Sch., Staveley. Rigger, Marine and Port Services Ltd, Pembroke Dock, 1977–92. Mem. (Lab) Dyfed CC, 1981–93. Branch Sec., TGWU, 1978–92. PPS to Sec. of State for Wales, 1997–2001; a Lord Comr, HM Treasury (Govt Whip), 2001–05; Parly Under-Sec. of State, Wales Office, 2005–07. *Address:* House of Commons, SW1A 0AA.

AINGER, Stephen David; Chief Executive, Partnership For Renewables, since 2007; *b* 27 Nov. 1951; *s of* Peter Jackson Ainger and Aileen (*née* Simpson); *m* 1992, Nicola Jane Corbett; one *s* one *d. Educ:* Towcester Grammar Sch.; Bath Univ. (BSc 1st cl. Hons (Physics) 1974). Exploration and Prodn posts with British Petroleum Co. Plc, London, Colombia, Brazil, Spain, Venezuela and Kuwait, 1974–98; Strategy and Business Develt Dir, Transco Plc, BG Gp, 1999–2000; Dir, Business Develt, Lattice Gp Plc, 2000–02; Chief Exec., Charities Aid Foundn, 2002–06. Trustee, Artsadmin, 2003–. FRSA. *Recreations:* classic cars, architectural heritage. *Address:* (office) 8th Floor, 3 Clements Inn, WC2A 2AZ. *T:* (020) 7171 7000, *Fax:* (020) 7171 7020; *e-mail:* stephen.ainger@carbontrust.co.uk.

AINLEY, (David) Geoffrey, CEng, FIMechE; FRAeS; AGAvA; Deputy Director (Projects and Research), Military Vehicles and Engineering Establishment, Chertsey, 1978–84; *b* 5 July 1924; *s of* Cyril Edward and Constance Ainley; *m* 1st, 1948, Dorothy Emily (*née* Roberts); one *s* one *d;* 2nd, 1959, Diana Margery Hill (*née* Sayles); one *d;* 3rd, 1988, Joyce Dinah (*née* Jessett). *Educ:* Brentwood Sch., Essex; Queen Mary Coll., London Univ. (BSc, 1st Cl. Hons). Engine Dept, RAE, Farnborough, 1943–44; Power Jets (R&D) Ltd, 1944–46; National Gas Turbine Estabt, Pyestock, 1946–66; idc 1967; Dir of Engine Develt, MoD (Procurement Exec.), 1968–78. George Stephenson Research Prize, IMechE, 1953. *Publications:* contrib. books and learned jls on gas turbine technology. *Recreations:* painting, sketching, golf. *Address:* 20 Hampton Close, Church Crookham, Fleet, Hants GU52 8LB.

AINLEY, Nicholas John; His Honour Judge Ainley; a Circuit Judge, since 2003; Vice President, Immigration Appeal Tribunal, 2003–05; *b* 18 March 1952; *s of* Edgar Ainley and Jean Olga Ainley (*née* Simister); *m* 1980, Susan Elizabeth Waugh; two *s* one *d. Educ:* Sevenoaks Sch. Called to the Bar, Lincoln's Inn, 1973; Supplementary Panel Counsel to the Crown (Common Law), 1995–2001; Asst Recorder, 1996–2000; a Recorder, 2000–03. *Publication:* (jtly) Disclosure and Confidentiality, 1996. *Recreations:* family, travel, books. *Address:* c/o The Law Courts, Altyre Road, Croydon CR9 5AB. *Clubs:* Sussex Yacht (Shoreham); Royal de Panne Sand Yacht (Belgium).

AINLEY, Vivien Lesley; Headmistress, South Hampstead High School, 2001–04; *b* 29 March 1950; *d of* Herbert John Matthews and Win Matthews; *m* 1975, Eric Michael Ainley; two *d. Educ:* Univ. of Durham (BA Econs 1971); Hughes Hall, Cambridge (PGCE with distinction 1979); Univ. of Maryland (MA Secondary Educn (Maths) 1982). CSIR, Pretoria, South Africa, 1972–73; Bank of England, 1973–77; UCNW, Bangor, 1976–77; CEGB, 1977–78; Teacher of Econs and Stats, 1985–91, Hd of Sixth Form, 1991–94, Haberdashers' Aske's Sch. for Girls; Sen. Mistress, Oundle Sch., 1994–96; Surmistress, St Paul's Girls' Sch., 1996–2001. *Recreations:* theatre, travel, gardening. *Address:* 52 Sterndale Road, W14 0HU.

AINSCOW, Robert Morrison, CB 1989; independent consultant, since 1996; Deputy Secretary, Overseas Development Administration, Foreign and Commonwealth Office, 1986–96; *b* 3 June 1936; *s of* Robert M. Ainscow and Hilda Ainscow (*née* Cleminson); *m* 1965, Faye Bider; one *s* one *d. Educ:* Salford Grammar School; Liverpool Univ. (BA Econ Hons). Statistician: Govt of Rhodesia and Nyasaland, 1957–61; UN Secretariat, New York, 1961–65 and 1966–68; Dept of Economic Affairs, London, 1965–66. Ministry of Overseas Development: Economic Adviser, 1968–70; Senior Economic Adviser, 1971–76; Head, South Asia Dept, 1976–79; Under Secretary, FCO (ODA), 1979–86. Chm., OECD (DAC) Working Party on Financial Aspects of Develt Assistance, 1982–86; Member: World Bank/IMF Develt Cttee Task Force on Concessional Flows, 1983–85, on Multilateral Develt Banks, 1994–96; Asian Develt Bank Inspection Panel, 1996–2002. Consultant to UN, World Bank, OECD, DFID, Ireland Aid, and Overseas Develt Council, Washington, 1996–. Mem. Bd Trustees, BRCS, 2000–06. *T:* and *Fax:* (020) 7435 2218; *e-mail:* robain@hotmail.co.uk.

AINSLEY, John Mark; tenor; *b* 9 July 1963; *s of* John Alwyn Ainsley and Dorothy Sylvia (*née* Anderson). *Educ:* Royal Grammar Sch., Worcester; Magdalen Coll., Oxford. Début in Stravinsky's Mass, RFH, 1984; subsequent débuts: USA, in NY and Boston, 1990; with Berlin Philharmonic Orch., 1992; Glyndebourne Fest., in Così fan Tutte, 1992; Aix-en-Provence, in Don Giovanni, 1993; San Francisco, in Don Giovanni, 1995; appears regularly with ENO, Royal Opera, and leading orchestras incl. LPO, LSO, Scottish Chamber Orch. and Orchestre de Paris. Has made numerous recordings. Grammy Award for best opera recording, 1995. *Recreation:* chocolate. *Address:* Askonas Holt Ltd, Lincoln House, 300 High Holborn, WC1V 7JH. *T:* (020) 7400 1700.

AINSLIE, Charles Benedict, (Ben), OBE 2005 (MBE 2001); professional yachtsman; *b* 5 Feb. 1977; *s of* Michael Roderick and Susan Linda Ainslie. *Educ:* Truro Sch.; Peter Symonds' Coll., Winchester. Laser Cl. World Champion, 1998 and 1999; Gold Medal, Laser Cl. Sailing, Sydney Olympics, 2000; Finn Cl. World Champion, 2002, 2003, 2004, 2005 and 2008; Gold Medal, Finn Cl. Sailing, Athens Olympics, 2004; Gold Medal, Finn Cl. Sailing, Beijing Olympics, 2008. ISAF World Sailor of the Year, 1998 and 2002. Hon. MSc UC Chichester, 2001; Hon. LLD Exeter, 2005; Hon. DSport Southampton Solent, 2007. *Publication:* The Laser Campaign Manual, 2002. *Recreations:* motor racing, cycling, flying. *Address:* Carne Vean, Manaccan, Helston, Cornwall TR12 6HD. *Clubs:* Royal Cornwall Yacht (Hon. Mem.), Stokes Bay Sailing (Gosport) (Hon. Mem.), Restronguet Sailing (Falmouth) (Hon. Mem.).

AINSWORTH, Sir Anthony (Thomas Hugh), 5th Bt *cr* 1916, of Ardanaiseig, co. Argyll; Director, Richard Glynn Consultants, since 2000; *b* 30 March 1962; *er s of* Sir David Ainsworth, 4th Bt and of Sarah Mary, *d of* Lt–Col H. C. Walford; *S* father, 1999; *m* 2003, Anong Pradith; one *d. Educ:* Harrow. Lt, Royal Hussars (PWO), 1982–85. Heir: *b* Charles David Ainsworth, *b* 24 Aug. 1966. *Address:* 208 Wireless Road, Lumpini, Bangkok 10330, Thailand; *e-mail:* anthony@rglynn.th.com.

AINSWORTH, James Bernard; restaurant consultant; Editor, Good Food Guide, 1994–2002 (Consultant Editor, 2003); *b* 1 Feb. 1944; *s of* Henry Bernard Ainsworth and Margaret Ainsworth (*née* Fletcher); *m* 2002, Valerie (*née* McCully); two step *d. Educ:* Duke St Primary Sch.; Chorley Grammar Sch.; Liverpool Univ. (BA Psychol.). Lectr in Psychol. and Educn, Chorley Coll. of Educn, 1970–78; Proprietor, Vineyard Restaurant, Northampton, 1979–84; drinks columnist, Punch, 1984–92; freelance wine writer and restaurant reviewer, 1984–. *Publications:* Mitchell Beazley Red Wine Guide, 1990; Mitchell Beazley White Wine Guide, 1990. *Recreations:* eating home produce including bacon and super-fresh eggs, playing the hymns in church. *Address:* Bicton Pool House, Bicton, Kingsland, Leominster, Herefordshire HR6 9PR.

AINSWORTH, Rev. Janina Helen Margaret; Chief Education Officer, Church of England, since 2007; General Secretary, National Society, since 2007; *b* 23 Dec. 1950; *d* of Paul and Isobel Brych; *m* 1974, Michael Ronald Ainsworth; two *s* two *d*. *Educ:* Nottingham High Sch. for Girls; Homerton Coll., Cambridge (Cert Ed 1972); Newnham Coll., Cambridge (BEd 1973); Lancaster Univ. (MA Religious Studies 1974); Ripon Coll., Cuddesdon. RE Teacher: Manor Sch., Arbury, 1974–75; Greaves Sch., Lancaster, 1975–78; pt-time Lectr and Warden, St Martin's Coll., Lancaster, 1978–82; Manchester Diocesan Board of Education: Children's Work Advr, 1986–91; RE and Schs Advr, 1991–98; Diocesan Dir of Educn, 1998–2007. Ordained deacon, 2005, priest, 2006; non-stipendiary Curate, E Farnworth and Kearsley, 2005–07. FRSA. *Publications:* (with Alan Brown) Moral Education, 1994; Clergy and Church Schools, 1995. *Recreations:* singing church music, cinema, crime novels. *Address:* c/o Church House, Great Smith Street, SW1P 3AZ. *T:* (020) 7898 1500; *e-mail:* janina.ainsworth@c-of-e.org.uk.

AINSWORTH, (Mervyn) John, OBE 2008; FCIS, FInstAM; Chief Executive and Secretary, Institute of Chartered Secretaries and Administrators, 1990–2007; *b* 28 Jan. 1947; *s* of late Gordon John Ainsworth and Eileen Ainsworth; *m* 1973, Marta Christina Marmolak; two *s* one *d*. *Educ:* Stanfields Technical High Sch., Stoke-on-Trent; Goldsmiths' Coll., Univ. of London (CertEd; DipEd). Asst Clerk to Govs and Bursar, Dulwich Coll., 1969–74; Principal Assistant, Sec. and Solicitors' Dept, CEGB, 1974–77; Secretarial Asst, BTDB, 1977–78; Sec., 1978–83, Sec. and Dir of Finance, 1983–84, BPIF; Sec. General, Inst. of Administrative Management, 1984–90. Director: ICSA Publishing, 1990–2007; ICSA Consultants, 1992–2007; ICSA Software, 1993–2007; Inst. of Business Administration, 1992–2007. Special Advr, Assets Reunited (UK) LLP, 2008–. Member: Bd, Nat. Examining Bd for Supervisory Management, 1984–99; Academic Bd, Greenwich Coll., 1984–97; Court, Cranfield Univ. (formerly Inst. of Technology), 1990–; Council for Admin (formerly Admin Lead Body), 1991–; Open and Distance Learning Quality Council (formerly Council for Certification of Correspondence Colls), 1994– (Chm., 1998–); City & Guilds Quality Standards Cttee, 1999–2005; Commonwealth Assoc. for Corporate Governance, 2000–. Mem. Ct of Assts, Worshipful Co. of Chartered Secs and Administrators, 2006–. Hon. Fellow, Canadian Inst. of Certified Administrative Managers, 1987; Hon. MCGI 2006. Hon. DBA Bournemouth, 1997; DUniv Anglia Ruskin, 2006. *Publications:* articles on management education and administrative systems. *Recreations:* golf, motoring, travel. *Address:* 3 Silverdale Drive, SE9 4DH.

AINSWORTH, Peter Michael; MP (C) Surrey East, since 1992; *b* 16 Nov. 1956; *s* of late Lt-Comdr Michael Lionel Yeoward Ainsworth, RN and of Patricia Mary Ainsworth (*née* Bedford); *m* 1981, Claire Alison Burnett; one *s* two *d*. *Educ:* Ludgrove, Wokingham; Bradfield Coll.; Lincoln Coll., Oxford (MA Eng. Lit. and Lang.). Res. Asst to Sir J. Stewart-Clark, MEP, 1979–81; Investment Analyst, Laing & Cruickshank, 1981–85; Sen. Investment Analyst, S. G. Warburg Securities, 1985–87; Asst Dir, 1987–89, Dir, 1989–92, S. G. Warburg Securities Corporate Finance. Mem., Wandsworth Borough Council, 1986–94 (Chm., Cons. Group, 1990–92). PPS to Chief Sec. to HM Treasury, 1994–95, to Sec. of State for Nat. Heritage, 1996; an Asst Govt Whip, 1996–97; Opposition Dep. Chief Whip, 1997–98; Shadow Secretary of State: for Culture, Media and Sport, 1998–2001; for Envmt, Food and Rural Affairs, 2001–02, 2005–. Member, Select Committee: on Envmt, 1993–94; on Public Affairs, 1996; on Envmtl Audit, 2003–05 (Chm., 2003–05). Sec., All-Party Conservation Gp, 1994–97. Mem. Council, Bow Group, 1984–86. Mem. Bd, Plantlife, 2003–. Chm., Elgar Foundn, 2005–. Presenter, Discord, Music and Dissent, radio, 2000. FRSA 1998. *Recreations:* family, music, doggerel. *Address:* House of Commons, SW1A 0AA. *Club:* MCC.

AINSWORTH, Rt Hon. Robert (William); PC 2005; MP (Lab) Coventry North East, since 1992; Minister of State, Ministry of Defence, since 2007; *b* 19 June 1952; *s* of late Stanley Ewart Ainsworth and Monica Pearl Ainsworth (later Mrs D. J. Scullion); *m* 1974, Gloria Jean Sandall; two *d*. *Educ:* Foxford Comprehensive School. Sheet metal worker and fitter, Jaguar, 1971–91 (Shop Steward, MSF, 1974–91; Sec., Joint Stewards, 1980–91). City Councillor, Coventry, 1984–93 (Dep. Leader, 1988–91; Chm., Finance, 1989–92). An Opposition Whip, 1995–97; a Lord Comr of HM Treasury (Govt Whip), 1997–2001; Parly Under-Sec. of State, DETR, 2001, Home Office, 2001–03; Treasurer of HM Household (Dep. Chief Whip), 2003–07. Mem., Select Cttee on environmental affairs, 1993–95. Vice-Chm., W Midlands Gp of Labour MPs, 1995–97. *Recreations:* walking, reading, chess. *Address:* House of Commons, SW1A 0AA. *T:* (020) 7219 4047. *Clubs:* Bell Green Working Men's (Coventry); Broad Street Old Boy's RFC (Coventry).

AINSWORTH, Prof. Roger William, DPhil; FRAeS; Master, St Catherine's College, Oxford, since 2002; Professor of Engineering Science, since 1998, and Pro Vice-Chancellor, since 2003, University of Oxford; *b* 17 Nov. 1951; *s* of Harold Ainsworth and Mary Ainsworth (*née* Reynolds); *m* 1978, Sarah Pilkington; one *s* two *d*. *Educ:* Lancaster Royal Grammar Sch.; Jesus Coll., Oxford (BA 1st Cl. 1973; DPhil 1976; Hon. Fellow, 2002). Research Section Leader: Aero Engines Div., Rolls-Royce Ltd, 1976–77; Engrg Scis Div., AERE Harwell, 1977–85; University of Oxford: Fellow and Tutor in Engrg, St Catherine's Coll., 1985–2002; Univ. Lectr in Fluid Mechanics, 1985–96; Reader in Engrg Sci., 1996–98; Sen. Proctor, 1998–99; Chairman: Faculty Bd of Mgt Studies, 1999–2001; Bd of Continuing Educn, 2004–; Mem., Council, 2002–05; Delegate, 1998–, Finance Delegate, 2001–, OUP. Vis. Prof., EPFL Lausanne, 1998–. Recorder, Engrg Section, BAAS, 1988–92. Trustee, Oxford Preservation Trust, 1989–95; Oxford Sch. of Drama, 2005–. Governor: Abingdon Sch., 1997–; Dragon Sch., Oxford, 2004–. Royal Society Esso Energy Award, 1996. Knight, Order of Danneborg (Denmark), 2006. *Publications:* various contribs related to turbomachinery in sci. jls. *Recreations:* Baroque music, technical pursuits and gadgetry. *Address:* The Master's Lodgings, St Catherine's College, Oxford OX1 3UJ. *T:* (01865) 271762. *Club:* Oxford and Cambridge.

AIPO RONGO, Bishop of; *see* Papua New Guinea, Archbishop of.

AIRD, Captain Sir Alastair (Sturgis), GCVO 1997 (KCVO 1984; CVO 1977; LVO 1969); Comptroller, 1974–2002, and Private Secretary and Equerry, 1993–2002, to Queen Elizabeth the Queen Mother; an Extra Equerry to the Queen, since 2003; *b* 14 Jan. 1931; *s* of Col Malcolm Aird; *m* 1963, Fiona Violet Myddelton (*see* F. V. Aird); two *d*. *Educ:* Eton; RMA Sandhurst. Commnd 9th Queen's Royal Lancers, 1951; served in BAOR; Adjt 9th Lancers, 1956–59; retd from Army, 1964. Equerry to Queen Elizabeth the Queen Mother, 1960; Asst Private Sec. to the Queen Mother, 1964. Mem. Council, Feathers Assoc. of Youth Clubs, 1973–93; Trustee, RSAS Develt Trust, 1986–99. Hon. Bencher, Middle Temple, 1991. *Recreations:* shooting, fishing, golf. *Address:* The Paddock, Lovells Court, Marnhull, Sturminster Newton, Dorset DT10 1JJ. *Clubs:* Cavalry and Guards; Eton Ramblers; I Zingari.

AIRD, Fiona Violet, (Lady Aird), CVO 2001 (LVO 1980); Extra Lady-in-Waiting to HRH Princess Margaret, Countess of Snowdon, 1963–2002; *b* 24 Sept. 1934; *d* of late Lt Col Ririd Myddelton, LVO, and of Lady Margaret Myddelton; *m* 1963, Capt. Sir Alastair Sturgis Aird, *qv*; two *d*. *Educ:* Westonbirt Sch.; in France. Lady-in-Waiting to HRH Princess Margaret, 1960–63. Mem. Council, UCL, 1987–97 (Hon. Fellow, 2003). Chm., Middx Hosp. League of Friends, 1987–2002; Vice-Pres., England, Nat. Assoc. of Hosp. and Community Friends, 2000–; Chm., Florence Nightingale Aid in Sickness Trust, 1994–. *Recreations:* reading, fishing. *Address:* The Paddock, Lovells Court, Marnhull, Sturminster Newton, Dorset DT10 1JJ.

AIRD, Sir (George) John, 4th Bt *cr* 1901; Chairman, Matcon plc, since 1980; Chairman and Managing Director, Sir John Aird & Co. Ltd, 1969–96; *b* 30 Jan. 1940; *e s* of Sir John Renton Aird, 3rd Bt, MVO, MC, and Lady Priscilla Aird, *yr d* of 2nd Earl of Ancaster; *S* father, 1973; *m* 1968, Margaret, *yr d* of Sir John Muir, 3rd Bt; one *s* two *d*. *Educ:* Eton; Oxford Univ.; Harvard Business Sch. MICE. Trainee, Sir Alexander Gibb & Partners, 1961–65; Manager, John Laing & Son Ltd, 1967–69. Dir, Healthcare Development Services Ltd, 1994–2006. *Recreations:* ski-ing, tennis, hunting. *Heir:* *s* James John Aird, *b* 12 June 1978. *Address:* Grange Farm, Evenlode, Moreton-in-Marsh, Glos GL56 0NT. *T:* (01608) 650607; *e-mail:* johnaird@aol.com.
See also Baroness Willoughby de Eresby.

AIREY, David Lawrence; Managing Director, Bunge & Co. Ltd, 1987–90, retired; *b* 28 April 1935; *s* of Samuel Airey and Helena Florence Lever; *m* 1961, Joan Mary Stewart; three *d*. *Educ:* Oldershaw Grammar Sch., Wallasey. J. Bibby & Sons Ltd: Management trainee, various sales/commercial management positions, 1952–74; Chief Exec., Edible Oils Div., 1974–78; Man. Dir, J. Bibby Edible Oils Ltd, 1979–86; Dep. Man. Dir, Bunge & Co. Ltd, 1986. Chm., Seed Crushers & Oil Processors Assoc., 1980–82. Trustee, Wiltshire and Swindon Community Foundn, 1996–2002. JP Liverpool, 1980–86. *Recreations:* Rugby Union football (Birkenhead Park FC, 1955–66, Cheshire, 1958–65, North West Counties, 1964, Barbarians, 1965), fishing, cooking, gardening, golf. *Address:* Darnley, Church Road, Woodborough, Pewsey, Wilts SN9 5PH. *T:* (01672) 851647. *Clubs:* Birkenhead Park FC; Upavon Golf.

AIREY, Dawn Elizabeth; Chairman and Chief Executive, Five, since 2008; *b* Preston, Lancs, 15 Nov. 1960; civil partnership 2006, Jacqueline Lawrence; one *d*. *Educ:* Kelly College; Girton College, Cambridge (MA Hons). Central TV: management trainee, 1985–86; Channel 4 Liaison Officer, 1987; Associate Producer, 1988; Controller, later Dir, Programme Planning, Central Broadcasting, 1988–93; Controller of Network Children's and Daytime Progs, ITV Network Centre, 1993–94; Controller of Arts and Entertainment, Channel 4, 1994–96; Dir of Progs, 1996–2000, Chief Exec., 2000–02, Channel 5; Man. Dir, Sky Networks, 2003–07, Man. Dir, Channels and Services, 2006–07, BSkyB; Man. Dir, Global Content, ITV, 2007–08. Non-exec. Dir, easyJet, 2004–. Member: Film Council, 1999–2002; Bd, Internat. Acad. of Television Arts and Scis, 2003–; British Liby Bd, 2007–. Patron, Birmingham Film and TV Festival, 1996–; Gov., Banff Fest., 1999–; Chm., Edinburgh Internat. Television Fest., 2000; Exec. Chm., Guardian Edin. Internat. Television Fest., 2002–06. Patron, Skillset, 2002–. Trustee, Media Trust, 2004–. FRSA 1996; FRTS 1999 (Vice-Pres., 2002–). *Recreations:* tennis, fine wines, cinema, TV, collecting antique maps. *Address:* Five, 22 Long Acre, WC2E 9LY.

AIREY, Janet Claire; *see* Bazley, J. C.

AIRLIE, 13th Earl of, *cr* 1639 (*de facto* 11th Earl, 13th but for the Attainder); **David George Coke Patrick Ogilvy,** KT 1985; GCVO 1984; PC 1984; Royal Victorian Chain, 1997; JP; Baron Ogilvy of Airlie, 1491; Captain late Scots Guards; Lord Chamberlain of HM Household, 1984–97; Lord-Lieutenant of Angus, 1989–2001; a Permanent Lord-in-Waiting to the Queen, since 1997; Chancellor, Order of the Thistle, since 2007; *b* 17 May 1926; *e s* of 12th Earl of Airlie, KT, GCVO, MC, and Lady Alexandra Marie Bridget Coke (*d* 1984), *d* of 3rd Earl of Leicester, GCVO; *S* father, 1968; *m* 1952, Virginia Fortune Ryan (*see* Countess of Airlie); three *s* three *d*. *Educ:* Eton. Lieutenant Scots Guards, 1944; serving 2nd Battalion Germany, 1945; Captain, ADC to High Comr and C-in-C Austria, 1947–48; Malaya, 1948–49; resigned commission, 1950. Ensign, 1975–85, Lieutenant, 1985–2000, Pres., 2000, Captain-Gen. and Gold Stick, 2004–, Queen's Body Guard for Scotland, Royal Company of Archers. Chancellor, Royal Victorian Order, 1984–97. Chairman: Schroders plc, 1977–84; Gen. Accident Fire & Life Assurance Corp., 1987–97 (Dir, 1962–97; Dep. Chm., 1975–87); Ashdown Investment Trust Ltd, 1968–82; Director: J. Henry Schroder Wagg & Co. Ltd, 1961–84 (Chm., 1973–77); Scottish & Newcastle Breweries plc, 1969–83; The Royal Bank of Scotland Gp, 1983–93; Baring Stratton Investment Trust (formerly Stratton Investment Trust), 1986–97. Chm., Historic Royal Palaces Trust, 1998–2002; Dep. Chm., Royal Collection Trust, 1992–97; Pres., NT for Scotland, 1998–2002; Trustee, Prince's Foundn for Built Envmt, 2003–06. Treasurer, Scout Assoc., 1962–86; Hon. Pres., Scottish Council of Scout Assoc., 1988–2001. Gov., Nuffield Nursing Homes Trust, 1985–89; Chancellor, Univ. of Abertay Dundee, 1994–. DL Angus, 1964; JP Angus, 1990. Hon. LLD Dundee, 1990. *Heir:* *s* Lord Ogilvy, *qv*. *Address:* Cortachy Castle, Kirriemuir, Angus DD8 4LX. *T:* (01575) 540231; 36 Sloane Court West, SW3 4TB. *T:* (020) 7823 6246.
See also Hon. J. D. D. Ogilvy, Sir H. Wake.

AIRLIE, Countess of; Virginia Fortune Ogilvy, DCVO 1995 (CVO 1983); Lady of the Bedchamber to the Queen since 1973; *b* 9 Feb. 1933; *d* of John Barry Ryan, Newport, RI, USA; *m* 1952, Lord Ogilvy (now Earl of Airlie, *qv*); three *s* three *d*. *Educ:* Brearley School, New York City. Founder Governor, Cobham School, Kent, 1958. Mem., Industrial Design Panel, British Rail, 1974–94; Comr, Royal Fine Arts Commn, 1975–88. Trustee: Tate Gallery, 1983–95 (Chm. Friends of Tate Gallery, 1978–83); Amer. Mus. in Britain, 1985–89 (Chm., 2001–); Nat. Gallery, 1989–95; Nat. Galls of Scotland, 1995 (Chm., 1997–2000). Pres., Angus Br., BRCS, 1988. *Address:* Cortachy Castle, Kirriemuir, Angus DD8 4LX; 36 Sloane Court West, SW3 4TB.

AIRS, Prof. Malcolm Russell, DPhil; FSA, FRHistS; Fellow, since 1991, and Vice-President, since 2006, Kellogg College (formerly Rewley House), Oxford; Professor of Conservation and the Historic Environment, University of Oxford, 2002–06; President, Institute of Historic Building Conservation, 2001–03 (Chairman, 1998–2001); *b* 7 March 1941; *s* of George William Laurence Airs and Gwendoline Elizabeth Airs (*née* Little); partner, 1971, Megan Parry; one *s*. *Educ:* Bushey Grammar Sch.; Oriel Coll., Oxford (BA Hons Modern Hist. 1963, MA, DPhil 1970). FSA 1980; IHBC 1998; FRHistS 2003. Historian, Historic Bldgs Div., GLC, 1966–73; Architectural Ed., Survey of London, 1973–74; Conservation Officer, S Oxfordshire DC, 1974–91; Lectr, 1991–96, Reader, 1996–2002, in Conservation and Historic Envmt, Univ. of Oxford. Member: Historic Bldgs and Areas Adv. Cttee, English Heritage, 1988–2003; Historic Buildings and Land Panel, Heritage Lottery Fund, 2004–05; Architectural Panel, NT, 2004–; Comr, RCHM, 1993–99. Trustee: Oxford Preservation Trust, 1993–; Standing Conf. on Trng of Architects in Conservation, 1996–2004; Landmark Trust, 2007–. Pres., Oxford Architectl and Histl Soc., 2001–05; Vice-Pres., Assoc. of Small Historic Towns and Villages, 2006–. *Publications:* The Making of the English Country House 1500–1640, 1975; The Buildings of Britain: Tudor and Jacobean, 1982; The Tudor and Jacobean Country House, 1995; numerous articles on architectural hist. and historic conservation. *Recreations:* visiting buildings, cultivating my allotment, following the lost cause of Oxford United. *Address:* 39 High Street, Dorchester on Thames, Wallingford OX10 7HN. *Club:* Oxford United Supporters.

AIRY, Maj.-Gen. Sir Christopher (John), KCVO 1989; CBE 1984; Private Secretary and Treasurer to TRH The Prince and Princess of Wales, 1990–91; an Extra Equerry to the Prince of Wales, since 1991; *b* 8 March 1934; *m* 1959, Judith Stephenson; one *s* two *d. Educ:* Marlborough Coll.; RMA Sandhurst. 2nd Lieut, Grenadier Guards, 1954; Scots Guards, 1974. PMA to Sec. of State for War, 1960; sc 1966; DAAG, Regtl Adjt, 1967; Bde Major, 4th Guards Armoured Bde, 1971; ndc 1973; CO, 1st Bn Scots Guards, 1974; Mil. Asst (GSO1) to Master Gen. of the Ordnance, 1976; Comdr 5th Field Force, 1979; rcds 1981; ACOS, HQ UKLF, 1982–83; Sen. Army Mem., RCDS, 1984–85; GOC London District and Maj.-Gen. Comdg Household Div., 1986; retd 1989. Chm., C. N. Unwin Ltd, 2006– (non-exec. Dir, 2003–06). Chairman: Not Forgotten Assoc., 1992–2001; Nat. Assoc. of Air Ambulance Services, 1999–2002; Comr, Royal Hosp., Chelsea, 1990–96; Mem., Prince of Wales's Council, 1990–91. Vice-Pres., Brainwave, 2000–. Trustee: Hedley Foundn, 1994–2002; The Voices Foundn, 2003–. Patron, Soc. of Mary and Martha, 1998–. *Recreations:* gardening, alpaca smallholder, churches. *Address:* c/o Headquarters Scots Guards, Wellington Barracks, Birdcage Walk, SW1E 6HQ.

AITCHISON, Sir Charles Walter de Lancey; *see* Aittchisen, Sir Lance Walter.

AITCHISON, Craigie (Ronald John), CBE 1999; RA 1988 (ARA 1978); painter; *b* 13 Jan. 1926; *yr s* of late Rt Hon. Lord Aitchison, PC, KC, LLD. *Educ:* Scotland; Slade Sch. of Fine Art. British Council Italian Govt Scholarship for painting, 1955; Edwin Austin Abbey Premier Scholarship, 1965; Lorne Scholarship, 1974–75. One-man Exhibitions: Beaux Arts Gall., 1959, 1960, 1964; Marlborough Fine Art (London) Ltd, 1968; Compass Gall., Glasgow, 1970; Basil Jacobs Gall., 1971; Rutland Gall., 1975; Knoedler Gall., 1977; Kettle's Yard Gall., Cambridge, 1979; Serpentine Gall. (major retrospective, 1953–81), 1981–82; Artis, Monte Carlo, Monaco, 1986; Albemarle Gall., 1987, 1989; Castlefield Gall., Manchester, 1990; Thomas Gibson Fine Art, London, 1993; Harewood House, Leeds (retrospective, 1954–94); Gall. of Modern Art, Glasgow (retrospective, 1956–96), 1996; Timothy Taylor Gall., Waddington Galls, 1998, 2001, 2004. Exhibited: Calouste Gulbenkian Internat. Exhibn, 1964; Il Tempo del imagine, 2nd Internat. Biennale, Bologna, 1967; Modern British Painters, Tokyo, Japan, 1969; 23rd Salon Actualité de l'Esprit, Paris, 1975; The Proper Study, British Council Lalit Kala Akademi, Delhi, 1984; Hard Won Image, Tate Gall., 1985; British Council Exhibn, Picturing People, Hong Kong and Zimbabwe, 1990; The Journey, Lincoln Cathedral, 1990; Nine Contemporary Painters, City of Bristol Mus. and Art Gall., 1990; British Council Exhibn, British Figurative Painting of 20th Century, Israel Mus., Jerusalem, 1992. Pictures in public collections: Tate Gall., Arts Council, Contemp. Art Soc., Scottish National Gall. of Modern Art, Glasgow Mus. and Art Gall., and Nat. Gall. of Melbourne, Australia; Truro Cathedral, Liverpool Cathedral and chapel of King's College, Cambridge. 1st Johnson Wax Prize, Royal Acad., 1982; Korn Ferry Internat. Award, Royal Acad., 1989 and 1991; 1st Jerwood Foundn Award, 1994; Nordstern Art Award, RA, 2000. *Address:* c/o Royal Academy of Arts, Burlington House, Piccadilly, W1V 0DS.

AITCHISON, Prof. Jean Margaret; Rupert Murdoch Professor of Language and Communication, University of Oxford, 1993–2003; Fellow, Worcester College, Oxford, 1993–2003, now Emeritus; *b* 3 July 1938; *d* of late John Frederick and Joan Eileen Aitchison; *m* 2000, John Robert Ayto. *Educ:* Wimbledon High Sch.; Girton Coll., Cambridge (BA 1st Cl. Hons Classics 1960; MA 1964); Radcliffe Coll., Harvard (AM Linguistics 1961). University of London: Asst Lectr in Ancient Greek, Bedford Coll., 1960–65; Lectr, 1965–82, Sen. Lectr, 1982–92, Reader, 1992, in Linguistics, LSE. Reith Lectr, BBC, 1996. *Publications:* Linguistics, 1972, 6th edn 2003; The Articulate Mammal: an introduction to psycholinguistics, 1976, 5th edn 2008; Language Change: progress or decay?, 1981, 3rd edn 2001; Words in the Mind: an introduction to the mental lexicon, 1987, 3rd edn 2003; The Seeds of Speech: language origin and evolution, 1996; The Language Web: the power and problem of words (Reith lectures), 1997; A Glossary of Language and Mind, 2003; (ed with Diana Lewis) New Media Language, 2003; The Word Weavers: newshounds and wordsmiths, 2007. *Recreation:* gardening. *Address:* 45 Malvern Road, E8 3LP. *T:* (020) 7249 3734; *e-mail:* jean.aitchison@worc.ox.ac.uk.

AITCHISON, June Rosemary, (Mrs T. J. Aitchison); *see* Whitfield, J. R.

AITCHISON, Thomas Nisbet, CBE 2005; Chief Executive, City of Edinburgh Council, since 1995; *b* 24 Feb. 1951; *s* of Thomas Aitchison and Mary (*née* Millar); *m* 1973, Kathleen Sadler; one *s* two *d. Educ:* Univ. of Glasgow (MA 1st Class Hons); Heriot-Watt Univ. (MSc). Lothian Regional Council: various posts, 1975–91; Depute Chief Exec., 1991–94; Chief Exec., 1994–95. Regl Returning Officer for Scotland Region, European elecns, 1999 and 2004. Chm., SOLACE Scotland, 2001–03. Mem. Court, Napier Univ., 1997–2002. Sec., Edinburgh Internat. Fest. Soc., 1996–. *Recreations:* hill-walking, football, music, fine wines and malt whiskies. *Address:* City of Edinburgh Council, Council Headquarters, Waverley Court, 4 East Market Street, Edinburgh EH8 8BG. *Fax:* (0131) 469 3010.

AITHRIE, Viscount; Charles Adrian Bristow William Hope; *b* 25 July 2001; *s* and *heir* of Earl of Hopetoun, *qv*.

AITKEN, family name of **Baron Beaverbrook**.

AITKEN, Cairns; *see* Aitken, R. C. B.

AITKEN, Gill; Director General, Legal Group, Department for Environment, Food and Rural Affairs, since 2007 (Director, Legal Services, 2004–07); *b* 23 March 1960; *d* of Bill and Pamela Parker; *m* 1998, Robert Aitken; one *s*, and two step *s. Educ:* St Hugh's Coll., Oxford (BA Hons Philosophy and Theol. 1982). Admitted solicitor, 1988; solicitor in private practice, 1988–93; lawyer in Govt Legal Service, 1993–. *Recreations:* family, cycling, art history, theatre, conversation and ideas.

AITKEN, Gillon Reid; literary agent; Chairman, Aitken Alexander Associates (formerly Gillon Aitken, then Aitken, Stone & Wylie, subsequently Aitken & Stone, latterly Gillon Aitken Associates) Ltd, since 1977; *b* 29 March 1938; *s* of James Aitken and Margaret Joane Aitken (*née* Simpson); *m* 1982, Cari Margareta Bengtsson (marr. diss. 2000); one *d. Educ:* Charterhouse Sch.; privately. Private schoolmaster, Surbiton, 1955–56; National Service, 1956–58: Somerset LI; Intelligence Corps; Jt Services Sch. for Linguists (Russian course); Royal Signal Corps, Berlin. Stuart's Advertising Agency Ltd, 1958–59; Editor: Chapman & Hall Ltd, 1959–66; Hodder & Stoughton Ltd, 1966–67; Dir, Anthony Sheil Associates Ltd, 1967–71; Man. Dir, Hamish Hamilton Ltd, 1971–74; Vice-Pres., Wallace, Aitken & Sheil, Inc. (NY), 1974–77; Chairman: Christy & Moore Ltd, 1977–; Hughes Massie Ltd, 1985–. *Publications:* translations from Russian: The Captain's Daughter & Other Stories by Alexander Sergeyevitch Pushkin, 1962; The Complete Prose Tales of Pushkin, 1966; One Day in the Life of Ivan Denisovich by Alexander Solzhenitsyn, 1970. *Recreations:* crossword puzzles, ping-pong. *Address:* c/o Aitken Alexander Associates Ltd, 18–21 Cavaye Place, SW10 9PT. *T:* (020) 7373 8672; The Garden Flat, 4 The Boltons, SW10 9TB. *T:* (020) 7373 7438. *Clubs:* Beefsteak, Brooks's.

AITKEN, Ian Levack; columnist, Tribune, since 1998; *b* 19 Sept. 1927; *s* of George Aitken and Agnes Levack Aitken; *m* 1956, Dr Catherine Hay Mackie (*d* 2006), *y d* of late Maitland Mackie, OBE; two *d. Educ:* King Alfred Sch., Hampstead; Regent Street Polytechnic; Lincoln Coll., Oxford (BA PPE; MA); LSE. Served Fleet Air Arm, 1945–48. HM Inspector of Factories, 1951; Res. Officer, CSEU, 1952; Industrial Reporter, Tribune, 1953–54; Industrial Reporter, subseq. Foreign Correspondent and Political Correspondent, Daily Express, 1954–64; political staff, The Guardian, 1964–92 (Political Editor, 1975–90; political columnist, 1990–92; columnist, 1992; contributor, 1992–); columnist and contributing editor, New Statesman, 1993–96. Gerald Barry Award for journalism, 1984. *Publication:* (with Mark Garnett) Splendid! Splendid!: the authorised biography of William Whitelaw, 2002. *Recreation:* music. *Address:* 8 Fitzwarren House, 12 Hornsey Lane, N6 5LX. *T:* (020) 7272 2314. *Club:* Garrick.

See also Baron Mackie of Benshie.

AITKEN, Jonathan William Patrick; *b* 30 Aug. 1942; *s* of late Sir William Aitken, KBE and Hon. Lady Aitken, MBE, JP; *m* 1st, 1979, Lolicia Olivera (marr. diss. 1998), *d* of Mr and Mrs O. Azucki, Zürich; one *s* twin *d*; one *d* by Soraya Khashoggi; 2nd, 2003, Hon. Elizabeth Harris, *d* of 1st Baron Ogmore, TD, PC. *Educ:* Eton Coll.; Christ Church, Oxford (MA Hons Law); HMPs Belmarsh and Standford Hill; Wycliffe Hall, Oxford (CTh Dist.). Private Sec. to Selwyn Lloyd, 1964–66; Foreign Corresp., London Evening Standard, 1966–71; Man. Dir, Slater Walker (Middle East) Ltd, 1973–75; Dep. Chm., Aitken Hume Internat. PLC, 1990–92 (Co-founder, 1981; Chm., 1981–90); Dir, TV-am PLC, 1981–88. MP (C) Thanet East, Feb. 1974–83, Thanet South, 1983–97; contested (C) Thanet South, 1997. Minister of State for Defence Procurement, MoD, 1992–94; PC, 1994–97; Chief Sec. to HM Treasury, 1994–95. Mem., Select Cttee on Employment, 1979–82. Dir, Prison Fellowship Internat., 2003–; Exec. Dir, Trinity Forum Europe, 2006–; Chm., Prison Reform Gp, Centre for Social Justice, 2007–. Pres., Christian Solidarity Worldwide, 2006–; Vice Pres., New Bridge Soc., 2007–. *Publications:* A Short Walk on the Campus, 1966; The Young Meteors, 1967; Land of Fortune: A Study of Australia, 1969; Officially Secret, 1970; Richard Nixon: a life, 1993; Pride and Perjury, 2000; Psalms for People under Pressure, 2004; Prayers for People under Pressure, 2004; Porridge and Passion, 2005; Charles W. Colson: a life redeemed, 2005; Heroes and Contemporaries, 2006; John Newton: from disgrace to amazing grace, 2007; articles in Spectator, Sunday Telegraph, Sunday Times, Guardian, American Spectator, Sydney Morning Herald, Washington Post, Independent, Daily Mail, Mail on Sunday, etc. *Address:* 83 Barkston Gardens, SW5 0EU; *e-mail:* jwpaitken@aol.com.

See also M. P. K. Aitken.

AITKEN, Maria Penelope Katharine; actress; Director, Dramatis Personae Co.; *b* 12 Sept. 1945; *d* of Sir William Traven Aitken, KBE and late Hon. Penelope Loader Maffey, MBE, JP; *m* 1st, 1968, Mark Durden-Smith (marr. diss.); 2nd, 1972, Arthur Nigel Davenport, *qv* (marr. diss.); one *s*; 3rd, 1991, Patrick McGrath, *qv. Educ:* Riddlesworth Hall, Norfolk; Sherborne Girls' Sch.; St Anne's Coll., Oxford. Associate Prof., Yale Sch. of Drama, 1990; Faculty Member: Juilliard Sch., NY, 1991–97; Drama Dept, NY Univ., 1995–96. *Stage includes:* first professional appearance, Belgrade Th., Coventry, 1967; rep., Th. Royal, Northampton, 1970–71; Travesties, RSC, 1974; A Little Night Music, Adelphi, 1975; Blithe Spirit, NT, 1976; Bedroom Farce, NT, 1977; Private Lives, Duchess, 1980; Design for Living, Queen's, 1982; Sister Mary Ignatius (also dir.), Ambassadors, 1983; Happy Family (dir.), Duke of York's, 1983; Private Lives (also dir.), 1984; After the Ball (dir.), Old Vic, 1985; The Rivals (dir.), Court, Chicago, 1985; Waste, RSC, 1985; The Women, Old Vic, 1986; The Vortex, Garrick, 1989; Other People's Money, Lyric, 1990; The Mystery of Irma Vep (dir.), Ambassadors, 1990; As You Like It (dir.), Regent's Park Open Air Th., 1992; Hay Fever, Albery, 1992; The Picture of Dorian Gray, Lyric, Hammersmith, 1994; Sylvia, Lyric, 1997; Easy Virtue (dir.), Chichester, 1999; Humble Boy, Gielgud, 2002; Man and Boy (dir.), Duchess, 2005; The 39 Steps (dir.), Criterion, 2006; *films:* A Fish Called Wanda, 1988; Fierce Creatures, 1997; Jinnah, 1998; producer, director and actor for TV and radio. *Publications:* A Girdle Round the Earth, 1986; Style: acting in high comedy, 1996.

See also J. W. P. Aitken.

AITKEN, Prof. Martin Jim, FRS 1983; FSA, FRAS, FInstP; Professor of Archaeometry, 1985–89, and Deputy Director, Research Laboratory for Archaeology, 1957–89, Oxford University; Fellow of Linacre College, Oxford, 1965–89; *b* 11 March 1922; *s* of Percy Aitken and Ethel Brittain; *m* Joan Killick; one *s* four *d. Educ:* Stamford Sch., Lincs; Wadham Coll. and Clarendon Lab., Oxford Univ. (MA, DPhil). Served War, RAF Radar Officer, 1942–46 (Burma Star, 1945). Mem., Former Physical Soc., 1951–; MRI, 1972–89. Editor, Archaeometry, 1958–89. *Publications:* Physics and Archaeology, 1961, 2nd edn 1974; Thermoluminescence Dating, 1985; Science-based dating in Archaeology, 1990; Introduction to Optical Dating, 1998. *Recreations:* sailing, dinghy-racing. *Address:* Le Garret, 63930 Augerolles, France.

AITKEN, Oonagh Melrose; sessional lecturer, project manager and researcher, McGill School of Social Work, Montreal, since 2006; *b* 11 March 1956. *Educ:* Paisley Grammar Sch.; Glasgow University (MA Hons, MEd). Teacher of modern languages, Linwood High Sch., Braidfield High Sch., and Garrion Acad., Wishaw (also Asst Head Teacher), 1982–90; Strathclyde Regional Council: Educn Officer, 1990–93; Brussels Officer, 1993–95; Actg Asst Chief Exec., 1995–96; Hd, Social Policy, Glasgow CC, 1996; Corporate Manager (Social Strategy), Fife Council, 1996–99; Chief Exec., COSLA, 1999–2001; Improvement and Development Agency: Regl Associate Dir, 2001–02, Regl Associate, 2002–03, South East; Acting Dir, Strategy, Inf. and Develt, 2003–04; Consultant, 2004–05. *Recreations:* literature, cinema, current affairs. *Address:* McGill School of Social Work, 3506 University, Montreal, QC H3A 2A7 , Canada.

AITKEN, Prof. (Robert) Cairns (Brown), CBE 1998; MD; FRCPE, FRCPsych; Chairman, Royal Infirmary of Edinburgh NHS Trust, 1993–97; *b* 20 Dec. 1933; *s* of late John Goold Aitken and Margaret Johnstone (*née* Brown); *m* 1959, Audrey May Lunn; one *s* one *d* (and one *d* decd). *Educ:* Cargilfield Sch., Edinburgh; Sedbergh Sch., Yorks; Univ. of Glasgow (MB, ChB 1957; MD 1965). FRCPE 1971; FRCPsych 1974. Univ. of Glasgow-McGill Univ. Exchange Schol., Montreal, 1958–59; RAF Inst. of Aviation Medicine, 1960–62; Registrar in Medicine, Orpington Hosp., Kent, 1962–64; Registrar, then Sen. Registrar, Maudsley Hosp., 1964–66; University of Edinburgh: Lectr and Sen. Lectr, Dept of Psychiatry, 1966–74; Prof. of Rehabilitation Studies and Hon. Consultant Physician, 1974–94; Dir, Disability Mgt Res. Gp, Assoc. of British Insurers, 1980–94; Dean, Faculty of Medicine, 1990–91; Vice-Principal (Planning and Budgeting), 1991–94. Visiting Professor: Univ. of Pennsylvania, 1971; Saragossa Univ., 1976; Monash Univ., 1982; Univ. of Malaya, 1993. Ed., Jl of Psychosomatic Res., 1979–86. Dir, Lothian Health Bd, 1991–93. Member: Council, RCPsych, 1972–74; Scottish Council on Disability, 1975–84; Council, Professions Supplementary to Medicine, 1983–90; Scottish Cttee for Hosp. Med. Services, 1985–87; GMC, 1991–96; Human Genetics Adv. Commn, 1996–99; Pres., Internat. Coll. of Psychosomatic Medicine, 1985–87. For. Associate Mem., Inst. of Medicine, Amer. Acad. of Sci., 1995. Hon. Fellow: Napier Poly. of Edinburgh, 1990; Internat. Coll. of Psychosomatic Medicine, 1994. Hon. DSc CNAA,

1992. Officers' Cross, Order of Merit (Poland), 1994. *Publications:* on stress in aircrew, measurement of mood and assessment and management of disability. *Recreations:* people, places and pleasures of Edinburgh, Scotland and beyond. *Address:* 11 Succoth Place, Edinburgh EH12 6BJ. *T:* (0131) 337 1550. *Club:* New (Edinburgh).

AITKEN, William Mackie; JP; DL; Member (C) Glasgow, Scottish Parliament, since 1999; *b* 15 April 1947; *s* of William Aitken and Nell Aitken. *Educ:* Allan Glen's Sch., Glasgow; Glasgow Coll. of Technol. ACII 1971. Underwriter and sales exec., insurance industry, 1965–98. Glasgow City Council: Mem. (C), 1976–99; Convenor, Licensing Cttee, 1977–80; Leader of Opposition, 1980–84 and 1992–96; Bailie of City, 1980–84, 1988–92 and 1996–99. Scottish Parliament: Dep. Opposition spokesman on justice, 2001–03; Vice Convenor, Justice 2 Cttee, 2000–03; Cons. Chief Whip and Parly Business Mgr, 2003–07; Shadow Sec. for Justice, 2007–; Convener, Justice Cttee, 2007–. JP 1985, DL 1992, Glasgow. *Publications:* contrib. articles to newspapers. *Recreations:* reading, walking, foreign travel, wining and dining with friends. *Address:* Scottish Parliament, Edinburgh EH99 1SP.

AITKIN, Prof. Donald Alexander, AO 1998; PhD; Chairman, Cultural Facilities Corporation, since 2002; Chief Executive Officer, Agrecon Pty Ltd, 2002–03 (Chairman, 1992–2002); *b* 4 Aug. 1937; *e s* of late Alexander George Aitkin and Edna Irene (*née* Taylor); *m* 1st, 1958, Janice Wood (marr. diss. 1977); one *s* three *d*; 2nd, 1977, Susan Elderton (marr. diss. 1991); one *s*; 3rd, 1991, Beverley Benger. *Educ:* Univ. of New England (MA 1961); ANU (PhD 1964). Postdoctoral Travelling Fellow, Nuffield Coll., Oxford, 1964; Australian National University: Res. Fellow in Pol Sci., 1965–68; Sen. Res. Fellow, 1968–71; Prof. of Politics (Foundn Prof.), Macquarie Univ., 1971–80; Institute of Advanced Studies, Australian National University: Prof. of Pol Sci., 1980–88; Chm. Bd, 1986–88; Vice-Chancellor, 1991–2002, Pres., 1997–2002, Prof. Emeritus, 2003–, Univ. of Canberra. Chairman: Aust. Res. Grants Cttee, 1986–87; Aust. Res. Council, 1988–90; ACT Schs Legislation Review, 1999–2000; Dep. Chm., ACT Sci. and Technol. Council, 1999–; Member: Aust. Sci. and Technol. Council, 1986–92; Tourism Ministerial Adv. Council, 2006–. Vice-Pres., Australian Vice-Chancellors' Cttee, 1994–95. Chairman: Aust. Maths Trust, 1995–2004; Nat. Olympiad Council, 1996–2004; NRMA/ACT Road Safety Trust, 2001–. Mem. Bd, Canberra Theatre Trust, 1993–97; Pres., Pro Musica Inc., 2002–; Dir, Artsound FM, 2004–06. FASSA 1975; FACE 1995; Hon. Fellow, Royal Aust. Planning Inst., 2001. DUniv Canberra, 2002; Hon. DLitt New England, 2004. *Publications:* The Colonel, 1969; The Country Party in New South Wales, 1972; Stability and Change in Australian Politics, 1977, 2nd edn 1982; The Second Chair (novel), 1977; (with B. Jinks) Australian Political Institutions, 1980 (trans. Japanese, 1985), 7th edn 2003; (ed) The Life of Politics, 1984; (ed) Surveys of Australian Political Science, 1985; What Was It All For? The Reshaping of Australia, 2005. *Recreations:* bushwalking, music, cooking. *Address:* 80 Banks Street, Yarralumla, ACT 2600, Australia.

AITTCHISEN, Sir Lance (Walter), 4th Bt *cr* 1938; *b* 27 May 1951; *er s* of Sir Stephen Charles de Lancey Aitchison, 3rd Bt, and (Elizabeth) Anne (Milburn), *er d* of late Lt-Col Edward Reed, Ghyllheugh, Longhorsley, Northumberland; changed name by Deed from Charles Walter de Lancey Aitchison, 2004; *S* father, 1958; *m* 1984, Susan, *yr d* of late Edward Ellis; one *s* one *d*. Lieut, 15/19th The King's Royal Hussars, 1974; RARO, 1974–78. MRICS. *Recreation:* fishing. *Heir: s* Rory Edward de Lancey Aitchison, *b* 7 March 1986.

AJAYI, Prof. (Jacob Festus) Ade, NNOM 1986; OFR 2000; Professor of History, University of Ibadan, 1963–89, now Emeritus; *b* 26 May 1929; *s* of late Chief E. Ade Ajayi and Mrs C. F. Bolajoko Ajayi; *m* 1956, Christie Aduke Martins; one *s* four *d*. *Educ:* University College, Ibadan; University College, Leicester; Univ. of London; BA 1st Cl. Hons, PhD (London). Research Fellow, Inst. of Historical Research, London, 1957–58; Lectr, Univ. of Ibadan, 1958–62, Sen. Lectr, 1962–63; Dean, Faculty of Arts, 1964–66; Asst to Vice-Chancellor, 1966–68. Fellow, Centre for Advanced Study in the Behavioural Sciences, Stanford, Calif, 1970–71; Vice-Chancellor, Univ. of Lagos, 1972–78; Pro-Chancellor, Ondo State Univ., Ado-Ekiti, 1984–88. Member: UN University Council, 1974–80 (Chm., 1975–77); Nat. Archives Cttee, Nigeria, 1961–72; Nat. Antiquities Commn, Nigeria, 1970–74; Exec. Council, Internat. African Inst. London, 1971– (Chm., 1975–87); Exec. Bd, Assoc. of African Univs, 1974–80; Admin. Bd, Internat. Assoc. of Univs, 1980–90; Pres., Historical Soc. of Nigeria, 1972–81; Pres., Internat. Congress of African Studies, 1978–85. Director: BCN plc, 1988–92; SOWSCO, 1994–. Chm., Jadeas Trust, 1989–. Mem. Governing Bd, Nigerian Nat. Order of Merit, 1996–2000. Hon. LLD Leicester, 1975; Hon. DLitt: Birmingham, 1984; Ondo State Univ., Ado-Ekiti, 1992. Hon. Fellow, SOAS, Univ. of London, 1994. Fellow, Hist. Soc. of Nigeria, 1980; Overseas FRHistS, 1982. Traditional titles, Bobapitan of Ikole-Ekiti and Onikoyi of Ife, 1983. *Publications:* Milestones in Nigerian History, 1962; (ed with Ian Espie) A Thousand Years of West African History, 1964; (with R. S. Smith) Yoruba Warfare in the Nineteenth Century, 1964; Christian Missions in Nigeria: the making of a new elite, 1965; (ed with Michael Crowder) A History of West Africa, vol. I, 1972; vol. II, 1974; (ed with T. N. Tamuno) The University of Ibadan, 1948–73, 1973; (ed with Bashir Ikara) Evolution of Political Culture in Nigeria, 1985; (ed with M. Crowder) A Historical Atlas of Africa, 1985; (ed) Africa in the Nineteenth Century until the 1880s, vol. VI of Unesco General History of Africa, 1989; History and the Nation, and other Addresses, 1990; (with Peter Pugh) Cementing a Partnership: the story of WAPCO 1960–1990, 1990; A Patriot to the Core: Samuel Ajayi Crowther, 1992, 2nd edn, subtitled Bishop Ajayi Crowther, 2001; History of the Nigerian Society of Engineers, 1995; (jtly) The African Experience with Higher Education, 1996; Kayode Eso: the making of a judge, 2002; contribs to Jl Historical Soc. of Nigeria, Jl of African History, etc. *Recreations:* dancing, tennis. *Address:* 1 Ojobadan Avenue, Bodija, Ibadan, Nigeria; PO Box 14617 UI, Ibadan, Nigeria; *e-mail:* jadeas@skannet.com.

AJEGBO, Sir Keith Onyema, Kt 2007; OBE 1994; education consultant; Headteacher, Deptford Green School, 1986–2006; *b* 31 Oct. 1946; *s* of Michael Ajegbo and Dorothy Ajegbo; *m* 1991, Deborah Caroline Fry; one *s* one *d*. *Educ:* Greenacres Primary Sch., Eltham; Eltham Coll.; Downing Coll., Cambridge (BA Eng. Lit. 1969); Univ. of Nottingham (PGCE 1970). Dep. Hd, Elliott Sch., Putney, 1981–86. Education consultant for: DFES, subseq. DCSF, 2006–, researched and wrote report for Sec. of State for Educn (Curriculum Review: Diversity and Citizenship, 2007); London Bor. of Newham, 2004–; UBS Investment Bank, 2006–; Future Leaders, 2006–. Governor: Nat. Coll. of Sch. Leadership, 2001–03; Goldsmiths, London, 2003–. Trustee: Citizenship Foundn, 2007–; Stephen Lawrence Trust, 2007. Hon. Fellow, Goldsmiths, London, 1997. Hon. DEd De Montfort, 2002. *Publications:* Black Lives, White Worlds, 1982; numerous articles for educn jls. *Recreations:* playing tennis (Capt., Cambridge Univ., 1969, Prentice Cup tour, 1968; Kent county team, 1966–82, county colours), reading novels, extensive library of pop music. *Club:* All England Lawn Tennis (Wimbledon).

AJIBOLA, Prince Bola Adesumbo, Hon. KBE 1989; CFR; SAN 1986; High Commissioner for Nigeria in the United Kingdom, 1999–2002; Leader of Nigerian Delegation, Cameroon-Nigeria Mixed Commision, since 2002; *b* 22 March 1934; *s* of Oba A. S. Ajibola and Adikatu Ashakun Ajibola; *m* 1961, Olu Olugbemi; three *s* two *d*. *Educ:* Owu Baptist Day Sch., Abeokuta, Nigeria; Baptist Boys' High Sch., Abeokuta. Called to the Bar, Lincoln's Inn, London, 1962. Principal Partner, Bola Ajobola & Co., Nigeria, 1967–85 (specialising in commercial law and internat. arbitration); Hon. Attorney-Gen. and Minister of Justice, Nigeria, 1985–91; Judge: Internat. Court of Justice, The Hague, 1991–94; World Bank Admin. Tribunal, 1994; Constitutional Court, Fedn of Bosnia and Herzegovina, 1995; delegate to numerous internat. confs. President: Nigerian Bar Assoc., 1984–85 (Chm., Human Rights Cttee, 1980–84); Pan African Council, London Court of Internat. Arbitration, 1994; Pres. and Founder, African Concern, 1995–; Chairman: Gen. Council of the Bar, Nigeria, 1985–91; Body of Sen. Advocates of Nigeria, 1985–91; Adv. Cttee of Prerogative of Mercy, Nigeria, 1989–91; Task Force for Revision of Laws, Nigeria, 1990; Member: Privileges Cttee, Nigerian Bar, 1985–91; Nigerian Police Council, 1989–91; Internat. Bar Assoc.; Internat. Chamber of Commerce; World Arbitration Inst.; Perm. Court of Arbitration, The Hague (also Mem., Bd of Trustees); Governing Bd, Internat. Maritime Law Inst., IMO; Internat. Law Commn, UN, 1986–91; Internat. Court of Arbitration, ICC (Vice Chm., Commn; arbitrator, numerous internat. cases); Internat. Maritime Arbitration Commn; Governing Body, African Soc. of Internat. and Comparative Law. Fellow, Nigerian Inst. of Advanced Legal Studies; FCIArb. Editor: All Nigeria Law Reports, 1961–90; Nigeria's Treaties in Force, 1970–90; Ed.-in-Chief, Justice; Gen. Editor, Federal Min. of Justice Law Review Series. *Publications:* Law Development and Administration in Nigeria, 1987; Towards a Better Administration of Justice System in Nigeria, 1988; Narcotics, Law and Policy in Nigeria, 1989; Compensation and Remedies for Victims of Crime, 1989; Banking Frauds and Other Financial Malpractices in Nigeria, 1989; Unification and Reform of Criminal Laws and Procedure Codes of Nigeria, 1990; Women and Children under Nigerian Law, 1990; Customary Law in Nigeria, 1991; Democracy and the Law; Dispute Resolution by International Court of Justice; papers and articles in learned jls. *Address:* c/o Nigeria High Commission, 9 Northumberland Avenue, WC2N 5BX. *T:* (020) 7839 1244. *Clubs:* Abeokuta (Abeokuta); Metropolitan (Lagos); Yoruba Tennis.

AKAM, Prof. Michael Edwin, DPhil; FRS 2000; FRES, FLS; Professor of Zoology, and Director, University Museum of Zoology, University of Cambridge, since 1997; Fellow, Darwin College, Cambridge, since 2006; *b* 19 June 1952; *s* of William Edwin Akam and Evelyn Warriner Akam (*née* Thorne); *m* 1979, Margaret Madeleine Bray; two *s*. *Educ:* King's Coll., Cambridge (BA Nat. Scis 1974); Magdalen Coll., Oxford (DPhil Genetics 1978). FRES 1985; FLS 1999. Australian Sci. Schol., Royal Instn, 1970. Coll. Lectr in Zoology, Magdalen Coll., Oxford, 1978; Res. Fellow, King's Coll., Cambridge, 1978–86; MRC Fellow, Lab. of Molecular Biology, Cambridge, 1978–79; Fellow, Dept of Biochemistry, Stanford Univ., 1979–81 (Damon-Runyan/Walter Winchell Fellow, 1979); Cambridge University: MRC Sen. Fellow, Dept of Genetics, 1982–90; Wellcome Principal Fellow, and Founding Mem., Wellcome/CRC Inst., 1990–97. Chm., British Soc. for Developmental Biology, 1989–94 (Waddington Medal, 2005). Mem., EMBO, 1987. FAAAS 2006. Kowalevsky Medal, St Petersburg Soc. of Naturalists, 2007. *Publications:* (ed jtly) The Evolution of Developmental Mechanisms, 1994; res. papers and reviews in jls, Proc. Royal Soc., etc. *Recreation:* the living world. *Address:* University Museum of Zoology, Downing Street, Cambridge CB2 3EJ. *T:* (01223) 336650.

AKENHEAD, Hon. Sir Robert, Kt 2007; **Hon. Mr Justice Akenhead;** a Judge of the High Court of Justice, Queen's Bench Division, since 2007; *b* 15 Sept. 1949; *s* of late Edmund and of Angela Akenhead; *m* 1972, Elizabeth Anne Jackson; one *s* three *d*. *Educ:* Rugby School; Exeter Univ. (LLB). Called to the Bar, Inner Temple, 1972, Bencher, 1997; in practice as barrister, 1973–; QC 1989; Head of Chambers, 2001–; Asst Recorder, 1991–94; Recorder, 1994–2007. Examiner, Dio. of Canterbury, 1991–. Ed., Building Law Reports, 1999–. *Publication:* Site Investigation and the Law, 1984. *Recreations:* theatre, cricket, ski-ing. *Address:* Royal Courts of Justice, Strand, WC2A 2LL.

AKERLOF, Prof. George Arthur, PhD; Professor of Economics, University of California at Berkeley, since 1980; Cassel Professor of Economics, London School of Economics and Political Science, 1978–81; *b* 17 June 1940; *s* of Gosta C. Akerlof and Rosalie C. Akerlof; *m* 1978, Janet Yellen; one *s*. *Educ:* Yale Univ. (BA 1962); MIT (PhD 1966). Fellowships: Woodrow Wilson, 1962–63; National Science Co-op., 1963–66; Fulbright, 1967–68; Guggenheim, 1973–74. Univ. of Calif, Berkeley: Asst Prof. of Econs, 1966–70; Associate Prof., 1970–77; Prof., 1977–78. Vis. Prof., Indian Statistical Inst., New Delhi, 1967–68. Sen. Economist, Council of Econ. Advisors, USA, 1973–74; Vis. Economist, Bd of Governors of Fed. Reserve System, USA, 1977–78. (Jtly) Nobel Prize for Economics, 2001. *Publications:* contrib. American Econ. Rev., Econ. Jl, Qly Jl Econs, Jl Polit. Econ., Rev. of Econ. Studies, Internat. Econ. Rev., Jl Econ. Theory, Indian Econ. Rev., and Rev. of Econs and Stats. *Address:* Department of Economics, University of California, Berkeley, CA 94720–3880, USA. *Club:* Piggy (Center Harbor, NH, USA).

AKERS, John Fellows; Chairman, International Business Machines Corp., 1986–93; *b* 1934; *m* 1960, Susan Davis; one *s* two *d*. *Educ:* Yale Univ. (BS). International Business Machines Corp., 1960–93: Pres., Data Processing Div., 1974–76; Vice Pres., Asst Gp Exec., plans and controls, Data Processing Product Gp, 1976–78; Vice Pres., Gp Exec., Data Processing Marketing Gp, 1978–81, Inf. Systems and Communications Gp, 1981–82, Sen. Vice Pres., 1982–83; Dir, 1983–93; Pres., 1983–89; Chief Exec. Officer, 1985–93. Director: New York Times Co., 1985; PepsiCo. Inc.; W. R. Grace; Lehmann Bros; Hallmark Cards. Formerly Mem., President's Educn Policy Adv. Cttee. Former Trustee, MMA; former Chm. Bd of Governors, United Way of America.

AKERS-DOUGLAS, family name of **Viscount Chilston**.

AKERS-JONES, Sir David, KBE 1985; CMG 1978; GBM 2002; Chief Secretary, Hong Kong, 1985–86; Acting Governor, Hong Kong, Dec. 1986–April 1987; *b* 14 April 1927; *s* of Walter George and Dorothy Jones; *m* 1951, Jane Spickernell (MBE 1988) (*d* 2002); one *d* (one *s* decd). *Educ:* Worthing High Sch.; Brasenose Coll., Oxford (MA; Hon. Fellow, 2005). British India Steam Navigation Co., 1945–49. Malayan Civil Service (studied Hokkien and Malay), 1954–57; Hong Kong Civil Service, 1957–86; Government Secretary: for New Territories, 1973–81; for City and New Territories, 1981–83; for Dist Admin, 1983–85; Advr to Gov., April–Sept. 1987. Chm., Hong Kong Housing Authy, 1988–93; Advr to China on Hong Kong Affairs, 1993–97; Hong Kong Chief Exec. Selection Cttee, 1996. Chm., Operation Smile China Medical Mission, 1992–; (Alternate) Chm., China Oxford Scholarship Fund, 1992–2007. Pres., Business and Professionals Fedn, 2005–. Pres., WWF Hong Kong, 1995–. Hon. Pres., Outward Bound Trust, Hong Kong, 1996– (Pres., 1986–95); Vice-Patron, Hong Kong Football Assoc. Hon. Member: RICS, 1991; HKIA, 2006. Hon. DCL Kent, 1987; Hon. LLD Chinese Univ. of Hong Kong, 1988; Hon. DSSc City Polytechnic of Hong Kong, 1993. *Recreations:* painting, gardening, walking, music. *Address:* Flat 1, 25th Floor, Bamboo Grove, 80 Kennedy Road, Hong Kong. *Clubs:* Royal Over-Seas League; Hong Kong, Kowloon, Dynasty, China, Gold Coast and Country (Hong Kong).

AKHTAR, Prof. Muhammad, FRS 1980; Professor of Biochemistry, University of Southampton, 1973–98, now Emeritus; *b* 23 Feb. 1933; *m* 1963, Monika E. Schurmann;

two *s. Educ:* Punjab Univ., Pakistan (MSc 1st class 1954); Imperial College, London (PhD, DIC 1959). Research Scientist, Inst. for Medicine and Chemistry, Cambridge, Mass, USA, 1959–63; University of Southampton: Lecturer in Biochemistry, 1963–66; Senior Lectr, 1966–68; Reader, 1968–73; Hd of Dept of Biochemistry, 1978–93; Chm., Sch. of Biochem. and Physiol. Scis, 1983–87; Dir, SERC Centre for Molecular Recognition, 1990–94. Chm., Inst. of Biomolecular Scis, 1989–90. Dist. Nat. Prof., Sch. of Biol Scis, Punjab Univ., Lahore, 2003–. Member: Chemical Soc. of GB; American Chemical Soc.; Biochemical Soc. of GB; Council, Royal Soc., 1983–85; Founding Fellow, Third World Acad. of Sciences, 1983 (Mem. Council and Treas., 1993–98; Vice-Pres., 1998–2004; Medal, 1996). Hon. DSc Karachi, 2002. Flintoff Medal, RSC, 1993. Sitara-I-Imtiaz (Pakistan), 1981. *Publications:* numerous works on: enzyme mechanisms; synthesis and biosynthesis of steroids and porphyrins; biochemistry of vision; synthesis of anti-microbial compounds. *Address:* School of Biological Sciences, University of Southampton, Southampton SO16 7PX. *T:* (023) 8059 4338.

AKIHITO, HM the Emperor of Japan; Collar, Supreme Order of Chrysanthemum, 1989; KG 1998; *b* Tokyo, 23 Dec. 1933; *e s* of Emperor Hirohito (Showa) and Empress Nagako (Kojun); *S* father, 1989; *m* 1959, Michiko Shoda; two *s* one *d. Educ:* Gakushuin Primary, Jun. and Sen. High Schs; Dept of Politics, Faculty of Politics and Econs, Gakushuin Univ. Official Investiture as Crown Prince of Japan, 1952. Res. Associate, Australian Mus.; Mem., Ichthyological Soc. of Japan; For. Member: Linnean Soc. of London; Zool Soc. of London, 1992. King Charles II Medal, Royal Soc., 1998. *Publications:* (contrib. jtly) Fishes of the Japanese Archipelago, 1984; (jtly) The Fresh Water Fishes of Japan, 1987; 30 papers on gobies. *Recreation:* tennis. *Heir: er s* Crown Prince Naruhito [*b* Tokyo, 23 Feb. 1960; *m* 1993, Masako Owada; one *d*]. *Address:* Imperial Palace, 1–1 Chiyoda, Chiyoda-ku, Tokyo 100–8111, Japan. *T:* (3) 32131111.

AKINKUGBE, Prof. Oladipo Olujimi, NNOM 1997; CON 1979; CFR 2004; Officier de l'Ordre National de la République de Côte d'Ivoire, 1981; MD, DPhil; FRCP, FWACP, FAS; Professor of Medicine, University of Ibadan, Nigeria, 1968–95, now Emeritus; *b* 17 July 1933; *s* of late Chief David Akinbobola and Chief (Mrs) Grace Akinkugbe; *m* 1965, Dr Folasade Modupeore Dina, *d* of late Chief I. O. Dina, CFR, OBE; two *s. Educ:* Univs of Ibadan (Fellow, 1998), London (MD), Liverpool (DTM&H) and Oxford (DPhil). FRCP 1968; FWACP 1975; FAS 1980. House Surg., London Hosp., 1958; House Phys., King's Coll. Hosp., London, 1959; Commonwealth Res. Fellow, Balliol Coll. and Regius Dept of Medicine, Oxford, 1962–64; Head of Dept of Medicine, 1972, Dean of Medicine, 1970–74, and Chm., Cttee of Deans, 1972–74, Univ. of Ibadan; Vice-Chancellor: Univ. of Ilorin, 1977–78 (Principal, 1975–77); Ahmadu Bello Univ., Zaria, 1978–79. Rockefeller Vis. Fellow, US Renal Centres, 1966; Vis. Fellow in Medicine, Univs of Manchester, Cambridge and London, 1969; Visiting Professor of Medicine: Harvard Univ., 1974–75; Univ. of Oxford (and Vis. Fellow, Balliol Coll.), 1981–82; Univ. of Cape Town, 1996. Adviser on Postgrad. Med. Educn to Fed. Govt of Nigeria, 1972–75; Chairman: Nat. Implementation Commn on Rev. of Higher Educn in Nigeria, 1992; Presidential Project on Revamping Teaching Hosps, 2003–07; Member: Univ. Grants Commn, Uganda Govt; OAU Scientific Panels on Health Manpower Develt; Council, Internat. Soc. of Hypertension, 1982–90; Bd of Trustees, African Assoc. of Nephrology, 1986–94; Bd of Trustees, Nigerian Educare Trust, 1997–; internat. socs of hypertension, cardiology, and nephrology; Med. Res. Soc. of GB; Scientific Adv. Panel, Ciba Foundn, 1970–98; WHO Expert Adv. Panels on Cardiovascular Diseases, 1973–78, on Health Manpower 1979–, on Health Sci. and Technol., 2003–; WHO Adv. Council on Health Res., 1990–95; Sec. to WHO 1984 Technical Discussions. Pro-Chancellor, and Chm. of Council, Univ. of Port-Harcourt, Nigeria, 1986–90; Chairman: Bd of Mgt, UCH, Ibadan, 2000–; Bd of Trustees, Ajayi Crowther Univ., Oyo, 2004–; Member: Governing Council and Bd of Trustees, Obafemi Awolowo Foundn, 1992; Governing Council, Nigeria Heart (formerly Heartcare) Foundn, 1994– (Chm., Bd of Trustees, 2000–); Exec. Council, World Innovation Foundn, 1998–; Bd of Trustees, Heritage Resources Conservation, 1999–; Bd, World Heart Fedn, 2004–; Chairman: Governing Council, Ajumogobia Science Foundn, 1997–; Bd of Trustees and Governing Council, Nigeria Soc. for Inf., Arts and Culture, 2002. President: Nigerian Assoc. of Nephrology, 1987–90; Nigerian Hypertension Soc., 1994; African Heart Network, 2001. Member, Editorial Bd: Jl of Hypertension, 1984–90; Jl of Human Hypertension, 1988–; Kidney International, 1990–98; Blood Pressure, 1991–; News in Physiological Scis, 1992–98. Hon. DSc: Ilorin, 1982; Fed. Univ. of Technol., Akure, 1992; Port Harcourt, 1997; Ogun State, 1998; Ibadan, 2006. Searle Dist. Res. Award, 1989; Boehringer Ingelheim Award, Internat. Soc. of Hypertension, 2004; Hallmarks of Labour Award, 2004; Life Achievement Award: Nigerian Acad. of Sci., 2004; Nat. Univs Commn, 2006. Traditional title, Atobase of Ife, 1991; Babalofin of Ijebu-Igbo, 1994; Adengbua of Ondo, 1995; Ikolaba Balogun Basegun of Ibadan, 1997. *Publications:* High Blood Pressure in the African, 1972; (ed) Priorities in National Health Planning, 1974; (ed) Cardiovascular Disease in Africa, 1976; (ed) Nigeria and Education: the challenges ahead, 1994; (ed jtly) Nigeria's Health in the 90s, 1996; (ed) Non-Communicable Diseases in Nigeria: final report of a national survey, 1997; (ed jtly) A Compendium of Clinical Medicine, 1999; (ed jtly) Clinical Medicine in the Tropics Series, 1987–; papers on hypertension and renal disease in African, Eur. and Amer. med. jls, and papers on med. and higher educn. *Recreations:* music, gardening, clocks, birdwatching, golf. *Address:* c/o Department of Medicine, University of Ibadan, Ibadan, Nigeria. *T:* 22317717; The Little Summit, Olubadan Aleshinloye Way, Iyaganku, Ibadan, Nigeria. *Clubs:* Dining (Ibadan); Oxford and Cambridge (Nigeria).

AKINOLA, Most Rev. Peter Jasper, CON 2003; Metropolitan, Archbishop and Primate of Nigeria, 2000–08; *b* 27 Jan. 1944; *m* 1969, Susan A. Akinola; three *s* three *d. Educ:* Diocesan Trng Centre, Wusasa; Theol Coll. of Northern Nigeria (Higher Dip. in Theol.); Virginia Theol Seminary, USA (MTS 1981). Catechist, Nguru, Nigeria, 1972; ordained deacon, 1978, priest, 1979; Vicar, St James, Suleija, Abuja, 1978–83; Canon (Missioner), Abuja, 1983–88; Bishop of Abuja, 1989–; Archbishop, Province Three, Nigeria, 1998–2000. Chairman: Global South, 2002; Conf. of Anglican Provinces in Africa, 2003–. *Address:* c/o Episcopal House, 24 Douala Street, Wuse, Zone 5, PO Box 212, ADCP, Abuja, Nigeria. *T:* (9) 5236950, *T:* (9) 5240496, *Fax:* (9) 5230986.

AKKER, John Richard; Executive Secretary, Council for Assisting Refugee Academics, since 1999; Visiting Professor, London South Bank University, since 2005; *b* 6 May 1943; *s* of Alec Louis Morris Akker and Ruby (*née* Bryant); *m* 1967, Jean-Anne Roxburgh (marr. diss. 1990); two *d. Educ:* SW Essex Tech. Coll.; Ruskin Coll., Oxford (L. C. White Schol.; Dip. Econ./Pol.); Univ. of York (BA Hons 1969); Cranfield Inst. of Technol. Mgt Sch. Clerical Officer, Ministry of Works, 1959–64; Asst Nat. Officer, 1969–71, Dep. Nat. Local Govt Officer, 1972–73, NALGO; Association of University Teachers: Asst Gen. Sec., 1973–77; Dep. Gen. Sec., 1978–94; Gen. Sec., NATFHE, 1994–97. Advr to EC, 1985–88. Exec. Dir, Network for Educn and Academic Rights, 2001–. Visiting Lecturer: CIT, 1970–74; Univ. of Wisconsin, 1977–78. Winston Churchill Fellowship, USA, 1976. Trustee: Refugee Council, 2000–; Immigration Adv. Service, 2002–. *Recreations:* motor sport, sailing, football. *Address:* CARA, London South Bank University, Technopark, 90 London Road, SE1 6LN; *e-mail:* akker.cara@lsbu.ac.uk. *Clubs:* National Liberal; Colchester United FC Supporters.

ALAGIAH, George Maxwell, OBE 2008; presenter, BBC TV 6 o'clock news, since 2003; *b* 22 Nov. 1955; *s* of Donald and Therese Alagiah; *m* 1984, Frances Robathan; two *s. Educ:* St John's Coll., Southsea; Van Mildert Coll., Durham Univ. South Magazine, 1982–89; BBC Foreign Affairs Correspondent, 1989–99, Africa Correspondent, 1994–99; News Presenter and journalist, BBC, 1999–2002. Monte Carlo TV Fest. Award; BAFTA commendation; awards as Journalist of the Year from: Amnesty Internat., 1994; BPG, 1994; James Cameron Meml Trust, 1995; Bayeux Award for War Reporting, 1996. *Publications:* A Passage to Africa, 2001; (jtly) The Day That Shook the World, 2001; A Home from Home, 2006. *Recreations:* sport, tennis, music, hiking. *Address:* BBC Television Centre, Wood Lane, W12 7RJ.

ALAGNA, Roberto; French tenor; *b* 7 June 1963; *m* 1st, Florence (*d* 1994); one *d*; 2nd, 1996, Angela Gheorghiu, *qv*. Worked as accountant, electrician and cabaret singer; studied under Rafael Ruiz; Pavarotti Internat. Voice Competition Prize, 1988. Débuts: Alfredo in La Traviata, Glyndebourne Touring Opera, 1988; Royal Opera, Covent Garden, 1992; La Scala, Milan, 1994; Théâtre du Chatelet, Paris, 1996; Metropolitan Opera, NY, 1996. Rôles include: Roméo in Roméo et Juliette (Laurence Olivier Award, Covent Garden, 1995); title rôle in Don Carlos; Rodolpho in La Bohème; Nemorino in L'elisir d'amore; Edgard in Lucia di Lammermoor; Cavaradossi in Tosca; Radamès in Aida; title rôle in Gounod's Faust. Film, Tosca, 2002. Numerous recordings. Officier des Arts et des Lettres (France), 2002 (Chevalier, 1996); Ordre Nat. du Mérite (France), 2003. *Address:* c/o M Levon Sayan, 76–78 avenue des Champs Elysées, 75008 Paris, France.

ALAIN, Marie-Claire Geneviève; organist; Lecturer, Conservatoire National de Région Rueil-Malmaison, Paris, 1978–98; *b* 10 Aug. 1926; *d* of Albert Alain and Magdeleine Alain (*née* Alberty); *m* 1950, Jacques Gommier (*d* 1992); one *s* one *d. Educ:* Institut Notre Dame, Saint-Germain-en-Laye; Conservatoire Nat. Supérieur de Musique, Paris. Lectr, Summer Acad. for Organists, Haarlem, Netherlands, 1956–72; Dir, Internat. Summer Acad. for Organists, Saint-Donat, 1978–92. Numerous concerts and recitals worldwide, 1955–; more than 250 recordings, incl. works of Jehan Alain, complete organ works of J. S. Bach, César Franck, Handel, Buxtehude and Mendelssohn. Prix Léonie Sonning, Copenhagen; Buxtehude Prize, Lübeck, 1976; Prix Franz Liszt, Budapest, 1987; 15 Grands Prix du Disque. Hon. doctorates: Colorado, 1972; Southern Methodist, Dallas, 1990; Sibelius Acad., 1997; Boston Conservatory, 1999. Commandeur: Légion d'honneur (France), 1997; Ordre Nat. du Mérite (France), 1998; Officier des Arts et des Lettres (France), 1999. *Address:* 4 rue Victor Hugo, 78230 Le Pecq, France.

ALANBROOKE, 3rd Viscount *cr* 1946; **Alan Victor Harold Brooke;** Baron Alanbrooke, 1945; *b* 24 Nov. 1932; *s* of 1st Viscount Alanbrooke, KG, GCB, OM, GCVO, DSO, and Benita Blanche (*d* 1968), *d* of Sir Harold Pelly, 4th Bt; *S* half-brother, 1972. *Educ:* Harrow; Bristol Univ. (BEd Hons 1976). Qualified teacher, 1975. Served Army, 1952–72; Captain RA, retired. *Heir:* none.

ALBANESE, Thomas; Chief Executive Officer, Rio Tinto plc, since 2007; *b* 9 Sept. 1957; *s* of Paul Albanese and Rosemarie Albanese (*née* Helm); *m* 1979, Mary Delane; two *d* (and one *d* decd). *Educ:* Univ. of Alaska (BS Mining Econs (*cum laude*) 1979; MS Mining Engrg 1981). Chief Operating Officer, Nerco Minerals Co., 1982–93; Rio Tinto plc, 1993–: Gen. Manager, Greeks Creek Mine, Alaska, 1993–95; Gp Exploration Exec., London, 1995–97; Vice Pres. Engrg and Gen. Manager Smelting and Refining, Kennecott Utah Copper, Salt Lake City, 1997–2000; Man. Dir, North Ltd, Australia, 2000–01; Chief Executive: Industrial Minerals Div., 2001–04; Copper, and Hd of Exploration, 2004–06; Dir, Gp Resources, 2006–07. *Recreations:* walking, swimming, canal boats. *Address:* Woodpeckers, Pachesham Park, Oxshott, Surrey KT22 0DJ.

ALBEE, Edward; American dramatist; *b* 12 March 1928. Has directed prodns of own plays, 1961–, mainly at English Th., Vienna, and Alley Th., Houston. *Publications: plays:* The Zoo Story, 1958; The Death of Bessie Smith, 1959; The Sandbox, 1959; Fam and Yam, 1959; The American Dream, 1960; Who's Afraid of Virginia Woolf?, 1962; (adapted from Carson McCullers' novella) The Ballad of the Sad Café, 1963; Tiny Alice, 1964; (adapted from the novel by James Purdy) Malcolm, 1965; A Delicate Balance, 1966 (Pulitzer Prize, 1967); (adapted from the play by Giles Cooper) Everything in the Garden, 1967; Box and Quotations from Chairman Mao Tse-Tung, 1968; All Over, 1971; Seascape, 1974 (Pulitzer Prize, 1975); Listening, 1975; Counting the Ways, 1976; The Lady from Dubuque, 1978; Lolita (adapted from V. Nabokov), 1979; The Man Who Had Three Arms, 1981; Finding the Sun, 1982; Marriage Play, 1986; Three Tall Women, 1991 (Pulitzer Prize, 1994); The Lorca Play, 1992; Fragments, 1993; The Play About the Baby, 1997; The Goat, or Who is Sylvia?, 2000; Occupant, 2001; Peter and Jerry, 2004; Me, Myself and I, 2007. *Address:* (office) 14 Harrison Street, New York, NY 10013, USA.

ALBEMARLE, 10th Earl of, *cr* 1696; **Rufus Arnold Alexis Keppel;** Baron Ashford, 1696; Viscount Bury, 1696; *b* 16 July 1965; *s* of Derek William Charles Keppel, Viscount Bury (*d* 1968), and Marina, *yr d* of late Count Serge Orloff-Davidoff; *S* grandfather, 1979; *m* 2001, Sally Claire Tadayon, *d* of Dr Jamal Tadion; one *s. Educ:* Central Sch. of Art (BA (Hons) Industrial Design, 1990). *Heir: s* Viscount Bury, *qv*. *Address:* Hurst Barns Farm, East Chiltington, Lewes, Sussex BN7 3QU.

ALBEMARLE, Diana, Countess of, (Diana Cicely), DBE 1956; Chairman: Development Commission, 1948–74; The Drama Board, 1964–78; *b* 6 Aug. 1909; *o c* of John Archibald Grove; *m* 1931, 9th Earl of Albemarle, MC (*d* 1979); one *d. Educ:* Sherborne Sch. for Girls. Norfolk County Organiser, WVS, 1939–44. Chairman: Exec. Cttee, Nat. Fedn of Women's Institutes, 1946–51; Departmental Cttee on Youth Service, 1958–60; Nat. Youth Employment Council, 1962–68. Vice-Chm., British Council, 1959–74. Member: Arts Council, 1951; Royal Commn on Civil Service, 1954; Harkness Fellowship Cttee of Award, 1963–69; UGC, 1956–70; Standing Commn on Museums and Galleries, 1958–71; English Local Govt Boundary Commn, 1971–77; Youth Develt Council, 1960–68; Council, Univ. of E Anglia, 1964–72. Life Trustee, Carnegie UK Trust (Chm., 1977–82); Trustee of: The Observer until 1977; Glyndebourne Arts Trust, 1968–80. RD Councillor, Wayland, Norfolk, 1935–46. Hon. DLitt Reading, 1959; Hon. DCL Oxon, 1960; Hon. LLD London, 1960. *Recreations:* gardening, reading. *Address:* Seymours, Melton, Woodbridge, Suffolk IP12 1LW. *T:* (01394) 382151.

See also Sir Hew Hamilton-Dalrymple.

ALBERTI, Sir (Kurt) George (Matthew Mayer), Kt 2000; DPhil; FRCP, FRCPE, FRCPath; Senior Research Fellow, Imperial College, London, since 2002; Professor of Medicine, University of Newcastle upon Tyne, 1985–2002 (Dean of Medicine, 1995–97); President, Royal College of Physicians, 1997–2002; *b* 27 Sept. 1937; *s* of late William Peter Matthew Alberti and Edith Elizabeth Alberti; *m* 1st, 1964; three *s*; *m* 2nd, 1998, Prof. Stephanie A. Amiel. *Educ:* Balliol Coll., Oxford (MA; DPhil 1964; BM, BCh 1965; Hon. Fellow 1999). FRCP 1978; FRCPath 1985; FRCPE 1988. Res. Fellow, Harvard Univ., Boston, USA, 1966–69; Res. Officer, Dept of Medicine, Oxford Univ., 1969–73; Prof.

of Chemical Pathology and Human Metabolism, 1973–78, Prof. of Clinical Biochemistry and Metabolic Medicine, 1978–85, Univ. of Southampton; Prof. of Medicine, ICSTM, 2000–02. Mem., WHO Expert Adv. Panel on Diabetes, 1979–. Nat. Clin. Dir for Emergency Access, 2002–08. Pres., Internat. Diabetes Fedn, 2000–03 (Vice-Pres., 1988–94); Vice-Chm., British Diabetic Assoc., 1996–99; Vice Pres., Diabetes UK, 2000–. Founder FMedSci 1998 (Mem. Council, 1998–2002). Hon. FRCPGlas 1999; Hon. FRCPI 1999. Hon. Member: Hungarian Diabetes Assoc., 1986; Argentinian Diabetes Assoc., 1991. Hon. MD: Aarhus, 1998; Athens, 2002; Hon. DM Southampton, 1999; Hon. DSc: Warwick, Cranfield, 2005. *Publications:* edited more than 30 medical books, including: Diabetes Annual, Vols 1–6; Internat. Textbook of Diabetes Mellitus, 1992, 2nd edn 1997; author of more than 1000 pubns in learned jls. *Recreations:* hill walking, jogging, crime fiction, opera.

ALBERTYN, Rt Rev. Charles Henry; a Bishop Suffragan, Diocese of Cape Town, 1983–93; *b* 24 Dec. 1928; *s* of Adam and Annie Albertyn; *m* 1965, Berenice Lategan; one *s* two *d*. *Educ:* Hewat Training College (Teacher's Diploma 1948); Diocesan Clergy School, Cape Town (LTh 1956). Teaching, 1948–52. Deacon 1955, priest 1956; Assistant, St Nicholas, Matroosfontein, 1955–60; Priest-in-charge, St Helena Bay, 1960–64; Assistant, St George's, Silvertown, 1965–70; Rector: Church of Holy Spirit, Heideveld, 1970–75; St Mary's, Kraaifontein, 1975–78; Church of Resurrection, Bonteheuwel, 1978–83; Canon of St George Cathedral, Cape Town, 1972–83; Archdeacon of Bellville, 1981–83. *Recreation:* watching soccer. *Address:* 7 Mynweg, Vanguard Estate, Athlone, Cape 7764, S Africa.

ALBERY, Ian Bronson; theatre consultant, UK and overseas, since 1968; *b* 21 Sept. 1936; *s* of Sir Donald Albery and Rubina Albery (*née* McGilchrist); *m* Barbara Yu Ling Lee (marr. diss.; she *d* 1997); two *s*; one *d* by Jenny Beavan; *m* 2003, Judy Monahan. *Educ:* Stowe; Lycée de Briançon, France. Stage, Production or Technical Manager for over 100 West End productions, 1958–70; Technical Dir, London Festival Ballet, 1964–68; Producer or Co-Producer for over 50 West End prodns, 1978–; Managing Director: Wyndham Theatres, Piccadilly Theatre, Donmar Productions, Omega Stage (Donmar Warehouse Th.), 1978–87; Theatre of Comedy, 1987–90; Dep. Chm., English Nat. Ballet, 1984–90; Dir, Ticketmaster (UK) Ltd, 1985–92; Chief Exec. and Producer, Sadler's Wells, Peacock and Lilian Baylis Theatres, 1994–2002; Chief Exec., Guildford Sch. of Acting Conservatoire, 2002–04. Consultant, Japan Satellite Broadcasting, 1991–92. Trustee, Theatres Trust, 1977–96. Pres., 1977–79, Vice-Pres., 1979–80, Soc. of West End Th. *Address:* Quartier de Chevrière, 26450 Roynac, France. *T:* (4) 75901221; *e-mail:* ian@albery.com.

ALBERY, John; *see* Albery, W. J.

ALBERY, Tim; theatre and opera director; *b* 20 May 1952. *Theatre* productions include: War Crimes, ICA, 1981; Secret Gardens, Amsterdam and ICA, 1983; Venice Preserv'd, Almeida, 1983; Hedda Gabler, Almeida, 1984; The Princess of Cleves, ICA, 1985; Mary Stuart, Greenwich, 1988; As You Like It, Old Vic, 1989; Berenice, NT, 1990; Wallenstein, RSC, 1993; Macbeth, RSC, 1996; Attempts on her Life, Royal Court, 1997; Nathan the Wise, Toronto, 2005; *opera* productions include: for English National Opera: Billy Budd, 1988; Beatrice and Benedict, 1990; Peter Grimes, 1991; Lohengrin, 1993; From the House of the Dead, 1997; La Bohème, 2000; War and Peace, 2001; for Opera North: The Midsummer Marriage, 1985; The Trojans, 1986; La finta giardiniera, 1989; Don Giovanni, 1991; Don Carlos, 1992; Luisa Miller, 1995; Così fan Tutte, 1997, 2004; Katya Kabanova, 1999; Idomeneo, 2003; King Croesus, Madama Butterfly, 2007; Macbeth, 2008; for Royal Opera: Chérubin, 1994; for Welsh National Opera: The Trojans, 1987; La finta giardiniera, 1994; Nabucco, 1995; for Scottish Opera: The Midsummer Marriage, 1988; The Trojans, 1990; Fidelio, 1994, 2005; The Ring Cycle, 2000–03; Don Giovanni, 2006; for Australian Opera: The Marriage of Figaro, 1992; for Netherlands Opera: Benvenuto Cellini, 1991; La Wally, 1993; Beatrice and Benedict, 2001; for Santa Fé Opera: Beatrice and Benedict, 1998; The Magic Flute, 2006; for Batignano Fest., Italy, The Turn of the Screw, 1983; for Bregenz Fest., Austria, La Wally, 1990; for Bayerische Staatsoper, Munich: Peter Grimes, 1991; Simon Boccanegra, 1995; Ariadne auf Naxos, 1996; for Metropolitan Opera, NY: A Midsummer Night's Dream, 1996; The Merry Widow, 2000; for Canadian Opera: Rodelinda, 2005; Götterdämmerung, 2006; for Glimmerglass Fest., Così fan Tutti, 2005; *musicals* include: Passion, Minnesota Opera, 2004; One Touch of Venus, Opera North, 2004; The Threepenny Opera, Toronto, 2007.

ALBERY, Prof. Wyndham John, FRS 1985; FRSC; Master, University College, Oxford, 1989–97; *b* 5 April 1936; *s* of late Michael James Albery, QC, and Mary Laughton Albery. *Educ:* Winchester Coll.; Balliol Coll., Oxford (MA, DPhil). Weir Jun. Research Fellow, 1962, Fellow, 1963–78, University Coll., Oxford; Lectr, Phys. Chem., Univ. of Oxford, 1964–78; Imperial College, London: Prof., Phys. Chemistry, 1978–89; Staff Orator, 1980–83; Dean, RCS, 1986–89. Vis. Fellow, Univ. of Minnesota, 1965; Vis. Prof., Harvard Univ., 1976. Tilden Lectr, RSC, 1979; Sherman Fairchild Schol., Calif. Inst. of Tech., 1985. Chairman: SERC Chemistry Cttee, 1982–85; Electrochem. Gp, RSC, 1985–89. Mem. Council, Royal Instn, 1985–88; Pres., Chemistry Section, British Assoc., 1992. Writer for television series That Was The Week That Was, 1963–64; also (with John Gould) two musicals, Who Was That Lady?, and On The Boil. Curator, Oxford Playhouse, 1974–78; Governor, Old Vic, 1979–89; Chm., Burton Taylor Theatre Management Cttee, 1990–93. Gov., Rugby Sch., 1987–2000; Fellow, Winchester Coll., 1989–2000. Hon. DSc Kent, 1990. *Publications:* Ring-Disc Electrodes, 1971; Electrode Kinetics, 1975; papers in jls: Faraday I, Nature, and Jls of Electrochemical Soc., Electroanalytical Chemistry, etc. *Recreations:* theatre, cruising. *Address:* 35 Falmouth House, Clarendon Place, Hyde Park Street, W2 2NT. *T:* (020) 7262 3909. *Club:* Garrick.

ALBRIGHT, Madeleine Korbel, PhD; Secretary of State, United States of America, 1997–2001; founder and Principal, Albright Group LLC, since 2001; *b* 15 May 1937; *m* Joseph Albright (marr. diss.); three *d*. *Educ:* Wellesley Coll. (BA Hons Pol Sci. 1959); Sch. of Advanced Internat. Studies, Johns Hopkins Univ.; Columbia Univ. (BA 1968; PhD 1976). Chief Legislative Asst to Senator Edmund Muskie, 1976–78; Staff Mem., Nat. Security Council and Mem., White House Staff, 1978–81; Sen. Fellow in Soviet and E European Affairs, Center for Strategic and Internat. Studies; Fellow, Woodrow Wilson Internat. Center for Scholars, 1981–82; Res. Prof. of Internat. Affairs and Dir, Women in Foreign Service Program, Georgetown Univ. Sch. of Foreign Service, 1982–92; Pres., Center for Nat. Policy, 1989–92 (Mem., Bd of Dirs); US Perm. Rep. to UN, 1993–96; Mem., Nat. Security Council, USA, 1993–2001. Member: Bd of Dirs, Atlantic Council of US; US Nat. Commn, UNESCO. Chm., Nat. Democratic Inst. for Internat. Affairs, 2001–. *Publications:* Poland: the role of the press in political change, 1983; Madam Secretary (autobiog.), 2003; articles in professional jls and chapters in books.

ALBROW, Susan Jane; *see* Owen, S. J.

ALBU, Sir George, 3rd Bt *cr* (UK) 1912, of Grosvenor Place, City of Westminster, and Johannesburg, Province of Transvaal, South Africa; farmer; *b* 5 June 1944; *o s* of Major Sir George Werner Albu, 2nd Bt, and Kathleen Betty (*d* 1956), *d* of Edward Charles Dicey, Parktown, Johannesburg; *S* father, 1963; *m* 1969, Joan Valerie Millar, London; two *d*. *Recreation:* horse racing. *Heir:* none. *Address:* Glen Hamish Farm, PO Box 62, Richmond, Natal, 3780, South Africa. *T:* (33) 2122587. *Clubs:* Victoria Country (Pietermaritzburg); Durban Country; Richmond (Natal) Country (Richmond).

ALCOCK, Air Chief Marshal Sir (Robert James) Michael, GCB 1996 (CB 1989); KBE 1992; FREng; Royal Air Force, retired; aerospace consultant, since 1997; Director, Cygnae Ltd, since 1997; Chairman, AMSS Ltd, since 2003; *b* 11 July 1936; *s* of late William George and Doris Alcock; *m* 1965, Pauline Mary Oades; two *d*. *Educ:* Victoria College, Jersey; Royal Aircraft Establishment. FIMechE; FRAeS. Commissioned, Engineer Branch, RAF, 1959; RAF Tech. Coll., Henlow, 1961; Goose Bay, Labrador, 1964; Units in Bomber Comd, 1959–69; RAF Staff Coll., Bracknell, 1970; PSO to DG Eng (RAF), 1971–73; OC Eng. Wing, RAF Coningsby, 1973–75; OC No 23 Maintenance Unit, RAF Aldergrove, 1975–77; Group Captain (Plans), HQ RAF Support Command, 1977–79; MoD, 1979–81; Dep. Comdt, RAF Staff Coll., Bracknell, 1981–84; RCDS, 1984; Dir Gen. of Communications, Inf. Systems and Orgn (RAF), 1985–88; AO Engrg, HQ Strike Comd, 1988–91; Chief Engr and Chief of Logistic Support, RAF, 1991–93; Air Mem. for Supply and Orgn, MoD, 1993–94; Air Member for Logistics and AOC-in-C, Logistics Comd, 1994–96. Trustee, RAF Benevolent Fund, 1996–2002. Chm., Bd of Mgt, Princess Marina Hse, 1996–2002. Pres., British Model Flyers' Assoc., 2000–. Governor, Victoria Coll., Jersey, 1995–2004. FREng (FEng 1995). Hon. DSc Cranfield, 1994. *Recreations:* golf, model aircraft, sailing. *Address:* c/o National Westminster Bank, PO Box 61, 2 Alexandra Road, Farnborough, Hants GU14 6YR. *Clubs:* Royal Air Force; Berkshire Golf, St Enodoc Golf.

ALDENHAM, 6th Baron *cr* 1896, of Aldenham, Co. Hertford, **AND HUNSDON OF HUNSDON,** 4th Baron *cr* 1923, of Briggens, Co. Hertford; **Vicary Tyser Gibbs;** *b* 9 June 1948; *s* of 5th Baron Aldenham and of Mary Elizabeth, *o d* of late Walter Parkyns Tyser; *S* father, 1986; *m* 1980, Josephine Nicola, *er d* of John Richmond Fell, Lower Bourne, Farnham, Surrey; three *s* one *d*. *Educ:* Eton; Oriel College, Oxford; RAC, Cirencester. Capel-Cure Myers Ltd, 1975–79; Dir, Montclare Shipping Co., 1986–. Chairman: Herts CLA, 1995–98; Watling Chase Community Forest, 1997–99. Freeman, City of London, 1979. *Heir:* *s* Hon. Humphrey William Fell Gibbs, *b* 31 Jan. 1989. *Address:* c/o Aldenham Estate Office, Home Farm, Aldenham Road, Elstree, Herts WD6 3AZ.

ALDER, Lucette, (Mrs Alan Alder); *see* Aldous, L.

ALDER, Michael; Controller, English Regional Television, British Broadcasting Corporation, 1977–86, retired; *b* 3 Nov. 1928; *s* of late Thomas Alder and Winifred Miller; *m* 1955, Freda, *d* of late John and Doris Hall; two *d*. *Educ:* Ranelagh Sch., Bracknell, Berks; Rutherford Coll., Newcastle-upon-Tyne. Newcastle Evening Chronicle, 1947–59; BBC North-East: Chief News Asst, Newcastle; Area News Editor, Newcastle; Representative, NE England, 1959–69; Head of Regional Television Development, BBC, 1969–77. Mem., Exec. Cttee, Relate (formerly Nat. Marriage Guidance Council), 1987–94 (Chm., S Warwicks, 1987–89; Chm., Appeals Cttee, 1988–94). Chm., Tanworth Educnl Foundn, 2004–08 (Vice Chm., 1994–2004). Mem., Incorporated Co. of Butchers, 1948. Freeman, City of Newcastle upon Tyne. *Recreations:* gardening, fishing, walking, country pursuits. *Address:* Red Roofs, Bates Lane, Tanworth-in-Arden, Warwicks B94 5AR. *T:* (01564) 742403.

ALDER, Prof. Roger William, DPhil, DSc; FRS 2006; CChem, FRSC; Professor of Organic Chemistry, University of Bristol, 1996–2002, now Professor Emeritus and Senior Research Fellow; *b* 26 April 1937; *s* of William John Alder and Mona Amelia Alder (*née* Nevitt); *m* 1961, Judy Anne Sweet; one *s* two *d*. *Educ:* Rendcomb Coll., Cirencester; Pembroke Coll., Oxford (MA, DPhil); DSc Bristol. CChem, FRSC, 1980. Lectr in Organic Chem., 1966–81, Reader, 1981–96, Univ. of Bristol. *Publications:* (jtly) Mechanism in Organic Chemistry, 1971; contrib. numerous papers on aspects of organic chem. *Address:* School of Chemistry, University of Bristol, Cantock's Close, Bristol BS8 1TS. *T:* (0117) 928 7657, *Fax:* (0117) 929 8611; *e-mail:* rog.alder@bris.ac.uk.

ALDERDICE, family name of **Baron Alderdice**.

ALDERDICE, Baron *cr* 1996 (Life Peer), of Knock, in the City of Belfast; **John Thomas Alderdice,** FRCPsych; consultant psychiatrist in psychotherapy, Belfast Health and Social Services Trust (formerly Eastern Health and Social Services Board, then South and East Belfast Health and Social Services Trust), since 1988; *b* 28 March 1955; *s* of Rev. David Alderdice and Helena Alderdice (*née* Shields); *m* 1977, Dr Joan Margaret Alderdice (*née* Hill), consultant pathologist; two *s* one *d*. *Educ:* Ballymena Acad.; Queen's Univ., Belfast (MB, BCh, BAO 1978). MRCPsych 1983; FRCPsych 1997; Jun. House Officer, Lagan Valley Hosp., 1978–79; Sen. House Officer, Belfast City Hosp., 1979–80; Registrar: Holywell and Whiteabbey Hosps, 1980–81; Shaftesbury Square Hosp., 1981–82; Lissue and Belfast City Hosps, 1982–83; Sen. Tutor and Sen. Registrar, Belfast City Hosp. and Queen's Univ., Belfast, 1983–87. Exec. Med. Dir, S and E Belfast HSS Trust, 1993–97. Hon. Lectr/Sen. Lectr, QUB, 1991–99; Hon. Prof., Univ. of San Marcos, Peru, 1999; Vis. Prof., Dept of Psychiatry and Neurobehavioral Scis, Univ. of Virginia, USA, 2006–. Dir, NI Inst. of Human Relns, 1991–94. Contested (Alliance): Belfast E, 1987, 1992; NI, European Parly Election, 1989. Alliance Party of Northern Ireland: Mem., Exec. Cttee, 1984–98; Chm., Policy Cttee, 1985–87; Vice-Chm., March–Oct. 1987; Leader, 1987–98; Leader: delegn at Inter-Party and Inter-Governmental Talks on the future of NI, 1991–98; delegn at Forum for Peace and Reconciliation, Dublin Castle, 1994–96; Mem., NI Forum, 1996–98; Speaker, NI Assembly, 1998–2004 (Mem. for Belfast East). European Liberal, Democrat and Reform Party (formerly Fedn of European Liberal, Democratic and Reform Parties): Mem., Exec. Cttee, 1987–2003; Treas., 1995–99; Vice-Pres., 1999–2003; Pres., Liberal International, 2005– (Mem. Bureau, 1996–; Vice Pres., 1992–99; Dep. Pres., 2000–05). Member: Ind. Monitoring Commn, 2004–; Commonwealth Commn on Respect and Understanding, 2006–07. Mem. (Vic. Area), Belfast City Council, 1989–97. Trustee, Ulster Museum, 1993–97. Hon. FRCPI 1997; Hon. FRCPsych 2001; Hon Mem., Peruvian Psychiatric Assoc., 2000; Hon. Affiliate, British Psychoanalytical Soc., 2001. Hon. DLitt UEL, 2008. Silver Medal, Congress of Peru, 1999; Medal of Honour, Coll. of Medicine, Peru, 1999; Erice Prize, World Fedn of Scientists, 2005; Extraordinarily Meritorious Service to Psychoanalysis Award, Internat. Psychoanalytical Assoc., 2005. Kt Comdr, Royal Order of Francis I, 2002. *Publications:* professional articles on psychology of terrorism and conflict; political articles. *Recreations:* reading, music, gastronomy. *Address:* House of Lords, SW1A 0PW. *T:* (020) 7219 5050, (Belfast) (028) 9079 3097, *Fax:* (028) 9022 5276; *e-mail:* alderdicej@parliament.uk. *Clubs:* National Liberal; Ulster Reform (Belfast).

See also D. K. Alderdice.

ALDERDICE, David King, OBE 1999; Consultant Dermatologist, Causeway Hospital, Coleraine, since 2002; Lord Mayor of Belfast, 1998–99; *b* 2 June 1966; *s* of Rev. David and Helena Alderdice; *m* 1989, Fiona Alison Johnston; one *s* two *d*. *Educ:* Queen's Univ.,

Belfast (MB BCh BAO 1989); Manchester Coll., Oxford (BA PPE 1994; MA 1998). MRCPI 1996. Jun., subseq. Sen., House Officer, Royal Victoria Hosp., Belfast, 1989–92; Specialist Registrar in Dermatology, Royal Victoria Hosp., Belfast and Belfast City Hosp., 1997–2002; Clin. Res. Fellow, Ulster Hosp., Dundonald, 1997–98. Contested (Alliance), N Antrim, Forum, 1996, parly elecns, 1997. Member (Alliance): Belfast CC, 1997–2005; N Down BC, 2005–. *Publications:* articles in dermatology, genitourinary and psychol learned jls. *Recreation:* squash racquets. *Address:* c/o Members' Room, North Down Borough Council, Town Hall, The Castle, Bangor BT20 4BJ. *T:* (028) 9127 0371.

See also Baron Alderdice.

ALDERMAN, Richard John; Director, Serious Fraud Office, since 2008; *b* 5 Aug. 1952; *s* of late John Edward Alderman and Patricia Eileen Alderman; *m* 1981, Joyce Sheelagh, *d* of Herrick Edwin and Joyce Hilda Wickens; one *d*. *Educ:* Woking Grammar Sch.; University College London (LLB). Called to the Bar, Gray's Inn, 1974; joined Solicitor's Office, Inland Revenue, 1975; seconded to Legal Secretariat to the Law Officers, 1991–93; Principal Asst Solicitor, 1996–2003, Dir, Special Compliance Office, 2003–05, Bd of Inland Revenue; Dir, Special Civil Investigations, HMRC, 2005–08. *Recreations:* family life, country walking. *Address:* Serious Fraud Office, Elm House, 10–16 Elm Street, WC1X 0BJ.

ALDERSLADE, Prof. Richard, FRCP, FFPH; Chief Executive, Children's High Level Group, since 2006; Special Professor of Health Policy, Nottingham University, since 1993; *b* 11 Aug. 1947; *s* of Herbert Raymond Alderslade and Edna F. Alderslade; *m* 1st, 1974, Elizabeth Rose (marr. diss. 1999); two *s* one *d* (and one *d* decd); 2nd, 1999, Angela Hendriksen; one step *d*. *Educ:* Chichester High Sch. for Boys; Christ Church, Oxford (BM BCh; MA); St George's Hosp. FFPH (FFPHM 1987); FRCP 1993. GP, 1974–76; Registrar in Community Medicine, 1976–78, Lectr, 1978–79; MO and SMO, DHSS, 1979–85; Specialist in Community Medicine, 1985–88 and Community Unit Gen. Manager, 1986–88, Hull HA; Regl Dir of Public Health and Regl MO, Trent RHA, 1988–94; Prof. of Community Care, Univ. of Sheffield, 1994–95; Regl Advr, Humanitarian Assistance, WHO Regl Office for Europe, Copenhagen, 1995–2001; Chief Officer, High Level Gp for Romanian Children and Advr to Prime Minister of Romania, 2001–02; Sen. External Relns Officer, WHO Office, UN, NY, 2002–06. *Publications:* articles on public health, BMJ and other jls. *Recreations:* walking, railways, photography. *Address:* Children's High Level Group, Hope House, 45 Great Peter Street, SW1P 3LT.

ALDERSON, Brian Wouldhave; freelance editor and writer; Children's Books Consultant, The Times, since 1995 (Children's Books Editor, 1967–95); *b* 19 Sept. 1930; *s* of John William Alderson and Helen Marjory Alderson; *m* 1953, Valerie Christine (*née* Wells) (*d* 2005); three *s* (and two *s* decd). *Educ:* Ackworth Sch.; University College of the South-West, Exeter (BA Hons). Work in the book trade, 1952–63; Tutor-librarian, East Herts Coll. of Further Educn, 1963–65; Sen. Lectr, (on Children's Literature and on the Book Trade), Polytechnic of N London, 1965–83. Visiting Professor: Univ. of Southern Mississippi, 1985; UCLA, 1986. Founder and first Chm., Children's Books Hist. Soc., 1969–78 and 1995–2001. Pres., Beatrix Potter Soc., 1995–. Exhibition organiser: (with descriptive notes): Early English Children's Books, BM, 1968; Looking at Picture Books, NBL, 1973; Grimm Tales in England, British Library, 1985–86; Randolph Caldecott and the Art of the English Picture Book, British Library, 1986–87; Be Merry and Wise: the early development of English children's books, Pierpont Morgan Library, NY, 1990–91; Childhood Re-Collected, Christ Church, Oxford, 1994; This Book Belongs To Me, Nat. Liby of Scotland, Edinburgh, 2002. DUniv Surrey, 2002. Eleanor Farjeon Award, 1968. *Publications:* Sing a Song for Sixpence, 1986; (with Iona and Robert Opie) Treasures of Childhood, 1989; The Arabian Nights, 1992; Ezra Jack Keats: artist and picture book maker, vol. 1, 1994, vol. 2, 2002; Edward Ardizzone: a bibliographic commentary, 2003; (with Felix de Marez Oyens) Be Merry and Wise: origins of children's book publishing in England 1650–1800, 2006; *translations:* Hürlimann: Three Centuries of Children's Books in Europe, 1967; Picture-book World, 1968; Grimm, Popular Folk Tales, 1978; Andersen, The Swan's Stories, 1997; *edited:* The Juvenile Library, 1966–74; The Colour Fairy Books, by Andrew Lang, 1975–82; Lear, A Book of Bosh, 1975; Children's Books in England, by F. J. Harvey Darton, 1982; Hans Christian Andersen and his Eventyr in England, 1982. *Recreations:* bibliography, dale-walking. *Address:* 28–30 Victoria Road, Richmond, North Yorks DL10 4AS. *T:* (01748) 823648.

ALDERSON, Daphne Elizabeth, (Mrs J. K. A. Alderson); *see* Wickham, D. E.

ALDERSON, (George) Lawrence (Hastings), CBE 2004; Chairman: Countrywide Livestock Ltd, since 1974; Rare Breeds Survival Trust, 2003–07; *b* 24 June 1939; *s* of late John Henry Alderson and Mary Hilda Alderson (*née* Hastings), Teesdale; *m* 2nd, 1971, Jacqueline Mary (marr. diss. 1983), *y d* of John Pasfield, OBE; one *s* one *d*; 4th, 1994, Marie Bridgette, *e d* of John Lynch. *Educ:* Barnard Castle Sch.; Selwyn Coll., Cambridge (BA 1962, MA; boxing blue). Farmer, 1968–92: created new breed, British Milksheep; Chm., Westwater Farm Partners, 1974–81. Consultant: on internat. genetic resources, 1974–90; EEC studies of endangered breeds, 1992–93. Dir, Traditional Breeds Meat Mktg Co., 1998–2000. Chm., Preserving Cttee, DEFRA Nat. Steering Cttee, 2003–06. Consultant, Internat. Evaluation Cttee, Danish Farm Animal Genetic Resources, 2001–02. Tech. Consultant, 1973–90, Dir, 1990–2000, Rare Breeds Survival Trust; Trustee and Founder Chm., Rare Breeds Internat., 1991–. Member: Council, Eur. Livestock Alliance, 2001–; Mgt Bd, PigBioDiv (Eur.), 2002–. Pres., White Park Cattle Soc., 1988–. Mem., Editl Adv. Bd, AGRI (FAO), 2003–. *Publications:* The Chance to Survive, 1978, 3rd edn 1994; Rare Breeds, 1984, 4th edn 2001; Genetic Conservation of Domestic Livestock, Vol. I 1990, Vol. II 1992; Saving the Breeds, 1994; Coloured Sheep, 1994; A Breed of Distinction, 1997; The Adaptation of Rare Breeds of British Livestock to Different Environments, 1998; Conservation Genetics of Endangered Horse Breeds, 2005. *Recreations:* sport, writing, genealogy, travel, breeding White Park cattle. *Address:* 6 Harnage, Shrewsbury, Shropshire SY5 6EJ; *e-mail:* alderson@clltd.demon.co.uk. *Club:* Farmers.

ALDERSON, Joanne Hazel; District Judge (Magistrates' Courts) (formerly Stipendiary Magistrate), Derbyshire, since 1997; *b* 18 March 1954; *d* of Colin and Joan Fleetwood; *m* 1983, Richard Alderson; two *s*. *Educ:* Wolverhampton Girls' High Sch.; Liverpool Univ. (LLB Hons); College of Law. Called to the Bar, Middle Temple, 1978. Legal Advr, W Midlands Prosecuting Solicitors' Dept, 1977–78; Court Clerk/Principal Asst, Wolverhampton Magistrates' Court, 1978–85; Deputy Clerk: to Warley Justices, 1985–86; to Wolverhampton Justices, 1986–97; Dep. Chief Exec., Wolverhampton Magistrates' Courts Cttee, 1995–97. *Recreations:* travel, bridge, swimming, reading. *Address:* Derby Magistrates' Court, St Mary's Gate, Derby DE1 3JR. *T:* (01332) 362000.

ALDERSON, John Cottingham, CBE 1981; QPM 1974; writer and commentator on police and penal affairs; Chief Constable of Devon and Cornwall, 1973–82; *b* 28 May 1922; *e s* of late Ernest Cottingham Alderson and Elsie Lavinia Rose; *m* 1948, Irené Macmillan Stirling; one *s*. *Educ:* Barnsley Elem. Schs and Techn. College. Called to Bar, Middle Temple. British Meml Foundn Fellow, Australia, 1956; Extension Certif. in Criminology, Univ. of Leeds. Highland LI, 1938–41 (Corp.); Army Phys. Trng Corps, N Africa and Italy, 1941–46 (Warrant Officer). West Riding Constabulary as Constable, 1946; Police Coll., 1954; Inspector, 1955; Sub-Divisional Comd, 1960; Sen. Comd Course, Police Coll., 1963–64; Dep. Chief Constable, Dorset, 1964–66; Metropolitan Police, Dep. Comdr (Admin and Ops), 1966; 2nd-in-comd No 3 Police District, 1967; Dep. Asst Comr (Trng), 1968; Comdt, Police Coll., 1970; Asst Comr (Personnel and Trng), 1973. Consultant on Human Rights to Council of Europe, 1981–. Member: BBC Gen. Adv. Council, 1971–78; Royal Humane Soc. Cttee, 1973–81; Pres., Royal Life-Saving Soc., 1974–78. Vis. Prof. of Police Studies, Strathclyde Univ., 1983–89; Res. Fellow, Inst. of Police and Criminol Studies, Univ. of Portsmouth, 1994–. External Examiner, Leadership Studies, Univ. of Exeter, 1994–. Fellow Commoner, Corpus Christi Coll., Cambridge, 1982; Fellow, Inst. of Criminology, Cambridge, 1982; Gwilym Gibbon Res. Fellow, Nuffield Coll., Oxford, 1982–83; Australian Commonwealth Fellow, Australian Govt, 1987; Hon. Res. Fellow, Centre for Police Studies, Univ. of Exeter, 1987–95. Contested (L) Teignbridge, Devon, 1983. Hon. LLD Exeter, 1979; Hon. DLitt Bradford, 1982. *Publications:* (contrib.) Encyclopedia of Crime and Criminals, 1960; (ed jtly) The Police We Deserve, 1973; Policing Freedom, 1979; Law and Disorder, 1984; Human Rights and the Police, 1984; Principled Policing, 1998; articles in professional jls and newspapers. *Recreations:* reading, writing, keeping fit.

ALDERSON, Lawrence; *see* Alderson, G. L. H.

ALDERSON, Margaret Hanne, (Maggie); journalist and novelist; *b* 31 July 1959; *d* of Douglas Arthur Alderson and Margaret Dura Alderson (*née* Mackay); *m* 1st, 1991, Geoffrey Francis Laurence (marr. diss. 1996); 2nd, 2002, Radenko Popovic; one *d*. *Educ:* Alleyne's Sch., Stone, Staffs; Univ. of St Andrews (MA Hons History of Art). Features Editor: Look Now, 1983; Honey, 1984; Commng Editor, You, 1985; Metropolitan Features Editor, Evening Standard, 1986; Editor: ES Magazine, 1988; Elle, 1989–92; Dep. Editor, Cleo magazine, 1993–94; Editor, Mode, 1994–95; sen. writer, Sydney Morning Herald, 1996–2001. Editor of the Year, Colour Supplements, British Soc. of Magazine Eds, 1989. *Publications:* Shoe Money, 1998; Pants On Fire, 2000; Handbag Heaven, 2001; (ed jtly) Big Night Out, 2002; Mad About the Boy, 2002; Handbags and Gladrags, 2004; (ed jtly) Ladies Night, 2005; Cents and Sensibility, 2006. *Address:* Bentinck House, Hastings, East Sussex. *Club:* Groucho.

ALDERSON, Martha, (Matti); international advisor on regulatory policy and strategy; Managing Director, FireHorses Ltd, since 2000; *b* 20 Dec. 1951; *d* of Edward Connelly and Helen Connelly (*née* Peacock); *m* 1970, Alan Alderson. *Educ:* Bearsden Acad., Dunbartonshire; Open Univ. (BA Hons 1994). Legal Exec., Scotland, 1970–72; Advertising Agency Poster Bureau, 1972–74; Advertising Standards Authority: Executive, 1975–80; Manager, 1980–89; Dep. Dir Gen., 1989–90; Dir Gen., 1990–2000. Vice Chm., European Advertising Standards Alliance, Brussels, 1991–2000. Member: Food Adv. Cttee, MAFF, 1997–2002; Better Regulation Task Force, 1998–2004; Doctors' and Dentists' Remuneration Review Body, 1998–2001; Press Complaints Commn, 2002–; Chm., Direct Mkting Commn (formerly Authy), 2007–; Removals Industry Ombudsman, 2008– (Mem. Bd, Removals Industry Ombudsman Scheme, 2004–08). Patron, Westminster Media Forum, 2001–. FCAM 1993; FRSA 1993. *Publications:* Report on Children, Advertising and Regulation in Europe, 2001; Alcohol Regulation in the Asia Pacific Region, 2006; columnist and contrib. numerous advertising and mktg textbooks, and jls in UK and EU. *Recreations:* design, cars, reading, studying. *Address:* Raglan House, Windsor Road, Gerrards Cross, Bucks SL9 7ND. *Club:* Commonwealth.

ALDERTON, John; actor (stage, films, television); *b* Gainsborough, Lincs, 27 Nov. 1940; *s* of Gordon John Alderton and Ivy Handley; *m* 1st, 1964, Jill Browne (marr. diss. 1970; she *d* 1991); 2nd, Pauline Collins, *qv*; two *s* one *d*. *Educ:* Kingston High Sch., Hull. *Stage:* 1st appearance (Rep.) Theatre Royal, York, in Badger's Green, 1961; cont. Rep.; 1st London appearance, Spring and Port Wine, Mermaid (later Apollo), 1965; Dutch Uncle, RSC, Aldwych, 1969; The Night I Chased the Women with an Eel, Comedy, 1969; Punch and Judy Stories, Howff, 1973; Judies, Comedy, 1974; The Birthday Party, Shaw, 1975; Confusions (4 parts), Apollo, 1976; Rattle of a Simple Man, Savoy, 1980; Special Occasions, Ambassadors, 1983; The Maintenance Man, Comedy, 1986; Waiting for Godot, NT, 1987; What the Butler Saw, RNT, 1995; Honeymoon Suite, Royal Court, 2004; *films:* (1962–): incl. Duffy, Hannibal Brooks, Zardoz, It Shouldn't Happen to a Vet, Please Sir, Calendar Girls; *television:* series: Please Sir, No Honestly, My Wife Next Door, P. G. Wodehouse, Thomas and Sarah, Father's Day, Forever Green and various plays. *Address:* c/o Curtis Brown, 28 Haymarket, SW1Y 4SP.

ALDHOUSE-GREEN, Prof. Miranda Jane, PhD; FSA; Professor of Archaeology, Cardiff University, since 2006; *b* 24 July 1947; *d* of Eric Aldhouse and Eunice Henriques; *m* 1970, Stephen Green (now Aldhouse-Green); one *d*. *Educ:* Cardiff Univ. (BA Hons Archaeol. 1969); Lady Margaret Hall, Oxford (MLitt 1974); Open Univ. (PhD 1981). FSA 1979. Pt-time Classical Studies Tutor, OU in Wales, 1982–94; Lectr, Cardiff Univ., 1990–94; University of Wales College, Newport, subseq. University of Wales, Newport: Sen. Lectr, 1994–97; Reader, 1997–98; Head, SCARAB Res. Centre, 1996–2006; Prof. of Archaeology, 1998–2006. Mem., Ancient Monuments Bd for Wales, 2001–. Pres., Prehistoric Soc., 2005 (Vice-Pres., 2002). Hon. Fellow, Centre for Advanced Welsh and Celtic Studies, Univ. of Wales, Aberystwyth, 1990–. *Publications:* The Gods of the Celts, 1986; Symbol and Image in Celtic Religious Art, 1989; The Sun Gods of Ancient Europe, 1991; Animals in Celtic Life and Myth, 1992; Dictionary of Celtic Myth and Legend, 1992; Celtic Goddesses, 1995; (ed) The Celtic World, 1995; Celtic Art, 1996; The World of the Druids, 1997; Dying for the Gods, 2001; An Archaeology of Images, 2004; (with S. Aldhouse-Green) The Quest for the Shaman in European Antiquity, 2005; Boudica Britannia, 2006; about 80 articles in learned archaeol. jls. *Recreations:* choral singing, wine, travel, early and baroque music, swimming, Burmese cats. *Address:* School of History and Archaeology, Cardiff University, Humanities Building, Colum Drive, Cardiff CF10 3EU. *T:* (029) 2087 0402; *e-mail:* Aldhouse-GreenMJ@cardiff.ac.uk.

ALDINGTON, 2nd Baron *cr* 1962; **Charles Harold Stuart Low;** Chairman: Deutsche Bank London, since 2002; Stramongate Ltd; *b* 22 June 1948; *s* of 1st Baron Aldington, KCMG, CBE, DSO, TD, PC and of Araminta Bowman, *d* of Sir Harold MacMichael, GCMG, DSO; *S* father, 2000; *m* 1989, Dr Regine, *d* of Erwin von Csongrady-Schopf and Liselotte (*née* Horstmann); one *s* twin *d*. *Educ:* Winchester Coll.; New Coll., Oxford (BA Hons); INSEAD. Citibank NA (NY), Hong Kong and Dusseldorf, 1971–77; Head of Ship Finance, then Head of UK Corporate Lending, then Dir, Continental Europe, Grindlays Bank, 1978–86; Deutsche Bank AG: Dir, Duisburg Br., 1986–87; Man. Dir, London, 1988–96; Man. Dir, Investment Banking, 1996–2002. Chairman: Eur. Vocational Coll., 1991–96; CENTEC, subseq. FOCUS Central London, Central London TEC, 1995–99; Member: Council, British-German Chamber of Commerce and Industry, 1995–; Chairman's Cttee, LIBA, 2003–; Chairman's Cttee, BBA, 2003–. Mem., Oxford Univ. Ct of Benefactors, 1990–. Trustee: English Internat., 1979–86; Whitechapel Art Gall. Foundn, 1991–96; Royal Acad. Trust, 2003–. Gov., Ditchley Foundn, 2006–. *Heir:* *s* Hon. Philip Toby Augustus Low, *b* 1 Sept. 1990. *Address:* 59 Warwick Square, SW1V

2AL. *Clubs:* Brooks's; Hong Kong.
See also Hon. P. J. S. Roberts.

ALDISS, Brian Wilson, OBE 2005; writer; critic; *b* 18 Aug. 1925; *s* of Stanley and Elizabeth May Aldiss; *m* 1965, Margaret Manson (*d* 1997); one *s* one *d*; and one *s* one *d* by previous *m*. *Educ:* Framlingham Coll.; West Buckland School. FRSL 1994. Royal Signals, 1943–47; book-selling, 1947–56; writer, 1956–; Literary Editor, Oxford Mail, 1958–69. Pres., British Science Fiction Assoc., 1960–64. Editor, SF Horizons, 1964–. Chairman, Oxford Branch Conservation Soc., 1968–69; Vice Pres., The Stapledon Soc., 1975–; Jt Pres., European SF Cttees, 1976–79; Society of Authors: Mem., Cttee of Management, 1976–78, Chm., 1978; Chm., Cultural Exchanges Cttee, 1979–; Member: Arts Council Literature Panel, 1978–80; Internat. PEN, 1983–; Pres., World SF, 1982–84; Vice-President: H. G. Wells Soc., 1983–; Soc. for Anglo-Chinese Understanding, 1987–91. Mem. Council, Council for Posterity, 1990–. Vice Pres., West Buckland Sch., 1996–. Hon. DLitt Reading, 2001. Observer Book Award for Science Fiction, 1956; Ditmar Award for Best Contemporary Writer of Science Fiction, 1969; first James Blish Award, for SF criticism, 1977; Pilgrim Award, 1978; first Award for Distinguished Scholarship, Internat. Assoc. for the Fantastic in the Arts, Houston, 1986; Prix Utopie, France, 1999; Grand Master of Science Fiction, Science Fiction Writers of America, 2000; Prix Européen, Grand Prix de l'Imaginaire, 2006. *Publications: science-fiction:* Space, Time and Nathaniel, 1957; Non-Stop, 1958 (Prix Jules Verne, 1977); Canopy of Time, 1959; The Male Response, 1961; Hothouse, 1962 (Hugo Award, 1961); Best Fantasy Stories, 1962; The Airs of Earth, 1963; The Dark Light Years, 1964; Introducing SF, 1964; Greybeard, 1964; Best SF Stories of Brian W. Aldiss, 1965; Earthworks, 1965; The Saliva Tree, 1966 (Nebula Award, 1965); An Age, 1967; Report on Probability A, 1968; Farewell, Fantastic Venus!, 1968; Intangibles Inc. and other Stories, 1969; A Brian Aldiss Omnibus, 1969; Barefoot in the Head, 1969; The Moment of Eclipse, 1971 (BSFA Award, 1972); Brian Aldiss Omnibus II, 1971; Frankenstein Unbound, 1973 (filmed, 1990); The Eighty-Minute Hour, 1974; (ed) Space Opera, 1974; (ed) Space Odysseys: an Anthology of Way-Back-When Futures, 1975; (ed) Hell's Cartographers, 1975; (ed) Evil Earths, 1975; Science Fiction Art: the fantasies of SF, 1975 (Ferrara Silver Comet, 1977); (ed with H. Harrison) Decade: the 1940s, 1976; (ed with H. Harrison) Decade: the 1950s, 1976; The Malacia Tapestry, 1976; (ed) Galactic Empires, vols 1 and 2, 1976; (ed with H. Harrison) The Year's Best Science Fiction No 9, 1976; Last Orders, 1977; (ed with H. Harrison) Decade: the 1960's, 1977; Enemies of the System, 1978; (ed) Perilous Planets, 1978; New Arrivals, Old Encounters, 1979; Moreau's Other Island, 1980; Helliconia Spring, 1982 (BSFA Award, John W. Campbell Meml Award); Helliconia Summer, 1983; Helliconia Winter, 1985; Helliconia Trilogy (boxed set of Helliconia Spring, Helliconia Summer, and Helliconia Winter), 1985; Cracken at Critical, 1987; Best SF Stories of Brian W. Aldiss, 1988; Science Fiction Blues, 1988; A Romance of the Equator, 1989; Dracula Unbound, 1991; A Tupolev Too Far, 1993; (with Roger Penrose) White Mars or, The Mind Set Free, 1999; Cultural Breaks, 2005; Sanity and the Lady, 2005; *fiction:* The Brightfount Diaries, 1955; The Hand-Reared Boy, 1970; A Soldier Erect, 1971; Brothers of the Head, 1977; A Rude Awakening, 1978; Life in the West, 1980; Foreign Bodies, 1981; Seasons in Flight, 1984; The Horatio Stubbs Saga, 1985; Ruins, 1987; Forgotten Life, 1988; Remembrance Day, 1993; Somewhere East of Life, 1994; The Secret of This Book, 1995; The Squire Quartet, 1998; Supertoys Last All Summer Long, 2001; Super-State, 2002; The Cretan Teat, 2002; Affairs at Hampden Ferrers, 2004; Jocasta, 2005; Harm, 2007; Walcot, 2007; *non-fiction:* Cities and Stones: A Traveller's Jugoslavia, 1966; The Shape of Further Things, 1970; Billion Year Spree: a history of science fiction, 1973 (Special BSFA Award, 1974; Eurocon Merit Award, 1976); This World and Nearer Ones, 1979; The Pale Shadow of Science, 1985; …And the Lurid Glare of the Comet, 1986; (with David Wingrove) Trillion Year Spree, 1986 (Hugo Award, 1987); Bury My Heart at W. H. Smith's, 1990; The Detached Retina, 1995; The Twinkling of an Eye (autobiog.), 1998; When the Feast is Finished, 1999; Art after Apogee, 2000; Researches and Churches in Serbia, 2002; *verse:* Home Life with Cats, 1992; At the Caligula Hotel, 1995; Songs from the Steppes of Central Asia, 1996; The Dark Sun Rises, 2002; Oedipus on Mars, 2004; The Prehistory of Mind, 2008. *Recreations:* fame, obscurity, trances. *Address:* Hambleden, 39 St Andrews Road, Old Headington, Oxford OX3 9DL. *Clubs:* Groucho; Writers in Oxford.

ALDOUS, Charles; QC 1985; *b* 3 June 1943; *s* of Guy Travers Aldous, QC and Elizabeth Angela Aldous (*née* Paul); *m* 1969, Hermione Sara de Courcy-Ireland; one *s* two *d* (and one *d* decd). *Educ:* Harrow; University College London (LLB). Called to the Bar, Inner Temple, 1967 (Bencher, 1994), Lincoln's Inn *ad eund*, 1967 (Bencher, 1993). *Address:* Ravensfield Farm, Bures Hamlet, Suffolk CO8 5DP.
See also Rt Hon. Sir W. Aldous.

ALDOUS, Prof. David John, PhD; FRS 1994; Professor of Statistics, University of California, Berkeley, since 1986; *b* 13 July 1952; *s* of Kenneth George Aldous and Joyce Minnie Aldous (*née* Finch); *m* 1986, Katy Edwards; one *s*. *Educ:* St John's Coll., Cambridge (BA 1973; PhD 1977). Res. Fellow, St John's Coll., Cambridge, 1977–79; University of California, Berkeley: Asst Prof., 1979–82; Associate Prof., 1982–86. *Publication:* Probability Approximations via the Poisson Clumping Heuristic, 1989. *Recreations:* volleyball, science fiction. *Address:* Department of Statistics, University of California, 367 Evans Hall #3860, Berkeley, CA 94720–3860, USA. *T:* (510) 6422781.

ALDOUS, Grahame Linley; QC 2008; a Recorder, since 2000; *b* London, 8 June 1956; *s* of Howard Aldous and Jocelyn Murray Aldous; partner, Vanessa Knapp, OBE; three *s*. *Educ:* Univ. of Exeter (LLB Hons 1978). Called to the Bar, Inner Temple, 1979; in practice at the Bar, specialising in clinical and professional negligence and personal injury. Contributing Ed., Kemp & Kemp Personal Injury Law Practice and Procedure, 2000–. *Publications:* (contrib.) Housing Law for the Elderly; contrib. Judicial Rev. *Recreations:* ocean racing, naval history. *Address:* 9 Gough Square, EC4A 3DG. *T:* (020) 7832 0500, *Fax:* (020) 7353 1344; *e-mail:* galdous@9goughsquare.co.uk. *Club:* Royal Ocean Racing.

ALDOUS, Hugh (Graham Cazalet), FCA; Partner, Grant Thornton UK LLP (formerly Robson Rhodes, then RSM Robson Rhodes LLP), 1976–2008; Member, Competition Commission (formerly Monopolies and Mergers Commission), 1998–2001; *b* 1 June 1944; *s* of Maj. Hugh Francis Travers Aldous and Emily Aldous; *m* 1967, Christabel Marshall. *Educ:* Leeds Univ. (BCom). ACA 1970, FCA 1976. Robson Rhodes, later RSM Robson Rhodes, then Grant Thornton, 1976–2008: on secondment to Depts of Transport and the Envmt, 1976–79; Man. Partner, 1987–97; DTI Inspector: House of Fraser Hldgs plc, 1987–88; TransTec plc, 2000–03. Chairman: RSM Internat., 1997–2000; Eastern European (formerly First Russian Frontiers) Trust plc, 2000– (Dir, 1995–); Protocol Associates NV, 2000–02; Craegmoor Ltd, 2001–05; Capita Sinclair Henderson Ltd, 2007–; Director: Freightliner Ltd, 1979–84; Sealink UK Ltd, 1981–84; British Waterways Bd, 1983–86; CILNTEC Ltd, 1991–96; FOCUS Ltd, 1996–98; Elderstreet VCT plc (formerly Gartmore Venture Capital Trust plc, then Millennium Venture Capital Trust), 1996–; Henderson TR Pacific Investment Trust plc, 2003–; Innospec Inc., 2005–; Polar Capital Holdings plc, 2007–; Melorio plc, 2007–. *Publications:* Guide to Government Incentives to Industry, 1979; Study of Businesses Financed under the Small Business Loan Guarantee Scheme, 1984; (with H. Brooke) Report into the affairs of House of Fraser Holdings plc, 1988; Review of the UK Financial and Professional Services Industry, 1992; (with R. Kaye) Report into the affairs of TransTec plc, 2003. *Recreation:* music. *Club:* Royal Automobile.

ALDOUS, Lucette; Senior Lecturer in Classical Ballet, Edith Cowan University, since 1994; Head of Classical Dance, Dance Department, Western Australian Academy of Performing Arts, 1984–99, now Senior Lecturer; Senior Adjudicator, National Eisteddfods, since 1979; *b* 26 Sept. 1938; *d* of Charles Fellows Aldous and Marie (*née* Rutherford); *m* 1972, Alan Alder; one *d*. *Educ:* Toronto Public Sch., NSW; Brisbane Public Sch., Qld; Randwick Girls' High Sch., NSW. Awarded Frances Scully Meml Schol. (Aust.) to study at Royal Ballet Sch., London, 1955; joined Ballet Rambert, 1957, Ballerina, 1958–63; Ballerina with: London Fest. Ballet, 1963–66; Royal Ballet, 1966–71; Prima Ballerina, The Australian Ballet, 1971; Master Teacher, Australian Ballet Sch., 1979; Guest Teacher: Australian Ballet, 1988–; Royal NZ Ballet Co., 1988–; West Australian Ballet Co., 1988–. Rep. Australia, 1st Internat. Ballet Competition, Jackson, Miss, USA, 1979; Guest, Kirov Ballet and Ballet School, Leningrad, 1975–76. Guest appearances: Giselle, with John Gilpin, NY, 1968; Lisbon, 1969; with Rudolf Nureyev, in Don Quixote: Aust., 1970, NY, Hamburg and Marseilles, 1971; Carmen, Johannesburg, 1970; The Sleeping Beauty: E Berlin, 1970, Teheran, 1970, 1975; partnered Edward Villela at Expo '74, Spokane, USA. *Television:* title rôle, La Sylphide, with Fleming Flindt, BBC, 1960. *Films:* as Kitri, in Don Quixote, with Rudolf Nureyev and Robert Helpmann, Aust., 1972; The Turning Point, 1977. Mem., Australia Council for the Arts, 1996–98. Patron, Australian Cecchetti Soc., 1991–. Hon. DLitt Edith Cowan, 1999. DStJ. *Recreations:* music, reading, gardening, breeding Burmese cats. *Address:* c/o Dance Department, Western Australian Academy of Performing Arts, 2 Bradford Street, Mount Lawley, Perth, WA 6050, Australia.

ALDOUS, Rt Hon. Sir William, Kt 1988; PC 1995; a Lord Justice of Appeal, 1995–2003; Justice of Appeal, Gibraltar, 2006; *b* 17 March 1936; *s* of Guy Travers Aldous, QC; *m* 1960, Gillian Frances Henson; one *s* two *d*. *Educ:* Harrow; Trinity Coll., Cambridge (MA). Barrister, Inner Temple, 1960, Bencher, 1985; Jun. Counsel, DTI, 1972–76; QC 1976; appointed to exercise appellate jurisdiction of BoT under Trade Marks Act, 1981–88; a Judge of the High Court, Chancery Div., 1988–95. Chm., Performing Rights Tribunal, 1986–88. Chm., British Eventing, 2005–06. *Address:* Layham Lodge, Lower Layham, Ipswich, Suffolk IP7 5RW.
See also C. Aldous.

ALDRED, Brian Gordon; Chief Executive, Lancashire Police Authority, 2003–07; *b* 27 April 1951; *s* of late James Bernard Aldred and of Jean Margaret Layton Aldred; *m* 1973, Miriam Constance Shaw; one *s* one *d*. *Educ:* Queen Elizabeth's Grammar Sch., Blackburn; Jesus Coll., Oxford (BA Modern Hist.; MA); Liverpool Poly. CIPFA. Cheshire CC, 1972–82; Dep. Dir of Finance, Bolton MBC, 1982–85; Lancashire County Council: Dep. County Treas., 1985–92; County Treas., 1992–2000; Dir of Resources, 2000–02. *Recreations:* cycling, fell-walking, archaeology.

ALDRED, Micheala Ann, PhD; Assistant Staff, Genomic Medicine Institute, Cleveland Clinic, and Assistant Professor, Department of Genetics, Case Western Reserve University School of Medicine, Cleveland, Ohio, since 2006; *b* 16 Oct. 1966; *d* of Spencer and Barbara Aldred; *m* 1991, Keith Niven Mitchell. *Educ:* University Coll. London (BSc Hons); Open Univ. (PhD 1993); DipRCPath 1998. Postdoctoral Research Associate: MRC Human Genetics Unit, Edinburgh, 1991–94; Univ. of Cambridge, 1994–96; University of Leicester: Lectr in Med. Molecular Genetics, 1996–2001; Res. Fellow, 2001–04; Sen. Lectr in Med. Molecular Genetics, 2004–06. Mem., Human Genetics Adv. Commn, 1997–99. Trustee, Retinoblastoma Soc., 1992–2001. *Publications:* papers in jls on human genetics. *Recreations:* charity work, photography, hiking.

ALDRIDGE, (Harold Edward) James; author; *b* 10 July 1918; *s* of William Thomas Aldridge and Edith Quayle Aldridge; *m* 1942, Dina Mitchnik; two *s*. With Herald and Sun, Melbourne, 1937–38; Daily Sketch, and Sunday Dispatch, London, 1939; subsequently Australian Newspaper Service and North American Newspaper Alliance (war correspondent), Finland, Norway, Middle East, Greece, USSR, until 1945; also correspondent for Time and Life, Teheran, 1944. Rhys Meml Award, 1945; Lenin Peace Prize, 1972. *Play:* The 49th State, Lyric, Hammersmith, 1947. *Publications:* Signed With Their Honour, 1942; The Sea Eagle, 1944; Of Many Men, 1946; The Diplomat, 1950; The Hunter, 1951; Heroes of the Empty View, 1954; Underwater Hunting for Inexperienced Englishmen, 1955; I Wish He Would Not Die, 1958; Gold and Sand (short stories), 1960; The Last Exile, 1961; A Captive in the Land, 1962; The Statesman's Game, 1966; My Brother Tom, 1966; The Flying 19, 1966; (with Paul Strand) Living Egypt, 1969; Cairo: Biography of a City, 1970; A Sporting Proposition, 1973; The Marvellous Mongolian, 1974; Mockery in Arms, 1974; The Untouchable Juli, 1975; One Last Glimpse, 1977 (adapted as stage play, Prague Vinohrady Th., 1981); Goodbye Un-America, 1979; The Broken Saddle, 1983; The True Story of Lilli Stubek, 1984 (Australian Children's Book of the Year, 1985); The True Story of Spit MacPhee, 1986 (Guardian Children's Fiction Prize; NSW Premier's Literary Award, 1986); The True Story of Lola MacKellar, 1993; The Girl from the Sea, 2003. *Recreations:* trout fishing, etc. *Address:* c/o Curtis Brown, 28/29 Haymarket, SW1Y 4SP.

ALDRIDGE, Dr John Frederick Lewis, OBE 1990, FRCP, FRCPEd, FFOM; consultant in occupational medicine, 1987–97; Civil Consultant in Occupational Medicine to the Royal Navy, 1983–92, Emeritus Consultant since 1992; *b* 28 Dec. 1926; *s* of Dr Frederick James Aldridge and Kathleen Marietta Micaela (*née* White); *m* 1955, Barbara Sheila Bolland; three *s* one *d*. *Educ:* Gresham's Sch.; St Thomas's Hosp. Med. Sch. (MB, BS 1951). DIH 1963; FRCPEd 1980; FFOM 1981; FRCP 1984. Served RAMC, 1953–60 (retd, Major). Indust. MO, Reed Paper Gp, 1960–63; CMO, IBM United Kingdom Ltd, 1963–87; part-time Hon. Clin. Asst, Dept of Psychol Medicine, UCH, 1970–76. Faculty of Occupational Medicine, Royal Coll. of Physicians: Vice-Dean, 1984–86; Dean, 1986–88; Chm., Ethics Cttee, 1991–96; Royal Soc. of Medicine: Fellow, 1964–2002; Hon. Sec., 1970–72 and Vice-Pres., 1974–77, Occupl Medicine Section; Soc. of Occupational Medicine: Mem., 1960–; Hon. Meetings Sec., 1969–71. Member: Specialist Adv. Cttee on Occupl Medicine, Jt Cttee of Higher Med. Trng, 1970–74; Nat. Occupl Health and Safety Cttee, RoSPA, 1979–81; Standing Med. Adv. Cttee, DHSS, 1986–88; Defence Med. Emergency Steering Cttee, 1986–88; Indust. Soc. Med. Adv. Cttee, 1986–89 (Chm., 1987–89); CEGB Med. Adv. Cttee, 1988–89. Mem., Council and Cttee of Management, Shipwrecked Mariners' Royal Benevolent Soc., 1987–96; Dir, Shipwrecked Mariners' Trading Ltd, 1999–2001. Chm., W Sussex Assoc. for the Disabled, 1995–97 (Mem. Council and Mgt Cttee, 1991–2006; Vice-Pres., 1997–); Vice Chm., Chichester DFAS, 2000–04 (Librarian, 1999–2003); Trustee, Southampton and Wessex Med. Sch. Trust, 1978–82. Liveryman, Worshipful Soc. of Apothecaries, 1984–. *Publications:* papers on occupl med. topics and occupl mental health. *Recreations:* 18th century English porcelain, watercolours, walking, shooting. *Address:* 2 Summersdale

Road, Chichester, W Sussex PO19 6PL. *T:* (01243) 784705. *Clubs:* Lansdowne; Vintage Sports Car.

ALDRIDGE, Stephen Charles, CB 2007; Director, Strategy Unit (formerly Prime Minister's Strategy Unit), Cabinet Office, since 2004; *b* 30 April 1957; *s* of Dennis and Pamela Aldridge; *m* 1995, Katie Iakovleva; one *d. Educ:* City Univ., London (BSc Econ 1978); University Coll. London (MSc Econ 1982). Public Services Econs Div., HM Treasury, 1991–93; Housing and Urban Econs, DoE, subseq. DETR, 1993–98; Cabinet Office: Chief Economist, Perf. and Innovation Unit, 1998–2002; Dep. Dir, Strategy Unit, 2002–04. *Address:* Strategy Unit, Cabinet Office, Admiralty Arch, The Mall, SW1A 2WH. *T:* (020) 7276 1470.

ALDRIDGE, Trevor Martin; solicitor; President: Special Educational Needs and Disability Tribunal (formerly Special Educational Needs Tribunal), 1994–2003; Protection of Children Act Tribunal, 1999–2001; *b* 22 Dec. 1933; *s* of Dr Sidney and Isabel Aldridge; *m* 1966, Joanna, *d* of C. J. v. D. Edwards; one *s* one *d. Educ:* Frensham Heights School; Sorbonne; St John's College, Cambridge (MA). Partner in Bower Cotton & Bower, 1962–84; Law Comr, 1984–93. Chairman: Conveyancing Standing Cttee, 1989 (Mem., 1985–89); Commonhold Working Gp, reported 1987. Hon. Vis. Prof., City Univ., 1994–95. Pres., Frensham Heights School, 1996– (Chm. Govs, 1977–95). Hon. QC 1992; Hon. Life Mem., Law Soc., 1995. General editor, Property Law Bulletin, 1980–84. *Publications:* Boundaries, Walls and Fences, 1962, 9th edn 2004; Finding Your Facts, 1963; Directory of Registers and Records, 1963, (consulting ed.) 5th edn 1993; Service Agreements, 1964, 4th edn 1982; Rent Control and Leasehold Enfranchisement, 1965, 11th edn as Aldridge's Residential Lettings, 1998; Betterment Levy, 1967; Letting Business Premises, 1971, 8th edn 2004; Your Home and the Law, 1975, 2nd edn 1979; (jtly) Managing Business Property, 1978; Criminal Law Act 1977, 1978; Guide to Enquiries of Local Authorities, 1978, 2nd edn 1982; Guide to Enquiries Before Contract, 1978; Guide to National Conditions of Sale, 1979, 2nd edn 1981; Leasehold Law, 1980; Housing Act, 1980, and as amended 1984, 2nd edn 1984; (ed) Powers of Attorney, 6th edn 1986 to 10th edn 2007; Guide to Law Society's Conditions of Sale, 1981, 2nd edn 1984; Questions of Law: Homes, 1982; Law of Flats, 1982, 3rd edn 1994; Practical Conveyancing Precedents, 1984; Practical Lease Precedents, 1987; Companion to Standard Conditions of Sale, 1990, 3rd edn 2003; Companion to Property Information Forms, 1990; First Registration, 1991; Companion to Enquiries of Local Authorities, 1991; Companion to the Law Society Business Lease, 1991; Implied Covenants for Title, 1995; Privity of Contract: Landlord and Tenant (Covenants) Act, 1995; Commonhold Law, 2002. *Address:* Birkitt Hill House, Offley, Hitchin, Herts SG5 3DB. *T:* (01462) 768261; *e-mail:* t.m.aldridge@btopenworld.com. *Club:* Oxford and Cambridge.

ALDRIN, Dr Buzz; President, Starcraft Enterprises International (research and development of space technology, manned flight to Mars), since 1988; *b* Montclair, NJ, USA, 20 Jan. 1930; *s* of late Col Edwin E. Aldrin, USAF retd, Brielle, NJ, and Marion Aldrin (*née* Moon); named Edwin Eugene, changed legally to Buzz, 1979; *m* 1988, Lois Driggs-Cannon; two *s* one *d* of former marriage. *Educ:* Montclair High Sch., Montclair, NJ (grad.); US Mil. Academy, West Point, NY (BSc); Mass Inst. of Technology (DSc in Astronautics). Received wings (USAF), 1952. Served in Korea (66 combat missions) with 51st Fighter Interceptor Wing. Aerial Gunnery Instr, Nellis Air Force Base, Nevada; attended Sqdn Officers Sch., Air Univ., Maxwell Air Force Base, Alabama; Aide to Dean of Faculty, USAF Academy; Flt Comdr with 36th Tactical Fighter Wing, Bitburg, Germany. Subseq. assigned to Gemini Target Office of Air Force Space Systems Div., Los Angeles, Calif; later transf. to USAF Field Office, Manned Spacecraft Center. One of 3rd group of astronauts named by NASA, Oct. 1963; served as back up pilot, Gemini 9 Mission and prime pilot, Gemini 12 Mission (launched into space, with James Lovell, 11 Nov. 1966), 4 day 59 revolution flight which brought Gemini Program to successful close; he established a new record for extravehicular activity and obtained first pictures taken from space of an eclipse of the sun; also made a rendezvous with the previously launched Agena; later assigned to 2nd manned Apollo flight, as back-up command module pilot; Lunar Module Pilot, Apollo 11 rocket flight to the Moon; first lunar landing with Neil Armstrong, July 1969; left NASA to return to USAF as Commandant, Aerospace Res. Pilots Sch., Edwards Air Force Base, Calif, 1971; retired USAF 1972. Mem., Soc. of Experimental Test Pilots; FAIAA; Tau Beta Pi, Sigma Xi. Further honours include Presidential Medal of Freedom, 1969; Air Force DSM with Oak Leaf Cluster; Legion of Merit; Air Force DFC with Oak Leaf Cluster; Air Medal with 2 Oak Leaf Clusters; and NASA DSM, Exceptional Service Medal, and Group Achievement Award. Various hon. memberships and hon. doctorates. *Publications:* Return to Earth (autobiography), 1973; Men From Earth: the Apollo Project, 1989; (jtly) Encounter with Tiber (science fiction), 1996; The Return (science fiction), 2000; Reaching for the Moon (for children), 2005. *Recreations:* athletics, scuba diving, ski-ing, golf, etc. *Address:* 10380 Wilshire Boulevard #703, Los Angeles, CA 90024, USA.

ALEKSANDER, Prof. Igor, PhD; FREng; Professor of Neural Systems Engineering, and Head of Department of Electrical Engineering, Imperial College of Science, Technology and Medicine, University of London, 1988–2002, now Emeritus; *b* 26 Jan. 1937. *Educ:* Marist Brothers' Coll., S Africa; Univ. of the Witwatersrand (BSc Eng); Univ. of London (PhD). Section Head of STC, Footscray, 1958–61; Lectr, Queen Mary Coll., Univ. of London, 1961–65; Reader in Electronics, Univ. of Kent, 1965–74; Prof. of Electronics and Head of Electrical Engrg Dept, Brunel Univ., 1974–84; Prof. of Information Technology Management, Computing Dept, Imperial Coll., 1984–88. FREng (FEng 1989); FCGI 1994. *Publications:* An Introduction to Logic Circuit Theory, 1971; Automata Theory: an engineering approach, 1976; The Human Machine, 1978; Reinventing Man, 1983 (USA 1984); Designing Intelligent Systems, 1984; Thinking Machines, 1987; An Introduction to Neural Computing, 1990; Neurons and Symbols: the stuff that mind is made of, 1993; Impossible Minds: my neurons, my consciousness, 1996; How to Build a Mind, 2000; The World in My Mind, 2005; *c* 120 papers on computing and human modelling. *Recreations:* tennis, ski-ing, music, architecture. *Address:* Imperial College of Science, Technology and Medicine, Exhibition Road, SW7 2AZ. *T:* (020) 7594 6176.

ALESSI, Dr Dario Renato, FRS 2008; FRSE; Principal Investigator, since 1997, and Deputy Director, since 2006, MRC Protein Phosphorylation Unit, University of Dundee; *b* Dec. 1967. *Educ:* Univ. of Birmingham (BSc 1st Cl. Hons Biochem. with Biotech. 1988; PhD 1991). Postdoctoral res., MRC Protein Phosphorylation Unit, Univ. of Dundee, 1991–96. Hon. Reader, 2001, Hon. Prof. of Signal Transduction, 2003, Univ. of Dundee. R. D. Lawrence Lectr, Diabetes UK, 2004; Francis Crick Prize Lectr, Royal Soc., 2006. Mem., EMBO, 2005. FRSE 2002. Colworth Medal, British Biochem. Soc., 1999; Eppendorf Young Eur. Investigator, 2000; Morgagni Young Investigator Prize, Servier Labs, 2002; Pfizer Acad. Award for Europe, 2002; Makdougall Brisbane Prize, RSE, 2002; Philip Leverhulme Prize, Leverhulme Trust, 2002; FEBS Anniv. Prize, 2003; Jun. Chamber Internat. Young Persons of Year Award, 2005; Gold Medal, EMBO, 2005. *Address:* MRC Protein Phosphorylation Unit, Sir James Black Centre, University of Dundee, Dundee DD1 5EH. *T:* (01382) 385602, *Fax:* (01382) 223778; *e-mail:* d.r.alessi@dundee.ac.uk.

ALEX; *see* Peattie, C. W. D. and Taylor, R. P.

ALEXANDER, family name of **Earl Alexander of Tunis** and **Earl of Caledon.**

ALEXANDER, Viscount; Frederick James Alexander; *b* 15 Oct. 1990; *s* and *heir* of Earl of Caledon, *qv.*

ALEXANDER OF TUNIS, 2nd Earl *cr* 1952; **Shane William Desmond Alexander;** Viscount, 1946; Baron Rideau, 1952; Lieutenant Irish Guards, retired, 1958; Director: International Hospitals Group and associated companies, since 1981; Pathfinder Financial Corporation, Toronto, since 1980; *b* 30 June 1935; *er s* of 1st Earl Alexander of Tunis, KG, PC, GCB, OM, GCMG, CSI, DSO, MC, and Lady Margaret Diana Bingham (Countess Alexander of Tunis), GBE, DStJ, DL (*d* 1977), *yr d* of 5th Earl of Lucan, PC, GCVO, KBE, CB; *S* father, 1969; *m* 1981, Hon. Davina Woodhouse (LVO 1991; Lady-in-Waiting to Princess Margaret, 1975–2002), *y d* of 4th Baron Terrington; two *d. Educ:* Ashbury Coll., Ottawa, Canada; Harrow. A Lord in Waiting (Govt Whip), 1974. Dir, Marketform Ltd, 1996–. Trustee, 1987–, and Chm., 1989–, Canada Meml Foundn; Pres., British-American-Canadian Associates, 1989–94. Patron, British-Tunisian Soc., 1979–99. Freeman, City of London, 1964; Liveryman, Mercers Company. Freedom, City of New Orleans, 1993. Order of Republic of Tunisia, 1995. *Heir:* *b* Hon. Brian James Alexander, *qv. Address:* 28 Clonmel Road, SW6 5BJ. *T:* (020) 7736 2604. *Clubs:* MCC; Quis Separabit.

ALEXANDER, Prof. Alan, FRSE; Chairman, Scottish Water, 2002–06; Professor of Local and Public Management, University of Strathclyde, 1993–2000, now Emeritus (Professor of Management in Local Government, 1987–93); Visiting Professor, University of Edinburgh Management School, since 2006; *b* 13 Dec. 1943; *s* of Alexander Alexander and Rose (*née* Rein); *m* 1964, Morag MacInnes (*see* M. Alexander); one *s* one *d. Educ:* Possil Secondary Sch., Glasgow; Albert Secondary Sch., Glasgow; Univ. of Glasgow (MA 1965). Lectr/Asst Prof. of Political Sci., Lakehead Univ., Ontario, 1966–71; Lectr in Politics, Univ. of Reading, 1971–87; Dir, Scottish Local Authorities Management Centre, 1987–93, and Hd, Dept of Human Resource Mgt, 1993–96, Univ. of Strathclyde. Scholar-in-Residence, Rockefeller Foundn, Villa Serbelloni, Bellagio, Italy, Feb.–March 1984; Fulbright Vis. Prof. of Politics, Randolph-Macon Woman's Coll., Virginia, 1986. Member: Board, Housing Corp., 1977–80; Council, Quarrier's, 1995–2000; Ind. Commn on Relations between Local Govt and the Scottish Parlt, 1998–99; Accounts Commn for Scotland, 2002–; ESRC, 2003–. Chairman: Glasgow Regeneration Fund, 1998–2001; W of Scotland Water Authy, 1999–2002; Distance Lab Ltd, 2006–; Postwatch Scotland, 2007–. Pres., Instn of Water Officers, 2005–06. Member: Reading BC, 1972–74; Berks CC, 1973–77. Member: Standing Res. Cttee on Local and Central Govt Relns, Joseph Rowntree Foundn, 1988–92; Adv. Bd, Edinburgh Univ. Mgt Sch., 2004–. Conducted independent inquiry into relations between Western Isles Islands Council and Bank of Credit and Commerce Internat., 1991. Contested (Lab) Henley, Feb. 1974. Pres., Raglan Housing Assoc., 1987– (Chm., 1975–87); Trustee, WaterAid, 2001–06. FRSE 2003. *Publications:* Local Government in Britain since Reorganisation, 1982 (Italian edn, revised, 1984); The Politics of Local Government in the United Kingdom, 1982; Borough Government and Politics: Reading 1835–1985, 1985; Managing the Fragmented Authority, 1994; articles in Local Govt Studies, Public Admin, Brit. Jl Pol. Sci. and others. *Recreations:* walking, theatre, opera, cinema, avoiding gardening.

ALEXANDER, Prof. Albert Geoffrey, FDSRCS; Professor of Conservative Dentistry, University of London, 1972–92, now Emeritus; *b* 22 Sept. 1932; *s* of William Francis Alexander and Muriel Katherine (*née* Boreham); *m* 1956, Dorothy Constance (*née* Johnson); one *d. Educ:* Bridlington Sch.; UCH Dental Sch., Univ. of London (BDS 1956; MDS 1968). LDSRCS 1955, FDSRCS 1961. Dental House Surgeon, Nat. Dental Hosp., 1955–56; Nat. Service, RADC, 1956–58; Clinical Asst, UCH Dental Dept, 1958; private dental practice, 1958–59; Lectr in Cons. Dentistry, 1959–62, Sen. Lectr in Cons. Dentistry and Periodontics, 1962–69, UCH Dental Sch.; Hon. Consultant, UCH Dental Hosp., 1967–92; Vice-Dean of Dental Studies, 1974–77, Dean, 1977–92, UCL Dental Sch., later UC and Middlesex Sch. of Dentistry; Vice-Dean, Faculty of Clinical Sciences, UCMSM, 1977–91; Prof. of Conservative Dentistry, Univ. of Hong Kong, 1992–94. Fellow, UCL, 1986; Member: Council, UCL, 1984–91; Senate, Univ. of London, 1987–91. Chm., Dental Educn Adv. Council, 1986–90; Member: GDC, 1986–92 (Treasurer, 1989–92); Bloomsbury HA, 1981–90. Fellow: Internat. Coll. of Dentists, 1975; Hong Kong Acad. of Medicine, 1993. *Publications:* (co-ed) The Prevention of Periodontal Disease, 1971; (jtly) Self-Assessment Manual, No 3, Clinical Dentistry, 1978; (co-ed) Companion to Dental Studies, Vol. 3, 1986, Vol. 2, 1988; scientific, technical and clinical articles on dentistry and dental research. *Recreations:* photography, blue and white Chinese ceramics.

ALEXANDER, Andrew Clive; columnist; City Editor, Daily Mail, 1984–2000; *b* 12 May 1935; *s* of Ronald and Doreen Alexander. *Educ:* Lancing College; Univ. of Life (2.2). Leader Writer, Yorkshire Post, 1960–65; Parly Sketch-Writer, Daily Telegraph, 1966–72; Parly Sketch-Writer and Columnist, Daily Mail, 1972–84. Director: Associated Newspapers plc, 1992–2000; Underoneroof Ltd, 2000–01; OneStopCarShop Ltd, 2000–02. Contested (C) Colne Valley, March 1963, 1964. Specialist Writer of the Year, British Press Awards, 1976 and 1977; Political Journalist of the Year, What the Papers Say awards, 1977; Jt Financial Journalist of the Year, Baltic Trent Award, 1986; Sen. Financial Journalist of the Year, Wincott Foundn, 1991. *Publication:* (with Alan Watkins) The Making of the Prime Minister, 1970. *Recreations:* music, gardening, history, weight training. *Address:* c/o Associated Newspapers plc, 2 Derry Street, W8 5TT. *T:* (020) 7938 6000. *Club:* Reform.

ALEXANDER, Anthony George Laurence; Deputy Chairman, Imperial Tobacco Group, since 1996; *b* 4 April 1938; *s* of George and Margaret Alexander; *m* 1962, Frances, *d* of Cyril Burdett; one *s* two *d. Educ:* St Edward's School, Oxford. FCA. Hanson plc: Dir, 1976–96; UK Chief Operating Officer, 1986–96. *Recreations:* tennis, golf. *Address:* Crafnant, Gregories Farm Lane, Beaconsfield, Bucks HP9 1HJ. *T:* (01494) 672882.

ALEXANDER, Bill, (William Alexander Paterson); Artistic Director, Birmingham Repertory Theatre, 1993–2000; Hon. Associate Director, Royal Shakespeare Company, since 1991 (Associate Director, 1984–91); *b* 23 Feb. 1948; *s* of Bill and Rosemary Paterson; *m* 1977, Juliet Harmer; two *d. Educ:* St Lawrence Coll., Ramsgate; Keele Univ. (BA Hons English/Politics). Seasons with The Other Company, Bristol Old Vic, Royal Court, 1972–78; Asst Dir, 1978–80, Resident Dir, 1980–84, RSC. Laurence Olivier award, Best Director, 1986. *Productions directed: Bristol Old Vic:* The Ride Across Lake Constance; Twelfth Night; Old Times; Butley; How the Other Half Loves; *Royal Court:* Sex and Kinship in a Savage Society, 1976; Amy and the Price of Cotton, 1977; Class Enemy, 1978; Sugar and Spice, 1979; *Royal Shakespeare Company:* Factory Birds, 1977; Shout Across the River, The Hang of the Gaol, Captain Swing, 1978; Men's Beano, 1979; Bastard Angel, Henry IV tour, 1980; Accrington Pals, 1981; Money, Clay, Molière, 1982;

Tartuffe, Volpone, 1983; Richard III, Today, The Merry Wives of Windsor, 1984; Crimes in Hot Countries, Downchild (co-dir), 1985; Country Dancing, A Midsummer Night's Dream, 1986; Cymbeline, Twelfth Night, The Merchant of Venice, 1987; The Duchess of Malfi, Cymbeline, 1989; Much Ado About Nothing, The Taming of the Shrew (dir, regional tour), 1990; The Bright and Bold Design, 1991; The Taming of the Shrew, The School of Night, 1992; Titus Andronicus, 2003; King Lear, 2004, transf. Albery, 2005; *Birmingham:* Othello, Volpone, Old Times, 1993; The Snowman, 1993, 1997, transf. Peacock Th., London, annually, 1997–; Awake and Sing, The Tempest, 1994; The Servant, Macbeth, The Way of the World, 1995; Divine Right, The Alchemist, 1996; The Merchant of Venice, 1997; Frozen, Hamlet, 1998; The Four Alice Bakers, Jumpers, Nativity, 1999; Quarantine, Twelfth Night, 2000; *National Theatre:* Mappa Mundi, Frozen, 2002; *other productions* include: Entertaining Mr Sloane, Nottingham Playhouse, 1977; The Gingerbread Lady, Ipswich, 1977; The Last of the Knuckle Men, Edin. Fest. Fringe, 1977; Julius Caesar, Newcastle upon Tyne, 1979; One White Day, Soho Poly, 1976; Mates, Leicester Square, 1976; Betrayal, 1980; Anna Christie, 1981, Cameri Th., Tel Aviv; Talk of the Devil, Watford Palace, 1986; Romeo and Juliet, Victory Theatre, NY, 1990; Troilus and Cressida, 1992, Henry IV, 2004, Shakespeare Theatre, Washington; The Importance of Being Earnest, Th. Royal, Northampton, 2002; Enemy of the People, Th. Clywd, 2002. *Recreation:* tennis. *Address:* Rose Cottage, Tunley, Glos GL7 6LP.

ALEXANDER, Hon. Brian (James), CMG 2000; Managing Director, Mustique Co., 1980–2008; *b* 31 July 1939; *s* of 1st Earl Alexander of Tunis, KG, GCB, OM, GCMG, CSI, DSO, MC, PC, and Lady Margaret Diana Bingham, GBE, DStJ, DL (*d* 1977), *yr d* of 5th Earl of Lucan, GCVO, KBE, CB, PC; *heir-presumptive* to brother, Earl Alexander of Tunis, *qv*; *m* 1999, Johanna Williamson Miller. *Educ:* Ashbury Coll., Ottawa; Harrow Sch.; Grenoble Univ. Served Irish Guards, 1958–61. Mgt trainee, Bowater Corp., 1961–62; Advertising Films Div., then Central Marketing Dept, subseq. Marketing Exec., Hotels Div., Rank Orgn, 1962–68; Manager, Previews Internat., 1968–71; self-employed, 1971–80; Mustique Co., 1980–2008. *Recreations:* windsurfing, tennis, golf, reading. *Address:* Sapphire House, Mustique, St Vincent, W Indies; e-mail: brian@mustique.vc; PO Box 349, Kingstown, St Vincent, W Indies. *Club:* White's.

ALEXANDER, Sir Charles G(undry), 2nd Bt *cr* 1945; MA, AIMarE; Chairman, Alexander Shipping Co. Ltd, 1959–87; *b* 5 May 1923; *s* of Sir Frank Alexander, 1st Bt, and Elsa Mary (*d* 1959), *d* of Sir Charles Collett, 1st Bt; *S* father, 1959; *m* 1st, 1944, Mary Neale, *o c* of S. R. Richardson; one *s* one *d*; 2nd, 1979, Eileen Ann Stewart. *Educ:* Bishop's Stortford College; St John's College, Cambridge. Served War as Lieut (E), RN, 1943–46. Chm., Governors Care Ltd, 1975–86; formerly Dep. Chm., Houlder Bros and Co. Ltd; Director: Furness–Houlder Insurance Ltd, until 1988; Furness–Houlder (Reinsurance Services) Ltd, until 1988; Inner London Region, National Westminster Bank Ltd, until 1987; Chm., Hull, Blyth & Co. Ltd, 1972–75. Chm., Bd of Governors, Bishop's Stortford College, until 1986. Mem. Court of Common Council, 1969; Alderman (Bridge Ward), 1970–76. Master, Merchant Taylors' Co., 1981–82; Prime Warden, Shipwrights' Co., 1983–84. *Heir:* s Richard Alexander [*b* 1 Sept. 1947; *m* 1971 (marr. diss.); two *s*]. *Address:* Newland House, 68 Newland, Sherborne, Dorset DT9 3AQ. *T:* (01935) 389758. *Club:* Royal Automobile.

ALEXANDER of Ballochmyle, Sir Claud Hagart-, 4th Bt *cr* 1886, of Ballochmyle; *b* 5 Nov. 1963; *s* of Sir Claud Hagart-Alexander of Ballochmyle, 3rd Bt and Hilda Etain Acheson; *S* father, 2006; *m* 1994, Elaine Susan, *d* of Vincent Park, Winnipeg; one *s*. *Educ:* Trinity Coll., Glenalmond; Glasgow Univ. (BSc). *Heir:* s Claud Miles Hagart-Alexander, *b* 28 Sept. 1998. *Address:* 514 Jeter Street, Redwood City, CA 94063, USA.

ALEXANDER, Daniel Grian; MP (Lib Dem) Inverness, Nairn, Badenoch and Strathspey, since 2005; *b* 15 May 1972; *s* of Dion Ralph Alexander and Jane Alexander; *m* 2005, Rebecca Louise Hoar; one *d*. *Educ:* St Anne's Coll., Oxford (BA Hons Philos., Politics and Econs). Researcher, Campaign for Freedom of Information, 1991; Press Officer, Scottish Lib Dems, 1993–96; Press Officer, 1996–97, Hd of Communications, 1997–2003, European Movt, subseq. Britain in Europe; Hd of Communications, Cairngorms Nat. Park, 2004–05. Lib Dem spokesman on disability, 2005–07; Lib Dem Shadow Sec. of State for Work and Pensions, 2007–. Chairman: All Party Gp on Media Literacy, 2006–08; Manifesto Gp, 2007–; Vice-Chm., All Party Gp on Citizens Advice, 2006–. Trustee, Joseph Rowntree Reform Trust, 2007–. *Recreations:* hill-walking, fishing, cricket. *Address:* House of Commons, SW1A 0AA. *T:* (020) 7219 2300; *e-mail:* danny@ highlandlibdems.org.uk.

ALEXANDER, David; see Alexander, J. D.

ALEXANDER, Maj.-Gen. David Crichton, CB 1976; Commandant, Scottish Police College, 1979–87, retired; *b* 28 Nov. 1926; *s* of James Alexander and Margaret (*née* Craig); *m* 1st, 1957, Diana Joyce (Jane) (*née* Fisher) (*d* 1995); one *s* two *d* and one step *s*; 2nd, 1996, Elizabeth Patricia (*née* Herrington). *Educ:* Edinburgh Academy. Joined RM, 1944; East Indies Fleet; 45 Commando, Malaya, Malta, Canal Zone, 1951–54; Parade Adjt Lympstone, 1954–57; Equerry and Acting Treasurer to Duke of Edinburgh, 1957–60; psc 1960; Directing Staff, Staff Coll., Camberley, 1962–65; 45 Commando (2IC), Aden, 1965–66; Staff of Chief of Defence Staff, incl. service with Sec. of State, 1966–69; CO 40 Commando, Singapore, 1969–70; Col GS to CGRM, 1970–73; ADC to the Queen, 1973–75; RCDS 1974; Comdr, Training Gp RM, 1975–77. Dir-Gen., English-Speaking Union, 1977–79. Governor, Corps of Commissionaires, 1978–97 (Pres., 1994–97); Member: Civil Service Final Selection Bd, 1978–88; MoD Police Review Cttee, 1985; Transport Users' Consultative Cttee for Scotland, 1989–93. Dir, Edinburgh Acad., 1980–89 (Chm., 1985–89). Pres., SSAFA, Fife, 1990–94. Freeman, City of London; Liveryman, Painter Stainers' Co., 1978. *Recreations:* fishing, gardening, golf. *Address:* Baldinnie, Park Place, Elie, Fife KY9 1DH. *T:* (01333) 330882. *Club:* Army and Navy.

ALEXANDER, Sir Douglas, 3rd Bt *cr* 1921; with Cowen & Co.; *b* 9 Sept. 1936; *s* of Lt-Comdr Archibald Gillespie Alexander (*d* 1978) (2nd *s* of 1st Bt), and of Margery Isabel, *d* of Arthur Brown Griffith; *S* uncle, 1983; *m* 1958, Marylon, *d* of Leonidas Collins Scatterday; two *s*. *Educ:* Rice Univ., Houston, Texas (MA 1961); PhD 1967 (Univ. of N Carolina). Formerly Assoc. Prof. and Chairman, French, State Univ. of New York at Albany. *Heir:* s Douglas Gillespie Alexander [*b* 24 July 1962; *m* 1993, Marsha Sue, *d* of Robert Fink]. *Address:* PO Box 369, Stowe, VT 05672–0369, USA.

ALEXANDER, Rt Hon. Douglas Garven; PC 2005; MP (Lab) Paisley and Renfrewshire South, since 2005 (Paisley South, Nov. 1997–2005); Secretary of State for International Development, since 2007; *b* 26 Oct. 1967; *s* of Rev. Douglas N. Alexander and Dr Joyce O. Alexander; *m* 2000, Jacqueline Christian; one *s* one *d*. *Educ:* Univ. of Edinburgh (MA 1st cl. Hons 1990; LLB (Dist.) 1993; DipLP 1994); Univ. of Pennsylvania. Admitted Solicitor, 1995; Brodies WS, 1994–96; Digby Brown, 1996–97. Minister of State: (Minister for E-Commerce and Competitiveness), DTI, 2001–02; Cabinet Office, 2002–03; Minister for the Cabinet Office and Chancellor of the Duchy of Lancaster, 2003–04; Minister of State: FCO and DTI, 2004–05; for Europe, 2005–06; Sec. of State

for Transport, and for Scotland, 2006–07. *Recreation:* fishing on the Isle of Mull. *Address:* c/o House of Commons, Westminster, SW1A 0AA.
    See also W. C. Alexander.

ALEXANDER, Fiona Jane, (Mrs Stanko Ilic); Director of Communications, University Hospital Birmingham NHS Foundation Trust, since 2006; *b* 18 July 1967; *d* of David Charles Alexander and Susan Margaret Heywood (*née* Lewis); *m* 2004, Stanko Ilic; one *d*. *Educ:* S Glamorgan Inst. of Higher Educn, Cardiff (NCTJ); DipM; ACIM. Asst Ed., MATCH mag., 1989–96; Editor: Leics Herald Post, 1996–97; Sunday Mercury, 1997–2000; Editor-in-Chief, Midland Independent Mags, 2000–02; Business Develt Dir, Trinity Mirror Midlands, 2002–03; Ed., Birmingham Post, 2003–06. *Recreations:* football clubs Arsenal and Birmingham City, fine food and wine. *Address:* University Hospital Birmingham NHS Foundation Trust, Queen Elizabeth Medical Centre, Edgbaston, Birmingham B15 2TH. *T:* (0121) 627 5977; *e-mail:* fiona_alexander@uhb.nhs.uk.

ALEXANDER, Helen Anne, CBE 2004; Chief Executive, Economist Group, 1997–2008; *b* 10 Feb. 1957; *d* of late Bernard Alexander and Tania Alexander (*née* Benckendorff); *m* 1985, Tim Suter; two *s* one *d*. *Educ:* Hertford Coll., Oxford (MA 1978; Hon. Fellow, 2002); INSEAD, France (MBA 1984); CDipAF. Gerald Duckworth, 1978–79; Faber & Faber, 1979–83; Economist Gp, 1985–. Non-executive Director: Northern Foods plc, 1994–2002; British Telecom plc, 1998–2002; Centrica plc, 2003–; Rolls-Royce Gp plc, 2007–. Advr, Bain Capital, 2008–. Vice-Pres., CBI, 2008–. Trustee, Tate, 2003–. Dir, INSEAD, 2005–. Gov., St Paul's Girls' Sch., 2003–.

ALEXANDER, Ian Douglas Gavin; QC 1989; **His Honour Judge Alexander;** a Circuit Judge, since 2002; *b* 10 April 1941; *s* of late Dr A. D. P. Alexander, MB ChB, and of Mrs D. Alexander; *m* 1969, Rosemary Kirkbride Richards; one *s* one *d*. *Educ:* Tonbridge; University College London (LLB). Called to Bar, Lincoln's Inn, 1964, Bencher, 1998; a Recorder, Midland and Oxford Circuit, 1982–2002. A Pres., Mental Health Review Tribunal, 2000–. Freemason; Grand Registrar of Craft and Chapter, United Grand Lodge of England, 2001–07. *Recreations:* horses, sailing, gardening, ski-ing, Church of England. *Address:* The Folly, Fifield, Chipping Norton, Oxon OX7 6HW. *Club:* Naval and Military.

ALEXANDER, Prof. (John) David, Hon. CBE 1998; DPhil; President Emeritus (formerly Trustees' Professor), Pomona College, since 1991 (President, 1969–91); *b* 18 Oct. 1932; *s* of John David Alexander, Sr and Mary Agnes McKinnon; *m* 1956, Catharine Coleman; one *s* two *d*. *Educ:* Southwestern at Memphis (BA); Louisville Presbyterian Theological Seminary; Oxford University (DPhil). Instructor to Associate Prof., San Francisco Theol Seminary, 1957–64; Pres., Southwestern at Memphis, 1965–69. Trustee, Teachers Insurance and Annuity Assoc., NY, 1970–2002; Director: Great Western Financial Corp., Beverly Hills, 1973–97; KCET (Community Supported TV of S Calif.), 1979–89; Amer. Council on Educn, Washington DC, 1981–84; National Assoc. of Indep. Colls and Univs, 1984–88; British Inst., 1979–87; Member: Nat. Panel on Academic Tenure, 1971–72; Assoc. of Amer. Med. Colls Panel on Gen. Professional Preparation of Physicians, 1981–84; Bd of Overseers, Huntington Library, Art Collections and Botanical Gardens, 1991–. Amer. Sec., Rhodes Scholarship Trust, 1981–98. Ed., The American Oxonian, 1998–2000. Dir, Children's Hosp. of Los Angeles, 1993–99. Trustee: Woodrow Wilson Nat. Fellowship Foundn, 1978–98; Seaver Inst., 1992–; Wenner-Gren Foundn for Anthropological Res., NY, 1995–2007; Emeriti Consortium, Inc., 2005–. Vice-Pres., Soc. of Fellows, Phi Beta Kappa, 2000–; Dist. Friend, Oxford Univ., 2000; Pres., American Friends of Nat. Portrait Gall. (London) Foundn, 2004–. Fellow, Amer. Acad. of Arts and Scis, 2006. Hon. LLD: Univ. of S California, 1970; Occidental Coll., 1970; Centre Coll. of Kentucky, 1971; Pepperdine Univ., Calif, 1991; Albertson Coll. of Idaho, 1992; Pomona Coll., Calif., 1996; Hon. LHD Loyola Marymount Univ., 1983; Hon. LittD Rhodes Coll., Memphis, 1986. *Publications:* (contrib.) History of the Rhodes Trust, 2001; The Goddess Pomona: a harvest of digressions, 2007; articles in Biblical studies; articles and chapters on higher educn in USA. *Recreations:* music, book collecting. *Address:* 406 Taylor Drive, Claremont, CA 91711–4137, USA. *T:* (909) 6247848. *Clubs:* Athenæum; Century Association (NY); California (Los Angeles); Bohemian (San Francisco).

ALEXANDER, Jonathan James Graham, DPhil; FBA 1985; FSA 1981; Sherman Fairchild Professor of Fine Arts, Institute of Fine Arts, New York, since 2002 (Professor of Fine Arts, since 1988); *b* 20 Aug. 1935; *s* of Arthur Ronald Brown and Frederica Emma Graham (who *m* 2nd, Boyd Alexander); *m* 1st, 1974, Mary Davey (marr. diss. 1995); one *s*; 2nd, 1996, Serita Winthrop (marr. diss. 2001). *Educ:* Magdalen Coll., Oxford (BA, MA, DPhil). Assistant, Dept of Western MSS, Bodleian Library, Oxford, 1963–71; Lecturer, 1971–73, Reader, 1973–87, History of Art Dept, Manchester Univ. Lyell Reader in Bibliography, Univ. of Oxford, 1982–83; Sen. Kress Fellow, Center for Adv. Study in Visual Arts, Nat. Gall. of Art, Washington DC, 1984–85; Sandars Reader in Bibliography, Cambridge Univ., 1984–85. Vis. Prof., UCL, 1991–93; John Simon Guggenheim Meml Fellow, 1995–96; Rio Tinto Distinguished Vis. Fellow, La Trobe Univ., Melbourne, 1997; Vis. Fellow, All Souls Coll., Oxford, 1998; J. Clawson Mills Art Hist. Fellowship, Met. Mus. of Art, NY, 2002; Samuel H. Kress Prof., Center for Advanced Study in the Visual Arts, Nat. Gall. of Art, Washington DC, 2004–05; J. Paul Getty Mus. Guest Scholar, 2006. Panizzi Lectures, BL, 2007–08. Fellow, Medieval Acad. of America, 1999. Hon. Fellow, Pierpont Morgan Liby, NY, 1995. *Publications:* (with Otto Pächt) Illuminated Manuscripts in the Bodleian Library, Oxford, 3 vols, 1966, 1970, 1973; (with A. C. de la Mare) Italian Illuminated Manuscripts in the Library of Major J. R. Abbey, 1969; Norman Illumination at Mont St Michel *c* 966–1100, 1970; The Master of Mary of Burgundy, A Book of Hours, 1970; Italian Renaissance Illuminations, 1977; Insular Manuscripts 6th–9th Century, 1978; The Decorated Letter, 1978; (with E. Temple) Illuminated Manuscripts in Oxford College Libraries, 1986; (ed with Paul Binski) Age of Chivalry: Art in Plantagenet England 1200–1400, 1987; Medieval Illuminators and Their Methods of Work, 1993; (ed) The Painted Page: Italian Renaissance book illumination 1450–1550, 1994; The Towneley Lectionary illuminated for Cardinal Alessandro Farnese by Giulio Clovio, 1997; Studies in Italian Manuscript Illumination, 2002; articles in Burlington Magazine, Arte Veneta, Pantheon, etc. *Recreation:* music. *Address:* Institute of Fine Arts, 1 East 78th Street, New York, NY 10021–0178, USA.

ALEXANDER, Lesley-Anne; Chief Executive, Royal National Institute of Blind People (formerly Royal National Institute of the Blind), since 2004; *b* 20 Sept. 1959; *d* of N. J. Davies and D. E. Davies; *m;* one *s;* m 1995, Colin James Reith. *Educ:* Thames Valley Univ. (MSc Ops Mgt). Housing Department: Ealing LBC, 1980–92; Enfield LBC, 1992–98; Dir of Ops, Peabody Trust, 1998–2003. Chm., British Judo Assoc., 1997–2001. *Recreation:* judo. *Address:* Royal National Institute of Blind People, 105 Judd Street, WC1H 9NE. *T:* (020) 7391 2200, *Fax:* (020) 7383 0508; *e-mail:* lesley-anne.alexander@rnib.org.uk.

ALEXANDER, McNeill; see Alexander, R. McN.

ALEXANDER, Rt Rev. Mervyn Alban Newman, DD; Bishop of Clifton, (RC), 1974–2001, now Bishop Emeritus; Parish Priest, St Joseph, Weston-super-Mare,

2001–07; *b* London, 29 June 1925; *s* of William Paul Alexander and Grace Evelyn Alexander (*née* Newman). *Educ:* Bishop Wordsworth School, Salisbury; Prior Park College, Bath; Gregorian University, Rome (DD 1951). Curate at Pro-Cathedral, Clifton, Bristol, 1951–63; RC Chaplain, Bristol University, 1953–67; Parish Priest, Our Lady of Lourdes, Weston-super-Mare, 1967–72; Auxiliary Bishop of Clifton and Titular Bishop of Pinhel, 1972–74; Vicar Capitular of Clifton, 1974. Hon. LLD Bristol, 2001. *Address:* St Angela's Convent, 5 Litfield Place, Bristol BS8 3LU. *T:* (0117) 973 0717.

ALEXANDER, Michael Richard, CEng, FIET; FIGEM; FIChemE; Chief Executive, British Energy plc, 2003–05; *b* 17 Nov. 1947; *s* of Humphrey and Pauline Alexander; *m* 1974, Clare Hollingsworth; two *s*. *Educ:* King George Grammar Sch., Southport; Univ. of Manchester Inst. of Sci. and Technol. (BSc 1st Cl. Hons Chem. Engrg; MSc Control Engrg). CEng 1975; MIChemE 1975, FIChemE 2004; FIGEM (FIGasE 1995); FIET (FIEE 2001). Dir, CIS, Eastern Europe, British Gas Exploration and Production Ltd, 1991–93; Managing Director: Public Gas Supply, British Gas plc, 1993–96; British Gas Trading Ltd, 1996–2001; Exec. Dir, 1996–2003, Chief Operating Officer, 2002–03, Centrica plc. Chairman: Goldfish Bank Ltd, 2002–03; TGE Marine Gp, 2008–; non-executive Director: Associated British Foods plc, 2002–07; Costain plc, 2007–; Adviser to: Marwyn Investment Mgt LLP, 2006–; Landis+Gyr Gp, 2007–. Ind. Dir, UK Payments Council, 2007–. Chm., Assoc. of Train Operating Cos, 2008–. *Recreations:* Rugby, walking, family. *Address:* c/o Costain plc, Costain House, Vanwall Business Park, Maidenhead, Berks SL6 4UB.

ALEXANDER, Morag, OBE 2001; Member and Scotland Commissioner, Equality and Human Rights Commission, since 2007; Convener, Scottish Social Services Council, 2001–07; *b* 10 Oct. 1943; *d* of Coll MacInnes and Sarah MacInnes (*née* Carberry); *m* 1964, Prof. Alan Alexander, *qv*; one *s* one *d*. *Educ:* Our Lady of Lourdes Sch., Glasgow; Glasgow Univ.; Lakehead Univ., Ont. (BA Hons). Res. Asst, ASTMS, 1971–73; editor and researcher, RIPA, 1973–82; freelance journalist and consultant, 1982–90; Founding Dir, TRAINING 2000 (Scotland) Ltd, Scottish Alliance for Women's Trng, 1990–92; Dir, EOC, Scotland, 1992–2001. Board Member: Children in Scotland, 1995–2000 (Chm., Early Years Adv. Gp, 1995–2002); Scottish Commn for Regulation of Care, 2001–07; Chairman: Fair Play Scotland, 2001–06; TOPSS UK Alliance, 2002–05. Member: Bd, Partnership for a Parliament, 1997; Scottish Senate, the Windsor Meetings, 1997–2000; Women's Adv. Gp to Scottish Exec. (formerly Scottish Office), 1997–2000; Expert Panel on Procedures and Standing Orders, Scottish Parlt, 1997–98; Bd, Turning Point Scotland, 1998–2006; Bd, Skills for Health, 2003–05; Skills for Care and Develt, 2005–07. Lay Mem., Scotland, Gen. Optical Council, 2007–. Mem., Cttee of Inquiry into Student Finance, 1999–2000. Member: Governing Body, Queen Margaret UC, 2001–07; Court, Queen Margaret Univ., Edinburgh, 2007–08. Founding Ed., Women in Europe, 1985–89; UK corresp., Women of Europe, 1987–92. *Recreations:* reading, walking, theatre, opera, spending time with family.

ALEXANDER, Pamela Elizabeth; Chief Executive, South East England Development Agency, since 2004; *b* 17 April 1954; *d* of late Reginald William Purchase Alexander and Marion Elizabeth Alexander (*née* Ross); *m* 1994, Dr Roger Booker; three step *s* one step *d*. *Educ:* Lady Eleanor Holles Sch.; Newnham Coll., Cambridge (MA Geog.). Department of the Environment, 1975–94: Asst Private Sec. to Minister for Housing, 1978–81; seconded to UK Rep., EC, Brussels, 1981–82; Hd, Publicity, 1987–90; Hd, Finance, Deptl Services, 1990–92; Hd, Housing Assocs Div., 1992–94; Dep. Chief Exec. (Ops), Housing Corp., 1995–97; Chief Exec., Historic Buildings and Monuments Commn (English Heritage), 1997–2001; Leader, Agency Policy Rev., Cabinet Office, 2001–02. Non-executive Director: Housing Finance Corp., 2001–; Quintain E&D plc, 2003. Dir, Brighton Dome and Festival Ltd, 2006–. Governor, Peabody Trust, 2000– (Chm., 2004–). Advr, Joseph Rowntree Foundn Res. Cttee, 1997–. Associate, New Economics Foundn, 2002–. FRSA 1998; FRGS 1999. *Recreations:* choral singing, tennis, walking, talking. *Address:* *e-mail:* pamalexander@seeda.co.uk.

ALEXANDER, Lt-Col Sir Patrick Desmond William C.; *see* Cable-Alexander.

ALEXANDER, Maj.-Gen. Paul Donald, CB 1989; MBE 1968; Policy Director (Army), Ministry of Defence, 1989–94; *b* 30 Nov. 1934; *s* of Donald Alexander and Alice Louisa Alexander (*née* Dunn); *m* 1958, Christine Winifred Marjorie Coakley; three *s*. *Educ:* Dudley Grammar Sch.; RMA Sandhurst; Staff Coll., Camberley; NDC; RCDS. Enlisted 1953; commissioned Royal Signals, 1955; served Hong Kong, E Africa, Germany; Comd 1st Div. Signal Regt, 1974–76; MoD, 1977–79; Comdr, Corps Royal Signals, 1st (Br) Corps, 1979–81; Dep. Mil. Sec. (B), 1982–85; Signal Officer in Chief (Army), 1985–89, retired. Col Comdt, RCS, 1989–95; Hon. Col, 35th Signal Regt, 1991–96. Chm., Royal Signals Assoc., 1990–95; Mem., E Anglian TA&VRA, 1991–2001 (County Chm., 1996–2000). Vice Pres., Lady Grover's Hosp. Fund, 2005– (Chm., 1998–2005). *Recreation:* gardening. *Clubs:* Army and Navy; Royal Signals Yacht (Adm., 1989–93).

ALEXANDER, Prof. Philip Stephen, DPhil; FBA 2005; Professor of Post-Biblical Jewish Literature, Manchester University, and Co-Director, Manchester University Centre for Jewish Studies, since 1995; *b* 10 March 1947; *s* of Robert and Priscilla Alexander; *m* 1973, Loveday Constance Anne Earl (Rev. Canon Prof. L. Alexander); one *s* one *d*. *Educ:* Pembroke Coll., Oxford (Hon. Mods Greek and Latin Lit. 1967; BA Oriental Studies 1969; DPhil Oriental Studies 1974; MA 1992). University of Manchester: Nathan Laski Lectr in Post-Biblical Jewish Studies, Dept of Near Eastern Studies, 1972–86; Sen. Lectr in Jewish Studies, 1986–91; Prof. of Post-Biblical Jewish Lit., Dept of Middle Eastern Studies, 1991–92; University of Oxford: Speaker's Lectr (pt-time), 1985–88; Pres., Oxford Centre for Hebrew and Jewish Studies, 1992–95; Hebrew Centre Lectr, Oriental Faculty, 1992–95; Fellow, St Cross Coll., 1992–95. *Publications:* Textual Sources for the Study of Judaism, 1984; (with G. Vermes) Serekh ha-Yahad and Two Related Texts, 1998; The Targum of Canticles: translated with a critical introduction, apparatus and notes, 2003; Companions to the Dead Sea Scrolls: the Mystical Texts, 2005; contrib. to major ref. works in field of Jewish studies; contribs to Jl Jewish Studies, Jl Semitic Studies. *Recreations:* hill-walking, swimming, Rembrandt, Bach, Shakespeare. *Address:* Religions and Theology, School of Arts, Histories and Cultures, Faculty of Humanities, University of Manchester, Manchester M13 9PL. *T:* (0161) 275 3977, *Fax:* (0161) 275 3151; *e-mail:* philip.s.alexander@man.ac.uk.

ALEXANDER, Prof. (Robert) McNeill, CBE 2000; FRS 1987; FIBiol; Professor of Zoology, University of Leeds, 1969–99; *b* 7 July 1934; *s* of Robert Priestley Alexander and Janet McNeill; *m* 1961, Ann Elizabeth Coulton; one *s* one *d*. *Educ:* Tonbridge School; Trinity Hall, Cambridge (MA, PhD); DSc Wales. Asst Lectr in Zoology, University Coll. of North Wales, 1958, Lectr 1961, Sen. Lectr 1968; Head, Dept of Pure and Applied Zoology, Univ. of Leeds, 1969–78 and 1983–87. Visiting Professor: Harvard, 1973; Duke, 1975; Nairobi, 1976, 1977, 1978; Basle, 1986; St Francis Xavier Univ. (NS), 1990; Univ. of Calif, Davis, 1992. Mem., Biological Scis Cttee, SRC, 1974–77. Sec., Zool Soc. of London, 1992–99 (Mem. Council, 1988–91; Vice Pres., 1990–91); President: Soc. for Experimental Biology, 1995–97 (Vice Pres., 1993–95); Internat. Soc. for Vertebrate Morphology, 1997–2001. Ed., Royal Soc. Proc. B, 1998–2004. Hon. Mem., Soc. for Integrative and Comparative Biol. (formerly Amer. Soc. of Zoologists), 1986; Member: Academia Europaea, 1996; European Acad. of Scis, 2004; Foreign Hon. Mem., Amer. Acad. of Arts and Scis, 2001. Hon. DSc Aberdeen, 2002; Hon. Dr Wageningen, 2003. Scientific Medal, Zoological Soc., 1969; Linnean Medal, Linnean Soc., 1979; Muybridge Medal, Internat. Soc. for Biomechanics, 1991; Borelli Award, Amer. Soc. for Biomechanics, 2003. *Publications:* Functional Design in Fishes, 1967, 3rd edn 1974; Animal Mechanics, 1968, 2nd edn 1983; Size and Shape, 1971; The Chordates, 1975, 2nd edn 1981; Biomechanics, 1975; The Invertebrates, 1979; Locomotion of Animals, 1982; Optima for Animals, 1982, 2nd edn 1996; Elastic Mechanisms in Animal Movement, 1988; Dynamics of Dinosaurs and other Extinct Giants, 1989; Animals, 1990; The Human Machine, 1992; Exploring Biomechanics, 1992; Bones, 1994; Energy for Animal Life, 1999; Principles of Animal Locomotion, 2003; Human Bones, 2005; papers on mechanics of human and animal movement. *Recreations:* history of natural history, history of tableware. *Address:* 14 Moor Park Mount, Leeds LS6 4BU. *T:* (0113) 275 9218.

ALEXANDER, Rosemary Anne, (Mrs G. L. S. Dobry); Founder and Principal, English Gardening School, since 1983; *b* 15 Dec. 1937; *d* of late Charles Sleigh and of Violet Allison (*née* Petrie); *m* 1st, 1956, Walter Ronald Alexander, CBE (marr. diss. 1975; he *d* 2006); two *s* two *d*; 2nd, 1982, His Honour George Leon Severyn Dobry, *qv*. *Educ:* Beacon Sch., Bridge of Allan, Stirlingshire. AIHort 1994. Trained as landscape architect; with Brian Clouston & Partners, Glasgow and London, 1973–79, then in private practice as garden designer. FSGD 1981. *Publications:* (with Tony Aldous) Landscape By Design, 1979; The English Gardening School, 1987; A Handbook for Garden Designers, 1994; Terraced, Town and Village Gardens, 1999; Garden Design, 2000; Caring for Your Garden, 2001; The Essential Garden Design Workbook, 2004; The Garden Maker's Manual, 2005; The Essential Garden Maintenance Workbook, 2006. *Recreations:* opera, fishing, walking. *Address:* Sandhill Farm House, Rogate, Petersfield, Hants GU31 5HU. *T:* (01730) 818373.

ALEXANDER, Steven; Chief Executive, Pre-School Learning Alliance, since 2004; *b* 23 Oct. 1954; *s* of late Louisa and James Alexander; two *s*. *Educ:* Bluecoat C of E Sch.; Coventry Univ. (CQSW; CSS; DMS; MBA); Putteridge Bury Business Sch. (PhD 1994). Operational Services Manager, Coventry Social Services, 1976–92; Asst Gen. Manager, S Birmingham Community NHS Trust, 1992–95; Dir of Ops, Sense, 1995–2001; CEO, British Dyslexia Assoc., 2001–04. Associate Consultant, Nat. Develt Team, 1992–94. Dir, Children's Workforce Develt Council, 2005–. Mem., Disability Employment Adv. Cttee, DWP, 2003–. Treas., Eur. Dyslexia Assoc. FRSA. *Recreations:* classic cars, antiques, supporting Coventry FC, music, horses. *Address:* Potfords Dam Farm, Coventry Road, Cawston, Rugby CV23 9JP. *T:* (020) 7697 2519; *e-mail:* stevealexander@pre-school.org.uk.

ALEXANDER, Thomas John; Senior Research Fellow, Department of Education (formerly of Educational Studies), University of Oxford, since 2000; Director for Education, Employment, Labour and Social Affairs (formerly Social Affairs, Manpower and Education), OECD, Paris, 1989–2000; *b* 11 March 1940; *s* of late John Alexander and of Agnes Douglas Stewart (*née* Creedican); *m* 1961, Pamela Mason; two *s* one *d*. *Educ:* Royal High Sch., Edinburgh. Entered FO, 1958; MECAS, 1961; Third Sec. (Commercial), Kuwait, 1963; Asst Private Sec. to the Minister of State, FO, 1965; Second Sec. (Commercial), Tripoli, 1967; seconded to industry (ICI), 1970; Vice Consul (Commercial), Seattle, 1970; First Sec., FCO, 1974; special unpaid leave to act as Private Sec. to Sec.-Gen. of OECD, Paris, 1977–82; Counsellor and Head of Chancery, Khartoum, 1982–83; Dep. Head of Planning, 1984, Head of Private Office of Sec.-Gen., 1984–89, OECD. Mem., Higher Educn Bd, 1999–, Gen. Educn Bd, 2002– (Chm., 2002–03, 2007–), Open Soc. Inst., Budapest. *Address:* *e-mail:* thomas.alexander@education.ox.ac.uk. *Club:* Oriental.

ALEXANDER, Wendy Cowan; Member (Lab) Paisley North, Scottish Parliament, since 1999; *b* 27 June 1963; *d* of Rev. Douglas N. Alexander and Dr Joyce O. Alexander; *m* 2003, Prof. Brian Ashcroft; one *s* one *d* (twins). *Educ:* Park Mains Sch., Erskine; Pearson Coll., Canada; Glasgow Univ. (MA Hons); Warwick Univ. (MA Econ); INSEAD, France (MBA). Research Officer, Scottish Lab. Party, 1988–92; with Booz Allen and Hamilton Internat., 1994–97; Advr to Sec. of State for Scotland, 1997–98. Scottish Executive, subseq. Scottish Government: Minister for Communities, 1999–2000; Minister for Enterprise and Lifelong Learning, 2000–02, and for Transport, 2001–02; Convenor, Finance Cttee, 2006–07; Lab Shadow Cabinet Sec. for Finance and Sustainable Growth, 2007–. Vis. Prof., Univ. of Strathclyde Business Sch., 2003–. *Address:* Scottish Parliament, Edinburgh EH99 1SP.

See also Rt Hon. D. G. Alexander.

ALEXANDER, William Gemmell, MBE 1945; *b* 19 Aug. 1918; *s* of Harold Gemmell Alexander and Winifred Ada Alexander (*née* Stott); *m* 1945, Janet Rona Page Alexander (*née* Elias); four *s* one *d*. *Educ:* Tre Arddur Bay Sch.; Sedbergh Sch.; Oxford Univ. (MA). Served War of 1939–45 (despatches, war stars and clasps): Driver Mechanic, 2nd Lieut, Lieut, Capt., Maj.; served in France, S Africa, Eritrea, Egypt, Middle East, Sicily, Italy, Algeria, NW Europe. HM Overseas Civil Service, 1946–59: Gilbert and Ellice Is, 1946–51; Mauritius, 1951–55; Cyprus, 1955–59; Man., Cooperative Wholesale Soc., Agricultural Dept, 1960–63; Dir, Internat. Cooperative Alliance, 1963–68; Dir-Gen., RoSPA, 1968–74; County Road Safety Officer, W Yorks MCC, 1974–78; Chm., W. H. Stott & Co. Ltd, 1979–83 (Dir, 1968–83). Mem., BSI Quality Assurance Council, 1975–83. Member: Bradford Dio. Bd of Finance, 1985–91; Ewecross Deanery Synod, 1985–99; Dent PCC, 1978–2008. Clerk, Dent Parish Council, 1980–86. Chm., Bd of Govs, Dent GS. ACMI (AMBIM 1963). *Recreations:* all sports, long distance walking. *Address:* Flat 2, Seedsgill Barn, Deepdale Road, Dent, Sedbergh, Cumbria LA10 5QL. *T:* (01539) 625228; *e-mail:* gemmell@dent228.fsnet.co.uk. *Club:* Royal Commonwealth Society.

ALEXANDER, William John, CBE 2005; FREng, FIMechE; Director, 1994–2005, Chief Executive, 1997–2005, RWE Thames Water plc (formerly Thames Water plc) (Group Managing Director, 1996–97); Chairman, Xansa plc, since 2004; *b* 15 Feb. 1947; *s* of John Fryer Alexander and Kathleen Mary (*née* Berry); *m* 1968, Dorothy Full; one *s* one *d*. FIMechE 1987; FREng (FEng 1996). British Coal: trng scheme, 1970; Chief Engr, Scottish Reg., 1982–86; Chief Mechanical Engr, 1986–87; Hd of Engrg, 1987–89; Thames Water Utilities: Engrg Dir, 1989–91; Technical Dir, 1991–92; Man. Dir, 1992–96. Non-executive Director: RMC, 2001–05; Perpetual Income and Growth Investment Trust, 2006–; Chairman: Henley Festival Ltd, 2003–; Clearview Traffic Ltd, 2006–. Mem. Bd, CBI, 2005–. Freeman, City of London, 1994; Liveryman, Engineers' Co., 1997–. Hon. FIMMM (Hon. FIMinE 1990); Hon. FCIWEM 2002. Hon. DSc: Cranfield, 2003; Reading, 2003. *Recreations:* classic cars, travel, swimming, walking; *Address:* Xansa, 420 Thames Valley Park Drive, Reading, RG6 1PU. *Clubs:* Mark's; Phyllis Court (Henley).

ALEXANDER-SINCLAIR of Freswick, Maj.-Gen. David Boyd, CB 1981; retired 1982; *b* 2 May 1927; *s* of late Comdr M. B. Alexander-Sinclair of Freswick, RN and late

Avril N. Fergusson-Buchanan; *m* 1958, Ann Ruth, *d* of late Lt-Col Graeme Daglish; two *s* one *d*. *Educ:* Eton. Commnd into Rifle Bde, 1946, served in Germany, Kenya, Cyprus; ADC to GOC South Malaya District and Maj.-Gen. Bde of Gurkhas, 1950–51; psc 1958; Bde Major, 6th Inf. Bde Gp, 1959–61; GSO2 (Dirg Staff) Staff Coll., 1963–65; comdg 3rd Bn Royal Green Jackets, 1967–69; MoD, 1965–67 and 1969–71; Comdr, 6th Armd Bde, 1971–73; Student, RCDS, 1974; GOC 1st Division, 1975–77; COS, UKLF, 1978–80; Comdt, Staff Coll., 1980–82.

AL FAYED, Mohamed; Chairman: Harrods Holdings Ltd, since 1994; Harrods Ltd, since 1985; Fulham Football Club, since 1997; Chairman and Owner, Ritz Hotel, Paris, since 1979; *b* Egypt, Jan. 1933; *m*; two *s* two *d* (and one *s* decd). *Educ:* Alexandria Univ. Hon. Mem., Emmanuel Coll., Cambridge, 1995. Officier, Légion d'Honneur, 1993 (Chevalier, 1985); La Grande Médaille de la Ville de Paris, 1985; Plaque de Paris, 1989; Commendatore, Order of Merit (Italy), 1990. *Address:* Harrods Ltd, Brompton Road, SW1 7XL.

ALFEROV, Prof. Zhores Ivanovich, DSc; Professor of Optoelectronics, since 1973, and Dean, Faculty of Physical Science and Technical Engineering, since 1988, St Petersburg State Polytechnical University (formerly V. I. Ulyanov Electrotechnical Institute, Leningrad); Director, A. F. Ioffe Physico-Technical Institute, St Petersburg (formerly Leningrad), since 1987; *b* Belorussia, USSR, 15 March 1930; *s* of Ivan Karpovich and Anna Vladimirovna; *m* 1967, Tamara Darskaya; two *c*. *Educ:* V. I. Ulyanov Electrotechnical Inst., Leningrad (DSc 1970). Jun. Researcher, 1953–64, Sen. Researcher, 1964–67, Head of Lab., 1967–87, A. F. Ioffe Physico-Technical Inst., Leningrad. Pres., St Petersburg Scientific Centre, 1989–. Mem., State Duma, 1995–. USSR, subseq. Russian, Academy of Science: Corresp. Mem., 1972, Mem., 1979; Vice-Pres., 1989–. (Jtly) Nobel Prize for Physics, 2000. *Publications:* four books; articles in jls on semiconductor technology. *Address:* St Petersburg State Polytechnical University, Polytechnicheskya 29, St Petersburg 195251, Russia; Ioffe Physico-Technical Institute, Polytechnicheskya 26, St Petersburg 194021, Russia.

ALFÖLDY, Tádé; Chairman and Chief Executive Officer, ATI Depo Rt, since 2005; Chairman: Preventiv Security Rt, since 2000; ATI Sziget Industrial Park Kft, since 2005; *b* 6 Aug. 1946; *s* of László Alföldy and Erzsébet (*née* Ujvári); *m* 1968, Orsolya Baraczka; two *d*. *Educ:* Karl Marx Univ. of Economics, Budapest. Hungarian Shipping Agency, 1968–70; Hungarian Youth Union, 1970–74; Sec.-Gen., Internat. Cttee, Children's and Adolescents' Movements, 1974–79; joined Ministry of Foreign Affairs, Hungary, 1979; Arab Desk Officer, 1979–80; 2nd, later 1st, Sec., Kuwait, 1980–85; British Desk Officer, 1985–89; Dir, N Atlantic Dept, 1989–90; Dep. State Sec., 1990–91; Ambassador: to Greece, 1991–94; to the UK, 1994–97. Jt Chm., Investor Holding Rt, 1997–2005. Vice Pres., 1997–2002, Mem. Bd of Auditors, 2002–, Hungarian Atlantic Council, Budapest. Mem., Foreign Policy Assoc., Budapest, 1991–. *Recreations:* family, tennis, gardening. *Address:* Investor Holding Rt, Budapest 1051, Szent István tér 11, Hungary.

ALFONSÍN, Dr Raúl Ricardo; President of Argentina, 1983–89; *b* 12 March 1927; *s* of Serafin Raúl Alfonsín and Ana María Foulkes; *m* 1949, María Lorenza Barreneche; three *s* three *d*. *Educ:* Regional Normal School, Chascomús; Gen. San Martín Mil. Acad.; Law Sch., Nat. Univ. of La Plata. Joined Radical Civic Union, 1945: Pres., 1983–91; Pres., Nat. Cttee, 1999–. Journalist, founder El Imparcial, Chascomús; Mem., Chascomús City Cttee, 1951, Mem. Council, 1954–55 (Pres., 1955 and 1959–61); Mem., Buenos Aires Provincial Legislature, 1952; Provincial Deputy, 1958–62; Deputy, Nat. Congress, 1963–66, 1973–76. Founder: Movimiento de Intransigencia y Renovación; Fundación Argentina para la Libre Información, 1992. Dr *hc*: New Mexico, New York, 1985; Bologna, Santiago de Compostela, Complutense de Madrid, 1988; Naples, 1990. Human Rights Prize (jtly), Council of Europe, 1986; numerous awards and foreign decorations. *Publications:* La Cuestión Argentina, 1980; Ahora, mi Propuesta Política, 1983; Que es el Radicalismo?, 1983; Alfonsín Responde, 1992; Democracia y Consenso, 1996. *Address:* Unión Cívica Radical, Alsina 1786, 1088 Buenos Aires, Argentina.

ALFORD, Richard Harding, CMG 2003; OBE 1988; British Council Director, Italy, 1996–2003; *b* 28 Dec. 1943; *s* of Jack Harding Alford and Sylvia Alford; *m* 1968, Penelope Jane Wort; one *s* two *d*. *Educ:* Dulwich Coll.; Keble Coll., Oxford (MA; Diploma in History and Philosophy of Science). Asst Cultural Attaché, British Embassy, Prague, 1969–72; posts in ME Dept, Policy Res. Dept, and Educnl Contracts Dept, British Council, 1972–77; Project Planning Centre, Bradford Univ., 1977; Inst. of Educn, London Univ., 1978; British Council: Asst Rep., New Delhi, 1978–81; Dir, E Europe and N Asia Dept, 1982–85; Rep., Poland, 1985–89; Dir of Personnel, 1989–93; Regl Dir, Central Europe, 1993–96. Sec., Charles Wallace India Trust, 2004–. Governor: Centre for Internat. Briefing, Farnham Castle, 1992–96; British Inst., Florence, 1996–2003; Atlantic Coll., 2005–. *Recreations:* tennis, theatre. *Address:* c/o British Council, 10 Spring Gardens, SW1A 2BN. *Club:* Friends of Dulwich College Sports.

ALFRED, (Arnold) Montague; Deputy Chairman: Ward Lock Educational Co. Ltd, 1985–88; BLA Publishing Ltd, 1985–88; Ling Kee (UK) Ltd, 1985–88; retired; *b* 21 March 1925; *s* of Reuben Alfred and Bessie Alfred (*née* Arbesfield); *m* 1947, Sheila Jacqueline Gold; three *s*. *Educ:* Central Foundation Boys' Sch.; Imperial Coll., London; London Sch. of Economics. Head of Economics Dept, Courtaulds Ltd, 1953–69; Director, Nylon Div., Courtaulds Ltd, 1964–69; Dir, BPC Ltd, 1969–81; Chairman: BPC Publishing Ltd, 1971–81; Caxton Publishing Holdings Ltd, 1971–81; Second Permanent Sec., and Chief Exec., PSA, DoE, 1982–84. *Publications:* Discounted Cash Flow (jointly), 1965; Business Economics (jointly), 1968. Numerous articles in: Accountant, Textile Jl, Investment Analyst, etc. *Recreation:* active in Jewish community affairs.

ALGOMA, Bishop of, since 1995; **Rt Rev. Ronald Curry Ferris;** *b* 2 July 1945; *s* of Herald Bland Ferris and Marjorie May Ferris; *m* 1965, Janet Agnes (*née* Waller); two *s* four *d*. *Educ:* Toronto Teachers' Coll. (diploma); Univ. of W Ontario (BA); Huron Coll., London, Ont. (MDiv); Pacific Sch. of Religion (DMin 1995). Teacher, Pape Avenue Elem. School, Toronto, 1965; Principal Teacher, Carcross Elem. School, Yukon, 1966–68. Incumbent, St Luke's Church, Old Crow, Yukon, 1970–72; Rector, St Stephen's Memorial Church, London, Ont., 1973–81; Bishop of Yukon, 1981–95. Hon. DD Huron Coll., London, Ont, 1982; Hon. STD Thorneloe Univ., Ont, 1995. *Address:* (office) PO Box 1168, 619 Wellington Street E, Sault Ste Marie, ON P6A 5N7, Canada.

ALGOSAIBI, Dr Ghazi Abdulrahman; Minister for Labour, Saudi Arabia, since 2004; *b* 2 March 1940; *s* of Abdul Rahman and Fatma; *m* 1968, Sigrid Presser; three *s* one *d*. *Educ:* primary and secondary schs, Bahrain; Cairo Univ. (LLB 1961); Univ. of Southern California (MA Internat Relations 1964); Univ. of London (PhD 1970). King Saud University, Riyadh: Lectr, Faculty of Commerce, 1965–70, Asst Prof., 1970–74; Dean, Faculty of Commerce, and Hd, Pol Sci. Dept, 1971–73; Dir Gen., Saudi Railways, 1974–75; Minister: Industry and Electricity, 1975–82; Health, 1982–84; Ambassador to Bahrain, 1984–92, to UK and Ireland, 1992–2002; Minister for Water, 2002–04. Numerous foreign awards. *Publications:* in Arabic: A Life in Poetry, 1980; From Here and There, 1981; Arabian Essays, 1982 (also in English); In My Humble Opinion, 1983; A Hundred Rose Petals, 1986; Development Face to Face, 1989; To Return to California as a Tourist, 1990; Cultural Invasion and Other Essays, 1991; Poems I Liked, 1992; The Gulf Crisis: an attempt to understand, 1992 (also in English); Poets Followed by Sinners: who are they?, 1994; An Apartment Called Freedom (novel), 1994 (trans. English 1996); The Dilemma of Development, 1995 (also in English); A Very Hot Political Dialogue, 1996; Al Asforiya, 1996; Conciliation, Fallacies and Other Issues, 1997; The Two of Them, 1997; The Myth, 1997; Voice from the Gulf, 1997; With Nagi and With Her, 1998; The Golden Cage (play), 1998; Yes, (Saudi) Minister!: a life in administration (autobiog.), 1999 (also in English); Seven (novel), 1999 (also in English); Thursday Break, 2000; Abu Shalaq, 2000; Dansko, 2000; *poetry:* Drops of Thirst; Battle Without Flag; Love Verses; You are Riyadh; Fever; Return to Old Places; The Complete Works of Poetry, 1960; Inside a Poet's Tent, 1988; Flowers in Sana's Braids, 1989; Necklace of Stones, 1991; Obituary of a Former Knight, 1992; Lyrics from Arabia, 1993 (also in English); From the Orient and the Desert, 1994; A Hundred Jasmine Flowers, 1995; Dusting the Colour from Roses, 1995 (also in English); Souhaim, 1996; Reading London's Face, 1997; Poems from the Pearl Islands; trans. Joseph Frankel, International Relations; anthologies. *Recreations:* swimming, fishing, table tennis. *Address:* Ministry of Labour, Omar bin Al-Khatab Street, Riyadh 11157, Saudi Arabia. *Clubs:* Brooks's, Travellers, Army and Navy (Hon. Mem.).

ALHAJI, Alhaji Abubakar, Hon. KBE 1989; Economic Adviser to Nigerian States of Sokoto, Kebbi and Zamfara, since 1999; High Commissioner for Nigeria in the United Kingdom, 1992–97; *b* 22 Nov. 1938; *m* Hajiya Amina Abubakar; three *s* three *d*. *Educ:* Univ. of Reading (BA Hons Political Economy); IMF Inst. course in public finance, 1974; Hague Inst. for Social Scis (course on industrialisation, 1970). Permanent Secretary, Ministries of: Trade, 1975–78; Industries, 1978–79; Finance, 1979–84; Nat. Planning, 1984–88; Hon. Minister, Ministries of: Budget and Planning, 1988–90; Finance and Economic Develt, 1990–92. Chm., Group 24 Cttee, 1991–92. Vice-Pres., Commonwealth Soc. for the Deaf. Sardauna of Sokoto, 1991. Hon. DSc Sokoto Univ., 1991. *Recreations:* horse riding, walking, reading. *Address:* c/o Government House, Sokoto State, Nigeria.

ALHEGELAN, Sheikh Faisal Al Abdul Aziz, Hon. GBE 1987; Grand Cross and Cordon, Order of King Abdul Aziz, Saudi Arabia; Saudi Arabian diplomat; Ambassador of Saudi Arabia to France, 1996–2003; *b* Jeddah, 7 Oct. 1929; *s* of Sheikh Abdulaziz Alhegelan and Fatima Al-Eissa; *m* 1961, Nouha Tarazi; three *s*. *Educ:* Faculty of Law, Fouad Univ., Cairo. Min. of Foreign Affairs, 1952–54; Saudi Arabian Embassy, Washington, USA, 1954–58; Chief of Protocol, Min. of Foreign Affairs, 1958–60; Polit. Adviser to King Sa'ud, 1960–61; Ambassador for Saudi Arabia to: Spain, 1961–68; Venezuela and Argentina (concurrently), 1968–75; Denmark, 1975–76; Court of St James's, 1976–79; USA, 1979–83; Minister of Health, Saudi Arabia, 1984–95. Chm. Bd of Dirs, Saudi Red Crescent Soc., 1984. Order of Isabel la Católica, Spain; Gran Cordon, Orden del Libertador, Venezuela; Grande Official, Orden Rio Branco, Brazil; May Grand Decoration, Argentina. *Recreations:* golf, bridge, collecting selective books and objets d'art.

ALI, (Abul Hassan) Mahmood; High Commissioner for People's Republic of Bangladesh in London, 1996–2001; *b* 6 Feb. 1943; *s* of late Hassan Ali and Zubaida Ali; *m* 1968, Shaheen Khaliq; two *s*. *Educ:* Dhaka Univ. (BA Hons Econs 1962; MA 1963). Lectr in Econs, Dhaka Univ., 1964–66; joined Pakistan Foreign Service, 1966: New York, 1968–71; joined Bangladesh Liberation War in NY, 1971, served in NY, 1971–75; involved in organising Bangladesh Community in USA and Canada; served in New Delhi, 1977–79; Dir-Gen., Foreign Ministry, 1979–82; Beijing, 1983–86; Ambassador to Bhutan, 1986–90; Additional Foreign Sec., 1991–92; Ambassador to Germany, 1992–95; Sec. and A-Grade Ambassador, 1993; Ambassador to Kingdom of Nepal, Feb.–Oct. 1996. *Publication:* (contrib.) American Response to Bangladesh Liberation War, 1996. *Recreations:* tennis (playing), interest in sports, music, art and literature. *Address:* c/o Ministry of Foreign Affairs, Topkhana, Dhaka, Bangladesh. *Club:* Kurmitola Golf (Dhaka).

ALI, Ebrahim Mahomed; Consultant, Freshfields Bruckhaus Deringer, since 2006; *b* 9 April 1951; *s* of Mahomed and Katija Ali; *m* 1981, Susan Linda Kirkby; two *s* one *d*. *Educ:* Morgan High Sch., Harare; Univ. of Zimbabwe (LLB); UCL (LLM); Columbia Univ., NY (LLM). Called to the Bar, Middle Temple, 1978; admitted as legal practitioner, Zimbabwe, 1982; Attorney Gen.'s Chambers, Zimbabwe, 1982–83; Kantor & Immerman, Zimbabwe, 1983–84; admitted solicitor, England and Wales, 1989; Solicitor, Inland Revenue: Principal Legal Officer, 1989–94; on secondment to Competition Br., Legal Dept, OFT, 1994–97; Asst Solicitor (special appeals, internat., EC, oil), 1997–2002; on secondment to Legal Dept, Ofgem, 2002–03; Principal Assistant Solicitor (Taxes), Bd of Inland Revenue, subseq. HMRC, 2003–06. *Recreations:* relaxing, sport. *Address:* Freshfields Bruckhaus Deringer, 65 Fleet Street, EC4Y 1HS.

ALI, Rt Rev. Dr Michael N.; *see* Nazir-Ali.

ALI, Monica; writer; *b* Dhaka, 20 Oct. 1967; *m* 2002, Simon Torrance; one *s* one *d*. *Educ:* Bolton Sch.; Wadham Coll., Oxford (BA Hons PPE). Mktg Manager, Verso, 1992–94; Account Dir, Newell & Sorrell (Interbrand), 1995–97; Gp Account Dir, Lambie-Nairn, 1997–98; freelance copy-writer, 1999–2001. *Publications:* Brick Lane, 2003; Alentejo Blue, 2006. *Recreations:* eating, cooking, yoga, riding, having baths. *Address:* c/o A. P. Watt, 20 John Street, WC1N 2DR.

ALI, Muhammad; former professional heavyweight boxer; *b* Cassius Marcellus Clay, Louisville, Ky, 17 Jan. 1942; *s* of Cassius Marcellus Clay, Sr and Odessa L. Clay (*née* Grady); changed name on conversion to Islam, 1964; *m* 1st, 1964, Sonji Roi (marr. diss. 1966); 2nd, 1967, Belinda Kalilah Boyd (marr. diss. 1977); one *s* three *d* (incl. twin *d*); 3rd, 1977, Veronica Porche (marr. diss. 1986); four *d*; 4th, 1986, Yolanda Williams; one *s*. *Educ:* Central High Sch., Louisville. Amateur boxer, 1954–60; Gold Medal, Light Heavyweight Boxing, Olympic Games, Rome, 1960; turned professional, 1960: 61 bouts; 37 knockouts; won 19 by decision; World Heavyweight Champion, 1964, 1974, 1978. Special Envoy of US Pres. to Africa, 1980, to Iraq, 1990; Messenger of Peace, UN, 2000. *Films:* The Greatest, 1977; Freedom Road, 1979. Lifetime Achievement Award, Amnesty Internat. US Presidential Medal of Freedom, 2005. *Publications:* (with Richard Durham) The Greatest: my own story, 1975; (with T. Hauser) Healing, 1996; (with Hana Ali) More than a Hero, 2000; (with Hana Ali) The Soul of a Butterfly, 2004. *Address:* PO Box 160, Berrien Springs, MI 49103, USA.

ALI, Tariq; writer; *b* 21 Oct. 1943; *s* of Tahira Hyat and Mazhar Ali Khan; partner, Susan Watkins; one *s* two *d*. *Educ:* Government Coll., Lahore (BA Hons); Exeter Coll., Oxford (PPE). Editor: The Black Dwarf, 1968–70; The Red Mole, 1970–73; Mem., Editorial Bd, New Left Review, 1982–; Series Producer, Channel Four TV: Bandung File, 1984–89; Rear Window, 1990–94; Editorial Dir, Verso Books, 2001–05. *Publications: non-fiction:* Pakistan: military rule or people's power, 1970; 1968 and After: inside the Revolution, 1978; Can Pakistan Survive?, 1982; Who's Afraid of Margaret Thatcher?, 1984; The Nehrus and the Gandhis: an Indian dynasty, 1985, 4th edn 2005; Streetfighting Years: an autobiography of the sixties, 1987, 2nd edn 2005; Revolution from Above: where is the

Soviet Union going?, 1988; The Clash of Fundamentalisms, 2002; Bush in Babylon, 2003; Speaking of Empire and Resistance (interviews with David Barsamian), 2005; Rough Music: Blair/bombs/Baghdad/London/terror, 2005; Pirates of the Caribbean: axis of hope, 2006; The Duel: Pakistan on the flight path of American power, 2007; *fiction:* Redemption, 1990; Shadows of the Pomegranate Tree, 1992; The Book of Saladin, 1998; Fear of Mirrors, 1998; The Stone Woman, 2000; A Sultan in Palermo, 2005; *plays:* Spinoza, 1993; Necklaces, 1994; The Illustrious Corpse, 2003; Zahra, 2007; with Howard Brenton: Iranian Nights, 1989; Moscow Gold, 1990; Ugly Rumours, 1998. *Recreations:* swimming, cinema, cricket, theatre. *Address:* 6 Meard Street, W1F 0EG. *T:* (020) 7437 3546, *Fax:* (020) 7734 0059; *e-mail:* tariq.ali3@btinternet.com. *Clubs:* Groucho, Blacks; Bolivarian Circle (Caracas).

ALIBHAI-BROWN, Yasmin; journalist; weekly columnist: The Independent, since 1998; Evening Standard, since 2005; *b* 10 Dec. 1949; *d* of Kassim Damji and Jena Ramji; *m* (marr. diss.); one *s*; *m* 1990, Colin Brown; one *d*. *Educ:* Makerere Univ., Uganda (BA Hons 1972); MPhil Oxon 1975. Arrived in UK from Uganda, 1972; journalist; contributions to: Guardian; Observer; NY Times; Time mag.; Newsweek; Daily Mail; radio and TV broadcaster. Res. Fellow, IPPR, 1996–2001. Advr to instns on race matters. Pres., Inst. Family Therapy. One-woman show, commnd and dir by RSC, 2005–06, UK and Indian tour, 2007. DUniv: Open, 1999; Oxford Brookes, 2004; Hon. Dr Liverpool John Moore's, 2003. Asia Award for achievement in writing, BBC, 1999; Special Award for outstanding contrib. to journalism, CRE, 2000; Media Personality of Year Award, 2000, Award for Journalism, 2004, Ethnic Minority Media Award; Windrush Outstanding Merit Award, 2000; GG2 Leadership and Diversity Award for Media Personality of Year, 2001; George Orwell Prize for political journalism, 2002. *Publications:* No Place Like Home, 1995; After Multiculturalism, 2000; Who Do We Think We Are?, 2001; Mixed Feelings, 2001; Some of My Best Friends Are, 2004. *Recreations:* theatre, reading, volunteering to assist children in need. *Address:* Independent House, 191 Marsh Wall, E14 9RS; *e-mail:* y.alibhai-brown@independent.co.uk.

ALKER, Doug; freelance management consultant; Chief Executive, Royal National Institute for Deaf People, 1995–97; *b* 23 Nov. 1940. *Educ:* London Univ. (BSc (external) 1967); Birmingham Univ. (MBA 1993). Analytical Chemist, Pilkington Bros, 1959–64; Exptl Officer, ICI, 1964–85; Researcher, BBC, 1985–87; Royal National Institute for Deaf People: Principal Regl Officer, 1987; Dir, Community Services, 1987–90; Dir, Quality and Res., 1990–94. Member: Nat. Disability Council, 1995–2000; Exec. Cttee, RADAR, 1997–2000; Chair: E Lancs Deaf Soc., 1980– (Dir, 2001–); Fedn of Deaf People, 1997–2001 (Pres., 2001–); BDA, 2002–. Chair, Kings Court (Blackburn) Ltd, 2000–. Indep. Assessor for DETR, 1999–. Hon. Fellow, Univ. of Central Lancashire, 1995. *Address:* PO Box 11, Darwen, Lancs BB3 3GH.

ALKER, Rt Rev. Mgr (John) Stephen, MBE 1997; QHC 2007; Principal Roman Catholic Chaplain and Vicar General to the Army, 2006–June 2009; Assistant Chaplain General, HQ Land Command, 2006–June 2009; *b* 1 July 1953; *s* of John Alker and Alice Alker (*née* Ashurst). *Educ:* St Joseph's Coll., Upholland, Wigan; St Cuthbert's Coll., Ushaw, Durham. Ordained priest, Liverpool Archdio., 1978; Assistant Priest: St Joseph's, Leigh, 1978–80; Metropolitan Cath., Liverpool, 1980–83; Chaplain, TA, 1981, Regular Army, 1983–, served Germany, NI, Australia, Cyprus, Bosnia, UK; first RC Asst Chaplain Gen., RAChD, 2003–06. Prelate of Honour, 2006. KHS 2002. *Recreations:* ornithology, country walks, classical music, ecclesiastical heraldry. *Address:* Headquarters Land Command, Erskine Barracks, Wilton, Salisbury, Wilts SP2 0AG. *T:* (01722) 433982, *Fax:* (01722) 433534; *e-mail:* john.alker593@land.mod.uk.

AL KHALIFA, Shaikh Abdul Aziz bin Mubarak; Assistant Under Secretary for Co-ordination and Follow-up, Ministry of Foreign Affairs, Bahrain, since 2002 (Assistant Under Secretary for Policy Co-ordination, 2001); *b* 10 Oct. 1962; *m* 1988, Shaikha Lamees Daij Al Khalifa. *Educ:* Wellington Sch., Som; Newbury Coll. (HND); Amer. Univ. Sch. of Internat. Service, Washington (BA); Inst. for Social and Economic Policy in Middle East, Harvard. Prime Minister's Court: Researcher on Political and Economic Affairs, 1987–90; Asst Dir of Information, 1990–94; acting Dir of Admin and Public Relations, 1994–96; Ambassador for Bahrain to UK, Denmark, Ireland, Holland, Norway and Sweden, 1996–2001. *Address:* Ministry of Foreign Affairs, POB 547, Government House, Manama, Bahrain.

AL KHALIFA, Shaikh Khalifa bin Abdullah; Head, National Security Agency, Bahrain, since 2008; *b* 4 March 1965; *m* 1989, Shaikha Mayar bint Khalifa Al Khalifa; three *s* one *d*. *Educ:* West Rifaa Sch. for Boys; Huston Tillotson Univ., Texas (BBA); South West Texas State Univ. (MBA). Ministry of Information, Bahrain: Tourism Sector, 1989–96; set up and expanded Foreign Media Affairs, 1996–2002; Asst Under Sec. for Foreign Media Affairs, 2002–06; Chief Exec., Bahrain Radio and TV Corp., 2006–07; Ambassador of Bahrain to the Court of St James's, 2007–08. Chm. of regl, nat. and internat. seminars and confs in media field. Shaikh Isa bin Salman Al Khalifa Medal 4th class. *Recreation:* reading about politics and social affairs. *Address:* National Security Agency, PO Box 2666, Kingdom of Bahrain.

AL-KHALILI, Prof. Jameel S., (Jim), OBE 2008; PhD; FInstP, FRAS; scientist, author and broadcaster; Professor of Physics and Professor of Public Engagement in Science, University of Surrey, since 2005; *b* Baghdad, 20 Sept. 1962; *s* of Sadik and Jean Al-Khalili; *m* 1986, Julie Frampton; one *s* one *d*. *Educ:* Univ. of Surrey (BSc Hons Physics 1986; PhD 1989). FInstP 2000; FRAS 2006. Res. Fellow, UCL, 1989–91; University of Surrey: Res. Fellow, 1991–92; Lectr in Physics, 1992–94; Advanced Res. Fellow, 1994–99; Sen. Lectr, 2000–05. Adjunct Prof., Michigan State Univ., 1999–2000. Sen. Advr on Sci. and Technol. to British Council, 2007–. British Association for Advancement of Science: Trustee, 2006–; Vice Pres., 2008–; Hon. Fellow, 2007. Michael Faraday Medal for Sci. Communication, Royal Soc., 2007. *Publications:* Black Holes, Wormholes and Time Machines, 1999; Nucleus: a trip into the heart of matter, 2001; Quantum: a guide for the perplexed, 2004; (ed) Lecture Notes in Physics: Nuclear Physics with Exotic Beams, vol I 2004, vol II 2006, vol III 2008; contrib. res. papers in jls, newspaper and mag. articles. *Recreations:* reading non-fiction (particularly history and philosophy), hiking, running, oil painting, playing guitar, following Leeds United FC. *Address:* Department of Physics, University of Surrey, Guildford, Surrey GU2 7XH. *T:* (01483) 686808, *Fax:* (01483) 686781; *e-mail:* j.alkhalili@surrey.ac.uk.

ALKIN, Lawrence Michael; Chairman, Metro Inns Ltd; *b* 16 June 1939; *s* of Henry and Phyllis Alkin. *Educ:* Mill Hill Sch.; University Coll. London (LLM). Sen. Partner, Alkin Colombotti and Partners, 1965–72; Managing Director: Filross Securities, 1972–; Holmes Place Ltd, 1979–96; Jt CEO, Holmes Place PLC, 1997–2000. *Recreations:* fishing (badly), cooking (moderately), dining out (well). *Address:* Flat 101, Block E, Montevetro Building, 100 Battersea Church Road, SW11 3YL.

ALLABY, (John) Michael; author, since 1973; *b* 18 Sept. 1933; *s* of Albert Theodore Allaby and Jessica May Allaby (*née* King); *m* 1957, Ailsa Marthe McGregor; one *s* one *d*. *Educ:* George Dixon Grammar Sch., Birmingham; Birmingham Sch. of Speech Training and Dramatic Art. Left sch. at 15, 1948; clerk, 1949; police cadet, Birmingham City Police, 1950–51; pilot, RAF, 1952–54; actor, 1955–64; Editorial Asst, Soil Assoc., 1964–72; Managing Editor, The Ecologist, 1972–73. *Publications:* The Eco-Activists, 1971; Who Will Eat?, 1972; (with Floyd Allen) Robots Behind the Plow, 1974; Ecology, 1975; (jtly) The Survival Handbook, 1975; Inventing Tomorrow, 1976; World Food Resources: actual and potential, 1977; (with Colin Tudge) Home Farm, 1977; (ed) A Dictionary of the Environment, 1977, 4th edn 1994; Making and Managing a Smallholding, 1979, 2nd edn 1986; Animals that Hunt, 1979; Wildlife of North America, 1979; (with Peter Bunyard) The Politics of Self-Sufficiency, 1980; A Year in the Life of a Field, 1981; (with Peter Crawford) The Curious Cat, 1982; Animal Artisans, 1982; (with James Lovelock) The Great Extinction, 1983; The Food Chain, 1984; (with James Lovelock) The Greening of Mars, 1984; (ed) The Oxford Dictionary of Natural History, 1985; Your Child and the Computer, 1985; (with Jane Burton) Nine Lives, 1985; 2040: our world in the future, 1985; (with Jane Burton) A Dog's Life, 1986; The Woodland Trust Book of British Woodlands, 1986; Ecology Facts, 1986, 2nd edn as Green Facts, 1989; The Ordnance Survey Outdoor Handbook, 1987; (with Jane Burton) A Pony's Tale, 1987; Conservation at Home, 1988; (ed) Thinking Green: an anthology of essential ecological writing, 1989; Guide to Gaia, 1989; Into Harmony with the Planet, 1990; Living in the Greenhouse, 1990; (ed with Ailsa Allaby) The Concise Oxford Dictionary of Earth Sciences, 1991, 3rd edn 2008; (ed) The Concise Oxford Dictionary of Zoology, 1991, 3rd edn 2009; (ed) The Concise Oxford Dictionary of Botany, 1992, 2nd edn as Oxford Dictionary of Plant Sciences, 1998; Elements: water, 1992; Elements: air, 1992; Elements: earth, 1993; Elements: fire, 1993; (with Neil Curtis) Planet Earth: a visual factfinder, 1993; (ed) The Concise Oxford Dictionary of Ecology, 1994, 3rd edn 2005; How the Weather Works, 1995; Facing the Future, 1995; Basics of Environmental Science, 1996, 2nd edn 2000; (with Michael Kent) Collins Pocket Reference Biology, 1996; How it Works: the environment, 1996; Ecosystem: temperate forests, 1999, 2nd edn 2007; Biomes of the World, 9 vols, 1999; DK Guide to Weather, 2000; Plants and Plant Life, 5 vols of 10-vol. series: Plant Ecology, Plants Used By People, Conifers, Flowering Plants - The Monocotyledons, Flowering Plants - The Dicotyledons, 2001; Ecosystem: deserts, 2001, 2nd edn 2007; Megabites: tornadoes and other dramatic weather systems, 2001; (with Derek Gjertsen) Makers of Science, 5 vols, 2001; Encyclopedia of Weather and Climate, 2 vols, 2002, 2nd edn 2007; How it Works: the world's weather, 2002; The Facts on File Weather and Climate Handbook, 2002; *series:* Dangerous Weather: Hurricanes, 1997, 2nd edn 2003, Tornadoes, 1997, 2nd edn 2003, Blizzards, 1997, 2nd edn 2003, Droughts, 1998, 2nd edn 2003, A Chronology of Weather, 1998, 2nd edn 2003, Floods, 1998, 2nd edn 2003, A Change in the Weather, 2003, Fog, Smog, and Poisoned Rain, 2003; Biomes of the Earth: Deserts, 2005, Grasslands, 2005, Temperate Forests, 2005, Tropical Forests, 2005; Countries of the World: India, 2005. *Recreations:* gardening, reading, watching movies. *Address:* Braehead Cottage, Tighnabruaich, Argyll PA21 2ED. *T:* and *Fax:* (01700) 811332; *e-mail:* m.allaby@btinternet.com.

ALLAIN, Prof. Jean-Pierre Charles, MD, PhD; FRCPath, FMedSci; Professor of Transfusion Medicine, University of Cambridge, since 1991; *b* 26 Jan. 1942; *s* of Jacques Louis Allain and Marthe Charlotte (*née* Petitjean); *m* 1st, 1962, DucDung Nguyen (marr. diss.); two *s* two *d*; 2nd, 1978, Helen Lee. *Educ:* Univ. of Paris (MD 1967; PhD 1986). FRCPath 1992. Asst Prof. of Haematol., Univ. of Paris, 1967–70; Dir, French Red Cross Haemophilia Centre, 1970–77; Head, Coagulation Res. Lab., Nat. Blood Transfusion Centre, Paris, 1977–81; Head, Dept of R&D Plasma Protein Derivatives, Nat. Blood Transfusion Centre, Paris, 1981–86; Dir of Med. Res., Diagnostic Div., Abbott Labs, Chicago, 1986–91; Dir, E Anglian Blood Transfusion Centre, 1991–94. FMedSci 2000. *Publications:* 140 papers in learned jls incl. N Engl. Jl Med., Lancet, Jl of Clin. Invest., Jl Lab. Clin. Med., BMJ, Blood, Transfusion. *Recreations:* tennis, ceramics.

ALLAIRE, Paul Arthur; Chairman, 1991–2001, and Chief Executive Officer, 1990–99 and 2000–01, Xerox Corporation; *b* 21 July 1938; *s* of late Arthur E. Allaire and of Mrs G. P. Murphy; *m* 1963, Kathleen Buckley; one *s* one *d*. *Educ:* Worcester Polytechnic Inst., USA (BS Elect. Eng., 1960); Carnegie-Mellon Univ., USA (MS Industrial Admin, 1966). Engineer, Univac, 1960–62; Project Manager, General Electric, 1962–64; Manager Financial Planning and Pricing, Xerox Corp., 1966–70; Financial Controller, Rank Xerox Ltd, 1970–73; Xerox Corporation: Dir, Internat. Finance, 1973–74; Dir, Internat. Ops, 1974–75; Rank Xerox Ltd: Chief Staff Officer, 1975–79; Dep. Man. Dir, 1979–80; Man. Dir, 1980–83; Mem., Bd of Dirs; Sen. Vice-Pres., 1983–86, Pres., 1986–91, Xerox Corp. Former Member, Board of Directors: Sara Lee Corp.; Glaxo SmithKline; Lucent Technologies; Priceline.com; Council on Competitiveness; Council on For. Relations. Mem., Bd of Dirs, NY City Ballet, 2000–. Member, Board of Trustees: Carnegie Mellon Univ. (Mem., Business Adv. Council, Grad. Sch. of Indust. Admin); Worcester Polytechnic Inst., Mass. Mem., Nat. Acad. of Engrg. *Recreations:* horse riding, tennis.

ALLAIS, Prof. Maurice; Commandeur de la Légion d'honneur, 1989; Officier des Palmes académiques, 1949; Chevalier de l'économie nationale, 1962; Grand Croix de l'Ordre National du Mérite, 1998; French economist and engineer; *b* 31 May 1911; *s* of Maurice Allais and Louise (*née* Caubet); *m* 1960, Jacqueline Bouteloup (decd); one *d*. *Educ:* Lycée Lakanal à Sceaux; Lycée Louis-le-Grand; Ecole Polytechnique; Ecole Nationale Supérieure des Mines de Paris. Engineer, Dept of Mines and Quarries, Nantes, 1937–43; Dir, Bureau de Documentation Minière, 1943–48; Prof. of Economic Analysis, Ecole Nationale Supérieure des Mines de Paris, 1944–88; Dir, Centre for Economic Analysis, 1946–; Prof. of Economic Theory, Inst. of Statistics, Univ. of Paris, 1947–68; research in economics, 1948–; Dir of Res., Centre National de la Recherche Scientifique, 1954–80; Prof., Graduate Inst. of Internat. Studies, Geneva, 1967–70; Dir, Clément Juglar Centre of Monetary Analysis, Univ of Paris, 1970–85. Fellow: Operations Res. Soc., 1958; Internat. Soc. of Econometrics, 1949. Mem. de l'Académie des Sciences Morales et Politiques, 1990; Hon. Mem., Amer. Econ. Assoc., 1976; Associate Foreign Member: US Nat. Acad. of Scis, 1989; Accademia Nazionale dei Lincei, Rome, 1991; l'Académie des Sciences de Russie, 1999. Dr *hc:* Univ. of Groningen, 1964; Univ. of Mons, 1992; Amer. Univ. of Paris, 1992; Univ. of Lisbon, 1993; Ecole des Hautes Etudes Commerciales, 1993. Prizes from: L'Académie des Sciences, 1933; L'Académie des Sciences Morales et Politiques, 1954, 1959, 1983, 1984. Gravity Res. Foundn, 1959; also Lanchester Prize, Amer. Economic Assoc., 1958; Prix Galabert, 1959; Grand Prix André Arnoux, 1968; Gold Medal, Centre National de la Recherche Scientifique, 1978; Nobel Prize for Economics, 1988. *Publications* include: A la recherche d'une discipline économique, 1943, 2nd edn as Traité d'Economie Pure, 1952, 3rd edn 1994; Abondance ou misère, 1946; Economie et Intérêt, 1947, 2nd edn 1997; Les fondements comptables de la macroéconomique, 1954, 2nd edn 1992; Manifeste pour une société libre, 1959; L'Europe unie, route de la prosperité, 1960; The Role of Capital in Economic Development, 1963; Growth without Inflation, 1968; Les théories de l'équilibre économique général et de l'éfficacité maximale, 1971; Inequality and Civilization, 1973; L'impôt sur le capital et la réforme monétaire, 1977, 2nd edn 1988; La théorie générale des surplus, 1980, 2nd edn 1989; Frequency, Probability and Chance, 1982; Determination of Cardinal Utility, 1985; Les conditions monétaires d'une économie de marchés, 1987; Autoportraits, 1989; Pour l'indexation, 1990; Pour la réforme de la fiscalité, 1990; L'Europe face à son avenir, que faire, 1991; Erreurs et impasses de la construction européenne, 1992; Combats pour l'Europe, 1994; Cardinalism, 1994; L'Anisotropie de l'espace, 1997; La Crise Mondiale d'aujourd'hui, 1999; L'Union européene: la mondialisation et le chômage, 1999; Des régularités significatives dans les observations interferométriques de Dayton C. Miller, 1997–2000; Fondements de la dynamique Monétaire, 2001; La Passion de la recherche, 2001; Un savant méconnu, 2002. *Address:* (office) 60 boulevard Saint Michel, 75006 Paris, France; *e-mail:* m.gendrot@clubinternet.fr.

ALLAM, Peter John; Architect Principal in private practice of Peter Allam, Chartered Architect, Dollar, 1964–68, 1971–78 and since 1981; *b* 17 June 1927; *er s* of late Leslie Francis Allam and Annette Farquharson (*née* Lawson); *m* 1961, Pamela Mackie Haynes; two *d. Educ:* Royal High Sch., Edinburgh; Glasgow Sch. of Architecture. War service, 1944–48, Far East; commnd in Seaforth Highlanders, 1946. Architectural trng, 1948–53. Bahrain Petroleum Co., Engrg Div., 1954–55; Asst in private architectural practices, 1956–64; Partner in private practice of Haswell-Smith & Partners, Edinburgh, 1978–79; Director, Saltire Soc., 1968–70; Dir of Sales, Smith & Wellstood Ltd, Manfg Ironfounders, 1979–81. ARIBA 1964; FRIAS 1985 (Associate, 1964). Sen. Observer, IAM, 1994. British Red Cross Trng Monitor, 2004–. VMSM 1999. *Recreations:* grandchildren, painting, singing in the bath. *Address:* 48 The Ness, Dollar, Clackmannanshire FK14 7EB. *T:* (01259) 742973.

ALLAM, Roger William; actor; *b* 26 Oct. 1953; *s* of Rev. William Sydney Allam and Kathleen Allam (*née* Service); partner, Rebecca Saire; two *s. Educ:* Christ's Hosp.; Univ. of Manchester (BA). With Royal Shakespeare Co., 1981–, Associate Artist, 1990–: rôles include: Mercutio in Romeo and Juliet, Oberon in Midsummer Night's Dream, 1984; Javert in Les Misérables, transf. Palace Th., 1985; Brutus in Julius Caesar, Duke Vincentio in Measure for Measure, Toby Belch in Twelfth Night, 1987; Benedick in Much Ado About Nothing, 1990; National Theatre, 1999–: rôles include: Graves in Money (Olivier Award for Best Supporting Actor, 2000), Ulysses in Troilus and Cressida (Clarence Derwent Award), Bassov in Summerfolk, 1999; Hitler in Albert Speer, Lophakin in The Cherry Orchard, 2000; Willy Brandt in Democracy, 2003, transf. Wyndham's, 2004; Reinhardt in Afterlife, 2008; West End includes: City of Angels, Prince of Wales, 1993; Arcadia, Haymarket, 1994; Importance of Being Earnest, Old Vic, 1995; Art, Wyndham's, 1997; Privates on Parade, Donmar, 2001 (Olivier Award for Best Actor, 2002); Aladdin, Old Vic, 2004, 2005; Boeing-Boeing, Comedy, 2007; other performances include: Blackbird, Edinburgh Fest., 2005, transf. Albery, 2006; Pravda, Chichester Festival Th., 2006; *films* include: A Cock & Bull Story, 2005; V for Vendetta, The Wind That Shakes the Barley, The Queen, 2006; Speed Racer, 2008. *Publications:* contrib. chapters to Players of Shakespeare, vol. II and vol. III. *Recreations:* playing and listening to music, cooking, drinking red wine. *Address:* c/o Claire Maroussas, Independent Talent Group Ltd, Oxford House, 76 Oxford Street, W1D 1BS. *T:* (020) 7636 6565, *Fax:* (020) 7323 9867. *Club:* 2 Brydges.

ALLAN; *see* Havelock-Allan.

ALLAN, Dr Alasdair James; Member (SNP) Western Isles, Scottish Parliament, since 2007; *b* Edinburgh, 6 May 1971; *s* of John H. Allan and Christine M. Allan. *Educ:* Selkirk High Sch.; Glasgow Univ. (MA Scottish Lang. and Lit.); Aberdeen Univ. (PhD Scots Lang. 1998). Sen. Vice Pres., Students' Rep. Council, Glasgow Univ., 1991–92. Teaching asst, English Dept, Aberdeen Univ., 1995–97; researcher, SNP HQ, 1998–99; Parliamentary Assistant: to Michael Russell, MSP, 1999–2002; to Alex Salmond, MP, 2002–04; Policy and Parly Affairs Manager, Carers Scotland, 2004–05; Sen. Media Relns Officer, Ch of Scotland, 2005–06; Parly Asst to Angus MacNeil, MP, 2006–07. Nat. Sec., SNP, 2003–06. Vice-Pres., Scots Lang. Soc., 1996–99. *Publication:* Talking Independence, 2001. *Recreations:* campaigning for independence, singing in local Gaelic choir (Mem., Back Gaelic Choir, Isle of Lewis). *Address:* (office) 31 Bayhead, Stornoway, Isle of Lewis HS1 2DU. *T:* (01851) 702272, *Fax:* (01851) 701767; *e-mail:* alasdair.allan.msp@scottish.parliament.uk; *web:* www.alasdairallanmsp.com.

ALLAN, Alexander Claud Stuart; Chairman, Joint Intelligence Committee and Head of Intelligence Assessment, Cabinet Office, since 2007; *b* 9 Feb. 1951; *s* of Lord Allan of Kilmahew, DSO, OBE and of Maureen (*née* Stuart Clark); *m* 1978, Katie Christine Clemson (*d* 2007). *Educ:* Harrow Sch.; Clare College, Cambridge; University College London (MSc). HM Customs and Excise, 1973–76; HM Treasury, 1976–92; secondments in Australia, 1983–84; Principal Private Sec. to Chancellor of the Exchequer, 1986–89; Under Sec. (Internat. Finance), 1989–90; Under Sec. (Gen. Expenditure Policy), 1990–92; Principal Private Sec. to PM, 1992–97; High Comr, Australia, 1997–99; UK Govt e-envoy, 1999–2000; Perm. Sec., DCA, subseq. MoJ, 2004–07. Mem., Premier's Science Council, WA, 2001–04. Mem., Senate, Univ. of WA, 2002–04. Mem., Royal S Beach Cycling Assoc., WA, 1983–. *Recreations:* Grateful Dead music, sailing, computers. *Address:* Cabinet Office, 70 Whitehall, SW1A 2AS; *e-mail:* alex.allan@whitegum.com. *Club:* Royal Ocean Racing.

ALLAN, Andrew Norman; Chairman, Codeworks, since 2005; *b* 26 Sept. 1943; *s* of Andrew Allan and Elizabeth (*née* Davison); *m*; two *s* three *d. Educ:* Birmingham Univ. (BA). Presenter, ABC Television, 1965–67; Producer: ITN, 1968; Thames Television, 1969–77; Head of News, Thames TV, 1977–78; Tyne Tees Television: Dir of Progs, 1978–82; Dep. Man. Dir, 1982–83; Man. Dir, 1983–84; Dir of Progs, Central Indep. TV, 1984–90; Managing Director: Central Broadcasting, 1990–93; Central Indep. TV, 1993–94; Chief Exec., 1994–95, Dir of Progs, 1996–98, Carlton TV. Chairman: Birmingham Rep. Theatre, 2000–05; Route4 plc, 2001–05. *Recreations:* theatre, music, reading, dining. *Address:* Cheviot View, Hedley, Stocksfield, Northumberland NE43 7SW.

ALLAN, Christopher David; QC 1995; a Recorder, since 1993; *b* 5 April 1952; *s* of Herbert Roy Allan and Joan (*née* Womersly); *m* 1977, Lynne Margaret Hosking; one *s* three *d. Educ:* Teignmouth Grammar Sch.; Manchester Univ. (LLB). Called to the Bar, Gray's Inn, 1974; Mem., Northern Circuit, 1975–. *Recreations:* tennis, theatre, walking. *Address:* 12 Byrom Street, Manchester M3 4PF. *T:* (0161) 829 2100; 22 Old Buildings, WC2A 3UJ.

ALLAN, Diana Rosemary, (Mrs R. B. Allan); *see* Cotton, D. R.

ALLAN, Douglas; *see* Allan, J. D.

ALLAN, Gary James Graham; QC (Scot.) 2007; Senior Advocate Depute (Crown Counsel), since 2007; *b* Aberdeen, 21 Jan. 1958; *s* of Stanley Gibson Allan and Margaret Harrison Allan (*née* Graham); *m* 1986, Margaret Muriel Glass; one *s* one *d. Educ:* Aberdeen Grammar Sch.; Univ. of Aberdeen (LLB Hons). Apprentice solicitor, McGrigor Donald and Co., Glasgow, 1980–82; Hughes Dowdall, Glasgow: Solicitor, 1982–86; Partner, 1986–93; admitted Faculty of Advocates, 1994. *Recreations:* watching sport, music, reading, food and drink with friends, the pursuit of opportunities to do absolutely nothing. *Address:* Advocates Library, Parliament House, Edinburgh EH1 1RF. *T:* (0131) 226 5071; *e-mail:* gary.allan@compasschambers.com.

ALLAN, George Alexander, MA; Headmaster, Robert Gordon's College, Aberdeen, 1978–96; *b* 3 Feb. 1936; *s* of William Allan and Janet Peters (*née* Watt); *m* 1962, Anne Violet Veevers; two *s. Educ:* Daniel Stewart's Coll., Edinburgh; Edinburgh Univ. (MA 1st Cl. Hons Classics; Bruce of Grangehill Scholar, 1957). Classics Master, Glasgow Acad., 1958–60; Daniel Stewart's College: Classics Master, 1960–63; Head of Classics, 1963–73; Housemaster, 1966–73; Schoolmaster Fellow, Corpus Christi Coll., Cambridge, 1972; Dep. Headmaster, Robert Gordon's Coll., 1973–77. Headmasters' Conference: Sec., 1980–86, Chm., 1988, 1989, Scottish Div.; Mem. Cttee, 1982, 1983; Mem., ISIS Scotland Cttee, 1984–93; Council Mem., Scottish Council of Indep. Schs, 1988–96, 1997–2002. Dir, Edinburgh Acad., 1996–2003; Governor: Welbeck Coll., 1980–89; Longridge Towers Sch., 2004–. Mem., Scottish Adv. Cttee, ICRF, 1996–97. *Recreations:* gardening, music. *Address:* Maxwiel, 5 Abbey View, Kelso TD5 8HX. *T:* (01573) 225128.

ALLAN, Rt Rev. Hugh James Pearson, DD; Assistant Bishop of Nova Scotia, 1991–94; *b* 7 Aug. 1928; *s* of Hugh Blomfield Allan and Agnes Dorothy (*née* Pearson); *m* 1955, Beverley Edith Baker; one *s* three *d. Educ:* St John's Coll., Univ. of Manitoba (LTh 1955, BA 1957). Deacon 1954, priest 1955; Assistant: St Aidan's, Winnipeg, 1954; All Saints, Winnipeg, 1955; Missionary, Peguis Indian Reserve, 1956–60; Rector, St Mark's, Winnipeg, 1960–68; Hon. Canon, Diocese of Rupert's Land, 1967; Rector, St Stephen's Swift Current, Sask., 1968–70; Rural Dean of Cypress, 1968–70; Dean of Qu'Appelle and Rector of St Paul's Cathedral, Regina, Sask., 1970–74; Bishop of Keewatin, 1974–91. Hon. DD, St John's Coll., Univ. of Manitoba, 1974. *Recreations:* ornithology, boating. *Address:* 235 One Snow Street, Winnipeg, MB R3T 2M4, Canada.

ALLAN, Ian, OBE 1995; Chairman, Ian Allan Group Ltd, since 1962; *b* 29 June 1922; *s* of George A. T. Allan, OBE, and Mary Louise (*née* Barnes); *m* 1947, Mollie Eileen (*née* Franklin); two *s. Educ:* St Paul's Sch. Joined Southern Railway Co., 1939. Founded Ian Allan Ltd, Publishers, 1945; other cos co-ordinated into Ian Allan Group Ltd, 1962. Dir, Dart Valley Light Railway PLC, 1968–2004 (Chm., 1976–87). Governor, Christ's Hosp., 1944–, Almoner, 1980–89; Chm., King Edward's Sch., Witley, 1983–95 (Governor, 1975–95); Treas., Bridewell Royal Hosp. 1983–95. Vice President: Transport Trust, 1979–; Assoc. of Indep. Rlys, 1997– (Chm., 1987–97); Heritage Rlys Assoc., 1996–; Mem., Transport Users Consultative Cttee for London, 1982–84. Pres., Main Line Steam Trust (Great Central Rly), 1995–. Patron, Mid Hants Rly plc, 1994–. Freeman, City of London, 1986. Hon. Freeman, Borough of Spelthorne, 2001. FCIT 1992. *Publications:* compiled and edited many books on railways and transport subjects, 1939–. *Recreations:* swimming, touring, miniature railways, Freemasonry. *Address:* Terminal House, Shepperton TW17 8AS. *T:* (01932) 255500; The Jetty, Middleton-on-Sea, Bognor Regis, W Sussex PO22 7TS. *T:* (01243) 593378.

ALLAN, James Nicholas, CMG 1989; CBE 1976; HM Diplomatic Service, retired; *b* 22 May 1932; *s* of late Morris Edward Allan and Joan Bach; *m* 1961, Helena Susara Crouse (*d* 2001); one *s* one *d. Educ:* Gresham's Sch.; London Sch. of Economics (BSc (Econ)). HM Forces, 1950–53. Asst Principal, CRO, 1956–58; Third, later Second Sec., Cape Town/Pretoria, 1958–59; Private Sec. to Parly Under-Sec., 1959–61; First Secretary: Freetown, 1961–64; Nicosia, 1964; CRO, later FCO, 1964–68; Head of Chancery, Peking, 1969–71; Luxembourg, 1971–73; Counsellor, seconded to Northern Ireland Office, Belfast, 1973–75; Counsellor, FCO, 1976; Head of Overseas Inf. Dept., FCO, 1978–81 (Governor's Staff, Salisbury, Dec. 1979–March 1980); High Comr in Mauritius, 1981–85, concurrently Ambassador (non-resident) to the Comoros, 1984–85; Ambassador to Mozambique, 1986–89; Sen. Directing Staff, RCDS, 1989–92. Mem., Commonwealth Observer Gp, S African elecns, 1994. *Address:* 7 The Orchard, SE3 0QS. *Club:* Athenæum.

See also Baron Bach.

ALLAN, Prof. James Wilson, DPhil; Professor of Eastern Art, University of Oxford, since 1996; Fellow of St Cross College, Oxford, 1990–2005, now Emeritus; *b* 5 May 1945; *s* of John Bellerby Allan and Evelyn Mary Allan; *m* 1970, Jennifer Robin Hawksworth; two *s* two *d. Educ:* Marlborough Coll.; St Edmund Hall, Oxford (MA 1966; DPhil 1976). Ashmolean Museum: Asst Keeper, 1966–88, Sen. Asst Keeper, 1988–91, Keeper, 1991–2005, Eastern Art Dept; Dir, Ashmolean Inter-Faith Exhibitions Service, 2005–06. *Publications:* Medieval Middle Eastern Pottery, 1971; Persian Metal Technology 700–1300 AD, 1978; Islamic Metalwork: the Nuhad Es-Said Collection, 1982; Nishapur: metalwork of the early Islamic period, 1982; Metalwork of the Islamic World: the Aron Collection, 1986; (ed) Creswell: A Short Account of Early Muslim Architecture, 1989; (with B. Gilmour) Persian Steel: the Tanavoli Collection, 2000. *Recreations:* music, ornithology, walking, travel. *Address:* Khalili Research Centre, 3 St John Street, Oxford OX1 2LG. *T:* (01865) 288355.

ALLAN, (John) Douglas, OBE 2006; Sheriff of Lothian and Borders at Edinburgh, since 2000; *b* 2 Oct. 1941; *s* of late Robert Taylor Allan and Christina Helen Blythe Reid or Allan; *m* 1966, Helen Elizabeth Jean Aiton or Allan; one *s* one *d. Educ:* George Watson's Coll.; Edinburgh Univ. (BL); Napier Coll., Edinburgh (DMS). Solicitor and Notary Public. Solicitor, 1963–67; Depute Procurator Fiscal, 1967–71; Sen. Legal Asst, Crown Office, 1971–76; Asst Procurator Fiscal, Glasgow, 1976–77; Sen. Asst Procurator Fiscal, Glasgow, 1978–79; Asst Solicitor, Crown Office, 1979–83; Regl Procurator Fiscal for Lothian and Borders and Procurator Fiscal for Edinburgh, 1983–88; Sheriff of South Strathclyde, Dumfries and Galloway at Lanark, 1988–2000. Bd Mem., Scottish Children's Reporter Admin, 1995–2003 (Dep. Chm., 2002–03); Mem., Judicial Appts Bd for Scotland, 2002–. Chm., Judicial Commn, Gen. Assembly of C of S, 1998–2003. Pres., Sheriffs' Assoc., 2000–02 (Vice Pres., 1997–2000; Sec., 1991–97); Regl Vice-Pres., Commonwealth Magistrates' and Judges' Assoc., 2003– (Mem., Council, 2000–03). *Recreations:* youth work, church work, walking. *Address:* Sheriff Court, 27 Chambers Street, Edinburgh EH1 1LB; Minard, 80 Greenbank Crescent, Edinburgh EH10 5SW. *T:* (0131) 447 2593.

ALLAN, John Murray, CBE 2005; Chief Financial Officer, Deutsche Post World Net, since 2007 (Member, Management Board, since 2006); *b* 20 Aug. 1948; *s* of Archibald John and Anna Allan; *m* 1st, 1970, Ewa Gaczol (marr. diss. 1998); two *d*; 2nd, 1999, Carole Thomas. *Educ:* Edinburgh Univ. (BSc Hons Mathematical Sci.). Brand Manager, Lever Bros, 1970–73; Mkting Manager, Bristol Myers, 1973–77; Fine Fare: Mkting Dir, 1977–83; Dir, 1980; Mkting and Buying Dir, 1983–84; Dir and Gen. Manager, 1984–85; BET: Divl Chm., 1985–87; Dir, 1987–94; Chief Exec., Ocean Gp, later Exel plc, 1994–2005; Chief Exec., DHL Logistics, 2006–07. Chm., CBI Transport Policy Cttee, 1998–2001; Mem., CBI President's Cttee, 2001–. Non-executive Director: Wolseley plc, 1999–2004; PHS plc, 2001–. Chm., Freight Forwarders Europe, 2006–07 (Vice Chm., 2002–06). Chm., Mkting Soc. of GB, 1983–84. Mem., Internat. Adv. Cttee, Singapore Economic Develt Bd, 2002–07. Trustee, Univ. of Edinburgh Develt Trusts, 1991–2000; Mem., Univ. of Edinburgh Campaign Bd, 2000–. FInstD 1986 (Mem. Council,

1991–99); CCMI (CIMgt 1995). FRSA 1995. *Recreations:* reading, conversation, history. *Address:* Deutsche Post World Net, Charles-de-Gaulle Strasse 20, 53113 Bonn, Germany.

ALLAN, Richard Andrew; Director, Regional Policy and Local Government, Office of the Deputy Prime Minister (formerly Department for Transport, Local Government and the Regions), 2001–05; *b* 28 Feb. 1948; *s* of late Kenneth and of Mary Allan; *m* 1975, Katharine Mary Tait; one *s* one *d. Educ:* Bolton Sch.; Balliol Coll., Oxford (MA Mod. Hist.). VSO, Nigeria, 1970. Asst Principal, DTI, 1970; Asst British Trade Comr, Hong Kong, 1973; Department of Industry: Private Sec. to Perm. Sec., 1974–75; Principal, 1975–79; First Sec. (Civil Aviation and Shipping), Washington, 1980–84; Department of Transport: Asst Sec., 1984; Principal Private Sec. to Sec. of State for Transport, 1985–87; Under Sec., 1988; seconded to BRB, 1988–90; Dir of Personnel, 1990–94; Head, Urban and Local Transport Directorate, 1994–97; Dir, London Transport Directorate, DETR, 1997–98; Dir, New London Governance, Govt Office for London, 1998–2000; Dir, Regl Policy and Regeneration, DETR, 2000–01. *Recreations:* choral singing, theatre, walking. *Address:* 1 Ellerton Road, SW18 3NG.

ALLAN, Richard Beecroft; Head of Government Relations, UK and Ireland, Cisco Systems, since 2005; *b* 11 Feb. 1966; *s* of John and Elizabeth Allan; *m* 1991, Louise Maria Netley (marr. diss. 2001); one *d. Educ:* Pembroke Coll., Cambridge (BA Hons Archaeology and Anthropology); Bristol Poly. (MSc IT). Archaeologist, 1988–90; NHS Computer Manager, 1991–97. MP (Lib Dem) Sheffield, Hallam, 1997–2005. Chm., Power of Inf. Task Force, 2008–. *Recreation:* visiting sites of historical interest and natural beauty. *Address: e-mail:* richard@richardallan.org.uk.

ALLAN, William Roderick Buchanan; formerly Arts Consultant to United Technologies Corporation, working with Tate Gallery, National Portrait Gallery and National Maritime Museum; *b* 11 Sept. 1945; *s* of James Buchanan Allan and Mildred Pattenden; *m* 1973, Gillian Gail Colgan (*d* 2004); two *s. Educ:* Stowe; Trinity Coll., Cambridge (MA Hons History, 1970). Joined staff of The Connoisseur, 1972, Editor 1976–80; Editorial Consultant to Ommific, 1980–83. Author of seven radio plays with nineteenth century historical themes. *Publications:* contrib. to several books dealing with British history; contrib. to History Today, The Connoisseur, and Antique Collector. *Recreations:* military history, cooking. *Address:* 52 Jamieson House, Edgar Road, Hounslow, Middlesex TW4 5QH.

ALLANBRIDGE, Hon. Lord; William Ian Stewart; a Senator of the College of Justice in Scotland, 1977–95; *b* 8 Nov. 1925; *s* of late John Stewart, FRIBA, and Mrs Maysie Shepherd Service or Stewart, Drimfearn, Bridge of Allan; *m* 1955, Naomi Joan Douglas (*d* 2005), *d* of late Sir James Boyd Douglas, CBE, and Lady Douglas, Barstibly, Castle Douglas; one *s* one *d. Educ:* Loretto; Glasgow and Edinburgh Univs. Sub-Lt, RNVR, 1944–46. Called to the Bar, 1951; QC (Scot.) 1965; Advocate-Depute, 1959–64; Mem., Criminal Injuries Compensation Bd, 1969–70, 1976–77; Home Advocate-Depute, 1970–72; Solicitor-General for Scotland, 1972–74; Temp. Sheriff-Principal of Dumfries and Galloway, April–Dec. 1974; Justice of Appeal, Republic of Botswana, 1996–99. *Address:* 60 Northumberland Street, Edinburgh EH3 6JE. *T:* (0131) 556 2823. *Club:* New (Edinburgh).

ALLASON, Lt-Col James Harry, OBE 1953; *b* 6 Sept. 1912; *s* of late Brigadier-General Walter Allason, DSO; *m* 1946, Nuala Elveen (marr. diss. 1974; she *d* 2008), *d* of late J. A. McArevey, Foxrock, Co. Dublin; two *s. Educ:* Haileybury; RMA, Woolwich. Commissioned RA, 1932; transferred 3rd DG, 1937; War Service India and Burma, 1939–44; retired 1953. Member Kensington Borough Council, 1956–65. Contested (C) Hackney Central, General Election, 1955; MP (C) Hemel Hempstead, 1959–Sept. 1974; PPS to Sec. of State for War, 1960–64. *Publication:* Ringside Seat, 2007. *Address:* 82 Ebury Mews, SW1W 9NX. *T:* (020) 7730 1576. *Clubs:* White's; Royal Yacht Squadron.

See also R. W. S. Allason.

ALLASON, Rupert William Simon; European Editor, World Intelligence Review (formerly Intelligence Quarterly), since 1985; *b* 8 Nov. 1951; *s* of Lt-Col J. H. Allason, *qv*; *m* 1979, Nicole Jane (marr. diss. 1996), *y d* of late M. L. Van Moppes; one *s* one *d. Educ:* Downside; Grenoble Univ.; London Univ. (external). Special Constable, 1975–82. BBC TV, 1978–82. Contested (C): Kettering, 1979; Battersea, 1983. MP (C) Torbay, 1987–97; contested (C) same seat, 1997. *Publications:* The Branch: A History of the Metropolitan Police Special Branch 1883–1983, 1983; *as Nigel West:* non-fiction: Spy! (with Richard Deacon), 1980; MI5: British Security Service Operations 1909–45, 1981; A Matter of Trust: MI5 1945–72, 1982; MI6: British Secret Intelligence Service Operations 1909–45, 1983; Unreliable Witnesses: espionage myths of World War II, 1984; Garbo (with Juan Pujol), 1985; GCHQ: The Secret Wireless War, 1986; Molehunt, 1987; The Friends: Britain's post-war secret intelligence operations, 1988; Games of Intelligence, 1989; Seven Spies Who Changed the World, 1991; Secret War, 1992; The Illegals, 1993; (ed) Faber Book of Espionage, 1993; (ed) Faber Book of Treachery, 1995; The Secret War for the Falklands, 1997; Counterfeit Spies, 1998; (with Oleg Tsarev) The Crown Jewels: the British secrets at the heart of the KGB archives, 1998; (ed) British Security Co-ordination: the secret history of British Intelligence in the Americas 1940–1945, 1998; Venona: the greatest secret of the Cold War, 1999; The Third Secret, 2000; Mortal Crimes, 2004; (ed) The Guy Liddell Diaries, 2005; Mask, 2005; Historical Dictionary of British Intelligence, 2005; On Her Majesty's Secret Service, 2006; Historical Dictionary of International Intelligence, 2006; Historical Dictionary of Cold War Counterintelligence, 2007; Historical Dictionary of World War II Intelligence, 2008; fiction: The Blue List, 1989; Cuban Bluff, 1990; Murder in the Commons, 1992; Murder in the Lords, 1994. *Recreations:* sailing, ski-ing. *Address:* 6 Burton Mews, SW1W 9EP. *Clubs:* White's, Special Forces; Royal Yacht Squadron (Cowes).

ALLCHIN, Rev. Canon Arthur Macdonald; Hon. Professor, University of Wales, Bangor, since 1992; *b* 20 April 1930; *s* of late Dr Frank Macdonald Allchin and Louise Maude Allchin. *Educ:* Westminster Sch.; Christ Church, Oxford (BLitt, MA); Cuddesdon Coll., Oxford. Curate, St Mary Abbots, Kensington, 1956–60; Librarian, Pusey House, Oxford, 1960–69; Warden, Community of Sisters of Love of God, Oxford, 1967–94; Res. Canon of Canterbury, 1973–87, Hon. Canon, 1988–. Programme Dir, St Theosevia Centre for Christian Spirituality, Oxford, 1987–96. Visiting Lecturer: General Theological Seminary, NY, 1967 and 1968; Catholic Theological Faculty, Lyons, 1980; Trinity Inst., NY, 1983; Vis. Prof., Nashotah House, Wisconsin, 1984, 1995. Editor, Sobornost, 1960–77; Jt Editor, Christian, 1975–80. Hon. DD: Bucharest Theol Inst., 1977; Nashotah House, 1985; Aarhus, 1992; Wales, 1993; Lambeth, 2006. *Publications:* The Silent Rebellion, 1958; The Spirit and the Word, 1963; (with J. Coulson) The Rediscovery of Newman, 1967; Ann Griffiths, 1976; The World is a Wedding, 1978; The Kingdom of Love and Knowledge, 1979; The Dynamic of Tradition, 1981; A Taste of Liberty, 1982; The Joy of All Creation, 1984, 2nd edn 1993; (with E. de Waal) Threshold of Light, 1986; Participation in God, 1988; The Heart of Compassion, 1989; Landscapes of Glory, 1989; Praise Above All, 1991; (ed with D. Jasper and contrib.) Heritage and Prophecy, 1993; God's Presence Makes the World, 1997; N. F. S. Grundtvig: an introduction to his life and work, 1997; Resurrection's Children, 1998; (with D. Morgan

and P. Thomas) Sensuous Glory: the poetic vision of D. Gwenallt Jones, 2000; (ed with S. Bradley and contrib.) Grundtvig in International Perspective, 2000; Friendship in God: Evelyn Underhill and Sorella Maria, 2003; The Gift of Theology, 2005; contrib. Studia Liturgica, Irenikon, Theology, Eastern Churches Review, Worship, One in Christ, Planet, Logos, Collectanea Cisterciensia. *Recreations:* music, poetry, enjoying hill country. *Address:* 1 Trem yr Wyddfa, Bangor LL57 2ER. *T:* (01248) 353744.

See also F. R. Allchin.

ALLCHIN, Frank Raymond, PhD; FBA 1981; Fellow of Churchill College, since 1963, and Reader in Indian Studies, 1972–90, University of Cambridge; Reader Emeritus, since 1990; *b* 9 July 1923; *s* of late Frank MacDonald Allchin and Louise Maude Wright; *m* 1951, Bridget Gordon; one *s* one *d. Educ:* Westminster Sch.; Regent Street Polytechnic; Sch. of Oriental and African Studies, London Univ. (BA, PhD 1954); MA Cantab. Lectr in Indian Archaeology, SOAS, 1954–59; Univ. Lectr in Indian Studies, Cambridge, 1959–72. Jt Dir, Cambridge Univ. (British) Archaeol Mission to Pakistan, 1975–92. Chairman: Ancient India and Iran Trust, 1995– (Treas., 1978–86, 1989–2001); British Assoc. for Conservation of Cultural Heritage of Sri Lanka, 1996–2003 (Vice Chm., 1982–91; Acting Chm., 1990–96); Dir, British Anuradhapura Project, Sri Lanka, 1989–93. Consultant: UNESCO, 1969, 1972, 1975; UNDP, 1971. Hon. DLitt Deccan Coll., Pune, India, 2007. *Publications:* Piklihal Excavations, 1960; Utnur Excavations, 1961; Neolithic Cattle Keepers of South India, 1963; Kavitāvalī, 1964; The Petition to Rām, 1966; (with B. Allchin) Birth of Indian Civilization, 1968; (with N. Hammond) The Archaeology of Afghanistan, 1978; (with D. K. Chakrabarti) Sourcebook of Indian Archaeology, vol. 1, 1979, vol 2, 1997, vol 3, 2003; (with B. Allchin) The Rise of Civilization in India and Pakistan, 1982; (jtly) The Archaeology of Early Historic South Asia, 1995; (with B. Allchin) The Origins of a Civilisation, 1997; contribs to learned journals. *Recreations:* gardening, walking, reading, bat watching, currently writing memoirs (with B. Allchin). *Address:* 2 Shepreth Road, Barrington, Cambridge CB22 7SB. *T:* (01223) 870494. *Club:* India International Centre (New Delhi).

See also Rev. Canon A. M. Allchin.

ALLCOCK, Stephen James, QC 1993; *b* 29 Jan. 1952; *s* of James Allcock and Pamela Eve Allcock. *Educ:* Bristol Grammar Sch.; Jesus Coll., Cambridge (BA). Called to the Bar, Gray's Inn, 1975; private practice, 1977–99; with PricewaterhouseCoopers, 2001–04. *Recreations:* motor cars, business, stock market, piano. *Club:* Groucho.

ALLDAY, Coningsby, CBE 1971; BSc (Hons); Chairman and Chief Executive, British Nuclear Fuels plc, 1983–86 (Managing Director, 1971–83); *b* 21 Nov. 1920; *s* of late Esca and Margaret Allday; *m* 1st, 1945, Iris Helena, (Bobbin), Adams (*d* 1990); one *s* one *d*; 2nd, 1993, Rosalind Roberts. *Educ:* Solihull Sch.; BSc (Hons) Chemistry, London. CEng, FIChemE 1979. ICI, 1939–59; UKAEA, 1959–71: Chief Chemist, Technical Dir, Commercial Dir, Dep. Man. Dir; Mem. UKAEA, 1976–86. Chairman, NIMTECH NW, 1986–90; Director: North Region, National Westminster Bank, 1985–92; Sonomatic Ltd, 1988–90. FRSA. Hon. DSc Salford, 1985. Chevalier, Légion d'Honneur, 1983.

ALLDEN, Alison; Deputy Registrar, Librarian and Director of Information Services, University of Bristol, since 2003; *b* 3 April 1954; *d* of Michael Allden and Jean Allden (*née* Reynolds); *m* 1989, David McCutcheon (*d* 2004); one *s* one *d. Educ:* Sch. of St Helen and St Katharine, Abingdon; Univ. of Bristol (BA Hons 1976); London Sch. of Econs (MSc Dist. 1988). MIFA 1985; MBCS 1988, FBCS; MCLIP 1992. Archaeologist, DoE, 1977–82; Co. Archaeologist, Glos CC, 1982–85; Researcher: BM, 1985–89; Nat. Maritime Mus., 1989–91; Computer Services Manager, Goldsmiths' Coll., Univ. of London, 1994–98; Dir, IT Services, Univ. of Warwick, 1998–2003. Member: Res. Resources Bd, ESRC, 2002–05; JISC Bd, HEFC, 2005– (Mem., 1998–, Chm., 2005–, JISC subcttees); Educn and Trng Forum, BCS, 2007–. Gov., Sch. of St Helen and St Katharine, Abingdon, 2002–. *Publications:* contrib. articles on archaeol., computing and mus. mgt to books and jls. *Recreations:* family, archaeology and culture, life-long learning. *Address:* University of Bristol, Senate House, Tyndall Avenue, Bristol BS8 1TH. *T:* (0117) 928 8106, *Fax:* (0117) 929 7547; *e-mail:* a.allden@bristol.ac.uk.

ALLDIS, Air Cdre Cecil Anderson, CBE 1962; DFC 1941; AFC 1956; RAF (retd); *b* 28 Sept. 1918; 2nd *s* of John Henry and Margaret Wright Alldis, Birkenhead; *m* 1942, Jeanette Claire Tarrant, *d* of Albert Edward Collingwood and Aida Mary Tarrant, Johannesburg; no *c. Educ:* Birkenhead Institute; Emmanuel Coll., Cambridge (MA). Served War, 1939–45 (despatches, DFC): Pilot, Wing Comdr, RAF, Bomber Command. Asst Air Attaché, Moscow, 1947–49; Flying and Staff appts, RAF, 1949–59; Dir of Administrative Plans, Air Ministry, 1959–62; Air Attaché, Bonn, 1963–66. Retd from RAF and entered Home Civil Service, 1966; MoD, 1966–69; seconded to HM Diplomatic Service, 1969; Counsellor (Defence Supply), HM Embassy, Bonn, 1969–80; retired from Home Civil Service, 1980. Sec. Gen., The Air League, 1982–90. *Recreations:* walking, reading. *Address:* Tudor Cottage, Oxshott Way, Cobham, Surrey KT11 2RU. *T:* (01932) 866092.

ALLDIS, John; conductor; *b* 10 Aug. 1929; *s* of W. J. and N. Alldis; *m* 1960, Ursula Margaret Mason; two *s. Educ:* Felsted School; King's Coll., Cambridge (MA). ARCO. Formed John Alldis Choir, 1962; Founder and Conductor, London Symphony Chorus, 1966–69; Conductor, London Philharmonic Choir, 1969–82; Joint Chief Conductor, Radio Denmark, 1971–77; Conductor, Groupe Vocal de France, 1979–83; Chorus Master, Hallé Choir, 1992–93. Choral Prof., Guildhall Sch. of Music, 1966–79 (FGSM 1976); Music Consultant, Israel Chamber Choir (Cameran Singers), 1989–91. Mem., Vaughan Williams Trust, 1976–2003. Fellow, Westminster Choir Coll., Princeton, NJ, 1978. Chevalier des Arts et des Lettres (France), 1984. *Address:* 3 Wool Road, Wimbledon, SW20 0HN. *T:* (020) 8946 4168.

ALLEN, family name of **Baron Croham**.

ALLEN, Anthony John, CBE 1994; public sector consultant; *b* 7 Oct. 1939; *s* of late Raymond Houghton Allen and Elsie Zillah Allen; *m* 1st, 1964, Suzanne Myfanwy Davies; two *s*; 2nd, 1987, Helen Leah Graney; two *s. Educ:* Battersea Grammar Sch.; Univ. of Exeter (LLB 1961). Admitted Solicitor, 1964. Asst Solicitor: Hendon Bor. Council, 1964–65; Barnet Bor. Council, 1965; Watford Bor. Council, 1966–68; Asst Town Clerk, Coventry CBC, 1968–71; Asst. Chief Exec., Lewisham Bor. Council, 1971–72; Solicitor to the Council and Dep. Town Clerk, Southwark Bor. Council, 1972–76; Chief Exec., Hammersmith and Fulham Bor. Council, 1976–86; Chief Exec., and Clerk to Lieutenancy, Royal Co. of Berks, 1986–93; Chief Exec., NHBC, 1994–96. Lay Inspector of Constabulary, 1997–2001. Non-exec. Dir, BSI, 1992–95. Vice Chm., London Youth Games Ltd, 1979–. Chm., Working Party on Social and Psychol Aspects of Major Disasters (report published, 1990). CCMI (CIMgt 1992). Chm., W Berks CAB, 2005–. Chm. Govs. Newbury Coll., 2003–; Dir, Assoc. of Colleges, 2006–. *Recreations:* golf, travel. *Address:* Appledown, School Lane, Frilsham, Berks RG18 9XB. *T:* (01635) 201445.

ALLEN, Benedict Colin; author, adventurer; *b* 1 March 1960; *s* of late Colin Allen and Virginia Stafford. *Educ:* Bradfield Coll.; Univ. of E Anglia (BSc Hons). Television programmes: Raiders of the Lost Lake, 1995; Great Railway Journeys: Mombasa to the Mts of the Moon, 1996; The Skeleton Coast, 1997; Edge of Blue Heaven, 1998; The Bones of Col Fawcett, 1998; Last of the Medicine Men, 2000; Icedogs, 2002; Adventure for Boys: the Lost Worlds of Rider Haggard, 2006; Traveller's Century, 2008. *Publications:* Mad White Giant, 1985; Into the Crocodile Nest, 1987; Hunting the Gugu, 1989; The Proving Grounds, 1991; Through Jaguar Eyes, 1994; (jtly) More Great Railway Journeys, 1996; The Skeleton Coast, 1997; Edge of Blue Heaven, 1998; Last of the Medicine Men, 2000; Faber Book of Exploration, 2002; Into the Abyss, 2006. *Recreations:* tending plants, reading biographies at home. *Address: e-mail:* info@benedictallen.com.

ALLEN, Brian, PhD; FSA; Director of Studies, Paul Mellon Centre for Studies in British Art, since 1993; *b* 3 Oct. 1952; *s* of Herbert and Mary Allen; *m* 1978, Katina Michael; two *s*. *Educ:* Univ. of East Anglia (BA 1974); Courtauld Inst. of Art, Univ. of London (MA 1975; PhD 1984). Research Asst, Witt Library, Courtauld Inst. of Art, 1975–76; Paul Mellon Centre for Studies in British Art: Asst Dir and Librarian, 1977–85, Dep. Dir of Studies, 1985–92. Adjunct Prof. of History of Art, Yale Univ., 1993–; Vis. Prof. of History of Art, Birkbeck Coll., Univ. of London, 1999–2004. Hon. Sec. and Editor, 1977–85, Chm., 1996–2003, Walpole Soc.; Pres., Johnson Club, 1993–97. Member: Paintings and Sculpture Cttee, Victorian Soc., 1981–84; Bd of Studies in History of Art, Univ. of London, 1986–93; Adv. Cttee, Yale Center for British Art, 1993–; Bd, Assoc. of Research Insts in Art History, 1993–; Council, Attingham Trust for Study of Country Houses and Collections, 1995–2005; Adv. Council, Sotheby's Inst. of Art, 2002–; Adv. Cttee, Getty Res. Inst. Provenance Index, 2002–04; Council, Tate Britain, 2003–; Internat. Adv. Bd, Ben Uri Gall., London Jewish Mus. of Art, 2003–; Adv. Council, NACF, 2004– (Mem. Exec. Cttee, 1998–2004; Chm., 2003–04); Appeal Cttee, Holburne Mus. of Art, Bath, 2005– (Trustee, 2000–03); Adv. Cttee, Chantrey Proj., Ashmolean Mus., Oxford, 2006–; Scientific Cttee, Vatican Museums Talman exhibn, 2007–. Trustee and Gov., Dr Johnson's House Trust, 1998; Trustee: Foundling Mus., 1998–2007; The Buildings Book Trust, 2002–; Gov., Gainsborough's House Trust, 2000–05; Member Committee: Friends of Strawberry Hill, 2000–03; American Friends of the Strawberry Hill Trust, 2007–; Co. Sec., UK Friends, Yale Charitable Corp., 2003–; Mem. Council, Academia Rossica, 2004–. Chm. Judging Panel, Sunday Times/Singer and Friedlander Watercolour Competition, 1997–; Judge, Garrick/Milne Prize, 2000. Chm., Works of Art Cttee, Garrick Club, 2005–. Chm., Modern Art Press, 2007–. Mem., Editorial Adv. Panel, Apollo, 1990–; Associate Editor, Oxford DNB, 1997–2004; Member: Panel of Specialist Advrs, Architectural Heritage, 1998–; Internat. Adv. Bd, British Art Jl, 1999–; Adv. Bd, Visual Culture in Britain, 2000–; Internat. Adv. Bd, Courtauld Inst. of Art Res. Forum, 2004–; Editl Bd, English Heritage Histl Rev., 2006–. FSA 2000. Hon. DLitt: Southampton Inst. (Nottingham Trent Univ.), 1999; Birmingham, 2006. *Publications:* Francis Hayman, 1987; (ed.) Towards a Modern Art World, 1995; (ed with L. Dukelskaya) British Art Treasures from Russian Imperial Collections in The Hermitage, 1996; numerous articles in Apollo, Burlington Mag., Jl RSA, etc. *Recreations:* watching association football, opera. *Address:* Paul Mellon Centre for Studies in British Art, 16 Bedford Square, WC1B 3JA. *T:* (020) 7580 0311; 7 Frances Road, Windsor, Berks SL4 3AE. *Club:* Garrick.

ALLEN, Charles Lamb, CBE 2003; FCMA; Chairman: Grandmet Management LLP, since 2007; Global Radio, since 2007; Chief Adviser to the Home Office, since 2007; *b* 4 Jan. 1957. *Educ:* Bell Coll., Hamilton. FCMA 1989. Accountant, British Steel, 1974–79; Dep. Audit Manager, Gallaghers plc, 1979–82; Dir, Management Services, Grandmet Internat. Services Ltd, 1982–85; Gp Man. Dir, Compass Vending, Grandmet Innovations Ltd, 1986–87; Man. Dir, Compass Gp Ltd, 1988–91; Chief Exec., Leisure Div., Granada Gp, 1991–92; Chief Exec., 1992–96, Chm., 1996–2006, Granada TV; Chief Exec., 1994–96, Chm., 1996–2006, LWT; Chief Exec., Granada Gp, 1996–2000; Exec. Chm., Granada Media, subseq. Granada plc, 2000–04; Chief Exec., ITV plc, 2004–06. Chairman: Granada Leisure and Services, 1993–2000; Boxclever, 1994–2000; Tyne Tees TV, 1997–2006; Yorkshire TV, 1997–2006; Anglia TV, 2000–06; Meridian TV, 2000–06; ITV Digital, 2001–02; Dep. Chm., 1994–96, Chm., 1996–2000, GMTV; non-exec. Dir, Tesco plc, 1999–. Dep. Chm., BITC, 1997–2007. Vice-Pres., RTS, 1996–. Chairman: British Commonwealth Games, 2000–02; Manchester 2002 Ltd, 2000–02; Vice-Chm., London 2012 Olympic Bid, 2004–05; Dir, London Organising Cttee of the Olympic Games, 2005–. Chm., Creative Industries Adv. Gp, 1999–2002; Mem., Talent and Enterprise Taskforce Adv. Gp, 2006–. Mem., Internat. Acad. of Television Arts and Scis, 1996. FRSA. Hon. DBA Manchester Metropolitan, 1999; Hon. DLitt Salford, 2002; Hon. DEcon Southampton Solent, 2006. *Recreations:* visual and performing arts, international travel.

ALLEN, Colin Mervyn Gordon, CBE 1978; General Manager, Covent Garden Market Authority, 1967–89; *b* 17 April 1929; *s* of late Cecil G. Allen and Gwendoline L. Allen (*née* Hutchinson); *m* 1953, Patricia, *d* of late William and late Doris Seddon; two *s* one *d*. *Educ:* King Edward's Sch., Bath. BA Open, 1985; MA London, 1986; MA London (Dist.), 1991. FCIPS (FInstPS 1967). Naval Store Dept, Admiralty, 1948–56; National Coal Board: London HQ, 1956–59; Area Stores Officer, NE Div., 1959–64; Covent Garden Market Authority: Planning Officer, 1964–66; Asst Gen. Man., 1967. President: Assoc. of Wholesale Markets within Internat. Union of Local Authorities, 1972–78; IPS, 1982–83. Chm., Vauxhall Cross Amenity Trust, 1982–83. *Publications:* Transplanting the Garden: the story of the relocation of Covent Garden Market, 1998; various papers on horticultural marketing and allied topics, supply and logistics matters, and ancient history and archaeology. *Recreation:* archaeology. *Address:* Grassington, 142 Gidley Way, Horspath, Oxford OX33 1TD. *T:* (01865) 872388.

ALLEN, David Charles Keith, AO 1990; Chairman, National Australia Bank Ltd, 2001–04 (Director, since 1992); *b* 3 April 1936; *s* of G. Keith Allen and Dorothy M. Allen; *m* 1st, 1964, Angela Mary Evatt (*d* 2001); two *s* one *d*; 2nd, 2002, Jocelyn Claire Searby. *Educ:* Oundle Sch.; Corpus Christi Coll., Cambridge (MA); Imperial Coll., London (MSc, DIC). Nat. Service, RE, Malaya, 1954–56. Joined Shell International, 1961: geophysicist, in Holland, NZ, Turkey and Nigeria, 1961–71; Chief Geophysicist, Shell Expro, London, 1971–74; Area Geologist, Shell Internat. Petroleum, The Hague, 1974–75; Western Division, Shell BP, Nigeria: Ops Manager, 1975–77; Divl Manager, 1977–79; Woodside Petroleum Ltd: Exec. Dir, 1980–82; Man. Dir, 1982–96; Chm., CSIRO, 1996–2001. Director: Amcor Ltd, 1996–2005; AGL, 1996–2008; Air Liquide (Aust.), 1997–2008 (Chm., 2005–08). Dir, Earthwatch Australia, 1994–2005. Hon. LLD Monash, 1994. *Recreations:* golf, travel. *Clubs:* MCC; Grannies Cricket (UK); Australian, Melbourne (Melbourne).

ALLEN, David Kenneth; a Senior Immigration Judge, Asylum and Immigration Tribunal (formerly a Vice-President, Immigration Appeal Tribunal), since 2000; *b* 23 Feb. 1950; *yr s* of late Philip Hernaman Allen and of Dorothy Allen (*née* Modral); *m* 1974, Joan Rosalind, *d* of late Rev. E. N. O. Gray and V. Gray; two *s* one *d*. *Educ:* Loughborough Grammar Sch.; Merton Coll., Oxford (BA Hons Juris; MA); McGill Univ., Montreal (LLM). Called to the Bar, Middle Temple, 1975; Lectr in Law, Inns of Court Sch. of Law, 1974–76; Department of Law, University of Leicester: Lectr, 1976–88; Sen. Lectr, 1988–99; Hd of Dept, 1993–96; Hon. Vis. Fellow, 1999–; in practice, Midland and Oxford Circuit, 1990–99. Immigration Adjudicator, 1989–2000 (pt-time, 1989–99). Vis. Prof., Dalhousie Univ., Halifax, NS, 1982–83. *Publications:* (jtly) Accident Compensation after Pearson, 1979; (jtly) Civil Liability for Defective Premises, 1982; (jtly) Fire, Safety and the Law, 1983, 2nd edn 1990; Misrepresentation, 1988; (jtly) Damages in Tort, 2000; essays; contrib. articles and notes in various jls. *Recreations:* golf, tennis, music. *Address:* Asylum and Immigration Tribunal, Field House, 15–25 Bream's Buildings, EC4A 1DZ.

See also P. R. H. Allen.

ALLEN, Prof. Deryck Norman de Garrs; Professor of Applied Mathematics in the University of Sheffield, 1955–80, now Emeritus; Warden of Ranmoor House, 1968–82; *b* 22 April 1918; *s* of Leonard Lincoln Allen and Dorothy Allen (*née* Asplin). *Educ:* King Edward VII School, Sheffield; Christ Church, Oxford. Messrs Rolls Royce, 1940; Research Asst to Sir Richard Southwell, FRS, 1941; Lectr in Applied Mathematics at Imperial Coll., London, 1945; Visiting Prof. in Dept of Mechanical Engineering, Massachusetts Inst. of Technology, 1949; Reader in Applied Mathematics at Imperial Coll. in Univ. of London, 1950. Pro-Vice-Chancellor, Sheffield Univ., 1966–70; Chm., Jt Matriculation Bd, 1973–76. *Publications:* Relaxation Methods, 1954 (US); papers on Applied Maths and Engineering Maths in: Proc. Royal Soc.; Philosophical Trans. of Royal Soc.; Quarterly Jl of Mechanics and Applied Maths; Jl of Instn of Civil Engineers. *Recreation:* travel. *Address:* Broomcroft House Nursing Home, 416 Ecclesall Road, Sheffield S11 9PY.

ALLEN, Donald F.; Founder and Partner, Down Office Equipment Co., since 1975; Chairman, Sports Council for Northern Ireland, 1990–2000; *b* 23 Sept. 1938; *m* 1969, Rosaline; three *d*. *Educ:* by Christian Brothers. Completed optician's trng course, 1964; mgt posts with Olivetti Ltd, 1964–75. Mem., UK Sports Council, 1997–2000. Pres., Belfast East Rotary Club. FInstD. *Recreations:* golf (playing), all sport (watching), theatre. *Address:* 49 Demesne Road, Holywood, Co. Down, Northern Ireland BT18 9EX. *Clubs:* Holywood Golf (Capt.; Trustee, 1986–), Royal Belfast Golf.

ALLEN, Edward; *see* Allen, F. E.

ALLEN, Elizabeth Martin, (Mrs T. Bennett), MA; Headteacher, Newstead Wood School for Girls, since 2001; *b* 5 March 1946; *d* of Alfred (David) Trory and Alvena Trory (*née* Fisk); *m* 1st, 1967, Trevor Winston Allen (marr. diss. 1985); two *d*; 2nd, 1999, Terence Bennett; three step *s*. *Educ:* Whitelands Coll. of Educn (Cert Ed Divinity); Birkbeck Coll., Univ. of London (BA Hons English); Inst. of Educn, Univ. of London (MA Curriculum Studies). Hd of Religious Studies, Wallington High Sch. for Girls, 1969–73; 2nd i/c English Dept, St Bede's Ecumenical Sch., Redhill, 1981–84; Hd of English, Court Lodge Sch., Horley, 1984–88; Dep. Headteacher, Carshalton High Sch. for Girls, 1988–93; Headteacher, Altwood C of E Sch., Maidenhead, 1993–2001. FRSA 2000. *Recreations:* literature, the theatre, the garden, adding to the porcelain collection, the children and grandchildren. *Address:* Newstead Wood School for Girls, Avebury Road, Orpington, Kent BR6 9SA. *T:* (01689) 853626, *Fax:* (01689) 853315.

ALLEN, Fergus Hamilton, CB 1969; ScD, MA, MAI; FRSL; First Civil Service Commissioner, Civil Service Department, 1974–81; *b* 3 Sept. 1921; *s* of late Charles Winckworth Allen and Marjorie Helen, *d* of F. J. S. Budge; *m* 1947, Margaret Joan, *d* of Prof. M. J. Gorman; two *d*. *Educ:* Newtown Sch., Waterford; Trinity Coll., Dublin. ScD 1966. Asst Engineer, Sir Cyril Kirkpatrick and Partners, 1943–48; Port of London Authority, 1949–52; Asst Director, Hydraulics Research Station, DSIR, 1952–58; Dir of Hydraulics Research, DSIR, 1958–65; Chief Scientific Officer, Cabinet Office, 1965–69; Civil Service Comr, 1969–74; Scientific and Technological Advr, CSD, 1969–72. Consultant, Boyden Internat. Ltd, 1982–86. Instn Civil Engrs: Mem., 1947–57; Fellow, 1957–86; Telford Gold Medal, 1958; Mem. Council, 1962–67, 1968–71. FRSL 2000. *Publications:* The Brown Parrots of Providencia (poems), 1993; Who Goes There? (poems), 1996; Mrs Power Looks Over the Bay (poems), 1999; Gas Light & Coke (poems), 2006; papers in technical journals. *Address:* Dundrum, Wantage Road, Streatley, Berks RG8 9LB. *T:* (01491) 873234. *Club:* Athenæum.

See also M. Allen.

ALLEN, Dr F(rederick) Edward, CMG 2004; JP; Senior Pastor, Abundant Life Bible Church, since 1979; *b* 2 Aug. 1929; *s* of Fred Allen and Bessie Allen (*née* Carey); *m* 1952, Iris Velma Archer; one *s* (one *d* decd). *Educ:* Eastern Sen. Sch.; private tutor; Trinity Theol Seminary (BTh; DD 1989). Evangelist to the Caribbean, N and S America, 1949–. Mem., Discharged Prisoners' Cttee, HM Prison, Nassau, 1964. JP Bahamas, 1991. Awards: Assoc. of Brethren, 1982; for Excellence in Gospel Broadcasting, Nat. Religious Broadcasters (Caribbean Chapter), 1990; Silver Jubilee (Bahamas), 1998; Sen. Citizen Award for Nation Building, 1999. *Recreations:* swimming, walking. *Address:* PO Box SS–5858, Nassau, Bahamas. *T:* (office) 3938134, *Fax:* 3938052; *e-mail:* eallen@albcm.org.

ALLEN, Gary James, CBE 1991; DL; Chairman, IMI plc, 2001–04 (Chief Executive, 1986–2001); *b* 30 Sept. 1944; *s* of Alfred and Alice Allen; *m* 1966, Judith Anne Nattrass; three *s*. *Educ:* King Edward VI Grammar School, Aston, Birmingham; Liverpool University (BCom). FCMA. Managing Dir, IMI Range, 1973–77; Dir, IMI, 1978–2004; Asst Man. Dir, IMI, 1985–86; Chairman: Optilon, 1979–84; Eley, 1981–85; (non-exec.) Nat. Exhibition Centre Ltd, 1989–; Dep. Chm., Marley, 1993–97 (Dir, 1989–97); non-executive Director: NV Bekaert SA, Belgium, 1987–; Birmingham European Airways, 1989–91; London Stock Exchange, 1994–; Temple Bar Investment Trust, 2001–. Mem. Council, CBI, 1986–99 (Mem., W Midlands Regional Council, 1983–89); Mem. Council, Birmingham Chamber of Industry & Commerce, 1983–98 (Pres., 1991–92). Lord's Taverners: Pres., W Midlands Regl Cttee, 1994–; Nat. Trustee, 1995–2001; Mem., Nat. Council, 1992–2001. Trustee, Industry in Educn, 1998–. Mem. Council, Univ. of Birmingham, 1985–90 (Hon. Life Mem., Court, 1984–). Mem. Bd, Birmingham Royal Ballet, 1993–2003. Pres., Midlands Club Cricket Conf., 1995–96. Chm., Birmingham Children's Hosp. Appeal, 1995–2000. DL 1993; High Sheriff, 2002–03, West Midlands. CCMI; FRSA. Hon. DSc Birmingham, 2003. Midland Businessman of the Year, 1989. Officer, Order of Leopold II (Belgium), 2002. *Recreations:* sport, reading, gardening. *Clubs:* Royal Automobile, Lord's Taverners.

ALLEN, Prof. Sir Geoffrey, Kt 1979; PhD; FRS 1976; FREng; FRSC; FInstP; Executive Adviser, Kobe Steel Ltd, 1990–2000; Head of Research, Unilever PLC, 1981–90 (Director, Unilever PLC and NV, 1982–90); *b* 29 Oct. 1928; *s* of John James and Marjorie Allen; *m* 1973, Valerie Frances Duckworth; one *d*. *Educ:* Clay Cross Tupton Hall Grammar Sch.; Univ. of Leeds (BSc, PhD). FInstP 1972; FPRI 1974; FRSC 1984; Hon. FIMMM 2002 (FIM 1991); FREng (FEng 1993). Postdoctoral Fellow, Nat. Res. Council, Canada, 1952–54; Lectr, Univ. of Manchester, 1955–65, Prof. of Chemical Physics, 1965–75; Prof. of Polymer Science, 1975–76, Prof. of Chemical Technology, 1976–81, Imperial Coll. of Science and Technology (Fellow, 1986); Vis. Fellow, Robinson Coll., Cambridge, 1980–. Non-exec. Dir, Courtaulds, 1987–93. Member: Science Research

Council, 1976, Chm., 1977–81; Royal Commn on Envmtl Pollution, 1991–99; Nat. Consumer Council, 1993–96; Council, Foundn for Sci. and Technol., 1995–2000; President: SCI, 1989–91; PRI, 1990–92; Inst. of Materials, 1994–95. A Vice-Pres., Royal Soc., 1991–93. Chancellor, UEA, 1994–2003. Fellow, St Catherine's Coll., Oxford, 1992. Hon. FUMIST 1993. Hon. FIChemE 1988; Hon. FCGI 1990. Hon. MSc Manchester; DUniv Open, 1981; Hon. DSc: Durham, East Anglia, 1984; Bath, Bradford, Loughborough, 1985; Essex, Keele, Leeds, 1986; Cranfield, 1988; Surrey, 1989; Sheffield, 1993; London Metropolitan, 1998. *Publications*: papers on chemical physics of polymers in Trans Faraday Soc., Polymer. *Recreations*: opera, walking, talking. *Address*: 18 Oxford House, 52 Parkside, Wimbledon, SW19 5NE.

ALLEN, Graham Leslie; consultant to local authorities on arts, museum and cultural services; *b* 27 May 1949; *s* of William Leslie Allen and Doris Allen (*née* Fraser). *Educ*: Ladywood Comprehensive Sch., Birmingham. Joined Birmingham City Council, 1973; Assistant Director: Museums Services, 1990–94; Mgt Services, 1994–95; acting Head of Museums Services, 1995; Asst Dir (Museums and Arts), 1995–2001; Sen. Asst Dir (Museums and Heritage Projects), 2001–04. Associate: 4ps Consultancy; Invigour Consultancy. Trustee, Birmingham Mus. Develt Trust; Trustee and Dir, Thinktank, Birmingham Mus. of Sci. and Industry. Chm., Selly Park Residents' Assoc. Mem., Lunar Soc., 1999–. FRSA 2000. *Recreations*: the arts, museums, hill walking. *Address*: 61 Sir Johns Road, Selly Park, Birmingham B29 7EP. *T*: (0121) 472 7953; *e-mail*: graham.allen11@btinternet.com.

ALLEN, Graham William; MP (Lab) Nottingham North, since 1987; *b* 11 Jan. 1953; *s* of William and Edna Allen. *Educ*: Robert Shaw Primary Sch.; Forest Fields Grammar Sch.; City of London Polytechnic; Leeds Univ. Warehouseman, Nottingham, 1971–72; Labour Party Res. Officer, 1978–83; Local Govt Officer, GLC, 1983–84; Trades Union National Co-ordinator, Political Fund Ballots Campaign, 1984–86; Regional Res. and Educn Officer, GMBATU, 1986–87. Opposition front bench spokesman on social security, 1991–92, on democracy and the constitution, 1992–94, on the media, 1994, on transport, 1995, on environment, 1996–97; a Lord Comr of HM Treasury (Govt Whip), 1997–98; Vice Chamberlain of HM Household, 1998–2001. Member: Public Accounts Cttee, 1988–91; Procedure Cttee, 1989–91; 1990 Financial Bill Cttee. Chm., PLP Treasury Cttee, 1990–91. Chm., One Nottingham, 2005–. *Publications*: Reinventing Democracy, 1995; The Last Prime Minister: being honest about the UK Presidency, 2002. *Recreations*: cricket, golf, painting, cooking. *Address*: House of Commons, SW1A 0AA. *T*: (020) 7219 4343. *Clubs*: Strelley Social, Beechdale Community Centre, Bulwell Community Centre, Basford Hall Miners Welfare (Nottingham).

ALLEN, Dame Ingrid (Victoria), (Dame Ingrid Barnes Thompson), DBE 2001 (CBE 1993); DL; MD, DSc, FRCPath, FMedSci; MRIA; Director of Research and Development, Health and Personal Social Services, Northern Ireland, 1997–2001; Professor of Neuropathology, Queen's University of Belfast, 1979–97, now Emeritus; *b* 30 July 1932; *d* of Rev. Robert Allen, MA, PhD, DD and Doris V. Allen; *m* 1st, 1972, Alan Watson Barnes, MA, ARIBA, Past Pres., RSUA (*d* 1987); 2nd, 1996, Prof. John Thompson. *Educ*: Cheltenham Ladies College; QUB. House Officer, Royal Victoria Hosp., Belfast, 1957–58; Musgrave Res. Fellow, Tutor in Path., Calvert Res. Fellow, QUB, 1958–64; Sen. Registrar, RVH, 1964–65; Sen. Lectr and Consultant in Neuropath., QUB/RVH, 1966–78; Reader and Consultant, 1978–79; Head, NI Regional Neuropath. Service, RVH, Belfast, 1979–97. Vis. Prof., Univ. of Ulster, 1988. Mem., MRC, 1989–92 (Chm., Neuroscis Bd, 1989–92); President: British Neuropathological Soc., 1993–95; Irish Neurological Assoc., 1993–; Vice-President: Internat. Soc. of Neuropath., 1988–92; RCPath, 1993–96 (Mem. Council and Coll. Cttees, 1990–97). MRIA 1993 (Fellow, 1993). Founder FMedSci 1998. DL Belfast 1989. Mem. editl bds of various scientific jls. *Publications*: (contrib.) Greenfield's Neuropathology, 1984; (contrib.) McAlpine's Multiple Sclerosis, 1990; contribs to jls on neuropathology, demyelinating diseases, neurovirology and neuro-oncology. *Recreations*: reading, playing the piano (badly), idling on an island in Donegal. *Address*: 95 Malone Road, Belfast BT9 6SP. *T*: (028) 9066 6662. *Club*: Athenæum.

ALLEN, James Hendricuss; QC 1995; a Recorder, since 1995; a Deputy High Court Judge, since 2000; *b* 19 Sept. 1949; *s* of James Ede Allen and Anna Catarina Allen; *m* 1st, 1974 (marr. diss. 1994); one *s* two *d*; 2nd, 1996, Melanie Jane Williamson; one *s* one *d*. *Educ*: Morley Grammar Sch.; Newcastle upon Tyne Poly. (BA Hons Law). Called to the Bar, Gray's Inn, 1973. *Recreations*: theatre, opera, foreign travel, shooting, tennis, bridge. *Address*: 6 Park Square East, Leeds LS1 2LW. *T*: (0113) 245 9763.

ALLEN, Janet Rosemary; Headmistress of Benenden School, Kent, 1976–85; *b* 11 April 1936; *d* of John Algernon Allen and Edna Mary Allen (*née* Orton). *Educ*: Cheltenham Ladies' Coll.; University Coll., Leicester; Hughes Hall, Cambridge. BA London 1958; CertEd Cambridge 1959. Asst Mistress, Howell's Sch., Denbigh, North Wales, 1959; Head of History Dept, 1961; in charge of First Year Sixth Form, 1968; Housemistress, 1968 and 1973–75. Acting Headmistress: Sch. of St Mary and St Anne, Abbots Bromley, Sept.–Dec. 1988; Selwyn Sch., Gloucester, 1989–90. Member: E-SU Scholarship Selection Panel, 1977–85; South East ISIS Cttee, 1978–84; Boarding Schs Assoc. Cttee, 1980–83; GSA Educnl sub-cttee, 1983–85; Gloucester Diocesan Bd of Educn, 1992–97; Mem., Winchcombe Ministry Leadership Team, 1997–. Vice-Pres., Women's Career Foundn (formerly Girls of the Realm Guild), 1981–. Governor: St Catherine's Sch., Bramley, 1986–91; The King's Sch., Worcester, 1996–2008. *Recreations*: music, theatre, pottery, helping to preserve national heritage. *Address*: Bourne Rise, Queen's Square, Winchcombe, Cheltenham, Glos GL54 5LR. *Club*: Royal Over-Seas League.

ALLEN, Prof. John Anthony, PhD, DSc; FIBiol; FRSE; Professor of Marine Biology, University of London, and Director, University Marine Biological Station, Millport, Isle of Cumbrae, 1976–91, now Professor Emeritus; Hon. Research Fellow, University Marine Biological Station, since 1991; *b* 27 May 1926; *s* of George Leonard John Allen and Dorothy Mary Allen; *m* 1st, 1952, Marion Ferguson Crow (marr. diss. 1983); one *s* one *d*; 2nd, 1983, Margaret Porteous Aitken; one adopted step *s*. *Educ*: High Pavement Sch., Nottingham; London Univ. (PhD, DSc). FIBiol 1969; FRSE 1968 (Mem. Council, 1970–73). Served in Sherwood Foresters, 1945–46, and RAMC, 1946–48. Asst Lectr, Univ. of Glasgow, 1951–54; John Murray Student, Royal Soc., 1952–54; Lectr/Sen. Lectr in Zool., then Reader in Marine Biol., Univ. of Newcastle upon Tyne, 1954–76. Post Doctoral Fellow and Guest Investigator, Woods Hole Oceanographic Instn, USA, 1965–2005; Vis. Prof., Univ. of Washington, 1968, 1970, 1971; Royal Soc. Vis. Prof., Univ. of West Indies, 1976. Member: NERC, 1977–83 (Chm., Univ. Affairs Cttee, 1978–83); Council, Scottish Marine Biol Assoc., 1977–83; Council, Marine Biol Assoc. UK, 1981–83, 1990–93; Life Sciences Bd, CNAA, 1981–84; Nature Conservancy Council, 1982–90 (Chm., Adv. Cttee Sci., 1984–90); British Nat. Cttee for Oceanic Res., 1988–90. Pres., Malacological Soc. of London, 1982–84. *Publications*: many papers on decapod crustacea and molluscs, and deep sea benthos, in learned jls. *Recreations*: travel, appreciation of gardens, pub-lunching. *Address*: Drialstone, Millport, Isle of Cumbrae, Scotland KA28 0EP. *T*: (01475) 530479.

ALLEN, Sir John (Derek), Kt 1994; CBE 1987; FCIOB; Board Member, since 1998, and Vice Chairman, 1998–2000, Welsh Development Agency; Member, Land Authority for Wales, 1976–98 (Deputy Chairman, 1988–98); *b* 6 Nov. 1928; *s* of late William Henry Allen and Lalla Dorothy Allen (*née* Bowen); *m* 1951, (Thelma) Jean Hooper; one *s*. *Educ*: Cardiff High Sch.; Cardiff Coll. of Technology (BA). FCIOB 1979. Civil Engr, then Chm. and Man. Dir, John Morgan Gp, Cardiff, 1947–79; Mgt Consultancy Practice, 1979–86. Dep. Chm., then Chm., Cwmbran Develt Corp., 1979–88; Chm., Housing for Wales, 1988–96. Pres., Nat. Fedn of Building Trade Employers, 1979 (Treas., 1980–83). FCMI (FIMgt 1980). Hon. Fellow, UWIC, 2000. Freeman, City of London, 1980. *Recreations*: fly-fishing, golf, gardening. *Address*: 5 Cotswold Court, Cyncoed Place, Cardiff CF23 6SL. *T*: (029) 2075 3688. *Club*: Cardiff Golf.

ALLEN, Very Rev. John Edward; Provost of Wakefield, 1982–97; *b* 9 June 1932; *s* of Rev. Canon Ronald and Mrs Isabel Allen; *m* 1957, Eleanor (*née* Prynne); one *s* three *d*. *Educ*: Rugby; University Coll., Oxford (MA); Fitzwilliam Coll., Cambridge (MA); Westcott House. Colonial Service, Kenya, 1957–63; Sales and Marketing, Kimberly-Clark Ltd, 1963–66; Theological College, 1966–68; Curate, Deal, Kent, 1968–71; Senior Chaplain to Univ. of Bristol and Vicar of St Paul's, Clifton, 1971–78; Vicar of Chippenham, Wilts, 1978–82. Mem., Gen. Synod of C of E, 1985–97. Vice Chm., Partnership for World Mission, 1987–96. Dir, Wakefield HA, 1991–97; Chm., Scarborough and NE Yorks Healthcare NHS Trust, 1997–2001. Chm., Local Research Ethics Cttee, 1992–97; Mem., Northern and Yorks Reg. Multi-Centre Res. Ethics Cttee, 1997–2001 (Vice-Chm., 1997–99). Religious Advr, Yorkshire TV, 1994–96. Gov., Queen Elizabeth GS, Wakefield, 1983–97; Chm. of Govs, Cathedral High Sch., 1993–97. Trustee and Dir, Public Arts, 1997–99. Pres., Scarborough Cavaliers Rotary Club, 2001–02. *Recreations*: walking, fishing and people. *Address*: The Glebe Barn, Sawdon, near Scarborough, N Yorks YO13 9DY. *T*: (01723) 859854; *e-mail*: jeallen70@btinternet.com.

See also R. G. B. Allen.

ALLEN, Maj.-Gen. John Geoffrey Robyn, CB 1976; Lay Observer attached to Lord Chancellor's Department, 1979–85; *b* 19 Aug. 1923; *s* of R. A. Allen and Mrs Allen (*née* Youngman); *m* 1959, Ann Monica (*née* Morford); one *s* one *d*. *Educ*: Haileybury. Commissioned KRRC, 1942; trans. RTR, 1947; Bt Lt-Col, 1961; Lt-Col, CO 2 RTR, 1963; Mil. Asst (GSO1) to CGS, MoD, 1965; Brig., Comd 20 Armd Bde, 1967; IDC, 1970; Dir of Operational Requirements 3 (Army), MoD, 1971; Maj.-Gen., Dir-Gen., Fighting Vehicles and Engineer Equipment, MoD, 1973–74; Dir, RAC, 1974–76; Sen. Army Directing Staff, RCDS, 1976–78; retired 1979. Col Comdt, RTR, 1976–80; Hon. Colonel: Westminster Dragoons, 1982–87; Royal Yeomanry, 1982–87. Member: Adv. Cttee on Legal Aid, 1979–86; Booth Cttee on Procedure in Matrimonial Causes, 1982–85; Mgt Cttee, Friends of Chichester Hosps, 1987–2002 (Chm., 1991–97; Pres., 1997–2002); Appeal Tribunals, FIMBRA, 1989–98; Membership and Disciplinary Tribunal, PIA, 1994–98. *Address*: Meadowleys, Charlton, Chichester, W Sussex PO18 0HU. *T*: (01243) 811638. *Club*: Army and Navy.

ALLEN, Prof. John Robert Lawrence, DSc; FRS 1979; Research Professor, Postgraduate Research Institute for Sedimentology, University of Reading, 1993–2001 (Director, 1988–93), Professor Emeritus and Visiting Professor, Department of Archaeology, since 2001; *b* 25 Oct. 1932; *s* of George Eustace Allen and Alice Josephine (*née* Formby); *m* 1959, Jean Mary (*née* Wood); four *s* one *d*. *Educ*: St Philip's Grammar Sch., Birmingham; Univ. of Sheffield (BSc; DSc 1972). Academic career in University of Reading, 1959–, Prof. of Geology, then of Sedimentology, 1972. Mem., NERC, 1992–94. FGS 1955; FSA 1991. Assoc. Mem., Royal Belgian Acad. of Scis, 1991. Hon. LLD Sheffield, 1994. Lyell Medal, Geolog. Soc., 1980; David Linton Award, British Geomorphological Research Group, 1983; Twenhofel Medal, Soc. of Economic Paleontologists and Mineralogists, 1987; G. K. Warren Prize, Nat. Acad. of Scis, USA, 1990; Sorby Medal, Internat. Assoc. of Sedimentologists, 1994; Penrose Medal, Geol Soc. of Amer., 1996. *Publications*: Current Ripples, 1968; Physical Processes of Sedimentation, 1970; Sedimentary Structures, 1982; Principles of Physical Sedimentology, 1985; numerous contribs to professional jls. *Recreations*: cooking, music, opera, pottery. *Address*: 17c Whiteknights Road, Reading RG6 7BY. *T*: (0118) 926 4621.

ALLEN, Jonathan Guy; HM Diplomatic Service; Head, Research, Information and Communications Unit, Foreign and Commonwealth Office, since 2007; *b* Nottingham, 5 March 1974; *s* of Jeremy and Maggie Allen. *Educ*: Nottingham High Sch.; St Catharine's Coll., Cambridge (BA 1996; MPhil 1997). Joined FCO, 1997; Second Sec. (Press/Pol), Cyprus, 1999–2002; Hd, Cyprus Section, FCO, 2002–03; Spokesman, UK Perm. Repn to the EU, Brussels, 2003–06; Asst Dir, Internat. Directorate, Home Office, 2006–07. *Recreations*: reading, theatre, walking, travelling, Nottingham Forest, Strollers Cricket Club, Yacht Club, eating and drinking well. *Address*: c/o Foreign and Commonwealth Office, King Charles Street, SW1A 2AH.

ALLEN, Joyce; see Moseley, J.

ALLEN, Katherine, (Kate); Director, Amnesty International UK, since 2000; *b* 25 Jan. 1955; *d* of William Allen and Patricia Allen (*née* Middleton). *Educ*: Brasenose Coll., Oxford (BA Hons PPE; Hon. Fellow, 2006). Policy Officer, GLC, 1977–79; Scientific Officer, SSRC, 1979–80; Policy Officer, Haringey LBC, 1980–81; Sen. Policy Officer (Social Services), ACC, 1981–87; Dep. Chief Exec., Refugee Council, 1987–99.

ALLEN, Kay; Group Head of Social Policy and Inclusion, Royal Mail Group, since 2007; *b* 31 Jan. 1964; *d* of Frank Garside Allen and Gladys Allen; *m* 2007, (Ivor) Philip Lever. *Educ*: Oldham Coll.; Huddersfield Univ. (BA Hons Business Studies 1989). CIPD 1991, MCIPD 1994. Personnel Manager, Shorrock Security, 1986–90; Dir of Human Resources, Royal Philharmonic Orch., 1990–95; Head of Diversity, B&Q, 1995–2000; Consultant, Grass Roots Gp, 2000–02; Head of Diversity, BSkyB, 2002–07. Commissioner: Disability Rights Commn, 2000–03; Commn for Equality and Human Rights, 2007–. Mem., Prime Minister's Council on Social Action, 2007–. Mem. Bd of Advrs, Helen Hamlyn Centre, 2004–. Mem., Editl Bd, Equal Opportunities Rev., 2003–. Owner, village pub. *Publication*: (jtly) Equality and Diversity, 2001. *Recreations*: passionate about Arabian horses (owner of two Arabian stallions), country pursuits. *Address*: Shaftesbury, Dorset. *T*: (01747) 851686; *e-mail*: kay@diverseadvice.com. *Club*: Royal Over-Seas League.

ALLEN, Sir Mark (John Spurgeon), Kt 2005; CMG 2002; HM Diplomatic Service, retired; Special Adviser to BP Group, since 2004; Senior Adviser to Monitor Group, since 2006; *b* 3 July 1950; *s* of Peter Muir Spurgeon Allen and Heather Anne Allen (*née* Roney); *m* 1976, Margaret Mary Watson; one *s* one *d*. *Educ*: Dragon Sch.; Downside; Exeter Coll., Oxford (MA). Entered FCO, 1973; MECAS, 1974; Third Secretary: Abu Dhabi, 1975–77; FCO, 1977–78; Second, later First, Sec., Cairo, 1978–82; First Secretary: Belgrade, 1982–86; FCO, 1986–90; Counsellor: Amman, 1990–94; FCO, 1994–2004. Sen. Advr, Palantir Technologies, Palo Alto, 2006–; Mem., Adv. Bd, Millennium Finance Corp., Private Equity Energy Fund, 2008–. Sen. Associate Mem., St Antony's Coll.,

Oxford, 2004–. Member: Adv. Council, London ME Inst., 2005–; IDEAS-CSWC, LSE, 2008–. *Publications:* Falconry in Arabia, 1980; (with Ruth Burrows) Letters on Prayer, 1999; First Holy Communion, 2002; Arabs, 2006. *Recreations:* falconry, Islamic calligraphy. *Address: e-mail:* mjsa@btinternet.com. *Clubs:* Travellers, Beefsteak; Leander.

ALLEN, Mary; executive coach and mentor; Chairman, Breast Cancer Campaign, 2002–06; *d* of Dr Fergus Hamilton Allen, *qv* and Joan Allen; *m* 1st, 1980, Robin George Woodhead, *qv* (marr. diss. 1990); 2nd, 1991, Nigel Pantling (marr. diss. 2004). *Educ:* School of St Helen and St Katherine; New Hall, Cambridge; UEA (MA Creative Writing 2002). Actress, West End and repertory, 1973–76; Agent, London Management, 1977–78; Arts, Sponsorship Manager, Mobil Oil Co., 1978–81; Assoc. for Business Sponsorship of the Arts, 1982–83; arts management consultant, 1983–90; Dir, Waterman's Arts Centre, 1990–92; Dir, Cheek by Jowl Theatre Co., 1989–92; Dep. Sec.-Gen., Arts Council of GB, 1992–94; Sec.-Gen., Arts Council of England, 1994–97; Chief Exec., Royal Opera House, Covent Garden, 1997–98. Director: City of London Fest., 2003–06; High Tide Fest., 2008–. Public Art Develt Trust: Trustee, 1983–92; Chm., 1987–92. *Publications:* Sponsoring the Arts: new business strategies for the 1990s, 1990; A House Divided, 1998. *Recreations:* opera, theatre, collecting contemporary art, gardening, playing the spoons.

ALLEN, Michael David Prior, FRICS; FCIArb; QC 2008; a Recorder, since 2005; *b* Liverpool, 24 March 1963; *s* of late Terence Roy Allen and of Margaret Prior Allen; *m* 1995, Lorraine Brown; one *s* one *d*. *Educ:* BSc Building Econs; LLB; LLM. ARICS 1987, FRICS 1992; FCIArb 2006. Called to the Bar, Gray's Inn, 1990; in practice at the Bar, 1990–. *Publication:* Company Law and the Human Rights Act, 2000. *Recreations:* playing and teaching squash, ski-ing, cheering the children on in their sports. *Address:* 7 King's Bench Walk, Temple, EC4Y 7DS. *T:* (020) 7583 0404, *Fax:* (020) 7583 0950; *e-mail:* dallen@7kbw.co.uk.

ALLEN, Paul Gardner; Chairman, Vulcan Inc., since 1983; *b* 21 Jan. 1953; *s* of late Kenneth Allen and of Faye Allen. *Educ:* Lakeside High Sch., Seattle; Washington State Univ. Programmer, Honeywell, Boston; Co-founder, Micro-Soft, later Microsoft Corp., 1975: Exec. Vice-Pres. of Res. and Product Develt, 1975–83; Dir, 1983–2000; Sen. Strategy Advr, 2000–. Founder: Asymetrix Corp., 1985; Vulcan Ventures, 1986; Starwave Corp., 1992; Interval Res., 1992; Paul Allen Group, 1994. Chairman: Portland Trailblazers, 1988–; Ticketmaster Hldgs Gp, 1993–; Seattle Seahawks, 1997–. *Address:* Vulcan Inc., 505 5th Avenue S, Suite 900, Seattle, WA 98104–3821, USA.

ALLEN, Hon. Sir Peter (Austin Philip Jermyn), Kt 1987; High Court Judge, Lesotho, 1987–89; *b* 20 Oct. 1929; *yr s* of late Donovan Jermyn Allen and Edith Jane Bates. *Educ:* Headlands School, Swindon; LLB London. Army service, 1947–55, Lieut RA, 1952–55. HM Overseas Police Service, Asst Supt Uganda Police, 1955–62; ADC to Governor of Uganda, 1957; called to the Bar, Gray's Inn, 1964; Lectr, 1962–64, Principal, 1964–70, Uganda Law School; Judicial Adviser, Buganda Kingdom, 1964; Advocate, High Court of Uganda, 1965; Chief Magistrate, Uganda, 1970–73; Judge, Uganda High Court, 1973–85; Chief Justice (Head of Uganda Judiciary, Chm., Judicial Service Commn), 1985–86. Member: Uganda Law Reform Commn, 1964–68; Foundn Cttee, Uganda YMCA, 1959; Dir, Mbarara Branch, YMCA, 1970–73; Chairman: Presidential Commn of Inquiry into Kampala City Council, 1971; Judicial Review of Caribbean Dependent Territories (Allen Report for FCO), 1990; Commn of Inquiry into Grand Cayman New Hospital Contracts, 1993; Mem., Uganda Law Soc., 1964–70. Uganda Independence Medal, 1962. *Publications:* An Introduction to the Law of Uganda (co-author), 1968; Days of Judgment, 1987; Interesting Times—Uganda Diaries 1955–1986, 2000; Inspector Beadle's Progress (fiction), 2007. *Address:* PO Box 38, Savannah, Grand Cayman KY1–1501, Cayman Islands, British West Indies. *Club:* Royal Commonwealth Society.

ALLEN, Peter William, FCA; Managing Partner, 1984–90, Deputy Chairman, 1990–94, Coopers & Lybrand; *b* 22 July 1938; *s* of late Alfred William Allen, Sittingbourne, Kent, and Myra Nora (*née* Rogers); *m* 1965, Patricia Mary, *d* of late Joseph Frederick Dunk, FCA, Sheffield; three *d*. *Educ:* Cambridge Univ. (MA). Served RAF, 1957–59. Joined Coopers & Lybrand, 1963; qualified CA, 1966; Partner, 1973; Chm., Internat. Personnel Cttee, 1975–78; Partner in Charge, London Office, 1983; Member: UK Bd, 1984–94; Internat. Exec. Cttee, 1988–90, 1992–94. Non-executive Director: Charter, 1994–2001; Schroder Ventures, 1994–; Bd Mem., Post Office, 1995–98. Mem. and Hon. Treas., Governing Bd, Lister Inst. of Preventive Medicine, 1998–2005; Bd Mem., BRCS, 1999–2000. CCMI (CIMgt 1993). Freeman, City of London, 1988; Liveryman, Co. of Glaziers and Painters of Glass, 1989–2003. *Recreations:* golf, painting. *Address:* John O'Gaddesden's House, Little Gaddesden, Berkhamsted, Herts HP4 1PF. *Club:* Reform.

ALLEN, (Philip) Richard (Hernaman), CB 2006; independent management and change consultant; *b* 26 Jan. 1949; *s* of late Philip Hernaman Allen and of Dorothy Allen (*née* Modral); *m* 1970, Vanessa (*née* Lampard); two *d*. *Educ:* Loughborough Grammar Sch.; Merton Coll., Oxford (BA (Hons) Mod. History). Asst Principal, HM Customs and Excise, 1970; Assistant Private Secretary: to Paymaster Gen., 1973; to Chancellor of the Duchy of Lancaster, 1974; HM Customs and Excise: Principal, 1975; Asst Sec., 1984; Comr of Customs and Excise, 1990; Director: Internal Taxes, 1990; Orgn, 1991; Dir, Policy, DSS, 1994; HM Customs and Excise: Comr, 1997–2001; Director: Ops (Compliance), 1997–98; Personnel and Finance, 1998–2000; Human Resources, 2000–01; Prin. Estabs Officer and Dir Reorgn Project, 2001; Dir, Corporate Services, DEFRA, 2001–05. FRSA. *Recreations:* music, badminton, running, writing.
See also D. K. Allen.

ALLEN, Richard Ian Gordon; Deputy Division Chief, Fiscal Affairs Department, International Monetary Fund, since 2005; *b* 13 Dec. 1944; *s* of Reginald Arthur Hill Allen and Edith Alice Allen (*née* Manger). *Educ:* Edinburgh Academy; Edinburgh Univ. (MA); York Univ. (BPhil). Consultant, UN Economic Commn for Europe, Geneva, 1970; Research Officer, NIESR, 1971–75; Economic Adviser: Dept of Energy, 1975–78; HM Treasury, 1978–81; Senior Economic Adviser, later Asst Sec., HM Treasury, 1981–85; Counsellor (Economic), Washington, 1985–87; Press Sec. to Chancellor of the Exchequer, 1987–88; Under Sec., HM Treasury, 1988–95; Financial Advr, Govt of Bahrain, 1995–96; Sen. Counsellor, SIGMA prog., OECD, Paris, 1996–2001; Sen. Advr on Governance, Asian Develt Bank, 2001; World Bank: Dir, Public Expenditure and Financial Accountability Prog., 2001–03; Lead Economist for Public Sector Issues, ME and N Africa Reg., 2003–05. Mem., Bd of Dirs, European Investment Bank, 1988–90. *Publications:* (with Daniel Tommasi) Managing Public Expenditure: a reference book for transition countries, 2001; (with Salvatore Schiavo-Campo and Thomas Columkill Garrity) Assessing and Reforming Public Financial Management, 2004. *Recreations:* collecting art, music, golf. *Club:* Royal Wimbledon Golf.

ALLEN, Prof. Robert Carson, PhD; FRSCan; FBA 2003; Professor of Economic History, University of Oxford, since 2002; Fellow, Nuffield College, Oxford, since 2001; *b* 10 Jan. 1947; *s* of Richard Carson Allen and Barbara Tudbury Allen; *m* 1990, Dianne Frank; one *s*. *Educ:* Carleton Coll. (BA 1969); Harvard Univ. (MA 1972; PhD 1975). FRSCan 1994. Asst Prof., Hamilton Coll., 1973–75; University of British Columbia: Asst Prof., 1975–80; Associate Prof., 1980–85; Prof., 1985–2000; Reader in Recent Social and Econ. Hist., Oxford Univ., 2001–02. Vis. Prof., Harvard Univ., 1993–94, 1999–2000. *Publications:* (with G. Rosenbluth) Restraining the Economy: social credit economic policies for BC in the Eighties, 1986; (with G. Rosenbluth) False Promises: the failure of conservative economics, 1992; Enclosure and the Yeoman: agrarian change and English economic development 1450–1850, 1992; Farm to Factory: a reinterpretation of the Soviet industrial revolution, 2003. *Recreations:* mountaineering, carpentry, gardening. *Address:* Nuffield College, New Road, Oxford OX1 1NF. *T:* (01865) 278589, *Fax:* (01865) 278621; *e-mail:* bob.allen@nuffield.oxford.ac.uk.

ALLEN, Robert Geoffrey Bruère, (Robin); QC 1995; a Recorder, since 2000; *b* 13 Feb. 1951; *s* of Rev. Canon R. E. T. Allen and Isabel (*née* Otter-Barry); *m* 1977, Elizabeth Gay Moon; two *s*. *Educ:* Rugby; University Coll., Oxford (BA PPE 1972). Called to the Bar, Middle Temple, 1974 (Bencher, 2004); in practice, specialising in discrimination, employment and public law, and human rights, 1976–; an Asst Recorder, 1997–2000; Hd of Chambers, 2002– (Jt Head, 2002–05). Co-organiser and first Treas., Free Representation Unit, 1973. Employment Law Advr to Legal Action Gp, 1978–80; Legal Advr to Local Govt Gp, Inst. Public Relns, 1988–90; expert advr to EC on law affecting most disadvantaged, 1993. Founder Mem. Cttee, Employment Law Bar Assoc., 1994–99 (Chm., 1997–99); Chairman: Bar in the Community, 2000–02; Bar Pro Bono Unit, 2000–02; Mem., Bar Council, 1999–2001; Chm., Bar Conf. Organising Bd, 2002. Mem., Home Office Human Rights Task Force, 1999–2001. Special Advr to Disability Rights Commn, 2002–07; Consultant, Age Concern and Age Europe, 2004–. Trustee, London Bombing Relief Charitable Fund, 2005–. Sec., Lambeth Central CLP, 1977. Chm., London Youth Adv. Centre, 1984–90. Chairman: Bd of Govs, Eleanor Palmer Primary Sch., 1988–91; Brandon Centre for Psychotherapy, 1991–93. *Publications:* How to Prepare a Case for an Industrial Tribunal, 1987; (ed and contrib) Home Office/Bar Council Study Guide to the Human Rights Act, 2000, rev. edn for Dept of Constitutional Affairs/Bar Council, 2004; Employment Law and Human Rights, 2002, 2nd edn 2007; contributed to: The Legal Framework and Social Consequences of Free Movement of Persons in the European Union, 1998; Women, Work and Inequality: the challenge of equal pay in a deregulated labour market, 1999; Anti-Discrimination: the way forward, 1999; Race Discrimination: developing and using a new legal framework, 2000; Bullen and Leake and Jacob's Precedents of Pleadings, 2000; The Legal Regulation of the Employment Relationship, 2001; Equality Law in an Enlarged Europe, 2007. *Recreations:* family life, fireworks, fishing. *Address:* Cloisters, 1 Pump Court, Temple, EC4Y 7AA. *T:* (020) 7827 4000, *Fax:* (020) 7827 4100. *Club:* Vincent's (Oxford).
See also Very Rev. J. E. Allen.

ALLEN, Sir Thomas, Kt 1999; CBE 1989; singer; *b* 10 Sept. 1944; *s* of Thomas Boaz Allen and Florence Allen; *m* 1st, 1968, Margaret Holley (marr. diss. 1986); one *s*; 2nd, 1988, Jeannie Gordon Lascelles. *Educ:* Robert Richardson Grammar Sch., Ryhope; Royal College of Music. ARCM; FRCM 1988. Welsh Nat. Opera, 1969–72; Principal Baritone, Royal Opera, Covent Garden, 1972–78; appearances include: Glyndebourne Fest. Opera; English Opera Group; Paris Opera; Florence; Teatro Colon, Buenos Aires; Met. Opera, NY; Hamburg; La Scala, Milan; BBC TV (The Gondoliers, The Marriage of Figaro); all major orchestras and various concert engagements abroad. Major rôles include: Figaro in Barber of Seville; Figaro and the Count in Marriage of Figaro; Papageno in The Magic Flute; Billy Budd; Marcello in La Bohême; Belcore in l'Elisir d'Amore; Sid in Albert Herring; Tarquinius in Rape of Lucretia; Guglielmo, and Don Alfonso, in Così fan Tutte; Demetrius in A Midsummer Night's Dream; Valentin in Faust; Dr Falke, and Eisenstein, in Die Fledermaus; King Arthur; The Count in Voice of Ariadne; Silvio in Pagliacci; Pelléas in Pelléas and Mélisande; Germont in La Traviata; Don Giovanni; Mandryka in Arabella; Malatesta in Don Pasquale; title rôle in Il ritorno d'Ulisse; Beckmesser in Die Meistersinger; Prosdocimo in The Turk in Italy; Music Master in Ariadne auf Naxos; title rôle in Sweeney Todd, and many others. Director: Albert Herring, RCM, 2002; Il Barbiere di Siviglia, Th. Royal, Glasgow, 2007; Don Giovanni, Sage, Gateshead, 2007; prod., Così fan Tutte, Sage, Gateshead. Hambro Vis. Prof. of Opera, Oxford Univ., 2000–01. Kammersänger, Bayerische Staatsoper, 2003. Patron, Samling Foundn. Hon. RAM, 1988. Hon. MA Newcastle, 1984; Hon. DMus Durham, 1988. *Publication:* Foreign Parts: a singer's journal, 1993. *Recreations:* gardening, golf, sailing, painting, ornithology. *Address:* c/o Askonas Holt Ltd, Lincoln House, 300 High Holborn, WC1V 7JH.

ALLEN, Twink; *see* Allen, W. R.

ALLEN, William Anthony; economic consultant; Chief Economist, Denholm Hall Group, since 2007; *b* 13 May 1949; *s* of Derek William Allen and Margaret Winifred Allen (*née* Jones); *m* 1972, Rosemary Margaret Eminson; one *s* two *d*. *Educ:* King's College Sch., Wimbledon; Balliol College, Oxford (BA); LSE (MScEcon). Joined Bank of England, 1972; Economic Intell. Dept, 1972–77; Gold and Foreign Exchange Office, 1977–78; seconded to Bank for Internat. Settlements, Basle, 1978–80; Bank of England: Asst Adviser, Economics Div. (working on monetary policy), 1980–82; Manager, Gilt-Edged Div., 1982–86; Hd of Money Market Operations Div., 1986–90; Hd of Foreign Exchange Div., 1990–94; Dep. Dir, 1994–2003; Dir for Europe, 2002–04; Econ. Advr, Brevan Howard Asset Mgt LLP, 2004–07. Pt-time Advr, Nat. Bank of Poland, 1990–2001. Vis. Sen. Fellow, Faculty of Finance, Cass Business Sch., 2004–. *Publications:* articles in economics jls. *Recreations:* gardening, jazz. *Address:* Denholm Hall Group, 28 Grosvenor Street, W1K 4QR.

ALLEN, Hon. Sir William (Clifford), KCMG 2000; JP; Minister of Finance and Planning, Bahamas, 1995–2002; *b* 15 March 1937; *m* 1960, Aloma Munnings; three *s* one *d*. *Educ:* St Augustine's Coll., Nassau; Rhodes Sch., NYC; NY Univ. (BSc Accounting); CUNY (MBA). Internal auditor, Stone and Webster Securities Corp., NY, 1965–68; budget supervisor, J. C. Penny Co., NY, 1968–70; Res. Manager, Bahamas Monetary Authy, 1970–74; Dep. Gov., 1974–80, Gov., 1980–87, Central Bank of Bahamas; Pres., Matrix Investment Ltd, 1987–92. Mem., Bahamas Senate, 1992–94; MP (Free Nat. Movt) Montagu, Bahamas, Nov. 1994–2002; Minister of State, Ministry of Finance and Planning, 1992–93; Minister of Planning and Public Service, 1993–95. *Address:* Prospect Ridge, POB CB10993, Nassau, Bahamas.

ALLEN, Sir William (Guilford), Kt 1981; Chairman, family group of companies; *b* 22 April 1932; *s* of Sir William Guilford Allen, CBE, and Mona Maree Allen; *m* 1959, Elaine Therese Doyle; two *s* one *d*. *Educ:* Downlands Coll., Toowoomba, Qld. In grazing industry, Merino sheep; Principal, Historic Malvern Hills Registered Merino Stud; stud Santa Gertrudis cattle breeder. Commercial broadcasting industry. Chm., Qld Transport and Technology Centre, 1984; Director: Qantas, 1981; Suncorp Building Soc., 1985–89; Power Brewing Co., 1989. Mem., Longreach Base Hosp. Bd, 1960–83. Treas., 1981, Trustee, 1989–, Nat. Party, Qld. Councillor, Longreach Shire, 1958. Fellow, GAPAN. *Recreation:* aviation. *Clubs:* Brisbane, Tattersalls, Australian, Longreach, Queensland Turf, Brisbane Amateur Turf (Brisbane); Australian, Royal Sydney Golf (Sydney).

ALLEN, Maj.-Gen. William Maurice, CB 1983; FCIT, FIMI, FILDM; MInstPet; Senior Military Consultant to Mondial Defence Systems (formerly Mondial & Co.), 1985–95; Regional Vice President and Senior Defence Adviser, Fortis Aviation Group, 1995–99; *b* 29 May 1931; *s* of William James Allen and Elizabeth Jane Henrietta Allen; *m* 1st, 1955, Patricia Mary (*née* Fletcher) (*d* 1998); one *d* decd; 2nd, 1998, Elizabeth (*née* Irving). *Educ:* Dunstable Sch. FCIT 1972; FIMI 1982; FILDM (FIPDM 1982); FCMI (FBIM 1983); MInstPet 1982. Commnd RASC, 1950; RCT, 1965; regtl and staff appts, Korea, Cyprus, Germany and UK; Student, Staff Coll., Camberley, 1961; Instructor, Staff Coll., Camberley and RMCS Shrivenham, 1968–70; Student, RCDS, 1976; Asst Comdt, RMA Sandhurst, 1979–81; Dir Gen. of Transport and Movements (Army), 1981–83. Dir of Educn and Trng, Burroughs Machines Ltd, 1983–85. Jt Man. Dir, Marina Moraira Yacht Brokers, 1989–92; Man. Dir, Fortis Internat. Ltd, 1991–92; Director: Govt Projects, Unisys Corp. (formerly Systems Develt Corp.), Heidelberg, 1985–86; Fortis Aviation Gp, Spain, 1988–89; European Management Information, 1989–92. Member, Council: IAM, 1982–85; NDTA, 1983–90. Chm., Milton Keynes Information Technol. Trng Centre, 1983–85. Associate, St George's House. Freeman, City of London, 1981; Hon. Liveryman, Worshipful Co. of Carmen, 1981. *Recreations:* economics, trout fishing, gardening, vigneron et oleiculteur de Languedoc. *Address:* c/o Royal Bank of Scotland, Holts Farnborough Branch, Lawrie House, 31–37 Victoria Road, Farnborough, Hants GU14 7NR.

ALLEN, Prof. William Richard, (Twink), CBE 2002; PhD, ScD; FRCVS; Jim Joel Professor of Equine Reproduction, Department of Veterinary Medicine (formerly Clinical Veterinary Medicine), University of Cambridge, 1995–2007; Fellow, Robinson College, Cambridge, 1995–2007, now Emeritus; Director, Thoroughbred Breeders' Association Equine Fertility Unit, Newmarket, 1989–2006; *b* 29 Aug. 1940; *s* of Francis Cecil Allen and Rose St Ledger Allen (*née* Sinclair); *m* 1965, Diana Margaret Emms; one *s* two *d*. *Educ:* Auckland Grammar Sch.; Univ. of Auckland; Univ. of Sydney (BVSc 1965); Univ. of Cambridge (PhD in Equine Reproductive Physiology 1970). FRCVS 2004. In vet. practice, Kaitaia, NZ, 1965; res. student, Dept of Clinical Vet. Medicine, Univ. of Cambridge, 1966–70; Post Doctoral Scientist, AFRC Unit of Reproductive Physiol. and Biochem., Cambridge, 1970–72; Prin. Vet. Res. Officer, Thoroughbred Breeders' Assoc. Equine Fertility Unit, Animal Res. Stn, Cambridge, 1972–89. *Publications:* (ed) Equine Reproduction, vols I–V, 1975–91; contrib. Proc. Internat. Symposia on Equine Reproduction; numerous papers in scientific jls and reference books. *Recreations:* fox hunting, horse racing, wildlife conservation. *Address:* Hare Park Stud House, London Road, Six-Mile-Bottom, near Newmarket, Suffolk CB8 0UZ. *T:* (01638) 572044; The Paul Mellon Laboratory of Equine Reproduction, 3 Tower Stables, Cheveley Park, Newmarket, Suffolk CB8 9DE. *T:* (01638) 730166, *Fax:* (05601) 533265.

See also L. Dettori.

ALLEN, Woody, (Allen Stewart Konigsberg); writer, actor, director; *b* Brooklyn, 1 Dec. 1935; *s* of late Martin and of Nettie Konigsberg; *m* 1966, Louise Lasser (marr. diss.); one *s* by Mia Farrow, *qv*; *m* 1997, Soon-Yi Previn. TV script writer, 1953–64, and appeared as a comedian in nightclubs and on TV shows. Sylvania Award, 1957. *Plays:* (writer) Don't Drink the Water, 1966; (writer and actor) Play It Again Sam, 1969 (filmed 1972); The Floating Light Bulb, 1990; (writer and dir) A Second Hand Memory, 2005. *Films:* (writer and actor) What's New Pussycat?, 1965; (actor): Casino Royale, 1967; Scenes from a Mall, 1991; (writer, actor and director): What's Up Tiger Lily?, 1966; Take the Money and Run, 1969; Bananas, 1971; Everything You Always Wanted to Know About Sex But Were Afraid to Ask, 1972; Sleeper, 1973; Love and Death, 1975; The Front, 1976; Annie Hall (Academy Award), 1977; Manhattan, 1979; Stardust Memories, 1980; A Midsummer Night's Sex Comedy, 1982; Zelig, 1983; Broadway Danny Rose, 1984; Hannah and her Sisters (Academy Award), 1986; New York Stories, 1989; Shadows and Fog, 1992; Husbands and Wives, 1992; Manhattan Murder Mystery, 1994; Mighty Aphrodite, 1995; Everyone Says I Love You, 1996; Deconstructing Harry, 1997; Small Time Crooks, 2000; The Curse of the Jade Scorpion, 2001; Hollywood Ending, 2002; Anything Else, 2003; (writer and director): Interiors, 1978; The Purple Rose of Cairo, 1985; Radio Days, 1987; September, 1988; Another Woman, 1989; Crimes and Misdemeanours, 1989; Alice, 1990; Bullets over Broadway, 1995; Celebrity, 1999; Sweet and Lowdown, 1999; Melinda and Melinda, 2005; Match Point, 2006; Cassandra's Dream, 2008. *Publications:* Getting Even, 1971; Without Feathers, 1975; Side Effects, 1981; Three One-Act Plays, 2004; Mere Anarchy (short stories), 2007; The Insanity Defense, 2007; contribs to New Yorker, etc.

ALLEN-JONES, Charles Martin; Senior Partner, Linklaters (formerly Linklaters & Paines), 1996–2001; Joint Chairman, Linklaters & Alliance, 1998–2001; *b* 7 Aug. 1939; *s* of late Air Vice-Marshal John Ernest Allen-Jones, CBE, and Margaret Allen-Jones (*née* Rix); *m* 1966, Caroline Beale; one *s* two *d*. *Educ:* Clifton Coll., Bristol. Admitted Solicitor, 1963. Articled Clerk: to the Clerk to the Justices, Uxbridge Magistrates Court, 1958–60; Vizard Oldman Crowder & Cash, London, 1960–63; Solicitor, Supreme Court, London, 1963; Linklaters & Paines, subseq. Linklaters: Solicitor, 1964; Partner, 1968–2001; Head, Hong Kong office, 1976–81; Head, Corporate Dept, 1985–91. Director: Caledonia Investments plc, 2001–; Hongkong Land Holdings Ltd, 2001–. Mem., Financial Reporting Council, 2001–07 (Member: Corporate Governance Cttee, 2004–; Financial Reporting Review Panel, 2006–). Trustee: BM, 2000–04; Asia House, 2001– (Chm., 2005–06). Member: Barbican Adv. Council, 1997–2005; Council, RCA, 2004– (Vice Chm., 2007–); Internat. Adv. Council, SOAS, 2007–. Mem., Cttee, Hong Kong Assoc., 2002–. Consultant Ed., CUP Law Practitioner Series, 2003–. *Recreations:* keeping in touch, Asia, travel, tennis, golf. *Address:* 6 Kensington Place, W8 7PT. *Clubs:* Brooks's; Cambridge University Real Tennis; Hong Kong (Hong Kong).

ALLENBY, family name of **Viscount Allenby**.

ALLENBY, 3rd Viscount *cr* 1919, of Megiddo and of Felixstowe; **Michael Jaffray Hynman Allenby;** Lieutenant-Colonel, The Royal Hussars, retired 1986; a Deputy Speaker, House of Lords, since 1993; *b* 20 April 1931; *s* of 2nd Viscount Allenby and of Mary Lethbridge Allenby (*d* 1988), *d* of Edward Champneys; *S* father, 1984; *m* 1965, Sara Margaret, *d* of Lt-Col Peter Milner Wiggin; one *s*. *Educ:* Eton; RMA Sandhurst. Commnd 2/Lieut 11th Hussars (PAO), 1951; served Malaya, 1953–56; ADC to Governor, Cyprus, 1957–58; Bde Major, 51 Brigade, Hong Kong, 1967–70; comd Royal Yeomanry (TA), 1974–77; GSO1 Instructor, Nigerian Staff Coll., Kaduna, 1977–79. Chm., Quickrest Ltd, 1987–90. Elected Mem., H of L, 1999. Vice Pres., Internat. League for Protection of Horses, 1999–2006 (Chm., 1997–99). *Recreations:* horses, sailing. *Heir:* *s* Hon. Henry Jaffray Hynman Allenby [*b* 29 July 1968; *m* 1997, Louise, *yr d* of Michael Green; two *s*].

ALLENDALE, 4th Viscount *cr* 1911; **Wentworth Peter Ismay Beaumont;** Baron 1906; *b* 13 Nov. 1948; *e s* of 3rd Viscount Allendale and of Hon. Sarah, 2nd *d* of 1st Baron Ismay, KG, GCB, CH, DSO, PC; *S* father, 2002; *m* 1975, Theresa Mary Magdalene (*née* More O'Ferrall); one *s* three *d*. *Educ:* Harrow. Landowner. *Recreations:* shooting, ski-ing, horseracing. *Heir:* *s* Hon. Wentworth Ambrose Ismay Beaumont, *b* 11 June 1979. *Address:* Bywell Castle, Stocksfield, Northumberland NE43 7AB. *T:* (01661) 842450, *Fax:* (01661) 842838. *Clubs:* Jockey, White's; Northern Counties, Recorders (Newcastle upon Tyne).

ALLENDE, Isabel; writer; *b* 2 Aug. 1942; *d* of Tomás Allende Pesce and Francisca Llona Barros; *m* 1st, 1962, Miguel Frías (marr. diss. 1987); one *s* (one *d* decd); 2nd, 1988, William C. Gordon. *Educ:* Ursulinas (German nuns), Chile; Dunalastaid Amer. Sch., La Paz; British Lebanese Trng Coll., Lebanon; La Maisonette, Chile. Journalist: Chile, 1964–74 (Paula (women's mag.), Mampato (children's mag.), TV programmes, film documentaries); El Nacional, Venezuela, 1975–84; Lecturer in Literature: Montclair Coll., USA; Univ. of Calif at Berkeley, 1988; Univ. of Virginia, 1988. Member: Academía de la Lengua, Chile, 1989; Academía de Artes y Ciencias, Puerto Rico, 1995. Hon. Prof. of Literature, Univ. of Chile, 1991. Lecture tours, N America and Europe. Work has been translated into more than 27 languages and has received numerous literary awards. Hon. DLitt: SUNY, 1991; Bates Coll., USA, 1994; Dominican Coll., USA, 1994; Columbia Coll., USA, 1996; Hon. DHL Florida Atlantic, 1996. Condecoración Gabriela Mistral (Chile), 1994; Chevalier, Ordre des Arts et des Lettres (France), 1994. *Plays:* El Embajador, 1971; La Balada del Medio Pelo, 1973; Los Siete Espejos, 1974. *Publications:* *novels:* La Casa de los Espíritus (The House of Spirits), 1982 (filmed; adapted for stage); De Amor y de Sombra (Of Love and Shadows), 1984 (filmed); Eva Luna, 1985 (adapted for stage); El Plan Infinito (The Infinite Plan), 1991; Paula, 1994 (adapted for stage); Hija de la Fortuna (Daughter of Fortune), 1999; Retrato en Sepia (Portrait in Sepia), 2000; La Ciudad de las Bestias (City of the Beasts), 2002; El reino del Dragón de Oro (Kingdom of the Golden Dragon), 2003; El Bosque de los Pigmeos (Forest of the Pygmies), 2005; Zorro, 2005; Inés del Alma Mía (Inés of My Soul), 2006; *short stories:* La Gorda de Porcelana, 1983; Cuentos de Eva Luna (Stories of Eva Luna), 1989 (adapted for theatre, opera, and ballet); Afrodita (Aphrodite), 1997; *memoirs:* Mi país inventado (My Invented Country), 2003; The Sum of Our Days, 2008; articles in jls in N America and Europe. *Address:* 116 Caledonia Street, Sausalito, CA 94965, USA.

ALLERTON, Air Vice-Marshal Richard Christopher, CB 1989; DL; Director General of Supply, Royal Air Force, 1987–90, retired; Chairman, Sharpe's of Aberdeen, 1995–98; *b* 7 Dec. 1935; *er s* of late Air Cdre Ord Denny Allerton, CB, CBE, and Kathleen Mary Allerton; *m* 1964, Marie Isobel Campbell Mackenzie, *er d* of Captain Sir Roderick Mackenzie, 11th Bt, CBE, DSC, RN, and Marie, Lady Mackenzie; two *s*. *Educ:* Stone House, Broadstairs; Stowe Sch. Commissioned RAF, 1954; served, 1955–78: RAF Hullavington, Oakington, Feltwell, Kinloss, RAF Unit HQ Coastal Command, Hereford, Little Rissington; Instructor, RAF Coll., Cranwell; Student, RAF Staff Coll., Bracknell; Staff, HQ RAF Germany; Chief Instructor, Supply and Secretarial Trng, RAF Coll., Cranwell; Student, Nat. Defence Coll., Latimer; MoD Harrogate; Dep. Dir, RAF Supply Policy, MoD, 1978–80; Station Comdr, RAF Stafford, 1980–82; RCDS 1983; Air Cdre, Supply and Movements, HQ Strike Comd, 1983–86. ADC to the Queen, 1980–82. Pres., RAF Cricket Assoc., 1987–89. Mem., St John Council for Cornwall, 1991–2000. DL Cornwall, 1995. *Recreations:* shooting, fishing, cricket. *Address:* c/o Lloyds TSB, 13 Broad Street, Launceston, Cornwall PL15 8AG. *Club:* Royal Air Force.

ALLEYNE, Sir George (Allanmore Ogarren), Kt 1990; OCC 2001; MD, FRCP; Director, Pan American Health Organization, 1995–2003 (Assistant Director, 1990–95), now Director Emeritus; Special Envoy of the UN Secretary-General for HIV/AIDS in the Caribbean, since 2003; *b* 7 Oct. 1932; *s* of Clinton O. Alleyne and Eileen A. Alleyne (*née* Gaskin); *m* 1958, Sylvan Ionie (*née* Chen); two *s* one *d*. *Educ:* Harrison College, Barbados; University College of the West Indies (MB BS London 1977, MD). Completed training as physician in Barbados and UCH, London, 1958–62; Sen. Med. Registrar, UCH, Jamaica, 1962–63; Res. Fellow, Sen. Res. Fellow, MRC Tropical Metabolism Res. Unit, 1963–72; Prof. of Medicine, Univ. of W Indies, 1972–81 (Chm., Dept of Medicine, 1976–81); Pan American Health Organization: Head of Res. Unit, 1981–83; Dir of Health Programs Develt, 1983–90. Chancellor, Univ. of W Indies, 2003–. Sir Arthur Sims Travelling Prof., 1977. Hon. FACP. Hon. DSc Univ. of W Indies, 1989. Jamaica Assoc. of Scientists Award, 1979. Jamaica Centenary Medal, 1980. *Publications:* contribs to learned jls on medicine, renal physiology and biochemistry, health and develt issues. *Recreations:* reading, gardening. *Address:* Pan American Health Organization, 525 23rd Street NW, Washington, DC 20037, USA. *T:* (202) 9743057.

ALLEYNE, Rev. Sir John (Olpherts Campbell), 5th Bt *cr* 1769; Rector of Weeke, Diocese of Winchester, 1975–93; *b* 18 Jan. 1928; *s* of Captain Sir John Meynell Alleyne, 4th Bt, DSO, DSC, RN, and Alice Violet (*d* 1985), *d* of late James Campbell; *S* father, 1983; *m* 1968, Honor, *d* of late William Albert Irwin, Belfast; one *s* one *d*. *Educ:* Eton; Jesus Coll., Cambridge (BA 1950, MA 1955). Deacon 1955, priest 1956; Curate, Southampton, 1955–58; Chaplain: Coventry Cathedral, 1958–62; Clare Coll., Cambridge, 1962–66; to Bishop of Bristol, 1966–68; Toc H Area Sec., SW England, 1968–71; Vicar of Speke, 1971–73, Rector, 1973–75. *Heir:* *s* Richard Meynell Alleyne, *b* 23 June 1972. *Address:* 2 Ash Grove, Guildford, Surrey GU2 8UT.

ALLEYNE, Selwyn Eugene, CBE 1986; Hong Kong Commissioner in London, 1987–89, retired; *b* 4 Dec. 1930; *s* of Gilbert Sydney Alleyne and Dorothy Alleyne; *m* 1956, Ellie Lynn Wong, MBE. *Educ:* Queen's Royal Coll., Trinidad; Jesus Coll., Oxford (MA). Joined Hong Kong Govt, 1956; Dep. Dir of Urban Services, 1974; Dep. Sec. for Civil Service, 1979; Dir of Social Welfare, and MLC, 1980; Dep. Financial Sec., 1983–87. *Recreations:* tennis, chess, collecting Chinese ceramics. *Clubs:* Civil Service; Hong Kong Jockey.

ALLI, Baron *cr* 1998 (Life Peer), of Norbury in the London Borough of Croydon; **Waheed Alli;** Chairman, Chorion Ltd, since 2003; *b* 16 Nov. 1964. *Educ:* Norbury Manor Sch. Formed televised production co., 24 Hour Productions, later Planet 24 Productions Ltd, with partner Charlie Parsons, Jt Man. Dir, 1992–99; Man. Dir, Carlton Productions, 1998–2000; Dir, Carlton Television, 1998–2000. Director: Shine Entertainment Ltd; Castaway Television; Chm., ASOS. Member: Teacher Trng Agency, 1997–98; Panel 2000; Creative Industry Taskforce; Bd, UK, UNICEF, 2002– (Vice Pres., 2002–). Gov., LSE, 2002–06. *Address:* House of Lords, SW1A 0PW.

ALLIANCE, Baron *cr* 2004 (Life Peer), of Manchester in the County of Greater Manchester; **David Alliance,** Kt 1989; CBE 1984; Chairman, N. Brown Group plc, since 1968; *b* June 1932. *Educ:* Iran. First acquisition, Thomas Hoghton (Oswaldtwistle), 1956; acquired Spirella, 1968, then Vantona Ltd, 1975, to form Vantona Group, 1975; acquired Carrington Viyella to form Vantona Viyella, 1983, Nottingham Manufacturing, 1985, Coats Patons to form Coats Viyella, 1986; Gp Chief Exec., 1975–90, Chm., 1989–99; Chm., Tootal Gp, 1991–99. Gov., Tel Aviv Univ., 1989–. CCMI (CBIM 1985); CompTI 1984. FRSA 1988. Hon. Fellow: UMIST 1988; Shenkar Coll. of Textile Tech. and Fashion, Israel, 1990. Hon. FCGI 1991. Hon. LLD: Victoria Univ. of Manchester, 1989; Liverpool, 1996; Hon. DSc Heriot-Watt, 1991. *Address:* House of Lords, SW1A 0PW.

ALLIES, Edgar Robin, (Bob); Partner, Allies and Morrison, architects, since 1983; *b* 5 Sept. 1953; *s* of Edgar Martyn Allies, MBE, DFC and Lily Maud Allies; *m* 1991, Jill Anne

Franklin; one *s* one *d. Educ:* Reading Sch.; Univ. of Edinburgh (MA Hons 1976; DipArch 1977). Rome Schol. in Architecture, 1981–82; Lectr, Univ. of Cambridge, 1984–88; George Simpson Vis. Prof., Univ. of Edinburgh, 1995; Vis. Prof., Univ. of Bath, 1996–99; Kea Dist. Vis. Prof., Univ. of Maryland, 1999. Mem., Faculty of Fine Arts, Brit. Sch. at Rome, 1997–2002. Mem. Council, AA, 2004–. With G. Morrison, founded Allies and Morrison, 1983; *completed projects* include: Clove Bldg, London, 1990 (RIBA Award 1991); Pierhead, Liverpool, 1995; Sarum Hall Sch., London, 1995 (RIBA Award 1996); Nunnery Sq., Sheffield, 1995 (RIBA Award 1996); British Embassy, Dublin, 1995 (RIBA Award 1997); Rosalind Franklin Bldg, Newnham Coll., Cambridge, 1995 (RIBA Award 1996); Abbey Mills Pumping Station, Stratford (RIBA Award), 1997; Rutherford Inf. Services Bldg, Goldsmiths Coll., London, 1997 (RIBA Award 1998); Extension to Horniman Mus., 2002 (RIBA Award 2004; Civic Trust Award 2004); One Piccadilly Gdns, Manchester, 2003 (RIBA Award 2004); 85 Southwark Street, 2003 (London Civic Trust Award 2004; RIBA London Bldg of the Year, 2004; Corporate Workplace Bldg Nat. Winner, British Council for Offices Awards, 2004); BBC Media Village, White City, 2004 (RIBA Award 2005); Fitzwilliam Coll. Gatehouse and Auditorium, 2004 (RIBA Award 2005); Girton Coll. Library, Cambridge, 2005 (RIBA Award 2006); British Council, Lagos, 2005 (RIBA Internat. Awards); Farnborough Business Park, 2006 (RIBA Award 2007); *exhibitions* include: New British Architecture, Japan, 1994; Allies and Morrison Retrospective, USA Schools of Architecture, 1996–98, Helsinki, Delft, Strasbourg, 1999. Edinburgh Architectural Assoc. Medal for Architecture, 1977; Allies and Morrison winner of Architectural Practice of the Year, Bldg Awards, 2004; Architect of the Year Award, Building Design Awards, 2007. *Publications:* Model Futures, 1983; Allies and Morrison, 1996. *Recreation:* contemporary music. *Address:* Allies and Morrison, 85 Southwark Street, SE1 0HX. *T:* (020) 7921 0100; 12 Well Road, NW3 1LH. *T:* (020) 7443 9309.

ALLIN, George, RCNC; Director General Ship Refitting, Ministry of Defence, 1989–93, retired; *b* 21 June 1933; *s* of late Henry Richard Allin and Mary Elizabeth Allin (*née* Wyatt); *m* 1st, 1956, Barbara May Short (marr. diss.); two *s*; 2nd, 1977, Janice Annette Richardson-Sandell. *Educ:* Devonport High Sch.; Devonport Dockyard Tech. Coll.; RNEC Manadon; RNC Greenwich. WhSch, BSc. Asst Elect. Engineer, 1957–59; HMS Belfast, 1959; Admiralty, Bath, 1959–62; Elect. Engineer, MoD (Navy), Bath, 1963–68; HM Dockyard, Devonport: Line Manager, 1968–70; Project Manager Frigates, 1970–71; Supt Elect. Engineer, Dep. Personnel Manager, 1971–74; Industrial Relations Manager, 1975; Org. and Develt. Div., Dockyard HQ, Bath, 1975–79; rcds 1979; HM Dockyard, Rosyth: Project Manager, SSBN Refit, 1980–81; Production Dir, 1981–83; Dockyard HQ, Bath: Management Systems and Audit Div., 1984–85; Principal Dir, Policy and Plans, 1985–86; Principal Dir, Ship Refitting, MoD (Navy), Bath, 1986–87; Dir, Aldermaston Projects, Brown & Root (on secondment), 1987–89. *Recreations:* chess, music, bowls, snooker, philately.

ALLINSON, Sir (Walter) Leonard, KCVO 1979 (MVO 1961); CMG 1976; HM Diplomatic Service, retired; *b* 1 May 1926; *o s* of Walter Allinson and Alice Frances Cassidy; *m* 1951, Margaret Patricia Watts; three *d* (of whom two are twins). *Educ:* Friern Barnet Grammar Sch.; Merton Coll., Oxford (First class in History, 1947; MA). Asst Principal, Ministry of Fuel and Power (Petroleum Div.), 1947–48; Asst Principal, later Principal, Min. of Education, 1948–58 (Asst Private Sec. to Minister, 1953–54); transf. CRO, 1958; First Sec. in Lahore and Karachi, 1960–62, Madras and New Delhi, 1963–66; Counsellor and Head of Political Affairs Dept, March 1968; Dep. Head, later Head, of Permanent Under Secretary's Dept, FCO, 1968–70; Counsellor and Head of Chancery, subsequently Deputy High Comr, Nairobi, 1970–73; RCDS, 1974; Diplomatic Service Inspectorate, 1975; Dep. High Comr and Minister, New Delhi, 1975–77; High Comr, Lusaka, 1978–80; Asst Under-Sec. of State (Africa), 1980–82; High Comr in Kenya and Ambassador to UN Environment Programme, 1982–86. Vice Pres., Royal African Soc., 1982–99; Mem. Council, East Africa Inst., 1986–92; Hon. Vice Chm., Kenya Soc., 1989–; Chm., Finance Cttee, Cornwall Red Cross, 1996–98. Gov., Wendron Voluntary Primary Sch., 1990–2003. *Address:* Tregarthen, Wendron, Helston, Cornwall TR13 0PY. *Club:* Oriental.

ALLIOT-MARIE, Dr Michèle Yvette Marie-Thérèse; Minister of the Interior, France, since 2007; *b* 10 Sept. 1946; *d* of Bernard Marie and Renée Leyko. *Educ:* Lycée Folie St-James, Neuilly-sur-Seine; Paris Sorbonne Univ. (BA Private Law, Pol Scis and Hist. of Law; Cert. Law and Econs in African Countries; MA Ethnol.; PhD Law and Politics). Sen. Lectr, Paris Sorbonne Univ., 1984–. Jun. Minister i/c teaching affairs, 1986–88; Mem. (RPR) EP, 1989–94; Minister of Youth and Sports, 1993–95. Deputy for Pyrénées-Atlantiques: (RPR), 1986, 1988, 1993, 1995, 1997; (UMP), 2002, 2007; Minister of Defence, 2002–07. Member: Municipal Council: Ciboure, 1983–88; Biarritz, 1989–91; and First Vice-Pres., Gen. Council, Pyrénées-Atlantiques, 1994–2001. Mayor, St-Jean-de-Luz, 1995–2002. Rassemblement pour la République: various posts including: Mem., Central Cttee, 1984–, Exec. Cttee, 1985–; Dep. Gen. Sec. i/c foreign affairs, 1990–93; Mem., Party Exec., 1991–; National Secretary: i/c social affairs, 1998–99; i/c elections, 1999; Party Chm., 1999–2002. Decorations include: Commandeur: Mérite de l'Educn Nat. and Croix de Comdr, Ordre Nat. (Ivory Coast); Ordre de la République (Egypt); Palmes magistrales 1st Cl. (Peru); Ordre de Stara Planina (Bulgaria); Grand Officier, Ordre Nat. du Lion (Senegal). *Publications:* La Décision Politique: attention! une République peut en cacher une autre, 1983; La Grande Peur des Classes Moyennes, 1996; Les Boursiers Étrangers en France: errements et potentialités, 1997; La République des Irresponsables, 1999; Le Chêne qu'on relève, 2005. *Address:* Ministère de l'Intérieur, Place Beauvau, 75008 Paris, France.

ALLIOTT, Sir John (Downes), Kt 1986; Judge of the High Court of Justice, Queen's Bench Division, 1986–2001; *b* 9 Jan. 1932; *er s* of late Alexander Clifford Alliott and Ena Kathleen Alliott (*née* Downes); *m* 1957, Patsy Jennifer, *d* of late Gordon Beckles Willson; two *s* one *d. Educ:* Charterhouse; Peterhouse, Cambridge (Schol., BA). Coldstream Guards, 1950–51; Peterhouse, 1951–54; called to Bar, Inner Temple, 1955, Bencher 1980; QC 1973. Dep. Chm., E Sussex QS, 1970–71; Recorder, 1972–86; Leader, 1983–86, Presiding Judge, 1989–92, SE Circuit. Member: Home Office Adv. Bd on Restricted Patients, 1983–86; Parole Bd, 1994–98 (Vice Chm., 1996–98). *Recreations:* rural pursuits, France and Italy, military history. *Address:* Park Stile, Love Hill Lane, Langley, Slough SL3 6DE.

ALLISON, Brian George; Operating Partner, Cognetas LLP (formerly Electra Partners Europe Ltd), since 2001; Director, Goodwood Estate Company Ltd, since 2007; *b* 4 April 1933; *s* of late Donald Brian Allison and Edith Maud Allison (*née* Humphries); *m* 1st, 1958, Glennis Mary Taylor (*d* 1993); one *s* one *d*; 2nd, 1996, Joanne Valerie Norman. *Educ:* Hele's Sch., Exeter; University Coll. London (BSc Econ). FCIM 1981. Flying Officer, RAF, 1955–58. Economist Statistician, Shell-Mex & BP, 1958; Marketing Res. Manager, Spicers, 1958–64; Business Intelligence Services, subseq. The BIS Group: Dir, 1964–91; Gen. Manager, 1964–69; Man. Dir and Dep. Chm., 1969–74; Chm. and Man. Dir, 1974–81; Chm. and Chief Exec., 1981–85; Exec. Chm., 1985–87. Director: NYNEX Inf. Solutions Gp, 1987–90; NYNEX Network Systems Co. (Brussels) SA, 1991–93; non-executive Director: English China Clays plc, subseq. ECC Gp, 1984–92; Brammer plc, 1988–97; Electra Corporate Ventures Ltd, 1989–96; Microgen Holdings plc, 1992–98; Unitech plc, 1993–96; Flexible Management Systems Ltd, 1998–2001; Mem., London Bd, Halifax Building Soc., 1991–95; Chm., Holt Lloyd Gp, 1995–97; Chm. and non-exec. Dir, Amtico Holdings Ltd, 1996–2006; Chm. and non-exec. Dir, Smith Gp Holdings, subseq. Detica Gp plc, 1997–2001. Mem., ESRC, 1986–90. University of Surrey: Vis. Prof., 1976–92, 1994–; Chm., Industrial Adv. Panel, Sch. of Mechanical and Materials Engrg, 1998–2001. Distinguished Scholar, QUB, 1989. *Recreations:* tennis, travel, motoring, restoring historic properties. *Clubs:* Reform; Goodwood Road Racing, Bentley Drivers, Rolls-Royce Enthusiasts.

ALLISON, Air Vice-Marshal Dennis, CB 1987; Chief Executive, North Western Regional Health Authority, 1990–94 (General Manager, 1986–90); *b* 15 Oct. 1932; *m* 1964, Rachel Anne, *d* of Air Vice-Marshal J. G. Franks, CB, CBE; one *s* four *d. Educ:* RAF Halton; RAF Coll., Cranwell; Manchester Univ. (MA 1994). Commnd, 1954; No 87 Sqdn, 1955–58; cfs 1958; Flying Instructor and Coll. Adjt, RAF Coll., 1958–61; CO, RAF Sharjah, 1961–62; Indian Jt Services Staff Coll., 1965; HQ 224 Gp, 1965–68; MoD Central Staffs, 1968–70; ndc, 1973; MoD Central Staffs, 1973–74; CO, RAF Coningsby, 1974–76; Canadian Nat. Defence Coll., 1977; MoD Central Staffs, 1978–79; Comdt, Central Flying Sch., 1979–83; Dir of Training (Flying), MoD, 1983–84; Dir of Management and Support of Intelligence, MoD, 1985–86; retired 1987. Chm., Family Health Service Computer Unit, 1992–94; Member: NHS Trng Authority, 1988–91; Standing Cttee on Postgrad. Medical Educn, 1988–93; Steering Cttee on Pharmacist Postgrad. Educn, 1991–94; Adv. Bd, NHS Estates, 1991–95; Nat. Blood Authority, 1993–2001 (Vice Chm., 1994–2001). Gov., Salford Coll. of Technology, 1987–89. QCVSA 1959. *Recreation:* following professional ladies' golf. *Address:* 5 Castlegate, Castle Bytham, Grantham, Lincs NG33 4RU. *T:* (01780) 410372. *Club:* Royal Air Force (Hon. Life Mem., 2004).

ALLISON, Gillian Margaret Clarkson; a District Judge (Magistrates' Courts), since 2005; *b* 23 Dec. 1960; *d* of Murray Penman Clarkson and Margaret Gladys Clarkson; *m* 1985, Glen Stuart Allison; two *s. Educ:* Merchant Taylors' Sch. for Girls; Surrey Univ.; Central London Poly. (Dip. Law, ext.); Inns of Court Sch. of Law. Called to the Bar, Gray's Inn, 1990; Bench Legal Manager, HM Courts Service, and Dep. Dist Judge, 2003–05. *Recreations:* family, friends, fitness training, Saracens RFC. *Address:* St Albans Magistrates' Court, St Peter's Street, St Albans AL1 3LB.

ALLISON, John, CBE 1975; company director; *b* 4 Oct. 1919; *m* 1st, 1948, Elvira Gwendoline Lewis (*d* 1992); one *s* two *d*; 2nd, 1997, Barbara Mary Tarrant. *Educ:* Morriston Elementary Sch.; Glanmor Secondary Sch.; Swansea Tech. Coll. In family business of quarrying to 1968, and musical instrument retailing, 1957–89. Mem. (Lab) Swansea City Council, 1957–74, Leader, 1967–74 (Dep. Mayor, 1966–67 and 1972–73); Mem. (Lab) W Glamorgan County Council, 1974–89, Leader, 1977–89 (Chm., 1975–76); Chm., ACC, 1986–88. Contested (Lab) Barry, 1970. Chm., S Wales Police Authority, 1987–89. DL W Glam, subseq. Swansea, 1975; JP Swansea, 1966. *Recreations:* fishing, gardening. *Club:* Morriston Golf.

ALLISON, John, PhD; Editor, Opera, since 2000; Music Critic, Sunday Telegraph, since 2005; *b* 20 May 1965; *s* of David Allison and Adele Myrtle Allison (*née* Kirby); *m* 1991, Nicole Galgut; one *s. Educ:* Rondebosch Boys' High Sch., Cape Town; Univ. of Cape Town (BMus 1986, PhD 1989); ARCO. Asst Organist, St George's Cathedral, Cape Town, 1985–89; Music Master, Culford Sch., 1990–91; Asst Ed., 1991–97, Co-ed., 1998–99, Opera mag.; Music Critic, The Times, 1995–2005. Ed., Glyndebourne Fest. prog., 1999–. *Publications:* Edward Elgar: sacred music, 1994; The Pocket Companion to Opera, 1994; (contrib.) New Grove Dictionary of Music and Musicians, 2nd edn 2001; (contrib.) Words on Music: essays in honour of Andrew Porter on the occasion of his 75th birthday, 2004. *Recreations:* travel, art. *Address:* Opera Magazine, 36 Black Lion Lane, W6 9BE. *T:* (020) 8563 8893; *e-mail:* john@opera.co.uk.

ALLISON, Air Chief Marshal Sir John (Shakespeare), KCB 1995; CBE 1986 (MBE 1971); Chairman, Hawk Associates Ltd, since 2007; *b* 24 March 1943; *o s* of Walter Allison and Mollie Emmie Allison (*née* Poole); *m* 1966, Gillian Patricia Middleton; two *s* three *d. Educ:* Royal Grammar Sch., Guildford; RAF College, Cranwell; psc, rcds. Commissioned 1964; flying and staff appts include: 5 Sqn; 226 OCU; 310 TFTS (USAF), Arizona; OC 228 OCU; Station Comdr, RAF Wildenrath; Sec., Chiefs of Staff Cttee; Dir, Air Force Plans and Programmes, 1987–89; ACDS Operational Requirements (Air), MoD, 1989–91; AOC No 11 Gp, 1991–94; COS and Dep. C-in-C, Strike Command, 1994–96; Air Member for Logistics and AOC-in-C, Logistics Comd, 1996–97; AOC-in-C, Strike Comd, 1997–99; Air ADC to Queen, 1997–99. Gentleman Usher to Sword of State, 2005–. Dir of Strategy, 2001–02, Ops Dir, 2002–04, Jaguar Racing Ltd; Project Dir, Filton Site Develt, Rolls-Royce plc, 2005–07. Mem., Criminal Injuries Compensation Appeals Panel, 2000–. Dir and Trustee, Shuttleworth Trust, 1999–. President: Europe Air Sports, 2004–; Popular Flying Assoc., 2006–. FRAeS 1995. *Recreations:* air display flying, gliding. *Address:* c/o National Westminster Bank, 24 Broadgate, Coventry CV1 1NB. *Club:* Royal Air Force.

ALLISON, Julia; General Secretary, 1994–97, Vice President, since 1997, Royal College of Midwives; *b* 26 Sept. 1939; *d* of Alfred Arthur Richley and Amelia (*née* Douglas); *m* 1960, Barrie Allison; one *s* one *d. Educ:* Lilley and Stone Foundn for Girls, Newark, Notts; Univ. of Nottingham (MA); Wolverhampton Poly. (CertEd (Dist.)). RM; ADM; MTD. Clerical officer, Civil Service, 1956–62; liby officer, Nottingham City Libraries, 1963–66; resident in Australia, 1966–68; liby officer, Nottingham City Libraries, 1968–79; direct entry pupil midwife, 1970–72; dist midwife, Nottingham Local Authy, 1972–76; midwifery sister, night duty, Nottingham AHA, 1976–77; registered foster mother, Nottingham Social Services, 1977–79; community midwife, Nottingham HA, 1979–86; midwife teacher, Kingsmill Hosp., 1986–89; Associate Researcher and Sen. Midwife Advr, Univ. of Nottingham, 1989–91; Head of Midwifery Educn, Norfolk Coll. of Nursing and Midwifery, 1991–94. Norwich Diocesan Pres., Mother's Union, 2001–06; Lay Canon, Norwich Cathedral, 2002–. *Publications:* Delivered at Home, 1996; The Organisation of Midwifery Care, 1998; (ed) First World War Diary of Robert Douglas, 2002; A Lifetime of Happiness, 2007; The Oldest Oriental Carpet Emporium, 2007. *Recreations:* painting, writing. *Address:* Victory Cottage, 6 Jermyns Road, Reydon, Southwold, Suffolk IP18 6QB.

ALLISON, Roderick Stuart, CB 1996; Joint Chairman and Head of UK Delegation, Channel Tunnel Safety Authority, 1997–2003; Member, Inter-Governmental Commission, 1997–2003; *b* 28 Nov. 1936; *s* of Stuart Frew Allison and Poppy (*née* Hodges); *m* 1968, Anne Sergeant; one *s* one *d. Educ:* Manchester Grammar Sch.; Balliol Coll., Oxford. Entered Ministry of Labour, 1959; Private Sec. to Perm. Sec., 1963–64; Principal, 1964; Civil Service Dept, 1969–71; Asst Sec., 1971, Under Sec., 1977, Dept of Employment; Health and Safety Executive, 1989–96: Dir, Safety Policy Div., 1992–94; Chief Exec., Offshore Safety Div., 1994–96; Mem., 1995–96. *Recreations:* reading, swimming, grandchildren. *Address:* c/o Channel Tunnel Safety Authority, 1 Kemble Street, WC2B 4AN.

ALLISON, Ronald William Paul, CVO 1978; journalist, author, broadcaster; television consultant; *b* 26 Jan. 1932; *o s* of Percy Allison and Dorothy (*née* Doyle); *m* 1st, 1956, Maureen Angela Macdonald (*d* 1992); two *d*; 2nd, 1993, Jennifer Loy Weider; one *s*. *Educ:* Weymouth Grammar Sch.; Taunton's Sch., Southampton. Reporter, Hampshire Chronicle, 1952–57; Reporter, BBC, 1957–67; freelance broadcaster, 1968–69; special correspondent, BBC, 1969–73; Press Sec. to Queen, 1973–78; regular presenter and commentator, Thames TV, 1978–90; Controller of Sport and Outside Broadcasts, 1980–85, Dir of Corporate Affairs, 1986–89, Thames TV; Chm. and Man. Dir, Grand Slam Sports, 1992–96; Dir, Corporate Affairs, BAFTA, 1993–98. Dir, Corporate Affairs, API Gp, 1996–98. Consultant on Royal Family to ITN, 1991–. Editor, BAFTA News, 1993–99. *Publications:* Look Back in Wonder, 1968; The Queen, 1973; Charles, Prince of our Time, 1978; The Country Life Book of Britain in the Seventies, 1980; (ed with Sarah Riddell) The Royal Encyclopedia, 1991; The Queen: 50 years—a celebration, 2001. *Recreations:* photography, watching football. *Clubs:* Lord's Taverners; Old Tauntonians (Southampton).

ALLISS, Peter; golfer; television commentator; golf course architect; writer; *b* 28 Feb. 1931; *s* of Percy Alliss and Dorothy Alliss (*née* Rust); *m* 1st, 1953, Joan; one *s* one *d*; 2nd, 1969, Jacqueline Anne; two *s* one *d* (and one *d* decd). *Educ:* Queen Elizabeth's Grammar Sch., Wimborne; Crosby House, Bournemouth. Nat. Service, RAF Regt, 1949–51. Professional golfer, 1946; played in 8 Ryder Cup matches and 10 Canada Cup (now World Cup) matches; winner of 21 major events; open championships of Spain, Portugal, Italy, Brazil. Past Pres., Ladies' PGA and British Green Keepers' Assoc.; twice Captain, British PGA. Hon. Member, Golf Clubs: Royal & Ancient, 2004; Royal Cinque Ports; Professional Golfers' Assoc.; Combe Hill; Moor Allerton; Beaconsfield; Trevose; Parkstone; Ferndown; Stoke Poges; W Cornwall; Peel; Muirfield Village; Wentworth; Guildford; Rosses Point; Lahinch; Broadstone; Chestfield; Auchterarder; Hindhead; Royal Porthcawl; President: Old Thorns; Remedy Oak. Hon. LLD St Andrews, 2005; Hon. DLitt Humberside, 1993; Bournemouth, 2002. *Publications:* Easier Golf (with Paul Trevillion), 1969; Bedside Golf, 1980; Shell Book of Golf, 1981; The Duke, 1983; Play Golf with Peter Alliss, 1983; The Who's Who of Golf, 1983; (with Michael Hobbs) The Open, 1984; Golfer's Logbook, 1984; Lasting the Course, 1984; More Bedside Golf, 1984; Peter Alliss' Most Memorable Golf, 1986; Peter Alliss' Supreme Champions of Golf, 1986; (ed) Winning Golf, 1986; Yet More Bedside Golf, 1986; Play Better Golf with Peter Alliss, 1989; (with Michael Hobbs) Peter Alliss' Best 100 Golfers, 1989; (with Bob Ferrier) The Best of Golf, 1989; The Lazy Golfers' Guide, 1995; Peter Alliss' Golf Heroes, 2002; Alliss's 19th Hole, 2005; *autobiography:* Alliss through the Looking Glass, 1964; Peter Alliss: an autobiography, 1981; My Life, 2004. *Recreation:* talking and taking wine with chums. *Address:* Bucklands, Hindhead, Surrey GU26 6HY. *Clubs:* Lansdowne, Crockfords, Ritz Casino.

ALLISTER, Ven. Donald Spargo; Archdeacon of Chester, since 2002; *b* 27 Aug. 1952; *s* of Charles and Barbara Allister; *m* 1976, Janice Reynolds; one *s* two *d*. *Educ:* Birkenhead Sch.; Peterhouse, Cambridge (BA 1974, MA 1977); Trinity Coll., Bristol. Ordained deacon, 1976, priest, 1977; Curate: St George's, Hyde, 1976–79; St Nicholas', Sevenoaks, 1979–83; Vicar, Christ Church, Birkenhead, 1983–89; Rector, St Mary's, Cheadle, 1989–2002. Chaplain, Arrowe Park Hosp., 1983–86; RD, Cheadle, 1999–2002. Chm., Church Soc., 1995–2000. Consultant Ed., C of E Newspaper, 1981–83. *Publications:* numerous articles in church and theol jls. *Address:* Church House, Lower Lane, Aldford, Chester CH3 6HP. *T:* (01244) 681973, ext. 253, *Fax:* (01244) 620456; *e-mail:* donald.allister@chester.anglican.org.

ALLISTER, James Hugh; QC (NI) 2001; Member for Northern Ireland, European Parliament, since 2004 (DemU, 2004–07, Traditional Unionist, since 2007); *b* 2 April 1953; *s* of Robert Allister and Mary Jane Allister (*née* McCrory); *m* 1978, Ruth McCullagh; two *s* one *d*. *Educ:* Regent House Grammar Sch., Newtownards; Queen's Univ., Belfast. Called to the NI Bar, 1976. Mem. (DemU) N Antrim, NI Assembly, 1982–86. *Address:* 139 Holywood Road, Belfast BT4 3BE. *T:* (028) 9065 5011; *e-mail:* jallister@europarl.eu.int.

ALLNUTT, Denis Edwin; former Director of Analytical Services, Department for Education and Employment; *b* 17 May 1946; *m* 1968, Patricia Livermore; one *s* one *d*. *Educ:* Hampton Sch., Middlesex; Univ. of Birmingham (BSc 1967). Statistician, Min. of Housing and Local Govt, DoE and Dept of Transport, 1967–82; Chief Statistician: Dept of Employment, 1982–88; DoE, 1988–90; Hd, subseq. Dir, Analytical Services, DES, then DFE, later DFEE, 1990–2000.

ALLNUTT, (Ian) Peter, OBE; MA; *b* 26 April 1917; *s* of Col E. B. Allnutt, CBE, MC, and Joan C. Gainsford; *m* 1st, 1946, Doreen Louise Lenagan (*d* 1995); four *d*; 2nd, 1997, Doreen Laven. *Educ:* Imperial Service Coll., Windsor; Sidney Sussex Coll., Cambridge. HM Colonial Service, 1939–46, Nigeria, with break, 1940–45, for service in World War II, Nigeria Regt, RWAFF (despatches). Service with the British Council in Peru, E Africa, Colombia, Argentina, Malta, London and Mexico, 1946–77. OBE 1976; Insignia of Aztec Eagle, 1975. *Recreations:* rowing, swimming, pre-Columbian America, the Hispanic world. *Club:* Leander (Henley-on-Thames).

ALLOTT, Air Cdre Molly Greenwood, CB 1975; *b* 28 Dec. 1918; *d* of late Gerald William Allott. *Educ:* Sheffield High Sch. for Girls. Served War of 1939–45: joined WAAF, 1941; served in: Egypt, Singapore, Germany. Staff of AOC-in-C: RAF Germany, 1960–63; Fighter Command, 1963–66; Training Command, 1971–73; Dir, WRAF, 1973–76; ADC 1973–76. Nat. Chm., Girls' Venture Corps, 1977–82; Member: Council, Union Jack Club, 1977–91; Main Grants Cttee, RAF Benevolent Fund, 1977–82. Raised funds for bldg of Battle of Britain Mus., Hendon, 1977–79. *Recreations:* travel, fine and decorative arts. *Address:* St George's, De La Warr Road, Milford-on-Sea, Lymington, Hants SO41 0NE. *Club:* Royal Air Force.

ALLOTT, Nicholas David; Managing Director, Cameron Mackintosh Ltd, since 2000; *b* 25 March 1954; *s* of late Brig. David Allott and of Shirley Allott; *m* 1989, Anneka Rice (separated 1993); two *s*; partner, Christa D'Souza; two *s*. *Educ:* Geelong Grammar Sch., Australia; Copthorne Sch., Sussex; Charterhouse, Surrey; Exeter Univ. Exec. Dir, Royal Th., Northampton, 1977–81; Cameron Mackintosh Ltd: Prodn Adminr, 1981–86; Exec. Producer, 1986–2000. Chm., Soho Th., 2005–. Trustee: Foundn for Sport and the Arts, 1996–; Oxford Sch. of Drama, 2000–; Roundhouse Trust, 2005–; Motivation Trust, 2005–. *Recreations:* ski-ing, shooting, sailing, keeping the peace. *Address:* 101 Gunterstone Road, W14 9BT. *T:* (020) 7602 0412, *Fax:* (020) 7610 4346; *e-mail:* nick@camack.co.uk. *Clubs:* Garrick, Groucho, Soho House.

ALLOTT, Prof. Philip James, LLD; FBA 2004; Professor of International Public Law, University of Cambridge, 2000–04, now Professor Emeritus; Fellow, Trinity College, Cambridge, since 1973; *b* Sheffield, 29 May 1937; of Reginald William Allott and Dorothy Allott (*née* Dobson). *Educ:* Downside Sch.; Trinity Coll., Cambridge (MA, LLM; LLD 1998). Called to the Bar, Gray's Inn, 1960; HM Diplomatic Service, 1960–73: Asst Legal Advr, then Legal Counsellor, 1965, FCO; Legal Advr, BMG, Berlin, 1965–68; Legal Counsellor, UK Perm. Repn to EC, Brussels, 1972–73; Law Faculty, University of Cambridge: Mem., 1976–; Lectr, 1980–97; Reader, 1997–2000. Bertha Wilson Dist. Vis. Prof., Dalhousie Univ. Law Sch., 1992; Ganshof van der Meersch Chair, Univ. Libre de Bruxelles, 1996; Faculty Mem., Hauser Global Law Sch. Prog., NY Univ. Law Sch., 1995–. Alternate Rep., UK Delegn to UN Law of the Sea Conf., 1976–80. *Publications:* Eunomia: new order for a new world, 1990, 2nd edn 2001; The Health of Nations: society and law beyond the state, 2002; Towards the International Rule of Law, 2005; Invisible Power: a philosophical adventure story, 2005; Invisible Power 2: a metaphysical adventure story, 2008. *Recreations:* high culture, the fine arts, gardening. *Address:* Trinity College, Cambridge CB2 1TQ; *e-mail:* pja1001@cam.ac.uk. *Club:* Oxford and Cambridge.

See also R. M. Allott.

ALLOTT, Robin Michael; Under-Secretary, Departments of Industry and Trade, 1978–80; *b* 9 May 1926; *s* of late Reginald William Allott and Dorothy (*née* Dobson). *Educ:* The Oratory Sch., Caversham; New Coll., Oxford; Sheffield Univ. Asst Principal, BoT, 1948; UK Delegn to OECD, Paris, 1952; Private Sec. to Sec. for Overseas Trade, 1953; Principal, Office for Scotland, Glasgow, 1954; UK Delegn to UN Conf. on Trade and Develt, Geneva, 1964; Asst Sec., BoT, 1965; Counsellor, UK Delegn to EEC, Brussels, 1971; sabbatical year, New Coll., Oxford, 1974–75; Dept of Industry (motor industry), 1975; Under-Sec., Dept of Trade, 1976. Member: European Sociobiol Soc., 1992; NY Acad. of Scis, 1995; AAAS, 1996. *Publications:* The Physical Foundation of Language, 1973; The Motor Theory of Language Origin, 1989; (ed) Studies in Language Origins 3, 1994; (ed jtly) Dorothy Dobson's Commonplace Book, 2000; The Natural Origin of Language, 2000; The Great Mosaic Eye, 2001; The Child and the World, 2005; contrib. Jl of Social and Evolutionary Systems; contrib. collections on lang. and origin of semiosis, sound symbolism, syntax, etc. *Recreations:* studying the evolutionary relation of language, perception and action and language acquisition. *Address:* 5 Fitzgerald Park, Seaford, East Sussex BN25 1AX. *T:* (01323) 4923000.

See also P. J. Allott.

ALLPORT, Denis Ivor; Chairman, 1979–85 and Chief Executive, 1977–85, Metal Box Ltd (Director, 1973–85, Managing Director, 1977–79, Deputy Chairman, 1979); *b* 20 Nov. 1922; *s* of late A. R. Allport and E. M. Allport (*née* Mashman); *m* 1949, Diana (*née* Marler); two *s* one *d*. *Educ:* Highgate School. Served War, Indian Army, 1941–46; joined Metal Box Ltd, 1946; various appts in UK, Singapore and Pakistan; Man. Dir, Metal Box Co. of India, 1969–70; Dir, Metal Box Overseas Ltd, 1970–74. Chairman: Castle Underwriting Agents Ltd, 1989–94 (Dir, 1988–94); Devonshire Underwriting Agents Ltd, 1991–93; Director: Beecham Gp plc, 1981–88; Marley plc, 1985–91. Member: Nat. Enterprise Bd, 1980–83; NRDC, 1981–83; Neill Cttee of Enquiry into Regulatory Arrangements at Lloyd's, 1986. Gov., Highgate Sch., 1981–94. CCMI (FBIM 1977). *Recreation:* golf. *Address:* 26 Great Maytham Hall, Rolvenden, Cranbrook, Kent TN17 4NE. *T:* (01580) 241909. *Clubs:* MCC, Oriental.

ALLSOP, Malcolm Vincent; Managing Director, Town House TV Productions Ltd, since 2004; *b* 9 Sept. 1950; *s* of Bernard and Irene Allsop; *m* 1975, Elaine Jessica Cox; one *s*. *Educ:* Highbury Grammar Sch., London. Reporter: Ormskirk Advertiser, Lancs, 1967–68; W Lancs Press Agency, 1968–70; and Producer, BBC Radio Merseyside, 1970–71; BBC TV Manchester, 1971–72; Anglia TV, Norwich, 1973; BBC TV East, Norwich, 1974–77; Anglia Television: Political Ed., 1978–84; Sen. Producer, Current Affairs, 1984–89; Controller, Current Affairs and Religion, 1990–94; Dep. Dir of Progs, 1994–96; Controller of Progs and Prodn, 1996–97; Dir of Progs and Prodn, 1998–2000; Controller of Factual Entertainment, Formats and Daytime, LWT/United Prodns, 2001–02; Dir, Anglia TV, until 2002; Controller, Format Sales and Acquisitions, Granada Media, 2002–03; Creative Dir, TéVé Media Gp, 2004; CEO, TéVé Partners, 2004. *Recreations:* painting, bird-watching, Victorian criminology, pipe-smoking. *Address:* Town House TV Productions Ltd, 7 Norwich Business Park, Whiting Road, Norwich, NR4 6DN.

ALLSOP, Peter Henry Bruce, CBE 1984; Publishing Consultant, Publishers' Management Advisers, 1983–2004; *b* 22 Aug. 1924; *s* of late Herbert Henry Allsop and Elsie Hilpern (*née* Whittaker); *m* 1950, Patricia Elizabeth Kingwell Bown; two *s* one *d*. *Educ:* Haileybury; Caius Coll., Cambridge (MA). Called to Bar, Lincoln's Inn, 1948, Bencher, 1989. Temp. Asst Principal, Air Min., 1944–48; Barrister in practice, 1948–50; Sweet & Maxwell: Editor, 1950–59; Dir, 1960–64; Man. Dir, 1965–73; Chm., 1974–80; Dir, Associated Book Publishers, 1963, Asst Man. Dir, 1965–67, Man. Dir, 1968–76, Chm., 1976–88. Chm., Teleordering Ltd, 1978–91; Trustee and Vice-Chm., Yale University Press, 1984–99 (Dir, 1981–84); Director: J. Whitaker & Sons, 1987–98; Lloyd's of London Press, 1991–95. Mem. Council, Publishers Assoc., 1969–81 (Treasurer, 1973–75, 1979–81; Pres., 1975–77; Vice-Pres., 1977–78; Trustee, 1982–95); Member: Printing and Publishing Industry Trng Bd, 1977–79; Publishers' Adv. Cttee, British Council, 1980–85; Chm., Management Cttee, Book House Training Centre, 1980–86. Chm., Social Security Appeal Tribunal, 1982–87 (Mem., 1979–82). Chm., Book Trade Benevolent Soc., 1986–92 (Trustee, 1976–85, 1994–98; Dir, 1985). Mem., St Albans City Council, 1955–58. Chm., DAC, Bath and Wells, 1985–94; Trustee, St Andrews Conservation Trust, Wells, 1987–99; Mem., Wells Cathedral Fabric Adv. Cttee, 1991–99. Chm. Council, King's Coll., Taunton, 1986–94 (Mem., 1983–86). Dir, Woodard Schools (Western Div.) Ltd, 1985–95. Editor, later Editor Emeritus: Current Law, 1952–90; Criminal Law Review, 1954–90. *Publications:* (ed) Bowstead's Law of Agency, 11th edn, 1951. *Recreations:* reading, theatre. *Clubs:* Garrick, Farmers'; Leander (Henley-on-Thames).

ALLSOP, Prof. Richard Edward, OBE 1997; PhD, DSc; CEng, FREng, FICE; Professor of Transport Studies, University College London, 1976–2005, now Professor Emeritus; *b* 2 May 1940; *s* of Edward James Allsop and Grace Ada Allsop (*née* Tacey); *m* 1990, Frances Elizabeth Killick. *Educ:* Bemrose Sch., Derby; Queens' Coll., Cambridge (MA Maths); University Coll. London (PhD Maths, DSc Engrg). CEng, FICE, 1990; FREng 1996; FCILT 1981; FIHT 1983. Scientific Officer, Road Res. Lab., 1964–66; Res. Fellow, 1967–69, Lectr in Transport Studies, 1970–72, UCL; Dir, Transport Ops Res. Gp, Univ. of Newcastle upon Tyne, 1973–76; Dean of Engrg, UCL, 1983–85. Visiting Professor: Univ. of Karlsruhe, 1977; Univ. of Natural Resources and Applied Life Scis, Vienna, 2002; Newcastle Univ., 2006–; Adjunct Prof., Qld Univ. of Technol., 2006–; Hon. Professor: Tech. Univ. of Cracow, 2000–; Moscow Automobile and Roads Inst. (State Tech. Univ.), 2001–; Vis. Fellow, Univ. of Osaka, 1981; Vis. Erskine Fellow, Univ. of Canterbury Christchurch, 1997. Ext. Res. Advr, Dept for Transport, 1993–; Dir, Parly Adv. Council for Transport Safety, 1995–. Mem., Road Traffic Law Rev., 1985–88. Visitor to Traffic Gp, Transport & Road Res. Lab., 1987–92. Bd Mem., Eur. Transport Safety Council, 2005–. Member: Northumberland and Newcastle Soc., 1973–; Chiltern Soc., 1977–. *Publications:* (with D. Zumkeller) Kleines Fachwörterbuch Verkehrswesen, 2003; (ed jtly) Transportation and Traffic Theory 2007, 2007; numerous papers in learned jls, edited proceedings. *Recreations:* photography, theatre, walking. *Address:* Centre for Transport Studies, University College London, Gower Street, WC1E 6BT. *T:* (020) 7679 1555, *Fax:* (020) 7679 1567; *e-mail:* rea@transport.ucl.ac.uk.

ALLSOPP, family name of **Baron Hindlip**.

ALLSOPP, Ven. Christine; Archdeacon of Northampton, since 2005; *b* 19 Jan. 1947; *d* of John Rupert Goddard and Phyllis May Goddard; *m* 1970, Dr Dennis Allsopp; two *s* one *d*. *Educ:* St Albans Grammar Sch. for Girls; Univ. of Aston (BSc (Chem.) 1968); Salisbury and Wells Theol Coll. Res. Chemist, 1968–70, Inf. Officer, 1970–72, Albright and Wilson; freelance scientific ed. and abstractor, 1977–86. Ordained deacon, 1989, priest, 1994; Asst Curate, Caversham and Mapledurham, 1989–94; Team Vicar, Bracknell, 1994–98; Team Rector, Bourne Valley, 1998–2005. RD, Alderbury, 1999–2005; Canon and Preb., Salisbury Cathedral, 2002–05; Hon. Canon, Peterborough Cathedral, 2005–. Mem., Gen. Synod of C of E, 2005–. *Recreations:* walking, swimming, Asian cooking. *Address:* Westbrook, 11 The Drive, Northampton NN1 4RZ. *T:* (01604) 714015, *Fax:* (01604) 792016; *e-mail:* archdeacon@aofn.wanadoo.co.uk.

ALLSOPP, Christopher John, CBE 2004; Director, Oxford Institute for Energy Studies, since 2006; Fellow of New College, 1967–2008, now Emeritus, and Senior Research Fellow, Department of Economics, since 2006, Oxford University; *b* 6 April 1941; twin *s* of late (Harold) Bruce Allsopp, FSA; *m* 1967, Marian Elizabeth Pearce. *Educ:* Balliol Coll., Oxford (MA 1967); Nuffield Coll., Oxford (BPhil Econs 1967). Econ. Asst, HM Treasury, 1966–67; Oxford University: Tutor in Econs, New Coll., 1967–2008; Lectr in Econs, 1968–97 (on leave to OECD, Paris, 1973–74); Reader in Econ. Policy, 1997–2006. Bank of England: Advr, 1980–83; Mem., Ct of Dirs, 1997–2000; Mem., Monetary Policy Cttee, 2000–03. Leader, indep. Review of Statistics for Economic Policymaking, 2003. Ed., Oxford Review of Econ. Policy, 1985–. *Address:* Oxford Institute for Energy Studies, 57 Woodstock Road, Oxford OX2 6FA.

ALLTHORPE-GUYTON, Marjorie; Director of Visual Arts, Arts Council England (formerly Arts Council of England), 1993–2006; *b* 29 July 1948; *d* of Maurice Jack Allthorpe-Guyton and Edith Florence (*née* Clark); *m* 1st, 1970, Brian Collison (marr. diss. 1977); 2nd, 1989, John Mullis (marr. diss. 2000); one *s* one *d*; 3rd, 2000, Paul Dale. *Educ:* Univ. of East Anglia (BA Hons Fine Art); Courtauld Inst. AMA 1974. Asst Keeper, Norwich Castle Mus., 1969–79; Researcher, Norwich Sch. of Art, 1980–82; Selector, British Art Show, Arts Council, 1982–84; Associate Ed., 1988–91, Ed., 1990–92, Artscribe. External Assessor, Fine Art degrees, 1988–95, Mem. Council, 1997–2005, Goldsmiths' Coll., London Univ.; External Assessor: Fine Art, Oxford Brookes Univ., 1998–2000; Art Theory, City Univ., 2003–07. FRSA 1994; FRCA 1999; RIBA 2003. Hon. Dr Anglia Ruskin Univ., 2005. Previews writer, Royal Acad. Mag. *Publications:* A Happy Eye: history of Norwich Sch. of Art 1845–1982, 1982; catalogues: Henry Bright, 1973; John Sell Cotman, 1975; John Thirtle, 1977; Norwich Castle Museum, 1979; many essays and articles on contemporary art. *Recreations:* cooking, yacht racing. *Address:* 1 Thornhill Road, N1 1HX. *Clubs:* Chelsea Arts, Blacks, Two Brydges.

ALLUM, Sarah Elizabeth Royle, (Mrs R. G. Allum); *see* Walker, S. E. R.

ALLWEIS, Martin Peter; His Honour Judge Allweis; a Circuit Judge, since 1994; Designated Family Judge for Greater Manchester, 1996–2005; *b* 22 Dec. 1947; *s* of late Jack Allweis and Iris Allweis (*née* Mosco); *m* 1984, Tracy Ruth, *d* of late Hyam Barr and of Bernice Barr; one *s* one *d*. *Educ:* Manchester Grammar Sch.; Sidney Sussex Coll., Cambridge (BA Hons 1969). Called to the Bar, Inner Temple, 1970; in practice on Northern Circuit, 1971–94; a Recorder, 1990–94. *Recreations:* family interests, football (Manchester City FC), squash. *Address:* c/o Manchester County Court, Manchester Civil Justice Centre, 1 Bridge Street, Manchester M60 9DJ.

ALLWOOD; *see* Muirhead-Allwood.

ALMOND, David John; novelist, short story writer and playwright for children and adults; *b* 15 May 1951; *s* of James Arthur Almond and Catherine Almond (*née* Barber); partner, Sara Jane Palmer; one *d*. *Educ:* St John's, Felling; St Aidan's, Sunderland; St Joseph's Hebburn; Univ. of E Anglia (BA Hons Eng. and American Lit.); Univ. of Newcastle upon Tyne (PGCE). Postman; teacher (primary, adults and special needs), Tyneside, 1976–98. Vis. Prof. of Creative Writing, Nottingham Trent Univ., 2007–. Commune mem., 1982–83. Ed., Panurge (fiction mag.), 1987–93. Hon. DLitt: Sunderland, 2001; Leicester, 2005. *Plays:* Wild Girl, Wild Boy, nat. tours, 2001, 2002; My Dad's a Birdman, Young Vic, 2003. *Publications:* Sleepless Nights, 1985; A Kind of Heaven, 1997; Counting Stars (short stories), 2000; *for children:* Skellig, 1998 (Library Assoc. Carnegie Medal, Whitbread Children's Book of the Year; Silver Pencil (Holland), 2000) (adapted for radio, and staged, Young Vic, 2003); Kit's Wilderness, 1999 (Smarties Silver Award, 1999; Silver Kiss (Holland), Michael L. Printz Award (USA), 2001; adapted for TV); Heaven Eyes, 2000 (adapted for radio, and staged, 2004); Secret Heart, 2001 (adapted for stage); Wild Girl, Wild Boy (play), 2002; The Fire-Eaters, 2003 (Smarties Gold Award, Whitbread Children's Book of the Year, 2003; Boston Globe-Horn Book Award (USA), 2004); Kate, the Cat and the Moon (illus. Stephen Lambert), 2004; Clay, 2005 (adapted for TV, 2008); My Dad's a Birdman, 2007; The Savage, 2008; Jackdaw Summer, 2008; The Boy who Climbed into the Moon, 2009; books trans. into more than 30 langs. *Recreation:* walking (Yorkshire Dales, Northumbrian beaches). *Address:* c/o Maggie Noach, The Maggie Noach Literary Agency, 22 Dorville Crescent, W6 0HJ.

ALMOND, George Haylock, CBE 2001 (MBE 1993); DL; Commander, St John Ambulance for Greater Manchester, since 2002; *b* 19 Jan. 1944; *s* of late Arthur Ernest Almond and of Mrs C. V. Almond; *m* 1968, Elizabeth Allcock; one *s* one *d*. *Educ:* Portsmouth Tech. High Sch.; Eastleigh Tech. Coll. Fireman, then Leading Fireman, and Sub-Officer, Hants Fire Service, 1962–70; Cheshire Fire Brigade: Station Officer, 1970–72; Asst Divl Officer, 1972–75; Divl Officer, Grade III, 1975–77; Divl Officer, Grade I, 1977–82; Divl Comdr, 1978–82; Greater Manchester County Fire Service: Asst County Fire Officer, 1982–90; Dep. County Fire Officer, 1990–95; County Fire Officer and Chief Exec., 1995–2002. Chairman: Fire Services Nat. Benevolent Fund, 2000; Emmaus North West Partnership, 2002–. FIFireE 1988 (Internat. Pres., 1996–97); FRSH 1989; FCIPD (FIPD 1991). Freeman, City of London, 1999. DL Greater Manchester, 1999. Hon. Fellow, Bolton Inst., 2000. Hon. MSc Salford, 2004. OStJ 2004 (SBStJ 2001). Fire Bde Long Service and Good Conduct Medal, 1982; Queen's Jubilee Medal, 2002. *Publications:* Accidents, Injuries and Illnesses to Firemen in Great Britain, 1972; (contrib.) Fire Service Drill Book, 1985; Preliminary Certificate Students Handbook, 1994; Elementary Fire Engineering Handbook, 2004; contrib. papers to technical jls. *Recreations:* music, reading, walking. *Address:* 4 Stonehouse, Chapeltown Road, Bromley Cross, Bolton, Lancs BL7 9NB. *Club:* Rotary (Manchester) (Pres., 2002–03).

ALMOND, Prof. Jeffrey William, PhD; FMedSci; Vice President, Discovery Research and External Research and Development, Sanofi Pasteur, since 1999; *b* 28 June 1951; *s* of Stanley Peter Almond and Joyce Mary Almond (*née* Fountain); *m* 1976, Karen Elizabeth Batley, BSc, PhD; two *s* one *d*. *Educ:* Univ. of Leeds (BSc); Downing Coll., Cambridge (PhD 1978). Lectr in Virology, Univ. of Leicester, 1979–85; Fellow, Lister Inst. of Preventive Medicine, 1985; University of Reading: Prof. of Microbiol., 1985–99; Hd, Sch. of Animal and Microbial Scis, 1991–95; Vis. Prof., 1999–. Mem., Spongiform Encephalopathies Adv. Cttee, UK Govt, 1995–99. Chm., Virology Div., Internat. Union of Microbiol Socs, 1996–99. Fellow, Amer. Acad. of Microbiol., 1996; FMedSci 2006. Ivanosky Medal for Virology, Russian Acad. Med. Scis, 1999. *Publications:* scientific papers, book chapters and rev. articles in jls. *Recreations:* Alpine sports, jardinage, golf, fitness centres, jogging. *Address:* Sanofi Pasteur, 1541 avenue Marcel Mérieux, 69280 Marcy l'Etoile, France. *T:* (4) 37379453, (mobile) 6033 60851, *Fax:* (4) 37373976; *e-mail:* jeffrey.almond@sanofipasteur.com.

ALMOND, Thomas Clive, OBE 1989; HM Diplomatic Service, retired; Consul-General, Bordeaux, 1992–98; *b* 30 Nov. 1939; *s* of late Thomas and Eveline Almond; *m* 1965, Auriol Gala Elizabeth Annette Hendry. *Educ:* Bristol Grammar Sch.; London Univ. Entered HM Diplomatic Service, 1967; Accra, 1968; Paris, 1971; FCO, 1975; Brussels, 1978; Jakarta, 1980; Brazzaville, 1983; Ambassador to People's Republic of the Congo, 1987–88; Asst Marshal of the Diplomatic Corps and Asst Head of Protocol Dept, 1988–92. *Recreations:* travelling, golf.

ALMUNIA AMANN, Joaquín; Member, European Commission, since 2004; *b* 17 June 1948; *m*; two *c*. *Educ:* Univ. of Deusto, Bilbao. Economist, Council Bureau, Spanish Chambers of Commerce, Brussels, 1972–75; Chief Economist, Unión Gen. de Trabajo, 1976–79. MP (PSOE), Spain, 1979–2004; Minister: of Employment and Social Security, 1982–86; of Public Admin, 1986–91. Parly Leader, 1994–97, Sec. Gen., 1997–2000, PSOE. *Publications include:* Memorias Políticas, 2001. *Address:* European Commission, Rue de la Loi 200, 1049 Brussels, Belgium.

ALPASS, John; Head of Fraud Strategy, Department for Work and Pensions (formerly Head of Fraud Intelligence, Department of Social Security), 2000–05. Security Service, 1973–95; Intelligence Co-ordinator, Cabinet Office, 1996–99. Member: Guildford Diocesan Adv. Cttee, 2003–; Bishop's Council, Dio. of Guildford, 2007–.

ALPHANDERY, Edmond Gérard; Member, General Council for Maine-et-Loire, since 1976; Mayor of Longué-Jumelles, since 1977; Chairman, CNP Assurances (formerly Caisse Nationale de Prévoyance), since 1998; Director: Calyon, since 2002; Suez, since 2003; Icade, since 2004; *b* 2 Sept. 1943; *m* 1972, Laurence Rivain; one *s*. *Educ:* Frédéric Mistral Lycée, Avignon; Inst. of Political Studies, Paris; Univs of Chicago and California at Berkeley. Asst Lectr, Univ. of Paris, IX, 1968–69; Lectr, Univ. of Aix-en-Provence, 1970–71; Sen. Lectr, and Dean, Faculty of Econ. Sci., Univ. of Nantes, 1971–74; Prof., Univ. of Angers, 1973; Associate Prof., Univ. of Pittsburgh, 1975; Prof. of Political Economy, Univ. of Paris II, 1974–92. Deputy (UDF-CDS) for Maine-et-Loire, French Nat. Assembly, 1978–93 (Mem., Finance Cttee, 1979–93); Minister of the Economy, France, 1993–95; Vice-Pres., 1991–94, Pres., 1994–95, Maine-et-Loire General Council. Vice-Pres., Centre des Démocrates Sociaux; numerous positions with economic and monetary bodies, incl. Mem., Governance Cttee, Caisse des Dépôts et Consignations, 2003– (Mem., Supervisory Bd, 1988–93); Mem., Consultative Cttee, Banque de France, 1998–; Mem., Adv. Bd, Lehman Brothers, 2007–08. Chm., Bd of Dirs, CNP Insurance SA, 1992–93; Chm., Electricité de France, 1995–98. Founder and Chm., Euro (50) Gp. Chm., Centre National des professions financières, 2003–. Mem., Trilateral Commn, 1996–. *Publications:* Les Politiques de stabilisation (with G. Delsupehe), 1974; Cours d'analyse macroéconomique, 1976; Analyse monétaire approfondie, 1978; 1986: le piège, 1985; La Rupture: le liberalisme à l'épreuve des faits (with A. Fourçans), 1987; La Reforme obligée: sous le soleil de l'euro, 2000. *Address:* CNP Assurances, 4 Place Raoul Dautry, 75716 Paris Cedex 15, France.

ALPTUNA, Akin, PhD; Ambassador of Turkey to the Court of St James's, 2003–07; *b* 23 May 1942; *s* of Huseyin Kamil Alptuna and Cahide Alptuna; *m* 1967, Esin Arman; two *s*. *Educ:* Ankara Univ. (BA; PhD in Internat. Relns). Joined Min. of Foreign Affairs, Turkey, 1967; Second, then First Sec., Copenhagen, 1972–75; First Sec., Nicosia, 1975–77; Hd of Section, Internat. Econ. Agreements Dept and Mem. of Cabinet for Minister of Foreign Affairs, 1977–79; Counsellor, Perm. Delegn of Turkey to EC, Brussels, 1979–81; Consul, Düsseldorf, 1981–83; Hd, Dept for Internat. Econ. Orgns, 1983–85; Dep. Hd of Mission, Turkish Perm. Delegn to UN, 1985–89; Dep. Dir Gen., Multilateral Political Affairs, 1989–93; Dir Gen., EU Dept, 1993–95; Ambassador: Helsinki, 1995–97; Perm. Repn of Turkey to OECD, 1997–2000; Dep. Under-Sec. for EU and W Europe, 1999–2003. *Address:* c/o Turkish Embassy, 43 Belgrave Square, SW1X 8PA. *T:* (020) 7393 0202, *Fax:* (020) 7393 9213. *Clubs:* Athenæum, Travellers, Cavalry and Guards.

AL SAUD, HRH Prince Mohammed Nawaf; Ambassador of the Kingdom of Saudi Arabia to the Court of St James's and to Ireland, since 2005; *b* 22 May 1953; *s* of HRH Prince Nawaf bin Abdulaziz and HH Princess Sharifa; *m* 1979, HH Princess Fadwa Khalid Abdullah; two *s* three *d*. *Educ:* Capital Institute High Sch., Riyadh; Sch. of Foreign Service, George Town Univ., Washington; John F. Kennedy Sch. of Govt, Harvard Univ. Diplomat; joined Royal Commn for Jubail and Yanbu, Saudi Arabia, 1981; joined Min. of Foreign Affairs, 1984, Minister's Cabinet; promoted to Inspector Gen.; Ambassador of Saudi Arabia to Italy and Malta, 1995; promoted to rank of Minister, 2005. Formerly: Dean, Arab Ambassadors in Italy; Chm., Islamic and Cultural Centre, Rome. Pres., Harvard Alumni Assoc., Saudi Arabia. *Recreations:* football, tennis. *Address:* Royal Embassy of Saudi Arabia, 30 Charles Street, W1J 5DZ. *T:* (020) 7917 3000, *Fax:* (020) 7917 3001. *Clubs:* Brooks's, Travellers.

AL SHAKAR, Karim Ebrahim; Ambassador of Bahrain to the People's Republic of China, since 2001, and concurrently (non-resident) to Malaysia, since 2001, to the Philippines, since 2002, to Thailand, since 2003, and to Singapore and Mongolia, since 2004; *b* 23 Dec. 1945; *m* 1979, Fatima Al Mansouri; three *d*. *Educ:* primary and secondary educn, Bahrain; Delhi Univ. (BA political science 1970). Attaché, Min. of Foreign Affairs, 1970; Mem., Perm. Mission to UN, later Min. of Foreign Affairs, 1972–76; First Sec., 1978; Counsellor, 1981; Perm. Rep. to UN, Geneva and Consul-Gen., 1982–87 (non-resident Ambassador to Germany and Austria and to UN, Vienna, 1984); Ambassador and Perm. Rep to UN, New York, 1987–90; Ambassador to UK, also to Republic of Ireland, the Netherlands and Denmark, 1992–95; Dir, Internat. Directorate, Ministry of Foreign Affairs, Bahrain, 1995–2001. *Recreation:* travelling. *Address:* Bahrain Embassy, C312 Lufthansa Center Office Building, 3rd Floor, 50 Liangmaqiao Road, Chaoyang District, Beijing 100016, People's Republic of China.

ALSOP, Marin; Music Director, Baltimore Symphony Orchestra, since 2007; *b* 16 Oct. 1956; *d* of K. LaMar Alsop and Ruth (*née* Condell). *Educ:* Juilliard Sch. (BM 1977, MM 1978). Music Director: Long Island Philharmonic Orch., 1989–96; Eugene SO, Oregon, 1989–96; Cabrillo Fest., 1992–; Colorado SO, 1993–2003 (Music Dir Laureate, 2003–); Principal Conductor, Bournemouth SO, 2002–08; Principal Guest Conductor: City of London Sinfonia, 2000–03; Royal Scottish Nat. Orch., 2000–03. Regular guest conductor: Philadelphia Orch.; Chicago SO; Los Angeles Philharmonic; NY

Philharmonic; LSO; LPO. MacArthur Foundn Fellow, 2005. *Recreations:* running, swimming, antique collecting, reading. *Address:* c/o Intermusica Artists, 16 Duncan Terrace, N1 8BZ. *T:* (020) 7278 5455.

ALSOP, William Allen, OBE 1999; RA 2000; Principal, SMC Alsop (formerly Alsop & Stormer, then Alsop) Architects, since 1979; *b* 12 Dec. 1947; *s* of Francis John Alsop and Brenda Hight; *m* 1972, Sheila E. Bean; two *s* one *d. Educ:* Architectural Association (DipAA). RIBA. Maxwell Fry, 1971; Cedric Price, 1973–77; Rodrick Ham, 1977–79. Prof. of Architecture, Technical Univ., Vienna, 1995–; Hon. Prof., Central St Martin's Coll. of Art and Design, 1997. Principal buildings: Hamburg Ferry Terminal; Cardiff Visitor Centre (RIBA Nat. Award, 1991); Cardiff Barrage; N Greenwich Underground station; Tottenham Hale Interchange station; Nat. Mus., Nuremberg; Govt HQ, Marseilles (RIBA Nat. Award, 1997); Peckham Library (RIBA Stirling Prize, 2000); Ontario Coll. of Art and Design, Toronto, 2004; Sch. of Medicine and Dentistry, QMW, 2004. Hamburgische Architektenkammer, 1992; Mem., Russian Architectl Inst., 1995. SADG 1973; FRSA. Hon. LLD Leicester, 1996; Hon. Dr (Design) Nottingham Trent, 2001; DUniv Sheffield Hallam, 2001. *Publications:* City of Objects, 1992; William Alsop Buildings and Projects, 1992; William Alsop Architect, Four Projects, 1993; Will Alsop and Jan Störmer, Architects, 1993; Le Grand Bleu-Marseille, 1994; Will Alsop, Book 1, 2001, Book 2, 2002. *Recreation:* fishing. *Address:* Parkgate Studio, 41 Parkgate Road, SW11 4NP. *T:* (020) 7978 7878.

ALSTON, David Ian; Arts Director, Arts Council of Wales, since 2005; *b* 26 June 1952; *s* of Cyril Alston and Dorothy Alston; *m* 1975, Christine Bodin (marr. diss. 1987); two *d*; partner Lesley Webster; one *s* one *d. Educ:* Corpus Christi Coll., Oxford (Open Exhibn, MA; Postgrad. Dip. in History of Art (Dist.)). Asst Curator of Pictures, Christ Church, Oxford, 1978–82; Asst Keeper of Art (Ruskin Collection), Sheffield, 1982; Dep. Dir of Arts, Sheffield MDC, 1982–93; Sen. Principal Keeper, Sheffield Arts and Museums, 1993–94; Keeper of Art, Nat. Museums and Galls of Wales, 1994–98; Galls Dir, 1998–2002, Acting Chief Exec., 2001–02, The Lowry. Co-Founder Ed., Oxford Art Jl, 1978. *Publications:* Under the Cover of Darkness: Night Prints, 1986; Piranesi's Prisons: a perspective, 1987; Graham Sutherland: nature into art, 2004; Into Painting: Brendan Stuart Burns, 2007; sundry exhibn texts and articles. *Recreations:* listening, looking, cooking, talking, drinking, walking, playing, loving, musing and other 'ings. *Address:* Arts Council of Wales, 9 Museum Place, Cardiff CF10 3NX; *e-mail:* david.alston@artswales.org.uk.

ALSTON, John Alistair, CBE 1988; DL; Chairman, Norfolk Health Authority, 1996–2002; *b* 24 May 1937; *s* of late David Alston and Bathia Mary (*née* Davidson). *Educ:* Orwell Park, Sherborne; RAC, Cirencester. Norfolk County Council: Mem., 1973–97; Leader, 1981–87 and 1989–93; Vice-Chm., 1987–88; Chm., 1988–89. Chairman: Norwich, then E Norfolk HA, subseq. Norfolk Health Commn, 1994–96; Chm., Broads Bill Steering Cttee, 1984–87; Member: Broads Authority, 1988–95; Council, Morley Res. Station, 1981–97; Council, UEA, 1986–2002 (Vice Chm., 1997–2002). Chairman: Norfolk Connections, 2000–02; Norfolk County Strategic Partnership, 2002–07. Pres., Norfolk Athletics Assoc., 1997–2007. DL 1991, High Sheriff, 2004–05, Norfolk. Hon. DCL UEA, 2004. *Recreations:* gardening, shooting, fishing. *Address:* Besthorpe Hall, Attleborough, Norfolk NR17 2LJ. *T:* (01953) 450300.

ALSTON, Rt Rev. Mgr J(oseph) Leo; Parish Priest, Sacred Heart Church, Ainsdale, Southport, 1972–98; *b* 17 Dec. 1917; *s* of Benjamin Alston and Mary Elizabeth (*née* Moss). *Educ:* St Mary's School, Chorley; Upholland College, Wigan; English Coll., Rome; Christ's College, Cambridge. Priest, 1942; Licentiate in Theology, Gregorian Univ., Rome, 1942; BA (1st Cl. Hons Classics) Cantab 1945. Classics Master, Upholland Coll., Wigan, 1945–52, Headmaster, 1952–64; Rector, Venerable English Coll., Rome, 1964–71. Protonotary Apostolic, 1988. Mem., Cambridge Soc. *Recreation:* music. *Address:* St Marie's House, 27 Seabank Road, Southport, Merseyside PR9 0EJ. *T:* (01704) 501361.

ALSTON, Richard John William, CBE 2001; choreographer; Artistic Director, The Place, and Richard Alston Dance Company, since 1994; *b* 30 Oct. 1948; *s* of late Gordon Walter Alston and Margot Alston (*née* Whitworth). *Educ:* Eton; Croydon Coll. of Art. Choreographed for London Contemporary Dance Theatre, 1970–72; founded Strider, 1972; worked in USA, 1975–77; Resident Choreographer, 1980–86, Artistic Dir, 1986–92, Ballet Rambert, subseq. Rambert Dance Co. Principal Ballets: Nowhere Slowly; Tiger Balm; Blue Schubert Fragments; Soft Verges; Rainbow Bandit; Doublework; Soda Lake; for Ballet Rambert: Rainbow Ripples, 1980; The Rite of Spring, 1981; Apollo Distraught, 1982; Dangerous Liaisons, 1985; Zansa, 1986; Dutiful Ducks, 1986; Pulcinella, 1987; Strong Language, 1987; Hymnos, 1988; Roughcut, 1990; Cat's Eye, 1992. Created: The Kingdom of Pagodas, for Royal Danish Ballet, 1982; Midsummer, for Royal Ballet, 1983; Le Marteau Sans Maitre, for Compagnie Chopinot, 1992; Delicious Arbour, for Shobana Jeyasingh Dance Co., 1993; Movements from Petrushka, Lachrymae, Rumours Visions, for Aldeburgh Festival, 1994; for Richard Alston Dance Co.: Shadow Realm, Something in the City, 1994; Stardust, 1995; Orpheus Singing and Dreaming, Beyond Measure, Okho, 1996; Brisk Singing, Light Flooding into Darkened Rooms, 1997; Red Run, Waltzes in Disorder, Sophisticated Curiosities, 1998; Slow Airs Almost All, A Sudden Exit, 1999; The Signal of a Shake, Tremor, 2000; Fever, Strange Company, Water Music, 2001; Touch and Go, Stampede, 2002; Overdrive, 2003; Shimmer, Gypsy Mixture, 2004; Such Longing, 2005. DUniv Surrey, 1993. Chevalier, Ordre des Arts et des Lettres (France), 1995. *Recreations:* music, reading. *Address:* The Place, 17 Duke's Road, WC1H 9AB.

ALSTON, Hon. Richard Kenneth Robert; High Commissioner for Australia in the United Kingdom, 2005–08; *b* 19 Dec. 1941; s of late Robert Bruce Alston and of Sheila Gertrude Alston; *m* 1973, Margaret Mary, (Megs), Kennedy; one *s* one *d. Educ:* Xavier Coll., Melbourne; Univ. of Melbourne (BA, LLB; BCom); Monash Univ. (LLM; MBA). Government of Australia: Senator (Lib) for Victoria, 1986–2004; Shadow Minister: for Communications, 1989–90 and 1993–96; for Social Security, Child Care and Retirement Incomes, 1990–92; for Superannuation and Child Care, 1992–93; for the Arts, 1994–96; Dep. Leader of the Opposition in Senate, 1993–96; Dep. Leader of Govt in Senate, 1996–2003; Minister for Communications, IT and the Arts, 1996–2003. Chm., Senate Select Cttees, 1991–96; Mem., Senate Standing Cttees on Finance and Public Admin, 1987–90, and Legal and Constitnl Affairs, 1989–90. Chm., Broadcasting Services Australia Ltd, 2004–05; Dir, Hansen Technologies Ltd, 2004–05. Adjunct Prof. of Information Technol., Bond Univ., 2004–. Centenary Medal (Australia), 2003. *Recreations:* Aboriginal art, modern literature, oriental rugs, jogging, pumping iron.

ALSTON, Robert John, CMG 1987; QSO 2004; DL; HM Diplomatic Service, retired; High Commissioner to New Zealand, Governor (non-resident) of Pitcairn, Henderson, Ducie and Oeno Islands, and High Commissioner (non-resident) to Western Samoa, 1994–98; *b* 10 Feb. 1938; *s* of late Arthur William Alston and of Rita Alston; *m* 1969, Patricia Claire Essex; one *s* one *d. Educ:* Ardingly Coll.; New Coll., Oxford (BA Mod. Hist.). Third Sec., Kabul, 1963; Eastern Dept, FO, 1966; Head of Computer Study Team, FCO, 1969; First Sec. (Econ.), Paris, 1971; First Sec. and Head of Chancery, Tehran, 1974; Asst Head, Energy Science and Space Dept, FCO, 1977; Head, Joint Nuclear Unit, FCO, 1978; Political Counsellor, UK Delegn to NATO, 1981; Head, Defence Dept, FCO, 1984; Ambassador to Oman, 1986–90; seconded to NI Office, 1990–92; Asst Under-Sec. of State (Public Depts), FCO, 1992–94. Chm., Link Foundn for UK-NZ Relations, 1999–2004; Advr, Internat. Trade & Investment Missions Ltd, 1999–2002; Trustees Rep., Commonwealth Inst., 2002–. Dir, Romney Resource Centre, 1999–2006. Consultant on Anglican Communion affairs to Archbishop of Canterbury, 1999–2002. Trustee, Antarctic Heritage Trust, 1998–; Mem. Cttee, Romney Marsh Historic Churches Trust, 2003–. Chairman of Governors: Ardingly Coll., 2005–; Marsh Acad., New Romney, 2007–. Mem. Ct, World Traders' Co., 2003– (Master, 2007–08). DL Kent, 2004. *Recreations:* gardening, travel, music. *Address:* 16 Carlisle Mansions, Carlisle Place, SW1P 1HX.

ALSTON, Prof. Robin Carfrae, OBE 1992; FSA; Professor of Library Studies, London University, 1990–98, now Professor Emeritus, University College London; Hon. Senior Research Fellow, English Studies, London University, since 1998; *b* 29 Jan. 1933; *s* of late Wilfred Louis Alston; *m* 1st, 1957, Joanna Ormiston (marr. diss. 1996); one *s* one *d* (and one *s* decd); 2nd, 1996, Janet Pedley-King (marr. diss. 1999). *Educ:* Rugby Sch.; Univs of British Columbia (BA 1954), Oxford (MA 1956), Toronto (MA 1958) and London (PhD 1964). Teaching Fellow, University Coll., Toronto, 1956–58; Lectr, New Brunswick Univ., 1958–60; Lectr in English Lit., Leeds Univ., 1964–76; Consultant to British Library, 1977–; Editor-in-Chief, 18th Century Short Title Catalogue, 1978–89; Advr to Develt and Systems Office, Humanities and Social Scis (formerly Ref. Div.), British Library, 1984–; Editl Dir, The Nineteenth Century, series of microfiche texts 1801–1900, 1985–. Dir, Sch. of Library, Archive and Information Studies, UCL, 1990–95; Course Dir, History of the Book, Sch. of Advanced Studies, London Univ., 1995–98. Hon. Res. Fellow, UCL, 1987–. Klein Vis. Prof., Univ of Texas, 1990; Vis. Prof., Univ. of Malta, 1994. David Murray Lectr, Univ. of Glasgow, 1983; Guest Lectr, Univ. of London, 1983, Sorbonne, 1984, Tokyo Symposium on micro-reproduction, 1984; Cecil Oldman Lectr, Leeds Univ., 1988, 1989; Morris Meml Lectr, Royal Instn, 1991. Jt Editor, Leeds Studies in English and Leeds Texts and Monographs, 1965–72; Editor, Studies in Early Modern English, 1965–72; Jt Editor, The Direction Line, 1976–; Editor: Special Pubns, Bibliographical Soc., 1983–; Libraries and Archives (series), 1991–. Founder, Chm. and principal Editor, Scolar Press Ltd, 1966–72, Man. Dir, 1984–; Founder, Janus Press, devoted to original art prints, 1973. Member: Adv. Cttee, British Library, 1975–; Adv. Cttee, MLA of America for the Wing Project, 1980–; Adv. Panel, Aust. Research Grants Cttee, 1983–; Adv. Bd, Cambridge Hist. of the Book in Britain, 1989–. Member: Organising Cttee, 18th Century Short Title Catalogue, 1976–; Cttee, British Book Trade Index, 1984–. Mem. Council, Bibliographical Soc., 1967– (Vice-Pres., 1978–88, Pres., 1988–90); Founding Mem. Council, Ilkley Literature Festival, 1973–; Jt Founder, Frederic Madden Soc., 1989–. Consultant, Consortium of Univ. Research Libraries, 1985–86; Adviser to: Govt of Pakistan on estabt of Nat. Liby of Pakistan, 1988; UC of Barbados, 2005–. FSA 1987; Hon. FLA 1986. Hon. DLitt London, 2005. Samuel Pepys Gold Medal, Ephemera Soc., 1984; Smithsonian Instn award, 1985; Walford Medal, Library Assoc., 1993; Gold Medal, Bibliographical Soc., 1996. *Publications:* An Introduction to Old English, 1961 (rev. edn 1966); A Catalogue of Books relating to the English Language (1500–1800) in Swedish Libraries, 1965; English Language and Medieval English Literature: a Select Reading-List for Students, 1966; A Bibliography of the English Language from the Invention of Printing to the Year 1800: Vol. I, 1965; Vols V and VIII, 1966; Vols VII and IV, 1967; Vol. II, 1968; Vol. VI, 1969; Vol. III, 1970; Vol. IX, 1971; Vol. X, 1972; Vol. XI, 1978; Vol. XII part 1, 1987; Vol. XII part 2, 1988; Vol. XIII, 1999; Vol. XIV, 2000; Vol. XV, 2001; Vol. XVI, 2002; Vol. XVII, 2003; Vol. XVIII, 2004–06; Vol. XIX, 2007; Alexander Gil's Logonomia Anglica (1619): a translation into Modern English, 1973; (jtly) The Works of William Bullokar, Vol. I, 1966; English Studies (rev. edn of Vol. III, Cambridge Bibl. Eng. Lit.), 1968; English Linguistics 1500–1800: a Collection of Texts in Facsimile (365 vols), 1967–72; European Linguistics 1500–1700: a Collection of Texts in Facsimile (12 vols), 1968–72; A Checklist of the works of Joseph Addison, 1976; Bibliography MARC and ESTC, 1978; Eighteenth-Century Subscription Lists, 1983; ESTC: the British Library Collections, 1983; The arrangement of books in the British Museum Library 1843–1973, and the British Library 1973–1985, 1987; The Nineteenth Century: subject scope and principles of selection, 1987; Index to Pressmarks in use in the British Museum Library and the British Library, 1987; Index to the Classification Schedules of the Map Collections in the British Library, 1987; Computers and Libraries, 1987; The British Library: past, present, future, 1989; Women Writers of Fiction, Verse and Drama: a checklist of works published between 1801 and 1900 in the collections of the British Library, 1990; Handlist of unpublished finding aids to the London Collections of the British Library, 1991; Handlist of catalogues and book lists in the Department of Manuscripts, British Library, 1991; Books with Manuscript: a catalogue, 1994; Books printed on vellum in The British Library, 1996; numerous articles, printed lectures, reviews, etc. *Recreations:* music, photography. *Address:* 67 Ocean City, St Philip, Barbados; *e-mail:* r_alston@sunbeach.net.

ALSTON-ROBERTS-WEST, Lt-Col George Arthur; *see* West.

ALT, Deborah; *see* Gribbon, D.

ALTARAS, Jonathan; Chairman and Managing Director, Jonathan Altaras Associates, since 1990; *b* 5 Aug. 1948; *s* of Leonard and Joy Altaras. *Educ:* Cheadle Hulme Sch.; Manchester Univ. (MA). Trustee, V&A Mus., 2003–06. Chm., Mus. of Performance, 2003–; Mem. Bd, Drama Centre, 1990–. *Recreation:* eating. *Address:* Jonathan Altaras Associates, 11 Garrick Street, WC2E 9AR. *T:* (020) 7836 8722; *e-mail:* dorothy@jaa.ndirect.co.uk. *Club:* Garrick.

ALTHORP, Viscount; Louis Frederick John Spencer; *b* 14 March 1994; *o s* and *heir* of Earl Spencer, *qv*.

ALTMAN, Brian; QC 2008; Senior Treasury Counsel, Central Criminal Court, since 2002; a Recorder, since 2003; *b* 16 Aug. 1957; *s* of late Stanley Altman and of Pauline Altman; *m* 1996, Charlotte Parkin; one *s* one *d* and one *s* one *d* from previous *m. Educ:* Chingford Sen. High Sch.; King's Coll. London (LLB); Univ. of Amsterdam (Dip. Eur. Int.). Called to the Bar, Middle Temple, 1981; Jun. Treasury Counsel, CCC, 1997–2002. *Recreations:* weight and fitness training, music, scuba diving. *Address:* (chambers) 2 Bedford Row, WC1R 4BU. *T:* (020) 7440 8888, *Fax:* (020) 7242 1738; *e-mail:* baltman@2bedfordrow.co.uk.

ALTMAN, John; His Honour Judge Altman; a Circuit Judge since 1991; Designated Family Judge for London, since 2007; *b* 21 June 1944; *s* of Lionel and Vita Altman; *m* 1968, Elizabeth Brown; two *d. Educ:* Bootham Sch., York; Univ. of Bristol (LLB); Council of Legal Education. Called to the Bar, Middle Temple, 1967; part-time Chm., Industrial Tribunals, 1983; Asst Recorder, 1985; Chm., Industrial Tribunals, 1986; a Recorder, 1989; Designated Family Judge: for Milton Keynes, 2003–07; for Oxford, 2005–07. Chm., W Yorks Family Mediation Service, 1997–2002. *Publications:* contribs to

Law Guardian. *Recreations:* reading, photography, music, theatre. *Address:* c/o Royal Courts of Justice, Strand, WC2A 2LL.

ALTMAN, Lionel Phillips, CBE 1979; special adviser to parliamentary and public bodies and to private sector; Chairman: European Cleaning Services Group, 1991–94; Hydro-Lock Europe (formerly Hydro-Lock UK), 1992–96; Equity & General plc, 1978–91; Westminster Consultancy, since 1998; *s* of late Arnold Altman and Catherine Phillips; *m* Diana; one *s* two *d* by previous marriages. *Educ:* University Coll. and Business Sch., also in Paris. FIMI; FCIM; FMI; MCIPR. Director: Carmo Holdings Ltd, 1947–63; Sears Holdings Motor Gp, 1963–72; Sears Finance, 1965–71; C. & W. Walker Holdings Ltd, 1974–77; H. P. Information plc, 1985–91; Motor Agents Assoc. Ltd, 1986–89 (Mem., Nat. Council, 1965–; Pres., 1975–77); Chm., Pre-Divisional Investments Ltd, 1972–95 (Chief Exec., 1972–94). Chairman: Motor Industry Educnl Consultative Council Industry Working Party, producing Altman Report on recruitment and training, 1968; Retail Motor Industry Working Party on Single European Market, 1988–92. Vice-Pres., and Mem. Council, Inst. of Motor Industry, 1970–78. Chairman: Publicity Club of London, 1961–62; Industry Taxation Panel, 1977–86; United Technologists Estabt, 1980–; Dep. Chm., Technology Transfer Assoc., 1984–90; Member: Council, CBI, 1977–88; CBI Industrial Policy Cttee, 1979–85; Dun & Bradstreet Industry Panel, 1982–86. Mem., Jt Consultative Cttee, London Ct of Internat. Arbitration, 1999–. Dep. Chm., Wallenberg Foundn, 1997–. Chairman: Automotive VIP Club, 1988–92; Barbican Assoc., 1995–98. Mem., Battle of Britain (London) Cttee, 2003–. Life Vice-Pres., Devon County Agricl Assoc., 1980. Gov., GSMD, 2000–. Trustee, Guildhall Sch. Trust, 2000–. Various TV and radio broadcasts. Mem., Court of Common Council, Corp. of London, 1996– (Member: Estabt Cttee, 2002–03; Policy and Resources Cttee, 2003–; Dep. Chm., Standards Cttee, 2001–04; Dep. Chm., 2001–03, Chm., 2003–, Libraries, Guildhall Art Gall. and Archives Cttee); Freeman: City of London, 1973; City of Glasgow, 1974; Liveryman and former Hon. Treas., Coachmakers' and Coach Harness Makers' Co.; Burgess Guild Brother, Cordwainers' Co. *Publications:* articles. *Address:* (office) 405 Gilbert House, Barbican, EC2Y 8BD. *T:* and *Fax:* (020) 7638 3023.

ALTMANN, Dr Rosalind Miriam; independent consultant on investment strategy, since 1993; Member, Lord Chancellor's Strategic Investment Board, since 2004; *b* 8 April 1956; *d* of Leo and Renate Altmann; *m* 1982, Paul Richer; one *s* two *d*. *Educ:* University Coll. London (BSc Econ 1st Cl. Hons); Harvard Univ. (Kennedy Schol.); London Sch. of Econs (PhD 1981). Investment Mgt Cert. Fund Manager, Prudential Assce, London, 1981–84; Hd, Internat. Equities, Chase Manhattan Bank, 1984–89; Director: Rothschild Asset Mgt, 1989–91; Natwest Investment Mgt, 1991–93; Consultant to HM Treasury on Pension Fund Investment, 2000; Policy Advr to Number 10 Policy Unit on pensions, investments and savings, 2000–05. Gov., 1989–, and non-exec. Dir, 2004–, LSE; Gov., Pensions Policy Inst. Trustee: Age Employment Network, 2004–; Trafalgar House Pension Trust, 2007–. Life Gov., Nightingale House for the Elderly, 1985. MSI 1992; MInstD 2000. *Publications:* articles in newspapers, jls and industry magazines, incl. Financial Times, The Times, Pensions Week, Financial Advr, Money Mktg, Pensions World, Wall St Jl, Professional Investor, Global Finance, Instnl Investor. *Recreations:* charity fund-raising, swimming, walking, table tennis. *Address:* *e-mail:* ros@rosaltmann.com.

ALTON, family name of **Baron Alton of Liverpool**.

ALTON OF LIVERPOOL, Baron *cr* 1997 (Life Peer), of Mossley Hill, in the Co. of Merseyside; **David Patrick Paul Alton;** Chairman, Banner Ethical Investment Fund, since 1999; Director, Merseyside Special Investment Fund, 2001–06; *b* 15 March 1951; *s* of Frederick and Bridget Alton; *m* 1988, Dilys Elizabeth, *yr d* of Rev. Philip Bell; three *s* one *d*. *Educ:* Edmund Campion Sch., Hornchurch; Christ's College of Education, Liverpool. Elected to Liverpool City Council as Britain's youngest City Councillor, 1972; CC, 1972–80; Deputy Leader of the Council and Housing Chairman, 1978; Vice-Pres., AMA, 1979–. MP Liverpool, Edge Hill (by-election), March 1979–83, Liverpool, Mossley Hill, 1983–97 (L, 1979–88, Lib Dem, 1988–97). Liberal Party spokesman on: the environment and race relations, 1979–81; home affairs, 1981–82; NI, 1987–88 (Alliance spokesman on NI, 1987); Chief Whip, Liberal Party, 1985–87; Member: Select Cttee on the Environment, 1981–85; H of C Privileges Cttee, 1994–97; cross-bencher, 1997. All-Party Groups: Treasurer: Pro-Life, 1993–2004; Landmines, 1996–2000; Friends of CAFOD; Chairman: Street Children, 1992–97; British-N Korea, 2003–; Vice Chm., Tibet Gp, 2005–; Sec., Sudan Gp, 2005–. Chm., Liberal Candidates Cttee, 1985. Nat. Pres., Nat. League of Young Liberals, 1979. Co-founder, Movement for Christian Democracy in Britain, 1990. Vis. Fellow, St Andrews Univ., 1996; Prof. of Citizenship, Liverpool John Moores Univ., 1997. Former Chm., Council for Educn in Commonwealth. Nat. Vice-Pres., Life; Pres., Liverpool Br., NSPCC; Vice-President: Liverpool YMCA; Crisis; Past Chairman: Forget-me-not Appeal (Royal Liverpool Hosp.); Merseyside CVS. Vice-Pres., Assoc. of Councillors. Patron: Jubilee Campaign for the release of prisoners of conscience, 1986–; Nat. Assoc. Child Contact Centres, 1997–. Mem., Catholic Writers' Guild; Trustee: Catholic Central Liby, 1998–2004; Partners In Hope, 1999–; Metta Educn Trust, 2002–. Columnist, The Universe, 1989–. Kt Comdr, Constantinian Order of St George, 2003. *Publications:* What Kind of Country?, 1987; Whose Choice Anyway?, 1988; Faith in Britain, 1991; Signs of Contradiction, 1996; Life After Death, 1997; Citizen Virtues, 1999; Citizen 21, 2001; Pilgrim Ways, 2001; Passion and Pain, 2003; Euthanasia: getting to the heart of the matter, 2005; Abortion: getting to the heart of the matter, 2005. *Recreations:* gardening, reading, walking. *Address:* House of Lords, SW1A 0PW; *e-mail:* davidalton@mail.com.

ALTON, Euan Beresford Seaton, MBE 1945; MC 1943; Under Secretary, Department of Health and Social Security, 1968–76; *b* 22 April 1919; *y s* of late William Lester St John Alton and Ellen Seaton Alton; *m* 1953, Diana Margaret Ede; one *s* one *d*. *Educ:* St Paul's Sch.; Magdalen Coll., Oxford (Exhibnr; MA). Served with Army, 1939–45; Major RA. Admin. Officer, Colonial Service and HM OCS, Gold Coast and Ghana, 1946–58; Admin. Officer, Class 1, 1957. Entered Civil Service as Asst Principal, Min. of Health, 1958; Principal, 1958; Asst Sec., 1961; Under Sec., 1968. *Recreations:* sailing, walking. *Address:* 19 Quay Courtyard, South Street, Manningtree, Essex CO11 1BA. *T:* (01206) 393419. *Club:* Stour Sailing (Manningtree).

ALTON, Roger; Editor, The Independent, since 2008; *b* 20 Dec. 1947; *s* of late Reginald Ernest Alton, MC and Jeannine Beatrice Alton (*née* Gentis); divorced; one *d*. *Educ:* Clifton Coll.; Exeter Coll., Oxford. Liverpool Post, 1969–74; The Guardian, 1974–98; Ed., The Observer, 1998–2007. Editor of the Year: What the Papers Say Awards, 2000; GQ Men of the Year Awards, 2005. *Recreations:* sports, films, ski-ing, climbing. *Address:* The Independent, Independent House, 191 Marsh Wall, E14 9RS. *Clubs:* Climbers', Soho House, Groucho.

ALTRINCHAM, 3rd Baron *cr* 1945, of Tormarton, co. Gloucester; **Anthony Ulick David Dundas Grigg;** *b* 12 Jan. 1934; *yr s* of 1st Baron Altrincham, KCMG, KCVO, DSO, MC, PC and Hon. Joan Dickson-Poynder; *S* brother, 2001; *m* 1965, Eliane, *d* of Marquis de Miramon; two *s* one *d*. *Educ:* Eton; New Coll., Oxford. *Heir:* *s* Hon. (Edward) Sebastian Grigg [*b* 18 Dec. 1965; *m* 1993, Rachel Sophia Kelly; three *s* two *d* (of whom one *s* one *d* are twins)]. *Address:* La Musclera, Tamariu 17212, Palafrugell, Girona, Spain.

ALVAREZ, Al(fred); poet and author; *b* London, 1929; *s* of late Bertie Alvarez and Katie Alvarez (*née* Levy); *m* 1st, 1956, Ursula Barr (marr. diss. 1961); one *s*; 2nd, 1966, Anne Adams; one *s* one *d*. *Educ:* Oundle Sch.; Corpus Christi Coll., Oxford (BA 1952, MA 1956; Hon. Fellow, 2001). Research Schol., CCC, Oxon, and Research Schol. of Goldsmiths' Company, 1952–53, 1954–55. Procter Visiting Fellowship, Princeton, 1953–54; Vis. Fellow of Rockefeller Foundn, USA, 1955–56, 1958; gave Christian Gauss Seminars in Criticism, Princeton, and was Lectr in Creative Writing, 1957–58; D. H. Lawrence Fellowship, New Mexico Univ., 1958; Poetry Critic and Editor, The Observer, 1956–66. Visiting Professor: Brandeis Univ., 1960; New York State Univ., Buffalo, 1966. Adv. Ed., Penguin Modern European Poets in Translation, 1966–78. Hon. DLitt East London, 1998. Vachel Lindsay Prize for Poetry (from Poetry, Chicago), 1961. *Publications:* The Shaping Spirit (US title, Stewards of Excellence), 1958; The School of Donne, 1961; The New Poetry (ed and introd), 1962; Under Pressure, 1965; Beyond All This Fiddle, 1968; Lost (poems), 1968; Penguin Modern Poets, No 18, 1970; Apparition (poems, with paintings by Charles Blackman), 1971; The Savage God, 1971; Beckett, 1973; Hers (novel), 1974; Hunt (novel), 1978; Autumn to Autumn and Selected Poems 1953–76, 1978; Life After Marriage, 1982; The Biggest Game in Town, 1983; Offshore, 1986; Feeding the Rat, 1988; Rain Forest (with paintings by Charles Blackman), 1988; Day of Atonement (novel), 1991; The Faber Book of Modern European Poetry (ed and introd.), 1992; Night, 1995; Where Did It All Go Right? (autobiog.), 1999; Poker: bets, bluffs and bad beats, 2001; New and Selected Poems, 2002; The Writer's Voice, 2005; Risky Business, 2007. *Recreations:* music, poker, cold water swimming. *Address:* c/o Aitken Alexander Associates, 18–21 Cavaye Place, SW10 9PT. *Clubs:* Beefsteak, Climbers', Alpine.

ALVES, Colin, OBE 1990; General Secretary: General Synod Board of Education, 1984–90; National Society for Promoting Religious Education, 1984–90; *b* 19 April 1930; *s* of Donald Alexander Alves and Marjorie Alice (*née* Marsh); *m* 1953, Peggy (*née* Kember); two *s* one *d*. *Educ:* Christ's Hospital, Horsham; Worcester Coll., Oxford (MA). School teaching, 1952–59; Lectr, King Alfred's Coll., Winchester, 1959–68; Head of Dept, Brighton Coll. of Educn, 1968–74; Dir, RE Centre, St Gabriel's Coll., 1974–77; Colleges Officer, General Synod Bd of Educn, 1977–84. Mem., Durham Commn on RE, 1967–70; Chm., Schs Council RE Cttee, 1971–77; Sec., Assoc. of Voluntary Colls, 1978–84; Member: Adv. Cttee on Supply and Educn of Teachers, 1980–85; Nat. Adv. Body for Public Sector Higher Educn, 1983–88; Voluntary Sector Consultative Council, 1984–88. Review Officer, Churches Together in England, 1993–94. Governor: Christ Church Coll., Canterbury, 1981–95; Haywards Heath Coll., 1982–99; Digby Stuart Coll., 1990–96; Trustee: Shoei Coll., Winchester, 1982–94; St Gabriel's Trust, 1984–; St Pierre Internat. Youth Trust, 1990–96; St Gregory's Trust, 1991–99. MLitt Lambeth, 1989. *Publications:* Religion and the Secondary School, 1968; The Christian in Education, 1972; The Question of Jesus, 1987; Free to Choose, 1991; contrib. various symposia on RE. *Recreations:* music, walking, gardening. *Address:* 9 Park Road, Haywards Heath, Sussex RH16 4HY. *T:* (01444) 454496.

ALVEY, John, CB 1980; FREng; Chairman, SIRA Ltd, 1987–94; *b* 19 June 1925; *s* of George C. V. Alvey and Hilda E. Alvey (*née* Pellatt); *m* 1955, Celia Edmed Marson; three *s*. *Educ:* Reeds Sch.; London Univ.; BSc (Eng), DipNEC. FIET. London Stock Exchange, to 1943. Royal Navy, 1943–46; Royal Naval Scientific Service, 1950; Head of Weapons Projects, Admiralty Surface Weapons Estabt, 1968–72; Dir-Gen. Electronics Radar, PE, MoD, 1972–73; Dir-Gen., Airborne Electronic Systems, PE, MoD, 1974–75; Dir, Admiralty Surface Weapons Estabt, 1976–77; Dep. Controller, R&D Estabts and Res. C, and Chief Scientist (RAF), MoD, 1977–80; Senior Dir, Technology, 1980–83, Man. Dir, Devlt and Procurement, and Engr-in-Chief, 1983–86, British Telecom. Dir (non-exec.), LSI Logic Ltd, 1986–91. Member Council: Fellowship of Engrg, 1985–92 (Vice-Pres., 1989–92); Foundn for Sci. and Technology, 1986–90; City Univ., 1985–93. Fellow, Queen Mary and Westfield Coll. (formerly QMC), London, 1988. FREng (FEng 1984). FRSA 1983. Hon. DSc City, 1984; Hon. DTech CNAA, 1991. *Recreations:* reading, Rugby, ski-ing, theatre going. *Address:* 9 Western Parade, Emsworth, Hants PO10 7HS.

ALVINGHAM, 2nd Baron *cr* 1929, of Woodfold; **Maj.-Gen. Robert Guy Eardley Yerburgh,** CBE 1978 (OBE 1972); DL; *b* 16 Dec. 1926; *s* of 1st Baron and Dorothea Gertrude (*d* 1927), *d* of late J. Eardley Yerburgh; *S* father, 1955; *m* 1952, Beryl Elliott, *d* of late W. D. Williams; one *s* one *d*. *Educ:* Eton. Commissioned 1946, Coldstream Guards; served UK, Palestine, Tripolitania, BAOR, Farelf, British Guiana; Head of Staff, CDS, 1972–75; Dep. Dir, Army Staff Duties, 1975–78; Dir of Army Quartering, 1978–81, retired. Patron: Royal British Legion, Oxfordshire; Henley and District Agricultural Assoc. DL Oxfordshire, 1996. *Heir:* *s* Captain Hon. Robert Richard Guy Yerburgh, 17th/21st Lancers, retired [*b* 10 Dec. 1956; *m* 1st, 1981, Vanessa, *yr d* of Captain Duncan Kirk (marr. diss. 1993); two *s*; 2nd, 1994, Karen, *er d* of Antony Baldwin; one *s* one *d*].

ALWARD, Peter Andrew Ulrich; Artistic Consultant: Cleveland Orchestra, since 2006; West-Eastern Divian Orchestra, since 2007; President, EMI Classics, 2002–05; *b* 20 Nov. 1950; *s* of late Herbert Andrew Alward and Marion Evelyne (*née* Schreiber). *Educ:* Mowden Prep. Sch., Hove; Bryanston; Guildhall Sch. of Music and Drama. Simrock Music Publishers, London, 1968–70; with EMI, 1970–2005: EMI Records UK, London, 1970–74; Eur. Co-ordinator, EMI Classical Div., Munich, 1975–83; Exec. Producer, with Herbert von Karajan, for all EMI recordings, 1976–89; Artists and Repertoire, UK: Manager, 1983–84; Internat. Dir, 1985–88; Vice-Pres., 1989–97; Sen. Vice-Pres., 1998–2001. Non-executive Director: Royal Opera/Opus Arte, 2007–; Opera Rara, 2007–. Member: Adv. Bd, Royal Opera House, Covent Garden, 1998–99; Bd of Trustees, Young Concert Artists Trust, 1999–2004; Artistic Cttee, Herbert von Karajan Stiftung, 2003–; Trustee, Masterclass Media Foundn, 2006–. Mem., Editl Adv. Bd, BBC Music, 2006–. *Recreations:* all classical music sectors, exhibitions of painting and sculpture, theatre, books, collecting stage designs and costume designs, cooking, travelling. *Address:* 24 Midway, Walton-on-Thames, Surrey KT12 3HZ. *T:* (01932) 248985; Reiteralpestrasse 19, 83395 Freilassing, Germany. *T:* (8654) 3558. *Club:* Arts.

AMANN, Prof. Ronald, PhD; Professor of Comparative Politics (formerly of Soviet Politics), University of Birmingham, 1986–2003, now Emeritus; *b* 21 Aug. 1943; *s* of George James Amann and Elizabeth Clementson Amann (*née* Towell); *m* 1965, Susan Frances Peters; two *s* one *d*. *Educ:* Heaton Grammar Sch., Newcastle upon Tyne; Univ. of Birmingham (MSocSc, PhD). Consultant, OECD, and Res. Associate, 1965–68; University of Birmingham: Asst Lectr, then Lectr and Sen. Lectr, 1968–83; Dir, Centre for Russian and E European Studies, 1983–89; Dean, Faculty of Commerce and Soc. Sci., 1989–91; Pro-Vice-Chancellor, 1991–94; Chief Exec. and Dep. Chm., ESRC, 1994–99; Dir-Gen., Centre for Mgt and Policy Studies, Cabinet Office, 1999–2002. Vis. Fellow, Osteuropa Inst., Munich, 1975. Special Advr, H of C Select Cttee on Sci. and Technol., 1976. Member: Technology Foresight Steering Cttee, 1995–2000; COPUS, 1996–1999; Adv. Bd, Centre for Analysis of Risk and Regulation, LSE, 2000–; Chm. Adv. Bd, Centre for Res. on Innovation and Competitiveness, Univ. of Manchester, 2001–. Ind. Mem., W Midlands Police Authy. Mem. Council, SSEES, London Univ., 1986–89. Founding AcSS, 1999. FRSA. *Publications:* jointly: Science Policy in the USSR, 1969; The Technological Level of Soviet Industry, 1977; Industrial Innovation in the Soviet Union, 1982; Technical Progress and Soviet Economic Development, 1986. *Recreations:* modern jazz, walking. *Address:* 26 Spring Road, Edgbaston, Birmingham B15 2HA. *T:* (0121) 440 6186.

AMARAL, Sergio Silva do, Hon. KBE 1997; Ambassador of Brazil to France, 2003–05; *b* 1 June 1944; *s* of Pedro Augusto do Amaral and Maria Aparecida Silva do Amaral; *m* Rosario Jorge do Amaral; two *d* ; one *s* one *d* from previous marriage. *Educ:* Univ. of Paris (Master in Pol Sci.); Rio Branco Inst.; Univ. of São Paulo (BSc Legal and Social Scis). Joined Brazilian Diplomatic Service, 1974; Paris, 1974–76; Bonn, 1977–80; Washington, 1984–87, 1992–93; Geneva, 1990–92; Sec. for Internat. Affairs, Min. of Finance, and Chief Debt Negotiator for Brazil, 1988–90; Dep. Rep. to GATT, Geneva, 1990–91; Vice-Minister for Envmt and the Amazon, 1993–94; COS to Minister of Finance, 1994; Exec. Sec., Federal Commn for Foreign Trade, 1995; Sec. of Social Communicn and Spokesman for Pres. of Brazil, 1995–99; Ambassador to UK, 1999–2001; Minister of Develt, Industry and Commerce, Brazil, 2001–02. Asst Prof. of Political Sci. and Internat. Relns, Univ. of Brasilia, 1981–99. Grand Cross, Order of Rio Branco (Brazil), 1996; Officer, Dienst Kreuz (Germany), 1980; Grand Cross: Order of Prince Henry (Portugal), 1995; Order of Merit (Italy), 1996; Order of Sacred Treasure 1st Cl. (Japan), 1996; Order of Merit (Portugal), 1997; Grand Officer, Légion d'honneur (France), 1998. *Publications:* articles in jls, papers, and conf. proceedings. *Recreations:* cycling, tennis.

AMARATUNGA, Prof. Gehan Anil Joseph, PhD; CEng, FREng, FIET; 1966 Professor of Engineering (Electrical), University of Cambridge, since 1998; Fellow, Churchill College, Cambridge, 1987–95 and since 1998; *b* 6 April 1956; *s* of Carl Hermen Joseph Amaratunga and Mallika Swarna (*née* Undugodage); *m* 1981, Praveen Dharshini Hitchcock; one *s* two *d*. *Educ:* Royal Coll., Colombo; Pelham Meml High Sch., NY; University Coll. Cardiff (BSc Hons); Wolfson Coll., Cambridge (PhD 1983). CEng, FREng 2004; FIET (FIEE 2004). University of Southampton: Res. Fellow in Microelectronics, 1983; Lectr in Electronics, 1984–86; Vis. Prof., Dept of Electronics and Computer Sci., 1998–; Lectr in Electrical Engrg, Univ. of Cambridge, 1987–95; Prof. of Electrical Engrg, Univ. of Liverpool, 1995–98. Founder, Chief Technol. Officer, and Dir, Cambridge Semiconductor Ltd, 2000–; Chm. and Dir, Wind Technologies Ltd, 2006–; Founder: Enecsys Ltd, 2004; Nanoinstruments Ltd, 2005. Royal Acad. Engrg Vis. Researcher, Stanford Univ., Calif, 1989. Silver Medal, Royal Acad. of Engrg, 2007. *Publications:* contrib. IEEE Trans, Physical Rev., Nature. *Recreations:* jazz, opera, cricket, classic cars, avant garde cinema. *Address:* Electrical Engineering Division, Engineering Department, Cambridge University, Cambridge CB3 0FA. *T:* (01223) 332648; *e-mail:* gaja1@cam.ac.uk.

AMBACHE, Jeremy Noel; management consultant in health and social care, since 2002; political adviser and campaigner, Liberal Democrats, since 2004; *b* 16 Dec. 1946; *s* of Nachman and Stella Ambache; *m* 1973, Ann Campbell; two *d*. *Educ:* Bedales Sch.; Sussex Univ. (BA); York Univ. (MPhil); Kingston Univ. (MA). Social worker, Birmingham Social Services, 1971–73; Team Manager, Hammersmith Social Services, 1974–80; Co-ordinator for Community Homes, Brent Social Services, 1981–84; Area Manager, Croydon Social Services, 1984–90; Divl Dir, Berks Social Services, 1990–91; Asst Dir, Bedfordshire Social Services, 1991–93; Dir of Social Services, Knowsley, 1993–2000; Dir of Social Services and Housing, Bromley, 2000–02. Contested (Lib Dem) Putney, 2005. *Recreations:* tennis, yoga, travel, walking. *Address:* 17 Hazlewell Road, Putney, SW15 6LT. *T:* (020) 8785 9650. *Club:* Putney Lawn Tennis.

AMBLER, John Doss; Vice-President, 1980–96, Vice-President, Human Resources, 1989–96, Texaco Inc.; *b* 24 July 1934; *m*; one *s* one *d*. *Educ:* Virginia Polytechnic Inst. and State Univ. (BSc Business Admin). Texaco Inc., USA: various assignments, Marketing Dept, Alexandra, Va, 1956–65; Dist Sales Manager, Harrisburg, Pa, 1965–67; Asst Divl Manager, Norfolk, Va, 1967–68; Staff Asst to Gen. Manager Marketing US, New York, 1968; various assignments, Chicago and New York, 1969–72; Gen. Manager, Texaco Olie Maatschappij BV, Rotterdam, 1972–75; Man. Dir, Texaco Oil AB, Stockholm, 1975–77; Asst to Pres., 1977, Asst to Chm. of the Bd, 1980, Texaco Inc.; Pres., Texaco Europe, New York, 1981–82; Chm. and Chief Exec. Officer, Texaco Ltd, 1982–89. *Recreations:* hunting, fishing, tennis, photography.

AMBO, Rt Rev. George Somboba, KBE 1988 (OBE 1978); Archbishop of Papua New Guinea, 1983–89; Bishop of Popondota, 1977–89; Chairman, South Pacific Anglican Council, 1986–89; *b* Gona, Nov. 1925; *s* of late J. O. Ambo, Gona; *m* 1946, Marcella O., *d* of Karau; two *s* two *d*. *Educ:* St Aidan's College, Dogura; Newton Theological Coll., Dogura. Deacon, 1955; Priest, 1958. Curate of: Menapi, 1955–57; Dogura, 1957–58; Priest in charge of Boianai, Diocese of New Guinea, 1958–63; Missionary at Wamira, 1963–69; an Asst Bishop of Papua New Guinea, 1960 (first Papuan-born Anglican Bishop). *Publication:* St John's Gospel in Ewage. *Recreations:* reading, carpentry. *Address:* c/o Anglican Diocesan Office, PO Box 26, Popondetta, Papua New Guinea.

AMBRASEYS, Prof. Nicholas, FREng; FICE; Professor of Engineering Seismology, University of London, at Imperial College, 1973–94, now Emeritus; Senior Research Fellow, since 1995, and Senior Research Investigator, since 1996, Imperial College; *b* 19 Jan. 1929; *s* of Neocles Ambraseys, Athens, and Cleopatra Jambany; *m* 1955, Xeni, *d* of A. Stavrou. *Educ:* National Technical Univ. of Athens (DipEng); Univ. of London (DIC; PhD; DSc 1980). Lectr in Civil Engineering, Imperial Coll., 1958–62; Associate Prof. of Civil Engrg, Univ. of Illinois, 1963; Prof. of Hydrodynamics, Nat. Tech. Univ., Athens, 1964; Imperial College: Lectr, 1965–68; Univ. Reader in Engrg Seismology, 1969–72; Hd, Engrg Seismology Sect., 1969–95. Chm., British Nat. Cttee for Earthquake Eng., 1961–71; Dir, Internat. Assoc. for Earthquake Engrg, 1961–77; Vice-Pres., European Assoc. for Earthquake Engrg, 1964–75; Mem., 1969–78, Vice-Chm., 1979–81, Unesco Internat. Adv. Cttee of Earthquake Risk; leader, UN/Unesco earthquake reconnaisance missions to Pakistan, Iran, Turkey, Romania, Jugoslavia, Italy, Greece, Algeria, Nicaragua, East and Central Africa; Chm., Internat. Commn for earthquake protection of historical monuments, 1977–81; consultant to UN/Unesco. Member: European Acad., 2002; Acad. of Athens, 2003. FREng (FEng 1985); FCGI 2000. Hon. Fellow, Internat. Assoc. for Earthquake Engrg, 1992; Hon. Mem., Earthquake Res. Inst., USA, 2001. Dr Eng *hc* Nat. Tech. Univ. of Athens, 1993. Decennial Award, European Assoc. for Earthquake Engrg, 1975; Busk Medal, RGS, 1975; William Smith Medal, Geological Soc. of London, 2002; Seismological Soc. of America Medal, 2006. Freedom of City of Skopje, 1999. *Publications:* (with C. Melville) A History of Persian Earthquakes, 1982; (with C. Melville) Seismicity of Arabia & Red Sea, 1994; (with C. Finkel) Seismicity of Turkey, 1995; papers on engrg seismology, soil mechanics, tectonics, historical seismicity. *Recreations:* history, philately. *Address:* Imperial College London, SW7 2BU. *T:* (020) 7589 5111; 19 Bede House, Manor Fields, SW15 3LT. *T:* (020) 8788 4219.

AMBROZIC, His Eminence Cardinal Aloysius Matthew; Archbishop of Toronto, (RC), 1990–2006; *b* 27 Jan. 1930; *s* of Aloysius Ambrozic and Helena (*née* Pecar). *Educ:* St Augustine's Seminary, Scarborough, Ont; Angelicum Rome (STL); Biblicum, Rome, 1957–60 (SSL); Univ. of Würzburg, Germany (ThD). Ordained, 1955; Curate, St Teresa's, Port Colborne, Ont, 1955–57; Professor: St Augustine's Seminary, Scarborough, Ont, 1960–67; Toronto Sch. of Theol., 1970–76; Auxiliary Bishop of Toronto, 1976–86; Coadjutor Archbishop of Toronto, 1986–90. Cardinal, 1998. *Publications:* The Hidden Kingdom, 1972; Remarks on the Canadian Catechism, 1974; Oče, posvečeno bodi tvoje ime, 1980; Oče, zgodi se tvoja volja, 1996; Če hoče kdo hoditi za menoj, 2001. *Recreations:* hiking, swimming.

AMERY, Colin Robert; architectural writer, critic and historian; Director, World Monuments Fund in Britain, since 1999 (Trustee, 1992–98); *b* 29 May 1944; *yr s* of late Kenneth George Amery and Florence Ellen Amery (*née* Young). *Educ:* King's College London; Univ. of Sussex (BA Hons). Editor and Inf. Officer, TCPA, 1968–70; Asst Editor and Features Editor, Architectural Review, 1970–79; Architecture Corresp., Financial Times, 1979–99. Advr for Sainsbury Wing, Nat. Gall., 1985–91; Arch. consultant to J. Sainsbury plc, 1985–2002. Vis. Fellow, Jesus Coll., Cambridge, 1989. Member: Arts Panel, Arts Council, 1984–86; Exec. Cttee, Georgian Gp, 1985–93; Adv. Cttee, Geffrye Mus., 1985–87; Architecture Panel, NT, 1986–; London Adv. Cttee, English Heritage, 1987–90; Building Cttee, Nat. Gallery, 1988–92; British Council, Visual Art Adv. Cttee, 1989–93; Chm., Fabric Adv. Cttee, St Edmundsbury Cathedral, 2001–. Dir, Sir John Soane Soc., 1987–2002; Dir of Develt, Prince of Wales's Inst. of Architecture, 1993–96; Pres., Lutyens Trust, 1999– (Chm., 1984–93); Chairman: Organising Cttee, Lutyens Exhibn, 1981–82; Duchy of Cornwall Commercial Property Develt Cttee, 1990–98; Perspectives on Architecture Ltd, 1994–98. Trustee: Spitalfields Trust, 1977–85; Brooking Collection, 1985–94; Nat. Museums and Galls on Merseyside, 1988–97; Architectural Heritage Fund, 1998–; Heather Trust for the Arts; War Memorials Trust, 2004–. Gov., Museum of London, 1992–99. Hon. FRIBA 1998. *Publications:* Period Houses and Their Details, 1974; (jtly) The Rape of Britain, 1975; Three Centuries of Architectural Craftsmanship, 1977; (jtly) The Victorian Buildings of London 1837–1887, 1980; (compiled jtly) Lutyens 1869–1944, 1981; (contrib.) Architecture of the British Empire, 1986; Wren's London, 1988; A Celebration of Art and Architecture: the National Gallery Sainsbury Wing, 1991; Bracken House, 1992; Architecture, Industry and Innovation: the early work of Nicholas Grimshaw & Partners, 1995; Vanishing Histories, 2001; (jtly) The Lost World of Pompeii, 2002; (jtly) St Petersburg, 2006; articles in professional jls. *Address:* 15 York House, Upper Montagu Street, W1H 1FR. *Clubs:* Brooks's, Pratt's, Arts.

AMESS, David Anthony Andrew; MP (C) Southend West, since 1997 (Basildon, 1983–97); *b* Plaistow, 26 March 1952; *s* of late James Henry Valentine Amess and of Maud Ethel Martin; *m* 1983, Julia Monica Margaret Arnold; one *s* four *d*. *Educ:* St Bonaventure's Grammar Sch.; Bournemouth Coll. of Technol. (BScEcon Hons 2.2, special subject Govt). Teacher, St John the Baptist Jun. Mixed Sch., Bethnal Green, 1970–71; Jun. Underwriter, Leslie & Godwin Agencies, 1974–77; Sen. Manager, Accountancy Personnel, 1977–80; Chm., Accountancy Aims, then Accountancy Ltd, 1990–96. Mem., Redbridge Council, 1982–86 (Vice Chm., Housing Cttee, 1982–85). Contested (C) Newham NW, 1979. Parliamentary Private Secretary: to Parly Under-Secs of State (Health), DHSS, 1987–88; to Minister of State and Parly Under-Sec. of State, Dept of Transport, 1988–90; to Minister of State, DoE, 1990–92; to Chief Sec. to the Treasury, 1992–94; to Sec. of State for Employment, 1994–95; to Sec. of State for Defence, 1995–97. Member: Broadcasting Select Cttee, 1994–97; Health Select Cttee, 1998–; Chairman's Panel, 2001–. All-Party Groups: Chairman: Solvent Abuse, 2000–; Fire Safety and Rescue, 2001–; Rheumatoid Arthritis, 2002–; Hepatology, 2004–; Holy See, 2006–; FRAME, 2006–; Jt Chm., Scouts, 1997–; Vice-Chairman: Guides, 2000; Hungary, 2003–; Obesity, 2003; Deep Vein Thrombosis Awareness, 2003–; Asthma, 2003–; Funerals and Bereavement, 2005–; Bermuda, 2005–; Warm Homes, 2005–; Thrombosis, 2006–; Lions Club Internat., 2006–; Sec., Eye Health and Visual Impairment, 2003–; Treasurer: ME (Myalgic Encephalomyelitis), 2001–; N Korea, 2004–. Chm., Cons. Back Bench Health Cttee, 1999–. Mem. Exec., 1922 Cttee, 2004–. Vice Pres., Nat. Lotteries Council, 1998. Dir, Parly Broadcasting Unit Ltd, 1997–99. Chm., 1912 Club, 1996–; Vice Chm., Assoc. of Cons. Clubs, 1997–. *Publications:* The Road to Basildon, 1993; Basildon Experience: Conservatives fight back, 1994; contrib. magazines and pamphlets. *Recreations:* gardening, music, sport, animals, theatre, travel. *Address:* c/o House of Commons, SW1A 0AA. *Clubs:* Carlton, St Stephen's; Kingswood Squash and Racketball (Basildon).

AMET, Hon. Sir Arnold (Karibone), Kt 1993; CBE 1987; MP (Nat. Alliance) Mandang, Papua New Guinea, since 2007; Chief Justice, Papua New Guinea, 1993–2003; *b* 30 Oct. 1952; *m* 1972, Miaru; three *s* two *d*. *Educ:* Univ. of PNG (LLB 1975); Legal Trng Inst., PNG. Joined Public Solicitor's Office, PNG, 1976; qualified as barrister and solicitor, 1977; Legal Officer and Sec., Nat. Airline Commn, 1979–80; Dep. Public Solicitor, 1980–81; Public Solicitor, 1981–83; Judge of National Trial Court and Supreme Court of Appeal, 1983–93. Hon. LLD PNG, 1993. *Recreations:* Christian Ministry, watching Rugby and cricket. *Address:* c/o Parliament House, Waigani, NCD, Papua New Guinea.

AMEY, Julian Nigel Robert; Chief Executive, Trinity College London, since 2006; *b* 19 June 1949; *s* of Robert Amey and Diana Amey (*née* Coles); *m* 1972, Ann Victoria Brenchley; three *d*. *Educ:* Wellingborough Sch.; Magdalene Coll., Cambridge (BA 1971, MA 1973). Longman Group: Exec. Trainee, 1971; Manager: Spain, 1972–76; Brazil, 1977–79; Latin America, 1979–83; Regional Manager, Asia Pacific Region, 1983–85; Dir, Internat. Sales and Mktg, 1985–89; Exec. Dir, BBC English, World Service, 1989–94; apptd to DTI, to assist in internat. promotion of British educn and media interest, 1994–96; Dir Gen., Canning House, 1996–2001; Chief Exec., CIBSE, 2001–06. Chm., Anglo-Chilean Soc., 2002–06. Governor: Bath Spa University Coll., 1996–; Trinity Coll., London, 2003–06. *Publications:* Spanish Business Dictionary, 1979; Portuguese Business Dictionary, 1981. *Recreations:* cricket, tennis, ornithology, travel. *Address:* Trinity College London, 89 Albert Embankment, SE1 7TP. *Clubs:* English-Speaking Union, Rumford; Hawks (Cambridge).

AMHERST OF HACKNEY, 4th Baron *cr* 1892; **William Hugh Amherst Cecil;** *b* 28 Dec. 1940; *s* of 3rd Baron Amherst of Hackney, CBE, and of Margaret Eirene Clifton Brown, *d* of late Brig.-Gen. Howard Clifton Brown; *S* father, 1980; *m* 1965, Elisabeth, *d* of Hugh Humphrey Merriman, DSO, MC, TD, DL; one *s* one *d*. *Educ:* Eton. Director: E. A. Gibson Shipbrokers Ltd, 1975–90; Seascope Sale and Purchase Ltd, 1994–97; Short Sea Europe plc, 1996–2002. Younger Brother, Trinity House, 1995. Member Council: New Forest Assoc., 1997–2000; RYA, 1999–2002. Patron: St John-at-Hackney; St John of Jerusalem, S Hackney. *Heir:* *s* Hon. Hugh William Amherst Cecil [*b* 17 July 1968; *m* 1996, Nicola Jane, *d* of Major Timothy Michels; one *s* two *d*]. *Address:* Hawthorn House, New Street, Lymington, Hampshire SO41 9BJ. *Clubs:* Royal Ocean Racing; Royal Yacht Squadron (Vice-Cdre, 1993–98, Cdre, 2001–05), Royal Cruising, Royal Lymington Yacht, Island Sailing.

AMIN, Prof. Ash, PhD; FBA 2007; Professor of Geography, since 1995, and Executive Director, Institute for Advanced Studies, since 2005, University of Durham; *b* 31 Oct. 1955; *s* of late Harish and Vilas Amin; *m* 1989, Lynne Marie Brown; one *s* two *d*. *Educ:* Reading Univ. (BA Hons Italian Studies 1979; PhD Geog. 1986). Newcastle University: Res. Associate, Centre for Urban and Regl Develt Studies, 1982–89; Lectr, then Sen. Lectr, Geog, 1989–94; Prof. of Geog., 1994–95. Visiting Professor: Naples, 1989; Rotterdam, 1995; Copenhagen, 1995; International Fellow: Naples, 1987; Uppsala, 1999. AcSS 2000. Corresp. Life Mem., Società Geografica Italiana, 1999. Edward Heath Award, RGS/IBG, 1998. *Publications:* (ed jtly) Technological Change, Industrial Restructuring and Regional Development, 1986; (ed jtly) Towards a New Europe?, 1991; (ed) Post-Fordism: a reader, 1994; (ed with N. Thrift) Globalisation, Institutions and Regional Development, 1994; (ed) Post-Fordism: a reader, 1994; (ed jtly) Behind the Myth of European Union, 1995; (ed with J. Hausner) Beyond Market and Hierarchy, 1997; (with D. Massey and N. Thrift) Cities for the Many not the Few, 2002 (trans. Italian); (with N. Thrift) Cities: reimagining the urban, 2002; (with A. Cameron and R. Hudson) Placing the Social Economy, 2002; (with D. Massey and N. Thrift) Decentering the Nation: a radical approach to regional inequality, 2003; (jtly) Organisational Learning: the role of communities, 2003; (ed jtly) The Blackwell Cultural Economy Reader, 2004; (with P. Cohendet) Architectures of Knowledge: firms, capabilities and communities, 2004; (ed jtly) Community, Economic Creativity and Organisation, 2008. *Recreations:* Bob Dylan, world music and ECM jazz, gardening, cooking. *Address:* Department of Geography, University of Durham, Durham DH1 3LE. *T:* (0191) 334 1850; *e-mail:* ash.amin@durham.ac.uk.

AMIS, Martin Louis; author; Professor of Creative Writing, Manchester University, since 2007; special writer for The Observer, since 1980; *b* 25 Aug. 1949; *s* of Sir Kingsley Amis, CBE, and Hilary Bardwell; *m* 1984, Antonia Phillips (marr. diss. 1996); two *s*; *m* 1998, Isabel Fonseca; two *d*. *Educ:* various schools; Exeter Coll., Oxford (BA Hons 1st cl. in English). Fiction and Poetry Editor, TLS, 1974; Literary Editor, New Statesman, 1977–79. *Publications:* The Rachel Papers, 1973 (Somerset Maugham Award, 1974); Dead Babies, 1975; Success, 1978; Other People: a mystery story, 1981; Money, 1984; The Moronic Inferno and Other Visits to America, 1986; Einstein's Monsters (short stories), 1987; London Fields, 1989; Time's Arrow, 1991; Visiting Mrs Nabokov and Other Excursions, 1993; The Information, 1995; Night Train, 1997; Heavy Water and Other Stories, 1998; Experience (memoir), 2000 (James Tait Black Meml Prize); The War Against Cliché: essays and reviews 1971–2000, 2001; Koba the Dread, 2002; Yellow Dog, 2003; House of Meetings, 2006; The Second Plane: September 11, 2001–2007, 2008. *Recreations:* tennis, chess, snooker. *Address:* c/o Wylie Agency (UK), 17 Bedford Square, WC1B 3JA; *e-mail:* mail@wylieagency.co.uk. *Club:* Oxford and Cambridge.

AMLOT, Roy Douglas; QC 1989; barrister; *b* 22 Sept. 1942; *s* of Douglas Lloyd Amlot and Ruby Luise Amlot; *m* 1969, Susan Margaret (*née* McDowell); two *s*. *Educ:* Dulwich Coll. Called to the Bar, Lincoln's Inn, 1963 (Bencher, 1986; Treas., 2007). Second Prosecuting Counsel to the Inland Revenue, Central Criminal Court and London Crown Courts, 1974; First Prosecuting Counsel to the Crown, Inner London Crown Court, 1975; Jun. Prosecuting Counsel to the Crown, Central Criminal Court, 1977, Sen. Prosecuting Counsel, 1981; First Sen. Prosecuting Counsel, 1987–89. Chairman: Criminal Bar Assoc., 1997; Bar Council, 2001; Mem., QC Appts Cttee, 2006–. *Publication:* (ed) 11th edn, Phipson on Evidence. *Recreations:* ski-ing, cycling, windsurfing, music. *Address:* 6 King's Bench Walk, Temple, EC4Y 7DR. *T:* (020) 7583 0410.

AMORIM, Celso; Minister of Foreign Affairs, Brazil, 1993–94 and since 2003; *b* 3 June 1942; *s* of Vicente Matheus Amorim and Beatriz Nunes Amorim; *m* 1966, Ana Maria Carvalho; three *s* one *d*. *Educ:* Brazilian Diplomatic Acad., Rio Branco Inst.; Diplomatic Acad. of Vienna (Postgrad. Dip. Internat. Relns 1967). Postgrad. work in Pol Sci./Internat. Relns, LSE, 1968–71. Chm., Brazilian Film Corp., 1979–82; Dep. Hd of Mission, Brazilian Embassy, Netherlands, 1982–85; Asst Sec., Min. of Sci. and Technol., 1985–88; Dir for Cultural Affairs, 1989, Dir for Econ. Affairs, 1990–91, Min. of Foreign Relns; Perm. Rep. to UN, GATT and Conf. on Disarmament, Geneva, 1991–93; Perm. Rep. to UN, NY, 1995–99; Perm. Rep. to UN and WTO, Geneva, 1999–2000; Ambassador to UK, 2001–02. Chairman: UN Security Council, 1999; Conf. on Disarmament, 2000; Gov. Body, ILO, 2000–01; Convention on Tobacco Control, 2000–01; WTO Council for Trade in Services, 2001. US Foreign Policy Assoc. Medal, 1999. Nat. and foreign decorations, incl. many Grand Crosses. *Publications:* articles in Brazilian and foreign pubns in fields of political theory, internat. relations, cultural policy, sci. and technological development. *Recreations:* reading, travelling, art, film. *Address:* Ministry of Foreign Affairs, Esplanada dos Ministérios, Bloco H, 70170–900, Brasilia DF, Brazil.

AMORY; *see* Heathcoat Amory and Heathcoat-Amory.

AMOS, Baroness *cr* 1997 (Life Peer), of Brondesbury in the London Borough of Brent; **Valerie Ann Amos;** PC 2003; *b* 13 March 1954; *d* of E. Michael Amos and Eunice Amos. *Educ:* Univ. of Warwick (BA Sociol.); Univ. of Birmingham (MA Cultural Studies); Univ. of E Anglia (doctoral research). With London Boroughs: Lambeth, 1981–82; Camden, 1983–85; Hackney, 1985–89 (Head of Trng; Head of Management Services); Management Consultant, 1984–89; Chief Exec., Equal Opportunities Commn, 1989–94; Dir, Amos Fraser Bernard, 1995–98. A Baroness in Waiting (Govt Whip), 1998–2001; Parly Under-Sec. of State, FCO, 2001–03; Sec. of State for Internat. Develt, 2003; Leader of H of L, 2003–07. Chairman: Bd of Govs, RCN Inst., 1994–98; Afiya Trust (formerly Black Heath Foundn), 1995–98. Member: Adv. Cttee, Centre for Educnl Develt Appraisal and Res., Univ. of Warwick, 1991–98; Gen. Council, King's Fund, 1992–98; Council, Inst. of Employment Studies, 1993–98; Trustee, IPPR, 1994–98. External Examiner: (MA Equal Opportunities), Univ. of Northumbria, at Newcastle (formerly Newcastle Poly.), 1989–93; Liverpool Univ., 1992–97. Dir, UCL Hosps NHS Trust, 1995–98; Fellow, UCL Hosps, 2000–. Dir, Hampstead Theatre, 1992–98; Dep. Chm., Runnymede Trust, 1990–98; Trustee: VSO, 1997–98; Project Hope, 1997–98; NPG, 2003–. Hon. LLD: Warwick, 2000; Staffordshire, 2000; Manchester, 2001; Bradford, 2006; Leicester, 2007. *Publications:* various articles on race and gender issues. *Address:* House of Lords, SW1A 0PW. *T:* (020) 7219 1863.

AMOS, Alan Thomas; investigator with Local Government Ombudsman, since 1993; Complaints Manager, Camden and Islington Health Authority, 2002–05; *b* 10 Nov. 1952; *s* of William Edmond Amos and Cynthia Florence Kathleen Amos. *Educ:* St Albans Sch.; St John's Coll., Oxford (MA(PPE) Hons); London Univ. Inst. of Educn (PGCE 1976). Pres., Oxford Univ. Cons. Assoc., 1974–75. Dir of Studies, Hd of Sixth Form, Hd of Econs and Politics Dept, Dame Alice Owen's Sch., Potters Bar, 1976–84; Hd of Agric. and Environment Sect., Cons. Res. Dept, 1984–86; Asst Prin., College of Further Educn, 1986–87. PA to Sec. of State for the Envmt, 1993. Councillor, 1978–90, Dep. Leader, and Chm. Educn Cttee, 1983–87, Enfield Bor. Council; Chm., London Boroughs Assoc. Educn Cttee, 1986–87; Member: (Lab), Tower Hamlets LBC, 1998–2008 (Chm., Overview and Scrutiny Cttee, 2002–08); Worcester CC, 2008–. Contested (C): Tottenham, GLC, 1981; Walthamstow, 1983; MP (C) Hexham, 1987–92; contested (Lab) Hitchin and Harpenden, 2001. Mem., Agriculture Select Cttee, 1989–92; Chairman: Cons. backbench Forestry Cttee, 1987–92; Parly ASH Gp, 1991–92; Secretary: Cons. backbench Transport Cttee, 1988–92 (Vice Chm., 1991–92); Cons. backbench Educn Cttee, 1989–92; British-Bulgarian All Party Gp, 1991–92; Chm., Northern Gp of Cons. MPs, 1991–92. Joined Labour party, 1994; Mem. Exec. Cttee, Poplar and Canning Town Lab Party, 1996– (Treas., 1997–); Chm., Millwall Lab Party, 2000–. Sec., Nat. Agricl and Countryside Forum, 1984–86. Lay Chm., NHS Indep. Review Panel, 1998–; Mem., Candidates Panel for appt to NHS Authorities, 1999–. A Vice-Pres., Gtr London YCs, 1981. Member: ESU, 1982–; ASH, 1987– (Mem. Council, 1991–); SPUC, 1987–. Hon. US Citizen, 1991. *Recreations:* travel, badminton, USA politics, bibliophilia.

AMOS, Timothy Robert, (Tim); QC 2008; *b* 13 Jan. 1964; *s* of Edward and Jean Miriam Amos; *m* 1995, Elke Mund, Cologne. *Educ:* King's Sch., Canterbury; Oriel Coll., Oxford (BA Hist. 1985); Poly. of Central London. Called to the Bar, Lincoln's Inn, 1987; in practice at the Bar, specialising in family law, esp. big money family finance cases, those with a foreign or internat. element and particularly Anglo-German cases. Standing Counsel to Queen's Proctor, 2001–08. *Recreations:* music and wine (separately and together). *Address:* Queen Elizabeth Building, Temple, EC4Y 9BS.

AMOS, William Bradshaw, (Brad), PhD; FRS 2007; biologist and optical designer; Research Staff, MRC Laboratory of Molecular Biology, Cambridge, since 1981; *b* 21 Nov. 1945; *s* of James and Edna Amos; *m* 1969, Linda Ann Richardson; two *s*. *Educ:* King Edward VII Sch., Sheffield; Queen Elizabeth's Hosp., Bristol; Queen's Coll., Oxford (MA Natural Scis 1966); Pembroke Coll., Cambridge (PhD 1970). University of Cambridge: Res. Fellow, King's Coll., 1970–74; Univ. Demonstrator and Balfour Student, Dept of Zoology, 1978–81. Chief Design Consultant, Bio-Rad Microsciences Ltd, 1986–2002. Principal Organiser, MRC Course in Advanced Optical Microscopy (annual), Plymouth, 2003–. Hon. FRPS 2002. Mullard Award, Royal Soc., 1994; Rank Prize for Optoelectronics, 1995; Ernst Abbe Award, NY Microscopical Soc., 2005. *Publications:* Molecules of the Cytoskeleton (with L. A. Amos), 1991; numerous articles in learned sci. jls; five patents in field of laser scanning microscopy. *Recreations:* aquatic microscopy, gemstone faceting, amateur dramatics, metalwork. *Address:* MRC Laboratory of Molecular Biology, Hills Road, Cambridge CB2 0QH. *T:* (01223) 411640, *Fax:* (01223) 213556; *e-mail:* ba@mrc-lmb.cam.ac.uk.

AMPHIPOLIS, Bishop of, since 2006; **Rt Rev. Basil Alfred Herbert Ernst Osborne;** Head of the Episcopal Vicariate of Orthodox Parishes of Russian Tradition in Great Britain and Ireland (Ecumenical Patriarchate), since 2006; *b* 12 April 1938; *s* of Alexander W. R. Osborne and Josephine Gerringer; *m* 1962, Rachel Vida Spitzer (*d* 1991); two *s* one *d*. *Educ:* State Univ. of New York at Buffalo (BA (Classics), 1963); Univ. of Cincinnati, Ohio (PhD (Classics), 1969). Ordained deacon, 1969, priest, 1973; consecrated bishop, 1993; Bishop of Sergievo, 1993–2006; Asst Bishop, 1993–2003, Administering Bishop, 2003–06, Russian Orthodox Dio. of Sourozh; VG, 1997–2003. A Pres., Churches Together in England, 1993–98; Chm., Oxfordshire Ecumenical Council, 1997–98. Chm. Bd of Dirs, Inst. for Orthodox Christian Studies, Cambridge, 1999–2003. Rep. of Russian Orthodox Church, Internat. Commn on Anglican-Orthodox Theol Dialogue, 2001–06. Editor: Sourozh: A Journal of Orthodox Life and Thought, 1980–2006; The Messenger, 2006–. Phi Beta Kappa, 1963. *Publications:* The Light of Christ, 1992, 2nd edn 1996; Speaking of the Kingdom, 1993. *Address:* 94a Banbury Road, Oxford OX2 6JT. *T:* (01865) 512701.

AMPLEFORTH, Abbot of; *see* Madden, Rt Rev. C.

AMPTHILL, 4th Baron *cr* 1881; **Geoffrey Denis Erskine Russell,** CBE 1986; PC 1995; Deputy Speaker, House of Lords, since 1983; Deputy Chairman: Express Newspapers, 1989–98 (Director, 1985–98); United Newspapers, 1991–96 (Director, 1981–96); *b* 15 Oct. 1921; *s* of 3rd Baron Ampthill, CBE, and Christabel, Lady Ampthill (*d* 1976); *S* father, 1973; *m* 1st, 1946, Susan Mary (marr. diss. 1971; she *d* 2001), *d* of late Hon. Charles John Frederic Winn; two *s* one *d* (and one *s* decd); 2nd, 1972, Elisabeth Anne Marie (marr. diss. 1987), *d* of late Claude Henri Gustave Mallon. *Educ:* Stowe. Irish Guards, 1941–46; 2nd Lt 1941, Captain 1944. Gen. Manager, Fortnum and Mason, 1947–51; Chairman, New Providence Hotel Co. Ltd, 1951–64; Dir, Dualvest plc, 1981–87. Managing Director of theatre owning and producing companies, 1953–81. Dep. Chm., 1980–92, Chm., 1992–94, of Cttees, H of L; Chairman: Select Cttee on Channel Tunnel Bill, 1987; Select Cttee on Channel Tunnel Rail Link Bill, 1996; elected Mem., H of L, 1999. Chm., London Helicopter Emergency Service, 1991–96. Dir, Leeds Castle Foundn, 1980–82. *Heir: s* Hon. David Whitney Erskine Russell [*b* 27 May 1947; *m* 1st, 1980, April McKenzie Arbon (marr. diss. 1998), *y d* of Paul Arbon, New York; two *d*; 2nd, 2002, Christia, *widow* of Prince Rostislav Romanoff and *d* of Harold Noregaard Ipsen]. *Address:* 6 North Court, Great Peter Street, SW1P 3LL.

AMRAN, Mohammed; Community Cohesion Manager, Greenhead High School, since 2004; *b* 20 Nov. 1975; *s* of Mohammed Ramzan and Rakhmat Jan; *m* 1998, Saima Tabassum; two *s* one *d*. *Educ:* Huddersfield Tech. Coll. (BTEC Nat. Public Services 1995); Bradford and Ilkley Community Coll. (DipHE 1998). Youth work, Grange Interlink Community Centre, Bradford, 1994–96; Play Scheme Leader, Manningham Sport Centre, 1994–97, and Girlington Action Gp, 1996, Bradford; Co-ordinator, Youth for Understanding UK, 1996–97; Recruitment Officer, Prince's Trust Volunteers, 1997–98; remand worker, Youth Offending Team, 1998–99; Outreach Manager, Prince's Trust, 1999–2002; Fundraiser, Yorks Air Ambulance Service Charity, 2002–04; Lay Visitor, Developing Policy Excellence, Central Police Trng Develt Authy, 2003–. Mem., CRE, 1998–2002. Chm., Courts Bd, DCA, subseq. MoJ, 2004–; Mem., Home Office Adv. Panel on Futurebuilders, 2005–. Mem. Panel, EC Cities Anti-Racism Project, 1996–97. Volunteer Trainer, Nat. Police Trng Sch., 1996–97. Member: Policy Action Team, DCMS, 1999–2000; IPPR (Criminal Justice Reform), 2000–02; Advr, Steering Gp, Holocaust Meml Day, Home Office, 2000–01. Mem., Duke of York's Community Initiative, Bradford, 2001–03; Mem., Police Liaison Cttee, Bradford and Dist Minority Ethnic Communities, 1998–; Dir, Bradford Youth Develt Partnership, 2000–. Eur. Rep., Prince's Trust Action, 1996–99. Mem. Court, Univ. of Leeds, 2002–. FRSA 2002. DUniv Bradford, 2002. Awards include: Imran Foundn Special Award in Recognition of Promotion of Asian Community, 2001; Gold Standard Winner, Arts and Community, Windrush Achievement Awards, 2001; Community and Campaigning Volunteer of Year, Whitbread Volunteers Action Awards, 2001; Beacon Prize (Community Builder), 2004. *Address:* 8 Highfield Drive, Heaton, Bradford, Yorks BD9 6HN.

AMWELL, 3rd Baron *cr* 1947, of Islington; **Keith Norman Montague;** independent consultant, since 2005; *b* 1 April 1943; *o s* of 2nd Baron Amwell and of Kathleen Elizabeth Montague (*née* Fountain); *S* father, 1990; *m* 1970, Mary, *d* of Frank Palfreyman; two *s*. *Educ:* Ealing Grammar Sch. for Boys; Nottingham Univ. BSc (Civil Engineering); CEng; FICE; CGeol, MIQA. Consulting civil engineer, 1965–96. Director: Thorburn Colquhoun Ltd, consulting engineers, 1994–96; Construction Industry Res. and Inf. Assoc., 1996–2005. *Publications:* papers to international construction confs. *Recreations:*

gardening, walking, photography, badminton. *Heir:* *s* Hon. Ian Keith Montague [*b* 20 Sept. 1973; *m* 2001, Amanda, *d* of George Sweetland; one *s* one *d*].

AMY, Dennis Oldrieve, CMG 1992; OBE 1984; HM Diplomatic Service, retired; Ambassador to the Democratic Republic of Madagascar, 1990–92, and Ambassador (non-resident) to Federal Islamic Republic of the Comoros, 1991–92; *b* 21 Oct. 1932; *s* of late George Arthur Amy and Isabella Thompson (*née* Crosby); *m* 1956, Helen Rosamunde (*d* 2005), *d* of late Wilfred Leslie Clemens; one *s* one *d*. *Educ:* Southall Grammar Sch. Served RM, 1951–53. Entered HM Foreign, later HM Diplomatic Service, 1949; FO, 1949–51 and 1953–58; Athens, 1958–61; Second Sec. and Vice Consul, Moscow, 1961–63; FO, 1963–65; DSAO, 1965; Second Sec. and Passport Officer, Canberra, 1966–70; First Sec., Ibadan, 1971–74; seconded to Dept of Trade, 1974–75; FCO, 1976–78; First Sec. (Commercial), Santiago, 1978–83 (Chargé d'Affaires, 1979); FCO, 1983–86 (Counsellor, 1985–86); Consul Gen., Bordeaux, 1986–89. *Recreation:* church, walking, badminton, gardening. *Address:* Timbers, Hambledon Road, Godalming, Surrey GU7 1PJ.

AMY, Ronald John, OBE 1998; FFA; Chairman: Aon Consulting, since 1998 (Chief Executive, 1998–2005); Review Body on Doctors' and Dentists' Remuneration, since 2007; *b* 17 June 1950; *s* of Ernest and Grace Amy; *m* 1st, 1975, Evelyn Morrison (marr. diss.); two *d*; 2nd, 1997, Patricia Groves. *Educ:* Glasgow Univ. (BSc Hons Pure Maths). FFA 1977. London Actuary, Scottish Mutual Assce Soc., 1978–80; UK Pensions Manager, Philips Electronics, 1980–84; Gp Pensions Dir, Metal Box Plc, 1984–86; Dir, New Business Devlt, BZW Investment Mgt, 1986–87; Gp Pensions Dir, 1987–88, Gp Compensation and Benefits Dir, 1988–96, Grand Metropolitan PLC; Chm. and Chief Exec., Alexander Clay, 1996–97. Member: Occupational Pensions Bd, 1989–97; Bd, OPRA, 1996–2003. Chm., Nat. Assoc. of Pension Funds, 1993–95. *Recreation:* golf. *Address:* Aon Consulting, 11 Devonshire Square, EC2M 4YR. *T:* (020) 7086 8000. *Clubs:* Royal Automobile, Caledonian; Cruden Bay Golf.

AMYOT, Léopold Henri, CVO 1990; Secretary to Governor General of Canada and Secretary General of Order of Canada and of Order of Military Merit, 1985–90; Herald Chancellor of Canada, 1988–90; *b* 25 Aug. 1930; *s* of S. Eugène Amyot and Juliette Gagnon; *m* 1958, (Marie Jeanne) Andrée Jobin; one *s* two *d*. *Educ:* Laval Univ., Québec (BLSc, BScSoc); Ottawa Univ. (BA); Geneva Univ. (course on Internat. Instns). Joined External Affairs, 1957; Second Secretary: Canberra, 1960; New Delhi, 1961; Counsellor, Paris, 1968; Amb. to Lebanon (with accredn to Syria, Jordan, Iraq), 1974; Dep. Sec. Gen., Agence de Co-opération culturelle et technique, Paris, 1976; Chief of Protocol, Ext. Affairs, Ottawa, 1980; Exec. Dir, Task Force, on Pope's Visit to Canada, 1983; Amb. to Morocco, 1983. Chm., Official Residences Collections (formerly Official Residences Arts) Adv. Cttee, 1985–. Member: Professional Assoc. of For. Service Officers, Ottawa, 1957–; Inst. canadien des Affaires internat., Québec, 1985–90. Prix d'honneur (Sect. de Québec), Inst. canadien des Affaires internat., 1985. *Recreations:* tennis, golf, swimming, contemporary art collector.

AMYOT, René; QC; barrister; former Counsel, Jolin, Fournier, Morisset; *b* Quebec City, 1 Nov. 1926; *s* of Omer Amyot and Caroline L'Espérance (*née* Barry); *m* 1954, Monique, *d* of Fernand Boutin; two *s* two *d*. *Educ:* Collège des Jésuites de Québec (BA 1946); Laval Univ. Law Sch. (LLL 1949); Harvard Univ. Grad. Sch. of Business Admin (MBA 1951). Called to Bar of Québec, 1949; QC Canada 1965. Joined Procter & Gamble, Montreal, 1951; Bouffard & Associates, Quebec, 1952; Asst Prof., Faculty of Admin. Scis, Laval Univ., 1954–69; Asst Prof., Fiscal Law, Laval Univ. Law Sch., 1960–70; Consul for Belgium, 1966–82. Dir, and Mem. Exec. Cttee, Centre de Recherche Industrielle de Québec, 1971–76; Pres., Quebec Dist Chamber of Commerce, 1972; Founding Pres., Centre Internat. Recherches et Etudes en Management, 1972; Chairman, Air Canada, 1981–83; Director: Bank of Nova Scotia, 1972–81; Logistec Corp.; Rothmans Inc.; Palmar Inc.; Fidusco Ltd; Ferme Charlevoix Inc.; Expand Images Canada Inc.; Cedar Gp Inc.; Dominion Bridge Inc.; Spearhead Management Canada Ltd. Dir, Council for Business and the Arts in Canada. Member: Canadian Bar Assoc.; Québec Bar Assoc.; Canadian Tax Foundn; Cttee, Internat. Chamber; Assoc. des MBA du Québec. Gov., Faculty of Administrative Scis, Laval Univ. Chevalier de l'Ordre de Léopold (Belgium), 1985. *Recreations:* ski-ing, swimming, tennis, farming. *Clubs:* Québec Garrison, Toronto.

ANANIA, Giorgio, PhD; Director, Cube Optics AG, since 2007; *b* 18 Oct. 1958; *s* of Spartaco and Fanny Anania; *m* 1979, Regine Boucher; two *d*. *Educ:* Princeton Univ. (MA, PhD); Magdalen Coll., Oxford (BA). Sen. Associate, Booz-Allen & Hamilton, New York, 1982–87; Strategic Marketing Man., and Gen. Man. Miniplex Product, Raychem Corp., California, 1987–91; Principal, OCC Strategy Consultants, Paris, 1991–93; Vice Pres., Sales, Marketing and Business Development, Flamel Technologies, Lyon, 1993–98; Sen. Vice Pres., Sales and Marketing, 1998–2000, Pres., 2000–07, CEO, 2001–07, Bookham Technology plc. *Recreations:* flying private planes, model building, most water sports, reading (non-fiction). *Address:* 22 The Chestnuts, Abingdon, Oxon OX14 3YN. *T:* (01235) 534427.

ANCRAM, Rt Hon. Michael; *see* Lothian, Marquess of.

ANDERSON, family name of **Viscount Waverley** and **Baron Anderson of Swansea**.

ANDERSON OF SWANSEA, Baron *cr* 2005 (Life Peer), of Swansea in the county of West Glamorgan; **Donald Anderson;** PC 2001; DL; barrister-at-law; *b* 17 June 1939; *s* of David Robert Anderson and Eva (*née* Mathias); *m* 1963, Dr Dorothy Trotman, BSc, PhD; three *s*. *Educ:* Swansea Grammar Sch.; University Coll. of Swansea (Hon. Fellow, 1985). 1st cl. hons Modern History and Politics, Swansea, 1960. Barrister; called to Bar, Inner Temple, 1969. Member of HM Foreign Service, 1960–64: Foreign Office, 1960–63; 3rd Sec., British Embassy, Budapest, 1963–64; lectured in Dept of Political Theory and Govt, University Coll., Swansea, 1964–66. Councillor, Kensington and Chelsea, 1971–75. MP (Lab): Monmouth, 1966–70; Swansea E, Oct. 1974–2005. Mem. Estimates Cttee, 1966–69; Vice-Chm., Welsh Labour Group, 1969–70, Chm., 1977–78; PPS to Minister of Defence (Administration), 1969–70; PPS to Attorney General, 1974–79; opposition front-bench spokesman on foreign affairs, 1983–92, on defence, 1993–94; Shadow Solicitor General, 1994–95. Member: Select Cttee on Welsh Affairs, 1980–83 (Chm., 1981–83); Select Cttee on Home Affairs, 1992–93; Speaker's Panel of Chairmen, 1995–99; Chm., Foreign Affairs Cttee, 1997–2005. Chairman: Parly Lab. Party Environment Gp, 1974–79; Welsh Lab. Gp, 1977–78. Former: Chm., British-French, -S African and -Norwegian Parly Gps; Vice Chm., British-German, -Spanish, -Netherlands, -Hungarian, Parly Gps; Mem. Exec., IPU, 1983–2001 (Vice-Chm. Exec., 1985–88; Treas., 1988–90, 1992); Chm., UK Br., CPA, 1997–2001 (Vice-Chm., 1986–97; Treas., 1990–93). Sen. Vice-Pres., Assoc. of European Parliamentarians for Africa (Southern), 1984–97; Member: North Atlantic Assembly, subseq. NATO Parly Assembly, 1992–2005 (Ldr, UK Delegn, 1997–98; Chm., Socialist Gp, 1997–2001); UK Delegn to OSCE, 1997–2001. Mem., H of L Sub-Cttee C (Foreign Affairs, Defence and Devlt Policy), EU Cttee, 2006–. Pres., Gower Soc., 1976–78. Chairman: Parly Christian Fellowship, 1990–93; Nat. Prayer Breakfast, 1989; President: Boys' Brigade of Wales, 1992–94; Swansea Male Choir; Mem. Bd, Mercy Ships. DL W Glam, 2006. Freeman, City and County of Swansea, 2000. Hon. Fellow, Swansea Inst. of Higher Educn, 2005. Commander's Cross, Order of Merit (FRG), 1986; Foreign Minister's Medal (Republic of Slovakia), 2004; Chevalier, Légion d'Honneur (France), 2005. *Recreations:* church work, walking and talking. *Address:* House of Lords, SW1A 0PW.

ANDERSON, Maj.-Gen. Alistair Andrew Gibson, CB 1980; *b* 26 Feb. 1927; *s* of Lt-Col John Gibson Anderson and Margaret Alice (*née* Scott); *m* 1953, Dr Margaret Grace Smith; one *s* two *d*. *Educ:* George Watson's Boys Coll., Edinburgh; University Coll. of SW of England, Exeter (Short Univ. Course, 1944); Staff Coll., Camberley; Jt Services Staff Coll., Latimer. Enlisted 1944; commnd Royal Corps of Signals, 1946; comd 18 Signal Regt, 1967–69; Defence Ops Centre, 1969–72; staff of Signal Officer-in-Chief, 1972–74; Comdt, Sch. of Signals, 1974–76; Signal Officer-in-Chief (Army), 1977–80, retired; Dir, Communications and Electronics Security Gp, GCHQ, 1980–85. Col Comdt, Royal Corps of Signals, 1980–86; Chm., Royal Signals Assoc., 1982–87. *Recreations:* walking, gardening. *Club:* Army and Navy.

ANDERSON, Dr Alun Mark; Senior Consultant, New Scientist, since 2005 (Editor 1992–99; Editor-in-Chief and Publishing Director, 1999–2005); *b* 27 May 1948; *s* of Peter Marchmont Anderson and Jane Watkin Anderson (*née* James). *Educ:* Univ. of Sussex (BSc 1968); Univ. of Edinburgh (PhD 1972). IBM Res. Fellow, 1972–74, Jun. Res. Fellow, Wolfson Coll., 1972–76, Oxford; Royal Soc. Res. Fellow, Kyoto Univ., 1977–79; Nature: News and Views Ed., 1980–83; Tokyo Bureau Chief, 1984–86; Washington Ed., 1986–90; Internat. Ed., Science, 1991–92. Dir, IPC Magazines Ltd, 1997–98. Member: Royal Soc. COPUS, 1997–2000; Royal Soc. Faraday Prize Cttee, 1999–2004; British Council Sci., Engrg and Envmt Adv. Cttee, 2001–. Member Council: Univ. of Sussex, 1998–2001; Royal Instn, 2005–. Trustee, St Andrews Prize, 1999–. Editor of the Year (Special Interest Magazines), BSME, 1993, 1995, 1997; Editors' Editor of the Year, BSME, 1997. *Publications:* Science and Technology in Japan, 1984, 2nd edn 1991. *Recreations:* mountain walking, travel. *Address:* New Scientist, RBI Ltd, Lacon House, 84 Theobald's Road, WC1X 8NS. *T:* (020) 7611 1204; *e-mail:* alun.anderson@gmail.com.

ANDERSON, Prof. Anne Harper, OBE 2002; PhD; Vice Principal, and Head, College of Art, Science and Engineering, University of Dundee, since 2006; *b* Glasgow, 19 Feb. 1954; *d* of James and Jean Thomson; *m* 1975, Ian Anderson; one *s* one *d*. *Educ:* Hutchesons' Girls' Grammar Sch., Glasgow; Univ. of Glasgow (MA Hons Psychol. 1976; PhD 1982). Res. Fellow, Univ. of Edinburgh, 1979–86; University of Glasgow: Lectr, 1986–97; Prof. of Psychol., 1997–2006; Dep. Dean, Faculty of Law, Business and Social Sci., 2005–06. Director: ESRC Cognitive Engrg Prog., 1995–2000; ESRC/EPSRC/DTI People at the Centre of Communication and Inf. Technols Prog., 2000–06; Mem., EPSRC, 2008–. *Publications:* (jtly) Teaching Talk, 1983; (with Tony Lynch) Listening, 1988; papers in learned jls incl. Jl of Memory and Lang., Lang. and Cognitive Processes, Computers in Human Behavior. *Recreations:* travel to nice places, good food, good fiction, relaxing with the family. *Address:* University of Dundee, Queen Mother Building, Dundee DD1 4HN. *T:* (01382) 386610, *Fax:* (01382) 386611; *e-mail:* a.h.anderson@dundee.ac.uk.

ANDERSON, Anthony John; QC 1982; a Recorder, 1995–99; *b* 12 Sept. 1938; *s* of late A. Fraser Anderson and Margaret Anderson; *m* 1970, Fenja Ragnhild Gunn. *Educ:* Harrow; Magdalen Coll., Oxford. MA. 2nd Lieut, The Gordon Highlanders, 1957–59. Called to the Bar, Inner Temple, 1964, Bencher, 1992; retired from practice, 2001. Chm. of Tribunals, SFA (formerly The Securities Assoc.), 1988–2001. *Recreations:* golf, fishing, gardening, choral singing. *Address:* Mariners, Mariners Lane, Bradfield, Berkshire RG7 6HU. *Clubs:* Garrick, MCC.

ANDERSON, Mrs Beverly Jean; educator; former journalist and broadcaster; *b* 9 Dec. 1940; *d* of Arthur Benjamin Phillpotts and Sylvia Phillpotts; *m* 1st, 1968, Angus Walker, *qv* (marr. diss. 1976); 2nd, 1976, Andrew Anderson (marr. diss. 1986); one *s*. *Educ:* Wellesley Coll., Mass (BA History, and Politics 1962); London Univ. (PGCE 1967). Jamaican Foreign Service, Kingston and Washington, 1963–66; primary sch. teacher, London, 1968–71, Oxfordshire primary schs, 1971–81; Headteacher, Berwood First Sch., Oxford, 1981–83; Sen. Lectr in Educn, Oxford Poly., 1985–89; Lectr in Educn, Warwick Univ., and educn consultant, 1989–93; Chief Exec., Book Trust, 1993–94; Head, Village Sch., Pacific Palisades, Calif, 1995–99; Middle School Principal, Trinity Sch., NY, 1999–2004. Dir, Railtrack, 1993–94. Chairman: Equal Opportunities Wkg Gp, NAB, 1987–88; CNAA Steering Cttee on Accesss Courses to HE Framework, 1988–89; Member: Nat. Curriculum Council, 1989–91; Council, ABSA, 1989–95; Arts Council, 1990–94; Governor: BFI, 1985–93; Oxford Stage Co. Bd, 1986–96; S Bank Bd, 1989–94. Mem., Nuffield Council on Bioethics, 1991–94; Chm. Council, Charter '88, 1989–93. Columnist, TES, 1989–93. Television includes: Presenter: Black on Black, 1982–83; Nothing but the Best; Sixty Minutes; After Dark, 1989–90; Behind the Headlines, 1990–91. FRSA 1991. Hon. Fellow, Leeds Metropolitan Univ., 1991. Hon. LLM Teesside, 1993. *Publications:* Learning with Logo: a teacher's guide, 1985; numerous articles on education, social issues and media education. *Recreations:* plays, paintings, poems, movies, dancing.

ANDERSON, Brian David Outram, AO 1993; PhD; FRS 1989; Distinguished Professor, Australian National University, since 2002 (Professor of Systems Engineering, 1981–2002); Distinguished Researcher, National ICT Australia, since 2006 (Chief Executive Officer and President, 2002–03; Chief Scientist, 2003–06); *b* 15 Jan. 1941; *s* of late David Outram Anderson and Nancy Anderson; *m* 1968, Dianne, *d* of M. Allen; three *d*. *Educ:* Sydney Univ.; Stanford Univ. (PhD 1966); California Univ. Res. Asst, Stanford Electronics Labs, 1964; Lectr in Electrical Engrg, Stanford Univ., 1965; Asst Prof. and Staff Consultant, Vidar Corp., Mount View, Calif., 1966; Hd of Dept, 1967–75, Prof., 1967–81, Dept of Electrical Engrg, Univ. of Newcastle; Dir, Res. Sch. of Information Scis and Engrg, ANU, 1994–2002. Mem., Scientific Adv. Bd, Rio Tinto (formerly CRA) Ltd, 1982–98; Director: Telectronics Hldgs Ltd, 1986–88; Nucleus Ltd, 1988–95; Cochlear Ltd, 1995–2005; Crasys Ltd, 1996–98; Anutech Pty Ltd, 1997–2000. Member: Aust. Res. Grants Cttee, 1972–77; Aust. Science and Technology Council, 1977–82; UNESCO Nat. Commn, 1982–83; Aust. Industrial Res. and Devlt Incentives Bd, 1984–86; Prime Minister's Sci. and Engrg Council, 1989–93; Prime Minister's Sci., Engrg and Innovation Council, 1998–2002; Aust. Res. Council, 2000–01; Aust. Res. Council Bd, 2001–03; Nat. Res. Priorities Standing Cttee, 2005–07; DEST e-Res. Co-ordinating Cttee, 2005–06. Member, Advisory Board: Inst. for Telecoms Res., 2004–07; Centre for Complex Dynamic Systems and Control, Univ. of Newcastle, NSW, 2004–; Centre for Applied Philos. and Public Ethics, 2005–. Pres., Australian Acad. of Sci., 1998–2002. FAA; FTS; FIEEE; Hon. FIE(Aust). For. Assoc., US NAE, 2002. Dr *hc:* Louvain, 1991; Swiss Federal Inst. of Technol., 1993; Hon. DEng: Sydney, 1995; Melbourne, 1997; Newcastle, NSW, 2005; Hon. DSc NSW, 2001. *Publications* include: Linear Optimal Control, 1971; Network Analysis and Synthesis, 1975; Optimal Filtering, 1980; Optimal Control, 1990. *Address:* Research School of Information Sciences and Engineering, Australian National University, Canberra, ACT 0200, Australia.

ANDERSON, Campbell McCheyne; Chairman, Southern Pacific Petroleum NL, since 2001; *b* 17 Sept. 1941; *s* of Allen Taylor Anderson and Ethel Catherine Rundle; *m* 1965, Sandra Maclean Harper; two *s* one *d*. *Educ:* The Armidale Sch., NSW, Aust.; Univ. of Sydney (BEcon). AASA. Trainee and General Administration, Boral Ltd, Australia, 1962–69; Gen. Manager/Man. Dir, Reef Oil NL, Australia, 1969–71; Asst Chief Representative, Burmah Oil Australia Ltd, 1972; Corporate Development, Burmah Oil Incorporated, New York, 1973; Corporate Development, 1974; Finance Director and Group Planning, Burmah Oil Trading Ltd, UK, 1975; Special Projects Dir, 1976, Shipping Dir, 1978, Industrial Dir, 1979, Man. Dir, 1982–84, Burmah Oil Co.; Man. Dir, 1985–93, Chief Exec. Officer, 1986–93, Renison Goldfields Consolidated; Man. Dir, North Ltd, 1994–98. Director: Consolidated Gold Fields, 1985–89; Ampolex Ltd, 1991–97 (Chm., 1991–96); Macquarie Direct Investments Ltd, 1999–2006; Aviva Australia Hldgs (formerly CGNU Australia), 1999–; IBJ Australia Bank, 2000–02; Reconciliation Australia Ltd, 2001–07; Clough Ltd, 2003–. Dir, Aust. Mines and Metals Assoc., 1985–93 (Pres., 1988–89); Councillor: Aust. Mining Industry Council, 1985–98 (Pres., 1991–93); Business Council of Aust., 1986–2000 (Pres., 1999–2000); Chm., Energy Resources Aust. Ltd, 1994–98. Pres., Australia-Japan Soc., Victoria, 1995–98. *Recreations:* golf, swimming, horse-racing, shooting. *Address:* 77 Drumalbyn Road, Bellevue Hill, NSW 2023, Australia. *Clubs:* Oil Industries; Australian (Sydney); Australian (Melbourne); Royal Sydney Golf, Royal Melbourne Golf; Australian Jockey; Elanora Country (NSW).

ANDERSON, Rear-Adm. (Charles) Courtney, CB 1971; Flag Officer, Admiralty Interview Board, 1969–71, retired; *b* 8 Nov. 1916; *s* of late Lt-Col Charles Anderson, Australian Light Horse, and Mrs Constance Powell-Anderson, OBE, JP; *m* 1940, Pamela Ruth Miles; three *s*. *Educ:* RNC, Dartmouth. Joined RN, 1930. Served War of 1939–45: in command of Motor Torpedo Boats, Destroyers and Frigates. Naval Intelligence, 1946–49 and 1955–57; Commanded HMS Contest, 1949–51; Comdr, 1952; BJSM, Washington, 1953–55; Capt., 1959; Naval Attaché, Bonn, 1962–65; Director, Naval Recruiting, 1966–68; ADC to Queen, 1968; Rear-Adm., 1969. Editor, The Board Bulletin, 1971–78. *Publications:* The Drum Beats Still, 1951; Seagulls in my Belfry, 1997; numerous articles and short stories. *Address:* 3 Lambourne Gardens, Breinton Lee, Hereford HR4 0TL.

ANDERSON, (Clarence) Eugene; business consultant; Chairman and Chief Executive, Ferranti International plc, 1990–94; *b* 31 Aug. 1938; *s* of Clarence Leslie Anderson and Wilda Faye Anderson; *m* 1977, Daniela Leopolda Proche; one *d*, and one *s* two *d* from a previous marriage. *Educ:* Univ. of Texas (BSc Chem. Engrg, 1961); Harvard Univ. (MBA 1963). Process Engr, New Orleans, 1961, Ops Analyst, Houston, 1963–66, Tenneco Oil Co.; Man. Dir, Globe Petroleum Sales Ltd, Lincs, 1966–69; Dir, Supply and Transportation, Houston, 1969–72, Dir, Operational Planning, Houston, 1972, Tenneco Oil Co.; Vice Pres., Tenneco International Co., Houston, 1973; Exec. Dir, Albright & Wilson Ltd, London, 1973–75; Vice Pres., Corporate Develt, Tenneco Inc., Houston, 1975–78; Dep. Man. Dir, Ops, Albright & Wilson Ltd, London, 1979–81; Pres., Celanese International Co., and Vice Pres., Celanese Corp., New York, 1981–85; Chief Exec., Johnson Matthey PLC, London, 1985–89. *Publication:* (jtly) report on microencapsulation. *Recreations:* music, literature, theatre, sailing, various sports.

ANDERSON, Clive Stuart; barrister; television and radio presenter and writer; *b* 10 Dec. 1952; *s* of Gordon Menzies Randall Anderson and late Doris Elizabeth Anderson; *m* 1981, Dr Jane Hughes; one *s* two *d*. *Educ:* Harrow County Sch. for Boys; Selwyn Coll., Cambridge (MA). Called to the Bar, Middle Temple, 1976. *Radio:* Host, Cabaret Upstairs, 1986–88; Chm., Whose Line is it Anyway?, 1988; Presenter: Devil's Advocate, 1991–92; Unreliable Evidence, 1998–; The Real…, 2002–; Clive Anderson's Chat Room, 2004–; *television:* Whose Line is it Anyway?, 1988–98; Clive Anderson Talks Back, 1989–95; Notes & Queries, 1993; Our Man In, 1995, 1996; Clive Anderson All Talk, 1996–99; If I Ruled the World, 1998–99; Clive Anderson Now, 2001–; various other progs. Pres., Woodland Trust, 2003–. *Publications:* (jtly) Great Railway Journeys, 1994; (with Ian Brown) Patent Nonsense, 1994; Our Man In, 1995; Our Man in Heaven & Hell, 1996. *Recreations:* history, comedy, football. *Address:* Curtis Brown, Haymarket House, 28–29 Haymarket, SW1Y 4SP. *T:* (020) 7393 4400; 6 King's Bench Walk, Temple, EC4Y 7DR. *T:* (020) 7583 0410.

ANDERSON, Courtney; *see* Anderson, (Charles) Courtney.

ANDERSON, Rev. David; Principal Lecturer in Religious Studies, Hertfordshire College of Higher Education (formerly Wall Hall College), Aldenham, Herts, 1974–84 (Senior Lecturer, 1970–74); *b* 30 Oct. 1919; *s* of William and Nancy Anderson, Newcastle upon Tyne; *m* 1953, Helen Finlay Robinson, 3rd *d* of Johnson and Eleanor Robinson, Whitley Bay, Northumberland; one *s* two *d*. *Educ:* Royal Grammar Sch., Newcastle upon Tyne; Selwyn Coll., Cambridge. Served in RA, 1940–42, Intelligence Corps, 1942–46, Lieut. Deacon, 1949, Priest, 1950; Curate of parish of St Gabriel, Sunderland, 1949–52; Tutor of St Aidan's Coll., Birkenhead, 1952–56; Warden of Melville Hall, Ibadan, Nigeria, 1956–58; Principal of: Immanuel Coll., Ibadan, Nigeria, 1958–62; Wycliffe Hall, Oxford, 1962–69. Examining Chaplain: to Bishop of Liverpool, 1969–75; to Bishop of St Albans, 1972–80. *Publications:* The Tragic Protest, 1969; Simone Weil, 1971; contrib: Religion and Modern Literature, 1975; William Golding: some critical considerations, 1978; The Passion of Man, 1980. *Recreations:* listening to music, hi-fi gramophones. *Address:* 16 Manor Park, Borrowash, Derby DE72 3LP. *T:* (01332) 664426.

ANDERSON, David; Chief Executive, Co-operative Financial Services Ltd, since 2005; *b* 23 Oct. 1955; *s* of Donald and Gweneth Anderson; *m* 1980, Fiona Ellen Hamilton; one *s* one *d*. *Educ:* Cheadle Hulme Sch.; St Edmund Hall, Oxford (MA PPE). Graduate trainee, Aveling Barford Ltd, construction equipment mfr, 1977–80; Dun and Bradstreet, 1980–83; PA Mgt Consultants, 1983–87; Dep. Gen. Manager (Mkting), 1987–90, Dir, 1990–2003, Chief Exec., 1996–2003, Yorkshire Building Soc.; Chief Exec., Jobcentre Plus, DWP, 2003–05. *Recreations:* golf, sailing. *Address:* Co-operative Financial Services Ltd, CIS Building, Miller Street, Manchester M60 0AL.

ANDERSON, David; MP (Lab) Blaydon, since 2005; *b* 2 Dec. 1953; *s* of Cyril and Janet Anderson; *m* 1973, Elizabeth Eva Jago. *Educ:* Doncaster and Durham Tech. Colls; Durham Univ. (DipSocSc); Moscow Higher Trade Union Sch. Colliery mechanic, 1969–89; care worker, 1989–2005. PPS to Minister of State, DIUS, 2007–. Trade Union Lay Official: NUM, 1978–89; UNISON, 1989–2005; Pres., UNISON, 2003–04; Mem., TUC Gen. Council, 2000–05. *Recreations:* walking, travel, music, caravanning. *Address:* House of Commons, SW1A 0AA. *T:* (020) 7219 4348; *e-mail:* andersonda@parliament.uk.

ANDERSON, David Heywood, CMG 1982; Judge of the International Tribunal for the Law of the Sea, 1996–2005; Barrister-at-Law; *b* 14 Sept. 1937; *s* of late Harry Anderson; *m* 1961, Jennifer Ratcliffe; one *s* one *d*. *Educ:* King James' Grammar Sch., Almondbury; LLB (Leeds); LLM (London). Called to Bar, Gray's Inn, 1963. HM Diplomatic Service, 1960–96: Asst Legal Adviser, FCO 1960–69; Legal Adviser, British Embassy, Bonn, 1969–72; Legal Counsellor, FCO, 1972–79; Legal Adviser, UK Mission to UN, NY, 1979–82; Legal Counsellor, 1982–87, Dep. Legal Advr, 1987–89, Second Legal Advr, 1989–96, FCO. Mem., Greenwich Forum, 1996–. *Publications:* Modern Law of the Sea - Selected Essays, 2007; (contrib.) International Maritime Boundaries, 1993–; contribs to British Yearbook of Internat. Law and learned jls. *Recreation:* gardening.

ANDERSON, David Munro; Chairman, Anderson Quantrend (formerly Allingham Anderson Roll Ross) Ltd, since 1990; *b* 15 Dec. 1937; *s* of Alexander Anderson and Jessica Anderson (*née* Vincent-Innes); *m* 1st, 1965, Veronica Jane (*née* Stevens) (marr. diss.); two *s* one *d*; 2nd, 1989, Ruth Lewis-Bowen. *Educ:* Morrison's Academy, Perthshire; Strathallan, Perthshire. Commissioned Black Watch; served W Africa; tea production with James Finlay & Co., India, 1959–62; London Chamber of Commerce and Industry, 1962–63; joined E. D. & F. Man Ltd, 1963; formed Anderson Man Ltd, 1981; formed E. D. & F. Man International Ltd, 1985, Chm., 1986–90; Man. Dir, Commodity Analysis Ltd, 1968; numerous directorships. Chairman, formation cttees: Internat. Petroleum Exchange; Baltic Internat. Freight Futures Exchange (jtly); former Vice-Chm., London Commodity Exchange; Dir, SIB, 1986–87. MSI. *Recreations:* ski-ing, shooting. *Address:* The Old Gardens, Kersey, Suffolk IP7 6ED. *Club:* Caledonian.

ANDERSON, David William Kinloch; QC 1999; a Recorder, since 2004; *b* 5 July 1961; *s* of Sir (William) Eric (Kinloch) Anderson, *qv* and Poppy (*née* Mason); *m* 1989, Margaret Beeton; two *d*. *Educ:* Eton Coll. (King's Schol.); New Coll., Oxford (Open Schol.; MA Ancient and Modern Hist. 1982); Downing Coll., Cambridge (BA Law 1984); Inns of Court Sch. of Law. Called to the Bar, Middle Temple, 1985, Bencher, 2007; Lawyer from Abroad, Covington & Burling, Washington, 1985–86; Stagiaire, Cabinet of Lord Cockfield, European Commn, 1987–88; in practice as barrister, Brick Court Chambers, 1988–. Vis. Lectr in European Law, 1989–95, Vis. Res. Fellow, 1995–99, Vis. Prof., 1999–, KCL. Ind. Expert to monitor freedom of expression and inf., Council of Europe, 2000–03. Mem. Exec. Cttee, Lord Slynn of Hadley European Law Foundn, 2002–. Member: Governing Body, British Assoc. for Central and Eastern Europe, 2002–08; Adv. Bd, SSEES, 2007–. Trustee, British Inst. of Internat. and Comparative Law, 2005–. *Publications:* References to the European Court, 1995, 2nd edn 2002; various articles in legal jls. *Recreations:* sailing, mountains, history. *Address:* Brick Court Chambers, 7–8 Essex Street, WC2R 3LD. *T:* (020) 7379 3550. *Clubs:* Athenæum; Ipswich Town Football.

ANDERSON, Prof. Declan John; Professor of Oral Biology, University of Bristol, 1966–85, now Professor Emeritus; Founder, The Oral and Dental Research Trust, 1989 (Director, 1989–92); *b* 20 June 1920; *s* of Arthur John Anderson and Katherine Mary Coffey; *m* 1947, Vivian Joy Dunkerton; four *s* three *d*. *Educ:* Christ's Hospital; Guy's Hospital Medical School, Univ. of London. BDS (London) 1942; LDSRCS 1943, BSc 1946, MSc 1947, PhD 1955. Prof. of Physiology, Univ. of Oregon, USA, 1957–58; Prof. of Physiology in Relation to Dentistry, Univ. of London, 1963–66. *Publications:* Physiology for Dental Students, 1952; (with R Buxton) How to Dissect and Understand Medical Terms, 1992; Introducing Silver, 2000; (with J. Flowerday) Introducing Silversmithing, 2002; scientific papers in professional jls. *Recreations:* silversmithing, forging, music. *Address:* Court House, 7 Court Lane, Edington, Westbury BA13 4PU.

ANDERSON, Dr Digby Carter; Director, Social Affairs Unit, 1980–2004; *b* 25 May 1944; *s* of late Donald Anderson and Elizabeth Nance Ethel Anderson; *m* 1965, Judith Harris. *Educ:* St Lawrence Coll.; Univ. of Reading (BA Hons); Brunel Univ. (MPhil, PhD). Lectr, then Sen. Lectr, Luton Coll. of Higher Educn, 1965–77; Tutor, Brunel Univ. Youth Work Trng Unit, 1974–78; Res. Fellow, Univ. of Nottingham, 1977–80; Associate Lectr, Brunel Univ., 1977–78. Mem., ESRC, 1989–93. Mem., Health Studies Cttee, CNAA, 1987–92. Columnist: The Times, 1984–88; Sunday Telegraph, 1988–89; Sunday Times, 1989–90; Spectator, 1984–2000; National Review, 1991–2000. Ordained deacon 1985, priest 1986; asst priest, St Saviour's, Luton, 1986–. Mem., Mont Pelerin Soc. *Publications:* (ed) Health Education in Practice, 1979; Evaluation by Classroom Experience, 1979; Evaluating Curriculum Proposals, 1980; (ed) The Ignorance of Social Intervention, 1980; Breaking the Spell of the Welfare State, 1981; (ed) The Kindness that Kills, 1984; (ed) A Diet of Reason, 1986; The Spectator Book of Imperative Cooking, 1987; (ed) Full Circle, 1988; (ed) Health, Lifestyle and Environment, 1992; (ed) The Loss of Virtue: moral confusion and social disorder in Britain and America, 1993; (ed) This Will Hurt: the restoration of civic order in America and Britain, 1995; (ed) Gentility Recalled: mere manners and the making of social order, 1996; (ed jtly) Faking It: the sentimentalisation of modern society, 1998; (compiler) The Dictionary of Dangerous Wars, 2000; Losing Friends, 2001; All Oiks Now, 2004; The English at Table, 2006; contrib. Sociology, Jl Curriculum Studies, Econ. Affairs, Social Policy Rev. *Recreations:* non-Germanic music, the seaside, dinner. *Address:* 17 Hardwick Place, Woburn Sands, Bucks MK17 8QQ. *T:* (01908) 584526.

ANDERSON, Prof. Donald Thomas, AO 1986; PhD, DSc; FRS 1977; Challis Professor of Biology, University of Sydney, 1984–91, Professor Emeritus, since 1992 (Professor of Biology, 1972–84); *b* 29 Dec. 1931; *s* of Thomas and Flora Anderson; *m* 1960, Joanne Trevathan (*née* Claridge). *Educ:* King's Coll., London Univ. DSc London, 1966; DSc Sydney, 1983. Lectr in Zoology, Sydney Univ., 1958–61; Sen. Lectr, 1962–66; Reader in Biology, 1967–71. Clarke Medal, Royal Soc. of NSW, 1979; Alexander Kowalevsky Medal, St Petersburg Soc. Naturalists, 2001. *Publication:* Embryology and Phylogeny of Annelids and Arthropods, 1973; Barnacles: structure, function, development and evolution, 1993; Atlas of Invertebrate Anatomy, 1996; Invertebrate Zoology, 1998, 2nd edn 2001; papers in zool. jls. *Recreations:* gardening, photography. *Address:* 5 Angophora Close, Wamberal, NSW 2260, Australia. *T:* (2) 43846670.

ANDERSON, Edmund John Seward; Chairman, Yorkshire Building Society, since 2007; *b* Singapore, 22 Dec. 1950; *s* of Dick and Irene Anderson; *m* 1982, Heather Medcalf; two *s* two *d*. *Educ:* Beaumont Coll.; Stonyhurst; Leeds Poly. (BSc Econs). CPFA 1973. Various local govt appts, 1973–87; Dep. Man. Dir, E Midlands Airport, 1987–90; Exec. Dir, Leeds CC, 1990–97; Man. Dir, Leeds Bradford Internat. Airport, 1997–2007. Non-exec. Dir, Kelda Gp plc, 2005–08. Chm., Airport Operators Assoc., 2001–02, 2008–. Leeds Chamber of Commerce: non-exec. Dir, 1998–; Pres., 2000–02; Chm., 2005–. Chm., Leeds Trinity and All Saints Coll., 2007–; Mem. Council, Univ. of Leeds, 2007–. Trustee: St Gemma's Hospice, 1999–; Leeds Internat. Pianoforte Competition, 2004–. *Recreations:* watching sport, music, walking in the Yorkshire Dales. *Address:* Yorkshire Building Society, Yorkshire House, Yorkshire Drive, Bradford, W Yorks BD5 8LJ. *Clubs:* Collingham and Linton Cricket; Scarcroft Golf.

ANDERSON, Sir Eric; *see* Anderson, Sir W. E. K.

ANDERSON, Eugene; *see* Anderson, C. E.

ANDERSON, Gerry, MBE 2001; film producer, director, and writer; Managing Director, Anderson Entertainment Ltd, since 2001; *b* 14 April 1929; *s* of Joseph and Deborah Anderson; *m* 1st, 1952, Betty Wrightman; two *d*; 2nd, 1961, Sylvia Thamm; one *s*; 3rd, 1981, Mary Robins; one *s*. *Educ:* Willesden County Secondary Sch. Entered film industry as Colonial Film Unit Trainee, 1943; Asst Editor, Gainsborough Pictures, 1945–47; dubbing editor, various indep. cos, 1949–53; Film Dir, Polytechnic Films, 1954–55; Co-Founder: Pentagon Films, 1955; AP Films, 1956; AP Merchandising, 1961; Chm., Century 21 Orgn, 1966–75; Dir of TV Commercials, 1961, 1988–92; Man. Dir, Inimitable Ltd, 1989–97. *Puppet films/series* include: director: The Adventures of Twizzle, 1956; Torchy the Battery Boy, 1957; producer: Four Feather Falls; Supercar, 1959–60; Fireball XL5, 1962; Stingray, 1963–65; Thunderbirds, 1966–67; Captain Scarlet and the Mysterons, 1967–68, re-make with computer-generated images as New Captain Scarlet, 2003; Joe 90, 1968–69; The Secret Service, 1969; Terrahawks, 1981–85; *live action series* include: UFO, 1969; The Protectors, 1971; Space: 1999, 1973–75, 1977–78; Space Precinct, 1993–95; *stop motion series:* Dick Spanner, 1987; Lavender Castle, 1997; *feature films:* executive producer: Thunderbirds are Go (puppet); Thunderbird 6 (puppet); producer, Journey to the far side of the Sun (live action). Hon. Fellow, BKSTS. *Recreations:* gardening, walking, DIY.

ANDERSON, Gordon Alexander, CBE 2000; CA, FCMA; Chartered Accountant; *b* 9 Aug. 1931; *s* of Cecil Brown Anderson and Janet Davidson Bell; *m* 1958, Eirené Cochrane Howie Douglas; two *s* one *d*. *Educ:* High School of Glasgow. Qualified as Chartered Accountant, 1955; FCMA 1984. National Service, RN, 1955–57. Partner: Moores Carson & Watson, 1958 (subseq. McClelland Moores & Co., Arthur Young McClelland Moores & Co., Arthur Young (Chm., 1987–89), and Ernst & Young (Dep. Sen. Partner, 1989–90)); McLintock Moores & Murray, 1963–69. Chairman: Bitmac Ltd, 1990–96 (Dir, 1984–96); TSB Bank Scotland, 1994–99 (Dir, 1991–99); Director: Douglas Firebrick Co. Ltd, 1961–70; Lloyds TSB Group (formerly TSB Group), 1993–99; Merchants House of Glasgow, 1996–2002. Mem., Scottish Milk Marketing Bd, 1979–85. Mem., Council on Tribunals, 1990–96 (Mem., Scottish Cttee, 1990–96). Institute of Chartered Accountants of Scotland: Mem. Council, 1980–84; Vice-Pres., 1984–86; Pres., 1986–87. Chm. of Govs, High Sch. of Glasgow, 1992–2001. *Recreations:* gardening, Rugby football. *Address:* 4 Manse Road Gardens, Bearsden, Glasgow G61 3PJ. *T:* (0141) 942 2803. *Clubs:* Western (Glasgow); Glasgow Golf; Buchanan Castle Golf (Captain 1979–80).

ANDERSON, James Frazer Gillan, CBE 1979; JP; DL; Member, Scottish Development Agency, 1986–89; *b* 25 March 1929; *m* 1956, May Harley; one *s* one *d*. *Educ:* Maddiston Primary Sch.; Graeme High Sch., Falkirk. Member: Stirling CC, 1958–75 (Convener, 1971–75); Central Regional Council, Scotland, 1974–96 (Convener, 1974–86). Mem., Health and Safety Commission, 1974–80. DUniv Stirling, 1987. OStJ. *Recreations:* gardening, walking.

ANDERSON, Sir (James) Iain (Walker), Kt 2008; CBE 2000; PhD; Director, Unilever PLC and NV, 1988–98; *b* Glasgow. 30 June 1938; *s* of John and Alice Anderson; *m* 1963, Katie McCrone; two *s*. *Educ:* King's Park Sch., Glasgow; Univ. of Glasgow (BSc Hons, PhD 1962). Res. Manager, Unilever, 1965–76; Chairman: Marine Harvest Ltd, 1976–79; Food Industries Ltd, 1979–80; PPF Ltd, 1980–82; Ops Dir, Unilever Chemicals Div., 1982–85; Chm., Batchelors Foods Ltd, 1985–88. Director: British Telecom plc, 1995–2001; BT Scotland, 1997–99 (Chm., 1999–2004); Scottish and Newcastle plc, 1998–2006. Chairman: Intense Photonics Ltd, 2000–06; Schs Enterprise Scotland Ltd, 2000–06. Special Advr to Prime Minister on Millennium Compliance (Y2K), 1998–2000; conducted indep. inquiry into Lessons to be Learned from 2001 outbreak of foot and mouth disease in UK, 2001–02; conducted indep. rev. of Govt's handling of foot and mouth outbreak in England in 2007, 2007–08. Gov., NIESR, 1992–98. Trustee: British Occupational Health Res. Foundn, 1996–98; Scottish Sci. Trust, 1997–2002; Leverhulme Trust, 1999–. *Recreations:* thinking about things, walking around, finding better restaurants, reading old newspapers, trying to hook fish, wine, food, boats, photography, travel, garden plants. *Address:* Burnbank, Acharn, by Aberfeldy, Perthshire PH15 2HU. *Club:* New (Edinburgh).

ANDERSON, Prof. Jan; *see* Anderson, J. M.

ANDERSON, Janet; MP (Lab) Rossendale and Darwen, since 1992; *b* 6 Dec. 1949; *d* of late Thomas Anderson and Ethel Pearson; *m*; two *s* one *d*. *Educ:* Kingsfield Comprehensive Sch.; Polytechnic of Central London; Univ. of Nantes (Dip. Bi-lingual Business Studies). Asst to Rt Hon. Barbara Castle, 1974–81, to Jack Straw, MP, 1981–87; Campaign Officer, PLP, 1988–89; Regl Organiser, Shopping Hours Reform Council, 1991–92. Contested (Lab) Rossendale and Darwen, 1987. PPS to Dep. Leader of Labour Party, 1992–93; an Opposition Whip, 1995–97; Vice Chamberlain of HM Household, 1997–98; Parly Under-Sec. of State, DCMS, 1998–2001. Member: H of C Commn, 1993–94; Select Cttee on Home Affairs, 1994–95 (Home Affairs Campaigns Co-ordinator, 1994–95). Secretary: All Party Footwear Gp, 1992–97; Tribune Gp of Lab MPs, 1993–97. *Recreations:* playing the piano, listening to opera. *Address:* House of Commons, SW1A 0AA. *T:* (020) 7219 5375; (office) 23 Bolton Road, Darwen, Lancs BB3 1DF. *T:* (01254) 704201, *Fax:* (01254) 762077; (office) King George Chambers, St James's Square, Burnley Road, Bacup, Lancs OL13 9AA. *T:* (01706) 877010, *Fax:* (01706) 870010. *Club:* Rosemount Working Men's (Stacksteads, Rossendale).

ANDERSON, Prof. Joan Mary, (Jan), FRS 1996; FAA; Honorary Research Fellow, Division of Plant Industry, Commonwealth Scientific and Industrial Research Organisation, since 1997; Adjunct Professor, Photobioenergetics Group, Research School of Biological Sciences, Australian National University, since 1996; *b* 12 May 1932; *d* of William Arthur Anderson, OBE and Mary Anderson (*née* Lee). *Educ:* Univ. of Otago, NZ (BSc 1954; MSc 1st Cl. Hons 1956); Univ. of California, Berkeley (PhD 1959). Div. of Plant Industry, CSIRO, 1962–, Chief Res. Scientist, 1962–97. Fellowships: King George VI Meml, NZ, 1956; Carnegie Inst., Stanford, 1966; Kettering, Dayton, Ohio, 1967; Harvard, 1973; Newnham Coll., Cambridge, 1973–74; Vis. Spring Prof., Univ. of California, Berkeley, 1982; Vis. Swedish Natural Sci. Res. Council Prof., Lund, 1986. FDhc Umeå, Sweden, 1998. Lemberg Medal, Aust. Soc. of Biochem., 1983. *Publications:* numerous articles on photosynthesis research. *Recreations:* music, art, water colour painting, bush walking. *Address:* Photobioenergetics Group, Research School of Biological Sciences, Australian National University, GPO Box 475, Canberra, ACT 2601, Australia. *T:* (2) 61255895, *Fax:* (2) 61258056; *e-mail:* jan.anderson@anu.edu.au.

ANDERSON, Prof. John, FRCP; FRCPGlas; FRCOG; Postgraduate Dean and Director, Postgraduate Institute for Medicine and Dentistry, and Professor of Medical Education, University of Newcastle upon Tyne, 1985–98, now Professor Emeritus; *b* 2 Feb. 1936; *s* of John and Norah Anderson, Newcastle upon Tyne; *m* Mary Bynon, Whitley Bay; one *s* one *d*. *Educ:* Royal Grammar Sch., Newcastle upon Tyne; Med. Sch., King's Coll., Univ. of Durham (MB, BS 2nd Cl. Hons). FRCP 1973 (MRCP 1961); FRCOG (*ad eundem*) 1983; FRCPGlas 1992. Med. Registrar, Royal Victoria Inf., Newcastle upon Tyne, 1962–64; Res. Fellow, Univ. of Virginia, Charlottesville, 1965–66; University of Newcastle upon Tyne: First Asst in Medicine 1967–68; Sen. Lectr in Medicine 1968–85; Academic Sub-Dean, Med. Sch., 1975–85. Hon. Cons. Phys., Royal Victoria Infirmary, 1968–. Mem. Council, RCP, 1974–77; Member: Assoc. of Phys of GB and Ire., 1976–; Exec. Cttee, ASME, 1979– (Hon. Treas., 1980–88; Gen. Sec., 1990–92; Chm. Council, 1992–95; Vice-Pres., 1996–); GMC, 1980–2001; GDC, 1986–99. *Publications:* The Multiple Choice Question in Medicine, 1976, 2nd edn 1982; numerous chapters in books, and papers in sci. jls on medicine, diabetes and med. educn. *Recreations:* listening to music, walking, watching cricket, reading, thinking. *Address:* 6 Wilson Gardens, Newcastle upon Tyne NE3 4JA. *T:* (0191) 285 4745. *Clubs:* Yorkshire CC, Durham CC.

ANDERSON, Sir John (Anthony), KBE 1994; FCA; Chief Executive and Director: South Pacific Merchant Finance Ltd, 1979–2005; National Bank of New Zealand Ltd, 1990–2005; ANZ National Bank Ltd, 2003–05; Chairman: Television New Zealand Ltd, since 2005; Capital & Coast Health Board, since 2007; *b* 2 Aug. 1945; *s* of Donald Ian Mogine Anderson and Elizabeth Grace Anderson (*née* Plummer); *m* 1970, Carol Margaret Tuck; two *s* one *d*. *Educ:* Christ's Coll.; Victoria Univ. of Wellington. ACA 1967, FCA 1991. With Deloitte Ross Tohmatsu, Wellington, 1962–69; Guest & Bell, Melbourne, 1969–72. Director: NZ Steel, 1986–87; Lloyds Merchant Bank (London), 1986–92; Lloyds Bank NZA, 1989–96; Commonwealth Bank of Australia, 2006–; Chm., Petroleum Corp. of NZ, 1986–88. Chairman: Adv. Bd, NZ Debt Mgt Office, 1989–2001; Prime Minister's NZ Employment Taskforce, 1994. Chairman: NZ Merchant Banks Assoc., 1982–89; NZ Bankers' Assoc., 1991–92 and 1999–2000; Pres., NZ Bankers' Inst., 1990. Bd Dir, ICC, 1997–; Chairman: NZ Cricket Bd, 1995–; NZ Sports Foundn, 1999–2002. First Blake Medal, Sir Peter Blake Trust, 2005. NZ Commemoration Medal, 1990. *Recreations:* cricket, tennis, golf, bridge. *Address:* 3 Bayview Terrace, Oriental Bay, Wellington, New Zealand. *T:* (4) 4990162. *Clubs:* Wellington, Wellesley (NZ).

ANDERSON, Hon. John (Duncan); Chairman, Eastern Star Gas, since 2007; Director, Crawford Fund; *b* 14 Nov. 1956; *s* of Duncan Anderson and Beryl Anderson (*née* Mann); *m* 1987, Julia Gillian Robertson; one *s* three *d*. *Educ:* Univ. of Sydney (MA). Farmer and grazier. MP (Nat.) Gwydir, NSW, 1989–2007; Minister for: Primary Industries and Energy, 1996–98; Transport and Regl Services, 1998–2005; Dep. Prime Minister, 1999–2005. Dep. Leader, 1993–99, Leader, 1999–2005, Nat. Party of Australia. *Address:* Eastern Star Gas, GPO Box 4526, Sydney, NSW 2001, Australia. *Club:* Australian (Sydney).

ANDERSON, John Ferguson; Chief Executive, Glasgow City Council, 1995–98; *b* 13 Dec. 1947; *s* of Charles and Isabella Anderson; *m* 1970, Sandra McFarlane; one *s* one *d*. *Educ:* Edinburgh Univ. (LLB Hons 1969). Legal Assistant, then Solicitor, later Asst Chief Solicitor, Glasgow Corp., 1969–75; Strathclyde Regional Council: Prin. Solicitor, 1975–78; Asst Dir of Admin, 1978–80; Sen. Exec. Officer, 1980–86; Prin. Exec. Officer, 1986–90; Dep. Chief Exec., 1990–95. *Recreations:* golf, watching football, transportation issues, church. *Address:* Balwearie, 41 Scott Brae, Kippen FK8 3DL.

ANDERSON, John Graeme, CBE 1989; CEng, FInstE; Deputy Chairman, Northern Engineering Industries plc, 1986–89; Director, Team General Partner, 1993–2002; *b* 3 June 1927; *s* of John Anderson and Ella (*née* Pusey); *m* 1953, Nancy Clarice Taylor Johnson; one *s* twin *d*. *Educ:* Merchant Taylors' Sch., Sandy Lodge; London Univ. (BScEng Hons). MIMechE. Served RN, Fleet Air Arm, 1945–48. International Combustion Ltd: graduate apprentice, 1952; Dir, 1968; Dep. Chief Exec., 1969; Man. Dir, 1974; Northern Engineering Industries: Man. Dir, NEI-Internat. Combustion Ltd, 1977; Managing Director: Mechanical Gp, 1980; Power Gp, 1982; Internat. and Projects Gp, 1984; Chm., NEI Pacific, 1984–88. Chm., Internat. Combustion-HUD Hong Kong, 1978–82; Dir, British Nuclear Associates, 1985–88; Alternate Dir, Nat. Nuclear Corp., 1986–88; Director: Tyne and Wear Develt Corp., 1987–93; The Newcastle Initiative, 1988–90. Mem., Duke of Kent's BOTB mission to Turkey, 1984. Chairman: Solid Waste Assoc., 1972–74; Watertube Boilermakers' Assoc., 1976–80; Member: Process Plant Assoc., 1968–87; Process Plant, EDC, 1972–76; Heavy Electrical, EDC, 1976–80. Gov., Derby Coll. of Technology, 1969–74. Chm., Upstage, 1977–79. *Recreations:* shooting, painting, music, fell walking. *Address:* Trinity Barns, Corbridge, Northumberland NE45 5HP. *T:* (01434) 633228.

ANDERSON, John Huxley Fordyce, FCIOB; Director: British Council for Offices, 1996–2003; Land Securities Properties, 2000–03; *b* 13 Jan. 1945; *s* of Alexander Robert Fordyce Anderson and Agnes Joan (*née* Huxley); *m* 1973, Tucker Lee Etherington; one *s* one *d*. *Educ:* Fan Court Sch.; Milton Abbey Sch.; Brixton Sch. of Building; Harvard Bus. Sch. (post-grad. PMD 1983). FCIOB 1988. Joined Higgs & Hill as indentured student, 1962; Project Planner on projects such as BBC TV Centre, RMA Sandhurst, 1966–69; Contract Manager, Sales and Marketing Manager then Dep. Man. Dir, Costains, Vale do Lobo, Portugal, 1969–74; with Town & City Properties in Holland, 1975–76; Develt Project Manager, Town & City Develts in London, 1976–83; Man. Dir, Town & City, then P&O, Develts, 1984–92; Director: Chelsea Harbour, 1984–92; P & O Property Hldgs, 1985–99; Managing Director: Bovis Construction Ltd, 1993–2000; Bovis Europe, 1996–2000; Jt Man. Dir, Bovis Construction Gp, 1997–2000 (Dir, 1988–). Man. Dir, PSA Building Mgt (on secondment to Govt), 1991–93. Non-exec. Dir, Maxxiom, 1997–2000. Director: Chelsfield plc, 2003–05; of Develt, Parkview (Battersea Power Station), 2006–07; SPV St Martin in the Fields Develts Ltd, 2006–; Buckingham Develts Ltd, 2007–08; of Projects and Develts, Tellesma LLP, 2008–. Chm., Export Gp for Construction Industries, 1999–2001. Hon. Property Consultant, Queen Elizabeth Foundn for the Disabled, 2001–. Chm., Lighthouse Club, 2005–08. Dir, Hambledon Village Shop. *Recreations:* parish council, golf, ski-ing, gardening, Rugby, opera, theatre, ballet, eating and drinking with friends. *Club:* Royal Automobile.

ANDERSON, Prof. John Kinloch, FSA; Professor of Classical Archaeology, University of California, Berkeley, 1958–93, now Emeritus; *b* 3 Jan. 1924; *s* of late Sir James Anderson, KCIE, and Lady Anderson; *m* 1954, Esperance (*d* 2000), *d* of late Guy Batham, Dunedin, NZ; one *s* two *d*. *Educ:* Trinity Coll., Glenalmond; Christ Church, Oxford (MA). Served War, in Black Watch (RHR) and Intelligence Corps, 1942–46 (final rank, Lieut). Student, British Sch. at Athens, 1949–52; Lecturer in Classics, Univ. of Otago, NZ, 1953–58. FSA 1976. Award for Distinction in Teaching, Phi Beta Kappa (N Calif. Chapter), 1988. *Publications:* Greek Vases in the Otago Museum, 1955; Ancient Greek Horsemanship, 1961; Military Theory and Practice in the Age of Xenophon, 1970; Xenophon, 1974; Hunting in the Ancient World, 1985; articles and reviews in Annual of British Sch. at Athens; Jl of Hellenic Studies, etc. *Recreation:* gardening. *Address:* 1020 Middlefield Road, Berkeley, CA 94708, USA. *T:* (510) 8415335.

ANDERSON, John M., PhD; FBA 1991; Professor of English Language, University of Edinburgh, 1988–2002, now Emeritus. *Educ:* Edinburgh Univ. (MA, PhD). Lectr until 1975, Reader, 1975–88, Edinburgh Univ. *Publications:* Grammar of Case: towards a localistic theory, 1971; An Essay Concerning Aspect, 1973; (ed with C. Jones) Historical Linguistics, 2 vols, 1974; (with R. Lass) Old English Phonology, 1975; On Case Grammar, 1977; (with C. Jones) Phonological Structure and the History of English, 1977; (with C. J. Ewen) Principles of Dependency Phonology, 1987; Linguistic Representation: structural analogy and stratification, 1992; Notional Theory of Syntactic Categories, 1997;

Modern Grammars of Case, 2006; The Grammar of Names, 2007. *Address:* Methoni, Messinias 24006, Greece.

ANDERSON, Prof. John Neil; (first) Professor of Dental Prosthetics, 1964–82 (now Emeritus), (first) Dean of Dentistry, 1972–76, 1980–82, University of Dundee; *b* 11 Feb. 1922; *m* 1945, Mary G. Croll; one *s* one *d. Educ:* High Storrs Gram. Sch., Sheffield; Sheffield Univ. Asst Lectr, Sheffield Univ., 1945–46; Lectr, Durham Univ., 1946–48; Lectr, Birmingham Univ., 1948–52; Sen. Lectr, St Andrews Univ., 1952–64. External Examiner, Univs of Malaya, Baghdad, Newcastle upon Tyne, Bristol, Birmingham, Liverpool, RCSI. *Publications:* Applied Dental Materials, 1956; (with R. Storer) Immediate and Replacement Dentures, 1966, 3rd edn, 1981; contribs to leading dental jls. *Recreations:* music, gardening, carpentry. *Address:* Wyndham, Derwent Drive, Baslow, Bakewell, Derbyshire DE45 1RS.

ANDERSON, Prof. John Russell, CBE 1980; Professor of Pathology at the Western Infirmary, Glasgow University, 1967–83, retired; *b* 31 May 1918; *s* of William Gregg Anderson and Mary Gordon Adam; *m* 1956, Audrey Margaret Shaw Wilson; two *s* one *d* (and one *d* decd). *Educ:* Worksop Coll.; St Andrews Univ. BSc (St Andrews) 1939, MB, ChB (St Andrews) 1942, MD (St Andrews) 1955; MRCP 1961; FRCPGlas 1965; FRCPath 1966; FRSE 1968. RAMC, 1944–47 (Emergency Commn). Lecturer and Senior Lecturer in Pathology, Glasgow Univ., 1947–65; George Holt Prof. of Pathology, Liverpool Univ., 1965–67. Rockefeller travelling fellowship in Medicine, at Rochester, NY, 1953–54. Pres., RCPath, 1978–81 (Vice-Pres., 1975). Hon. FRCPI, 1981. Hon. LLD Dundee, 1981. *Publications:* Autoimmunity, Clinical and Experimental (jtly), 1967; (ed) Muir's Textbook of Pathology, 9th edn 1971 to 12th edn 1985; various papers on immunopathology in scientific jls. *Recreations:* golf, arboriculture, gardening. *Address:* 3 Connell Crescent, Milngavie, Glasgow G62 6AR.

ANDERSON, Dame Josephine; *see* Barstow, Dame J.

ANDERSON, Julian Anthony; Director General, Country Landowners' Association, 1990–2000; *b* 12 June 1938; *s* of Sir Kenneth Anderson, KBE, CB. *Educ:* King Alfred Sch.; Wadham Coll., Oxford (MA). Entered MAFF as Asst Principal, 1961; Asst Private Sec. to Minister of Agriculture, 1964–66; Principal, 1966; seconded to FCO, 1970–73; Asst Sec., 1973, Under Sec., 1982–90, MAFF; seconded as Minister (Food and Agriculture), UK Perm. Rep. to EEC, 1982–85. *Recreations:* music, sport, travel, photography, gardening, DIY. *Clubs:* Oxford and Cambridge, Civil Service.

ANDERSON, Julian David; composer; *b* 6 April 1967. *Educ:* Royal Coll. of Music (BMus London 1st cl.); Gonville and Caius Coll., Cambridge, 1990–91; King's Coll., Cambridge, 1992–94 (MPhil Composition). Prof. of Composition, Harvard Univ.; Daniel R. Lewis Young Composer Fellow, Cleveland Orch., 2005–07. Works performed by numerous ensembles and orchestras in Europe and USA, incl. Cleveland Orch., Boston SO, Schoenberg and Asko Ensembles. Broadcast talks on music on BBC and Swiss Radio. *Compositions* include: Symphony, 2003; Book of Hours, 2004; commissions from: London Sinfonietta, 1994 (Khorovod) and 1999; BBC Proms, 1998 (The Stations of the Sun); Cheltenham Festival, 1997 (The Crazed Moon). *Publications:* articles on music in Musical Times, Tempo, The Independent. *Recreations:* films, reading, poetry, swimming. *Address:* c/o Faber Music, 3 Queen Square, WC1N 3AU.

ANDERSON, Kenneth Walter; Managing Director, UBS Investment Bank, since 2006; *b* 22 Feb. 1960; *s* of late Walter Anderson and of Barbara Anderson; *m* 1983, Pamela Davison; three *s. Educ:* American Community Sch., London; Texas A&M Univ. Director: of Strategic Investment, MG Technologies AG, Germany, 2000–01; of Healthcare, Amey plc, 2001–02; Department of Health: Dir, Contract Procurement Prog., 2002–03; Commercial Dir Gen., 2003–06. Adjunct Prof. of Mgt, Tanaka Business Sch., Imperial Coll. London, 2005–. *Recreations:* ski-ing, reading, fishing. *Address:* UBS Investment Bank, 1 Finsbury Avenue, EC2M 2PP. *T:* (020) 7567 8000; *e-mail:* ken.anderson@ubs.com.

ANDERSON, Lesley Jane, (Mrs C. Crawford); QC 2006; a Recorder, since 2006; *b* 6 April 1963; *d* of Ian Anderson and late Rosemary Campbell Anderson; *m* 1996, Colin Crawford; one step *s* one step *d. Educ:* King Edward VI Camp Hill Sch. for Girls, Birmingham; Univ. of Manchester (LLB Hons 1984). CEDR Accredited Mediator, 2000. Lectr in Law, Univ. of Manchester, 1984–89; called to the Bar, Middle Temple, 1989; Trng Manager, Norton Rose M5 Gp of Legal Practices, 1989–91; barrister, 40 King St Chambers, subseq. Kings Chambers, Manchester, 1991–. *Publications:* articles in legal and professional jls. *Recreations:* food, wine, theatre, cinema, modern jazz, Scottish folk music, literature. *Address:* Kings Chambers, 36 Young Street, Manchester M3 3FT. *T:* (0161) 819 8261, *Fax:* (0161) 835 2139; *e-mail:* anderson.lesley@ntlworld.com.

ANDERSON, Prof. Malcolm Grove; Professor of Physical Geography, since 1989, and Pro-Vice-Chancellor, since 2005, University of Bristol; *b* 27 June 1949; *s* of Wilfred Roy Anderson and Frances Betty Anderson; *m* 1972, Elizabeth Ann Roger; one *d. Educ:* Univ. of Nottingham (BSc); Univ. of Cambridge (PhD); Univ. of Bristol (DSc). FICE 1996. Research Fellow, Sidney Sussex Coll., Cambridge, 1972; University of Bristol: Lectr, 1973; Reader, 1985; Head, Dept of Geography, 1990–96, 2002–05; Dir, Inst. for Advanced Studies, 1997–2000 (Vice-Provost, 2000–02). Res. Hydrologist, US Corps of Engrs, 1981–82; Sen. Res. Geotechnical Engr, Hong Kong Govt, 1982–83; Nuffield Foundn, Sen. Science Fellowship, 1988–89; Quater Centenary Vis. Fellowship, Emmanuel Coll., Cambridge, 1989. Technical Advr, Poverty Reduction Fund, 2004–, Chm., Management of Slope Stability in Communities (MoSSaiC) Cttee, 2004–, Govt of St Lucia, WI. Natural Environment Research Council: Mem., AAPS Cttee, 1990–93; Chm., Land-Ocean Interaction Study Steering Cttee, 1998–2001; Member: Council, 2002–07; Audit Cttee, 2003–07; Mem., Science Grants Panel, Nuffield Foundn, 1992–2007; Scholarship Assessor, ACU, 1993–97. Mem., Bristol Cathedral Council, 2002–. Editor-in-Chief, Hydrological Processes, 1986–. Life Fellow, Indian Assoc. of Hydrologists, 1995. Gill Meml Award, RGS, 1986; Trevithick Premium Award, ICE, 1996, 2007. *Publications:* edited jointly: Hydrological Forecasting, 1985; Slope Stability: geotechnical engineering and geomorphology, 1987; Modelling Geomorphological Systems, 1988; Process Studies in Hillslope Hydrology, 1990; Floodplain Processes, 1996; Advances in Hillslope Processes, 1996; Model Validation: perspectives in hydrological science, 2001; Encyclopaedia of Hydrological Sciences, 2005; Landslides: hazard and risk, 2005; numerous res. pubns in hydrological scis and geotechnics. *Recreation:* Anse la Voutte Bay, West Indies. *Address:* Senate House, University of Bristol, Bristol BS8 1TH. *T:* (0117) 928 8275.

ANDERSON, Prof. Michael, OBE 1999; FRSE; FBA 1989; Professor of Economic History, University of Edinburgh, since 1979; *b* 21 Feb. 1942; *s* of Douglas Henry and Rose Lillian Anderson; *m* 1st, 1966, Rosemary Elizabeth Kitching (marr. diss.); one *s* one *d*; 2nd, 2007, Elspeth Catriona MacArthur. *Educ:* Kingston Grammar Sch.; Queens' Coll., Cambridge (BA 1964; MA 1968; PhD 1969). FRSE 1990. University of Edinburgh: Department of Sociology: Asst Lectr, 1967; Lectr, 1969; Reader, 1975; Department of Economic and Social History, 1979; Dean, Faculty of Social Scis, 1985–89; Vice-Principal, 1989–93, 1997–2000; Acting Principal, April–Aug. 1994; Sen. Vice-Principal, 2000–07. Member: Economic and Social History Cttee, SSRC, 1974–78; Computing Cttee, SSRC, 1980–82; Scot. Records Adv. Council, 1984–93; ESRC, 1990–94 (Member: Res. Resources and Methods Cttee, 1982–84; Society and Politics Res. Devlt Gp, 1989–92; Chm., Res. Resources Bd, 1992–94); History of Medicine Cttee, Wellcome Trust, 1988–92; BL Bd, 1994–2003 (Dep. Chm., 2000–03); Council, British Acad., 1995–98; Res. Information Network Adv. Bd, 2005–; HEFCE Res. Cttee, 2006–; Adv. Cttee, Nat. Statistics Centre for Demography, 2006–. Chm., Res. Support Libraries Programme, 1998–2003. Curator, RSE, 1997–99. Chm., Bd of Trustees, Nat. Library of Scotland, 2000– (Trustee, 1998–). Hon. FFA. Dr *hc* Edinburgh, 2007. *Publications:* Family Structure in Nineteenth Century Lancashire, 1971; (ed) Sociology of the Family, 1972; Approaches to the History of the Western Family 1500–1914, 1981; The 1851 Census: a national sample of the enumerators returns, 1987; Population Change in Northwestern Europe 1750–1850, 1988; (ed) Social and Political Economy of the Household, 1995; (ed) British Population History, 1996. *Recreations:* natural history, gardening, study of ancient civilizations.

ANDERSON, Michael James; Director General, Climate Change Group, Department for Environment, Food and Rural Affairs, since 2007; *b* 3 April 1961; *s* of James and Beryl Anderson; *m* 1987, Julie Dickens; two *s* one *d. Educ:* Newcastle Royal Grammar Sch.; Hymers Coll., Hull; Trinity Coll., Cambridge (BA Hons Law 1983). Law Lectr, Univ. of Ill, Urbana-Champaign, 1983–84; Foreign and Commonwealth Office, 1984–2003: Moscow, 1988–89; UK Delegn to Conf. on Disarmament, Geneva, 1992–97; Private Secretary: to Sir David Spedding, 1997–99; to Sir Richard Dearlove, 1999–2000; UK Mission to UN, NY, 2000–03; Prin. Private Sec. to the Lord Chancellor and Sec. of State for Constitutional Affairs, 2003–06; Dir of Strategy and Communication, DCA, 2006–07. *Recreations:* doing, thinking, family, sports. *Address:* (office) Nobel House, 17 Smith Square, SW1P 3JR; *e-mail:* mike.anderson@defra.gsi.gov.uk.

ANDERSON, Vice Adm. Sir Neil (Dudley), KBE 1982 (CBE 1976); CB 1979; Chief of Defence Staff (NZ), 1980–83; *b* 5 April 1927; *s* of Eric Dudley Anderson and Margaret Evelyn (*née* Craig); *m* 1951, Barbara Lillias Romaine Wright; one *s* (and one *s* decd). *Educ:* Hastings High Sch.; BRNC. Joined RNZN, 1944; trng and sea service with RN, 1944–49; Korean War Service, 1950–51; qual. as navigation specialist; Navigator: HMS Vanguard, 1952–53; HMNZS Lachlan, 1954; HMS Saintes, 1958–59; Commanding Officer, HMNZS: Taranaki, 1961–62; Waikato, 1968–69; Philomel, 1969–70; Dep. Chief of Def. Staff, 1976–77; Chief of Naval Staff, 1977–80. Lieut 1949, Lt-Comdr 1957, Comdr 1960, Captain 1968, Cdre 1972, Rear Adm. 1977, Vice Adm. 1980. *Recreations:* croquet, fishing. *Address:* 2/248 Oriental Parade, Wellington 6001, New Zealand. *T:* and *Fax:* (4) 3858494. *Club:* Wellington (Wellington, NZ).

ANDERSON, Paul James; journalist and author; Lecturer in Journalism, City University, since 2000; *b* 3 Oct. 1959; *s* of James George Anderson and Marjorie Rosemary Anderson (*née* Thorpe). *Educ:* Ipswich Sch.; Balliol Coll., Oxford (BA Hons PPE 1981); London College of Printing. Dep. Ed., European Nuclear Disarmament Jl, 1984–87; Reviews Ed., 1986–91, Editor, 1991–93, Tribune; Dep. Ed., New Statesman, 1993–96; News Ed., Red Pepper, 1997–99; Dep. Ed., New Times, 1999–2000. Dir, People's Europe 98, 1998. *Publications:* (ed jtly) Mad Dogs: The US Raid on Libya, 1986; (with Nyta Mann) Safety First: the making of New Labour, 1997; (ed) Orwell in Tribune: 'As I Please' and other writings, 2006. *Address:* 119 Woodbridge Road, Ipswich IP4 2NJ.

ANDERSON, Prof. Philip Warren; Joseph Henry Professor of Physics, Princeton University, New Jersey, 1975–96, now Emeritus; *b* 13 Dec. 1923; *s* of Prof. H. W. Anderson and Mrs Elsie O. Anderson; *m* 1947, Joyce Gothwaite; one *d. Educ:* Harvard Univ. BS 1943; MA 1947; PhD 1949, Harvard. Naval Res. Lab., Washington, DC, 1943–45 (Chief Petty Officer, USN). Mem., Technical Staff, 1949–76, Dir, 1976–84, Bell Telephone Labs. Fulbright Lectr, Tokyo Univ., 1953–54; Overseas Fellow, Churchill Coll., Cambridge, 1961–62; Vis. Prof. of Theoretical Physics, Univ. of Cambridge, 1967–75, and Fellow of Jesus College, Cambridge, 1969–75, Hon. Fellow, 1978–; Cherwell-Simon Meml Lectureship, 1979–80, George Eastman Prof., 1993–94, Oxford Univ. Member: Amer. Acad. of Arts and Sciences, 1966; Nat. Acad. of Sciences, US, 1967; Amer. Philosophical Soc., 1991; Foreign Member: Royal Society, London, 1980; Japan Acad., 1988; Indian Nat. Acad. of Scis, 1990; Russian Nat. Acad. of Sci., 1994; Foreign Associate: Accademia Lincei, Rome, 1985; Indian Acad. of Sci., 1996. Hon. FInstP, 1986. Hon. DSc: Illinois, 1978; Rutgers, 1991; Ecole Normale Supérieure, Paris, 1995; Gustavus Adolphus Coll., Minn, 1995; Sheffield, 1996; Hon. PhD Tokyo, 2002. O. E. Buckley Prize, Amer. Phys. Soc., 1964; Dannie Heinemann Prize, Akad. Wiss. Göttingen, 1975; (jtly) Nobel Prize for Physics, 1977; Guthrie Medal, Inst. of Physics, 1978; Centennial Medal, Harvard, 1996; John Bardeen Prize, 1997. Nat. Medal of Science, US, 1984. *Publications:* Concepts in Solids, 1963; Basic Notions of Condensed Matter Physics, 1984; A Career in Theoretical Physics, 1994; The Theory of Superconductivity in the High Tc Cuprates, 1996; numerous articles in scholarly jls. *Recreations:* go (Japanese game), rank sho-dan, walking. *Address:* 74 Aunt Molly Road, Hopewell, NJ 08525, USA.

ANDERSON, Ray Thomas, OAM 2005; Chairman, Educang Pty Ltd, since 2006; Board Member, Epic Employment Service Inc., since 2000; *b* 23 Nov. 1936; *s* of late Thomas James Anderson and Daisy Eva D'Arcy-Irvine (*née* Woodhouse); *m* 1962, Margaret, *d* of Ronald George Geach; one *s* three *d. Educ:* State Commercial High Sch., Brisbane; Univ. of Queensland (BCom Hons); Macquarie Univ. (BLegS). Public servant, Brisbane, 1956–60; RAAF Psychologist, Brisbane, 1961–62; Trainee Trade Comr, Canberra, 1963; First Sec. and Asst Trade Comr, Australian High Commn, Singapore, 1964–67; Trade Commissioner: Johannesburg, 1968; Cape Town, 1969–70; Counsellor (Commercial) and Sen. Trade Comr, Aust. High Commn, New Delhi, 1971–73; Regl Dir, DTI, Brisbane, 1974–76; Counsellor (Commercial) and Trade Comr (Mktg), Aust. Embassy, Tokyo, 1977–80; Asst Sec., Dept. of Trade, 1980–82; First Asst Sec., Depts of Foreign Affairs and Trade, Trade, Immigration and Ethnic Affairs, 1982–87; Manager, Nat. Ops, AUSTRADE, 1987–89; Minister (Marketing) and Sen. Trade Comr, London and Minister (Commercial), The Hague, 1990–91; Agent-Gen. for Qld in London, 1991–95; Exec. Dir, 1996, Asst Dir-Gen. 1997, Dept of Econ. Devlt and Trade, Qld; Gen. Manager, Evans Deakin Industries, 1997–99; Exec. Dir, Anglicare, 1999–2005. Admitted Barrister, Supreme Court, NSW and High Court of Australia, and Barrister and Solicitor, Supreme Court, ACT, 1989. Dir, EAC Ltd, 2000–05. Diocese of Brisbane: Member: Diocesan Council, 1999–. Freeman, City of London, 1991. Flying Officer, RAAF Reserve. Hon. FAIEx. Centenary Medal, Australia, 2003. *Recreations:* tennis, reading, travel, theatre. *Address:* Box 464, PO Tugan, Qld 4224, Australia. *Clubs:* Singapore Town; United Services, Queensland (Brisbane).

ANDERSON, Reginald, CMG 1974; *b* 3 Nov. 1921; *s* of late Herbert Anderson and Anne Mary (*née* Hicks); *m* 1945, Audrey Gabrielle Williams; two *d. Educ:* Palmers, Grays, Essex. Cabinet Office, 1938–40. Served War, RAF, Flt Lt, 1941–46. Ministry of: Supply, 1947–57; Supply Staff, Australia, 1957–59; Aviation, 1960–67; Counsellor, British

Embassy, Washington, 1967–70; Asst Under-Sec. of State, 1970–76, Dep. Under-Sec. of State, 1976–81, MoD. *Address:* Reynosa, Heronway, Shenfield, Essex CM13 2LX. *T:* (01277) 213077. *Club:* Royal Air Force.

ANDERSON, Robert Edward; QC 2006; barrister; *b* 12 Nov. 1963; *s* of Edward and Ivy Anderson; one *s*. *Educ:* Oundle Sch.; Pembroke Coll., Cambridge (BA Hons Law 1985). Called to the Bar, Gray's Inn and Middle Temple, 1986; in practice, specialising in commercial, sports and entertainment law, 1986–. *Recreation:* Lucifer Star Machine. *Address:* Blackstone Chambers, Temple, EC4Y 9BW. *T:* (020) 7583 1770, *Fax:* (020) 7822 7350; *e-mail:* robertanderson@blackstonechambers.com. *Club:* Home House.

ANDERSON, Robert Geoffrey William; Fellow, Clare Hall, Cambridge, since 2006; *b* 2 May 1944; *er s* of Herbert Patrick Anderson and Kathleen Diana Anderson (*née* Burns); *m* 1st, 1973, Margaret Elizabeth Callis Lea (marr. diss. 2003); two *s*; 2nd, 2005, Jane Virginia Portal. *Educ:* Woodhouse Sch., London; St John's Coll., Oxford (Casberd exhibitioner; BSc, MA, DPhil; Hon. Fellow, 2000). FRSC 1984; FSA 1986; FRSE 1990. Assistant Keeper: Royal Scottish Museum, 1970–75; Science Museum, 1975–78; Dep. Keeper, Wellcome Museum of History of Medicine, and Sec., Adv. Council, Science Museum, 1978–80; Keeper, Dept of Chemistry, Science Mus., 1980–84; Director: Royal Scottish Mus., 1984–85; Nat. Museums of Scotland, 1985–92; British Mus., 1992–2002; Fellow, IAS, Princeton, 2002–03; By Fellow, Churchill Coll., Cambridge, 2003–04; Vis. Fellow, CCC, Cambridge, 2004–05. Sec., Royal Scottish Soc. of Arts, 1973–75; Member Council: Soc. for History of Alchemy and Chemistry, 1978–; Gp for Scientific, Technological and Medical Collections, 1979–83; British Soc. History of Science, 1981–84 (Pres., 1988–90); Scottish Museums, 1984–91; Museums Assoc., 1988–92; Mem., British Nat. Cttee for Hist. of Science, 1985–89; Pres., Scientific Instrument Commn, IUHPS, 1982–97. Member Editorial Board: Annals of Science, 1981–; Annali di Storia della Scienza, 1986–. Trustee, Boerhaave Mus., Leiden, 1994–99. Hon. FSAScot 1991. Hon. DSc: Edinburgh, 1995; Durham, 1998. Dexter Prize, Amer. Chemical Soc., 1986. *Publications:* The Mariner's Astrolabe, 1972; Edinburgh and Medicine, 1976; (ed) The Early Years of the Edinburgh Medical School, 1976; The Playfair Collection and the Teaching of Chemistry at the University of Edinburgh, 1978; (contrib.) The History of Technology, Vol. VI, ed T. I. Williams, 1978; Science in India, 1982; (ed) Science, Medicine and Dissent: Joseph Priestley (1733–1804), 1987; Scientific Instrument Makers Trade Catalogues, 1990; (ed) A New Museum for Scotland, 1990; (with G. Fyffe) Joseph Black: a Bibliography, 1992; (ed) Making Instruments Count, 1993; The Great Court at the British Museum, 2000. *Recreation:* books. *Address:* Honey Hill House, Honey Hill, Cambridge CB3 0BG. *T:* (01223) 328049. *Club:* Athenæum.

ANDERSON, Prof. Robert Henry; Joseph Levy Professor of Paediatric Cardiac Morphology, Institute of Child Health, University College London, 1999–2007 (at National Heart and Lung Institute, Imperial College School of Medicine, 1979–99), University of London; *b* 4 April 1942; *s* of Henry Anderson and Doris Amy Anderson (*née* Callear); *m* 1966, Christine (*née* Ibbotson); one *s* one *d*. *Educ:* Wellington Grammar Sch., Shropshire; Manchester Univ. BSc (Hons); MD; FRCPath. House Officer, Professorial Surgical Unit, 1966, Medical Unit, 1967, Manchester Royal Infirmary; Asst Lectr in Anatomy, 1967–69, Lectr, 1969–73, Manchester Univ.; MRC Travelling Fellow, Dept of Cardiology, Univ. of Amsterdam, 1973–74; Cardiothoracic Institute, now National Heart and Lung Institute, University of London: British Heart Foundn Sen. Res. Fellow and Sen. Lectr in Paediatrics, 1974–77; Joseph Levy Reader, 1977–79, Joseph Levy Prof., 1979–2007, Paediatric Cardiac Morphology. Hon. Consultant: Royal Brompton & Harefield NHS Trust, 1974–99; Gt Ormond St Hosp., 1999–2007. Hon. Prof. of Surgery, Univ. of N Carolina, USA, 1984–; Visiting Professor: Univ. of Pittsburgh, Pa, 1985–; Liverpool Univ., 1989–; St George's Hosp. Med. Sch., 2000–; Univ. of Newcastle, 2007–. Excerpta Medica Travel Award, 1977; British Heart Foundn Prize for Cardiovascular Research, 1984. Associate Editor, Internat. Jl of Cardiology, 1985–91; Ed.-in-Chief, Cardiology in the Young, 1997–2007 (Exec. Ed., 1992–97). *Publications:* (ed jtly) Paediatric Cardiology, 1977, vol. 3, 1981, vol. 5, 1983, vol. 6, 1986; (with A. E. Becker) Cardiac Anatomy, 1980; (with E. A. Shinebourne) Current Paediatric Cardiology, 1980; (with A. E. Becker) Pathology of Congenital Heart Disease, 1981; (with M. J. Davies and A. E. Becker) Pathology of the Conduction Tissues, 1983; (jtly) Morphology of Congenital Heart Disease, 1983; (with A. E. Becker) Cardiac Pathology, 1984; (with G. A. H. Miller and M. L. Rigby) The Diagnosis of Congenital Heart Disease, 1985; (with B. R. Wilcox) Surgical Anatomy of the Heart, 1985, 3rd edn 2004; (jtly) Paediatric Cardiology, 2 vols, 1987, 2nd edn 2002; (with P. J. Oldershaw and J. R. Dawson) Clinician's Illustrated Dictionary of Cardiology, 1988; (jtly) Atlas of the Heart, 1988; (jtly) Transoesophageal Echocardiography in Clinical Practice, 1991; (with A. E. Becker) The Heart Structure in Health and Disease, 1992; over 250 invited chapters in published books and over 600 papers in jls. *Recreations:* golf, music, wine. *Address:* 60 Earlsfield Road, SW18 3DN. *T:* (020) 8870 4368. *Clubs:* Saintsbury, Roehampton; Walton Heath Golf.

ANDERSON, Robert (Woodruff); playwright; *b* NYC, 28 April 1917; *s* of James Hewston Anderson and Myra Esther (*née* Grigg); *m* 1st, 1940, Phyllis Stohl (*d* 1956); 2nd, 1959, Teresa Wright (marr. diss. 1978). *Educ:* Phillips Exeter Acad.; Harvard Univ. AB (*magna cum laude*) 1939, MA 1940. Served USNR, 1942–46 (Lt); won prize (sponsored by War Dept) for best play written by a serviceman overseas, Come Marching Home, 1945, subseq. prod, Univ. of Iowa and Blackfriars Guild, NY. Rockefeller Fellowship, 1946; taught playwrighting, American Theatre Wing Professional Trng Prog., 1946–50; organized and taught Playwright's Unit, Actors Studio, 1955; Writer in Residence, Univ. of N Carolina, 1969; Faculty: Salzburg Seminar in Amer. Studies, 1968; Univ. of Iowa Writers' Workshop, 1976. Member: Playwrights Co., 1953–60; Bd of Governors, American Playwrights Theatre, 1963–; Council, Dramatists Guild, 1954– (Pres., 1971–73); New Dramatists Cttee, 1949– (Pres., 1955–57); Vice-Pres., Authors' League of America; Chm., Harvard Bd of Overseers' Cttee to visit the Performing Arts, 1970–76. Wrote and adapted plays for TV and Radio, 1948–53. Elected to Theater Hall of Fame, 1980. Connecticut Commn on the Arts Award, 1992. *Plays:* Eden Rose, 1948; Love Revisited, 1952; Tea and Sympathy, 1953; All Summer Long, 1954; Silent Night, Lonely Night, 1959; The Days Between, 1965; You Know I Can't Hear You When the Water's Running (four short plays), 1967; I Never Sang For My Father, 1968; Solitaire/Double Solitaire, 1971; Free and Clear, 1983; The Kissing was Always the Best, 1987; The Last Act is a Solo, 1989; *screenplays:* Tea and Sympathy, 1956; Until They Sail, 1957; The Nun's Story, 1959; The Sand Pebbles, 1965; I Never Sang For My Father, 1970 (Writers Guild Award for Best Screenplay, 1971); The Patricia Neal Story, TV, 1981; Absolute Strangers, TV, 1991; The Last Act is a Solo, TV, 1991 (ACE Award). *Publications: novels:* After, 1973; Getting Up and Going Home, 1978; *anthology:* (jtly) Elements of Literature, 6 vols, 1988. *Recreations:* photography, tennis. *Club:* Harvard (New York City).

ANDERSON, Rodney Brian; Director of Marine and Fisheries, Department for Environment, Food and Rural Affairs, since 2006 (Director of Fisheries, 2004–06); *b* 12 July 1948; *s* of Guy and Phyllis Anderson; *m* 1974, Mavis Barker; two *d*. ACIS 1972. Local Govt career, 1964–89; various posts, DoE, subseq. DETR, then DEFRA, 1989–; Hd, Water Supply and Regulation, 2000–04. *Recreations:* reading, walking, travelling, angling. *Address:* Department for Environment, Food and Rural Affairs, Nobel House, 17 Smith Square, SW1P 3JR. *T:* (020) 7238 4259; *e-mail:* rodney.anderson@defra.gsi.gov.uk.

ANDERSON, Rolande Jane Rita; Director-General for Transformation, Office for National Statistics, since 2008; *b* 10 Oct. 1955; *d* of late Arthur Ingham Anderson and of Rolande Marie Anderson. *Educ:* Lycée Français de Londres; Newnham Coll., Cambridge (BA Hons Mod. and Mediaeval Langs, MA Mod. Langs). Fast Stream Admin Trainee, Depts of Industry and of Prices and Consumer Protection, 1976–79; HEO, Dept of Trade, 1979–83; Principal and Hd of Section, DTI, 1983–89; Grade 7, Eur. Secretariat, Cabinet Office, 1989–91; Hd (Asst Sec.), Policy and Planning, Insolvency Service Exec. Agency, 1991–92; Dir, Aerospace and Defence Industries Policy, 1992–96, Regl Eur. Funds, 1996–99, Competition Policy, 1999–2002, DTI; Chief Exec., Radiocommunications Agency, 2002–03; Dep. Dir Gen., Innovation Gp, DTI, 2003–05; Regl Dir, Govt Office for the SE, 2006–08. Mem., panel of assessors for Fast Stream recruitment, CSSB, 1988–91; DTI Member, Steering Board: Patent Office, 2004–05; Nat. Weights and Measures Lab., 2004–05. Non-exec. Dir, Genesis Housing Gp, 2005–. Associate Fellow, Newnham Coll., Cambridge, 2004–07. *Address:* Office for National Statistics, Cardiff Road, Newport, S Wales NP10 8XG.

ANDERSON, Prof. Ross John, PhD; FIMA, FIET; Professor of Security Engineering, University of Cambridge, since 2003; computer security consultant, since 1984; *b* 1956; *s* of William and Anne Anderson; *m* Shireen; one *d*. *Educ:* High Sch. of Glasgow; Trinity Coll., Cambridge (BA 1978; MA 1982; PhD 1995). FIMA 1993; FIET (FIEE 2000). University of Cambridge: Lectr, 1995–2000, Reader, 2000–03; Mem. Council, 2003–. Ed., Computer and Communications Security Reviews, 1992–99. Chm., Foundn for Information Policy Research, 1998–. *Publications:* Fast Software Encryption, 1993; Security in Clinical Information Systems, 1996; Information Hiding, 1996; Personal Medical Information: security, engineering and ethics, 1997; Security Engineering: a guide to building dependable distributed systems, 2001, 2nd edn 2008. *Recreation:* music. *Address:* Computer Laboratory, University of Cambridge, J. J. Thomson Avenue, Cambridge CB3 0FD. *T:* (01223) 334733; *e-mail:* info@ross-anderson.com.

ANDERSON, Prof. Sir Roy (Malcolm), Kt 2006; FRS 1986; Professor of Infectious Disease Epidemiology, since 2000 (Head of Department, 2000–04), Rector, since 2008, Imperial College London; Chief Scientific Adviser, Ministry of Defence, 2004–08; *b* 12 April 1947; *s* of James Anderson and Betty Watson-Weatherburn; *m* 1st, 1975, Dr Mary Joan Anderson (marr. diss. 1989); 2nd, 1990, Dr Claire Baron. *Educ:* Duncombe Sch., Bengeo; Richard Hale Sch., Hertford; Imperial Coll., London (BSc, ARCS, PhD, DIC). CBiol, FIBiol. IBM Research Fellow, Univ. of Oxford, 1971–73; Lectr, King's Coll., London, 1973–77; Lectr, 1977–80, Reader, 1980–82, Prof., 1982–93, Head of Dept of Biology, 1984–93, Imperial Coll., London Univ.; University of Oxford: Linacre Prof. of Zoology, 1993–2000, and Hd, Zoology Dept, 1993–98; Dir, Wellcome Trust Centre for Epidemiology of Infectious Diseases, 1994–2000; Fellow, Merton Coll., Oxford, 1993–2000. Vis. Prof., McGill Univ., 1982–; Alexander Langmuir Vis. Prof., Harvard, 1990–; Genentech Vis. Prof., Univ. of Washington, 1998; James McLaughlin Vis. Prof., Univ. of Texas, 1999. Nuffield Medal Lect., RSocMed, 2002. Member: NERC, 1988–91 (Chm., Services and Facilities Cttee, 1989–90); ACOST, 1989–93 (Chm., Standing Cttee on Envmt, 1990–93); Spongiform Encephalopathy Adv. Cttee, 1998–2003; EPSRC, 2004–08; Chm., Sci. Adv. Council, DEFRA, 2004–. Chm., Oxford Biologica Ltd (formerly IBHSC Ltd), 1999–2001; Dir, GlaxoSmithKline, 2007–. Member, Scientific Advisory Board: IMS, 1997–99; deCode, 1998–2002; Bill & Melinda Gates Foundn Initiative on Grand Challenges in Global Health, 2003–. Member, Council: Zoological Soc., 1988–90; Royal Soc., 1989–91; RSTM&H, 1989–92; RPMS, 1994–97; Mem. Ct, LSHTM, 1993–. Gov., Wellcome Trust Ltd, 1992–2000 (Trustee, Wellcome Trust, 1991–92; Chairman: Infection and Immunity Grant Panel, 1990–92; Population Studies Panel). For. Mem., Inst. of Medicine, NAS, USA, 1999. Founder FMedSci 1998. Hon. FIA 2000; Hon. FRCPath 2000; Hon. FSS 2002; Hon. FRAgS 2002. Hon. Fellow, Linacre Coll., Oxford, 1993. Hon. DSc: East Anglia, 1997; Stirling, 1998. Zoological Soc. Scientific Medal, 1982; Huxley Meml Medal, Imperial Coll., London, 1983; Wright Meml Medal, British Soc. of Parasitology, 1986; David Starr Jordan Medal, Univs of Stanford, Cornell and Indiana, 1986; Chalmers Medal, RSTM&H, 1988; Weldon Medal, Oxford Univ., 1989; John Hill Grundy Medal, Royal Army Med. Coll., 1990; Frink Medal, Zoological Soc. of London, 1993; Joseph Smadel Medal, Infectious Diseases Soc. of Amer., 1994; Distinguished Statistical Ecologist Award, 1998; Dist. Parasitologists Award, Amer. Soc. of Parasitology, 1999. *Publications:* (ed) Population Dynamics of Infectious Disease Agents: theory and applications, 1982; (ed jtly) Population Biology of Infectious Diseases, 1982; (with R. M. May) Infectious Diseases of Humans: dynamics and control, 1991. *Recreations:* hill walking, croquet, natural history. *Address:* Faculty Building, Imperial College London, Exhibition Road, SW7 2AZ. *Club:* Athenæum.

ANDERSON, Roy William; District Judge (Magistrates' Courts) (formerly Stipendiary Magistrate), West Yorkshire, since 1999; *b* 10 Feb. 1950; *s* of William Patterson Bruce Anderson and Thirza Elizabeth Anderson (*née* Wakeham); *m* 1974, Pauline Mary Rylands; two *s*. *Educ:* King Edward VI Sch., Stratford-upon-Avon; University Coll. London (LLB). Articled clerk, City of Swansea, 1972–74; Prosecuting Solicitor, W Midlands CC, 1974–80; Solicitor, Jacobs Bird & Co., Birmingham, 1980–84; Sole Principal, Roy Anderson Solicitor, Birmingham, 1984–99. *Recreations:* reading, theatre, tennis, golf. *Address:* Leeds District Magistrates' Court, PO Box 97, Westgate, Leeds LS1 3JP. *Club:* Silsden Golf.

ANDERSON, Rupert John; QC 2003; *b* 5 Aug. 1958; *s* of John David Bennett Anderson and Roberta Elizabeth Anderson. *Educ:* Cambridgeshire County High Sch.; Hills Road Sixth Form Coll., Cambridge; Pembroke Coll., Cambridge (MA). Called to the Bar, Inner Temple, 1981. Mem., Attorney-Gen.'s A panel of Counsel to Crown, 2000–03. *Publications:* (specialist ed) Copinger and Skone James on Copyright, 14th edn 1999; (contrib.) Weinberg and Blank on Takeovers and Mergers, 2000; (contrib.) PLC Competition Manual, 2002; contrib. to various jls. *Recreations:* classical history, baroque and choral music, dogs. *Address:* Prospect House, 92 North End, Bassingbourn, Royston, Herts SG8 5PD. *T:* (01763) 245932; *e-mail:* randerson@monckton.com.

ANDERSON, Air Vice-Marshal Timothy Michael, DSO 1999; Assistant Chief of the Air Staff, since 2007; *b* 2 Feb. 1957; *s* of George Anderson and Beatrice Anderson; *m* 1979, Ursula Henderson; two *d*. *Educ:* Belfast Royal Acad.; King's Coll. London (MA 1994). Ops Flight Comdr No 1 Sqn, RAAF, 1988–90; Mil. Asst to DCDS (Systems), 1996–98; OC No 14 Sqdn, RAF, 1999–2000; CO RAF Bruggen, 2000–01; Dir, Equipment Capability (Deep Target Attack), MoD, 2003–05; Comdt, RAF Air Warfare Centre, 2005–07. FRAeS 2002. *Recreations:* cycling, military history, golf, Asian cooking, motor sport. *Club:* Royal Air Force.

ANDERSON, Victor Frederick; Higher Economic Analyst, Sustainable Development Commission, since 2006; *b* 7 Feb. 1952; *s* of Tom and Iris Anderson; *m* 1987, Joan Rawlinson; one *s*. *Educ:* Whitgift Sch.; Brasenose Coll., Oxford (BA). Lectr, 1980–88, at Paddington Coll. of FE, 1982–88; Researcher: New Econs Foundn, 1987–92; Plaid

Cymru Gp of MPs, 1992–2000 and 2004–05; Sen. Researcher, Policy Develt Unit, Plaid Cymru, 2004. Mem. (Green), London Assembly, GLA, 2000–03. Mem. Bd, London Develt Agency, 2000–04. Envmt Advr to Mayor of London, 2001–04; Mem., London Sustainable Develt Commn, 2002–04. Develt Manager, Green Econs Inst., 2005. Mem. Editl Bd, Internat. Jl of Green Economics, 2006–. *Publications:* Alternative Economic Indicators, 1991; Energy Efficiency Policies, 1993; Greens and the New Politics, 2001. *Recreations:* dancing, visiting museums. *Address:* 12 Glynwood Court, Dartmouth Road, Forest Hill, SE23 3HU.

ANDERSON, Sir (William) Eric (Kinloch), KT 2002; MA, MLitt, DLitt, FRSE; Provost of Eton College, 2000–Feb. 2009; *b* 27 May 1936; *er s* of late W. J. Kinloch Anderson and Margaret (*née* Harper), Edinburgh; *m* 1960, Poppy, *d* of late W. M. Mason, Skipton; one *s* one *d*. *Educ:* George Watson's Coll.; Univ. of St Andrews (MA); Balliol Coll., Oxford (MLitt; Hon. Fellow, 1989). Asst Master: Fettes Coll., 1960–64; Gordonstoun, 1964–66; Asst Master, Fettes Coll., and Housemaster, Arniston House, 1967–70; Headmaster: Abingdon Sch., 1970–75; Shrewsbury Sch., 1975–80; Eton Coll., 1980–94; Rector, Lincoln Coll., Oxford, 1994–2000 (Hon. Fellow, 2000). Chairman: King George VI and Queen Elizabeth Foundn of St Catharine's, Cumberland Lodge, 1997–2008; Nat. Heritage Meml Fund, 1998–2001 (Trustee, 1996–2001). President: Edinburgh Sir Walter Scott Club, 1981; Johnson Soc., 1992; Mem., DCMS Adv. Panel for Public Appointments, 1997–2004. Trustee: Karim Rida Said Foundn, 1994–98, 2004–; Wordsworth Trust, 1996–97; Royal Collection, 2000–06; Shakespeare Birthplace Trust, 2001–; Farmington Trust, 2005–. Mem. Visiting Cttee, Harvard Meml Church, 2001–07. Council Mem., Royal Holloway, London Univ. (formerly RHBNC), 1990–95; Gov., Shrewsbury Sch., 1994–2000; Visitor, Harris Manchester Coll., Oxford Univ., 2001–. Chm. of Judges, Whitbread Book Awards, 2000. FRSE 1985. Hon. DLitt: St Andrews, 1981; Hull, 1994; Siena, 1999. *Publications:* The Written Word, 1964; (ed) The Journal of Sir Walter Scott, 1972, rev. edn 1998; (ed) The Percy Letters, vol IX, 1988; (ed) The Sayings of Sir Walter Scott, 1995; articles and reviews. *Recreations:* theatre, golf, fishing. *Address:* (until Feb. 2009) Provost's Lodge, Eton College, Windsor, Berks SL4 6DH.

See also D. W. K. Anderson.

ANDERSSON, Hilary Harper; correspondent, Panorama, BBC, since 2006; *b* 23 Sept. 1967; *d* of Alfred McRae Andersson and Zosha Mary Andersson; one *s*. *Educ:* Cheltenham Ladies' Coll.; Univ. of Edinburgh (MA Hons Politics). Joined BBC, 1991: producer, World Service, 1992–94; sen. broadcast journalist, 1994–96; Lagos Corresp., 1996–99; Jerusalem Corresp., 1999–2001; Africa Corresp., 2001–05; special reports for Panorama: Secrets of the Camps, 2005; The New Killing Fields, 2005; Climate of Fear, 2006. *Publication:* Mozambique: a war against the people, 1992. *Recreations:* ski-ing, windsurfing, writing. *Address:* c/o BBC, Television Centre, Wood Lane, W12 7RJ. *T:* (020) 8743 8000; *e-mail:* Hilary.Andersson.01@bbc.co.uk.

ANDERTON, Prof. Brian Henry, PhD; FMedSci; Director, MRC Centre for Neurodegeneration Research, since 2005, and Professor of Neuroscience, Institute of Psychiatry, since 1989, at King's College London; *b* 25 Dec. 1945; *s* of Henry Anderton and Mary Anderton (*née* Ashcroft); *m* 1969, Thérèse L. F. Loviny; one *s*. *Educ:* Allsop High Sch. for Boys, Liverpool; University College London (BSc 1967; PhD 1970). MRC Biophysics Unit, KCL, 1970–72; Lectr in Biochem., Poly. of Central London, 1972–77; Lectr in Biochem. and Immunology, Chelsea Coll., Univ. of London, 1977–79; St George's Hospital Medical School, University of London: Lectr in Immunology, 1979–81; Sen. Lectr in Immunology, 1981–86; Reader in Molecular Pathology, 1986–88. FMedSci 2007. *Publications:* contribs to sci. jls on nervous system and molecular pathology of Alzheimer's disease and other neurodegenerative diseases. *Recreations:* hill walking, cycling, general reading, theatre, cinema, listening to music. *Address:* Department of Neuroscience, Institute of Psychiatry, King's College London, De Crespigny Park, SE5 8AF. *T:* (020) 7848 0258.

ANDERTON, Sir (Cyril) James, Kt 1991; CBE 1982; QPM 1977; DL; Chief Constable, Greater Manchester Police Force, 1976–91 (Deputy Chief Constable, 1975); *b* 24 May 1932; *o s* of late James Anderton and Lucy Anderton (*née* Occleshaw); *m* 1955, Joan Baron; one *d*. *Educ:* St Matthew's Church Sch., Highfield; Wigan Grammar Sch. Certif. Criminology, Manchester Univ., 1960; Sen. Comd Course, Police Coll., 1967. Corps of Royal Mil. Police, 1950–53; Constable to Chief Inspector, Manchester City Police, 1953–67; Chief Supt, Cheshire Constab., 1967–68; Asst Chief Constable, Leicester and Rutland Constab., 1968–72; Asst to HM Chief Inspector of Constab. for England and Wales, Home Office, London, 1972–75; Dep. Chief Constable, Leics Constabulary, 1975. Mem., ACPO, 1968–91 (Pres., 1986–87). FCO lect. tour, FE and SE Asia, 1973. UK Govt deleg., UN Congress on Prevention of Crime, Budapest, 1974. British Institute of Management: Pres., Manchester Br., 1984–93; Chm., 1986–90, Mem., 1985–90, NW Regl Bd; Cert. of Merit, 1990. President: Manchester NSPCC Jun. League, 1979–93; Christian Police Assoc., 1979–81; Manchester and Dist RSPCA, 1984–2000 (Vice-Pres., 1981–84); Wigan and Dist RSPCA, 1999–2000 (Patron, 1986–99); Wythenshawe Hosp. League of Friends, 1991–2004; Altrincham Town Centre Partnership, 1994–2003; Disabled Living, Manchester, 1995–2005 (Patron, 1991–; Hon. Life Mem., 2006); Bolton Outward Bound Assoc., 1995–2002 (Vice-Pres., 1991–95); NW Reg., YMCA, 1996–2002; Manchester YMCA, 2000–02 (Vice-Pres., 1976–2000); Greater Manchester Fedn of Clubs for Young People (formerly Boys' Clubs), 2001–05 (Vice-Pres., 1984–2001; Patron, 2005–). Member: Manchester Adv. Bd, Salvation Army, 1977–2001 (Chm., 1993–2001; Hon. Life Mem., Salvation Army Adv. Bd, 2000); Salvation Army Territorial Adv. Bd, 1996–2001; Exec. Cttee, Manchester NSPCC, 1979–93; Bd, Henshaws Soc. for the Blind, 1991–95; Royal Soc. of St George, 1992–; CCJ, 1992–; Friends of Israel Assoc., 1992–; Broughton Catholic Charitable Soc., 1996–; Nat. Adv. Gp, YMCA, 1997–2002 (Chm., Prisons Steering Gp, 1994–2002). Comdr, St John Amb., Greater Manchester, 1989–96 (County Dir, 1976–89); Vice-President: Manchester and District RLSS, 1976–2000; Adelphi Lads' Club, Salford, 1979–2006; Sharp Street Ragged Sch., Manchester, 1982–2002; Manchester Schools Football Assoc., 1976–91; Greater Manchester East Scout Council, 1977–91; 318 (Sale) Sqn, ATC, 1985–; Wigan Hospice, 1990–; Greater Manchester West Scout Council, 1992–; Manchester and Dist NSPCC, 1994–. Boys' Brigade: Pres., Leics Bn, 1972–76; Hon. Nat. Vice-Pres., 1983–. Patron: NW Counties Schs ABA, 1980–91; NW Campaign for Kidney Donors, 1983–; NW Eye Res. Trust, 1982–91; N Manchester Hosp. Broadcasting Service, 1983–; Internat. Spinal Res. Trust (Greater Manchester Cttee), 1983–91; Sale RNLI, 1986–; Stockport Canal Trust, 1989–; The British Trust, 1991–; Stockport Lourdes Gp HCPT (formerly ACROSS), 1993–; Trafford Multiple Sclerosis Soc., 1994–2004; Mottram and Hattersley ABC, 1994–2003; Rhodes Foundn Scholarship Trust, 1996–; Lancashire and Cheshire (formerly Gtr Manchester) Lupus Gp, 1996–2005; Gtr Manchester Youth Field Gun Assoc., 1996–2003 (Pres., 1992–96); Police Boxing Assoc. of England, 1997–2003; Manchester Stedfast Assoc., 1999–. British College of Accordionists: Chm., Governing Council, 1972–77; Vice-Pres., 1977–84; Pres., 1984–91; Patron, 1991–2002. Trustee, Manchester Olympic Bid Cttee, 1985–93; Chm. of Trustees, S Manchester Accident Rescue Team, 1996–2001; Chm., Manchester Concerts Cttee, Sargent Cancer Care for Children, 1992–2003. Hon. FBCA 1976; Hon. RNCM 1984. Member: Catholic Union of GB; NT; Wigan Little Theatre; Royal Exchange Th., Manchester; Garrick Th., Altrincham; Corps of Royal Mil. Police Assoc. Mancunian of The Year, 1980. DL Greater Manchester, 1989. Freeman, City of London, 1990. KStJ 1989 (OStJ 1978; CStJ 1982; Mem., Chapter-Gen., 1993–99). KMLJ 1998; KHS 1999. Cross Pro Ecclesia et Pontifice, 1982. Chevalier de la Confrérie des Chevaliers du Tastevin, 1985. *Recreations:* opera, theatre, fell-walking; Rugby League supporter. *Address:* 9 The Avenue, Sale, Cheshire M33 4PB.

ANDERTON, Hon. James Patrick, (Jim); MP Wigram, New Zealand, since 1996 (MP Sydenham, 1984–96) (Lab 1984–89, NewLab, then Alliance, 1989–2002, Progressive since 2002); Minister of Forests, since 2004, and of Agriculture, of Fisheries and for Biosecurity, since 2005, New Zealand; *b* 21 Jan. 1938; *m* 1st, Joan Caulfield (marr. diss.); three *s* one *d*; 2nd, Carole Anne. *Educ:* Seddon Meml Technical Coll.; Auckland Teachers' Trng Coll. Formerly: teacher; Child Welfare Officer, Educn Dept, Wanganui; Export Manager, UEB Textiles, 1969–70; Man. Dir, Anderton Hldgs, 1971. Member: Manukau CC, 1965–68; Auckland CC, 1974–77; Auckland Regl Authy, 1977–80. Dep. Prime Minister of NZ, 1999–2002; Minister for Econ. Develt, and for Industry and Regl Develt, 1999–2005. Labour Party, 1963–89: Pres., 1979–84; Mem., Policy Council, 1979–89; Leader, NewLabour Party, 1989–2002; Jt Founder, 1991, Leader, 1992–2001, Alliance; Leader, Progressive Party, 2002–. Organiser, Catholic Youth Movt, 1960–65; Sec., Catholic Diocesan Office, Auckland, 1967–69. *Address:* Parliament Buildings, Wellington, New Zealand.

ANDO, Tadao, Hon. RA 2002; architect; Director, Tadao Ando Architect and Associates, since 1969; *b* 13 Sept. 1941; *s* of Mitsugu Kitayama and Asako Kitayama; adopted by grandparents Hikoichi Ando and Kikue Ando; *m* 1970, Yumiko Kato. *Educ:* self-educated in architecture. Visiting Professor: Yale Univ., 1987; Columbia Univ., 1988; Harvard, 1990. *Works include:* Row House, Sumiyoshi (Azuma House), 1975; Rokko Housing I and II, 1978–89; Kidosaki House, 1982; Church of The Light, Osaka, 1987; Japanese Pavilion, Expo '92, Seville, 1989. *Exhibitions include:* Mus. of Modern Art, NY, 1991; Centre Georges Pompidou, Paris, 1993; Basilica Palladiana, Vicenza, 1994; RA, 1998. Hon. FAIA 1991; Hon. FRIBA 1993. Chevalier, Ordre des Arts et des Lettres (France), 1995. Alvar Aalto Medal, Finnish Assoc. Architects, 1986; Gold Medal of Architecture, French Acad. Architecture, 1989; Arnold W. Brunner Meml Prize, AAIL, 1991; Carlsberg Architectural Prize, 1992; Pritzker Architecture Prize, 1995; Royal Gold Medal, RIBA, 1997. *Publications:* Tadao Ando Monographies, 1982; Tadao Ando: buildings, projects, writings, 1984; Tadao Ando Complete Works, 1995; (with Richard Pare) The Colours of Light, 1996. *Address:* 5–23 Toyosaki 2–chome, Kita-ku, Osaka 531–0072, Japan. *T:* (6) 63751148.

ANDOVER, Viscount; Alexander Charles Michael Winston Robsahm Howard; Managing Director: guntrader.co.uk Ltd, since 1997; Peer2Peer Ltd, 2001; Visa Systems, since 2005; *b* 17 Sept. 1974; *s* and *heir* of 21st Earl of Suffolk and Berkshire, *qv*. *Educ:* Eton Coll.; Bristol Univ. *Address: e-mail:* andover@charltonpark.com.

ANDRE, Carl; sculptor; *b* 16 Sept. 1935; *s* of George Hans Andre and Margaret Andre (*née* Johnson). First exhibn, 1964; represented in collections in: Tate Gall.; Mus. of Modern Art, NYC; Guggenheim Mus., NYC; La Jolla Mus. Contemporary Art; Mönchengladbach Mus., Germany; Kunstmuseum Basel, Switzerland; Stedelijk Mus., Amsterdam; Musée Nationale d'Art Moderne, Paris; Nat. Gall. of Canada, Ottawa; Seattle Art Mus.; Musèo de Arte Moderno, Bogotá; *solo exhibitions:* Tibor de Nagy Gall., NY, 1965; Konrad Fischer Gall., Düsseldorf, 1967, 2006; Guggenheim Mus., 1970; Univ. Art Mus., Berkeley, Calif, 1979; Paula Cooper Gall., NY, 1983; (retrospective) Whitechapel Art Gall., 2000; Sadie Coles HQ, London, 2001; Ace Gall., LA, 2002; Galerie Tschudi, Switzerland, 2003; Galerie Arnaud Lefebvre, Paris, 2004; Kunsthalle Basel, Switzerland, 2005; Andrea Rosen Gall., NY, 2007; Yvon Lambert, Paris, 2008. *Address:* c/o Konrad Fischer, Platanenstrasse 7, 40233 Düsseldorf, Germany; c/o Paula Cooper, 534 W 21 St, New York, NY 10011, USA.

ANDREAE, Sophie Clodagh Mary, (Mrs D. E. Blain); *b* 10 Nov. 1954; *d* of Herman Kleinwort (Sonny) Andreae and Clodagh Mary (*née* Alleyn); *m* 1984, Douglas Ellis Blain; three *s* one *d*. *Educ:* St Mary's, Ascot; Newnham Coll., Cambridge. SAVE Britain's Heritage: Sec., 1976–84; Chm., 1984–88; Head, London Div., English Heritage (Historic Bldgs and Monuments Commn for England), 1988–93. Member: Royal Fine Art Commn, 1996–99; CABE, 1999–2004 (Chm., CABE Educn Foundn, 2002–06); English Heritage/CABE Urban Panel, 2004–07; Places of Worship Forum, English Heritage, 2005–; Council, Nat. Trust, 2006–. Trustee: Heritage of London Trust, 1985–2003; Greenwich Foundn, 2007–; Member: London DAC, 1988–2001; St Paul's Cathedral Fabric Adv. Cttee, 1991–; Exec. Cttee, Georgian Gp, 1993–; Council, London Historic Parks and Gardens Trust, 1993–2002. Vice Chm., Patrimony Cttee, RC Bishops' Conf., 2002–. Dir, Action for Mkt Towns, 1998–2003. High Sheriff, Powys, 2002–03. Pres., Offa's Dyke Assoc., 2003–. Chm., Friends of St Andrew's Church, Presteigne, Powys, 1998–; Trustee, Judge's Lodging Mus., Presteigne, Powys, 2007–. *Publications:* (contrib.) Preserving the Past: the rise of heritage in modern Britain, 1996; ed and contrib. to numerous SAVE Britain's Heritage reports. *Address:* 23 Brompton Square, SW3 2AD.

ANDREAE-JONES, William Pearce; QC 1984; a Recorder of the Crown Court, since 1982; *b* 21 July 1942. *Educ:* Canford Sch.; Corpus Christi Coll., Cambridge (MA Hons). Called to the Bar, Inner Temple, 1965. *Address:* Citadel Chambers, 190 Corporation Street, Birmingham B4 6QD; 1 Chancery Lane, WC2A 1LF; King's Bench Chambers, Wellington House, 175 Holdenhurst Road, Bournemouth, Dorset BH8 8DQ.

ANDREOTTI, Giulio; Life Senator, Chamber of Deputies, since 1992; Prime Minister (President of the Council of Ministers) of Italy, 1972–73, 1976–79 and 1989–92; *b* 14 Jan. 1919; *s* of Filippo and Rosa Andreotti; *m* 1945, Livia Danese; two *s* two *d*. *Educ:* Univ. of Rome. Mem. for Rome Latina Viterbo Frosinone, Chamber of Deputies, 1946–92. Under Sec. of State, Council of Ministers, 1947–54; Minister of Interior, 1954; Minister of Finance, 1955–58; Minister of the Treasury, 1958–59; Minister of Defence, 1959–65; Minister of Industry and Commerce, 1966–68; Chm., Christian Democrats, 1968–72; Minister of Defence, March–Oct. 1974; Minister for Budget and Economic Planning, 1974–76; Minister of Foreign Affairs, 1983–89. Founder, and Editor, Concretezza (political weekly), 1955–76. Hon. Dr: Sorbonne; Loyola Univ., Chicago; Copernican Univ. of Torun, Poland; La Plata; Salamanca; St John's, NY; Warsaw; Univ. of Sci. and Technol., Beijing; New York; Jewish Theol Seminary, NY. Bancarella Prize, 1985. *Publications* include: Pranzo di magro per il cardinale, 1954; De Gasperi e il suo tempo, 1965; La Sciarada di Papa Mastai, 1967; Ore 13: il Ministro deve morire, 1975; Ad Ogni morte di Papa, 1980; Il diario 1976–79, 1981; De Gasperi visto da vicino, 1986; Visti da vicino (4 vols of profiles): Onorevole, stia zitto, 1987, vol II, 1992; L'URSS vista da vicino, 1988, Gli USA visti da vicino, 1989; Il potere logora … ma è meglio non perderlo, 1990; Governare con la crisi, 1991; The USA Up Close, 1992; Cosa Loro, 1995; De Prima Repubblica, 1996; many articles. *Address:* Senato della Repubblica, Palazzo Giustiniani, Via della Dogana Vecchia 29, 00816 Rome, Italy.

ANDRES, Clare; *see* Tickell, C.

ANDRESEN GUIMARÃES, Fernando; Ambassador of Portugal to the Court of St James's, 2003–06; *b* 13 Nov. 1941; *s* of Fernando João Andresen Guimarães and Maria Carlota da Rocha Vasconcelos Meireles de Lacerda Andresen Guimarães; *m* 1984, Graça Trocado; two *s* from a previous marriage. *Educ:* Univ. of Lisbon (Econs degree). Joined Portuguese Diplomatic Service, 1969; Sec., Malawi, 1970–73; First Sec., London, 1973–76; Min. of Foreign Affairs, 1976–77; NATO Defence Coll., Rome, 1977–78; Counsellor, UN, NY, 1978–82; Consul Gen., Angola, 1982–86; Ambassador to: Iraq, 1986–88; Algeria, 1988–91; Dir Gen., Aid to Develt, 1991–92; Pres., Interministerial Commn on Macau and Portuguese-Chinese Jt Liaison Gp, 1992–95; Ambassador to USA, 1995–99; Perm. Rep. to NATO, 1999–2003. Decorations include: Grand Cross, Order of Christ (Portugal); Grand Cross, Order Infante D. Henrique (Portugal); Naval Cross, 1st cl. (Portugal). *Recreations:* reading, golf, opera (as spectator).

ANDREW, Prof. Christopher Maurice, PhD; FRHistS; Professor of Modern and Contemporary History, 1993–2008, Director of Research, Department of History, since 2008, University of Cambridge; Fellow, Corpus Christi College, Cambridge, since 1967; *b* 23 July 1941; *s* of Maurice Viccars Andrew and Freda Mary (*née* Sandall); *m* 1962, Jennifer Ann Alicia Garratt; one *s* two *d*. *Educ:* Norwich Sch.; Corpus Christi Coll., Cambridge (MA, PhD). FRHistS 1976. Res. Fellow, Gonville and Caius Coll., Cambridge, 1965–67; Dir of Studies in History, 1967–81 and 1988–, Sen. Tutor, 1981–87, Corpus Christi Coll., Cambridge; Univ. Lectr in History, 1972–89, Reader in Mod. and Contemp. Hist., 1989–93, Univ. of Cambridge. Ext. Examr in History, NUI, 1977–84. Specialist Adviser, H of C Select Cttee on Educn, Science and the Arts, 1982–83. Visiting Professor: Univ. of Toronto, 1991; Harvard Univ., 1992. Visiting Fellow: ANU, 1987; Wilson Center, Washington, 1987. TV Presenter: The Fatal Attraction of Adolf Hitler, 1989; Hess: an edge of conspiracy, 1990; The Cambridge Moles, 1990; All the King's Jews, 1990; A Cold War, 1991; BBC Radio Presenter (series): Tampering with the Past, 1990; What if?, 1990–94; Hindsight, 1993–95. Editor: The Historical Journal, 1976–85; Intelligence and National Security, 1986–. *Publications:* Théophile Delcassé and the making of the Entente Cordiale, 1968; The First World War: causes and consequences, 1970 (vol. 19 of Hamlyn History of the World); (with A. S. Kanya-Forstner) France Overseas: the First World War and the climax of French imperial expansion, 1981; (ed with Prof. D. Dilks) The Missing Dimension: governments and intelligence communities in the Twentieth Century, 1984; Secret Service: the making of the British Intelligence Community, 1985; Codebreaking and Signals Intelligence, 1986; (ed with Jeremy Noakes) Intelligence and International Relations 1900–1945, 1987; (with Oleg Gordievsky) KGB: the inside story of its foreign operations from Lenin to Gorbachev, 1990; (with Oleg Gordievsky) Instructions from The Centre: top secret files on KGB foreign operations, 1991; (with Oleg Gordievsky) More Instructions from The Centre, 1992; For The President's Eyes Only: secret intelligence and the American presidency from Washington to Bush, 1995; (with Vasili Mitrokhin) The Mitrokhin Archive: the KGB in Europe and the West, 1999, vol. II: the KGB and the world, 2005; broadcasts and articles on mod. history, Association football, secret intelligence, internat. relations. *Address:* 67 Grantchester Meadows, Cambridge CB3 9JL. *T:* (01223) 353773.

ANDREW, Christopher Robert, (Rob), MBE 1995; Elite Rugby Director, Rugby Football Union, since 2006; *b* 18 Feb. 1963; *m* 1989, Sara; three *d*. *Educ:* Barnard Castle; St John's Coll., Cambridge (BA 1985; MA 1989; Rugby blue, cricket blue). MRICS (ARICS 1988). Chartered surveyor with Debenham, Tewson & Chinnocks, until 1995; Develt Dir, Newcastle RFC, then Dir of Rugby, Newcastle Falcons, 1995–2006. Played for: Nottingham RFC, 1984–87; Wasps FC, 1987–91, 1992–96; Toulouse RFC, 1991–92; Barbarians RFC, and Newcastle RFC, 1996–99; England, 1985–97 (over 71 caps); World Cup team 1987, 1991, 1995; Grand Slam side, 1991, 1992, 1995; British Lions tour, Australia, 1989, NZ 1993. *Publication:* A Game and a Half, 1994. *Address:* c/o Rugby Football Union, Rugby House, Rugby Road, Twickenham TW1 1DS.

ANDREW, Prof. Colin; Professor of Manufacturing Engineering, 1986–94, and Chairman of Council, School of Technology, 1993–94, Cambridge University; Fellow, Christ's College, Cambridge, 1986–94; *b* 22 May 1934; *s* of Arnold Roy and Kathleen Andrew; *m* 1952, Ruth E. Probert; two *s* two *d*. *Educ:* Bristol Grammar Sch.; Christ's Coll., Cambridge Univ. MA; PhD. Res. Engr, Rolls-Royce, 1955–58; research, Cambridge, 1958–60; Develt Engr, James Archdale & Co., 1960–61; Bristol University: Lectr, 1961–68; Reader, 1968–71; Prof. of Applied Mechanics, 1971–82; Hon. Prof., 1982–86. Managing Director: Flamgard Ltd, 1982–85; Bristol Technical Develts Ltd, 1985–94. Chairman: Engrg Processes Cttee, SERC, 1981–83; Production Cttee, SERC, 1983–84; Main Engrg Panel, and Mech., Aeronautical and Manufacturing Panel, UFC Res. Assessment Exercise, 1992; Mech., Aeronautical and Manufacturing Panel, HEFCE Res. Assessment Exercise, 1996; Member: Technology Sub-Cttee, UGC, 1986–89; Engrg Council, 1990–94 (Chm., Bd of Engrs Registration, 1992–94). *Publications:* (jtly) Creep Feed Grinding, 1985; papers in scientific jls. *Address:* Hybank, Itton, Chepstow NP16 6BZ.

ANDREW, Douglas Robert; Lead Infrastructure Specialist, World Bank; *b* 14 June 1951; *s* of Douglas Robert Lawson Andrew and Patricia Eleanor (*née* Thorp). *Educ:* Princeton Univ. (MPA); Auckland Univ. (MCom Hons). Various posts in NZ Treasury, 1975–97 (Dep. Sec., 1995–97); Bd Mem. and Gp Dir, Economic Regulation, CAA, 1997–2003. Member: Eurocontrol Performance Review Commn, 1998–2003; Regulatory Cttee, Eurocontrol, 2003. *Publication:* (jtly) The Caucasian Tiger: policies to sustain growth in Armenia, 2007. *Recreation:* tennis. *Address:* c/o World Bank, 1818 H Street NW, Washington, DC 20433, USA.

ANDREW, His Honour Herbert Henry; QC 1982; a Circuit Judge, 1984–99; *b* 26 July 1928; *s* of Herbert Henry Andrew and Nora Andrew (*née* Gough); *m* 1966, Annette Josephine Colbert; two *s* two *d*. *Educ:* Preston Grammar Sch.; Queens' Coll., Cambridge (BA). Called to the Bar, Gray's Inn, 1952; practised on Northern Circuit, 1953–84; a Recorder, 1978–84. *Recreation:* fell walking. *Club:* Liverpool Racquet.

ANDREW, Hon. (John) Neil, AO 2008; Speaker, House of Representatives, Australia, 1998–2004; Chairman, Crawford Fund, Australian Academy of Technological Sciences and Engineering, since 2005; *b* 7 June 1944; *s* of Jack Clover Andrew and Elsie Mavis Andrew; *m* 1971, Carolyn Ann Ayles; two *s* one *d*. *Educ:* Waikerie High Sch.; Urrbrae Agricl Coll.; Australian Nuffield Schol. in Agric., UK, 1975. Horticulture (fruit and vineyards), 1964–83. MP (L) Wakefield, SA, 1983–2004; Dep. Opposition Whip, 1985–89, 1990–93; Chief Govt Whip, House of Reps, 1997–98. *Recreations:* horticulture, camping, reading, aviation. *Address:* c/o Australian Academy of Technological Sciences and Engineering, 197 Royal Parade, Parkville, Vic 3052, Australia.

ANDREW, Rob; *see* Andrew, C. R.

ANDREW, Sir Robert (John), KCB 1986 (CB 1979); civil servant, retired; *b* 25 Oct. 1928; *s* of late Robert Young Andrew and Elsie (*née* Heritage); *m* 1963, Elizabeth Bayley (OBE 2000); two *s*. *Educ:* King's College Sch., Wimbledon; Merton Coll., Oxford (MA; Hon. Fellow 2005). Intelligence Corps, 1947–49. Joined Civil Service, 1952: Asst Principal, War Office, Principal, 1957; Min. of Defence, 1963; Asst Sec., 1965; Defence Counsellor, UK Delegn to NATO, 1967–70; Private Sec. to Sec. of State for Defence, 1971–73; Under-Sec., CSD, 1973–75; Asst Under-Sec. of State, MoD, 1975–76; Dep. Under-Sec. of State, Home Office, 1976–83; Perm. Under-Sec. of State, NI Office, 1984–88; Cabinet Office, Review of Govt Legal Services, 1988. Dir, Esmée Fairbairn Charitable Trust, 1989–94. Conservator of Wimbledon and Putney Commons, 1973–. Governor, King's College Sch., 1975–2000 (Chm., 1990–2000; Hon. Fellow 2003). Mem. Council, Royal Holloway, Univ. of London (formerly RHBNC), 1989–99 (Chm., 1992–99; Hon. Fellow, 2000). Trustee, BBC Children in Need Appeal, 1993–99. FRSA 1992. *Recreations:* reading, walking, carpentry. *Address:* 8 High Cedar Drive, Wimbledon, SW20 0NU. *Club:* Oxford and Cambridge.

ANDREW, Her Honour Sandra Christine; a Circuit Judge, 1999–2004; Designated Family Judge, Canterbury Combined Court, 2000–04; a Deputy Circuit Judge, since 2004; *b* 5 Nov. 1941; *d* of Albert Hugh Dudley Tyas and Anne Florence (*née* Preston); *m* 1963, John Andrew (*d* 2001); two *s*. *Educ:* various prep. schools; E Grinstead Co. Grammar Sch. Admitted Solicitor, 1964; in private practice, 1964–83; Registrar, SE Circuit, Bromley Co. Court, 1983, transf. to Maidstone, 1990; Trng Registrar, then Dist Judge, 1986–99; Care Dist Judge, 1991–99. Member: President's Ancillary Relief Adv. Gp (formerly Lord Chancellor's Adv. Cttee on Ancillary Relief), 1993–2004; Family Proceedings Rules Cttee, 1993–97; Litigant Inf. Sub-Cttee, Civil Justice Council, 1998–2001; Tutor team for Dep. Dist Judges, Judicial Studies Bd, 1998–2001. Chm., SE Circuit Assoc. Dist Judges, 1992–95; SE Circuit (S) Rep., Nat. Cttee, Assoc. Dist Judges, 1996–99 (Co-opted Mem., Family Sub-Cttee, 1993–96). *Recreations:* music, bridge, travel, reading. *Address:* c/o The Law Courts, Chaucer Road, Canterbury, Kent CT1 1ZA. *Club:* Army and Navy.

ANDREW, Sydney Percy Smith, FRS 1976; FREng, FIChemE, MIMechE; consultant chemical engineer; ICI Senior Research Associate, 1976–88; *b* 16 May 1926; *s* of Harold C. Andrew and Kathleen M. (*née* Smith); *m* 1986, Ruth Harrison Kenyon (*née* Treanor). *Educ:* Barnard Castle Sch.; King's Coll., Durham Univ. (Open Schol.; BSc); Trinity Hall, Cambridge (Schol. and Prizeman; MA). Joined ICI Billingham Div., 1950; Chemical Engrg Res., 1951; Plant Engr, 1953; Section Manager: Reactor Res., 1955; Process Design, 1959; Gp Man., Catalysts and Chemicals Res., 1963–76. Vis. Prof., Univ. of Bath, 1988–. Chm., Res. Cttee, IChemE. FREng (FEng 1976). Hon. DSc Leeds, 1979. Soc. of Chemical Industry Medal, 1989. *Publications:* Catalyst Handbook, 1970; various papers in chemical engrg, applied chemistry and plant physiology. *Recreations:* archaeology, ancient and medieval history. *Address:* 1 The Wynd, Stainton in Cleveland, Middlesbrough TS8 9BP. *T:* (01642) 596348.

ANDREWS, Baroness *cr* 2000 (Life Peer), of Southover in the co. of East Sussex; **Elizabeth Kay Andrews,** OBE 1998; DPhil; Parliamentary Under-Secretary of State, Department for Communities and Local Government (formerly Office of the Deputy Prime Minister), since 2005; *b* 16 May 1943; *d* of Clifford and Louisa Andrews; *m* 1970, Prof. Roy MacLeod (marr. diss. 1992); one *s*. *Educ:* Univ. of Wales (BA 1964); Univ. of Sussex (MA 1970; DPhil 1975). Res. Fellow, Science Policy Res. Unit, Univ. of Sussex, 1968–70; Res. Clerk, then Sen. Res. Clerk, H of C, 1970–85; Special Advr, Rt Hon. Neil Kinnock, MP, Leader of the Opposition, 1985–92; Dir, Education Extra (nat. charity for out-of-sch. learning), 1992–2002. A Baroness in Waiting (Govt Whip), 2002–05. *Publications:* (with J. B. Poole) The Government of Science, 1972; (with John Jacobs) Punishing the Poor, 1990; Good Practice & Policy for After School, 1997; Extra Learning, 2001; articles in history, science policy and social policy jls. *Recreations:* opera, walking, friends. *Address:* House of Lords, SW1A 0PW.

ANDREWS, Ann; *see* Beynon, A.

ANDREWS, Anthony Peter Hamilton; Chairman, Scottish Country Alliance Educational Trust, since 2003; Executive Director, Atlantic Salmon Trust, since 2008; *b* 23 Dec. 1946; *s* of Col Peter Edward Clinton Andrews and Jean Margaret Hamilton (*née* Cooke); *m* 1973, Alison Margaret Dudley Morgan; one *s* two *d*. *Educ:* King's Sch., Worcester; Univ. of St Andrews (MA); UCNW, Bangor (Dip. TEFL). Served RM, 1964–71. Land agent, 1975–76; with British Council, 1976–2002: Kano, Nigeria, 1976–78; Belgrade, 1979–81; Muscat, Oman, 1981–85; Recife, Brazil, 1985–89; Director: Scotland, 1989–95; Russia and Central Asia, 1996–2000; Germany, 2000–02; Chief Exec., Scottish Countryside Alliance, 2002–08. *Recreations:* angling, river management, sailing, the arts. *Address:* Milton of Finavon House, by Forfar, Angus DD8 3PY. *T:* (01307) 850275; (office) King James VI Building, Friarton Road, Perth PH2 8DG. *T:* (01738) 472032. *Club:* New (Edinburgh).

ANDREWS, David; Member of the Dáil (TD) (FF) for Dún Laoghaire, 1965–2002; Minister for Foreign Affairs, Republic of Ireland, 1997–2000; *b* 15 March 1935; *s* of Christopher Andrews and Mary Coyle; *m* Annette Cusack; two *s* three *d*. *Educ:* Colaiste Mhuire, Christian Brothers' Sch.; Cistercian College, Roscrea; University College Dublin (BCL). Called to the Bar, King's Inns, 1962; Senior Counsel. Parly Sec. to Taoiseach, and Govt Chief Whip, 1970–73; opposition frontbench spokesman on justice and social welfare, 1973–77; Minister of State: Dept of Foreign Affairs, 1977–79; Dept of Justice, 1978–79; Minister: for Foreign Affairs, 1992–93; for Defence and the Marine, 1993–94; opposition spokesman on tourism and trade, 1995–97; Minister for Defence, 1997. Member: Cttee on the Constitution, 1967; New Ireland Forum, 1983–84. Mem., British-Irish Interparly Body, 1990–92. Chevalier, Légion d'Honneur, 2006. *Recreations:* fly fishing, walking, theatre.

ANDREWS, Prof. David John, PhD; FREng, FIMechE; FRINA; Professor of Engineering Design, Department of Mechanical Engineering, University College London, since 2000; *b* 9 Aug. 1947; *m* 1970, Philippa Vanette Whitehurst; one *s* one *d*. *Educ:* Stationers' Co. Sch.; University Coll. London (BSc Eng 1970; MSc 1971; PhD 1984). FRINA 1987; FREng 2000; FIMechE 2002. RCNC Cadetship, 1965; Constructor Lieut, RCNC, 1971; Ministry of Defence: professional design on in-service and new build submarines, Submarine Design Section, Ship Dept, Bath, 1972–75; Constructor Grade, working on Invincible carrier design and subseq. Forward Design Gp, 1975–80; Lectr in Naval Architecture, UCL, 1980–84; Ministry of Defence: Hd, Trident Submarine Hull Design Section, Bath, 1984–86; Hd, Amphibious Gp (Chief Constructor), Replacement Amphibious Shipping Prog., 1986–90; Hd, Concept Design Div., Future Projects (Naval), Whitehall, 1990–93; Prof. of Naval Architecture, UCL, 1993–98; Dir, Frigates and Mine Countermeasures, Defence Procurement Agency, then Integrated Project Team Leader, Future Surface Combatant, MoD, Bristol, 1998–2000. Royal Institution of Naval Architects: Chm., Membership Cttee, 1993–2000; Chm., Future Directions Cttee, 2000–; Vice Pres., 2005–; Mem. Council and Exec. Cttee, 2005–. Mem., Panel 28, 2008 RAE. Freeman, Co. of Engrs, 2007. FRSA 1996. *Publications:* Synthesis in Ship Design (thesis), 1984; (contrib.) Finite Element Methods Applied to Thin Walled Structures, 1987; (contrib.) Technology and Naval Combat in the

Twentieth Century and Beyond, 2001; (contrib.) Ship Design and Construction, 2004; contrib. numerous papers on ship design published by RINA, Royal Soc., etc, and in conf. proc. *Recreations:* painting and sketching, reading, cinema and theatre going, re-exploring London with my wife. *Address:* Department of Mechanical Engineering, University College London, Torrington Place, WC1E 7JE. *T:* (020) 7679 3874; *e-mail:* d_andrews@meng.ucl.ac.uk.

ANDREWS, David Roger Griffith, CBE 1981; Chairman, Gwion Ltd, 1986–95; *b* 27 March 1933; *s* of C. H. R. Andrews and G. M. Andrews; *m* 1963, Dorothy Ann Campbell; two *s* one *d. Educ:* Abingdon Sch.; Pembroke Coll., Oxford (MA). FCMA. Pirelli-General, 1956–59; Ford Motor Company, 1960–69: Controller: Product Engrg, 1965–66; Transmission and Chassis Div., 1967; European Sales Ops, 1967–69; Asst Controller, Ford of Europe, 1969; BLMC: Controller, 1970; Finance Dir, Austin Morris, 1971–72; Man. Dir, Power and Transmission Div., 1973–75; British Leyland Ltd: Man. Dir, Leyland International, 1975–77; Exec. Vice Chm., BL Ltd, 1977–82; Chm., Leyland Gp and Land Rover Gp, 1981–82; Chm. and Chief Exec., Land Rover-Leyland, 1982–86. Director: Clarges Pharmaceutical Trustees Ltd, 1983–91; Glaxo Trustees Ltd, 1983–91; Ex-Cell-O Ltd, 1987–88; Foundn for Sci. and Technology, 1990–95 (Mem. Council, 1990–95, and Hon. Treas., 1990–95; Foundn Medal, 1996). Member: CBI Council, 1981–86; Exec. Cttee, SMMT, 1981–86; Open Univ. Visiting Cttee, 1982–85. FRSA. *Recreation:* reading.

ANDREWS, Sir Derek (Henry), KCB 1991 (CB 1984); CBE 1970; Permanent Secretary, Ministry of Agriculture, Fisheries and Food, 1987–93, retired; Chairman, Residuary Milk Marketing Board, 1994–2002; *b* 17 Feb. 1933; *s* of late Henry Andrews and Emma Jane Andrews; *m* 1st, 1956, Catharine May (*née* Childe) (*d* 1982); two *s* one *d*; 2nd, 1991, Alison Margaret Blackburn, *d* of Sir William Nield, GCMG, KCB. *Educ:* LSE (BA (Hons) 1955). Ministry of Agriculture, Fisheries and Food: Asst Principal, 1957; Asst Private Sec. to Minister of Agriculture, Fisheries and Food, 1960–61; Principal, 1961; Asst Sec., 1968; Private Sec. to Prime Minister, 1966–70; Harvard Univ., USA, 1970–71; Under-Sec., 1973; Dep. Sec., 1981. FRGS. *Clubs:* Reform; Aldeburgh Yacht.

ANDREWS, Finola Mary Lucy; *see* O'Farrell, F. M. L.

ANDREWS, Geraldine Mary; QC 2001; a Recorder, since 2001; a Deputy High Court Judge, since 2006; *b* 19 April 1959; *d* of Walter and Mary Andrews. *Educ:* King's Coll. London (LLB 1st Cl. Hons 1980, LLM 1982; AKC; Dip.). Called to the Bar, Gray's Inn, 1981, Bencher, 2004; barrister, 1983–, specialising in commercial law, esp. banking; called to Irish Bar, 1993. *Publications:* (with S. Gee) Mareva Injunctions, 1988; (with R. Millett) The Law of Guarantees, 1992, 5th edn 2007. *Recreations:* keen violinist, theatre, music, sport, reading, learning modern languages. *Address:* Essex Court Chambers, 24 Lincoln's Inn Fields, WC2A 3EG. *T:* (020) 7813 8000.

ANDREWS, Sir Ian (Charles Franklin), Kt 2007; CBE 1992; TD 1989; Second Permanent Under-Secretary of State, Ministry of Defence, 2002–08; *b* 26 Nov. 1953; *s* of Peter Harry Andrews and Nancy Gwladys Andrews (*née* Franklin); *m* 1985, Moira Fraser McEwan; two *s* one *d. Educ:* Solihull Sch.; Univ. of Bristol (BSc Social Sci.). Joined Ministry of Defence, 1975: Private Sec. to 2nd Perm. Under Sec. of State, 1979–81; short service volunteer commn, RRF, 1981–82; Principal, 1982; NATO Defence Coll., 1984–85; Asst Private Sec. to Sec. of State for Defence, 1986–88; Head: Defence Lands, 1988–90; Resources and Prog. (Army), 1990–93; Civil Sec., British Forces Germany/BAOR, 1993–95; Man. Dir (Facilities), DERA, 1995–97; Chief Exec., Defence Estates Agency, 1998–2002. Served TA in rank of Major, 1972–93. FRGS 1996. *Recreations:* travel, ski-ing.

ANDREWS, Prof. John Albert, CBE 2000; Chairman, Board of Governors and Pro Chancellor, University of Glamorgan, since 2008; *b* 29 Jan. 1935; *s* of late Arthur George Andrews and Hilda May Andrews (*née* Banwell); *m* 1960, Elizabeth Ann Mary Wilkes; two *d. Educ:* Newport High Sch.; Wadham Coll., Oxford (MA, BCL). Called to the Bar, Gray's Inn, 1960, Bencher, 1991. Asst Lectr, Univ. of Manchester, 1957–58; Lectr in English Law, Univ. of Birmingham, 1958–67; University College of Wales, Aberystwyth: Prof. of Law, 1967–92; Hon. Prof., 1992–2000; Emeritus Prof., 2000–; Head of Dept of Law, 1970–92; Vice-Principal, 1985–88. Chief Exec., FEFCW and HEFCW, 1992–2000; Chm., Gen. Teaching Council for Wales, 2000–04. Visiting Professor: Thessaloniki, 1974, 1990; Cracow, 1978; Maryland, 1983. Former chm. or mem., numerous educnl, police and adv. bodies; Member: Police Trng Council, 1987–2002 (Academic Advr, 1997–2002); Lord Chancellor's Adv. Cttee on Legal Educn, 1987–90; Welsh Econ. Council, 1994–96; Criminal Injuries Compensation Appeals Panel, 2000–06; Police Skills and Standards Orgn, 2001–04; Police Accreditation and Licensing Bd, 2002–06; Justice Sector Skills Council, Policing Cttee, 2004–06; Actuarial Profession Disciplinary Panel, 2004–; Chairman: Council of Validating Universities, 1987–90 (Vice Chm., 1982–87); Police Promotions Exams Bd, 1987–2002; Agricl Wages Bd, 1999–2003. Member Council: Cardiff Univ., 2000–; Univ. of Wales Coll. of Medicine, 2000–04; Member, Court of Governors: Univ. of Wales, 1969–92, 2001–04; Nat. Liby of Wales, 1979–92; Member, Board of Governors: Penglais Sch., 1974–80; Llanishen High Sch., 2005–; Mem., Bd of Dirs, Royal Welsh Coll. of Music and Drama, 2006–. Hon. Fellow: Univ. of Wales Coll., Newport, 2000; Cardiff Univ., 2008. Trustee: SLS (formerly SPTL), 1990–2004 (Pres., SPTL, 1988–89); Hamlyn Trust, 1969–2000; AHRB, 2001–05. Mem., Welsh Cttee, NCH, 2004–. FRSA 1992. JP N Ceredigion, 1975–91. Editor, Legal Studies, 1981–93. *Publications:* (ed) Welsh Studies in Public Law, 1970; (ed) Human Rights in Criminal Procedure, 1982; (with L. G. Henshaw) The Welsh Language in the Courts, 1984; (with W. D. Hines) Keyguide to the International Protection of Human Rights, 1987; (with D. M. Hirst) Criminal Evidence, 1987, 3rd edn 1997; Criminal Evidence: statutes and materials, 1990; contribs to legal and educnl books and jls. *Recreations:* walking, theatre, food, opera. *Address:* 7 Maeshendre, Aberystwyth, Ceredigion SY23 3PR. *T:* (01970) 623921; The Croft, 110 Mill Road, Lisvane, Cardiff CF14 0UG. *T:* (029) 2075 3980; Faculty of Law, University of Wales, Hugh Owen Building, Penglais, Aberystwyth, Ceredigion SY23 3DY. *T:* (01970) 622712. *Club:* Brynamlwg (Aberystwyth).

ANDREWS, Rev. John Robert; General Secretary, Professional Association of Teachers, 1992–97 (Assistant General Secretary, 1982–91); Local Minister, Parish of Farewell, Diocese of Lichfield, since 2004; *b* 15 June 1942; *s* of late John Henry Andrews, ERD, MA, FCCA, and Marjorie Andrews (*née* Kirkman); *m* 1966, Minna D. L. Stevenson; two *d. Educ:* Nottingham High Sch.; Nottingham Coll. of Educn (CertEd 1963). ACP 1973; FCollP 1982; DipSMS 1982. Teacher in primary and secondary schs, 1963–72; Headteacher, Birmingham LEA, 1972–81; Professional Association of Teachers: Mem. Council, 1972–81; Chairman: Educn Cttee, 1975–77; Pay and Conditions Cttee, 1977–81. Mem., Council, Managerial and Professional Staffs, later Managerial and Professional Staffs Assoc., 1988–2000 (Pres., 1990–92; Chm., 1997–2000). Mem., Econ. and Social Cttee, EU, 1994–98. Chm., Indep. Unions Trng Council, 1989–96; Vice-Pres., European Confedn of Indep. Trade Unions, 1992–94; Bd Mem., 1994–2002, Treas., 1996–2002, Confédération Européenne des Cadres; Bd Mem. and Treas., Eur. Managers Inst., 2000–02; Chartered Management Institute: Chm., 2001–04, Pres., 2004–, Derby Br.; Mem., Chartered Manager Assessment Panel, 2002–. Mem., Schs Orgn Cttee for Staffordshire, 1999–. Dir, GTC (England & Wales) Trust, 1992–99. Member: Lichfield Deanery Synod, 1970–; Lichfield Diocesan Synod, 1979–2003; Exec. Cttee, Lichfield Diocesan Bd of Finance, 1987–2003; Lichfield Diocesan Bd of Educn, 1998– (Chm. Cttee for Mgt and Finance of Dio. Schs, 1998–; Mem. Exec. Cttee, 2001–); Bishop's Council, 1999–2003; Reader, Lichfield Diocese (Gentleshaw and Farewell), 1967–2004. Ordained deacon, 2004, priest, 2005. Mem., Parish Council, Longdon, Staffs, 1973– (Chm., 1991–93, 2003–06). Governor, Gentleshaw Sch., 1993–97, 1999– (Chm. Govs, 1996–97, 2006–, Vice-Chm., 2004–06). FCMI (FIMgt 1992; MBIM 1982); FRSA 1992. *Publications:* (contrib.) Butterworth's Law of Education, 1997; contribs to various jls on multi-cultural educn, general educnl issues and educn law. *Recreations:* hill walking, foreign travel, listening to music. *Address:* 1 Chaseley Gardens, Burntwood, Staffs WS7 9DJ. *T:* (01543) 674354. *Club:* Royal Commonwealth Society.

ANDREWS, Dame Julie (Elizabeth), DBE 2000; actress; *b* 1 Oct. 1935; *m* 1st, Anthony J. Walton (marr. diss. 1968); one *d*; 2nd, 1969, Blake Edwards; one step *s* one step *d*, and two adopted *d. Educ:* Woodbrook Girls' Sch., Beckenham and private governess. Appeared in The Boy Friend, NY, 1954; My Fair Lady: New York, 1956, London, 1958; Camelot, New York, 1960; Victor/Victoria, New York, 1995; directorial début, The Boy Friend, Bay Street Th., NY, 2003. *Films:* (Walt Disney) Mary Poppins, 1963 (Academy Award, 1964); Americanisation of Emily, 1964; Sound of Music, 1964; Hawaii, 1965; Torn Curtain, 1966; Thoroughly Modern Millie, 1966; Star, 1967; Darling Lili, 1970; The Tamarind Seed, 1973; "10", 1980; Little Miss Marker, 1980; S.O.B., 1981; Victor/Victoria, 1982; The Man Who Loved Women, 1983; Duet for One, 1987; That's Life, 1987; Relative Values, 2000; The Princess Diaries, 2001; The Princess Diaries II, 2004; Shrek II, 2004; Shrek III, 2007; *television:* Cinderella, 1957; Julie & Carol at Carnegie Hall, 1961; An Evening with Julie Andrews and Harry Belafonte, 1969; Julie & Carol at Lincoln Center, 1971; The Julie Andrews Hour, 1972–73 (7 Emmy Awards); Julie & Dick at Covent Garden, 1973–74; Julie & Jackie—How Sweet it is, 1973–74; Julie & Perry & The Muppets, 1973–74; My Favourite Things, 1975; The Puzzle Children, 1976; ABC's Silver Anniversary Celebration, 1978; Julie Andrews… One Step into Spring, 1978; The Sound of Christmas (Emmy Award), 1987; Julie & Carol Together Again, 1989; Great Performances Live in Concert, 1990; Our Sons, 1991; The Julie Show, 1992; One Special Night, 1999; On Golden Pond, 2001; Eloise at the Plaza, 2003; Eloise at Christmastime, 2003. *Publications:* (as Julie Andrews Edwards) Mandy, 1972; Last of the Really Great Whangdoodles, 1973; Little Bo, 1999; Little Bo in France, 2002; (with Emma Walton Hamilton): Dumpy the Dump Truck, 2000; Dumpy at School, 2000; Dumpy Saves Christmas, 2001; Dumpy and the Big Storm, 2002; Dumpy and the Firefighters, 2003; Simeon's Gift, 2003; Dragon, 2004; The Great American Mousical, 2006; Home: a memoir of my early years, 2008. *Recreations:* gardening, boating, writing.

ANDREWS, Prof. Kenneth Raymond, FBA 1986; Professor of History, University of Hull, 1979–88 (part-time, 1986–88), now Emeritus; *b* 26 Aug. 1921; *s* of Arthur Walter and Marion Gertrude Andrews; *m* 1969, Ottilie Kalman, Olomouc, Czechoslovakia; two step *s. Educ:* Henry Thornton Sch., Clapham; King's College London (BA 1948, PhD 1951). Lectr, Univ. of Liverpool, 1963–64; Lectr and Sen. Lectr, Univ. of Hull, 1964–79. *Publications:* English Privateering Voyages to the West Indies, 1959; Elizabethan Privateering, 1964; Drake's Voyages, 1967; The Last Voyage of Drake and Hawkins, 1972; The Spanish Caribbean, 1978; Trade, Plunder and Settlement, 1984; Ships, Money and Politics, 1991; articles in learned jls.

ANDREWS, Leighton Russell; Member (Lab) Rhondda, National Assembly for Wales, since 2003; *b* 11 Aug. 1957; *s* of Len and Peggy Andrews; *m* 1996, Ann Beynon, *qv*; one step *s* one step *d. Educ:* University Coll. of N Wales, Bangor (BA Hons English and Hist.); Univ. of Sussex (MA Hist.). Vice-Pres., NUS, 1980–81; Parly Officer, Age Concern, 1982–84; Campaign Dir, Internat. Year of Shelter, 1984–87; Dir, then Man. Dir, Sallingbury Casey, subseq. Rowland Sallingbury Casey, 1988–93; Hd, Public Affairs, BBC, 1993–96; Chm., Political Context, 1996–99; Dir, then Man. Dir, Westminster Strategy, 1999–2001; Man. Dir, Smart Co., 2001–02; Lectr, Sch. of Journalism, Cardiff Univ., 2002–03. Vis. Prof., Univ. of Westminster, 1997–; Hon. Prof., Cardiff Univ., 2004–. Dep. Minister for Social Justice and Public Service Delivery, 2007, for Regeneration, 2007–, Welsh Assembly Govt. *Publications:* Wales Says Yes, 1999; contrib. various articles and chapters. *Recreations:* watching Cardiff City FC, winding up nationalists, music, cinema, theatre, reading literature, history and political biography. *Address:* National Assembly for Wales, Cardiff Bay, Cardiff CF99 1NA. *T:* (029) 2089 8784, *Fax:* (029) 2089 8299; *e-mail:* leighton.andrews@wales.gov.uk. *Club:* Ferndale Rugby.

ANDREWS, Mark Björnsen; Partner (formerly Deputy Chairman), Denton Wilde Sapte, solicitors, since 2000; *b* 12 July 1952; *s* of Harry Field Andrews and Ruth Margaret Andrews (*née* Legge). *Educ:* Reading Grammar Sch.; Hertford Coll., Oxford (BA Jurisp.). Articled Clerk, Clarks, solicitors, Reading, 1974–76; Wilde Sapte, subseq. Denton Wilde Sapte: Asst Solicitor, 1976–79; Partner, 1979–2000; Head of Insolvency Gp, 1989–2000; Sen. Partner, 1996–2000; Head, Restructuring and Insolvency Gp, 2000–. Trustee, Pimlico Opera, 1991–; Chm. Trustees, Grange Park Opera Endowment Fund, 2005–. *Recreations:* music, history, ornithology, walking. *Address:* Denton Wilde Sapte, 1 Fleet Place, EC4M 7WS. *T:* (020) 7320 6702.

ANDREWS, Nigel John; Film Critic, Financial Times, since 1973; *b* 3 April 1947; *s* of Francis Yardley Andrews and Marguerite Joan Andrews. *Educ:* Lancing Coll., Sussex; Jesus Coll., Cambridge (MA English). Contributor and reviewer, Sight and Sound and Monthly Film Bulletin, 1969–73; Asst Ed., Cinema One books and Sight and Sound mag., 1972–73; regular broadcaster, BBC Radio; writer and presenter, Kaleidoscope, Radio 4, and other arts programmes, 1975–. Mem., BFI, 1971–. Critic of Year, British Press Awards, 1985, 2002. FRSA 2002. *Publications:* (contrib.) The Book of the Cinema, 1979; Horror Films, 1985; True Myths: the life and times of Arnold Schwarzenegger, 1995; Travolta: the life, 1998; Jaws, 1999. *Address:* c/o Curtis Brown, Haymarket House, 28–29 Haymarket, SW1Y 4SP.

ANDREWS, Peter John; QC 1991; a Recorder of the Crown Court, since 1990; a Deputy High Court Judge, Queen's Bench Division, since 1998; *b* 14 Nov. 1946; *s* of Reginald and Dora Andrews; *m* 1976, Ann Chavasse; two *d. Educ:* Bishop Vesey Grammar Sch.; Bristol Univ. (Undergraduate Scholar; LLB); Christ's Coll., Cambridge (DCrim). Called to the Bar, Lincoln's Inn (Hardwicke Scholar), 1970, Bencher, 1999; barrister specialising in catastrophic personal injury and clinical negligence litigation; Junior, Midland and Oxford Circuit, 1973–74; Asst Recorder, 1986–90. Chm., Fountain Court Chambers (Birmingham) Ltd, 1994–2004; Head of Chambers, 199 Strand, 1997–2000. Mem., Professional Conduct Cttee, GMC, 2001–; Legal Mem., Mental Health Rev. Tribunals, 2007–. Contributing Ed. and Mem., Editl Bd, The Quantum of Damages, 2004–. *Publications:* Catastrophic Injuries: a guide to compensation, 1997; (contrib.)

Personal Injury Handbook, 1997, 3rd edn 2005; (contrib.) Kemp and Kemp, The Quantum of Damages, 1998–. *Address:* 7 Bedford Row, WC1R 4BS.

ANDREWS, Robert Graham M.; *see* Marshall-Andrews.

ANDREWS, Rt Rev. Rodney Osborne; *see* Saskatoon, Bishop of.

ANDREWS, Stuart Morrison; Head Master of Clifton College, 1975–90; *b* 23 June 1932; *s* of William Hannaford Andrews and Eileen Elizabeth Andrews; *m* 1962, Marie Elizabeth van Wyk; two *s. Educ:* Newton Abbot Grammar Sch.; St Dunstan's Coll.; Sidney Sussex Coll., Cambridge (MA). Nat. service with Parachute Bde, 1952–53. Sen. History Master and Librarian, St Dunstan's Coll., 1956–60; Chief History Master and Librarian, Repton Sch., 1961–67; Head Master, Norwich Sch., 1967–75. Chm., Direct-grant Sub-cttee, HMC, 1974–75; Dep. Chm., Assisted Places Cttee, 1982–91; Nat. Rep., HMC, 1987–89; HMC Lead Inspector of Schs, 1994–96. Trustee, Glastonbury Abbey Develt Trust, 1992–96; Chm. Trustees and Managers, Wells & Mendip Mus., 1999–2004. Chm., Emmott Foundn, 1999–2006. Editor, Conference, 1972–82. *Publications:* Eighteenth-century Europe, 1965; Enlightened Despotism, 1967; Methodism and Society, 1970; Rediscovery of America, 1998; British Periodical Press and the French Revolution, 2000; Unitarian Radicalism: political rhetoric 1770–1814, 2003; Irish Rebellion: Protestant polemic 1798–1900, 2006; articles in various historical jls. *Recreations:* walking, writing. *Address:* 34 St Thomas Street, Wells, Somerset BA5 2UX.

ANDREWS, William Denys Cathcart, CBE 1980; WS; Partner, Shepherd & Wedderburn, WS, Edinburgh, 1962–91; *b* 3 June 1931; *s* of Eugene Andrews and Agnes Armstrong; *m* 1955, May O'Beirne; two *s* two *d. Educ:* Girvan High Sch.; Worksop Coll.; Edinburgh Univ. (BL). Served RASC, 1950–52. Law Society of Scotland: Mem. Council, 1972–81; Vice Pres., 1977–78; Pres., 1978–79. Examr in Conveyancing, Edinburgh Univ., 1974–77. Pt-time Mem., Lands Tribunal for Scotland, 1980–91. Fiscal to Soc. of Writers to HM Signet, 1987–91. *Recreation:* gardening. *Address:* Auchairne, Ballantrae, South Ayrshire KA26 0NX. *T:* (01465) 831344.

ANDRIESSEN, Prof. Frans, (Franciscus H. J. J.), Kt, Order of Dutch Lion; Grand Cross, Order of Orange-Nassau; LLD; Member, 1981–92, Vice-President, 1985–92, the European Commission (responsible for external relations); *b* Utrecht, 2 April 1929; *m*; four *c. Educ:* Univ. of Utrecht (LLD). Served at Catholic Housing Institute, latterly as Director, 1954–72. Member: Provincial States of Utrecht, 1958–67; Lower House of the States-General (Netherlands Parliament), initially as specialist in housing matters, 1967–77; Chairman, KVP party in Lower House, 1971–77; Minister of Finance, Netherlands, 1977–80; Member, Upper House of States-General (Senate), 1980. Prof. of European Integration, Rijksuniversiteit, Utrecht, 1989–99, now Emeritus. Grand Cross: Order of Leopold II (Belgium); Order of Isabel the Catholic (Spain); Order of Merit (Austria); Order of the Falcon (Iceland); Order of the Finnish Lion (Finland). *Address:* H. Vaesgaarde 1, 1950 Kraainem, Belgium.

ANDRUS, Francis Sedley, LVO 1982; Beaumont Herald of Arms Extraordinary, since 1982; *b* 26 Feb. 1915; *o s* of late Brig.-Gen. Thomas Alchin Andrus, CMG, JP, and Alice Loveday (*née* Parr); unmarried. *Educ:* Wellington Coll.; St Peter's Hall (now Coll.), Oxford (MA). Entered College of Arms as Member of Staff, 1938; Bluemantle Pursuivant of Arms, 1970–72; Lancaster Herald of Arms, 1972–82. Freeman, City of London, 1988. Lord of the Manor of Southfleet, Kent, 1952–. *Address:* 8 Oakwood Rise, Longfield, Kent DA3 7PA. *T:* (01474) 705424.

ANELAY OF ST JOHNS, Baroness *cr* 1996 (Life Peer), of St Johns in the county of Surrey; **Joyce Anne Anelay,** DBE 1995 (OBE 1990); JP; *b* 17 July 1947; *d* of late Stanley Charles Clarke and of Annette Marjorie Clarke; *m* 1970, Richard Alfred Anelay, *qv. Educ:* Merryhills Primary Sch., Enfield; Enfield Co. Sch.; Bristol Univ. (BA Hons Hist.); London Univ. Inst. of Educn (Cert Ed); Brunel Univ. (MA Public and Social Admin). Teacher, St David's Sch., Ashford, Middx, 1969–74; Voluntary Advr, Woking CAB, 1976–85 (Chm., 1988–93; Pres., 1996–). Member: Social Security Appeal Tribunal, 1983–96; Social Security Adv. Cttee for GB and NI, 1989–96. Opposition spokesman on agriculture, 1997–98, on culture, media and sport, 1998–2002, on Home Affairs, 2002–07; an Opposition Whip, 1997–98, Opposition Chief Whip, 2007–, H of L. Mem., Procedure Cttee, 1997–2000, 2007–. Conservative Women's Committee: Chm., SE Area, 1987–90; Vice-Chm., SE Area Exec. Cttee, 1990–93; Chm., Nat. Cttee, 1993–96; Member: Nat. Union of Cons. Party, 1987–97 (Vice-Pres., 1996–97); Women's Nat. Commission, 1990–93. Trustee: UNICEF UK, 2004–07; Just a Drop, 2004–06. JP NW Surrey, 1985–97. Chm. Govs, Hermitage First and Middle Schs, 1981–88. FRSA 1991. Hon. DSocSc Brunel, 1997. *Recreations:* golf, reading. *Address:* House of Lords, SW1A 0PW. *Club:* Woking Golf.

ANELAY, Richard Alfred; QC 1993; a Recorder, since 1992; a Deputy High Court Judge, Family Division, since 1995; *b* 26 March 1946; *s* of late Maurice Alfred Anelay and Bertha Anelay; *m* 1970, Joyce Anne Clarke (*see* Baroness Anelay of St Johns). *Educ:* Dodmire Primary Sch., Darlington; Queen Elizabeth Grammar Sch., Darlington; Bristol Univ. (BA Classics and Philosophy); Council of Legal Educn. Called to the Bar, Middle Temple, 1970, Bencher, 2003; Asst Recorder, 1987. Hd of Chambers, 2006–. Dir, Bar Mutual Indemnity Fund, 2005–. Consulting Ed., Encyclopedia of Financial Provision in Family Matters, 1998–. *Recreation:* golf. *Address:* 1 King's Bench Walk, Temple, EC4Y 7DB. *T:* (020) 7936 1500. *Club:* Woking Golf.

ANFOM, Emmanuel E.; *see* Evans-Anfom.

ANGEL, Anthony Lionel; Head of Europe, Middle East and Africa, Standard & Poor's, since 2008; *b* 3 Dec. 1952; *s* of William and Frances Angel; *m* 1975, Ruth Hartog; two *s. Educ:* Haberdashers' Aske's Sch., Elstree; Queens' Coll., Cambridge (MA). Admitted Solicitor, 1978. Linklaters: Articled Clerk, 1976; Partner, 1984–2008; Head of Tax, 1994–98; Man. Partner, 1998–2007. *Recreations:* ski-ing, tennis, theatre. *Address:* Standard & Poor's, 20 Canada Square, E14 5LH.

ANGEL, Gerald Bernard Nathaniel Aylmer; Senior District Judge, Family Division of the High Court, 1991–2004 (Registrar, 1980–90; District Judge, 1991); *b* 4 Nov. 1937; *s* of late Bernard Francis and Ethel Angel; *m* 1968, Lesley Susan Kemp; three *s* one *d* (and one *s* decd). *Educ:* St Mary's Sch., Nairobi. Served Kenya Regt, 1956–57. Called to Bar, Inner Temple, 1959, Bencher 1992; Advocate, Kenya, 1960–62; practice at Bar, 1962–80. Member: Judicial Studies Bd, 1989–90 (Mem., Civil and Family Cttee, 1985–90); Supreme Ct Procedure Cttee, 1990–95; Matrimonial Causes Rule Cttee, 1991; Family Proceedings Rule Cttee, 1991–2003. *Publications:* (ed) Industrial Tribunals Reports, 1966–78; (contrib.) Atkin's Court Forms (Adv. Editor), 1988–2003. *Recreations:* reading, walking. *Address:* Garden House, 12 Aylsham Road, North Walsham, Norfolk NR28 0BH. *T:* (01692) 402401.

ANGEL, Heather, FRPS, FBIPP; professional wildlife photographer, author and lecturer; *b* 21 July 1941; *d* of Stanley Paul Le Rougetel and Hazel Marie Le Rougetel (*née* Sherwood); *m* 1964, Martin Vivian Angel; one *s. Educ:* 14 schools in England and NZ; Bristol Univ. (BSc Hons (Zoology) 1962; MSc 1965). FRPS 1972; FBIPP 1974. One-man Exhibitions: The Natural History of Britain and Ireland, Sci. Mus., 1981; Nature in Focus, Natural Hist. Mus., 1987; The Art of Wildlife Photography, Gloucester, 1989; Natural Visions, UK tour, 2000–04, Cairo, 2002, Kuala Lumpur, 2002, Beijing, 2003. Television: demonstrating photographic techniques, Me and My Camera I, 1981; Me and My Camera II, 1983; Gardener's World, 1983; Nature, 1984; Nocon on Photography, 1988. Led British Photographic Delegn to China, 1985. Photos used worldwide in books, magazines, on TV, advertising, etc, 1972–. Special Prof., Dept of Life Sci., Nottingham Univ., 1994–. Hon. FRPS 1986 (Pres., 1984–86). Hon. DSc Bath, 1986. Hood Medal, RPS, 1975; Médaille de Salverte, Soc. Française de Photographie, 1984; Louis Schmidt Award, Biocommunications Assoc., 1998. *Publications:* Nature Photography: its art and techniques, 1972; All Colour Book of Ocean Life, 1975; Photographing Nature: Trees, 1975, Insects, 1975, Seashore, 1975, Flowers, 1975, Fungi, 1975; Seashore Life on Rocky Shores, 1975; Seashore Life on Sandy Beaches, 1975; Seashells of the Seashore, 1976; Wild Animals in the Garden, 1976; Life in the Oceans, 1977; Life in our Estuaries, 1977; Life in our Rivers, 1977; British Wild Orchids, 1977; The Countryside of the New Forest, 1977; The Countryside of South Wales, 1977; Seaweeds of the Seashore, 1977; Seashells of the Seashore, Book 1, 1978, Book 2, 1978; The Countryside of Devon, 1980; The Guinness Book of Seashore Life, 1981; The Natural History of Britain and Ireland, 1981; The Family Water Naturalist, 1982; The Book of Nature Photography, 1982; The Book of Close-up Photography, 1983; Heather Angel's Countryside, 1983; A Camera in the Garden, 1984; Close-up Photography, 1986; Kodak Calendar, The Thames, 1987; A View from a Window, 1988; Nature in Focus, 1988; Landscape Photography, 1989; Animal Photography, 1991; Kew: a world of plants, 1993; Photographing the Natural World, 1994; Outdoor Photography: 101 tips and hints, 1997; How to Photograph Flowers, 1998; Pandas, 1998; How to Photograph Water, 1999; Natural Visions, 2000; Giant Pandas, 2006; Puffins, 2007; *for children:* Your Book of Fishes, 1972; The World of an Estuary, 1975; Fact Finder—Seashore, 1976; The World of a Stream, 1976; Fungi, 1979; Lichens, 1980; Mosses and Ferns, 1980. *Recreation:* travelling to remote parts of the world to photograph wilderness areas and unusual aspects of animal behaviour. *Fax:* (01252) 727464; *web:* www.heatherangel.co.uk.

ANGEL, Prof. James Roger Prior, FRS 1990; Regents Professor of Astronomy, since 1990, Director, Steward Observatory Mirror Laboratory, since 1985, and Director, Center for Astronomical Adaptative Optics, since 1996, University of Arizona; *b* 7 Feb. 1941; *s* of James Lee Angel and Joan Angel; *m* 1965, Ellinor M. Goonan; one *s* one *d. Educ:* St Peter's Coll., Oxford (Hon. Schol.; BA 1963; Hon. Fellow, 1993); Calif. Inst. of Technology (MS 1966); DPhil Oxon 1967. FRAS 1993. Post Doctoral Assistant, then Asst Prof., later Associate Prof. of Physics, Columbia Univ., 1967–72; Alfred P. Sloan Res. Fellow, 1970–74; Associate Prof. and Prof. of Astronomy, Arizona Univ., 1973–90. MacArthur Fellow, John D. and Catherine T. MacArthur Foundn, 1996–2001. Vice-Pres., Amer. Astronomical Soc., 1987–90 (Pierce Prize, 1976); Fellow, Amer. Acad. of Arts and Scis, 1990. MNAS 2000. *Publications:* numerous papers on white dwarf stars, quasars, the search for extra-solar planetary systems, astronomical mirrors, telescopes and their instruments, and adaptive optics. *Recreation:* planting trees. *Address:* Steward Observatory, University of Arizona, Tucson, AZ 85721–0065, USA. *T:* (520) 6216541.

ANGELOU, Marguerite Annie, (Maya); writer, singer and actress; *b* St Louis, 4 April 1928; *d* of Bailey Johnson and Vivian Baxter Johnson; one *s. Educ:* George Washington High Sch., San Francisco; California Labor Sch. Yale Univ. Fellowship, 1970; Rockefeller Foundn Scholar, 1975; Reynolds Prof. of Amer. Studies, Wake Forest Univ., 1981–. Writer, director, or actor: *stage:* Cabaret for Freedom, 1960; Medea, 1966; The Least of These, 1966; Gettin' Up Stayed On My Mind, 1967; Ajax, 1974; And Still I Rise, 1976; Look Away, 1975; Moon and Rainbow Shawl, 1988; *films:* Georgia, Georgia, 1972; All Day Long, 1974; Poetic Justice, 1993; How to Make an American Quilt, 1996; *television:* Black, Blue, Black, 1968; Roots, 1977; Sister, Sister, 1982. Awards include: Amer. Revolution Bicentennial, 1975; Woman of the Year in Communications, 1976; Horatio Alger, 1992. *Publications: autobiography:* I Know Why the Caged Bird Sings, 1970 (televised, 1979); Gather Together in My Name, 1974; Singin' and Swingin' and Gettin' Merry Like Christmas, 1976; The Heart of a Woman, 1981; All God's Children Need Travelling Shoes, 1986; Wouldn't Take Nothing for my Journey Now, 1993; (jtly) My Painted House, My Friendly Chicken and Me, 1994; A Song Flung to Heaven, 2002; Hallelujah! the Welcome Table, 2005; *essays:* Lessons in Life, 1993; *poetry:* Just Give Me a Cool Drink of Water 'Fore I Diiie, 1971; Oh Pray My Wings are Gonna Fit Me Well, 1975; Shaker, Why Don't You Sing?, 1983; Now Sheba Sings the Song, 1987; I shall not be Moved, 1990; On the Pulse of Morning, 1993 (delivered personally at Presidential Inauguration); Complete Collected Poems of Maya Angelou, 1995; Amazing Peace, 2005; *fiction:* Even the Stars Look Lonesome, 1998; *short stories:* All Day Long. *Address:* c/o Dave La Camera, Lordly and Dame Inc., 51 Church Street, Boston, MA 02116–5417, USA.

ANGIOLINI, Rt Hon. Elish Frances; PC 2006; Lord Advocate, Scottish Government (formerly Scottish Executive), since 2006; *b* 24 June 1960; *d* of James McPhilomy and Mary McPhilomy (*née* Magill); *m* 1985, Domenico Angiolini; two *s. Educ:* Notre Dame Sch., Glasgow; Univ. of Strathclyde (LLB Hons; DipLP). Admitted solicitor, 1985; Depute Procurator Fiscal, Airdrie; Mgt Services Gp, Crown Office; Sen. Depute Procurator Fiscal, Asst Procurator Fiscal 1995–97, Glasgow; with Crown Office, 1997–2000; Regl Procurator Fiscal, Grampian, Highlands and Is, 2000–01; QC (Scot.) 2001; Solicitor Gen. for Scotland, 2001–06. *Recreations:* walking, picking wild mushrooms, cinema, eating out. *Address:* Crown Office, 25 Chambers Street, Edinburgh EH1 1LA. *T:* (0131) 247 2665.

ANGLESEY, 7th Marquess of, *cr* 1815; **George Charles Henry Victor Paget;** Baron Paget, of Beau Desert, 1549; Earl of Uxbridge, 1784; Bt 1730; Lord-Lieutenant of Gwynedd, 1983–89; *b* 8 Oct. 1922; *o s* of 6th Marquess of Anglesey, GCVO, and Lady Victoria Marjorie Harriet Manners (*d* 1946), *d* of 8th Duke of Rutland; *S* father, 1947; *m* 1948, Elizabeth Shirley Vaughan Morgan (*see* Marchioness of Anglesey); two *s* three *d. Educ:* Wixenford, Wokingham; Eton Coll. Major, RHG, 1946. Div. Dir, Wales, Nationwide Building Soc., 1973–89. President: Anglesey Conservative Assoc., 1948–83; Nat. Museum of Wales, 1962–68; Friends of Friendless Churches, 1966–84; Ancient Monuments Soc., 1979–84. Treasurer, Danilo Dolci Trust (Britain), 1964–86. Vice-Chm., Welsh Cttee, Nat. Trust, 1975–85; Member: Historic Buildings Council for Wales, 1953–92 (Chm., 1977–92); Royal Fine Art Commn, 1965–71; Redundant Churches Fund, 1969–78; Royal Commn on Historical Manuscripts, 1984–92; Council, Soc. of Army Historical Research; Trustee: Nat. Portrait Gall., 1979–91; Nat. Heritage Memorial Fund, 1980–92. Hon. Prof., UCW, 1986. FSA 1952; FRSL 1969; Hon. FRIBA, 1971; FRHistS, 1975. Anglesey: CC, 1951–67; JP, 1959–68, 1983–89; DL, 1960, Vice-Lieut, 1960. Hon. Fellow, Royal Cambrian Acad. Freeman of the City of London. Hon. DLitt Wales, 1984. Octavia Hill Bronze Medal, Nat. Trust, 2002. CStJ 1984. *Publications:* (ed) The Capel Letters, 1814–1817, 1955; One-Leg: the Life and Letters of 1st Marquess of Anglesey, 1961, repr. 1996; (ed) Sergeant Pearman's Memoirs, 1968; (ed) Little Hodge, 1971; A History of the British Cavalry 1816–1919 (Chesney Gold Medal, RUSI, 1997):

vol. I, 1816–1850, 1973; vol. II, 1851–1871, 1975; vol. III, 1872–1898, 1982 (Templer Medal, Nat. Army Mus., 1982); vol. IV, 1899–1913, 1986; vol. V, 1914–1919: Egypt, Palestine and Syria, 1995; vol. VI, 1914–1918: Mesopotamia, 1996; vol. VII, 1914: The Curragh Incident and the Western Front, 1996; vol. VIII, The Western Front, 1915–1918, and Epilogue, 1919–1939, 1997. *Recreations:* gardening, music. *Heir: s* Earl of Uxbridge, *qv. Address:* Plâs-Newydd, Llanfairpwll, Anglesey LL61 6DZ. *T:* (01248) 714330.

ANGLESEY, Marchioness of; (Elizabeth) Shirley Vaughan Paget, DBE 1983 (CBE 1977); LVO 1993; Member of Board, British Council, 1985–95 (Chairman, Drama and Dance Advisory Committee, 1981–91); Vice-Chairman, Museums and Galleries Commission, 1989–96 (Member, 1981–96); *b* 4 Dec. 1924; *d* of late Charles Morgan and Hilda Vaughan (both novelists); *m* 1948, Marquess of Anglesey, *qv;* two *s* three *d. Educ:* Francis Holland Sch., London; St James', West Malvern; Kent Place Sch., USA. Personal Secretary to Gladwyn Jebb, FO, until marriage. Chm., Broadcasting Complaints Commn, 1987–91. Dep. Chm., Prince of Wales Cttee, 1970–80. Member: Civic Trust for Wales, 1967–76; Arts Council, 1972–81 (Chm., Welsh Arts Council, 1975–81); Royal Commn on Environmental Pollution, 1973–79; IBA, 1976–82; Radioactive Waste Management Adv. Cttee, 1981–92; Vice-Chm., Govt Working Party on Methods of Sewage Disposal, 1969–70. Chm., NFWI, 1966–69. A Vice-Pres., C&G, 1998– (Hon. FCGI 2003). Mem., Theatres Trust, 1992–95. Trustee, Pilgrim Trust, 1982–2001. Hon. Fellow, UCNW, Bangor, 1990. Hon. LLD Wales, 1977. *Address:* Plâs-Newydd, Llanfairpwll, Gwynedd LL61 6DZ. *T:* (01248) 714330.

See also R. H. V. C. Morgan.

ANGLIN, Prof. Douglas (George); Professor of Political Science, Carleton University, Ottawa, Canada, 1958–89, Adjunct Research Professor, 1989–93, Professor Emeritus, since 1993; *b* Toronto, Canada, 16 Dec. 1923; *s* of George Chambers Anglin, MD, and Ruth Cecilia Cale, MD; *m* 1948, Mary Elizabeth Watson; two *d. Educ:* Toronto Univ.; Corpus Christi and Nuffield Colls, Oxford Univ. BA Toronto; MA, DPhil Oxon. Lieut, RCNVR, 1943–45. Asst (later Associate) Prof. of Political Sci. and Internat. Relations, Univ. of Manitoba, Winnipeg, 1951–58; Associate Prof. (later Prof.), Carleton Univ., 1958–89. Vice-Chancellor, Univ. of Zambia, Lusaka, Zambia, 1965–69; Associate Research Fellow, Nigerian Inst. of Social and Economic Research, Univ. of Ibadan, Ibadan, Nigeria, 1962–63; Research Associate, Center of Internat. Studies, Princeton Univ., 1969–70. Canadian Association of African Studies: Pres., 1973–74; Distinguished Africanist Schol., 1989. Consultant, Educn for Democracy Prog., South African Council of Churches, Johannesburg, 1992–94. *Publications:* The St Pierre and Miquelon Affaire of 1941: a study in diplomacy in the North Atlantic quadrangle, 1966, repr. 1999; Zambia's Foreign Policy: studies in diplomacy and dependence, 1979; Zambian Crisis Behaviour: confronting Rhodesia's unilateral declaration of independence 1965–1966, 1994; Confronting Rwandan Genocide: the military options, 2002; edited jointly: Africa: Problems and Prospects 1961; Conflict and Change in Southern Africa, 1978; Canada, Scandinavia and Southern Africa, 1978; articles on Internat. and African affairs in a variety of learned jls. *Address:* Carleton University, 1125 Colonel By Drive, Ottawa, Ontario K1S 5B6, Canada.

ANGLO, Margaret Mary, (Mrs Sydney Anglo); *see* McGowan, M. M.

ANGLO, Prof. Sydney, PhD; FBA 2005; Professor of the History of Ideas, 1981–86, Research Professor, 1986–99, now Professor Emeritus, University of Wales Swansea (formerly University College of Swansea); *b* 1 March 1934; *s* of Harry Anglo and Ray (*née* Pelter); *m* 1964, Margaret Mary McGowan, *qv. Educ:* Pinner Co. Grammar Sch.; London Sch. of Economics (BA 1955; PhD 1959). Sen. Res. Fellow, Univ. of Reading, 1958–61; Lectr in the Hist. of Ideas, 1961–69, Sen. Lectr, 1969–75, Reader, 1975–81, UC of Swansea. Sen. Fellow, Warburg Inst., 1970–71. Mem., Adv. Cttee, Ref. Div., BL, 1975–84. Sec., 1967–70, Chm., 1986–89, Soc. for Renaissance Studies. FSA 1965. Numerous contribs to BBC Radio; features include: The Leonardo Cylinders, 1989; The Big Fight Fiasco of 1467, 1992; Piping the Blues, 1992; The Great Snooker Final, 1994; Great Spy, Lousy Tapdancer, 1996; Cheese, 1997. Arms and Armour Soc. Medal, 2002. *Publications:* The Great Tournament Roll of Westminster, 1968; Spectacle, Pageantry and Early Tudor Policy, 1969, 2nd edn 1997; Machiavelli, a Dissection, 1969; La tryumphante Entrée de Charles Prince des Espargnes, 1974; (ed) The Damned Art: essays in the literature of witchcraft, 1977; (ed) Chivalry in the Renaissance, 1990; Images of Tudor Kingship, 1992; The Martial Arts of Renaissance Europe, 2000; Machiavelli - the First Century: studies in enthusiasm, hostility and irrelevance, 2005; numerous contribs to learned jls, periodicals and collaborative vols. *Recreations:* telephone conversation with friends, listening to and reading about pianists past and present. *Address:* 59 Green Ridge, Brighton BN1 5LU. *Club:* East India.

ANGUS, Sir Michael (Richardson), Kt 1990; DL; Chairman, Whitbread PLC, 1992–2000 (Director, 1986–2000; Deputy Chairman, 1992); Deputy Chairman, The Boots Company PLC, 1998–2000 (Chairman, 1994–98); *b* 5 May 1930; *s* of William Richardson Angus and Doris Margaret Breach; *m* 1952, Eileen Isabel May Elliott; two *s* one *d. Educ:* Marling Sch., Stroud, Glos; Bristol Univ. (BSc Hons; Hon. Fellow, 1998). CCMI (CBIM 1979). Served RAF, 1951–54. Unilever, 1954–92: Marketing Dir, Thibaud Gibbs, Paris, 1962–65; Man. Dir, Res. Bureau, 1965–67; Sales Dir, Lever Brothers UK, 1967–70; Toilet Preparations Co-ordinator, 1970–76; Chemicals Co-ordinator, 1976–80; Regional Dir, N America, 1979–84; Chairman and Chief Executive Officer: Unilever United States, Inc., New York, 1980–84; Lever Brothers Co., New York, 1980–84; Chm., Unilever PLC, 1986–92 (Dir, 1970–92; Vice Chm., 1984–86); Vice Chm., Unilever NV, 1986–92 (Dir, 1970–92). Dir, Nat. Westminster Bank, 1991–2000 (a Dep. Chm., 1991–94); Chm., RAC Holdings Ltd, 1999; Jt Dep. Chm., 1989–93, Dep. Chm., 1993–2000, British Airways (Dir, 1988–2000); non-executive Director: Thorn EMI plc, 1988–93; Halcrow Gp Ltd, 2000–06. Jt Chm., Netherlands-British Chamber of Commerce, 1984–89; Internat. Counsellor, The Conference Board, 1984–96, Emeritus, 1996. Pres., CBI, 1992–94 (Dep. Pres., 1991–92, 1994–95). Vis. Fellow, Nuffield Coll., Oxford, 1986–92. Dir, Ditchley Foundn, 1994–. Trustee, Leverhulme Trust, 1984– (Chm. Trustees, 1999–). Chairman of Governors: Ashridge Management Coll., 1991–2002 (Governor, 1974–2002; Pres., 2002–); RAC, Cirencester, 1992–2006 (Vice Pres., 2006–); Mem. Court of Govs, LSE, 1985–95. DL Gloucestershire, 1997. Hon. DSc: Bristol, 1990; Buckingham, 1994; Hon. LLD Nottingham, 1996. Holland Trade Award, 1990. Comdr, Order of Oranje-Nassau (Netherlands), 1992. *Recreations:* countryside, wine, mathematical puzzles. *Address:* Cerney House, North Cerney, Cirencester, Glos GL7 7BX. *Clubs:* Athenæum, Brooks's; University (New York).

ANGUS, Robert James Campbell; Social Security and Child Support Commissioner, 1995–2007; *b* 7 Feb. 1935; *s* of James Angus and Jessie Macrae Angus; *m* 1968, Jean Anne Martin. *Educ:* Shawlands Acad.; Univ. of Glasgow (BL 1957). Nat. service, RA, 1958–60. Admitted solicitor, Scotland, 1960; in private practice, 1960–71; Legal Asst, Office of Solicitor to Sec. of State for Scotland, 1972–74, Sen. Legal Asst, 1974; on secondment as Administrator, SHHD, 1974–78; Solicitor's Office, 1978–82; Inquiry Reporter, Scottish Office, 1982–84; Chairman: Social Security, Medical and Vaccine Damage Appeal Tribunals, 1984–95; Child Support Appeal Tribunals, 1992–95. *Recreations:* history, music, history and mechanics of pianos, rough gardening. *Address:* Hunter Gap, Keenley, Allendale, Northumberland NE47 9NT. *Clubs:* Royal Scots (Edinburgh); Glasgow Art (Glasgow).

ANHOLT, Trudy Frances Charlene; *see* Mackay, T. F. C.

ANNALY, 6th Baron *cr* 1863; **Luke Richard White;** a Lord in Waiting (Government Whip), 1994; *b* 29 June 1954; *o s* of 5th Baron Annaly and Lady Marye Isabel Pepys (*d* 1958), *d* of 7th Earl of Cottenham; *S* father, 1990; *m* 1983, Caroline Nina, *yr d* of Col Robert Garnett, MBE; one *s* three *d. Educ:* Eton; RMA Sandhurst. Commnd Royal Hussars, 1974–78, RARO, 1978–86. Freeman, Haberdashers' Co., 1997. *Heir: s* Hon. Luke Henry White, *b* 20 Sept. 1990.

ANNAN, Kofi Atta, Hon. GCMG 2007; President, Global Humanitarian Forum, since 2007; Secretary-General, United Nations, 1997–2006; *b* 1938; *m;* one *s* two *d. Educ:* Univ. of Sci. and Technol., Kumasi, Ghana; Macalester Coll., St Paul, Minnesota, USA; Institut des Hautes Etudes Internationales, Geneva, Switzerland; MIT (Alfred P. Sloan Fellow, 1971–72). Various posts in UN, Addis Ababa and NY, and WHO, Geneva, 1962–71; Admin. Officer, UN, Geneva, 1972–74; Chief Civilian Personnel Officer, UNEF, Cairo, 1974; Man. Dir, Ghana Tourist Develt Co., 1974–76; Dep. Chief of Staff Services, 1976–80, Dep. Dir, Div. of Admin and Hd, Personnel Service, 1980–83, UNHCR, Geneva; UN, New York: Dir of Admin Mgt Services, then of Budget, 1984–87; Asst Sec.-Gen., Human Resources Mgt, 1987–90; Controller, Programme Planning, Budget and Finance, 1990–92; Under Sec.-Gen., 1993–95, Dept of Peace Keeping Ops; UN Special Envoy to former Yugoslavia, 1995–96. Hon. DCL Oxford, 2001. Nobel Peace Prize, 2001. *Publication:* (with Elie Wiesel) Confronting Anti-Semitism (essays), 2006. *Address:* c/o Global Humanitarian Forum, Villa Rigot, Avenue de la Paix 9, 1202 Geneva, Switzerland.

ANNAND, John Angus; Under Secretary, Welsh Office, 1975–85; *b* 13 May 1926; *s* of James Annand and Lilias Annand (*née* Smith); *m* 1971, Julia Dawn Hardman (marr. diss. 1986). *Educ:* Hillhead High Sch., Glasgow; Glasgow Univ. (MA, 1st Cl. Hons); Brasenose Coll., Oxford (MLitt). Lecturer: Univ. of Ceylon; Univ. of South Australia, 1951–53; Asst Dir, Civil Service Commn, 1953–57; Principal, 1957, Asst Sec., 1967, HM Treasury; Civil Service Dept, 1968; Welsh Office, 1971; Under Sec., Health and Social Work Dept, Welsh Office, 1975; Economic Policy Gp, 1978. Mem., GMC, 1986–90. *Address:* 21 Fairwater Road, Llandaff, Cardiff CF5 2LD.

ANNANDALE AND HARTFELL, 11th Earl of, *cr* 1662 (S) with precedence to 1643; **Patrick Andrew Wentworth Hope Johnstone of Annandale and of that Ilk;** Earl of the territorial earldom of Annandale and Hartfell, and of the Lordship of Johnstone; Hereditary Steward of the Stewartry of Annandale; Hereditary Keeper of the Castle of Lochmaben; Chief of the Name and Arms of Johnstone; landowner; Vice-Lord Lieutenant, Dumfries and Galloway Region, districts of Nithsdale, Annandale and Eskdale, since 1992; *b* 19 April 1941; *s* of Major Percy Wentworth Hope Johnstone of Annandale and of that Ilk, TD (*d* 1983) (*de jure* 10th Earl) and Margaret Jane (*d* 1998), *d* of Herbert William Francis Hunter-Arundell; claim to earldom admitted by Committee for Privileges, House of Lords, 1985; *m* 1969, Susan Josephine, *d* of late Col Walter John Macdonald Ross, CB, OBE, MC, TD, Netherhall, Castle Douglas; one *s* one *d. Educ:* Stowe School; RAC, Cirencester. Member: Dumfries CC, 1970–75; Dumfries and Galloway Regional Council, 1974–86; Scottish Valuation Advisory Council, 1983–85. Director: Bowring Members Agency, 1985–88; Murray Lawrence Members Agency, 1988–92; Solway River Purification Bd, 1970–86; Chm., Royal Jubilee and Prince's Trusts for Dumfries and Galloway, 1984–88. Underwriting Member of Lloyds, 1976–2004. DL Nithsdale and Annandale and Eskdale, 1987. *Recreations:* golf, shooting. *Heir: s* Lord Johnstone, *qv. Address:* Annandale Estates Office, St Ann's, Lockerbie, Dumfriesshire DG11 1HQ. *Club:* Puffin's (Edinburgh).

ANNESLEY, family name of **Earl Annesley** and **Viscount Valentia**.

ANNESLEY, 11th Earl *cr* 1789, of Castelwellan, co. Down; **Philip Harrison Annesley;** Baron Annesley 1758; Viscount Glerawly 1766; *b* 29 March 1927; 2nd *s* of 9th Earl Annesley and Nora, *y d* of Walter Harrison; *S* brother, 2001; *m* 1951, Florence Eileen (*d* 1995), *o d* of John Arthur Johnston. *Heir: b* Hon. Michael Robert Annesley [*b* 4 Dec. 1933; *m* 1956, Audrey Mary Goodwright; two *s* one *d*].

ANNESLEY, (Arthur) Noël (Grove); Hon. Chairman, Christie's International UK Ltd, since 2003; *b* 28 Dec. 1941; *s* of late E. P. Grove Annesley, OBE and Ruth, *d* of A. Norman Rushforth; *m* 1968, Caroline Lumley; two *s. Educ:* Harrow Sch. (entrance schol.); Worcester Coll., Oxford (Open Schol. in classics; MA). Joined Christie Manson & Woods Ltd, fine art auctioneers, 1964; founded Dept of Prints, Drawings and Watercolours; auctioneer, 1967–; holds world record for Old Master Drawings (Michelangelo and Leonardo da Vinci) and British watercolours (J. M. W. Turner); authority on Old Master Drawings; discoveries incl. drawings by Michelangelo, Sebastiano del Piombo, Raphael and Rubens; Dep. Chm., 1985–91; Dir, Christie's Internat. plc, 1989–98 (Dep. Chm., 1992–98); Dep. Chm., Christie's Fine Art Ltd, 1998–2000; Chairman: Christie's Fine Art Specialist Gp, 2000–03; Christie's Educn, 2000–. Mem. Adv. Panel, Nat. Heritage Meml Fund, 2006–. Mem. Council, American Mus. in Britain, 1988–; Trustee: Villiers David Foundn, 1996–; Dulwich Picture Gall., 1999– (Dep. Chm., 2006–); Yehudi Menuhin Sch., 2000– (Chm., Appeal Cttee to raise funds for concert hall, 2000–05). *Publications:* contribs to specialist books and jls. *Recreations:* music (especially chamber), exploring classical sites, gardening. *Address:* c/o Christie's, 8 King Street, St James's, SW1Y 6QT. *T:* (020) 7389 2241, *Fax:* (020) 7389 2520. *Clubs:* Brooks's, Garrick, MCC.

ANNESLEY, Sir Hugh (Norman), Kt 1992; QPM 1986; Chief Constable, Royal Ulster Constabulary, 1989–96; *b* 22 June 1939; *s* of late William Henry Annesley and of Agnes Annesley (*née* Redmond); *m* 1970, Elizabeth Ann (*née* MacPherson); one *s* one *d. Educ:* St Andrew's Prep. Sch., Dublin; Avoca Sch. for Boys, Blackrock. Joined Metropolitan Police, 1958; Chief Supt, 1974; Police Staff College: Special Course, 1963; Intermed. Comd Course, 1971; Sen. Comd Course, 1975; Asst Chief Constable, Personnel and Ops, Sussex Police, 1976; RCDS 1980; Metropolitan Police, Deputy Assistant Commissioner: Central and NW London, 1981; Personnel, 1983; Dir, Force Re-organisation Team, 1984; Assistant Commissioner: Personnel and Training, 1985; Specialist Ops, 1987. Graduate: Nat. Exec. Inst., FBI, 1986; Mem. Exec. Cttee, Interpol (British Rep.), 1987–90, and 1993–94. Bd of Govs, Burgess Hill Sch. for Girls, 1997 (Chm. Govs, 2000–05). *Recreations:* hockey, sailing.

ANNESLEY, Noël; *see* Annesley, A. N. G.

ANNETTS, Deborah Claire; Chief Executive, Incorporated Society of Musicians, since 2008; Interim Chief Executive, Parenting UK, 2008; *b* 7 Oct. 1960; *d* of Robert John Annetts and Patricia Margaret Annetts; partner, Simon Thomsett. *Educ:* St Albans Girls' Grammar Sch.; St Hilda's Coll., Oxford (BA PPE 1983). Admitted solicitor, 1989; Hd, Employment Law, 1994–99, Partner, 1998–99, Stephens Innocent, solicitors; Partner and Hd, Employment Law, Tarlo Lyons, Solicitors, 1999–2000; Asst Dir, Public Concern at Work, 2000–01; Chief Executive: Voluntary Euthanasia Soc., subseq. Dignity in Dying, 2001–07; YWCA, 2007. Board Member: London Museums Agency, 2001–03; Medic Alert, 2003–07 (Vice Chair, 2005–07); Law Soc. Charity, 2003–. Pres., Young Fabians, 1984–85. FRSA 2003; FRSocMed 2006. *Recreations:* theatre, film, social history, coastal path walking, tennis. *Address:* Annetts Consulting Ltd, 5 Jupiter House, Calleva Park, Aldermaston, Reading, Berks RG7 8NN.

ANNING, Raymon Harry, CBE 1982; QPM 1975; Commissioner of Police, The Royal Hong Kong Police Force, 1985–90; *b* 22 July 1930; *s* of Frederick Charles Anning and Doris Mabel Anning (*née* Wakefield); *m* 1949, Beryl Joan Boxall; one *s* one *d*. *Educ:* Richmond and East Sheen Grammar School. Army (East Surrey Regt and Royal Military Police), 1948–50. Metropolitan Police, 1952–79: Constable to Chief Supt, Divisions and Headquarters, 1952–69; Officer i/c Anguilla Police Unit, W Indies, 1969; Chief Supt i/c Discipline Office, New Scotland Yard, 1970–72; Commander i/c A 10 (Complaints Investigation) Branch, NSY, 1972–75; seconded to Hong Kong Govt, 1974; Dep. Asst Commissioner C (CID) Dept, 1975–78; Inspector of Metropolitan Police (Dep. Asst Comr), 1979; HM Inspector of Constabulary for England and Wales, 1979–83; Dep. Comr of Police, Hong Kong, 1983–85. Graduate of Nat. Exec. Inst., FBI Academy, Quantico, Virginia, USA, 1979. *Recreation:* walking. *Clubs:* Royal Automobile; Hong Kong Golf.

ANNIS, Francesca; actress; *b* 1945. *Theatre:* Royal Shakespeare Company: Romeo and Juliet, 1976; Troilus and Cressida, 1976; Luciana in Comedy of Errors, 1976; Natalya in A Month in the Country, Nat. Th., 1981; Masha in Three Sisters, Albery, 1987; Melitta in Mrs Klein, NT, 1988; Rosmersholm, Young Vic, 1992; Lady Windermere's Fan, Albery, 1994; Hamlet, Hackney Empire, 1995; Ghosts, Comedy, 2001; The Vortex, Donmar Warehouse, 2002; Blood, Royal Court, 2003; Henry IV, Donmar Warehouse, 2004; The Shoreditch Madonna, Soho Th., Epitaph for George Dillon, Comedy, 2005. *Films* include: Penny Gold, 1972; Macbeth, 1973; Krull, 1983; Dune, 1984; The Golden River; Under the Cherry Moon; The Debt Collector, 1999; The Libertine, 2004; Revolver, 2005. *Television:* A Pin to see the Peepshow, 1973; Madame Bovary, 1975; Stronger than the Sun, 1977; The Ragazza, 1978; Lillie (series), 1978; Partners in Crime (series), 1983; Inside Story (series), 1986; Parnell and the Englishwoman, Absolute Hell, 1991; The Gravy Train Goes East (series), 1991; Between the Lines (series), 1993; Reckless (series), 1997; Deadly Summer, 1997; Wives and Daughters, Milk, 1999; Deceit, 2000; Jericho, 2005; Cranford, 2007. *Address:* c/o Independent Talent Group Ltd, Oxford House, 76 Oxford Street, W1D 1BS.

ANSARI, Gholamreza; Ambassador of Iran to Russia, since 2005; *b* 22 Nov. 1955; *m* 1981, Shahin K. Shirazi; four *d*. *Educ:* Allameh Tabatabaee Univ., Tehran (BSc Physics). Ministry of Interior, 1980–88: Gov., Piranshar City, 1980–81; Dep. Gov. Gen., 1981–87, Supt of Governor Generalship, 1987–88, Azerbaijan Province; Dep. Dir, Foreign Nationals and Refugees Dept, 1987–88; Ministry of Foreign Affairs, 1988–: Dep. Dir, Europe Dept, 1988–90; Dir, W Europe Dept, 1990–92; Chargé d'Affaires, London, 1992–99; Ambassador to UK, 1999–2000; Director General: Consular Affairs Dept, 2001–04; E Asia and Oceania Affairs Dept, 2004–05. *Recreations:* reading, walking, jogging, horse-riding, swimming, listening to Iranian traditional music, spending time with the family. *Address:* Embassy of Iran, Pokrovsky Boulevard No7, Moscow, Russia.

ANSBRO, David Anthony; Chairman, SFL Ltd, since 2006; *b* 3 April 1945; *s* of late David T. Ansbro and Kathleen Mary Ansbro (*née* Mallett); *m* 1967, Veronica Mary (*née* Auton); two *d*. *Educ:* Xaverian Coll., Manchester; Leeds Univ. (LLB Hons). Articled to Town Clerk, Leeds, 1966–69; admitted Solicitor, 1969; Solicitor, Leeds City Council, 1969–73; Asst Dir of Admin, 1973–77, Dep. Dir of Admin, 1977–81, W Yorks County Council; Town Clerk and Chief Exec., York City Council, 1981–85; Chief Exec., Kirklees Council, 1985–87; Rees & Co., Solicitors, Huddersfield, 1987–88; Chief Exec., Leeds City Council, 1988–91; Partner, Hepworth & Chadwick, then Eversheds, 1991–2003, Managing Partner, 2000–03; Managing Partner, Eversheds, Leeds and Manchester, 1995–2000. Consultant, Grant Thornton, 2003–. Mem., Local Govt Commn for England, 1992–95. Dir, Leeds TEC, 1990–99; Chm., Leeds Renaissance Partnership, 2005–. Pro-Chancellor, Leeds Univ., 2000–07. Trustee: Henry Moore Foundn, 2003–; Nat. Centre for Early Music, 2003–. Hon. LLD Leeds, 2007. Papal Medal Pro Ecclesia et Pontifice, 1982. *Recreations:* family, friends, golf, watching Manchester City. *Address:* The Green, Airton, Skipton, N Yorks BD23 4AH. *T:* (01729) 830451. *Clubs:* Honley Cricket; Skipton Golf; Wharfedale Rugby Union Football.

ANSELL, Anthony Ronald Louis; His Honour Judge Ansell; a Circuit Judge, since 1995; a Judge of Employment Appeal Tribunal, since 2002; *b* 9 Sept. 1946; *s* of Samuel Ansell and Joan Ansell; *m* 1970, Karen Kaye; one *s* one *d*. *Educ:* Dulwich Coll.; University Coll. London (LLB). Called to the Bar, Gray's Inn, 1968; in practice at the Bar, 1968–80; admitted Solicitor, 1980; in practice as solicitor, 1980–95; Asst Recorder, 1987–91; Recorder, 1991–95. Mem., Sentencing Adv. Panel, 2005–. Vice-Pres., United Synagogue, 1992–97. *Publication:* (jtly) A Time for Change: the Kalms review of United Synagogue, 1992. *Recreations:* walking, opera, Chelsea Football Club. *Address:* c/o Gee Street Courthouse, 29/41 Gee Street, EC1V 3RE. *T:* (020) 7250 7200.

ANSELL, Maj.-Gen. Nicholas George Picton, CB 1992; OBE 1980; JP, DL; Clerk of the Course, Exeter Racecourse, 1995–2002; Director, Devon and Exeter Steeplechases Ltd, 1997–2007; *b* 17 Aug. 1937; *s* of Col Sir Michael Ansell, CBE, DSO and Victoria Jacintha Fleetwood Fuller; *m* 1961, Vivien, *e d* of Col Anthony Taylor, DSO, MC; two *s* one *d*. *Educ:* Wellington Coll.; Magdalene Coll., Cambridge (MA). Commnd into 5th Royal Inniskilling Dragoon Guards, 1956; served BAOR, Libya, Cyprus; sc Camberley, 1970; Bde Major RAC HQ 1 (BR) Corps, 1971–72; Instructor Staff Coll., 1976–77; CO 5th Royal Inniskilling Dragoon Guards, 1977–80; Col GS Staff Coll., 1980–81; comd 20 Armd Bde, 1982–83; RCDS, 1984; Dep. Chief of Staff HQ BAOR, 1985–86; Dir, RAC, 1987–89; Sen. DS, Army, RCDS, 1990–92. JP N Devon, 1994; DL Devon, 1996; High Sheriff, Devon, 2002–03. *Recreations:* fishing, bird watching. *Address:* The Potting Shed, Pillhead, Bideford, Devon EX39 4NF.

ANSIP, Andrus; Prime Minister of Estonia, since 2005; *b* Jartu, Estonia, 1 Oct. 1956; *m*; three *d*. *Educ:* Tartu Univ. (Dip. Chem. 1979); York Univ., Toronto (Business Mgt 1992). Hd, Jartu Regl Office, Jt Venture Estkompexim, 1989–93; Mem., Bd of Dirs, Rahvapank (People's Bank), 1993–95; Chairman, Management Board: Radio Jartu Ltd, 1994–98; Fondijuhtide AS (Fundmanager Ltd), 1995–96; Livonia Privatization IF, 1995–96; Bankruptcy Trustee, Tartu Commercial Bank, 1995–98; Mayor of Jartu, 1998–2004; Minister of Econ. Affairs and Communications, Estonia, 2004–05. Mem., Estonia Reform Party. Order of White Star, 3rd Cl. (Estonia), 2005; Officer, Nat. Order of Merit (Malta), 2001. *Address:* Office of the Prime Minister, Stenbocki Maja, Rahukohtu 3, 15161 Tallinn, Estonia. *T:* 6935701, *Fax:* 6935704; *e-mail:* peaminister@riik.ee.

ANSON, family name of **Earl of Lichfield**.

ANSON, Charles Vernon, CVO 1996 (LVO 1983); Vice Chairman, Cubitt Consulting PR, since 2002; *b* 11 March 1944; *s* of Philip Vernon Anson and Stella Anson; *m* 1976, Clarissa Rosamund Denton (marr. diss. 2005); one *s* one *d*. *Educ:* Lancing College; Jesus College, Cambridge (BA History). Joined Diplomatic Service, 1966; Third, later Second Sec. (Commercial), Washington, 1968–71; FCO, 1971–74; Asst Private Sec. to Minister of State, 1974–76; Second Sec. (Commercial), Tehran, 1976–79; seconded to Press Office, 10 Downing St., 1979–81; First Sec. (Inf.), Washington, 1981–85; FCO, 1985–87; Dir of Public Relations, Kleinwort Benson, 1987–90; Press Sec. to the Queen, 1990–97; Gp Corporate Relns Dir, Grand Metropolitan, later Diageo plc, 1997–98; Hd of Communications, EBU, 1998–2000; Dir of Corporate Commns, Hilton Gp, 2000–01; Communications Advr, The Queen's Golden Jubilee Weekend Trust, 2001–02. Trustee: Elizabeth Finn Trust, 2002–; Brogdale Horticultural Trust, 2002–. *Address:* c/o Cubitt Consulting, 30 Coleman Street, EC2R 5AL. *T:* (020) 7367 5100. *Club:* Hurlingham.

ANSON, Vice-Adm. Sir Edward (Rosebery), KCB 1984; FRAeS 1982; Senior Naval Adviser, British Aerospace plc, 1989–91, retired; Aerospace Consultant (part-time), I.A.D. Aerospace Ltd, Worthing, 1991–93; *b* 11 May 1929; *s* of Ross Rosebery Anson and Ethel Jane (*née* Green); *m* 1960, Rosemary Anne Radcliffe; one *s* one *d*. *Educ:* Prince of Wales Sch., Nairobi, Kenya; BRNC, Dartmouth; Empire Test Pilots Sch., Farnborough (grad. 1957). Served, 1952–64: Naval Air Sqdns, and 700X and 700Z Flts (Blackburn Aircraft Ltd, 1959–61); comd HMS Eskimo, 1964–66; Commander (Air): RNAS Lossiemouth, 1967–68; HMS Eagle, 1969–70; comd Inter Service Hovercraft Trials Unit, 1971; Naval and Air Attaché, Tokyo and Seoul, 1972–74; comd HMS Juno and Captain F4, 1974–76; comd HMS Ark Royal, 1976–78; Flag Officer, Naval Air Command, 1979–82; C of S to C-in-C Fleet, 1982–84, retired. Exec. Dir, Sales, BAe Bristol Div., 1985–86; Pres. and Chief Exec. Officer, BAe, Washington, 1986–89. *Recreations:* walking, golf, photography. *Address:* c/o Lloyds TSB, High Street, Yeovil, Somerset.

ANSON, Dame Elizabeth (Audrey), (Lady Anson), DBE 1995; JP, DL; Chairman, Independent Appeals Authority for School Examinations, 1990–99; Independent Monitor to Parliament on Entry Clearance Refusals, 1994–2000; *b* 9 Jan. 1931; *d* of late Rear-Adm. Sir Philip Clarke, KBE, CB, DSO, and Audrey (*née* White); *m* 1955, Rear-Adm. Sir Peter Anson, Bt, *qv*; two *s* two *d*. *Educ:* Weirfield Sch., Taunton; Royal Naval Sch., Haslemere; King's Coll., London (LLB). Called to Bar, Inner Temple, 1953; joined Western Circuit, 1953; practice at Bar, 1952–56; part-time Adjudicator, 1979–87, an Adjudicator, 1987–91, Immigration Appeals. Councillor, Waverley Bor. Council, 1974–95, Mayor, 1987–88. Association of District Councils of England and Wales: Mem., 1983–95; Vice-Chm., 1989–91; Chm., 1991–93; Dep. Chm., and Chm. Exec. Cttee, 1993–95; Chm., Housing and Environmental Health Cttee, 1987–89. Dep. Chm., Local Govt Management Bd, 1991–93; Member: Local Govt Audit Commn, 1987–90; Cons. Nat. Local Govt Adv. Cttee, 1991–95; Nat. Union Exec. Cttee, 1992–95; Local and Central Govt Relations Res. Cttee, Joseph Rowntree Meml Trust, 1992–96; EU Cttee of the Regions, 1993–98; Packaging Standards Council, 1992–96. Chm., Eagle Radio (formerly Surrey and NE Hampshire Radio Ltd, then County Sound Radio Network Ltd), 1993–2006. Chm., Nat. Mobility Scheme, 1987–88. Chm. W Surrey Br., IoD, 2002–05; Chair of Judges, Surrey Business Awards, 2005–. Vice President: Inst. of Envmtl Health Officers, 1989–2001; Assoc. of Drainage Authorities, 1995–. Pres., SW Surrey Conservative Assoc., 2003–06. Mem. Schs Forum, Hants CC, 2005–. Chm. Governors, Rowledge C of E Primary Sch., 1995–2003. FRSA 1992. JP 1977, DL 1984, Surrey. *Recreations:* travel, needlecraft. *Address:* Rosefield, Rowledge, Farnham, Surrey GU10 4AT. *T:* (01252) 792724.

ANSON, Sir John, KCB 1990 (CB 1981); Second Permanent Secretary (Public Expenditure), HM Treasury, 1987–90; *b* 3 Aug. 1930; *yr s* of Sir Edward Anson, 6th Bt, and Alison (*née* Pollock) (*d* 1997); *m* 1957, Myrica Fergie-Woods; one *s* two *d* (and one *s* decd). *Educ:* Winchester, Magdalene Coll., Cambridge (MA; Smith's Prize). Served in HM Treasury, 1954–68; Financial Counsellor, British Embassy, Paris, 1968–71; Asst Sec., 1971–72, Under-Sec., 1972–74, Cabinet Office; Under-Sec., 1974–77, Dep. Sec., 1977–87, HM Treasury; Economic Minister, British Embassy, Washington, and UK Exec. Dir, IMF and World Bank, 1980–83. Chairman: Public Finance Foundn, 1991–94; Retirement Income Inquiry, 1994–96. Hon. Treas., Council of Churches for Britain and Ireland, 1990–92; Chair, House of Laity, Southwark Diocesan Synod, 1996–97.

See also Sir Peter Anson, Bt.

ANSON, Rear-Adm. Sir Peter, 7th Bt, *cr* 1831; CB 1974; DL; CEng, FIET; Chairman, IGG Component Technology Ltd, 1992–97; *b* 31 July 1924; *er s* of Sir Edward R. Anson, 6th Bt, and Alison (*d* 1997), *o d* of late Hugh Pollock; *S* father 1951; *m* 1955, Elizabeth Audrey Clarke (*see* Dame Elizabeth Anson); two *s* two *d*. *Educ:* RNC, Dartmouth. Joined RN 1938; Lieut 1944. Served War of 1939–45, HMS Prince of Wales, HMS Exeter. Lieut-Comdr, 1952; Comdr 1956. Commanding Officer, HMS Alert, 1957–58; Staff of RN Tactical Sch., Woolwich, 1959–61; Commanding Officer, HMS Broadsword, 1961–62; Captain, 1963; Director Weapons, Radio (Naval), 1965–66 (Dep. Director, 1963–65); CO HMS Naiad and Captain (D) Londonderry Squadron, 1966–68; Captain, HM Signal School, 1968–70; Commodore, Commander Naval Forces Gulf, 1970–72; ACDS (Signals), 1972–74, retired 1975. Marconi Space and Defence Systems, later Marconi Space Systems: Divl Manager, Satellites, 1977–84; Man. Dir, 1984–85; Chm., 1985–91. Chm., UK Industrial Space Cttee, 1980–82. FIERE 1972. High Sheriff, Surrey, 1993. DL Surrey, 1993. *Heir: s* Philip Roland Anson, *b* 4 Oct. 1957. *Address:* Rosefield, Rowledge, Farnham, Surrey GU10 4AT. *T:* and *Fax:* (01252) 792724.

See also Sir John Anson.

ANSTEE, Eric Edward, FCA, FFA; non-executive Director: Insight Investment Funds Management Ltd, since 2006; Insight Investment Management (Global) Ltd, since 2006; Vision Media Group (International) plc, 2007; Financial Reporting Council, since 2007; Chairman of Council, Institute of Financial Accountants, since 2007; *b* 1 Jan. 1951; *s* of Reginald Thomas Anstee and Margaret Doris Anstee (*née* Hampshire); *m* 1982, Suzanne Joy Piller; one *s* three *d*. *Educ:* St Albans Sch. FCA 1974. Ernst and Young: London and Singapore, 1974–83; on secondment as Commercial Accountancy Advr to HM Treasury, 1983–86; Partner, London, 1986–93; Gp Finance Dir, Eastern Electricity plc, 1993–95; Advr to Lord Hanson, Hanson plc, 1995–96; Group Finance Director: Energy Gp plc, 1996–98; Old Mutual plc, 1998–2000; Chief Executive: Old Mutual Financial Services plc, 2000–01; Old Mutual Asset Management Inc., 2000–01; non-exec. Chm., Mansell plc, 2001–03; Chief Exec., ICAEW, 2003–06. Non-exec. Dir, Severn Trent plc, 1999–2003. Chm., Eastern Reg. Industrial Develt Bd, DTI, 1993–99. Mem., Takeover Panel Appeals Bd, 2006–. *Recreations:* tennis, golf, gardening. *Club:* Athenæum.

ANSTEE, Dame Margaret (Joan), DCMG 1994; lecturer, writer and consultant on UN issues and peacekeeping training; Adviser to: President and Government of Bolivia (*ad honorem*), 1993–97 and 2002–05; Under-Secretary-General of the United Nations,

1987–93; *b* 25 June 1926; *d* of Edward Curtis Anstee and Anne Adaliza (*née* Mills). *Educ:* Chelmsford County High Sch. for Girls; Newnham Coll., Cambridge (MA; 1st cl. Hons, Mod. and Med. Langs Tripos; Hon. Fellow, 1991); BSc(Econ) London. Lectr in Spanish, QUB, 1947–48; Third Sec., FO, 1948–52; Admin. Officer, UN Technical Assistance Bd, Manila, Philippines, 1952–54; Spanish Supervisor, Cambridge Univ., 1955–56; UN Technical Assistance Board: O i/c Bogotá, Colombia, 1956–57; Resident Rep., Uruguay, 1957–59; Resident Rep., UN Tech. Assistance Bd, Dir of Special Fund Progs, and Dir of UN Inf. Centre, Bolivia, 1960–65; Resident Rep., UNDP, Ethiopia, and UNDP Liaison Officer with UN Econ. Commn for Africa, 1965–67; Sen. Econ. Adviser, Prime Minister's Office, UK, 1967–68; Sen. Asst to Comr i/c Study of Capacity of UN Develt System, 1968–69; Resident Rep., UNDP, Morocco, 1969–72; Resident Rep., UNDP, Chile, and UNDP Liaison Officer with UN Econ. Commn for Latin America, 1972–74; Dep. to UN Under Sec.-Gen. i/c UN Relief Operation to Bangladesh, and Dep. Co-ordinator of UN Emergency Assistance to Zambia, June–Dec. 1973; United Nations Development Programme, New York: Dep. Asst Adminr, and Dep. Reg Dir for Latin America, 1974–76; Dir, Adminr's Unit for Special Assignments, Feb.–July 1976; Asst Dep. Adminr, July–Dec. 1976; Asst Adminr and Dir, Bureau for Prog. Policy and Evaluation, 1977–78; Asst Sec.-Gen. of UN (Dept of Technical Co-operation for Develt), NY, 1978–87; Dir-Gen., UN Office, Vienna, and Head, Centre for Social Develt and Humanitarian Affairs, 1987–92. Special Representative of Secretary-General: for Bolivia, 1982–92; for co-ordination of internat. assistance to Mexico following the earthquake, 1985–87; for UN Conf. for adoption of convention against illicit traffic in narcotic drugs and psychotropic substances, 1988; for Peru, 1991–92; Special Rep. of Sec.-Gen. for Angola, and Head, UN Angola Verification Mission (UNAVEM II), 1992–93; Sec.-Gen.'s Personal rep., to co-ordinate UN efforts, Kuwait (burning oil wells and envmtl impact of Gulf war in whole reg.), 1991–92. Chm., Adv. Gp on review of World Food Council, UN, 1985–86; Special Co-ordinator of UN Sec.-Gen. to ensure implementation of Gen. Assembly resolution on financial and admin. reform of UN, 1986–87; Co-ordinator for all UN Drug-Control-Related Activities, 1987–90; UN Co-ordinator of Internat. Co-operation for Chernobyl, 1991–92; Chm., Expert Adv. Gp to Lessons Learned Unit, UN Dept of Peacekeeping Ops, 1996–2001. Sec.-Gen., 8th UN Congress on Prevention of Crime and Treatment of Offenders, 1990. Vice Pres., UN Assoc. of UK, 2002–. Member: Bd of Trustees, HelpAge Internat., 1993–96; Council of Advisers, Yale Univ. UN Studies, 1996–; Adv. Council, Oxford Res. Gp, 1997–; Adv. Bd, British-Angola Forum, 1998–; Internat. Adv. Council, UN Intellectual Hist. Project, 1999–; President Jimmy Carter's Internat. Council on Conflict Resolution, 2001–; Editorial Bd, Global Governance, 2004–. DU Essex, 1994; Hon. LLD: Westminster, 1996; Cambridge, 2004; Hon. DSc (Econ) London, 1998. Reves Peace Prize, Coll. of William and Mary, Williamsburg, USA, 1993. Comdr, Order of Ouissam Alaouite, Morocco, 1972; Dama Gran Cruz, Condor of the Andes, Bolivia, 1986; Grosse Goldene Ehrenzeichen am Bande, Austria, 1992; Gran Caballero, Orden de Bernardo O'Higgins, Chile, 2006. *Publications:* The Administration of International Development Aid, USA 1969; Gate of the Sun: a prospect of Bolivia, 1970 (USA 1971); (ed with R. K. A. Gardiner and C. Patterson) Africa and the World (Haile Selassie Prize Trust Symposium), 1970; Orphan of the Cold War; the inside story of the collapse of the Angolan peace process 1992–93, 1996 (USA 1996; Portugal, 1997); Never Learn to Type: a woman at the United Nations, 2003; numerous articles and chapters in books on UN reform, peacekeeping, economic and social development. *Recreations:* writing, gardening, hill-walking (preferably in the Andes), bird-watching, swimming. *Address:* c/o PNUD, Casilla 9072, La Paz, Bolivia; c/o The Walled Garden, Knill, near Presteigne, Powys LD8 2PR. *T:* (01544) 267411. *Club:* Oxford and Cambridge.

ANSTEE, Nicholas John, FCA; Senior Director, S J Berwin LLP, since 2007; *b* 27 May 1958; *s* of Wing Comdr Peter John Anstee and Ann Tudor Anstee (*née* Price); *m* 1983, Claire Mary Carson Cooper; three *d. Educ:* Stamford Sch. ICAEW 1982; FCA 1987. Dearden Farrow, 1984–86; Binder Hamlyn, 1987–94; Partner, Andersen, 1994. Dir, London Marathon, 2004–. Common Councilman, City of London, 1987–96; Alderman, Aldersgate Ward, 1996–; Sheriff, City of London, 2003–04; Liveryman: Butchers' Co., 1996–; Plaisterers' Co., 2005–. Governor: City of London Sch. for Girls, 1993–2003; Christ's Hosp., 1996–; King Edward Sch., 1996–. *Recreations:* marathon running, cricket, tennis. *Address:* 8 Wallside, Monkwell Square, Barbican, EC2Y 8BH. *T:* (020) 7588 6851; *e-mail:* nick.anstee@btinternet.com. *Clubs:* Aldersgate Ward, MCC.

ANSTEY, Edgar, MA, PhD; Deputy Chief Scientific Officer, Civil Service Department, and Head of Behavioural Sciences Research Division, 1969–77; *b* 5 March 1917; British; *s* of late Percy Lewis Anstey and Dr Vera Anstey; *m* 1939, Zoë Lilian Robertson (*d* 2000); one *s. Educ:* Winchester Coll.; King's Coll., Cambridge. Assistant Principal, Dominions Office, 1938; Private Sec. to Duke of Devonshire, 1939. 2nd Lieut Dorset Regt, 1940; Major, War Office (DSP), 1941. Founder-Head of Civil Service Commission Research Unit, 1945; Principal, Home Office, 1951; Senior Principal Psychologist, Min. of Defence, 1958; Chief Psychologist, Civil Service Commn, 1964–69. Pres., N Cornwall Liberal Democrat Assoc., 1988–90 (N Cornwall Liberal Assoc., 1985–88). *Publications:* Interviewing for the Selection of Staff (with Dr E. O. Mercer), 1956; Staff Reporting and Staff Development, 1961; Committees - How they work and how to work them, 1962; Psychological Tests, 1966; The Techniques of Interviewing, 1968; (with Dr C. A. Fletcher and Dr J. Walker) Staff Appraisal and Development, 1976; An Introduction to Selection Interviewing, 1978; articles in Brit. Jl of Psychology, Occupational Psychology, etc. *Recreations:* fell-walking, surfing, bridge. *Address:* Sandrock, 3 Higher Tristram, Polzeath, Wadebridge, Cornwall PL27 6TF. *T:* (01208) 863324. *Club:* Royal Commonwealth Society.

ANSTRUTHER of that Ilk, Sir Sebastian Paten Campbell, 9th Bt *cr* 1694 (NS), of Balcaskie, and 14th Bt *cr* 1700 (NS) of Anstruther; *b* 13 Sept. 1962; *s* of Sir Ian Fife Campbell Anstruther of that Ilk, 8th, 13th and 10th Bt and Susan Margaret Walker (*née* Paten); *S* to father's NS Baronetcies, 2007, but his name does not appear on the Official Roll of the Baronetage; *m* 1992, Pornpan Pinitwong, Thailand; one *s* one *d. Heir: s* Maximilian Sengtawan Pinitwong Anstruther, *b* 26 Jan. 1995. *Address:* The Estate Office, Barlavington, Petworth, W Sussex GU28 0LG.

ANSTRUTHER-GOUGH-CALTHORPE, Sir Euan (Hamilton), 3rd Bt *cr* 1929; property manager; *b* 22 June 1966; *s* of Niall Hamilton Anstruther-Gough-Calthorpe (*d* 1970) and of Martha Rodman (who *m* 2nd, 1975, Sir Charles C. Nicholson, Bt, *qv*), *d* of Stuart Warren Don; *S* grandfather, 1985; *m* 2002, Anna Joan Wright; one *s* one *d. Educ:* Hawtreys, Savernake Forest; Harrow School; Royal Agricultural Coll., Cirencester (Dip. in Estate Mgt). Pres., Birmingham Botanical Gdns, 1985–99. Director: STG Hldgs plc, 1999–2004; HTTP Technol. Inc., 2000–03. *Heir: s* Barnaby Charles Anstruther-Gough-Calthorpe, *b* 28 Oct. 2005. *Clubs:* Brooks's; Edgbaston Priory (Pres., 1985–); Hartley Wintney Golf (Pres., 1985–99).

ANTALPÉTER, Tibor; Director: Hungarian Investment Company Ltd, 1995–2001; Linamar Hungary Rt (formerly Mezőgép) Orosháza, since 1997; *b* 4 Feb. 1930; *s* of late István Antalpéter and Viktória Dobai; *m* 1956, Adél Máthé; two *d. Educ:* Univ. of Economics, Budapest; graduated 1954. Importtex, foreign trade co., 1954; Commercial Sec. in London, 1956–60; Department of International Commercial Relations, Ministry of Foreign Trade: Head of Section, 1960; Dir of Dept, 1964; Dep. Dir-Gen., 1968–73; Dir-Gen. of Dept, 1977–88; Commercial Counsellor, London, 1973–77, 1988–90; Ambassador to UK, 1990–94. Mem., 2000–02, Chm., 2002–, Supervisory Bd, Danubius Hotels Gp (Dir, 1996–2000); Mem., Supervisory Bd, Weslin, Oroszlány, 2000–03. Vice-Chm., CAB Internat., 1992–94. Internat. volley-ball player, 1947–56; Chm., Hungarian Volley-ball Assoc. and Mem., Hungarian Olympic Cttee, 1980–86. Hon. FRSA 1992. Order of Merit for Labour, Bronze 1966, Gold 1979; Order of Merit of Hungarian Republic, Middle Cross, 1995. Order of the Finnish Lion, 1st Cl., 1969; Comdr, Order of Prince Henry the Navigator (Portugal), 1979; Order of Merit, Grand Silver Grade (Austria), 1983. *Recreations:* sport, music. *Address:* Kavics u. 11, 1025 Budapest, Hungary.

ANTANANARIVO, Bishop of; *see* Rabenirina, Rt Rev. R. J.

ANTHONY, Rear Adm. Derek James, MBE 1983; Clerk to the Shipwrights' Company, since 2003; *b* 2 Nov. 1947; *s* of late James Kenwood Anthony and Nora Evelyn Anthony (*née* Honnor); *m* 1970, Denyse Irene Hopper Wright; two *d. Educ:* New Beacon Prep. Sch., Sevenoaks; Eastbourne Coll.; BRNC, Dartmouth. Joined Royal Navy, 1966: sea-going appts, HM Ships Opossum, Revenge, Andrew, Oxley, Oberon, Sovereign, 1970–80; CO, HMS Onslaught, 1981–82; Exchange Service, USN, 1982–84; jsdc, 1985; CO, HMS Warspite, 1986–88, Submarine Comd Course, 1988–90; Head, RN Seaman Officers Policy, MoD, 1990–91; CO, HMS Cumberland, 1991–93; Dir, Naval Service Conditions, 1993–96; hcsc, Camberley, 1996; Dep. Flag Officer Submarines, 1996–97; Naval Attaché, Asst Defence Attaché, Washington, and UK Nat. Liaison Rep. to SACLANT, 1997–2000; FO Scotland, Northern England and NI, 2000–03. Chairman: Assoc. of RN Officers, 2004–; RN Benevolent Soc. for Officers, 2005–. Mem., Incorp. of Wrights of Glasgow, 2002–. *Recreations:* golf, tennis, music, clarinet, history, family. *Address:* Bolton House, Faversham Road, Boughton Lees, Ashford, Kent TN25 4HS. *Clubs:* Army and Navy, Royal Navy of 1765 and 1785.

ANTHONY, Rt Hon. Douglas; *see* Anthony, Rt Hon. J. D.

ANTHONY, Evelyn Bridget Patricia, (Mrs Michael Ward-Thomas); DL; author; *b* 3 July 1928; *d* of Henry Christian Stephens, inventor of the Dome Trainer in World War II, and Elizabeth (*née* Sharkey); *g g d* of Henry Stephens of Cholderton, Wilts, inventor of Stephens Ink; *m* 1955, Michael Ward-Thomas (*d* 2004); four *s* one *d* (and one *d* decd). *Educ:* Convent of Sacred Heart, Roehampton. Freeman, City of London, 1987; Liveryman, Needlemakers' Co., 1987. High Sheriff, Essex, 1994–95, DL Essex, 1995. *Publications:* Imperial Highness, 1953; Curse Not the King, 1954; Far Fly the Eagles, 1955; Anne Boleyn, 1956 (US Literary Guild Award); Victoria, 1957 (US Literary Guild Award); Elizabeth, 1959; Charles the King, 1961; Clandara, 1963; The Heiress, 1964; Valentina, 1965; The Rendezvous, 1967; Anne of Austria, 1968; The Legend, 1969; The Assassin, 1970; The Tamarind Seed, 1971; The Poellenberg Inheritance, 1972; The Occupying Power, 1973 (Yorkshire Post Fiction Prize); The Malaspiga Exit, 1974; The Persian Ransom, 1975; The Silver Falcon, 1977; The Return, 1978; The Grave of Truth, 1979; The Defector, 1980; The Avenue of the Dead, 1981; Albatross, 1982; The Company of Saints, 1983; Voices on the Wind, 1985; No Enemy But Time, 1987; The House of Vandekar, 1988; The Scarlet Thread, 1989; The Relic, 1991; The Dolls' House, 1992; Exposure, 1993; Bloodstones, 1994; The Legacy, 1997. *Recreations:* racing (National Hunt), gardening, going to sale rooms (Christie's or Sotheby's).

ANTHONY, Graham George, CEng; Director, Industry and Regions, Engineering Council, 1983–90; *b* 25 Oct. 1931; *s* of George Alfred and Dorothy Anthony; *m* 1957, Thelma Jane Firmstone; two *s* one *d. Educ:* Fletton Grammar Sch.; King's College London (BSc Eng). Projects Manager, ICI Fibres, 1956; Works Engineer, ICI India, 1964; Chief Engineer, Ilford Ltd, 1968; Gen. Manager, Bonded Structures, 1975; Commercial Dir, Ciba-Geigy (UK) Ltd, 1979. FRSA. *Recreations:* offshore sailing, woodworking. *Address:* 11 North Terrace, Cambridge CB5 8DJ. *T:* (01223) 360553.

ANTHONY, Guy; *see* Anthony, M. G.

ANTHONY, Rt Hon. (John) Douglas, AC 2003; CH 1982; PC 1971; company director and farmer; Director: John Swires & Sons Pty Ltd (Australia), since 1987; Clyde Agriculture Ltd, since 1988; *b* 31 Dec. 1929; *s* of late H. L. Anthony; *m* 1957, Margot Macdonald Budd; two *s* one *d. Educ:* Murwillumbah Primary and High Schs, The King's Sch., Parramatta; Queensland Agricultural Coll. (QDA). MP, Country Party, later National Party, Richmond, NSW, 1957–84, (Mem., Exec. Council, 1963–72, 1975–83). Minister for Interior, 1964–67; Minister for Primary Industry, 1967–71; Dep. Prime Minister and Minister for Trade and Industry, 1971–72; Minister for Overseas Trade, Minerals and Energy, Nov.–Dec. 1975; Dep. Prime Minister and Minister for Trade and Resources, 1975–83. Dep. Leader, Aust. Country Party, 1966–71; Leader, Nat. Country Party, later Nat. Party, 1971–84. Chairman: Pan Australian Mining Ltd, then Mt Leyshon Gold Mines, 1986–92; Resource Finance Corp., 1986–2003; Commonwealth Regl Telecommunications Infrastructure Fund, then Networking Nation, 1997–2002; Dir, Normandy Mining Ltd, 1992–2000. Chm. Governing Council, Old Parlt House, 1998–. Hon. Fellow, AATSE, 1990. Hon. LLD Victoria Univ. of Wellington, NZ, 1983; DUniv Sydney, 1997. Council Gold Medal, Qld Agricl Coll., 1985. Canberra Medal, 1989; NZ Commemorative Medal, 1990. *Recreations:* golf, tennis, fishing, swimming. *Address:* Sunnymeadows, Murwillumbah, NSW 2484, Australia. *Clubs:* Union, Royal Sydney Golf (Sydney); Queensland (Brisbane).

ANTHONY, (Michael) Guy; His Honour Judge Anthony; a Circuit Judge, since 1998; *b* 5 March 1950; *s* of Kenneth Anthony and June Anthony (*née* Gallifent); *m* 1974, Jane Farrer; one *s. Educ:* St Paul's Sch.; Magdalen Coll., Oxford (BA 1971; MA). Called to the Bar, Middle Temple, 1972; in practice at the Bar, 1972–98; an Asst Recorder, 1989–93; a Recorder, 1993–98; SE Circuit. Mem., Mental Health Review Tribunal, 2002–. *Recreations:* travel, reading, spending time with family, Rugby and other sports. *Address:* Lewes Combined Crown and County Court Centre, The Law Courts, High Street, Lewes, E Sussex BN7 1YB. *T:* (01273) 480400.

ANTHONY, Ronald Desmond; consultant in safety and engineering, since 1986; Chief Inspector of Nuclear Installations, Health and Safety Executive, 1981–85; *b* 21 Nov. 1925; *s* of William Arthur Anthony and Olive Frances Anthony (*née* Buck); *m* 1948, Betty Margaret Croft; four *d. Educ:* Chislehurst and Sidcup Grammar School; City and Guilds Coll., Imperial Coll. of Science and Technology (BSc, ACGI). CEng, FIMechE, MRAeS. Vickers Armstrongs (Supermarine), 1950; Nuclear Power Plant Co., 1957; Inspectorate of Nuclear Installations, 1960; Deputy Chief Inspector, 1973; Dir, Safety Policy Div., 1977, Hazardous Installations Gp, 1981–82, Health and Safety Exec. *Publications:* papers in technical journals. *Recreation:* golf. *Address:* 2 Perry House, Chislehurst Road, Sidcup, Kent DA14 6BE. *T:* (020) 8302 6090.

ANTHONY, Vivian Stanley; educational consultant; Reporting Inspector of Independent Schools, 1994–2007; Secretary, Headmasters' and Headmistresses' (formerly Headmasters') Conference, 1990–2000; *b* 5 May 1938; *s* of Captain and Mrs A. S. Anthony; *m* 1969, Rosamund Anne MacDermot Byrn; one *s* one *d*. *Educ:* Cardiff High Sch.; LSE (1st Div. 2nd Cl. Hons BSc Econ); Fitzwilliam Coll., Cambridge (DipEd); Merton Coll., Oxford (schoolmaster student). Asst Master, Leeds Grammar Sch., 1960–64; Asst Master and Housemaster, Tonbridge Sch., 1964–69; Lectr in Educn, Univ. of Leeds, 1969–71; Dep. Headmaster, The King's Sch., Macclesfield, 1971–76; Headmaster, Colfe's Sch., London, 1976–90. Asst Examr, Econ. Hist., London Univ., 1964–71; Asst Examr, Econs, Oxford and Cambridge Bd, 1970–76, Chief Examr (Awarder), Econs, 1976–92; Ext. Examr, Educn, Univs of Manchester, 1972–75, Birmingham, 1975–78, and Lancaster, 1977–79. Mem., DFEE Wkg Gp on Sch. Security, 1996–2000. Chm., Econs Assoc., 1974–77; Member: Schools Council Social Science Cttee, 1976–83; London Univ. Schs Examinations Cttee, 1981–85; Secondary Examinations Council Economics Panel, 1984–89; CBI/Schools Panel, 1984–88. Sabbatical tour, US indep. schools, 1983. Chm., London Area, 1988–89, Mem. Council, 1989–2000, SHA; Headmasters' Conference: elected, 1980; Chm., Academic Policy Cttee, 1988–90 (Mem., 1983–2000); Mem., Professional Develt Cttee, 1985–2004, Teacher Shortage Wkg Party, 1987–88, Assisted Places Cttee, 1987–89; Chm., Records of Achievement Wkg Party, 1987–90; Trng Co-ordinator, 2000–04; Hon. Associate, 2000. Member: Exec. Cttee, Nat. Professional Qualification for Headship (E Midlands), 1996–99; Exec., Boarding Schs Assoc., 2000–04. Mem., Admiralty Interview Bd, 1980–2004. Comr, Inland Revenue, 1989–90. Mem. Court, Univ. of Kent, 1985–90; Governor: Stamford Sch., 1992– (Chm. of Educn, 1996–); King's Sch., Macclesfield, 1993–96; Bromsgrove Sch., 1995– (Chm. of Educn, 2001–); Uppingham Sch., 1996–2006; British Sch. in Colombo, 1999–2007. Chairman: Allexton Parish Meeting, 2005–; Three Villages Conservation Trust, 2005–. Mem., Uppingham Local Hist. Soc., 2005–. Hon. Freeman, Leathersellers' Co., 1990. Hon. FCP 1991. Hon. DEd De Montfort, 1999. *Publications:* Monopoly, 1968, 3rd edn 1976; Overseas Trade, 1969, 4th edn 1981; Banks and Markets, 1970, 3rd edn 1979; Objective Tests in A Level Economics, 1971, 2nd edn 1974; Objective Tests in Introductory Economics, 1975, 3rd edn 1983; History of Rugby Football at Colfe's, 1980; US Independent Schools, 1984; 150 Years of Cricket at Colfe's, 1986; (ed) Head to Head, 1993; (ed) Manual of Guidance, 1995; (ed) Head to HoD, 1998; (ed) Head to House, 2000; Allexton Church Guide, 2007; *contributor:* The Teaching of Economics in Secondary Schools, 1970; Curriculum Development in Secondary Schools, 1973; Control of the Economy, 1974; Comparative Economics in Teaching Economics, 1984; The Search for Standards, 1992; Access and Affordability, 1994; Uppingham in Peacetime, 2007; articles in Economics, Leicestershire & Rutland Life. *Recreations:* choral singing (Chm., 1998–2004, Pres., 2007–, Leics Chorale), Rugby football (Leicester FC), local and family history. *Address:* Bridge House, Allexton, Leics LE15 9AB. *T:* (01572) 717400. *Clubs:* East India, Devonshire, Sports and Public Schools, English-Speaking Union, Old Colfeians' Association.

ANTON, Alexander Elder, CBE 1973; FBA 1972; *b* 2 July 1922; *m* 1949, Doris May Lawrence; one *s*. *Educ:* Aberdeen Univ. (MA, LLB with dist.; Hon. LLD 1993). Solicitor, 1949; Lectr, Aberdeen, 1953–59; Prof. of Jurisprudence, Univ. of Glasgow, 1959–73. Hon. Vis. Prof., 1982–84, Hon. Prof., 1984, Aberdeen Univ. Mem., Scottish Law Commission, 1966–82. Literary Dir, Stair Soc., 1960–66; Chm., Scottish Rights of Way Soc., 1988–92. *Publications:* Private International Law, 1967, 2nd edn (with P. R. Beaumont), 1990; Civil Jurisdiction in Scotland, 1984; The Speyside Way, 2002; contribs to legal and historical jls. *Recreation:* hill walking. *Address:* 5 Seafield Drive West, Aberdeen AB15 7XA.

ANTRIM, 14th Earl of, *cr* 1620; **Alexander Randal Mark McDonnell;** Viscount Dunluce; Keeper of Conservation, 1975–95, and Director (formerly Head) of Collection Services, 1990–95, Tate Gallery; *b* 3 Feb. 1935; *er s* of 13th Earl of Antrim, KBE, and Angela Christina (*d* 1984), *d* of Sir Mark Sykes, 6th Bt; *S* father, 1977 (but continued to be known as Viscount Dunluce until 1995); *m* 1963, Sarah Elizabeth Anne (marr. diss. 1974), 2nd *d* of St John Harmsworth; one *s* two *d*; *m* 1977, Elizabeth, *d* of late Michael Moses Sacher; one *d*. *Educ:* Downside; Christ Church, Oxford; Ruskin Sch. of Art. Restorer: the Ulster Museum, 1969–71; Tate Gall., 1965–75. Dir, Ulster Television, 1982–2000; Chm., Northern Salmon Co. Ltd, 2000–. Mem., Exec. Cttee, City and Guilds Art School, 1983–. FRSA 1984. Prime Warden, Fishmongers' Co., 1995–96. *Recreations:* painting, vintage cars. *Heir: s* Viscount Dunluce, *qv*. *Address:* Deerpark Cottage, Castle Lane, Glenarm, Ballymena, Co. Antrim BT44 0BQ. *Club:* Beefsteak.

ANTROBUS, Sir Edward (Philip), 8th Bt *cr* 1815, of Antrobus, Cheshire; *b* 28 Sept. 1938; *er s* of Sir Philip Coutts Antrobus, 7th Bt and his 1st wife, Dorothy Margaret Mary (*d* 1973), *d* of Rev. W. G. Davis; *S* father, 1995; *m* 1st, 1966, Janet Sarah Elizabeth (*d* 1990), *d* of Philip Sceales, Johannesburg; one *s* one *d* (and one *d* decd); 2nd, 1996, Rozanne Penelope, *d* of Neville Simpson. *Educ:* Witwatersrand Univ. (BSc Mining Engrg); Magdalene Coll., Cambridge (MA). *Heir: s* Francis Edward Sceales Antrobus, BSc Eng Cape Town, *b* 24 Oct. 1972. *Address:* 54A 3rd Avenue, Parktown North, 2193 Johannesburg, South Africa.

ANWYL, Her Honour Shirley Anne; QC 1979; a Circuit Judge, 1995–2008; Resident Judge, Woolwich Crown Court, 1999–2007; *b* 10 Dec. 1940; *d* of James Ritchie and Helen Sutherland Ritchie; *m* 1969, Robin Hamilton Corson Anwyl; two *s*. *Educ:* St Mary's Diocesan Sch. for Girls, Pretoria; Rhodes Univ., S Africa (BA, LLB). Called to the South African Bar, 1963; called to the Bar, Inner Temple, 1966, Bencher, 1985. A Recorder, 1981–95. Member: Senate of Inns of Court and Bar, 1978–81; Gen. Council of the Bar, 1987; Criminal Injuries Compensation Bd, 1980–95; Mental Health Review Tribunal, 1983–99. Chm., Barristers' Benevolent Assoc., 1989–95. FRSA 1989. Freeman, City of London, 1994; Liveryman, Fruiterers' Co., 1996. *Recreations:* theatre, sailing. *Club:* Guild of Freemen of City of London.

ANYAOKU, Eleazar Chukwuemeka, (Emeka), CFR 2003; CON 1982; Hon. GCVO 2000; Ndichie Chief Adazie of Obosi; Ugwumba of Idemili; Secretary-General of the Commonwealth, 1990–2000; *b* 18 Jan. 1933; *e s* of late Emmanuel Chukwuemeka Anyaoku, Ononukpo of Okpuno Ire, Obosi, Nigeria, and Cecilia Adiba (*née* Ogbogu); *m* 1962, Ebunola Olubunmi, *yr d* of late barrister Olusola Akanbi Solanke, of Abeokuta, Nigeria; three *s* one *d*. *Educ:* Merchants of Light Sch., Oba; Univ. of Ibadan (Schol.), Nigeria; courses in England and France. Exec. Asst, Commonwealth Develt Corp., in London and Lagos, 1959–62. Joined Nigerian Diplomatic Service, 1962; Mem. Nigerian Permanent Mission to the UN, New York, 1963–66; seconded to Commonwealth Secretariat as Asst Dir, 1966–71, and Dir, 1971–75, Internat. Affairs Div.; Asst Sec.-Gen., 1975–77, Dep. Sec.-Gen. (Political), 1977–83 and 1984–90, of the Commonwealth. Minister of External Affairs, Nigeria, Nov.–Dec. 1983. Served as Secretary: Review Cttee on Commonwealth inter-governmental organisations, June–Aug., 1966; Commonwealth Observer Team for Gibraltar Referendum, Aug.–Sept., 1967; Anguilla Commn, WI, Jan.–Sept. 1970; Leader, Commonwealth Mission for Mozambique, 1975; Commonwealth Observer, Zimbabwe Talks, Geneva, 1976; accompanied Commonwealth Eminent Persons Gp, SA, 1986. Pres., Royal Commonwealth Society, London, 2000– (Vice-Pres., 1975–2000); Mem. Council, Overseas Develt Inst., 1979–90. Trustee, BM, 2005–. Mem., Governing Council: SCF, 1984–90; IISS, London, 1987; Mem., Governing Bd, South Centre, Geneva, 2002–; Hon. Mem., Club of Rome, 1992–. Internat. Pres., WWF, 2002–. FRSA 1984. Hon. Fellow, Inst. of Educn, Univ. of London, 1994. Hon. DLitt: Ibadan, 1990; Buckingham, 1994; Bradford, 1995; Hon. DPhil Ahmadu Bello, 1991; Hon. LLD: Nigeria, 1991; Aberdeen, Reading, 1992; Bristol, Oxford Brookes, 1993; Leeds, South Bank, 1994; New Brunswick, North London, 1995; Liverpool, London, 1997; Nottingham. Livingstone Medal, RSGS, 1996. Freeman, City of London, 1998. *Publications:* The Missing Headlines, 1997; The Inside Story of the Modern Commonwealth, 2004; essays in various pubns. *Recreations:* tennis, swimming, reading. *Address:* 36 Lugard Avenue, PO Box 56236, Ikoyi, Lagos, Nigeria. *Clubs:* Royal Commonwealth Society, Africa Centre, Travellers; Metropolitan (Lagos).

AOTEAROA, NEW ZEALAND AND POLYNESIA, Archbishops and Co-Presiding Bishops of; *see* Polynesia, Bishop in; Waikato, Bishop of.

APEL, Dr Hans Eberhard; Member (SPD) of Bundestag, 1965–90; Minister of Defence, Germany, 1978–82; *b* Hamburg, 25 Feb. 1932; *m* 1956, Ingrid Schwingel; two *d*. *Educ:* Hamburg Univ. Diplom-Volkswirt, 1957, Dr.rer.pol, 1960. Apprentice in Hamburg export and import business, 1951–54; Sec., Socialist Group in European Parlt, 1958–61; Head of Economics, Finance and Transportation Dept of European Parlt, 1962–65. MEP, 1965–69; Chm., Bundestag Cttee on Transportation, 1969–72; Parly Sec. of State, Min. for Foreign Affairs, Germany, 1972–74; Federal Minister of Finance, 1974–78. Joined Social Democratic Party (SPD), 1955: Dep. Chm., Parly Gp, 1969–72; Mem. Nat. Bd, 1970–88. Hon. Prof. in Econ. Dept, Rostock Univ., 1993. *Publications:* Edwin Cannan und seine Schüler (Doct. Thesis), 1961; Raumordnung der Bundesrepublik, in: Deutschland 1975, 1964; Europas neue Grenzen, 1964; Der deutsche Parlamentarismus, 1968; Bonn, den Tagebuch eines Bundestagsabgeordneten, 1972; Der Abstieg, 1990; Die deformierte Demokratie, 1991; Der kranke Koloss, 1994. *Recreations:* sailing, soccer. *Address:* Rögenfeld 42c, 22359 Hamburg, Germany.

APPLEBY, Bernadette Joan; *see* Kenny, B. J.

APPLEBY, His Honour Brian John; QC 1971; a Circuit Judge, 1988–2003, a Deputy Circuit Judge, since 2003; *b* 25 Feb. 1930; *s* of Ernest Joel and Gertrude Appleby; *m* 1st, 1958, Rosa Helena (*née* Flitterman) (*d* 1996); one *s* one *d*; 2nd, 1998, Lynda Jane Eaton. *Educ:* Uppingham; St John's Coll., Cambridge (BA). Called to Bar, Middle Temple, 1953; Bencher, 1980. Dep. Chm., Notts QS, 1970–71; a Recorder, 1972–88. Mem., Nottingham City Council, 1955–58 and 1960–63. District Referee, Nottinghamshire Wages Conciliation Board, NCB, 1980–88. President, Court of Appeal: St Helena, 1998–; Falkland Is, 2002–; Indian Ocean Territory, 2002–. *Recreations:* watching good football (preferably Nottingham Forest: Mem. Club Cttee, 1965–82, Life Mem., 1982; Vice-Chm., 1972–75, Chm., 1975–78); swimming, reading and enjoying, when possible, company of wife and children. *Address:* The Briars, Old Melton Road, Normanton on the Wolds, Nottingham NG12 5NN.

APPLEBY, Douglas Edward Surtees; farmer; retired Managing Director, The Boots Co. Ltd; *b* 17 May 1929; *s* of Robert Appleby, MSc and Muriel (*née* Surtees); *m* 1952; one *s* one *d*. *Educ:* Durham Johnston Sch.; Univ. of London (BSc); Univ. of Nottingham (BSc). Chartered Accountant, 1957. Commissioned, RAF, Cranwell, 1950–54. Moore, Stephens & Co., Chartered Accountants, London, 1954–57; Distillers Co. Ltd, 1957–58; Corn Products Co., New York, 1959–63; Wilkinson Sword Ltd, 1964–68; The Boots Co. Ltd, 1968–81 (Finance Dir, 1968–72, Man. Dir, 1973–81). Regional Dir, Nat. Westminster Bank, 1979–88; Chairman: John H. Mason Ltd, 1982–96; Meadow Farm Produce plc, 1984–86; Sims Food Gp plc, 1987–89. Member Council: Inst. Chartered Accountants, 1971–75; Loughborough Univ., 1973–75; CBI, 1977–81. *Address:* Hathersage Park, Hope Valley, Derbys S32 1DQ.

APPLEBY, Elizabeth; *see* Appleby, L. E.

APPLEBY, Dame Hazel Gillian; *see* Genn, Dame H. G.

APPLEBY, Prof. (James) Louis (John), CBE 2006; MD; FRCP, FRCPsych; Professor of Psychiatry, University of Manchester, since 1996; National Director for Mental Health, Department of Health, since 2000; *b* 27 Feb. 1955; *s* of James and Doris May Appleby; *m* 1992, Juliet Haselden; two *s* two *d*. *Educ:* Bathgate Acad.; Univ. of Edinburgh (BSc Hons; MB ChB; MD 1995). MRCP 1983, FRCP 1995; MRCPsych 1986, FRCPsych 1997. Sen. Lectr, Univ. of Manchester, 1991–96. Dir, Nat. Confidential Inquiry into suicide and homicide by people with mental illness, 1996–. *Publications:* A Medical Tour Through the Whole Island of Great Britain, 1994, 2nd edn 1995; contrib. numerous res. pubns on suicide and postnatal mental illness. *Recreations:* spending time with my family, clarinet, astronomy, birdwatching, Manchester United. *Address:* Department of Health, Richmond House, 79 Whitehall, SW1A 2NS; Centre for Suicide Prevention, University Place, University of Manchester, Oxford Road, Manchester M13 9PL.

APPLEBY, John Laurence; Chief Economist, King's Fund, since 1998; *b* 26 April 1958; *s* of Will Appleby and Margaret Sheila Appleby; partner, Claire Helen Melamed; three *s* one *d*. *Educ:* Univ. of Essex (BA Hons Econs 1979); Univ. of York (MSc Health Econs 1981). Economist in NHS, Birmingham and London, 1981–88; Manager of Res., NAHAT, 1988–93; Senior Lecturer in Health Economics: Univ. of Birmingham, 1993–95; Univ. of East Anglia, 1995–98. Hon. Vis. Prof., Dept of Econs, City Univ., London, 2002–. *Publications:* Financing Health Care in the 1990s, 1992; (jtly) The Reorganised NHS, 5th edn 1995, 6th edn 1998; numerous book chapters and peer-reviewed papers. *Recreations:* when not painting, reading, iPodding or DIYing, slumped in front of TV with a bottle of wine. *Address:* King's Fund, 11–13 Cavendish Square, W1G 0AN. *T:* (020) 7307 2400, *Fax:* (020) 7307 2807.

APPLEBY, John Montague; His Honour Judge Appleby; a Circuit Judge, Northern Circuit, since 2003; *b* 8 Nov. 1945; *s* of Montague Eric Appleby and Carmen Irene Appleby; *m* 1970, Barbara Joan Plumb; one *s*. *Educ:* Dauntsey's; Univ. of Nottingham (LLB Hons). Admitted solicitor, 1970; Asst Solicitor, Leicester, 1970–72; joined Truman & Appleby, later Truman Close Kendall & Appleby, 1972: Partner, 1974–88; Man. Partner, 1988–98; merged to form Nelsons, 1999: Mem., Mgt Bd, 1999–2000; Partner, 1999–2003; Asst Recorder, 1993–99; Recorder, 1999–2003. Mem. Council, Law Soc., 1984–99; Pres., Notts Law Soc., 1997. Pres., Notts Hockey Assoc., 1994–96. *Publication:* (contrib.) Professional Management of a Solicitor's Practice, 1980. *Recreations:* golf, travel, wine, theatre. *Address:* Manchester Civil Justice Centre, 1 Bridge Street West, Manchester M60 9DJ. *Clubs:* Nottingham Hockey (Vice-Pres.), Bacchanalians Hockey (Midlands); Nottingham Cricket (Vice-Pres.); Hale Golf.

APPLEBY, (Lesley) Elizabeth, (Mrs Michael Kenneth Collins), QC 1979; barrister-at-law; a Deputy High Court Judge, since 1985; a Recorder, since 1989; *b* 12 Aug. 1942; *o d* of late Arthur Leslie Appleby and Dorothy Evelyn Appleby (*née* Edwards); *m* 1978,

Michael Kenneth Collins, OBE, BSc, MICE; one *s* one *d*. *Educ:* Dominican Convent, Brewood, Staffs; Wolverhampton Girls' High Sch.; Manchester Univ. (LLB Hons). Called to Bar, Gray's Inn, 1965 (Richardson Schol.); *ad eundem* Lincoln's Inn, 1975, Bencher, 1986; in practice at Chancery Bar, 1966–; inspector of five cos, Dept of Trade, 1983; Chm., Inquiry into Lambeth BC, 1993. Member, Senate of Inns of Court and Bar, 1977–80, 1981–82. Chm., Ethics and Integrity Cttee, Cons. Party, 1998–. *Recreations:* swimming, gardening. *Address:* 4/5 Gray's Inn Square, Gray's Inn, WC1R 5AY. *T:* (020) 7404 5252; Glebe House, West Grinstead, Horsham, West Sussex RH13 8LR. *T:* (01403) 711228.

APPLEBY, Louis; *see* Appleby, J. L. J.

APPLEBY, Malcolm Arthur; engraver designer; *b* 6 Jan. 1946; *s* of James William and Marjory Appleby; *m* 2000, Philippa Swann; one *d*. *Educ:* Haws Down County Secondary Modern School for Boys; Beckenham Sch. of Art; Ravensbourne Coll. of Art and Design; Central Sch. of Arts and Crafts; Sir John Cass Sch. of Art; Royal Coll. of Art. Set up trade, 1968; bought Crathes station, 1970; moved workshop to Perthshire, 1996; developed fresh approaches to engraving on silver, forging after engraving; created first pure gold and pure silver pieces to bear Scottish hallmark, 1999; works designed and executed include: engraving on Prince of Wales coronet; model of moon (subseq. gift to first moon astronauts); steel and gold cylinder box for Goldsmiths' Co.; steel, gold, ivory and silver chess set, 1977; 500th anniv. silver for London Assay Office; King George VI Diamond Stakes trophy, 1978; seal for the Board of Trustees, V & A; silver condiment set for 10 Downing Street, commnd by Silver Trust; major silver commn for Royal Mus. of Scotland; silver table centre for new Scottish Parlt; gold Royal Medal for RSE, 2000; sporting guns (product designer, Holland & Holland, gunmakers, 1991–97), silver bowls, jewels, prints. Work in collections: Aberdeen Art Gallery; Royal Scottish Museum; Scottish Craft Collection; East Midlands Arts; Fitzwilliam Mus., Cambridge; BM; Goldsmiths' Co.; V&A; Crafts Council; Contemporary Arts Soc.; Tower of London Royal Armouries; Nat. Mus. of Finland; Åland Maritime Mus.; S Australia Maritime Mus.; Perth Art Gall. and Mus.; Ashmoleum Mus. One-man retrospective, Aberdeen Art Gall., 1998; (contrib.) Creation exhibn, Goldsmiths' Hall, 2004; (jt retrospective) Precious Statements, Goldsmiths' Hall, 2006. Founder, British Art Postage Stamp Soc., 1986; Mem., British Art Medal Soc., 1987–. Chm., Crathes Drumoak Community Council, 1981. Life Member: NT for Scotland, 1971; SPAB, 1989; British Dragon Fly Soc., 2001; Orkney Boat Mus.; Cluny Gardens. Member: Silver Soc.; Butterfly Conservation Soc.; John Muir Trust. Hon. Mem., Grandtully and Strathtay Br., Women's Rural Inst., 1997; non-specialist resident, Dun Coillich Steering Cttee, 2001–02. Liveryman, Goldsmiths' Co. Hon. DLitt Heriot-Watt, 2000. *Recreations:* work, walking, garden design, drinking herbal tea with friends, acting in pantomime, conservation matters, breeding silver spangled Hamburg bantams, tree planting with Philippa Swann. *Address:* Aultbeag, Grandtully, by Aberfeldy, Perthshire PH15 2QU. *T:* (01887) 840484.

APPLEBY, Dom Raphael, OSB; Member, School Chaplaincy Team, Downside, since 2003; *b* 18 July 1931; *s* of Harold Thompson Appleby and Margaret Morgan. *Educ:* Downside; Christ's Coll., Cambridge (MA). Downside novitiate, 1951; Housemaster at Downside, 1962–75, Head Master, 1975–80; Nat. Chaplain, Catholic Students' Council, 1974–94; Parish Priest, St Joseph's, Great Malvern, 1996–2003. Nat. Co-ordinator for RC Chaplains in Higher Educn, 1980–87; Diocesan Youth Chaplain, Clifton Dio., 1983–89. *Publications:* Dear Church, What's the Point?, 1984; Glimpses of God, 1993. *Recreations:* books, music. *Address:* Downside Abbey, Bath BA3 4RH.

APPLEBY, Rt Rev. Richard Franklin; Bishop of the Northern Region and an Assistant Bishop, Diocese of Brisbane, 1999–2006; *b* 17 Nov. 1940; *s* of Julian Paul Leonard Appleby and Lilian Margaret Appleby (*née* Pragnell); *m* 1966, Elizabeth Clark; two *d*. *Educ:* Eltham High Sch.; Univ. of Melbourne (BSc); St John's Coll., Morpeth (ThL (Hons)). Curate of Glenroy, 1967–68; Curate of N Balwyn and Chaplain to Apprentices and Probation Hostels, 1969–70; Chaplain to Christchurch Grammar Sch., 1970–71; Warden of Wollaston Coll. and Chaplain to the Archbishop of Perth, 1972–75; Rector of Belmont, 1975–80; Dean of Bathurst and Examining Chaplain to the Bishop of Bathurst, 1980–83; Auxiliary Bishop of Newcastle, 1983–92; Bishop of the Northern Territory (Australia), 1992–99. President: NSW Ecumenical Council, 1987–89; Qld Churches Together, 2004–05; Nat. Council of Churches of Australia, 2006–. *Recreations:* gardening, walking, listening to music. *Address:* PO Box 112, Waratah, NSW 2298, Australia. *T:* (2) 49674628; *e-mail:* rfappleby@gmail.com.

APPLEGARTH, Adam John; Chief Executive, Northern Rock plc, 2001–07; *b* 3 Aug. 1962; *s* of John Speed Applegarth and Mary Applegarth; *m* 1984, Patricia Catherine Killeen; two *s*. *Educ:* Sedbergh Sch.; Grey Coll., Durham Univ. (BA). Gen. Manager, 1993–96, Exec. Dir, 1996–97, Northern Rock Building Soc.; Exec. Dir, Northern Rock plc, 1997–2007; Dir, Northern Rock (Guernsey) Ltd, 1996–2001; non-exec. Dir, Persimmon, 2006–07. Trustee, Internat. Centre for Life Trust, 1997–2001. Gov., RGS, Newcastle, 2002–. *Recreation:* cricket. *Club:* Ashbrooke Sporting.

APPLEGATE, Ven. John, PhD; Course Director, Learning for Mission and Ministry, Southern North-West Training Partnership, since 2008; Archdeacon of Bolton, 2002–08, now Emeritus; *b* 1956. *Educ:* Bristol Univ. (BSc 1975); Trinity Coll., Bristol (DipHE; PhD). Ordained deacon, 1984, priest, 1985; Curate: Collyhurst, dio. Manchester, 1984–87; Higher Broughton, and St Clement with St Matthias, Lower Broughton, 1987–92; St James with St Clement and St Matthias, Broughton, 1992–94; Rector, 1994–96, Team Rector, 1996–2002, Broughton. Area Dean, Salford, 1996–2002. Pt-time Lectr and Hon. Res. Fellow, Univ. of Manchester, 2001–.

APPLEGATE, Lt Gen. Richard Arthur David, OBE 1996; Chief of Materiel (Land), Defence Equipment and Support Organisation, and Quartermaster General, since 2007; *b* 20 March 1955; *s* of late Arthur Applegate and of Elsie Applegate; *m* 1979, Rachael Bridgeman; two *d*. *Educ:* Chislehurst and Sidcup Grammar Sch.; Manchester Univ. (BA Hons Politics and Mod. Hist.); Staff Coll., Camberley (psc† 1987); Joint Staff Coll., Bracknell (hcsc(j) 1998). Service in Bosnia, Kosovo, NI, Belize, Hong Kong, Kenya, Germany, Belgium and UK; Mil. Asst/Speechwriter to SACEUR, 1992–94; Comdr UN and European Rapid Reaction Bde Artillery Gps, Mount Igman/Sarajevo, 1995; CO 19th Regt RA (Highland Gunners), 1994–96; Col Force Develt, 1996–98; CRA 3rd (UK) Div., 1998–2000; Director: Indirect Battlefield Engagement; Deep Target Attack, 2000–03; Capability Manager (Battlespace Manoeuvre), MoD, 2003–06, and Master Gen. of the Ordnance, 2006. Col Comdt, RA, 2006–. Légionnaire 1st cl. d'Honneur, Légion Étrangère, 1996; Legion of Merit (USA), 2007. *Publications:* numerous articles in RUSI Jl, Defense Analysis and in-house jls; winner, Thales essay competition, 2002. *Recreations:* walking, coarse gardening, unpaid taxi driving for my daughters, military history. *Address:* Maple 2, NH 2, Abbey Wood, Bristol BS34 8JH.

APPLETON, John Fortnam; His Honour Judge Appleton; a Circuit Judge, since 1992; Designated Civil Judge, Lancashire and Cumbria (formerly Preston) Group of Courts, since 1999; *b* 8 April 1946; *s* of late George Fortnam Appleton, OBE, TD, JP, DL and Patricia Margaret Appleton; *m* 1983, Maureen Sellers; one *s*. *Educ:* Harrow; Bristol Univ. (LLB Hons). Called to the Bar, Middle Temple, 1969; a Recorder of the Crown Court, 1985–92. *Recreations:* family, country pursuits. *Address:* The Court Service, Lancashire and Cumbria Group of Courts, Sessions House, Lancaster Road, Preston PR1 2PD. *T:* (01772) 821451, *Fax:* (01772) 884767.

APPLETON, Brig. John Roper, OBE 2000; CEng, FIMechE; Director and Trustee: Smallpeice Trust, since 1998 (Chairman, 2001–07); Arkwright Scholarships Trust, since 2000 (Chairman, 2001–07); *b* 29 April 1938; *s* of late John Jackson Appleton and Ada Mary Appleton (*née* Roper); *m* 1st, 1959, Jenifer Jane Worman; one *s* one *d*; 2nd, 1978, Elizabeth Ann Cullen; two *d*. *Educ:* Liverpool Collegiate Sch.; Alun Grammar Sch., Mold; RMA Sandhurst; RMC Shrivenham. BScEng. Commnd REME, 1958; regtl and staff appts in UK, BAOR, Cyprus, Canada, 1961–78; MoD, 1978–79; Comdr REME, 1st Armd Div., BAOR, 1979–82; British Liaison Officer, HQ US Army, Pentagon, 1982–83; MoD, 1983–84; Asst Dir, Defence Commitments Staff, MoD, 1984–87, retired 1987. Fellowship, subseq. Royal Academy, of Engineering: Head of Engineering Affairs, 1987; Head of Corporate Affairs, 1991; Exec. Sec., 1993–2000; Hon. FREng 2000. Liveryman, Engineers' Co., 1996–. *Recreations:* gardening, garden construction. *Address:* Chatterton House, The Park, Great Bookham, Surrey KT23 3LN.

APPLEYARD, James; *see* Appleyard, W. J.

APPLEYARD, Joan Ena, (Lady Appleyard); Headmistress, St Swithun's School, Winchester, 1986–94; *b* 15 Aug. 1946; *d* of William Jefferson and Ruth Ena Leake; *m* 1994, Sir Leonard Appleyard, *qv*. *Educ:* Univ. of Newcastle (BA Hons History); Westminster Coll., Oxford (Dip Ed). Asst Mistress, 1968–70, Head of History, 1970–73, Scarborough Girls' High Sch.; Head of Humanities, Graham Sch., Scarborough, 1973–75; Dep. Head, 1975–79, Headmistress, 1979–86, Hunmanby Hall Sch., Filey. Pres., GSA, 1992–93. Dep. Chm., ESU, 1999–2005. *Recreations:* drama, opera, reading, cooking.

APPLEYARD, Sir Leonard (Vincent), KCMG 1994 (CMG 1986); Pro Chancellor, Bournemouth University; *b* 2 Sept. 1938; *s* of Thomas William Appleyard; *m* 1st, 1964, Elizabeth Margaret West (marr. diss. 1994); two *d*; 2nd, 1994, Joan Ena Jefferson (*see* J. E. Appleyard). *Educ:* Read School, Drax, W Yorks; Queens' Coll., Cambridge (MA). Foreign Office, 1962; Third Secretary, Hong Kong, 1964; Second Secretary, Peking, 1966; Second, later First, Secretary, Foreign Office, 1969; First Secretary, Delhi, 1971, Moscow, 1975; HM Treasury, 1978; Financial Counsellor, Paris, 1979–82; Head of Economic Relations Dept, FCO, 1982–84; Principal Private Sec. to Sec. of State for Foreign and Commonwealth Affairs, 1984–86; Ambassador to Hungary, 1986–89; Dep. Sec., Cabinet Office, 1989–91 (on secondment); Political Dir and Dep. Under-Sec. of State, FCO, 1991–94; Ambassador to People's Republic of China, 1994–97. Vice-Chm., Barclays Capital, 1998–2003. Chm., Council, Winchester Cathedral. *Recreations:* music, shooting, fishing.

APPLEYARD, Sir Raymond (Kenelm), KBE 1986; PhD; Director-General for Information Market and Innovation, Commission of the European Communities, 1981–86; *b* 5 Oct. 1922; *s* of late Maj.-Gen. K. C. Appleyard, CBE, TD, DL, and Monica Mary Louis; *m* 1947, Joan Greenwood; one *s* two *d*. *Educ:* Rugby; Cambridge. BA 1943, MA 1948, PhD 1950. Instructor, Yale Univ., 1949–51; Fellow, Rockefeller Foundn, California Inst. of Technology, 1951–53; Research Officer, Atomic Energy of Canada Ltd, 1953–56; Sec., UN Scientific Cttee on effects of atomic radiation, 1956–61; Dir, Biology Services, Commn of European Atomic Energy Community, 1961–73; Dir-Gen. for Scientific and Tech. Information and Information Management, EEC Commn, 1973–80. Exec. Sec., European Molecular Biology Organisation, 1965–73; Sec., European Molecular Biology Conf., 1969–73; President: Inst. of Information Scientists, 1981–82; Inst. of Translation and Interpreting, 1989–94. Hon. Dr.med Ulm, 1977. *Publications:* contribs to: Nature, Jl Gen. Microbiol., Genetics. *Recreations:* bridge, tennis. *Clubs:* Athenæum; Fondation Universitaire (Brussels).

APPLEYARD, Dr (William) James, FRCP; Dean of Clinical Sciences, Kigesi International School of Medicine, Uganda, 2000–04; Consultant Paediatrician, 1971–98, Hon. Consultant Paediatrician, 1998–99, and Clinical Director, Paediatric Directorate, 1992–98, Kent and Canterbury Hospitals NHS Trust (formerly Canterbury and Thanet Health District); *b* 25 Oct. 1935; *s* of late E. R. Appleyard and Maud Oliver Collingwood (*née* Marshall); *m* 1964, Elizabeth Anne Ward; one *s* two *d*. *Educ:* Canford Sch.; Exeter College, Oxford (BM BCh, MA); Guy's Hosp. Med. Sch., Univ. of London. DObstRCOG; FRCP 1978; FRCPCH 1998. Junior paediat. posts, Guy's and Gt Ormond St; Resident in Pediat., Univ. of Louisville, 1964–65; Dyers' Co. Res. Registrar, St Thomas' Hosp., 1968–69. British Medical Association: Treas., 1996–2002; Member: Jt Consultants Cttee, 1976–95; Consultants Cttee, 1971–2002 (Dep. Chm., 1979–83); Dep. Chm., 1989–91, Chm., 1992–95, Rep. Body. Treasurer, BPA, 1983–88; Mem., GMC, 1984–2003 (Mem., Educn Cttee, 1993–96); Member Council: RCP, 1988–91 (Member: Standing Cttee, 1970–72; Res. Cttee, 1971–74; Paed. Cttee, 1987–91; Examng Bd, 1992–98); World Med. Assoc., 1995–2005 (Chm., Med. Ethics Cttee, 1996–99; Pres., 2003–04; immed. Past Pres., 2005); Chm. Ethics Cttee and Site Visitor, Internat. Assoc. of Med. Colls, 2006– (Hon. Sec. to Bd of Trustees, 2007). Member: Health Service Inf. Steering Gp, Korner Cttee, 1985; DoH Inf. Adv. Gp, 1986–90; Nat. Specialist Commissioning Adv. Gp, DoH, 1995–96; London Univ. Nominee, Kent AHA, 1974–78. Mem. Bd, Urbani Internat., Geneva, 2004–. Hon. Tutor in Paed., Guy's Hosp.; Hon. Lectr in Paed., St Thomas' Hosp.; Dean of Clin. Studies, (UK), St George's Univ. Sch. of Medicine, Grenada, 1995–97 (Associate Prof., 1985–90; Prof. of Paediatrics, 1991–95; Chm., Senate, 1991–93). Hon. Treas., Kent Postgrad. Med. Centre, Canterbury, 1998–2000. Patron, Dyspraxia Trust, 1988–. Liveryman, Apothecaries' Soc., 1983. Hon. FRCPCH 2002. Hon. DM Kent at Canterbury, 1999; Hon. DHL St George's, Grenada, 2000. Alumnus Award for Paed. Res., Univ. of Louisville, 1965. Mem., Ed. Bd, Jl Chinese Med. Assoc., 2003–06. *Publications:* contribs to med. jls. *Recreations:* lawn tennis, photography, erstwhile allotment digger. *Address:* Thimble Hall, Blean Common, Blean, Kent CT2 9JJ. *T:* (01227) 781771. *Club:* Athenæum.

APSLEY, Lord; Allen Christopher Bertram Bathurst; *b* 11 March 1961; *s* and *heir* of 8th Earl Bathurst, *qv*; *m* 1st, 1986, Hilary (marr. diss. 1995), *d* of John F. George, Weston Lodge Albury, Guildford; one *s* one *d*; 2nd, 1996, Sara, *d* of Christopher Chapman. *Educ:* Harrow Sch.; Wye Coll., London Univ.; RAC, Cirencester. Gov., Royal Agric. Coll., Cirencester, 2003–. Chm., NFU, Glos Co., 2003–04; Pres., Glos Farming Wildlife Adv. Gp, 2006–. *Heir:* *s* Hon. Benjamin George Henry Bathurst, *b* 6 March 1990. *Address:* Cirencester Park, Cirencester, Glos GL7 2BT.

APTED, Michael David, CMG 2008; director and producer of television and films; *b* 10 Feb. 1941; *m* (marr. diss.); two *s*; *m* Jo; one *s*. *Educ:* Downing Coll., Cambridge (BA 1963). With Granada TV, 1963–70: researcher, 1963; dir, episodes of Coronation Street; investigative reporter, World in Action, incl. research, 1964, on 7 Up, which became first of series (director: Seven Plus Seven, 1970; 21 Up, 1977; 28 Up, 1985; 35 Up, 1991; 42 Up, 1998; 49 Up, 2005). Director: *television:* series: Big Breadwinner Hog, 1969; The

Lovers, 1970; Folly Foot (for children), 1972; My Life and Times, 1991; plays and films: Slattery's Mounted Foot, 1970; The Mosedale Horseshoe, 1971; The Reporters, 1972; Kisses at Fifty, 1972; Another Sunday and Sweet FA, 1972; The Collection, 1975; Stronger than the Sun, 1977; P'tang Yang Kipperbang, 1982; The Long Way Home, 1989; Always Outnumbered, 1998; Nathan Dixon, 1999; *films include*: Triple Echo, 1973; Stardust, 1975; The Squeeze, 1977; Agatha, 1979; Coal Miner's Daughter, 1980; Continental Divide, 1981; Gorky Park, 1983; Firstborn, 1984; Bring on the Night, 1985; Critical Condition, 1987; Gorillas in the Mist, 1988; Class Action, 1991; Incident at Oglala, 1992; Thunderheart, 1992; Blink, 1994; Moving the Mountain, 1994; Nell, 1995; Extreme Measures, 1997; (also prod) Inspirations (documentary), 1997; The World is Not Enough, 1999; Me and Isaac Newton, 1999; Enigma, 2001; Enough, 2002; Amazing Grace, 2007; *executive producer:* The River Rat, 1984; Dracula, 1992. *Publication:* 7 Up, 1999. *Address:* c/o United Agents, 12-26 Lexington Street, W1F 0LE.

APTHORP, John Dorrington, OBE 1999; Chairman, Majestic Wine Warehouses (formerly Wizard Wine), 1989–2005; *b* 25 April 1935; *s* of late Eric and Mildred Apthorp; *m* 1959, Jane Frances Arnold; three *s* one *d. Educ:* Aldenham School. Sub-Lieut RNVR, 1953–55. Family business, Appypak, 1956–68; started Bejam Group, 1968, Exec. Chm., 1968–87, non-exec. Chm., 1987–88. Mem., Tay River Bd. Councillor, London Bor. of Barnet, 1968–74. Liveryman: Butchers' Co., 1974–; Vintners' Co., 1999–. Gov., London Acad., 2004–. FCMI (FBIM 1977); FInstD 1978; FIGD 1981. Guardian Young Business Man of Year, 1974. Commandeur d'Honneur pour Commanderie du Bontemps de Medoc et des Graves, 1977. *Recreations:* shooting, wine. *Address:* The Field House, Newlands Avenue, Radlett, Herts WD7 8EL. *T:* (01923) 855201. *Clubs:* St Hubert's (Pres.), Radlett Tennis and Squash.

AQUINO, Maria Corazón Cojuangco, (Cory); President of the Philippines, 1986–92; *b* 25 Jan. 1933; *d* of late José and Demetria Cojuangco; *m* 1954, Benigno S. Aquino (*d* 1983); one *s* four *d. Educ:* St Scholastica's Coll. and Assumption Convent, Manila; Ravenhill Acad., Philadelphia; Notre Dame Sch., NY; Mount St Vincent Coll., NY (BA); Far Eastern Univ., Manila. Numerous honours, awards and hon. degrees from Philippine and overseas bodies. *Address:* 25 Times Street, Quezon City, Philippines.

ARAD, Prof. Ron, RDI 2002; architect and designer; Professor of Product Design, Royal College of Art, since 1998; *b* 24 April 1951; *s* of Grisha and Itai Arad; *m* 1975, Dr Alma Erlich; two *d. Educ:* Jerusalem Acad. of Art; Architectural Assoc. (dip. 1979). Professor: of Product Design, Hochschule für Angewandte Kunst, Vienna, 1994–97; of Furniture Design, RCA, 1997. Guest Ed., Internat. Design Yearbook, 1994. Designer of Year, Salon du Meuble, Paris, 1994; Barcelona Primavera Internat. Award for Design, 2001; Gio Ponti Internat. Design Award, Denver, 2001; Oribe Art and Design Award, Japan, 2001; Architektur und Wohnen Designer of the Year Award, 2004; FX Mag. Designer of the Year Award, 2005; Visionary Award, Mus. of Arts & Design, NY, 2006; Laureate, Contemporary Art Prize, French Friends of Tel Aviv Mus. of Art, 2007. *Recreations:* tennis, ping-pong. *Address:* 62 Chalk Farm Road, NW1 8AN. *T:* (020) 7284 4963, *Fax:* (020) 7379 0499; *e-mail:* info@ronarad.com; *web:* www.ronarad.com.

ARAGONA, Giancarlo, Hon. KCVO 2005; Ambassador of Italy to the Court of St James's, since 2004; *b* 14 Nov. 1942; *s* of late Giovanni Aragona and of Bianca Maria Aragona (*née* Vinci); *m* 1968, Sandra Pauline Jackson; two *d. Educ:* Messina Univ., Italy (degree in Internat. Law). Entered Italian Diplomatic Service, 1969: served in Vienna, Freiburg im Breisgau and Lagos, 1969–80; Foreign Ministry, Rome, 1980–84; First Counsellor (Political), London, 1984–87; First Counsellor, then Minister-Counsellor and Dep. Perm. Rep., Delegn to NATO, 1987–92; Diplomatic Advr to Defence Minister, Rome, 1992–95; Dir of Cabinet of Foreign Minister, 1995–96; Sec. Gen., OSCE, 1996–99; Ambassador to Russian Fedn, 1999–2001; Dir Gen., Political Multilateral Affairs and Human Rights, Min. of Foreign Affairs, 2001–04. Cavaliere di Gran Croce dell'Ordine al Merito della Repubblica Italiana, 2007. *Address:* Italian Embassy, 14 Three Kings Yard, Davies Street, W1K 4EH. *T:* (020) 7312 2200, *Fax:* (020) 7312 2230; *e-mail:* ambasciata.londra@esteri.it.

ARAM, Zeev, FCSD; Chairman, Aram Designs Ltd and Aram Store, since 2002; *b* 5 Oct. 1931; *s* of Aaron and Palma Ungar; *m* 1958, Elizabeth Bunzl; one *s* three *d. Educ:* Central Sch. of Arts and Design (NDD). Worked in architects practices of Ernő Goldfinger, RIBA, Sir Basil Spence & Partners and Andrew Renton Associates, 1960–63; estabd own design practice, Zeem Aram and Associates, 1963; founded Aram Designs, 1964; opened furniture and design showroom in Chelsea, 1964, 2nd showroom in Hampstead, 1991; design and furniture showrooms, Aram Store, Drury Lane, opened 2002. Estabd Grad. Show of Young Designers, 1987. FCSD 1973; FRSA 1982. Hon. FRIBA 2006; Hon. FRCA 1992; Hon. Fellow, Univ. of the Arts, London, 2004. Arts Bicentenary Medal, RSA, 1996. *Recreations:* walking, music, sailing. *Address:* c/o Aram Designs Ltd, 110 Drury Lane, Covent Garden, WC2B 5SG. *T:* (020) 7240 3933, *Fax:* (020) 240 3697; *e-mail:* admin@aram.co.uk. *Club:* Chelsea Arts.

ARAUCARIA; *see* Graham, Rev. J.G.

ARBER, Prof. Werner; Professor of Molecular Microbiology, Basle University, 1971–96. President, International Council of Scientific Unions, 1996–99. Discovered restriction enzymes at Geneva in 1960's; Nobel Prize in Physiology or Medicine (jointly), 1978. *Address:* Department of Microbiology, Biozentrum der Universität Basel, 70 Klingelbergstrasse, 4056 Basel, Switzerland.

ARBIB, Sir Martyn, Kt 2003; DL; FCA; Founder and Chairman, Perpetual plc, 1973–2000; *b* 27 June 1939; *s* of late Richard Arbib and Denise Arbib; *m* 1969, Anne Hermione Parton; two *s* two *d. Educ:* Felsted Sch. FCA 1962. Trained with Spicer & Pegler, 1956–62; qualified Chartered Accountant, 1962; Kelsey Industries PLC, 1966–72 (non-exec. Dir, 1975–2000). Dir, Perpetual Income & Growth Investment Trust, 1996–. Trustee: Arbib Foundn, 1987–; Langley Acad. Trust, 2006–; Dir, 1991–, Dep. Chm., 1994–2001, Chm., 2001–, River and Rowing Mus. Foundn, Henley on Thames; Dir, 1992, Jt Chm., 1994–2003, Henley Fest. of Music and the Arts. DL Oxon, 2001. *Recreations:* golf, dry fly fishing, flat racehorse owner and breeder. *Address:* The Old Rectory, 17 Thameside, Henley on Thames, Oxon RG9 1LH. *Clubs:* Huntercombe Golf, Queenwood Golf.

ARBOUR, Anthony Francis; JP; Member (C) South West, London Assembly, Greater London Authority, since 2000; *b* 30 Aug. 1945; *s* of late Charles Foster Arbour and of Magdalen Arbour; *m* 1970, Caroline Anne Cooper; three *s* one *d. Educ:* St Andrew's Sch., Ham Common; Surbiton Co. Grammar Sch.; Kingston Coll. of Technol. (BSc Econ); City Univ. Business Sch. (MBA). Admitted to the Bar, Gray's Inn, 1967. Sen. Lectr, Kingston Univ. Business Sch., 1967–2000 (Vis. Hon. Fellow, 2000–). Mem., Employment Tribunals, London Central (formerly Industrial Tribunals, London North), 1993–. Member (C): Richmond upon Thames BC, 1968– (Chm., Planning Cttee, 1974–80; Leader, Cons. Gp, 1996–2002; Leader of Council, 2002–06); Surbiton, GLC, 1983–87. London Assembly, GLA: Chm., Planning Cttee, 2000–02; Cons. spokesman on planning and standards, 2004–; Chm., Planning and Spatial Develt Cttee, 2005–. Vice-Chm., Kingston and Richmond FHSA, 1990–96; Mem., Metropolitan Police Authy, 2000–. JP Richmond upon Thames, 1974. Chm., Hampton Wick United Charity, 1972–. Governor: Kingston Poly., 1988–90; Tiffin Sch., 1988–92. *Recreations:* book collecting, watching TV soap operas, car booting, eBaying. *Address:* 3 Holmesdale Road, Teddington, Middx TW11 9LJ; Greater London Authority, City Hall, Queen's Walk, SE1 2AA.

ARBUCKLE, Andrew, FRASE; Member (Lib Dem) Scotland Mid and Fife, Scottish Parliament, Jan. 2005–2007; *b* 12 April 1944; *s* of John and Lydia Arbuckle; *m* Margaret Elizabeth Arbuckle (marr. diss. 1985); two *d. Educ:* Bell Baxter High Sch., Cupar; Elmwood Coll., Cupar (NDA). Farmer, E Fife; Agricl Ed., Dundee Courier & Advertiser, 1986–2005. Lib Dem spokesman on finance, Scottish Parlt, 2005–07. Member (Lib Dem): Fife Regl Council, 1986–95; Fife Council, 1995–. Mem., Tay Bridge Bd, 1996–. Pres., Fife NFU, 1989–91. Mem. Ct, St Andrews Univ., 1990–95. Chm., Fife Athletic Club, 1980–81. FRASE 2000. *Recreations:* sport, reading, music. *Address:* Fliskmillan Cottage, Newburgh, Cupar, Fife KY14 6HN.

ARBUTHNOT, Rev. Andrew Robert Coghill; Missioner, London Healing Mission, 1983–95; Director, Sun Alliance and London Insurance Ltd, 1970–91; *b* 14 Jan. 1926; *s* of Robert Wemyss Muir Arbuthnot and Mary Arbuthnot (*née* Coghill); *m* 1952, Audrey Dutton-Barker; one *s* one *d. Educ:* Eton; Southwark Ordination Course. Served 1944–47, Captain, Scots Guards, wounded. Dir, Arbuthnot Latham & Co. Ltd, 1953–82; Chm. and Chief Exec., Arbuthnot Latham Holdings, 1974–81; Chm., Arbuthnot Insurance Services, 1968–83. Contested (C) Houghton-le-Spring, 1959. Ordained Deacon, 1974; Priest, 1975. *Publications:* (with Audrey Arbuthnot) Love that Heals, 1986; Christian Prayer and Healing, 1989; All You Need is More and More of Jesus, 1993. *Recreations:* water colour painting, operas. *Address:* Monksfield House, Tilford, Farnham, Surrey GU10 2AL. *T:* (01252) 782233.

ARBUTHNOT, Emma Louise; a District Judge (Magistrates' Courts), since 2005; a Recorder, since 2002; *b* 9 Jan. 1959; *d* of (John) Michael Broadbent, *qv*; *m* 1984, Rt Hon. James Norwich Arbuthnot, *qv*; one *s* three *d. Educ:* Lycée Français de Londres; Queen Mary Coll., Univ. of London (BA); City Univ. (Dip. Law); Coll. of Legal Educn. Called to the Bar, Inner Temple, 1986, Bencher, 2007; Tenant, 6 King's Bench Walk, 1988–2005; a Dep. Dist Judge, 2000–05. Member: Cttee, Criminal Bar Assoc., 1996–2002; Bar Council, 1998– (Mem., Professional Conduct and Complaints Cttee, 1998–2005; Vice-Chm., Public Affairs Cttee, 2003–05). Chm., Earl's Court Youth Club, 1987–; Dir, Feathers' Clubs Assoc., 1999–. Judge, Asian Women of Achievement Awards, 2004–. *Recreations:* cycling, su doku, weeding, reading. *Address:* c/o Westminster Magistrates' Court, Horseferry Road, SW10 2AX.

ARBUTHNOT, Rt Hon. James (Norwich); PC 1998; MP (C) North East Hampshire, since 1997 (Wanstead and Woodford, 1987–97); barrister; *b* 4 Aug. 1952; 2nd *s* of Sir John Arbuthnot, 1st Bt, MBE, TD and of Margaret Jean, *yr d* of late Alexander G. Duff; *heir pres.* of Sir William Arbuthnot, Bt, *qv*; *m* 1984, Emma Louise Broadbent (*see* E. L. Arbuthnot); one *s* three *d. Educ:* Wellesley House, Broadstairs; Eton Coll. (Captain of School); Trinity Coll., Cambridge (MA). Called to the Bar, 1975; practising barrister, 1977–92 and 2002–03. Councillor, Royal Bor. of Kensington and Chelsea, 1978–87. Contested (C) Cynon Valley, 1983, May 1984. PPS to Minister of State for Armed Forces, 1988–90, to Sec. of State, DTI, 1990–92; an Asst Govt Whip, 1992–94; Parly Under-Sec. of State, DSS, 1994–95; Minister of State for Defence Procurement, MoD, 1995–97; Opposition Chief Whip, 1997–2001; Shadow Sec. of State for Trade, 2003–05. Chm., Defence Select Cttee, 2005–. Pres., Cynon Valley Cons. Assoc., 1983–92. *Recreations:* playing guitar, ski-ing, cookery, computers. *Address:* House of Commons, SW1A 0AA. *T:* (020) 7219 3000.

ARBUTHNOT, Sir Keith Robert Charles, 8th Bt *cr* 1823, of Edinburgh; *b* 23 Sept. 1951; *s* of Sir Hugh Fitz-Gerald Arbuthnot, 7th Bt and Elizabeth Kathleen (*d* 1972), *d* of late Sqdn-Ldr G. G. A. Williams; *S* father, 1983; *m* 1st, 1982, Anne (marr. diss. 2001), *yr d* of late Brig. Peter Moore; two *s* one *d*; 2nd, 2003, Alison Jane, *d* of John Warner and Ann Casson. *Educ:* Wellington; Univ. of Edinburgh. BSc (Soc. Sci.). *Heir: s* Robert Hugh Peter Arbuthnot, *b* 2 March 1986. *Address:* Ivy House, High Street, Edgmond, Newport, Shropshire TF10 8JX.

ARBUTHNOT, Sir William (Reierson), 2nd Bt *cr* 1964, of Kittybrewster, Aberdeen; *b* 2 Sept. 1950; *s* of Sir John Sinclair-Wemyss Arbuthnot, 1st Bt, MBE, TD, sometime MP (C) Dover Div. of Kent, and of (Margaret) Jean, *yr d* of late Alexander Gordon Duff; *S* father, 1992. *Educ:* Eton; Coll. of Law, London. Arbuthnot Latham Holdings, 1970–76; Joynson-Hicks & Co., solicitors, 1978–81. Dir, Assoc. of Lloyd's Members, 1997–2005. Dep. Chm., High Premium Gp, 1994–. Liveryman, Grocers' Co., 1981. *Recreations:* genealogy; webmaster, Arbuthnott Family Assoc. and Kittybrewster.com. *Heir: b* Rt Hon. James Norwich Arbuthnot, *qv. Address:* 37 Cathcart Road, SW10 9JG. *T:* (020) 7795 0707, *Fax:* (020) 7823 3344; *e-mail:* wra@kittybrewster.com.

ARBUTHNOTT, family name of **Viscount of Arbuthnott**.

ARBUTHNOTT, 16th Viscount of, *cr* 1641; **John Campbell Arbuthnott,** KT 1996; CBE 1986; DSC 1945; FRSE 1984; Lord-Lieutenant, Grampian Region (Kincardineshire), 1977–99; Her Majesty's Lord High Commissioner to General Assembly, Church of Scotland, 1986, 1987; *b* 26 Oct. 1924; *e s* of 15th Viscount of Arbuthnott, CB, CBE, DSO, MC, and Ursula Collingwood (*d* 1989); *S* father, 1966; *m* 1949, Mary Elizabeth Darley (*née* Oxley); one *s* one *d. Educ:* Fettes Coll.; Gonville and Caius Coll., Cambridge. Served RNVR (Fleet Air Arm), 1942–46; Near and Far East, British Pacific Fleet, 1945. Cambridge University, 1946–49 (Estate Management), MA 1967. Chartered Surveyor and Land Agent; Agricultural Land Service, 1949–55; Land Agent (Scotland), The Nature Conservancy, 1955–67. Chm., Aberdeen and Northern Marts, 1986–91 (Dir, 1973–91); Director: Scottish Widows' Fund and Life Assurance Soc., 1978–94 (Dep. Chm., 1982–84, 1987–88; Chm., 1984–87); Scottish Northern Investment Trust, 1979–85; Clydesdale Bank, 1985–92 (Northern Area, 1975–85); Britoil, 1988–90; Scottish Adv. Bd, BP, 1990–96. Member: Countryside Commn for Scotland, 1967–71; Aberdeen Univ. Court, 1978–84; Royal Commn on Historical MSS, 1987–94; Chm., Red Deer Commn, 1969–75; President: British Assoc. for Shooting and Conservation (formerly Wildfowlers Assoc. of GB and Ireland), 1973–92; The Scottish Landowners' Fedn, 1974–79 (Convener, 1971–74); Royal Zool Soc. of Scotland, 1976–96; Scottish Agricl Orgn Soc., 1980–83; RSGS, 1983–87; Fedn of Agricl Co-operatives (UK) Ltd, 1983–87; Dep. Chm., Nature Conservancy Council, 1980–85, Chm., Adv. Cttee for Scotland, 1980–85. Hon. Air Cdre, 612 Co. of Aberdeen Sqn, RAuxAF, 1998–. FRSA. Hon. LLD Aberdeen, 1995. GCStJ 1994; Prior of Scotland, OStJ, 1983–95. *Recreations:* countryside activities, historical research. *Heir: s* Master of Arbuthnott, *qv. Address:* Arbuthnott House, by Laurencekirk, Kincardineshire, Scotland AB30 1PA. *T:* (01561) 361226. *Clubs:* Army and Navy; New (Edinburgh).

ARBUTHNOTT, Master of; Hon. John Keith Oxley Arbuthnott, DL; *b* 18 July 1950; *s* and *heir* of 16th Viscount of Arbuthnott, *qv*; *m* 1974, Jill Mary, *er d* of Captain Colin Farquharson, *qv*; one *s* two *d*. *Educ:* Fettes College; Aberdeen Univ. Mem., Grampian Health Bd, 1993–97; Vice-Convenor, Scottish Landowners' Fedn, 2003–05; Chm., Scottish Rural Property and Business Assoc., 2005–. DL Kincardineshire, 2000. *Address:* Kilternan, Arbuthnott, Laurencekirk, Kincardineshire AB30 1NA. *T:* (01561) 320417.

ARBUTHNOTT, Hugh James, CMG 1984; HM Diplomatic Service, retired; *b* 27 Dec. 1936; *m*; two *s* (and one *s* decd). *Educ:* Ampleforth Coll., Yorks; New Coll., Oxford. Nat. Service, Black Watch, 1955–57. Joined Foreign (subseq. Diplomatic) Service, 1960; 3rd Sec., Tehran, 1962–64; 2nd, later 1st Sec., FO, 1964–66; Private Sec., Minister of State for Foreign Affairs, 1966–68; Lagos, 1968–71; 1st Sec. (Head of Chancery), Tehran, 1971–74; Asst, later Head of European Integration Dept (External), FCO, 1974–77; Counsellor (Agric. and Econ.), Paris, 1978–80; Head of Chancery, Paris, 1980–83; Under Sec., Internat. Div., ODA, 1983–85; Ambassador to Romania, 1986–89, to Portugal, 1989–93, to Denmark, 1993–96. Chm., Martin Currie Eur. Investment Trust, 1997–2004. Chm., Charities Evaluation Services, 1997–2003. Chm., Iran Soc., 2006–. Trustee, Children at Risk Foundn (UK), 1997–2007. *Publication:* Common Man's Guide to the Common Market (ed with G. Edwards), 1979, 2nd edn (co-author with G. Edwards), 1989. *Address:* Ashwood House, Caldbec Hill, Battle, E Sussex TN33 0JY.

ARBUTHNOTT, Sir John (Peebles), Kt 1998; PhD, ScD; FRCPath, FMedSci; FRSE; FIBiol; Chairman, Greater Glasgow and Clyde (formerly Greater Glasgow) NHS Board, 2002–07; *b* 8 April 1939; *s* of James Anderson Arbuthnott and Jean (*née* Kelly); *m* 1962, Elinor Rutherford Smillie; one *s* two *d*. *Educ:* Univ. of Glasgow (BSc 1960; PhD 1964); Trinity Coll., Dublin (ScD 1984; Hon. FTCD 1992). FIBiol 1988; FRSE 1993; FIIB 1993; FRCPath 1995. University of Glasgow: Lectr, Dept of Bacteriology, 1963–67; Alan Johnston, Lawrence and Moseley Res. Fellow of Royal Soc., 1968–72; Sen. Lectr, Dept of Microbiol., 1972–73; Sen. Lectr, Dept of Bacteriol., 1973–75; Professor of Microbiology: TCD, 1976–88 (Bursar, 1983–86); Univ. of Nottingham, 1988–91; Prin. and Vice Chancellor, Strathclyde Univ., 1991–2000. Vis. Lectr, Dept of Microbiol., New York Univ. Med. Centre, 1966–67. Sec. and Treas., Carnegie Trust for Univs of Scotland, 2000–04. Chair, External Adv. Bd, Wolfson Inst. for Health & Wellbeing, Univ. of Durham, 2000–08. Bd Mem., Food Standards Agency and Chm., Scottish Food Adv. Cttee, 2000–02; Member: Bd, PHLS, 1991–97; Bd, Glasgow Development Agency, 1995–2000; Bd, British Council Educn Counselling Service, 1995–96; Cttee, DTI Multimedia Industry Adv. Gp, 1995–97; Nat. Cttee of Inquiry into Higher Educn, 1996–97; Chm., Commn on Boundary Changes and Voting Systems, 2004–05. Chm., Jt Inf. Systems Cttee, HEFC, 1994–98; Convenor, Cttee of Scottish Higher Educn Principals, 1994–96. Pres., Scottish Assoc. of Marine Sci., 2005–. Treasurer, Soc. for Gen. Microbiol., 1987–92. Chairman: Nat. Review of allocation of health resources in Scotland, 1998–2000; Standing Cttee on resource allocation to health services in Scotland, 2001–03. Hon. Sec., UK Bioscis Fedn, 2002–06. Founder FMedSci 1998. Hon. FRCPSGlas 1997. MRIA 1985. Hon. Fellow, Internat. Med. Univ., Kuala Lumpur; Hon. Principal Fellow, Dept of Clinical Pharmacol., Univ. of Oxford. Hon. DSc: Łódź, 1995; Univ. Teknologi, Malaysia, 1997; Glasgow, 1999; Durham, 2007; Hon. LLD: QUB, 1996; Aberdeen, 1998; Hon. DEd Queen Margaret's UC, 2000. *Publications:* edited: (jtly) Isoelectric Focusing, 1975; (jtly) The Determinants of Bacterial and Viral Pathogenicity, 1983; (jtly) Foodborne Illness: a Lancet review, 1991; more than 100 in prestigious scientific learned jls and books. *Recreations:* golf, birdwatching. *Address:* 9 Curlinghall, Broomfield Crescent, Largs KA30 8LB. *Club:* Western (Glasgow).

ARBUTHNOTT, Robert, CBE 1991; Minister (Cultural Affairs), India, British Council, 1988–93; *b* 28 Sept. 1936; *s* of late Archibald Arbuthnott, MBE, ED, and Barbara Joan (*née* Worters); *m* 1962, Sophie Robina (*née* Axford); one *s* two *d*. *Educ:* Sedbergh Sch. (scholar); Emmanuel Coll., Cambridge (exhibnr; BA Mod Langs, MA). Nat. service, 1955–57 (2nd Lieut The Black Watch RHR). British Council, 1960–94: Karachi, 1960–62; Lahore, 1962–64; London, 1964–67; Representative, Nepal, 1967–72; London Inst. of Education, 1972–73; Representative, Malaysia, 1973–76; Director, Educational Contracts Dept, 1976–77; Controller, Personnel and Staff Recruitment Div., 1978–81; Representative, Germany, 1981–85; RCDS, 1986; Controller, America, Pacific and S Asia Div., 1987. Member: Adv. Panel, Nehru Centre, 1998–2002; Council, Royal Soc. of Asian Affairs, 2006–. Member: Mgt Cttee, St Anthony's Cheshire Home, Wolverhampton, 1995–2000; English Haydn Fest. Cttee, Bridgnorth, 1995–2000; Internat. Cttee, Leonard Cheshire Foundn, 1997–2003. FRAS 1995 (Mem. Council, 1996–2000). *Recreations:* music-making, the arts, historic buildings. *Club:* Oxford and Cambridge.

ARCAYA, Ignacio; Ambassador of Venezuela to the United States of America, 2001–02; *b* Caracas, 3 June 1939; *s* of Ignacio Luis Arcaya and Antonieta (*née* Smith); *m* 1966, Lydia Vincenti; one *s* one *d*. *Educ:* Central Univ. of Venezuela (Internat. Affairs, 1964; Law, 1968). Third Sec., Perm. Mission of Venezuela in Geneva, 1966–68; Second Sec., Min. for Foreign Affairs, 1968–69; First Sec., Mission to OAS, Washington, 1969–72; Counsellor, Inst. of Foreign Trade, Min. for Foreign Affairs, 1972–75; Minister Counsellor of Econ. Affairs, Paris, 1975–78; Ambassador to Australia and non-resident Ambassador to NZ, Fiji and Philippines, 1978–84; Sec. Gen., Assoc. of Iron Ore Exporting Countries, 1984–88; Ambassador-at-large, Min. for Foreign Affairs, 1988; Ambassador: to Chile, 1989–92; to UK, 1992–95 and (non-resident) to Ireland, 1994–95; to Argentina, 1995–98; Perm. Rep. to UN, 1998–99 and 2000–01; Minister of Govt and Justice, 1999–2000; acting Pres. of Venezuela, Oct. 1999. Venezuelan orders: Order of Liberator, 1992; Orden Francisco de Miranda, 1995; Orden Andrés Bello, 1995; Orden al Merito en el Trabajo, 1998; Orden J. C. Falcón, 1999; numerous foreign orders. *Recreations:* polo, golf, tennis, fencing (sabre), ski-ing. *Address:* Arcaya & Associates, Suite 610, 2699 South Bayshore Drive, Coconut Grove, FL 33133, USA. *T:* (305) 8602589, *Fax:* (305) 2859227; MCEDE, Torre Miranda A Oficina 82-A, Avenida Francisco de Miranda, Caracas 1060, Venezuela. *T:* (212) 2634716, 2631526, *Fax:* (212) 2661608; *e-mail:* ia@arcaya.com. *Clubs:* Caracas Country; Royal Berkshire Polo; Royal & Ancient Golf (St Andrews); Chantilly Polo (Paris).

ARCHDALE, Sir Edward (Folmer), 3rd Bt *cr* 1928; DSC 1943; Captain, RN, retired; *b* 8 Sept. 1921; *s* of Vice-Adm. Sir Nicholas Edward Archdale, 2nd Bt, CBE, and Gerda (*d* 1969), 2nd *d* of late F. C. Sievers, Copenhagen; *S* father, 1955; *m* 1954, Elizabeth Ann Stewart (marr. diss. 1978), *d* of late Maj.-Gen. Wilfrid Boyd Fellowes Lukis, CBE; one *s* one *d* (and one *d* decd). *Educ:* Royal Naval Coll., Dartmouth. Joined Royal Navy, 1935; served War of 1939–45 (despatches, DSC). *Recreation:* civilization. *Heir: s* Nicholas Edward Archdale, *b* 2 Dec. 1965. *Address:* Albury House, 6 Albury Road, Guildford GU1 2BT.

ARCHER, family name of **Barons Archer of Sandwell** and **Archer of Weston-super-Mare**.

ARCHER OF SANDWELL, Baron *cr* 1992 (Life Peer), of Sandwell in the County of West Midlands; **Peter Kingsley Archer;** PC 1977; QC 1971; a Recorder of the Crown Court, 1982–98; *b* 20 Nov. 1926; *s* of Cyril Kingsley Archer and May (*née* Baker); *m* 1954, Margaret Irene (*née* Smith); one *s*. *Educ:* Wednesday Boys' High Sch.; LSE; University Coll., London (Fellow 1978). Called to Bar, Gray's Inn, 1952; Bencher, 1974; commenced practice, 1953. MP (Lab) Rowley Regis and Tipton, 1966–74, Warley West, 1974–92. PPS to Attorney-Gen., 1967–70; Solicitor General, 1974–79; chief Opposition spokesman on legal affairs, 1979–82, on trade, 1982–83, on N Ireland, 1983–87. UK Deleg. to UN Gen. Assembly (Third Cttee), 1969. Chairman: Council on Tribunals, 1992–99; Enemy Property Claims Assessment Panel, 1999–; Inquiry into Contaminated Blood, 2007–08; Mem., Privy Council Review of Intercept Evidence, 2007–08. Chairman: Amnesty International (British Section), 1971–74; Parly gp for World Govt, 1970–74; Soc. of Labour Lawyers, 1971–74, 1979–93 (Jt Pres., 1993–); Mem., Exec. Cttee, Fabian Soc., 1974–86 (Chm., 1980–81; Pres., 1993–). Ombudsman for Mirror Group Newspapers, 1989–90. President: World Disarmament Campaign, 1993–; One World Trust, 1993–. Pres., Methodist Homes for the Aged, 1992–. *Publications:* The Queen's Courts, 1956; ed Social Welfare and the Citizen, 1957; Communism and the Law, 1963; (with Lord Reay) Freedom at Stake, 1966; Human Rights, 1969; (jtly) Purpose in Socialism, 1973; The Role of the Law Officers, 1978; contributions to: Trends in Social Welfare, 1965; Atkin's, Court Forms, 1965; The International Protection of Human Rights, 1967; Renewal, 1983; Fabian Centenary Essays, 1984; (ed) More Law Reform Now, 1984. *Recreations:* music, writing, talking. *Address:* House of Lords, SW1A 0PW.

ARCHER OF WESTON-SUPER-MARE, Baron *cr* 1992 (Life Peer), of Mark in the County of Somerset; **Jeffrey Howard Archer;** politician and author; *b* 15 April 1940; *s* of late William Archer and Lola Archer (*née* Cook); *m* 1966, Mary Weeden (*see* M. D. Archer); two *s*. *Educ:* by my wife since leaving Wellington Sch., Somerset; Brasenose Coll., Oxford. Athletics Blues, 1963–65, Gymnastics Blue, 1963, Pres. OUAC 1965; ran for Great Britain (never fast enough); Oxford 100 yards record (9.6 sec.), 1966. Mem. GLC for Havering, 1966–70; MP (C) Louth, Dec. 1969–Sept. 1974. Dep. Chm., Cons. Party, 1985–86. Former Pres., Somerset AAA; Pres., World Snooker Assoc. (formerly World Professional Billiards & Snooker Assoc.), 1997–99. Co-ordinator, Simple Truth Campaign, 1991. *Plays:* Beyond Reasonable Doubt, Queen's, 1987; Exclusive, Strand, 1990; The Accused (and acted), Haymarket Theatre Royal, 2000. *Publications:* Not a Penny More, Not a Penny Less, 1975 (televised, 1990); Shall We Tell the President?, 1977; Kane and Abel, 1979 (televised, 1986); A Quiver Full of Arrows (short stories), 1980; The Prodigal Daughter, 1982; First Among Equals, 1984 (televised, 1986); A Matter of Honour, 1986; A Twist in the Tale (short stories), 1988; As the Crow Flies, 1991; Honour Among Thieves, 1993; Twelve Red Herrings (short stories), 1994; The Fourth Estate, 1996; The Collected Short Stories, 1997; The Eleventh Commandment, 1998; To Cut a Long Story Short (short stories), 2000; A Prison Diary, vol. I, Hell, 2002, vol. II, Purgatory, 2003, vol. III, Heaven, 2004; Sons of Fortune, 2003; Paths of Glory (screenplay), 2005; False Impression (also screenplay), 2006; Cat O'Nine Tales (short stories), 2006; (with Francis J. Moloney) The Gospel according to Judas, 2007; A Prisoner of Birth, 2008. *Recreations:* theatre, watching Somerset play cricket and Cambridge play Rugby, charity auctioneer. *Address:* 93 Albert Embankment, SE1 7TY.

ARCHER OF WESTON-SUPER-MARE, Lady; *see* Archer, M. D.

ARCHER, Albert, MBE 1980; Member, Royal Commission on Environmental Pollution, 1981–85; *b* 7 March 1915; *s* of Arthur Archer and Margaret Alice Norris; *m* 1st, 1939; two *s*; 2nd, 1975, Peggy, *widow* of John F. Marsh; two step *s*. *Educ:* Manchester Grammar Sch.; Manchester Coll. of Technology. Fellow, Instn of Environmental Health Officers, 1961. Chief Public Health Inspector, Bor. of Halesowen, 1943–73; City of Birmingham: Environmtl Protection Officer, 1973–75; Dep. City Environmtl Officer, 1975–76; City Environmtl Officer, 1976–80. Mem., govt working parties on air pollution. Pres., Inst. of Environmental Health Officers, 1979–83. *Publications:* articles on air pollution in technical jls. *Recreation:* watching cricket. *Address:* 10 Peppard Road, Maidenbower, Crawley, West Sussex RH10 7QS. *T:* (01293) 884068.

ARCHER, Anthony William; Partner, Odgers Ray & Berndtson, since 1995; *b* 17 Jan. 1953; *s* of George William Frederic Archer and Mary Archer (*née* Deeming); *m* 1979, Louise Marion Rhodes; one *s* two *d*. *Educ:* St Edward's Sch., Oxford; Univ. of Birmingham (LLB Hons 1975). ACA 1979. Asst Manager, Tax, Price Waterhouse & Co., 1975–80; Asst Manager, Corporate Finance, S. G. Warburg & Co. Ltd, 1980–83; various posts in London and NY, County NatWest Ltd, 1983–88 (Dir, 1988); Man. Dir, MacLennan & Partners, 1988–92; Principal, TASA Ltd, 1992–95. Mem., Crown Nominations Commn, 2005–07. Mem., Gen. Synod of C of E, 1993–. Mem. Council, Wycliffe Hall, Oxford, 2000–. Freeman, City of London, 2001; Liveryman, Wheelwrights' Co., 2001–. *Recreations:* gardening, running half-marathons, grandparenting. *Address:* Barn Cottage, Little Gaddesden, Berkhamsted, Herts HP4 1PH. *T:* (01442) 842397; *e-mail:* aw.archer@btinternet.com.

ARCHER, Gilbert Baird; Vice Lord-Lieutenant for Tweeddale, since 2008; Chairman, Tods of Orkney Ltd (oatcake and biscuit manufacturers), since 1970; *b* Edinburgh, 24 Aug. 1942; *s* of late John Mark Archer, CBE and Marjorie Carmichael (*née* Baird); *m* 1967, Irené, *er d* of late Rev. Dr John C. M. Conn and Jess (*née* Stewart); two *d*. *Educ:* Melville Coll. Chairman: John Dickson & Son Ltd, 1985–97; Borders 1996 Ltd, 1996–98; Dir, EPS Moulders Ltd, 1985–88. Dir, Scottish Council Develt and Industry, 1993–96. Chm., Leith Chamber of Commerce, 1986–88; Pres., Edinburgh Chamber of Commerce, 1990–92; Chm., Assoc. of Scottish Chambers of Commerce, 1993–96; Dep. Pres., British Chambers of Commerce, 1995–96. Chm., Edinburgh Common Purpose, 1991–94. Dir, Scottish Council of Indep. Schs, 1988–91; Mem. Council, Governing Bodies Assoc. of Indep. Schs, 1988–91. Chm., St Columba's Hospice, 1998–2004 (now Hon. Vice Pres.). Vice Convener, George Watson's Coll., 1978–80; Governor: Fettes Coll., 1986–90; Napier Univ., 1991–97. Master: Co. of Merchants of the City of Edinburgh, 1997–99; Gunmakers' Co., 2006–07. Moderator, High Constables of Port of Leith, 1990–91. DL Tweeddale, 1994. *Recreations:* previously flying, now country pursuits. *Address:* 12 Broughton Place, Edinburgh EH1 3RX. *T:* (0131) 556 4518, *Fax:* (0131) 557 8650. *Clubs:* Army and Navy; New (Edinburgh).

ARCHER, Graham Robertson, CMG 1997; HM Diplomatic Service, retired; High Commissioner to Malta, 1995–99; *b* 4 July 1939; *s* of late Henry Robertson Archer and Winifred Archer; *m* 1963, Pauline Cowan; two *d*. *Educ:* Judd School, Tonbridge. Joined Commonwealth Relations Office, 1962; British High Commission, New Delhi, 1964; Vice Consul, Kuwait, 1966; CRO (later FCO), 1967; Second Secretary (Commercial), Washington, 1970; First Secretary: FCO, 1972; Wellington, NZ, 1975; FCO, 1979; Counsellor: Pretoria, 1982; The Hague, 1986; FCO, 1990. Chm., Commonwealth Soc. for the Deaf, 2001–03; Dep. Chm. Cttee, SE Reg., NT. KStJ 1999. *Club:* Royal Over-Seas League (Mem., Exec. Cttee).

ARCHER, Mrs Jean Mary; Under-Secretary, Ministry of Agriculture, Fisheries and Food, 1973–86; *b* 24 Aug. 1932; *e d* of late Reginald R. and D. Jane Harvey, Braiseworth Hall, Tannington, Suffolk; *m* 1954, G. Michéal D. Archer, MB, BChir, FFARCS, *er s* of Maj.-Gen. G. T. L. Archer, CB; two *d*. *Educ:* Fleet House, Felixstowe; St Felix Sch.,

Southwold; Newnham Coll., Cambridge (MA Econs 1954). Asst Principal, Min. of Agriculture, 1954; Private Sec. to successive Perm. Secs, MAFF, 1956–59; Principal 1960; Sec., Reorganisation Commn for Eggs, 1967; Asst Sec. 1968; Under-Sec. i/c Food Policy Gp, MAFF, 1973; Under-Sec., Dept of Prices and Consumer Protection, 1974–76; returned to MAFF, as Under-Sec., Milk and Marketing Group, 1976; Under-Sec., Meat, Poultry and Eggs Div., 1980. *Recreations:* travel, music, tennis, watching sport, swimming administration (Team Man., Chelsea/Kensington Swimming Club; Hon. Sec., Swimmers' Parents' and Supporters' Assoc.). *Club:* Hurlingham.

ARCHER, John Francis Ashweek; QC 1975; a Recorder of the Crown Court, 1974–97; *b* 9 July 1925; *s* of late George Eric Archer, FRCSE, and Frances Archer (*née* Ashweek); *m* 1995, Vivienne Frances Weatherhead (*née* Ecclestone). *Educ:* Winchester Coll., 1938–43; New Coll., Oxford, 1947–49 (BA 1949). Served War of 1939–45, 1944–47; Lieut RA, 1948. Called to Bar, Inner Temple, 1950, Bencher, 1984. Mem., Criminal Injuries Compensation Bd, 1987–2000. *Recreations:* motoring, bridge. *Address:* The Cottage, 68 High Street, Wicken, Cambs CB7 5XR.

ARCHER, Malcolm David, FRCO; Director of Chapel Music, Winchester College, since 2007; *b* 29 April 1952; *s* of Gordon Austin Archer and Joan Eddleston Archer; *m* 1994, Alison Jane Robinson; one *s* one *d*. *Educ:* King Edward VII Sch., Lytham; Royal Coll. of Music (ARCM 1971); Jesus Coll., Cambridge (Organ Schol.; MA, CertEd). FRCO 1974. Asst Dir of Music, Magdalen Coll. Sch., Oxford, 1976–78; Asst Organist, Norwich Cathedral, 1978–83; Organist and Master of the Choristers, Bristol Cathedral, 1983–90; freelance organist, conductor and composer, 1990–96; music staff, 1990–96, Head of Chapel Music, 1994–96, Clifton Coll.; Organist and Master of the Choristers, Wells Cathedral, 1996–2004; Organist and Dir of Music, St Paul's Cathedral, 2004–07. Founder and Musical Dir, City of Bristol Choir, 1991–2000; Conductor, Wells Cathedral Oratorio Soc., 1996–2004. Hon. FNMSM, 2002; Hon. FGCM, 2005. *Publications:* A Year of Praise, 1991; (ed jtly) Carols Old and New, 1991; After the Last Verse, 1995; (ed jtly) Advent for Choirs, 1999; (ed jtly) Epiphany to All Saints for Choirs, 2004; over 200 compositions; major works include: Love Unknown, 1992; Requiem, 1993; The Coming of the Kingdom, 1999; Three Psalms of David, 2000; Veni Creator Spiritus, 2004; The Garden of Love, 2004. *Recreations:* watercolour painting, cooking, classic cars, antique clocks. *Address:* Winchester College, College Street, Winchester SO23 9NA.

ARCHER, Dr Mary Doreen; Chairman, Cambridge University Hospitals NHS Foundation Trust (formerly Addenbrooke's NHS Trust), since 2002 (Director, since 1992; Vice-Chairman, 1999–2002); *b* 22 Dec. 1944; *d* of late Harold Norman Weeden and Doreen Weeden (*née* Cox); *m* 1966, Jeffrey Howard Archer (*see* Baron Archer of Weston-super-Mare); two *s*. *Educ:* Cheltenham Ladies' College; St Anne's Coll., Oxford (Nuffield Schol.; MA 1972); Imperial Coll., London Univ. (PhD 1968); MA Cantab 1976. FRSC 1987. Junior Res. Fellow, St Hilda's Coll., Oxford, 1968–71; temp. Lectr in Chemistry, Somerville Coll., Oxford, 1971–72; Res. Fellow, Royal Instn of GB, 1972–76 (Dewar Fellow, 1975–76); Lector in Chemistry, Trinity Coll., Cambridge, 1976–86; Fellow and Coll. Lectr in Chem., Newnham Coll., Cambridge, 1976–86 (Bye-Fellow, 1987–2002). Sen. Academic Fellow, De Montfort Univ. (formerly Leicester Polytechnic), 1990–; Vis. Prof., Dept of Biochem., 1991–99, Centre for Energy Policy and Technol., 2000–03, Imperial Coll., London; Visitor, Univ. of Hertfordshire, 1993–2005. Member: Renewable Energy Adv. Gp, Dept of Energy/DTI, 1991–92; Energy Adv. Panel, DTI, 1992–98; COPUS, 1995–2000; Energy Policy Adv. Gp, Royal Soc., 1998–2004. Chm., E of England Stem Cell Network Steering Gp, 2004–. Trustee: Science Mus., 1990–2000; UK Stem Cell Foundn, 2005–. Mem. Council, Cheltenham Ladies' Coll., 1991–2000. Mem. Bd of Dirs, Internat. Solar Energy Soc., 1975–81 (Sec., UK Section, 1973–76); Manager, 1982–84, Mem. Council, 1984–85 and 1997–2002, Royal Instn; Chm., Nat. Energy Foundn, 1990–2000 (Pres., 2000–); Pres., Solar Energy Soc., 2001–. Director: Anglia Television Gp, 1987–95; Mid Anglia Radio, 1988–94; Q103 (formerly Cambridge & Newmarket FM Radio), 1988–97. Mem. Council of Lloyd's, 1989–92. Pres., Guild of Church Musicians, 1989–. Hon. DSc Hertfordshire, 1994. Melchett Medal, Inst. of Energy, 2002; Eva Philbin Award, Inst. of Chem. of Ireland, 2007. *Publications:* Rupert Brooke and the Old Vicarage, Grantchester, 1989; (ed jtly) Clean Electricity from Photovoltaics, 2001; (ed jtly) Molecular to Global Photosynthesis, 2004; (ed jtly) Transformation and Change: the 1702 Chair of Chemistry at Cambridge, 2004; (ed jtly) Solar Photon Conversion in Nanostructured and Photoelectrochemical Systems, 2008; contribs to chem. jls. *Recreations:* reading, writing, singing. *Address:* The Old Vicarage, Grantchester, Cambridge CB3 9ND. *T:* (01223) 840213.

ARCHER, Nicholas Stewart, MVO 2001; HM Diplomatic Service; Ambassador to Denmark, since 2008; *b* 24 Dec. 1960; *s* of Thomas Stewart Archer and Marjorie Anne Archer (*née* Mackenzie); *m* 1999, Erica Margaret Power; two *s*. *Educ:* Denstone Coll.; Univ. of Durham (BA 1982). With Sotheby's, 1983; entered FCO, 1983: Third, later Second Sec., Amman, 1986–89; FCO, 1989–92; Private Sec. to Minister of State, FCO, 1992–94; First Sec., Oslo, 1995–97; Asst Private Sec. to the Prince of Wales, 1997–2000; Head: NE Asia and Pacific Dept, FCO, 2001–02; Near East and N Africa Dept, FCO, 2002–05; High Comr, Malta, 2006–08. Trustee, St Catherine Foundn, 1997–2000. *Address:* c/o Foreign and Commonwealth Office, King Charles Street, SW1A 2AH.

ARCHER, Timothy John; Consultant, Reed Smith Richards Butler (formerly Richards Butler), since 2001 (Partner, 1973–2001; Senior Partner, 1991–2000); *b* 9 Feb. 1943; *s* of Jack Valentine Archer and Phyllis Emma Archer (*née* Cotton); *m* 1972, Gillian Karen Davies; one *s* one *d*. *Educ:* Sutton Valence Sch.; Merton Coll., Oxford (MA); Coll. of Law. Alfred Syrett Prizeman, Law Soc., 1966; admitted Solicitor, 1969. Richards Butler, Solicitors, subseq. Reed Smith Richards Butler, 1965–. Part-time Chm., Employment Tribunals, 2002–06. Director: Royal Philharmonic Orch., 1993–95; Philharmonia Orch. Trust, 1997–; Harefield Res. Foundn, 2002–03. Mem., Management Cttee, Univ. of Exeter Centre for Legal Practice, 1993–96. *Publications:* (contrib.) International Handbook on Contracts of Employment, 1988, 2nd edn 1991; (jtly) Trade Unions, Employers and the Law, 1991; (jtly) Collective Labour Law, 2000. *Recreations:* sport, travel, music, art. *Club:* City of London.

ARCHER, William Ernest; Chairman, Focus DIY Ltd (formerly Focus DIY, then Focus Do It All, subseq. Focus Wickes Group), since 1992 (Chief Executive Officer, 1992–2002); *b* 6 May 1944; *s* of Joseph and Elizabeth Archer; *m* 1963, Shirley Patricia Clarke; one *s* two *d*. *Educ:* Wellington Sch. for Boys. Sales Manager Nat. Accounts, Crown Dec. Prod., Reed Internat. Ltd, 1968–83; Man. Dir, Signpost/Ashfield Paints, 1983–87; (with business partner) acquired retailer Choice DIY Ltd, 1987; Man. Dir, Choice DIY Ltd, subseq. Focus DIY, 1987–92. MInstD; MCIM. *Recreations:* golf, swimming, walking, reading, football, tennis. *Address:* Focus DIY Ltd, Gawsworth House, Westmere Drive, Crewe, Cheshire CW1 6XB; *e-mail:* vicki.rigby@focusdiy.co.uk. *Clubs:* Pleasington Golf; La Manga.

ARCHIBALD, Liliana, OBE 1997; Chairman: Adam Brothers Contingency Ltd, 1991–92 (Director, 1957–73 and 1977–85); Wilton Park Academic Council, 1992–99; *b* 25 May 1928; *d* of late Noah and Sophie Barou; *m* 1951, George Christopher Archibald (marr. diss. 1965). *Educ:* Kingsley Sch.; Geneva University. Univ. Lectr, Otago Univ., 1952–55; Director: Const & Co. Ltd, 1955–73, 1977–83; Credit Consultants Ltd, 1957–73, 1977–85; Fenchurch Gp Internat., 1985–88; Holman Wade, 1989–92; CLM Insurance Fund, 1993–99. Head of Division (Credit Insurance and Export Credit), EEC, 1973–77; EEC Advr to Lloyd's and the British Insurance Brokers Assoc., 1978–85; Internat. Affairs Advr to Lloyd's, 1981–85; Advr to Internat. Gp of Protection & Indemnity Clubs, 1980–85. Frequent lecturer on insurance-related problems. Member: Liberalisation of Trade in Services Cttee, British Invisible Exports Council, 1981–95; British Export Finance Adv. Council, 1982–91; Action Resource Centre, 1986–91; Govt Inquiry into Shops Act - Sunday and Late-Night Trading, 1984–85; Review Cttee, Banking Law Services, 1987–88; Lord Chancellor's Adv. Cttee on Legal Educn and Conduct, 1991–94; Vice-Chm., ICC Insurance Commn, 1982–87; Chm., Insurance Cttee, British Nat. Cttee, ICC, 1983–87. Member of Lloyd's, 1973–94. *Publications:* (trans. and ed) Peter the Great, 1958; (trans. and ed) Rise of the Romanovs, 1970; contrib. Bankers Magazine. *Recreations:* driving fast cars, ski-ing, gardening. *Address:* 21 Langland Gardens, NW3 6QE.

ARCULUS, Sir David; *see* Arculus, Sir T. D. G.

ARCULUS, Sir Ronald, KCMG 1979 (CMG 1968); KCVO 1980; HM Diplomatic Service, retired; *b* 11 Feb. 1923; *s* of late Cecil Arculus, MC and Ethel L. Arculus; *m* 1953, Sheila Mary Faux; one *s* one *d*. *Educ:* Solihull; Exeter Coll., Oxford (MA; Hon. Fellow, 1989). 4th Queen's Own Hussars (later Queen's Royal Hussars), 1942–45 (Captain). Joined HM Diplomatic Service, 1947; FO, 1947; San Francisco, 1948; La Paz, 1950; FO, 1951; Ankara, 1953; FO, 1957; Washington, 1961; Counsellor, 1965; New York, 1965–68; IDC, 1969; Head of Science and Technology Dept, FCO, 1970–72; Minister (Economic), Paris, 1973–77; Ambassador and Permt Leader, UK Delegn to UN Conf. on Law of the Sea, 1977–79; Ambassador to Italy, 1979–83. Dir, 1983–91, Trustee, 1986–93, Consultant, 1992–95, Glaxo Hldgs. Special Advr to Govt on Channel Tunnel trains, 1987–88. Consultant: Trusthouse Forte, 1983–86; London and Continental Bankers Ltd, 1985–90. Dir of Appeals, King's Med. Res. Trust, 1984–88. Pres., Kensington Soc., 2001– (Chm., 1999–2001). Governor, British Institute, Florence, 1983–94. FCMI (FBIM 1984). Freeman, City of London, 1981. Kt Grand Cross, Order of Merit, Italy, 1980. *Recreations:* travel, music, fine arts, antiques. *Address:* 20 Kensington Court Gardens, W8 5QF. *Clubs:* Hurlingham; Cowdray Park Polo.

ARCULUS, Sir (Thomas) David (Guy), Kt 2005; non-executive Director: Telefónica O_2 Europe plc, since 2006; Telefónica SA, since 2006; Chairman, O_2 plc (formerly mmO_2), 2004–06; *b* 2 June 1946; *s* of Thomas Guy Arculus and Mary (*née* Barton); *m* 1973, Anne Murdoch Sleeman; two *s* one *d*. *Educ:* Bromsgrove Sch.; Oriel Coll., Oxford (MA 1968); London Graduate Sch. of Business Studies (MSc 1972). VSO, 1964–65. BBC Producer, 1968–70; EMAP plc: Publisher, 1972–84; Dep. Man. Dir, 1984–89; Gp Man. Dir, 1989–97; Chief Operating Officer, United News and Media plc, 1997–98; Chairman: ipc Gp, 1998–2001; Severn Trent plc, 1998–2004; Earls Court and Olympia Ltd, 2002–04. Non-executive Director: Norcros, 1993–96; Barclays plc, 1997–2006; Guiton Gp, 2000–02; Pearson plc, 2006–. Chm., Better Regulation Task Force, Cabinet Office, 2002–05. Mem., President's Cttee, 2003–, Dep. Pres., 2005–06, CBI. Chairman: PPA, 1988–90; NCC, 1993–96. Deleg., Finance Cttee, OUP, 2000–06; Chm., Investment Cttee, Oriel Coll., Oxford, 2000–04. A Comr, Public Works Loan Bd, 2001–02. Trustee, Industry and Parliament Trust, 2006– (Fellow, 1994). Freeman, City of London, 1989. DUniv Central England, 2003. Marcus Morris Award, PPA, 1993. *Recreations:* cricket, hill walking, reading. *Address:* O_2, 5th Floor, Abbey Business Centre, 16 St Martins Le Grand, St Paul's, EC1A 4NA; *e-mail:* david.arculus@o2.com. *Clubs:* Oxford and Cambridge, Groucho, Thirty, MCC.

ARDAGH AND CLONMACNOISE, Bishop of, (RC), since 1983; **Most Rev. Colm O'Reilly;** *b* 11 Jan. 1935; *s* of John and Alicia O'Reilly. Ordained priest, 1960. *Address:* St Michael's, Longford, Ireland. *T:* (43) 46432.

ARDEE, Lord; Anthony Jacques Brabazon; *b* 30 Jan. 1977; *o s* of Earl of Meath, *qv*; *m* 2004, Fionnuala, *d* of Joseph Aston; one *d*. *Educ:* Harrow Sch.

ARDEN, Andrew Paul Russel; QC 1991; *b* 20 April 1948; *m* 1991, Joanne Leahy; one *d*. *Educ:* Stowe; University College Sch.; University Coll. London (LLB). MCIH 2002. Called to the Bar, Gray's Inn, 1974; Dir, Small Heath Community Law Centre, Birmingham, 1976–78. Local government inquiries/reviews: for GLC, 1982–83; for Bristol CC, 1985; for Hackney LBC, 1985–87, 1993–94; for Camden LBC, 1992. Founder, Arden Chambers, 1993. Vis. Prof. of Law, Faculty of Devel t and Soc., Sheffield Hallam Univ., 2001–. General Editor: Encyclopaedia of Housing Law, 1978–; Housing Law Reports, 1981–; Jl of Housing Law, 1997–; Consultant Ed., Local Government Law Reports, 2000–01 (Gen. Ed., 1999–2000). *Publications:* Manual of Housing Law, 1978, 8th edn (with Andrew Dymond), 2007; Housing Act 1980 (annotations), 1980; (with Prof. M. Partington) Quiet Enjoyment, 1980, 6th edn (with D. Carter and A. Dymond) 2002; (with Prof. M. Partington) Housing Law, 1983, 2nd edn (also with C. Hunter), 1994; (with Prof. J. T. Farrand) Rent Acts & Regulations, amended and annotated, 1981; (with C. Cross) Housing & Building Control Act 1984 (annotations), 1984; Private Tenants Handbook, 1985, 2nd edn 1989; Public Tenants Handbook, 1985, 2nd edn 1989; (with S. McGrath) Landlord & Tenant Act 1985 (annotations), 1986; Housing Act 1985 (annotations), 1986; (with J. Ramage) Housing Associations Act 1985 (annotations), 1986; Homeless Persons Handbook, 1986, 2nd edn 1988; (with C. Hunter) Housing Act 1988 (annotations), 1989; (with Sir Robert Megarry) Assured Tenancies, Vol. 3, The Rent Acts, 11th edn 1989; (with C. Hunter) Local Government & Housing Act 1989 (annotations), 1990; (with C. Hunter) Local Government Finance Law, 1994; (with C. Hunter) Housing Act 1996 (annotations), 1996; (with C. Hunter) Housing Grants, Construction and Renewal Act 1996 (annotations), 1996; Homeless Persons Act, 1982, 5th edn (with C. Hunter) Homelessness and Allocations, 1997, 7th edn (with C. Hunter and L. Johnson) 2007; (jtly) Local Government Constitutional and Administrative Law, 1999, 2nd edn 2008; *fiction:* The Motive Not The Deed, 1974; No Certain Roof, 1985; The Object Man, 1986; The Programme, 2001; four thrillers under pseudonym Bernard Bannerman, 1990–91. *Recreations:* Southern Comfort, Hill Street Blues, Camel cigarettes, Manzi's Lunch Club. *Address:* Arden Chambers, 2 John Street, WC1N 2ES. *T:* (020) 7242 4244, *Fax:* (020) 7242 3224; *e-mail:* Andrew.Arden@Ardenchambers.com.

ARDEN, Rt Rev. Donald Seymour, CBE 1981; Hon. Assistant Bishop of London, since 1981, and voluntary assistant priest, St Alban's, North Harrow, since 1986; *b* 12 April 1916; *s* of Stanley and Winifred Arden; *m* 1962, Jane Grace Riddle; two *s*. *Educ:* St Peter's Coll., Adelaide; University of Leeds (BA); College of the Resurrection, Mirfield. Deacon, 1939; Priest, 1940. Curate of: St Catherine's, Hatcham, 1939–40; Nettleden with Potten End, 1941–43; Asst Priest, Pretoria African Mission, 1944–51; Director of Usuthu Mission, Swaziland, 1951–61; Bishop of Nyasaland, 1961 (name of diocese changed, when Nyasaland was granted independence, July 1964); Bishop of Malaŵi, 1964–71, of Southern Malaŵi, 1971–81; Archbishop of Central Africa, 1971–80; Priest-in-charge of St Margaret's, Uxbridge, 1981–86. *Publication:* Out of Africa Something New, 1976.

Recreation: photography. *Address:* 6 Frobisher Close, Pinner, Middx HA5 1NN. *T:* (020) 8866 6009; *e-mail:* ardendj@yahoo.co.uk.

ARDEN, John; novelist and playwright; *b* 26 Oct. 1930; *s* of C. A. Arden and A. E. Layland; *m* 1957, Margaretta Ruth D'Arcy; four *s* (and one *s* decd). *Educ:* Sedbergh Sch.; King's Coll., Cambridge; Edinburgh Coll. of Art. *Plays produced include:* All Fall Down, 1955; The Life of Man, 1956; The Waters of Babylon, 1957; Live Like Pigs, 1958; Serjeant Musgrave's Dance, 1959; Soldier, Soldier, 1960; Wet Fish, 1962; The Workhouse Donkey, 1963; Ironhand, 1963; Armstrong's Last Goodnight, 1964; Left-Handed Liberty, 1965; The True History of Squire Jonathan and his Unfortunate Treasure, 1968; The Bagman, 1970; Pearl, 1978; To Put It Frankly, 1979; Don Quixote, 1980; Garland for a Hoar Head, 1982; The Old Man Sleeps Alone, 1982; Little Novels of Wilkie Collins, 1997; Woe Alas, the Fatal Cashbox, 1999; Wild Ride to Dublin, 2003; Poor Tom, Thy Horn is Dry, 2003; Scam, 2007; *with Margaretta D'Arcy:* The Business of Good Government, 1960; The Happy Haven, 1960; Ars Longa Vita Brevis, 1964; Friday's Hiding, 1966; The Royal Pardon, 1966; The Hero Rises Up, 1968; Island of the Mighty, 1972; The Ballygombeen Bequest, 1972; The Non-Stop Connolly Cycle, 1975; Vandaleur's Folly, 1978; The Little Gray Home in the West, 1978; The Manchester Enthusiasts, 1984; Whose is the Kingdom?, 1988; A Suburban Suicide, 1994. *Publications:* (with Margaretta D'Arcy) To Present the Pretence (essays), 1977; Silence Among the Weapons (novel), 1982; Books of Bale (novel), 1988; (with Margaretta D'Arcy) Awkward Corners (essays, etc.), 1988; Cogs Tyrannic (novellas), 1991; Jack Juggler and the Emperor's Whore (novel), 1995; The Stealing Steps (short stories), 2003. *Recreations:* antiquarianism, mythology. *Address:* c/o Casarotto Ramsay Ltd, Waverley House, 7–12 Noel Street, W1F 8GQ.

ARDEN, Rt Hon. Dame Mary (Howarth), DBE 1993; PC 2000; **Rt Hon. Lady Justice Arden;** a Lady Justice of Appeal, since 2000; *b* 23 Jan. 1947; *d* of late Lt-Col E. C. Arden, LLB, TD and M. M. Arden (*née* Smith); *m* 1973, Jonathan Hugh Mance (*see* Baron Mance); one *s* two *d*. *Educ:* Huyton College; Girton College, Cambridge (MA, LLM; Hon. Fellow, 1995); Harvard Law School (LLM). Called to the Bar, Gray's Inn, 1971 (Arden and Birkenhead Scholarships, 1971); admitted *ad eundem* to Lincoln's Inn, 1973 (Bencher, 1993); QC 1986; Attorney Gen., Duchy of Lancaster, 1991–93; a Judge of the High Ct of Justice, Chancery Div., 1993–2000; UK *ad hoc* Judge, Eur. Ct of Human Rights, 2000; Judge i/c of Internat. Judicial Relns, 2005–. Chm., Law Commn, 1996–99. Bar Mem., Law Society's Standing Cttee on Company Law, 1976–2007; Member: Financial Law Panel, 1993–2000; Steering Gp, Company Law Review Project, 1998–2001; Chairman: Wking Party of Judges' Council on Constitutional Reform, 2004–06; Papers Cttee, Commonwealth Law Conf., 2005. DTI Inspector, Rotaprint PLC, 1988–91. Mem. Council, Statute Law Soc., 2001–07. Member: Exec. Cttee, 2004–05, Advr to Bd of Trustees, 2005–, British Inst. of Internat. and Comparative Law; Ext. Adv. Bd, Faculty of Modern History, Univ. of Oxford, 2000–06; Amer. Law Inst., 2003–; Adv. Bd, Centre of European Law, KCL, 2008–; Visitor, Royal Holloway, Univ. of London, 2008. Acad. Trustee, Kennedy Meml Trust, 1995–2005. Pres., Assoc. of Women Barristers, 1994–98. Chair, CAB, Royal Cts of Justice, 1994–97; Patron, Free Repn Unit, 2007–. Hon. Fellow, Liverpool John Moores Univ., 2006. DUniv Essex, 1997; Hon. LLD: Liverpool, 1998; Warwick, 1999; RHBNC, 1999; Nottingham, 2002. Editor, Chancery Guide, 1995, 1999. *Publications:* Negligence and the Public Accountant (contrib.), 1972; Legal Editor, Current Accounting Law and Practice, by Robert Willott, 1976; (with George Eccles) Tolley's Companies Act 1980, 1980; Legal Consultant Editor: Tolley's Companies Act 1981, 1981; Tolley's Accounting Problems of the Companies Acts, 1984; Accounting Provisions of the Companies Act 1985, 1985; Coopers & Lybrand Deloitte Manual of Accounting, vols 1 and 2, 1990, 1995; Jt Gen. Editor and Contributor, Buckley on the Companies Acts, 14th edn: Special Bulletin, 1990, 15th edn 2000 (updated biannually); (contrib.) Accounting and the Law, 1992; (contrib.) Perspectives on Company Law, 1995; (contrib.) Law, Society and Economy, 1997; articles in legal jls. *Recreations:* travel, reading, theatre. *Address:* Royal Courts of Justice, Strand, WC2A 2LL.

ARDEN, Peter Leonard; QC 2006; *b* 5 April 1960; *s* of Surgeon Captain Leonard Arden and Ann Arden; *m* 1999, Zia Kurban Bhaloo; one *d*. *Educ:* University Coll. London (LLB); Queens' Coll., Cambridge (LLB 1982). Called to the Bar, Gray's Inn, 1983.

ARFIELD, John Alan; University Librarian, University of Western Australia, since 1996; *b* 15 March 1949; *s* of Donald Sidney Arfield and Barbara Winifred Arfield (*née* Alderton); *m* 1st, 1970, Paula May Perrin (marr. diss. 1998); one *s* two *d*; 2nd, 2004, Susan June Henshall. *Educ:* Kingston Grammar Sch.; Jesus Coll., Cambridge (BA 1971; MA 1975); Univ. of Sheffield (MA 1973). Cambridge University Library: Asst Liby Officer, 1973–78; Asst Under-Librarian, 1978–79; Under-Librarian, 1979–81; Sub-Librarian (Tech. Services), UC, Cardiff, 1981–88; Dep. Librarian, Reading Univ., 1988–92; University Librarian, Loughborough Univ., 1992–96. *Publications:* articles in librarianship. *Recreations:* squash, cricket, theatre, music. *Address:* University Library, University of Western Australia, Crawley, WA 6009, Australia.

ARFON-JONES, Elisabeth, (Mrs B. Watkins); DL; Deputy President, Asylum and Immigration Tribunal, since 2005; *b* 2 July 1950; *d* of late Arfon Arfon-Jones and Margaret Arfon-Jones (*née* Price); *m* 1982, Brian Watkins, *qv*; one *d*. *Educ:* University Coll. London (LLB 1971). Called to the Bar, Gray's Inn, 1972 (William Shaw Schol.; Fellow, 2008); in practice at the Bar, 1973–77; Sen. Prosecuting Solicitor, Cheshire, 1977–80; Crown Counsel, Bermuda, 1980–81; Registrar, Supreme Court, Bermuda, 1981–83; an Immigration Adjudicator, 1997–2005; Dep. Chief Immigration Adjudicator, 2001–04; Acting Chief Immigration Adjudicator, 2004–05. A Civil Service Comr, 2007–. A Lay Chm., NHS Complaints Rev. Panels in Wales, 1995–2006. US Liby of Congress Rep. (pt-time), Islamabad, 1984–86; Chm., Internat. Cttee, BC Red Cross, Vancouver, 1986–90; Founding Chm., Swaziland Hospice at Home, 1990–93. Mem. Bd, Community Fund (formerly National Lottery Charities Bd), 1998–2004 (Chm., Wales Cttee, 2000–02). Member: Ministerial Adv. Gp on Community Volunteering, 1999–2004; Multi-Centre Res. Ethics Cttee for Wales, 2001–03. Lay Mem., Lord Chancellor's Adv. Cttee for Appointment of JPs in Gwent, 2000–. Hon. Sec., Assoc. of Women Barristers, 1999–2001. Mem. Council, Barnardo's, 2001–08 (Chm., Wales Cttee, 2007–08). DL Gwent, 2006. *Recreations:* 'laughter and the love of friends' (worldwide), theatre, ski-ing. *Address:* c/o Coutts & Co., 440 Strand, WC2R 0QS; *e-mail:* watb@compuserve.com. *Clubs:* Athenæum, Royal Over-Seas League.

ARGENT, Malcolm, CBE 1985; Deputy Chairman, Civil Aviation Authority, 1995–98; *b* 14 Aug. 1935; *s* of Leonard James and Winifred Hilda Argent; *m* 1st, 1961, Mary Patricia Addis Stimson (marr. diss. 1983); one *s* one *d*; 2nd, 1986, Thelma Hazel Eddleston. *Educ:* Palmer's Sch., Grays, Essex. General Post Office, London Telecommunications Region: Exec. Officer, 1953–62; Higher Exec. Officer, 1962–66; Principal, PO Headquarters, 1966–70; Private Sec., Man. Dir, Telecommunications, 1970–74; Personnel Controller, External Telecommun. Exec., 1974–75; Dir, Chairman's Office, PO Central Headquarters, 1975–77; Dir, Eastern Telecommun. Region, 1977; Secretary: of the Post Office, 1978–81; British Telecommunications Corp., 1981–94; British Telecommunications plc, 1984–94 (Dir, 1989–98); Chm., NATS, 1996–98. Trustee, British Telecommunications Staff Superannuation Fund, 1981–94. Director: McCaw Cellular Communications Inc., 1989–94; Westminster Health Care plc, 1992–99; Clerical, Medical & Gen. Assce Soc., 1994–2001; Clerical Medical Investment Gp, 1997–2001; Chm., Envision Licensing Ltd, 1999. Member: Council, CBI, 1994–95; Cttee, Essex Magistrates' Courts, 2000–04. Freeman, City of London, 1987. CCMI (CIMgt 1992; CBIM 1991; FBIM 1980). Hon. DSc Aston, 2004. *Recreation:* golf. *Address:* Chestnuts, Fryerning Lane, Ingatestone, Essex CM4 0GF.

ARGENTA, Nancy Maureen; soprano; *b* Nelson, Canada, 17 Jan. 1957; *d* of Hugh and Agnes Herbison; adopted Argenta as professional name. *Educ:* Vancouver Community Coll.; Univ. of Western Ontario (Artist Dip. in Performance). Début, Hippolyte and Aricie, Fest. d'Aix en Provence, 1983; has performed in Australia, Europe, Japan, N America, S America, with major orchestras and companies, including Boston SO, Leipzig Gewandhaus Orch., Montreal SO, LPO and Philharmonia Orch; also tours as a recitalist. Has made over 50 recordings. *Recreations:* walking, gardening, cycling, woodwork. *Address:* c/o Askonas Holt Ltd, Lincoln House, 300 High Holborn, WC1V 7JH. *T:* (020) 7400 1700.

ARGENTINA, Bishop of, since 2002; **Most Rev. Gregory James Venables;** Presiding Bishop (Primate) of the Province of the Southern Cone of America, since 2001; *b* 6 Dec. 1949; *s* of Rev. Dudley James Venables and May Norah Venables (*née* Saddington); *m* 1970, Sylvia Margaret Norton; one *s* two *d*. *Educ:* Chatham House; Kingston Univ.; Christchurch Coll., Canterbury. Computer Systems Officer, Sterling Winthrop, 1971–72; English master, Holy Cross Sch., Broadstairs, 1974–77; Headmaster, St Andrews Coll., Asuncion, Paraguay, 1978–89; ordained deacon, March 1984, priest, Nov. 1984; Asst Curate, St Helen's and St Giles, Rainham with St Mary's, Wennington, dio. of Chelmsford, 1990–93; Asst Bishop, dio. of Peru and Bolivia, 1993–95; Bishop of Bolivia, and Vice-Primate, Province of the Southern Cone of America, 1995–2000; Coadjutor Bishop of Argentina, 2000–02. *Publication:* Look to the Scars, 1973. *Recreations:* reading, music, walking. *Address:* 25 de Mayo 282, 1001 Buenos Aires, Argentina. *T:* (11) 43424618, *Fax:* (11) 43310234; *e-mail:* diocesisanglibue@fibertel.com.ar.

ARGERICH, Martha; pianist; *b* Buenos Aires, 5 June 1941; *m* 1st, 1963, Robert Chen (marr. diss.); one *d*; 2nd, 1969, Charles Dutoit, conductor (marr. diss.); one *d*. Studied with Vincenzo Scaramuzza, Madeleine Lipatti, Nikita Magaloff, Friedrich Gulda, Arturo Benedetti Michelangeli, Stefan Askenase. Début in Buenos Aires, 1949, in London, 1964; soloist with leading orchestras. Numerous recordings. First Prize: Ferruccio Busoni Internat. Competition, Bolzano, Italy, 1957; Internat. Music Competition, Geneva, 1957; Internat. Chopin Competition, Warsaw, 1965. *Address:* c/o Jacques Thelen Agence Artistique, 15 avenue Montaigne, 75008 Paris, France.

ARGUS, Donald Robert, AO 1998; Chairman, BHP Billiton (formerly BHP Ltd), since 1999 (Director, since 1996); *b* 1 Aug. 1938; *s* of Dudley Francis and Evelyn Argus; *m* 1961, Patricia Anne Hutson; three *d*. *Educ:* C of E GS, Brisbane; RMIT; Harvard Univ. FAIB; FCPA; FAICD. National Australia Bank: General Manager: Credit Bureau, 1984–87; Gp Strategic Develt, 1987–89; Chief Operating Officer, 1989–90; Man. Dir and Chief Exec., 1990–99. Chm., Brambles Ltd (formerly Brambles Industries), 1999– (Dir, 1999–); Director: Southcorp Ltd, 1999–2003; Australian Foundn Investment Co., 1999–; Member: Allianz Internat. Adv. Bd, 2000–; Internat. Adv. Bd, NYSE, 2005–. Hon. LLD Monash; DUniv Griffith. *Recreations:* golf, reading, hockey. *Address:* c/o BHP Billiton, 180 Lonsdale Street, Melbourne, Vic 3000, Australia. *T:* (3) 96093891, *Fax:* (3) 96093588. *Clubs:* Australian, Melbourne (Melbourne); Kingston Heath Golf; Queensland Cricketers (Brisbane).

ARGYLL, 13th Duke of, *cr* 1701 (Scotland), 1892 (UK); **Torquhil Ian Campbell;** Marquess of Lorne and Kintyre; Earl of Campbell and Cowal; Viscount Lochow and Glenyla; Baron Inveraray, Mull, Morvern and Tiry, 1701; Baron Campbell, 1445; Earl of Argyll, 1457; Baron Lorne, 1470; Baron Kintyre, 1633 (Scotland); Baron Sundridge, 1766; Baron Hamilton of Hameldon, 1776; Bt 1627; 37th Baron and 47th Knight of Lochow; Celtic title, Mac Cailein Mor, Chief of Clan Campbell; Hereditary Master of the Royal Household, Scotland; Hereditary High Sheriff of the County of Argyll; Admiral of the Western Coast and Isles; Keeper of the Great Seal of Scotland and of the Castles of Dunstaffnage, Dunoon, and Carrick and Tarbert; *b* 29 May 1968; *s* of 12th Duke of Argyll, and Iona Mary, *d* of Capt. Sir Ivar Colquhoun, 8th Bt; *S* father, 2001; *m* 2002, Eleanor Mary, *d* of Peter H. G. Cadbury; two *s*. *Educ:* Craigflower; Cargilfield; Glenalmond Coll.; Royal Agricultural Coll., Cirencester. A Page of Honour to the Queen, 1981–83. *Heir: s* Marquess of Lorne, *qv*. *Address:* Inveraray Castle, Inveraray, Argyll PA32 8XF.

ARGYLL AND THE ISLES, Bishop of, since 2004; **Rt Rev. (Alexander) Martin Shaw;** *b* 22 Sept. 1944; *s* of James D. D. Shaw, MBE and Jean Shaw; *m* 1971, Elspeth Longden; one *s* one *d* (and one *s* decd). *Educ:* Trinity Coll., Glenalmond; KCL (AKC 1967); Glasgow Univ. (Dip. Social Psych. 1969). Ordained deacon, 1968, priest, 1969; Curate: St Oswald's, Glasgow, 1968–70; Old St Paul's, Edinburgh, 1970–75; Chaplain, King's Coll., Cambridge, 1975–77; Principal, Inst. of Christian Studies, All Saints, Margaret St, W1, 1977–78; Rector, Holy Trinity, Dunoon, 1978–81; Succentor, Exeter Cathedral, 1981–83; Diocesan Missioner, Exeter Dio., 1983–89; Res. Canon, Precentor and Sub-Dean, St Edmundsbury Cathedral, 1989–2004; Temp. Dean, King's Coll., Cambridge, 2002. Broadcaster on radio and television; writer of poetry; singer (baritone), song recitals and oratorios. *Publications:* First Light, 2001; My Father's Arms, song cycle for soprano and string trio, 2002; Christ's Winter Pilgrimage, 2006. *Recreations:* walking, movies, photography, opera, reading, avoiding gardening. *Address:* The Pines, Ardconnel Road, Oban, Argyll PA34 5DR. *T:* (01631) 566912; *e-mail:* alexandermartin.shaw@virgin.net.

ARGYLL AND THE ISLES, Bishop of, (RC), since 1999; **Rt Rev. Ian Murray;** *b* 15 Dec. 1932; *s* of John Murray and Margaret Murray (*née* Rodgers). *Educ:* Blairs Coll., Aberdeen; Royal Scots Coll., Valladolid, Spain; BA Hons Open Univ. 1991. Ordained priest, 1956; Curate: Lochore, Fife, 1956–61; St Columba, Edinburgh, 1961–63; Vice-Rector, Royal Scots Coll., Spain, 1963–70; Chaplain, Stirling Univ., 1970–78; Parish Priest: St Bride, Cowdenbeath, 1978–85; St Ninian, Edinburgh, 1985–87; Rector, Royal Scots Coll., Valladolid, 1987–88, Salamanca, 1988–94; Parish Priest: Galashiels, 1994–96; St Francis Xavier, Falkirk, 1996–99; VG, Archdio. of St Andrews and Edinburgh, 1996–99. Prelate of Honour, 1989. *Address:* Bishop's House, Esplanade, Oban PA34 5AB. *T:* (01631) 571395.

ARGYLL AND THE ISLES, Dean of; *see* MacCallum, Very Rev. N. D.

ARGYLL AND THE ISLES, Provost in; *see* Maclean, Very Rev. A. M.

ARGYRIS, Nicholas John; Director, Communications Services: policy and regulatory framework (formerly Telecommunications Trans European Networks and Services and Postal Services), European Commission, 1993–2001; *b* 22 March 1943; *s* of late Costas

Argyris and Eileen Argyris (*née* Pollard); *m* 1st, 1966, Carol Bartlett (marr. diss. 1991); one *s* two *d*; 2nd, 1992, Danielle Canneel. *Educ:* St Paul's Sch.; Clare Coll., Cambridge (BA Hons Econs 1965; Cert. Ed. 1966). Schoolmaster, 1966–68; with Govt Econ. Service, in Depts of Econ. Affairs, Technol. and Trade and Ind., 1969–73; joined European Commission, 1973: worked in Directorate General for: Competition, 1973–84 (State Aids); Develt, 1985–86 (Trade and Private Investment Issues); Competition, 1987–91 (Head of Div., Transport and Tourist Industries); Dir for internal market, DG for Energy, 1991–93. Former Mem., England junior chess team (London junior champion, 1960). *Publications:* articles on air transport, energy and telecommunications policy. *Recreations:* reading, walking, music, circle dancing, gardening, chess problems.

ARIAS-SALGADO Y MONTALVO, Fernando; Ambassador of Spain to Morocco, 2001–04; Barrister-at-Law; *b* 3 May 1938; *s* of Gabriel Arias-Salgado y Cubas and Maria Montalvo Gutierrez. Mem., Illustrious Coll. of Lawyers of Madrid. Entered Diplomatic Sch., 1963; Sec., Permanent Rep. of Spain to UN, 1966; Advr, UN Security Council, 1968–69; Asst Dir Gen., Promotion of Research, 1971, Asst Dir Gen., Internat. Co-operation, 1972, Min. of Educn and Science; Legal Advr (internat. matters), Legal Dept, Min. of Foreign Affairs, 1973; Counsellor, Spanish Delegn to Internat. Court of Justice, 1975; Tech. Sec. Gen., Min. of Foreign Affairs, 1976; Dir Gen., Radiotelevisión Española, 1977; Ambassador to the Court of St James's, 1981–83; Dir, Internat. Legal Dept, Min. of Foreign Affairs, 1983–85; Consul-Gen. for Spain in Zürich, 1985–90; Ambassador and Perm. Rep. of Spain to Internat. Orgns in Vienna, 1990–93; Ambassador: to Tunisia, 1993–96; to Switzerland and Liechtenstein, 1996–2001. Comendador: Orden de Isabel la Católica; Orden del Merito Civil; Orden de San Raimundo de Peñafort; Caballero, Orden de Carlos III.

ARIAS SÁNCHEZ, Oscar, PhD; President of Costa Rica, 1986–90 and since 2006; President, Arias Foundation for Peace, since 1990; *b* 13 Sept. 1940; *m* Margarita; one *s* one *d*. *Educ:* Univ. of Costa Rica; Univ. of Essex. Prof., Sch. of Political Sciences, Univ. of Costa Rica, 1969–72; Minister of Nat. Planning and Economic Policy, 1972–77; Gen. Sec., 1979–86, Liberación Nacional Party; Congressman, 1978–82. Formulated Central American Peace Agreement, 1986–87. Member: Stockholm Internat. Peace Res. Inst.; Carter Center; Inst. for Internat. Studies, Stanford Univ.; ILD Rockefeller Foundn; Internat. Centre for Human Rights and Democratic Develt; Inter Press Service; Bd of Dirs, WWF. Hon. PhD: Harvard, 1988; Essex, 1988; Dartmouth, 1992. Nobel Peace Prize, 1987; Martin Luther King Peace Prize, Martin Luther King Foundn, 1987; Prince of Asturias Prize, 1988; Nat. Audubon Soc. Prize, 1988; Liberty Medal, Univ. of Pennsylvania, 1991. *Publications:* Pressure Groups in Costa Rica, 1970; Who Governs in Costa Rica?, 1976; Latin American Democracy, Independence and Society, 1977; Roads for Costa Rica's Development, 1977; New Ways for Costa Rican Development, 1980. *Address:* Casa Presidencial, 520–2010 Zapote, San José, Costa Rica; c/o Arias Foundation/Center for Peace, PO Box 8–6410–1000, San José, Costa Rica. *T:* 2552955, *Fax:* 2552244.

ARIE, Prof. Thomas Harry David, CBE 1995; FRCPsych, FRCP, FFPH; Foundation Professor of Health Care of the Elderly, University of Nottingham, 1977–95, now Professor Emeritus, and Hon. Consultant Psychiatrist, Nottingham Health Authority, 1977–95; *b* 9 Aug. 1933; *s* of late Dr O. M. Arie and Hedy Arie; *m* 1963, Eleanor, FRCP, *yr d* of Sir Robert Aitken, FRCP, FRACP; two *d* one *s*. *Educ:* Reading Sch.; Balliol Coll., Oxford (Open Exhibnr in Classics; 1st cl. Hons, Classical Mods); MA, BM 1960; DPM. Training, Radcliffe Infirmary, Oxford, and Maudsley and London Hosps; Consultant Psychiatrist, Goodmayes Hosp., 1969–77; Sen. Lectr in Social Medicine, London Hosp. Med. Coll.; Hon. Sen. Lectr in Psychiatry, UCH Med. Sch. Royal College of Psychiatrists: Mem. Council, 1975–79, 1981–86, 1991–97; Vice-Pres., 1984–86; Chm., Specialist Section on Psychiatry of Old Age, 1981–86; Jt Cttee on Higher Psychiatric Training, 1978–84; Hon. FRCPsych 2001; Royal College of Physicians: Geriatrics Cttee, 1984–90; Examining Bd for Dipl. in Geriatric Medicine, 1983–92. Member: Central Council for Educn and Trng in Social Work, 1975–81; Standing Med. Adv. Cttee, DHSS, 1980–84; Cttee on Review of Medicines, 1981–90; Res. Adv. Council, Nat. Inst. for Social Work, 1982–90; Med. Adv. Cttee to Registrar General, 1990–93; Council, AgeCare, Royal Surgical Aid Soc., 1995– (Vice-Chm., 1998–2007; Vice-Pres., 2008). Fotheringham Lectr, Univ. of Toronto, 1979; Vis. Prof., NZ Geriatrics Soc., 1980; Dozor Vis. Prof., Univ. of the Negev, Israel, 1988; Fröhlich Vis. Prof., UCLA, 1991; Vis. Prof., Keele Univ., 1997. Chm., Geriatric Psych. Section, World Psych. Assoc., 1989–93. Governor, Centre for Policy on Ageing, 1992–98. Founders' Medal, British Geriatrics Soc., 2005. *Publications:* (ed) Health Care of the Elderly, 1981; (ed) Recent Advances in Psychogeriatrics, Vol. 1 1985, Vol. 2 1992; articles in med. jls and chapters in other people's books. *Address:* Cromwell House, West Church Street, Kenninghall, Norfolk NR16 2EN. *T:* (01953) 887375.

ARIS, Aung San Suu Kyi, (Mrs M. V. Aris); *see* Aung San Suu Kyi.

ARIS, John Bernard Benedict, TD 1967; with IMPACT Programme, 1990–99 (Director, 1990–95); *b* 6 June 1934; *s* of John (Jack) Woodbridge Aris and Joyce Mary (*née* Williams). *Educ:* Eton (King's Schol.); Magdalen Coll., Oxford (MA). FBCS; CITP. LEO Computers, 1958–63; English Electric Computers, 1963–69; ICL, 1969–75; Imperial Group, 1975–85 (Man., Gp Management Services, 1982–85); Dir, NCC, 1985–90. Non-exec. Dir, NCC, 1981–85; Chairman: FOCUS Private Sector Users Cttee (DTI), 1984–85; Alvey IT User Panel, 1985–88; Mem., IT 86 Cttee, 1986. Founder Freeman, Co. of Information Technologists, 1987 (Liveryman, 1992). FInstD; FRSA. *Publication:* (jtly) User Driven Innovation, 1996. *Recreations:* travel, music, art, scuba diving, gastronomy.

ARKELL, John Hardy, MA; Headmaster, Gresham's School, Holt, 1991–2002; *b* 10 July 1939; *s* of Hardy Arkell and Vivienne (*née* Le Sueur); *m* 1963, Jean Harding, JP; two *s* one *d*. *Educ:* Stowe Sch.; Selwyn Coll., Cambridge (BA Hons English Tripos; MA). National Service, HM Submarines, 1958–60 (Sub Lieut). Asst Master, Abingdon Sch., 1963–64; Head of VI form English, Framlingham Coll., 1964–70; Fettes College, 1970–83: Head of English Dept, 1971–73, 1976–78; Founder Headmaster, Fettes Jun. Sch., 1973–79; Housemaster, Glencorse House, 1979–83; Headmaster, Wrekin Coll., 1983–91. Chm., ISIS, Central England, 1989–91; Sec., HMC Midland Div., 1990–91; HMC Rep., ISC (formerly ISJC) Special Needs Cttee, 1991–2002. Governor: Oakham Sch., 2001–; Beeston Hall Prep. Sch., 2003–. Lay Reader, Benefice of Weybourne, 2006–. *Recreations:* tennis, sailing, motor cars, drama. *Address:* Church Farm House, Lower Bodham, Holt, Norfolk NR25 6PS. *T:* (01263) 712137.

ARKLEY, Alistair Grant, CBE 2006; DL; Chairman, New Century Enterprises (formerly New Century Inns) Ltd, since 1999; *b* 13 May 1947; *s* of Alexander Arkley and Victoria Margaret Arkley (*née* Grant); *m* 1972, Kathleen Ann Raeburn; three *s*. *Educ:* Aberdeen Acad.; Aberdeen Univ. (BSc Engrg). Engrg Officer, R&D, ICI, 1971–72; various posts, selling and mktg, Procter & Gamble, 1972–79; Sales and Mktg Dir, Scottish Breweries, Scottish & Newcastle plc, 1979–85; Man. Dir, J. W. Cameron & Co. Ltd, 1985–91; Chief Exec., Century Inns plc, 1991–99. Chairman: Passionate Pub Co., 1999–; Chameleon Pub. Co., 1999–; Steelite Internat. plc, 2006–; non-exec. Dir, Belhaven plc, 1999–2005. Mem. Bd, One North East RDA, 1999–2004. Chairman: Tees Valley Partnership, 1999–2005; Northern Business Forum, 2005–07. Dir, British Beer and Pub Assoc., 1991–2007. DL Co. Durham, 2007. *Recreations:* countryside, gardening, football (spectating). *Address:* New Century Enterprises Ltd, Belasis Business Centre, Coxwold Way, Billingham, Tees Valley TS23 4EA. *T:* (office) (01642) 343415, *Fax:* (01642) 345729; *e-mail:* a.arkley@new-century.co.uk. *Club:* Royal Automobile.

ARLINGTON, Baroness (11th in line), *cr* 1664; **Jennifer Jane Forwood;** *b* 7 May 1939; *er d* of Maj.-Gen. Sir John Nelson, KCVO, CB, DSO, OBE, MC, and Lady Jane Nelson; *S* in 1999 to Barony of uncle, 9th Duke of Grafton, which had fallen into abeyance in 1936; *m* 1964, Rodney Forwood (*d* 1999); two *s*. *Educ:* Downham. *Recreations:* horse racing, bridge, gardening. *Heir: s* Hon. Patrick John Dudley Forwood [*b* 23 April 1967; *m* 2001, Alexandra, *yr d* of late Anthony Psychopulos and of Mrs Neil Maconochie].

ARMAGH, Archbishop of, and Primate of All Ireland, since 2007; **Most Rev. Alan Edwin Thomas Harper,** OBE 1996; *b* Tamworth, 20 March 1944; *m* 1967, Helen Louise McLean; one *s* three *d*. *Educ:* Leeds Univ. (BA 1965); C of I Theol Coll. Sen. Insp. of Historic Monuments, Archaeol Survey of NI, 1966–74; Asst Prin. Planning Officer, Staffs CC, 1974–75. Ordained deacon, 1978, priest, 1979; Curate Asst, Ballywillan, 1978–80; Incumbent: Moville with Greencastle, 1980–82; Christ Church, Londonderry, 1982–86; St John's, Malone, 1986–2002; Precentor, Belfast Cathedral, 1996–2002; Archdeacon of Connor, 1996–2002; Bishop of Connor, 2002–07. Preb. of St Audoen, Nat. Cathedral and Collegiate Church of St Patrick, Dublin, 1990–2001. Founder Trustee and first Chm., Ulster Historic Churches Trust, 1995–2000; Mem., 1980–95, Chm., 1988–95, Historic Monuments Council for NI. *Address:* 5 Beresford Road, Armagh, Co. Armagh BT61 9AU. *T:* (office) (028) 3752 7144; *e-mail:* archbishop@armagh.anglican.org.

ARMAGH, Archbishop of, (RC), and Primate of All Ireland, since 1996; **His Eminence Cardinal Seán Brady;** *b* 16 Aug. 1939. *Educ:* St Patrick's Coll., Cavan; St Patrick's Coll., Maynooth (BA 1960; HDipEd 1967); Irish Coll., Rome; Lateran Univ., Rome (STB 1964; DCL 1967). Ordained priest, 1964; teacher, High Sch., St Patrick's Coll., Cavan, 1967–80; Vice Rector, 1980–87, Rector, 1987–93, Pontifical Irish Coll., Rome; Parish Priest, Castletara, Co. Cavan, 1993–95; Coadjutor Archbishop of Armagh, 1995–96. Cardinal, 2007. *Address:* Ara Coeli, Armagh, Ireland BT61 7QY; *e-mail:* admin@aracoeli.com.

ARMAGH, Dean of; *see* Rooke, Very Rev. P. W.

ARMANI, Giorgio; Italian fashion designer; *b* 11 July 1934; *s* of late Ugo Armani and of Maria Raimondi. *Educ:* Univ. of Milan. Mil. Service, 1957. La Rinascente, Milan, 1957–64; Designer and Product Developer, Nino Cerruti, 1964–70; freelance designer, 1970–; founded Giorgio Armani SpA, 1975 and created own-label ready-to-wear clothing; has since introduced other Armani lines, incl. accessories, fragrances and eyewear. Dr *hc* RCA, 1991. Numerous fashion awards. Gran Cavaliere dell'ordine al merito della Repubblica Italiana, 1987 (Commendatore, 1985; Grand'Ufficiale, 1986). *Address:* Giorgio Armani SpA, Via Borgonuovo, 11 20121 Milan, Italy. *T:* (02) 723181; Giorgio Armani Corporation, 114 Fifth Avenue, New York, NY 10011, USA.

ARME, Prof. Christopher, PhD, DSc; CBiol, FIBiol; Professor of Zoology, University of Keele, 1979–2007, now Emeritus; *b* 10 Aug. 1939; *s* of Cyril Boddington and Monica Henrietta Arme; *m* 1962; three *s*. *Educ:* Heanor Grammar Sch.; Univ. of Leeds (BSc 1961; PhD 1964); Univ. of Keele (DSc 1985). FIBiol 1980; CBiol 1980. SRC/NATO Res. Fellow, Univ. of Leeds, 1964–66; Res. Associate, Rice Univ., Texas, 1966–68; Lectr, later Reader, QUB, 1968–76; Head of Biology Gp, N Staffs Polytechnic, 1976–79; Head, Dept of Biol Scis, 1981–88, Dean of Natural Scis, 1998–2001, Univ. of Keele; Dir of Terrestrial and Freshwater Scis, NERC, 1993–95 (on leave of absence from Keele Univ.). British Society for Parasitology: Hon. Gen. Sec., 1980–83; Silver Jubilee Lectr, 1987; Vice Pres., 1988–90; Pres., 1990–92; Hon. Mem., 1992. Chm., Heads of Zool. Depts of Univs Gp, 1981–82; Institute of Biology: Hon. Treas. and Chm., Finance Cttee, 1986–93; Chm., Staffing Cttee, 1993–99; Treas., Europ. Fedn of Parasitologists, 1992–2000. Mem., Biol Scis Cttee, and Chm., Animal Scis and Psychol. Sub-Cttee, SERC, 1989–92; Chairman: Steering Cttee, NERC special topic prog. on wildlife diseases, 1992–93; Policy Adv. Cttee, Envmtl Res. Prog., DFID (formerly ODA), 1995–99; Molecular Genetics in Ecology Initiative, Aberdeen Univ./Inst. of Terrestrial Ecology, Banchory, 1995–99; Mem., Adv. Cttee, Centre for Ecology and Hydrology, NERC, 1998–2002. Mem. Bd of Govs, Harper Adams Agricl Coll., 1996–2002. Hon. Member: Czechoslovakian Parasitological Soc., 1989; All-Russia Soc. of Helminthologists, 1992; Bulgarian Soc. for Parasitology, 1995. Jt Editor, Parasitology, 1987–2006; Ed.-in-Chief, Parasites and Vectors, 2008–. Hon. DSc Slovak Acad. of Scis, 1995. K. I. Skryabin Medal, All-Russian Soc. of Helminthologists, 1994; Hovorka Medal, Slovak Acad. of Scis, 1995; Charter Award Medal, Inst. of Biology, 1995. *Publications:* (ed jtly) Biology of the Eucestoda, Vols I and II, 1983; (ed) Molecular Transfer across Parasite Membranes, 1988; (ed jtly) Toxic Reactions of the Liver, 1992; contribs to parasitological jls. *Address:* School of Life Sciences, University of Keele, Keele, Staffs ST5 5BG. *T:* (01782) 583025.

ARMFIELD, Diana Maxwell, (Mrs Bernard Dunstan), RA 1991 (ARA 1989); RWS 1983 (ARWS 1977); RWA; RCA; painter, since 1965; *b* 11 June 1920; *d* of Joseph Harold Armfield and Gertrude Mary Uttley; *m* 1949, Bernard Dunstan, *qv*; two *s* (and one *s* decd). *Educ:* Bedales; Bournemouth Art Sch.; Slade Sch.; Central School of Arts and Crafts. MCSD. Textile/wallpaper designer, 1949–65; work in Fest. of Britain, 1951, and Permanent Collection, V&A Mus. One woman exhibitions: Browse & Darby (London), regularly, 1979–; RCA Conwy, and Cardiff, 2001; other exhibitions include: Friends' Room, RA, also Cardiff and Llanbedrog, 1995; Bala, 1996; Wassenaar, Holland, 1998; Nat. Mus. of Cardiff, 1998; Bedales Art & Design Centenary Exhibn, 1999; Kentucky, USA, 2005; Arts Club, London, 2006; Curwen & New Acad. Gall. 50th Anniv. Show, 2008. Artist in Residence: Perth, WA, 1985; Jackson, Wyoming, 1989. Work in Permanent Collections: Govt picture collection, RWA; Yale Center for British Art; Nat. Trust; Contemporary Art Soc. for Wales; Lancaster City Mus.; RWS collection, BM; Faringdon Trust; RWS Queen's birthday collection, 1996; Commissions: Reuters, Nat. Trust, 1989; Prince of Wales, 1989; Royal Acad. diploma collection. RWA 1975, now Hon. Retired RWA; RCA 1991, now Hon. Retired RCA; Hon. Mem., Pastel Soc., 1988; Hon. NEAC 2000. *Publications:* (jtly) Painting in Oils, 1982; (jtly) Drawing, 1982; *relevant publication:* The Art of Diana Armfield, by Julian Halsby, 1995. *Recreations:* music, gardening, travel. *Address:* 10 High Park Road, Kew, Richmond, Surrey TW9 4BH; Llwynhir, Parc, Bala, Gwynedd, North Wales LL23 7YU. *Club:* Arts.

ARMIDALE, Bishop of, since 2000; **Rt Rev. Peter Robert Brain,** DMin; *b* 2 April 1947; *s* of Paul W. and Doris J. Brain; *m* 1973, Christine Charlton; three *s* one *d*. *Educ:* North Sydney Tech. High Sch.; Moore Theol Coll. (ThL, DipA, DipRE); Fuller Seminary, Pasadena (DMin 1994). Worked in Accounts, and Investments, Australian Mutual Provident Soc., 1963–70. Ordained deacon and priest, 1975; Curate: Sans Souci,

Sydney, 1975–76; Holy Trinity, Adelaide, 1977–80; Rector: Maddington, Perth, 1980–88; Wanneroo, Perth, 1988–99. *Publication:* Going the Distance in Ministry, 2004. *Recreations:* golf, walking, woodwork. *Address:* 206 Allingham Street, Armidale, NSW 2350, Australia. *T:* (2) 67724491.

ARMITAGE, Edward, CB 1974; Comptroller-General, Patent Office and Industrial Property and Copyright Department, Department of Trade (formerly Trade and Industry), 1969–77; *b* 16 July 1917; *s* of Harry and Florence Armitage; *m* 1st, 1940, Marjorie Pope (*d* 1997); one *s* two *d*; 2nd, 1999, Marjorie Malby. *Educ:* Huddersfield Coll.; St Catharine's Coll., Cambridge. Patent Office, BoT: Asst Examr 1939; Examr 1944; Sen. Examr 1949; Principal Examr 1960; Suptg Examr 1962; Asst Comptroller 1966. Governor, Centre d'Etudes Internationales de la Propriété Industrielle, Strasbourg, 1975–85; Mem. Council, Common Law Inst. of Intellectual Property, 1981–97; Pres., Internat. Assoc. for Protection of Industrial Property, 1983–86. *Recreations:* bowls, bridge, gardening. *Address:* Richmond House, Plud Street, Wedmore, Somerset BS28 4BE. *T:* (01934) 712756.

See also P. Armitage.

ARMITAGE, (Ernest) Keith; QC 1994; **His Honour Judge Armitage;** a Circuit Judge, since 2001; *b* 15 May 1949; *s* of Selwyn and Marjorie Armitage; *m* 1972, Anita Sharples; one *s* one *d*. *Educ:* Trent Coll., Notts; Univ. of Liverpool (LLB Hons). Called to the Bar, Middle Temple, 1970; in practice, Northern Circuit, 1971–2001; a Recorder, 1989–2001. *Recreations:* travel, gliding (soaring). *Address:* Court of Justice, Crown Square, Manchester M3 3FL.

ARMITAGE, John Vernon, PhD; Principal, 1975–97, and Hon. Senior Fellow in Mathematical Sciences, since 1997, College of St Hild and St Bede, Durham; *b* 21 May 1932; *s* of Horace Armitage and Evelyn (*née* Hauton); *m* 1963, Sarah Catherine Clay; two *s*. *Educ:* Rothwell Grammar Sch., Yorks; UCL (BSc, PhD); Cuddesdon Coll., Oxford. Asst Master: Pontefract High Sch., 1956–58; Shrewsbury Sch., 1958–59; Lectr in Maths, Univ. of Durham, 1959–67; Sen. Lectr in Maths, King's Coll., London, 1967–70; Prof. of Mathematical Educn, Univ. of Nottingham, 1970–75; Special Prof., Nottingham Univ., 1976–79. Chm., Math. Instruction Sub-Cttee, Brit. Nat. Cttee for Maths, Royal Soc., 1975–78. *Publications:* (with H. B. Griffiths) A Companion to Advanced Mathematics, 1969; (with W. F. Eberlein) Elliptic Functions, 2006; papers on theory of numbers in various jls. *Recreations:* railways, cricket and most games inexpertly. *Address:* 7 Potters Close, Potters Bank, Durham DH1 3UB.

ARMITAGE, Keith; *see* Armitage, E. K.

ARMITAGE, Air Chief Marshal Sir Michael (John), KCB 1983; CBE 1975; Commandant, Royal College of Defence Studies, 1988–89; *b* 25 Aug. 1930; *m* 1st, 1955 (marr. diss. 1969); three *s*; 2nd, 1970, Gretl Renate Steinig. *Educ:* Newport Secondary Grammar Sch., IW; Halton Apprentice; RAF Coll., Cranwell. psc 1965, jssc 1970, rcds 1975. Commnd 1953; flying and staff appts, incl. 28 Sqn, Hong Kong, and No 4 and No 1 Flying Trng Schools; Personal Staff Officer to Comdr 2ATAF, 1966; OC 17 Sqdn, 1967–70; Directing Staff, JSSC and NDC, 1971–72; Stn Comdr, RAF Luqa, Malta, 1972–74; Dir Forward Policy, Ministry of Defence (Air Force Dept), 1976–78; Dep. Comdr, RAF Germany, 1978–80; Senior RAF Mem., RCDS, 1980–81; Dir of Service Intelligence, 1982; Dep. Chief of Defence Staff (Intelligence), 1983–84; Chief of Defence Intelligence and Dep. Chm., Jt Intelligence Cttee, 1985–86; Air Mem. for Supply and Orgn, Air Force Dept, MoD, 1986–87. Mem. Council, RUSI, 1986. Trustee: RAF Mus., 1986–87; Headley Ct, 1986–87; Chm., Mus. of E Asian Art, Bath, 1996–2000. Lectures on air power, defence and military history. Freeman, City of London, 1996. *Publications:* (jtly) Air Power in the Nuclear Age, 1982; Unmanned Aircraft, 1988; The Royal Air Force: an illustrated history, 1993, 3rd edn 1999; (ed) Great Air Battles of the Royal Air Force, 1996; contrib. prof. jls. *Recreations:* military history, shooting, reading, writing, lecturing on cruise ships. *Address:* c/o Lloyds TSB, Cox & King's Branch, 7 Pall Mall, SW1Y 5NA. *Club:* Royal Air Force.

ARMITAGE, Prof. Peter, CBE 1984; Professor of Applied Statistics (formerly of Biomathematics), 1976–90, now Emeritus, and Fellow, St Peter's College, University of Oxford, 1976–90, now Emeritus Fellow; *b* 15 June 1924; *s* of Harry and Florence Armitage, Huddersfield; *m* 1st, 1947, Phyllis Enid Perry (*d* 2001), London; one *s* two *d*; 2nd, 2003, Cecil Dione Rowlatt, Abingdon. *Educ:* Huddersfield Coll.; Trinity Coll., Cambridge (Wrangler, 1947; MA 1952); PhD London, 1951. Ministry of Supply, 1943–45; National Physical Laboratory, 1945–46; Mem. Statistical Research Unit of Med. Research Council, London Sch. of Hygiene and Trop. Med., 1947–61; Prof. of Medical Statistics, Univ. of London, 1961–76. President: Biometric Soc., 1972–73 (Hon. Life Mem., 1998); Royal Statistical Soc., 1982–84 (Hon. Sec., 1958–64); Internat. Soc. for Clinical Biostatistics, 1990–91; Mem., International Statistical Institute, 1961. Hon. FFPM 1991. Hon. DSc De Montfort, 1998. (Jtly) J. Allyn Taylor Prize, John P. Robarts Res. Inst., London, Ont, 1987; Guy Medals in bronze, silver and gold, Royal Statistical Soc., 1962, 1978, 1990. Editor, Biometrics, 1980–84. *Publications:* Sequential Medical Trials, 1960, 2nd edn 1975; Statistical Methods in Medical Research, 1971, 4th edn (jtly), 2001; (ed with H. A. David) Advances in Biometry, 1996; (ed with T. Colton) Encyclopedia of Biostatistics, 1998, 2nd edn 2005; papers in statistical and medical journals. *Recreations:* music, genealogy. *Address:* 2 Reading Road, Wallingford, Oxon OX10 9DP. *T:* (01491) 835840.

See also E. Armitage.

ARMITAGE, Simon Robert; poet, novelist, playwright, song-lyricist, screen-writer and broadcaster; *b* 26 May 1963. Writer of song-lyrics for film, Feltham Sings, 2002 (BAFTA and Ivor Novello Awards, 2004). *Publications: poetry:* Zoom!, 1989; Xanadu, 1992; Kid, 1992; Book of Matches, 1993; (with G. Maxwell) Moon Country, 1995; The Dead Sea Poems, 1996; CloudCuckooLand, 1997; Killing Time, 1999; Selected Poems, 2001; The Universal Home Doctor, 2002; Travelling Songs, 2002; Tyrannosaurus Rex Versus the Corduroy Kid, 2006; *prose:* All Points North, 1998; *plays:* Mister Heracles, 2000; Jerusalem, 2005; Gig, 2008; *novels:* Little Green Man, 2001; The White Stuff, 2004; *dramatisation:* The Odyssey, 2005; *libretto:* The Assassin Tree, 2006; *translation:* Sir Gawain and the Green Knight, 2007. *Address:* c/o DGA, 55 Monmouth Street, WC2H 9DG.

ARMITSTEAD, Claire Louise, (Mrs J. C. Yandell); Literary Editor, The Guardian, since 1999; *b* 2 Dec. 1958; *d* of Charles Henry Wilfrid Armitstead and Gillian Louise Armitstead (*née* Bartley); *m* 1983, John Christopher Yandell; one *s* one *d*. *Educ:* Zaria Children's Sch., Nigeria; Bedales Sch.; St Hilda's Coll., Oxford (BA). Reporter, S Wales Argus, 1980–84; sub-ed. and Theatre Critic, Hampstead and Highgate Express, 1984–88; Theatre Critic, Financial Times, 1988–92; Theatre Critic, 1992–95, Arts Ed., 1995–99, Guardian. *Recreations:* reading, writing, gardening, trying to play the piano. *Address:* The Guardian, Kings Place, 90 York Way, N1 9AG.

ARMITT, John Alexander, CBE 1996; FREng, FICE; Chairman: Olympic Delivery Authority, since 2007; Engineering and Physical Sciences Research Council, since 2007; *b* 2 Feb. 1946; *s* of Alexander Walter Armitt and Lily Irene (*née* Dunce); *m* 1969, Mavis Dorothy Sage (marr. diss.); one *s* one *d*. *Educ:* Portsmouth Northern Grammar Sch.; Portsmouth Coll. of Technology. FREng (FEng 1993); FICE 1989. John Laing Construction, 1966–93; Jt Man. Dir, 1988–93; Chairman: J. Laing Internat., 1988–93; Laing Civil Engrg, 1988–93; Chief Executive: Union Railways, 1993–97; Costain Gp, 1997–2001; Railtrack plc, 2001–02; Network Rail, 2002–07. Non-exec. Dir, Berkeley Gp, 2007–. Council Member: ICE, 1989–92 (Chm., Mgt Bd, 1989–92); FCEC, 1986–93 (Chm., European Affairs Cttee, 1989–92). Pres., Export Gp for Constructional Inds, 1992–93; Member: Overseas Project Bd, DTI, 1992–93; Export Guarantees Adv. Council, 2001–04; Commn for Integrated Transport, 2004–07. Mem. Bd, Major Projects Assoc., 1994–2004. *Recreations:* sailing, golf, theatre, music. *Address: e-mail:* john.armitt@london2012.com.

ARMOND, Ralph Peter; Director General, Zoological Society of London, since 2004; *b* 30 May 1957; *s* of John Walter Armond and Helene Maria Armond; *m* 1984, Jane Caroline Everitt; one *s* one *d*. *Educ:* King's Coll. Sch., Wimbledon; Emmanuel Coll., Cambridge (BA Geog. 1978). Retail Mktg, Boots Co. Plc, 1978–84; Mktg Manager, Dixons Stores Gp, 1984–88; Tussauds Group Ltd, 1988–2004: Mktg Manager, Chessington World of Adventures, 1988–91; Gen. Manager, Warwick Castle, 1991–95; Divl Dir, Alton Towers Resort, 1995–2004. Outstanding Personal Contribn to Tourism award, Heart of England Tourist Bd, 2003. *Recreations:* mountain biking, jogging, learning to play the saxophone. *Address:* Zoological Society of London, Regent's Park, NW1 4RY. *T:* (020) 7449 6207.

ARMOUR, Prof. Sir James, Kt 1995; CBE 1989; FRSE; FRCVS; FMedSci; Vice-Principal, 1990–95, and Professor of Veterinary Parasitology, 1976–95, now Emeritus, University of Glasgow; Chairman, Glasgow Dental Hospital and School NHS Trust, 1995–98; *b* 17 Sept. 1929; *s* of James Angus Armour and Margaret Brown Roy; *m* 1st, 1953, Irene Morris (*d* 1988); two *s* two *d*; 2nd, 1992, Christine Strickland. *Educ:* Marr Coll., Troon; Univ. of Glasgow (PhD 1967). MRCVS 1952, FRCVS 1995; FRSE 1991. Colonial Service, Nigeria: Vet. Officer, 1953–57; Vet. Parasitologist, 1957–60; Parasitologist, Cooper Technical Bureau, Berkhamsted, 1960–63; University of Glasgow: Research Fellow, 1963–67; Lectr, 1967–70; Sen. Lectr, 1970–73; Reader, 1973–76; Dean, Vet. Faculty, 1986–91. Chairman: Vet. Products Cttee, Medicines Commn, 1987–96; Governing Body, Inst. of Animal Health, Compton, 1991–97; Member: Adv. Bd, Inst. of Aquaculture, Univ. of Stirling, 1997–2003; Bd, Hannah Res. Inst., Ayr, 1999–. Chairman: Moredun Foundn for Animal Health and Welfare, 2000–04; St Andrews Clinics for Children in Africa, 1996–; Trustee, Scottish Sci. Trust, 1999–2001. Vice-Pres., RSE, 1998–2000. Founder FMedSci 1998. Hon. FIBiol 2001. Dr *hc* Utrecht, 1981; DVM&S Edinburgh, 1995; DU: Glasgow, 2001; Stirling, 2005. Bicentenary Medal, RSE, 2002. *Publications:* (with Urquhart and Duncan) Veterinary Parasitology, 1988; numerous contribs to vet. and parasitology jls. *Recreations:* golf (British Boys Golf Champion, Hoylake, 1947), watching soccer and Rugby. *Address:* 4b Towans Court, Prestwick KA9 2AY. *Clubs:* Royal Troon Golf (Captain, 1990–92; Hon. Pres., 2007–), Turnberry Golf; Atlanta Athletic (USA).

ARMOUR, Prof. John Hamish; Lovells Professor of Law and Finance, Oxford University, since 2007; Fellow, Oriel College, Oxford, since 2007; *b* Nottingham, 24 Dec. 1971; *s* of Edward and Suzanne Armour; *m* 2007, Rebecca Ann Williams. *Educ:* Pembroke Coll., Oxford (BA 1994; BCL 1995); Yale Law Sch. (LLM 1996). University of Nottingham: Lectr in Law, 1996–2000; Norton Rose Lectr in Corporate and Financial Law, 2000–01; University of Cambridge: Res. Fellow, Centre for Business Res., 1999–2000; Sen. Res. Fellow, 2001–02; Lectr in Law, 2002–05; Sen. Lectr in Law, 2005–07. *Publications:* (ed) Vulnerable Transactions in Corporate Insolvency, 2003; (ed) After Enron: modernising corporate and securities law in Europe and the US, 2006; contrib. to academic jls. *Recreations:* film, cars, hill-walking. *Address:* Oriel College, Oxford OX1 4EW. *T:* (01865) 286544; *e-mail:* john.armour@law.ox.ac.uk.

ARMOUR, Nicholas Hilary Stuart; HM Diplomatic Service; Consul-General, Toronto, and Director, UK Trade and Investment, Canada, since 2005; *b* 12 June 1951; *s* of late Brig. William Stanley Gibson Armour and of Penelope Jean Armour; *m* 1982, Georgina Elizabeth Fortescue (*d* 2003); two *d*. *Educ:* Ampleforth Coll.; Exeter Univ. (BA). FCO, 1974; MECAS: Lebanon, Beaconsfield, Jordan, 1975; Beirut, 1977; FCO, 1980; Head of Chancery, Athens, 1984; Asst Head of Dept, FCO, 1989; Counsellor, Muscat, 1991; on loan to DTI, 1994–97; Consul-Gen., Dubai and the Northern Emirates, 1997–99; on loan to Royal Mail ViaCode, 2000; Head, North America Dept, FCO, 2000–03; Sen. DS (Civil), RCDS, 2003–05 (on secondment). Mem., Madrigal Soc., 1995–. *Recreations:* music, singing, sailing. *Address:* c/o Foreign and Commonwealth Office, King Charles Street, SW1A 2AH.

ARMSON, (Frederick) Simon (Arden); clinical psychotherapist and development coach, since 2004; *b* 11 Sept. 1948; *s* of late Frank Gerald Arden Armson and Margaret Fenella Armson (*née* Newton); *m* 1975, Marion Albinia (*née* Hamilton-Russell); one *s* two *d*. *Educ:* Denstone Coll.; MSc (Mental Health Studies) Guy's Hosp. Med. Sch., London, 1996; Dip. Clin. Psychotherapy, CAT, 2002; Dip. Neuro-linguistic programming, Internat. Neuro-linguistic Programming Trainers' Assoc., 2007; registered UKCP, 2005. Various administrative and managerial posts, NHS, 1970–84; Asst Gen. Sec. 1984–89, Gen. Sec. 1989, Chief Exec., 1990–2004, The Samaritans. Dir, The Samaritans Enterprises Ltd, 1996–2004. Chair: BBC Radio Helpline Adv. Gp, 1995–98; Telephone Helplines Gp, 1992–96; Develt Adv. Cttee, Cancer Bacup Service, 1998–2001. UK Rep., 1996–2005, Chm., Nat. Delegs, 2001–03, Mem. Exec. Cttee, 2001–03, Internat. Assoc. for Suicide Prevention; Member: Suicide Prevention Sub-Gp, DoH Wider Health Wkg Gp, 1995–97; RCN Men's Health Forum, 1995–97; Steering Cttee for Structure Review of British Red Cross, 1995; Adv. Cttee, Inst. of Volunteer Research, 1996–2002; Wkg Gp, Rev. of BACUP Cancer Counselling Service, 1997; Cttee, ICSTIS, 2001–; Lay Mem., Mental Health Rev. Tribunal, 2006–. Mental Health Act Comr, 2002– (Mem. Bd, 2004–). Trustee: ChildLine, 1999–2006; Broadcasting Support Services, 2003–; Mental Health Media Trust, 2004–; National Nightline, 2005–06; Maytree Respite Centre, 2005–; CLIC Sargent, 2006–. Hon. Mem., Telephone Helplines Assoc., 1999. Chairman of Judges: Guardian Jerwood Award, 1995–99; Guardian Charity Award, 2000–03; Mem. Cttee, Ringel Award, 2001–03. CCMI (CIMgt 1995; Pres., Mid Thames Br., 2006–). FRSA 1993. *Publications:* (contrib.) International Handbook of Suicide and Attempted Suicide, 2000; (contrib.) Every Family in the Land, 2004; (contrib.) Prevention and Treatment of Suicidal Behaviour, 2005. *Recreations:* music, cycling (cross country), walking, sailing, ski-ing. *Address:* Broad Oak, Hurley, Maidenhead, Berkshire SL6 5LW. *T:* (01628) 824322. *Club:* Reform.

ARMSON, Rev. Canon John Moss, PhD; Member, Hengrave Ecumenical Community, 2001–03; *b* 21 Dec. 1939; *s* of Arthur Eric Armson and Edith Isobel Moss. *Educ:* Wyggeston Sch.; Selwyn Coll., Cambridge (MA); St Andrews Univ. (PhD); College of the Resurrection, Mirfield. Curate, St John, Notting Hill, 1966; Chaplain and Fellow, Downing Coll., Cambridge, 1969; Chaplain, 1973–77, Vice-Principal, 1977–82, Westcott House, Cambridge; Principal, Edinburgh Theol Coll., 1982–89; Canon

Residentiary, Rochester Cathedral, 1989–2001, Canon Emeritus, 2001–. *Recreations:* music, theatre, gardening, landscaping. *Address:* Mill Bank, Rowlestone, Herefords HR2 0DS.

ARMSON, Simon; *see* Armson, F. S. A.

ARMSTRONG, family name of **Baron Armstrong of Ilminster**.

ARMSTRONG OF ILMINSTER, Baron *cr* 1988 (Life Peer), of Ashill in the county of Somerset; **Robert Temple Armstrong,** GCB 1983 (KCB 1978; CB 1974); CVO 1975; Secretary of the Cabinet, 1979–87, and Head of the Home Civil Service, 1983–87 (Joint Head, 1981–83), retired; director of companies; *b* 30 March 1927; *o s* of Sir Thomas (Henry Wait) Armstrong, DMus, FRCM; *m* 1st, 1953, Serena Mary Benedicta (marr. diss. 1985; she *d* 1994), *er d* of Sir Roger Chance, 3rd Bt, MC; two *d*; 2nd, 1985, (Mary) Patricia, *d* of late C. C. Carlow. *Educ:* Dragon Sch., Oxford; Eton; Christ Church, Oxford (Hon. Student 1985). Asst Principal, Treasury, 1950–55; Private Secretary to: Rt Hon. Reginald Maudling, MP (when Economic Sec. to Treasury), 1953–54; Rt Hon. R. A. Butler, CH, MP (when Chancellor of the Exchequer), 1954–55; Principal, Treasury, 1955–57; Sec., Radcliffe Cttee on Working of Monetary System, 1957–59; returned to Treasury as Principal, 1959–64; Sec., Armitage Cttee on Pay of Postmen, 1964; Asst Sec., Cabinet Office, 1964–66; Sec. of Kindersley Review Body on Doctors' and Dentists' Remuneration and of Franks Cttee on Pay of Higher Civil Service, 1964–66; Asst Sec., Treasury, 1967–68; Jt Prin. Private Sec. to Rt Hon. Roy Jenkins, MP (Chancellor of the Exchequer), 1968; Under Secretary (Home Finance), Treasury, 1968–70; Principal Private Sec. to Prime Minister, 1970–75; Dep. Sec., 1973; Dep. Under-Sec. of State, Home Office, 1975–77, Permt Under Sec. of State, 1977–79. Director: BAT Industries, 1988–97; Inchcape, 1988–95; Bristol and West plc (formerly Bristol and West Building Soc.), 1988–97 (Chm., 1993–97); N. M. Rothschild & Sons, 1988–97; RTZ Corporation, 1988–97; Shell Transport & Trading Co., 1988–97; Lucas Industries, 1989–92; Biotechnology Investments Ltd, subseq. 3i Bioscience Investment Trust, 1989–2002 (Chm., 1989–2001); Carlton Television, 1991–95; IAMGold Ltd, 1996–2003; Bank of Ireland, 1997–2001; Chm., Forensic Investigative Associates, 1997–2003; Mem., Supervisory Bd, Robeco Gp, 1988–97. Chancellor, Univ. of Hull, 1994–2006. Chairman: Bd of Trustees, V & A Museum, 1988–98; Hestercombe Gardens Trust, 1996–2005; Bd of Govs, RNCM, 2000–05; Sir Edward Heath Charitable Foundn, 2005–; Trustee: Leeds Castle Foundn, 1988–2007 (Chm., 2001–07); Wells Cathedral Sch. Foundn, 2007–; Dir, RAM, 1975–98 (Hon. Fellow 1985); Member: Council of Management, Royal Philharmonic Soc., 1975–2002; Rhodes Trust, 1975–97; Bd of Dirs, Royal Opera House, Covent Garden, 1988–93 (Sec., 1968–88); Royal Acad. of Music Foundn, 1988–2000. Fellow of Eton Coll., 1979–94. Hon. Bencher, Inner Temple, 1986. *Recreation:* music. *Address:* House of Lords, SW1A 0PW.

ARMSTRONG, Alan Gordon; Senior Lecturer in Economics, University of Bristol, 1977–97; *b* 11 Feb. 1937; *s* of late Joseph Gordon Armstrong and Evelyn Armstrong (*née* Aird); *m* 1963, Margaret Louise Harwood; one *s* one *d*. *Educ:* Bede Grammar Sch., Sunderland; Queens' Coll., Cambridge (MA). Economist, Reed Paper Gp, 1960–62; Res. Officer, Dept of Applied Econs, Univ. of Cambridge, 1962–69; Fellow, Selwyn Coll., Cambridge, 1967–69; Lectr in Econs, Univ. of Bristol, 1970–77. Part-time Mem., Monopolies and Mergers Commn, 1989–95; Consultant on Economic Statistics to: UN Statistical Office, OECD, EEC, ONS, DTI, NEDO, various times, 1970–2001; Member: EC Adv. Cttee on Econ. and Social Statistics, 1992–97; UK Central Statistical Office (formerly Central Statistical Office Users') Adv. Cttee, 1992–96. *Publications:* Input-Output Tables and Analysis, 1973; Structural Change in UK, 1974; Review of DTI Statistics, 1989; res. papers and jl articles on input-output, nat. accounts and the motor industry. *Recreations:* gardening (by necessity), family history, cricket, church affairs. *Address:* Rock House, King's Hill, Nailsea, Bristol BS48 2AU. *T:* (01275) 853197.

ARMSTRONG, Very Rev. Christopher John; Dean of Blackburn, since 2001; *b* 18 Dec. 1947; *s* of John Armstrong and Susan Elizabeth Armstrong; *m* 1976, Geraldine Anne Clementsen; two *s* one *d*. *Educ:* Dunstable Grammar Sch.; Bede Coll., Univ. of Durham (Cert Ed 1969); Kelham Theol Coll.; Univ. of Nottingham (BTh 1975). Ordained deacon, 1975, priest, 1976; Asst Curate, All Saints, Maidstone, 1975–79; Chaplain, Coll. of St Hild and St Bede, Univ. of Durham, 1979–85; Domestic Chaplain to Archbp of York and Diocesan Dir of Ordinands, Dio. York, 1985–91; Vicar, St Martin, Scarborough, 1991–2001. *Recreations:* sport, mountaineering, gardening, theatre and cinema, travel. *Address:* The Deanery, Preston New Road, Blackburn, Lancs BB2 6PS. *T:* (01254) 52502.

ARMSTRONG, Lt-Col Sir Christopher (John Edmund Stuart), 7th Bt *cr* 1841, of Gallen Priory, King's County; MBE 1979; *b* 15 Jan. 1940; *s* of Sir Andrew Clarence Francis Armstrong, 6th Bt, CMG and Laurel May (*née* Stuart; *d* 1988); *S* father, 1997; *m* 1972, Georgina Elizabeth Carey, *d* of Lt-Col W. G. Lewis; three *s* one *d*. *Educ:* Ampleforth; RMA, Sandhurst. Lt-Col, RCT. *Heir: s* Charles Andrew Armstrong, *b* 21 Feb. 1973.

ARMSTRONG, Prof. (Christopher) Mark, DPhil; FBA 2007; Professor of Economics, University College London, since 2003; *b* 26 Dec. 1964; *s* of John Armstrong and Jane Armstrong; *m* 1999, Carli Coetzee; one *s* one *d*. *Educ:* Bedales Sch., Petersfield; Queens' Coll., Cambridge (BA Hons Math. 1987); St John's Coll., Oxford (DPhil Econs 1992). Lectr in Econs, Univ. of Cambridge, 1992–94; Eric Roll Prof. of Econ. Policy, Univ. of Southampton, 1994–97; Fellow in Econs, Nuffield Coll., Oxford, 1997–2003. Editor: Rev. of Econ. Studies, 1999–2003; Rand Jl of Econs, 2005–. *Publications:* articles in academic jls on industrial economics, competition policy and consumer behaviour. *Recreations:* playing the piano, cooking, keeping up with my children Harriet and Joseph. *Address:* Department of Economics, University College London, Gower Street, WC1E 6BT; *e-mail:* mark.armstrong@ucl.ac.uk.

ARMSTRONG, Douglas; *see* Armstrong, R. D.

ARMSTRONG, Dr Ernest McAlpine, CB 2005; FRCSE, FRCPE, FRCPGlas, FRCGP, FFPH; Chief Medical Officer, Scottish Executive Department of Health, 2000–05; *b* 3 June 1945; *s* of Ernest Armstrong and Mary Brownlie McLean Armstrong (*née* McAlpine); *m* 1970, Dr Katherine Mary Dickson Young; two *s*. *Educ:* Hamilton Acad.; Glasgow Univ. (BSc (Hons) 1968; MB ChB (Hons) 1970). MRCP 1975; FRCGP 1987; FRCPGlas 1988; FRCPE 1996; FFPH (FFPHM 2001); FRCSE 2001. Lectr in Pathology, Glasgow Univ., 1971–74; Trainee Assistant, Douglas, 1974–75; Principal in gen. practice, Argyll, 1975–93; Sec., BMA, 1993–2000. *Publications:* articles on ultrastructure, clinical immunology and med. politics. *Recreations:* church music, opera, sailing, travelling. *Address:* 29/1 Inverleith Place, Edinburgh EH3 5QD. *Club:* Caledonian.

ARMSTRONG, Frank William, FREng; FIMechE; FRAeS; independent technical consultant, since 1991; *b* 26 March 1931; *s* of Frank Armstrong and Millicent L. Armstrong; *m* 1957, Diane T. Varley; three *d*. *Educ:* Stretford Grammar Sch.; Royal Technical Coll., Salford; Queen Mary Coll., Univ. of London (BSc Eng; MSc Eng 1956). FIMechE 1981; FRAeS 1981; FREng (FEng 1991). Massey-Harris Ltd, 1947–51; De Havilland Engine Co., 1956–58; Admiralty Engineering Lab., 1958–59; NGTE, 1959–78; Engine Div., MoD (PE), 1978–81; Dep. Dir, R&D, NGTE, 1981–83; Royal Aircraft, later Royal Aerospace, Establishment: Head of Propulsion Dept, 1983–87; Dep. Dir (Aircraft), 1987–88; Dep. Dir (Aerospace Vehicles), 1988–90; Dir (Aerospace Vehicles), 1990–91. *Publications:* contribs on aeronautics research, gas turbines and aircraft propulsion to learned jls. *Recreations:* mountaineering, music, aviation history. *Address:* 6 Corringway, Church Crookham, Fleet, Hants GU52 6AN. *T:* (01252) 616526.

ARMSTRONG, Rt Hon. Hilary (Jane); PC 1999; MP (Lab) Durham North West, since 1987; *b* 30 Nov. 1945; *d* of Rt Hon. Ernest Armstrong, PC and of Hannah P. Lamb; *m* 1992, Dr Paul Corrigan. *Educ:* Monkwearmouth Comp. Sch., Sunderland; West Ham Coll. of Technology (BSc Sociology); Univ. of Birmingham (Dip. in Social Work). VSO, Murray Girls' High Sch., Kenya, 1967–69; Social Worker, Newcastle City Social Services Dept, 1970–73; Community Worker, Southwick Neighbourhood Action Project, Sunderland, 1973–75; Lectr, Community and Youth Work, Sunderland Polytechnic, 1975–86. Frontbench spokesperson on education, 1988–92 (under-fives, primary, and special educn), on Treasury affairs, 1994–95; PPS to Leader of the Opposition, 1992–94; Minister of State, DETR, 1997–2001; Parly Sec. to HM Treasury (Govt Chief Whip), 2001–06; Chancellor of the Duchy of Lancaster and Minister for the Cabinet Office, 2006–07. *Recreations:* reading, theatre, football. *Address:* House of Commons, Westminster, SW1A 0AA. *T:* (020) 7219 5076; (constituency) (01388) 767065.

ARMSTRONG, Iain Gillies; QC (Scot.) 2000; *b* 26 May 1956; *s* of John Gillies Armstrong and June Bell Black; *m* 1977, Deirdre Elizabeth Mary Mackenzie; one *s* one *d*. *Educ:* Inverness Royal Acad., Glasgow Univ. Called to Scottish Bar, 1986; Clerk of Faculty of Advocates, 1995–99 (Vice Dean, 2008–); Standing Jun. Counsel in Scotland, DSS, 1998–2000; Crown Counsel, 2000–03. Mem., Jt Standing Cttee on Legal Educn in Scotland, 1995–99. Gov., Fettes Coll., 2000–. *Address:* 2 Ramsay Garden, Edinburgh EH1 2NA. *T:* (0131) 225 2292; Advocates' Library, Parliament House, Edinburgh EH1 1RF. *T:* (0131) 226 5071. *Club:* New (Edinburgh).

ARMSTRONG, Prof. Isobel Mair, PhD; FBA 2003; Professor of English, Birkbeck College, University of London, 1989–2002, now Professor Emeritus, and Hon. Fellow, 2002; *b* 25 March 1937; *d* of Richard Aneurin Jones and Marjorie Jackson; *m* 1961, John Michael Armstrong; two *s* one *d*. *Educ:* Friends' Sch., Saffron Walden; Univ. of Leicester (BA 1959; PhD 1963). Asst Lectr and Lectr in English, UCL, 1963–70; Lectr and Sen. Lectr in English, Univ. of Leicester, 1971–79; Prof. of English, Univ. of Southampton, 1979–89. Vis. Prof., Princeton Univ., 1983–84; Frank and Eleanor Griffiths Chair, Bread Loaf Sch. of English, 1990, Robert Frost Chair, 2002, Middlebury Coll.; Vis. Prof., Harvard Univ., 1995–96, 1999, 2004, 2008; Sen. Res. Fellow, Inst. of English Studies, 2002; John Hinkley Vis. Prof., Johns Hopkins Univ., 2005. Hon. DLitt Leicester, 2005. Jt Editor, Women: a cultural review, 1990–; Gen. Editor, Writers and their Work, British Council, 1992–2006. *Publications:* Victorian Scrutinies: reviews of poetry 1830–70, 1972; Language as Living Form in Nineteenth Century Poetry, 1982; Victorian Poetry, 1993; Nineteenth Century Women Poets, 1996; (ed with Virginia Blain) Women's Poetry in the Enlightenment, 1999; (ed with Virginia Blain) Women's Poetry, Late Romantic to Late Victorian, 1999; The Radical Aesthetic, 2000; Victorian Glassworlds: glass culture and the imagination, 1830–1880, 2008. *Recreation:* drawing in pen and ink. *Address:* Department of English and Humanities, Birkbeck College, Malet Street, WC1E 7HX. *T:* (020) 7631 6078.

ARMSTRONG, Jack; *see* Armstrong, J. A.

ARMSTRONG, John Archibald, (Jack), OC 1983; retired; Chief Executive Officer, 1973–82, and Chairman, 1974–82, Imperial Oil Ltd; *b* Dauphin, Manitoba, 24 March 1917. *Educ:* Univ. of Manitoba (BSc Geol.); Queen's Univ. at Kingston (BSc Chem. Engrg). Worked for short time with Geol Survey of Canada and in mining industry; joined Imperial Oil Ltd as geologist, Regina, 1940; appts as: exploration geophysicist, western Canada, and with affiliated cos in USA and S America; Asst Reg. Manager, Producing Dept, 1949; Asst Co-ordinator, Producing Dept of Standard Oil Co. (NJ), New York; Gen. Man., Imperial's Producing Dept, Toronto, 1960; Dir, 1961; Dir resp. for Marketing Ops, 1963–65; Exec. Vice-Pres., 1966, Pres. 1970, Chief Exec. Officer, 1973, Chm., 1974. Chm., Commonwealth Study Conf. Assoc. Life Mem., Fraser Inst. Hon. LLD: Winnipeg, 1978; Calgary, 1980.

ARMSTRONG, Rear Adm. John Herbert Arthur James, (Louis), CBE 2004; Chief Executive, Royal Institution of Chartered Surveyors, since 1998; *b* 4 Sept. 1946; *s* of John William Armstrong and Marie Helen (*née* Clark); *m* 1973, Marjorie Anne Corbett (marr. diss. 2006); one *s* one *d*; partner, Sibley Pyne. *Educ:* King's Sch., Canterbury; BRNC Dartmouth; Magdalen Coll., Oxford (MA Law). Served in HM Ships Fife, Intrepid and Zulu, 1970–75; called to the Bar, Middle Temple, 1976; Staff Legal Advr to Flag Officer, Plymouth, 1977–79; HM Yacht Britannia, 1979–81; Comdr 1981; HMS Raleigh, 1981–83; Naval Secretary's Staff, 1983–85; HMS Illustrious, 1985–87; Capt. 1987; seconded to Cabinet Office, 1987–89; Asst Dir, Sea Systems' Operational Requirements, MoD, 1989–91; RCDS 1992; Director: Naval Manpower Planning, 1993; Naval Personnel Plans and Progs, 1994; Cdre, 1994; Comdt, RNSC, Greenwich, 1994–95; Rear Adm., 1996; Sen. Naval Directing Staff, RCDS, 1996–98. Dir, Inst. of Leadership and Mgt, 2006–. Mem. Council, C&G, 2005–. FRSA 1998. Liveryman, Co. of Chartered Surveyors, 2007–. *Recreations:* the arts, ski-ing, tennis, parties. *Address:* Royal Institution of Chartered Surveyors, 12 Great George Street, Parliament Square, SW1P 3AD. *T:* (020) 7334 3707. *Club:* Reform.

ARMSTRONG, Karen Andersen; writer, since 1982; *b* 14 Nov. 1944; *d* of John Oliver Seymour Armstrong and Eileen Hastings Armstrong (*née* McHale). *Educ:* Convent of Holy Child Jesus, Edgbaston; St Anne's Coll., Oxford (MA; MLitt). Mem., Soc. of the Holy Child Jesus, 1962–69. Tutorial Res. Fellow, Bedford Coll., Univ. of London, 1973–76; Hd of English, James Allen's Girls' Sch., Dulwich, 1976–82. *Publications:* Through the Narrow Gate, 1981; Beginning the World, 1983; The First Christian, 1984; Tongues of Fire, 1985; The Gospel According to Woman, 1986; Holy War: the Crusades and their impact on today's world, 1988; Muhammad: a biography of the Prophet, 1991; A History of God, 1993; In the Beginning, 1996; Jerusalem, One City, Three Faiths, 1996; The Battle for God: a history of Fundamentalism, 2000; Islam: a short history, 2000; Buddha, 2001; The Spiral Staircase: a memoir, 2004; A Short History of Myth, 2005; The Great Transformation: the world at the time of Buddha, Socrates, Confucius and Jeremiah, 2006; Muhammad: a prophet for our time, 2006; The Bible: a biography, 2007. *Recreations:* literature, music, theatre. *Address:* c/o Felicity Bryan, 2A North Parade, Banbury Road, Oxford OX2 6LX. *T:* (01865) 513816, *Fax:* (01865) 310055; *e-mail:* paolachurchill@yahoo.co.uk.

ARMSTRONG, Lance; professional cyclist, retired 2005; *b* Plano, Texas, 18 Sept. 1971; *s* of Linda Armstrong (*née* Walling); *m* 1998, Kristin Richard (marr. diss. 2003); one *s* twin *d.* Nat. Amateur Champion, USA, 1991; Member: US Olympic Team, 1992, 1996, 2000 (Bronze Medal); Motorola Team, 1993–96; Cofidis Team, 1996–97; US Postal Service, subseq. Discovery Channel, Pro Cycling Team, 1998–2005. Winner, numerous races, including: World Cycling Championships, Oslo, 1993; Tour DuPont, 1995, 1996; Tour de Luxembourg, 1998; Tour de France, 1999, 2000, 2001, 2002, 2003, 2004, 2005 (1st person to win 7 consecutive races); Grand Prix du Midi Libre, 2002. Founder, Lance Armstrong Foundn for Cancer, 1996. *Publications:* It's Not About the Bike: my journey back to life, 2000; (jtly) The Lance Armstrong Performance Program, 2001; (with S. Jenkins) Every Second Counts, 2003. *Address:* c/o Capital Sports & Entertainment, Suite 430, 98 San Jacinto Boulevard, Austin, TX 78701, USA; c/o Lance Armstrong Foundation, PO Box 13026, Austin, TX 78711, USA.

ARMSTRONG, Lisa, (Mrs P. Hadaway); Fashion Editor, The Times, since 1998; Contributing Editor, Vogue, since 1999; *b* 12 Oct. 1961; *d* of Royston Myers and Rosalind Armstrong, and step *d* of Clement Armstrong; *m* 1988, Paul Hadaway; two *d.* *Educ:* Dorchester Grammar Sch. for Girls; Bristol Univ. (BA Hons English Lit.); City Univ. (Postgrad. Dip. Journalism). Asst Ed., Fitness Mag., 1985–86; Insight Ed., Elle, 1986–88; Dep. Features Ed., Vogue, 1988–91; Fashion Ed., The Independent and Independent on Sunday, 1991–93; Fashion Features Dir, Vogue, 1993–98. Judge, Good Business Awards, RSPCA, 2004–. Fashion Writer of the Year, British Fashion Council, 2001. *Publications:* Front Row, 1998; Dead Stylish, 2001; Bad Manors, 2003; Deja View, 2004. *Recreations:* reading, riding, needlepoint, finding places to put finished needlepoint. *Address:* The Times, 1 Pennington Street, E98 1TT.

ARMSTRONG, Mark; *see* Armstrong, C. M.

ARMSTRONG, Neil A.; Chairman, EDO Corporation, 2000–02, now Emeritus; formerly NASA Astronaut (Commander, Apollo 11 Rocket Flight to the Moon, 1969); *b* Wapakoneta, Ohio, USA, 5 Aug. 1930; *s* of Stephen and Viola Armstrong, Wapakoneta; *m* 1956. *Educ:* High Sch., Wapakoneta, Ohio; Univ. of Southern California (MS); Purdue Univ. (BSc). Served in Korea (78 combat missions) being a naval aviator, 1949–52. He joined NASA's Lewis Research Center, 1955 (then NACA Lewis Flight Propulsion Lab.) and later transf. to NASA High Speed Flight Station at Edwards Air Force Base, Calif, as an aeronautical research pilot for NACA and NASA; in this capacity, he performed as an X-15 project pilot, flying that aircraft to over 200,000 feet and approximately 4,000 miles per hour; other flight test work included piloting the X-1 rocket airplane, the F-100, F-101, F-102, F-104, F5D, B-47, the paraglider, and others; as pilot of the B-29 "drop" aircraft, he participated in the launches of over 100 rocket airplane flights. Selected as an astronaut by NASA, Sept. 1962; served as backup Command Pilot for Gemini 5 flight; as Command Pilot for Gemini 8 mission, launched 16 March 1966; he performed the first successful docking of 2 vehicles in space; served as backup Command Pilot for Gemini 11 mission; assigned as backup Comdr for Apollo VIII Flight, 1969; Dep. Associate Administrator of Aeronautics, NASA HQ, Washington, 1970–71; University Prof. of Aerospace Engrg, Univ. of Cincinnati, 1971–79; Chairman: Cardwell International Ltd, 1980–82; AIL Systems Inc., 1989–2000. Mem., Nat. Acad. of Engrg. Fellow, Soc. of Experimental Test Pilots; FRAeS. Honours include NASA Exceptional Service Medal, and AIAA Astronautics Award for 1966; RGS Gold Medal, 1970. Presidential Medal for Freedom, 1969.

ARMSTRONG, Sir Patrick (John), Kt 2002; CBE 1989; JP; Chairman, Police Authority of Northern Ireland, 1996–2001; *b* 16 Sept. 1927; *s* of Andrew and Hannah Armstrong; *m* 1949, Agnes Carson; two *s* two *d.* *Educ:* Ruskin Coll., Oxford (DipEcon and Pol Sci.); Queen's Univ., Belfast (BA, Dip. Social Studies); Univ. of Newcastle upon Tyne (Dip. Applied Social Studies). Factory worker, 1947–57; Dep. Co. Welfare Officer, 1966–71, Chief Welfare Officer, 1971–73, Co. Antrim; Dep. Chief Inspector of Social Services for NI, 1973–83, Chief Inspector of Social Services, 1983–89. Vice-Chm., Police Authy for NI, 1994–96. JP 1994. *Recreations:* walking, cycling, reading. *Address:* 13 North Parade, Belfast BT7 2GF. *T:* (028) 9064 3616. *Club:* Ulster Reform (Belfast).

ARMSTRONG, Prof. Peter; Professor of Diagnostic Radiology, St Bartholomew's Hospital, 1989–2005; President, Royal College of Radiologists, 1998–2001; *b* 31 Aug. 1940; *s* of Alexander Armstrong and Ada Armstrong (*née* Lapidas); *m* 1967, Carole J. Gray; one *s* one *d* (and one *s* decd). *Educ:* Marylebone Grammar Sch.; Middlesex Hosp. Med. Sch. (MB BS 1963). Jun. hosp. posts, Middlesex Hosp. and Guy's Hosp., 1963–70; Consultant Radiologist, KCH, 1970–77; Prof. of Radiology and Dir, Diagnostic Radiology Dept, Univ. of Virginia, 1977–89. Ed., Clinical Radiology, 1990–94. Warden for Clinical Radiology, RCR, 1994–98. *Publications:* (with M. Wastie) Diagnostic Imaging, 1981, 5th edn 2004; (jtly) Imaging Diseases of the Chest, 1990, 4th edn 2005; contrib. numerous articles on radiological topics to med. jls and books. *Recreations:* reading, theatre, opera. *Address:* Academic Department of Radiology, St Bartholomew's Hospital, Dominion House, 59 Bartholomew's Close, EC1A 7ED. *Club:* Shadows Radiology.

ARMSTRONG, Peter John Bowden; His Honour Judge Armstrong; a Circuit Judge, since 2000; *b* 19 Dec. 1951; *s* of late William David Armstrong, MBE and Kathleen Mary Armstrong; *m* 1976, Joanna Cox; two *d.* *Educ:* Durham Johnston Grammar Technical Sch.; Trinity Coll., Cambridge (MA). Called to the Bar, Middle Temple, 1974; in practice at the Bar, Middlesbrough, 1976–2000; Asst Recorder, 1990–94; a Recorder, 1994–2000; North Eastern Circuit. *Recreations:* golf, cricket, Rugby, music. *Address:* c/o Teesside Court Centre, Russell Street, Middlesbrough TS1 2AE. *Clubs:* Eaglescliffe Golf (Stockton-on-Tees); Durham CC.

ARMSTRONG, Sir Richard, Kt 2004; CBE 1993; FRSE; conductor; Music Director, Scottish Opera, 1993–2005; *b* 7 Jan. 1943. *Educ:* Wyggeston School, Leicester; Corpus Christi College, Cambridge (Hon. Fellow, 1994). Music staff, Royal Opera House, Covent Garden, 1966–68; Welsh National Opera: head of music staff, 1968–73; Musical Director, 1973–86; Principal Guest Conductor, Frankfurt Opera, 1987–90. FRSE 2002. Hon. DMus: De Montfort, 1992; Glasgow, 2001; Aberdeen, 2002; St Andrews, 2004. Janáček Medal, 1978. *Recreations:* walking, food. *Address:* c/o Ingpen & Williams, 7 St George's Court, 131 Putney Bridge Road, SW15 2PA.

ARMSTRONG, (Robert) Douglas; QC (Scot.) 2005; *m* Sally Grossart; two *d.* *Educ:* Aberdeen Univ. (LLB Hons 1986; DipLP 1987). Admitted Faculty of Advocates, 1990; called to the Bar, Inner Temple, 1999; in practice as barrister, 1999–, specialising in planning, envmt and admin. and constitutional law. *Address:* Advocates' Library, Parliament House, Edinburgh EH1 1RF.

ARMSTRONG, Sheila Ann; soprano; *b* 13 Aug. 1942; *m* 1980, Prof. David Edward Cooper, *qv* (marr. diss. 1998). *Educ:* Hirst Park Girls' Sch., Ashington, Northumberland; Royal Academy of Music, London. Debut Sadler's Wells, 1965, Glyndebourne, 1966, Covent Garden, 1973. Sings all over Europe, Far East, N and S America; has made many recordings. K. Ferrier and Mozart Prize, 1965; Hon. RAM 1970, FRAM 1973. Hon. MA Newcastle, 1979; Hon. DMus Durham, 1991. *Recreations:* interior decoration, collecting antique keys, gardening, flower arranging.

ARMSTRONG-JONES, family name of **Earl of Snowdon**.

ARMYTAGE, Captain David George, CBE 1981; Royal Navy, retired; Secretary General, British Diabetic Association, 1981–91; *b* 4 Sept. 1929; *e s* of late Rear-Adm. Reginald William Armytage, GC, CBE and Sylvia Beatrice Armytage; *heir* to Sir (John) Martin Armytage, Bt, *qv*; *m* 1954, Countess Cosima Antonia de Bosdari; two *s* one *d.* *Educ:* RNC, Dartmouth. Comd Motor Torpedo Boats, 1952–53; Direction Officer: 809 Sqn, 1956–58; HMS Chichester, 1958–59; Action Data Automation Project Team, 1959–64; Direction Officer, HMS Eagle, 1964–66; Directorate, Navigation and Tactical Control, 1966–68; comd HMS Minerva, 1968–70; Defence Policy Staff, 1970–72; Naval Asst to First Sea Lord, 1972–74; Internat. Mil. Staff, Brussels, 1975–76; comd, HMS Scylla, 1976 and HMS Jupiter, 1977–78; Capt., 7th Frigate Sqn, 1976–78; Dep. Dir, Naval Warfare, 1978–80; comd, NATO Standing Naval Force Atlantic, 1980–81. ADC to the Queen, 1981. Master Mariner, 1967. *Recreations:* sailing, gardening, shooting. *Address:* Sharcott Manor, Pewsey, Wilts SN9 5PA. *T:* (01672) 563485. *Clubs:* Oriental, Royal Naval Sailing Association; Royal Channel Islands Yacht.

ARMYTAGE, John McDonald G.; *see* Green-Armytage.

ARMYTAGE, Sir (John) Martin, 9th Bt *cr* 1738, of Kirklees, Yorkshire; *b* 26 Feb. 1933; *s* of Sir John Lionel Armytage, 8th Bt, and of Evelyn Mary Jessamine, *d* of Edward Herbert Fox, Adbury Park, Newbury; *S* father, 1983. *Educ:* Eton; Worcester Coll., Oxford. *Heir:* *cousin* Captain David George Armytage, *qv*. *Address:* 5 St James's Place, Cheltenham, Glos GL50 2EG. *T:* (01242) 525869.

ARNAULT, Bernard Jean Etienne; President, since 1984, and Chairman, Christian Dior; President, since 1989, and Chairman, since 1992, Louis Vuitton Moët Hennessy; *b* Roubaix, 5 March 1949; *s* of Jean Arnault and Marie-Jo (*née* Savinel); *m* 1991, Hélène Mercier; three *s*; one *s* one *d* by former marriage. *Educ:* Ecole Polytechnique, Paris. Qualified as engineer, 1971. President: Ferret Savinel, 1978–84; Financière Agache SA, 1984–89. Man of the Year, NY, 1991. Officier, 2001, Commandeur, 2007, Légion d'Honneur; Commandeur, Ordre des Arts et des Lettres, 2002. *Recreations:* music, piano, tennis. *Address:* 22 avenue Montaigne, 75008 Paris, France. *T:* (1) 44132222.

ARNELL, Prof. Nigel William, PhD; FRGS; Professor of Climate Systems Science, and Director, Walker Institute for Climate System Research, University of Reading, since 2007; *b* Newport, IoW, 10 Dec. 1959; *s* of Roy and Audrey Arnell; *m* 1993, Hilary Kathryn Stevens (*née* Burn); one *d*, and one step *s* one step *d.* *Educ:* W Kidlington Primary Sch.; Gosford Hill Secondary Sch.; Univ. of Southampton (BSc Hons Geog.; PhD Geog.). Hydrologist, Inst. of Hydrol., 1984–94; University of Southampton: Reader in Geog., 1995–99; Prof. of Geog., 1999–2007; Hd, Sch. of Geog., 2003–07. Vis. Prof., NUI, Maynouth, 2007–. *Publications:* Global Warming, River Flows and Water Resources, 1996; Hydrology and Global Environmental Change, 2002; lead author, 2nd, 3rd and 4th Assessment Reports of InterGovtl Panel on Climate Change; contrib. jls incl. Climatic Change, Jl Hydrol., Jl Geophysical Res. *Recreations:* walking in the country, especially the remoter parts of the British Isles, gardening, badminton, old maps. *Address:* Walker Institute for Climate System Research, University of Reading, Earley Gate, Reading RG6 6BB; *e-mail:* n.w.arnell@reading.ac.uk.

ARNELL, Richard Anthony Sayer; Hon. FTCL; composer; conductor; poet; Principal Lecturer, Trinity College of Music, 1981–87 (Teacher of Composition, 1949–81); *b* 15 Sept. 1917; *s* of late Richard Sayer Arnell and Hélène Marie Scherf; *m* 1992, Joan Heycock; one *s* three *d* from former marriages. *Educ:* The Hall, Hampstead; University Coll. Sch., NW3; Royal Coll. of Music. Music Consultant, BBC North American Service, 1943–46; Lectr, Royal Ballet Sch., 1958–59. Editor, The Composer, 1961–64, 1991–93; Chairman: Composers' Guild of GB, 1965, 1974–75 (Vice-Pres., 1992–); Young Musicians' Symph. Orch. Soc., 1973–75. Vis. Lectr (Fulbright Exchange), Bowdoin Coll., Maine, 1967–68; Vis. Prof. Hofstra Univ., New York, 1968–70. Music Dir and Board Mem., London Internat. Film Sch., 1975–89 (Chm., Film Sch. Trust, 1981–87; Chm., Friends of LIFS, 1982–87, Vice-Pres., 1988–); Music Dir, Ram Filming Ltd, 1980–91; Director: Organic Sounds Ltd, 1982–87; A plus A Ltd, 1984–89. Chm., Friends of TCM Junior Dept, 1986–87 (Vice-Pres., 1987–). Chairman: Tadcaster Civic Soc. Music and Arts Cttee, 1988–91; Saxmundham Music and Arts, 1992–95 (Pres., 1995–). Composer of the Year, 1966 (Music Teachers Assoc. Award); Tadcaster Town Council Merit Award, 1990. *Compositions include:* 7 symphonies; 2 concertos for violin; concerto for harpsichord; 2 concertos for piano; string trio; 6 string quartets; 2 quintets; piano trio; piano works; songs; cantatas; organ works; music for string orchestra, wind ensembles, brass ensembles, song cycles; electronic music; *opera:* Love in Transit; Moonflowers; *music theatre:* Ça Va, 2004; *ballet scores:* Punch and the Child, for Ballet Soc., NY, 1947; Harlequin in April, for Arts Council, 1951; The Great Detective, 1953, The Angels, 1957, for Sadler's Wells Theatre Ballet; Giselle (Adam) re-orchestrated, for Ballet Rambert, 1965; *film scores:* The Land, 1941; The Third Secret, 1963; The Visit, 1964; The Man Outside, 1966; Topsail Schooner, 1966; Bequest for a Village, 1969; Second Best, 1972; Stained Glass, 1973; Wires Over the Border, 1974; Black Panther, 1977; Antagonist, 1980; Dilemma, 1981; Doctor in the Sky, 1983; Toulouse Lautrec, 1984; Light of the World, 1990; *other works:* Symphonic Portrait, Lord Byron, for Sir Thomas Beecham, 1953; Landscapes and Figures, for Sir Thomas Beecham, 1956; Petrified Princess, puppet operetta (libretto by Bryan Guinness), for BBC, 1959; Robert Flaherty, Impression for Radio Eireann, 1960; Musica Pacifica for Edward Benjamin, 1963; Festival Flourish, for Salvation Army, 1965; 2nd piano concerto, for RPO, 1967; Overture, Food of Love, for Portland Symph. Orch., 1968; My Ladye Greene Sleeves, for Hofstra Univ., 1968; Life Boat Voluntary, for RNLI, 1974; Call, for LPO, 1980; Ode to Beecham, for RPO, 1986; War God II, 1987; Con Amore, 1990; Xanadu, 1993; *mixed media:* Nocturne: Prague, 1968; I Think of all Soft Limbs, for Canadian Broadcasting Corp., 1971; Combat Zone, for Hofstra Univ., 1971; Astronaut One, 1973; Not Wanted on Voyage, 1990; 24 Hours in TR Scale, 1995; "B"—Queen Boudicca, 2004; Ode for Mandela, 2004. *Club:* Savage.

ARNEY, Claudia Isobel; Director, Enterprise and Growth Unit, HM Treasury, 2006–08; *b* 25 Jan. 1971; *d* of Hon. Martin Jay, *qv*; *m* 2000, John Arney; one *s* two *d.* *Educ:* Hertford Coll., Oxford (BA English Lit.); INSEAD (MBA). Business Analyst, McKinsey and Co., 1992–94; Strategy and Develt Exec., Pearson plc, 1994–97; Product Develt Manager, FT, 1997–99; Man. Dir, thestreet.co.uk, 1999–2000; Exec. Dir, Goldman Sachs, 2000–06.

ARNISON, Maj.-Gen. Peter Maurice, AC 2001 (AO 1992); CVO 2002; Governor of Queensland, Australia, 1997–2003; Chancellor, Queensland University of Technology, since 2004; *b* 21 Oct. 1940; *s* of Frank and Norma Arnison; *m* 1964, Barbara Ruth Smith; one *s* one *d.* *Educ:* Lismore High Sch.; Royal Mil. Coll., Duntroon; Army Staff Coll., Queenscliff; Univ. of Queensland (BEc 1976); Securities Inst. of Australia (Grad. Dip. in Applied Finance and Investment 1993). CO 5th 7th Bn Royal Aust. Regt, 1981–82; COS HQ 1st Div., Brisbane, 1983–84; Comdt Land Warfare Centre, Canungra, Qld, 1985–86; Comdr 3rd Bde, Townsville, Qld, 1987–88; RCDS 1989; Dir-Gen. Jt Ops and Plans, HQ Aust. Defence Force, Canberra, 1990; Comdr 1st Div., Brisbane, Qld, 1991–94; Land Comdr Australia, Sydney, 1994–96. Exec. Dir, Allied Rubber Products (Qld), 1996–97.

DUniv: Griffith, 1998; Qld Univ. of Technology, 1999; Hon. DLit Southern Qld, 2001; Hon. LLD Qld, 2002. KStJ 1997. *Publication:* Australia's Security Arrangements in the South West Pacific, 1989. *Recreations:* golf, watching Rugby and cricket, theatre, reading, computing. *Address:* 86 Yabba Street, Ascot, Qld 4007, Australia. *Clubs:* Queensland, United Service (Brisbane); Royal Queensland Golf.

ARNOLD, Anne Mary; a District Judge (Magistrates' Courts), Hampshire, since 2006; a Recorder, since 2005; *b* 16 March 1958; *d* of late Lt Comdr Stanley Hugh Childs Plant, RNR, RD, and of Enid Edith Plant (*née* Morgan); *m* 1987, Peter Roderick Arnold. *Educ:* Talbot Heath, Bournemouth; Dorset Inst. Higher Educn and Université de Caen (BA Hons); Univ. of Birmingham (MBA Public Service); Homerton Coll., Cambridge (AdvDip Professional Trng and Develt). Called to the Bar, Inner Temple, 1981; Dorset Magistrates' Courts, 1979–99: Legal Advr, 1980–82; Principal Legal Advr, 1982–92; Dep. Justices' Trng Officer, 1991–94; Bench Legal Advr, 1992–94; Dir of Legal Services, 1994–99; Jt Staff Trng Officer, 1995–99; Associate Inspector, HM Magistrates' Courts Inspectorate, 1998; Actg Provincial Stipendiary Magistrate, E and W Sussex Commn Areas, 1997–99; a Provincial Stipendiary Magistrate, then District Judge (Magistrates' Cts), E Sussex, 1999–2006. Adjudicator, Prison Rule 53(A)2 and Young Offender Instn Rule 58(A)2, 2002–. *Publication:* (contrib.) Atkin's Court Forms, vol. 5, 2nd edn, 2001, vol. 25, 2002, vol. 5(i) 2nd edn, 2004, vol. 19(1A) and 19(1B), 2005, vol. 25(1), 2007. *Recreations:* sailing, running, swimming, cycling, gardening. *Address:* The Law Courts, Winston Churchill Avenue, Portsmouth, Hants PO1 2DQ. *T:* (023) 9281 9421. *Clubs:* Bar Yacht; Itchenor Sailing.

ARNOLD, Dr Bruce, OBE 2003; Chief Critic, Irish Independent, Dublin, since 1986; *b* 6 Sept. 1936; *s* of George Croft Arnold and Margaret Shaw; *m* 1959, Ysabel Mavis Cleave; two *s* one *d*. *Educ:* Kingham Hill Sch., Oxon; Trinity Coll., Dublin (MA); National Univ. of Ireland (DLitt 2000). Political commentator and arts journalist: Irish Times, 1961–67; Sunday Independent, 1967–70; Irish Independent, 1972–; Literary Ed., Irish Indep., 1986–2001. *Publications:* A Concise History of Irish Art, 1969, rev. edn 1998; Coppinger quartet: A Singer at the Wedding, 1978; The Song of the Nightingale, 1980; The Muted Swan, 1981; Running to Paradise, 1983; Orpen: mirror to an age, 1981; What Kind of Country, 1984; Margaret Thatcher: a study in power, 1984; An Art Atlas of Britain and Ireland, 1991; The Scandal of Ulysses, 1991, rev. edn 2004; Mainie Jellett and the Modern Movement in Ireland, 1991 (Amer. Conf. for Irish Studies Prize); Haughey: his life and unlucky deeds, 1993, rev. edn 2007; Jack Yeats, 1998; Jonathan Swift: an illustrated life, 1999; Jack Lynch: hero in crisis, 2001; The Spire and other essays in Irish culture, 2003; He That Is Down Need Fear No Fall, 2008. *Recreations:* camellias, snowdrops, singing madrigals. *Address:* e-mail: brucea@gofree.indigo.ie. *Club:* Athenæum.

ARNOLD, Prof. Dana Rebecca, PhD; FSA, FRHistS; Professor of Architectural History, since 1999 and Head of Research, School of Humanities, since 2003, University of Southampton; *b* 22 June 1961; *d* of late Edward Cyril Arnold and of Josephine Arnold; *m* 1989, Dr Kenneth Haynes (marr. diss. 2007). *Educ:* Westfield Coll., London (BA 1983); Bartlett Sch. of Architecture, UCL (MSc 1984; PhD 1997). Sen. Lectr, Dept of Fine Art, Univ. of Leeds, 1994–99. Research Fellow: Yale Univ., 1997 and 2005; Getty Res. Inst., Calif, 2002; Univ. of Cambridge, 2003. Mem., AHRC (formerly AHRB), 2004–. FRSA 2000; FSA 2006; FRHistS 2007. Ed., Art History jl, 1997–2002; Gen. Ed., New Interventions in Art History (book series), 2002–. *Publications include:* (ed) Belov'd by Ev'ry Muse: Richard Boyle, 3rd Earl of Burlington and 4th Earl of Cork (1694–1753), 1994; (ed) Squandrous and Lavish Profusion: George IV, his image and patronage of the arts, 1995; (ed) The Georgian Villa, 1995, 2nd edn 1998; (ed) The Georgian Country House, 1998, 2nd edn 2003; (ed) The Metropolis and its Image, 1999; Re-presenting the Metropolis: architecture, urban experience and social life in London 1800–1840, 2000; Reading Architectural History, 2002; (ed jtly) Tracing Architecture, 2003; (ed jtly) Art and Thought, 2003; Art History: a very short introduction, 2004; (ed) Cultural Identities and the Aesthetics of Britishness, 2004; (ed jtly) Architecture as Experience, 2004; Rural Urbanism: London landscapes in the early nineteenth century, 2006; (ed jtly) Re-thinking Architectural Historiography, 2006; (ed jtly) Biographies and Space, 2007. *Address:* School of Humanities, University of Southampton, Highfield, Southampton SO17 1BJ.

ARNOLD, David George; film composer, songwriter and record producer; *b* 23 Jan. 1962; *s* of George and Rita Arnold; *m* 1996, Eleanor Pole; one *s* twin *d*. Composer: for *films* including: The Young Americans, 1993; Stargate, 1994; Last of the Dogmen, 1995; Independence Day (Grammy Award for Best Film Score), 1996; Tomorrow Never Dies, A Life Less Ordinary, 1997; Godzilla, 1998; The World is not Enough, 1999 (Ivor Novello Award for Best Film Score, 2003); Shaft, 2000; Zoolander, Baby Boy, 2001; Enough, Changing Lanes, Die Another Day, 2002; 2 Fast 2 Furious, 2003; Stepford Wives, 2004; Stoned, Four Brothers, 2005; Casino Royale, Venus, Amazing Grace, 2006; Hot Fuzz, 2007; How to Lose Friends and Alienate People, 2008; for *television* including: The Visitor (series), 1997; Randall & Hopkirk Deceased (series), 2000; Little Britain (series), 2003 (RTS Award for Best Music, 2005). Composer and producer of numerous recordings. Fellow, British Acad. of Composers & Songwriters, 2005. *Recreations:* watching cooking on TV, wandering round streets in a daze. *Address:* Air Studios, Lyndhurst Road, NW3 4DJ. *T:* (020) 7794 0660, *Fax:* (020) 7794 8518; *e-mail:* davidgarnold@gmail.com.

ARNOLD, Prof. David John, DPhil; FBA 2004; Professor of Asian and Global History, University of Warwick, since 2006; *b* 1 Oct. 1946; *s* of Mansel John and May Arnold; *m* 1988, Juliet Elizabeth Miller. *Educ:* Univ. of Exeter (BA Hons (Hist.) 1968); Univ. of Sussex (DPhil 1973). Lectr in History, Univ. of Dar es Salaam, 1972–75; Res. Fellow, Flinders Univ., Australia, 1975–77; Res. Fellow, SOAS, 1977–78; Lectr in History, Univ. of Lancaster, 1979–88; Prof. of S Asian Hist., 1988–2006, Hd, Dept of Hist., 1992–96, Pro-Dir for Res., 1999–2002, SOAS. *Publications:* The Age of Discovery 1400–1600, 1983, 2nd edn 2002; Famine: social crisis and historical change, 1988; Colonizing the Body: state medicine and epidemic disease in nineteenth-century India, 1993; The Problem of Nature: environment, culture and European expansion, 1996; Science, Technology and Medicine in Colonial India, 2000; Gandhi, 2001; The Tropics and the Travelling Gaze: India, landscape and science 1800–1856, 2005. *Recreations:* travel, gardening. *Address:* Department of History, University of Warwick, Coventry CV4 7AL. *T:* (024) 7652 3315; *e-mail:* d.arnold@warwick.ac.uk.

ARNOLD, Rev. Duane Wade-Hampton, PhD; Principal, St Chad's College, University of Durham, 1994–97; *b* 5 Aug. 1953; *s* of Wade H. Arnold and Louise Elizabeth (*née* Hensley); *m* 1980, Janet Lee Drew. *Educ:* Univ. of State of New York (BA 1979); Concordia Seminary (MA 1981); St Chad's Coll., Durham (PhD 1989); STh (Lambeth Dip. in Theol.), 1984. Minister, First Church, Detroit, Michigan, 1985–87; Precentor, St Paul's Cathedral, Detroit, 1987; Chaplain, Wayne State Univ., Detroit, 1988–91; Curate, St Thomas Church, Fifth Ave, NY, 1991–93. Tutor, St Chad's Coll., Durham, 1983–85; Adjunct Lecturer: in Religious Studies, Univ. of Detroit, 1985–88; in Church History, Ashland Seminary, Ohio, 1987–91. Fellow, Coll. of Preachers, Washington Nat. Cathedral, 1991. ChStJ 1990. Governor's Award, Michigan, 1988. *Publications:* A Lutheran Reader, 1982; The Way, the Truth and the Life, 1982; Francis, A Call to Conversion, 1990; Prayers of the Martyrs, 1991; The Early Episcopal Career of Athanasius of Alexandria, 1991; Praying with John Donne and George Herbert, 1992; *De Doctrina Christiana*, Classic of Western Civilization, 1995; (with R. Hudson) Beyond Belief: what the Martyrs said to God, 2002; (with R. Hudson) Más allá de la Fe, 2004; contribs to learned jls. *Recreation:* shooting. *Club:* Columbia (Indianapolis).

ARNOLD, Eve, Hon. OBE 2003; photographer and writer; *b* Philadelphia, 1925; *m* (marr. diss.); one *s*. Took a 6-week photography class with Alexei Brodovitch, at New Sch. for Social Research, NY, 1948, after receiving a $40 Rolleicord as her first camera; first photographs in Picture Post, followed by Ladies Home Jl, Life, Time, Look, Stern, Paris Match, Harpers, Queen, Sunday Times; joined Magnum Photos agency, 1951; works in USA, UK, Africa, China, Russia, Afghanistan, Arab countries; portrait photographs include Royalty, film stars and politicians. Exhibitions: Brooklyn Mus., NY, 1980; Nat. Portrait Gall., 1991; (retrospective) Barbican, 1996; Marilyn Monroe by Eve Arnold, Halcyon Gall., London, 2005; In China, Asia House, London, 2007. *Films:* Behind the Veil, 1973; special production photographer on 31 films. *Publications:* The Unretouched Woman, 1976; Flashback!: the 50s, 1978; In China, 1980; In America, 1984; Marilyn Monroe: an appreciation, 1987; Private View: inside Baryshnikov's American Ballet Theatre, 1988; All in a Day's Work, 1989; Eve Arnold in Britain, 1991; Eve Arnold: in retrospect, 1996; Eve Arnold: Film Journal, 2002; Handbook (with Footnotes), 2004; Marilyn Monroe, 2005. *Address:* Flat 3, 26 Mount Street, W1K 2RS.

ARNOLD, Glynis, (Mrs Elliott Arnold); *see* Johns, G.

ARNOLD, Jacques Arnold; consultant on Latin America; *b* London, 27 Aug. 1947; *s* of late Samuel Arnold and Eugenie (*née* Patentini); *m* 1976, Patricia Anne, *er d* of late Dennis Maunder, Windsor; one *s* two *d*. *Educ:* schools in Brazil and by correspondence; London School of Economics (BSc (Econ) 1972). Asst Gp Rep., Midland Bank, São Paulo, 1976–78; Regl Dir, Thomas Cook Gp, 1978–84; Asst Trade Finance Dir, Midland Bank, 1984–85; Dir, American Express Europe Ltd, 1985–87; Adviser for Latin America: GEC plc, 1998–2000; BAE Systems, 2000–04; FIRST Mag., 2006–; has travelled to over 90 countries on business. County Councillor for Oundle, Northants, 1981–85. Contested (C) Coventry SE, 1983. MP (C) Gravesham, 1987–97; contested (C) same seat, 1997, 2001. PPS to Minister of State: for Envmt and Countryside, 1992–93; Home Office, 1993–95. Member: Educn, Arts and Sci. Select Cttee, 1989–92; Treasury and CS Select Cttee, 1997; Sec., Cons. Backbench Cttee on Foreign and Commonwealth Affairs, 1990–92, 1995–97; Vice-Chm., 1995–96, Chm., 1996–97, Cons. Backbench Cttee on Constitutional Affairs. Secretary: British-Latin-American Parly Gp, 1987–97; Scout Assoc. Parly Gp, 1987–97; Chairman: British Brazilian Parly Gp, 1992–97; British Portuguese Parly Gp, 1995–97. Chm., LSE Cons. Soc., 1971–72; Treasurer, Nat. Assoc. of Cons. Graduates, 1974–76; Chm., Hyde Park Tories, 1975–76; Vice-Chairman: Croydon NE Cons. Assoc., 1974–76; Corby Cons. Assoc., 1983–85. Chm., Kent County Scout Council, 1998–2000. Trustee, Environment Foundn, 1989–2003. Grand Official, Order of Southern Cross (Brazil), 1993. *Publications:* Democracy for Europe, 1977; (ed) Royal Houses of Europe (series), 1998–2008; (ed) History of Britain's Parliamentary Constituencies, 2008. *Recreations:* family life, gardening, genealogy. *Address:* Fairlawn, 243 London Road, West Malling, Kent ME19 5AD. *T:* and *Fax:* (01732) 848388. *Club:* Carlton.

ARNOLD, Jennette; Member (Lab), since July 2000 (London, 2000–04, North East, since 2004), and Chairman, since 2008, London Assembly, Greater London Authority. Formerly: nurse; health visitor; Regl Dir, RCN. Mem. (Lab) Islington BC, 1994–2002 (Dep. Mayor, 1999–2000). Chair: Cultural Strategy Gp for London, 2000–04; London Health Commn, 2004–; Vice-Chair, London Cultural Commn, 2005–. Member: Metropolitan Police Authy, 2000–; Mayor of London's Adv. Cabinet, 2000–; UK Delegn to EU Cttee of the Regions, 2002–. Mem. Bd, Arts Council England - London, 2002–06. *Address:* Greater London Authority, City Hall, Queen's Walk, SE1 2AA.

ARNOLD, Prof. John André, FCA; Director, Manchester Business School, and KPMG Professor of Accounting and Financial Management, University of Manchester, 1994–2006; *b* 30 April 1944; *s* of André Eugene Arnold and May Arnold (*née* Vickers); *m* 1997, Sylvia Bailey; two *d*. *Educ:* London Sch. of Econs (MSc 1969). FCA 1967. Teaching Fellow, LSE, 1967–69; Lectr in Accounting, Univ. of Kent, 1969–71; Lectr, 1971–75, Sen. Lectr, 1975–77, Prof. of Accounting, 1977–94, Univ. of Manchester. Vis. Prof., Grad. Sch. of Business, Univ. of Washington, 1981–82. Chm., pro.manchester, 2007–08. Pres., Manchester Soc. of Chartered Accountants, 1991–92. CCMI 1995. *Publications:* Pricing and Output Decisions, 1973; Accounting for Management Decisions, 1983, 3rd edn 1996; Financial Accounting, 1985, 2nd edn 1994; contrib. numerous articles to learned jls. *Recreations:* squash, tennis, watching Stockport County FC. *Address:* 3 Green Meadows, Marple, Stockport, Cheshire SK6 6QF. *T:* (0161) 449 9432; *e-mail:* john.arnold@mbs.ac.uk. *Clubs:* Marple Cricket and Squash, Hazel Grove Lawn Tennis (Stockport).

ARNOLD, Very Rev. John Robert, OBE 2002; Dean of Durham, 1989–2002, now Emeritus; *b* 1 Nov. 1933; *s* of John Stanley and Ivy Arnold; *m* 1963, Livia Anneliese Franke; one *s* two *d*. *Educ:* Christ's Hospital; Sidney Sussex Coll., Cambridge (MA); Westcott House Theol College. Curate of Holy Trinity, Millhouses, Sheffield, 1960–63; Sir Henry Stephenson Fellow, Univ. of Sheffield, 1962–63; Chaplain and Lectr, Univ. of Southampton, 1963–72; Secretary, Board for Mission and Unity, General Synod of the Church of England, 1972–78; Dean of Rochester, 1978–89. Pt-time Lectr, Univ. of Durham, 1992–2002. Hon. Canon of Winchester Cathedral, 1974–78; Mem., General Synod, 1980–2002. Mem., European Ecumenical Commn for Church and Society, 1986–98; Pres., Conference of European Churches, 1986–2001 (Vice-Chm., 1986–92; Chm., 1993–97). Pres., Anglican-Lutheran Soc., 1999–. Hon. Fellow, St Chad's Coll., Univ. of Durham, 2002. DD Lambeth, 1999; Hon. DD Dunelm, 2002. Order of Saint Vladimir (Russian Orthodox Church), 1977. Officers' Cross, Order of Merit (Germany), 1991. *Publications:* (trans.) Eucharistic Liturgy of Taizé, 1962; (contrib.) Hewitt, Strategist for the Spirit, 1985; Rochester Cathedral, 1987; (contrib.) Cathedrals Now, 1996; (contrib.) Preaching from Cathedrals, 1998; Life Conquers Death, 2007; contribs to Theology, Crucible, St Luke's Journal of Theology. *Recreations:* music, European languages and literature. *Address:* 26 Hawks Lane, Canterbury CT1 2NU.

ARNOLD, Rt Rev. John Stanley Kenneth; Auxiliary Bishop of Westminster, (RC), since 2006; *b* 12 June 1953; *s* of Stanley Kenneth Arnold and Mary Arnold (*née* Murray). *Educ:* Ratcliffe Coll., Leics; Trinity Coll., Oxford (MA Juris.); Council of Legal Educn, London; Gregorian Univ., Rome (DCL 1985). Barrister, 1976; ordained priest, 1983; Chaplain, 1985–89, Sub-Adminr, 1989–93, Westminster Cathedral; Parish Priest, Our Lady of Mt Carmel and St George, Enfield, 1993–2001; Westminster Diocese: VG and Chancellor, 2001–06; Moderator of the Curia and Chancellor, 2005–. *Publication:* Quality of Mercy: a fresh look at the Sacrament of Reconciliation, 1993. *Address:* Archbishop's House, Ambrosden Avenue, SW1P 1QJ. *T:* (020) 7931 6062; *e-mail:* johnarnold@rcdow.org.uk.

ARNOLD, Rt Rev. Keith Appleby; Hon. Assistant Bishop, Diocese of Oxford, since 1996; *b* 1 Oct. 1926; *s* of Dr Frederick Arnold, Hale, Cheshire, and Alice Mary Appleby Arnold (*née* Holt); *m* 1955, Deborah Noreen Glenwright; one *s* one *d*. *Educ*: Winchester; Trinity Coll., Cambridge (MA); Westcott House, Cambridge. Served as Lieut, Coldstream Guards, 1944–48. Curate: Haltwhistle, Northumberland, 1952–55; St John's, Princes St, Edinburgh, 1955–61; Chaplain, TA, 1956–61; Rector of St John's, Edinburgh, 1961–69; Vicar of Kirkby Lonsdale, Cumbria, 1969–73; Team Rector of Hemel Hempstead, 1973–80; Bishop Suffragan of Warwick, 1980–90; Hon. Asst Bishop, dio. of Newcastle, 1991–96. Vice-Pres., Abbeyfield Soc., 1981–91; Chairman: Housing Assocs Charitable Trust, 1980–86; English Villages Housing Assoc., 1987–. Pres., S Warwicks Marriage Guidance Council, subseq. Relate, 1980–90. *Recreations*: 19th century history, gardening. *Address*: 9 Dinglederry, Olney, Bucks MK46 5ES. *T*: (01234) 713044.

ARNOLD, Hon. Lynn Maurice Ferguson, AO 2004; Chief Executive Officer, Anglicare SA, since 2008; *b* 27 Jan. 1949; *s* of Maurice and Jean Arnold; *m* 1978, Elaine Palmer; two *s* three *d*. *Educ*: Adelaide Boys' High Sch.; Univ. of Adelaide (BA, BEd; PhD 2003). Dip. en la Alta Dirección de Empresas, ESADE, 1996. Teacher, Salisbury N High Sch., 1971–74; Adv. Teacher, Health Educn Project Team, 1975–76; Personal Assistant to MHR, 1977–79; MHA (ALP) Salisbury, 1979–87; MP (ALP) Ramsay, 1987–93; Taylor, 1993–94; Minister of: Education, 1982–85; Technology, 1982–87; Children's Services, 1985; Employment and Further Educn, and State Develt, 1985–89; Industry, Trade & Technol., also Agriculture, Fisheries, and Ethnic Affairs, 1989–92; Economic Develt, and Multicultural and Ethnic Affairs, 1992–93; Premier of S Australia, 1992–93; Leader of the Opposition and Shadow Minister of Econ. Develt and of Multicultural and Ethnic Affairs, 1993–94; Vis. Scholar, Univ. of Oviedo, Spain, 1994–95; student, Escuela Superior de Administración y Dirección de Empresas, Barcelona, 1995–96; CEO, World Vision Australia, 1997–2003; Regl Vice-Pres. (Asia/Pacific), World Vision Internat., 2003–08. Sec. and Pres., Campaign for Peace in Vietnam, 1970–73. Mem. Council, Univ. of Adelaide, 1979–82. Trustee, Cttee for the Economic Develt of Australia, 1997–2003. Mem., Australian Inst. of Co. Dirs, 1997–. *Publications*: Nigeria-Biafra Conflict, 1968; (jtly) Hoa Binh Third Force in Vietnam, 1970; (jtly) You and Me, 1975; (jtly) All Together, 1976. *Recreations*: sociolinguistics, history. *Address*: c/o Anglicare SA, 18 King William Road, Adelaide, SA 5000, Australia.

ARNOLD, Dr Richard Bentham; Executive Vice-President, International Federation of Pharmaceutical Manufacturers' Associations, 1984–97; *b* 29 Aug. 1932; *s* of George Benjamin and Alice Arnold; *m* 1956, Margaret Evelyn Racey; one *s* one *d*. *Educ*: Stamford Sch.; King Edward VII Sch., King's Lynn; Nottingham Univ. BSc, PhD. Joined May & Baker Ltd, 1959; Commercial Manager, Pharmaceuticals Div., 1974–76; Dir Designate, 1976, Dir, 1977–83, Assoc. of British Pharmaceutical Industry. *Recreations*: golf, fishing, bird watching.

ARNOLD, Hon. Sir Richard David, Kt 2008; **Hon. Mr Justice Arnold;** a Judge of the High Court of Justice, Chancery Division, since 2008; *b* 23 June 1961; *s* of late Francis Arnold and of Ann Arnold (*née* Churchill); *m* 1990, Mary Elford; two *d*. *Educ*: Highgate Sch.; Magdalen Coll., Oxford (BA Nat. Sci. 1983, MA 1986); Univ. of Westminster (Dip. Law 1984). Called to the Bar, Middle Temple, 1985. QC 2000; Dep. High Court Judge, 2004–08. Chm. Cttee, Code of Practice for Promotion of Animal Medicines, Nat. Office of Animal Health, 2002–. Apptd to hear Trade Mark appeals, 2003–08; Mem., Panel of Chairmen, Competition Appeal Tribunal, 2008–. Ed., Entertainment and Media Law Reports, 1993–2004. *Publications*: Performers' Rights, 1990, 4th edn 2008; (jtly) Computer Software: legal protection in the UK, 2nd edn 1992; (ed) Halsbury's Laws— Trade Marks, 4th edn reissue. *Recreations*: collecting contemporary British abstract paintings and ceramics, music, cinema, theatre, opera, cooking. *Address*: Royal Courts of Justice, Strand, WC2A 2LL. *Club*: MCC.

ARNOLD, Simon Rory; Deputy Chairman, Aon Group (formerly Bain Hogg Group) plc, 1995; Chairman, Octavian Syndicate Management Services Ltd, 1995; *b* 10 Sept. 1933; *s* of R. W. Arnold and R. A. Arnold; *m* 1960, (Janet) Linda May; one *s* one *d*. *Educ*: Diocesan Coll., Cape Town. J. H. Minet & Co. Ltd: S Africa, 1952; London, 1955; Chm. and Chief Exec., 1979; Gp Man. Dir, Minet Holdings, 1983; Chief Exec., Bain Dawes Ltd, 1984; Chm. and Chief Exec., Bain Clarkson Ltd, 1986–95; Main Bd Dir, Inchcape plc, 1988–94. Member: Lloyd's Brokers Cttee, 1979–91 (Chm., 1986–91); Council, Lloyd's, 1991–94; Insurance Brokers' Registration Council, 1995– (Chm., 1998); Chm., BIIBA, 1994. *Recreations*: ski-ing, walking, golf, tennis.

ARNOLD, Sir Thomas (Richard), Kt 1990; theatre producer; publisher; consultant in Middle East affairs; *b* 25 Jan. 1947; *s* of late Thomas Charles Arnold, OBE and Helen Breen; *m* 1984, Elizabeth Jane (marr. diss. 1993), *widow* of Robin Smithers; one *d*. *Educ*: Bedales Sch.; Le Rosey, Geneva; Pembroke Coll., Oxford (MA). Contested (C): Manchester Cheetham, 1970; Hazel Grove, Feb. 1974. MP (C) Hazel Grove, Oct. 1974–1997. PPS to Sec. of State for NI, 1979–81, to Lord Privy Seal, FCO, 1981–82; Chm., Treasury and CS Select Cttee, 1994–97 (Mem., 1992–94). Vice-Chm., Conservative Party, 1983–92. *Address*: No 1 Knightsbridge, SW1X 7LX.

ARNOLD, Wallace; *see* Brown, C. E. M.

ARNOLD, William; Chief Executive, Law Commission, since 2008; *b* 13 May 1953; *s* of Rev. William and Mrs Ruth Arnold; *m* 1992, Elizabeth Anne McLellan; twin *s*. *Educ*: Bury Grammar Sch.; King's Coll., Cambridge (MA Classics). Joined Lord Chancellor's Department, 1974: Asst Private Sec. to Lord Chancellor, 1977–79; Principal, 1979; Head of Legal Services Div., 1987; Head of Remuneration and Competition Div., 1988; Head, Courts and Legal Services Bill Div., 1989; Dir of Corporate Services and Principal Estabt and Finance Officer, PRO, 1991–92; on loan to Dept of PM and Cabinet, Canberra, Australia, 1993–94; Hd, Family Policy Div., LCD, 1994–99; Hd of Govt Offices and Regl Policy, then Regl Policy and Regeneration, Div. 1, DETR, 1999–2001; Dir, Regl Develt Agency Policy, Finance and Sponsorship, DTI, 2001–03; Hd, Criminal Justice System Confidence Unit, Home Office, 2003; Sec. to the Judicial Appointments Comrs, 2004–06; Interim Chief Exec., Family Justice Council, 2006; Hd, Court Broadcasting Unit, Min. of Justice, 2006–07. Reader: St Margaret's Church, Putney, 1989–2008; All Saints, East Sheen, 2008–. FRSA 2000. *Recreations*: ski-ing, swimming, long-distance trekking, opera, ballet. *Address*: Law Commission, Steel House, 11 Tothill Street, SW1H 9LJ.

ARNOLD-BAKER, Charles, OBE 1966; Chairman, Longcross Press, since 1968; Consultant Lecturer, 1978, and Visiting Professor, 1985–94, City University; *b* 25 June 1918; *s* of Baron Albrecht v. Blumenthal and Alice Wilhelmine (*née* Hainsworth); adopted surname of mother's second husband, Percival Richard Arnold Baker, 1938; *m* 1943, Edith (*née* Woods); one *s* one *d*. *Educ*: Winchester Coll.; Magdalen Coll., Oxford. BA 1940. Called to Bar, Inner Temple, 1948. Army (Private to Captain), 1940–46. Admty Bar, 1948–52; Sec., Nat. Assoc. of Local Councils, 1953–78; Dep. Eastern Traffic Comr, 1978–90. Editor, Road Law, 1992–96. Mem., Royal Commn on Common Lands, 1955–58; Mem. European Cttee, Internat. Union of Local Authorities, 1960–78; a Deleg.

to European Local Govt Assembly, Strasbourg, 1960–78. Occasional broadcaster, Radio 4, 1987–92. Gwylim Gibbons Award, Nuffield Coll., Oxford, 1959. King Haakon's Medal of Freedom (Norway), 1945. *Publications*: Norway (pamphlet), 1946; Everyman's Dictionary of Dates, 1954; Parish Administration, 1958; New Law and Practice of Parish Administration, 1966; The 5000 and the Power Tangle, 1967; The Local Government Act 1972, 1973; Local Council Administration, 1975, 6th edn 2001; The Local Government, Planning and Land Act 1980, 1981; Practical Law for Arts Administrators, 1983, 3rd edn 1992; The Five Thousand and the Living Constitution, 1986; The Companion to British History, 1996, 2nd edn 2001; For He is An Englishman: memoirs of a Prussian nobleman, 2007; Quacks and Quotes, 2008; many contribs to British and European local govt and legal jls. *Recreations*: travel, history, writing, music, cooking, journalism, wine, doing nothing. *Address*: Top Floor, 2 Mitre Court Buildings, Temple, EC4Y 7BX. *T*: (020) 7353 3490. *Club*: Union (Oxford).

ARNOT, Prof. Madeleine Mary, (Lady Young), PhD; Professor of Sociology of Education, University of Cambridge, since 2004; Fellow, Jesus College, Cambridge, since 1990; *b* 9 Jan. 1950; *d* of Eric Maxwell-Arnot and Marie Madeleine (*née* Rzewuska); *m* 1st, 1973, Neil MacDonald (marr. diss. 1980); 2nd, 1982, R. Allan Drummond (*d* 1994); one *s* one *d*; 3rd, 1998, Sir Robin Urquhart Young, *qv*. *Educ*: More House Convent, London; Univ. of Edinburgh (MA 1st Cl. Hons 1972); Univ. of London Inst. of Educn; PhD Open 1989; MA Cantab 1998. Lectr, Open Univ., 1975–88; Lectr, 1988–2000, Reader, 2000–04, Cambridge Univ.; Leverhulme Trust Res. Fellow, 1996–97; Dir of Studies in Educn, Jesus Coll., Cambridge, 1990–. Noted Schol., Univ. of BC, 1993; George A. Miller Vis. Prof., Univ. of Illinois, Champagne Urbana, 2000; Visiting Professor: Univ. of Porto, 2001–; Aristotle Univ. of Thessaloniki, 2003–; Univ. of Stockholm, 2005. Member: Wkg Gp on Initial Teacher Educn, SCAA, 1996; Wkg Gp on Citizenship and Initial Teacher Educn, 2000, DfEE; Gender Policy Gp, QCA, 1998–99; Consultative Gp, EOC, 1999–2002; Steering Gp Global Monitoring Report, UNESCO, 2003; Gender expert for Council of Europe Jt Cttee on Human Rights and Educn, 1999. FRSA 1996; AcSS 2004. Hon. Mem., Sen. Common Room, Lucy Cavendish Coll., Cambridge, 1997. FilDr *hc* Uppsala. *Publications*: (jtly) Educational Reforms and Gender Equality in Schools, 1996; (jtly) Recent Research on Gender and Educational Performance, 1998; (jtly) Closing the Gender Gap: post-war education and social change, 1999; Reproducing Gender?: essays on educational theory and feminist politics, 2002; (jtly) Consultation in the Classroom: developing dialogue about teaching and learning, 2004; anthologies: as M. M. MacDonald: (ed jtly) Schooling and Capitalism, 1977; Education and the State, Vol. 1: Schooling and the National Interest, 1981, Vol. 2: Politics, Patriarchy and Practice, 1981; as M. Arnot: (ed) Race and Gender: equal opportunities policies in education, 1985; edited jointly: Gender and the Politics of Schooling, 1987; Gender Under Scrutiny: new inquiries in education, 1987; Voicing Concerns: sociological perspectives on contemporary education reforms, 1992; Feminism and Social Justice in Education: international perspectives, 1993; Challenging Democracy?: international perspectives on gender, education and citizenship, 2000; Gender Education and Equality in a Global Context: conceptual frameworks and policy perspectives, 2008. *Address*: Jesus College, Cambridge CB5 8BL. *T*: (01223) 339339, *Fax*: (01223) 339313.

ARNOTT, Sir Alexander John Maxwell, 6th Bt *cr* 1896, of Woodlands, Shandon, Co. Cork; *b* 18 Sept. 1975; *s* of Sir John Robert Alexander Arnott, 5th Bt, and of Ann Margaret, *d* of late T. A. Farrelly, Kilcar, Co. Cavan; *S* father, 1981. *Heir*: *b* Andrew John Eric Arnott, *b* 20 June 1978. *Address*: 11 Palmerston Road, Dublin 6, Ireland.

ARNOTT, Deborah; Director, Action on Smoking and Health, since 2003; *b* 23 June 1955; *d* of Michael MacMillan Arnott and Felicity Arnott (*née* Hugh-Jones); *m* 1996, Jon Davies; two *s*. *Educ*: Brunel Univ. (BSc Hons Govt, Politics and Mod. Hist. 1977); Cranfield (MBA 1981). Grad. trainee and Industrial Relns Officer, Triumph Cars, 1977–80; business consultant, planning, research and systems, 1981–82; journalist, Management Today, 1982–83; LWT Factual Programmes: researcher, 1984–86; producer director, 1986–93; series producer and prog. editor, 1993–98; Hd, Consumer Educn, Financial Services Authy, 1998–2002. Equality Officer and Shop Steward, ACTT, later BECTU, at LWT, 1983–93; Mem., Nat. Exec. and Standing Orders Cttees, ACTT, 1984–86. Chair, Mgt Cttee, and Special Advr to Bd, Personal Finance Educn Gp, 1998–2002; Mem., Govt Task Force on Tackling Over-indebtedness, 2000–02. Mem. Cttee, Kingsway workplace nursery, 1983–94; Governor: Walnut Tree Walk Primary Sch., 1995–2001; Pimlico Comprehensive, Westminster, 2002–06. Alwyn Smith prize for most outstanding contrib. to public health, FPH, 2007. *Publications*: reports and papers for public bodies, campaigning gps and journals. *Recreations*: cycling, choral singing, watching TV with my children. *Address*: Action on Smoking and Health, 144–145 Shoreditch High Street, E1 6JE. *T*: (020) 7739 5902; *e-mail*: deborah.arnott@ash.org.uk.

ARNOTT, Edward Ian W.; *see* Walker-Arnott.

ARNOTT, Geoffrey; *see* Arnott, W. G.

ARNOTT, Prof. Struther, CBE 1996; FRS 1985; Principal and Vice-Chancellor, University of St Andrews, 1986–2000, now Emeritus; *b* 25 Sept. 1934; *s* of Charles McCann and Christina Struthers Arnott; *m* 1970, Greta Edwards, BA, DLitt; two *s*. *Educ*: Hamilton Academy, Lanarkshire; Glasgow Univ. (BSc, PhD). FRSC 1970; FRSE 1988. King's College London: scientist, MRC Biophysics Research Unit, 1960–70; demonstrator in Physics. 1960–67; dir of postgraduate studies in Biophysics, 1967–70; FKC 1997; Purdue University: Prof. of Molecular Biology, 1970–; Head, Dept of Biol Scis, 1975–80; Vice-Pres. for Research and Dean, Graduate Sch., 1980–86; Oxford University: Sen. Vis. Fellow, Jesus Coll., 1980–81; Nuffield Res. Fellow, Green Coll., 1985–86. Haddow Prof., Inst. of Cancer Res., 2000–03; Vis. Prof. and Sen. Res. Fellow, Imperial Coll., London, 2002–; Vis. Prof., Sch. of Pharmacy, Univ. of London, 2003–. Guggenheim Meml Foundn Fellow, 1985. Hon. ScD St Andrews, Laurinburg, USA, 1994; Hon. DSc Purdue, USA, 1998; Hon. LLD St Andrews, 1999. *Publications*: papers in learned jls on structures of fibrous biopolymers, especially nucleic acids and polysaccharides, and techniques for visualizing them. *Recreations*: bird watching, botanizing. *Address*: Cancer Research UK Biomolecular Structure Group, School of Pharmacy, University of London, 29–39 Brunswick Square, WC1N 1AX; *e-mail*: struther.arnott@pharmacy.ac.uk. *Clubs*: Athenæum; Caledonian; Royal and Ancient (St Andrews).

ARNOTT, Prof. W(illiam) Geoffrey, PhD; FBA 1999; Professor of Greek Language and Literature, University of Leeds, 1968–91, now Emeritus; *b* 17 Sept. 1930; *s* of late Bertie Arnott and Edith May Arnott (*née* Smith); *m* 1955, Vera Hodson; three *d*. *Educ*: Bury Grammar Sch.; Pembroke Coll., Cambridge (Schol.); BA 1952; Porson Prize, 1952; MA 1956; PhD 1960). Asst Master, Bristol Grammar Sch., 1952–53; Carrington-Coe Res. Student, Univ. of Cambridge, 1953–54; Asst Lectr in Greek, Bedford Coll., London Univ., 1955–59; Asst Dir of Exams, Civil Service Commn, 1959–60; Asst Lectr in Classics, Univ. of Hull, 1950–61; Lectr in Classics, King's Coll., Univ. of Durham, 1960–63; Lectr in Classics, 1963–66, Sen. Lectr in Classics, 1966–67, Univ. of Newcastle upon Tyne. Vis. Mem., Inst. of Advanced Studies, Princeton, 1973; Vis. Schol., Univ. of

British Columbia, 1982; Visiting Professor: Univ. of Wellington, 1982; Univ. of Alexandria, 1983; Univ. of Queensland, 1987; Univ. of Bologna, 1998; Vis. Fellow, Gonville and Caius Coll., Cambridge, 1987–88. Lectr, NADFAS, 1980–2004. Pres., Leeds Birdwatchers Club, 1981–84. Member: Classical Jls Bd, 1970–94; Bd of Mgt, Greece & Rome, 1981–89. Fellow, Italian Soc. for Study of Classical Antiquity, 1981. *Publications:* Menander's Dyskolos: a translation, 1960; Menander, Plautus, Terence, 1975; Menander, vol. I, 1979, vol. II, 1996, vol. III, 2000; Alexis: a commentary, 1996; Birds in the Ancient World from A–Z, 2007; papers and reviews in classical jls, etc. *Recreations:* birds and 19th century bird painting, crosswords, photography, travel. *Address:* 35 Arncliffe Road, Leeds LS16 5AP. *T:* (0113) 275 2751.

ARON, Michael Douglas; HM Diplomatic Service; Ambassador to Kuwait, since 2008; *b* 22 March 1959; *s* of late Maurice Aron and of Sheila Aron (née Torrens); *m* 1986, Rachel Ann Golding Barker (*see* R. A. G. Aron); two *s* two *d*. *Educ:* Exeter Sch.; Leeds Univ. (BA Hons Arabic and French); Poly. of Central London. English lang. teacher, Sudan, 1981–83; joined FCO, 1984: Conf. Support Officer, UK Mission to UN, NY, 1985; on secondment to EC, 1986; Second, later First Sec., FCO, 1986–88; First Secretary: (Commercial and Econ.), Brasilia, 1988–91; FCO, 1991–93; UK Mission to UN, 1993–96; Dep. Hd, ME Dept, FCO, 1996–97; Head: Comprehensive Spending Review Unit, FCO, 1997–98; Mgt Consultancy Services, FCO, 1998–99; Counsellor and Dep. Hd of Mission, Amman, Jordan, 1999–2002; Political Counsellor, UK Repn to EU, Brussels, 2002–06; EU Dir and Hd, Scottish Govt (formerly Exec.) EU Office, Brussels (on secondment), 2006–08. *Recreations:* football, Arsenal, tennis, walking, France. *Address:* c/o Foreign and Commonwealth Office, King Charles Street, SW1A 2AH.

ARON, Rachel Ann Golding, PhD; HM Diplomatic Service; Ambassador to Belgium, since 2007; *b* 18 July 1951; *d* of Guy Barker and Ailsa Barker (née Gladdish); *m* 1986, Michael Douglas Aron, *qv*; two *s* two *d*. *Educ:* Ashford Sch. for Girls; Westfield Coll., Univ. of London (BA Hons Hist. 1973; PGCE 1974); Darwin Coll., Cambridge (PhD 1978). Res. Asst to Sir Frederick Catherwood, MEP, 1979–84; joined FCO, 1984; First Sec. and Cyprus Desk Officer, 1984–86; Privileges and Immunities Desk Officer, 1987–88; Hd of Chancery, Brasilia, 1988–91; Asst Hd, Eastern Dept, 1991–93; First Sec. (Pol), UK Mission to UN, NY, 1993–96; FCO Chair, CSSB, 1997–99; remote project work for HR Directorate in Amman and Brussels, 2000–03. Chair, Parents' Assoc., 2003–05; Bd of Govs, 2005–07, British Sch. of Brussels. *Publication:* Conscience, Government and War, 1978. *Recreations:* walking, gardening. *Address:* c/o Foreign and Commonwealth Office, King Charles Street, SW1A 2AH; *e-mail:* rachel.aron@fco.gov.uk.

ARONSOHN, Lotte Therese; *see* Newman, L. T.

ARONSON, Hazel Josephine; *see* Cosgrove, Rt Hon. Lady.

ARRAN, 9th Earl of, *cr* 1762, of the Arran Islands, Co. Galway; **Arthur Desmond Colquhoun Gore;** Bt 1662; Viscount Sudley, Baron Saunders, 1758; Baron Sudley (UK), 1884; *b* 14 July 1938; *er s* of 8th Earl of Arran and of Fiona Bryde, *er d* of Sir Iain Colquhoun of Luss, 7th Bt, KT, DSO; *S* father, 1983; *m* 1974, Eleanor, (MBE 2008), *er d* of Bernard van Cutsem and Lady Margaret Fortescue; two *d*. *Educ:* Eton; Balliol College, Oxford. 2nd Lieutenant, 1st Bn Grenadier Guards (National Service). Asst Manager, Daily Mail, 1972–73; Man. Dir, Clark Nelson, 1973–74; Asst Gen. Manager, Daily and Sunday Express, June–Nov. 1974. Dir, Waterstone & Co. Ltd, 1984–87. A Lord in Waiting (Govt Whip), 1987–89; Parliamentary Under-Secretary of State: for the Armed Forces, MoD, 1989–92; NI Office, 1992–94; Parly Under-Sec. of State, DoE, 1994; Captain of the Yeomen of the Guard (Dep. Govt Chief Whip), 1994–95; elected Mem., H of L, 1999. Director: HMV, 1995–98; Bonham's, 1997–2000; Weather World, 2005. Chm., Waste Mgt Industry NTO, 2000–. Co-Chm., Children's Country Holidays Fund. Trustee, Chelsea Physic Garden, 1994–. *Recreations:* tennis, shooting, gardening, croquet. *Address:* c/o House of Lords, SW1A 0PW. *Clubs:* White's, Pratt's, Turf, Beefsteak.

ARRAN, Graham Kent; His Honour Judge Arran; a Circuit Judge, since 2007; *b* Manchester, 13 April 1947; *s* of Carl and Dorothy Arran; *m* 1st, 1973, Carol Quellmalz (d 1986); one *s* two *d*; 2nd, 1992, Susan Duncan. *Educ:* N Manchester Grammar Sch.; London Sch. of Econs and Pol Sci. (LLB). Called to the Bar, Lincoln's Inn, 1969; in practice at the Bar, London, specialising in criminal law, 1969–2007; Asst Recorder, 1990–94; Recorder, 1994–2007. *Recreations:* being taken for walks by the dogs, collecting antique silver and glass occasionally, going on holiday. *Address:* Harrow Crown Court, Hailsham Drive, Harrow HA1 4TU. *T:* (020) 8424 2294.

ARRAND, Ven. Geoffrey William; Archdeacon of Suffolk, since 1994; *b* 24 July 1944; *s* of Thomas Staniforth Arrand and Alice Ada Arrand; *m* 1st, 1968, Mary Marshall (marr. diss.); one *s* two *d*; 2nd, 2005, Margaret Elizabeth Frost. *Educ:* King's Coll., London (BD 1966, AKC). Ordained deacon, 1967, priest, 1968; Assistant Curate: Washington, dio. of Durham, 1967–70; S Ormsby Gp, 1970–73; Team Vicar, Great Grimsby, 1973–79; Team Rector, Halesworth, 1979–85; Dean of Bocking and Rector of Hadleigh with Layham and Shelley, 1985–94; RD of Hadleigh, 1986–94. Hon. Canon, St Edmundsbury Cathedral, 1991–. Mem., Gen. Synod, 2005–. OStJ 1994 (County Chaplain, Suffolk, 1995–). *Recreation:* golf. *Address:* Glebe House, Ashfield cum Thorpe, Stowmarket, Suffolk IP14 6LX. *T:* (01728) 685497, *Fax:* (01728) 685969. *Club:* Fynn Valley Golf (Ipswich).

ARRINDELL, Sir Clement Athelston, GCMG 1984; GCVO 1985; Kt 1982; QC; Governor-General, St Christopher and Nevis, 1983–95 (Governor, St Kitts-Nevis, 1981–83); *b* Basseterre, 19 April 1931. *Educ:* private school; Basseterre Boys' Elementary Sch.; St Kitts-Nevis Grammar Sch. (Island Scholar). Called to the Bar, Lincoln's Inn, 1958. Post-grad. studies; in practice as barrister and solicitor, 1959–66; Acting Magistrate, 1964–66; Magistrate, 1966–71; Chief Magistrate, 1972–78; Judge, WI Associated States Supreme Court, 1978–81. *Recreations:* piano-playing, classical music, gardening. *Address:* The Lark, Bird Rock, St Kitts, West Indies.

ARROW, Kenneth Joseph; Professor of Economics and Operations Research, Stanford University, 1979–91, Professor Emeritus, 1991; *b* 23 Aug. 1921; *s* of Harry I. and Lillian Arrow; *m* 1947, Selma Schweitzer; two *s*. *Educ:* City College (BS in Social Science 1940); Columbia Univ. (MA 1941, PhD 1951). Captain, US AAF, 1942–46. Research Associate, Cowles Commn for Research in Economics, Univ. of Chicago, 1947–49; Actg Asst Prof., Associate Prof. and Prof. of Economics, Statistics and Operations Research, Stanford Univ., 1949–68; Prof. of Econs, later University Prof., Harvard Univ., 1968–79. Staff Mem., US Council of Economic Advisers, 1962. Consultant, The Rand Corp., 1948–. Fellow, Churchill Coll., Cambridge, 1963–64, 1970, 1973, 1986. President: Internat. Economic Assoc., 1983–86; Internat. Soc. for Inventory Res., 1984–90; Member: Inst. of Management Sciences (Pres., 1963); Nat. Acad. of Sciences; Amer. Inst. of Medicine; Amer. Philosoph. Soc.; Pontifical Acad. of Social Scis; Fellow: Econometric Soc. (Pres., 1956); Amer. Acad. of Arts and Sciences (Vice Pres., 1979–80, 1991–94); Amer. Assoc. for Advancement of Science (Chm., Section K, 1982); Amer. Statistical Assoc.; Amer. Financial Assoc.; Dist. Fellow: Amer. Econ. Assoc. (Pres., 1972); Western Econ. Assoc.

(Pres., 1980–81); Corresp. Fellow, British Acad., 1976; Foreign Mem., Royal Soc., 2006; Foreign Hon. Mem., Finnish Acad. of Sciences. Hon. LLD: Chicago, 1967; City Univ. of NY, 1972; Univ. of Pennsylvania, 1976; Washington Univ., St Louis, Missouri, 1989; Ben-Gurion Univ., 1989; Hon. Dr. Soc. and Econ. Sciences, Vienna, 1971; Hon. ScD Columbia, 1973; Hon. DSocSci Yale, 1974; Hon. Dr: Paris, 1974; Hebrew Univ. of Jerusalem, 1975; Helsinki, 1976; Aix-Marseille III, 1985; Sacro Cuore, Milan, 1994; Uppsala, 1995; Buenos Aires, 1999; Cyprus, 2000; Tel Aviv, 2001; Hon. LittD Cambridge, 1985. John Bates Clark Medal, American Economic Assoc., 1957; Nobel Meml Prize in Economic Science, 1972; von Neumann Prize, Inst. of Management Scis and Ops Res. Soc. of America, 1986; US Nat. Medal of Science, 2004. Order of the Rising Sun (2nd class), Japan, 1984. *Publications:* Social Choice and Individual Values, 1951, 2nd edn 1963; (with S. Karlin and H. Scarf) Studies in the Mathematical Theory of Inventory and Production, 1958; (with M. Hoffenberg) A Time Series Analysis of Interindustry Demands, 1959; (with L. Hurwicz and H. Uzawa) Studies in Linear and Nonlinear Programming, 1959; Aspects of the Theory of Risk Bearing, 1965; (with M. Kurz) Public Investment, the Rate of Return, and Optimal Fiscal Policy, 1971; Essays in the Theory of Risk-Bearing, 1971; (with F. Hahn) General Competitive Analysis, 1972; The Limits of Organization, 1974; (with L. Hurwicz) Studies in Resource Allocation Processes, 1977; Collected Papers, Vols 1–6, 1984–86; (with H. Raynaud) Social Choice and Multicriterion Decision-Making, 1986; 230 articles in jls and collective vols. *Address:* Department of Economics, Stanford University, Stanford, CA 94305–6072, USA.

ARROWSMITH, Amanda Jane Elizabeth; Chair, Eastern Region Committee, Heritage Lottery Fund, 2001–04; *b* 28 Dec. 1947; *d* of late Michael St George Arrowsmith and Elizabeth Arrowsmith (née Bartlett). *Educ:* Lady Margaret Hall, Oxford (MA); MBA Open Univ. Archive trng, Bodleian Liby, Oxford, 1971–72; asst, sen. asst and dep. archivist posts, Northumberland and Suffolk CCs, 1972–79; Co. Archivist, Berks, 1979–82, Suffolk, 1982–87; Dep. Dir of Arts and Libraries, 1987–90, Dir of Libraries and Heritage, 1990–2001, Suffolk. Comr, RCHME, 1994–98; Mem., Hist. Bldgs and Monuments Commn (Eng. Heritage), 1998–2001. Member: Adv. Council on Public Records, 1995–2000; Eastern Reg. Cttee, SE Museums Service, 1999–2003; Exec. Cttee, Friends of Nat. Libraries, 1993–96 and 1999–2003; Reviewing Cttee on Export of Works of Art, 2002–06 (Chm., Manuscripts and Documents Wkg Gp, 2002–06); Pres., 1996–99, Vice-Pres., 2002–, Soc. of Archivists. Dir, Victim Support Suffolk, 2002–03 (Chm., Magistrates' Courts Witness Support Service Cttee, 2002–03). Mem. Bd, Living East, 1999–2002. Hon. Ed., Chapels Soc., 2004–07. *Publications:* contrib. articles to Archives, Jl Soc. Archivists, New Liby World. *Address:* 56 Bury Street, Stowmarket, Suffolk IP14 1HF.

ARROWSMITH, Pat; peace activist and socialist; on staff of Amnesty International, 1971–94, retired; *b* 2 March 1930; *d* of late George Ernest Arrowsmith and late Margaret Vera (née Kingham); *m* Mr Gardner, 11 Aug. 1979, separated 11 Aug. 1979; lesbian partnership with Wendy Butlin, 1962–76. *Educ:* Farringtons; Stover Sch.; Cheltenham Ladies' Coll.; Newnham Coll., Cambridge (BA history); Univ. of Ohio; Liverpool Univ. (Cert. in Social Science). Has held many jobs, incl.: Community Organizer in Chicago, 1952–53; Cinema Usher, 1953–54; Social Caseworker, Liverpool Family Service Unit, 1954; Child Care Officer, 1955 and 1964; Nursing Asst, Deva Psychiatric Hosp., 1956–57; Reporter for Peace News, 1965; Gardener for Camden BC, 1966–68; Researcher for Soc. of Friends Race Relations Cttee, 1969–71; Case Worker for NCCL, 1971; and on farms, as waiter in cafes, in a factory, as a toy demonstrator, as a 'temp' in numerous offices, as asst in children's home, as newspaper deliverer and sales agent, as cleaner, as bartender, and in a holiday camp. Organizer for Direct Action Cttee against Nuclear War, Cttee of 100 and Campaign for Nuclear Disarmament, 1958–68; gaoled 11 times as political prisoner, 1958–85 (adopted twice as Prisoner of Conscience by Amnesty International); awarded: Holloway Prison Green Band, 1964; Girl Crusaders knighthood, 1940; Americans Removing Injustice, Suppression and Exploitation peace prize, 1991; Unsung Woman award, Haringey Council, 2001. Contested: Fulham, 1966 (Radical Alliance) and 1970 (Hammersmith Stop the SE Asia War Cttee), on peace issues; Cardiff South East (Independent Socialist), 1979. Member: War Resisters' Internat.; Campaign for Nuclear Disarmament (Vice-Pres.). *Publications:* Jericho (novel), 1965; Somewhere Like This (novel), 1970; To Asia in Peace, 1972; The Colour of Six Schools, 1972; Breakout (poems and drawings from prison), 1975; On the Brink (anti-war poems with pictures), 1981; The Prisoner (novel), 1982; Thin Ice (anti-nuclear poems), 1984; Nine Lives (poems and pictures), 1990; I Should Have Been a Hornby Train (fiction-cum-memoirs), 1995; Many are Called (novel), 1998; Drawing to Extinction (poems and pictures), 2000; Going On (poems), 2005. *Recreations:* water colour painting (has held and contrib. exhibns), swimming, writing poetry. *Address:* 132c Middle Lane, N8 7JP. *T:* (020) 8340 2661.

ARROYO, Gloria M.; *see* Macapagal-Arroyo.

ARSCOTT, John Robert Dare; Director, Airspace Policy, Civil Aviation Authority, since 1999; *b* 19 April 1947; *s* of Richard Arscott and Janet Arscott (née Knibbs); *m* 1971, Kyrle Margaret Bradley; one *d* and one *s* decd. *Educ:* Lindisfarne Coll. RAF, 1966; jsdc 1984; awc 1987; posts in NATS and Mil. Air Traffic Ops, 1990–95; AOC Mil. Air Traffic Ops, 1996–99; retired in rank of Air Vice-Marshal, 2001. *Recreations:* aviation, railways, walking, DIY, 3-day eventing. *Address:* CAA House, 45–59 Kingsway, WC2B 6TE. *T:* (020) 7453 6500. *Club:* Royal Air Force.

ARSHAD, Rowena, (Mrs M. Q. Parnell), OBE 2001; Director, Centre for Education for Racial Equality in Scotland, since 1994, and Senior Lecturer, since 1997, University of Edinburgh; *b* 27 April 1960; *d* of Zainal Arshad bin Zainal Abidin and Teoh Phaik Choo; *m* 1985, Malcolm Quarrie Parnell; one *s* one *d*. *Educ:* Methodist Girls' Sch., Penang, W Malaysia; St Francis Coll., Letchworth; Bulmershe Coll. of Higher Educn (Cert. in Youth and Community Work 1985); Moray House, Heriot-Watt Univ. (MEd 1995); Univ. of Edinburgh. Scottish Educn and Action for Develt, 1985–88; Multicultural Educn Centre, Edinburgh, 1988–91; Lectr, Moray House Inst. of Educn, Edinburgh, 1991–97. Member: SHEFC, 1999–2005; Independent Inquiry into Student Finance, 1999; Working Party on Guidelines in Sex Educn in Scottish Schs, 2000; Equal Opportunities Commn, 2001–07; SFC, 2005–; Convenor Educn Sub Gp, Race Equality Adv. Forum, Scottish Exec., 1999–2001. Board Member: Telford Coll., Edinburgh, 2001–; Inspectorate of Educn, 2001–; Member: Governance Adv. Team, British Council, 2002–; Inst. of Contemporary Scotland, 2002–. Mem. Editl Bd, Scottish Affairs jl, 1992–. *Publication:* (contrib.) Tomorrow's Scotland, 2002. *Recreations:* reading political literature on Scotland, equity, justice, travelling (particularly to favourite city Toronto), cooking for family and friends, playing with border collie Perry. *Address:* Charteris Building, Moray House School of Education, University of Edinburgh, Holyrood Road, Edinburgh EH8 8AQ. *T:* (0131) 651 6371, *Fax:* (0131) 651 6511; *e-mail:* Rowena.Arshad@ed.ac.uk.

ARTAZA-ROUXEL, Mario; Adjunct Professor, Institute of International Studies, University of Chile; *b* 2 Sept. 1937; *s* of Osvaldo Artaza and Guillermina Rouxel; *m* 1982, Anita Valsasnini; one *s* two *d*. *Educ:* Law Sch., Univ. of Chile; Univ. of Virginia (MA (Foreign Affairs) 1962); American Univ., Washington (Internat. Relations). Entered

Foreign Service of Chile, 1958; Third Sec., Chilean Embassy, Washington, 1964; Second, subseq. First Sec., Chilean Mission to OAS, 1968–69; Dir, Inst. of Political Science, Catholic Univ. of Chile, 1970; Counsellor, Chilean Embassy, Peru, 1971–73; Chargé d'Affaires, Chilean Embassy, Washington, 1973; Prof., Univ. of the Pacific, Calif, 1973–74; World Bank: Public Affairs Officer, 1974–75; Loan Officer for Pakistan, 1976–82, for Argentina, Uruguay and Paraguay, 1982–87; Sen. Ops Officer, Infrastructure Projects, Latin Amer. Reg., 1988–90; Alternate Ambassador of Chile, Internat. Orgns, Geneva, 1990–92; Ministry of Foreign Affairs, Santiago: Director: Multilateral Affairs, 1992–93; Policy Planning, 1994–96; Ambassador of Chile: to UK, 1996–99; to USA, 1999–2000; Dir. Gen. of Foreign Policy, 2000–02; Exec. Dir, Asia-Pacific Economic Co-operation Secretariat, 2004–05. Comendador, Orden del Sol (Peru), 1972; Grand Cross: Orden de Miranda (Venezuela), 1999; Order of Merit (Paraguay), 2000; Orden del Libertador (Argentina), 2002; Grand Officer (Uruguay), 2001. *Publications:* (contrib.) The Overall Development of Chile, ed M. Zañartu, 1968; (contrib.) America 70, ed A. Naudon, 1970. *Recreations:* music, theatre, reading, travel. *Address:* Institute of International Studies, University of Chile, Avenida Condell 249, Providencia, Santiago, Chile.

ARTHANAYAKE, Nihal; BBC Radio 1 Disc Jockey, since 2002; Member Board, British Council, since 2006; *b* 1 June 1971; *s* of Tilak Arthanayake and Rohini Arthanayake; *m* 2005, Eesha. *Educ:* St Mary's Coll., Strawberry Hill (BA Hons). Television presenter: The Drop, 2001; Saturday Show Extra; Whitey Blighty (documentary), 2003; Desi DNA, 2004–07; Where's Your F***ing Manners (documentary), 2004; God is a DJ for Heaven and Earth Show, 2007; jt programmer, with Radio 1, London Flavas stage, 2004–; promoter and creator, Bombay Bronx clubnight. Mem. Bd, Metal Arts Think Tank, 2007–. Cultural Ambassador, London 2012 Olympics, 2004–; Ambassador, Football Aid Charity, 2007–. *Recreations:* walking my Staffordshire Bull Terrier, Luna, swimming, going to see the mighty Tottenham Hotspur, listening to music, DJing, looking at my My Space page, messageboards. *Address:* e-mail: dj.nihal@bbc.co.uk.

ARTHUIS, Jean Raymond Francis Marcel; Member for Mayenne, Senate, France; *b* 7 Oct. 1944; *m* 1971, Brigitte Lafont; one *s* one *d*. *Educ:* Ecole Supérieure de Commerce, Nantes; Institut d'Etudes Politiques, Paris. Sen. consultant in internat. auditing office; Founder of a soc. for accounting expertise and auditors. Senator, Mayenne, 1983–86, 1988–95 and 1997– (President: Gpe de l'Union Centriste, 1998–2002; Finance Commn, 2002–); Pres., Gen. Council of Mayenne, 1992– (Rapporteur général of budget to Senate, 1992–95). Secretary of State: Ministry of Social Affairs and Employment, 1986–87; for competition and consumption, Ministry of Economy, Finance and Privatization, 1987–88; Minister of: Economic Development and Planning, May–Aug. 1995; the Economy, Finance and Planning, Aug.–Nov. 1995; the Economy and of Finance, 1995–97. Mayor, Château-Gontier, Mayenne, 1971–2001. *Publications:* (with H. Haenel) Justice Sinistrée: démocratie en danger, 1991; Les Délocalisations et l'emploi, 1993; Dans les coulisses de Bercy, 1998; Mondialisation: la France à contre emploi, 2007. *Recreation:* horse-riding. *Address:* Sénat, 15 rue de Vaugirard, 75006 Paris, France; 8 rue René Homo, 53200 Château-Gontier, France.

ARTHUR, family name of **Baron Glenarthur**.

ARTHUR, Adrian; Editor, The Courier, Dundee, 1993–2002; *b* 28 Sept. 1937; *s* of Alastair and Jean Arthur, Kirkcaldy; *m* 1962, Patricia Mill; one *s* two *d*. *Educ:* Harris Academy, Dundee; Univ. of St Andrews (BL). Sub-Editor, People's Journal, 1954–56; Nat. Service, RAF, 1956–58; editorial staff, The Courier, Dundee, 1958–2002 (Dep. Editor, 1978–93). Hon. Fellow, Univ. of Abertay, Dundee, 2003. *Recreations:* golf, reading, travel, Rotary. *Address:* 33 Seaforth Crescent, West Ferry, Dundee DD5 1QD. *T:* (01382) 776842. *Clubs:* Carnoustie; Dalhousie Golf; Royal Tay Yacht.

ARTHUR, Sir Gavyn (Farr), Kt 2004; **His Honour Judge Sir Gavyn Arthur;** a Circuit Judge, since 2007; Lord Mayor of London, 2002–03; *b* 13 Sept. 1951; *s* of late Maj. the Hon. Leonard Arthur, sometime Chm., Natal Provincial Assembly, and Raina Arthur (*née* Farr). *Educ:* Harrow Sch.; Christ Church, Oxford (MA Jurisprudence). Called to the Bar, Middle Temple, 1975 (Bencher, 2001); in practice as barrister, 1977–2007; Recorder, 2002–07. Mem. Cttee, Western Circuit, 1985–88. Common Councilman, Ward of Farringdon Without, 1988–91; Alderman, Cripplegate Ward, 1991–2007; Sheriff, City of London, 1998–99; HM Lieut, City of London, 2002–; Chief Magistrate, City of London, 2002–03; Admiral, Port of London, 2002–03. Freeman, City of London, 1979; Liveryman: Co. of Gardeners, 1990– (Master, 2007–08); Co. of Wax-Chandlers, 1996– (Mem., Ct of Assts). Mem., Guild of Public Relations Practitioners, 2000– (Mem., Ct of Assts). Chm., Arab Financial Forum, 2004–. Vice-President: British Red Cross, 1993–; Inst. of Export, 1999–. Member: Anglo-Austrian Soc.; British Assoc. for Cemeteries in SE Asia; British Lebanese Soc.; British Tunisia Soc.; British Ukrainian Law Assoc.; City of London Sheriffs Soc. (Patron); Cttee, Save the Children; Council, Imperial Soc. of Knights Bachelor, 2005–; Gov., 2004–07; Vice-Adm. of the Northern Waters, 2004–, Hon. the Irish Soc. Trustee: Sir John Soane Mus., 1996–2004; Cripplegate Foundn; Lord Kitchener Nat. Meml Fund; St Paul's Cathedral. Patron: Royal Soc. of St George; Three Faiths Forum; Vice-Patron, Treloar Coll. Appeal. Chancellor, City Univ., 2002–03; Vice-Patron, London Metropolitan Univ. Governor: Christ's Hosp., 1991–2007; King Edward's Sch., Witley, 1991–2007; City of London Sch. for Girls, 1991–2007; City of London Freemen's Sch., 1994–2007. Hon. DCL City, 2002. KStJ 2002. Order of Honour (Georgia), 2003; Kt Comdr, Royal Order of Francis I, 2006. *Recreations:* travel, Alpine walking. *Address:* c/o 2 Harcourt Buildings, Temple, EC4Y 9DB. *Club:* Brooks's.

ARTHUR, Prof. James Greig, FRS 1992; FRSC 1981; University Professor, since 1987, and Professor of Mathematics, since 1979, University of Toronto; *b* 18 May 1944; *s* of John Greig Arthur and Katherine Mary Patricia Scott; *m* 1972, Dorothy Pendleton Helm; two *s*. *Educ:* Upper Canada Coll.; Univ. of Toronto (BSc, MSc); Yale Univ. (PhD). Instructor, Princeton Univ., 1970–72; Asst Prof., Yale Univ., 1972–76; Prof., Duke Univ., 1976–79. Sloan Fellowship, 1976; E. W. R. Steacie Meml Fellowship, 1982. Synge Award, RSC, 1987. *Publication:* Simple Algebras, Base Change and the Advanced Theory of the Trace Formula (with Laurent Clozel), 1989. *Recreations:* tennis, golf. *Address:* 23 Woodlawn Avenue W, Toronto, Ontario M4V 1G6, Canada. *T:* (416) 9640975.

ARTHUR, James Stanley, CMG 1977; HM Diplomatic Service, retired; British High Commissioner in Bridgetown, 1978–82, also British High Commissioner (non-resident) to Dominica, 1978–82, to St Lucia and St Vincent, 1979–82, to Grenada, 1980–82, to Antigua and Barbuda, 1981–82, and concurrently British Government Representative to West Indies Associated State of St Kitts-Nevis; retired 1983; *b* 3 Feb. 1923; *s* of Laurence and Catherine Arthur, Lerwick, Shetland; *m* 1950, Marion North; two *s* two *d*. *Educ:* Trinity Academy, Edinburgh; Liverpool Univ. (BSc). Scientific Civil Service, 1944–46; Asst Principal, Scottish Educn Dept, 1946; Min. of Educn/Dept of Educn and Science, 1947–66: Private Sec. to Parly Sec., 1948–50; Principal Private Sec. to Minister, 1960–62; Counsellor, FO, 1966; Nairobi, 1967–70; Dep. High Comr, Malta, 1970–73; High Comr, Suva, 1974–78, and first High Comr (non-resident), Republic of Nauru, 1977–78. Mem. Court, Liverpool Univ., 1987–. *Recreations:* walking the dog, music. *Address:*

Moreton House, Longborough, Moreton-in-Marsh, Glos GL56 0QQ. *T:* (01451) 830774.

ARTHUR, Lt-Gen. Sir (John) Norman (Stewart), KCB 1985; CVO 2007; Lord-Lieutenant, Stewartry of Kirkcudbright (Dumfries and Galloway Region), 1996–2006; General Officer Commanding Scotland and Governor of Edinburgh Castle, 1985–88, retired; *b* 6 March 1931; *s* of Col Evelyn Stewart Arthur, DL, and Mrs E. S. Arthur (*née* Burnett-Stuart); *m* 1960, Theresa Mary Hopkinson; one *s* one *d* (and one *s* decd). *Educ:* Eton Coll.; RMA, Sandhurst. rcds, jssc, psc. Commnd Royal Scots Greys, 1951; commanded: Royal Scots Dragoon Guards, 1972–74 (despatches, 1974); 7th Armoured Bde, 1976–77; Brig., Gen. Staff, Intelligence, MoD, 1978–80; GOC 3rd Armoured Div., 1980–82; Dir of Personal Services (Army), MoD, 1983–85. Col Comdt, Military Provost Staff Corps, 1985–88; Col, The Royal Scots Dragoon Gds (Carabiniers and Greys), 1984–92; Hon. Col, 205 (Scottish) Gen. Hosp., RAMC(V), 1988–93. The Scottish Yeomanry, 1993–97. Chm., Cavalry Colonels, 1987–92. Officer, Royal Co. of Archers, Queen's Body Guard for Scotland. Chairman: Scotland, Army Benevolent Fund, 1988–2000; Leonard Cheshire Services, SW Scotland, 1994–2000; President: Combined Cavalry Old Comrades Assoc., 1995–2000; Lowland RFCA, 2001–06; Vice Pres., Edinburgh and Borders, Riding for the Disabled Assoc., 1988–94; Dir, Edinburgh Mil. Tattoo Co., 1988–91; Pres., Scottish Conservation Projects, 1989–94; Mem., Automobile Assoc. Cttee, 1990–98. Humanitarian aid work to Balkans, 1992–. Mem., British Olympic Team, Equestrian Three-Day Event, 1960. DL Stewartry, 1989; JP 1996. *Recreations:* field and country sports and pursuits, horsemanship, military history. *Address:* Newbarns, Dalbeattie, Kirkcudbrightshire DG5 4PY. *T:* (01556) 630227.

ARTHUR, His Honour John Rhys, DFC 1944; JP; a Circuit Judge, 1975–93; *b* 29 April 1923; *s* of late John Morgan Arthur and Eleanor Arthur; *m* 1951, Joan Tremearne Pickering; two *s* one *d*. *Educ:* Mill Hill; Christ's Coll., Cambridge (MA). Commnd RAF, Bomber Command, 1943, demobilised 1946. Cambridge, 1946–48; called to Bar, Inner Temple, 1949. Asst Recorder, Blackburn QS, 1970; Dep. Chm., Lancs County QS, 1970–71; a Recorder, 1972–75. JP Lancs, 1970. *Address:* Orovales, 135 Caldy Road, Wirral CH48 1LP. *T:* (0151) 625 8624. *Clubs:* MCC, Old Millhillians; Athenæum (Liverpool); Cardiff Athletic.

ARTHUR, Sir Michael (Anthony), KCMG 2004 (CMG 1992); HM Diplomatic Service; Ambassador to the Federal Republic of Germany, since 2007; *b* 28 Aug. 1950; *s* of late John Richard Arthur and of Mary Deirdre (*née* Chaundy); *m* 1974, Plaxy Gillian Beatrice (*née* Corke); two *s* two *d*. *Educ:* Watford GS; Rugby; Balliol Coll., Oxford. Entered HM Diplomatic Service, 1972; UK Mission to UN, NY, 1972; FCO, 1973; 3rd, later 2nd Sec., UK Perm. Representation to Eur. Communities, 1974–76; 2nd Sec., Kinshasa, 1976–78; FCO, 1978–83; Private Secretary: to Lord Privy Seal, 1981; to Minister of State, FCO, 1982; 1st Sec., Bonn, 1984–88; Hd, EC Dept (Internal), FCO, 1988–93; Sen. Associate Mem., St Antony's Coll., Oxford, 1993; Counsellor and Hd of Chancery, Paris, 1993–97; Dir (Resources) and Chief Inspector, FCO, 1997–99; Minister and Dep. Hd of Mission, Washington, 1999–2000; Econ. Dir, then Dir-Gen., EU and Econ., FCO, 2001–03; High Comr, India, 2003–07. *Recreations:* music, travel, books. *Address:* c/o Foreign and Commonwealth Office, King Charles Street, SW1A 2AH.

ARTHUR, Prof. Michael James Paul, DM; FRCP, FMedSci; Vice-Chancellor, University of Leeds, since 2004; *b* 3 Aug. 1954; *s* of Reginald Alfred John Arthur and Patricia Margaret Arthur; *m* 1979, Elizabeth Susan McCaughey; one *s* two *d*. *Educ:* Burnt Mill Comprehensive Sch., Harlow; Sch. of Medicine, Univ. of Southampton (BM 1977; DM 1986). FRCP 1993. Med. Registrar, Wessex Reg., 1980–82; University of Southampton: Lectr in Medicine, 1982–89; Sen. Lectr, 1989–92; Prof. of Medicine, 1992–2004; Hd, Sch. of Medicine, 1998–2001; Dir of Res., Sch. of Medicine, 2001–02; Dean, Faculty of Medicine, Health and Life Scis, 2003–04. Fogarty Internat. Travelling Fellow, Liver Center Lab., Univ. of Calif, San Francisco, 1986–88; Fulbright Dist. Scholar, Mount Sinai Sch. of Medicine, NY, 2002. Mem., Adv. Gp on Hepatitis, DoH, 1998–2004; Mem., Molecular and Cell Panel, Wellcome Trust, 1998–2002 and 2003–04 (Vice-Chm., 2000); Chm., 2003–04). Pres., British Assoc. for Study of the Liver, 2001–03. Chair, Nat. Student Survey Steering Gp, 2006–; Mem. Bd, QCA, 2007–. Board Member: Yorkshire Forward, 2007–; Opera North, 2007–. FMedSci 1998; FRSA 2006. Hon. Fellow, Assoc. of Physicians of GB and Ireland, 2006. Res. Prize, Amer. Liver Foundn, 1987; Linacre Medal, RCP, 1994. *Publications:* (ed jtly) Wright's Liver and Biliary Disease, 3rd edn 1992; numerous contribs to biomed. jls relating to liver disease and the pathogenesis of liver fibrosis. *Recreation:* sailing and yacht racing in the Solent. *Address:* Vice-Chancellor's Office, University of Leeds, Leeds LS2 9JT. *T:* (023) 8079 6886. *Club:* Royal Southern Yacht (Hamble).

ARTHUR, Lt-Gen. Sir Norman; see Arthur, Lt-Gen. Sir J. N. S.

ARTHUR, Rt Hon. Owen Seymour; PC 1995; MP (Lab) Barbados, since 1984; Prime Minister of Barbados, also Minister of Finance and Economic Affairs, Defence and Security and the Civil Service, 1994–2008; *b* 17 Oct. 1949; *m* 1st, 1978, Beverley Jeanne Batchelor (marr. diss.); 2nd, 2006, Julie Ann Price. *Educ:* Harrison Coll., Barbados; Univ. of West Indies at Cave Hill (BA) and at Mona (MSc). Research Asst, UWI, Jamaica, 1973; Asst Economic Planner, then Chief Econ. Planner, Nat. Planning Agency, Jamaica, 1974–79; Dir of Econs, Jamaica Bauxite Inst., 1979–81; Chief Project Analyst, Min. of Finance, Barbados, 1981–83; Lectr, Dept of Management, UWI, Cave Hill, 1986, Res. Fellow, 1993. Mem., Barbados Senate, 1983–84; Parly Sec., Min. of Finance, 1985–86; Chm., Barbados Labour Party, 1993–96, 1998–99; Leader of Opposition, 1993–94. *Publications:* The Commercialisation of Technology in Jamaica, 1979; Energy and Mineral Resource Development in the Jamaica Bauxite Industry, 1981; The IMF and Economic Stabilisation Policies in Barbados, 1984. *Recreations:* cooking, gardening.

ARTHUR, Richard Andrew; Director and Chairman, Audit Committee, Assettrust Housing Ltd, since 2003; Chairman: Renaissance Bedford, since 2005; Child Support Agency, 2006–08; *b* 24 March 1944; *s* of late Cyril Stuart Arthur and Cicely Arthur; *m* 1st, 1968, Diana Thompson (marr. diss.); one *s* one *d*; 2nd, 1986, Akiko Shindo; one step *s*. *Educ:* King's Sch., Canterbury; Christ's Coll., Cambridge (MA Econs); London Business Sch. (MSc Business). Commonwealth Development Finance Co.: Regl Dir, SE Asia, 1976–80; Chief Exec., Australia, 1981–82; Hd of Ops, 1982–86; Exec. Dir, Scimitar Develt Capital, 1986–93. Mem., Audit Commn, 1995–2003; Bd Mem., Housing Corp., 2000–04 (Chm., Regulation and Supervisory Cttee, 2001–04). Dir, 1998–2002, Chm., 1998–2000, Vice-Chm., 2000–02, Public Private Partnerships Prog.; Vice-Chm., Central London Partnership, 1998–2000. Dir, Accord plc, 2000–07. London Borough of Camden: Mem. (Lab), 1971–76 and 1990–2002; Chm. of Staff, 1975–76; Chm., Social Services, 1991–93; Leader, 1993–2000. Vice-Chm., Assoc. of London Govt, 2000–02 (Chm., Community Safety and Policing Panel, 2000–02). Mem. Regl Exec., Greater London Lab Party, 2000–02. Mem. Ct, Middlesex Univ., 1996–2000. *Recreations:* gardening, reading, travel. *Address:* 11d Highgate West Hill, N6 6JR. *T:* (020) 8341 9148. *Club:* Singapore Cricket.

ARTHUR, Sandra Joy; Midwife Lecturer, School of Nursing and Midwifery Studies, Cardiff University, since 1998; *b* 16 April 1957; *d* of William Chapman and Evelyn Joy Chapman; *m* 1981, Stephen Laurence Arthur; two *s. Educ:* Queen Elizabeth Hosp., Birmingham (SRN 1979); Good Hope Hosp., Sutton Coldfield (SCM 1980); Cardiff Univ. (PGCE; LLM Legal Aspects in Med. Practice). Midwife, S Glamorgan, Cardiff and Vale NHS Trust, 1980. Hon. Supervisor of Midwives, 1996–. Mem. Council, Royal Coll. of Midwives, 1993–98; President: Assoc. of Supervisors of Midwives, 2002–; Nursing and Midwifery Council, 2006–07. *Recreations:* tennis, sailing, gardening. *Address:* Cardiff School of Nursing and Midwifery Studies, Neuadd Meirionnydd, Heath Park Campus, Cardiff CF14 4YS; *e-mail:* Arthursj@cf.ac.uk. *Clubs:* Penarth Yacht, Penarth Lawn Tennis.

ARTHUR, Sir Stephen (John), 6th Bt *cr* 1841, of Upper Canada; *b* 1 July 1953; *s* of Hon. Sir Basil Malcolm Arthur, 5th Bt, MP, and of Elizabeth Rita, *d* of late Alan Mervyn Wells; *S* father, 1985; *m* 1978, Carolyn Margaret (marr. diss.), *d* of Burney Lawrence Daimond, Cairns, Queensland; one *s* two *d. Educ:* Timaru Boys' High School. *Heir: s* Benjamin Nathan Arthur, *b* 27 March 1979.

ARTHURS, Prof. Harry William, OC 1989; OOnt 1995; FRSC 1982; University Professor, Osgoode Hall Law School, York University, Canada, 1995–2005 (Professor of Law, 1968–95); *b* 9 May 1935; *s* of Leon and Ellen Arthurs; *m* 1974, Penelope Geraldine Ann Milnes; two *s. Educ:* Univ. of Toronto (BA, LLB); Harvard Univ. (LLM). Barrister and Solicitor, 1961. York University: Asst Prof. 1961, Associate Prof. 1964, Associate Dean 1967, Dean 1972–77, Osgoode Hall Law Sch.; Pres., 1985–92, Pres. Emeritus, 1992–. Mem., Economic Council of Can., 1978–82; Bencher, Law Soc. of Upper Can., 1979–84; Chm., Consultative Gp on Res. and Educn in Law, 1981–84; Arbitrator, Mediator in Labour Disputes, 1962–84; Chair, Council of Ontario Univs, 1987–89; a Dir, Internat. Centre for Human Rights and Democratic Develt, 1999–2002; Commissioner: Rev. of Federal Labour Standards, 2004–06; Rev. of Ontario Pensions Legislation, 2006–. Visiting Professor: Univ. of Toronto, 1965; McGill, 1967; Visiting Scholar: Clare Hall, Cambridge, 1971; Inst. for Socio-Legal Res., Oxford, 1977–78; Vis. Research Prof., UCL, 1984, 2003. Killam Laureate, 2002. Corresp. FBA 2003. Hon. LLD: Sherbrooke, 1986; Brock, 1986; Law Soc. of Upper Can., 1987; McGill, 1995; Montreal, 2002; Toronto, 2002; Hon. DLitt Lethbridge, 1991; Hon. DCL Windsor, 2004. *Publications:* Law and Learning, 1983; (jtly) Industrial Relations and Labour Law in Canada, 1979, 3rd edn 1988; Without the Law, 1985. *Address:* Osgoode Hall Law School, York University, 4700 Keele Street, Toronto, Ontario M3J 1P3, Canada. *T:* (416) 7365407.

ARTHURSON, Paul Andrew; QC (Scot.) 2005; All Scotland Floating Sheriff, since 2005; *b* 16 Dec. 1964; *s* of Dr Iain Hayden Arthurson and Margaret Arthurson; *m* 1997, Dr Sharon Elizabeth McAuslane; two *d. Educ:* Daniel Stewart's and Melville Coll., Edinburgh; Univ. of Edinburgh (LLB Hons 1986); Worcester Coll., Oxford (Dip Law 1990). Advocate, 1991–2005; Temp. Sheriff, 1999; Pt-time Sheriff, 2003–05. *Recreations:* family life, golf, hill-walking. *Club:* Bruntsfield Links Golfing Society (Edinburgh).

ARTIS, Prof. Michael John, FBA 1988; Director, Manchester Regional Economics Centre, Institute for Political and Economic Governance, and Professor of Economics, Manchester University, since 2005; *b* 29 June 1938; *s* of Cyril John and Violet Emily Artis; *m* 1st, 1961, Lilian Gregson (marr. diss. 1982); two *d*; 2nd, 1983, Shirley Knight. *Educ:* Baines Grammar Sch., Poulton-le-Fylde, Lancs; Magdalen Coll., Oxford. BA Hons (PPE) Oxon. Assistant Research Officer, Oxford Univ., 1959; Lectr in Economics, Adelaide Univ., 1964; Lectr and Sen. Lectr in Economics, Flinders Univ., 1966; Research Officer and Review Editor, Nat. Inst. of Economic and Social Research, London, 1967; Prof. of Applied Economics, Swansea Univ. Coll., 1972; Prof. of Econs, Manchester Univ., 1975–99 (on leave of absence, 1995–99); Prof. of Econs, 1995–2003, Professorial Fellow, 2004–, European Univ. Inst., Florence. *Publications:* Foundations of British Monetary Policy, 1964; (with M. K. Lewis) Monetary Control in the United Kingdom, 1981; Macroeconomics, 1984; (with S. Ostry) International Economic Policy Co-ordination, 1986; (with M. K. Lewis) Money in Britain, 1991; contribs on economics, economic policy to books and learned jls. *Recreation:* eating out. *Address:* 76 Bexton Road, Knutsford, Cheshire WA16 0DX. *Club:* Reform.

ARTON, Simon Nicholas B.; *see* Bourne-Arton.

ARTRO MORRIS, John Evan; District Judge, Principal Registry of the Family Division (formerly a Registrar of the Supreme Court, Family Division), 1977–95; *b* 17 Feb. 1925; *s* of Tudor and Mabel Artro Morris; *m* 1961, Karin Ilsa Alida Russell (*d* 1999); two *s. Educ:* Liverpool Coll.; The Queen's Coll., Oxford (MA). Served RN, 1943–47; Acting Stores Chief Petty Officer. Called to the Bar, Middle Temple, 1952; practised at the Bar, 1952–77. *Recreations:* television, reading, contemplation. *Address:* 48 Seymour Avenue, East Ewell, Surrey KT17 2RR.

ARUNDEL AND BRIGHTON, Bishop of, (RC), since 2001; **Rt Rev. Kieran Thomas Conry;** *b* 1 Feb. 1951. *Educ:* Cotton Coll., N Staffs; Ven. English Coll., Rome; Gregorian Univ., Rome (PhB, STB). Ordained 1975; Teacher, Cotton Coll., 1976–80; Private Sec. to Apostolic Delegate to the Court of St James's, 1980–88; Parish Priest, Leek, 1988–90; Administrator, St Chad's Cathedral, 1990–94; Dir, Catholic Media Office, 1994–2001; Parish Priest, St Austin's, Stafford, 2001. Mem., 1988–93, Vice-Chm., 1992–93, Nat. Conf. of Priests; Chm., Birmingham City Centre Churches, 1992–93. *Address:* High Oaks, Old Brighton Road North, Pease Pottage, W Sussex RH11 9AJ.

ARUNDEL AND SURREY, Earl of; Henry Miles Fitzalan-Howard; *b* 3 Dec. 1987; *s* and *heir* of Duke of Norfolk, *qv. Educ:* Radley College. Formula BMW UK Rookie Champion, 2006.

ARUNDELL; *see* Monckton-Arundell, family name of Viscount Galway.

ARUNDELL, family name of **Baron Talbot of Malahide**.

ARVILL, Robert; *see* Boote, R. E.

ASANTE, Kwaku Baprui, GM 1976; MOV 1978; High Commissioner for Ghana in London, 1991–93; *b* 26 March 1924; *s* of Kweku Asante and Odorso Amoo; *m* 1958, Matilda Dzagbele Anteson; three *s* two *d. Educ:* Achimota Coll.; Durham Univ. (BSc); Final Exam., Inst. Statisticians (AIS), London. Sen. Maths Master, Achimota, 1954–56; joined Ghana Foreign Service, 1956; Hd, African Dept of Foreign Ministry, 1957–60; 2nd Sec., London, 1957–58; Chargé d'Affaires, Tel Aviv, 1958–60; Principal Sec., African Affairs Secretariat, Office of Pres., 1960–66; Head of Admin, OAU, 1966–67; Ambassador to Switzerland and Austria and Permanent Delegate to UN Office, Geneva, 1967–72; Principal Sec., Min. of Foreign Affairs, 1972; Sen. Principal Sec., Ministries of Trade and Tourism, and Economic Planning, 1973–76; Ambassador to Belgium, Luxembourg and EEC, 1976–79; Sec.-Gen., Social Democratic Front, 1979–81; Sec. (Minister) for Trade and Tourism, 1982; Private Consultant, 1982–88; Sec. (Minister) for Educn, 1988–91. Chairman: Unimax Macmillan, 2001–; La Community Bank, 2006–. Pres., Gadangme Council, 1998–. Columnist, Daily Graphic. Hon. LLD Ghana, 1999; Hon. DLit Univ. of Develt Studies, Tamale, 2004. *Publications:* Foreign Policy Making in Ghana, 1997; Voice From Afar: a Ghanaian experience, 2003; articles in Ghanaian and foreign newspapers and jls. *Recreations:* music, cricket. *Address:* Asanteson, Palm Wine Junction, La, PO Box 6616, Accra, Ghana. *T:* (21) 774344; CT 4075, Accra, Ghana.

ASANTE-MENSAH, Evelyn Justina, OBE 2006; Strategic Adviser on Community Cohesion and Diversity, Government Office for the North West, since 2006, on secondment; Chief Executive, Black Health Agency, since 1999; *b* 11 Oct. 1965; *d* of late Kwaku Asante-Mensah and of Beatrice Gyamfi (*née* Amoo-Mensah); step *d* of Alfred Gyamfi; partner, Yoni Ejo; one *s* three *d. Educ:* Nicholls Ardwick High Sch., Manchester; Manchester Metropolitan Univ. (MA 2001). Joined Black Health Agency, 1992. Non-exec. Dir, Manchester HA, 1998–2000; Chm., Manchester (formerly Central Manchester) PCT, 2000–. Chairman: Race for Health, 2002–; Appt Commn, Black and Minority Ethnic Adv. Gp, 2004–; Brook, 2007–; Mem., Equal Opportunities Commn, 2004–07. Hon. DLitt Manchester Metropolitan, 2003. *Recreations:* reading, gardening, cooking, spending time with family. *Address:* Government Office for the North West, Home Office Group, City Tower, Piccadilly Plaza, Manchester M1 4BE. *T:* (0161) 952 4220, (0161) 952 4196; *e-mail:* evelyn.asante-mensah@gonw.gsi.gov.uk.

ASBIL, Rt Rev. Walter Gordon; Bishop of Niagara, 1991–97; *b* 3 Oct. 1932; *m* 1957, Mavis Asbil; three *s* one *d. Educ:* Concordia Univ., Montreal (BA); McGill Univ. (BD, STM). Ordained deacon, 1957, priest, 1957; Rector: Aylwin River Desert, 1957–60; Montreal South Shore, 1960–65; St Stephen's, Montreal, 1965–67; St George, St Anne de Bellevue, 1967–70; St George, St Catharine's, 1970–86; Rector and Dean, Christ Church Cathedral, Ottawa, 1986–90; Co-adjutor Bishop of Niagara, 1990–91. Hon. DD Montreal Dio. Theol Coll., 1991. *Address:* 1107, 3 Towering Heights Boulevard, St Catharines, ON L2T 4A4, Canada.

ASBRIDGE, Sir Jonathan (Elliott), Kt 2006; Director of Nursing and Clinical Services, Clinicenta Ltd, since 2007; *b* 16 Feb. 1959; *s* of late Roy Derek Asbridge and Doris Enid Asbridge; *m* 1986, Helen Catherine Lewis-Smith; two *s* two *d. Educ:* Nightingale Sch., St Thomas' Hosp., London (SRN 1980); UC Swansea (DipN 1987). Dir, Clinical Care Services, Addenbrooke's Hosp., 1989–92; Executive Nurse Director: Llandough Hosp., Cardiff, 1992–94; Oxford Radcliffe Hosp., 1994–97; Chief Nurse, Barts and the London NHS Trust, 1997–2003; Nat. Clinical Dir, Emergency Care, DoH, 2003–06. Pres., Nursing and Midwifery Council, 2001–06. Mem., Council for Health Regulatory Excellence, 2002–06 (Vice Chm., 2004–05). Chm., Eur. Health Wkg Gp, Conseil Européen des Professions Libérales, 2004–; Mem., Internat. Council of Nurses Observatory of Licensure and Regulation, 2004–. Council Mem., Florence Nightingale Foundn, 2002–06; Life Vice Pres., Nightingale Fellowship, 2005–. Hon. DSc City, 2004. *Recreations:* tennis, walking, biographies, aviation. *Address:* Clinicenta Ltd, Suite 7, Hampden House, Monument Business Park, Chalgrove, Oxon OX44 7RW.

ASCHERSON, (Charles) Neal; journalist and author; *b* 5 Oct. 1932; *s* of late Stephen Romer Ascherson and Evelyn Mabel Ascherson; *m* 1st, 1958, Corinna Adam (marr. diss. 1982); two *d*; 2nd, 1984, Isabel Hilton; one *s* one *d. Educ:* Eton College; King's College, Cambridge (MA; Hon. Fellow, 1993). Served RM, 1950–52. Reporter and leader writer, Manchester Guardian, 1956–58; Commonwealth corresp., Scotsman, 1959–60; The Observer: reporter, 1960–63; Central Europe corresp., 1963–68; Eastern Europe corresp., 1968–75; foreign writer, 1979–85; columnist, 1985–90; Associate Editor, 1985–89; columnist, The Independent on Sunday, 1990–98. Scottish politics corresp., Scotsman, 1975–79. Asst Lectr, Inst. of Archaeology, UCL, 1998–. Hon. DLitt: Strathclyde, 1988; Bradford, 2006; Hon. DSc(SocSci) Edinburgh, 1990; DUniv Open, 1991; Hon. LLD St Andrews, 1999; DUniv Paisley, 2003. Reporter of the Year 1982, Journalist of the Year 1987, Granada Awards; James Cameron Award, 1989; David Watt Meml Prize, 1991; (jtly) George Orwell Award, Political Qly, 1993; Saltire Award for Literature, 1995. Golden Insignia, Order of Merit (Poland), 1992. *Publications:* The King Incorporated, 1963; The Polish August, 1981; The Struggles for Poland, 1987; Games with Shadows, 1988; Black Sea, 1995; Stone Voices, 2002. *Address:* 27 Corsica Street, N5 1JT. *Club:* Ognisko Polskie (Polish Hearth Club).

ASFARI, Ayman; Group Chief Executive, Petrofac plc, since 2002; *b* 8 July 1958; *s* of Dr Adeeb Asfari and Lamia Haroun; *m* 1983, Sawsan El-Himani; four *s. Educ:* Villanova Univ. (BSc Civil Engrg 1979); Univ. of Pennsylvania (MSc Civil and Urban Engrg 1980). Resident Engr, Conser Consulting Gp, 1980–81; Man. Dir, Desert Line Projects (DLP), Muscat, Oman, 1982–91; Man. Dir, Petrofac UK Ltd, Chm. and Chief Exec., Petrofac Internat. Ltd, and Dir in all other Petrofac cos, 1991–2002. *Recreations:* tennis, golf, ski-ing, boating. *Address:* Petrofac plc, 4th Floor, 117 Jermyn Street, SW1Y 6HH. *T:* (020) 7811 4900. *Clubs:* Royal Automobile, Institute of Directors.

ASGHAR, Mohammad; Member (Plaid Cymru) South Wales East, National Assembly for Wales, since 2007; *b* Peshawar, 30 Sept. 1945; *s* of M. Aslam Khan and Zubaza Aslam; *m* 1983, Firdaus; one *d. Educ:* Peshawar Univ. (BA 1968). Asst to Principal, chartered accountants, 1972–83; Principal, MA Associates, accountants, 1983–. *Recreations:* holder of Private Pilot's Licence, keen sportsman, cricket, athletics, badminton. *Address:* National Assembly for Wales, Cardiff Bay, Cardiff CF99 1NA. *T:* (029) 2089 8321, *Fax:* (029) 2089 8726; *e-mail:* mohammad.asghar@wales.gov.uk.

ASH, Brian Maxwell; QC 1990; *b* 31 Jan. 1941; *s* of late Carl Ash and of Irene Ash (*née* Atkinson); *m* 1971, Barbara Anne Maxwell, creator and founding editor of BBC TV Question Time; two *s* one *d. Educ:* Mercers' Sch.; City of London Sch.; New Coll., Oxford (Open Exhibnr; BA). BBC TV Current Affairs Producer, Reporter and Programme Presenter, 1967–73; called to the Bar, Gray's Inn, 1975. Chm. of Panel, Examination in Public of First Alteration to Devon Structure Plan, 1986; Sec., Local Govt, Planning and Envmtl Bar Assoc., 1990–92. *Recreations:* golf, sailing, ski-ing, music. *Address:* 4–5 Gray's Inn Square, WC1R 5AH. *T:* (020) 7404 5252. *Clubs:* Royal Mid-Surrey Golf; Royal Norwich Golf.

ASH, Daniel Victor, FRCP, FRCR; Consultant in Clinical Oncology, Cookridge Hospital, Leeds, since 1979; President, Royal College of Radiologists, 2001–04 (Dean, Faculty of Clinical Oncology, 1998–2000); *b* 18 Oct. 1943; *s* of Vivien and Isidore Ash; *m* 1969, Deirdre Meikle; one *s* one *d. Educ:* Royal London Hosp. Medical Coll. (MB BS). FRCR 1976; FRCP 1992. Lectr in Medicine, Makerere Univ., Kampala, 1971–72; Registrar in Radiotherapy, Churchill Hosp., Oxford, 1973–76; Lectr in Radiotherapy, Royal Marsden Hosp., London, 1976–79. President: British Oncology Assoc., 1994–97; European Brachytherapy Gp, 1995–98. *Publications:* (jtly) Practical Radiotherapy Planning, 1985, 3rd edn 2000; (jtly) Effective Treatment of Prostate Cancer, 2002; clinical res. papers on radiation sensitisers, photodynamic therapy and brachytherapy. *Recreations:* music (classical and jazz), walking, ceramics. *Address:* Cookridge Hospital, Hospital Lane, Leeds LS16 6QB.

ASH, Prof. Sir Eric (Albert), Kt 1990; CBE 1983; FRS 1977; FREng; Professor of Electrical Engineering, University College London, 1993–97, now Emeritus; *b* 31 Jan. 1928; *s* of Walter and Dorothea Ash; *m* 1954, Clare (*née* Babb); five *d*. *Educ:* University College Sch.; Imperial Coll. of Science and Technology. BSc(Eng), PhD, DSc; FCGI, DIC. FREng (FEng 1978); FIET; FIEEE; FInstP. Research Fellow: Stanford Univ., Calif, 1952–54; QMC, 1954–55; Res. Engr, Standard Telecommunication Laboratories Ltd, 1955–63; Sen. Lectr, 1963–65, Reader, 1965–67, Prof., 1967–85, Pender Prof. and Head of Dept, 1980–85, Dept of Electronic and Electrical Engrg, UCL (Hon. Fellow, 1985); Rector, Imperial Coll., London Univ., 1985–93 (Hon. Fellow, 1995). Dir (non-exec.), BT (formerly British Telecom), 1987–93; Chm., Hydroventuri Ltd, 2001–03. Pres., IEE, 1987–88 (Vice-Pres., 1980–83; Dep. Pres., 1984–86); Treas. and Vice-Pres., Royal Soc., 1997–2002; Mem., Exec. Bd, Fellowship of Engrg, 1981–84. Chm., BBC Science Advisory Cttee, 1987–90. Trustee: Science Mus., 1987–91; Wolfson Foundn, 1988–. Sec., Royal Instn, 1984–88 (Vice Pres., 1980–82; Manager, 1980–84; Vice Pres. and Chm. of Council, 1995–99). Foreign Member: NAE, US, 2001; Russian Acad. of Sci., 2003. Marconi International Fellowship, 1984. Dr *hc*: Aston, 1987; Leicester, 1987; Institut National Polytechnique de Grenoble, 1987; Edinburgh, 1988; Polytechnic Univ., NY, 1988; Westminster, 1992; Sussex, 1993; Glasgow, 1994; Chinese Univ. of Hong Kong, 1994; City Univ. of Hong Kong, 1998; Surrey, 2001; Nanyan Technol Univ., Singapore, 2002. Faraday Medal, IEE, 1980; Royal Medal, Royal Soc., 1986. National Order of Merit (France), 1990. *Publications:* patents; papers on topics in physical electronics in various engrg and physics jls. *Recreations:* music, ski-ing, swimming. *Address:* 11 Ripplevale Grove, N1 1HS.

ASH, Dame Margaret; *see* Barbour, Dame M.

ASH, Raymond; former Director, Business Statistics Office, retired from Civil Service, 1986; Director, Business and Trade Statistics Ltd, since 1986; *b* 2 Jan. 1928; *s* of late Horace Ash and Gladys Ash; *m* 1947, Mavis (*née* Wootton); two *s* one *d*. *Educ:* Wolverhampton Grammar Sch. Civil Service, 1949–86: professional statistician and senior manager working on health, labour, overseas trade, and business statistics. *Publications:* contrib. learned jls. *Recreations:* country walks, tourism, historical studies. *Address:* 20 Taliesin Close, Rogerstone, Newport, Gwent NP10 0DD. *T:* (01633) 663814.

ASH, Timothy John G.; *see* Garton Ash.

ASHBEE, Paul; Archaeologist, University of East Anglia, 1969–83; *b* 23 June 1918; *s* of Lewis Ashbee and Hannah Mary Elizabeth Ashbee (*née* Brett); *m* 1952, Richmal Crompton Lamburn Disher (*d* 2005); one *s* one *d*. *Educ:* sch. in Maidstone, Kent; Univ. of London; Univ. of Leicester (MA; DLitt 1984). Post-grad. Dip. Prehistoric Archaeology, London. Royal W Kent Regt and REME, 1939–46; Control Commn for Germany, 1946–49; Univ. of London, Univ. of Bristol (Redland Coll.), 1949–54; Asst Master and Head of History, Forest Hill Sch., 1954–68. Excavation of prehistoric sites, mostly barrows both long and round for then Min. of Works, 1949–76; Co-dir with R. L. S. Bruce-Mitford of BM excavations at Sutton-Hoo, 1964–69; Mem., Sutton Hoo Research Cttee, 1982–2002. Mem. Council and Meetings Sec., Prehistoric Soc., 1960–74; Sec. (Wareham Earthwork), British Assoc. Sub-Cttee for Archaeological Field Experiment, 1961–; one-time Sec., Neolithic and Bronze Age Cttee, Council for British Archaeology; Mem. Royal Commn on Historical Monuments (England), 1975–85; Mem., Area Archaeological Adv. Cttee (DoE) for Norfolk and Suffolk, 1975–79. Pres., Cornwall Archæol Soc., 1976–80, Vice-Pres., 1980–84; Chm., Scole Cttee for E Anglian Archaeology, 1979–84. Patron, Kent Archaeol Soc., 2002–. FSA 1958; FRSAI 1987. *Publications:* The Bronze Age Round Barrow in Britain, 1960; The Earthen Long Barrow in Britain, 1970, 2nd edn 1984; Ancient Scilly, 1974; The Ancient British, 1978; chapter in Sutton Hoo, Vol. I, 1976; Wilsford Shaft, 1989; Halangy Down, Isles of Scilly, 2000; Kent in Prehistoric Times, 2005; numerous papers, articles and reviews in Archaeologia, Antiquaries Jl, Archaeological Jl, Proc. Prehistoric Soc., Antiquity, Cornish Archaeology, Arch. Cantiana, Proc. Dorset Arch. and Nat. Hist. Soc., Proc. Hants FC, Wilts Archaeol Magazine, Yorks Arch. Jl, etc. *Recreations:* East Anglia, historical architecture, bibliophilia. *Address:* The Old Rectory, Chedgrave, Norfolk NR14 6ND. *T:* (01508) 520595. *Club:* Norfolk (Norwich).

ASHBERG, Judith; *see* Piatkus, J.

ASHBOURNE, 4th Baron *cr* 1885; **Edward Barry Greynville Gibson;** Lieut-Comdr RN, retired; *b* 28 Jan. 1933; *s* of 3rd Baron Ashbourne, CB, DSO, and Reta Frances Manning (*d* 1996), *e d* of E. M. Hazeland, Hong Kong; *S* father, 1983; *m* 1967, Yvonne Georgina, *d* of Mrs Flora Ham, of Malin, County Donegal; three *s*. *Educ:* Rugby. RN, 1951–72; Kitcat and Aitken, stockbrokers, 1972–73, 1976–79; Vickers, da Costa & Co. Ltd, stockbrokers, 1973–76; Save & Prosper Gp, 1979–81; GT Management, 1981–88; MoD, 1989–93. Pres., Christian Broadcasting Council, 1998–. Pres., Harting and Dist Br., Chichester Cons. Assoc.; Pres., Hampshire Autistic Soc. *Heir: s* Hon. Edward Charles d'Olier Gibson [*b* 31 Dec. 1967; *m* 2001, Tanya Louise, *d* of Bryan Beckett, OBE; one *s* one *d*]. *Address:* Colebrook Barn, East Harting Farm, Petersfield, Hants GU31 5LU.

ASHBOURNE, (Kenneth) John (Turner); public sector consultant and company chairman; *b* 16 July 1938; *s* of Ernest John Ashbourne and Phyllis Ashbourne; *m* 1959, Valerie Anne Sado; one *s* one *d*. *Educ:* St Dunstan's Coll.; London Sch. of Econs (BSc Econs 1959). Teacher, then lectr, 1959–68; Mgt Develt Officer, BAC, 1968–71; Hd, Corporate Planning, London Borough of Lewisham, 1971–74; Asst Chief Exec., Suffolk CC, 1974–77; Chief Exec., Royal Borough of Kingston-upon-Thames, 1977–80; Dep. Man. Dir, Express Newspaper Gp, 1980–83; Sen. Consultant, Hay-MSL, 1983–85; Chief Executive: Cambridge HA, 1985–91; Addenbrooke's Hosp., then Addenbrooke's NHS Trust, 1991–98; E Anglian Ambulance NHS Trust, 1999. Chairman: Chapter Ltd, 1999–; Enterprise Cradle Ltd, 2001–. Sen. Mem., Hughes Hall, 1992–2000, and Associate Lectr, Clinical Sch., 1994–2000, Univ. of Cambridge. Chm., UK Univ. Hosps Forum, 1998–2000. Founder and Hon. Dir, Shelby Transplant Trust, 1994–2000. Mem. Nat. Council, British Falconers' Club, 1977–88; Mem., 1980–86, Vice-Chm., 1983–86, Hawk Bd. Gov., Anglia Poly. Univ., 1996–2000. *Recreations:* music, cars, birds of prey, wood. *Address:* 248400 5th Side Road Mono, RR#5, Orangeville, ON L9W 2Z2, Canada; Eadon House, 1 Easton Lane, Bozeat, Northants NN29 7NN.

ASHBROOK, 11th Viscount *cr* 1751 (Ire.); **Michael Llowarch Warburton Flower;** JP; DL; Baron Castle Durrow 1733; landowner; Vice Lord-Lieutenant, Cheshire, since 1990; *b* 9 Dec. 1935; *s* of 10th Viscount Ashbrook and Elizabeth, *er d* of Capt. John Egerton-Warburton and Hon. Mrs Waters; *S* father, 1995; *m* 1971, Zoë Mary Engleheart; two *s* one *d*. *Educ:* Eton; Worcester Coll., Oxford (MA Mod. Hist.). 2nd Lieut, Grenadier Guards, 1955. Solicitor, 1963; Partner, Farrer & Co., Solicitors, 1966–76; Partner, then Consultant, Pannone & Partners (formerly March Pearson & Skelton), 1985–96. Chm., Taxation Sub-Cttee, 1984–86, Pres., Cheshire Branch, 1990–99, CLA. DL 1982, JP 1983, Cheshire. *Recreations:* gardening, the countryside, shooting. *Heir: s* Hon. Rowland Francis Warburton Flower [*b* 16 Jan. 1975; *m* 2004, Annika Jane, *d* of Julian Beavan; one *s*]. *Address:* The Old Parsonage, Arley Green, Northwich, Cheshire CW9 6LZ. *T:* (01565) 777277. *Club:* Brooks's.
See also Sir C. J. Hoare, Bt.

ASHBROOK, Kate Jessie; General Secretary, Open Spaces Society, since 1984; *b* 1 Feb. 1955; *d* of John Ashbrook and Margaret Balfour; lives with Christopher Myles Hall, *qv*. *Educ:* Benenden Sch., Kent; Exeter Univ. (BSc). Member, Executive Committee: Open Spaces Soc., 1978–84; Ramblers' Assoc., 1982– (Vice-Chm., 1993–95; Chm., 1995–98, 2006–; Chm., Access Cttee, 1997–; Footpath Sec., Bucks and W Middx, 1986–); Council for National Parks, 1983– (Vice-Chm., 1998–2003; Chm., 2003–); Member: Common Land Forum, 1984–86; Countryside Agency, 1999–2006; Nat. Parks Review Adv. Panel, DEFRA, 2002; Common Land Stakeholder Wkg Gp, DEFRA, 2002–03; Adv. Mem., Thames Basin Heaths Special Protection Area Jt Strategic Partnership Bd, 2007–. Chm., Central Rights of Way Cttee, 1991–98; Sec., Countryside Link, 1989–92; Pres., Dartmoor Preservation Assoc., 1995– (Hon. Sec., 1981–84). Mem., Inst. of Public Rights of Way Officers, 1999–. Chm., Turville Sch. Trust, 1994–95. Editor, Open Space, 1984–. *Publications:* (contrib.) The Walks of South-East England, 1975; (contrib.) Severnside: a guide to family walks, 1976; pamphlets; contribs to The Countryman and various jls. *Recreations:* pedantry, finding illegally blocked footpaths, learning British birdsong. *Address:* Telfer's Cottage, Turville, Henley-on-Thames RG9 6QL. *T:* (01491) 638396.

ASHBURNER, Prof. Michael, PhD, ScD; FRS 1990; Professor of Biology, University of Cambridge, since 1991; Fellow, Churchill College, Cambridge, since 1980; *b* 23 May 1942; *s* of Geoffrey Staton Ashburner and Diane Ashburner (*née* Leff); *m* 1963, Francesca Ryan, *d* of Desmond Francis Ryan and Isabel Ryan; one *s* two *d*. *Educ:* Royal Grammar Sch., High Wycombe; Churchill Coll., Cambridge (BA 1964, PhD 1968, ScD 1978). FRES 1975. University of Cambridge: Asst in Research, 1966–68; Univ. Demonstrator, 1968–73; Univ. Lectr, 1973–80; Reader in Developmental Genetics, 1980–91. Gordon Ross Res. Fellow, Calif Inst. of Technology, 1968–69; Visiting Professor: Univ. of California Sch. of Medicine, San Francisco, 1977–78; Univ. of Crete, 1985; Univ. of Pavia, Italy, 1990–96; Miller Vis. Prof., Univ. of California at Berkeley, 1986. Lectures: Goldschmidt, Hebrew Univ., Jerusalem, 1985; Osborne, Edinburgh Univ., 1991; Dacre, Peterhouse, Cambridge, 1992. Res. Co-ordinator, EMBL, 1994–98; Jt Hd, EMBL-European Bioinformatics Inst., 1998–2001. Member: EMBO, 1977, Council, 1988–91; Governing Council, Internat. Centre for Insect Physiology and Ecology, Nairobi, 1991–96; Council, Royal Soc., 2001–03. Pres., Genetical Soc., 1997–2000. Mem., Academia Europaea, 1989; Fellow, Japan Soc. for Promotion of Sci., 1992. Hon. Foreign Mem., Amer. Acad. of Arts and Scis, 1993. Hon. Dr Biol Crete, 2002; Hon. DSc Edinburgh, 2003. *Publications:* (ed) The Genetics and Biology of Drosophila, 1976–86, 12 vols; (ed) Insect Cytogenetics, 1980; (ed) Heat Shock: from bacteria to man, 1982; Drosophila: a laboratory handbook, 1989, (jtly) 2nd edn 2005; Won for All: how the Drosophila genome was sequenced, 2006; contribs to scientific jls. *Recreations:* walking, watching birds. *Address:* 5 Bateman Street, Cambridge CB2 1NB. *T:* (01223) 364706; Department of Genetics, Downing Street, Cambridge CB2 3EH. *T:* (01223) 333969.

ASHBURNHAM, Sir James Fleetwood, 13th Bt *cr* 1661, of Broomham, Sussex; *b* 17 Dec. 1979; *s* of John Anchitel Fleetwood Ashburnham (*d* 1981) and of Corinne Ashburnham (*née* O'Brien, now Merricks); *S* grandfather, 1999. *Educ:* Sherborne; King's Coll., London. *Address:* 70 Charlwood Street, SW1V 4PQ.

ASHBURTON, 7th Baron *cr* 1835; **John Francis Harcourt Baring,** KG 1994; KCVO 1990 (CVO 1980); Kt 1983; DL; Chairman: Barings plc, 1985–89 (non-executive Director, 1989–94); Baring Brothers & Co. Ltd, 1974–89 (a Managing Director, 1955–74); BP Co. plc, 1992–95 (Director, 1982–95); *b* 2 Nov. 1928; *er s* of 6th Baron Ashburton, KG, KCVO, DL and Hon. Doris Mary Thérèse Harcourt (*d* 1981), *e d* of 1st Viscount Harcourt; *S* father, 1991; *m* 1st, 1955, Susan Mary Renwick (marr. diss. 1984), *e d* of 1st Baron Renwick, KBE, and Mrs John Ormiston; two *s* two *d*; 2nd, 1987, Mrs Sarah Crewe, *d* of late J. G. Spencer Churchill. *Educ:* Eton (Fellow, 1982–97); Trinity Coll., Oxford (MA; Hon. Fellow 1989). Dep. Chm., Royal Insurance Co. Ltd, 1975–82 (Dir, 1964–82); Chairman: Outwich Investment Trust Ltd, 1968–86; Baring Stratton Investment Trust, 1986–97; Director: Trafford Park Estates Ltd, 1964–77; Dunlop Holdings Ltd, 1981–84; Bank of England, 1983–91; Jaguar, 1989–91. Receiver-Gen., 1974–90, Lord Warden of the Stannaries, 1990–94, Duchy of Cornwall. Vice-Pres., British Bankers' Assoc., 1977–81; Pres., Overseas Bankers' Club, 1977–78. Chm., Accepting Houses Cttee, 1977–81; Chm., Cttee on Finance for Industry, NEDC, 1980–86. Member: British Transport Docks Bd, 1966–71; President's Cttee, CBI, 1976–79; Trustee and Hon. Treas., Police Foundn, 1989–2001; Member: Council, Baring Foundn, 1971–98 (Chm., 1987–98); Exec. Cttee, NACF, 1989–99. Trustee: Rhodes Trust, 1970–99 (Chm., 1987–99); Southampton Univ. Develt Trust, 1986–96 (Chm., 1989–96); Nat. Gall., 1981–87; Winchester Cathedral Trust, 1989– (Chm., 1993–2006). High Steward, Winchester Cathedral, 1991–. DL Hants, 1994. Hon. Fellow, Hertford Coll., Oxford, 1976. *Heir: s* Hon. Mark Francis Robert Baring [*b* 17 Aug. 1958; *m* 1983, Miranda Caroline, *d* of Captain Charles St John Graham Moncrieff; two *s* two *d*]. *Address:* Lake House, Northington, Alresford, Hants SO24 9TG; 42A Caithness Road, W14 0JD. *Clubs:* Pratt's, Flyfishers', Beefsteak.

ASHBY, David Glynn; barrister; *b* 14 May 1940; *s* of Robert M. Ashby and Isobel A. Davidson; *m* 1965, Silvana Morena (marr. diss. 1998); one *d*. *Educ:* Royal Grammar Sch., High Wycombe; Bristol Univ. (LLB Hons). Called to the Bar, Gray's Inn, 1963; formerly in practice on SE Circuit. Member: Hammersmith Bor. Council, 1968–71; for W Woolwich, GLC, 1977–81; ILEA, 1977–81. MP (C) NW Leics, 1983–97. *Recreations:* gardening, sailing (Transatlantic 2003–04, Mediterranean 2005–06), music. *Address:* 7B Westleigh Avenue, SW15 6RF.

ASHBY, Francis Dalton, OBE 1975; Director, National Counties Building Society, 1980–90; retired; *b* 20 Jan. 1920; *s* of late John Frederick Ashby and late Jessie Ashby; *m* 1948, Mollie Isabel Mitchell (*d* 1999); one *s* one *d* (and one *d* decd). *Educ:* Watford Grammar Sch. Diploma in Govt Admin. War Service, Royal Signals, 1940–46: POW, Far East, 1942–45. National Debt Office: Exec. Officer, 1938; Asst Comptroller and Estabt Officer, 1966–76; Comptroller-General, 1976–80. Hon. Treas., Cedars Village Residents' Assoc., 1998–2000. *Recreations:* listening to music, retirement village activities. *Address:* 21 Badgers Walk, Chorleywood, Herts WD3 5GA.

ASHBY, Rt Rev. Godfrey William Ernest Candler; Assistant Bishop of George, South Africa, 1995–2008; an Honorary Assistant Bishop, Diocese of Portsmouth, since 2008; *b* 6 Nov. 1930; *s* of late William Candler Ashby and Vera Fane Ashby (*née* Hickey); *m* 1957, Sally Hawtree; four *s* two *d*. *Educ:* King's School, Chester; King's Coll., London (BD, AKC, PhD). Deacon 1955, priest 1956; Assistant Curate: St Peter, St Helier, Morden, 1955–57; Clydesdale Mission, 1958; Priest-in-charge, St Mark's Mission, 1958–60; Subwarden, St Paul's Coll., Grahamstown, 1960–65; Rector of Alice and Lectr, Federal Theological Seminary, 1966–68; Sen. Lecturer, Old Testament and Hebrew, Rhodes Univ., Grahamstown, 1969–75; Assoc. Professor, 1974–75; Overseas Visiting Scholar, St John's Coll., Cambridge, 1975; Dean and Archdeacon, Cathedral of St Michael and St George, Grahamstown, 1976–80; Bishop of St John's (Transkei and S Africa), 1980–84;

Prof. of Divinity, Univ. of Witwatersrand, Johannesburg, 1985–88; Asst Bp of Leicester, 1988–95; Priest-in-Charge, Newtown Linford, 1992–95. Hon. Canon, Leicester Cathedral, 1994–. *Publications:* Theodoret of Cyrrhus as Exegete of the Old Testament, 1970; Sacrifice, 1988; Exodus (commentary), 1998; articles in theological jls. *Recreations:* ornithology, French literature. *Address:* 12 Jay Close, Horndean, Hants PO8 9DJ.

ASHBY, Prof. Michael Farries, CBE 1997; FRS 1979; FREng; Royal Society Research Professor, Department of Engineering, University of Cambridge, since 1989 (Professor of Engineering Materials, 1973–89); *b* 20 Nov. 1935; *s* of Baron Ashby, FRS; *m* 1962, Maureen Stewart; two *s* one *d*. *Educ:* Campbell Coll., Belfast; Queens' Coll., Cambridge (BA, MA, PhD). Post-doctoral work, Cambridge, 1960–62; Asst, Univ. of Göttingen, 1962–65; Asst Prof., Harvard Univ., 1965–69; Prof. of Metallurgy, Harvard Univ., 1969–73. Mem., Akad. der Wissenschaften zu Göttingen, 1980–. FREng (FEng 1993). Hon. MA Harvard, 1969. Editor: Acta Metallurgica, 1974–96; Progress in Materials Science, 1995–. *Publications:* Deformation Mechanism Maps, 1982; Engineering Materials, pt 1 1986, pt 2 1996; Materials Selection in Design, 1992, 3rd edn 2004; Cellular Solids, 1997; Materials and Design, 2002; Materials: engineering, properties, science, design, 2007. *Recreations:* music, design. *Address:* 51 Maids Causeway, Cambridge CB5 8DE. *T:* (01223) 301333.

ASHCOMBE, 4th Baron *cr* 1892; **Henry Edward Cubitt;** late RAF; Chairman, Cubitt Estates Ltd; *b* 31 March 1924; *er s* of 3rd Baron Ashcombe; *S* father, 1962; *m* 1955, Ghislaine (marr. diss. 1968), *o d* of Cornelius Willem Dresselhuys, Long Island, New York; *m* 1973, Hon. Virginia Carington, *yr d* of Baron Carrington, *qv*; *m* 1979, Mrs Elizabeth Dent-Brocklehurst. *Educ:* Eton. Served War of 1939–45, RAF. Consul-General in London for the Principality of Monaco, 1961–68. *Heir: cousin* Mark Edward Cubitt [*b* 29 Feb. 1964; *m* 1992, Melissa Mary, *o d* of Maj. Charles Hay; two *s*]. *Address:* Sudeley Castle, Winchcombe, Cheltenham, Glos GL54 5JD. *Club:* White's.

See also Earl of Harrington.

ASHCROFT, Baron *cr* 2000 (Life Peer), of Chichester in the County of West Sussex; **Michael Anthony Ashcroft,** KCMG 2000; international businessman and entrepreneur; Chairman, BB Holdings, since 1987; a Deputy Chairman, Conservative and Unionist Party, since 2005; *b* 4 March 1946; *s* of Frederic Parker Ashcroft and Mary Lavinia Long; *m* 1st, 1972, Wendy Mahoney (marr. diss. 1984); two *s* one *d*; 2nd, 1986, Susi Anstey. *Educ:* King Edward VI Grammar Sch., Norwich; Royal Grammar Sch., High Wycombe; Mid-Essex Tech. Coll., Chelmsford. Varied business interests in public and private cos in UK, USA and Caribbean. Former Chairman: Hawley Group; ADT Ltd; Dir, Tyco Internat., 1984–2002. Ambassador from Belize to the UN, 1998–2000. Party Treas., Conservative Party, 1998–2001; Treas., Internat. Democratic Union, 2007–. Founder and Chm., Crimestoppers Trust, 1988–. Chm., Ashcroft Technology Acad. (formerly ADT Coll.), 1991–; Chancellor, Anglia Ruskin Univ., 2001–. *Publications:* Smell the Coffee: a wake up call to the Conservative Party, 2005; Dirty Politics, Dirty Times, 2005; Victoria Cross Heroes, 2006. *Recreations:* researching the Victoria Cross, entertaining friends, trying something new, messing about in boats. *Address:* House of Lords, SW1A 0PW.

ASHCROFT, Andrew Richard; HM Diplomatic Service, retired; Chief Executive, Ambassador Communications, since 2008; *b* 28 May 1961; *s* of Ivor John Ashcroft and Amy Joan Ashcroft; *m* 2001, Dr Amanda Sives (marr. diss. 2006). *Educ:* Worle Sch., Weston-super-Mare; Millfield Sch. Entered FCO, 1980; Finance Dept, then S Asian Dept, FCO, 1980–82; 3rd Sec. (Commercial), Muscat, 1982–86; 3rd, later 2nd Sec. (Chancery), Tel Aviv, 1987–91; Asst Private Sec. to Minister of State (ME, Near East, N Africa and Former Soviet Union and Central Eastern Europe), FCO, 1991–95; 1st Sec. (Commercial), Harare, 1996–99; Hd, Caribbean Section, FCO, 1999–2001; Ambassador, Dominican Republic and Haiti, 2002–06; FCO, London, 2006–07. *Recreations:* music (trumpet and piano), cricket, golf, tennis. *Club:* Royal Harare Golf.

ASHCROFT, Emma Georgina Annalies; *see* Fielding, E. G. A.

ASHCROFT, Prof. Frances Mary, PhD, ScD; FRS 1999; Royal Society GlaxoSmithKline Research Professor, University of Oxford, since 2001; Fellow, Trinity College, Oxford, since 1992; *b* 15 Feb. 1952; *d* of John and Kathleen Ashcroft. *Educ:* Talbot Heath Sch., Bournemouth; Girton Coll., Cambridge (BA 1974; MA 1978; PhD 1979; ScD 1996). MRC Trng Fellow, Physiol., Leicester Univ., 1978–82; Oxford University: Demonstrator in Physiol., 1982–85; EPA Cephalosporin Jun. Res. Fellow, Linacre Coll., 1983–85; Royal Soc. 1983 Univ. Res. Fellow, Physiol., 1985–90; Lecturer in Physiology: Christ Church, 1986–87; Trinity Coll., 1988–89; Univ. Lectr in Physiol., 1990–96; Tutorial Fellow in Medicine, St Hilda's Coll., 1990–91; Prof. of Physiol., 1996–2001. Grass Foundn Fellow, 1978; Muscular Dystrophy Assoc. Fellow, Physiol., UCLA, 1981–82. G. L. Brown Prize Lectr, 1997; Peter Curran Lectr, Yale Univ., 1999; Charitable Infirmary Lectr, RCSI, 2003. FMedSci 1999. DUniv Open, 2003; Hon. DSc Leicester, 2007. Frank Smart Prize, Cambridge Univ., 1974; Andrew Cudworth Meml Prize, 1990; G. B. Morgagni Young Investigator Award, 1991; Charter Award, Inst. of Biology, 2004; Walter Cannon Award, Amer. Physiol. Soc., 2007; Albert Renold Prize, Eur. Assoc. for the Study of Diabetes, 2007. *Publications:* (with S. J. H. Ashcroft) Insulin-Molecular Biology to Pathology, 1992; Ion Channels and Disease, 1999; Life at the Extremes: the science of survival, 2000; res. papers in Nature, Jl Physiology, etc. *Recreations:* reading, writing, walking. *Address:* University Laboratory of Physiology, Parks Road, Oxford OX1 3PT.

ASHCROFT, Hon. John David, JD; Attorney General of the United States of America, 2001–04; *b* Chicago, 9 May 1942; *m* Janet Elise; two *s* one *d*. *Educ:* Yale Univ.; Univ. of Chicago (JD 1967). Admitted: Missouri State Bar; US Supreme Court Bar. In private practice, Springfield, Mo, 1967–73; Associate Prof., SW Missouri State Univ., Springfield, 1967–72; State Auditor, 1973–75, Asst Attorney Gen., 1975–77, Attorney Gen., 1977–84, Gov., 1985–93, Missouri; Attorney, Suelthaus and Kaplan, 1993–94; US Senator Missouri, 1995–2001. *Publications:* (with Janet E. Ashcroft) College Law for Business; (with Janet E. Ashcroft) It's the Law, 1979; Lessons From a Father to his Son, 1998.

ASHCROFT, John Kevin, CBE 1990; Crabtree Consultancy Group Ltd, since 1990; *b* 24 Dec. 1948; *s* of Cumania Manion and late John Ashcroft; *m* 1972, Jennifer Ann (*née* King); two *s* one *d*. *Educ:* Upholland Grammar School; LSE (BSc Econ Hons); PhD Manchester Metropolitan Univ., 1996. Marketing Trainee, Tube Investments, 1970; Brand Manager, Crown Wallcoverings Internat. Div., 1974; Marketing Dir, Crown Wallcoverings French Subsidiary, 1976; Man. Dir, Coloroll, 1978–82, Dep. Chm. and Chief Exec., 1982–86, Chm., 1986–90. Young Business Man of the Year, The Guardian, 1987. *Recreations:* fine arts, opera, sports, wine.

ASHCROFT, Noel Graham; Agent General for Western Australia in London, since 2005; *b* 2 May 1944; *s* of Arthur Joseph Ashcroft and late Eileen May Ashcroft; *m* 1st, 1968, Penelope Anthea Edwards (marr. diss. 2000); four *d*; 2nd, 2003, Susan Mary Feeney (*née* Zanco); two step *s*. *Educ:* St Francis Xavier Coll., Bunbury; St Ildephonsis Coll., New Norcia; Australian National Univ. (BSc Forestry 1967); Linacre Coll., Oxford (MSc 1974). Divl Forest Officer, 1968–80, Regl Forest Manager, 1980–83, Forests Dept, WA; Project Manager, Govt of WA Functional Review Cttee, 1983–86; Associate Dir, Barrack House Gp Pty, Ltd, 1986–89; Government of Western Australia: Dir, Dept of Resources Develt, 1989–2001; Exec. Dir, Office of Major Projects, 2001–03; Dep. Dir Gen., Dept of Industry and Resources, 2003–05. Mem., 2005–, Mem. Bd of Mgt, 2006–, Britain-Australia Soc.; Mem., Cook Soc., 2005–. *Recreations:* building, furniture restoration, golf, fishing, sightseeing. *Address:* Government of Western Australia, European Office, Australia Centre, Corner of Strand and Melbourne Place, WC2B 4LG. *T:* (020) 7395 0562, *Fax:* (020) 7379 0865; *e-mail:* noel.ashcroft@wago.co.uk. *Club:* Lord's Taverners.

ASHCROFT, Philip Giles; Solicitor, British Telecommunications, 1981–87; *b* 15 Nov. 1926; *s* of Edmund Samuel Ashcroft and Constance Ruth Ashcroft (*née* Giles); *m* 1st, 1968, Kathleen Margaret Senior (marr. diss. 1983); one *s*; 2nd, 1985, Valerie May Smith, *d* of late E. T. G. Smith. *Educ:* Royal Grammar Sch., Newcastle upon Tyne; Durham Univ. Admitted solicitor, 1951. Joined Treasury Solicitor's Dept, 1955; Asst Legal Adviser, Land Commn, 1967; Asst Treasury Solicitor, 1971; Under-Sec. (Legal), DTI, 1973; Legal Adviser, Dept of Energy, 1974–80; Dep. Solicitor to the Post Office, 1980–81. Legal Consultant, Registry of Friendly Socs and Building Socs Commn, 1988–96. *Recreations:* reading, listening to music. *Address:* 24A Rudd's Lane, Haddenham, Aylesbury, Bucks HP17 8JP. *T:* (01844) 291921.

ASHCROFT, Wendy Cowan, (Mrs B. Ashcroft); *see* Alexander, W. C.

ASHDOWN, family name of **Baron Ashdown of Norton-sub-Hamdon**.

ASHDOWN OF NORTON-SUB-HAMDON, Baron *cr* 2001 (Life Peer), of Norton-sub-Hamdon in the County of Somerset; **Jeremy John Durham Ashdown, (Paddy),** GCMG 2006; KBE 2000; PC 1989; High Representative of the International Community and EU Special Representative in Bosnia and Herzegovina, 2002–06; *b* 27 Feb. 1941; *s* of late John W. R. D. Ashdown and Lois A. Ashdown; *m* 1962, Jane (*née* Courtenay); one *s* one *d*. *Educ:* Bedford Sch. Served RM, 1959–71: 41 and 42 Commando; commanded 2 Special Boat Section; Captain RM; HM Diplomatic Service, 1st Sec., UK Mission to UN, Geneva, 1971–76; Commercial Manager's Dept, Westlands Gp, 1976–78; Sen. Manager, Morlands Ltd, 1978–81; employed by Dorset CC, 1982–83. Contested (L) Yeovil, 1979; MP Yeovil, 1983–2001 (L 1983–88, Lib Dem 1988–2001); Leader, Liberal Democrats, 1988–99. L spokesman for Trade and Industry, 1983–86; Lib/SDP Alliance spokesman on education and science, 1987; Lib Dem spokesman on NI, 1988–97. *Publications:* Citizen's Britain, 1989; Beyond Westminster, 1994; Making Change our Ally, 1994; The Ashdown Diaries, vol. 1, 2000, vol. 2, 2001; Swords and Ploughshares: bringing peace to the 21st century, 2007. *Recreations:* walking, gardening, wine making. *Address:* House of Lords, SW1A 0PW. *Club:* National Liberal.

ASHE, (Thomas) Michael; QC 1994; QC (NI) 1998; SC (Ire.) 2000; a Recorder, since 2000; *b* 10 March 1949; *s* of John Ashe and Nancy (*née* O'Connor); *m* 1977, Helen Morag Nicholson. *Educ:* Finchley Catholic Grammar Sch. Called to the Bar, Middle Temple, 1971, Bencher, 1998; called to Irish Bar, 1975, Northern Irish Bar, 1993. Estate Duty Office, CS, 1967–70; merchant banking, 1971–76; practice at the Bar, 1978–. Dep. Public Prosecutor, Min. of Finance, Singapore, 1988–90; an Asst Recorder, 1998–2000. Editor, Company Lawyer, 1983–2007. Hon. General Counsel to Brit. Inst. of Securities Laws, 1980–; Hon. Consultant to Commercial Crime Unit, Commonwealth Secretariat, 1980–84. Mem. Bd, Centre for Internat. Documentation on Organised and Economic Crime, Cambridge, 1990–; Guest Lectr, Fac. of Laws, Univ. of Cambridge, 1990–95. Auditor and Notary, Dio. of Brentwood, 1997–. *Publications:* (jtly) Insider Trading, 1990, 2nd edn 1994; (jtly) Insider Dealing (Ireland), 1992; (jtly) Insider Crime, 1994; (jtly) Money Laundering, 2000, 2nd edn 2007; contrib. Money, 1980, and (jtly) Injunctions, 1991, in Halsbury's Laws of England, 4th edn; articles in legal periodicals. *Recreations:* walking, railways, Gregorian Chant, classical music, Irish traditional music. *Address:* 9 Stone Buildings, Lincoln's Inn, WC2A 3NN. *T:* (020) 7404 5055.

ASHER, Bernard Harry; Director and Vice-Chairman, Legal & General Group plc, 1998–2004; Chairman, Liontrust Asset Management plc, since 2004; *b* 9 March 1936; *s* of Samuel Asher and Rebecca (*née* Fisher); *m* 1961, Batia Sislin; one *s* two *d*. *Educ:* LSE (BSc). S. Japhet & Co., 1957–59; English Electric Co., 1960–67; ITT Inc., 1967–74 and 1978–80; on secondment to NEDO, 1975–78; Hong Kong Bank, 1980–92; Chairman: HSBC Investment Bank Ltd, 1992–98; James Capel & Co., 1991–98; Samuel Montagu, 1993–98; Lonrho Africa, 1998–2004. Non-executive Director: Rémy Cointreau SA, 1992–95; The China Fund Inc., 1995–99; Randgold Resources Ltd, 1997–; Morgan Sindall plc, 1998–; China Shoto, 2005–. Investment Advr, RCP, 1998–. Trustee, The Health Foundn (formerly Healthcare Med. Trust, then PPP Foundn), 1998–. Vice Chm. Governors, LSE, 1998–. *Recreations:* opera, walking. *Address:* Liontrust Asset Management, 2 Savoy Court, Strand, WC2R 0EZ. *Clubs:* Reform; Hong Kong, Hong Kong Jockey.

ASHER, Jane; actress and writer; *b* 5 April 1946; *d* of late Richard A. J. Asher, MD, FRCP and of Margaret Asher (*née* Eliot); *m* Gerald Scarfe, *qv*; two *s* one *d*. *Educ:* North Bridge House; Miss Lambert's PNEU. *Stage:* Will You Walk a Little Faster, Duke of York's, 1960; Wendy in Peter Pan, Scala, 1961; Bristol Old Vic, 1965; Romeo and Juliet and Measure for Measure, NY, 1967; Look Back in Anger, Royal Court, 1969; The Philanthropist, Mayfair and NY, 1970; Treats, Royal Court, 1975; National Theatre, 1976; Whose Life is it Anyway?, Mermaid and Savoy, 1978; Before the Party, Queen's, 1978; Blithe Spirit, Vaudeville, 1986; Henceforward, Vaudeville, 1988; The School for Scandal, NT, 1990; Making it Better, Criterion, 1992; The Shallow End, Royal Court, 1997; Things We Do For Love, Gielgud, 1998; House, and Garden, RNT, 2000; What the Butler Saw, tour, 2001; Festen, Almeida, transf. Lyric, 2004; The World's Biggest Diamond, Royal Court, 2005; *films include:* Mandy, 1951; Greengage Summer, 1961; Alfie, 1966; Deep End, 1970; Henry VIII and his Six Wives, 1970; Runners, 1984; Dream Child, 1985; Paris by Night, 1988; The Maidens' Conspiracy, 2005; Death at a Funeral, 2007; *television includes:* Brideshead Revisited, 1981; The Mistress, 1986; Wish Me Luck, 1987–89; Eats for Treats, 1990; Tonight at 8.30, Murder Most Horrid, 1991; Closing Numbers, 1993; The Choir, 1995; Good Living, 1997, 1998; Crossroads, 2003; Miss Marple, 2004; New Tricks, 2005; A For Andromeda, 2006; Holby City, 2007; The Palace (series), 2008; numerous plays for radio; Radio Actress of the Year Award, 1986. Member: BBC Gen. Adv. Council, 1991–; BAFTA, 1985; Forum, 1993–. President: Nat. Autistic Soc., 1997– (Vice Pres., 1990–97); Arthritis Care, 2003–; Parkinson's Disease Soc.; Vice-Pres., Nat. Deaf Children's Soc., 2003–; Trustee: WWF; Child Accident Prevention Trust; Ford Martin Trust for Cancer in Children; Children in Need. Governor, Molecule Theatre. Started business, Jane Asher Party Cakes, London, 1990; designer and consultant for Sainsbury's cakes, 1992–99; Consultant, Debenhams, 1999–2004. Columnist: Today newspaper, 1994–95; The Express, 1998–2001. FRSA 1989. Hon. LLD Bristol, 2001. *Publications:* Jane Asher's Party Cakes, 1982; Jane Asher's Fancy Dress, 1983; Silent Nights for You and Your Baby, 1984; Jane Asher's Quick Party Cakes, 1986; Moppy is Happy, 1987; Moppy is Angry, 1987; Easy Entertaining, 1987; Keep Your Baby Safe, 1988; Children's Parties, 1988; Calendar of Cakes, 1989; Eats for Treats, 1990; Jane Asher's Book of Cake Decorating Ideas, 1993; Round the World Cookbook, 1994; Time to Play,

1995; The Longing, 1996; 101 Things I wish I'd known before…, 1996; The Best of Good Living, 1998; The Question, 1998; Good Living at Christmas, 1998; Tricks of the Trade, 1999; Losing It, 2002; Cakes For Fun, 2005; Moppy is Calm, 2005; Moppy is Sad, 2005; Beautiful Baking, 2007; journalism for newspapers and magazines. *Recreations:* reading, The Times crossword. *Address:* c/o United Agents, 12-26 Lexington Street, W1F 0LE. *T:* (020) 3214 0800.

ASHFORD, Ronald, CBE 1992; CEng, FIMechE, FRAeS; aviation and safety consultant; *b* 24 Aug. 1932; *s* of Russell Sutcliffe Ashford and Dorothy Ashford (*née* Shorland); *m* 1955, Françoise Louisa Gabrielle Génestal du Chaumeil; two *s*. *Educ:* St Edward's Sch., Oxford; De Havilland Aeronautical Tech. Sch. Flight Develt Engr, De Havilland Aircraft Co., 1953–56; Pilot Officer, RAF, 1956–58; Flight Develt Engr and Sen. Aerodynamicist, De Havilland/Hawker Siddeley Aviation, 1958–68; Design Surveyor, Air Registration Bd, 1968–72; Civil Aviation Authority: Surveyor and Head, Flight Dept, 1972–83; Dir-Gen., Airworthiness, 1983–88; Group Dir, Safety Regulation, and Board Mem., 1988–92; Sec. Gen., Eur. Jt Aviation Authorities, 1992–94. Wakefield Gold Medal, 1989, Hodgson Prize, 1991, RAeS; Dist. Service Award, Flight Safety Foundn, 1992; Award for Dist. Service, US Fed. Aviation Admin, 1992; Cumberbatch Trophy, GAPAN, 1992; James Clayton Prize, IMechE, 1995. *Publications:* papers in Jl RAeS. *Recreations:* walking, gardening. *Address:* Sheeplands, 17 Granville Road, Limpsfield, Oxted, Surrey RH8 0BX. *T:* (01883) 382917. *Club:* Royal Air Force.

ASHFORD, William Stanton, OBE 1971; HM Diplomatic Service, retired; *b* 4 July 1924; *s* of Thomas and May Ashford; *m* 1957, Rosalind Anne Collett; two *s*. Served RAF, 1943–47; Air Ministry, 1948; Commonwealth Relations Office, 1961; Director of British Information Services, Sierra Leone, 1961, Ghana, 1962; Acting Consul-General, Tangier, 1965; Regional Information Officer, Bombay, 1966; Head of Chancery, British Government Office, Montreal, 1967; seconded to Northern Ireland Office, 1972; FCO, 1974; Consul-General, Adelaide, 1977; High Comr, Vanuatu, 1980–82. *Recreations:* 18th Century music, gardening. *Address:* c/o Lloyds TSB, PO Box 770, St Helier, Jersey JE4 8ZZ. *T:* (01534) 59655.

ASHIOTIS, Costas, Hon. MBE 1952; High Commissioner of Cyprus in London, 1966–79; Cyprus Ambassador to Denmark, Sweden, Norway and Malta, 1966–79; *b* 1908; *m*. *Educ:* Pancyprian Gymnasium, Nicosia; London Sch. of Economics. Journalist and editor; joined Govt Service, 1942; Asst Comr of Labour, 1948; Dir-Gen., Min. of Foreign Affairs, 1960. Mem. Cyprus delegns to UN and to internat. confs. Retired from Foreign Service, 1979. *Publications:* Labour Conditions in Cyprus during the War Years, 1939–45; literary articles. *Address:* 10 Ev. Pallikarides Street, Nicosia, Cyprus.

ASHKEN, Kenneth Richard, CB 1996; JP; Director (Policy), Crown Prosecution Service, 1990–95; *b* 13 June 1945; *s* of Karol and Dulcinea Ashken; *m* 1st, 1969, Linda Salemink (marr. diss.); two *s* one *d*; partner, 1986; 2nd, 1996, Patricia Almond (*d* 1996); one *d*. *Educ:* Whitgift Sch., Croydon; London Univ. (LLB Hons); Cambridge Inst. of Criminology (DipCrim). Admitted solicitor, 1972. Office of Director of Public Prosecutions, 1972; Asst Dir of Public Prosecutions, 1984; Hd of Policy and Inf. Div., 1986, Dir, Policy and Communications Gp (Grade 3), 1990, Crown Prosecution Service. UK Govt consultant to S African Ministry of Justice, 1998–99. Lay Chm., indep. review panels, NHS, 1998–2001; non-exec. Dir, Bromley Primary Care NHS Trust, 2001–04. Member: Cttee, SE London Probation Service, 1997–2001; London Area Bd, Nat. Probation Service, 2001–07. Mem., Funding Panel, Victim Support, 1997– (Vice-Chair, 2006–). FRSA 1990. JP SE London, 2000. *Recreation:* travel. *Club:* Royal Automobile.

ASHKENAZY, Vladimir; concert pianist; conductor; Music Director, European Union Youth Orchestra, since 2002; *b* Gorky, Russia, 6 July 1937; *m* 1961, Thorunn Johannsdottir, *d* of Johann Tryggvason, Iceland; two *s* three *d*. *Educ:* Central Musical Sch., Moscow; Conservatoire, Moscow. Studied under Sumbatyan; Lev Oborin class, 1955: grad 1960. Internat. Chopin Comp., Warsaw, at age of 17 (gained 2nd prize); won Queen Elisabeth Internat. Piano Comp., Brussels, at age of 18 (gold medal). Joint winner (with John Ogdon) of Tchaikovsky Piano Comp., Moscow, 1962. London debut with London Symph. Orch. under George Hurst, and subseq., solo recital, Festival Hall, 1963. Music Dir, RPO, 1987–94; Chief Conductor, Berlin Radio SO, subseq. Deutsches Symphonie-Orchester Berlin, 1989–99; Music Dir and Chief Conductor, Czech Philharmonic Orchestra, 1998–2003; Music Dir, NHK SO, Tokyo, 2004–07. Has played in many countries. Makes recordings. Hon. RAM 1972. Icelandic Order of the Falcon, 1971. *Publication:* (with Jasper Parrott) Beyond Frontiers, 1985. *Address:* Pilatusstrasse 13, 6045 Meggen, Switzerland.

ASHLEY, family name of **Baron Ashley of Stoke**.

ASHLEY OF STOKE, Baron *cr* 1992 (Life Peer), of Widnes in the County of Cheshire; **Jack Ashley,** CH 1975; PC 1979; *b* 6 Dec. 1922; *s* of John Ashley and Isabella Bridge; *m* 1951, Pauline Kay Crispin (*d* 2003); three *d*. *Educ:* St Patrick's Elem. Sch., Widnes, Lancs; Ruskin Coll., Oxford; Gonville and Caius Coll., Cambridge (Hon. Fellow). Labourer and cranedriver, 1936–46; Shop Steward Convenor and Nat. Exec. Mem., Chemical Workers' Union, 1946; Scholarship, Ruskin Coll., 1946–48 and Caius Coll., 1948–51 (Chm. Cambridge Labour Club, 1950; Pres. Cambridge Union, 1951); BBC Radio Producer, 1951–57; Commonwealth Fund Fellow, 1955; BBC Senior Television Producer, 1957–66; Mem., General Advisory Council, BBC, 1967–69, 1970–74. Councillor, Borough of Widnes, 1945. MP (Lab) Stoke-on-Trent, South, 1966–92. Parliamentary Private Secretary: to Sec. of State for Econ. Affairs, 1967–68; to Sec. of State, DHSS, 1974–76. Mem., Lab. Party Nat. Exec. Cttee, 1976–78. Co-Chm., All-Party Disablement Gp. President: Deafness Res. UK (formerly Hearing and Speech, subseq. Defeating Deafness, Trust), 1985–; RNID, 1987–; Royal Coll. of Speech and Language Therapists, 1995–2001. Chancellor, Staffordshire Univ., 1993–2002. Holds 13 hon. degrees. *Publications:* Journey into Silence (autobiog.), 1973; Acts of Defiance (autobiog.), 1992. *Address:* House of Lords, SW1A 0PW.

See also J. Ashley.

ASHLEY, Sir Bernard (Albert), Kt 1987; Founder, Laura Ashley Holdings plc, 1993 (Chairman, 1985–93; non-executive Director, 1991–98); Founder, designer and colourist, Elanbach, since 2000; *b* 11 Aug. 1926; *s* of Albert Ashley and Hilda Maud Ashley; *m* 1st, 1949, Laura Mountney (*d* 1985); two *s* two *d*; 2nd, 1990, Mme Regine Burnell. *Educ:* Whitgift Middle Sch., Croydon, Surrey. Army commission, 1944; Royal Fusiliers, 1944–46, seconded 1 Gurkha Rifles, 1944–45. Incorporated Ashley, Mountney Ltd, 1954; Chm., Ashley, Mountney Ltd, later Laura Ashley Ltd, 1954–93. Hon. DScEcon Wales, 1986. *Recreations:* sailing, flying. *Address:* Llangoed Hall, Llyswen, Brecon, Powys LD3 0YP. *Clubs:* Royal Thames Yacht (Southampton); Army Sailing Association.

ASHLEY, Cedric, CBE 1984; PhD; CEng, FIMechE; automotive engineering and e-learning consultant; Chairman: Cedric Ashley and Associates, since 1989; Euromotor Autotrain LLP, since 2006; Kingsgate Property (Mgt) Ltd, since 2008; Managing Director, Steyr Power Technology, since 1992; *b* 11 Nov. 1936; *s* of Ronald Ashley and Gladys Fincher; *m* 1st, 1960, Pamela Jane Turner (decd); one *s*; 2nd, 1965, (Marjorie) Vivien Gooch (marr. diss. 1991); one *s* one *d*; 3rd, 1991, Auriol Mary Keogh. *Educ:* King Edward's Sch., Birmingham; Mech. Engrg Dept, Univ. of Birmingham (BSc 1958, PhD 1964). CEng 1972; FIMechE 1978. Rolls-Royce Ltd, Derby, 1955–60; Univ. of Birmingham, 1960–73: ICI Res. Fellow, 1963; Lectr, 1966; Internat. Technical Dir, Bostrom Div., Universal Oil Products Ltd, 1973–77; Dir, Motor Industry Res. Assoc., 1977–87; Man. Dir, Lotus Engineering, 1987; Chief Exec., BICERI, 1989–91. Dir, Euromotor, Univ. of Birmingham, 1992–2006. Chairman: SEE, 1970–72; RAC Tech. Cttee, 1980–87; Member: SMMT Technical Bds, 1977–87; Board, Assoc. Ind. Contract Res. Orgns, 1977–86 (Pres., 1982–84); Automobile Div., IMechE, 1978–93 (Chm., 1990–91); Court, Cranfield Inst. of Technol., 1977–87; Engine and Vehicles Cttee, DTI, 1980–88; Three-Dimensional Design Bd, CNAA, 1981–87. Trustee, Sir Henry Royce Foundn, 2006–. Liveryman, Carmen's Co., 1987. FRSA 1983. Cementation Muffelite Award, SEE, 1968; Design Council Award, 1974. TA, 1959–68. *Publications:* (contrib.) Infrasound and Low Frequency Vibration, ed Tempest, 1976; papers on electro-hydraulics, vehicle ride, and effect of vibration and shock on man and buildings, in learned jls. *Recreations:* travel, reading. *Address:* (office) Euromotor Autotrain LLP, 148 Clydesdale Tower, Birmingham B1 1UH. *T:* (0121) 622 7476; *e-mail:* c.ashley@autotrain.org.

ASHLEY, Jacqueline; political interviewer and columnist, The Guardian, since 2002; *b* 10 Sept. 1954; *d* of Lord Ashley of Stoke, *qv*; *m* 1987, Andrew William Stevenson Marr, *qv*; one *s* two *d*. *Educ:* Rosebery Grammar Sch., Epsom; St Anne's Coll., Oxford (MA PPE). Producer and Newsreader, Newsnight, BBC TV, 1980–83; Producer and Reporter, TV-am, 1983–84; Politics Producer, Channel 4 News, 1984–87; Editor, Their Lordships' House, Channel 4, 1987–88; Presenter, The Parliament Programme, Channel 4, 1988–89; Political Corresp., ITN, 1989–98; Presenter, People and Politics, BBC World Service, 1998–2000; Political Editor, New Statesman, 2000–02. Presenter: The Week in Westminster, BBC Radio 4, 1999–. *Recreations:* reading, swimming. *Address:* The Guardian, Kings Place, 90 York Way, N1 9AG.

ASHLEY, Neil; Chairman, Heritage Property Group, since 1997; *b* 14 Nov. 1936; *s* of late Bernard Stephenson Ashley and of Nora Ashley (*née* Dixon); *m* 1st, 1961, Jane Evelyn Victoria (*d* 1995), *d* of late Granville Canty and of Vera Canty; two *s*; 2nd, 2002, Dr Shirley Anne, *d* of late Col George Frederick Preston Bradbrooke and Lillian (*née* Sibley). *Educ:* Barton-on-Humber Grammar Sch.; Battersea Poly.; Ashridge Mgt Coll. Man. Dir, ARC Construction Ltd, 1971–79; Dir, Balfour Beatty Construction Ltd, 1979–84; Man. Dir, Balfour Beatty Internat. Ltd, 1984–88; Jt Man. Dir, Balfour Beatty plc, 1985–89; Chairman: Balfour Beatty Projects Ltd, 1985–88; Balfour Beatty Canada Ltd, 1986–89; Balfour Beatty Malaysia SND BYD, 1986–88; Balfour Beatty Inc., 1987–89; Heery Internat. Inc. USA, 1987–89; Amey plc, 1989–2000; Amey Construction Ltd, 1989–98; Amey Facilities Mgt Ltd, 1990–98; Amey Homes Ltd, 1991–98; Amey Building Ltd, 1992–98; Amey Railways Ltd, 1996–98. Chairman: Energy Power Resources, 1997–2003; Courtenay Develts, 1998–2004; BPO Gp, 1999–2004; Oxford Radcliffe Hospitals NHS Trust, 2000–03; Vectra Gp, 2003–07; BPOSS Ltd, 2005–. Non-exec. Dir, Volvere plc, 2002–. Mem., Nat. Council, 1994–2000, Chm., Southern Regl Council, 1995–97, CBI. Mem. Bd, British Road Fedn, 1993–98. Indep. Gov., Oxford Brookes Univ., 1997–2005 (Chm., Audit Cttee, 1999–2005); Member: Med. Scis Bd, Oxford Univ., 2000–03; Inst. of Cancer Res., 2004 (Dep. Chm., Develt Bd, 2004–). Vice Pres. and Mem. Council, Lighthouse Club (Construction Ind. Charity), 1991– (Chm., 1998–2001); Chairman: Oxford Radcliffe Charities and Radcliffe Med. Foundn, 2000–03; Oxford Radcliffe Hospitals NHS Trust Cancer Campaign, 2007–. Chm. Trustees, Occtopus, 2004–; Trustee, Ashley (formerly Jane Ashley) Charitable Trust, 1995–; Patron: Mulberry Bush Sch. (for care and educn of troubled children), 1998–; Dorchester Abbey Appeal, 1999–; Vice-Patron, Purley Park Trust, 2003–07. FRSA 1993. Freeman, City of London, 1979; Liveryman, and Mem. Ct, Paviors' Co., 1979–. DUniv Oxford Brookes, 2006. *Publications:* contrib. numerous technical and commercial papers to jls and presentations on wide range of business topics. *Recreations:* boating, shooting, dogs, pyrotechnics. *Address:* Burcot Grange, Burcot, Oxon OX14 3DJ. *T:* (01865) 407106, *Fax:* (01865) 409969; 52 Upper Montagu Street, W1H 1SJ. *T:* and *Fax:* (020) 7569 8595; *e-mail:* neil@bpogroup.com. *Clubs:* Royal Automobile; Leander (Henley); Clifton Hampton Cricket; Henley Rugby.

ASHLEY-COOPER, family name of **Earl of Shaftesbury**.

ASHLEY-MILLER, Dr Michael, CBE 1995; DPH; FFPH; FRCPE; FRCP; Secretary, Nuffield Provincial Hospitals Trust, London, 1986–95; *b* 1 Dec. 1930; *s* of Cyril and Marjorie Ashley-Miller; *m* 1958, Yvonne Townend; three *d*. *Educ:* Charterhouse; Oxford Univ.; King's Coll. Hosp.; London Sch. of Hygiene and Tropical Med. MA Oxon; BM BCh; DObstRCOG. FFPH (FFCM 1977); FRCPE 1985; FRCP 1990. Ho. Surg., Ho. Phys., King's Coll. Hosp., 1956–57; SMO, Dulwich Hosp., 1957; MO/SMO, RAF, 1958–61; SMO, IoW CC, 1961–64; MO/SMO, MRC (HQ Staff), 1964–74; PMO, SPMO, Scottish Home and Health Dept, 1974–86. Mem. Council, RSocMed, 1998–2002 (Pres., Gen. Practice Sect., 1994–95). Mem. Council, Stroke Assoc., 1997–2006. Hon. MRCP 1986; Hon. FRCGP 1994. FRSocMed 1996. *Publications:* (contrib.) Textbook of Public Health, Vol. III, 1985; (ed jtly) Screening for Risk of Coronary Heart Disease, 1987. *Recreations:* theatre, reading, visiting cathedrals. *T:* (020) 7272 7017. *Club:* Royal Society of Medicine.

ASHLEY-SMITH, Jonathan, PhD; FMA; Secretary General, International Institute for Conservation, 2003–06; *b* 25 Aug. 1946; *s* of Ewart Trist and Marian Tanfield Ashley-Smith; *m* 1967, Diane Louise (*née* Wagland); one *s* one *d*. *Educ:* Sutton Valence Public Sch.; Bristol Univ. (BSc (Hons), PhD). FMA 1988. Post-doctoral research, Cambridge Univ., 1970–72; Victoria and Albert Museum, 1973–2004: Hd of Conservation, 1977–2002; Sen. Res. Fellow (Conservation Studies), 2002–04. Leverhulme Fellow, 1995; Sen. Mem., Wolfson Coll., Cambridge, 1995. Member: UKIC, 1974– (Accredited Mem., 1999; Mem., Exec Cttee, 1978–; Vice-Chm., 1980; Chm., 1983–84); Crafts Council, 1980–83 (Mem., Conservation Cttee, 1978–83); Council for Care of Churches Conservation Cttee, 1978–85; Board of Governors, London Coll. of Furniture, 1983–85. Vis. Prof., RCA, 1999. FRSC 1987; FIIC 1985; Hon. FRCA 1992; FRSA 2000. Scientific Editor, Science for Conservators (Crafts Council series), 1983–84. Plowden Medal, Royal Patentholders Assoc., 2000. *Publications:* Risk Assessment for Object Conservation, 1999; articles in learned jls on organometallic chemistry, conservation risk, spectroscopy and scientific examination of art objects. *Recreations:* loud music, strong cider. *Address:* *e-mail:* ashley@jonsmith.demon.co.uk.

ASHMOLE, (Harold) David; Head of Boys, London Studio Centre, since 2002; Senior Principal Dancer, 1984–93, Guest Artist, since 1994, Australian Ballet; *b* 31 Oct. 1949; *s* of Richard Thomas Ashmole and Edith Ashmole. *Educ:* Sandye Place, Beds; Royal Ballet Sch.; Grad. Dip Visual and Performing Arts, Melbourne Univ. Solo Seal, Royal Acad. of Dancing; ARAD. Joined Royal Ballet Co., 1968; Soloist, 1972; Principal, 1975; transf. to Sadler's Wells Royal Ballet, 1976, Sen. Principal, 1978–84; Dir, Australian Ballet Foundn, 1995–99. Lectr in Classical Dance, Victorian Coll. of the Arts, Univ. of Melbourne,

1998–2001; Guest Teacher: London Studio Centre, 1999–2000, 2001; K Ballet UK, 2000; Singapore Dance Theatre, 2000; Birmingham Royal Ballet, 2001–; Winter Sch., Universal Ballet Acad., Korea, 2006. Appeared in: Dame Alicia Markova's Master Classes, BBC Television, 1980; Maina Gielgud's Steps, Notes and Squeaks, Aberdeen Internat. Festival, 1981. Guest appearances with Scottish Ballet, 1981, with Bolshoi (for UNESCO Gala), 1986, with Sadler's Wells Royal Ballet at Royal Opera House, 1986 (season) and in Japan, Germany, S Africa and France. *Classical ballets include:* La Bayadère, Coppélia, Daphnis and Chloe, Giselle, Nutcracker, Raymonda, The Seasons, Sleeping Beauty, Swan Lake, La Sylphide; *other ballets include:* (choreography by Ashton): Cinderella, The Two Pigeons, La Fille Mal Gardée, Les Rendezvous, The Dream, Lament of the Waves, Symphonic Variations, Birthday Offering; (Balanchine): Apollo, Prodigal Son, Serenade, The Four Temperaments, Agon, Tchaikovsky Pas de Deux; (Béjart): Gaîté Parisienne, Webern Opus 5, Songs of a Wayfarer, Le Concours; (Bintley): Night Moves, Homage to Chopin, The Swan of Tuonela; (Cranko): Brouillards, Pineapple Poll, The Taming of the Shrew, Onegin; (Darrell): The Tales of Hoffmann; (de Valois): Checkmate, The Rake's Progress; (Fokine): Les Sylphides, Petrushka; (Hynd): Papillon; (Lander): Etudes; (Lifar): Suite en Blanc; (MacMillan): Concerto, Elite Syncopations, Romeo and Juliet, Quartet, Song of the Earth, Symphony; (Massine): La Boutique Fantasque; (Miller-Ashmole): Snugglepot-and-Cuddlepie; (Nijinska): Les Biches; (Nureyev): Don Quixote; (Robbins): Dances at a Gathering, Requiem Canticles, In the Night, Concert; (Seymour): Intimate Letters, Rashomon; (Samsova): Paquita; (Tetley): Gemini, Laborintus, Orpheus; (van Manen): Grosse Fugue, 5 Tangos; (Wright): Summertide; (Prokovsky): The Three Musketeers; (Seregi): Spartacus. *Recreations:* Moorcroft pottery collection, gardening, fishing. *Address:* London Studio Centre, 42–50 York Way, N1 9AB.

ASHMORE, Dr Alick, CBE 1979; Director, Daresbury Laboratory, Science Research Council, 1970–81; *b* 7 Nov. 1920; *s* of Frank Owen Ashmore and Beatrice Maud Swindells; *m* 1947, Eileen Elsie Fuller; two *s* three *d*. *Educ:* King Edward VII Sch., Lytham; King's Coll., London. Experimental Officer, RRDE, Malvern, 1941–47; Lecturer in Physics, University of Liverpool, 1947–59; Queen Mary Coll., London: Reader in Experimental Physics, 1960–64; Prof. of Nuclear Physics, 1964–70, also Head of Physics Dept, 1968–70. *Publications:* research publications on nuclear and elementary-particle physics in Proc. Phys. Soc., Nuclear Physics, Physical Review. *Recreations:* walking, travel. *Address:* Farnham House, Hesket Newmarket, Wigton, Cumbria CA7 8JG. *T:* (01697) 478414.

ASHMORE, Admiral of the Fleet Sir Edward Beckwith, GCB 1974 (KCB 1971; CB 1966); DSC 1942; *b* 11 Dec. 1919; *er s* of late Vice-Admiral L. H. Ashmore, CB, DSO and late Tamara Vasilevna Schutt, St Petersburg; *m* 1942, Elizabeth Mary Doveton Sturdee, *d* of late Rear-Admiral Sir Lionel Sturdee, 2nd Bt, CBE; one *s* one *d* (and one *d* decd). *Educ:* RNC, Dartmouth. Served HMS Birmingham, Jupiter, Middleton, 1938–42; qualified in Signals, 1943; Staff of C-in-C Home Fleet, Flag Lieut, 4th Cruiser Sqdn, 1944–45; qualified Interpreter in Russian, 1946; Asst Naval Attaché, Moscow, 1946–47; Squadron Communications Officer, 3rd Aircraft Carrier Squadron, 1950; Commander 1950; comd HMS Alert, 1952–53; Captain 1955; Chief Signal Officer, AFNORTH, 1956; Captain (F) 6th Frigate Sqdn, and CO HMS Blackpool, 1958; Director of Plans, Admiralty and Min. of Defence, 1960–62; Commander British Forces Caribbean Area, 1963–64; Rear-Adm., 1965; Asst Chief of the Defence Staff, Signals, 1965–67; Flag Officer, Second-in-Command, Far East Fleet, 1967–68; Vice-Adm. 1968; Vice-Chief, Naval Staff, 1969–71; Adm. 1970; C-in-C Western Fleet, Sept.-Oct. 1971; C-in-C, Fleet, 1971–74; Chief of Naval Staff and First Sea Lord, 1974–77; First and Principal Naval Aide-de-Camp to the Queen, 1974–77; CDS, Feb.-Aug. 1977. Dir, Racal Electronics plc, 1978–97. Gov., Suttons Hosp. in Charterhouse, 1976–2000. *Publication:* The Battle and the Breeze: the naval reminiscences of Admiral of the Fleet Sir Edward Ashmore, 1997. *Recreations:* usual.

See also Sir John Sykes, Bt.

ASHMORE, Gillian Margaret; Recording Clerk, Society of Friends (Quakers), since 2007; *b* 14 Oct. 1949; *d* of John Oxenham and Joan Oxenham; *m* 1971, Frederick Scott Ashmore; two *s* two *d*. *Educ:* Walthamstow Hall, Sevenoaks; Winchester Co. High Sch. for Girls; Newnham Coll., Cambridge (BA Hons Hist.). Depts of the Envmt and Tspt, 1971–86; seconded to Housing Corp., 1974; Dep. Dir, Enterprise and Deregulation Unit, Dept of Employment, 1986–87, then DTI, 1987–89; Head, Central Finance Div., Dept of Transport, 1990–92; Dir, Privatisation Studies, BRB, 1992–94; Regl Dir, Govt Office for SE, 1994–98; Principal, Mulberry Consulting, 1999–2007. Chief Exec., EOC, 2001–02. Chair: Kingston Victim Support, 1998–2001; Refugee Housing Assoc., 1999–2006; Exec. Dir, Fostering Network, 2003; Trustee: Metropolitan Housing Trust, then Metropolitan Housing Partnership, 1999–2006; Victim Support London, 1999–2001. Gov., Richmond Adult and Community Coll., 2000–06. Associate, Newnham Coll., Cambridge, 1998–. FRSA 1995. *Recreations:* Society of Friends, novels, history, talking. *Address:* 47 Lower Teddington Road, Hampton Wick, Kingston, Surrey KT1 4HQ.

ASHMORE, Prof. Jonathan Felix, PhD; FRS 1996; Bernard Katz Professor of Biophysics, University College London, since 1996; *b* 16 April 1948; *s* of late Eric Peter Ashmore, theatre director, and Rosalie Sylvia Crutchley, actress; *m* 1974, Sonia Elizabeth Newby; one *s* one *d*. *Educ:* Westminster; Univ. of Sussex (BSc 1st cl. Mathematical Physics); Imperial Coll., London (PhD); University College London (MSc Physiology). Vis. Scientist, Internat. Centre for Theoretical Physics, Trieste, Italy, 1971–72; Nuffield Biological Scholar, 1972–74; Res. Asst, Dept of Biophysics, UCL, 1974–77; Fulbright Scholar, and Vis. Physiologist, Ophthalmology Dept, Univ. of California, San Francisco, 1977–80; Lectr, Univ. of Sussex, 1980–83; Lectr, 1983–88, Reader in Physiology, 1988–93, Prof. of Biophysics, 1993–96, Univ. of Bristol; Dir, UCL Ear Inst., 2004. G. L. Brown Lectr, Physiological Soc., 1992. Chief Scientific Advr, Defeating Deafness, subseq. Deafness Res. UK, 2002–07. Acted in film, A Kid for Two Farthings, 1955. FMedSci 2001. *Publications:* contribs to learned jls on cellular basis of hearing. *Recreation:* travel. *Address:* Department of Physiology, University College London, Gower Street, WC1E 6BT. *T:* (020) 7679 6080, *Fax:* (020) 7387 6368; *e-mail:* j.ashmore@ucl.ac.uk.

ASHRAWI, Hanan; Media Director and spokesperson, Arab League, since 2001; Member, Palestinian Legislative Council, since 1996; *b* 1946; *m* Emile Ashrawi; two *d*. *Educ:* American Univ., Beirut; Univ. of Virginia. Prof. of English Literature, Chm. of English Dept, and Dean of Arts, Birzeit Univ., West Bank, 1973–90; Dir Gen., Human Rights Instn, Jerusalem. Joined Fatah, PLO; official spokesperson, Palestinian Delegn, 1991–93; Mem., and former Head, Palestinian Independent Commn for Palestinian Republic; Minister of Higher Educn, Palestinian Legislative Council, 1996–98. *Publications:* A Passion for Peace, 1994; This Side of Peace, 1995. *Address:* c/o Palestinian Legislative Council, Jerusalem, West Bank, via Israel.

ASHTON, family name of **Baron Ashton of Hyde**.

ASHTON OF HYDE, 4th Baron *cr* 1911; **Thomas Henry Ashton;** Chief Executive Officer: Faraday Underwriting Ltd, since 2005 (Director, since 1999); Faraday Reinsurance Co. Ltd, since 2005 (Director, since 2002); *b* 18 July 1958; *s* of 3rd Baron Ashton of Hyde and of Pauline Trewlove Ashton (*née* Brackenbury); *S* father, 2008; *m* 1987, Emma Louise, *d* of Colin Allinson; four *d*. *Educ:* Eton; Trinity Coll., Oxford (BA 1980). Late Lt Royal Hussars (PWO), Royal Wessex Yeo. Vice Pres., Guy Carpenter & Co., Inc., 1990–92; Director: C. T. Bowring Reinsurance Ltd, 1992–93; D. P. Mann Ltd, 1996–99. Jt Master, Heythrop Hunt, 2007–. *Heir:* *b* Hon. John Edward Ashton, *b* 30 Jan. 1966. *Address:* Broadwell Hill, Moreton-in-Marsh, Glos GL56 0UD. *Club:* Boodle's.

ASHTON OF UPHOLLAND, Baroness *cr* 1999 (Life Peer), of St Albans in the county of Hertfordshire; **Catherine Margaret Ashton;** PC 2006; Member, European Commission, since 2008; *b* 20 March 1956; *d* of late Harold and Clare Margaret Ashton; *m* 1988, Peter Jon Kellner, *qv*; one *s* one *d*. *Educ:* Upholland Grammar Sch.; Bedford Coll., Univ. of London (BSc 1977). Admin. Sec., CND, 1977–79; Business Manager, The Coverdale Orgn, 1979–81; Dir of Public Affairs, BITC, 1983–89; freelance policy advr, 1989–99; on secondment from London First to Home Office, 1998–2001. Chm., E and N Herts, subseq. Herts, HA, 1998–2001. Parliamentary Under-Secretary of State: DFES, 2001–04; DCA, subseq. MoJ, 2004–07; Leader of the H of L, 2007–08. Vice Pres., Nat. Council for One-Parent Families. Trustee, Verulamium Mus. Chm. Governors, Spencer Jun. Sch., 1995–2001. *Recreations:* theatre, family. *Address:* European Commission, 200 Rue de la Loi, 1049 Brussels, Belgium. *Club:* Royal Commonwealth Society.

ASHTON, Rt Rev. Cyril Guy; *see* Doncaster, Bishop Suffragan of.

ASHTON, George Arthur, CEng; FIMechE; engineering and management consultant, retired; *b* 27 Nov. 1921; *s* of Lewis and Mary Ashton; *m* 1st, 1948, Joan Rutter (decd); one *s*; 2nd, 1978, Pauline Jennifer Margett. *Educ:* Llanidloes Grammar Sch.; Birmingham Central Tech. Coll. Student Engrg Apprentice, Austin Motor Co., 1939–42. HM Forces, 1943–47 (Major, REME). Works Dir, Tubes Ltd, 1958; Tech. Dir, 1962, Dep. Man. Dir, 1966, TI Steel Tube Div.; Dir, Tube Investments, 1969; Man. Dir, Machine Div., 1974, Technical Dir and Business Area Chm., 1978–84, TI Group plc; Chm., Seamless Tubes Ltd, 1983–86. Dir, A. Lee & Sons plc, 1981–91. Consultant, Welsh Develt Agency, 1984–87. Pres., BISPA, 1974–75; Vice-Pres., AMTRI, 1986– (Chm. Council, 1982–86). FRSA 1981. *Recreation:* theatre-going. *Address:* Barn Cottage, Longford, Ashbourne, Derbys DE6 3DT. *T:* (01335) 330561. *Club:* Royal Over-Seas League.

ASHTON, John; Foreign Secretary's Special Representative for Climate Change, Foreign and Commonwealth Office, since 2006; *b* 7 Nov. 1956; *s* of Prof. John Ashton and Prof. Heather Ashton; *m* 1983, Kao Fengning, (Judy); one *s*. *Educ:* Royal Grammar Sch., Newcastle upon Tyne; St John's Coll., Cambridge (MA). Radio Astronomy Gp, New Cavendish Lab., Cambridge, 1977–78; FCO 1978; Science Officer, Peking, 1981–84; Head, China Section, FCO, 1984–86; Cabinet Office, 1986–88; Rome, 1988–93; Dep. Political Advr to Governor, Hong Kong, 1993–97; Vis. Fellow, Green Coll., Oxford, 1997–98; Hd of Envmt, Sci. and Energy, then Envmt Policy, Dept, FCO, 1998–2002; Dir for Strategic Partnerships, LEAD Internat., 2002–04; Founder and Chief Exec., E3G (Third Generation Environmentalism), 2004–06. Vis. Prof., Imperial Coll. London, 2006–. Member, Advisory Board: Climate Inst., Washington, 1998–; Climate Care, 2002–; Climate Change Capital, 2003–; Bren Sch. of Envmtl Sci. and Mgt, Univ. of California, 2006–. FRSA; Mem., ICA. *Recreations:* cricket, nature. *Address:* Foreign and Commonwealth Office, King Charles Street, SW1A 2AH. *Clubs:* MCC; Kew Cricket; Kowloon Cricket.

ASHTON, Prof. John Richard, CBE 2000; Professor of Public Health Policy and Strategy, University of Liverpool, since 1993; Director of Public Health and County Medical Officer, Cumbria Primary Care Trust and Cumbria County Council, since 2007; *b* Liverpool, 27 May 1947; *s* of Edward Ashton and Irene Ashton (*née* Pettit); *m* 1st, 1968, Pamela Scott (marr. diss. 2001); three *s*; 2nd, 2004, Catherine Benedicte, (Maggi), Morris; one *s*, and two step *s*. *Educ:* Quarry Bank High Sch., Liverpool; Univ. of Newcastle upon Tyne (MB BS 1970); London Sch. of Hygiene and Trop. Medicine (MSc Soc. Med. 1978). FFPHM 1986; FRCPsych 1993; MFFP 1993; FRCPE 2003; FRCP 2004. House physician and surgeon, Newcastle Univ. Hosps, 1970–71; Registrar in Psychiatry and Family Practitioner, Newcastle, 1971–75; Lectr in Primary Care, Southampton Univ., 1975–76; Sen. Lectr in Preventive Medicine, LSHTM, 1980–82; Sen. Lectr in Public Health, Univ. of Liverpool, 1983–93; Regional Director of Public Health and Regional Medical Officer: Mersey, 1993–94; Govt Office for NW (formerly NW RHA, then NW Region, NHS Exec., DoH), 1994–2006. Visiting Professor: Valencia Inst. Public Health, 1988; Liverpool John Moores Univ., 1998; Med. Sch., Univ. of Manchester, 2001–; Univ. of Central Lancs, 2004–; Univ. of Cumbria, 2008–; Professorial Fellow, Liverpool Sch. of Trop. Medicine, 1994; Fellow, Liverpool John Moores Univ., 2003. Advr on Urban Health, Health Policy, Public Health Educn and Violence, WHO; Neighbourhood Renewal Advr to UK govt. Member: Liverpool Med. Instn, 1990–; Manchester Med. Soc., 1995–. Member: John Snow Soc.; Duncan Soc., 1998–; Chm., Woolton Soc., 2001–03. Ed., Jl of Epidemiology and Community Health, 1997–2008. *Publications:* Everyday Psychiatry, 1980; The New Public Health, 1988; Esmedune 2000, 1988; Healthy Cities, 1992; (ed) The Epidemiological Imagination, 1994; The Pool of Life, 1997; contrib. articles on medical, public health and social issues. *Recreations:* Liverpool FC, fell walking, cycling, keeping chickens, dogs, alpacas, contributing to regenerating Liverpool. *Address:* 8 Church Road, Much Woolton, Liverpool L25 5JF. *T:* (0151) 428 1563. *Club:* Athenæum (Liverpool).

ASHTON, Joseph William, OBE 2007; journalist; *b* 9 Oct. 1933; *s* of Arthur and Nellie Ashton, Sheffield; *m* 1957, Margaret Patricia Lee; one *d*. *Educ:* High Storrs Grammar Sch.; Rotherham Technical Coll. Engineering Apprentice, 1949–54; RAF National Service, 1954–56; Cost Control Design Engineer, 1956–68; Sheffield City Councillor, 1962–69. MP (Lab) Bassetlaw Div. of Notts, Nov. 1968–2001. PPS to Sec. of State for Energy, formerly Sec. of State for Industry, 1975–76; an Asst Govt Whip, 1976–77; Opposition Spokesman on Energy, 1979–81. Member, Select Committee: on Trade and Industry, 1987–92; on Home Affairs, 1989–92; on Nat. Heritage, 1992–97; on Modernising the House, 1997–98; Chm., Parly All-Party Football Cttee, 1992–2001. Dir, Sheffield Wednesday, 1990–99. Founder and Chm., Assoc. of Former Members of Parliament, 2001–. Columnist for: Sheffield Star, 1970–75, 1979–80, 1990–91; Labour Weekly, 1971–82; Daily Star, 1979–87; Sunday People, 1987–88; Plus magazine, 1988–89. Columnist of the Year, What the Papers Say, Granada TV, 1984. *Publications:* Grass Roots, 1977; A Majority of One (stage play), 1981; Red Rose Blues (memoirs), 2000. *Recreations:* football, reading, do-it-yourself, motoring, travel, films, theatre. *Address:* 16 Ranmoor Park Road, Sheffield S10 3GX. *T:* (0114) 230 7175.

ASHTON, Prof. Robert, PhD; Professor of English History, University of East Anglia, 1963–89, now Emeritus; *b* 21 July 1924; *s* of late Joseph and late Edith F. Ashton; *m* 1946, Margaret Alice Sedgwick; two *d*. *Educ:* Magdalen Coll. Sch., Oxford; University Coll., Southampton (1942–43, 1946–49); London Sch. of Economics (1949–52). BA 1st Cl. hons (London) 1949; PhD (London) 1953. Asst Lecturer in Economic History, Univ. of Nottingham, 1952; Lecturer, 1954; Senior Lecturer, 1961; Vis. Associate Prof. in History, Univ. of California, Berkeley, 1962–63; Prof. of English History, 1963, and Dean of Sch.

of English Studies, 1964–67, Univ. of East Anglia. Vis. Fellow, All Souls Coll., Oxford, 1973–74 and 1987; James Ford Special Lectr in History, Oxford, 1982; Leverhulme Emeritus Fellow, 1989–91. FRHistS 1960 (Vice-Pres., 1983–86). *Publications:* The Crown and the Money Market, 1603–1640, 1960; Charles I and the City, in Essays in the Economic and Social History of Tudor and Stuart England in honour of R. H. Tawney (ed F. J. Fisher), 1961; James I by his Contemporaries, 1969; The Civil War and the Class Struggle, in The English Civil War and After 1642–1658 (ed R. H. Parry), 1970; The English Civil War: Conservatism and Revolution 1603–49, 1978, 2nd edn 1989; The City and the Court 1603–1643, 1979; Reformation and Revolution 1558–1660, 1984; Counter-Revolution: the second Civil War and its origins, 1646–8, 1994; articles in learned periodicals. *Recreations:* music, looking at old buildings, exploring Italy and things Italian, wine. *Address:* The Manor House, Brundall, Norwich NR13 5JY. *T:* (01603) 713368.

ASHTON, Robin James; Chief Executive, London Scottish Bank plc, since 2007; *b* 19 Jan. 1958; *s* of late Frederick James Ashton and of Florence Mary Ashton; *m* 1st, 1985, Elizabeth Miles (marr. diss. 2002); one *s* one *d;* 2nd, 2004, Jasna Mozetič; one *s. Educ:* Bradford Grammar Sch.; Durham Univ. (BA Hons Econs and Law). ACA. Coopers & Lybrand, 1979–83; Finance Dir, Provident Insurance plc, 1983–85; Finance Dir and Dep. Man. Dir, H. T. Greenwood Ltd, 1986–88; Man. Dir, Provident Investments Ltd, 1989; Provident Financial plc: Gp Treas., 1989–93; Finance Dir, 1993–99; Dep. Chief Exec., 1999–2001; Chief Exec., 2001–06. *Address:* London Scottish Bank plc, 201 Deansgate, Manchester M3 3NW.

ASHTON, Prof. Rosemary Doreen, OBE 1999; FRSL; FBA 2000; Quain Professor of English Language and Literature, University College London, since 2002; *b* 11 April 1947; *d* of late David Thomson and of Doreen Sidley Thomson (*née* Rose); *m* 1971, Gerard Ashton (*d* 1999); two *s* one *d. Educ:* Univ. of Aberdeen (MA Hons English and German 1969); Newnham Coll., Cambridge (PhD 1974). Temp. Lectr, English Dept, Univ. of Birmingham, 1973–74; Lectr, 1974–86, Reader, 1986–91, Prof., 1991–2002, English Dept, UCL. FRSL 1999; Founding Fellow, English Assoc., 1999. FRSA 2002. *Publications:* The German Idea: four English writers and the reception of German thought 1800–1860, 1980; Little Germany: exile and asylum in Victorian England, 1986; The Mill on the Floss: a natural history, 1990; G. H. Lewes: a life, 1991; The Life of Samuel Taylor Coleridge: a critical biography, 1996; George Eliot: a life, 1996; Thomas and Jane Carlyle: portrait of a marriage, 2002; 142 Strand: a radical address in Victorian London, 2006. *Recreations:* gardening, table tennis, listening to music. *Address:* English Department, University College London, Gower Street, WC1E 6BT. *T:* (020) 7679 3143.

ASHTON, Ruth Mary, (Mrs E. F. Henschel), OBE 1991; RN, RM, MTD; non-executive Director and Vice-Chairman, Bromley Primary Care NHS Trust, 2001–07; *b* 27 March 1939; *d* of Leigh Perry Ashton and Marion Lucy Ashton (*née* Tryon); *m* 1984, E. Fred Henschel. *Educ:* Kenya High Sch. for Girls; Clarendon Sch. (lately Abergele); London Hosp. and Queen Mother's Hosp., Glasgow; High Coombe Midwife Teachers' Training College (RN 1964; RM 1967; MTD 1970). Staff Midwife and Midwifery Sister, Queen Mother's Hosp., Glasgow, 1967–69; Nursing Officer and Midwifery Tutor, King's College Hosp., 1971–75; Tutor, 1975–79, Professional Officer, 1979, Gen. Sec., 1980–94, Royal College of Midwives. Non-executive Director: Optimum Health Services NHS Trust, 1994–99; Community Health S London NHS Trust, 1999–2000. Chm., Workforce Develt Confedn, NHS SE London, 2002–06. Temp. Advr on Midwifery, WHO, 1995. Treas., Internat. Confedn of Midwives, 1997–2002. Temp. Prof. March of Dimes, Los Angeles, 1982. Lay Mem., London Deanery Sch. of Gen. Practice Bd, 2007–. ACIArb 1995. OStJ 1988. *Publications:* midwifery related articles. *Recreations:* gardening, sailing, travel. *Address:* c/o National Westminster Bank, PO Box 192, 116 Fenchurch Street, EC3M 5AN. *T:* (home) (020) 8851 7403; *e-mail:* ruhens@tiscali.co.uk.

ASHTON, William Michael Allingham, MBE 1978; Musical Director, National Youth Jazz Orchestra of Great Britain, since 1968; *b* Blackpool, 6 Dec. 1936; *s* of Eric Sandiford Ashton and Zilla Dorothea (*née* Miles); *m* 1966, Kay Carol Watkins; two *s* one *d. Educ:* Rossall Sch., Fleetwood; St Peter's Coll., Oxford (BA Hons Mod. Langs 1961; DipEd 1962). Nat. Service, RAF, 1955–57. Professional musician, 1962–63; teacher of French in London schs, 1963–73. Founded London Schs Jazz Orch., 1965; became Nat. Youth Jazz Orch., 1968. Editor, News from NYJO, 1988–. Appeared in Royal Variety Perf., 1978; visits to America, Russia, Australasia, France, Poland, Portugal, Germany, Bulgaria, Turkey, Malta, Spain, Italy, etc.; appearances at festivals, film premières, etc. Numerous recordings. Has written over 60 recorded songs, incl. Wait and See, Much Too Much, It's Over, Accident Prone, Thought I'd Ask, Let's Settle Down, Why Don't They Write Songs Like This Any More?, Don't Go to Her. Member: Arts Sub-cttee, Internat. Year of the Child, 1979; Cttee, Assoc. British Jazz Musicians, 1988–. Fellow, City of Leeds Coll. of Music, 1995. BP ABSA Award, 1991; Music Retailers Assoc. Annual Awards for Excellence, 1984, 1990; NYJO voted Best British Big Band, British Jazz Awards, 1993, 1995, 1998, 2002; BBC R2 Award for services to British jazz, 1995; Silver Medal for Jazz, Musicians' Co., 1996. *Recreations:* song writing, snorkelling, reading. *Address:* 11 Victor Road, Harrow, Middx HA2 6PT. *T:* (020) 8863 2717, *Fax:* (020) 8863 8685; *e-mail:* bill.ashton@virgin.net.

ASHTOWN, 7th Baron *cr* 1800; **Nigel Clive Cosby Trench,** KCMG 1976 (CMG 1966); HM Diplomatic Service, retired; *b* 27 Oct. 1916; *s* of Clive Newcome Trench (*d* 1964), *g s* of 2nd Baron, and Kathleen (*d* 1979), 2nd *d* of Major Ivar MacIvor, CIE; *S* cousin, 1990; *m* 1st, 1939, Marcelle Catherine Clotterbooke Patyn (*d* 1994); one *s;* 2nd, 1997, Mary, Princess of Pless, *d* of late Lt Col and Mrs R. G. E. Minchin. *Educ:* Eton; Univ. of Cambridge. Served in KRRC, 1940–46 (despatches). Appointed a Member of the Foreign (subseq. Diplomatic) Service, 1946; Lisbon, 1946; First Secretary, 1948; returned Foreign Office, 1949; First Secretary (Commercial), Lima, 1952; transf. Foreign Office, 1955; Counsellor, Tokyo, 1961; Counsellor, Washington, 1963; Cabinet Office, 1967; HM Ambassador to Korea, 1969–71; CS Selection Board, 1971–73; Ambassador to Portugal, 1974–76. Mem., Police, Prison and Fire Service Selection Bds, 1977–86. Sungrye Medal, Order of Diplomatic Service Merit (Korea), 1984. *Heir:* s Hon. Roderick Nigel Godolphin Trench [*b* 17 Nov. 1944; *m* 1st, 1967, Janet (*d* 1971), *d* of Harold Hamilton-Faulkner; one *s;* 2nd, 1973, Susan Barbara, *d* of L. F. Day, FRCS, DLO; one *d*].

ASHURST, (Kenneth William) Stewart; DL; Chief Executive and Clerk, Essex County Council, 1995–2005; Partner, Odgers Ray & Berndtson, 2006–07; *b* 19 May 1945; *s* of Kenneth Latham Ashurst, OBE and Helen Ferguson Ashurst (*née* Rae); *m* 1984, Catherine Mary Sample; two *s* one *d. Educ:* Royal Grammar Sch., Newcastle upon Tyne; King Edward VI Grammar Sch., Lichfield; Exeter Coll., Oxford Univ. (MA); Guildford Coll. of Law; Birmingham Univ. (MSocSc). Trainee solicitor, Leicester and Newcastle upon Tyne CBCs, 1967–68; Assistant Solicitor: Newcastle upon Tyne, 1968–71; Cumberland CC, 1972–73; Asst Co. Clerk, Cumbria CC, 1973–79; Dep. Co. Sec., 1979–81, Co. Solicitor and Dep. Co. Clerk, 1981–85, Suffolk CC; Dep. Chief Exec. and Clerk, Essex CC, 1985–94. Clerk to: Essex Police Authy, 1995–2002; Essex Fire Authy, 1998–2004;

Essex Lieutenancy, 1995–2004; River Crouch Harbour Authy, 1995–2004; Secretary: Lord Chancellor's Adv. Cttee in Essex, 1995–2004; Stansted Airport Consultative Cttee, 1995–2004 (Chm., 2007–); Mem., Essex TEC Bd, 1995–2001. Director: Disability Essex, 2005–07; Children's Legal Centre, Essex Univ., 2006–07. Nat. Chm., ACCE, 2003–04. Law Society: Council Mem., 1989–97; Chm., Local Govt Gp, 1986–87. Mem. Council, Industrial Soc., 1997–2001. Dir, Year of Opera and Musical Theatre, 1996–97. DL Essex, 2004. FCMI (FIMgt 1982). FRSA 1998. *Recreations:* wine, opera, food. *Address:* Oaklands Lodge, Valletta Close, Coval Park, Chelmsford, Essex CM1 2PT.

ASHURST, Stephen John; His Honour Judge Ashurst; a Circuit Judge, since 2004; Resident Judge, York Crown Court, since 2007; *b* 19 April 1957; *s* of John Anthony Ashurst and Doris Ashurst; *m* 1981, Deborah Ann Sherwin; one *s* one *d. Educ:* South Hunsley Sch., E Yorks; Univ. of Newcastle upon Tyne (LLB). Called to the Bar, Inner Temple, 1979; in practice as barrister, Leeds and Middlesbrough, 1979–2004; an Asst Recorder, 1994–98, Recorder, 1998–2004. Judicial Mem., N Yorks Probation Bd, 2006–. Hon. Recorder, City of York, 2008. *Recreation:* music. *Address:* York Crown Court, The Castle, York YO1 9WZ.

ASHWIN, Mary Christine; see Vitoria, M. C.

ASHWORTH, Prof. Alan, PhD; FRS 2008; Professor of Molecular Biology, Institute of Cancer Research, University of London, since 1997; Director, Breakthrough Breast Cancer Research Centre, since 1999; *b* 26 Aug. 1960; *s* of Arthur and Dorothy Ashworth; partner, Dr Amanda McGuigan. *Educ:* Thornleigh Salesian Coll., Bolton; Imperial Coll. London (BSc Hons 1981); UCL (PhD 1984). Gp Leader, 1988–, Chm., Section of Gene Function, 1997–99, Inst. Cancer Res. Mem., EMBO, 1999. FMedSci 2002. *Publications:* contribs to scientific jls. *Recreations:* cinema, theatre, reading, writing. *Address:* Breakthrough Breast Cancer Research Centre, Institute of Cancer Research, 237 Fulham Road, SW3 6JB; *e-mail:* alan.ashworth@icr.ac.uk.

ASHWORTH, Prof. Andrew John, PhD, DCL; FBA 1993; Vinerian Professor of English Law, University of Oxford, since 1997; Fellow of All Souls College, Oxford, since 1997; *b* 11 Oct. 1947; *s* of late Clifford Ashworth and Amy Ashworth (*née* Ogden); *m* 1st, 1971, Gillian Frisby (marr. diss. 2002); two *d;* 2nd, 2006, Veronica Bagnall. *Educ:* London Sch. of Economics (LLB 1968); New Coll., Oxford (BCL 1970; DCL 1993); Manchester Univ. (PhD 1973). Lectr, then Sen. Lectr, in Law, Manchester Univ., 1970–78; Fellow and Tutor in Law, Worcester Coll., Oxford, 1978–88; Edmund-Davies Prof. of Criminal Law and Criminal Justice, KCL, 1988–97. Mem., Sentencing Adv. Panel, 1999–. Editor, Criminal Law Rev., 1975–99. Hon. QC 1997. Hon. LLD De Montfort, 1998; Hon. DJur Uppsala, 2003. *Publications:* Sentencing and Penal Policy, 1983; Principles of Criminal Law, 1991, 5th edn 2006; Sentencing and Criminal Justice, 1992, 4th edn 2005; The Criminal Process, 1994, 3rd edn (with Mike Redmayne) 2005; (with Ben Emmerson) Human Rights and Criminal Justice, 2001, 2nd edn 2007; Human Rights, Serious Crime and Criminal Procedure, 2002. *Recreations:* bridge, travel. *Address:* All Souls College, Oxford OX1 4AL.

ASHWORTH, Anne Mary Catherine; Assistant Editor (Property), The Times, since 2006; *b* 13 June 1954; *d* of Peter Ashworth and Joan Ashworth (*née* Kay); *m* 1985, Tom Maddocks; one *s. Educ:* Ursuline Convent High Sch., Wimbledon; King's Coll. London (BA Hons French and German). Reporter: Sunday Express, 1982–86; Today, 1986; Daily Mail, 1986–87; Personal Finance Editor: Mail on Sunday, 1987–94; The Times, 1994–2006. *Recreations:* art, architecture, cinema. *Address:* The Times, Pennington Street, E98 1TA. *T:* (020) 7782 5083; *e-mail:* anne.ashworth@thetimes.co.uk.

ASHWORTH, Auriol, (Lady Ashworth); see Stevens, A.

ASHWORTH, Prof. Graham William, CBE 1980; DL; Visiting Professor: of Environmental Policy, University of Salford, since 2004; International Baptist Theological Seminary, Prague, since 2003; *b* 14 July 1935; *s* of Frederick William Ashworth and Ivy Alice Ashworth; *m* 1960, Gwyneth Mai Morgan-Jones; three *d. Educ:* Devonport High Sch., Plymouth; Univ. of Liverpool (Master of Civic Design, BArch). RIBA, PPRTPI, FRSA, FInstEnvSci, FCMI. LCC (Hook New Town Project), 1959–61; consultancy with Graeme Shankland, 1961–64; architect to Civic Trust, 1964–65; Dir, Civic Trust for North-West, 1965–73 (Chm., Exec. Cttee, 1973–87); Prof. of Urban Envmtl Studies, Univ. of Salford, 1973–87; Director: Univ. of Salford Environmental Inst., 1978–87; CAMPUS (Campaign to Promote Univ. of Salford), 1981–87; Dir Gen., Keep Britain Tidy, then Tidy Britain, Gp, 1987–2000. Chairman: Going for Green, 1994–2000; World of Glass, 2000–; Envmtl Campaigns, 2000–03. Member: Skeffington Cttee on Public Participation in Planning, 1969; North-West Adv. Council of BBC, 1970–75 (Chm.); NW Economic Planning Council (and Sub-gp Chm.), 1968–79; Countryside Commn, 1974–77; Merseyside Urban Develt Corp., 1981–92; (non-exec.) North Western Electricity Bd, 1985–88; Chairman: Ravenhead Renaissance, 1988–2002; Rural Recovery Trust, 2002–04. Governor, Northern Baptist Coll., 1966–82; President: RTPI, 1973–74; Foundn for Envmtl Educn, 1988–2004 (Pres., 1996–2004); Chm., Instn of Environmental Sciences, 1980–82. Member: Council, St George's House, Windsor, 1982–88; Council, Baptist Union, 1983– (Pres., 2000–01). Trustee, Manchester Mus. of Science and Industry, 1988–90. Editor, Internat. Jl of Environmental Educn, 1981–2001. DL Lancs, 1991. *Publications:* An Encyclopædia of Planning, 1973; Britain in Bloom, 1991; The Role of Local Government in Environmental Protection, 1992. *Recreations:* gardening, painting, church and social work. *Address:* Spring House, Preston New Road, Samlesbury, Preston PR5 0UP; *e-mail:* g_ashworth@btconnect.com. *Club:* Athenæum.

ASHWORTH, Ian Edward; Planning Inspector, Department of the Environment, 1987–95; *b* 3 March 1930; *s* of late William Holt and Cicely Ashworth, Rochdale; *m* Pauline, *er d* of late Maurice James Heddle, MBE, JP, and Gladys Heddle, Westcliff-on-Sea; two *s* one *d. Educ:* Manchester Grammar Sch.; The Queen's Coll., Oxford (BCL, MA). Admitted Solicitor, 1956; FGA 1983. Asst Solicitor, Rochdale, 1956–58; Dep. Town Clerk, Dep. Clerk of Peace, Canterbury, 1958–63; Town Clerk, Clerk of Peace, Deal, 1963–66; Town Clerk, Rugby, 1966–70; Circuit Administrator, Western Circuit, Lord Chancellor's Dept (Under Sec.), 1970–87. *Recreations:* music, gemmology, gardening. *Address:* Westdale Edge, Beer Road, Seaton, Devon EX12 2PT. *T:* (01297) 21212. *Club:* Oxford and Cambridge.

ASHWORTH, Sir John (Michael), Kt 2008; DSc; FIBiol; Chairman, Barts and the London NHS Trust, 2003–07; *b* 27 Nov. 1938; *s* of late Jack Ashworth and late Constance Mary Ousman; *m* 1st, 1963, Ann Knight (*d* 1985); one *s* three *d;* 2nd, 1988, Auriol Stevens, *qv. Educ:* West Buckland Sch., N Devon; Exeter Coll., Oxford (MA, DSc; Hon. Fellow, 1983); Leicester Univ. (PhD). FIBiol 1974. Dept of Biochemistry, Univ. of Leicester: Res. Demonstr, 1961–63; Lectr, 1963–71; Reader, 1971–73; Prof. of Biology, Univ. of Essex, 1974–79 (on secondment to Cabinet Office, 1976–79); Under-Sec., Cabinet Office, 1979–81 and Chief Scientist, Central Policy Review Staff, 1976–81; Vice-Chancellor, Univ. of Salford, 1981–90; Dir, LSE, 1990–96; Chm., British Liby Bd, 1996–2001. Harkness Fellow of Commonwealth Fund, NY, at Brandeis Univ. and Univ.

of Calif, 1965–67. NEDO: Chm., Information Technology EDC, 1983–86; Mem., Electronics EDC, 1983–86. Chairman: Nat. Accreditation Council for Certification Bodies, BSI, 1984–88; NCC, 1983–92. Director: Granada TV, 1987–89; Granada Group, 1990–2002; J. Sainsbury, 1993–97; London First, 1993–98. Mem. Council, Inst. of Cancer Res., 2000–. Pres., Council for Assisting Refugee Academics, 2002–. Colworth Medal, Biochem. Soc., 1972. *Publications:* Cell Differentiation, 1972; (with J. Dee) The Slime Moulds, 1976; over 100 pubns in prof. jls on biochem., genet., cell biolog. and educnl topics. *Recreation:* sailing. *Address:* Garden House, Wivenhoe, Essex CO7 9BD. *Club:* Wivenhoe Sailing.

ASHWORTH, Lance Dominic Piers; QC 2006; a Recorder of the Crown Court, since 2002 and of the County Court, since 2007; *b* 13 June 1964; *s* of Piers Ashworth, QC and of Iolene Jennifer Scholes (*née* Foxley); *m* 1989, Sally Elizabeth Downs; two *s* one *d*. *Educ:* Oundle Sch.; Pembroke Coll., Cambridge (BA 1986, MA 1990). Called to the Bar, Middle Temple, 1987; specialises in commercial and insolvency law. *Publication:* (contrib.) Mithani: Directors' Disqualification, nos 8 to 27, 1995–2007. *Recreations:* tennis (Ilmington 1st Team), golf, Rugby, cricket (Earlswood CC). *Address:* St Philips Chambers, 55 Temple Row, Birmingham B2 5LS. *T:* (0121) 246 7000, *Fax:* (0121) 246 7001; *e-mail:* lashworth@st-philips.com.

ASHWORTH, Peter Anthony Frank; Director, Leeds Permanent Building Society, 1971–92 (President, 1978); *b* 24 Aug. 1935; *s* of Peter Ormerod and Dorothy Christine Ashworth; *m* 1964, Elisabeth Crompton; one *s* one *d*. *Educ:* Leeds Grammar School. Articled to Hollis & Webb, Chartered Surveyors, Leeds (later Weatherall, Green & Smith, now Sanderson Weatherall), 1953–56; Partner, 1961–80. *Recreations:* golf, gardening. *Address:* 4 Bridge Paddock, Collingham, Wetherby LS22 5BN. *T:* (01937) 572953. *Club:* Alwoodley Golf (Leeds).

ASHWORTH, Richard James; Member (C) South East Region, European Parliament, since 2004; *b* 17 Sept. 1947; *s* of late Maurice Ashworth and Eileen Ashworth; *m* 1972, Sally Poulton; three *d*. *Educ:* King's Sch., Canterbury; Seale-Hayne Coll., Devon (DipAgr; Dip. in Farm Mgt; NDA). Farmer, 1970–2001. Chairman: United Milk Plc, 1996–2002; NFU Corporate, 2000–02. Contested (C) Devon North, 1997. European Parliament: Member: Industry Cttee, 2004–; Employment and Social Affairs Cttee, 2004–; PPS to delegn leader, 2004–. *Recreations:* sport, music, theatre, country pursuits. *Address:* The Heights, Hospital Hill, Folkestone, Kent CT20 3TL. *T:* (01303) 237736; *e-mail:* rashworth@europarl.eu.int. *Club:* Farmers.

ASHWORTH, Thomas Leslie, MSc; Head Master, Ermysted's Grammar School, Skipton, 1998–2008; *b* 17 Sept. 1949; *s* of late William Leslie Ashworth and Katharine Elizabeth Ashworth; *m* 1979, Roslyn Williams; two *d*. *Educ:* Birkenhead Inst.; Queen Mary Coll., London (BSc Hons Maths 1971); Univ. of Liverpool (MSc Maths 1973). Maths teacher, Birkenhead Sch., 1973–83; Sen. Teacher and Hd of Maths, Ripon GS, 1983–88; Dep. Head Master, Reading Sch., 1988–98. *Recreations:* Rugby (RFU panel referee, 1988–2000), philately, ICT, travel. *Address:* 22 Cross Bank, Skipton, N Yorks BD23 6AH; *e-mail:* tla179@aol.com.

ASIM, Dr Mohamed; High Commissioner of the Maldives in the United Kingdom, since 2007; *b* 1960; *m* Mariyam Ali Manik; one *s* one *d*. *Educ:* American Univ. of Beirut (BA Public Admin); California State Univ., Sacramento (MA Internat. Relns); Australian National Univ. (PhD Pol Sci. and Internat. Relns 1999). Government of the Maldives: admin. officer, Min. of Educn, 1982–83; President's Office, 1983–96; Dir Gen., Employment Affairs, 1996–99; Dir Gen., Public Service Div., President's Office, 1999–2004; High Comr, Sri Lanka and concurrently to Bangladesh and Pakistan, 2004–07. *Publications:* contrib. articles on public admin and public sector reform in the Maldives to Labour and Mgt in Develt Jl and Public Admin and Develt Jl. *Address:* High Commission of the Republic of Maldives, 22 Nottingham Place, W1V 5NJ.

ASKARI, Hasan; Chief Executive, Old Mutual Financial Services plc, 2003–07 (Director, 1999–2003); Adviser: Old Mutual plc, since 2007; Kotak Mahindra Bank, Mumbai, since 2008; *b* 29 June 1945; *s* of late Syed Mohammad and Kishwar Jahan Askari; *m* 1976, Nasreen Hassam Ismail; one *s* one *d*. *Educ:* University Coll., Oxford (MA 1975). S. G. Warburg & Co. Ltd, London, 1975–80; Chase Manhattan Bank: Dir, Hong Kong, 1981–85; Man. Dir, Tokyo, 1985–89; Man. Dir, Barclays de Zoete Wedd Ltd, Tokyo, 1989–92, London, 1992–99. Dir, Gt Ormond St Hosp. for Children NHS Trust, 1999–2007. Trustee, BM, 1999–2007. Mem., RSAA, 1979; FRAS 1979. *Recreations:* cricket, South Asian art, walking (preferably in solitude). *Address:* 22 Ovington Square, SW3 1LR. *T:* (020) 7002 6108, *Fax:* (020) 7002 6199; *e-mail:* hasan.askari@omg.co.uk. *Clubs:* Oriental; American (Tokyo).

ASKE, Sir Robert John Bingham, 3rd Bt *cr* 1922; *b* 12 March 1941; *s* of late Robert Edward Aske (*yr s* of Sir Robert Aske, 1st Bt) and of Joan, *o d* of late Capt. Eric Bingham Ackerley; *S* uncle, 2001. *Educ:* King's Sch., Canterbury. *Heir:* none. *Address:* 5 Bicton Place, Heavitree, Exeter EX1 2PF.

ASKEW, Barry Reginald William; journalist, broadcaster and public relations consultant; *b* 13 Dec. 1936; *s* of late Reginald Ewart Askew and Jane Elizabeth Askew; *m* 1st, 1958, June Roberts (marr. diss. 1978), *d* of late Vernon and Betty Roberts; one *s* one *d*; 2nd, 1980, Deborah Parker (marr. diss. 1989), *d* of Harold and Enid Parker. *Educ:* Lady Manners Grammar Sch., Bakewell, Derbys. Trainee reporter upwards, Derbyshire Times, 1952–57; Reporter and sub-ed., Sheffield Telegraph, 1957–59; reporter, feature writer and broadcaster, Raymonds News Agency, Derby, 1959–61; Editor, Matlock Mercury, 1961–63; Industrial Correspondent, Asst Ed., Dep. Ed., Sheffield Telegraph, later Morning Telegraph, Sheffield, 1964–68; Associate Ed., The Star, Sheffield, 1968; Editor, 1968–81, Dir, 1978–81, Lancashire Evening Post; Editor, News of the World, 1981. Presenter and anchor man: ITV, 1970–81; BBC Radio 4, 1971–72; BBC1, 1972; BBC2, 1972–76. Consultant in TV, radio, PR and commerce, 1982–95. Mem., Davies Cttee to reform hosp. complaints procedures in UK, 1971–73. Campaigning Journalist of 1971, IPC Nat. Press Awards; Journalist of 1977, British Press Awards; Crime Reporter of 1977, Witness Box Awards. *Recreations:* Rugby, chess, reading military history. *Address:* 14 Sunningdale, Woodplumpton Road, Broughton, Preston, Lancs PR4 0AX. *T:* (01772) 863021.

ASKEW, Sir Bryan, Kt 1989; Personnel Director, Samuel Smith Old Brewery (Tadcaster), 1982–95; Chairman, Yorkshire Regional Health Authority, 1983–94; *b* 18 Aug. 1930; *s* of John Pinkney Askew and Matilda Askew; *m* 1955, Millicent Rose Holder; two *d*. *Educ:* Wellfield Grammar Sch., Wingate, Co. Durham; Fitzwilliam Coll., Cambridge (MA Hons History). ICI Ltd, 1952–59; Consett Iron Co. Ltd (later part of British Steel Corporation), 1959–71; own consultancy, 1971–74; Samuel Smith Old Brewery (Tadcaster), 1974–95. Chm., Advanced Digital Telecom Ltd, 1997–99. Member, Consett UDC, 1967–71; contested (C) General Elections: Penistone, 1964 and 1966; York, 1970. Mem., Duke of Edinburgh's Third Commonwealth Study Conf., Australia, 1968. Mem., Working Gp on Young People and Alcohol, Home Office Standing Conf. on Crime Prevention, 1987. Chm., British Polio Fellowship, 2004–08. Mem. Court, 1985–2006, Mem. Council, 1988–2000, Univ. of Leeds. Chm., Burgage Holders of Alnmouth Common, 2003–. FRSA 1986 (Chm., Yorks Region, 1997–99); FRSocMed 1988. Hon. LLD Hull, 1992. *Recreations:* listening to music, reading, writing to The Times. *Address:* 27 Golf Links Avenue, Tadcaster LS24 9HF. *T:* (01937) 833216; Flat 1, The Manor House, Alnmouth, Northumberland NE66 2RJ. *T:* (01665) 830047.

ASKEW, Rev. Canon Reginald James Albert; Dean of King's College, London, 1988–93; Canon Emeritus, Salisbury Cathedral, since 1988; *b* 16 May 1928; *s* of late Paul Askew and Amy Wainwright; *m* 1953, Kate, *yr d* of late Rev. Henry Townsend Wigley; one *s* two *d*. *Educ:* Harrow; Corpus Christi Coll., Cambridge (MA); Lincoln Theological College. Curate of Highgate, 1957–61; Tutor and Chaplain of Wells Theol Coll., 1961–65, Vice-Principal 1966–69; Priest Vicar of Wells Cath., 1961–69; Vicar of Christ Church, Lancaster Gate, London, 1969–73; Principal, Salisbury and Wells Theol Coll., 1973–87; Canon of Salisbury Cathedral and Prebendary of Grantham Borealis, 1975–87. Proctor in Convocation for London Univ., Gen. Synod of C of E, 1990–93. Chaplain, Merchant Taylors' Co., 1996–97. Trustee, Christian Evidence Soc., 1988–2002. Mem., Corrymeela Community, 1990–. Pres., Bath and Wells Clerical Soc., 1998–. *Publications:* The Tree of Noah, 1971; Muskets and Altars: Jeremy Taylor and the last of the Anglicans, 1997. *Recreations:* music, gardening, making wood-cuts and lino-cuts. *Address:* Carters Cottage, North Wootton, Shepton Mallet, Somerset BA4 4AF. *T:* (01749) 890728. *Club:* Athenæum.

ASKONAS, Brigitte Alice, PhD; FRS 1973; with Weatherall Institute of Molecular Medicine (Molecular Immunology), John Radcliffe Hospital, Oxford, since 1989 (part-time); Visiting Professor, Department of Molecular and Cellular Biology (formerly Department of Biology, subseq. of Biological Sciences), Imperial College London, since 1995 (part-time); *b* 1 April 1923; *d* of late Charles F. Askonas and Rose Askonas. *Educ:* McGill Univ., Montreal (BSc, MSc); Cambridge Univ. (PhD; Hon. Fellow, New Hall and Girton Coll.). Research student, Sch. of Biochemistry, Univ. of Cambridge, 1949–52; Immunology Div., NIMR, 1953–89 (Head of Div., 1977–88); Dept of Bacteriology and Immunology, Harvard Med. Sch., Boston, 1961–62; Basel Inst. for Immunology, Basel, Switzerland, 1971–72. Vis. Prof., Dept of Medicine, St Mary's Hosp. Med. Sch., London, 1988–94. Mem. Council, Royal Soc., 1988–90 and 2002–03 (Vice Pres., 1989–90). Founder FMedSci 1998; FIC 2000. Hon. Member: Amer. Soc. of Immunology; Soc. française d'Immunologie; German Ges. für Immunologie; Foreign Associate, US NAS, 2007. Hon. DSc McGill, 1987. Robert Koch Gold Medal, Robert Koch Foundn, 2007. *Publications:* contrib. scientific papers to various biochemical and immunological jls and books. *Recreations:* art, travel. *Address:* 23 Hillside Gardens, N6 5SU. *T:* (020) 8348 6792; Department of Molecular and Cellular Biology, Imperial College London, Sir Alexander Fleming Building, Imperial College Road, SW7 2AZ. *T:* (020) 7594 5405, *Fax:* (020) 7584 2056.

ASLET, Clive William; Editor-at-Large, Country Life, since 2006 (Deputy Editor, 1989–92; Editor, 1993–2006); Editor in Chief, Country Life Books, 1994–2006; *b* 15 Feb. 1955; *s* of Kenneth and Monica Aslet; *m* 1980, Naomi Roth; three *s*. *Educ:* King's College Sch., Wimbledon; Peterhouse, Cambridge. Joined Country Life, 1977, Architectural Editor, 1984–88; Ed. in Chief, New Eden, 1999–. Dir, Country and Leisure Media Ltd, 1999–. Founding Hon. Sec., Thirties Soc., 1979–87. Gov., St Peter's Eaton Sq. C of E Sch., 1999–. FRSA. *Publications:* The Last Country Houses, 1982; (with Alan Powers) The National Trust Book of the English House, 1985; Quinlan Terry, the Revival of Architecture, 1986; The American Country House, 1990; Countryblast, 1991; (introd.) The American Houses of Robert A. M. Stern, 1991; Anyone for England? a search for British identity, 1997; (with Derry Moore) The House of Lords, 1998; The Story of Greenwich, 1999; Greenwich Millennium, 2000; A Horse in the Country: a diary of a year in the heart of England, 2001; The Landmarks of Britain, 2005. *Recreations:* children, challenging parking tickets. *Address:* c/o Country Life, King's Reach Tower, Stamford Street, SE1 9LS. *T:* (020) 7261 6969. *Club:* Garrick.

ASPEL, Michael Terence, OBE 1993; broadcaster and writer; *b* 12 Jan. 1933; *s* of late Edward and of Violet Aspel; *m* 1st, 1957, Dian; one *s* (and one *s* decd); 2nd, 1962, Ann; twin *s* and *d*; 3rd 1977, Elizabeth; two *s*. *Educ:* Emanuel School. Tea boy, publishers, 1949–51. Nat. Service, KRRC and Para Regt, TA, 1951–53. Radio actor, 1954–57; television announcer, 1957–60, newsreader, 1960–68; freelance broadcaster, radio and TV, 1968–; presenter: Aspel and Company, 1984–93; This is Your Life, 1988–2003; Antiques Roadshow, 2000–08; occasional stage appearances. Vice-President: BLISS (Baby Life Support Systems), 1981–; ASBAH (Assoc. for Spina Bifida and Hydrocephalus), 1985–; Patron, Plan International, 1986–. Member: Equity, 1955–; Lord's Taverners; RYA. Hon. Fellow, Cardiff Univ., 2002. Mem., RTS Hall of Fame, 1996. *Publications:* Polly Wants a Zebra (autobiog.), 1974; Hang On! (for children), 1982; (with Richard Hearsey) Child's Play, 1985; regular contribs to magazines. *Recreations:* water sports, theatre, cinema, eating, travel. *Address:* c/o Shepherd Management, 4th Floor, 45 Maddox Street, W1S 2PE.

ASPIN, Norman, CMG 1968; HM Diplomatic Service, retired; Adviser and Secretary, East Africa Association, 1981–84; *b* 9 Nov. 1922; *s* of Thomas and Eleanor Aspin; *m* 1948, Elizabeth Irving; three *s*. *Educ:* Darwen Grammar Sch.; Durham Univ. (MA). War Service, 1942–45, Lieut RNVR. Demonstrator in Geography, Durham Univ., 1947–48; Asst Principal, Commonwealth Relations Office, 1948; served in India, 1948–51; Principal, Commonwealth Relations Office, 1952; served in Federation of Rhodesia and Nyasaland, 1954–57; HM Treasury, 1958–60; British Deputy High Commissioner in Sierra Leone, 1961–63; Commonwealth Relations Office, 1963–65; British Embassy, Tel Aviv, 1966–69; IDC 1970; Head of Personnel Policy Dept, FCO, 1971–73; Under-Sec., FCO, 1973–76; Comr, British Indian Ocean Territory, 1976; British High Comr in Malta, 1976–79; Asst Under-Sec. of State, FCO, 1979–80. *Recreations:* sailing, tennis. *Address:* Mounsey Bank, Dacre, Cumbria CA11 0HL.

ASPINALL, John Michael; QC 1995; a Recorder, 1990–98; *b* 19 Feb. 1948; *s* of Kenneth James Aspinall and Joan Mary Aspinall; *m* 1980, Frances Helen Parks. *Educ:* Kampala Kindergarten; Wigan and Dist Mining and Tech. Coll.; Liverpool Univ. (LLB Hons). Called to the Bar, Inner Temple, 1971; Asst Recorder, 1985–90. RAC Motor Sports Council: Mem., 1990, Chm., 1994, Judicial Cttee; Mem., 1994. Winner, Observer Mace Nat. Debating Comp., 1971. *Recreations:* motor sports, being with my wife and friends at the Drax Arms. *Address:* 3 Paper Buildings, 30 Christchurch Road, Bournemouth BH1 3PD. *T:* (01202) 292102. *Club:* Savile.

ASPINALL, Most Rev. Phillip John; *see* Brisbane, Archbishop of.

ASPINALL, Wilfred; European Union policy and strategy adviser; Director: Aspinall & Associates, since 1988; Eversheds Financial Services Forum, since 1998; European Parliament Forum for Construction, since 2002; The Strategy Centre, Brussels, since 2004; *b* 14 Sept. 1942; *s* of late Charles Aspinall and Elizabeth Aspinall; *m* 1973, Judith Mary (*d* 2005), *d* of late Leonard James Pimlott and Kathleen Mary Pimlott; one *d*. *Educ:*

Poynton Secondary Modern; Stockport Coll. for Further Educn. Staff, National Provincial Bank Ltd, 1960–69; Asst Gen. Sec., National Westminster Staff Assoc., 1969–75; Dep. Sec. (part-time), Council of Bank Staff Assocs, 1969–75; Mem., Banking Staff Council, 1970–77; Gen. Sec., Confedn of Bank Staff Assocs, 1975–79; Exec. Dir, Fedn of Managerial, Professional and Gen. Assocs, 1978–94. Mem., EU Economic and Social Consultative Assembly, 1986–99. Vice-Pres., Confédération Internat. des Cadres, 1979–94. Member: N Herts DHA, 1981–86; NW Thames RHA, 1986–88; Hammersmith and Queen Charlotte's SHA, 1981–90; Professions Allied to Medicine, Whitley Management Negotiating Cttee, 1983–87. *Recreations:* motoring, travel - particularly to places of historical interest, social affairs and political history. *Address:* The Coach House, Shillington Road, Pirton, Hitchin, Herts SG5 3QJ. *T:* 07872 953922; (Brussels private office) Rue Wiertz 31, 1050 Brussels, Belgium. *T:* (2) 2308510, *Fax:* (2) 2307818; *e-mail:* wa@wilfredaspinall.eu.

ASPINWALL, Jack Heywood; author; company director; *b* 5 Feb. 1933; *m* 1954, Brenda Jean Aspinwall; one *s* two *d*. *Educ:* Prescot Grammar School, Lancs; Marconi College, Chelmsford. Served RAF, 1949–56. Director: family retail business, 1956–66; food distbn co., 1966–71; investment co., 1971–96. Mem., Avon CC, 1973–80. Contested (L) Kingswood, Feb. and Oct. 1974; MP (C) Kingswood, 1979–83, Wansdyke, 1983–97. *Publications:* (comp.) Kindly Sit Down!: best after-dinner stories from both Houses of Parliament, 1983; Hit Me Again, 1992; Tell Me Another, 1994. *Address:* 156 Bath Road, Willsbridge, Bristol BS30 6EF.

ASPLIN, Sarah Jane, (Mrs N. A. Sherwin); QC 2002; *b* 16 Sept. 1959; *d* of Raymond Asplin and Florence Grace Asplin; *m* 1986, Nicholas Adrian Sherwin; two *d*. *Educ:* Southampton Coll. for Girls; Fitzwilliam Coll., Cambridge (MA); St Edmund Hall, Oxford (BCL). Called to the Bar, Gray's Inn, 1984, Bencher, 2006; in practice as barrister, specialising in Chancery and pensions law and life assurance, 1985–; Dep. High Court Judge, Chancery Div. Member: Chancery Bar Assoc., 1985–; Assoc. Pension Lawyers, 1990– (Mem., Litigation Sub-Cttee, 2000–); Fees Collection Cttee and Implementation Cttee, Bar Council. *Recreations:* playing the violin, classical music. *Address:* (chambers) 3 Stone Buildings, Lincoln's Inn, WC2A 3XL. *T:* (020) 7242 4937, *Fax:* (020) 7405 3896; *e-mail:* Sasplin@3sb.law.co.uk.

ASPRAY, Rodney George, FCA; Managing Director, Worthbase Ltd, 1990–2000; *b* 1934. Secretary, Manchester and Salford Cooperative Society, 1965–69; Chief Exec. Officer, Norwest Co-op. Soc., 1969–91. Director: Co-operative Bank, 1980–89 (Chm., 1986–89); Co-operative Wholesale Soc. Ltd, 1980–89; Mersey Docks & Harbour Co., 1987–94; Piccadilly Radio Plc, 1989–90. Mem., Monopolies and Mergers Commn, 1975–81. FCA 1960.

ASQUITH, family name of **Earl of Oxford and Asquith**.

ASQUITH, Viscount; Raymond Benedict Bartholomew Michael Asquith, OBE 1992; Director: JKX Oil & Gas plc, since 1997; Zander Corporation Ltd, since 2002; Europa Capital Emerging Europe Ltd, since 2007; *b* 24 Aug. 1952; *er s* and *heir* of Earl of Oxford and Asquith, *qv*; *m* 1978, Mary Clare, *e d* of Francis Pollen; one *s* four *d*. *Educ:* Ampleforth; Balliol College, Oxford. HM Diplomatic Service, 1980–97: FCO, 1980–83; First Sec., Moscow, 1983–85; Cabinet Office and FCO, 1985–92; Counsellor, Kiev, 1992–97. *Heir: s* Hon. Mark Julian Asquith, *b* 13 May 1979. *Address:* Branch Farm, Mells, Frome, Somerset BA11 3RE.

See also Hon. D. A. G. Asquith.

ASQUITH, Hon. Dominic (Anthony Gerard), CMG 2004; HM Diplomatic Service; Ambassador to Egypt, since 2007; *b* 7 Feb. 1957; *y s* of Earl of Oxford and Asquith, *qv*; *m* 1988, Louise Cotton; two *s* two *d*. Joined HM Diplomatic Service, 1983; FCO, 1983–86; Second Sec., Damascus, 1986–87; First Secretary: Muscat, 1987–89; FCO, 1989–92; Washington, 1992–96; Minister and Dep. Hd of Mission, Argentina, 1997–2001; Dep. Hd of Mission and Consul Gen., Saudi Arabia, 2001–04; Dep. Special Rep. and Dep. Head of Mission, Iraq, 2004; Dir, Iraq Directorate, FCO, 2004–06; Ambassador to Iraq, 2006–07. *Address:* c/o Foreign and Commonwealth Office, King Charles Street, SW1A 2AH.

See also Viscount Asquith.

ASSCHER, Sir (Adolf) William, Kt 1992; MD, FRCP; Principal (formerly Dean) and Professor of Medicine, St George's Hospital Medical School, London University, 1988–96; Consultant Physician, St George's Hospital; *b* 20 March 1931; *s* of William Benjamin Asscher and Roosje van der Molen; *m* 1st, 1959, Corrie van Welt (*d* 1961); 2nd, 1962, Dr Jennifer Lloyd, (*d* 2006), *d* of Wynne Llewelyn Lloyd, CB; two *d*. *Educ:* Maerlant Lyceum, The Hague; London Hosp. Med. Coll. BSc 1954; MB 1957; MD 1963; MRCP 1959, FRCP 1971; FFPM 1992. Nat. service, Lieut RE, 1949–51. Jun. appts, London Hosp., 1957–59; Lectr in Medicine, London Hosp. Med. Coll., 1959–64; Welsh National School of Medicine, later University of Wales College of Medicine: Sen. Lectr, 1964–70, and Hon. Cons. Physician, Royal Inf., Cardiff; Reader, 1970–76; Prof. of Medicine, 1976–80; Head of Dept of Renal Medicine, 1980–88. Chairman: Cttee on Review of Medicines, DHSS, 1985–87; Cttee on Safety of Medicines, Dept of Health (formerly DHSS), 1987–92 (Mem., 1984–87); Member: Medicines Commn, DHSS, 1981–84; SW Thames RHA, 1987–90; Jt Consultants Cttee, 1992–96; Med. Adv. Cttee, Royal Hosp. for Neuro-Rehabilitation, Putney, 1995–97; Welsh Arts Council, 1985–88. Chm., Morriston Hosp. NHS Trust, Swansea, 1996–99; non-executive Director: Wandsworth DHA, 1991–93; St George's Health Care Trust, 1993–96; Vanguard Media plc, 1996–2002; Cancer Research Ventures, 1999–2001. Chairman: Med. Benefit Risk Foundn UK, 1993–96; Welsh Med. Technology Forum, 1993–; BMA Bd of Sci. and Educn, 1998–2002; UK Co-ordinating Cttee on Cancer Res., 1998–2002; Working Party on Therapeutic Uses of Cannabinoids, RPharmS, 1998–2000. Royal College of Physicians: Regl Advr, 1976–79; Mem. Council, 1977–80; Pres., Faculty of Pharmaceutical Medicine, 1995–97. Examnr, Final MB, Wales, London, Bristol and Edinburgh. Pres., Renal Assoc., 1986–89. Hon. Fellow: St George's Hosp. Med. Sch., 1996; QMW, 1998. DUniv Kingston, 1996. Gold Medal, BMA, 2002. *Publications:* (with W. Brumfitt) Urinary Tract Infection, 1973; The Challenge of Urinary Tract Infections, 1980; (with D. B. Moffat and E. Sanders) Nephrology Illustrated, 1982; (with D. B. Moffat) Nephro-Urology, 1983; (with W. Brumfitt) Microbial Diseases in Nephrology, 1986; (with S. R. Walker) Medicines and Risk-Benefit Decisions, 1986; (with J. D. Williams) Clinical Atlas of the Kidney, 1991; papers on nephrology and drug regulation in learned jls. *Recreation:* visual arts. *Address:* 10 The Paddock, Cowbridge, Vale of Glamorgan CF71 7EJ. *Club:* Cardiff and County (Cardiff).

ASSHETON, family name of **Baron Clitheroe**.

ASSHETON, Hon. Nicholas, CVO 2002; FSA; Treasurer and Extra Equerry to the Queen Mother, 1998–2002; *b* 23 May 1934; *yr s* of 1st Baron Clitheroe, KCVO, PC, FSA and Sylvia Benita Frances, Lady Clitheroe, FRICS (*d* 1991), *d* of 6th Baron Hotham; *m* 1960, Jacqueline Jill, *d* of Marshal of the Royal Air Force Sir Arthur Harris, 1st Bt, GCB, OBE, AFC; one *s* two *d*. *Educ:* Eton; Christ Church, Oxford (MA). FSA 1984. 2nd Lieut, Life Guards, 1954; Lieut, Inns of Court Regt, 1954–57. Joined Montagu, Loebl, Stanley & Co. (Stockbrokers), 1957: Partner, 1960; Sen. Partner, 1978–86; Chm., 1986–87; Coutts & Co.: Dir, 1987–99; Dep. Chm., 1993–99; Chm., SG Hambros Bank & Trust Ltd, 2000–07. Mem., Stock Exchange, 1960–92 (Mem. Council, 1969–87). Dir, United Services Trustee, 1981–2002, Chm., 1997–2002. Treas., Corp. of Church House, 1988–2002. Vice Chm., 2004–07, Vice Pres., 2007–, Heritage of London Trust. Mem. Council, Soc. of Antiquaries, 1998–2001. Chief Hon. Steward, Westminster Abbey, 2002–06. Liveryman, Vintners' Co., 1955. *Address:* 15 Hammersmith Terrace, W6 9TS. *Clubs:* White's, Pratt's, Beefsteak.

ASSIRATI, Robert; Projects Director, Office of Government Commerce, HM Treasury, since 2001; *b* 27 May 1947; *s* of late Frederick Louis Assirati and Mary Violet Assirati (*née* Dillon); *m* 1968, Lynne Elizabeth Yeend; one *s* one *d*. *Educ:* Stationers' Company's Sch., London; Hertford Coll., Oxford (MA PPE). MCIPS 1997; CITP 2007. Nat. Coal Bd, 1968; Data Processing Manager, Eli Lilly & Co., 1972; Management Services Manager, British Carpets, 1976; Company Dir, C Squared, 1984; Commercial Dir, Inland Revenue IT Office, 1986; Chief Exec., CCTA, 1996–2001. Vice Pres. and Trustee, British Computer Soc., 2007–. Freeman, City of London; Liveryman, Co. of Information Technologists, 2003. MCMI; FRSA; FBCS. Hon. FAPM. *Recreations:* bridge, tennis, travel, theatre. *Address:* The Alders, Capel, Tonbridge, Kent TN12 6SU. *T:* (01892) 836609.

ASTAIRE, Jarvis Joseph, OBE 2004; Chairman: GRA (formerly Greyhound Racing Association), 1993–2005; First Artist Corporation plc, since 2006; *b* 6 Oct. 1923; *s* of late Max and Esther Astaire; *m* 1st, 1948, Phyllis Oppenheim (*d* 1974); one *s* one *d*; 2nd, 1981, Nadine Hyman (*d* 1986). *Educ:* Kilburn Grammar Sch., London. Dir, Lewis & Burrows Ltd, 1957–60; Managing Director: Mappin & Webb Ltd, 1958–60; Hurst Park Syndicate, 1962–71; Dep. Chm., Wembley Stadium, 1984–99; Director: Perthpoint Investments Ltd, 1959–70; Associated Suburban Properties Ltd, 1963–81; Anglo-Continental Investment & Finance Co. Ltd, 1964–75; William Hill Org., 1971–82; First Artists Prodns Inc. (USA), 1976–79; Wembley PLC (formerly GRA Gp), 1987–99; Revlon Group Ltd, 1991–98. Mem. Bd, British Greyhound Racing, 1991–2004. Introduced into UK showing of sporting events on large screen in cinemas, 1964. Pres., Royal Free Hosp. and Med. Sch. Appeal Trust, 1991–97 (Chm., 1974); Hon. Treas., 1976–, and Vice Pres., 1982–, Fedn of London Youth Clubs (formerly London Fedn of Boys' Clubs); Chm., Police Dependants' Trust Appeal, 1999–; Trustee: Nightingale House Home for Aged Jews, 1984–; Bowles Outdoor Centre, 1985–; Royal Free Cancer Res. Trust, 2001–. Chm., Associated City Properties, 1981–2001. Chief Barker (Pres.), Variety Club of GB, 1983; Pres., Variety Clubs Internat. (Worldwide), 1991–93. Mem. Adv. Council, LSO, 1996–2004. Freeman, City of London, 1983. *Recreations:* playing tennis, watching cricket and football. *Address:* One Great Cumberland Place, W1H 7AL. *T:* (020) 7723 3900. *Clubs:* East India, MCC, Queen's; Friars (USA).

ASTBURY, Prof. Alan, PhD; FRS 1993; FRS(Can) 1988; R. M. Pearce Professor of Physics, University of Victoria, British Columbia, 1983–2000, now Emeritus; Director, TRIUMF Laboratory, Vancouver, 1994–2001; *b* 27 Nov. 1934; *s* of Harold Astbury and Jane Astbury (*née* Horton); *m* 1964, Kathleen Ann Stratmeyer; two *d*. *Educ:* Nantwich and Acton Grammar Sch.; Univ. of Liverpool (BSc, PhD). Leverhulme Research Fellow, Univ. of Liverpool, 1959–61; Res. Associate, Lawrence Radiation Lab., Berkeley, Calif., 1961–63; Res. Physicist, Rutherford Appleton Lab., UK, 1963–83. Vis. Scientist, CERN, Geneva, 1970–74 and 1980–83. Pres., IUPAP, 2005–08. Hon. DSc: Liverpool, 2003; Victoria, BC, 2003; Simon Fraser, BC, 2006. Rutherford Medal, Inst. Physics, 1986; Gold Medal, Canadian Assoc. of Physics, 2002. *Publications:* numerous in learned jls. *Recreations:* ski-ing, jazz, playing piano. *Address:* Department of Physics and Astronomy, University of Victoria, PO Box 3055, Station Commercial Service Centre, Victoria, BC V8W 3P6, Canada. *T:* (250) 7217725; 1383 St Patrick Street, Victoria, BC V8S 4Y5, Canada.

ASTBURY, Nicholas John, FRCS, FRCOphth, FRCP; Consultant Ophthalmic Surgeon, Norfolk and Norwich University Hospital NHS Trust (formerly West Norwich Hospital), since 1983; President, Royal College of Ophthalmologists, 2003–06; *b* 21 Feb. 1949; *s* of late Dr John Schonberg Astbury and of Dr Noel Hope Astbury (*née* Gunn); *m* 1970, Susan Patricia Whall; two *s* two *d*. *Educ:* Rugby Sch.; Guy's Hosp. Med. Sch. (MB BS 1972). LRCP 1972; MRCS 1972, FRCS 1977; DO 1974; FRCOphth 1989; FRCP 2005. Sen. Registrar, KCH and Moorfields Eye Hosp., 1981–83. Vice-Pres. and Chm., Professional Standards Cttee, Royal Coll. of Ophthalmologists, 2000–03. *Recreations:* hill walking, blue water sailing, horology, photography, making automata. *Address:* Rectory Farmhouse, The Street, Shotesham, Norwich NR15 1YL. *T:* (01508) 550377; *e-mail:* nick.astbury@virgin.net.

ASTBURY, Nicholas Paul; HM Diplomatic Service; Ambassador to Eritrea, since 2006; *b* 13 Aug. 1971; *s* of Nigel Astbury and Yvonne Susan Astbury (*née* Harburn). *Educ:* Hills Rd Sixth Form Coll., Cambridge; University Coll. London (BA Internat. Historical Studies; MA Legal and Political Theory). Entered FCO, 1994; Second Secretary: Colombo, 1995–99; FCO, 1999–2001; Private Sec. to Parly Under-Sec. of State, 2001–02; Deputy Head: UKvisas, 2002–04; Drugs Team, Kabul, 2005. *Recreations:* photography, diving, numismatics, beer. *Address:* c/o Foreign and Commonwealth Office, King Charles Street, SW1A 2AH. *Club:* Bentham Boat.

ASTILL, Hon. Sir Michael (John), Kt 1996; a Judge of the High Court of Justice, Queen's Bench Division, 1996–2004; *b* 31 Jan. 1938; *s* of Cyril Norman Astill and Winifred Astill; *m* 1968, Jean Elizabeth, *d* of Dr J. C. H. Mackenzie; three *s* one *d*. *Educ:* Blackfriars School, Laxton, Northants. Admitted solicitor, 1962; called to the Bar, Middle Temple, 1972, Bencher, 1996; a Recorder, 1980–84; a Circuit Judge, 1984–96; a Pres., Mental Health Tribunals, 1986–96; Presiding Judge, Midland and Oxford Circuit, 1999–2002. Mem., Judicial Studies Bd, 1995–99 (Chm., Magisterial Cttee, 1995–99). *Recreations:* music, reading, sport. *Address:* c/o Royal Courts of Justice, Strand, WC2A 2LL.

ASTLEY, family name of **Baron Hastings**.

ASTLEY, Neil Philip; Editor and Managing Director, Bloodaxe Books Ltd, since 1978; *b* 12 May 1953; *s* of Philip Thomas Astley and late Margaret Ivy Astley (*née* Soleman); *Educ:* Price's Sch., Fareham; Alliance Française, Paris; Univ. of Newcastle upon Tyne (BA 1st Cl. Hons). Journalist, England and Australia, 1972–74. Hon. DLitt Newcastle upon Tyne, 1996. Eric Gregory Award, Soc. of Authors, 1982. *Publications:* (ed) Ten North-East Poets, 1980; The Speechless Act, 1984; (ed) Bossy Parrot, 1987; Darwin Survivor (Recommendation, Poetry Book Soc.), 1988; (ed) Poetry with an Edge, 1988, 2nd edn 1993; (ed) Tony Harrison (critical anthology), 1991; Biting My Tongue, 1995; (ed) New Blood, 1999; The End of My Tether (novel), 2002; (ed) Staying Alive: real poems for unreal times, 2002; (ed) Pleased to See Me, 2002; (ed) Do Not Go Gentle, 2003; (ed) Being Alive: the sequel to Staying Alive, 2004; The Sheep Who Changed the World (novel), 2005; (ed) Passionfood: 100 love poems, 2005; (ed) Bloodaxe Poetry

Introductions: vol. 1, 2006, vol. 2, 2006, vol. 3, 2007; (ed jtly) Soul Food: nourishing poems for starved minds, 2007; (ed) Earth Shattering: ecopoems, 2007; (ed jtly) In Person: 30 poets filmed by Pamela Robertson-Pearce, 2008. *Recreations:* reading, enjoying countryside, folklore, sheep. *Address:* Bloodaxe Books Ltd, Highgreen, Tarset, Northumberland NE48 1RP. *T:* (01434) 240500.

ASTLEY, Philip Sinton, CVO 1999 (LVO 1979); HM Diplomatic Service, retired; Ambassador to Denmark, 1999–2003; *b* 18 Aug. 1943; *s* of Bernard Astley and Barbara Astley (*née* Sinton); *m* 1966, Susanne Poulsen; two *d. Educ:* St Albans Sch.; Magdalene Coll., Cambridge (BA 1965). Asst Representative, British Council, Madras, 1966–70; British Council, London, 1970–73; First Sec., FCO, 1973–76, Copenhagen, 1976–79; First Sec. and Head of Chancery, East Berlin, 1980–82; First Sec., FCO, 1982–84; Counsellor and Head of Management Review Staff, FCO, 1984–86; Econ. Counsellor and Consul Gen., Islamabad, 1986–90; Dep. Head of Mission, Copenhagen, 1990–94; Counsellor, and Hd of Human Rights Policy Dept, FCO, 1994–96; Asst Under-Sec. of State, FCO, and HM Vice-Marshal of the Diplomatic Corps, 1996–99. Freeman, City of London, 1999. Grand Cross, Order of Dannebrog (Denmark), 2000. *Recreations:* oriental textiles, gardening. *Address:* Lark Hill, Egerton, Ashford, Kent TN27 9BG.

ASTLEY, Rita Ann; *see* Clifton, R. A.

ASTLING, (Alistair) Vivian, OBE 2005; DL; Chairman, National Forest Co., 1999–2005; *b* 6 Sept. 1943; *s* of late Alec William Astling, MBE and Barbara Grace Astling; *m* 1967, Hazel Ruth Clarke. *Educ:* Glyn Grammar Sch., Epsom; Sheffield Univ. (LLB 1965; LLM 1967); Birmingham Univ. (MSocSci 1973). West Bromwich County Borough Council: articled clerk, 1967; Asst Solicitor, 1971; Asst Town Clerk, 1973; Walsall Metropolitan Borough Council: Corporate Planner, 1974; Chief Exec. and Town Clerk, 1982–88; Chief Exec., Dudley MBC, 1988–99. Clerk to W Midlands Police Authy, 1988–99; Sec. to Shareholders' Forum, 1988–97, Chm., Consultative Cttee, 2002–, Birmingham Internat. Airport. Member Board: Midlands Arts Centre, 1999–; Artsites, 2002–06; Dudley Coll. Corp., 2003– (Chm., 2004–). Trustee, Heart of the Nat. Forest Foundn, 2005–. DL W Midlands, 2008. Hon. MBA Wolverhampton, 1999. *Recreations:* squash, sculpture, theatre, music. *Address:* 16 Knighton Drive, Sutton Coldfield, W Midlands B74 4QP.

ASTON, Bishop Suffragan of; *no new appointment at time of going to press.*

ASTON, Archdeacon of; *see* Russell, Ven. B. K.

ASTON, Sir Harold (George), Kt 1983; CBE 1976; Chairman and Chief Executive, Bonds Coats Patons Ltd, 1981–87 (Deputy Chairman, 1970–80); Director, Central Sydney Area Health Service, 1988–92; *b* Sydney, 13 March 1923; *s* of Harold John Aston and Annie Dorothea McKeown; *m* 1947, Joyce Thelma Smith (decd); one *s* one *d. Educ:* Crown Street Boys' Sch., Sydney, Australia. Manager, Buckinghams Ltd, Sydney, 1948–55; Bonds Industries Ltd: Merchandising Manager, 1955–63; Gen. Man., 1963–67; Man. Dir, 1967–70; Director: Bonds Coats Patons Ltd (formerly Bonds Industries Ltd); Manufacturers Mutual Insurance, 1982– (Vice Chm., 1987–); Downard-Pickfords Pty Ltd, 1983–89 (Chm.); Australian Guarantee Corp. Ltd, 1983–88; Australian Manufacturing Life Assce Ltd, 1984–88; Rothmans Hldgs Ltd, 1986– (Dep. Chm., 1989–); Westpac Banking Corp., 1988–92; Chm., Television and Telecasters Ltd, 1991–92; Consultant, Pacific Dunlop Ltd, 1987–. President: Textile Council of Australia, 1973–80 (Life Mem., 1984); Confedn of Aust. Industry, 1980–82; Hon. Trustee, Cttee for Econ. Develt of Australia, 1988–; Governor: Aesop Foundn, 1988–; (Founding), Heart Inst. of Australia, 1986–93. CompTI 1984; FCFI 1986; CStJ 1993 (Dep. Receiver-Gen., Finance Cttee, 1985–). *Recreations:* walking, gardening, travelling. *Address:* 58/129 Surf Parade, Broadbeach, Qld 4218, Australia. *Clubs:* American, Australian, Royal Sydney Yacht Squadron (Sydney); Concord Golf.

ASTON, Dr Margaret Evelyn, (Hon. Mrs Buxton), FSA, FRHistS; FBA 1994; historian; *b* 9 Oct. 1932; *d* of 1st Baron Bridges, KG, GCB, GCVO, MC, PC, FRS and of late Katharine Dianthe, *d* of 2nd Baron Farrer; *m* 1st, 1954, Trevor Henry Aston (marr. diss. 1969; he *d* 1985); 2nd, 1971, Paul William Jex Buxton, *qv*; one *d* (and one *d* decd). *Educ:* Downe House; Lady Margaret Hall, Oxford (BA, MA; DPhil 1962). FRHistS 1962; FSA 1987. Lectr, St Anne's Coll., Oxford, 1956–59; Theodor Heuss Schol., W Germany, 1960–61; Res. Fellow, Newnham Coll., Cambridge, 1961–66; Res. Fellow, Folger Shakespeare Liby, and teaching post, Catholic Univ. of America, Washington, 1966–69; Hon. Sen. Res. Fellow, QUB, 1984–85. Pres., Ecclesiastical History Soc., 2000–01. DUniv York, 2001. *Publications:* Thomas Arundel: a study of church life in the reign of Richard II, 1967; The Fifteenth Century: the prospect of Europe, 1968, repr. 1994; Lollards and Reformers: images and literacy in late medieval religion, 1984; England's Iconoclasts: laws against images, 1988; Faith and Fire: popular and unpopular religion 1350–1600, 1993; The King's Bedpost: reformation and iconography in a Tudor group portrait, 1994; (ed) The Panorama of the Renaissance, 1996; (ed jtly) Lollardy and Gentry in the Later Middle Ages, 1997; (ed jtly) Much Heaving and Shoving: late-medieval gentry and their concerns, 2005; contrib. learned jls. *Address:* Castle House, Chipping Ongar, Essex CM5 9JT. *T:* (01277) 362642.

ASTON, Prof. Michael Antony, FSA; Professor of Landscape Archaeology, University of Bristol, 1996–2004, now Emeritus; *b* 1 July 1946; *s* of Harold and Gladys Aston; one *s. Educ:* Univ. of Birmingham (BA 1967). FSA 1976; MIFA 1983. Field Officer, Oxford City and County Mus., 1970–74; County Archaeologist, Somerset CC, 1974–78; Tutor, Ext. Studies Dept, Univ. of Oxford, 1978–79; University of Bristol: Staff Tutor in Archaeol., 1979–89; Reader in Archaeol., 1989–96. Hon. Prof., Dept of Archaeol., Univ. of Durham, 2004–; Hon. Vis. Prof., Dept of Archaeol., Univ. of Exeter, 2004–. Jt Presenter, Time Team series, TV, 1994–. Hon. DLitt UC Winchester, 2004; Hon. MA Worcester, 2007. *Publications:* (with Trevor Rowley) Landscape Archaeology, 1974; (with James Bond) The Landscape of Towns, 1976; Interpreting the Landscape, 1985; Mick's Archaeology, 2000; Monasteries in the Landscape, 2000; (with Victor Ambrus) Recreating the Past, 2001; (with Tony Robinson) Archaeology is Rubbish, 2002; Interpreting the Landscape from the Air, 2002; (with Christopher Gerrard) The Shapwick Project, Somerset: a rural landscape explored, 2007. *Recreations:* walking, camping in my camper van, music (classical concerts), pottery, painting, landscape gardening, visiting archaeological sites, churches, etc. *Address:* Department of Archaeology and Anthropology, University of Bristol, 43 Woodland Road, Bristol BS8 1UU.

ASTON, Prof. Peter George, DPhil; Professor and Head of Music, University of East Anglia, 1974–98, Professor Emeritus, since 2001; *b* 5 Oct. 1938; *s* of late George William Aston and Elizabeth Oliver Aston (*née* Smith); *m* 1960, Elaine Veronica Neale; one *s. Educ:* Tettenhall Coll.; Birmingham Sch. of Music (GBSM); Univ. of York (DPhil); FTCL, ARCM. Lectr in Music, 1964–72, Sen. Lectr, 1972–74, Univ. of York; Dean, Sch. of Fine Arts and Music, 1981–84, Professorial Fellow, 1998–2001, UEA. Dir, Tudor Consort, 1958–65; Conductor: English Baroque Ensemble, 1968–70; Aldeburgh Festival Singers, 1975–88; Principal Guest Conductor: Sacramento Bach Fest., USA, 1993–2001; Incontri

Corali Internat. Choral Fest., Italy, 1996; Schola Cantorum Gedanensis, Poland, 1999; Jt Artistic Dir, Norwich Fest. of Contemporary Church Music, 1981–; Chorus Master, Norfolk and Norwich Triennial Fest., 1982–88. Composer-in-residence, Combe Bank Sch., Kent, 2006–. Chairman: Eastern Arts Assoc. Music Panel, 1976–81; Norfolk Assoc. for the Advancement of Music, 1990–93 (Pres., 1993–98); Acad. Bd, Guild of Church Musicians, 1996–; President: Trianon Music Gp, 1984–96; Bury St Edmunds Bach Soc., 2005–. Royal School of Church Music: Chm., Norfolk and Norwich Area Cttee, 1998–2006; Mem., Adv. Bd, 2000–, Press Editl Bd, 2003–. Patron, Lowestoft Choral Soc., 1986–. Gen. Editor, UEA Recording Series, 1979–98; Editor, Peter Aston Editl Liby, Pavane Publishing, USA, 2001–. Hon. Lay Canon and Mem. Council, Norwich Cathedral, 2002–. FRSA 1980; FRSCM 1999. Hon. Fellow, Curwen Inst., 1987; Hon. RCM 1991; Hon. FGCM 1995. *Compositions:* song cycles, chamber music, choral and orchestral works, church music, opera. *Publications:* George Jeffreys and the English Baroque, 1970; The Music of York Minster, 1972; Sound and Silence (jtly), 1970, German edn 1972, Italian edn 1979, Japanese edn 1982; (ed) The Collected Works of George Jeffreys, 3 vols, 1977; (jtly) Music Theory in Practice, vol. 1, 1992, vols 2 and 3, 1993; contrib. to internat. music jls. *Recreations:* Association football, cricket, bridge, chess. *Address:* University of East Anglia, Music Centre, School of Music, Norwich NR4 7TJ. *T:* (01603) 592452. *Clubs:* Athenæum; Norfolk (Norwich).

ASTOR, family name of **Viscount Astor** and **Baron Astor of Hever**.

ASTOR, 4th Viscount *cr* 1917, of Hever Castle; **William Waldorf Astor;** Baron 1916; *b* 27 Dec. 1951; *s* of 3rd Viscount Astor; *S* father, 1966; *m* 1976, Annabel Sheffield, *d* of T. Jones; two *s* one *d. Educ:* Eton Coll. A Lord in Waiting (Govt Whip), 1990–93. Parliamentary Under-Secretary of State: DSS, 1993–94; Dept of Nat. Heritage, 1994–95; an Opposition spokesman, H of L, 1996–; elected Mem., H of L, 1999; Director: Networkers Internat. plc, 1996–; Chorion plc, 1997–. Trustee, Sir Stanley Spencer Gall., Cookham, 1975–. *Heir: s* Hon. William Waldorf Astor, *b* 18 Jan. 1979. *Address:* Ginge Manor, Wantage, Oxon OX12 8QT. *Club:* White's.

ASTOR OF HEVER, 3rd Baron *cr* 1956, of Hever Castle; **John Jacob Astor;** DL; *b* 16 June 1946; *s* of 2nd Baron Astor of Hever and Lady Irene Haig, *d* of Field Marshal 1st Earl Haig, KT, GCB, OM, GCVO, KCIE; *S* father, 1984; *m* 1st, 1970, Fiona Diana Lennox Harvey (marr. diss. 1990), *d* of Captain Roger Harvey; three *d;* 2nd, 1990, Hon. Elizabeth, *d* of 2nd Viscount Mackintosh of Halifax, OBE, BEM; one *s* one *d. Educ:* Eton College. Lieut Life Guards, 1966–70, Malaysia, Hong Kong, Ulster. Director: Terres Blanches Services Sarl, 1975–77; Valberg Plaza Sarl, 1977–82; Managing Director: Honon et Cie, 1982–; Astor France Sarl, 1989–; Pres., Astor Enterprises Inc., 1983–. An Opposition Whip, H of L, 1998–; elected Mem., H of L, 1999. Vice-Chairman: Thames Gateway Parly Gp, 1998–; British-Malaysia Parly Gp, 2000–; Secretary: Anglo-Swiss Parly Assoc., 1992–; All Party Motor Gp, 1998–; All Party Gp on Autism, 2000–; All Party Gp on Shooting and Conservation, 2002–; Joint Treasurer: British-S African Parly Assoc., 1994; Franco-British Parly Relations Cttee. Trustee: Rochester Cathedral Trust; Canterbury Cathedral Trust; Astor Foundn; Astor of Hever Trust; Patron: Edenbridge Music and Arts Trust; Bridge Trust, 1993–; Kent Assoc. of Youth Clubs, 1994–; Eden Valley Mus. Trust, 1998–; President: Sevenoaks Westminster Patrons Club; Earl Haig Br., and Kent Br., 2003–, Royal British Legion; Motorsport Industry Assoc., 1995–; Kent Fedn of Amenity Socs, 1995–; RoSPA, 1996–99. Gov., Cobham Hall Sch., 1993–96. DL Kent, 1996. Chm., Council of St John, Kent, 1987–97; KStJ 1998. *Heir: s* Hon. Charles Gavin John Astor, *b* 10 Nov. 1990. *Address:* Frenchstreet House, Westerham, Kent TN16 1PW. *Clubs:* White's; Riviera Golf.

ASTOR, David Waldorf, CBE 1994; DL; farmer, since 1973; Director, Priory Investments Ltd, 1990–2007; *b* 9 Aug. 1943; *s* of late Michael Langhorne Astor and Barbara Mary (*née* McNeill); *m* 1968, Clare Pamela St John; two *s* two *d. Educ:* Eton Coll.; Harvard Univ. Short service commn in Royal Scots Greys, 1962–65. United Newspapers, 1970–72; Housing Corp., 1972–75; Head of Develt, National Th., 1978–79; Dir, Jupiter Tarbutt Merlin, 1985–91. Chairman: CPRE, 1983–93; Southern Arts Bd, 1998–2002. Chairman: Action for Prisoners' Families, 2003–; Turn2Us, 2007–. Trustee: Glyndebourne Arts Trust, 1995–2005; Elizabeth Finn Care (formerly Elizabeth Finn Trust), 2004–. Contested (SDP/Alliance) Plymouth Drake, 1987. FRSA. DL Oxon, 2007. *Recreations:* books, sport. *Address:* Bruern Grange, Milton under Wychwood, Oxford OX7 6HA. *T:* (01993) 830413. *Clubs:* Brooks's, Beefsteak, MCC.

ASTWOOD, Hon. Sir James (Rufus), KBE 1994; Kt 1982; JP; President, Court of Appeal: Bermuda, 1994–2003; Turks and Caicos Islands, 1997–2002; *b* 4 Oct. 1923; *s* of late James Rufus Astwood, Sr, and Mabel Winifred Astwood; *m* 1952, Gloria Preston Norton; one *s* two *d. Educ:* Berkeley Inst., Bermuda; Univ. of Toronto, Canada. Called to the Bar, Gray's Inn, London, Feb. 1956, Hon. Bencher, 1985; admitted to practice at Jamaican Bar, Oct. 1956; joined Jamaican Legal Service, 1957; Dep. Clerk of Courts, 1957–58; Clerk of Courts, Jamaica, 1958–63; Stipendiary Magistrate and Judge of Grand Court, Cayman Islands (on secondment from Jamaica), 1958–59; Resident Magistrate, Jamaica, 1963–74; Puisne Judge, Jamaica, during 1971 and 1973; retd from Jamaican Legal Service, 1974; Sen. Magistrate, Bermuda, 1974–76; Solicitor General, 1976–77; Acting Attorney General, during 1976 and 1977; Acting Dep. Governor for a period in 1977; Chief Justice, 1977–93, Justice of Appeal, 1993–94, Bermuda. Has served on several cttees, tribunals and bds of enquiry, both in Bermuda and Jamaica. *Recreations:* golf, cricket, photography, reading, bridge, travel. *Address:* The Pebble, 7 Astwood Walk, Warwick WK08, Bermuda; PO Box HM 1674, Hamilton HMGX, Bermuda. *Clubs:* Bermuda Senior Golfers Society, Coral Beach and Tennis, Mid Ocean, Riddell's Bay Golf and Country (Bermuda).

ATCHERLEY, Sir Harold Winter, Kt 1977; Chairman: Suffolk and North Essex Branch, European Movement, 1995–98 (President, 1998–2002); Aldeburgh Foundation, 1989–94 (Deputy Chairman, 1988–89); Toynbee Hall, 1985–90 (Member, Management Committee, 1979–90); *b* 30 Aug. 1918; *s* of L. W. Atcherley and Maude Lester (*née* Nash); *m* 1st, 1946, Anita Helen (*née* Leslie) (marr. diss. 1990); one *s* two *d;* 2nd, 1990, Mrs Elke Jessett (*d* 2004), *d* of late Dr Carl Langbehn; 3rd, 2005, Mrs Sarah, (Sally), Mordant. *Educ:* Gresham's Sch.; Heidelberg and Geneva Univs. Joined Royal Dutch Shell Gp, 1937. Served War: Queen's Westminster Rifles, 1939; commissioned Intelligence Corps, 1940; served 18th Infty Div., Singapore; POW, 1942–45. Rejoined Royal Dutch Shell Gp, 1946: served Egypt, Lebanon, Syria, Argentina, Brazil, 1946–59. Personnel Co-ordinator, Royal Dutch Shell Group, 1964–70, retd. Recruitment Advisor to Ministry of Defence, 1970–71. Chm., Tyzack & Partners, 1979–85; Dir, British Home Stores Ltd, 1973–87. Chairman: Armed Forces Pay Review Body, 1971–82; Police Negotiating Bd, 1983–86 (Dep. Chm., 1982); Member: Top Salaries Review Body, 1971–87; Nat. Staff Cttee for Nurses and Midwives, 1973–77; Cttee of Inquiry into Pay and Related Conditions of Service of Nurses, 1974; Cttee of Inquiry into Remuneration of Members of Local Authorities, 1977. Vice-Chm., Suffolk Wildlife Trust, 1987–90; Mem. Management Cttee, Suffolk Rural Housing Assoc., 1984–87. Empress Leopoldina Medal (Brazil), 1958. *Recreations:* music, good food and wine with family and friends.

ATHA, Bernard Peter, CBE 2007 (OBE 1991); Principal Lecturer in Business Studies, Huddersfield Technical College, 1973–90; Lord Mayor, City of Leeds, 2000–01; *b* 27 Aug. 1928; *s* of Horace Michael Atha and Mary Quinlan; unmarried. *Educ:* Leeds Modern Sch.; Leeds Univ. (LLB Hons). Barrister-at-law, Gray's Inn. Commn, RAF, 1950–52. Variety artist on stage; Mem. Equity; films and TV plays. Elected Leeds City Council, 1957; Chm., Leeds Leisure Services Cttee, 1988–99; former Chairman: Watch Cttee; Social Services Cttee; Educn Cttee. Vice-Chm., W Leeds HA, 1988–90. Contested (Lab): Penrith and the Border, 1959; Pudsey, 1964. Pres., Leeds Co-op. Soc., 1976–96; Chairman: Leeds Playhouse, 1974–2007; Northern Ballet Theatre, 1995–. Member: Arts Council, 1979–82; Ministerial Working Party on Sport and Recreation, 1974, on Sport for the Disabled, 1989; EU (formerly EC) Sport for Disabled Cttee, 1992–99 (Vice-Chm., 1997–99); Internat. Paralympic Cttee, 1993–98; Sports Lottery Bd, 1995–2003; Vice-Chm., Sports Council, 1976–80; Chairman: Yorks and Humberside Reg. Sports Council, 1966–76; Nat. Water Sports Centre, 1978–84; UK Sports Assoc. for People with Mental Handicap, 1980– (Pres., INASFMH, 1993–2007); British Paralympics Assoc., 1989. Vice-Chairman: St James' Univ. Hosp. NHS Trust, 1993–98 (Dir, 1990–98); United Leeds Teaching Hosps NHS Trust, subseq. United Leeds Hosps Charitable Foundn, 2001– (Mem., 2000–). Chairman: Disability Sports Develt Trust (formerly British Paralympic Trust), 1990–; English Fedn Disability Sport, 1999–. Chairman: Yorks Dance Centre Trust, 1987–2007; Red Ladder Theatre Co., 1987–; Craft Centre and Design Gall., Leeds, 1988–; Liz Dawn Cancer Appeal; Yorkshire Youth Ballet (formerly Yorkshire Youth Dance), 2006–08. Governor, Sports Aid Foundn. FRSA. Hon. Fellow, Leeds Coll. of Music, 2002. *Recreations:* sport, the arts, travel. *Address:* 25 Moseley Wood Croft, Leeds, West Yorks LS16 7JJ. *T:* (0113) 267 2485.

ATHABASCA, Archbishop of, since 2003; **Most Rev. John Robert Clarke;** Metropolitan of the Ecclesiastical Province of Rupert's Land, since 2003; *b* 27 July 1938; *s* of Rt Rev. Neville and Alice Clarke; *m* 1964, Nadia Juliann Slusar; one *s* two *d. Educ:* Univ. of W Ontario (BA); Huron Coll., London, Ontario (LTh; DD *jure dignitatis,* 1992). Ordained: deacon, 1963; priest, 1964; Curate, St Michael and All Angels, Toronto, 1964–66; Priest-in-charge, Church of the Apostles, Moosonee, 1966–84; Exec. Archdeacon and Treas., Dio. of Athabasca, 1984–91; Bishop of Athabasca, 1992–. *Recreations:* woodworking, travelling, canoeing, gardening. *Address:* PO Box 6868, Peace River, Alberta T8S 1S6, Canada. *T:* (home) (780) 6241008; (office) (780) 6242767.

ATHERTON, Alan Royle, CB 1990; Director, The Argyll Consultancies PLC, 1991–2002 (Deputy Chairman, 1992–94; Chairman, 1994–99); *b* 25 April 1931; *s* of Harold Atherton and Hilda (*née* Royle); *m* 1959, Valerie Kemp (marr. diss. 1996); three *s* one *d. Educ:* Cowley Sch., St Helens; Sheffield Univ. (BSc (Hons Chem.)). ICI Ltd, 1955–58; Department of Scientific and Industrial Research: SSO, 1959–64; Private Sec. to Permanent Sec., 1960–64; PSO, Road Res. Lab., 1964–65; Principal, Min. of Housing and Local Govt, 1965–70; Asst Sec., Ordnance Survey, 1970–74; Under-Sec., 1975–87, Dep. Sec., 1987–91, DoE. Chm., Local Govt Staff Commn (Eng.), 1993–98. Vice Chm., CS Med. Assoc., then CS Healthcare, 1987–98. Chm., Queen Elizabeth II Conf. Centre Bd, 1990–93; Dir, Internat. Centre for Facilities, Canada, 1993–2001; Member: Letchworth Garden City Corp., 1991–94; Historic Royal Palaces Agency Adv. Gp, 1991–98. *Recreations:* walking, gardening, ballet, Rugby. *Club:* Athenæum.

ATHERTON, Candice Kathleen, (Candy); freelance journalist, since 1980; political consultant, since 2005; Managing Director, Atherton Associates, since 2007; *b* 21 Sept. 1955; *d* of late Denis G. W. Atherton and of Pamela A. M. Osborne; *m* 2002, Broderick Ross. *Educ:* Poly. of N London (BA Hons Applied Social Studies). Journalist, Portsmouth News, 1974; West Sussex Probation Service, 1975–76; Founder, Women's Aid Refuge, 1977; Co-Founder, Everywoman Magazine, 1984; freelance journalist, 1980–. Member: (Lab), Islington LBC, 1986–92 (Mayor, 1989–90); Islington HA, 1986–90. Contested (Lab), Chesham and Amersham, 1992. MP (Lab) Falmouth and Camborne, 1997–2005; contested (Lab) same seat, 2005. Member: Select Committee: on Educn and Employment, 1997–2001; on Envmt, Food and Rural Affairs, 2002–05. Chair: All-Party (formerly Associate) Parly Water Gp, 1997–2005; Rural Housing Adv. Gp, 2007–. Treas., Parly Waterways Gp, 1999–2005; Sec., All-Party Parly Objective 1 Areas Gp, 2000–05. Mem. Bd, Housing Corp., 2005–. Freeman, City of London, 1989. *Recreations:* bird-watching, canal boats. *Address:* Pinkmoors Cottage, Pinkmoors, St Day, Cornwall TR16 5NL.

ATHERTON, David, OBE 1999; Founder and Artistic Director, Mainly Mozart Festival, Southern California and Northern Mexico, since 1989; Conductor Laureate, Hong Kong Philharmonic Orchestra, since 2000 (Music Director, 1989–2000); *b* 3 Jan. 1944; *s* of Robert and Lavinia Atherton; *m* 1970, Ann Gianetta Drake; one *s* two *d. Educ:* Cambridge Univ. (MA). LRAM, LTCL. Music Dir, London Sinfonietta, 1967–73 and 1989–91 (Co-Founder, 1967); Repetiteur, Royal Opera House, Covent Garden, 1967–68; Resident Conductor, Royal Opera House, 1968–80; Principal Conductor and Artistic Advr, 1980–83, Principal Guest Conductor, 1983–86, Royal Liverpool Philharmonic Orch.; Music Dir and Principal Conductor, San Diego Symphony Orch., 1980–87; Artistic Dir and Conductor: London Stravinsky Fest., 1979–82; Ravel/Varèse Fest., 1983–84; Principal Guest Conductor: BBC SO, 1985–89; BBC Nat. Orch. of Wales, 1994–97. Co-Founder, Pres. and Artistic Dir, Global Music Network, 1998–2002. Became youngest conductor in history of Henry Wood Promenade Concerts at Royal Albert Hall, and also at Royal Opera House, 1968; Royal Festival Hall debut, 1969; from 1970 performances in Europe, Middle East, Far East, Australasia, N America. Adapted and arranged Pandora by Roberto Gerhard for Royal Ballet, 1975. Conductor of the year award (Composers' Guild of GB), 1971; Edison award, 1973; Grand Prix du Disque award, 1977; Koussevitzky Award, 1981; Internat. Record Critics Award, 1982; Prix Caecilia, 1982. *Publications:* (ed) The Complete Instrumental and Chamber Music of Arnold Schoenberg and Roberto Gerhard, 1973; (ed) Pandora and Don Quixote Suites by Roberto Gerhard, 1973; contrib., The Musical Companion, 1978, The New Grove Dictionary, 1981. *Recreations:* travel, computers, theatre. *Address:* Askonas Holt Ltd, Lincoln House, 300 High Holborn, WC1V 7JH. *T:* (020) 7400 1700, *Fax:* (020) 7400 1799.

ATHERTON, James Bernard; Secretary-General, British Bankers' Association, 1982–85; *b* 3 Dec. 1927; *s* of late James Atherton and Edith (*née* Atkinson); *m* 1953, Eileen Margaret Birch; two *s. Educ:* Alsop High Sch., Liverpool. Served RAF, 1946–48; Martins Bank, 1943–46 and 1948–69 (Asst Chief Accountant, 1966–69); Barclays Bank, 1969–82 (Chief Clearing Manager, 1969–73, Asst Gen. Manager, 1973–78, Divl Gen. Manager, 1978–82). *Recreations:* opera, gardening. *Address:* c/o Barclays Bank, 10 The Square, Petersfield, Hants GU32 3HW.

ATHERTON, Brig. Maurice Alan, CBE 1981; JP; Vice Lord-Lieutenant, Kent, 2000–02; *b* 9 Oct. 1926; *s* of late Rev. Harold Atherton and Beatrice Atherton (*née* Shaw); *m* 1954, Guendolene Mary Upton; one *s* one *d. Educ:* St John's Sch., Leatherhead; Staff Coll., Camberley (psc). Commnd E Yorks Regt, 1946 (served in Egypt, Sudan, Malaya, Austria, Germany, UK); MA to Comdr British Forces, Hong Kong, 1959–62; coll. chief instructor, RMA Sandhurst, 1964–67; CO 1 Green Howards, 1967–69; GSO 1, NI, 1969–71; defence advr, Ghana, 1971–73; Comdr, Dover Shorncliffe Garrison and Dep. Constable, Dover Castle, 1976–81. Co. Pres., Kent, RBL, 1982–91; Chm., Kent Cttee, Army Benevolent Fund, 1984–96. Gov., Christ Church UC, Canterbury, 1985–99 (Chm. Govs, 1993–99); Comr, Duke of York's Royal Mil. Sch., 1992–2003. JP 1982–91, High Sheriff 1983–84, DL 1984, Kent. Hon. DCL Kent, 1996. *Recreations:* gardening, shooting. *Address:* Digges Place, Barham, Canterbury, Kent CT4 6PJ. *T:* (01227) 831420. *Club:* Lansdowne.

ATHERTON, Michael Andrew, OBE 1997; sports commentator and broadcaster; *b* 23 March 1968; *s* of Alan and Wendy Atherton; one *s. Educ:* Manchester Grammar Sch.; Downing Coll., Cambridge (BA Hons History; MA). 1st class début, Cambridge *v* Essex, 1987; played for Lancashire CCC, 1987–2001; Captain: Young England, Sri Lanka 1987, Australia 1988; Cambridge Univ., 1988–89; Combined Universities, 1989; Mem., England Test team, 115 matches, 1989–2001; captained 54 Test matches, 1993–98 and 2001; scored 16 Test centuries. Mem., Editl Board, Wisden Cricket Monthly, 1993–2003; columnist: Sunday Telegraph, 2001–07; The Times, 2008–. Cricket commentator: Channel 4, 2001–05; BSkyB, 2006–. *Publications:* Opening Up: my autobiography, 2002; Gambling: a story of triumph and disaster, 2007. *Recreations:* golf, reading; is cricket still a recreation?! *Address:* c/o Jon Holmes Media Ltd, 5th Floor, Holborn Gate, 26 Southampton Buildings, WC2A 1PQ. *Club:* Groucho.

ATHERTON, Rt Rev. Mgr Richard, OBE 1989; Chaplain to the Archbishop of Liverpool, 1996–2002; *b* 15 Feb. 1928; *s* of Richard Atherton and Winifred Mary Atherton (*née* Hurst). *Educ:* St Francis Xavier's Coll., Liverpool; Upholland Coll., Wigan; Dip. Criminology, London Univ., 1979; BA Hons Maryvale Inst., Birmingham, 1995; MA Durham, 1997. Ordained priest, 1954; Curate: St Cecilia's, Tuebrook, Liverpool, 1954–60; St Philip Neri's, Liverpool, 1960–65; Prison Chaplain: Walton, Liverpool, 1965–75; Appleton Thorne, Warrington, 1975–77; Principal RC Prison Chaplain, 1977–87; Parish Priest, St Joseph's, Leigh, Lancs, 1987–89; Pres., Ushaw Coll., 1991–96. *Publications:* Summons to Serve, 1987; New Light on the Psalms, 1993; Praying the Prayer of the Church, 1998; Praying the Sunday Psalms, Year A, 2001, Year B, 2003, Year C, 2004; Let's Meet the Prophets, 2008. *Recreations:* walking, reading. *Address:* 8 Lindley Road, Elland, W Yorks HX5 0TE. *T:* (0151) 724 6398.

ATHERTON, Robert Kenneth; His Honour Judge Atherton; a Circuit Judge, since 2000; *b* 22 June 1947; *s* of late John and Evelyn Atherton; civil partnership 2006, Michael Montgomery. *Educ:* Boteler Grammar Sch., Warrington; Univ. of Liverpool (LLB Hons). Called to the Bar, Gray's Inn, 1970; in practice at the Bar, 1971–2000; Asst Recorder, 1994–99; a Recorder, 1999–2000. Legal Mem., Mental Health Review Tribunal, 1989–2000. Asst Comr, Parly Boundary Commn, 1993–95. *Recreations:* travel, music, gardening. *Address:* Civil Justice Centre, PO Box 4239, 1 Bridge Street West, Manchester M60 1UR.

ATHERTON, Stephen Nicholas; QC 2006; barrister; *b* 6 May 1966; *s* of James Alan Atherton and late Ann Margaret Atherton; *m* 1992, Lucy-Jane Coppock; one *d. Educ:* West Park Sch.; Univ. of Lancaster (LLB Hons); Magdalene Coll., Cambridge (LLM 1988). Called to the Bar, Middle Temple, 1989, and Gray's Inn. Barrister specialising in domestic and internat. corporate insolvency and restructuring, and civil aspects of domestic and internat. commercial fraud. *Publications:* various legal texts and articles. *Recreations:* Rugby Union, Rugby League, cricket, films, food, family, collecting ancient Chinese ceramics and British watercolours and drawings. *Address:* 3–4 South Square, Gray's Inn, WC1R 5HP. *T:* (020) 7696 9900; *e-mail:* stephenatherton@southsquare.com; Old Isleworth, Middlesex; Hinton St George, Somerset. *Club:* Hinton St George Cricket.

ATHOLL, 11th Duke of *cr* 1703; **John Murray;** Lord Murray of Tullibardine 1604; Earl of Tullibardine 1606; Earl of Atholl 1629; Marquess of Atholl, Viscount of Balquhidder, Lord Murray, Balvenie and Gask, 1676; Marquess of Tullibardine, Earl of Strathtay and Strathardle, Viscount Glenalmond and Glenlyon, 1703 – all in the peerage of Scotland; professional land surveyor; *b* 19 Jan. 1929; *s* of Maj. George Murray (*d* 1940), and Joan (*d* 2000), *d* of William Eastwood; *S* cousin, 1996; *m* 1956, Margaret Yvonne, *o d* of Ronald Leonard Leach; two *s* one *d. Heir: s* Marquess of Tullibardine, *qv.*

ATIYAH, Sir Michael (Francis), OM 1992; Kt 1983; MA, PhD Cantab; FRS 1962; FRSE 1985; President, Royal Society of Edinburgh, 2005–08; Master of Trinity College, Cambridge, 1990–97, Fellow since 1997; Director, Isaac Newton Institute for Mathematical Sciences, Cambridge, 1990–96; *b* 22 April 1929; *e s* of late Edward Atiyah and Jean Levens; *m* 1955, Lily Brown; two *s* (and one *s* decd). *Educ:* Victoria Coll., Egypt; Manchester Grammar Sch.; Trinity Coll., Cambridge. Research Fellow, Trinity Coll., Camb., 1954–58, Hon. Fellow, 1976–97; First Smith's Prize, 1954; Commonwealth Fund Fellow, 1955–56; Mem. Inst. for Advanced Study, Princeton, 1955–56, 1959–60, 1967–68, 1987; Asst Lectr in Mathematics, 1957–58, Lectr 1958–61, Univ. of Cambridge; Fellow, Pembroke Coll., Cambridge, 1958–61 (Hon. Fellow, 1983); Reader in Mathematics, Univ. of Oxford, and Professorial Fellow of St Catherine's Coll., Oxford, 1961–63 (Hon. Fellow, 1992); Savilian Prof. of Geometry, and Fellow of New College, Oxford, 1963–69 (Hon. Fellow 1999); Prof. of Mathematics, Inst. for Advanced Study, Princeton, NJ, 1969–72; Royal Soc. Res. Prof., Mathematical Inst., Oxford, and Professorial Fellow, St Catherine's Coll., Oxford, 1973–90. Hon. Prof., Univ. of Edinburgh, 1997–. Visiting Lecturer, Harvard, 1962–63 and 1964–65. Member: Exec. Cttee, Internat. Mathematical Union, 1966–74; SERC, 1984–89; ACOST, 1991–93; President: London Mathematical Soc., 1975–77; Mathematical Assoc., 1981–82; Royal Soc., 1990–95; Chm., European Mathematical Council, 1978–90. Pres., Pugwash, 1997–2002. Chancellor, Univ. of Leicester, 1995–2005. Freeman, City of London, 1996. Fellow, Univ. of Wales Swansea, 1999. Founder FMedSci 1998 (Hon. FMedSci 2001). Hon. FREng (Hon. FEng 1993). Foreign Member: Amer. Acad. of Arts and Scis; Swedish Royal Acad.; Leopoldina Acad.; Nat. Acad. of Scis, USA; Acad. des Sciences, France; Royal Irish Acad.; Czechoslovak Union of Mathematicians and Physicists; Amer. Philos. Soc.; Indian Nat. Science Acad.; Australian Acad. of Scis; Ukrainian Acad. of Scis; Russian Acad. of Scis; Georgian Acad. of Scis; Venezuelan Acad. of Scis; Accad. Nazionale dei Lincei, Rome; Moscow Mathematical Soc.; Royal Norwegian Acad. of Sci. and Letters, 2001; Spanish Royal Acad. of Sci., 2002. Hon. Prof., Chinese Acad. of Scis; Hon. Fellow, Darwin Coll., Cambridge, 1992; Hon. Dist. Fellow, Leicester Univ., 2007. Hon. FFA 1999. Hon. DSc: Bonn, 1968; Warwick, 1969; Durham, 1979; St Andrew's, 1981; Dublin, Chicago, 1983; Edinburgh, 1984; Essex, London, 1985; Sussex, 1986; Ghent, 1987; Reading, Helsinki, 1990; Leicester, 1991; Salamanca, Rutgers, 1992; Wales, Montreal, Waterloo, 1993; Lebanese Univ., Birmingham, Keele, Queen's (Ontario), 1994; UMIST, Chinese Univ. of Hong Kong, 1996; Brown, 1997; Oxford, Prague, 1998; Heriot-Watt, 1999; Mexico, 2001; York, 2005; Harvard, 2006; Hon. ScD Cantab, 1984; DUniv: Open, 1995; Scuola Normale, Pisa, 2007; Poly. Univ. of Catalonia, 2008; Hon. DHumLit American Univ. of Beirut, 2004. Fields Medal, Internat. Congress of Mathematicians, Moscow, 1966; Royal Medal, Royal Soc., 1968; De Morgan Medal, London Mathematical Soc., 1980; Antonio Feltrinelli Prize for mathematical sciences, Accademia Nazionale dei Lincei, Rome, 1981; King Faisal Foundn Internat. Prize for Science, Saudi Arabia, 1987; Copley Medal, Royal Soc., 1988; Gunning Victoria Jubilee

Prize, RSE, 1990; Nehru Meml Medal, INSA, 1993; Franklin Medal, Amer. Phil. Soc., 1993; Royal Medal, RSE, 2003; (jtly) Abel Prize, Norwegian Acad. of Sci. and Letters, 2004; President's Medal, Inst. of Physics, 2008. Commander, Order of Cedars (Lebanon), 1994; Mem. (1st Class), Order of Andrés Bello (Venezuela), 1997; Mem. (1st class), Golden Order of Merit (Lebanon), 2004. *Publications:* Collected Works, 5 vols, 1988, vol. 6, 2004; The Geometry and Physics of Knots, 1990; papers in mathematical journals. *Recreation:* gardening. *Address:* 3/8 West Grange Gardens, Edinburgh EH9 2RA.
See also P. S. Atiyah.

ATIYAH, Prof. Patrick Selim, DCL; QC 1989; FBA 1978; Professor of English Law, and Fellow of St John's College, Oxford University, 1977–88, Hon. Fellow, 1988; *b* 5 March 1931; *s* of Edward Atiyah and D. J. C. Levens; *m* 1951, Christine Best; three *s* (and one *s* decd). *Educ:* Woking County Grammar Sch. for Boys; Magdalen Coll., Oxford (MA 1957, DCL 1974). Called to the Bar, Inner Temple, 1956. Asst Lectr, LSE, 1954–55; Lectr, Univ. of Khartoum, 1955–59; Legal Asst, BoT, 1961–64; Fellow, New Coll., Oxford, 1964–69; Professor of Law: ANU, 1970–73; Warwick Univ., 1973–77; Visiting Professor: Univ of Texas, 1979; Harvard Law Sch., 1982–83; Duke Univ., 1985. Lectures: Lionel Cohen, Hebrew Univ., Jerusalem, 1980; Oliver Wendell Holmes, Harvard Law Sch., 1981; Cecil Wright Meml, Univ. of Toronto, 1983; Viscount Bennett, Univ. of New Brunswick, 1984; Chorley, LSE, 1985; Hamlyn, Leeds Univ., 1987. Hon. LLD Warwick, 1989. General Editor, Oxford Jl of Legal Studies, 1981–86. *Publications:* The Sale of Goods, 1957, 8th edn 1990, 10th edn (ed John Adams), 2000; Introduction to the Law of Contract, 1961, 6th edn (ed Stephen Smith), 2007; Vicarious Liability, 1967; Accidents, Compensation and the Law, 1970, 6th edn (ed Peter Cane), 1999; The Rise and Fall of Freedom of Contract, 1979; Promises, Morals and Law, 1981 (Swiney Prize, RSA/RSP, 1984); Law and Modern Society, 1983, 2nd edn 1995; Essays on Contract, 1987; Pragmatism and Theory in English Law, 1987; (with R. S. Summers) Form and Substance in Anglo-American Law, 1987; The Damages Lottery, 1997; articles in legal jls. *Recreations:* gardening, cooking. *Address:* 65 Seaview Road, Hayling Island, Hants PO11 9PD. *T:* (023) 9246 2474.
See also Sir M. F. Atiyah.

ATKIN, Alec Field, CBE 1978; FREng; FRAeS; Managing Director, Marketing, Aircraft Group, British Aerospace, 1981–82, retired; Director, AWA (Consultancy) Ltd, since 1983; *b* 26 April 1925; *s* of Alec and Grace Atkin; *m* 1948, Nora Helen Darby (marr. diss. 1982); two *s* one *d*; *m* 1982, Wendy Atkin (marr. diss. 1998); *m* 2006, Lynn Tonkinson. *Educ:* Riley High Sch.; Hull Technical Coll. (DipAe); Hull Univ. (BSc (Hons) Maths, ext. London). FIMechE 1945–2000; FRAeS 1952; FREng (FEng 1979). English Electric Co., Preston: Aerodynamicist, 1950; Dep. Chief Aerodyn., 1954; Head of Exper. Aerodyns, 1957; Asst Chief Engr, then Proj. Manager, 1959; Warton Div., British Aircraft Corporation Ltd: Special Dir, 1964; Dir, 1970; Asst Man. Dir, 1973–75; Dep. Man. Dir, 1975–76; Man. Dir, 1976–77; Man. Dir (Mil.), Aircraft Gp of British Aerospace, and Chm., Warton, Kingston-Brough and Manchester Divs, 1978–81. FRSA. Hon. DSc Hull, 1997. *Recreation:* sailing. *Address:* Les Fougères d'Icart, Icart Road, St Martin, Guernsey GY4 6JG.

ATKIN, Gavin Mark; freelance journalist; Editor, The Practitioner, 2000–06; *b* 2 Jan. 1956; *s* of Alistair Brian and Sunya Mary Atkin; one *s* one *d*; partner, Julie Arnott. *Educ:* Univ. of Newcastle upon Tyne (BSc Gen. Scis). Man. Editor, The Practitioner, 1994–2000. Chm., Kent Gathering of Traditional Music, 2007–. *Publication:* Ultrasimple Boatbuilding, 2007. *Recreations:* being a dad, traditional music, contemporary country dance music, sailing, designing and building small boats.

ATKINS, Andrew Windham; Executive Director, Friends of the Earth (England, Wales and Northern Ireland), since 2008; *b* Eastleigh, Hants, 9 Oct. 1960; *s* of Rev. Roger Atkins and Diana Atkins (*née* Gilbard); *m* 1985, Sarah Witts; one *s* two *d*. *Educ:* University Coll. London (BA Hons Geog. 1982); Inst. of Latin American Studies, Univ. of London (MA Latin American Studies 1983). Nat. Coordinator, 1985, Gen. Sec., 1986–88, Chile Cttee for Human Rights; Partnership Scheme Coordinator, CAFOD, 1988–90; Latin America Desk Officer, Catholic Inst. for Internat. Relns, 1990–97; Tearfund: Public Policy Advr, 1997–98; Public Policy Team Leader, 1998–2000; Advocacy (Policy and Campaigns) Dir, 2000–08. Board Member: Make Poverty Hist. Campaign, 2004–06; Micah Challenge Campaign, 2004–08. FRSA. *Recreations:* landscape painting, cycling, world literature, theatre. *Address:* Friends of the Earth, 26–28 Underwood Street, N1 7JQ. *T:* (020) 7490 0336, *Fax:* (020) 7490 0881; *e-mail:* andy.atkins@foe.co.uk.

ATKINS, Charlotte; MP (Lab) Staffordshire Moorlands, since 1997; *b* 24 Sept. 1950; *d* of Ronald and Jessie Atkins; *m* 1990, Gus Brain; one *d*. *Educ:* Colchester County High Sch.; LSE (BSc(Econ)); MA London Univ. Asst Community Relations Officer, Luton CRC, 1974–76; Res. Officer, then Hd of Res., UCATT, 1976–80; Res. and Political Officer, AUEW (TASS), 1980–83; Press Officer, 1983–92, Parly Officer, 1992–97, COHSE, then UNISON. PPS to Minister of State for Trade, DTI and FCO, 2001–02; an Asst Govt Whip, 2002–05; Parly Under-Sec. of State, DfT, 2004–05. Member: Select Cttee on Educn and Employment, 1997–2001; Cttee of Selection, 1997–2000; Select Cttee on Health, 2005–. Mem., PLP Parly Cttee, 1997–2000. Contested (Lab) Eastbourne, Oct. 1990. *Address:* House of Commons, SW1A 0AA.

ATKINS, Charlotte Elizabeth Mary; *see* Voake, C. E. M.

ATKINS, Dame Eileen, DBE 2001 (CBE 1990); actress and writer; *b* 16 June 1934; *d* of Arthur Thomas Atkins and late Annie Ellen (*née* Elkins); *m* Bill Shepherd. *Educ:* Latymer Grammar Sch., Edmonton; Guildhall Sch. of Music and Drama. *Stage appearances include:* Twelfth Night, Richard III, The Tempest, Old Vic, 1962; The Killing of Sister George (Best Actress, Standard Awards), Bristol Old Vic, transf. Duke of York's, 1965; The Cocktail Party, Wyndham's, transf. Haymarket, 1968; Vivat! Vivat Regina! (Variety Award), Piccadilly, 1970; Suzanne Andler, Aldwych, 1973; As You Like It, Stratford, 1973; St Joan, Old Vic, 1977; Passion Play, Aldwych, 1981; Medea, Young Vic, 1986; The Winter's Tale, and Cymbeline (Olivier Award), Mountain Language, NT, 1988; A Room of One's Own, Hampstead, 1989; Exclusive, Strand, 1989; Prin, NY, 1990; The Night of the Iguana, NT, 1992; Vita and Virginia, Ambassadors, 1993, NY, 1994; Indiscretions, NY, 1995; John Gabriel Borkman, NT, 1996; A Delicate Balance, Haymarket (Best Actress, Evening Standard Awards), 1997; The Unexpected Man, RSC, transf. Duchess (Best Actress, Olivier Awards), 1998; Honour, NT, 2003; The Retreat from Moscow, NY, 2003; The Birthday Party, Duchess, 2005; Doubt, NY, 2006; There Came a Gypsy Riding, Almeida, 2007; The Sea, Haymarket, 2008; The Female of the Species, Vaudeville, 2008; *films include:* Equus, 1974; The Dresser, 1984; Let Him Have It, 1990; Wolf, 1994; Women Talking Dirty, 2001; Gosford Park, 2002; What a Girl Wants, 2003; Vanity Fair, 2005; Evening, 2007; *TV appearances include:* The Duchess of Malfi; Sons and Lovers; Smiley's People; Nelly's Version; The Burston Rebellion; Breaking Up; The Vision; Mrs Pankhurst in In My Defence (series), 1990; A Room of One's Own, 1990; The Lost Language of Cranes, 1993; The Maitlands, 1993; Cold Comfort Farm, 1995 (film, 1997); Talking Heads 2, 1998; Madame Bovary, 2000; Bertie and Elizabeth, 2002; Love Again, 2003; Waking the Dead, Cranford, 2007 (Best Actress, BAFTA, 2008). Co-created television series: Upstairs Downstairs; The House of Eliott; *screenplay:* Mrs Dalloway (Best Screenplay, Evening Standard British Film Awards), 1998. *Address:* c/o Paul Lyon Maris, Independent Talent Group Ltd, Oxford House, 76 Oxford Street, W1D 1BS.

ATKINS, Prof. Madeleine Julia, PhD; Vice-Chancellor, Coventry University, since 2004; *b* 2 July 1952; *d* of Harold and Julia Dunkerley; *m* 1975, John Michael Atkins; two *s*. *Educ:* Girton Coll., Cambridge (BA Hons 1974); Lady Margaret Hall, Oxford (PGCE); Nottingham Univ. (PhD 1982). Teacher, Hinchinbrooke Comprehensive Sch., 1975–79; post-doctoral res., Nottingham Univ., 1982–83; University of Newcastle upon Tyne: Lectr, 1984–88; Sen. Lectr, 1988–2004; Head, Dept of Educn, 1991–96; Dean, Faculty of Educn, 1996–98; Pro-Vice-Chancellor, 1998–2004. *Publications:* (with G. A. Brown) Effective Teaching in Higher Education, 1988; contrib. numerous articles on mgt in higher educn and on use of multimedia applications in learning to jls. *Recreations:* theatre, walking. *Address:* Coventry University, Priory Street, Coventry CV1 5FB. *T:* (024) 7688 8212, *Fax:* (024) 7688 8638; *e-mail:* m.atkins@coventry.ac.uk.

ATKINS, Rev. Dr Martyn David; General Secretary, Methodist Church of Great Britain, and Secretary, Methodist Conference, since 2008; *b* 16 June 1955; *s* of Raymond and Marion Atkins; *m* 1980, Helen Claire Robinson; three *s*. *Educ:* Victoria Univ. of Manchester (BA; PhD 1990). Ordained Methodist Minister, 1981; Leeds (S) Methodist circuit, 1981–86; Shipley and Bingley Methodist circuit, 1986–91; Chaplain, Edgehill Coll., Bideford, Devon, 1991–96; Postgrad. Tutor, 1996–2004, Principal, 2004–08, Cliff Coll., Sheffield. Pres., Methodist Conference, 2007–08. *Publications:* Preaching in a Cultural Context, 2001; Sermon on the Mount, 2002; Resourcing Renewal, 2007. *Recreations:* supporting Leeds United Football Club, book collecting, reading. *Address:* Methodist Church House, 25 Marylebone Road, NW1 5JR. *T:* (020) 7486 5502.

ATKINS, Rt Rev. Peter Geoffrey; Bishop of Waiapu, 1983–90; Dean, Theological College of St John the Evangelist, Auckland, 1991–96; *b* 29 April 1936; *s* of late Lt-Col Owen Ivan Atkins and Mrs Mary Atkins; *m* 1968, Rosemary Elizabeth (*née* Allen); one *d*. *Educ:* Merchant Taylors' School, Crosby, Liverpool; Sidney Sussex Coll., Cambridge; St John's Coll., Auckland, NZ. MA (Cantab), BD (Otago), LTh (NZ). Deacon 1962, priest 1963; Curate, Karori Parish, Wellington, 1962–66; Priest-Tutor, St Peter's Theological Coll., Siota, Solomon Is, 1966–67; Curate, Dannevirke Parish, dio. Waiapu, 1968–70; Vicar of Waipukurau Parish, 1970–73; Diocesan Sec. and Registrar, Diocese of Waiapu, 1973–79; Canon of St John's Cathedral, Napier, 1974–79; Vicar of Havelock North, 1979–83; Archdeacon of Hawkes Bay, 1979–83; Vicar-Gen., Diocese of Waiapu, 1980–83; Commissary to Archbishop of NZ, 1983; Lectr in Liturgy and Evangelism, Univ. of Auckland and Melbourne Coll. of Divinity, 1991–97. Hon. Sen. Res. Fellow, Univ. of Birmingham, 1996. Contributor, Reviews in Religion and Theology, 1997–2006; Mem., Editl Bd, Rural Theology, 2006–. *Publications:* Good News in Evangelism, 1992; (contrib.) Counselling Issues and South Pacific Communities, 1997; Worship 2000, 1999; Soul Time, 2000; (jtly) Personality Type and Scripture: exploring Luke's gospel, 2000, exploring Matthew's gospel, 2001, exploring Mark's gospel, 2002; Soul Care, 2001; Ascension Now, 2001; (jtly) Family Prayers, 2003; Memory and Liturgy, 2004; (jtly) Cool Prayers, 2004; (jtly) Prayer Kids, 2008. *Recreations:* writing, gardening, music. *Address:* 9A Paunui Street, St Helier's Bay, Auckland 1071, New Zealand. *T:* (9) 5754775, *Fax:* (9) 5750477.

ATKINS, Prof. Peter William, PhD; FRSC; Professor of Chemistry, University of Oxford, 1998–2007; Fellow and Tutor, Lincoln College, Oxford, 1965–2007, now Supernumerary Fellow (Acting Rector, 2007); *b* 10 Aug. 1940; *s* of William Henry Atkins and Ellen Louise Atkins; *m* 1st, 1964, Judith Ann Kearton (marr. diss. 1983); one *d*; 2nd, 1991, Susan Adele Greenfield (*see* Baroness Greenfield) (marr. diss. 2005); 3rd, 2008, Patricia Jean Nobes. *Educ:* Dr Challoner's Sch., Amersham; Univ. of Leicester (BSc 1961; PhD 1964); MA Oxon 1965. FRSC 2002. Harkness Fellow, UCLA, 1964–65; Lectr, Univ. of Oxford, 1965–2007. Vis. Prof. in China, Japan, France, NZ and Israel. Nyholm Lectr, 1999; Hon. Prof., Mendeleyev Univ., Moscow, 2006. Chairman: Davy-Faraday Lab. Cttee, 1999–2005; Educn Strategy Develt Cttee, 2000, Cttee on Chemistry Educn, 2002–05, IUPAC. Mem. Council, Royal Instn, 1999–2005; Mem. Ct, Leicester Univ., 2000–. Hon. Associate, Rationalist Press Assoc., 1993. Hon. DSc: Utrecht, 1992; Leicester, 2002. Meldola Medal, RSC, 1969. *Publications:* The Structure of Inorganic Radicals, 1967; Tables for Group Theory, 1970; Molecular Quantum Mechanics, 1970, 4th edn 2005; Physical Chemistry, 1978, 8th edn 2006; Solutions Manual for Physical Chemistry, 1978, 8th edn 2006; Quanta: a handbook of concepts, 1974, 2nd edn 1991; Principles of Physical Chemistry, 1981; The Creation, 1981; Quantization, 1981; Solutions Manual for Molecular Quantum Mechanics, 1983, 2nd edn 1997; The Second Law, 1984; Molecules, 1987, 2nd edn as Atkins' Molecules, 2003; General Chemistry, 1987, 2nd edn 1992; Chemistry: principles and applications, 1988; Inorganic Chemistry, 1990, 4th edn 2006; Atoms, Electrons and Change, 1991; The Elements of Physical Chemistry, 1992, 4th edn 2005; Creation Revisited, 1992; The Periodic Kingdom, 1995; Concepts of Physical Chemistry, 1995; Chemistry: molecules, matter, and change, 1997, 4th edn 1999; Chemical Principles, 1999, 4th edn 2007; Galileo's Finger: the ten great ideas of science, 2003; Four Laws that Drive the Universe, 2007. *Recreation:* working. *Address:* Lincoln College, Oxford OX1 3DR. *Club:* Athenæum.

ATKINS, Rt Hon. Sir Robert (James), Kt 1997; PC 1995; Member (C) North West Region, England, European Parliament, since 1999; *b* 5 Feb. 1946; *s* of late Reginald Alfred and of Winifred Margaret Atkins; *m* 1969, Dulcie Mary (*née* Chaplin); one *s* one *d*. *Educ:* Highgate School. Councillor, London Borough of Haringey, 1968–77; Vice-Chm., Greater London Young Conservatives, 1969–70, 1971–72. Contested (C) Luton West, Feb. 1974 and Oct. 1974 general elections. MP (C) Preston North, 1979–83, South Ribble, 1983–97; contested (C) South Ribble, 1997. PPS to Minister of State, DoI, then DTI, 1982–84, to Minister without Portfolio, 1984–85, to Sec. of State for Employment, 1985–87; Parly Under Sec. of State, DTI, 1987–89, Dept of Transport, 1989–90, DoE (Minister for Sport), 1990, DES (Minister for Sport), 1990–92; Minister of State, NI Office, 1992–94; Minister of State for the Environment and the Countryside, DoE, 1994–95. Vice-Chm., Cons. Aviation Cttee, 1979–82; Jt Sec., Cons. Defence Cttee, 1979–82. Chm., NW Cons. MPs, 1996–97; Dep. Leader, British Cons. MEPs, 2004–07. President: Cons. Trade Unionists, 1984–87; Wyre & Preston N Cons. Assoc., 2007–. Member: Victorian Soc.; Sherlock Holmes Soc. of London; English Heritage; Historic Churches Preservation Trust; Nat. Trust. Chm., Lancs CCC Develt Assoc., 2002–. Freeman, City of London, 1989. *Publication:* (contrib.) Changing Gear, 1981. *Recreations:* cricket, ecclesiology, wine, Holmesiana. *Address:* European Parliament, Rue Wiertz, 1047 Brussels, Belgium; Manor House, Lancaster Road, Garstang, Lancs PR3 1JA. *Clubs:* Carlton, MCC, Lord's Taverners; Middlesex County Cricket, Lords and Commons Cricket, Lancashire County Cricket (Vice-Pres., 2005–), Garstang Cricket (Pres., 2007–), Preston Grasshoppers Rugby Fooball (Vice-Pres., 1990–), Garstang Rugby Union Football (Vice-Pres., 2007–).

ATKINS, Ronald Henry; b Barry, Glam, 13 June 1916; s of Frank and Elizabeth Atkins; m; three s two d. Educ: Barry County Sch.; London Univ. (BA Hons). Teacher, 1949–66 (latterly Head, Eng. Dept, Halstead Sec. Sch.); Lectr, Accrington Coll. of Further Educn, 1970–74. Member: Braintree RDC, 1952–61; (Lab) Preston Dist Council, 1974–76, 1980–. Contested (Lab) Lowestoft, 1964; MP (Lab) Preston North, 1966–70 and Feb. 1974–1979. Recreations: jazz, dancing, walking. Address: 38 James Street, Preston, Lancs PR1 4JU. T: (01772) 251910.

ATKINS, Rosemary Jean, (Rosie), FLS; Curator, Chelsea Physic Garden, since 2002; b 9 Oct. 1947; m 1973, Eric James Brown; one s one d. Educ: St Michael's Sch. for Girls, Limpsfield; Ravensbourne Sch. of Art. Sunday Times, 1968–82; freelance journalist and gardening writer, 1982–; gardening corresp., Today, 1985–92; Editor, Gardens Illustrated Mag., 1993–2002. Produced jointly, In the Air, BBC Radio 4, 1983. Royal Horticultural Society: Judge, Woody Plants (formerly Floral B) Cttee, 2004–; Mem., Horticl Bd, 2006–. FLS 2004. Editor's Editor Award, BSME, 1996. Publications: (jtly) The Sunday Times Book of the Countryside, 1978; (contrib.) Making a Garden: the history of the National Garden Scheme, 2001; (ed) Gardens Illustrated Plant Profiles, 2003; Roses, 2004. Recreations: gardening, writing, painting, travel, photography. Address: Chelsea Physic Garden, 66 Royal Hospital Road, SW3 4HS. Club: Chelsea Arts.

ATKINS, Dr Susan Ruth Elizabeth; Service Complaints Commissioner for the Armed Forces, since 2007; b 4 March 1952; d of late Victor Charles Rodney Prickett and of Marian Sarah Gertrude Prickett; m 1977, Stephen Thomas Atkins; one s one d. Educ: Manchester High Sch. for Girls; Univ. of Birmingham (LLB Hons); Univ. of Calif, Berkeley (Master of Criminol.); Univ. of Southampton (PhD 1986). Admitted solicitor, 1977. Articled clerk, GLC, 1974–77; Lectr in Law, Univ. of Southampton, 1977–89; Principal, Home Office, 1989–93; Dep. Chief Exec., EOC, 1993–95; Home Office: Head: of Extradition, 1995–96; of Personnel Policy, 1996–99; of Probation, 1999–2000; Dir, Women and Equality Unit, Cabinet Office, 2000–02; Chief Exec., Ind. Police Complaints Commn, 2003–06; Interim Chief Exec., Appts Commn, 2007. Vis. Fellow, 1989–95, Vis. Prof., 1995–2001, Univ. of Southampton. Non-exec. Bd Mem., HMP Manchester, 1994–95; Bd Mem., QAA, 2004–; non-exec. Dir, Leadership Foundn for Higher Educn, 2007–. Publications: (with B. Hoggett) Women and the Law, 1984; contribs to legal jls, mainly on sex discrimination and European law. Recreations: reading, travel, tapestry.

ATKINSON, Sir Alec; see Atkinson, Sir J. A.

ATKINSON, Sir Anthony Barnes, (Sir Tony), Kt 2000; FBA 1984; Professor of Economics, University of Oxford, since 2007; Senior Research Fellow, Nuffield College, Oxford, since 2005 (Warden, 1994–2005); b 4 Sept. 1944; s of Norman Joseph Atkinson and Esther Muriel Atkinson; m 1965, Judith Mary (née Mandeville); two s one d. Educ: Cranbrook Sch.; Churchill Coll., Cambridge (MA). Fellow, St John's Coll., Cambridge, 1967–71; Prof. of Econs, Univ. of Essex, 1971–76; Prof. and Hd of Dept of Political Economy, UCL, 1976–79; Prof. of Econs, LSE, 1980–92; Prof. of Political Economy, and Fellow, Churchill Coll., Cambridge, 1992–94. Vis. Prof., MIT, 1973; Chaire Blaise Pascal, Paris Sch. of Econs, 2005–07. Member: Royal Commn on Distribution of Income and Wealth, 1978–79; Retail Prices Index Adv. Cttee, 1984–90; Pension Law Review Cttee, 1992–93; Social Justice Commn, 1992–94; Conseil d'Analyse Economique, France, 1997–2001. Editor, Jl of Public Economics, 1972–97. President: European Econ. Assoc., 1989 (Vice-Pres., 1986–88); Internat. Econ. Assoc., 1989–92; Vice-Pres., British Acad., 1988–90. Fellow, Econometric Soc., 1975 (Vice-Pres., 1986–87, Pres., 1988). Hon. Mem., Amer. Econ. Assoc., 1985. Fellow, Centre for Econ. Studies, Munich, 1995. Hon. Fellow, LSE, 2005. Hon. Dr Rer. Pol. Univ. of Frankfurt, 1987; Hon. Dr en Sci. Econ., Univ. of Lausanne, 1988; Hon. Dr: Univ. of Liège, 1989; Athens Univ. of Econs, 1991; Stirling, 1992; Edinburgh, 1994; Essex, Bologna, and Ecole Normale Supérieure, Paris, 1995; South Bank and Univ. Catholique, Louvain, 1996; Nottingham, 2000; London Metropolitan, 2002; Gent, Antwerp, and European Univ. Inst., Florence, 2004; Molise, 2006. Scientific Prize, Union des Assurances de Paris, 1986; Frank E. Seidman Dist. Award in Pol. Econ., Rhodes Coll., Tenn, 1995; A.SK Social Sci. Award, WZB, Berlin, 2007. Chevalier, Légion d'Honneur (France), 2001. Publications: Poverty in Britain and the Reform of Social Security, 1969; Unequal Shares, 1972; The Tax Credit Scheme, 1973; Economics of Inequality, 1975; (with A. J. Harrison) Distribution of Personal Wealth in Britain, 1978; (with J. E. Stiglitz) Lectures on Public Economics, 1980; Social Justice and Public Policy, 1982; (jtly) Parents and Children, 1983; (with J. Micklewright) Unemployment Benefits and Unemployment Duration, 1985; Poverty and Social Security, 1989; (with J. Micklewright) Economic Transformation in Eastern Europe and the Distribution of Income, 1992; Public Economics in Action, 1995; Incomes and the Welfare State, 1996; The Economic Consequences of Rolling Back the Welfare State, 1999; (jtly) Social Indicators, 2002; (jtly) The EU and Social Inclusion, 2006; The Changing Distribution of Earnings in OECD Countries, 2008; articles in Rev. of Econ. Studies, Econ. Jl, Jl of Public Econs, Jl of Econ. Theory. Address: Nuffield College, Oxford OX1 1NF.

ATKINSON, Arthur Kingsley Hall, CB 1985; Chief Executive, Intervention Board for Agricultural Produce, 1980–86; b 24 Dec. 1926; er s of Arthur Hall Atkinson and Florence (née Gerrans). Educ: Priory Sch., Shrewsbury; Emmanuel Coll., Cambridge (MA). RAF, 1948; MAFF: Asst Principal 1950; Private Sec. 1953; Principal 1956; Asst Sec. 1965; Under Sec., 1973; Cabinet Office, 1976–78; MAFF, 1978–80. Recreations: travel, music, gardening.

ATKINSON, Prof. Bernard, OBE 2001; FREng, FIChemE; Director-General, BRF International (formerly Director, Brewing Research Foundation), 1981–96; b 17 March 1936; s of late Thomas Atkinson and of Elizabeth Ann (née Wilcox); m 1957, Kathleen Mary Richardson; two s. Educ: Farnworth Grammar Sch.; Univ. of Birmingham (BSc); Univ. of Manchester Inst. of Science and Technology; PhD Univ. of Manchester. FREng (FEng 1980). Post-Doctoral Fellow and Asst Prof., Rice Univ., Houston, Texas, 1960–63; Lectr, Sen. Lectr in Chem. Engrg, and latterly Reader in Biochem. Engrg, University Coll. of Swansea, 1963–74 (Hon. Fellow, 1991); Prof. and Head of Dept of Chem. Engrg, UMIST, 1974–81; Visiting Professor: UMIST, 1981–86; Swansea, 1986–; Heriot-Watt, 1991–96. European Brewery Convention: Mem.; Management Cttee and Council, 1990–97; Vice Pres., 1991–97. Mem., BBSRC, 1996–2001. Gov., Queen Victoria Hosp. NHS Foundn Trust, 2004– (Gov. Rep., Bd of Dirs, 2007–). Editor, Biochemical Engineering Journal, 1983–93. Senior Moulton Medal, IChemE, 1976; Gairn EEC Medal, Soc. of Engrs, 1985; Presidential Award, Master Brewers' Assoc. of the Americas, 1988; Donald Medal, IChemE, 1996. Publications: Biochemical Reactors, 1974, trans. Japanese, Russian, Spanish; (with P. F. Cooper) Biological Fluidised Bed Treatment of Water and Waste Water, 1981; (with F. Mavituna) Biochemical Engineering and Biotechnology Handbook, 1982, 2nd edn 1991; (ed) Research and Innovation in the 1990s: the chemical engineering challenge, 1986; (with C. Webb and G. M. Black) Process Engineering Aspects of Immobilised Cell Systems, 1986; numerous contribs to chemical engrg and biochemical engrg jls. Recreations: cycling, sailing, walking. Address:

Little Mieders, Borers Arms Road, Copthorne, Crawley, West Sussex RH10 3LJ. T: (01342) 713181. Club: Square Rigger (Sec., 2007–).

ATKINSON, Prof. Bruce Wilson, PhD; Professor of Geography, Queen Mary and Westfield College (formerly at Queen Mary College), University of London, 1983–2004, now Emeritus; b 28 Sept. 1941; s of J. and S. A. Atkinson. Educ: University Coll., London (BSc, PhD). Queen Mary, subseq. Queen Mary and Westfield College, University of London: Lectr, 1964–78; Reader, 1978–83; Hd, Dept of Geog., 1985–89; Dean of Social Scis, 1991–94; Mem., Senate and Acad. Council, Univ. of London, 1991–94. Natural Environment Research Council: Mem., 1982–85, Chm., 1988–91, Aquatic & Atmospheric Phys. Sci. Cttee; Mem., Atmos. Sci., Marine Sci., Terrestrial and Freshwater Sci. and Higher Educn Affairs Cttees, 1988–91. Member: Meteorol and Atmos. Phys. Sub-cttee, Nat. Cttee on Geodesy and Geophysics, 1988–90; Scientific Adv. Cttee, Meteorol Office, 1996–2004. Mem. Council and cttees, and Editor, Weather, RMetS, 1972–79; Chm., Pubns Cttee, 1992–98, Mem. Council, 1993–95, RGS-IBG (formerly RGS); Mem., Assoc. Brit. Climatologists, 1970– (Chm., 1976–78). Ed., Progress in Physical Geography, 1977–. Hugh Robert Mill Medal, RMetS, 1974; Back Award, RGS, 1981. Publications: Weather Business, 1968; (ed) Dynamical Meteorology, 1981; Mesoscale Atmospheric Circulations, 1981; Weather: Review of UK Statistical Sources, 1985; (ed jtly) Encyclopædic Dictionary of Physical Geography, 1986; (with A. Gadd) Weather: a modern guide to forecasting, 1986; articles in Qly Jl RMetS, Jl Applied Met., Boundary Layer Meteorol., Monthly Weather Rev., Revs of Geophysics, Jl of Geophysical Res., Trans IBG, Geog., Weather, Canadian Geog. Recreations: walking, music. Clubs: Athenæum, Geographical.

ATKINSON, Carol Lesley, (Mrs C. A. Kinch); Her Honour Judge Atkinson; a Circuit Judge, since 2007; b N Yorks, 29 Sept. 1962; d of George Atkinson and Maureen Atkinson (née Heslop); m 1994, Christopher Anthony Kinch, qv; one s two d. Educ: Cleveland Girls Grammar Sch.; Rye Hills Sch., Redcar; Sir William Turner's Sixth Form Coll.; Lancaster Univ. (LLB Hons); Inns of Court Sch. of Law. Called to the Bar, Gray's Inn, 1985 (Karmel Schol. 1986); Recorder, 2001–07. Mem., Bar Council, 1997–2007. Sec., Family Law Bar Assoc., 2004–07. Recreations: my children, running, swimming, music, Middlesbrough FC; Black Belt, 1st Dan, Karate. Address: Gee Street Courthouse, Clerkenwell and Shoreditch County Court, 29–41 Gee Street, EC1V 3RE.

ATKINSON, David Anthony; b 24 March 1940; s of late Arthur Joseph Atkinson and of Joan Margaret Atkinson (née Zink); m 1968, Susan Nicola Pilsworth; one s one d. Educ: St George's Coll., Weybridge; Coll. of Automobile and Aeronautical Engrg, Chelsea. Diplomas in Auto. Engrg and Motor Industry Management. Member: Southend County Borough Council, 1969–72; Essex CC, 1973–78. MP (C) Bournemouth East, Nov. 1977–2005. PPS, 1979–87, to Rt Hon. Paul Channon, MP (Minister of State, Civil Service Dept, 1979–81, Minister for the Arts, 1981–83, Minister of State, DTI, 1983–86, Sec. of State for Trade and Industry, 1986–87). Introduced Licensing (Occasional Permissions) Act 1983. Mem., Council of Europe and WEU, 1979–86, 1987–2005 (Leader, Conservative delgn, 1997–2005; Chm., EDG, 1998–2005). Nat. Chm., Young Conservative Orgn, 1970–71; Life Vice Pres., Christian Solidarity Internat. (UK), 1996 (Chm., 1979–83; Pres., 1983–96). Recreations: mountaineering, art and architecture, travel. Address: c/o Bournemouth East Conservative Association, Haviland Road West, Bournemouth BH1 4JW.

ATKINSON, Rt Rev. David John; see Thetford, Bishop Suffragan of.

ATKINSON, David Rowland; Regional Chairman, British Gas East Midlands, 1987–92; b 18 June 1930; s of late Rowland Hodgson Atkinson and Nora Marian (née Coleman); m 1956, Marian Eileen Sales; one d. Educ: Wrekin College. FCA, CCMI, CompIGasE. National Coal Board: NW Div., 1955; E Midlands Div., 1961; Chief Accountant, W Midlands Gas, 1969; Dir of Finance, E Midlands Gas, 1977; Dep. Chm., SE Gas, 1983; Dir of Finance, British Gas, 1985. Recreations: Rugby, gardening, ciné photography. Address: Russetts, 124 The Ridings, Rothley, Leics LE7 7SL.

ATKINSON, Air Marshal Sir David (William), KBE 1982; FFOM; FRCPE; FFPH; Director-General, Stroke (formerly Chest, Heart and Stroke) Association, 1985–93; Director-General, RAF Medical Services, 1981–84; b 29 Sept. 1924; s of late David William Atkinson and Margaret Atkinson; m 1948, Mary (née Sowerby) (separated); one s. Educ: Edinburgh Univ. (MB, ChB 1948). DPH and DIH, London; FFPH (FFCM 1976); MFOM 1978, FFOM 1983; FRCPE 1983. Joined RAF, 1949; med. officer appts, UK, Jordan and Egypt, 1949–63; Student, RAF Staff Coll., 1963–64; SMO, RAF Brüggen, Germany, 1964–67; Dep. PMO, HQ Air Support Comd, 1967–70; PMO, HQ Brit. Forces Gulf, Bahrain, 1970–71; OC RAF Hosp., Wegberg, Germany, 1971–73; Dir of Health and Research (RAF), 1974–78; QHP 1977–84; PMO, RAF Strike Command, 1978–81. Freeman, City of London, 1984; Liveryman, Soc. of Apothecaries. CStJ 1981. Publication: (jtly) Double Crew Continuous Flying Operations: a study of aircrew sleep patterns, 1970. Recreations: walking, gardening, reading, looking at pictures. Address: Rosedene, Woodside Lane, Lymington, Hants SO41 8FJ. Club: Royal Air Force.

ATKINSON, Frank, CBE 1995 (OBE 1980); FSA; FMA; Director, Beamish North of England Open Air Museum, 1970–87; b 13 April 1924; s of Ernest Atkinson and Elfrida (née Bedford); m 1953, Joan Peirson; three s. Educ: Holgate Grammar Sch., Barnsley; Sheffield Univ. (BSc). Director: Wakefield City Art Gall. and Mus., 1949; Halifax Museums, 1951; Bowes Mus. and Durham Co. Mus. Service, 1958. Member: Working Party on Preservation of Technolog. Material, 1970–71; Wright Cttee on Provincial Museums and Galls, 1971–73; Working Party of Standing Commn on Museums and Galls (Drew Report), 1975–78; Museums and Galleries Commn, 1987–94 (Chm., Registration Cttee, 1988–94). Chairman: Thomas Bewick Birthplace Trust, 1985–91; Northumbrian Tourism Co-ordination Gp, 1989–93; Thomas Bewick (Newcastle) Trust, 1996–2001; Juvenile Autism in the NE Wkg Gp, 1996–99; Friends of Beamish Mus. Ltd, 1996–. Pres., Museums Assoc., 1974–75. Hon. MA Newcastle upon Tyne, 1971; Hon. DCL Durham, 1987. Publications: Aspects of the 18th century Woollen and Worsted Trade, 1956; The Great Northern Coalfield, 1966, 3rd edn 1979; Industrial Archaeology of North East England, 1974; Life and Traditions in Northumberland and Durham, 1977, 3rd edn 2001; North East England: people at work 1860–1950, 1980; Victorian Britain: North East England, 1989; Northern Life, 1991; The Man Who Made Beamish: an autobiography, 1999; The Story of Ovingham on Tyne, 2001; contribs to Trans Newcomen Soc., Procs of British Spel. Soc., Antiquaries Jl, Museums Jl, etc. Recreations: pot-holing (now only in retrospect), computer programming, village history. Address: e-mail: frankatk@btinternet.com. T: (01661) 835445.

ATKINSON, Sir Frederick John, (Sir Fred), KCB 1979 (CB 1971); Hon. Fellow of Jesus College, Oxford, since 1979; b 7 Dec. 1919; s of George Edward Atkinson and of late Elizabeth Sabina Cooper; m 1947, Margaret Grace Gibson; two d. Educ: Dulwich Coll.; Jesus Coll., Oxford. Lectr, Jesus and Trinity Colls, Oxford, 1947–49; Economic Section, Cabinet Office, 1949–51; British Embassy, Washington, 1952–54; HM Treasury, 1955–62; Economic Adviser, Foreign Office, 1962–63; HM Treasury, 1963–69 (Dep.

Dir, Economic Section, Treasury, 1965–69); Controller, Economics and Statistics, Min. of Technology, 1970; Chief Econ. Adviser, DTI, 1970–73; an Asst Sec.-Gen., OECD, Paris, 1973–75; Dep. Sec. and Chief Econ. Advr, Dept of Energy, 1975–77; Chief Economic Adviser, HM Treasury, and Head of Govt Econ. Service, 1977–79. *Publication:* (with S. Hall) Oil and the British Economy, 1983. *Recreation:* reading. *Address:* 26 Lee Terrace, Blackheath, SE3 9TZ. *T:* (020) 8852 1040; Tickner Cottage, Aldington, Kent TN25 7EG. *T:* (01233) 720514.

ATKINSON, Brig. Geoffrey Arthur; Executive Secretary, Royal Academy of Engineering (formerly Fellowship of Engineering), 1990–93; *b* 17 March 1931; *s* of Arthur Vivian Atkinson and Flora Muriel Atkinson (*née* Lucas); *m* 1952, Joyce Eileen Pavey; one *s* one *d. Educ:* Berkhamsted Sch.; Royal Military College of Science (BScEng); Manchester Business Sch. CEng, FIMechE. Commnd REME, 1950; Regtl and technical employment, UK, Malaya, BAOR, 1950–60; EME, Queen's Own Hussars, 1960; Instr, RMA Sandhurst, 1962; Technical Staff trng, RMCS, 1963; BEME 20 Armd Bde, 1965; Weapons Staff, Army Sch. of Transport, 1967; CO 7 Armd Workshop, 1970; GSO1(W) DGFVE, 1972; ADEME 1/3 HQ DEME, 1975; Mil. Dir of Studies, Weapons and Vehicles, RMCS, 1977; CCREME HQ 1 BR Corps, BAOR, 1978; Dir of Equipment Engrg, HQ DGEME, 1981; Comdr HQ REME TA, 1983, retired 1984. Hon. Col REME Specialist Units TA, 1986–89. Dep. Sec., Fellowship of Engineering, 1984. Member: Council, Parly and Scientific Cttee, 1991–93; Cttee, Parly Gp for Engrg Develt, 1991–93. Freeman, City of London, 1990; Liveryman, Co. of Engineers, 1991–2003.

ATKINSON, Harry Hindmarsh, PhD; consultant; Under Secretary, Director (Special Responsibilities), Science and Engineering Research Council, 1988–92; *b* 5 Aug. 1929; *s* of late Harry Temple Atkinson and Constance Hindmarsh Atkinson (*née* Shields); *m* 1958, Anne Judith Barrett; two *s* one *d. Educ:* Nelson Coll., Nelson, NZ; Canterbury University Coll., NZ (BSc, sen. schol.; MSc (1st cl. Hons)), 1948–52. Asst Lectr, Physics, CUC, 1952–53; Research Asst, Cornell Univ., USA, 1954–55; Corpus Christi Coll. and Cavendish Laboratory, Cambridge Univ., 1955–58 (PhD); Sen. Research Fellow, AERE, Harwell, 1958–61; Head, General Physics Group, Rutherford Laboratory, 1961–69; Staff Chief Scientific Adviser, Cabinet Office, 1969–72; Dep. Chief Scientific Officer and Head of Astronomy, Space and Radio Division, SRC, 1972–78; Dir (Astronomy, Space and Radio, and Nuclear Physics), SRC later SERC, 1979–83; Dir Science, SERC, 1983–88. Chm. Council, ESA, 1984–87 (Vice-Chm., 1981–84, UK Deleg., 1974–87); UK Member: EISCAT Council, 1976–86; Bd, Anglo-Aust. Telescope, 1979–88; Cttee, S African Astronomical Observatory, 1979–83; Council, European Synchrotron Radiation Facility, 1986–88; Chairman: Cttee on Netherlands/UK Astronomy Collaboration, 1981–88; Steering Cttee, Inst. Laue-Langevin, Grenoble, 1984 and 1987 (UK deleg., 1983–88); UK Govt Task Force on Potentially Hazardous Near-Earth Objects, 2000; Mem., Working Gp on Near Earth Objects, ESF, 2001. Assessor, UGC, 1987–89; Member: NI Cttee, UFC, 1989–93; Working Gp on Internat. Collaboration (Cabinet Office), ACOST, 1989; Co-ordinator, UK, Australia, NZ sci. collaboration, 1989–94. Chief Scientist, Loss Prevention Council, 1990–98. Consultant: UGC of HK Govt, 1993–95; Oxford Univ. Commn on future of the Univ., 1995–96. Trustee, Trans-Antarctic Assoc., 1993–. *Publications:* papers on various branches of physics, science and higher education policy, international comparisons. *Address:* Bampton, Oxon. *Club:* Athenæum.

ATKINSON, Prof. Helen Valerie, PhD; CEng, FREng, FIMMM, FIMechE; Professor of Materials Processing, since 2002, and Head, Mechanics of Materials Group, Department of Engineering, since 2004, University of Leicester; *b* Portadown, NI, 29 April 1960; *d* of Arthur and Sheila Bavister; *m* 1984, Ven. Richard William Bryant Atkinson, *qv*; one *s* two *d. Educ:* South Park High Sch., Lincoln; Girton Coll., Cambridge (BA 1981); Imperial Coll. of Sci. and Technol., Univ. of London (PhD 1986; DIC 1986). MIM 1985, FIMMM 1998; CEng 1986; FIMechE 2004; FREng 2007. SO, 1981–83, HSO, 1983–87, SSO, 1987, Materials Develt Div., UKAEA, Harwell; Sen. Lectr in Materials, Sheffield City Poly., 1987–89; Lectr, 1989–96, Sen. Lectr, 1996–2000, Reader, 2000–02, in Materials, Univ. of Sheffield. Member: UK Foresight Panel on Materials, 1994–99; Action Gp on Sensors, Office of Sci. and Technol., 1996–97; British Transport Police Cttee, 1998–2003; Chem. and Materials Task Force, UK Foresight Crime Prevention Panel, 1999–2001; Lord Chancellor's Adv. Cttee for Appt of Magistrates in Rotherham, 2000–02; Implementation Gp for Govt's Strategy on Women in Sci., Engrg and Technol., DTI, 2004–07. Member: Bd of Dirs, Eur. Soc. of Material Forming, 2007–; Educn and Trng Panel, Engrg and Technol. Bd, 2008–; Standing Cttee on Educn and Trng, RAE, 2008–. Jt Chm., Engrg Professors' Council/Engrg and Technol. Bd Cttee on costs of teaching engrg degrees, 2007–08. Member, Council: Inst. of Metals, 1989–91; Inst. of Materials, 1992–96. Mem. Cttee, Engrg Professors' Council, 2004–. Member: Oxford Diocesan Bd of Social Responsibility, 1986–87; Sheffield Diocesan Bd of Social Responsibility, 1990–91. Member, Editorial Board: Jl Fatigue and Fracture of Engrg Materials and Structures, 1996–2002; Internat. Jl Microstructure and Material Properties, 2004–. Plowden Prize, British Nuclear Energy Soc., 1985; (jtly) Williams Prize, IMMM, 2002. *Publications:* (with B. A. Rickinson) Hot Isostatic Processing, 1991; (ed) Modelling of Semi-Solid Processing, 2008; contrib. papers on metallurgy and materials sci. *Recreations:* gardening, singing, walking. *Address:* Department of Engineering, University of Leicester, University Road, Leicester LE1 7RH. *T:* (0116) 252 2598.

ATKINSON, Prof. James; Founder Director, Centre for Reformation Studies, Sheffield, 1983–2006; Professor of Biblical Studies, University of Sheffield, 1967–79, now Emeritus; *b* 27 April 1914; *s* of Nicholas Ridley Atkinson and Margaret (*née* Hindhaugh); *m* 1939, Laura Jean Nutley (decd); one *s* one *d. Educ:* Tynemouth High Sch.; Univ. of Durham. MA 1939, MLitt 1950 Durham; DrTheol, Münster, Germany, 1955. Curate, Newcastle upon Tyne, 1937; Precentor, Sheffield Cath., 1941; Vicar, Sheffield, 1944; Fellow, Univ. of Sheffield, 1951; Canon Theologian: Leicester, 1954–70; Sheffield, 1971–93; Reader in Theology, Univ. of Hull, 1956; Vis. Prof., Chicago, 1966; Public Orator, Univ. of Sheffield, 1972–79; Consultant Prof. with Evangelical Anglican Res. Centre, Latimer House, Oxford, 1981–84; Special Prof. in Reformation Theol., Univ. of Nottingham, 1993–2001. Examining Chaplain to: Bp of Leicester, 1968–79; Bp of Derby, 1978–95. Member: Anglican-Roman Catholic Preparatory Commission, 1967–72; Gen. Synod of Church of England, 1975–80; Marriage Commn, 1976–78. Pres., Soc. for Study of Theology, 1978–80; Mem., Acad. Internat. des Sciences Religieuses, 1980–2006. Hon. DD Hull, 1997. *Publications:* Library of Christian Classics, Vol. XVI, 1962; Rome and Reformation, 1965; Luther's Works, Vol. 44, 1966; Luther and the Birth of Protestantism, 1968; (trans. Spanish 1971, Italian 1983); The Reformation, Paternoster Church History, Vol. 4, 1968; The Trial of Luther, 1971; Martin Luther: Prophet to the Church Catholic, 1983; The Darkness of Faith, 1987; (contrib.) The Bible, the Reformation and the Church, ed W. P. Stephens, 1994; Faith Lost-Faith Regained, 2005; Understanding the Incarnation, 2008; contribs to learned jls, also essays and parts of books. *Recreations:* gardening, music. *Address:* Leach House, Hathersage, Derbyshire S32 1BA. *T:* (01433) 650570.

See also Sir Robert Atkinson.

ATKINSON, Sir John Alexander, (Sir Alec), KCB 1978 (CB 1976); DFC 1943; Second Permanent Secretary, Department of Health and Social Security, 1977–79; *b* 9 June 1919; *yr s* of late Rev. R. F. Atkinson and late Harriet Harrold Atkinson, BSc (*née* Lowdon); *m* 1945, Marguerite Louise Pearson, MA (*d* 2004); one *d. Educ:* Kingswood Sch.; Queen's Coll., Oxford. Served in RAF, 1939–45. Asst Prin., 1946, Prin., 1949, Min. of Nat. Insce; Cabinet Office, 1950–52; Prin. Private Sec. to Minister of Pensions and Nat. Insce, 1957–58; Asst Sec., 1958; Under-Sec., Min. of Social Security, later DHSS, 1966–73; Dep. Sec., DHSS, 1973–76. Member: Panel of Chairmen, CSSB, 1979–88; Occupational Pensions Bd, 1981–88. Chm., Working Gp on Pensions and Divorce, Pensions Management Inst. with Law Soc., 1992–93. Pres., Kingswood Assoc., 1983. *Address:* Bleak House, The Drive, Belmont, Sutton, Surrey SM2 7DH. *T:* (020) 8642 6479. *Club:* Oxford and Cambridge.

ATKINSON, Kenneth Neil, FCIPD; Managing Director, Travel Training Co. Ltd, 1995 (Dir, then Chief Executive, ABTA National Training Board, 1989–94); *b* 4 April 1931; *s* of William Atkinson and Alice Reid. *Educ:* Kingussie High Sch., Inverness-shire; BA Hons Open Univ. 2001. ARCM 1961; FCIPD (FIPM 1986). Various appts, Min. of Labour and Dept of Employment, 1948–67; Dep. Chief Conciliation Officer, Dept of Employment, 1968–72; Dir, Industry Trng Bd Relations, MSC, 1973–78; Manpower Services Dir, Scotland, 1979–82; Dir of Youth Training, Training Agency (formerly Manpower Services/Training Commn), 1983–89. Chm., Prince's Trust Community Venture, 1989–92; Mem. Bd, Prince's Trust Volunteers, 1993–94. Mem., Council, CGLI, 1991–98. Musical Dir, Ruislip Operatic Soc., 1994–. FRSA 2003. *Recreations:* tennis, choral and solo singing, conducting. *Address:* 14/7 St Margaret's Place, Edinburgh EH9 1AY. *T:* (0131) 447 5975; 4 Morford Close, Ruislip, Middlesex HA4 8SW. *T:* and *Fax:* (020) 8866 2581. *Club:* Royal Automobile.

ATKINSON, (Michael) Kent; Group Finance Director, Lloyds TSB Group plc, 1995–2002 (non-executive Director, 2002–03); *b* 19 May 1945; *s* of late Carl Kent Atkinson and Edith Atkinson (*née* Gilbert); *m* 1970, Eufemia Alexandra Alarcón; two *s. Educ:* Blundell's Sch. Entered Bank of London & South America Ltd, 1964: sen. appts, Bank of London/Lloyds Bank Internat. Ltd in Colombia, Ecuador, Panama, Bahrain, Dubai, Paraguay and Argentina, 1967–86; Gen. Manager, Argentina, Chile, Peru, Bolivia, Paraguay and Uruguay, 1987–89; Lloyds Bank plc: Regl Exec. Dir, 1989–94; Gen. Manager, Retail Ops, 1994–95. Director: Lloyds Bank Subsidiaries Ltd, 1995–2002; Lloyds Commercial Properties Ltd, 1995–98; Lloyds Bank, then Lloyds TSB, Financial Services (Hldgs) Ltd, 1995–2001; TSB Bank Ltd, 1995–99; Lloyds TSB Bank plc, 1995–2002; Three Copthall Avenue Ltd, 2000–02. Non-executive Director: Coca-Cola HBC SA (formerly Coca-Cola Beverages), 1998–; telent plc (formerly Marconi Corp.), 2002–07; Cookson Gp plc, 2003–05; Standard Life plc (formerly Standard Life Assurance Co.), 2005–; Gemalto (formerly Axalto) NV, 2005–; Millicom Internat. SA, 2007–; Northern Rock plc, 2008–; Chairman: Standard Life Bank Ltd, 2007; Link Plus Corp., 2006–08. *Recreations:* tennis, golf, Rugby, soccer, opera, personal computers. *Clubs:* Effingham Golf, Horsley Sports.

ATKINSON, Michael William, CMG 1985; MBE 1970; HM Diplomatic Service, retired; *b* 11 April 1932; *m* 1963, Veronica Bobrovsky; two *s* one *d. Educ:* Purley County Grammar School; Queen's College, Oxford (BA Hons). Served FO, Vientiane, Buenos Aires, British Honduras, Madrid; FCO 1975; NATO Defence Coll., 1976; Counsellor, Budapest, 1977–80, Peking, 1980–82; Hd of Consular Dept, FCO, 1982–85; Ambassador: to Ecuador, 1985–89; to Romania, 1989–92; Personnel Assessor, FCO, 1992–98.

ATKINSON, Nigel John Bewley; Vice Lord-Lieutenant of Hampshire, since 2007; non-executive Chairman, Ocean Radio Group, since 2001; non-executive Director, Fuller, Smith & Turner plc, since 2006; *b* London, 25 Dec. 1953; *s* of John Bewley Atkinson, MBE and Jean Margaret Atkinson; *m* 1987, Christine Pamela Oliver; one *d* and one step *s* one step *d. Educ:* Haileybury Coll.; RMA Sandhurst. Served RGJ, Captain and Adjt, 1973–79. Sales Dir, Courage Ltd, 1979–90; Chief Exec., George Gale & Co. Ltd, 1990–2006. Non-exec. Chm., S E Hants Enterprise Agencies, 1992–2003. Chm., St John Ambulance, Hants, 2001–; Vice-Pres., Duke of Edinburgh Award, Hants, 1998–. Trustee, HMS Warrior, 2001–. DL Hants, 1999. CStJ 2007. *Recreations:* tennis, ski-ing. *Address:* c/o Fuller, Smith & Turner plc, The Griffin Brewery, Chiswick Lane South, W4 2QB. *Clubs:* Lansdowne, Royal Green Jackets.

ATKINSON, Norman; *b* 25 March 1923; *s* of George Atkinson, Manchester; *m* 1948, Irene Parry. *Educ:* elementary and technical schs. Served apprenticeship, Metropolitan Vickers Ltd, Trafford Park. Member of Manchester City Council, 1945–49. Chief Design Engineer, Manchester University, 1957–64. Contested (Lab) Wythenshawe, 1955, Altrincham and Sale, 1959. MP (Lab) Tottenham, 1964–87. Treasurer, Labour Party, 1976–81. Mem., Governing Body, Imperial Coll., London, 1975–89. Hon. MA Manchester, 1997. *Publications:* Sir Joseph Whitworth: the world's best mechanician, 1996; Old Merypebbles (play), 2005; political pamphlets. *Recreations:* walking, cricket, football, oil painting. *Club:* Arts.

ATKINSON, Very Rev. Peter Gordon; Dean of Worcester, since 2007; *b* 26 Aug. 1952; *m* 1983, Lynne Wilcock; two *s* one *d. Educ:* St John's Coll., Oxford (BA 1974; MA 1978); Westcott House, Cambridge. Ordained: deacon, 1979; priest, 1980; Asst Curate, Clapham Old Town Team Ministry, 1979–83; Priest-in-charge, St Mary, Tatsfield, 1983–90; Rector, Holy Trinity, Bath, 1990–91; Principal, Chichester Theol Coll., 1991–94; Rector, Lavant, 1994–97; Bursalis Preb., 1991–97, Canon Residentiary and Chancellor, 1997–2007, Chichester Cathedral; Dio. Warden of Readers, Chichester, 2001–03. Mem., Gen. Synod of C of E, 2000–05. Vice-Chm., 2002–07, Chm., 2007–, Cathedral Libraries and Archives Assoc.; Mem., Cathedrals Fabric Commn for England, 2001–05. Master, St Oswald's Hosp., Worcester, 2007–. FRSA 2006. *Publications:* (contrib.) Stepping Stones: joint essays on Anglican Catholic and Evangelical Unity, ed C. Baxter, 1987; Friendship and the Body of Christ, 2005. *Recreations:* reading, travel. *Address:* The Deanery, 10 College Green, Worcester WR1 2LH. *T:* (01905) 27821.

ATKINSON, Peter Landreth; MP (C) Hexham, since 1992; *b* 19 Jan. 1943; *s* of Major Douglas Wilson Atkinson, RTR (*d* Burma, 1945) and of Amy Landreth; *m* 1976, Brione, *d* of late Comdr Arthur Darley, RN and Elspeth Darley; two *d. Educ:* Cheltenham Coll. Journalist, 1961–87 (formerly News Editor, Evening Standard); Dep. Dir, British Field Sports Soc., 1987–92. Councillor: London Borough of Wandsworth, 1978–82; Suffolk County Council, 1989–92. PPS to Chm. of Cons. Pty, 1994–95, 1997–98, to Sec. of State for Transport, 1996–97; an Opposition Whip, 1999–2002, 2003–05. Member: Select Cttee on Scottish Affairs, 1992–2002; Speaker's Panel of Chairmen, 1997–99, 2005–; Procedure Cttee, 2003–05. *Recreations:* shooting, racing, gardening. *Address:* House of Commons, SW1A 0AA. *Clubs:* Albert Edward (Hexham); Northern Counties (Newcastle).

ATKINSON, Reay; *see* Atkinson, W. R.

ATKINSON, Ven. Richard William Bryant, OBE 2002; Archdeacon of Leicester, since 2002; *b* 17 Dec. 1958; *s* of William and Eileen Atkinson; *m* 1984, Helen Valerie Bavister (*see* H. V. Atkinson); one *s* two *d. Educ:* St Paul's Sch.; Magdalene Coll., Cambridge (MA); Ripon Coll., Cuddesdon. Ordained deacon, 1984, priest, 1985; Asst Curate, Abingdon, 1984–87; Team Vicar, 1987–91, Team Rector, 1991–96, Sheffield Manor; Vicar of Rotherham, 1996–2002. Hon. Canon, Sheffield Cathedral, 1998–2002. Mem., Gen. Synod of C of E, 1991–; Church Comr, 2001–. Hon. Tutor, Ripon Coll., Cuddesdon, 1987–92. Mem., Carnegie UK Trust Commn. Dep. Chm., Places for People, 1998–2005; Chm., Braunstone Community Assoc., 2002–06. Chm., St Philips Centre for Study and Engagement in a Multi Faith Society, 2005–. Trustee, Church Urban Fund, 2003–. *Recreations:* cooking, biography and history, walking, watching Rugby Union, housing and regeneration, The Archers. *Address:* 46 Southernhay Road, Stoneygate, Leicester LE2 3TJ. *T:* (0116) 270 4441; *e-mail:* richard.atkinson@lecCofE.org.

ATKINSON, Sir Robert, Kt 1983; DSC 1941; RD 1947; FREng; Chairman, British Shipbuilders, 1980–84; *b* 7 March 1916; *s* of Nicholas and Margaret Atkinson; *m* 1st, 1941, Joyce Forster (*d* 1973); one *s* one *d*; 2nd, 1977, Margaret Hazel Walker. *Educ:* London Univ. (BSc(Eng) Hons). FIMechE, CEng, FREng (FEng 1983); FIMarEST. Served War 1939–45 (DSC 1941 and two Bars, 1st, 1943, 2nd, 1944, mentioned in Despatches, 1943). Managing Director: Wm Doxford, 1957–61; Tube Investments (Eng), 1961–67; Unicorn Industries, 1967–72; Chm., Aurora Holdings, Sheffield, 1972–84; Dir, Stag Furniture Hldgs, 1973–92. Chm., Engrg and Shipbuilding Cttee, BSI, 1984–87. James Clayton Medal, NECInst, 1961. *Publications:* The Design and Operating Experience of an Ore Carrier Built Abroad, 1957; The Manufacture of Doxford Crankshafts, 1960; Some Crankshaft Failures: investigations into causes and remedies, 1960; British Shipbuilders Offshore Division, 1982; booklets: The Development and Decline of British Shipbuilding; Some Experiences of an Ancient Mariner; pamphlets and technical papers. *Recreations:* salmon fishing, walking, gardening. *Address:* Southdowns, 1 Little Hayes Lane, Itchen Abbas, Winchester SO21 1XA. *Club:* Royal Thames Yacht.

See also Prof. James Atkinson.

ATKINSON, Rowan Sebastian; actor and writer; *b* 6 Jan. 1955; *s* of late Eric Atkinson and of Ella May Atkinson; *m* 1990, Sunetra Sastry; one *s* one *d. Educ:* Durham Cathedral Choristers' Sch.; St Bees Sch.; Newcastle Univ.; Oxford Univ. (BSc, MSc). *Stage:* Beyond a Joke, Hampstead, 1978; Oxford Univ. Revues at Edinburgh Festival Fringe; youngest person to have a one-man show in the West End of London, 1981; The Nerd, 1984; The New Revue, 1986; The Sneeze, 1988; *television:* Not the Nine O'clock News, 1979–82; The Black Adder, 1983; Blackadder II, 1985; Blackadder the Third, 1987; Blackadder goes Forth, 1989; Mr Bean, The Return of Mr Bean, The Curse of Mr Bean, 1990–94; The Thin Blue Line, 1995; *films:* The Tall Guy, The Appointment of Dennis Jennings, 1989; The Witches, 1990; Hot Shots—Part Deux, 1993; Four Weddings and a Funeral, The Lion King, 1994; Bean—The Ultimate Disaster Movie, 1997; Blackadder—Back and Forth, Maybe Baby, 2000; Rat Race, Scooby Doo, 2002; Johnny English, Love Actually, 2003; Keeping Mum, 2005; Mr Bean's Holiday, 2007. *Recreations:* motor cars, motor sport. *Address:* c/o PBJ Management Ltd, 7 Soho Street, W1D 3DQ. *T:* (020) 7287 1112; *e-mail:* general@pbjmgt.co.uk.

ATKINSON, Dr Susan, (Sue), CBE 2002; FFPH; Visiting Professor, Department of Epidemiology and Public Health, University College London, since 2002; non-executive Director, University College London Hospital NHS Foundation Trust, since 2007; Chairman, Greater London Alcohol and Drug Alliance, since 2007; *b* 10 Aug. 1946; *d* of Fredrick Booth Atkinson and Jay Atkinson (*née* Carruthers); *m*; one *d. Educ:* Merchant Taylors' Sch. for Girls; UCNW (BSc Zoology); New Hall, Cambridge (MA 1976; MB BChir 1975); Middlesex Hosp. Med. Sch. DCH 1977; FFPH (FFPHM 1989). Res. Associate in animal behaviour/zool., Univ. of Cambridge, 1969–70; Registrar and SHO posts, Paediatrics, Bristol Children's Hosp. and Addenbrooke's Hosp., 1976–78; Registrar in Public Health Medicine, Avon Area HA, 1979–80; Res. Fellow, NH and MRC Perinatal Epidemiology Unit, Univ. of WA, 1980–81; GP, Bristol, 1981–82; Sen. Registrar in Public Health Medicine, Bristol and Weston HA, 1982–84; Public Health Consultant, Bristol HA, 1985–87; Dir, Public Health, and Chief Exec., SE London HA, 1987–93; Regional Director of Public Health: Wessex, then Wessex and SW RHA, 1993–94; S Thames RHA, then S Thames Regl Office, NHS Exec., 1994–99; Med. Dir, 1999–2003, Regl Dir of Public Health, 1999–2006, London, DoH; Health Advr to Mayor of London and GLA, 2000–06. Special Advr to Health Select Cttee, 1991–92. Mem. Bd, FSA, 2008–. Mem., London Sports Bd, 2003–. Mem. Bd and Ct, LSHTM, 2001–. *Publications:* articles and chapters on spastic diplegia, vision screening, public health in UK and health impact assessment. *Recreations:* cinema, art, music. *Address: e-mail:* sue@sueatkinson.com. *T:* 07884 473280.

ATKINSON, Prof. Thomas, PhD, DSc, DEng; FREng; Professor and Head of Department of Mining Engineering, Nottingham University, 1977–88, now Emeritus; Adjunct Professor, University of British Columbia, since 1997; *b* 23 Jan. 1924; *s* of Thomas Bell and Elizabeth Atkinson; *m* 1948, Dorothy; one *d. Educ:* Imperial Coll., London. DIC; PhD London, 1973; DSc Nottingham, 1988; DEng Witwatersrand, 1989. FREng (FEng 1987); FIMMM, FIMinE, FIET, FIMechE. Served RN, 1942–46. Charlaw and Sacriston Collieries Ltd, Durham, 1938–42; NCB, 1946–49; Andrew Yule, India, 1949–53; KWPR, Australia, 1953–56; Mining Engr, Powell Duffryn Technical Services Ltd, 1956–68; Sen. Lectr, Imperial Coll., 1968–73; Head of Coal Mining Div., Shell Internat. Petroleum Maatschappij BV, Holland, 1973–77. Dir, British Mining Consultants Ltd, 1969–88; Chm., Consolidated Coalfields Ltd, 1986–91. Chm., Nat. Awards Tribunal, British Coal (formerly NCB), 1984–92. FRSA. *Publications:* contribs to Mining Engrg, Mineral Econs, Mine Electrics, etc. *Recreation:* painting. *Address:* # 212, 5683 Hampton Place, Vancouver, BC V6T 2H3, Canada. *Club:* Chaps.

ATKINSON, (William) Reay, CB 1985; FBCS; Under Secretary, 1978–86, and Regional Director, North Eastern Region, 1981–86, Department of Industry; *b* 15 March 1926; *s* of William Edwin Atkinson and Lena Marion (*née* Haselhurst); *m*; one *s* two *d*; *m* 1983, Rita Katherine (*née* Bunn). *Educ:* Gosforth Grammar Sch., Newcastle upon Tyne; King's Coll., Durham Univ.; Worcester Coll., Oxford. Served RNVR, 1943–46. Entered Civil Service as Inspector of Taxes, 1950; Principal, 1958, Asst. Sec., 1965; Secretaries Office, Inland Revenue, 1958–61 and 1962–69; Asst Sec., Royal Commn on the Press, 1961–62; Civil Service Dept, 1969; Under Sec., and Dir, Central Computer Agency, CSD, 1973–78. Chm., Northern Development Co. Ltd, 1986–90; Director: English Estates Corp., 1986–94; Northern Rock Building Soc., 1987–96; Belasis Hall Technol. Park, 1989–98; Maryport Develt Co. Ltd, 1989–95. Chm., Northern Rock Foundn, 1997–2000. Chm. of Governors, Univ. of Northumbria at Newcastle (formerly Newcastle-upon-Tyne Polytechnic), 1989–96 (Hon. Fellow, 1987). Hon. Fellow, Univ. of Newcastle upon Tyne, 2005. Hon. DCL Northumbria at Newcastle, 1998. *Recreations:* gentle walking, reading, music. *Address:* 1 Greencroft Avenue, Corbridge, Northumberland NE45 5DW. *T:* (01434) 632351.

ATKINSON, Sir William (Samuel), Kt 2008; Headteacher, Phoenix High School, Hammersmith and Fulham, since 1995; *b* St Ann, Jamaica, 9 April 1950; *s* of late William Benjamin Atkinson and Sara Jane Atkinson; *m* 1974, Jacqueline Ann Burley; three *s* one *d. Educ:* King's Coll. London (MA 1981). Teacher, Portsmouth Modern Boys' Sch., 1971–72; Asst Hd of Year, Islington Green Sch., 1973–74; Hd of Year, Holloway Boys' Sch., 1974–81; Deputy Head: Henry Thornton Sch., 1981–83; White Hart Lane Sch., Haringey, 1983–86; Headteacher: Copland Community Sch., Brent, 1986–87; Cranford Community Sch., 1987–95. Member: Spot Measures Action Recovery Team, 1997, Standards Task Force, 1997–2001, DfEE; Justice Task Force, 1999, London Youth Crime Reduction Task Force, 2003–04, Home Office; London Black and Minority Ethnic Communities Cracking Crime Partnership Bd, until 2006; Adv. Panel on Children's Viewing, BBFC. Nat. Judge, 2002–, Dep. Chm., Nat. Judging Panel, 2006, Teaching Awards; Chm., London Teaching Awards Panel, 2003. Mem., Fulham Sch. Commn 2007; Chm., Hammersmith and Fulham Youth Task Force, 2007. Trustee: Inst. for Citizenship, 2001–06; Shaftesbury Homes and Arethusa, 2001–06. Mem. Council, Industrial Soc. FRSA (Mem., Council, 2004–). Media roles and appearances incl. contribs to wide range of TV and radio progs; role of headteacher in The Unteachables (documentary series), 2005. Hon. Dr North London, 2002. *Recreations:* Rugby, theatre, family. *Address:* Phoenix High School, The Curve, Shepherds Bush, W12 0RQ.

ATTALI, Jacques; Member, Conseil d'Etat, France, 1981–90 and since 1993; Président: Attali et Associés, since 1994; PlaNet Finance, since 1999; *b* 1 Nov. 1943. *Educ:* Ecole Polytechnique; Inst. d'Etudes Politiques de Paris; Ecole des Mines; Ecole Nat. d'Admin. Dr d'Etat en Sci. Econ. Conseil d'Etat: Auditeur, 1970; Maître des Requêtes, 1977; Conseiller, 1989; Special Advr to President of French Republic, 1981–91; Founding Pres., EBRD, 1991–93. *Publications:* Analyse économique de la vie politique, 1972; Modèles Politiques, 1973; (with Marc Guillaume) L'Anti-Economique, 1974; La Parole et l'outil, 1975; Bruits, 1976; La nouvelle Economie Française, 1977; L'Ordre Cannibale, 1979; Les Trois Mondes, 1981; Histoire du Temps, 1982; La figure de Fraser, 1984; Un homme d'influence, 1985; Au propre et au figuré, 1988; Lignes d'Horizon, 1990; 1492, 1991; Verbatim, 1993; Europe(s), 1994; L'Economie de l'Apocalypse, 1995; Verbatim II, 1995; Verbatim III, 1996; Chemins de Sagesse: traité du labyrinthe, 1996; Mémoire de Sabliers, 1997; Dictionnaire du XXIe siècle, 1998; Fraternités, 1999; Blaise Pascal, 2000; Economic History of the Jewish People, 2002; L'homme nomade, 2003; La Voie humaine, 2004; La confrérie des éveillés, 2004; Karl Marx ou l'esprit du monde, 2005; C'était François Mitterrand, 2005; *fiction:* La vie éternelle, 1989; Le premier Jour après moi, 1990; Il viendra, 1994; Manuel, l'Enfant Rêve (for children), 1994; Au-delà de nulle part, 1997; La femme du menteur, 1999; *play:* Les portes du Ciel, 1999. *Address:* 27 rue Vernet, 75008 Paris, France.

ATTALIDES, Michalis A.; Rector, University of Nicosia (formerly Intercollege), since 2006 (Dean, School of Humanities, Social Sciences and Law, 2003–06); *b* 15 Nov. 1941; *s* of Antonis Attalides and Katina Loizou; *m* 1991, Alexandra Alexandrou; one *s* one *d* from previous marriages. *Educ:* London Sch. of Econs (BSc Econ); Princeton Univ. (PhD 1975). Lectr in Sociology, Univ. of Leicester, 1966–68; sociologist, Cyprus Town and Country Planning Project, 1968–70; Counterpart of UNESCO Expert, Social Research Centre, Cyprus, 1971 and 1973–74; mil. service, 1972; Guest Lectr, Otto Suhr Inst., Free Univ. of Berlin, 1974–75; journalist, 1975–76; Internat. Relns Service, House of Representatives of Cyprus, 1977–89 (Dir, 1979–89); Dir, Pol Affairs Div. B (Cyprus Question) (with rank of Ambassador), Min. of Foreign Affairs, 1989–91; Ambassador to France, also accredited to Morocco, Portugal and Spain, 1991–95; Perm. Delegate to EU, also accredited to Belgium and Luxembourg, 1995–98; High Comr in London, 1998–2000; Perm. Sec., Min. of Foreign Affairs, Cyprus, 2000–01; Rep. of Govt of Cyprus, Eur. Convention, 2002–03. *Publications:* Social Change and Urbanization in Cyprus: a study of Nicosia, 1971; Cyprus: nationalism and international politics, 1980. *Address:* University of Nicosia, 46 Makedonitissas Avenue, PO Box 24005, 1700 Nicosia, Cyprus; *e-mail:* attalides.m@unic.ac.cy.

ATTALLAH, Naim Ibrahim; Book Publisher and Proprietor: Quartet Books, since 1976; The Women's Press, since 1977; Robin Clark, since 1980; *b* 1 May 1931; *s* of Ibrahim and Genevieve Attallah; *m* 1957, Maria Attallah (*née* Nykolyn); one *s. Educ:* Battersea Polytechnic. Foreign Exchange Dealer, 1957; Financial Consultant, 1966; Dir of cos, 1969–; Financial Dir and Jt Man. Dir, Asprey of Bond Street, 1979–92; Gp Chief Exec., Asprey PLC, 1992–96; Managing Director: Mappin & Webb, 1990–95; Watches of Switzerland, 1990–95; Exec. Dir, Garrard, 1990–95; Magazine Proprietor: The Literary Review, 1981–2001; The Wire, 1984–2000; The Oldie, 1991–2001. Proprietor, Academy Club, 1989–96. Launched Parfums Namara, Avant l'Amour and Après l'Amour, 1985, Naïdor, 1987, l'Amour de Namara, 1990; launched Namara Fine Art, 1997. *Theatre:* co-presenter, Happy End, Lyric, 1975; presented and produced, The Beastly Beatitudes of Balthazar B, Duke of York's, 1981; co-prod, Trafford Tanzi, Mermaid, 1982; *films:* co-prod (with David Frost), The Slipper and the Rose, 1974–75; exec. producer, Brimstone and Treacle, 1982; also prod and presented TV docs. MUniv Surrey, 1993. *Publications:* Women, 1987; Singular Encounters, 1990; Of a Certain Age, 1992; More of a Certain Age, 1993; Speaking for the Oldie, 1995; A Timeless Passion (novel), 1995; Asking Questions, 1996; Tara & Claire (novel), 1996; A Woman a Week, 1998; In Conversation with Naim Attallah, 1998; Insights, 1999; Dialogues, 2000; The Old Ladies of Nazareth, 2004; The Boy in England, 2005; In Touch With His Roots, 2006; Fulfilment & Betrayal, 2007; contrib. Literary Review, Oldie, and most nat. newspapers. *Recreations:* classical music, opera, theatre, cinema, photography. *Address:* 25 Shepherd Market, W1J 7PP. *T:* (020) 7499 2901, *Fax:* (020) 7499 2914; *e-mail:* nattallah@aol.com.

ATTANASIO, Prof. Orazio Pietro, PhD; FBA 2004; Professor of Economics, University College London, since 1995; *b* 31 Oct. 1959. *Educ:* Univ. of Bologna; London Sch. of Econs and Pol Sci. (MSc 1984; PhD 1988). Asst Prof. of Econs, 1988–94, Fellow, Hoover Instn, 1993–94, Stanford Univ.; Associate Prof. of Econs, Univ. of Bologna, 1993–95; Res. Fellow, Inst. for Fiscal Studies, 1995–; Dir, Centre for the Evaluation of Develt Policies, UCL and Inst. for Fiscal Studies, 2002–. *Publications:* contrib. learned jls. *Address:* Department of Economics, University College London, Gower Street, WC1E 6BT; Institute for Fiscal Studies, 7 Ridgmount Street, WC1E 7AE.

ATTENBOROUGH, family name of **Baron Attenborough**.

ATTENBOROUGH, Baron *cr* 1993 (Life Peer), of Richmond upon Thames, in the London Borough of Richmond upon Thames; **Richard Samuel Attenborough,** Kt 1976; CBE 1967; actor, producer and director; Goodwill Ambassador for UNICEF, since 1987; Chancellor, University of Sussex, since 1998 (Pro-Chancellor, 1970–98); *b* 29 Aug. 1923; *s* of late Frederick L. Attenborough; *m* 1945, Sheila Beryl Grant Sim; one *s* one *d* (and one *d* decd). *Educ:* Wyggeston Grammar Sch., Leicester. Leverhulme Schol. to Royal Acad. of Dramatic Art, 1941 (Bancroft Medal). First stage appearance as Richard Miller in Ah Wilderness, Intimate Theatre, Palmers Green, 1941; Ralph Berger in Awake and Sing, Arts Theatre (West End début), 1942; Sebastian in Twelfth Night, Ba in Holy Isle, Murder in the Red Barn, Arts Theatre; The Little Foxes, Piccadilly Theatre, 1942; Brighton Rock,

Garrick, 1943. Joined RAF 1943; seconded to RAF Film Unit for Journey Together, 1944; demobilised, 1946. Returned to stage in The Way Back (Home of the Brave), Westminster, 1949; To Dorothy, a Son, Savoy, 1950, Garrick, 1951; Sweet Madness, Vaudeville, 1952; The Mousetrap, Ambassadors, 1952–54; Double Image, Savoy, 1956–57, St James's, 1957; The Rape of the Belt, Piccadilly, 1957–58. *Film: appearances:* In Which We Serve (screen début), 1942; School for Secrets, The Man Within, Dancing With Crime, Brighton Rock, London Belongs to Me, The Guinea Pig, The Lost People, Boys in Brown, Morning Departure, Hell is Sold Out, The Magic Box, Gift Horse, Father's Doing Fine, Eight O'Clock Walk, The Ship That Died of Shame, Private's Progress, The Baby and the Battleship, Brothers in Law, The Scamp, Dunkirk, The Man Upstairs, Sea of Sand, Danger Within, I'm All Right Jack, Jet Storm, SOS Pacific; The Angry Silence (also co-prod), 1959; The League of Gentlemen, 1960; Only Two Can Play, All Night Long, 1961; The Dock Brief, The Great Escape, 1962; Séance On a Wet Afternoon (also prod; Best actor, San Sebastian Film Fest. and British Film Acad.), The Third Secret, 1963; Guns at Batasi (Best actor, British Film Acad.), 1964; The Flight of the Phœnix, 1965; The Sand Pebbles (Hollywood Golden Globe), 1966; Dr Dolittle (Hollywood Golden Globe), The Bliss of Mrs Blossom, 1967; Only When I Larf, 1968; The Last Grenade, A Severed Head, David Copperfield, Loot, 1969; 10 Rillington Place, 1970; And Then There Were None, Rosebud, Brannigan, Conduct Unbecoming, 1974; The Chess Players, 1977; The Human Factor, 1979; Jurassic Park, 1993; Miracle on 34th Street, 1994; The Lost World: Jurassic Park, 1997; Elizabeth, 1998; Puckoon, 2001; *produced:* Whistle Down the Wind, 1961; The L-Shaped Room, 1962; *directed:* Young Winston (Hollywood Golden Globe), 1972; A Bridge Too Far (Evening News Best Drama Award), 1976; Magic, 1978; A Chorus Line, 1985; In Love and War, 1997; Closing the Ring, 2007; *produced and directed:* Oh! What a Lovely War (16 Internat. Awards incl. Hollywood Golden Globe and SFTA UN Award), 1968; Gandhi (8 Oscars, 5 BAFTA Awards, 5 Hollywood Golden Globes, Dirs' Guild of America Award for Outstanding Directorial Achievement), 1980–81; Cry Freedom (Berlinale Kamera; BFI Award for Technical Achievement), 1987; Chaplin, 1992; Shadowlands, 1993 (Alexander Korda Award for Outstanding British Film of the Year, BAFTA); In Love and War, 1997; Grey Owl, 2000. Formed: Beaver Films with Bryan Forbes, 1959; Allied Film Makers, 1960. Chairman: Goldcrest Films & Television Ltd, 1982–87; Channel Four Television, 1987–92 (Dep. Chm., 1980–86); Capital Radio, 1972–92 (Life Pres., 1992–); Duke of York's Theatre, 1979–92. Dir, Chelsea Football Club, 1969–82 (Life Vice Pres., 1993–). Chairman: Actor's Charitable Trust, 1956–88 (Pres., 1988–); Combined Theatrical Charities Appeals Council, 1964–88 (Pres., 1988–); BAFTA (formerly SFTA), 1969–70 (Vice-Pres., 1971–94; Chm. Trustees, 1970–); RADA, 1972–2002 (Mem. Council, 1963–; Pres., 2002–); UK Trustees, Waterford-Kamhlaba Sch., Swaziland, 1976– (Gov., 1987–); BFI, 1981–92; Cttee of Inquiry into the Arts and Disabled People, 1983–85; British Screen Adv. Council, 1987–96 (Hon. Pres., 1996); European Script Fund, 1988–96 (Hon. Pres., 1996); Member: British Actors' Equity Assoc. Council, 1949–73; Cinematograph Films Council, 1967–73; Arts Council of GB, 1970–73. Trustee: Tate Gall., 1976–82 and 1994–96 (Tate Foundn, 1986–); Foundn for Sport and the Arts, 1991–. Pres., Nat. Film Sch., 1997– (Gov., 1970–81); Dir, Young Vic, 1974–84. Pres., Muscular Dystrophy Gp of GB, 1971– (Vice-Pres., 1962–71); Chm., Help a London Child; Gov., Motability, 1977–. Patron: Kingsley Hall Community Centre, 1982–; RA Centre for Disability and the Arts, Leicester, 1990–. President: The Gandhi Foundn, 1983–; Brighton Festival, 1984–95; British Film Year, 1984–86; Arts for Health, 1989–; Gardner Centre for the Arts, Sussex Univ., 1990– (Patron, 1969–90). Fleming Meml Lect., RTS, 1989; Cameron Mackintosh Vis. Prof. of Contemporary Theatre, Oxford Univ., 1996. Fellow: BAFTA, 1983; BFI, 1992. Freeman, City of Leicester, 1990. FKC 1993; Hon. Fellow: Univ. of Wales, 1997; Nat. Film and Television Sch., 2001. Hon. DLitt: Leicester, 1970; Kent, 1981; Sussex, 1987; Hon. DLit Amer. Internat. Univ., London, 1994; Hon. DCL Newcastle, 1974; Hon. LLD Dickinson, Penn., 1983. Evening Standard Film Award, 40 years service to British Cinema, 1983; Award of Merit for Humanitarianism in Film Making, European Film Awards, 1988; Shakespeare Prize, FVS Foundn, Hamburg, 1992; Praemium Imperiale, Japan Art Assoc., 1998. Martin Luther King, Jr Peace Prize, 1983. Padma Bhushan (India), 1983; Commandeur, Ordre des Arts et des Lettres (France), 1985; Chevalier, Légion d'Honneur (France), 1988. *Publications:* In Search of Gandhi, 1982; (with Diana Carter) Richard Attenborough's Chorus Line, 1986; Cry Freedom, A Pictorial Record, 1987. *Recreations:* collecting paintings and sculpture, listening to music, watching football. *Address:* Old Friars, Richmond Green, Surrey TW9 1NQ. *Clubs:* Garrick, Beefsteak.

See also Sir D. F. Attenborough, Hon. M. J. Attenborough.

ATTENBOROUGH, Sir David (Frederick), OM 2005; CH 1996; Kt 1985; CVO 1991; CBE 1974; FRS 1983; FLS; FSA; broadcaster and naturalist; *b* 8 May 1926; *s* of late Frederick Levi Attenborough; *m* 1950, Jane Elizabeth Ebsworth Oriel (*d* 1997); one *s* one *d. Educ:* Wyggeston Grammar Sch. for Boys, Leicester; Clare Coll., Cambridge (Hon. Fellow, 1980). Served in Royal Navy, 1947–49. Editorial Asst in an educational publishing house, 1949–52; joined BBC Television Service as trainee producer, 1952; undertook zoological and ethnographic filming expeditions to: Sierra Leone, 1954; British Guiana, 1955; Indonesia, 1956; New Guinea, 1957; Paraguay and Argentina, 1958; South West Pacific, 1959; Madagascar, 1960; Northern Territory of Australia, 1962; the Zambesi, 1964; Bali, 1969; Central New Guinea, 1971; Celebes, Borneo, Peru and Colombia, 1973; Mali, British Columbia, Iran, Solomon Islands, 1974; Nigeria, 1975; Controller, BBC2, BBC Television Service, 1965–68; Dir of Programmes, Television, and Mem., Bd of Management, BBC, 1969–72. Writer and presenter, BBC series: Tribal Eye, 1976; Wildlife on One, annually 1977–2004; Life on Earth, 1979; The Living Planet, 1984; The First Eden, 1987; Lost Worlds, Vanished Lives, 1989; The Trials of Life, 1990; Life in the Freezer, 1993; The Private Life of Plants, 1995; The Life of Birds, 1998; State of the Planet, 2000; The Life of Mammals, 2002; Life in the Undergrowth, 2005; Life in Cold Blood, 2008. Huw Wheldon Meml Lecture, RTS, 1987. President: BAAS, 1990–91; RSNC, 1991–96; Mem., Nature Conservancy Council, 1973–82. Trustee: WWF UK, 1965–69, 1972–82, 1984–90; WWF Internat., 1979–86; British Museum, 1980–2001; Science Museum, 1984–87; Royal Botanic Gardens, Kew, 1986–92 (Kew Award, 1996). Corresp. Mem., Amer. Mus. Nat. Hist., 1985. Fellow, BAFTA 1980; FRSE 2006; FLS 2007 (Hon. FLS 1998); FSA 2008. Hon. Fellow: Manchester Polytechnic, 1976; UMIST, 1980; Hon. FRCP 1991; Hon. FIBiol 2000. Special Award, SFTA, 1961; Silver Medal, Zool Soc. of London, 1966; Silver Medal, RTS, 1966; Desmond Davis Award, SFTA, 1970; Cherry Kearton Medal, RGS, 1972; Kalinga Prize, UNESCO, 1981; Washburn Award, Boston Mus. of Sci., 1983; Hopper Day Medal, Acad. of Natural Scis, Philadelphia, 1983; Founder's Gold Medal, RGS, 1985; Internat. Emmy Award, 1985; Encyclopaedia Britannica Award, 1987; Livingstone Medal, RSGS, 1990; Franklin Medal, RSA, 1990; Gold Medal, RTS, 1991; Golden Kamera Award, Berlin, 1993; Edinburgh Medal, Edinburgh Sci. Fest., 1998; Internat. Cosmos Prize, Osaka, 2000; Michael Faraday Prize, Royal Soc., 2003; Raffles Medal, Zool Soc. of London, 2004; Caird Medal, Nat. Maritime Mus., 2004; Bicentennial Medal, Smithsonian Instn, 2004; Petersen Medal, Harvard, 2004; Descartes Prize, EC, 2004. Hon. DLitt: Leicester, 1970; City, 1972; London, 1980; Birmingham, 1982; Hon. DSc: Liverpool, 1974; Heriot-Watt, 1978; Sussex, 1979; Bath, 1981; Ulster, Durham, 1982; Keele, 1986; Oxford, 1988; Plymouth,

1992; Bradford, 1998; Nottingham, 1999; UWE, Iceland, Guelph, 2003; UEA, 2005; Uppsala, 2007; Hon. LLD: Bristol, 1977; Glasgow, 1980; DUniv: Open Univ., 1980; Essex, 1987; Antwerp, 1993; Hon. ScD Cambridge, 1984; Hon. DVetMed Edinburgh, 1994. Hon. Freeman, City of Leicester, 1990. Comdr of Golden Ark (Netherlands), 1983. *Publications:* Zoo Quest to Guiana, 1956; Zoo Quest for a Dragon, 1957; Zoo Quest in Paraguay, 1959; Quest in Paradise, 1960; Zoo Quest to Madagascar, 1961; Quest under Capricorn, 1963; The Tribal Eye, 1976; Life on Earth, 1979; The Living Planet, 1984; The First Eden, 1987; The Trials of Life, 1990; The Private Life of Plants, 1994; The Life of Birds, 1998; Life on Air (memoirs), 2002; The Life of Mammals, 2002; Life in the Undergrowth, 2005; Life in Cold Blood, 2007. *Recreations:* music, tribal art, natural history. *Address:* 5 Park Road, Richmond, Surrey TW10 6NS.

See also Baron Attenborough.

ATTENBOROUGH, (Hon.) Michael John; Artistic Director, Almeida Theatre, since 2002; *b* 13 Feb. 1950; *s* of Baron Attenborough, *qv; m* 1st, 1971, Jane Seymour (*née* Joyce Frankenberg) (marr. diss. 1976); 2nd, 1984, Karen Lewis; two *s. Educ:* Westminster Sch.; Sussex Univ. (BA Hons English). Associate Director: Mercury Theatre, Colchester, 1972–74; Leeds Playhouse, 1974–79; Young Vic Theatre, 1979–80; Artistic Director: Palace Theatre, Watford, 1980–84; Hampstead Theatre, 1984–89; Turnstyle Gp, 1989–90; Exec. Producer, 1990–95, Principal Associate Dir, 1995–2002, RSC. Vice-Chm., RADA, 2005–. Hon. DLitt Sussex, 2005. *Recreations:* music, football, reading, being with my family. *Address:* Almeida Theatre, Almeida Street, N1 1TA.

ATTENBOROUGH, Peter John; Director of Educational and Community Care Projects, 1994–2004, Administrator, Leadership and Fellowship Schemes, 2004–06, The Rank Foundation; Headmaster of Charterhouse, 1982–93; *b* 4 April 1938; *m* 1967, Alexandra Deidre Campbell Page; one *s* one *d. Educ:* Christ's Hospital; Peterhouse, Cambridge. BA Classics 1960, MA 1964. Asst Master, Uppingham Sch., 1960–75 (Housemaster, Senior Classics Master); Asst Master, Starehe Boys' Centre, Nairobi, 1966–67; Headmaster, Sedbergh Sch., 1975–81. Chairman: Common Entrance Cttee of Independent Schs, 1983–88; Schools Arabic Project, 1986–87; Mem., HMC Cttee, 1986–90. Almoner, Christ's Hosp., 1987–2001; Governor: Ashdown House, 1983–93; Haslemere Prep. Sch., 1986–93; St Edmund's Sch., 1986–94; Brambletye Sch., 1989–99; Caldicott Sch., 1990–93; Haberdashers' Monmouth Schs, 1996–2007; Trustee, Uppingham Sch., 1993–2002. Trustee: Inner City Young People's Project, 1989–98; Starehe Endowment Fund (UK), 1995–. Freeman, City of London, 1965; Liveryman, Skinners' Co., 1978. *Address:* Rawmarsh Cottage, Linton, near Ross-on-Wye, Herefords HR9 7RX.

ATTEWELL, Brian; HM Diplomatic Service, retired; *b* 29 May 1937; *s* of late William John Geldard Attewell and Marie Evelyn Attewell; *m* 1st, 1963, Mary Gillian Tandy (*d* 2000); two *s* one *d;* 2nd, 2002, Angelika Pathak. *Educ:* Dulwich Coll.; London School of Economics and Political Science (BScEcon 1961); Birkbeck Coll., London (Dip. Hist. of Art, 2006). BoT, 1956–58, 1961–66; Private Sec. to Parly Sec., 1964–66; transf. to Diplomatic Service, 1966: Washington, 1967–70; Buenos Aires, 1970–73; FCO, 1974–78; Canberra, 1978–80; FCO, 1980–83; Dubai, 1984–87; Brussels, 1988–92; High Comr, Bahamas, 1992–96. *Recreations:* golf, walking, listening to music (classical and jazz), watercolours, following fortunes of Charlton Athletic. *Club:* Wimbledon Park Golf (Dir, 2006–).

ATTLEE, family name of **Earl Attlee.**

ATTLEE, 3rd Earl *cr* 1955; **John Richard Attlee;** Viscount Prestwood, 1955; *b* 3 Oct. 1956; *s* of 2nd Earl Attlee and Anne Barbara, *er d* of late James Henderson, CBE; *S* father, 1991. *Educ:* Stowe. Engrg and automotive industries until 1993; British Direct Aid: Bosnia, 1993–94; Rwanda, 1995. TA officer, Maj. REME (V), Op. Lodestar, 1997–98, OC 150 Recovery Company, 1998–2000; Op. TELIC, 2003. Opposition Whip, H of L, 1997–99; spokesman, in H of L, for transport, 1997 and 1999–2001, for NI, 1997 and 1998–99, for energy, 1998, and for defence, 1998–2001, for transport and defence, 2002–03, for trade and industry, 2003–05; for maritime and shipping, 2007–; elected Mem., H of L, 1999. Pres., Heavy Transport Assoc., 1994–. *Address:* House of Lords, SW1A 0PW. *T:* (020) 7219 6071; *e-mail:* attleej@parliament.uk.

ATTLEE, Air Vice-Marshal Donald Laurence, CB 1978; LVO 1964; DL; fruit farmer, 1977–95, retired; *b* 2 Sept. 1922; *s* of Major Laurence Attlee; *m* 1952, Jane Hamilton Young; one *s* two *d. Educ:* Haileybury. Pilot trng in Canada, 1942–44; Flying Instructor, 1944–48; Staff, Trng Comd, 1949–52; 12 Sqdn, 1952–54; Air Ministry, Air Staff, 1954–55; RAF Staff Coll., 1956; 59 Sqdn, 1957–59; CO, The Queen's Flight (W/Cdr), 1960–63; HQ, RAF Germany, 1964–67; CO, RAF Brize Norton, 1968–69; IDC, 1970; MoD Policy Staff, 1971–72; Dir of RAF Recruiting, 1973–74; Air Cdre, Intell., 1974–75; AOA Trng Comd, 1975–77, retired. Chm., Mid-Devon Business Club, 1985–87; Mem. Bd, Mid-Devon Enterprise Agency, 1983–93. Mem., Mid-Devon DC, 1982–2003 (Vice-Chm., 1987–89; Chm., 1989–91; Leader, 2002–03; Hon. Alderman, 2003). DL Devon, 1991. *Recreations:* genealogy, gardening. *Address:* Wintergold, 31 Longmead, Hemyock, Devon EX15 3SG. *T:* (01823) 680317. *Club:* Royal Air Force.

ATTRIDGE, Prof. Derek, PhD; FBA 2007; Professor of English and Related Literature, University of York, since 1998 (Head, Department of English and Related Literature, 2004–07); *b* 6 May 1945; *s* of Henry Lester Attridge and Marjorie Julia Attridge (*née* Lloyd); *m* 1st, 1969, Anna Mary Ridehalgh (marr. diss. 1976); 2nd, 1986, Suzanne Hall; two *d. Educ:* Scottsville Govt Sch., S Africa; Maritzburg Coll., S Africa; Univ. of Natal (BA Hons English 1966); Clare Coll., Cambridge (BA English 1968; PhD 1972). Res. Lectr, Christ Church, Oxford, 1971–73; Lectr, then Sen. Lectr in English, Univ. of Southampton, 1973–84; Prof. of English Studies, 1984–88, Hd of Dept, 1985–86, Univ. of Strathclyde; Prof. of English, 1988–98, Dir of Grad. Studies, 1994–98, Rutgers Univ.; Leverhulme Res. Prof., Univ. of York, 1998–2003. Visiting Professor: Univ. of Illinois, 1979; Univ. of Orléans, 1990; Vis. Prof., 1984, 1987, Dist. Vis. Prof., 1998–2006, Rutgers Univ.; Vis. Scholar, New Hall, Cambridge, 1993–97; S. W. Brooks Fellow, Univ. of Qld, 2007. Mem., Scottish Adv. Bd, British Council, 1985–88. Mem., Bd of Trustees, Internat. James Joyce Foundn, 1986–96, 2007–. Member, Editorial Board: Derrida Today; Interventions; James Joyce Qly; Joyce Studies Annual; Jl of Narrative Theory; Language and Literature; Modern Fiction Studies, etc. *Publications:* Well-weighed Syllables: Elizabethan verse in classical metres, 1974; The Rhythms of English Poetry, 1982; (ed with D. Ferrer) Post-structuralist Joyce: essays from the French, 1984; (ed jtly) Post-structuralism and the Question of History, 1987; (ed jtly) The Linguistics of Writing: arguments between language and literature, 1987; Peculiar Language: literature as difference from the Renaissance to James Joyce, 1988, 2nd edn 2004; (ed) The Cambridge Companion to James Joyce, 1990, 2nd edn 2004; (ed) Jacques Derrida: acts of literature, 1992; Poetic Rhythm: an introduction, 1995; (ed with R. Jolly) Writing South Africa: literature, apartheid, and democracy 1970–1995, 1998; Joyce Effects: on language, theory, and history, 2000; (ed with M. Howes) Semicolonial Joyce, 2000; (with T. Carper) Meter and Meaning: an introduction to rhythm in poetry, 2003; The Singularity of Literature, 2004; J. M. Coetzee and the Ethics of Reading: literature in the event, 2004; (ed) James

Joyce's Ulysses: a casebook, 2004; How to Read Joyce, 2007; articles in Essays in Criticism, Jl of Postcolonial Writing, MLN, Modernism/Modernity, New Literary History, Novel, Paragraph, PMLA, Poetics Today, South Atlantic Quarterly, etc. *Address:* Department of English and Related Literature, University of York, Heslington, York YO10 5DD. *T:* (01904) 433361, *Fax:* (01904) 433372.

ATTRIDGE, Elizabeth Ann Johnston, (Mrs John Attridge); Senior Clerk/Adviser, European Legislation Committee, House of Commons, 1994–98; *b* 26 Jan. 1934; *d* of late Rev. John Worthington Johnston, MA, CF, and Mary Isabel Giraud (*née* McFadden); *m* 1956, John Attridge; one *s*. *Educ:* Richmond Lodge Sch., Belfast; St Andrews Univ., Fife. Assistant Principal, Min. of Education, NI, 1955, reappointed on marriage (marriage bar), MAFF, London, 1956; assisted on Agriculture Acts, 1957 and 1958; Head Plant Health Br., 1963–66, Finance, 1966–69, External Relations (GATT) Br., 1969–72; Assistant Secretary: Animal Health I, 1972–75; Marketing Policy and Potatoes, 1975–78; Tropical Foods Div., 1978–83; Under Secretary: European Community Group, 1983–85; Emergencies, Food Quality and Pest Control, 1985–89; Animal Health Gp, 1989–91; Agricl Inputs, Plant Protection and Emergencies Gp, 1991–94. Chairman, International Coffee Council, 1982–83. *Recreations:* collecting fabric, opera. *Address:* Croxley East, The Heath, Weybridge, Surrey KT13 0UA.

ATTWELL, Prof. David Ian, PhD; FMedSci; FRS 2001; Jodrell Professor of Physiology, University College London, since 1995; *b* 18 Feb. 1953; *s* of Arthur Attwell and Vera Eileen Attwell (*née* Slade); *m* 1988, Ulrike Schmidt; one *s*. *Educ:* Magdalen Coll., Oxford (BA 1st Cl. Physics 1974; BA 2nd Cl. Physiological Scis 1975; PhD Physiol. 1979). Fellow, Magdalen Coll., Oxford, 1977–79 and 1980–81; University College London: Lectr in Physiol., 1981–88; Reader, 1988–91; Prof. of Physiol., 1991–95. SRC Postdoctoral Fellow, Berkeley, Calif, 1979–80; Henry Head Fellow, Royal Soc., 1984–89. FMedSci 2000. *Publications:* contribs to learned jls on neuroscience. *Recreation:* travel. *Address:* Department of Physiology, University College London, Gower Street, WC1E 6BT. *T:* (020) 7679 7342.

ATTWOOD, Jonathan F.; *see* Freeman-Attwood.

ATTWOOD, Thomas Jaymril; management and marketing consultant; Chairman, Cargill, Attwood and Thomas Ltd, Management Consultancy Group, 1965–97; Associate Professor of Strategic Management, International Management Centres, 1997–2004; *b* 30 March 1931; *s* of George Frederick Attwood and Avril Sandys (*née* Cargill, NZ); *m* 1963, Lynette O. E. Lewis; one *s* one *d*. *Educ:* Haileybury and Imperial Service Coll.; RMA Sandhurst; Harvard Grad. Sch. of Business Admin; INSEAD, Fontainebleau. Pres., Internat. Consultants' Foundn, 1978–81. Conducted seminars for UN Secretariat, European Commn and World Council of Churches, 1970–80; presented papers to Eur. Top Management Symposium, Davos, Internat. Training Conf. and to World Public Relations Conf. Mem. Exec. Cttee, Brit. Management Training Export Council, 1978–85; Chm., Post Office Users National Council, 1982–83. Mem. Court, Worshipful Company of Marketors, 1985–93 (Liveryman, 1980). FCIM; FIMC; FCMI, FInstD. Mem., Richmond upon Thames Borough Council, 1969–71. *Publications:* (jtly) Bow Group pubn on United Nations, 1961; contrib. to reference books, incl. Systems Thinking, Innovation in Global Consultation, Handbook of Management Development, and Helping Across Cultures; articles on marketing, management and business topics. *Recreations:* travel, music, chess, City of London, cricket. *Address:* 48 Alder Lodge, Stevenage Road, SW6 6NR. *T:* (020) 7381 3301; *e-mail:* tom.@attwood.@tiscali.co.uk. *Clubs:* City Livery, MCC, Lord's Taverners, Hurlingham.

ATTWOOLL, David John; Director, Attwooll Associates Ltd, since 2002; *b* 22 April 1949; *s* of Derek Attwooll and Dorothy Attwooll (*née* Hunt); *m* 1979, Trish Cowan; two *s* one *d*. *Educ:* Lancing Coll.; Pembroke Coll., Cambridge (BA 1970; MA). Editorial Dir, Reference and Gen., OUP, 1985–89; Random House: Man. Dir, Paperback Div., 1989–90; Man. Dir, Reference Div., 1990–92; Man. Dir, Helicon Publishing, 1992–2002. Chairman: Liverpool Univ. Press, 2004–; Oxfordshire Artweeks, 2006–; Heritage House Gp, 2007–; non-executive Director: Duncan Baird Publishing, 1992–; Oxford Inspires, 2004–; Associate Publisher, Oxford Internat. Centre for Publishing Studies, Oxford Brookes Univ., 1995–. FRSA. *Recreations:* music (particularly jazz), travel, cricket, reading. *Address:* Attwooll Associates Ltd, 90 Divinity Road, Oxford OX4 1LN. *T:* (01865) 422230, *Fax:* (01865) 791192; *e-mail:* david@attwoollassociates.com. *Club:* QI (Oxford); Southfield Cricket.

ATTWOOLL, Elspeth Mary-Ann Muncy; Member (Lib Dem) Scotland, European Parliament, since 1999; *b* 1 Feb. 1943; *d* of Hugh Robert Rhind Attwooll and Joan Attwooll (*née* Fidler); *m* 1990, Donald Gordon Henry. *Educ:* Tiffin Girls' Sch., Kingston upon Thames; St Andrews Univ.; Queen's Coll., Dundee (LLB, MA Hons Politics and Philosophy). University of Glasgow: Asst Lectr, Lectr, Sen. Lectr in Jurisp., 1966–98; ILO, Geneva, 1968–69. *Publications:* The Tapestry of the Law, 1997; articles and essays on legal philosophy. *Recreation:* reading, particularly detective fiction. *Address:* 2A Whitton Street, Glasgow G20 0AN. *T:* (0141) 946 1370.

ATWELL, Very Rev. James Edgar; Dean of Winchester, since 2006; *b* 3 June 1946; *s* of Joseph Norman Edgar Atwell and Sybil Marion Atwell (*née* Burnett); *m* 1976, Lorna Goodwin; one *s* two *d*. *Educ:* Dauntsey's Sch.; Exeter Coll., Oxford (MA, BD); Harvard Univ. (ThM). Ordained deacon, 1970, priest, 1971; Assistant Curate: St John the Evangelist, E Dulwich, 1970–74; Great St Mary's, Cambridge, 1974–77; Chaplain, Jesus Coll., Cambridge, 1977–81; Vicar of Towcester, 1981–95; RD, Towcester, 1983–91; Provost, subseq. Dean, of St Edmundsbury, 1995–2006. Member: Cathedral Fabric Commn for England, 2006–; Bd of Overseers, Harvard Meml Ch., USA, 2006–. *Publications:* Sources of the Old Testament, 2004; (contrib.) Dreaming Spires?, 2005; contrib. to Jl Theol Studies. *Recreations:* countryside, walking, driving a Land Rover, travel, fairground organs, theology. *Address:* The Deanery, The Close, Winchester, Hants SO23 9LS. *T:* (01962) 857203, *Fax:* (01962) 857264.

ATWELL, Rt Rev. Robert Ronald; *see* Stockport, Bishop Suffragan of.

ATWOOD, Barry Thomas; public and European Community law consultant, since 1995; Principal Assistant Solicitor (Under Secretary), Ministry of Agriculture, Fisheries and Food, 1989–95; *b* 25 Feb. 1940; *s* of Percival Atwood and Vera Fanny Atwood (*née* Stoneham); *m* 1965, Jennifer Ann Burgess; two *s*. *Educ:* Bristol Grammar Sch.; Bristol Univ. (LLB); University College London. Solicitor. Articled John Robinson and Jarvis, Isle of Wight, 1961; Solicitor with Robert Smith & Co., Bristol, 1965; Legal Dept, Ministry of Agriculture, Fisheries and Food: conveyancing, 1966; food legislation, 1970; Common Agricultural Policy, 1977; i/c European Court litigation, 1982; Agricultural Commodities and Food Safety Bill, 1986; Legal Gp B (domestic and EC litigation and commercial work), 1989–92; Legal Gp A (legislation and adv. work), 1992–95. *Publications:* (contrib.) Law of the European Communities, 1999; Butterworth's Food Law, 2nd edn 2000, 3rd edn as Food Law (with K. Thompson and C. Willett) 2008. *Recreations:* family, music, walking, France, Italy. *Address:* 10 Box Ridge Avenue, Purley, Surrey CR8 3AP.

ATWOOD, Margaret, CC (Can.) 1981; FRSC 1987; writer; *b* Ottawa, 18 Nov. 1939; *m* Graeme Gibson; one *d*. *Educ:* Univ. of Toronto (BA 1961); Radcliffe Coll., Cambridge, Mass (AM 1962); Harvard Univ., Cambridge, Mass. Lectr in English, Univ. of BC, Vancouver, 1964–65; Instructor in English: Sir George Williams Univ., Montreal, 1967–68; Univ. of Alberta, 1969–70; Asst Prof. of English, York Univ., Toronto, 1971–72; Writer-in-Residence: Univ. of Toronto, 1972–73; Macquarie Univ., Australia, 1987; Hon. Chair, Univ. of Alabama, Tuscaloosa, 1985; Berg Prof., New York Univ., 1986. Holds hon. degrees from univs and colls; recipient of awards, medals and prizes for writing. TV scripts: The Servant Girl, 1974; Snowbird, 1981; (with Peter Pearson) Heaven on Earth, 1986; radio script, The Trumpets of Summer, 1964. *Publications: poetry:* The Circle Game, 1966; The Animals in That Country, 1969; The Journals of Susanna Moodie, 1970 (illus. edn, 1997); Procedures for Underground, 1970; Power Politics, 1971; You Are Happy, 1974; Selected Poems, 1976; Two-Headed Poems, 1978; True Stories, 1981; Notes Towards a Poem that Can Never be Written, 1981; (ed) The New Oxford Book of Canadian Verse in English, 1982; Snake Poems, 1983; Interlunar, 1984; Selected Poems II: poems selected and new 1976–1986, 1986; Selected Poems 1966–1984, 1990; Margaret Atwood Poems 1965–1975, 1991; Poems 1976–1986, 1992; Morning in the Burned House, 1995; The Door, 2007; also poetry in art and small press edns; *fiction:* The Edible Woman, 1969; Surfacing, 1972; Lady Oracle, 1976; Dancing Girls (short stories), 1977; Up in the Tree (for children), 1978; Anna's Pet (for children), 1980; Life Before Man, 1979; Bodily Harm, 1981; Encounters with the Element Man, 1982; Murder in the Dark (short stories), 1983; Bluebeard's Egg (short stories), 1983; Unearthing Suite, 1983; The Handmaid's Tale, 1985 (Governor General's Award, 1986; filmed 1990); (ed with Robert Weaver) The Oxford Book of Canadian Short Stories in English, 1986, new edn as The New Oxford Book of Canadian Short Stories in English, 1995; Cat's Eye, 1989; (ed with Shannon Ravenel) The Best American Short Stories, 1989; For the Birds (for children), 1990; Wilderness Tips (short stories), 1991; Good Bones (short stories), 1992; The Robber Bride, 1993; Princess Prunella and the Purple Peanut (for children), 1995; Alias Grace (Giller Prize, Giller Foundn, Canada; Canadian Booksellers Assoc. Author of the Year; Nat. Arts Club Medal of Honor for Literature), 1996; The Blind Assassin (Booker Prize), 2000; Oryx and Crake, 2003; Rude Ramsay and the Roaring Radishes (for children), 2003; Bashful Bob and Doleful Dorinda (for children), 2004; The Penelopiad, 2005; The Tent (short stories), 2006; Moral Disorder (short stories), 2006; *non-fiction:* Survival: a thematic guide to Canadian literature, 1972; Days of the Rebels 1815–1840, 1977; Second Words: selected critical prose, 1982; Strange Things: the malevolent North in Canadian literature, 1995; Negotiating with the Dead: a writer on writing, 2002; Moving Targets: writing with intent 1982–2004, 2004; Curious Pursuits: occasional writing, 2005. *Address:* c/o McClelland & Stewart, 75 Sherbourne Street, 5th Floor, Toronto, Ont M5A 2P9, Canada.

AUBREY, David John; QC 1996; a Recorder, since 1998; *b* 6 Jan. 1950; *s* of Raymond John Morgan Aubrey and Dorothy Mary (*née* Griffiths); *m* 1980, Julia Catherine Drew; one *d*. *Educ:* Cathays High Sch., Cardiff; University Coll., Cardiff (LLB Hons); Inns of Court Sch. of Law. Called to the Bar, Middle Temple, 1976, Bencher, 2002; Hd of Chambers, Temple Chambers, Cardiff and Newport. Treas., Wales and Chester Circuit, 2000–03. Member: Criminal Bar Assoc., 1988–; Bar Council, 1998–. Pres., Boys' Brigade in Wales, 2004– (Vice Pres., 2002–04). *Recreations:* gardening, music, cricket, collecting Boys' Brigade memorabilia, genealogy. *Address:* 32 Park Place, Cardiff CF10 3BA. *T:* (029) 2039 7364; *e-mail:* dj.aubreyqc@virgin.net.

AUBREY-FLETCHER, family name of **Baroness Braye**.

AUBREY-FLETCHER, Sir Henry (Egerton), 8th Bt *cr* 1782, of Clea Hall, Cumberland; farmer and company director; Lord-Lieutenant of Buckinghamshire, since 2006 (Vice Lord-Lieutenant, 1997–2006); *b* 27 Nov. 1945; *s* of Sir John Henry Lancelot Aubrey-Fletcher, 7th Bt and Diana Mary Fynvola (*d* 1996), *o c* of Lt-Col Arthur Egerton; *S* father, 1992; *m* 1976, Sara Roberta, *d* of late Major Robert Gilliam Buchanan and Mrs Margaret Ogden-White; three *s*. *Educ:* Eton. Chm., Chilton House Nursing Home, 1987–. Chm., Fox FM ILR, 2000 (Dir, 1989–). Dep. Chm., NT, 2003–; Member: Landscape Adv. Cttee, Dept of Transport, 1990–94. Pres., CLA, 2007–. Chm., Berks, Bucks and Oxon Wildlife (formerly Naturalist) Trust, 1995–2001; Trustee, Chequers Trust, 1997–. High Sheriff, Bucks, 1995–96. *Recreations:* IT, media and rural affairs. *Heir:* *s* John Robert Aubrey-Fletcher, *b* 20 June 1977. *Address:* Estate Office, Chilton, Aylesbury, Bucks HP18 9LR. *T:* (01844) 265201.

AUCHINCLOSS, Louis Stanton; author; Partner, Hawkins Delafield and Wood, NYC, 1957–86 (Associate, 1954–57); *b* NY, 27 Sept. 1917; *s* of J. H. Auchincloss and P. Stanton; *m* 1957, Adèle Lawrence; three *s*. *Educ:* Groton Sch.; Yale Univ.; Univ. of Virginia (LLB). Lieut USNR; served, 1941–45. Admitted to NY Bar, 1941; Associate Sullivan and Cromwell, 1941–51. Mem. Exec. Cttee, Assoc. of Bar of NY City. Pres., Museum of City of NY, 1967; Trustee, Josiah Macy Jr Foundn. Mem., Nat. Inst. of Arts and Letters. *Publications:* The Indifferent Children, 1947; The Injustice Collectors, 1950; Sybil, 1952; A Law for the Lion, 1953; The Romantic Egoists, 1954; The Great World and Timothy Colt, 1956; Venus in Sparta, 1958; Pursuit of the Prodigal, 1959; The House of Five Talents, 1960; Reflections of a Jacobite, 1961; Portrait in Brownstone, 1962; Powers of Attorney, 1963; The Rector of Justin, 1964; Pioneers and Caretakers, 1966; The Embezzler, 1966; Tales of Manhattan, 1967; A World of Profit, 1969; Second Chance: tales to two generations, 1970; Edith Wharton, 1972; I Come as a Thief, 1972; Richelieu, 1972; The Partners, 1974; A Writer's Capital, 1974; Reading Henry James, 1975; The Winthrop Covenant, 1976; The Dark Lady, 1977; The Country Cousin, 1978; The House of the Prophet, 1980; The Cat and the King, 1981; Watch Fires, 1982; Honourable Men, 1986; Diary of a Yuppie, 1987; The Golden Calves, 1989; (ed) Hone and Strong Diaries of Old Manhattan, 1989; Fellow Passengers, 1990; J. P. Morgan, 1990; House of the Prophet, 1991; Lady of Situations, 1991; False Gods, 1992; Three Lives, 1993; Tales of Yesteryear, 1994; The Style's the Man, 1994; Collected Stories, 1994; The Education of Oscar Fairfax, 1995; The Man Behind the Book, 1996; La Gloire, 1996; The Atonement, 1997; The Anniversary, 1999; Her Infinite Variety, 2000; Woodrow Wilson, 2000; Theodore Roosevelt, 2002; Manhattan Monologues, 2002; pamphlets on American writers. *Address:* 1111 Park Avenue, New York, NY 10128–1234, USA. *Club:* Century Association (NY).

AUCKLAND, 10th Baron *cr* 1789 (Ire.), 1793 (GB); **Robert Ian Burnard Eden;** *b* 25 July 1962; *s* of 9th Baron Auckland and Dorothy Margaret, *d* of H. J. Manser; *S* father, 1997; *m* 1986, Geraldine Caroll; one *d*. *Educ:* Blundell's Sch., Tiverton. *Heir: cousin* Henry Vane Eden [*b* 11 March 1958; *m* 1988, Alice Claire Needham; one *s* two *d* (and one *s* decd)].

AUCKLAND (Dio. Durham), **Archdeacon of;** *see* Barker, Ven. N. J. W.

AUCKLAND (NZ), Bishop of, since 1995; **Rt Rev. John Campbell Paterson;** Primate and Presiding Bishop of the Anglican Church in Aotearoa, New Zealand and Polynesia, 1998–2004; *b* 4 Jan. 1945; *s* of Thomas Paterson and Lucy Mary Paterson; *m* 1968, Marion Reid Anderson; two *d. Educ:* King's Coll., Auckland; Auckland Univ. (BA); St John's Coll., Auckland (LTh (Hons)); Dip. Public Speaking (NZ Speech Bd), 1969. Ordained, deacon, 1969, priest, 1970; Assistant Curate, Whangarei, 1969–71; Vicar, Waimate North Maori Pastorate, 1971–76; Co-Missioner, Auckland Maori Mission, 1976; Chaplain, Queen Victoria Sch., 1976–82; TF Chaplain, 1976–84; Sec., Te Pihopatanga o Aotearoa, 1978–86; Provincial Sec., Church of the Province of NZ, 1986–92; Gen. Sec., Anglican Church in Aotearoa, NZ and Polynesia, 1992–95. Chm., ACC, 2002– (Mem., 1990–96; Vice-Chm., 1996–2002). *Publication:* (ed) He Toenga Whatiwhatinga, 1983. *Recreations:* music, sport, literature. *Address:* PO Box 37–242, Parnell 1033, Auckland, New Zealand. *T:* (9) 3027202.

AUCKLAND (NZ), Bishop of, (RC), since 1994; **Most Rev. Patrick James Dunn;** *b* London, 5 Feb. 1950; *s* of Hugh Patrick Dunn and June Mary (*née* Grevatt). *Educ:* Sacred Heart Coll., Auckland; Canterbury Univ. (BA); Otago Univ. (BTheol); Melbourne Coll. of Divinity, Australia (MTheol 1989). Ordained priest, 1976; Catholic Maori Mission, Auckland, 1976–77; Assistant Priest: Mangere E, 1978–79; Takapuna, 1980–84; Co-Pastor, Pakuranga, 1985; Dir, First Year Formation House, Dio. of Auckland, 1986–87; Parish Priest, Northcote, 1990–92; Pastoral Asst to RC Bp of Auckland, and VG, 1993–94. *Publication:* Priesthood, 1990. *Address:* Pompallier Diocesan Centre, Private Bag 47904, Ponsonby, Auckland 1144, New Zealand. *T:* (9) 3603002.

AUCKLAND, Mary Josephine, OBE 2002; independent consultant and trainer; *b* 22 Nov. 1950; *d* of Reginald George Auckland and Annie Auckland (*née* Sullivan); *m* 2003, Terence John Beck. *Educ:* Poly of N London (LA Professional Exams 1971); University Coll. London (BSc Hons Anthropol. 1977); London Sch. of Econs (MSc Industrial Relns and Personnel Mgt 1986). MCLIP (ALA 1973). Res. Asst, Sch. of Librarianship and Inf. Studies, Poly. of N London, 1971–72; Res. Librarian, Liby and Learning Resources Service, City of London Poly., 1972–74; Asst Librarian, 1979–88, Sub-Librarian, 1988–89, British Liby of Pol and Econ. Sci., LSE; Dep. Librarian and Hd, User Services, Univ. of Southampton Liby, 1990–92; Librarian, SOAS, Univ. of London, 1992–98; Dir of Liby and Learning Resources, London Inst., subseq. Univ. of the Arts London, 1998–2005. Conf. Dir, Computers in Libraries Internat., 1993–95. Member: Cttee for Inf. Envmt (formerly for Electronic Inf.), Jt Inf. Systems Cttee, 1996–2003 (Chair, Content Wkg Gp, 1999–2000); UK Office for Liby Networking Mgt Cttee, 1999–2001; UKOLN Strategic Adv. Gp, 2002–03; British Council Knowledge and Inf. Adv. Cttee, 2002–; Artifact Exec. Bd, 2002–05; ARLIS Nat. Co-ordinating Cttee, 2004–05. Mem., Higher Educn/British Liby Task Force, 2000–01. Mem. Council, LA, 1991–99 (Chm. Council, 1997–99; Chm., Acad. and Res. Libraries Cttee, 1993–95). Acad. Gov., Ct of Govs, SOAS, 1996–98; Acad. Bd Gov., Ct of Govs, London Inst. (later Univ. of the Arts London), 1999–2005. Mem. Trustees, CLIP Benevolent Fund, 2004–. Hon. FCLIP 2002. Cawthorne Prize, LA, 1970. *Publications:* contrib. various articles, chapters, etc. in professional pubns, and conf. papers. *Recreations:* good company, travel. *Club:* Reform.

AUDET, Daniel; Senior Vice-President, Conseil du patronat du Québec, since 2007; *b* 6 April 1961; *s* of Marc Audet and Gisèle (*née* Bédard); *m*; one *d. Educ:* Univ. of Ottawa (philosophy); Univ. of Montreal (law); Montreal Bar school. Freelance journalist, Montreal, 1986–90; attorney, Lapointe Rosenstein, Montreal, 1990–94; COS for Quebec Dep. Premier and Minister of State for Economy and Finance, Quebec, 1994–97; Vice Pres., Corporate Affairs, Videotron Inc., Montreal, 1997–2000. Member Board: Canadian Customs and Revenue Agency, 1999–2000; Horizon Scis and Technologies Inc., 1999–2000; Agent Gen. of Quebec in London, 2000–03; Man. Partner, Nat. Public Relations Inc., Montreal, 2003–07. Chm. Bd, Fondation jeunesse du monde, 1998–2000; Mem. Exec., Montreal Internat. Ambassador Club, 1999–2000. *Recreations:* arts in general, economics and the digital revolution. *Address:* Conseil du patronat du Québec, Suite 510, 1010 Sherbrooke Street W, Montreal, QC H3A 2R7, Canada.

AUDLAND, Sir Christopher (John), KCMG 1987 (CMG 1973); DL; HM Diplomatic Service and Commission of the European Communities, retired; *b* 7 July 1926; *s* of late Brig. Edward Gordon Audland, CB, CBE, MC, and Violet Mary, *d* of late Herbert Shepherd-Cross, MP; *m* 1955, Maura Daphne Sullivan; two *s* one *d. Educ:* Winchester Coll. RA, 1944–48 (Temp. Capt.). Entered Foreign (subseq. Diplomatic) Service, 1948; served in: Berlin and Bonn; British Representation to Council of Europe, Strasbourg; Washington; UK Delegn to negotiations for British Membership of European Communities, Brussels, 1961–63; Buenos Aires; Head of Science and Technology Dept, FCO, 1968–70; Counsellor (Head of Chancery), Bonn, 1970–73; seconded to Commn of Eur. Communities, 1973: Dep. Sec.-Gen., 1973–81; Dir-Gen. for Energy, 1981–86. Head, UK Delegn to 1st UN Conf. on Seabed and Ocean Floor, 1968; Dep. Head, UK Delegn to Four-Power Negotiations on Berlin, 1970–72. Hon. Fellow, Faculty of Law, and Vis. Lectr on European Instns, Edinburgh Univ., 1986–. Vice President: Europa Nostra, 1988–91; Internat. Castles Inst., 1988–90 (Pres., 1990–91); Europa Nostra united with Internat. Castles Inst., 1991–96 (Exec. Pres., 1992; Hon. Pres., 1997–). Member: NW Regl Cttee, National Trust, 1987–95; European Strategy Bd, ICL, 1988–96; Lake District Nat. Park Authority, 1989–95; Pro-Chancellor, Lancaster Univ., 1990–97 (Mem., Council, 1988–97; Hon. Fellow, 2007). Trustee: Peter Kirk Meml Fund, 1989–96; Ruskin Foundn, 1994–2001; European Opera Centre, 1996–2002. DL Cumbria, 1996. *Publication:* Right Place, Right Time (autobiog.), 2004. *Address:* The Old House, Ackenthwaite, Milnthorpe, Cumbria LA7 7DH. *T:* (015395) 62202, *Fax:* (015395) 64041; *e-mail:* cja_ack@btinternet.com. *Club:* Oxford and Cambridge.

AUDLEY, Barony *cr* 1312–13; in abeyance. *Co-heiresses:* Hon. Patricia Ann Mackinnon [*b* 10 Aug. 1946; *m* 1969, Carey Leigh Mackinnon; one *s* one *d*]; Hon. Jennifer Michelle Carrington [*b* 23 May 1948; *m* 1978, Michael William Carrington; two *s* one *d*]; Hon. Amanda Elizabeth Souter [*b* 5 May 1958; one *d*].

AUDLEY, Prof. Robert John, PhD; FBPsS; Professor of Psychology, University College London, 1965–94, now Professor Emeritus; *b* 15 Dec. 1928; *s* of Walter Audley and Agnes Lilian (*née* Baker); *m* 1st, 1952, Patricia Mary Bannister (marr. diss. 1977); one *s* (and one *s* decd); 2nd, 1990, Vera Elyashiv Bickerdike. *Educ:* Battersea Grammar Sch.; University Coll. London (BSc 1st Cl. Hons Psychology, 1952; PhD 1955). Fulbright Scholar and Res. Asst, Washington State Univ., 1952; University College London: Res. Worker, MRC Gp for Exptl Investigation of Behaviour, 1955–57; Lectr in Psychology, 1957–64; Reader in Psychology, 1964; Head, Psychology Dept, 1979–93; Dean, Faculty of Science, 1985–88; Vice-Provost, 1988–94; Fellow, 1989. Vis. Prof., Columbia Univ., NY, 1962; Vis. Miller Prof., Univ. of Calif, Berkeley, 1971; Vis Fellow, Inst. for Advanced Study, Princeton, 1970. Member: UGC Social Studies Sub-Cttee, 1975–82; UGC Equipment Sub-Cttee, 1982–89; Computer Bd for Univs and Res. Councils, 1986–90; MRC/RN Personnel Res. Cttee, 1984 (Chm., Psychology Sub-Cttee, 1984–95); Chm., Jt Wkg Gp, ESRC/HEFC Jt Inf. Systems Cttee, 1990–99 (Mem., New Technology Sub-Cttee, Jt Inf. Systems Cttee, 1993–95). President: British Psychological Soc., 1969–70; Exptl Psychology Soc., 1975–76. Editor, British Jl of Math. and Stat. Psychology, 1965–70. *Publications:* papers on choice, judgement, medical mishaps. *Recreations:* crosswords, cooking, the arts. *Address:* 22 Keats Grove, NW3 2RS. *T:* (020) 7435 6655.

AUDLEY-CHARLES, Prof. Michael Geoffrey, PhD; Yates-Goldsmid Professor of Geology, 1982–93, now Emeritus Professor, and Head of the Department of Geological Sciences, 1982–92, University College London; *b* 10 Jan. 1935; *s* of Laurence Geoffrey Audley-Charles and Elsie Ada (*née* Ustonson); *m* 1965, Brenda Amy Cordeiro; one *s* one *d. Educ:* Royal Wanstead Sch.; Chelsea Polytechnic (BSc); Imperial Coll., London (PhD). Geologist with mining and petroleum cos, Canada and Australia, 1957–62; Imperial Coll. of Science and Technology, London: research in geology, 1962–67; Lectr in Geol., 1967–73; Reader in Geol., 1973–77; Prof. of Geol. and Head of Dept of Geol Sciences, Queen Mary Coll., London, 1977–82. Hon. Fellow, UCL, 1995. *Publications:* geological papers dealing with stratigraphy of British Triassic, regional geol. of Indonesia and Crete and evolution of Gondwanaland, in learned jls. *Recreation:* gardening. *Address:* La Serre, St Pantaléon, 46800 Montcuq, France. *T:* 565318067.

AUDUS, Prof. Leslie John, MA, PhD, ScD Cantab; FIBiol; Hildred Carlile Professor of Botany, Bedford College, University of London, 1948–79; *b* 9 Dec. 1911; English; *m* 1938, Rowena Mabel Ferguson (*d* 1987); two *d. Educ:* Downing Coll., Cambridge Univ. Downing Coll. Exhibitioner, 1929–31; Frank Smart Research Student (Cambridge Univ.), 1934–35; Lecturer in Botany, University Coll., Cardiff, 1935–40. Served War of 1939–45: RAFVR (Technical, Radar, Officer), 1940–46; PoW South Pacific, 1942–45. Scientific Officer, Agricultural Research Council, Unit of Soil Metabolism, Cardiff, 1946–47; Monsanto Lecturer in Plant Physiology, University Coll., Cardiff, 1948. Recorder, 1961–65, Pres., 1967–68, Section K, British Assoc. for the Advancement of Science. Vis. Prof. of Botany: Univ. of California, Berkeley, 1958; Univ. of Minnesota, Minneapolis, 1965. Vice-Pres. Linnean Soc. of London, 1959–60 (Hon. FLS 1995); Life Mem. New York Academy of Sciences, 1961. Editor, Journal Exp. Botany, 1965–74. *Publications:* Plant Growth Substances, 1953, 3rd edn 1972; (ed) The Physiology and Biochemistry of Herbicides, 1964; (ed) Herbicides: physiology, biochemistry and ecology, 1976; Spice Island Slaves, 1996; original research on plant respiration, hormones, responses to gravity, soil micro-biology in relation to pesticides, etc. in Annals of Botany, New Phytologist, Nature, Journal of Experimental Botany, Weed Research, etc. *Recreations:* furniture construction and restoration, electronics, amateur radio. *Address:* 11 Crossborough Hill, Basingstoke, Hants RG21 4AG.

AUERBACH, Frank Helmuth; painter; *b* 29 April 1931; *s* of Max Auerbach, lawyer, and Charlotte Norah Auerbach; *m* 1958, Julia Wolstenholme; one *s. Educ:* privately; St Martin's Sch. of Art; Royal Coll. of Art. *One-man exhibitions:* Beaux Arts Gallery, 1956, 1959, 1961, 1962, 1963; Marlborough Fine Art, 1965, 1967, 1971, 1974, 1983, 1987, 1990, 1997, 2004; Marlborough Gall., New York, 1969, 1982, 1994, 1998, 2006; Villiers, Sydney, Australia, 1972; Bergamini, Milan, 1973; Univ. of Essex, 1973; Mun. Gall. of Modern Art, Dublin, 1975; Marlborough, Zurich, 1976; Anthony D'Offay, London, 1978; Arts Council Retrospective, Hayward Gall., Fruit Market Gall., Edinburgh, 1978; Jacobson, NY, 1979; Anne Berthoud, London, 1983; Venice Biennale, British Pavilion, 1986 (Golden Lion Prize); Kunstverein, Hamburg; Museum Folkwang, Essen; Centro de Arte Reina Sofia, Madrid, 1986–87; Rijksmuseum Vincent van Gogh, Amsterdam, 1989; Yale Center for British Art, New Haven, 1991; Nat. Gall., 1995; Campbell-Thiebaud Gall., San Francisco, 1995; Rex Irwin, Woollahra, 1996; Charlottenborg, Copenhagen, 2000; RA 2001; Marlborough, Madrid, 2002. *Mixed exhibitions:* Carnegie International, Pittsburgh, 1958, 1961; Dunn International, Fredericton, 1963; Gulbenkian International, Tate Gallery, 1964; Peter Stuyvesant Foundn Collection, London, 1967; The Human Clay, Hayward Gall., 1976; European Painting in the Seventies, Los Angeles County Mus. and tour, 1976; Annual Exhbn, part I, Hayward Gall., 1977; Westkunst, Cologne, 1981; New Spirit in Painting, RA, 1981; Internat. Survey, Moma, NY, 1984; The Hard Won Image, Tate Gall., 1984; The British Show, Art Gall. of WA, Perth, and tour, 1985; British Art in the Twentieth Century, RA, 1987; Current Affairs, Mus. of Modern Art, Oxford, and tour, 1987; A School of London, Kunstnernes Hus., Oslo, and tour, 1987–88; Pursuit of the Real, Manchester City Art Gall., 1990; British Figurative Painting of the Twentieth Century, Israel Mus., Jerusalem, 1992–93; From London, Scottish Nat. Gall. of Modern Art, Edinburgh, and tour, 1995–96; School of London, Fondation Dina Vierny, Musée Maillol, Paris, and tour, 1998–99. *Public collections:* Arts Council; Brit. Council; Brit. Museum; Tate Gallery, London; Metropolitan Museum, NY; Mus. of Modern Art, NY; National Gallery of Victoria, Melbourne; Nat. Galls of Australia, W Australia and NSW; County Museum of LA, Calif; Cleveland Mus., Ohio; Art Inst., Chicago; Univ. of Cincinnati; St Louis Art Mus.; Yale Center for British Art, New Haven; Tamayo Mus., Mexico; Aberdeen, Bedford, Bolton, Cambridge, Edinburgh, Hartlepool, Huddersfield, Hull, Leeds, Leicester, Manchester, Nottingham, Oldham, Rochdale, Sheffield, Southampton Galls; Contemporary Art Soc., etc. *Address:* c/o Marlborough Fine Art, 6 Albemarle Street, W1S 4BY.

AUGIER, Sir Fitzroy (Richard), Kt 1996; Professor of History, University of the West Indies, 1989–95, now Professor Emeritus; *b* 17 Dec. 1924; *s* of Frank John Augier and Lucie Lastique; *m* 1959, Leila Yvette Gibbs; two *s* one *d. Educ:* St Mary's Coll., Castries; Univ. of St Andrews (MA 1949; PhD 1954); London Univ. Inst. of Educn (DipEd 1950); Inst. Commonwealth Studies. Served RAF, 1942–46. Pres., West Indian Students' Union, 1952–54; University of the West Indies: Jun. Res. Fellow, 1954; Lectr, Dept of Hist., 1955–65; Sen. Lectr, 1965–89; Dean, Faculty of Arts and Gen. Studies, 1967–72; Pro Vice Chancellor, 1972–90. Rockefeller Fellow, Inst. of Historical Res., London Univ., 1962. Chairman: Caribbean Exams Council, 1986–96; Drafting Cttee, UNESCO Gen. Hist. of Caribbean, 1981. Fellow, Inst. of Jamaica, 2003. Medal, Internat. Council on Archives, 1980; Musgrave Medal (Gold), Council, Inst. of Jamaica, 1996. Chevalier, Ordre des Arts et des Lettres (France), 1989. *Publications:* (jtly) The Making of the West Indies, 1960; (jtly) Sources of West Indian History: documents with commentary, 1962; contrib. to Caribbean Qly, New World Qly, Jl Caribbean Hist. *Recreation:* gardening. *Address:* Department of History, University of the West Indies, Mona, Kingston 7, Jamaica, West Indies. *T:* 9271922; *e-mail:* history@uwimona.edu.jm; 70 Donhead Close, Kingston 6, Jamaica, West Indies. *T:* 9275385.

AUKIN, David; Director: David Aukin Productions Ltd, since 2003; Chief Executive Officer: Daybreak Pictures Ltd, since 2006; Artichoke Productions Ltd, since 2005; *b* 12 Feb. 1942; *s* of late Charles and Regina Aukin; *m* 1969, Nancy Meckler, theatre director; two *s. Educ:* St Paul's Sch., London; St Edmund Hall, Oxford (BA). Admitted Solicitor, 1965. Literary Advr, Traverse Theatre Club, 1970–73; Administrator, Oxford Playhouse Co., 1974–75; Administrator, 1975–79, Dir, 1979–84, Hampstead Theatre; Dir, Leicester Haymarket Theatre, 1984–86; Exec. Dir, NT, 1986–90; Hd of Drama, 1990–97, Hd of Film, 1997–98, Channel 4 Television; Jt Chief Exec., HAL Films, 1998–2000; Dir, Act Prodns Ltd, 2001–04; Hd of Drama, Mentorn, 2003–06. Chm., Soho Theatre and Writers' Centre, 1994–2005. *Recreation:* golf. *Address:* 27 Manor House Court, Warrington Gardens, W9 2PZ. *Club:* Century.

AULD, Alasdair Alpin, FMA; Director, Glasgow Museums and Art Galleries, 1979–88, retired; *b* 16 Nov. 1930; *s* of Herbert Bruce Auld and Janetta Isabel MacAlpine; *m* 1959, Mary Hendry Paul; one *s* one *d. Educ:* Shawlands Acad., Glasgow; Glasgow Sch. of Art (DA). FMA 1971. Glasgow Museums and Art Galleries: Asst Curator, 1956–72; Keeper of Fine Art, 1972–76; Depute Dir, 1976–79. Pres., Scottish Fedn of Museums and Art Galls, 1981–84. Hon. Curator, RCPSG, 1991–. Hon. FRCPSGlas 2001. *Publications:* catalogues; articles on museum subjects. *Recreations:* golf, travel, painting. *Address:* 3 Dalziel Drive, Pollokshields, Glasgow G41 4JA. *T:* (0141) 427 1720.

AULD, Margaret Gibson, RGN, RM, RMT; FRCN; MPhil; Chief Nursing Officer, Scottish Home and Health Department, 1977–88, retired; *b* 11 July 1932; *d* of late Alexander John Sutton Auld and Eleanor Margaret Ingram. *Educ:* Glasgow; Cardiff High Sch. for Girls; Radcliffe Infirm., Oxford (SRN 1953); St David's Hosp., Cardiff; Queen's Park Hosp., Blackburn (SCM 1954). Midwife Teacher's Dipl., 1962; Certif. of Nursing Admin, 1966, MPhil 1974, Edinburgh. Queen's Park Hosp., Blackburn, 1953–54; Staff Midwife, Cardiff Maternity Hosp., 1955, Sister, 1957; Sister, Queen Mary Hosp., Dunedin, NZ, 1959–60; Deptl Sister, Cardiff Maternity Hosp., 1960–66; Asst Matron, Simpson Meml Maternity Pavilion, Edinburgh, 1966–68, Matron, 1968–73; Actg Chief Reg. Nursing Officer, S-Eastern Reg. Hosp. Bd, Edinburgh, 1973; Chief Area Nursing Off., Borders Health Bd, 1973–76. Life Vice Pres., Royal Coll. of Midwives of UK, 1988. Chm., CRAG/SCOTMEG Review of Maternity Services in Scotland, 1992–96; Member: GNC (Scotland), 1973–76; Central Midwives Bd (Scotland), 1972–76; Cttee on Nursing (Briggs), 1970–72; Maternity Services Cttee, Integration of Maternity Work (Tennent Report), 1972–73; Human Fertilization and Embryol. Authy, 1990–93; Cttee on Ethics of Gene Therapy, 1990–93; Nuffield Council on Bioethics, 1991–94. Vice-Chm., Eildon Housing Assoc., 2001– (Mem., 1989–). Patron, Queen Margaret Univ. (formerly Queen Margaret Coll., subseq. Queen Margaret UC), Edinburgh, 1999– (Gov., 1989–2000; Chm. Bd of Govs, 1997–2000). FRCN 1981; CCMI (CBIM 1983). Hon. DSc CNAA, 1987. *Recreations:* reading, music, entertaining. *Address:* Staddlestones, Neidpath Road, Peebles EH45 8NN. *T:* (01721) 729594.

AULD, Rt Hon. Sir Robin (Ernest), Kt 1988; PC 1995; a Lord Justice of Appeal, 1995–2007; Vice-Chairman, Judicial Appointments Commission, 2006–07; a Justice of the Court of Appeal, Bermuda, since 2008; *b* 19 July 1937; *s* of late Ernest Auld and Adelaide Mackie; *m* 1963 (marr. diss. 2005); one *s* one *d. Educ:* Brooklands Coll.; King's Coll., London (LLB 1st cl. Hons 1958; PhD 1963; FKC 1987). Called to Bar, Gray's Inn, 1959 (first in order of merit, Bar finals; Macaskie Schol., Lord Justice Holker Sen. Schol.), Bencher, 1984; in practice at English Bar, 1959–87; admitted to Bar: State of NY, USA, 1984; NSW, Australia, 1986. QC 1975; a Recorder, 1977–87; a Judge of the High Court of Justice, QBD, 1987–95; Presiding Judge, Western Circuit, 1991–94; Sen. Presiding Judge for England and Wales, 1995–98. Sen. Res. Scholar, Yale Law Sch., 2001; Vis. Prof., KCL, 2007–. Legal Assessor, GMC and GDC, 1982–87. Mem., Judicial Studies Bd, 1989–91. Mem., Commn of Inquiry into Casino Gambling in the Bahamas, 1967; Chm., William Tyndale Schools' Inquiry, 1975–76; Dept of Trade Inspector, Ashbourne Investments Ltd, 1975–79; Counsel to Inquiry into Brixton Disorders, 1981; Chm., Home Office Cttee of Inquiry into Sunday Trading, 1983–84; conducted Criminal Courts Review, 1999–2001. Master, Woolmen's Co., 1984–85. Hon. LLD Hertfordshire, 2002. *Address:* Lamb Chambers, Lamb Building, Temple, EC4Y 7AS. *T:* (020) 7797 8301; *e-mail:* robin.auld@lambchambers.co.uk. *Clubs:* Athenæum; Yale (New York).

AUMANN, Prof. Robert John, PhD; Professor of Mathematics, 1968–2001, now Emeritus, and Member, Centre for Study of Rationality, since 1991, Hebrew University of Jerusalem; *b* Frankfurt am Main, 8 June 1930; *m* 1st, 1955, Esther Schlesinger (*d* 1998); four *c* (and one *s* decd); 2nd, 2005, Batya Cohn. *Educ:* Yeshiva High Sch., NY; City Coll. of New York (BS 1950); Mass Inst. of Technol. (SM 1952; PhD 1955). Mathematics Department, Hebrew University of Jerusalem: Instructor, 1956–58; Lectr, 1958–61; Sen. Lectr, 1961–64; Associate Prof. 1964–68. Corresp. FBA 1995. (Jtly) Nobel Prize in Econs, 2005. *Publications:* (with L. S. Shapley) Values of Non-Atomic Games, 1974; (with Y. Tauman and S. Zamir) Game Theory (2 vols), 1989; (ed jtly) Handbook of Game Theory with Economic Applications, vol. 1, 1992, vol. 2, 1994, vol. 3, 2002; (with M. Maschler) Repeated Games with Incomplete Information, 1995; Collected Papers (2 vols), 2000; articles in learned jls. *Address:* Center for Rationality, Hebrew University, 91904 Jerusalem, Israel.

AUNG SAN SUU KYI; Co-Founder and General Secretary, National League for Democracy, Burma, since 1988; Burmese prisoner of conscience, 1989–95; *b* Rangoon, 19 June 1945; *d* of U Aung San (assassinated, 19 July 1947) and late Daw Khin Kyi; *m* 1972, Michael Vaillancourt Aris (*d* 1999); two *s. Educ:* St Francis Convent, Rangoon; Methodist English High Sch., Rangoon; Lady Shri Ram Coll., Delhi Univ.; St Hugh's Coll., Oxford (BA PPE 1967; MA; Hon. Fellow, 1990). Asst Sec., Adv. Cttee on Admin. and Budgetary Questions, UN Secretariat, NY, 1969–71; Res. Officer, Min. of Foreign Affairs, Bhutan, 1972. Vis. Schol., Centre for SE Asian Studies, Kyoto Univ., Japan, 1985–86. Fellow, Indian Inst. of Advanced Studies, Simla, 1987. Hon. Mem., World Commn on Culture and Develt, Unesco, 1992–95; Mem., Acad. Universelle des Cultures, Paris, 1993. Hon. Pres., LSE Students' Union, 1992; Hon. Life Mem., Univ. of London Union, 1992. Hon. doctorates: Thammasat Univ., Bangkok, 1992; Toronto Univ., 1993; Vrije Univ., Brussels, 1994; Queen's Univ., Kingston, 1995. Thorolf Rafto Award for Human Rights, Norway, 1990; Nobel Peace Prize, 1991; Sakharov Prize for Freedom of Thought, European Parlt, 1991; Annual Award, Internat. Human Rights Law Group, USA, 1992; Simón Bolívar Prize, Unesco, 1992; Prix Littéraire des Droits de l'Homme, Paris, 1992; Rose Prize, Internat. Forum of Danish Lab. Movement, 1993; Victor Jara Internat. Human Rights Award, Center for Human Rights and Constitutional Law, LA, 1993; Bremen Solidarity Prize, 1993; Liberal Internat. Prize for Freedom, 1995; Jawaharlal Nehru Award for Internat. Understanding, 1995; Freedom Award of Internat. Rescue Cttee, 1995. *Publications:* (ed with Michael Aris) Tibetan Studies in Honour of Hugh Richardson, 1980; Aung San, 1984, 2nd edn as Aung San of Burma: a biographical portrait by his daughter, 1990; (contrib.) Burma and Japan: basic studies on their cultural and social structure, 1987; Burma and India: some aspects of intellectual life under colonialism, 1990; Freedom from Fear and Other Writings, 1991, 2nd edn 1995; Towards a True Refuge (Joyce Pearce Meml Lect.), 1993; numerous speeches. *Address:* 54–6 University Avenue, Rangoon, Burma.

AUNG, U Win; Minister for Foreign Affairs, Myanmar, 1998–2005; *b* 28 Feb. 1944; *m* 1972, Daw San Yone; two *s* one *d. Educ:* Yangon Univ. (BSc). 2nd Lieut, 1964; Major 1978; joined Foreign Service, 1985; Chargé d'Affaires: Laos, 1986–88; Singapore, 1988–90; Ambassador to Germany, 1990–96; Ambassador to the Court of St James's, 1996–98. Naing Ngan Daw Sit Smu Htan Tazeik; Pyi Thu Wun Htan Gaung Tazeik. *Publications:* Nation of the Gold and Selected Articles, 1996; articles in periodicals in Myanmar. *Recreation:* music. *Address:* c/o Ministry of Foreign Affairs, Pyay Road, Yangon, Union of Myanmar.

AUST, Anthony Ivall, CMG 1995; international law consultant, writer and teacher; *b* 9 March 1942; *s* of Ivall George Aust and Jessie Anne Salmon; *m* 1st, 1969, Jacqueline Antoinette Thérèse Paris (marr. diss. 1987); two *d*; 2nd, 1988, Dr Kirsten Kaarre Jensen. *Educ:* London Sch. of Econs and Pol Science (LLB 1963, LLM 1967). Admitted Solicitor, 1967. Asst Legal Adviser, FCO (formerly CO), 1967–76; Legal Adviser, British Mil. Govt, Berlin, 1976–79; Asst Legal Adviser, FCO, 1979–84; Legal Counsellor, FCO, 1984–88 and 1991–2000; Counsellor (Legal Advr) UK Mission to UN, NY, 1988–91; Dep. Legal Advr, FCO, 2000–02. Visiting Professor: UCL, 2002–; LSE, 2003–. *Publications:* Modern Treaty Law and Practice, 2000, Chinese edn 2005, 2nd edn 2007; Handbook of International Law, 2005. *Recreations:* architecture, cinema, gardening, parlour games. *Address:* 5 Coulter Road, W6 0BJ; *e-mail:* aiaust@aol.com.

AUSTEN, Patrick George; Operating Partner, Nova Capital Management Ltd, since 2003; *b* 22 Sept. 1943; *m* 1968, Margaret; three *s* one *d. Educ:* Bristol Coll. of Commerce; Leicester Sch. of Textiles; Leicester Poly.; Centre d'Etudes Industrielles, Geneva. ICI Fibres, 1961–83: commercial apprentice, British Nylon Spinners (later ICI Fibres), 1961–65; mgt trainee, 1965–67; Trade Sales Manager, 1967–70; Fibres Manager, Republic of Ireland, 1970–73; Business Area Manager, 1974–79; Commercial Manager, Textile Fibres, 1979–83; BTR, 1983–93; Managing Director: Pretty Polly, 1983–85; Pretty Polly and Dunlopillo, 1985–87; Chief Exec., Liberty plc, 1993–96. *Recreations:* golf, motor-racing. *Address:* Nova Capital Management Ltd, 11 Strand, WC2N 5HR.

AUSTEN, Richard Bertram G.; *see* Godwin-Austen.

AUSTEN, Richard James, MBE 1996; HM Diplomatic Service; Ambassador to Panama, since 2006; *b* 25 May 1955; *s* of late Capt. George Albert Austen, MN and Joyce Margaret Austen. *Educ:* Steyning Grammar Sch.; Univ. of Bristol (BA Hons (Theol.) 1977). Grad. trainee, Midland Bank, 1977–81; joined FCO, 1981; Desk Officer, Consular Dept, 1981–82, ME Dept, 1982–83, FCO; Attaché, Dar Es Salaam, 1983–87; 3rd Sec., Ottawa, 1987–90; Desk Officer, Protocol Dept, FCO, 1990–93; Dep. High Comr, Banjul, 1993–96; Desk Officer, Perm. Under-Sec.'s Dept, FCO, 1996–97; Dep. Hd, Conference Dept, FCO, 1997–98; Hd of Section, Latin America and Caribbean Dept, FCO, 1998–2001; Dep. High Comr, Port Louis, 2001–03; Ambassador to Mongolia, 2004–06. *Recreations:* walking, cycling, religion, travelling, family history. *Address:* c/o Foreign and Commonwealth Office, King Charles Street, SW1A 2AH.

AUSTEN-SMITH, Air Marshal Sir Roy (David), KBE 1979; CB 1975; CVO 1994; DFC 1953; retired; a Gentleman Usher to HM the Queen, 1982–94, an Extra Gentleman Usher, since 1994; *b* 28 June 1924; *m* 1951, Ann (*née* Alderson); two *s. Educ:* Hurstpierpoint College. Pilot trng, Canada, 1943–44; No 41 Sqn (2 TAF), 1945; No 33 Sqdn, Malaya, 1950–53; Sqn Comdr, RAF Coll., Cranwell, 1953–56; OC No 73 Sqdn, Cyprus, 1956–59; Air Min., 1960–63; OC No 57 Sqdn, 1964–66; HQ 2 ATAF, 1966–68; CO, RAF Wattisham, 1968–70; MoD, 1970–72; AOC and Comdt, RAF Coll., Cranwell, 1972–75; SASO Near East Air Force, 1975–76; Comdr British Forces, Cyprus, AOC Air HQ Cyprus and Administrator, Sovereign Base Areas, Cyprus, 1976–78; Hd of British Defence Staff, Washington, and Defence Attaché, 1978–81. *Recreation:* golf. *Address:* c/o National Westminster Bank, Swanley, Kent BR8 7WL. *Club:* Royal Air Force.

AUSTIN, Sir Anthony Leonard, 6th Bt *cr* 1894, of Red Hill, Castleford, West Riding; *b* 30 Sept. 1930; *yr s* of Sir William Ronald Austin, 4th Bt (*d* 1989) and his 1st wife, Dorothy Mary (*d* 1957), *d* of L. A. Bidwell, FRCS; *S* brother, 1995; *m* 1st, 1956, Mary Annette (marr. diss. 1966), *d* of Richard Kelly; two *s* one *d*; 2nd, 1967, Aileen Morrison Hall, *d* of William Hall Stewart; one *d. Educ:* Downside. *Heir: s* Peter John Austin [*b* 29 July 1958; *m* 1988, Jane Clare Dracup]. *Address:* Stanbury Manor, Morwenstow, Bude, Cornwall EX23 9JQ.

AUSTIN, Brian Patrick; HM Diplomatic Service, retired; *b* 18 March 1938; *s* of Edward William Austin and Winifred Alice Austin (*née* Villiger); *m* 1st, 1968, Gusti Lina (*d* 2002); one *s* one *d*; 2nd, 2007, Dr Mary Laurie-Pile. *Educ:* St Olave's Grammar Sch.; Clare Coll., Cambridge. National Service, 1956–58. Joined CRO, 1961; Central African Office, 1962; Lagos, 1963; The Hague, 1966; First Sec., FCO, 1969; Montreal, 1973; FCO, 1978; Dep. High Comr, Kaduna, 1981–84; Counsellor: FCO, 1984–88; Stockholm, 1989–93; Consul-Gen., Vancouver, 1993–98. *Recreation:* birdwatching. *Address:* Clinton, Nightingale Avenue, West Horsley, Surrey KT24 6PB.

AUSTIN, Prof. Colin François Lloyd, DPhil; FBA 1983; Fellow, Trinity Hall, Cambridge, 1965–2008, now Emeritus (Director of Studies in Classics, 1965-2005); Professor of Greek, University of Cambridge, 1998–2008; *b* Melbourne, Australia, 26 July 1941; *s* of Prof. Lloyd James Austin, FBA; *m* 1967, Mishtu Mazumdar, Calcutta, India; one *s* one *d. Educ:* Lycée Lakanal, Paris; Manchester Grammar Sch.; Jesus Coll., Cambridge (Scholar; MA 1965); Christ Church, Oxford (Sen. Scholar; MA, DPhil 1965); Freie Universität, West Berlin (Post-grad. Student). University of Cambridge: John Stewart of Rannoch Scholar in Greek and Latin, 1960; Battie Scholar, Henry Arthur Thomas Scholar and Hallam Prize, 1961; Sir William Browne Medal for a Latin Epigram, 1961; Porson Prize, 1962; Prendergast Greek Student, 1962; Res. Fellow, Trinity Hall, 1965–69; Asst Univ. Lectr in Classics, 1969–73, Lectr, 1973–88; Reader in Greek Lang. and Lit., 1988–98; Leverhulme Res. Fellow, 1979 and 1981. Treas., Cambridge Philological Soc., 1971–. *Publications:* De nouveaux fragments de l'Erechthée d'Euripide, 1967; Nova Fragmenta Euripidea, 1968; (with Prof. R. Kassel) Papyrus Bodmer XXV et XXVI, 2 vols, 1969; Menandri Aspis et Samia, 2 vols, 1969–70; Comicorum Graecorum Fragmenta in papyris reperta, 1973; (with Prof. R. Kassel) Poetae Comici Graeci: vol. IV, Aristophon–Crobylus, 1983, vol. III 2, Aristophanes, Testimonia et Fragmenta, 1984, vol. V, Damoxenus–Magnes, 1986, vol. VII, Menecrates–Xenophon, 1989, vol. II, Agathenor–Aristonymus, 1991, vol. VIII, Adespota, 1995, vol. VI 2, Menander, Testimonia et Fragmenta apud scriptores servata, 1998, vol. I, Comoedia Dorica, Mimi, Phlyaces, 2001; (jtly) Posidippo di Pella Epigrammi, 2001; (with Prof. G. Bastianini) Posidippi Pellaei quae supersunt omnia, 2002; (with Prof. S. D. Olson) Aristophanes, Thesmophoriazusae, 2004; notes and reviews in classical periodicals. *Recreations:* cycling, philately, wine tasting. *Address:* 7 Park Terrace, Cambridge CB1 1JH. *T:* (01223) 362732; Trinity Hall, Cambridge CB2 1TJ.

AUSTIN, David Charles Henshaw, OBE 2007; VMH 2002; farmer, since 1943; Chairman, David Austin Roses Ltd, since 1970; *b* 16 Feb. 1926; *s* of Charles Frederick Austin and Lilian Austin; *m* 1956, Patricia Josephine Braithwaite (*d* 2007); two *s* one *d. Educ:* Shrewsbury Sch. Non-professional rose breeder, 1946–70; nurseryman and professional rose breeder, developing new race, English Roses, 1970–. Hon. MSc East London, 1997. Veitch Meml Medal, RHS, 1994; Queen Mary Commemoration Medal, 1994, Dean Hole Medal, 2000, Royal Nat. Rose Soc.; Landscape Gardening Award, Franco-British Soc., 1995. *Publications:* The Heritage of the Rose, 1988; Old Roses and English Roses, 1992; Shrub Roses and Climbing Roses, 1993; David Austin's English Roses, 1993 (Gardening Book of Year Award, Garden Writers' Guild, 1994); The English Rose, 1998. *Recreations:* reading and writing poetry, current affairs, swimming, gardens, the countryside. *Address:* (office) David Austin Roses Ltd, Bowling Green Lane, Albrighton, Wolverhampton, W Midlands WV7 3HB. *T:* (01902) 376300; Bowling Green House, Bowling Green Lane, Albrighton, Wolverhampton, W Midlands WV7 3HB.

AUSTIN, Gary Ronald; Chief Executive, a^{2}om International, since 2008 (Managing Director, a^{2}om academy, 2006–08); *b* 28 May 1956; *s* of late Ronald Austin and of Doris Austin (*née* Pearce); *m* 1980, Susan Ann Horridge; one *s* one *d. Educ:* Univ. of Nottingham (BSc Hons (Geog.) 1978); City Univ. Business Sch. (MBA 1984). Bank clerk, Nat. Westminster Bank, 1974–75; Econ. Planning Asst. N. Lichfield & Partners, 1978–79; Manpower Planner, City Area, 1980–84, City Dist, 1984–86, British Telecom plc; Dep. Regl Personnel Dir, SW Regl HA, 1986–92; Chief Exec., Blood Services SW, 1992–94; Exec. Dir, Nat. Blood Service, 1994–99; Chief Exec., Driving Standards Agency, 2000–06. Non-exec. Dir, E Midlands Ambulance Service NHS Trust, 2006–. CCMI 2003. *Recreations:* Bath Rugby, family, cultivating *prunus laurocerasus. Address:* a^{2}om, 3000 Cathedral Hill, Guildford, Surrey GU2 7YB; *e-mail:* gaustin@a2om.com.

AUSTIN, Ven. George Bernard; Archdeacon of York, 1988–99, now Emeritus; broadcaster, writer; *b* 16 July 1931; *s* of Oswald Hulton Austin and Evelyn Austin; *m* 1962, Roberta Anise Thompson; one *s. Educ:* St David's Coll., Lampeter (BA); Chichester Theological Coll. Deacon 1955, priest 1956; Assistant Curate: St Peter's, Chorley, 1955–57; St Clement's, Notting Dale, 1957–59; Asst Chaplain, Univ. of London, 1960; Asst Curate, Dunstable Priory, 1961–64; Vicar: St Mary the Virgin, Eaton Bray, 1964–70; St Peter, Bushey Heath, 1970–88. Hon. Canon, St Albans, 1978–88; Canon, York, 1988–99, now Emeritus. Proctor in Convocation, 1970–95; a Church Commr, 1978–95. *Publications:* Life of our Lord, 1960; WCC Programme to Combat Racism, 1979; (contrib.) When will ye be Wise?, 1983; (contrib.) Building in Love, 1990; Journey to Faith, 1992; Affairs of State, 1995; (contrib.) Quo Vaditis, 1996; But This I Know, 1996; contrib. to national press. *Recreations:* cooking, theatre. *Address:* North Back House, Main Street, Wheldrake, York YO19 6AG. *T:* (01904) 448509; *e-mail:* george.austin@virgin.net.

AUSTIN, Ian; MP (Lab) Dudley North, since 2005; an Assistant Government Whip, and Minister for the West Midlands, since 2008; *b* 8 March 1965; *s* of Alfred and Margaret Austin; *m* 1993, Catherine Miles; two *s* one *d. Educ:* Dudley Sch.; Univ. of Essex (BA Hons Govt). Communications Manager, Focus Housing, 1989–94; Press Officer, Labour Party, 1995–98; Dep. Dir of Communications, Scottish Labour Party, 1998–99; political advr to Chancellor of Exchequer, 1999–2005. Mem. (Lab) Dudley MBC, 1991–95. PPS to Prime Minister, 2007–08. *Recreations:* reading, watching football, cycling. *Address:* House of Commons, SW1A 0AA. *T:* (020) 7219 8012, *Fax:* (020) 7219 4408; Turner House, 157/185 Wrens Nest Road, Dudley DY1 3RU. *T:* (01384) 342503/4, *Fax:* (01384) 342523.

AUSTIN, Hon. Jacob, (Jack); PC (Canada) 1981; QC (British Columbia) 1970; Member of the Senate, 1975–2007, and Minister and Leader of the Government in the Senate, 2003–06, Canadian Parliament; *b* 2 March 1932; *s* of Morris Austin and Clara Edith (*née* Chetner); *m* (marr. diss.); three *d; m* 1978, Natalie Veiner Freeman. *Educ:* Univ. of British Columbia (BA, LLB); Harvard Univ. (LLM). Barrister and Solicitor, BC and Yukon Territory. Asst Prof. of Law, Univ. of Brit. Columbia, 1955–58; practising lawyer, Vancouver, BC, 1958–63; Exec. Asst to Minister of Northern Affairs and Nat. Resources, 1963–65; contested (Liberal) Vancouver-Kingsway, Can. Federal Election, 1965; practising lawyer, Vancouver, BC, 1966–70; Dep. Minister, Dept of Energy, Mines and Resources, Ottawa, 1970–74; Principal Sec. to Prime Minister, Ottawa, May 1974–Aug. 1975; Minister of State, 1981–82; Minister of State for Social Develt, responsible for Canada Develt Investment Corp., and Minister for Expo '86, 1982–84; Chm., Ministerial Sub-Cttee on Broadcasting and Cultural Affairs, 1982–84. Pres., Internat. Div., Bank of British Columbia, 1985–86; Associate Counsel: Swinton & Co., 1986–92; Boughton Peterson & Co., 1992–2002; Chm. Board and Dir, Elite Insurance Management Ltd, 1986–90. Pres., Canada China Business Council, 1993–2001. Hon. DSocSc Univ. East Asia, 1987. *Publications:* articles on law and public affairs in Canadian Bar Rev., Amer. Soc. of Internat. Law and other publns. *Recreations:* sailing, golf, reading, theatre. *Address:* Suite 2900, 650 West Georgia Street, Vancouver, BC V6B 4N8, Canada. *Clubs:* Rideau (Ottawa); Vancouver (Vancouver, BC).

AUSTIN, John Eric; MP (Lab) Erith and Thamesmead, since 1997 (Woolwich, 1992–97); *b* 21 Aug. 1944; *s* of late Stanley George Austin and Ellen Elizabeth (*née* Day); adopted surname Austin-Walker, 1965, reverted to Austin, 1997; *m* 1965, Linda Margaret Walker (marr. diss. 1998); two *s* one *d. Educ:* Glyn Grammar Sch., Epsom; Goldsmiths' Coll., Univ. of London (Cert. Community and Youth Work 1972); Sch. for Advanced Urban Studies, Univ. of Bristol (MSc Policy Studies 1990). Hosp. lab. technician, 1961–63; Labour Party organiser, 1963–70; social worker/community worker, Bexley, 1972–74; Race Equality Officer (Dir, Bexley Council for Racial Equality), 1974–92. London Borough of Greenwich Council: Mem., 1970–94; Vice-Chm., 1971–74, Chm., 1974–78, Social Services; Dep. Leader, 1981–82; Leader, 1982–87; Mayor of Greenwich, 1987–88 and 1988–89. Vice-Chairman: ALA, 1983–87 (Envmt Spokesperson, 1989–92); London Strategic Policy Unit, 1986–88; Chaiman: London Ecology Unit, 1990–92; London Emergency Planning Inf. Centre, 1990–92. Chairman: British Youth Council, 1969–71; Assoc. CHCs for England and Wales, 1986–88. Contested (Lab) Woolwich, 1987. Mem., Select Cttee on Health, 1994–2005. Jt Chm., All Party Osteoporosis Gp, 1996–; Treasurer: Parly Human Rights Gp, 1997–98; Parly Gibraltar Gp, 1997–98; Secretary: British/Czech and Slovak Parly Gp, 1997–; British/Hungary Parly Gp, 1997–; Chairman: British/Slovenia Parly Gp, 1997–; British/Albania Parly Gp, 1997–; All Party UK Overseas Territories Parly Gp, 1998–; All Party Trinidad and Tobago Gp, 2005–; Vice-Chm., British Falkland Is Gp, 1997–2006. Vice Chm., London Gp of Labour MPs, 1992–97; Chm., Socialist Campaign Gp of Labour MPs, 1992–98. Deleg., Parly Assembly, Council of Europe and WEU, 2004– (Vice-Chm., Sub-Cttee on Human Trafficking); Vice-Chm., UK br., CPA, 2004–05 (Mem. Exec. Cttee, 1997–); Mem., Internat. Exec., IPU, 2004–07 (Mem. Exec. Cttee, British Gp, 1997– (Chm., 2002–05); Pres., 12+ (Geopolitical Gp), 2006–). Hon. Chm., British Caribbean Assoc., 1997–. Dir, London Marathon Charitable Trust; Trustee, Crossness Engines Trust. *Recreations:* cooking, gardening, marathon running, travel. *Address:* House of Commons, SW1A 0AA. *T:* (020) 7219 5195, *Fax:* (020) 7219 2706; (constituency office) *T:* (020) 8311 4444. *Clubs:* St Patrick's Social (Plumstead); Woolwich Catholic.

AUSTIN, Mark; Presenter, ITV Evening News, since 2003 and ITV News at Ten, since 2008 (ITV News at 10.30pm, 2006–08); *b* 1 Nov. 1958; *m* 1991; one *s* two *d. Educ:* Bournemouth Sch.; Highbury Coll., Portsmouth. Reporter, Bournemouth Evening Echo, 1976–80; newsroom writer, 1980–82, news reporter, 1982–85, sports reporter, 1985–86, BBC; joined ITV News as sports correspondent, 1986; Asia correspondent, 1990–93, 1996–98; Africa correspondent, 1993–96; Sen. Correspondent, 1998–2002. Presenter, TV series, Survivor, 2001. *Address:* Independent Television News Ltd, 200 Gray's Inn Road, WC1X 8XZ.

AUSTIN, Sir Roger (Mark), KCB 1992; AFC 1973; aviation and defence consultant, since 1998; *b* 9 March 1940; *s* of Mark and Sylvia Joan Austin. *Educ:* King Alfred's Grammar Sch., Wantage. FRAeS. Commissioned in RAF, 1957; flying appts as Qualified Flying Instructor and with Nos 20 and 54 Sqns, 1960–68; commanded No 54 Sqn, 1969; flying appt with No 4 Sqn, 1970–72; Staff Coll., Camberley, 1973; commanded 233 OCU, 1974–77; PSO to AOC-in-C Strike Command, 1977–80; commanded RAF Chivenor, 1980–82; ADC to the Queen, 1980–82; Staff of HQ Strike Command, 1982–84; Dir of Op. Requirements, 1984–85; RCDS, 1986; AO i/c Central Tactics and Trials Orgn, 1987; DG Aircraft 1, MoD (PE), 1987–89; AOC and Comdt, RAF Coll., Cranwell, 1989–92; DCDS (Systems), MoD, 1992–94; Controller Aircraft, MoD, 1994–96; Dep. Chief of Defence Procurement (Ops), MoD (PE), 1995–96; Air Marshal, retd 1997. FO RAFVR (T), 1997. President: RBL, 1997–2000; Victory Services Assoc., 2002– (Chm., 1997–2001); Trustee, RAF Benevolent Fund, 2000–. *Recreations:* flying, transport systems, photography. *Address:* 10 Cleveland Grove, Newbury, Berks RG14 1XF. *Club:* Royal Air Force.

AUSTIN-SMITH, Michael Gerard; QC 1990; a Recorder, since 1986; *b* 4 Sept. 1944; *s* of late Cyril John Austin-Smith and Joyce Austin-Smith; *m* 1971, Stephanie Maddocks; one *s* one *d. Educ:* Hampton Grammar Sch.; Exeter Univ. (LLB Hons). Called to the Bar, Inner Temple, 1969, Bencher, 2002. DTI Inspector, 1988–89 and 1989–90. *Address:* 23 Essex Street, WC2R 3AA. *T:* (020) 7413 0353. *Clubs:* Royal Corinthian Yacht, Island Sailing, Cowes Corinthian, Baat (Cowes).

AUSTIN-WALKER, John Eric; *see* Austin, J. E.

AUSTRALIA, Primate of; *see* Brisbane, Archbishop of.

AUSTRALIA, North West, Bishop of, since 2004; **Rt Rev. David Gray Mulready;** *b* 13 Sept. 1947; *s* of Norman Benson Mulready and Edna Faith Mulready (*née* Osborne); *m* 1971, Maureen Jane Mulready (*née* Lawrie); two *s* one *d. Educ:* Newington Coll., Sydney; Moore Theol Coll., Sydney (ThL 1971); Melbourne Coll. of Divinity (DipRE 1973). Ordained deacon and priest, 1971; Assistant Minister: Camden, 1971–73; Eastwood, 1973–74; Rector: Tambar Springs, 1974–77; Walgett, 1977–81; Manilla, 1981–85; Gunnedah, 1985–89; State Dir, Bush Ch Aid Soc., 1989–93; Rector, Penrith, 1993–2000; Rector and Sen. Canon, St John's Cathedral, Parramatta, 2000–04. *Recreations:* family, gardening, photography, travel, reading. *Address:* PO Box 2783, Geraldton, WA 6531, Australia. *T:* (8) 99214653; *e-mail:* david@anglicandnwa.org.

AUSTWICK, Prof. Kenneth; JP; Professor of Education, Bath University, 1966–91, now Emeritus; *b* 26 May 1927; *s* of Harry and Beatrice Austwick; *m* 1956, Gillian Griffin; one *s* one *d. Educ:* Morecambe Grammar Sch.; Sheffield Univ. BSc Maths, DipEd, MSc, PhD Sheffield. Schoolmaster, Bromsgrove, Frome and Nottingham, 1950–59; Lectr/Sen. Lectr, Sheffield Univ., 1959–65; Dep. Dir, Inst. of Educn, Reading Univ., 1965–66; Pro-Vice-Chancellor, Bath Univ., 1972–75. Vis. Lecturer: Univ. of BC, 1963; Univ. of Michigan, 1963; Univ. of Wits., 1967. Consultant, OECD, 1965; Adviser, Home Office, 1967–81; Chm., Nat. Savings SW Regional Educn, 1975–78. JP Bath 1970. FRSA. *Publications:* Logarithms, 1962; Equations and Graphs, 1963; (ed) Teaching Machines and Programming, 1964; (ed) Aspects of Educational Technology, 1972; Maths at Work, 1985; Mathematics Connections, 1985; Level by Level Mathematics, 1991; (ed) Working Science, 1991; (ed) Working English, 1991; articles and contribs on maths teaching and educnl technology. *Recreations:* gardening, bridge. *Address:* Laundry Cottage, Combe Hay, Bath BA2 7EG. *T:* (01225) 832541.

AUTON, Sylvia Jean; Chief Executive, IPC Media Ltd, since 2003 (Director, since 1998); Executive Vice President, Time Inc., since 2007; *b* 8 June 1949; *m* 1978, William Auton; two *s. Educ:* Southampton Univ. (BSc Jt Hons). Publishing Dir, New Scientist, 1990–98; Man. Dir, IPC Country & Leisure Media, 1998–2003; Trustee, 1998–, Chm., 2000–, IPC Media Pension Trustee Ltd; Dir, PPA Ltd, 2003–. *Recreations:* walking, travel. *Address:* IPC Media Ltd, Blue Fin Building, 110 Southwark Street, SE1 0SU. *T:* (020) 3148 5102; *e-mail:* sylvia_auton@ipcmedia.com.

AVEBURY, 4th Baron *cr* 1900; **Eric Reginald Lubbock;** Bt 1806; *b* 29 Sept. 1928; *s* of Hon. Maurice Fox Pitt Lubbock (6th *s* of 1st Baron) (*d* 1957), and Hon. Mary Katherine Adelaide Stanley (*d* 1981), *d* of 5th Baron Stanley of Alderley; *S* cousin, 1971; *m* 1953, Kina Maria (marr. diss. 1983) (*see* Kina, Lady Avebury); two *s* one *d*; 2nd, 1985, Lindsay Stewart; one *s. Educ:* Upper Canada Coll.; Harrow Sch.; Balliol Coll., Oxford (BA Engineering; boxing blue; Hon. Fellow, 2004). MIMechE, CEng; FBCS. Welsh Guards (Gdsman, 2nd Lieut); 1949–51; Rolls Royce Ltd, 1951–56; Grad. Apprentice; Export Sales Dept; Tech. Assistant to Foundry Manager. Management Consultant: Production Engineering Ltd, 1953–60; Charterhouse Group Ltd, 1960. MP (L) Orpington, 1962–70; Liberal Whip in House of Commons, 1963–70; elected Mem., H of L, 1999. Dir, C. L. Projects Ltd, 1966–; Consultant, Morgan-Grampian Ltd, 1970–. President: Data Processing Management Assoc., 1972–75; Fluoridation Soc., 1972–84; Conservation Soc., 1973–83. Member: Council, Inst. of Race Relations, 1972–74; Royal Commn on Standards of Conduct in Public Life, 1974–76; Chm., British Parly Human Rights Gp, 1976–97 (Vice Pres., 1997–). Member: Information Cttee, H of L, 2001–; Select Cttee on the EU, H of L, 2002–. Vice Pres., London Bach Soc., 1998– (Pres., 1984–98); Pres., Steinitz Bach Players, 1984–. Patron, Buddhist Prison Chaplaincy, 1992–. *Recreations:* listening to music, reading. *Heir: s* Hon. Lyulph Ambrose Jonathan Lubbock [*b* 15 June 1954; *m* 1977, Susan (*née* MacDonald); one *s* one *d*]. *Address:* House of Lords, SW1A 0PW; 26 Flodden Road, SE5 9LH.

AVEBURY, Kina, Lady; Kina-Maria Lubbock; consultant on health and social policy; *b* 2 Sept. 1934; *d* of late Count Joseph O'Kelly de Gallagh and Mrs M. Bruce; *m* 1953, 4th Baron Avebury, *qv* (marr. diss. 1983); two *s* one *d. Educ:* Convent of the Sacred Heart, Tunbridge Wells; Goldsmiths' College (BScSoc Hons) and LSE, Univ. of London. Lectr, Royal Coll. of Nursing, 1970–74; campaign organizer, European Movement, 1975; Asst Dir, Nat. Assoc. for Mental Health, 1976–82; Sociologist, Dept of Psychiatry, London Hosp. Med. Coll., 1983–85; Mental Health Planner, Tower Hamlets Social Services, 1986–94. Chairman: Nat. Marriage Guidance Council, 1975–82; Family Service Units, 1984–87; Avebury Working Party, 1982–84 (produced Code of Practice for Residential Care for DHSS); Working Party for A Better Home Life, 1996, Working Party on Nat. Required Standards for Long Term Care, 1998–99, Centre for Policy on Ageing; Mem., Central Council for Educn and Trng in Social Work, 1986–90. JP Kent, 1974–79. *Publications:* Volunteers in Mental Health, 1985; (with R. Williams) A Place in Mind, 1995; (jtly) The Substance of Young Needs, 1996; articles on mental health and related social policy. *Recreations:* painting, opera, cooking.

AVERY, Brian Stuart, FDSRCS; FRCSE; Consultant Oral and Maxillofacial Surgeon, James Cook University Hospital, Middlesbrough, since 1983; Dean, Faculty of Dental Surgery, Royal College of Surgeons of England, since 2004; *b* 15 Feb. 1947; *s* of Stuart and Edna Avery; *m* 1972, Fiona Gibson; two *s* two *d. Educ:* Fox Primary Sch., Notting Hill Gate; Abingdon Sch.; Guy's Hosp. Med. Sch., Univ. of London (BDS Hons 1970;

MB BS 1974). LDSRCS 1970, FDSRCS 1976; LRCP 1974; MRCS 1974, Hon. FRCS 2005; FRCSE 1985. House officer posts, Guy's Hosp., 1974–75; Registrar in Oral and Maxillofacial Surgery: Eastman Dental Hosp., 1975; Queen Mary Hosp., Roehampton and Westminster Hosp., 1976–78; Sen. Registrar in Oral and Maxillofacial Surgery, Canniesburn Hosp., Glasgow, 1978–83. Hon. Prof. of Oral and Maxillofacial Surgery, Univ. of Teesside, 2002–. Consultant to the Army, 1995–. Pres., BAOMS, 2005. Member: Council, RCS, 2003–; Acad. of Med. Royal Colls, 2004–. Hon. Fellow: Indian Assoc. Oral and Maxillofacial Surgery, 1992; Amer. Assoc. Oral and Maxillofacial Surgery, 2005. *Publications:* with G. Dimitroulis: Maxillofacial Injuries: a synopsis of basic principles, diagnosis and management, 1994; Oral Cancer: a synopsis of pathology and management, 1998; contrib. book chapters and articles related to oral and maxillofacial surgery. *Recreations:* reading, dining, travelling, keeping children's cars on the road, cursing inefficiency of the National Health Service. *Address:* Mordon House, Mordon, Sedgefield, Stockton-on-Tees TS21 2EY. *T:* (01740) 620634, *Fax:* (01740) 623702; *e-mail:* Avery@mordonhouse.fsnet.co.uk.

AVERY, (Francis) John; Chairman, Averys of Bristol, since 2002 (Managing Director, 1975–2002); *b* 27 Dec. 1941; *s* of Ronald Avery and Linda Avery (*née* Jackson); *m* 1967, Sarah Midgley; one *s* three *d*. *Educ:* Clifton Coll.; Lincoln Coll., Oxford (MA Agricl Sci. 1965). MW 1975. Mem., Wine Selection Cttee for Govt Hospitality, 1997–; Wine Advr to Grocers' Co., 1997–. Chairman: Internat. Wine and Food Soc., 1996–2000; Inst. of Masters of Wine, 2000–01. Liveryman, Vintners' Co. (Master, 2004–05); Master: Soc. of Merchant Venturers, Bristol, 1995–96; Antient Soc. of St Stephen's Ringers, Bristol, 1994–95; Pres., Anchor Soc. of Bristol, 1990. Judge, Australian and NZ Wine Shows, 1978–; Chief Judge, Winpac Wine Comp., Hong Kong, 1989–2003. *Recreations:* ski-ing, cricket, Rugby (watching only!). *Address:* Apartment 10, The Grove, West Hay Road, Wrington, Bristol BS40 5NS. *Clubs:* Garrick, MCC; Ski Club of GB; Marden's, Kandahar Ski.

AVERY, Gillian Elise, (Mrs A. O. J. Cockshut); writer; *b* 1926; *d* of late Norman and Grace Avery; *m* 1952, A. O. J. Cockshut; one *d*. *Educ:* Dunottar Sch., Reigate. Chm., Children's Books History Soc., 1987–90; Mem., American Antiquarian Soc., 1988. *Publications: children's fiction:* The Warden's Niece, 1957; Trespassers at Charlcote, 1958; James without Thomas, 1959; The Elephant War, 1960; To Tame a Sister, 1961; The Greatest Gresham, 1962; The Peacock House, 1963; The Italian Spring, 1964; The Call of the Valley, 1966; A Likely Lad, 1971 (Guardian Award, 1972); Huck and her Time Machine, 1977; *adult fiction:* The Lost Railway, 1980; Onlookers, 1983; *non-fiction:* 19th Century Children: heroes and heroines in English children's stories (with Angela Bull), 1965; Victorian People in Life and Literature, 1970; The Echoing Green: memories of Regency and Victorian youth, 1974; Childhood's Pattern, 1975; Children and Their Books: a celebration of the work of Iona and Peter Opie (ed with Julia Briggs), 1989; The Best Type of Girl: a history of girls' independent schools, 1991; Behold the Child: a history of American children and their books 1622–1922, 1994; (ed with Kimberley Reynolds) Representations of Childhood Death, 2000; Cheltenham Ladies: a history of Cheltenham Ladies' College 1853–2003, 2003; ed, Gollancz revivals of early children's books, 1967–70, and anthologies of stories and extracts from early children's books. *Address:* 32 Charlbury Road, Oxford OX2 6UU.

AVERY, Graham John Lloyd; Secretary General, Trans European Policy Studies Association, since 2006; Senior Adviser, European Policy Centre, since 2006; Hon. Director General, European Commission, since 2006; *b* 29 Oct. 1943; *s* of Rev. Edward Avery and Alice Avery; *m* 1st, 1967, Susan Steele (marr. diss.); two *s*; 2nd, 2002, Annalisa Cecchi; one *s*. *Educ:* Kingswood Sch., Bath; Balliol Coll., Oxford (MA). Joined MAFF, 1965; Principal responsible for negotiations for British entry to European Communities, 1969–72; PPS to Ministers, Fred Peart, John Silkin, 1976; Commission of the European Communities, subseq. European Commission, Brussels: Member of Cabinets: of President, Roy Jenkins, 1977–80; of Vice-Pres. for External Relns, Christopher Soames, 1973–76; of Comrs for Agric., Finn Gundelach 1981, Poul Dalsager 1981, Frans Andriessen 1985–86; served: in Directorate Gen. for Agric. as Hd of Div. for Econ. Affairs and Gen. Problems, 1981–84, as Dir for Rural Develt, 1987–90; in Directorate Gen. for External Relations as Dir for relns with USA, Canada, Australia and NZ, 1990–92, as Dir for relns with Austria, Switzerland, Iceland, Norway, Sweden and Finland, 1992–93, in Task Force for Enlargement as Dir, 1993–94; in Directorate Gen. for External Political Relations, as Head of Policy Planning, 1995, as Chief Advr for Enlargement, 1996–98; Inspector Gen., 1998–2000; Chief Advr, Directorate Gen. for Enlargement, 2000–03; Chief Advr, subseq. Dir for Strategy, Co-ordination and Analysis, Directorate Gen. for External Relations, 2004–06. Vis. Prof., Coll. of Europe, 2003–05; Sen. Mem., St Antony's Coll., Oxford, 2005–. Fellow: Center for Internat. Affairs, Harvard Univ., 1986–87; Eur. Univ. Inst., Florence, 2002–03. *Publications:* (with Fraser Cameron): The Enlargement of the European Union, 1998; The Future of Europe: enlargement and integration, 2004; articles in Internat. Affairs, World Today, Europ. Affairs, Prospect, Jl of Agricl Econs, Europ. Environment Rev., etc. *Address:* 65 Southmoor Road, Oxford OX2 6RE.

AVERY, James Royle, (Roy); Headmaster, Bristol Grammar School, 1975–86; *b* 7 Dec. 1925; *s* of Charles James Avery and Dorothy May Avery; *m* 1954, Marjorie Louise (*née* Smith); one *s* one *d*. *Educ:* Queen Elizabeth's Hosp., Bristol; Magdalen Coll., Oxford; Bristol Univ. MA Oxon, CertifEd Bristol; FRSA. Asst History Master, Bristol Grammar Sch., 1951–59; Sen. History Master, Haberdashers' Aske's Sch. at Hampstead, then Elstree, 1960–65; Head Master, Harrow County Boys' Sch., 1965–75. Mem. Council, Bristol Univ., 1982–95. Hon. MLitt Bristol, 1996. *Publications:* The Story of Aldenham House, 1961; The Elstree Murder, 1962; The History of Queen Elizabeth's Hospital 1590–1990, 1990; The Sky's the Limit: the story of Bristol philanthropist John James, 1906–1996, 2001; contrib. Dictionary of World History, 1973; articles, reviews in educnl jls. *Recreations:* reading, walking, sport, music, the ecumenical movement, international studies. *Address:* First Floor Flat, 4 Rockleaze, Sneyd Park, Bristol BS9 1ND. *T:* (0117) 968 6805.

AVERY, John; *see* Avery, F. J.

AVERY, John Ernest, CB 1997; Deputy Parliamentary Commissioner for Administration, 1990–2000; *b* 18 April 1940; *s* of Ernest Charles Avery and Pauline Margaret Avery; *m* 1966, Anna Meddings; two *d*. *Educ:* Plymouth Coll.; Leeds Univ. (BSc). Called to the Bar, Gray's Inn, 1972. Patent Examiner, Bd of Trade, 1964–72; Office of Fair Trading, 1972–76; Dept of Industry, later DTI, 1976–89; Dir of Investigations, Office of Parly Comr for Admin (Ombudsman), 1989–90. *Recreations:* squash, theatre.

AVERY, Roy; *see* Avery, J. R.

AVERY JONES, Dr John Francis, CBE 1987; a Special Commissioner of Income Tax, since 2002 (Deputy, 1991–2001); Chairman, VAT and Duties Tribunals, since 2002 (part-time, 1991–2001); *b* 5 April 1940; *s* of Sir Francis Avery Jones, CBE, FRCP; *m* 1994, Catherine Susan Bobbett. *Educ:* Rugby Sch.; Trinity Coll., Cambridge (MA, LLM, PhD 1993). Solicitor, 1966; Partner in Bircham & Co., 1970; Sen. Partner, Speechly Bircham, 1985–2001. Member: Meade Cttee, 1975–77; Keith Cttee, 1980–84. Pres., Inst. of Taxation, 1980–82 (Hon. FTII 2002); Chm., Law Soc.'s Revenue Law Cttee, 1983–87; Member Council: Law Soc., 1986–90; Inst. for Fiscal Studies, 1988–; Exec. Cttee, Internat. Fiscal Assoc., 1988–94 (1st Vice-Pres., 1993–94; Chm., British Br., 1989–91); Mem., Bd of Trustees, Internat. Bureau of Fiscal Documentation, 1989– (Chm., 1991–2002). Vis. Prof. of Taxation, LSE, 1988–; Atax Cliffbrook Vis. Schol., Univ. of NSW, 1995. David R. Tillinghast Lectr on Internat. Taxation, New York Univ., 1997. Mem., Steering Cttee, Tax Law Rewrite, 1996–; Mem., Tax Law Review Cttee, 1997– (Chm., 1997–2005). Member, Board of Governors: Voluntary Hosp. of St Bartholomew, 1984–; LSE, 1995– (Chm., Audit Cttee, 1996–2003); Chm., Addington Soc., 1985–87. Master: Co. of Barbers, 1985–86; City of London Solicitors' Co., 1997–98. Consulting Editor: Encyclopedia of VAT, 1989–93 (Gen. Ed., 1972–89); British Tax Review, 1997– (Jt Ed., 1974–97); Mem. Editl Bd, Simon's Taxes, 1977–2001. Frans Banninck Cocq Medal, City of Amsterdam, 2002. *Publications:* (ed) Tax Havens and Measures Against Tax Avoidance and Evasion in the EEC, 1974; numerous articles on tax. *Recreations:* music, particularly opera. *Address:* c/o Finance and Tax Tribunals, 15–19 Bedford Avenue, WC1B 3AS. *T:* (020) 7612 9700, *Fax:* (020) 7436 4151. *Club:* Athenæum.

AVIS, Rev. Preb. Dr Paul David Loup; General Secretary, Church of England Council for Christian Unity, since 1998; Chaplain to the Queen, since 2008; *b* 21 July 1947; *s* of Peter George Hobden Avis and Diana Joan (*née* Loup); *m* 1970, Susan Janet Haywood; three *s*. *Educ:* London Bible Coll. (BD Hons London Univ. (ext.) 1970; PhD 1976); Westcott House, Cambridge. Deacon 1975, priest 1976; Curate, South Molton, dio. Exeter, 1975–80; Vicar, Stoke Canon, Poltimore with Huxham, Rewe with Netherexe, 1980–98. Preb. of Exeter Cathedral, 1993–2008; Sub Dean of Exeter Cathedral, 1997–2008; Canon Theologian of Exeter Cathedral, 2008–. Hon. Dir, Centre for Study of Christian Church, Univ. of Exeter, 1997–. Jt Ed., Internat. Jl for Study of the Christian Church, 2001–; Convening Ed., Ecclesiology, 2004–. *Publications:* The Church in the Theology of the Reformers, 1982; Ecumenical Theology, 1986; The Methods of Modern Theology, 1986; Foundations of Modern Historical Thought, 1986; Gore: Construction and Conflict, 1988; (ed and contrib.) The Threshold of Theology, 1988; Eros and the Sacred, 1989; Anglicanism and the Christian Church, 1989, 2nd edn 2002; Authority, Leadership and Conflict in the Church, 1992; (ed and contrib.) The Resurrection of Jesus Christ, 1993; (ed and contrib.) Divine Revelation, 1997; Faith in the Fires of Criticism, 1997; God and the Creative Imagination, 1999; The Anglican Understanding of the Church, 2000; Church, State and Establishment, 2001; (ed and contrib.) The Christian Church: an introduction to the major traditions, 2002; A Church Drawing Near, 2003; (ed and contrib.) Public Faith?, 2003; (ed and contrib.) Seeking the Truth of Change in the Church, 2003; (ed and contrib.) Paths to Unity, 2004; A Ministry Shaped by Mission, 2005; Beyond the Reformation?: authority, primacy and unity in the conciliar tradition, 2006; The Identity of Anglicanism: essentials of Anglican ecclesiology, 2008. *Recreations:* walking, literature, writing theology. *Address:* Church House, Great Smith Street, SW1P 3AZ. *T:* (020) 7898 1470; *e-mail:* paul.avis@c-of-e.org.uk; Lea Hill, Membury, Axminster, Devon EX13 7AQ. *T:* (01404) 881881; *e-mail:* reception@leahill.co.uk.

AVISON, Dr Gerald; Co-Founder, 1988, and Chairman, since 2007, TTP Group plc (Chief Executive, 1988–2007); *b* 23 Nov. 1940; *s* of Fred and Edith Avison; *m* 1971, Jean Margaret Mizen; one *s* one *d*. *Educ:* Manchester Grammar Sch.; Univ. of Bristol (BSc; PhD 1967). Engr, Guided Weapons Div., 1968–71, Manager, Electron Beam Welding Dept, 1971–73, BAC; PA Technology: Sen. Engr, 1973–75; Consultant, 1975–78, Sen. Consultant, 1978–85; Man. Dir, Cambridge Lab., 1985–87; Chm., TTP Communications plc, 2000–06. Director: TTP Venture Managers Ltd, 1999–; Cambridge Network, 2002–. Trustee, Hirsch Trust for Camlab Employees, 2001–. *Recreations:* travel, family, curiosity. *Address:* 59 Victoria Park, Cambridge CB4 3EJ. *T:* (01223) 354553, *Fax:* (01763) 261582; *e-mail:* ga@ttpgroup.com.

AVISS, Derek William; 'cellist; Principal, Trinity College of Music, since 2007; Joint Principal, Trinity Laban Conservatoire of Music and Dance, since 2007; *b* 21 Aug. 1948; *s* of Arthur William Archibald and Joan Gladys Aviss; *m* 1994, Jennifer Jane Smith; one *s* from previous marriage. *Educ:* Trinity Coll. of Music (LTCL 1970; Hon. FTCL 1986). FLCM 1979. Free-lance professional 'cellist, performing with Ariosti Piano Trio, Cantilena Ensemble, 1970–. Trinity College of Music: Professor of 'Cello, Jun. Dept, 1976–90, Sen. Dept, 1979–; Sen. Lectr in 'Cello and Chamber Music, 1986–; Head: String Dept, 1990–94; Performance Studies, 1992–94; Dep. Principal, 1994–2005; Dir, 2005–07. FRSA 2000. *Recreations:* motor cars, cricket, literature, music, theatre, travel. *Address:* The Clock House, The Dower Court, Somerford Keynes, Glos GL7 6DN. *T:* (01285) 861974, *Fax:* (01285) 862492; *e-mail:* daviss@tcm.ac.uk.

AWDRY, Daniel (Edmund), TD; DL; *b* 10 Sept. 1924; *s* of late Col Edmund Portman Awdry, MC, TD, DL, Coters, Chippenham, Wilts, and Mrs Evelyn Daphne Alexandra Awdry, JP (formerly French); *m* 1950, Elizabeth Cattley (*d* 2007); three *d*. *Educ:* Winchester Coll. RAC, OCTU, Sandhurst, 1943–44 (Belt of Honour). Served with 10th Hussars as Lieut, Italy, 1944–45; ADC to GOC 56th London Div., Italy, 1945; Royal Wilts Yeo., 1947–62; Major and Sqdn Comdr, 1955–62. Qualified Solicitor, 1950. Mayor of Chippenham, 1958–59; Pres., Southern Boroughs Assoc., 1959–60. MP (C) Chippenham, Wilts, Nov. 1962–1979; PPS to Minister of State, Board of Trade, Jan.–Oct. 1964; PPS to Solicitor-Gen., 1973–74. Director: BET Omnibus Services, 1966–80; Sheepbridge Engineering, 1968–79; Rediffusion Ltd, 1973–85; Colonial Mutual Life Assurance Ltd, 1974–89. DL Wilts, 1979. *Recreation:* chess. *Address:* Old Manor, Beanacre, near Melksham, Wilts SN12 7PT. *T:* (01225) 702315.

AX, Emanuel; concert pianist, since 1974; *b* 8 June 1949; *m* Yoko Nazaki; one *s* one *d*. *Educ:* Juilliard Sch. (studied with Mieczylaw Munz); Columbia Univ. Regular solo appearances with symphony orchs, incl. NY Philharmonic, National Symphony, Philadelphia Orch., Boston SO, Chicago SO, Cleveland Orch., Berlin Philharmonic, LPO, etc.; recitals at Carnegie Hall, Concertgebouw, Amsterdam, Barbican Centre, Théâtre des Champs Elysées, etc.; has played duo recitals with cellist Yo-Yo Ma annually since 1976; performed world premières of piano concertos by: Joseph Schwantner, 1988; Ezra Laderman, 1992; John Adams, 1997; Christopher Rouse, 1999; Bright Sheng, 2000, 2003; Krzysztof Penderecki, 2002; Melinda Wagner, 2003. Numerous recordings; Grammy Awards, 1985–86, 1992–95. First Prize, Arthur Rubinstein Internat. Piano Competition, 1974; Michael's Award, Young Concert Artists, 1975; Avery Fisher Prize, 1979. *Address:* c/o ICM Artists Inc., 40 West 57th Street, New York, NY 10019, USA. *T:* (212) 5565600.

AXEL, Prof. Richard, MD; Professor of Biochemistry and Molecular Biophysics, Columbia University, since 1999; *b* 2 July 1946; two *s*. *Educ:* Columbia Univ. (AB 1967); Johns Hopkins Univ. (MD 1970). Res. Associate, NIH, 1972–74; Columbia University: Asst Prof., Inst. of Cancer Res., 1974–78; Prof. of Pathol. and Biochem., 1978; Investigator, Howard Hughes Medical Inst., 1984–. (Jtly) Nobel Prize in Physiology or

Medicine, 2004. *Address:* Axel Laboratory, Howard Hughes Medical Institute, Columbia University, Room 1014, 701 West 168th Street, New York, NY 10032, USA.

AXFORD, David Norman, PhD; CMet, CEng, FIET; international consultant meteorologist; Adviser to Earthwatch Europe, Oxford, 1996–2000; *b* 14 June 1934; *s* of Norman Axford and Joy Alicia Axford (*née* Williams); *m* 1st, 1962, Elizabeth Anne (*née* Stiles) (marr. diss. 1980); one *s* two *d*; 2nd, 1980, Diana Rosemary Joan (*née* Bufton); three step *s* one step *d*. *Educ:* Merchant Taylors' School, Sandy Lodge; Plymouth Coll.; St John's Coll., Cambridge (Baylis Open Scholarship in Maths; BA 1956, MA 1960, PhD (Met.) 1972); MSc (Electronics) Southampton 1963; Advanced Dip. (English Local Hist.) Oxford Univ., 2004. FIET (FIEE 1982). Entered Met. Office, 1958; Flying Officer, RAF, 1958–60; Meteorological Office: Forecasting and Research, 1960–68; Met. Research Flight, and Radiosondes, 1968–76; Operational Instrumentation, 1976–80; Telecommunications, 1980–82; Dep. Dir, Observational Services, 1982–84; Dir of Services, 1984–89; Dep. Sec.-Gen., WMO, 1989–95; Special Exec. Advr to Sec.-Gen., WMO, 1995. Chm., Cttee on Operational World Weather Watch Systems Evaluation, N Atlantic (CONA), 1985–89. Pres., N Atlantic Observing Stations (NAOS) Bd, 1983–86; Vice Pres., RMetS, 1989–91 (Mem. Council and Hon. Gen. Sec., 1983–88; Mem., 1998–2004, Chm., 1999–2004, Accreditation Bd); European Meteorological Society: Chm., Accreditation Cttee, 2001–06; Vice Pres. and Treas., 2002–05. Mem., Exec. Cttee, British Assoc. of Former UN Civil Service, 1996– (Vice Chm., 1998–99; Chm., 1999–2004; Vice-Pres., 2004–). Clerk/Correspondent of Trustees, Stanford-in-the-Vale Public Purposes Charity, 2002– (Chm., 2000–02); Chm., Stanford-in-the-Vale Local and Dist History Soc., 2004–. Trustee: Thames Valley Hospice, 1996–98; Friends of the Ridgeway, 2008–. L. G. Groves 2nd Meml Prize for Met., 1970. *Publications:* papers in learned jls on met. and aspects of met. instrumentation in GB and USA. *Recreations:* home and garden, music, travel, good food, family history research, local English history, 12 grandchildren. *Address:* Honey End, 14 Ock Meadow, Stanford-in-the-Vale, Oxon SN7 8LN. *T:* (01367) 718480.

AXFORD, Sir (William) Ian, Kt 1996; PhD; FRS 1986; Director, Max Planck Institut für Aeronomie, Katlenburg-Lindau, Germany, 1974–82 and 1985–2001, now Emeritus; *b* 2 Jan. 1933; *s* of John Edgar Axford and May Victoria Axford; *m* 1955, Catherine Joy; two *s* two *d*. *Educ:* Univ. of Canterbury, NZ (MSc Hons, ME Dist.); Univ. of Manchester (PhD); Univ. of Cambridge. NZ Defence Science Corps, 1957–63; seconded to Defence Res. Bd, Ottawa, 1960–62; Associate Prof. of Astronomy, 1963–66, Prof. of Astronomy, 1966–67, Cornell Univ., Ithaca, NY; Prof. of Physics and Applied Physics, Univ. of Calif at San Diego, 1967–74; Vice-Chancellor, Victoria Univ. of Wellington, NZ, 1982–85. Pres., COSPAR, 1986–94; Vice-Pres., Scientific Cttee on Solar-Terrestrial Physics, 1986–90. Hon. Prof., Göttingen Univ., 1978; Regents Prof., Univ. of Calif., Riverside, 2003; Pei-Ling Chan Prof. of Physics, Univ. of Alabama, 2002–04; Adjunct Prof., Auckland Univ. of Technology, 2004–. Appleton Meml Lectr, URSI, 1969. Chm. Bd, NZ Foundn for Res., Sci. and Technol., 1992–95. Chm., Marsden Fund, 1994–98. Pres., European Geophysical Soc., 1990–92 (Hon. Mem., 1996); Vice Pres., Asia Oceania Geoscis Soc., 2004–05 (First Hon. Mem., 2006). Fellow, Amer. Geophysical Union, 1971; ARAS 1981; For. Associate, US Nat. Acad. of Scis, 1983; Member: Internat. Acad. of Astronautics, 1985; Academia Europaea, 1989. Hon. FRSNZ 1993. Hon. DSc: Canterbury, 1996; Victoria Univ. of Wellington, 1999. Space Science Award, AIAA, 1970; John Adam Fleming Medal, Amer. Geophysical Union, 1972; Tsiolkovsky Medal, Kosmonautical Fedn, USSR, 1987; Chapman Medal, RAS, 1994; NZ Sci. and Technol. Gold Medal, 1994; NZ Scientist of the Year, New Zealander of the Year, We Care Foundn, 1995. Freedom, City of Napier, NZ, 1999. *Publications:* (with T. K. Breus) In Soso's Web, 2004; about 300 articles in scientific jls on aspects of space physics and astrophysics. *Address:* 2 Gladstone Road, Napier, New Zealand. *T:* (6) 8352188, *Fax:* (6) 8352176.

AXON, Prof. Anthony Thomas Roger, MD; FRCP; Consultant Physician and Gastroenterologist, Leeds General Infirmary, since 1975; Hon. Professor of Gastroenterology, University of Leeds, since 1995; *b* 21 Nov. 1941; *s* of Robert and Ruth Axon; *m* 1965, Jill Coleman; two *s* one *d*. *Educ:* Woodhouse Grove Sch., W Yorks; St Bartholomew's Hosp. Med. Coll., London (MB BS Hons, Dist. in Medicine, MD 1973). FRCP 1980. Hse Physician and Resident in Pathology, St Bartholomew's Hosp., 1965–68; Registrar, 1968–70, Sen. Registrar, 1971–75, St Thomas' Hosp., London. Mem. Council, RCP, 1992–94. Vice-Pres. Endoscopy, British Soc. Gastroenterol., 1989–91; President: N of England Gastroenterol. Soc., 1999–2000; British Soc. of Gastroenterol., 2000–01; Eur. Soc. of Gastrointestinal Endoscopy, 2000–02; World Orgn of Gastrointestinal Endoscopy, 2005–09; United European Gastroenterology Fedn, 2006–; Mem., Educn Cttee, World Orgn of Gastroenterology, 1999–2004. *Publications:* contrib. numerous original papers on wide variety of gastrointestinal subjects, specifically inflammatory bowel disease, intestinal permeability, endoscopic retrograde cholangio-pancreatography, safety in endoscopy, Helicobacter pylori, cancer surveillance, aetiology of gastric cancer, to peer review jls and other pubns. *Recreations:* travel, gardening. *Address:* Leeds General Infirmary, Great George Street, Leeds LS1 3EX. *T:* (0113) 392 2125; Upwood, Woodlands Drive, Rawdon, Leeds LS19 6JZ. *T:* (0113) 250 3452.

AXWORTHY, Hon. Lloyd; PC (Can.) 1980; OC 2003; OM; PhD; President and Vice-Chancellor, University of Winnipeg, since 2004; *b* 21 Dec. 1939; *s* of Norman Joseph and Gwen Anne Axworthy; *m* 1984, Denise Ommanney; two *s* one *d*. *Educ:* Univ. of Winnipeg (BA 1961); Princeton Univ. (MA 1963; PhD 1972). Asst Prof. of Pol Sci., 1969–79, and Dir, Inst. of Urban Studies, 1970–79, Univ. of Winnipeg. MLA(L) Manitoba, 1973–79; MP (L): Winnipeg-Fort Garry, 1979–88; Winnipeg S Centre, 1988–2001; Minister of State for Status of Women, Canada, 1980–81; Minister of Employment and Immigration, 1980–83; Minister of Transportation, 1983–84; Opposition spokesman on internat. trade, 1984–88; Liberal spokesman on external affairs, 1988–93; Minister of Human Resources Develt, and of Western Econ. Diversification, 1993–96; Minister for Foreign Affairs, 1996–2001; Dir, Liu Inst. for Global Issues, Univ. of BC, 2001–04 (Sen. Associate, 2004–). Mem., Commn for the Legal Empowerment of the Poor, UN Develt Prog., 2006–; Head, OAS Electoral Observation Mission to Peru, 2006. *Publication:* Navigating a New World: Canada's global future, 2003. *Recreation:* golf. *Address:* President's Office, University of Winnipeg, 515 Portage Avenue, Winnipeg, MB R3B 2E9, Canada.

AYALA, Jaime Z. de; *see* Zobel de Ayala.

AYALA-LASSO, José; Ambassador of Ecuador to France, 2002–03; *b* 29 Jan. 1932; *m* Monique Wiets de Ayala-Lasso; one *s* three *d*. *Educ:* Catholic Univ. of Leuven, Belgium; Catholic Univ. of Ecuador; Central Univ. of Ecuador. Ministry of Foreign Affairs, Ecuador, 1955; served Tokyo, Lima, Rome and Min. of Foreign Affairs, to 1974; Ambassador of the Foreign Service, 1975; Under-Sec.-Gen., Min. of Foreign Affairs, 1975; Minister of Foreign Affairs, 1977; Ambassador to Belgium, Luxembourg and EC, 1979, to Peru, 1983; Ambassador and Perm. Rep. of Ecuador to UN, 1989–94; UN High Comr for Human Rights, 1994–97; Minister of Foreign Affairs, Ecuador, 1997–99; Ambassador to Holy See, 1999–2001. Order Al Mérito (Ecuador); numerous orders from foreign counties. *Recreation:* classical music. *Address:* c/o Ministry of Foreign Affairs, Avenida 10 de Agosto y Carrión, Quito, Ecuador.

AYCKBOURN, Sir Alan, Kt 1997; CBE 1987; playwright; Artistic Director, Stephen Joseph Theatre, Scarborough, 1972–March 2009; *b* 12 April 1939; *s* of Horace Ayckbourn and Irene Maude (*née* Worley); *m* 1st, 1959, Christine Helen (*née* Roland); two *s*; 2nd, 1997, Heather Stoney. *Educ:* Haileybury. Worked in repertory as Stage Manager/Actor at Edinburgh, Worthing, Leatherhead, Oxford, and with late Stephen Joseph's Theatre-in-the-Round Co., at Scarborough. Founder Mem., Victoria Theatre, Stoke-on-Trent, 1962. BBC Radio Drama Producer, Leeds, 1964–70; Co. Dir, NT, 1986–87. Vis. Prof. of Contemporary Theatre, and Fellow, St Catherine's Coll., Oxford, 1991–92. Has written numerous full-length plays. London productions: Mr Whatnot, Arts, 1964; Relatively Speaking, Duke of York's, 1967, Greenwich, 1986 (televised, 1969, 1989); How the Other Half Loves, Lyric, 1970, Duke of York's, 1988; Time and Time Again, Comedy, 1972 (televised, 1976); Absurd Person Singular, Criterion, 1973 (Evening Standard Drama Award, Best Comedy, 1973) (televised, 1985); The Norman Conquests (Trilogy), Globe, 1974 (Evening Standard Drama Award, Best Play; Variety Club of GB Award; Plays and Players Award) (televised, 1977); Jeeves (musical, with Andrew Lloyd Webber), Her Majesty's, 1975, reworked as By Jeeves, Duke of York's, transf. Lyric, 1996, NY, 2001; Absent Friends, Garrick, 1975 (televised, 1985); Confusions, Apollo, 1976; Bedroom Farce, Nat. Theatre, 1977 (televised, 1980); Just Between Ourselves, Queen's, 1977 (Evening Standard Drama Award, Best Play) (televised, 1978); Ten Times Table (dir), Globe, 1978; Joking Apart, Globe, 1979 (Shared Plays and Players Award); Sisterly Feelings, Nat. Theatre, 1980; Taking Steps, Lyric, 1980; Suburban Strains (musical with Paul Todd), Round House, 1981; Season's Greetings, Apollo, 1982; Way Upstream (dir), Nat. Theatre, 1982 (televised, 1987); Making Tracks (musical with Paul Todd), Greenwich, 1983; Intimate Exchanges, Ambassadors, 1984; A Chorus of Disapproval (dir), Nat. Theatre, 1985 (Evening Standard Drama Award, Best Comedy; Olivier Award, Best Comedy; DRAMA Award, Best Comedy, 1985), transf. Lyric, 1986 (filmed, 1989); Woman in Mind (dir), Vaudeville, 1986; A Small Family Business (dir), Nat. Theatre, 1987 (Evening Standard Drama Award, Best Play); Henceforward… (dir), Vaudeville, 1988 (Evening Standard Drama Award, Best Comedy, 1989); Man of the Moment (dir), Globe, 1990 (Evening Standard Drama Award, Best Comedy, 1990); The Revengers' Comedies (dir), Strand, 1991; Time of My Life (dir), Vaudeville, 1993; Wildest Dreams (dir), RSC, 1993; Communicating Doors (dir), Gielgud, 1995, transf. Savoy, 1996 (Writers' Guild of GB Award, Best West End Play, 1996); Things We Do For Love (dir), Gielgud, 1998 (Lloyds Pvte Banking Playwright of the Year); adapt. Ostrovsky's The Forest, RNT, 1999; Comic Potential (dir), Lyric, 1999; House & Garden (dir), RNT, 2000; Damsels in Distress (trilogy: GamePlan; FlatSpin; RolePlay), (dir), Duchess, 2002; Scarborough: Body Language, 1990; Dreams from a Summer House (play with music by John Pattison), 1992; Haunting Julia, 1994; A Word from our Sponsor (musical with John Pattison), 1995; Snake in the Grass, 2002; Sugar Daddies, 2003; Drowning on Dry Land, 2004; Private Fears in Public Places, 2004 (filmed, 2007); Improbable Fiction, 2005; If I Were You, 2006; Life and Beth, 2008; other plays directed: Tons of Money, Nat. Theatre, 1986; A View from the Bridge, Nat. Theatre, transf. Aldwych, 1987; 'Tis Pity she's a Whore, Nat. Theatre, 1988; Two Weeks with the Queen, Nat. Theatre, 1994; Conversations with my Father, Old Vic, 1995; The Safari Party, Scarborough, 2002, Hampstead, 2003. *Plays for children:* Callisto 5, 1990; My Very Own Story, 1991; This Is Where We Came In, 1991; Invisible Friends (dir), Nat. Theatre, 1991; Mr A's Amazing Maze Plays, Nat. Theatre, 1993; The Musical Jigsaw Play, 1994; The Champion of Paribanou, 1996; The Boy Who Fell Into A Book, 1998; Gizmo, RNT, 1999; Callisto #7, 1999; (with music by Denis King) Whenever, 2000; The Jollies, 2002; (with music by D. King) Orvin—Champion of Champions, 2003; The Ten Magic Bridges, 2003; My Sister Sadie, 2003; Miss Yesterday, 2004; Miranda's Magic Mirror, 2004; The Girl Who Lost Her Voice, 2005. Hon. DLitt: Hull, 1981; Keele, 1987; Leeds, 1987; York, 1992; Bradford, 1994; Univ. of Wales Coll. of Cardiff, 1995; Manchester, 2003; DUniv Open, 1998. Sunday Times Award for Literary Achievement, 2000. *Publications:* The Norman Conquests, 1975; Three Plays (Absurd Person Singular, Absent Friends, Bedroom Farce), 1977; Joking Apart and Other Plays (Just Between Ourselves, Ten Times Table), 1979; Sisterly Feelings, and Taking Steps, 1981; A Chorus of Disapproval, 1986; Woman in Mind, 1986; A Small Family Business, 1987; Henceforward…, 1988; Mr A's Amazing Maze Plays, 1989; Man of the Moment, 1990; Invisible Friends (play for children), 1991; The Revengers' Comedies, 1991; Time of My Life, 1993; Wildest Dreams, 1993; Callisto 5, This is Where We Came In, My Very Own Story, 1995; Communicating Doors, 1995; A Word from our Sponsor, 1998; Things We Do For Love, 1998; Alan Ayckbourn: Plays 2, 1998; The Forest, 1999; Comic Potential, 1999, new edn 2006; House & Garden, 2000; Whenever, 2002; The Crafty Art of Playmaking, 2002; Damsels in Distress, 2002; The Jollies, 2002; Orvin—Champion of Champions, 2003; My Sister Sadie, 2003; Snake in the Grass, 2004; Alan Ayckbourn: Plays 3, 2005; Drowning on Dry Land, 2006; Improbable Fiction, 2007. *Recreations:* music, reading, cricket, films. *Address:* c/o Casarotto Ramsay & Associates Ltd, Waverley House, 7–12 Noel Street, W1F 8QG. *T:* (020) 7287 4450.

AYERS, John Gilbert; Keeper, Far Eastern Department, Victoria and Albert Museum, 1970–82; *b* 27 July 1922; *s* of H. W. Ayers, CB, CBE; *m* 1957, Bridget Elspeth Jacqueline Fanshawe; one *s* two *d*. *Educ:* St Paul's Sch.; St Edmund Hall, Oxford. Served in RAF, 1941–46 (Sgt). Asst Keeper, Dept of Ceramics, Victoria and Albert Museum, 1950, Dep. Keeper 1963. Pres., Oriental Ceramic Soc., 1984–87. *Publications:* The Seligman Collection of Oriental Art, II, 1964; The Baur Collection: Chinese Ceramics, I–IV, 1968–74, Japanese Ceramics, 1982; (with R. J. Charleston) The James A. de Rothschild Collection: Meissen and Oriental Porcelain, 1971; Oriental Ceramics, The World's Great Collections: Victoria and Albert Museum, 1975; (with J. Rawson) Chinese Jade throughout the Ages, exhbn catalogue, 1975; (with D. Howard) China for the West, 2 vols, 1978; (with D. Howard) Masterpieces of Chinese Export Porcelain, 1980; Oriental Art in the Victoria and Albert Museum, 1983; (ed) Chinese Ceramics in the Topkapi Saray Museum, Istanbul, 3 vols, 1986; (with O. Impey and J. V. G. Mallet) Porcelain for Palaces: the fashion for Japan in Europe 1650–1750, 1990; Chinese Ceramic Tea Vessels: the K. S. Lo Collection, Hong Kong, 1991; A Jade Menagerie: creatures real and imaginary from the Worrell Collection, 1993; Chinese Ceramics in the Baur Collection, Geneva, 2 vols, 1999; Blanc de Chine: divine images in porcelain, exhbn catalogue, China Inst., NY, 2002; The Chinese Porcelain Collection of Marie Vergottis, Lausanne, 2004. *Address:* 3 Bedford Gardens, W8 7ED. *T:* (020) 7229 5168.

AYERS, Prof. Michael Richard, PhD; FBA 2001; Professor of Philosophy, University of Oxford, 1996–2002; Fellow of Wadham College, Oxford, 1965–2002, now Emeritus; *b* 27 June 1935; *s* of Dick Ayers and Sybil Kerr Ayers (*née* Rutherglen); *m* 1962, Delia Mary Bell; one *s* one *d*. *Educ:* Battersea Grammar Sch.; St John's Coll., Cambridge (BA 1959; MA, PhD 1965). Jun. Res. Fellow, St John's Coll., Cambridge, 1962–65; Tutor in Philosophy, Wadham Coll., Oxford, 1965; CUF Lectr in Philosophy, 1965–94, Reader in Philosophy, 1994–2002, Univ. of Oxford. Vis. Lectr, 1964–65, Vis. Prof., 1979, 2007, Univ. of Calif, Berkeley; Vis. Prof., Univ. of Oregon, 1970–71; Vis. Fellow, Res. Sch. of Social Scis, ANU, 1993; Ida Beam Dist. Vis. Prof., Univ. of Iowa, 1995. MAE 2006. *Publications:* The Refutation of Determinism, 1968; (with J. Ree and A. Westoby) Philosophy and its Past, 1978; Locke: vol. 1, Epistemology, vol. 2, Ontology, 1991; Locke: ideas and things, 1997; (ed with D. Garber) The Cambridge History of Seventeenth Century Philosophy, 2 vols, 1998; contrib. to jls, collections and works of reference. *Recreations:* walking, gardening, natural history. *Address:* Wadham College, Oxford OX1 3PN.

AYERST, Rev. Edward Richard; Chaplain to the Queen, 1987–95; *b* 21 Oct. 1925; *m* 1959, Pauline Clarke; one *s* two *d*. *Educ:* Coopers' Company's School; Leeds Univ. (BA Hons 1951); College of the Resurrection, Mirfield. Vicar of St Mary with St John, Edmonton, N18, 1960–66; Rector of East Cowes with Whippingham, IoW, 1966–77; Vicar of Bridgwater, 1977–90. Mem., Philosophical Soc., 1981. *Recreations:* sailing; helping the Sea Cadet Corps. *Address:* 56 Maple Drive, Burnham-on-Sea, Somerset TA8 1DH. *T:* (01278) 780701.

AYKROYD, Sir James (Alexander Frederic), 3rd Bt *cr* 1929, of Birstwith Hall, Hampsthwaite, co. York; Chairman, Speyside Distillers Co. Ltd, since 2001; *b* 6 Sept. 1943; *s* of Bertram Aykroyd (*d* 1983), *y s* of Sir Frederic Alfred Aykroyd, 1st Bt, and his 1st wife, Margôt (later Dame Margôt Smith, DBE), *d* of Leonard Graham Brown; *S* uncle, 1993; *m* 1973, Jennifer Marshall; two *d*. *Educ:* Eton Coll.; Univ. of Aix en Provence; Univ. of Madrid. Sen. Export Dir, James Buchanan & Co. Ltd, 1965–83; Export Man. Dir, Martini & Rossi SpA, 1983–87; Chm., Alexander Muir & Son Ltd, 1993–. *Recreations:* active sports esp. tennis and golf. *Heir: half b* Toby Nigel Bertram Aykroyd, *b* 13 Nov. 1955. *Address:* Birstwith Hall, near Harrogate, Yorks HG3 2JW. *T:* (01423) 770250. *Club:* Alwoodley Golf.

AYKROYD, Sir Michael David, 4th Bt *cr* 1920, of Lightcliffe, Yorks; *b* 14 June 1928; *s* of George Hammond Aykroyd, TD, and Margaret (*née* Aykroyd); *S* cousin, 2007; *m* 1952, Gillian, *o d* of Donald George Cowling, MBE; one *s* three *d*. *Educ:* USA. *Recreation:* shooting. *Heir: s* Henry Robert George Aykroyd [*b* 4 April 1954; *m* 1975, Lucy Merlin Brown; two *s* three *d* (incl. twin *d*)]. *Address:* The Homestead, Killinghall, Harrogate, N Yorks HG3 2BQ. *T:* (01423) 506437; *e-mail:* michael.aykroyd@ruralmail.net.

AYLARD, Richard John, CVO 1994; External Affairs and Environment Director, Thames Water, since 2004 (Corporate Social Responsibility Director, 2002–04); Extra Equerry to the Prince of Wales, since 1996; *b* 10 April 1952; *s* of John and Joy Aylard; *m* 1st, 1977, Sally Williams (marr. diss. 1984); 2nd, 1984, Suzanne Walker (marr. diss. 1998); two *d*; 3rd, 1998, Jennifer Jones; one *s* one *d*. *Educ:* Queen Elizabeth's Grammar Sch., Barnet; Reading Univ. (BSc Hons Applied Zoology with Maths). Joined RN as university cadet, 1972; served HM Ships Shavington, Ark Royal, Fox, 1974–77; Staff of Flag Officer Submarines, 1977–79; Flag Lieut to Dep. SACLANT, Norfolk, USA, 1979–81; Capt's Sec., HMS Invincible, 1981–83; Supply Officer, HMS Brazen, 1984–85; Equerry to the Princess of Wales, 1985–88; Comdr RN, 1987; Asst Private Sec. and Comptroller to the Prince and Princess of Wales, 1988–91; RN retd, 1989; Private Sec. and Treas. to the Prince of Wales, 1991–96; consultant on envmtl issues and public affairs, 1996–2002. *Recreations:* sailing, fishing, gardening, ski-ing.

AYLEN, Walter Stafford; QC 1983; a Deputy High Court Judge, 1993–2005; *b* St Helena, 21 May 1937; *s* of late Rt Rev. Charles Arthur William Aylen and Elisabeth Margaret Anna (*née* Hills); *m* 1967, Peggy Elizabeth Lainé Woodford; three *d*. *Educ:* Summer Fields Sch.; Winchester Coll. (schol.); New Coll., Oxford (schol., sen. schol.; BCL; MA). Commnd 2nd Lieut KRRC, 1956–57. Called to the Bar, Middle Temple, 1962 (Bencher 1991); Head of Chambers, Hardwicke Bldg, 1991–2000; Mem., ADR Chambers, 2000–. Asst Recorder, 1982; Recorder, 1985–2003. Mem., Internat. Panel, Alternative Dispute Resolution Gp, 2001–. Mem., Bar Council, 1994–96 (Chm., Bar Services and IT Cttee, 1994; Vice-Chm., Finance Cttee, 1995–96). MCIArb 1999. FRSA 1989. *Recreations:* reading novels (especially his wife's), theatre, music. *Address:* 24 Fairmount Road, SW2 2BL. *T:* (020) 8671 7301; Hardwicke Building, New Square, Lincoln's Inn, WC2A 3SB. *T:* (020) 7242 2523; 15 New Bridge Street, EC4V 6AU. *T:* (020) 7842 1900.

AYLESFORD, 12th Earl of, *cr* 1714; **Charles Heneage Finch-Knightley;** Baron Guernsey, 1703; Vice Lord-Lieutenant for West Midlands, since 1990; *b* 27 March 1947; *s* of 11th Earl of Aylesford and Margaret Rosemary Tyer; *S* father, 2008; *m* 1971, Penelope Anstice, *y d* of Kenneth A. G. Crawley; one *s* four *d* (incl. twin *d*). *Educ:* Oundle; Trinity Coll., Cambridge. DL West Midlands, 1986. *Recreations:* shooting, fishing, Real tennis, cricket. *Heir: s* Lord Guernsey, *qv*. *Address:* Packington Hall, Meriden, Coventry CV7 7HF. *T:* (01676) 522274.

AYLETT, Crispin David William; QC 2008; Senior Treasury Counsel, Central Criminal Court, since 2006; *b* 13 Aug. 1961; *s* of late David Leonard Nankivell Aylett and of Freda Emily Aylett (*née* Montague, now Whitehead); *m* 1989, Louise Sheppard; two *s* two *d*. *Educ:* Dulwich Coll.; Bristol Univ. (BA Hons 1983); City Univ., London (Dip Law 1984). Called to the Bar, Inner Temple, 1985 (Scarman Schol.). Jun. Treasury Counsel, Central Criminal Court, 2001–06. Sec., Cakemaker's Dozen, 1985–2002. *Recreations:* theatre, cricket, football, True Crime. *Address:* 3 Raymond Buildings, Gray's Inn, WC1R 5BH. *T:* (020) 7400 6400.

AYLING, Peter William, OBE 1989; BSc, CEng, FRINA; Secretary, Royal Institution of Naval Architects, 1967–89; *b* 25 Sept. 1925; *s* of late William Frank and Edith Louise Ayling; *m* 1949, Sheila Bargery; two *s* two *d*. *Educ:* Royal Dockyard Sch., Portsmouth; King's Coll., Univ. of Durham (BSc). Shipwright apprentice, HM Dockyard, Portsmouth, 1942–47; King's Coll., Univ. of Durham, 1947–50; Research and Principal Research Officer, British Ship Research Assoc., London, 1950–65; Principal Scientific Officer, Ship Div., Nat. Physical Laboratory, Feltham (now British Maritime Technology Ltd), 1965–67. *Publications:* papers on ship strength and vibration, Trans RINA, NECInst and IESS. *Recreations:* music, gardening, walking, motoring. *Address:* Oakmead, School Road, Camelsdale, Haslemere, Surrey GU27 3RN. *T:* (01428) 644474.

AYLING, Robert John; Chief Executive, British Airways, 1996–2000; *b* 3 Aug. 1946; *m* 1972, Julia Crallan; two *s* one *d*. *Educ:* King's Coll. Sch., Wimbledon. Admitted solicitor, 1968; joined Elborne, Mitchell & Co., Solicitors, 1969, Partner, 1971; Department of Trade, later of Trade and Industry: Legal Advr, 1974 (work on UK accession to EEC, 1974–77); Asst Solicitor and Head, Aviation Law Br., 1979 (legislation to privatise British Airways Bd); UK deleg., UN Commn for Internat. Trade Law, 1979–83; Under Sec. (Legal), 1983; British Airways: Legal Dir, 1985; Company Sec., 1987; Human Resources Dir, 1988; Marketing and Ops Dir, 1991; Gp Man. Dir, 1993. Chairman: New Millennium Experience Co., 1997–2000; Holidaybreak plc, 2003–; Sanctuary Group plc, 2006–07. Non-executive Director: Royal & Sun Alliance, 1994–2004; Dyson Ltd, 2001– (Vice-Chm., 2005–); Glas Cymru (Welsh Water), 2008–. Gov., King's Coll. Sch., 1996–2006. Hon. LLD Brunel, 1996. *Recreation:* hillwalking. *Club:* Brooks's.

AYLING, Tracy Jane, (Mrs C. A. Hutton); QC 2006; *b* 27 April 1960; *d* of Rex John Ayling and Doreen Ayling (*née* Matthews); *m* 2004, Charles Adrian Hutton. *Educ:* Horndean Comprehensive Sch.; Durham Univ. (BA Hons 1982). Called to the Bar, Inner Temple, 1983. *Recreations:* cuisine, travel, shoes. *Address:* 2 Bedford Row, WC1R 4BU. *T:* (020) 7440 8888, *Fax:* (020) 7242 1738.

AYLMER, family name of **Baron Aylmer**.

AYLMER, 14th Baron *cr* 1718; **(Anthony) Julian Aylmer;** Bt 1662; Partner, Reynolds Porter Chamberlain LLP, since 1982; *b* 10 Dec. 1951; *o s* of 13th Baron Aylmer and Countess Maddalena Sofia, *d* of late Count Arbeno Attems; *S* father, 2006; *m* 1990, Belinda Rosemary, *e d* of Major Peter Henry Parker; one *s* one *d*. *Educ:* Westminster; Trinity Hall, Cambridge (MA). Admitted solicitor, 1976. *Recreations:* history, genealogy, architecture. *Heir: s* Hon. Michael Henry Aylmer, *b* 21 March 1991. *Address:* 16 Edgarley Terrace, SW6 6QF. *Club:* Brooks's.

AYLMER, Sir Richard John, 16th Bt *cr* 1622, of Donadea, Co. Kildare; writer; *b* 23 April 1937; *s* of Sir Fenton Gerald Aylmer, 15th Bt and Rosalind Boultbee (*d* 1991), *d* of J. Percival Bell; *S* father, 1987; *m* 1962, Lise, *d* of Paul Demers; one *s* one *d*. *Educ:* Lower Canada Coll., Montreal; Western Ontario, London, Canada; Harvard Univ., Cambridge, Mass, USA. *Heir: s* Fenton Paul Aylmer [*b* 31 Oct. 1965; *m* 1989, Pina Mastromonaco; one *s*]. *Address:* 4460 Francis Peninsula Road, Madeira Park, BC V0N 2H0, Canada. *T:* (604) 8832130.

AYLWARD, Adrian John Francis; Headmaster, St Antony's Leweston School, since 2006; *b* 12 Nov. 1957; *s* of John James and Cynthia Aylward; *m* 1990, Caroline Cramer; one *s* two *d*. *Educ:* Worth Sch., Sussex; Exeter Coll., Oxford (BA); King's Coll. London (PGCE). Formerly investment banker; Royal Sovereign Group (Chief Exec., 1986–91); Dir, EMESS plc, 1990–91; Housemaster and Head of Religious Studies, Downside Sch., 1992–96; Headmaster, Stonyhurst Coll., 1996–2006. Mem., Irish Assoc. Knight of Malta. *Recreations:* fishing, philosophy, sport, travel. *Address:* St Antony's Leweston School, Sherborne, Dorset DT9 6EN. *T:* (01963) 210691, *Fax:* (01963) 210786. *Club:* Brooks's.

AYLWARD, (George) William, MD; FRCS, FRCOphth; Consultant Ophthalmic Surgeon, since 1994, Medical Director, since 2002, Moorfields Eye Hospital; *b* 23 Dec. 1957; *s* of James Ernest Aylward and Martha Harvey Aylward; *m* 1983, Catherine Joy Otty; one *s* one *d*. *Educ:* Malvern Coll.; Corpus Christi Coll., Cambridge (MB BChir); Addenbrooke's Hosp. (Cambridge Univ. Med. Sch. (MD 1990)). FRCS 1987; FRCOphth 1989. SHO, Western Eye Hosp., London, 1985–86; Lectr, Sydney Univ., 1987–89; Sen. Registrar, 1989–92, Fellow in Vitreoretinal Surgery, 1992–93, Moorfields Eye Hosp. Fellow in Med. Retina, Bascom Palmer Eye Inst., Miami, 1993–94. Vice Pres., Eur. Soc. of Retina Specialists, 2007–. Member: Club Jules Gonin, Lausanne, 1998–; Ophthalmic Club, 1999–. *Publications:* contrib. chapters to books, including: Ophthalmology, 1997; Clinical Retina, 2002; Ryan's Retina, 2005; numerous contribs to peer-reviewed ophthalmic jls. *Recreations:* sailing, cooking. *Address:* Moorfields Eye Hospital, City Road, EC1V 2PD; 114 Harley Street, W1G 7JJ. *T:* (020) 7566 2039, *Fax:* (020) 7224 1752; *e-mail:* bill.aylward@moorfields.nhs.uk.

AYLWARD, Prof. Mansel, CB 2002; FRCP, FFPM, FFOM; Professor, Centre for Psychosocial and Disability Research, Cardiff University, since 2004 (part-time, School of Psychology, Cardiff University and University of Wales College of Medicine, 2002–04); Chair, Wales Centre for Health, Welsh Assembly, since 2004; *b* 29 Nov. 1942; *s* of John Aylward and Cora Doreen Aylward (*née* Evans); *m* 1963, Angela Bridget Besley; one *s* one *d*. *Educ:* Cyfarthfa Castle Grammar Sch., Merthyr Tydfil; London Hosp. Med. Coll., Univ. of London (BSc 1964; MB BS Hons 1967); FFPM 1991; DDAM RCP 2001; FFOM 2003; FRCP 2003. MRC Clin. Res. Fellow in Exptl Surgery, London Hosp., 1968–70; Lectr in Surgery, London Hosp. Med. Coll., 1969; GP, Merthyr Tydfil, 1970–73; Clin. Assistant in Dermatol. and Minor Surgery, St Tydfil's Hosp., 1970–76; Res. Physician, Singleton Hosp., Swansea and Merthyr and Cynon Valleys, 1973–76; Chm. and Man. Dir, Simbec Research Ltd, 1974–84; Dir of Clin. Res., Berk Pharmaceuticals, 1974–76; Dir, Women's Health Concern, London, 1976–86; Pres., Simbec Research (USA) Inc., 1980–84; Dir of Clin. Res., Lyonnaise Industrielle Pharmaceutique, France, 1982–84; Regl MO, DHSS, Cardiff, 1985–88; SMO, DSS, London, 1988–90; Sec. to Attendance Allowance Bd, London, 1991; PMO and Dir of Med. Policy, R&D, Benefits Agency, London, 1991–95; CMO and Chief Scientist, DSS, subseq. DWP, 1995–2005. Chief Med. Advr, War Pensions, later Veterans, Agency, MoD, 2001–05; Civilian Med. Advr in Disability Medicine to Army, 2004–. Expert Agrée Medicine Interne, France, 1982. Vis. Prof., Harvard Univ., 2004–. Lectures include: Thakrah, Soc. Occ. Med., 2006; Edward Jones, Cardiff Univ., 2006; Dynamics of Disability Keynote, FLA, USA, 2008. Chm., Standards Cttee, Merthyr Tydfil CB, 2002–; Chair: Health Commn Wales Rev., 2007–08; All Wales Public Mental Health Network, 2007–; Member: Health Honours Cttee UK, 2005–; Industrial Injuries Adv. Cttee, 2005–. Director: Elision Gp Ltd UK, 2005–07; Arkaga Health & Technology Ltd, 2008–. Patron, Vocational Rehabilitation Assoc. (UK), 2005–. FRSocMed 1981 (Academic Dean (Wales), 2001–; Hon. Treas. and Dir, 2005–07). Hon. FFPH 2008. *Publications:* Management of the Menopause and Post-Menopausal Years, 1975; The Disability Handbook, 1991, 2nd edn 1998; Back Pain: an international review, 2002; (contrib.) Malingering and Illness Deception, 2003; Scientific Concepts and Basis of Incapacity Benefits, 2005; The Power of Belief, 2006; (contrib.) Fitness for Work, 3rd edn 2007; contribs on disability assessment, rehabilitation, and social security issues to learned jls. *Recreations:* military history, travel, theatre, video-making, grandchildren. *Address:* UnumProvident Centre for Psychosocial and Disability Research, Cardiff University, Cardiff CF10 3YG; (home) Cefn Cottage, Cefn Coed, Merthyr Tydfil CF48 2PH. *Club:* Athenæum.

AYLWARD, William; *see* Aylward, G. W.

AYNSLEY-GREEN, Sir Albert, Kt 2006; DPhil; FRCP, FRCPE, FRCPCH, FMedSci; Children's Commissioner for England, since 2005; Nuffield Professor of Child Health, Institute of Child Health, University College London, 1993–2005, now Emeritus; *b* 30 May 1943; *m* 1967, Rosemary Anne Boucher; two *d*. *Educ:* Glyn Grammar Sch., Epsom; Guy's Hosp. Med. Sch., Univ. of London (MB BS); Oriel Coll., Oxford (MA, DPhil; Hon. Fellow, 2007). MRCS 1967; FRCP 1982; FRCPE 1987; FRCPCH 1997 (Hon. FRCPCH 2008). House Officer posts at Guy's Hosp., London, St Luke's Hosp., Guildford, Radcliffe Infirmary, Oxford and RPMS, Hammersmith Hosp., London, 1967–70; Radcliffe Infirmary, Oxford: Wellcome Res. Fellow, 1970–72; Clinical Lectr in Internal Medicine, 1972–73; Sen. House Officer and Registrar posts in Paediatrics, Radcliffe Infirmary and John Radcliffe Hosp., Oxford, 1973–74; European Sci. Exchange Fellow, Royal Soc. and Swiss Nat. Res. Council, Univ. Children's Hosp., Zurich, 1974–75; University of Oxford: Clinical Lectr in Paediatrics, 1975–78; Univ. Lectr,

1978–83; Fellow, Green Coll., 1980–83; Hon. Consultant Paediatrician, Oxford AHA, 1978–83; University of Newcastle upon Tyne: James Spence Prof. of Child Health and Hd of Dept, 1984–93; Hd, Sch. of Clinical Med. Scis, 1991–93; Hon. Consultant Paediatrician: Royal Victoria Infirmary, Newcastle upon Tyne, 1984–93; Gt Ormond St Hosp. and UCL, 1993–2005; Vice-Dean for Clin. Res., Inst. of Child Health, Univ. of London, at UCL, 1999–2003; Dir, Clinical R&D, Gt Ormond St Hosp. for Children, 1993–2003; NHS Nat. Clin. Dir for Children and Chm., NHS Nat. Children's Taskforce, DoH, 2001–05. Non-exec. Mem., Bd of Govs, Hosp. for Sick Children, Gt Ormond St, 1990–93; Exec. Mem., Trust Bd, Gt Ormond St Hosp. for Children NHS Trust, 1993–2003; non-exec. Dir, Salisbury Foundn NHS Trust, 2007–08. Chm., Adv. Gp on NHS Priorities for R&D in Mother and Child Health, DoH, 1994–95; Mem., Central R&D Cttee, DoH, 1999–2002. Hon. Mem. Council, NSPCC, 2006–; Pres., Contact a Family, 2007–. Visiting Professor: Univ. of Ulm, FRG, 1986; Harvard Univ., 1987; Columbus Children's Hosp., Ohio State Univ., 1991; Vis. Paediatrician in Residence, Royal Children's Hosp., Univ. of Qld, 1989; Vis. Lectr, Children's Hosp., Camperdown, Sydney, 1992; Queen Elizabeth the Queen Mother Fellow, Nuffield Trust, 2004–05. Numerous lectures in Europe, USA and Australia including: Lockyer, RCP, 1988; Assoc. of Paediatric Anaesthetists of GB and Ire. (and Medal), 1990; Niilo Hallman, Univs of Helsinki and Tampere, Finland (and Medal), 1991. External Examiner in Paediatrics: Univ. of Malaya, 1990; Chinese Univ. of Hong Kong, 1994–98; Univ. of Kuwait, 1996. European Society for Paediatric Endocrinology: Sec., 1982–87; Pres., 1994–95; Pres., Assoc. of Clin. Profs of Paediatrics, 1999–2002. Founder FMedSci, 1998; Millennium Fellow, Paediatric Soc. NZ, 2000; Hon. FFPH 2007. Hon. Member: Hungarian Paediatric Assoc., 1988 (Silver Medal, 2004); S African Paediatric Assoc., 1998; Finnish Paediatric Soc., 2006. Dr *hc* Pécs, 1998; Hon. DCL Northumbria, 2005; Hon. MD Liverpool, 2006; DUniv: Northampton, 2007; York, 2008. Andrea Prader Prize and Medal, 1991, (jtly) Henning Andersen Prize, 1999, European Soc. for Paediatric Endocrinology. *Publications:* papers and articles on children in society, child health and childhood, and scientifically on endocrinology and metabolism in infancy. *Recreations:* family, walking, music, photography. *Address:* (office) 1 London Bridge, SE1 9BG. *Club:* Athenæum.

AYONG, Most Rev. James Simon; *see* Papua New Guinea, Archbishop of.

AYOUB, Fouad; Ambassador of the Hashemite Kingdom of Jordan to Canada, 2002–05; *b* 15 Aug. 1944; *m* 1974, Marie Vernazza; two *s* one *d*. *Educ:* California State Univ., San Francisco (BA; MA philosophy 1974). Press Secretary to King Hussein, 1977–91; Mem., Jordanian Delegn to Madrid Peace Conf., 1991; Ambassador of Jordan to UK, 1991–99, and (non-resident) to Iceland and Ireland, 1992–99; Ambassador of Jordan to Switzerland, 1999–2001. Fellow, Centre for Internat. Affairs, Harvard, 1983–84. Order of El Istiqlal (Jordan), 1991; numerous foreign orders. *Recreation:* reading.

AYRES, Gillian, OBE 1986; RA; painter, artist; *b* 3 Feb. 1930; *d* of Stephen and Florence Ayres; *m* Henry Mundy (marr. diss.); two *s*. *Educ:* St Paul's Girls' Sch.; Camberwell Sch. of Art. Student, 1946–50; taught, 1959–81 (incl. Sen. Lectr, St Martin's Sch. of Art, and Head of Painting, Winchester Sch. of Art, 1978–81). ARA 1982, RA 1991–97 (resigned), rejoined 2000. One-woman Exhibitions include: Gallery One, 1956; Redfern Gall., 1958; Moulton Gall., 1960 and 1962; Kasmin Gall., 1965, 1966 and 1969; William Darby Gall., 1976; Women's Internat. Centre, New York, 1976; Knoedler Gall., 1979, 1982, 1987; Mus. of Mod. Art, Oxford, 1981; Alan Cristea Gall., 2007; retrospective exhibitions: Serpentine Gall., 1983; RA Sackler Gall., Yale British Art Center, and Iowa Mus., 1997; also exhibited: Redfern Gall., 1957; 1st Paris Biennale, 1959; Hayward Gall., 1971; Silver Jubilee Exhibn, RA, 1977; Knoedler Gall., NY, 1985; Tate Gall., 1995. Works in public collections: Tate Gall.; Mus. of Mod. Art, NY; Olinda Mus., Brazil; Gulbenkian Foundn, Lisbon; V&A Mus.; British Council. Hon. DLit London, 1994. Prize winner: Tokyo Biennale, 1963; John Moores Prize, 1982; Indian Trienale, Gold Medal, 1991. *Address:* c/o Alan Cristea Gallery, 31 Cork Street, W1S 3NU.

AYRES, Ian Leslie; Head, Business Operations, BUPA Commissioning, since 2008; *b* 14 Nov. 1954; *s* of Dennis Albert Walter Ayres and Patience Ayres; *m* 1980, Catherine Tucker; two *s* one *d*. *Educ:* Univ. of Surrey (BSc Hons Psychol. and Philosophy); Univ. of Warwick (MBA). Pres., Univ. of Surrey Students' Union, 1976–77. BP Oil UK: Asst Manpower Planner, 1977–80; Business Controller, 1980–84; Sales Manager, 1984–88; Project Manager, Business Process Re-engrg, 1990–94; Project Manager, Queen Mary's Christian Care Foundn, 1994–95; National Health Service: Chief Executive Officer: SW London Total Purchasing Project, 1995–99; Nelson PCG, 1999–2000; Nelson and W Merton PCT, 2000–02; Sutton and Merton PCT, 2002–06; Hillingdon PCT, 2006; Dir, Downsview Ltd, 2007. *Recreations:* church going, ski-ing, reading. *Address:* 3 Cornwall Road, Cheam, Surrey SM2 6DR. *T:* (020) 8296 8645; *e-mail:* IanLAyres@aol.com.

AYRES, Pamela, (Mrs D. Russell), MBE 2004; writer, broadcaster and entertainer; *b* 14 March 1947; *d* of Stanley William Ayres and Phyllis Evelyn Loder; *m* 1982, Dudley Russell; two *s*. *Educ:* Stanford-in-the-Vale Village Primary Sch., Berks; Faringdon Secondary Modern Sch., Berks. Served WRAF, 1965–69. Writer and performer: *television:* début on Opportunity Knocks, 1975; The World of Pam Ayres (series), 1977; TV specials in UK, Hong Kong and Canada, 1978–79; *radio:* Pam Ayres Radio Show (series), 1995; presenter: Pam Ayres on Sunday, 1996–99; Pam Ayres' Open Road, 2000–01; Ayres on the Air (series), 2004, 2006; appeared in Royal Variety Show, Palladium, 1977; annual UK concert tours; regular concert tours in Australia and NZ; also perf. in Canada, France, Ireland, Hong Kong and Kenya. *Publications:* Some of Me Poetry, 1976; Some More of Me Poetry, 1976; Thoughts of a Late-Night Knitter, 1978; All Pam's Poems, 1978; The Ballad of Bill Spinks' Bedstead and Other Poems, 1981; Dear Mum, 1985; Pam Ayres: The Works, 1992; With These Hands, 1997; Surgically Enhanced: the new collection, 2006; *for children:* Bertha and the Racing Pigeon, 1979; Guess Who?, 1987; Guess What?, 1987; When Dad Fills In The Garden Pond, 1988; When Dad Cuts Down The Chestnut Tree, 1988; Piggo and the Nosebag, 1990; Piggo has a Train Ride, 1990; Piggo and the Fork-lift Truck, 1991; The Bear Who Was Left Behind, 1991; Jack Crater, 1992; Guess Why?, 1994; Guess Where?, 1994; The Nubbler, 1997 (trans. Japanese, 1999). *Recreations:* gardening, bee-keeping, drawing, wildlife. *Address:* PO Box 64, Cirencester, Glos GL7 5YD. *T:* (01285) 644622; *web:* www.pamayres.com.

AYRIS, Dr Paul; Director of UCL Library Services, University College London, since 1997; *b* 27 April 1957; *s* of Walter Roy Ayris and Irene Ayris (*née* Ball). *Educ:* Selwyn Coll., Cambridge (BA, MA); Gonville and Caius Coll., Cambridge (PhD 1984); Univ. of Sheffield (MA). Sir Henry Stephenson Fellow, Univ. of Sheffield, 1982–84; Cambridge University Library: Asst Librarian, Scientific Periodicals Liby, 1985–89; Automation Div., 1989–96; Hd, IT Services, 1994–96; Dep. Librarian, UCL, Jan.–Sept. 1997. Exec. Ed., Reformation & Renaissance Rev., 1999–2006. *Publication:* (ed with D. Selwyn) Thomas Cranmer, Churchman and Scholar, 1993, 2nd edn 1999. *Recreations:* ecclesiastical architecture, visiting foreign cities, classical music, sailing. *Address:* UCL Library Services, UCL, Gower Street, WC1E 6BT. *T:* (020) 7679 7834; *e-mail:* p.ayris@ucl.ac.uk.

AYRTON, Norman Walter; international theatre and opera director; Dean, British American Drama Academy, London, 1986–96; *b* London, 25 Sept. 1924. Served War of 1939–45, RNVR. Trained as an actor at Old Vic Theatre School under Michael Saint Denis, 1947–48; joined Old Vic Company, 1948; repertory experience at Farnham and Oxford, 1949–50; on staff of Old Vic Sch., 1949–52; rejoined Old Vic Company for 1951 Festival Season; opened own teaching studio, 1952; began dramatic coaching for Royal Opera House, Covent Garden, 1953; apptd Asst Principal of London Academy of Music and Dramatic Art, 1954; taught at Shakespeare Festival, Stratford, Ont, and Royal Shakespeare Theatre, Stratford-upon-Avon, 1959–62; apptd GHQ Drama Adviser to Girl Guide Movement, 1960–74; Principal, LAMDA, 1966–72; Dean, World Shakespeare Study Centre, Bankside, 1972; Nat. Inst. of Dramatic Art, Sydney, 1973–74; Faculty, Juilliard Sch., NY, 1974–85; Dir of Opera, Royal Acad. of Music, 1986–90. *Director:* Artaxerxes, for Handel Opera Soc., Camden Festival, 1963; La Traviata, Covent Garden, 1963; Manon, Covent Garden, 1964; Sutherland-Williamson Grand Opera Season, in Australia, 1965; Twelfth Night at Dallas Theatre Center, Texas, 1967; The Way of the World, NY, 1976; Lakmé, Sydney Opera House, 1976; Der Rosenkavalier, Sydney Opera House, 1983; *Guest Director:* Australian Council for Arts, Sydney and Brisbane, 1973; Loeb Drama Center, Harvard (and teacher), 1974, 1976, 1978; Melbourne Theatre Co., 1974–; Vancouver Opera Assoc., 1975–83; Sydney Opera House, 1976–81, 1983; Williamstown Festival, USA, 1977; Hartford Stage Co. and Amer. Stage Fest., 1978–; Missouri Rep. Theatre, 1980–81; Nat. Opera Studio, London, 1980–81; Spoleto Fest., USA, 1984; Sarah Lawrence Coll., NY, 1993, 1997, 2001; Utah Shakespeare Fest., 1994; BADA Midsummer Conservatory, Oxford, 2006–08; *Resident Stage Director:* Amer. Opera Center, NY, 1981–85; Vassar Coll., NY, 1990–2001; Cornell Univ., 1995, 1998; Florida State Univ., 1997–; Asolo Theatre, Sarasota, 2002. Hon. RAM 1989. *Recreations:* reading, music, gardens, travel. *Address:* 40A Birchington Road, NW6 4LJ.

AZA, Alberto; Head of the Royal Household, Spain, since 2002; *b* 22 May 1937; *s* of Alberto Aza and Marcela Arias; *m* 1963, María Eulalia Custodio Martí; two *s* four *d*. *Educ:* Univ. de Oviedo; Law Faculty of Madrid (Law Degree); BA, BSc. Joined Diplomatic Service, 1965; served Libreville, Algiers, Rome, Madrid; Dir, Cabinet of the Spanish Prime Minister, 1977–83; Chief Dir, OAS, Latin-America Dept, Min. of Foreign Affairs, 1983; Minister Counsellor, Lisbon, 1983–85; Ambassador: to OAS, Washington, 1985–89; to Belize (resident in Washington), 1985–89; to Mexico, 1990–92; to UK, 1992–99; Dir, Office of Diplomatic Inf., 1999–2002; Sec. Gen., Royal Household, Spain, 2002. Hon. DLitt Portsmouth, 1997. Gran Cruz del Mérito Civil (Spain), 1979; Gran Cruz del Mérito Naval (Spain), 1996. *Recreations:* fishing, golf, walking. *Address:* Casa del Rey, Palacio de la Zarzuela, 28071 Madrid, Spain. *Clubs:* Puerta de Hierro, Nuevo (Madrid).

AZIZ, Mohammed Abdul; Director, FaithWise Ltd, since 2003; *b* 28 Feb. 1971; *s* of Moinul Islam and Sundora Khatun; *m* 1998, Duaa Izzidien; one *s* one *d*. *Educ:* UCL (LLB Hons (Law), LLM (Jurisprudence and Human Rights Law)). Called to the Bar, Gray's Inn, 1997. London Borough of Tower Hamlets: Policy Officer, 1997–2000; Lawyer, 1998–99; Chief Executive Officer: Forum Against Islamophobia and Racism, 2000–02; British Muslim Res. Centre, 2002–04. Mem., Treasury Counsel Rev. Team, 2005. Member: CRE, 2004–07; EOC, 2005–07; Commission for Equality and Human Rights: Member: Govt Task Force, 2003–04; Govt Steering Gp, 2004–; Equalities Reference Gp, 2005–. Member: Mgt Cttee, UK Race & Europe Network, 2003–; Bd, European Network Against Racism, 2004–; Council, Liberty, 2004–. Mem., Honours Cttees for State and Community, Voluntary and Local Service, 2005–. Trustee: E London Mosque and London Muslim Centre, 1992–; Book Foundn, 2000–. *Recreations:* swimming, gardening, travelling. *T:* (020) 7093 4300, *Fax:* (020) 7093 4700; *e-mail:* maziz@faithwise.co.uk.

AZIZ, Shaukat; Member for Attock, National Assembly, Pakistan, 2004–07; Prime Minister of Pakistan, 2004–07, and Minister of Finance, 1999–2007; *b* 6 March 1949; *m*; three *c*. *Educ:* Gordon Coll., Rawalpindi (BSc 1967); Univ. of Karachi (MBA 1969). With Citibank, 1969–99, posts included: Hd of Corporate and Investment Banking for Asia Pacific Reg., then for Central and Eastern Europe; ME and Africa Corporate Planning Officer, Citicorp; Man. Dir, Saudi American Bank; Global Hd, Private Banking, Citigroup; Vice-Pres., 1992. Senator, Pakistan, 2002.

AZIZ, Suhail Ibne; international management consultant, since 1981; Chairman and Managing Director, Brettonwood Partnership Ltd, since 1990; *b* Bangladesh (then India), 3 Oct. 1937; permanently resident in England, since 1966; *s* of Azizur Rahman and Lutfunnessa Khatoon; *m* 1960, Elizabeth Ann Pyne, Dartmouth, Devon; two *d*. *Educ:* Govt High Sec. Sch., Sylhet; Murarichand Coll., Dacca Univ., Sylhet (Intermed. in Science, 1954); Jt Services Pre-Cadet Trng Sch., Quetta; Cadet Trng Sch., PNS Himalaya, Karachi; BRNC, Dartmouth (Actg Sub-Lieut 1958); (mature student) Kingston upon Thames Polytechnic and Trent Polytech., Nottingham (Dipl. in Man. Studies, 1970); (ext. student) London Univ. (BScEcon Hons 1972); (internal student) Birkbeck Coll., London Univ., (MScEcon 1976); Michigan Business Sch., USA (mgt courses, 1992). FCMI (FIMgt 1981); FIMC 1991; CMC 1994. Sub-Lieut and Lieut, Pakistan Navy Destroyers/Mine Sweeper (Exec. Br.), 1954–61. Personnel and indust. relations: Unilever (Pakistan); Royal Air Force; Commn on Indust. Relations, London; Ford Motor Co. (GB); Mars Ltd, 1963–78; Dir of Gen. Services Div., CRE, 1978–81; Dep. Dir of Econ. Develt, London Borough of Lewisham, 1984–89; Management Consultant, Fullemploy Consultancy Ltd, 1989–90; Mem. Exec. Sub-Cttee, and Bd Mem., Tower Hamlets, Education Business Partnership, 1993–. Mem., London Electricity Consumer Cttee, 1991–95. Chairman: Lambeth Healthcare NHS Trust, 1998–99; S London Community Health NHS Trust, 1999–2000; London Probation Bd, Nat. Probation Service, 2001–07. Leading Mem., Bangladesh Movement in UK, 1971. Member: Exec., Standing Conf. of Asian Orgs in UK, 1972–90; N Metropol. Conciliation Cttee, Race Relations Bd, 1971–74; Exec., Post Conf. Constituent Cttee, Black People in Britain - the Way Forward, 1975–76; Adv. Cttee to Gulbenkian Foundn on Area Resource Centre and Community Support Forum, 1976–81; Exec., Nottingham and Dist Community Relations Council, 1975–78; Dept of Employment Race Relations Employment Adv. Gp, 1977–78; BBC Asian programme Adv. Cttee, 1977–81; Industrial Tribunals, 1977–95; Exec., Nat. Org. of African, Asian and Caribbean Peoples, 1976–77; Home Sec.'s Standing Adv. Council on Race Relations, 1976–78; Steering Cttee, Asian Support Forum, 1984–86; Steering Cttee, Develt Policy Forum, DFID, 1998–2000; Jt Consultative Cttee with Ethnic Minorities, Merton BC, 1985–87; Plunkett Foundn for Co-operative Studies, 1985–97; "One World", 1986–90; Adv. Gp, City of London Polytechnic Ethnic Minority Business Develt Unit, 1987–94; Res. Adv. Bd, QMW, London Univ., 1988–99; (co-opted), Exec. Cttee, Tower Hamlets Assoc. for Racial Equality, 1988–91 (Mem., Action Tower Hamlets, 1987); Bangladeshis in Britain - a Response Forum, 1987–89; Tower Hamlets Consortium, 1994–97; Exec. Mem. and Trustee, Docklands Forum, 1991–99; Chairman: Jalalabad Overseas Orgn in UK, 1983–; London Boroughs Bangladesh Assoc., 1984–; Founder Chm., East London Bangladeshi Enterprise Agency, 1985–. CRE Bursary to study Minority Business Develt initiatives in

USA, 1986. Mem., Labour Econ. Finance Taxation Assoc., 1973–80; Institute of Management Consultants: Chm., Third World Specialist Gp, 1984–92; Mem. Council, 1995–. Jt Trustee, United Action–Bangladesh Relief Fund, 1971–90; Trustee: Brixton Neighbourhood Assoc., 1979–82; Trust for Educn and Devel, 1992–2004; Community Develt Foundn, 1999–; pact (Prison Advice & Care Trust), 2006–; Advr and Trustee, SE London Community Foundn, 1996–. Comr, Commonwealth Scholarship Commn, 1996–2002. Governor: London Guildhall Univ., 1995–2003; Lambeth Coll., 1999–. Deeply interested in community and race relations and believes profoundly that future health of Brit. society depends on achieving good race relations. *Recreations:* travelling, seeing places of historical interest, meeting people, reading (*eg* political economy). *Clubs:* Royal Air Force; Sudan (Khartoum).

AZNAR LÓPEZ, José María; Prime Minister of Spain, 1996–2004; Distinguished Scholar, Georgetown University, USA, since 2004; *b* Madrid, 1953; *m* 1977, Ana Botella; two *s* one *d*. *Educ:* Univ. Complutense, Madrid (LLB). Tax Inspector, 1976. Mem., Cortes, 1982–2004; Chief Exec., Castile-León Reg.; Premier, Castilla y León Autonomous Reg., 1987. Joined Alianza Popular, later Partido Popular, 1978: Dep. Sec. Gen., 1982; Pres., 1990–2004; Vice-Pres., European Popular Party, 1993. Dir, News Corp., 2006–. Pres., Fundación para el Análisis y los Estudios Sociales, Madrid. *Publications:* Libertad y solidaridad, 1991; España: la segunda transición, 1994; La España en que yo creo, 1995; Ocho años de Gobierno, 2004; Retratos y Perfiles: de Fraga a Bush, 2005. *Recreations:* reading, sports, music.

B

BABINGTON, His Honour Robert John, DSC 1943; QC (NI) 1965; appointed County Court Judge for Fermanagh and Tyrone, 1978; *b* 9 April 1920; *s* of David Louis James Babington and Alice Marie (*née* McClintock); *m* 1952, Elizabeth Bryanna Marguerite Alton, *d* of Dr E. H. Alton, Provost of Trinity College, Dublin; two *s* one *d*. *Educ:* St Columba's Coll., Rathfarnham, Dublin; Trinity Coll., Dublin (BA). Called to the Bar, Inn of Court of NI, 1947. MP North Down, Stormont, 1968–72. *Recreations:* golf, bird-watching. *Address:* c/o Royal Courts of Justice, Chichester Street, Belfast BT1 3JF. *Clubs:* Special Forces; Tyrone County (Omagh); Fermanagh County (Enniskillen); Royal Belfast Golf.

BABINGTON, Roger Vincent, FREng; FRINA; Director General Ships and Chief Executive, Ships Support Agency, Ministry of Defence, 1996–97; *b* 6 April 1943; *s* of late George Cyril Babington and Rita Mary Babington (*née* Simpkins); *m* 1967, Susan Wendy Eaton; two *s* two *d*. *Educ:* King Edward's Sch., Bath; Univ. of Birmingham (BSc); University Coll. London (MSc). RCNC. Asst Constructor, MoD, 1965–73; Constructor, MoD, Bath, 1973–76; Naval Constructor Overseer, MoD, Barrow-in-Furness, 1976–81; HM Dockyard, Rosyth: Constructor, 1981–82; Chief Constructor, 1982–86; Dir of Progs and Planning, 1986–87; Ministry of Defence, Bath: Dir, Surface Ships D, 1987–89; Dir, SSN20, 1989–91; Dir, Submarines, 1991–93; Dir-Gen., Ship Refitting, 1993; Dir-Gen., Fleet Support (Ships), 1993–95; Dir-Gen. Ships, 1995–96; Managing Director: BMT Marine Procurement Ltd, 1998–99; BMT Defence Services Ltd, 1999–2001. FREng (FEng 1995). *Recreations:* badminton, golf, house, garden and vehicle maintenance, watching sport, listening. *Address:* Shoscombe Lodge, Shoscombe, Bath BA2 8LU. *T:* and *Fax:* (01761) 432436.

BABINGTON-BROWNE, Gillian Brenda, (Mrs K. J. Wilson); a District Judge (Magistrates' Courts) (formerly Metropolitan Stipendiary Magistrate), 1991–2008; *b* 20 May 1949; *d* of Derek Keith Babington-Browne and Olive Maude (*née* Seymour); *m* 1983, Kenneth John Wilson. *Educ:* Rochester Girls' Grammar Sch.; Coll. of Law, London. Admitted Solicitor, 1973; Asst Solicitor with Arnold, Tuff & Grimwade, Rochester, 1973–74; Assistant with Ronald A. Prior, 1974, with Edward Lewis Possart, London, 1974–78; own practice, 1978–89; freelance advocate and consultant, 1989–91. Hon. Mem., London Criminal Courts Solicitors' Assoc. (Pres., 1990–91; Associate Mem., 1991–2005). *Publications:* contribs to legal jls. *Recreations:* gardening, interior design/decorating, reading.

BACALL, Betty Joan, (Lauren Bacall); actress; *b* NYC, 16 Sept. 1924; *d* of William Perske and Natalie Perske (*née* Weinstein, later Bacal); adopted stage name, Lauren Bacall; *m* 1st, 1945, Humphrey Bogart (*d* 1957); one *s* one *d*; 2nd, 1961, Jason Robards (marr. diss. 1969; he *d* 2000); one *s*. *Educ:* Julia Richman High Sch., NY; Amer. Acad. of Dramatic Arts, NY. *Plays:* on Broadway: Franklin Street, 1942; Goodbye Charlie, 1959; Cactus Flower, 1965; Applause, 1970 (Tony Award for Best Actress in a Musical, 1970), London, 1972; Wonderful Town, 1977; Woman of the Year, 1981 (Tony Award for Best Actress in a Musical, 1981); Sweet Bird of Youth, 1983, London, 1985; Waiting in the Wings, 1999; Visit, Chichester Fest., 1995; *films* include: To Have and Have Not, 1944; Confidential Agent, 1945; The Big Sleep, 1946; Dark Passage, 1947; Key Largo, 1948; Young Man with a Horn, Bright Leaf, 1950; How to Marry a Millionaire, 1953; Woman's World, 1954; The Cobweb, Blood Alley, 1955; Written on the Wind, 1956; Designing Woman, 1957; The Gift of Love, 1958; North West Frontier, 1959; Shock Treatment, Sex and the Single Girl, 1964; Harper, 1966; Murder on the Orient Express, 1974; The Shootist, 1976; Health, 1980; The Fan, 1981; Appointment with Death, Mr North, 1988; Tree of Hands, 1989; Misery, 1990; A Star for Two, All I Want for Christmas, 1991; A Foreign Field, 1993; Prêt-à-Porter, 1994; The Mirror Has Two Faces (Screen Actors Guild Award, Golden Globe Award, 1997), My Fellow Americans, 1996; Day and Night, 1997; Diamonds, The Venice Project, Presence of Mind, 1999; The Limit, Dogville, 2003; Birth, 2004; Manderlay, 2005; These Foolish Things, 2006; The Walker, 2007; numerous television appearances. Cecil B. DeMille Award, Golden Globe Awards, 1993. Comdr, Ordre des Arts et Lettres (France), 1995. *Publications:* Lauren Bacall By Myself, 1978; Lauren Bacall Now, 1994; By Myself and Then Some, 2005. *Address:* c/o HarperCollins Publishers, 10 East 53rd Street, New York, NY 10022, USA.

BACH, family name of **Baron Bach**.

BACH, Baron *cr* 1998 (Life Peer), of Lutterworth in the co. of Leicestershire; **William Stephen Goulden Bach;** Parliamentary Under-Secretary of State, Ministry of Justice, since 2008; *b* 25 Dec. 1946; *s* of late Stephen Craine Goulden Bach, CBE and Joan Bach; *m* 1984, Caroline Jones, *er d* of Eric and Cynthia Smeaton; one *d*, and one *s* one *d* from former marriage. *Educ:* Westminster Sch.; New Coll., Oxford (BA). Called to the Bar, Middle Temple, 1972; Midland and Oxford Circuit; Hd of Chambers. Member (Lab): Leicester City Council, 1976–87; Harborough DC, 1995–99; Mayor, Lutterworth, 1993–94. Labour Party: Treas., Leics W Const., 1974–87; Chm., Harborough Dist., 1989–95; Chm., Northants and Blaby Euro. Const., 1992–99. Member: Lab Party Econ. Commn, 1998–99; Lab Party Nat. Policy Forum, 1998–99. Government spokesman: Home Office, DfEE, LCD, 1999–2000; FCO, BERR, MoJ, 2007–; a Lord in Waiting (Govt Whip), 1999–2000, 2007–08; Parly Sec., LCD, 2000–01; Parliamentary Under-Secretary of State: MoD, 2001–05; DEFRA, 2005–06. Contested (Lab): Gainsborough, 1979; Sherwood, 1983 and 1987. Mem. Council, Leicester Univ., 1980–99. *Recreations:* playing and watching football and cricket, Leicester City FC supporter, music, reading hard-boiled American crime fiction. *Address:* House of Lords, SW1A 0PW.

See also J. N. Allan.

BACHE, Andrew Philip Foley, CMG 1992; JP; HM Diplomatic Service, retired; Ambassador to Denmark, 1996–99; *b* 29 Dec. 1939; *s* of late Robert Philip Sidney Bache, OBE and Jessie Bache; *m* 1963, Shân Headley; two *s* one *d*. *Educ:* Shrewsbury Sch.; Emmanuel Coll., Cambridge (MA). Joined HM Diplomatic Service, 1963; 3rd Sec., Nicosia, 1964–66; Treasury Centre for Admin. Studies, 1966; 2nd Sec., Sofia, 1966–68; FCO, 1968–71; 1st Sec., Lagos, 1971–74; FCO, 1974–78; 1st Sec. (Commercial), Vienna, 1978–81; Counsellor and Head of Chancery, Tokyo, 1981–85; Counsellor and Dep. Hd of Mission, Ankara, 1985–87; Hd of Personnel Services Dept, FCO, 1988–90; on secondment as Diplomatic Service Chm. to CSSB, 1990–91; Ambassador, Romania, 1992–96. Chief Exec., Westminster Foundn for Democracy, 2001–02. Chm., Hospices of Hope Romania Trust, 2001–. JP West London, 2001. Dr *hc*: Technical Univ., Cluj, 1994; Sibiu Univ., 1995. *Recreations:* diverse, including travel, history, ornithology, fine arts, squash, tennis, cricket, Real tennis. *Clubs:* Oxford and Cambridge, Royal Commonwealth Society, MCC.

BACHER, Dr Aron, (Ali); Executive Director, Wits Foundation, 2003–06; Chairman: Seniors' Finance, since 2007; Stella Vista, since 2007; *b* 24 May 1942; *s* of Rose and Koppel Bacher; *m* 1965, Shira Ruth Teeger; one *s* two *d*. *Educ:* Yeoville Boys' Primary Sch.; King Edward VII High Sch.; Witwatersrand Univ. (MB BCh). Junior appts, Baragwanath and Natalspruit Hosps, 1968–69; private practice, Rosebank, Johannesburg, 1970–79. Managing Director: Delta Distributors, 1979–81; Transvaal Cricket Council, 1981–86; South African Cricket Union, 1986–91; United Cricket Bd of S Africa, 1991–2000; Exec. Dir, 2003 ICC Cricket World Cup, 2001–03. International Cricket Council: Mem. Exec. Bd, 1997–2000; Chm., Internat. Develt Cttee, 1996–2000. Cricket début for Transvaal, 1959–60; captained S Africa, 1970; played 12 Test matches, made 120 1st cl. appearances, 7,894 runs, 18 centuries, 110 catches, one stumping; retired, 1974; Transvaal and Nat. Selectors' Panels, 1976–83; Dir S African Cricket Develt Club, 1986. Numerous awards include Jack Cheetham Meml, 1990, for doing the most to normalise sport in S Africa. *Recreation:* jogging. *Address:* PO Box 55041, Northlands 2116, South Africa. *T:* (11) 7831263.

BACK, Kenneth John Campbell, AO 1984; MSc, PhD; higher education consultant; *b* 13 Aug. 1925; *s* of J. L. Back; *m* 1950, Patricia, *d* of R. O. Cummings; two *d*. *Educ:* Sydney High Sch.; Sydney Univ. (MSc); Univ. of Queensland (PhD). Res. Bacteriologist, Davis Gelatine (Aust.) Pty Ltd, 1947–49; Queensland University: Lectr in Bacteriology, 1950–56; Sen. Lectr in Microbiology, 1957–61; Actg Prof. of Microbiology, 1962; Warden, University Coll. of Townsville, Queensland, 1963–70; Vice-Chancellor, James Cook Univ. of N Queensland, 1970–85, Prof. Emeritus, 1986–; Exec. Dir, Internat. Develt Program of Australian Univs and Colls Ltd, 1986–90. Vis. Fellow, ANU, 1996–2000. Chm., Standing Cttee, Australian Univs Internat. Develt Prog. (formerly Australian-Asian Univs Co-operation Scheme), 1977–85. Hon. DSc: Queensland, 1982; James Cook, 1995; DUniv: South Pacific, 1992; Nat. Univ. of Samoa, 1998. *Publications:* papers on microbiological metabolism, international education. *Recreation:* bridge. *Address:* 205/36 Bunker Road, Victoria Point, Qld 4165, Australia.

BACKETT, Prof. (Edward) Maurice; Foundation Professor of Community Health, University of Nottingham, 1969–81, now Professor Emeritus; *b* 12 Jan. 1916; *o s* of late Frederick and Louisa Backett; *m* 1940, Shirley Paul-Thompson; one *s* two *d*. *Educ:* University Coll., London; Westminster Hospital. Operational Research with RAF; Nuffield Fellow in Social Medicine; Research Worker, Medical Research Council; Lecturer, Queen's Univ., Belfast; Senior Lecturer, Guy's Hospital and London Sch. of Hygiene and Tropical Medicine; Prof. and Head of Dept of Public Health and Social Medicine, Univ. of Aberdeen, 1958–69. Hon. Member: Internat. Epidemiol Assoc., 1984; Soc. for Social Medicine, 1986. *Publications:* The Risk Approach to Health Care, 1984; papers in scientific journals. *Address:* Harvey Cottage, Fore Street, Totnes, Devon TQ9 5NJ. *T:* (01803) 865241; *e-mail:* c/o james.cowie@btinternet.com.

BACKHOUSE, Sir Alfred (James Stott), 5th Bt *cr* 1901; *b* 7 April 2002; *s* of Sir Jonathan Roger Backhouse, 4th Bt and of Sarah Ann, *o d* of J. A. Stott; S father, 2007.

BACKHOUSE, David, FRBS, RWA; sculptor; *b* 5 May 1941; *s* of late Joseph and Jessie Backhouse; *m* 1975, Sarah Barber; one *s* two *d*. *Educ:* Lord Weymouth Sch.; W of England Coll. of Art. RWA 1978; FRBS 1983. Numerous one-man exhibns, London and NY; public sculptures include: Meml to Merchant Seamen, Bristol, 2001; Animals in War Meml, London, 2004; sculptures in public and private collections internationally. *Recreation:* habitat improvement. *Address:* The Old Post Office, Lullington, Frome, Som BA11 2PW. *T:* (01373) 831318; *e-mail:* info@backhousesculptures.com.

BACKHOUSE, David Miles; Chairman: South Farm Products Ltd, since 1964; Leo Consult Ltd, since 1986; *b* 30 Jan. 1939; *s* of late Jonathan Backhouse and Alice Joan (*née* Woodroffe); *m* 1969, Sophia Ann (*née* Townsend); one *s* one *d*. *Educ:* Summerfields, Oxford; Eton Coll. Commenced career in banking with Schroders PLC, 1966; Chief Exec. Officer, Dunbar Gp, 1973–84; Chm., Henderson Admin Gp, 1990–92; Chm., Johnson Fry Hldgs, 1995–2000. Non-executive Director: Hambro Life Assce, 1982–84; TSB Group, 1985–92; Witan Investment Company, 1985–92; Royal Agricl Coll., 1987–2005. *Recreations:* tennis, riding. *Address:* South Farm House, Hatherop, Glos GL7 3PN. *T:* (01285) 712225.

BACKHOUSE, Roger Bainbridge; QC 1984; *b* 8 March 1938; *s* of late Leslie Bainbridge Backhouse and of Jean Backhouse; *m* 1962, Elizabeth Constance, *d* of Comdr J. A. Lowe, DSO, DSC; two *s* one *d*. *Educ:* Liverpool Coll.; Trinity Hall, Cambridge (History Tripos parts I & II). Nat. Service, RAF, 1956–58 (Pilot Officer). Worked in family business, 1961–62; Schoolmaster, 1962–64; called to the Bar, Middle Temple, 1965. *Recreations:* shooting, golf, opera. *Address:* 14 Parchment Street, Winchester, Hants SO23 8AZ. *T:* (01962) 863053. *Clubs:* Royal Air Force; Hockley Golf.

BACKLER, Dr Gary George; Director, Rail Service Delivery, Department for Transport, since 2005; *b* 19 July 1955; *s* of Robert and Barbara Backler; *m* 1990, Elizabeth Ann Edes; two *d.* *Educ:* Merton Coll., Oxford (MA Modern Hist.); Univ. of BC (MSc Commerce & Business Admin); Leeds Univ. (PhD Econ. Studies 1987). Traffic mgt trainee, British Rail, 1976–78; res. asst, Centre for Transportation Studies, Vancouver, 1978–81; Sen. Associate, Booz, Allen & Hamilton, 1985–90; Supervising Consultant, Price Waterhouse, 1990–94; Asst Dir, Office of Passenger Rail Franchising, 1994–98; Dir, Franchise Mgt, Shadow Strategic Rail Authy, 1998–2000; Exec. Dir, Regl Networks, 2000–02, Franchise Dir, N & W, 2002–05, Strategic Rail Authy. MCMI. *Publications:* contribs to logistics jls. *Recreation:* keeping fit. *Address:* Department for Transport Rail Group, Great Minster House, 76 Marsham Street, SW1P 4DR. *T:* (020) 7944 8031, *Fax:* (020) 7944 2177; *e-mail:* gary.backler@dft.gsi.gov.uk.

BACKUS, Rear Adm. Alexander Kirkwood, CB 2003; OBE 1989; Chief of Staff (Warfare) and Rear Admiral Surface Ships, 2002–03; *b* 1 April 1948; *s* of late Jake Kirkwood Backus and Jean Backus (*née* Stobie); *m* 1971, Margaret Joan Pocock; two *s* one *d.* *Educ:* Sevenoaks Sch., Kent; BRNC, Dartmouth. Joined RN, 1966; served HM Ships Fiskerton, Intrepid, Eastbourne, Cavalier, Bacchante, Blake, Arrow, Cleopatra, and Torquay, 1967–84; CO, Arethusa, 1984; JSDC Greenwich, 1986; Comdr Sea Training, 1988; Capt. 6th Frigate Sqn, HMS Hermione, 1990; Comdr British Forces Falkland Islands, 1995–96; ACOS (Policy) to C-in-C Fleet, 1996–99; Flag Officer Sea Trng, 1999–2001; Flag Officer Surface Flotilla, 2001–02. Chm., Devon Rural Skills Trust, 2002–. Silver Jubilee Medal, 1977; Golden Jubilee Medal, 2002. *Recreations:* ornithology, photography, shooting, fishing, rural skills, tennis, ski-ing. *Clubs:* Royal Naval (Argyll); Western Isles Yacht.

BACON, Gareth Andrew; Member (C) London Assembly, Greater London Authority, since 2008; *b* Hong Kong, 7 April 1972; *s* of Robert and Helen Bacon; *m* 2004, Cheryl Cooley; one *d.* *Educ:* Univ. of Kent, Canterbury (BA Hons Pols and Govt 1996; MA Eur. Pols 1997). Mem. (C), Bexley LBC, 1998– (Dep. Mayor, 2001–02; Cabinet Mem. for Envmt, 2006–). Contested (C) Greenwich and Lewisham, GLA, 2004. Cons. spokesman on envmt, GLA, 2008–. Hd, public sector div., Martin Ward Anderson, 2004–. *Recreations:* former Rugby player, current squash player, season ticket holder at Manchester United Football Club. *Address:* Greater London Authority, City Hall, The Queen's Walk, SE1 2AA. *T:* (020) 7983 5784; *e-mail:* gareth.bacon@london.gov.uk.

BACON, Prof. George Edward, MA, ScD Cantab, PhD London; Professor of Physics, University of Sheffield, 1963–81, now Emeritus; *b* 5 Dec. 1917; *s* of late George H. Bacon and Lilian A. Bacon, Derby; *m* 1945, Enid Trigg (*d* 2003); one *s* one *d.* *Educ:* Derby Sch.; Emmanuel Coll., Cambridge (Open and Sen. Schol.). CPhys. Air Ministry, Telecommunications Research Estabt, 1939–46. Dep. Chief Scientific Officer, AERE, Harwell, 1946–63; Dean, Faculty of Pure Science, Sheffield Univ., 1969–71. Leverhulme Emeritus Fellow, 1988. FInstP (Guthrie Medal, 1999). Hon. DSc Sheffield, 1998. *Publications:* Neutron Diffraction, 1955; Applications of Neutron Diffraction in Chemistry, 1963; X-ray and Neutron Diffraction, 1966; Neutron Physics, 1969; Neutron Scattering in Chemistry, 1977; The Architecture of Solids, 1981; Fifty Years of Neutron Diffraction, 1987; many scientific pubns on X-ray and neutron crystallographic studies in Proc. Royal Society, Acta Cryst., etc. *Recreations:* gardening, photography, genealogy. *Address:* Windrush Way, Guiting Power, Cheltenham GL54 5US. *T:* (01451) 850631.

BACON, Jennifer Helen, CB 1995; Director-General, Health and Safety Executive, 1995–2000; *b* 16 April 1945; *d* of Dr Lionel James Bacon and Joyce Bacon (*née* Chapman). *Educ:* Bedales Sch., Petersfield; New Hall, Cambridge (BA Hons 1st cl.; Hon. Fellow, 1997). Joined Civil Service as Asst Principal, Min. of Labour, 1967; Private Sec. to Minister of State for Employment, 1971–72; Principal, 1972–78, worked on health and safety and industrial relations legislation; Principal Private Sec. to Sec. of State for Employment, 1977–78; Asst Sec., Controller of Trng Services, MSC, 1978–80; sabbatical, travelling in Latin America, 1980–81; Asst Sec., Machinery of Govt Div., CSD, later MPO, 1981–82; Under Sec., Dir of Adult (formerly Occupational) Trng, MSC, 1982–86; Under Sec., School Curriculum and Exams, DES, 1986–89; Department of Employment: Prin. Finance Officer (Grade 3), 1989–91; Dir of Resources and Strategy (Grade 2), 1991–92; Dep. Dir-Gen. (Policy), HSE, 1992–95; Head, Animal, Health and Envmt Directorate, MAFF, then DEFRA, 2000–01. Mem., External Review Gp, Water UK, 2004–. Mem., Adv. Cttee on Degree Awarding Powers, QAA, 1998–2004. Mem. Bd, Sheffield Develt Corp., 1992–95. Vis. Fellow, Nuffield Coll., Oxford, 1989–97. Gov., Bedales Sch., 2002–05. Hon. DSc Aston, 2000. *Recreations:* classical music especially opera, travelling, walking.

BACON, John William, CB 2006; FCCA; healthcare consultant; *b* 1 Nov. 1950; *s* of late William Bacon and of Joy Bacon; *m* 1975, Margaret Clapson; one *d.* *Educ:* Cambridgeshire High Sch.; Univ. of Kent (BA). FCCA 1975. UKAEA, 1972–83: Chief Finance Officer, Culham Lab., 1979–82; Head of Finance, Harwell Lab., 1983; NHS, 1983–94; Department of Health: Dir of Finance and Performance, London Reg., 1995–2000; Dir, Health and Social Care, London, 2000–03; Dir of Service Delivery, 2003–05. Associate Consultant, Grant Thornton Internat., 2007–; Healthcare Consultant, Health Works, 2006–. Sec., London Old Tablers Soc., 2007–. *Address:* 3 Ventnor Villas, Hove BN3 3DD.

BACON, Sir Nicholas (Hickman Ponsonby), 14th Bt of Redgrave, *cr* 1611, and 15th Bt of Mildenhall, *cr* 1627; Premier Baronet of England; DL; Lord Warden of the Stannaries and Keeper of the Privy Seal, Duchy of Cornwall, since 2006; *b* 17 May 1953; *s* of Sir Edmund Castell Bacon, 13th and 14th Bt, KG, KBE, TD and Priscilla Dora, *d* of Col Sir Charles Edward Ponsonby, 1st Bt, TD; *S* father, 1982; *m* 1981, Susan, *d* of Raymond Dinnis, Edenbridge, Kent; four *s.* *Educ:* Eton; Dundee Univ. (MA). Barrister-at-law, Gray's Inn. A Page of Honour to the Queen, 1966–69. DL Norfolk, 1998. *Heir:* *s* Henry Hickman Bacon, *b* 23 April 1984. *Address:* Raveningham Hall, Norfolk NR14 6NS. *Club:* Pratt's.

BACON, Peter James; HM Diplomatic Service, retired; Consul-General, Houston, 1995–2001; *b* 17 Sept. 1941; *s* of Alfred J. Bacon and Mildred (*née* Randall); *m* 1963, Valerie Ann Colby; one *s* one *d.* *Educ:* Huish's Grammar Sch., Taunton. GPO, 1958–63; joined HM Diplomatic Service, 1963; CRO, 1963–64; Nicosia, 1964–66; Kota Kinabalu, 1967–70; Brussels, 1970–71; Beirut, 1971–75; Asst Private Sec. to Minister of State, FCO, 1975–78; Suva, 1978–80; First Sec. (Energy), Washington, 1980–84; Hd, Parly Relns Dept, FCO, 1984–88; Consul (Commercial), Johannesburg, 1988–92; Counsellor (Commercial and Develt), Jakarta, 1992–95. *Recreations:* golf, travel. *Address:* The Pines, Blagdon Hill, Taunton, Somerset TA3 7SL.

BACON, Richard Michael; MP (C) Norfolk South, since 2001; *b* 3 Dec. 1962; *s* of Michael Edward Bacon and Sheila Margaret Bacon (*née* Taylor, now Campbell); *m* 2006, Victoria Louise Panton; one *s.* *Educ:* King's Sch., Worcester; LSE (BSc 1st cl. Hons 1986); Goethe Inst., Berlin. Investment banker, Barclays de Zoete Wedd Ltd, 1986–89; financial journalist, principally with Euromoney Publications, 1993–94; Dep. Dir, Mgt Consultancies Assoc., 1994–96; Associate Partner, Brunswick Public Relations, 1996–99; Founder, English Word Factory, 1999–. Member: Public Accounts Cttee, H of C, 2001–; European Scrutiny Cttee, 2003–07; Public Accounts Commn, 2005–. Chm., Hammersmith Cons. Assoc., 1995–96. Co-founder, Cons. Party Geneva project, 2000. Contested (C) Vauxhall, 1997. *Recreation:* playing the bongos. *Address:* House of Commons, SW1A 0AA. *T:* (01379) 643728. *Club:* Ronnie Scott's.

BACON, Sir Sidney (Charles), Kt 1977; CB 1971; BSc(Eng); CEng, FREng, FIMechE, FIET; Managing Director, Royal Ordnance Factories, 1972–79; Deputy Chairman, Royal Ordnance Factories Board, 1972–79; *b* 11 Feb. 1919; *s* of Charles and Alice Bacon. *Educ:* Woolwich Polytechnic; London Univ. Military Service, 1943–48, Capt. REME. Royal Arsenal, Woolwich, 1933–58; Regional Supt of Inspection, N Midland Region, 1958–60; Asst Dir, ROF, Nottingham, 1960–61; Director, ROF: Leeds, 1961–62; Woolwich, 1962–64; Birtley, 1965; idc, 1964; Dir of Ordnance Factories, Weapons and Fighting Vehicles, 1965–66; Dep. Controller, ROFs, 1966–69; Controller, ROFs, 1969–72. Dir, Short Brothers, 1980–89. Pres., IProdE, 1979; Mem. Council, CGLI, 1979–91. Hon. FCGI 1991. *Recreations:* golf, listening to music. *Address:* 228 Erith Road, Bexleyheath, Kent DA7 6HP. *Club:* Shooters Hill Golf.

BADAWI, Zeinab Mohammed-Khair; broadcaster and journalist, BBC, since 1998; *d* of Mohammed-Khair Badawi and Asia Malik; *m* 1991, David Antony Crook; two *s* two *d.* *Educ:* St Hilda's Coll., Oxford (BA Politics, Philosophy, Econs); Sch. of Oriental and African Studies, London Univ. (MA Middle East Hist.). Broadcast journalist: Yorkshire TV, 1982–86; BBC Manchester, 1986–87; News Reporter and Presenter, Channel 4 News, ITN, 1988–98. Chm., Article 19 (Internat. Centre Against Censorship), 1998–2002; Vice-Pres., UNA, 1998–; Council Member: ODI, 1990–; Bd, Inst. of Contemporary History, 2001–; Board Member: British Council, 2004–; NPG, 2004–. Chm., Africa Medical Partnership Fund, 2004–. Trustee: Africa Centre, 2001–03; BBC World Service Trust, 2002–. *Recreations:* family, theatre, music. *Address:* BBC Television Centre, Wood Lane, W12 7RJ. *T:* (020) 8743 8000.

BADCOCK, Maj.-Gen. John Michael Watson, CB 1976; MBE 1959; DL; Chairman, S. W. Mount & Sons, 1982–86; *b* 10 Nov. 1922; *s* of late R. D. Badcock, MC, JP and Mrs J. D. Badcock; *m* 1948, Gillian Pauline (*née* Attfield) (*d* 2007); one *s* two *d.* *Educ:* Sherborne Sch.; Worcester Coll., Oxford. Enlisted in ranks (Army), 1941; commnd Royal Corps of Signals, 1942; war service UK and BAOR; Ceylon, 1945–47; served in UK, Persian Gulf, BAOR and Cyprus; Comdr 2 Inf. Bde and Dep. Constable of Dover Castle, 1968–71; Dep. Mil. Sec., 1971–72; Dir of Manning (Army), 1972–74; Defence Advr and Head of British Defence Liaison Staff, Canberra, 1974–77; retired. psc, jssc, idc. Col Comdt, Royal Signals, 1974–80 and 1982–90; Master of Signals, 1982–90; Hon. Col, 31 (London) Signal Regt (Volunteers), 1978–83. Chm., SE TA&VRA, 1979–85. Chief Appeals Officer, CRC, 1978–82. DL Kent, 1980. *Recreations:* watching Rugby football, cricket, hockey, most field sports less horsemanship. *Address:* c/o RHQ Royal Signals, Blandford Camp, Blandford, Dorset DT11 8RH. *T:* (01258) 482076.

BADDELEY, Prof. Alan David, CBE 1999; PhD; FRS 1993; FBA 2008; Professor of Psychology, University of York, since 2003; *b* 23 March 1934; *s* of Donald and Nellie Baddeley; *m* 1964, Hilary Ann White; three *s.* *Educ:* University Coll., London (BA; Fellow, 1998); Princeton Univ. (MA). PhD Cantab, 1962. Walker Fellow, Princeton Univ., 1956–57; Scientist, MRC Applied Psychology Unit, Cambridge, 1958–67; Lectr then Reader, Sussex Univ., 1969–72; Prof. of Psychology, Stirling Univ., 1972–74; Dir, Applied Psychology Unit, MRC, Cambridge, 1974–95; Sen. Res. Fellow, Churchill Coll., Cambridge, 1988–95; Hon. Prof. of Cognitive Psychology, Cambridge Univ., 1991–95; Prof. of Psychology, Univ. of Bristol, 1995–2003. Vis. Fellow, Univ. of California, San Diego, 1970–71; Visiting Professor: Harvard Univ., 1984; Univ. of Queensland, 1990; Univ. of Texas, Austin, 1991; Fellow, Center for Advanced Study in Behavioral Scis, Stanford, 2001–02. President: Experimental Psychology Soc., 1984–86; European Soc. for Cognitive Psychology, 1986–90. Founder FMedSci 1998. Hon. FBPsS 1995. Mem., Academia Europaea, 1989; Hon. For. Mem., Amer. Acad. of Arts and Scis, 1996. Hon. DPhil Umeå, Sweden, 1991; DUniv: Stirling, 1996; Essex, 1999; Plymouth, 2000; Dr *hc* Edinburgh, 2005. Aristotle Prize, 2001; Dist. Scientific Contrib. Award, Amer. Psycholog. Assoc., 2001. *Publications:* The Psychology of Memory, 1976; Your Memory: a user's guide, 1982; Working Memory, 1986; Human Memory: theory and practice, 1990; Essentials of Human Memory, 1999. *Recreations:* walking, reading, travel. *Address:* Department of Psychology, University of York, Heslington, York YO10 5DD. *T:* (01904) 432882.

BADDELEY, Sir John (Wolsey Beresford), 4th Bt *cr* 1922; *b* 27 Jan. 1938; *s* of Sir John Beresford Baddeley, 3rd Bt, and Nancy Winifred (*d* 1994), *d* of late Thomas Wolsey; *S* father, 1979; *m* 1st, 1962, Sara Rosalind Crofts (marr. diss. 1992); three *d*; 2nd, 1998, Mrs Carol Quinlan (*née* Greenham). *Educ:* Bradfield College, Berks. FCA. Qualified as Chartered Accountant, 1961. *Recreations:* inland waterways, tennis, squash, gardening. *Heir:* *kinsman* Paul Allan Baddeley [*b* 15 Aug. 1948; *m* 1977, Lesley Springett; two *s*]. *Address:* Springwood, Sandgate Lane, Storrington, Sussex RH20 3HJ. *T:* (01903) 743054.

BADDELEY, Ven. Martin James; Archdeacon of Reigate, 1996–2000; *b* 10 Nov. 1936; *s* of Walter Hubert and Mary Katharine Baddeley; *m* 1962, Judith Clare Hill (*d* 2005); two *s* one *d.* *Educ:* Keble Coll., Oxford (BA 1960; MA 1964); Lincoln Theol Coll. Ordained deacon, 1962, priest, 1963; Asst Curate, St Matthew, Stretford, 1962–64; staff, Lincoln Theol Coll., 1965–69; Chaplain, 1969–74, Fellow, 1972–74, Fitzwilliam Coll., Cambridge; Chaplain, New Hall, Cambridge, 1969–74; Canon Residentiary, Rochester Cathedral, 1974–80; Principal, Southwark Ordination Course, 1980–94; Jt Principal, SE Inst. for Theol Educn, 1994–96. *Recreations:* walking, reading. *Address:* 2 Glendower, Fossil Bank, Upper Colwall, Malvern, Worcs WR13 6PJ.

BADDELEY, Stephen John; Director of National Sport, Sport England, since 2004; *b* 28 March 1961; *s* of William Baddeley and Barbara Isobel Baddeley (*née* Dufty); *m* 1984, Deirdre Ilene Sharman (marr. diss. 1997); one *s* one *d*; partner, Kirsten Irene Gwerder; one *s.* *Educ:* Chelsea Coll., Univ. of London (BSc 1982); Open Univ. (BA 1990). Professional badminton player, 1982–90; Dir of Coaching and Develt, Scottish Badminton Union, 1990–92; (pt-time) Manager, British Badminton Olympic Team, 1990–92; Head Coach, Nat. Badminton Centre, Lausanne, and Asst Nat. Coach for Switzerland, 1992–96; Dir of Elite Play, 1996–97, Performance Dir, 1997–99, Chief Exec., 1998–2004, Badminton Assoc. of England Ltd. *Publications:* Badminton in Action, 1988; Go and Play Badminton, 1992. *Recreation:* jogging. *Address:* Sport England, 3rd Floor, Victoria House, Bloomsbury Square, WC1B 4SE.

BADDILEY, Prof. Sir James, Kt 1977; PhD, DSc, ScD; FRS 1961; FRSE 1962; Professor of Chemical Microbiology, 1977–83, now Emeritus, and Director, Microbiological Chemistry Research Laboratory, 1975–83, University of Newcastle upon Tyne; SERC Senior Research Fellow, and Fellow of Pembroke College, University of Cambridge, 1981–85, now Emeritus; *b* 15 May 1918; *s* of late James Baddiley and Ivy Logan Cato; *m* 1944, Hazel Mary (*d* 2007), *yr d* of Wesley Wilfrid Townsend and Ann Rayner Townsend (*née* Kilner); one *s.* *Educ:* Manchester Grammar Sch.; Manchester

University (BSc (1st Class Hons., Chem.) 1941, PhD 1944, DSc 1953; Sir Clement Royds Meml Schol., 1942, Beyer Fellow, 1943–44); MA 1981, ScD 1986, Cantab. Imperial Chemical Industries Fellow, Pembroke Coll., Cambridge, 1945–49; Swedish Medical Research Council Fellow, Wenner-Grens Institute for Cell Biology, Stockholm, 1947–49; Mem. of Staff, Dept of Biochemistry, Lister Institute of Preventive Medicine, London, 1949–55; Rockefeller Fellowship, Mass Gen. Hosp., Harvard Med. Sch., 1954; Prof. of Organic Chem., King's Coll., Univ. of Durham, 1954–77 (later Univ. of Newcastle upon Tyne); Head of Sch. of Chemistry, Newcastle upon Tyne Univ., 1968–78. Member: Council, Chemical Soc., 1962–65; Cttee, Biochemical Soc., 1964–67; Council, Soc. of Gen. Microbiol., 1973–75; Council, SERC (formerly SRC), 1979–81 (Mem., Enzyme Chem. and Technol Cttee, 1972–75, Biol Scis Cttee, 1976–79; Mem., Science Bd, 1979–81); Council, Royal Soc., 1977–79; Adv. Cttee, CIBA (later CIBA-GEIGY) Fellowships, 1966–88; Editorial Boards, Biochemical Preparations, 1960–70, Biochimica et Biophysica Acta, 1970–77, Cambridge Studies in Biotechnology, 1985–. Trustee, EPA Cephalosporin Fund, 1979–2004; Patron, Alzheimer's Res. Trust, 1993–. Karl Folkers Vis. Prof. in Biochem., Illinois Univ., 1962; Tilden Lectr, Chem. Soc., 1959; Special Vis. Lectr, Dept of Microbiology, Temple Univ., Pa, 1966; Leeuwenhoek Lectr, Royal Society, 1967; Pedler Lectr, Chem. Soc., 1978; Endowment Lectr, Bose Inst., Calcutta, 1980. Founder Mem., Interdisciplinary Cttee, Consejo Cultural Mundial. Hon. Mem., Amer. Soc. Biochem. and Molecular Biol. Hon. DSc Heriot Watt, 1979; Bath, 1986. Meldola Medal, RIC, 1947; Corday-Morgan Medal, Chem. Soc., 1952; Davy Medal, Royal Soc., 1974. Responsible for first chemical synthesis (structure definitive) of ADP and ATP; discovery of teichoic acids in bacterial cell walls and membranes. *Publications:* numerous contribs on chemistry and biochemistry of co-enzymes, bacterial cell walls and membranes in Journal of the Chemical Society, Nature, Biochemical Journal, etc; articles in various microbiological and biochemical reviews. *Recreations:* mountaineering, swimming, photography, music, fine arts. *Address:* 21 Grange Court, Pinehurst, Grange Road, Cambridge CB3 9BD; Department of Biochemistry, University of Cambridge, Tennis Court Road, Cambridge CB2 1QW. *T:* (01223) 333600.

BADEN, (Edwin) John, CA; Director, 1987–98, and Deputy Chairman, 1989–90 and 1996–98, Girobank plc; *b* 18 Aug. 1928; *s* of Percy Baden and Jacoba (*née* de Blank); *m* 1952, Christine Irene (*née* Grose) (*d* 2003); one *s* three *d* (and one *s* decd). *Educ:* Winchester Coll.; Corpus Christi Coll., Cambridge (MA Econ and Law). Audit Clerk, Deloitte Haskins & Sells, CA, 1951–54; Financial Dir/Co. Sec., H. Parrot & Co., Wine Importer, 1954–61; Dir of various subsids, C & A Modes, 1961–63; a Man. Dir, Samuel Montagu & Co. Ltd, 1963–78; Man. Dir/Chief Exec., Italian International Bank Plc, 1978–89; Girobank: Chief Exec., 1989–91; Man. Dir, 1990–91; Chm., 1995–96. Dir, 1990–98, Dep. Chm., 1997–98, Alliance & Leicester Building Soc., then Alliance & Leicester PLC (Chm., Gp Credit Policy Cttee, 1998–2001). Member, Management Committee: Pan European Property Unit Trust, 1973–2001; N American Property Unit Trust, 1975–93 (Chm., 1980–93). Sec. Gen., Eurogiro (formerly European Post/Giro Dirs Gp), 1993–97 (Chm., 1990–92); Mem., EU Payment Systems Technical Develt Gp, 1990–97. Institute of Chartered Accountants of Scotland: Mem., Council, 1984–90; Mem., Res. Cttee, 1966–74, 1985–88, 1991–95. Trustee, Internat. Centre for Res. in Accounting, Univ. of Lancaster, 1975–96. Mem., Review Panel, Financial Reporting Council, 1990–95. Chm., Stammerham Amenity Assoc., 1998–2001; Dir, Rosebery Housing Assoc., 1999–2005. Liveryman, Co. of Information Technologists, 1992–. Cavaliere Ufficiale, Order of Merit, Italian Republic, 1986. *Publications:* (contrib.) Making Corporate Reports Valuable, 1988; Auditing into the 21st Century, 1993; Post Giro Banking in Europe, 1993; Internal Control and Financial Reporting, 1994; articles in professional magazines. *Recreations:* reading, sailing, shooting. *Address:* Lanaways Barn, Two Mile Ash, Horsham, W Sussex RH13 0LA. *T:* (01403) 733834, *Fax:* (01403) 732860.

BADEN-POWELL, family name of **Baron Baden-Powell.**

BADEN-POWELL, 3rd Baron *cr* 1929, of Gilwell; **Robert Crause Baden-Powell;** Bt 1922; Vice-President, Scout Association, since 1982; Chairman, Quarter Horse Racing UK, since 1985; *b* 15 Oct. 1936; *s* of 2nd Baron and Carine Crause Baden-Powell (*née* Boardman) (*d* 1993); *S* father, 1962; *m* 1963, Patience Hélène Mary Batty (*see* Lady Baden-Powell). *Educ:* Bryanston (Blandford). Money broker, 1964–84; Director: City Share Trust, 1964–70; Bolton Bldg Soc., 1974–88; Managing Director: Fieldguard Ltd, 1984–; Highline Estates Ltd, 1986–95. Chief Scouts Comr, 1965–82; Pres., West Yorks Scout Council, 1972–88; Mem., 1965–, Mem. Cttee, 1972–78, Council, Scout Assoc. Mem. Council, British Quarter Horse Assoc., 1984–90 (Chm., 1990); Chm., Quarter Horse Racing UK, 1985–88. Vice Pres., Camping and Caravanning Club, 2002– (Pres., 1992–2002). *Recreation:* breeding racing Quarter Horses. *Heir: b* Hon. David Michael Baden-Powell [*b* 11 Dec. 1940; *m* 1966, Joan Phillips, *d* of H. W. Berryman, Melbourne, Australia; three *s*]. *Address:* Weston Farmhouse, The Street, Albury, Surrey GU5 9AY. *T:* (01483) 205087.

BADEN-POWELL, Lady; Patience Hélène Mary Baden-Powell, CBE 1986; DL; Vice President, The Girl Guides Association, 1990–2000; President, Commonwealth Youth Exchange Council, 1982–86; *b* 27 Oct. 1936; *d* of Mr and Mrs D. M. Batty, Zimbabwe; *m* 1963, Baron Baden-Powell, *qv. Educ:* St Peter's Diocesan Sch., Bulawayo. Internat. Comr, 1975–79, Chief Comr, 1980–85, Girl Guides Assoc. Director: Laurentian Financial Gp, 1981–94; Fieldguard Ltd, 1986–. President: Woodlarks Camp Site for the Disabled, 1978–; Nat. Playbus Assoc., 1979–2004; Surrey Council for Voluntary Youth Services, 1986–; Patron: Surrey Antiques Fair, 1969–2003; E Africa Women's League UK, 2005–; Walton Firs Campsite and Activity Centre, 2006–. DL Surrey, 2004. *Address:* Weston Farmhouse, The Street, Albury, Surrey GU5 9AY. *T:* (01483) 205087.

BADENOCH, David Fraser, DM; FRCS; Hon. Consultant Urological Surgeon, St Bartholomew's and Royal London Hospitals, since 2000 (Consultant, 1988–2000); Urological Surgeon, King Edward VII Hospital for Officers, since 1996; *b* 7 Feb. 1949; 3rd *s* of late Alec Badenoch, MD, ChM, FRCS and Dr Jean Badenoch; *m* 1981, Michele Patricia Howard; two *s* two *d. Educ:* Marlborough Coll.; Lincoln Coll., Oxford (Rugby blue 1971; BA Animal Physiology 1970; BM BCh 1975; MA 1975; DM 1988; MCh 1988); Med. Coll.; St Bartholomew's Hosp. FRCS 1979. House Surgeon, Registrar and Lectr in Surgery, St Bartholomew's Hosp., London, 1976–82; Sen. Registrar in Urology, London Hosp., 1982–87; Sen. Lectr in Urology, London Hosp. Med. Coll., London Univ., 1988–99. Surg. Lt Comdr, RNR, 1978–91. Hon. Surg., Royal Scottish Corp., 1993–2006. Vis. Prof. of Urology, Mayo Clinic, 2001. Member: British Assoc. of Urological Surgeons; Amer. Urological Assoc.; European Urological Assoc.; Société Internationale d'Urologie; British Fertility Soc.; RSocMed (Hon. Sec., 1997–99, Hon. Treas., 2000–05, Pres., 2008–Oct. 2009, Section of Urology); British Prostate Gp; Hon. Sec., Chelsea Clin. Soc., 2000–08. Fellow, Eur. Bd of Urology, 1995. Creevy Meml Lect., Minnesota Soc. of Urology, 2001. Trustee, Orchid Cancer Charity, 2006–. Surgitek Prize, British Assoc. of Urological Surgeons, 1987; Grand Prix, European Urological Assoc., 1988. *Publications:* Aids to Urology, 1987; contribs to textbooks and jls in urology and infertility. *Recreations:* reading, piano, Rugby, opera, company of good friends.

Address: 101 Harley Street, W1G 6AH. *T:* (020) 7935 3881. *Clubs:* Garrick, Lansdowne; Vincent's (Oxford).

BADENOCH, (Ian) James (Forster); QC 1989; a Recorder, since 1987; a Deputy High Court Judge, since 1994; a President, Mental Health Review Tribunal, since 2000; *b* 24 July 1945; *s* of Sir John Badenoch and of Anne, *d* of Prof. Lancelot Forster; *m* 1979, Marie-Thérèse Victoria Cabourn-Smith; two *s* one *d. Educ:* Dragon Sch., Oxford; Rugby Sch.; Magdalen Coll., Oxford (Open Scholar, Demyship; MA). MCIArb 2004. Called to the Bar, Lincoln's Inn, 1968 (Bencher, 2000); Mem., Inner Temple; admitted (*ad eundem*) Hong Kong Bar, 1999. Accredited Mediator, 2003–. Chm., Expert Witness Inst., 2004–. Member: Medico-Legal Soc.; Harveian Soc.; London Common Law Bar Assoc.; Professional Negligence Bar Assoc.; Assoc. of Regulatory and Disciplinary Lawyers; Human Rights Lawyers Assoc. FRSocMed 2005. *Publications:* (contrib.) Medical Negligence, 1990, 3rd edn 2000; Urology and the Law, 2007. *Recreations:* fossil hunting, travel, wildlife photography, the study of herons. *Address:* 1 Crown Office Row, Temple, EC4Y 7HH. *T:* (020) 7797 7500.

BADER, Dr Alfred, Hon. CBE 1998; President, Alfred Bader Fine Arts, since 1992; *b* Vienna, 28 April 1924; *s* of Alfred and Elisabeth Bader; *m* 1st, 1952, Helen Daniels (marr. diss.); two *s*; 2nd, 1982, Isabel Overton. *Educ:* Queen's Univ., Kingston, Ont. (BSc 1945, BA 1946, MSc 1947); Harvard Univ. (MA 1949, PhD 1950). Res. chemist, 1950–53, Gp Leader, 1953–54, Pittsburgh Plate Glass Co.; Aldrich Chemical Co.: Chief Chemist, 1954–55; Pres., 1955–81; Chm., 1981–91; Pres., 1975–80, Chm., 1980–91, Sigma-Aldrich Corp. (Chm. Emeritus, 1991–92). Guest Curator, Milwaukee Art Mus., 1976 and 1989. FRSA 1989. Honorary Fellow: RSC, 1990; UCL, 2006. Numerous hon. degrees, including: DSc: Wisconsin, Milwaukee, 1980; Purdue, 1984; Wisconsin-Madison, 1984; Northwestern, 1990; Edinburgh, 1998; Glasgow, 1999; Masaryk, 2000; Simon Fraser, 2005; Ottawa, 2006; LLD Queen's, Kingston, 1986; DUniv Sussex, 1989. Awards include: J. E. Purkyne Medal, Czech Acad. Scis, 1994; Charles Lathrop Parsons Award, 1995, Distinguished Contributors Award, 1998, ACS; Gold Medal, Amer. Inst. Chemists, 1997. *Publication:* Adventures of a Chemist Collector, 1995. *Address:* 2961 N Shepard Avenue, Milwaukee, WI 53211, USA. *T:* (414) 9625169.

BADER, David John; Director, Social Justice and Regeneration, Welsh Assembly Government, 2003–05; *b* 26 July 1945; *s* of Erling David Bader and Sybil Mary Bader (*née* Lewis); *m* 1969, Hilary Mary Organ; one *s* one *d. Educ:* Newport High Sch. for Boys. FCIH 1975. Dir, Housing and Architectural Services, Newport CBC, 1972–89; Dep. Chief Exec., Housing for Wales (Tai Cymru), 1989–98; Dir, Housing, Welsh Assembly Govt, 1998–2003. Mem., Ind. Remuneration Panel for Wales, 2008–. Trustee: Wales Community Fire Safety Trust, 2003–05; Somer Housing Trust, 2005– (Chm., 2005–). *Recreations:* golf, classic car restoration, bidding on eBay, gardening, cinema, reading. *Address:* 20 Groves Road, Newport NP20 3SP; *e-mail:* johnbader@ukonline.co.uk. *Club:* Newport Golf.

BADGE, Sir Peter (Gilmour Noto), Kt 1998; Chief Metropolitan Stipendiary Magistrate, 1992–97; a District Judge (Magistrates' Courts) (formerly Stipendiary Magistrate, Devon), 1997–2002; *b* 20 Nov. 1931; *s* of late Ernest Desmond Badge, LDS and Marie Benson Badge (*née* Clough); *m* 1956, Mary Rose Noble; four *d. Educ:* Univ. of Liverpool (LLB). National Service, 1956–58: RNVR, lower deck and commnd; UK, ME and FE; RNR, 1958–62. Solicitor, 1956; Mem., Solicitor's Dept, New Scotland Yard, 1958–61; Asst Solicitor and later Partner, 1961–75, Kidd, Rapinet, Badge & Co.; Notary Public; Metropolitan Stipendiary Magistrate, 1975–97; a Recorder, 1980–92, 1997–99; a Chm., Inner London Juvenile Panel, 1979–97; Pres., Mental Health Review Tribunals, 1997–2003. Member: Lord Chancellor's Adv. Cttee for Inner London, 1983–97; Magisterial Cttee, Judicial Studies Bd, 1985–90; Chm., Legal Cttee, Magistrates' Assoc., 1990–93. Mem., Basket Makers' Assoc., 1987–2002; Pres., Coracle Soc., 1997– (Chm., 1985–97); Chm., Binney Meml Awards Cttee, 1992–97. Mem. Bd of Green Cloth, Verge of the Palaces of St James's, Whitehall etc, 1992–2003. Liveryman, Co. of Basket Makers, 1995–2001. Contested (L) Windsor and Maidenhead, 1964. *Publications:* articles on coracles.

BADGE, Robin Howard L.; *see* Lovell-Badge.

BADGER, Prof. Anthony John, PhD; Master of Clare College, Cambridge, since 2003; Paul Mellon Professor of American History, Cambridge University, since 1992; *b* 6 March 1947; *s* of Kenneth Badger and Iris G. (*née* Summerill); *m* 1979, Ruth Catherine Davis; two *s. Educ:* Cotham Grammar Sch.; Sidney Sussex Coll., Cambridge (BA, MA; Hon. Fellow, 2003); Hull Univ. (PhD). Department of History, Newcastle University: Lectr, 1971–81; Sen. Lectr, 1981–91; Prof., 1991; Fellow, Sidney Sussex Coll., Cambridge, 1992–2003. Hon. DLitt Hull, 1999. *Publications:* Prosperity Road: the New Deal, North Carolina and tobacco, 1980; North Carolina and the New Deal, 1981; The New Deal: the Depression years, 1989; (ed jtly) The Making of Martin Luther King and the Civil Rights Movement, 1996; (ed jtly) Southern Landscapes, 1996; Race and War: Lyndon Johnson and William Fulbright, 2000; (ed jtly) Contesting Democracy: substance and structure in American political history 1775–2000, 2001; New Deal/New South, 2007; FDR: the first hundred days, 2008. *Recreations:* walking, supporting Bristol Rovers. *Address:* The Master's Lodge, Clare College, Cambridge CB2 1TL. *T:* (01223) 333207; *e-mail:* ajb1001@cam.ac.uk.

BADHAM, Prof. Paul Brian Leslie; Professor of Theology and Religious Studies, University of Wales, Lampeter, since 1991; *b* 26 Sept. 1942; *s* of Rev. Leslie Badham, QHC and Effie (*née* Garrett); *m* 1969, Dr Linda Frances Elson; one *s. Educ:* Reading Sch.; Jesus Coll., Oxford (BA 1965; MA 1969); Jesus Coll., Cambridge (BA 1968; MA 1972); Westcott House, Cambridge; Univ. of Birmingham (PhD 1973). Divinity Master, Churcher's Coll., Petersfield, 1965–66; ordained deacon, 1968, priest, 1969; Curate: Edgbaston, 1968–69; Rubery, 1969–73; St David's University College, Lampeter, then University of Wales, Lampeter: Lectr, 1973–83; Sen. Lectr, 1983–88; Reader, 1988–91; Chm. of Church History, 1982–86; Chm. of Religion and Ethics, 1987–91; Dean, Faculty of Theology, 1991–97; Hd, Dept of Theology and Religious Studies, 1991–99; Hd, Sch. of Anthropology, Classics, Philosophy, Theology and Religious Studies, 1999–2002. Chm., Subject Panel for Theology and Religious Studies, Univ. of Wales, 1998–2003; Sec., Assoc. of Univ. Depts of Theology and Religious Studies, 1990–94. Sen. Res. Fellow, Ian Ramsey Centre, Oxford, 2004–. Member: Res. Panel for Philosophy, Law and Religious Studies, AHRB, 1999–2003; Benchmarking Panel for Theology and Religious Studies, QAA, 1999–2000 (Subject Reviewer, 2000–02). Dir, Alister Hardy Centre for Study of Religious Experience, 2002– (Trustee, 1997–2002). Vice-Pres., Modern Churchpeople's Union, 2001– (Mem. Council, 1974–95). Patron, Dignity in Dying, 2006–. FRSocMed 2007. Ed., Modern Believing, 2006–. *Publications:* Christian Beliefs about Life after Death, 1976; (with Linda Badham) Immortality or Extinction?, 1982; (ed jtly) Death and Immortality in the Religions of the World, 1987; (ed jtly) Perspectives on Death and Dying, 1987; (ed) Religion, State and Society in Modern Britain, 1989; (ed) A John Hick Reader, 1990; (ed) Ethics on the Frontier of Human Existence, 1992; The Christian Understanding of God and Christ in Relation to True

Pure-Land Buddhism, 1994; (ed jtly) Facing Death, 1996; The Contemporary Challenge of Modernist Theology, 1998; (ed jtly) Religious Experience in Contemporary China, 2007; contribs to jls. *Address:* Department of Theology and Religious Studies, University of Wales, Lampeter, Ceredigion SA48 7ED. *T:* (01570) 424708; *e-mail:* p.badham@lamp.ac.uk.

BADIAN, Ernst, FBA 1965; Professor of History, 1971–82, John Moors Cabot Professor of History, 1982–98, Harvard University, now Emeritus; *b* 8 Aug. 1925; *m* 1950, Nathlie Anne (*née* Wimsett); one *s* one *d*. *Educ:* Christchurch Boys' High Sch.; Canterbury Univ. Coll., Christchurch, NZ; University Coll., Oxford (Hon. Fellow 1987). MA (1st cl. hons), NZ, 1946; LitD, Victoria, NZ, 1962. University of Oxford: Chancellor's Prize for Latin Prose, 1950; Craven Fellow, 1950; Conington Prize, 1959; BA (1st cl. hons Lit. Hum.) 1950; MA 1954; DPhil 1956. Asst Lectr in Classics, Victoria University Coll., Wellington, 1947–48; Rome Scholar in Classics, British Sch. at Rome, 1950–52; Asst Lectr in Classics and Ancient History, Univ. of Sheffield, 1952–54; Lectr in Classics, Univ. of Durham, 1954–65; Prof. of Ancient History, Univ. of Leeds, 1965–69; Prof. of Classics and History, State Univ. of NY at Buffalo, 1969–71. Editor, Amer. Jl of Ancient History, 1976–2001. John Simon Guggenheim Fellow, 1985; Fellow, Nat. Humanities Center, 1988. Visiting Professor: Univs of Oregon, Washington and California (Los Angeles), 1961; Univ. of S Africa, 1965, 1973; Harvard, 1967; State Univ. of NY (Buffalo), 1967–68; Heidelberg, 1973; Univ. of California (Sather Prof.), 1976; Univ. of Colorado, 1978; Univ. of Tel-Aviv, 1981; Martin Classical Lectr, Oberlin Coll., 1978; lecturing visits to Australia, Canada, France, Germany, Holland, Israel, Italy, NZ, Switzerland, and S Africa. Fellow: Amer. Acad. of Arts and Sciences, 1974; Amer. Numismatic Soc., 1987; Corresponding Member: Austrian Acad. of Scis, 1975; German Archaeol Inst., 1981; Foreign Mem., Finnish Acad. of Sci. and Letters, 1985. Hon. Mem., Soc. for Promotion of Roman Studies, 1983. Hon. LitD: Macquarie, 1993; Canterbury, NZ, 1999. Austrian Cross of Honour for Sci. and Art, 1999. *Publications:* Foreign Clientelae (264–70 BC), 1958; Studies in Greek and Roman History, 1964; (ed) Ancient Society and Institutions, 1966; (ed) Polybius (The Great Histories Series), 1966; Roman Imperialism in the Late Republic, 1967 (2nd edn 1968); Publicans and Sinners, 1972 (trans. German (expanded) 1997); (ed) Sir Ronald Syme, Roman Papers, Vols 1–2, 1979; From Plataea to Potidaea, 1993; contribs to collections, dictionaries and encyclopaedias and to classical and historical journals. *Recreation:* parrots. *Address:* Department of History, Harvard University, Cambridge, MA 02138, USA.

BAER, Sir Jack (Mervyn Frank), Kt 1997; independent fine art consultant, since 2001; *b* 29 Aug. 1924; *yr s* of late Frank and Alix Baer; *m* 1st, 1952, Jean St Clair (marr. diss. 1969; she *d* 1973), *o c* of late L. F. St Clair and Evelyn Synnott; one *d*; 2nd, 1970, Diana Downes Baillieu, *yr d* of late Aubrey Clare Robinson and Mollie Panter-Downes; two step *d*. *Educ:* Bryanston; Slade Sch. of Fine Art, University Coll., London. Served RAF (Combined Ops), 1942–46. Proprietor, Hazlitt Gallery, 1948 until merger with Gooden & Fox, 1973; Man. Dir, 1973–92, Chm., 1992–94, Consultant, 1994–2001, Hazlitt, Gooden & Fox. Chm., Fine Arts and Antiques Export Adv. Cttee to Dept of Trade, 1971–73 (Vice-Chm., 1969–71). Member: Reviewing Cttee on Export of Works of Art, 1992–2001; Museums and Galls Commn, 1993–98 (Chm., Acceptance in Lieu of Tax Panel, 1993–2000). Pres., Fine Art Provident Institution, 1972–75. Chm., Soc. of London Art Dealers, 1977–80 (Vice Chm., 1974–77). Trustee: Burlington Magazine Foundn, 1991–2003; Nat. Mus and Galls on Merseyside Develt Trust, 1998–; Campaign for Museums, 1998–. *Publications:* numerous exhibition catalogues; articles in various jls. *Recreation:* drawing. *Address:* 9 Phillimore Terrace, W8 6BJ. *T:* (020) 7937 6899. *Club:* Brooks's.

BAGGE, Sir (John) Jeremy (Picton), 7th Bt *cr* 1867, of Stradsett Hall, Norfolk; DL; *b* 21 June 1945; *s* of Sir John Bagge, 6th Bt, ED, DL and Elizabeth Helena (*d* 1996), *d* of late Daniel James Davies, CBE; *S* father, 1990; *m* 1979, Sarah Margaret Phipps, *d* of late Maj. James Shelley Phipps Armstrong; two *s* one *d*. *Educ:* Eton. FCA 1968. DL Norfolk, 1996; High Sheriff, Norfolk, 2003–04. *Heir: s* Alfred James John Bagge, *b* 1 July 1980. *Address:* Stradsett Hall, King's Lynn, Norfolk PE33 9HA.

BAGIER, Gordon Alexander Thomas; DL; *b* 7 July 1924; *m* 1949, Violet Sinclair; two *s* two *d*. *Educ:* Pendower Secondary Technical Sch., Newcastle upon Tyne. Served RM, 1941–45. Signals Inspector, British Railways; Pres., Yorks District Council, NUR, 1962–64. Mem. of Keighley Borough Council, 1956–60; Mem. of Sowerby Bridge Urban Council, 1962–65. MP (Lab) Sunderland South, 1964–87. PPS to Home Secretary, 1968–69. Chm., Select Cttee on Transport, 1985–87. DL Tyne and Wear, 1988. *Recreation:* golf. *Address:* Nesta, 89 Whaggs Lane, Whickham, Newcastle upon Tyne NE16 4PQ. *Clubs:* Victory Services; Westerhope Golf (Newcastle upon Tyne).

BAGLIN, Richard John; Chairman, Greenwich Healthcare NHS Trust, 1995–2000 (Director, 1993–2000); *b* 30 Oct. 1942; *s* of F. W. and C. C. Baglin; *m* 1964, Anne Christine; one *d*. *Educ:* Preston Manor County Grammar Sch.; St John's Coll., Cambridge (MA). Various posts with Abbey National BS, later Abbey National plc, 1964–93: Gen. Man., 1981–88; Dir, various subsidiaries, 1987–93; Man. Dir, New Businesses, 1988–92. Mem., SE London Probation Service Cttee, 1993–95. Gov., Greenwich Univ., 2001–. *Recreations:* theatre, the arts. *Address:* 2 Feathers Place, Greenwich, SE10 9NE. *T:* (020) 8858 9895.

BAGNALL, Air Chief Marshal Sir Anthony (John Crowther), GBE 2003 (OBE 1982); KCB 1998 (CB 1994); Vice-Chief of Defence Staff, 2001–05; *b* 8 June 1945; *s* of Maurice Arthur Bagnall and Marjorie (*née* Crowther); *m* 1970, Pamela Diane Wilson; one *s* two *d*. *Educ:* Stretford Grammar Sch. RAF Coll., Cranwell, 1964; Flight Comdr, 5 Sqn, 1975; Advanced Staff College, 1978; Sqn Comdr, 43 Sqn, 1983, 23 Sqn, 1985; Dir, Air Staff Briefing and Co-ordination, 1985; Station Comdr, RAF Leuchars, 1987; RCDS 1990; Dir, Air Force Staff Duties, 1991; ACAS, 1992; AOC No 11 Gp, 1994; Dep. C-in-C, AFCENT, 1996–98; Air Mem. for Personnel, and AOC-in-C, Personnel and Trng Comd, 1998–2000; C-in-C Strike Comd, 2000–01; Air ADC to the Queen, 2000–01. Mem., Ct, St Andrews Univ., 2005–. *Recreations:* golf, bridge, fell walking. *Address:* c/o Lloyds TSB, 53 King Street, Manchester M60 2ES. *Club:* Royal Air Force.

BAGNALL, Kenneth Reginald; QC 1973; QC (Hong Kong) 1983; Chairman, The New Law Publishing Co. plc, 1993; Editor-in-Chief, New Property Cases, 1986; *b* 26 Nov. 1927; *s* of Reginald and Elizabeth Bagnall; *m* 1st, 1955, Margaret Edith Wall; one *s* one *d*; 2nd, 1963, Rosemary Hearn; one *s* one *d*. *Educ:* King Edward VI Sch., Birmingham; Univ. of Birmingham (LLB Hons). Yardley Scholar. Served Royal Air Force; Pilot Officer, 1947, Flt Lt, 1948. Called to the Bar, Gray's Inn, 1950; a Dep. Judge of Crown Court, 1975–83. Co-founder, 1980, Chm., 1980–82, and Life Gov., 1983, Anglo-American Real Property Inst. Mem., Crafts Council, 1982–85; Co-founder, Bagnall Gall., Crafts Council, 1982. Founder: The New Law Fax Reporting Service, 1992; Internat. Legal Index Online, 2006; Founder and Designer, New Law Online, 1995; Co-founder and Consultant, Law Alert Ltd, 1999. Mem., Inst. of Dirs. Freeman, City and Corp. of London, 1972; Freeman and Liveryman, Barber-Surgeons' Co., 1972. *Publications:* Guide to Business Tenancies, 1956; Atkins Court Forms and Precedents (Town Planning), 1973; (with K. Lewison) Development Land Tax, 1978; Judicial Review, 1985. *Recreations:* yachting, motoring, travel. *Address:* Flat 16, Eversley Court, St Anne's Road, Eastbourne BN21 2BS. *Clubs:* 1900, United and Cecil.

BAGNALL, Peter Hill, CBE 1999; DL; Chairman, Oxford Radcliffe Hospitals NHS Trust, 1993–2000; *b* 8 Oct. 1931; *s* of Reginald Stuart Bagnall and Mary Adelaide (*née* Hill); *m* 1st, 1955, Edith Ann Wood (marr. diss. 1979); one *s* one *d* (and one *s* decd); 2nd, 1979, Diana Elizabeth Rayner. *Educ:* Newcastle-under-Lyme Sch.; St Catharine's Coll., Cambridge (MA). Nat. Service and TA Commns, N Staffs Regt. Dir, W. H. Smith & Son Ltd, 1968–88; Dir and Man. Dir, W. H. Smith PLC, 1974–88, retd; Chm., Book Club Associates, 1972–88; Director: Book Tokens Ltd, 1975–2000; W. H. Smith Pension Trustees Ltd, 1979–2002; TSB/Trustcard, 1986–89; The Book Trust, 1986–93 (Chm., 1989–91); Longman/Ladybird Books, 1987–90; British Museum Co., 1988–2000; Blackwell Ltd, Oxford, 1989–96. Dir, Oxon HA, 1989–93. Trustee, Radcliffe Med. Foundn, 1993–2003; Chm., Oxford Radcliffe Hosps Charitable Funds, 2003–. Mem., Vis. Cttee, Open Univ., 1988–92; Chm. Govs and Pro-Chancellor, Oxford Brookes Univ., 1993–98 (Gov., 1988–98). Churchwarden, St Mary's, Buckland. Mem. Council, St Luke's Hospital, Oxford, 2003–. DL Oxfordshire, 1995. Hon. LLD Oxford Brookes, 1998. *Recreations:* book collecting, theatre, travel, local affairs. *Address:* Orchard House, Buckland, Faringdon, Oxon SN7 8QW. *Clubs:* Garrick, Sloane.

BAGOT, family name of **Baron Bagot**.

BAGOT, 10th Baron *cr* 1780, of Bagot's Bromley, co. Stafford; **Charles Hugh Shaun Bagot;** Bt 1627; *b* 23 Feb. 1944; *s* of 9th Baron Bagot and of Muriel Patricia (*née* Moore-Boyle); *S* father, 2001; *m* 1986, Mrs Sally A. Stone, *d* of D. G. Blunden; one *d*. *Heir: kinsman* Richard Charles Villiers Bagot, *b* 26 April 1941. *Address:* 16 Barclay Road, SW6 1EH.

BAGRI, family name of **Baron Bagri**.

BAGRI, Baron *cr* 1997 (Life Peer), of Regent's Park in the City of Westminster; **Raj Kumar Bagri,** CBE 1995; Founder, and Chairman, since 1970, Metdist Ltd; *b* 24 Aug. 1930; *m* 1954, Usha Maheshwary; one *s* one *d*. Chairman: Metdist group of cos, 1981–; Bagri Foundation, 1990–. Hon. Pres., London Metal Exchange, 2003–06 (Dir, 1983; Vice Chm., 1990; Chm., 1993–2002). Mem., Governing Body, SOAS, 1997–2007. Chm. Trustees, Rajiv Gandhi (UK) Foundn, 1997–. Hon. Fellow, London Business Sch., 2004. Hon. DSc: City, 1999; Nottingham, 2000. *Address:* Metdist Ltd, 80 Cannon Street, EC4N 6EJ.

See also Hon. A. Bagri.

BAGRI, Hon. Apurv; Managing Director, Metdist Group, since 1980; *b* 11 Nov. 1959; *s* of Baron Bagri, *qv*; *m* 1982, Alka Rakyan; two *d*. *Educ:* University Coll. Sch., London; Cass Business Sch., London (BSc Business Admin 1980); Wharton Univ. (AMP 1993). Dir, Bagri Foundn, 1990–. Mem., Crown Estate Paving Commn, 1996–; non-exec. Dir and Mem., Adv. Bd, Royal Parks, 2003–. Mem. Bd, Dubai FSA, 2004–. Mem. Bd, Internat. Wrought Copper Council, 2000– (Chm., 2002–04). Vis. Prof., Cass Business Sch., London, 2004–. Member: Governing Council, City Univ., 2002–; Bd of Govs, London Business Sch., 2003– (Dep. Chm., 2006–); Corp., University Coll. Sch., 1992–. Trustee: The Indus Entrepreneurs (UK) Ltd (TiE-UK), 2000– (Founding Pres.); TiE Inc., 2002– (Chm., 2005–); Asia House, 2000–; Royal Parks Foundn, 2003–. Mem. Bd, UK India Business Council, 2004–. Hon. DSc City, 2006. *Recreations:* watching cricket, travel, reading. *Address:* Metdist Ltd, 80 Cannon Street, EC4N 6EJ. *T:* (020) 7280 0000, *Fax:* (020) 7606 6650; *e-mail:* rbarnett@metdist.com. *Club:* MCC.

BAGSHAW, (Charles) Kerry, CMG 1998; OBE 1992; Director, Arial Associates, since 2006; *b* 5 Oct. 1943; *s* of Harry Bagshaw and Frances Bagshaw (*née* Mackay); *m* 1st, 1965, Janet Bond (marr. diss.); one *d*; 2nd, 1970, Pamela Georgina Slater; two *d*. *Educ:* White Fathers. Joined RM, 1961; commnd 1965; RM Commandos (43, 40 and 45), 1963–68; SBS, 1969–74. HM Diplomatic Service, 1974–98: First Secretary: Gaborone, 1977–79; FCO, 1979–82; UK Mission to UN, Geneva, 1982–86; FCO, 1986–87; Moscow, 1988–91; Counsellor, FCO, 1992–98. De Beers: Gen. Manager, Gp Security, 2000–03; Gp Manager, Internat. Industry Analysis, 2003–04. *Recreations:* mountains (winter and summer), music, wine and food, cycling.

BAGSHAW, Prof. Michael, FFOM; FRAeS; Professor of Aviation Medicine, King's College London, 2005–08, now Emeritus; *b* 9 July 1946; *s* of Robert and Alice Bagshaw; *m* 1970, Penelope Isaac; two *d*. *Educ:* Welsh Nat. Sch. of Medicine, Cardiff (MB BCh 1973); MRCS, LRCP 1973; DAvMed 1980; MFOM 1982, FFOM 2003; DFFP 1995; FRAeS 1995. Airline Transport Pilot's Licence; CAA Flying Examr. Clerical Asst, Architect's Dept, Swansea BC, 1966; Technical Photographer, Univ. of Swansea, 1967; medical student, Cardiff, 1967–70; RAF, 1970–86: Med. Br., 1970–75; Fast Jet Pilot (Hunter, Jaguar), 1975–78; Flying Instr, RAF Coll., Cranwell, 1978–80; Sen. Med. Officer Pilot, RAF Inst. of Aviation Medicine, 1980–86; Locum Consultant in Neuro-Otology, St George's Hosp., London, 1987; Principal, General Practice, Crowthorne, 1987–90; Estabt MO, DERA, Farnborough, 1990–92; Sen. Aviation Physician, 1992–97, Hd of Med. Services, 1997–2004, British Airways. Hon. civilian consultant advr in aviation medicine to the Army, 2003–. Vis. Prof., Cranfield Univ., 2005–. Pres., Aerospace Med. Assoc., 2005–06. Technology lecture, Royal Society, 1996. Liveryman, GAPAN, 1992– (Award of Merit, 1997). Clarkson Trophy, RAF, 1978; Buchanan Barbour Award, RAeS, 1984. *Publications:* Human Performance and Limitations in Aviation, 1991; (contrib.) Principles and Practice of Travel Medicine, 2001; (contrib.) Oxford Textbook of Medicine, 2002; (contrib.) Ernsting's Aviation Medicine, 2007; (contrib.) Fundamentals of Aerospace Medicine, 2008; papers and articles on aviation medicine. *Recreations:* violinist, Crowthorne Orchestra; bass singer, Royal Meml Chapel, Sandhurst; general aviation (flying instructor and examiner; corporate jet pilot). *Address:* 3 Bramley Grove, Crowthorne, Berks RG45 6EB. *T:* (01344) 775647. *Club:* Royal Air Force.

BAGSHAWE, Prof. Kenneth Dawson, CBE 1990; MD; FRCP, FRCOG; FRCR; FRS 1989; Professor of Medical Oncology in the University of London at Imperial College School of Medicine (formerly Charing Cross Hospital Medical School, later Charing Cross and Westminster Medical School), 1974–90, now Emeritus; Hon. Consultant Physician, Charing Cross Hospital, since 1990 (Consultant Physician, 1961–90); *b* 17 Aug. 1925; *s* of Harry Bagshawe and Gladys (*née* Dawson); *m* 1st, 1946, Ann Kelly (marr. diss. 1976; she *d* 2000); one *s* one *d*; 2nd, 1977, Sylvia Dorothy Lawler (*née* Corben) (*d* 1996); 3rd, 1998, Surinder Kanta Sharma. *Educ:* Harrow County Sch.; London Sch. of Econs and Pol Science; St Mary's Hosp. Med. Sch. (MB, BS 1952; MD 1964). FRCP 1969; FRCR 1983; FRCOG *ad eundem* 1978. Served RN, 1942–46. Fellow, Johns Hopkins Univ., Baltimore, USA, 1955–56; Sen. Registrar, St Mary's Hosp., 1956–60. Visiting Professor: Down State Univ., NY, 1977; Univ. of Hong Kong, 1982, 1994. Chm., DHSS Wkg Gp on Acute Cancer Services, 1980–84. Cancer Research Campaign: Chm., Scientific Cttee, 1983–88; Chm., Exec. Cttee, 1988–90; Vice Chm.

Bd, 1988–2002. Chm., Aepact Ltd, 1996–2000. Hon. FRSocMed 1993. Hon. DSc Bradford, 1990. Galen Medal, London Soc. of Apothecaries, 1993. *Publications:* Choriocarcinoma, 1969; Medical Oncology, 1975; 300 papers on cancer chemotherapy, tumour markers, drug targeting, etc. *Recreations:* (passive) music, art; (active) demolition, conservation. *Address:* 115 George Street, W1H 7HF. *T:* (020) 7262 6033, (office) (020) 8846 7517. *Club:* Athenæum.

BAHL, Kamlesh, (Mrs N. Lakhani), CBE 1997; Vice-President, Law Society, 1999–2000; *b* 28 May 1956; *d* of Swinder Nath Bahl and Leela Wati Bahl; *m* 1986, Dr Nitin Lakhani. *Educ:* Univ. of Birmingham (LLB 1977). Admitted Solicitor, 1980. GLC, 1978–81; BSC, 1981–84; Texaco Ltd, 1984–87; Data Logic Ltd: Legal and Commercial Manager, 1987–89; Company Sec. and Manager, Legal Services, 1989–93. Chm., EOC, 1993–98. Mem., Barnet HA, 1989–90; non-exec. Dir, Parkside HA, 1990–93. Law Society: Chm., Commerce and Industry Gp, 1988–89; Mem. Council, 1990–2000 and 2003–. Member: Justice Sub-Cttee on Judiciary, 1991–92; Ethnic Minorities Adv. Cttee and Tribunals Cttee (Cttees of Lord Chancellor's Judicial Studies Bd), 1991–94; Council and Standing Cttee on HAs, NAHAT, 1993–94; Council, Justice, 1993–94. Indep. Mem., Diplomatic Service Appeal Bd, FCO, 1993–. Bd Mem., London Transport, 1999. EC Rep., EC Consultative Commn on Racism and Xenophobia, 1994–; Vice Pres., Eur. Adv. Cttee on Equal Opportunities, 1998. Mem. Council, Scout Assoc., 1996–. Mem. Council, Open Univ., 1999–; Gov., Univ. of Westminster, 1997–2003. FRSA. Hon. Fellow, Liverpool John Moores Univ., 1998. Hon. MA North London, 1997; Hon. LLD: De Montfort, 1998; Birmingham, 1999; Hon. DCL Northumbria, 1999. *Publication:* (ed) Managing Legal Practice in Business, 1989. *Recreations:* swimming, dancing, travelling, theatre.

BAILES, Alyson Judith Kirtley, CMG 2001; Visiting Professor, Department of Political Science, University of Iceland, since 2007; *b* 6 April 1949; *d* of John-Lloyd Bailes and Barbara (*née* Martin). *Educ:* Belvedere Sch., Liverpool; Somerville Coll., Oxford (MA Modern Hist.). HM Diplomatic Service, 1969–2002: Budapest, 1970–74; UK Delgn to NATO, 1974–76; FCO, 1976–78; Asst to EC 'Cttee of Wise Men' (which reported on ways of improving functioning of EC instns), 1979; on loan to MoD, 1979–81; Bonn, 1981–84; Dep. Head of Planning Staff, FCO, 1984–86; Counsellor, Peking, 1987–89; on attachment to RIIA, 1990; Consul-Gen. and Dep. Head of Mission, Oslo, 1990–93; Head of Security Policy Dept, FCO, 1994–96; Vice-Pres., Inst. of East West Studies, NY, 1996–97 (on special leave); Political Dir, WEU, Brussels, 1997–2000; Ambassador to Finland, 2000–02. Dir, Stockholm Internat. Peace Res. Inst., 2002–07. Comdr, Royal Order of the Polar Star (Sweden), 2008. *Recreations:* music, nature, travel. *Address:* Department of Political Science, Faculty of Social Science, University of Iceland, Oddi, 101 Reykjavik, Iceland.

BAILEY, family name of **Baron Glanusk**.

BAILEY, Adrian Edward; MP (Lab and Co-op) West Bromwich West, since Nov. 2000; *b* 11 Dec. 1945; *s* of Edward Arthur Bailey and Sylvia Alice Bailey; *m* 1989, Jill Patricia Millard (*née* Hunscott); one step *s*. *Educ:* Cheltenham Grammar Sch.; Univ. of Exeter (BA Hons Econ. Hist.); Loughborough Coll. of Librarianship (Post Grad. DipLib). Librarian, Cheshire CC, 1971–82; Pol Organiser, Co-op Party, 1982–2000. Mem. (Lab), Sandwell MBC, 1991–2000 (Dep. Leader, 1997–2000). Contested (Lab): S Worcs, 1970; Nantwich, Feb. and Oct. 1974; Wirral, March 1976; Cheshire W, EP, 1979. *Recreations:* supporting Cheltenham Town FC, cricket, dog walking. *Address:* House of Commons, SW1A 0AA; 181 Oakham Road, Tividale, Oldbury, W Midlands B69 1PZ.

BAILEY, Sir Alan (Marshall), KCB 1986 (CB 1982); Permanent Secretary, Department of Transport, 1986–91; *b* 26 June 1931; *s* of John Marshall Bailey and Muriel May Bailey; *m* 1st, 1959, Stella Mary Scott (marr. diss. 1981); three *s*; 2nd, 1981, Shirley Jane Barrett. *Educ:* Bedford Sch.; St John's and Merton Colls, Oxford (MA, BPhil; Hon. Fellow, St John's Coll., 1991). Harmsworth Senior Scholarship, 1954; Harkness Commonwealth Fellowship, USA, 1963–64. Principal Private Sec. to Chancellor of the Exchequer, 1971–73; Under-Sec., HM Treasury, 1973–78, Dep. Sec., 1978–83 (Central Policy Review Staff, Cabinet Office, 1981–82), 2nd Perm. Sec., 1983–85. Board Mem., London Transport, 1991–2000. Hon. Treas., Hist. of Parliament Trust, 1994–. *Address:* 56 Greenfell Mansions, Glaisher Street, SE8 3EU.

BAILEY, Prof. Allen Jackson, FRSC; Professor of Biochemistry, University of Bristol, 1980–96, now Emeritus; *b* 31 Jan. 1931; *s* of late Horace Jackson Bailey and Mabel Bailey (*née* Young); *m* 1956, Beryl Lee; twin *s* two *d*. *Educ:* Eccles Grammar Sch.; BSc London (Chem.) 1954; MSc (Physics) 1958, PhD (Chem.) 1960, Birmingham; MA 1967, ScD 1973, Cambridge. FIFST. Shell Chemicals, 1954–57; Low Temp. Res. Station, Univ. of Cambridge, 1960–67; Harkness Fellow, Commonwealth Fund, Biol. Dept, CIT, 1963–65; joined AFRC Meat Res. Inst., Bristol, 1967: SPSO (Special Merit), 1972; Head of Biochem. Dept, 1977–79; Director (DCSO), 1979–85; Hd of Lab., AFRC Inst. of Food Res., Bristol, 1985–90; Hd of Collagen Res. Gp, Bristol Univ., 1991–2001. Visiting Professor: São Paulo Univ., 1991; UCL, 2004–. Scott Robertson Meml Lectr, QUB, 1986; Proctor Meml Lectr, Leeds, 1991. Hon. Fellow, British Connective Tissue Soc.; Hon. FRCP 2003. Senior Medal Food Science, RSC, 1987; Internat. Lectureship Award, Amer. Meat Sci. Assoc., 1989. Mem. Editl Bds, sci. jls. *Publications:* Recent Advances in Meat Science, 1985; Collagen as a Food, 1987; Connective Tissue in Meat and Meat Products, 1989; Elastomeric Proteins, 2003; sci. papers in learned jls. *Recreations:* travel, photography, painting. *Address:* Seasons, Bridgwater Road, Winscombe, Avon BS25 1NA. *T:* (01934) 843447. *Club:* Farmers'.

BAILEY, Sir Brian (Harry), Kt 1983; OBE 1976; JP; DL; Chairman, Television South West Ltd, 1980–93; Director: Channel Four Television, 1985–91 (Deputy Chairman, 1989–91); Oracle Teletext Ltd, 1983–93; *b* 25 March 1923; *s* of Harry Bailey and Lilian (*née* Pulfer); *m* 1948, Nina Olive Sylvia (*née* Saunders); two *d*. *Educ:* Lowestoft Grammar Sch. RAF, 1941–45. SW Dist Organisation Officer, NALGO, 1951–82; South Western Reg. Sec., TUC, 1968–81. Chairman: South Western RHA, 1975–82; Health Educn Council, 1983–87; Health Educn Authority, 1987–89; Member: Somerset CC, 1966–84; SW Econ. Planning Council, 1969–79; Central Health Services Council, 1978–80; MRC, 1978–86; Adv. Cttee on Severn Barrage, Dept of Energy, 1978–81; Business Educn Council, 1980–84; NHS Management Inquiry Team, 1983–84. Chm. Council, Indep. Television Assoc., 1991; Vice-Chm., BBC Radio Bristol Adv. Council, 1971–78; Member: BBC West Reg. Adv. Council, 1973–78; Council, ITCA, 1982–86; South and West Adv. Bd, Legal and General Assurance Soc. Ltd, 1985–87. Director: Independent Television Publications Ltd, 1985–90; Bournemouth Orchs (formerly Western Orchestral Soc. Ltd), 1982–96 (Vice Pres., 1996–). SW Regl Pres., MENCAP, 1984–90; Nat. Pres., Hosp. Caterers Assoc., 1987–2004. Trustee, EEC Chamber Orchestra, 1987–97. Gen. Governor, British Nutrition Foundn, 1987–91. Chm. of Govs, Dartington Coll. of Arts, 1992–2003. JP Somerset, 1964 (Chm., Taunton Deane Magistrates Bench, 1987–92); DL Somerset, 1988. Hon. LLD Plymouth, 2003. *Recreations:* football, cricket and tennis (watching), music. *Address:* Runnerstones, 32 Stonegallows, Taunton, Somerset TA1 5JP. *T:* (01823) 461265.

BAILEY, Colin Frederick, QPM 1993; Chief Constable, Nottinghamshire Constabulary, 1995–2000; *b* 17 Oct. 1943; *s* of late Fred Bailey and of Mary (*née* Sivill); *m* 1966, Christine Lound; one *s* one *d*. *Educ:* Queen Elizabeth's GS, Horncastle, Lincs; Univ. of Sheffield (LLB Hons). Lincolnshire Constab., 1960–86; Asst Chief Constable (Crime Ops), W Yorks Police, 1986–90; Dep. Chief Constable, Nottinghamshire Constab., 1990–95. Chairman: ACPO Race and Community Relns Sub Cttee, 1995–2000; ACPO Crime Prevention Sub Cttee, 1997–2000. Pres., Nottingham Br., RLSS, 1995–2000; Chm., E Midlands RLSS, 1998–2000. Chm., Police History Soc., 1998–2001. Pres., Carlton Male Voice Choir, 2005–. *Recreations:* antique porcelain, wildlife, gardening, wine, foreign travel. *Address:* c/o Nottinghamshire Police Headquarters, Sherwood Lodge, Arnold, Notts NG5 8PP. *T:* (0115) 967 0999, *Fax:* (0115) 967 0900.

BAILEY, David, CBE 2001; FCSD; photographer, film maker; *b* 2 Jan. 1938; *s* of William Bailey and Agnes (*née* Green); *m* 1st, 1960, Rosemary Bramble; 2nd, 1967, Catherine Deneuve, *qv* (marr. diss.); 3rd, 1975, Marie Helvin (marr. diss. 1985); 4th, 1986, Catherine Dyer; two *s* one *d*. *Educ:* self taught. FRPS 1972 (Hon. FRPS 1999); FSIAD 1975. Photographer for Vogue, 1959–; dir of television commercials, 1966–, of documentaries, 1968–; director and producer: Who Dealt? (TV film), 1992; Models Close-Up (TV documentary), 1998; dir, The Intruder (film), 1999. Exhibitions: Nat. Portrait Gall., 1971; one-man retrospective, V&A, 1983; Internat. Centre of Photograph, NY, 1984; Photographs from the Sudan, ICA and tour, 1985; Bailey Now!, Nat. Centre of Photography, Bath, 1989; Hamilton's Gall., annually, 1995–; Camerawork, Berlin, 1997; Carla Sozzani Gall., Milan, 1997; Galerie Claire Fontaine, Luxembourg, 1997; A Gallery for Fine Photography, New Orleans; painting exhibn, Well Hung Gall., 1997; Barbican, 1999; Nat. Mus. of Photography, Film & TV, 1999; Modern a Museet, Stockholm, 2000; Helsinki City Art Mus., 2000. FRSA. Hon. FCGI. Hon. DLitt Bradford, 1999. D&AD President's Award, for outstanding contrib. to creativity, 1998; awards for commercials including Clios, D&AD Gold Award, Cannes Golden Lion and Emmy. RPS Centenary Medal, 2005. *Publications:* Box of Pinups, 1964; Goodbye Baby and Amen, 1969; Warhol, 1974; Beady Minces, 1974; Papua New Guinea, 1975; Mixed Moments, 1976; Trouble and Strife, 1980; David Bailey's London NW1, 1982; Black and White Memories, 1983; Nudes 1981–84, 1984; Imagine, 1985; If We Shadows, 1992; The Lady is a Tramp, 1995 (TV film, 1995); Rock & Roll Heroes, 1997; Models Close-Up, 1998; Archive One, 1957–69, 1999; Chasing Rainbows, 2001; (with Kate Kray) The Art of Violence, 2003; Archive Two: locations, 2003; Bailey's Democracy, 2005; Havana, 2006; NY JS DB 62, 2007; Pictures That Mark Can Do, 2007. *Recreations:* aviculture, photography, travelling, painting.

BAILEY, David John; QC 2006; *b* 6 March 1965; *s* of John Hardy Bailey and Joyce Marion de Havilland; *m* 1993, Catherine Crick; two *s* and one step *s*. *Educ:* Oundle Sch.; Mansfield Coll., Oxford (Eldon Schol.; BA 1st Cl. Hons); Univ. of Calif, Los Angeles (LLM). Called to the Bar, Gray's Inn, 1989; specialising in commercial law. Chm. and Dir, English Sinfonia, 2003–. Trustee, Menat Trust, 2003–. Mem., Old Oundelian Club. *Publication:* (contrib.) Insurance Disputes, 1999, 2nd edn 2003. *Recreations:* shooting, skiing, music, theatre. *Address:* 7 King's Bench Walk, Temple, EC4Y 7DS. *T:* (020) 7583 0404, *Fax:* (020) 7583 0950; *e-mail:* dbailey@7kbw.co.uk. *Clubs:* Royal Automobile, MCC.

BAILEY, Dennis, RDI 1980; ARCA; graphic designer and illustrator; Partner, Bailey and Kenny, since 1988; *b* 20 Jan. 1931; *s* of Leonard Charles Bailey and Ethel Louise Funnell; *m* 1985, Nicola Anne Roberts; one *s* one *d*. *Educ:* West Sussex Sch. of Art, Worthing; Royal College of Art. Asst Editor, Graphis magazine, Zürich, 1956; free-lance design practice, London, 1957–87; Paris, 1961–64; Art Dir, Town magazine, London, 1964–66; Lectr in graphic design, Chelsea Sch. of Art, 1970–81, Middlesex Polytechnic, 1985–89. *Clients and work include:* Economist Newspaper: covers and typographic advisor; Economist Publications: The World in 1987–2006; Architectural Assoc.: art dir of journal AA Files; Arts Council of GB: design of exhibn catalogues and posters for Dada and Surrealism Reviewed, 1978, Picasso's Picassos, 1981, Renoir, 1985, Torres-Garcia, 1985, Le Corbusier, 1987, Art in Latin America, 1989, Dali: the early years, 1994; Royal Academy: catalogue and graphics for Pompeii AD 79, 1977, graphics for The Genius of Venice, 1984, Inigo Jones, 1989, Frans Hals, 1990, Egon Schiele, 1990, Mantegna, 1992; RSA: housestyle, 1989; A. d'Offay Gallery: catalogues, 1990–91; design of business print for Cons. Gold Fields, London Merchant Securities and N. M. Rothschild & Sons. Design of BMJ, 1997; illustrations for The Economist, Esquire, Harpers Bazaar (USA), Illustrated London News, Listener, Nova, Observer, Olympia (Paris), Town; book jackets for Jonathan Cape, Penguin Books and Anglo-German Foundn. Books designed: Bonnard, 1995; Francis Bacon's Studio, 2005; Performing Architecture, 2006. *Address:* Cunningham Place, NW8 8JU. *T:* (studio) (020) 7721 7705.

BAILEY, Sir Derrick Thomas Louis, 3rd Bt *cr* 1919; DFC; *b* 15 Aug. 1918; 2nd *s* of Sir Abe Bailey, 1st Bt, KCMG; *S* half-brother, 1946; *m* 1st, 1946, Katharine Nancy Stormonth Darling (marr. diss.; she *d* 1998); four *s* one *d*; 2nd, 1980, Mrs Jean Roscoe (marr. diss. 1990; she *d* 1996). *Educ:* Winchester. Engaged in farming. *Recreations:* all sports, all games. *Heir:* *s* John Richard Bailey [*b* 11 June 1947; *m* 1977, Jane, *o d* of John Pearson Gregory; two *s* one *d*]. *Address:* Bluestones, Alderney, CI GY99 9ZZ. *Club:* Rand (Johannesburg).

BAILEY, Edward Henry; His Honour Judge Bailey; a Circuit Judge, since 2000; *b* 24 May 1949; *s* of Geoffrey Henry Bailey and Ninette Bailey; *m* 1983, Claire Dorothy Ann From; two *d*. *Educ:* King's Sch., Canterbury; Gonville and Caius Coll., Cambridge (MA, LLB). Called to the Bar, Middle Temple, 1970; Lectr, Inns of Court Sch. of Law, 1970–72; in practice as barrister, 1972–2000. *Publications:* Personal Insolvency: law and practice, 1987, 4th edn 2008; Corporate Insolvency: law and practice, 1992, 3rd edn 2007; Law of Voluntary Arrangements, 2003, 2nd edn 2007; (contrib.) Halsbury's Laws of England, 4th edn 1989. *Recreations:* music, gardening.

BAILEY, Glenda Adrianne, OBE 2008; Editor-in-Chief, Harper's Bazaar, since 2001; *b* 16 Nov. 1958; *d* of John Ernest Bailey and Constance Groome. *Educ:* Noel Baker Sch., Derby; Kingston Poly. (BA Fashion Design; Hon. MA). Editor: Honey Magazine, 1986; Folio Magazine, 1987; Marie Claire (UK edn), 1988–96; Editor-in-Chief, Marie Claire (US edn), 1996–2001. Women's Magazine Editor of the Year, 1989, 1992, Editor's Editor of the Year, 1992, BSME; Amnesty Internat. Award, 1997; Mediaweek Editor of the Year Award. Hon. PrD Derby, 2001. *Address:* (office) 300 West 57th Street, New York, NY 10019, USA.

BAILEY, Harold William; Chairman, Associated British Foods, 2000–02; *b* 16 Nov. 1935; *s* of Harold Wilfred Bailey and Winifred Bailey (*née* Pollard); *m* 1955, Barbara Eileen Stringer (*d* 1999); two *s* one *d*; *m* 2001, Susan Alice Miller. *Educ:* John Ruskin Grammar Sch., Croydon. CA 1959. With Thomson McLintock & Co., 1953–62; Associated British Foods plc, 1962–2002: Financial Dir, 1978–97; Dep. Chm., 1997–99. *Recreations:* sailing, diving, reading, gardening. *Club:* Royal Automobile.

BAILEY, Jack Arthur; Secretary, MCC, 1974–87; Secretary, International Cricket Conference, 1974–87; *b* 22 June 1930; *s* of Horace Arthur and Elsie Winifred Bailey; *m* 1st, 1957, Julianne Mary Squier (marr. diss.); one *s* two *d*; 2nd, 1991, Vivian Mary Robins. *Educ:* Christ's Hospital; University Coll., Oxford (BA). Asst Master, Bedford Sch., 1958–60; Reed Paper Group, 1960–67; Rugby Football Correspondent, Sunday Telegraph, 1962–74; Asst Sec., MCC, 1967–74. Regular contributor to The Times, 1987–. Mem., Cricket Writers' Club. *Publications:* Conflicts in Cricket, 1989; Trevor Bailey: a life in cricket, 1993. *Recreations:* cricket (played for Essex and for Oxford Univ.), golf. *Address:* Wickets, Dippenhall Street, Crondall, Farnham, Surrey GU10 5NX. *T:* (01252) 851870. *Clubs:* Farmers', MCC; Harlequins Cricket (Pres., 1988–), XL (Pres., 1997–99); Vincent's (Oxford).

BAILEY, Jessica Lois; *see* Corner, J. L.

BAILEY, John; *see* Bailey, W. J. J.

BAILEY, Sir John Bilsland, KCB 1987 (CB 1982); Chief Adjudicator, 1989–2000, and Director, 1998–2002, Independent Committee for Supervision of Standards of Telephone Information Services; Chairman, Disciplinary Tribunal of Personal Investment Authority, 1994–2001; *b* 5 Nov. 1928; *o s* of late Walter Bailey and Ethel Edith Bailey, FRAM (who *m* 2nd, Sir Thomas George Spencer); *m* 1952, Marion Rosemary (*née* Carroll); two *s* one *d*. *Educ:* Eltham Coll.; University Coll., London (LLB). Solicitor of Supreme Court. Under-Sec. (Legal), Dept of HM Procurator General and Treasury Solicitor, 1973–77; Legal Dir, Office of Fair Trading, 1977–79; Dep. Treasury Solicitor, 1979–84; HM Procurator Gen. and Treasury Solicitor, 1984–88. Pres., Disciplinary Cttee, 1994, Public Interest Dir, 1993–94, LAUTRO; Dir, PIA, 1994–97. Gov., Anglo-European Coll. of Chiropractic, 1990–94. Chm., Westminster Soc., 1994–2000. *Recreation:* historical perambulations.

BAILEY, Maj. Gen. Jonathan Bernard Appleton, CB 2005; MBE 1980; PhD; Director, Boeing Defence UK, since 2007; *b* 12 April 1951; *m* 1976, Deborah Smith; two *s* one *d*. *Educ:* Charterhouse; Univ. of Sussex (BA 1972); Univ. of Cranfield (PhD 2004). Commnd RA 1972; served NI; comd Assembly Place "ROMEO" (ZIPRA guerillas), Rhodesia, 1979–80; OC troops, MV Baltic Ferry, sailing to S Atlantic, then Ops Officer, 4th Field Regt RA, Falklands War, 1982; psc 1983; HCSC 1994; Chief Fire Co-ordination, ARRC, 1997–99; Chief Jt Implementation Commn, HQ Kosovo Force, and Chief Liaison Officer, Yugoslav Gen. Staff and Kosovo Liberation Army, 1999; Dir, RA, 2000–01; Dir Gen. Devlt and Doctrine, MoD, 2002–05. Dir, Centre for Defence and Internat. Security Studies, 2005–06; defence analyst and consultant, 2005–07. Consultant, Leverhulme prog. on Changing Character of War, Oxford Univ., 2005–. Col Comdt, RA, 2003–08. QCVS 1999. *Publications:* Field Artillery and Firepower, 1989; Great Power Strategy in Asia 1905–2005, 2007; contributor: British Fighting Methods in the Great War, 1996; The Emerging Strategic Environment, 1999; The Dynamics of Military Revolution 1300–2050, 2001; The Past as Prologue, 2006; Contemporary Operations: reflections on and of Empire, 2007; contrib professional jls.

BAILEY, Rt Rev. Jonathan Sansbury, KCVO 2005; Bishop of Derby, 1995–2005; Clerk of the Closet to the Queen, 1996–2005; Hon. Assistant Bishop, Diocese of Gloucester, since 2005; *b* 24 Feb. 1940; *s* of late Walter Eric and of Audrey Sansbury Bailey; *m* 1965, Rev. Susan Mary Bennett-Jones; three *s*. *Educ:* Quarry Bank High School, Liverpool; Trinity College, Cambridge (MA). Assistant Curate: Sutton, St Helens, Lancs, 1965–68; St Paul, Warrington, 1968–71; Warden, Marrick Priory, 1971–76; Vicar of Wetherby, Yorks, 1976–82; Archdeacon of Southend and Bishop's Officer for Industry and Commerce, dio. of Chelmsford, 1982–92; Suffragan Bishop of Dunwich, 1992–95. Chm., Churches Main Cttee, 2002–05. Entered H of L, 1999. DUniv Derby, 2006. *Recreations:* theatre, music, carpentry. *Address:* 28 Burleigh Way, Wickwar, Wotton-under-Edge, Glos GL12 8LR. *T:* (01454) 294112; *e-mail:* jonathan.s.bailey@gmail.com.

BAILEY, Mark David, PhD; Headmaster, The Grammar School at Leeds (formerly Leeds Grammar School), since 1999; *b* 21 Nov. 1960; *s* of Ronald Bailey and Maureen Bailey (*née* Oates); *m* 1989, Julie Margaret Noy; one *s* one *d*. *Educ:* Univ. of Durham (BA Econ. Hist. 1982); Corpus Christi Coll., Cambridge (PhD History 1986; Rugby blue, 1982–85). Fellow, Gonville and Caius Coll., Cambridge, 1986–96; Lectr in Local History, Bd of Continuing Educn, Univ. of Cambridge, 1991–96; Fellow, Corpus Christi Coll., Cambridge, 1996–99. Mem. Council, RFU, 1994–98. Played Rugby Union for England, 1984–90 (7 caps); Captain, Suffolk CCC, 1988–90. Mem. Council, Sir Winston Churchill Meml Trust, 2007–. FRHistS 1999. T. S. Ashton Award, British Econ. Hist. Soc., 1988, 1994. *Publications:* A Marginal Economy?: East Anglian Breckland in the later Middle Ages, 1989; (ed) The Bailiffs' Minute Book of Dunwich 1404–1430, 1992; (with J. Hatcher) Modelling the Middle Ages: the history and theory of England's Economic Development, 2001; The English Manor *c* 1200–*c* 1500, 2002; Medieval Suffolk: an economic and social history 1200–1500, 2007; various articles in learned jls and contribs to collections of essays on medieval England. *Recreations:* local history, walking, sport, food, music. *Address:* The Grammar School at Leeds, Alwoodley Gates, Leeds LS17 8GS. *T:* (0113) 229 1552. *Clubs:* East India (Hon. Mem.); Hawks (Cambridge).

BAILEY, Michael John; Group Chief Executive, Compass Group plc, 1999–2006; *b* 14 Oct. 1948; *s* of Sidney William Bailey and Joyce Mary Bailey; *m* (separated); two *d*. *Educ:* Westminster Coll., London. Gardner Merchant: various posts, from Food Service Manager to Exec. Dir, UK South, 1964–85; Pres., US subsidiary, 1985–91; Man. Dir, UK contract feeding business, 1991–92; Exec. Vice Pres., Nutrition Mgt Food Services Co., 1992; Compass Group plc: Gp Devolt Dir, 1993–94; Chief Exec., N America Div., 1994–99. FHCIMA 1995. *Recreations:* music, watching sports, cooking. *Address:* c/o Compass Group plc, Compass House, Guildford Street, Chertsey, Surrey KT16 9BQ. *T:* (01932) 573000.

BAILEY, Norman Stanley, CBE 1977; operatic and concert baritone; *b* Birmingham, 23 March 1933; *s* of late Stanley and Agnes Bailey; *m* 1st, 1957, Doreen Simpson (marr. diss. 1983); two *s* one *d*; 2nd, 1985, Kristine Ciesinski. *Educ:* Rhodes Univ., S Africa; Vienna State Academy. BMus; Performer's and Teacher's Licentiate in Singing; Diplomas, opera, lieder, oratorio. Principal baritone, Sadler's Wells Opera, 1967–71; regular engagements at world's major opera houses and festivals, including: La Scala, Milan; Royal Opera House, Covent Garden; Bayreuth Wagner Festival (first British Hans Sachs in Meistersinger, 1969); Vienna State Opera (first British Wanderer in Siegfried, 1976); Metropolitan Opera, NY; Chicago Opera; Paris Opera; Edinburgh Festival; Hamburg State Opera; Munich State Opera; Opera North; Glyndebourne Fest. BBC Television performances in Falstaff, La Traviata, The Flying Dutchman, Macbeth. Recordings include The Ring (Goodall); Meistersinger and Der Fliegende Holländer (Solti); Walküre (Klemperer), among others. Hon. RAM, 1981; Hon. DMus Rhodes, 1986. *Recreations:* Mem., Baha'i world community; chess, notaphily, golf, microcomputing, indoor rowing (Mem. 16 million meter club; Winner, N American Rowing Challenge, 2004). *Address:* PO Box 655, Victor, ID 83455, USA.

BAILEY, Patrick Edward Robert; Director, Dan-Air Associated Services, 1985–92; *b* 16 Feb. 1925; *s* of late Edward Bailey and Mary Elizabeth Bailey; *m* 1947, Rowena Evelyn Nichols (*d* 1995); two *s* three *d*. *Educ:* Clapham Coll.; St Joseph's Coll., Mark Cross; LSE. BSc(Econ). MIPM; FCILT (FCIT 1971) (Mem. Council, 1982–85 and 1987–89). RAPC and RAEC (Captain), 1943–48; Labour Management, Min. of Supply and Army Department: ROF Glascoed, 1951–54; RAE Farnborough, 1954–58; RSAF Enfield, 1958–59; ROF Radway Green, 1959–61; ROFs Woolwich, 1961–66. British Airports Authority: Dep. Personnel Dir, 1966; Personnel Dir, 1970; Airport Services Dir, 1974; Dir, Gatwick and Stansted Airports, 1977–85. Chm. Trustees, British Airports Authority Superannuation Scheme, 1975–86. Mem., Air Transport and Travel Industry Trng Bd, 1971–76; Mem. Bd, Internat. Civil Airports Assoc., 1974–77. Mem., Mid-Sussex DC, 1986–99 (Chm., 1991–93). *Address:* 17 Lucastes Lane, Haywards Heath, W Sussex RH16 1LE.

BAILEY, Paul, (christened **Peter Harry**); freelance writer, since 1967; radio broadcaster; *b* 16 Feb. 1937; *s* of Arthur Oswald Bailey and Helen Maud Burgess. *Educ:* Sir Walter St John's Sch., London; Central School of Speech and Drama. Actor, 1956–64: appeared in first productions of Ann Jellicoe's The Sport of My Mad Mother, 1958, and John Osborne's and Anthony Creighton's Epitaph for George Dillon, 1958. Literary Fellow at Univ. of Newcastle and Univ. of Durham, 1972–74; Bicentennial Fellowship, 1976; Visiting Lectr in English Literature, North Dakota State Univ., 1977–79. Frequent radio broadcaster, mainly on Radio 3; has written and presented programmes on Karen Blixen, Henry Green, I. B. Singer and Primo Levi, among others. FRSL, 1982–84. E. M. Forster Award, 1974; George Orwell Meml Prize, 1978, for broadcast essay The Limitations of Despair. *Publications:* At the Jerusalem, 1967 (Somerset Maugham Award, 1968; Arts Council Prize, 1968); Trespasses, 1970; A Distant Likeness, 1973; Peter Smart's Confessions, 1977; Old Soldiers, 1980; An English Madam, 1982; Gabriel's Lament, 1986; An Immaculate Mistake: scenes from childhood and beyond (autobiog.), 1990; Sugar Cane, 1993; (ed) The Oxford Book of London, 1995; (ed) First Love, 1997; Kitty and Virgil, 1998; (ed) The Stately Homo: a celebration of the life of Quentin Crisp, 2000; Three Queer Lives (Fred Barnes, Naomi Jacob and Arthur Marshall), 2001; Uncle Rudolf (novel), 2002; A Dog's Life (memoir), 2003; contribs to Independent, TLS, Daily Telegraph, Guardian. *Recreations:* wandering in Eastern Europe, visiting churches, chamber music, watching tennis. *Address:* 79 Davisville Road, W12 9SH. *T:* (020) 8749 2279, *T:* and *Fax:* (020) 8248 2127.

BAILEY, Sir Richard (John), Kt 1984; CBE 1977; Chairman, British Ceramic Research Limited, 1982–83 and 1987–90; Director, Central Independent Television plc, 1986–94; *b* 8 July 1923; *s* of Philip Bailey and Doris Margaret (*née* Freebody); *m* 1945, Marcia Rachel Cureton Webb; one *s* three *d*. *Educ:* Shrewsbury. FICeram 1955. Served RNVR 1942–46 (Lieut). Doulton Fine China Ltd: Technical Dir, 1955–63; Man. Dir, 1963–72; Dir, Doulton & Co. Ltd, 1967–82; Chairman: Royal Crown Derby Porcelain Co. Ltd, 1983–87; Royal Doulton Ltd, 1983–87. Jt Chm., Ceramics Industry Nat. Jt Council, 1969–84; Mem., Ceramic Industry Training Bd, 1967–70; Dir, W Midlands Industrial Devolt Assoc., 1983–87; President: BCMF, 1973–74; British Ceramic Soc., 1980–81; Chm., North Staffs Business Initiative, 1981–91. Pres., North Staffs Med. Inst., 1987–99. Hon. Freeman, City of Stoke-on-Trent, 1987. FRSA 1977. Hon. Fellow, Staffordshire Univ. (formerly Poly.), 1988. MUniv Keele, 1983. *Recreations:* golf, walking, gardening.

BAILEY, Ronald William, CMG 1961; HM Diplomatic Service, retired; *b* 14 June 1917; *o s* of William Staveley Bailey and May Eveline (*née* Cudlipp), Southampton; *m* 1946, Joan Hassall (*d* 2001), *d* of late A. E. Gray, JP, Stoke-on-Trent; one *s* one *d*. *Educ:* King Edward VI Sch., Southampton; Trinity Hall, Cambridge (Wootton Isaacson Scholar in Spanish). Probationer Vice-Consul, Beirut, 1939–41; HM Vice-Consul, Alexandria, 1941–45; Asst Oriental Sec., British Embassy, Cairo, 1945–48; 1st Sec., Foreign Office, 1948–49; British Legation, Beirut, 1949–52 (acted as Chargé d'Affaires, 1949, 1950 and 1951); British Embassy, Washington, 1952–55; Counsellor, Washington, 1955–57; Khartoum, 1957–60 (acted as Chargé d'Affaires in each of these years); Chargé d'Affaires, Taiz, 1960–62; Consul-Gen., Gothenburg, 1963–65; Minister, British Embassy, Baghdad, 1965–67; Ambassador to Bolivia, 1967–71; Ambassador to Morocco, 1971–75. Mem. Council, Anglo-Arab Assoc., 1978–85. Vice-Pres., 1975–87, Pres., 1987–89, Hon. Vice-Pres., 1989–2001, Soc. for Protection of Animals Abroad; Chm., Black Down Cttee, Nat. Trust, 1982–87; Founder, 1975, Hon. Pres., 1989–98, British-Moroccan Soc. *Publication:* (ed) Records of Oman 1867–1960 (12 vols), 1989–92. *Recreations:* walking, photography. *Address:* 3 Strand Court, Topsham, Exeter EX3 0AZ. *T:* (01392) 879538. *Club:* Oriental.

BAILEY, Sly; *see* Bailey, Sylvia.

BAILEY, Sylvia, (Sly); Chief Executive, Trinity Mirror plc, since 2003; *b* 24 Jan. 1962; *d* of Thomas Lewis Grice and Sylvia Grice (*née* Bantick); *m* 1998, Peter Bailey. *Educ:* St Saviour's and St Olave's Grammar Sch. for Girls. IPC Magazines, 1989–2002: Ad Sales Dir, 1990–97; Bd Dir, 1994–2002; Man. Dir, TX, 1997–99; Chief Exec., IPC Media, 1999–2002; non-executive Director: Littlewoods plc, April–Sept. 2002; EMI, 2004–07 (Sen. Ind. Dir, and Chm., Remco, 2007). Mem., Press Assoc. Bd, 2003–. Pres., NewstrAid, 2003–. Bd Mem., NSPCC Stop Organised Abuse Appeal, 2005–. Marcus Morris Award, PPA, 2002. *Recreation:* family. *Address:* Trinity Mirror plc, 1 Canada Square, E14 5AP. *T:* (020) 7293 2203, *Fax:* (020) 7293 3225. *Club:* Women's Advertising.

BAILEY, (William) John (Joseph); journalist; Editor, Northern Cross, since 1981; *b* 11 June 1940; *s* of Ernest Robert Bailey and Josephine Smith; *m* 1963, Maureen Anne, *d* of James Gibbs Neenan and Marjorie Dorema Wrigglesworth; five *s* three *d*. *Educ:* St Joseph's, Stanford-le-Hope, Essex; Campion Hall, Jamaica; St George's Coll., Kingston, Jamaica; St Chad's Coll., Wolverhampton. Reporter: Southend Standard, Essex, and Essex and Thurrock Gazette, 1960–63; Northern Daily Mail, 1963–64; Chief Reporter, Billingham and Stockton Express, 1964–72; Sub-Editor, Mail, Hartlepool, 1972–75; Features Editor, Echo, Sunderland, 1975–97; Media Officer, Sunderland City Council, 1998–2005. Mem., Press Council, 1974–80 (Mem., Cttee for Evidence to Royal Commission on Press, 1975–76). National Union of Journalists: Mem., Nat. Exec. Council, 1966–82; Pres., 1973–74; Gen. Treasurer, 1975–82; Mem. of Honour, 1999. Sec., Hartlepool People Ltd, 1983–2002. Provincial Journalist of the Year (jtly with Carol Roberton), British Press Awards, 1977 (commended, 1979); Special award Northern Cross, Tom Cordner North East Press Awards, 1984–85, 1989, 1992, 1996, 1997. *Address:* 225 Park Road, Hartlepool TS26 9NG. *T:* (01429) 264577. *Clubs:* Press (Glasgow); Iona (Hartlepool); Tyneside Irish Centre (Newcastle upon Tyne).

BAILHACHE, Sir Philip (Martin), Kt 1996; Bailiff of Jersey, since 1995 (Deputy Bailiff, 1994–95); a Judge of the Court of Appeal, Jersey, since 1994, and Guernsey, since 1996; *b* 28 Feb. 1946; *s* of late Jurat Lester Vivian Bailhache (Lieut-Bailiff of Jersey, 1980–82) and Nanette Ross (*née* Ferguson); *m* 1st, 1967 (marr. diss. 1982); two *s* two *d*; 2nd, 1984, Linda (*née* Le Vavasseur dit Durell); one *s* one *d*. *Educ:* Charterhouse; Pembroke Coll., Oxford (Hon. Fellow, 1995). Called to the Bar, Middle Temple, 1968, Hon. Bencher, 2003; called to the Jersey Bar, 1969; QC (Jersey) 1989. In private practice as Advocate, Jersey, 1969–74; States of Jersey Dep. for Grouville, 1972–74; Solicitor-Gen., Jersey,

1975–85; Attorney Gen. for Jersey, 1986–93. Chm., Jersey Arts Council, 1987–89. Editor, Jersey and Guernsey Law Review (formerly Jersey Law Review), 1997–. *Recreations:* books, wine, gardening, the arts. *Address:* L'Anquetinerie, Grouville, Jersey, Channel Islands JE3 9UX. *T:* (01534) 852533. *Clubs:* Reform; United (Jersey).

See also W. J. Bailhache.

BAILHACHE, William James; QC 2000; HM Attorney General for Jersey, since 2000; *b* 24 June 1953; *s* of late Jurat Lester Vivian Bailhache, sometime Lieut Bailiff of Jersey, and Nanette Ross Bailhache (*née* Ferguson); *m* 1975, Jennifer Laura Nudds; one *s* one *d*. *Educ:* Charterhouse; Merton Coll., Oxford (MA). Called to the Bar, Middle Temple, 1975; Advocate, Royal Court of Jersey, 1976; Partner, Bailhache & Bailhache, 1977–94, Bailhache Labesse, 1994–99. Chm., Barclays Bank Finance Co. (Jersey) Ltd, 1996–99 (Dir, 1982–99); Dir, Jersey Gas Co. Ltd, 1992–94. *Recreations:* golf, ski-ing, reading, opera. *Address:* Seymour House, La Rocque, Jersey JE3 9BB. *T:* (01534) 854708. *Clubs:* Oxford and Cambridge; Vincent's (Oxford); Royal Jersey Golf (Captain, 1995–96).

See also Sir P. M. Bailhache.

BAILIE, Robert Ernest, (Roy), OBE 1995; Chairman, W. & G. Baird (Holdings) Ltd, since 1982; *b* 2 June 1943; s of Robert and Rosetta Bailie; *m* 1971, Paddy Clark; two *s* one *d*. *Educ:* Belfast High Sch.; Queen's Univ., Belfast; Harvard Sch. of Business (grad. 1985). MSO Ltd, 1958–65; joined W. & G. Baird, 1965, Man. Dir, 1972, led mgt buy-out, 1977; Director: W. & G. Baird Ltd, 1977–; Graphic Plates Ltd, 1977–; MSO Ltd, 1984–; Textflow Services Ltd, 1987–; Biddles Ltd, 1989–; Blackstaff Press Ltd, 1995–; Thanet Press Ltd, 1995–; Corporate Document Services Ltd, 2000–; Court, Bank of Ireland, 1999–2006 (Mem., NI Adv. Bd, 1994–98); Bank of Ireland UK Financial Services PLC, 2006–; non-executive Director: UTV, 1997–; Bank of England, 1998–2003. Pres., BPIF, 1999–2001 (Mem., Exec. Bd of Mgt, 1978–80, Chm., 1980–84, NW Reg.; Vice-Pres., 1997–99). Member: NI Council for Higher Educn, 1985–90; IDB for NI, 1990–95; Adv. Council on Alcohol and Drug Educn, 1990–99; Chairman: CBI (NI), 1992–94; NI Tourist Bd, 1996–2002. *Recreations:* sailing, golf, walking. *Address:* 60 Ballymena Road, Doagh, Ballyclare, Co. Antrim BT39 0QR. *T:* (028) 9334 0383.

BAILIE, Rt Hon. Robin John; PC (NI) 1971; Solicitor of the Supreme Court of Judicature, Northern Ireland, since 1961; *b* 6 March 1937; *m* 1961, Margaret F. (*née* Boggs); one *s* three *d*. *Educ:* Rainey Endowed Sch. Magherafelt, Co. Londonderry; The Queen's Univ. of Belfast (LLB). MP (NI) for Newtonabbey, 1969–72; Minister of Commerce, Govt of NI, 1971–72. *Recreations:* wine drinking, ski-ing, squash, golf, tennis. *Address:* Calle del Cieruo 18, Los Monteros, Marbella 29600, Spain. *T:* (34) 52775568.

BAILIE, Roy; *see* Bailie, Robert E.

BAILLIE, family name of **Baron Burton.**

BAILLIE, Sir Adrian (Louis), 8th Bt *cr* 1823, of Polkemmet, Linlithgowshire; *b* 26 March 1973; *o s* of Sir Gawaine George Hope Baillie, 7th Bt and of (Lucile) Margot Baillie; *S* father, 2003; *m* 2006, Amber Rose Laine. *Educ:* Eton Coll.; Manchester Univ. (BA); City Univ. (Dip. Law); Inns of Court Sch. of Law; London Business Sch. (MBA). Called to the Bar, Middle Temple, 1999. Company Director. *Address:* Freechase, Warninglid, Haywards Heath, West Sussex RH17 5SZ.

BAILLIE, Alastair Turner; HM Diplomatic Service, retired; Deputy High Commissioner in Calcutta, 1987–91; *b* 24 Dec. 1932; *s* of late Archibald Turner Baillie and Margaret Pinkerton Baillie; *m* 1st, 1965, Wilma Noreen Armstrong (marr. diss. 1974); one *s*; 2nd, 1977, Irena Maria Gregor; one step *s* one step *d*. *Educ:* Dame Allan's Sch., Newcastle upon Tyne; Christ's Coll., Cambridge (BA). National Service, commissioned Queen's Own Cameron Highlanders, 1951–53. HMOCS: North Borneo, subseq. Sabah, Malaysia, 1957–67; joined HM Diplomatic Service, 1967; FCO, 1967–73; Consul (Commercial), Karachi, 1973–77; First Sec. and Head of Chancery, Manila, 1977–80; Counsellor, Addis Ababa, 1980–81; Counsellor (Commercial), Caracas, 1981–83; Governor of Anguilla, 1983–87. *Recreations:* sport, reading, travelling.

BAILLIE, Alexander; 'cellist; *b* 1956; *m* Christel; one *s* two *d*. *Educ:* Royal Coll. of Music; Hochschule für Musik, Vienna; studied with Jacqueline du Pré. Soloist with LSO, BBC SO, CBSO and orchestras worldwide; premières of works include Colin Matthew's Cello Concerto, 1984, Penderecki's 2nd Cello Concerto, and concerti by H. K. Gruber and Andrew MacDonald; recitals include Bach's Cello Suites (unaccompanied), Wigmore Hall, 1997; also appears with chamber music ensembles; Member: Villiers Piano Quartet; Heveningham Hall Piano Trio; Alia Musica, Berlin; formerly Mem., The Fires of London. Vis. Prof., Royal Coll. of Music; Prof. of Cello, Bremen Hochschule.

BAILLIE, Andrew Bruce; QC 2001; a Recorder, since 1989; *b* 17 May 1948; *s* of Edward Oswald Baillie and Molly Eva (Renée) Baillie (*née* Andrews); *m* 1976, Mary Lou Meech Palmer (*d* 1988); one *s* two *d*. *Educ:* King's Coll. Sch., Wimbledon; Univ. de Besançon; Univ. of Kent at Canterbury (BA Social Scis 1969). called to the Bar, Inner Temple, 1970. *Recreations:* played Rugby for Univ. of Kent, E Kent and London Scottish; now various from triathlons to flower arranging. *Address:* 9 Gough Square, EC4A 3DE. *T:* (020) 7832 0500; *e-mail:* abaillie@9goughsquare.co.uk.

BAILLIE, Ian Fowler, CMG 1966; OBE 1962; Director, The Thistle Foundation, Edinburgh, 1970–81; *b* 16 Feb. 1921; *s* of late Very Rev. John Baillie, CH, DLitt, DD, LLD and Florence Jewel (*née* Fowler); *m* 1951, Sheila Barbour (*née* Mathewson); two *s* one *d*. *Educ:* Edinburgh Acad.; Corpus Christi Coll., Oxford (MA). War service, British and Indian Armies, 1941–46. HM Overseas Civil Service (formerly Colonial Service), 1946–66: Admin. Officer (District Comr), Gold Coast, 1946–54; Registrar of Co-operative Socs and Chief Marketing Officer, Aden, 1955; Protectorate Financial Sec., Aden, 1959; Dep. British Agent, Aden, 1962; Brit. Agent and Asst High Comr, Aden, 1963; Dir, Aden Airways 1959–66; Sen. Research Associate and Administrative Officer, Agricultural Adjustment Unit, Dept of Agricultural Economics, Univ. of Newcastle upon Tyne, 1966–69. *Publication:* (ed with S. J. Sheehy) Irish Agriculture in a Changing World, 1971. *Recreation:* angling. *Address:* Flat 4, 61 Grange Loan, Edinburgh EH9 2EG. *T:* (0131) 667 2647.

BAILLIE, Jacqueline, (Jackie); Member (Lab) Dumbarton, Scottish Parliament, since 1999; *b* Hong Kong, 15 Jan. 1964; *d* of Frank and Sophie Barnes; *m* 1982, Stephen, *s* of James and Margaret Baillie; one *d*. *Educ:* Glasgow Univ. (MSc). Resource Centre Manager, Strathkelvin DC, 1990–96; Community Economic Develt Manager, E Dumbartonshire Council, 1996–99. Scottish Parliament: Dep. Minister for Communities, 1999–2000; Minister for Social Justice, 2000–01. Chair, Scottish Labour Party, 1997–98 (Mem., Exec. Cttee, 1990–99). *Address:* Scottish Parliament, Edinburgh EH99 1SP.

BAILLIE, Prof. John, CA; Chairman: Accounts Commission for Scotland, since 2007 (Member, since 2003); Audit Scotland, since 2007 (Member of Board, since 2004); Visiting Professor of Accountancy: University of Glasgow, since 1996; Heriot-Watt University, 1989–2004, now Honorary Professor; *b* 7 Oct. 1944; *s* of Arthur and Agnes

Baillie; *m* 1972, Annette Alexander; one *s* one *d*. *Educ:* Whitehill Sch. CA 1967 (Gold Medal and Distinction in final exams). Partner: Thomson McLintock & Co., later KPMG Peat Marwick, 1978–93; Scott-Moncrieff, 1993–2001. Johnstone-Smith Prof. of Accountancy, Univ. of Glasgow, 1983–88. Member: Reporting Panel, Competition Commn, 2002–; Ind. Local Govt Finance Review Cttee, 2004–07. Convenor, Res. Cttee, 1995–99, and Mem. various technical and professional affairs cttees, Inst. of Chartered Accountants of Scotland. FRSA 1996. Hon. MA Glasgow, 1983. *Publications:* Systems of Profit Measurement, 1985; Consolidated Accounts and the Seventh Directive, 1985; technical and professional papers; contribs to Accountants' Magazine and other professional jls. *Recreations:* keeping fit, reading, music, golf. *Address:* The Glen, Glencairn Road, Kilmacolm, Renfrewshire PA13 4PB. *T:* (01505) 873254. *Clubs:* Western (Glasgow); Kilmacolm Golf (Captain, 2002).

BAILLIE, William James Laidlaw, CBE 1998; PPRSA (RSA 1979; ARSA 1968); PPRSW (PRSW 1974; RSW 1963); painter; President, Royal Scottish Academy, 1990–98 (Treasurer, 1980–90); *b* 19 April 1923; *s* of James and Helen Baillie; *m* 1961, Helen Gillon; one *s* two *d*. *Educ:* Dunfermline High Sch.; Edinburgh College of Art (Andrew Grant Schol., 1941–50; Dip. Drawing and Painting 1950). Studies interrupted by war service with Royal Corps of Signals, mainly in Far East, 1942–47. Taught in Edinburgh schools, 1951–60; Mem., Teaching Staff, Edin. College of Art, 1960–88, Sen. Lectr, 1968–88; Visiting Tutor, National Gallery of Canada Summer Sch., near Ottawa, 1955. Exhibits at Albemarle Gall., London, but mostly in Scotland, mainly at Scottish Gall., Edinburgh; first retrospective exhibn in Kirkcaldy Art Gallery, 1977; numerous private commns. HRA; RGI. Hon. DLitt Heriot-Watt, 1997. *Recreations:* music, travel. *Address:* 6A Esslemont Road, Edinburgh EH16 5PX. *T:* (0131) 667 1538.

BAILLIE-HAMILTON, family name of **Earl of Haddington.**

BAILLIEU, family name of **Baron Baillieu.**

BAILLIEU, 3rd Baron *cr* 1953, of Sefton, Australia and Parkwood, Surrey; **James William Latham Baillieu;** Director, Anthony Baillieu and Associates (Hong Kong) Ltd, since 1992; Managing Director, Bank NIKoil, since 2000; *b* 16 Nov. 1950; *s* of 2nd Baron Baillieu and Anne Bayliss, *d* of Leslie William Page, Southport, Queensland; *S* father, 1973; *m* 1st, 1974, Cornelia Masters Ladd (marr. diss. 1985), *d* of William Ladd; one *s*; 2nd, 1986, Clare Stephenson (marr. diss. 1995), *d* of Peter Stephenson; 3rd, 2004, Olga Vladimirovna; one *s*. *Educ:* Radley College; Monash Univ., Melbourne (BEc 1977). Short Service Commission, Coldstream Guards, 1970–73. Banque Nationale de Paris, 1978–80; Asst Dir, Rothschild Australia Ltd, 1980–88; Dir, Manufacturers Hanover Australia Ltd, 1988–90; Dir, Standard Chartered Asia Ltd, 1990–92; Asst Dir, Credit Lyonnais Asia Ltd, 1992–94; Asst Dir, Nomura International (Hong Kong) Ltd, 1995; Gen. Dir, Regent European Securities, 1995–96; Dir, CentreInvest Gp, Moscow, 1996–99. *Heir: s* Hon. Robert Latham Baillieu, *b* 2 Feb. 1979. *Clubs:* Boodle's; Hong Kong (Hong Kong); Australian (Melbourne).

BAILLIEU, Christopher Latham, MBE 1977; Chairman, British Swimming, since 2001; *b* 12 Dec. 1949; *s* of Hon. Edward Baillieu and Betty Anne Baillieu (*née* Bowie); *m* 1984, Jane Elizabeth Bowie; two *s* one *d*. *Educ:* Jesus Coll., Cambridge (BA 1990). Called to the Bar, Lincoln's Inn, 1976. Represented Great Britain in rowing, 1973–83; winner: Silver Medal, double sculls, Olympic Games, 1976; Gold Medal, World Championships, 1977; competed Olympic Games, 1980. Chm., The Olympians, 2004–; Vice Chairman: SportsAid, 2000–; Torch Trophy Trust, 2002–. Steward, Henley Royal Regatta (Mem., Mgt Cttee, 1986–; Trustee, Henley Stewards' Trust, 1992–). *Recreations:* exploring old buildings, hills, valleys and waterways. *Address:* 11 Woodthorpe Road, Putney, SW15 6UQ. *Clubs:* Hawks' (Cambridge); Leander.

BAILLIEU, Colin Clive; Lecturer: European Business School, London, since 1995; London College of Printing, since 1998; Member, Monopolies and Mergers Commission, 1984–93; *b* 2 July 1930; *s* of Ian Baillieu and Joanna Baillieu (*née* Brinton); *m* 1st, 1955, Diana Robinson (marr. diss. 1968); two *d*; 2nd, 1968, Renata Richter; two *s*. *Educ:* Dragon Sch.; Eton. Commissioned Coldstream Guards, 1949. Local newspaper, Evening Standard, 1951–52; British Metal Corp., 1952–58; British Aluminium, 1958–60; Monsanto Fibres, 1960–66; Arthur Sanderson, 1966–68; Ultrasonic Machines, 1968–76. Chm., Gresham Underwriting Agencies, 1990–92. Mem., Council of Lloyd's, 1983–88. Contested (C) Rossendale, Lancs, 1964 and 1966. Dir, Orchestra of St John's, Smith Square, 1999–2000. Dist Comr, Cowdray Pony Club, 1998–2001. *Publication:* The Lion and the Lamb, 1996. *Recreations:* ski-ing, teaching boys to play polo, 17th Century history. *Address:* Hoyle Farm, Heyshott, Midhurst, West Sussex GU29 0DY. *T:* (01798) 867230. *Clubs:* Travellers, Beefsteak, Shikar, MCC.

BAIN, Andrew David, OBE 1997; FRSE 1980; Visiting Professor of Political Economy, University of Glasgow, 1991–98; *b* 21 March 1936; *s* of Hugh Bain and Kathleen (*née* Eadie); *m* 1st, 1960, Anneliese Minna Frieda Kroggel (marr. diss. 1988); three *s*; 2nd, 1989, Eleanor Riches. *Educ:* Glasgow Academy; Christ's Coll., Cambridge; PhD Cantab 1963. Junior Res. Officer, Dept of Applied Econs, Cambridge Univ., 1958–60; Res. Fellow, Christ's Coll., Cambridge, 1960; Instructor, Cowles Foundn, Yale Univ., 1960–61; Lectr, Cambridge, 1961–66; Fellow, Corpus Christi Coll., Cambridge, 1962; on secondment to Bank of England, 1965–67; Prof. of Econs, 1967–70, Esmee Fairbairn Prof. of Econs of Finance and Investment, 1970–77, Univ. of Stirling; Walton Prof. of Monetary and Financial Econs, Univ. of Strathclyde, 1977–84; Gp Econ. Advr, Midland Bank, 1984–90. Member: Cttee to Review the Functioning of Financial Institutions, 1977–80; (part-time) Monopolies and Mergers Commn, 1981–82; TEC Nat. Council, 1994–97; (part-time) Appeal Panel, Competition Commn, 2000–03; Competition Appeal Tribunal, 2003–. Bd Mem., Scottish Enterprise, 1991–98. *Publications:* The Growth of Television Ownership in the United Kingdom (monograph), 1964; The Control of the Money Supply, 1970; Company Financing in the UK, 1975; The Economics of the Financial System, 1981, 2nd edn 1992; articles on demand analysis, monetary policy and other subjects.

See also Colin D. Bain.

BAIN, Christopher Derek; Director, Catholic Agency for Overseas Development, since 2003; *b* 27 Nov. 1953; *s* of Derek Bain and Mary Bain (*née* Hill). *Educ:* Leicester Univ. (BA); Middlesex Univ. (MBA); Open Univ. (MSc Develt Mgt). VSO develt worker, Fiji, 1975–77; VSO Field Officer, S Pacific, 1977–79; Dir, Churches' Housing Trust, Fiji, 1979–82; London Area Coordinator, Christian Aid, 1982–89; Oxfam: Sen. Campaigns Advr, 1989–93; Hd of Campaigns, 1993–96; Hd of Progs, VSO, 1996–2003. Hon. Dir, Disaster Emergency Cttee, 2003–; Chm., British Overseas Aid Gp, 2005–. *Recreations:* long distance pilgrimages, ale and malt whiskey appreciation, friends. *Address:* 4 Penton Place, SE17 3JT. *T:* (020) 7735 7500; *e-mail:* cdb@cafod.org.uk.

BAIN, Prof. Colin David, PhD; Professor of Chemistry, since 2005, Director, Institute for Advanced Studies, since 2008, University of Durham; *b* 2 Jan. 1963; *s* of Andrew David Bain, *qv; m* 1992, Emma Victoria Claudia Kauffmann; one *s* two *d*. *Educ:* Dollar Acad.; Corpus Christi Coll., Cambridge (BA 1983); Harvard Univ. (PhD 1989). Mr & Mrs John

Jaffe Res. Fellow, Univ. of Cambridge, and Fellow, Christ's Coll., Cambridge, 1988–91; Univ. Lectr, Univ. of Oxford, 1991–2005; Fellow, Magdalen Coll., Oxford, 1991–2005, Emeritus, 2005–. Director: Magdalen Develt Co. Ltd, 1998–2005; GTE for Oxfordshire Ltd, 1999–2004; Member, Scientific Advisory Board: Oxford Capital Partners, 2005–; Max Planck Institute for Colloid and Interface Research, 2007–. Mem., Faraday Council, RSC, 2006–08. *Publications:* approx. 100 book chapters and articles in learned jls. *Recreations:* hill-walking, cycling, sailing. *Address:* Department of Chemistry, Durham University, South Road, Durham DH1 3LE. *T:* (0191) 334 2138, *Fax:* (0191) 334 2051; *e-mail:* c.d.bain@dur.ac.uk.

BAIN, Douglas John; Industrial Adviser to the Secretary of State for Scotland, 1983–85; *b* 9 July 1924; *s* of Alexander Gillan Bain and Fanny Heaford; *m* 1946, Jean Wallace Fairbairn; three *d. Educ:* Pollokshields Secondary School; Royal Technical Coll. (now Strathclyde Univ.), Glasgow (DRTC). ATI. Royal Tech. Coll., 1941–43 and 1948–51. RAF, 1943–48. J. & P. Coats Ltd, 1951–83: graduate trainee, 1951–55; overseas management, 1955–60; central management, 1960–68; Director, 1968–83; seconded to Scottish Office (Scottish Econ. Planning Dept) as Under Sec., 1979–82. *Recreations:* golf, walking, geology, flying. *Address:* 49 Bimbadeen Crescent, Yallambie, Melbourne, Vic 3085, Australia.

BAIN, Prof. Sir George (Sayers), Kt 2001; DPhil; President and Vice-Chancellor, Queen's University Belfast, 1998–2004, now Professor Emeritus; *b* 24 Feb. 1939; *s* of George Alexander Bain and Margaret Ioleen Bamford; *m* 1st, 1962, Carol Lynn Ogden White (marr. diss. 1987); one *s* one *d*; 2nd, 1988, Frances Gwynneth Rigby (*née* Vickers). *Educ:* Univ. of Manitoba (BA Hons 1961, MA 1964); Oxford Univ. (DPhil 1968). Lectr in Econs, Univ. of Manitoba, 1962–63; Res. Fellow, Nuffield Coll., Oxford, 1966–69; Frank Thomas Prof. of Indust. Relations, UMIST, 1969–70; University of Warwick: Dep. Dir, 1970–74, Dir, 1974–81, SSRC Industrial Relations Res. Unit; Pressed Steel Fisher Prof. of Industrial Relations, 1979–89; Chm., Sch. of Industrial and Business Studies, 1983–89; Principal, London Business Sch., 1989–97. Sec., British Univs Indust. Relations Assoc., 1971–74. Member: Mech. Engrg Econ. Develt Cttee, NEDO, 1974–76; Cttee of Inquiry on Indust. Democracy, Dept of Trade (Chm., Lord Bullock), 1975–76; Council: ESRC, 1986–91; Nat. Forum for Management Educn and Develt, 1987–90; Chm. Council, Univ. Management Schs, 1987–90. Member: Bd of Trustees, 1990–96, and Exec. Vice-Pres., 1991–95, European Foundn for Management Develt; Internat. Affairs Cttee, 1990–92, Bd of Dirs, 1992–94, Amer. Assembly of Collegiate Schs of Business; Council, Foundn for Mgt Educn, 1991–95; Council, IMgt (formerly BIM), 1991–93; Senior Salaries Review Body, 1993–96; Internat. Council, Amer. Mgt Assoc., 1993–95; Foundn for Canadian Studies in UK, 1993–2001, 2004–06; Exec. Cttee, Co-operation Ireland GB, 1994–97 (Dep. Chm., 1996–97); Bd of Dirs, Grad. Mgt Admission Council, 1996–97; Bd of Co-operation Ireland, 1998–2004; Educn Honours Cttee, 2005–; Trustee: Navan at Armagh, 1999–2003; Scotch-Irish Trust, 1999–2007; Council for Advancement and Support of Educn, (CASE), 2004–08; CASE Europe, 2004–07. Chairman: Food Sector Wkg Gp, NEDO, 1991–92; Commn on Public Policy and British Business, 1995–97; Low Pay Commn, 1997–2002; NI Meml Fund, 1998–2002; Conf. of Univ. Rectors in Ireland, 2000–01; Work and Parents Task Force, DTI, 2001; Pensions Policy Inst., 2002–04; Indep. Review of Fire Service, ODPM, 2002; ACU, 2002–03; NI Legal Services Review Gp, 2005–06; Advr on Royal Mail to Sec. of State for Trade and Industry, 2005–06; NI Independent Strategic Review of Educn, 2006; NI Rev. on Location of Public Sector Jobs, 2007–08. Pres., Involvement and Participation Assoc., 2002–06. Director: Blackwell Publishers Ltd (formerly Basil Blackwell Ltd), 1990–97; The Economist Gp, 1992–2001; Canada Life Gp (UK) Ltd, 1994–; Canada Life Assce Co., 1996–2003; Electra Private Equity (formerly Electra Investment Trust PLC), 1998–2008; Bombardier Aerospace Shorts Brothers Plc, 1998–2007; NI Sci. Park Foundn, 1999–2004; NI Adv. Bd, Bank of Ireland, 2000–02; Canada Life Capital Corp., 2003–; Iain More Associates, 2004–07; Entertainment One, 2007–. Consultant: Royal Commn on Trade Unions and Employers' Assocs (Donovan Commn), 1966–67; NBPI, 1967–69; Canadian Task Force on Labour Relns, 1968; Dept of Employment; Manitoba and Canada Depts of Labour; arbitrator and mediator in indust. disputes. Vice-Chm., Bd and Chm., Develt Trust, Lyric Theatre, Belfast, 2006–. Patron, Somme Assoc., 2004–. FRSA 1987; CCMI (CIMgt 1991); Companion, Assoc. Business Schs, 2007; Fellow: British Acad. of Mgt, 1994; London Business Sch., 1999. AcSS 2000. Hon. Fellow, Nuffield Coll., Oxford, 2002. Hon. DBA De Montfort, 1994; Hon. LLD: NUI, 1998; Guelph, UC of Cape Breton, 1999; Manitoba, Warwick, 2003; Queen's, Canada, 2004; QUB, 2005; Hon. DLitt: Ulster, 2002; New Brunswick, 2003; Hon. DSc Cranfield, 2005. *Publications:* Trade Union Growth and Recognition, 1967; The Growth of White-Collar Unionism, 1970; (jtly) The Reform of Collective Bargaining at Plant and Company Level, 1971; (jtly) Social Stratification and Trade Unionism, 1973; (jtly) Union Growth and the Business Cycle, 1976; (jtly) A Bibliography of British Industrial Relations, 1979; (jtly) Profiles of Union Growth, 1980; (ed) Industrial Relations in Britain, 1983; (jtly) A Bibliography of British Industrial Relations 1971–1979, 1985; contrib. prof. and learned jls. *Recreations:* reading, genealogy, piano playing, Western riding. *Address:* Vice-Chancellor's Office, Queen's University Belfast, University Road, Belfast BT7 1NN. *Club:* Reform.

BAIN, Iain Andrew; Editor, Nairnshire Telegraph, since 1987; *b* 25 Feb. 1949; *s* of Alastair I. R. Bain and late Jean R. Forrest; *m* 1974, Maureen Beattie; three *d. Educ:* Nairn Acad.; Univ. of Aberdeen (MA). Research, Univ. of Durham, 1971–74; Sub-editor, 1974, Asst Editor, 1980, Editor, 1981–87, The Geographical Magazine. Chm. Trustees, Nairn Mus., 1998–; Pres., Nairn Lit. Inst., 2002–05. *Publications:* Mountains and People, 1982; Water on the Land, 1983; Mountains and Earth Movements, 1984; various articles. *Recreations:* reading, walking, photography. *Address:* Rosebank, Leopold Street, Nairn IV12 4BE. *Club:* Nairn Golf.

BAIN, Janet; *see* Rossant, J.

BAIN, John; *see* Bain, K. J.

BAIN, Ven. (John) Stuart; Archdeacon of Sunderland, since 2002; Priest in charge, Parish of Hedworth, since 2003 (Assistant Priest, 2002–03); *b* 12 Oct. 1955; *s* of John and Doris Bain; *m* 1978, Angela Forster; two *s* one *d. Educ:* Van Mildert Coll., Univ. of Durham (BA Theol. 1977); Westcott House, Cambridge. Ordained deacon, 1980, priest, 1981; Assistant Curate: Holy Trinity, Washington, 1980–84; St Nicholas, Dunston, 1984–86; Vicar, Shiney Row and Herrington, 1986–92; Priest-in-charge: Whitworth and Spennymoor, 1992–97; Merrington, 1994–97; Vicar, Spennymoor, Whitworth and Merrington, 1997–2002. Area Dean, Auckland, 1996–2002; Hon. Canon, 1998–2002, (supernumerary) Non-Residentiary Canon, 2002–, Durham Cathedral. Chm., DFW Adoption (formerly Durham Family Welfare), 1999–. *Recreations:* music (very eclectic tastes), cycling, cooking, enjoying good wines, surfing the net, enjoying mountains. *Address:* St Nicholas' Vicarage, Hedworth Lane, Boldon Colliery NE35 9JA. *T:* (0191) 536 2300, *Fax:* (0191) 519 3369; *e-mail:* Archdeacon.of.Sunderland@durham.anglican.org.

BAIN, (Kenneth) John, OBE 2000; MA; Headmaster, The Purcell School, 1983–99; *b* 8 July 1939; *s* of Allan John and Hetty Bain; *m* 1962, Cynthia Mary Spain; one *s* one *d. Educ:* Bancroft's School; St Peter's College, Oxford (MA). Assistant Master, Stanbridge Earls School, 1962–70; Assistant Master and Housemaster, Cranleigh School, 1970–83. Gov., Arts Educnl Sch., Tring, 1999–2002. Dir, Endymion Ensemble, 1999–2003. Hon. RCM 1999. *Publications:* occasional articles in educational jls. *Recreations:* Spanish language and culture, music, golf, walking, rough gardening. *Address:* Candida House, Whitechurch Canonicorum, Bridport, Dorset DT6 6RQ. *T:* (01297) 489629.

BAIN, Neville Clifford, FCA, FCIS; Chairman, Hogg Robinson plc, 1997–2007; Chairman, Institute of Directors, since 2006; *b* 14 July 1940; *s* of Charles Alexander Bain and Gertrude Mae Bain; *m* 1987, Anne Patricia (*née* Kemp); one step *d*, and one *s* one *d* by previous marriage. *Educ:* King's High Sch., Dunedin, NZ; Otago Univ., Dunedin (BCom Acctcy 1964; BCom Econ 1966; MCom Hons 1968). CMA; ACA 1959, FCA 1989; FCIS 1962. Trainee Inspector, Inland Revenue, NZ, 1957–59; Manager, Anderson & Co., Chartered Accountants, NZ, 1960–62; Cadbury Schweppes Hudson: Cost Accountant, subseq. Financial Controller, and Co. Sec., NZ, 1963–68; Finance Dir, NZ, 1968–75; Cadbury Schweppes: Group Chief Exec., S Africa, 1975–80; Group Strategic Planning Dir, 1980–83 (apptd to Main Bd, 1981); Managing Director: Cadbury Ltd, 1983–86; Cadbury World Wide, 1986–89; Dep. Group Chief Exec. and Finance Dir, Cadbury Schweppes Plc, 1989–90; Gp Chief Exec., Coats Viyella PLC, 1990–97; Chm., Post Office, then Consignia, 1997–2001. Chairman: SHL Gp, 1998–2003 (non-exec. Dir, 1997–2003); Gartmore Split Capital Opportunities Trust, 1999–2001; Hogg Robinson Pension Fund, 2000–; Scottish Newcastle Pension Trustees, 2007–; Director: London Internat. Gp, 1988–93; Gartmore Scotland Investment Trust, 1992–2001; Safeway plc (formerly Argyll Group), 1993–2000; Scottish & Newcastle, 1997–; non-executive Director: Biocon Ltd, 2000–; Provexis Ltd, 2003–. FInstD 1995 (Councillor, 1997–; Chm., Audit Cttee, 1999–). Hon. LLD Otago, NZ, 1993. *Publications:* Successful Management, 1995; (with D. Band) Winning Ways through Corporate Governance, 1996; (with Bill Mabey) The People Advantage, 1999; The Effective Director, 2009. *Recreations:* sport, walking, music. *Address:* Institute of Directors, 116 Pall Mall, SW1Y 5ED. *T:* (020) 7451 3120.

BAIN, Ven. Stuart; *see* Bain, Ven. J. S.

BAINBRIDGE, Dame Beryl, DBE 2000; FRSL; actress, writer; *b* 21 Nov. 1934; *d* of Richard Bainbridge and Winifred Baines; *m* 1954, Austin Davies (marr. diss.); one *s* one *d*; and one *d* by Alan Sharp. *Educ:* Merchant Taylors' Sch., Liverpool; Arts Educational Schools, Ltd, Tring. Weekly columnist, Evening Standard, 1987–93. FRSL 1978; Fellow, Hunterian Soc., 1997. Hon. LittD Liverpool, 1986. (Jtly) David Cohen Prize, Arts Council, 2003. *Plays:* Tiptoe Through the Tulips, 1976; The Warrior's Return, 1977; Its a Lovely Day Tomorrow, 1977; Journal of Bridget Hitler, 1981; Somewhere More Central (TV), 1981; Evensong (TV), 1986. *Publications:* A Weekend with Claud, 1967, rev. edn 1981; Another Part of the Wood, 1968, rev. edn 1979; Harriet Said…, 1972; The Dressmaker, 1973 (film, 1989); The Bottle Factory Outing, 1974 (Guardian Fiction Award); Sweet William, 1975 (film, 1980); A Quiet Life, 1976, repr. 1999; Injury Time, 1977 (Whitbread Award); Young Adolf, 1978; Winter Garden, 1980; English Journey, 1984 (TV series, 1984); Watson's Apology, 1984; Mum and Mr Armitage, 1985; Forever England, 1986 (TV series, 1986); Filthy Lucre, 1986; An Awfully Big Adventure, 1989 (staged, 1992; filmed, 1995); The Birthday Boys, 1991; Something Happened Yesterday (essays), 1993; Every Man for Himself, 1996 (Whitbread Award); Master Georgie, 1998 (James Tait Black Meml Prize, W. H. Smith Award); According to Queeney, 2001; Front Row, 2005. *Recreations:* painting, sleeping. *Address:* 42 Albert Street, NW1 7NU. *T:* (020) 7387 3113.

BAINBRIDGE, Cyril, FCIJ; author and journalist; *b* 15 Nov. 1928; *o s* of late Arthur Herman and Edith Bainbridge; *m* 1953, Barbara Hannah (*née* Crook); one *s* two *d. Educ:* privately (Negus Coll., Bradford). Served Army, staff of CGS, WO, 1947–49. Entered journalism as Reporter, Bingley Guardian, 1944–45; Telegraph and Argus, and Yorkshire Observer, Bradford, 1945–54; Press Assoc., 1954–63; joined The Times, 1963: Asst News Editor, 1967; Dep. News Editor, 1967–69; Regional News Editor, 1969–77; Managing News Editor, 1977–82; Asst Managing Editor, 1982–86; Editorial Data Manager, Times Newspapers, 1986–88. Vice-Pres., 1977–78, Pres., 1978–79, Fellow, 1986, Chartered Inst. of Journalists; Member: Press Council, 1980–90; Nat. Council for Trng of Journalists, 1983–86. *Publications:* Taught With Care: a Century of Church Schooling, 1974; The Brontës and their Country, 1978, 3rd edn 1993; Brass Triumphant, 1980; North Yorkshire and North Humberside, 1984, 2nd edn 1989; (ed) One Hundred Years of Journalism, 1984; Pavilions on the Sea, 1986; (jtly) The News of the World Story, 1993; contrib. to various magazines. *Recreations:* reading, brass bands, water colour painting. *Address:* 6 Lea Road, Hemingford Grey, Huntingdon, Cambs PE28 9ED.

BAINBRIDGE, Prof. Janet Mary, OBE 2000; PhD; Global Research and Development Specialist, UK Trade and Investment, since 2007; Chief Executive, European Process Industries Competitiveness Centre, 2001–04; *b* 14 April 1947; *d* of Henry George Munn and Vera Doreen Munn; *m* 1st, 1970, Geoffrey Stathers Tuffnell (marr. diss. 1985); 2nd, 1987, Dr George Bainbridge; one *s* one *d. Educ:* Gravesend Girls' Grammar Sch.; Univ. of Newcastle upon Tyne (BSc Hons); Univ. of Leeds (PGCE); Univ. of Durham (PhD 1986). Microbiol. Res., Head Office, J. Sainsbury Ltd, 1968–70; NHS, 1970–71; secondary teaching, 1971–72; lectr, further educn, 1972–80; Teesside Polytechnic, then University: Lectr, then Sen. Lectr, 1980–85; Prin. Lectr, 1985–92; Divl Leader, 1992–98; Prof., 1996–2007, now Emeritus; Dir, Sch. of Sci. and Technol., 1998–2002; Tutor Counsellor, Sci. Foundn Degree, 1989–99, and Tutor, genetics, 1990–92, Open Univ. Sen. Specialist Advr (Govt and Europe), One Northeast, 2004–07. Mem., EPSRC, 2000–; Chair: Govt Adv. Cttee on novel foods and processes, 1997–2003; Scientific Adv. Cttee on Genetic Manipulation (Contained Use), 2004–; Mem. Council, British Potato Council, 2003– (Chair, R&D Cttee, 2003–); mem., other expert cttees and foresight panels. MSOFHT 1994; MILT 2000; FRSA 1998. *Publications:* numerous contribs to learned jls; expert papers for parly cttees, enquiries, etc. *Recreations:* family, gardening, travel.

BAINBRIDGE, Prof. Simon; freelance composer, conductor and lecturer; Professor and Head of Composition, Royal Academy of Music, University of London, 2001–07 (Senior Lecturer, 1999–2001 and since 2007); *b* 30 Aug. 1952; *s* of John Bainbridge and Nan Knowles; *m* 1997, Lynda Richardson; one *d. Educ:* Central Tutorial Sch. for Young Musicians; Highgate Sch.; Royal Coll. of Music. Freelance composer, 1973–; Margaret Lee Crofts Fellowship (studying with Gunther Schuller), Berkshire Music Center, Tanglewood, USA, 1973; Leonard Bernstein Fellowship, 1974; Forman Fellow in Composition, Edinburgh Univ., 1976–78; US-UK Bicentennial Fellowship, 1978–79; Music Dir, Royal Nat. Theatre, 1980–82; Composer in residence, Southern Arts, 1982–86; Professor of Composition: RCM, 1989–99; GSMD, 1991–99; Composer in residence, Univ. of Wales Coll. of Cardiff, 1993–94. Hon. RAM 2002. Gemini Prize in Composition, Musicians' Co., 1988. *Compositions include:* Viola Concerto, 1978; Fantasia for Double Orchestra, 1984; Ad ora Incerta: four orchestral songs from Primo Levi, 1994 (Grawemeyer Award for Music Composition, Univ. of Louisville, 1997); Landscape and Memory, 1995; Four Primo Levi settings, 1996; (for orchestra) Diptych, 2007; Music Space Reflection, 2007. *Recreations:* films, reading, cooking, swimming, walking. *Address:* c/o Novello & Co. (Music Sales Ltd), 14–15 Berners Street, W1T 3LJ. *Club:* Royal Over-Seas League.

BAINES, (John) Christopher; independent environmental consultant; Director, Baines Environmental Ltd, since 1979; *b* Sheffield, S Yorks, 4 May 1947; *s* of Stuart and Winifred Baines; partner, 1988, Nerys Jones. *Educ:* Ecclesfield Grammar Sch.; Wye Coll., Univ. of London (BSc Hons Horticulture); City of Birmingham Poly. (Postgrad. Dip. Landscape Architecture). MInstBiol 1979. Landscape architect, Blakedown Landscapes Ltd, 1969–74; Sen. Lectr in Landscape Design and Mgt, City of Birmingham Poly., 1974–88; Partner, Landscape Design Gp, 1974–79. Presenter, TV progs incl. The Wild Side of Town, The ARK, Pebble Mill at One, Countryfile, Saturday Starship, The Big E, That's Gardening, throughout 1980s. Hon. Prof., UCE, 1986. Member: Rural Affairs Adv. Bd, 1998–2001, Breathing Places Adv. Bd, 2006–, BBC; Adv. Gp, CABE Space, 2004–; Urban Regeneration Panel, City of Bath, 2004–; Expert Panel, Heritage Lottery Fund, 2005–; Indep. Envmtl Rev. Panel, Stratford City and 2012 Olympic Village, 2007–; Chm., indep. design panel, Barking Riverside, London, 2007–. Nat. Vice Pres., Royal Soc. for Nature Conservation, 1997–. Hon. President: Assoc. for Envmt-Conscious Bldg, 1994–; Wildside Centre, Wolverhampton, 1997–; Urban Wildlife Partnership, 2000–; Thames Estuary Partnership, 2001–; Essex Wildlife Trust, 2004–; Hon. Vice President: Wildlife Trust for Brimingham and the Black Country, 1990–; Bankside Open Spaces Trust, 1999–. Trustee, Nat. Heritage Meml Fund, 1998–2004. Patron, Landscape Design Trust, 2001–. FRSA. Hon. FCIWEM 2000. Hon. Dr Envmtl Mgt Sheffield Hallam, 1998. Medal of Honour, RSPB, 2004. *Publications:* How to Make a Wildlife Garden, 1985, 2nd edn 2000; The Wild Side of Town, 1987 (Nat. Conservation Book Prize, Royal Soc. of Wildlife Trusts, 1987); A Guide to Habitat Creation, 1988, 2nd edn 1992; *for children:* The Old Boot, The Nest, The Flower, The Picnic, 1996, 2nd edn 2002. *Recreations:* cooking, gardening, walking, nature conservation, watercolour painting, ski-ing. *Address:* Baines Environmental Ltd, PO Box 35, Wolverhampton WV1 4XJ. *T:* (01902) 424820; *e-mail:* chris.baines@blueyonder.co.uk.

BAINES, Prof. John Robert, MA, DPhil; Professor of Egyptology, Oxford University and Fellow of Queen's College, Oxford, since 1976; *b* 17 March 1946; *o s* of late Edward Russell Baines and of Dora Margaret Jean (*née* O'Brien); *m* 1971, Jennifer Christine Ann, *e d* of S. T. Smith; one *s* one *d*. *Educ:* Winchester Coll.; New Coll., Linacre Coll., Worcester Coll., Oxford (BA 1967, MA, DPhil 1976). Lectr in Egyptology, Univ. of Durham, 1970–75; Laycock Student, Worcester Coll., Oxford, 1973–75. Visiting Professor: Univ. of Arizona, 1982, 1988; Univ. of Michigan, 1989; Ecole Pratique des Hautes Etudes, Paris, 1994, 2003; Harvard Univ., 1995–96, 1999–2000; Univ. of Basel, 2003; Dist. Vis. Prof., Amer. Univ., Cairo, 1999; Freehling Prof., Univ. of Michigan, 2002–03; Fellow, Humboldt-Stiftung, 1982, 1989, 1996. Corresp. Mem., German Archaeol Inst., 1999. *Publications:* (trans. and ed) H. Schäfer, Principles of Egyptian Art, 1974, rev. edn 1986; (with J. Malek) Atlas of Ancient Egypt, 1980 (trans. 11 langs), 2nd edn as Cultural Atlas of Ancient Egypt, 2000; (trans. and ed) E. Hornung, Conceptions of God in Ancient Egypt, 1982; Fecundity Figures, 1985; (ed jtly) Pyramid Studies and Other Essays presented to I. E. S. Edwards, 1988; (jtly) Religion in Ancient Egypt (ed B. Shafer), 1991; (ed) Stone Vessels, Pottery and Sealings from the Tomb of Tut'ankhamūn, 1993; (ed jtly) Civilizations of the Ancient Near East, 4 vols, 1995; (contrib.) Ancient Egyptian Kingship, 1995; Die Bedeutung des Reisens im alten Ägypten, 2004; Visual and Written Culture in Ancient Egypt, 2007; articles in collections and in Acta Orientalia, American Anthropologist, Art History, Encyclopaedia Britannica, Jl Egypt. Archaeol., Man, Orientalia, Studien altägypt. Kultur, etc. *Address:* Oriental Institute, Pusey Lane, Oxford OX1 2LE.
See also P. J. Baines.

BAINES, Rt Rev. Nicholas; *see* Croydon, Area Bishop of.

BAINES, Priscilla Jean, CB 2004; Librarian, House of Commons, 2000–04; *b* 5 Oct. 1942; *d* of late Edward Russell Baines and of (Dora Margaret) Jean Baines (*née* O'Brien). *Educ:* Tonbridge Girls' Grammar Sch.; Somerville Coll., Oxford (BA Agric. 1963; MA 1967); Linacre Coll., Oxford (BLitt 1969). Adminr, Chelsea Coll., Univ. of London, 1965–68; House of Commons: Library Clerk, 1968–77; Head: Economic Affairs Section, 1977–88; Science and Envmt Section, 1988–91; Parly Div., 1991–93; Dep. Librarian and Dir of Human Resources, 1993–99. Associate, Hist. of Parlt, 2005–. *Publications:* (contrib.) New Select Committees, 1985, (contrib.) Westminster and Europe, 1996, 2004, and other pubns of Study of Parlt Gp. *Recreations:* food, travel, opera. *Address:* 11 Ravensdon Street, SE11 4AQ.
See also J. R. Baines.

BAINS, Lawrence Arthur, CBE 1983; DL; formerly Director: Bains Brothers Ltd; Crowland Leasings Ltd; Bains Finance Management Ltd; *b* 11 May 1920; *s* of late Arthur Bains and Mabel (*née* Payn); *m* 1954, Margaret, *d* of late Sir William and Lady Grimshaw; two *s* one *d*. *Educ:* Stationers' Company's School. Served War, 1939–46: Middlesex Yeomanry, 1939; N Africa, 1940; POW, 1942, escaped Italy, 1943. Hornsey Borough Council: Mem., 1949–65; Dep. Leader, 1958–64; Mayor, 1964–65; Council, London Borough of Haringey: Mem., 1964–74; Finance Chm., 1968–71; Greater London Council: Chm., 1977–78; Mem. for Hornsey/Haringey, 1967–81; Chm., South Area Planning Bd, 1970–73; Dep. Leader, Housing Policy Cttee, 1979–81; Chm., GLC/Tower Hamlets Jt Housing Management Cttee, 1979–81; Mem., Lee Valley Regional Park Authority, 1968–81 (Chm., 1980–81); Chm., Haringey DHA, 1982–93. Chm., N London Coll. of Health Studies, 1991–95. Trustee, Help the Homeless, 1979–. Liveryman, Basketmakers' Co., 1978– (Mem., Ct of Assts, 1995–). DL Greater London, 1978 (Rep. DL for Borough of Barnet, 1983–95). Officer, Order of St Lazarus of Jerusalem. *Recreation:* being a grandfather. *Address:* 12 Abbotts Road, New Barnet EN5 5DP. *T:* (020) 8440 3499.

BAIRD, Sir Andrew; *see* Baird, Sir J. A. G.

BAIRD, Anthony; *see* Baird, E. A. B.

BAIRD, Charles Fitz; Chairman and Chief Executive Officer, Inco Ltd, 1980–87, retired; *b* 4 Sept. 1922; *s* of George White and Julia (Fitz) Baird; *m* 1947, Norma Adele White; two *s* two *d*. *Educ:* Middlebury Coll. (BA); New York Univ. (Grad. Sch. of Bus. Admin); Harvard Univ. (Advanced Management Program). US Marine Corps, 1943–46, 1951–52 (Capt.). Standard Oil Co. (NJ), now Exxon, 1948–65: Dep. European Financial Rep., London, 1955–58; Asst Treas., 1958–62; Dir, Esso Standard SA Française, 1962–65; Asst Sec., Financial Man., US Navy, 1965–67, Under Secretary, 1967–69; Internat. Nickel Co. of Canada Ltd (Inco Ltd): Vice Pres. Finance, 1969–72, Sen. Vice Pres., 1972–76; Dir, 1974–93; Vice Chm., 1976–77; Pres., 1977–80. Director: Bank of Montreal, 1975–93; Aetna Life and Casualty Co., 1982–93. Nat. Advr, Council on Oceans and Atmosphere, 1972–74; Member: Presidential Commn on Marine Sci. Engrg and Resources, 1967–69; Council on Foreign Relations. Mem., Bd of Trustees, Bucknell Univ., 1969–95 (Chm., 1976–82); Trustee, Center for Naval Analyses, 1990–2002 (Chm., 1992–97). Hon. LLD Bucknell Univ. 1976. US Navy Distinguished Civilian Service Award, 1969. *Recreations:* tennis, platform tennis, golf. *Clubs:* Chevy Chase (Washington, DC); Maidstone (E Hampton, NY); Bridgehampton (NY).

BAIRD, Sir Charles William Stuart, 6th Bt *cr* 1809, of Newbyth, Haddingtonshire; *b* 8 June 1939; *s* of Robert William Stuart Baird and Maxine Christine, *o c* of Rupert Darrell, NY; *S* uncle, 2000; *m* 1965, Jane Joanna, *e d* of late Brig. A. Darley Bridge; three *d*. *Educ:* Switzerland. *Heir: kinsman* Andrew James Baird, *b* 23 Oct. 1970. *Address:* 12 Falstaff Street, Sunnybank Hills, Brisbane, Qld 4109, Australia.

BAIRD, Prof. David Tennent, CBE 2000; FRCP, FRCOG, FMedSci; Medical Research Council Clinical Research Professor of Reproductive Endocrinology, Edinburgh University, 1985–2000, now Emeritus; *b* 13 March 1935; *s* of Sir Dugald Baird, MD, FRCOG and Lady (May) Baird (*née* Tennent), CBE; *m* 1st, 1965, Frances Diana Lichtveld (marr. diss. 1995); two *s*; 2nd, 2000, Anna Frances Glasier. *Educ:* Aberdeen Grammar Sch., Aberdeen Univ.; Trinity Coll., Cambridge (BA); Edinburgh Univ. (MB, ChB; DSc). Junior med. posts, Royal Infirmary, Edinburgh, 1959–65; MRC Travelling Research Fellow, Worcester Foundn of Experimental Biology, USA, 1965–68; Lectr, later Sen. Lectr, Dept of Obstetrics, Univ. of Edinburgh, 1968–72; Dep. Dir, MRC Unit of Reproductive Biology, Edinburgh, 1972–77; Prof. of Obst. and Gyn., Univ. of Edinburgh, 1977–85. Consultant Gynaecologist, Royal Infirmary, Edinburgh, 1970–2000. FRSE 1990. Founder FMedSci 1998. Hon. MD Nottingham, 2002. *Publications:* Mechanism of Menstrual Bleeding, 1985; contribs in med. and sci. jls on reproductive endocrinology and contraception. *Recreations:* ski mountaineering, golf. *Address:* 22 India Street, Edinburgh EH3 6HB. *T:* (0131) 225 3962.

BAIRD, (Eric) Anthony (Bamber); Director, Institute for Complementary Medicine, 1980–2002; *b* 11 Dec. 1920; *s* of Oswald Baird and Marion Bamber; *m* 1st, 1952, Margareta Toss (marr. diss. 1957); 2nd, 1959, Inger Bohman (marr. diss. 1977); two *d*. *Educ:* LSE (BScEcon). Served RA, 1941–46. Swedish Broadcasting Corp., 1950–65; Public Relations Ltd, 1965–72; Civil Service, 1973–78; Inst. for Complementary Medicine, 1979–2002. Chm., British Council of Complementary Medicine, 1997–2002. FRSA 1992; FRSocMed 1999. *Publications:* Notes on Canada, 1962; (jtly) The Charm of Sweden, 1962. *Recreations:* writing children's stories, gardening. *Address:* 24 Backwoods Lane, Lindfield, Haywards Heath, West Sussex RH16 2ED. *T:* (01444) 482018. *Club:* Reform.

BAIRD, Guy Martin, FCA; Senior Adviser, European Investment Bank, Brussels, 2001–06; *b* 3 Jan. 1948; *s* of late Thomas Herbert Mertens Baird and Kathleen Florence Baird (*née* Mapley, later Ballard); *m* 1969, Juliet Hope Mears (marr. diss. 1984); two *d*. *Educ:* Wellington College. ACA 1970, FCA 1975. Bland Fielden & Co., 1966–69; Cooper Brothers & Co., subseq. Coopers & Lybrand, 1970–72; Manager, Fidital, Coopers & Lybrand SpA, Rome, 1972–74; Vice Pres. Finance, Italicor Inc., Atlanta and Milan, 1975–77; Manager, Andrew Moore & Co., 1978–79; Sen. Loan Officer, Luxembourg, 1980–83, Head of London Office, 1983–2001, EIB. Mem., Rolls-Royce Enthusiasts' Club, 2006–. *Recreations:* riding, sailing, Wagner. *Club:* East India.

BAIRD, Sir (James) Andrew (Gardiner), 11th Bt *cr* 1695 (NS), of Saughton Hall, Edinburgh; *b* 2 May 1946; *s* of Sir James Baird, 10th Bt, MC and of Mabel Ann, (Gay), *d* of A. Gill; *S* father, 1997, but his name does not appear on the Official Roll of the Baronetage; *m* 1984, Jean Margaret (marr. diss. 1988), *yr d* of Brig. Sir Ian Jardine, 4th Bt, OBE, MC; one *s*. *Educ:* Eton. *Heir: s* Alexander William Gardiner Baird, *b* 28 May 1986.

BAIRD, James Hewson; Chief Executive and Company Secretary, British Veterinary Association, 1987–2002; *b* 28 March 1944; *s* of James Baird, MBE, MRCVS and Ann Sarah Baird (*née* Hewson); *m* 1969, Clare Rosalind (*née* Langstaff); three *d*. *Educ:* Austin Friars; Creighton, Carlisle; Newcastle upon Tyne Univ. (BSc Hons Agric). Hydrologist, Essex River Authy, 1968–75; Policy Officer, Nat. Water Council, 1975–80. Institution of Civil Engineers: Asst Dir, 1980–81; Dir of Admin., 1981–86; Mem., Infrastructure Planning Gp, 1982–86; Dir, Assoc. of Municipal Engineers, 1984–86; Dir, External Affairs, Fedn of Civil Engineering Contractors, 1986–87. *Recreations:* Rugby, gardening, farming, countryside. *Address:* Bowered Green Cottage, Church Street, Boxted, Colchester CO4 5SY. *Club:* Farmers'.

BAIRD, Air Marshal Sir John (Alexander), KBE 1999; DL; Surgeon General to the Armed Forces, 1997–2000; *b* 25 July 1937; *s* of late Dr David Alexander Baird, CBE and Isobel T. Baird; *m* 1963, Mary Clews. *Educ:* Merchiston Castle Sch.; Edinburgh Univ. (MB ChB). FFOM; FRCPE 1998; FRCSE 1999; DAvMed; FRAeS. Western Gen. Hosp., Edinburgh, 1961–62; MO Sarawak, 1962–63; commnd RAF, 1963; RAF Stations, UK and Singapore, 1963–80; exchange post, USA, 1970–73; HQ Strike Comd, 1980–83; MoD, 1983–86; OC Princess of Wales RAF Hosp., Ely, 1987–88; PMO, RAF Germany, 1988–91; PMO, HQ RAF Strike Comd, 1991–94; Dir Gen., RAF Med. Services, 1994–97. QHP 1991–2000. Mem., Internat. Acad. of Aviation and Space Medicine, 1993. FRSocMed 1983; Fellow: Aerospace Med. Assoc., 1992; Assoc. of Med. Secs, 2001. DL Cambs, 1998. CStJ 1997. *Publications:* contribs to med. jls on aviation medicine subjects. *Recreations:* ornithology, wild-life conservation, cricket, music. *Address:* Braeburn, Barway, Ely, Cambs CB7 5UB. *Club:* Royal Air Force.

BAIRD, Joyce Elizabeth Leslie, OBE 1991; Joint General Secretary, Assistant Masters and Mistresses Association, 1978–90; *b* 8 Dec. 1929; *d* of Dr J. C. H. Baird and Mrs J. E. Baird. *Educ:* The Abbey School, Reading; Newnham College, Cambridge (MA); secretarial training. FEIS 1987. Sec. to Ernö Goldfinger, architect, 1952; Secretary to Sir Austin Robinson and editorial assistant, Royal Economic Soc., 1952–60; Senior Geography Mistress, Hertfordshire and Essex High School, Bishop's Stortford, 1961–77 (Dep. Head, 1973–75). President: Assoc. of Assistant Mistresses, 1976–77; Internat. Fedn of Secondary Teachers, 1981–85; Vice Pres., NFER, 1991–. Mem., Cambridge City Council, 1992–96. Bd Mem., Granta Housing Soc., 1992–2006. Trustee, Cambridge Preservation Soc., 1998–. Gov., Alleyn's Sch., Dulwich, 1993–2003. *Recreations:* opera, thinking about gardening, travel. *Address:* 26 Fulbrooke Road, Cambridge CB3 9EE. *T:* (01223) 354909. *Club:* Royal Commonwealth Society.

BAIRD, Kenneth William; Project Director/Managing Director, European Opera Centre, since 1994; *b* 14 July 1950; *s* of William and Christine Baird. *Educ:* Uppingham School; St Andrews Univ. (MA); Royal College of Music; Royal Sch. of Church Music. LRAM, ARCM. English National Opera, 1974–82; Gen. Manager, Aldeburgh Foundn, 1982–88; Music Dir, Arts Council, 1988–94. Sec., New Opera Co., 1981–82. Member: NW Arts Bd, 1998–2002; Arts Council NW, 2002–04; Bd, Huddersfield Contemporary Music Fest., 1997–2004; Birmingham Contemp. Music Gp, 2000–. Adv. Dir, Sonic Arts Network (Chm., 2003–). Chairman: Snape Historical Trust, 1986–2001; British Arts Fests

Assoc., 1988. Trustee, R. A. Vestey Meml Trust, 1991–2004. *Address:* c/o European Opera Centre, Hope at Everton, 1 Haigh Street, Liverpool L3 8QP. *Club:* Chelsea Arts.

BAIRD, Nicholas Graham Faraday, CVO 2008; HM Diplomatic Service; Ambassador to Turkey, since 2006; *b* 15 May 1962; *s* of Colin and Elizabeth Baird; *m* 1985, Caroline Jane Ivett; one *s* two *d*. *Educ:* Dulwich Coll.; Emmanuel Coll., Cambridge (MA English Lit.). Joined FCO, 1983; Third Sec., Kuwait, 1986–89; First Sec., UK Repn to EU, Brussels, 1989–93; Private Sec. to Parly Under-Sec. of State, FCO, 1993–95; Hd, Amsterdam Intergovtl Conf. Unit, FCO, 1995–97; Counsellor and Dep. Hd of Mission, Muscat, 1997–98; Counsellor, UK Repn to EU, Brussels, 1998–2002; Hd, EU Dept (Internal), FCO, 2002–03; Sen. Dir, Internat., Immigration and Nationality Directorate, 2003–04, Policy, Immigration and Nationality Directorate, 2004–06, Home Office (on secondment). *Recreations:* reading, theatre, cycling, travel. *Address:* c/o Foreign and Commonwealth Office, SW1A 2AH.

BAIRD, Shiona Elizabeth; Member (Green) Scotland North East, Scottish Parliament, 2003–07; *b* 14 Sept. 1946; *d* of Iain Fraser MacKenzie and Jean MacKenzie; *m* 1968, John, (Iain), Lambie Baird; four *s* one *d*. *Educ:* Edinburgh Univ. (BSc Soc. Sci. 1968; Dip. Soc. Admin 1969). Social worker, 1969–71; mother and farmer, 1971–. Bd Dir, Tayside Foundn for Conservation of Resources, 1997–. *Recreation:* enjoying the outdoors.

BAIRD, Susan, CBE 1991; JP; Vice Lord-Lieutenant, City of Glasgow, since 1996; Member (Lab), City of Glasgow Council (formerly Glasgow District Council, then Glasgow City Council), since 1974; *b* 26 May 1940; *d* of Archie and Susan Reilly; *m* 1957, George Baird; three *s* one *d*. *Educ:* St Mark's Secondary School, Glasgow. Mem. Labour Party, 1969; City of Glasgow Council (formerly Glasgow District Council, then Glasgow City Council): Bailie of the City, 1980–84; Convener, Manpower Cttee, 1980–84; Vice-Convener: Parks and Recreation Cttee, 1984–88; Strathclyde Fire and Rescue, 2006–. Lord Provost and Lord-Lieutenant of Glasgow, 1988–92. JP 1977, DL 1992, Glasgow. DUniv Glasgow, 1990. St Mungo Prize, St Mungo Trust, 1991. OStJ. *Recreations:* reading, walking. *Address:* 138 Downfield Street, Parkhead, Glasgow G32 8RZ. *T:* (0141) 778 7641.

BAIRD, Vice-Adm. Sir Thomas (Henry Eustace), KCB 1980; DL; *b* Canterbury, Kent, 17 May 1924; *s* of Geoffrey Henry and Helen Jane Baird; *m* 1953, Angela Florence Ann Paul, Symington, Ayrshire; one *s* one *d*. *Educ:* RNC, Dartmouth. Served HM Ships: Trinidad, in support of convoys to Russia, 1941, Midshipman; Bermuda, Russian convoys and landings in N Africa, and Orwell, Russian convoys and Atlantic escort force, 1942; Howe, E Indies, 1943, Sub-Lt; Rapid, E Indies, 1944 until VJ Day, Lieut; St James, Home Fleet, 1946; Ganges, Ratings' New Entry Trng, 1948; Plucky, Exec. Officer, mine clearance in Mediterranean, 1950; Lt Comdr 1952; Veryan Bay, Exec. Officer, W Indies and Falkland Is., 1953; O-in-C, Petty Officers' Leadership Sch., Malta, 1954; Exec. Officer, HMS Whirlwind, Home Fleet and Med., for Suez Op., 1956; Comd, HMS Acute, Dartmouth Trng Sqdn, 1958; Comdr 1959; Comd, HMS Ulysses, Home Fleet, 1960; Staff, C-in-C, Home Fleet, Northwood, 1961; Exec. Officer, Jt Anti-Sub. Sch., Londonderry, 1963; EO, HMS Bulwark, Far East, 1965; Ch. Staff Officer to Cdre, Naval Drafting, 1966; Captain 1967; Dep. Dir, Naval Equipment, Adm., Bath, 1967; Captain: Mine Countermeasures; Fishery Protection and HMS Lochinvar (comd), 1969; Comd, HMS Glamorgan, Far East, W Indies, S Amer., Med., and UK Waters, 1971; Captain of the Fleet, 1973; Rear Adm. 1976; Chief of Staff to C-in-C Naval Home Comd, 1976–77; Dir Gen., Naval Personal Services, 1978–79; Vice-Adm. 1979; Flag Officer Scotland and NI, 1979–82. Chm. Exec. Cttee, Erskine Hosp., 1986–95. DL Ayrshire and Arran, 1982. *Recreations:* cricket, golf, shooting, fishing. *Address:* Craigrethill, Symington, Ayrshire KA1 5QN. *Club:* Prestwick Golf (Prestwick).

BAIRD, Vera; QC 2000; MP (Lab) Redcar, since 2001; Solicitor General, since 2007; *d* of Jack Thomas and Alice (*née* Marsland); *m* 1st, 1972, David John Taylor-Gooby (marr. diss. 1978); 2nd, 1978, Robert Brian Baird (*d* 1979); two step *s*. *Educ:* Newcastle Polytechnic (LLB Hons 1972); Open Univ. (BA 1982). Called to the Bar, Gray's Inn, 1975, Bencher, 2004. Parly Under-Sec. of State, DCA, then MoJ, 2006–07. Vis. Law Fellow, St Hilda's Coll., Oxford, 1999. *Publications:* Rape in Court, 1998; Defending Battered Women Who Kill, 2000. *Address:* 14 Tooks Court, Cursitor Street, EC4A 1LB.

BAIRD, William; Under Secretary, Scottish Home and Health Department, 1978–87; *b* 13 Oct. 1927; *s* of Peter and Christina Baird, Airdrie; *m* 1954, Anne Templeton Macfarlane; two *d*. *Educ:* Airdrie Academy; Glasgow Univ. Entered Scottish Home Dept, 1952; Private Sec. to Perm. Under-Sec. of State, Scottish Office, 1957; Principal, Scottish Educn Dept, 1958–63; Private Sec. to Minister of State and successive Secs of State for Scotland, 1963–65; Asst Sec., Scottish Educn Dept, 1965–66; Dept of Agriculture and Fisheries for Scotland, 1966–71; Scottish Office Finance Div., 1971–73; Registrar General for Scotland, 1973–78. *Address:* 8 Strathearn Road, North Berwick EH39 5BZ. *T:* (01620) 893190.

BAIRSTO, Air Vice-Marshal Nigel Alexander, CB 2007; MBE 1991; CEng, FIMechE, FRAeS; Associate Partner, IBM Global Business Services, and European Director Logistic Solutions, Defence and Security, since 2007; *b* 27 Aug. 1953; *s* of Air Marshal Sir Peter Edward Bairsto, *qv*; *m* 1976, Alison Margaret Philippe; one *s* one *d*. *Educ:* King's Sch., Ely; Portsmouth Poly. (BSc 1975); RAF Coll., Cranwell; Cranfield Inst. of Technol. (MSc 1986); Cranfield Univ. (MDA 1999). CEng 1989; FIMechE 1997; FRAeS 2000. Commnd RAF Eng. Officer, 1971; RAF Leuchars, 1978–80; RAF Cottesmore, 1980–82; MoD, London, 1982–87; Sen. Engr Officer 14 Sqn, RAF Bruggen, 1987–91; RAF Staff Coll., Bracknell, 1991; Wing Comdr, Tornado, Strike Command, 1992–93; OC Eng & Supply, RAF Leeming, 1993–95; Gp Capt., Logistics, Strike Command, 1996–98; Station Comdr, Sealand, and Electronics Dir, DARA, 1998–2000; rcds 2000; ACOS Ops (Force Protection), Strike Command, and Comdt Gen., RAF Regt, 2001–03; Defence Logistics Organisation, Ministry of Defence: Tornado Integrated Project Team Leader, 2003–05; 1 Gp Cluster Leader, 2005; Dir Gen. Defence Logistics Transformation, 2005–07. Northern Area Pres., RAFA, 2007–. FCMI 1997. *Recreations:* golf, shooting, ski-ing, private flying, gardening. *Address:* Swayfield, Lincs. *T:* (01476) 550097; *e-mail:* bears178@aol.com. *Clubs:* Royal Air Force; Royal and Ancient Golf; Luffenham Heath Golf; West Rheine Golf.

BAIRSTO, Air Marshal Sir Peter (Edward), KBE 1981 (CBE 1973); CB 1980; AFC 1957; DL; *b* 3 Aug. 1926; *s* of late Arthur Bairsto and Beatrice (*née* Lewis); *m* 1947, Kathleen (*née* Clarbour); two *s* one *d*. *Educ:* Rhyl Grammar Sch. Pilot, FAA, 1944–46; 1946–62: FO RAF Regt, Palestine, Aden Protectorate; Flying Instr; Fighter Pilot, Fighter Comd and Near East; Flight Comdr, 43 Sqdn, and Leader, RAF Aerobatic Team; Sqdn Comdr, 66 Sqdn; RAF Staff Coll.; Wing Comdr, Flying, Nicosia, 1963–64; Op. Requirements, MoD, 1965–67; JSSC Latimer, 1967; Instr, RAF Staff Coll., 1968–70; Stn Comdr, RAF Honington, 1971–73; Dir, Op. Requirements, MoD, 1974–77; AOC Training Units, Support Command, 1977–79; Comdr, Northern Maritime Air Region, 1979–81; Dep. C-in-C, Strike Command, 1981–84. Vice-Chm. (Air), Highland TAVRA, 1984–90. Hon. Col, Northern Gp Field Sqns RE (Airfield Damage Repair) (Vol.), 1989–92. Mem., Scottish Sports Council, 1985–90. HM Comr, Queen Victoria Sch., Dunblane, 1984–93; Chm. Management Bd, RAF Benevolent Fund Home, Alastrean House, Tarland, 1984–94. Mem., St Andrews Links Trust, 1989–95 (Chm., 1993–95). Queen's Commendation for Valuable Services in the Air, 1955 and 1960. CCMI. DL Fife, 1992. *Recreations:* golf, fishing, shooting, gardening. *Address:* Bearwood, Hepburn Gardens, St Andrews, Fife KY16 9LT. *T:* (01334) 475505. *Clubs:* Royal Air Force; Royal and Ancient Golf.

See also Air Vice-Marshal N. A. Bairsto.

BAIRSTOW, John; Founder, 1968, Chairman, 1972–93, Queens Moat Houses PLC (formerly Queens Modern Hotels Ltd); *b* 25 Aug. 1930; *m*; four *d*. *Educ:* City of London Sch. FSVA. Founded Bairstow, Eves and Son, Valuers and Estate Agents, 1953. *Relevant publication:* Corporate Hijack? The John Bairstow Story, by Brian Lynch, 2005. *Recreation:* salmon fishing.

BAISTER, Stephen, PhD; Chief Bankruptcy Registrar of the High Court, Royal Courts of Justice, since 2004 (Bankruptcy Registrar, 1996–2004); *b* 15 Feb. 1952; *s* of John Norman Baister and Bridget Baister. *Educ:* Merton Coll., Oxford (BA Mod. Langs 1974); Birkbeck Coll., London (MA German 1978); University Coll. London (PhD Law 1992). Admitted solicitor, 1981; solicitor in private practice, 1981–96. Trustee, Condor Trust for Educn, 2005–. *Publications:* with Chris Patrick: Guide to East Germany, 1990; Latvia: the Bradt travel guide, 1999, 5th edn 2007; Riga: the Bradt city guide, 2005; William Le Queux: master of mystery, 2007; *contributions to:* Atkin's Court Forms; Butterworth's Encyclopaedia of Forms and Precedents; Civil Procedure; Muir Hunter on Personal Insolvency. *Address:* Bankruptcy Chambers, Royal Courts of Justice, Strand, WC2A 2LL.

BAKER, family name of **Baron Baker of Dorking**.

BAKER OF DORKING, Baron *cr* 1997 (Life Peer), of Iford in the Co. of East Sussex; **Kenneth Wilfred Baker,** CH 1992; PC 1984; Chairman: Graphite Resources plc, since 2007; Clear Communications, since 2007; *b* 3 Nov. 1934; *s* of late W. M. Baker, OBE and of Mrs Baker (*née* Harries); *m* 1963, Mary Elizabeth Gray-Muir; one *s* two *d*. *Educ:* St Paul's Sch.; Magdalen Coll., Oxford. Nat. Service, 1953–55: Lieut in Gunners, N Africa; Artillery Instructor to Libyan Army. Oxford, 1955–58 (Sec. of Union). Served Twickenham Borough Council, 1960–62. Contested (C): Poplar, 1964; Acton, 1966. MP (C): Acton, March 1968–1970; St Marylebone, Oct. 1970–1983; Mole Valley, 1983–97; Parly Sec., CSD, 1972–74; PPS to Leader of Opposition, 1974–75; Minister of State and Minister for Information Technology, DTI, 1981–84; Minister for Local Govt, DoE, 1984–85; Sec. of State for the Environment, 1985–86; Sec. of State for Educn and Sci., 1986–89; Chancellor of the Duchy of Lancaster, 1989–90; Chm., Conservative Party, 1989–90; Sec. of State for Home Dept, 1990–92. Mem., Public Accounts Cttee, 1969–70; Chm., H of L Inf. Cttee, 2002–06; Mem., House Cttee, H of L, 2007–. Mem. Exec., 1922 Cttee, 1975–81. Chm., Hansard Soc., 1978–81. Sec. Gen., UN Conf. of Parliamentarians on World Population and Development, 1978. Pres., Royal London Soc. for the Blind, 1999–; Vice Chm., Cartoon Art Trust, 2003–. *Publications:* (ed) I Have No Gun But I Can Spit, 1980; (ed) London Lines, 1982; (ed) The Faber Book of English History in Verse, 1988; (ed) Unauthorized Versions: poems and their parodies, 1990; (ed) The Faber Book of Conservatism, 1993; The Turbulent Years: my life in politics, 1993; The Prime Ministers: an irreverent political history in cartoons, 1995; (ed) The Faber Book of War Poetry, 1996; The Kings and Queens: an irreverent cartoon history of the British monarchy, 1996; (ed) A Children's English History in Verse, 2000; (ed) The Faber Book of Landscape Poetry, 2000; George IV: a life in caricature, 2005; George III: a life in caricature, 2007. *Recreation:* collecting books and political caricatures. *Address:* House of Lords, Westminster, SW1A 0PW. *Clubs:* Athenæum, Garrick.

BAKER, Prof. Alan, FRS 1973; Professor of Pure Mathematics, University of Cambridge, 1974–2006, now Professor Emeritus; Fellow of Trinity College, Cambridge, since 1964; *b* 19 Aug. 1939; *o c* of Barnet and Bessie Baker. *Educ:* Stratford Grammar Sch.; University Coll. London; Trinity Coll., Cambridge. BSc (London); MA, PhD (Cantab). Mem., Dept of Mathematics, UCL, 1964–65 and Fellow, UCL, 1979; Research Fellow, 1964–68, and Dir of Studies in Mathematics, 1968–74, Trinity Coll., Cambridge; Mem., Dept of Pure Maths and Math. Statistics, Univ. of Cambridge, 1966–2006; Reader in Theory of Numbers, 1972–74. Visiting Professor: Univs of Michigan and Colorado, 1969; Stanford Univ., 1974; Royal Soc. Kan Tong Po Prof., Univ. of Hong Kong, 1988; ETH, Zürich, 1989; Mem., Inst. for Advanced Study, Princeton, 1970; Mathematical Scis Res. Inst., Berkeley, 1993; First Turán Lectr, J. Bolyai Math. Soc. Hungary, 1978. MAE 1998. Foreign Fellow: Indian Nat. Sci. Acad., 1980; Nat. Acad. of Scis, India, 1993; Hon. Mem., Hungarian Acad. of Scis, 2001. Hon. Dr Univ. Louis Pasteur, Strasbourg, 1998. Fields Medal, Internat. Congress of Mathematicians, Nice, 1970; Adams Prize of Univ. of Cambridge, 1971–72. *Publications:* Transcendental Number Theory, 1975; (ed jtly) Transcendence Theory: advances and applications, 1977; A Concise Introduction to the Theory of Numbers, 1984; (ed) New Advances in Transcendence Theory, 1988; (with G. Wüstholz) Logarithmic Forms and Diophantine Geometry, 2007; papers in various mathematical jls. *Recreation:* travel. *Address:* Centre for Mathematical Sciences, Wilberforce Road, Cambridge CB3 0WB. *T:* (01223) 337999; Trinity College, Cambridge CB2 1TQ. *T:* (01223) 338400.

BAKER, Alistair James; Managing Director, Microsoft Ltd, 2004–06; Vice President, Microsoft EMEA, 2004–06; *b* 26 July 1962; one *s* two *d*. *Educ:* BSc Hons Computing and Informatics; Postgrad. DipM. Joined IBM, 1985; various rôles, IBM, Hewlett Packard, Morse Computers, 1985–96; joined Microsoft, 1996; Country Manager, Scotland, 1996–2000; Gp Dir, Microsoft Services Orgn, 2000–02; Gen. Manager, Small and Mid-Mkt Solutions and Partners, 2002–04. FCIM; FRSA. *Recreations:* cycling, snow-boarding, guitar.

BAKER, Andrew William; QC 2006; *b* 21 Dec. 1965; *s* of Gordon Baker and Ann Baker (now Williamson); *m* 1986, Philippa Jane Ghaut; four *s*. *Educ:* Lenzie Acad., Strathclyde; Merton Coll., Oxford (BA Maths 1986; MA 1990); City Univ. (PGDipLaw 1987). Called to the Bar, Lincoln's Inn, 1988 (Hardwicke, Wolfson and Kennedy Scholar); Tutor, law of internat. trade, 1988–89; in practice at the Bar, 1989–. CEDR Accredited Mediator, 2008. Gov., Busbridge C of E (Aided) Jun. Sch., 2005–. *Publication:* (jtly) Time Charters, 6th edn 2008. *Recreations:* time with Philippa and the Fabulous Baker Boys, golf, football, Lotus cars, playing trumpet, music, films. *Address:* 20 Essex Street, WC2R 3AL. *T:* (020) 7842 1200, *Fax:* (020) 7842 1270; *e-mail:* abaker@20essexst.com.

BAKER, Ann Maureen, (Mrs D. R. Baker); *see* Jenner, A. M.

BAKER, Anthony Thomas; aviation consultant; Director, International Aviation Negotiations, Department for Transport, retired 2004; *b* 1944; *s* of Charles Arthur Baker and Ivy Louvain Baker; *m* 1969, Alicia Veronica Roberts; two *s* one *d*. *Educ:* Chatham House Grammar Sch., Ramsgate; Lincoln Coll., Oxford (BA Hons Modern History). Ministry of Transport: Asst Principal, 1965–70; Principal, 1970–75; Principal, HM Treasury, 1975–78; Asst Sec., 1978–88, and 1991–96, MOT; Dir, Internat. Aviation

Negotiations, DoE, then DETR, subseq. DTLR, later DfT, 1996–2004. Dir, County NatWest Ltd, 1988–91. Freeman, City of London. *Recreations:* theatre, opera, reading. *Address:* 68 Talbot Road, N6 4RA.

BAKER, Sir Bryan (William), Kt 1997; Chairman, West Midlands Region, NHS Executive, Department of Health, 1996–97 (Chairman, West Midlands Regional Health Authority, 1993–96); *b* 12 Dec. 1932; *m* 1954, Christine Margaret (*née* Hole); one *d.* Joined Tarmac, 1952; Gp Man. Dir, Tarmac plc, 1983–92. Non-executive Director: Volvo Truck & Bus Ltd, 1992; Birse Group PLC, 1993–; Pemberstone PLC, 1995; Benson Gp PLC, 1996; Chm., Bruntcliffe Aggregates PLC, 1996–97.

BAKER, Cecil John; Director, Alliance & Leicester Building Society (formerly Alliance Building Society), 1970–92 (Chairman, 1981–91); *b* 2 Sept. 1915; *s* of late Frederick William Baker and Mildred Beatrice Palmer; *m* 1st, 1942, Kathleen Cecilia Henning (marr. diss. 1965); one *s*; 2nd, 1971, Joan Beatrice Barnes; one *d. Educ:* Whitgift Sch.; LSE (LLB 1939; BSc(Econ) 1949); Inst. of Actuaries. FIA 1948; ACII 1937. Sec., Insurance Inst. of London, 1945–49; Investment Manager, London Assurance, 1950–64; Investment Consultant, Hambros Bank Ltd, 1964–74; Chairman: Pension Fund Property Unit Trust, 1966–87; Charities Property Unit Trust, 1967–87; Agricl Property Unit Trust for Pension Funds and Charities, 1976–87; Victory Insurance Holdings Ltd, 1979–85; British American Property Unit Trust, 1982–87; United Real Property Trust plc, 1983–86 (Dir, 1982–86); Hunting Gate Group, 1980–90; Dir, Abbey Life Group plc, 1985–88. *Recreations:* golf, travel. *Address:* 3 Tennyson Court, 12 Dorset Square, NW1 6QB. *T:* (020) 7724 9716.

BAKER, Charles A.; *see* Arnold-Baker.

BAKER, Air Vice-Marshal Christopher Paul, CB 1991; Chairman, Taylor Curnow Ltd, since 1994; *b* 14 June 1938; *er s* of late Paul Hocking Baker, FCA and Kathleen Minnie Florence Baker; *m* 1st, 1961, Heather Ann Laity (decd), *d* of late Cecil Henry Laity and Eleanor Hocking Laity; three *s*; 2nd, 1981, Francesca R. Aghabi, *er d* of late George Khalil Aghabi and Elizabeth Maria Regina Aghabi; two *s. Educ:* Bickley Hall, Kent; Tonbridge School. Commnd RAF, 1958; served 1958–61: RAF Khormaksar (Air Movements), Aden; Supply Sqdn, RAF Coll., Cranwell; RAF Labuan, N Borneo; No 389 Maintenance Unit, RAF Seletar, Singapore; MoD Harrogate; student, RAF Staff Coll., Bracknell; OC Supply Sqdn, RAF Linton-on-Ouse; SHAPE, Two ATAF; ndc; Directing Staff, RAF Staff Coll., Bracknell; HQ RAF Support Comd; Dep. Dir, RAF Supply Systems, MoD; Comd Supply Movements Officer, HQ Strike Comd, RAF High Wycombe, 1982–84; RCDS, 1985; Dir, Supply Systems, MoD, 1986–87; Dir, Supply Policy and Logistics Plans, MoD, 1988–89; Dir Gen. of Support Management, RAF, 1989–93. Gen. Manager, Defence Sector Business Gp, TNT Express (UK) Ltd, 1993–94. Freeman, City of London; Liveryman, Bakers' Co. *Publications:* papers on the crisis of authority, oil potential of the Arctic Basin, and German reunification. *Recreations:* Rugby, rowing, ski-ing, modern history. *Address:* Lloyds TSB, Cox's & King's Branch, PO Box 1190, 7 Pall Mall, SW1Y 5NA.

BAKER, Claire Josephine, PhD; Member (Lab) Scotland Mid and Fife, Scottish Parliament, since 2007; *b* Dunfermline, 4 March 1971; *d* of James Brennan and Margaret Brennan (*née* Edgar); *m* 2004, Richard James Baker, *qv*; one *d. Educ:* Edinburgh Univ. (MA Hons English Lang. and Lit.); Glasgow Univ. (PhD English Lit. 1997). Labour researcher, Scottish Parlt, 1999–2002; Amicus researcher, 2002–04; Res. and Information Manager, RCN Scotland, 2004–05; Policy Manager, SCVO, 2005–07. *Publication:* Critical Guide to the Poetry of Sylvia Plath, 1998. *Address:* 219 Wellesley Road, Methil, Fife KY8 3BN. *T:* (01333) 300974, *Fax:* (01333) 300413; *e-mail:* claire.baker.msp@scottish.parliament.uk.

BAKER, David Brian, OBE 2001; FSA; consultant, historic environment conservation, since 1997; *b* 20 Jan. 1941; *s* of Henry and Maie Baker; *m* 1963, Evelyn Amos; one *s. Educ:* Hertford Coll., Oxford (BA Hons Mod. Hist. 1963); Inst. of Educn, London (PGCE 1964). FSA 1972; MIFA 1982; IHBC 1998. Asst Hist. Master, Bedford Sch., 1964–68; Lectr in Hist., Portsmouth Poly., 1968–71; Conservation and Archaeol. Officer, Beds County Planning Dept, 1972–97. Member: various adv. cttees, English Heritage, 1990–; Council, NT, 1998–2006; Vice-Pres., Council for British Archaeol., 1999–2008. Chm., Adv. Bd for Redundant Churches, C of E, 2005–08 (Mem., 2001–08); Member: St Albans DAC, 1973–; Rochester Fabric Adv. Cttee, 2007–. *Publications:* Living with the Past, 1983; numerous papers in conservation and archaeol jls. *Recreations:* photography, music, gardening. *Address:* 3 Oldway, Bletsoe, Bedford MK44 1QG. *T:* (01234) 781179, *Fax:* (01234) 782645; *e-mail:* dbb@suttons.org.uk.

BAKER, Derek; *see* Baker, L. G. D.

BAKER, Derek Alexander; Director, Central Personnel Group, Department of Finance and Personnel, Northern Ireland, since 2006; *b* 3 Nov. 1957; *s* of Alexander James Baker and Sarah Beatrice Baker; *m* 1989, Barbara Anne Haggan; one *s* two *d. Educ:* Queen's Univ., Belfast (BA Hons French and German). Joined NICS, 1980; Dept for Econ. Develt, 1980–84, and 1987–93; Harland & Wolff Shipbuilders (on secondment), 1985–87; Asst Sec., Dept of Health and Social Services, 1993–2002; Dep. Sec., Dept for Social Develt, 2002–06. *Address:* Central Personnel Group, Department of Finance and Personnel, Royston House, Upper Queen Street, Belfast BT1 6FD. *T:* (028) 9054 7479, *Fax:* (028) 9054 7433; *e-mail:* derek.baker@dfpni.gov.uk.

BAKER, Dick; *see* Baker, F. E.

BAKER, Dr Edward James, FRCP, FRCPCH; Medical Director, Guy's and St Thomas' NHS Foundation Trust (formerly Guy's and St Thomas' Hospital NHS Trust), since 2003; *b* 2 May 1956; *s* of late Christopher Baker and of Dr Hazel Baker; *m* 1982, Patricia Hudswell; two *d. Educ:* Trinity Coll., Cambridge (MB BChir 1979; MA; MD 1986); St Thomas's Hosp. Med. Sch. FRCP 1994; FRCPCH 1997. Hon. Consultant Paediatric Cardiologist, Guy's Hosp., 1987–; Sen. Lectr, KCL, 1987–. Editor-in-Chief, Cardiology in the Young, 2007–. *Publication:* (ed jtly) Paediatric Cardiology, 1986, 2nd edn 2002. *Address:* St Thomas' Hospital, Westminster Bridge Road, SE1 7EH. *T:* (020) 7188 3734.

BAKER, Elizabeth Margaret; Headmistress, Wimbledon High School, 1992–95, retired; *b* 13 Sept. 1945; *d* of Walter and Betty Gale; *m*; one *d. Educ:* University College of Wales, Swansea (BA, DipEd). Lectr, Derby Coll. of Further Educn, 1968–71; Classics Teacher: West Monmouth Sch., 1971–74; Cheltenham Bournside, 1974–81; Cheltenham Ladies' Coll., 1981–88; Headmistress, Ellerslie, Malvern, 1988–92. *Recreations:* wine, letter-writing, keeping the classics alive. *Address:* 35 Blackbarn Lane, Usk NP15 1BP. *T:* (01291) 671231.

BAKER, Hon. Francis Edward N.; *see* Noel-Baker.

BAKER, Francis Eustace, (Dick), CBE 1984 (OBE 1979); business interests in property, farming and the automotive industry; Partner, Crossroads Motors, since 1988; *b* 19 April 1933; *s* of Stephen and Jessica Wilhelmina Baker; *m* 1957, Constance Anne Shilling; two *s* two *d. Educ:* Borden Grammar Sch.; New Coll., Oxford (MA). Nat. Service, RN, 1955–57 (Sub Lieut). Admin. Officer, HMOCS, 1957; Solomon Is, 1958–63; farming, 1963–67; Admin. Officer, Condominium of New Hebrides, 1967–79; Chief Sec. to Falkland Is Govt, 1979–83; Gov. and C-in-C, St Helena and Dependencies, 1984–88. Silver Jubilee Medal, 1977. *Recreations:* swimming, reading, farming, interesting motor cars. *Address:* Fairway, Bannister Hill, Borden, Sittingbourne, Kent ME9 8HT. *T:* (01795) 423301.

BAKER, Francis Raymond, OBE 1997; HM Diplomatic Service; Counsellor (Foreign and Security Policy), Washington, since 2004; *b* 27 Jan. 1961; *s* of late Raymond Albert Baker and Pamela Annis Baker; *m* 1983, Maria Pilar Fernandez; one *s* one *d. Educ:* Dartford Grammar Sch. Entered FCO, 1981: Third Sec., Panama City, 1983–86; Third, later Second Sec., Buenos Aires, 1986–91; Second Sec., FCO, 1991–93; First Secretary: Ankara, 1993–96; on secondment to US State Dept, Washington, 1996–97; FCO, 1997–98; Private Sec. to Minister of State, FCO, 1998–2000; Head, Africa Dept (Equatorial), FCO, 2000–03; Counsellor (Pol/Mil.), Washington, 2003–04. *Recreations:* golf, cricket, watching football (Charlton Athletic FC), rock music, sailing, rallying. *Address:* c/o Foreign and Commonwealth Office, King Charles Street, SW1A 2AH.

BAKER, Gordon Meldrum; HM Diplomatic Service, retired; Associate Fellow and Chairman, Caribbean Study Group, Royal Institute of International Affairs, 2001–07; *b* 4 July 1941; *o s* of Walter John Ralph Gordon Baker and Kathleen Margaret Henrietta Dawe Baker (*née* Meldrum); *m* 1978, Sheila Mary Megson. *Educ:* St Andrew's Sch., Bawdrip, near Bridgwater. MSc Bradford 1976. Lord Chancellor's Dept, 1959–66; transf. to HM Diplomatic Service, 1966; Commonwealth Office, 1966–68; FO (later FCO), 1968–69; Lagos, 1969–72; First Sec., FCO, 1973–75 (Resident Clerk, 1974–75); sabbatical at Postgrad. Sch. of Studies in Industrial Technol., Univ. of Bradford, 1975–76; FCO, 1976–78 (Res. Clerk, 1976–78); First Sec. (Chancery/Information), subseq. First Sec., Head of Chancery and Consul, Brasilia, 1978–81; Asst Head, Mexico and Central America Dept, FCO, 1982–84; Counsellor, 1984; on secondment to British Aerospace, 1984–86; Counsellor, Head of Chancery then Dep. Hd of Mission, and Consul-General, Santiago, 1986–89, Chargé d'Affaires, 1986, 1987 and 1989; RCDS, 1990–91; Head of W Indian and Atlantic Dept, FCO, 1991–94; High Commissioner: Belize, 1995–98; Barbados and Eastern Caribbean States, 1998–2001; Inquiry Sec., Competition Commn, 2002; Temp. Sen. Clerk, Cttee Office, H of L, 2002–06; Clerk, Sub-Cttee G (Social Policy and Consumer Affairs), EU Select Cttee, 2004–06. Mem., Exec. Cttee, Anglo-Chilean Soc., 2002–06. Trustee, Friends of Georgian Soc. of Jamaica, 2003–05. Patron, Age Activity Centre, Wandsworth, 2001–. Member: Exec. Cttee, Westcombe Soc. (local community assoc.), 2002– (Chm., 2007–); Cttee, Ramphal Centre, 2007–. *Publication:* (ed) No Island is an Island: the impact of globalization on the Commonwealth Caribbean, 2007. *Recreations:* walking, watching birds, browsing. *Address:* 78 Foyle Road, Blackheath, SE3 7RH. *T:* (020) 8858 3675.

BAKER, Howard Henry, Jr; Senior Counsel, Baker, Donelson, Bearman, Caldwell & Berkowitz, PC, since 2005; Senior Advisor, Citigroup, since 2005; *b* 15 Nov. 1925; *s* of Howard H. Baker and Dora Ladd; *m* 1st, 1951, Joy Dirksen (*d* 1993); one *s* one *d*; 2nd, 1996, Hon. Nancy Landon Kassebaum. *Educ:* McCallie Sch.; Tulane Univ.; Univ. of Tennessee (LLB 1949). Served USN, 1943–46. Dir, Pennzoil; Chm. of Bd, Newstar Inc. US Senate: Senator from Tennessee 1967–85; Minority Leader, 1977–81; Majority Leader, 1981–85; former Co-Chm., Senate Select Cttee on Presidential Campaign Activities, and mem. other Senate cttees; Chief of Staff, White House, 1987–88. Senior Partner: Baker, Worthington, Crossley, Stansberry & Woolf, Knoxville, Tenn, 1985–87 and 1988–95; Baker, Donelson, Bearman & Caldwell, Washington, 1995–2001; US Ambassador to Japan, 2001–05. Mem., Bd of Regents, Smithsonian Instn. Mem., Amer. Bar Assoc. Presidential Medal of Freedom, 1984. *Publications:* No Margin for Error, 1980; Howard Baker's Washington, 1982; Big South Fork Country, 1993; Scott's Gulf, 2000. *Address:* (office) Lincoln Square, 555 Eleventh Street NW, Sixth Floor, Washington, DC 20004, USA.

BAKER, Ian Michael; a District Judge (Magistrates' Courts) (formerly Metropolitan Stipendiary Magistrate), since 1990; a Recorder, since 2002; *b* 8 May 1947; *s* of late David Ernest Baker and Phyllis Hinds; *m* 1st, 1976, Sue Joel (marr. diss. 1985); one *s*; 2nd, 1991, Jill Sack (*d* 2001); 3rd, 2005, Jane Hinde. *Educ:* Cynffig Grammar Sch., Mid Glam; St Catharine's Coll., Cambridge (MA). Travelled, New England, Latin America and Asia, 1969–71. Articled, then Asst Solicitor to John Clitheroe, Kingsley Napley, 1972–76; Partner, Heninghem, Ambler & Gildener, York, 1976–79; Assistant Solicitor: Claude, Hornby & Cox, 1979; Seifert Sedley, 1980–83; Clinton Davis, 1984–87; Partner, T. V. Edwards, 1987–90. Mem., Equal Treatment Adv. Cttee, Judicial Studies Bd, 2002–. Trustee, Nat. Council for Welfare of Prisoners Abroad, 1986–99 (Chm., 1993–99). *Recreations:* travel, clarinet and saxophone, theatre, music, art, gardening, bird watching. *Address:* Highbury Corner Magistrates' Court, 51 Holloway Road, N7 8JA. *Club:* Ronnie Scott's.

BAKER, James Addison, III; Senior Partner, Baker & Botts, since 1993; Founder, 1993, and Hon. Chairman, James A. Baker III Institute for Public Policy; *b* 28 April 1930; *s* of James A. Baker, Jr and late Bonner Means Baker; *m* 1973, Susan Garrett; eight *c. Educ:* Princeton Univ. (BA); Univ. of Texas at Austin (law degree). Served US Marine Corps, 1952–54. Practised law, firm of Andrews, Kurth, Campbell and Jones, Houston, Texas, 1957–75, 1977–81. Under Sec. of Commerce, US Govt, 1975; National Chairman: President Ford's re-elecn campaign, 1976; George Bush for President Cttee, 1979–80; Dep. Dir, Reagan-Bush Transition and Sen. Advr to 1980 Reagan-Bush Cttee, 1980–Jan. 1981; Chief of Staff to US President, 1981–85; Sec. of US Treasury, 1985–88; Sec. of State, USA, 1989–92; COS and Sen. Counsellor to Pres. of USA, 1992–93. Personal Envoy of UN Sec. Gen. for Western Sahara, 1997–2004; Co-Chm., Iraq Study Gp, US, 2006. Numerous hon. degrees. US Presidential Medal of Freedom, 1992. *Publications:* The Politics of Diplomacy, 1995; Work Hard, Study… And Keep Out of Politics! (memoir), 2006. *Recreations:* hunting, fishing, tennis, golf. *Address:* Baker & Botts, 1 Shell Plaza, 910 Louisiana, Houston, TX 77002–4995, USA; James A. Baker III Institute for Public Policy, 6100 Main Street, Rice University, Baker Hall, Suite 120, Houston, TX 77005, USA. *Clubs:* numerous social, civic and paternal.

BAKER, Col James Henry, MBE 1999; Head of Conservation, Ministry of Defence, 1986–2003; *b* 15 Feb. 1938; *s* of late Lt-Col George Baker, TD, and Gwladys Joan Baker (*née* Russell), Dickhurst, Haslemere; *m* 1961, Lally Moss; one *s* one *d. Educ:* Harrow Sch. Commnd Irish Guards, 1957; served BAOR, Cyprus, Aden, Belize; ADC to Maj.-Gen. comdg Household Bde, 1965–67; CO, 1st Bn, Irish Guards, 1977–79; MA to QMG, 1979–81; Regtl Lt Col, Irish Guards, 1981–85. Standard Bearer, HM Body Guard of Hon. Corps of Gentlemen-at-Arms, 2003–08 (Harbinger, 2000–03). Commandeur, Order of Adolf-Nassau (Luxembourg), 1985. *Recreations:* fishing, shooting, archaeology. *Address:* Rovehurst, Chiddingfold, Surrey GU8 4SN. *T:* (01428) 644463. *Clubs:* White's, MCC.

BAKER, Dame Janet (Abbott), CH 1994; DBE 1976 (CBE 1970); professional singer; *b* 21 Aug. 1933; *d* of Robert Abbott Baker and May (*née* Pollard); *m* 1957, James Keith Shelley. *Educ:* The College for Girls, York; Wintringham, Grimsby. Mem., Munster Trust. Chancellor, Univ. of York, 1991–2004. Trustee, Foundn for Sport and the Arts, 1991–. Daily Mail Kathleen Ferrier Award, 1956; Queen's Prize, Royal College of Music, 1959; Shakespeare Prize, Hamburg, 1971; Copenhagen Sonning Prize, 1979. Hon. DMus: Birmingham, 1968; Leicester, 1974; London, 1974; Hull, 1975; Oxon, 1975; Leeds, 1980; Lancaster, 1983; York, 1984; Hon. MusD Cantab, 1984; Hon. LLD Aberdeen, 1980; Hon. DLitt Bradford, 1983. Hon. Fellow: St Anne's Coll., Oxford, 1975; Downing Coll., Cambridge, 1985. FRSA 1979. Gold Medal, Royal Philharmonic Soc., 1990. Comdr, Order of Arts and Letters (France), 1995. *Publication:* Full Circle (autobiog.), 1982. *Recreations:* reading, walking.

BAKER, Jeremy Russell; QC 1999; a Recorder, since 2000; *b* 9 Feb. 1958. Called to the Bar, Middle Temple, 1979. *Address:* Paradise Chambers, 26 Paradise Square, Sheffield S1 2DE; Thomas More Chambers, 7 Lincoln's Inn Fields, WC2A 3BP.

BAKER, His Honour John Arnold; DL; a Circuit Judge, 1973–98; *b* Calcutta, 5 Nov. 1925; *s* of late William Sydney Baker, MC and Hilda Dora Baker (*née* Swiss); *m* 1954, Edith Muriel Joy Heward; two *d*. *Educ:* Plymouth Coll.; Wellington Sch., Somerset; Wadham Coll., Oxford (MA, BCL). Served RNVR, 1943–44. Treas., Oxford Union, 1948. Admitted Solicitor, 1951; called to Bar, Gray's Inn, 1960. A Recorder, 1972–73. Chm., Nat. League of Young Liberals, 1952–53; contested (L): Richmond, 1959 and 1964; Dorking, 1970; Vice-Pres., Liberal Party, 1968–69; Chm., Liberal Party Exec., 1969–70. Pres., Medico-Legal Soc., 1986–88. Trustee, 2002–06, Patron, 2006–, The Apex Trust. DL Surrey, 1986. *Publication:* Ballot Box to Jury Box (memoir), 2005. *Recreations:* music, watching sport. *Address:* c/o The Crown Court, 6–8 Penrhyn Road, Kingston upon Thames, Surrey KT1 2BB. *T:* (020) 8240 2500. *Clubs:* National Liberal (Trustee), MCC; Nothing (Richmond).

BAKER, Rt Rev. John Austin; Bishop of Salisbury, 1982–93; Hon. Assistant Bishop, diocese of Winchester, since 1994; *b* 11 Jan. 1928; *s* of George Austin Baker and Grace Edna Baker; *m* 1974, Gillian Mary Leach (MBE 1997). *Educ:* Marlborough; Oriel Coll., Oxford (MA, MLitt). Asst Curate, All Saints', Cuddesdon, and Lectr in Old Testament, Cuddesdon Theol Coll., 1954–57; Priest 1955; Asst Curate, St Anselm's, Hatch End, and Asst Lectr in NT Greek, King's Coll., London, 1957–59; Official Fellow, Chaplain and Lectr in Divinity, Corpus Christi Coll., Oxford, 1959–73, Emeritus Fellow, 1977; Lectr in Theology, Brasenose and Lincoln Colls, Oxford, 1959–73; Hebrew Lectr, Exeter Coll., Oxford, 1969–73; Canon of Westminster, 1973–82; Treas., 1974–78; Sub-Dean and Lector Theologiae, 1978–82; Rector of St Margaret's, Westminster, and Speaker's Chaplain, 1978–82. Governor of Pusey House, Oxford, 1970–78; Exam. Chaplain to Bp of Oxford, 1960–78, to Bp of Southwark, 1973–78. Governor: Westminster Sch., 1974–81; Ripon Coll., Cuddesdon, 1974–80; Westminster City Sch., 1978–82; Dorset Inst. of Higher Educn, 1982–86; Bishop Wordsworth's Sch., 1982–93; Sherborne Sch., 1982–93; Salisbury & Wells Theological Coll., 1982–93; Pres. of Council, Marlborough Coll., 1982–93; Trustee, Harold Buxton Trust, 1973–79. Dorrance Vis. Prof., Trinity Coll., Hartford, Conn, USA, 1967; Vis. Prof., King's Coll., London, 1974–77; Hulsean Preacher, Univ. of Cambridge, 1979; Select Preacher, Univ. of Oxford, 1983; Stephenson Lectr, Univ. of Sheffield, 1994; Warburton Lectr, Inns of Court, 1994. Chairman: Defence Theol Working Party, C of E Bd for Social Responsibility, 1980–82; C of E Doctrine Commn, 1985–87 (Mem. 1967–76, 1977–81, 1984–87); House of Bps Working Party on Nature of Christian Belief, 1985–86, on Issues in Human Sexuality, 1990–91; Member: Faith and Order Advisory Gp, C of E Bd for Mission and Unity, 1976–81; Cttee for Theological Education, 1982–85; Standing Commn, WCC Faith and Order Commn, 1983–87; Exec. Cttee, CCJ, 1995–97; Vice-President: Nat. Family Mediation, 1993–; Sudan Church Assoc., 1994–. Pres., Anglican Soc. for Welfare of Animals, 1998–2008. Chaplain, Playing Card Makers' Co., 1977. DD Lambeth, 1991. *Publications:* The Foolishness of God, 1970; Travels in Oudamovia, 1976; Prophecy in the Church, 1976; The Living Splendour of Westminster Abbey, 1977; The Whole Family of God, 1981; The Right Time, 1981; Evidence for the Resurrection, 1986; Christian Civilisation and Common Security, 1990; The Faith of a Christian, 1996; Faith: the country between doubt and hope, 2009; contrib. to: Man: Fallen and Free (ed Kemp), 1969; Thinking about the Eucharist (ed Ramsey), 1972; Church Membership and Intercommunion (ed Kent and Murray), 1973; What about the New Testament? (ed Hooker and Hickling), 1975; Man and Nature (ed Montefiore), 1975; Studia Biblica I, 1978; Religious Studies and Public Examinations (ed Hulmes and Watson), 1980; Believing in the Church, 1981; Hospice: the living Idea (ed Saunders, Summers and Teller), 1981; Darwin: a Commemoration (ed R. J. Berry), 1982; Unholy Warfare (ed D. Martin and P. Mullen), 1983; The Challenge of Northern Ireland, 1984; Lessons before Midnight (ed J. White), 1984; Feminine in the Church (ed M. Furlong), 1984; Dropping the Bomb (ed J. Gladwin), 1985; Theology and Racism, I (ed K. Leech), 1985; Peace Together (ed C. Barrett), 1986; Working for the Kingdom (ed J. Fuller), 1986; Faith and Renewal (ed T. F. Best), 1986; Church, Kingdom, World (ed G. Limouris), 1986; Women Priests? (ed A. Peberdy), 1988; For the Love of Animals (ed B. and M. Annett), 1989; Liberating Life (ed S. McFague *et al*), 1990; The Extended Circle (ed J. Wynne Tyson), 1990; Praying for Peace (ed M. Hare Duke), 1991; The Church, Medicine and the New Age (ed J. Watt), 1995; The Warburton Lectures 1985–94, 1995; Community-Unity-Communion: essays in honour of Mary Tanner (ed C. Podmore), 1998; Act of Synod—Act of Folly? (ed M. Furlong), 1998; *translations:* W. Eichrodt, Theology of the Old Testament, vol. 1 1961, vol. 2 1967; T. Bovet, That They May Have Life, 1964; J. Daniélou, Theology of Jewish Christianity, 1964; H. von Campenhausen, Ecclesiastical Authority and Spiritual Power, 1969; H. von Campenhausen, The Formation of the Christian Bible, 1972; J. Daniélou, Gospel Message and Hellenistic Culture, 1973; (with David Smith) J. Daniélou, The Origins of Latin Christianity, 1977. *Recreation:* music. *Address:* 4 Mede Villas, Kingsgate Road, Winchester, Hants SO23 9QQ. *T:* (01962) 861388, *Fax:* (01962) 843089.

BAKER, Prof. Sir John Hamilton, Kt 2003; LLD; FBA 1984; Downing Professor of the Laws of England, Cambridge University, since 1998; Fellow, St Catharine's College, Cambridge, since 1971 (President, 2004–07); *b* 10 April 1944; *s* of Kenneth Lee Vincent Baker, QPM and Marjorie (*née* Bagshaw); *m* 1st, 1968, Veronica Margaret (marr. diss. 1997), *d* of Rev. W. S. Lloyd; two *d*; 2nd, 2002, Fiona Rosalind Holdsworth (*née* Cantlay) (*d* 2005). *Educ:* King Edward VI Grammar School, Chelmsford; UCL (LLB 1965 (Andrews Medal), PhD 1968; Fellow 1990); MA Cantab 1971, LLD 1984, Yorke Prize, 1975. FRHistS 1980. Called to the Bar, Inner Temple, 1966 (Hon. Bencher 1988), *aeg* Gray's Inn, 1978. Asst Lectr, Faculty of Laws, UCL, 1965–67, Lectr, 1967–71; Cambridge University: Librarian, Squire Law Library, 1971–73; Univ. Lectr in Law, 1973–83; Reader in English Legal History, 1983–88; Prof. of English Legal Hist., 1988–98; Junior Proctor, 1980–81; Chm., Faculty of Law, 1990–92. Visiting Professor: European Univ. Inst., Florence, 1979; Yale Law Sch., 1987; NY Univ. Sch. of Law, 1988–; Vis. Lectr, Harvard Law Sch., 1982; Mellon Senior Res. Fellow, H. E. Huntington Lib., San Marino, Calif., 1983; Ford Special Lectr, Oxford Univ., 1984; Vis. Fellow, All Souls Coll., Oxford, 1995. Corresp. Fellow, Amer. Soc. Legal History, 1993; Hon. Fellow, Soc. for Advanced Legal Studies, 1997. Literary Dir, Selden Soc., 1981– (Jt Dir, 1981–90). Hon. QC 1996. Hon. LLD Chicago, 1992. Ames Prize, Harvard, 1985. *Publications:* An Introduction to English Legal History, 1971, 4th edn 2002; English Legal Manuscripts, vol. I, 1975, vol. II, 1978; The Reports of Sir John Spelman, 1977–78; (ed) Legal Records and the Historian, 1978; Manual of Law French, 1979, 2nd edn 1990; The Order of Serjeants at Law, 1984; English Legal Manuscripts in the USA, vol. I 1985, vol. II 1991; The Legal Profession and the Common Law, 1986; (with S. F. C. Milsom) Sources of English Legal History, 1986; The Notebook of Sir John Port, 1986; (ed) Judicial Records, Law Reports and the Growth of Case Law, 1989; Readings and Moots in the Inns of Court, vol. II, 1990; Cases from the lost notebooks of Sir James Dyer, 1994; Catalogue of English Legal MSS in Cambridge University Library, 1996; Spelman's Reading on Quo Warranto, 1997; Monuments of Endlesse Labours, 1998; The Reports of John Caryll, 1999; The Common Law Tradition, 2000; The Law's Two Bodies, 2001; Readers and Readings at the Inns of Court, 2001; Oxford History of the Laws of England, vol. 6, 2003; articles in legal and hist. jls. *Address:* St Catharine's College, Cambridge CB2 1RL. *T:* (01223) 338317.

BAKER, Sir John (William), Kt 2007; CBE 2000; Chairman: The Maersk Company, since 2003; Renewable Energy Holdings plc, since 2005; *b* 5 Dec. 1937; *s* of Reginald and Wilhelmina Baker; *m* 1st, 1962, Pauline (*née* Moore); one *s*; 2nd, 1975, Gillian (*née* Bullen). *Educ:* Harrow Weald County Grammar Sch.; Oriel Coll., Oxford. Served Army, 1959–61. MoT, 1961–70; DoE, 1970–74; Dep. Chief Exec., Housing Corp., 1974–78; Sec., 1979–80, Bd Mem., 1980–89, Corporate Man. Dir, 1986–89, CEGB; Chief Exec., 1990–95, Chm., 1995–97, National Power; Dir, 1995–2003, Dep. Chm., 2002–03, Royal and Sun Alliance Insurance Gp; Chm., Medeva PLC, 1996–2000; Dep. Chm., Celltech Gp, 2000–03. Chairman: Globeleq, 2003–07; Momenta Hldgs, 2006–07; Greatfleet, 2007–; Mem. Business Adv. Council, A. P. Moller Gp, 1996–. Chm., Sen. Salaries Rev. Body, 2002–08. Chairman: ENO, 1996–2001; Associated Bd, Royal Schs of Music, 2000–06; Trustees, Oxford Philomusica, 2007–. Chairman: Exec. Assembly, World Energy Council, 1995–98; Groundwork Foundn, 1996–2001. Chm., Governing Body, Holland Park Sch., 2003–. *Recreations:* tennis, golf, bridge, music, theatre.

See also Rev. J. M. R. Baker.

BAKER, Jonathan Leslie; QC 2001; a Recorder, since 2000; a Deputy High Court Judge, since 2003; *b* 6 Aug. 1955; *s* of late Leslie Baker and Isobel Baker; *m* 1980, Helen Sharrock; one *s* one *d*. *Educ:* St Albans Sch.; St John's Coll., Cambridge (MA). Called to the Bar, Middle Temple, 1978; barrister, specialising in Family Law, 1979–; Hd, Harcourt Chambers, 2004–. Mem. Cttee, Family Law Bar Assoc., 2005–. Chm., Relate, Oxon, 1998–. Gov., Magdalen College Sch., Oxford, 2005–. *Publication:* (jtly) Contact: the new deal, 2006. *Recreations:* music, history, family life. *Address:* Harcourt Chambers, 2 Harcourt Buildings, Temple, EC4Y 9DB.

BAKER, Rev. Jonathan Mark Richard; Principal, Pusey House, Oxford, since 2003; Assistant Curate, St Thomas with St Frideswide, Oxford, and Binsey, since 2008; *b* 6 Oct. 1966; *s* of Sir John William Baker, *qv*; *m* 1992, Jacqueline Norton; two *s* one *d*. *Educ:* Merchant Taylors' Sch., Northwood; St John's Coll., Oxford (BA 1988, MPhil 1990, MA (Eng. Lit.)); St Stephen's House, Oxford (BA Theol. 1992). Ordained deacon, 1993, priest, 1994; Asst Curate, All Saints, Ascot Heath, 1993–96; Priest i/c, 1996–99, Vicar, 1999–2003, Holy Trinity, Reading and St Mark, Reading. *Publications:* (ed) Consecrated Women?, 2004; (ed jtly) Who Is This Man?, 2006. *Recreations:* music, theatre, poetry, crime fiction, continental holidays. *Address:* Pusey House, Oxford OX1 3LZ. *T:* (01865) 278415; *e-mail:* jonathan.baker@stx.ox.ac.uk.

BAKER, Prof. (Leonard Graham) Derek, MA, BLitt; Professor of History, 1986–95, Director, Institute for Medieval Renaissance and Hispanic Studies, 1989–95, Director, Centre for Undergraduate Study and Research, 1990–95, University of Texas; *b* 21 April 1931; *s* of Leonard and late Phoebe Caroline Baker; *m* 1970, Jean Dorothy Johnston; one *s* one *d*. *Educ:* Christ's Hospital; Oriel Coll., Oxford (1st Class Hons Modern History 1955, MA, BLitt). Captain, Royal Signals, 1950–52. Senior History Master, The Leys School, 1956–66; Lecturer in Medieval History, Univ. of Edinburgh, 1966–79; Headmaster, Christ's Hosp., 1979–85. Vis. Prof., Univ. of Houston, 1993. Dir/Editor, Academia Publishing and Media, 1991. Editor, Ecclesiastical History Soc., 1969–80; Pres., British Sub-Commn, Commn Internat. d'Histoire Ecclésiastique Comparée, 1971–80. Dir, Exec. Cttee, Haskins Soc., 1990 (Ed., 1995). FRHistS 1969. *Publications:* Portraits and Documents, Vol. 1 1967, Vol. 2 1969; (ed) Studies in Church History, 7–17, 1970–80 (subsidia 1–2, 1978–79); Partnership in Excellence, 1974; Women of Power, vol. 1, 1993; Feminea Medievalia, vol. 1, 1993; numerous articles in historical jls. *Recreations:* singing; climbing, mountaineering, pot-holing, camping; good company; food and wine; travel. *Address:* New House, The Street, Nutbourne, Pulborough, W Sussex RH20 2HE. *T:* (01798) 813033. *Clubs:* National Liberal; Leander (Henley-on-Thames).

BAKER, Mark Alexander Wyndham, CBE 1998; Chairman, Magnox Electric plc, 1996–98; *b* 19 June 1940; *s* of late Lt-Comdr Alexander Arthur Wyndham Baker, RN and Renée Gavrelle Stenson (*née* Macnaghten); *m* 1964, Meriel, *yr d* of late Capt. Hugh Chetwynd-Talbot, MBE and of Cynthia Chetwynd-Talbot; one *s* one *d*. *Educ:* Prince Edward Sch., Salisbury, S Rhodesia; University Coll. of Rhodesia & Nyasaland (Beit Schol.; BA London); Christ Church, Oxford (Rhodes Schol.; MA). United Kingdom Atomic Energy Authority, 1964–89: Sec., 1976–78, Gen. Sec., 1978–81, AERE, Harwell; Dir of Personnel and Admin, Northern Div., 1981–84; Authority Personnel Officer, 1984–86; Authority Sec., 1986–89; Exec. Dir, Corporate Affairs and Personnel, Nuclear Electric plc, 1989–96. Chm., Electricity Pensions Ltd, 1996–2006; non-exec. Dir, Pension Protection Fund, 2004–. Deputy Chairman: Police Negotiating Bd, 2000–04; Police Adv. Bd, 2001–04. Mem., Sen. Salaries Review Body, 2004–. Mem., Adv. Cttee, Envmtl Change Inst., Oxford Univ., 1999–2004. Mem. Bd of Trustees, Save the Children, 1998–2004. FInstE 1996 (Pres., 1998–99). *Recreations:* gardening, golf, walking, poetry, words. *Address:* The Old School, Fyfield, Abingdon OX13 5LR. *T:* (01865) 390724; *e-mail:* MarkWBaker@aol.com. *Clubs:* Oxford and Cambridge; Antrobus Dining (Cheshire); Old Fogeys Golf (Dulwich).

BAKER, Martin John; Master of Music, Westminster Cathedral, since 2000; recitalist; *b* 26 July 1967. *Educ:* Royal Northern Coll. of Music Jun. Sch.; Chetham's Sch. of Music; Downing Coll., Cambridge (Organ Scholar; BA 1988). Organ Scholar, Westminster Cathedral, 1988–90; Assistant Organist: St Paul's Cathedral, 1990–91; Westminster Abbey, 1992–2000. Recitals include improvisations. *Address:* Clergy House, Westminster Cathedral, 42 Francis Street, SW1P 1QW.

BAKER, Martyn Murray; Director of Economic Development (formerly of Economic Development and Education), City of London Corporation, 1999–2008; *b* 10 March 1944; *s* of late Norman and Constance Baker; *m* 1970, Rosemary Caroline Holdich. *Educ:* Dulwich Coll.; Pembroke Coll., Oxford (MA). Asst Principal, Min. of Aviation, 1965–67; Private Sec. to Ministers, Min. of Technology, Min. of Aviation Supply, and DTI, 1968–71; Principal, 1971; Principal Private Sec. to Sec. of State for Trade, 1977–78; Counsellor, Civil Aviation and Shipping, Washington, 1978–82; Department of Trade and Industry: Asst Sec., Air Div., 1982–85; Projects and Export Policy Div., 1985–86;

Under Sec., 1986; Regl Dir, NW, 1986–88; Dir, Enterprise and Deregulation Unit, 1988–90; Head of Overseas Trade Div., 1990–93; Head of Exports to Asia, Africa and Australasia Div., 1993–96; Hd of Chemicals and Biotechnology Directorate, 1996–99, and Hd of Consumer Goods, Business and Postal Services Directorate, 1997–99. Member: Export Guarantees Advisory Council, 1985–86; Cttee for ME Trade, 1990–96; Council, China Britain Trade Gp, 1993–96; Asia Pacific Adv. Gp, 1993–96; BBSRC, 1996–99. Leader, Manchester-Salford City Action Team, 1986–88; Chm., City Fringe Partnership Exec. Team, 1999–2005. FRSA 1988.

BAKER, Mary Geraldine, MBE 1995; President: European Parkinson's Disease Association, since 1992; European Federation of Neurological Associations, since 2002; *b* 27 Oct. 1936; *d* of George and Emily Wheeler; *m* 1960, Robert William John Baker; three *s*. *Educ:* Bromley High Sch.; Leeds Univ. (BA); Inst. of Almoners. AIMSW. Almoner, St Thomas' Hosp., 1959–61; housewife and mother, 1961–75; Social Worker, 1975–82; Principal Med. Social Worker, Frimley Park Hosp., 1982–83; Parkinson's Disease Society of UK: National Welfare Dir, 1984–91, 1992; Acting Chief Exec., 1991–92; Dir of Welfare Develt, 1994; Nat. and Internat. Develt Consultant, 1995–99; Chief Exec., 1999–2001. Mem., Adv. Gp on Rehabilitation, DoH, 1992–94; Chm., WHO Cttee of NGOs concerned with neurol disorders, 1998–2002. Vice-Pres., European Brain Council, 2002–; World Federation of Neurology: Mem., Med. Educn Res. Gp, 1998–; Mem., PR and WHO Liaison Cttee, 2002–. Patient Ed., BMJ, 2004– (Mem., Edtl Bd, 2000–). Hon. FCSLT 1991. Paul Harris Fellow, Rotary Foundn, 1997. DUniv. Surrey, 2003. *Publications:* Speech Therapy in Practice, 1988; (with B. McCall) Care of the Elderly, 1990; (with P. Smith) The Role of the Social Worker in the Management of Parkinson's Disease, 1991; (jtly) The Wall between neurology and psychiatry, 2002; Practical Neurology: destigmatizing stigma in people with neurological problems, 2003; contribs to learned jls incl. BMJ. *Recreations:* music, theatre, reading, bridge, caravanning. *Address:* Kailua, Maybourne Rise, Mayford, Woking, Surrey GU22 0SH. *T:* (01483) 763626. *Club:* Soroptimists'.

BAKER, Michael Findlay; QC 1990; **His Honour Judge Findlay Baker;** DL; a Circuit Judge, since 1995; Resident Judge, St Albans Crown Court, since 2000; *b* 26 May 1943; *s* of Rt Hon. Sir George Baker, PC, OBE; *m* 1973, Sarah Hartley Overton; two *d*. *Educ:* Haileybury; Brasenose Coll., Oxford. Called to the Bar, Inner Temple, 1966; a Recorder, 1991–95. Sec., Nat. Reference Tribunals for Coal-mining Industry, 1973–95. Chairman: Herts Criminal Justice Strategy (Liaison) Cttee, 1998–2003; Herts Area Judicial Forum, 2002–; Vale House Stabilisation Services, 2003–; Mem. Bd, Herts Probation Cttee, 1998–. Gov., Univ. of Hertfordshire, 2008. DL Herts, 2008. *Recreations:* mountain climbing and walking. *Address:* The Crown Court, Bricket Road, St Albans, Herts AL1 3HY. *Clubs:* Alpine, Climbers'; Thames Hare and Hounds.
See also Rt Hon. Sir T. S. G. Baker.

BAKER, Prof. Michael John, TD 1971; Professor of Marketing, Strathclyde University, 1971–99, now Emeritus; Chairman, Westburn Publishers Ltd, since 1984; *b* 5 Nov. 1935; *s* of John Overend Baker and Constance Dorothy (*née* Smith); *m* 1959, Sheila (*née* Bell); one *s* two *d*. *Educ:* Worksop Coll.; Gosforth and Harvey Grammar Schs; Durham Univ. (BA); London Univ. (BScEcon); Harvard Univ. (CertITP, DBA); DipM. FRSE 1995; FCIM 1971; FCAM 1983; FScotvec 1988; FSQA 1997. 2nd Lieut, RA, 1956–57. Salesman, Richard Thomas & Baldwins (Sales) Ltd, 1958–64; Asst Lectr, Medway Coll. of Technology, 1964–66; Lectr, Hull Coll. of Technology, 1966–68; Foundn for Management Educn Fellow, 1968–71, Res. Associate, 1969–71, Harvard Business Sch.; Dean, Strathclyde Bus. Sch., 1978–84; Dep. Principal, 1984–91, Sen. Advr to Principal, 1991–94, Strathclyde Univ. Mem., Vice Chm. and Chm., Scottish Bus. Educn Council, 1973–85; Pres., Acad. of Marketing (formerly Marketing Educn Gp), 1986–2005 (Chm., 1973–86); Member: Food and Drink, EDC, 1976–78; SSRC Management and Industrial Relns Cttee, 1976–80; Nat. Councillor, Inst. of Marketing, 1977, Vice Chm. 1984–86, Chm. 1987; Trustee, CIM, 2008–. Member: Scottish Hosps Endowment Res. Trust, 1983–96; Chief Scientist's Cttee, SHHD, 1985–96; Bus. and Management Sub-Cttee, UGC, 1985–89. Chairman: Scottish Marketing Projects Ltd, 1986–2005; IBEX Ltd, 1991–2005; Director: Stoddard Sekers International (formerly Stoddard Hldgs) PLC, 1983–97; Scottish Transport Gp, 1986–90; ARIS plc, 1990–94; Reid Gp, 1989–91; SGBS Ltd, 1990–97; STAMP Ltd, 1992–96. Dir, Scottish Med. Res. Fund, 1992–96. Visiting Professor: Univ. of Surrey, 1995–; Nottingham Trent Univ., 1999–2001; Hon. Prof., Univ. of Wales, Aberystwyth, 1999–; Adjunct Prof., Monash Univ., 2000–; Special Prof., Nottingham Univ., 2001–07. Governor, Lomond Sch., 1984–96. Dean, Senate, CIM, 1994–2002. Founding Editor: Jl of Marketing Management, 1985; Jl of Customer Behaviour, 2002. FRSA 1986. Hon. FCIM 1989; Hon. FAM 1997; Hon. FEMAC 2004. Hon. LLD Portsmouth, 2000; DUniv Surrey, 2003. *Publications:* Marketing, 1971, 7th edn 2006; Marketing New Industrial Products, 1975; (with R. McTavish) Product Policy, 1976; (ed) Marketing in Adversity, 1976; (ed) Marketing Theory and Practice, 1976, 3rd edn 1995; (ed) Industrial Innovation, 1979; Market Development, 1983; (ed) Dictionary of Marketing, 1984, 3rd edn 1998; Marketing Strategy and Management, 1985, 4th edn 2007; (with S. T. Parkinson) Organisational Buying Behaviour, 1986; (ed) The Marketing Book, 1987, 6th edn 2008; (with D. Ughanwa) The Role of Design in International Competitiveness, 1989; (with S. Hart) Marketing and Competitive Success, 1989; Research for Marketing, 1991; (ed) Perspectives on Marketing Management, vol. 1, 1991, vol. 2, 1992, vol. 3, 1993, vol. 4, 1994; Companion Encyclopedia of Marketing, 1995; The Marketing Manual, 1998; (with S. Hart) Product Strategy and Management, 1998, 2nd edn 2007; (ed) The Encyclopedia of Marketing, 1999; (ed) Marketing Theory, 2000; (ed) Marketing: critical perspectives, 5 vols, 2001; Business and Management Research, 2003, 2nd edn (with Anne Foy) 2008. *Recreations:* hill walking, sailing, foreign travel, building bridges and mending fences. *Address:* Westburn, Helensburgh G84 9NH. *T:* (01436) 674686. *Club:* Royal Over-Seas League.

BAKER, His Honour Michael John David; a Circuit Judge, 1988–99; *b* 17 April 1934; *s* of late Ernest Bowden Baker and Dulcie Baker; *m* 1958, Edna Harriet Lane; one *s* one *d*. *Educ:* Trinity Sch. of John Whitgift; Bristol Univ. (LLB Hons). Admitted solicitor, 1957. Flying Officer, RAF, 1957–60. Joined firm of Glanvilles, Solicitors, Portsmouth, 1960; Partner, 1963–88; a Recorder, 1980–88. Coroner, S Hampshire, 1973–88 (Asst Dep. Coroner, 1971; Dep. Coroner, 1972). Pres., Southern Coroners Soc., 1975–76; Mem. Council, Coroners Soc. of England and Wales, 1979–88 (Jun. Vice-Pres., 1987–88). Mem., Council of Mgt, Music at Boxgrove, 1997–; Hon. Patron, Chichester Festival Th., 2002–; Mem., Cttee, Friends of Arundel Castle CC, 2003–. Churchwarden, St Margaret's Ch, Eartham, 2004–. Trustee, Leonard Hawkins Trust, 2004–. *Recreations:* walking, tennis, watching cricket, the theatre, music (particularly choral singing), photography. *Address:* c/o Glanvilles, Solicitors, Langstone Gate, Solent Road, Havant, Hants PO9 1TR. *T:* (023) 9249 2300. *Clubs:* Royal Over-Seas League; Law Society; Emsworth Sailing.

BAKER, Nigel Marcus, MVO 2003; HM Diplomatic Service; Ambassador to Bolivia, since 2007; *b* 9 Sept. 1966; *s* of late Clive Baker and of Mary (*née* Appleyard, now Berg); *m* 1997, Alexandra Čechova. *Educ:* Dulwich Coll.; Gonville and Caius Coll., Cambridge (BA Hons 1st cl. Hist. 1988; MA 1992). Researcher, Cons. Res. Dept, 1989; Third Sec., FCO, 1989; Third, later Second Sec., Prague, 1992–93; Dep. Hd of Mission, Bratislava, 1993–95; First Sec., FCO, 1998; Hd of Eur. Defence Section, Security Policy Dept, FCO, 1998–2000; Asst Private Sec. to Prince of Wales, 2000–03; Dep. Hd of Mission, Havana, 2003–06. Writer and histl researcher, Verona, 1996–97. Trustee, St Catherine's Foundn, 2000–03; Mem. Cttee, Friends of Royal Opera House, 2000–03. *Publications:* articles in British and Eur. pubns on Byron, Palmerston, Italian history, European security and defence. *Recreations:* history in all its forms, good food and drink, mountains, civilisation, escaping. *Address:* c/o British Embassy, La Paz, Bolivia; *e-mail:* baker.sn@gmail.com.

BAKER, Nigel Robert James; QC 1988; a Recorder, since 1985; a Deputy High Court Judge, Queen's Bench Division, since 1994; *b* 21 Dec. 1942; *s* of late Herbert James Baker and Amy Beatrice Baker; *m* 1973, Stephanie Joy Stephenson; one *s*. *Educ:* Norwich Sch.; Univ. of Southampton (BA Law 1st cl.); Queens' Coll., Cambridge (LLM). Lectr in Law, Univ. of Leicester, 1968–70; called to the Bar, Middle Temple, 1969, Bencher, 1997; practice in London and on Midland Circuit. Mem., Bar Council, 1985. *Recreations:* football (supporting Barnet FC), fell walking, gardening. *Address:* 7 Bedford Row, WC1R 4BU. *T:* (020) 7242 3555.

BAKER, Norman John; MP (Lib Dem) Lewes, since 1997; *b* 26 July 1957. *Educ:* Royal Holloway Coll., London Univ. (BA Hons). Our Price Records, 1978–83; teacher, 1985–97. Member: Lewes DC, 1987–99 (Leader of Council, 1991–97); E Sussex CC, 1989–97. Contested (Lib Dem) Lewes, 1992. *Address:* House of Commons, SW1A 0AA.

BAKER, His Honour Paul Vivian; a Circuit Judge, 1983–96; *b* 27 March 1923; *er s* of Vivian Cyril Baker and Maud Lydia Baker; *m* 1957, Stella Paterson Eadie, *d* of William Eadie, MD; one *s* one *d*. *Educ:* City of London Sch.; University Coll., Oxford (BCL, MA). RAF Wireless Operator and Navigator, 1941–46. Called to Bar, Lincoln's Inn, 1950, Bencher, 1979; QC 1972. Editor, Law Quarterly Review, 1971–87. Chm., Incorporated Council of Law Reporting for England and Wales, 1992–2001. *Publication:* (ed) Records of the Hon. Society of Lincoln's Inn, vol. 6 (1914–1965), 2001. *Recreation:* growing old gracefully. *Address:* 6 Redgrave Court, Patron's Way East, Denham Garden Village, Uxbridge, Middx UB9 5NT. *T:* (020) 7242 2633. *Clubs:* Athenæum, Authors'.

BAKER, His Honour Peter Maxwell; QC 1974; a Circuit Judge, 1983–2000; *b* 26 March 1930; *s* of late Harold Baker and of Rose Baker; *m* 1st, 1954, Jacqueline Mary Marshall (*d* 1986); three *d*; 2nd, 1988, Sandra Elizabeth Hughes. *Educ:* King Edward VII Sch., Sheffield; Exeter Coll., Oxford (MA). Called to Bar, Gray's Inn, 1956 (Holker Senior Exhibitioner); Junior, NE Circuit, 1960; a Recorder of the Crown Court, 1972–83. *Recreations:* fishing, shooting, yachting, music, watching others garden. *Address:* c/o North-Eastern Regional Director, 18th Floor, West Riding House, Albion Street, Leeds LS1 5AA.

BAKER, Philip Woolf, OBE 1997; QC 2002; *b* 14 July 1955; *s* of Lionel Baker and Frances Baker (*née* Roth); *m* 1992, Bing-Sum Lau; two *s* one *d*. *Educ:* Haberdashers' Aske's Sch., Elstree; Emmanuel Coll., Cambridge (MA); Balliol Coll., Oxford (BCL); University Coll., London (LLM); SOAS, London (PhD 1985); London Business Sch. (MBA). Called to the Bar, Gray's Inn, 1979; Lectr in Law, SOAS, London Univ., 1979–87; in practice as barrister, 1987–. Vis. Prof., Queen Mary Coll., Univ. of London, 1997–2008; Vis. Fellow, Inst. of Advanced Legal Studies, Univ. of London. *Publications:* Double Taxation Conventions and International Tax Law, 1991, 3rd edn 2001; contrib. articles on internat. tax law, Chinese law, Islamic law and human rights. *Recreations:* sinology, my family. *Address:* Gray's Inn Tax Chambers, 3rd Floor, Gray's Inn Chambers, Gray's Inn, WC1R 5JA. *T:* (020) 7242 2642, *Fax:* (020) 7831 9017; *e-mail:* pb@taxbar.com.

BAKER, Piers Howard Burton, PhD; HM Diplomatic Service, retired; Director, International Office, Imperial College London, since 2007; *b* 23 July 1956; *s* of late Dr Donald Burton Baker and Marjorie Winifred Baker; *m* 1979, Maria Eugenia Vilaincour; three *s*. *Educ:* King's Sch., Canterbury; Corpus Christi Coll., Cambridge (MA 1981, PhD 1983). Joined HM Diplomatic Service, FCO, 1983; First Sec., Brussels, 1985–88; FCO, 1988–93; First Sec., UK Repn, Brussels, 1993–96; FCO, 1996–2001; Dep. Hd of Mission, Consul-Gen. and Dir, Trade Promotion, then Trade and Investment, Vienna, 2001–06. *Publication:* Shahr-i Zohak and the History of the Bamiyan Valley, Afghanistan, 1991. *Recreations:* music, walking. *Address:* Imperial College London, S Kensington Campus, SW7 2AZ.

BAKER, Prof. Raymond, CBE 2002; PhD; FRS 1994; Chief Executive, Biotechnology and Biological Sciences Research Council, 1996–2001; *b* 1 Nov. 1936; *s* of Alfred Baker and May (*née* Golds); *m* 1960, Marian Slater; one *s* two *d*. *Educ:* Ilkeston Grammar Sch.; Leicester Univ. (BSc, PhD). Postdoctoral Fellow, UCLA, 1962–64; University of Southampton: Lectr in Organic Chem., 1964–72; Sen. Lectr, 1972–74; Reader, 1974–77; Prof., 1977–84; Dir, Wolfson Unit of Chemical Entomology, 1976–84; Dir 1984–89, Exec. Dir, 1989–96, of Medicinal Chem., Merck Sharp & Dohme Res. Labs. *Publications:* Mechanism in Organic Chemistry, 1971; contrib. numerous articles to Jl Chemical Soc., Jl Medicinal Chem., and other scientific jls. *Recreations:* golf, gardening. *Address:* Angeston Court, Uley, Dursley, Glos GL11 5AL. *T:* (01453) 861017.

BAKER, Richard Andrew; non-executive Chairman, Virgin Active Ltd, since 2008; *b* 6 Aug. 1962; *s* of John and Mary Baker; *m* Suzanne; two *d*. *Educ:* Bishop Vesey's Grammar Sch., Sutton Coldfield; Downing Coll., Cambridge (BA 1984). Nat. Account Manager, Brand Mktg and Hd of Sales, UK Multiples, Mars Confectionery, 1986–95; Gp Mktg Dir, then Chief Operating Officer, ASDA, 1995–2003; CEO, Alliance Boots (formerly Boots Gp) plc, 2003–07. *Recreations:* keen sportsman playing competitive hockey, tennis and golf. *Club:* Royal Automobile.

BAKER, Richard Douglas James, OBE 1976; RD 1979; broadcaster and author; Member, Broadcasting Standards Council, 1988–93; *b* Willesden, London, 15 June 1925; *s* of Albert and Jane Isobel Baker; *m* 1961, Margaret Celia Martin; two *s*. *Educ:* Kilburn Grammar Sch.; Peterhouse, Cambridge (MA). Served War, Royal Navy, 1943–46. Actor, 1948; Teacher, 1949; Third Programme Announcer, 1950–53; BBC TV Newsreader, 1954–82; Commentator for State Occasion Outside Broadcasts, 1967–70; TV Introductions to Promenade Concerts, 1960–95; Panellist on BBC2's Face the Music, 1966–79; Presenter, Omnibus, BBC TV, 1983; on Radio 4: presenter of Start the Week with Richard Baker, 1970–87; These You Have Loved, 1972–77; Baker's Dozen, 1978–87; Rollercoaster, 1984; Music in Mind, 1987–88; Richard Baker Compares Notes, 1987–95; The Musical Directors, 1998; on Radio 3: Mainly for Pleasure, 1986–92; In Tune, 1992–95; Rush Hour concerts, 1994–95; Sound Stories, 1998–99; on Radio 2: presenter of Melodies for You, 1986–95 and 1999–2003; Friday Night is Music Night, 1998–2005; Your 100 Best Tunes, 2003–07; on Classic FM: presenter, Classic Countdown, 1996; Evening Concerts, 1997–98; Baker's Choice, 1998–99. Columnist, Now! Magazine, 1979–80. Mem., Council, Friends of Covent Garden; Trustee, D'Oyly Carte Opera Co., 1985–98; Governor, NYO of GB, 1985–2001. TV Newscaster of the Year (Radio Industries Club), 1972, 1974, 1979; BBC Radio Personality of the Year

(Variety Club of GB), 1984; Sony Gold Award for Lifetime Achievement in Radio, 1996. Hon. FLCM 1974; Hon. RCM 1988. Hon. LLD: Strathclyde, 1979; Aberdeen, 1983. *Publications:* Here is the News (broadcasts), 1966; The Terror of Tobermory, 1972; The Magic of Music, 1975; Dry Ginger, 1977; Richard Baker's Music Guide, 1979; Mozart, 1982, rev. edn 1991; London, a theme with variations, 1989; Richard Baker's Companion to Music, 1993; Schubert: an illustrated biography, 1997; (ed) Music of the Sea, 2005. *Address:* c/o Stephannie Williams Artists, 16 Swanfold, Wilmcote, Stratford upon Avon CV37 9XH. *T:* (01789) 266272.

BAKER, Richard Hugh; HM Diplomatic Service, retired; *b* 22 Oct. 1935; *s* of late Hugh Cuthbert Baker and (Muriel) Lovenda Baker (*née* Owens); *m* 1963, Patricia Marianne Haigh Thomas; one *s* three *d. Educ:* Marlborough Coll.; New Coll., Oxford. Army (2nd Lieut RA), 1954–56. Plebiscite Officer, UN Plebiscite, S Cameroons, 1960–61; joined Diplomatic Service, 1962; 3rd, later 2nd, then 1st Sec., Addis Ababa, 1963–66; Foreign Office, 1967; Private Sec. to Permanent Under-Sec. of State, Foreign Office (later FCO), 1967–70; 1st Sec. and Head of Chancery, Warsaw, 1970–72; FCO, 1973–76; RCDS 1977; Econ. and Financial Counsellor, and Dep. Head, UK Perm. Delegn to OECD, Paris, 1978–82; Dep. High Comr, Ottawa, 1982–86; Asst Under-Sec. of State, and Civilian Mem., Sen. Directing Staff, RCDS, 1986–89. *Recreations:* music, painting, literature, pottery, printmaking, writing. *Address:* 1 The Thatched Cottages, Water Lane, Radwinter, Saffron Walden CB10 2TX.

BAKER, Richard James; Member (Lab) Scotland North East, Scottish Parliament, since 2003; *b* 29 May 1974; *s* of Rev. Canon James Baker, MBE and Rev. Anne Baker; *m* 2004, Claire Josephine Brennan (*see* C. J. Baker); one *d. Educ:* Aberdeen Univ. (MA English Lit.). Pres., NUS Scotland, 1998–2000; Scottish Press Officer, Help the Aged, 2000–02. *Recreations:* choral singing, football, cinema, reading. *Address:* Scottish Parliament, Edinburgh EH99 1SP. *T:* (constituency office) (01224) 641171, *Fax:* (01224) 641104; *e-mail:* richard.baker.msp@scottish.parliament.uk.

BAKER, Sir Robert George Humphrey S.; *see* Sherston-Baker.

BAKER, Dr Robin William, CMG 2005; Vice-Chancellor, University of Chichester, since 2007; *b* 4 Oct. 1953; *s* of late William John David Baker and Brenda Olive Baker (*née* Hodges); *m* 1974, Miriam Joy Turpin (marr. diss. 1997); two *s. Educ:* Bishop Wordsworth's Sch., Salisbury; Sch. of Slavonic and East European Studies, Univ. of London (BA 1976); Univ. of East Anglia (PhD 1984). MoD, 1976–80; res. student, 1980–84; British Council: S Africa, 1984–89; Head of Recruitment, 1989; Hungary, 1990–93; Thessaloniki, Greece, 1994–96; Russia, 1996–99; Director: W and S Europe, 1999; Europe, 1999–2002; Dep. Dir-Gen., 2002–05; Pro-Vice-Chancellor, Univ. of Kent, 2005–07. Sen. Vis. Fellow, Inst. for Balkan Studies, Thessaloniki, 1995–; Vis. Fellow, SSEES, 1995–97, 1999. Member: Council for Assisting Refugee Academics, 2003–; Council, Univ. of Kent, 2003–05; Internat. Policy Cttee, Royal Soc., 2003–05; Jamestown 2007 British Cttee, 2006–07. Member, Advisory Council: Inst. of Romance Studies, Univ. of London, 1999–2002; SSEES, 2000–. Trustee and Dir, Chichester Festival Th., 2007–. Fellow, UCL, 2004. FRSA 1998. *Publications:* The Development of the Komi Case System: a dialectological investigation, 1985; papers on history and languages of E Europe. *Recreations:* jazz, opera, South-East Europe. *Address:* University of Chichester, College Lane, Chichester, W Sussex PO19 6PE. *Club:* Travellers.

BAKER, Roger, QPM 2008; Chief Constable, Essex Police, since 2005; *b* 15 Nov. 1958; *s* of William Ernest Baker and Norah Margaret Baker; *m* 1999, Patricia Anne O'Callaghan; two *d* (and one *d* decd). *Educ:* Shirebrook Comp. Sch., Mansfield; Univ. of Derby (MBA 1998); Univ. of Manchester (MA Organisational Mgt 2000). Derbyshire Constabulary, 1977–2001, Chief Supt, 1999; Asst Chief Constable, Staffs Police, 2001–03; Dep. Chief Constable, N Yorks Police, 2003–05. *Recreations:* equestrian pursuits, golf, walking the dogs. *Address:* Essex Police, PO Box No 2, Police Headquarters, Springfield, Chelmsford, Essex CM2 6DA. *T:* (01245) 452110, *Fax:* (01245) 452123; *e-mail:* chief.constable@essex.pnn.police.uk.

BAKER, Samantha Jayne, (Sam); Editor, Red, since 2006; *b* 7 July 1966; *d* of Cliff Baker and Di (*née* Riglar); *m* 1993, Jon Courtenay Grimwood; one step *s. Educ:* Winton Sch.; Cricklade Coll.; Birmingham Univ. (BSocSc Pol Sci.). Chat mag., 1988–92; writer, Take a Break, 1992–93; Features Ed., then Dep. Ed., New Woman, 1993–96; Editor: Just Seventeen, 1996–97; Minx, 1997–98; Company, 1998–2003; Cosmopolitan, 2004–06. *Publications:* Fashion Victim, 2005; This Year's Model, 2008. *Recreations:* work, reassembling my entire past on iPod, Friday night curries, sleeping. *Address:* Red, 64 North Row, W1K 7LL. *T:* (020) 7150 7641, *Fax:* (020) 7150 7684; *e-mail:* sam.baker@hf-co.uk. *Clubs:* Black's, Shoreditch House.

BAKER, Rt Hon. Sir Scott; *see* Baker, Rt Hon. Sir T. S. G.

BAKER, Stuart William; His Honour Judge Stuart Baker; a Circuit Judge, since 1998; *b* 1 June 1952; *s* of Henry Baker and Elizabeth Baker (*née* Hooker); *m* 1975, Christine Elizabeth Bennett; (one *s* decd). *Educ:* Univ. of Newcastle upon Tyne (LLB Hons 1973). Called to the Bar, Inner Temple, 1974; in practice at the Bar, 1975–98; Asst Recorder, 1991–94; a Recorder, 1994–98; Northern Circuit. Mem., Legal Aid Area Appeal Cttee, 1991–98; Legal Mem., Mental Health Review Tribunal, 1996–98. *Recreations:* fell walking, theatre, woodturning, playing viola. *Address:* Preston Combined Court Centre, Openshaw Place, Ringway, Preston PR1 2LL.

BAKER, Rt Hon. Sir (Thomas) Scott (Gillespie), Kt 1988; PC 2002; **Rt Hon. Lord Justice Scott Baker;** a Lord Justice of Appeal, since 2002; *b* 10 Dec. 1937; *s* of late Rt Hon. Sir George Baker, PC, OBE and Jessie McCall Baker; *m* 1973, (Margaret) Joy Strange; two *s* one *d. Educ:* Haileybury; Brasenose Coll., Oxford (Hon. Fellow 2003). Called to the Bar, Middle Temple, 1961 (Astbury Schol.), Bencher 1985, Treasurer 2004; a Recorder, 1976–88; QC 1978; a Judge of the High Court, Family Div., 1988–92, QBD, 1993–2002; Family Div. Liaison Judge (Wales and Chester Circuit), 1990–92; Presiding Judge, Wales and Chester Circuit, 1991–95; Lead Judge, Administrative Ct, 2000–02. Member: Senate, Inns of Court, 1977–84; Bar Council, 1988. Member: Govt Cttee of Inquiry into Human Fertilisation (Warnock Cttee), 1982–84; Parole Bd, 1999–2002 (Vice-Chm., 2000–02). Asst Dep. Coroner for Inquest into the deaths of Diana, Princess of Wales and Dodi Al Fayed, 2007–08. Mem., Chorleywood UDC, 1965–68. Dep. Chm., Cricket Council Appeals Cttee, 1986–88. Gov., Caldecott Sch., 1991–2005 (Chm., 1996–2003). *Recreations:* golf, fishing, shooting. *Address:* Royal Courts of Justice, Strand, WC2A 2LL. *Clubs:* MCC; Denham Golf (Captain, 1992, Chm., 1995–2001).

See also M. F. Baker.

BAKER-BATES, Merrick Stuart, CMG 1996; HM Diplomatic Service, retired; Historical Records Adviser, Foreign and Commonwealth Office, since 2000; *b* 22 July 1939; *s* of late E. T. Baker-Bates, MD, FRCP, and of Norah Stuart (*née* Kirkham); *m* 1963, Chrystal Jacqueline Goodacre; one *s* one *d. Educ:* Shrewsbury Sch.; Hertford Coll., Oxford (MA); College of Europe, Bruges. Journalist, Brussels, 1962–63; entered HM Diplomatic Service, 1963; 3rd, later 2nd Sec., Tokyo, 1963–68; 1st Secretary: FCO, 1968–73; (Inf.), Washington, 1973–76; (Commercial), Tokyo, 1976–79; Counsellor (Commercial), Tokyo, 1979–82. Dir, Cornes & Co., Tokyo, 1982–85; Representative Dir, Gestetner Ltd (Japan), 1982–85; Dep. High Comr and Counsellor (Commercial/ Econ.), Kuala Lumpur, 1986–89; Hd of S Atlantic and Antarctic Dept, FCO, and Comr, British Antarctic Territory, 1989–92; Consul-Gen., Los Angeles, 1992–97. Youth Offending Team mentor, Leicester Probation, 2002–07. Mem., Mgt Cttee, British-Malaysia Soc., 2004–. Comdr, 1998–2005, Pres., 2005–08, St John Ambulance (Northants). Shakespeare's Globe Trust: Mem., Develt Council, 1998–2003; Chm., Internat. Cttee, 1999–2005; Bd Mem., 2001–05; Mem. Council, 2005–. Trustee, Oxford Univ. Soc., 2001–08. OStJ 2000. *Recreations:* photography, golf. *Address:* *e-mail:* merrick@bakerbates.com. *Club:* Tokyo (Tokyo).

See also R. P. Baker-Bates.

BAKER-BATES, Rodney Pennington; Chairman: Helphire Group plc, since 2005; Britannia Building Society, since 2008 (Member of Board, since 2007); *b* 25 April 1944; *s* of Eric Tom Baker-Bates and Norah Stuart (*née* Kirkham); *m* 1972, Gail Elizabeth Roberts; one *s. Educ:* Shrewsbury Sch.; Hertford Coll., Oxford (MA History). FICA 1975; AIMC 1975; FCIB 1991. Glyn Mills & Co., 1966–68; Arthur Andersen & Co., 1968–77; Chase Manhattan Bank, 1977–84; Midland Bank, 1984–92; Dir of Finance and IT, BBC, 1993–98; Man. Dir, Corporate Pensions Business, Prudential Corp., 1998–99; Chief Exec., Gp Pensions, 1999–2000, Prudential Financial Services, 2000–01, Consultant, 2001–02, Prudential plc. Director: Dexia Municipal Bank, 1997–2000; Aspen Group, 1997–99; Lloyds Register of Shipping, 1998–2007; Prudential Assce Co. Ltd, 2000–01; Bedlam Asset Mgt plc, 2003–; Chairman: Change Partnership Ltd, 1998–2001; Hydra Associates, 1999–2001; CoralEurobet plc, 1999–2002; Burns e-Commerce Solutions, 2002–04; Stobart Gp plc (formerly Westbury Property Fund), 2002–; EG Consulting Ltd, 2003–; First Assist Gp Ltd, 2003–; The Music Solution Ltd, 2004–; Cabot Financial Hldgs Gp, 2004–06; G's Mktg Gp Ltd, 2006–; Consultant to Bd, C. Hoare & Co., 2001– (Chm., Exec. Man. Partners, 2001–06). Dir, City of London Fest., 2001–04; Gov., RSC, 2003–. Governor, Bedales Sch., 1993–2002. Trustee: Royal Nat. Pension Fund for Nurses, 2000–01; Burdett Trust for Nursing, 2001–; Dolphin Square Trust, 2001–; Mem. Audit Cttee, Wellcome Trust, 2005–07. *Recreations:* gardening, performing arts, country pursuits. *Address:* c/o C. Hoare & Co, 37 Fleet Street, EC4P 4DQ. *T:* (020) 7353 4522. *Club:* Brooks's.

See also M. S. Baker-Bates.

BAKER WILBRAHAM, Sir Richard, 8th Bt *cr* 1776; DL; Director, J. Henry Schroder Wagg & Co. Ltd, 1969–89; Chairman, Bibby Line Group, 1992–97 (Deputy Chairman, 1989–92); *b* 5 Feb. 1934; *s* of Sir Randle Baker Wilbraham, 7th Bt, and Betty Ann, CBE (*d* 1975), *d* of W. Matt Torrens; *S* father, 1980; *m* 1962, Anne Christine Peto, *d* of late Charles Peto Bennett, OBE; one *s* three *d. Educ:* Harrow. Welsh Guards, 1952–54. J. Henry Schroder Wagg & Co. Ltd, 1954–89. Director: Westpool Investment Trust, 1974–92; Brixton Estate, 1985–2001 (Dep. Chm., 1994–2001); The Really Useful Group plc, 1985–90; Charles Barker Group, 1986–89; Grosvenor Estates Hldgs, 1989–99 (Dep. Chm., 1989–99); Severn Trent, 1989–94; Majedie Investments, 1989–2001; Christie Hosp. NHS Trust, 1990–96. Mem., Gen. Council, King Edward's Hosp. Fund for London, 1986–98. Gov., Nuffield Hosps, 1990–2001. A Church Comr, 1994–2001. Trustee, Grosvenor Estate, 1981–99. Governor: Harrow Sch., 1982–92; The King's Sch., Macclesfield, 1986–2006; Manchester Metropolitan Univ., 1998–2001. Upper Bailiff, Weavers' Co., 1994–95. High Sheriff, Cheshire, 1991–92; DL Cheshire, 1992. *Recreations:* field sports. *Heir:* *s* Randle Baker Wilbraham [*b* 28 May 1963; *m* 1997, Amanda, *e d* of Robert Glossop; one *s* two *d*]. *Address:* Rode Hall, Scholar Green, Cheshire ST7 3QP. *T:* (01270) 882961. *Club:* Brooks's.

BAKEWELL, Dame Joan (Dawson), DBE 2008 (CBE 1999); broadcaster and writer; *b* 16 April; *d* of John Rowlands and Rose Bland; *m* 1st, 1955, Michael Bakewell (marr. diss. 1972); one *s* one *d*; 2nd, 1975, Jack Emery (marr. diss. 2001). *Educ:* Stockport High Sch. for Girls; Newnham Coll., Cambridge (BA History and Econs). Associate, 1980–91, Associate Fellow, 1984–87, Newnham Coll., Cambridge. TV critic, The Times, 1978–81; columnist: Sunday Times, 1988–90; Guardian, 2003–05; Independent, 2006–. Gov., BFI, 1994–2003 (Dep. Chm., 1997–99; Chm., 1999–2003). Mem. Bd, RNT, 1996–2003. Chm., Nat. Campaign for the Arts, 2004–. Pres., Soc. of Arts Publicists, 1984–90. Mem. Council, Aldeburgh Foundn, 1985–99. Hon. Prof., Dept of Film and Media, Univ. of Stirling, 2006–. Hon. FRCA 1994; Hon. Fellow, RHBNC, 1997. Hon. DLitt: Queen Margaret UC, Edinburgh, 2005; Chester, 2007; Univ. of Arts, London, 2008. *Television:* BBC Television includes: Meeting Point, 1964; The Second Sex, 1964; Late Night Line Up, 1965–72; The Youthful Eye, 1968; Moviemakers at the National Film Theatre, 1971; Film 72, and Film 73, 1972–73; For the Sake of Appearance, Where is Your God?, Who Cares?, and The Affirmative Way (series), 1973; Holiday '74, '75, '76, '77 and '78 (series); What's it all About? (2 series) and Time Running Out (series), 1974; The Shakespeare Business, The Brontë Business, and Generation to Generation (series), 1976; My Day with the Children, 1977; Arts UK: OK?, 1980; Arts Correspondent, 1981–87; The Heart of the Matter, 1988–2000; Travels with Pevsner: Derbyshire, 1998; My Generation, 2000; Taboo (series), 2001; ITV includes: Sunday Break, 1962; Home at 4.30, 1964; (writer and producer) Thank You, Ron (documentary), 1974; Fairest Fortune and Edinburgh Festival Report, 1974; Reports Action (4 series), 1976–78. *Radio:* Away from it All, 1978–79; PM, 1979–81; Artist of the Week, 1998–2000; Chm., The Brains Trust, 1998–2001; Belief, 2001–; Midsummer Sins, 2004; Radio 4 plays: There and Back; Parish Magazine: 3 editions; Brought to Book, 2005. *Theatre:* Brontës: The Private Faces, Edinburgh Fest., 1979. *Publications:* (with Nicholas Garnham) The New Priesthood: British television today, 1970; (with John Drummond) A Fine and Private Place, 1977; The Complete Traveller, 1977; The Heart of Heart of the Matter, 1996; The Centre of the Bed (autobiog.), 2003; Belief, 2005; The View from Here, 2006. *Recreations:* theatre, travel, cinema. *Address:* Knight Ayton Management, 114 St Martin's Lane, WC2N 4BE. *T:* (020) 7836 5333.

BAKHURST, Kevin Alexander; Controller, News 24, BBC, since 2006; *b* 10 Dec. 1965; *s* of Christopher and Elizabeth Bakhurst; *m* 1990, Barbara King; two *s* one *d. Educ:* Haberdashers' Aske's Sch. for Boys, Elstree; St John's Coll., Cambridge (BA Modern Langs 1988). Audit Asst, Price Waterhouse, 1988–89; BBC: researcher and asst producer, Business Breakfast, 1989–90; Producer, Nine O'Clock News, 1990–94; Europe Producer, Brussels, 1994–95; Asst Ed., News, 1996–2001; Evenings Ed., News 24, 2001–03; Ed., Ten O'clock News, BBC TV, 2003–06. JP St Albans, 2000–06. *Recreations:* travel, speaking French, film and cinema, watching Chelsea, reading and political autobiography, local history. *Address:* c/o BBC TV Centre, Wood Lane, W12 7RJ; *e-mail:* kevin.bakhurst@bbc.co.uk.

BALÁZS, Prof. Péter; Professor of Political Science, Center for EU Enlargement Studies, Central European University, Budapest, since 2005; *b* 5 Dec. 1941; *s* of Sándor Balázs and Klára Pecz. *Educ:* Budapest Sch. of Econs (Dip. in Econs 1963; Dr habil 2000); Hungarian Acad. of Scis (Dr 2003). Economist, Elektroimpex Hungarian Foreign Trading Co.,

1963–68; Desk Officer, then Dir, Min. of Foreign Trade, 1969–82; Counsellor i/c EC, Hungarian Embassy, Brussels, 1982–87; Prime Minister's Office, 1987–88; Dir Gen. for multilateral relns, Min. of Internat. Econ. Relns, 1988–92; Perm. State Sec., Min. of Industry and Trade, 1992–93; Ambassador of Hungary: to Denmark, 1994–96; to Germany, 1997–2000; Prof., Budapest Univ. of Econs and Public Admin, 2000–02; State Sec. for Integration and Ext. Econ. Relns, Min. of Foreign Affairs, 2002–03; Ambassador, Perm. Repn to EU, 2003–04; Mem., European Commn, 2004. *Publications:* Az Európai Unió külkapcsolatai és Magyarország, 1996; (contrib.) Enlarging the European Union, 1997; (contrib.) Öszinte Könyv az Európai Unióról, 1999; (contrib.) Az Európai Unió politikái, 2000; (contrib.) Európai Közjog és politika, 2000; (contrib.) Unser Europa-Gemeinsam stärker: die kooperation der Klein- und Mittelstaaten im EU-Konvent, 2004. *Recreations:* classical music, horse riding.

BALCHIN, Sir Robert (George Alexander), Kt 1993; DL; Knight Principal, Imperial Society of Knights Bachelor, since 2006; *b* 31 July 1942; *s* of late Leonard George Balchin and Elizabeth Balchin (*née* Skelton); *m* 1970, Jennifer, OStJ, *d* of late Bernard Kevin Kinlay, Cape Town; twin *s* (of whom one decd). *Educ:* Bec Sch.; Univ. of London; Univ. of Hull. Teacher, 1964–69; Res., Univ. of Hull Inst. of Educn, 1969–71; Headmaster, Hill Sch., Westerham, 1972–80; Chairman: HSW Ltd, 1980–2000; Pardoe-Blacker (Publishing) Ltd, 1989–99; Blacker Publishing Ltd, 2003–; Grant-Maintained Schs Foundn and Centre, 1989–99; Centre for Educn Mgt, 1994–2002; Centre for Educn Finance Ltd, 2002–. Chairman: Educn Commn, 2003–; Commn on Special Educn Needs, 2006–. St John Ambulance: Asst Dir-Gen., 1982–84; Dir-Gen., 1984–90; Mem. Chapter-Gen., Order of St John, 1984–99. Mem. Council, 1995–, Registrar, 1998–2006, Imperial Soc. of Kts Bachelor. Mem., FAS, 1994–97 (Chairman: New Schs Cttee, 1994–97; Schs Improvement Cttee, 1996–97); Jt Founder/Treas., Catch 'em Young Project Trust, 1984–98; President: English Schs Orch., 1998–; League of Mercy, 1999–; Dep. Patron, Nat. Assoc. for Gifted Children, 1999–; Patron: Gateway Training Centre for Homeless, 1999–; Nat. Centre for Volunteering, 1999–2004. Chm., Balchin Family Soc., 1993–. Mem., Surrey CC, 1981–85. Member: Court, Univ. of Leeds, 1995–2000; Council, Goldsmiths' Coll., London, 1997–2005 (Dep. Chm. Council, 1999–2005); Pro-Chancellor, Brunel Univ., 2006–. Freeman, 1980, Liveryman, 1987, Goldsmiths' Co. (Mem., Educn Cttee, 1995–2002); Freeman and Liveryman, Broderers' Co., 2004. Hon. Col, Humberside & S Yorks ACF, 2004–. DL Greater London, 2001. FCP 1971 (Hon. FCP 1987); Hon. FHS 1987; Hon. FCGI 1998. Hon. DPhil Northland Open Univ., Canada, 1985; Hon. DLitt Hull, 2006. KStJ 1984. Cross of Merit (Comdr), SMO Malta, 1987. *Publications:* Emergency Aid in Schools, 1984; New Money, 1985, 2nd edn 1989; (jtly) Choosing a State School, 1989; numerous articles on educn/politics. *Address:* New Place, Lingfield, Surrey RH7 6EF. *T:* (01342) 834543; 88 Marsham Court, Westminster, SW1P 4LA. *Clubs:* Athenæum, Beefsteak.

BALCOMBE, David Julian; QC 2002; a Recorder, since 2000; *b* 4 Feb. 1958; s of Rt Hon. Sir (Alfred) John Balcombe and of Jacqueline Rosemary, (Lady Balcombe); *m* 1992, Sally Jane Spence; two *s*. *Educ:* Winchester Coll.; Univ. of Kent at Canterbury (BA). Called to the Bar, Lincoln's Inn, 1980. *Address:* 1 Crown Office Row, Temple, EC4Y 7HH. *T:* (020) 7797 7500.

BALDERSTONE, Sir James (Schofield), AC 1992; Kt 1983; company director, now retired; Chairman: Australian Mutual Provident Society, 1990–93 (Director, 1979–93); Chase AMP Bank, 1990–91 (Director, 1985–91); Broken Hill Proprietary Co. Ltd, 1984–89 (Director, 1971–89); Stanbroke Pastoral Co., 1982–93 (Managing Director, 1964–81); *b* 2 May 1921; *s* of late James Schofield and Mary Essendon Balderstone; *m* 1946, Mary Henrietta Tyree; two *s* two *d*. *Educ:* Scotch College, Melbourne. Service with RANR, WWII, 1940–45. General Manager for Aust., Thos Borthwick & Sons, 1953–67; Dep. Chm., Westpac Banking Corp., 1992–93 (Dir, 1981–84); Director: NW Shelf Develt Pty, 1976–83; Woodside Petroleum, 1976–83; ICI (Australia), 1981–84. Founding Chm., Australian Meat Exporters' Fed. Council, 1963–64; Mem., Australian Meat Bd, 1964–67. Chairman: Commonwealth Govt Policy Discussion Gp on Agriculture, 1981–82; Scotch Coll. Council, 1991–95. Mem. Council, Aust. War Meml, 1994–99; Dir, Aust. War Meml Foundn, 1996–99. Pres., Inst. of Public Affairs (Vic.), 1981–84. DUniv Newcastle, NSW, 1985. Commander's Cross, Order of Merit (Germany), 1991. *Recreations:* farming, reading, sport. *Address:* 115 Mont Albert Road, Canterbury, Vic 3126, Australia. *T:* (3) 98363137. *Clubs:* Australian, Melbourne (Melbourne); Union (Sydney); Queensland (Brisbane).

BALDING, Clare Victoria; sports presenter, BBC, since 1998; *b* 29 Jan. 1971; *d* of Ian Balding, LVO, and Lady Emma Balding, *sister* of Earl of Huntingdon, *qv*. *Educ:* Downe House; Newnham Coll., Cambridge (BA 2nd Cl. Hons English; Pres., Cambridge Union, 1992). Racing reporter, BBC Radio 5 Live, 1993–94; sports presenter, BBC Radio, 1994–; presenter: BBC horse-racing coverage, incl. Royal Ascot; Badminton, Burghley and Gatcombe Horse Trials; BBC Grandstand and Sunday Grandstand, 2000–07; Sydney Olympics and Paralympics, 2000; Salt Lake City Winter Olympics, 2002; Athens Olympics and Paralympics, 2004; Crufts, 2005, 2007, 2008; Beijing Olympics and Paralympics, 2008. Sports columnist: Evening Standard, 1997–2003; Observer, 2004–. Presenter, Ramblings, BBC Radio 4, 1998–. Judge, Whitbread Book Awards, 2001. Racing Journalist of the Year, 2003, Racing Broadcaster of the Year, 2004, Horserace Writers and Photographers Assoc.; Sports Presenter of the Year, RTS, 2004. *Recreations:* riding, tennis, ski-ing, theatre, cinema, travel. *Address:* Park House, Kingsclere, Newbury, Berks RG20 5PY. *T:* (01635) 297648.

BALDOCK, Brian Ford, CBE 1997; Chairman, Mencap, since 1998; *b* 10 June 1934; *s* of Ernest A. and Florence F. Baldock; *m* 1st, 1956, Mary Lillian Bartolo (marr. diss. 1966); two *s*; 2nd, 1968, Carole Anthea Mason; one *s*. *Educ:* Clapham Coll., London. Army Officer, 1952–55. Procter & Gamble, 1956–61; Ted Bates Inc., 1961–63; Rank Orgn, 1963–66; Smith & Nephew, 1966–75; Revlon Inc., 1975–78; Imperial Group, 1978–86; Guinness PLC: Dir, 1986–96; Gp Man. Dir, 1989–96; Dep. Chm., 1992–96. Chairman: Portman Group, 1989–96; Wellington Investments Ltd, 1997–2002; Dalgety, later Sygen Internat., 1998–2005 (Dir, 1992–2005); Marks & Spencer plc, 1999–2000 (non-exec. Dir, 1996–2004); First Artist Corp., 2001–03; Dir, Cornhill Insurance, 1996–2002. Freeman, City of London, 1989. CInstM 1991 (FInstM 1976); Fellow, Marketing Soc., 1988. FRSA 1987. *Recreations:* theatre (opera), cricket. *Address:* Chairman's Office, Royal Mencap Society, 123 Golden Lane, EC1Y 0RT. *Clubs:* Garrick, MCC, Lord's Taverners (Mem. Council; Chm., 1992–95).

BALDOCK, Lionel Trevor; Agent-General for Victoria, 1990–93; *b* 26 Nov. 1936; *s* of late Lionel Vernon Baldock and Alice Thelma Baldock; *m* 1st, 1967, Carolynne Cutting (marr. diss.); one *s* one *d*; 2nd, 1993, Aude L. S. Jaffrézo; one *s* one *d*. *Educ:* Melbourne Univ. (BCom). Man. Dir, Evasoft Leather Co., 1958–73; General Manager: Tecnicast Pty Ltd, 1974–80; (also Dir) Centrifugal Castings Australia Pty Ltd, 1974–80; J. C. & Howard Wright Pty Ltd, 1983–84; Pacific Dunlop Ltd (NSW), 1984–85; Sen. Trade Comr, Australian Trade Commn, Paris, 1985–90. *Recreations:* swimming, ski-ing, sailing, walking.

BALDOCK, (Richard) Stephen; High Master, St Paul's School, 1992–2004; *b* 19 Nov. 1944; *s* of John Allan Baldock and Marjorie Procter Baldock; *m* 1969, Dr Janet Elizabeth Cottrell; one *s* three *d*. *Educ:* St Paul's Sch.; King's Coll., Cambridge (John Stewart of Rannoch schol. in Greek and Latin 1964; BA 1967 Part I Classics, Part II Theology, MA 1970). St Paul's School: Asst Master, 1970–77; Housemaster, School House, 1977–84; Surmaster, 1984–92. Council Mem. and Educnl Advr, Overseas Missionary Fellowship, 1989–. Trustee: Combined Trusts Scholarship Trust, 2004–; Indep. Schs' Christian Alliance, 2005–; South Square Trust, 2007–. Governor: Monkton Combe Sch., Bath, 2003–; Gordonstoun Sch., 2006–; Visitor, Collingham coll., SW London, 2004–. *Recreations:* family, computers, sport. *Address:* c/o Old Pauline Club, St Paul's School, Lonsdale Road, Barnes, SW13 9JT. *Clubs:* Naval, MCC.

See also S. R. Baldock.

BALDOCK, Sarah Ruth, (Mrs David Hurley), FRCO; Organist and Master of the Choristers, Chichester Cathedral, since 2008; *b* Wembley, 5 April 1975; *d* of (Richard) Stephen Baldock, *qv*; *m* 2002, David Hurley. *Educ:* St Paul's Girls' Sch., London; Pembroke Coll., Cambridge (BA 1996). FRCO 1997. Organist-in-Residence, Tonbridge Sch., 1996–98; Asst Organist and Dir of Girls' Choir, 1998–2002, Asst Dir of Music, 2002–08, Winchester Cathedral. *Recreations:* cooking and eating, gardening. *Address:* c/o The Royal Chantry, Cathedral Cloisters, Chichester, W Sussex PO19 1PX. *T:* (01243) 782595, *Fax:* (01243) 812499; *e-mail:* organist@chichestercathedral.org.uk.

BALDRY, Antony Brian, (Tony); MP (C) Banbury, since 1983; *b* 10 July 1950; *e s* of Peter Edward Baldry and Oina (*née* Paterson); *m* 1st, 1979, Catherine Elizabeth (marr. diss. 1996), 2nd *d* of Captain James Weir, RN and Elizabeth Weir; one *s* one *d*; 2nd, 2001, Pippa Isbell, *e d* of Lt Col Penny Payne and Betty Payne. *Educ:* Leighton Park Sch., Reading; Univ. of Sussex (MA, LLB). Called to the Bar, Lincoln's Inn, 1975; barrister. Director: New Opportunity Press, 1975–90; Newpoint Publishing Gp, 1983–90; Transense Technologies plc, 1998–2008; Chairman: Black Rock Oil & Gas plc, 2005–; Westminster Oil Ltd, 2007–. Contested (C) Thurrock, 1979. PPS to Minister of State for Foreign and Commonwealth Affairs, 1986–87, to Lord Privy Seal and Leader of the House, 1987–89, to Sec. of State for Energy, 1989–90; Parliamentary Under-Secretary of State: Dept of Energy, 1990; DoE, 1990–94; FCO, 1994–95; Minister of State, MAFF, 1995–97. Mem., Parly Select Cttee on Employment, 1983–86; on Trade and Industry, 1997–2001; on Standards and Privileges, 2001; on Internat. Develt, 2001–05 (Chm., 2001–05). Joined Sussex Yeomanry, 1971; TA Officer, resigned 1990; Hon. Col, RLC (TA), 1997–. Robert Schuman Silver Medal, Stiftung FVS Hamburg, 1978. *Recreations:* walking in the country, reading historical biography, gardening, cricket. *Address:* House of Commons, SW1A 0AA. *Clubs:* Carlton, Farmers', Garrick, Brass Monkey.

BALDRY, Lorraine; Chairman, London Thames Gateway Development Corporation, since 2004; *b* 22 May 1949; *m* 1973, Don Baldry. Prudential Corp. plc, 1990–98; Man. Dir, Regus plc, 1999–2000; Sen. Advr, Investment Banking Div., Morgan Stanley, 2000–02; Chief Exec., Chesterton plc, 2002–03. Chairman: Central London Partnership, 1998–; Inventa Partners, 2002–; Dir, Tri-Air Developments Ltd, 2006–. Mem. Bd and Chm., Planning, Olympic Delivery Authy, 2006–. *Address:* London Thames Gateway Development Corporation, 9th Floor, South Quay Plaza 3, 189 Marsh Wall, E14 9SH. *T:* (020) 7517 4732; *e-mail:* lorraine.baldry@ltgdc.org.uk.

BALDRY, Tony; *see* Baldry, A. B.

BALDWIN, family name of **Earl Baldwin of Bewdley**.

BALDWIN OF BEWDLEY, 4th Earl *cr* 1937; **Edward Alfred Alexander Baldwin;** Viscount Corvedale, 1937; *b* 3 Jan. 1938; *o s* of 3rd Earl Baldwin of Bewdley and Joan Elspeth, *y d* of late C. Alexander Tomes, New York, USA; *S* father, 1976; *m* 1970, Sarah MacMurray (*d* 2001), *er d* of Evan James, *qv*; three *s*. *Educ:* Eton; Trinity Coll., Cambridge (MA, PGCE). Chm., British Acupuncture Accreditation Bd, 1990–98. Jt Chm., Parly Gp for Alternative and Complementary Medicine, 1992–2002; elected Mem., H of L, 1999; Mem., H of L Select Cttee inquiry into complementary and alternative medicine, 2000. *Publication:* (ed jtly) Baldwin Papers: a Conservative statesman 1908–47, 2004. *Heir:* *s* Viscount Corvedale, *qv*. *Address:* 2 Scholar Place, Cumnor Hill, Oxford OX2 9RD. *Club:* MCC.

BALDWIN, Alan Charles; a District Judge (Magistrates' Courts) (formerly Metropolitan Stipendiary Magistrate), since 1990; *b* 14 April 1948; *s* of Frederick Baldwin and Millicent Baldwin (*née* McCarthy); *m* 1974, Denise Maureen Jagger; two *s*. Admitted Solicitor, 1976. *Address:* Camberwell Green Magistrates' Court, D'Eynsford Road, SE5 7UP.

BALDWIN, Brian Paul; HM Diplomatic Service, retired; British High Commissioner, Solomon Islands, 2001–04; *b* 7 Dec. 1944; *s* of late Dennis and Violet Baldwin; *m* 1966, Elizabeth Mary Evans; three *s* one *d*. *Educ:* St Albans Grammar Sch. Joined Diplomatic Service, 1967; Vice Consul (Commercial), Johannesburg, 1970–72; Third Sec., Belgrade, 1973–75; Vice Consul (Political), Johannesburg, 1979–83; First Sec., Muscat, 1988–93; Dep. High Comr, Port Moresby, 1993–97; Administrator, Tristan Da Cunha, 1998–2001. *Recreations:* athletics, golf, tennis, photography. *Address:* PO Box 470, Noordhoek 7979, South Africa.

BALDWIN, David Arthur, CBE 1990; CEng, FIET; Director Emeritus, Hewlett-Packard Ltd, since 1996 (Chairman, 1988–96); *b* 1 Sept. 1936; *s* of late Isaac Arthur Baldwin and Edith Mary Baldwin (*née* Collins); *m* 1961, (Jacqueline) Anne Westcott; one *s* one *d*. *Educ:* Twickenham Technical Coll.; Wimbledon Technical Coll. (qualified electronic engineer). CEng; FIET (FIEE 1989). R&D Engineer, EMI, 1954–63; Sales Engineer, Solartron, 1963–65; Hewlett-Packard: Sales Engineer and Sales Manager, 1965–73; European Marketing Manager, 1973–78; Man. Dir, Hewlett-Packard Ltd, 1978–88. Man. Dir, Hewlett-Packard Europ. Multi-Country Region, 1990; Pres., Hewlett-Packard Belgium, 1991; Chm., Hewlett-Packard Spain, 1991; Dir, Hewlett-Packard Finland, Sweden, Denmark, Netherlands and Austria, 1991–96. Mem., BOTB, 1994–98 (Chm., European Trade Cttee, 1994–98); Chm., Thames Action and Res. Gp for Educn and Trng Ltd, 1996–. Mem. Council, RSA, 1994–. Member, Court: Cranfield Univ. (formerly Inst. of Technol.), 1987–; Brunel Univ., 1988–. CCMI; FInstD; FIMktg. Freeman City of London, 1988; Liveryman, Guild of Inf. Technologists, 1994. DUniv Strathclyde, 1990. *Recreations:* golf, ski-ing, photography, painting, sailing. *Address:* c/o Hewlett-Packard Ltd, Cain Road, Bracknell, Berks RG12 1HN. *T:* (01344) 360000.

BALDWIN, Sir Jack (Edward), Kt 1997; PhD; FRS 1978; Waynflete Professor of Chemistry and Fellow of Magdalen College, University of Oxford, 1978–2006, now Professor Emeritus and Hon. Fellow; *b* 8 Aug. 1938; *s* of Frederick Charles Baldwin and Olive Frances Headland; *m* 1977, Christine Louise, *d* of William B. Franchi. *Educ:* Lewes County Grammar Sch.; Imperial Coll., London Univ. (BSc, DIC, PhD). ARCS. Asst Lectr in Chem., Imperial Coll., 1963, Lectr, 1966; Asst Prof. of Chem., Pa State Univ., 1967, Associate Prof., 1969; Alfred P. Sloan Fellow, 1969–70, Associate Prof. of Chem., 1970, Prof., 1972, MIT; Daniell Prof. of Chem., King's Coll., London, 1972; Prof. of

Chem., MIT, 1972–78. Dir, Oxford Centre for Molecular Sciences, 1988–98. Mem., BBSRC, 1994–97. Lectures: Tilden, RSC, 1979; Simonsen, RSC, 1982. Corresp. Mem., Academia Scientiarum Gottingensis, Göttingen, 1988; For. Mem., Amer. Acad. of Arts and Scis, 1993. Hon. DSc: Warwick, 1988, Strathclyde, 1989. Corday Morgan Medal and Prize, Chem. Soc., 1975; Medal and Prize for Synthetic Organic Chemistry, RSC, 1980; Paul Karrer Medal and Prize, Zürich Univ., 1984; Medal and Prize for Natural Product Chemistry, RSC, 1984; Hugo Müller Medal, RSC, 1987; Max Tischler Award, Harvard Univ., 1987; Dr Paul Jansen Prize for Creativity in Organic Synthesis, Belgium, 1988; Davy Medal, 1994, Leverhulme Medal, 1999, Royal Soc.; Nakanishi Prize, Chem. Soc. of Japan, 2002. *Publications:* res. pubns in Jl of Amer. Chem. Soc., Jl of Chem. Soc., Tetrahedron. *Address:* Chemistry Research Laboratory, Mansfield Road, Oxford OX1 3TA.

BALDWIN, Prof. John Evan, PhD; FRS 1991; Professor of Radioastronomy, 1989–99, now Emeritus, and Fellow of Queens' College, since 1989, University of Cambridge; Head of Mullard Radio Astronomy Observatory, Cavendish Laboratory, 1987–97; *b* 6 Dec. 1931; *s* of Evan Baldwin and Mary Wild; *m* 1969, Joyce Cox. *Educ:* Merchant Taylors', Crosby; Queens' Coll., Cambridge (MA; Clerk Maxwell Student, 1955–57; PhD 1956). FInstP 1997. Cambridge University: Research Fellow, later Fellow, Queens' Coll., 1956–74; Univ. Demonstrator in Physics, 1957–62; Asst Dir of Research, 1962–81; Reader, 1981–89. Guthrie Medal, Inst. of Physics, 1997; Hopkins Prize, Cambridge Philosophical Soc., 1997; Jackson Gwilt Medal, RAS, 2001. *Publications:* contribs to scientific jls. *Recreations:* gardening, mountain walking. *Address:* Cavendish Laboratory, 19 J. J. Thomson Avenue, Cambridge CB3 0HE. *T:* (01223) 337294.

BALDWIN, John Paul; QC 1991; barrister; a Recorder, since 2004; *b* 15 Aug. 1947; *s* of late Frank Baldwin and Marjorie Baldwin (*née* Jay); *m* 1981, Julie Campbell; two *d.* *Educ:* Nelson Grammar Sch.; Univ. of Leeds (BSc 1st Cl. Hons 1968); St John's Coll., Oxford (DPhil 1972). Res. Fellow, Univ. of Oxford, 1972–75; called to the Bar, Gray's Inn, 1977, Bencher, 2000. Judge, Patents County Court, 2006–. *Publications:* numerous scientific pubns, 1969–75. *Recreations:* tennis, gardening. *Address:* 8 New Square, Lincoln's Inn, WC2A 3QP. *T:* (020) 7405 4321. *Clubs:* Queen's, Harbour, Campden Hill Lawn Tennis.

BALDWIN, Mark Phillip; founder and choreographer, Mark Baldwin Dance Co., since 1992; Artistic Director, Rambert Dance Company, since 2002; *b* 16 Jan. 1954; *s* of late Ronald William Baldwin and Rose Theresa Evans. *Educ:* St Kentigerns Coll., NZ; Pakuranga Coll., NZ; Suva Grammar Sch., Fiji; Elam Sch. of Fine Arts, Univ. of Auckland. Founder Dancer, Limbs Dance Co., NZ, New Zealand Ballet, Australian Dance Theatre, Rambert Dance Co., 1979–92; choreographer-in-residence, Sadler's Wells, 1993; resident artist, The Place, 1995–96; choreographer-in-residence, Scottish Ballet, 1996. Works choreographed for Rambert Dance Co. include: Island to Island, 1991; Gone, 1992; Spirit, 1994; Banter Banter, 1994; Constant Speed, 2005; for Scottish Ballet: Haydn Pieces, 1995; Ae Fond Kiss, 1996; More Poulenc, 1996; for Staatsoper, Berlin: Labyrinth, 1997; The Demon, 1998; The Man with a Moustache (for City Ballet of London), 1998; Towards Poetry (for Royal Ballet), 1999; Pointe Blank (for TV), 1999; Frankenstein (for BBC4), 2003; The Wedding (for Royal NZ Ballet), 2006. *Address:* Rambert Dance Company, 94 Chiswick High Road, W4 1SH.

BALDWIN, Nicholas Peter, CEng, FIMechE, FIET; Chief Executive, Powergen UK plc, 2001–02; *b* 17 Dec. 1952; *s* of Desmond Stanley Frederick Baldwin and Beatrix Marie Baldwin (*née* Walker); *m* 2002, Adrienne Ann Plunkett; one *s* one *d.* *Educ:* City Univ. (BSc Mechanical Engrg); Birkbeck Coll., Univ. of London (MSc Econs). CEng 1979; FIMechE 1996; FIET (FIEE 2002); CDir 2007. Metropolitan Water Bd, 1971–74; Thames Water Authy, 1974–80; CEGB, 1980–89, Sen. Energy Analyst, 1986–89; PowerGen plc, 1989–; Econ. Studies Manager, 1989–90; Business Planning Manager, 1990–92; Head of Strategic Planning, 1992–94; Director: Strategy, 1994–95; Generation, 1995–96; Man. Dir, UK Electricity Prodn, 1996–98; Exec. Dir, UK Ops, 1998–2001. Non-executive Director: Energy Gp Advisory Bd, DTI, 2002–06; Forensic Sci. Service, 2004–; Nuclear Decommng Authy, 2004– (Chm., 2007–08); Scottish and Southern Energy, 2006–. Chm., Public Weather Service Customer Gp, 2007–. FRSA 1998. *Publications:* articles in Energy Policy and Energy Economics. *Recreations:* long distance walking, jazz and rock music, reading, family activities. *Club:* Worcester County Cricket.

BALDWIN, Air Vice-Marshal Nigel Bruce, CB 1996; CBE 1992; Chairman, RAF Historical Society, since 1997; *b* 20 Sept. 1941; *s* of Peter William Baldwin and Doris Baldwin; *m* 1963, Jennifer; one *d* (and one *d* decd). *Educ:* Peter Symonds' Sch., Winchester; RAF Coll., Cranwell. Pilot, Vulcans, 9/35 Sqns, 1963–68; ADC to AOC 11 Gp, 1968–70; Sqn Ldr, Vulcans, 35 Sqn, Cyprus, 1970–73; Staff Coll., Bracknell, 1974; HQ Strike Command, 1975–76; OC 50 Sqn, Vulcans, 1977–79; US Air War Coll. and Faculty, US Air Command and Staff Coll., 1979–82; Gp Captain and Station Comdr, Wyton, 1983–85; Internat. Fellow, Nat. Defense Univ., Washington, 1986; Asst Dir of Defence Policy, MoD, 1986–88; Air Cdre Plans, HQ Strike Command, 1989–92; ACDS (Overseas), 1993–96. Vice-Pres., Ex-Services Mental Welfare Soc. (Chm., 1997). FRAeS 1997. *Recreations:* hill walking, Schubert, Nelson. *Club:* Royal Air Force.

BALDWIN, Maj.-Gen. Peter Alan Charles, CBE 1994; Company Secretary, Television Corporation, 1997–2006 (Consultant, 1996); *b* 19 Feb. 1927; *s* of Alec Baldwin and Anne Dance; *m* 1st, 1953, Judith Elizabeth Mace; 2nd, 1982, Gail J. Roberts. *Educ:* King Edward VI Grammar Sch., Chelmsford. Enlisted 1942; commnd R Signals 1947; early service included Berlin, 1948–49 (during airlift), and Korean War, 1950; Staff Coll., 1960; JSSC, 1964; Borneo operations (despatches, 1967); Directing Staff, Staff Coll., 1967–69; Comdr, 13 Signal Regt, BAOR, 1969–71; Sec. for Studies, NATO Defence Coll., 1971–74; Comdr, 2 Signal Group, 1974–76; ACOS Jt Exercises Div., Allied Forces Central Europe, 1976–77; Maj.-Gen. and Chief Signal Officer, BAOR, 1977–79. Dep. Dir of Radio, 1979–87, Dir of Radio, 1987–90, IBA; Chief Exec., Radio Authy, 1991–95. Mem., Bd, Crimestoppers, 2003–06. Trustee: Eyeless Trust, 1996–2007 (Chm., 2002–07); CSV, 1997–; D'Oyly Carte Opera Co., 2000–. Fellow, Radio Acad., 1992; FRSA 1993. *Recreations:* cricket, music, theatre. *Address:* c/o Lloyds TSB, 7 Pall Mall, SW1Y 5NA. *Club:* Army and Navy.

BALDWIN, Sir Peter (Robert), KCB 1977 (CB 1973); MA; Chairman, Help For All Trust, since 2002; *b* 10 Nov. 1922; *s* of Charles Baldwin and Katie Baldwin (*née* Field); *m* 1951, Margaret Helen Moar; two *s.* *Educ:* City of London Sch.; Corpus Christi Coll., Oxford (Hon. Fellow, 1980). Foreign Office, 1942–45; Gen. Register Office, 1948–54; HM Treasury, 1954–62; Cabinet Office, 1962–64; HM Treasury, 1964–76; Principal Private Sec. to Chancellor of Exchequer, July 1966–Jan. 1968; Under-Sec., HM Treasury, 1968–72; Dep. Sec., HM Treasury, 1972–76; Second Permanent Sec., DoE, 1976; Permanent Sec., Dept of Transport, 1976–82. Dir, Mitchell Cotts, 1983–87; Chairman: SE Thames RHA, 1983–91; Rural Village Develt Foundn, 1983–85 (Vice-Chm., 1985–90); Brent Dial-a-Ride, 1983–85; Westminster Dial-a-Ride, 1984–87; Community Transport, 1985–87; Disabled Persons Transport Adv. Cttee, 1986–93; President: Readibus, 1981–84; Disability Action Westminster, 1986–95 (Chm., 1983–86); Tripscope 1994–2006 (Chm., 1986–94); AFASIC, 1995–; Charities Aid Foundn, 1999–2003 (Mem.

Bd, 1988–99; Vice Chm., 1993; Chm., 1994–99); Vice-President: RNID, 1983–91; Mobilise (formerly Disabled Drivers Motoring Club), 1985–; Hearing Dogs for Deaf People, 1986– (Chm., 1983–86); PHAB, 1988– (Vice-Chm., 1981, Chm., 1982–88; Vice-Pres., N Ireland, 1990–); RADAR, 1998– (Mem., 1983–96, Chm., 1992–96, Exec. Cttee); Right from the Start, 2007–. Automobile Association: Vice-Pres., 1993–; Mem. Cttee, 1983–93, Vice-Chm. Cttee, 1990–93; AA Road Safety Research Foundation: Mem. Cttee, 1986–90; Chm., 1990–94; Mem., Chm's Res. Adv. Gp, 1994–2005. Member: Nat. Rly Mus. Cttee, 1983–87; Railway Heritage Trust Tech. Panel, 1984–; Bd, Public Finance Foundn, 1984–98; Compact Wkg Gp, 1998–2002; Adv. Cttee, Air Ambulance Assoc., 2000–02; Chairman: Kent Air Ambulance Trust, 1992–94; Pets As Therapy, 1997–2006 (Trustee, 1990–2006); Pres., 2007–); Motorway Archive Trust, 2000–06. Royal Society of Arts: FRSA; Mem., 1983–94, Chm., 1985–87; Council; Vice-Pres., 1987–94; Emeritus Vice-Pres., 1994–. Chm. Delegacy, KCH Med. and Dental Sch., 1991–98; Member: Bd, City Lit. Inst., 1990–95; Council, KCL, 1992–2003; Bd of Govs, UMDS of Guy's and St Thomas' Hosp., 1993–98. Chm., St Catherine's Home and Sch., Ventnor, 1961–78; Gov., Eltham Coll., 1984–85. Trustee, Flanders Club, 2002–04. Life Vice-Pres., CS Sports Council, 1982 (Vice-Chm., 1974–78; Chm., 1978–82). Freeman, City of London, 1992. FKC; FCILT; Hon. FIHT; CCMI. *Publications:* (ed with R. C. D. Baldwin) The Motorway Achievement: the British motorway system: visualisation, policy and administration, 2004; (ed with R. C. D. Baldwin and M. M. Chrimes) Visions of Reconstruction 1940–1948, 2005; (ed with R. C. D. Baldwin) The Motorway Achievement: the motorways of Southern and Eastern England, 2007. *Recreations:* painting, watching cricket. *Address:* 2 Stokes Cottages, Burwash Common, near Etchingham, E Sussex TN19 7LR. *T:* (01435) 883550. *Club:* Reform.

BALDWIN, Prof. Thomas Raymond, PhD; Professor of Philosophy, University of York, since 1995; *b* 10 April 1947; *s* of Raymond Baldwin and Penelope Baldwin (*née* Barlow); *m* 1973, Anna Barber; two *d.* *Educ:* Trinity Coll., Cambridge (BA (Moral Scis) 1968; PhD (Philos.) 1971). Lectr in Philos., Makerere Univ., Kampala, 1971–72; Jun. Res. Fellow, Churchill Coll., Cambridge, 1973–74; Lecturer: Univ. of York, 1974–84; Philos. Faculty, Cambridge Univ., 1984–95; Fellow, Clare Coll., Cambridge, 1984–95. Ed., Mind, 2005–. Member: Nuffield Council on Bioethics, 2000–06; HFEA, 2001–05 (Dep. Chm., 2002–05). *Publications:* G. E. Moore, 1990; Contemporary Philosophy, 2001; Cambridge History of Philosophy, 2003. *Recreations:* walking, visiting gardens. *Address:* Department of Philosophy, University of York, York YO10 5DD. *T:* (01904) 433252; *e-mail:* trb2@york.ac.uk.

BALES, Kenneth Frederick, CBE 1990; Regional Managing Director, West Midlands Regional Health Authority, 1984–92; *b* 2 March 1931; *s* of Frederick Charles Bales and Deborah Alice Bales; *m* 1958, Margaret Hazel Austin; two *s* one *d.* *Educ:* Buckhurst Hill Grammar Sch.; LSE; Univ. of Manchester. BScSoc; DipSocAdmin; AHSM. Hosp. Sec., Newhall & Hesketh Park Hosps, 1958–62; Regional Trng Officer, Birmingham Regional Hosp. Bd, 1962–65; Regional Staff Officer, Birmingham Regional Staff Cttee, 1965–68; Group Sec., W Birmingham HMC, 1968–73; Regional Administrator, W Midlands RHA, 1973–84. Vice Pres., Disability W Midlands, 1999–2006 (Chm., 1996–98). *Recreations:* painting, sport, bridge. *Address:* Stronefield, 4 St Catherine's Close, Blackwell, near Bromsgrove, Worcestershire B60 1BG. *T:* (0121) 445 1424.

BALFE, Richard Andrew; President, European Parliament Members Pension Fund, since 2004; *b* 14 May 1944; *s* of Dr Richard J. Balfe and Mrs Dorothy L. Balfe (*née* de Cann); *m* 1986, Susan Jane Honeyford; one *s* one *d*, and one *s* by a previous marriage. *Educ:* Brook Secondary Sch., Sheffield; LSE (BSc Hons 1971). Fellow Royal Statistical Soc., 1972. HM Diplomatic Service, 1965–70; Res. Officer, Finer Cttee on One Parent Families, 1970–73; Political Sec., RACS, 1973–79; Dir, RACS and associated cos, 1978–85. European Parliament: Mem. (Lab 1979–2001, C 2002–04) London S Inner, 1979–99, London Reg., 1999–2004; Quaestor, 1994–2004; Member: Foreign Affairs Cttee, 1981–99; Security Cttee, 1989–99; Econ. and Monetary Cttee, 1999–2004; Petitions Cttee, 2001–04. Parly Candidate (Lab), Paddington South, 1970; contested (Lab) Southwark and Bermondsey, 1992. Mem., GLC for Southwark/Dulwich, 1973–77; Chairman: Thamesmead New Town Cttee, 1973–75; GLC Housing Cttee, 1975–77. Member: Exec. Cttee, Fabian Soc., 1981–82; London Labour Party Exec., 1973–95 (Chair, Policy Cttee, 1983–85); Chair, Political Cttee, Royal Arsenal Co-op (CWS), 1984–95. Mem., Ct of Governors, LSE, 1973–91. *Recreations:* collecting books and pamphlets on political and social history topics, opera, Wagner, walking. *Address:* (office) 8B/24 European Parliament, Rue Wiertz, 1047 Brussels, Belgium; (home) The Old Rectory, 10 Fitzroy Street, Newmarket CB8 0JW; *e-mail:* richard.balfe@balfes.com. *Club:* Reform.

BALFOUR, family name of **Earl of Balfour** and **Barons Balfour of Inchrye, Kinross** and **Riverdale**.

BALFOUR, 5th Earl of, *cr* 1922; **Roderick Francis Arthur Balfour;** Viscount Traprain 1922; *b* 9 Dec. 1948; *s* of Eustace Arthur Goschen Balfour and Anne (*née* Yule); *S* cousin, 2003; *m* 1971, Lady Tessa Mary Isabel Fitzalan-Howard, *e d* of 17th Duke of Norfolk, KG, GCVO, CB, CBE, MC; four *d.* *Educ:* Eton; London Business Sch. Mem., London Stock Exchange, 1975–81; Dir, Union Discount Co. of London plc, 1983–90; Dir, Rothschild Trust Corp. Ltd, 1990–2005; Founder and Dir, Virtus Trust Gp, 2005–. Non-executive Director: Bateman Engrg NV, 2005–; Nikanor plc, 2006–. Liveryman, Clothworkers' Co., 1986. *Heir:* *b* Hon. Charles George Yule Balfour [*b* 23 April 1951; *m* 1st, 1978, Audrey Margaret Hoare; 2nd, 1987, Svea Maria Cecily Lucrezia von Goëss; one *s* one *d*]. *Address:* *e-mail:* EofBPrivate@aol.com. *Club:* White's, Walbrook.

BALFOUR OF BURLEIGH, Lord *cr* 1607 (*de facto* 8th Lord, 12th but for the Attainder); **Robert Bruce,** CEng, FIET; FRSE; Chancellor, Stirling University, 1988–98; Vice Lord-Lieutenant, Clackmannan, 1995–2001; *b* 6 Jan. 1927; *e s* of 11th Lord Balfour of Burleigh and Dorothy (*d* 1976), *d* of late R. H. Done; *S* father, 1967; *m* 1st, 1971, Mrs Jennifer Brittain-Catlin (marr. diss. 1993), *d* of late E. S. Manasseh; two *d*; 2nd, 1993, Janet Morgan (*see* Lady Balfour of Burleigh). *Educ:* Westminster Sch. Served Home Guard, 1944–45 as Private, 2nd Herefordshire Bn; RN, 1945–48, as Ldg Radio Electrician's Mate. Joined English Electric Co. Ltd, 1951; graduate apprentice, 1951–52; Asst Foreman, Heavy Electrical Plant Dept, Stafford Works, 1952–54; Asst Superintendent, Heavy Electrical Plant Dept, Netherton Works, Liverpool, 1954–57; Manager, English Electric Co. of India (Pvt) Ltd, Madras, 1957–60; Dir and Gen. Manager, English Electric Co. India Ltd, 1960–64; Dep. Gen. Manager, English Electric Co. Ltd, Netherton, Liverpool, 1964–65, Gen. Manager 1965–66; Dir and Gen. Manager, D. Napier & Son Ltd, 1966–68; Dep. Gov., Bank of Scotland, 1977–91 (Dir, 1968–91). Chairman: Viking Oil, 1971–80; NWS Bank (formerly North West Securities), 1978–91; Capella Nova, 1988–; Canongate Press, 1991–93; United Artists Communications (Scotland), 1993–96; Director: Scottish Investment Trust, 1971–97; Tarmac, 1981–90; William Lawson Distillers Ltd, 1984–97; Television Educnl Network, 1990–96; UAPT Infolink, 1991–94; Member: British Railways (Scottish) Board, 1982–93; Forestry Commn, 1971–74. Chm., Fedn of Scottish Bank Employers, 1977–86. Chairman: Scottish Arts Council, 1971–80;

NBL Scotland, 1981–85; Turing Inst., 1983–91; Scottish Cttee, ABSA, 1990–94 (Mem. Council, 1976–94); Dir, Edinburgh Book Fest., 1981–97 (Chm., 1981–87). Pres., Friends of Vellore, 1973–. Vice-Pres., RNID, 1987–2004; Treasurer: Royal Scottish Corp., 1967–2004; RSE, 1989–94; Trustee: John Muir Trust, 1989–96; Bletchley Park Trust, 2000–; Dir, Eur. Brandenburg Ensemble, 2007–. Hon. FRIAS, 1982. DUniv Stirling, 1988; Hon. DLitt Robert Gordon, 1995. *Recreations:* music, climbing, woodwork, open air ice-skating. *Heir: d* Hon. Victoria Bruce-Winkler [*b* 7 May 1973; *m* 2002, Michail Winkler; one *d*]. *Address:* Brucefield, Clackmannanshire FK10 3QF.

See also G. J. D. Bruce.

BALFOUR OF BURLEIGH, Lady; Janet Bruce, CBE 2008; writer and company director; *b* 5 Dec. 1945; *e d* of Frank Morgan and Shiela Sadler; *m* 1993, Lord Balfour of Burleigh, *qv*. *Educ:* Newbury Co. Girls Grammar Sch.; St Hugh's Coll., Oxford. MA, DPhil Oxon, MA Sussex. FSAScot 1992; FRSE 1999. Kennedy Meml Scholar, Harvard Univ., 1968–69; Student, Nuffield Coll., Oxford, 1969–71; Res. Fellow, Wolfson Coll., Oxford and Res. Officer, Univ. of Essex, 1971–72; Res. Fellow, Nuffield Coll., Oxford, 1972–74; Lectr in Politics, Exeter Coll., Oxford, 1974–76; Dir of Studies, St Hugh's Coll., Oxford, 1975–76 and Lectr in Politics, 1976–78; Mem., Central Policy Rev. Staff, Cabinet Office, 1978–81. Mem. Bd, British Council, 1989–99. Vis. Fellow, All Souls Coll., Oxford, 1983. Dir, Satellite Television PLC, 1981–83; Special Advr to Dir-Gen., BBC, 1983–86; Advr to Bd, Granada Gp, 1986–89; Mem., London Adv. Bd, Nat. and Provincial Bldg Soc., 1988–89; Chairman: Cable & Wireless Flexible Resource Ltd, 1993–97; Nuclear Liabilities Fund (formerly Nuclear Generation Decommissioning Co.), 2003– (Dir, 1996–2003); non-executive Director: Cable & Wireless, 1988–2004; W. H. Smith, 1989–95; Midlands Electricity, 1990–96; Pitney Bowes, 1991–93; Scottish American Investment Trust, 1991–2008; Scottish Med. Res. Fund, 1993–96; Scottish Life, 1995–2001; Scottish Oriental Smaller Cos Investment Trust, 1995–; NMT Group, 1997–2004; BPB, 2000–05; Stagecoach Gp, 2001–; Murray Internat. Investment Trust, 2003–; Close Enterprise VCT, 2006–. Vice-Pres., Videotext Industries Assoc., 1985–91; Dir, Hulton Deutsch Collection, 1988–90. Member: Lord Chancellor's Adv. Council on Public Records, 1982–86; Scottish Museums Council Develt Resource, 1988–96; Adv. Council, Inst. for Advanced Studies in the Humanities, Univ. of Edinburgh, 1988–96; Ancient Monuments Bd for Scotland, 1990–97; Book Trust (Scotland), 1992–99; Scottish Econ. Council, 1993–96; Chairman: Scotland's Book Campaign, 1994–96; Readiscovery Touring Ltd, 1996–99. Trustee: Amer. Sch. in London, 1985–88; Fairground Heritage Trust, 1987–90; Cyclotron Trust, 1988–90; Scottish Hosp. Endowments Res. Trust, 1992–96; Carnegie Endowment for Univs of Scotland, 1994–; Nuclear Trust, 1996–; Scottish Science Trust, 1997–99; Nat. Library of Scotland, 2002–; Trusthouse Charitable Foundn, 2006–; Chairman: Dorothy Burns Charitable Trust, 1992–2002; Scottish Cultural Resources Access Network Ltd, 1996–2004; Scottish Mus. of Year Awards, 1999–2004. Mem., Editorial Bd, Political Quarterly, 1980–90. Hon. LLD Strathclyde, 1999; Hon. DLitt Napier, 1999. *Publications:* (as Janet Morgan): The House of Lords and the Labour Government 1964–70, 1975; Reinforcing Parliament, 1976; (ed) The Diaries of a Cabinet Minister 1964–70 by Richard Crossman, 3 vols 1975, 1976, 1977; (ed) Backbench Diaries 1951–63 by Richard Crossman, 1980; (ed with Richard Hoggart) The Future of Broadcasting, 1982; Agatha Christie: a biography, 1984; Edwina Mountbatten: a life of her own, 1991; The Secrets of rue St Roch, 2004. *Recreations:* music of Handel, sea-bathing, ice-skating out of doors, pruning. *Address:* Brucefield, Clackmannanshire FK10 3QF. *T:* (01259) 730228.

BALFOUR OF INCHRYE, 2nd Baron *cr* 1945, of Shefford; **Ian Balfour;** *b* 21 Dec. 1924; *s* of 1st Baron Balfour of Inchrye, PC, MC and Diana Blanche (*d* 1982), *d* of Sir Robert Grenville Harvey, 2nd Bt; *S* father, 1988; *m* 1953, Josephine Maria Jane (*d* 2007), *d* of late Morogh Percy Wyndham Bernard and of the Hon. Mrs Bernard; one *d*. *Educ:* Eton, spasmodically, and Magdalen College, Oxford (MA). Business consultant, author and composer of 9 operas, and numerous orchestral and instrumental works. Performances include: In Memoriam II (oboe, harp, percussion and strings), Dublin, 1982; Suite No 1 for 'Cello, Edinburgh, 1984, London, 1986; Oxford Memories (orch.), Oxford, London, 1996; Millennium Surprise (orch.), Esterhazy, Leipzig, Moscow, Prague, 2000. *Publication:* Famous Diamonds, 1987, 4th edn 2000. *Recreations:* watching cricket and Association football, walking, writing, thinking, drinking, dreaming. *Address:* 4 Marsh End, Ferry Road, Walberswick, Suffolk IP18 6TH. *Club:* Garrick.

BALFOUR, Alexander William; Head of New Media, London Organising Committee of the Olympic Games Ltd, since 2006; *b* 26 Feb. 1971; *s* of Peter Edward Gerald Balfour, *qv* and Diana Rosemary Balfour; *m* 2000, Samantha, (Sam), Walker; one *s* one *d*. *Educ:* St John's Coll., Cambridge (BA 1993). Reporter, Euromoney mag., 1994–95; freelance journalist, 1995–97; Editor, GE '97, 1997; Content Dir, UK Citizens Online Democracy, 1998; Producer, The Guardian, 1998–99; Dir, Business Develt, 2000–01, Chm., 2001–06, CricInfo Ltd. Mem., Haddock Club. *Recreations:* riding fixed gear bicycles, being bullied by my children, swimming in the sea, reading, watching cricket, DJing, surfing the Interweb. *Address:* c/o LOCOG, 1 Churchill Place, E14 5LN. *T:* (020) 3201 2000; *e-mail:* alex.balfour@london2012.com. *Clubs:* Lansdowne, MCC; London Dynamo, Rye Wheelers.

BALFOUR, Comdr Colin James, RN; DL; Vice Lord-Lieutenant of Hampshire, 1996–99; *b* 12 June 1924; *s* of late Maj. Melville Balfour, MC, Wintershill Hall, Hants and Margaret, (Daisy), Mary Balfour (*née* Lascelles); *m* 1949, Prudence Elizabeth, JP, *d* of Adm. Sir Ragnar Colvin, KBE, CB; one *s* one *d*. *Educ:* Eton. Joined RN, 1942: served HMS Nelson, Mediterranean, 1943; D-Day and N Russia Convoys, 1944–45; HMS Cossack, Korean War, 1950–52; RNSC, 1955; 1st Lt, HM Yacht Britannia, 1956–57; Comdr 1957; Capt., HMS Finisterre, 1960–62; resigned 1965. Mem., Hants Local Valuation Panel, 1971–81 (Chm., 1977–81). Country Landowners' Association: Chm., 1980–81, Pres., 1987–94, Hants Br.; Chm., Legal and Parly Sub-cttee and Mem., Nat. Exec. Cttee, 1982–87; Chm., Charitable Trust, 1988–96. Pres., Hants Fedn of Young Farmers' Clubs, 1982. Liaison Officer (Hants), Duke of Edinburgh's Award Scheme, 1966–76. Governor: and Vice-Chm., Larkhills Special Sch., Winchester, 1975–80; Durley C of E Primary Sch., 1966–97 (Chm., 1980–96). High Sheriff 1972, DL 1973, Hants. Freeman, City of London, 1982; Liveryman, Farmers' Co., 1983–2005. *Recreations:* shooting, small woodland management. *Address:* Wintershill Farmhouse, Durley, Hants SO32 2AH. *Clubs:* Brooks's, Pratt's.

See also J. M. J. Balfour.

BALFOUR, (Elizabeth) Jean, CBE 1981; FRSE 1980; FRSA; FICFor; FIBiol; JP; Chairman, Countryside Commission for Scotland, 1972–82; *b* 4 Nov. 1927; 2nd *d* of late Maj.-Gen. Sir James Syme Drew, KBE, CB, DSO, MC, and late Victoria Maxwell of Munches; *m* 1950, John Charles Balfour, *qv*; three *s*. *Educ:* Edinburgh Univ. (BSc). Partner/Owner, Balbirnie Home Farms; Dir, A. & J. Bowen & Co. Ltd; Chm., Loch Duart Ltd, 1999–2006; Mem. Bd, Scottish Quality Salmon, 2005–06. Pres., Royal Scottish Forestry Soc., 1969–71; Mem., Fife CC, 1958–70; Chm., Fife County and City and Royal Burgh of Dunfermline Joint Probation Cttee, 1967–69; Governor, East of Scotland Coll. of Agriculture, 1958–88, Vice Pres. 1982–88; Dir, Scottish Agricl Colls, 1987–88, Dir, Council, 1974–87; Member: Scottish Agric. Develt Council, 1972–77; Verney Working Party on Natural Resources, 1971–72; Nature Conservancy Council, 1973–80; Oil Develt Council, 1973–78; Scottish Economic Council, 1978–83; Forth River Purification Bd, 1992–96; Council, Scottish Landowners Fedn, 1996–99 (Chm., Forestry Cttee, 1997–99); Chairman: Regional Adv. Cttee, East (Scotland) Forestry Commn, 1976–85; Regional Adv. Cttee, Mid (Scotland) Forestry Commn, 1987–2000; Food and Farming Adv. Cttee, Scottish Cons. and Unionist Assoc., 1985–88; Crarae Gardens Charitable Trust, 1986–93; W Sutherland Fisheries Trust, 1996–99; Hon. Vice Pres., Scottish Wildlife Trust (Vice-Chm., 1968–72; Founder Council Mem.). Deputy Chairman: Seafish Industry Authority, 1987–90; Cttee on Women in Science, Engrg and Technol., OST, Cabinet Office, 1993–94. Member: Cttee of Enquiry on handling of geographical information, 1985–87; RSE Foot and Mouth Enquiry, 2001–02. Trustee: Buckland Foundn, 1989–94; Royal Botanic Gdns, Edinburgh, 1992–98. Mem. Council, RSE, 1983–86; Mem. Council and Chm., Policy and Legislation Cttee, Inst. of Chartered Foresters, 1986–88; Council Mem. and Chm., Mid Scotland Timber Growers' Assoc., 2000–02. Hon. Vice-Pres., Scottish YHA, 1983–. Mem. Court, St Andrews Univ., 1983–87 (Chm. Ct Cttee, Estates and Buildings, 1983–87); Gov., Duncan of Jordanstone Coll. of Art, 1992–96. JP Fife, 1963. FRSA 1981; FRZSScot 1983; FIBiol 1988; FRSGS 1997. Hon. DSc St Andrews, 1977; DUniv Stirling, 1991. Forestry Medal, Inst. of Chartered Foresters, 1996. Order of the Falcon (Iceland), 1994. Report to Government, A New Look at the Northern Ireland Countryside, 1984–85. *Recreations:* hill walking, fishing, painting, exploring arctic vegetation, shooting. *Address:* Kirkforthar House, Markinch, Fife KY7 6LS. *T:* (01592) 752233; Scourie, by Lairg, Sutherland IV27 4TH. *Clubs:* Farmers'; (Assoc. Mem.) New (Edinburgh).

BALFOUR, Maj. Gen. James Melville John, CBE 2001 (OBE 1992); Director General, Winston Churchill Memorial Trust, since 2007; *b* 6 May 1951; *s* of Comdr Colin James Balfour, *qv*; *m* 1981, Carolyn Laing; one *s* two *d*. *Educ:* Eton Coll.; Mons Officer Cadet Sch.; Army Staff Coll. Commnd 3rd Bn RGJ, 1970; ADC to CGS, 1977; Capt., 1978–82; Defence Services Staff Coll., India, 1983; Major, Mil. Ops, MoD, 1984–85; Co. Comdr, 3rd Bn RGJ, 1986–88; JSDC, Greenwich, 1988; Directing Staff, Army Staff Col., Camberley, 1988–90; CO, 3rd Bn, RGJ, 1990–92; MA to QMG, 1993; HCSC 1994; Col, Mil. Ops, MoD, 1994–95; Comdr, 3rd Inf. Bde, 1996–97; RCDS 1998; COS, HQ NI, 1999–2001; Comdr, British Forces, Bosnia, 2001; Dir, Infantry, MoD, 2002–04; Co-ordinator, Kosovo Protection Corps, 2005–06; Pres., Gen. Court Martial, 2006–07. Chm., Youth Clubs Hants and IoW, 2007; County Chairman: Game and Wildlife Conservancy Trust, 2008; ABF, 2008. *Recreations:* field sports, gardening. *Address:* Winston Churchill Memorial Trust, 15 Queensgate Terrace, SW7 5PR.

BALFOUR, Jean; *see* Balfour, E. J.

BALFOUR, John Charles, OBE 1978; MC 1943; JP; Vice Lord-Lieutenant for Fife, 1988–96; Chairman, Fife Area Health Board, 1983–87 (Member, 1981–87); *b* 28 July 1919; *s* of late Brig. E. W. S. Balfour, CVO, DSO, OBE, MC, and Lady Ruth Balfour, CBE; *m* 1950, (Elizabeth) Jean Drew (*see* (Elizabeth) Jean Balfour); three *s*. *Educ:* Eton Coll.; Trinity Coll., Cambridge (BA). Served war, Royal Artillery, 1939–45 (Major), N Africa and Europe. Member, Royal Company of Archers, Queen's Body Guard for Scotland, 1949–. Member: Inter-departmental Cttee on Children and Young Persons, Scotland (Chm., Lord Kilbrandon), 1961–64; Scottish Council on Crime, 1972–75; Chairman: Children's Panel, Fife County, 1970–75, Fife Region 1975–77; Scottish Assoc. of Youth Clubs, 1968–79. JP 1957, DL 1958, Fife. *Address:* Kirkforthar House, Markinch, Glenrothes, Fife KY7 6LS. *T:* (01592) 752233, *Fax:* (01592) 610314. *Club:* New (Edinburgh).

See also P. E. G. Balfour.

BALFOUR, Michael William, OBE 2008; FCA; Founder, and Co-Chairman, since 2006, Fitness First Holdings Ltd (Chief Executive Officer, 1992–2004; Deputy Chairman, 2005–06); *b* 3 May 1949; *s* of Alexander and Winifred Balfour; *m* 1978, Margaret; one *s* one *d*. Gen. Manager, Lucas (Latina America) Inc., 1978–81; Man. Dir, Bytex Ltd, 1982–85; Dir, Mannai Investment Co., 1985–92. Director: Fitness Industry Assoc., 2003–; Skills Active, 2005–. Hon. DBA Bournemouth, 2004. *Recreations:* sailing, golf. *T:* (01202) 707300, *Fax:* (01202) 709127; *e-mail:* mikebalfour@fitnessfirst.com.

BALFOUR, Neil Roxburgh; Chairman: Mermaid Holdings Ltd, since 1991; KP Capital Sp. z.o.o., since 2005; *b* 12 Aug. 1944; *s* of Archibald Roxburgh Balfour and Lilian Helen Cooper; *m* 1st, 1969, HRH Princess Elizabeth of Yugoslavia; one *s*; 2nd, 1978, Serena Mary Spencer-Churchill Russell; two *s* one *d*. *Educ:* Ampleforth Coll., Yorks; University Coll., Oxford Univ. (BA History). Called to the Bar, Middle Temple, 1969. Baring Brothers & Co., 1968–74; European Banking Co. Ltd, 1974–83 (Exec. Dir, 1980–83). Chm., York Trust Group plc, 1986–91; Pres., and CEO, Mostostal Warszawa SA, 2000–02. Mem. (C) N Yorks, European Parlt, 1979–84. *Publication:* Paul of Yugoslavia (biography), 1980. *Recreations:* bridge, golf, tennis, shooting, fishing. *Address:* 55 Warwick Square, SW1V 2AJ. *Clubs:* Turf, Pratt's, White's; Royal St George's (Sandwich), Sunningdale; Arcangues (Biarritz).

BALFOUR, Peter Edward Gerald, CBE 1984; Chairman, Charterhouse plc, 1985–90; a Vice-Chairman, Royal Bank of Scotland, 1985–90 (Director, 1971–90); Director, 1978–91, Vice-Chairman, 1981–91, Royal Bank of Scotland Group; *b* 9 July 1921; *y s* of late Brig. Edward William Sturgis Balfour, CVO, DSO, OBE, MC and Lady Ruth Balfour, CBE, MB; *m* 1st, 1948, Grizelda Davina Roberta Ogilvy (marr. diss. 1967); two *s* one *d*; 2nd, 1968, Diana Rosemary Wainman; one *s* one *d*. *Educ:* Eton College. Scots Guards, 1940–54. Joined Wm McEwan & Co. Ltd, 1954; Chm. and Chief Exec., Scottish & Newcastle Breweries, 1970–83. Director: British Assets Trust Ltd, 1962–91; Selective Assets Trust (formerly Edinburgh American Assets Trust), 1962–92 (Chm., 1978–92); First Charlotte Assets Trust, 1980–92 (Chm., 1981–92). Chm., Scottish Council for Develt and Industry, 1978–85. Mem., Hansard Soc. Commn on Electoral Reform, 1975–76. *Address:* Scadlaw House, Humbie, East Lothian EH36 5PH. *T:* (01875) 833252. *Club:* Cavalry and Guards.

See also A. W. Balfour, J. C. Balfour.

BALFOUR, Raymond Lewis, LVO 1965; HM Diplomatic Service, retired; Counsellor, Kuwait, 1979–83; *b* 23 April 1923; *s* of Henry James Balfour and Vera Alice (*née* Dunford); *m* 1975, Vanda Gaye Crompton. RMA Sandhurst, 1942; commnd RAC; served with IV Queen's Own Hussars, 1942–47. Diplomatic Service, 1947–87; served at Munich, Beirut, Gdansk (Poland), Baghdad, Khartoum, Geneva, Damascus; Counsellor, Tripoli, 1976–79. Order of the Blue Nile, Sudan, 1965. *Recreations:* travel, gardening. *Address:* 25 Chenery Drive, Sprowston, Norwich, Norfolk NR7 8RR.

BALFOUR, Richard Creighton, MBE 1945; retired; *b* 3 Feb. 1916; *s* of Donald Creighton Balfour and Muriel Fonçeca; *m* 1943, Adela Rosemary Welch (*d* 2004); two *s*. *Educ:* St Edward's Sch., Oxford (Pres., Sch. Soc., 1985–86). FIB. Joined Bank of England, 1935; Agent, Leeds, 1961–65; Deputy Chief Cashier, 1965–70; Chief Accountant, 1970–75. Dir, Datasaab Ltd, 1975–81. Naval Service, Lt-Comdr RNVR, 1939–46.

President: Royal National Rose Soc., 1973 and 1974; World Fedn of Rose Socs, 1983–85 (Vice-Pres. for Europe, 1981–83; Chm., Classification Cttee, 1981–88); Chairman: 1976—The Year of the Rose; Internat. Rose Conf., Oxford, 1976; organiser and designer of the British Garden at Montreal Floralies, 1980. Master, Worshipful Co. of Gardeners, 1991–92; Freeman, City of London. DHM 1974. Gold Medal, World Fedn of Rose Socs, 1985; Australian Rose Award, 1989. *Publications:* articles in many horticultural magazines and photographs in many publications. *Recreations:* roses, gardening, photography, dancing, sea floating, collecting rocks and hat pins, travel, watching sport. *Address:* Albion House, Little Waltham, Chelmsford, Essex CM3 3LA. *T:* (01245) 360410.

BALKWILL, Prof. Frances Rosemary, OBE 2008; PhD; Professor of Cancer Biology, Queen Mary, University of London, and Head, Centre for Cancer and Inflammation (formerly Centre for Translational Oncology), Institute of Cancer (formerly Cancer Research UK Translational Oncology Laboratory), Barts and The London School of Medicine and Dentistry (formerly Barts and The London, Queen Mary's Medical School), since 2000; *b* 18 March 1952; *d* of late Elson Howard Lucas Leach and of Rosemary Emily Leach; *m* 1973, Lewis Balkwill (marr. diss. 1987); one *s* one *d*. *Educ:* Surbiton High Sch.; Bristol Univ. (BSc); Univ. of London (PhD). Prin. Scientist and Lab. Hd, ICRF, 1979–2000; Dir, Centre of the Cell (sci. centre for children), Barts and The London Sch. of Medicine and Dentistry (formerly Barts and the London, Queen Mary's Med. Sch.), 2002–. Non-Parly Bd Mem., POST, 2000–. Series Ed., Making Sense of Science, 1995–. FMedSci 2006. Award for Communication in the Life Scis, EMBO, 2004; Michael Faraday Prize, Royal Soc., 2005. *Publications:* Cytokines in Cancer Therapy, 1989; (ed) Cytokines: a practical approach, 1991, 3rd edn 2000; (ed jtly) Interleukin 2, 1992; (ed) Frontiers in Molecular Biology: the cytokine network, 2000; *books for children* (designed and illustrated by Mic Rolph): Cells are Us, 1990; Cell Wars, 1990; DNA is Here to Stay, 1992; Amazing Schemes within your Genes, 1993; The Egg and Sperm Race, 1994; Microbes, Bugs, and Wonder Drugs, 1995; Enjoy Your Cells (series), 2001–02; Staying Alive: fighting HIV/AIDS, 2002; SuperCells, 2003; You, Me and HIV, 2004; approx. 200 pubns in scientific jls. *Recreations:* writing, travel, bird watching. *Address:* Centre for Cancer and Inflammation, Institute of Cancer and the Cancer Research UK Clinical Centre, Barts and The London School of Medicine and Dentistry, Charterhouse Square, EC1M 6BQ. *T:* (020) 7882 6108, *Fax:* (020) 7882 6110; *e-mail:* frances.balkwill@cancer.org.uk.

BALL, Air Marshal Sir Alfred (Henry Wynne), KCB 1976 (CB 1967); DSO 1943; DFC 1942; Vice-Chairman (Air), Council of Territorial, Auxiliary and Volunteer Reserve Associations, 1979–84; *b* 18 Jan. 1921; *s* of Captain J. A. E. Ball, MC, BA, BE, Chief Engineer, Bengal Nagpur Railway, 1937; *m* 1942, Nan McDonald (*d* 2006); three *s* one *d*. *Educ:* Campbell Coll., Belfast; RAF Coll., Cranwell; idc, jssc, psc, pfc. Served War of 1939–45 (despatches twice; US Air Medal 1943); Sqdn Ldr 1942; Wing Comdr 1944; air operations, Lysanders, Spitfires, Mosquitoes; commanded: 4 Photo. Reconn. Unit; 682, 542, 540 and 13 Photo. Reconn. Sqdns in N Africa, UK, France and Middle East; E Africa, 1947; RAF Staff Coll., 1952; Canberras, RAF Wyton, 1953; RAF Flying Coll., Bomber Comd, 1956; jssc 1959; BJSM, Washington, 1959; Comdr, Honington V Bomber Base, 1963–64; Air Officer, Administration, Aden, 1965; IDC, 1967; Dir of Operations, (RAF), MoD, 1967–68; Air Vice-Marshal, 1968; ACOS, Automatic Data Processing Div., SHAPE, 1968–71; Dir-Gen. Organisation (RAF), 1971–75; Air Marshal, 1975; UK Rep., Perm. Mil. Deputies Gp, Cento, 1975–77; Dep. C-in-C, RAF Strike Command, 1977–79, retired 1979. Mil. Affairs Advr, Internat. Computers Ltd, 1979–83. Hon. Air Cdre, No 2624 (Co. of Oxford) RAuxAF Regt Sqdn, 1984–90. Hon. FBCS 1984 (Hon. MBCS 1974). *Recreations:* golf, bridge. *Clubs:* Royal Air Force; Phyllis Court.

BALL, Alison; QC 1995; a Recorder, since 1998; *b* 12 Jan. 1948; *d* of Winifred Alice Ball and Hilary Noble Ball; *m* 1980, Richard; two *d*. *Educ:* Bedales Sch.; King's Coll., London (LLB Hons). Called to the Bar, Middle Temple, 1972, Bencher, 2002; founded Specialist Family Law Chambers, 1989, Joint Head, 1990–. *Recreations:* my family and other animals. *Address:* 1 Garden Court, Temple, EC4Y 9BJ. *T:* (020) 7797 7900.

BALL, Anthony George, (Tony), MBE 1986; FCIM; FIMI; FCGI; Founder, 1983, and Chairman, 1983–2006, Tony Ball Associates (TBA) plc; *b* 14 Nov. 1934; *s* of Harry Ball and Mary Irene Ball, Bridgwater; *m* 1st, 1957, Ruth Parry Davies (marr. diss. 1997); two *s* one *d*; 2nd, 2000, Ms Jan Kennedy. *Educ:* Grammar Sch., Bridgwater. Indentured engineering apprentice, Austin Motor Co., 1951–55; responsible for launch of Mini, 1959; UK Car and Commercial Vehicle Sales Manager, 1961–66, Austin Motor Co.; Sales and Marketing Exec., British Motor Corp., 1966–67; Chm. and Man. Dir, Barlow Rand UK Motor Gp, 1967–78; Managing Director: Barlow Rand Ford, S Africa, 1971–73; Barlow Rand European Operations, 1973–78; returned to British Leyland as Man. Dir, Overseas Trading Operations, 1978; Dep. Man. Dir, Austin Morris Ltd, 1979; Chm. and Man. Dir, British Leyland Europe & Overseas, 1979–82; Director, 1979–82: BL Cars Ltd (World Sales Chief, 1979–82; responsible for launch of the Austin Metro in 1980); Austin Morris Ltd; Rover Triumph Ltd; Jaguar Rover Triumph Inc. (USA); Dir, Jaguar Cars Ltd, 1979–82; Chief Exec., Henlys plc, 1981–83. Dep. Chm., Lumley Insce Gp, 1983–95; Director: Jetmaster UK, 1989–97; Theatrical Agents Billy Marsh Associates Ltd, 1993–; Royal Carlton Hotel, Blackpool, 1998–2007. Dir, producer and stager of 'Industrial Theatre' Motivational confs, sponsorship, marketing, promotions, special events and new product launches, 1983–. Responsible for: staging new product launches for British Leyland, Austin, Rover, MG, Jaguar, General Motors, Vauxhall, Proton, Mercedes-Benz, Daihatsu, LDV, Land Rover, Bedford trucks, Optare buses, Pioneer-UK, Fiat and Gillette; production and staging of opening ceremony of Rugby World Cup, Twickenham, 1991; DoH European drug abuse prevention campaign, 1992. Apptd Marketing Adviser: to Sec. of State for Energy, 1984–87; to Sec. of State for Wales, 1988–91; to SMMT for producing and promoting: British Internat. Motor Show, 1992–96; Scottish Motor Show, 1997–2001; to FA for producing opening and closing ceremonies of European Football Championships, Wembley, 1996, FA Cup Finals, 1996–2000 and promotional and presentation work for England World Cup Bid, 2006; to RFU for 125th Anniversary celebrations, 1996, for 5 Nations Championship activities, Twickenham, 1997–; to RFU Français for prodn of opening ceremony at Stade de France, Paris, 1998; to Welsh RU for producing opening and closing ceremonies, Rugby World Cup, Millennium Stadium, Cardiff Arms Park, 1999; to ECB for producing opening ceremony, Cricket World Cup, Lord's, 1999; responsible for: promoting London Zoo relaunch, 1993; creating and producing Lloyds Bank's Playwright of the Year Award, annually 1994–2003. Vice-Chm., Fellowship of Motor Industry, 2007–. Pres., Austin Ex-Apprentices Assoc., 2006–. Lectr, public and after dinner speaker; TV and radio broadcasts on motivation, marketing, public speaking and industrial subjects; producer, The Birth of Rugby (TV); panellist, Any Questions (TV and radio). Mason Meml Lecture, Birmingham Univ., 1983. Governor, N Worcs Coll., 1984–91. Patron, Wordsworth Trust, 2004–. Freeman of City of London, 1980; Liveryman: Worshipful Co. of Coach Makers and Coach Harness Makers, 1980; Worshipful Co. of Carmen, 1982. Fellowship of Inst. of Marketing awarded 1981, for services to Brit. Motor Industry; FCGI 1999; Hon. Mem. CGLI, 1982, for services to technical and vocational educn; Prince Philip Medal, CGLI, 1984, for outstanding lifetime contribution to British marketing. Benedictine Award, Business After-Dinner Speaker of the Year, 1992, 1993. *Publications:* (contrib.) Metro: the book of the car, 1981; (contrib.) Tales out of School: misdeeds of the famous, 1983; A Marketing Study of the Welsh Craft Industry (Welsh Office report, 1988); (contrib.) Making Better Business Presentations, 1988; (contrib.) Men and Motors of 'The Austin', 2000; contribs to numerous industrial, management, marketing and public speaking books and jls. *Recreations:* theatre, British military history, sharing good humour. *Address:* 76a Grove End Road, St John's Wood, NW8 9ND. *T:* (020) 7449 6930; Silverhowe, Red Bank Road, Grasmere, Cumbria LA22 9PX. *Club:* Lord's Taverners.

See also M. A. Ball.

BALL, Arthur Beresford, OBE 1973; HM Diplomatic Service, retired; history teacher, 1989–91, language teacher, 1991–97, Gresham's School; *b* 15 Aug. 1923; *s* of Charles Henry and Lilian Ball; *m* 1961, June Stella Luckett; one *s* two *d*. *Educ:* Bede Collegiate Boys' Sch., Sunderland; Univ. of E Anglia (BA Hons 1987; MA 1989). Joined HM Diplomatic Service, 1949: Bahrain, 1949; Tripoli, 1950; Middle East Centre for Arab Studies, 1952; Ramullah, 1953; Damascus, 1954; Foreign Office, 1957; Kuwait, 1959; HM Consul, New Orleans, 1963; Jedda, 1965; FO, 1967; São Paulo, 1969; Lisbon, 1972; Ankara, 1975; Consul-Gen., Perth, WA, 1978–80. *Recreations:* bookbinding, historical studies.

BALL, Sir Christopher (John Elinger), Kt 1988; MA; Chancellor, University of Derby, 1995–2003; *b* 22 April 1935; *er s* of late Laurence Elinger Ball, OBE, and Christine Florence Mary Ball (*née* Howe); *m* 1958, Wendy Ruth Colyer, *d* of late Cecil Frederick Colyer and of Ruth Colyer (*née* Reddaway); three *s* three *d*. *Educ:* St George's School, Harpenden; Merton College, Oxford (Harmsworth Scholar 1959; Hon. Fellow, 1987); 1st Cl. English Language and Literature, 1959; Dipl. in Comparative Philology, 1962; MA Oxon, 1963. 2nd Lieut, Parachute Regt, 1955–56. Lectr in English Language, Merton Coll., Oxford, 1960–61; Lectr in Comparative Linguistics, Sch. of Oriental and African Studies (Univ. of London), 1961–64; Fellow and Tutor in English Language, Lincoln Coll., Oxford, 1964–79 (Bursar, 1972–79; Hon. Fellow, 1981); Warden, Keble College, Oxford, 1980–88 (Hon. Fellow, 1989). Founding Fellow, Kellogg Forum for Continuing Educn, Univ. of Oxford, 1988–89; Vis. Prof. in Higher Educn, Leeds Poly., 1989–91; Fellow in Continuing Educn, 1989–92, Dir of Learning, 1992–97, RSA. Sec., Linguistics Assoc. of GB, 1964–67; Pres., Oxford Assoc. of University Teachers, 1968–71; Publications Sec., Philological Soc., 1969–75; Chairman: Oxford Univ. English Bd, 1977–79; Bd of NAB, 1982–88; Higher Educn Inf. Services Trust, 1987–90; Member: General Bd of the Faculties, 1979–82; Hebdomadal Council, 1985–89; CNAA, 1982–88 (Chm., English Studies Bd, 1973–80, Linguistics Bd, 1977–82); BTEC, 1984–89 (Chm., Quality Assurance & Control Cttee, 1989–90); IT Skills Shortages Cttee (Butcher Cttee), 1984–85; CBI IT Skills Agency, 1985–88; CBI Task Force, 1988–89. Chairman: NICEC, 1989–93; Pegasus, 1989–92; Strategic Educn Fora for Kent, 1992–97, Oxfordshire, 1992–97, and Gtr Peterborough, 1992–95; Educn Policy Cttee, RSA Exams Bd, 1993–96; Patron, Campaign for Learning, RSA, 1998– (Chm., 1996–98). Vice-Chm., Jigsaw Gp, 1998–2004; founding Chm., The Talent Foundn, 1999–2004 (Patron, 2004–); Chm., Global Univ. Alliance, 2000–04. Member: Council and Exec., Templeton Coll., Oxford, 1981–92; Centre for Medieval and Renaissance Studies, Oxford, 1987–90; Brathay Hall Trust, 1988–91 (Chm, 1990–91; Fellow, 2003–); Manchester Polytechnic, 1989–91 (Hon. Fellow, 1988). President: ACFHE, 1990–92; SEAL, 2000–05. Gov., St George's Sch., Harpenden, 1985–89. Jt Founding Editor (with late Angus Cameron), Toronto Dictionary of Old English, 1970; Member Editorial Board: Oxford Rev. of Education, 1984–96; Science and Public Affairs, 1989–94. FRSA 1987. Hon. Fellow: Univ. of Westminster (formerly Poly. of Central London), 1991; Auckland Inst. of Technol., NZ, 1992; NE Wales Inst., Wrexham, 1996; Oxford Brookes Univ.; Millennium Fellow, Auckland Univ. of Technol., NZ, 2000. Hon. DLitt CNAA, 1989; DUniv: N London, 1993; Open, 2002; Derby, 2003; Hon. DEd Greenwich, 1994. *Publications:* Fitness for Purpose, 1985; Aim Higher, 1989; (ed jtly) Higher Education in the 1990s, 1989; More Means Different, 1990; Learning Pays, 1991; Sharks and Splashes, 1991; Profitable Learning, 1992; Start Right, 1994; poetry (as John Elinger), pamphlets and various contributions to philological, linguistic and educational jls. *Address:* 45 Richmond Road, Oxford OX1 2JJ. *T:* and *Fax:* (01865) 310800.

BALL, Christopher John Watkins; Deputy Chairman, PG Bison Ltd, 1999; *b* 2 Nov. 1939; *s* of late Clifford George and of Cynthia Lindsay Watkins-Ball; *m* 1968, Susan Anne Nellist; one *s* two *d*. *Educ:* St John's Coll., Johannesburg; Univ. of the Witwatersrand (Dipl. Iuris 1963); Jesus Coll., Cambridge (MA Econs 1967). Outwich South Africa Ltd, 1968–72, Dir 1970; Barclays Group, 1972–89: Barclays Nat. Merchant Bank, S Africa, 1972–78; Manager, Corporate Finance, 1972–75; Gen. Manager, 1975–78; Man. Dir, Barclays Nat. Western Bank, S Africa, 1978–80; Regional Gen. Manager, London, Barclays Bank, 1980–83; Barclays Nat. Bank Ltd (now First Nat. Bank of Southern Africa), S Africa, 1983, Man. Dir, 1984–89; Chief Exec., Pvte Bank & Trust Co., 1989–93; Chm., SA Housing Trust, 1994–95; CEO, Cape Town 2004 Olympic Bid, 1995–97. Director: Medbank Ltd; Premier Foods Ltd; Chairman: Century City Ltd; Canal Walk Ltd. Pres., Clearing Bankers' Assoc. of S Africa, 1985. Trustee: Nelson Mandela Childrens' Fund; READ Orgn. *Recreations:* golf, tennis. *Address:* Buitensig, 4 Gardenia Lane, Constantia, Cape Town, 7806, South Africa. *T:* (21) 7941422, *Fax:* (21) 7944294; *e-mail:* buitcon@iafrica.com. *Club:* Leander.

BALL, Colin George; Director, Commonwealth Foundation, 2000–04 (Deputy Director, 1998–99); *b* 22 July 1943; *s* of George Heyward Ball and Bessie Margaret Ball (*née* Henry); *m* 1st, 1968, Maureen Sheelagh Bryan (marr. diss. 1996); one *s* one *d*; 2nd, 1998, Susan Helen Armstrong. *Educ:* Sevenoaks Sch.; Univ. of Keele (BA (Hons)). Teaching, Malaysia, Ghana, Nigeria, UK, 1961–62, 1966–70; Dir Schs Adv. Service, CSV, 1970–72; Asst Principal, Birstall Community Coll., 1973–74; Principal, Home Office and MSC, 1975–79; Founder, Chm. and CEO, Centre for Employment Initiatives, 1980–88; freelance researcher, consultant and writer, 1988–97. Chm., Commonwealth Assoc. for Local Action and Econ. Develt, 1990–96. *Publications:* Education for a Change, 1973; Community Service and the Young Unemployed, 1977; Fit for Work?, 1979; Whose Business is Business, 1980; Locally Based Responses to Long-term Unemployment, 1988; Towards an Enterprising Culture, 1989; Non-governmental Organisations: guidelines for good policy and practice, 1995. *Recreations:* music, reading, writing, Italy. *Address:* 1/41 Griffith Street, New Farm, Qld 4005, Australia. *Club:* Royal Commonwealth Society.

BALL, Denis William, MBE 1971; industrial and financial consultant; *b* 20 Oct. 1928; *er s* of late William Charles Thomas and Dora Adelaide Ball, Eastbourne; *m* 1972, Marja Tellervo Lumijärvi (*d* 1987), *er d* of late Osmo Kullervo and Leila Tellervo Lumijärvi, Toijala, Finland; two *s* one *d*. *Educ:* Brunswick Sch.; Tonbridge Sch. (Scholar); Brasenose Coll., Oxford (MA). Sub-Lt, RNR, 1953; Lieut 1954; Lt-Comdr 1958. Asst Master, 1953–72, Housemaster, 1954–72, The King's Sch., Canterbury; Headmaster, Kelly Coll., 1972–85 (Governor, 1997–2004). Director: Perkins Foods, 1987–96 (founder Dir); James Wilkes, 1987–88; Western Bloodstock, 1987–92; Redbridge Properties, 1990–96; Kelly Enterprises, 1997–2002; Bamboo Travel, 2008–; Cons., Throgmorton Investment Management, 1977–78. Trustee, Tavistock Sch., 1972–85; Vice-Chm. of Governors, St Michael's Sch., Tawstock Court, 1974–93 (Hon. Gov., 1993–; Headmaster during interregnum, 1986); Mem., Political and PR Sub-Cttee, HMC, 1979–84. Hon. Treas., Ickham PCC, 1990–. Mem., Johnson Club, 1987–98. *Recreations:* Elizabethan history, cryptography, literary and mathematical puzzles, cricket, Real tennis (played for MCC and Jesters), squash (played for Oxford Univ. and Kent), golf, ballet, poverty in Uganda. *Address:* Ickham Hall, Ickham, Canterbury, Kent CT3 1QT. *Clubs:* MCC, Jesters.

BALL, Dr Harold William; Keeper of Palæontology, British Museum (Natural History), 1966–86; *b* 11 July 1926; *s* of Harold Ball and Florence (*née* Harris); *m* 1955, Patricia Mary (*née* Silvester); two *s* two *d. Educ:* Yardley Gram. Sch.; Birmingham Univ. BSc 1947, PhD 1949, Birmingham. Geologist, Nyasaland Geological Survey, 1949–51; Asst Lectr in Geology, King's Coll., London, 1951–54; Dept of Palæontology, British Museum (Nat. Hist.), 1954–86: Dep. Keeper, 1965; Keeper, 1966. Adrian Vis. Fellow, Univ. of Leicester, 1972–77. Sec., 1968–72, Vice-Pres., 1972–73, 1984–86, Geological Soc. of London; Pres., 1981–84, Vice-Pres., 1984–86, Soc. for the History of Natural History. Wollaston Fund, Geological Soc. of London, 1965. *Publications:* papers on the stratigraphy of the Old Red Sandstone and on the palæontology of the Antarctic in several scientific jls. *Recreations:* music, gardening. *Address:* Wilderbrook, Dormans Park, East Grinstead, West Sussex RH19 2LT. *T:* (01342) 870426.

BALL, Sir James; *see* Ball, Sir R. J.

BALL, Prof. John Geoffrey, CEng; consultant metallurgist; Professor of Physical Metallurgy, Imperial College, University of London, 1956–80, now Emeritus (Head of Metallurgy Department, 1957–79; Senior Research Fellow, 1980–86); *b* 27 Sept. 1916; *s* of late I. H. Ball and late Mrs E. M. Ball; *m* 1941, Joan C. M., *d* of late Arthur Wiltshire, JP, Bournemouth. *Educ:* Wellington (Salop) High Sch.; Univ. of Birmingham. British Welding Res. Assoc., 1941–49; Sen. Metallurgist, 1945–49; AERE, Harwell, 1949–56; Head of Reactor Metallurgy, 1953–56. Min. of Tech. Visitor to British Non-Ferrous Metals Res. Assoc., 1962–72. Dean, Royal Sch. of Mines, Imperial Coll., 1962–65 and 1971–74; Dean, Faculty of Engineering, Univ. of London, 1970–74. Chairman: Res. Bd, 1964–74, and Mem. of Council Br. Welding Res. Assoc., 1964–81; Engrg Physics Sub-Cttee, Aeronautical Res. Council, 1964–68; Metallurgy Bd, CNAA, 1965–71; Metallurgy and Materials Cttee and Univ. Science and Technology Bd, SRC, 1967–70; Engrg Bd, SRC, 1969–71; Manpower Utilisation Working Party, 1967–69; Mem., Light Water Reactor Pressure Vessel Study Gp, Dept of Energy, 1974–77. Consultant on Materials, SERC, 1983–84. President: Inst. of Welding, 1965–66; Instn of Metallurgists, 1966–67 (Mem. Council 1951–56, 1958–70); Member: Council, Br. Nuclear Forum, 1964–71; Manpower Resources Cttee, 1965–68; Council, Inst. of Metals, 1965; Council, Iron and Steel Inst., 1965; Council, City Univ., 1966–90; Brain Drain Cttee, 1966–67; Public Enquiry into loss of "Sea Gem", 1967; Materials and Structures Cttee, 1967–70; Technology Sub-Cttee of UGC, 1968–73; Chartered Engineer Section Bd, CEI, 1978–83; Mem., Group IV Exec. Cttee, Engineering Council, 1983–94. Governor, Sir John Cass Coll., 1958–67. Hon. ARSM 1961. Brooker Medal, Welding Inst., 1979; Freedom of Inst. and Distinguished Service Award, Indian Inst. of Technology, Delhi, 1985. *Address:* 3 Sylvan Close, Limpsfield, Surrey RH8 0DX. *T:* (01883) 713511.

BALL, Sir John (Macleod), Kt 2006; DPhil; FRS 1989; FRSE; FIMA; Sedleian Professor of Natural Philosophy, since 1996, and Director, Oxford Centre for Nonlinear PDE, since 2007, University of Oxford; Fellow, Queen's College, Oxford, since 1996; *b* 19 May 1948; *s* of Ernest Frederick Ball and Dorothy Forbes Ball; *m* 1st, 1973, Mary Judith Hodges (marr. diss. 1977); 2nd, 1992, Sedhar Chozam; two *s* one *d. Educ:* Mill Hill Sch.; St John's Coll., Cambridge (BA Maths, 1969; Hon. Fellow, 2005); Univ. of Sussex (DPhil 1972). FRSE 1980; FIMA 2003. SRC Postdoctoral Res. Fellow, Dept of Maths, Heriot-Watt Univ., and Lefschetz Center for Dynamical Systems, Brown Univ., USA, 1972–74; Lectr in Maths, 1974–78, Reader in Maths, 1978–82, SERC Sen. Fellow, 1980–85, Prof. of Applied Analysis, 1982–96, Heriot-Watt Univ. Visiting Professor: Dept of Maths, Univ. of Calif, Berkeley, 1979–80; Laboratoire d'Analyse Numérique, Université Pierre et Marie Curie, Paris, 1987–88, 1994; Inst. for Advanced Study, Princeton, 1993–94, 2002–03; Univ. Montpellier II, 2003; Hon. Prof., Heriot-Watt Univ., 1998–. Member Council: EPSRC, 1994–99; Edinburgh Mathematical Soc., 1972– (Pres., 1989–90); London Math. Soc., 1982– (Pres., 1996–98); Amer. Math. Soc., 1987–; Soc. for Nat. Phil., 1978–; Pres., IMU, 2003–06. Member: Programme Cttee, Internat. Centre for Mathematical Scis, Edinburgh, 1996– (Mem. Exec. Cttee, 1991–96, Chm., 1991–93); Bd of Govs, Weizmann Inst., 1998–. Delegate, OUP, 1998–. Associé Etranger, Acad. des Sciences, Paris, 2000; Foreign Member: Instituto Lombardo, 2005; Norwegian Acad. of Sci. and Letters, 2007; MAE, 2008; Hon. Mem., Edinburgh Math. Soc., 2008. Hon. DSc: Ecole Polytechnique Fédérale, Lausanne, 1992; Heriot-Watt, 1998; Sussex, 2000; Montpellier II, 2003; Edinburgh, 2004. Whittaker Prize, Edinburgh Math. Soc., 1981; Jun. Whitehead Prize, 1982, Naylor Prize, 1994, London Math. Soc.; Keith Prize, RSE, 1990; Theodore von Karman Prize, SIAM, 1999; David Crighton Medal, LMS/IMA, 2003; Royal Medal, RSE, 2006. Mem. Editorial Boards of various math. and scientific jls and book series. *Publications:* articles in math. and scientific jls. *Recreations:* travel, music, chess. *Address:* Mathematical Institute, 24–29 St Giles', Oxford OX1 3LB. *T:* (01865) 273577.

BALL, Michael Ashley; actor and singer; *b* 27 June 1962; *s* of Anthony George Ball, *qv*; partner, Cathy McGowan. *Educ:* Plymouth Coll.; Farnham Sixth Form Coll.; Guildford Sch. of Acting (Dip. Acting). *Theatre* includes: first professional rôle as Judas/John the Baptist, Godspell, 1984; first starring rôle, Frederick, The Pirates of Penzance, Manchester Opera House, 1985; West End début: created rôle of Marius, Les Misérables, Barbican and Palace, 1985; other major rôles include: Raoul, Phantom of the Opera, Her Majesty's, 1987; created rôle of Alex, Aspects of Love, Prince of Wales, 1989, NY 1990; Giorgio, Passion, Queen's, 1996; Alone Together, Divas Season, Donmar Warehouse, 2001; Caractacus Potts, Chitty Chitty Bang Bang, Palladium, 2002–03; Count Fosco, Woman in White, Palace, 2005; Kismet, ENO, 2007; Hairspray, Shaftesbury, 2007 (Laurence Olivier Award, 2008); *film:* England My England, 1996; *television* includes: GB rep., Eurovision Song Contest, 1992; two series of Michael Ball, 1993, 1994; Royal Variety Performances; numerous nat. and internat. concert tours; has made numerous recordings. Patron and Co-Founder, charity, Res. into Ovarian Cancer (ROC). Most Promising Artiste Award, 1989, Best Recording Artiste, 1998, Variety Club of GB; Most Popular Musical Actor, Theatregoers Club of GB, 1999. *Recreations:* collecting graphic novels and single malt whiskeys, country walking, music, theatre. *Address:* c/o Dalzell and Beresford, 26 Astwood Mews, SW7 4DE.

BALL, Rt Rev. Michael Thomas; Bishop of Truro, 1990–97; *b* 14 Feb. 1932; *s* of Thomas James Ball and Kathleen Bradley Ball. *Educ:* Lancing Coll., Sussex; Queens' Coll., Cambridge (BA 1955; MA 1959). Schoolmastering, 1955–76; Co-Founder, Community of the Glorious Ascension, 1960; Prior at Stroud Priory, 1963–76; Curate, Whitehall, Stroud, Glos, 1971–76; Priest-in-charge of Stanmer with Falmer, and Senior Anglican Chaplain to Higher Education in Brighton, including Sussex Univ., 1976–80; Bishop Suffragan of Jarrow, 1980–90. Mem., H of L, 1996–97. Advr to Tyne Tees Television, 1983–89. Mem. Council, St Luke's Hosp. for the Clergy, 1994–2006. *Publications:* So There We Are, 1997; Foolish Risks of God, 2002. *Recreations:* music, housework. *Address:* Manor Lodge, Aller, Langport, Somerset TA10 0QN.

See also Rt Rev. P. J. Ball.

BALL, Rt Rev. Peter John, CGA; Bishop of Gloucester, 1992–93; *b* 14 Feb. 1932; *s* of Thomas James and Kathleen Obena Bradley Ball. *Educ:* Lancing; Queens' Coll., Cambridge; Wells Theological College. MA (Nat. Sci.). Ordained, 1956; Curate of Rottingdean, 1956–58; Co-founder and Brother of Monastic Community of the Glorious Ascension, 1960 (Prior, 1960–77); Suffragan Bishop of Lewes, 1977–92; Prebendary, Chichester Cathedral, 1978, Canon Emeritus, 2000. Fellow of Woodard Corporation, 1962–71; Member: Archbishops' Council of Evangelism, 1965–68; Midlands Religious Broadcasting Council of the BBC, 1967–69; Admin. Council, Royal Jubilee Trusts, 1986–88. Archbishop of Canterbury's Adviser to HMC, 1985–90. Governor: Wellington Coll., 1985–93; Radley Coll., 1986–93; Lancing Coll., 1972–82, 1990–. Freeman, Bor. of Eastbourne, 1992. DUniv Sussex, 1992. *Recreations:* squash (Cambridge Blue, 1953) and music. *Address:* Manor Lodge, Aller, Langport, Somerset TA10 0QN.

See also Rt Rev. M. T. Ball.

BALL, Rev. Canon Peter William; Canon Emeritus, St Paul's Cathedral, since 1990 (Residentiary Canon, 1984–90); Public Preacher, diocese of Salisbury, since 1990; *b* 17 Jan. 1930; *s* of Leonard Wevell Ball and Dorothy Mary Ball; *m* 1956, Angela Jane Dunlop (*d* 2004); one *s* two *d. Educ:* Aldenham School; Worcester Coll., Oxford (MA); Cuddesdon Coll., Oxford. Asst Curate, All Saints, Poplar, 1955; Vicar, The Ascension, Wembley, 1961; Rector, St Nicholas, Shepperton, 1968; Area Dean of Spelthorne, 1972–83; Prebendary of St Paul's Cathedral, 1976. Dir, Post Ordination Trng and Continuing Ministerial Educn, Kensington Episcopal Area, 1984–87. Chaplain: Rediffusion Television, 1961–68; Thames Television, 1970–93. First Dir, Brent Samaritans, 1965–68; Dep. Dir, NW Surrey Samaritans, 1973–79. Mem., European Conf. on the Catechumenate, 1975– (Chm., 1983). *Publications:* Journey into Faith, 1984; Adult Believing, 1988; Adult Way to Faith, 1992; Journey into Truth, 1996; Anglican Spiritual Direction, 1998; (with Ven. Malcolm Grundy) Faith on the Way, 2000; Introducing Spiritual Direction, 2003. *Recreations:* gardening, walking, music. *Address:* Whittonedge, Whittonditch Road, Ramsbury, Marlborough, Wilts SN8 2PX.

BALL, Sir Richard Bentley, 5th Bt *cr* 1911, of Merrion Square, Dublin and Killybegs, Donegal; *b* 29 Jan. 1953; *o s* of Sir Charles Ball, 4th Bt and Alison Mary (*née* Bentley); *S* father, 2002; *m* 1991, Beverley Ann, *d* of late Bertram Joffre Wright; one *d. Educ:* Sherborne; Leicester Univ. ACA. *Heir: cousin* Christopher Nigel Morton Ball [*b* 3 Nov. 1951; *m* 1974, Melanie Fenner; one *s* one *d*].

BALL, Prof. Sir (Robert) James, Kt 1984; MA, PhD; Professor of Economics, 1965–97, now Emeritus, Principal, 1972–84, London Business School; Chairman, Legal and General Group Plc, 1980–94 (Director, 1978–94); *b* 15 July 1933; *s* of Arnold James Hector Ball; *m* 1st, 1954, Patricia Mary Hart Davies (marr. diss. 1970); three *d* (and one *s* one *d* decd); 2nd, 1970, Lindsay Jackson (*née* Wonnacott); one step *s. Educ:* St Marylebone Grammar Sch.; The Queen's College, Oxford; Styring Schol.; George Webb Medley Junior Schol. (Univ. Prizeman), 1956; BA 1957 (First cl. Hons PPE), MA 1960; PhD Univ. of Pennsylvania, 1973. RAF 1952–54 (Pilot-Officer, Navigator). Research Officer, Oxford University Inst. of Statistics, 1957–58; IBM Fellow, Univ. of Pennsylvania, 1958–60; Lectr, Manchester Univ., 1960, Sen. Lectr, 1963–65; London Business School: Governor, 1969–84; Dep. Principal, 1971–72; Fellow, 1998. Chm., Royal Bank of Canada Holdings (UK) Ltd, 1995–98; Director: Ogilvy and Mather Ltd, 1969–71; Economic Models Ltd, 1971–72; Barclays Bank Trust Co., 1973–86; Tube Investments, 1974–84; IBM UK Hldgs Ltd, 1979–95; LASMO plc, 1988–94; Royal Bank of Canada, 1990–98; IBM UK Pensions Trust Ltd, 1994–2004; Part-time Mem., NFC, 1973–77. Economic Advr, Touche Ross & Co., 1984–95; Mem., Adv. Bd, IBM UK Ltd, 1995–98. Member: Cttee to Review National Savings (Page Cttee), 1971–73; Economics Cttee of SSRC, 1971–74; Cttee on Social Forecasting, SSRC, 1971–72; Cttee of Enquiry into Electricity Supply Industry (Plowden Cttee), 1974–75; Chm., Treasury Cttee on Policy Optimisation, 1976–78. Marshall Aid Commemoration Comr, 1987–94. Governor, NIESR, 1973–. Vice-Pres., Chartered Inst. of Marketing, 1991–94; Member Council: REconS, 1973–79; BIM, 1974–82 (Chm., Economic and Social Affairs Cttee, 1979–82); British-N American Cttee, 1985–98. Pres., Sect. F, BAAS, 1990–91. Vice-Pres., CAM Foundn, 1983–92; Trustee: Foulkes Foundn, 1984–2006; Civic Trust, 1986–91; The Economist, 1987–99; Re Action Trust, 1991–93. Fellow, Econometric Soc., 1973; CCMI (CBIM 1974); FIAM 1985. Freeman, City of London, 1987. Hon. DSc Aston, 1987; Hon. DSocSc Manchester, 1988. *Publications:* An Econometric Model of the United Kingdom, 1961; Inflation and the Theory of Money, 1964; (ed) Inflation, 1969; (ed) The International Linkage of National Economic Models, 1972; Money and Employment, 1982; (with M. Albert) Toward European Economic Recovery in the 1980s (report to European Parliament), 1984; (ed) The Economics of Wealth Creation, 1992; The British Economy at the Crossroads, 1998; articles in professional jls. *Recreations:* gardening, chess. *Address:* London Business School, Sussex Place, Regent's Park, NW1 4SA. *T:* (020) 7262 5050. *Club:* Royal Automobile.

BALL, Simon Peter; Group Finance Director, 3i Group plc, since 2005; *b* 2 May 1960; *s* of Peter Terence Ball and Maureen Eleanor Ball (*née* Bishop); *m* 1992, Sandra Marie Cameron; two *d. Educ:* Chislehurst and Sidcup Grammar Sch.; UCL (BSc (Econ)). ACA 1985; MSI. Price Waterhouse & Co., 1981–85; Kleinwort Benson Group plc, 1985–98: Finance Dir, Kleinwort Benson Securities Ltd, 1990–93; Finance Dir, Kleinwort Benson Ltd, 1994–95; Chief Operating Officer, 1995–98; Robert Fleming Holdings Ltd, 1998–2000: Gp Finance Dir, 1998–2000; Chm., Robert Fleming Inc., 1999–2000; Exec. Dir, Intelligent Energy Ltd, 2001–02; Dir Gen., Finance, DCA, 2003–05. Non-executive Director: Leica Geosystems AG, Switzerland, 2001–05; Cable & Wireless, 2006–. FRSA 2003. *Recreations:* golf, cinema, running, theatre, cooking. *Address: e-mail:* simon.ball@3i.com. *Club:* Roehampton.

BALL, Prof. Stephen John, DPhil; FBA 2006; Karl Mannheim Professor of Sociology of Education, since 2001, and Associate Director, Centre for Critical Education Policy Studies, since 2005, Institute of Education, University of London; *b* 21 Jan. 1950; *s* of John and Betty Flora Joan Ball; *m* 1975, Trinidad Fructuoso-Gallego. *Educ:* Univ. of Essex (BA Hons Sociol. 1972); Univ. of Sussex (MA Sociol Studies 1975; DPhil Sociol. 1978). Lectr in Educn, Univ. of Sussex, 1975–85; King's College, London: Tutor in Urban Educn, 1985–89; Reader in Sociol. of Educn, 1990–91; Prof. of Educn, 1991–2001. AcSS 2000. Hon. Dr Turku, 2003. *Publications:* Beachside Comprehensive, 1981; The Micropolitics of the School, 1987; Politics and Policy-making in Education, 1990; Education Reform, 1994; Class Strategies in the Education Market, 2003; Education Policy and Social Class: selected works, 2006. *Recreations:* film, novels, walking, horse-riding. *Address:* Centre for Critical Education Policy Studies, Institute of Education, 20 Bedford Way, WC1H 0AL. *T:* (020) 7612 6973; *e-mail:* s.ball@ioe.ac.uk.

BALL, Tessa; *see* Hilton, T.

BALLADUR, Edouard; Chevalier, Légion d'Honneur; Deputy (RPR subsequently UMP) for Paris, French National Assembly, 1986–2007 (re-elected 1988, 1993, 1995, 1997 and 2002); Prime Minister of France, 1993–95; *b* 2 May 1929; *s* of Pierre Balladur and Emilie Latour; *m* 1957, Marie-Josèphe Delacour; four *s. Educ:* Lycée Thiers, Marseilles; Faculté de Droit, Aix-en-Provence; Inst. d'etudes Politiques; Ecole Nat. d'Admin. Jun. Auditeur, 1957, Maître des Requêtes, 1963, Conseil d'Etat; Adviser to Dir-Gen., ORTF, 1962–63 (Mem. Admin Council, 1967–68); Tech. Adviser, Office of Prime Minister Pompidou, 1966–68; Pres., French Co. for routier tunnel under Mont Blanc, 1968–81; Mem., Admin Council, Nat. Forestry Office, 1968–73; Asst Sec. Gen., later Sec. Gen., French President's Office, 1969–74; Chm. and Chief Exec., Générale de Service Informatique, 1977–86; Chm. and Chief Exec., Co. européene d'accumulateurs, 1980–86; Mem., Conseil d'Etat, 1984–; Minister for Economy, Finance and Privatization, 1986–88; Mem., Paris City Council, 1989–. Numerous medals and awards, incl. Jacques Rueff Prize, NY, 1986; Euromoney Prize, IMF, 1987; Gold Medal for patronage, French Acad., 1988; Louise Michel Prize, 1993. *Publications:* l'Arbre de mai, 1979; Je crois en l'homme plus qu'en l'Etat, 1987; (jtly) Passion et longueur de temps, 1989; Douze lettres aux Français trop tranquilles, 1990; Des modes et des convictions, 1992; Le dictionnaire de la réforme, 1992; Deux ans à Matignon, 1995; Caractère de la France, 1997; Avenir de la différence, 1999; Renaissance de la droite, pour une alternance décomplexée, 2000. *Address:* Conseil d'Etat, 75100 Paris, France.

BALLANCE, Chris(topher); playwright; Member (Green) Scotland South, Scottish Parliament, 2003–07; *b* 7 July 1952; *s* of Howard and Gwyneth Ballance; *m* 2005, Alis Taylor; one *s. Educ:* Alderman Newton's Sch., Leicester; Reigate Grammar Sch.; St Andrews Univ. Work in anti-nuclear power and public transport campaigns; Co-founder, First of May Radical Bookshop, Edinburgh, 1977; self-employed writer for theatre and radio, 1990–; jt-owner, secondhand bookshop, Wigtown, 2000–; Member: Scottish Soc. of Playwrights, 1992–; Writers Guild of GB, 1995–. Mem., Equity, 1994–. *Recreations:* film, theatre, hill-walking, swimming.

BALLANTINE, (David) Grant, FFA; Directing Actuary, Government Actuary's Department, 1991–2004; *b* 24 March 1941; *s* of James Williamson Ballantine and Robertha (*née* Fairley); *m* 1969, Marjorie Campbell Brown; one *s* one *d. Educ:* Daniel Stewart's Coll.; Edinburgh Univ. (BSc 1st Cl.). Scottish Widows' Fund, 1963–68; Asst Vice-Pres., Amer. Insce Gp (Far East), 1968–73; Government Actuary's Department, 1973–2004: Actuary, 1973–82; Chief Actuary, 1983–90. Mem. Council, Faculty of Actuaries, 1991–94. *Publications:* articles in trade and professional jls.

BALLANTYNE, Fiona Catherine; Principal, Ballantyne Mackay Consultants, since 1990; *b* Bristol, 9 July 1950; *d* of James Douglas and Marjorie Mackay; *m* 1973, (Andrew) Neil Ballantyne. *Educ:* Univ. of Edinburgh (MA). FCIM 2004. Scottish Development Agency: Hd, Small Business Services, 1984–88; Dir, Tayside and Fife, 1988–90. Chm., Essentia Gp, 1997–2001; Dir, 4-consulting Ltd, 2001–; Mem. Bd, Edinburgh Print Studios Ltd, 2004–. Vice Chm., BBC Broadcasting Council for Scotland, 1991–96; Member: Bd, Edinburgh Healthcare Trust, 1994–96; Consumer Panel, OFCOM, 2004–; Bd, Office of the Scottish Charity Regulator, 2008–; Chm., Museums Galls Scotland, 2007–. Chm., Edinburgh Br., IoD, 2002–06. Vice Chairman: Duncan of Jordanstone Coll. of Art, 1988–94; Queen Margaret University, 2002–05. *Recreations:* walking, gardening, reading. *Address:* c/o Ballantyne Mackay Consultants, 2–8 Millar Crescent, Edinburgh EH10 5HW.

BALLANTYNE, Sir Frederick (Nathaniel), GCMG 2002; Governor General, St Vincent and the Grenadines, since 2002; *b* 5 July 1936; *s* of Samuel and Olive Ballantyne; *m* 1996, Sally Ann; eight *c* (and one *c* decd). *Educ:* Syracuse Univ., NY (MD); Bd Certified Internal Medicine Cardiology. Med. Dir, Kingstown Gen. Hosp., 1970–83; CMO, St Vincent and Grenadines, 1983–88. *Recreations:* sailing, tennis, bridge. *Address:* Government House, Montrose, St Vincent and the Grenadines, West Indies. *T:* 4561401, *Fax:* 4579710; *e-mail:* govthouse@vincysurf.com.

BALLARD, Ven. Andrew Edgar; Archdeacon of Manchester, since 2005; *b* 14 Jan. 1944; *s* of Arthur Henry and Phyllis Marian Ballard; *m* 1970, Marian Caroline Conolly; one *s* two *d. Educ:* Rossall Sch.; St John's Coll., Durham Univ. (BA Hons Theol. 1966); Westcott House, Cambridge. Ordained deacon 1968, priest 1969; Asst Curate, St Mary, Bryanston Sq., and Asst Chaplain, Middlesex Hosp., London, 1968–72; Sen. Asst Curate, St Mary, Portsea, 1972–76; Vicar: St James, Haslingden with St Stephen, Haslingden Grane, 1976–82; St Paul, Walkden, 1982–93; Team Rector, St Paul, Walkden with St John the Baptist, Little Hulton, 1993–98; Area Dean, Farnworth, 1990–98; Priest in charge, 1998–2000, Team Rector, 2000, Rochdale Team Ministry; Archdeacon of Rochdale, 2000–05. Hon. Canon, Manchester Cathedral, 1998–2000. *Recreations:* church music, playing the organ. *Address:* 2 The Walled Garden, Ewhurst Avenue, Swinton, Manchester M27 0FR. *T:* (0161) 794 2401.

BALLARD, Jacqueline Margaret, (Jackie); Chief Executive, Royal National Institute for Deaf People, since 2007; *b* 4 Jan. 1953; *d* of late Alexander Mackenzie and of Daisy Mackenzie (*née* Macdonald); *m* 1975, Derek Ballard (marr. diss. 1989); one *d. Educ:* Monmouth Sch. for Girls; London Sch. of Economics (BSc Social Psychology). Social Worker, Waltham Forest, 1974–76; Further Educn Lectr, Yeovil Coll., 1982–90. Member: (L then Lib Dem) S Somerset DC, 1987–91 (Leader, 1990–91); (Lib Dem) Somerset CC, 1993–97 (Dep. Leader, 1993–95); Council Support Officer, Assoc. of Lib Dem Councillors, 1993–97. MP (Lib Dem) Taunton, 1997–2001. Contested (Lib Dem) Taunton, 2001. Dir Gen., RSPCA, 2002–07. Mem., Youth Justice Bd, 2003–05. *Address:* RNID, 19–23 Featherstone Street, EC1Y 8SL; *e-mail:* jackie.ballard@rnid.org.uk.

BALLARD, James Graham; novelist and short story writer; *b* 15 Nov. 1930; *s* of late James Ballard and Edna Ballard (*née* Johnstone); *m* 1954, Helen Mary Matthews (*d* 1964); one *s* two *d. Educ:* Leys School, Cambridge; King's College, Cambridge. *Publications:* The Drowned World, 1963; The 4-Dimensional Nightmare, 1963 (re-issued as The Voices of Time, 1985); The Terminal Beach, 1964; The Drought, 1965; The Crystal World, 1966; The Disaster Area, 1967; The Atrocity Exhibition, 1970; Crash, 1973 (filmed 1997); Vermilion Sands, 1973; Concrete Island, 1974; High Rise, 1975; Low-Flying Aircraft, 1976; The Unlimited Dream Company, 1979; Myths of the Near Future, 1982; Empire of the Sun, 1984 (filmed, 1988); The Venus Hunters, 1986; The Day of Creation, 1987; Running Wild, 1988; War Fever, 1990; The Kindness of Women, 1991; Rushing to Paradise, 1994; A User's Guide to the Millennium, 1996; Cocaine Nights, 1996; Super-Cannes, 2000; Millennium People, 2003; Kingdom Come, 2006; Miracles of Life: Shanghai to Shepperton (autobiog.), 2008. *Address:* 36 Old Charlton Road, Shepperton, Middlesex TW17 8AT. *T:* (01932) 225692.

See also M. A. Richardson.

BALLARD, John Frederick, CB 2001; non-executive Director, Northern Ireland Water, since 2007; *b* 8 Aug. 1943; *s* of Frederick and Margaret Ballard; *m* 1st, 1975, Ann Helm (marr. diss. 1999); one *s* two *d*; 2nd, 2000, Helena (*née* Rose). *Educ:* Roundhay Grammar Sch., Leeds; Ifield Grammar Sch., W Sussex; Southampton Univ. (BA); Exeter Univ. (CertEd). Academic Registrar's Dept, Univ. of Surrey, 1965–69; Asst Principal, MoT, 1969; Principal, DoE, 1972; Treasury, 1976; Asst Sec. 1978, Sec., Top Salaries Review Body and Police Negotiating Bd; DoE, 1979; Prin. Private Sec. to Sec. of State for the Environment, 1983–85; Under Sec., DoE and Dept of Transport, and Regl Dir, Yorks and Humberside Region, 1986; Dir, Housing Assocs and the Private Sector, DoE, 1990–92; Dir, Maxwell Pensions Unit, DSS, 1992–93 (on secondment); Dir, Town and Country Planning, DoE, 1993–97; Dir Finance, and Principal Finance Officer, DoE, subseq. DETR, 1997–2001; Dir, Water and Land, DETR, subseq. DEFRA, 2001–03. Dir, British Water, 2004–06. Mem. Steering Bd, Marine Fisheries Agency, 2005–. Trustee, Maxwell Pensioners Trust, 1993–97; Associate Special Trustee, 1992–99, Special Trustee, 1999–, Gt Ormond St Hosp. for Sick Children; Chm., Gt Ormond St Hosp. Children's Charity, 2006–08. Gov., Brooklands Sch., Blackheath, 2005–. *Recreations:* trekking, tennis, singing, reading. *Address:* 81 Humber Road, Blackheath, SE3 7LR.

BALLARD, Mark; Communications Manager, Scottish Council for Voluntary Organisations; *b* 27 June 1971; *s* of Roger and Cathy Ballard; *m* 2002, Heather Stacey; one *s. Educ:* Edinburgh Univ. (MA Hons (Econ. and Social Hist.) 1994). Various positions, European Youth Forest Action, Edinburgh and Amsterdam, 1994–98; Ed., Reforesting Scotland Jl, 1998–2001; estd and ran EMBE Environmental Communications, consultancy co., 2002–03. Scottish Green Party: spokesperson on internat. develt, 1999–2000; Convener, Nat. Council, 2000–02; Nat. Sec., 2002–03. Mem. (Green) Lothians, Scottish Parlt, 2003–07. Rector, Edinburgh Univ., 2006–. *Recreations:* cycling, Indian cookery.

BALLARD, Ven. Peter James; Archdeacon of Lancaster, since 2006; *b* 10 March 1955; *m* 1978, Helen Lees; two *d. Educ:* Grammar Sch. for Boys, Chadderton; St Hild and St Bede's Coll., Durham (BEd 1978); DipTheol London (ext.) 1985; Sarum and Wells Theol Coll. Various posts with TEC, then BTEC, 1978–85; ordained deacon, 1987, priest, 1988; Asst Curate, Grantham, 1987–91; Vicar, Christ Ch, Lancaster, 1991–98; RD Lancaster, 1995–98; Canon Residentiary, Blackburn Cathedral, 1998–2006; Diocesan Dir of Educn, Blackburn, 1998–. Mem., Gen. Synod of C of E, 2000–. Consulting Ed., Internat. Jl of Comparative Religious Educn and Values, 2001–. Gov., St Martin's Coll. of Higher Educn, 1999–2007 (Actg Chm., 2005); Chm. and Pro Chancellor, Univ. of Cumbria, 2007– (Vice Chm., 2006–07). *Publications:* (with Brian Boughton) Construction Mathematics, vols I and II, 1983; (contrib.) Mission Shaped Youth, 2007. *Recreations:* bad golf, electronic gardening, watching most sports, spending time with the family. *Address:* Wheatfield, 7 Dallas Road, Lancaster LA1 1TN. *T:* (01524) 32897, *Fax:* (01524) 66095; *e-mail:* peter.j.ballard@btinternet.com.

BALLARD, Dr Robert Duane; oceanographer and marine explorer; Founder and President, Institute for Exploration, since 1995; *b* 30 June 1942; *s* of Chester P. Ballard and Harriett N. Ballard; *m* 1991, Barbara Earle; two *s* one *d. Educ:* Univ. of California, Santa Barbara (BS 1965); Univ. of Hawaii; Univ. of Southern California; Univ. of Rhode Island (PhD 1974). 2nd Lieut, US Army Intelligence, 1965–67; USN, 1967–70, served Vietnam War; Comdr, USNR, 1987–2001. Woods Hole Oceanographic Institution: Res. Associate, 1969–74; Asst Scientist, 1974–76; Associate Scientist, 1976–83; Founder, Deep Submergence Lab., and Sen. Scientist, Dept of Applied Ocean Physics and Engrg, 1983–; Dir, Center for Marine Exploration, 1989–95; Scientist Emeritus, 1997–. Founder, Jason Project (use of remotely operated vehicles for deep-sea exploration), 1989; Founder, 1989, and Chm. of Bd, 1990–95, Jason Foundn for Educn. Expeditions include: exploration of Mid-ocean Ridge, 1974, of Galapagos Rift, 1977; discovery of polymetallic sulphides, 1979; Titanic, 1985; German battleship Bismarck, 1989; warships from lost fleet of Guadalcanal, 1992; Lusitania, 1994; Roman ships off coast of Tunisia, 1997; USS Yorktown, 1998; Black Sea, 2000. Presenter, Nat. Geographic Explorer TV prog., 1989–91; award-winning films for television incl. Secrets of the Titanic, 1985, and Last Voyage of the Lusitania, 1994. Many scientific, academic and multi-media awards and honours. *Publications:* Photographic Atlas of the Mid-Atlantic Ridge Rift Valley, 1977; (jtly) The Discovery of the Titanic, 1987 (trans. 10 langs); The Discovery of the Bismarck, 1990 (trans. 8 langs); Bright Shark (novel), 1992 (trans. 6 langs); The Lost Ships of Guadalcanal, 1993 (trans. 5 langs); (jtly) Exploring the Lusitania, 1995 (trans. 2 langs); Explorations (autobiog.), 1995 (trans. 2 langs); Lost Liners, 1997 (trans. 5 langs); History of Deep Submergence Science and Technology, 1998; At the Water's Edge: coastal images of America, 1998; Return to Midway, 1999; The Eternal Darkness: a personal history of deep-sea exploration, 2000; *for children:* Exploring the Titanic, 1988 (trans. 7 langs); The Lost Wreck of the Isis, 1990 (trans. 5 langs); Exploring the Bismarck, 1991 (trans. 2 langs); Explorer, 1992; Ghost Liners, 1998; contrib. many learned jls. *Address:* Institute for Exploration, 55 Coogan Blvd, Mystic, CT 06355, USA.

BALLARD, Ronald Alfred; Head of Technical Services of the Central Computers and Telecommunications Agency, HM Treasury (formerly Civil Service Department), 1980–85; consultant, 1985–95; voluntary work, Help the Aged, 1989–2007; *b* 17 Feb. 1925; *s* of Joseph William and Ivy Amy Ballard; *m* 1948, Eileen Margaret Edwards; one *d. Educ:* Univ. of Birmingham (BSc (Hons) Physics). National Service, RN, 1945–47. Admiralty Surface Weapons Establishment, Portsmouth: Scientific Officer, then Sen. Scientific Officer, Research and Development Seaborne Radar Systems, 1948–55; Application of Computers to Naval Comd and Control Systems, 1955–69; PSO, 1960, responsibilities for Action Data Automation (ADA), on HMS Eagle and destroyers; SPSO, to Head Computer Systems and Techniques in Civil Service Dept (Central Computers Agency in 1972), 1969; Head of Central Computers Facility, 1972–76; DCSO, to Head Technical Services Div. of Central Computers Agency, 1977; CSO(B), 1980–85. Treasurer: Sutton Assoc. for the Blind, 1985–98; Carshalton Assoc. for the Elderly, 2000–04; Asst Treas., League of Friends, Queen Mary's Hosp., Carshalton, 1986–95.

BALLENTYNE, Donald Francis, CMG 1985; HM Diplomatic Service, retired; Consul-General, Los Angeles, 1985–89; *b* 5 May 1929; *s* of late Henry Q. Ballentyne and Frances R. MacLaren; *m* 1950, Elizabeth Heywood, *d* of late Leslie A. Heywood; one *s* one *d. Educ:* Haberdashers' Aske's Hatcham Sch. FO, 1950–53; Berne and Ankara, 1953–56; Consul: Munich, 1957; Stanleyville, 1961; Cape Town, 1962; First Secretary: Luxembourg, 1965–69; Havana, 1969–72; FCO, 1972–74; Counsellor (Commercial), The Hague, 1974–78; Bonn, 1978–81; Counsellor, E Berlin, 1982–84. *Address:* Orford, Suffolk.

BALLESTEROS, Severiano; professional golfer, 1974–2007; *b* Santander, Spain, 9 April 1957; *s* of Baldomero Ballesteros; *m* 1988, Carmen Botin; two *s* one *d.* Won Spanish Young Professional title, 1975, 1978; French Open, 1977, 1982, 1985, 1986; Japan Open, 1977, 1978; Swiss Open, 1977, 1978, 1989; German Open, 1978, 1988; Open Champion, Lytham St Anne's, 1979 and 1988, St Andrews, 1984; won US Masters, 1980, 1983; World Matchplay Champion, Wentworth, 1981, 1982, 1984, 1985; Australian PGA Championship, 1981; Spanish Open, 1985, 1995; Dutch Open, 1986; British Masters, 1991; PGA Championship, 1991; Internat. Open, 1994; numerous other titles in Europe, USA, Australasia; Mem. Ryder Cup team, 1979, 1983, 1985, 1987, 1989, Captain, 1997. Prince of Asturias prize for sport, 1989. *Publications:* (with Robert Green): Troubleshooting, 1996; Seve: My Life and Golf, 2002. *Address:* c/o Fairway SA, C1 Pasaje de Peña, 2–4ª Planta, 39008 Santander, Spain.

BALLMER, Steve; Chief Executive Officer, Microsoft Corporation, since 2000; *b* March 1956; *m* Connie; three *c. Educ:* Harvard Univ. (BA); Stanford Univ. Graduate Sch. of Business. Asst Product Manager, Procter & Gamble Co.; joined Microsoft Corp., 1980; Vice-Pres., Marketing; Sen. Vice-Pres., Systems Software; Exec. Vice-Pres., Sales and Support, until 1998; Pres., 1998–2000. Dir, Accenture, 2001–. *Address:* Microsoft Corporation, 1 Microsoft Way, Redmond, WA 98052–8300, USA.

BALLS, Alastair Gordon, CB 1995; Chairman, The International Centre for Life, since 2007 (Chief Executive, 1998–2007); *b* 18 March 1944; *s* of late Dr Ernest George Balls and Elspeth Russell Balls; *m* 1978, Beryl May Nichol; one *s* one *d. Educ:* Hamilton Acad.; Univ. of St Andrews (MA); Univ. of Manchester (MA). Economist: Treasury, Govt of Tanzania, 1966–68; Min. of Transport, UK, 1969–74; Sec., Adv. Cttee on Channel Tunnel, 1974–75; Sen. Econ. Adviser, HM Treasury, 1976–79; Asst Sec., Dept of Environment, 1979–83; Regl Dir, Depts of Environment and Transport (Northern Region), 1984–87; Chief Exec., Tyne and Wear Develt Corp., 1987–98. Chairman: Newcastle Gateshead Initiative, 2004–07; Northern Rock Foundn, 2006–. Non-executive Director: Northumbrian Water Ltd, 2002–; N Star Venture Capital, 2004–. Mem. Bd, HEFCE, 2006–. Mem., ITC, 1998–2003. Chm., Alzheimer's Soc., 2007–. Vice-Chm., Council, Univ. of Newcastle upon Tyne, 1994–2000. *Recreations:* sailing, fishing, maintaining rusty old cars. *Address:* The International Centre for Life Trust, Times Square, Newcastle upon Tyne NE1 4EP.

BALLS, Rt Hon. Edward (Michael); PC 2007; MP (Lab and Co-op) Normanton, since 2005; Secretary of State for Children, Schools and Families, since 2007; *b* 25 Feb. 1967; *s* of Prof. Michael Balls and Carolyn Janet Balls; *m* 1998, Rt Hon. Yvette Cooper, *qv*; one *s* two *d. Educ:* Bawburgh Co. Primary Sch.; Crossdale Drive Primary Sch., Keyworth; Nottingham High Sch.; Keble Coll., Oxford (BA 1st Cl. Hons PPE); John F. Kennedy Sch. of Govt, Harvard Univ. (Kennedy Scholar; MPA). Teaching Fellow, Dept. of Econs, Harvard Univ., and Nat. Bureau of Econ. Res., 1989–90; econs leader writer and columnist, Financial Times, 1990–94; Econ. Advr to Shadow Chancellor, 1994–97; Sec., Labour Party Econ. Policy Commn, 1994–97; Econ. Advr to Chancellor of the Exchequer, HM Treasury, 1997–99; Chief Econ. Advr, HM Treasury, 1999–2004. Chm., Cttee of Deputies, IMF, 2002–04. Sen. Res. Fellow, Smith Inst., 2004–05. Econ. Sec. to HM Treasury, 2006–07. Chm., Fabian Soc., 2007. Mem. Council, REconS, 1997–2002. Hon. LLD Nottingham, 2003. *Publications:* (Principal Ed.) World Bank Development Report, 1995; (ed with Gus O'Donnell) Reforming Britain's Economic and Financial Policy, 2002; (ed with Joe Grice and Gus O'Donnell) Reforming Britain's Microeconomic Policy, 2004; contribs to learned jls, incl. Scottish Jl Pol. Econ., World Economics, and to reports published by Fabian Soc. and Social Justice Commn. *Recreations:* playing football, the violin and with daughters Ellie and Maddy and son Joe. *Address:* House of Commons, SW1A 0AA. *T:* (020) 7219 4115.

BALLS, Rt Hon. Yvette; *see* Cooper, Rt Hon. Y.

BALLYEDMOND, Baron *cr* 2004 (Life Peer), of Mourne in the County of Down; **Edward Haughey,** OBE 1987; JP; Chairman, Norbrook Laboratories Ltd and Norbrook Holdings BV, since 1980; Member, Senate of Ireland, since 1994 (Government spokesman for Northern Ireland); *b* 5 Jan. 1944; *s* of Edward Haughey and Rose Haughey (*née* Traynor); *m* 1972, Mary Gordon Young; two *s* one *d. Educ:* Christian Brothers Sch., Dundalk, Ireland. Bd Mem., Warrenpoint Harbour Authy, 1986–89; Dir, Adv. Bd, Bank of Ireland, 1987–; Chairman: Ballyedmond Castle Farms Ltd, 1991–; Haughey Airports, 2000–; Haughey Air, 2000–. Member: Forum for Peace and Reconciliation, 1996–; Oireachtas Cttee for For. Affairs, 1997–; British-Irish Inter-Parly Body, 1997–; Inst. of British/Irish Studies, 2000–. Trustee: Dublin City Univ., 1995–; RCVS, 2001– (Perm. Vice-Pres.; Hon. ARCVS). Perm. Vice-Pres., Anglo-Chilean Soc., 1995; Hon. Consul for Chile in NI, 1992. JP NI 1986. FInstD; FIAM. Dist. Fellow, Griffith Coll., Dublin; Fellow Entrepreneurship, RVC, Univ. of London, 2004. Hon. Associate: BVA, 2004; NI Veterinary Assoc., 2008. Hon. Fellow, Irish Mgt Inst.; Hon. FRCSI 1998. Hon. DBA Internat. Mgt Centres, 1992; Hon. LLD NUI, 1997. Order of Bernardo O'Higgins (Chile), 1995. *Recreations:* fishing, shooting, walking. *Address:* Ballyedmond Castle, Rostrevor, Co. Down, Northern Ireland BT34 3AF. *T:* (028) 3026 9824; Corby Castle, Great Corby, Cumbria CA4 8LR; 64 Fitzwilliam Square, Dublin 2, Ireland; 9 Belgrave Square, SW1X 8PH. *Clubs:* Savage; Reform (Belfast); Kildare Street and University (Dublin).

BALMER, Colin Victor, CB 2001; Managing Director, Cabinet Office, 2003–06; *b* 22 Aug. 1946; *s* of Peter Lionel Balmer and Adelaide Currie Balmer; *m* 1978, Frances Mary Montrésor (marr. diss. 2006); two *s* one *d*; *m* 2006, Lesley Ann Pasricha. *Educ:* Liverpool Inst. High Sch. War Office, 1963, later Ministry of Defence: Asst Private Sec. to Minister of State, 1972; Private Sec. to Parly Under-Sec. of State (RAF), 1973; Civil Advr to GOC N Ireland, 1973; Cabinet Office, 1977; Private Sec. to Minister of State (Defence Procurement), 1980; UK Delegn to NATO, 1982; MoD 1984; Minister (Defence Materiel), Washington, 1990; Ministry of Defence: Asst Under-Sec. of State, 1992–96; Dep. Under-Sec. of State (Resources, Programmes and Finance), 1996–98; Finance Dir, 1998–2003. Non-executive Director: QinetiQ Gp plc, 2006–; Royal Mint, 2007–. *Recreations:* golf, tennis, bridge, rock and roll music, playing guitar (badly). *Address: e-mail:* colinbalmer@btinternet.com.

BALMER, Derek Rigby, RWA 1970; painter and photographer; President, Royal West of England Academy, since 2001; *b* 28 Dec. 1934; *s* of Geoffrey Johnstone Balmer and Barbara Winifred Balmer (*née* Rigby); *m* 1962, Elizabeth Mary Rose Hawkins; one *s* one *d. Educ:* Waterloo House Sch.; Sefton Park Sch.; West of England Coll. of Art. *One-man exhibitions* include: Fimbarrus Gall., Bath, 1960; Arnolfini Gall., Bristol, 1966, 1968; City Art Gall., Bristol, 1975; Sharples Gall., RWA, 1980; Anthony Hepworth Fine Art, Bath, 1992, 1994, 2005, London, 1994, 2000; Gisela van Beers, London, 1992; Montpelier Sandelson, London, 1995; Smelik and Stokking Galls, Holland, 1996, 1998, 2000, 2001; New Gall., RWA, 2003; Campden Gall., Chipping Campden, 2005, 2008; *retrospective exhibition:* President's Eye: 1950–2007, RWA Galls, 2007; *group exhibitions* include: Arnolfini Gall., Bristol, 1963, 1964, 1983; Arts Council Touring Exhibn, 1967; Leicester Galls, London, 1968, 1969, 1970; Victoria Art Gall., Bath, 1970; New Art Centre, London, 1982; Louise Hallet Gall., London, 1985; London Contemp. Art Fair, annually 1990–; Campden Gall., Chipping Campden, 2004. Chm., RWA, 1997–2000. Pro-Chancellor, UWE, 2003–. Hon. DArts UWE, 2001. Hon. RA 2003. *Recreations:* art history, reading, cricket, walking Newfoundland dogs. *Address:* Mulberry House, 12 Avon Grove, Sneyd Park, Bristol BS9 1PJ. *T:* (0117) 968 2953; c/o Anthony Hepworth Fine Art, 1 Margaret Buildings, Bath BA1 2LP. *T:* (01225) 447480. *Club:* Chelsea Arts.

BALMFORTH, Ven. Anthony James; Archdeacon of Bristol, 1979–90, now Archdeacon Emeritus; *b* 3 Sept. 1926; *s* of Joseph Henry and Daisy Florence Balmforth; *m* 1952, Eileen Julia, *d* of James Raymond and Kitty Anne Evans; one *s* two *d. Educ:* Sebright School, Wolverley; Brasenose Coll., Oxford (BA 1950, MA 1951); Lincoln Theological Coll. Army service, 1944–48. Deacon 1952, priest 1953, dio. Southwell; Curate of Mansfield, 1952–55; Vicar of Skegby, Notts, 1955–61; Vicar of St John's, Kidderminster, Worcs, 1961–65; Rector of St Nicolas, King's Norton, Birmingham, 1965–79; Hon. Canon of Birmingham Cathedral, 1975–79; RD of King's Norton, 1973–79; Examining Chaplain to: Bishop of Birmingham, 1978–79; Bishop of Bristol, 1981–90. Hon. Canon of Bristol Cathedral, 1979–. Mem., Gen. Synod of C of E, 1982–90. *Recreations:* cricket, gardening. *Address:* Slipper Cottage, Stag Hill, Yorkley, near Lydney, Glos GL15 4TB. *T:* (01594) 564016.

BALNIEL, Lord; Anthony Robert Lindsay; Director, J. O. Hambro Investment Management, since 1987 (Chief Executive Officer, 2004–07); *b* 24 Nov. 1958; *s* and *heir* of Earl of Crawford and Balcarres, *qv*; *m* 1989, Nicola A., *y d* of Antony Bicket; two *s* two *d. Educ:* Eton Coll.; Univ. of Edinburgh. *Heir: s* Master of Lindsay, *qv. Address:* 6 Pembridge Place, W2 4XB. *Clubs:* New (Edinburgh); XII.

BALOGUN-LYNCH, Christopher Charles, FRCSE, FRCOG; Consultant Obstetrician and Gynaecological Surgeon, Milton Keynes General Hospital, since 1984; *b* 1 Oct. 1947; *s* of late Prof. Prince E. Balogun-Lynch and Jane A. Balogun-Lynch; *m* 1986, Julia Caroline Klinner; one *s* three *d. Educ:* Christ Church, Oxford (MA); St Bartholomew's Hosp., London (MB BS 1974). FRCSE 1979; FRCOG 1991; MCIArb 1999; QDR 1994. Surgeon in private practice, Harley St, 1984–. Royal Coll. Tutor and Trainer in Minimal Access Surgery, 1995–. Hon. Vis. Gynaecological Cancer Surgeon, Northampton Gen. Hosp., 2001. Introduced carbon dioxide laser, YAG laser and keyhole surgery techniques to Milton Keynes Hosp., 1985–2003; innovator of new technology and obstetric and gynaecological surgical techniques incl. the control of post-partum haemorrhage now in worldwide application. Vis. Prof., Cranfield Univ., 2006–; has lectured in Sydney, Cape Town, USA, Italy and various centres in UK, 1988–. Obstetrics and gynaecol. undergrad. Trainer and Examiner, Oxford Univ., 2007–. Publications Referee: British Jl Obstetrics and Gynaecol.; Eur. Jl Obstetrics and Gynaecol.; Internat. Jl Obstetrics and Gynaecol.; American Jl Obstetrics and Gynaecol. Founder and Chair, Myrtle Peach Trust for Gynaecological Cancer Prevention and Res., 1985–. Liveryman, Soc. of Apothecaries, 1983–. MAE 1992; FLLA 1997. Fellow, Royal Soc. of St George, 2002. DUniv Open, 1997. Serono Labs (UK) Award for Assisted Conception, 1987. Grand Commanding Officer, Republic of Sierra Leone, 2007. *Publications:* (jtly) The Surgical Management of Post Partum Haemorrhage, 2005; (ed jtly) A Textbook of Postpartum Hemorrhage, 2006; numerous contribs to medical, surgical, scientific, clinical, endoscopic surgery, medico-legal and educational papers in leading jls. *Recreations:* Rugby, cricket, occasional golf, family outings. *Address:* Linford Court, Church Lane, Little Linford, Bucks MK19 7EB. *T:* and *Fax:* (01908) 615717; *e-mail:* enquiries@cblynch.com. *Clubs:* Athenæum, Royal Automobile.

BALSHAW, Maria Jane, DPhil; Director, Whitworth Art Gallery, University of Manchester, since 2006; *b* 24 Jan. 1970; *d* of Walter and Colette Balshaw; one *s* one *d* with Liam Kennedy. *Educ:* Univ. of Liverpool (BA Hons Eng. and Cultural Studies 1991); Univ. of Sussex (MA Critical Theory 1992; DPhil African American Visual Culture and Lit. 1997). Lectr in Cultural Studies, UC Northampton, 1993–97; Res. Fellow in American Urban Culture, Univ. of Birmingham, 1997–2002; Dir, Creative Partnerships Birmingham, 2002–05; Dir of External Relns and Develt, Arts Council England, W Midlands, 2005–06. Clore Leadership Fellow, 2004–05. *Publications:* Urban Space and Representation (ed with Liam Kennedy), 1999; Looking for Harlem: African American urban culture, 2000; (ed jtly) City Sites: multimedia essays on Chicago and New York, 2000. *Recreations:* dancing (especially in kitchen with my kids), gardening, travelling anywhere, visiting art galleries, cooking, eating out. *Address:* The Whitworth Art Gallery, University of Manchester, Oxford Road, Manchester M15 3ER. *T:* (0161) 275 5740; *e-mail:* maria-balshaw@manchester.ac.uk.

BALSOM, Alison Louise; classical trumpet soloist, since 2001; Professor of Trumpet, Guildhall School of Music and Drama, since 2006; *b* 7 Oct. 1978; *d* of William and Zena Balsom. *Educ:* Tannery Drift Primary Sch.; Greneway Middle Sch.; Meridian Sch., Royston; Hills Rd Sixth Form Coll., Cambridge; Guildhall Sch. of Music and Drama (BMus Hons 2001); Paris Conservatoire. Has appeared as soloist with all BBC orchestras and ensembles incl. LA Philharmonic, Acad. of St Martin-in-the-Fields. Young Concert Artists Trust Artist, 2001–04; BBC New Generation Artist, 2004–06. Brass Winner, BBC Young Musician of Year, 1998; Gramophone Award, Classic FM Listeners' Choice, 2006; Young British Classical Performer, Classical Brit Awards, 2006; Echo Klassik Award, 2007. *Recreations:* catamaran dinghy sailing, photography, exploring. *Address:* c/o Maggie O'Herlihy, HarrisonParrott Artists Management, 12 Penzance Place, W11 4PA; *e-mail:* maggie.oherlihy@harrisonparrott.co.uk.

BALSTON, His Honour Antony Francis; a Circuit Judge, 1985–2005; *b* 18 Jan. 1939; *s* of late Comdr E. F. Balston, DSO, RN, and D. B. L. Balston (*née* Ferrers); *m* 1966, Anne Marie Judith Ball; two *s* one *d. Educ:* Downside; Christ's Coll., Cambridge (MA). Served Royal Navy, 1957–59; Univ. of Cambridge, 1959–62; admitted Solicitor, 1966. Partner, Herington Willings & Penry Davey, Solicitors, Hastings, 1967–85; a Recorder of the Crown Court, 1980–85; Hon. Recorder, Hastings, 1984–2005. *Recreation:* gardening. *Club:* Farmers.

BALTIMORE, David, PhD; Robert Andrews Millikan Professor of Biology, California Institute of Technology, since 2006 (President, 1997–2006); *b* New York, 7 March 1938; *s* of Richard and Gertrude Baltimore; *m* 1968, Alice Huang; one *d. Educ:* Swarthmore Coll. (BA 1960); Rockefeller Univ. (PhD 1964). Postdoctoral Fellow, MIT, 1963–64; Albert Einstein Coll. of Med., NY, 1964–65; Research Associate, Salk Inst., La Jolla, Calif, 1965–68; Massachusetts Institute of Technology: Associate Prof., 1968–72; Amer. Cancer Soc. Prof. of Microbiol., 1973–83; Prof. of Biology, 1972–90; Dir, Whitehead Inst., 1982–90; Prof., 1990–94, Pres., 1990–91, Rockefeller Univ.; Ivan R. Cottrell Prof. of Molecular Biol. and Immunol., MIT, 1994–97. FAAAS 1980 (Pres., 2007–08; Chm., 2008–Feb. 2009). Chm., AIDS Vaccine Adv. Cttee, NIH, 1996–2002. Member: Nat. Acad. of Scis, 1974; Amer. Acad. of Arts and Scis, 1974; Pontifical Acad. of Scis, 1978; Foreign Mem., Royal Soc., 1987. Eli Lilly Award in Microbiology and Immunology, 1971; US Steel Foundn Award in Molecular Biology, 1974; (jtly) Nobel Prize for Physiology or Medicine, 1975; US Nat. Medal of Science, 1999; Warren Alpert Foundn Prize, 2000; AMA Scientific Achievement Award, 2002. *Address:* California Institute of Technology, 147–75, 1200 E California Boulevard, Pasadena, CA 91125, USA.

BAMBER, Helen, OBE 1997; Co-founding Director, Helen Bamber Foundation, since 2005. Mem., Relief and Rehabilitation Assoc., UN, 1945–47; Mem., Cttee for the Care of Children from Concentration Camps, 1947; health and social work in various hospitals and orgns; joined Amnesty Internat., 1961 (Mem. Exec. Council, and Sec., Med. Gp, 1974, British section); Founder and Dir, Med. Foundn for the Care of Victims of Torture, 1985–2002. Consultant and supervisor, Family Trauma Centre, Belfast. Hon. DCL Oxon, 2000. *Address:* Helen Bamber Foundation, 5 Museum House, 25 Museum Street, WC1A 1JT.

BAMBERG, Harold Rolf, CBE 1968; FRAeS; Chairman: Glos Air Ltd, since 1985; Via Nova Properties Ltd, since 1985; Bamberg Farms Ltd, since 1996; *b* 17 Nov. 1923; *m* 1957 (marr. diss. 1990); one *s* two *d*, and one *s* one *d* of a former marriage. *Educ:* Hampstead. Former Chm., British Independent Air Transport Assoc.; Life Vice Pres., British Business and Gen. Aviation (formerly GAMTA) (formerly Chm.); former Director: Cunard Steamship Co.; BOAC Cunard, etc; Founder: British Eagle International Airlines, 1948; Lunn Poly Ltd, 1956. Mem., NFU. FRAeS 1993. Kt, Order of Merit, Italian Republic, 1960. *Recreations:* horses, agriculture. *Address:* 18 Cheniston Court, Ridgemount Road, Ascot, Berks SL5 9SF. *T:* (01344) 625950, *Fax:* (01344) 872285; *e-mail:* h.bamberg489@btinternet.com. *Club:* Guards' Polo (Life Mem.).

BAMBOROUGH, John Bernard; Principal of Linacre College, Oxford, 1962–88; Pro-Vice-Chancellor, Oxford University, 1966–88; *b* 3 Jan. 1921; *s* of John George Bamborough; *m* 1947, Anne, *d* of Olav Indrehus, Indrehus, Norway; one *s* one *d*. *Educ:* Haberdashers' Aske's Hampstead Sch. (Scholar); New College, Oxford (Scholar). 1st Class, English Language and Literature, 1941; MA 1946. Service in RN, 1941–46 (in Coastal Forces as Lieut RNVR; afterwards as Educ. Officer with rank of Instructor Lieut, RN). Junior Lectr, New Coll., Oxford, 1946; Fellow and Tutor, Wadham Coll., Oxford, 1947–62 (Dean, 1947–54; Domestic Bursar, 1954–56; Sen. Tutor, 1957–61); Univ. Lectr in English, 1951–62; Mem. Hebdomadal Council, Oxford Univ., 1961–79. Hon. Fellow: New Coll., Oxford, 1967; Linacre Coll., Oxford, 1988; Wadham Coll., Oxford, 1988. Clerk of the Market, Oxford Univ., 1997–2002. Editor, Review of English Studies, 1964–78. Cavaliere Ufficiale, Order of Merit (Italy), 1991. *Publications:* The Little World of Man, 1952; Ben Jonson, 1959; (ed) Pope's Life of Ward, 1961; Jonson's Volpone, 1963; The Alchemist, 1967; Ben Jonson, 1970; (ed) Burton's Anatomy of Melancholy, vols iv–vi, 1998–2000. *Address:* 18 Winchester Road, Oxford OX2 6NA. *T:* (01865) 559886.

BAMERT, Matthias; conductor; Principal Conductor and Artistic Advisor, Malaysian Philharmonic Orchestra, since 2004; Chief Conductor, West Australian Symphony Orchestra, since 2004; *b* Switzerland, 5 July 1942; *m* 1969, Susan Exline; one *s* one *d*. Asst conductor to Leopold Stokowski, 1970–71; Resident Conductor, Cleveland Orch., USA, 1971–78; Music Director: Swiss Radio Orch., Basel, 1977–83; London Mozart Players, 1993–2000. Principal Guest Conductor: Scottish Nat. Orch., 1985–90; NZ SO, 2000–02; Associate Guest Conductor, RPO, 2001–. Director: Musica Nova fest., Glasgow, 1985–90; Lucerne Fest., 1992–98. Has worked with orchestras incl. LPO, BBC Philharmonic, BBC SO, CBSO, Orchestre de Paris, Rotterdam Philharmonic, Cleveland Orchestra, Pittsburgh Symphony, Houston Symphony, Montreal Symphony, and appears regularly at Promenade concerts; tours each season in Europe, N America, Australia, NZ, Hong Kong and Japan, and has made over 60 recordings. *Address:* IMG Artists, The Light Box, 111 Power Road, Chiswick, W4 5PY.

BAMFORD, Alan George, CBE 1985; Principal, Homerton College, Cambridge, 1985–91; *b* 12 July 1930; *s* of James Ross and Margaret Emily Bamford; *m* 1954, Joan Margaret, *e d* of Arthur W. Vint; four *s*. *Educ:* Prescot Grammar School; Borough Road College, London; Liverpool University (DipEd, MEd); MA Cantab; Cert. Ed. London. Teacher and Dep. Headmaster, Lancashire primary schs, 1952–62; Lectr in Primary Educn, Liverpool Univ., 1962–63; Sen. Lectr in Educn, Chester Coll., 1963–66; Principal Lectr and Head of Educn Dept, S Katharine's Coll., Liverpool, 1966–71; Principal, Westhill Coll., Birmingham, 1971–85. Pres., Birmingham Council of Christian Educn, 1972–74, Vice-Pres., 1974–91; Vice-Pres., Colls of Educn Christian Union, 1965–86, Pres., 1966–67, 1972–73; Chm., Birmingham Assoc. of Youth Clubs, 1972–85, Vice-Pres., 1985–; Member: Standing Conf. on Studies in Educn, 1974–91 (Exec. Cttee and Editl Bd, 1978–87, Sec., 1982–84); Council of Nat. Youth Bureau, 1974–80 (Exec. Cttee, 1978–80); Adv. Cttee on religious broadcasts, BBC Radio Birmingham, 1972–80; Educn Cttee, Free Church Fed. Council, 1978–89; BCC Standing Cttee on Theol Educn, 1979–82; Council, British and Foreign School Soc., 1979–85; Exec. Cttee, Assoc. of Voluntary Colls, 1979–86; Standing Cttee on Educn and Training of Teachers, 1985–91 (Vice-Chm., 1988; Chm., 1989); Cttee, Standing Conf. of Principals and Dirs of Colls and Insts of Higher Educn, 1986–91; Voluntary Sector Consultative Council, 1987–88; Cambridge HA, 1987–90 (Trustee, 1988–90); Chairman: Colls Cttee, NATFHE, 1981–82; Central Register and Clearing House Cttee, 1981–82 (Mem. Council of Management, 1982–92). Gov., London Bible Coll., 1981–89. JP Birmingham 1977–85. Hon. MA Birmingham, 1981. *Publications:* articles on educn and church-related subjects. *Recreations:* travel, photography.

BAMFORD, Sir Anthony (Paul), Kt 1990; DL; Chairman and Managing Director, J. C. Bamford Group, since 1975; *b* 23 Oct. 1945; *s* of late Joseph Cyril Bamford, CBE; *m* 1974, Carole Gray Whitt (OBE 2006); two *s* one *d*. *Educ:* Ampleforth Coll.; Grenoble Univ. FIAgrE 2003. Joined JCB, 1962. Dir, Tarmac, 1987–95. Member: Design Council, 1987–89; President's Cttee, CBI, 1986–88. Pres., Staffs Agricl Soc., 1987–88. Pres., Burton on Trent Cons. Assoc., 1987–90. High Sheriff, Staffs, 1985–86. DL Staffs, 1989. Hon. FCGI 1993. Hon. MEng Birmingham, 1987; DUniv Keele, 1988; Hon. DSc Cranfield, 1994; Hon. DTech: Staffordshire, 1998; Loughborough, 2002; Hon. DBA Robert Gordon, 1996. Young Exporter of the Year, 1972; Young Businessman of the Year, 1979; Top Exporter of the Year, 1995; Entrepreneurial Award, British Amer. Business Inc., 2003. Chevalier, l'Ordre National du Mérite (France), 1989; Commendatore al merito della Repubblica Italiana, 1995. *Recreations:* farming, gardening. *Address:* c/o J. C. Bamford Excavators Ltd, Rocester, Uttoxeter, Staffs ST14 5JP. *Clubs:* Pratt's, White's, British Racing Drivers'.

BAMFORD, Louis Neville Jules; Legal Executive with Margetts & Ritchie, Solicitors, Birmingham, since 1960; *b* 2 July 1932; *s* of Neville Barnes Bamford and Elise Marie Bamford; unmarried. *Educ:* local schools in Birmingham. Member (Lab): Birmingham CC, 1971–74; W Midlands CC, 1974–86 (Chm., 1981–82); Birmingham CC, 1986–2002 (Chm., Gen. Purposes Cttee; Chief Whip, Lab Gp; Hon. Alderman, 2002). *Recreations:* sport, music. *Address:* 15 Chilton Court, Park Approach, Erdington, Birmingham B23 7XY; (office) Coleridge Chambers, 177 Corporation Street, Birmingham B4 6RL.

BAMPFYLDE, family name of **Baron Poltimore**.

BANATVALA, Prof. Jehangir Edalji, CBE 1999; MD; FRCP, FRCPath, FMedSci; Professor of Clinical Virology, Guy's, King's College and St Thomas' Hospitals Medical and Dental School, 1975–99, now Emeritus; Hon. Consultant Virologist, Guy's and St Thomas' Hospital Trust, 1975–99; *b* 7 Jan. 1934; *s* of Dr Edal Banatvala and Ratti Banatvala (*née* Shroff); *m* 1959, Roshan (*née* Mugaseth); three *s* (one *d* decd). *Educ:* Forest Sch., London; Gonville and Caius Coll., Cambridge (MA, MB BChir 1958; MD (Whitby Medal) 1964); London Hosp. Med. Coll. DPH London 1961; DCH 1961; MRCPath 1965, FRCPath 1977; MRCP 1986, FRCP 1995. Polio Fund Res. Fellow, Univ. of Cambridge, 1961–64; Fulbright Schol. and Amer. Thoracic Soc. Fellow, Yale Univ., 1964–65; Sen. Lectr, 1965–71, Reader, 1971–75, St Thomas' Hosp. Med. Sch., then UMDS of Guy's and St Thomas' Hosp.; Chm., St Thomas' Hosp. Mgt Team and Med. Adv. Cttee, 1983–84. Royal College of Pathologists: Registrar, 1985–87; Vice Pres., 1987–90; Mem. Council, 1993–96; Member: Council, Med. Defence Union, 1987–2004; Jt Cttee on Vaccination and Immunisation, DoH, 1986–95; PHLS Bd, 1995–2001; Chairman: Adv. Gp on Hepatitis, DoH, 1990–98; Mem., European Soc. of Clin. Virology, 1997–; Pres., European Assoc. Against Virus Disease, 1981–83. Hon. Cons. Microbiologist to the Army, 1992–97. Dir, Clinical Pathology Accreditation (UK) Ltd, 1997–2002. Examiner, Univs of London, Cambridge, Colombo, West Indies and Riyadh. Mem. Senate, London Univ., 1987–94; Governor: Forest Sch., E17, 1993–; Mill Hill Sch., 2001–. Founder FMedSci 1998. Freeman, City of London, 1987; Liveryman, Co. of Apothecaries, 1986. *Publications:* (ed) Current Problems in Clinical Virology, 1971; (ed jtly) Principles and Practice of Clinical Virology, 1987, 5th edn 2004; (ed) Viral Infections of the Heart, 1993; papers in gen. and specialised med. jls on intrauterine and perinatal infections, blood-borne virus infections, viral vaccines, etc. *Recreations:* watching sports in which one no longer performs (rowing, cricket), playing tennis, music, good company in good restaurants. *Address:* Little Acre, Church End, Henham, Bishop's Stortford, Herts CM22 6AN. *T:* (01279) 850386. *Clubs:* Athenæum, MCC; Leander (Henley-on-Thames); Hawks (Hon. Mem.) (Cambridge).

BANBURY, family name of **Baron Banbury of Southam**.

BANBURY OF SOUTHAM, 3rd Baron *cr* 1924, of Southam; **Charles William Banbury;** Bt 1902; *b* 29 July 1953; *s* of 2nd Baron Banbury of Southam and of Hilda Ruth, *d* of late A. H. R. Carr; *S* father, 1981; *m* 1st, 1984, Lucinda Trehearne (marr. diss. 1986); 2nd, 1989, Inger Marianne Norton; three *d*. *Educ:* Eton College. *Heir:* none. *Address:* The Mill, Fossebridge, Glos GL54 3JN.

BAND, Adm. Sir Jonathon, GCB 2008 (KCB 2002); Chief of Naval Staff and First Sea Lord, since 2006; First and Principal Naval Aide-de-Camp to the Queen, since 2006; *b* 2 Feb. 1950; *s* of Victor and Muriel Band; *m* 1979, Sarah Asbury; two *d*. *Educ:* Brambletye Sch.; Haileybury Coll.; Exeter Univ. (BA 1972). Served: HMS Soberton, 1979–81; Fleet HQ, 1981–83; HMS Phoebe, 1983–85; MoD, 1986–89; HMS Norfolk and Ninth Frigate Sqn, 1989–91; MoD, 1991–95; HMS Illustrious, 1995–97; ACNS, MoD, 1997–99; Team Leader, Defence Trng and Educn Study, MoD, 2000–01; Dep. C-in-C Fleet, 2001–02; C-in-C Fleet, 2002–05; Comdr Allied Naval Forces N, 2002–04; Comdr Allied Maritime Component Comd Northwood, 2004–06. Younger Brother, Trinity House, 1998–. Liveryman, Shipwrights' Co., 2006–. Comp. ILM; FRSA. *Recreations:* family dominated, including boating, tennis. *Address:* Ministry of Defence, Main Building, Whitehall, SW1A 2HB. *Club:* Royal Naval and Royal Albert Yacht (Portsmouth).

BAND, His Honour Robert Murray Niven, MC 1944; QC 1974; a Circuit Judge, 1978–91; *b* 23 Nov. 1919; *s* of Robert Niven Band and Agnes Jane Band; *m* 1948, Nancy Margery Redhead; two *d*. *Educ:* Trinity Coll., Glenalmond; Hertford Coll., Oxford (MA). Served in Royal Artillery, 1940–46. Called to the Bar, Inner Temple, 1947; Junior Treasury Counsel in Probate Matters, 1972–74; Chm. Family Law Bar Assoc., 1972–74; a Recorder of the Crown Court, 1977–78. Chm., St Teresa's Hosp., Wimbledon, 1969–83. *Recreations:* the countryside, gardens, old buildings, treen.

BAND, Thomas Mollison, FSAScot; Chairman, Perthshire Housing Association, since 2003 (Director, since 1994); *b* 28 March 1934; *s* of late Robert Boyce Band and Elizabeth Band; *m* 1959, Jean McKenzie Brien; one *s* two *d*. *Educ:* Perth Academy. National Service, RAF, 1952–54. Joined Civil Service, 1954; Principal, BoT, 1969; Sen. Principal, Dept of Industry, 1973; Scottish Econ. Planning Dept, 1975, Asst Sec., 1976; Scottish Development Dept, 1978; Scottish Office, Finance, 1981; Dir, Historic Bldgs and Monuments, Scottish Develt Dept, 1984–87; Chief Exec., Scottish Tourist Bd, 1987–94. Chairman: Made in Scotland Ltd, 1994–95; Anderson Enterprises Ltd, 1994–98; Edinburgh Europa Ltd, 1994–98; Perth Repertory Th. Ltd, 1995–2002. Dir, Edinburgh Telford Coll., 1989–98. Chm., Industrial Cttee, Napier Univ. (formerly Napier Poly. of Edinburgh), 1989–95. Gov., Queen Margaret UC, Edinburgh, 1995–2002. President: Perthshire Soc. of Natural Sci., 2004–07; Scots Lang. Soc., 2004–; Eur. Bureau of Lesser Used Langs (UK), 2005–. FRSA 1993. *Recreations:* ski-ing, gardening. *Address:* Heathfield, Pitcairngreen, Perthshire PH1 3LS. *T:* (01738) 583403.

BANDA, Prof. Enric, DSc; Director, Catalan Research and Innovation Foundation, since 2004; *b* 21 June 1948; *s* of Emilio and Maria Banda; *m* 1st, 1973 (marr. diss. 1982); 2nd, 1983, Gemma Lienas, writer. *Educ:* Univ. of Barcelona (BSc Physics 1974; DSc Physics 1979). Researcher, ETH-Zürich, 1980–83; Head, Geophysical Survey, Catalan Govt, 1983–87; Res. Prof., Consejo Superior de Investigaciones Científicas, 1987; Head, Inst. of Earth Sciences, Barcelona, 1988–91; Sec. Gen., Nat. Plan R&D, Spain, 1994; Sec. of State for Universities and Research, Spain, 1995–96; Sec. Gen., ESF, 1998–2003. Pres., Euroscience. Chevalier de la Légion d'Honneur (France), 1997. *Publications:* more than 150 scientific papers. *Address:* Catalan Research and Innovation Foundation, Passeig Lluís Companys 23, 08010 Barcelona, Spain.

BANERJEE, Urmila, (Millie), CBE 2002; Member, Office of Communications, since 2002; *b* Calcutta, 30 June 1946; *d* of late Shankar Ray-Chaudhuri and of Maya Ray-Chaudhuri; *m* 1st, 1970, Pradip Banerjee (marr. diss. 1985); 2nd, 1991, Christopher Anthony Seymour. *Educ:* University Coll. London (BSc Zool.); Poly. of N London (DMS); Massachusetts Inst. of Technol. (Sen. Exec. Prog.). Post Office Telecommunications: Operational Manager, Internat. Telephones, 1970–76; Tutor, Telecoms Mgt Coll., 1976–79; Exec. Asst to MD Telecoms, 1979–84; British Telecommunications: Dep. Gen. Manager, London SW, 1984–88; Dist Gen. Manager, London Networks, 1988–90; Director: Personnel, Worldwide Networks, 1990–92; Integrated Systems, 1992–95; Pricing, 1995; Vice Pres., Prog. Mgt, 1995–97, Exec. Vice Pres., Ops, 1997–2000, ICO Global Communications. Non-exec. Dir, Channel 4 TV, 2000–02. Chm., Postwatch, 2005–; Non-executive Director: Prison Service Agency, 1990–95; Focus Central London, 1997–2000; Cabinet Office Bd, 1999–2005; Sector Skills Develt Agency, 2001–04; Strategic Rail Authy, 2002–05; Member: Nurses and Allied Professions Pay Rev. Bd, 1999–2002; Judicial Appts Commn, 2001–05. Gov., S Bank Univ., 1993–98; Mem. Adv. Bd, Tanaka Imperial Business Sch., 2003–07. Trustee, 2001–07, and Chm., 2005–07, Carnegie Trust UK. *Recreations:* cooking, France. *Address:* 14 Marlborough Street, SW3 3PS. *T:* (020) 7581 1399, *Fax:* (020) 7581 5155; *e-mail:* millie.banerjee@btinternet.com.

BANFIELD, Ven. David John; Archdeacon of Bristol, 1990–98; *b* 25 June 1933; *s* of Norman Charles Banfield and Muriel Gladys Honor Banfield (*née* Pippard); *m* 1967, Rita (*née* Woolhouse); three *d*. *Educ:* Yeovil Sch.; London Coll. of Divinity, London Univ. (ALCD). RAF, 1951–53. Deacon 1957, priest 1958; Curate, Middleton, Manchester, 1957–62; Chaplain and Asst Warden, Scargill House, Yorks, 1962–67; Vicar of Addiscombe, Croydon, 1967–80; Vicar of Luton, Beds, 1980–90; RD, Luton, 1989–90; Hon. Canon, St Alban's, 1989–90. *Recreations:* travel, walking, music, gardening. *Address:* 47 Avon Way, Stoke Bishop, Bristol BS9 1SL. *T:* (0117) 968 4227.

BANFIELD, John Martin, FEI; Director, Mobil Europe, 1996–2001; *b* 15 Nov. 1947; *s* of Jack Banfield and Peggy Winifred Banfield (*née* Parker); *m* 1978, Mary Gerrey Morton; one *s* one *d*. *Educ:* Haberdashers' Aske's; St John's Coll., Cambridge (MA Geography). FEI

(FInstPet 1996). Joined Mobil Oil Co., 1969; Man. Dir, Mobil Cyprus, 1986–87; Director: Mobil Benelux, 1988–89; Mobil Oil Co., 1990–91; Pres., Mobil Benelux, 1992; Dir, Mobil Germany, 1993; Chm., Mobil Oil Co., 1994–96. Vice-Pres., Inst. of Petroleum, 1996–99; Pres., Oil Industries Club, 1997–98. *Recreations:* music, sailing, travel. *Address:* Garden Corner, Mickleham, Surrey. *Club:* MCC.

BANGAY, Deborah Joanna Janet; QC 2006; *b* 29 Nov. 1957; *d* of Joe and Janet Bangay; *m* (marr. diss. 2001); two *s* (twins). *Educ:* Cranwell Primary Sch.; Sleaford High Sch.; Wycombe High Sch.; Univ. of Exeter (LLB Hons 1979); Council of Legal Educn. Called to the Bar, Gray's Inn, 1981; in practice, specialising in family law. *Recreations:* fly fishing, football, cooking, gardening, theatre, ballet. *Address:* 1 Hare Court, Temple, EC4Y 7BE. *T:* (020) 7797 7070, *Fax:* (020) 7797 7435; *e-mail:* bangay@1hc.com. *Clubs:* Soho House, 2 Brydges Place.

BANGEMANN, Dr Martin; a Member, European Commission (formerly Commission of the European Community), 1989–99 (a Vice-President, 1989–93); Senior Adviser, Telefónica, 2000–05; *b* 15 Nov. 1934; *s* of Martin Bangemann and Lotte Telge; *m* 1962, Renate Bauer; three *s* two *d*. *Educ:* Univ. of Tübingen; Univ. of Munich (DJur). Lawyer, 1964–. Mem., Bundestag, 1972–80 and 1986–89; Mem., European Parliament, 1973–84; Minister of Econs, FRG, 1984–88. Freie Demokratische Partei: Mem., 1963–; Chm., 1985–88. Fed. Cross of Merit with star (Germany); Bavarian Order of Merit.

BANGHAM, Alec Douglas, MD; FRCP; FRS 1977; retired; Research Worker, Agricultural Research Council, Institute of Animal Physiology, Babraham, 1952–82 and Head, Biophysics Unit, 1971–82; *b* 10 Nov. 1921; *s* of Dr Donald Hugh and Edith Bangham; *m* 1943, Rosalind Barbara Reiss; three *s* one *d*. *Educ:* Bryanston Sch.; UCL and UCH Med. Sch. (MD). FRCP 1997. Captain, RAMC, 1946–48. Lectr, Dept of Exper. Pathology, UCH, 1949–52; Principal Scientific Officer, 1952–63, Senior Principal Scientific Officer (Merit Award), 1963–82, ARC, Babraham. Fellow, UCL, 1981–. *Publications:* contrib. Nature, Biochim. Biophys. Acta, and Methods in Membrane Biol. *Recreations:* horticulture, photographic arts, sailing. *Address:* 17 High Green, Great Shelford, Cambridge CB2 5EG. *T:* (01223) 843192; *e-mail:* alecbangham@wwr.co.uk; *web:* www.bangham.org.uk.

BANGOR, 8th Viscount *cr* 1781 (Ire.); **William Maxwell David Ward;** Baron 1770 (Ire.); antiquarian bookseller; *b* 9 Aug. 1948; *s* of 7th Viscount Bangor and his 3rd wife, Leila Mary Heaton (*d* 1959); *S* father, 1993; *m* 1976, Sarah Mary Malet Bradford, *qv*. *Educ:* University Coll., London. *Recreations:* history, music, antiquity, Bolton Wanderers. *Heir: presumptive: b* Hon. (Edward) Nicholas Ward [*b* 16 Jan. 1953; *m* 1985, Rachel Mary, *d* of Hon. Hugh Waldorf Astor; two *d*]. *Address:* 31 Britannia Road, SW6 2HJ. *Club:* Chelsea Arts.

BANGOR, Viscountess; *see* Bradford, S. M. M. W.

BANGOR, Bishop of; *no new appointment at time of going to press.*

BANGOR, Dean of; *see* Hawkins, Very Rev. A. J.

BANHAM, Mrs Belinda Joan, CBE 1977; JP; Independent Assesor, Office of the Commissioner for Public Appointments, since 2000; independent consultant, health care services, since 1996; *d* of late Col Charles Unwin and Winifred Unwin; *m* 1939, Terence Middlecott Banham (*d* 1995); two *s* two *d*. *Educ:* privately; West Bank Sch.; Brussels; BSc Hons, Dip. Social Studies London; Dip. PhilMed Soc. of Apothecaries. RGN. Work in health services, 1937–; work in theory and practice on aspects of social deviance and deprivation, Cornwall CC, 1954–67; Mem., SW RHB, 1965–74; Chairman: Cornwall and Isles of Scilly HMC, 1967–74 (Mem., 1964–77); Cornwall and Isles of Scilly AHA, 1974–77; Kensington, Chelsea and Westminster FPC, 1979–85 (Mem. 1977–79); Paddington and N Kensington DHA, 1981–86; Mem., Lambeth, Southwark and Lewisham FPC, 1987–90; Chm., Lambeth, Southwark and Lewisham FHSA, 1993–96 (Vice-Chm., 1990–93); Vice-Chm., Lambeth, Southwark and Lewisham Health Commn, 1993–96. Lay Chm., and Convenor, NHS Complaints Procedure, London Reg., 1999–2003; Chm., Prof. Adv. Gp, Enfield, Barking, Haringay and Camden PCTs, 2003–05. Mem., MRC, 1980–87 (Chm., Standing Cttee on Use of Medical Inf. in Research, 1980–87). Mem., Industrial Tribunals, 1974–87. Marriage Guidance Councillor, 1960–72. A Vice-Chm., Disabled Living Foundn, 1984–91 (Dir, then Hon. Dir, 1977–83); Vice President: Friends of St Mary's Hosp., Paddington, 2000– (Pres., 1983–90); KIDS, 1987– (Chm., 1982–87); AFASIC, 1990–. Mem. Delegacy, KCH Med. Sch., 1996–99. Pres., Wytham Hall, 2005– (Trustee, 1985–97; Vice Chm., 1990–99). Mem. Bd of Trustees, Carrick CAB; Member and caseworker: RBL; SSAFA, Cornwall. JP Cornwall, 1972. Special interests: social deprivation and deviance, Health Service management and use of resources. *Publications:* Snapshots in Time: some experiences in health care 1936–1991, 1991; General Practice in the NHS: or, football round the mulberry bush 1918–1995, 1995; (jtly) (paper) Systems Science in Health Care (NATO Conf., Paris, 1977); (jtly) (report) Partnership in Action: a study of healthcare services for elderly and physically handicapped in Newcastle, 1989. *Recreations:* gardening, plant biology, medical ethics, theatre. *Address:* 21 Bosvigo Road, Truro, Cornwall TR1 3DG.

See also Sir J. M. M. Banham.

BANHAM, Sir John (Michael Middlecott), Kt 1992; DL; Chairman, Johnson Matthey plc, since 2006; *b* 22 Aug. 1940; *s* of late Terence Middlecott Banham, FRCS and of Belinda Joan Banham, *qv*; *m* 1965, Frances Barbara Molyneux Favell; one *s* two *d*. *Educ:* Charterhouse; Queens' Coll., Cambridge (Foundn Schol.; BA 1st cl. in Natural Scis, 1962; Hon. Fellow, 1989). Asst Principal, HM Foreign Service, 1962–64; Dir of Marketing, Wallcoverings Div., Reed International, 1965–69; McKinsey & Co. Inc.: Associate, 1969–75; Principal, 1975–80; Dir, 1980–83. Controller, Audit Commn, 1983–87; Dir-Gen., CBI, 1987–92; Chm., Local Govt Commn for England, 1992–95. Chm., Retail and Consumer Affairs Foresight Panel, 1997–2001. Chairman: John Labatt (Europe), subseq. Labatt Breweries of Europe, 1992–95; Westcountry Television, 1992–95; Tarmac, 1994–2000 (Dir, 1992–2000); Kingfisher, 1996–2001; ECI Ventures, 1992–2005; Whitbread, 2000–05 (Dir, 1999–2005); Geest, 2002–05; Cyclacel Ltd, 2002–06; Spacelabs Healthcare Inc., 2005–08; Director: National Westminster Bank, 1992–98; National Power, 1992–98; Merchants Trust, 1992–; Cyclacel Therapeutics Inc., 2006–; Sen. Indep. Dir, Invesco Inc. (formerly Amvescap plc), 1999–. Mem., BOTB, 1989–92; Dir and Mem. Bd, Business in the Community, 1989–92. Member Council: PSI, 1986–92; Forum for Management Educn and Develt, 1988–93; BESO, 1991–92. Member: Council of Management, PDSA, 1982–93; Governing Body, London Business Sch., 1987–92; Managing Trustee, Nuffield Foundn, 1988–97; Hon. Treas., Cancer Res. Campaign, 1991–2002. DL Cornwall, 1999. Hon. LLD Bath, 1987; Hon. DSc: Loughborough, 1989; Exeter, 1993; Strathclyde, 1995. *Publications:* Future of the British Car Industry, 1975; Realizing the Promise of a National Health Service, 1977; The Anatomy of Change: blueprint for a new era, 1994; numerous reports for Audit Commn on education, housing, social services and local government finance, 1984–87, and for CBI on UK economy, skills, transport, the infrastructure, urban regeneration and manufacturing. *Recreations:* walking, ground clearing, gardening. *Address:* Penberth, St Buryan, Penzance, Cornwall TR19 6HJ. *Fax:* (01736) 810722. *Club:* Travellers.

BANISTER, Prof. David John, PhD; Professor of Transport Studies, University of Oxford, and Fellow of St Anne's College, Oxford, since 2006; *b* 10 July 1950; *s* of late Stephen Michael Alvin Banister and of Rachel Joan Banister; *m* 1985, Elizabeth Dawn Bucknell; three *d*. *Educ:* Royal Grammar Sch., Guildford; Nottingham Univ. (BA 1st Cl. Hons Geog.); Leeds Univ. (PhD Transport Studies 1976). CMILT (MCIT 1976; MILT 1999). Lectr in Geog., Univ. of Reading, 1975–78; University College London: Lectr in Transport Policy, 1979–88; Sen. Lectr, 1988–90; Reader in Transport Planning, 1990–95; Prof. of Transport Planning, 1995–2006. Vis. VSB Prof., Tinbergen Inst., Amsterdam, 1994–97; Vis. Prof., Univ. of Bodenkultur, Vienna, 2007. Jt Ed., Built Envmt, 1992–; Ed., Transport Reviews, 2001–; Mem., editl bds of several jls. Non-exec. Dir, Taylor and Francis Gp PLC, 1990–2004. Dir, Res. Prog. on Transport and Envmt, ESRC, 1992–96; Member: Adv. Gps on Future Integrated Transport, Inland Surface Transport, Cities and Sustainability, EPSRC, 1994–2004; Team for Town and Country Planning, RAE 2001 and 2008, HEFCE. Chm., Econ. Commn for Europe's Task Force on Urban Transport Patterns and Land Use Planning, UN, 2000–02. FRSA 1988. Trustee: Ferguson Charitable Trust, 1979–; Civic Trust, 2005– (Chm., Policy Cttee, 2006–). Editor, Spon series on Transport, Development and Sustainability, 1999–2006. *Publications:* Transport Mobility and Deprivation in Inter-Urban Areas, 1980; (jtly) Transport and Public Policy Planning, 1981; Rural Transport and Planning, 1985; (jtly) Urban Transport and Planning, 1989; (jtly) Transport in a Free Market Economy, 1991; (jtly) Transport in Unified Europe: policies and challenges, 1993; (jtly) Transport, the Environment and Sustainable Development, 1993; Transport Planning, 1994, 2nd edn 2002; Transport and Urban Development, 1995; (jtly) European Transport and Communications Networks: policy evolution and change, 1995; (jtly) Telematics and Transport Behaviour, 1996; Transport Policy and the Environment, 1998; (jtly) Environment, Land Use and Urban Policy, 1999; (jtly) European Transport Policy and Sustainable Mobility, 2000; (jtly) Encouraging Transport Alternatives: good practice in reducing travel, 2000; (jtly) Transport Investment and Economic Development, 2000; Unsustainable Transport, 2005; (jtly) Land Use and Transport: European perspectives on integrated policies, 2007; contrib. books and internat. jls. *Recreations:* gardening, farming, walking, good company and conversation. *Address:* Transport Studies Unit, Oxford University Centre for the Environment, South Parks Road, Oxford OX1 3QY. *T:* (01865) 275984.

BANKS, (Arthur) David; journalist and broadcaster; *b* 13 Feb. 1948; *s* of Arthur Banks and Helen (*née* Renton); *m* 1975, Gemma Newton; one *s* one *d*. *Educ:* Boteler Grammar Sch., Warrington. Asst Man. Editor, NY Post, 1979–81; Night Editor, then Asst Editor, The Sun, 1981–86; Dep. Man. Editor, NY Daily News, 1986–87; Dep. Editor, The Australian, 1987–89; Editor: Daily Telegraph Mirror (Sydney), 1989–92; Daily Mirror, 1992–94; Editl Dir, Mirror Gp Newspapers, 1994–97; Consultant Ed., Sunday Mirror, 1997–98; Dir of Information, Mirror Gp, 1998–99. Presenter, Breakfast Show, Talk Radio, 1999–2000. *Recreation:* celebrating my second life. *Address:* c/o The Roseman Organisation, 51 Queen Anne Street, W1G 9HS.

BANKS, Caroline; non-executive Director, Financial Ombudsman Service, since 2005; Director, Consumer Regulation Enforcement Division, Office of Fair Trading, 1998–2003; *b* 24 April 1950; *d* of Geoffrey Banks and Pamela Dane Banks. *Educ:* Kitwe Girls' High Sch., Zambia; Middlesex Poly. (BA Hons). Office of Fair Trading: various posts, 1975–82; Head, Consumer Credit Licensing Bureau, 1982–88; Principal Estabt and Finance Officer, 1988–97. Member: Code Panel, Energy Retail Assoc., 2003–; CSAB, 2004–. *Recreations:* gardening, tapestry. *Address:* 40 Meadowcroft Road, Palmers Green, N13 4EA.

BANKS, Charles Augustus, III; Clayton, Dubilier & Rice Inc., since 2006; *b* Greensboro, N Carolina, 20 Dec. 1940; *s* of late Charles Augustus Banks, Jr and Madge McMillan Banks; *m* 1962, Marie Ann Sullivan; two *s* one *d*. *Educ:* Brown Univ. (BA 1962); Young Exec. Inst. of Professional Mgt, Univ. of N Carolina; Wharton Sch., Univ. of Pennsylvania, (AMP 1989). Ensign/ Lt, USNR (Active), 1962–64. Plant manager, Minerals Recovery Corp., 1964–65; mortgage banker, Cameron-Brown Co., 1965–67; Ferguson Enterprises Inc.: Peebles Supply Div., 1967–69; Outside Sales, Lenz Supply Div., 1969–70; Vice-Pres. and Gen. Manager, Alexandria, Va, 1970–77; Pres. and Gen. Manager, Herndon, Va, 1977–81; Dir, 1977; Regl Manager, 1981–87; Sen. Exec. Vice-Pres., 1987–89; Pres. and Chief Ops Officer, 1989–93; Pres. and CEO, 1993–2001; Chm., 2001–06; Dir, Wolseley plc (parent co. of Ferguson Enterprises), 1992–2006, Chief Exec., 2001–06. Non-exec. Dir, Bunzl PLC, 2002–. *Address:* PO Box 2778, 12500 Jefferson Avenue, Newport News, VA 23602, USA.

BANKS, Christopher Nigel, CBE 2003; Chairman, Learning and Skills Council, since 2004; Founder, Big Thoughts Ltd, since 2001; *b* 1 Sept. 1959; *s* of James Nigel Alexander and Pamela Ethel Banks; *m* 1982, Karen Jane Dauber; one *s* two *d*. *Educ:* Bristol Cathedral Sch.; Birmingham Univ. (BA Combined Hons Latin and French); Aston Univ. (MBA). Client Services, A. C. Nielsen, 1983–85; Marketing Manager, Mars Inc., 1985–89; Marketing Dir, H. P. Bulmer, 1989–92; Man. Dir, URM Agencies, part of Allied Domecq, 1992–95; CEO, Justerini & Brooks, part of Grand Metropolitan, 1996–97; Man. Dir, Coca-Cola GB, 1997–2001. Mem., Women and Work Commn, 2004–07. Chm., London Employer Coalition, 1999–2004; Mem., Nat. Council, and Chm., Young People's Learning Cttee, LSC, 2000–04; Dep. Chm., Nat. Employment Panel, 2001–08. Pres., British Soft Drinks Assoc., 2003–05. *Address:* Learning and Skills Council, Centre Point, 103 New Oxford Street, WC1A 1DR; *e-mail:* chris.banks@lsc.gov.uk.

BANKS, David; *see* Banks, A. D.

BANKS, Frank David, DPhil; FCA; Chairman, H. Berkeley (Holdings) Ltd, 1984–90; *b* 11 April 1933; *s* of Samuel and Elizabeth Banks; *m* 1st, 1955, Catherine Jacob; one *s* two *d*; 2nd, 1967, Sonia Gay Coleman; one *d*. *Educ:* Liverpool Collegiate Sch.; Carnegie Mellon Univ. (PFE); Open Univ. (BA 1988); Univ. of Sussex (MA 1992; DPhil 2003). British Oxygen Co. Ltd, 1957–58; Imperial Chemical Industries Ltd, 1959–62; English Electric Co. Ltd, 1963–68; Finance Dir, Platt International Ltd, 1969–71; Industrial Advr, DTI, 1972–73; Constructors John Brown Ltd, 1974–80; Man. Dir, Agribusiness Div., Tate & Lyle Ltd, 1981–83. *Recreations:* music, history. *Address:* 3 Adams Close, Ampthill, Beds MK45 2UB.

BANKS, Mrs Gillian Theresa, CB 1990; *b* 7 Feb. 1933; *d* of Percy and Enid Brimblecombe; *m* 1960, John Anthony Gorst Banks (marr. diss. 1993); one *s* two *d*. *Educ:* Walthamstow Hall Sch., Sevenoaks; Lady Margaret Hall, Oxford (BA). Asst Principal, Colonial Office, 1955; Principal, Treasury, 1966; Department of Health and Social Security: Asst Sec., 1972; Under Sec. 1981; Dir, Health Authy Finance, 1985; Dir, OPCS and Registrar Gen. for Eng. and Wales, 1986; Dir, Carnegie Inquiry into the Third Age, 1990; led Functions, Manpower and Sen. Management Review of Wider DoH, 1994; Dir, Retirement Income Inquiry, 1994; Mem., Camden and Islington HA, 1995; non-exec. Dir, Royal Free Hampstead NHS Trust, 1997–2004. Policy Consultant, Age

Concern, England, 1996; Hon. Treas., Age Concern Camden, 1997–2002. Lay Mem., Council, RPSGB, 1996–2001. *Recreation:* hill walking. *Address:* Flat 3, Andrew Court, 2 Wedderburn Road, NW3 5QE. *T:* (020) 7435 4973.

BANKS, Gordon Raymond; MP (Lab) Ochil and South Perthshire, since 2005; *b* 14 June 1955; *s* of William Banks and Patricia Marion Banks (*née* Macknight); *m* 1981, Lynda Nicol; one *s* one *d*. *Educ:* Univ. of Stirling (BA Hons Hist. and Politics); Glasgow Coll. of Building and Printing (Construction Technician). Chief Buyer: Barratt (Edinburgh) Ltd, 1975–84; Barratt (Falkirk) Ltd, 1984–86; Man. Dir, Cartmore Bldg Supply Co. Ltd, 1986–. Parly Officer for Dr Richard Simpson, MP, 1999–2003; researcher for Martin O'Neill, MP, 2003–05. Mem., Nat. Policy Forum, and Quality of Life Policy Forum, Lab. Party, 2002–05. PPS to Minister for Pension Reform, DWP, 2006–07, to Sec. of State for Culture, Media and Sport, 2007–08, to Sec. of State for Work and Pensions, 2008–. *Recreations:* music (song-writing), motor sport, football. *Address:* (constituency office) 49–51 High Street, Alloa, Clackmannanshire FK10 1JF. *T:* (01259) 721536, *Fax:* (01259) 216761; *e-mail:* banksgr@parliament.uk.

BANKS, Iain; writer; *b* Fife, Scotland, 16 Feb. 1954. *Educ:* Stirling Univ. Technician: British Steel, 1976; IBM, Greenock, 1978; Costing Clerk, Denton, Hall & Burgin, London, 1980. *Publications:* The Wasp Factory, 1984; Walking on Glass, 1985; The Bridge, 1986; Espedair Street, 1987; Canal Dreams, 1989; The Crow Road, 1992 (televised, 1996); Complicity, 1993 (filmed, 2000); Whit, 1995; A Song of Stone, 1997; The Business, 1999; Dead Air, 2002; The Steep Approach to Garbadale, 2007; *as Iain M. Banks*: Consider Phlebas, 1987; The Player of Games, 1988; Use of Weapons, 1990; The State of the Art, 1991; Against a Dark Background, 1993; Feersum Endjinn, 1994; Excession, 1996; Inversions, 1998; Look to Windward, 2000; The Algebraist, 2004; Matter, 2008; *non-fiction:* Raw Spirit, 2003. *Address:* c/o Little, Brown, 100 Victoria Embankment, EC4Y 0DY.

BANKS, John, FREng, FIET; Chairman, Adacom 3270 Communications Ltd, 1986–90; *b* 2 Dec. 1920; *s* of John Banks and Jane Dewhurst; *m* 1943, Nancy Olive Yates; two *s*. *Educ:* Univ. of Liverpool (BEng Hons; MEng). FREng (FEng 1983); FIET (FIEE 1959). Chief Engr, Power Cables Div., BICC, 1956–67; Divl Dir and Gen. Man., Supertension Cables Div., BICC, 1968–74; Exec. Dir, 1975–78, Chm., 1978–84, BICC Research and Engineering Ltd; Exec. Dir, BICC, 1979–84. Vis. Prof., Liverpool Univ., 1987–. Pres., IEE, 1982–83. *Recreations:* golf, swimming, music and the arts. *Address:* Flat B1 Marine Gate, Marine Drive, Brighton BN2 5TQ. *T:* (01273) 690756. *Club:* Seaford Golf.

BANKS, Lynne Reid; writer; *b* 1929; *d* of Dr James Reid-Banks and Muriel (Pat) (*née* Marsh); *m* 1965, Chaim Stephenson, sculptor; three *s*. *Educ:* schooling mainly in Canada; RADA. Actress, 1949–54; reporter for ITN, 1955–62; English teacher in kibbutz in Western Galilee, Israel, 1963–71; full-time writer, 1971–; writing includes plays for stage, television and radio. *Publications: plays:* It Never Rains, 1954; All in a Row, 1956; The Killer Dies Twice, 1956; Already, It's Tomorrow, 1962; (for children) Travels of Yoshi and the Tea-Kettle, 1993; *fiction:* The L-Shaped Room, 1960 (trans. 10 langs; filmed 1962); An End to Running, 1962 (trans. 2 langs); Children at the Gate, 1968; The Backward Shadow, 1970; Two is Lonely, 1974; Defy the Wilderness, 1981; The Warning Bell, 1984; Casualties, 1986; Fair Exchange, 1998; *biographical fiction:* Dark Quartet: the story of the Brontes, 1976 (Yorks Arts Lit. Award, 1977); Path to the Silent Country: Charlotte Bronte's years of fame, 1977; *history:* Letters to my Israeli Sons, 1979; Torn Country, USA 1982; *for young adults:* One More River, 1973; Sarah and After, 1975; My Darling Villain, 1977 (trans. 3 langs); The Writing on the Wall, 1981; Melusine, 1988 (trans. 3 langs); Broken Bridge, 1994 (trans. 2 langs); *for children:* The Adventures of King Midas, 1976 (trans. 4 langs); The Farthest-Away Mountain, 1977; I, Houdini, 1978 (trans. 4 langs); The Indian in the Cupboard, 1980 (trans. 24 langs) (Pacific NW Choice Award, 1984; Calif. Young Readers Medal, 1985; Va Children's Choice, 1988; Mass. Children's Choice, 1988; Rebecca Caudill Award, Ill, 1989; Arizona Children's Choice, 1989; filmed, 1995); Maura's Angel, 1984 (trans. 2 langs); The Fairy Rebel, 1985 (trans. 3 langs); Return of the Indian, 1986 (trans. 5 langs); The Secret of the Indian, 1989 (trans. 4 langs); The Magic Hare, 1992; Mystery of the Cupboard, 1993 (trans. 3 langs); Harry the Poisonous Centipede, 1996; Angela and Diabola, 1997 (trans. 2 langs); The Key to the Indian, 1999; Moses in Egypt, 1998 (trans. 3 langs); Alice-by-Accident, 2000; Harry the Poisonous Centipede's Big Adventure, 2000; The Dungeon, 2002; Stealing Stacey, 2004; Tiger, Tiger, 2004; Harry the Poisonous Centipede Goes to Sea, 2005; short stories; articles in The Times, The Guardian, Sunday Telegraph, Observer, TES, TLS, Independent on Sunday, Sunday Times, Spectator, Saga Magazine, and in overseas periodicals. *Recreations:* theatre, gardening, visiting schools overseas and at home. *Address:* c/o Watson, Little Ltd, 48–56 Bayham Place, NW1 0EU.

BANKS, Matthew Richard William; *see* Gordon Banks, M. R. W.

BANKS, Richard Lee; Director, since 1998, and Managing Director, Wholesale Banking, since 2002, Alliance & Leicester plc (Distribution Operations Director, 2000–02); *b* 15 June 1951; *s* of Richard Cyril Banks and Mary Banks; *m* 1978, Elaine Helena Kret; two *s*. *Educ:* Stockport Secondary Technical High Sch.; Manchester Poly. (BA Hons Business Studies). Joined Midland Bank, 1974, various mgt posts, 1978–87; Girobank: Gen. Manager, 1987–91; Sen. Gen. Manager, 1991–94; Dir, Corporate Banking, 1994–96; Man. Dir, 1996–2000. *Recreations:* reading, cottage renovation. *Address:* (office) Carlton Park, Narborough, Leics LE19 0AL.

BANKS, Robert George; *b* 18 Jan. 1937; *s* of late George Walmsley Banks, MBE, and of Olive Beryl Banks (*née* Tyler); *m* 1967, Diana Margaret Payne Crawfurd (marr. diss. 2004); four *s* one *d* (of whom one *s* one *d* are twins). *Educ:* Haileybury. Lt-Comdr RNR. Jt Founder Dir, Antocks Lairn Ltd, 1963–67. Mem., Alcohol Educn and Res. Council, 1982–88. Mem., Paddington BC, 1959–65. MP (C) Harrogate, Feb. 1974–97. PPS to Minister of State and to Under-Sec. of State, FCO, 1979–82. Member: Select Cttee on Foreign Affairs (and its Overseas Develt Sub-Cttee), 1982; Select Cttee on Trade and Industry, 1994–97; Jt Sec., Cons. Defence Cttee, 1976–79; Chairman: British-Sudan All Party Parly Gp, 1984–97; All-Party Tourism Gp, 1992–97 (Sec., 1973–79; Vice-Chm., 1979–92); Vice-Chm., Yorks Cons. Mems' Cttee, 1983–97. Member: Council of Europe, 1977–81; WEU, 1977–81; N Atlantic Assembly, 1981–95. Introd Licensing (Alcohol Educn and Res.) Act, 1981; sponsored Licensing (Restaurants Meals) Act, 1987. Reports: for Mil. Cttee of WEU, Report on Nuclear, Biol. and Chem. Protection, adopted by WEU Assembly April 1980; North Atlantic Assembly document, The Technology of Military Space Systems, 1982. *Publications:* (jtly) Britain's Home Defence Gamble (pamphlet), 1979; New Jobs from Pleasure, report on tourism, 1985; Tories for Tourism, 1995. *Recreations:* travel, architecture, contemporary art. *Address:* Brett House, 305 Munster Road, SW6 6BJ.

BANN, Prof. Stephen, CBE 2004; PhD; FBA 1998; Professor of History of Art, University of Bristol, since 2000; *b* 1 Aug. 1942; *s* of Harry Bann, OBE and Edna Bann (*née* Pailin). *Educ:* Winchester Coll. (schol.); King's Coll., Cambridge (schol.; BA Hist. 1963; MA; PhD 1967). State Res. Studentship, 1963–66, in Paris, 1964–65; University of Kent: Lectr, 1967–75, Sen. Lectr, 1975–80, in History; Reader in Modern Cultural Studies, 1980–88; Prof. of Modern Cultural Studies, 1988–2000; Sen. Fellow, 2003–08, Beattrix Farrand Distinguished Sen. Fellow, 2009, Dumbarton Oaks Res. Liby, Washington; Sen. Mellon Fellow, Canadian Centre for Architecture, Montreal, 2003. Visiting Professor: Rennes Univ., 1994; Johns Hopkins Univ., 1996–98; Bologna Univ., 1998; Warburg Foundn, Hamburg, 2002; Inst Nat. d'Histoire de l'Art, Paris, 2003; Edmond J. Safra Prof., Center for Advanced Studies in the Visual Arts, Washington, 2005. Getty Lectures, Univ. of Southern Calif, 2004. Member: Art Panel, Arts Council of GB, 1975–78; Humanities Res. Bd, British Acad., 1997–98; Chm. Res. Cttee, AHRB, 1998–2000; Res. Awards Adv. Cttee, Leverhulme Trust, 1998–2005. Pres., Comité Internat. d'Histoire de l'Art, 2000–04. Mem. Council, Friends of Canterbury Cathedral, 1990–2000. Trustee, Little Sparta Trust, 1994–. Dep. Ed., then Ed., 20th Century Studies, 1969–76; Adv. Ed., Reaktion Books, 1985–. R. H. Gapper Prize for French Studies, Soc. for French Studies, 2002. *Publications:* Experimental Painting, 1970; (ed) The Tradition of Constructivism, 1974; The Clothing of Clio, 1984; The True Vine: on visual representation and the Western tradition, 1989; The Inventions of History, 1990; Under the Sign: John Bargrave as collector, traveler and witness, 1994; The Sculpture of Stephen Cox, 1995; Romanticism and the Rise of History, 1995; Paul Delaroche: history painted, 1997; Parallel Lines: printmakers, painters and photographers in nineteenth-century France, 2001; Jannis Kounellis, 2003; (ed) The Reception of Walter Pater in Europe, 2004; Ways Around Modernism, 2007; (ed) The Coral Mind: Adrian Stokes' engagement with architecture, art history, criticism and psychoanalysis, 2007. *Recreations:* travel, collecting. *Address:* 2 New Street, St Dunstan's, Canterbury, Kent CT2 8AU. *T:* (01227) 761135; Department of History of Art, University of Bristol, Bristol BS8 1UU. *Club:* Savile.

BANNATYNE, (Walker) Duncan, OBE 2004; Chairman: Bannatyne Fitness Ltd, since 1996; Bannatyne Hotels Ltd, since 1996; Bannatyne Casinos Ltd, since 2003; Bannatyne Housing Ltd, since 2005; *b* 2 Feb. 1949; one *s* five *d*. RN, 1964–68. Started own business, Duncan's Super Ices; established: Quality Care Homes, 1986, sold 1996; Just Learning, 1996, sold 2002. Funded Bannatyne Hospices for Children with HIV and Aids, Romania and Colombia. *Address:* Bannatyne Fitness Ltd, Power House, Haughton Road, Darlington, Co. Durham DL1 1ST. *T:* (01325) 382565, *Fax:* (01325) 355588.

BANNENBERG, Jennifer Bridget; *see* Tanfield, J. B.

BANNER, Rev. Prof. Michael Charles, DPhil; Dean of Chapel, Director of Studies, and Fellow, Trinity College, Cambridge, since 2006; *b* 19 April 1961; *s* of Maurice Banner and Maureen (*née* Ince); *m* 1st, 1983, Elizabeth Jane Wheare (marr. diss. 2001); two *d*; 2nd, 2007, Sally-Ann Gannon. *Educ:* Bromsgrove Sch.; Balliol Coll., Oxford (BA Philos. and Theol. 1st cl. 1983; MA 1985; DPhil 1986). Ordained deacon 1986, priest 1987. Bampton Res. Fellow, St Peter's Coll., Oxford, 1985–88; Dean, Chaplain, Fellow and Dir of Studies in Philosophy and Theol., 1988–94, Tutor 1989–94, Peterhouse, Cambridge; F. D. Maurice Prof. of Moral and Social Theology, KCL, 1994–2004; Prof. of Public Policy and Ethics in the Life Scis, Univ. of Edinburgh, 2004–06; Dir, ESRC Genomics Policy and Res. Forum, 2004–06. Vis. Res. Fellow, Merton Coll., Oxford, 1993. Chairman: HM Govt Cttee of Enquiry on Ethics of Emerging Technologies in Breeding of Farm Animals, 1993–95; Home Office Animal Procedures Cttee, 1998–2006; CJD Incidents Panel, DoH, 2000–04; Shell Panel on Animal Testing, 2002–. Member: Royal Commn on Envmtl Pollution, 1996–2002; Agric. and Envmt Biotech. Commn, 2000–03; Human Tissue Authy, 2005–; Cttee of Reference, F&C Asset Mgt, 2007–. Asst Curate, Balsham, W Wratting, Weston Colville and W Wickham, 2000–04. Member: C of E Bd for Social Responsibility, 1995–2001; C of E Doctrine Commn, 1996–99. Trustee, Scott Holland Fund, 1996–99. Baron de Lancey Lectr, Cambridge Univ., 1998. Consultant Editor, Studies in Christian Ethics, 1996–2007; Corresp. Editor, Jl of Ethical Theory and Moral Practice, 1997–2004; Mem. Editl Bd, Internat Jl of Systematic Theology, 1998–2004. *Publications:* The Justification of Science and the Rationality of Religious Belief, 1990; The Practice of Abortion: a critique, 1999; Christian Ethics and Contemporary Moral Problems, 1999; The Doctrine of God and Theological Ethics, 2006; A Brief History of Christian Ethics, 2009; various articles in learned jls. *Recreations:* galleries, tennis, mountain biking, cross country ski-ing, horse riding. *Address:* Trinity College, Cambridge CB2 1TQ. *Club:* National.

BANNERMAN, Bernard; *see* Arden, A. P. R.

BANNERMAN, Sir David (Gordon), 15th Bt *cr* 1682 (NS), of Elsick, Kincardineshire; OBE 1977; Ministry of Defence, 1963–97; *b* 18 Aug. 1935; *s* of Lt-Col Sir Donald Arthur Gordon Bannerman, 13th Bt and Barbara Charlotte, *d* of late Lt-Col Alexander Cameron, OBE, IMS; *S* brother, Sir Alexander Patrick Bannerman, 14th Bt, 1989; *m* 1960, Mary Prudence, *d* of Rev. Philip Frank Ardagh-Walter; four *d*. *Educ:* Gordonstoun; New Coll., Oxford (MA); University Coll. London (MSc 1999). 2nd Lieut Queen's Own Cameron Highlanders, 1954–56. HMOCS (Tanzania), 1960–63. Chm., Gordonstoun Assoc., 1997–2000. *Recreations:* painting, ornithology, architecture. *Address:* 3 St George's Road, St Margaret's, Twickenham, Middlesex TW1 1QS.

See also M. A. O'Neill.

BANNISTER, (Richard) Matthew; broadcaster and journalist; presenter, The Last Word, Radio 4, since 2006; Chairman, Trust the DJ, since 2001; *b* 16 March 1957; *s* of late Richard Neville Bannister and of Olga Margaret Bannister; *m* 1st, 1984, Amanda Gerrard Walker (*d* 1988); one *d*; 2nd, 1989, Shelagh Margaret Macleod (*d* 2005); one *s*. *Educ:* King Edward VII Sch., Sheffield; Nottingham Univ. (LLB Hons). Presenter, BBC Radio Nottingham, 1978–81; Reporter/Presenter: Capital Radio, 1981–83; Newsbeat, Radio 1, 1983–85; Dep. Head, 1985–87, Head, 1987–88, News and Talks, Capital Radio; BBC 1988–2000: Man. Ed., Gtr London Radio, 1988–91; Project Co-ordinator: Charter Renewal, 1991–93; Prog. Strategy Review, 1993; Controller, BBC Radio 1, 1993–98; Dir, BBC Radio, 1996–98; Chief Exec., BBC Prodn, 1999–2000; Dir of Mkting and Communications, BBC, 2000; presenter, BBC Radio 5 Live, 2002–05. Mem. Bd, Chichester Fest. Theatre, 1999–. Fellow, Radio Acad., 1998. *Recreations:* rock music, theatre, collecting P. G. Wodehouse first editions. *Address:* Studio 131, Rosden House, 372 Old Street, EC1V 9AU.

BANNISTER, Sir Roger (Gilbert), Kt 1975; CBE 1955; DM (Oxon); FRCP; Master of Pembroke College, Oxford, 1985–93; Hon. Consultant Physician, National Hospital for Neurology and Neurosurgery, Queen Square, WC1 (non-executive Director, 1992–96; formerly Consultant Physician, National Hospital for Nervous Diseases); Hon. Consultant Neurologist: St Mary's Hospital and Western Ophthalmic Hospital, W2 (formerly Consultant Neurologist); Oxford Regional and District Health Authorities, 1985–95; *b* 23 March 1929; *s* of late Ralph and of Alice Bannister, Harrow; *m* 1955, Moyra Elver, *d* of late Per Jacobsson, Chairman IMF; two *s* two *d*. *Educ:* City of Bath Boys' Sch.; University Coll. Sch., London; Exeter and Merton Colls, Oxford; St Mary's Hospital Medical Sch., London. Amelia Jackson Studentship, Exeter Coll., Oxford, 1947; BA (hons) Physiology, Junior Demonstrator in Physiology, Harmsworth Senior Scholar, Merton Coll., Oxford, 1950; Open and State Schol., St Mary's Hosp., 1951; MSc Thesis in Physiology, 1952; MRCS, LRCP, 1954; BM, BCh Oxford, 1954; DM Oxford, 1963. William Hyde Award for research relating physical education to medicine; MRCP 1957. Junior Medical Specialist, RAMC, 1958; Radcliffe Travelling Fellowship from Oxford Univ., at Harvard, USA, 1962–63. Correspondent, Sunday Times, 1955–62. Chm., Hon. Consultants, King Edward VII Convalescent Home for Officers, Osborne, 1979–87. Chm., Medical Cttee, St Mary's Hosp., 1983–85; Deleg., Imperial Coll., representing St Mary's Hosp. Med. Sch., 1988–92; Trustee, St Mary's Hosp. Med. Sch. Develt Trust, 1994–98 (Chm. Trustees, 1998–2006). Inaugural Annual Sir Roger Bannister Lecture, Eur. Autonomic Soc., 2004. President: National Fitness Panel, NABC, 1956–59; Alzheimer's Disease Soc., 1982–84; Sports Medicine Sect., RSM, 1994–95; Gen. Sect., BAAS, 1995; Founder and Chm., Clinical Autonomic Res. Soc., 1982–84. Mem. Council, King George's Jubilee Trust, 1961–67; Pres., Sussex Assoc. of Youth Clubs, 1972–79; Chm., Res. Cttee, Adv. Sports Council, 1965–71; Mem., Min. of Health Adv. Cttee on Drug Dependence, 1967–70; Chm., Sports Council, 1971–74; Pres., Internat. Council for Sport and Physical Recreation, 1976–83. Mem., Management Cttee, 1979–84, Council, 1984–, King Edward's Hosp. Fund for London; Trustee: King George VI and Queen Elizabeth Foundn of St Catharine's, Cumberland Lodge, Windsor, 1985–2005; Leeds Castle, 1989–2006; Henry and Proctor Amer. Fellowships, 1987–99; Winston Churchill Fellowships, 1988–2006; Med. Commn on Accident Prevention, 1994–99; Mem. of Commn, Marshall Fellowships, 1986–94; Steering Cttee, Fulbright Fellowships, 1996–97. Patron, British Assoc. of Sport and Medicine, 1996–. Pres., Bath Inst. of Biomedical Engrg, 1998–2004; Governor: Atlantic Coll., 1985–93; Abingdon Sch., 1985–93; Sherborne Sch., 1989–93. Winner Oxford v Cambridge Mile, 1947–50; Pres. OUAC, 1948; Capt. Oxford & Cambridge Combined American Team, 1949; Finalist, Olympic Games, Helsinki, 1952; British Mile Champion, 1951, 1953, 1954; World Record for One Mile, 1954 (3 mins 59.4 secs); British Empire Mile winner and record, 1954; European 1500 metres title and record, 1954. Hon. Freeman: City of Oxford, 2004; London Bor. of Harrow, 2004. Hon. FUMIST 1972; Hon. Fellow: Exeter Coll., Oxford, 1979; Merton Coll., Oxford, 1986; Pembroke Coll., Oxford, 1994; Harris Manchester Coll., Oxford, 2007; Brunel Univ., 2008; Hon. FIC 1999. Hon. FRCSE 2002. Hon. LLD Liverpool, 1972; Hon. DLitt Sheffield, 1978; hon. doctorates: Jyvaskyla, Finland, 1982; Bath, Grinnell, 1984; Rochester, NY, 1985; Pavia, Italy, 1986; Williams Coll., USA, 1987; Victoria Univ., Canada, 1987; Wales, Cardiff, 1994; Loughborough, 1996; UEA, 1997; Cranfield, 2002; Manchester Combined Univs, 2002. Hans-Heinrich Siegbert Prize, 1977; First Lifetime Achievement Award, Amer. Acad. Neurol., 2005. Chm. Editorial Bd, Clinical Autonomic Res., 1991–97; Mem., Editorial Bd, Jl of the Autonomic Nervous System, 1980–95; Associate Editor, Jl Neurol Sci., 1985–95. Publications: First Four Minutes, 1955, 50th Anniversary edn 2004; (ed) Brain's Clinical Neurology, 3rd edn 1969 to 6th edn 1985, 7th edn 1992 (as Brain and Bannister's Clinical Neurology); (ed) Autonomic Failure, 1983 to 3rd edn 1992, (ed with C. J. Mathias) 4th edn 1999 and 5th edn 2008; papers on physiology of exercise, heat illness and neurological subjects. Address: 21 Bardwell Road, Oxford OX2 6SU. T: (01865) 511413. Clubs: Athenæum; Vincent's (Oxford).

BANNON, Michael Joseph, FRCPI, FRCPCH; Postgraduate Dean, Department of Postgraduate Medical and Dental Education, Oxford, since 2003; b 2 May 1954; s of Christopher Bannon and Ann (née Kelly); m 1988, Yvonne Helen Carter, qv; one s. Educ: Trinity Coll., Dublin (MB BCh, BAO 1978; MA 1992; DCH 1979); MA Oxon; Univ. of Keele (MSc). FRCPI 1993; FRCPCH 1993. Consultant Paediatrician: City Gen. Hosp., N Staffs, 1990–92; Warwick Hosp., 1992–96; Northwick Park Hosp., 1996–2003. Sen. Lectr, Warwick Univ., 1992–96. Publications: Protecting Children from Abuse and Neglect in Primary Care, 2003; contrib. papers on child protection and med. educn. Recreation: Irish folk music. Address: Department of Postgraduate Medical and Dental Education, The Triangle, Roosevelt Drive, Headington, Oxford OX3 3XP. T: (01865) 740605.

BANNON, Yvonne Helen; see Carter, Y. H.

BANO, (Ernest) Andrew (Louis); Social Security and Child Support Commissioner, since 2000; b 7 May 1944; s of late Imre Bano and Susanne Bano; m 1985, Elizabeth Anne Sheehy; three s one d. Educ: Cardinal Vaughan Meml Sch.; Inns of Court Sch. of Law. Trng Consultant, 1966–69; Trng Develt Officer, BEA, 1969–72; called to the Bar, Gray's Inn, 1973; in practice at Common Law Bar, 1973–88; Head of Chambers, 1986–88; Chm. (part-time), Industrial Tribunals, 1984–88; Chm., Employment Tribunals, 1988–2000; Dep. Social Security Comr, 1996–2000; Legal Chm. (part-time), Pensions Appeal Tribunals, 2001–05; Pension Appeal Comr, 2005–. Sec., Industrial Tribunals Adv. Cttee on Legislation and Rules, 1992–95. Recreations: opera, private flying, woodwork. Address: Office of the Social Security and Child Support Commissioners, 83 Farringdon Street, EC4A 4DH. T: (020) 7395 3347.

BANTING, Ven. (Kenneth) Mervyn (Lancelot Hadfield); Archdeacon of the Isle of Wight, 1996–2003, now Archdeacon Emeritus; b 8 Sept. 1937; s of late Rev. Canon H. M. J. Banting and P. M. Banting; m 1970, Linda (née Gick); four d. Educ: Pembroke Coll., Cambridge (MA, 1965); Cuddesdon Coll., Oxford. Ordained deacon, 1965, priest, 1966; Chaplain, Winchester Coll., 1965–70; Asst Curate, St Francis, Leigh Park, Portsmouth, 1970–73; Team Vicar, Highfield, Hemel Hempstead, 1973–79; Vicar, Goldington, Bedford, 1979–88; Priest-in-charge, Renhold, 1980–82; RD, Bedford, 1984–87; Vicar, St Cuthbert's, Portsmouth, 1988–96; RD, Portsmouth, 1994–96. Recreations: sailing, horology. Address: Furzend, 38A Bosham Hoe, W Sussex PO18 8ET. T: (01243) 572340; e-mail: merlinbanting@f2s.com.

BANTON, Prof. Michael Parker, CMG 2001; JP; PhD, DSc; Professor of Sociology, 1965–92, now Emeritus, and Pro-Vice-Chancellor, 1985–88, University of Bristol; b 8 Sept. 1926; s of Francis Clive Banton and Kathleen Blanche (née Parkes); m 1952, Rut Marianne (née Jacobson), Luleå; one s two d (and one s decd). Educ: King Edward's Sch., Birmingham; London Sch. of Economics. BSc Econ. 1950; PhD 1954; DSc 1964. Served RN, 1944–47 (Sub-Lieut, RNVR). Asst, then Lecturer, then Reader, in Social Anthropology, University of Edinburgh, 1950–65. Dir, SSRC Res. Unit on Ethnic Relations, 1970–78. Visiting Professor: MIT, 1962–63; Wayne State Univ., Detroit, 1971; Univ. of Delaware, 1976; ANU, 1981; Duke Univ., 1982. Editor, Sociology, 1966–69. President: Section N, 1969–70 and Section H, 1985–86, BAAS; Royal Anthropological Inst., 1987–89; Mem., Vetenskapssocieteten, Lund, Sweden, 1972; Member: Royal Commn on Criminal Procedure, 1978–80; Royal Commn on Bermuda, 1978; UK National Commn for UNESCO, 1963–66 and 1980–85; UN Cttee for the Elimination of Racial Discrimination, 1986–2001 (Chm., 1996–98); Ethnic Minorities Adv. Cttee, Judicial Studies Bd, 1993–96; SW Regl Hosp. Board, 1966–70. JP Bristol, 1966. FRSA 1981. FilDr hc Stockholm, 2000. Publications: The Coloured Quarter, 1955; West African City, 1957; White and Coloured, 1959; The Policeman in the Community, 1964; Roles, 1965; Race Relations, 1967; Racial Minorities, 1972; Police-Community Relations, 1973; (with J. Harwood) The Race Concept, 1975; The Idea of Race, 1977; Racial and Ethnic Competition, 1983; Promoting Racial Harmony, 1985; Investigating Robbery, 1985; Racial Theories, 1987, 2nd edn 1998; Racial Consciousness, 1988; Discrimination,

1994; International Action Against Racial Discrimination, 1996; Ethnic and Racial Consciousness, 1997; The International Politics of Race, 2002. Address: Fairways, Luxted Road, Downe, Orpington BR6 7JT. T: (01959) 576828; e-mail: michael@ banton.demon.co.uk.

BANVILLE, John; writer; b Wexford, 8 Dec. 1945; s of Martin and Agnes Banville; two s with Janet Dunham Banville; two d with Patricia Quinn. Educ: Christian Brothers' Schs; St Peter's Coll., Wexford, Ireland. Journalist, 1970–99; Literary Ed., Irish Times, 1988–99. Theatre: The Broken Jug, Abbey Th., Dublin, 1994; God's Gift, Dublin Th. Fest. and tour, 2000; The Book of Evidence, Kilkenny Th. Fest., 2002 and Gate Th., Dublin, 2003; television play: Seachange, 1994; radio includes: Stardust, series of monologues, 2004; plays: Kepler, 2004; Todtnauberg, 2005. Publications: Long Lankin (short stories), 1970; novels: Nightspawn, 1971; Birchwood, 1974; Doctor Copernicus (James Tait Black Meml Prize), 1976; Kepler (Guardian Fiction Prize), 1980; The Newton Letter, 1982 (filmed for TV as Reflections); Mefisto, 1986; The Book of Evidence, 1989 (Guinness Peat Aviation Award, Premio Ennio Flaiano, Italy, 1991); Ghosts, 1993; Athena, 1995; The Untouchable, 1997; Eclipse, 2000; Shroud, 2002; The Sea (Man Booker Prize), 2005; non-fiction: Prague Pictures: portraits of a city, 2003; adaptations of dramas by Heinrich von Kleist: The Broken Jug, 1994; God's Gift, 2000; Love in the Wars, 2005; as Benjamin Black: Christine Falls, 2006; The Silver Swan, 2007. Recreation: work. Address: c/o Ed Victor Ltd, 6 Bayley Street, Bedford Square, WC1B 3HE. T: (020) 7304 4100, Fax: (020) 7304 4111. Clubs: Kildare Street and University, St Stephen's Green (Dublin).

BAPTISTA DA SILVA, Dr Carlos Boaventura; Counsellor to Chairman, Board of Trustees, Calouste Gulbenkian Foundation, since 2005 (Secretary, 1974–2005); b 13 Feb. 1935; s of Fernando Baptista da Silva and Virginia Boaventura Baptista da Silva; m 1961, Emilia de Almeida Nadal; two s one d. Educ: Univ. of Lisbon (Lic. in Law). Lawyer, 1968–. Counsellor, Lisbon Mint Consulting Cttee. Dir, Gremio Literario, Lisbon, 2001–. Mem., Gen. Cttee, Oliveira Martins Foundn, Lisbon, 1980–. Counsellor, FIDEM, 2007–. Comdr, Order of Public Instruction (Portugal), 1968. Publications: several texts on medal art. Recreations: collector of medals and modern art, music, reading. Address: Rua dos Navegantes 53–5° DT°, 1200–730 Lisbon, Portugal. T: and Fax: 213974242; e-mail: cbsilva935@metcabo.com.

BAR-HILLEL, Mira; Property and Planning Correspondent, Evening Standard, since 1986; b 30 Sept. 1946; d of late Prof. Yehoshua Bar-Hillel and Shulamit (née Aschkenazy). Educ: Hebrew Gymnasia, Jerusalem; Hebrew Univ., Jerusalem (BA Soviet Studies 1972). Military Service, Israel Defence Forces, 1963–65. News reporter: Voice of Israel, 1965–72; Building mag., 1973–82 (News Editor, 1978–82); freelance writer on property and also architecture and planning, 1982–. LBC Radio Property Expert, 1993–94. Internat. Bldg Press Award, 1979, 1980, 1983, 1988, 1994, 1995, 1996; RICS Award, 1985; Incorporated Soc. Valuers and Auctioneers Award, 1986, 1996; Laing Homes Award, 1989, 1991, 1993. Recreations: cats, fighting Modernism. Address: Evening Standard, Northcliffe House, 2 Derry Street, High Street, Kensington, W8 5EE. T: (020) 7938 6000; e-mail: mira.barhillel@standard.co.uk.

BARAK, Jeff(rey); Editor-in-Chief, Ynetnews.com, since 2007; b 26 April 1961; s of Malcolm and Estelle Barak; m 1989, Yemima Rabin; two s one d. Educ: Leeds Grammar Sch.; Univ. of Newcastle upon Tyne (BA Hons English Lit.). Formerly ME analyst for assorted media; Ed.-in-Chief, Jerusalem Post, 1996–2002; Dep. Ed., 2002–05, Man. Ed., 2005–06, Jewish Chronicle. Recreation: watching televised sport. Address: PO Box 85285, Mevnsseret Zion 90805, Israel. T: 526453637; e-mail: jeff-ba@y-i.co.il.

BARAŃSKI, Prof. Zygmunt Guido; Serena Professor of Italian, University of Cambridge, and Fellow, New Hall (from May 2009, Murray Edwards College), Cambridge, since 2002; b 13 April 1951; s of Henryk Barański and Sonia Mariotti; m 1979, Margaret Ellen Watt; one s one d. Educ: St Bede's Coll., Manchester; Hull Univ. (BA 1973). Lectr in Italian, Univ. of Aberdeen, 1976–79; University of Reading: Lectr, 1979–89, Sen. Lectr, 1989–92, in Italian Studies; Prof. of Italian Studies, 1992–2002. Visiting Professor: McGill Univ., 1988, 1997; Univ. of Virginia, Charlottesville, 1991; Univ. of Connecticut, 1993; Yale Univ., 1995; Univ. of Notre Dame, 1996, 1998, 2004, 2007; Univ. of Bari, 2001; Univ. of California, Berkeley, 2002. Pres., Internat. Dante Seminar, 2003–08. Commendatore, Ordine della Stella della Solidarietà (Italy), 2005. Publications: (ed) Libri poetarum in quattuor species dividuntur: essays on Dante and genre, 1995; Luce nuova, sole nuovo: saggi sul rinnovamento culturale in Dante, 1996; Pasolini Old and New, 1999; Dante e i segni, 2000; Chiosar con altro testo: leggere Dante nel trecento, 2001; contribs to learned jls. Recreations: following Manchester United, cycling, music. Address: New Hall (from May 2009, Murray Edwards College), Cambridge CB3 0DF. T: (01223) 762263, Fax: (01223) 763110; e-mail: zgb20@cam.ac.uk.

BARBACK, Ronald Henry; Professor of Economics, University of Hull, 1965–76 (Dean, Faculty of Social Sciences and Law, 1966–69); b 31 Oct. 1919; s of late Harry Barback and Winifred Florence (née Norris); m 1950, Sylvia Chambers (d 2004); one s one d. Educ: Woodside Sch., Glasgow; UC, Nottingham (BScEcon); Queen's and Nuffield Colls, Oxford (MLitt). Asst Lectr in Econs, Univ. of Nottingham, 1946–48; Lectr in Econs, subseq. Sen. Lectr, Canberra University Coll., Australia, 1949–56; Univ. of Ibadan (formerly University Coll., Ibadan): Prof. of Econs and Social Studies, 1956–63; Dean, Faculty of Arts, 1958–59; Dean, Faculty of Econs and Social Studies, 1959–63; Dir, Nigerian (formerly W African) Inst. of Social and Econ. Res., 1956–63; Sen. Res. Fellow, Econ. Res. Inst., Dublin, 1963–64; Prof. of Econs, TCD, 1964–65; Vis. Prof., Brunel Univ., 1984–86. Dep. Econ. Dir and Head, Econ. Res., CBI, 1977–81, Consultant, 1981–82. Nigeria: Mem., Ibadan Univ. Hosp. Bd of Management, 1958–63; Mem., J t Econ. Planning Cttee, Fedn of Nigeria, 1959–61; Sole Arbitrator, Trade Disputes in Ports and Railways, 1958; Chm., Fed. Govt Cttee to advise on fostering a share market, 1959. UK Official Delegate, FAO meeting on investment in fisheries, 1970; Mem., FAO mission to Sri Lanka, 1975. Consultant, Div. of Fisheries, Europ. Commn Directorate-Gen. of Agriculture, 1974; Specialist Advr, H of L Select Cttee on Eur. Communities, 1980–83; Commonwealth Scholarships Commn Adviser on Econs, 1971–76. Mem., Schools Council Social Sciences Cttee, 1971–80; Chm., Schs Council Econs and Business Studies Syllabus Steering Gp, 1975–77. Member: Hull and Dist Local Employment Cttee, 1966–73; N Humberside Dist Manpower Cttee, 1973–76; CNAA Business and Management Studies Bd, 1978–81, Economics Bd, 1982–86; Ct, Brunel Univ., 1979–83; Gov., Tunbridge Wells Girls' GS, 1996–98. Chm., Royal Tunbridge Wells Civic Soc., 1991–93 (Vice-Pres., 1994–96). Member: Editorial Bd, Bull. of Economic Research (formerly Yorks Bull. of Social and Economic Research), 1965–76 (Jt Editor, 1966–67); Editorial Adv. Bd, Applied Economics, 1969–80; Editor, Humberside Statistical Bull., nos 1–3, 1974, 1975, 1977. Publications: (contrib.) The Commonwealth in the World Today, ed J. Eppstein, 1956; (ed with Prof. Sir Douglas Copland) The Conflict of Expansion and Stability, 1957; (contrib.) The Commonwealth and Europe (EIU), 1960; The Pricing of Manufactures, 1964; (contrib.) Insurance Markets of the World, ed M. Grossmann 1964; (contrib.) Webster's New World Companion to English and American Literature, 1973;

Forms of Co-operation in the British Fishing Industry, 1976; (with M. Breimer and A. F. Haug) Development of the East Coast Fisheries of Sri Lanka, 1976; The Firm and its Environment, 1984; contrib. New Internat. Encyc., FAO Fisheries Reports, and jls. *Recreations:* walking, music.

BARBARITO, Most Rev. Luigi, Hon. GCVO 1996; DD, JCD; Titular Archbishop of Fiorentino; Apostolic Nuncio (formerly Pro-Nuncio) to the Court of St James's, 1986–97; *b* Atripalda, Avellino, Italy, 19 April 1922; *s* of Vincenzo Barbarito and Alfonsina Armerini. *Educ:* Pontifical Seminary, Benevento, Italy; Gregorian Univ., Rome (JCD); Papal Diplomatic Academy, Rome (Diploma). Priest, 1944; served Diocese of Avellino, 1944–52; entered Diplomatic Service of Holy See, 1953; Sec., Apostolic Delegn, Australia, 1953–59; Secretariat of State of Vatican (Council for Public Affairs of the Church), 1959–67; Counsellor, Apostolic Nunciature, Paris, 1967–69; Archbishop and Papal Nuncio to Haiti and Delegate to the Antilles, 1969–75; Pro-Nuncio to Senegal, Bourkina Fasso, Niger, Mali, Mauritania, Cape Verde Is and Guinea Bissau, 1975–78; Apostolic Pro-Nuncio to Australia, 1978–86. Mem., Mexican Acad. of Internat. Law. Grand Cross, National Order of Haiti, 1975; Grand Cross, Order of the Lion (Senegal), 1978; Knight Commander, Order of Merit (Italy), 1966, (Portugal), 1967. *Recreations:* music, walking. *Address:* c/o Suore Francescane, via Bravetta 518, 00164 Rome, Italy. *T:* (6) 66166354.

BARBER OF TEWKESBURY, Baron *cr* 1992 (Life Peer), of Gotherington in the County of Gloucestershire; **Derek Coates Barber,** Kt 1984; Chairman: Booker Countryside Advisory Board, 1990–96; Countryside Commission, 1981–91; *s* of Thomas Smith-Barber and Elsie Coates; 1st marr. diss. 1981; *m* 2nd, 1983, Rosemary Jennifer Brougham, *o d* of late Lt-Comdr Randolph Brougham Pearson, RN, and Hilary Diana Mackinlay Pearson (*née* Bennett). *Educ:* Royal Agricl Coll., Cirencester (MRAC; Gold Medal, Practical Agriculture; FRAC 1999). Served War: invalided, Armed Forces, 1942. Farmed in Glos Cotswolds; Mem., Cheltenham Rural District Council, 1948–52; Dist Adv. Officer, National Agricl Adv. Service, MAFF, 1946–57; County Agricl Advisor, Glos, 1957–72; Environment Consultant to Humberts, Chartered Surveyors, 1972–93; MAFF Assessor: Pilkington Cttee on Agric. Educ., 1966; Agric. and Hort. Trng Bd, 1968. Member: H of L Sub-Cttee D (Food and Agric.), 1992–96; H of L Select Cttee on Sustainable Devel, 1994–95. Chairman: BBC's Central Agricl Adv. Cttee, 1974–80 (*ex officio* Mem., BBC's Gen. Adv. Council, 1972–80); New National Forest Adv. Bd, 1991–95. Royal Soc. for Protection of Birds: Mem., 1970–75, Chm., 1976–81, Council; Chm., Educn Cttee, 1972–75; Vice-Pres., 1982; Pres., 1990–91. President: RASE, 1991–92; Rare Breeds Survival Trust, 1991–95, 1997–99 (Mem. Council, 1987–99); Hawk and Owl Trust, 1992–96; British Pig Assoc., 1995–96 (Vice-Pres., 1997–99); Glos Naturalists' Soc., 1981–; Vice-Pres., Ornithol Soc. of Mid-East, 1987–97; Mem. Council, British Trust for Ornithology, 1987–90; Founder Mem., 1969, Farming and Wildlife Adv. Gp of landowning, farming and wildlife conservation bodies; Member: Ordnance Survey Adv. Bd, 1982–85; Bd, RURAL Council, 1983–94; Bd, CEED, 1984–98; Centre for Agricl Strategy, 1985–91; Arable Res. Insts Assoc., 1991–95; Long Ashton Res. Stn Cttee, 1991–95. Dep. Chm., Bd, Groundwork Foundn, 1985–91; Patron, Woodland Trust, 1991–. FRAgS 1992; FIAgrM 1992. Hon. FRASE 1986. Hon. DSc Bradford, 1986. First Recipient, Summers Trophy for services to agric. in practice or science, 1955; Bledisloe Gold Medal for distinguished service to UK agriculture, 1967; RSPB Gold Medal for services to bird protection, 1982; Massey-Ferguson Award for services to agric., 1989; RASE Gold Medal, for distinguished service to UK agric., 1991. Silver Jubilee Medal, 1977. Editor, Humberts Commentary, 1973–88; columnist, Power Farming, 1973–91; Spec. Correspondent, Waitaki NZR Times, 1982–88. *Publications:* (with Keith Dexter) Farming for Profits, 1961, 2nd edn 1967; (with J. G. S. and Frances Donaldson) Farming in Britain Today, 1969, 2nd edn 1972; (ed) Farming with Wildlife, 1971; A History of Humberts, 1980; contrib. farming and wildlife conservation jls. *Recreations:* birds, wildlife conservation, farming. *Address:* House of Lords, SW1A 0PW. *Club:* Farmers'.

BARBER, Alan Vincent Heys; freelance consultant in urban greenspace management, since 1992; Member, Commission for Architecture and the Built Environment, since 2003; *b* 11 June 1942; *s* of late Harold Heys Barber and of Mary McLean Barber; *m* 1965, Angela Janice Alton; two *d*. *Educ:* King George V Grammar Sch., Southport; Royal Botanic Gdns, Kew. Parks Manager, Bristol CC, 1974–92. Mem., Govt Urban Green Spaces Taskforce, 2000–02. Simon Res. Fellow, Univ. of Manchester, 2003–. Pres., Inst. of Leisure and Amenity Mgt, 1997–98 (Hon. Fellow, 2004); Hon. ALI 1995. DUniv Essex, 2005. *Publication:* Green Future: a study of the management of multifunctional urban green spaces in England, 2005. *Recreations:* walking, music, grandchildren. *Address:* 9 Shipham Close, Nailsea, Bristol BS48 4YB. *T:* (01275) 854851; *e-mail:* alan.barber@blueyonder.co.uk.

BARBER, Brendan Paul; General Secretary, Trades Union Congress, since 2003; Member of Court, Bank of England, since 2003; *b* 3 April 1951; *s* of John and Agnes Barber; *m* 1981, Mary Rose Gray; two *d*. *Educ:* St Mary's Coll., Crosby; City Univ., London (BSc Hons; Pres. Students Union, 1973–74). Volunteer teacher, VSO, Ghana, 1969–70; Researcher, ceramics, glass and mineral products, ITB, 1974–75; Trades Union Congress: Asst, Orgn Dept, 1975–79; Hd, Press and Information Dept, 1979–87; Hd, Orgn Dept, 1987–93; Dep. Gen. Sec., 1993–2003. Member Council: ACAS, 1995–2004; Sport England, 1999–2002. *Recreations:* golf, football (Mem., Everton Supporters' Club, London Area), theatre, cinema. *Address:* Trades Union Congress, Congress House, Great Russell Street, WC1B 3LS. *T:* (020) 7467 1231; *e-mail:* bbarber@tuc.org.uk. *Club:* Muswell Hill Golf.

BARBER, Chris; *see* Barber, D. C.

BARBER, Sir David; *see* Barber, Sir T. D.

BARBER, (Donald) Chris(topher), OBE 1991; band leader, The Chris Barber Band; *b* 17 April 1930; *s* of Henrietta Mary Evelyn Barber, MA Cantab and Donald Barber, CBE, BA Cantab; *m*; one *s* one *d*; *m* Kate; one step *d*. *Educ:* King Alfred School; St Paul's School. Formed first amateur band, 1949; present band commenced on professional basis, 1954; plays trombone, baritone horn, double bass and trumpet. Hon. Citizen, New Orleans. Numerous recordings, including over 150 LPs and 100 CDs, with records in the hit parade of over 40 countries world wide. *Recreations:* antique collecting and collecting jazz and blues records, snooker, motor racing. *Address:* c/o ENTEC Ltd, 517 Yeading Lane, Northolt, Middlesex UB5 6LN. *T:* (020) 8842 4044, *Fax:* (020) 8842 3310; *e-mail:* dc@Entec-soundandlight.com.

BARBER, Edward Simon Dominic, RDI 2007; Founding Director and Co-owner: BarberOsgerby, since 1996; Universal Design Studio, since 2001; *b* Shrewsbury, 6 April 1969; *s* of Simon Barber and Penelope Barber (*née* Baldock). *Educ:* Leeds Poly. (BA Hons Interior Design); Royal Coll. of Art (MA Arch. and Interior Design). Tutor: Ravensbourne Coll., 1996–2000; Ecole cantonale d'art de Lausanne, 2003–. Dir, workshop, Vitra Design Mus., 2004. FRSA 2005. Jerwood Applied Arts Prize (jtly), Jerwood Foundn, 2004. *Address:* BarberOsgerby, 35–42 Charlotte Road, EC2A 3PG. *T:* (020) 7033 3884, *Fax:* (020) 7033 3882; *e-mail:* mail@barberosgerby.com.

BARBER, Frank; Senior Partner, Morgan, Fentiman & Barber, 1993–97; Deputy Chairman of Lloyd's, 1983, 1984; *b* 5 July 1923; *s* of Sidney Barber and Florence (*née* Seath); *m* 1st, 1945, Gertrude Kathleen Carson (decd); one *s* one *d* (and one *s* decd); 2nd, 1994, Elizabeth Joan Charvet. *Educ:* West Norwood Central School. RAFVR, 1942–46. Entered Lloyd's, 1939; Underwriter, Lloyd's syndicate, Frank Barber & others, 1962–81; Member: Cttee of Lloyd's, 1977–80, 1982–85 and 1987; Council of Lloyd's, 1983–85 and 1987; Dep. Chm., Lloyd's Underwriters' Non-Marine Assoc., 1971, Chm., 1972; Dep. Chm., British Insurers' European Cttee, 1983. Partner: Morgan, Fentiman & Barber, 1968–97; G. S. Christensen & Partners, 1985–2000; Chairman: A. E. Grant (Underwriting Agencies) Ltd, 1991–96; Frank Barber Underwriting Ltd, 2000–. *Recreations:* music, walking, sailing. *Address:* Doiley Hill Lodge, Hurstbourne Tarrant, Andover, Hants SP11 0ER.

BARBER, Giles Gaudard; Librarian, Taylor Institution, University of Oxford, 1970–96; Fellow, Linacre College, Oxford, 1963–96, now Emeritus (Vice-Principal, 1988–90); *b* 15 Aug. 1930; *s* of Eric Arthur Barber and Madeleine Barber (*née* Gaudard); *m* 1st, 1958, Monique Fluchère (*d* 1969); one *d*; 2nd, 1970, Gemma Miani (marr. diss. 1997); two *s* one *d*; 3rd, 1997, Lisa Jefferson; one step *d*. *Educ:* Dragon Sch., Oxford; Leighton Park Sch.; St John's Coll., Oxford (MA, BLitt). Asst, Bodleian Library, 1954–70; Univ. Lectr in Continental Bibliography, Oxford, 1969–96. Pres., Oxford Bibliographical Soc., 1992–96 and 1999–2000; Vice-Pres., Bibliographical Soc., 1983–93; Chm., Voltaire Foundn, 1987–89; Mem. Council, Internat. Soc. for 18th Century Studies, 1979–83. Vis. Lectr, Univ. of Paris IV (Sorbonne), 1980; Lectures: 1st Graham Pollard Meml, 1984; Moses Tyson Meml, Manchester Univ., 1985; Panizzi, British Library, 1988; First Founders' Library Lectr, Univ. of Wales, Lampeter, 1996; Sandars Reader in Bibliography, Cambridge Univ., 1997–98. Corresp. Mem., Soc. Archéologique du Midi de la France, 2004. Gordon Duff Prize in Bibliography, 1962. Commandeur, Ordre des Arts et des Lettres (France), 2002 (Officier, 1992). *Publications:* (ed jtly) Fine Bindings 1500–1700, 1968; A checklist of French printing manuals, 1969; Textile and embroidered bookbindings, 1971; (ed) Book making in Diderot's Encyclopédie, 1973; (ed) Contat, Anecdotes typographiques, 1980; (ed jtly) Buch und Buchhandel in Europa im achtzehnten Jahrhundert, 1981; Daphnis and Chloe, 1989; Studies in the booktrade of the European Enlightenment, 1994; Arks for Learning, 1995; Les Rues de Saint-Girons, 2004; articles in learned jls. *Recreations:* book-collecting, gardening. *Address:* La Mandro, 09420 Lescure, France; *e-mail:* giles.barber@wanadoo.fr.

BARBER, Prof. James, PhD; FRS 2005; FRSC; Ernst Chain Professor of Biochemistry, Imperial College London (formerly Imperial College of Science, Technology and Medicine), since 1989 (Head of Department of Biochemistry, 1989–99); *b* 16 July 1940; *s* of Stanley William George Barber and Sophia Helen Barber; *m* 1965, Marilyn Jane Emily Tyrrell; one *s* one *d*. *Educ:* Portsmouth Southern Grammar Sch.; Univ. of Wales (BSc Hons Chem.); Univ. of East Anglia (MSc, PhD Biophys.). FRSC 1983. Unilever Biochem. Soc. European Fellow, Univ. of Leiden, 1967–68; Imperial College: Lectr, Dept of Botany, 1968–74; Reader in Plant Physiology, 1974–79, Prof., 1979–89; Dean, Royal Coll. of Science, 1989–91. Miller Prof., Univ. of Calif at Berkeley, 1989–90, 2001; Burroughs Wellcome Fund Prof., Univ. of Calif, 2000. Lectures: Brookhaven Sci. Assoc. Dist., 2005; Drummond, Queen Mary, London, 2005; Arnon, UC Berkeley, 2008. Selby Fellow, Australian Acad. of Scis, 1996; Foreign Mem., Swedish Royal Acad. of Scis, 2003. Mem., Academia Europaea, 1989. Hon. Dr Univ. of Stockholm, 1992. Flintoff Medal, RSC, 2002; Italgas Prize for Energy and Envmt, Academia Europaea, 2005; Novartis Medal and Prize, Biochem. Soc., 2006; Wheland Medal and Prize, Univ. of Chicago, 2007. *Publications:* The Intact Chloroplast, 1976; Primary Processes in Photosynthesis, 1977; Photosynthesis in Relation to Model Systems, 1979; Electron Transport and Photophosphorylation, 1982; Chloroplast Biogenesis, 1984; Photosynthetic Mechanisms and the Environment, 1986; The Light Reactions, 1987; The Photosystems: structure, function and molecular biology, 1992; Molecular Processes of Photosynthesis, 1994; Molecular to Global Photosynthesis, 2004; articles and reviews. *Recreations:* running, sailing, gardening. *Address:* Wolfson Laboratories, Division of Molecular Sciences, Imperial College London, SW7 2AZ. *T:* (020) 7594 5266; *e-mail:* j.barber@imperial.ac.uk.

BARBER, Prof. James Peden, PhD; Master, Hatfield College, Durham, 1980–96; Professor of Politics, Durham University, 1992–96, now Emeritus; Associate Fellow, Centre of International Studies, Cambridge University, since 1996; Research Fellow, South African Institute of International Affairs, since 1996; *b* 6 Nov. 1931; *s* of John and Carrie Barber; *m* 1955, Margaret June (*née* McCormac); three *s* one *d*. *Educ:* Liverpool Inst. High Sch.; Pembroke Coll., Cambridge (MA, PhD); The Queen's Coll., Oxford. Served RAF, 1950–52 (Pilot Officer). Colonial Service, Uganda: Dist Officer, subseq. Asst Sec. to Prime Minister and Clerk to the Cabinet, 1956–63; Lectr, Univ. of NSW, Australia, 1963–65; Lectr in Govt, Univ. of Exeter, 1965–69 (seconded to University Coll. of Rhodesia, 1965–67); Prof. of Political Science, Open Univ., 1969–80; Pro-Vice-Chancellor, 1987–92 and Sub-Warden, 1990–92, Durham Univ. Advr, Commons Select Cttee on Foreign Affairs, 1990–91. Mem. RIIA; Part-time Dir, Chatham House study, Southern Africa in Conflict, 1979–81. Mem., Amnesty International. President: Durham Univ. Soc. of Fellows, 1988; Durham Univ. Hockey Club, 1981–96. JP Bedford, 1977–80. *Publications:* Rhodesia: the road to rebellion, 1967; Imperial Frontier, 1968; South Africa's Foreign Policy, 1973; European Community: vision and reality, 1974; The Nature of Foreign Policy, 1975; Who Makes British Foreign Policy?, 1977; The West and South Africa, 1982; The Uneasy Relationship: Britain and South Africa, 1983; South Africa: the search for status and security, 1990; The Prime Minister since 1945, 1991; Forging the New South Africa, 1994; South Africa in the Twentieth Century: a political history, 1999; Mandela's World, 2004. *Recreations:* choral music, golf, bowls, walking. *Address:* 14 North Terrace, Midsummer Common, Cambridge CB5 8DJ. *T:* (01223) 313453. *Club:* Menzies Golf (Cambridge).

BARBER, Prof. Karin Judith, PhD; FBA 2003; Professor of African Cultural Anthropology, Centre of West African Studies, University of Birmingham, since 1999; *b* 2 July 1949; *d* of Charles and Barbara Barber; partner, Dr Paulo Fernando de Moraes Farias. *Educ:* Lawnswood High Sch., Leeds; Girton Coll., Cambridge (BA English 1st cl., MA); UCL (Dip. in Soc. Anthropol.); Univ. of Ife (PhD). Lectr, Dept of African Langs and Lits, Univ. of Ife, 1977–84; Centre of West African Studies, University of Birmingham: Lectr, 1985–93; Sen. Lectr, 1993–97; Reader, 1997–99; Dir, 1998–2001. Vis. Preceptor, Inst. for Adv. Study and Res. in African Humanities, 1993–94, Melville J. Herskovits Vis. Chair in African Studies, 1999, Northwestern Univ., Illinois. *Publications:* Yorùbá Dùn ún So: a beginners' course in Yorùbá, 1984, 2nd edn 1990; (ed with P. F. de Moraes Farias) Discourse and its Disguises: the interpretation of African oral texts, 1989; (ed with P. F. de Moraes Farias) Self-assertion and Brokerage: early cultural nationalism in West Africa, 1990; I Could Speak Until Tomorrow: Oríkì, women and the past in a Yorùbá town (Amaury Talbot Prize, RAI), 1991; (with Bayo Ogundijo) Yorùbá Popular

Theatre: three plays by the Oyin Adejobi Company, 1994; (jtly) West African Popular Theatre, 1997; (ed) Readings in African Popular Culture, 1997; (with Akin Oyetade) Yorùbá Wuyì, 1999; The Generation of Plays: Yorùbá popular life in theater (Herskovits Award, African Studies Assoc., USA), 2000; (ed) Africa's Hidden Histories: everyday literacy and making the self, 2006; The Anthropology of Texts, Persons and Publics, 2007. *Recreations:* theatre, music. *Address:* Centre of West African Studies, University of Birmingham, Edgbaston, Birmingham B15 2TT. *T:* (0121) 414 5125, *Fax:* (0121) 414 3228; *e-mail:* k.j.barber@bham.ac.uk.

BARBER, Lionel; Editor, Financial Times, since 2005; *b* 18 Jan. 1955; *s* of Frank Douglas Barber and Joan Elizabeth Barber (*née* Nolan); *m* 1986, Victoria Greenwood; one *s* one *d*. *Educ:* Dulwich Coll.; St Edmund Hall, Oxford (BA Jt Hons German and Modern Hist.). Reporter, Scotsman, 1978–81; business reporter, Sunday Times, 1981–85; Financial Times: UK company news reporter, 1985–86; Washington Corresp., 1986–92; Brussels Bureau Chief, 1992–98; News Ed., 1998–2000; European Ed., 2000–02; US Managing Ed., 2002–05. *Publications:* (jtly) The Delorean Tapes, 1984; (jtly) The Price of Truth: the story of Reuter's millions, 1985; (jtly) Not with Honour, 1986. *Recreations:* cycling, tennis, working out, reading American history, watching Rugby. *Address:* Financial Times, Number One, Southwark Bridge, SE1 9HL. *T:* (020) 7873 4045.

BARBER, Prof. Sir Michael (Bayldon), Kt 2005; Expert Partner, Global Public Sector Practice, McKinsey & Company, since 2005; *b* 24 Nov. 1955; *s* of Christopher and Anne Barber; *m* 1982, Karen Alderman; three *d*. *Educ:* Bootham Sch., York; Queen's Coll., Oxford (BA Hons 1977); Georg-August Univ., Göttingen; Westminster Coll., Oxford (PGCE 1979); Inst. of Educn, London Univ. (MA 1991). History Teacher: Watford, 1979–83; Zimbabwe, 1983–85; Policy and Res. Officer, 1985–89, Education Officer, 1989–93, NUT; Professor of Education: Keele Univ., 1993–95; Inst. of Educn, London Univ., 1995–97; Dir, Standards and Effectiveness Unit, and Chief Advr to Sec. of State on Sch. Standards, DFEE, 1997–2001; Chief Advr to Prime Minister on Delivery, and Hd, Prime Minister's Delivery Unit, 2001–05. Vis. Prof., Univ. of London, 2001–. Mem. (Lab), Hackney LBC, 1986–90 (Chair, Educn Cttee, 1988–89). Contested (Lab) Henley-on-Thames, 1987. FRSA 1993. Hon. EdD Wolverhampton, 2003. *Publications:* Education and the Teacher Unions, 1992; The Making of 1944 Education Act, 1994; The National Curriculum: a study in policy, 1996; The Learning Game: arguments for an education revolution, 1996, revd edn 1997; High Standards and High Expectations for All No Matter What: creating a world class education service in England, 2000; The Very Big Picture: the possibility of global education reform, 2001; The Virtue of Accountability, 2005; Instruction to Deliver: Tony Blair, reform of public services and achievement of targets, 2007; (with Mona Mowshed) How the World's Best Performing Education Systems Come Out on Top, 2007. *Recreations:* mountain walking, Liverpool Football Club, chess, reading history books. *Address:* 62 Lawford Road, N1 5BL. *T:* (020) 7249 7689.

BARBER, Nicholas Charles Faithorn, CBE 2004; Chairman, Bolero International Ltd, since 1998; *b* 7 Sept. 1940; *s* of Bertram Harold and Nancy Lorraine Barber; *m* 1966, Sheena Macrae Graham; two *s* one *d*. *Educ:* Ludgrove Sch.; Shrewsbury Sch.; Wadham Coll., Oxford (MA; Fellow 2007); Columbia Univ., New York, 1969–71 (MBA). Lectr, Marlboro Coll., Vermont, USA, 1963–64; joined Ocean Steam Ship, subseq. Ocean Transport and Trading, later Ocean Group, 1964; Dir, 1980–94; Chief Exec., 1986–94. Divl Dir, NEB, 1977–79. Chairman: IEC Gp plc, 1996–99; Orion Publishing Gp, 1997–98; Kappa IT Ventures, 1998–2007; Director: Costain Gp, 1990–93; Royal Insurance Hldgs plc, 1991–96 (Dep. Chm., 1994–96); Royal & Sun Alliance Insurance Gp plc, 1996–2003; Barings plc, 1994–95; Bank of Ireland UK Financial Services plc (formerly Bristol & West Bldg Soc., then Bristol and West plc), 1994–2003 (Dep. Chm., 2001–03); Albright & Wilson plc, 1995–99; Fidelity Japanese Values PLC, 2000–; The Maersk Co., 2004–. Mem., NW Industrial Develt Bd, 1982–85; Gov., NIESR, 1991– (Mem., Exec. Cttee, 2001–). Dir, Liverpool Playhouse, 1982–87; Mem., Adv. Cttee, Tate Gall., Liverpool, 1988–92; Trustee: Nat. Museums and Galls on Merseyside, 1986–94; Shrewsbury Sch. Foundn, 1990–2006; British Mus., 1993–2003; Country Houses Foundn, 2004–; Chairman: British Mus. Friends (formerly British Mus. Soc.), 1992–2003; British Mus. Co. Ltd, 1996–2003; Ashmolean Mus., 2003–. Governor: Shrewsbury Sch., 1983–2003 (Dep. Chm., 1997–2003); London Business Sch., 1993–2001; Vice-Pres., Liverpool Sch. of Tropical Medicine, 1988–; Chm., Huron Univ. USA in London Ltd, 1998–2007; Member Council: Liverpool Univ., 1985–88; Industrial Soc., 1993–99; Mem., Adv. Council, Asia House, 1996–; Dir, Hult Internat. Business Sch., Boston, 2008–. FRSA 1994. Hon. DHL Marlboro Coll., Vermont, 2005. *Recreations:* mountain walking, cricket, woodland gardening, museums, reading. *Address:* 6 Lytton Court, 14 Barter Street, WC1A 2AH. *Clubs:* Brooks's, MCC; Denham Golf.

BARBER, Pamela Gay; DL; Headteacher, Lancaster Girls' Grammar School, 1987–2007; *b* 8 May 1947; *d* of Harold and Muriel Nunwick; *m* Paul Barker. *Educ:* N Western Poly., London (BA Hons Geog.); Leeds Univ. (PGCE). Class teacher, then Hd of Geog. and Hd of Sixth Form, Belle Vue Girls' Sch., Bradford, 1969–80; Deputy Head: Crossley and Porter Sch., Halifax, 1980–85; Crossley Heath Sch., Halifax, 1985–86. Boarding Headteacher, Admiralty Interview Bd, 1992–2005. Non-exec. Dir, Lancaster HA, 1990–93. Mem. Bd, Bay Radio, 1999–2003. DL Lancs, 2007. Mem. Council, Lancaster Univ., 1989–95. Mem., Adv. Cttee, Arkwright Trust, 1998–2007. *Recreations:* foreign travel, horse riding, donkey keeping, gardening, fell-walking.

BARBER, Rt Rev. Paul Everard; Bishop Suffragan of Brixworth, 1989–2001; Hon. Assistant Bishop, Diocese of Bath and Wells, since 2001; *b* 16 Sept. 1935; *s* of Cecil Arthur and Mollie Barber; *m* 1959, Patricia Jayne Walford; two *s* two *d* (and one *s* decd). *Educ:* Sherborne School; St John's Coll., Cambridge (BA 1958, MA 1966); Wells Theological College. Deacon 1960, priest 1961, dio. Guildford; Curate of St Francis, Westborough, 1960–66; Vicar: Camberley with Yorktown, 1966–73; St Thomas-on-The Bourne, Farnham, 1973–80; Rural Dean of Farnham, 1974–79; Archdeacon of Surrey, 1980–89; Hon. Canon: of Guildford, 1980–89; of Peterborough, 1997–2001. General Synod, 1979–85; Member, Council of College of Preachers, 1969–98. Archbp of Canterbury's Advr to HMC, 1993–2001. Gov., Millfield Sch., 2002–. *Recreations:* sport, theatre, cinema, walking. *Address:* 41 Somerton Road, Street, Somerset BA16 0DR. *T:* (01458) 442916.

BARBER, Stephen James; social services consultant; Chief Children's Officer, and Director of Social Services, London Borough of Barnet, 1999–2000; *b* 15 Nov. 1946; *s* of John Barber and Jenny Barber (*née* Roshan Mirza); *m* 1972, Mary Margaret Hoffman; three *d*. *Educ:* Hall Sch., Hampstead; Uppingham Sch., Rutland; Trinity Coll., Cambridge (BA, MA); Brunel Univ. (MA, CQSW). Res. student, 1970–73; nursing asst, Cassell Hosp., 1973–74; social worker, 1974–79, Team Leader, 1979–85, Principal Officer, 1985–88, RBK&C; Asst Dir (Children and Families), London Borough of Ealing, 1988–93; Controller of Community Services, London Borough of Barnet, 1993–99. Child Protection Adviser, dio. of Oxford, 2003–. Chm., Springboard Family Project, 2004–. Trustee: British Assoc. (formerly Agencies) for Adoption and Fostering, 1999–2000; Parents and Children Together, 2004–05; Hampshire and Thames Valley Circles of Support and Accountability, 2008–. Treas., Charles Williams Soc., 2001–. *Publications:* contrib. reviews and articles to TES, Community Care, Adoption and Fostering, etc. *Recreations:* playing the piano, collecting books and CDs, visiting cathedral cities. *Address:* c/o Diocesan Church House, North Hinksey, Oxford OX2 0NB.

BARBER, Sir (Thomas) David, 3rd Bt *cr* 1960, of Greasley, Nottingham; self-employed philatelist; *b* 18 Nov. 1937; *o s* of Col Sir William Francis Barber, 2nd Bt and his 1st wife, Diana Constance Barber (*née* Lloyd) (*d* 1984); *S* father, 1995; *m* 1st, 1971, Amanda Mary Healing (*née* Rabone) (marr. diss. 1976); one *s*; 2nd, 1978 Jeannine Mary Boyle (*née* Gurney); one *s* one *d*. *Educ:* Eton; Trinity Coll., Cambridge (MA). 2nd Lieut, RA, 1958–61. *Heir: s* Thomas Edward Barber [*b* 14 March 1973; *m* 2004, Davina Alice, *o d* of Anthony Duckworth-Chad, OBE; two *d* (twins)]. *Address:* Windrush House, Inkpen, Hungerford, Berks RG17 9QY. *Clubs:* Free Foresters.

BARBER, Trevor Wing; His Honour Judge Barber; a Circuit Judge, since 1992; *b* 10 June 1943; *s* of Robert and Margaret Barber; *m* 1967, Judith Penelope Downey; one *s* one *d*. *Educ:* Worksop Coll.; Newcastle Univ. (LLB). Called to the Bar, Inner Temple, 1967; practice in Sheffield, 1967–92. *Recreations:* gardening, golf, reading. *Address:* Juniper Lodge, Hillfoot Road, Totley, Sheffield S17 3AX.

BARBER, Prof. William Joseph, Hon. OBE 1981; Professor of Economics, Wesleyan University, Middletown, Conn, USA, 1965–93; *b* 13 Jan. 1925; *s* of Ward Barber; *m* 1955, Sheila Mary Marr; three *s*. *Educ:* Harvard Univ. (AB); Balliol Coll., Oxford (BA 1st Cl. Hons, 1951, MA 1955); DPhil (Nuffield Coll.) 1958. Served War, US Army, 1943–46. Lectr in Econs, Balliol Coll., Oxford, 1956; Wesleyan University: Dept of Economics, 1957–93; Asst Prof., 1957–61; Associate Prof., 1961–65; Prof., 1965–93; Andrews Prof., 1972–93; Andrews Prof. Emeritus, 1994–; Acting Pres., Aug.–Oct. 1988. Research Associate: Oxford Univ. Inst. of Economics and Statistics, 1962–63; Twentieth Century Fund, South Asian Study, 1961–62. Amer. Sec., Rhodes Scholarship Trust, 1970–80. Pres., Hist. of Econs Soc., 1989–90 (Distinguished Fellow, 2002). Hon. DLitt Wesleyan, 2005. *Publications:* The Economy of British Central Africa, 1961; A History of Economic Thought, 1967; contributor to Asian Drama: an inquiry into the poverty of nations (with Gunnar Myrdal and others), 1968; British Economic Thought and India 1600–1858, 1975; (jtly) Exhortation and Controls: the search for a wage-price policy, 1975; Energy Policy in Perspective, 1981; From New Era to New Deal: Herbert Hoover, the economists, and American economic policy 1921–1933, 1985; (ed, and jt author) Breaking the Academic Mould: economists and American higher learning in the nineteenth century, 1988; (ed) Perspectives on the History of Economic Thought, vols V and VI, 1991; Designs within Disorder: Franklin D. Roosevelt, the economists, and the shaping of American economic policy 1933–1945, 1996; (ed) Works of Irving Fisher, 14 vols, 1997; (ed) Early American Economic Thought series, 6 vols, 2004; Gunnar Myrdal: an intellectual biography, 2007; contribs to professional jls. *Address:* 306 Pine Street, Middletown, CT 06457, USA. *T:* (860) 3462612.

BARBIERI, Margaret Elizabeth, (Mrs M. E. Barbieri-Webb); freelance ballet teacher and coach, since 1990; Artistic Director, Images of Dance, since 1990; *b* 2 March 1947; *d* of Ettore Barbieri and Lea Barbieri; *m* 1982, Iain Webb, Artistic Dir, Sarasota Ballet Co.; one *s*. *Educ:* Convent High Sch., Durban, S Africa. Trained with Iris Manning and Brownie Sutton, S Africa; Royal Ballet Sen. Sch., 1963; joined Royal Ballet, 1965; Principal, 1970; Sen. Principal, SWRB, 1974–89. Dir, Classical Graduate Course, London Studio Centre, 1990–; guest teacher, Royal Ballet Sch., 1990–94. Gypsy Girl, Two Pigeons, 1966; 1st Giselle, Covent Garden, 1968; 1st Sleeping Beauty, Leeds, 1969; 1st Swan Lake, Frankfurt, 1977, Covent Garden, 1983; 1st Romeo and Juliet, Covent Garden, 1979; 1st Sleeping Beauty, Covent Garden, 1985. Other roles with Royal Ballet: La Fille mal Gardée, Two Pigeons, The Dream, Façade, Wedding Bouquet, Rendezvous (Ashton); Lady and the Fool, Card Game, Pineapple Poll (Cranko); The Invitation, Solitaire, (Summer) The Four Seasons (MacMillan); Checkmate, The Rake's Progress (de Valois); Grosse Fugue, Tilt (van Manen); Lilac Garden (Tudor); Fête Etrange (Howard); Grand Tour (Layton); Summer Garden (Hynd); Game Piano (Thorpe), 1978; Cinderella (Killar), 1978; Cinderella (Rodrigues), 1979; Papillon, The Taming of the Shrew, 1980; Coppélia, Les Sylphides, Raymonda Act III, Spectre de la Rose; La Vivandière, 1982; Petrushka, 1984. Roles created: Knight Errant (Tudor), 1968; From Waking Sleep (Drew), 1970; Ante-Room (Cauley), 1971; Oscar Wilde (Layton), 1972; Sacred Circles and The Sword (Drew), 1973; The Entertainers (Killar), 1974; Charlotte Brontë (Hynd), 1974; Summertide (Wright), 1977; Metamorphosis (Bintley), 1984; Flowers of the Forest (Bintley), 1985; The Wand of Youth (Corder), 1985. Recreated: Pavlova's Dragonfly Solo, 1977; The Dying Swan, produced by Dame Alicia Markova after Fokine, 1985. Guest artist, 1990–92, guest teacher, 1991–92, Birmingham Royal Ballet. Staged for Images of Dance: Les Sylphides, Façade, 1991; Rake's Progress, 1992; Pineapple Poll, La Bayadère, 1993; Raymonda, 1994; Swan Lake, 1995; Paquita, 1996; staged: Façade and Raymonda Act 3 for K Ballet Co., Japan, 2003; Façade for Oregon Ballet Th. Co., Portland, 2004; The Two Pigeons for K Ballet Co., Japan and State Ballet of Georgia, Tbilisi, 2006. Travelled with Royal Ballet to Australia, Canada, China, Egypt, Far East, France, Germany, Greece, Holland, Israel, Italy, Japan, New Zealand, Portugal, Spain, Switzerland, Yugoslavia, India and North and South America; guest appearances, USA, Germany, S Africa, France, Norway, Czechoslovakia. TV Appearances in: Spectre de la Rose; Grosse Fugue; Giselle; Coppelia; Checkmate; Metamorphosis; Markova master classes. Gov., Royal Ballet, 1991–. *Recreations:* music (classical), theatre, gardening. *Address:* Chiswick.

BARBOSA, Rubens Antonio, Hon. GCVO 1997 (Hon. LVO 1969); President and Chief Executive officer, Rubens Barbosa & Associates, since 2004; *b* 13 June 1938; *s* of José Orlando Barbosa and Lice Farina Barbosa; *m* 1969, Maria Ignez Correa da Costa Barbosa; one *s* one *d*. *Educ:* Univ. of São Paulo, Brazil (Law graduate); LSE (MA); other degrees in economics, finance and politics. Exec. Sec., Brazilian Trade Commn with socialist countries of Eastern Europe, 1976–84; Head of Staff, Min. of External Relations, 1985–86; Under-Sec. Gen., Multilateral and Special Pol Affairs, 1986; Head, Internat. Affairs, Min. of Economy, 1987–88; Ambassador and Perm. Rep. to Latin-Amer. Integration Assoc., 1988–91; Under-Sec. Gen., Regl Integration, Econ. Affairs and Foreign Trade, Min. of External Relations, and Co-ordinator for Mercosur, Brazil, 1991–93; Ambassador: to UK, 1994–99; to USA, 1999–2004. Pres., Assoc. of Coffee Producing Countries, 1993–99. Grand Cross, Order of Rio Branco (Brazil); French Legion of Honour; orders from Argentina and Mexico; honours from Germany, Belgium, Italy, Iran, Portugal. *Publications:* America Latina em Perspectiva: a integração regional da retórica à realidade, 1991; The Mercosur Codes, 2000; articles in newspapers and learned jls. *Recreations:* tennis, classical music. *Address:* (office) Avenida Brigadeiro Faria Lima 2055, 9º andar, São Paulo, SP, Brazil.

BARBOUR, James Jack, OBE 1992; Chief Executive, Lothian NHS Board, since 2001; *b* 16 Jan. 1953; *s* of late Thomas Jack Barbour and Flora Jean Barbour (*née* Murray); one *s* two *d*; partner, Julie Barnes. *Educ:* Madras Coll., St Andrews; Univ. of Strathclyde (BA Jt

Hons Politics, Sociol., Econs). MHSM 1983. Grad. Mgt Trainee, NHS in Scotland, 1977–79; Administrator, Gtr Glasgow Health Bd, 1979–83; EEC Exchange scholarship in Germany, 1981; Unit Administration, Gt Ormond St Gp of Hosps, 1983–86; General Manager: Royal Manchester Children's Hosp., 1986–87; Aberdeen Royal Infirmary, 1987–92; Chief Executive: Aberdeen Royal Hosps NHS Trust, 1992–94; Central Manchester Healthcare NHS Trust, 1994–98; Sheffield HA, 1998–2001. Alumnus, London Business Sch. Develt Prog., 1989. Hon. Prof., Queen Margaret Univ. (formerly Queen Margaret UC), 2002. Burgess, City of Aberdeen, 1992. *Recreation:* trying to stay fit! *Address:* Lothian NHS Board, Deaconess House, 148 Pleasance, Edinburgh EH8 9RS. *T:* (0131) 536 9000. *Club:* Royal Northern (Aberdeen).

BARBOUR, Dame Margaret, DBE 2002 (CBE 1991); DL; Chairman, J. Barbour & Sons Ltd, since 1972 (Director, 1969–72); *b* 1 Feb. 1940; *d* of David and Mary Ann Davies; *m* 1st, 1964, John Malcolm Barbour (*d* 1968); one *d* ; 2nd, 1991, David William Ash. *Educ:* Middlesborough High Sch.; Battersea Poly. (DipEd). Teacher: Elliot Sch., Putney, 1961–64; Church High Sch., Newcastle upon Tyne, 1964–66. DL Tyne and Wear, 1992. Hon. DBA Sunderland, 1994; Hon. DCL Newcastle, 1998. *Recreations:* swimming, bridge, collecting antiques. *Address:* J. Barbour & Sons Ltd, Simonside, South Shields, Tyne and Wear NE34 9PD. *T:* (0191) 455 4444, *Fax:* (0191) 427 4259.

BARBOUR, Muriel Janet; *see* Gray, M. J.

BARBOUR, Very Rev. Prof. Robert Alexander Stewart, KCVO 1991; MC 1945; Professor of New Testament Exegesis, University of Aberdeen, 1971–82; Master of Christ's College, Aberdeen, 1977–82; an Extra Chaplain to the Queen in Scotland since 1991 (Chaplain-in-Ordinary to the Queen, 1976–91); Dean of the Chapel Royal in Scotland, 1981–91; Prelate of the Priory of Scotland of the Order of St John, 1977–93; *b* 11 May 1921; *s* of George Freeland Barbour and Helen Victoria (*née* Hepburne-Scott); *m* 1950, Margaret Isobel Pigot; three *s* one *d. Educ:* Rugby Sch.; Balliol Coll., Oxford (MA 1946); Univ. of St Andrews (BD 1952); Yale Univ. (STM 1953). Sec., Edinburgh Christian Council for Overseas Students, 1953–55; Lectr and Sen. Lectr in NT Lang., Lit. and Theol., Univ. of Edinburgh, 1955–71. Hensley Henson Lectr, Univ. of Oxford, 1983–84. Moderator, Gen. Assembly of Church of Scotland, 1979–80. Chm., Scottish Churches' Council, 1982–86. Hon. Sec., Studiorum Novi Testamenti Societas, 1970–77. Chm. Governors, Rannoch Sch., 1973–79. Hon. DD St Andrews, 1979. *Publications:* The Scottish Horse 1939–45, 1950; Traditio-Historical Criticism of the Gospels, 1972; What is the Church for?, 1973; articles in various jls. *Recreations:* music, walking, forestry. *Address:* Old Fincastle, Pitlochry, Perthshire PH16 5RJ. *T:* (01796) 473209. *Club:* New (Edinburgh).

BARCLAY, Prof. (Alan) Neil, DPhil; Scientific Staff, Medical Research Council, Sir William Dunn School of Pathology, University of Oxford, since 1978; Titular Professor of Molecular Immunology, University of Oxford, since 1998; *b* 12 March 1950; *s* of Frank Rodney Barclay and late Betty Cowie Barclay (*née* Watson); *m* 1975, Ella Geraldine Quinn; two *s* one *d. Educ:* Hardye's Sch., Dorchester; Oriel Coll., Oxford (DPhil Biochem 1976). Res. Fellow, Inst. of Neurobiology, Univ. of Göteborg, Sweden, 1976–78; Scientific Staff, MRC Cellular Immunol. Unit, Oxford, 1978–99. Academic Advr, Oxford Univ. Bioinformatics Centre, 1990–2000. Chm., Everest Biotech Ltd, 1999–. Hon. Mem., Scandinavian Soc. of Immunology, 1993. *Publications:* (jtly) The Leucocyte Antigen Factsbook, 1993, 2nd edn 1997; contribs to scientific jls. *Recreations:* literature, listening to music, writing stories (unpublished). *Address:* Sir William Dunn School of Pathology, Oxford University, South Parks Road, Oxford OX1 3RE. *T:* (01865) 275598.

BARCLAY, Christopher Francis Robert, CMG 1967; Secretary, Government Hospitality Fund, 1976–80; *b* 8 June 1919; *s* of late Captain Robert Barclay, RA (retired) and late Annie Douglas Dowdeswell Barclay (*née* Davidson); *m* 1st, 1950, Clare Justice Troutbeck (marr. diss., 1962); two *s* one *d*; 2nd, 1962, Diana Elizabeth Goodman; one *s* one *d. Educ:* Eton Coll.; Magdalen Coll., Oxford (MA). 2nd Lieut The Rifle Bde, 1940; Capt. 1942; Major 1943; served in Middle East; Political Officer, Northern Iraq, 1945; Brit. Embassy, Baghdad, 1946. Foreign Office, 1946; Second Sec., British Embassy, Cairo, 1947; First Sec., Foreign Office, 1950; Brit. Embassy, Bonn, 1953; FO, 1956; Regional Information Officer, Beirut, 1960; FO, 1961; Counsellor and Head of Information Research Dept, 1962–66; Head of Personnel Dept (Training and General), FCO, 1967–69; Asst Sec., CSD, 1969–73; DoE, 1973–76. Chm., Jt Nat. Horse Educn and Trng Council, 1988–90. Mem. Council, City Univ., 1976–84. Master, Saddlers' Co., 1983–84. FRSA 1984. *Address:* Croft Edge, Painswick, Glos GL6 6XH. *T:* (01452) 812332.

BARCLAY, Sir Colville Herbert Sanford, 14th Bt *cr* 1668; painter; *b* 7 May 1913; *s* of late Rt Hon. Sir Colville Adrian de Rune Barclay, 3rd *s* of 11th Bt, and Sarita Enriqueta, *d* of late Herbert Ward; *S* uncle, 1930; *m* 1949, Rosamond Grant Renton Elliott; three *s. Educ:* Eton, Trinity Coll., Oxford. Third Sec., Diplomatic Service, 1937–41; enlisted in Navy, Nov. 1941; Sub-Lieut RNVR 1942; Lieut 1943; Lieut Commander 1945; demobilised, 1946. Exhibitor: Royal Academy, RBA, London Group, Bradford City and Brighton Art Galleries. Chm. Royal London Homoeopathic Hospital, 1970–74 (Vice-Chm., 1961–65; Chm., League of Friends, 1974–84). Plant-hunting expedns to Crete, Turkey, Cyprus, Réunion, Mauritius and Nepal, 1966–81. *Publications:* Crete: checklist of the vascular plants, 1986; articles in botanical jls. *Recreation:* gardening. *Heir: s* Robert Colraine Barclay [*b* 12 Feb. 1950; *m* 1980, Lucilia Saboia (marr. diss. 1986), *y d* of Carlos Saboia de Albuquerque, Rio de Janeiro; one *s* one *d*]. *Address:* 23 High Street, Broughton, near Stockbridge, Hants SO20 8AE.

BARCLAY, Sir David (Rowat), Kt 2000; Joint Proprietor: Littlewoods, since 2002; The Daily Telegraph, Sunday Telegraph, Spectator magazine and Apollo and business magazines, since 2004. Joint Proprietor: Howard Hotel, 1975–2000; Mirabeau Hotel, Monaco, 1979–; The European, 1992–98; Scotsman Publications, 1995–2006; Ritz Hotel, 1995–; Cavendish Hotel, London, 2006–. Mem., Chief Pleas, Sark, 1993–. Jt Founder and Trustee, David and Frederick Barclay Foundn. Hon. Dr Glasgow, 1998. Officier, Ordre de Saint Charles (Monaco), 2000.

See also Sir F. H. Barclay.

BARCLAY, Sir Frederick (Hugh), Kt 2000; Joint Proprietor: Littlewoods, since 2002; The Daily Telegraph, Sunday Telegraph, Spectator magazine and Apollo and business magazines, since 2004. Former estate agent. Joint Proprietor: Howard Hotel, 1975–2000; Mirabeau Hotel, Monaco, 1979–; The European, 1992–98; Scotsman Publications, 1995–2006; Ritz Hotel, 1995–; Cavendish Hotel, London, 2006–. Jt Founder and Trustee, David and Frederick Barclay Foundn. Hon. Dr Glasgow, 1998. Officier, Ordre de Saint Charles (Monaco), 2000.

See also Sir D. R. Barclay.

BARCLAY, Hugh Maben, CB 1992; Clerk of Public Bills, House of Commons, 1988–91; *b* 20 Feb. 1927; *s* of late William Barclay, FRCS, and late Mary Barclay; *m* 1956, Hilda Johnston; one *s* one *d. Educ:* Fettes Coll., Edinburgh (exhbnr); Gonville and Caius

Coll., Cambridge (schol.). Served Royal Artillery, 1948. House of Commons: Asst Clerk, 1950; Sen. Clerk, 1955; Dep. Principal Clerk, 1967; Principal Clerk, 1976; Clerk of Standing Cttees, 1976; Clerk of Private Bills, 1982. *Address:* 29 Gheluvelt Court, Brook Street, Barbourne, Worcester WR1 1JB. *T:* (01905) 330296.

BARCLAY, James Christopher, OBE 2006; Chairman: M & G Equity Investment Trust PLC, since 1998 (Director, since 1996); LTP Trade PLC, since 2000; *b* 7 July 1945; *s* of late Theodore David Barclay and Anne Barclay; *m* 1974, Rolleen Anne, *d* of late Lt-Col Arthur Forbes and Joan Forbes; one *s* one *d. Educ:* Harrow. Served 15th/19th The King's Royal Hussars, 1964–67. Dep. Chm., 1981–85, Chm., 1985–98, Cater Allen Hldgs PLC; Chm., Cater Ryder & Co. Ltd, 1981. Director: Abbey National Treasury Services plc, 1997–98; Abbey National Offshore Hldgs Ltd, 1998–2000; Thos Agnew & Sons Ltd, 1998–; New Fulcrum Investment Trust plc, 1999–2006; Liontrust Knowledge Economy Trust PLC, 2001–03; Rathbone Brothers PLC, 2003–. Dir, UK Debt Mgt Office, 2000–05. Chm., London Discount Market Assoc., 1988–90. *Recreations:* fresh air pursuits. *Address:* Rivers Hall, Waldringfield, Woodbridge, Suffolk IP12 4QX. *Clubs:* Boodle's, Pratt's.

BARCLAY, John Alistair; Executive Director, Royal Bank of Scotland Group plc, retired; *b* 5 Dec. 1933; *m* 1963, Mary Tierney (*née* Brown); three *d. Educ:* Banff Academy. FCIBS. Joined Royal Bank of Scotland, 1949; Chief City Manager, 1982–84; seconded to Williams & Glyn's Bank (Asst Gen. Manager), 1984–85; Exec. Vice-Pres., NY, 1985–88; Sen. Gen. Manager, UK Banking, 1988–89; Exec. Dir, International, 1989–90; Man. Dir, Corporate and Institutional Banking, 1990–92; Dep. Gp Chief Exec., 1992–94. *Recreations:* travel, golf, reading, gardening, curling, photography, good food and wine.

BARCLAY, Prof. John Martyn Gurney, PhD; Lightfoot Professor of Divinity, Durham University, since 2003; *b* 31 July 1958; *s* of Oliver and Dorothy Barclay; *m* 1981, Diana Knox; two *s* one *d. Educ:* Queens' Coll., Cambridge (BA 1981; PhD 1986). University of Glasgow: Lectr, 1984–96; Sen. Lectr, 1996–2000; Prof., 2000–03. *Publications:* Obeying the Truth: Paul's ethics in Galatians, 1988; Jews in the Mediterranean Diaspora, 1996; Colossians and Philemon, 1997; Flavius Josephus: translation and commentary, Vol. 10, Against Apion, 2007. *Recreations:* cycling, walking. *Address:* Kimblesworth House, Kimblesworth, Chester-le-Street DH2 3QP. *T:* (0191) 371 0388; *e-mail:* john.barclay@durham.ac.uk.

BARCLAY, Neil; *see* Barclay, A. N.

BARCLAY, Patrick; football columnist, Sunday Telegraph, since 1996; *b* 15 Aug. 1947; *s* of Guy Deghy and Patricia Wighton; one *s* one *d. Educ:* Dundee High Sch. Sub-editor, 1966–77, football writer, 1977–86, The Guardian; football columnist: Today, 1986; The Independent, 1986–91; The Observer, 1991–96. *Recreations:* reading, travel. *Address:* c/o The Sunday Telegraph, 111 Buckingham Palace Road, SW1W 0DT.

BARCLAY, Paul Robert; His Honour Judge Barclay; a Circuit Judge, since 1998; *s* of late John Alexander Barclay and of Mabel Elizabeth Barclay; *m* 1972, Sarah Louise Jones; two *s* two *d. Educ:* Nottingham High Sch.; St John's Coll., Cambridge (MA 1971). Called to the Bar, Middle Temple, 1972; in practice at the Bar, 1972–98; an Asst Recorder, 1992–96; a Recorder, 1996–98. *Recreation:* village cricket. *Address:* Bristol County Court, Small Street, Bristol BS1 1DA.

BARCLAY, Sir Peter (Maurice), Kt 1992; CBE 1984; Chairman, 1996–2001, Trustee, 1972–2001, Joseph Rowntree Foundation (formerly Joseph Rowntree Memorial Trust); *b* 6 March 1926; *s* of George Ronald Barclay and Josephine (*née* Lambert); *m* 1953, Elizabeth Mary Wright; one *s* two *d. Educ:* Bryanston Sch.; Magdalene Coll., Cambridge (MA). Served RNVR, 1944–46. Admitted Solicitor, 1952; Senior Partner, 1964–74, Partner, 1974–88, Beachcroft & Co. Chm., The Family Fund Trust, 1973–97. Chairman: Cttee on Roles and Tasks of Social Workers, 1981–82; Social Security Adv. Cttee, 1984–93; Nat. Family Mediation, 1994–96. Non-exec. Mem., DSS Deptl Bd, 1994–97. Pres., National Inst. for Social Work, 1988 (Chm., 1973–85); Chm., Horticultural Therapy, 1989–94; Pres., St Pancras and Humanist Housing Assoc., 2000– (Vice Pres., St Pancras Housing Assoc., 1994–2000; Mem., 1971–93, Chm., 1983–91, Management Cttee). Governor, Bryanston Sch., 1972–88; Council Mem., PSI, 1989–95; Trustee, Nat. Family and Parenting Inst., 1999–2005. DUniv: Stirling, 1994; York, 1996. *Recreations:* gardening, painting. *Address:* Mulberry House, Sion Hill, Bath BA1 2UL. *T:* (01225) 424868; *e-mail:* peterbarclay@tiscali.co.uk.

BARCLAY, Yvonne Fay, (Mrs William Barclay); *see* Minton, Y. F.

BARDA, Clive Blackmore; freelance photographer, since 1968; *b* 14 Jan. 1945; *s* of Gaston Barda and Marjorie (*née* Blackmore); *m* 1970, Rosalind Mary Whiteley; three *s. Educ:* Bryanston Sch.; Birkbeck Coll., London (BA Hons Modern Langs). Photographer, specialising in performing arts, esp. classical music, opera and theatre. Exhibitions: RFH, London, 1979; Science Museum, London, 1985; RNCM, Manchester, 1980; Perth, Australia, 1981; RPS, Bath, 1985; Nat. Mus. of Photography, Film and TV, Bradford, 1988; Nagaoka, Japan, 1996; Tokyo, 1998; Edinburgh, 2001; Paris, 2002. FRSA 1996. *Publications:* The Sculpture of David Wynne, 1975; The Complete Phantom of the Opera, 1988; The Complete Aspects of Love, 1990; Celebration!, 1996; Performance!, 2001; The Power of the Ring, 2007. *Recreations:* cooking, fell-walking, singing in the church choir, classical music, opera, theatre, dance, watching cricket. *T:* (020) 8579 5202, *Fax:* (020) 8840 1083; *e-mail:* clivebarda@pobox.com. *Clubs:* Garrick, MCC.

BARDEN, Prof. Laing, CBE 1990; PhD, DSc; Vice-Chancellor, University of Northumbria at Newcastle, 1992–96 (Director, Newcastle upon Tyne Polytechnic, 1978–92); *b* 29 Aug. 1931; *s* of Alfred Eversfield Barden and Edna (*née* Laing); *m* 1956, Nancy Carr; two *s* one *d. Educ:* Washington Grammar Sch.; Durham Univ. (BSc, MSc). R. T. James & Partners, 1954–59. Liverpool Univ., 1959–62 (PhD); Manchester Univ., 1962–69 (DSc); Strathclyde Univ., 1969–74; Newcastle upon Tyne Polytechnic, subseq. Univ. of Northumbria at Newcastle, 1974–96. Director: Microelectronics Applications Res. Inst. Ltd, 1980–90; Tyne and Wear Enterprise Trust Ltd, 1982–96; Newcastle Technology Centre Ltd, 1985–90; Newcastle Initiative, 1988–96. Chm., Bubble Foundn UK, 1997–2006. Mem., Council for Industry and Higher Educn, 1987–96. *Publications:* contribs to Geotechnique, Proc. ICE, Jl Amer. Soc. CE, Qly Jl Eng. Geol. *Recreations:* cricket, soccer, snooker. *Address:* 7 Westfarm Road, Cleadon, Tyne and Wear SR6 7UG. *T:* (0191) 536 2317. *Clubs:* Mid Boldon (Boldon), Boldon Cricket.

BARDER, Sir Brian (Leon), KCMG 1992; HM Diplomatic Service, retired; High Commissioner to Australia, 1991–94; *b* 20 June 1934; *s* of Harry and Vivien Barder; *m* 1958, Jane Maureen Cornwell; two *d* one *s. Educ:* Sherborne; St Catharine's Coll., Cambridge (BA). 2nd Lieut, 7 Royal Tank Regt, 1952–54. Colonial Office, 1957; Private Sec. to Permanent Under-Sec., 1960–61; HM Diplomatic Service, 1965; First Secretary, UK Mission to UN, 1964–68; FCO, 1968–70; First Sec. and Press Attaché, Moscow, 1971–73; Counsellor and Head of Chancery, British High Commn, Canberra, 1973–77; Canadian Nat. Defence Coll., Kingston, Ontario, 1977–78; Head of Central and

Southern, later Southern African Dept, FCO, 1978–82; Ambassador to Ethiopia, 1982–86; Ambassador to Poland, 1986–88; High Comr to Nigeria, and concurrently Ambassador to Benin, 1988–91. Mem., Commonwealth Observer Mission for Namibian elections, 1994. ODA Consultant on Diplomatic Trng, Eastern and Central Europe, 1996. Panel of Chairs, CSSB, 1995–96. Member: Bd of Management, Royal Hosp. for Neuro-disability, 1996–2003; Cttee, ESU Centre for Speech and Debate (formerly Internat. Debate and Communication Trng), 1996–; Special Immigration Appeals Commn, 1998–2004. Editl Consultant, Dictionary of Diplomacy, 2001 and 2003. CON 1989. *Publications:* (contrib.) Fowler's Modern English Usage, 3rd edn 1996; contrib. Pol Qly, London Rev. of Books, Guardian, etc. *Recreations:* computer, music, campaigning, cycling, writing letters to the newspapers. *Address:* 20 Victoria Mews, Earlsfield, SW18 3PY; *e-mail:* brianbarder@compuserve.com; *web:* www.barder.com. *Club:* Oxford and Cambridge.

See also O. M. Barder, E. L. Wen.

BARDER, Owen Matthew; Director, International Finance and Development Effectiveness (formerly Global Development Effectiveness), Department for International Development, since 2006; *b* 20 Feb. 1967; *s* of Sir Brian Leon Barder, *qv*; partner, Grethe Petersen. *Educ:* Sevenoaks Sch.; New Coll., Oxford (BA Hons PPE 1988); London Sch. of Econs (MSc Econs 1991). HM Treasury, 1988–96, Private Sec. to the Chancellor of the Exchequer, 1991–94; Dept of Finance, S Africa, 1997–99; Private Sec., Econ. Affairs, to the Prime Minister, 1999–2000; Department for International Development: Hd, Africa Policy, 2000–02; Dir, Inf., Communications, Knowledge, 2002–04; Center for Global Develt, Washington (on special leave), 2004–06. Vis. Scholar, Univ. of Calif, Berkeley, 2004–06. Non-exec. Dir, One World International, 2000–04. *Publications:* Making Markets for Vaccines (jtly), 2004; Running for Fitness, 2002; Get Fit Running, 2004. *Recreations:* running, information technology, cycling. *Address:* Department for International Development, 1 Palace Street, SW1E 5HE. *T:* 07825 053467; *e-mail:* owen@barder.com; *web:* www.owen.org. *Club:* Serpentine Running.

BARDSLEY, Andrew Tromlow; JP; General Manager and Chief Executive, Harlow Development Corporation, 1973–80; *b* 7 Dec. 1927; *o s* of Andrew and Gladys Ada Bardsley; *m* 1954, June Patricia (*née* Ford); one *s* one *d*. *Educ:* Ashton-under-Lyne Grammar Sch.; Manchester Coll. of Art. CEng, FICE. Royal Navy, 1947–49. Entered Local Govt (Municipal Engrg), 1950; various appts leading to Borough Engr and Surveyor, Worksop MB, 1962–69; Director of Technical Services: Corby New Town, 1969–71; Luton CBC, 1971–73; Principal, Westgate Develt Consultancy, 1981–93. Gen. Comr. of Taxes in England and Wales, 1987–92. JP Essex, 1975 (Dep. Chm., Harlow Bench, 1987–92). *Recreations:* golf, music, gardening, most spectator sports. *Address:* 2 Carrbridge Gardens, Talbot Woods, Bournemouth, Dorset BH3 7EL. *T:* (01202) 537954. *Club:* Bournemouth Bowling (Past Pres.).

BAREAU, Peter John, CBE 2002; Senior Adviser, Corporate Value Associates, since 2003; Chief Executive, National Savings and Investments (formerly National Savings), 1996–2002; *b* 1 June 1942; *s* of late Paul Bareau, OBE and Kitty Bareau (*née* Gibson); *m* 1st, 1967, Irene Nelson (marr. diss.); one *s* one *d*; 2nd, 1976, Karen Giesemann (*d* 2001); one *s* two *d*; 3rd, 2003, Ruth Holyoak (*née* Hardy); two step *s*. *Educ:* Eton Coll.; Queens' Coll., Cambridge (MA). With Bank of London & S America in UK, USA, Paraguay and Spain, 1966–72; with Lloyds Bank Internat. in UK and Brazil, 1973–84; Lloyds Bank PLC: General Manager: Strategic Planning, 1985–86; Europe, ME and Internat. Pvte Banking, 1987–91; Personnel, 1992–96. Chm., Surrey and Sussex SHA, 2003–06. Indep. Mem., Energy Gp Adv. Bd, DTI, 2004–06. Trustee, Breast Cancer Campaign, 2002–06. Hon. FCMC 2003. *Address:* Old Coach House, Alldens Lane, Godalming, Surrey GU8 4AP. *T:* (01483) 415010.

BARENBLATT, Prof. Grigory Isaakovich, PhD; ScD; Professor of Mathematics, University of California at Berkeley, since 1997; G. I. Taylor Professor of Fluid Mechanics, University of Cambridge, 1992–94, now Emeritus, and Hon. Fellow, Gonville and Caius College, Cambridge, 1999 (Fellow, 1994–99); *b* 10 July 1927; *s* of Isaak Grigorievich Barenblatt and Nadezhda Veniaminovna (*née* Kagan); *m* 1952, Iraida Nikolaevna Kochina; two *d*. *Educ:* Moscow Univ. (MSc 1950; PhD 1953; ScD 1957); Univ. of Cambridge (MA 1993). Res. Scientist, Inst. of Petroleum, USSR Acad. of Sci., Moscow, 1953–61; Prof. and Hd, Dept of Mechanics of Solids, Inst. of Mechanics, Moscow Univ., 1961–75; Hd, Theoretical Dept, Inst. of Oceanology, USSR Acad. of Sci., Moscow, 1975–92. Foreign Member: Amer. Acad. of Arts and Scis, 1975; Royal Soc., 2000; Foreign Associate: US Nat. Acad. of Engrg, 1992; US Nat. Acad. of Sci., 1997; MAE, 1993. Hon. DTech Royal Inst. of Technol., Stockholm, 1989; Hon. Dr Civil Engrg Torino Polytechnic Inst., 2005. Laureate, Panetti Gold Medal and Prize, 1995; Lagrange Medal, Accademia dei Lincei, 1995; G. I. Taylor Medal, Amer. Soc. of Engrg Sci., 1999; J. C. Maxwell Prize, Internat. Congress on Industrial and Applied Maths, 1999; S. P. Timoshenko Medal, ASME, 2005. *Publications:* Similarity, Self-Similarity, and Intermediate Asymptotics, 1979; Dimensional Analysis, 1987; (jtly) Theory of Fluid Flows in Porous Media, 1990; Scaling, Self-Similarity, and Intermediate Asymptotics, 1996; Scaling, 2003; contrib. Jl Applied Maths and Mechanics, Physics of Atmosphere and Ocean, Jl Fluid Mechanics. *Recreation:* historical reading. *Address:* Department of Mathematics, University of California, Berkeley, CA 94720–3840, USA.

BARENBOIM, Daniel; pianist and conductor; Musical Director: Chicago Symphony Orchestra, 1991–2006; Berlin State Opera, since 1992; Principal Guest Conductor, La Scala, Milan, since 2006; *b* Buenos Aires, 15 Nov. 1942; *s* of Enrique Barenboim and late Aida Barenboim (*née* Schuster); *m* 1st, 1967, Jacqueline du Pré (*d* 1987); 2nd, 1988, Elena Bashkirova; two *s*. *Educ:* Santa Cecilia Acad., Rome; studied with his father; coached by Edwin Fischer, Nadia Boulanger, and Igor Markevitch. Debut as pianist with: Israel Philharmonic Orchestra, 1953; Royal Philharmonic Orchestra, 1956; Berlin Philharmonic Orchestra, 1963; NY Philharmonic Orchestra, 1964; Musical Dir, Orchestre de Paris, 1975–88; tours include: Australia, North and South America, Far East; regular appearances at Bayreuth, Edinburgh, Lucerne, Prague and Salzburg Festivals. Many recordings as conductor and pianist. BBC Reith Lectr, 2006. Beethoven Medal, 1958; Paderewski Medal, 1963; subsequently other awards. Legion of Honour (France), 1987. *Publications:* A Life in Music, 1991; Parallels and Paradoxes, 2002; Everything is Connected, 2008. *Address:* c/o Agence de Concerts Cæcilia, 29 rue de la Coulouvrenière, 1204 Genève, Switzerland.

BARFIELD, Julia Barbara, MBE 2000; Director, Marks Barfield Architects, since 1989; *b* 15 Nov. 1952; *d* of Arnold Robert Barfield and Iolanthe Mary Barfield; *m* 1981, David Joseph Marks, *qv*; one *s* two *d*. *Educ:* Godolphin and Latymer Sch.; AA Sch. of Architecture. Dir, Tetra Ltd, 1978–79; Architectural Asst, Richard Rogers Partnership, 1979–81; Project Architect, Foster Associates, 1981–88; Founding Dir, London Eye Co., 1994–2006. Member: Council, AA, 2001–06; Design Review Panel, CABE, 2004–; Council, Guy's and St Thomas' Hosp., 2005–; Gov., Godolphin and Latymer Sch., 2006–. *Recreation:* family, travel, arts. *Address:* Marks Barfield Architects, 50 Bromells Road, SW4 0BG. *T:* (020) 7501 0180; *e-mail:* jbarfield@marksbarfield.com.

BARFIELD, Richard Arthur; *b* 5 April 1947; *s* of Arthur Victor Harold Barfield and Margaret Hilda Barfield; *m* 1969, Alison Helen Hamilton; one *s* one *d*. *Educ:* Gt Yarmouth Grammar Sch.; Edinburgh Univ. (BSc Maths). Standard Life Assce Co., 1970–96 (Chief Investment Manager, 1988–96). Chm., Synergy G P Ltd, 1999–. Non-executive Director: Baillie Gifford Japan Investment Trust, 1998–; Merchants Investment Trust, 1999–; Edinburgh Investment Trust, 2001–; J. P. Morgan Fleming Overseas Investment Trust, 2001–; Standard Life Investments Property Income Trust, 2003–. Mem., Investment Adv. Panel, Strathclyde Pension Fund, 2004–; Chm., Investment Sub-Cttee, Rio Tinto Pension Fund, 2007–. Mem., Public Oversight Bd (formerly Public Oversight Bd for Accountancy), 2004–. FFA 1974. *Recreations:* walking, music, good food and wine. *Club:* Sloane.

BARFORD, Prof. David, DPhil; FRS 2006; FMedSci; Professor of Molecular Biology, and Co-chair, Section of Structural Biology, Institute of Cancer Research, since 1999; *b* 17 Aug. 1963; *s* of Jack and Mai Barford. *Educ:* Univ. of Bristol (BSc 1984); DPhil Oxford 1988. Research Fellow: Univ. of Oxford, 1988–90; Univ. of Dundee, 1990–91; Cold Spring Harbor Lab., NY, 1991–94; Lectr, Univ. of Oxford and Tutorial Fellow, Somerville Coll., Oxford, 1994–99. Mem. Scientific Adv. Bd, Ceptyr Corp., Seattle, 1996–2004. Mem. EMBO, 2003. FMedSci 2003. *Publications:* contribs to scientific jls. *Recreations:* classical music, reading. *Address:* Institute of Cancer Research, 237 Fulham Road, SW3 6JB. *T:* (020) 7153 5420, *Fax:* (020) 7153 5457; *e-mail:* david.barford@icr.ac.uk.

BARGERY, (Bruno Philip) Robert; Director, The Georgian Group, since 2002; *b* 4 April 1966; *s* of Geoffrey Maxwell Bargery and Barbara Ann Hill. *Educ:* Hinchley Wood Sch.; Kingston Coll.; Exeter Univ.; Exeter Coll., Oxford. DoE, 1991–95; Researcher, Royal Fine Art Commn, 1995–99; Head, Policy and Res., CABE, 1999–2001. FRSA 2003. *Address:* 33 Merganser Court, Star Place, St Katharine Docks, E1W 1AQ; *e-mail:* robert@georgiangroup.org.uk.

BARHAM, Geoffrey Simon; His Honour Judge Barham; a Circuit Judge, since 1993; *b* 23 Dec. 1945; *s* of late Denis Patrick Barham and Pleasance (*née* Brooke); *m* 1976, Sarah Seebold; one *s* one *d*. *Educ:* Malvern Coll.; Christ's Coll., Cambridge (MA). Called to the Bar, Lincoln's Inn, 1968; Asst Recorder, 1983; Recorder, 1987. *Recreation:* golf. *Club:* Norfolk (Norwich).

BARI, Dr Muhammad Abdul, MBE 2003; Secretary General, Muslim Council of Great Britain, since 2006; *b* 2 Oct. 1953; *s* of Muhammad Manikuddin and Karmunnesa Bari; *m* Sayeda Akhter; three *s* one *d*. *Educ:* King's Coll., London (PhD; PGCE). Specialist Teacher, London Bor. of Tower Hamlets. Chm., E London Mosque/London Muslim Centre. Trustee, Muslim Aid. Non-exec. Dir, LOCOG, 2005–. *Publications:* The Greatest Gift: a guide to parenting from an Islamic perspective, 2002; Building Muslim Families: challenges and expectations, 2002; Race, Religion and Muslim Identity in Britain, 2005; Marriage and Family Building in Islam, 2007. *Recreations:* reading, travelling, playing with children. *Address:* Muslim Council of Britain, PO Box 57330, London E1 2WJ. *T:* 0845 262 6786, *Fax:* (020) 7247 7079; *e-mail:* sg@mcb.org.uk.

BARING, family name of **Baron Ashburton**, of **Earl of Cromer**, of **Baron Howick of Glendale**, of **Baron Northbrook**, and of **Baron Revelstoke**.

BARING, Sir John (Francis), 3rd Bt *cr* 1911, of Nubia House, Isle of Wight; Member, Mercator Management LLC, since 1999; *b* 21 May 1947; *s* of Raymond Alexander Baring (*d* 1967) (2nd *s* of 1st Bt) and Margaret Fleetwood Baring (who *m* 1991, 6th Earl of Malmesbury, TD; she *d* 1994), *d* of late Col R. W. P. C. Campbell-Preston; *S* uncle, 1990; *m* 1st, 1971, Elizabeth Anne (marr. diss. 2004), MS, ATR (BC), Certified Psychoanalyst, *yr d* of Robert D. H. Pillitz; two *s* one *d*; 2nd, 2007, Penelope Ann Roberts. Citibank NA, 1971–72; Chemical Bank, 1972–84; Kidder, Peabody & Co. Inc., 1984–89; GPA Group Ltd, 1989; Hackman, Baring & Co., 1991–97; PricewaterhouseCoopers Securities LLC, 1997–99; Managing Partner, Mercator Capital LLC, 1999–2004. Director: Camphill Foundn, 2002–; Camphill Village USA, 2004–. Chm. Trustees, Rudolf Steiner Sch., 2002–. *Recreations:* gardening, fishing. *Heir:* *s* Julian Alexander David Baring, *b* 10 Feb. 1975. *Address:* 328 Arcadia Drive, Ancramdale, NY 12503, USA.

BARING, Nicholas Hugo, CBE 2003; Chairman, Council of Management, Baring Foundation, 1998–2004 (Member, 1973–2004); *b* 2 Jan. 1934; *er s* of Francis Anthony Baring (killed in action, 1940) and Lady Rose Baring, DCVO; *m* 1972, (Elizabeth) Diana, *d* of late Brig. Charles Crawfurd; three *s*. *Educ:* Eton (King's Schol.); Magdalene Coll., Cambridge (exhibnr, BA). Nat. service, 2nd Lieut Coldstream Guards, 1952–54. ADC to Governor of Kenya, 1957–58; joined Baring Brothers, 1958; Man. Dir, Baring Brothers & Co., 1963–86; Dir, Barings plc, 1985–94 (Dep. Chm., 1986–89). Dir, Commercial Union plc, 1968–98 (Chm., 1990–98). Mem., City Capital Markets Cttee, 1983–89 (Chm., 1983–87). Vice Pres., Liverpool Sch. of Tropical Medicine, 1982–89, 1996– (Pres., 1989–96); Chm., Bd of Trustees, Nat. Gall., 1992–96 (Trustee, 1989–96); Trustee, Fitzwilliam Museum Develt Trust (formerly Fitzwilliam Museum Trust), 1997– (Chm., 2004–). National Trust: Mem. Exec. Cttee, 1965–69 and 1979–2002; Mem. Council, 1978–2002; Chm., Finance Cttee, 1980–91. Mem. Council of Management, Architectl Heritage Fund, 1987–. Hon. LLD Liverpool, 1995; Hon. DCL: Kent, 1998; Northumbria, 2004. *Address:* The Old Rectory, Ham, Marlborough, Wilts SN8 3QR. *T:* (01488) 668081. *Club:* Brooks's, Beefsteak.

See also P. Baring.

BARING, Peter; *b* 28 Oct. 1935; *yr s* of Francis Anthony Baring (killed in action, 1940) and Lady Rose Baring, DCVO; *m* 1960, Teresa Anne Bridgeman (CBE 1998); three *s*. *Educ:* Magdalene College, Cambridge (MA English). Joined Baring Brothers & Co., 1959, Director, 1967; Chairman: Barings plc, 1989–95; Baring Asset Management, 1993–95. Dir, Inchcape, 1978–96. Dep. Chm., Provident Mutual Life Assurance Assoc., 1989–95. Chm., London Investment Banking Assoc., 1991–94. Gov., London Business Sch., 1991–95. Chm., Glyndebourne Arts Trust, 1994–96.

See also N. H. Baring.

BARKER, family name of **Baroness Trumpington**.

BARKER, Baroness *cr* 1999 (Life Peer), of Anagach in Highland; **Elizabeth Jean Barker;** management consultant, since 2008; *b* Outwood, W Yorks, 31 Jan. 1961. *Educ:* Dalziel High Sch., Motherwell; Broadway Sch., Oldham; Univ. of Southampton (BSc(SocSci) Hons Psychology). Pres., Union of Liberal Students, 1982–83. Age Concern England: Project Co-Ordinator, Opportunities for Volunteering Programme, 1983–88; Grants Officer, 1988–92; Field Officer, 1992–2008. Member: Liberal Party Nat. Exec., 1982–83; Liberal Assembly Cttee, 1984–88; Lib Dem Federal Conf. Cttee, 1988– (Chm., 1997–2004); Lib Dem Federal Policy Cttee, 1997–2003. Mem., T&GWU (ACTSS). Trustee, Andy Lawson Meml Fund. *Address:* House of Lords, SW1A 0PW.

BARKER, Prof. Andrew Dennison, PhD; FBA 2005; Professor of Classics, University of Birmingham, since 1998; *b* 24 April 1943; *s* of Edwin Barker and Nancy Ethel Barker;

m 1st, Susan Margaret Hough (marr. diss. 1976); two *s*; 2nd, 1978, Jill Davida Newman; two *s* one *d*. *Educ:* Christ's Hosp.; Queen's Coll., Oxford (BA); Australian Nat. Univ. (PhD). Lectr in Philosophy, 1970–87, Sen. Lectr, 1987–92, Univ. of Warwick; Asst Lectr in Classics, Univ. of Cambridge, 1976–78, and Fellow and Dir of Studies in Classics and Philosophy, Selwyn Coll., Cambridge, 1977–78 (on leave from Univ. of Warwick); Sen. Lectr in Classics, 1992–95, Prof., 1995, Univ. of Otago; Reader in Classics, Univ. of Birmingham, 1996–98. *Publications:* Greek Musical Writings, vol. 1, 1984, vol. 2, 1989; Scientific Method in Ptolemy's Harmonics, 2000; Euterpe: ricerche sulla musica Greca e Romana, 2002; Psicomusicologia Nella Grecia Antica, 2005; The Science of Harmonics in Classical Greece, 2007; articles on ancient Greek music and philosophy. *Recreations:* negotiations with dogs, horse, family; DIY building and land-maintenance, natural history, listening to music. *Address:* Institute of Archaeology and Antiquity, University of Birmingham, Birmingham B15 2TT. *T:* (01926) 428286; *e-mail:* andrewqbarker@hotmail.com.

BARKER, Hon. Dame Anne Judith; *see* Rafferty, Dame A. J.

BARKER, Anthony; QC 1985; a Recorder, since 1985; *b* 10 Jan. 1944. *Educ:* Newcastle-under-Lyme High Sch.; Clare Coll., Cambridge (BA Hons). Called to the Bar, Middle Temple, 1966, Bencher, 1997. Asst Recorder, 1981. Mem. Faculty, Nat. Inst. for Trial Advocacy, Gainesville, Houston, Berkeley and Colorado, USA, 1985–90. Mem., Internat. Soc. of Barristers, 2000. *Recreations:* gardening, walking, music. *Address:* Hilderstone House, Hilderstone, near Stone, Staffs ST15 8SF. *T:* (01889) 505331.

BARKER, Barry, MBE 1960; FCIS; Secretary and Chief Executive, Institute of Chartered Secretaries and Administrators (formerly Chartered Institute of Secretaries), 1976–89; *b* 28 Dec. 1929; *s* of late Francis Walter Barker and Amy Barker; *m* 1954, Dr Vira Dubash; two *s*. *Educ:* Ipswich Sch.; Trinity Coll., Oxford (MA Class. Greats). Secretary: Bombay Chamber of Commerce and Industry, 1956–62; The Metal Box Co. of India Ltd, 1962–67. Dir, Shipbuilding Industry Bd, 1967–71; Consultant at Dept of Industry, 1972; Sec., Pye Holdings Ltd, 1972–76. Chairman: Consultative Council of Professional Management Orgns, 1981–90; Nat. Endorsement Bd, Management Charter Initiative, 1990–94. Member: BTEC, 1985–94; RSA Exams Bd, 1987–94; NCVQ, 1989–92; Bd of Management, Young Vic Co., 1984–90. *Recreations:* the theatre and the arts. *Address:* 82 Darwin Court, Gloucester Avenue, NW1 7BQ. *T:* (020) 7911 0570.

BARKER, Brian John; QC 1990; **His Honour Judge Barker;** a Senior Circuit Judge, since 2000; Common Serjeant, City of London, since 2005; *b* 15 Jan. 1945; *s* of William Barker and Irene Barker (*née* Gillow); *m* 1977, Anne Judith Rafferty (*see* Dame A. J. Rafferty); three *d* (and one *d* decd). *Educ:* Strode's School, Egham; Univ. of Birmingham (LLB); Univ. of Kansas (MA). Called to the Bar, Gray's Inn, 1969, Bencher, 1999. A Recorder, 1985–2000. Mem., Senate and Bar Council, 1976–79. A Pres., Mental Health Review Tribunals, 1993–. Chm., Criminal Bar Assoc., 1998–2000. Course Dir, Criminal Continuation Seminars, Judicial Studies Bd, 2003–07. Governor: Strode's Coll., Egham; Sir John Cass Foundn, Aldgate, 2003– (Treas., 2005–07). Freeman, City of London; Liveryman, Coopers' Co., 1989– (Mem., Ct of Assts, 1995–; Master Warden, 2008–June 2009). *Recreations:* sheep rearing, golf. *Address:* Central Criminal Court, Old Bailey, EC4M 7EH. *Clubs:* Bishopsgate Ward; Rye Golf.

BARKER, Rt Rev. Clifford Conder, TD 1970; Bishop Suffragan of Selby, 1983–91; Hon. Assistant Bishop of York, since 1991; *b* 22 April 1926; *s* of Sidney and Kathleen Alice Barker; *m* 1952, Marie Edwards (*d* 1982); one *s* two *d*; 2nd, 1983, Mrs Audrey Gregson; two step *s* one step *d*. *Educ:* Oriel Coll., Oxford (BA 1950, MA 1955); St Chad's Coll., Durham (Dip. in Theol. 1952). Emergency Commn, The Green Howards, 1944–48; deacon 1952, priest 1953; Curate: All Saints', Scarborough, 1952–55; Redcar, 1955–57; Vicar: All Saints', Sculcoates, Hull, 1957–63; Rudby-in-Cleveland, 1963–70; RD of Stokesley, 1965–70; Vicar, St Olave with St Giles, York, 1970–76; RD of York, 1971–76; Canon of York, 1973–76; Bishop Suffragan of Whitby, 1976–83. CF (TA), 1958–74. *Recreations:* travel, reading, crosswords, gardening, music. *Address:* Wylde Green, 15 Oak Tree Close, Strensall, York YO32 5TE. *T:* (01904) 490406.

BARKER, Sir Colin, Kt 1991; Chairman, British Technology Group Ltd, 1983–93 (Chief Executive, 1983–85); *b* 20 Oct. 1926; *m* 1951, Beryl; three *s* one *d*. *Educ:* Hull Grammar Sch.; London and Edinburgh Univs. Ford UK, 1960–67 (Finance Dir, 1967); Finance Director: Blue Circle, 1968–70; STC, 1970–80; British Steel Corp., 1980–83. Chairman: CIN Management, 1985–93; British Investment Trust, 1985–93; MCD (UK), 1990–95; Anglian Group (formerly Anglian Windows), 1991–95; Director: Reed Internat., 1983–92; British Coal Corp., 1984–91; Edinburgh Fund Managers, 1988–93. *Address:* 12 Clune Court, Hutton Road, Shenfield, Essex CM15 8NQ.

BARKER, David; QC 1976; a Recorder of the Crown Court, 1974–98; *b* 13 April 1932; *s* of late Frederick Barker and of Amy Evelyn Barker; *m* 1957, Diana Mary Vinson Barker (*née* Duckworth); one *s* three *d*. *Educ:* Sir John Deane's Grammar Sch., Northwich; University Coll., London; Univ. of Michigan. 1st cl. hons LLB London; LLM Michigan. RAF, 1956–59. Called to Bar, Inner Temple, 1954, Bencher, 1985; practised Midland and Oxford Circuit; a Dep. High Court Judge, 1993–98. Mem., Senate of Inns of Court and the Bar, 1981–84. Member: Criminal Injuries Compensation Bd, 1990–2000; Criminal Injuries Compensation Appeals Panel, 1997–2007. Mem., Woodhouse Parish Council, 2003– (Chm., 2005–). Contested (Lab) Runcorn, 1955. *Recreations:* gardening, walking, sailing. *Address:* 17 Nanhill Drive, Woodhouse Eaves, Leics LE12 8TL. *T:* (01509) 890224. *Club:* Reform.

BARKER, Prof. David (Faubert), MA, DPhil, DSc; Professor of Zoology, University of Durham, 1962–87, now Professor Emeritus; *b* 18 Feb. 1922; *s* of Faubert and Doreen Barker; *m* 1st, 1945, Kathleen Mary Frances Pocock; three *s* two *d*; 2nd, 1978, Patricia Margaret Drake (*see* P. M. Barker); one *s* one *d*. *Educ:* Bryanston Sch.; Magdalen Coll., Oxford. DSc 1972. Senior Demy of Magdalen Coll., 1946; Leverhulme Research Scholar, Royal Coll. of Surgeons, 1946; Demonstrator in Zoology and Comparative Anatomy, Oxford, 1947; DPhil 1948; Rolleston Prizeman, 1948; Prof. of Zoology, Univ. of Hong Kong, 1950–62; led scientific expeditions to Tunisia, 1950, North Borneo, 1952; Dean of Faculty of Science, Hong Kong, 1959–60; Public Orator, Hong Kong, 1961; Sir Derman Christopherson Fellow, Durham Univ. Research Foundn, 1984–85. Emeritus Fellow, Leverhulme Trust, 1989–92. *Publications:* (Founder) Editor, Hong Kong Univ. Fisheries Journal, 1954–60; Editor, Symposium on Muscle Receptors, 1962; scientific papers, mostly on muscle innervation. *Address:* 10 The Avenue, Durham DH1 4ED. *T:* (0191) 384 0908.

BARKER, Prof. David James Purslove, CBE 2006; MD, PhD, DSc; FRCP; FRS 1998; Professor of Clinical Epidemiology, University of Southampton, since 1979 (Director, Medical Research Council Environmental Epidemiology Unit, 1983–2003); *b* 29 June 1938; *s* of Hugh Purslove and Joye Frances Barker; *m* 1st, 1960, Angela Beatrice Coddington (*d* 1980); three *s* two *d*; 2nd, 1983, Janet Elizabeth Franklin; one step *s* two step *d*. *Educ:* Oundle Sch.; Guy's Hosp. Med. Sch., London Univ. (BSc 1st Cl. Hons, 1959; MB BS 1962; PhD 1966; MD 1973). FRCP 1979. University of Birmingham: Research Fellow in Social Medicine, 1963–66; Lectr in Medicine, 1966–69; Lectr in Preventive Medicine, Makerere Univ., Uganda, 1969–72; Sen. Lectr in Clinical Epidemiology and Consultant Physician, Univ. of Southampton, 1972–79. Founder FMedSci 1998. Hon. FRCOG 1993; Hon. FRCPCH 2003. Hon. DSc Birmingham 2003. Royal Soc. Wellcome Gold Medal, 1994; Prince Mahidol Award, Prince Mahidol Award Foundn, Thailand, 2001; Danone Internat. Nutrition Award, 2005; Archbp Gandarillas Medal, Chile, 2006; Fondation Ipsen Award, Paris, 2007. *Publications:* Practical Epidemiology, 1973, 4th edn 1992; (with G. Rose) Epidemiology in Medical Practice, 1976, 5th edn (with C. Cooper and G. Rose) 1998; (with G. Rose) Epidemiology for the Uninitiated, 1979, 5th edn 2003; Fetal and Infant Origins of Adult Disease, 1992; Mothers, Babies and Disease in Later Life, 1994, 2nd edn 1998; The Best Start in Life, 2003. *Recreations:* writing, drawing, golf, fishing, craic. *Address:* Manor Farm, East Dean, near Salisbury, Wilts SP5 1HB. *T:* (01794) 340016.

BARKER, Prof. Eileen Vartan, OBE 2000; PhD; FBA 1998; Professor of Sociology with Special Reference to the Study of Religion, London School of Economics, 1992–2003, now Emeritus; Leverhulme Emeritus Fellow, 2004–07; *b* 21 April 1938; *d* of Calman MacLennan and Mary Helen MacLennan (*née* Muir); *m* 1958, Peter Johnson Barker, MBE; two *d*. *Educ:* Cheltenham Ladies' Coll.; Webber Douglas Sch. of Singing and Dramatic Art; London Sch. of Econs (BSc 1st Cl. Hons Sociol. 1970; PhD 1984). London School of Economics: Lectr, 1970–85; Sen. Lectr, 1985–90; Reader, 1990–92; Dean, Undergrad. Studies, 1982–86. Leonard Greenberg Distinguished Vis. Fellow, Trinity Coll., Hertford, USA, 2000. Founder and Chm., INFORM, 1988–. President: Soc. for Scientific Study of Religion, 1991–93; Assoc. for Sociol. of Religion, 2001–02. PhD *hc* Copenhagen, 2000. Martin E. Marty Award for Public Understanding of Religion, Amer. Acad. of Religion, 2000. *Publications:* (ed) Of Gods and Men, 1982; (ed) New Religious Movements: a perspective for understanding society, 1982; The Making of a Moonie: brainwashing or choice?, 1984 (SSSR Dist. Book Award 1985); New Religious Movements: a practical introduction, 1989; (ed jtly) Secularization, Rationalism and Sectarianism, 1993; (ed jtly) Twenty Years On: changes in new religious movements, 1995; (ed) LSE on Freedom, 1995; (ed jtly) New Religions and New Religiosity, 1998; (ed) Freedom and Religion in Eastern Europe, 2003; numerous contribs to scholarly jls and books. *Address:* London School of Economics, Department of Sociology, Houghton Street, WC2A 2AE. *T:* (020) 7955 7289.

BARKER, Prof. Graeme William Walter, FSA; FBA 1999; Disney Professor of Archaeology and Director, McDonald Institute for Archaeological Research, University of Cambridge, since 2004; Fellow, St John's College, Cambridge, since 2004; *b* 23 Oct. 1946; *s* of Reginald Walter Barker and Kathleen (*née* Walton); *m* 1976, Sarah Miranda Buchanan (marr. diss. 1991); one *d* (and one *s* decd). *Educ:* Alleyn's Sch., Dulwich; St John's Coll., Cambridge (Henry Arthur Thomas Schol., 1965–67; MA; PhD 1973). FSA 1979. Rome Schol. in Classical Studies, British Sch. at Rome, 1969–71; Lectr, 1972–81, Sen. Lectr, 1981–88, in Prehist. and Archaeol., Sheffield Univ.; Dir., British Sch. at Rome, 1984–88; Leicester University: Prof. and Hd, Sch. of Archaeol Studies, 1988–2000; Graduate Dean, 2000–03; Pro-Vice-Chancellor, 2003–04. Dir, Niah Cave Project, Sarawak, 2000–. Member: Exec. Cttee, UK Council for Graduate Educn, 2001–03; AHRB, subseq. AHRC, 2003–. Pres., Prehistoric Soc., 2001–05. Dan David Prize, 2005. *Publications:* Landscape and Society: Prehistoric Central Italy, 1981, Italian edn 1984; (with R. Hodges) Archaeology and Italian Society, 1981; Prehistoric Communities in Northern England, 1981; (jtly) La Casatico di Marcaria, 1983; (jtly) Cyrenaica in Classical Antiquity, 1984; Prehistoric Farming in Europe, 1985; (with C. S. Gamble) Beyond Domestication in Prehistoric Europe: Investigations in Subsistence Archaeology and Social Complexity, 1985; (with J. A. Lloyd) Roman Landscapes, 1991; (with R. Maggi and R. Nisbet) Archeologia della Pastorizia nell'Europa Meridionale, 1993; A Mediterranean Valley: landscape archaeology and *Annales* history in the Biferno Valley, 1995; The Biferno Valley Survey: the archaeological and geomorphological record, 1995; (jtly) Farming the Desert: the UNESCO Libyan valleys survey, 2 vols, 1996; (with T. Rasmussen) The Etruscans, 1998; (ed) The Companion Encyclopedia of Archaeology, 2 vols, 1999; (with D. Gilbertson) The Archaeology of Drylands: living at the margin, 2000; (jtly) The Human Use of Caves in Peninsular and Island Southeast Asia, 2005; The Agricultural Revolution in Prehistory: why did foragers become farmers?, 2006; (ed jtly) Archaeology and Desertification: the Wadi Faynan landscape survey, Southern Jordan, 2007; contribs, esp. on landscape archaeol. and ancient agric., to learned jls. *Address:* McDonald Institute for Archaeological Research, Downing Street, Cambridge CB2 3ER. *T:* (01223) 339284.

BARKER, Gregory; MP (C) Bexhill and Battle, since 2001; *b* Sussex, 8 March 1966; *m* 1992, Celeste Harrison (marr. diss. 2008); two *s* one *d*. *Educ:* Steyning Grammar Sch.; Lancing Coll.; RHBNC (BA 1987). Researcher, Centre for Policy Studies, 1987–88 (Associate, 1988–); Equity Analyst, Gerrard Vivian Gray, 1988–90; Dir, Internat. Pacific Securities, 1990–97; Associate Partner, Brunswick Gp Ltd, 1997–98; Hd, Investor Communications, Siberian Oil Co., 1998–2000. Dir, Daric plc, 1998–2001. An Opposition Whip, 2003–05; opposition spokesman on climate change and envmt, 2005–. Mem., H of C Envmtl Audit Select Cttee, 2001–05. Contested (C) Eccles, 1997. *Address:* c/o House of Commons, SW1A 0AA.

BARKER, Harold; retired; Keeper, Department of Conservation and Technical Services, British Museum, 1975–79; Member: Council for Care of Churches, 1976–81; Crafts Council, 1979–80; *b* 15 Feb. 1919; *s* of William Frampton Barker and Lily (*née* Pack); *m* 1942, Everilda Alice Whittle; one *s* one *d*. *Educ:* City Secondary Sch., Sheffield Univ. (BSc). Experimental Asst, 1940, Experimental Officer, 1942, Chemical Inspectorate, Min. of Supply; British Museum: Experimental Officer, Research Lab., 1947; Sen. Experimental Officer, 1953; Chief Experimental Officer, 1960; Principal Scientific Officer, 1966; Acting Keeper, 1975. *Publications:* papers on radiocarbon dating and scientific examination of antiquities in various jls. *Recreations:* music, walking, videography. *Address:* 27 Westbourne Park, Falsgrave, Scarborough, N Yorks YO12 4AS. *T:* (01723) 353273.

BARKER, Howard; playwright and poet; *b* 28 June 1946. *Educ:* Univ. of Sussex (MA). Theatre productions, 1970–, include: *Royal Court:* No End of Blame, 1981; Victory, 1983; version of Thomas Middleton's Women Beware Women, 1986; The Last Supper, 1988; Golgo, 1990; Hated Nightfall, 1995; *RSC* at The Pit: The Castle, 1985; Downchild: a fantasy, 1985; The Bite of the Night, 1988; *Leicester:* The Last Supper, 1989; Seven Lears, 1990; Judith, 1995; (Uncle) Vanya, 1996; other productions: A Passion in Six Days, Crucible, Sheffield, 1983; The Power of the Dog, Hampstead, 1985; Possibilities, Almeida, 1988. TV and radio plays include: Scenes from an Execution, Radio 3, 1984 (Best Drama Script, Sony Radio Awards, 1985; Prix Italia, 1985; perf. Almeida, 1990); Pity in History, BBC 2, 1985; A Hard Heart, Radio 3, 1992 (perf. Almeida, 1992); The Early Hours of a Reviled Man, Radio 3, 1992; A House of Correction, Albertina, Radio 3, 1999; Knowledge and a Girl, Radio 4, 2001; The Moving and The Still, Radio 3, 2003. Opera (with Nigel Osborne) Terrible Mouth, ENO, Almeida, 1992. Formed The

Wrestling School (company to perform own work), 1989: The Europeans, 1993; Wounds to the Face, 1997; Ursula, 1998; Und, 1999; The Ecstatic Bible, He Stumbled, 2000; A House of Correction, 2001; Gertrude - the Cry, 2002; 13 Objects, 2003; Dead Hands, 2004. *Publications: plays:* Stripwell, and Claw, 1977; Fair Slaughter, 1978; Love of a Good Man, and All Bleeding, 1981; That Good Between Us, and Credentials of a Sympathiser, 1981; No End of Blame: scenes of overcoming, 1981; Two Plays for the Right: Birth on a Hard Shouder, and The Loud Boy's Life, 1982; Hang of the Gaol, 1982; Victory: choices in reaction, 1983; The Castle, and Scenes from an Execution, 1984; Crimes in Hot Countries, and Fair Slaughter, 1984; Power of the Dog, 1985; A Passion in Six Days, and Downchild, 1985; The Last Supper: a New Testament, 1988; Lullabies for the Impatient, 1988; Possibilities, 1988; Pity in History, 1989; Seven Lears, and Golgo, 1990; Europeans, and Judith, 1990; Collected Plays, vol. I, 1990, vol. II, 1993, vol. III, 1996, vol. IV, 1997, vol. V, 1999; A Hard Heart, 1992; The Early Hours of a Reviled Man, 1992; Gertrude, and Knowledge and a Girl, 2002; Death: the one and the art of theatre, 2004; The Ecstatic Bible, 2004; *poetry:* Don't Exaggerate (Desire and Abuse), 1985; Breath of the Crowd, 1986; Gary the Thief/Gary Upright, 1987; The Ascent of Monte Grappa, 1991; The Tortmann Diaries, 1996; *essays:* Arguments for a Theatre, 1989. *Address:* c/o Judy Daish Associates, 2 St Charles Place, W10 6EG.

BARKER, Hon. Sir Ian; *see* Barker, Hon. Sir R. I.

BARKER, John Alan, CB 2003; CPsychol 1988; Deputy Chair, Civil Service Appeal Board, since 2007; *b* 5 Oct. 1945; *s* of Alan Gilbert Foster Barker and Gwendoline Margery Barker; *m* 1977, Vivienne Frances Cook; one *s* one *d. Educ:* Denstone Coll., Uttoxeter; St Andrews Univ. (MA Econs and Psychol.); Birkbeck Coll., London (MSc Occupational Psychol.). AFBPsS. Sen. Psychologist, CSD, 1974–80; Principal Psychologist, CSSB, 1980–85; Administrative Principal, CSSB, 1985–86 ; Principal, Personnel Mgt, MPO then HM Treasury, 1986–89; HM Treasury: Head: Allowances Div., 1989–91; Mgt Services, 1991–95; Cabinet Office: Hd, Sen. CS Div., 1995–97; Director: CS Employer Gp, 1997–99; CS Corporate Mgt, 1999–2002; Corporate Develt Gp, 2002–07. NE Dir, Whitehall and Ind. Gp, 2002–. Trustee, Employers' Forum for Age, 2002–05. *Recreations:* choral singing, sport (spectator), reading, wine. *Address:* 42 Hurstdene Avenue, Hayes, Bromley, Kent BR2 7JJ; *e-mail:* johnbarker45@hotmail.co.uk.

BARKER, John Francis Holroyd, CB 1984; Consultant, Cabinet Office, 1985–93; *b* 3 Feb. 1925; *s* of Rev. C. H. Barker and B. A. Barker (*née* Bullivant); *m* 1954, Felicity Ann (*née* Martindale); three *d. Educ:* King Edward's School, Stourbridge; Oriel College, Oxford. RNVR, 1943–46. Director of Music, Abingdon School, 1950–54; War Office/Ministry of Defence, 1954–85. *Recreation:* music. *Address:* c/o Coutts & Co., 440 Strand, WC2R 0QS. *Club:* Athenæum.

BARKER, Katharine Mary, (Mrs P. R. Donovan), CBE 2006; Member, Monetary Policy Committee, Bank of England, since 2001; *b* 29 Nov. 1957; *d* of Wilfred Barker and Eileen May (*née* Pinhorn); *m* 1982, Peter Richard Donovan; two *s. Educ:* St Hilda's Coll., Oxford (BA Hons PPE). Investment analyst, PO Pension Fund, 1979–81; Res. Officer, NIESR, 1981–85; Chief Economist, Ford of Europe, 1985–94; Chief Econ. Advr, CBI, 1994–2001. Mem., Panel of Independent Advrs, HM Treasury, 1996–97. Non-exec. Dir, Yorkshire Bldg Soc., 1999–2001. Mem. Bd, Housing Corp., 2005–. Chairman: Indep. Review of UK Housing Supply, 2003–04; Financial Adv. Cttee, FA, 2003–06; Indep. Review of Land Use Planning, 2005–06; Mem., Football Regulatory Authy, 2006–. Mem., 1999–2007, Chm., 2007–, Bd of Govs, Anglia Ruskin (formerly Anglia Poly.) Univ. *Publications:* contribs to jls. *Recreation:* bell-ringing. *Address:* Bank of England, Threadneedle Street, EC2R 8AH. *T:* (020) 7601 4271.

BARKER, Prof. Kenneth, CBE 1994; Vice-Chancellor, Thames Valley University, 1999–2003; *b* 26 June 1934; *s* of Thomas William and Lillian Barker; *m* 1958, Jean Ivy Pearl; one *s* one *d. Educ:* Royal Coll. of Music (ARCM); King's Coll., London (BMus); Sussex Univ. (MA). GRSM, FTCL, FLCM. Schoolmaster, 1958–62; lectr and university teacher, 1962–75; Principal, Gipsy Hill Coll., 1975; Pro-Dir, Kingston Polytechnic, 1975–86; Dep. Dir/Dir Designate, 1986–87, Dir, 1987–92, Leicester Poly., then Chief Exec. and Vice-Chancellor, De Montfort Univ., 1992–99. Chm., Postgrad. Initial Trng Bd, 1975–80, Chm., Music Bd and Chm., Cttee for Creative Arts, 1980–90, CNAA. Board Member: London West LSC, 2001–03; London NHS Workforce Confedn, 2001–03. Trustee, Richmond Amer. Internat Univ. in London, 1997–2004. FRSA; CCMI. Hon. DSc Moscow State Tech. Univ., 1995; DUniv: St Petersburg Univ. of Design and Technology, 1997; De Montfort, 1999; Thames Valley, 2004; Hon. DEd Kingston, 2003. *Publications:* contribs to jls. *Recreations:* music, theatre, watching Rugby. *Address:* Bramshott, Church Road, Surbiton, Surrey KT6 5HH. *T:* (020) 8398 4700. *Clubs:* Athenæum, Reform, Institute of Directors.

BARKER, Ven. Nicholas John Willoughby; Archdeacon of Auckland, since 2007; Priest-in-Charge, Holy Trinity, Darlington, since 2007; *b* 12 Dec. 1949; *s* of Rev. Arthur Barker and Peggy Barker; *m* 1980, Katherine Pritchard; three *s* one *d. Educ:* Sedbergh Sch.; Oriel Coll., Oxford (MA Metallurgy 1973; MA Theol. 1975). Ordained deacon, 1977, priest, 1978; Curate, St Mary's, Watford, 1977–80; Team Vicar, St James & Emmanuel, Didsbury, 1980–86; Rector, St George's, Kidderminster, 1986–2007; Rural Dean, Kidderminster, 2001–07. Hon. Canon, Worcester Cathedral, 2003–07; Hon. Supernumerary Canon, Durham Cathedral, 2007–. *Recreations:* bee-keeping, hill-walking, sailing, gardening. *Address:* 45 Milbank Road, Darlington DL3 9NL. *T:* (01325) 480444, *Fax:* (01325) 354027; *e-mail:* Archdeacon.of.Auckland@durham.anglican.org.

BARKER, Nicolas John, OBE 2002; FBA 1998; Editor, Book Collector, since 1965; *b* 6 Dec. 1932; *s* of Sir Ernest Barker, FBA, and Olivia Stuart Horner; *m* 1962, Joanna Mary Sophia Nyda Cotton; two *s* three *d. Educ:* Westminster Sch.; New Coll., Oxford (MA). With Bailliere, Tindall & Cox, 1958 and Rupert Hart-Davis, 1959; Asst Keeper, National Portrait Gallery, 1964; with Macmillan & Co. Ltd, 1965; with OUP, 1971; Dep. Keeper, British Library, 1976–92. William Andrews Clark Vis. Prof., UCLA, 1986–87; Scholar, Getty Center for History of Art and the Humanities, 1996; Sandars Reader in Bibliography, Cambridge Univ., 1999–2000. Panizzi Lectr, BL, 2001; Rosenbach Lectr, Univ. of Pennsylvania, 2002. President: Amici Thomae Mori, 1978–89; Double Crown Club, 1980–81; Bibliographical Soc., 1981–85; Chm., London Liby, 1994–2004 (Mem. Cttee, 1971–2004; a Vice-Pres., 2005–); Member: Publication Bd of Dirs, RNIB, 1969–92; BBC and ITV Appeals Adv. Cttee, 1977–86; Nat. Trust Arts Panel, 1979–91 (Libraries Advr, 1991–99); Liby Cttee, RHS, 1996– (Chm., 1996–2004). Trustee: The Pilgrim Trust, 1977–2007; York Glaziers Trust, 1990– (Chm., 2004–); Chm., Laurence Sterne Trust, 1984–; Chm. Trustees, Type Mus., 1995–. DUniv York, 1994. *Publications:* The Publications of the Roxburghe Club, 1962; The Printer and the Poet, 1970; Stanley Morison, 1972; (ed) Essays and Papers of A. N. L. Munby, 1977; (ed) The Early Life of James McBey: an autobiography, 1883–1911, 1977; Bibliotheca Lindesiana, 1977; The Oxford University Press and the Spread of Learning 1478–1978, 1978; (with John Collins) A Sequel to an Enquiry, 1983; Aldus Manutius and the Development of Greek Script and Type, 1985; The Butterfly Books, 1987; Two East Anglian Picture Books, 1988; (ed) Treasures of the British Library, 1989; (ed) S. Morison, Early Italian Writing-Books, 1990; (with Sir Anthony Wagner and A. Payne) Medieval Pageant, 1993; Hortus Eystettensis: the Bishop's Garden and Besler's Magnificent Book, 1994; The Great Book of Thomas Trevilian, 2000; Form and Meaning in the History of the Book, 2002; The Devonshire Inheritance, 2003; The Library of Thomas Tresham and Thomas Brudenell, 2006. *Address:* 22 Clarendon Road, W11 3AB. *T:* (020) 7727 4340. *Clubs:* Garrick, Beefsteak, Roxburghe; Roxburghe (San Francisco); Zamorano (Los Angeles).

BARKER, Pamela Gay; *see* Barber, P. G.

BARKER, Patricia Margaret, CBE 2000; novelist, since 1982; *b* 8 May 1943; *d* of Moyra Drake; *m* 1978, David Faubert Barker, *qv*; one *s* one *d. Educ:* Grangefield GS; London School of Economics (BScEcon; Hon. Fellow, 1998); Durham Univ. (DipEd). Teacher, until 1982. Hon. MLitt Teesside, 1994; Hon. DLitt: Napier, 1996; Durham, 1998; Hertfordshire, 1998; London, 2002; DUniv Open, 1997. Author of the Year Award, Booksellers' Assoc., 1996. *Publications:* Union Street (Fawcett Prize), 1982; Blow Your House Down, 1984; The Century's Daughter, 1986 (retitled Liza's England, 1996); The Man Who Wasn't There, 1989; The Regeneration Trilogy: Regeneration, 1991 (filmed 1997); The Eye in the Door, 1993 (Guardian Fiction Prize, Northern Electric Special Arts Award, 1994); The Ghost Road (Booker Prize), 1995; Another World, 1998; Border Crossing, 2001; Double Vision, 2003; Life Class, 2007. *Address:* c/o Aitken Alexander Associates, 18–21 Cavaye Place, SW10 9PT. *T:* (020) 7373 8672.

BARKER, Paul; writer and broadcaster; *b* 24 Aug. 1935; *s* of Donald and Marion Barker; *m* 1960, Sally, *e d* of James and Marion Huddleston; three *s* one *d. Educ:* Hebden Bridge Grammar Sch.; Calder High Sch.; Brasenose Coll., Oxford (Hulme Exhibr), MA. Intell. Corps (commn), 1953–55. Lecteur, Ecole Normale Supérieure, Paris, 1958–59; The Times, 1959–63; New Society, staff writer, 1964; The Economist, 1964–65; New Society: Dep. Editor, 1965–68; Editor, 1968–86; Social Policy Ed., Sunday Telegraph, 1986–88; Associate Ed., The Independent Magazine, 1988–90. Evening Standard: townscape and arts columnist, 1987–92; social commentary, 1992–2007; social and political columnist, Sunday Times, 1990–91; townscape columnist, New Statesman, 1996–99. A Dir, Pennine Heritage, 1978–86. Mem., UK Adv. Cttee, Harkness Fellowships, 1995–97. Vis. Fellow, Centre for Analysis of Social Policy, Univ. of Bath, 1986–2000; Leverhulme Res. Fellow, 1993–95; Res. Fellow in Architecture, Royal Commn for Exhibn of 1851, 2000–02. Institute of Community Studies: Chm., 2000–01 (Trustee, 1991–2001); Fellow, 1992, Sen. Fellow, 1995, Sen. Res. Fellow, 2000–05; Sen. Res. Fellow, Young Foundn, 2005–. FRSA 1990. (Jtly) BPG Award for outstanding radio prog., My Country, Right or Wrong, 1988. *Publications:* (contrib.) Youth in New Society, 1966; (contrib.) Your Sunday Paper, 1967; (contrib. and ed) One for Sorrow, Two for Joy, 1972; (ed) A Sociological Portrait, 1972; (ed) The Social Sciences Today, 1975 (Spanish edn, 1979); (contrib. and ed) Arts in Society, 1977, rev. edn 2006; (contrib. and ed) The Other Britain, 1982; (ed) Founders of the Welfare State, 1985; (contrib.) Britain in the Eighties, 1989; (contrib.) Towards a New Landscape, 1993; (contrib.) Young at Eighty, 1995; (contrib. and ed) Gulliver and Beyond, 1996; (contrib. and ed) Living as Equals, 1996 (Spanish edn, 2000); (ed jtly) A Critic Writes, 1997; (contrib.) Town and Country, 1998; (contrib.) Non-Plan, 2000; (jtly) The Meaning of the Jubilee, 2002; (contrib.) From Black Economy to Moment of Truth, 2004; (contrib.) Porcupines in Winter, 2006; (contrib.) The Rise and Rise of Meritocracy, 2006; numerous essays and articles in magazines and newspapers, incl. TLS and Prospect. *Recreation:* driving to a baroque church, with the radio on. *Address:* 15 Dartmouth Park Avenue, NW5 1JL. *T:* (020) 7485 8861. *Club:* Architecture.

BARKER, Peter William, CBE 1988; DL; Chairman, Fenner (formerly J. H. Fenner (Holdings)) PLC, 1982–93; *b* 24 Aug. 1928; *s* of William Henry George and Mabel Irene Barker; *m* 1961, Mary Rose Hainsworth, MBE, JP, DL; one *s* one *d. Educ:* Royal Liberty Sch., Romford; Dorking County High Sch.; South London Polytechnic. CCMI; FInstD; FCIM. J. H. Fenner & Co., 1953–67; Jt Managing Dir, Fenner International, 1967–71; Chief Exec., J. H. Fenner (Holdings), 1971–82. Dir, Neepsend plc, 1984–93; Chm., Hartingdon Ltd, 1997–99. Member: Yorks and Humberside Regional Council, CBI, 1981–94 (Chm., 1991–93); National Council, CBI, 1985–95; Yorks and Humberside Regional Indust. Develt Bd, 1981–95 (Chm., 1992–95). Pro-Chancellor, Univ. of Hull, 1993–2002, now Emeritus. Hon. DSc (Econ) Hull, 1992. FRSA. DL E Yorks (formerly Humberside), 1990; High Sheriff, Humberside, 1993–94. *Recreations:* sailing, ski-ing, tennis, music. *Address:* Swanland Rise, West Ella, East Yorks HU10 7SF. *T:* (01482) 653050. *Clubs:* Royal Yorkshire Yacht, Royal Thames Yacht.

BARKER, Hon. Sir (Richard) Ian, Kt 1994; arbitrator and mediator; Senior Judge, High Court of New Zealand, 1991–97; Chairman, Banking Ombudsman Commission, New Zealand, since 1997; *b* 17 March 1934; *s* of Archibald Henry Barker and Kate Dorothy Barker (*née* Humphrys); *m* 1965, Mary Christine Allardyce; two *s* three *d. Educ:* Auckland Univ. (BA, LLB, 1958). FCIArb; FAMINZ(Arb/Med). Called to the Bar, NZ, 1958; Partner, Morpeth, Gould & Co., solicitors, Auckland, 1968–80; Barrister, 1968–76; QC (NZ) 1973; Judge, High Court of NZ, 1976–97; Member, Court of Appeal: Cook Is, 1990–; Fiji, 1997–; Samoa and Vanuatu, 1998–2001; Pitcairn, 2004–. Door Tenant, Essex Ct Chambers, London, 1998–. Vis. Schol., Wolfson Coll., Cambridge, 2006. Chancellor, Univ. of Auckland, 1991–99. Nominee of NZ Govt on ICSID Panel of Arbitrators, 1999–. President: Legal Res. Foundn of NZ, 1981–90; Arbitrators' and Mediators' Inst. of NZ, 2000–02. Hon. LLD Auckland Univ., 1999. *Publications:* contrib. articles to NZ and Australian jls. *Recreations:* walking, reading, music, railways. *Address:* 10 Seaview Road, Auckland 5, New Zealand. *Club:* Northern (Auckland).

BARKER, Richard Philip; Headmaster, Sevenoaks School, 1981–96; *b* 17 July 1939; *s* of late Philip Watson Barker and Helen May Barker; *m* 1966, Imogen Margaret Harris; two *s* one *d. Educ:* Repton; Trinity Coll., Cambridge (MA 1962); Bristol Univ. (Cert. Ed. 1963). Head of Geography, Bedales Sch., 1963–65; Founder Dir, A level business studies project, 1966–73; Lectr, Inst. of Education, London Univ., 1973–74; Housemaster, Marlborough Coll., 1973–81. Resident Gov., British Sch., Colombo, Sri Lanka, 1996–97; Governor: Epsom Coll., 1996–2002; Chm. of Govs, Worth Sch., 1999–2002. Chm., Friends of Yehudi Menuhin Sch., 1996–2002. Mem., RSA. *Publications:* (ed) Understanding Business Series, 1976–98. *Recreations:* educational interests, beekeeping, croquet, fishing, repairing buildings, travelling. *Address:* Slyfield Farm House, Stoke D'Abernon, Cobham, Surrey KT11 3QE. *T:* (01932) 862634; *e-mail:* barker@slyfieldfh.freeserve.co.uk.

BARKER, Dr Richard William; Director General, Association of British Pharmaceutical Industry, since 2004; *b* 18 Oct. 1948; *s* of late William Barker and Florence Barker; *m* 1969, Jennifer Ruth (marr. diss. 2000); two *s* one *d. Educ:* Alleyn's Sch.; Exeter Coll., Oxford (MA; DPhil 1973). Partner, Healthcare Practice Leader, McKinsey & Co., 1980–93; Gen. Manager, Healthcare Solutions, IBM, 1993–96; President: Chiron Diagnostics, 1996–2000; New Medicine Partners, 2001–03; Chm. and CEO, Molecular Staging, 2003–06. Chm., Stem Cells for Safer Medicines, 2007–; non-executive Director: Sunquest, 1997–2001; Exact Scis, 1999–2005; Adlyfe, 2004–; Internat. Health Partners, 2005–; iCo Therapeutics, 2006–. Member: Ministerial Industry Strategy Gp, 2005–; NHS Stakeholder Forum (formerly NHS Nat. Leadership Network), 2006–; UK Clin. Res.

Consortium, 2006–; e-Health Res. Bd, OSCHR, 2007–. Europ. Fedn of Pharmaceutical Industry Assocs, 2004–; Internat. Fedn of Pharmaceutical Manufacturers and Assocs, 2004–. *Recreations:* hiking, kayaking, music. *Address:* Association of British Pharmaceutical Industry, 12 Whitehall, SW1A 2DY. *T:* (020) 7747 1427; *e-mail:* rbarker@abpi.org.uk.

BARKER, Ronald Hugh, PhD; BSc; CEng, FIET, FIMechE; Deputy Director, Royal Armament Research and Development Establishment, 1965–75, retired; *b* 28 Oct. 1915; *s* of E. W. Barker and L. A. Taylor; *m* 1943, W. E. Hunt; two *s*. *Educ:* University of Hull. Physicist, Standard Telephones and Cables, 1938–41; Ministry of Supply, 1941–59; Dep. Dir, Central Electricity Research Laboratories, 1959–62; Technical Dir, The Pullin Group Ltd, 1962–65. *Publications:* various, on servomechanisms and control systems.

BARKER, Simon George Harry, FCA; QC 2008; a Recorder, since 1995; *b* London, 1950; *s* of Edgar John Harry and Dorothy Joan Barker; *m* 1972, Eva-Marie; one *s* one *d*. *Educ:* Westminster Sch.; Ealing Tech. Coll. (BA Hons). ACA 1976, FCA 1981. Called to the Bar, Lincoln's Inn, 1979. *Recreations:* rowing, water sports, ski-ing, art, theatre, films, music, football. *Address:* Maitland Chambers, 7 Stone Buildings, Lincoln's Inn, WC2A 3SZ. *T:* (020) 7406 1200. *Clubs:* London Rowing; Leander (Henley-on-Thames).

BARKER, Thomas Christopher; HM Diplomatic Service, retired; *b* 28 June 1928; *m* 1960, Griselda Helen Cormack; two *s* one *d*. *Educ:* Uppingham (Schol.); New Coll., Oxford (Schol.; MA, Lit Hum, 1952; Gaisford Prize for Greek Verse). 2nd Lt, 1st Bn, The Worcestershire Regt, 1947–48. HM Foreign Service, 1952; Third Sec., Paris, 1953–55; Second Sec., Baghdad, 1955–58; FO, 1958–62; First Sec., Head of Chancery and Consul, Mexico City, 1962–67; FO, 1967–69; Counsellor and Head of Chancery, Caracas, 1969–71; FCO, 1971–75; seconded as Under Sec., NI Office, Belfast, 1976. Curator, 1978–87, Secretary to Trustees, 1987–93, Scottish Nat. War Meml, Edinburgh.

BARKER, Timothy Gwynne; Chairman, Robert Walters plc, 2001–07; *b* 8 April 1940; *s* of late Lt Col Frank Richard Peter Barker and Hon. Olwen Gwynne (*née* Philipps); *m* 1964, Philippa Rachel Mary Thursby-Pelham; one *s* one *d*. *Educ:* Eton Coll.; McGill Univ., Montreal; Jesus Coll., Cambridge (MA). Dir, 1973–2000 and Hd of Corporate Finance, 1986–90, Kleinwort Benson Ltd; Kleinwort Benson Group plc, subseq. Dresdner Kleinwort Benson: Dir, 1988–93; Dep. Chief Exec., 1990–93; Vice Chm., 1993–2000; Chm., Kleinwort Benson Private Bank Ltd, 1997–2004. Director-General: City Panel on Take-overs and Mergers, 1984–85; Council for the Securities Industry, 1984–85. Non-executive Director: Electrocomponents plc, 2000–; Drax Gp plc, 2004–. Mem., Professional Oversight Bd, Financial Reporting Council, 2004–. *Address:* 58 Winchester Street, SW1V 4NH. *T:* (020) 7630 8700.

BARKER, Trevor; Chairman, Alpha Consolidated Holdings Ltd, 1988–2003; *b* 24 March 1935; *s* of Samuel Lawrence Barker and Lilian Barker (*née* Dawson); *m* 1957, Joan Elizabeth Cross; one *s* one *d*. *Educ:* Acklam Hall Grammar School. FCA. Price Waterhouse & Co., 1957–58; Cooper Brothers, 1958–62; sole practitioner, 1962–70; Chm. and Chief Exec., Gold Case Travel, 1964–77; Dir, Ellerman Wilson Lines, 1977–80; Chairman: John Crowther Gp, 1980–88; William Morris Fine Arts, 1981–88; Micklegate Gp, 1989–95; Drew Scientific Gp, 1993–95; Dep. Chm., Blanchards, 1988–94; Dir, Darlington Bldg Soc., 1994–2000. FRSA 1989. Liveryman, Co. of Woolmen, 1986. *Recreations:* grandchildren, breeding and racing thoroughbred horses, opera, music, literature, the arts. *Address:* PO Box 711, Como, WA 6952, Australia.

BARKING, Area Bishop of, since 2002; **Rt Rev. David John Leader Hawkins;** *b* 30 March 1949; *s* of John Mitchell and Monica Mary Hawkins; *m* 1973, Carole Gladwin; three *d*. *Educ:* Kingsmead Sch.; Wrekin Coll.; St John's Coll., Nottingham; Nottingham Univ. (BTh, LTh 1973); London Coll. of Divinity (ALCD 1973). Teacher, Mbiruri Secondary Sch., Embu, Kenya, 1968–69. Ordained deacon, 1973, priest, 1974; Curate, St Andrew's, Bebington, 1973–76; Founding Warden, Bida Bible Trng Centre, Northern Nigeria, 1976–82; Vicar, St John's, Bida, and Acting Archdeacon, Bida Archdeaconry, 1979–82; Priest i/c, St Matthew's with St Luke's, Oxford, 1983–86; Vicar, 1986–99, Team Rector, 1999–2002, St George's, Leeds. Diocese of Chelmsford: Hd Bishop for Mission and Parish Develt, 2004; Hd Bishop for Youth, 2005; Archbp's Advr for Black Majority Churches, 2006–. Canon Emeritus, Kaduna, Nigeria, 1982. Chaplain, Yorks CCC, 1986–2002. Dir, Ashlar House, 1986–2001; Exec. Trustee, St George's Crypt, 1986–2002; Chair, Leeds Faith in Schs, 1993–2002. Pres., Bardsey Bird and Field Observatory, 2008. *Recreations:* painting, music, mountain walking, sailing, running, poetry. *Address:* Barking Lodge, Verulam Avenue, Walthamstow, E17 8ES.

BARKSHIRE, John; *see* Barkshire, R. R. St J.

BARKSHIRE, Robert Renny St John, (John), CBE 1990; TD; JP; DL; banker; *b* 31 Aug. 1935; *s* of late Robert Hugh Barkshire, CBE; *m* 1st, 1960, Margaret Elizabeth Robinson (marr. diss. 1990); two *s* one *d*; 2nd, 1990, Audrey Mary Anne Witham. *Educ:* Bedford School. ACIB. Served Duke of Wellington's Regt, 2nd Lieut, 1953–55; HAC, 1955–74 (CO, 1970–72; Regtl Col, 1972–74). Joined Cater Ryder & Co., 1955, Jt Man. Dir, 1963–72; Chm., Mercantile House Holdings plc, 1972–87; Non-exec. Dir, Extel Gp PLC, 1979–87 (Dep. Chm., 1986–87); Chairman: CL-Alexanders Laing & Cruickshank Hldgs Ltd, 1984–88; Internat. Commodities Clearing House Ltd, 1986–90. Chm., Financial Futures Wkg Pty, 1980, later LIFFE Steering Cttee, 1981–82; Dir, LIFFE, 1982–91 (Chm., 1982–85); Member: Adv. Bd, Internat. Monetary Market Div., Chicago Mercantile Exchange, 1981–84; London Adv. Bd, Bank Julius Baer, 1988–91. Chairman: Uplink Ltd (EPN Satellite Service), 1988–90; Chaco Investments Ltd, 1994–2001; non-executive Director: Household Mortgage Corp., 1985–94 (Chm., 1993–94); Savills, 1988–95; Sun Life and Provincial Holdings plc, 1988–99; TR Property Investment Trust plc, 1993–2002. Chm., Eastbourne Hosps NHS Trust, 1993–99. Chm., Cttee on Market in Single Properties, 1985–2000. Gen. Comr for Income Tax, City of London, 1981–. Chairman: Reserve Forces Assoc., 1983–87; Sussex TA Cttee, 1983–85; SE TAVRA, 1985–91; Dep. Chm., TA Sport Bd, 1983–95 (Mem., 1979–95). Financial Advisor: Victory Services Assoc. (formerly Club), 1981–95; RE Central Mgt Investments Policy Cttee, 1988–2007; RBL Mgt Bd, 1991–2005; Army Central Fund, 1995–2007; Royal Signals Trustees Ltd, 1996–2005; Dir, Officers' Pensions Soc. Investment Co. Ltd, 1982–95; Member: Regular Forces Employment Assoc. Council, 1986–95; SSAFA Council (Trustee and Mem. Exec. and Finance Cttee), 1996–2008; Adv. Bd, Army Common Investment Fund, 2002–04; Chm., Nat. Meml Arboretum, 2003–; Trustee: Regtl Assoc., Duke of Wellington's Regt, 1990–; Army Benevolent Fund (Pres., E Sussex Br., 1999–); RBL, 2005– (Co-opted Mem., Nat. Council, 1991–2005; Chm., Chiddingly and Dist, 1982–87); Yorks Regt, 2006–. Chairman: E Sussex Br., Magistrates' Assoc., 1986–91; E Sussex Magistrates' Courts Cttee, 1993–97 and 1999–2001; Sussex Magistrates' Courts Cttee, 2001–02. Mem., Chiddingly Parish Council, 1979–86; Treas., Burwash PCC, 1999–. Governor: Harpur Trust, 1984–89 (Chm., Bedford Sch. Cttee, 1984–89); Eastbourne Coll., 1980–95 (Vice Chm., 1983–92); Roedean Sch., 1984–89; Burwash Primary C of E Sch., 1999– (Chm., 2002–); Comr, Duke of York's Royal Military Sch., 1986–95. Freeman, City of London, 1973; Liveryman, Worshipful Co. of Farmers, 1981. JP Lewes, 1980; DL E Sussex, 1986. *Recreations:* sailing, shooting. *Address:* Denes House, High Street, Burwash, East Sussex TN19 7EH. *T:* (01435) 882646. *Clubs:* City of London, Cavalry and Guards, MCC; Royal Fowey Yacht (Cornwall).

BARLING, Hon. Sir Gerald (Edward), Kt 2007; **Hon. Mr Justice Barling;** a Judge of the High Court of Justice, Chancery Division, since 2007; President, Competition Appeal Tribunal, since 2007; *b* 18 Sept. 1949; *s* of Banks Hubert Barling and Barbara Margarita (*née* Myerscough); *m* 1983, Myriam Frances (*née* Ponsford); three *d*. *Educ:* St Mary's Coll., Blackburn; New Coll., Oxford (Burnett Open Exhibnr in Classics, 1968; Hons Sch. of Jurisprudence (1st Cl.), 1971; MA). Called to the Bar, Middle Temple, 1972 (Harmsworth Entrance Exhibnr, 1971; Astbury Law Scholar, 1973; Bencher, 2001). Practised at Common Law Bar, Manchester, 1973–81; practising in UK and EC Law, Brick Court Chambers, London, 1981–2007; Asst Recorder, 1990–93; QC 1991; Recorder, 1993–2007; Actg Deemster, I of M Court of Appeal, 2000–. Lectr in Law, New Coll., Oxford, 1972–77. Chairman: Western European Sub-Cttee, Bar Council, 1991–92; Bar European Gp, 1994–96 (Vice-Chm., 1992–94). *Publications:* (contrib.) Butterworth's European Court Practice, 1991; (co-ed) Practitioner's Handbook of EC Law, 1998; papers on different aspects of EC Law. *Recreation:* countryside pursuits. *Address:* Royal Courts of Justice, Strand, WC2A 2LL.

BARLOW, Celia Anne; MP (Lab) Hove, since 2005; *b* 28 Sept. 1955; *m* Robert Harvey Jaffa; two *s* one *d*. *Educ:* King Edward High Sch. for Girls, Birmingham; New Hall, Cambridge (BA 1976); University Coll., Cardiff; Central St Martin's Coll. of Art and Design. Reporter, Telegraph and Argus, Bradford, 1979–82; reporter and Asst Ed., Asia TV HK, 1982–83; journalist and Home News Ed., BBC TV News, 1983–95; freelance video producer, 1998–2000; Lectr in Video Prodn, Chichester Coll. of Arts, Sci. and Technol., 2000–05. Contested (Lab) Chichester, 2001. *Publication:* Spray of Pearls, 1993. *Address:* (office) 1 Blatchington Road, Hove, E Sussex BN3 3YP; House of Commons, SW1A 0AA.

BARLOW, Sir Christopher Hilaro, 7th Bt *cr* 1803; architect; *b* 1 Dec. 1929; *s* of Sir Richard Barlow, 6th Bt, AFC, and Rosamund Sylvia, *d* of late F. S. Anderton (she *m* 2nd, 1950, Rev. Leonard Haslet Morrison, MA); *S* father, 1946; *m* 1st, 1952, J. C. de M. Audley (*d* 2002), *e d* of late J. E. Audley, Cheshire; one *s* two *d* (and one *s* decd); 2nd, 2003, Mrs Jeane Gage, *e d* of Douglas Stevens, Hamilton. *Educ:* Eton; McGill Univ., Montreal. BArch. MRAIC. Past Pres., Newfoundland Architects' Assoc. Lt Governor's Silver Medal, 1953. *Heir: s* Crispian John Edmund Audley Barlow, Chief Ranger, Ibhubesi Wildlife Service, S Africa [*b* 20 April 1958; *m* 1st, 1981, Anne Waiching Siu (marr. diss. 2005); one *d*; 2nd, 2006, Christi Lane, Philadelphia, Penn]. *Address:* 40 St James Place, Hamilton, ON L8P 2N4, Canada.

BARLOW, Prof. David Hearnshaw, MD; Executive Dean, Faculty of Medicine, University of Glasgow, since 2005; *b* 26 Dec. 1949; *s* of Archibald and Anne Barlow; *m* 1973, Norma Christie Woodrow; one *s* one *d*. *Educ:* Clydebank High Sch.; Univ. of Glasgow (BSc Hons Biochem. 1971; MB ChB 1975; MD 1982); MA Oxon 1985. FRCOG 1993; MRCP 2005; FRCPGlas 2006. MRC Trng Fellowship, 1977–78; Hall Tutorial Fellow, Univ. of Glasgow, 1979–81; Sen. Registrar, Queen Mother's Hosp., Glasgow, 1981–84; Oxford University: Clinical Reader in Obstetrics and Gynaecology, 1984–90; Nuffield Professor of Obstetrics and Gynaecology, 1990–2004; Fellow: Green Coll., 1984–90; Oriel Coll., 1990–2004, Hon. Fellow, 2006; Hon. Consultant Obstetrician and Gynaecologist, The Women's Centre, Oxford Radcliffe Hosps NHS Trust (formerly John Radcliffe Hosp.), Oxford, 1984–2004. Lectures: Blair Bell Meml, 1985, Simpson Oration, 2006, RCOG; Haward Jacobs, British Fertility Soc., 2005. Chairman: DoH Adv. Gp on Osteoporosis (report published, 1995); NICE Guideline Develt Gp on Fertility, 2002–04; NICE Guideline Develt Gp on Osteoporosis, 2003–08. Mem. Bd, Acad. Medicine for Scotland, 2005–. Mem., HFEA, 1998–2006. Mem., FIGO Expert Panel on the Menopause, 1998–. Mem. Council, RCOG, 1996–2002. Chm., British Menopause Soc., 1999–2001; Trustee: Nat. Osteoporosis Soc., 1995–2006 (Chm., 2002–04); Nat. Endometriosis Soc., 1997–2000. Pres., Eur. Menopause and Andropause Soc., 2007– (Vice-Pres., 2004–06). Chm., Oxford NHS R & D Consortium, 2001–04. Member: Medical Scis Divisional Bd, Univ. of Oxford, 2000–04; RAE 2001 and RAE 2008 Panels, HEFCE. Internat. Trustee, Susan Mubarak Foundn for Women's Health, Egypt, 2006–. Founder FMedSci 1998. Mem., Editl Bd, Best Practice in Obstetrics and Gynaecology, 1995–2004; Ed., Menstrual Disorders & Subfertility Gp, Cochrane Collaboration, 1996–; Editor-in-Chief, Human Reproduction Jl, 2000–06. *Publications:* (ed) Clinical Guidelines on the Prevention and Treatment of Osteoporosis, 1999; scientific publications in field of reproduction, particularly on endometriosis, the menopause and IVF. *Recreations:* wide-ranging interest in music, painting. *Address:* Faculty of Medicine, Wolfson Medical School Building, University Avenue, Glasgow G12 8QQ. *T:* (0141) 330 33625921.

BARLOW, David John; broadcasting consultant; Adviser on International Relations, BBC, since 1993; *b* 20 Oct. 1937; *s* of Ralph and Joan Barlow; *m* 2001, Stella M. Waterman (*née* Hewer); one step *s* one step *d*, and five *s* one *d* of previous marriages. *Educ:* Leighton Park Sch.; The Queen's Coll., Oxford; Leeds Univ. MA, DipEd (Oxon); DipESL (Leeds). British Council, 1962–63; BBC, 1963–: Producer, African Service; Schools Broadcasting, 1965–67; Programme Organiser, Hindi, Tamil, Nepali and Bengali Service, 1967–70; Further Educn Radio, 1970–71; UNESCO, British Council Consultancies, 1970–73; Head of Liaison Internat. Relations, 1974–76; Chief Asst Regions, 1977–79; Gen. Sec., ITCA, 1980–81; BBC: Sec., 1981–84; Controller: Public Affairs and Internat. Relations, 1984–86; Public Affairs, 1986–87; Regional Broadcasting, 1987–90; seconded to EBU as Co-ordinator for Audio Visual Eureka Project, 1990–91; Controller, Information Services and Internat. Relns, 1991–92. Non-exec. Dir, Bedford Hosp. NHS Trust, 2002–04. Mem., RTS, 1980–. Trustee, Children in Need, 1986–92. Chm., Govs, Sharnbrook Upper Sch., 2002–03 (Vice-Chm., 2001–02). *Recreations:* bird watching, mountains, books. *Address:* 6 Rue des Ecoles, 79120 Chenay, France. *T:* (5) 49293899; *e-mail:* davidbarlow1@wanadoo.fr.

BARLOW, David Michael Rigby, CB 1996; Under Secretary, Government Legal Service, 1989–96; *b* 8 June 1936; *s* of late Samuel Gordon Barlow and Eunice Hodson Barlow; *m* 1973, Valeree Elizabeth Rush-Smith; one *s*; one *d* by previous marr. *Educ:* Shrewsbury Sch.; Christ Church, Oxford (MA Law). National Service: Midshipman RNVR in Submarine Br. of RN, 1954–56; Sub-Lieut and Lieut in permanent RNR, 1956–61. Solicitor, England and Wales, 1965, NI, 1991. Appointments as a lawyer in the public service, 1965–73; Asst Sec. in Govt Legal Service, 1973–89. *Recreations:* Spanish language and culture, ski-ing, cinema.

BARLOW, Francis; *see* Barlow, R. F. D.

BARLOW, Prof. Frank, CBE 1989; MA, DPhil; FBA 1970; FRSL 1971; FRHistS; Professor of History and Head of Department, University of Exeter, 1953–76, now Emeritus Professor; *b* 19 April 1911; *e s* of Percy Hawthorn and Margaret Julia Barlow; *m* 1936, Moira Stella Brigid Garvey; two *s*. *Educ:* Newcastle High Sch.; St John's Coll., Oxford (Open Schol., 1930; 1st Cl. Hons Sch. of Modern History, 1933; Bryce Student,

1933; BLitt 1934; Hon. Fellow, 2001); DPhil Oxon 1937. Oxford Senior Student, 1934; Fereday Fellow, St John's Coll., Oxford, 1935–38; Asst Lecturer, University Coll., London, 1936–40; War service in the Army, 1941–46, commissioned into Intelligence Corps, demobilised as Major; Lecturer 1946, Reader 1949, Dep. Vice-Chancellor, 1961–63, Public Orator, 1974–76, University of Exeter. Hon. DLitt Exon, 1981. *Publications:* The Letters of Arnulf of Lisieux, 1939; Durham Annals and Documents of the Thirteenth Century, 1945; Durham Jurisdictional Peculiars, 1950; The Feudal Kingdom of England, 1955; (ed and trans.) The Life of King Edward the Confessor, 1962; The English Church, 1000–1066, 1963; William I and the Norman Conquest, 1965; Edward the Confessor, 1970; (with Martin Biddle, Olof von Feilitzen and D. J. Keene) Winchester in the Early Middle Ages, 1976; The English Church 1066–1154, 1979; The Norman Conquest and Beyond (selected papers), 1983; William Rufus, 1983; Thomas Becket, 1986; Introduction to Devonshire Domesday Book, 1991; English Episcopal Acta, xi–xii (Exeter 1046–1257), 1996; (ed and trans.) Carmen de Hastingae Proelio, 1999; The Godwins, 2002. *Recreation:* gardening. *Address:* Middle Court Hall, Kenton, Exeter EX6 8NA. *T:* (01626) 890438.

BARLOW, Sir Frank, Kt 1998; CBE 1993; Chairman, Logica, 1995–2002; *b* 25 March 1930; *s* of John and Isabella Barlow; *m* 1950, Constance Patricia Ginns (*d* 2000); one *s* two *d*. *Educ:* Barrow Grammar Sch., Cumbria. Nigerian Electricity Supply Corp., 1952–59; Daily Times, Nigeria, 1960–62; Managing Director: Ghana Graphic, 1962–63; Barbados Advocate, 1963; Trinidad Mirror Newspapers, 1963–64; Gen. Manager, Daily Mirror, 1964–67; Man. Dir, King & Hutchings, 1967–75; Dir and Gen. Manager, Westminster Press, 1975–83; Dir, Economist, 1983–99; Chief Executive: Financial Times Group, 1983–90 (Chm., 1993–96); Westminster Press Group, 1985–90; Man. Dir, Pearson plc, 1990–96; Chairman: BSkyB, 1991–95; Thames Television, 1995–97; Channel 5, 1997. Pres., Les Echos, Paris, 1988–90; Director: Elsevier (UK), 1991–94; Soc. Européene des Satellites SA, 2000–02; Chm., Lottery Products Ltd, 1997–. Dir, Press Assoc., 1985–93. Chm., Printers' Charitable Corp., 1995–2000, Pres. Emeritus, 2006. Dir, Royal Philharmonic Orch., 1988–93. *Recreations:* golf, fell walking, angling. *Address:* Tremarne, Marsham Way, Gerrards Cross, Bucks SL9 8AW. *Club:* Carlton.

BARLOW, Gavin Galbraith; Director General Management and Organisation, Ministry of Defence, since 2006; *b* 5 May 1964; *s* of Peter John Barlow and Elizabeth Findlay Barlow; *m* 1991, Dr Alice Rebecca Chishick; three *s* two *d*. *Educ:* Univ. of Bristol (BSc Soc. Sci. 1986); Imperial Coll., London (MBA, DIC, 1997). Ministry of Defence, 1987–: Asst Private Sec. to Minister of State (Armed Forces), 1989–91; Administrative Sec., Sovereign Base Areas Admin, Cyprus, 1999–2002; Dir Policy Planning, 2002–06. *Recreations:* cooking, cycling, books. *Address:* Ministry of Defence, Main Building, Whitehall, SW1A 2HB. *T:* (020) 7218 4096.

BARLOW, George Francis, OBE 1998; FRICS; Chairman, London Development Agency, 2000–03; Chief Executive (formerly Director), Peabody Trust, 1987–99; *b* 26 May 1939; *s* of late George and Agnes Barlow; *m* 1969, Judith Alice Newton; one *s* two *d*. *Educ:* Wimbledon Coll.; Hammersmith Sch. of Art and Building; Polytechnic of Central London. Surveyor, Building Design Partnership, 1962–67; Develt Surveyor, GLC Housing Dept, 1967–70; The Housing Develt Officer, London Borough of Camden, 1970–76; Dir/Sec., Metropolitan Housing Trust, 1976–87. External Examiner, Polytechnic of Central London, 1989–90. Mem., Housing Cttee, 1986–91, Chm., Housing Policy Panel, 1996–99, RICS; Chm., London Housing Assocs Council, 1978–82; Dep. Chm., London Develt Partnership, 1998–2000; Member: Central YMCA Housing Assoc., 1982–85; Council, Nat. Fedn of Housing Assocs, 1985–89; Cttee, Community Self Build Agency, 1989–94; Cttee, Broomleigh Housing Assoc., 1989–95; Trustee: Kent Community Housing Trust, 1989–92; William Sutton Trust, 1999–2001; Mem. Bd, East London Partnership, 1991–99. Chm., Youth Homelessness Cttee, Prince's Trust/BITC, 1994–98. Gov., Univ. of E London, 1996–2000. Sen. Associate, King's Fund, 1999–2004. Hon. DLitt: Westminster, 2001; London South Bank, 2004. *Recreations:* theatre, horseracing.

BARLOW, Sir (George) William, Kt 1977; BSc Tech, FREng, FIMechE, FIET; President, Royal Academy of Engineering (formerly Fellowship of Engineering), 1991–96; *b* 8 June 1924; *s* of Albert Edward and Annice Barlow; *m* 1948, Elaine Mary Atherton (*née* Adamson); one *s* one *d*. *Educ:* Manchester Grammar Sch.; Manchester Univ. (Kitchener Schol., Louis Atkinson Schol.; BSc Tech. 1st cl. Hons Elec Engrg, 1944). Served as Elec. Lt, RNVR, 1944–47. Various appts, The English Electric Co. Ltd (in Spain, 1952–55, Canada, 1958–62); Gen. Manager, Liverpool and Netherton, 1964–67; Managing Director: English Electric Domestic Appliance Co. Ltd, 1965–67; English Electric Computers Ltd, 1967–68; Gp Chief Exec., 1969–77, Chm., 1971–77, Ransome Hoffman Pollard Ltd; Chm. and Chief Exec., Post Office, 1977–80, organized separation of Post Office and British Telecom, 1980; Chairman: Thorn EMI Engrg Gp, 1980–84; Ericsson, 1981–94; BICC, 1984–91 (Dir, 1980–91); SKF (UK), 1990–92; Barking Power Ltd, 1992–93; Kennedy and Donkin, then Parsons Brinckerhoff, 1997–2002; Director: Vodafone Group, 1988–98; Chemring Gp, 1994–97. Chm., NICG, 1980. Member: Industrial Develt Adv. Bd, 1972–79; Council, IEE, 1969–72 (Vice-Pres., 1978–80, Dep. Pres., 1983–84; Hon. Fellow, 1990); Council, IMechE, 1971–74; National Electronics Council, 1982–94; President: BEAMA, 1986–87; ORGALIME, 1990–92; Vice Pres., City and Guilds of London Inst., 1982–92. Chairman: Design Council, 1980–86; Engineering Council, 1988–90. Pres., Assoc. of Lancastrians in London, 1981 and 1992. Trustee, Brain Res. Trust, 1987–99. Governor, London Business Sch., 1979–92 (Hon. Fellow, 1991). Master, Worshipful Company of Engineers, 1986–87. FREng (FEng 1979). Hon. FUMIST 1978; Hon. FIET (Hon. FIEE 1990); Hon. FICE 1991; Hon. FIMechE 1993; Hon. FCGI 1996. Hon. DSc: Cranfield, 1979; Bath, 1986; Aston, 1988; City, 1989; Hon. DTech: CNAA, 1988; Loughborough, 1993; Hon DEng UMIST, 1996. *Recreations:* golf, racing. *Address:* 4 Parkside, Henley-on-Thames, Oxon RG9 1TX. *T:* (01491) 410550; *e-mail:* barlow@oviedo.demon.co.uk. *Clubs:* Brooks's; Leander (Henley-on-Thames); Huntercombe Golf.

BARLOW, Dr Horace Basil, FRS 1969; Royal Society Research Professor, Physiological Laboratory, Cambridge University, 1973–87; *b* 8 Dec. 1921; *s* of Sir (James) Alan (Noel) Barlow, 2nd Bt, GCB, KBE and Nora Barlow (*née* Darwin); *m* 1st, 1954, Ruthala (marr. diss., 1970), *d* of late Dr M. H. Salaman; four *d*; 2nd, 1980, Miranda, *d* of John Weston Smith; one *s* two *d*. *Educ:* Winchester; Trinity Coll., Cambridge. Research Fellow, Trinity Coll., 1950–54, Lectr, King's Coll., Cambridge, 1954–64. Demonstrator and Asst Dir of Research, Physiological Lab., Cambridge, 1954–64; Prof. of Physiological Optics and Physiology, Univ. of Calif, Berkeley, 1964–73. Australia Prize, 1993; Royal Medal, Royal Soc., 1993; Lashley Award, Amer. Philosophical Soc., 2003. *Publications:* several, on neurophysiology of vision in Jl of Physiology, and elsewhere. *Address:* Trinity College, Cambridge CB2 1TQ.

BARLOW, Sir James (Alan), 4th Bt *cr* 1902, of Wimpole Street, St Marylebone, co. London; communications consultant, Bell Canada, Vancouver, since 2002; *b* 10 July 1956; *s* of Sir Thomas Erasmus Barlow, 3rd Bt and of Isabel Barlow (*née* Body); *S* father, 2003; *m* 2004, Sylvia Lois Mann. *Educ:* Highgate Sch.; Manchester Univ. (BSc). US Steel Res. Center, Penn, USA, 1978; The Welding Inst., Cambridge, UK, 1979–82; Harland & Wolff, Shipbuilders, Belfast, 1982–84; Glassdrumman Lodge Hotel, Newcastle, Ire., 1985–92; Galgorm Manor Hotel, Ballymena, 1992–95; Covenant Life Coll., Fort St John, BC, 1996–98; IBM Canada, Vancouver, 1999–2002. Pres., Interjab Computer Support Services, Vancouver, 2002–. Vice Pres., Abbotsford Chamber of Commerce, BC, 2001–. Patron, Galapagos Conservation Trust, London, 2004–; Vice Chm., Bd of Trustees, Abbotsford Christ the King, 2006–. *Recreations:* ornithology, the countryside, the Bible, technology. *Address:* 1652 King Crescent, Abbotsford, BC V2S 7M7, Canada. *T:* (604) 5042412, *Fax:* (604) 5042413; *e-mail:* jabathome@aol.com. *Clubs:* Savile, Royal Over-Seas League.

BARLOW, Jan; Chief Executive, Battersea Dogs & Cats Home, since 2006; *b* 28 Sept. 1965; *d* of Peter and Joan Barlow; partner, Dr Gavin Alexander. *Educ:* Corpus Christi Coll., Cambridge (BA 1989, MA 1992); South Bank Univ., London (MSc 1998). Manager, GP Postgrad. Educn, East Anglian RHA, 1990–92; Jt Planning and Business Manager, Croydon HA and Croydon FHSA, 1992–94; Hd, Corporate Mgt, Croydon HA, 1994–97; Hd, Corporate Affairs, Save the Children, 1997–2001; Chief Exec., Brook Adv. Centres, then Brook, 2001–06. *Recreation:* horses, specifically dressage. *Address:* Battersea Dogs & Cats Home, 4 Battersea Park Road, SW8 4AA. *T:* (020) 7622 3626, *Fax:* (020) 7627 9200; *e-mail:* j.barlow@dogshome.org.

BARLOW, Sir John (Kemp), 3rd Bt *cr* 1907, of Bradwall Hall, Sandbach; merchant banker and farmer; Director: Thomas Barlow and Bro. Ltd; Majedie Investments plc, since 1978; Director of other companies; *b* 22 April 1934; *s* of Sir John Denman Barlow, 2nd Bt and Hon. Diana Helen (*d* 1986), *d* of 1st Baron Rochdale, CB and *sister* of 1st Viscount Rochdale, OBE, TD; *S* father, 1986; *m* 1st, 1962, Susan (marr. diss. 1998), *er d* of Col Sir Andrew Horsbrugh-Porter, 3rd Bt, DSO; four *s*; 2nd, 1998, Mrs Pauline Windsor. *Educ:* Winchester; Trinity Coll., Cambridge (MA 1958). Chm., Rubber Growers' Assoc., 1974. Steward of the Jockey Club, 1988–90. High Sheriff, Cheshire, 1979. *Recreations:* steeplechasing, hunting, shooting. *Heir:* *s* John William Marshall Barlow [*b* 12 March 1964; *m* 1991, Sarah Nobes; three *s*]. *Clubs:* Brooks's, City of London, Jockey.

BARLOW, Prof. Martin Thomas, ScD; FRS 2005; FRSC 1998; Professor of Mathematics, University of British Columbia, since 1992; *b* 16 June 1953; *s* of late Andrew Dalmahoy Barlow and of Yvonne Rosalind Barlow; *m* 1994, Colleen Patricia McLaughlin. *Educ:* Sussex House Sch., London; St Paul's Sch., London; Trinity Coll., Cambridge (BA 1975; ScD 1993); University Coll. of Swansea (PhD). Fellow, Trinity Coll., Cambridge, 1979–92. *Publications:* contrib. to learned jls. *Address:* Department of Mathematics, University of British Columbia, Vancouver, BC V6T 1Z2, Canada. *T:* (604) 8226377, *Fax:* (604) 8226074.

BARLOW, Patrick; actor, writer, director; *b* 18 March 1947; *s* of Edward Morgan and Sheila Maud Barlow; two *s* one *d*. *Educ:* Uppingham Sch.; Birmingham Univ. (BA 1968). Founder mem., Inter-Action Community Arts, 1968–72; Dir, Lancaster Young People's Theatre, 1972–74; Founder Dir, Solent People's Theatre, 1974–76; created Henrietta Sluggett and appeared nationwide in clubs, streets, theatres, incl. Crucible, Sheffield, Haymarket, Leicester and NT, 1976–79; created *National Theatre of Brent*, 1980, appeared in and wrote jointly: stage: Charge of the Light Brigade, 1980; Zulu!, 1981; Black Hole of Calcutta, 1982; Götterdämmerung, 1982; The Messiah, 1983; Complete Guide to Sex, 1984; Greatest Story Ever Told, 1987; Mysteries of Sex, 1997; Love Upon the Throne, 1998; The New Messiah, 2000; The Wonder of Sex, 2001; television: Messiah, 1983; Mighty Moments from World History, Lawrence of Arabia, Dawn of Man, Boadicea, Arthur and Guinevere, 1985; Revolution!!, 1989; created Royal Dingle Co. for Oh Dear Purcell!, 1995; Massive Landmarks of the Twentieth Century, Queen Victoria, Russian Revolution, Edward VIII and Mrs Simpson, Cuban Missile Crisis, First Man on the Moon, Clinton and Monica, 1999; *other stage appearances* incl.: Truscott, in Loot, Manchester Royal Exchange, 1987; Humphry, in Common Pursuit, Phoenix, 1988; Pseudolus, in A Funny Thing Happened on the Way to the Forum, Manchester Liby Th., 1988; Sidney, in Silly Cow, Haymarket, 1991; Toad, in Wind in the Willows, RNT, 1994; *television* incl.: Talk to Me, 1983; Victoria Wood: As Seen on TV, 1985; All Passion Spent, 1986; Thank You Miss Jones, 1987; Absolutely Fabulous, 1994, 2004; Aristophanes, 1995; Is It Legal?, 1995, 1996, 1998; Cows, 1996; Goodbye Mr Steadman, 1999; The Nearly Complete and Utter History of Everything, 2002; Hans Christian Anderson, 2002; Murder in Suburbia, 2004; Shakespeare's Happy Endings, 2005; Marple: By the Pricking of My Thumbs, 2006; Jam and Jerusalem, 2006, 2008; Sensitive Skin, 2007; regular appearances on French & Saunders; *films* incl.: Shakespeare in Love, 1999; Notting Hill, 1999; Girl from Rio, 2001; Bridget Jones's Diary, 2001; Nanny McPhee, 2005; Scoop, 2006; *radio* incl.: All the World's a Globe, Midsummer Wedding, 1990; Noah, 1991; Desmond Dingle's Compleat Life and Works of William Shakespeare, 1995; Rent, 1996, 1997, 1998; The Patrick and Maureen Maybe Music Experience, 1999; Just Plain Gardening, 2002, 2005; National Theatre of Brent's Complete and Utter History of the Mona Lisa, 2004 (Sony Gold for Best Comedy, Gold award, NY Fests, 2005); The Furniture Play, 2004; Volpone, 2004; Small Gods, 2006; National Theatre of Brent's Messiah, 2006; National Theatre of Brent's The Arts and How They Was Done, 6 episodes, 2007; Desmond Dingle's Entire History of the Theatre, 2007; regular contrib., Looking Forward to the Past, Quote Unquote. Writer: for television: The Ghost of Faffner Hall (jtly), 1989; adaptation, The Growing Pains of Adrian Mole, 1986; screenplay, Van Gogh (Prix Futura, Berlin Film Fest.), 1990; Scarfe on Sex, 1991; The True Adventures of Christopher Columbus (also actor and dir), 1992; Queen of the East, 1994 (also actor); adaptation, The Young Visiters, 2003 (also actor); for theatre: libretto, Judgement of Paris, Garden Venture, Royal Opera, 1991; How to Deal with Getting Dumped, GogMagog Theatre Co., 2002; The 39 Steps, W Yorks Playhouse, 2005, transf. Criterion, 2006 (Best Comedy, Olivier Awards, 2007), transf. NY, 2008. *Publications:* All the World's a Globe, 1987 (adapted for radio) (Sony Radio award, 1990; Premier Ondas award, 1991); Shakespeare: The Truth, 1993; Love Upon the Throne, 1998; The Messiah, 2001; The Wonder of Sex, 2001; Desmond Olivier Dingle's Complete History of the Whole World, 2002. *Address:* (as writer/director) Casarotto and Associates, Waverley House, 7–12 Noel Street, W1F 8GQ; (as actor) JAA, 11 Garrick Street, WC2E 9AR. *Clubs:* Groucho, Two Brydges, Adam Street.

BARLOW, (Richard) Francis (Dudley); QC 2006; barrister; *b* 9 Oct. 1938; *y s* of late Dudley Barlow and Ruby Barlow (*née* Brews); *m* 1966, Helen Mary, *er d* of late Wilfrid Gawthorne and of Maureen Gawthorne (*née* Nelson); three *s*. *Educ:* Dauntsey's Sch.; Christ Church, Oxford (BA 1962; MA 1966). Nat. Service, RN, 1957–59; Lt-Comdr RNR. Called to the Bar, Inner Temple, 1965; Bencher, Lincoln's Inn, 1994; in practice at Chancery Bar. *Address:* 10 Old Square, Lincoln's Inn, WC2A 3SU. *T:* (020) 7405 0758. *Club:* Garrick.

BARLOW, Roy Oxspring; solicitor; a Recorder of the Crown Court, 1975–97; *b* 13 Feb. 1927; *s* of George and Clarice Barlow; *m* 1957, Kathleen Mary Roberts; two *s* one *d*. *Educ:* King Edward VII Sch., Sheffield; Queen's Coll., Oxford; Sheffield Univ. (LLB). Local

Government, 1952–62; solicitor in private practice, 1962–. Asst Comr, Parly Boundary Commn, 1992–95. *Recreations:* farming, walking, reading. *Address:* The Cottage, Oxton Rakes, Barlow Dronfield, NE Derbys S18 7TH. *T:* (0114) 289 0652.

BARLOW, Stephen William, FGSM, FRCO; conductor, composer and pianist; *b* 30 June 1954; *s* of George William Barlow and Irene Catherine Barlow (*née* Moretti); *m* 1986, Joanna Lamond Lumley, *qv*. *Educ:* Canterbury Cathedral Choir Sch.; King's Sch., Canterbury; Trinity Coll., Cambridge (BA 1975); Guildhall Sch. of Music and Drama. FRCO 1971; FGSM 1986. Associate Conductor, Glyndebourne Fest. Opera, 1980–81; Resident Conductor, ENO, 1980–83; Music Director: Opera 80, 1987–90 (co-founder, 1979); Queensland Philharmonic, 1996–99; Artistic Dir, Opera Northern Ireland, 1996–99. Début as conductor, Royal Opera House, Covent Garden, 1989, then San Francisco, Melbourne, Sydney, Detroit, Miami, Berlin, Auckland, Singapore, Vancouver, Amsterdam, Chicago, Copenhagen, Aarhus, Belgrade, Catania, Toronto, etc. *Publications:* String Quartet, 2000; The Rainbow Bear (for children), 2000; Pas de Deux for Flute and Piano, 2002; King (opera for Canterbury Cathedral), 2004; Clarinet Concerto, 2008. *Recreations:* wine, driving, cricket, composing and playing chamber music. *Address:* c/o Musichall, Ivydene, Vicarage Way, Ringmer, Lewes, E Sussex BN8 5LA. *T:* (01273) 814240; *e-mail:* info@musichall.uk.com.

BARLOW, Sir William; *see* Barlow, Sir G. W.

BARLTROP, Roger Arnold Rowlandson, CMG 1987; CVO 1982; HM Diplomatic Service, retired; Ambassador to Fiji, 1988–89 (High Commissioner, 1982–88) and High Commissioner (non-resident) to Republic of Nauru and to Tuvalu, 1982–89; *b* 19 Jan. 1930; *s* of late Ernest William Barltrop, CMG, CBE, DSO, and Ethel Alice Lucy Barltrop (*née* Baker); *m* 1st, 1962, Penelope Pierrepont Dalton (marr. diss.); two *s* two *d*; 2nd, 1998, Bojana Komadina (*née* Jovanovic). *Educ:* Solihull Sch.; Leeds Grammar Sch.; Exeter Coll., Oxford. MA. Served RN, 1949–50, RNVR/RNR, 1950–64 (Lt-Comdr 1962). Asst Principal, CRO, 1954–56; Second Sec., New Delhi, 1956–57; Private Sec. to Parly Under-Sec. of State and Minister of State, CRO, 1957–60; First Sec., E Nigeria, 1960–62; Actg Dep. High Comr, W Nigeria, 1962; First Sec., Salisbury, Rhodesia, 1962–65; CRO, Commonwealth Office and FO, later FCO, 1965–69; First Sec. and Head of Chancery, Ankara, 1969–70; Dep. British Govt Rep., WI Associated States, 1971–73; Counsellor and Head of Chancery, Addis Ababa, 1973–77; Head of Commonwealth Coordination Dept, FCO, 1978–82. Mem., Commonwealth Observer Gp for elections in Bangladesh, Feb. 1991, and in St Kitts/Nevis, 1995; Mem., UK/OSCE Observer Gp for elections in Bosnia, 1996; Foreign Affairs Trng Advr, Solomon Is, 1994. Chm., Pacific Is Soc. of UK and Ireland, 1992–98. *Publications:* contribs to Round Table (Commonwealth jl of internat. affairs). *Recreations:* sailing, genealogy, opera. *Address:* 35 Highfield Drive, Hurstpierpoint, West Sussex BN6 9AU. *Club:* Royal Commonwealth Society.

BARNA, Prof. Tibor, CBE 1974; Professor of Economics, University of Sussex, 1962–82, Professor Emeritus 1984; Member, Monopolies and Mergers Commission, 1963–78; *b* 1919. *Educ:* London School of Economics. Lecturer, London School of Economics, 1944; Official Fellow, Nuffield College, Oxford, 1947; senior posts in UN Economic Commission for Europe, 1949; Assistant Director, National Institute of Economic and Social Research, London, 1955. *Publications:* Redistribution of Income through Public Finance in 1937, 1945; Investment and Growth Policies in British Industrial Firms, 1962; Agriculture towards the Year 2000, 1979; European Process Plant Industry, 1981; papers in Jl Royal Statistical Soc., Economic Jl, European Econ. Review.

BARNARD, 11th Baron *cr* 1698; **Harry John Neville Vane,** TD 1960; landowner; Lord-Lieutenant and Custos Rotulorum of County Durham, 1970–88; a Vice-Chairman, Council, British Red Cross Society, 1987–93 (Member Council 1982–85; Hon. Vice President, since 1999); Chairman, Teesdale Mercury Ltd, since 1983; *b* 21 Sept. 1923; *er s* of 10th Baron Barnard, CMG, OBE, MC, TD, and Sylvia Mary (*d* 1993), *d* of Herbert Straker; *S* father, 1964; *m* 1952, Lady Davina Mary Cecil, DStJ (marr. diss. 1992), *e d* of 6th Marquess of Exeter, KCMG; one *s* four *d*. *Educ:* Eton; MSc Durham, 1986. Served War of 1939–45, RAFVR, 1942–46 (Flying Officer, 1945). Northumberland Hussars (TA), 1948–66; Lt-Col Commanding, 1964–66. Vice-Pres., N of England TA&VRA, 1970 and 1977–88, Pres., 1974–77. Hon. Col, 7 (Durham) Bn The Light Infantry, 1979–89. County Councillor, Durham, 1952–61. Member: Durham Co. AEC, 1953–72 (Chm., 1970–72); N Regional Panel, MAFF, 1972–76; CLA Council, 1950–80; Dir, NE Housing Assoc., 1964–77. President: Farmway Ltd (formerly Teesside Farmers), 1965–2003; Durham Co. Br., CLA, 1965–89; Durham Co. St John Council, 1971–88; Durham Co. Scouts Assoc., 1972–88; Durham and Cleveland Co. Br. RBL, 1973–92; Durham Wildlife Trust (formerly Durham Co. Conservation Trust), 1984–95; Durham Co. Fedn of Young Farmers Clubs, 1991–92; Vice-Pres., Game Conservancy Trust, 1997–. Patron: Durham Co. Br., BRCS, 1993– (Pres., 1969–87); Durham Co. RBL, 2001–. DL Durham, 1956, Vice-Lieutenant, 1969–70; JP Durham, 1961. Joint Master of Zetland Hounds, 1963–65. Sen. Grand Warden, United Grand Lodge of England, 1970–71; Provincial Grand Master for Durham, 1969–98. Queen's Badge of Honour, BRCS, 1991. KStJ 1971. *Heir: s* Hon. Henry Francis Cecil Vane [*b* 11 March 1959; *m* 1998, Kate, *yr d* of Christopher Robson; one *s* two *d*]. *Address:* Raby Castle, PO Box 50, Staindrop, Darlington, Co. Durham DL2 3AY. *T:* (01833) 660751. *Clubs:* Brooks's; Durham County (Durham); Northern Counties (Newcastle upon Tyne).

BARNARD, David; *see* Barnard, J. D. W.

BARNARD, Prof. Eric Albert, PhD; FRS 1981; Visiting Professor, Department of Pharmacology, University of Cambridge, since 1999; Director, Molecular Neurobiology Unit, and Professor of Neurobiology, Royal Free and University College Medical School (formerly Royal Free Hospital School of Medicine), London University, 1992–98, Emeritus Professor, since 1999; *m* 1956, Penelope J. Hennessy; two *s* two *d*. *Educ:* Davenant Foundn Sch.; King's Coll., London. BSc, PhD 1956. King's College, London: Nuffield Foundn Fellow, 1956–59; Asst Lectr, 1959–60; Lectr, 1960–64. State University of New York at Buffalo: Associate Prof. of Biochemical Pharmacol., 1964–65; Prof. of Biochemistry, 1965–76; Head of Biochemistry Dept, 1969–76; Imperial College of Science and Technology, London: Rank Prof. of Physiol Biochemistry, 1976–85; Chm., Div. of Life Sciences, 1977–85; Head, Dept of Biochem., 1979–85; Dir, MRC Molecular Neurobiol. Unit, Cambridge, 1985–92. Rockefeller Fellow, Univ. of Calif, Berkeley, 1960–61; Guggenheim Fellow, MRC Lab. of Molecular Biol., Cambridge, 1971. Visiting Professor: Univ. of Marburg, Germany, 1965; Tokyo Univ., 1993; Vis. Scientist, Inst. Pasteur, France, 1973. Member: British Pharmacol Soc.; Biochem. Soc.; Soc. for Neurosci., USA; Internat. Soc. Neurochem; EMBO; Cttee, Internat. Union of Pharmacology, 1991–2000; Cttee Mem., CNRS, France. UK rep., EC Cttee on Decade of the Brain, 1987–92. Foreign Mem., Polish Acad. of Scis, 2000. Josiah Macy Faculty Scholar Award, USA, 1975; Ciba Medal and Prize, 1985; Eastman Kodak Award, USA, 1988; Erspamer Internat. Award for Neuroscience, 1991; ECNP-Synthélabo Award for Neuroscience Res., 1996; Eli Lilly Prize for European Neuroscience, 1998; Thudicum Medal for Molecular Neuroscience, Biochem. Soc., 2007. Editor-in-Chief, Receptors and Channels, 1993–2000; mem. editl bd, three other scientific jls. *Publications:* editor of eight scientific books; several hundred papers in learned jls. *Recreation:* the pursuit of good claret. *Address:* Department of Pharmacology, University of Cambridge, Tennis Court Road, Cambridge CB2 1PD. *T:* (01223) 847876, 334043; *e-mail:* eb247@cam.ac.uk.

BARNARD, Surg. Rear Adm. Ernest Edward Peter, DPhil; FFCM; Surgeon Rear Admiral, Operational Medical Services, 1982–84; retired 1984; *b* 22 Feb. 1927; *s* of Lionel Edward Barnard and Ernestine (*née* Lethbridge); *m* 1955, Dr Joan Barnard (*née* Gunn); one *s* one *d*. *Educ:* schools in England and Australia; Univ. of Adelaide; St Mary's Hosp., Univ. of London (MB, BS 1955); St John's Coll., Univ. of Oxford (student, 1966–68; DPhil 1969). MRCS, LRCP 1955; MFOM 1979; FFCM 1980. After house appts, joined RN, 1956; served, 1957–76: HMS Bulwark, Reclaim and Dolphin; RN Physiol Lab.; RN Med. Sch.; Inst. of Naval Medicine; Dept of Med. Dir Gen. (Naval); exchange service with US Navy at Naval Med. Res. Inst., Bethesda, Md, 1976–78; Inst. of Naval Medicine, 1978–80; QHP 1980–84; Dep. Med. Dir Gen. (Naval), 1980–82; Surgeon Rear-Adm., Inst. of Naval Medicine, and Dean of Naval Medicine, 1982. FRSocMed 1962. *Publications:* papers on underwater medicine and physiology. *Recreations:* gardening, genealogy, photography. *Address:* c/o Barclays Bank, PO Box 6, Portsmouth PO6 3DH.

BARNARD, Hermione; *see* Lee, H.

BARNARD, (John) David (William), CBE 2000; FRCS, FDSRCS; Consultant Oral and Maxillofacial Surgeon, Queen Alexandra Hospital, Portsmouth Hospitals NHS Trust, 1979–2005; *b* 5 March 1943; *s* of Dr George Edward Barnard and Gwenllian Mary Barnard (*née* Thomas); *m* 1980, Cheryl Barlow. *Educ:* St Marylebone Grammar Sch.; Guy's Hosp. Dental Sch. (BDS London 1966). FDSRCS 1974; FDSRCPSGlas 1974. Hse surgeon, Guy's Hosp., 1967; RN Dental Service, 1967–72; Asst Dental Surgeon, Queen Victoria Hosp., E Grinstead, 1973–75; Sen. Registrar, Oxford Hosps, 1975–79. Civil Consultant, Royal Hosp. (formerly Royal Naval Hosp.), Haslar, 1983–2005; Consultant Advr in Oral and Maxillofacial Surgery, RN, 2002–05 Leverhulme Fellow in Oral Surgery, Univ. of California, 1978; Hunterian Prof., RCS, 1978. Clifford Ballard Meml Lecture, Consultant Orthodontists' Gp, British Orthodontic Soc., 2004. Member: Central Cttee, Hosp. Dental Services, 1988–99 (Chm., 1995–98); Jt Consultants Cttee, 1995–2001; Central Consultants and Specialists Cttee, BMA, 1995–2001; Standing Dental Adv. Cttee, 1998–2004. Mem., GDC, 1998–2004 (Chm., Postgrad. Sub Cttee, 2001–03; Chm., Educn Cttee, 2003–04); Hosps Gp Pres., 1985, Chm., Gp Cttee, 1988–99, Mem., Council and Rep. Bd, 1995–98, Fellow, 2004, BDA; Mem. Council, 1987–92, Hon. Treas., 1989–92, Pres., 2004, BAOMS; Odontological Section, Royal Society of Medicine: Mem. Council, 1990–99; Hon. Treas., 1993–96; Vice-Pres., 1996–99; Royal College of Surgeons of England: Bd Mem., 1995–2002, Dean, 1998–2001, Faculty of Dental Surgery; Mem. Council, 1998–2002; Trustee, Hunterian Collection, 2008. FDSRCSE (*ad hominem*) 1998; FRCS (by election) 2000; FFGDP(UK) 2008. Hon. Fellow, Amer. Assoc. of Oral and Maxillofacial Surgeons, 2004. Colyer Gold Medal, Faculty of Dental Surgery, RCS, 2004. *Publications:* contrib. chapters in books and articles to learned jls. *Recreations:* motor sport (sports car racing), general aviation, my dogs. *Address:* 31 Bath Road, Emsworth, Hants PO10 7ER. *T:* (01243) 372987. *Clubs:* Goodwood Flying; Emsworth Sailing.

BARNARD, Prof. John Michael; Professor of English Literature, School of English, University of Leeds, 1978–2001, now Emeritus; *b* Folkestone, 13 Feb. 1936; *s* of John Claude Southard Barnard and Dora Grace Barnard; *m* 1st, 1961, Katherine Duckham (marr. diss. 1975); one *s* two *d*; partner, 1975, *m* 2nd, 1991, Hermione Lee, *qv*. *Educ:* Wadham Coll., Oxford (BA (Hons) Eng. Lang. and Lit.; BLitt; MA). Res. Asst, English Dept, Yale Univ., 1961–64; Vis. Lectr, English Dept, Univ. of California at Santa Barbara, 1964–65; Post-doctoral Fellow, William Andrews Clark Meml Liby, UCLA, 1965; Leeds University: Lectr and Sen. Lectr, Sch. of English, 1965–78; Dir, Inst. of Bibliography and Textual Criticism, Sch. of English, 1996–2001 (Actg Dir, 1982–96). Res. Fellow, William Andrews Clark Meml Liby, UCLA, and Huntington Liby, 1994. Mem., British Cttee, Eighteenth Century Short Title Catalogue, 1983–89; Vice-Pres., Bibliographical Soc., 1998– (Mem. Council, 1989–94). Mem., English Panel, 1996 RAE, Chm., English Panel, 2001 RAE, HEFCE. Lectures: British Academy Warton, 1989; Friends of Bodleian Quatercentenary, 2002; D. F. McKenzie, Oxford Univ., 2005. Internat. expert Verkenningscommissie Moderne Letteren, Netherlands, 1992–93. FEA 2000. General Editor: Longman Annotated Poets, 1976–, with Paul Hammond, 2001–; The Cambridge History of The Book, Vols 1–2 and 5–7, 2003–; Member, Editorial Board: English Poetry Full Text Database, 1991–93; English Verse Drama Full Text Database, 1993–95; English Prose Drama Full Text Database, 1994–96. *Publications:* (ed) William Congreve, The Way of the World, 1972; (ed) Pope: The Critical Heritage, 1973; (ed) John Keats: the complete poems, 1973, 3rd edn 1988; (ed) Etherege: The Man of Mode, 1979, rev. edn 2007; John Keats, 1987; (ed) John Keats: selected poems, 1988; (jtly) The Early Seventeenth-Century York Book Trade and John Foster's Inventory of 1616, 1994; (ed) The Folio Society John Keats, 2001; (ed jtly) The Cambridge History of the Book in Britain, Vol. 4 1557–1695, 2002; (ed) Selected Poems: John Keats, 2007; chapters in books, articles in Brit. and Amer. learned jls, occasional reviews, etc. *Recreations:* travel, walking. *Address:* Lane End, Weeton Lane, Weeton, Leeds LS17 0AN.

BARNARD, Sir Joseph (Brian), Kt 1986; DL; Director, Financial Consultancy Services Ltd, 2000–03; *b* 22 Jan. 1928; *s* of Joseph Ernest Barnard and Elizabeth Loudon (*née* Constantine); *m* 1959, Suzanne Hamilton Bray; three *s* (incl. twins). *Educ:* Bramcote School, Scarborough; Sedbergh School. Served Army, 1946–48, commissioned KRRC. Director: Joseph Constantine Steamship Line, 1952–66; Teesside Warehousing Co., 1966–97. Farms at East Harsley. Dir, Northern Electric (formerly NE Electricity Bd), 1986–90; Chm., NE Electricity Cons. Council, 1986–90; Mem., Electricity Consumers' Council, 1986–90. Vice-Chm., 1988–91, Chm., 1991–92, Nat. Union of Cons. and Unionist Assocs (Chm., Yorks Area, 1983–88); Chm., Cons. Assoc. for Cleveland and Yorks N Euro Constituency, 1993–94; Pres., Richmond Cons. Assoc., 2007–. Life Vice President: Yorkshire Conservative Clubs, 1994; Conservatives at Work, 1994. Chm. Governors, Ingleby Arncliffe C of E Primary School, 1979–91; Patron, St Oswald's, E Harlsey. JP Northallerton, 1973–94; Chm., Northallerton (formerly Allertonshire PSD), 1981–93; Mem., N Yorks Magistrates' Courts Cttee, 1981–93. DL N Yorks, 1988. *Recreations:* walking, shooting, gardening. *Address:* Harlsey Hall, Northallerton, N Yorks DL6 2BL. *T:* (01609) 882203. *Club:* Carlton.

BARNARD, Toby Christopher, DPhil; FBA 2007; Lecturer in History, University of Oxford, since 1976; Fellow and Tutor in History, since 1976, and Archivist and Fellow Librarian, since 2005, Hertford College, Oxford; *b* 17 April 1945; *s* of Robert John Barnard and Gina Barnard (*née* Motta). *Educ:* Torquay Boys' Grammar Sch.; Brighton, Hove and Sussex Grammar Sch.; Queen's Coll., Oxford (BA 1966; DPhil 1972). Bryce Sen. Scholar in Hist., Oxford Univ., 1968–69; Tutor in Hist., Univ. of Exeter, 1969–70; Lectr in Hist., Royal Holloway Coll., Univ. of London, 1970–76. Historical advr, Carroll Inst. of Irish Hist., 1991–94; British Acad. Res. Reader, 1997–99; Vis. Fellow, Archbishop Narcissus Marsh's Liby, Dublin, 2001–02; Leverhulme Sen. Res. Fellow, 2006–. Hon. MRIA 2001. FRHistS 1977. *Publications:* Cromwellian Ireland: English government and reform in Ireland 1649–1660, 1975, 2nd edn 2000; The English Republic 1649–1660, 1982, 2nd edn 1997; The Abduction of a Limerick Heiress: social and political relations in mid-eighteenth-century Ireland, 1998; A New Anatomy of Ireland: the Irish protestants 1641–1770, 2003; Making the Grand Figure: lives and possessions in Ireland 1641–1770, 2004; Irish Protestant Ascents and Descents 1641–1770, 2004; The Kingdom of Ireland 1641–1760, 2004; Guide to the Sources for the History of Material Culture in Ireland 1500–2000, 2005; Improving Ireland?: projectors, prophets and profiteers, 1641–1786, 2008; *edited:* (with Jane Clark) Lord Burlington: architecture, art and life, 1995; (with D. Ó. Crónín and K. Simms) A Miracle of Learning: studies in manuscripts and Irish learning: essays in honour of William O'Sullivan, 1998; (with Jane Fenlon) The Dukes of Ormonde 1610–1745, 2000; (with W. G. Neely) The Clergy of the Church of Ireland 1000–2000: messengers, watchmen and stewards, 2006; articles in historical jls and book reviews in TLS, Irish Times, English Historical Review, etc. *Recreations:* pugs (Member, Pug Dog Club), collecting, West Cork. *Address:* Hertford College, Oxford OX1 3BW. *T:* (01865) 279400. *Club:* Oxford and Cambridge.

BARNE, Major Nicholas Michael Lancelot, CVO 2003 (LVO 1996); Extra Equerry to the Duke and Duchess of Gloucester, since 2004 (Private Secretary, Comptroller and Equerry, 1989–2004); *b* 25 Nov. 1943; *m* 1974, Hon. Janet Elizabeth, *d* of Baron Maclean, KT, GCVO, KBE, PC; two *s. Educ:* Eton Coll. Regular officer, Scots Guards, 1965–79; fruit farming, 1979–84. Hon. Col, Norfolk ACF, 1989–2001 (Co. Comdt, 1985–89). Private Sec., Comptroller and Equerry, 1989–2004, Extra Equerry, 2004, to Princess Alice, Duchess of Gloucester. Freeman, City of London, 2001; Liveryman, Co. of Broderers, 2002–. *Recreation:* shooting. *Address:* Blofield House, Blofield, Norwich, Norfolk NR13 4RW.

BARNEBY, Col Michael Paul; Clerk to the Salters' Company, 1990–2006; *b* 29 March 1939; *m* 1973, Bridget, *d* of Col A. G. Roberts, DSO, Crickhowell; three *d. Educ:* Radley Coll. Commissioned into 15th/19th King's Royal Hussars, 1958; served Germany, NI, Hong Kong; commanded Royal Hong Kong Regt (Volunteers), 1981–83; retired from Army, 1988; Dir of Planning and Admin, Clark Whitehill, 1988–89. *Recreations:* hunting, shooting, racing. *Address:* Patience House, Steventon, Hants RG25 3BD. *Club:* Boodle's.

BARNES; *see* Oppenheim-Barnes.

BARNES, family name of **Baron Gorell**.

BARNES, Adrian Francis Patrick, CVO 1996; DL; Remembrancer of the City of London, 1986–2003; *b* 25 Jan. 1943; *s* of late Francis Walter Ibbetson Barnes and of Heather Katherine (*née* Tamplin); *m* 1980, Sally Eve Whatley; one *s* one *d. Educ:* St Paul's School; MA City of London Polytechnic 1981. Called to the Bar, Gray's Inn, 1973, Bencher, 2000 (Doyen, Seniors in Hall, 1992–2000); Solicitor's Dept, DTI, 1975; Dep. Remembrancer, Corp. of London, 1982. Wimbledon Civic Forum: Founder, Mem. Exec. and Adv. Council, 1999–2003; Chm., Gen. Meetings on Constitution, 1999, Educn Forums and on Strategy, 2000–03. Chm., Wimbledon Guild of Social Welfare, 2004– (Mem., Exec. Cttee, 2003–; Chairman: Counselling Mgt Cttee, 2004–; Centenary Cttee, 2004–). Chm. Govs, The Music Therapy Charity, 1997–2003 (Gov., 1995–). Freeman: City of London, 1982; Guild of Arts Scholars, Dealers and Collectors, 2007– (Mem. Court of Assts, 2007–); Liveryman, Merchant Taylors' Co., 1989–. DL Greater London, 2002. *Recreations:* music, cricket, rowing, chess, biography, City lore. *Address:* 18 Clare Court, SW19 4RZ. *Clubs:* Garrick, Guildhall, MCC.

BARNES, Alan Robert, CBE 1976; JP; Headmaster, Ruffwood School, Kirkby, Liverpool, 1959–87; Field Officer and Consultant, Secondary Heads Association, 1987–2000; *b* 9 Aug. 1927; *s* of Arthur Barnes and Ida Barnes; *m* 1951, Pearl Muriel Boughton; (two *s* decd). *Educ:* Enfield Grammar Sch.; Queens' Coll., Cambridge (MA). National Service, RAEC. Wallington County Grammar Sch., 1951–55; Churchfields Sch., West Bromwich, 1955–59. Pres., Headmasters' Assoc., 1974, Treas., 1975–77; Chm., Jt Four Secondary Assocs, 1978; Treas., Secondary Heads Assoc., 1978–82; Vice-Chm., British Educn Management and Admin Soc., 1980–82, Chm. 1982–84. Schools Liaison Officer, Univ. of Essex, 1988–92. Chm., HMA Benevolent Fund, 1975–2005. Treasurer, HiPACT, 2000–04. JP Knowsley, Merseyside, 1967. *Publications:* (contrib.) Going Comprehensive (ed Halsall), 1970; (contrib.) Management and Headship in the Secondary School (ed Jennings), 1978; contrib. to: Education, BEMAS Jl, SHA publications. *Recreation:* bridge. *Address:* 2 Lark Valley Drive, Fornham St Martin, Bury St Edmunds, Suffolk IP28 6UF; *e-mail:* AlanBarnes@Larkvalley.fsnet.co.uk.

BARNES, Anthony Hugh, FSA; Director, Redundant Churches Fund, 1984–92; *b* 16 June 1931; *s* of Sir George Barnes and Anne Barnes; *m* 1st, 1956, Susan Dempsey; two *s* one *d*; 2nd, 1984, Jennifer Carey. *Educ:* King's Coll., Cambridge (MA). FCIPD. Schweppes Ltd, 1954–66; Royal Opera House, 1966–70; ICI, 1970–82; self-employed, 1982–84. Trustee: Norfolk Churches Trust, 1995–2002 (Sec., 1992–95); Norwich Historic Churches Trust, 2001–. Vice-Pres., Norwich Labour Party, 2000–01. FSA 2004. *Address:* 1 Dixon's Court, 52 Bethel Street, Norwich NR2 1NR. *T:* (01603) 666783.

BARNES, Barbara Lucinda; a District Judge (Magistrates' Courts), since 2004; *b* 28 Nov. 1953; *d* of Arthur Frederick Barnes and Barbara Barnes (*née* Willisford). *Educ:* Blackheath High Sch.; St George's Sch., Harpenden; KCL (LLB 1975). Called to the Bar, Gray's Inn, 1976; Inner London Magistrates' Courts Service: Dep. Chief Clerk, 1979–88; Dep. Trng Officer, 1988–91; Justices' Clerk, Greenwich, 1998–2003. Ed., Archbold: Magistrates' Courts Criminal Practice, 2004–. *Recreations:* amateur dramatics, theatre, travel, reading. *Address:* c/o Uxbridge Magistrates' Court, Harefield Road, Uxbridge, Middx UB8 1PQ.

BARNES, Most Rev. Brian James, KBE 2003 (MBE 1983); OFM; Archbishop of Port Moresby, (RC), 1997–2008, now Emeritus; Bishop for Disciplinary Forces, 1999–2008; *b* 23 March 1933; *s* of Arthur Keith Barnes and Eileen Victoria (*née* Whereat). *Educ:* Greyfriars, Mornington, Vic; St Paschal's Coll., Box Hill, Vic. Ordained priest, 1958; Missionary, Aitape dio., PNG, 1959–68; Police Chaplain, Port Moresby, 1968–88; Bishop of Aitape, 1988–97. Pres., Catholic Bps' Conf., PNG and Solomon Is, 1993–96; Chm., Heads of Churches' Cttee, 2005–08 (for Service chaplaincies) (Vice Chm., 1998–2005); Member: Nat. Disaster Cttee, 1998–2008; Senate for Priestly Formation, 1999–2008. Chairman: Police Promotion Bd, 1999–2000 and 2006–07; Deputy Chairman: St Mary's Medical Centre Bd, 1999–; NCD Commn Liquor Licensing Cttee, 2000–01; Mem., NCD Physical Planning Bd, 2003–05. Chancellor, and Chm. Governing Council, Catholic Theol Inst., 1999–2008; Chairman: Holy Spirit Seminary Bd, 1999–2008; Council, Nat. Res. Inst., 2001–06. *Recreation:* golf. *Address:* c/o Archbishop's House, PO Box 1032, Boroko, NCD 111, PNG. *T:* (office) 3251192, *Fax:* (office) 3256731; *e-mail:* archpom@daltron.com.pg.

BARNES, Christopher John Andrew, CB 1996; Assessor for Department for Environment, Food and Rural Affairs (formerly Ministry of Agriculture, Fisheries and Food), Office of the Commissioner for Public Appointments, since 1996; Senior Associate, Res Consortium, since 2005; *b* 11 Oct. 1944; *s* of late Eric Vernon Barnes and Joan Mary Barnes; *m* 1st, 1978, Carolyn Elizabeth Douglass Johnston (*d* 1990); two *s*; 2nd, 1990, Susan Elizabeth Bird; two *s. Educ:* City of London Sch.; London School of Economics (BScEcon). Ministry of Agriculture, Fisheries and Food: Exec. Officer, 1962; Asst Principal, 1967; Private Sec. to Parly Sec., 1969–71; Principal, 1971; Sec. to Northfield Cttee on Agricultural Land Ownership and Occupancy, 1977–79; Asst Sec., 1980; Chief Reg. Officer, Nottingham and Reading, 1980–83; Hd of Personnel and R&D Requirements Divs, 1983–90; 'Barnes Review' of near market R&D, 1988; Under Sec. (Grade 3), 1990–96; Arable Crops and Hortic., later Arable Crops and Alcoholic Drinks Gp, 1990–95; Dir of Estabs, 1995–96, retired. A Chm., CSSB, 1995–97. Sen. Consultant, Andersons, 1996–98; Associate Dir, Andersons Chamberlain Recruitment, 1996–98; Dir, Drew Associates Ltd, 1996–98; Exec. Search Consultant, Rundle Brownswood, 2002–. Chairman: Assured Produce Ltd, 1999–2001; Chris Barnes Ltd (formerly Modernising Skills Ltd), 1999–; Assured Food Standards Ltd, 2000–03; Man. Dir, Currency Connect UK, 2004–05; Dir, Horticultural Business, Huntington Gp, 2003–05; non-exec. Dir, Booker Food Services, 1987–90. Chm., Governing Body, CMi plc, 2005– (Mem., 2003–). Mem. Management Cttee, CS Healthcare, 1992–99 (Vice-Chm., 1997–99); Chm., Bucks HA, 1999–2000 (non-exec. Dir, 1996–99). FRSA 1999; FIHort 2002. *Recreations:* off-road vehicles, country living, France. *Club:* Farmers'.

BARNES, Clive Alexander, CBE 1975; Associate Editor and Chief Drama and Dance Critic, New York Post, since 1977; *b* London, 13 May 1927; *s* of Arthur Lionel Barnes and Freda Marguerite Garratt; *m* 1958, Patricia Winckley; one *s* one *d. Educ:* King's Coll., London; St Catherine's Coll., Oxford. Served RAF, 1946–48. Admin. Officer, Town Planning Dept, LCC, 1952–61; concurrently freelance journalist; Chief Dance Critic, The Times, 1961–65; Exec. Editor, Dance and Dancers, Music and Musicians, and Plays and Players, 1961–65; a London Correspondent, New York Times, 1963–65, Dance Critic, 1965–77, Drama Critic (weekdays only), 1967–77; a NY correspondent, The Times, 1970–. Knight of the Order of Dannebrog (Denmark), 1972. *Publications:* Ballet in Britain since the War, 1953; (ed, with others) Ballet Here and Now, 1961; Frederick Ashton and his Ballets, 1961; Dance Scene, USA (commentary), 1967; (ed with J. Gassner) Best American Plays, 6th series, 1963–67, 1971, and 7th series, 1974; (ed) New York Times Directory of the Theatre, 1973; Nureyev, 1983; contribs to jls, inc. Punch, The New Statesman, The Spectator, The New Republic. *Recreations:* eating, drinking, walking, theatre-going. *Address:* c/o New York Post, 1211 6th Avenue, New York, NY 10036, USA. *Club:* Century (NY).

BARNES, Sir David; *see* Barnes, Sir J. D. F.

BARNES, David John; Head Master, Pate's Grammar School, Cheltenham, 1986–2000; *b* 6 Nov. 1939; *s* of David Alan Barnes and Norah Barnes (*née* Fleming); *m* 1961, Jan Crofts; one *s* one *d. Educ:* The Grammar Sch., Wolstanton, Staffs; Queen's Coll., Oxford (Open Schol.; MA); DipEd London; Post Grad. Cert. in Architectural Hist., Oxford, 2003. Assistant Master: Pocklington Sch., York, 1962–66; Nottingham High Sch., 1966–68; Vice-Principal, Newcastle-under-Lyme Sch., 1968–86. *Publications:* A Parent's Guide to GCSE, 1988; various check-lists and guides to students' reading, 1991. *Recreations:* fly-fishing, Homer, digging holes and other honest labour. *Address:* 32 Gretton Road, Gotherington, Cheltenham, Glos GL52 9QU.

BARNES, (David) Michael (William); QC 1981; a Recorder, since 1985; *b* 16 July 1943; *s* of David Charles Barnes and Florence Maud Barnes; *m* 1970, Susan Dorothy Turner; three *s. Educ:* Monmouth Sch.; Wadham Coll., Oxford. Called to Bar, Middle Temple, 1965, Bencher, 1989. Hon. Research Fellow, Lady Margaret Hall, Oxford, 1979; Vis. Fellow, Univ. of Auckland, NZ, 1995. Chm., Hinckley Point 'C' Public Inquiry, 1988. *Publications:* Leasehold Reform Act 1967, 1967; Hill and Redman's Law of Landlord and Tenant, 15th edn 1970 to 18th edn 1988; Hill and Redman's Guide to Rent Review, 2001. *Recreations:* walking, crime fiction. *Address:* Wilberforce Chambers, 8 New Square, WC2A 3QP. *Club:* Beefsteak.

BARNES, Edward Campbell; independent television producer/director and television consultant, since 1986; Head of Children's Programmes, BBC Television, 1978–86; *b* 8 Oct. 1928; *s* of Hubert Turnbull Barnes and Annie Mabel Barnes; *m* 1950, Dorothy Smith (*d* 1992); one *s* two *d. Educ:* Wigan Coll. British Forces Network, Vienna, 1946–49; stage management, provincial and West End theatre, 1949–55; BBC Television: studio management, 1955–62; Producer, Blue Peter, 1962–70; Dep. Head of Children's Progs, 1970–78, incl.: original Editor, John Craven's Newsround; Producer: Blue Peter Royal Safari with Princess Anne; 6 series of Blue Peter Special Assignments; Producer and Director: Treasure Houses, 1986; All Our Children, 1987–90; Boxpops, 1992; The Lowdown, 1992. Mem. Bd, Children's Film and Television Foundn Ltd, 1983–97; Dir, Christian Children's Fund, 1995–2002. Consultant, St Paul's Multi-media, 1995–96. Mem., RTS (Mem., Awards Cttee, 1989–91). Trustee, EveryChild, 2002–03. SFTA Award, 1969; RTS Silver Medal, 1986; Pye Television Award, 1986. *Publications:* 25 Blue Peter Books and 8 Blue Peter Mini Books, 1964–; 6 Blue Peter Special Assignment Books, 1973–75; Blue Peter Royal Safari, 1971; Petra: a dog for everyone, 1977; Blue Peter: the inside story, 1989; numerous articles for nat. press. *Recreations:* cricket, music, birding, walking, Venice, Bali.

See also S. J. C. Barnes.

BARNES, Rt Rev. Edwin Ronald; Bishop Suffragan of Richborough, Episcopal Visitor for the Province of Canterbury, 1995–2001; Hon. Assistant Bishop, Diocese of Winchester, since 2001; *b* 6 Feb. 1935; *s* of Edwin and Dorothy Barnes; m 1963, Jane Elizabeth (*née* Green); one *s* one *d. Educ:* Plymouth College; Pembroke Coll., Oxford (MA). Rector of Farncombe, Surrey, 1967–78; Vicar of Hessle, dio. York, 1978–87; Principal, St Stephen's House, Oxford, 1987–95. Proctor in Convocation, Canterbury 1975–78, York 1985–87; Mem., General Synod of C of E, 1990–95 (Mem. Standing Cttee, 1992–95). Hon. Canon: Christ Church, Oxford, 1994–95; St Albans Cathedral, 1997–2001. President: Guild of All Souls, 1997–2004; English Church Union, 2005–. *Address:* 1 Queen Elizabeth Avenue, Lymington, Hants SO41 9HN.

BARNES, Eric Charles, CBE 1992; GBS 2005; High Court Judge, Hong Kong, 1981–91; *b* 12 Sept. 1924; *m* 1st, Estelle Fay Barnes (*née* Darnell); four *s* one *d*; 2nd, 1978, Judianna Wai Ling Barnes (*née* Chang); one *s* one *d. Educ:* Univ. of Queensland (LLB). Chief Adjudicator, Immigration Tribunal, Hong Kong, 1993–2004; Chm., Appeal Bd on Public Meetings and Demonstrations, Hong Kong, 1995–99. Mem., Australian Assoc., Hong Kong, 1994–. *Recreations:* tennis, racing (horse), sports. *Address:* House 52, Manderly Garden, 48 Deep Water Bay Road, Hong Kong. *Clubs:* United Services Recreation, Kowloon Cricket, Hong Kong Jockey (Hong Kong); Tattersall's (Brisbane).

BARNES, Geoffrey Thomas, CBE 1989; HM Overseas Civil Service, retired; *b* 18 Aug. 1932; *s* of late Thomas Arthur Barnes and Ethel Maud (*née* Walker); *m* 1962, Agnete Scot Madsen; three *s* one *d. Educ:* Dover College; St Catharine's College, Cambridge (MA). Nat. Service, 2nd Lieut QO Royal West Kent Regt; served Malaya, 1951–52; Lieut, Royal Warwickshire Regt, TA, 1952–55. Admin Officer, HMOCS Sarawak, 1956–68; City and Guilds of London, 1968–70; HMOCS Hong Kong: Asst Defence Sec., 1970–72;

Police Civil Sec., 1972–76; Asst Dir, Commerce and Industry Dept, 1976–77; Dep. Sec. for Security, 1977–81, for Health and Welfare, 1981–84; Comr, Indep. Commn Against Corruption, 1985–88; Sec. for Security, Hong Kong Govt, and Official Mem., Legislative Council, 1988–90. Consultant to FCO on anti-corruption measures in Jamaica, 1990, Peru, 1991, Venezuela, 1992 and Ecuador, 1993. Pres., ICAC Assoc., 1993–98. JP Hong Kong, 1980. *Publications:* Mostly Memories (autobiog.), 1996, rev. edn 1999; With the Dirty Half-Hundred in Malaya (autobiog.), 2001. *Recreations:* sailing, painting, golf, gardening. *Address:* Alloways, Cranleigh Road, Ewhurst, Surrey GU6 7RJ. *T:* (01483) 276490. *Clubs:* Royal Over-Seas League; Hong Kong (Hong Kong) (Life Mem.).

See also K. J. Barnes.

BARNES, Harold, (Harry); *b* 22 July 1936; *s* of late Joseph and Betsy Barnes; *m* 1963, Elizabeth Ann Stephenson; one *s* one *d. Educ:* Ruskin Coll., Oxford (Dip. Econs and Political Science); Hull Univ. (BA Philosophy and Political Studies). National Service, 1954–56. Railway clerk, 1952–54 and 1956–60; adult student, 1960–65; further educn lectr, 1965–66; Lectr, Sheffield Univ., 1966–87. MP (Lab) Derbys NE, 1987–2005. Joint President: New Dialogue (Britain), 1992– (Chm., 1990–92); Labour Friends of Iraq, 2004–. Mem., National Admin. Council, Ind. Labour Publications, 1977–80 and 1982–85. *Publications:* pamphlets on local govt and on the public face of Militant; articles and reviews in Labour Leader, London Labour Briefing, Tribune, Morning Star, Local Socialism, New Socialist, Derbyshire Miner, Leeds Weekly Citizen, Sheffield Forward, Industrial Tutor, Political Studies. *Clubs:* Dronfield Contact; Chesterfield Labour.

BARNES, Jack Henry; Director of Administration, British Society for Allergy and Clinical Immunology, 2002–05; *b* 11 Dec. 1943; *s* of James Barnes and Joan Ivy (*née* Sears); *m* 1966, Nicola Pearse; two *d. Educ:* Hatfield Sch., Herts; Univ. of Sussex (BA); LSE (MSc). Dep. Chief Inspector, Social Services Inspectorate, DHSS, 1983–88; Department of Health: Dep. Chief Scientist and Dir, Res. Management, 1988–91; Under Sec. 1991–99; Head: Primary Care Div., NHS Exec., 1991–95; Internat. and Industry Div., 1995–99; Dir of Res. and Policy, Nat. Asthma Campaign, 2000–03. Non-exec. Dir, E Sussex Downs and Weald PCT. Trustee, Mental Health Foundn, 1997–2003. Gov., Goldsmiths, Univ. of London. *Address:* c/o British Society for Allergy and Clinical Immunology, 17 Doughty Street, WC1N 2PL.

BARNES, Sir (James) David (Francis), Kt 1996; CBE 1987; Deputy Chairman, AstraZeneca PLC, 1999–2001; *b* 4 March 1936; *s* of Eric Cecil Barnes, CMG, and of Jean Margaret Barnes; *m* 1963, Wendy Fiona Mary (*née* Riddell); one *s* one *d. Educ:* Shrewsbury Sch.; Liverpool Univ. National Service, commnd 'N' Battery (Eagle Troop), 2nd Regt RA, 1958–60 (Malaya). ICI Pharmaceuticals Division: Overseas Dir 1971–77, Dep. Chm. 1977–83; Chm., ICI Paints Div., 1983–86; Exec. Dir, ICI, 1986–93; CEO, Zeneca Group PLC, 1993–99. Non-executive Director: Thorn EMI, 1987–94; Redland, 1994–98; Prudential, 1999–2003; non-exec. Chm., Imperial Cancer Res. Technol., 1999–2002; Dep. Chm., Syngenta AG, 2000–04. Chairman: Pharmaceuticals EDC, NEDO, 1983–92; Biotechnology Industries Working Party, NEDO, 1989–91. Vice-Pres., Thames Valley Hospice, 1986–. Mem. Council, VSO, 1996–99; a Dep. Chm., BITC, 1996–2000 (Chm., Economic Regeneration Leadership Team, 1996–2000). Mem. Bd of Governors, Ashridge (Bonar Law Meml) Trust, 1993–2006; Gov. and Bd Mem., Intellectual Property Inst., 1994–2000; Member: Governing Body, Shrewsbury Sch., 1997–2006; Bd of Trustees, BRCS, 1998–2004. FInstD; CCMI; FRSA 1988; Hon. Associate, BVA, 1995 (Wooldridge Meml Medal, 1995). Hon. LLD Liverpool, 1996; Hon. DSc UMIST, 1998. Centenary Medal, SCI, 2000. *Recreations:* fishing, shooting, walking.

BARNES, James Frederick, CB 1982; Deputy Chief Scientific Adviser, and Head of Profession for the Science Group, Ministry of Defence, 1987–89; *b* 8 March 1932; *s* of Wilfred and Doris M. Barnes; *m* 1957, Dorothy Jean Drew; one *s* two *d. Educ:* Taunton's Sch., Southampton; Queen's Coll., Oxford. BA 1953, MA 1957. CEng, FRAeS. Bristol Aeroplane Co. (Engine Div.), 1953; Min. of Supply, Nat. Gas Turbine Estabt: Sci. Officer 1955; Sen. Sci. Off. 1957; Principal Sci. Off. 1962; Sen. Principal Sci. Off. (Individual Merit) 1965; Min. of Aviation Supply, Asst Dir, Engine R&D, 1970; seconded to HM Diplomatic Service, Counsellor (Science and Technology), British Embassy, Washington, 1972; Under-Sec., MoD, 1974; Dir Gen. Res. (C), MoD (Procurement Exec.), 1974–77; Dep. Dir (Weapons), RAE, 1978–79; Dep. Chief Scientific Adviser (Projs), MoD, 1979–82; Dep. Controller, Establishments Resources and Personnel, MoD, 1982–84; Dep. Controller, Estabts and Res., MoD, 1984–86. Chm., MoD Individual Merit Promotion Panel, 1990–98. Stewardship Advr, dio. of Monmouth, 1989–96; Dir, Monmouth Diocesan Bd of Finance, 1999–2000; Mem., Monmouth Dio. Trng for Ministry Cttee, 1989–2004; Sec., Monmouth DAC for Care of Churches, 1994–96; Chm., CCBI Stewardship Network, 1993–96; Member: Council on Christian Approaches to Defence and Disarmament, 1980–2006; Member, Church in Wales Working Gps on Ecclesiastical Exemption, Charities Act 1993 and status of PCCs, 1995–96. Lay Member: Guildford Diocesan Synod, 1978–84; Winchester Diocesan Synod, 1985–89; Chm., Deanery Finance Cttee, Alton, Hants, 1987–89; Bishop's Nominee, Monmouth Diocesan Conf., 1990–2004; Mem., Hereford Diocesan Bd of Finance, 2007–, Diocesan Pastoral Cttee, 2007–; Churchwarden, All Saints', Farringdon, 1985–89; Sub-Warden, Trellech PCC, 1997–2003. Chm., Tymawr Convent Appeals Gp, 1997–2003. Member: Monmouth & Llandaff Housing Assoc., 1991–93; Gwerin (Cymru) Housing Assoc., 1993–94; Trustee: Roger Williams & Queen Victoria Almshouses, Newport, 1990–99; Babington Educnl Trust, 1997–2003; Founder Trustee, Friends of Trellech Church & Churchyard, 2002–04. Chm. of Govs, Yateley Manor Prep. Sch., 1981–89. Secretary: Ledbury Ch Stewardship Cttee, 2005–; Ledbury Deanery, 2007–; Treas., Ledbury Probus Club, 2006–. James Clayton Fund Prize, IMechE, 1964. *Publications:* (contrib.) Trellech Millennium book; contrib. books and learned jls on mech. engrg, esp. gas turbine technology, heat transfer and stress analysis. *Recreation:* making things. *Address:* 15 Kempley Brook Drive, Ledbury, Herefordshire HR8 2FJ.

BARNES, Janet; Chief Executive, York Museums Trust, since 2002; *b* 23 April 1952; *d* of Frederick George Hagan and Margaret Hagan (*née* Wilson); *m* 1970, Philip Barnes. *Educ:* Sheffield Univ. (BA Hons English Lit.); Manchester Univ. (Postgrad. Dip. Mus and Art Gall. Studies). Keeper, Ruskin Gall. and Ruskin Craft Gall., 1985–94; Sen. Curator, Sheffield Galls and Museums, 1995–99; Dir, Crafts Council, 1999–2002. Chm., Yorks, Arts Council England, 2005–. Hon. Curator, Turner Mus. of Glass, Univ. of Sheffield, 1979–99. Dir, Guild of St George, 1994–. Hon. LLD Sheffield, 2000; DUniv Sheffield Hallam, 2001. *Publications:* Percy Horton: 1897–1970 Artist and Absolutist, 1982; Ruskin and Sheffield, 1985, 2nd edn 1996; Catalogue of the Turner Museum of Glass, 1993. *Recreation:* husband. *Address:* c/o York Museums Trust, St Mary's Lodge, Museum Gardens, York YO30 7DR.

BARNES, John; a Senior Immigration Judge, Asylum and Immigration Tribunal (formerly a Vice-President, Immigration Appeal Tribunal), 2000–06; *b* 13 March 1938; *s* of Frederick Walter John Barnes, MBE, LLB and Phyllis Edna Barnes (*née* Brooks); *m* 1992, Frances (*née* Broadrick); three *s* by a previous marriage. *Educ:* Brentwood Sch., Essex; Univ. of London (LLB Hons ext.). Admitted solicitor, 1961; engaged in private practice, 1961–97. Part-time Chm., Industrial Tribunals, 1993–99; Immigration Adjudicator, part-time, 1995–97, full-time, 1997–2000. Mem., Internat. Assoc. of Refugee Law Judges, 2004–. *Publication:* A Manual for Refugee Law Judges, 2007; contrib. to Internat. Jl of Refugee Law. *Recreations:* learning to enjoy retirement, theatre, history, art. *Address:* Orchard Place, Triq ta' Sansuna, Xaghra XRA 1652, Gozo, Malta. *T:* 21561647. *Club:* Athenæum.

BARNES, John Alfred, CBE 1993; Director-General, City and Guilds of London Institute, 1985–93; *b* 29 April 1930; *s* of John Joseph and Margaret Carr Barnes; *m* 1954, Ivy May (*née* Walker); two *d. Educ:* Bede Boys Grammar Sch., Sunderland; Durham Univ. (MA, BSc, MEd). Teacher, Grangefield Grammar Sch., Stockton-on-Tees, 1953–57; Asst Educn Officer, Barnsley, 1957–61; Dep. Dir, then Dir of Educn, City of Wakefield, 1963–68; Chief Educn Officer, City of Salford, 1968–84. Mem. Council, Assoc. of Colls of Further and Higher Educn, 1976–82 (Chm. 1980–81); Chairman: Northern Examining Assoc., 1979–82; Associated Lancs Schs Examg Bd, 1972–84; Member: Associated Examg Bd, Nat. Exams Bd for Supervisory Studies, 1985–93; Further Educn Unit Management Bd, 1986–89; YTS Certification Bd, 1986–89; various ind. trng bds, 1969–78, and MSC cttees, 1978–84; Review of Vocational Qualifications Working Gp, 1985–86; Task Gp on Assessment and Testing, 1987–88; Exec. Mem., Standing Conf. on Sch. Sci. and Technol., 1985–89 (Chm., Exec. Cttee, 1988–89). Mem., Nat. Exec. Cttee, Soc. of Educn Officers, 1979–84; Sec., Assoc. of Educn Officers, 1977–84; Treas., NFER, 1979–84; Pres., Educnl Develt Assoc., 1980–85. Chm., Sir Isaac Pitman Ltd, 1990–93; Sec., UK Skills, 1990–93. Mem. Council, City Technology Colls Trust, 1990–93; Gov., Imperial Coll., 1987–93; Mem. Court, Reading Univ., 1994–97. Mem. (C), Bucks CC, 1993–97 (Chm., Personnel Cttee, 1994–97; Vice-Chm., 1994–96, Chm., 1996–97, Educn Cttee). Mem., Thames Valley (formerly Bucks and Oxon) Valuation Tribunals Gp, 1997–2001. Chm., Bournemouth and Poole NT (formerly Bournemouth NT), 2004–. Trustee, City Parochial Foundn and Trust for London, 1993–2005 (Chm., Grants Cttee, 2004–05). Mem., Probus. FRSA 1973; FITD 1986 (Hon. FITD 1993); FCollP 1991; Hon. FCGI 1993; Hon. CIPD 1994. *Publications:* occasional papers in educnl press. *Recreations:* cultural activities, foreign travel. *Address:* 1 Seapoint, 8 Martello Park, Canford Cliffs, Poole, Dorset BH13 7BA. *T:* (01202) 701768. *Club:* Athenæum.

BARNES, Prof. John Arundel, DSC 1944; FBA 1981; Professor of Sociology, University of Cambridge, 1969–82, now Emeritus; Fellow of Churchill College, Cambridge, since 1969; *b* Reading, 9 Sept. 1918; *s* of T. D. and M. G. Barnes, Bath; *m* 1942, Helen Frances, *d* of Charles Bastable; three *s* one *d. Educ:* Christ's Hosp.; St John's Coll., Cambridge; Sch. of African Studies, Univ. of Cape Town; Balliol Coll., Oxford. Fellow, St John's Coll., Cambridge, 1950–53; Simon Research Fellow, Manchester Univ., 1951–53; Reader in Anthropology, London Univ., 1954–56; Prof. of Anthropology, Sydney Univ., 1956–58; Prof. of Anthropology, Inst. of Advanced Studies, ANU, Canberra, 1958–69; Overseas Fellow, Churchill Coll., Cambridge, 1965–66. Australian National University: Vis. Fellow, 1978–79, 1985–92; Program Visitor, Sociology, Res. Sch. of Social Scis, 1992–98. *Publications:* Marriage in a Changing Society, 1951; Politics in a Changing Society, 1954; Inquest on the Murngin, 1967; Sociology in Cambridge, 1970; Three Styles in the Study of Kinship, 1971; Social Networks, 1972; The Ethics of Inquiry in Social Science, 1977; Who Should Know What?, 1979; Models and interpretations, 1990; A Pack of Lies, 1994. *Address:* Churchill College, Cambridge CB3 0DS.

BARNES, John Nigel; Conservation & Learning Director, Historic Royal Palaces, since 2001; *b* 24 June 1961; *s* of Geoffrey Philip Barnes and Shirley Anne (*née* Eaton); partner, Lauren Kathleen Agnew; two *d. Educ:* Judd Sch., Tonbridge; S Bank Poly. (BA Hons, Postgrad. DipArch). Registered Architect; ARB (ARC 1989); RIBA 1989–2006. In private practice in architecture, 1984–94; English Heritage: Hd, Architecture and Survey, 1994–95; Director: Professional Services, 1995–98; Major Projects, 1998–2001. *Recreations:* karate, life drawing. *Address:* Historic Royal Palaces, Hampton Court Palace, Surrey KT8 9AU. *T:* (020) 3166 6363, *Fax:* (020) 3166 6365; *e-mail:* john.barnes@hrp.org.uk.

BARNES, Prof. Jonathan, FBA 1987; Professor of Ancient Philosophy, University of Paris-Sorbonne, 2002–06; *b* 26 Dec. 1942; *s* of late A. L. Barnes and K. M. Barnes; *m* 1965, Jennifer Postgate; two *d. Educ:* City of London Sch.; Balliol Coll., Oxford. Oxford University: Fellow, Oriel Coll., 1968–78; Fellow, 1978–94, Emeritus Fellow, 1994–, Balliol Coll.; Prof. of Ancient Philosophy, 1989–94; Prof. of Ancient Philosophy, Univ. of Geneva, 1994–2002. Visiting posts at: Inst. for Advanced Study, Princeton, 1972; Univ. of Texas, 1981; Wissenschaftskolleg zu Berlin, 1985; Univ. of Alberta, 1986; Univ. of Zurich, 1987; Istituto Italiano per gli studi filosofici, Naples, 1988, 1998; Ecole Normale Supérieure, Paris, 1996 (Condorcet Medal, 1996); Scuola Normale Superiore di Pisa, 2002. Fellow, Amer. Acad. Arts and Scis, 1999. Hon. Fellow, Oriel Coll., Oxford, 2007. *Publications:* The Ontological Argument, 1972; Aristotle's Posterior Analytics, 1975; The Presocratic Philosophers, 1979; Aristotle, 1982; Early Greek Philosophy, 1987; The Toils of Scepticism, 1991; The Cambridge Companion to Aristotle, 1995; Logic and the Imperial Stoa, 1997; Porphyry: introduction, 2003; Truth, etc, 2007; Coffee with Aristotle, 2008. *Address:* Les Charmilles, 36200 Ceaulmont, France.

See also J. P. Barnes.

BARNES, Joseph Harry George; Chairman, Baxters of Speyside, 1994–98; Director, 1969–93, Joint Managing Director, 1988–90, J. Sainsbury plc; *b* 24 July 1930; *s* of William Henry Joseph Barnes and Dorothy Eleanor Barnes; *m* 1958, Rosemary Gander; two *s. Educ:* John Ruskin Grammar Sch., Croydon. FCA 1963. Articled clerk, Lever Honeyman & Co., 1946–52. National Service, 2nd Lieut RAPC, 1953–55. Joined J. Sainsbury plc, 1956. *Recreations:* tennis, fishing. *Address:* Tudor Court, 29 Grimwade Avenue, Croydon, Surrey CR0 5DJ. *T:* (020) 8654 5696.

BARNES, Julian Patrick; writer; *b* 19 Jan. 1946; *m* Pat Kavanagh. *Educ:* City of London Sch.; Magdalen Coll., Oxford. Lexicographer, OED Supplement, 1969–72; freelance journalist; Contributing Ed., New Review, 1977; Asst Literary Ed., 1977–79, TV Critic, 1977–81, New Statesman; Dep. Literary Ed., Sunday Times, 1980–82; TV Critic, Observer, 1982–86; London correspondent, The New Yorker, 1990–95. E. M. Forster Award, US Acad. of Arts and Letters, 1986; Shakespeare Prize, Germany, 1993; Austrian State Prize for European Literature, 2004. Commandeur de l'Ordre des Arts et des Lettres (France), 2004. *Publications:* Metroland, 1980 (Somerset Maugham Award, 1981); Before She Met Me, 1982; Flaubert's Parrot, 1984 (Geoffrey Faber Meml Prize, 1985; Prix Médicis, 1986; Grinzane Cavour Prize (Italy), 1988); Staring at the Sun, 1986; A History of the World in 10½ Chapters, 1989; Talking it Over, 1991 (Prix Femina, 1992); The Porcupine, 1992; Letters from London (essays), 1995; Cross Channel (short stories), 1996; England, England, 1998; Love, etc, 2000; Something to Declare (essays), 2002; trans. Daudet, In the Land of Pain, 2002; The Pedant in the Kitchen, 2003; The Lemon Table (short stories), 2004; Arthur & George, 2005; Nothing to be Frightened of (non-fiction), 2008; (as Dan Kavanagh): Duffy, 1980; Fiddle City, 1981; Putting the Boot In, 1985;

Going to the Dogs, 1987. *Address:* c/o United Agents, 12–26 Lexington Street, W1F 0LE.
See also Jonathan Barnes.

BARNES, Sir Kenneth, KCB 1977 (CB 1970); Permanent Secretary, Department of Employment, 1976–82; *b* 26 Aug. 1922; *s* of Arthur and Doris Barnes, Accrington, Lancs; *m* 1948, Barbara Ainsworth (*d* 2001); one *s* two *d. Educ:* Accrington Grammar Sch.; Balliol Coll., Oxford. Lancs Fusiliers, 1942–45. Entered Ministry of Labour, 1948; Under-Sec., Cabinet Office, 1966–68; Dep. Sec., Dept of Employment, 1968–75. *Address:* South Sandhills, Sandy Lane, Betchworth, Surrey RH3 7AA. *T:* (01737) 842445.

BARNES, Kenneth James, CBE 1969 (MBE 1964); Advisor (Finance), Directorate General for Development, Commission of the European Communities, 1982–87; *b* 8 May 1930; *s* of late Thomas Arthur Barnes and Ethel Maud Barnes; *m* 1st, 1953, Lesley Dawn Grummett Wright (*d* 1976); two *s* one *d*; 2nd, 1981, Anna Elisabeth Gustaf Maria Vanoorlé (marr. diss. 1988). *Educ:* Guilford and Hale Schs, Perth, WA; Dover Coll.; St Catharine's Coll., Cambridge (Crabtree exhibnr; MA); London Univ. Pilot Officer, RAF, 1949–50; Flying Officer, RAFVR, 1950–53. Administrative Officer, HMOCS Eastern Nigeria, 1954–60; Asst Sec., Min. of Finance, Malaŵi, 1960–64, Sen. Asst Sec., 1965, Dep. Sec., 1966, Permanent Sec., 1967–71; Asst Sec., British Steel Corp., 1971–73; EEC: Principal Administrator, Directorate-Gen. for Develt, 1973–75; Head of Div. for Ind. Co-operation, Trade Promotion and Regional Co-operation, 1976–78; Hd of Div. for Caribbean, Indian and Pacific Oceans, 1979–80; Advr (Political), 1981–82; Advr (Finance), 1983–87. Chairman: Newbury Dist Liaison Group on Disablement, 1990–97; Internat. Cttee, RADAR, 1993–2001; Member: Council, Anti-Slavery Internat., 1991–98 (Jt Treas., 1992–97); Council, John Grooms Assoc. for Disabled, 1994–97 (Advr, 1997–). *Publications:* Polio and ME in Nigeria, Malawi, Belgium, England and Other Places, 1998; (contrib.) Palm Wine & Leopard's Whiskers, 1999; A Rough Passage: memories of Empire, vols I and II, 2006. *Recreations:* reading, esp. history, listening to music, mediaeval fortifications, strengthening European Community links, charities for the disabled. *Address:* 29 Bearwater, Charnham Street, Hungerford, Berks RG17 0NN. *T:* (01488) 684329, *Fax:* (01488) 681733; *e-mail:* kjbarnes@29bearwater.freeserve.co.uk. *Club:* Royal Over-Seas League.
See also G. T. Barnes.

BARNES, Mark Richard Purcell; QC 1992. Called to the Bar, Lincoln's Inn, 1974. *Address:* 1 Essex Court, Temple, EC4Y 9AR. *T:* (020) 7583 2000; *e-mail:* mbarnes@oeclaw.co.uk.

BARNES, Melvyn Peter Keith, OBE 1990; MCLIP; Guildhall Librarian and Director of Libraries and Art Galleries, Corporation of London, 1984–2002; *b* 26 Sept. 1942; *s* of Harry and Doris Barnes; *m* 1965, Judith Anne Leicester; two *s. Educ:* Chatham House Sch., Ramsgate; North-Western Polytechnic, London. MCLIP (ALA 1965); DMA 1972; FCMI (FBIM 1980). Public library posts in Kent, Herts and Manchester, 1958–68; Dep. Bor. Librarian, Newcastle-under-Lyme, 1968–72; Chief Librarian, Ipswich, 1972–74; Bor. Librarian and Arts Officer, Kensington and Chelsea, 1974–80; City Librarian, Westminster, 1980–84. Hon. Librarian to Clockmakers' Co., and Gardeners' Co., 1984–2002. Member: LA Council, 1974–98 (Chm. Exec. Cttee, 1987–92; Vice-Pres., 1991–93; Pres., 1995); Liby and Inf. Services Council, 1984–89; Brit. Liby Adv. Council, 1986–91; Brit. Liby SRIS Adv. Cttee, 1986–91. Pres., Internat. Assoc. of Metropolitan City Libraries, 1989–92; Dep. Chm., Liby Services Trust and Liby Services Ltd, 1983–93. Hon. Treas., Victoria County History of Inner Middlesex, 1979–90. Gov., St Bride Inst., 1984–2002. Liveryman, Clockmakers' Co., 1990–2002; Hon. Freeman, Gardeners' Co., 1995. Editorial Cons., Journal of Librarianship, 1980–94; Editorial Advr, Librarianship & Information Work Worldwide, 1991–99. *Publications:* Youth Library Work, 1968, 2nd edn 1976; Best Detective Fiction, 1975; Murder in Print, 1986; Dick Francis, 1986; Root and Branch: a history of the Worshipful Company of Gardeners of London, 1994; (ed) Deerstalker series of classic crime fiction reprints, 1977–82; contributor to numerous books and jls in fields of librarianship and crime fiction criticism. *Recreations:* reading and writing, going to the theatre, studying the history of the movies and stage musicals, performing amateur operatics.

BARNES, Michael; *see* Barnes, D. M. W.

BARNES, Michael Cecil John, CBE 1998; Legal Services Ombudsman for England and Wales, 1991–97; *b* 22 Sept. 1932; *s* of late Major C. H. R. Barnes, OBE and of Katherine Louise (*née* Kennedy); *m* 1962, Anne Mason; one *s* one *d. Educ:* Malvern; Corpus Christi Coll., Oxford. Nat. Service, 2nd Lieut, Wilts Regt, served in Hong Kong, 1952–53. MP (Lab) Brentford and Chiswick, 1966–Feb. 1974; an Opposition Spokesman on food and food prices, 1970–71; Chairman: Parly Labour Party Social Security Group, 1969–70; ASTMS Parly Cttee, 1970–71; Jt Hon. Sec., Labour Cttee for Europe, 1969–71; Mem., Public Accounts Cttee, 1967–74. Contested (Lab): Wycombe, 1964; Brentford and Isleworth, Feb. 1974; Mem. Labour Party, 1957–79; helped form SDP, 1981; rejoined Labour Party, 1983–2001. Chm., Electricity Consumers' Council, 1977–83; Dir, UKIAS, 1984–90. Member: Council of Management, War on Want, 1972–77; Nat. Consumer Council, 1975–80; Arts Council Trng Cttee, 1977–83; Energy Commn, 1977–79; Internat. Cttee of Nat. Council for Voluntary Organisations, 1977–83; Advertising Standards Authority, 1979–85; Direct Mail Services Standards Bd, 1983–86; Data Protection Tribunal, 1985–90; Investigation Cttee, Solicitors' Complaints Bureau, 1987–90; Legal Services Commn (formerly Legal Aid Bd), 1998–2001; Financial Ombudsman Service Bd (formerly Financial Services Ombudsman Bd), 1999–2002, Ind. Assessor, 2002–. Chm., British and Irish Ombudsman Assoc., 1995–98. Chairman: UK Adv. Cttee on EEC Action Against Poverty Programme, 1975–76; Notting Hill Social Council, 1976–79; West London Fair Housing Gp Ltd, 1980–87; Vice Chm., Bangabandhu Soc., 1980–90; Organising Secretary: Gulbenkian Foundn Drama Trng Inquiry, 1974–75; Music Trng Inquiry, 1976–77; Sec., Nat. Council for Drama Trng, 1976–84; Chm., Hounslow Arts Trust, 1974–82; Trustee, Project Hand Trust, 1974–77; Governor, Internat. Musicians Seminar, Prussia Cove, 1978–81. *Recreations:* walking, reading. *Address:* 45 Ladbroke Grove, W11 3AR. *T:* (020) 7727 2533.

BARNES, Prof. Michael Patrick; Professor of Scandinavian Studies, University College London, 1995–2005, now Professor Emeritus (Professor of Scandinavian Philology, 1983–94); *b* 28 June 1940; *s* of William Edward Clement Barnes and Gladys Constance Barnes (*née* Hooper); *m* 1970, Kirsten Heiberg (*née* Røer); one *s* three *d. Educ:* University College London (BA, MA); Univ. of Oslo. Asst Lectr, Lectr and Reader in Scandinavian Philology, UCL, 1964–83. Visiting Professor: Tórshavn, Faroe Islands, 1979 and 1990; Uppsala Univ., 1984. Member: Gustav Adolfs Akademien, Uppsala, 1984 (Corresp. Mem., 1977); Det norske Videnskaps-Akademi, Oslo, 1997. Jt Ed., North-Western European Language Evolution, 1989– (Mem. Adv. Bd, 1981–88); Member, Editorial Board: Fróðskaparrit, 1995–; Maal og Minne, 1996–; Norsk lingvistisk tidsskrift, 1997–; Nordic Jl of Linguistics, 2000–; Beiträge zur nordischen Philologie, 2000–; Jt Hon. Sec., Viking Soc. for Northern Research, 1983–2006 (Mem. Editl Bd, 1970–76, Chief Editor, 1977–83, Saga Book of the Viking Soc.). Hon. DPhil Uppsala, 2002. Knight: Order of the Falcon (Iceland), 1992; 1st Cl., Royal Norwegian Order of Merit, 2008. *Publications:* Draumkvæde: an edition and study, 1974; The Runic Inscriptions of Maeshowe, Orkney, 1994; (jtly) The Runic Inscriptions of Viking Age Dublin, 1997; The Norn Language of Orkney and Shetland, 1998; A New Introduction to Old Norse, vol. I: Grammar, 1999; Faroese Language Studies, 2001; (jtly) Introduction to Scandinavian Phonetics, 2005; (jtly) The Scandinavian Runic Inscriptions of Britain, 2006; articles in learned jls. *Recreations:* badminton, being with family, walking disused railways. *Address:* 93 Longland Drive, N20 8HN. *T:* (020) 8445 4697.

BARNES, Prof. Peter John, DM, DSc; FRCP, FMedSci; FRS 2007; Professor of Thoracic Medicine, Imperial College, London (National Heart and Lung Institute) and Hon. Consultant Physician, Royal Brompton Hospital, since 1987; Head of Respiratory Medicine, Imperial College, London, since 1997; *b* 29 Oct. 1946; *s* of late John Barnes and Eileen Gertrude Barnes (*née* Thurman); *m* 1976, Olivia Harvard-Watts; three *s. Educ:* Leamington Coll.; St Catharine's Coll., Cambridge (open schol., BA (1st class); MA); Worcester Coll., Oxford (DM, DSc). FRCP 1985. Jun. med. posts, then Registrar, Oxford and UCH, London; MRC fellowships, Univ. of Calif, San Francisco, and RPMS, London; Hammersmith Hospital, London: Sen. Registrar, 1979–82; Sen. Lectr and Consultant Physician, RPMS, 1982–85; Prof. of Clinical Pharmacol., Cardiothoracic Inst., London, 1985–87. Vis. Prof., RSocMed, 1993. Lectures: Linacre, RCP, 1994; Amberson (and Prize), Amer. Thoracic Soc., 1996; Sadoul, Eur. Respiratory Soc., 1999. Founder FMedSci 1998. Hon. MD: Ferarra, Italy, 1997; Athens, 2001. Dutch Med. Fedn Prize, 1995; Ariens Prize, Dutch Pharmacol. Soc., 2005; Quintiles Prize, British Pharmacol. Soc., 2005; Presidential Award, Eur. Respiratory Soc., 2007; Medal, British Thoracic Soc., 2007. *Publications:* New Drugs for Asthma, 1982, 3rd edn 1998; Asthma: basic mechanisms and clinical management, 1989, 3rd edn 1998; (ed jtly) The Lung: scientific foundations, 1991, 3rd edn 1998; Recent Advances in Respiratory Medicine, 1993; (jtly) Conquering Asthma, 1994; (jtly) Molecular Biology of Lung Disease, 1994; Asthma (2 vols), 1997; (ed jtly) Antonomic Control of the Respiratory System, 1997; (jtly) Asthma Therapy, 1998; Managing Chronic Obstructive Pulmonary Disease, 1999; (jtly) Asthma and Chronic Obstructive Pulmonary Disease, 2002; over 1,000 pubns on lung pharmacol. and airway disease. *Recreations:* travel, ethnic art collecting, gardening, film and theatre going. *Address:* Airway Disease Section, National Heart and Lung Institute (Imperial College), Dovehouse Street, SW3 6LY. *T:* (020) 7351 8174.

BARNES, Richard Michael; Member (C) Ealing and Hillingdon, since 2000, and Deputy Mayor, since 2008, London Assembly, Greater London Authority; *b* 1 Dec. 1947; *s* of late John William Barnes and of Kate (Kitty) Barnes (*née* Harper). *Educ:* UWIST, Cardiff (BSc Hons Econs). Mem. (C) Hillingdon BC, 1982– (Leader, Cons. Gp, 1992–2000; Leader, 1998–2000). Mem., Metropolitan Police Authority, 2000–. London Assembly, Greater London Authority: Chm., Safer London Cttee, 2004, 7 July Rev. Cttee; Leader, Cons. Gp. Non-exec. Dir, NW London Strategic HA. Advr, Book Trust. *Recreations:* gardening, chelonia, opera, bibliophile. *Address:* 280 Northwood Road, Harefield, Middx UB9 6PU. *T:* (020) 7983 4387. *Club:* Hayes and Harlington Conservative.

BARNES, Dr Robert Sandford; Chairman, Robert S. Barnes Consultants, since 1978; Principal, Queen Elizabeth College, Kensington, London University, 1978–85; *b* 8 July 1924; *s* of William Edward and Ada Elsie Barnes (*née* Sutherst); *m* 1952, Julia Frances Marriott Grant; one *s* three *d. Educ:* Univ. of Manchester (BSc Hons 1948, MSc 1959, DSc 1962). FInstP 1961; FIMMM (FIM 1965); CEng 1977; CPhys 1985. Radar Research, Admiralty Signals Estab., Witley, Surrey, 1944–47; AERE, Harwell: Metallurgical Research on nuclear materials, 1948–62; Head of Irradiation Branch, 1962–65; Vis. Scientist, The Science Center, N Amer. Aviation Co., Calif, 1965; Head of Metallurgy Div., AERE, Harwell, 1966–68; Dep. Dir, BISRA, 1968–69; Dir, BISRA, 1969–70; Dir R&D, British Steel Corp., 1970–75; Chief Scientist, BSC, 1975–78. Technical Adviser: Bd of BOC Ltd, 1978–79; Bd of BOC International Ltd, 1979–81; Bd of New Ventures Secretariat, 1978–80. Chm., Ruthner Continuous Crop Systems Ltd, 1976–78. Member: CBI Res. and Technol. Cttee, 1968–75; Adv. Council on R&D for Iron and Steel, 1970–75; Materials Science and Technol. Cttee, SRC, 1975–79; European Industrial Res. Management Assoc., 1970 (Vice-Pres., 1974–78); Parly and Scientific Cttee, 1970–80, 1983–85; Foundn for Science and Technology, 1984– (Mem., Membership Cttee, 1987–98); Chm., Materials Technology Panel, Internat. Tin Res. Inst., 1988–94. Member: Council, Welding Inst., 1970–75; Council, Instn of Metallurgists, 1970–75 and 1979–85 (Vice Pres., 1979; Sen. Vice Pres., 1982; Pres., 1983–85); Council, Metals Soc., 1974–80, 1982–85 (Chm., Coordinating Cttee, 1976–78; Mem., Executive Cttee, 1976–80). Institute of Metals: Mem., Steering Gp, 1983–84; Mem. Council, 1985–92; Mem. Exec. Cttee, 1985–92; Past Pres., 1985–; Chm., Professional Bd, 1985–92; Institute of Materials Members Trust: Trustee, 1984–2003; Mem., 1986–2002; Chm., 1992–99. Chairman: Combined Operations Working Party, 1980–81; European Nuclear Steel-making Club, 1973–76; UK Mem., Conseil d'Association Européenne pour la Promotion de la Recherche Technique en Sidérurgie, 1972–78; Member: Adv. Council on Energy Conservation, Industry Group, 1977–78; Council, Nat. Backpain Assoc., 1979–98. Hon. Mem. Council, Iron and Steel Inst., 1969–73. Governor, Sheffield Polytechnic, 1968–72; Member: Court of Univ. of Surrey, 1968–80; Collegiate Council, Univ. of London, 1978–85; Jt Finance and Gen. Purposes Cttee, Univ. of London, 1978–85; Senate, Univ. of London, 1980–85; Member Council: King's Coll. London, 1982–85; Chelsea Coll., 1983–85; Bd Mem., CSTI, 1984–88. Mem., Supporters of Nuclear Energy. Numerous lectures at home and overseas including: Hatfield Meml, Iron and Steel Inst., 1973; John Player, IMechE, 1976. Freeman, City of London, 1984; Liveryman, Worshipful Co. of Engrs, 1985. Rosenhain Medallist, Inst. of Metals, 1964. FRSA 1976; FKC 1985; Life Member: RYA, 1976; Royal Instn, 1986; Nat. Trust, 1986. *Publications:* chapters in specialist books of science; scientific papers in various learned jls on the effects of atomic radiation on materials, on the rôle of energy in the production of engineering materials, etc. *Recreations:* cruising in the Mediterranean on sailing yacht Bombero, coupled with archaeology. *Address:* One The Mansion, Ashwood Place, Woking, Surrey GU22 7JR. *T:* (01483) 761529. *Clubs:* Athenæum, Cruising Association.

BARNES, Roger Anthony; Director, Hambros Bank Ltd, 1993–97; Assistant Director, Bank of England and Head of Banking Supervision Division, 1988–93; *b* 29 May 1937; *s* of Kenneth Ernest Barnes and Lilian Agnes (*née* King); *m* 1961, Tessa Margaret Soundy; two *s* two *d. Educ:* Malvern College; St John's College, Oxford (BA). Bank of England, 1961–93. Mem. Council of Management, European Sch. of Management, 1994–2003. Trustee, CAF, 1999–2003. *Recreations:* golf, music, English folk dancing. *Address:* 40 Battlefield Road, St Albans, Herts AL1 4DD. *T:* (01727) 851987. *Club:* City of London.

BARNES, Rosemary Susan, (Rosie); Chief Executive, Cystic Fibrosis Trust, since 1996; *b* 16 May 1946; *d* of Alan Allen and Kathleen (*née* Brown); *m* 1967, Graham Barnes; two *s* one *d. Educ:* Bilborough Grammar Sch.; Birmingham Univ. (BSocSci Hons). Management Trainee, Research Bureau Ltd, 1967–69; Product Manager, Yardley of London Ltd, 1969–72; primary teacher (briefly), 1972; freelance market researcher, 1973–87. MP Greenwich, Feb. 1987–1992 (SDP, 1987–90, Social Democrat, 1990–92);

contested (Soc. Dem.) Greenwich, 1992. Dir, Birthright, subseq. WellBeing, 1992–96. *Recreations:* gardening, cooking, reading, travelling, walking, yoga, my dogs. *Address:* (office) 11 London Road, Bromley, Kent BR1 1BY.

BARNES, Shani Estelle; Her Honour Judge Barnes; a Circuit Judge, since 2004; *b* 24 Sept. 1955; *d* of late Sidney Hurst and of Renée Hurst; *m* 1994, David Thomas Howker, *qv*; two *s* three *d*. *Educ:* Central Foundn Grammar Sch. for Girls; Middlesex Univ. (BA 1st cl. Hons 1984). Called to the Bar, Middle Temple, 1986; Asst Recorder, 1999–2000; Recorder, 2000–04. *Address:* c/o Circuit Secretariat, Rose Court, 2 Southwark Bridge, SE1 9HS.

BARNES, Simon John Campbell; writer; chief sports writer, The Times, since 2002 (sports columnist, 1982–2002); *b* 22 July 1951; *s* of Edward Campbell Barnes, *qv* and late Dorothy Elsie Barnes (*née* Smith); *m* 1983, Cindy Lee Wright; two *s*. *Educ:* Emanuel Sch.; Bristol Univ. (BA Hons). Surrey and S London Newspapers, 1974–78; contributor to S China Morning Post, Asian Business and Asian Finance, based in Asia, 1978–82; wildlife writer, RSPB Birds magazine, 1994–; sports columnist, The Spectator, 1995–2002. Patron, Spinal Research, 2000–. Sports Writer of Year: British Press Awards, 1987, What the Papers Say Awards, 2003; Sports Feature Writer of Year, Sports Council, 1988 and 1998; Sports Columnist of the Year: Sports Writers' Assoc., 2001, Sports Journalists' Assoc., 2007; Football Writer of Year, Football Supporters' Assoc., 1991. *Publications:* Phil Edmonds: a singular man, 1986; Horsesweat and Tears, 1988; A Sportswriter's Year, 1989; A la Recherche du Cricket Perdu, 1989; Sportswriter's Eye, 1989; Flying in the Face of Nature, 1991; Tiger!, 1994; Planet Zoo, 2000; On Horseback, 2000; How to be a Bad Birdwatcher, 2004; A Bad Birdwatcher's Companion, 2005; The Meaning of Sport, 2006; How to be Wild, 2007; *novels*: Rogue Lion Safaris, 1997; Hong Kong Belongers, 1999; Miss Chance, 2000. *Recreations:* Africa, horses, birdsong, Bach. *Address:* c/o The Times, 1 Pennington Street, E98 1TT. *T:* (020) 7782 5000, *Fax:* (020) 7782 5211. *Club:* Tewin Irregulars Cricket.

BARNES, Timothy Paul; QC 1986; a Recorder, since 1987; *b* 23 April 1944; *s* of late Arthur Morley Barnes and Valerie Enid Mary Barnes; *m* 1969, Patricia Margaret Gale; one *s* three *d*. *Educ:* Bradfield Coll., Berkshire; Christ's Coll., Cambridge (MA). Called to Bar, Gray's Inn, 1968 (Hilbery Exhibn; Bencher, 2004); practises Midland and Oxford Circuit; Asst Recorder, 1983. Chm., Greenwich Soc., 2001–. *Recreations:* gardening, theatre. *Address:* The White House, Crooms Hill, SE10 8HH. *T:* (020) 8858 1185, *Fax:* (020) 8858 0788. *Club:* MCC.

BARNES JONES, Deborah Elizabeth Vavasseur; HM Diplomatic Service; Governor, Montserrat, 2004–07; *b* 6 Oct. 1956; *née* Barnes; *m* 1986, Frederick Richard Jones; twin *d*. Joined FCO, 1980; Moscow, 1983–85; First Secretary: on loan to Cabinet Office, 1985–86; (Chancery), Israel, 1988–92; FCO, 1992–96; Dep. Hd of Mission, Uruguay, 1996–2001; Ambassador to Georgia, 2001–04. *Address:* c/o Foreign and Commonwealth Office, King Charles Street, SW1A 2AH.

BARNES THOMPSON, Dame Ingrid Victoria; *see* Allen, Dame I. V.

BARNETT, family name of **Baron Barnett**.

BARNETT, Baron *cr* 1983 (Life Peer), of Heywood and Royton in Greater Manchester; **Joel Barnett;** PC 1975; JP; chairman and director of a number of companies; *b* 14 Oct. 1923; *s* of Louis and Ettie Barnett, both of Manchester; *m* 1949, Lilian Goldstone; one *d*. *Educ:* Derby Street Jewish Sch.; Manchester Central High Sch. Certified accountant. Served RASC and British Military Govt in Germany. Mem. of Prestwich, Lancs, Borough Council, 1956–59; Hon. Treas. Manchester Fabian Society, 1953–65. Contested (Lab) Runcorn Div. of Cheshire, Oct. 1959; MP (Lab) Heywood and Royton Div., Lancs, 1964–83. Member: Public Accounts Cttee, 1965–71 (Chm., 1979–83); Public Expenditure Cttee, 1971–74; Select Cttee on Tax Credits, 1973–74; Chm. Parly Labour Party Economic and Finance Group, 1967–70 and 1972–74 (Vice-Chm., 1966–67); Opposition Spokesman on Treasury matters, 1970–74; Chief Sec. to the Treasury, 1974–79 (Cabinet Mem., 1977–79); Opposition spokesman on the Treasury in House of Lords, 1983–86. Vice-Chm., Bd of Govs, BBC, 1986–93. Chm., British Screen Finance Ltd (formerly British Screen Finance Consortium), 1985–97. Mem., Internat. Adv. Bd, Unisys, 1989–96. Chm., Building Societies' Ombudsman Council, 1987–96. Trustee, V&A Museum, 1984–97. Mem., Hallé Cttee, 1982–93. Chm., Birkbeck Coll. Appeal Cttee, 1990–96; Trustee, Open Univ. Foundn, 1994–. Chm., Hansard Soc. for Parly Govt, 1984–90. Pres., RIPA, 1989–92. Hon. Fellow, Birkbeck Coll., London, 1992. JP Lancs 1960. Hon. LLD Strathclyde, 1983. *Publication:* Inside the Treasury, 1982. *Recreations:* walking, conversation and reading, good food. *Address:* Flat 92, 24 John Islip Street, SW1P 4LG; 7 Hillingdon Road, Whitefield, Manchester M45 7QQ.

BARNETT, Andrew; *see* Barnett, J. A.

BARNETT, Andrew John; His Honour Judge Andrew Barnett; a Circuit Judge, since 2004; *b* 19 Sept. 1953; *s* of Rev. Canon Norman Barnett and Dorette Barnett; *m* 1978, Gillian Lindsey, *d* of Patrick Leonard James, *qv*; three *s* one *d*. *Educ:* Marlborough Coll.; KCL (BD). Called to the Bar, Gray's Inn, 1977; Asst Recorder, 1992–96; Recorder, 1996–2004. Mem. Cttee, Council of Circuit Judges, 2006–. *Recreations:* most outdoor activities, including golf. *Address:* Winchester Combined Court Centre, The Law Courts, Winchester, Hants SO23 9DL. *T:* (01962) 814100. *Clubs:* Lansdowne; High Post Golf.

BARNETT, Charles Henry; Chief Executive, Ascot Racecourse, since 2007; *b* 15 July 1948; *s* of late Major B. G. Barnett and D. Barnett; *m* 1978, Georgina Greig; one *s* two *d*. *Educ:* Eton Coll.; Christ Church, Oxford (BA 2nd Cl. Hons Jurisprudence; MA). Chief Executive: Haydock Park Racecourse, 1984–93; Chester Race Co. Ltd, 1996–2000; Man. Dir, Aintree Racecourse Co. Ltd, 1993–2007. *Recreation:* country pursuits. *Address:* Ascot Racecourse, Ascot, Berks SL5 7JX. *T:* (01344) 621093.

BARNETT, Dr Christopher Andrew; Headmaster, Whitgift School, Croydon, since 1991; *b* 1 Feb. 1953; *s* of Peter Alan Barnett and Joan Barnett (*née* Cullis); *m* 1976, Hon. Laura Miriam Elizabeth, *o c* of Baron Weidenfeld, *qv*; three *s* one *d*. *Educ:* Cedars Sch., Leighton Buzzard; Oriel Coll., Oxford (Exhibnr; BA Hons History 1974; MA 1978; DPhil 1981). Lectr in Econs, Brunel Univ., 1975–77; Head of History Dept, Bradfield Coll., Berks, 1978–87; Second Master, Dauntsey's Sch., Wilts, 1987–91. Fellow Commoner, Downing Coll., Cambridge, 1987; Evelyn Wrench Scholar, ESU, 1990. Pres., Croydon Music Fest., 1992–. *Recreations:* opera, political Victoriana, hill-walking, travel, horse-racing. *Address:* Whitgift School, Haling Park, South Croydon CR2 6YT. *T:* (020) 8688 9222. *Club:* Athenæum.

BARNETT, His Honour Christopher John Anthony; QC 1983; a Deputy Circuit Judge, since 2003 (a Circuit Judge, 1988–2003); Designated Family Judge, Suffolk, 1991–2003; *b* 18 May 1936; *s* of Richard Adrian Barnett and Phyllis Barnett (*née* Cartwright); *m* 1959, Sylvia Marieliese (*née* Pritt); two *s* one *d*. *Educ:* Repton Sch., Derbyshire; College of Law, London. Called to the Bar, Gray's Inn, 1965. Volunteer, Kenya Regt, 1954–55; District Officer (Kikuyu Guard) and Kenya Government Service, 1955–60; a District Officer in HM Overseas Civil Service, serving in Kenya, 1960–62; in practice as barrister, 1965–88; a Recorder, 1982–88; Jt Hd of Chambers, 4 Paper Buildings, 1985–88; a Dep. High Court Judge, QBD, 1991–97. A Pres., Mental Health Review Tribunal Restricted Patients Panel, 2002–. Mem., Wine Cttee, SE Circuit, 1984–88; Chm., SE Circuit Area Liaison Cttee, 1985–88; Mem. Cttee, Council of Circuit Judges, 1992–2003; a Chm., Bar Disciplinary Tribunal, 2006–. Chm., Suffolk Community Alcohol Services, 1993–95; a Patron, Relate, W Suffolk, 1998–. Mem., Court of Essex Univ., 1983–. Pres., Old Reptonian Soc., 2002. *Recreations:* cricket, tennis, walking, travel, gardening under instruction. *Address:* c/o Judicial Secretariat, 2nd Floor, Rose Court, 2 Southwark Bridge, SE1 9HS. *Club:* Kenya Kongonis Cricket.

BARNETT, Cindy; *see* Barnett, L. J.

BARNETT, Clive Durac, MA; HM Inspector of Schools, since 2002; *b* 22 July 1949; *s* of Edgar Thomas Barnett and Betty Marian Barnett; *m* 1981, Patricia Michelle Morrissey. *Educ:* King's Coll. Sch., Wimbledon; Magdalen Coll., Oxford (BA Hons, MA, PGCE). Asst Teacher of History, Kingston GS, 1971–79; Head, History and Politics Depts, Watford Boys' GS, 1979–86; Dep. Headmaster, Portsmouth GS, 1986–92; Headmaster, Bishop Wordsworth's Sch., Salisbury, 1992–2002. Mem., Salisbury Diocesan Bd of Educn, 1998–2002; Lay Canon, Salisbury Cath., 2007–. Trustee, Trade Aid, 1996–2006 (Chm., 1996–2002); Mem. Cttee, Bloxham Project, 1998–2005 (Vice-Chm., 1999–2002); Patron, EdUKaid, 2007–. *Publication:* (jtly) Smike (a musical), 1973 (televised 1974). *Recreations:* cricket, cycling, walking, listening to most forms of music, travelling, spending time with my wife! *Address:* Office for Standards in Education, South Region Education, Learning and Skills, Freshford House, Redcliffe Way, Bristol BS1 6NL. *T:* (0117) 945 6293. *Club:* MCC.

BARNETT, Colin Michael; international business consultant, since 1990; Regional Secretary, North-West Regional Council of the Trades Union Congress, 1976–85; Divisional Officer, North-West Division of the National Union of Public Employees, 1971–84; *b* 27 Aug. 1929; *s* of Arthur Barnett and Kathleen Mary Barnett; *m* 1st, 1953, Margaret Barnett (marr. diss. 1980); one *s* one *d*; 2nd, 1982, Hilary Carolyn Hodge, PhD; one *s* one *d*. *Educ:* St Michael's Elem. Sch., Southfields; Wandsworth Grammar Sch.; London Sch. of Econs and Polit. Science; WEA classes. Area Officer, NUPE, 1959, Asst Divl Officer 1961. Chm. Gp H, Duke of Edinburgh Conf. on Industry and Society, 1974. Secretary: NW Peace Council, 1979–; NW Cttee Against Racism, 1980–. Chm., MSC Area Bd, Gtr Manchester and Lancashire, 1978–83. Member: Merseyside District Manpower Bd, 1983–86; Industrial Tribunal, Manchester, 1974–99; Liverpool Social Security Appeal Tribunal, 1986–99. Dir, AT4 Community Prog. Agency, 1986–89. Debt and Industrial Advr, St Helens CAB, 1984–92; Marriage Guidance Counsellor, 1984–92. Organised: People's March for Jobs, 1981; (jtly) People's March for Jobs, 1983. British Representative: NW Russia Agency for Internat. Co-operation and Develt; St Petersburg British-Russia Soc.; Co-ordinator, UK projects for St Petersburg Health Dept. Employment Advr, This is Your Right, Granada TV, 1970–89. Governor, William Temple Foundn, 1980–87; Chm. Governors, Broadway Community High Sch., St Helens, 1999–2004. Chm. Trustees, Prescot and St Helens Victim Support Service. Chm., Sedbergh Book Town Cttee Ltd, 2004. *Recreations:* reading, promoting values of socialist ethics. *Address:* 17 Bainbridge Road, Sedbergh, Cumbria LA10 5AU. *T:* (01539) 620314; *e-mail:* hchodge@virgin.net.

BARNETT, Correlli (Douglas), CBE 1997; author; Fellow, Churchill College, Cambridge, since 1977; Keeper of the Churchill Archives Centre, 1977–95; *b* 28 June 1927; *s* of D. A. Barnett; *m* 1950, Ruth Murby; two *d*. *Educ:* Trinity Sch., Croydon; Exeter Coll., Oxford. Second class hons, Mod. Hist. with Mil. Hist. and the Theory of War as a special subject; MA 1954. Intell. Corps, 1945–48. North Thames Gas Bd, 1952–57; Public Relations, 1957–63. Vice-Pres., E Arts Assoc., 1978–91 (Chm. Literature Panel, and Mem. Exec. Cttee, 1972–78); Pres., East Anglian Writers, 1969–88; Member: Council, Royal Utd Services Inst. for Defence Studies, 1973–85; Cttee, London Library, 1977–79 and 1982–84. Leverhulme Res. Fellowship, 1976; apptd Lectr in Defence Studies, Univ. of Cambridge, 1980; resigned in order to devote more time to writing, 1983. Winston Churchill Meml Lectr, Switzerland, 1982. Hon. Pres., Western Front Assoc., 1998–. FRSL; FRHistS; FRSA. Hon. FCGI 2003. Hon. DSc Cranfield, 1993. Chesney Gold Medal, RUSI, 1991. *Publications:* The Hump Organisation, 1957; The Channel Tunnel (with Humphrey Slater), 1958; The Desert Generals, 1960, new enlarged edn, 1983; The Swordbearers, 1963; Britain and Her Army, 1970 (RSL award, 1971); The Collapse of British Power, 1972; Marlborough, 1974; Bonaparte, 1978; The Great War, 1979; The Audit of War, 1986 (US edn as The Pride and the Fall, 1987); Engage the Enemy More Closely: the Royal Navy in the Second World War, 1991 (Yorkshire Post Book of the Year Award, 1991); The Lost Victory: British dreams, British realities 1945–1950, 1995; The Verdict of Peace: Britain between her yesterday and the future, 2001; (historical consultant and writer to) BBC Television series: The Great War, 1963–64; The Lost Peace, 1965–66; The Commanders, 1972–73; reviews Mil. Hist. for The Spectator and The Sunday Telegraph; contrib. to: The Promise of Greatness (a symposium on the Great War), 1968; Governing Elites (a symposium), 1969; Decisive Battles of the Twentieth Century, 1976; The War Lords, 1976; The Economic System in the UK, 1985; Education for Capability, 1986; (ed) Hitler's Generals, 1989. *Recreations:* gardening, interior decorating, idling, eating, mole-hunting, travelling through France. *Address:* Catbridge House, East Carleton, Norwich NR14 8JX. *T:* (01508) 570410. *Club:* Beefsteak.

BARNETT, Prof. David Braham, CBE 2007; MD; FRCP; Professor of Clinical Pharmacology, University of Leicester Medical School, since 1984 (Head, Department of Medicine, 1999); *b* 17 July 1944. *Educ:* Sheffield Univ. Med. Sch. (MB ChB Hons 1967; MD 1979). FRCP 1981. Merck Internat. Travelling Fellow, 1975–76; Sen. Lectr, Univ. of Leicester, 1976–84; Hon. Consultant Physician, Leicester Royal Infirmary, 1976–. Non-exec. Dir, Leicester Royal Infirmary NHS Trust, 1993–2000. Chairman: Appraisals Cttee, NICE, 1999–. *Publications:* original research, rev. articles and book chapters in fields of molecular pharmacology and general cardiovascular clinical pharmacology, with specialist interest in ischaemic heart disease. *Recreations:* golf, reading, theatre. *Address:* Department of Cardiovascular Sciences, Level 4, Robert Kilpatrick Clinical Sciences Building, Leicester Royal Infirmary, Leicester LE2 7LX. *T:* (0116) 252 3126.

BARNETT, Geoffrey Grant Fulton, OBE 2001; Trustee, since 2001, Chair of Council, since 2006, Barnardo's (Hon. Treasurer, 2002–06); *b* 9 March 1943; *s* of Air Chief Marshal Sir Denis H. F. Barnett, GCB, CBE, DFC; *m* 1968, Fiona Katharine Milligan; two *s* two *d*. *Educ:* Winchester; Clare Coll., Cambridge (MA). Courtaulds Ltd, 1964–67; The Economist Intelligence Unit, 1967–70; British Printing Corp., 1970–71; Baring Brothers & Co. Ltd, 1971–95 (Dir, 1979–95); Man. Dir, Baring Brothers Asia, Hong Kong, 1979–83; seconded as Dir Gen., Panel on Takeovers and Mergers, 1989–92. Dir, Language Line Ltd, 1996–99; Trustee: Castelnau Centre Project, 2002– (Chm., 2002–); StartHere, 2000–05; St Michael's Fellowship, 2002–06; Baring Foundn, 2005–. Hon.

Treas., VSO, 1984–2000; Mem., Governing Bd, London and Quadrant Housing Trust, 1985–2000. Lay Chm., Richmond and Barnes Deanery Synod, 2002–07; Lay Reader, C of E, 2003–. FRSA 1992. *Recreations:* Scotland, walking, music, bird watching. *Address:* 2 Mill Hill Road, SW13 0HR. *T:* (020) 8878 6975.

BARNETT, Dame Jenifer W.; *see* Wilson-Barnett.

BARNETT, Jeremy John, OBE 1982; independent tour consultant, since 1999; *b* 26 Jan. 1941; *s* of late Audrey Wickham Barnett and Lt-Comdr Charles Richard Barnett, RN; *m* 1968, Maureen Janet Cullum; one *s* one *d*. *Educ:* St Edward's Sch., Oxford; St Andrews Univ. (MA); Leeds Univ. (Dip TEFL); SOAS, London Univ. (MA 1994). Joined British Council, 1964; teaching, Victory Coll., Cairo, 1965–67; Lectr, Inst. of Educn, Istanbul, 1967–69; MECAS, Lebanon, 1969–70; Dir of Studies, Turco-British Assoc., Ankara, 1970–72; British Council Rep., Riyadh, 1972–75; Dir, ME Dept, 1975–78; Counsellor for British Council and Cultural Affairs, Ankara, 1978–82; British Council Rep., Warsaw, 1982–85; Dir, E Europe and N Asia Dept, 1985–88; Controller, S and W Asia Div., 1988–89; British Council Rep., later Dir, and Cultural Counsellor, British Embassy, Cairo, 1989–93. Westminster Classic Tours, 1995–99 (Man. Dir, 1998–99). *Recreation:* hill walking. *Address:* Oakdene Station Road, Groombridge, Tunbridge Wells, Kent TN3 9NB. *T:* and *Fax:* (01892) 864626.

BARNETT, (John) Andrew; Director, The Policy Practice Ltd, since 2004; *b* Repton, 1 Dec. 1946; *s* of William Gordon Barnett and Margaret Action Barnett (*née* Wain); *m* 1977, Mary Jane Smith; two *d*. *Educ:* Repton Sch.; Univ. of Sussex (MA Develt Studies 1970). Economist, ODA, 1971–72; University of Sussex: Res. Officer, Inst. of Develt Studies, 1974–77; Prog. Officer, Internat. Develt Res. Centre, Canada, 1977–85; Fellow, 1985–96, Leader, Technol. and Develt Gp, 1987–93, Sci. Policy Res. Unit, subseq. Sci. and Technol. Policy Res. Unit (Hon. Fellow, 1996–); Dir of Res., Intermediate Technol. Develt Gp, 1994–98. Partner, Sussex Development Project Consultants Ltd, 1973–78; Dir, Sussex Research Associates Ltd, 1985–. Specialist Adviser: Select Cttee on Sci. and Technol., H of L, 1989; Select Cttee on Sci. and Technol., H of C, 2003–04; Mem., Ind. Tech. Adv. Gp, Energy Sector Mgt Assistance Prog., World Bank, 1996–2007. Member Board: Womankind Worldwide, London, 1999– (Chm., 2006–07); ODI, 2000–; Small Scale Sustainable Infrastructure Develt Fund, Cambridge, Mass, 2002–08. *Publications:* articles in learned jls, books and reports on energy policy, technol. policy and res. policy in developing countries. *Recreations:* sailing, walking, cooking. *Address:* c/o The Policy Practice Ltd, 33 Southdown Avenue, Brighton BN1 6EH. *T:* (01273) 330331.

BARNETT, Joseph Anthony, CBE 1983 (OBE 1975); Director (formerly Representative), British Council, Tokyo, 1983–91, retired; *b* 19 Dec. 1931; *s* of Joseph Edward Barnett and Helen Johnson; *m* 1960, Carolina Johnson Rice (*d* 1998); one *s* one *d*. *Educ:* St Albans Sch.; Pembroke Coll., Cambridge (BA (Hons) English and Psychology); Edinburgh Univ. (Diploma in Applied Linguistics). Served Army, 1950–51 (2nd Lieut). Teaching, Aylesford House, St Albans, 1954–55; Unilever Ltd, 1955–58; apptd British Council, 1958; Asst Educn Officer, Dacca, Pakistan, 1958; trng at Sch. of Applied Linguistics, Edinburgh Univ., 1960; Educn Officer, Dacca, 1961; seconded to Inst. of Educn, London Univ., 1963; Head, English Language Teaching Inst., London, 1964; Dir of Studies, Regional Inst. of English, Bangalore, India, 1968; Representative, Ethiopia, 1971; Controller, English Language Teaching Div., 1975; Representative, Brazil, 1978–82. *Publications:* (jtly) Getting on in English, 1960; Success with English (language laboratory materials), Books 1–3, 1966–69. *Recreation:* sport (tennis, armchair cricket, Rugby). *Address:* The Thatch, Stebbing Green, Dunmow, Essex CM6 3TE. *T:* (01371) 856014. *Club:* Athenæum.

BARNETT, Kenneth Thomas, CB 1979; Deputy Secretary, Department of the Environment, 1976–80; *b* 12 Jan. 1921; *yr s* of late Frederick Charles Barnett and Ethel Barnett (*née* Powell); *m* 1943, Emily May Lovering; one *d*. *Educ:* Howard Gardens High Sch., Cardiff. Entered Civil Service (Min. of Transport), 1937; Sea Transport Office, Port Said, 1951–54; Asst Sec., 1965; Under-Sec., Cabinet Office (on secondment), 1971–73; Under-Sec., DoE, 1970–76. Dir, Abbey Data Systems Ltd, 1984–2005. *Recreations:* gardening, watching Rugby football. *Address:* 5 Redan Close, Highcliffe-on-Sea, Christchurch, Dorset BH23 5DJ. *T:* (01425) 276945.

BARNETT, Kevin Edward; His Honour Judge Kevin Barnett; a Circuit Judge, since 1996; *b* 2 Jan. 1948; *s* of Arthur and Winifred Barnett; *m* 1972, Patricia Margaret Smith; one *d*. *Educ:* Wellesbourne Sch.; Tudor Grange Grammar Sch.; London Univ. (LLB Hons ext.). Called to the Bar, Gray's Inn, 1971; Wales and Chester Circuit. *Recreations:* painting, photography, cooking. *Address:* Court Service, Wales and Chester Circuit, 2nd Floor, Churchill House, Churchill Way, Cardiff CF1 4HH. *Club:* Lansdowne.

BARNETT, Lucinda Jane, (Cindy); JP; Chairman, Magistrates' Association, 2005–08; *b* 21 March 1951; *d* of late Richard William Gilbert and of Margaret Gwenllian Gilbert (*née* Edwards); *m* 1976, William Evans Barnett, *qv*; two *s*. *Educ:* Croydon High Sch. (GDST); King's Coll. London (Inglis studentship; BA 1st Cl. Hons 1972; MA 1973; PGCE 1974). ARCM 1971. Civil servant, DoE, 1974–77; teacher (pt-time), in schs. and private coaching, 1978–94. Member: Lord Chancellor's Adv. Cttee (SE London), 1993–2001; SE London Probation Cttee, 1998–2001; Magistrates' Courts' Sentencing Guidelines Wkg Party, 2002–03; Magisterial and Family Sub-cttee, 2005–07, Magisterial Cttee, 2007–08, Judicial Studies Bd; Judges' Council, 2005–08; Jt Chm., Nat. Offender Mgt Service/Sentencer Consultation Gp, 2005–08. Member, Board of Visitors: HMP Downview, 1994–2002 (Chm., 1997–2000); HMP Wandsworth, 2002. Member: Croydon Area Child Protection Cttee, 1994–2000 (Chm., Registration Appeals Panel); Croydon Magistrates' Courts' Cttee, 1999–2001; Chm., Croydon Family Panel, 2000–02. Magistrates' Association: Mem. Council, 2001–; Chm., Criminal Justice System, subseq. Judicial Policy and Practice, Cttee, 2002–05; Dep. Chm., 2002–05. JP Croydon, 1986. Gov., Croydon High Sch., 1993–2005 (Chm. Govs, 2000–05). *Publications:* contrib. Magistrate mag. *Recreations:* music, reading, computing. *Address:* c/o Magistrates' Association, 28 Fitzroy Square, W1T 6DD. *T:* (020) 7387 2353, *Fax:* (020) 7383 4020.

BARNETT, Rt Rev. Paul William, PhD; Bishop of North Sydney, and an Assistant Bishop, Diocese of Sydney, 1990–2001; *b* 23 Sept. 1935; *s* of William and Edna Barnett; *m* 1963, Anita Janet Simpson; two *s* two *d*. *Educ:* Univ. of London (BD Hons 1963, PhD 1978); Univ. of Sydney (MA Hons 1975). Deacon, 1963; priest, 1965; Lectr, Moore Theol Coll., 1964–67; Rector, St Barnabas, Broadway, 1967–73; Rector, Holy Trinity, Adelaide, 1973–79; Master, Robert Menzies Coll., Macquarie Univ., 1980–90. Lecturer, part time: Macquarie Univ., 1980–86; Univ. of Sydney, 1982–92. Vis. Prof., 1987, 1991, 1993, 1995, Res. Prof., 1996–, Regent Coll., Vancouver; Vis. Fellow in History, 1987–, Sen. Fellow in Ancient History Documentary Res., 2002–, Macquarie Univ.; Kingham Fellow, Oak Hill Theol Coll., 1996; Fellow, Inst. of Biblical Res., 2000. Highly commended author, Christian Booksellers Conf., 1990. *Publications:* Is the New Testament History?, 1986; The Message of 2 Corinthians, 1988; Bethlehem to Patmos, 1989; Apocalypse Now and Then, 1990; The Two Faces of Jesus, 1990; The Servant King, 1991; The Truth About Jesus, 1994; Jesus and the Logic of History, 1997;

Commentary on 2 Corinthians, 1997; Jesus and the Rise of Early Christianity, 1999; Commentary on 1 Corinthians, 2000; Commentary on Romans, 2003; Birth of Christianity, 2005; Shepherd King, 2005; First Peter, 2006; Paul, Missionary of Jesus, 2008. *Recreations:* tennis, swimming, fishing, fine music. *Address:* 59 Essex Street, Epping, NSW 2121, Australia.

BARNETT, Prof. Richard Robert, PhD; Vice Chancellor, since 2006, and Professor of Public Finance and Management, since 1990, University of Ulster; *b* 17 Oct. 1952; *s* of late Sidney Barnett and of Joyce Barnett (*née* Stocker). *Educ:* St Ivo Sch., St Ives; Abbey Sch., Ramsey; Univ. of Salford (BSc 1974; PhD 1983). Lecturer in Economics: Univ. of Salford, 1977–78; Univ. of York, 1978–90; University of Ulster: Dean, Faculty of Business and Mgt, 1994–2000; Pro Vice Chancellor, 2000–05; Actg Vice Chancellor, 2004–06. Vivienne Stewart Fellow, Univ. of Cambridge, and Vis. Scholar, Wolfson Coll., Cambridge, 1988; Vis. Prof. of Econs, Queen's Univ., Ontario, 1989–90. Non-exec. Dir, United Hosps HSS Trust, 1996–2004; Director: ILEX Urban Regeneration Co. Ltd, 2005–; NI Sci. Park Foundn Ltd, 2006–; non-exec. Dir, Bombadier-Shorts Aerospace (Belfast) Ltd, 2007–. Member: NI Adv. Cttee, British Council, 2000–; NIHEC, 2004–. Trustee, Daphne Jackson Trust, 2008–. CCMI 2007. *Publications:* contrib. learned jls and chapters in books in area of econ. policy and public finance. *Recreations:* contemporary fiction, motor sport. *Address:* University of Ulster, Cromore Road, Coleraine, Co. Londonderry BT52 1TA. *T:* (028) 7032 4329, *Fax:* (028) 7032 4901; *e-mail:* rr.barnett@ulster.ac.uk. *Club:* Ulster Reform.

BARNETT, Robert William, OBE 1993; HM Diplomatic Service, retired; Head of Science and Technology Unit, Foreign and Commonwealth Office, 2001–02; *b* 25 May 1954; *s* of late Harry Frederick Barnett, Wells-next-the-Sea, Norfolk and Dorothy Anne Barnett (*née* Williamson); *m* 1979, Caroline Sara Weale; two *s*. *Educ:* Wymondham Coll., Norfolk; St Catharine's Coll., Cambridge (BA Hons Mod. & Med. Langs 1977; MA 1979). Joined FCO, 1977: Japanese lang. trng, 1979; Third Sec., Tokyo, 1980–83; Policy Planning Staff, FCO, 1984; Asst Private Sec. to Minister of State, 1984–86; First Secretary: Western European Dept, FCO, 1986–88; Bonn, 1988–91; seconded to Saxony State Govt as Inward Investment Advr, 1992; Asst Hd, Eastern Adriatic Unit, FCO, 1993–94; Ambassador to Bosnia-Herzegovina, 1994–95; Counsellor (Sci., Technol. and Envmt), Bonn, 1995–99; Counsellor, Review of FCO Internat. Sci. and Technol. Work, 1999–2001. Mem. (Ind.), Cotswold DC, 2003. *Recreations:* walking, photography, gardening.

BARNETT, Robin Anthony, CMG 2006; HM Diplomatic Service; Ambassador to Romania, since 2006; *b* 8 March 1958; *s* of Bryan Anderson Barnett and Marion Barnett; *m* 1st, 1989, Debra Marianne Bunt (marr. diss. 1999); one *s*, and one step *s*; 2nd, 1999, Tesca Marie Osman; one step *s* one step *d*. *Educ:* Birmingham Univ. (LLB Hons 1979). Joined FCO, 1980: Second Secretary: Warsaw, 1982–85; FCO, 1985–90; First Secretary: UK Delegn to conventional forces in Europe negotiations, Vienna, 1990–91; UK Mission to UN, NY, 1991–95; FCO, 1996–98; Counsellor and Dep. Hd of Mission, Warsaw, 1998–2001; Hd, UKvisas, FCO, 2002–06. *Recreations:* travel, football (Manchester United), reading, film, cooking. *Address:* c/o Foreign and Commonwealth Office, King Charles Street, SW1A 2AH.

BARNETT, Prof. Stephen Mark, PhD; FRS 2006; CPhys; FRSE; Professor of Quantum Optics, University of Strathclyde, since 1996; *b* 20 Feb. 1961; *s* of Peter Symon Barnett and Rita Barnett; partner, Dr Claire Rosalie Gilson; one *s* one *d*. *Educ:* Imperial Coll., London (BSc, PhD 1985). Postdoctoral Res. Fellow, Imperial Coll., London, 1985–87; Harwell-Wolfson Res. Fellow, 1987–88; GEC and Fellowship of Engrg Fellow, Univ. of Oxford, 1988–90; Lectr in Physics, KCL, 1990–91; RSE Res. Fellow, 1991–94, Reader, 1994–96, Univ. of Strathclyde. FRSE 1996. *Publication:* (with Dr P. M. Radmore) Methods in Theoretical Quantum Optics, 1997. *Recreations:* croquet, playing the viola. *Address:* Department of Physics, University of Strathclyde, 107 Rottenrow, Glasgow G4 0NG. *T:* (0141) 548 3457, *Fax:* (0141) 552 2891; *e-mail:* steve@phys.strath.ac.uk.

BARNETT, William Evans; QC 1984; **His Honour Judge William Barnett;** a Circuit Judge, since 1994; *b* 10 March 1937; *s* of late Alec Barnett and Esmé (*née* Leon); *m* 1976, Lucinda Jane Gilbert (*see* L. J. Barnett); two *s*. *Educ:* Repton; Keble Coll., Oxford (BA Jurisprudence, 1961; MA 1965). National Service, RCS, 1956–58. Called to the Bar, Inner Temple, 1962; Major Scholarship, Inner Temple, 1962. A Recorder, 1981–94. Mem., Personal Injuries Litigation Procedure Wkg Pty, 1976–78; Judicial Mem., Mental Health Rev. Tribunal, 1993–2004. Mem., Whitgift Sch. Cttee, 1996–2002; Gov., Whitgift Foundn, 2004–. *Recreations:* golf, photography, gardening. *Address:* c/o Croydon Combined Court Centre, The Law Courts, Altyre Road, Croydon, Surrey CR9 5AB. *T:* (020) 8410 4700. *Club:* Royal Automobile.

BARNEVIK, Percy; Chairman of the Board: AstraZeneca PLC, 1999–2004; ABB (formerly ABB Asea Brown Boveri) Ltd, Zürich, Switzerland, 1996–2001 (President and Chief Executive Officer, 1988–96); *b* Simrishamn, Sweden, 1941. *Educ:* Sch. of Econs, Gothenburg, Sweden (MBA 1964); Stanford Univ. Johnson Group, 1966–69; Sandvik AB: Group Controller, 1969–75; Pres. of Sandvik, USA, 1975–79; Exec. Vice Pres., 1979–80, Chm., 1983–2002, Hon. Chm., 2002–, Sandvik AB Sweden; Pres. and Chief Exec. Officer, Asea, 1980–87. Chm. Bd, Investor AB, 1997–2002 (Bd Mem., Providentia, subseq. Investor, 1987–2002); Bd Mem., General Motors, 1996–. Hon. Fellow London Business Sch., 1996. Hon. FREng 1998. Hon. DTech Linköping, Sweden, 1989; Hon. DEcons Gothenburg, 1991; Hon. DLaws Babson Coll., Mass, USA, 1995; Hon. DSc Cranfield, 1997; Hon. Dr UMIST with Manchester, 1999. *Address:* 10 Hill Street, W1J 5NQ.

BARNEWALL, family name of **Baron Trimlestown.**

BARNEWALL, Sir Reginald Robert, 13th Bt *cr* 1622; cattle breeder and orchardist at Mount Tamborine; *b* 1 Oct. 1924; *o s* of Sir Reginald J. Barnewall, 12th Bt and of Jessie Ellen, *d* of John Fry; *S* father, 1961; *m* 1st, 1946, Elsie Muriel (*d* 1962), *d* of Thomas Matthews-Frederick, Brisbane; three *d* (one *s* decd); 2nd, 1962, Maureen Ellen, *d* of William Joseph Daly, South Caulfield, Vic; one *s*. *Educ:* Xavier Coll., Melbourne. Served War of 1939–45, overseas with RAE, AIF. Served with Citizen Military Forces Unit, 8/13 Victorian Mounted Rifles, Royal Australian Armoured Corps, 1948–58 (Lieut, acting Major). Managing Dir, Southern Airlines Ltd of Melbourne, 1953–58; Founder, and Operations Manager, Polynesian Airlines, Apia, Western Samoa, 1958–62; Managing Dir, Orchid Beach (Fraser Island) Pty Ltd, 1962–71; Dir, Island Airways Pty Ltd, Pialba, Qld, 1964–68; owner and operator, Coastal-Air Co. (Qld), 1971–76; Dir and Vice-Chm., J. Roy Stevens Pty Ltd, to 1975. *Heir:* *s* Peter Joseph Barnewall [*b* 26 Oct. 1963; *m* 1988, Kathryn Jane, *d* of Hugh Carroll; two *s* one *d*]. *Address:* Innisfree House, Normandie Court, Mount Tamborine, Queensland 4272, Australia. *Clubs:* United Service (Brisbane); RSL (Surfers Paradise); Royal Automobile (Queensland).

BARNICOAT, Thomas Humphry; Chief Operating Officer, Endemol Group, 2005–07; *b* 21 Oct. 1952; *s* of John Barnicoat and Jane Barnicoat (*née* Selby, now Wright); *m* 1980, Katrina Noelle Chalmers; three *d*. *Educ:* Lycée Français de Londres; St John's Coll., Oxford (BA Hist. and French). Ed., Isis, 1976; joined BBC, 1977: grad. trainee, 1977–79; scriptwriter, TV News, 1979–81; producer and dir, TV Current Affairs, 1981–86; Producer, Crown TV, 1986; Dir, Public Affairs, Sotheby's, 1986–87; Producer, Business TV, 1987–89; Dir, Corporate Devlt, 1990–93, Dep. Chief Exec., 1993–95, Broadcast Communications plc; Chief Exec., Broadcast Communications plc, subseq. Endemol UK, 1995–2004. Mem., Scotch Malt Whisky Soc. *Recreations:* swimming, driving, sleeping, military history. *Address:* *e-mail:* tbarnicoat@mac.com. *Clubs:* Reform, Hurlingham.

BARNIER, Michel Jean; Conseiller d'Etat; Minister for Agriculture, France, since 2007; *b* 9 Jan. 1951; *m* 1982, Isabelle Altmayer; two *s* one *d*. *Educ:* Ecole Supérieure de Commerce de Paris (Dip. 1972). Govt service, 1973–78. Mem. (RPR) for Savoie, Nat. Assembly, 1978–93; Minister of the Environment, France, 1993–95; Minister of State for European Affairs, 1995–97; Minister of Foreign Affairs, 2004–05. Mem., Eur. Commn, 1999–2004. Corporate Vice Pres., Internat. Develt, Mérieux Alliance, 2005–07. Mem., 1973–99, Chm., 1982–99, Deptl Council of Savoie; Senator for Savoie, 1997–99; Pres., Senate Delegn for EU, 1998. Jt Pres., Organising Cttee, Olympic Games, Albertville and Savoie, 1987–92. *Publications:* Vive la politique, 1985; Chacun pour tous: le défi écologique, 1990; Atlas des risques majeurs, 1992; Vers une mer inconnue, 1994; Notre contrat pour l'alternance, 2001. *Address:* 19 chemin des Jardins, 73200 Albertville, France; Ministry of Agriculture, 78 rue de Varenne, 75349 Paris 07 SP, France.

BARNISH, Alan Joseph; consultant, Cambridgeshire County Council, since 2003 (Chief Executive, 1997–2003); *b* 13 Oct. 1949; *s* of Sydney and Dora Barnish; *m* 1972, Elizabeth Sanders; one *s* one *d*. *Educ:* Leeds Univ. (BCom); IPFA. Mid Glam CC, 1975–90; Chief Exec. and Co. Treas., Powys CC, 1990–93; Chief Exec., Shropshire CC, 1993–97.

BARNSLEY, John Corbitt; company director; Chief Executive Officer, Business Process Outsourcing, PricewaterhouseCoopers, 1998–2001; *b* 25 May 1948; *s* of William C. Barnsley, consultant thoracic surgeon, and Hilda C. Barnsley (*née* Robson); *m* (marr. diss.); one *s* one *d* (and one *d* decd); civil partnership 2006, James Ian Mackenzie. *Educ:* Heaton Grammar Sch., Newcastle upon Tyne; Newcastle upon Tyne Univ. (LLB 1st Cl. Hons 1969; Reynoldson Meml Prize). Joined Price Waterhouse, Newcastle, 1970: Sen. Tax Partner, UK, 1990–93; European Leader for Audit and Business Services, 1993–95; Managing Partner, UK, 1995–98; Joint Global Dir of Ops, 1996–98; company merged with Coopers & Lybrand, 1998. Sen. Ind. non-exec. Dir, LMS Capital (formerly Leo Capital) plc, 2006–; non-executive Director: Northern Investors Co. PLC, 2002–; Grainger Trust PLC, 2003–; American Appraisal Associates, 2003–; Chairman: American Appraisal Associates UK, 2005–; Creswell Medical Ltd, 2006–. Chm., London (formerly N Thames) R & D Cttee, NHS Exec., 1997–. *Recreations:* Chinese porcelain, antique furniture. *Address:* 8 Montpelier Terrace, Knightsbridge, SW7 1JP. *Club:* Reform.

BARNSLEY, Victoria, (Hon. Mrs Nicholas Howard); Chief Executive and Publisher, HarperCollins UK, since 2000; *b* 4 March 1954; *d* of late T. E. Barnsley, OBE and Margaret Gwyneth Barnsley (*née* Llewellin); *m* 1992, Hon. Nicholas Howard; one *d*, and one step *s*. *Educ:* University Coll. London (BA Hons English; Hon. Fellow, 2005); Univ. of York (MA French and English 19th Century Novel). Founder, and Chm. and Chief Exec., Fourth Estate Ltd, 1984–2000. Trustee: Tate Gall., 1998–2007; Nat. Gall., 2005–07; Tate Foundn, 2007–; Dir, Tate Enterprises (formerly Tate Gall. Pubns) Ltd, 1998–2007. *Address:* HarperCollins, 77–85 Fulham Palace Road, Hammersmith, W6 8JB. *Club:* Groucho.

BARNSTAPLE, Archdeacon of; *see* Gunn-Johnson, Ven. D. A.

BARON, Hon. Dame Florence (Jacqueline), DBE 2004; **Hon. Mrs Justice Baron;** a Judge of the High Court of Justice, Family Division, since 2003; Liaison Judge, South Eastern Circuit, since 2008; *b* 7 Oct. 1952; *d* of Jose Baron and Ellen Elizabeth Jane Baron (*née* McLennan). *Educ:* Jersey Coll. for Girls; St Hugh's Coll., Oxford (BA Juris.; Hon. Fellow 2004). Called to the Bar, Middle Temple, 1976; QC 1995; a Recorder, 1999–2003; a Dep. High Court Judge, 2000–03. *Recreation:* relaxing. *Address:* Royal Courts of Justice, Strand, WC2A 2LL.

BARON, Franklin Andrew Merrifield; Permanent Representative of Commonwealth of Dominica to United Nations and to Organisation of American States, 1982–95; Dominican High Commissioner to London, 1986–92; *b* 19 Jan. 1923; *m* 1973, Sybil Eva Francisca McIntyre. *Educ:* Portsmouth Govt Sch., St Mary's Acad., Dominica Grammar Sch. A. A. Baron & Co.: entered firm, 1939; Partner, 1945; sole owner, 1978–. Member: Roseau Town Council, 1945–47 and 1956–58; Legislative and Exec. Councils, 1954–61; Founder and Leader, United People's Party, 1954–56; Minister of Trade and Production, 1956–60; Chief Minister and Minister of Finance, 1960–61. Ambassador to USA, 1982–86. Chairman: National Commercial Bank, 1986–90; Fort Young Hotel Co., 1986–89; The New Chronicle, 1989–96 (Dir, 1984–96); Proprietor: Paramount Printers Ltd, 1992–; The Chronicle, 1996–. Member: Public Service Commn, 1976–78; Electoral Commn, 1979–90; Dominica Boundaries Commn, 1979–90; Bd, Dominica Electricity Services, 1981–91 (Chm., 1983–91); Bd, Industrial Develt Corp., 1984–89; Chm., Dominica Public Library, 1985–89. Highest Award of Honour (Dominica), 2006. *Recreations:* horticulture, reading, travel. *Address:* 14 Cork Street, Roseau, Dominica. *T:* 4488151, 4480415, *Fax:* 4405295.

BARON, Prof. Jean-Claude, MD; FMedSci; Professor of Stroke Medicine, Department of Clinical Neurosciences (formerly Departments of Medicine and Neurology), University of Cambridge, since 2000; *b* 25 March 1949; *s* of Marcel and Yolaine Baron (*née* Bonan); *m* 1974, Annik Arnette de la Charlonny; one *s* two *d*. *Educ:* Univ. of Paris (MD). Asst Lectr in Biophysics, 1979–82, then in Neurol., 1982–86, Univ. of Paris; Sen. Registrar in Nuclear Medicine, 1979–82, then in Neurol., 1982–86, Salpêtrière Hosp., Paris; Director: of Res., INSERM, France, 1986–2000; INSERM Res. Unit # 320, Caen, 1989–2000; Scientific Dir, CYCERON Neuroimaging Res. Centre, Univ. of Caen, 1987–2000; Hon. Consultant in Neurol., Addenbrooke's Hosp., Cambridge, 2000–. FMedSci 2003. Johann Jacob Wepfer Award, Eur. Stroke Conf., 2005. *Publications:* (ed jtly) The Ischemic Penumbra, 2007; contrib. numerous peer-reviewed articles to learned jls, incl. Lancet, Brain, Annals of Neurol., Stroke; numerous book chapters and refereed abstracts. *Recreations:* music (playing the guitar), classic blues, J. S. Bach, Mozart. *Address:* Department of Clinical Neurosciences, R3, Box 83, Addenbrooke's Hospital, Cambridge CB2 2QQ. *T:* (01223) 217806.

BARON, John Charles; MP (C) Billericay, since 2001; *b* 21 June 1959; *s* of Raymond Arthur Ernest Baron and Kathleen Ruby Baron; *m* 1992, Thalia Anne Mayson Laird; two *d*. *Educ:* Jesus Coll., Cambridge (MA). Capt., RRF, 1984–88. Director: Henderson Private Investors, 1988–99; Rothschild Asset Mgt, 1999–2001. *Recreations:* tennis, walking, cycling, family. *Address:* c/o House of Commons, SW1A 0AA. *T:* (constituency office) (01268) 520765.

BARON, Dr (Ora) Wendy, OBE 1992; Director (formerly Curator), Government Art Collection, 1978–97; *b* 20 March 1937; *d* of late Dr S. B. Dimson and Gladys Felicia Dimson, CBE; *m* 1st, 1960, Jeremy Hugh Baron (marr. diss.); one *s* one *d*; 2nd, 1990, David Joseph Wyatt, *qv*. *Educ:* St Paul's Girls' Sch.; Courtauld Institute of Art (BA, PhD). Trustee: Public Art Commns Agency, 1990–99; Contemp. Art Soc., 1997–2001; Arts Res. Ltd, 1998–2004; NACF, 1998–. Has selected, researched and catalogued exhibitions, including: Sickert, Fine Art Soc., 1973; Camden Town Recalled, Fine Art Soc., 1976; The Camden Town Group, New Haven, USA, 1980; Late Sickert, Hayward Gall., 1981; Sickert, Royal Acad., 1992, Amsterdam, 1993. FRSA 1993; FSA 2006. *Publications:* Sickert, 1973; Miss Ethel Sands and her Circle, 1977; The Camden Town Group, 1979; Perfect Moderns, 2000; Sickert: paintings and drawings, 2006; articles and reviews in professional jls in the field of modern British art.

BARON, Sir Thomas, Kt 1992; CBE 1983. FRICS 1948. *Address:* Lightoaks Hall, Glazebury, Warrington WA3 5PX.

BARÓN CRESPO, Enrique Carlos; lawyer; Member, European Parliament, since 1986 (President, 1989–92); *b* Madrid, 27 March 1944; *m*; one *s*. *Educ:* Univ. of Madrid (LLL); Inst. Católico de Dirección de Empresas (Lic. en Ciencias Empresariales); Ecole Supérieure des Scis Econ. et Commerciales, Paris (Dip.). Lectr in Agricl Econs, Inst. Nacional de Estudios Agrarios, Valladolid, and in Structural Econs, Univ. of Madrid, 1966–70; lawyer in private practice, 1970–77. Mem. (PSOE), Congress of Deputies, Spain, 1977–87; spokesman on econ. and budgetary affairs, 1977–82; Minister of Transport, Tourism and Communications, 1982–85. European Parliament: a Vice-Pres., 1986–89; Pres., Gp of Party of European Socialists, 1999–2004. Pres., Internat. European Movt, 1987–89. *Publications:* Población y Hambre en el Mundo; El Fin del Campesinado; La Civilización del Automóvil; Europa 92: el rapto del futuro; Europe at the Dawn of the Millennium, 1997; contribs on economic and social questions to major Spanish periodicals. *Address:* European Parliament, Rue Wiertz 60, 1047 Brussels, Belgium; Oficina Parlamento Europeo, Paseo de la Castellana 46, 28046 Madrid, Spain.

BARR, Clare Elizabeth; *see* Pelham, C. E.

BARR, Danielle; Member, Broadcasting Standards Commission, 1994–99; *b* 7 Aug. 1940; *d* of Michael and Helen Brachfeld; *m* 1966, Marvin Stein; one *d*, and one step *s*. *Educ:* Tichon Hadash High Sch., Tel Aviv. Nat. Service, Israeli Army, 1958–60; Account Exec., Crane Advertising, 1961–64; Asst Advertising Manager, Goya, 1964–67; Brand Manager, 1967–76, Mktg Manager, 1976–80, Elida Gibbs; Dir, Geers Gross Advertising, 1980–84; Head of Advertising, Natwest Bank, 1984–87; Man. Dir, 1987–89, Chm., 1989–91, Publicis; Man. Dir, Third Age Mktg, 1993–95. Mem., Mktg Gp of GB, 1986–. *Recreations:* theatre, music, quilting. *Address:* 20 Jameson Street, W8 7SH. *T:* (020) 7221 2632. *Club:* Women's Advertising of London (Pres., 1985–86).

BARR, David; a Metropolitan Stipendiary Magistrate, 1976–96; *b* Glasgow, 15 Oct. 1925; *s* of late Walter and Betty Barr; *m* 1960, Ruth Weitzman; one *s* one *d*. *Educ:* Haberdashers' Aske's Hampstead Sch.; Largs Higher Grade Sch.; Brookline High Sch., Boston, USA; Edinburgh Univ.; University Coll., London (LLB). Royal Navy, 1943–47. Solicitor, 1953; private practice, 1953–76 (Partner, Pritchard Englefield & Tobin). JP Inner London Area, 1963–76; Chm., Inner London Juvenile Panel, 1969–76; Dep. Chm., N Westminster PSD, 1968–76. Manager, Finnart House Sch., Weybridge, 1955–73 (Trustee, 1973–96, Chm., 1985–96). Mem., Moorfields and Whittington Hosp. NHS Local Regl Ethics Cttee, 2002–. Pres., David Isaacs Fund, 1986–94. Trustee, London Action Trust, 2001–03. Governor: Haverstock Comp. Sch., 1997–2001; Richard Cobden Primary Sch., 1997–. *Recreations:* collecting 'Alice', bridge. *Address:* 19 St Mark's Crescent, NW1 7TU. *Clubs:* Garrick, MCC.

BARR, Maj.-Gen. John Alexander James Pooler, CB 1993; CBE 1989; Engineer-in-Chief (Army), 1991–93; *b* 29 Jan. 1939. 2nd Lieut, RE, 1960; Lt-Col, 1978; GSO1 (DS) SC, 1978; Brig. 1983; Comdt, Royal Sch. of Mil. Engrg, Chatham, 1983–87; Dir of Army Staff Duties, MoD, 1987–89; DCS (Support), HQ Allied Forces Northern Europe, 1989–91; Maj.-Gen., 1991. Col Comdt, RE, 1993–2002. CompICE 1992. *Address:* c/o Lloyds TSB, Cox's & King's Branch, PO Box 1190, 7 Pall Mall, SW1Y 5NA.

BARR, Kenneth Glen; Sheriff of South Strathclyde, Dumfries and Galloway at Dumfries, since 1976; *b* 20 Jan. 1941; *o s* of late Rev. Gavin Barr and Catherine McLellan Barr (*née* McGhie); *m* 1970, Susanne Crichton Keir (*d* 1996). *Educ:* Ardrossan Acad.; Royal High Sch.; Edinburgh Univ. (MA, LLB). Admitted to Faculty of Advocates, 1964. *Address:* Sheriff Court House, Dumfries DG1 2AN.

BARR, Prof. Nicholas Adrian, PhD; Professor of Public Economics, European Institute, London School of Economics and Political Science, since 2002; *b* London, 23 Nov. 1943; *s* of Herman and Edith Barr; *m* 1991, Gillian Lee (*née* Audigier); two step *s*. *Educ:* London Sch. of Econs and Political Sci. (BSc (Econ) 1965; MSc (Econ) 1967); Univ. of Calif, Berkeley (PhD 1971). Lectr in Econs, 1971–88, Sen. Lectr in Econs, 1988–2000, Reader, 2000–02, LSE. Vis. Schol., Fiscal Affairs Dept, IMF, 2000. World Bank: Consultant, Europe and Central Asia Reg., Central and Southern Eur. Depts, HR Ops Div., 1990–92; Principal Author, World Develt Report, 1995–96. Trustee, HelpAge Internat., 2004–. FRSA 1997. *Publications:* (jtly) Self-Assessment for Income Tax, 1977; (with A. Prest) Public Finance in Theory and Practice, 6th edn 1979, 7th edn 1985; The Economics of the Welfare State, 1987, 4th edn 2004 (trans. French, Greek, Hungarian, Korean and Polish); (with J. Barnes) Strategies for Higher Education: the alternative White Paper, 1988; Student Loans: the next steps, 1989; (ed with D. Whynes) Current Issues in the Economics of Welfare, 1993; (ed) Labor Markets and Social Policy in Central and Eastern Europe: the transition and beyond, 1994 (trans. Hungarian, Romanian and Russian); (contrib.) World Development Report 1996: from plan to market, 1996 (trans. Arabic, Chinese, French, German, Japanese, Russian and Spanish); The Welfare State as Piggy Bank: information, risk, uncertainty and the role of the State, 2001 (trans. Japanese); (ed) Economic Theory and the Welfare State, Vol. I: theory, Vol. II: income transfers, Vol. III: benefits in kind, 2001; (with I. Crawford) Financing Higher Education: answers from the UK, 2005; (ed) Labor Markets and Social Policy in Central and Eastern Europe: the accession and beyond, 2005; (with P. Diamond) Reforming Pensions: principles and policy choices, 2008; contrib. jls incl. Jl Econ. Lit., Econ. Jl, Economica, Oxford Rev. of Econ. Policy, Educn Econs, Econs of Transition, Internat. Social Security Rev., British Tax Rev., Public Money and Mgt, Jl Public Policy, Jl Social Policy, Political Qly. *Recreations:* cricket, computers, grandchildren. *Address:* European Institute, London School of Economics, Houghton Street, WC2A 2AE. *T:* (020) 7955 7482, *Fax:* (020) 7955 7546; *e-mail:* N.Barr@lse.ac.uk. *Club:* Middlesex County Cricket.

BARR YOUNG, His Honour Gavin Neil; a Circuit Judge, 1988–2005; *b* 14 Aug. 1939; *s* of Dr James Barr Young and Elsie Barr Young (*née* Hodgkinson); *m* 1969, Barbara

Elizabeth Breckon; two *d*. *Educ:* Loretto Sch., Musselburgh; Leeds Univ. (LLB). Called to the Bar, Gray's Inn, 1963; Member, North Eastern Circuit, 1964–88 (North Eastern Circuit Junior, 1968); a Recorder of the Crown Court, 1979–88. Part-time Legal Pres., Mental Health Rev. Tribunals, 2001–. *Recreations:* gardening, music. *Address:* Flaxbourne House, Great Ouseburn, York YO26 9RG.

BARRACK, William Sample, Jr; Senior Vice-President, Texaco Inc., NY, 1983–92; *b* 26 July 1929; *s* of William Sample Barrack and Edna Mae Henderson; *m* 1953, Evelyn Irene Ball; one *s* one *d*. *Educ:* Pittsburgh Univ. BSc (Eng) 1950. Comdr, USN, 1950–53. Joined Texaco Inc., 1953; marketing and management positions in USA, 1953–67; in Europe, 1967–71; Vice-President: in NY, 1971–80; Marketing Dept, Europe, 1971–76; Producing Dept, Eastern Hemisphere, 1976–77; Personnel and Corporate Services Dept, 1977–80; Chm. and Chief Exec., Texaco Ltd, London, 1980–82. Director: Caltex Petroleum Corp.; Texaco Foundn Inc.; Standard Commercial Corp.; Consolidated Natural Gas Corp. Governor, Foreign Policy Assoc.; Member: US Naval War College Foundn; Bd of Visitors, Univ. of Pittsburgh. Trustee, Manhattanville College. *Clubs:* Woodway Country; Ox Ridge Hunt; Ida Lewis Yacht; North Sea Yacht (Belgium); Clambake (Newport, RI); New York Yacht.

BARRACLOUGH, Richard Michael; QC 2003; *b* 29 April 1953; *s* of Michael Alfred William Barraclough and Doreen Barraclough; *m* 1982, Lindsey Elsa Petronella Taylor; two *s* three *d*. *Educ:* St Michael's Coll., Leeds; St Catherine's Coll., Oxford (MA). Solicitor of the Supreme Court, 1978; called to the Bar, Inner Temple, 1980. Legal Assessor, GMC, 1997–. Chm., Disability Cttee, Bar Council, 2004–. *Recreations:* motor-cycling, cellist, opera-singing, morganeering, Scottish dancing. *Address:* 6 Pump Court, Temple, EC4Y 7AR. *T:* (020) 7797 8400, *Fax:* (020) 7797 8401; *e-mail:* facutvivas@hotmail.com; Stella Maris, Port Bannatyne, Island of Bute, Scotland. *Clubs:* Royal Automobile; Hog.

BARRAN, Sir John (Napoleon Ruthven), 4th Bt *cr* 1895; Head of Information Technology, Central Office of Information, 1985–87, retired; *b* 14 Feb. 1934; *s* of Sir John Leighton Barran, 3rd Bt, and Hon. Alison Mary (*d* 1973), 3rd *d* of 9th Baron Ruthven, CB, CMG, DSO; *S* father, 1974; *m* 1965, Jane Margaret, *d* of Sir Stanley Hooker, CBE, FRS; one *s* one *d*. *Educ:* Heatherdown Sch., Ascot; Winchester Coll.; University Coll., London (BA 1994). National Service, 1952–54, Lieut, 5th Roy. Inniskilling Dragoon Guards; served Canal Zone. Asst Account Executive: Dorland Advertising Ltd, 1956–58; Masius & Fergusson Advertising Ltd, 1958–61; Account Executive, Ogilvy, Benson & Mather (New York) Inc., 1961–63; Overseas TV News Service, COI, 1964; First Sec. (Information), British High Commission, Ottawa, 1965–67; Central Office of Information: Home Documentary Film Section, 1967–72; Overseas TV and Film News Services, 1972–75; TV Commercials and Fillers Unit, 1975–78; Head of Viewdata Unit, 1978–85. Founded Video History to make documentaries, 1986. *Recreations:* entertaining, gardening, shooting. *Heir: s* John Ruthven Barran, *b* 10 Nov. 1971. *Address:* 17 St Leonard's Terrace, SW3 4QG. *T:* (020) 7730 2801; The Hermitage, East Bergholt, Suffolk CO7 6RB; Middle Rigg Farm, Sawley, North Yorks HG4 3HA.

BARRASS, Gordon Stephen, CMG 1992; HM Diplomatic Service, retired; *b* 5 Aug. 1940; *s* of James and Mary Barrass; *m* 1st, 1965, Alice Cecile Oberg (*d* 1984); 2nd, 1992, Dr Kristen Clarke Lippincott, *qv*. *Educ:* Hertford Grammar Sch.; LSE (BSc (Econs)); SOAS (postgrad.). FCO, 1965–67; Chinese Language student, Hong Kong Univ., 1967–69; in Office of HM Chargé d'Affaires, Peking, 1970–72; Cultural Exchange Dept, FCO, 1972–74; UKMIS Geneva, 1974–78; Planning Staff, FCO, 1979–82; RCDS, 1983; seconded to MoD, 1984, Cabinet Office, 1987; Under Sec., 1991–93. Advr, Internat. Affairs, Coopers & Lybrand, then PricewaterhouseCoopers, 1993–2002. Mem., Bd, IDEAS, 2008–. Guest Curator, Brushes with Surprise exhibn, BM, 2002. *Publication:* The Art of Calligraphy in Modern China, 2002. *Recreations:* Chinese and Western art, classical archaeology, opera, travel, books. *Address:* 3 Mount Vernon, NW3 6QS.

BARRASS, Kristen Clarke; *see* Lippincott, K. C.

BARRATT, Francis Russell, CB 1975; Deputy Secretary, HM Treasury, 1973–82; *b* 16 Nov. 1924; *s* of Frederick Russell Barratt; *m* 1st, 1949, Janet Mary Sherborne (marr. diss. 1978); three *s*; 2nd, 1979, Josephine Norah Harrison (*née* McCririck) (*d* 2005). *Educ:* Durban High Sch., SA; Clifton; University Coll., Oxford. War Service, 1943–46; Captain, Intelligence Corps, 1946. Asst Principal, HM Treasury, 1949; Principal, 1953; First Sec., UK High Commission, Karachi, 1956–58; Asst Sec., 1962, Under Sec., 1968, HM Treasury. Dir, Amdahl (UK), 1983–93; Trustee, Amdahl (UK) Pension Fund, 1984–95. Mem., Rev. Bd for Govt Contracts, 1984–93. *Address:* Little Paddocks, Smallhythe Road, Tenterden, Kent TN30 7LY. *T:* (01580) 763734.

BARRATT, Gilbert Alexander; Master of the Supreme Court, Chancery Division, 1980–97; *b* 7 Aug. 1930; *s* of Arthur Walter Barratt and Frances Erskine Barratt (*née* Scott); *m* 1964, Fiona MacDermott; one *s* one *d*. *Educ:* Winchester; New Coll., Oxford. BA Modern History. Qualified as Solicitor, 1957; Partner: Stitt & Co., 1960–63; Thicknesse & Hull, 1963–67; Lee Bolton & Lee, 1967–78; Winckworth & Pemberton, 1978–80. *Recreation:* travel. *Address:* The Old School House, Clungunford, Craven Arms, Shropshire SY7 0QE. *Club:* Travellers.

BARRATT, Sir Lawrence Arthur, (Sir Lawrie), Kt 1982; FCIS; Life President, Barratt Developments PLC, and subsidiary companies, 1989–91 and since 1997 (Managing Director, 1962–88; Chairman, 1962–88 and 1991–97); *b* Newcastle, 14 Nov. 1927; *m* 1st, 1951 (marr. diss. 1984); two *s*; 2nd, 1984, Mary Sheila (*née* Brierley). Founded Barratt Developments, as a private co., 1958. *Recreations:* golf, shooting, sailing. *Address:* Barratt Developments, Rotterdam House, 116 Quayside, Newcastle upon Tyne NE1 3DA.

BARRATT, Michael Fieldhouse; communications consultant; broadcaster on radio and television; Chairman: Michael Barratt Ltd, 1977–97; Commercial Video Ltd, since 1981; *b* 3 Jan. 1928; *s* of late Wallace Milner Barratt and Doris Barratt; *m* 1st, 1952, Joan Francesca Warner (marr. diss.; she *d* 1995); three *s* three *d*; 2nd, 1977, Dilys Jane Morgan; two *s* one *d*. *Educ:* Rossall and Paisley Grammar Sch. Entered journalism, Kemsley Newspapers, 1944; Editor, Nigerian Citizen, 1956; *television:* Reporter, Panorama, 1963; Presenter: 24 Hours, 1965–69; Nationwide, 1969–77; Songs of Praise, 1977–82; Reporting London, 1983–88; *radio:* Question-Master, Gardeners' Question Time, 1973–79. Dir, Career Best Ltd, 1995–97. Chm. of Trustees, People to Places, 1996–; Trustee, Temple Holdings, 1992–96. Rector, Aberdeen Univ., 1973. FRSA. Hon. LLD Aberdeen, 1975. *Publications:* Michael Barratt, 1973; Michael Barratt's Down-to-Earth Gardening Book, 1974; Michael Barratt's Complete Gardening Book, 1977; Golf with Tony Jacklin, 1978; Making the Most of the Media, 1996; Making the Most of Retirement, 1999. *Recreations:* golf, cricket, listening. *Address:* 9 Andrews Reach, Bourne End, Bucks SL8 5GA. *T:* (01628) 530895; *e-mail:* michael@mbarratt.co.uk.

BARRATT, Prof. Michael George; Professor of Mathematics, Northwestern University, Illinois, 1974–99, now Emeritus; *b* 26 Jan. 1927; *e s* of George Bernard Barratt and Marjorie Holloway Barratt (*née* Oldham); *m* 1st, 1952, Jenepher Hudson (marr. diss. 1972); one *s* four *d*; 2nd, 1974, Eileen Saxon (*née* Hough). *Educ:* Stationers' Company's Sch.; Magdalen Coll., Oxford. Junior Lecturer, Oxford Univ., 1950–52; Fellow, Magdalen Coll., Oxford, 1952–56; Lectr, Brasenose Coll., Oxford, 1955–59; Sen. Lectr and Reader, 1959–63, Prof. of Pure Maths, 1964–74, Manchester Univ. Visiting Professor: Chicago Univ., 1963–64; Princeton Univ., 1979. Fellow, IAS, Jerusalem, 1982. *Publications:* papers in mathematical jls. *Address:* 1350 Shilhon Road, Duluth, MN 55804–8635, USA.

BARRATT, Nicholas David, PhD; Chief Executive Officer: Firebird Media, since 2007 (Co-Founder, 2005); Sticks Research Agency, since 2007 (Founder, 2000); *b* Chiswick, London, 16 May 1970; *s* of late David Frank Ernest Barratt and of Daphne June Barratt (*née* Miller); *m* 1999, Sarah Ward. *Educ:* Newland House Prep. Sch.; Hampton Sch.; King's Coll. London (BA 1st cl. Hons Hist. 1991; PhD Medieval Hist. 1996). Reader advr and Co-ordinator of Academic Inductions, PRO, 1996–2000; Specialist Researcher, BBC, 2000–02, incl. House Detectives, House Detectives at Large, Invasion, One Foot in the Past and Britain's Best Buildings. Freelance broadcaster; television: on-screen document specialist, House Detectives, 1997–98; presenter: Small Piece of History, 2002; Family History Project, 2003; Secrets From the Attic, 2008–; specialist researcher: Wreck Detectives, 2003–04; Seven Wonders of the Industrial World, 2003; consultant and specialist researcher: Who Do You Think You Are?, BBC, 2004–07 (and co-presenter, 2004), SBS Australia, 2008–, RTÉ, 2008–; Not Forgotten, 2007; co-presenter: History Mysteries, 2005; Hidden House History, 2006; So You Think You're Royal, 2007; radio: co-presenter, Tracing Your Roots, 2007–. Columnist, Daily Telegraph, 2005–08. Co-creator, Nation's Memorybank personal heritage website, 2007; Principal Consultant and Co-founder, National History Show, featuring Who Do You Think You Are? Live, 2007–. Mem., Exec. Cttee, Fedn of Family History Socs, 2005–06. Julian Bickersteth Meml Medal, Inst. of Heraldic and Genealogical Studies, 2008. *Publications:* Tracing the History of Your House, 2001, 2nd edn 2006; Receipt Rolls, 4, 5, 6, Henry III, 2003; Receipt Rolls, 7, 8, Henry III, 2007; (jtly) Who Do You Think You Are?, 2, 2005, 3, 2006; The Family Detective, 2006; (jtly) Genealogy for Dummies, 2006; The Who Do You Think You Are? Encyclopaedia of Family History, 2008; *contributions to:* King John: new interpretations, 1999; Crises, Revolutions and Self-Sustained Growth, 1999; Family and Dynasty in Late Medieval England, 2003; English Government in the Thirteenth Century, 2004; Thirteenth Century X, 2005; The Story of Where You Live, 2005; Henry II: new interpretations, 2007; How to Trace Your Family History on the Internet, 2008; contrib. English Historical Rev., Internat. History Rev. *Recreations:* football (playing and managing), running (completed two London marathons). *Address:* c/o HHB Agency Ltd, 122 Arlington Road, NW1 7HP. *T:* (020) 7485 0044; *e-mail:* admin@sra-uk.com.

BARRATT, Sir Richard (Stanley), Kt 1988; CBE 1981; QPM 1974; HM Chief Inspector of Constabulary, 1987–90; *b* 11 Aug. 1928; *s* of Richard Barratt and Mona Barratt; *m* 1952, Sarah Elizabeth Hale; one *s* two *d*. *Educ:* Saltley Grammar Sch., Birmingham. CCMI. Birmingham City Police (Constable to Chief Inspector), 1949–65; Dir, Home Office Crime Prevention Centre, Stafford, 1963; seconded to Home Office (Res. and Develt), 1964; Sen. Comd Course, Police Coll., 1964; Supt, Cheshire Constab., 1965, Chief Supt, 1966; Asst Chief Constable, Manchester City Police, 1967; Asst Chief Constable, Manchester and Salford Police, 1968, Dep. Chief Constable, 1972; Dep. Chief Constable, Greater Manchester Police, 1974; Chief Constable, S Yorks Police, 1975–78; HM Inspector of Constabulary, 1978–87. Review of the Royal Bahamas Police, 1985. Led Police delegns to China, 1987, Pakistan, 1990. Assessor, Guildford and Woolwich Inquiry, 1990–94. Mem., Gaming Bd for GB, 1991–95. CStJ 1996. *Recreations:* reading, gardening, golf.

BARRATT, Robin Alexander; QC 1989; **His Honour Judge Barratt;** a Circuit Judge, since 1998; *b* 24 April 1945; *s* of Harold and Phyllis Barratt; *m* 1972, Gillian Anne Ellis (marr. diss. 1999); one *s* three *d*. *Educ:* Charterhouse; Worcester Coll., Oxford (Exhibnr; BA Hons, MA). Harmsworth Entrance Exhibnr, 1965, Schol. 1969; called to the Bar, Middle Temple, 1970. Lectr in Law, Kingston Polytechnic, 1968–71; Western Circuit, 1971; Asst Recorder, 1990; a Recorder, 1993–98. Councillor (C), London Bor. of Merton, 1978–86. *Recreations:* fell walking, music. *Address:* Chichester Combined Court Centre, Southgate, Chichester PO19 1SX.

BARRELL, Dr Anthony Charles, CB 1994; FREng; Chief Executive, North Sea Safety, Health and Safety Executive, 1991–94; *b* 4 June 1933; *s* of William Frederick Barrell and Ruth Eleanor Barrell (*née* Painter); *m* 1963, Jean, *d* of Francis Henry Hawkes and Clarice Jean (*née* Silke); one *s* one *d*. *Educ:* Friars Sch., Bangor; Kingston Grammar Sch.; Birmingham Univ.; Imperial Coll. BSc Hons chem. eng. CEng; FREng (FEng 1990); FIChemE 1984; Eur Ing 1988. Chemist, Ministry of Supply, later War Dept, 1959–64; Commissioning Engineer, African Explosives and Chemical Industries, 1964–65; Shift Manager, MoD, 1965–66; Chemical Inspector, then Supt. Specialist Inspector, HM Factory Inspectorate, 1966–78; Head of Major Hazards Assessment Unit, HSE, 1978–85; Dir, Technology, HSE, 1985–90; Chief Exec., N Sea Safety, Dept of Energy, 1990–91. Non-executive Director: BAA, 1994–2001; Lloyd's Register (formerly Lloyd's Register of Shipping), 1998–; Partner, TBP, 1994–; Special Advr, NATS, 2000–. Member, Council: IChemE, 1989–94 (Pres., 1993–94); Royal Acad. of Engrg, 1994–97. Hon. DEng Birmingham, 1995. *Publications:* papers on assessment and control of major hazards, on offshore safety and on fire and explosion risks. *Recreations:* walking, reading, boating, golf. *Address:* c/o Lloyd's Register, 71 Fenchurch Street, EC3M 4BS. *T:* (020) 7423 2612. *Clubs:* Royal Dart Yacht (Cdre, 2000–03); Churston Golf (Chm., 2004–06).

BARRELL, Prof. John Charles, PhD; FBA 2001; Professor of English, University of York, since 1993; *b* 3 Feb. 1943; *s* of John Ellis Barrell and Beatrice Mary Barrell; *m* 1st, 1965, Audrey Jones (marr. diss. 1975); two *s*; 2nd, 1975, Jania Miller (marr. diss. 1978); 3rd, 1992, Prof. Harriet Guest; one *d*. *Educ:* Trinity Coll., Cambridge (BA 1964; MA 1967); Univ. of Essex (PhD 1971). Lectr, Dept of Lit., Univ. of Essex, 1968–72; University of Cambridge: Lectr in English, and Fellow, King's Coll., 1972–85; Lectr, Newnham Coll., 1972–84; Prof. of English, Univ. of Sussex, 1986–93. British Acad. Reader, 1991–93; Vis. Fellow, Inst. of Advanced Study, Indiana Univ., 2002; Schaffner Vis. Prof., Chicago Univ., 2002; Leverhulme Major Res. Fellow, 2002–04. FEA 2001. *Publications:* The Idea of Landscape and the Sense of Place 1730–1840: an approach to the poetry of John Clare, 1972; The Dark Side of the Landscape: the rural poor in English painting 1730–1840, 1980; English Literature in History 1730–1780: an equal, wide survey, 1983; The Political Theory of Painting from Reynolds to Hazlitt, 1986; Poetry, Language and Politics, 1988; The Infection of Thomas De Quincey: a psychopathology of imperialism, 1991; The Birth of Pandora and the Division of Knowledge, 1992; Imagining the King's Death: figurative treason, fantasies of regicide 1793–1796, 2000; The Spirit of Despotism: invasions of privacy in the 1790s, 2006; *edited:* S. T. Coleridge, On the Constitution of the Church and State, 1972; (with John Bull) The Penguin Book of Pastoral Verse, 1972; Painting and the Politics of Culture: new essays on British Art 1700–1850, 1992; Exhibition Extraordinary!! Radical Broadsides of the Mid 1790s, 2001; (with Jon Mee) Trials for Treason and Sedition 1792–1794, 8 vols, 2006–07. *Recreations:*

gardening, playing cricket, book-collecting. *Address:* Centre for Eighteenth Century Studies, University of York, King's Manor, York YO1 7EP. *T:* (01904) 434981.

BARRETT, Angela Jane; illustrator; *b* 23 Aug. 1955; *d* of Donald and Dinah Patricia Barrett. *Educ:* Coborn Sch. for Girls, Bow; Maidstone Coll. of Art; Royal Coll. of Art. Mem., Art Workers' Guild. *Publications:* illustrated: The King, the Cat and the Fiddle, by Yehudi Menuhin and Christopher Hope, 1983; Naomi Lewis, The Wild Swans, 1984; Susan Hill, Through the Kitchen Window, 1984; James Riordan, The Woman in the Moon, 1984; Christopher Hope, The Dragon Wore Pink, 1985; Susan Hill, Through the Garden Gate, 1986, Can it be true?, 1988 (Smarties Award); Naomi Lewis, The Snow Queen, 1988; Proud Knight, Fair Lady, trans. Naomi Lewis, 1989; Martin Waddell, The Hidden House, 1990 (W. H. Smith Award 1991); Susan Hill, The Walker Book of Ghost Stories, 1990; Snow White, re-told by Josephine Poole, 1991; Jenny Nimmo, The Witches and the Singing Mice, 1993; Susan Hill, Beware Beware, 1993; Geraldine McCaughrean, The Orchard Book of Stories from the Ballet, 1994; Angela McAllister, The Ice Palace, 1994; Candide, Voltaire, trans. Christopher Thacker, 1996; Naomi Lewis, The Emperor's New Clothes, 1997 (IBBY Award 2000); Josephine Poole, Joan of Arc, 1998; Rocking Horse Land and other classic tales of dolls and toys, compiled by Naomi Lewis, 2000; The Orchard Book of Shakespeare Stories, retold by Andrew Matthews, 2001; Sharon Darrow, Through the Tempests Dark and Wild, 2003; Josephine Poole, Anne Frank, 2005; Beauty and the Beast, re-told by Max Eilenberg, 2006; Paul Gallico, The Snow Goose, 2007; Leo Tolstoy, Anna Karenina, 2008. *Recreations:* reading, needlework, roaming about London. *Address:* c/o Caradoc King, A. P. Watt Ltd, 20 John Street, WC1N 2DR. *T:* (020) 7405 6774.

BARRETT, Prof. Ann, MD; FRCP, FRCR; FMedSci; Professor of Oncology, School of Medicine, University of East Anglia, since 2002; *b* 27 Feb. 1943; *d* of Robert Douglas and Elsie Mary Brown; *m* 1989, Adrian Bell. *Educ:* St Bartholomew's Hosp. (MD). Junior posts, St Bartholomew's, UCH, Middlesex, Mount Vernon and Westminster Hosps, 1968–76; Chef de Clinique, Hôpital Tenon, Paris, 1976; Sen. Lectr and Consultant, Royal Marsden Hosp., 1977–86; Prof. of Radiation Oncology, Glasgow Univ., 1986–2002; Dir, Beatson Oncology Centre, Glasgow, 1987–91. Member: Cttee on Med. Aspects of Radiation in the Envmt, NRPB, 1988–93; Molecular and Cellular Med. Bd, MRC, 1991–94; Nat. Radiotherapy Adv. Gp, 2005–; Psychosocial Gp, NCRI, 2005–. Chm., Standing Scottish Cttee, 1992–95, Registrar, 2000–02, Dean, 2002–04, Faculty of Clin. Oncology, RCR; Pres., Scottish Radiological Soc., 1995–97; Pres., Eur. Soc. for Therapeutic Radiation Oncology, 1997–99. Founder FMedSci 1998. *Publications:* Practical Radiotherapy Planning, 1985, 3rd edn 1999; Cancer in Children, 1986, 5th edn 2005. *Recreations:* hill walking, the Arts. *Address:* School of Medicine, Health Policy and Practice Institute of Health, University of East Anglia, Norwich NR4 7TJ. *T:* (01603) 591105.

BARRETT, Prof. Anthony Gerard Martin, FMedSci; FRS 1999; Glaxo Professor of Organic Chemistry, and Director, Wolfson Centre for Organic Chemistry in Medical Science, since 1993, and Sir Derek Barton Professor of Synthetic Chemistry, since 1999, Imperial College London; *b* Exeter, Devon, 2 March 1952; *s* of Claude E. V. Barrett and Margaret Teresa Barrett (*née* Bannon); naturalised US citizen. *Educ:* Imperial Coll. of Science and Technology (BSc 1st Cl. Hons Chemistry 1973; PhD 1975; DIC 1975; SRC Student, 1973–75). Lectr, 1975–82, Sen. Lectr, 1982–83, Imperial Coll. of Science and Technology; Professor of Chemistry: Northwestern Univ., 1983–90; Colorado State Univ., 1990–93. Dir of Chemistry, Argenta Discovery (formerly ChemMedICa), 1998–. Fellow, Japan Soc. for Promotion of Science, 1989. Mem., Chemicals Panel, Technology Foresight Prog., Office of Sci. and Technology, 1994. FMedSci 2003. Lectureships: Tilden, RSC, 1994; Backer, Univ. of Groningen, 1996; Glaxo Wellcome, E Carolina Univ., 1998; Organic Divl Interim, Royal Aust. Chem. Inst., 1999; Eaborn-Cornforth, Sussex Univ., 1999; Allelix Dist., Queens Univ., Ont., 1999; Sir Robert Price, CSIRO, 1999; Novo Nordisk, Tech. Univ. of Denmark, 2000; Upper Rhine, 2001; AstraZeneca Pharmaceuticals, Ohio State Univ., 2002; Pattison, Univ. of Western Ont., 2002; Boehringer Ingelheim, Univ. of New Orleans, 2002; Weissberger-Williams, Kodak, NY, 2002; Novartis Chemistry, Basel, 2002; Troisième Cycle, Geneva, Fribourg, Bern and Lausanne, 2002; GlaxoSmithKline and Celltech, Univ. of Bristol, 2003; Pedler, RSC, 2004; Mich. Chemistry, 2005; Simonsen, RSC, 2006. Dist. Schol., Hope Coll., Mich. 2003. Meldola Medal, 1980, Harrison Medal, 1982, Corday-Morgan Medal, 1986, Award in Natural Products Chemistry, 2001, RSC; Armstrong Medal, Imperial Coll., 1981; Glaxo Wellcome Award, 2000; Innovation Award, Specialised Organic Sector Assoc., 2000; iAc Award for Applied Catalysis, 2001; Royal Soc. Wolfson Res. Merit Award, 2002. *Address:* Department of Chemistry, Imperial College London, SW7 2AZ. *T:* (020) 7594 5766, *Fax:* (020) 7594 5805; *e-mail:* agmb.barrett@imperial.ac.uk.

BARRETT, Rev. Prof. Charles Kingsley, DD; FBA 1961; Professor of Divinity, Durham University, 1958–82; *b* 4 May 1917; *s* of Rev. F. Barrett and Clara (*née* Seed); *m* 1944, Margaret E. Heap, Calverley, Yorks; one *s* one *d*. *Educ:* Shebbear Coll.; Pembroke Coll., Cambridge (Hon. Fellow, 1995); Wesley House, Cambridge. DD Cantab, 1956. Asst Tutor, Wesley Coll., Headingley, 1942; Methodist Minister, Darlington, 1943; Lecturer in Theology, Durham Univ., 1945. Lectures: Hewett, USA, 1961; Shaffer, Yale, 1965; Delitzsch, Münster, 1967; Cato, Australia, 1969; Tate-Willson, Dallas, 1975; McMartin, Ottawa, 1976; Sanderson, Melbourne, and West-Watson, Christchurch, NZ, 1983; Alexander Robertson, Univ. of Glasgow, 1984; K. W. Clark, Duke, USA, 1987; Ryan, Asbury Seminary, Kentucky, 1988; Dominion-Chalmers, Ottawa, 1990; Woodruff Vis. Prof., Emory Univ., Atlanta, 1986; Gunning Fellow, Edinburgh Univ., 1994. Vice-Pres., British and Foreign Bible Soc.; Pres., Studiorum Novi Testamenti Societas, 1973; Mem., Royal Norwegian Soc. of Scis and Letters, 1991; Hon. Mem., Soc. of Biblical Literature, USA. Hon. DD: Hull, 1970; Aberdeen, 1972; Hon. DrTheol Hamburg, 1981. Burkitt Medal for Biblical Studies, 1966; von Humboldt Forschungspreis, 1988. *Publications:* The Holy Spirit and the Gospel Tradition, 1947; The Gospel according to St John, 1955, 2nd edn 1978; The New Testament Background: Selected Documents, 1956, 2nd edn 1987; Biblical Preaching and Biblical Scholarship, 1957; The Epistle to the Romans, 1957, 2nd edn 1991; Westcott as Commentator, 1959; Yesterday, Today and Forever: The New Testament Problem, 1959; Luke the Historian in Recent Study, 1961; From First Adam to Last, 1962; The Pastoral Epistles, 1963; Reading Through Romans, 1963; History and Faith: the Story of the Passion, 1967; Jesus and the Gospel Tradition, 1967; The First Epistle to the Corinthians, 1968; The Signs of an Apostle, 1970; Das Johannesevangelium und das Judentum, 1970; The Prologue of St John's Gospel, 1971; New Testament Essays, 1972; The Second Epistle to the Corinthians, 1973; The Fourth Gospel and Judaism, 1975; (ed) Donum Gentilicium, 1978; Essays on Paul, 1982; Essays on John, 1982; Freedom and Obligation, 1985; Church, Ministry and Sacraments in the New Testament, 1985; The Acts of the Apostles, vol. I (Internat. Critical Commentary series), 1994, vol. II, 1998; Paul: an introduction to his thought, 1994; Jesus and The Word, 1995; (jointly) Jesus, Paul and John, 1999; (jtly) Conflicts and Challenges in Early Christianity, 1999; The Acts of the Apostles: a shorter commentary, 2002; On Paul, 2003; contributions to learned journals and symposia in Britain, the Continent, Australia and USA. *Address:* 22 Rosemount, Durham DH1 5GA. *T:* (0191) 386 1340.

BARRETT, David, OC 2005; broadcaster, writer and political commentator on national and provincial media, since 1985; Premier and Minister of Finance, Province of British Columbia, Canada, 1972–75; *b* Vancouver, 2 Oct. 1930; *s* of Samuel Barrett and Rose (*née* Hyatt); father a business man in East Vancouver, after war service; *m* 1953, Shirley Hackman, West Vancouver; two *s* one *d*. *Educ:* Britannia High Sch., Vancouver; Seattle Univ. (BA(Phil) 1953); St Louis Univ. (Master of Social Work 1956). Personnel and Staff Trng Officer, Haney Correctional Inst., 1957–59; also gained experience in a variety of jobs. Fellow, Inst. of Politics, Harvard Univ., 1987; Adjunct Prof., Simon Fraser Univ.; Visiting Scholar: McGill Univ., 1988; Western Washington Univ. Elected: MLA for Dewdney, Sept. 1960 and 1963; to re-distributed riding of Coquitlam 1966, 1969 and 1972; Vancouver East, by-election 1976, 1979; New Democratic Party Leader, June 1970–1984 (first Social Democratic Govt in history of Province); Leader, Official Opposition, British Columbia, 1970–72 and 1975–84; MP (NDP) Esquimalt-Juan de Fuca, 1988–93. Chm., BC Royal Commn on the Construction Industry, 1998–99. Dr of Laws, *hc*, St Louis Univ., 1974; Hon. DPhil Simon Fraser Univ., BC, 1986. *Publication:* Barrett (memoirs), 1995. *Address:* 1179 Monro Street, Victoria, BC V9A 5P5, Canada.

BARRETT, Edmond Fox, OBE 1981; HM Diplomatic Service, retired; First Secretary, Foreign and Commonwealth Office, 1986–88; *b* 24 Aug. 1928; *s* of late Edmond Henry Barrett and Ellen Mary Barrett (*née* Fox); *m* 1959, Catherine Wendy Howard (*née* Slater). *Educ:* St Brendan's Coll., Bristol. Dominions Office, 1946; Royal Navy, 1947–49; CRO, 1949–50; Karachi, 1950–52; New Delhi, 1952–54; CRO, 1954–55; Admiralty, 1955–60; Foreign Office, 1960–63; Bucharest, 1963–65; Rio de Janeiro, 1965–68; Boston, 1968–70; Mexico City, 1971–73; FCO, 1973–76; Santo Domingo, 1976–79; Tehran, 1979–81; Consul Gen., Bilbao, 1981–86. *Recreations:* reading, gardening. *Address:* 10 Greenheys Place, Woking, Surrey GU22 7JD.

BARRETT, John; MP (Lib Dem) Edinburgh West, since 2001; *b* 11 Feb. 1954; *s* of Andrew Barrett and Elizabeth Mary (*née* Benert); *m* 1975, Carol Pearson; one *d*. *Educ:* Forrester High Sch., Edinburgh; Napier Poly., Edinburgh. Director: ABC Productions, 1985–; Edinburgh Internat. Film Fest., 1995–2001; EDI Group, 1997–99; Edinburgh and Borders Screen Industries, 1997–2001; Edinburgh Film House, 1997–2001. Mem. (Lib Dem) Edinburgh CC, 1995–2001. Lib Dem spokesman on internat. develt, 2003–. *Recreations:* travel, film, theatre, music (playing and listening). *Address:* House of Commons, SW1A 0AA. *T:* (020) 7219 8224.

BARRETT, Rev. John Charles Allanson; Headmaster, The Leys School, Cambridge, 1990–2004; Principal, ACS (International), Singapore, since 2004; *b* 8 June 1943; *s* of Leonard Wilfred Allanson Barrett and Marjorie Joyce Barrett; *m* 1967, Sally Elisabeth Hatley; one *s* one *d*. *Educ:* Culford Sch.; Univ. of Newcastle upon Tyne (BA Hons); Fitzwilliam Coll., Cambridge; Wesley House, Cambridge. MA Cantab. Ordained Methodist Minister. Chaplain and Lectr in Divinity, Westminster Coll., Oxford, 1968–69; Asst Tutor, Wesley Coll., Bristol, 1969–71; Circuit Minister, Hanley Trinity Circuit, Stoke on Trent, and actg Hd of Religious Studies, Birches High Sch., Hanley, 1971–73; Chaplain and Hd of Religious and Gen. Studies, Kingswood Sch., Bath, 1973–83; Headmaster, Kent Coll., Pembury, 1983–90. Mem., HMC Cttee, 1997–98 (Sec., 1997, Chm., 1998, Eastern Div., HMC; Chm., HMC Working Party on Alcohol and Drug Abuse, 1996–99). World Methodist Council: Mem. Exec. Cttee, 1981– (Vice Chm., 2001–06; Chm., 2006–); Chairman: Educn Cttee, 1991–2001; Prog. Cttee, 1992–96; Brit. Cttee, 1999– (Sec., 1986–97); Mem., Presidium, 1996–. Vice-Pres., Internat. Assoc. of Methodist Schs, Colls and Univs, 1998–2006. Bloxham Project: Mem. Steering Cttee, 1986–92; Trustee, 2002–. Governor, Queenswood Sch., 1997–2004. FRSA 1996. Hon. DD Florida Southern, 1992. *Publications:* What is a Christian School?, 1981; Family Worship in Theory and Practice, 1983; Methodist Education in Britain, 1990; Methodists and Education: from roots to fulfilment, 2000; (contrib.) Serving God with Heart and Mind, 2001; sections on Methodism in Encyc. Britannica Year Books, 1988–98. *Address:* Tudor Lodge, 151 High Street, Harston, Cambridge CB22 7QD. *T:* (01223) 872842; *e-mail:* jcabarrett@aol.com.

BARRETT, John Edward, MBE 2007; tennis commentator and journalist; *b* 17 April 1931; *s* of Alfred Edward Barrett and Margaret Helen Barrett (*née* Walker); *m* 1967, (Florence) Angela (Margaret) Mortimer; one *s* one *d*. *Educ:* University College Sch., Hampstead; St John's Coll., Cambridge (MA History). Joined Slazengers as management trainee, 1957; Tournament Dir, 1975; Dir, 1978; Consultant, 1981–95 (latterly Dunlop Slazenger International). Tennis career: RAF champion, 1950, 1951; Captain of Cambridge, 1954; Nat. Indoor Doubles champion (with D. Black), 1953; Davis Cup, 1956–57, non-playing Captain, 1959–62; Dir, LTA Trng Squad (Barrett Boys), 1965–68; qualified LTA coach, 1969; Founded: BP Internat Tennis Fellowship, 1968–80 (and directed); BP Cup (21-and-under), 1973–80; Junior Internat. Series, 1975–79. Financial Times: tennis corresp., 1963–; crossword contribs, 1986–. TV tennis commentator: BBC, 1971–2006; Australian networks, 1981–; USA. *Publications:* Tennis and Racket Games, 1975; Play Tennis with Rosewall, 1975; 100 Wimbledon Championships, 1986; (with Dan Maskell) From Where I Sit, 1988; (with Dan Maskell) Oh, I Say, 1989; Wimbledon: the official history of The Championships, 2001; (ed and contrib.) World of Tennis, annually, 1969–2001. *Recreations:* music, theatre, reading. *Address:* All England Lawn Tennis Club, Church Road, Wimbledon, SW19 5AE. *Clubs:* All England Lawn Tennis (Vice-Pres.), International Lawn Tennis, Queen's.

BARRETT, Lorraine Jayne; Member (Lab) Cardiff South and Penarth, National Assembly for Wales, since 1999; *b* 18 March 1950; *m* 1972, Paul Franklyn Barrett; one *s* one *d*. *Educ:* Porth County Sch. for Girls. Nursing, 1966–70; secretarial work, 1970–74; Personal and Political asst to Alun Michael, MP, 1987–99. Mem. (Lab), Vale of Glamorgan UA, 1995–99. *Recreations:* reading horror and thriller books, walking, cinema. *Address:* National Assembly for Wales, Cardiff CF99 1NA. *T:* (029) 2089 8376.

BARRETT, Matthew W., OC 1995; Chairman, Barclays PLC, 2004–06 (Group Chief Executive, 1999–2004); *b* Co. Kerry, 20 Sept. 1944. *Educ:* Christian Brothers Sch., Kells; Harvard Univ. (AMP 1981). Joined Bank of Montreal, 1962; Chief Operating Officer, 1987–89; Chief Exec. Officer, 1989–99; Chm., 1990–99. *Address:* c/o Barclays PLC, One Churchill Place, E14 5HP.

BARRETT, Michael Paul, OBE 1987; Chief Executive Officer, Great Britain Sasakawa Foundation, 2000–06; *b* 30 July 1941; *s* of William James Barrett and Irene (*née* Beynon); *m* 1966, Marie-Thérèse Françoise Juliette Lombard; two *s*. *Educ:* Westminster City Sch.; Univ. of Durham (BA Hons Classics). Asst Tutor in English to Overseas Students, Univ. of Birmingham, 1963–64; British Council: Asst Dir, Port Harcourt, 1964–65; Asst Rep., Addis Ababa, 1966–69; Educnl Television Officer, Tokyo, 1970–72; Dir, Films Dept, 1972–75; Educnl Technologist, Media Dept, 1975–77; Non-Formal Educn Specialist, Nairobi, 1977–80; Dep. Rep., Japan, 1980–84; Cultural Attaché, Washington, 1984–87; Dir, PR, 1987–88; Consultant, Goddard Kay Rogers & Associates Ltd, 1989; Man. Dir, GKR Japan Ltd, 1989–93; Dir, British Council, Japan, 1993–99. Vice-Pres., British Chamber of Commerce in Japan, 1992–99. Non-exec. Dir, S London & Maudsley NHS Trust, 2001–07. Mem. Council, Japan Soc., 2000–06; Mem. Culture Cttee, Asia House,

2001–; Mem. Mgt Cttee, Sainsbury Inst. for Japanese Art & Culture, 2006–. Trustee, British Sch. in Tokyo, 1992–99 (Chm., 1992–95). FRGS 1989. Order of the Rising Sun (Japan), 2006. *Recreations:* contemporary art and music, fishing, sailing, Celtic culture. *Address:* 25 Offerton Road, SW4 0DJ; Rosalbert, Roullens 11290, France.

BARRETT, Nicholas James; Chief Executive, Outward Bound Trust, since 2006; *b* 3 Sept. 1960; *s* of Sir Stephen Jeremy Barrett, *qv*; *m* 2001, Fiona Lewis; one *s* four *d*. *Educ:* Christ Church, Oxford (BA Mod. Hist.; PGCE). Volunteer, VSO, Bhutan and Kenya, 1983–87; Regl Organiser, ActionAid, 1987–89; Voluntary Service Overseas: Prog. Dir, W Kenya, 1989–91; Head, New Services, 1991–95; Dir, Recruitment, 1995–2000; Chief Exec., Ramblers' Assoc., 2000–05. *Recreations:* climbing small mountains, family, reading. *Address:* Outward Bound Trust, Hackthorpe Hall, Hackthorpe, Penrith, Cumbria LA10 2HX. *Clubs:* Alpine; Ausable (NY).

BARRETT, Paul Michael, CMG 2001; OBE 1993; Chairman (non-executive): Medreich PLC, since 1997; Medreich Ltd, Bangalore, India, since 2005; *b* 9 Nov. 1945; *s* of Thomas Barrett and Gladys Barrett (*née* Cook); *m* 1970, Mary Elizabeth Tuthill; one *s* one *d*. *Educ:* Sir Roger Manwood's Sch., Sandwich; Grey Coll., Univ. of Durham (BA Hons Modern Hist. 1967); Templeton Coll., Oxford (AMP 1985). VSO, Starene Boys' Centre, Nairobi, 1968–69; Beecham Gp Ltd, 1969–76: Gen. Manager, Nigeria, 1973–74; Regl Mktg Manager, Africa/Caribbean, 1974–76; Nat. Sales Manager, Servier Labs, 1976–78; Manager, Francophone Africa, Beecham Gp, 1978–89, Smithkline Beecham, 1989–93; Dir and Vice-Pres., Africa, Smithkline Beecham, 1993–2000. Chm., Microsulis PLC, 1999–2002. Chm., Tropical Africa Adv. Gp, DTI, 1989–2000. Chm., British Francophone Business Gp, 1981–88. Vice-Chm., Harpsden Hall Trust, 2002–; Chm., John Hodges' Trust for Harpsden Hall, 2005–08; Mem. Cttee, 2001–02, Chm., 2002–, S Oxon Mencap; Mem., Major Gifts Cttee, African Med. and Res. Foundn, 2001–03; Chm., Chiltern Centre for Disabled Children Ltd, 2003–. Churchwarden, St Margaret's Ch, Harpsden, 2001–07. *Recreations:* reading, theatre, opera, walking, keep fit, jogging. *Address:* 1 Leicester Close, Henley-on-Thames, Oxon RG9 2LD. *T:* (01491) 578051; *e-mail:* paulandmarybarrett@tiscali.co.uk.

BARRETT, Rt Rev. Peter Francis; Bishop of Cashel and Ossory, 2003–06; *b* 8 Feb. 1956; *s* of Alexander Barrett and Kathleen (*née* Aldred); *m* 1980, Anne (*née* Davidson); two *s* one *d*. *Educ:* Avoca Kingstown Sch.; TCD (BA 1978, MA 1981, DipTh 1981, MPhil 1984). Ordained deacon, 1981, priest, 1982; Curate Assistant: Drumachose, 1981–83; St Ann and St Mark with St Stephen, 1983–85; Rector: Conwal Union with Gartan, 1985–90; St George's, Belfast, 1990–94; Dean of Residence and Chaplain, TCD, 1994–98; Dean of Waterford, 1998–2003. Reviews Ed., Search: a C of I Jl, 1994–98. *Publications:* Love's Redeeming Work (Irish Consultant), 2001; The Measure and the Pledge of Love, 2003; Symbols of Service, 2004; contrib. jl Scripture in the Church. *Recreations:* music, ornithology, sport, especially hockey. *Clubs:* Kildare Street and University (Dublin); Monkstown Hockey.

BARRETT, Prof. Spencer Charles Hilton, PhD; FRS 2004; FRSC; Professor of Botany, since 1977, Canada Research Chair in Evolutionary Genetics, since 2001, University of Toronto; *b* 7 June 1948; *s* of Arthur Charles and Doris Barrett; *m* 1973, Suzanne Whittaker; two *s*. *Educ:* Univ. of Reading (BSc Hons (Horticultural Botany) 1971); Univ. of Calif, Berkeley (PhD (Botany) 1977). FRSC 1988. Member, Expert Panel: on Predicting Invasions, Nat. Res. Council, USA, 1999–2001; on Future of Food Biotechnol., RSC, 2000–01. Member: British Ecol Soc.; Soc. for Study of Evolution; Botanical Soc. of America; European Evolutionary Biol. Soc. *Publications:* (ed) Evolution and Function of Heterostyly, 1992; (ed) Floral Biology: studies on floral evolution in animal-pollinated plants, 1996; (ed) Ecology and Evolution of Flowers, 2006; numerous book chapters and articles in learned jls. *Recreations:* plant exploration, travel, gardening, photography, music of Brian Eno. *Address:* 182 Humbervale Boulevard, Toronto, ON M8Y 3P8, Canada. *T:* (416) 2341871; Department of Ecology and Evolutionary Biology, University of Toronto, 25 Willcocks Street, Toronto, ON M5S 3B2, Canada. *T:* (416) 9784151, *Fax:* (416) 9785878; *e-mail:* barrett@eeb.utoronto.ca.

BARRETT, Sir Stephen (Jeremy), KCMG 1991 (CMG 1982); HM Diplomatic Service, retired; Ambassador to Poland, 1988–91; *b* 4 Dec. 1931; *s* of late W. P. Barrett and Dorothy Barrett; *m* 1958, Alison Mary Irvine; three *s*. *Educ:* Westminster Sch.; Christ Church, Oxford (MA). FO, 1955–57; 3rd, later 2nd Sec., Political Office with Middle East Forces, Cyprus, 1957–59; Berlin, 1959–62; 1st Sec., FO, 1962–65; Head of Chancery, Helsinki, 1965–68; 1st Sec., FCO, 1968–72; Counsellor and Head of Chancery, Prague, 1972–74; Head of SW European Dept, FCO, later Principal Private Sec. to Foreign and Commonwealth Sec., 1975; Head of Science and Technology Dept, FCO, 1976–77; Fellow, Center for Internat. Affairs, Harvard, 1977–78; Counsellor, Ankara, 1978–81; Head of British Interests Section, Tehran, 1981; Asst Under-Sec. of State, FCO, 1981–84; Ambassador to Czechoslovakia, 1985–88. *Recreations:* climbing small mountains, reading. *Address:* 9 Redgrave Court, Patron's Way East, Denham Garden Village, Uxbridge UB9 5NT. *Club:* Ausable (St Huberts, NY).

See also N. J. Barrett.

BARRETT-LENNARD, Sir Peter John, 7th Bt *cr* 1801, of Belhus, Essex; *b* 26 Sept. 1942; *s* of Roy Barrett-Lennard and Joyce Christine Elizabeth (*née* Drinkwater); *S* cousin, 2007, but his name does not appear on the Official Roll of the Baronetage; *m* 1979, Sonja, *d* of Vladimir Belačič, Zagreb; one *s*. *Heir:* *s* Simon James Barrett-Lennard, *b* 12 Aug. 1980. *Address:* Forest House, Forest Road, East Horsley, Surrey KT24 5BX.

BARRICK, Jonathan; Chief Executive Officer, Stroke Association, since 2004; *b* 14 Jan. 1954; *s* of Jack William Barrick and Audrey Joan Barrick (*née* Cook); *m* 1988, Susan Skinner; two *d*; partner, Olivia Belle. *Educ:* Davenant Foundn Grammar Sch.; Bath Univ. (BSc Sociol. 1978); Kent Univ.; Middlesex Univ. (PG Dip. Housing 1993); Henley Mgt Coll. (MBA 2002). MCIH; FCMI. DHSS, 1979–81; Inspector Taxes, 1981–83; London Bor. of Haringay, 1983–89; RNIB, 1989–2004, Dir, Community Services, 1996–2004. Trustee: Neurological Alliance, 2004–; AMRC, 2006–; Stroke Alliance for Europe, 2006–. *Publications:* (jtly) Building Sight, 1995; contribs to jls in vision impairment and inclusive access. *Recreations:* Tottenham Hotspur FC, travel, family interests, studying leadership and strategy issues. *Address:* The Stroke Association, Stroke House, 240 City Road, EC1V 2PR. *T:* (020) 7566 0305; *e-mail:* jbarrick@stroke.org.uk.

BARRIE, (Charles) David (Ogilvy); Director, The Art Fund, since 1992; *b* 9 Nov. 1953; *s* of late Alexander Ogilvy Barrie and Patricia Mary Tucker; *m* 1978, Mary Emily, *d* of Rt Hon. Sir Ralph Gibson, PC; two *d*. *Educ:* Bryanston Sch.; Brasenose Coll., Oxford (Phil and Exp. Psych.). HM Diplomatic Service, 1975; served FCO 1975–76; Dublin, 1976–80; seconded to Cabinet Office, 1980–81; FCO, 1981–87; transf. Cabinet Office, 1988; seconded to Japan Festival 1991, as Exec. Dir, 1989–92; resigned from Cabinet Office, 1992. Bd Mem., MLA (formerly Resource: Council for Mus, Archives, and Libraries), 2000–06 (Mem., Acceptance-in-Lieu Panel, 2000–06). Companion and Dir, Guild of St George, 1992–2004. Trustee: Civitella Ranieri Foundn, 1995–99; Ruskin Foundn, 1996–; Chm., Ruskin To-Day, 1999–. Trustee, Butterfly Conservation, 2003–. *Publications:* (ed) John Ruskin's Modern Painters, 1987, 2nd edn 2000; numerous articles and reviews. *Recreation:* sailing. *Address:* The Art Fund, Millais House, 7 Cromwell Place, SW7 2JN. *T:* (020) 7225 4800. *Clubs:* Arts; Royal Cruising; Emsworth Sailing.

BARRIE, Herbert, MD, FRCP, FRCPCH; Consultant Paediatrician, Charing Cross Hospital, 1966–84 (Physician in charge, 1984–86); *b* 9 Oct. 1927; *m* 1963, Dinah Barrie, MB, BS, FRCPath; one *s* one *d*. *Educ:* Wallington County Grammar School; University College and Med. Sch., London. MB, BS 1950; MD 1952; MRCP 1957, FRCP 1972; FRCPCH 1997. Registrar, Hosp. for Sick Children, Gt Ormond St, 1955–57; Research Fellow, Harvard Univ., Children's Med. Center, 1957; Sen. Registrar and Sen. Lectr, Dept of Paediatrics, St Thomas' Hosp., 1959–65. Vis. Prof., Downstate Univ. Med. Center, NY, 1976. Member: British Assoc. of Perinatal Paediatrics; Vaccine Damage Tribunal Panel. *Publications:* contribs to books and jls on paediatric and neonatal topics, esp. resuscitation of newborn and neonatal special care. *Recreations:* tennis, writing, wishful thinking. *Address:* 3 Burghley Avenue, New Malden, Surrey KT3 4SW. *T:* (020) 8942 2836.

BARRIE, Lesley; General Manager and Member, Tayside Health Board, 1993–97, retired; *b* 20 Sept. 1944. *Educ:* Glasgow High Sch. for Girls; Univ. of Glasgow (DPA). MHSM; DipHSM. NHS admin. trainee, 1963–66; hosp. mgt, 1966–77; District General Manager: Inverclyde Dist, 1977–81; Glasgow SE, 1981–83; Dir, Admin Services, Glasgow Royal Infirmary, Royal Maternity Hosp. and Glasgow Dental Hosp., 1983–87; Unit Gen. Manager, Stirling Royal Infirmary, 1987–91; Gen. Manager and Mem., Forth Valley Health Bd, 1991–93. Chm., Social Security Appeal Tribunals, 1978–90; Mem., Industrial Tribunal, 1992–98. Hon. Sen. Lectr, Dept of Epidemiology and Public Health, Dundee Univ., 1994–97. MCMI. *Recreations:* table tennis (Scottish International, 1963–70), badminton, reading.

BARRIE, (Thomas) Scott; Member (Lab) Dunfermline West, Scottish Parliament, 1999–2007; *b* 10 March 1962; *s* of William Barrie and Helen McBain Barrie (*née* Scott). *Educ:* Auchmuty High Sch., Glenrothes; Edinburgh Univ. (MA Hons 1983); Stirling Univ. (CQSW 1986). Fife Regional Council: Social Worker, 1986–90; Sen. Social Worker, 1990–91; Team Manager, Social Work Dept, 1991–96; Team Leader, Social Work Service, Fife Council, 1996–99. Mem. (Lab), Dunfermline DC, 1988–92. *Recreations:* hill walking, supporter of Dunfermline Athletic.

BARRINGTON, Sir Benjamin, 8th Bt *cr* 1831, of Limerick; *b* 23 Jan. 1950; *s* of Major John William Barrington and his 1st wife, Annie, *d* of Florian Wetten; *S* cousin, 2003, but his name does not appear on the Official Roll of the Baronetage; *m* 1980, Carola Christel Mogck; one *s* one *d*. *Heir:* *s* Patrick Benjamin Barrington, *b* 5 May 1988. *Address:* 44 Cherovan Drive SW, Calgary, AB T2P 2P1, Canada.

BARRINGTON, Donal; Judge of the Supreme Court of Ireland, 1996–2000; President, Irish Commission on Human Rights, 2000–02; *b* 28 Feb. 1928; *s* of Thomas Barrington and Eileen Barrington (*née* Bracken); *m* 1959, Eileen O'Donovan; two *s* two *d*. *Educ:* Belvedere Coll.; University Coll., Dublin (MA, LLB). Called to the Bar, King's Inns, 1951, Bencher, 1978; called to Inner Bar, 1968; Judge, High Court of Ireland, 1979–89; Judge, Court of First Instance of European Communities, 1989–96. Chairman: Commn on Safety at Work, 1983–84; Stardust Compensation Tribunal, 1985–86. Chm., Gen. Council of the Bar, Ireland, 1977–79. Pres., Irish Centre for European Law, 1996–2000. *Publications:* contribs to learned jls. *Recreations:* music, gardening. *Address:* 8 St John's Park, Dun Laoghaire, Co. Dublin, Republic of Ireland. *T:* (1) 2841817.

BARRINGTON, Edward John, (Ted); Irish Ambassador to the Court of St James's, 1995–2001; *b* 26 July 1949; *s* of Edward Barrington and Sarah Barrington (*née* Byrne); *m* 1972, Clare O'Brien; one *s*. *Educ:* University College Dublin (BA). Entered Irish Diplomatic Service, 1971; 3rd Sec., 1971, 1st Sec., 1973; Perm. Rep. to EEC, 1975–80; 1st Sec., Press and Information, 1980; Counsellor, Political, 1980–85; Assistant Secretary: Admin, 1985–89; EC Div., 1989–91; Political Div. and Political Dir, 1991–95; Dep. Sec., 1995. Vis. Prof., Res. Inst. for Irish and Scottish Studies, Univ. of Aberdeen; Vis. Res. Fellow, Inst. for British-Irish Studies, UC Dublin. DUniv N London. *Recreations:* bird-watching, cinema, hiking, theatre, jazz. *Address:* Sun Villa, Mauritiustown, Rosslare Strand, Co. Wexford, Ireland. *T:* (53) 32880.

BARRINGTON, Jonah, MBE; Consultant, England Squash (formerly Squash Rackets Association), since 1996; *b* 29 April 1941; *m* 1973, Madeline Ibbotson (*née* Wooller); two *s*. *Educ:* Cheltenham Coll.; Trinity Coll., Dublin. Professional squash rackets player, 1969–83; winner: British Open, 1967–68, 1970–73; Egyptian Open, 1968; Canadian Open, 1983. Coach, English Squash Rackets Team; Dir of Excellence, 1988–93, Pres., 1994, Squash Rackets Assoc. *Publications:* On Squash, 1973; (jtly) Tackle Squash, 1977; Murder in the Squash Court, 1982.

BARRINGTON, Sir Nicholas (John), KCMG 1990 (CMG 1982); CVO 1975; HM Diplomatic Service, retired; Ambassador, 1987–89, subsequently High Commissioner, 1989–94, to Pakistan; non-resident Ambassador to Afghanistan, 1994; *b* 23 July 1934; *s* of late Eric Alan Barrington and Mildred (*née* Bill). *Educ:* Repton (Pres., Old Reptonian Soc., 1995–96); Clare Coll., Cambridge (MA 1957; Hon. Fellow 1992). HM Forces, RA, 1952–54. Joined Diplomatic Service, 1957; Tehran (language student), 1958; Oriental Sec., Kabul, 1959; FO, 1961; 2nd Sec., UK Delegn to European Communities, Brussels, 1963; 1st Sec., Rawalpindi, 1965; FO, 1967; Private Sec. to Permanent Under Sec., Commonwealth Office, April 1968; Asst Private Sec. to Foreign and Commonwealth Sec., Oct. 1968; Head of Chancery, Tokyo, 1972–75 (promoted Counsellor and for a period apptd Chargé d'Affaires, Hanoi, 1973); Head of Guidance and Information Policy (subsequently Information Policy) Dept, FCO, 1976–78; Counsellor, Cairo, 1978–81; Minister and Head of British Interests Section, Tehran, 1981–83; Supernumerary Ambassador attached to UK Mission to UN, NY, for Gen. Assembly, autumn 1983; Co-ordinator for London Econ. Summit, 1984; Asst Under-Sec. of State (Public Depts), FCO, 1984–87. Chm., Management Cttee, Southwold Summer Theatre, 1995–2001; Co-Pres., Clare Coll. Develt Prog., 1995–2002; Member: Develt Cttee, Cambridge Univ. Divinity Faculty, 1994–97; Standing Cttee on Schs and Insts, British Acad., 1995–96; Special Projs Cttee, Sadler's Wells Th., 1996–2001; Friends of New River Walk, Islington, 1995–2002; Cttee to restore spire of St Stephen's Ch, Canonbury, 1998–2002. Member: Exec. Cttee, Asia House, 1994–2000 (originator and Exhibn Comr, 50 Years of Painting and Sculpture in Pakistan, Brunei Gall., 2000); Pakistan Soc., 1995–2002 (acting Chm., 2001); Council: Royal Soc. for Asian Affairs, 1995–2000; British Inst. of Persian Studies, 1996–2001 (Mem., Adv. Council, 2002–); British Assoc. for Cemeteries in S Asia, 1996–. Trustee: Ancient India and Iran Trust, 1993–; Mus. of Empire and Commonwealth, Bristol, 1996– (first Pres. of Friends, 1996–2002); Patron, Hindu Kush Conservation Assoc., 1995–2000. FRSA 1984. 3rd Cl., Order of the Sacred Treasure, Japan, 1975. *Publications:* (foreword and asst ed.) Old Roads, new Highways: 50 years of Pakistan, 1997; (jtly) A Passage to Nuristan, 2005. *Recreations:* theatre, drawing, prosopography, Persian poetry. *Address:* 2 Banhams Close, Cambridge CB4 1HX. *Clubs:* Athenæum, Royal Commonwealth Society, Nikaean.

BARRINGTON, Ted; *see* Barrington, E. J.

BARRINGTON-WARD, Rt Rev. Simon, KCMG 2001; Bishop of Coventry, 1985–97; Hon. Assistant Bishop, Diocese of Ely, since 1998; Prelate of the Most Distinguished Order of St Michael and St George, 1989–2005; *b* 27 May 1930; *s* of Robert McGowan Barrington-Ward and Margaret Adele Barrington-Ward; *m* 1963, Jean Caverhill Taylor; two *d. Educ:* Eton; Magdalene Coll., Cambridge (MA; Hon. Fellow, 1987). Lektor, Free Univ., Berlin, 1953–54; Westcott House, Cambridge, 1954–56; Chaplain, Magdalene Coll., Cambridge, 1956–60; Asst Lectr in Religious Studies, Univ. of Ibadan, 1960–63; Fellow and Dean of Chapel, Magdalene Coll., Cambridge, 1963–69; Principal, Crowther Hall, Selly Oak Colls, Birmingham, 1969–74; Gen. Sec., CMS, 1975–85; Hon. Canon of Derby Cathedral, 1975–85; a Chaplain to the Queen, 1984–85. Chairman: Partnership for World Mission, 1987–91; Internat. Affairs Cttee, Bd for Social Responsibility of Gen. Synod, 1986–96. Pres., St John's Coll., Nottingham, 1987–2000. FRAI. Hon. DD Wycliffe Coll., Toronto, 1984; Hon. DLitt Warwick, 1998. *Publications:* CMS Newsletter, 1975–85; Love Will Out (anthology of news letters), 1988; Why God?, 1993; The Jesus Prayer, 1996; (jtly) Praying the Jesus Prayer Together, 2001; *contributor to:* Christianity in Independent Africa (ed Fasholé Luke and others), 1978; Today's Anglican Worship (ed C. Buchanan), 1980; Renewal—An Emerging Pattern, by Graham Pulkingham and others, 1980; A New Dictionary of Christian Theology (ed Alan Richardson and John Bowden), 1983; Christianity Today, 1988; The World's Religions, 1988; The Weight of Glory (ed D. W. Hardy and P. H. Sedgwick), 1991. *Address:* 4 Searle Street, Cambridge CB4 3DB.

BARRITT, Rev. Dr Gordon Emerson, OBE 1979; Principal, National Children's Home, 1969–86; President of the Methodist Conference, 1984–85; *b* 30 Sept. 1920; *s* of Norman and Doris Barritt; *m* 1947, Joan Mary Alway (*d* 1984); two *s* one *d*; *m* 1993, Karen Lesley Windle (marr. diss. 1999); *m* 2003, Eileen Marjorie Smith. *Educ:* William Hulme's Grammar Sch., Manchester; Manchester Univ.; Cambridge Univ. (Wesley House and Fitzwilliam Coll.). Served War, RAF, 1942–45 (despatches). Methodist Minister: Kempston Methodist Church, Bedford, 1947–52; Westlands Methodist Church, Newcastle-under-Lyme, 1952–57; Chaplain, Univ. of Keele, 1953–57. Dir, Enfield Counselling Service, 1986–89; Treasurer, 1969–86, Chm., 1970–72, Nat. Council of Voluntary Child Care Organisations; Member: Home Office Adv. Council on Child Care, 1968–71; Brit. Assoc. of Social Workers, 1960–95; Nat. Children's Bureau, 1963–2000 (Treasurer, 1989–95; Vice Pres., 1997–2000); Internat. Union for Child Welfare, 1969–86; Chm., Kids, 1986–93; Gov., CAF, 1996–2000. Vice Chm. of Council, Selly Oak Colls, Birmingham, 1991–2000 (Fellow, 1987); Governor: Farringtons Sch., 1986–94 (Chm. of Govs, 1986–93); Queenswood Sch., 1986–93. DUniv Keele, 1985. *Publications:* The Edgworth Story, 1972; (ed) Many Pieces—One Aim, 1975; (ed) Family Life, 1979; Residential Care, 1979; contrib.: Caring for Children, 1969; Giving Our Best, 1982; Thomas Bowman Stephenson, 1996. *Recreations:* music, walking. *Address:* 10 Cadogan Gardens, Grange Park, N21 1ER. *T:* and *Fax:* (020) 8360 8687.

BARRON; *see* Shepherd-Barron.

BARRON, Brian Munro, MBE 2007; New York News Correspondent, BBC Television News and Current Affairs, since 2005; *b* 28 April 1940; *s* of Albert and Norah Barron; *m* 1974, Angela Lee, MA; one *d. Educ:* Bristol Grammar School. Junior Reporter, Western Daily Press, Bristol, 1956–60; Dep. Chief Sub-editor, Evening World, Bristol, 1960–61; Sub-editor, Daily Mirror, 1961–63; Dep. Chief Sub-editor, Evening Post, Bristol, 1963–65; Sub-editor, BBC External Services, London, 1965–67; Correspondent, BBC Radio: Aden, 1967–68; ME, Cairo, 1968–69; SE Asia, Singapore, 1969–71; Reporter, BBC TV News, 1971–73; Correspondent, BBC TV: Far East, Hong Kong, 1973–76; Africa, Nairobi, 1976–81; Ireland, 1981–83; Washington, 1983–86; Asia, 1986–94; New York, 1994–2000; Rome, 2000–04. Royal Television Society: Journalist of the Year, 1979–80; Internat. Reporting Award, 1985. *Recreations:* opera, cinema, running, tennis. *Address:* British Broadcasting Corporation, 450 West 33rd Street, New York, NY 10001, USA. *Clubs:* Oriental, Travellers.

BARRON, Prof. Caroline Mary, PhD; FRHistS, FSA; Professor of the History of London, 2000–05 and Dean of the Graduate School, 1999–2003, Royal Holloway, University of London; *b* 7 Dec. 1939; *d* of late William David Hogarth, OBE and Grace Allen Hogarth; *m* 1962, Prof. John Penrose Barron (*d* 2008); two *d. Educ:* North London Collegiate Sch.; Somerville Coll., Oxford (Exhibnr; MA Mod. Hist. 1966); Westfield Coll., London (PhD 1970). Bedford College, subseq. Royal Holloway and Bedford New College, University of London: Asst Lectr, 1967, Lectr, 1968–83, Sen. Lectr, 1983–91, in Hist.; Dean, Faculty of Arts, 1983–85; Reader in Hist. of London, 1991–99; Mem. Council, 1984–87. Reader, British Academy, 1988–90. Member: Cttee, Victoria County Hist., 1970–95; Council, London Record Soc., 1973–76, 1996– (Chm., 2005–); Royal Commn on Historical Manuscripts, 1999–2003; Adv. Council on Nat. Records and Archives, 2003–05. Chm., Hilda Martindale Trust, 1984–87. Mem. Council, GPDST, 1979–94 (Chm. Educn Cttee, 1992–94); Chm. Govs, Wimbledon High Sch., 1985–88; Gov., NLCS, 1985–91. Pres., Assoc. of Senior Mems, Somerville Coll., 1994–99; Chm. Friends, PRO, 1999–2002. Mem. Editorial Bd, Hist. of Parliament, 1988–. FRHistS (Mem. Council, 1989–94). Corresp. Fellow, Medieval Acad. of America, 2007. *Publications:* (ed and contrib.) The Reign of Richard II, 1971; The Medieval Guildhall of London, 1974; The Parish of St Andrew Holborn, 1979; Revolt in London 11th to 15th June 1381, 1981; (ed and contrib.) The Church in the Century before the Reformation, 1985; Hugh Alley's Caveat: markets of London in 1598, 1988; (ed and contrib.) Widows of Medieval London, 1994; (ed and contrib.) England and the Low Countries in the Late Middle Ages, 1995; (ed and contrib.) The Church and Learning in Later Medieval Society, 2001; London in the Later Middle Ages: government and people, 2004; *contributions to:* British Atlas of Historic Towns, 1990; New Cambridge Medieval History, 1999; Cambridge Urban History of England, 2000; St Paul's, the Cathedral Church of London, 2004; contrib. Oxford DNB. *Recreations:* travel, people. *Address:* Alhambra Cottage, 9 Boundary Road, NW8 0HE. *Club:* University Women's.

BARRON, Derek Donald; Chairman and Chief Executive, Ford Motor Co. Ltd, 1986–91; Chairman, Ford Motor Credit Co., 1986–91; *b* 7 June 1929; *s* of Donald Frederick James Barron and Hettie Barbara Barron; *m* 1963, Rosemary Ingrid Brian; two *s. Educ:* Beckenham Grammar School; University College London. Joined Ford Motor Co. Sales, 1951; Tractor Group, 1961; Tractor Manager, Ford Italiana 1963; Marketing Associate, Ford Motor Co. USA, 1970; Gen. Sales Manager, Overseas Markets, 1971; Man. Dir, Ford Italiana, 1973; Group Dir, Southern European Sales, Ford of Europe, 1977; Sales and Marketing Dir, Ford Brazil, 1979; Vice-Pres., Ford Motor de Venezuela, 1982; Dir-Vice-Pres., Operations, Ford Brazil, 1985. DUniv Essex, 1989.

BARRON, Sir Donald (James), Kt 1972; DL; Chairman, Joseph Rowntree Foundation, 1981–96; *b* 17 March 1921; *o s* of Albert Gibson Barron and Elizabeth Macdonald, Edinburgh; *m* 1956, Gillian Mary, *o d* of John Saville, York; three *s* two *d. Educ:* George Heriot's Sch., Edinburgh; Edinburgh Univ. (BCom). Member, Inst. Chartered Accountants of Scotland. Joined Rowntree Mackintosh Ltd, 1952; Dir, 1961; Vice-Chm., 1965; Chm., 1966–81. Dir, 1972, Vice-Chm., 1981–82, Chm., 1982–87, Midland Bank plc. Dep. Chm., CLCB, 1983–85; Chm., Cttee of London and Scottish Bankers, 1985–87. Director: Investors in Industry, subseq. 3i, Gp, 1980–91; Canada Life Assurance Co. of GB Ltd, 1980–96 (Chm., 1991–94; Dep. Chm., 1994–96); Canada Life Unit Trust Managers Ltd, 1980–96 (Chm., 1982–96); Canada Life Assurance Co., Toronto, 1980–96; Canada Life Assce (Ireland), 1992–96; Clydesdale Bank, 1986–87. Mem., Bd of Banking Supervision, 1987–89. Dir, BIM Foundn, 1977–80 and Mem. Council, BIM, 1978–80; Trustee, Joseph Rowntree Foundn (formerly Meml Trust), 1966–73, 1975–96 (Chm., 1981–96); Treasurer, 1966–72, a Pro-Chancellor, 1982–95, York Univ.; Member: Council of CBI, 1966–81 (Chm., CBI Educn Foundn, 1981–85); SSRC, 1971–72; UGC, 1972–81; Council, PSI, 1978–85; Council, Inst. of Chartered Accountants of Scotland, 1980–81; NEDC, 1983–85. Governor, London Business Sch., 1982–88. Chm., York Millennium Bridge Trust, 1997–2003. DL N Yorks (formerly WR Yorks and City of York), 1971–96. Hon. doctorates: Loughborough, 1982; Heriot-Watt, 1983; CNAA, 1983; Edinburgh, 1984; Nottingham, 1985; York, 1986. *Recreations:* travelling, golf, tennis, gardening. *Address:* Greenfield, Sim Balk Lane, Bishopthorpe, York YO23 2QH. *T:* (01904) 705675, *Fax:* (01904) 700183. *Club:* Athenæum.

BARRON, Henry Denis; Judge of the Supreme Court, Ireland, 1997–2000; *b* 25 May 1928; *s* of Harrie and Lena Barron; *m* 1958, Rosalind Scheps (*d* 1997); two *s* two *d. Educ:* Castle Park Sch., Dalkey; Coll. of St Columba, Rathfarnham, Dublin; Trinity Coll., Dublin (BA, LLB); King's Inns, Dublin (BL). Called to the Irish Bar, 1951, Sen. Bar, 1970; called to the Bar, Middle Temple, 1953; Judge of the High Court, Ireland, 1982–97. Mem. (sole), Commn of Inquiry into bombings in Dublin, Monaghan, 1974, and Dundalk, 1975, 2000–05. Visitor, Univ. of Dublin, 1983–2003. *Recreations:* bridge, travel. *Club:* Kildare Street and University (Dublin).

BARRON, Iann Marchant, CBE 1994; Chairman, Division Group plc, 1990–99; *b* 16 June 1936; *s* of William Barron; *m* 1962, Jacqueline Almond (marr. diss. 1989); two *s* two *d*; one *s. Educ:* University College School; Christ's College, Cambridge (exhibitioner; MA). Elliott Automation, 1961–65; Managing Director: Computer Technology Ltd, 1965–72; Microcomputer Analysis Ltd, 1973–78; Exec. Dir, 1978–89, Chief Strategic Officer, 1984–89, INMOS International; Man. Dir, INMOS, 1981–88. Vis. Prof., Westfield Coll., London, 1976–78; Vis. Indust. Prof., Bristol Univ., 1985–; Vis. Fellow: QMC, 1976; Science Policy Res. Unit, 1977–78. Exec. Trustee, The Exploratory, 1992–98; Dir, Bristol 2000, 1995–2000. Mem. Council, UCS, 1983–2002. Distinguished FBCS, 1986. FIET (FIEE 1994). Hon. DSc: Bristol Polytechnic, 1988; Hull, 1989. R. W. Mitchell Medal, 1983; J. J. Thompson Medal, IEE, 1986; IEE Achievement Medal for computing and control, 1996. *Publications:* The Future with Microelectronics (with Ray Curnow), 1977; technical papers. *Address:* Barrow Court, Barrow Gurney, Somerset BS48 3RP.

BARRON, Rt Hon. Kevin (John); PC 2001; MP (Lab) Rother Valley, since 1983; *b* 26 Oct. 1946; *s* of Richard Barron; *m* 1969; one *s* two *d. Educ:* Maltby Hall Secondary Modern Sch.; Ruskin Coll., Oxford. NCB, 1962–83. PPS to Leader of the Opposition, 1985–87; Opposition spokesman on energy, 1988–92, on employment, 1993–95, on health, 1995–97. Member: Select Cttee on Energy, 1983–85; Select Cttee on Environmental Affairs, 1992–93; Parly Intelligence and Security Cttee, 1997–2005; Standards and Privileges Cttee, 2005–; Liaison Cttee, 2005–; Chm., Select Cttee on Health, 2005–. Chm., Yorkshire Labour MPs, 1987–. Pres., Rotherham and Dist TUC, 1982–83. Trustee and Dir, Nat. Coal Mining Mus. for England. Vice Pres., RSH. *Address:* House of Commons, SW1A 0AA.

BARRON, Prof. Laurence David, DPhil; FRS 2005; FRSE; FInstP, FRSC; Gardiner Professor of Chemistry, University of Glasgow, since 1998; *b* 12 Feb. 1944; *s* of Gerald Landon Barron and Stella Barron (*née* Gertz); *m* 1969, Sharon Aviva Wolf; one *s* one *d. Educ:* King Edward VI Grammar Sch., Southampton; Northern Poly. (BSc); Lincoln Coll., Oxford (DPhil 1969). FInstP 2005; FRSC 2005. Chemistry Department, University of Cambridge: SRC Fellow, 1969; Res. Asst, 1971; Ramsay Meml Fellow, 1974; University of Glasgow: Lectr in Physical Chem., 1975–80; Reader, 1980–84; Prof. of Physical Chem., 1984–98; EPSRC Sen. Fellow, 1995–2000. Vis. Miller Res. Prof., Univ. of Calif, Berkeley, 1995; Vis. Prof., Univ. Paul Sabatier, Toulouse, 2003. Lectures: Schmidt Meml, Weizmann Inst., Israel, 1984; Conover Meml, Vanderbilt Univ., USA, 1987; Guest Review, Assoc. of Physicians of GB and Ireland, 1997; Chem. Soc. of Zürich, 1998. FRSE 1992. Corday-Morgan Medal and Prize, Chem. Soc., 1977; Sir Harold Thompson Award for Molecular Spectroscopy, 1992. *Publications:* Molecular Light Scattering and Optical Activity, 1982, 2nd edn 2004; contrib. res. papers to chemistry, physics and life sci. jls. *Recreations:* walking, listening to music (classical and jazz), water-colour painting, building and flying radio control model aircraft. *Address:* Department of Chemistry, University of Glasgow, Glasgow G12 8QQ. *T:* (0141) 330 5168, *Fax:* (0141) 330 4888; *e-mail:* laurence@chem.gla.ac.uk.

BARRON, Peter Scott; Head of Communications and Public Affairs, UK, Ireland and Benelux, Google, since 2008; *b* Belfast, 16 Oct. 1962; *s* of Wilson and Greta Barron; *m* 1996, Julia Stroud; two *s* one *d. Educ:* Royal Belfast Academical Instn; Univ. of Manchester Inst. of Sci. and Technol. (BSc Hons Eur. Studies and Mod. Langs). Ed., Algarve News, 1987–88; news trainee, BBC News, 1988–90; Producer, BBC Newsnight, 1990–97; Deputy Editor: Channel 4 News, 1997–2002; Tonight with Trevor McDonald, 2002–03; Editor: If..., BBC Current Affairs, 2003–04; Newsnight, BBC, 2004–08. Adv. Chm., Edinburgh TV Fest., 2007. *Recreations:* playing the guitar, collecting records, visiting Spain. *Address:* c/o Google UK Ltd, Belgrave House, Buckingham Palace Road, SW1W 9TQ.

BARRON, Maj.-Gen. Richard Edward, CB 1993; *b* 22 Nov. 1940; *s* of John Barron and Lorna Frances Barron; *m* 1968, Margaret Ann Eggar; one *s* one *d. Educ:* Oundle; RMA. Commissioned Queen's Royal Irish Hussars, 1962; Staff College, 1973; DAA&QMG 7th Armoured Brigade, 1974–76; Instructor, Staff Coll., 1978–81; CO, QRIH, 1981–84; Comdr, 7th Armoured Brigade, 1984–86; RCDS 1987; QMG's Staff, 1988–89; Dir, RAC, 1989–92. Col, Queen's Royal Hussars, 1993–99. *Recreations:* restoration, gardening, fishing. *Address:* Middle Burrow, Timberscombe, Som TA24 7UD. *Clubs:* MCC, Cavalry and Guards.

BARRONS, John Lawson; Director, Century Newspapers Ltd, Belfast, 1989–98 (Chief Executive, 1989–97); *b* 10 Oct. 1932; *s* of late William Cowper Barrons, MBE and Amy Marie Barrons (*née* Lawson); *m* 1st, 1957, Caroline Anne (marr. diss. 1986), *d* of late George Edward Foster; three *s*; 2nd, 1987, Lauren Ruth, *d* of late Robert Z. Friedman. *Educ:* Caterham Sch. Nat. Service, 1st Bn Northamptonshire Regt, 1952–54. Journalist, UK and USA, 1950–57; Gen. Manager, Nuneaton Observer, 1957; Managing Editor, Northampton Chronicle & Echo, 1959; Gen. Manager, Edinburgh Evening News, 1961; Gen. Manager, 1965–76, Man. Dir, 1976–85, Westminster Press. Director: Pearson Longman, 1979–83; Stephen Austin Newspapers, 1986–91; Northern Press, 1986–91; Lincolnshire Standard Gp plc, 1987–88; President: Westminster (Florida) Inc., 1980–85; Westminster (Jacksonville) Inc., 1982–85. Dir, Evening Newspaper Advertising Bureau,

1978–81 (Chm. 1979–80); Dir, The Press Association Ltd, 1985–86; Chm., Printing Industry Res. Assoc., 1983–85 (Mem. Council, 1978, a Vice-Chm., 1979–83); Mem. Bd of Management, Internat. Electronic Publishing Res. Centre, 1981–85. Member, Council: Newspaper Soc., 1975–87 (Pres., 1981–82; Hon. Vice-Pres., 1983–); CPU, 1970–86. Director: BITC, NI, 1994–2006; City West Action Ltd, Belfast, 1995–2008. *Recreations:* walking, watching wolfhounds, fishing. *Address:* 8 Harberton Avenue, Belfast BT9 6PH. *Clubs:* Flyfishers', MCC.

See also R. L. Barrons.

BARRONS, Maj.-Gen. Richard Lawson, CBE 2003 (OBE 1999; MBE 1993); Deputy Commanding General Multinational Corps (Iraq), since 2008; *b* Northampton, 17 May 1959; *s* of John Lawson Barrons, *qv*; *m* 1988, Cherry Louise Dedow; two *d*. *Educ:* Merchant Taylors Sch., Northwood; Queen's Coll., Oxford (BA); Cranfield Inst. of Technol. (MBA). Psc 1991; COS, 11 Armd Bde, 1992–93; Battery Comdr, B Battery, RHA, 1994–96; MA to CGS, 1997–99; CO, 3rd Regt, RHA, 1999–2001; COS 3(UK) Div., 2002–03; HCSC(J) 2003; Comdr, 39 Infantry Bde, 2004–06; ACOS Commitments, HQ Land, 2006–07. QCVS 2004 and 2006. *Publication:* (with Deborah Tom) The Business General, 2006. *Recreations:* ski-ing, cycling, garden labouring, keeping the dog sharp, the search for the perfect cappuccino. *Address:* c/o Military Secretary, Army Personnel Centre, Kentigern House, 65 Brown Street, Glasgow G2 8EX; *e-mail:* 825barro@armymail.mod.uk. *Club:* Army and Navy.

BARROS MELET, Cristián; Ambassador of Chile to Peru, since 2006; *b* 19 Oct. 1952; *s* of Diego Barros and Tencha Melet; *m* 1976, Mary Florence Michell Nielsen; one *s*. *Educ:* St Gabriel's Sch.; Sagrados Corazones Padres Franceses; Sch. of Law, Univ. of Chile; Diplomatic Acad. Andrés Bello; Catholic Univ., Santiago. Entered Diplomatic Service, Consular Div., Chile, 1974; Legal Dept, 1975–78; Protocol Dept, 1978; Admin. Dept, 1978–79; Consul: Mendoza, Argentina, 1979; Bariloche, Argentina, 1980–83; Bilateral Policy Dept, America Div., 1983–85; Consul and Consul Gen., Chicago, 1985–88; First Sec., Canada, 1989–90; Hd of Cabinet for Dir Gen. of Foreign Policy, 1990; Dir of Personnel, 1990–91; Ambassador, Dir Gen., Admin. Dept, 1991–93; Ambassador to Denmark, 1993–96; Dir Gen., Admin. Dept, 1996–98; Dir Gen., Foreign Policy, 1998–99; Ambassador to UK, 2000–02; Vice Minister of Foreign Affairs, 2002–06. Grand Cross: Order of Merit (Portugal), 1993; Order of Dannebrog (Denmark), 1996; Order of May (Argentina), 1998; Order of El Sol (Peru), 1999; Grand Order, Order of Merit (Brazil), 1999. *Address:* Embassy of Chile, Avenida Javier Prado Oeste 790, San Isidro, Lima 27, Peru.

BARROSO, José Manuel D.; *see* Durão Barroso.

BARROT, Jacques; Member and Vice-President, European Commission, since 2004; *b* 3 Feb. 1937; *s* of Noël Barrot and Marthe Barrot (*née* Pivot); *m*; one *s* two *d*. *Educ:* Coll. d'Yssingeaux; Faculté de Droit, Paris; Inst. d'Etudes Politiques, Paris. Deputy for Haute-Loire, National Assembly, France: (Union Centriste) 1967–78; (UDF) 1981–2002; (Union pour un mouvement populaire) 2002–04. Sec. of State, Min. of Equipment, 1974–78; Minister: of Commerce and Wkg Classes, 1978–79; of Health and Social Security, 1979–81; of Labour, Social Dialogue and Participation, 1995; of Labour and Social Affairs, 1995–97. Mem., 1974–2004, Pres., 1976–2004, Conseil-Gen., Haute-Loire; Mayor of Yssingeaux, 1989–2001. *Publications:* Les Pierres de l'avenir, 1978; (jtly) Notre contrat pour l'alternance, 2002; L'Europe n'est pas ce que vous croyez, 2007. *Address:* European Commission, Rue de la Loi 200, 1049 Brussels, Belgium.

BARROW, Colin, CBE 2004; Chairman, Alpha Strategic plc, since 2005; *b* 18 June 1952; *s* of Reginald Barrow and Margaret (*née* Jones); *m* 1994, Angelica Bortis (marr. diss. 2007); two *s*; partner, Ana Smaldon. *Educ:* Dulwich Coll.; Clare Coll., Cambridge (BA Moral Scis & Law 1974). John Brown Gp, 1974–83; Man. Dir, Funds Mgt Div., ED&F Man, 1983–96; Chm., Sabre Fund Mgt, 1996–2005. Member (C): Suffolk CC, 1997–2002; Westminster CC, 2002– (Dep. Leader, 2005–). Chm., Improvement and Develt Agency for Local Govt, 2000–04. Director: Rambert Dance Co., 1997–2003; Policy Exchange, 2002–05. Chm., Nat. Autistic Soc., 2005– (Treas., 2004). *Recreations:* inexpert skier, scuba diver, bridge player. *Address:* Alpha Strategic plc, 66 Buckingham Gate, SW1E 6AU. *T:* (020) 7222 2223, *Fax:* (020) 7222 5129; *e-mail:* mail@cbarrow.com.

BARROW, Prof. Geoffrey Wallis Steuart, FBA 1976; Sir William Fraser Professor of Scottish History and Palæography, University of Edinburgh, 1979–92, now Professor Emeritus; *b* Headingley, Leeds, 28 Nov. 1924; *s* of late Charles Embleton Barrow and Marjorie, *d* of Donald Stuart; *m* 1951, Heather Elizabeth, *d* of James McLeish Lownie; one *s* one *d*. *Educ:* St Edward's Sch., Oxford; Inverness Royal Acad.; St Andrews Univ.; Pembroke Coll., Oxford. FRSE 1977. Lecturer in History, University Coll., London, 1950–61; Prof. of Mediaeval Hist., King's Coll., Univ. of Durham, later Univ. of Newcastle upon Tyne, 1961–74; Prof. of Scottish History, Univ. of St Andrews, 1974–79. Mem., Royal Commn on Historical MSS, 1984–90. Ford's Lectr, Univ. of Oxford, 1977; Rhind Lectr, Soc. of Antiquaries of Scotland, 1985. Vice Pres., Commn Internationale de Diplomatique, 1994–2005. Hon. DLitt: Glasgow, 1988; Newcastle, 1994. *Publications:* Feudal Britain, 1956; Acts of Malcolm IV, King of Scots, 1960; Robert Bruce and the Community of the Realm of Scotland, 1965; Acts of William I, King of Scots, 1971; Kingdom of the Scots, 1973; (ed) The Scottish Tradition, 1974; The Anglo-Norman Era in Scottish History, 1980; Kingship and Unity, 1981; Scotland and its Neighbours, 1992; The Charters of David I, 1999; contrib. Scottish Historical Review, etc. *Address:* 12A Lauder Road, Edinburgh EH9 2EL.

BARROW, Jill Helen; Director, Leadership Consultancy, Big Blue Experience, since 2006; *b* 26 April 1951; *d* of Philip Eric Horwood and Mavis Mary (*née* Handscombe); *m* (marr. diss.); two *d*. *Educ:* Durham Univ. (Cert Ed 1972; MA Ed 1983); Open Univ. (BA 1980). Teaching in secondary, special and further educn, 1972–86; educn mgt and inspection, 1986–90; Dep. Dir of Educn, Essex CC, 1990–93; Dir of Educn, Surrey CC, 1993–95; Chief Exec., Lincs CC, 1995–98; Chief Exec., SW of England RDA, 1999–2001; Bd Mem. for England, New Ops Fund, 1999–2004; Dir, Consultancy and Develt, GatenbySanderson, 2004–06. *Recreations:* walking, outdoor activities, travelling, reading.

BARROW, Dame Jocelyn (Anita), DBE 1992 (OBE 1972); Development Director, Focus Consultancy Ltd, 1996–2002; Deputy Chairman, Broadcasting Standards Council, 1989–95; *b* 15 April 1929; *d* of Charles Newton Barrow and Olive Irene Barrow (*née* Pierre); *m* 1970, Henderson Downer. *Educ:* Univ. of London. Mem., Taylor Cttee on School Governors; Gen. Sec., later Vice-Chm., Campaign Against Racial Discrimination, 1964–69; Vice-Chm., Internat. Human Rights Year Cttee, 1968; Member: CRC, 1968–72; Parole Bd, 1983–87. A Governor, BBC, 1981–88. Chairman: Independent Cttee of Management, Optical Consumer Complaints Service, 1992–; Independent Equal Opportunities Inquiry into Ethnicity and Trng and Assessment on Bar Vocational Course, 1993–94; Non-exec. Dir, Whittington Hosp. NHS Trust, 1993–99. Mem., Econ. and Social Cttee, EC, 1990–98. Nat. Vice-Pres., Nat. Towns-women's Guilds, 1978–80, 1987–; Pres. and Founder, Community Housing Assoc.; Governor: Farnham Castle, 1977–93; BFI, 1991–97. Patron: Blackliners, 1989–; Unifem UK, 1998–. FRSA. Hon. DLitt E London, 1992. *Recreations:* theatre, music, cooking, reading. *Address:* c/o Focus Consultancy Ltd, 38 Grosvenor Gardens, SW1W 0EB. *Club:* Reform.

BARROW, Prof. John David, DPhil; FRS 2003; FRAS, FInstP; Professor of Mathematical Sciences, Department of Applied Mathematics and Theoretical Physics, University of Cambridge, since 1999; Fellow, Clare Hall, Cambridge, since 1999 (Vice President, 2004–07); Director, Millennium Mathematics Project, Cambridge, since 1999; *b* 29 Nov. 1952; *s* of Walter Henry Barrow and Lois Miriam Barrow (*née* Tucker); *m* 1975, Elizabeth Mary East; two *s* one *d*. *Educ:* Van Mildert Coll., Durham Univ. (BSc Hons 1974); Magdalen Coll., Oxford (DPhil Astrophysics 1977). FRAS 1981; FInstP 1998. Res. Lectr, Christ Church and Dept of Astrophysics, Oxford Univ., 1977–80; Lindemann Fellow, Dept of Astronomy, 1977–78, Miller Fellow, Dept of Physics, 1980–81, Univ. of Calif, Berkeley; Astronomy Centre, University of Sussex: Lectr, 1981–88; Sen. Lectr, 1988–89; Prof., 1989–99; Dir, 1989–90 and 1995–99. Gordon Godfrey Vis. Prof., Univ. of NSW, Sydney, 1998, 2000, 2003. Gresham Prof. of Astronomy, Gresham Coll., 2003–07, now Emeritus. Hon. Prof., Nanjing Univ., 2005. Lectures: Centenary Gifford, Glasgow, 1989; Scott, Leuven, 1989; Collingwood, Durham, 1990; George Darwin, London, 1992; Spinoza, Amsterdam, 1993; Spreadbury, London, 1994; Benedum, Va, 1997; Kelvin, Glasgow, 1999; Flamsteed, Derby, 2000; Tyndall, Bristol, 2001; Whitrow, London, 2002; Brasher, Kingston, 2002; Newton, Grantham, 2003; Gresham, London, 2003; Hubert James, Purdue, 2004; Carl Von Weizsäcker, Hamburg, 2004; McCrea Centenary, Sussex, 2004; Wood, Newcastle, 2005; Hamilton, Dublin, 2005; Boyle, St Mary-le-Bow, 2007; Roscoe, Liverpool, 2007; Borderlands, Durham, 2007; Källen, Lund, 2007; Si-Wei, Taiwan, 2008; Sciama, Oxford and Trieste, 2008; Phillips, Cardiff, 2008. Forum Fellow, World Econ. Forum, 1999–2000. FRSA 1999. Hon. DSc: Herts, 1999; Szczecin, 2007; Durham, 2008. Locker Prize, Birmingham Univ., 1989; Kelvin Medal, Royal Glasgow Philosophical Soc., 1999; Lacchini Medal, Union Astrofili Italiani, 2005; Templeton Prize, Templeton Foundn, 2006; Queen's Anniversary Prize, 2006. *Publications:* The Left Hand of Creation, 1983, 2nd edn 1995; L'Homme et le Cosmos, 1984; The Anthropic Cosmological Principle, 1986, 2nd edn 1996; The World Within the World, 1988, 2nd edn 1995; Theories of Everything, 1991, 2nd edn 1994; Pi in the Sky, 1992, 2nd edn 1994; Perché il Mondo è Matematico?, 1992, 2nd edn 2001; The Origin of the Universe, 1993, 2nd edn 2001; The Artful Universe, 1995, 2nd edn 1997; Impossibility, 1998, 2nd edn 2000; Between Inner Space and Outer Space, 1999; The Universe that Discovered Itself, 2000; The Book of Nothing, 2000, 2nd edn 2002; The Constants of Nature, 2002; Science and Ultimate Reality, 2004; The Artful Universe Expanded, 2005; The Infinite Book, 2005; New Theories of Everything, 2007; Cosmic Imagery, 2008; *theatre script:* Infinities, 2002 (Premi Ubu Italian Theatre Award, 2002; Italgas Prize, 2003); contrib. to works of reference and numerous scientific articles to learned jls. *Recreations:* athletics, books, travelling, throwing things away. *Address:* Centre for Mathematical Sciences, Cambridge University, Wilberforce Road, Cambridge CB3 0WA. *Fax:* (01223) 765900; *e-mail:* J.D.Barrow@damtp.cam.ac.uk.

BARROW, Captain Michael Ernest, CVO 2002; DSO 1982; RN; *b* 21 May 1932; *s* of late Captain Guy Runciman Barrow, OBE, RN and late Barbara Barrow (*née* Heinekey); *m* 1962, Judith Ann (*née* Cooper); two *s* one *d*. *Educ:* Wellesley House; RNC, Dartmouth. Served in HM Ships: Devonshire, Liverpool; Agincourt, Euryalus, 1950–54; HM Yacht Britannia, 1954–56; Camperdown, 1958–59; Flag Lt to Cdre Hong Kong, 1956–58; commanded: Caunton, 1960; Laleston, 1961–62; Mohawk, 1963–64; Torquay, 1967–69; Diomede, 1973–75; Glamorgan, 1980–83 (Falkland Is conflict); RN Staff Course, 1966; Staff Flag Officer, Malta, 1970–71; Comdr RNC, Dartmouth, 1971–73; Dep. Dir, Recruiting, 1975–77; Asst Chief of Staff (Ops) to Comdr, Allied Naval Forces Southern Europe, Naples, 1978–80; ADC to the Queen, 1982–83; retired RN 1983. Clerk to the Worshipful Co. of Haberdashers, 1983–95, Hon. Assistant, 1995–. Gentleman Usher to Her Majesty, 1984–2002, Extra Gentleman Usher, 2002–. Trustee, Falkland Is Meml Chapel, 1992–2006; Dir, Union Jack Club, 1996–. *Recreations:* sailing, gardening. *Address:* Heathfield, Shear Hill, Petersfield, Hampshire GU31 4BB. *T:* (01730) 264198. *Clubs:* Army and Navy; Royal Naval Sailing.

BARROW, Captain Sir Richard John Uniacke, 6th Bt *cr* 1835; *b* 2 Aug. 1933; *s* of Sir Wilfrid John Wilson Croker Barrow, 5th Bt and (Gwladys) Patricia (*née* Uniacke); *S* father, 1960; *m* 1961, Alison Kate (marr. diss. 1974), *yr d* of late Capt. Russell Grenfell, RN, and of Mrs Lindsay-Young; one *s* two *d*. *Educ:* Abbey Sch., Ramsgate; Beaumont Coll., Old Windsor. Commnd 2nd Lieut Irish Guards, 1952; served: Germany, 1952–53; Egypt, 1953–56; Cyprus, 1958; Germany, 1959–60; retired, 1960; joined International Computers and Tabulators Ltd; resigned 1973. *Heir: s* Anthony John Grenfell Barrow [*b* 24 May 1962; *m* 1st, 1990, Rebecca Mary Long (marr. diss. 1996); one *d*; 2nd, 2001, Elisa Isabel Marzo Pérez]. *Address:* 2 Underwood House, Sycamore Gardens, W6 0AR.

BARROW, Timothy Earle, CMG 2006; LVO 1994; MBE 1994; HM Diplomatic Service; UK Representative to Political and Security Committee, European Union, since 2008; *b* 15 Feb. 1964; *m* Alison; two *s* one *d*. Entered FCO, 1987; Second Sec. (Chancery), Moscow, 1989–93; First Sec., FCO, 1993–94; Pvte Sec. to Minister of State, FCO, 1994–96; First Sec., UK Rep. to EU, Brussels, 1996–98; Pvte Sec. to Sec. of State, FCO, 1998–2000; Hd, Common Foreign and Security Policy Dept, FCO, 2000–03; Asst Dir, EU (Ext.), FCO, 2003–06; Ambassador to Ukraine, 2006–08. *Address:* c/o Foreign and Commonwealth Office, King Charles Street, SW1A 2AH.

BARROW, Ursula Helen, (Viscountess Waverley), PhD; Wisbech Schools Co-ordinator, Cambridgeshire Advisory Service, since 2002; *b* 31 Oct. 1955; *d* of Raymond Hugh and Rita Helen Barrow; *m* 1994, Viscount Waverley, *qv*; one *s*. *Educ:* Newnham Coll., Cambridge (BA Hons 1977; MA 1981; PhD 1988; Fellow, 1999–2000); Jesus Coll., Cambridge (LLM 1992). Econ. Develt Planner, Planning Unit, Govt of Belize, 1978; consultant for small business affairs, urban planning and marketing, Frazier & Assocs, 1979–85; Counsellor and Dep. High Comr, London, 1988–89; Perm. Rep. to UN, 1989–90; Asst Dir (Pol), Commonwealth Secretariat, 1991–93; High Comr for Belize in London, 1993–98, also Ambassador to EU, Belgium, France, Germany and Holy See. Dir, Belize Telecommunications Ltd, 2004–05.

BARRY, Prof. Brian Michael, FBA 1988; Lieber Professor of Political Philosophy, Columbia University, New York, 1998–2005, now Emeritus; *b* 7 Aug. 1936; *s* of James Frederick and Doris Rose Barry; *m* 1st, 1960, Joanna Hill Scroggs (marr. diss. 1988); one *s*; 2nd, 1991, Anni Parker. *Educ:* Taunton's Sch., Southampton; Queen's Coll., Oxford (MA; DPhil 1965). Lloyd-Muirhead Res. Fellow, Univ. of Birmingham, 1960–61; Rockefeller Fellow in Legal and Political Philosophy, and Fellow of Harvard College, 1961–62; Asst Lectr, Keele Univ., 1962–63; Lectr, Univ. of Southampton, 1963–65; Tutorial Fellow, University Coll., Oxford, 1965–66; Official Fellow, Nuffield Coll., Oxford, 1966–69 and 1972–75; Prof., Univ. of Essex, 1969–72 (Dean of Social Studies, 1971–72); Prof., Univ. of British Columbia, 1975–76; Fellow, Center for Advanced Study in the Behavioral Scis, 1976–77; Professor: Univ. of Chicago, 1977–82; California Inst. of Technology, 1982–86; European Univ. Inst., Florence, 1986–87; Prof. of Pol Sci., LSE,

1987–98, now Emeritus. Founding Editor, British Jl of Political Science, 1971–72; Editor, Ethics, 1979–82. *Publications:* Political Argument, 1965; Sociologists, Economists and Democracy, 1970; The Liberal Theory of Justice, 1973; (with Russell Hardin) Rational Man and Irrational Society?, 1982; Democracy, Power and Justice: collected essays, 1989, rev. edn 1991; Theories of Justice, 1989; Justice as Impartiality, 1995; Culture and Equality, 2001; Why Social Justice Matters, 2005; articles in learned jls. *Recreations:* theatre, cooking.

BARRY, Daniel, CB 1988; Permanent Secretary, Department of the Environment for Northern Ireland, 1983–88; *b* 4 March 1928; *s* of William John Graham Barry and Sarah (*née* Wilkinson); *m* 1951, Florence (*née* Matier); two *s* one *d. Educ:* Belfast Mercantile Coll. FCIS, FSCA, FIHT. Local Government Officer with various NI Councils, 1944–68; Town Clerk, Carrickfergus Borough Council, 1968–73; Asst Sec. (Roads), Dept of the Environment for NI, 1973–76, Dep. Sec., 1976–80; Dep. Sec., Dept of Educn for NI, 1980–83. *Recreations:* golf, gardening, painting.

BARRY, David; *see* Barry, J. D.

BARRY, Sir Edward; *see* Barry, Sir L. E. A. T.

BARRY, Edward Norman, CB 1981; Under Secretary, Northern Ireland Office, 1979–81, retired 1981; *b* 22 Feb. 1920; *s* of Samuel and Matilda (*née* Legge); *m* 1952, Inez Anna (*née* Elliott); one *s* two *d. Educ:* Bangor Grammar Sch. Northern Ireland Civil Service: Department of Finance: Establishment Div., 1940–51; Works Div., 1951–60; Treasury Div., 1960–67; Establishment Officer, 1967–72; Min. of Home Affairs, 1972–74; Asst Sec., N Ireland Office, 1974–79. *Recreations:* golf, football (Hon. Treas., 1977–96, and Life Mem., Irish Football Association).

BARRY, Hilary Alice S.; *see* Samson-Barry.

BARRY, Prof. (James) David, PhD; Professor of Molecular Parasitology, since 1996, and Director, Wellcome Trust Centre for Molecular Parasitology, since 1999, University of Glasgow; *b* Glasgow, 13 Dec. 1949; *s* of James Barry and Helen Barry (*née* Cairns); *m* 1st, 1973, Mary Mowat (*d* 1992); one *s* three *d*; 2nd, 2001, Olwyn Byron; one *d. Educ:* Univ. of Glasgow (BSc Combined Biol.; PhD 1977). Res. Fellow, Univ. of Glasgow, 1977–86; Scientist, Internat. Lab. for Res. on Animal Diseases, Nairobi, 1978–80; Sen. Lectr, 1986–92, Reader, 1992–96, Univ. of Glasgow. Consultancy appts with scientific research funding bodies. *Publications:* 100 scientific contribs. *Recreations:* drawing and painting, reflection. *Address:* Wellcome Trust Centre for Molecular Parasitology, Glasgow Biomedical Research Centre, 120 University Place, Glasgow G12 8TA. *T:* (0141) 330 4875, *Fax:* (0141) 330 5422; *e-mail:* j.d.barry@bio.gla.ac.uk.

BARRY, His Honour James Edward; a Circuit Judge, 1994–2006; *b* 27 May 1938; *s* of James Douglas Barry and Margaret (*née* Thornton); *m* 1963, Pauline Pratt; three *s. Educ:* Merchant Taylors' Sch., Crosby; Brasenose Coll., Oxford (schol.; MA Jurisp.). Called to the Bar, Inner Temple, 1963; in practice, NE Circuit, 1963–85; Stipendiary Magistrate for S Yorks, 1985–94; a Recorder, 1985–94. Part-time Chm., Industrial Tribunals, 1983–85. *Recreations:* reading, eating and drinking.

BARRY, John; *see* Prendergast, J. B.

BARRY, Sir (Lawrence) Edward (Anthony Tress), 5th Bt *cr* 1899; Baron de Barry in Portugal *cr* 1876; *b* 1 Nov. 1939; *s* of Sir Rupert Rodney Francis Tress Barry, 4th Bt, MBE, and Diana Madeline (*d* 1948), *o d* of R. O'Brien Thompson; *S* father, 1977; *m* 1st, 1968, Fenella Hoult (marr. diss. 1991); one *s* one *d*; 2nd, 1992, (Elizabeth) Jill Dawe, *d* of G. Bradley, Fishtoft. *Educ:* Haileybury. Formerly Captain, Grenadier Guards. *Heir: s* William Rupert Philip Tress Barry [*b* 13 Dec. 1973; *m* 2004, Diana, d of Antoni Leidner, Germany; one *s* one *d*]. *Address:* Swinstead Cottage, High Street, Swinstead, Grantham NG33 4PA.

BARRY, Michael; *see* Bukht, M. M. J.

BARRY, Rt Rev. (Noel) Patrick, OSB; Abbot of Ampleforth, 1984–97; *b* 6 Dec. 1917; 2nd *s* of Dr T. St J. Barry, Wallasey, Cheshire. *Educ:* Ampleforth Coll.; St Benet's Hall, Oxford. Housemaster, Ampleforth Coll., 1954–64, Headmaster 1964–79. First Asst to Abbot Pres. of English Benedictine Congregation, 1985–97. Chairman: Conference of Catholic Colleges, 1973–75; HMC, 1975; Union of Monastic Superiors, 1989–95. *Address:* St Louis Abbey, 500 South Mason Road, St Louis, MO 63141–8500, USA; Ampleforth Abbey, York YO6 4EN.

BARRY, Peter; *b* Cork, 10 Aug. 1928; *s* of Anthony Barry and Rita Costello; *m* 1958, Margaret O'Mullane; four *s* two *d. Educ:* Christian Brothers' Coll., Cork. Alderman of Cork Corp., 1967–73; Lord Mayor of Cork, 1970–71. TD: Cork City SE, 1969–82; Cork South Central, 1982–97; opposition spokesman on labour and public services, 1972–73; Minister for: Transport and Power, 1973–76; Education, 1976–77; opposition spokesman on finance and economic affairs, 1977–81; Minister for the Environment, 1981–82; opposition spokesman on the environment, 1982; Minister for Foreign Affairs, 1982–87; opposition spokesman on foreign affairs, 1987–91, on industry and commerce, 1991–92. Dep. Leader of Fine Gael Party, 1979–87, 1991; Chm., Nat. Exec., 1982–84. Co-Chm., Anglo-Irish Conf., 1982–87; negotiated Anglo-Irish Agreement, 1986. Established: An Bórd Gais, 1976; Housing Finance Agency, 1982. *Address:* 150 Blackrock Road, Cork, Republic of Ireland.

BARSTOW, Dame Josephine (Clare), DBE 1995 (CBE 1985); opera singer, free-lance since 1971; *b* Sheffield, 27 Sept. 1940; *m* 1969, Ande Anderson (*d* 1996); no *c. Educ:* Birmingham Univ. (BA). Debut with Opera for All, 1964; studied at London Opera Centre, 1965–66; Opera for All, 1966; Glyndebourne Chorus, 1967; Sadler's Wells Contract Principal, 1967–68, sang Cherubino, Euridice, Violetta; *Welsh National Opera:* Contract Principal, 1968–70, sang Violetta, Countess, Fiordiligi, Mimi, Amelia, Simon Boccanegra; Don Carlos, 1973; Jenufa, 1975; Peter Grimes, 1978, 1983; Tatyana in Onegin, 1980; Tosca, 1985; Un Ballo in Maschera, 1986; The Makropoulos Case, 1994; *Covent Garden:* Denise, world première, Tippett's The Knot Garden, 1970 (recorded 1974); Falstaff, 1975; Salome, 1982; Santuzza, 1982; Peter Grimes, 1988 and 1995; Attila, 1990; Fidelio, 1993; Katya Kabanova, 2000; Queen of Spades, 2001; *Glyndebourne:* Lady Macbeth (for TV), 1972; Idomeneo, 1974; Fidelio, 1981; *English National Opera:* has sung all parts in Hoffman, Emilia Marty (Makropulos Case), Natasha (War and Peace) and Traviata; Der Rosenkavalier, 1975, 1984; Salome, 1975; Don Carlos, 1976, 1986; Tosca, 1976, 1987; Forza del Destino, 1978, 1992; Aida, 1979; Fidelio, Arabella, 1980; The Flying Dutchman, La Bohème, 1982; The Valkyrie, 1983; Don Giovanni, 1986; Lady Macbeth of Mtsensk, 1987, 1991; Street Scene, 1993; Jenufa, 1994; The Carmelites, 1999, 2005; *Opera North:* Gloriana, 1993, 1997, 2001; Jenufa, 1995; Medea, Wozzeck, 1996; Aida, 1997; Falstaff, 2000; Albert Herring, 2002. Other appearances include: Alice in Falstaff, Aix-en-Provence Festival, 1971; Nitocris in Belshazzar, Geneva, 1972; Jeanne, British première, Penderecki's The Devils, 1973; Marguerite, world première, Crosse's The Story of Vasco, 1974; Fidelio, Jenufa, Scottish Opera, 1977; Gayle, world première, Tippett's The Ice Break, 1977; US début as Lady Macbeth, Miami, 1977; Musetta in La Bohème, NY Met., 1977; Salome, East Berlin, 1979 (Critics Prize), San Francisco, 1982; Abigaille in Nabucco, Miami, 1981; début in Chicago as Lady Macbeth, 1981; new prod. of Jenufa, Cologne, 1981; La Voix Humaine and Pagliacci, Chicago, 1982; The Makropulos Case (in Italian), Florence, 1983; Gutrune, Göterdämmerung, Bayreuth, 1983; Die Fledermaus, San Francisco, 1984; Peter Grimes, 1984, La Traviata, 1985, Salome, 1987, Der Rosenkavalier, 1990, Houston; Benigna, world première, Penderecki's Die Schwarze Maske, Salzburg, 1986, Vienna Staatsoper, 1986; Manon Lescaut, USA, 1986; Tosca, Bolshoi, Tbilisi, 1986; Tosca, and Macbeth, Bolshoi, Riga, 1986; Macbeth, Zurich, 1986, Munich, 1987; Medea, Boston, 1988; Prokofiev's The Fiery Angel, Adelaide, 1988; Un Ballo in Maschera, Salzburg, 1989, 1990; Fanciulla del West, Toulouse, 1991; Chrysothemis, Houston, 1993; Fidelio, 1992, Salome, 1994, Amsterdam; Peter Grimes, Tokyo, 1998; first Jenufa in Czech, Antwerp, 1999; debut at Wigmore Hall, 2007. Sings in other opera houses in USA, Canada and Europe. Recordings include: Un Ballo in Maschera; Verdi arias; scenes from Salome, Médée, Makropulos Case and Turandot; Kiss Me Kate; Kurt Weill's Street Scene, Gloriana; Albert Herring; Wozzeck; Jenufa. Runs business of Arabian stud farm, Devon. Fidelio medal, Assoc. of Internat. Opera Directors, 1985. *Recreations:* gardening, walking. *Address:* c/o Musichall Ltd, Vicarage Way, Ringmer, E Sussex BN8 5LA.

BARSTOW, Prof. Martin Adrian, PhD; CPhys, FInstP; CSci; FRAS; Professor of Astrophysics and Space Science, since 2003, and Head, Department of Physics and Astronomy, since 2005, University of Leicester; *b* Scunthorpe, 18 May 1958; *s* of Brian Thomas Barstow and Marjorie Anona Barstow (*née* Willans); *m* 1981, Rachel Ann Howes; one *s* one *d. Educ:* Carlinghow Primary Sch.; Batley Boys' Grammar Sch.; Univ. of York (BA Physics 1979); Univ. of Leicester (PhD 1983). FRAS 1987; FInstP 1998; CSci 2004. Department of Physics and Astronomy, University of Leicester: Res. Associate, 1983–90; SERC/PPARC Advanced Fellow, 1991–98; Lectr, 1994–98; Reader, 1998–2003. Member: Public Understanding of Sci. Judges Panel, PPARC, 1996–2000 (Chm., 1997–2000); Public Understanding of Sci. Adv. Panel, PPARC, 1997–2000. Consultant on Space Educn to BNSC, 2005. Chm., Educn Adv. Bd, Nat. Space Centre, 2001–; Member: Adv. Gp, Near Earth Object Inf. Centre, 2002–; Mgt Bd, E Midlands Regl Sci. Learning Centre, 2003–. Mem., Time Allocation Cttee, 2001, 2003, 2006, Users' Cttee, 2004–, Hubble Space Telescope. Mem., Wakeham Panel, Res. Councils UK Rev. of Physics, 2008. Mem., Organizing Cttee, Physics Olympiad 2000, 1997–2000. Mem., 2005–08, Sec., 2008–, Council, RAS. Mem., Adv. Bd, Physics Rev., 1998–. *Publications:* (ed) White Dwarfs: advances in observation and theory, 1993; (with J. B. Holberg) Extreme Ultraviolet Astronomy, 2003; (ed jtly) UV Astronomy: stars from birth to death, 2007; contrib. astronomical and instrumentation jls. *Recreations:* choral singing with my family, Morris dancing, allotment and home gardening, church organ playing, folk music. *Address:* Department of Physics and Astronomy, University of Leicester, University Road, Leicester LE1 7RH. *T:* (0116) 252 3492, *Fax:* (0116) 252 3311; *e-mail:* mab@star.le.ac.uk.

BARSTOW, Stan, FRSL; writer; *b* 28 June 1928; *s* of Wilfred Barstow and Elsie Gosnay; *m* 1951, Constance Mary Kershaw; one *s* one *d. Educ:* Ossett Grammar Sch. Employed in Engineering Industry, 1944–62, mainly as Draughtsman. Best British Dramatisation, Writers' Guild of GB, 1974; Royal TV Soc. Writers' Award, 1975. FRSL 1999; Fellow, Welsh Acad., 2008. Hon. Fellow, Bretton Coll., 1985. Hon. MA Open Univ., 1982. *Radio: dramatisations:* A Kind of Loving, 1964; The Pity of it All, 1967; Bright Day, 1968; The Watchers on the Shore, 1971; We could always fit a sidecar, 1974; The Right True End, 1978; The Apples of Paradise, 1988; Foreign Parts, 1990; My Son, my Son, 1993. *Television: dramatisations:* A Raging Calm, 1974; South Riding, 1974; Joby, 1975; The Cost of Loving, 1977; Travellers, 1978; A Kind of Loving (from A Kind of Loving, The Watchers on the Shore, The Right True End), 1982; A Brother's Tale, 1983; The Man Who Cried, 1993; (with Diana Griffiths) Calon Gaeth (A Small Country), 2007. *Publications:* A Kind of Loving, 1960; The Desperadoes, 1961; Ask Me Tomorrow, 1962; Joby, 1964; The Watchers on the Shore, 1966; A Raging Calm, 1968; A Season with Eros, 1971; The Right True End, 1976; A Brother's Tale, 1980; A Kind of Loving: The Vic Brown Trilogy, 1982; The Glad Eye, 1984; Just You Wait and See, 1986; B-Movie, 1987; Give Us This Day, 1989; Next of Kin, 1991; In My Own Good Time, 2001; *plays:* Listen for the Trains, Love, 1970; Joby (TV script), 1977; An Enemy of the People (ad. Ibsen), 1978; The Human Element, and Albert's Part (TV scripts), 1984; (with Alfred Bradley): Ask Me Tomorrow, 1966; A Kind of Loving, 1970; Stringer's Last Stand, 1972. *Address:* c/o The Agency, 24 Pottery Lane, W11 4LZ.

BARTELL, family name of **Baroness Gibson of Market Rasen**.

BARTER, Nicholas Arthur Beamish; Principal, Royal Academy of Dramatic Art, 1993–2008; *b* 12 Sept. 1940; *s* of Paul André Valentine Spencer and Sylvia Theadora Essex Barter; *m* 1961, Brigid Alice Panet (marr. diss. 1981); one *s* one *d*; *m* 1998, Noriko Sasaki; one *d. Educ:* Cheltenham Coll.; Pembroke Coll., Cambridge (BA Hons, MA). ABC TV Trainee Directors Award, 1963; Asst Dir, Phoenix Th., Leicester, 1963–65; Dir of Prodns, Lincoln Theatre Royal, 1965–68; Dep. Artistic Dir, RSC Theatregoround, 1968; Dir, Ipswich Arts Th., 1968–71; Asst Drama Dir, Arts Council of GB, 1971–75; Artistic Dir, Unicorn Th., 1977–86 (Best Prodn for Young People Award, Drama mag., 1982, for Beowulf); Children's Th. Consultant, Los Angeles, 1986; Course Dir, and Dep. Principal, RADA, 1988–93. Chm., Dharma Trust, 1990–97. *Publications:* Playing with Plays, 1979; contrib. Theatre Qly, Theatre Internat.

BARTER, Sir Peter (Leslie Charles), Kt 2001; OBE 1986; *b* Sydney, Australia, 26 March 1940; *s* of late John Frank Barter and of Wyn Emily Barter; *m* 1970 Janet Ellen Carter; one *s. Educ:* Newington Coll.; Wellington Coll., Sydney. MP (People's Progress) 1992–97, (Nat. Alliance), 2002–07, Madang, PNG. Gov., Madang Province, 1992–94; Minister for Health, PNG, 1994–96; Minister for Provincial Affairs and Bougainville, 1996–97; Provincial Minister, 1997–98; Minister for Intergovt Relns and Bougainville Affairs, 2002–06; Minister for Health and Bougainville Affairs, 2006–07. Work in aviation and tourism develt in Papua New Guinea: Chairman: Melanesian Foundn, 1980–2008; Mgt Gp, PNG Incentive Fund, 1997–2002; PNG Nat. Events Council, 2000–07; Nat. Aids Council, 2008; Dep. Chm., PNG Tourist Authy, 1998–2000. Licensed commercial pilot of both fixed and rotary wing, 1967–. *Recreation:* sailing in motor yacht Kalibobo Spirit. *Address:* PO Box 707, Madang 511, Papua New Guinea. *T:* 8522766, *Fax:* 8523543.

BARTFIELD, Robert; His Honour Judge Bartfield; a Circuit Judge, since 1996; *b* 30 Dec. 1949; *s* of Isaac and Emily Bartfield; *m* 1977, Susan Eleanor Griffin; one *s* one *d. Educ:* Leeds Grammar Sch.; Queen Mary Coll., London (LLB). Called to the Bar, Middle Temple, 1971; in practice as barrister, 1971–96; a Recorder, 1993–96. *Recreations:* tennis, football.

BARTHOLOMEW, Prof. David John, PhD; FBA 1987; Professor of Statistics, London School of Economics, 1973–96, then Emeritus (Pro-Director, 1988–91); *b* 6 Aug. 1931; *s* of Albert and Joyce Bartholomew; *m* 1955, Marian Elsie Lake; two *d. Educ:* University

College London (BSc, PhD). Scientist, NCB, 1955–57; Lectr in Stats, Univ. of Keele, 1957–60; Lectr, then Sen. Lectr, UCW, Aberystwyth, 1960–67; Prof. of Stats, Univ. of Kent, 1967–73. Pres., Royal Statistical Soc., 1993–95 (Hon. Sec., 1976–82; Treas., 1989–93); Vice-Pres., Manpower Soc., 1987–95. Chm., Science and Religion Forum, 1997–2000. *Publications:* (jtly) Backbench Opinion in the House of Commons 1955–1959, 1961; Stochastic Models for Social Processes, 1967, 3rd edn 1982; (jtly) Let's Look at the Figures: the quantitative approach to human affairs, 1971; (jtly) Statistical Inference Under Order Restrictions, 1972; (jtly) Statistical Techniques for Manpower Planning, 1979, 2nd edn 1991; Mathematical Methods in Social Science, 1981; God of Chance, 1984; Latent Variable Models and Factor Analysis, 1987, 2nd edn (jtly) 1999; Uncertain Belief, 1996; The Statistical Approach to Social Measurement, 1996; (jtly) The Analysis and Interpretation of Multivariate Data for Social Scientists, 2002, 2nd edn 2008; Measuring Intelligence: facts and fallacies, 2004; Measurement (4 vols), 2006; God, Chance and Purpose, 2008; papers in statistical, theological and social science jls. *Recreations:* gardening, steam railways, theology. *Address:* 6 Beaconsfield Close, Sudbury, Suffolk CO10 1JR. *T:* (01787) 372517.

BARTLE, Philip Martyn; QC 2003; a Recorder, since 2004; *b* 24 Dec. 1952; *s* of Leslie Bartle and Zena Bartle (*née* Unger). *Educ:* Manchester Grammar Sch.; Christ Church, Oxford (MA, BCL). Called to the Bar, Middle Temple, 1976, Bencher, 2006; in practice, specialising in law of professional negligence. *Publication:* (contrib.) ADR and Commercial Disputes, 2002. *Recreations:* theatre, classical music, travel, reading. *Address:* Littleton Chambers, 3 King's Bench Walk North, EC4Y 7HR. *T:* (020) 7797 8600, *Fax:* (020) 7797 8699.

BARTLE, Ronald David; a Metropolitan Stipendiary Magistrate, 1972–99; Deputy to Chief Magistrate, 1992–99; *b* 14 April 1929; *s* of late Rev. George Clement Bartle and Winifred Marie Bartle; *m* 1st, 1963; one *s* one *d;* 2nd, 1981, Hisako (*née* Yagi) (*d* 2004). *Educ:* St John's Sch., Leatherhead; Jesus Coll., Cambridge (MA). Nat. Service, 1947–49 (Army Athletic Colours). Called to Bar, Lincoln's Inn, 1954; practised at Criminal Bar, 1954–72; a Dep. Circuit Judge, 1975–79; a Chm., Inner London Juvenile Courts, 1975–79. Member: Home Office Council on Drug Abuse, 1987–; Home Office Cttee on Magistrates' Court Procedure, 1989–. Lectr on Advocacy, Council of Legal Educn, 1984–89. Contested (C) Islington N, 1958, 1959; Mem., Essex CC, 1963–66. Freeman, City of London, 1976; Liveryman, Basketmakers' Co., 1976– (Steward, 1990; Mem. Ct, 1997–; Prime Warden, 2005–06). Patron, Pathway to Recovery Trust. Governor: Corp. of Sons of the Clergy, 1995–; RNLI, 1997–. Church Warden, St Mary the Boltons, Kensington, 1992–95; Church Warden and Trustee, St Margaret Pattens, 1999–; Member: City of London Deanery Synod, 2000–; Friends of City of London Churches, 2001–; Guild of Freemen, City of London; Royal Soc. of St George. *Publications:* Introduction to Shipping Law, 1958; The Police Officer in Court, 1984; Crime and the New Magistrate, 1985; The Law and the Lawless, 1987; Bow Street Beak, 1999; The Police Witness, 2002; (contrib.) Atkin's Court Forms and Precedents; contrib. to legal jls. *Recreations:* music, reading, swimming. *Clubs:* Garrick, City Pickwick, City Livery.

BARTLES-SMITH, Ven. Douglas Leslie; Archdeacon of Southwark, 1985–2004, now Emeritus; Chaplain to the Queen, 1996–2007; *b* 3 June 1937; *s* of late Leslie Charles and Muriel Rose Bartles-Smith; *m* 1967, Patricia Ann Coburn; two *s* one *d. Educ:* Shrewsbury School; St Edmund Hall, Oxford (MA); Wells Theol Coll. Nat. Service (2nd Lieut, RASC), 1956–58. Curate of St Stephen's, Rochester Row, SW1, 1963–68; Curate-in-charge, St Michael and All Angels with Emmanuel and All Souls, Camberwell, 1968–72; Vicar, 1972–75; Vicar of St Luke, Battersea, 1975–85; RD of Battersea, 1981–85. Hon. Freeman, London Bor. of Southwark, 2004. *Publications:* (co-author) Urban Ghetto, 1976; Opportunities for a Strong Church, 1993; Fighting Fundamentalism, 2007. *Recreations:* Shrewsbury Town Football Club, reading, walking, travel. *Address:* 18 Vane Road, Shrewsbury SY3 7HB.

BARTLETT, Sir Andrew (Alan), 5th Bt *cr* 1913, of Hardington Mandeville, Somerset; *b* 26 May 1973; *er s* of Sir John Hardington David Bartlett, 4th Bt and of his 2nd wife, Elizabeth Joyce (*née* Raine); *S* father, 1998. *Heir: b* Stephen Bartlett, *b* 5 July 1975.

BARTLETT, Andrew Vincent Bramwell; QC 1993; a Recorder, since 2004; chartered arbitrator; *b* 7 Oct. 1952; *s* of John Samuel Bartlett and Doris Jean Bartlett; *m* 1974, Elisabeth Jefferis. *Educ:* Jesus Coll., Oxford (BA). Called to the Bar, Middle Temple, 1974, Bencher, 2005. Chm., Financial Services and Mkts Tribunal, 2001–; Dep. Chm., Information Tribunal, 2004–. Chm., Technol. and Construction Bar Assoc., 2007–. FCIArb. *Address:* Crown Office Chambers, 2 Crown Office Row, Temple, EC4Y 7HJ. *T:* (020) 7797 8100.

BARTLETT, Charles; *see* Bartlett, H. C.

BARTLETT, Dr Christopher Leslie Reginald, FRCP, FFPH; Director, Public Health Laboratory Service Communicable Disease Surveillance Centre, 1988–2000; *b* 20 Dec. 1940; *s* of Reginald James Bartlett and Dorothea Amelia Bartlett; *m* 1979, Alicia Teresa Tower; one *s* two *d. Educ:* Milton Sch., Bulawayo, Southern Rhodesia; Lysses Sch., Hants; St Bartholomew's Hosp. Med. Coll. (MB, BS 1965); MSc LSHTM 1977. MRCS 1965; LRCP 1965, FRCP 1991; MFCM 1978, FFPH (FFPHM 1983). RAF SSC, 1967–72. Registrar, Wessex RHA, seconded to LSHTM, 1975–77; Public Health Laboratory Service: Sen. Registrar, 1977–79; Consultant Epidemiologist, 1979–88. Consultant Med. Epidemiologist, Caribbean Epidemiol. Centre, 1984–85. Hon. Lectr, Dept of Envmtl and Preventative Medicine, St Bartholomew's Hosp. Med. Coll., 1980; Hon. Sen. Lectr, Dept of Epidemiol. and Med. Stats, Royal London Hosp., 1990; Vis. Prof., LSHTM, 1997–. Chm., PHLS Cttee on Legionnaire's Disease, 1989; Member: DHSS Cttee on Aspects and Use of Biocides, 1986; Registrar-Gen's Med. Adv. Cttee, DoH, 1988–90; Expert Gp on Cryptosporidium in Water Supplies, DoE and DoH, 1989–90; Steering Gp on Microbiol Safety of Food, MAFF and DoH, 1991–95; CMO's Health of Nation Cttee, DoH, 1992–2000. Faculty of Public Health Medicine: Member: Bd, 1988–91; Educn Cttee, 1988–94; Pres., Sect. of Epidemiol. and Public Health, RSocMed. 1996 (Mem., Council, 1990–94); Mem. Council, RIPH&H, 1991–94. Member: Scientific Steering Cttee, Réseau Nat. de Santé Publique, France, 1992; Steering Gp, European Prog. for Intervention Epidemiol. Trng, 1994; PROMED Steering Cttee, Fedn of Amer. Scientists, 1995; Communicable Diseases Wkg Gp, G7 Nations Global Healthcare Applications Project, 1995; MRC CJD Epidemiol. Subcttee, 1996; EU/USA Task Force on Communicable Diseases, 1996 (Co-Chm., Surveillance and Response Wkg Gp, 1996); Project Leader, European Surveillance of Travel Associated Legionnaire's Disease, 1993; Jt Project Leader, SALMNET (EU Surveillance of Salmonella Infections), 1994; Chm., Charter Gp of Heads of Instns with responsibilities in nat. surveillance of disease in EU countries, 1994. Specialist Advr, Editl Bd, Jl Infection, 1991–. *Publications:* chapters, articles and papers in med. and scientific texts on aspects of epidemiology and prevention of infectious diseases. *Recreations:* family, walking, ski-ing, travelling. *Club:* Royal Society of Medicine.

BARTLETT, George Robert; QC 1986; President of the Lands Tribunal, since 1998; a Deputy High Court Judge, since 1994; *b* 22 Oct. 1944; *s* of late Commander H. V. Bartlett, RN and Angela (*née* Webster); *m* 1972, Dr Clare Virginia, *y d* of G. C. Fortin; three *s. Educ:* Tonbridge Sch.; Trinity Coll., Oxford (MA). Called to the Bar, Middle Temple, 1966, Bencher, 1995. A Recorder, 1990–2000; an Asst Parly Boundary Comr, 1992–98. Ed., Ryde on Rating, 1990. Hon. RICS 2000. *Address:* Lands Tribunal, Procession House, 55 Ludgate Hill, EC4M 7JW.

BARTLETT, (Harold) Charles, RE 1961 (ARE 1950); RWS 1970 (ARWS 1959); President, Royal Society of Painters in Water Colours, 1987–92; painter and printmaker; *b* Grimsby, 23 Sept. 1921; *s* of Charles Henry and Frances Kate Bartlett; *m;* one *s; m* 1970, Olwen Jones, RE, RWS. *Educ:* Eastbourne Grammar Sch.; Eastbourne Sch. of Art; Royal College of Art (ARCA 1949). Sen. Lectr in Drawing and Painting, Harrow College of Art, 1960–70. First one man exhibition in London, 1960; major retrospective, Bankside Gall., London, 1997. *Recreations:* music, sailing. *Address:* St Andrews, Fingringhoe, near Colchester, Essex CO5 7BG. *T:* (01206) 729406.

BARTLETT, Henry Francis, CMG 1975; OBE 1964; HM Diplomatic Service, retired; *b* 8 March 1916; *s* of F. V. S. and A. G. Bartlett, London; *m* 1940, A. D. Roy (*d* 2004). *Educ:* St Paul's Sch.; Queen's Coll., Oxford; Ruskin Sch. of Drawing; Univ. of California (Commonwealth Fellow). Min. of Inf., 1940–45; Paris, 1944–47; Vice-Consul Lyons, 1948–49; FO, 1949–50; Vice-Consul, Szczecin, 1950; Second, later First, Sec., Warsaw, 1951–53; FO, 1953–55; First Sec. (Commercial), Caracas, 1955–60; First Sec. (Inf.), Mexico City, 1960–63; Consul, Khorramshahr, 1964–67; Dep. High Comr, Brisbane, 1967–69; Counsellor, Manila, 1969–72 (Chargé d'Affaires, 1971); Ambassador to Paraguay, 1972–75. Hon. Prof., Nat. Univ. of Asunción, 1975. Exec. Officer, Utah Foundation, Brisbane, 1976–89. Exhibitions of painting: Paris, 1947; London, 1950; Caracas, 1957, 1959; Mexico City, 1962; Brisbane, 1969, 1978, 1981, 1983, 1985, 1988, 1990, 1992, 1994, 1996. Represented: Commonwealth Art Bank; Queensland and S Aust. State Galleries; Queensland Univ. of Technol.; Brisbane Civic Art Gall.; Bendigo Art Gall. Trustee: Queensland Art Gallery, 1977–87; Qld Cultural Centre Trust, 1980–87. *Recreation:* painting. *Address:* 14 Bowen Place, 341 Bowen Terrace, New Farm, Brisbane, Qld 4005, Australia.

BARTLETT, John Vernon, CBE 1976; MA; FREng, FICE; consulting engineer, retired; *b* 18 June 1927; *s* of late Vernon F. Bartlett and Olga Bartlett (*née* Testrup); *m* 1951, Gillian, *d* of late Philip Hoffmann, Sturmer Hall, Essex; four *s. Educ:* Stowe; Trinity Coll., Cambridge. Served 9th Airborne Squadron, RE, 1946–48; Engineer and Railway Staff Corps, TA, 1978; Col 1986. Engineer with John Mowlem & Co. Ltd, 1951–57; joined staff of Mott, Hay & Anderson, 1957; Partner, 1966–88; Chm., 1973–88. Pres., ICE, 1982–83 (Vice-Pres., 1979–82; Mem. Council, 1974–77); Chm., British Tunnelling Soc., 1977–79. Gov., Imperial Coll., 1991–95. FRSA 1975. Mem. Council, Fellowship of Engrg, 1982–86. Master, Engineers' Co., 1992–93 (Mem., Court of Assts, 1986–2004). Telford Gold Medal, (jointly) 1971, 1973; S. G. Brown Medal, Royal Soc., 1973. *Publications:* Tunnels: Planning Design and Construction (with T. M. Megaw), vol. 1, 1981, vol. 2, 1982; Ships of North Cornwall, 1996; contrib. various papers to ICE, ASCE, etc. *Recreations:* sailing, maritime history (Founder, Bartlett Library, Nat. Maritime Mus. Cornwall, 2002). *Address:* 6 Cottenham Park Road, SW20 0RZ. *T:* (020) 8946 9576. *Clubs:* Hawks (Cambridge); Harlequin Football; Royal Engineers Yacht.

BARTLETT, Neil Vivian, OBE 2000; writer, director; Artistic Director, Lyric Theatre, Hammersmith, 1994–2004; *b* 23 Aug. 1958; *s* of Trevor and Pam Bartlett; partner, James Gardiner. *Educ:* Magdalen Coll., Oxford (BA Hons Eng. Lit.). Works written, adapted and directed include: *theatre:* More Bigger Snacks Now, 1985; A Vision of Love Revealed in Sleep, 1987; Sarrasine, 1990; A Judgement in Stone, 1992; Night After Night, 1993; The Picture of Dorian Gray, 1994; Lady into Fox, 1996; The Seven Sacraments of Nicholas Poussin, 1997; *television:* That's What Friends are For, 1987; Where is Love?, 1988; Pedagogue, 1989; That's How Strong My Love Is, 1990; *film:* Now That It's Morning, 1992; major productions directed: Romeo and Juliet, 1994; The Letter, 1995; Mrs Warren's Profession, A Christmas Carol, 1996; Then Again, Treasure Island, 1997; Cause Célèbre, Seven Sonnets of Michaelangelo, Cinderella, 1998; The Dispute, 1999; The Servant, 2001; The Prince of Homburg, The Island of Slaves, 2002; Pericles, 2003; Oliver Twist, Don Juan, 2004; Dido, Queen of Carthage, Amer. Rep. Co., Boston, 2005; The Rake's Progress, Aldeburgh Fest., 2006; The Maids, The Pianist, Twelfth Night, RSC, 2007; An Ideal Husband, Romeo and Juliet, RSC, 2008; has performed at RNT, Royal Court, Blackpool Grand and Vauxhall Tavern. *Publications:* Who Was That Man?, 1988; Ready to Catch Him Should He Fall, 1989; A Vision of Love Revealed in Sleep, 1990; (trans.) Berenice/The Misanthrope/School for Wives, 1991; (trans.) The Game of Love and Chance, 1992; Night After Night, 1993; Mr Clive and Mr Page, 1995; (trans.) Splendid's, 1995; (trans.) The Dispute, 1999; (trans.) The Threesome, 2000; In Extremis, 2000; (trans.) The Prince of Homburg, 2002; (trans.) The Island of Slaves, 2002; (trans.) Don Juan, 2005; Solo Voices, 2005; Skin Lane, 2007; adaptations for stage: Camille, 2003; A Christmas Carol, 2003; Oliver Twist, 2004; Great Expectations, 2007. *Recreations:* weight training, bull terriers, tree peonies, HIV and breast cancer charity work. *Address:* c/o The Agency, 24 Pottery Lane, W11 4LZ. *T:* (020) 7727 1346; *e-mail:* info@theagency.co.uk; *web:* www.neil-bartlett.com.

BARTLETT, Prof. Robert John, FBA 1997; FRSE, FSA, FRHistS; Professor of Mediaeval History, University of St Andrews, since 1992; *b* 27 Nov. 1950; *s* of Leonard Frederick Bartlett and Mabel Emily Adams; *m* 1979, Honora Elaine Hickey; one *s* one *d. Educ:* Peterhouse, Cambridge (BA 1972; MA 1976); St John's Coll., Oxford (DPhil 1978). Lectr in History, Edinburgh Univ., 1980–86; Prof. of Medieval History, Univ. of Chicago, 1986–92; British Acad. Reader, 1995–97. Junior Fellow, Univ. of Michigan Soc. of Fellows, 1979–80; Mem., Inst. for Advanced Study and Fellow, Davis Center, Princeton, 1983–84; von Humboldt Fellow, Göttingen, 1988–89. Presenter, Inside the Medieval Mind, BBC4, 2008. *Publications:* Gerald of Wales 1146–1223, 1982; Trial by Fire and Water, 1986; The Making of Europe, 1993; England under the Norman and Angevin Kings, 2000; (ed) Medieval Panorama, 2001; (ed) Geoffrey of Burton, Life and Miracles of St Modwenna, 2002; (ed) The Miracles of St Æbbe of Coldingham and St Margaret of Scotland, 2003; The Hanged Man, 2004; The Natural and the Supernatural in the Middle Ages, 2008; contribs to learned jls. *Address:* Department of Mediaeval History, University of St Andrews, St Andrews, Fife KY16 9AL. *T:* (01334) 463308.

BARTLETT, Timothy Conn; Director, Tourism and Hotel Advisory Services, since 2006; *b* 15 Dec. 1944; *s* of Gordon Thomas Bartlett and Margaret Decima Bartlett; *m* 1st, 1970, Deira Janis Vacher (marr. diss.); one *s* one *d;* 2nd, 1988, Xochitl Alicia Quintanilla; two *d. Educ:* Cranleigh Sch.; Pembroke Coll., Oxford (Hons French and Spanish). Morgan Grampian Books, 1967–68; British Tourist Authority: London, 1968–70 and 1974–77; Sydney, 1970–74; Manager: Mexico, 1977–82; Western USA, based in LA, 1982–87; France, 1987–88; General Manager: S Europe, 1988–91; Asia Pacific, 1991–94; Europe, based in Brussels, 1994–95; Acting Chief Exec., 1995–96, Chief Exec., 1996–99, English Tourist Bd; Chief Exec., British Assoc. of Leisure Parks, Piers and Attractions,

1999–2001; Dir, Tourism Div., 1999–2001 and Dir, Spain, Portugal and Latin America, 2001–05, TRI Hospitality Consulting; Chief Exec., Newcastle-Gateshead Initiative, 2005. *Recreations:* tennis, reading, music, travel. *Address:* Playa de Fuenterrabia 10, Las Rozas, Madrid 28290, Spain; *e-mail:* timcbartlett@hotmail.com.

BARTOLI, Cecilia; mezzo soprano; *b* Rome, 4 June 1966; *d* of Pietro Angelo Bartoli and Silvana Bartoli (*née* Bazzoni). *Educ:* Acad. of Santa Cecilia, Rome. Début, Barber of Seville, Teatro dell'opera, Rome, 1986; has performed at La Scala, Milan, Opéra Bastille, Carnegie Hall, Maggio Musicale Fest., Florence, Salzburg Fest., Wigmore Hall, Aix-en-Provence Fest., NY Metropolitan Opera, Royal Opera House, Covent Garden; also with major orchs, incl. Vienna Philharmonic and Berlin Philharmonic, and major period instrument ensembles. Numerous recordings. Hon. RAM; Academician, Santa Cecilia, Rome. Knight: Order of Merit (Italy); Fine Arts (France).

BARTON, Alan Burnell; Head of Resource Management and Finance Division (formerly Under Secretary), Department of Health, 1993–98; *b* 2 May 1943; *s* of Charles Henry Barton and Rose Edith Barton; *m* 1969, Jirina Klapstova; one *s* one *d*. *Educ:* Glyn Grammar Sch., Ewell; Bristol Univ. (BSc Chem.). Operational Research Exec., NCB, 1966–73; Department of Health and Social Security: Principal, 1973–78; Asst Sec., 1979–90; Dir, Medical Devices Directorate, DoH, 1990–93. Advr, Rickmansworth CAB, 2000–; Social Policy Advr, Citizens Advice (formerly NACAB), 2000–; Mem., Low Incomes Tax Reform Gp, 2005–. *Recreations:* jazz, theatre, country houses, walking. *Address:* 67 Heronsgate Road, Chorleywood, Rickmansworth, Herts WD3 5PA.

BARTON, Prof. (Barbara) Anne, PhD; FBA 1991; Professor of English, Cambridge University, 1984–2000; Fellow of Trinity College, Cambridge, since 1986; *b* 9 May 1933; *d* of Oscar Charles Roesen and Blanche Godfrey Williams; *m* 1st, 1957, William Harvey Righter; 2nd, 1969, John Bernard Adie Barton, *qv*. *Educ:* Bryn Mawr College, USA. BA 1954 (*summa cum laude*); PhD Cantab 1960. Lectr in History of Art, Ithaca Coll., NY, 1958–59; Girton College, Cambridge: Rosalind Lady Carlisle Research Fellow, 1960–62; Official Fellow in English, 1962–72; Dir of Studies in English, 1963–72; Univ. Asst Lectr, later Univ. Lectr in English, Cambridge, 1962–72; Hildred Carlile Prof. of English and Head of Dept, Bedford Coll., London, 1972–74; Fellow and Tutor in English, New Coll., Oxford and CUF Lectr, 1974–84. Lectures: British Acad. Chatterton, 1967; Alexander Meml, Univ. Coll., Toronto, 1983; British Acad. Shakespeare, 1991; Northcliffe, UCL, 1994; Clark, Cambridge, 2003. MAE 1995. Hon. Fellow: Shakespeare Inst., Univ. of Birmingham, 1982; New Coll., Oxford, 1989. Member Editorial Advisory Boards: Shakespeare Survey, 1972–99; Shakespeare Quarterly, 1981–2004; Studies in English Literature, 1976–; Romanticism, 1995–. *Publications:* Shakespeare and the Idea of the Play, 1962, 4th edn 1977, trans. Japanese 1982; Ben Jonson, Dramatist, 1984; The Names of Comedy, 1990; Byron: Don Juan, 1992; Essays, Mainly Shakespearean, 1994; essays and studies in learned jls. *Recreations:* opera, fine arts. *Address:* Trinity College, Cambridge CB2 1TQ. *T:* (01223) 338466.

BARTON, Ven. (Charles) John Greenwood; Archdeacon of Aston, 1990–2003; Priest-in-charge, St Peter, Bickenhill, 2002–03; *b* 5 June 1936; *s* of Charles William Greenwood Barton and Doris Lilian Leach; *m* 1972 (marr. diss. 1981); one *s*. *Educ:* Battersea Grammar Sch.; London Coll. of Divinity (ALCD). Asst Curate, St Mary Bredin, Canterbury, 1963–66; Vicar, Whitfield with West Langdon, dio. Canterbury, 1966–75; Vicar, St Luke, South Kensington, 1975–83; Area Dean, Chelsea, 1980–83; Chief Broadcasting Officer, Church of England, 1983–90. Communications Advr to Archbishop of York, 2005–06; Acting Chief of Staff to Archbishop of York, 2007. Mem., Gen. Synod of C of E, 2000–03. Chm., BBC W Midlands Regl Adv. Council, 1995–98; Mem., English Nat. Forum, 1995–98. Member, Council: Corp. of Church House, 1989–; St Luke's Hosp. for Clergy, 2000–03. Chm., 2000–02, Trustee, 2002–03, Midlands Ethnic Albanian Foundn. *Address:* 3 Stuart Court, Puckle Lane, Canterbury, Kent CT1 3LA. *T:* (01227) 379688; *e-mail:* johnbarton@waitrose.com. *Club:* National Liberal.

BARTON, Maj.-Gen. Eric Walter, CB 1983; MBE 1966; FRGS; Director, Caravan Club Ltd, 1984–93; *b* 27 April 1928; *s* of Reginald John Barton and Dorothy (*née* Bradfield); *m* 1st, 1955, Rowena Ulrica Riddell (marr. diss. 1960); 2nd, 1963, Margaret Ann (*née* Jenkins) (marr. diss. 1983); two *s*; 3rd, 1984, Mrs Pamela Clare Frimann, *d* of late Reginald D. Mason and of Doris Mason, Winchelsea. *Educ:* St Clement Danes Sch., London; Royal Military Coll. of Science (BScEng 1955). Dip. in Photogrammetry, UCL, 1960. FCMI (FBIM 1979); FRGS 1979. Commnd RE, 1948; served Mid East, 1948–50; Arab Legion, 1951–52; seconded to Dir, Overseas Surveys, E Africa, 1957–59; Sen. Instr, Sch. of Mil. Survey, 1961–63; OC 13 Fd Survey Sqn, Aden, 1965–67; Dir, Surveys and Prodn, Ordnance Survey, 1977–80; Dir of Mil. Survey, 1980–84. Major 1961, Lt-Col 1967, Col 1972, Brig. 1976, Maj.-Gen. 1980. Col Comdt, RE, 1982–87; Hon. Col, Field Survey Sqn, later 135 Indep. Topographic Sqn RE (V) TA, 1984–89. Pres., Defence Surveyors' Assoc. (formerly Field Survey Assoc.), 1991–2004 (Chm., 1984–86); Member: Council, Photogrammetric Soc., 1979–82; Nat. Cttee for Photogrammetry, 1979–84; Council, RGS, 1980–83; Council, British Schs Exploring Soc., 1980–84; Nat. Cttee for Geography, 1981–84. *Recreations:* swimming, water sports, numismatics. *Address:* c/o Barclays Bank, Lewes, E Sussex BN7 2JP.

BARTON, Rev. Prof. John, DPhil, DLitt; FBA 2007; Oriel and Laing Professor of the Interpretation of Holy Scripture, University of Oxford, since 1991; Fellow of Oriel College, Oxford, since 1991; *b* 17 June 1948; *s* of Bernard Arthur Barton and Gwendolyn Harriet Barton; *m* 1973, Mary Burn; one *d*. *Educ:* Latymer Upper Sch., Hammersmith; Keble Coll., Oxford (MA; DPhil 1974; DLitt 1988). Deacon and priest, 1973. University of Oxford: Jun. Res. Fellow, Merton Coll., 1973–74; Official Fellow, St Cross Coll., 1974–91; University Lectr in Theology (OT), 1974–89; Reader in Biblical Studies, 1989–91; Chaplain, St Cross Coll., 1979–91. Canon Theologian, Winchester Cathedral, 1991–2003. Hon. Dr theol. Bonn, 1998. *Publications:* Amos's Oracles against the Nations, 1980; Reading the Old Testament: method in biblical study, 1984, 2nd edn 1996; Oracles of God: perceptions of ancient prophecy in Israel after the Exile, 1986; People of the Book?—the authority of the Bible in Christianity, 1988, 2nd edn 1993; Love Unknown: meditations on the Death and Resurrection of Jesus, 1990; What is the Bible?, 1991, 2nd edn 1997; Isaiah 1–39, 1995; The Spirit and the Letter: studies in the biblical canon, 1997; Making the Christian Bible, 1997; Ethics and the Old Testament, 1998; (ed) The Cambridge Companion to Biblical Interpretation, 1998; (ed jtly) The Oxford Bible Commentary, 2001; Joel and Obadiah, 2001; (ed) The Biblical World, 2002; Understanding Old Testament Ethics, 2003; (with J. L. V. Bowden) The Original Story: God, Israel and the World, 2004; Living Belief: being Christian, being human, 2005; The Nature of Biblical Criticism, 2007; The Old Testament: canon, literature, theology, 2007. *Address:* Oriel College, Oxford OX1 4EW.

BARTON, John Bernard Adie, CBE 1981; Advisory Director, Royal Shakespeare Company, since 1991 (Associate Director, 1964–91); *b* 26 Nov. 1928; *s* of late Sir Harold Montague Barton and Joyce Wale; *m* 1968, Anne Righter (*see* B. A. Barton). *Educ:* Eton Coll.; King's Coll., Cambridge (BA, MA). Fellow, King's Coll., Cambridge, 1954–60 (Lay Dean, 1956–59). Joined Royal Shakespeare Company, 1960; Associate Dir, 1964. Has adapted texts and directed or co-directed many plays for Royal Shakespeare Company, including: The Taming of the Shrew, 1960; The Hollow Crown, 1961; The Art of Seduction, 1962; The Wars of the Roses, 1963–64; Henry IV, Parts I and II, and Henry V, 1964–66; Love's Labour's Lost, 1965; Coriolanus and All's Well That Ends Well, 1967; Julius Caesar and Troilus and Cressida, 1968; Twelfth Night and When Thou Art King, 1969; Measure for Measure and The Tempest, 1970; Richard II, Henry V, and Othello, 1971; Richard II, 1973; King John, Cymbeline, and Dr Faustus, 1974; Perkin Warbeck, 1975; Much Ado About Nothing, The Winter's Tale, and Troilus and Cressida, 1976; A Midsummer Night's Dream, Pillars of the Community, 1977; The Way of the World, The Merchant of Venice, Love's Labour's Lost, 1978; The Greeks, 1979; Hamlet, 1980; The Merchant of Venice, Titus Andronicus and The Two Gentlemen of Verona, 1981; La Ronde, 1982; Life's a Dream, 1983; The Devils, 1984; Waste, Dream Play, 1985; The Rover, 1986; Three Sisters, 1988; Coriolanus, 1989; Peer Gynt, 1994; Cain, 1995. Directed: The School for Scandal, Haymarket, 1983, Duke of York's, 1983; The Vikings at Helgeland, Den Nationale Scene, Bergen, 1983; Peer Gynt, 1990, Measure for Measure, As You Like It, 1991, Oslo. Wrote and presented Playing Shakespeare, LWT, 1982, Channel 4, 1984; narrated Morte d'Arthur, BBC2, 1984; wrote The War that Never Ends, BBC2, 1990. *Publications:* The Hollow Crown, 1962 (and 1971); The Wars of the Roses, 1970; The Greeks, 1981; Playing Shakespeare, 1982; Tantalus, 2000. *Recreations:* travel, chess, work. *Address:* 14 de Walden Court, 85 New Cavendish Street, W1W 6XD.

BARTON, Ven. John Greenwood; *see* Barton, Ven. C. J. G.

BARTON, Prof. Leonard Francis; Professor of Inclusive Education, Institute of Education, London University, 2001, now Emeritus; *b* 20 April 1941. *Educ:* Liverpool Univ. (BA Hons); Manchester Univ. (MEd). Prof. of Educn, Bristol Poly., 1986–90; Sheffield University: Head of Res. Degrees, and Dir of Inclusive Educn Res. Centre; Prof. of Educn, 1990–2001. Sir Allan Sewell Fellow, Griffiths Univ., Australia, 1995–96. Founder and Editor, Disability and Society, 1985–. *Publications:* (ed) Disability and Society: emerging issues and insights, 1996; (ed) Disability, Politics and the Struggle for Change, 2001. *Recreations:* swimming, walking, listening to music. *Address:* c/o Institute of Education, 20 Bedford Way, WC1H 0AL.

BARTON, Prof. Nicholas Hamilton, PhD; FRS 1994; Professor, Institute for Evolutionary Biology (formerly Institute of Cell, Animal and Population Biology), University of Edinburgh, since 1994. *Educ:* Peterhouse, Cambridge (BA 1976; MA 1980); Univ. of E Anglia (PhD). Cambridge University: Res. Fellow, Girton Coll., 1980; Demonstrator, Dept of Genetics, 1980–82; Lectr, then Reader, Dept of Genetics and Biometry, UCL, 1982–90; Darwin Trust Fellow, Inst. of Cell, Animal and Population Biol., Edinburgh Univ., 1990. FRSE 1995. *Address:* Institute for Evolutionary Biology, Ashworth Laboratories, University of Edinburgh, West Mains Road, Edinburgh EH9 3JT. *T:* (0131) 650 5509, *Fax:* (0131) 667 3210.

BARTON, Philip Robert, CMG 2007; OBE 1997; HM Diplomatic Service; Director, South Asia, Foreign and Commonwealth Office, since 2008; *b* 18 Aug. 1963; *s* of late Geoffrey Howard Barton and of Katharine Anne (*née* Stubbings); *m* 1999, Amanda Joy Bowen; one *s* one *d*. *Educ:* Warwick Univ. (BA Econs and Politics); London Sch. of Econs (MSc Econs). Joined FCO, 1986: Third, then Second, Sec., Caracas, 1987–91; Cabinet Office (on secondment), 1991–93; First Secretary: FCO, 1993–94; New Delhi, 1994–96; Private Sec. to Prime Minister (on secondment), 1997–2000; Dep. High Comr, Cyprus, 2000–04; Dep. Gov., Gibraltar, 2005–08. *Recreations:* football, tennis, hiking, travel, reading. *Address:* c/o Foreign and Commonwealth Office, King Charles Street, SW1A 2AH.

BARTON, Roger; owns and runs Llama Trekking, Sheffield, since 2007; *b* 6 Jan. 1945; *s* of late Joseph and Doreen Barton; *m* 1965; two *s*. *Educ:* Burngreave Secondary Modern Sch.; Granville Coll. (Engrg Technician's Cert.). Fitter, 1961–81; Sheffield TUC and Labour Party Sec., 1981–89. Mem., Sheffield CC, 1971–90. Mem. (Lab) Sheffield, Eur. Parlt, 1989–99; contested (Lab) Yorkshire and the Humber Region, 1999. Former Dir, Insight Dynamics. *Recreations:* walking, gentle cycling, water sports. *Address:* 50 Hartley Brook Avenue, Sheffield S5 0HN. *Clubs:* Trades and Labour, Wortley Hall Labour (Sheffield).

BARTRAM, Christopher John, FRICS; Chairman, Orchard Street Investment Management, since 2004; *b* Cambridge, 8 April 1949; *s* of John and Irene Bartram; *m* 1974, Carolyn Bates; one *s* one *d*. *Educ:* Oundle Sch.; Downing Coll., Cambridge (BA 1972). FRICS 1989. In private practice, London, 1972; Asst Surveyor, Equitable Life Assce, 1974–78; Property Investment Manager, Scottish Amicable Life, 1978–85; Partner, Jones Lang Wootton, 1985–95, Man. Partner, 1991–94; CEO, Haslemere NV, 1995–2004. A Crown Estate Comr, 2007–. Chm., Bank of England Property Forum, 2002–05. Pres., British Property Fedn, 2000–01. Associate Fellow, Downing Coll., Cambridge, 2005–. *Recreation:* golf. *Address:* 15 Trumpington Road, Cambridge CB2 8AJ; *e-mail:* cbartram@orchard-street.co.uk. *Clubs:* Reform; Royal West Norfolk Golf, Royal Worlington Golf, Royal and Ancient Golf.

BARTRAM, Prof. Clive Issell, FRCS, FRCP, FRCR; Professor of Gastrointestinal Radiology, Imperial College, University of London, since 1999; *b* 30 June 1943; *s* of Henry George and Muriel Barbara Bartram; *m* 1966, Michele Juliette François; two *s*. *Educ:* Dragon Sch., Oxford; St Edward's Sch., Oxford; Westminster Hosp. Med. Sch. (MB BS 1966). FRCR 1972; FRCP 1985; FRCS 1999. Consultant Radiologist, St Bartholomew's Hosp., 1974–94; Consultant Radiologist, 1974–2004, Clinical Dir, 2001–04, St Mark's Hosp.; Dir, Radiology, Princess Grace Hosp., 1990–. Hon. Consultant Radiologist, Hammersmith Hosp., 1994–99. *Publications:* Radiology in Inflammatory Bowel Disease, 1983; Handbook of Anal Endosonography, 1997; Imaging of Pelvic Floor Disorders, 2003; contrib. articles on gastrointestinal radiology and pelvic floor disorders. *Recreations:* walking, theatre, music, reading, some gardening. *Address:* Pelhams, Maplefield Lane, Chalfont St Giles, Bucks HP8 4TY. *T:* (01494) 766303; *e-mail:* cibartram@aol.com. *Club:* Royal Society of Medicine.

BARTRAM, George Christopher, TD 1960; Vice Lord-Lieutenant of Co. Durham, 1997–2002; *b* 23 Aug. 1927; *s* of Robert Appleby Bartram and Winifred Hannah (*née* Murray); *m* 1969, Josephine Anne Ker Staveley; two *s*. *Educ:* Rugby Sch.; St Catharine's Coll., Cambridge (MA). Served DLI, 1945–48; TA service, DLI, 1948–64; Hon. Col, 7th Bn (Durham) LI, 1989–94. Bartram & Sons Ltd, Ship Builders, 1952–63; Colvilles Ltd, Steel Mfrs, 1964–72; trainee, Paddington Churches Housing Assoc., 1974; Chief Exec., Endeavour Housing Assoc., 1975–92. Pres., Co. Durham SSAFA Forces Help, 1987–2002. High Sheriff, 1982, DL 1990, Co. Durham. *Recreations:* unskilled gardening, reading, family history research. *Address:* Eldon House, Heighington, Newton Aycliffe, Co. Durham DL5 6PP. *T:* (01325) 312270. *Club:* Victory Services.

BARTTELOT, Col Sir Brian Walter de Stopham, 5th Bt *cr* 1875; OBE 1983; psc; Vice Lord-Lieutenant for West Sussex, since 1994; Member, HM Body Guard of the

Honourable Corps of Gentlemen at Arms, since 1993; *b* 17 July 1941; *s* of Lt-Col Sir Walter de Stopham Barttelot, 4th Bt, and Sara Patricia (who *m* 2nd, 1965, Comdr James Barttelot, RN retd; she *d* 1998), *d* of late Lieut-Col H. V. Ravenscroft; *S* father, 1944; *m* 1969, Hon. Mary Angela Fiona Weld Forester, (MBE 2001; DL, DStJ), *y d* of 7th Baron Forester, and of Marie Louise Priscilla, CStJ, *d* of Sir Herbert Perrott, 6th Bt, CH, CB; four *d*. *Educ*: Eton; RMA, Sandhurst. Commnd Coldstream Guards, 1961; Temp. Equerry to HM the Queen, 1970–71. Camberley Staff Coll., 1974; GSO2, Army Staff Duties Directorate, MoD, 1975–76; Second in comd, 2nd Bn, Coldstream Guards, 1977–78; Mil. Sec. to Maj.-Gen. comdg London Dist and Household Div., 1978–81; GSO1, MoD, 1981–82; CO 1st Bn Coldstream Gds, 1982–85; GSO1, HQ BAOR, 1985–86; Regtl Lt-Col Comdg Coldstream Guards, 1986–92. Col, Foot Guards, 1989–92; Hon. Col, Sussex ACF, 1996–2007. President: W Sussex Scout Council, 1993–; S of England Agricl Soc., 2001–02. Chm. Exec. Cttee, Standing Council of the Baronetage, 1996–2001; Chm., Baronet's Trust, 2002–. Liveryman, Gunmakers' Co., 1981. DL W Sussex, 1988, High Sheriff, W Sussex, 1997–98. *Heir*: *b* Robin Ravenscroft Barttelot [*b* 15 Dec. 1943; *m* 1987, Theresa, *er d* of late Kenneth Greenlees; one *s* one *d*]. *Address*: Stopham Park, Pulborough, W Sussex RH20 1DY. *Clubs*: Cavalry and Guards, Pratt's, Farmers'.

BARWELL, David John Frank; international business consultant; *b* 12 Oct. 1938; *s* of James Howard and Helen Mary Barwell; *m* 1968, Christine Sarah Carter; one *s*. *Educ*: Lancing College; Trinity College, Oxford; Institut des Hautes Etudes Internationales, Geneva. FCO, 1965; served: Aden, 1967; Baghdad, 1968; Bahrain, 1971; Cairo, 1973; FCO, 1976; Nicosia, 1982; Paris, 1985; FCO, 1989–93; Consultant, Control Risks Gp, 1994–2002; FCO Regl Advr, Central Africa, 2002–03; Dir, Coalition Provisional Authy, Baghdad, 2003. Mem., Methodology Soc., 2002–. Trustee, Kidnap Victim Support, 2002–07. *Recreations*: gardening, singing. *Club*: Athenæum.

BARWICK, Brian Robert; Chief Executive, Football Association, 2005–08; *b* 21 June 1954; *s* of John Leonard Barwick and Jean Ellen Barwick; *m* 1982, Geraldine Lynch; two *s*. *Educ*: Rudston Rd Co. Primary Sch.; Quarry Bank Comprehensive Sch.; Liverpool Univ. (BA Hons Econs). Journalist/sub-editor, North Western Evening Mail, Barrow-in-Furness, 1976–79; BBC Television (Sport): Asst Producer, 1979–84; Producer, Football Focus, 1982–84; Asst Ed., Grandstand, 1984–88; Editor: Match of the Day, 1988–95; Sportsnight, 1990–94; World Cup coverage, 1990 and 1994; Olympics, 1992 and 1996; Sports Rev. of the Year, 1991–95; Hd, Sport (Prodn), 1995–97; Controller, ITV Sport, 1998–2004; Dir of Programming, ITV2, 1998–2001. *Publication*: (with G. Sinstadt) The Great Derbies: Everton *v* Liverpool, 1988. *Recreations*: watching sport, football, boxing and cricket; British TV comedy, sports and comedy memorabilia collecting, contemporary music, holidaying with family.

BARWISE, Stephanie Nicola, (Mrs N. P. O'Donohoe); QC 2006; *b* 17 Feb. 1964; *d* of Frank Barwise and Dorothy Carlyle Barwise (*née* Armstrong); *m* 2003, Nicholas Peter O'Donohoe; one *s* two *d*, and two step *d*. *Educ*: Downing Coll., Cambridge (BA Law 1986; LLM 1987). Called to the Bar, Middle Temple, 1988; in practice as barrister, specialising in commercial and construction law, 1989–. *Recreations*: scuba-diving, ski-ing, dog sledding in Lapland, contortion (in the form of pilates). *Address*: 1 Atkin Building, Gray's Inn, WC1R 5AT. *Clubs*: Leander (Henley-on-Thames); Ospreys (Cambridge).

BARWISE, Prof. (Thomas) Patrick, PhD; Professor of Management and Marketing, London Business School, 1990–2007, now Emeritus; *b* 26 June 1946; *s* of (Henry) Balfour and Lily Barwise (*née* Abeles); *m* 1973, Mary Campbell (separated 2002); one *s* one *d*; partner, Dr Catherine Horwood (*née* Galitzine). *Educ*: Lincoln Coll., Oxford (Old Members' Scholar; BA Engrg Sci. with Econs 1968; MA 1973); London Business Sch. (MSc with Dist. Business Studies 1973; PhD 1985). Systems Engr, IBM, 1968–71; Asst to Chief Exec., Austin-Hall Gp, 1973–74; Mktg Manager, Graphic Systems Internat., 1974–76; London Business School: Sen. Res. Officer, 1976–82; Lectr, then Sen. Lectr in Mktg, 1982–90. Mem. Council, Consumers' Assoc., 1995–2000, 2006– (Dep. Chm., 1998–2000); conducted mktg audit for Nat. Audit Office of award of Nat. Lottery to Camelot, 1995; Chm., task force on commercial activities in schs (for Consumers' Assoc. and ISBA), 2000–01; led indep. review of BBC digital television services, DCMS, 2004; Advr, Ofcom, 2004–. Mem., Hansard Soc. Commn on Parlt and the Public, 2004–05. Fellow: Sunningdale Inst., 2005–; Marketing Soc., 2006–. *Publications*: Online Searching, 1979; Managing Strategic Investment Decisions, 1988; Television and its Audience, 1988; Accounting for Brands, 1989; Children, Advertising and Nutrition, 1994; Strategic Decisions, 1997; Predictions: Media, 1998; Advertising in a Recession, 1999; Market Metrics: what should we tell the shareholders?, 2001; Marketing and the Internet, 2002; Marketing Expenditure Trends, 2002, 2nd edn 2003; Simply Better, 2004 (Berry-AMA Prize, 2005); (with S. Meehan) Customer Insights That Matter, 2009; contrib. numerous articles to Jl Mktg, Jl Consumer Res., Mktg Sci., Harvard Business Rev., etc. *Recreation*: talking. *Address*: London Business School, Regent's Park, NW1 4SA.

BARYSHNIKOV, Mikhail; dancer, actor, producer; Co-Founder (with Mark Morris) and Director, White Oak Dance Project, 1990–2002; *b* 27 Jan. 1948; *s* of Nicolai Baryshnikov and Alexandra (*née* Kisselov). *Educ*: Ballet Sch. of Riga, Latvia; Kirov Ballet Sch., Leningrad. Soloist, Kirov Ballet Co., 1969–74; Principal Dancer, NY City Ballet, 1978–79; Artistic Dir, 1980–89, Principal Dancer, 1974–78 and 1980–89, American Ballet Theater. Guest Artist, 1974–, with: Royal Ballet; National Ballet of Canada; Hamburg Ballet; Ballet Victoria, Aust.; Stuttgart Ballet; Alvin Ailey Dance Co., and Eliot Feld Ballet, New York; Spoleto Festival. Repertoire includes: Shadowplay (Tudor); Le Jeune Homme et la Morte (Petit); Sacré du Printemps (Tetley); Prodigal Son, Apollo, Theme and Variations (Balanchine); Afternoon of a Faun (Robbins); Romeo and Juliet, Wild Boy (MacMillan); Configurations (Choo San Goh); Les Patineurs, A Month in the Country (Ashton); Spectre de la Rose, Le Pavillon d'Armide, Petrouchka (Fokine); Santa Fe Saga (Feld); La Sylphide, La Bayadère, Coppélia, La Fille mal gardée (Bournonville); Swan Lake (Sergeyev and Bruhn); The Nutcracker, Don Quixote (own choreography). Works created: Medea (Butler), 1975; Push Comes to Shove, and, Once More Frank (Tharp), Connotations on Hamlet (Neumeier), Pas de Duke (Ailey), Other Dances (Robbins), 1976; Variations on America (Feld), 1977; Rubies (Balanchine), Opus Nineteen (Robbins), 1979; Rhapsody (Ashton), 1980. Over 50 works commissioned by White Oak Dance Project and Baryshnikov Dance Foundn including: Waiting for the Sunrise (Lubovitch); Three Preludes (Morris); Punch and Judy (Gordon); Pergolesi (Tharp); Unspoken Territory (Reitz); Journey of a Poet (Hawkins); Heartbeat:mb (Janney and Rudner); Blue Heron (Schlömer); The Good Army (O'Day); Piano Bar (Béjart); See Through Knot (Jasperse); Single Duet (Hay); Chacony (Childs); The Show/Achilles Heels (Move); Yazoo (Feld). Gold Medal: Varna Competition, Bulgaria, 1966; 1st Internat. Ballet Comp., Moscow, 1968 (also awarded Nijinsky Prize by Paris Acad. of Dance); Dance Magazine Award, NYC, 1978; Kennedy Center Honors, 2000; Nat. Medal of Arts, 2000; Nijinsky Award for choreographic work Past Forward, 2002; Chubb Fellowship Award, Yale Univ., 2003; Liberty Prize, 2004; Jerome Robbins Award, 2004; Nixon Center Award, 2004; Arison Award, 2005. *Films*: The Turning Point, 1978; White Nights, 1986; Dancers, 1987; Company Business, 1991; The Cabinet of Dr Ramirez, 1991. *Television*: Sex in the City, 2004. *Publications*: (with Charles Engell France,

photographs by Martha Swope) Baryshnikov at Work, 1976; (with John Fraser, photographs by Eve Arnold) Private View: inside Baryshnikov's American Ballet Theatre, 1988; Baryshnikov in Black and White, 2002. *Recreations*: fishing, golf, photography.

BARZUN, Jacques; University Professor Emeritus, Columbia University; *b* 30 Nov. 1907; *s* of Henri Barzun and Anna-Rose Martin; *m* 1936, Mariana Lowell (*d* 1979); two *s* one *d*; *m* 1980, Marguerite Davenport. *Educ*: Lycée Janson de Sailly; Columbia Univ. Instructor in History, Columbia Univ., 1929; Research Fellow, American Council of Learned Socs, 1933–34; Columbia University: Asst Prof., 1938; Associate Prof., 1942; Prof. of History, 1945–75; University Prof., 1967; Dean of Grad. Faculties, 1955–58; Dean of Faculties and Provost, 1958–67. Dir Emeritus, Council for Basic Educn; Dir, NY Soc. Library; Mem. Adv. Council, Univ. Coll. at Buckingham. Membre Associé de l'Académie Delphinale, Grenoble, 1952; Member: Amer. Acad. of Arts and Letters, USA (President, 1972–75, 1977–79); Amer. Acad. of Arts and Sciences; American Historical Assoc.; Amer. Philos. Soc.; FRSA, USA (Benjamin Franklin Fellow); FRSL. Seth Low Prof. of History, Columbia Univ., 1960; Extraordinary Fellow, Churchill Coll., Cambridge, 1961–. Literary Advisor, Charles Scribner's Sons Ltd, 1975–93; Mem. Bd of Editors, Encyclopaedia Britannica, 1962–. Chevalier de la Légion d'Honneur. *Publications*: The French Race: Theories of its Origins, 1932; Race: A Study in Superstition, 1937 (revd, 1965); Of Human Freedom, 1939 (revd, 1964); Darwin, Marx, Wagner, 1941 (revd, 1958); Teacher in America, 1945 (revd, 1981); Berlioz and the Romantic Century, 1950, 4th edn 1982; Pleasures of Music, 1951, rev. edn 1977; Selected Letters of Byron, 1953, 2nd edn 1957; Nouvelles Lettres de Berlioz, 1954, 2nd edn 1974; God's Country and Mine, 1954; Music in American Life, 1956; The Energies of Art, 1956; The Modern Researcher (with Henry F. Graff), 1957, 5th edn 1993; The House of Intellect, 1959, 2nd edn 1961; Classic, Romantic and Modern, 1961; Science: The Glorious Entertainment, 1964; (ed) Follett's Modern American Usage, 1967; The American University, 1968, 3rd edn 1992; (with W. H. Taylor) A Catalogue of Crime, 1971, rev. edn 1989; On Writing, Editing and Publishing, 1971; Berlioz's Evenings with the Orchestra, 1956, 2nd edn 1973; The Use and Abuse of Art, 1974; Clio and the Doctors, 1974; Simple and Direct, 1975; Critical Questions, 1982; A Stroll with William James, 1983; A Word Or Two Before You Go, 1986; The Culture We Deserve, 1989; Begin Here, 1991; An Essay on French Verse for Readers of English Poetry, 1991; From Dawn to Decadence, 2001; What is a School?, 2002; A Jacques Barzun Reader, 2002; contrib. to leading US journals. *Address*: 18 Wolfeton Way, San Antonio, TX 78218–6045, USA. *Club*: Century (New York).

BASBAUM, Prof. Allan Irwin, PhD; FRS 2006; Professor, since 1984, and Chairman, Department of Anatomy, since 1977, University of California, San Francisco. *Educ*: McGill Univ. (BS 1968); Univ. of Penn (PhD 1972). Postdoctoral research: in neurophysiol., UCL, 1972–74; in neuroanatomy, UCSF, 1974–76; Associate Prof., Depts of Anatomy and of Physiol., UCSF, 1980–84. Co-founder and Mem., Scientific Adv. Bd, BiPar Sciences Inc. Chm., French American Internat. Sch. (Mem. Bd, 1988–; Pres., until 2004). FMedSci 2007. *Publications*: articles in jls. *Address*: Department of Anatomy, University of California, 1550 4th Street, Rock Hall, San Francisco, CA 94143, USA.

BĂSESCU, Traian; President of Romania, since 2004; *b* 4 Nov. 1951; *s* of Dimitru and Elena Traian; *m* 1975, Maria; two *d*. *Educ*: Mircea cel Bătrân Naval Inst. (grad 1976); Norwegian Acad. (schol.); advanced courses Mgt in Shipping Ind. 1995). Naval Officer, NAVROM, 1976–81; Captain, Comdr, Arges, Crisana and Biruinta ships, 1981–87; Chief, NAVROM Agency, Belgium, 1987–89; Gen. Manager, State Inspectorate for Civil Navigation, 1989–90, Under-Sec. of State and Chief, Shipping Dept, 1990–91, Min. of Transportation; Minister of Transportation, 1991–92; Deputy (Democratic), Vaslui, 1992–96; Minister of Transportation, 1996–2000; Mayor of Bucharest, 2000–04. Democratic Party (PD): Bucharest Orgn, 2000–01; Pres., 2001–04; Co-Pres., DA (Justice and Truth) Alliance, 2001–04. Hon. Dr Pol Scis Hankuk, Seoul, 2005; Hon. Dr Diplomatic and Strategic Centre of Studies, Paris, 2005. Comdr, Nat. Order of Merit (Romania), 2000; Medal of Renaissance, 1st Cl. (Jordan), 2005. *Recreations*: spending time with my family, taking long walks in nature. *Address*: Cotroceni Palace, Cotroceni Boulevard No 1, Sector 1, Bucharest, Romania. *T*: 213121159, 214306195, *Fax*: 214113131, 214139303; *e-mail*: procetatean@presidency.ro.

BASHAM, Brian Arthur; *b* 30 July 1943; *s* of late Arthur Edgar Basham and Gladys Florence Alice (*née* Turner); *m* 1st, 1968, Charlotte Blackman; two *d*; 2nd, 1988, Eileen Wise (marr. diss. 1996); 3rd, 1998, Lynne Goodson. *Educ*: Brownhill Road Primary Sch., Catford; Catford Secondary Sch. GEC Export Clerk, 1961; Daily Mail City Office: Stock Exchange prices collector, 1962; City Press reporter, then chief sub-editor, 1963; Prodn Editor, Daily Mail City Page, 1964; Financial Journalist: Daily Telegraph, 1966; The Times, 1968; Fund Man., Regent Fund Managers, 1971; Associate Dir, John Addey Associates, 1973; Founder, 1976, subseq. Dep. Chm., Broad Street Gp; Co-Founder and Dep. Chm., Primrose Care, 1993–98; Chairman: Intershare, 1995–; Equity Development, 2006–; G-PAP, 2006–. *Publication*: (with Craig Pickering) Tomorrow's Giants, 1998. *Recreations*: politics, reading, constitutional reform, motorcycling, gardening, walking. *Address*: 14 Elsworthy Rise, NW3 3SH. *T*: (office) (020) 7405 7777.

BASHIR, Prof. Marie Roslyn, AC 2001 (AO 1988); CVO 2005; FRANZCP; Governor of New South Wales, Australia, since 2001; *d* of M. Bashir; *m* 1957, Sir Nicholas Michael Shehadie, *qv*; one *s* two *d*. *Educ*: Sydney Girls' High Sch.; Univ. of Sydney (MB, BS 1956). Taught at Univs of Sydney and of NSW; Clinical Prof. of Psychiatry, Univ. of Sydney, 1993–2001; Area Dir, Mental Health Services, Central Sydney, 1994–2001; Sen. Consultant, Aboriginal Med. Services, Redfern and Kempsey, 1996–2001. Chancellor, Univ. of Sydney, 2007–. *Address*: (office) Macquarie Street, Sydney, NSW 2000, Australia.

BASHMET, Yuri Abramovich; viola player; Principal Conductor, Symphony Orchestra of New Russia, since 2002; *b* 24 Jan. 1953; *m* Natalia Timofeevna; one *s* one *d*. *Educ*: Moscow State Conservatory. Winner, Munich International Viola Competition, 1976; Founder and Dir, Chamber Orchestra Moscow Soloists, 1989–; Artistic Dir, Sviatoslav Richter's December Nights Fest., Moscow. Has performed with the world's major orchestras including: Berlin Philharmonic; Boston Symphony; Concertgebouw; LSO; Los Angeles Philharmonic; Montreal Symphony; first performance of viola concerti by Alfred Schnittke, Aleksander Tchaikovsky, Poul Ruders, Sofia Gubaidulina, Mark-Anthony Turnage, Giya Kancheli and Alexander Raskatov. Founder, Yuri Bashmet Internat. Foundn, 1994. *Address*: c/o Van Walsum Management, The Tower Building, 11 York Road, SE1 7NX. *T*: (020) 7902 0520; Apartment 16, Nezhdanovoy str. 7, 103009, Moscow, Russia.

BASIL OF AMPHIPOLIS, Bishop; *see* Amphipolis, Bishop of.

BASING, 6th Baron *cr* 1887; **Stuart Anthony Whitfield Sclater-Booth;** *b* 18 Dec. 1969; *s* of 5th Baron Basing and of Patricia Ann, *d* of late George Bryan Whitfield, New Haven, Conn; *S* father, 2007; *m* 1997, Kirsten Erica, *d* of Eric Henry Oxboel; two *s* one *d*. *Educ*: Collegiate Sch.; Vassar Coll.; Boston Univ. (MA). *Heir*: *s* Hon. Luke Waters Sclater-Booth, *b* 1 Sept. 2000.

BASINGSTOKE, Bishop Suffragan of, since 2002; **Rt Rev. Trevor Willmott;** *b* 29 March 1950; *s* of Frederick and Phyllis Willmott; *m* 1973, Margaret Anne Hawkins; one *d*. *Educ:* St Peter's Coll., Oxford (MA); Fitzwilliam Coll., Cambridge (DipTh); Westcott House, Cambridge. Ordained deacon, 1974, priest, 1975; Asst Curate, St George's, Norton, 1974–78; Asst Chaplain, Oslo with Trondheim, 1978–79; Chaplain of Naples with Capri, Bari and Sorrento, 1979–83; Rector of Ecton, 1983–89; Diocesan Dir of Ordinands and Post Ordination Training, Peterborough, 1986–97; Canon Residentiary of Peterborough Cathedral, 1989–97; Archdeacon of Durham, 1997–2002. *Recreations:* travel, cooking, the appreciation of good wine, sport, music. *Address:* Bishopswood End, 40 Kingswood Rise, Four Marks, Alton, Hants GU34 5BD. *T:* (01420) 562925, *Fax:* (01420) 561251; *e-mail:* trevor.willmott@dial.pipex.com.

BASKER, Prof. Robin Michael, OBE 2001; DDS; Professor of Dental Prosthetics, University of Leeds, 1978–2000, now Emeritus; Consultant in Restorative Dentistry, United Leeds Teaching Hospitals NHS Trust (formerly Leeds Western Health Authority), 1978–2000; *b* 26 Dec. 1936; *s* of Caryl Ashbourne Basker and Edna Crowden (*née* Russell); *m* 1961, Jacqueline Mary Bowles; two *d*. *Educ:* Wellingborough Sch.; London Hosp. Med. Coll., Univ. of London (BDS 1961); Birmingham Univ. (DDS 1969). LDSRCS 1961, MGDSRCS 1979. General dental practice, 1961–63; Lectr and Sen. Lectr, Univ. of Birmingham, 1963–78; Leeds University: Dean, Sch. of Dentistry, 1985–90; Chm., Bd of Faculty of Medicine and Dentistry, 1990–93. Hon. Scientific Advr, British Dental Jl, 1980–96; British Standards Expert Advr, ISO TC/106, 1982–2005. Mem., Nuffield Foundn Inquiry into trng and educn of personnel auxiliary to dentistry, 1992–93. Member: Dental Cttee, Med. Defence Union, 1985–95; GDC, 1986–99 (Treas., 1992–94; Chm., Registration Sub-Cttee, 1994; Chm., Educn Cttee, 1994–99); President: British Soc. for Study of Prosthetic Dentistry, 1988 (Mem. Council and Sec., 1978–81); Yorks Br., BDA, 1991–92; British Soc. of Gerodontology, 1999; Chm., Lindsay Soc. for the History of Dentistry, 2008. Ext. Examr in Dental Subjects, Univs of Birmingham, Bristol, Dundee, London, Manchester, Malaya, Newcastle upon Tyne, Sheffield, Wales, UC, Cork and Univ. Kebangsaan, Malaysia; Examr for Membership of Gen. Dental Surgery, RCS, 1979–84 (Chm. Examrs, 1987–92). Life Mem., British Soc. of Gerodontol., 2001; Hon. Mem., British Soc. for Study of Prosthetic Dentistry, 2001. FRSocMed; Hon. FDSRCSE 2000. John Tomes Medal, BDA, 2000. *Publications:* Prosthetic Treatment of the Edentulous Patient, 1976, 4th edn 2002; Overdentures in General Dental Practice, 1983, 3rd edn 1993; A Colour Atlas of Removable Partial Dentures, 1987; Clinical Guide to Removable Partial Dentures, 2000; Clinical Guide to Removable Partial Denture Design, 2000. *Recreations:* choral singing, guiding people around Fountains Abbey.

BASS; *see* Hastings Bass, family name of Earl of Huntingdon.

BASS, Bryan Geoffrey; Headmaster, City of London School, 1990–95; *b* 23 March 1934; *s* of Leslie Horace Bass and Mary Joyce Light; *m* 1956, Cecilia Manning; one *s* two *d*. *Educ:* Wells Cathedral School; Christ Church, Oxford (BA Hons English 1956; MA 1983). Teacher, Manchester Grammar School; Headmaster, Hymers College, Hull, 1983–90. Mem., NE London Educn Assoc., 1995–96. *Recreations:* making music, cooking with friends. *Address:* 32 Newland Park, Hull HU5 2DW.

BASS, Rear-Adm. Paul Eric, CB 1981; CEng, FIMechE, MIMarEST; *b* 7 March 1925; *s* of C. H. P. Bass, Ipswich; *m* 1948, Audrey Bruce Tomlinson (*d* 2002); one *s*. *Educ:* Northgate School, Ipswich; Royal Naval Engineering Coll., Keyham. Served as Midshipman in HM Ships Cambrian, Mauritius, Premier and Rodney; Lieut in Belfast, Phoebe and Implacable; Lt Comdr in Ulysses; Comdr in Lion and Tiger; Naval Staff Course, 1962; Captain, Weapons Trials, 1969–72; NATO Defense Course, 1972–73; Asst Chief of Staff (Intelligence), SACLANT, 1973–75; Dir, Naval Manning and Training (Engineering), 1975–78; Flag Officer, Portsmouth and Port Admiral, Portsmouth, 1979–81, retired 1981. *Recreation:* sailing. *Clubs:* Royal Yacht Squadron; Royal Naval Sailing Association; Royal Naval and Royal Albert Yacht (Portsmouth).

BASSAM OF BRIGHTON, Baron *cr* 1997 (Life Peer), of Brighton in the co. of East Sussex; **John Steven Bassam;** Captain of the Honourable Corps of Gentlemen at Arms (Government Chief Whip in the House of Lords), since 2008 (a Lord in Waiting (Government Whip), 2001–08); *b* 11 June 1953; *s* of late Sydney Stevens and Enid Bassam; partner, Jill Whittaker; one *s* two *d* (and one *s* decd). *Educ:* Univ. of Sussex (BA Hons History 1975; Hon. Fellow, 2001); Univ. of Kent (MA Social Work 1979). Social Worker, E Sussex CC, 1976–77; Legal Advr, N Lewisham Law Centre, 1979–83; Policy Adviser: LB Camden, 1983–84; GLC (Police Cttee), 1984–86; London Strategic Policy Unit (Policing), 1986–87; Asst Sec., Police, Fire, Envmntl Health and Consumer Affairs, AMA, 1988–97; Consultant Advr, KPMG, 1997–99. Parly Under-Sec. of State, Home Office, 1999–2001. Member (Lab): Brighton BC, 1983–97 (Leader, 1987–97); Brighton & Hove Unitary Council, 1996–99 (Leader, 1996–99). Fellow, Brighton Coll., 2002–. *Publications:* articles for local govt pubns. *Recreations:* cricket (plays for Preston Village CC), walking, running, watching football, reading, history of churches. *Address:* Longstone, 25 Church Place, Brighton BN2 5JN. *T:* (01273) 609473.

BASSET, Bryan Ronald, CBE 1988; Chairman, Royal Ordnance plc, 1985–87; *b* 29 Oct. 1932; *s* of late Ronald Lambart Basset and Lady Elizabeth Basset, DCVO; *m* 1960, Lady Carey Elizabeth Coke, *d* of 5th Earl of Leicester; three *s*. *Educ:* Eton; RMA Sandhurst. Captain, Scots Guards, 1952–57. Stockbroker, Toronto, Canada, 1957–59; Panmure Gordon & Co., Stockbrokers, 1959–72; Managing Director, Philip Hill Investment Trust, 1972–85. *Recreations:* shooting, fishing. *Address:* Quarles, Wells-next-the-Sea, Norfolk NR23 1RY. *T:* (01328) 738105. *Club:* White's.

BASSETT, Douglas Anthony; Director, National Museum of Wales, 1977–86, now Senior Research Fellow; *b* 11 Aug. 1927; *s* of Hugh Bassett and Annie Jane Bassett; *m* 1955, Elizabeth Menna Roberts; three *d*. *Educ:* Llanelli Boys' Grammar Sch.; University Coll. of Wales, Aberystwyth. Asst Lectr and Lectr, Dept of Geology, Glasgow Univ., 1952–59; Keeper, Dept of Geology, Nat. Museum of Wales, 1959–77. Member: Water Resources Bd, 1965–73 (Chm., Adv. Cttee for Wales, 1967–73); Nature Conservancy Council (and Chm., Adv. Cttee for Wales), 1973–85; Secretary of State for Wales' Celtic Sea Adv. Cttee, 1974–79; Ordnance Survey Rev. Cttee, 1978–79; Adv. Cttee for Wales, British Council, 1983–90; Founder Mem. and first Chm., Assoc. of Teachers of Geology, 1967–68; Chm., Royal Soc. Cttee on History of Geology, 1972–82. Dir, Nat. Welsh-American Foundn, 1980– (Vice-Pres., 1996–99). Prince of Wales' Cttee, 1977–86. Hon. Professorial Fellow, University Coll., Cardiff, 1977. Editor: Nature in Wales, 1982–87; Manual of Curatorship, Museums Assoc., 1983–. Aberconway Medal, Instn of Geologists, 1985; Silver Medal, Czechoslavakian Soc. for Internat. Relns, 1985. Mem. White Order of Bards of GB, 1979; Officier de l'Ordre des Arts et des Lettres (received from Min. of Culture, Paris), 1983; American Order of Ivorites Award, 2007. *Publications:* Bibliography and Index of Geology and Allied Sciences for Wales and the Welsh Borders, 1897–1958, 1961; A Source-book of Geological, Geomorphological and Soil Maps for Wales and the Welsh Borders (1800–1966), 1967; Wales in Miniature, 1993; contribs to various geological, museum and historical jls and to biographical dictionaries. *Recreations:* bibliography, chronology. *Address:* 4 Romilly Road, Cardiff CF5 1FH.

BASSETT, John Anthony Seward, FRICS; Consultant, Jones Lang LaSalle (formerly Jones, Lang, Wootton), since 1997 (Senior Partner, 1991–97); *b* 8 Sept. 1936; *s* of Roger Seward and Marjorie Bassett; *m* 1st, 1960, Jean Margaret Cooper (marr. diss. 1993); one *s* one *d*; 2nd, 1994, Jennifer David (marr. diss. 2003). *Educ:* Blundell's Sch.; Coll. of Estate Management, London Univ. FRICS 1972. Joined Folkard & Hayward, 1957; Donaldson & Sons, 1960–63; joined Jones, Lang, Wootton, 1963, Partner 1967–97. Chairman: MWB Leisure Funds, 1996–2003; X-Leisure (Gen. Partner) Ltd, 2004–. Hon. Treas., Westminster Property Owners' Assoc., 1989–98. Trustee, Chatham Historic Dockyard Trust, 1997–. *Recreations:* ocean racing, ski-ing, travel, fly fishing. *Address:* 6 Ranelagh Grove, SW1W 8PD. *Clubs:* Pilgrims; Royal Thames Yacht, Royal Ocean Racing.

BASSETT, Nigel F.; *see* Fox Bassett.

BASSETT CROSS, Alistair Robert Sinclair; District Judge, Principal Registry, Family Division, High Court of Justice, since 1991; *b* 25 Aug. 1944; *s* of late Edward Bassett Cross and Marguerite Sinclair Bassett Cross (*née* Mitchell); *m* 1977, Margaret Victoria Janes; one *s* one *d*. *Educ:* Bishop Challoner Sch., Shortlands; Coll. of Law, Lancaster Gate. FInstLEx 1971. Legal Exec. with Lawrence Graham, 1964–77; solicitor, 1980; Legal Exec. and Solicitor, Payne Hicks Beach, 1977–91 (Partner, 1988–91); Dep. County Court and Dist Registrar, 1990. Mem., Solicitors' Family Law Assoc., 1984; Mem., Family Mediators' Assoc., 1989; Accredited Family Mediator, 1990; Mem., Adv. Bd of Mediation Service, Inst. of Family Therapy, 1995–98; Trustee, Mediation for Families (London E and City), 1999–2001. HAC, 1965, commnd, 1969; Mem., Co. of Pikemen and Musketeers, Lord Mayor's Bodyguard, 1993 (Elder Serjeant, 2003–06). Freeman, City of London, 1993; Liveryman, Poulters' Co., 1996. *Publications:* (ed) Supreme Court Practice, 1994–99; Civil Procedure, 2000–06; (ed) The Family Court Practice, 2004–06. *Recreations:* family, anything and everything. *Address:* Principal Registry (Family Division), First Avenue House, 42–49 High Holborn, WC1V 6NP. *Club:* Naval and Military.

BASSEY, Dame Shirley (Veronica), DBE 2000 (CBE 1994); singer; *b* Tiger Bay, Cardiff, 8 Jan. 1937; *d* of late Henry and Eliza Jane Bassey; one *d*; *m* 1st, 1961, Kenneth Hume (marr. diss. 1965; decd); 2nd, 1971, Sergio Novak (marr. diss. 1981); one adopted *s* (one *d* decd). Appeared in Such is Life, 1955; *recordings* include: *singles:* Burn My Candle; Banana Boat Song, 1957; As I Love You, 1959; Kiss Me Honey; Reach for the Stars/ Climb Every Mountain, 1961; What Now My Love; I Am What I Am; I (Who Have Nothing); Goldfinger, 1964; Diamonds Are Forever, 1971; Something; For All We Know; Never Never Never; Moonraker, 1979; *albums:* Born to Sing the Blues, 1958; And I Love You So, 1972; Live at Carnegie Hall, 1973; Magic Is You, 1978; Sassy Bassey, 1985; La Mujer, 1989; New York, New York, 1991; Great Shirley Bassey, 1999; numerous concerts and tours; series, BBC TV; appeared in film, La Passione, 1996. Artist for Peace, UNESCO, 2000; Internat. Ambassador, Variety Club, 2001. Britannia Award for Best Female Singer, 1977; Lifetime Achievement Award, Nat. Music Awards, 2003. Légion d'Honneur (France), 2003. *Address:* c/o Victoria Settepassi, 31 Avenue Princess Grace, MC 98000, Monaco.

BASSINGTHWAIGHTE, His Honour Keith; a Circuit Judge, 1991–2003; Resident Judge, Guildford Crown Court Centre, 2000–03; a Deputy Circuit Judge, 2003–05; *b* 19 Jan. 1943; *s* of Reginald and Barbara Bassingthwaighte; *m* 1966, Olwyn Burn. *Educ:* Ashford (Middx) County Grammar Sch. Admitted solicitor, 1967. Served RAF Legal Branch as Flt Lt, 1968, Sqdn Ldr 1973, Wing Comdr 1978 and Gp Capt. 1981; retired 1984. Chm., Industrial Tribunals (London Central and S regions), part-time 1984–85, full-time 1985–91; a Recorder of the Crown Court, 1987–91. Pres., Social Security Appeal, Medical Appeal, Disability Appeal, Child Support Appeal and Vaccine Damage Tribunals, 1994–98; a Judge, Employment Appeal Tribunal, 1996. Mem., Parole Bd, 2004–. *Recreations:* golf, tennis, scuba diving, bridge, opera. *Address:* c/o Barclays Bank, Sloane Square, SW1W 8AF. *Clubs:* Royal Air Force; Worplesdon Golf (Woking); Tiverton Golf.

BASSNETT, Prof. Susan Edna, PhD; FRSL; writer; Professor of Comparative Literature, since 1992, Pro-Vice-Chancellor, 1997–2003 and since 2005, University of Warwick; *b* 21 Oct. 1945; *d* of Raymond George Bassnett and Anne Eileen Bassnett (*née* Hardwick); one *s* three *d*. *Educ:* Denmark, Portugal, Italy and UK; Univ. of Manchester (BA 1st Cl. Hons English and Italian 1968); Univ. of Lancaster (PhD French 1975). Lecturer: Univ. of Rome, 1968–72; Univ. of Lancaster, 1972–76; Univ. of Warwick, 1976–: estabd Centre for Translation and Comparative Cultural Studies, 1985; Reader, 1989–92. Has held Vis. Prof. posts at univs worldwide; Vis. Lectr, Michigan State Univ., 1974–75. Member: Arts Adv. Bd, British Council, 2002–06; W Midlands Culture, 2002–; Arts Council England, W Midlands, 2003–; QAA, 2003–. Mem. Bd, SOAS, 2003–. FCIL (FIL 2000); MAE 2006. *Publications:* Translation Studies, 1980, 3rd edn 2002; Luigi Pirandello, 1983; Sylvia Plath: an introduction to the poetry, 1987, 2nd edn 2004; (jtly) The Actress in Her Time: Bernhardt, Terry, Duse, 1988; Magdalena: women's experimental theatre, 1989; (ed) Knives and Angels: Latin American women's writing, 1990; Shakespeare: the Elizabethan plays, 1993; Comparative Literature: a critical introduction, 1993; (jtly) Three Tragic Actresses: Siddons, Rachel, Ristori, 1996; (with A. Lefevere) Constructing Cultures, 1998; (ed with H. Trivedi) Postcolonial Translation: theory and practice, 1999; Exchanging Lives, 2002; (ed with P. Bush) The Translator as Writer, 2006. *Recreations:* reading, walking with dogs, textiles, writing. *Address:* Centre for Translation and Comparative Cultural Studies, University of Warwick, Coventry CV4 7AL. *T:* (024) 7652 3655; *e-mail:* s.bassnett@warwick.ac.uk.

BASTIN, Prof. John Andrew, MA, PhD; FRAS; Professor, 1971–84, now Emeritus, and Head of Department of Physics, 1975–80, Queen Mary College, London University; *b* 3 Jan. 1929; *s* of Lucy and Arthur Bastin; *m*; one *s* one *d*; *m* 1985, Aida Baterina Delfino. *Educ:* George Monoux Grammar Sch., London; Corpus Christi Coll., Oxford (MA, PhD). Univ. of Ibadan, Nigeria, 1952–56; Univ. of Reading, 1956–59; Queen Mary Coll., Univ. of London, 1959–84. Initiated a group in far infrared astronomy at Queen Mary College, 1960–70. *Publications:* papers on far infrared astronomy and lunar evolution. *Recreations:* English water colours, architecture, Renaissance and Baroque music. *Address:* 5 The Clockhouse, Redlynch Park, Bruton, Somerset BA10 0NH.

BASTON, Ven. Caroline; Archdeacon of the Isle of Wight, since 2006; *b* 17 Oct. 1956; *d* of Dr John Baston, MB ChB, DPM, FRCGP and Dr Daphne Baston, MB ChB, MRCGP. *Educ:* Birmingham Univ. (BSc 1978); Birmingham Poly. (Cert Ed 1979); Ripon Coll., Cuddesdon. Teacher, Shireland High Sch., Smethwick, 1979–87. Ordained deacon, 1989, priest, 1994; Asst Curate, Thornhill St Christopher, Southampton, 1989–95; Rector, All Saints', Winchester, with St Andrew, Chilcomb, with St Peter, Chesil, 1995–2006; Communications Officer, 1995–98, Dir of Ordinands, 1999–2006, Dio. Winchester. Hon. Canon, Winchester Cathedral, 2000–06, Canon Emeritus, 2006–. *Address:* 5 The Boltons, Kite Hill, Wootton Bridge, Isle of Wight PO33 4PB. *T:* (01983) 884432; *e-mail:* adiow@portsmouth.anglican.org.

BATCHELOR, Prof. (John) Richard; Professor of Immunology, Royal Postgraduate Medical School, Hammersmith Hospital, 1979–94, now Professor Emeritus; *b* 4 Oct. 1931; *s* of B. W. Batchelor, CBE and Mrs C. E. Batchelor; *m* 1955, Moira Ann (*née* McLellan); two *s* two *d*. *Educ:* Marlborough Coll.; Emmanuel Coll., Cambridge; Guy's Hospital, London. MB, BChir Cantab, 1955; MD Cantab 1965. FRCPath 1991; FRCP 1995. Nat. Service, RAMC, 1957–59; Dept of Pathology, Guy's Hospital: Res. Fellow, 1959–61; Lectr and Sen. Lectr, 1961–67; Prof. of Transplantation Research, RCS, 1967; Dir, McIndoe Res. Unit, Queen Victoria Hosp., East Grinstead, 1967–78. European Editor, Transplantation, 1964–97. Pres., Transplantation Soc., 1988–90 (Hon. Sec., then Vice-Pres. (E Hemisphere), 1976–80); Member Council, Nat. Kidney Res. Fund, 1979–86; Chm., Scientific Co-ord. Cttee, Arthritis and Rheumatism Council, 1988–96. Trustee: Kennedy Inst. for Rheumatology Trust, 1997– (Dep. Chm., 1997–); Sir Jules Thorn Charitable Trust, 1999–2004. MRSocMed. Mem. Court, Skinners' Company. Hon. Fellow, Faculty of Medicine, Imperial Coll. London, 2002. *Publications:* scientific articles upon tissue transplantation research in various special jls. *Recreations:* tennis, walking. *Address:* Little Ambrook, Nursery Road, Walton-on-the-Hill, Tadworth, Surrey KT20 7TU. *T:* (01737) 812028. *Club:* Queen's.

BATE, Prof. (Andrew) Jonathan, CBE 2006; PhD; FBA 1999; FRSL; Professor of Shakespeare and Renaissance Literature, University of Warwick, since 2003; *b* 26 June 1958; *s* of Ronald Montagu Bate and Sylvia Helen Bate; *m* 1st, 1984, Hilary Gaskin (marr. diss. 1995); 2nd, 1996, Paula Jayne Byrne; two *s* one *d*. *Educ:* Sevenoaks Sch., Kent; St Catharine's Coll., Cambridge (MA; PhD 1984; Hon. Fellow, 2000). Harkness Fellow, Harvard Univ., 1980–81; Research Fellow, St Catharine's Coll., Cambridge, 1983–85; Fellow, Trinity Hall, Cambridge and Lectr, Trinity Hall and Girton Coll., 1985–90; King Alfred Prof. of English Lit., Univ. of Liverpool, 1991–2003; Research Reader, British Acad., 1994–96; Leverhulme Personal Res. Prof., 1999–2004. Vis. Prof., UCLA, 1989, 1996. Mem., AHRC, 2007–. Gov., 2002–, Mem. Board, 2003–, RSC. FRSL 2004. *Publications:* Shakespeare and the English Romantic Imagination, 1986; (ed) Lamb, Essays of Elia, 1987; Shakespearean Constitutions, 1989; Romantic Ecology, 1991; (ed) The Romantics on Shakespeare, 1992; Shakespeare and Ovid, 1993; The Arden Shakespeare: Titus Andronicus, 1995; (ed) Shakespeare: an illustrated stage history, 1996; The Genius of Shakespeare, 1997; The Cure for Love (novel), 1998; The Song of the Earth, 2000; John Clare: a biography, 2003 (Hawthornden Prize, James Tait Black Meml Prize, 2004); (ed) I Am: the selected poetry of John Clare, 2003; (ed) The RSC Shakespeare: complete works, 2007; Soul of the Age: the life, mind and world of William Shakespeare, 2008. *Recreations:* gardening, fine art, opera, walking. *Address:* Department of English, University of Warwick, Coventry CV4 7AL. *T:* (024) 7652 3341.

BATE, Anthony John; His Honour Judge Bate; a Circuit Judge, since 2007; *b* Leamington Spa, 30 Nov. 1961; *er s* of Terence and Mary Bate; *m* 1988, Sally Trower; two *s*. *Educ:* Queen Elizabeth's Grammar Sch., Blackburn; Christ's Coll., Cambridge (BA 1983; VetMB 1986). MRCVS 1986. Called to the Bar, Lincoln's Inn (Denning Schol.), 1987; in practice as barrister specializing in criminal and common law, E Anglian Chambers, Norwich, 1988–2007; Mem., Regl Civil Panel of Counsel instructed by Treasury Solicitor, 2000–07; a Recorder, 2003–07. Trustee, Welfare Fund for Companion Animals, 1999–. *Recreations:* browsing second-hand bookshops, badminton, rambling, railway and military history. *Address:* c/o The Crown Court, 83 East Road, Cambridge CB1 1BT. *T:* (01223) 488321.

BATE, Prof. Christopher Michael, PhD; FRS 1997; Royal Society Professor of Developmental Neurobiology (formerly Professor of Developmental Neurobiology), since 1998, and Fellow of King's College, since 1992, University of Cambridge. *Educ:* Trinity Coll., Oxford (BA 1966); PhD Cantab 1976. Cambridge University: Lectr in Zoology, until 1994; Reader in Develtl Biol., 1994–98. *Address:* Department of Zoology, Downing Street, Cambridge CB2 3EJ. *T:* (01223) 336639, *Fax:* (01223) 336676; King's College, Cambridge CB2 1ST.

BATE, David Christopher; QC 1994; a Recorder, since 1991; *b* 2 May 1945; *s* of late Robert Leslie Bate and Brenda Mabel Bate (*née* Price); *m* 2003, Fiona Adele Graham; three *s* one *d* from previous marriage. *Educ:* Hendon Co. Grammar Sch.; Manchester Univ. (LLB Hons). Called to the Bar, Gray's Inn, 1969; VSO (UNA) with Melanesian Mission, 1969–70; Crown Counsel, British Solomon Is Protectorate, 1971. *Recreations:* swimming, cycling, trying to sing in tune with 'The Seven Deadly Sins'. *Address:* Hollis Whiteman Chambers, Queen Elizabeth Building, Temple, EC4Y 9BS. *T:* (020) 7583 5766.

BATE, Sir David (Lindsay), KBE 1978 (CBE 1968); Chief Judge, Benue and Plateau States of Nigeria, 1975–77; Senior Puisne Judge, High Court of Justice, Northern States of Nigeria, 1968–75 (Puisne Judge, 1957–68); *b* 3 March 1916; *m* 1948, Thadeen June, *d* of late R. F. O'Donnell Peet; two *s*. *Educ:* Marlborough; Trinity Coll., Cambridge. Called to Bar, Inner Temple, 1938. Commissioned, Royal Artillery, 1939 and served, Royal Artillery, 1939–46. Entered Colonial Legal Service, 1947; Crown Counsel, Nigeria, 1947–52; Senior Crown Counsel, Nigeria, 1952–54; Senior Crown Counsel, Northern Nigeria, 1954–56; Solicitor-Gen., Northern Nigeria, 1956. *Recreations:* shooting, fishing. *Address:* PO Box 1339, Howick 3290, Natal, South Africa.

BATE, Jennifer Lucy, OBE 2008; FRCO; classical concert organist, since 1969; composer, since 1972; *b* 11 Nov. 1944; *d* of Horace Alfred Bate and Dorothy Marjorie Alice Bate (*née* Hunt). *Educ:* Bristol Univ. (BA Hons 1966). ARCM 1961; LRAM 1963; FRCO 1967. Shaw Librarian, LSE, 1966–69. Vice-Pres., British Music Soc., 1996–. Vice-Pres., N London Fest., 2003. Has played in over 40 countries, incl. tours in S America, France and Italy; first organist to open a BBC Prom Concert with solo performance, 1974; world expert on organ works of Olivier Messiaen; has lectured worldwide, incl. A Guide to the King of Instruments (an educn prog. for all age gps); masterclasses and teaching projects for British Council; TV appearances and performances; has made numerous recordings, incl. world première recording of Messiaen's Livre du Saint Sacrement, 1987 (Grand Prix du Disque; Record of Year, Sunday Times; Pick of Year, Times), complete organ works of Mendelssohn, 2005, complete organ works of Peter Dickinson, 2008. FRSA 2002. Hon. DMus Bristol, 2007. Personnalité de l'Année (France), 1989; Award for Early Instrumental Music, Music Retailers' Assoc., 1991. *Compositions:* Toccata on a theme of Martin Shaw, 1972; Introduction and Variations on an old French Carol, 1979; Four Reflections: No 3 1981, No 2 1982, No 1 1986, No 4 1986; Homage to 1685, 1985; Lament, 1995; An English Canon, 1996; Variations on a Gregorian Theme, 1998; Four Handel-inspired Miniatures, 2007; Five Hymn-Tune Preludes, 2008. *Publication:* (contrib.) Grove's Dictionary of Music and Musicians, 6th edn 1974– (incl. New Grove's Dictionary of Music and Musicians, 1998–99). *Recreation:* gardening. *Address:* 35 Collingwood Avenue, Muswell Hill, N10 3EH. *T:* (020) 8883 3811, *Fax:* (020) 8444 3695; *e-mail:* jenniferbate@classical-artists.com.

BATE, Jonathan; see Bate, A. J.

BATELY, Prof. Janet Margaret, (Mrs L. J. Summers), CBE 2000; FBA 1990; Sir Israel Gollancz Professor of English Language and Medieval Literature, King's College, University of London, 1995–97, now Emeritus (Professor of English Language and Medieval Literature, 1977–95); *b* 3 April 1932; *d* of late Alfred William Bately and Dorothy Maud Bately (*née* Willis); *m* 1964, Leslie John Summers (*d* 2006), sculptor; one *s*. *Educ:* Greenhead High Sch., Huddersfield; Westcliff High Sch. for Girls; Somerville Coll., Oxford (Shaw Lefevre Scholar; Eileen Gonner Meml Prize, 1953; BA 1st cl. hons English 1954, Dip. in Comparative Philology (with distinction) 1956, MA 1958; Hon. Fellow, 1997); FKC 1986. Asst Lectr in English, Birkbeck Coll., Univ. of London, 1955–58, Lectr, 1958–69, Reader, 1970–76. Lectures: Sir Israel Gollancz Meml, British Acad., 1978; Toller Meml, Manchester Univ., 1987; Dark Age, Univ. of Kent, 1991. Chm., Scholarships Cttee, Univ. of London, 1988–91. Member: Council, EETS, 1981–; Exec. Cttee, Fontes Anglo-Saxonici, 1985–; Adv. Cttee, Internat. Soc. of Anglo-Saxonists, 1986–91; Adv. Cttee, Sources of Anglo-Saxon Lit. and Culture, 1987–; Humanities Res. Bd, British Acad., 1994–95; Adv. Bd, Inst. for Histl Study of Lang., Glasgow Univ., 1998–. Mem. Hon. Develt Bd, Book Trust, 2002–. Governor: Cranleigh Sch., 1982–88; King's Coll. Sch., Wimbledon, 1991–94; Notting Hill and Ealing High Sch., 1998–2002. FRSA 2000. Gen. Ed., King's Coll. London Medieval Studies, 1987–2001. *Publications:* The Old English Orosius, 1980; The Literary Prose of King Alfred's Reign: Translation or Transformation, 1980; (ed) The Anglo-Saxon Chronicle: MS.A, 1986; The Anglo-Saxon Chronicle: texts and textual relationships, 1991; The Tanner Bede, 1992; Anonymous Old English Homilies: a preliminary bibliography, 1993; (ed jtly) Ohthere's Voyages: a late 9th century account of voyages along the coast of Norway and Denmark and its cultural context, 2006; contribs to: England Before the Conquest, 1971; Saints, Scholars and Heroes (ed M. H. King and W. M. Stevens), 1979; Five Hundred Years of Words and Sounds (ed E. G. Stanley and Douglas Grey), 1983; Learning and Literature in Anglo-Saxon England (ed M. Lapidge and H. Gneuss), 1985; Medieval English Studies (ed D. Kennedy, R. Waldron and J. Wittig), 1988; Words for Robert Burchfield's Sixty-Fifth Birthday (ed E. G. Stanley and T. F. Hoad), 1988; From Anglo-Saxon to Early Middle English (ed M. Godden *et al.*), 1994; Medieval English Language Scholarship (ed A. Oizumi and T. Kubouchi), 2005; Leeds Studies in English, Reading Medieval Studies, Eichstätter Beiträge, Medium Aevum, Rev. of English Studies, Anglia, English Studies, Essays and Studies, Classica et Mediaevalia, Scriptorium, Studies in Philology, Mediev. Arch., Notes and Queries, Archaeologia, Anglo-Saxon England, The Dickensian, Jl Soc. of Archivists, Bull. John Rylands Library, etc. *Recreations:* music, gardening. *Address:* 86 Cawdor Crescent, W7 2DD. *T:* (020) 8567 0486.

BATEMAN, Mary-Rose Christine, (Mrs R. D. Farley), MA; Headmistress, Perse School for Girls, Cambridge, 1980–89; *b* 16 March 1935; *d* of late Comdr G. A. Bateman, RN, and Mrs G. A. Bateman; *m* 1990, Richard Dashwood Farley (*d* 1996). *Educ:* The Abbey, Malvern Wells, Worcs; St Anne's Coll., Oxford (MA); CertEd Cambridge. Assistant English Mistress: Westonbirt Sch., Tetbury, Glos, 1957–60; Ashford Sch., Kent, 1960–61; Lady Eleanor Holles Sch., Middx, 1961–64; Head of English Department: Westonbirt Sch., Glos, 1964–69; Brighton and Hove High Sch., GPDST, 1969–71; Headmistress, Berkhamsted School for Girls, Herts, 1971–80. Administrator, Women's Nat. Cancer Control Campaign, 1989. *Address:* Harrow Hill Cottage, Long Compton, Shipston on Stour, Warwickshire CV36 5JJ. *T:* (01608) 684231.

BATEMAN, Paul Terence; Chairman, JP Morgan Asset Management, since 2007 (Chief Executive Officer, 2002–07); *b* 28 April 1946; *s* of Nelson John Bateman and Frances Ellen (*née* Johnston); *m* 1970, Moira (*née* Burdis); two *s*. *Educ:* Westcliff High Sch. for Boys; Univ. of Leicester (BSc). Save and Prosper Gp Ltd, 1967: graduate, secretarial dept, 1967–68; asst to Gp Actuary, 1968–73; Marketing Manager, 1973–75; Gp Marketing Manager, 1975–80; Gp Marketing and Develt Manager, 1980–81; Exec. Dir, Marketing and Develt, 1981–88; Chief Exec., 1988–95; Chm., Robert Fleming Asset Management, 1995–2001; Hd, Asset Mgt for Europe, Asia and Japan, JP Morgan Fleming Asset Mgt, 2001–02. Chm., Barts City Lifesavers, 1998–. *Recreation:* yachting. *Address:* JP Morgan Asset Management, Finsbury Dials, 20 Finsbury Street, EC2Y 9AQ. *T:* (020) 7742 6000. *Club:* Royal Burnham Yacht.

BATEMAN, Peter; HM Diplomatic Service; Ambassador to Luxembourg, since 2007; *b* 23 Dec. 1955; *s* of Sqdn Ldr Ralph Edwin Bateman, MBE and Alma Bateman (*née* Laws); *m* 1985, Andrea Henriette Subercaseaux; two *s* one *d*. *Educ:* Carre's Grammar Sch., Sleaford, Lincs; St Peter's Coll., Oxford (MA). Conf. interpreter, EC, 1979–84; joined HM Diplomatic Service, 1984: First Secretary: Tokyo, 1986–90; FCO, 1991–93; (Commercial), Berlin, 1993–97; FCO, 1997–98; Commercial Counsellor, Tokyo, 1998–2002; Counsellor, FCO, 2002–03; on secondment as Dep. Chief Exec., Internat. Financial Services, 2003–05; Ambassador to Bolivia, 2005–07. *Recreations:* family life, golf, travel. *Address:* c/o Foreign and Commonwealth Office, King Charles Street, SW1A 2AH; 44 The Drive, Sevenoaks, Kent TN13 3AF. *Club:* Queen's.

BATEMAN, Richard George Saumarez La T.; see La Trobe-Bateman.

BATEMAN, Richard Mark, PhD; DSc; Head of Policy, Biosciences Federation, since 2006 (Member, Executive Council, since 2004); *b* Bradford, 27 May 1958; *s* of William Horace Roy Bateman and Joan Mary Lund (*née* Laban); *m* (marr. diss. 2002). *Educ:* Luton Coll. of Higher Educn (BSc (Commendation) 1982); Birkbeck Coll., London (BSc 1st Cl. Hons 1984); PhD (Palaeozoic Palaeobotany) London 1988; DSc (Systematic Botany) London 2001. Asst SO, Sect. for Quaternary Studies, Rothamsted Exptl Station, 1977–84; Lindemann Res. Fellow and Vis. Scientist, Dept of Paleobiol., Smithsonian Instn, Washington, 1988–91; Sen. NERC Res. Fellow (Palaeobotany), Depts of Earth and Plant Scis, Oxford Univ., 1991–94; PSO, Royal Botanic Gdn, Edinburgh, and Nat. Museums of Scotland, 1994–96; Dir of Sci. and SPSO, Royal Botanic Gdn, Edinburgh, 1996–99; Keeper of Botany, 1999–2004, Individual Merit Researcher (Evolution), 2005–06, Natural History Mus. Hon. Research Fellow: Edinburgh Univ., 1997–2002; Royal Botanic Gardens, Kew, 2003–; Vis. Prof., Reading Univ., 2000–. Member, Council: Systematics Assoc., 1992– (Pres., 2006–); UK Systematics Forum, 1997–2001; Linnean Soc., 1999– (Vice-Pres., 2004–); Bot. Soc. Br. Isles, 2002– (Vice-Pres., 2004–08); Mem., Awards Cttee III, Royal Soc., 2003–. Pres., UK Hardy Orchid Soc., 2000–08. President's Award, Geol Soc. of GB, 1988; Bicentenary Medal, Linnean Soc., 1994. *Publications:* (jtly) Molecular Systematics and Plant Evolution, 1999; (jtly) Developmental Genetics and Plant Evolution, 2002; contrib. over 100 papers to scientific jls. *Recreations:* natural history, travel, film, pontificating while drinking decent beer. *Address:* c/o Jodrell Laboratory, Royal Botanic Gardens Kew, Richmond, Surrey TW9 3DS. *T:* (020) 8332 5342.

BATEMAN, Richard Montague; Executive Secretary, Geological Society, 1980–97; *b* 27 Nov. 1943; *s* of late Gordon Montague Bateman and Joan Rhoda Bateman (*née* Puddifoot); *m* Gillian Elizabeth, *er d* of late Noel Leslie Costain, OBE; one *d*. *Educ:* Lyme Regis Grammar Sch.; Greenwich Maritime Inst., Univ. of Greenwich (MA 2002). Entered Civil Service, 1964, MoD (Air), 1965–69; Chamber of Shipping of UK, 1969–75, Asst Sec., 1973–75; Gen. Council of British Shipping, 1975–80. Sec., Assoc. of European Geol Socs, 1987–92. Mem., Envmt Council, 1994–97. Mem. Council, Haslemere Educnl Mus., 1998–. Member: Ocean Liner Soc., 1992; Sci., Technol., Engrg and Med. PR Assoc., 1993; Geologists' Assoc., 1997–2004 (Mem. Council, 2008–); Soc. for Nautical

Res., 1997 (Mem. Council, 2003–07 and 2008–); British Titanic Soc., 1998; Steamship Historical Soc. of America, 1999; Council, Greenwich Forum, 2008–. Associate, ACENVO, then ACEVO, 1998–2001. *Recreations:* maritime history, classical music. *Club:* Royal Naval and Royal Albert Yacht.

BATES; *see* Baker-Bates.

BATES, family name of **Baron Bates**.

BATES, Baron *cr* 2008 (Life Peer), of Langbaurgh in the County of West Yorkshire; **Michael Walton Bates;** Managing Director, Walton Bates Associates Ltd, since 2006; Director, Vardy Group of Companies, since 2006; *b* 26 May 1961; *s* of John Bates and Ruth Walton; *m* 1983, Carole Whitfield (separated 2005), *d* of Sydney and late Irene Whitfield; two *s*. *Educ:* Heathfield Sen. High Sch.; Gateshead Coll.; Wadham Coll., Oxford (MBA 1998). Young Conservatives: Mem., Nat. Adv. Cttee, 1984–87; Chm., Northern Area, 1984–87. Sen. Vice-Pres., later Dir of Consultancy and Res., 1998–2006, Sen. Advr, 2006–07, Oxford Analytica Inc. Director: estandardsforum.com Inc., 2001–07; Financial Standards Foundn (Bermuda) Ltd, 2001–03; non-exec. Dir, Congregational & General plc, 2001–06. Assoc. Chm., Northern Area Develt Initiative, 1990–92. Contested (C): Tyne Bridge, 1987; Langbaurgh, Nov. 1991. MP (C) Langbaurgh, 1992–97; contested (C) Middlesbrough South and Cleveland East, 1997. PPS to Minister of State, DSS, 1992–93, NI Office, 1994; an Asst Govt Whip, 1994–95; a Lord Comr, HM Treasury, 1995–96; HM Paymaster Gen., 1996–97. Member: Select Cttee on Social Security, 1992; Select Cttee on Health, 1994. Dep. Chm., Cons. Party (North), 2007–. Shell Fellow, Industry and Parlt Trust, 1997–. Mem., RIIA, 1998–. Member: Business Adv. Forum, Saïd Business Sch. (formerly Mem. Council, Sch. of Mgt Studies), Oxford Univ., 2000–; Caux Round Table, 2001– (Trustee, 2006–); European Ideas Network, 2002–. *Address:* 42 Old Dryburn Way, Durham DH1 5SE; *e-mail:* michael@waltonbates.com.

BATES, Alfred; Research Assistant, Union of Shop, Distributive and Allied Workers, 1991–2000; *b* 8 June 1944; *s* of Norman and Alice Bates; single. *Educ:* Stretford Grammar Sch. for Boys; Manchester Univ. (BSc); Corpus Christi Coll., Cambridge. Lectr in Maths, De La Salle Coll. of Educn, Middleton, 1967–74. MP (Lab) Bebington and Ellesmere Port, Feb. 1974–1979; PPS to Minister of State for Social Security, 1974–76; Asst Govt Whip, 1976–79; a Lord Comr, HM Treasury, 1979. Researcher and presenter, 1980–87, and an assistant producer, 1983–87, BBC TV; freelance media consultant, 1987–91. Mem., Trafford MBC, 1992–2000 (Chm., Licensing Cttee, 1996–97, 1998–2000; Chm., Public Protection Cttee, 1997–98). Mem., Exec. Cttee, Assoc. of Former Members of Parlt, 2007–. Mem. Bd of Dirs, Hallé Concerts Soc., 1996–98. *Recreation:* cricket umpiring. *Address:* 116 Jackson Street, Stretford, Manchester M32 8BB.

BATES, Clive David Nicholas; Head of Environmental Policy, Environment Agency, since 2005; *b* 16 Feb. 1961; *s* of David and Patricia Bates. *Educ:* Wilmslow Grammar Sch., Cheshire; Emmanuel Coll., Cambridge (BA Hons Engrg 1983); Imperial Coll., London (MSc Envmtl Technol. 1992). Marketing computers for IBM (UK) Ltd, 1983–91; envmtl campaigner, Greenpeace, 1992–95; Programme Manager, Internat. Inst. for Energy Conservation, 1996–97; Dir, ASH, 1997–2003; Team Leader, Prime Minister's Strategy Unit, Cabinet Office, 2003–05. FRSA 1998. *Publications:* reports and papers for campaigning groups. *Recreations:* cycling, mountains, blogging http://baconbutty.blogspot.com. *Address:* Environment Agency, Millbank Tower, 21–24 Millbank, SW1P 4XL; 42 Allerton Road, N16 5UF. *Club:* Black's.

BATES, Air Vice-Marshal David Frank, CB 1983; RAF retired; *b* 10 April 1928; *s* of late S. F. Bates, MusB, FRCO, and N. A. Bates (*née* Story); *m* 1954, Margaret Winifred (*née* Biles); one *s* one *d*. *Educ:* Warwick Sch.; RAF Coll., Cranwell. Commnd, 1950; served Egypt, Innsworth, UKSLS Australia, HQ Transport Comd, RAF Technical Coll., Staff Coll., Lyneham, El Adem, Staff Coll., Jt Services Staff Coll., Innsworth, and RCDS, 1950–73; Stn Comdr, Uxbridge, 1974–75; Dir of Personnel Ground, 1975–76; Dir of Personnel Management (ADP), 1976–79; AOA, RAF Support Comd, 1979–82. Bursar, Warwick Sch., 1983–85. Pres., Adastrian Cricket Club, 1977–82. *Recreations:* cricket, most sports, gardening, model railways. *Address:* Meadow Cottage, Calf Lane, Chipping Campden, Glos GL55 6JQ. *Clubs:* Royal Air Force, MCC.

BATES, Prof. David Richard, PhD; FRHistS, FSA; Professor of Medieval History, University of East Anglia, since 2008; *b* 30 April 1945; *s* of Jack Bates and Violet Anne Bates (*née* Swain); *m* 1971, Helen Mary Fryer; one *s* one *d*. *Educ:* King Edward VI Grammar Sch., Nuneaton; Univ. of Exeter (BA 1966; PhD 1970). FRHistS 1985; FSA 1993. Lectr, then Sen. Lectr and Reader in Hist., UC, Cardiff, subseq. Univ. of Wales, Cardiff, 1973–94; Edwards Prof. of Medieval Hist., Univ. of Glasgow, 1994–2003; Prof. of Hist. and Dir, Inst. of Historical Res., Univ. of London, 2003–08. Huntington Library Fellow, 1984; Prof. Invité, Ecole Nat. des Chartes, Paris, 1999; British Acad. Marc Fitch Res. Reader, 2001–03; Vis. Fellow Commoner, Trinity Coll., Cambridge, 2002–03; Dir d'Etudes Invité, Ecole Pratique des Hautes Etudes, Paris, 2003. A Vice-Pres., RHistS, 2003–06. Founding Fellow, Inst. of Contemp. Scotland, 2000; Centenary Fellow, Historical Assoc., 2006. Dr *hc* Caen, 2000. *Publications:* Normandy before 1066, 1982; A Bibliography of Domesday Book, 1986; William the Conqueror, 1989; Bishop Remigius of Lincoln 1067–1092, 1992; (ed jtly) England and Normandy in the Middle Ages, 1994; (ed jtly) Conflict and Coexistence, 1997; Regesta Regum Anglo-Normannorum: the Acta of William I 1066–1087, 1998; Reordering the Past and Negotiating the Present in Stenton's First Century (Stenton Lect.), 2000; (ed jtly) Domesday Book, 2001; (ed jtly) Writing Medieval Biography 750–1250: essays in honour of Frank Barlow, 2006; (ed jtly) Liens personnels, réseaux, solidarités en France et dans les îles britanniques, 2006; contribs to various books and many articles in historical jls incl. English Historical Rev., Speculum, Histl Res. and Annales de Normandie. *Address:* School of History, University of East Anglia, Norwich NR4 7TJ. *T:* (01603) 592070.

BATES, Django Leon; jazz keyboardist and composer; *b* 2 Oct. 1960; *s* of Ralf Bates and Frances Sinker (*née* Roseveare); one *s* two *d*. *Educ:* ILEA Centre for Young Musicians; Morley Coll. A founder mem., Loose Tubes; band leader: Humans, subseq. Human Chain, 1980–; Delightful Precipice, 1991–; stoRMChaser, 2005–. Performances worldwide. Artistic Dir, Fuse Fest., Leeds, March 2004. Resident composer: Molde Internat. Jazz Fest., 1995; European City of Culture, Copenhagen, 1996; Harrogate Internat. Fest., 1997. ALCM; Fellow, Leeds Coll. of Music, 2005; Hon. RAM 2000. Danish Jazzpar Prize, 1997. *Compositions include:* Out There (music theatre prodn), 1993; What it's Like to be Alive (piano concerto), 1996; 1 in a Million, 1997; 2000 Years Beyond Undo (electronic keyboard concerto), 2000; Umpteenth Violin Concerto, 2004. *Recordings include:* Music for the Third Policeman, 1990; summer fruits (and unrest), 1993; autumn fires (and green shoots), 1994; winter truce (and homes blaze), 1995; Good Evening…here is the news, 1996; Like Life, 1998; Quiet Nights, 1998; You Live and Learn (apparently), 2004. *Address:* c/o Jeremy Farnell, 21 St Johns Church Road, E9 6EJ; *e-mail:* management@djangobates.co.uk.

BATES, Prof. Gillian Patricia, PhD; FRS 2007; Professor of Neurogenetics, King's College London School of Medicine (formerly Guy's, King's College and St Thomas' Hospitals School of Medicine), since 1998; *b* 19 May 1956; *d* of Alan Richard Bates and Joan Mabel Bates. *Educ:* Kenilworth Grammar Sch.; Sheffield Univ. (BSc 1979); Birkbeck Coll., London (MSc 1984); St Mary's Hosp. Med. Sch., Univ. of London (PhD 1987). Postdoctoral Fellow, ICRF, 1987–93; Sen. Lectr in Molecular Biology, UMDS of Guy's and St Thomas' Hosps, 1994–98. FMedSci 1999. Nat. Med. Res. Award, Nat. Health Council, USA, 1993; Milton Wexler Award for Res. into Huntington's Disease, Huntington's Disease Soc. of America, 1998; Glaxo Wellcome Gold Medal, Royal Soc., 1998; Pius XI Medal, 1998; Klaus Joachim Zulch Prize, 2001. *Publications:* papers in genetics, molecular biology, and neurosci. jls; contribs to scientific and med. reference books. *Recreations:* reading, contemporary arts and design. *Address:* Department of Medical and Molecular Genetics, Guy's, King's College London School of Medicine, 8th Floor, Guy's Tower, Guy's Hospital, SE1 9RT. *T:* (020) 7188 3722.

BATES, Rt Rev. Gordon; Hon. Assistant Bishop, Dioceses of Carlisle and Blackburn, since 1999; *b* 16 March 1934; *s* of Ernest and Kathleen Bates; *m* 1960, Betty (*née* Vaux); two *d*. *Educ:* Kelham Theological Coll. (SSM). Curate of All Saints, New Eltham, 1958–62; Youth Chaplain in Gloucester Diocese, 1962–64; Diocesan Youth Officer and Chaplain of Liverpool Cathedral, 1965–69; Vicar of Huyton, 1969–73; Canon Residentiary and Precentor of Liverpool Cathedral and Diocesan Director of Ordinands, 1973–83; Bp Suffragan of Whitby, 1983–99. Mem., House of Bishops, Gen. Synod, 1988–99. Mem., Central Religious Adv. Council to BBC and ITV, 1990–93. Chm., Cumbria, RSCM, 2002–04. Trustee, Sandford St Martin Trust, 1990–93. *Recreations:* golf, music, writing. *Address:* Caedmon House, 2 Loyne Park, Whittington, via Carnforth, Lancs LA6 2NL. *T:* (01524) 272010.

BATES, Sir James Geoffrey, 7th Bt *cr* 1880, of Bellefield, co. Lancaster; *b* 14 March 1985; *s* of Richard Geoffrey Bates, *yr s* of 5th Bt and Diana Margaret Rankin; *S* uncle, 2007. *Heir: kinsman* Hugh Percy Bates [*b* 9 Jan. 1953; *m* 1977, Angela Roberta Wall; one *s* one *d*].

BATES, John Gerald Higgs; Solicitor, Office of Inland Revenue, 1990–96; *b* 28 July 1936; *o s* of Thomas William Bates and Winifred Alice Higgs; *m* 1971, Antoinette Lotery (*d* 1984); two *s*; *m* 1992, Alba Heather Phyllida Whicher. *Educ:* Kettering Grammar Sch.; St Catharine's Coll., Cambridge (MA); Harvard Law Sch. (LLM). Called to the Bar, Middle Temple, 1959. Practised at the Bar, 1962–66; Office of Solicitor of Inland Revenue, 1966–96: Under Sec. (Legal), 1990. *Recreations:* cooking, wine, music.

BATES, Kenneth; Chairman, Leeds United Football Club, since 2005; *b* 4 Dec. 1931; *m* Suzannah. Ready-mix concrete business; dairy farmer; Chairman: Oldham Athletic FC; Wigan Athletic FC, 1981; Chelsea FC, 1982–2004; Wembley Nat. Stadium Ltd, until 2000 (Dir, 1997–2001). *Address:* Leeds United Football Club, Elland Road, Leeds LS11 0ES.

BATES, Sir Malcolm (Rowland), Kt 1998; Chairman: Premier Farnell plc, 1997–2005; HHG plc, 2003–05; *b* 23 Sept. 1934; *s* of late Rowland Bates and Ivy Bates (*née* Hope); *m* 1960, Lynda Margaret Price; three *d*. *Educ:* Portsmouth Grammar Sch.; Univ. of Warwick (MSc); Harvard Business Sch. FCIS 1963; FRAeS 1993; CCMI (CIMgt 1983). Flying Officer, RAF, 1956–58. Delta Group plc, 1959–68 (Man. Dir, Elkington & Co. plc, 1966–68); Adwest Gp plc, 1968–69; Industrial Reorgn Corp., 1969–70; Man. Dir, Spey Investments, 1970–72; Jt Man. Dir, Wm Brandt & Sons Ltd, 1972–75; General Electric Co. plc: Sen. Commercial Dir, 1976–80; Dir, 1980–97; Dep. Man. Dir, 1985–97. Special Advr to Paymaster General, HM Treasury, 1997–99. Chairman: AMP (UK) plc, 1996–2003; London Transport, 1999–2003. Non-executive Director: Enterprise Oil, 1991–95; Pearl Assurance, 1996–2005; London Life, 1996–2005; BICC plc, 1997–99; Wavetek, Wandel & Goltermann Inc. (formerly Wavetek Corp.) (USA), 1997–99; AMP Ltd (Australia), 1998–2003; Grass Valley Group (USA), 1999–2002; The New Theatre Royal Trustees (Portsmouth) Ltd, 1999–2001; NPI Ltd, 1999–2005. Advr, DLJ Phoenix Equity Partners II, 1997–2004. Chm., Engrg Deregulation Task Force, 1993–94; Member: Industrial Develt Adv. Bd, 1993–99; Private Finance Panel, 1993–96; IMRO, 1995–96; Finance Bd, RAeS, 1997–99. Chm., Business in the Arts, 1996–99; Mem. Council, ABSA, 1996–99; Advr, Nat. Musicians SO, 2001–; Dir and Trustee, Oxford Philomusica Trust, 2006–. Vice-Pres., London Playing Fields Soc., 2001– (Chm., Gen. Purposes Cttee, 1995–2001). Gov., Univ. of Westminster, 1995–2002 (Dep. Chm., 1999–2002). Freeman: City of London, 1985; Painter-Stainers' Co., 1985. Hon. FICPD, 1998. Hon. DLitt Westminster, 2002. *Recreations:* classical music, reading. *Address:* Mulberry Close, Croft Road, Goring-on-Thames, Oxon RG8 9ES. *T:* (01491) 872214. *Club:* Royal Air Force.

BATES, Margaret Patricia; *see* Munn, M. P.

BATES, Michael, (Mick); Member (Lib Dem) Montgomeryshire, National Assembly for Wales, since 1999; *b* 24 Sept. 1947; *s* of George William Bates and Lilly (*née* Stevens); *m* 1972, Buddug Thomas; one *s* one *d*. *Educ:* Open Univ. (BA Educn and Sci. 1970). Science teacher, Humphrey Perkins Jun. High Sch., Barrow on Soar, and Belvidere Secondary Sch., Shrewsbury, 1970–75; Head of Gen. Sci., Grove Sch., Market Drayton, 1975–77; farmer, 1977–99. Mem. (Lib Dem) Powys CC, 1994–95. National Farmers' Union: Chm., Llanfair Caereinion Br., 1983–85; Chm., Co. Livestock Cttee, 1988–91; Mem., Co. Public Affairs Cttee, 1990–; County Chm., Powys, 1991; NFU delegate, 1995. Lib Dem Br. Sec., 1988, Election Sub Agent, 1992. Mem., Eisteddfod Finance Cttee, 1989. Gov., Llanfair Co. Primary Sch., 1994–95. Chm., Llanfair Forum Community Regeneration Project. *Recreations:* all sports, especially Rugby, charity work, painting, walking, music. *Address:* National Assembly for Wales, Cardiff Bay, Cardiff CF99 1NA. *T:* (029) 2089 8340.

BATES, Michael Charles, OBE 1994; HM Diplomatic Service, retired; Consul-General, Atlanta, 2001–05; *b* 9 April 1948; *s* of late Stanley Herbert Bates and of Winifred (*née* Watkinson); *m* 1971, Janice Kwan Foh Yin; one *s* one *d*. *Educ:* Stratton Grammar Sch. Joined HM Diplomatic Service, 1966: Attaché, New Delhi, 1971–74; Third Sec., Moscow, 1974–77; FCO, 1977–79; Second, later First Sec., Singapore, 1979–83; First Sec., Brussels, 1983–87; Press Officer to Prime Minister, 1987–89; Head, Parly Relns Unit, FCO, 1989–91; Dep. Head of Mission, Riga, 1991–92; Chargé d'Affaires, Bratislava, 1993–94; Ambassador, Slovak Republic, 1994–95; Dep. Head, News Dept, FCO, 1995–96; Dep. High Comr, Bombay, 1996–2001. *Recreations:* music, reading, travel.

BATES, Patricia Ann; *see* Stewart, P. A.

BATES, Sir Richard (Dawson Hoult), 3rd Bt *cr* 1937, of Magherabuoy, co. Londonderry; *b* 12 May 1956; *er s* of Sir Dawson Bates, 2nd Bt, MC and of Mary Murray (*née* Hoult); *S* father, 1998; *m* 2001, Harriet Domenique, *yr d* of Domenico Scaramella; one *s* one *d*. *Heir: s* Dominic Dawson Bates, *b* 21 Jan. 2006.

BATES, Wendy Elizabeth; *see* Sudbury, W. E.

BATESON, John Swinburne, FIHT; Chairman, Country Holiday Parks Ltd, since 2002; *b* 11 Jan. 1942; *s* of William Swinburne Bateson and Katherine Urquart (*née* Lyttle); *m* Jean Vivien Forsyth; one *s* two *d*. *Educ:* Appleby Grammar Sch.; Lancaster Royal Grammar Sch. FIHT 1986. Family business and associated activities, 1959–61; Harbour & General Works Ltd: Trainee Quantity Surveyor, 1961; Quantity Surveyor, 1966; Site Quantity Surveyor, Marples Ridgway Ltd, 1966–68; Leonard Fairclough Ltd: Site Quantity Surveyor, 1969; Contracts Surveyor, 1971; Chief Quantity Surveyor, Scotland, 1974; Fairclough Civil Engineering Ltd: Asst to Chief Exec., 1977; Man. Dir, Southern Div., 1979; Fairclough Construction Group Ltd: Asst to Chief Exec., 1980; Dir, 1981–95; AMEC plc: Dir, 1982–86; Dep. Chief Exec., 1986–88; Gp Chief Exec., 1988–95. Chairman: Bateson's Hotels (1958) Ltd, 1986–2002; Indep. Radio Gp, 1995–99; Merewood Gp Ltd, 1997–2003. *Recreations:* gardening, aviation, reading, photography, chess, bridge, antiques.

BATESON, Prof. Sir (Paul) Patrick (Gordon), Kt 2003; FRS 1983; Professor of Ethology, University of Cambridge, 1984–2005, now Emeritus Professor; Provost of King's College, Cambridge, 1988–2003 (Fellow, 1964–84; Professorial Fellow, 1984–88; Life Fellow, since 2003); *b* 31 March 1938; *s* of Richard Gordon Bateson and Sölvi Helene Berg; *m* 1963, Dusha Matthews; two *d*. *Educ:* Westminster Sch.; King's Coll., Cambridge (BA 1960, PhD 1963, MA 1965, ScD 1977). Harkness Fellow, Stanford Univ. Medical Centre, Calif, 1963–65; Sen. Asst in Res., Sub-Dept of Animal Behaviour, Univ. of Cambridge, 1965–69; Lectr in Zoology, Univ. of Cambridge, 1969–78; Dir, Sub-Dept of Animal Behaviour, 1976–88; Reader in Animal Behaviour, 1978–84. Pres., Assoc. for the Study of Animal Behaviour, 1977–80; Member: Council for Sci. and Soc., 1989–92; Museums and Galls Commn, 1995–2000 (Vice-Chm., 1998–2000). Biological Sec., Royal Soc., 1998–2003; Pres., Zool Soc. of London, 2004– (Mem. Council, 1989–92). Mem., UK Panel for Res. Integrity in Health and Biomed. Scis, 2006–. Trustee, Inst. for Public Policy Research, 1988–95. Rutherford Meml Lect., Australia and NZ, 2007. For. Mem., Amer. Philos. Soc., 2006; Mem., Sigma Xi, 2006. Hon. Fellow, QMW. Hon. FZS. Hon. DSc St Andrews, 2001. Scientific Medal, Zool Soc. of London, 1976; Medal Assoc. for Study of Animal Behaviour, 2001. *Publications:* (ed with P. H. Klopfer) Perspectives in Ethology, Vols 1–8, 1973–89; (ed with R. A. Hinde) Growing Points in Ethology, 1976; (ed) Mate Choice, 1983; (contrib.) Defended to Death, 1983; (with Paul Martin) Measuring Behaviour, 1986, 3rd edn 2007; (ed with D. S. Turner) The Domestic Cat: the biology of its behaviour, 1988, 2nd edn 2000; (ed) The Development and Integration of Behaviour, 1991; (with P. Martin) Design for a Life: how behaviour develops, 1999. *Recreation:* turning wilderness into garden. *Address:* The Old Rectory, Rectory Street, Halesworth, Suffolk IP19 8BL. *T:* (01986) 873182.

BATEY, Mavis Lilian, MBE 1986; FSA; President, Garden History Society, 1985–2000; *b* 5 May 1921; *d* of Frederick Lever and Lily Lever; *m* 1942, Keith Batey; one *s* two *d*. *Educ:* Convent of Ladies of Mary, Croydon; University Coll. London. Worked at Bletchley Park, breaking German Enigma codes, 1940–45. Tutor (part time), Oxford Dept of External Studies, 1970–92. Mem., Historic Parks and Gardens Panel, English Heritage, 1984–94. Hon. Sec., Garden History Soc., 1971–85. FSA 2002. Veitch Meml Medal, RHS, 1985. *Publications:* Alice's Adventures in Oxford, 1980; Oxford Gardens, 1982; Historic Gardens of Oxford and Cambridge, 1989; (with D. Lambert) The English Garden Tour, 1990; Arcadian Thames, 1994; Privy Garden at Hampton Court, 1995; Regency Gardens, 1995; Jane Austen and the English Landscape, 1996; Alexander Pope: the poet and the landscape, 1999; (jtly) Indignation!, 2000. *Recreations:* walking, bird-watching, reading.

BATH, 7th Marquess of, *cr* 1789; **Alexander George Thynn;** Bt 1641; Viscount Weymouth and Baron Thynne, 1682; Director: Cheddar Caves, since 1956; Longleat Enterprises, since 1964; *b* 6 May 1932; *s* of 6th Marquess of Bath and his 1st wife, Hon. Daphne Winifred Louise (*d* 1997), *d* of 4th Baron Vivian; *S* father, 1992; *m* 1969, Anna Gael Gyarmathy; one *s* one *d*. *Educ:* Eton College; Christ Church, Oxford (BA, MA). Lieutenant in the Life Guards, 1951–52, and in Royal Wilts Yeomanry, 1953–57. Contested (Wessex Regionalist): Westbury, Feb. 1974; Wells, 1979; contested (Wessex Regionalist and European Federal Party) Wessex, European Election 1979. Permanent exhibn of paintings since 1949 and murals since 1964, first opened to the public in 1962 in private apartments at Longleat House. Record, I Play the Host, singing own compositions, 1974. *Publications:* (as Alexander Thynn) (before 1976 Alexander Thynne) The Carry-cot, 1972; Lord Weymouth's Murals, 1974; A Regionalist Manifesto, 1975; The King is Dead, 1976; Pillars of the Establishment, 1980; The New World Order of Alexander Thynn, 2000; A Plateful of Privilege, vol. 1, the Early Years, vol. 2, Top Hat and Tails, vol. 3, Two Bites of the Apple, 2003, vol. 4, A Degree of Instability: the Oxford years, 2005. *Heir: s* Viscount Weymouth, *qv*. *Address:* Longleat, Warminster, Wilts BA12 7NN. *T:* (01985) 844300.

BATH and WELLS, Bishop of, since 2002; **Rt Rev. Peter Bryan Price;** *b* 17 May 1944; *s* of Alec Henry Price and Phyllis Evelyn Mary Price; *m* 1967, Edith Margaret Burns; four *s*. *Educ:* Redland Coll., Bristol (Cert Ed 1966); Oak Hill Theol Coll. (Dip. in Pastoral Studies, 1974). Asst Master, Ashton Park Sch., Bristol, 1966–70; Tutor, Lindley Lodge, Nuneaton, 1970; Head of Religious Studies, Cordeaux Sch., Louth, 1970–72; ordained, 1974; Community Chaplain, Crookhorn, Portsmouth and Asst Curate, Christ Church, Portsdown, 1974–78; Chaplain, Scargill House, Kettlewell, 1978–80; Vicar, St Mary Magdalene, Addiscombe, Croydon, 1980–88; Canon Residentiary and Chancellor, Southwark Cathedral, 1988–91, Canon Emeritus, 1992–97; Gen. Sec., USPG, 1992–97; Area Bp, Kingston-upon-Thames, 1997–2002. Visitor, Wadham Coll., Oxford, 2002–. *Publications:* The Church as Kingdom, 1987; Seeds of the Word, 1996; Telling it as it is, 1998; Living Faith in the World through Word and Action, 1998; To Each their Place, 1999; Mark Today, 1999; Jesus Manifesto: reflections on St Luke's gospel, 2000; Undersong: listening to the soul, 2001; Playing the Blue Note, 2002; (with Jeanne Hinton) Changing Communities, 2003. *Recreations:* painting, swimming, walking, conversation. *Address:* The Palace, Wells, Somerset BA5 2PD. *T:* (01749) 672341, *Fax:* (01749) 679355; *e-mail:* bishop@bathwells.anglican.org.

BATH, Archdeacon of; *see* Piggott, Ven. A. J.

BATHER, John Knollys; Lord-Lieutenant of Derbyshire, since 1994; *b* 5 May 1934; *m* 1960, Elizabeth Barbara Longstaff; one *s* two *d*. *Educ:* Shrewsbury Sch.; Nat. Foundry Coll. High Sheriff, Derbys, 1990–91. Freeman, City of London; Liveryman, Founders' Co. *Recreations:* gardening, shooting, watercolours. *Address:* Longford Grange, Longford, Ashbourne, Derbys DE6 3AH. *T:* (01335) 330429. *Club:* Boodle's.

BATHERSBY, Most Rev. John Alexius; *see* Brisbane, Archbishop of, (RC).

BATHO, James; *see* Batho, W. J. S.

BATHO, Sir Peter (Ghislain), 3rd Bt *cr* 1928, of Frinton, Essex; *b* 9 Dec. 1939; *s* of Sir Maurice Benjamin Batho, 2nd Bt and Antoinette Marie (*d* 1994), *d* of Baron d'Udekem d'Acoz; *S* father, 1990; *m* 1966, Lucille Mary, *d* of Wilfrid F. Williamson; three *s*. *Educ:* Ampleforth Coll.; Writtle Agricl Coll. Career in agriculture. Mem., Suffolk CC, 1989–93. *Heir: s* Rupert Sebastian Ghislain Batho [*b* 26 Oct. 1967; *m* 1995, Jo-Anne Louise, *e d* of Rodney Frank Hellawell]. *Address:* Park Farm, Saxmundham, Suffolk IP17 1DQ. *T:* (01728) 602132.

BATHO, (Walter) James (Scott), CBE 1998; Chairman: London and Quadrant Housing Trust, 1989–98; Crown Housing Association, 1996–2003; *b* 13 Nov. 1925; *er s* of Walter Scott Batho and Isabella Laidlaw Batho (*née* Common); *m* 1951, Barbara Kingsford; two *s* two *d*. *Educ:* Epsom County Grammar Sch.; Univ. of Edinburgh (MA Eng. Lit. and Lang.). Served War, RNVR, 1943–46. Air Min., 1950–53; WO, 1953–63 (Private Sec. to Perm. Under Sec. of State, 1956–57); MPBW, 1963–70; DoE, 1970–85, Under Sec., 1979–85 (Regl Dir and Chm., Regl Bd for Eastern Region, DoE and Dept of Transport, 1983–85). Chm., Noise Review Wkg Party, DoE, 1990. Pres., Ashtead Choral Soc., 1990–. *Recreations:* singing, reading, gardening. *Address:* Bushpease, 16 Grays Lane, Ashtead, Surrey KT21 1BU. *T:* (01372) 273471. *Clubs:* Naval, MCC.

BATHURST, family name of **Earl Bathurst** and **Viscount Bledisloe**.

BATHURST, 8th Earl *cr* 1772; **Henry Allen John Bathurst;** DL; Baron Bathurst of Battlesden, Bedfordshire, 1712; Baron Apsley of Apsley, Sussex, 1771; Earl Bathurst of Bathurst, Sussex, 1772; Capt. Royal Gloucestershire Hussars (TA); TARO, 1959; *b* 1 May 1927; *s* of Lord Apsley, DSO, MC, MP (killed on active service, 1942) and Lady Apsley, CBE, MP for Bristol Central 1943–45 (*d* 1966); *g s* of 7th Earl; *S* grandfather, 1943; *m* 1st, 1959, Judith Mary (marr. diss. 1977; she *d* 2001), *d* of Mr and Mrs A. C. Nelson, Springfield House, Foulridge, Lancs; two *s* one *d*; 2nd, 1978, Gloria, *widow* of David Rutherston and *o d* of Harold Edward Clarry, Vancouver, BC. *Educ:* Ridley Coll., Canada; Eton; Christ Church, Oxford, 1948–49. Lieut 10th Royal Hussars (PWO), 1946–48. Capt., Royal Glos. Hussars, TA, 1949–57. Hon. Sec. Agricultural Cttee (Conservative), House of Lords, 1957; a Lord-in-Waiting, 1957–61; Joint Parliamentary Under-Sec. of State, Home Office, 1961–July 1962. Governor, Royal Agricultural Coll.; Pres. Glos Branch CPRE. Chancellor, Primrose League, 1959–61. Dir, Forestor Gp, 1986–92. Member: CLA Council, 1965 (Chm., Glos Branch of CLA, 1968–71); Timber Growers' Organisation (TGO) Council, 1966; President: Royal Forestry Soc., 1976–78; InstSMM, 1982–92; Assoc. of Professional Foresters, 1983–87, 1995–98. Master, 1950–64, Jt Master, 1964–66, Vale of White Horse (Earl Bathurst's) Hounds. DL County of Gloucester, 1960. *Heir: s* Lord Apsley, *qv*. *Clubs:* White's, Cavalry and Guards.

BATHURST, Admiral of the Fleet Sir (David) Benjamin, GCB 1991 (KCB 1987); First Sea Lord and Chief of Naval Staff, and First and Principal Naval Aide-de-Camp to the Queen, 1993–95; Vice Lord-Lieutenant, Somerset, since 1999; *b* 27 May 1936; *s* of late Group Captain Peter Bathurst, RAF and Lady Ann Bathurst; *m* 1959, Sarah Peto; one *s* three *d*. *Educ:* Eton College; Britannia RN College, Dartmouth. Joined RN, 1953; qualified as Pilot, 1960, as Helicopter Instructor, 1964; Fleet Air Arm appts incl. 2 years' exchange with RAN, 723 and 725 Sqdns; Senior Pilot, 820 Naval Air Sqdn; CO 819 Naval Air Sqdn; HMS Norfolk, 1971; Naval Staff, 1973; CO, HMS Ariadne, 1975; Naval Asst to First Sea Lord, 1976; Captain, 5th Frigate Sqdn, HMS Minerva, 1978; RCDS 1981; Dir of Naval Air Warfare, 1982; Flag Officer, Second Flotilla, 1983–85; Dir.-Gen., Naval Manpower and Training, 1985–86; Chief of Fleet Support, 1986–89; C-in-C Fleet, Allied C-in-C Channel, and C-in-C Eastern Atlantic Area, 1989–91; Vice Chief of Defence Staff, 1991–93. FRAeS. Younger Brother, Trinity House. Liveryman, GAPAN. DL Somerset, 1996. *Recreations:* gardening, shooting, fishing. *Address:* c/o Coutts and Co., 440 Strand, WC2R 0QS. *Clubs:* Boodle's, Army and Navy, MCC.

BATHURST, Sir (Frederick) John (Charles Gordon) Hervey-, 7th Bt *cr* 1818, of Lainston, Hants; *b* 23 April 1934; *o s* of Sir Frederick Peter Methuen Hervey-Bathurst, 6th Bt and of Maureen Eley (*née* Gordon); *S* father, 1995; *m* 1957, Caroline, *d* of Lt-Col Sir William Starkey, 2nd Bt; one *s* two *d*. *Educ:* Eton; Trinity Coll., Cambridge (MA). Grenadier Guards, 1952–54. Lazard Brothers & Co. Ltd, 1957–91. *Heir: s* Frederick William John Hervey-Bathurst [*b* 18 Sept. 1965; *m* 1991, Annabel Warburg; one *s* one *d*]. *Address:* Somborne Park, Stockbridge, Hants SO20 6QT. *T:* (01794) 388322.
See also Sir J. F. Portal, Bt.

BATHURST NORMAN, His Honour George Alfred; a Senior Circuit Judge, 1997–2004 (a Circuit Judge, 1986–2004); *b* 15 Jan. 1939; *s* of Charles Phipps Bathurst Norman and Hon. Doreen Albinia de Burgh Norman (*née* Gibbs); *m* 1973, Susan Elizabeth Ball; one *s* one *d*. *Educ:* Harrow Sch.; Magdalen Coll., Oxford (BA). Called to the Bar, Inner Temple, 1961; SE Circuit, 1962; Dep. Circuit Judge, 1975; a Metropolitan Stipendiary Magistrate, 1981–86; a Recorder, 1986. Mem., Home Office Working Party on Coroners Rules, 1976–81. Mem., Gen. Council of the Bar, 1968–70. Mem., Middlesex Probation Cttee, 1994–99. Chm., Lord Chancellor's Adv. Cttee on JPs for Middlesex, 1996–2004 (Dep. Chm., 1994–96). *Publications:* research papers on drugs and drug smuggling. *Recreations:* wildlife, ornithology, cricket, travel. *Address:* c/o 2 Bedford Row, WC1R 4BU. *Club:* MCC.

BATISTE, Spencer Lee; solicitor since 1970; a Senior Immigration Judge, Asylum and Immigration Tribunal (formerly a Vice-President, Immigration Appeal Tribunal), since 2002 (Immigration Adjudicator, 1997–2002); *b* 5 June 1945; *m* 1969, Susan Elizabeth (*née* Atkin); one *s* one *d*. *Educ:* Carmel Coll.; Sorbonne, Paris; Cambridge Univ. (MA). MP (C) Elmet, 1983–97; contested (C) same seat, 1997. PPS to Minister of State for Industry and IT, 1985–87, to Minister of State for Defence Procurement, 1987–89, to Sir Leon Brittan, Vice-Pres. of EC Commn, 1989–97. Member: Select Cttee on Energy, 1985; Select Cttee on Information, 1991–97; Select Cttee on Sci. and Technology, 1992–97; Vice-Chairman: Cons. Space Cttee, 1986–97 (Sec., 1983–85); Cons. Trade and Industry Cttee, 1989–97. Pres., Yorks Cons. Trade Unionists, 1984–87 (Nat. Pres., 1990). Vice-Chm., Small Business Bureau, 1983–92. Law Clerk to Sheffield Assay Office, 1974–2000. Mem., British Hallmarking Council, 1988–2000. *Recreations:* gardening, reading, photography. *Address:* c/o Asylum and Immigration Tribunal, Field House, 15–25 Bream's Buildings, EC4A 1DZ.

BATLEY, John Geoffrey, OBE 1987; CEng; Consultant, Dan-Rail, Copenhagen, 1988–92; Transport Consultant, Carl Bro (UK), 1993–96; *b* 21 May 1930; *s* of John William and Doris Batley; *m* 1953, Cicely Anne Pindar; one *s* (one *d* decd). *Educ:* Keighley Grammar School. MICE. British Rail: trained and qualified as a chartered engineer in NE Region, 1947–53; Asst Divl Engr, Leeds, 1962; Management Services Officer, BR HQ, London, 1965; Dep. Principal, British Transport Staff Coll., Woking, 1970; Divl Manager, Leeds, 1976; Dep. Chief Secretary, BRB, London, 1982; Sec., BRB, 1984–87; Project Co-ordinator, World Bank/Tanzanian Railway Corp., 1988–92. *Recreations:* walking, golf, gardening. *Club:* Farmers'.

BATT, Christopher, OBE 1998; Director, Chris Batt Consulting Ltd, since 2007; Chief Executive, Museums, Libraries and Archives Council, 2003–07; *b* 3 July 1947; *s* of Charles and Ethel Batt; *m* 2004, Adrienne Billcliffe. *Educ:* Henry Thornton Grammar Sch.; Open Univ. (BA 1st Cl. Hons). FCLIP (FLA 1985; Hon. Fellow 1998). London Borough of

Croydon: Dep. Chief Librarian, 1978–91; Bor. Libraries and Mus Officer, 1991–96; Dir, Leisure Services, 1996–99; Chief Network Advr, Liby and Inf. Commn, 1999–2000; Dir, Libraries and Inf. Soc. Team, Resource: Council for Mus, Archives and Libraries, 2000–03. FRSA 2001. *Publications:* Information Technology in Public Libraries, 1985, 6th edn 1998; contribs to Public Liby Jl. *Recreations:* flying light aircraft, photography, history of science and technology, music. *Address:* e-mail: cbatt@mac.com.

BATTARBEE, Prof. Richard William, DPhil, DSc; FRS 2006; Professor of Environmental Change, University College London, since 1991; *b* 30 May 1947; *s* of Halstead and Ethel Battarbee; *m* 1972, Gill Parkes. *Educ:* University Coll. London (BA); DPhil NUU 1973; DSc London 1997. Royal Soc. Eur. Res. Fellow, Uppsala Univ., 1971–73; Res. Fellow, NUU, 1973–76; Lectr, 1976–82, Reader, 1982–91, in Geog., UCL. Foreign Mem., Norwegian Acad. of Sci. and Letters. *Publications:* Palaeolimnology and Lake Acidification, 1990; Global Change in the Holocene, 2003. *Recreation:* silent piano playing. *Address:* 25 Ormonde Mansions, 110A Southampton Row, WC1B 4BS; *e-mail:* r.battarbee@ucl.ac.uk.

BATTEN, Gerard; Member (UK Ind) London Region, European Parliament, since 2004; *b* 27 March 1954. Hand bookbinder, 1972–76; Manager, BT, 1976–2004. UK Independence Party: Founder Mem., 1993–; Mem., NEC, 1993–97, 2002–; Party Sec., 1994–97. *Address:* PO Box 51542, London, SE1 3XS; European Parliament, Rue Wiertz, 1047 Brussels, Belgium.

BATTEN, Sir John (Charles), KCVO 1987; MD, FRCP; Physician to the Queen, 1974–89 (Physician to HM Royal Household, 1970–74), and Head of HM Medical Household, 1982–89; Physician: King Edward VII Hospital for Officers, 1968–89; King Edward VII Hospital, Midhurst, 1969–89; Hon. Physician to: St George's Hospital, since 1980; Royal Brompton Hospital (formerly Brompton Hospital), since 1986; *b* 11 March 1924; *s* of late Raymond Wallis Batten, JP and Gladys (*née* Charles); *m* 1950, Anne Mary Margaret (*d* 2007), *d* of late John Oriel, CBE, MC; one *s* two *d* (and one *d* decd). *Educ:* Mill Hill School; St Bartholomew's Medical School. MB, BS 1946 London Univ.; MRCP 1950; MD London 1951; FRCP 1964. Junior appts, St George's Hosp. and Brompton Hosp., 1946–58. Surgeon Captain, Royal Horse Guards, 1947–49. Physician: St George's Hospital, 1958–79; Brompton Hosp., 1959–86. Dep. Chief Med. Referee, 1958–74, CMO, 1974–95, Confederation Life. Dorothy Temple Cross Research Fellow, Cornell Univ. Medical Coll., New York, 1954–55. Examiner in Medicine, London Univ., 1968; Marc Daniels Lectr, RCP, 1969; Croonian Lectr, RCP, 1983. Member: Board of Governors, Brompton Hosp., 1966–69; St George's Hosp. Medical School Council, 1969; Council, RSocMed, 1970; Royal College of Physicians: Censor, 1977–78; Senior Censor, 1980–81; Vice-Pres., 1980–81. President: Cystic Fibrosis Trust, 1986–2003; British Lung Foundn, 1987–95; Medical Protection Soc., 1988–97. Life Vice-Pres., RNLI, 2000. *Publications:* contributions to medical books and journals. *Recreations:* music, sailing. *Address:* 7 Lion Gate Gardens, Richmond, Surrey TW9 2DF. *T:* (020) 8940 3282.

BATTEN, Stephen Duval; QC 1989; barrister; a Recorder, since 1988; *b* 2 April 1945; *s* of Brig. Stephen Alexander Holgate Batten, CBE and of Alice Joan Batten, MBE, *d* of Sir Ernest Royden, 3rd Bt; *m* 1976, Valerie Jean Trim; one *s* one *d*. *Educ:* Uppingham; Pembroke Coll., Oxford (BA). Called to the Bar, Middle Temple, 1968, Bencher 1998. *Recreations:* golf, equestrianism. *Address:* 3 Raymond Buildings, Gray's Inn, WC1R 5BH. *T:* (020) 7831 3833.

BATTERBURY, His Honour Paul Tracy Shepherd, TD 1972 (2 bars); DL; a Circuit Judge, 1983–99; *b* 25 Jan. 1934; only *s* of late Hugh Basil John Batterbury and of Inez Batterbury; *m* 1962, Sheila Margaret, *d* of John Watson; one *s* one *d*. *Educ:* St Olave's Grammar Sch., Southwark; Univ. of Bristol (LLB). Served RAF, 1952–55, TA, 1959–85 (Major, RA). Called to Bar, Inner Temple, 1959; practising barrister, 1959–83. Councillor: Chislehurst and Sidcup UDC, 1960–62; London Borough of Greenwich, 1968–71 (Chm., Housing Cttee, 1970–71). Founder Trustee, St Olave's Sch., SE9, 1970–2001; Founder Chm., Gallipoli Meml Lects, 1986–89. Vice-Pres., SE London, SJAB, 1988–91. DL Greater London, 1986–2001; rep. DL, London Borough of Havering, 1989–95. *Recreations:* walking, caravanning. *Address:* 5 Paper Buildings, Temple, EC4Y 9HB. *T:* (020) 7583 9275.

BATTERHAM, Robin John, AO 2004; PhD; FREng; FTSE; President, Australian Academy of Technological Sciences and Engineering, since 2005; Group Chief Scientist, Rio Tinto, since 2006; *b* 3 April 1941; *s* of Maurice Samuel and Marjorie Kate Batterham. *Educ:* Brighton Grammar Sch.; Melbourne Univ. (BE; PhD 1969). FTSE 1988; FAustIMM 1989; FIChemE 1998; FIEAust 1999; FAIM 1999; FAA 2001; FAICD 2001; FREng 2004. Res. Scientist, later Chief Res. Scientist and Chief of Minerals Res. Div., CSIRO, 1970–88; various positions incl. Man. Dir, R&D, then Global Practice Leader, Innovation, Rio Tinto, 1988–2006; Chief Scientist of Australia, 1999–2005. Professorial Fellow, Univ. of Melbourne, 2004–. Pres., IChemE, 2004. Corresp. Mem., Swiss Acad. Engrg Scis, 2002; For. Associate, NAE, US, 2004. Hon. DLitt Melbourne, 2004; Hon. DSc Sydney Univ. of Technol., 2006. Centenary Medal (Australia), 2001. *Publications:* The Chance to Change, 2000; jl, conf. and patent pubns. *Recreations:* music (organist Scots Ch, Melbourne), ski-ing, cycling. *Address:* 153 Park Drive, Parkville, Vic 3052, Australia. *T:* (3) 9347 0576; *e-mail:* robin.batterham@gmx.net.

BATTERSBY, Sir Alan (Rushton), Kt 1992; MSc, PhD, DSc, ScD; FRS 1966; Professor of Organic Chemistry, Cambridge University, 1969–92, now Emeritus; Fellow of St Catharine's College, Cambridge, 1969–92, Emeritus Fellow, 1992–2000, Hon. Fellow, 2000; *b* Leigh, 4 March 1925; *s* of William and Hilda Battersby; *m* 1949, Margaret Ruth (*d* 1997), *d* of Thomas and Annie Hart, Whaley Bridge, Cheshire; two *s*. *Educ:* Grammar Sch., Leigh; Univ. of Manchester (Mercer and Woodiwis Schol.; MSc); Univ. of St Andrews (PhD); DSc Bristol; ScD Cantab. Asst Lectr in Chemistry, Univ. of St Andrews, 1948–53; Commonwealth Fund Fellow at Rockefeller Inst., NY, 1950–51 and at Univ. of Illinois, 1951–52; Lectr in Chemistry, Univ. of Bristol, 1954–62; Prof. of Organic Chemistry, Univ. of Liverpool, 1962–69. Mem. Council, Royal Soc., 1973–75. Mem. Deutsche Akademie der Naturforscher Leopoldina, 1967; MAE 1990. Pres., Bürgenstock Conf., 1976. Chm., Exec. Council, 1983–90, Trustee, 1993–2000, Novartis (formerly Ciba) Foundn. Foreign Fellow: Nat. Acad. of Scis, India, 1990; Indian Nat. Science Acad., 1993. Honorary Member: Soc. Royale de Chimie, Belgium, 1987; Amer. Acad. of Arts and Scis, 1988; Soc. Argentina de Investigaciones en Quimica Organica, 1997. Lectures: Treat Johnson, Yale, 1969; Pacific Coast, USA, 1971; Karl Folkers, Wisconsin, 1972; N-E Coast, USA, 1974; Andrews, NSW, 1975; Middle Rhine, 1976; Tishler, Harvard, 1978; August Wilhelm von Hoffmann, Ges. Deutscher Chem., 1979; Pedler, Chem. Soc., 1980–81; Rennebohm, Wisconsin, 1981; Kharasch, Chicago, 1982; Bakerian, Royal Soc., 1984; Baker, Cornell, 1984; Lady Masson Meml, Melbourne, 1987; Atlantic Coast, USA, 1988; Nehru Centenary, Seshadri Meml and Zaheer Meml, India, 1989; Marvel, Illinois, 1989; Gilman, Iowa, 1989; Alder, Cologne, 1991; Dauben, Berkeley, 1994; Alexander Cruickshank, Gordon Confs, 1994; Linus Pauling, Oregon, 1996; IAP, Columbia, 1999; Univ. Lectr, Ottawa, 1993; Visiting Professor: Cornell Univ., 1969; Virginia Univ., 1971; Tohoku Univ., Japan, 1974; ANU, 1975; Technion, Israel, 1977; Univ. of Canterbury, NZ, 1980; Melbourne Univ., 1987; Univ. of Auckland, NZ, 1989, 1993; Univ. of NSW, 1990. Chemical Society: Corday-Morgan Medal, 1959; Tilden Medal and Lectr, 1963; Hügo Müller Medal and Lectr, 1972; Flintoff Medal, 1975; Award in Natural Product Chemistry, 1978; Longstaff Medal, 1984; Robert Robinson Lectr and Medal, 1986. Paul Karrer Medal and Lectr, Univ. Zürich, 1977; Davy Medal, 1977, Royal Medal, 1984, Copley Medal, 2000, Royal Soc.; Roger Adams Award in Organic Chemistry, ACS, 1983; Havinga Medal, Holland, 1984; Antoni Feltrinelli Internat. Prize for Chemistry, Rome, 1986; Varro Tyler Lect. and Award, Purdue, 1987; Adolf Windaus Medal, Göttingen, 1987; Wolf Prize, Israel, 1989; Arun Guthikonda Meml Award, Columbia, 1991; Hofmann Meml Medal, Ges. Deutscher Chem., 1992; Tetrahedron Prize for creativity in org. chem., 1995; Hans Herloff Inhoffen Medal, Univ. Braunschweig, 1997; Robert A. Welch Award in Chemistry, USA, 2000; Robert B. Woodward Award, USA, 2004. Hon. LLD St Andrews, 1977; Hon. DSc: Rockefeller Univ., USA, 1977; Sheffield, 1986; Heriot-Watt, 1987; Bristol, 1994; Liverpool, 1996. *Publications:* papers in chemical jls, particularly Jl Chem. Soc. *Recreations:* music, hiking, camping, sailing, fly fishing, gardening. *Address:* University Chemical Laboratory, Lensfield Road, Cambridge CB2 1EW. *T:* (01223) 336400.

BATTISCOMBE, Christopher Charles Richard, CMG 1992; JP; Director General (formerly Secretary General), Society of London Art Dealers, since 2001; Secretary, British Art Market Federation, since 2001; *b* 27 April 1940; *s* of late Lt-Col Christopher Robert Battiscombe and Karin Sigrid (*née* Timberg); *m* 1972, Brigid Melita Theresa Lunn; one *s* one *d*. *Educ:* Wellington Coll.; New Coll., Oxford (BA Greats). Entered FO, 1963; ME Centre for Arabic Studies, Shemlan, Lebanon, 1963–65; Third/Second Sec., Kuwait, 1965–68; FCO, 1968–71; First Secretary: UK Delegn, OECD, Paris, 1971–74; UK Mission to UN, New York, 1974–78; Asst Head, Eastern European and Soviet Dept, FCO, 1978–80; Commercial Counsellor: Cairo, 1981–84; Paris, 1984–86; Counsellor, FCO, 1986–90; Ambassador to Algeria, 1990–94; Asst Under-Sec. of State, then Dir (Public Depts), FCO, 1994–97; Ambassador to Jordan, 1997–2000. Chm., Anglo Jordanian Soc., 2002–. JP Wimbledon, 2002–07. *Recreations:* golf, ski-ing, tennis. *Clubs:* Kandahar; Temple Golf.

BATTISHILL, Sir Anthony (Michael William), GCB 1997 (KCB 1989); Chairman, Board of Inland Revenue, 1986–97 (Deputy Chairman, 1985); *b* 5 July 1937; *s* of William George Battishill and Kathleen Rose Bishop; *m* 1961, Heather Frances Lawes; one *d*. *Educ:* Taunton Sch.; Hele's Sch., Exeter; London Sch. of Economics. BSc (Econ). 2nd Lieut, RAEC, 1958–60. Inland Revenue, 1960–63; HM Treasury, 1963–65; Inland Revenue, 1965–76, Asst Sec., 1970; Central Policy Review Staff, 1976–77; Principal Private Sec. to Chancellor of the Exchequer, HM Treasury, 1977–80; Under Sec., HM Treasury, 1980–82, 1983–85, Inland Revenue, 1982–83. Chm., Student Loans Co. Ltd, 1998–2001. Mem. Ct of Governors, LSE, 1987– (Vice-Chm., 2003–). CCMI. *Recreations:* gardening, old maps. *Address:* 4 Highfield Close, West Byfleet, Surrey KT14 6QR.

BATTLE, Dennis Frank Orlando; consultant on public sector reform, strategic management and human resource management, since 1998; *b* 17 Dec. 1942; *s* of Frank William Orlando and Marion Kathleen Battle; *m* 1965, Sandra Moule; one *s* one *d*. *Educ:* Bedford Modern School. Joined Customs and Excise as Exec. Officer, 1962; Higher Exec. Officer, NBPI, 1967; Sen. Exec. Officer, CS Coll., 1972; returned to Customs and Excise, 1975: Grade 7 1978, Asst Sec. 1985; Comr, 1990–98; Dir of Personnel, 1990–94, Dir of Personnel and Finance, 1994–98. Non-exec. Dir, Sentinel Housing Assoc., 1998–. FCIPD (FIPD 1998). *Recreation:* watching Aldershot FC and Sussex CCC.

BATTLE, Rt Hon. John Dominic; PC 2002; MP (Lab) Leeds West, since 1987; *b* 26 April 1951; *s* of John and late Audrey Battle; *m* 1977, Mary Meenan; one *s* two *d*. *Educ:* Leeds Univ. (BA Hons (1st cl.) 1976). Training for RC Priesthood, Upholland Coll., 1969–72; Leeds Univ., 1973–77; Res. Officer to Derek Enright, MEP, 1979–83; Nat. Co-ordinator, Church Action on Poverty, 1983–87. Opposition front-bench spokesman on housing, 1992–94, on science and technology, 1994–95, on energy, 1995–97; Minister of State: (Minister for Energy and Industry), DTI, 1997–99; FCO, 1999–2001. Mem., Internat. Develt Select Cttee, 2001–. Chairman, All Party Parliamentary Group: on Epilepsy, 1993–97; on Overseas Develt, 2005– (Vice-Chm., 1992–97); on Columbia, 2005–; on Poverty, 2006–. *Recreations:* walking, poetry, supporting Leeds United FC. *Address:* House of Commons, SW1A 0AA. *T:* (020) 7219 4201.

BATTLE, Susan, (Sue), CBE 2006 (OBE 1995); Chief Executive, Birmingham Chamber of Commerce and Industry, 1999–2006; *b* 7 Aug. 1946; *d* of Harry and Beryl Sagar; *m* 1969, George Henry Battle. *Educ:* Old Hall Sch., Norfolk; Newcastle upon Tyne Coll. of Commerce (HND Business Studies). Statistical Asst to Sales Dir, Procter & Gamble Ltd, 1967–72; Adminr, M & R Internat., Riyadh, 1972–75; Birmingham Chamber of Commerce and Industry: Asst Sec., 1977–80; Head of Home and Economic Dept, 1980–84; Asst Dir, 1984–88; Dep. Chief Exec., 1989–99. *Recreations:* ornithology, the countryside, Islamic history and culture. *Address:* 8 Brookfield House, Hackmans Gate Lane, Belbroughton, Stourbridge, Worcs DY9 0DL.

BATTY, Prof. (John) Michael, CBE 2004; PhD; FBA 2001; FRTPI, FCILT; Bartlett Professor of Planning (formerly Professor of Spatial Analysis and Planning), and Director, Centre for Advanced Spatial Analysis, University College London, since 1995; *b* 11 Jan. 1945; *s* of Jack Batty and Nell Batty (*née* Marsden); *m* 1969, Susan Elizabeth Howell; one *s*. *Educ:* Quarry Bank Grammar Sch., Liverpool; Univ. of Manchester (BA 1966); UWIST (PhD 1984). FRTPI 1983; FCILT (FCIT 1990). Asst Lectr, Univ. of Manchester, 1966–69; University of Reading: Res. Asst, 1969–72; Lectr, 1972–74 and 1975–76; Reader, 1976–79; Prof. of City and Regl Planning, 1979–90, Dean, Sch. of Envmtl Design, 1983–86, UC Cardiff; Prof. of Geog., 1990–95, Dir, Nat. Center for Geographic Inf. and Analysis, 1990–95, SUNY, Buffalo. Vis. Asst Prof., Univ. of Waterloo, Ont, 1974; Vis. Fellow, Univ. of Melbourne, 1982; Croucher Fellow, Univ. of Hong Kong, 1986; Vis. Prof., Univ. of Illinois at Urbana-Champaign, 1986; Sir Edward Youde Meml Foundn Vis. Prof., Univ. of Hong Kong, 2001. Ed., Envmt and Planning B, 1981–. Mem., Res. Bd, 1980–82, Chm., Planning Cttee, 1980–82, SSRC; Vice-Chm., Envmt and Planning Cttee, ESRC, 1982–84; Mem., Jt Transport Cttee, 1982–85, Mem., Scientific Computing Adv. Panel, 1989–90, SERC; Mem., Cttee on Scientific Computing, NERC, 1988–90; Mem., Computer Bd for Univs and Res. Councils, 1988–90. FRSA 1983. Award for Technol Progress, Assoc. Geographic Inf., 1998; Back Award, RGS, 1999. *Publications:* Urban Modelling, 1976; (ed) Systems Analysis in Urban Policy-Making and Planning, 1983; (ed) Optimization and Discrete Choice in Urban Systems, 1985; (ed) Advances in Urban Systems Modelling, 1986; Microcomputer Graphics, 1987; (ed) Cities of the 21st Century, 1991; Fractal Cities, 1994; (ed) Cities in Competition, 1995; (ed) Spatial Analysis, 1996; (ed) Advanced Spatial Analysis, 2003; Cities and Complexity, 2005. *Recreations:* discovering America, reading, Indian food, Georgian architecture. *Address:* Centre for Advanced Spatial Analysis, University College London, 1–19 Torrington Place, WC1E 6BT. *T:* (020) 7679 1781; 9 White Horse House, 1 Little Britain, EC1A 7BX. *T:* (020) 7600 8186.

BATTY, Paul Daniel; QC 1995; **His Honour Judge Batty;** a Circuit Judge, since 2003; *b* 13 June 1953; *s* of late Vincent Batty and of Catherine Batty; *m* 1986, Angela Jane Palmer; one *d*. *Educ:* St Aidan's Grammar Sch., Sunderland; Newcastle upon Tyne Univ. (LLB). Called to the Bar, Lincoln's Inn, 1975, Bencher, 2003; Junior, NE Circuit, 1985; Bar Mess Junior, 1982–85; Asst Recorder, 1991; a Recorder, 1994–2003. *Recreations:* boating, angling, Rugby. *Address:* Carlisle Crown Court, Earl Street, Carlisle CA1 1DJ. *T:* (01228) 590588. *Club:* Northern Counties (Newcastle upon Tyne).

BATTY, Peter Wright; television and film producer, director and writer; Chief Executive, Peter Batty Productions, since 1970; *b* 18 June 1931; *s* of late Ernest Faulkner Batty and Gladys Victoria Wright; *m* 1959, Anne Elizabeth Stringer (*d* 2000); two *s* one *d*. *Educ:* Bede Grammar Sch., Sunderland; Queen's Coll., Oxford. Feature-writer, Financial Times, 1954–56; freelance journalist, USA, 1956–58; Producer, BBC TV, 1958–64: mem. original Tonight team, other prodns incl. The Quiet Revolution, The Big Freeze, The Katanga Affair, Sons of the Navvy Man; Editor, Tonight, 1963–64; Exec. Producer and Associate Head of Factual Programming, ATV, 1964–68: prodns incl. The Fall and Rise of the House of Krupp (Grand Prix for Documentary, Venice Film Fest., 1965; Silver Dove, Leipzig Film Fest., 1965), The Road to Suez, The Suez Affair, Vietnam Fly-in, Battle for the Desert; freelance work for BBC TV, ITV and Channel 4, 1968–. Progs dir., prod and scripted incl. The Plutocrats, The Aristocrats, Battle for Cassino, Battle for the Bulge, Birth of the Bomb, Farouk: last of the Pharaohs, Operation Barbarossa, Superspy, Sunderland's Pride and Passion, A Rothschild and his Red Gold, Search for the Super, Spy Extraordinary, Story of Wine, World of Television, The Rise and Rise of Laura Ashley, The Gospel According to St Michael, Battle for Warsaw, Battle for Dien Bien Phu, Nuclear Nightmares, A Turn Up in a Million, Il Poverello, Swindle!, The Algerian War, Fonteyn and Nureyev: the perfect partnership, The Divided Union, A Time for Remembrance, Swastika over British Soil, Tito: Churchill's man?, Tito: his own man; prod and scripted 6 episodes (incl. pilot) World at War series. *Publications:* The House of Krupp, 1966; (with Peter Parish) The Divided Union, 1987; La Guerre d'Algérie, 1989. *Recreations:* walking, reading, listening to music. *Address:* Claremont House, Renfrew Road, Kingston, Surrey KT2 7NT. *T:* (020) 8942 6304. *Club:* Garrick.

BATY, Robert John, OBE 2002; CEng, FREng, FICE; Chief Executive, South West Water Ltd, 1996–2006; *b* 1 June 1944; *s* of late Robert George Baty and of Sarah Baty (*née* Hall); *m* 1975, Patricia Fagan; two *d*. *Educ:* Calday Grange Grammar Sch.; Liverpool Coll. of Building. CEng 1970; FCIWEM 1981; FIWO 1990; FICE 1992; FREng 2000. North West Water: Resident Engr, then Principal Engr, 1974–83; Area Manager, 1983–85; Regl Manager, 1985–88; Engrg and Scientific Dir, SW Water Ltd, 1988–96. Exec. Dir, Pennon plc, 1996–2006. Non-exec. Dir, Royal Devon and Exeter NHS Foundn Trust, 2004–. CCMI 2001. *Recreations:* Rugby and sport generally, recreational flying, classic car restoration. *Address:* Nanparah Lodge, Higher Broad Oak Road, West Hill, Ottery St Mary, Devon EX11 1XJ. *T:* (01404) 812327.

BAUCKHAM, Prof. Richard John, PhD; FBA 1998; FRSE; Professor of New Testament Studies, 1992–2007, and Bishop Wardlaw Professor, 2000–07, St Mary's College, University of St Andrews; *b* 22 Sept. 1946; *s* of John Robert Bauckham and Stephania Lilian Bauckham (*née* Wells). *Educ:* Enfield GS; Clare Coll., Cambridge (BA Hons Hist. 1st cl. 1969; MA 1972; PhD 1973). FRSE 2002. Fellow, St John's Coll., Cambridge, 1972–75; Lectr in Theol., Leeds Univ., 1976–77; Lectr, 1977–87, Reader, 1987–92, in Hist. of Christian Thought, Manchester Univ. Member: Doctrine Commn, C of E, 1990–2003; Doctrine Cttee, Scottish Episcopal Ch, 1997–2002. *Publications:* Tudor Apocalypse, 1978; Jude, 2 Peter (commentary), 1983; Moltmann: Messianic theology in the making, 1987; The Bible in Politics, 1989; Word Biblical Themes: Jude, 2 Peter, 1990; Jude and the Relatives of Jesus in the Early Church, 1990; The Theology of the Book of Revelation, 1993; The Climax of Prophecy, 1993; The Theology of Jürgen Moltmann, 1995; The Fate of the Dead, 1998; James: Wisdom of James, Disciple of Jesus the Sage, 1999; God Crucified: monotheism and Christology in the New Testament, 1999; (with Trevor Hart) Hope Against Hope: Christian eschatology in contemporary context, 1999; Gospel Women, 2002; God and the Crisis of Freedom, 2002; Bible and Mission, 2003; The MacBears of Bearloch, 2006; Jesus and the Eyewitnesses, 2006; The Testimony of the Beloved Disciple, 2007; Jesus and the God of Israel, 2008; The Jewish World and the New Testament, 2008; *edited:* (jtly) Scripture, Tradition and Reason, 1988; (jtly) The Nuclear Weapons Debate: theological and ethical issues, 1989; The Book of Acts in its Palestinian Setting, 1995; The Gospels for All Christians, 1997; God will be All in All: the eschatology of Jürgen Moltmann, 1999; many articles in books and learned jls. *Recreations:* gardening, walking, novels. *Address:* 11 Archway Court, Barton Road, Cambridge CB3 9LW.

BAUGH, John Trevor; Director General of Supplies and Transport (Naval), Ministry of Defence, 1986–93; *b* 24 Sept. 1932; *s* of late Thomas Harold Baugh and Nellie Baugh (*née* Machin); *m* 1st, 1956, Pauline Andrews (decd); three *s*; 2nd, 1981, Noreen Rita Rosemary Sykes; two step *s*. *Educ:* Queen Elizabeth's Hospital, Bristol. CMILT (MCIT 1956). Asst Naval Store Officer, Devonport, 1953; Dep. Naval Store Officer, Admiralty, 1959; Armament Supply Officer, Alexandria, 1966; Principal, MoD, Bath, 1970; Supt, RN Store Depot, Copenacre, 1974; Asst Sec., MoD (Navy), 1976, Exec. Dir, 1979; MoD (Army), 1983, Asst Under Sec. of State 1985. *Recreations:* bridge, golf. *Address:* Treetops, North Road, Bath, Avon BA2 6HB. *Clubs:* Athenæum; Bath Golf; Christchurch (NZ).

BAUGHAN, Julian James; QC 1990; a Recorder, since 1985; *b* 8 Feb. 1944; *s* of late Prof. E. C. Baughan, CBE, and Mrs E. C. Baughan. *Educ:* Eton Coll. (King's Schol.); Balliol Coll., Oxford (Brassey Italian Schol.; BA History). Called to Bar, Inner Temple, 1967 (Profumo Schol., Philip Teichman Schol., Major Schol.); Prosecuting Counsel to DTI, 1983–90. *Address:* 13 King's Bench Walk, Temple, EC4Y 7EN.

BAUGHEN, Rt Rev. Michael Alfred; Bishop of Chester, 1982–96; Assistant Bishop, diocese of Guildford, since 2006; *b* 7 June 1930; *s* of Alfred Henry and Clarice Adelaide Baughen; *m* 1956, Myrtle Newcomb Phillips; two *s* one *d*. *Educ:* Bromley County Grammar Sch.; Univ. of London; Oak Hill Theol Coll. BD (London). With Martins Bank, 1946–48, 1950–51. Army, Royal Signals, 1948–50. Degree Course and Ordination Trng, 1951–56; Curate: St Paul's, Hyson Green, Nottingham, 1956–59; Reigate Parish Ch., 1959–61; Candidates Sec., Church Pastoral Aid Soc., 1961–64; Rector of Holy Trinity (Platt), Rusholme, Manchester, 1964–70; Vicar of All Souls, Langham Place, W1, 1970–75; Rector, 1975–82; Area Dean of St Marylebone, 1978–82; a Prebendary of St Paul's Cathedral, 1979–82; Asst Bp, dio. of London, 1996–2006; Priest-in-charge, St James's, Clerkenwell, 1997–98. Hon. LLD Liverpool, 1994. *Publications:* Moses and the Venture of Faith, 1979; The Prayer Principle, 1981; II Corinthians: a spiritual health-warning to the Church, 1982; Chained to the Gospel, 1986; Evidence for Christ, 1986; Getting through to God, 1992; (with Myrtle Baughen) Your Marriage, 1994; Grace People: rooted in God's covenant love, 2006; Editor: Youth Praise, 1966; Youth Praise II, 1969; Psalm Praise, 1973; consultant editor, Hymns for Today's Church, 1982; gen. ed, Sing Glory, 1999. *Recreations:* music, railways, touring. *Address:* 42 Rookwood Court, Guildford, Surrey GU2 4EL.

BAULCOMBE, Prof. David Charles, PhD; FRS 2001; Professor of Botany, and Royal Society Research Professor, Department of Plant Sciences, University of Cambridge, since 2007; *b* 7 April 1952; *s* of William (Jim) and Joan Baulcombe; *m* 1976, Rose Eden; one *s* three *d*. *Educ:* Leamington Coll., Leamington Spa; Leeds Univ. (BSc Botany); Edinburgh Univ. (PhD 1977). Postdoctoral Fellow: McGill Univ., Montreal, 1977–78; Univ. of Georgia, Athens, 1979–80; res. scientist, Plant Breeding Inst., Cambridge, 1981–88; Sen. Scientist, Sainsbury Lab., John Innes Centre, Norwich, 1988–2007; Prof., Dept of Biological Scis, UEA, 2002–07 (Hon. Prof., 1998–2002). Pres., Internat. Soc. of Plant Molecular Biology, 2003–04. Mem., EMBO, 1998; MAE, 2003; Foreign Associate Mem., Nat. Acad. of Scis, USA, 2005. Prix des Céréalières de France, 1990; Kumho Sci. Internat. Award, Kumho Cultural Foundn, S Korea, 2002; (jtly) Wiley Internat. Prize in Biomedicine, 2003; Beijerinck Prize for Virology, Royal Dutch Acad. Arts and Scis, 2004; Royal Medal, Royal Soc., 2006; (jtly) Franklin Medal, Franklin Inst., USA, 2008. *Publications:* contrib. res. papers and articles on plant genetics, virology and genetic engrg in Nature, Science, Cell, and specialist jls. *Recreations:* sailing, hill-walking, music. *Address:* Department of Plant Sciences, University of Cambridge, Downing Street, Cambridge CB2 3EA. *T:* (01223) 333900. *Club:* Norfolk Punt (Barton, Norfolk).

BAUM, Prof. Michael, ChM; FRCS; Professor of Surgery, 1996–2000, now Emeritus, and Visiting Professor of Medical Humanities, since 2000, University College London; Consultant Surgeon, UCL Hospitals NHS Trust, since 1996; *b* 31 May 1937; *s* of Isidor and Mary Baum; *m* 1965, Judith (*née* Marcus); one *s* two *d*. *Educ:* Univ. of Birmingham (MB, ChB; ChM). FRCS 1965. Lecturer in Surgery, King's College Hosp., 1969–72; Research Fellow, Univ. of Pittsburgh, USA, 1971–72; Reader in Surgery, Welsh National Sch. of Medicine, Cardiff, 1972–78; Hon. Cons. Surgeon, King's College Hosp., 1978–80; Professor of Surgery: KCH Med. Sch., London, 1980–90; Inst. of Cancer Res., Royal Marsden Hosp., 1990–96, Prof. Emeritus, 1996–; Vis. Prof., UCL, 1995–96. Chairman: SE Thames Regional Cancer Organisation, 1988–90; British Breast Gp, 1989–91; Breast Cancer Cttee, UK Co-ordinating Cttee for Cancer Research, 1989–96; Psychosocial Oncology Cttee, Nat. Cancer Res. Network, 2004–06; Mem., Adv. Cttee on Breast Cancer Screening, DHSS, 1987–95; Specialist Advr, Select Cttee on Health, 1996–98. President: British Oncological Assoc., 1996–98; Eur. Breast Cancer Conf., 2000–02. Chm., Med. Cttee, AVMA, 2000–05. Karl Popper Meml Lect., LSE, 2007. FRSA 1998. Hon. FRCR 1998. Hon. MD Göteborg, 1986. Gold Medal, Internat. Coll. of Surgeons, 1994; Celebrating Survival award, Univ. of Texas, San Antonio, 2000; William McGuire Prize, Univ. of Texas, 2002; Internat. Soc. for Breast Cancer Res. Prize, 2003; St Gallen Prize, Univ. of Gallen, 2007; Galen Medal for Therapeutics, Soc. of Apothecaries. *Publications:* Breast Cancer—The Facts, 1981, 3rd edn 1994; Classic Papers in Breast Disease, 2003; multiple pubns on breast cancer, cancer therapy, cancer biology and the philosophy of science. *Recreations:* painting, sculpting, theatre, reading, philosophizing. *Address:* 2 Cotman Close, NW11 6PT. *T:* (020) 8905 5069. *Clubs:* Athenæum, Royal Society of Medicine.

BAUMAN, Robert Patten; Chairman, BTR, 1998–99 (Deputy Chairman, 1997–98); *b* 27 March 1931; *s* of John Nevan Bauman Jr and Lucille Miller Patten; *m* 1961, Patricia Hughes Jones; one *s* one *d*. *Educ:* Ohio Wesleyan Univ. (BA); Harvard Sch. of Business (MBA). Served USAF, 1955–57. General Foods Corp., 1958–81: Corp. Vice-Pres., 1968; Group Vice-Pres., 1970; Exec. Vice-Pres. and Corp. Dir, 1972–81; Pres., Internat. Ops, 1974–81; Dir, Avco Corp., 1980, Chm. and Chief Exec., 1981–85; Vice-Chm. and Dir, Textron Inc., 1985–86; Chm. and Chief Exec., Beecham Gp, 1986–89; Chief Exec., SmithKline Beecham, 1989–94; Chm., BAe, 1994–98. Director: Cap Cities/ABC Inc., 1986–96; Union Pacific Corp., 1987–2001; CIGNA Corp., 1990–2001; Reuters Holdings, 1993–2000; Russell Reynolds Associates Inc., 1994–; Morgan Stanley Gp Inc., 1996–2004; Hathaway Holdings Inc., 1996–2001; Invensys, 1999–2002. Mem., MRC, 1991–95. Trustee: Ohio Wesleyan Univ., 1982–; Royal Botanic Gardens, Kew, 1990–2000. *Publications:* Plants as Pets, 1982; (jtly) From Promise to Performance, 1996. *Recreations:* growing orchids, tennis, photography, golf. *Clubs:* Queen's; Blind Brook (New York); Walton Heath Golf; Wisley Golf.

BAUMBERG, Prof. Jeremy John, DPhil; FInstP; Professor of Nanoscience, University of Cambridge, since 2007; *b* 14 March 1967; *s* of late Prof. Simon Baumberg, OBE and of Ruth Elizabeth Baumberg; *m* 1994, Melissa Murray; two *d*. *Educ:* Jesus Coll., Cambridge (BA Hons Natural Scis 1988); Jesus Coll., Oxford (DPhil 1993). FInstP 1999. Jun. Res. Fellow, Jesus Coll., Oxford, 1992–94; IBM Res. Fellow, UCSB, USA, 1994–95; Researcher, Hitachi Cambridge Lab., 1995–98; Prof. of Nano-scale Physics, Univ. of Southampton, 1998–2007. Founder, Mesophotonics Ltd, 2001–. Fellow: Inst. of Nanotechnology, 1999; Optical Soc. of America, 2006. *Recreations:* fell walking, pianist, drinking saké, stone carving, kinetic sculptures, tennis, choral singing, clock making. *Address:* Cavendish Laboratory, University of Cambridge, J. J. Thompson Avenue, Cambridge CB3 0HE. *T:* (01223) 337429; *e-mail:* j.j.baumberg@phy.cam.ac.uk.

BAUME, Jonathan Edward; General Secretary, FDA (formerly Association of First Division Civil Servants), since 1997; *b* 14 July 1953; *s* of late George Frederick Baume and Mary Louisa Baume (*née* Hardwick). *Educ:* Queen Elizabeth Grammar Sch., Wakefield; Keble Coll., Oxford (BA Hons 1974; MA). Oxfordshire CC, 1974–76; Dept of Employment Gp, 1977–87; Orgn and Indust. Relns Dept, TUC, 1987–89; Asst Gen. Sec., 1989–94, Dep. Gen. Sec., 1994–97, FDA. Mem., TUC Gen. Council, 2001–. Member: Ministerial Adv. Gp on Openness in Public Sector, 1998–99; Ministerial Adv. Gp on Implementation of Freedom of Information Act, 2001–04; Age Adv. Gp, DTI, 2004–. *Recreations:* yoga, post-war jazz, world music, rambling. *Address:* FDA, 2 Caxton Street, SW1H 0QH. *T:* (020) 7343 1111. *Club:* Athenæum.

BAUR, Christopher Frank; writer and publisher; Executive Chairman, Editions Publishing Ltd, since 2004; *b* 28 May 1942; *s* of Mrs Marty Stewart (*née* Sigg) and Frank Baur; *m* 1965, Jaqueline Gilchrist; four *s*. *Educ:* Dalhousie Prep. Sch.; Strathallan Sch., Perthshire. Joined Scotsman as copy boy, 1960; trained as journalist; Scotsman's Industrial Reporter, 1963, additionally Scottish Politics, 1972; Financial Times, Scottish corresp., 1973; Scottish political corresp., BBC, 1976; The Scotsman: Asst Editor, 1978, writing on politics and economic affairs; Dep. Editor, 1983–85; Editor, 1985–87; Editor, Scottish Business Insider, 1990–94; Dir, Insider Gp, 1994–2003; Man. Dir, Insider Custom Publishing, 1997–99. *Recreation:* creating. *Address:* 29 Edgehead Village, near Pathhead, Midlothian EH37 5RL. *T:* (01875) 320476.

BAVIN, Rt Rev. Timothy John, FRSCM; OSB; *b* 17 Sept. 1935; *s* of Edward Sydney Durrance and Marjorie Gwendoline Bavin. *Educ:* Brighton Coll.; Worcester Coll., Oxford (2nd Cl. Theol., MA); Cuddesdon Coll. Curate, St Alban's Cathedral Pretoria, 1961–64; Chaplain, St Alban's Coll., Pretoria, 1965–68; Curate of Uckfield, Sussex, 1969–71; Vicar of Good Shepherd, Brighton, 1971–73; Dean and Rector of Cathedral of St Mary the Virgin, Johannesburg, 1973–74; Bishop of Johannesburg, 1974–84; Bishop of Portsmouth, 1985–95; monk, OSB, 1996–. Mem., OGS, 1987–97; FRSCM 1991. ChStJ 1975. *Publication:* Deacons in the Ministry of the Church, 1987. *Recreations:* music, gardening. *Address:* Alton Abbey, Alton, Hants GU34 4AP.

BAWDEN, Prof. Charles Roskelly, FBA; Professor of Mongolian, University of London, 1970–84, now Emeritus Professor; *b* 22 April 1924; *s* of George Charles Bawden and Eleanor Alice Adelaide Bawden (*née* Russell); *m* 1949, Jean Barham Johnson; three *s* one *d*. *Educ:* Weymouth Grammar School; Peterhouse, Cambridge (MA, PhD, Dipl. in Oriental Languages). War Service, RNVR, 1943–46. Asst Principal, German Section, Foreign Office, 1948–49; Lectr in Mongolian, SOAS, 1955; Reader in Mongolian, 1962, and Prof., 1970, Univ. of London; Head of Dept of Far East, SOAS, 1970–84; Pro-Director, SOAS, 1982–84. FBA 1971–80, 1985; Mem. corresp., Soc. Finno-Ougrienne 1975. Hon. Mem., Societas Uralo-Altacca, 2003. Friendship Medal, Mongolia, 1997; Order of the Pole Star, Sweden, 2007. *Publications:* The Mongol Chronicle Altan Tobči, 1955; The Jebtsundamba Khutukhtus of Urga, 1961; The Modern History of Mongolia, 1968, 2nd edn 1989; The Chester Beatty Library: a catalogue of the Mongolian Collection, 1969; Shamans Lamas and Evangelicals: the English missionaries in Siberia, 1985; Confronting the Supernatural: Mongolian traditional ways and means, 1994; Mongolian-English Dictionary, 1997; Tales of an Old Lama, 1997; Mongolian Traditional Literature: an anthology, 2003; articles and reviews in SOAS Bull., Central Asiatic Jl, Zentralasiatische Studien and other periodicals. *Address:* 19 Richings Way, Iver, Bucks SL0 9DA.

BAWDEN, Nina Mary, (Mrs A. S. Kark), CBE 1995; MA; FRSL; JP; novelist; *b* 19 Jan. 1925; *d* of Charles and Ellalaine Ursula May Mabey; *m* 1st, 1946, Henry Walton Bawden; one *s* (and one *s* decd); 2nd, 1954, Austen Steven Kark, CBE (*d* 2002); one *d*. *Educ:* Ilford County High Sch.; Somerville Coll., Oxford (BA; Hon. Fellow, 2001). Asst, Town and Country Planning Assoc., 1946–47. JP Surrey, 1968. Mem., ALCS. Pres., Soc. of Women Writers and Journalists. *Publications: novels:* Who Calls the Tune, 1953; The Odd Flamingo, 1954; Change Here for Babylon, 1955; The Solitary Child, 1956; Devil by the Sea, 1958, 2nd edn 1972 (abridged for children, 1976); Just Like a Lady, 1960; In Honour Bound, 1961; Tortoise by Candlelight, 1963; Under the Skin, 1964; A Little Love, a Little Learning, 1965; A Woman of My Age, 1967; The Grain of Truth, 1969; The Birds on the Trees, 1970; Anna Apparent, 1972; George beneath a Paper Moon, 1974; Afternoon of a Good Woman, 1976 (Yorkshire Post Novel of the Year, 1976); Familiar Passions, 1979; Walking Naked, 1981; The Ice House, 1983; Circles of Deceit, 1987 (televised, 1990); Family Money, 1991 (televised, 1997); A Nice Change, 1997; Ruffian on the Stair, 2001; *for children:* The Secret Passage, 1963; On the Run, 1964; The White Horse Gang, 1966; Squib, 1966; A Handful of Thieves, 1967; The Witch's Daughter, 1968; The Runaway Summer, 1969; Carrie's War, 1975 (Phoenix Award, 1995); The Peppermint Pig, 1975 (Guardian award, 1976); Rebel on a Rock, 1978; The Robbers, 1978; Kept in the Dark, 1982; The Finding, 1985; Princess Alice, 1985; Keeping Henry, 1987; The Outside Child, 1989; Humbug, 1992; The Real Plato Jones, 1993; Granny the Pag, 1995; Off the Road, 1998; *non-fiction:* Dear Austen, 2005; *autobiography:* In My Own Time, 1994. *Recreations:* travelling, reading, politics, friends. *Address:* 22 Noel Road, N1 8HA. *T:* (020) 7226 2839; 19 Kapodistriou, Nauplion 21100, Greece. *Clubs:* Oriental, PEN, Society of Authors.

BAWTREE, Rear Adm. David Kenneth, CB 1993; DL; CEng, FIMechE, FIET; Chairman and Chief Executive, Future Ship Project for 21st Century (FSP21), since 2001; *b* 1 Oct. 1937; *s* of Kenneth Alfred Bawtree and Dorothy Constance Bawtree (*née* Allen); *m* 1962, Ann Cummins; one *s* one *d*. *Educ:* Christ's Hospital; Royal Naval Engineering College. BSc(Eng). Served in HM Ships Maidstone, Jutland, Diamond, Defender, Rothesay, Bristol, and MoD, 1965–76; Staff of C-in-C Fleet, 1979, of DG Weapons, 1981; Dep. Dir, Naval Analysis, 1983; RCDS 1985; Dep. Dir, Op. Requirements (Navy), 1986; Dir, Naval Engrg Training, 1987–90; Flag Officer, and Naval Base Comdr, Portsmouth, 1990–93; Civil Emergencies Advr, Home Office, 1993–97. Dir, Flagship Portsmouth, 1997 (Chm., 2000–05). Advr in Civil Emergencies, Visor Consultants, 1998–; Project Manager: MMI (Research), 2001–02; Stargate Technologies, 2002–04; SeaCell, 2004–07. Dir, Portsmouth Healthcare NHS Trust, 1993–96; Chm., Portsmouth Hosps NHS Trust, 1996–2001. Pres., Portsmouth Model Boats Display Team., 1992–. Past President: Royal Naval and Royal Albert Yacht Club, Portsmouth; Naval Home Club; RN & RM Children's Home; Royal Naval Squash Rackets Assoc.; Chm., Portsmouth Dockyard Industries, 1997; Past Member: Victory Technical Adv. Cttee; Mary Rose Trust; Portsmouth Naval Base Heritage Trust; Royal Naval Mus.; Trustee: St Mary's Music Foundn, 1990–2001 (Chm., 1990–2001); Portsmouth News Snowball Appeal, 1992–94; HMS Warrior 1860, 1993– (Chm., 1997–); Chm., Hants Foundn for Young Musicians, 1993–2003. Patron, CP Centre, 2002–; former Patron, Portsmouth MacMillan Appeal. Almoner, Christ's Hospital, 1998–2004. Governor: Portsmouth Grammar Sch., 1990– (Chm., 1993–); Penhale First Sch., 1991–2002. Guildsman, St Bride's, Fleet St, 1997–; Consultant to Bishop of London, 1998–2006. Freeman, City of London; Liveryman, Engineers' Co. (Master, 2007–08). FRSA 2006. DL Hants, 1997. *Recreations:* fives (Nat. Masters' Champion, 2003, 2004 and 2005), squash, organs and their music, miniature furniture, tropical fish.

BAX, Martin Charles Owen, DM; FRCP; FRSL; Senior Lecturer, Imperial College School of Medicine, 1997–2001, now Emeritus Reader; *b* 13 Aug. 1933; *s* of Cyril E. O. Bax and E. C. M. Bayne; *m* 1956, Judith Mary Osborne; three *s*. *Educ:* Dauntsey's Sch., Wilts; New Coll., Oxford (MA, BM BCh, DM); Guy's Hosp., London. Lectr, Guy's Med. Sch., 1961–74; Res. Paediatrician, Thomas Coram Res. Unit, St Mary's Hosp., London, 1974–82; Dir, Community Paediatric Res. Unit, St Mary's Hosp. Med. Sch., 1982–85; Med. Dir, Community Paediatric Res. Unit, Westminster Hosp. Med. Sch., later Charing Cross and Westminster Med. Sch., subseq. Imperial Coll. Sch. of Medicine, 1985–. Editor, Ambit Literary & Arts Magazine, 1959–; Sen. Ed., Mac Keith Press, 1978–2004. Folke Bernadette Lectr, Sweden, 1984. FRSL 2002. Anderson-Aldrich Award, Amer. Acad. of Paediatrics, 1990; Dist. Service Award, Amer. Acad. for Cerebral Palsy & Develt Medicine, 1994. *Publications:* The Hospital Ship (novel), 1975; Edmond Went Far Away (for children), 1990; (jtly) Child Development and Child Health, 1990; Love on the Borders (novel), 2005; Memoirs of a Gone World (short stories), 2008. *Recreations:* tennis, walking. *Address:* 17 Priory Gardens, Highgate, N6 5QY. *T:* (020) 8340 3566. *Clubs:* Chelsea Arts, Royal Society of Medicine.

BAXENDALE, Leo; freelance artist; *b* 27 Oct. 1930; *s* of Leo Baxendale and Gertrude Baxendale (*née* Dickinson); *m* 1955, Peggy Green; three *s* two *d*. *Educ:* Preston Catholic Coll. Created: Little Plum, Minnie the Minx and Bash St Kids for The Beano, 1953, drew them and their siblings, Three Bears and Banana Bunch, 1953–64; WHAM! comic (Grimly Feendish, Barmy Army, *et al*), 1964; characters for Fleetway/IPC comics, 1966–75; set up Reaper Books, 1987; created I LOVE You Baby Basil!, The Guardian, 1990; stopped drawing due to arthritis, 1992. Publisher, The Strategic Commentary, by Terence Heelas, 1965–67. *Publications:* Willy the Kid, Book 1, 1976, Book 2, 1977, Book 3, 1978; A Very Funny Business (autobiog.), 1978; The Encroachment, 1988; On Comedy: the Beano and ideology, 1989, 2nd edn 1993; I LOVE You Baby Basil!, 1991; Pictures in the Mind, 2000; The Worst of Willy the Kid, 2002; The Beano Room, 2005. *Recreation:* seeping into the woodwork and rotting it. *Address:* 11 Brockley Acres, Eastcombe, Stroud, Glos GL6 7DU; *e-mail:* romics@reaper.co.uk.

BAXENDALE, Presiley Lamorna, (Mrs R. K. FitzGerald); QC 1992; *b* 31 Jan. 1951; *d* of late Geoffrey Arthur Baxendale and Elizabeth (*née* Stevenson); *m* 1978, Richard Kieran FitzGerald; one *s* one *d*. *Educ:* St Mary's Sch., Wantage; St Anne's Coll., Oxford (BA). Called to the Bar, Lincoln's Inn, 1974, Bencher, 1999; Jun. Counsel to Crown, Common Law, 1991. Member: ICSTIS, 1986–90; Council, Justice, 1994–2002. Mem., Ct of Govs, LSE, 1988–. Counsel to Scott Inquiry, 1992–95. *Address:* Blackstone Chambers, Blackstone House, Temple, EC4Y 9BW. *T:* (020) 7583 1770, *Fax:* (020) 7822 7350. *Club:* CWIL.

BAXENDELL, Sir Peter (Brian), Kt 1981; CBE 1972; FREng; FIC; Director, Shell Transport and Trading Co., 1973–95 (Chairman, 1979–85); *b* 28 Feb. 1925; *s* of Lesley Wilfred Edward Baxendell and Evelyn Mary Baxendell (*née* Gaskin); *m* 1949, Rosemary (*née* Lacey); two *s* two *d*. *Educ:* St Francis Xavier's, Liverpool; Royal School of Mines, London (ARSM, BSc; FIC 1983). FREng (FEng 1978). Joined Royal Dutch/Shell Group, 1946; Petroleum Engr in Egypt, 1947, and Venezuela, 1950; Techn. Dir, Shell-BP Nigeria, 1963; Head of SE Asia Div., London, 1966; Man. Dir, Shell-BP Nigeria, 1969; Chm., Shell UK, 1974–79; Man. Dir, 1973, Chm., Cttee of Man. Dirs, 1982–85, Royal Dutch/Shell Gp of Cos; Chm., Shell Canada Ltd, 1980–85; Dir, Shell Oil Co., USA, 1982–85; Chm., Hawker Siddeley Gp, 1986–91 (Dir, 1984–91; Dep. Chm., Jan.–April 1986); Director: Sun Life Assurance Co. of Canada, 1986–97; Inchcape, 1986–93. Mem., UGC, 1983–89. Mem., Governing Body, Imperial Coll., London, 1983–99 (Vice Chm., 1991–99). Hon. DSc: Heriot-Watt, 1982; QUB, 1986; London, 1986; Loughborough, 1987. Commander, Order of Orange-Nassau, 1985. *Publications:* articles on petroleum engrg subjects in scientific jls. *Recreations:* tennis, fishing. *Address:* c/o Shell Centre, SE1 7NA.

BAXTER, Canon Dr Christina Ann, CBE 2005; Principal, St John's College, Nottingham, since 1997 (Dean, 1988–97); Chairman of House of Laity, General Synod of Church of England, since 1995 (Vice-Chairman, 1990–95); *b* 8 March 1947; *d* of Leslie John David and Madge Adeline Baxter. *Educ:* Walthamstow Hall, Sevenoaks, Kent; Durham Univ. (BA, PhD); Bristol Univ. (Cert Ed). Asst Teacher, 1969–73, Head of Religious Educn, 1973–76, John Leggott Sixth Form Coll., Scunthorpe; part-time tutor, St John's Coll., Durham, and Durham research student, 1976–79; Lectr in Christian Doctrine, St John's Coll., Nottingham, 1979–. Canon Theologian, Coventry Cath., 1996–2006; Lay Canon, Southwell Minster, 2000–. Mem., Archbishops' Council, 1998–. *Publication:* Wounds of Jesus, 2005. *Recreation:* swimming. *Address:* St John's College, Chilwell Lane, Bramcote, Nottingham NG9 3DS. *T:* (0115) 925 1114; 18 St Michael's Square, Bramcote, Nottingham NG9 3HG. *T:* (0115) 922 4087.

BAXTER, Glen; artist; *b* 4 March 1944; *s* of Charles Baxter and Florence Baxter; *m* 1991, Carole Suzanne Elsa Agis; one *s* one *d*. *Educ:* Leeds Coll. of Art. *Exhibitions:* Gotham Book Mart, NYC, 1974, 1976, 1979; Anthony Stokes Gall., London, 1978, 1980; ICA, 1981; Mus. of Modern Art, Oxford, 1981; Nigel Greenwood Gall., London, 1983, 1985, 1990; Holly Solomon Gall., NY, 1985; Sydney Biennale, Australia, 1986; Samia Saouma, Paris, 1987, 1991; Musée de l'Abbaye Sainte-Croix, Les Sables d'Olonne, France, 1987; Seita Mus., Paris, 1990; Adelaide Fest., 1992; Tanya Rumpff Galerie, Haarlem, 1992; Ginza Art Space, Tokyo, 1994; Wilkinson Fine Art, London, 1994; Les Entrepôts Laydet, Paris, 1995; Nagy Fine Art, Sydney, 1996; Modernism, San Francisco, 1998, 2002, 2006, 2008; Gal. de la Châme, Paris, 1998, 2004, 2008; Artothèque Gal., Angoulême, and Gal. de la Châtre, Palais de Congrès, Paris, Chris Beetles Gall., and Anthony Wilkinson Gall., London, 1999; Lombard Freid Fine Arts, NY, 2001; Galerie Daniel Blau, Munich, 2001; Le Salon d'Art, Brussels, 2003, 2008; Wetering Gal., Amsterdam, 2004; Flowers Central Gall., London, 2004, 2006; Gal. Martine et Thibault de la Châtre, Paris, 2006. *Works in collections:* Tate Gall.; De Young Mus., San Francisco; V&A. Histl tapestry (commnd by French Min. of Culture, 1999), Contemporary Art Mus., Rochechouart, France. *Publications:* The Works, 1977; Atlas, 1979; The Impending Gleam, 1981; Glen Baxter: his life, 1983; Jodhpurs in the Quantocks, 1986; The Billiard Table Murders, 1990; Returns to Normal, 1992; The Wonder Book of Sex, 1995; 1936 at the Hotel Furkablick, 1997; Glen Baxter's Gourmet Guide, 1997; Blizzards of Tweed, 1999; Trundling Grunts, 2002; Loomings over the Suet, 2004; (with Clark Coolidge) Speech with Humans, 2007. *Recreations:* marquetry, snood retrieval. *Clubs:* Groucho, Chelsea Arts; Ale and Quail (New York).

BAXTER, Maj.-Gen. Ian Stuart, CBE 1982 (MBE 1973); antiques dealer, since 1990; *b* 20 July 1937; *s* of Charles Baxter and Edith (*née* Trinder); *m* 1961, Meg Bullock; three *d*. *Educ:* Ottershaw Sch. Commissioned RASC, 1958; RCT, 1965; regtl and staff appts UK, NI, Kenya, India, Germany and Falkland Is; sc, Camberley, 1970; ndc, Latimer, 1974; DS, Staff Coll., Camberley, 1975–78; CO, 2nd Armoured Div., Regt RCT, 1978–80; Col AQ Commando Forces, RM, 1980–83 (incl. Falklands Campaign); RCDS, 1984; Dir, Army Recruiting, 1985–87; ACDS (Logistics), 1987–90, retd. Col Comdt, RCT, 1989–93. Dir (non-exec.), Cornwall Community Healthcare NHS Trust, 1990–93; Vice-Chm. (non-exec.), Cornwall HealthCare NHS Trust, 1993–95. Dir (non-exec.), Curnow Care, 1995–2001. Pres., RCT/RASC Instn, 1993–98. Chm. Govs, Quethiock Sch., 2001–06. *Recreations:* antique restoration, Rugby. *Address:* Weston House, Callington, Cornwall PL17 7JJ.

BAXTER, John, FREng; FRSE; FIMarEST, FIMechE, FIET; Group Engineering Director, BP plc, since 2004; *b* 26 March 1951; *s* of late Robert Baxter and Ruth Baxter (*née* Baxter); *m* 1996, Margaret Helen Carnell; two *s* from a previous marriage. *Educ:* Queen's Park Sch., Glasgow; Strathclyde Univ. (BSc Hons); RNC, Greenwich (Postgrad. Dip.). FIMechE 1993; FIET (FIEE 2001); FREng 2003; FIMarEST 2007. Hd, Nuclear Reactors, Harwell, 1988–90; Director: Engrg, UKAEA, 1990–94; Dounreay, 1994–96; Mem., UKAEA, 1994–98; Chief Engr, 1998–2001, Gp Engrg Dir, 2001–04, Powergen plc. Pres., IMechE, 2007–08. FRSE 2008; FRSA 1996. Lt Col, 2003–07, Col, 2007–, Engr & Logistic Staff Corps, RE (V). Liveryman, Co. of Engrs, 2001; Freeman, Tallow Chandlers' Co., 2008. Hon. DTech Robert Gordon, 2008. *Recreations:* sailing, ski-ing, walking. *Address:* BP plc, Chertsey Road, Sunbury-on-Thames, Middx TW16 7LN. *T:* (01932) 762000. *Club:* Institute of Directors.

BAXTER, John Lawson; Vice Lord-Lieutenant of County Londonderry, since 2002; *b* 25 Nov. 1939; *s* of John Lawson Baxter and Enid Maud Taggart; *m* 1967; three *s*. *Educ:* Trinity Coll., Dublin; Queen's Univ., Belfast; BA, BComm, LLB; LLM Tulane Univ., New Orleans. Solicitor. Mem. (U) N Ireland Assembly, for N Antrim, 1973–75; Minister of Information, N Ireland Executive, 1974. Chm. (part-time), Industrial Tribunals (NI), 1980–83; Member: Northern Health and Social Services Board, 1982–; Criminal Injury Appeals Panel, 2002–. Mem. Council, Ulster Univ., 2002–. DL Co. Londonderry, 1988. *Recreations:* golf, fishing. *Address:* Beardiville, Cloyfin, Coleraine, N Ireland. *T:* (028) 2073 1552.

BAXTER, John Stephen; Head Master, Wells Cathedral School, 1986–2000; *b* 7 Sept. 1939; *s* of George Baxter and Muriel (*née* Firman); *m* 1965, Priscilla Candy; two *s*. *Educ:* Magdalen Coll. Sch., Oxford; Merton Coll., Oxford; Grey Coll., Durham. BA Modern History, Durham; DipEd Oxford. Assistant Master: Cranleigh Sch., 1964–67; Christ's

Coll., NZ, 1967–70; Westminster Sch., 1971–86 (Hd of Hist., 1974–79; Hse Master, 1979–86). Educn Consultant, Emergent Dynamics (formerly Breakthrough), 2000–05. Ecclesiastical Insce Gp Scholar, 1993; Korea Foundn Fellow, 1993. Res. Asst, H of C, 1971–79; Reader, Edward Arnold, 1980–83. Mem., Admiralty Interview Bd, 1988–2005. Chairman: SW Div., HMC, 1991; Choir Schs Assoc., 1995–97; Nat. Assoc. of Music and Ballet Schs, 1998–2000; Mem., Music and Dance Scheme Adv. Gp, DfES, 2001–07. Governor: St Aubyn's Sch., 1978–95; Truro Sch., 2000–07 (Chm., 2002–07); Trustee: Commonwealth Linking Trust, 1972–95; Wells Cath. Sch. Foundn, 2007–; Member, Board of Management: MusicSpace, 1988–2000; British Sch. of Brussels, 2000– (Trustee, 2006–). Mem. (ex-officio), NYO, 1986–2000. Page Schol., 1998, Chm., Cornwall Br., 2003–, ESU. MCMI (MIMgt 1991); FRSA 1990 (Mem., SW Region Cttee, 2001–04). Freeman, City of London, 1991; Liveryman, Musicians' Co., 1991–. *Publications:* (contrib.) History of Lords and Commons Cricket, 1989; The Three Churches of St Minver, 2003; papers and articles in educn jls. *Recreations:* music, Cornish history, golf, sport (GB Olympic Hockey Squad, Oxon; Capt., Oxon U19 Rugby; Minor Counties Cricket, Cornwall Veterans Cricket). *Address:* Lowerdale, Daymer Lane, Trebetherick, Cornwall PL27 6SA. *T:* (01208) 863613. *Clubs:* MCC (Mem., Indoor Sch. Cttee, 1976–86); Vincent's (Oxford); St Enodoc Golf, (Cornwall).

BAXTER, Kenneth Peter; Director, Baxter & Associates Pty Ltd, since 2000; Chairman, TFG International Pty Ltd, since 2001; Policy Adviser to the Chief Secretary, Papua New Guinea, since 2000; *b* 23 Oct. 1943; *s* of P. F. Baxter; *m* 1973, Pamela Annabel Marr; two *s* one *d*. *Educ:* Fort St Boys' High Sch.; Univ. of Sydney (BEc). Farming columnist and press sec., 1972–80; Dir, Corporate Affairs, Philip Morris Ltd and Asst Man. Dir, Philip Morris Aust. Ltd, 1981–82; Cllr, Aust. Rural Adjustment Unit, 1982–87; Mem., Aust. Egg Bd, 1983–85; Man. Dir, NSW Egg Corp., 1983–88; Dir, Grain Handling Authy, NSW, 1986–89; Chairman: Good Food Products Aust. Pty Ltd, 1986–88; Aust. Dairy Res. Council, 1986–; Darling Harbour Authy, 1989–90; Dairy R&D Corp., 1990–92; Aust. Dairy Ltd, 1992–; Aust. Dairy Corp., 1992–98; Thai Dairy Ind. Co. Ltd, 1998–99 (Dir, 1992–98); Director: KPMG, 1996–2000; Hydro Tas (formerly Hydro Electric Corp. of Tasmania), 1996–; Pan Pharmaceuticals Ltd, 2000–. Dep. Dir-Gen., Premier's Dept, NSW, 1988–92; Sec., Dept of the Premier and Cabinet, Vic, 1992–95; Dir-Gen., Premier's Dept, NSW, 1995–96. Mem., Sydney Orgng Cttee for Olympic Games, 1995–96. Comr, Aust. Nat. Rlys Commn, 1997–98. Dir, Baker Med. Res. Foundn, 1996–98. FAICD 1980; FAIM 1985. *Publications:* Wool Marketing in New Zealand, 1967, 2nd edn 1972; Statutory Marketing Authorities, 1988. *Recreations:* rowing, sailing, surf life-saving, reading. *Address:* TFG International, Level 14, Norwich House 6–10 O'Connell Street, Sydney NSW 2000, Australia. *Clubs:* Melbourne (Victoria); Royal Sydney Yacht Squadron (Sydney); Mosman Rowing.

BAXTER, Prof. Murdoch Scott, PhD, CChem, FRSC; FRSE; scientific consultant; Founding Editor, Journal of Environmental Radioactivity, since 1983; *b* 12 March 1944; *s* of John Sawyer Napier Baxter and Margaret Hastie Baxter (*née* Murdoch); *m* 1968, Janice Henderson; one *s*. *Educ:* Univ. of Glasgow. BSc Hons Chem. 1966, PhD Geochem. 1969. Research Fellow, State Univ. of NY (Noble gas history of lunar rocks and meteorites), 1969–70; Lectr, Dept of Chemistry, Univ. of Glasgow (geochem., radiochem. and envmtl radioactivity), 1970–85; Vis. Consultant, IAEA (nuclear waste disposal), 1981–82; Dir, Scottish Univs Res. and Reactor Centre, 1985–90; Dir, Marine Envmt Lab. (formerly Internat. Lab. of Marine Radioactivity), IAEA, 1990–97; Personal Chair, Univ. of Glasgow, 1985–95. Member: Challenger Soc. for Marine Sci., 1975–; Scottish Assoc. for Marine Sci. (formerly Scottish Marine Biology Assoc.), 1975–. FRSE 1989; Fellow, Internat. Union of Eco-Ethics, 1998; Hon. Mem. and Advr, Internat. Union of Radioecol., 1999–; Advr, Inst. Nuclear Technol., Portugal, 2000–. Mem., Scotch Malt Whisky Soc. Ed., Radioactivity in the Environment book series, 1999–. Chevalier, Order of St Charles (Monaco), 1997. *Publications:* numerous papers to professional jls. *Recreations:* hill walking, golf, sailing, sport watching, Queen's Park FC. *Address:* Ampfield House, Clachan Seil, Argyll PA34 4TL. *T:* and *Fax:* (01852) 300351; *e-mail:* baxter@isleofseil.demon.co.uk.

BAXTER, Prof. Rodney James, FRS 1982; FAA 1977; Professor in the Department of Theoretical Physics, Institute of Advanced Studies, and in the School of Mathematical Sciences, 1981–2002, Visiting Fellow in the School of Mathematical Sciences, since 2002, Australian National University; *b* 8 Feb. 1940; *s* of Thomas James Baxter and Florence A. Baxter; *m* 1968, Elizabeth Phillips; one *s* one *d*. *Educ:* Bancroft's Sch., Essex; Trinity Coll., Cambridge; Australian National Univ. Reservoir Engineer, Iraq Petroleum Co., 1964–65; Research Fellow, ANU, 1965–68; Asst Prof., Mathematics Dept, Massachusetts Inst. of Technology, 1968–70; Fellow, ANU, 1970–81; Royal Soc. Res. Prof., 1992, Sen. Fellow, 1992–, Isaac Newton Inst. for Mathematical Scis, Cambridge Univ. Pawsey Medal, Aust. Acad. of Science, 1975; Boltzmann Medal, IUPAP, 1980; Heineman Prize, Amer. Inst. of Physics, 1987; Harrie Massey Medal, Inst. of Physics, 1994; Onsager Prize, Amer. Physical Soc., 2006; Onsager Medal, Norwegian Univ. of Sci. and Technol., 2006. *Publications:* Exactly Solved Models in Statistical Mechanics, 1982; contribs to Proc. Royal Soc., Jl of Physics A, Physical Rev., Statistical Physics, Annals of Physics. *Recreation:* theatre. *Address:* Centre for Mathematics and its Applications, Building 27, Australian National University, Canberra, ACT 0200, Australia. *T:* (2) 62492968.

BAXTER, Roger George, PhD; FRAS; UK boarding school consultant; Partner, Select Education (formerly Select Education and Select Consultants), since 1995; *b* 21 April 1940; *s* of late Rev. Benjamin George Baxter and Gweneth Muriel Baxter (*née* Causer); *m* 1967, Dorothy Ann Cook; one *s* one *d*. *Educ:* Handsworth Grammar Sch., Birmingham; Univ. of Sheffield (BSc, PhD). Junior Research Fellow, Univ. of Sheffield, 1965–66, Lectr, Dept of Applied Mathematics, 1966–70; Asst Mathematics Master, Winchester Coll., 1970–81, Under Master, 1976–81; Headmaster, Sedbergh Sch., 1982–95. Governor: Bramcote Sch., Scarborough, 1982–95; Hurworth Hse Sch., Darlington, 1982–95; Cathedral Choir Sch., Ripon, 1984–95; Mowden Hall Sch., Northumberland, 1984–96; Cundall Manor Sch., York, 1988–98; Durham Sch., 1995–2005; Bow Sch., Durham, 1995–2005; Chetwynde Sch., Barrow, 2003– (Chm. Govs, 2005–). Member: HMC Academic Policy Cttee, 1985–90; Common Entrance Board, 1989–94. Mem. Ct, Univ. of Lancaster, 1994–95. Overseas Mem., British Business Gp Dubai & Northern Emirates, 1999–2008. Church Warden, Cartmel Priory, 1997–. Freeman, City of London, 1992; Liveryman, Gunmakers' Co., 1992–. *Publications:* various papers on numerical studies in magnetoplasma diffusion with applications to the F-2 layer of the ionosphere. *Recreations:* opera, music, cooking, wine. *Address:* The Rivelin, Lindale, Grange-over-Sands, Cumbria LA11 6LJ. *T:* and *Fax:* (01539) 535129; *e-mail:* baxterrg@aol.com.

BAYCROFT, Rt Rev. John Arthur; Bishop of Ottawa, 1993–99; *b* 2 June 1933; *s* of Robert Baycroft and Mary Alice (*née* Williams); *m* 1955, Joan, *d* of V. Lake; one *s* two *d*. *Educ:* Sir William Turner Sch.; Christ's Coll., Cambridge (Synge Schol.) (BA 1954; MA 1958); Ripon Hall, Oxford; Trinity Coll., Toronto (BD 1959). Ordained deacon, 1955, priest, 1956; Rector, Loughborough, Ont, 1955–57; Asst Rector, St Matthew's, Ottawa, 1957–62; Rector: Perth, Ont, 1962–67; St Matthias, Ottawa, 1967–84; Christchurch Cathedral, and Dean of Ottawa, 1984–86; Suffragan Bishop of Ottawa, 1985–93; Dir, Anglican Centre in Rome, and Archbp of Canterbury's Rep. to the Holy See, 1999–2001; Dir, Ecumenical Relns and Studies, Anglican Communion, 2002–03. Mem., ARCIC, 1982–2004. Hon. DD: Montreal Diocesan Theol Coll., 1988; Huron Coll., 1997; Wycliffe Coll., Toronto, 2004; DSLitt (*jur. dig.*) Thornloe Univ., 1991; DUniv St Paul, Ottawa, 2002. *Publications:* The Anglican Way, 1980; The Eucharistic Way, 1982; The Way of Prayer, 1983; numerous articles in jls. *Recreations:* theatre, art, ballet. *Address:* 97 Java Street, Ottawa, ON K1Y 3L5, Canada. *Clubs:* National Press, Rideau (Ottawa).

BAYDA, Hon. Edward Dmytro; Chief Justice of Saskatchewan, 1981–2006; *b* 9 Sept. 1931; *s* of Dmytro Andrew Bayda and Mary Bilinski; *m* 1953, Marie-Thérèse Yvonne Gagné (decd); one *s* five *d*; *m* 2002, Lorraine Bethell. *Educ:* Univ. of Saskatchewan (BA 1951, LLB 1953). Called to the Bar, Saskatchewan, 1954; QC (Sask) 1966. Senior Partner, Bayda, Halvorson, Scheibel & Thompson, 1966–72. Judge, Court of Queen's Bench, 1972; Justice, Court of Appeal, 1974. Hon. LLD: Saskatchewan, 1989; Regina, 2006. KM 1975. *Address:* 3000 Albert Street, Regina, SK S4S 3N7, Canada. *T:* (306) 5862126.

BAYFIELD, Rabbi Anthony Michael; Head of Movement, Movement for Reform Judaism, since 2005 (Chief Executive, Reform Movement and Reform Synagogues of Great Britain, 1994–2005); *b* 4 July 1946; *s* of Ronald Bayfield and Sheila (*née* Mann); *m* 1969, Linda Gavinia (*née* Rose) (*d* 2003); one *s* two *d*. *Educ:* Royal Liberty Sch., Gidea Park; Magdalene Coll., Cambridge (MA (Hons) Law); Leo Baeck Coll., London (Rabbinic degree). Rabbi, NW Surrey Synagogue, 1972–82; Dir, Sternberg Centre for Judaism (Manor House Trust), 1983–. Dir, Advancement of Jewish Educn Trust, 1987–93; Co-ordinator of Supervisors, 1987–93, Lectr in Homiletics, Leo Baeck Coll., 1992–96. Chairman: Assembly of Rabbis, Reform Synagogues of GB, 1980–82; Council of Reform and Liberal Rabbis, 1984–86. Co-Pres., CCJ, 2004–. Founder Editor, Manna (Qly Jl of Progressive Judaism), 1983–. DD Lambeth, 2006. *Publications:* Churban: the murder of the Jews of Europe, 1981; (ed) Dialogue with a Difference, 1992; Sinai, Law and Responsible Autonomy: Reform Judaism and the Halakhic tradition, 1993; (ed jtly) He Kissed Him and They Wept, 2001; articles in European Judaism, Brit. Jl of Religious Educn, Church Times. *Recreations:* family life, reading, walking, Essex CCC, suffering with West Ham United FC. *Address:* Movement for Reform Judaism, Sternberg Centre for Judaism, 80 East End Road, Finchley, N3 2SY. *T:* (020) 8349 5645.

BAYLEY, Hagan; *see* Bayley, J. H. P.

BAYLEY, Hugh; MP (Lab) City of York, since 1997 (York, 1992–97); *b* 9 Jan. 1952; *s* of Michael and Pauline Bayley; *m* 1984, Fenella Jeffers; one *s* one *d*. *Educ:* Haileybury Sch.; Univ. of Bristol (BSc); Univ. of York (BPhil). Dist Officer, 1975–77, Nat. Officer, 1977–82, NALGO; Gen. Sec., Internat. Broadcasting Trust, 1982–86; Lectr in Social Policy, 1986–87, Res. Fellow in Health Econs, 1987–92, Univ. of York. Councillor, London Bor. of Camden, 1980–86. Mem., York HA, 1988–90. PPS to Sec. of State for Health, 1997–98; Parly Under-Sec. of State, DSS, 1999–2001. Mem., Select Cttee on Health, 1992–97, on Internat. Develt, 2001–. Chairman: Public Bill Cttees; Africa All Party Parly Gp, 2003–; PLP Internat. Develt Cttee, 2001–. UK delegate to: N Atlantic Assembly, 1997–99; NATO Parly Assembly, 2001– (Rapporteur, Econs and Security Cttee, 2006–). Chairman: Westminster Foundn for Democracy, 2005–; UK Br., Commonwealth Parly Assoc., 2006–. *Publication:* The Nation's Health, 1995. *Address:* 59 Holgate Road, York YO24 4AA. *T:* (01904) 623713.

BAYLEY, Prof. (John) Hagan (Pryce), PhD; Professor of Chemical Biology, University of Oxford, since 2003; Fellow, Hertford College, Oxford, since 2003; *b* 13 Feb. 1951; *s* of David and Nora Bayley; *m* 1988, Orit Braha; two *s*. *Educ:* King's Sch., Chester; Uppingham Sch.; Balliol Coll., Oxford (BA, MA); Harvard Univ. (PhD Chem. 1979). Postdoctoral res., Depts of Chem. and Biol., MIT, 1979–81; Asst Prof. of Biochem., Columbia Univ., 1981–84; Lectr in Organic Chem., and Fellow, Brasenose Coll., Oxford Univ., 1984–85; Columbia University: Asst Investigator, Howard Hughes Med. Inst., 1985–88; Associate Prof., Center for Neurobiol. and Behavior, 1987–88; Sen. Scientist, 1988–94, Principal Scientist, 1994–96, Worcester Foundn; Associate Prof. of Biochem. and Molecular Biol., 1991–96, and of Physiol., 1995–96, Univ. of Mass Med. Center; Associate Prof. of Chem., Clark Univ., 1996; Prof. of Chem., Texas A&M Univ., 1997–2003; Prof. and Hd, Dept of Med. Biochem. and Genetics, Texas A&M Univ. System Health Sci. Center, 1997–2003. *Address:* Department of Chemistry, University of Oxford, Chemistry Research Laboratory, Mansfield Road, Oxford OX1 3TA. *T:* (01865) 285100, *Fax:* (01865) 275708; *e-mail:* hagan.bayley@chem.ox.ac.uk.

BAYLEY, Prof. John Oliver, CBE 1999; FBA 1990; Warton Professor of English Literature, and Fellow of St Catherine's College, University of Oxford, 1974–92; *b* 27 March 1925; *s* of F. J. Bayley; *m* 1st, 1956, Dame Jean Iris Murdoch, DBE, CLit (*d* 1999); 2nd, 2000, Audhild Villers. *Educ:* Eton; New Coll., Oxford. 1st cl. hons English Oxon 1950. Served in Army, 1943–47. Mem., St Antony's and Magdalen Colls, Oxford, 1951–55; Fellow and Tutor in English, New Coll., Oxford, 1955–74. *Publications:* The Romantic Survival: A Study in Poetic Evolution, 1956; The Characters of Love, 1961; Tolstoy and the Novel, 1966; Pushkin: A Comparative Commentary, 1971; The Uses of Division: unity and disharmony in literature, 1976; An Essay on Hardy, 1978; Shakespeare and Tragedy, 1981; The Order of Battle at Trafalgar, 1987; The Short Story: Henry James to Elizabeth Bowen, 1988; Housman's Poems, 1992; Iris: a memoir of Iris Murdoch, 1998; Iris and the Friends: a year of memories, 1999; Widower's House, 2001; Hand Luggage (anthology), 2001; The Power of Delight: a lifetime in literature, 2005; *fiction:* In Another Country, 1954; trilogy: Alice, 1994; The Queer Captain, 1995; George's Lair, 1996; The Red Hat, 1997.

BAYLEY, Nicola Mary; writer, artist and illustrator; *b* 18 Aug. 1949; *d* of Percy Harold Bayley and Ann Barbara Crowder; *m* 1978, Alan John Howard Hilton, *qv*; one *s*. *Educ:* Farnborough Hill Convent College; St Martin's Sch. of Art (DipAD); Royal College of Art (MA Illus.). *Publications: written and illustrated:* Nicola Bayley's Book of Nursery Rhymes, 1975; One Old Oxford Ox, 1977; Copy Cats (5 books), 1984; As I was Going Up and Down, 1985; Hush-a-bye Baby, 1985; *compiled and illustrated:* The Necessary Cat, 1998; *illustrated:* Tyger Voyage, 1976; Puss in Boots, 1976; La Corona and the Tin Frog, 1979; The Patchwork Cat, 1981; The Mouldy, 1983; Merry Go Rhymes (4 books), 1987; The Mousehole Cat, 1990; (with Jan Mark) Fun with Mrs Thumb, 1993; Katje the Windmill Cat, 2001; The Jungle Book: Mowgli's story, 2005. *Recreations:* watching the garden, opera, sleeping, cats. *Address:* c/o Walker Books, 87 Vauxhall Walk, SE11 5HJ. *Club:* Art Workers Guild.

BAYLEY, Lt-Comdr Oswald Stewart Morris, (Oscar); RN retd; *b* 15 April 1926; *s* of late Rev. J. H. S. Bayley; *m* Pamela Margaret Harrison; one *s* one *d* by a former marriage. *Educ:* St John's Sch., Leatherhead; King James's Grammar Sch., Knaresborough. Called to Bar, Lincoln's Inn, 1959. Entered RN, 1944: Ceylon, 1956–58; Supply Off., HMS Narvik and Sqdn Supply Off., 5th Submarine Div., 1960–62; Sec. to Comdr British Forces Caribbean Area, 1962–65; retd from RN at own request, 1966. Legal Asst (Unfair Competition), The Distillers Co. Ltd, 1966–68; Clerk, Fishmongers' Co., 1968–73; Accountant, Hawker Siddeley Gp, 1978–81, John Lewis Partnership, 1981–82. Dir, Seed

Oysters (UK) Ltd. Clerk to Governors of Gresham's Sch., Holt; Hon. Sec., Salmon and Trout Assoc. and of Shellfish Assoc. of Great Britain; Vice-Chm., National Anglers' Council; Secretary: Atlantic Salmon Research Trust; City and Guilds of London Art Sch. Ltd, 1968–73; Nat. Assoc. of Pension Funds Investment Protection Cttee, 1974–75. Dir and Chief Sec., The Royal Life Saving Soc., 1976–78. Reader: All Saints Church, Footscray, 1989; St Andrew's Church, Orpington, Kent, 1994; St Botolph's Ch, Lullingstone, Kent, 1999; Chm., Sidcup Council of Churches, 1990–92. *Address:* 244 Bexley Lane, Sidcup, Kent DA14 4JG.

BAYLEY, Peter Charles; Emeritus Professor, University of St Andrews; Emeritus Fellow, University College, Oxford; *b* 25 Jan. 1921; *y s* of late William Charles Abell Bayley and Irene Evelyn Beatrice (*née* Heath); *m* 1951, Patience (marr. diss. 1980), *d* of late Sir George (Norman) Clark and Lady Clark; one *s* two *d*. *Educ:* Crypt Sch., Gloucester; state scholarship, 1939; University Coll., Oxford (Sidgwick Exhibnr; MA 1st Cl. Hons English, 1947). Served RA (anti-tank) and Intell. Corps (India), 1941–46. Jun. Res. Fellow, University Coll., Oxford, 1947; Fellow and Praelector in English, 1949–72 (at various times Keeper of Coll. Buildings, Domestic Bursar, Tutor for Admissions, Librarian; Editor of University Coll. Record, 1949–70); Univ. Lectr in English, 1952–72; Proctor, 1957–58; Founder Master of Collingwood Coll. and Lectr, Dept of English, Univ. of Durham, 1971–78; Berry Prof. and Head of Dept of English, Univ. of St Andrews, 1978–85. Vis. Reader, Birla Inst., Pilani, Rajasthan, India, 1966; Vis. Lectr, Yale Univ., and Robert Bates Vis. Fellow, Jonathan Edwards Coll., 1970; Brown Distinguished Vis. Prof., Univ. of the South, Sewanee, Tenn, 1978; Brown Distinguished Vis. Lectr in British Studies, Vanderbilt Univ., Univ. of the South, Sewanee, etc, 1985. Oxford Univ. Corresp., The Times, 1960–63. Sen. Mem., OUDS, 1958–69; Chairman: Oxford Univ. Theatre Fund, 1959–61; Oxford Playhouse Mgt Cttee, 1961–65; Founder Mem., Cherwell Family Housing Trust, later Cherwell Housing Trust, Oxford, 1967. *Publications:* Edmund Spenser, Prince of Poets, 1971; 'Casebook' on Spenser's The Faerie Queene, 1977; Poems of Milton, 1982; An ABC of Shakespeare, 1985; University College, Oxford: a guide and brief history, 1992; edited: Spenser, The Faerie Queene: Book II, 1965; Book I, 1966; Loves and Deaths: short stories by 19th century novelists, 1972; contributed to: Patterns of Love and Courtesy, 1966; Oxford Bibliographical Guides, 1971; C. S. Lewis at the Breakfast Table, 1979; Encyclopaedia of Oxford, 1988; Literature East and West, 1995; Sir William Jones 1746–94, 1998; Fancy's Images: 'faerie' and romance in Chaucer, Spenser and Shakespeare, in Festschrift for Prof. V. Kostić, Belgrade Univ., 2000; articles in TLS, Rev. of English Studies, Essays in Criticism, Critical Qly. *Recreations:* nature, art. *Address:* 63 Oxford Street, Woodstock, Oxford OX20 1TJ.

BAYLEY, Prof. Peter James; Drapers Professor of French, since 1985, and Fellow of Gonville and Caius College, since 1971, Cambridge University; *b* 20 Nov. 1944; *s* of John Henry Bayley and Margaret Burness, Portreath, Cornwall. *Educ:* Redruth County Grammar Sch.; Emmanuel Coll., Cambridge (Kitchener Schol., 1963–66; 1st cl. Hons Mod. and Med. Langs Tripos, 1964 and 1966; MA 1970; PhD 1971); Ecole Normale Supérieure, Paris (French Govt Schol., 1967–68). Cambridge University: Fellow of Emmanuel Coll., 1969–71; Coll. Lectr, Gonville and Caius Coll., 1971–85; Tutor, 1973–79; Praelector Rhetoricus, 1980–86; Univ. Asst Lectr in French, 1974–78; Univ. Lectr, 1978–85; Head, Dept of French, 1983–96; Mem., Gen. Bd of Faculties, 1999–2003; Chm., Sch. of Arts and Humanities, 2001–03. Hon. Sen. Res. Fellow, Inst. of Romance Studies, London Univ., 1990. Vice-Pres., Assoc. of Univ. Profs of French, 1989–97. Pres., Soc. for French Studies, 1990–92; deleg., and Mem. Exec., Univ. Council for Modern Langs, 1994–96. Officier des Palmes Académiques, 1988. *Publications:* French Pulpit Oratory 1598–1650, 1980; (ed with D. Coleman) The Equilibrium of Wit: essays for Odette de Mourgues, 1982; (ed) Selected Sermons of the French Baroque, 1983; (ed) Présences du Moyen Âge et de la Renaissance en France au XVIIe siècle, 2003; contributions to: Critique et création littéraires en France (ed Fumaroli), 1977; Bossuet: la Prédication au XVIIe siècle (ed Collinet and Goyet), 1980; Catholicism in Early Modern History: a guide to research (ed O'Malley), 1988; Convergences: rhetoric and poetic in Seventeenth-Century France (ed Rubin and McKinley), 1989; New Oxford Companion to Literature in French (ed France), 1995; Actes de Tulane, 2001; Actes de Tempe, 2002; Actes de Charlottesville, 2003; Cambridge Rev., Dix-Septième Siècle, French Studies, Mod. Lang. Rev., Studies on Voltaire and the Eighteenth Century, etc. *Recreations:* Spain, food and wine, gardening, English ecclesiastical history. *Address:* Gonville and Caius College, Cambridge CB2 1TA. *T:* (01223) 332439; (vacations) The White House, Hackleton, Northants NN7 2AD. *T:* (01604) 870059.

BAYLEY, Stephen Paul; design consultant and writer; Principal, EYE-Q Ltd, since 1990; Architecture and Design Critic, The Observer, since 2006; *b* 13 Oct. 1951; *s* of late Donald and Anne Bayley; *m* 1981, Flo Fothergill; one *s* one *d*. *Educ:* Quarry Bank Sch., Liverpool; Manchester Univ.; Liverpool Univ. Sch. of Architecture. Lecturer: Hist. of Art, Open Univ., 1974–76; Hist. and Theory of Art, Univ. of Kent, 1976–80; Dir, Conran Foundn, 1981–89; Dir, Boilerhouse Project, in V&A Mus., 1982–86; Founding Dir, later Chief Exec., Design Mus., 1986–89. A Contributing Editor: GQ, 1991–; Car, 1996–; Management Today, 1999–; The Erotic Review, 2001–; Waitrose Food Illustrated, 2005–. Mem., Design Cttee, LRT, 1989–91. Has lectured at: Nat. Inst. of Design, Ahmedabad; India Inst. of Technol., Bombay; Art Gall. of WA, Perth; Nat. Gall. of Victoria, Melbourne; Salon de l'Automobile, Geneva; Sony Design Center, Tokyo; Internat. Expo, Nagoya; Art Coll. Center of Design (Europe), La Tour-de-Peilz, Switzerland; École Supérieure des Sciences et Études Commerciales, Paris; RIBA; RSA; RCA; and at univs, colls and museums throughout Britain and Europe. Honorary Fellow: Liverpool Inst. of Performing Arts, 2001; UWIC, 2007. Magazine Columnist of the Year, PPA, 1995. Chevalier de l'Ordre des Arts et des Lettres (France), 1989. *Publications:* In Good Shape, 1979; The Albert Memorial, 1981; Harley Earl and the Dream Machine, 1983; The Conran Directory of Design, 1985; Sex, Drink and Fast Cars, 1986; Twentieth Century Style and Design, 1986; Commerce and Culture, 1989; Taste, 1991; Beefeater 2-Day Guide to London, 1993; Labour Camp: the failure of style over substance, 1998; Moving Objects, 1999; General Knowledge, 2000; Sex: an intimate history, 2001; Dictionary of Idiocy (with an Appendix by Gustave Flaubert), 2003; Life's A Pitch, 2007; Intelligence Made Visible, 2007; numerous Open Univ. books, and Boilerhouse/Design Mus. catalogues inc. Art and Industry, 1982; Sony Design, 1982; Taste, 1983; Robots, 1984; National Characteristics, 1985; Coke, 1986. *Recreations:* indistinguishable from work, but both involve words, pictures, food, drink, sport and travel. *Address:* (office) 176 Kennington Park Road, SE11 4BT. *T:* (020) 7820 8899. *Club:* Hurlingham.

BAYLIS, Prof. Peter Howard, MD; FRCP, FMedSci; Dean of Medicine, 1997–2005, Provost of Faculty of Medical Sciences, 2002–05, University of Newcastle upon Tyne; *b* 9 Sept. 1943; *s* of late Derek Baylis and of Lore Baylis; *m* 1968, Dr Susan Mary While; one *s* two *d*. *Educ:* Wallington Grammar Sch.; Univ. of Bristol (BSc, MB ChB, MD). FRCP 1983. Trng in medicine, endocrinology and research, Queen Elizabeth Hosp., Birmingham, 1970–76; Clinical Endocrinology Fellow, Univ. of Indiana, 1976–78; Lectr in Medicine, Univ. of Birmingham, 1978–80; Consultant Physician and Sen. Lectr in Medicine, Royal Victoria Infirmary, Newcastle, 1980–90; Prof. of Exptl Medicine and Clinical Sub-Dean, Med. Sch., Univ. of Newcastle upon Tyne, 1990–97. Founder FMedSci, 1998. *Publications:* (with P. Padfield) The Posterior Pituitary: hormone secretion in health and disease, 1985; (jtly) Case Presentations in Endocrinology and Diabetes, 1988; Salt and Water Homeostasis in Health and Disease, 1989; book chapters and over 130 original articles. *Recreations:* long-distance running, classical music, reading. *Address:* 53 The Rise, Darras Hall, Ponteland, Newcastle upon Tyne NE20 9LQ.

BAYLIS, Rear-Adm. Robert Goodwin, CB 1984; OBE 1963; Chief Executive, R. G. Baylis & Associates, since 1984; *b* 29 Nov. 1925; *s* of Harold Goodwin Baylis and Evelyn May (*née* Whitworth); *m* 1949, Joyce Rosemary Churchill (*d* 1995); two *s* one *d*. *Educ:* Highgate Sch.; Edinburgh Univ.; Loughborough Coll.; RN Engrg Coll.; Trinity Coll., Cambridge. MA Cantab. MRAeS. Joined Royal Navy, 1943; various appts at sea in Far East and Home Fleet and ashore in research and develt and trng establishments; Staff of C-in-C, S Atlantic and S America, 1958; British Navy Staff, Washington, and Special Projects (Polaris), 1964; Defence Fellow, Southampton Univ., 1969; Naval ADC to HM the Queen, 1978; Staff of Vice Chief of Defence Staff, 1979; President, Ordnance Board, 1981–84. Comdr 1961, Captain 1970, Rear-Adm. 1979. Dir, 1988–2000, Associate, 2000–, British Maritime Technol. Reliability Consultants. Mem., Nuffield Theatre Bd, 1988– (Chm., 1989–93, 1995–97). Mem. (Emeritus), Australian Ordnance Council; Mem. Council, IEE, 1984–86. Vice-Patron, CP Centre, 2003–. *Recreations:* painting, playwriting. *Address:* Broadwaters, 4 Cliff Road, Hill Head, Fareham, Hants PO14 3JS. *Club:* Lansdowne.

BAYLIS, Trevor Graham, OBE 1997; inventor; Chairman, Trevor Baylis Brands plc, since 2004; *b* 13 May 1937; *s* of Cecil Archibald Walter Baylis and Gladys Jane Brown. *Educ:* Dormer's Wells Secondary Modern Sch. Represented Britain in swimming competitions at age of 15; Soil Mechanics Lab., 1953–59; Phys. Trng Instr, NS, 1959–61; Technical Salesman, Purley Pools, 1961 (also designed 50 products for swimming pools); professional swimmer and stuntman; founded Shotline Displays, 1970 (appeared on TV with Peter Cook and Dudley Moore, Dave Allen, and David Nixon); underwater escape artiste, Berlin Circus, Dec. 1970; founded Shotline Steel Swimming Pools, 1971 (built over 300 pools in schs in UK); developed 200 products for the disabled, Orange Aids, 1985; invented clockwork radio, 1990; jt Founder, Baygen, 1995; Co-founded The Electric Shoe Co. and The Personal Power Co. (to power mobile 'phone batteries through walking), 1999. Vis. Prof., Buckingham Univ., 1998–. Vice-President: Techknowlogy charity, 2001–; Women of Achievement Awards, 2002–. Patron: Spelthorne Farm Project for the Handicapped, 2004; Mus. of Sci. and Industry, Manchester, 2004; Dormer Wells Infant Sch., 2004; LEPRA, 2005; Wessex Round Table of Inventors, 2005. Hon. Fellow: UWIST, 1998; Univ. of Wolverhampton, 1999; Hon. Res. Fellow, Sch. of Journalism, Cardiff Univ., 1999. Hon. MSc: Brunel, 1997; UEA, 1997; Teesside, 1998; Hon. DTech: Nottingham Trent, 1998; Southampton Inst., 1998; DUniv: Open, 2001; Middlesex, 2002; Oxford Brookes, 2004; Hon. MBA Luton, 2001; Hon. DSc Heriot-Watt, 2003. Presidential Gold and Silver Medals, IMechE, 1997; Paul Harris Fellow, Rotary Club. *Publication:* Clock This: my life as an inventor, 1999. *Recreations:* swimming, diving, underwater swimming, boating, after dinner speaking; enthusiastic owner of Jaguar E-type. *Address:* Haven Studio, Eel Pie Island, Twickenham TW1 3DY.

BAYLISS, David, OBE 1992; FREng; Eur Ing; Director: Halcrow Consulting (formerly Halcrow Fox), since 1999; Blackpool Urban Regeneration Co., since 2005; *b* 9 July 1938; *s* of Herbert and Annie Esther Bayliss; *m* 1961, Dorothy Christine Crohill; two *s* one *d*. *Educ:* Arnold Sch., Blackpool; UMIST (BSc Tech 1961); Manchester Univ. (Dip TP 1966). CEng, FICE, 1980; FITE 1984; FIHT 1972; FRTPI 1972; FREng (FEng 1993); Eur Ing 1991. Manchester Corp., 1961–66; GLC, 1966–68; Centre for Environmental Studies, 1968–69; GLC, 1969–84 (Asst Divl Engr; Head, Transport Studies; Chief Transport Planner); Dir of Planning, London Transport, 1984–99. Chairman: SERC/DoT LINK Transport Infrastructure and Ops Steering Gp, 1991–96, Inland Surface Transport Prog. Adv. Gp, 1996–; UITP Internat. Commn on Transport Econs, 1996–98; Fifth Framework Expert Adv. Gp on Sustainable Mobility and Intermodality, EC, 1998–2002. Vis. Prof., ICSTM, 1999–. Chm., Regional Studies Assoc., 1978–81; Member Council: CIT, 1978–82; IHT, 1992–94; ICE, 1996–98; Royal Acad. of Engrg, 1999–2002. President: British Parking Assoc., 1987–89; Transport Studies Soc., 1989–90; UK Vice Pres., Internat. Union of Public Transport, 1997–98. Chm., Rees Jeffreys Road Fund, 2004–. Member: Transit Res. Analysis Cttee, NAE, 2004–; Public Policy Cttee, RAC Foundn, 2005–. *Recreations:* writing, travel, wine. *Address:* 37 Ledborough Lane, Beaconsfield, Bucks HP9 2DB. *T:* (01494) 673313.

BAYLISS, Frederic Joseph; Special Professor, Department of Continuing Education (formerly Adult Education), University of Nottingham, 1988–97; *b* 15 April 1926; *s* of Gordon and Gertrude Bayliss; *m* 1948, Mary Provost; one *d* (and one *d* decd). *Educ:* Ashby de la Zouch Grammar Sch.; Hertford Coll., Oxford. PhD Nottingham 1960. RAF, 1944–47. Tutor in Economics, Oxford Univ. Tutorial Classes Cttee, 1950–57; Lectr in Industrial Relations, Dept of Adult Education, Univ. of Nottingham, 1957–65; Industrial Relations Advr, NBPI, 1965–69; Asst Sec., CIR, 1969–71; Sen. Economic Advr, Dept of Employment, 1971–73; Under Sec., Pay Board, 1973–74; Sec., Royal Commn on the Distribution of Income and Wealth, 1974–77; Acct Gen., Dept of Employment, 1977–86. Chairman: Campaign for Work, 1988–92; Employment Policy Inst., 1992–95. *Publications:* British Wages Councils, 1962; The Standard of Living, 1965; Making a Minimum Wage Work, 1991; (with S. Kessler) Contemporary British Industrial Relations, 1992, 3rd edn 1998; Does Britain still have a Pay Problem?, 1993. *Recreations:* gardening, walking. *Address:* 37 Rufus Close, Lewes, East Sussex BN7 1BG. *T:* (01273) 474317.

BAYLISS, Jeremy David Bagot, FRICS; Chief Executive, The Foundation, Royal Botanic Gardens, Kew, 1997–2002; President, Royal Institution of Chartered Surveyors, 1996–97; *b* 27 March 1937; *s* of Edmund Bayliss and Marjorie Clare (*née* Thompson); *m* 1962, Hon. Mary Selina Bridgeman (*see* Hon. M. S. Bayliss); three *s*. *Educ:* Harrow; Sidney Sussex Coll., Cambridge (MA). ARICS 1962, FRICS 1971. 2nd Lieut, Coldstream Guards, 1956–57. Partner, Gerald Eve, Chartered Surveyors, 1967–97 (Sen. Partner, 1988–97); Chm., Gerald Eve Financial Services, 1989–96. Royal Institution of Chartered Surveyors: Chm., various cttees, 1983–; Mem., Gen. Council, 1987–; Pres., Planning and Develt Div., 1989–90. Chm., CBI Land Use Panel, 1992–95. Mem., Adv. Panel to Secs of State for the Envmt and for Wales on Standards for Planning Inspectorate, 1993–96. Hon. Co. Organiser (Berks), Nat. Gardens Scheme, 2002–07. Trustee: Royal Merchant Navy Sch. Foundn, 2003–07; Soc. for Horticl Therapy, 2004–. Gov., Bearwood Coll., 1999– (Chm., 2003–). Chm., Reading S Cons. Assoc., 1975–78. *Recreations:* gardening, country pursuits. *Address:* Loddon Lower Farm, Swallowfield, near Reading, Berks RG7 1JE. *T:* (0118) 988 3218. *Club:* Boodle's.

BAYLISS, John; Chairman, Affinity (formerly Broomleigh Charitable) Trust, 1999–2004; Director, Downland Affinity Group Ltd, 2003–04; *b* 22 Jan. 1934; *s* of late Athol Thomas Bayliss and Elizabeth Rose Bayliss; *m* 1954, Maureen (*née* Smith); one *d*. *Educ:* Haberdashers' Aske's, Hatcham. Westminster Bank, 1950; Abbey National Building Society, then Abbey National plc, 1957–93: Regional Man., 1969; Personnel Man., 1972;

Asst Gen. Man., 1974; General Manager: Field Operations, 1976; Housing, 1981; Marketing, 1983; Man. Dir (Retail Ops), 1988; Dep. Chm., 1991–93. Chairman: Broomleigh Housing Assoc. Ltd, 1990–96; Richmount Mgt Ltd, 1994–2000. *Recreation:* France. *Address:* Lyndhurst, Broad Oak, Brenchley, Kent TN12 7NN.

BAYLISS, John Francis Temple; an Assistant Judge Advocate General, since 1996; a Recorder, since 1999; *b* 11 Aug. 1942; *s* of Capt. Horace Temple Taylor Bayliss, DSO, RN and Patricia Bayliss (*née* Loftus); *m* 1981, Annelize Kors; one *s* one *d*. *Educ:* Ampleforth Coll.; BRNC, Dartmouth. Joined Royal Navy, 1960; called to the Bar, Gray's Inn, 1974, NSW, 1981; Comd Legal Officer, Sydney, RAN, 1980–82; Captain, 1986; Sec. to C-in-C Fleet, 1986–88; IMS, Brussels, 1988–92; Chief Naval Judge Advocate, 1992–95; an Asst Recorder, 1994–99. *Recreation:* golf. *Address:* Office of the Judge Advocate General, 81 Chancery Lane, WC2A 1BQ. *T:* (020) 7218 8085.

BAYLISS, Hon. Mary Selina; JP; Lord Lieutenant of Berkshire, since 2008; *b* Bramham Park, Yorks, 14 Jan. 1940; *d* of 2nd Viscount Bridgeman, KBE, CB, DSO, MC and Mary Kathleen (*née* Lane Fox); *m* 1962, Jeremy David Bagot Bayliss, *qv*; three *s*. *Educ:* St Mary's Sch., Wantage. Mem., Reading Minster Appeal Cttee, 2005–; Gov., Chiltern Nursery Trng Coll., 1970–95; Patron, Reading Mencap, 2006–. Pres., Swallowfield Horticl Soc., 2006–. Berkshire: JP 1978 (Chairman: Family Panel, 1994–97; Bench, 1998–2001); High Sheriff 2005–06; DL 2007. *Recreations:* music, gardening, travel. *Address:* Loddon Lower Farm, Lamb's Lane, Swallowfield, Berks RG7 1JE.

BAYLISS, Rev. Roger Owen; Principal Chaplain, Church of Scotland and Free Churches, and Director, Chaplaincy Services, Royal Air Force, 1998–2001; *b* 21 July 1944; *s* of Stanley John Bayliss and Joyce Audrey Bayliss; *m* 1976, Pauline Jones; two *s*. *Educ:* Westminster Coll., Oxford (DTh 1999). RMN 1966; SRN 1969; SRN for Mentally Subnormal, 1975; Dip. Counselling. Nurse training: Saxondale Hosp., 1963–66; Nottingham Gen. Hosp., 1966–69; Lea Castle Inst., 1973–75; ordained, 1981; entered Chaplains' Branch, RAF, 1981: served at stations: Lyneham, Marham, Stanley (Falkland Is), Bruggen, N Luffenham, Cottesmore, Leeming, Coningsby; HQ RAF Germany; 2 Gp HQ; RAF Support Comd; HQ PTC. QHC, 1998–2001. *Recreations:* classic cars, fly fishing, squash, music (rock and blues), reading. *Address:* 25 Kingswood Heights, Kingswood, Bristol BS15 1TD. *T:* (0117) 961 3710. *Club:* Royal Air Force.

BAYLISS, Thomas William Maxwell; QC 2003; a Recorder, since 2000; *b* 24 June 1954; *s* of Thomas Maxwell Bayliss and Dorothy Vera Bayliss; *m* 1977, Caroline Jane Allpress; one *s* one *d*. *Educ:* King's Sch., Gloucester; Leeds Univ. (LLB Hons). Called to the Bar, Inner Temple, 1977; Standing Counsel to Inland Revenue, 1991–2003. *Recreations:* bridge, tennis, theatre. *Address:* Park Court Chambers, 16 Park Place, Leeds LS1 2SJ. *T:* (0113) 243 3277, *Fax:* (0113) 242 1285.

BAYLISS, Valerie June, CB 1996; education and training consultant; Associate Professor of Education, University of Sheffield, 1996–2001; *b* 10 June 1944; *d* of George and Ellen Russell; *m* 1971, Derek Andrew Bayliss; one *s*. *Educ:* Wallington County Grammar Sch. for Girls; Univ. of Wales (1st cl. hons History, BA 1965; MA 1967). Research Student, LSE, 1966–68; Dept of Employment, 1968; Manpower Services Commission, subseq. Training Agency: Head of Job Centre Services, 1978–82; Head, YTS Policy, 1982–85; Dir, Field Ops, 1985–87; Under Sec., and Dir, Resources and Personnel, 1987–90; Dir of Educn Progs, later of Youth and Educn Policy, Dept of Employment, subseq. Dept for Educn and Employment, 1991–95. Sheffield University: Mem. Council, 1988–95 and 2002–; Dir, Management Sch., 1991–96. Director: Sheffield Futures Ltd (formerly Sheffield Careers Guidance Services Ltd), 1997–2004 (Chm., 1999–2004); Connexions South Yorkshire Ltd, 2001–04. Mem. Bd, Sheffield Develt Corp., 1996–97. Dep. Chm., Nat. Adv. Council for Careers and Educnl Guidance, 1996–2000. Mem. Council, RSA, 2002–07; Director, RSA projects: Redefining Work, 1996–98; Redefining Schooling, 1998–99; Opening Minds, 2000–05. Mem. Council, 1996–, Mem. Exec., 1999–, Jt Hon. Sec., 2005–, C&G; Gov., Barnsley Coll., 1996–2002. Chm., S Yorks Reg., Victorian Soc., 1997–. Trustee, Brathay Hall Trust, 2001–. Patron, Nat. Youth Agency, 1996–. Hon. Fellow, Inst. of Careers Guidance, 1996. FRSA 1990; FCGI 2005. *Publications:* Key Views on the Future of Work, 1997; Redefining Work, 1998; Redefining Schooling, 1998; Redefining the Curriculum, 1999; Opening Minds: education for the 21st Century, 1999; What Should Our Children Learn?, 2000; Opening Minds: Taking Stock, 2003. *Recreations:* walking, reading, listening to music. *T:* (0114) 230 7693.

BAYLY, Sir Christopher (Alan), Kt 2007; LittD; FRHistS; FRSL; FBA 1990; Vere Harmsworth Professor of Imperial and Naval History, since 1992 and Fellow of St Catharine's College, since 1970, Cambridge University; *b* 18 May 1945; *s* of Roy Ernest and Elfreda Madeleine Bayly; *m* 1981, Susan Banks Kaufmann. *Educ:* Skinners' School, Tunbridge Wells; Balliol College, Oxford (MA); St Antony's, Oxford (DPhil 1970); LittD Cantab. FRSL 2006. Stanhope Prize, Oxford, 1965. Cambridge University: Dir of Studies in History, St Catharine's Coll., 1970–92 (Tutor, 1977–80); Smuts Reader in Commonwealth Studies, 1981–87; Reader in Modern Indian History, 1988–91; Prof. of Modern Indian Hist., 1991–92. Sen. Scholar, Kluge Center, Library of Congress, Washington, 2006. Directeur d'Etudes associé, CNRS, Ecole des Hautes Etudes, Paris, 1986. Vis. Prof., Univ. of Virginia, Charlottesville, 1975. MAE. Wolfson Prize for History, Wolfson Foundn, 2005. *Publications:* The Local Roots of Indian Politics: Allahabad 1880–1920, 1975; Rulers, Townsmen and Bazaars: North Indian society in the age of British Expansion 1770–1870, 1983, 2nd edn 1988; Indian Society and the Making of the British Empire, 1988; Imperial Meridian: the British Empire and the world 1780–1830, 1989; (ed) The Raj: India and the British 1600–1947, 1990; Empire and Information: intelligence gathering and social communication in India 1780–1870, 1996; Origins of Nationality in South Asia, 1998; The Birth of the Modern World: global connections and comparisons 1780–1914, 2003; (with Tim Harper) Forgotten Armies: the fall of British Asia 1941–1945, 2004; (with Tim Harper) Forgotten Wars: the end of Britain's Asian Empire, 2007; contribs to jls. *Recreation:* travelling. *Address:* St Catharine's College, Cambridge CB2 1RL. *T:* (01223) 338321. *Club:* Reform.

BAYLY, Richard Dion; Deputy Regional Director, Government Office for the South West, since 2007; *b* 25 Feb. 1951; *s* of Edward Hugh Bayly and Denise Bayly (*née* Dudley); *m* 1986, Dr Lea Diane Jones; two *d*. *Educ:* Rugby Sch.; Bristol Univ. (BScEcon). Entered Civil Service, 1974: DoE, 1974–79; Dept of Transport, 1979–97 (on secondment to BRB, as Dir, Privatisation Studies, 1990–91); DETR, 1997–2001 (on secondment to Cabinet Office, 1997–99; Acting Chief Exec., CS Coll., 1998–99); Dir, Devon and Cornwall, Govt Office for SW, 1999–2007; DfT (formerly DTLR), 2001–. *Address:* (office) Mast House, Shepherds Wharf, 24 Sutton Road, Plymouth PL4 0HJ. *T:* (01752) 635050.

BAYNE, Prof. Brian Leicester, OBE 1998; PhD; FIBiol; Visiting Professor, Centre for Research on Ecological Impacts of Coastal Cities, University of Sydney, since 2001 (Research Professor, 1997–2001); *b* 24 July 1938; *s* of John Leonard and Jean Leicester Bayne; *m* 1960, Marianne Middleton; two *d*. *Educ:* Ardingly Coll.; Univ. of Wales (BSc, PhD). Post-doctoral res., Univ. of Copenhagen and Fisheries Laboratory, Conwy, 1963–68; Lectr, Sch. of Biology, Univ. of Leicester, 1968–73; Institute for Marine Environmental Research, Plymouth: Res. Scientist, 1973–83; Dir, 1983–88; Plymouth Marine Laboratory, NERC: Dir, 1988–94; Dir, Centre for Coastal and Marine Scis, 1994–97. Fellow, Univ. of Wales, 1996. *Publications:* Marine Mussels: ecology and physiology, 1976; res. papers in marine sci. jls, *eg* Jl of Experimental Marine Biol. and Ecol. *Recreation:* sailing. *Address:* 16 Lockington Avenue, Plymouth, Devon PL3 5QR; Centre for Research on Ecological Impacts of Coastal Cities, Marine Ecology Labs A11, University of Sydney, NSW 2006, Australia.

BAYNE, Sir Nicholas (Peter), KCMG 1992 (CMG 1984); HM Diplomatic Service, retired; High Commissioner to Canada, 1992–96; *b* 15 Feb. 1937; *s* of late Captain Ronald Bayne, RN and Elisabeth Ashcroft; *m* 1961, Diana Wilde; two *s* (and one *s* decd). *Educ:* Eton Coll.; Christ Church, Oxford (MA, DPhil). Entered Diplomatic Service, 1961; served at British Embassies in Manila, 1963–66, and Bonn, 1969–72; seconded to HM Treasury, 1974–75; Financial Counsellor, Paris, 1975–79; Head of Financial, later Economic Relations, Dept, FCO, 1979–82; attached to RIIA, 1982–83; Ambassador to Zaire, 1983–84, also accredited to the Congo, Rwanda and Burundi, 1984; seconded to CSSB, 1985; Ambassador and UK Perm. Rep. to OECD, Paris, 1985–88; Dep. Under-Sec. of State, FCO, 1988–92. Chm., Liberalisation of Trade in Services Cttee, British Invisibles, 1996–2000. Fellow, Internat. Relns Dept, LSE, 1997–. *Publications:* (with R. D. Putnam) Hanging Together: the Seven-Power Summits, 1984, rev. edn 1987 (trans. German, Japanese, Italian); Hanging in There: the G7 and G8 summit in maturity and renewal, 2000; The Grey Wares of North-West Anatolia and their Relation to the Early Greek Settlements, 2000; (with S. Woolcock) The New Economic Diplomacy, 2003, 2nd edn 2007; Staying Together: the G8 summit confronts the 21st century, 2005. *Recreations:* reading, sightseeing. *Address:* 2 Chetwynd House, Hampton Court Green, East Molesey, Surrey KT8 9BS. *Club:* Travellers.

BAYNE, Shenagh Irvine; a District Judge (Magistrates' Courts), since 2004; *b* 30 April 1953; *d* of David Morton Bayne and Katherine Clementine Bayne; partner, S. A. Gibson. *Educ:* English Sch. of Paris; Berkhamsted Sch. for Girls; Edinburgh Univ. (BA). Admitted solicitor, 1980; Trevor Hamlyn & Co., Solicitors, 1980–82; Deacons, Hong Kong, 1982–84; Simmons & Simmons, Solicitors, 1984–85; EMI Music, 1985–86; Freelance Solicitor Advocate, 1986–92, 1997–2004; CPS, 1992–97; Stipendiary Magistrate, subseq. Dep. Dist Judge, 1998–2004. Immigration Adjudicator (pt-time), 2002–04. *Recreations:* golf, hill-walking, ski-ing, contemporary literature, film and theatre going, travel. *Address:* South Western Magistrates' Court, Lavender Hill, SW11 1JU. *Club:* Hong Kong Football.

BAYNES, Sir Christopher (Rory), 8th Bt *cr* 1801, of Harefield Place, Middlesex; *b* 11 May 1956; *s* of Sir John Baynes, 7th Bt and of Shirley Maxwell Baynes (*née* Dodds); *S* father, 2005; *m* 1992, Sandra Finuala Merriman; two *s* one *d*. *Heir: s* Alasdair William Merriman Baynes, *b* 3 Dec. 1993.

BAYNHAM, Prof. Alexander Christopher; strategic technical consultant, since 1996; Principal, Cranfield University (formerly Cranfield Institute of Technology) (Shrivenham Campus), 1989–96, now Emeritus Professor; *b* 22 Dec. 1935; *s* of Alexander Baynham and Dulcie Rowena Rees; *m* 1961, Eileen May Wilson; two *s* one *d*. *Educ:* Marling Sch.; Reading Univ. (BSc); Warwick Univ. (PhD); Royal Coll. of Defence Studies (rcds). Joined Royal Signals and Radar Estab., Malvern, 1955; rejoined, 1961 (univ. studies, 1958–61); Head, Optics and Electronics Gp, 1976; RCDS, 1978; Scientific Adviser to Asst Chief Adviser on Projects, 1979; Dep. Dir, 1980–83, Dir, 1984–86, RSRE; Dir, RARDE, 1986–89. *Publications:* Plasma Effects in Semi-conductors, 1971; assorted papers in Jl of Physics, Jl of Applied Physics and in Proc. Phys. Soc. *Recreations:* church activities, music. *Address:* c/o Cranfield University, Shrivenham Campus, Swindon, Wilts SN6 8LA.

BAYNHAM, Dr John William, CBE 1994; Chairman, Lothian Health Board, 1990–97; *b* 20 Jan. 1929; *s* of Rev. Albert J. Baynham and Euphemia Baynham; *m* 1959, Marcella Bridget (Marié) Friel; one *d*. *Educ:* Bathgate Academy; Aberdeen Univ. (BSc, PhD); Imperial College London (DIC). Scottish Agricultural Industries: res. develt chemist, 1955–62; Production Planning/ Techno Commercial, 1962–70; Trade Union negotiating and gen. management, 1970–80; Dir, Sales and Marketing, 1980–84; overall Agribusiness Dir, 1984–87. Founder Dir, Leith Enterprise Trust, 1984 (Chm., 1987–90). Chm., Salary Cttee, Conf. of Scottish Centrally Funded Colls, 1997–99. Chm., Bd of Govs, Moray House Inst. of Educn, Heriot-Watt Univ., 1991–95; Gov., Queen Margaret Coll., Edinburgh, 1995–99. Dr *hc*: Edinburgh, 1995; Queen Margaret UC, 1999. *Publications:* contribs to learned jls and seminars. *Recreations:* good food and wine, grandchildren. *Club:* Royal Burgess Golfing Society (Edinburgh).

BAYS, Rt Rev. Eric; Bishop of Qu'Appelle, 1986–97; *b* 10 Aug. 1932; *s* of Rev. Canon P. C. Bays and Hilda (*née* Harper); *m* 1967, Patricia Ann Earle; one *s* one *d*. *Educ:* Univ. of Manitoba (BSc 1955); Univ. of Saskatchewan (BA 1959): Univ. of Emmanuel College (LTh 1959); Christian Theological Seminary (MMin 1974). Flight Lieut, RCAF (Reserve), 1955. Asst Curate, All Saints', Winnipeg, 1959–61; Lecturer, Emmanuel Coll., 1961–62; Priest-in-charge: Burns Lake, BC, 1962–63; Masset, BC, 1963–64; Novice, Community of the Resurrection, Mirfield, 1964–65; Vicar, St Saviour's, Winnipeg with Bird's Hill, 1965–68; Rector, All Saints', Winnipeg, 1968–76; Professor, Coll. of Emmanuel and St Chad, 1976–86, Vice-Principal, 1981–86. Canon of St John's Cathedral, Winnipeg, 1971–86. Hon. DD Coll. of Emmanuel and St Chad, 1987. *Recreations:* golf, curling. *Address:* 700 Roosevelt Avenue, Ottawa, ON K2A 2A7, Canada.

BAYTON, Rt Rev. John, AM 1983; Master Iconographer, St Peter's Icon School, since 1999; *b* 24 March 1930; *s* of Ernest Bayton and Jean Bayton (*née* Edwards); *m* 1959, Elizabeth Anne, *d* of Rt Rev. J. A. G. Housden; one *s* two *d*. *Educ:* Aust. Coll. of Theology, ACT (ThL (Hons)); St Francis Theol Coll., Brisbane. Ordained deacon 1956, priest 1957; Rector, Longreach, Qld, 1958–63; Rector and Sub-dean, Thursday Island (Canon in Residence), 1963–65; Rector, Auchenflower, 1965–68; Dean of St Paul's Cathedral, Rockhampton, 1968–79; Vicar, St Peter's, Eastern Hill, 1980–89; Archdeacon of Malvern, 1986–89; Bishop of Geelong (Asst Bishop, dio. of Melbourne), 1989–95; Episcopal Chaplain, St George's Coll., Jerusalem, 1995–96, 1998 (Chm., Australasian Cttee, 2003–; Vis. Chaplain and Lectr, 2003–); Assisting Bishop in Chicago, Chaplain-in-Residence and Vis. Prof., Seabury-Western Seminary, Evanston, 1997; Adminr, St John's Cathedral, Brisbane, 1998–99. Founder, 1981, Patron, 1993–, Inst. for Spiritual Studies, Melbourne. Solo Art Exhibitions: Brisbane 1967, 1976, 1978, 1998; Rockhampton 1975, 1976; Melbourne 1981, 1984, 1986, 1987; Jerusalem, 1995, 1996; Chicago, 1997; Raffles Artfolio Gall., Singapore, 1999; Bishopscourt, Melbourne, 2001. Represented in public and private collections Australia, Chicago, USA, Jerusalem and UK. Prelate, Aust. Priory, Order of St John of Jerusalem and Knights Hospitaler, 1990; GCSJ 1995; ChLJ 2000; OMLJ 2003. *Publications:* Cross over Carpentaria, 1965; Coming of the Light, 1971; The Icon, 1980; (ed) Anglican Spirituality, 1982. *Recreations:* painting, sketching, sculpting, reading, walking. *Address:* 219 Canterbury Road, Blackburn, Vic 3130, Australia. *Club:* Melbourne (Melbourne).

BAYÜLKEN, Ümit Halûk, Hon. GCVO 1967; President: Turkish Atlantic Treaty Association, since 1984; Turkish Parliamentarians' Union, 1992-97, now Hon. President;

Atlantic Treaty Association, Paris, 1994–97, now Patron; *b* 7 July 1921; *s* of Staff Officer H. Hüsnü Bayülken and Mrs Melek Bayülken; *m* 1952, Mrs Valihe Salci; one *s* one *d*. *Educ*: Lycée of Haydarpasa, Istanbul; Faculty of Political Science (Diplomatic Sect.), Univ. of Ankara. Joined Min. of For. Affairs, 1944; 3rd Sec., 2nd Political Dept; served in Private Cabinet of Sec.-Gen.; mil. service as reserve Officer, 1945–47; Vice-Consul, Frankfurt-on-Main, 1947–49; 1st Sec., Bonn, 1950–51; Dir of Middle East Sect., Ankara, 1951–53; Mem. Turkish Delegn to UN 7th Gen. Assembly, 1952; Political Adviser, 1953–56, Counsellor, 1956–59, Turkish Perm. Mission to UN; rep. Turkey at London Jt Cttee on Cyprus, 1959–60; Dir-Gen., Policy Planning Gp, Min. of Foreign Affairs, 1960–63; Minister Plenipotentiary, 1963; Dep. Sec.-Gen. for Polit. Affairs, 1963–64; Sec.-Gen. with rank of Ambassador, 1964–66; Ambassador to London, 1966–69, to United Nations, 1969–71; Minister of Foreign Affairs, 1971–74; Secretary-General, Cento, 1975–77; Sec.-Gen., Presidency of Turkish Republic, 1977–80; Senator, 1980; Minister of Defence, 1980–83; MP, Antalya, 1983–87. Mem., Turkish Delegns to 8th–13th, 16th–20th Gen. Assemblies of UN; rep. Turkey at internat. confrs, 1953–66; Leader of Turkish Delegn: at meeting of For. Ministers, 2nd Afro-Asian Conf., Algiers, 1965; to Ministerial Councils of NATO, OECD, Cento and Regl Co-operation for Develt, 1971–74; Turkey and EEC Jt Assoc., 1971–74; to Cttee of Ministers, Council of Europe, 1972; at Conf. on European Security and Co-operation, 1973; Mem., Parly Assembly of European Council, 1984–87. Univ. of Ankara: Mem., Inst. of Internat. Relations; Lectr, Faculty of Polit. Scis, 1963–66. Hon. Gov., Sch. of Oriental and African Studies, London; Hon. Mem., Mexican Acad. of Internat. Law. Isabel la Católica (Spain), 1964; Grand Cross of Merit (Germany), 1965; Sitara-i-Pakistan (Pakistan), 1970; Star, Order One (Jordan), 1972; Sirdar-i-Ali (Afghanistan), 1972. Tunisia, 1973; UAR, 1973; UN, 1975; Turkish Pres., 1980; Order of Madara Horseman (Bulgaria), 1997; Chevalier de la Légion d'Honneur (France), 2002. *Publications*: lectures, articles, studies and essays on subject of minorities, Cyprus, principles of foreign policy, internat. relations and disputes. *Recreations*: music, painting, reading. *Address*: Nergiz, Sokak no 15/20, Çankaya, Ankara 06680, Turkey.

BAZALGETTE, Peter Lytton, Chairman, Endemol UK plc, 2002–07; Chief Creative Officer, Endemol Group, 2005–07; *b* 22 May 1953; *s* of late Paul Bazalgette and Diana (*née* Coffin); *m* 1985, Hilary Jane Newiss; one *s* one *d*. *Educ*: Dulwich Coll.; Fitzwilliam Coll., Cambridge (Pres., Cambridge Union, 1975; BA Hons Law 1976). BBC News Trainee, 1977; Man. Dir, Bazal, 1987–98; Creative Dir, GMG Endemol Entertainment, 1998–2002. Non-executive Director: Channel 4, 2001–04; Victoria Real; Zeppotron. TV formats created, 1984–, incl. Food and Drink, Ready Steady Cook, Changing Rooms, Ground Force; formats sold to 30 countries; UK producer, Big Brother. Dep. Chm., National Film & Television Sch., 2002–. MacTaggart Lectr, Edinburgh TV Fest., 1998; Wheldon Lectr, RTS, 2001. Mem. Cttee. ESU Centre for Internat. Debate, 1996–; Co-Chm., British Acad. of Gastronomes, 1993–. Non-exec. Dir, YouGov.com, 2005–. Trustee: Crossness Engines Trust, 1994– (Chm., 1999); ENO, 2004–. Fellow, BAFTA, 2000; FRTS 2002. Judges Award, RTS, 2003. *Publications*: Billion Dollar Game, 2005; jointly: BBC Food Check, 1989; The Food Revolution, 1991; The Big Food & Drink Book, 1993; You Don't Have to Diet, 1994. *Recreations*: cricket, gluttony. *Address*: e-mail: peter.bazalgette@newbaz.com. *Clubs*: Beefsteak, Hurlingham.

BAZLEY, Rt Rev. Colin Frederick; Bishop of Chile, 1977–2000; Hon. Assistant Bishop, diocese of Chester, since 2000; *b* 27 June 1935; *s* of Reginald Samuel Bazley and Isabella Davies; *m* 1960, Barbara Helen Griffiths; three *d*. *Educ*: Birkenhead School; St Peter's Hall, Oxford (MA); Tyndale Hall, Bristol. Deacon 1959, priest 1960; Assistant Curate, St Leonard's, Bootle, 1959–62; Missionary of S American Missionary Society in Chile, 1962–69; Rural Dean of Chol-Chol, 1962–66; Archdeacon of Temuco, 1966–69; Assistant Bishop for Cautin and Malleco, Dio. Chile, Bolivia and Peru, 1969–75; Assistant Bishop for Santiago, 1975–77; Bishop of Chile, Bolivia and Peru, 1977; diocese divided, Oct. 1977; Bishop of Chile and Bolivia until Oct. 1981, when diocese again divided; Presiding Bishop of the Anglican Council for South America, 1977–83; Primate, Province of S Cone of America, 1989–95. Warden of Readers, dio. of Chester, 2000–05. Mem., Inter-Anglican Theol and Doctrinal Commn, 1994–97. *Recreations*: football (Liverpool supporter) and fishing on camping holidays. *Address*: 121 Brackenwood Road, Higher Bebington, Wirral CH63 2LU.

BAZLEY, Janet Claire, (Mrs I. F. Airey); QC 2006; a Recorder, since 2000; *d* of John Harold Bazley and Loukia Bazley; *m* 1987, Ian Frank Airey; one *s* two *d*. *Educ*: Lady Eleanor Holles Sch.; University Coll. London (LLB Hons 1979). Called to the Bar, Lincoln's Inn, 1980; in practice as a barrister, 1980–; Asst Recorder, 1998–2000. Member: Family Law Bar Assoc., 1992–; Law Reform Cttee, Bar Council, 2001–. *Publications*: Money Laundering for Lawyers (with David Winch), 2004; contrib. to Halsbury's Laws. *Recreations*: foreign languages and travel, opera, hill walking. *Address*: 1 Garden Court, Temple, EC4Y 9BJ. *T*: (020) 7797 7900, *Fax*: (020) 7797 7929; *e-mail*: bazley@1gc.com.

BAZLEY, Dame Margaret (Clara), DNZM 1999; Chair, New Zealand Fire Service Commission, since 1999; *b* 23 Jan. 1938. *Educ*: Registered Comprehensive Nurse; Dip. Nursing, DoH and Victoria Univ.; Dip. Health Admin., Massey Univ. Nursing, 1956–78, including: Matron, Sunnyside Psych. Hosp., Christchurch, 1965–73; Dep. Matron in Chief, Auckland Hosp. Bd, 1974–75; Chief Nursing Officer, Waikato Hosp. Bd, 1975–78; Dir, Div. of Nursing, NZ Dept of Health, 1978–84; State Services Commission: Comr, 1984–87; Dep. Chm., 1987–88; Sec. for Transport, 1988–93; Dir-Gen., Dept of Social Welfare, 1993–99; Chief Exec., Min. of Social Policy, NZ, 1999–2001. Mem., NZ delegns to OECD, ISSA, WHO, Internat. Council of Nursing, etc, in Australia, USA and Europe. Chair, Foundn for Res., Sci. and Technol., 2004– (Dep. Presiding Mem., 2002–04). Member: Waitangi Tribunal, 2001–; Commn of Inquiry into Police Conduct, 2004–07; Registrar of Pecuniary Interests of Mems of Parlt, 2006–; Royal Commn of Inquiry on Auckland Governance, 2007–. Trustee, Westpactrust Stadium, 2000–05. Business Woman of the Year, More/AirNZ, 1987. *Recreations*: gardening, reading, cooking, music. *Address*: (office) PO Box 2133, Wellington, New Zealand.

BAZLEY, Sir (Thomas John) Sebastian, 4th Bt *cr* 1869, of Hatherop, co. Gloucester; *b* 31 Aug. 1948; *s* of Sir Thomas Bazley, 3rd Bt and of Carmen, *o d* of James Tulla; *S* father, 1997. *Educ*: St Christopher Sch., Letchworth; Magdalen Coll., Oxford (BA Hons Maths). *Heir*: *b* Anthony Martin Christopher Bazley [*b* 23 Feb. 1958; *m* 1996, Claudia Patricia Montoya Cano; one *s* one *d*].

BEACH; see Hicks Beach, family name of Earl St Aldwyn.

BEACH, Prof. David Hugh, PhD; FRS 1996; Professor of Stem Cell Biology, Queen Mary, University of London, since 2004; *b* 18 May 1954; *s* of Gen. Sir Hugh Beach, *qv*. *Educ*: Peterhouse, Cambridge (BA); Univ. of Miami (PhD 1977). Postdoctoral Fellow, Univ. of Sussex, 1978–82; Cold Spring Harbor Laboratory: Postdoctoral Fellow, 1982–83; Jun. Staff Investigator, then Sen. Staff Investigator, 1984–89; Tenured Scientist, 1992–; Sen. Staff Scientist, 1989–97; Investigator, Howard Hughes Med. Inst., 1990–97; Adjunct Investigator, Cold Spring Harbour Lab., 1997–2000; Hugh and Catherine Stevenson Prof. of Cancer Biology, UCL, 1997–2002. Adjunct Associate Prof., SUNY, Stony, 1990–97. Founder, Mitotix Inc., 1992; Founder and Pres., Genetica Inc., 1996–2004. Eli Lilly

Research Award, 1994; Bristol-Myers Squibb Award, 2000; Raymond Bourgine Award for cancer research, 2001. *Publications*: numerous papers in reviewed jls, incl. Nature and Cell and Science. *Recreations*: flying, scuba diving, ski-ing, shooting, fly fishing, writing fiction. *Address*: Institute of Cell and Molecular Biology, Barts and the London, Queen Mary's School of Medicine and Dentistry, 4 Newark Street, E1 2AT. *T*: 07799 620947. *Club*: Royal Lymington Yacht.

BEACH, Gen. Sir (William Gerald) Hugh, GBE 1980 (OBE 1966); KCB 1976; MC 1944; *b* 20 May 1923; *s* of late Maj.-Gen. W. H. Beach, CB, CMG, DSO; *m* 1951, Estelle Mary Henry (*d* 1989); three *s* one *d*. *Educ*: Winchester; Peterhouse, Cambridge (MA; Hon. Fellow 1982). Active service in France, 1944 and Java, 1946; comd: 4 Field Sqn, 1956–57; Cambridge Univ. OTC, 1961–63; 2 Div. RE, 1965–67; 12 Inf. Bde, 1969–70; Defence Fellow, Edinburgh Univ. (MSc), 1971; Dir, Army Staff Duties, MoD, 1971–74; Comdt, Staff Coll., Camberley, 1974–75; Dep. C-in-C, UKLF, 1976–77; Master-Gen. of the Ordnance, 1977–81; Chief Royal Engr, 1982–87; Warden, St George's House, Windsor Castle, 1981–86. Dir, Council for Arms Control, 1986–89. Vice Lord-Lieut for Greater London, 1981–87. Kermit Roosevelt Vis. Lectr to US Armed Forces, 1977; Mountbatten Lectr, Edinburgh Univ., 1981; Gallipoli Meml Lectr, 1985; Wilfred Fish Meml Lectr, GDC, 1986. Colonel Commandant: REME, 1976–81; RPC, 1976–80; RE, 1977–87; Hon. Colonel, Cambridge Univ. OTC, TAVR, 1977–87; Chm., CCF Assoc., 1981–87; Chm., MoD Study Gp on Censorship, 1983. Mem., Security Commn, 1982–91. Chairman: Rochester Cathedral Develt Trust, 1986–99; Winchester DAC for Care of Churches, 1988–97; Hampshire and the Islands Historic Churches Trust, 1993–2003; Winchester Cathedral Fabric Adv. Cttee, 1996–; Member, Committee of Management: Council for Christian Approaches to Defence and Disarmament, 1988–; Verification Res., Trng and Inf. Centre, 1990–; Acronym Inst., 2004–. Chairman: SPCK, 1994–99; Foundation Trustees, Church Army, 1996–2001. Chm. Govs, Bedales Sch., 1989–96. CCMI; FRSA. Hon. Fellow CIBSE, 1988. Hon. DCL Kent, 1990. *Publications*: numerous articles, reviews and chapters in books on military matters and arms control. *Recreation*: ski-ing. *Address*: Flat 12, Roberts Court, 45 Barkston Gardens, SW5 0ES. *T*: (020) 7835 1219. *Club*: Farmers'.

See also D. H. Beach.

BEACHAM, Prof. Arthur, OBE 1961; MA, PhD; Deputy Vice-Chancellor, Murdoch University, Western Australia, 1976–79 (Acting Vice-Chancellor, 1977–78); *b* 27 July 1913; *s* of William Walter and Maud Elizabeth Beacham; *m* 1938, Margaret Doreen Moseley (*d* 1979); one *s* one *d*. *Educ*: Pontywaun Grammar Sch.; University Coll. of Wales (BA 1935); Univ. of Liverpool (MA 1937); PhD Belfast 1941. Jevons Res. Student, Univ. of Liverpool, 1935–36; Leon Res. Fellow, Univ. of London, 1942–43; Lectr in Economics, Queen's Univ. of Belfast, 1938–45; Sen. Lectr, University Coll. of Wales, 1945–47; Prof. of Indust. Relations, University Coll., Cardiff, 1947–51; Prof. of Economics, University Coll. of Wales, Aberystwyth, 1951–63; Vice-Chancellor, Univ. of Otago, Dunedin, New Zealand, 1964–66; Gonner Prof. of Applied Econs, Liverpool Univ., 1966–75. Chairman: Mid-Wales Industrial Develt Assoc., 1957–63; Post Office Arbitration Tribunal, 1972–73; Member: Advisory Council for Education (Wales), 1949–52; Transp. Consultative Cttee for Wales, 1948–63 (Chm. 1961–63); Central Transp. Consultative Cttee, 1961–63; Economics Cttee of DSIR, 1961–63; North West Economic Planning Council, 1966–74; Merseyside Passenger Transport Authority, 1969–71; Council, Royal Economic Soc., 1970–74. Chm., Cttees on Care of Intellectually Handicapped, Australia, 1982–85; Dir, Superannuation Scheme for Aust. Univs, 1982–83. Hon. LLD Otago, 1969; Hon. DUniv Murdoch, 1982. *Publications*: Economics of Industrial Organisation, 1948 (5th edn 1970); Industries in Welsh Country Towns, 1950. Articles in Econ. Jl, Quarterly Jl of Economics, Oxford Econ. Papers, etc. *Recreations*: golf, gardening. *Address*: 10 Mannersley Street, Carindale, Qld 4152, Australia. *T*: (7) 33986630. *Clubs*: Dunedin (Dunedin, NZ); Cricketers' (Qld).

BEADLE, (John) Nicholas, CMG 2006; Fellow, Harvard University, 2007–08; *b* 20 Aug. 1957; *s* of Lt-Col (retd) George Colin Beadle and late Gillian Beadle; *m* 1990, Linda Rose Davidson; one *d*. *Educ*: Grangefield GS, Stockton; Newcastle upon Tyne Poly. (LLB); Heriot-Watt Univ. (MBA). Thomson Newspapers, 1978–83; Proprietor, Accommodation Ltd, 1984–90; Dir, cos of late Jack Calvert, 1990–97; Ministry of Defence, 1997–: UK Hydrographic Office, 1997–2001; RCDS 2002; NATO Policy, 2003; EU and UN Policy, 2004; Sen. Advr to Iraqi MoD, Baghdad, 2004–05; Private Sec. to Sec. of State for Defence, 2005–07. *Recreations*: fly-fishing, painting, sport, dabbling. *Address*: e-mail: nickbeadle@yahoo.co.uk.

BEADLES, Anthony Hugh, MA; Headmaster of Epsom College, 1993–2000; *b* 18 Sept. 1940; *s* of late O. H. R. Beadles, OBE and N. K. Beadles; *m* 1970, Heather Iona McFerran; two *s* one *d*. *Educ*: Epsom Coll.; Christ Church, Oxford (MA). Head of History, Ellesmere Coll., 1963–67; Head of History and Asst Housemaster, Harrow Sch., 1967–85; Headmaster, King's Sch., Bruton, 1985–93. *Recreations*: cricket, mountains, golf. *Address*: Chaff Barn, Downyard, Compton Pauncefoot, Yeovil, Somerset BA22 7EL. *Clubs*: MCC; Vincent's (Oxford).

BEAKE, Ven. Stuart Alexander; Archdeacon of Surrey, since 2005; *b* 18 Sept. 1949; *s* of Ernest Alexander and Pamela Mary Beake; *m* 1987, Sally Anne Williams; one *s* one *d*. *Educ*: King's Coll. Sch., Wimbledon; Emmanuel Coll., Cambridge (BA 1972, MA 1975); Cuddesdon Coll., Oxford. Ordained deacon, 1974, priest, 1975; Asst Curate, Hitchin St Mary, 1974–79; Team Vicar, St Mary, Hemel Hempstead, 1979–85; Domestic Chaplain to Bishop of Southwell, 1985–87; Vicar, St Andrew, Shottery, 1987–2000; RD, Fosse Deanery, 1992–99; Diocesan Dir of Ordinands and Hd, Vocations and Trng Dept, Coventry Dio., 1995–2000; Sub-Dean and Canon Residentiary, Coventry Cathedral, 2000–05 (Hon. Canon, 1999). *Recreations*: reading, gardening, music, model railway, old jokes. *Address*: c/o Diocesan House, Quarry Street, Guildford, Surrey GU1 3XG.

BEAL, Peter George, PhD; FBA 1993; FSA; Database Compiler, Catalogue of English Literary Manuscripts 1450–1700, since 2005; Consultant, Department of Books and Manuscripts, Sotheby's, London, since 2005; *b* Coventry, 16 April 1944; *s* of William George Beal and Marjorie Ena Owen; *m* 1st, 1974, Gwyneth Morgan (marr. diss. 1980); 2nd, 1982, Sally Josephine Taylor (marr. diss. 1994); one step *s*; 3rd, 1998, Grace Janette Ioppolo. *Educ*: King Henry VIII Grammar Sch., Coventry; Leeds Univ. (BA Hons English, 1966; PhD 1974). Res. editor, Bowker/Mansell Publishing, 1974–79; Manuscript Expert, 1980–2005, Dep. Dir, 1990–95, Dir, 1996–2005, Printed Books and MSS, subseq. Dept of Books and MSS, Sotheby's, London. Lyell Reader in Bibliography, Oxford Univ., 1995–96. Vis. Prof., Dept of English, Reading Univ., 2000–02; Sen. Res. Fellow, Inst. of English Studies, Univ. of London, 2002–. FSA 2007. *Publications*: Index of English Literary Manuscripts, vol. I, parts 1 and 2, 1450–1625 (2 vols), 1980, vol. II, parts 1 and 2, 1625–1700 (2 vols), 1987, 1993; (gen. ed.) English Verse Miscellanies of the Seventeenth Century (5 vols), 1990; In Praise of Scribes: manuscripts and their makers in 17th century England, 1998; A Dictionary of English Manuscript Terminology 1450–2000, 2008; (co-founded and co-ed) English Manuscript Studies 1100–1700, annually, 1989–; contribs, mainly on 16th and 17th century literary MSS, to learned jls.

Recreations: reading, films, travel. *Address:* Institute of English Studies, Senate House, Malet Street, WC1E 7HU. *T:* (020) 7664 4864; *e-mail:* Peter.Beal@sas.ac.uk.

BEAL, Rt Rev. Robert George; Bishop of Wangaratta, 1985–94; *b* 17 Aug. 1929; *s* of Samuel and Phyllis Beal; *m* 1956, Valerie Francis Illich; two *s* four *d*. *Educ:* Sydney Grammar School; St Francis' College, Brisbane, Qld; Newcastle Univ., NSW (BA, ThL). Ordained, 1953; Priest, Asst Curate, St Francis', Nundah, Brisbane, 1953–55; Rector: South Townsville, 1955–59; Auchenflower, Brisbane, 1959–65; Dean of Wangaratta, 1965–72; Rector of Ipswich, Brisbane, and Residentiary Canon of St John's Cathedral, 1974–75; Dean of Newcastle, NSW, 1975–83; Archdeacon of Albury, 1983–85. *Recreation:* gardening. *Address:* 1 Pangari Place, New Lambton Gardens, Newcastle, NSW 2299, Australia.

BEALE, Anthony John; Solicitor and Legal Adviser, Welsh Office, 1980–91; Under Secretary (Legal), Welsh Office, 1983–91; *b* 16 March 1932; *o s* of late Edgar Beale and Victoria Beale; *m* 1969, Helen Margaret Owen-Jones; one *s* one *d*. *Educ:* Hitchin Grammar Sch.; King's Coll. London (LLB; AKC); BA Hons Open 1999. Solicitor of the Supreme Court, 1956. Legal Asst, 1960, Sen. Legal Asst, 1966, Min. of Housing and Local Govt and Min. of Health; Consultant, Council of Europe, 1973; Asst Solicitor, DoE 1974. ARPS. *Recreations:* photography, golf, collecting old cheques.

BEALE, Prof. Geoffrey Herbert, MBE 1947; PhD; FRS 1959; FRSE; Royal Society Research Professor, Edinburgh University, 1963–78; *b* 11 June 1913; *s* of Herbert Walter and Elsie Beale; *m* 1949, Betty Brydon McCallum (marr. diss. 1969); three *s*. *Educ:* Sutton County Sch.; Imperial Coll. of Science, London. Scientific Research Worker, John Innes Horticultural Institution, London, 1935–40. Served in HM Forces (1941–46). Research worker, Department of Genetics, Carnegie Institute, Cold Spring Harbor, New York, 1947; Rockefeller Fellow, Indiana Univ., 1947–48; Lecturer, Dept of Animal Genetics, 1948–59, Reader in Animal Genetics, 1959–63, Edinburgh Univ. Research Worker (part-time), Chulalongkorn Univ., Bangkok, 1976. FRSE 1966. Hon. DSc Chulalongkorn, 1996. *Publications:* The Genetics of Paramecium aurelia, 1954; (with Jonathan Knowles) Extranuclear Genetics, 1978; (with S. Thaithong) Malaria Parasites, 1992.

BEALE, Prof. Hugh Gurney, FBA 2004; Professor of Law, University of Warwick, since 1987; *b* 4 May 1948; *s* of Charles Beale and Anne Freeland Beale (*née* Gurney-Dixon); *m* 1970, Jane Wilson Cox; two *s* one *d*. *Educ:* Leys Sch., Cambridge; Exeter Coll., Oxford (BA Jurisp. 1969). Called to the Bar, Lincoln's Inn, 1971 (Hon. Bencher, 1999). Lecturer in Law: Univ. of Connecticut, 1969–71; UCW, Aberystwyth, 1971–73; Univ. of Bristol, 1973–86; Reader, Univ. of Bristol, 1986–87. Visiting Professor: Univ. of N Carolina, 1982–83; Univ. of Paris I, 1995; Univ. of Utrecht, 1996; Univ. of Oxford, 2007–. A Law Comr, 2000–07. Hon. QC 2002. Hon. LLD: Miskolc, 1995; De Montfort, 2003; Antwerp, 2005. *Publications:* Remedies for Breach of Contract, 1980; (jtly) Contract Cases and Materials, 1985, 5th edn 2007; (ed jtly) Principles of European Contract Law, Part I, 1995, Parts I and II, 2000; (Gen. Ed.) Chitty on Contracts, 28th edn 1999, 29th edn 2004; (ed jtly) Casebooks on the Common Law of Europe: Contract Law, 2001. *Recreations:* fishing, music, walking. *Address:* School of Law, University of Warwick, Coventry CV4 7AL. *T:* (024) 7657 3844.

BEALE, James Patrick; Senior Programme Manager, Maxwell Stamp plc, since 2008; *b* 14 Nov. 1959; *s* of Patrick Ashton Beale and Janet Margaret Beale; *m* 1991, Mary Elizabeth Wilson; two *d*. *Educ:* Sch. of Oriental and African Studies, Univ. of London (BA Hons Geog.); Univ. of Reading (MSc Agricl Econs 1986). Data analyst, Kestrel Gp, Tripoli, Libya, 1982–84; Project Manager, Agric. and Fisheries Div., Crown Agents, 1986–88; Sight Savers International: Programme Manager, E Asia and Pacific, 1988–93; Regl Dir, Thailand and Bangladesh, 1993–95; Chief Exec., Ockenden Venture, subseq. Ockenden Internat., 1995–2008. *Address:* c/o Maxwell Stamp plc, Abbot's Court, Farringdon Lane, EC1R 3AX. *T:* (020) 7251 0147.

BEALE, Lt-Gen. Sir Peter (John), KBE 1992; FRCP; Hon. Consultant, British Red Cross, since 2000 (Chief Medical Adviser, 1994–2000); *b* 18 March 1934; *s* of Basil and Eileen Beale; *m* 1st, 1959, Julia Mary Winter, MB BS (*d* 2000); four *s* one *d* (and one *d* decd); 2nd, 2001, Mary Elisabeth Williams. *Educ:* St Paul's Cathedral Choir Sch.; Felsted Sch. (Music Schol.); Gonville and Caius Coll., Cambridge (Choral Schol.; BA); Westminster Hosp. MB BChir 1958. DTM&H; FFCM; FFOM. Commissioned RAMC, 1960; medical training, 1964–71; Consultant Physician, Army, 1971; served Far East, Middle East, BAOR; Community Physician, Army, 1981; served BAOR and UK; Comdr Medical, HQ UKLF, 1987–90; DGAMS, 1990–93; Surg. Gen., MoD, 1991–94. QHP 1987–94. President: Old Felstedian Soc., 1998–2001; Army Officer Golfing Soc., 2001–05; Captain, Old Felstedian Golfing Soc., 2001–03. Gov., Yehudi Menuhin Sch., 1995–. OStJ. *Publications:* contribs to professional jls on tropical and military medicine. *Recreations:* music (conductor, tenor, pianist, French Horn player), sport (golf, squash, tennis), bridge. *Address:* The Old Bakery, Avebury, Marlborough, Wilts SN8 1RF. *T:* (01672) 539315. *Club:* Tidworth Garrison Golf (Pres., 1989–2002).

See also S. R. Beale.

BEALE, Simon Russell, (Simon Russell Beale), CBE 2003; actor; *b* 12 Jan. 1961; *s* of Lt-Gen. Sir Peter Beale, *qv*. *Educ:* St Paul's Cathedral Choir Sch.; Clifton Coll., Bristol; Gonville and Caius Coll., Cambridge (BA 1st Cl. Hons English 1982; Hon. Fellow, 2008); Guildhall Sch. of Music and Drama. Royal Shakespeare Co., 1985–93 (Associate Artist); Royal National Theatre, 1995–98 (Associate Artist). *Theatre:* Look to the Rainbow, Apollo, 1983; Women Beware Women, Royal Court, 1985; Royal Shakespeare Company: A Winter's Tale, The Fair Maid of the West, 1985; Restoration, Man of Mode, 1987; Troilus and Cressida, The Seagull, Edward II, 1989; Richard III, 1990; Ghosts, 1993; The Tempest, 1993–94; Royal National Theatre: Volpone, 1995 (best supporting actor, Olivier Award, 1996); Rosencrantz and Guildenstern are Dead, 1995; Othello, 1997; Candide (best actor in a musical, Olivier Award, 2000), Money, Summerfolk, Battle Royal, 1999; Hamlet (best actor, Evening Standard Award, best Shakespearean perf., Critics' Circle Award), 2000; Humble Boy, 2001; Jumpers, 2003; The Life of Galileo, 2006; The Alchemist, 2006; Much Ado About Nothing, 2007; Major Barbara, 2008; A Slight Ache, 2008; Uncle Vanya, Twelfth Night, Donmar Warehouse, 2002 (best actor, Evening Standard Award, Critics' Circle Award, and Olivier Award, 2003); Macbeth, Almeida, 2005; Julius Caesar, Barbican, 2005; The Philanthropist, Donmar Warehouse, 2005 (best actor, Evening Standard Theatre Award, and Critics' Circle Award, 2005); Spamalot, NY, 2005, Palace Th., 2007; *television:* Persuasion, 1995; A Dance to the Music of Time, 1997 (best actor, RTS Award, 1997, BAFTA Award, 1998); presenter, Sacred Music, 2008; *films:* Hamlet, 1997; The Temptation of Franz Schubert, 1997; An Ideal Husband, 1999; performances on radio. *Recreations:* music, history, history of religion, crosswords. *Address:* Richard Stone Partnership, 25 Whitehall, SW1A 2BS. *T:* (020) 7839 6421.

BEALES, Prof. Derek Edward Dawson, PhD, LittD; FRHistS; FBA 1989; Professor of Modern History, University of Cambridge, 1980–97, now Emeritus; Fellow of Sidney Sussex College, Cambridge, since 1958; *b* 12 June 1931; *s* of late Edward Beales and Dorothy Kathleen Beales (*née* Dawson); *m* 1964, Sara Jean (*née* Ledbury); one *s* one *d*. *Educ:* Bishop's Stortford Coll.; Sidney Sussex Coll., Cambridge (MA, PhD, LittD). Sidney Sussex College, Cambridge: Research Fellow, 1955–58; Tutor, 1961–70; Vice-Master, 1973–75; Cambridge University: Asst Lectr, 1962–65, Lectr, 1965–80; Chairman: Faculty Board of History, 1979–81; Mgt Cttee, Internat. Studies, 1992–95; Member: Liby Syndicate, 1982–88; Gen. Bd of Faculties, 1987–89. Vis. Lectr, Harvard Univ., 1965; Lectures: Founder's Meml, St Deiniol's Liby, Hawarden, 1990; Stenton, Univ. of Reading, 1992; Birkbeck, Trinity Coll., Cambridge, 1993. Vis. Prof., Central Eur. Univ., Budapest, 1995–. Fellow, Collegium Budapest, 1995; Leverhulme Emeritus Fellowship, 2000. British rep., Humanities Standing Cttee, ESF, 1994–99. Mem. Council, RHistS, 1984–88. Editor, 1971–75, Mem. Editl Bd, Historical Jl, 1976–2002 (Chm., 1990–97). *Publications:* England and Italy 1859–60, 1961; From Castlereagh to Gladstone, 1969; The Risorgimento and the Unification of Italy, 1971, 2nd edn (with E. F. Biagini), 2002; History and Biography, 1981; (ed with Geoffrey Best) History, Society and the Churches, 1985; Joseph II: in the shadow of Maria Theresa 1741–80, 1987; Mozart and the Habsburgs, 1993; (ed with H. B. Nisbet) Sidney Sussex Quatercentenary Essays, 1996; (Gen. Ed.) Cassell's Companions to 18th and 20th Century Britain, 2001; Prosperity and Plunder: European Catholic monasteries in the Age of Revolution, 2003 (Paolucci/Bagehot Book Award, Intercollegiate Studies Inst., 2004); Enlightenment and Reform in the Eighteenth Century, 2005; Joseph II: against the world 1780–1790, 2008; articles in learned jls. *Recreations:* playing keyboard instruments and bridge, walking, not gardening. *Address:* Sidney Sussex College, Cambridge CB2 3HU. *T:* (01223) 338833. *Club:* Athenæum.

BEALES, Peter Leslie, MBE 2005; Chairman and Managing Director, Peter Beales Roses, since 1967; *b* 22 July 1936; *s* of E. M. Howes; *m* 1961, Joan Elizabeth Allington; one *s* one *d*. *Educ:* Aldborough School, Norfolk; Norwich City Tech. Coll. FIHort. Apprenticed E. B. LeGrice Roses (1st apprentice, Horticultural Apprentice Scheme), 1952–57; Nat. Service, RA, 1957–59; Manager, Rose Dept, Hillings Nurseries, Chobham, 1959–66; founded Peter Beales Roses, 1967. Lecturer, UK and overseas, 1985–. Pres., Royal Nat. Rose Soc., 2003–05. Chm., Attleborough Chamber of Commerce, 1988–89. Chm., Norfolk and Norwich Horticultural Soc., 1998–2001 (Pres., 1997–98); President: Norfolk Br., Gardening with Disabilities, 1999–; Attleborough Horticl Soc., 2000–. Hon. Life Mem., Bermuda Rose Soc., 1987; Life Mem., N Ireland Rose Soc., 1985. Freeman, City of London; Liveryman, Gardeners' Co. Lester E. Harrell Award for significant contrib. to heritage roses, USA, 1988; DHM, Royal Nat. Rose Soc., 1997; VMH 2003; Queen Mother's Internat. Rose Award, Royal Nat. Rose Soc., 2006; Gold Medal, World Fedn of Rose Societies, 2006. *Publications:* Georgian and Regency Roses, 1981; Early Victorian Roses, 1981; Late Victorian Roses, 1981; Edwardian Roses, 1981; Classic Roses, 1985; Twentieth-Century Roses, 1988; Roses, 1992; Visions of Roses, 1996; New Classic Roses, 1997; A Passion for Roses, 2004. *Recreations:* photography, rose breeding, travelling, sport, book collecting. *Address:* Peter Beales Roses, London Road, Attleborough, Norfolk NR17 1AY. *T:* (01953) 454707.

BEALEY, Prof. Frank William; Professor of Politics, University of Aberdeen, 1964–90, now Emeritus; *b* Bilston, Staffs, 31 Aug. 1922; *er s* of Ernest Bealey and Nora (*née* Hampton), both of Netherton, Dudley; *m* 1960, Sheila Hurst; one *s* two *d*. *Educ:* Hill Street Elem. Sch.; King Edward VI Grammar Sch., Stourbridge; London Sch. of Economics (BSc Econ 1948); DSc Econ London, 1990. Able Seaman in RN, 1941–46. Finnish Govt Scholar, 1948–49; Research Asst for Passfield Trust, 1950–51; Extra-Mural Lectr, University of Manchester (Burnley Area), 1951–52; Lectr, then Sen. Lectr, University of Keele, 1952–64. Vis. Fellow, Yale, 1980. Treas., Soc. for Study of Labour Hist., 1960–63. Organiser, Parly All-Party Gp, Social Sci. and Policy, 1984–89. Trustee, Jan Hus Educnl Foundn, 1981–2003; Co-ordinator of Jt European Project 0276 (Political Sci. in Czechoslovakia), 1991–93. FRHistS 1974. *Publications:* (with Henry Pelling) Labour and Politics, 1958, 2nd edn 1982; (with J. Blondel and W. P. McCann) Constituency Politics, 1965; The Social and Political Thought of the British Labour Party, 1970; The Post Office Engineering Union, 1976; (with John Sewel) The Politics of Independence, 1981; Democracy in the Contemporary State, 1988; (jtly) Elements in Political Science, 1999; The Blackwell Dictionary of Political Science, 1999; Power in Business and the State, 2001; articles in academic jls. *Recreations:* reading poetry, eating and drinking, watching football and cricket. *Address:* 11 Viewforth Terrace, Edinburgh EH10 4LH. *T:* (0131) 229 8313. *Clubs:* Economicals Association Football, Economicals Cricket.

BEAMISH, Sir Adrian (John), KCMG 1999 (CMG 1988); HM Diplomatic Service, retired; Lecturer, History Department, University College, Cork, since 1999; *b* 21 Jan. 1939; *s* of Thomas Charles Constantine Beamish and Josephine Mary (*née* Lee); *m* 1965, Caroline Lipscomb (marr. diss. 1991); two *d*; *m* 1994, Antonia Cavanagh; one *d*, and one step *s* one step *d*. *Educ:* Christian Brothers' Coll., Cork; Prior Park Coll., Bath; Christ's Coll., Cambridge (MA); Università per gli Stranieri, Perugia. Third, later Second Secretary, Tehran, 1963–66; Foreign Office, 1966–69; First Sec., UK Delegn, OECD, Paris, 1970–73; New Delhi, 1973–76; FCO, 1976–78; Counsellor, Dep. Head, Personnel Operations Dept, FCO, 1978–80; Counsellor (Economic), Bonn, 1981–85; Hd, Falkland Is Dept, FCO, 1985–87; Ambassador to Peru, 1987–89; Asst Under-Sec. of State (Americas), FCO, 1989–94; Ambassador to Mexico, 1994–99. *Recreations:* books, plants. *Address:* The Parochial House, Inniscarra, Co. Cork, Ireland. *T:* (21) 4871239.

BEAMISH, David Richard; Clerk Assistant, House of Lords, since 2007; *b* 20 Aug. 1952; *s* of late Richard Ludlow Beamish and Heather Margaret Ensor Beamish (*née* Lock); *m* 1989, (Fiona) Philippa Tudor, *d* of James Brian Tudor; one *d*. *Educ:* Marlborough Coll.; St John's Coll., Cambridge (MA, LLM). House of Lords: Clerk, 1974; Sen. Clerk, 1979; Chief Clerk, 1987; Principal Clerk, 1993; seconded to Cabinet Office as Private Sec. to Leader of H of L and Govt Chief Whip, 1983–86; Clerk of the Journals, 1993–95 and 2002–05; Clerk of Cttees and Clerk of Overseas Office, 1995–2002; Reading Clerk, 2003–07. BBC TV Mastermind Champion, 1988. *Publication:* (ed jtly) The House of Lords at Work, 1993. *Recreations:* church bell ringing, family history. *Address:* House of Lords, SW1A 0PW. *T:* (020) 7219 3151, *Fax:* (020) 7219 0329; *e-mail:* beamishdr@parliament.uk.

BEAMISH, Sarah Frances, (Sally); composer; *b* 26 Aug. 1956; *d* of William Anthony Alten Beamish and Ursula Mary (*née* Snow); *m* 1988, Robert Irvine; two *s* one *d*. *Educ:* Camden Sch. for Girls; Nat. Youth Orch.; Royal Northern Coll. of Music (GRNCM); Staatliche Hochschule für Musik, Detmold. Viola player, Raphael Ensemble, Acad. of St Martin-in-the-Fields, London Sinfonietta, Lontano, 1979–90; Composer's Bursary, Arts Council, 1989; Composer-in-Residence: Swedish Chamber Orch., 1998–2002; Scottish Chamber Orch., 1998–2002. Recordings: River ('Cello, Viola and Oboe Concertos); The Imagined Sound of Sun on Stone (Saxophone Concerto, etc); Bridging the Day ('cello and piano), 2001; String Quartets, 2006; The Seafarer, 2008. *Compositions include:* 1st Symphony (first perf., Iceland SO, 1993); Knotgrass Elegy (oratorio), 2001; Monster (opera), 2001; Viola Concerto No 2, 2002; Trumpet Concerto, 2003; Percussion Concerto, 2005; Shenachie (stage musical), 2006; Accordion Concerto, 2006. Hon.

DMus Glasgow, 2001. *Recreations:* painting, writing. *Address:* City Halls, Candleriggs, Glasgow G1 1NQ. *T:* (0141) 552 5222.

BEAN, Basil, CBE 1985; Vice Chairman, Barratt Developments Plc, 1997–2001; Vice President, National House Building Council, since 1994 (Director General, then Chief Executive, 1985–94 and 1996–97); *b* 2 July 1931; *s* of Walter Bean and Alice Louise Bean; *m* 1956, Janet Mary Brown; one *d. Educ:* Archbishop Holgate Sch., York. Mem. CIPFA. York City, 1948–53; West Bromwich Borough, 1953–56; Sutton London Bor., 1957–62; Skelmersdale Develt Corp., 1962–66; Havering London Bor., 1967–69; Northampton Develt Corp., 1969–80 (Gen. Manager, 1977–80); Chief Exec., Merseyside Develt Corp., 1980–85; overseas consultancies. Chm., Admiral Homes Ltd, 1996–97. Mem., British Waterways Bd, 1985–88. Hon. FABE 1980. *Publications:* financial and technical papers. *Recreations:* reading, walking, travel. *Address:* 4 Paget Close, Great Houghton, Northampton NN4 7EF. *T:* (01604) 765135. *Club:* Northampton and County (Northampton).

BEAN, Dr Charles Richard; Deputy Governor, Bank of England, since 2008; *b* 16 Sept. 1953; *s* of Charles Ernest Bean and Mary (*née* Welsh). *Educ:* Emmanuel Coll., Cambridge (BA 1975); MIT (PhD 1981). Economist, HM Treasury, 1975–79 and 1981–82; London School of Economics: Lectr, 1982–86; Reader, 1986–90; Prof., 1990–2000; Chief Economist and Exec. Dir, Bank of England, 2000–08. Visiting Professor: Stanford Univ., 1990; Reserve Bank of Australia, 1999. *Publications:* contrib. learned jls. *Recreations:* cricket, opera. *Address:* Bank of England, Threadneedle Street, EC2R 8AH. *T:* (020) 7601 4999.

BEAN, Hon. Sir David (Michael), Kt 2004; **Hon. Mr Justice Bean;** a Judge of the High Court of Justice, Queen's Bench Division, since 2004; a Presiding Judge, South Eastern Circuit, since 2007; *b* 25 March 1954; *s* of late George Joseph Bean and of Zdenka White; *m* 1st, 1986 (marr. diss. 1996); two *s*; 2nd, 2004, Ruth Thompson, *qv. Educ:* St Paul's Sch., Barnes; Trinity Hall, Cambridge (1st Cl. Hons Law). Called to the Bar, Middle Temple, 1976, Bencher, 2001; a Recorder, 1996–2004; QC 1997. Chairman: Gen. Council of the Bar, 2002 (Vice-Chm, 2001); Employment Law Bar Assoc., 1999–2001; Immigration Services Tribunal, 2001–04. Lay Mem., GMC, 2003–04; Mem., Civil Justice Council, 2003–05. *Publications:* Injunctions, 1979, 9th edn 2006; (with Anthony Nigel Fricker) Enforcement of Injunctions and Undertakings, 1991; (ed) Law Reform for All, 1996. *Recreations:* opera, hill-walking, books. *Address:* Royal Courts of Justice, Strand, WC2A 2LL. *Club:* Reform.

BEAN, Rev. Canon John Victor; Vicar, St Mary, Cowes, Isle of Wight, 1966–91, and Priest-in-charge, All Saints, Gurnard, IoW, 1978–91; Chaplain to the Queen, 1980–95; *b* 1 Dec. 1925; *s* of Albert Victor and Eleanor Ethel Bean; *m* 1955, Nancy Evelyn Evans; two *s* one *d* (and one *d* died in infancy). *Educ:* local schools; Grammar Sch., Gt Yarmouth; Downing Coll., Cambridge (MA); Salisbury Theological Coll., 1948. Served War, RNVR, 1944–46; returned to Cambridge, 1946–48. Assistant Curate: St James, Milton, Portsmouth, 1950–55; St Peter and St Paul, Fareham, 1955–59; Vicar, St Helen's, IoW, 1959–66. Rural Dean of West Wight, 1968–73; Clergy Proctor for Diocese of Portsmouth, 1973–80; Hon. Canon, Portsmouth Cathedral, 1970–91, Canon Emeritus, 1991. *Recreations:* photography, boat-watching, tidying up. *Address:* 23 Seldon Avenue, Ryde, Isle of Wight PO33 1NS. *Club:* Gurnard Sailing (Gurnard).

BEAN, Leonard, CMG 1964; MBE (mil.) 1945; MA; Secretary, Southern Gas Region, 1966–79, retired; *b* 19 Sept. 1914; *s* of late Harry Bean, Bradford, Yorks, and late Agnes Sherwood Beattie, Worcester; *m* 1938, Nancy Winifred (*d* 1990), *d* of Robert John Neilson, Dunedin, NZ; one *d. Educ:* Canterbury Coll., NZ; Queens' Coll., Cambridge. Served War of 1939–45: Major, 2nd NZ Div. (despatches, MBE). Entered Colonial Service, N Rhodesia, 1945; Provincial Comr, 1959; Perm. Sec. (Native Affairs), 1961; acted as Minister for Native Affairs and Natural Resources in periods, 1961–64; Permanent Secretary: to Prime Minister, 1964; also to President, 1964. Adviser to President, Zambia, 1964–66. *Recreations:* golf, gardening. *Clubs:* MCC; Bramshaw Golf.

BEAN, Marisa; *see* Robles, M.

BEAN, Prof. Philip Thomas, PhD; Professor of Criminology and Director, Midlands Centre for Criminology and Criminal Justice, Department of Social Sciences, Loughborough University, 1990–2003, now Emeritus Professor; *b* 24 Sept. 1936; *s* of Thomas William Bean and Amy Bean; *m* 1st, 1964, Anne Elizabeth Sellar (marr. diss. 1968); 2nd, 1969, Valerie Winifred Davis (*d* 1999); two *s. Educ:* Bedford Modern Sch.; Univ. of London (BSc Soc (ext.), MSc Econ); Univ. of Nottingham (PhD). Probation Officer, Inner London Probation Service, 1963–69; Res. Officer, MRC, 1969–72; Lectr and Sen. Lectr in Social Sci., Univ. of Nottingham, 1972–90; Reader in Criminology, Univ. of Loughborough, 1990. Vis. Prof. at American, Canadian and Australian univs. Pres., British Soc. of Criminology, 1996–99; Associate, GMC, 2000–05. *Publications include:* The Social Control of Drugs, 1974; Rehabilitation and Deviance, 1976; Compulsory Admissions to Mental Hospitals, 1980; Punishment, 1981; Mental Disorder and Legal Control, 1987; Mental Disorder and Community Safety, 2000; Drugs and Crime, 2004; Madness and Crime, 2007; numerous contribs to learned jls. *Recreations:* poetry, music, esp. New Orleans jazz and opera. *Address:* 41 Trevor Road, West Bridgford, Notts NG2 6FT. *T:* (0115) 923 3895.

BEAN, Shaun Mark, (Sean); actor; *b* Sheffield, 17 April 1959; *s* of Brian and Rita Bean; *m* 1st, 1981, Debra James (marr. diss.); 2nd, 1990, Melanie Hill (marr. diss. 1997); two *d*; 3rd, 1997, Abigail Cruttenden (marr. diss. 2000); one *d*; 4th, 2008, Georgina Sutcliffe. *Educ:* RADA. Stage début, Tybalt in Romeo and Juliet, Watermill Th., Newbury, 1983; *other theatre includes:* Romeo and Juliet, The Fair Maid of the West, A Midsummer Night's Dream, RSC, 1986–87; Killing the Cat, Royal Court Th., 1990; Macbeth, Albery Th., 2002. *Television includes:* Troubles, 1988; The Fifteen Streets, 1989; Small Zones, Lorna Doone, 1990; Tell Me That You Love Me, My Kingdom for a Horse, Clarissa, Prince, 1991; Fool's Gold, 1992; Lady Chatterley, A Woman's Guide to Adultery, 1993; Sharpe (series), 1993–97; Scarlett, Jacob, 1994; Bravo Two Zero, Extremely Dangerous, 1999; Henry VIII, 2003; Sharpe's Challenge, 2006. *Films include:* Caravaggio, 1986; Stormy Monday, 1988; War Requiem, How to Get Ahead in Advertising, 1989; Windprints, The Field, 1990; In the Border Country, 1991; Patriot Games, 1992; Shopping, Black Beauty, 1994; Goldeneye, 1995; When Saturday Comes, 1996; Anna Karenina, 1997; Airborne, Ronin, 1998; Essex Boys, 2000; The Lord of the Rings: The Fellowship of the Ring, 2001; Don't Say a Word, Tom and Thomas, Equilibrium, 2002; The Big Empty, 2003; Troy, National Treasure, 2004; The Island, Flightplan, 2005; North Country, The Dark, Silent Hill, 2006; Outlaw, The Hitcher, Far North, 2007. *Address:* c/o Independent Talent Group Ltd, Oxford House, 76 Oxford Street, W1D 1BS.

BEANEY, Jan, (Mrs S. Udall); textile artist; author; *b* 31 July 1938; *d* of Jack and Audrey Beaney; *m* 1967, Stephen Udall; one *s* one *d. Educ:* Southampton Coll. of Art; W Sussex Coll. of Art (NDD Painting/Lithography); Hornsey Coll. of Art (ATC); City & Guilds of London Inst. (Licentiate). Lecturer in Art and Embroidery: grammar/technical sch., Northolt, 1959–64; Whitelands Coll. of Educn, 1964–68; Associate Lectr in Embroidery and Design, Windsor and Maidenhead Coll., subseq. E Berks Coll., 1976–2000, Artist-in-Residence, 2000–. Freelance lectr and teacher in design/stitched textiles, UK, USA, Australia, NZ, Canada, Israel and Germany, 1966–. Work exhibited in UK, Europe, Israel and Japan; work in private and public collections, GB and worldwide. Co-founder, Double Trouble Enterprises (publishers), 1997. Presenter, BBC TV series, Embroidery, 1980; contribs to TV progs, 1984–95. Examr, then Jt Chief Examr, Creative Studies, C&G, 1979–95. Member: 62 Gp of Textile Artists, 1962– (Hon. Mem., 1998); Embroiderers' Guild, 1963– (Hon. Mem., 2001); Hon. Mem., C&G, 1996. MUniv Surrey, 1995. *Publications:* The Young Embroiderer, 1966; Fun with Collage, 1970; Fun with Embroidery, 1975; Landscapes in Picture, Collage and Design, 1976; Buildings in Picture, Collage and Design, 1976; Textures and Surface Patterns, 1978; Embroidery: new approaches, 1978; Stitches: new approaches, 1985; The Art of the Needle, 1988; Vanishing Act, 1997; with Jean Littlejohn: A Complete Guide to Creative Embroidery, 1971; Stitch Magic, 1998; Bonding and Beyond, Transfer to Transform, 1999; Gardens and More, Conversations with Constance, 2000; Trees as a Theme, Giving Pleasure, 2001; New Dimensions, Double Vision, 2002; A Tale of Two Stitches, A Sketch in Time, 2003; No Stone Unturned, Connections, 2004; Colour Explorations, Over the Line, 2005; Grids to Stitch, Seductive Surfaces, 2006; Red, Embellish and Enrich, 2007; Location, Location, Seeing Double, 2008; contrib. numerous articles on stitching and textile design. *Recreations:* entertaining friends, travel, reading, painting, gardening. *Address:* Double Trouble Enterprises, PO Box 348, Maidenhead, Berks SL6 6XB. *Fax:* (01628) 675699.

BEAR, Michael David, CEng; JP; Chief Executive, Spitalfields Development Group, since 1991; Managing Director: Balfour Beatty Property Ltd, since 1993; Michael Bear Developments Ltd, since 1996; Regeneration Director, Hammerson UK Properties plc, since 2007; *b* Nairobi, 21 Jan. 1953; *s* of Lionel Meyer Bear and Rebecca Bear; *m* 1979, Barbara Anne Sandler; one *s* one *d. Educ:* Clifton Coll. Sch.; Univ. of Witwatersrand (BSc Eng 1974); Cranfield Inst. of Technol. (MBA 1981). CEng 1978; MICE 1979. Aid worker, S African Voluntary Service, 1970–74; Project Engineer: Hawkins Hawkins & Osborne, 1974–78; Sir Frederick Snow Ltd, 1978–81; Business Analyst, Taylor Woodrow, 1981–82; Internat. Business Develt Manager, Balfour Beatty Engrg Ltd, 1982–88; Man. Dir, Iberia Develts Ltd, 1988–89; Dir, LET Europe BV, 1989–93. Director: Avatar Ltd, 1993–2000; White City Centre Ltd, 1994–98; British Urban Develt Ltd, 1995–99; Cityside Regeneration Ltd, 1997–2003. Chm., Bethnal Green City Challenge, 1993–97. Director: Spitalfields Fest., 1991–2006 (Hon. Advr, 2007–); Spitalfields Mkt Community Trust, 1991–; Metropolitan Drinking Fountain and Cattle Trough Assoc., 2005–; CRASH, 2006–; City Arts Trust, 2007–. MInstD 1997. Governor: London Metropolitan Univ., 2000–03; London South Bank Univ., 2004–; Christ's Hosp., 2005–; Sir John Cass Primary Sch., 2006–; Clifton Coll., 2007–; Sir John Cass Foundn, 2008–. Liveryman: Co. of Paviors, 2002– (Mem., Ct of Assts, 2006–); Co. of Chartered Surveyors, 2006– (Mem., Ct of Assts, 2007–). City of London, Portsoken Ward: Councilman, 2003–04; Dep. Alderman, 2004–05; Alderman, 2005–. JP 2005, Sheriff, 2007–08, City of London. SBStJ 2008. *Recreations:* small business ventures, scuba diving, tennis, opera, theatre, international travel, supporting the England Rugby team. *Address:* Spitalfields Development Group, 65 Brushfield Street, E1 6AA. *T:* (020) 7377 1496, *Fax:* (020) 7377 1783; *e-mail:* michael.bear@hammerson.com. *Club:* Reform.

BEARD, Allan Geoffrey, CB 1979; CBE 1994; Under Secretary, Department of Health and Social Security, 1968–79 (Ministry of Social Security 1966–68); *b* 18 Oct. 1919; *s* of late Major Henry Thomas Beard and Florence Mercy Beard; *m* 1945, Helen McDonagh; one *d. Educ:* Ormskirk Grammar Sch. Clerical Officer, Air Min., 1936; Exec. Off., Higher Exec. Off., Asst Principal, Assistance Board, 1938–47; Army Service, 1940–46 (Capt., RE); Principal, Nat. Assistance Board, 1950; Asst Sec., 1962. Life Vice-Pres., Motability, 2000– (Governor, 1981–99, Hon. Treasurer, 1985–98). *Publication:* Motability: the road to freedom, 1998. *Recreation:* gardening. *Address:* 51 Rectory Park, Sanderstead, Surrey CR2 9JR. *T:* (020) 8916 0744.

BEARD, (Christopher) Nigel; *b* 10 Oct. 1936; *o s* of Albert Leonard Beard, Castleford, Yorks, and Irene (*née* Bowes); *m* 1969, Jennifer Anne, *d* of T. B. Cotton, Guildford, Surrey; one *s* one *d. Educ:* Castleford Grammar Sch., Yorks; University Coll. London. BSc Hons, Special Physics. Asst Mathematics Master, Tadcaster Grammar Sch., Yorks, 1958–59; Physicist with English Electric Atomic Power Div., working on design of Hinckley Point Nuclear Power Station, 1959–61; Market Researcher, Esso Petroleum Co., assessing future UK Energy demands and market for oil, 1961; Ministry of Defence: Scientific Officer, later Principal Scientific Officer, in Defence Operational Analysis Estabt (engaged in analysis of central defence policy and investment issues), 1961–68, and Supt of Studies pertaining to Land Ops; responsible for policy and investment studies related to Defence of Europe and strategic movement of the Army, Dec. 1968–72; Chief Planner, Strategy, GLC, 1973–74; Dir, London Docklands Develt Team, 1974–79; Sen. Consultant, ICI, 1979–93; Sen. Man., ICI-Zeneca Ltd, 1993–97. Mem., SW Thames RHA, 1978–86; Mem. Bd, Royal Marsden Hosp., 1982–90. Mem., Lab. Pty Nat. Constitutional Cttee, 1995–98. MP (Lab) Bexleyheath and Crayford, 1997–2005; contested (Lab) same seat, 2005. Member: Select Cttee on Science and Technol., 1997–2000; Ecclesiastical Cttee, 1997–2005; Treasury Select Cttee, 2000–05; Speaker's Panel of Chairmen, 2001–05. Chm., All-Party Gp on the City, 2003–05. Vice-Chm., PLP Defence Cttee, 2001–05. Contested (Lab): Woking, 1979; Portsmouth N, 1983; Erith and Crayford, 1992. FRSA. *Publication:* The Practical Use of Linear Programming in Planning and Analysis, 1974 (HMSO). *Recreations:* reading, walking, the theatre. *Address:* Lanquhart, The Ridgway, Pyrford, Woking, Surrey GU22 8PW; *e-mail:* nigel.beard@btinternet.com. *Club:* Athenæum.

BEARD, Mary; *see* Beard, W. M.

BEARD, Nigel; *see* Beard, C. N.

BEARD, Peter Hill; American photographer; *b* 22 Jan. 1938; *s* of Anson Beard; *m* 1st, 1967, Minnie Cushing (marr. diss. 1971); 2nd, 1978, Cheryl Tiegs (marr. diss. 1984); 3rd, 1986, Nejma Khanum; one *d. Educ:* Yale Univ. (grad 1961). Career of escapism through collage, books, diaries and anthropology. Major exhibitions include: Blum-Helman, NY, 1975 (first exhibn); ICP, NY, 1977 (first one man exhibn); Diary, 1979, African Wallpaper, 1993, Seibu Mus., Japan; Carnets Africains, Paris, 1996–97; Pettiness and Futility, LA, 1998; 50 Years of Portraits, Toronto, LA, New Orleans, 1998–99; Stress and Density, Berlin, Vienna, 1999; 28 Pieces, Paris, 1999; Living Sculpture, London, 2004–05; Time's Up, London, 2006–07. *Publications:* The End of the Game, 1965; Eyelids of Morning: the mingled destinies of crocodiles and men, 1973; Longing for Darkness: Kamante's tales from Out of Africa, 1975; Zara's Tales from Hog Ranch, 2004; exhibition catalogues: Diary, 1993; Photo poche, 1996; Carnets Africains, 1997; Peter Beard: 50 Years of Portraits, 1999; Stress and Density, 1999; Peter Beard, 2006. *Address:* Driftwood Cove, Box 603, Montauk Point, Long Island, NY 11954, USA. *Club:* White Rhino (Nyeri, Kenya).

BEARD, Prof. Richard William, MD 1971; FRCOG 1972; Professor and Head of Department of Obstetrics and Gynaecology, St Mary's Hospital Medical School, 1972–96, now Emeritus Professor of Obstetrics and Gynaecology, Imperial College School of Medicine; *b* 4 May 1931; *s* of late William and Irene Beard; *m* 1st, 1957, Jane; two *s*; 2nd, 1979, Irène Victoire Marie de Marotte de Montigny; one *s*. *Educ:* Westminster Sch.; Christ's Coll., Cambridge (MA, MB BChir); St Bartholomew's Hosp. Obstetrician and Gynaecologist, RAF Changi, Singapore, 1957–60; Chelsea Hosp. for Women, 1961–62; UCH, 1962–63; Senior Lecturer/Hon. Consultant: Queen Charlotte's and Chelsea Hosps, 1964–68; King's Coll. Hosp., 1968–72. Dir, Pelvic Pain Clinic, Northwick Park Hosp., 1996–2000. Advr to Social Services Select Cttee, H of C (2nd Report on Perinatal and Neonatal Mortality), 1978–80; Civilian Consultant in Obstetrics and Gynaecology to RAF, 1983–2001; Consultant Advr in Obsts and Gynaecol. to DoH (formerly DHSS), 1985–91. Pres., Eur. Bd and Coll. of Obsts and Gynaecol., 1996–99. Mem., Acad. Royale de Médecine de Belgique, 1983. *Publications:* Fetal Physiology and Medicine, 1976, 2nd edn 1983; contribs to learned jls. *Recreations:* tennis, sailing, Chinese history. *Address:* 64 Elgin Crescent, W11 2JJ. *T:* (020) 7727 3129; Lough Ine House, Ballyisland, Skibbereen, Co. Cork, Eire. *T:* (28) 21934. *Club:* Garrick.

BEARD, Prof. (Winifred) Mary, (Mrs R. S. Cormack), PhD; Professor of Classics, University of Cambridge, since 2004; Fellow, Newnham College, Cambridge, since 1984; *b* 1 Jan. 1955; *d* of Roy Whitbread Beard and Joyce Emily (*née* Taylor); *m* 1985, Robin Sinclair Cormack, *qv*; one *s* one *d*. *Educ:* Newnham Coll., Cambridge (BA Classics 1977, MA 1980; PhD 1982). Lectr in Classics, KCL, 1979–83; University of Cambridge: Lectr in Classics, 1984–99; Reader in Classics, 1999–2004. Classics Ed. (pt-time), TLS, 1992–. *Publications:* (with M. Crawford) Rome in the Late Republic, 1985, 2nd edn 1999; The Good Working Mother's Guide, 1989; (ed jtly) Pagan Priests: religion and power in the ancient world, 1990; (with J. Henderson) Classics: a very short introduction, 1995, 2nd edn 2000; (jtly) Religions of Rome I and II, 1998; The Invention of Jane Harrison, 2000; (with J. Henderson) Classical Art: from Greece to Rome, 2001; The Parthenon, 2002; (with K. Hopkins) The Colosseum, 2005; The Roman Triumph, 2007. *Address:* Newnham College, Cambridge CB3 9DF. *T:* (01223) 335700; *e-mail:* mb127@cam.ac.uk.

BEARDMORE, Prof. John Alec, CBiol, FIBiol; Emeritus Professor and Consultant in Aquacultural Genetics, Swansea University (formerly University of Wales, Swansea), since 2000; *b* 1 May 1930; *s* of George Edward Beardmore and Anne Jean (*née* Warrington); *m* 1953, Anne Patricia Wallace; three *s* one *d* (and one *s* decd). *Educ:* Burton on Trent Grammar Sch.; Birmingham Central Tech. Coll.; Univ. of Sheffield. BSc (1st Cl. Botany) 1953, PhD (Genetics) 1956. Research Demonstrator, Dept of Botany, Univ. of Sheffield, 1954–56; Commonwealth Fund Fellow, Columbia Univ., 1956–58; Vis. Asst Prof. in Plant Breeding, Cornell Univ., 1958; Lectr in Genetics, Univ. of Sheffield, 1958–61; Prof. of Genetics and Dir, Genetics Inst., Univ. of Groningen, 1961–66; Nat. Science Foundn Senior Foreign Fellow, Pennsylvania State Univ., 1966; University College of Swansea, subseq. University of Wales, Swansea: Prof. of Genetics, 1966–97; Dean of Science, 1974–76; Vice-Principal, 1977–80; Dir, Inst. of Marine Studies, 1983–87; Hd, Sch. of Biol Scis, 1988–95; Professorial Fellow in Genetics, 1997–2000. Manager, DFID (formerly ODA) Fish Genetics Res. Prog., 1990–2001; Man. Dir, 1995–2005, Chm., 2005–, Fishgen Ltd. Chm., Univ. of Wales Validation Bd, 1994–97; Mem., Univ. of Wales Vice Chancellors' Bd, 1993–96. Vis. Prof., Univ. of Ghent, 1992–2002. Member: NERC Aquatic Life Scis Cttee, 1982–87 (Chm., 1984–87); CNAA: Life Scis Cttee, 1979–85; Cttee for Science, 1985–87; Bd, Council of Sci. and Technology Insts, 1983–85 (Chm., 1984–85); Council, Galton Inst. (formerly Eugenics Soc.), 1980–96, 2002– (Chm., Res. Cttee, 1979–87; Vice-Pres., 2005–); British Nat. Cttee for Biology, 1983–87; Council, Linnean Soc., 1989–93; Cttee, Heads of Univ. Biol Scis (Treas., 1989–91, Chm., 1991–94); Adv. Bd, Internat. Foundn for Sci., 1992–; Vice-Pres., Inst. of Biol., 1985–87 (Mem. Council, 1976–79; Hon. Sec., 1980–85); UK rep., Council of European Communities Biologists Assoc., 1980–87. Hon. Treas., Gower Soc., 2005–. FRSA; FAAAS; FRSocMed. Darwin Lectr, Inst. of Biol. and Eugenics Soc., 1984. Univ. of Helsinki Medal, 1980. *Publications:* (ed with B. Battaglia) Marine Organisms: genetics ecology and evolution, 1977; (ed jtly) Artemia: basic and applied biology, 2002; articles on evolutionary genetics, human genetics and applications of genetics to aquaculture. *Recreations:* bridge, walking. *Address:* 153 Derwen Fawr Road, Swansea SA2 8ED. *T:* (01792) 206232.

BEARDSWORTH, Maj.-Gen. Simon John, CB 1984; *b* 18 April 1929; *s* of late Paymaster-Captain Stanley Thomas Beardsworth, RN and Pearl Sylvia Emma (Biddy) Beardsworth (*née* Blake); *m* 1954, Barbara Bingham Turner; three *s*. *Educ:* RC Sch. of St Edmund's Coll., Ware; RMA Sandhurst; RMCS. BSc. Commissioned Royal Tank Regt, 1949; Regtl service, staff training and staff appts, 1950–69; CO 1st RTR, 1970–72; Project Manager, Future Main Battle Tank, 1973–77; Student, Royal Naval War College, 1977; Dir of Projects, Armoured Fighting Vehicles, 1977–80; Dep. Comdt, RMCS, 1980–81; Vice Master Gen. of the Ordnance, 1981–84; consultant in defence procurement, 1984–97. *Recreations:* theatre, sudoku. *Address:* c/o Lloyds TSB, Crewkerne, Somerset TA18 7LR. *Club:* Army and Navy.

BEARE, Stuart Newton; Consultant, Richards Butler, Solicitors, 1996–2002 (Partner, 1969–96, Senior Partner, 1988–91); *b* 6 Oct. 1936; *s* of Newton Beare and Joyce (*née* Atkinson); *m* 1974, Cheryl Wells. *Educ:* Clifton Coll.; Clare Coll., Cambridge (MA, LLB). Nat. Service, commnd Royal Signals, attached RWAFF, 1956–57. Plebiscite Supervisory Officer, N Cameroons, 1960–61; admitted solicitor, 1964. Clerk, Ward of Portsoken, 1993–96 (Hon. Ward Clerk, 1996–). Master, City of London Solicitors' Co. and Pres., City of London Law Soc., 1995–96. *Recreations:* mountain walking, ski-ing. *Address:* 24 Ripplevale Grove, N1 1HU. *T:* (020) 7609 0766. *Clubs:* Alpine, City of London, Oriental.

BEARMAN, Prof. Peter William, FREng; Professor of Experimental Aerodynamics, Imperial College of Science, Technology and Medicine, 1986–2004, now Emeritus; *b* 8 Oct. 1938; *s* of William Stanley Bearman and Nana Joan Bearman; *m* 1969, Marietta Neubauer; one *s* one *d*. *Educ:* Jesus Coll., Cambridge (MA 1962; PhD 1965). SSO, Nat. Phys. Lab., 1965–69; Department of Aeronautics, Imperial College, London: Lectr, 1969–81; Reader, 1981–86; Head of Dept, 1989–98; Pro-Rector, Projects, 1999–2001, Dep. Rector, 2001–04, ICSTM. FRAeS 1990; FCGI 1997; FREng (FEng 1997). *Publications:* (ed) Flow-induced Vibration, 1995; around 170 sci. papers. *Recreations:* cycling, gardening, ski-ing. *Address:* Imperial College, SW7 2AZ. *T:* (020) 7594 5055.

BEARN, Prof. Alexander Gordon, MD; FRCP, FRCPEd, FACP; Executive Officer, American Philosophical Society, 1997–2002, now Emeritus; Professor of Medicine, Cornell University Medical College, 1966–79, now Professor Emeritus (Stanton Griffis Distinguished Medical Professor, 1977–79); Attending Physician, The New York Hospital, since 1966; *b* 29 March 1923; *s* of E. G. Bearn, CB, CBE; *m* 1952, Margaret, *d* of Clarence Slocum, Fanwood, NJ, USA; one *s* one *d*. *Educ:* Epsom Coll.; Guy's Hosp., London. Postgraduate Medical Sch. of London, 1949–51. Rockefeller Univ., 1951–66; Hon. Research Asst, University Coll. (Galton Laboratory), 1958–59; Prof. and Sen. Physician, Rockefeller Univ., 1964–66; Chm., Dept of Medicine, Cornell Univ. Med. Coll., 1966–77; Physician-in-Chief, NY Hosp., 1966–77; Sen. Vice Pres., Medical and Scientific Affairs, Merck Sharp and Dohme Internat., 1979–88. Woodrow Wilson Foundn Vis. Fellow, 1979–80; Dist. Vis. Fellow, 1996–97, Fellow Commoner, 1997–, Christ's Coll., Cambridge; Adjunct and Vis. Prof., Rockefeller Univ., 1966– (Hon. Physician, 1988–); Adjunct Prof., Univ. of Pennsylvania Sch. of Medicine, 1998–. Trustee: Rockefeller Univ., 1970–98; Howard Hughes Medical Inst., 1987–2005; Dir, Josiah Macy Jr Foundn, 1981–98. Mem. Editorial Bd, several scientific and med. jls. Lectures: Lowell, Harvard, 1958; Medical Research Soc., 1969; Lilly, RCP, 1973; Harvey, 1975; Lettsomian, Med. Soc., 1976. Macy Faculty Scholar Award, 1974–75. Alfred Benzon Prize, Denmark, 1979; Benjamin Franklin Medal, 2000; David Rockefeller Award, 2002. Member: Nat. Acad. Science; Amer. Philosophical Soc. (Exec. Officer, 1997–2002); Foreign Mem., Norwegian Acad. Science and Letters. Hon. MD Catholic Univ., Korea, 1968; Docteur *hc* Paris, 1975. *Publications:* Archibald Garrod and the individuality of man, 1993; Sir Clifford Allbutt, Scholar and Physician, 2007; Sir Francis Richard Fraser: a canny Scot shapes British medicine, 2008; articles on human genetics and liver disease, 1950–; (Co-Editor) Progress in Medical Genetics, annually, 1962–85; (Associate Editor) Cecil and Loeb: Textbook of Medicine. *Recreations:* biography, collecting snuff-mulls, aristology. *Address:* 241 South 6th Street, Philadelphia, PA 19106, USA. *T:* (215) 9252666; 31 Clarendon Street, Cambridge CB1 1JX. *Clubs:* Philadelphia (Pa); Knickerbocker, Century (NY); Hawks (Cambridge); Crail Golf (Scotland).

BEARN, Rev. Hugh William; Vicar, St Anne's Church, Tottington, since 1996; Chaplain to the Queen, since 2006; *b* 31 March 1962; *s* of John Hugh Bearn and Gladys Eileen Bearn (*née* Saint); *m* 1990, Alison Margaret (*neé* Cooper); two *s*. *Educ:* Oxford Sch.; Manchester Univ. (BA 1984; MA 1998); St John's Coll., Durham (CTh 1988). Schoolmaster, St Edmund's Sch., Canterbury; ordained deacon, 1989, priest, 1990; Asst Curate, Christ Church, Heaton, 1989–92; Chaplain, RAF, 1992–96. Chaplain: RAChD, TA, 1996–2002; Bury Hospice, 1999–2004; Manchester County ACF, 2006–; Chaplain to the Bishop, RBL Fest. of Remembrance, 2002–. Member: Fraternity, CR, Mirfield, 1991–; Sen. Common Room, St Anselm Hall, Univ. of Manchester, 2002– (Hon. Chaplain). Vice-Pres., Manchester Br., Prayer Bk Soc., 2003–. Sec., Old Boys' Soc., Oxford Sch., 1983; Gov., Tottington High Sch., 1996–2001. Bk Reviewer, Contact, 1997. *Publications:* History of Tottington St Anne, 1999; On the Way… a journey into faith, 2007. *Recreations:* family, all things French, marathon running, keep fit, all sport, supporting the varied social, musical and sporting life of my boys, regimental history of the Bearn family. *Address:* The Vicarage, Chapel Street, Tottington, Bury, Lancs BL8 4AP. *T:* (01204) 883713; *e-mail:* hughbearn@aol.com. *Clubs:* Royal Air Force; Royal Irish Officers (Belfast); Manchester Dio. Cricket.

BEARSTED, 5th Viscount *cr* 1925, of Maidstone, Kent; **Nicholas Alan Samuel;** Bt 1903; Baron 1921; *b* 22 Jan. 1950; *s* of 4th Viscount Bearsted, MC, TD and Hon. Elizabeth Adelaide (*d* 1983), *d* of Baron Cohen, PC; *S* father, 1996; *m* 1975, Caroline Jane, *d* of Dr David Sacks; one *s* four *d*. *Educ:* Eton; New Coll., Oxford. *Heir: s* Hon. Harry Richard Samuel, *b* 23 May 1988. *Address:* The Estate Office, Farley Hall, Castle Road, Farley Hill, Berks RG7 1UL.

BEASHEL, John Francis; His Honour Judge Beashel; DL; a Circuit Judge, since 1993; Resident Judge, Dorchester Crown Court, 1994–2006; *b* 3 Aug. 1942; *s* of late Nicholas Beashel and Margaret Rita Beashel, JP; *m* 1966, Kay Dunning; three *s* one *d*. *Educ:* Coll. of Law. Called to the Bar, Gray's Inn, 1970, NSW, 1989; Asst Recorder, 1983–89; Recorder, 1989–93; Liaison Judge to Dorset Justices, 1994–2006. Pres., Dorset Br., Magistrates' Assoc., 1998–2006. DL Dorset, 2007. *Recreations:* golf, travel, reading, walking, cooking. *Address:* Courts of Justice, Deansleigh Road, Bournemouth, Dorset BH7 7DS. *T:* (01202) 502800. *Club:* Ferndown Golf.

BEASLEY, Ann, (Ann Beasley Manders); Director of Finance, HM Prison Service, since 2003; *b* 13 Sept. 1958; *d* of Albert Beasley and Joyce Shirley Beasley (*née* Hodgson); marr. diss.; two *s*. *Educ:* Manchester Univ. (BSc Maths, MSc Stats); Kingston Univ. (MBA). Asst Statistician, HM Customs & Excise, 1980–82; Sen. Asst Statistician and Statistician, CAA, 1982–88; joined Metropolitan Police Service, 1988; Hd, Performance Inf., 1988–92; Hd, Equal Opportunities, 1992–94; Area Business Manager, 1994–2000; Hd, Business Develt and Support, then Dir, Business Change, 2000–02; Hd, Planning Gp, HM Prison Service, 2002–03. *Recreations:* theatre, original art, DIY, cats, gardening, chocolate. *Address:* HM Prison Service Headquarters, Cleland House, Page Street, SW1P 4LN. *T:* (020) 7217 6822, *Fax:* (020) 7217 6746; *e-mail:* ann.beasley@hmps.gsi.gov.uk.

BEASLEY, Dame Christine Joan, DBE 2008 (CBE 2002); Chief Nursing Officer, Department of Health, since 2004; *b* 13 June 1944; *d* of Clifford and Muriel de'Ath; *m* 1st, 1967, John Wills; three *s*; 2nd, 1989, Jack Beasley. *Educ:* Royal London Hosp. (SRN); W London Inst. (Registered Dist Nurse; DMS; DipN). Chief Nurse, Riverside Hosps, 1989–94; Regl Dir of Nursing, N Thames and London, 1994–2002; Partnership Develt Dir, Modernisation Agency, 2002–04. Fellow, Queen's Nursing Inst., 2004. Trustee, Marie Curie Cancer Care, 2000–. Gov., Thames Valley Univ., 2000–. *Recreations:* theatre, entertaining, travel. *Address:* 80 Mayfield Avenue, Ealing, W13 9UX. *T:* (020) 7210 5598; *e-mail:* Christine.beasley@doh.gsi.gov.uk.

BEASLEY, Michael Charles, IPFA, FCA, FCCA; County Treasurer, Royal County of Berkshire, 1970–88; *b* 20 July 1924; *y s* of late William Isaac Beasley and Mary Gladys (*née* Williams), Ipswich, Suffolk; *m* 1955, Jean Anita Mary, *o d* of late Reginald John Shedrick Webber and Margaret Dorothy (*née* Rees), Penarth, S Glamorgan; one *s*. *Educ:* Northgate Grammar Sch., Ipswich; BScEcon London. Treasurer's Dept, East Suffolk County Council, 1940–48; served Royal Navy, 1943–46; Treasurer's Dept, Staffordshire CC, 1948–51; Educn Accountant, Glamorgan CC, 1951–54; Asst County Treasurer, Nottinghamshire CC, 1954–61; Dep. County Treasurer, Royal County of Berkshire, 1961–70, Acting Chief Exec., 1986. Examiner, CIPFA, 1963–66; Financial Adviser, Assoc. of County Councils and former County Councils Assoc., 1971–87; Hon. Treasurer, Soc. of County Treasurers, 1984–88 (Hon. Sec., 1972–80, Vice-Pres., 1980–81, Pres., 1981–82); member of various central and local govt cttees. Member Council: Local Authorities Mutual Investment Trust, 1974–75; RIPA, 1976–82. *Publications:* (ed) Charging for Local Authority Services, 1984; contribs to jls on local govt finance and computers. *Recreations:* cultivating indolence, pottering and pondering, encouraging anti-theism. *Address:* 239 Hyde End Road, Spencers Wood, Berkshire RG7 1BU. *T:* (0118) 988 3868.

BEASLEY-MURRAY, Rev. Dr Paul; Senior Minister, Central Baptist (formerly Baptist) Church, Victoria Road South, Chelmsford, since 1993; *b* 14 March 1944; *s* of late Rev. Dr George R. Beasley-Murray; *m* 1967, Caroline (*née* Griffiths); three *s* one *d*. *Educ:* Trinity School of John Whitgift; Jesus Coll., Cambridge (MA); Northern Baptist Coll. and Manchester Univ. (PhD); Baptist Theol Seminary, Rüschlikon and Zürich Univ. Baptist Missionary Soc., Zaire (Professor at National Univ., Theol. Faculty), 1970–72; Pastor of Altrincham Baptist Church, Cheshire, 1973–86; Principal, Spurgeon's Coll., 1986–92.

Chm., Ministry Today (formerly Richard Baxter Inst. for Ministry), 1994–. Patron, Soc. of Mary and Martha, Sheldon, Exeter, 2008–. Editor, Ministry Today, 1994–. *Publications:* (with A. Wilkinson) Turning the Tide, 1981; Pastors Under Pressure, 1989; Dynamic Leadership, 1990; (ed) Mission to the World, 1991; Faith and Festivity, 1991; Radical Believers, 1992; (ed) Anyone for Ordination?, 1993; A Call to Excellence, 1995; Radical Disciples, 1996; Happy Every After?: a guide to the marriage adventure, 1996; Radical Leaders, 1997; Power for God's Sake, 1998; The Message of the Resurrection, 2000; Fearless for Truth, 2002; Building for the Future, 2003; A Loved One Dies, 2005; Joy to the World, 2005; Transform Your Church, 2005. *Recreations:* music, parties, cooking. *Address:* The Old Manse, 3 Roxwell Road, Chelmsford, Essex CM1 2LY. *T:* (01245) 352996, *Fax:* (01245) 267203; *e-mail:* pbeasleymurray@btclick.com. *Club:* Chelmsford Rivermead Rotary.

BEASTALL, John Sale, CB 1995; Head of Local Government Group, HM Treasury, 1993–95; *b* 2 July 1941; *s* of Howard and Marjorie Betty Beastall (*née* Sale). *Educ:* St Paul's School; Balliol College, Oxford (BA 1963). Asst Principal, HM Treasury, 1963–67 (Asst Private Sec. to Chancellor of the Exchequer, 1966–67); Principal: HM Treasury, 1967–68 and 1971–75 (Private Sec. to Paymaster General, 1974–75); CSD, 1968–71; Assistant Secretary: HM Treasury, 1975–79 and 1981–85; CSD, 1979–81; DES, 1985–87; Treasury Officer of Accounts, 1987–93. Receiver, Met. Police Dist, 1995; Develt Dir, St Paul's Sch., 1996–2000. Chairman: Outward Housing, 2002–07; LAMB Health Care Foundn, 2004–; Feltham Community Chaplaincy Trust, 2008–. *Club:* Oxford and Cambridge.

BEATON, James Wallace, GC 1974; CVO 1992 (LVO 1987); JP; security manager, now retired; Chief Superintendent, Metropolitan Police, 1985–92; *b* St Fergus, Aberdeenshire, 16 Feb. 1943; *s* of J. A. Beaton and B. McDonald; *m* 1965, Anne C. Ballantyne; two *d. Educ:* Peterhead Acad., Aberdeenshire. Joined Metropolitan Police, 1962: Notting Hill, 1962–66; Sergeant, Harrow Road, 1966–71; Station Sergeant, Wembley, 1971–73; Royalty Protection Officer, 'A' Division, 1973; Police Officer to The Princess Anne, 1973–79; Police Inspector, 1974; Chief Inspector, 1979; Superintendent, 1983; Queen's Police Officer, 1983–92. JP E Yorks, 2004. Director's Honor Award, US Secret Service, 1974. *Recreations:* reading, keeping fit, golf, hill walking. *Address:* 57 Carter Drive, Beverley, East Yorkshire HU17 9GL.

BEATSON, Hon. Sir Jack, Kt 2003; FBA 2001; **Hon. Mr Justice Beatson;** a Judge of the High Court of Justice, Queen's Bench Division, since 2003; *b* 3 Nov. 1948; *s* of late John James Beatson and Miriam Beatson (*née* White); *m* 1973, Charlotte, *y d* of Lt-Col J. A. Christie-Miller; one *d* (one *s* decd). *Educ:* Whittingehame Coll., Brighton; Brasenose Coll., Oxford (BCL, MA; DCL 2000); LLD Cantab 2001. Called to the Bar, Inner Temple, 1972, Hon. Bencher, 1993; a Law Comr, 1989–94; a Recorder, 1994–2003; QC 1998; a Dep. High Court Judge, 2000–03. Lectr in Law, Univ. of Bristol, 1972–73; Fellow and Tutor in Law, Merton Coll., Oxford, 1973–94 (Hon. Fellow, 1995); University of Cambridge: Rouse Ball Prof. of English Law, 1993–2003; Fellow, St John's Coll., 1994–2003 (Hon. Fellow, 2005); Dir, Centre for Public Law, 1997–2001; Chm., Faculty of Law, 2001–03. Visiting Professor: Osgoode Hall Law Sch., Toronto, 1979; Univ. of Virginia Law Sch., 1980, 1983; Vis. Sen. Teaching Fellow, Nat Univ. of Singapore, 1987; Vis. Fellow, Univ. of WA, 1988; Dist. Vis. Prof., Univ. of Toronto, 2000. Mem., Competition (formerly Monopolies and Mergers) Commn, 1995–2000. Pres., British Acad. Forensic Scis, 2007. *Publications:* (ed jtly) Chitty on Contract, 25th edn 1982 to 28th edn 1999; (with M. H. Matthews) Administrative Law: Cases and Materials, 1983, 2nd edn 1989; The Use and Abuse of Unjust Enrichment, 1991; (ed jtly) Good Faith and Fault in Contract Law, 1995; (ed jtly) European Public Law, 1998; (ed) Anson's Law of Contract, 27th edn 1998, 28th edn 2002; (jtly) Human Rights: the 1998 Act and the European Convention, 2000; (ed with R. Zimmermann) Jurists Uprooted: German-speaking émigré lawyers in twentieth century Britain, 2004; articles on administrative law, contract, and restitution in legal jls. *Recreations:* trying to relax, amateur gardening. *Address:* Royal Courts of Justice, Strand, WC2A 2LL.

BEATTIE, Anthony; *see* Beattie, G. A.

BEATTIE, David, CMG 1989; HM Diplomatic Service, retired; Personnel Assessor, Foreign and Commonwealth Office, 1998–2008; *b* 5 March 1938; *s* of late George William David Beattie and Norna Alice (*née* Nicolson); *m* 1966, Ulla Marita Alha, *d* of late Allan Alha and Brita-Maja (*née* Tuominen), Helsinki, Finland; two *d. Educ:* Merchant Taylors' Sch., Crosby; Lincoln Coll., Oxford (BA 1964, MA 1967). National Service, Royal Navy, 1957–59; Sub-Lieut RNR, 1959; Lieut RNR 1962–67. Entered HM Foreign (now Diplomatic) Service, 1963; FO, 1963–64; Moscow, 1964–66; FO, 1966–70; Nicosia, 1970–74; FCO, 1974–78; Counsellor, later Dep. Head, UK Delegn to Negotiations on Mutual Reduction of Forces and Armaments and Associated Measures in Central Europe, Vienna, 1978–82; Counsellor (Commercial), Moscow, 1982–85; Head of Energy, Science and Space Dept, FCO, 1985–87; Min. and Dep. UK Perm. Rep. to NATO, Brussels, 1987–92; Ambassador to Swiss Confedn, and concurrently (non-resident) to Principality of Liechtenstein, 1992–97. Principal Sec., Royal Stuart Soc., 1997–2002; Vice-Pres., Anglo-Swiss Soc., 2000–06. Hon. Life Mem., British-Swiss Chamber of Commerce, 2000. Trustee, Chiswick House Friends, 1998–. Freeman, City of London, 1989; Mem. Ct Assts, Masons' Co., 2000– (Master, 2006–07). Commander's Cross, Order of Merit (Liechtenstein), 2007. *Publication:* Liechtenstein: a modern history, 2004, trans. German, 2005. *Recreations:* bridge, walking, history. *Address:* PO Box 13609, W4 4GU. *Club:* Travellers.

BEATTIE, (George) Anthony; UK Permanent Representative to the UN Food and Agriculture Agencies in Rome, 1997–2004, with personal rank of Ambassador, 2002–04; *b* 17 April 1944; *s* of James Ellison Beattie and Christine Beattie; *m* 1973, Janet Frances Dring; one *s. Educ:* Stationers' Company's Sch., London; Trinity Coll., Cambridge (MA). Economic Planning Div., Office of the President, Malawi, 1966–69; Overseas Development Administration: Economic Planning Staff, 1969–78; Admin. Group, 1978; Dir, Tropical Develt and Res. Inst., 1986; Dir, Overseas Develt Natural Resources Inst., 1987–90; Chief Exec., Natural Resources Inst., 1990–96; seconded to Efficiency and Effectiveness Gp, OPS, Cabinet Office, 1996–97; Internat. Div., Dept for Internat. Develt, 1997; Minister (UN Agencies and Aid Affairs), Rome, 1997 (on secondment). *Recreations:* music, pottering in the country, Border terriers. *Address:* Middle Standen, Benenden, Cranbrook, Kent TN17 4LA.

BEATTIE, Hon. Dame Heather; *see* Steel, Hon. Dame A. H.

BEATTIE, Hon. Peter (Douglas); MLA (ALP) Brisbane Central, 1989–2007; Premier of Queensland, 1998–2007; Minister for Trade, 2001–07; *b* 18 Nov. 1952; *s* of Arthur and Edna Beattie; *m* 1975, Heather Scott-Halliday; twin *s* one *d. Educ:* Atherton High Sch.; Univ. of Queensland (BA, LLB); Qld Univ. of Technol. (MA). Admitted Solicitor, Supreme Court of Qld, 1978. Minister for Health, 1995–96; Leader, State Opposition, 1996–98. *Publications:* In the Arena, 1990; The Year of the Dangerous Ones, 1994. *Recreations:* walking, biotechnology history, reading, swimming. *Address:* Level 15, Executive Building, 100 George Street, Brisbane, Qld 4000, Australia.

BEATTIE, Trevor Stephen; Creative Director, Beattie McGuinness Bungay, since 2005; *b* 24 Dec. 1958; *s* of late John Vincent Beattie and of Ada Alice Beattie. *Educ:* Wolverhampton Poly. (BA Hons). Copywriter, advertising: ABM 1981–83; BMP, 1987–90; joined TBWA/HKR, 1990; Creative Dir, 1993–2005, Chm., 2001–05, TBWA/London (Advertising). Notable ad campaigns: Labour Party, French Connection (fcuk), Sony PlayStation, Wonderbra. Hon. DA Wolverhampton, 2000. *Recreations:* flying, gardening, fighting the forces of conservatism, flying to space with Virgin Galactic in 2008. *Address:* (office) 16 Shorts Gardens, Covent Garden, WC2H 9AU. *T:* (020) 7632 0400.

BEATTY, 3rd Earl *cr* 1919; **David Beatty;** Viscount Borodale of Wexford, Baron Beatty of the North Sea and of Brooksby, 1919; *b* 21 Nov. 1946; *s* of 2nd Earl Beatty, DSC, and of Dorothy Rita, *d* of late M. J. Furey, New Orleans, USA; *S* father, 1972; *m* 1971, Anne (marr. diss. 1983), *d* of A. Please, Wokingham; two *s*; *m* 1984, Anoma Corinne Wijewardene (marr. diss. 2000). *Educ:* Eton. *Heir: s* Viscount Borodale, *qv*.

BEATTY, Hon. (Henry) Perrin; PC (Can) 1979; President and Chief Executive Officer, Canadian Chamber of Commerce, since 2007; *b* 1 June 1950; *m* 1974, Julia Kenny; two *s. Educ:* Upper Canada College; Univ. of Western Ontario (BA 1971). MP (Progressive C) Wellington–Grey–Dufferin–Simcoe, Canada, 1972–93; Minister of State for Treasury Bd, 1979; Minister of Nat. Revenue and for Canada Post Corp., 1984; Solicitor General, 1985; Minister of Nat. Defence, 1986–89; Minister of Nat. Health and Welfare, 1989–91; Minister of Communications, 1991–93; Minister for External Affairs, 1993; Pres. and CEO, Canadian Broadcasting Corp., 1995–99; Pres. and CEO, Canadian Manufacturers and Exporters, 1999–2007. Hon. Vis. Prof., Univ. of Western Ontario, 1994–95. *Address:* Canadian Chamber of Commerce, 360 Albert Street, Suite 420, Ottawa, ON K1R 7X7, Canada.

BEAUCHAMP, Sir Christopher Radstock Proctor-, 9th Bt *cr* 1744; solicitor with Gilbert Stephens, Exeter, retired; *b* 30 Jan. 1935; *s* of Rev. Sir Ivor Cuthbert Proctor-Beauchamp, 8th Bt, and Caroline Muriel (*d* 1987), *d* of late Frank Densham; *S* father, 1971; *m* 1965, Rosalind Emily Margot, 3rd *d* of G. P. Wainwright, St Leonards-on-Sea; two *s* one *d. Educ:* Rugby; Trinity College, Cambridge (MA). *Heir: s* Charles Barclay Proctor-Beauchamp [*b* 7 July 1969; *m* 1996, Harriet, *e d* of Anthony Meacock; one *s* twin *d*]. *Address:* The Coach House, 4 Balfour Mews, Sidmouth, Devon EX10 8XL.

BEAUCHAMP, Brig. Vernon John; Chief Executive, The National Autistic Society, 2000–08; *b* 19 Sept. 1943; *s* of late Herbert George Beauchamp and Vera Helena (*née* Daly); *m* 1971, Annemarie, *d* of Evert Teunis van den Born; two *s. Educ:* Portsmouth Grammar Sch.; RMA Sandhurst. Commnd Royal Warwickshire Fusiliers, 1963; transferred 2nd KEO Gurkha Rifles, 1969; served Germany, Borneo, Hong Kong, Brunei, Malaysia and Nepal; Army Staff Coll., 1976; Bde Major, 20 Armoured Bde, 1977–79; NDC, 1981; Comdt, 2 Bn 2nd KEO Gurkha Rifles, 1981–84; sen. staff appts, MoD and HQ BAOR, 1984–87; Comdr, 48 Gurkha Inf. Bde, 1987–89; RCDS, 1990; Comdt, Sch. of Infantry, 1991–93. Chief Exec., Royal Hosp. for Neuro-disability, 1993–2000. *Recreations:* golf, running. *Address:* 20 Castle Street, Farnham, Surrey GU9 7JA. *Club:* Fadeaways.

BEAUCLERK, family name of **Duke of St Albans**.

BEAUFORT, 11th Duke of, *cr* 1682; **David Robert Somerset;** Earl of Worcester, 1514; Marquess of Worcester, 1642; Chairman, Marlborough Fine Art Ltd, since 1977; *b* 23 Feb. 1928; *s* of late Captain Henry Robert Somers Fitzroy de Vere Somerset, DSO (*d* 1965) (*g g s* of 8th Duke) and late Bettine Violet Somerset (*née* Malcolm) (*d* 1973); *S* cousin, 1984; *m* 1st, 1950, Lady Caroline Jane Thynne (*d* 1995), *d* of 6th Marquess of Bath and of Hon. Daphne Vivian; three *s* one *d*; 2nd, 2000, Miranda Morley. *Educ:* Eton. Formerly Lieutenant, Coldstream Guards. Pres., British Horse Soc., 1988–90. *Heir: s* Marquess of Worcester, *qv*. *Address:* Badminton, Glos GL9 1DB.

BEAUFOY, Simon Roger Barton; screenwriter and director; *b* Keighley, 26 Dec. 1966; *s* of Roger and Madeleine Beaufoy; *m* Jane Garwood; one *s* one *d. Educ:* Malsis Prep. Sch., Yorks; Ermysted's Grammar Sch., Skipton; Sedbergh Sch.; St Peter's Coll., Oxford; Bournemouth & Poole Coll. of Art and Design (film course 1992). *Television:* (dir) Shattered Dream, 1993; (dir and writer) Physics for Fish, 1994–95; (writer) Burn Up, 2008; *films:* (co-writer and dir) Yellow; writer: The Full Monty, 1997; Among Giants, 1998; (and co-dir) The Darkest Light, 1999; This is not a Love Song, 2003; Yasmin, 2004; Miss Pettigrew Lives for a Day, 2008; Slumdog Millionaire, 2008. *Recreations:* barge-driving, ski-touring, climbing, river swimming. *Address:* c/o Charlotte Knight, Rodd Hall Agency, 6th floor, Fairgate House, 78 New Oxford Street, WC1A 1HB. *T:* (020) 7079 7987; *e-mail:* office@rodhallagency.com.

BEAUMONT, family name of **Viscount Allendale**.

BEAUMONT, Bill; *see* Beaumont, W. B.

BEAUMONT, David Colin Baskcomb; HM Diplomatic Service, retired; High Commissioner, Botswana, 1995–98; *b* 16 Aug. 1942; *s* of Colin Baskcomb Beaumont and Denise Heather Smith; *m* 1965, Barbara Enid Morris; two *s* one *d. Educ:* St Benedict's Sch., Ealing. Joined CRO, 1961; Private Sec. to Special Rep. in Africa, Nairobi, 1965; Third Sec., Bahrain, 1967; Second Sec., FCO, 1970; Second Sec. (Commercial), Accra, 1974; First Sec., FCO, 1977; First Sec. (Develt), Kathmandu, 1981; First Sec. and Dep. Head of Mission, Addis Ababa, 1982; First Sec., later Counsellor, FCO, 1986; Head of Protocol Dept, 1989–94, and First Asst Marshal of the Diplomatic Corps, 1993–94, FCO. Dir, Guildford Crossroads Care, 1999–2002. *Recreations:* tennis, walking, cooking. *Address:* 42 Harvey Road, Guildford, Surrey GU1 3SE. *T:* (01483) 539577. *Clubs:* MCC; Pirbright Tennis Association.

BEAUMONT, Captain Hon. Sir (Edward) Nicholas (Canning), KCVO 1994 (CVO 1986; LVO 1976); DL; Vice Lord-Lieutenant of Berkshire, 1989–94; *b* 14 Dec. 1929; 3rd *s* of 2nd Viscount Allendale, KG, CB, CBE, MC and Violet (*d* 1979), *d* of Sir Charles Seely, 2nd Bt; *m* 1953, Jane Caroline (*d* 2007), *d* of Alexander Lewis Paget Falconer Wallace, of Candacraig, Strathdon, Aberdeenshire; two *s. Educ:* Eton. Joined Life Guards, 1948; Captain 1956; retired 1960. Assistant to Clerk of the Course, Ascot, 1964; Clerk of the Course and Sec. to Ascot Authy, 1969–94. Pres., Berks SJAB, 1988–94. DL Berks 1982; DL Northumberland, 1996. KStJ. *Address:* Low Shield House, Sparty Lea, Allendale, Northumberland NE47 9UD. *T:* (01434) 685037.

BEAUMONT, Sir George Howland Francis, 12th Bt, *cr* 1661; late Lieutenant 60th Rifles; *b* 24 Sept. 1924; *s* of 11th Bt and Renée Muriel (*d* 1987), 2nd *d* of late Maj.-Gen. Sir Edward Northey, GCMG, CB; *S* father, 1933; *m* 1949, Barbara Singleton (marr. annulled, 1951); *m* 1963, Henrietta Anne (marr. diss. 1986), *d* of late Dr A. Waymouth and Mrs J. Rodwell, Riverside Cottage, Donnington, Berks; twin *d. Educ:* Stowe Sch. *Address:* Stretton House, Stretton-on-Fosse, near Moreton-in-Marsh, Glos GL56 9SB. *T:* (01608) 662845. *Club:* Lansdowne.

BEAUMONT, Rt Rev. Gerald Edward; Vicar, Parish of St John's, Camberwell, Diocese of Melbourne, since 2004; *b* 18 Feb. 1940; *s* of John Beaumont and Marjorie Beaumont; *m* 1967, Elsa Lynette Sampson; two *d*. *Educ:* Australian Coll. of Theology (LTh); Royal Melbourne Inst. of Technology (BA Fine Arts). Deacon 1968, priest 1969, Melbourne; Curate: St Andrew's, Brighton, Vic., 1968–70; Geelong W, 1970–71; Vicar of Mooroolbark, 1971–74; Priest/Pilot, Carpentaria Aerial Mission, Dio. Carpentaria, Qld, 1974–75; Vicar, Armadale-Hawksburn, Vic., 1975–81; Priest-in-Charge, Kooyong, Vic., 1982–86; Vicar, E Melbourne, 1986–92; Canon Pastor, St George's Cathedral, Perth, WA, 1992–94; Rector, Ascension, Alice Springs, NT, and Hon. Canon, Christ Church Cathedral, Darwin, 1995–98; an Asst Bishop, Dio. of Perth, WA (Bp of Goldfields-Country Region), 1998–2004. *Recreations:* painting (exhibiting professional artist), motorcycling. *Address:* 15 The Grove, Camberwell, Vic 3124, Australia. *T:* (3) 98896456; *e-mail:* gebart@stjohnscamberwell.org.au. *Club:* Ulysses (Melbourne).

BEAUMONT, (John) Michael, OBE 2001; Seigneur of Sark, since 1974; *b* 20 Dec. 1927; *s* of late Lionel (Buster) Beaumont and Enid Beaumont (*née* Ripley), and *g s* of Dame Sibyl Hathaway, Dame of Sark; *m* 1956, Diana (*née* La Trobe-Bateman); two *s*. *Educ:* Loughborough Coll. (DLC). Aircraft Design Engr, 1952–70; Chief Techn. Engr, Beagle Aircraft, 1969–70; Design Engr, BAC GW Div., 1970–75. *Recreations:* theatre, music, gardening. *Heir:* *s* Christopher Beaumont, *b* 4 Feb. 1957. *Address:* La Seigneurie, Sark, Channel Islands. *T:* (01481) 832017.

BEAUMONT, John Richard; President, Beaumont Partners sprl, since 2007; *b* 24 June 1957; *s* of Jim Beaumont and Betty Marie (*née* Jarratt); *m* 2000, Annie Margaret (*née* Jupp); two *d* by a previous marriage. *Educ:* Univ. of Durham (BA Geog.). Res. Asst, Univ. of Leeds, 1978–80; Lectr, Univ. of Keele, 1980–83; Consultant, Coopers & Lybrand (London and NY), 1983–85; Jt Man. Dir, Pinpoint Analysis Ltd, London, 1985–87; ICL Prof. of Applied Management Information Systems and Dir, European Centre for Inf. Resource Management, Univ. of Stirling, 1987–90; Prof. and Hd of Sch. of Management, Bath Univ., 1990–92. Man. Dir, Stratatech, 1986–93; Energis Communications Ltd: Strategy Planning Manager, 1993–94; Head of Corporate Strategy and Affairs, 1994–95; Dir of Marketing, 1995–96; Dir of Strategy and Business Develt, 1996–99; Man. Dir, Planet Online Ltd, subseq. Energis^2, 1998–2002; Dir, Energis plc, 2001–02; CEO, UK eUniversities Worldwide Ltd, 2002–04; Partner, Beaumont and Beaumont Ltd, 2004–05; CEO, QA plc, 2005–06; Man. Dir and Hd of UK Public Services, BearingPoint Ltd, 2006–07. Chm., Ision AG, 2001–02; Dep. Chm. Supervisory Bd, Business Online AG, 1999–2000; Dir, Metro Hldgs Ltd, 1998–2002; non-executive Director: WorldPay Ltd, 1999–2002; European Telecommunications and Technology Ltd, 1999–2003; Novia Financials plc, 2007–. Non-executive Director: Office of Nat. Statistics, 1996–99; UK Health Educn Partnership, 2003–04. Hon. Professor: QUB, 1990–93; City Univ., 1994–98. Mem. Council, ESRC, 1989–93. *Publications:* (with P. Keys) Future Cities, 1982; (with S. Williams) Projects in Geography, 1983; (with E. Sutherland) Information Resources Management, 1992; (jtly) Managing our Environment, 1993. *Recreations:* family, good wine and food, travel, golf, watching Rugby (League and Union), reading fiction. *Address:* Allée du Bois de Bercuit 129, 1390 Grez-Doiceau, Belgium.

BEAUMONT, John Richard; Regional Chairman of Employment Tribunals (North West Region), 1999–2002; *b* 22 June 1947; *s* late Stanley and Winifred Beaumont; *m* 1986, Susan Margaret (*née* Blowers); one *s* two *d*, and one step *s*. *Educ:* Wolverhampton Grammar Sch.; Merton Coll., Oxford (BA 1969; MA 1973). Schoolmaster, Buckingham Coll., Harrow, 1969–71; Regl Organiser, W Midlands, 1971–73, Nat. Dir of Projects, 1973–74, Shelter; Senior Legal Officer: Alnwick DC, 1974; Thurrock BC, 1974–75; called to the Bar, Inner Temple, 1976; in practice at the Bar, Northern Circuit, 1976–94; Chm., Industrial, then Employment, Tribunals, subseq. Employment Judge, 1994–2008 (pt-time, 1992–94); Chm., Reserve Forces Appeal Tribunal, 1999–2008. Gov., Knutsford High Sch., 1999– (Vice-Chm., 2000–02; Chm., 2002–07). *Recreations:* walking, reading (especially Victorian history and literature), family picnics, non-league football (League Rep., Unibond Northern Premier League). *Address:* Carlton House, Seymour Chase, Knutsford, Cheshire WA16 9BY.

BEAUMONT, Martin Dudley, FCA; Chairman, Skillsmart Retail Ltd, since 2007; *b* 6 Aug. 1949; *s* of Patrick Beaumont, DL and late Lindesay Beaumont; *m* 1976, Andrea Wilberforce; three *d*. *Educ:* Stowe Sch.; Magdalene Coll., Cambridge (MA Econs/Land Economy). FCA 1975. Dir, 1980–83, Partner, 1983–87, Thomson McLintock, subseq. KPMG; Gp Finance Dir, Egmont Publishing Gp, 1987–90; Chief Financial Officer, 1990–92, Chief Exec., 1992–2002, United Co-operatives; Dir, 1996–07, Dep. Chm., 2000–07, Co-operative Bank; Gp Chief Exec., Co-operative Gp, 2002–07; Dep. Chm., Co-operative Financial Services, 2002–07; Dir, CIS, 2002–07. Dir, Chester Race Course Co., 2007–. Mem. Council, Duchy of Lancaster, 2007–. Dir, 2005–07, Dep. Chm., 2006–07, NW Business Leadership Team. *Recreations:* family, fishing, tennis, reading.

BEAUMONT, Michael; *see* Beaumont, J. M.

BEAUMONT, Hon. Sir Nicholas; *see* Beaumont, Hon. Sir E. N. C.

BEAUMONT, Peter John Luther, QC 1986; **His Honour Judge Beaumont;** a Circuit Judge, since 1989; Recorder of London, since 2004; *b* 10 Jan. 1944; *s* of S. P. L. Beaumont, OBE, and D. V. Beaumont; *m* 1970, Ann Jarratt; one *s* one *d*. *Educ:* Peterhouse, Zimbabwe; Univ. of Zimbabwe (BScEcon Hons). Called to the Bar, Lincoln's Inn, 1967 (Bencher, 2001); practised South Eastern Circuit; a Recorder, 1986; Common Serjeant, City of London, 2001–04. Member: Parole Bd, 1992–97; Criminal Cttee, Judicial Studies Bd, 2000–03; Sentencing Guidelines Council, 2004–. Governor, Felsted Sch., 1990–2002 (Chm., 1993–98). *Recreations:* golf, tennis, gardening. *Address:* Central Criminal Court, Old Bailey, EC4M 7EH. *T:* (020) 7248 3277. *Club:* Travellers.

BEAUMONT, Sir Richard Ashton, KCMG 1965 (CMG 1955); OBE 1949; HM Diplomatic Service, retired; *b* 29 Dec. 1912; *s* of A. R. Beaumont, FRCS, Uppingham, and Evelyn Frances (*née* Rendle); *m* 1st, 1942, Alou (*d* 1985), *d* of M. Camran, Istanbul; one *d*; 2nd, 1989, Melanie Anns, *d* of Major H. Brummell. *Educ:* Repton; Oriel Coll., Oxford. Joined HM Consular Service, 1936; posted Lebanon and Syria, 1936–41. Served War, 1941–44. Returned to Foreign Office, 1944; served in London, Iraq, Venezuela; Imperial Defence Coll., 1958; Head of Arabian Department, Foreign Office, 1959; Ambassador: to Morocco, 1961–65; to Iraq, 1965–67; Dep. Under-Sec. of State, FO, 1967–69; Ambassador to the Arab Republic of Egypt, 1969–72. Dir-Gen., Middle East Assoc., 1973–77; Chairman: Arab British Centre, 1976–77; Anglo-Arab Assoc., 1979–99; Arab-British Chamber of Commerce, 1980–96. Governor, SOAS, 1973–78. Trustee, Thomson Foundn, 1974–2000. *Address:* 82 Peterborough Road, SW6 3EB.

BEAUMONT, Prof. Steven Peter, OBE 2002; PhD; CEng, FREng; FRSE; Professor of Nanoelectronics, since 1989, and Vice Principal for Research and Enterprise, since 2005, University of Glasgow; *b* Norwich, 20 Feb. 1952; *s* of Albert Reginald Beaumont and Joyce Margaret Beaumont (later Churchard) and step *s* of Arthur Robert Churchard; *m* 1977, Joanne Mary Beaumont; one *s* two *d*. *Educ:* Norwich Sch.; Corpus Christi Coll., Cambridge (BA 1974; PhD 1979). CEng 1987, MIET 1987; FREng 2007; FRSE 2000. University of Glasgow: Res. Fellow, 1978–83; Barr & Stroud Lectr, then Sen. Lectr, 1983–89; Hd, Dept of Electronics and Electrical Engrg, 1994–98; Dir, Inst. for System Level Integration, 1999–2004. Tech. Dir, Intellemetrics Ltd, 1982–90; Director: Photonix Ltd, 2003–; GU Hldgs Ltd, 2005–; Kelvin Nanotechnology Ltd, 2005–. Mem., Scottish Sci. Adv. Cttee, Scottish Govt, 2005–. *Publications:* contrib. papers to learned jls and at major academic confs. *Recreations:* crofting, reading, listening to music, Chair, 1st Glasgow Scout Group. *Address:* Research & Enterprise, 10 The Square, University of Glasgow, Glasgow G12 8QQ. *Fax:* (0141) 330 2112; *e-mail:* steve.beaumont@enterprise.gla.ac.uk.

BEAUMONT, William Anderson, CB 1986; OBE (mil.) 1961; AE 1953; Speaker's Secretary, House of Commons, 1982–86; *b* 30 Oct. 1924; *s* of late William Lionel Beaumont and Mrs E. Taverner; *m* 1st, 1946, Kythé (*d* 1988), *d* of late Major K. G. Mackenzie, Victoria, BC; one *d*; 2nd, 1989, Rosalie, *widow* of Judge Michael Underhill, QC. *Educ:* Terrington Hall, York; Cranleigh Sch. (Entrance Exhibnr); Christ Church, Oxford (MA (Hons) 1950, DipEd (Dist.) 1951). Served RAF, Navigator, 1942–47, 355 Sqdn, 232 Sqdn, SEAC (FO). Asst Master, Bristol Grammar Sch., 1951–54; Beaumont and Smith Ltd, Pudsey, 1954–66 (Man. Dir, 1958–66); Henry Mason (Shipley) Ltd (Man. Dir, 1966–76); Principal, Welsh Office, 1976–79; Asst Sec., Welsh Office, 1979–82. RAuxAF 3507 (Co. of Somerset) FCU, 1948–54; 3609 (W Riding) FCU, 1954–61 (Wing Comdr CO, 1958–61); Observer Comdr, No 18 (Leeds) Gp, Royal Observer Corps, 1962–75 (ROC Medal 1975). A Chm. of Assessors, CSSB, 1988–92. Dir, St David's Forum, 1986–92; Sec., Prince of Wales Award Gp, 1987–90; Mem., Awards Cttee, RAF Benevolent Fund, 1990–; Vice-Chm., Franco-British Soc., 1991–98. *Recreations:* pontificating, watching gardening. *Address:* Apartment 31, Albury Park Mansion, Guildford, Surrey GU5 9BB. *T:* (01483) 209231. *Clubs:* Royal Air Force, Civil Service; United Services Mess (Cardiff); Nothing (Richmond).

BEAUMONT, William Blackledge, (Bill), CBE 2008 (OBE 1982); Rugby Union footballer, retired; sports broadcaster and writer; Managing Director, Bill Beaumont Textiles Ltd; *b* 9 March 1952; *s* of Ronald Walton Beaumont and Joyce Beaumont; *m* 1977, Hilary Jane Seed; three *s*. *Educ:* Ellesmere Coll., Shropshire. Joined family textile business, 1971; Dir, J. Blackledge & Son Ltd, 1981. First played Rugby Union for England, 1975; 34 caps (20 caps as Captain); Mem., British Lions, NZ tour, 1977; Captain, British Lions, S Africa tour, 1980; played for Lancashire Barbarians, retd 1982. Chm., British Lions, NZ tour, 2005. Television includes A Question of Sport (BBC TV), 1982–96. *Publications:* Thanks to Rugby, 1982; Bill Beaumont's Tackle Rugby, 1983; Bill Beaumont's Sporting Year Book, 1984; Bill Beaumont: the autobiography, 2003; (with Mark Baldwin) Beaumont's Up and Under, 2005. *Recreations:* tennis, golf, water ski-ing. *Clubs:* East India, MCC; Fylde Rugby Union Football; Royal Lytham St Anne's Golf.

BEAUREPAIRE, Dame Beryl (Edith), AC 1991; DBE 1981 (OBE 1975); *b* 24 Sept. 1923; *d* of late E. L. Bedggood; *m* 1946, Ian Francis Beaurepaire, CMG (*d* 1996); two *s*. *Educ:* Fintona Girls' Sch., Balwyn, Victoria; Univ. of Melbourne. ASO, WAAAF, 1942–45. Mem. Nat. Exec., YWCA Australia, 1969–77. Liberal Party of Australia: Chm., Victorian Women's Sect., 1973–76; Chm., Federal Women's Sect., 1974–76; Vice-Pres., Victorian Div., 1976–86. Mem., Federal Women's Adv. Cttee Working Party, 1977. Pres., Victorian Assoc. of Order of British Empire, 1988–90. Vice Pres., Citizen's Welfare Service, Vic, 1970–86; Convenor, Nat. Women's Adv. Council, Australia, 1978–82. Member: Council, Australian War Memorial, 1982–93 (Chm., 1985–93; Chm., Fund Raising Cttee, 1993–96); Australian Children's Television Foundation Bd, 1982–88; Bd, Victoria's 150th Authy, 1982–87; Australian Bi-centennial Multicultural Foundn, 1989–92. Chm., Bd of Management, Fintona Girls' Sch., 1973–87; Patron: Portsea (formerly Portsea Children's) Camp, 1996–; Peninsula Health (formerly Peninsula Health Care Network) Foundn, 1996–; Alliance of Girls' Schs Australasia, 1996–; Palliative Care Victoria, 1997–; Epilepsy Foundn of Victoria Inc., 1999–; Australians Against Child Abuse, 1999–; Children First Foundn, 2000–; Child & Family Care Network, 2000–. Silver Jubilee Medal, 1977; Centenary Medal, 2003. *Address:* 18 Barton Drive, Mount Eliza, Vic 3930, Australia. *T:* (3) 97871129, *Fax:* (3) 97879389. *Clubs:* Alexandra, Naval and Military (Melbourne); Peninsula Country Golf (Frankston).

BEAVER, Dr Sarah Ann; Fellow and Academic Administrator/Domestic Bursar, All Souls' College, Oxford, since 2008; *b* 5 Feb. 1952; *d* of John Maurice Wilks and Ida Elizabeth Wilks (*née* Clements); *m* 1979, Rev. Dr William Carpenter Beaver, *qv*; two *s*. *Educ:* Bath High Sch., GPDST; Somerville Coll., Oxford (MA Modern Hist.); Sheffield Univ. (Cert Ed); Wolfson Coll., Oxford (DPhil 1979). Asst Mistress, Lord Williams's Sch., Thame, 1974–76; Jun. Res. Fellow, Wolfson Coll., Oxford, 1978–80; Lectr, Balliol Coll., Oxford, 1979–80; Ministry of Defence, 1980–: Principal, 1985; Hd, Materiel Co-ordination (Navy), 1994; Dir, Procurement Finance, 1995–98; on loan to Nat. Assembly for Wales as Dir, NHS Finance, 1998–2002; Dir, EU and UN, 2002–04; Dir Gen., Internat. Security Policy, 2004–07; Command Sec., Perm. Jt HQ (UK), MoD, 2007–08. Trustee, Marie Curie Cancer Care, 2007–. *Recreations:* cycling, gardening. *Address:* Ministry of Defence, Permanent Joint HQ (UK), Northwood HQ, Sandy Lane, Northwood, Middx HA6 3HP. *T:* (01923) 837526; *e-mail:* sarah.beaver@all-souls.ox.ac.uk. *Club:* Colston (Bristol).

BEAVER, Rev. Dr William Carpenter, II; Office of the Lord Mayor of London, since 2003; *b* 17 Sept. 1945; *s* of late William Carpenter Beaver, MD and Margaret Edith Beaver, MD (*née* Nelson); *m* 1979, Sarah Ann Wilks (*see* S. A. Beaver); two *s*. *Educ:* Colorado Coll., USA (BA 1967; Benezet Distinguished Alumnus, 2000); US Army Comd and Staff Coll. (psc 1980); Wolfson Coll., Oxford (Beit Sen. Schol., Rhodes House; DPhil 1976); St Stephen's House, Oxford (CertTh 1982). Served US Army, 1967–71 (Bronze Star (valour, thrice); Meritorious Service Medal; Air Medal; Combat Infantry Badge), Reserves, 1971–96. Exec. Dir, Univ. of Oxford Develt Records Project, and Jun. Res. Fellow, Wolfson Coll., Oxford, 1977–80; Dep. Hd, Corporate and Community Communications, J. Walter Thompson, 1980–83; Dir, Publicity, Barnardo's, 1983–89; Group Director: Public Affairs, Pergamon AGB Internat. Res., 1989–90; Corporate Affairs, Nat. Westminster Bank, 1990–92; Dir, Marketing, The Industrial Soc., 1992–97; Director of Communications: C of E, 1997–2002; BRCS, 2002–03. Ordained deacon, 1982, priest, 1983; Assistant Curate: St John the Divine, Kennington, 1982–95; St Mary Redcliffe, Bristol, 1995–; St Andrew, Holborn, 2001–04; Hon. Priest-in-charge, St Andrew's, Avonmouth, 1995–98. Chaplain, Mercers' Co., 2002–. Vice Chm., Charles Edward Brooke Sch., Brixton, 1992–2002. FCIPR (FIPR 2003). *Recreation:* bicycling. *Address:* Mansion House, EC4N 8BH. *Club:* Nikaean.

BEAVERBROOK, 3rd Baron *cr* 1917, of Beaverbrook, New Brunswick, and of Cherkley, Surrey; **Maxwell William Humphrey Aitken;** Bt 1916; Chairman: Beaverbrook Foundation, since 1985; Net Integration Inc., since 2000; Pine Ventures plc, since 2007; *b* 29 Dec. 1951; *s* of Sir (John William) Max Aitken, 2nd Bt, DSO, DFC, and of Violet, *d* of Sir Humphrey de Trafford, 4th Bt, MC; *S* to disclaimed barony of father, 1985; *m* 1974, Susan Angela More O'Ferrall; two *s* two *d*. *Educ:* Charterhouse; Pembroke Coll., Cambridge. Beaverbrook Newspapers Ltd, 1973–77; Dir, Ventech, 1983–86; Chm.,

Ventech Healthcare Corp. Inc., 1986, 1988–92. Govt spokesman for Home Office and DTI, H of L, 1986; a Lord in Waiting (Government Whip), 1986–88; Dep. Treas., 1988–90, Treas., 1990–92, Cons. Party; Treas., European Democratic Union, 1990–92. Chm., Nat. Assoc. of Boys' Clubs, 1989–92. Mem. Council, Homeopathic Trust, 1986–92. Hon. Air Cdre, 4624 Sqn, RAuxAF, 2004–. *Recreations:* motor sport (Eur. GT Champion, 1998), offshore powerboat racing (winner, Harmsworth Trophy, 2004). *Heir: s* Hon. Maxwell Francis Aitken [*b* 17 March 1977; *m* 2007, Inés Nieto Gómez-Valencia]. *Address:* Nelson's Place, Fawley, Southampton SO45 1AA. *Clubs:* White's, Royal Air Force; Royal Yacht Squadron; British Racing Drivers'; British Powerboat Racing (Chm., 2003–).

BEAVIS, Air Chief Marshal Sir Michael (Gordon), KCB 1981; CBE 1977 (OBE 1969); AFC 1962; Director, Skye Pharma PLC (formerly Tubular Edgington Group, then Black & Edgington Group), 1989–2006; *b* 13 Aug. 1929; *s* of Walter Erle Beavis and Mary Ann (*née* Sarjantson); *m* 1950, Joy Marion (*née* Jones); one *s* one *d*. *Educ:* Kilburn Grammar Sch. Joined RAF 1947; commnd 1949; served Fighter Comd Squadrons 1950–54, RNZAF 1954–56; flew Vulcan aircraft, Bomber Comd, 1958–62; Staff Coll., 1963; MoD, 1964–66; OC No 10 Squadron (VC10s), 1966–68; Group Captain Flying, Akrotiri, Cyprus, 1968–71; Asst Dir, Defence Policy, MoD, 1971–73; RCDS, 1974; RAF Germany, 1975–77 (SASO 1976–77); Dir Gen. RAF Training, 1977–80; Comdt, RAF Staff Coll., 1980–81; AOC-in-C, RAF Support Comd, 1981–84; Dep. C-in-C, AFCENT, 1984–86. Dir, Alliance Aircraft Co., USA, 2000–03. CCMI. Freeman, City of London, 1980; Liveryman, GAPAN, 1983. *Recreations:* golf, bridge, travel. *Address:* c/o Lloyds TSB, 202 High Street, Lincoln LN5 7AP. *Club:* Royal Air Force.

BEAZER, Brian Cyril; Chairman and Chief Executive, Beazer (formerly C. H. Beazer (Holdings)) PLC, 1983–91; Chairman, Beazer Homes USA Inc., since 1992; *b* 22 Feb. 1935; *s* of late Cyril Henry George Beazer and of Ada Vera Beazer; *m* 1958, Patricia (*née* White); one *d*. *Educ:* Wells Cathedral School. Joined C.H. Beazer, 1958; Man. Dir, 1968; apptd Chm. and Chief Exec. on death of his father in 1983. *Recreations:* walking, reading. *Address:* The Weavers House, Castle Combe, Wiltshire SN14 7HX.

BEAZLEY, Christopher John Pridham; Member (C) Eastern Region, England, European Parliament, since 1999; *b* 5 Sept. 1952; *s* of late Peter George Beazley, CBE; *m* 1978, Christiane Marie Elyane (*née* Dillemann); two *s* one *d*. *Educ:* Shrewsbury; Bristol Univ. Former Nuffield Research Fellow, School of European Studies, Sussex Univ. Vice Chm., Lewes and Eastbourne branch, European Movement, 1980; Wealden DC, 1979–83. MEP (C) Cornwall and Plymouth, 1984–94; contested (C) Cornwall and W Plymouth, Eur. Parly elecns, 1994; European Parliament: spokesman on regl policy, 1984–89, on justice and home affairs, 1992–94, on constitutional affairs, 1999–2001, on educn and culture, 2001–; Vice-Chairman: Transport Cttee, 1989–91; Baltic States Delegn, 1991–94; Chairman: Estonian Delegn, 2001–04; Baltic States Intergp, 2004–. *Club:* Oriental.

BEAZLEY, Hon. Kim Christian; MP (ALP) Brand, Perth, Australia, 1996–2007 (Swan, Perth, 1980–96); Leader of the Opposition, Australia, 1996–2001 and 2005–06; Leader of the House of Representatives, Australia, 1988–96 (Vice-President, Executive Council, 1988–91); *b* 14 Dec. 1948; *s* of late Hon. Kim Edward Beazley and of Betty Beazley; *m* 1st, 1974, Mary Paltridge (marr. diss. 1989); two *d*; 2nd, 1990, Susanna Annus; one *d*. *Educ:* Univ. of Western Australia (MA); Oxford Univ. (Rhodes Scholar; MPhil). Tutor in Social and Political Theory, Murdoch Univ., WA, 1976–79, Lectr 1980. Minister of State for Aviation, and Minister Assisting the Minister for Defence, 1983–84; Special Minister of State, 1983–84; Minister of State for Defence, 1984–90; Minister for Transport and Communications, 1990–91, for Finance, 1991, for Employment, Educn and Training, 1991–93, for Finance, 1993–96; Dep. Prime Minister, 1995–96. Mem., Jt Parly Cttee on Foreign Affairs and Defence, 1980–83, 2002–05, on Aust. Security Intelligence Orgn, ASIS and DSD, 2002–05. Mem. Nat. Exec., ALP, 1991–94, 1996–2001. *Publication:* (with I. Clark) The Politics of Intrusion: the Super-Powers in the Indian Ocean, 1979. *Recreations:* swimming, reading. *Address:* c/o Parliament House, Canberra, ACT 2600, Australia.

BEAZLEY, Thomas Alan George; QC 2001; *b* 2 March 1951; *s* of late Derek Edwin George Beazley and of Rosemary Janet Beazley; *m* 1980, Ingrid Ann Marrable; two *d*. *Educ:* Emmanuel Coll., Cambridge (BA; LLB). Called to the Bar, Middle Temple, 1979. *Recreations:* reading, travelling, cooking. *Address:* Blackstone Chambers, Blackstone House, Temple, EC4Y 9BW.

BEBB, Gordon Montfort; QC 2002; a Recorder, since 2001; *b* 1 May 1952; *s* of Simon and Adonia Montfort Bebb; *m* 1978, Rachel Millington; one *s* one *d*. *Educ:* Winchester Coll.; Magdalen Coll., Oxford (MA). Called to the Bar, Middle Temple, 1975; Asst Recorder, 1997–2001. *Recreations:* theatre, art, music, sport. *Address:* Outer Temple Chambers, The Outer Temple, 222 Strand, WC2R 1BA. *T:* (020) 7353 6381, *Fax:* (020) 7583 1786. *Club:* Jesters.

BECHER, Sir John (William Michael) Wrixon-, 6th Bt *cr* 1831, of Ballygiblin, co. Cork; Principal, Becher Ford Reynolds, since 2006; *b* 29 Sept. 1950; *s* of Sir William Fane Wrixon-Becher, 5th Bt, MC and Hon. Vanda (who later *m* 9th Earl of Glasgow), *d* of 4th Baron Vivian; *S* father, 2000. *Educ:* Ludgrove; Harrow; Neuchâtel Univ. Lloyds Non-Marine Underwriter, 1971–74; Lloyds Broker, Eckersley Hicks Ltd, 1974–82; Hutchison Craft Financial Services Ltd, 1982–87; Dir, Wise Speke Financial Services Ltd, 1987–93; Financial Consultant, HSBC Actuaries and Consultants Ltd, 1993–2000; Partner, Ford Reynolds and Associates Ltd, 2000–05. Director: Old Street Productions Ltd, 2001–03; Wind Energy Ltd, 2002–04. Mem., Personal Finance Soc., 2005–. *Recreations:* golf, shooting, fishing, all field sports. *Address:* Cork and Bottle House, Mansel Lacy, Herefordshire HR4 7HP. *Clubs:* White's, Annabel's, MCC; I Zingari; Swinley Forest.

BECHTEL, Stephen Davison, Jr; Chairman Emeritus: Bechtel Group, Inc., since 1990; Fremont Group, since 1995; *b* 1925; *s* of Stephen Davison Bechtel and Laura Peart. Joined Bechtel Group, Inc. (Engineers and Constructors), 1941; Pres., 1960; Chm., 1973–90. Mem., Bd of Trustees, CIT, 1967–96 (Life Trustee, 1997). Chairman: Business Council, 1987–88; Nat. Acad. of Engrg, 1982–86. Mem., President's Council, Purdue Univ., 1984–; Mem. Adv. Council, 1991–, Vice Chm. and Mem. Bd of Visitors, 1992–, Inst. for Internat. Studies, Stanford Univ. Numerous awards including: Herbert Hoover Medal, 1981; Chairman's Award, 1982, Nat. Engrg Award, 1997, Amer. Assoc. of Engrg Socs; President's Award, 1985, OPAL Award for Lifetime Achievement in Construction, 2000, ASCE; Nat. Medal of Technology, 1991; Founders Award, NAE, 1999; Engr of Distinction Award, Univ. of Colorado, 2000. Officer, Legion of Honour (France), 1979. *Address:* c/o Bechtel Group, Inc., PO Box 193965, San Francisco, CA 94119–3965, USA.

BECK, Rev. Brian Edgar, MA; President of the Methodist Conference, 1993–94; Secretary of the Conference, 1984–98; *b* 27 Sept. 1933; *o s* of late A. G. and C. A. Beck; *m* 1958, Margaret Ludlow; three *d*. *Educ:* City of London School; Corpus Christi College, Cambridge (1st Cl. Classical Tripos pts 1 and 2); Wesley House, Cambridge (1st Cl. Theol. Tripos pt 2). BA 1955, MA 1959. Ordained Methodist Minister, 1960; Asst Tutor, Handsworth Coll., 1957–59; E Suffolk Circuit Minister, 1959–62; St Paul's United Theological Coll., Limuru, Kenya, 1962–68; Tutor, Wesley House, Cambridge, 1968–80, Principal 1980–84. Sec., E African Church Union Consultation Worship and Liturgy Cttee, 1963–68; Mem., World Methodist Council, 1966–71, 1981–98; Co-Chm., Oxford Inst. of Methodist Theol. Studies, 1976–2002. Hon. Chaplain, Guild of St Bride, Fleet Street, 1994–. Fernley-Hartley Lectr, 1978; Vis. Prof., Wesley Theol Seminary, Washington, 1999. DD Lambeth, 1998. *Publications:* Reading the New Testament Today, 1977; Christian Character in the Gospel of St Luke, 1989; Gospel Insights, 1998; Exploring Methodism's Heritage, 2004; (ed jtly) Unmasking Methodist Theology, 2004; contributor to: Christian Belief, a Catholic-Methodist statement, 1970; Unity the Next Step?, 1972; Suffering and Martyrdom in the New Testament, 1981; Rethinking Wesley's Theology, 1998; Community-Unity-Communion, 1998; Managing the Church?, 2000; Apostolicity and Unity, 2002; Reflections on Ministry, 2004; articles in NT Studies, Epworth Review. *Recreations:* walking, DIY, cross-stitch. *Address:* 26 Hurrell Road, Cambridge CB4 3RH. *T:* and *Fax:* (01223) 312260.

BECK, Clive; *b* 12 April 1937; *s* of Sir Edgar Charles Beck, CBE, and Mary Agnes Beck; *m* 1960, Philippa Flood; three *s* three *d*. *Educ:* Ampleforth College. 2nd Lieut, The Life Guards, 1956–57; John Mowlem & Co., 1957–67; SGB Group, 1967–86; Dep. Chm., John Mowlem & Co., 1986–92. Director: London Management Ltd, 1990–; Pioneer Concrete Holdings plc, 1990–97. *Recreation:* golf. *Address:* 8 Atherton Drive, Wimbledon, SW19 5LB. *Clubs:* Royal Wimbledon Golf, Swinley Forest Golf.
See also Sir E. P. Beck.

BECK, Sir (Edgar) Philip, Kt 1988; Chairman: John Mowlem & Co., 1979–95; Railtrack, 1999–2001; *b* 9 Aug. 1934; *s* of Sir Edgar Charles Beck, CBE, and Mary Agnes Beck; *m* 1st, 1957, Thomasina Joanna Jeal (marr. diss.); two *s*; 2nd, 1991, Bridget Cockerell (*née* Heathcoat-Amory). *Educ:* Ampleforth College; Jesus College, Cambridge (MA). Dir, John Mowlem, 1964, Dep. Chm., 1978–79. Chairman: FCEC, 1982–83; Export Group for Constructional Industries, 1986–88. Non-executive Director: Invensys, 1992–2003; Delta, 1993–2004. *Address:* Pylle Manor, Shepton Mallet, Somerset BA4 6TD. *Club:* Royal Yacht Squadron.
See also C. Beck.

BECK, Lydia Helena; *see* Lopes Cardozo Kindersley, L. H.

BECK, Peter, MD; FRCP; Lord-Lieutenant for South Glamorgan, since 2008; *b* Leicester, 4 July 1941; *s* of Frank Beck and Kittie Eileen Beck (*née* Clark); *m* 1964, Lyn Davies; one *s* one *d*. *Educ:* Wyggeston Boys' Sch., Leicester; St Mary's Hosp. Med. Sch., London (MB BS Hons 1965; MD 1976); MA Wales 1989. FRCP 1980. Jun. posts, St Mary's and Hammersmith Hosps, 1965–67; SHO, then Registrar, Cardiff Royal Infirmary, 1967–70; Lectr, Welsh Nat. Sch. of Medicine, Cardiff, 1970–71; MRC Clin. Res. Fellow, Cardiff, 1971–73; Wellcome Travelling Fellow, Harvard Med. Sch., 1974–75; Consultant Physician, Cardiff Teaching Hosps, 1974–2003. DL S Glamorgan, 1994. OStJ 2006. *Publications:* contrib. papers on haemophilia, angio-oedema, immuno-assay, diabetes and med. ethics. *Recreations:* golf, Rugby, family, art. *Address:* Tyla Teg, 46 Ty Gwyn Road, Penylan, Cardiff CF23 5JG. *T:* (029) 2048 5982; *e-mail:* pandlbeck@tiscali.co.uk. *Clubs:* Army and Navy; Cardiff and County; Royal Porthcawl Golf.

BECK, Sir Philip; *see* Beck, Sir E. P.

BECKE, Prof. Axel Dieter, PhD; FRS 2006; FRSC; Killam Professor of Computational Science, Dalhousie University, since 2006; *b* Esslingen, Germany, 10 June 1953. *Educ:* Queen's Univ., Kingston, Ont (BSc 1975); McMaster Univ. (MSc 1977; PhD 1981). FRSC 2000. Postdoctoral Fellow, Dalhousie Univ., 1981–84; NSERC Univ. Res. Fellow, Queen's Univ., 1984–94; Prof. of Chemistry, Queen's Univ., until 2006. Killam Res. Fellow, Canada Council for the Arts, 2005–07. Mem., Internat. Acad. of Quantum Molec. Sci. *Publications:* articles in scientific jls. *Address:* Department of Chemistry, Dalhousie University, Halifax, NS B3H 4J3, Canada.

BECKE, Mrs Shirley Cameron, OBE 1974; QPM 1972; Vice-Chairman, 1976–83 and Regional Administrator, London Region, 1974–79, Women's Royal Voluntary Service, retired; *b* 29 April 1917; *er d* of late George L. Jennings, AMIGasE and Marion Jennings; *m* 1954, Rev. Justice Becke, MBE, TD, FCA (*d* 1990); no *c*. *Educ:* privately; Ealing Co. Gram. Sch. Trained in Gas Engineering, 1935–40. Joined Metropolitan Police as Constable, 1941; served in various ranks; Woman Commander, 1969–74. OStJ 1975. *Recreations:* reading, bridge. *Address:* 4 North Close, St Martin's Square, Chichester PO19 1NU. *T:* (01243) 784295.

BECKE, Lt-Col William Hugh Adamson, CMG 1964; DSO 1945; *b* 24 Sept. 1916; *er s* of late Brig.-Gen. J. H. W. Becke, CMG, DSO, AFC, and late Mrs A. P. Becke (*née* Adamson); *m* 1945, Mary Catherine, 3rd *d* of late Major G. M. Richmond, Kincairney, Murthly, Perthshire. *Educ:* Charterhouse; RMC Sandhurst. Commissioned in The Sherwood Foresters, 1937. British Military Mission to Greece, 1949–52; Asst Military Adviser to the High Commissioner for the UK in Pakistan, 1957–59; Military Attaché, Djakarta, 1962–64; retd 1966. Private Sec. and Comptroller to Governor of Victoria, 1969–74; Personnel Officer, Gas and Fuel Corp. of Vic, 1974–82. *Address:* 3 Chambers Street, South Yarra, Vic 3141, Australia. *Clubs:* Army and Navy; Melbourne, Victoria Racing (Melbourne).

BECKER, Boris; former professional tennis player; entrepreneur; *b* 22 Nov. 1967; *s* of late Karl-Heinz and Elvira Becker; *m* Barbara Feltus (marr. diss. 2001); two *s*; one *d*. West German Junior Champion, 1983; wins include: Young Masters' Junior Tournament, 1985; Wimbledon, 1985 (youngest winner), 1986, 1989; US Open, 1989; Australian Open, 1991, 1996; ATP World Champion, 1992, 1995; Davis Cup winner, 1988, 1989; retired as professional tennis player, 1999. *Publication:* Boris Becker - The Player: the autobiography, 2004. *Address:* Boris Becker & Co., Grafenauweg 4, 6300 Zug, Switzerland.

BECKER, Prof. Gary Stanley, PhD; University Professor, Departments of Economics and Sociology, Graduate School of Business, University of Chicago, since 1983; *b* 2 Dec. 1930; *s* of Louis William Becker and Anna (*née* Siskind); *m* 1st, 1954, Doria Slote (decd); two *d*; 2nd, 1979, Guity Nashat; two *s*. *Educ:* Princeton Univ. (AB *summa cum laude* 1951); Univ. of Chicago (AM 1953; PhD 1955). Asst Prof., Univ. of Chicago, 1954–57; Columbia University: Asst and Associate Prof of Econs, 1957–60; Prof. of Econs, 1960–68; Arthur Lehman Prof. of Econs, 1968–69; University of Chicago: Ford Foundn Vis. Prof. of Econs, 1969–70; Prof., 1970–83, Chm., 1984–85, Dept of Econs. Member: Domestic Adv. Bd, Hoover Instn, 1973–91 (Sen. Fellow, 1990–); Acad. Adv. Bd, Amer. Enterprise Inst. for Public Policy Res., 1987–91; Associate Mem., Inst. Fiscal and Monetary Policy, Min. of Finance, Japan, 1988–; Res. Associate, Econs Res. Center, Nat. Opinion Res. Center, 1980–; Affiliate, Lexecon Corp., 1990–2002; Dir, UNext.com, 1999–2003. Columnist, Business Week, 1985–2004. Member: American Economic

Association: Vice-Pres., 1974; Pres., 1987; Distinguished Fellow, 1988; Mont Pelerin Society, 1971–: Exec. Bd, 1985–96; Vice-Pres., 1989–90; Pres., 1990–92; Editl Bd, Amer. Econ. Rev., 1968–71; Amer. Statistical Assoc. (Fellow 1965); Econometric Soc. Member: Nat. Acad. Scis, 1975–; Internat. Union for Scientific Study of Population, 1982–; Amer. Philosophical Soc., 1986–; Founding Mem., Nat. Acad. Educn (Vice-Pres., 1965–67). Fellow: Amer. Acad. Arts and Scis, 1972; Nat. Assoc. of Business Economists, 1993; Pontifical Acad. of Sci., 1997. Hon. degrees: PhD: Hebrew Univ., Jerusalem, 1985; Palermo, 1993; LLD: Knox Coll., Ill, 1985; Harvard, 2003; Dr of Arts, Illinois, 1988; DSc: SUNY, 1990; Rochester, 1995; DHL: Princeton, 1991; Columbia, 1993; Hofstra, 1997; DBA: Miami, 1995; Aix-Marseilles, 1999; DEconSc Warsaw Sch. of Econs, 1995; Dr: Prague Univ. of Econs, 1995; Athens, 2002. John Bates Clark Medal, Amer. Econ. Assoc., 1967; Frank E. Seidman Dist. Award in Pol Econ., 1985; Merit Award, NIH, 1986; John R. Commons Award, Omicron Delta Epsilon, 1987; Nobel Prize for Economics, 1992; US Nat. Medal of Sci., 2000; Phoenix Prize, Univ. of Chicago, 2001; Amer. Acad. of Achievement, 2001; Heartland Prize, Chicago Tribune, 2002; Nat. Inst. of Child Health and Human Develt Hall of Honor, 2003; Hayek Award, Frederic A. von Hayek-Gesellschaft Awards, Germany, 2003; Von Neumann Lecture Award, Rajk Coll., Corvinus Univ., Budapest, 2004; Arrow Award, Internat. Health Econs Assoc., 2005; Provost's Teaching Award, Univ. of Chicago, 2006. Medal of the Italian Presidency, 2004; Presidential Medal of Freedom (USA), 2007. *Publications:* The Economics of Discrimination, 1957, 2nd edn 1971; Human Capital, 1964, 3rd edn 1993 (trans. Japanese 1975, Spanish 1984, Chinese 1987, Romanian 1997); Human Capital and the Personal Distribution of Income: an analytical approach, 1967; Economic Theory, 1971 (trans. Japanese, 1976); (ed jtly) Essays in the Economics of Crime and Punishment, 1974; (with G. Ghez) The Allocation of Time and Goods Over the Life Cycle, 1975; The Economic Approach to Human Behaviour, 1976 (trans. German 1982, Polish 1990, Chinese 1993, Romanian 1994, Italian 1998); A Treatise on the Family, 1981, expanded edn 1991 (trans. Spanish 1987, Chinese 1988); Accounting for Tastes, 1996; (with Guity Nashat) The Economics of Life, 1996 (trans. Chinese 1997, Czech 1997, German 1998, Japanese 1998, Spanish 2002); (with Kevin M. Murphy) Social Economics, 2000; contrib. chaps in numerous books and articles in jls incl. Jl Pol Econ., Qly Jl Econs, Amer. Econ. Rev., Jl Law and Econs, Jl Labor Econs, Business Econs, etc. *Address:* Department of Economics, University of Chicago, 1126 East 59th Street, Chicago, IL 60637, USA. *T:* (773) 7028168; 1308 East 58th Street, Chicago, IL 60637, USA.

BECKER, Judith Myfanwy Sarah; *see* Hall, J. M. S.

BECKERLEG, John; Director of Resources, National Policing Improvement Agency, since 2006; *b* 12 Aug. 1956; *s* of Lewis Beckerleg and Doris (*née* Bundy); *m* 1983, April Cornelia Saunders; two *s* one *d*. *Educ:* Emmanuel Coll., Cambridge (MA 1981); MBA Henley Mgt Coll. 1998. CIPFA 1981. Chief Accountant, Cambs CC, 1985–87; Sen. Asst Co. Treas., Herts CC, 1987–91; Buckinghamshire County Council: Dep. Co. Treas., 1991–93; Dir of Finance, 1993–96; Dir of Corporate Services, 1996–98; Dir of Social Services, 1998–2000; Strategic Manager, 2000–04; Mgt Consultant, Management Options Ltd, 2004–06. *Recreations:* theatre, genealogy. *Address:* Daffodil Cottage, Main Street, Grendon Underwood, Bucks HP18 0ST.

BECKERMAN, Wilfred, PhD; Fellow of Balliol College, Oxford, 1975–92, now Emeritus; Reader in Economics, Oxford University, 1978–92; *b* 19 May 1925; *s* of Morris and Mathilda Beckerman; *m* 1st, 1952, Nicole Geneviève Ritter (*d* 1979); one *s* two *d*; 2nd, 1991, Joanna Pasek; one *d*. *Educ:* Ealing County Sch.; Trinity Coll., Cambridge (MA, PhD). RNVR, 1943–46. Trinity Coll., Cambridge, 1946–50; Lecturer in Economics, Univ. of Nottingham, 1950–52; OEEC and OECD, Paris, 1952–61; National Inst. of Economic and Social Research, 1962–63; Fellow of Balliol Coll., Oxford, 1964–69; Economic Advr to Pres. of BoT (leave of absence from Balliol), 1967–69; Prof. of Political Economy, Univ. of London, and Head of Dept of Political Economy, UCL, 1969–75. Mem., Royal Commn on Environmental Pollution, 1970–73. Member: Exec. Cttee, NIESR, 1973–96; Council, Royal Economic Soc., 1990–93. Elie Halévy Vis. Prof. Institut d'Etudes Politiques, Paris, 1977; Resident Scholar, Woodrow Wilson Internat. Center for Scholars, Washington, DC, 1982; Vis. Prof. of Econs, UCL, 2005–. Consultant: World Bank; OECD; ILO. Pres., Section F (Economics), BAAS, 1978. *Publications:* The British Economy in 1975 (with associates), 1965; International Comparisons of Real Incomes, 1966; An Introduction to National Income Analysis, 1968; (ed and contrib.) The Labour Government's Economic Record, 1972; In Defence of Economic Growth, 1974; Measures of Leisure, Equality and Welfare, 1978; (ed and contrib.) Slow Growth in Britain: Causes and Consequences, 1979; Poverty and the Impact of Income Maintenance Programmes, 1979; (with S. Clark) Poverty and the Impact of Social Security in Britain since 1961, 1982; (ed and contrib.) Wage Rigidity and Unemployment, 1986; Small is Stupid, 1995; Growth, the Environment and the Distribution of Incomes, 1995; (with J. Pasek) Justice, Posterity and the Environment, 2001; A Poverty of Reason: sustainable development and economic growth, 2003; articles in Economic Jl, Economica, Econometrica, Review of Economic Studies, Review of Economics and Statistics, etc. *Recreations:* various. *Address:* 1c Norham Gardens, Oxford OX2 6PS.

BECKETT, family name of **Baron Grimthorpe**.

BECKETT, Prof. Arnold Heyworth, OBE 1983; Professor of Pharmacy, Chelsea College (University of London), 1959–85, now Emeritus; *b* 12 Feb. 1920; *m* 1991, Prof. Bozena W. Hadzija. *Educ:* Baines Grammar Sch., Poulton-le-Fylde; Sch. of Pharmacy and Birkbeck Coll., University of London. FRPharmS (FPS 1942); BSc 1947; PhD 1950; DSc London, 1959. Head, Dept of Pharmacy, Chelsea Coll. of Sci. and Technology, 1959–79. Chm., Med. Commn, Internat. Tennis Fedn, 1985–93; Mem., Med. Commn, Internat. Olympic Cttee, 1968–93; Mem., British Olympic Assoc. Med. Commn, until 1986; Chm., Bd of Pharmaceutical Sciences, Fédération Internat. Pharmaceutique, 1960–80; Mem. Council, Pharmaceutical, later Royal Pharmaceutical, Soc. of GB, 1965–90 (Pres., 1981–82). Jt Founder, Biovail Corp. Internat., 1978; Chairman: Bio-Dis, 1982–; Vitabiotics Ltd, 1994–. Vis. Prof. to Univs, USA and Canada. Examr in Pharmaceut. Chem., univs in UK, Nigeria, Ghana, Singapore. Internat. pharmaceutical and nutraceutical consultant. Pereira Medal, 1942; STAS Medal, Belg. Chem. Soc., 1962; Hanbury Meml Medal, 1974; Charter Gold Medal, 1977; Mem. of Olympic Order, Silver Medal, 1980. Hon. DSc: Heriot-Watt, 1976; Uppsala, 1977; Leuven, 1982. *Publications:* (co-author) Practical Pharmaceutical Chemistry, 1962; Part 1, 3rd edn, 1975, Part 2, 3rd edn, 1976; founder Co-editor, Jl of Medicinal Chemistry; research contribs to 450 jls. *Recreations:* travel, sport, photography. *Address:* 20 Braybrooke Gardens, Upper Norwood, SE19 2UN.

BECKETT, Bruce Probart, FRIBA, FRIAS, FRTPI, FCIOB; Chartered Architect, Town and Country Planner and Building Consultant in private practice, 1984–97; *b* 7 June 1924; *s* of J. D. L. Beckett and Florence Theresa (*née* Probart); *m* 1957, Jean McDonald; two *s* three *d* (incl. twin *s* and *d*). *Educ:* Rondebosch Boys' High Sch., Cape Town; Univ. of Cape Town (BArch with distinction, 1950); University Coll. London (Diploma in Town Planning, 1963). Active Service SA Navy, 1943; Midshipman, 1943; Sub-Lieut, 1944; seconded RN, 1944; Lieut, 1946. ARIBA 1950, FRIBA 1968; FRIAS 1968. Mem. Inst. S African Architects, 1950; FRTPI (AMTPI 1966); FCIOB 1979. Private practice in S Africa, 1952–59, London, 1960. Sen. Architect, War Office, 1961; Superintending Grade Arch., Directorate-Gen. of Res. and Development, 1963–67; Chief Architect, 1967–84 and Dir of Bldg, 1978–84, Scottish Office, retd. Partner, Hutchison Locke & Monk, 1984–87. Dep. Leader, Timber Trade Mission to Canada, 1964. A Vice-Pres., RIBA, 1972–73, 1975–76, 1976–77; Hon. Librarian, 1976–78. Sec. of State for Scotland's nominee on ARCUK, 1970–85, RIBA nominee, 1985–97; Member Council: EAA, 1970–78; RIAS, 1971–78, 1984–87; RIBA, 1972–78; Member: Sec. of State for Environment's Construction and Housing Res. Adv. Council, 1968–79; Building Res. Estabt Adv. Cttees in England and Scotland, 1970–84; York Adv. Cttee for continuing educn for building professions, 1975–80. Assessor, to Scottish Cttee of Design Council, 1974–84; Civic Trust Adjudicator, 1985–87. *Publications:* papers on industrialised building, contract procedure, etc, in various jls; HMSO publications on Scottish housing, educational and health buildings. *Recreations:* sailing, walking. *Address:* 20 Thamespoint, Fairways, Teddington, Middx TW11 9PP. *T:* (020) 8943 8843; 15 Mayville Gardens, Edinburgh EH5 3DB. *T:* (0131) 556 2867. *Clubs:* Arts; New (Edinburgh); Kelvin (Kelvin Grove, Cape Town).

BECKETT, Maj.-Gen. Denis Arthur, CB 1971; DSO 1944; OBE 1960; *b* 19 May 1917; *o s* of late Archibald Beckett, Woodford Green, Essex; *m* 1946, Elizabeth (marr. diss. 1974), *er d* of late Col Guy Edwards, Upper Slaughter, Glos; one *s*; *m* 1978, Nancy Ann Hitt. *Educ:* Forest Sch.; Chard Sch. Joined Hon. Artillery Co., 1939; commnd into Essex Regt, 1940; served in W Africa, Middle East, Italy and Greece, 1940–45; DAA & QMG and Bde Major, Parachute Bdes, 1948–50; Instructor, RMA Sandhurst, 1951–53; Directing Staff, Staff Coll., Camberley, 1953–56; Second in Comd 3rd Bn Para. Regt, 1956–58; comd 2nd Bn Para. Regt, 1958–60; Directing Staff, JSSC, 1960–61; comd 19 Bde, 1961–63; idc 1964; DAG, BAOR, 1965–66; Chief of Staff, Far East Land Forces, 1966–68; Dir of Personal Services (Army), 1968–71, retired 1971. Liveryman, Coopers' Co., 1962–. *Address:* 2217 Allen Creek Road, West Palm Beach, Florida, FL 33411–5777, USA. *Clubs:* Army and Navy, Lansdowne.

BECKETT, Maj.-Gen. Edwin Horace Alexander, CB 1988; MBE 1974; Head of British Defence Staff, Washington, 1988–91, retired; *b* 16 May 1937; *s* of William Alexander Beckett and Doris Beckett; *m* 1963, Micaela Elizabeth Benedicta, *d* of Col Sir Edward Malet, Bt, OBE; three *s* one *d*. *Educ:* Henry Fanshawe School; RMA Sandhurst; ndc, psc, sq. Commissioned 1957 West Yorks Regt; regtl service in Aden (despatches 1968), Gibraltar, Germany and N Ireland; DAA&QMG 11 Armd Brigade, 1972–74; CO 1 PWO, 1976–78 (despatches 1977); GSO1 (DS) Staff Coll., 1979; Comdt Junior Div., Staff Coll., 1980; Comdr UKMF and 6 Field Force, 1981; Comdr UKMF, 1 Inf. Brigade and Tidworth Garrison, 1982; Director: Concepts, MoD, 1983–84; Army Plans and Programmes, MoD, 1984–85; C of S, HQ BAOR, 1985–88. Col Comdt, The King's Div., 1988–94; Col, PWO, 1996–2001. Dir, Corporate Affairs, IDV Ltd, 1991–96; Founder and Chm., British Brands Gp, 1992–96 (Pres., 1997–99). Chairman: Calvert Trust Exmoor, 1994–2000 (Trustee, 1994–2003); Exmoor Trust, 1999–; Trustee, Directory of Social Change, 2002– (Vice-Chm., 2004). *Recreations:* fishing, picture framing, farming for fun. *Clubs:* Army and Navy, Pilgrims.

BECKETT, Frances Mary, OBE 2006; Chief Executive, Church Urban Fund, 2002–08; *b* 20 Nov. 1951. *Educ:* Trent Poly. (CQSW); LSE (MSc Vol. Sector Orgn). Social Worker, Somerset CC, 1972–76; Student Advr, UCCF, 1976–80; Community Worker, 1981–86; Shaftesbury Society, 1986–2002: Social Work Advr, Community Care Co-ordinator, Urban Action Dir; Chief Exec., 1995–2002. Chairman: ACEVO, 2003–05; Voluntary and Community Sector Adv. Gp, Home Office, 2003–05, Cabinet Office, 2005–; Restore (Peckham), 2003–; Nat. Poverty Campaign, 2007–. Member of Board: Faith Based Regeneration Network, 2004–; NCVO, 2006–07; LDA, 2008–. FRSA 2000. *Publications:* Called to Action, 1989; Rebuild, 2001. *Recreations:* Church involvement, theatre, cinema, reading. *Address:* c/o Church Urban Fund, Church House, Great Smith Street, SW1P 3NZ.

BECKETT, Prof. John Vincent, PhD; FRHistS, FSA; Professor of English Regional History, University of Nottingham, since 1990; on secondment as Director, Victoria County History, University of London, since 2005; *b* 12 July 1950; *s* of William Vincent Beckett and Kathleen Amelia Beckett (*née* Reed); *m* 1979, Christine Sylvia Campbell; one *s*. *Educ:* Univ. of Lancaster (BA 1971; PhD 1975). FRHistS 1981. Lord Adams Res. Fellow, Univ. of Newcastle upon Tyne, 1974–76; Lectr in Hist., Wroxton Coll. of Fairleigh Dickinson Univ., Banbury, 1976–78; Lectr in Econ. and Social Hist., Univ. of Hull, 1979; University of Nottingham: Lectr in Hist., 1979–87; Reader in English Regl Hist., 1987–90. Chm., Editl Bd, Midland Hist., 2001–. Chm., British Agricl Hist. Soc., 2001–05. Chairman: Hist. of Lincs Cttee, 1988–; Thoroton Soc. of Notts, 1992–. FSA 1992. *Publications:* Coal and Tobacco: the Lowthers and the economic development of West Cumberland 1660–1760, 1981; The Aristocracy in England 1660–1914, 1986, rev. edn 1989; The East Midlands from AD1000, 1988; A History of Laxton: England's last open-field village, 1989; The Agricultural Revolution, 1990; The Rise and Fall of the Grenvilles, Dukes of Buckingham and Chandos 1710–1921, 1994; (jtly) Agricultural Rent in England 1690–1914, 1997; (ed) A Centenary History of Nottingham, 1997; (jtly) Farm Production in England 1700–1914, 2001; Byron and Newstead: the aristocrat and the Abbey, 2001; (ed) Nottinghamshire Past: essays in honour of Adrian Henstock, 2003; City Status in the United Kingdom 1830–2002, 2005; Writing Local History, 2007; contrib. numerous articles and reviews to jls incl. Agricl Hist., Agricl Hist. Rev., Archives, Bull. Inst. Histl Res., Bull. John Rylands Liby, Byron Jl, Econ. Hist. Rev., English Histl Rev., History Today, Jl British Studies. *Recreations:* sport, walking, local history. *Address:* Institute of Historical Research, University of London, WC1E 7HU. *T:* (020) 7862 8772; *e-mail:* john.beckett@sas.ac.uk.

BECKETT, Rt Hon. Margaret (Mary), (Mrs L. A. Beckett); PC 1993; MP (Lab) Derby South, since 1983; Minister of State, Department for Communities and Local Government, since 2008; *b* 15 Jan. 1943; *d* of late Cyril and Winifred Jackson; *m* 1979, Lionel A. Beckett; two step *s*. *Educ:* Notre Dame High Sch., Norwich; Manchester Coll. of Sci. and Technol. Formerly: engrg apprentice (metallurgy), AEI, Manchester; exptl officer, Manchester Univ.; Labour Party res. asst, 1970–74; political adviser, Minister for Overseas Develt, 1974; Principal Researcher, Granada TV, 1979–83. Contested (Lab) Lincoln, Feb. 1974; MP (Lab) Lincoln, Oct. 1974–1979; PPS to Minister for Overseas Develt, 1974–75; Asst Govt Whip, 1975–76; Parly Under-Sec. of State, DES, 1976–79; Opposition front bench spokesman on health and social security, 1984–89; Mem., Shadow Cabinet, 1989–97; Shadow Chief Sec. to the Treasury, 1989–92; Shadow Leader, H of C, 1992–94; Campaigns Co-ordinator and Dep. Leader, Lab Party, 1992–94; Actg Leader, Lab Party, May–July 1994; opposition front bench spokesman on health, 1994–95, on trade and industry, 1995–97; Pres., BoT, and Sec. of State for Trade and Industry, 1997–98; Pres. of the Council and Leader, H of C, 1998–2001; Secretary of State: for Envmt, Food and Rural Affairs, 2001–06; for Foreign and Commonwealth Affairs,

2006–07. Mem. NEC, Labour Party, 1980–81, 1985–86, 1988–97. *Recreations:* cooking, reading, caravanning. *Address:* c/o House of Commons, SW1A 0AA.

BECKETT, Nikaila Susan; non-executive Chairman, Technetix Group Ltd, since 2008; *b* 16 June 1961; two *s*. IBM, UK, USA and Europe, 1979–95; Founder, 1995, Chief Exec., 1997–2007, NSB Retail Systems Plc. Non-exec. Dir, Victoria plc, 2007–. *Recreations:* sailing, scuba diving, tennis, eating out.

BECKETT, Sir Richard (Gervase), 3rd Bt *cr* 1921; QC 1988; barrister; *b* 27 March 1944; *s* of Sir Martyn Gervase Beckett, 2nd Bt, MC, RIBA and Hon. Priscilla, *d* of 3rd Viscount Esher, GBE; *S* father, 2001; *m* 1976, Elizabeth Ann, *d* of Major Hugo Waterhouse; one *s* three *d*. *Educ:* Eton. Diploma in Economics (Oxford). Called to the Bar, Middle Temple, 1965; practice at the Bar, 1966–. *Recreation:* landscape. *Heir: s* Walter Gervase Beckett, *b* 16 Jan. 1987. *Address:* 51 Lennox Gardens, SW1X 0DF. *Clubs:* Pratt's, Portland.

BECKETT, Samantha Mary Constance, (Mrs I. D. Mason), OBE 1999; Director, Fiscal Policy, HM Treasury, since 2008; *b* Camberley, 19 Dec. 1966; *d* of Bill Beckett and Connie Beckett (*née* McKenna); *m* 1994, Ian David Mason; two *d*. *Educ:* St Wilfrid's RC Comprehensive Sch., Crawley; New Coll., Oxford (BA Hons PPE); London Sch. of Econs (MSc Econs). Joined HM Treasury, 1988; Mem., Econ. Briefing and Analysis teams, 1988–96; Chancellor of the Exchequer's Speechwriter, 1996–98; Sec. to Diana, Princess of Wales Meml Cttee, 1998; Head: Productivity Team, 1999–2000; Competition and Econ. Regulation Team, 2000–04; Director: Ops, 2004–07; Policy and Planning, 2007. *Address:* HM Treasury, 1 Horseguards Road, SW1A 2HQ.

BECKETT, Sir Terence (Norman), KBE 1987 (CBE 1974); Kt 1978; DL; Managing Director and Chief Executive, 1974–80 and Chairman, 1976–80, Ford Motor Co. Ltd; Director General, Confederation of British Industry, 1980–87 (Member, Council, 1976–80); *b* 13 Dec. 1923; *s* of late Horace Norman Beckett, MBE and late Clarice Lillian (*née* Allsop); *m* 1950, Sylvia Gladys Asprey; one *d*. *Educ:* Wolverhampton and S Staffs Tech. Coll. (Engrg Cadetship Diploma); London Sch. of Econs (BScEcon, Hon. Fellow, 1994). FIMechE, CEng, FIMI, FREng. Captain REME, British Army (UK, India, Malaya), 1945–48; RARO, 1949–62. Company Trainee, Ford Motor Co. Ltd, 1950; Asst in office of Dep. Chm. and Man. Dir, 1951; Man., Styling, Briggs Motor Bodies Ltd (Ford subsid.), 1954; Admin Man., Engrg, Briggs, 1955; Manager, Product Staff, 1955; Gen. Man., Product Planning Staff, 1961 (responsible for Cortina, Transit Van, 'D' series truck); Manager, Marketing Staff, 1963; Dir, Car Div., 1964; Exec. Dir, Ford Motor Co. Ltd, 1966 and Dir of Sales, 1968; Vice-Pres., European and Overseas Sales Ops, Ford of Europe Inc., 1969–74; Chm., Ford Motor Credit Co. Ltd, 1976–80; Director: ICI, 1976–80; Automotive Finance Ltd, 1974–77. Dep. Chm., CEGB, 1990 (Dir, 1987–90). Advr to Jt Cttee of MMB and Dairy Trade Fedn, 1987–94. Member: NEDC, 1980–87; Engineering Industries Council, 1975–80; BIM Council, 1976–77; Top Salaries Review Body, 1987–92; Grand Council, Motor and Cycle Trades Benevolent Fund (BEN), 1976–80; SMMT Council and Exec. Cttee, 1974–80; Council, Automobile Div., IMechE, 1979–80; Vice Pres. and Hon. Fellow, Inst. of the Motor Industry, 1974–80; Vice-Pres., Conference on Schs, Sci. and Technol., 1979–80; Chm., Governing Body, London Business Sch., 1979–86; Mem. Court, Cranfield Inst. of Technology, 1977–82; Governor, NIESR, 1978–; Governor and Mem. Court, LSE, 1978–99; Pro-Chancellor, Univ. of Essex, 1989–98 (Mem. Court, 1985–; Chm. Council, 1989–95). Mem. Court of Assts, Worshipful Co. of Engineers, 1983–85. DL Essex, 1991. Pres., IVCA, 1987–91. Patron: MSC Award Scheme for Disabled People, 1979–80; AIESEC, 1985. Lectures: Stamp, London Univ., 1982; Pfizer, Kent at Canterbury Univ., 1983. CCMI; FRSA 1984. Hon. Fellow: Sidney Sussex Coll., Cambridge, 1981; London Business Sch., 1988; Hon. DSc: Cranfield, 1977; Heriot-Watt, 1981; Hon. DSc (Econ.) London, 1982; Hon. DTech: Brunel, 1991; Wolverhampton, 1995; DU Essex, 1995; Hon. DLitt Anglia Poly., 1998. Hambro Businessman of the Year, 1978; BIM Gold Medal, 1980. *Recreations:* travel, music. *Address:* c/o Barclays Bank plc, 74 High Street, Ingatestone, Essex CM4 9BW.

BECKETT, William Cartwright, CB 1978; LLM; Solicitor to the Corporation of Lloyd's, 1985–93; *b* 21 Sept. 1929; *s* of late William Beckett and Emily (*née* Cartwright); *m* 1st, 1956, Marjorie Jean Hoskin; two *s*; 2nd, 1974, Lesley Margaret Furlonger. *Educ:* Salford Grammar Sch.; Manchester Univ. (LLB 1950, LLM 1952). Called to Bar, Middle Temple, 1952. Joined Treasury Solicitor's Dept, 1956; Board of Trade, 1965; Asst Solicitor, DEP, 1969; Under-Sec., DTI, 1972; Dep.-Sec. 1977; Legal Secretary, Law Officers' Dept, 1975–80; Solicitor, DTI, 1980–84. *Recreations:* music, golf. *Address:* Stocks Farm, New Road, Rayne, Essex CM7 8SY.

BECKFORD, Prof. James Arthur, PhD, DLitt; FBA 2004; Professor of Sociology, University of Warwick, 1989–2007, now Emeritus; *b* 1 Dec. 1942; *s* of late John Henry Beckford and Elisabeth Alice May Beckford; *m* 1965, Julia Carolyn Hanson; one *s* twin *d*. *Educ:* Alma Rd Sch.; Tottenham Grammar Sch.; Univ. of Reading (BA 1965; PhD 1972; DLitt 1985). Lectr in Sociol., Univ. of Reading, 1966–73; Lectr, then Sen. Lectr, Sociol., Univ. of Durham, 1973–87; Prof. of Sociol., Loyola Univ. of Chicago, 1987–89. Directeur d'études invité: Ecole des Hautes Etudes en Sciences Sociales, Paris, 2001; Ecole Pratique des Hautes Etudes, Paris, 2004. *Publications:* The Trumpet of Prophecy: a sociological study of Jehovah's Witnesses, 1975; Religious Organization: a trend report and bibliography, 1975; Cult Controversies: societal responses to new religious movements, 1985; (ed) New Religious Movements and Rapid Social Change, 1986; (ed jtly) The Changing Face of Religion, 1989; Religion and Advanced Industrial Society, 1989; (ed jtly) Secularization, Rationalism and Sectarianism, 1993; (with S. Gilliat) Religion in Prison: equal rites in a multi-faith society, 1998; (ed jtly) Challenging Religion: essays in honour of Eileen Barker, 2003; Social Theory and Religion, 2003; (jtly) Muslims in Prison: challenge and change in Britain and France, 2005; (ed jtly) Theorising Religion: classical and contemporary debates, 2006; (ed jtly) The Sage Handbook of the Sociology of Religion, 2007; numerous scholarly articles and chapters. *Recreations:* owls, Japanese language, playing the clarinet and bagpipes. *Address:* Department of Sociology, University of Warwick, Coventry CV4 7AL. *T:* (01926) 851252, *Fax:* (024) 7652 3497; *e-mail:* j.a.beckford@warwick.ac.uk.

BECKHAM, David Robert Joseph, OBE 2003; professional footballer, Los Angeles Galaxy, since 2007; Captain, England Football Team, 2000–06; *b* Leytonstone, 2 May 1975; *s* of Ted and Sandra Beckham; *m* 1999, Victoria Adams; three *s*. Manchester United Football Club: trainee, 1991; team member, 1992–2003; Premier League début, 1995; member, winning team: FA Premier League, 1996, 1997, 1999, 2000, 2001, 2003; FA Cup, 1996, 1999; Charity Shield, 1996, 1997; UEFA Champions League, 1999; team mem., Real Madrid FC, 2003–07, mem., winning team, La Liga, 2007. Internat. appearances for England, 1996–; mem., World Cup team, 1998, 2002 and 2006. Opened David Beckham children's football acad., London and LA, 2005. Bobby Charlton Soccer Skills Award, 1987; Manchester United Player of the Year, 1996–97; Young Player of the Year, PFA, 1996–97; Sky Football Personality of the Year, 1997; Sportsman of the Year, Sport Writers' Assoc., 2001; BBC Sports Personality of the Year, 2001. *Publications:* (with Neil Harman) David Beckham: my story, 1999; David Beckham: my world (autobiog.), 2000; (with Tom Watt) My Side (autobiog.), 2003. *Address:* c/o Los Angeles Galaxy, 18400 Avalon Boulevard, Suite 200, Carson, CA 90746, USA.

BECKINGHAM, Peter; HM Diplomatic Service; Ambassador to the Philippines, since 2005; *b* 16 March 1949; *s* of late Rev. Leslie Beckingham and Eileen Beckingham (*née* Grimsey); *m* 1975, Jill Mary Trotman; two *d*. *Educ:* Chigwell Sch.; Selwyn Coll., Cambridge (MA). MIEx 1998. Argo Record Co., 1970–1974; BOTB, 1974–79; Dir, British Inf. Services, NY, 1979–84; News Dept, FCO, 1984 (Hd, Press Centre, G7 Summit); Energy, Sci. and Space Dept, FCO, 1984–86; Hd, Horn of Africa Section, E Africa Dept, FCO, 1986–88; First Sec. (Commercial), Stockholm, 1988–92; Hd, Political Section, Canberra, 1992–96; Dir, Jt Export Promotion Directorate, FCO/DTI, 1996–99; Consul Gen., Sydney, and Dir Gen., Trade and Investment Promotion, Australia, 1999–2004. *Publications:* (ed) Australia and Britain: the evolving relationship, 1993; (ed) Our Shared Future, UK-Australia Dialogue, 2004. *Recreations:* music, golf, tennis. *Address:* c/o Foreign and Commonwealth Office, King Charles Street, SW1A 2AH. *Clubs:* Manila Golf, Manila Polo.

BECKLAKE, (Ernest) John (Stephen), PhD; CEng; Senior Research Fellow, Science Museum, since 1994; *b* 24 June 1943; *s* of Ernest and Evelyn Becklake; *m* 1965, Susan Elizabeth (*née* Buckle), BSc; two *s*. *Educ:* Bideford Grammar Sch.; Exeter Univ. (BSc, PhD). CEng 1988; FRAeS 1996. Engr, EMI Electronics, Wells, 1967–69; Post-Doctoral Fellow, Victoria Univ., BC, Canada, 1969–70; Sen. Scientist, Marconi Space and Def. Systems, Frimley, 1970–72; Science Museum: Asst Keeper, Dept of Earth and Space Sciences, 1972–80; Keeper, Dept of Elect. Engrg, Communications and Circulation, 1980–85; Keeper, Dept of Engrg, subseq. Head of Technology Gp, 1985–94. Mem., Internat. Acad. of Astronautics, 1988– (Chm., Hist. Cttee, 1996–). Man. Ed., DERA Hist. Project, DERA Farnborough, 1995–2001. Consultant, German Rocketry, Aerospace Mus., Cosford, 1997–2002. MBIS. *Publications:* Man and the Moon, 1980; The Climate Crisis, 1989; The Population Explosion, 1990; Pollution, 1990; (ed) History of Rocketry and Astronautics, vol. XVI, 1995; (series editor) Exploration and Discovery, 1980–; technical pubns in Electronics Letters, Jl of Physics D, Jl of British Interplanetary Soc., and Spaceflight. *Recreations:* gardening, golf, Rugby. *Address:* Tree Wood, Robin Hood Lane, Sutton Green, Guildford, Surrey GU7 4QY. *T:* (01483) 766931. *Club:* Puttenham Golf.

BECKMAN, Michael David; QC 1976; *b* 6 April 1932; *s* of Nathan and Esther Beckman; *m*; two *d*. *Educ:* King's Coll., London (LLB (Hons)). Called to the Bar, Lincoln's Inn, 1954. Qualified mediator, CEDR, 2004, ADR, 2006. *Recreations:* various. *Address:* Bullards, Widford, Herts SG12 8SG. *T:* (01279) 842669; (chambers) 11 Stone Buildings, Lincoln's Inn, WC2A 3TG; (chambers) 4 King's Bench Walk, Temple, EC4Y 7DL; 12 North Pallant, Chichester PO19 1TQ.

BECKWITH, Prof. Athelstan Laurence Johnson, AO 2004; FRS 1988; FAA; FRACI; Professor of Organic Chemistry, Research School of Chemistry, Australian National University, 1981–96, now Emeritus (Dean, 1989–91); *b* 20 Feb. 1930; *s* of Laurence Alfred Beckwith and Doris Grace Beckwith; *m* 1953, Phyllis Kaye Marshall, Perth, WA; one *s* two *d*. *Educ:* Perth Modern Sch.; Univ. of WA (BSc Hons); Oxford Univ. (DPhil 1956). FAA 1973; FRACI 1973. Lectr in Chemistry, Adelaide Univ., 1953; CSIRO Overseas Student, 1954; Res. Officer, CSIRO Melbourne, 1957; Adelaide University: Lectr in Organic Chemistry, 1958; Prof., 1965–81; Dean of Science, 1972–73. Temp. Lectr, Imperial Coll., London, 1962–63; Vis. Lectr, Univ. of York, 1968; Carnegie Fellow, 1968. Federal Pres., RACI, 1965 (Rennie Medal, 1960; H. G. Smith Meml Medal, 1981; Organic Chemistry Medal, 1992; Leighton Medal, 1997); Treas., Aust. Acad. of Sci., 1997–2001. *Publications:* numerous articles in Jl of Chem. Soc., Jl of Amer. Chem. Soc., etc. *Recreations:* golf, music, walking. *Address:* 3/9 Crisp Circuit, Bruce, ACT 2617, Australia. *T:* (2) 62493234, (2) 62530696.

BECKWITH, Sir John (Lionel), Kt 2002; CBE 1996; FCA; Chairman, Pacific Investments, since 1993; Founder Chairman, London & Edinburgh Trust PLC, 1971–92; *b* 19 March 1947; *s* of Col Harold Beckwith and Agnes Camilla McMichael (*née* Duncan); *m* 1975, Heather Marie Robbins (marr. diss. 2001); two *s*; one *d* with Hélène Aubry. *Educ:* Harrow Sch. FCA 1970; ATII 1970. Arthur Andersen & Co., 1969–71; with London & Edinburgh Trust PLC, 1971–92. Founder Chm., Rutland Trust plc, 1986–91; Chairman: Riverside PLC, 1993–97; Barbican Healthcare PLC, 1996–98; Red River Capital Hldgs, 2006–. Director: Frontiers Gp, 1996–; Harlequin FC, 1996–97. Member: Develt Bd, Cancer Relief Macmillan Fund; NCH Action for Children's 125th Anniversary Appeal Cttee. Vice-President: RNIB; Youth Clubs UK; Founder, and Chm. Bd of Trustees, Youth Sport Trust; Patron, Teenage Cancer Trust. Hon. DLitt Loughborough, 2000. Duke of Edinburgh Arthur Bell Trophy, 1999. *Recreations:* sport, music, ballet. *Address:* (office) 124 Sloane Street, SW1X 9BW. *Clubs:* MCC, Annabel's, Queen's; Old Harrovian Football; Royal Berkshire Golf; Thurlestone Golf; Sunningdale Golf; Riverside Racquet Centre.

See also P. M. Beckwith.

BECKWITH, Peter Michael, OBE 2007; Chairman, PMB Holdings Ltd, since 1992; Deputy Chairman, Ambassador Theatre Group Ltd, since 1992; *b* 20 Jan. 1945; *s* of Col Harold Andrew Beckwith and Agnes Camilla McMichael Beckwith; *m* 1968, Paula Gay Bateman; two *d*. *Educ:* Harrow School; Emmanuel College, Cambridge (MA Hons; Hon. Fellow, 1999). Qualified Solicitor, 1970; Asst Solicitor, Norton Rose Botterell & Roche; London & Edinburgh Trust: Joint Founder and shareholder, 1972; Managing Director, 1983–86; Dep. Chm., 1987; Chm., 1992. Pres., Harbour Club, Milan, 1999–. Vice Patron, Cambridge Foundn, 1992– (Trustee, 1997–2002). Gov., Harrow Sch., 1992. Hon. LLD Cantab, 2000. *Recreations:* tennis, ski-ing, Association football, theatre, dogs, cycling. *Address:* PMB Holdings Ltd, Hill Place House, 55A High Street, SW19 5BA. *Clubs:* Riverside Racquets, Harbour, Chelsea Football; Downhill Only (Wengen); Harbour (Milan); Austria Haus (Vail).

See also Sir J. L. Beckwith.

BECTIVE, Earl of; Thomas Rupert Charles Christopher Taylour; *b* 18 June 1989; *s* and *heir* of Marquis of Headfort, *qv*. *Educ:* Radley Coll. *Recreation:* rowing (Mem., GB Junior Rowing Team, 2007).

BEDBROOK, Jack Harry, CEng, FRINA; FIMgt; RCNC; Managing Director, HM Dockyard, Devonport, 1979–84; *b* 8 Aug. 1924; *s* of Harry Bedbrook and Emma Bedbrook; *m* (marr. diss. 1989); three *d*; *m* 1996, Sylvia. *Educ:* Technical Coll., Portsmouth; RNC, Greenwich. Dir Gen. Ships Dept, Admiralty, 1946–51; Asst Constructor, Devonport, 1951–54; Dockyard Dept, Bath, 1954–56; Constructor, Gibraltar Dockyard, 1956–58; Admiralty Exptl Works, Haslar, 1958–62; Dir Gen. Ships Dept, 1962–65; Chief Constructor, Portsmouth, 1965–71; Project Manager, Rosyth, 1971–74; Prodn Dir, Devonport, 1974–77; Man. Dir, HM Dockyard, Rosyth, 1977–79. *Recreations:* gardening, music. *Address:* Laxtons, Cargreen, Saltash, Cornwall PL12 6PA. *T:* (01752) 844519.

BEDDARD, His Honour Nicholas Elliot; a Circuit Judge, 1986–2003; *b* 26 April 1934; *s* of Terence Elliot Beddard and Ursula Mary Hamilton Howard; *m* 1964, Gillian Elisabeth Vaughan Bevan, 2nd *d* of Llewellyn and Molly Bevan; two *s* one *d*. *Educ:* Eton. National Service, 1952–54; commissioned, Royal Sussex Regt, 1953; TA (Royal Sussex Regt), 1955–64. United Africa Co., 1955–58; Asst Public Policy Executive, RAC, 1958–68; called to the Bar, Inner Temple, 1967; a Recorder, 1986. *Recreations:* choral singing, skiing, golf. *Address:* The Old School, Sudbourne, Woodbridge, Suffolk IP12 2BE. *T:* (01394) 450468. *Clubs:* Lansdowne; Aldeburgh Golf.

BEDDINGTON, Prof. John Rex, CMG 2004; PhD; FRS 2001; Chief Scientific Adviser to the Government and Head of the Government Office for Science, Department for Innovation, Universities and Skills, since 2008; *b* 13 Oct. 1945; *s* of Harry Beddington and Mildred (*née* Weale); *m* 1st, 1968, Sarah West (marr. diss. 1972); one *s*; 2nd, 1973, Prof. Sally Baldwin (marr. diss. 1979); one *d*; 3rd, 1990, Caroline Hiller. *Educ:* Monmouth Sch.; London Sch. of Econs (BSc Econ, MSc); Edinburgh Univ. (PhD). Res. Asst, Edinburgh Univ., 1968–71; Lectr on Population Biol., York Univ., 1971–84; Imperial College, London: Reader in Applied Population Biol., 1984–91; Prof. of Applied Population Biol., 1991–2007; Dir, Centre for Envmtl Technol., 1994–97; Dir, T. H. Huxley Sch. of Envmt, Earth Scis and Engrg, 1998–2001; Hd, Dept of Envmtl Sci. and Technol., 2001–04. Sen. Fellow, Internat. Inst. for Envmt and Develt, 1980–83; Hd, UK Scientific Delegn, Commn for Conservation of Antarctic Living Marine Resources, 1983–2007; Dir, Fisheries Mgt Sci. Prog., DFID (formerly ODA), 1989–2006; Chairman: Scientific Cttee, Indian Ocean Tuna Commn, 1998; Sci. Adv. Council, DEFRA, 2005–2007; Member: NERC, 2000–06 (Mem. Exec. Bd, 2002–05); Council, Zool Soc. of London, 2003–07. Chairman Trustees: People's Trust for Endangered Species, 1984–2007; Marine Educn and Conservation Trust, 1987–2007. Pres., Resource Modelling Assoc., 1992–94. Heidelberg Award for Envmtl Excellence, 1997. *Publications:* articles on ecology, population biol. and fisheries mgt. *Recreations:* hill-walking, art, birdwatching. *Address:* Government Office for Science, Department for Innovation, Universities and Skills, Kingsgate House, 66–74 Victoria Street, SW1E 6SW. *Club:* Travellers.

BEDDOE; *see* Rowe-Beddoe.

BEDDOE, Martin William Denton; His Honour Judge Beddoe; a Circuit Judge, since 2007; *b* Abyad, Egypt, 7 July 1955; *s* of late Lt Col Arthur Beddoe and of Jane Beddoe; *m* 1993, Prof. Mary Margaret Anne McCabe, *qv*; two *d*. *Educ:* Peterhouse, Cambridge (BA Hons 1977). Called to the Bar, Gray's Inn, 1979; in practice at the Bar, 1980–2007; Recorder, 2002–07; Standing Counsel to HMRC Prosecutions Office, 2005–07. *Recreations:* golf, cycling, cricket, birdwatching. *Address:* c/o Southwark Crown Court, 1 English Grounds (off Battlebridge Lane), Southwark, SE1 2HU. *T:* (020) 7522 7200. *Clubs:* Royal Worlington and Newmarket Golf; Philanderers Cricket.

BEDDOW, Prof. Michael; Professor of German, University of Leeds, 1986–98; *b* 3 Sept. 1947; *s* of Austin Beddow and Ivy Beddow; *m* 1976, Helena Hajzyk; one *s*. *Educ:* West Park Grammar Sch., St Helens; St John's Coll., Cambridge. Trinity Hall, Cambridge: Res. Fellow, 1973–75; Staff Fellow, 1975–79; Lectr in German, KCL, 1979–86. Vice Chm. Governors, Silcoates Sch., Wakefield, 1993–2001. *Publications:* The Fiction of Humanity, 1982; Goethe's Faust I: a critical guide, 1986; Thomas Mann: Dr Faustus, 1994; articles and reviews in Jl European Studies, London German Studies, TLS, Publications of English Goethe Soc. *Recreations:* walking, choral singing, computer construction and programming. *Address:* 3 Oakwood Park, Leeds LS8 2PJ. *T:* (0113) 240 1561.

BEDELL, Elaine; Controller, Entertainment Commissioning, BBC, since 2007; *d* of Albert and Iris Bedell; *m* 1990, Clive Brill; one *s* one *d*. *Educ:* Valentines High Sch., Ilford; Leeds Univ. (BA 1st Cl. Hons English). Producer, BBC, 1987–93 (productions include: Start the Week (radio); Clive James Talk Shows; Clive James on the 90s (BAFTA award 1991); Postcards; New Year's Eve Shows; Assignment: Bill Clinton's election campaign); Hd, Factual Entertainment, Tiger Aspect Prodns, and Exec. Producer, Bill Hicks, It's Just a Ride, 1993–94; Managing Director: Watchmaker Prodns, 1994–2000; Chrysalis Entertainment, 2000–02; Exec. Dir, Royal Shakespeare Co. Enterprises, 2002–03; Indep. Exec., 2003–04, Commng Ed., Factual Entertainment, 2004–06, BBC. *Recreation:* dancing. *Address:* c/o BBC Television Centre, Wood Lane, W12 7RJ; *e-mail:* Elaine.Bedell@bbc.co.uk.

BEDFORD, 15th Duke of, *cr* 1694; **Andrew Ian Henry Russell;** Marquess of Tavistock, 1694; Earl of Bedford, 1550; Baron Russell, 1539; Baron Russell of Thornhaugh, 1603; Baron Howland of Streatham, 1695; Partner, Bloomsbury Stud, since 1985; Director: Tattersalls Ltd, since 1992; Woburn Enterprises Ltd, since 2003; *b* 30 March 1962; *e s* of 14th Duke of Bedford and of Henrietta, *d* of late Henry F. Tiarks; *S* father, 2003; *m* 2000, Louise, *d* of late Donald Crammond and of Dowager Lady Delves Broughton; one *s* one *d*. *Educ:* Heatherdown; Harrow; Harvard. *Recreation:* country pursuits. *Heir: s* Marquess of Tavistock, *qv*. *Address:* Woburn Abbey, Woburn, Beds MK17 9WA. *T:* (01525) 290333, *Fax:* (01525) 290191. *Clubs:* Jockey; AD (Cambridge, Mass); Brook (New York).

BEDFORD, Bishop Suffragan of, since 2003; **Rt Rev. Richard Neil Inwood;** *b* 4 March 1946; *s* of Cyril and Sylvia Inwood; *m* 1969, Elizabeth Joan Abram; three *d*. *Educ:* University Coll., Oxford (MA, BSc Chem.); Univ. of Nottingham (BA Theol.). Teacher, Uganda, 1969; Works R & D chemist, Dyestuffs Div., ICI, 1970–71; ministerial trng, St John's Coll., Nottingham, 1971–74; ordained deacon, 1974, priest, 1975; Curate: Christ Church, Fulwood, Sheffield, 1974–78; All Souls, Langham Place, W1, 1978–81; Vicar, St Luke's, Bath, 1981–89; Hon. Chaplain, Dorothy House Foundn, Bath, 1984–89; Rector, Yeovil with Kingston Pitney, 1989–95; Prebendary of Wells, 1990–95; Archdeacon of Halifax, 1995–2003; Central Chaplain, Mothers' Union, 2004–. *Publications:* Biblical Perspectives on Counselling, 1980; (jtly) The Church, 1987. *Recreations:* fell walking, gardening, music, family. *Address:* Bishop's Lodge, Bedford Road, Cardington, Bedford, MK44 3SS. *T:* (01234) 831432, *Fax:* (01234) 831484.

BEDFORD, Archdeacon of; *see* Hughes, Ven. P. V.

BEDFORD, David, FRAM, FTCL; Composer in Association, English Sinfonia, 1993–2005 (Youth Music Director, 1986–93); *b* 4 Aug. 1937; *s* of late Leslie Herbert Bedford and Lesley Florence Keitley Duff; *m* 1st, 1958, Maureen Parsonage; two *d*; 2nd, 1969, Susan Pilgrim; two *d*; 3rd, 1994, Allison Powell; one *s* two *d*. *Educ:* Lancing College; Royal Acad. of Music (ARAM; FRAM 1997); Trinity Coll. London (LTCL; FTCL 1998). Guy's Hosp. porter, 1956; teacher, Whitefield Sch., Hendon, 1965; teacher, 1968–80, and composer-in-residence, 1969–81, Queen's Coll., London; Assoc. Vis. Composer, Gordonstoun, 1983–88; Imogen Holst Composer in Residence, Dartington Coll. of Arts, 1996–97. Mem. Exec. Cttee, SPNM, 1982–88; Pres., British Music Information Centre, 1988–89; Chm., Assoc. of Professional Composers, 1991–93; Chairman: PRS, 2002–04 (Dep. Chm. (writer), 1999–2001); PRS Foundn, 2000–02. Patron, Barnet Schs Music Assoc., 1987. Numerous compositions, many commissioned by major London orchestras and BBC; numerous recordings. *Recreations:* tennis, table tennis, cricket, astronomy, ancient history, philosophy, horror films. *Address:* 12 Oakwood Road, Bristol BS9 4NR. *T:* (0117) 962 4202; *e-mail:* dvbmus@aol.com.

See also S. J. R. Bedford.

BEDFORD, Steuart John Rudolf; freelance conductor; Artistic Director, English Sinfonia, 1981–1990; *b* 31 July 1939; *s* of late L. H. Bedford and Lesley Florence Keitley Duff; *m* 1st, 1969, Norma Burrowes, *qv*; 2nd, 1980, Celia, *er d* of Mr and Mrs G. R. Harding; two *d*. *Educ:* Lancing Coll., Sussex; Royal Acad. of Music. Fellow, RCO; FRAM; BA. Artistic Dir, 1974–98, and Exec. Artistic Dir, 1987–98, Aldeburgh Festival; Co-Artistic Dir, English Music Theatre Co., 1976–79. Royal Acad. of Music, 1965; English Opera Gp, now English Music Theatre, 1967–. Debut at Metropolitan, NY, 1974 (Death in Venice); new prodn of The Marriage of Figaro, 1975. Has conducted with English Opera Gp, Welsh National Opera, Florentine Opera, Luxembourg Philharmonic, Royal Scottish Nat. Orch., Bordeaux Opera, Opera Theatre of St Louis, NY City Opera; also at Royal Opera House, Covent Garden (operas incl. Owen Wingrave and Death in Venice, by Benjamin Britten, and Cosi Fan Tutte); also in Santa Fe, Buenos Aires, France, Belgium, Holland, Canada, Vienna, Denmark, etc. Recordings include a series of works by Benjamin Britten. *Recreations:* golf, gardening. *Address:* c/o HarrisonParrott Ltd, 12 Penzance Place, W11 4PA.

See also D. Bedford.

BEDFORD-JONES, Rt Rev. Michael Hugh Harold; a Suffragan Bishop of Toronto, 1994–2008 (Area Bishop of Trent-Durham, 2006–08); *b* 29 Sept. 1942; *s* of Rev. Canon Hugh Bedford-Jones and Gretchen Flagler Bedford-Jones (*née* Gray); *m* 1967, Jeanne Yvonne Soules. *Educ:* Toronto Univ. (BA 1965; MA 1979); Univ. of Trinity Coll., Toronto (STB 1968). Ordained deacon, 1967, priest, 1968; St James' Cathedral, Toronto: Asst Curate, 1968–70; Dir of Christian Educn, 1970–74; Sen. Asst, 1974–75; Rector, Ch. of the Epiphany, Scarborough, 1976–83; Regl Dean, Scarborough, 1980–83; Rector, St Aidan, Toronto, 1983–88; Regl Dean, Toronto East, 1985–88; Exec. Asst to Bishop of Toronto, 1988–91; Canon, St James' Cathedral, 1990; Dean of Dio. of Ontario and Rector of St George's Cathedral, Kingston, Ont, 1991–94; Area Bishop of York Scarborough, 1994–2006. Hon. DD Univ. of Trinity Coll., Toronto, 1997; Hon. STD Thorneloe, 2004. *Recreations:* sailing, music, cottage life. *Address:* 384 Lakebreeze Drive, Newcastle, ON L1B 1P5, Canada; *e-mail:* mbjhome@sympatico.ca.

BEDI, Prof. Raman, DDS; DSc; FDSRCSE, FDSRCS, FFPH, FFGDP(UK); Professor of Transcultural Oral Health, King's College, London, since 2002; Director, Global Child Dental Health Taskforce, since 2006; *b* 20 May 1953; *s* of Satya-Paul Bedi and Raj Bedi (*née* Kaur); *m* 1986, Kathryn Jane Walter; three *s*. *Educ:* Headlands Sch.; Univ. of Bristol (BDS 1976, DDS 1993; DSc 2003); Trinity Coll., Bristol (DipHE Theol. 1979); Univ. of Manchester (MSc 1986). FDSRCSE 1982; FDSRCS 2002; FFPH 2003; FFGDP(UK) 2004. Lecturer in Paediatric Dentistry: Univ. of Manchester, 1979–82; Univ. of Hong Kong, 1983–86; Univ. of Edinburgh, 1988–91; Sen. Lectr in Paediatric Dentistry, Univ. of Birmingham, 1991–96; Prof. and Head of Dept of Transcultural Oral Health, Eastman Dental Inst., UCL, 1996–2002; Chief Dental Officer for England, DoH, 2002–05. Co-Dir, WHO Collaborating Centre for Disability, Culture and Oral Health, 1998–. Member: NHS/DoH Top Team, 2002–05; Strategic Wider Participation Cttee, HEFCE, 2003–; Bd, Higher Educn Leadership Foundn, 2003–06; Founding Mem., Nat. Health and Social Care Leadership Network, 2004–05. President: British Soc. for Disability and Oral Health, 2002; Educn Res. Gp, Internat. Assoc. for Dental Res., 2002–04 (Chm., Regl Develt Cttee, 2002–04); Chm., British Assoc. of Physicians of Indian Origin, 2006–. Trustee, Children's Soc., 2006–. Mem., Gen. Synod of C of E, 1995–2005. *Publications:* (ed with P. Jones) Betel-quid and Tobacco Chewing Among the Bangladeshi Community in the United Kingdom: usage and health issues, 1995; (with P. Jones) Embracing Goodwill: establishing healthy alliances with black organisations, 1996; (ed jtly) Dentists, Patients and Ethnic Minorities: towards the new millennium, 1996; (with P. A. Lowe) Best Practise in Primary Healthcare: oral healthcare delivery in a multi-ethnic society, 1997; (with J. Sardo Infirri) The Root Cause: oral health care in disadvantaged communities, 1999; contribs to scientific jls. *Recreations:* chess, tennis, travelling. *Address:* Oak Cottage, 12 Manor Way, Potters Bar, Herts EN6 1EL. *Club:* Athenæum.

BEDINGFELD, Sir Edmund George Felix P.; *see* Paston-Bedingfeld.

BEDINGFELD, Henry Edgar Paston-; York Herald of Arms, since 1993; *b* 7 Dec. 1943; *s and heir* of Sir Edmund Paston-Bedingfeld, Bt, *qv*; *m* 1968, Mary Kathleen, *d* of Brig. R. D. Ambrose, CIE, OBE, MC; two *s* two *d*. *Educ:* Ampleforth College, York. Chartered Surveyor. Rouge Croix Pursuivant of Arms, 1983–93. Genealogist, British Assoc. of SMO Malta, 1995–2000. Founder Chairman, 1975–80, Vice-Pres., 1980–2006, Pres., 2006–, Norfolk Heraldry Soc.; Member Council: Heraldry Soc., 1976–85, and 1990–99; Norfolk Record Soc., 1986– (Vice-Pres., 2003–); Royal Soc. of St George, 2000–; Sec., Standing Council of the Baronetage, 1984–88; Vice-President: Cambridge Univ. Heraldic and Genealogical Soc., 1988–; Suffolk Family Hist. Soc., 1991–. Rep. of Duke of Norfolk, Commn d'Inf. et de Liaison des Assocs Nobles d'Europe, 1994. Freeman of the City of London; Liveryman: Scriveners' Co. (Mem. Ct of Assts, 2003–); Bowyers' Co. Kt of Sovereign Mil. Order of Malta. *Publications:* Oxburgh Hall, The First 500 Years, 1982; (jtly) Heraldry, 1993. *Address:* The College of Arms, Queen Victoria Street, EC4V 4BT. *T:* (020) 7236 6420; Oxburgh Hall, Norfolk PE33 9PS. *T:* (01366) 328269. *Club:* Boodle's.

BEDINGFIELD, Julian Peter; HM Diplomatic Service, retired; First Secretary and Deputy Head of Mission, Ljubljana, 1999–2004; *b* 23 July 1945; *s* of Thomas William Bedingfield and Eileen Bedingfield (*née* Neves); *m* 1975, Margery Mary Jones Davies; one *s* two *d*. *Educ:* Sir Joseph Williamson's Mathematical Sch., Rochester. Joined Foreign Office, 1964: lang. trng, 1968; Scientific Attaché, Moscow, 1969–70; FCO, 1970–71; Düsseldorf, 1971–73; Bonn, 1973–75; Second Secretary: (Commercial), Dhaka, 1975–76; Dep. Hd of Mission, Ulan Bator, 1976–78; FCO, 1978–82; (Admin) and Consul, Berne, 1982–86; (Chancery/Inf.), Rabat, 1986–91; First Secretary: FCO, 1991–94; UK Delegn, NATO, Brussels, 1994–99. *Recreations:* travel, photography.

BEDNORZ, Johannes-Georg, PhD; Physicist at IBM Research Laboratory, Zürich, since 1982; *b* 16 May 1950. *Educ:* Swiss Federal Institute of Technology, Zürich. (Jtly) Nobel Prize for Physics, 1987. *Publications:* papers in learned jls on new super-conducting materials. *Address:* IBM Zürich Research Laboratory, Säumerstrasse 4, 8803 Rüschlikon, Switzerland.

BEDSER, Sir Alec (Victor), Kt 1997; CBE 1982 (OBE 1964); Chairman, England Cricket Selection Committee, 1968–81 (Member, 1961–85); *b* 4 July 1918; twin *s* of late Arthur and Florence Beatrice Bedser. *Educ:* Monument Hill Secondary Sch., Woking. Served with RAF in UK, France (BEF), N Africa, Sicily, Italy, Austria, 1939–46. Joined Surrey County Cricket Club, as Professional, 1938; awarded Surrey CCC and England caps, 1946, 1st Test Match v India, created record by taking 22 wickets in first two Tests; toured Australia as Member of MCC team, 1946–47, 1950–51, 1954–55; toured S Africa with MCC, 1948–49; held record of most number of Test wickets (236), since beaten,

1953; took 100th wicket against Australia (first English bowler since 1914 to do this), 1953; Asst Man. to Duke of Norfolk on MCC tour to Australia, 1962–63; Manager: MCC team to Australia, 1974–75; England team tour of Australia and India, 1979–80; Mem., MCC Cttee, 1982–85. Pres., Surrey CCC, 1987–88. Founded own company (office equipment and supplies) with Eric Bedser, 1955. Freeman, City of London, 1968; Liveryman, Worshipful Co. of Environmental Cleaners, 1988. *Publications:* (with E. A. Bedser) Our Cricket Story, 1951; Bowling, 1952; (with E. A. Bedser) Following On, 1954; Cricket Choice, 1981; (with Alex Bannister) Twin Ambitions (autobiog.), 1986. *Recreations:* cricket, golf. *Clubs:* MCC (Hon. Life Mem., 1962; Hon. Life Vice Pres., 1999), East India, Devonshire, Sports and Public Schools (Hon. Life Mem.); Surrey County Cricket (Hon. Life Mem.); West Hill Golf (Hon. Life Mem.; Pres., 2006–).

BEECH, Jacqueline Elaine; Her Honour Judge Beech; a Circuit Judge, since 2007; *b* Coventry, 8 Jan. 1958; *d* of Deric Charles Beech and Maureen Mary Beech (*née* Clooney). *Educ:* Wolston High Sch. Sec. Mod.; Tile Hill Coll. of Further Educn; Preston Poly. (BA Hons 1980). Called to the Bar, Middle Temple, 1981; a Recorder, 2002–07. Chairman: Transport Tribunal, 2000–; London Bus Permits Appeal Panel, 2002–. *Publication:* (contrib. transport section) Atkins Court Forms, vol. 39, 2nd edn 2006. *Recreations:* fell walking and all things Cumbrian, arts and literature, fine food and wine (Higher Cert. in Wine and Spirits, Wine & Spirit Education Trust). *Address:* Snaresbrook Crown Court, 75 Hollybush Hill, E11 1QW. *T:* (020) 8530 0000.

BEECHAM, Sir Jeremy (Hugh), Kt 1994; DL; Member, Newcastle upon Tyne City Council, since 1967 (Leader, 1977–94); Consultant, Beecham Peacock, since 2002; *b* 17 Nov. 1944; *s* of Laurence and Florence Beecham; *m* 1968, Brenda Elizabeth (*née* Woolf); one *s* one *d*. *Educ:* Royal Grammar Sch., Newcastle upon Tyne; University Coll., Oxford (First Cl. Hons Jurisprudence; MA). Chm., OU Labour Club, 1964. Admitted Solicitor, 1968; Partner, Allan Henderson Beecham & Peacock, subseq. Beecham Peacock, 1968–2002. Dir, Northern Develt Co., 1986–91. Newcastle upon Tyne City Council: Chairman: Social Services Cttee, 1973–77; Policy and Resources Cttee, 1977–94; Finance Cttee, 1979–85; Develt Cttee, 1995–97; Newcastle City Challenge, 1992–97. Chairman: AMA, 1991–97 (Dep. Chm., 1984–86; Vice Chm., 1986–91); Local Govt Assoc., 1995–2004 (Vice Chm., 2004–); Review of Local Public Services in Wales, 2005–06; Vice Chm., Northern Regl Councils Assoc., 1986–91. Labour Party: Member: Local and Regl Govt Sub-Cttee, NEC, 1971–83, 1991–; NEC/Shadow Cabinet Wkg Pty on Future of Local Govt, 1984–87; Domestic and Internat. Policy Cttee, 1992–; Jt Policy Cttee, 1992–; NEC, 1998– (Chm., 2005–06). Member: RTPI Working Party on Public Participation in Planning, 1980–82; Historic Bldgs and Monuments Commn for England, 1983–87; Local and Central Govt Relns Res. Cttee, Joseph Rowntree Meml Trust, 1987–96; President's Cttee, Business in the Community, 1988–; Bd of Trustees, NE Civic Trust, 1989–92; NHS Modernisation Bd, 2000–04; Community Voluntary and Local Services Honours Cttee, 2005–. Pres., BURA, 1996–. Participant, Königswinter Conf., 1986. Member: Council of Management, Neighbourhood Energy Action, 1987–89; Council, Common Purpose, 1989–; President: Age Concern Newcastle, 1995–; Newcastle Choral Soc., 1997–; Newcastle People to People, 1998–2007; Vice President: Community Foundn, 2000–; Newcastle CVS, 2001–. Mem. Adv. Bd, Harold Hartog Sch. of Govt, Tel Aviv Univ., 2005–; Mem. Bd, New Israel Fund, 2007. Trustee, Trusthouse Charitable Foundn, 1999–. Contested (Lab) Tynemouth, 1970. DL Tyne and Wear, 1995. Hon. Freeman Newcastle upon Tyne, 1995. Hon. Fellow, Univ. of Northumbria (formerly Newcastle upon Tyne Poly.), 1989. Hon. DCL Newcastle, 1992. *Recreations:* reading, history, music, very amateur photography, the Northumbrian countryside. *Address:* (office) 7 Collingwood Street, Newcastle upon Tyne NE1 1JE; 39 The Drive, Gosforth, Newcastle upon Tyne NE3 4AJ. *T:* (0191) 285 1888.

BEECHAM, Sir John Stratford Roland, 4th Bt *cr* 1914; *S* father, 1982, but his name does not appear on the Official Roll of the Baronetage. *Heir:* *b* Robert Adrian Beecham [*b* 6 Jan. 1942; *m* 1969, Daphne Mattinson; one *s* one *d*].

BEEDHAM, Brian James, CBE 1989; Associate Editor, The Economist, 1989–2002; *b* 12 Jan. 1928; *s* of James Victor Beedham and Nina Beedham (*née* Zambra); *m* 1960, Barbara Zollikofer. *Educ:* Leeds Grammar Sch.; The Queen's Coll., Oxford. RA, 1950–52. Asst Editor, Yorkshire Post, 1952–55; The Economist, 1955–2002: Washington correspondent, 1958–61; Foreign Editor, 1964–89. Commonwealth Fellowship, 1956–57. Fellow, Royal Geographical Society. *Recreations:* hillwalking, music, Kipling and Wodehouse. *Address:* 9 Hillside, SW19 4NH. *T:* (020) 8946 4454. *Club:* Travellers.

BEEDHAM, Trevor, FRCOG; Consultant Gynaecologist and Obstetrician, The Royal London and St Bartholomew's Hospitals, since 1981; Deputy Medical Director, since 2006, and Divisional Director, since 2008, Barts and The London NHS Trust; Associate Dean, since 2006, and Hon. Professor, since 2008, Institute of Health Sciences Education, Barts and the London (formerly Queen Mary) School of Medicine and Dentistry, since 2006; *b* 30 July 1942; *s* of Herbert and Olive Beedham (*née* Spikings); *m* 1966, Anne Darnbrough-Cameron; two *s* one *d*. *Educ:* High Pavement Grammar Sch., Nottingham; Royal Dental Hosp., and London Hosp. Med. Sch., Univ. of London (BDS 1965; MB BS Hons 1972). MRCOG 1977, FRCOG 1989. Careers Officer, 1994–98, Chm., Contg Med. Educn Cttee, 1998–2002, RCOG; Clin. Dir, Barts and The London NHS Trust, 2003–08; Hon. Sen. Lectr, Queen Mary Sch. of Medicine and Dentistry, 2006–08. Regional Advr and Chm., NE Thames Obs and Gynae. Higher Trng Cttee, 1991–94; Mem., Appeals Panel, Specialist Trng Authy, subseq. Postgraduate Med. Educn and Trng Bd, 1999–. Examr, MB BS, DRCOG, FRCOG, 1981–; PLAB Part 1 Panel and Med. Sch. Visitor, GMC, 2001–. Asst, Soc. of Apothecaries, 1996– (Chm., Exam. Bd, 2004–; Sen. Warden, 2008–Aug. 2009). *Publications:* contrib. and ed text books in obstetrics and gynaecology; referee for BJOG, Obstetrician and Gynaecologist, Jl of RSM, etc. *Recreation:* swimming. *Address:* The Royal London Hospital, Whitechapel, E1 1BB. *T:* (020) 7377 7295; *e-mail:* trevor.beedham@bartsandthelondon.nhs.uk.

BEELS, Jonathan Sidney Spencer, CMG 1998; HM Diplomatic Service, retired; Consultant, Ministry of Defence, 1998–99; *b* 19 Jan. 1943; *s* of Sidney Beels and Joan Constance Beels (*née* Groves); *m* 1st, 1966, Patricia Joan Mills (marr. diss. 1982); one *s* one *d*; 2nd, 1983, Penelope Jane Aedy (marr. diss. 1998). *Educ:* Ardingly Coll.; St John's Coll., Cambridge (MA 1969). Entered Diplomatic Service, 1965; Prague, 1970–73; FCO, 1973–77; on loan to Northern Ireland Office, 1977–78; resigned from Diplomatic Service, 1979; Govt Service, Sultanate of Oman, 1979–83; Man. Dir, Control Risks (GS) Ltd, 1983–88; rejoined Diplomatic Service, 1988; Counsellor, Nicosia, 1992–93; FCO, 1994–98. *Recreations:* golf, shooting, tennis, motorcycling.

BEENSTOCK, Prof. Michael, PhD; Pinhas Sapir Professor of Economics, Hebrew University, Jerusalem, since 1996; *b* 18 June 1946; *s* of Sidney and Taubie Beenstock; *m* 1968, Ruchi Hager; one *s* four *d*. *Educ:* London Sch. of Econs and Political Science (BSc, MSc; PhD 1976). Econ. Advisor, HM Treasury, 1970–76; Economist, World Bank, Washington, DC, 1976–78; Sen. Res. Fellow, London Business Sch., 1978–81; Esmée Fairbairn Prof. of Finance and Investment, City Univ. Business Sch., 1981–87; Prof. of Econs, Hebrew Univ., Jerusalem, 1987–96 (Lady Davis Prof., 1987–89). *Publications:* The Foreign Exchange Market, 1978; A Neoclassical Analysis of Macroeconomic Policy, 1980; Health, Migration and Development, 1980; The World Economy in Transition, 1983, 2nd edn 1984; Insurance for Unemployment, 1986; Work, Welfare and Taxation, 1986; (jtly) Insurance for Unemployment, 1986; (ed) Modelling the Labour Market, 1988; (jtly) Modelling the World Shipping Markets, 1993. *Recreation:* music. *Address:* Kefar Etzion 35/4, Jerusalem, Israel. *T:* (2) 6723184.

BEER, Dame Gillian (Patricia Kempster), DBE 1998; FBA 1991; FRSL; King Edward VII Professor of English Literature, University of Cambridge, 1994–2002; President, Clare Hall, Cambridge, 1994–2001 (Fellow, 2001–02, Hon. Fellow, 2002); *b* 27 Jan. 1935; *d* of Owen Kempster Thomas and Ruth Winifred Bell; *m* 1962, John Bernard Beer, *qv*; three *s*. *Educ:* St Anne's Coll., Oxford (MA, BLitt; Hon. Fellow, 1989); LittD Cambridge. Asst Lectr, Bedford Coll., London, 1959–62; part-time Lectr, Liverpool Univ., 1962–64; Cambridge University: Asst Lectr 1966–71, Lectr, subseq. Reader in Literature and Narrative, 1971–89; Prof. of English, 1989–94; Fellow, Girton Coll., 1965–94 (Hon. Fellow, 1994). Vice-Pres., British Acad., 1994–96; Pres., Hist. of Science Sect., BAAS, 1998. Trustee, BM, 1992–2002. Chm., Poetry Book Soc., 1992–96; Pres., British Comparative Lit. Soc., 2003–. Chm. Judges, Booker Prize, 1997. FRSL 2006. Hon. Fellow, Univ. of Wales, Cardiff, 1996. Foreign Hon. Mem., Amer. Acad. of Arts and Scis, 2001. Hon. LittD: Liverpool, 1995; Anglia Poly., 1997; Leicester, 1999; London, 2001; Sorbonne, 2001; QUB, 2005; Hon. DLitt Oxford, 2005. *Publications:* Meredith: a change of masks, 1970; The Romance, 1970; Darwin's Plots, 1983, 2nd edn 2000; George Eliot, 1986; Arguing with the Past, 1989; Open Fields, 1996; Virginia Woolf: the Common Ground, 1996. *Recreations:* music, travel, conversation. *Address:* Clare Hall, Herschel Road, Cambridge CB3 9AL. *T:* (01223) 356384 and 332360.

BEER, Ian David Stafford, CBE 1992; MA; JP; Head Master of Harrow, 1981–91; Founder and Trustee, since 1993, and Chairman of Trustees, since 2005, SPIRE Rugby Trust (formerly SPIRE); Chairman of Trustees, RFU Charitable Trust, 2005–08; *b* 28 April 1931; *s* of late William Beer and Doris Ethel Beer; *m* 1960, Angela Felce, *d* of Col E. S. G. Howard, MC, RA and F. D. Howard; two *s* one *d*. *Educ:* Whitgift Sch.; St Catharine's Coll., Cambridge (Exhibitioner). E-SU Walter Page Scholar, 1968. Second Lieut in 1st Bn Royal Fusiliers, 1950. Bursar, Ottershaw Sch., 1955; Guinness Ltd, 1956–57; House Master, Marlborough Coll., Wilts, 1957–61; Head Master: Ellesmere Coll., Salop, 1961–69; Lancing Coll., Sussex, 1969–81. Chairman: HMC Academic Cttee, 1977–79; HMC, 1980; Physical Educn Working Gp for Nat. Curriculum, 1990–91; ISJC, then ISC, 1997–2001 (Vice-Chm., 1994–97; Chm., Adv. Cttee, 1988–91); Vice-Chm., GBA, 1994–2001; Founder Mem., Gen. Teaching Council, 2000–01. Mem., Sports Council, 1992–94. Chm. Council, Winston Churchill Meml Trust, 1997–2006 (Mem., 1990–2006; Trustee, 1998–2006); Trustee, RMC Group plc Welfare Trust, 1983–2006. Evelyn Wrench Lectr, ESU, 1988, 1990. Governor: Whitgift Sch., 1986–91; Charterhouse Sch., 1991–93; Malvern Coll., 1991–2001; Mem. Council, Univ. of Buckingham, 1992–96; Chm. of Trustees, Lancing Coll. Chapel Trust, 1996–. Chm. Editorial Bd, Rugby World and Post (formerly Rugby World, then Rugby Post), 1977–93. JP Shropshire, 1963–69, W Sussex, 1970–81, Middx, 1981–91, Glos, 1992. Hon. FCP 1990. *Publication:* But Headmaster!, 2001. *Recreations:* Rugby Football Union (Mem. Exec. Cttee, 1984–95; Vice Pres., 1991–93; Pres., 1993–94) (formerly: played Rugby for England; CURFC (Capt.), Harlequins, Old Whitgiftians), carpentry, reading, zoology, meeting people. *Address:* c/o SPIRE, 41 Station Road, North Harrow, Middx HA2 7SX. *Clubs:* East India, Devonshire, Sports and Public Schools; Hawks (Cambridge).

BEER, Prof. Janet, PhD; Vice Chancellor, Oxford Brookes University, since 2007; *b* 1 Aug. 1956; *d* of Derek Stanley John Beer and Jean Patricia Beer; *m* 1996, David Woodman; one *s* one *d*. *Educ:* Univ. of Reading (BA Hons); Univ. of Warwick (MA; PhD 1984). Pt-time Lectr, Univ. of Warwick, 1979–80 and 1981–83; Yale Fellow, Yale Univ., 1980–81; Educn Adminr, ILEA, 1983–89; Sen., then Principal Lectr, Univ. of Surrey, Roehampton, later Univ. of Roehampton, 1989–97; Hd, Dept of English, 1998–2002, Pro Vice Chancellor and Dean of Faculty, 2002–07, Manchester Metropolitan Univ. *Publications:* Edith Wharton: traveller in the land of letters, 1990, 2nd edn 1995; Kate Chopin, Edith Wharton and Charlotte Perkins Gilman: studies in short fiction, 1997, 2nd edn 2005; Edith Wharton, 2002; (ed jtly) Special Relationships: Anglo-American antagonisms and affinities 1854–1936, 2002. *Recreations:* swimming, walking, theatre, family. *Address:* Office of the Vice Chancellor, Oxford Brookes University, Headington Hill Hall, Oxford OX3 0BP. *T:* (01865) 484801, *Fax:* (01865) 484809; *e-mail:* vc@brookes.ac.uk.

BEÉR, Prof. János Miklós, DSc, PhD; FREng; Professor of Chemical and Fuel Engineering, Massachusetts Institute of Technology (MIT), 1976–93, now Emeritus; Scientific Director, MIT Combustion Research Facilities, since 1980; *b* Budapest, 27 Feb. 1923; *s* of Sándor Beér and Gizella Trismai; *m* 1944, Marta Gabriella Csató. *Educ:* Berzsenyi Dániel Gymnasium, Budapest; Univ. of Budapest (Dipl-Ing 1950); PhD Sheffield, 1960, DSc(Tech) Sheffield, 1967. Heat Research Inst., Budapest: Research Officer, 1949–52; Head, Combustion Dept, 1952–56; Princ. Lectr (part-time), University of Budapest, 1953–56; Research Engr, Babcock & Wilcox Ltd, Renfrew, 1957; Research Bursar, University of Sheffield, 1957–60; Head, Research Stn, Internat. Flame Research Foundn, Ijmuiden, Holland, 1960–63; Prof., Dept of Fuel Science, Pa State Univ., 1963–65; Newton Drew Prof. of Chemical Engrg and Fuel Technology and Head of Dept, Univ. of Sheffield, 1965–76; Dean, Faculty of Engineering, Univ. of Sheffield, 1973–75; Programme Dir for Combustion, MIT Energy Lab., 1976–86. Hon. Supt of Res., Internat. Flame Res. Foundn, 1991. Member: Adv. Council on R&D for Fuel and Power, DTI, later Dept of Energy, 1973–76; Adv. Bd, Safety in Mines Research, Dept of Energy, 1974–76; Clean Air Council, DoE, 1974–76; Bd of Directors, The Combustion Inst., Pittsburgh, USA, 1974–86; Mem., Adv. Cttee, Italian Nat. Res. Council, 1974–; Chm., Clean Coal Utilization Project, US Nat. Acad. of Scis, 1987–88; Mem., US Nat. Coal Council (Adv. Council to Energy Sec.), 1993–. Gen. Superintendent of Research, Internat. Flame Research Foundn, 1972–89 (Hon. Supt of Res., 1990–). Editor, Fuel and Energy Science Monograph Series, 1966–. Australian Commonwealth Vis. Fellow, 1972; Fellow ASME, 1978 (Moody Award, 1964; Percy Nicholls Award, 1988); FREng (FEng 1979). Hon. Member: Hungarian Acad. of Scis, 1986; Hungarian Acad. of Engrng, 1991. Foreign Mem., Finnish Acad. of Technology, 1989. Dr *hc* Miskolc, Hungary, 1987; Budapest Tech. Sci., Hungary, 1997. Melchett Medal, Inst. Energy, London, 1985; Coal Science Gold Medal, BCURA, 1986; Alfred Edgerton Gold Medal, Combustion Inst., 1986; Axel Axelson Johnson Medal, Swedish Acad. of Engrg Scis, 1995; Energy System Award, AIAA, 1998; George Westinghouse Gold Medal, ASME, 2001; Homer H. Lowry Award, US Dept of Energy, 2003. *Publications:* (with N. Chigier) Combustion Aerodynamics, 1972; (ed with M. W. Thring) Industrial Flames, 1972; (ed with H. B. Palmer) Developments in Combustion Science and Technology, 1974; (ed with N. Afgan) Heat Transfer in Flames, 1975; contribs to Nature, Combustion and Flame, Basic Engrg Jl, Amer. Soc. Mech. Engrg, Jl Inst. F, ZVDI, Internat. Gas Wärme, Proc. Internat. Symposia on Combustion, etc. *Recreations:* swimming, rowing, reading, music. *Address:* Department of Chemical Engineering, Massachusetts Institute of Technology, Cambridge, MA 02139, USA. *T:* (617) 2536661.

BEER, Prof. John Bernard, LittD; FBA 1994; Professor of English Literature, University of Cambridge, 1987–93, Professor Emeritus, since 1993; Fellow of Peterhouse, Cambridge, 1964–93, Emeritus Fellow, since 1993; *b* 31 March 1926; *s* of John Bateman Beer and Eva Chilton; *m* 1962, Gillian Patricia Kempster Thomas (*see* Dame G. P. K. Beer); three *s*. *Educ:* Watford Grammar Sch.; St John's Coll., Cambridge (MA, PhD); LittD Cantab 1995. Research Fellow, St John's Coll., Cambridge, 1955–58; Lectr, Manchester Univ., 1958–64; Univ. Lectr, Cambridge, 1964–78; Reader in English Literature, Cambridge, 1978–87. British Acad. Chatterton Lectr, 1964; Vis. Prof., Univ. of Virginia, 1975; Leverhulme Emeritus Fellowship, 1995–96; Stanton Lectureship in Philos. of Religion, 2006–07; numerous lecture tours abroad. Pres., Charles Lamb Soc., 1989–2002. Gen. Ed., Coleridge's Writings, 1990–. *Publications:* Coleridge the Visionary, 1959; The Achievement of E. M. Forster, 1962; (ed) Coleridge's Poems, 1963, new edn 1999; Blake's Humanism, 1968; Blake's Visionary Universe, 1969; (ed) Coleridge's Variety: bicentenary studies, 1974; Coleridge's Poetic Intelligence, 1977; Wordsworth and the Human Heart, 1978; Wordsworth in Time, 1979; (ed with G. K. Das) E. M. Forster: a human exploration, 1979; (ed) A Passage to India: essays in interpretation, 1985; (ed) Aids to Reflection, 1993; Romantic Influences: contemporary, Victorian, modern, 1993; Against Finality, 1993; (ed) Questioning Romanticism, 1995; (ed) Selected Poems of Arthur Hugh Clough, 1998; Providence and Love: studies in Wordsworth, Channing, Myers, George Eliot and Ruskin, 1998; (ed) Coleridge's Writings: On Religion and Psychology, 2002; Romantic Consciousness: Blake to Mary Shelley, 2003; Post-Romantic Consciousness: Dickens to Plath, 2003; William Blake: a literary life, 2005; numerous articles and reviews. *Recreations:* music, travel, walking in town and country. *Address:* Peterhouse, Cambridge CB2 1RD. *T:* (home) (01223) 356384. *Club:* Royal Over-Seas League.

BEER, Ven. John Stuart; Archdeacon of Cambridge (formerly Ely), since 2004; Bye Fellow, Fitzwilliam College, Cambridge, since 2001; *b* 15 March 1944; *s* of late John Gilbert Beer and May (*née* Scott); *m* 1970, Susan, *d* of late Gordon and Jessie Spencer; two *s* one *d*. *Educ:* Roundhay Sch.; Pembroke Coll., Oxford (MA (Theol.) 1968); Westcott House, Cambridge (MA 1976). Advertising and Finance, Rowntree & Co. Ltd, York, 1965–69; ordained deacon, 1971, priest, 1972; Asst Curate, St John the Baptist, Knaresborough, 1971–74; Fellow and Chaplain, Fitzwilliam Coll., Cambridge, and Chaplain, New Hall, 1974–80; Rector of Toft with Hardwick, Caldecote and Childerley, 1980–87; Dir of Post Ordination Training and Dir of Studies for Readers, dio. of Ely, and Vicar of Grantchester, 1987–97; Dir of Ordinands, 1987–2002, Co-Dir, 1993–2002, dio. Ely; Archdeacon of Huntingdon, 1997–2004, and of Wisbech, 2003–04. Mem., Ethics Cttee, Dunn Res. Inst., 1987–2001. Chm., Cathedral Pilgrims Assoc. Conf., 1987–97. *Publications:* Who is Jesus?, 1982; contribs to theol jls. *Recreations:* tennis, golf, music, wine. *Address:* St Botolph's Rectory, 1a Summerfield, Cambridge CB3 9HE. *T:* (01223) 350424, *Fax:* (01223) 360929; *e-mail:* archdeacon.cambridge@ely.anglican.org.

BEER, Air Vice-Marshal Peter George, CB 1995; CBE 1987 (OBE 1979); LVO 1974; Fellow and Home Bursar, Jesus College, Oxford, 1997–2006, now Emeritus Fellow; *b* 16 July 1941; *s* of Herbert George Beer and Kathleen Mary Beer; *m* 1975, Fiona Georgina Hamilton Davidson; two *s*. *Educ:* Hugh Sexey's Sch., Bruton; MA Oxon 1997. Equerry to HM the Queen, 1971–74; Officer Commanding: No 55 Sqdn, 1977–79; RAF Brize Norton, 1984–86; Dir, RAF Plans and Programmes, 1989–91; Comdr British Forces, Falkland Is, 1991–92; Dir-Gen. Training and Personnel, RAF, 1992–94; COS, Personnel and Training Comd, RAF, 1994–95, retd. Non-exec. Dir, Oxford Radcliffe Hosps NHS Trust, 1997–2003. Vice-Pres., RAF Hockey Assoc. *Recreations:* cricket, opera. *Address:* Southfield, Stonehill Lane, Southmoor, Oxon OX13 5HU. *Clubs:* Royal Air Force, MCC.

BEERLING, John William; freelance media consultant, film director, and writer, since 1994; *b* 12 April 1937; *s* of Raymond Starr and May Elizabeth Julia Beerling; *m* 1st, 1959, Carol Ann Reynolds (marr. diss. 1991); one *s* one *d*; 2nd, 1993, Celia Margaret Potter (marr. diss. 1998); 3rd, 1999, Susan Patricia Armstrong. *Educ:* Sir Roger Manwood's Grammar Sch., Sandwich, Kent. National Service, RAF, 1955–57. Joined BBC, 1957; Studio Manager, 1958; Producer, 1962; Head of Radio 1 Programmes, 1983; Controller, Radio 1, 1985–93. Chm., Radio Data Systems Forum, Geneva, 1993–; Dir, Stereo Pair, 1997–98; Partner, The Great Outdoor Picture Co., 1998–2002; Man. Dir, Classic Gold Digital Radio, 2000–02. Gov., Brits Sch. for Performing Arts and Technology, 1995–2006. Pres., TRIC, 1992–93. Fellow, Radio Acad., 2005. *Publications:* Emperor Rosko's D. J. Handbook, 1976; Radio 1—The Inside Scene, 2008. *Recreations:* photography, fishing, ski-ing. *Address:* Rockfield, 62 Raikeswood Drive, Skipton, N Yorks BD23 1LY.

BEESLEY, Ian Blake; Official Historian, Cabinet Office, since 2007; Chairman, Wisdom of the Ancients Consulting Ltd, since 2003; Commissioner for National Statistics, since 2004; *b* 11 July 1942; *s* of Frank and Catherine Beesley; *m* 1st, 1964, Birgitte (*née* Smith) (marr. diss. 1982); 2nd, 1983, Elizabeth (*née* Wigley) (marr. diss. 1998); one *s* two *d*; 3rd, 2000, Edna (*née* Chivers) (CBE 2006); one step *s*. *Educ:* Manchester Grammar School; St Edmund Hall, Oxford (PPE). MA; Cert. in Statistics. Central Statistical Office, 1964–76; Chief Statistician, HM Treasury, 1976–78; Dep. Head, Unit supporting Lord Rayner, PM's adviser on efficiency, 1981–83; Under Sec. and Official Head of PM's Efficiency Unit, 1983–86; Partner, Price Waterhouse, subseq. PricewaterhouseCoopers, 1986–2003. Alternate Mem., Jarratt Cttee on efficiency in universities, 1984–85; Mem., Croham Cttee to review function and operation of UGC, 1985–87. Member: Employment Service Adv. Gp, 1992–98; Expert Gp advising Govt on Nat. Experience Corps, 2000–01; Home Sec.'s Expert Gp on compilation and publication of crime statistics, 2006. Mem., Council, Surrey Univ., 1986–92. FSS 1966; FRSA 1990. Freeman: Co. of Mgt Consultants, 2003; City of London, 2003. *Publications:* Policy analysis and evaluation in British Government (RIPA seminar papers), 1983; (contrib.) Straight from the CEO, 1998; contribs to Jl Royal Statistical Soc.; articles on value for money in the arts. *Address:* (office) 5A China Wharf, 29 Mill Street, SE1 2BQ. *Club:* Savile.

BEESLEY, Peter Frederick Barton; Registrar: Faculty Office of the Archbishop of Canterbury, since 1981; Diocese of Guildford, since 1981; Diocese of Ely, since 2002 (Joint, 1978–2002); Diocese of Hereford, since 2007 (Joint, 1983–2007); Senior Partner, Lee Bolton & Lee, since 2000 (Partner, since 1969); *b* 30 April 1943; *s* of Ronald Fitzgerald Barton Beesley and Mary Kurczyn (*née* Parker); *m* 1974, Elizabeth Jane Grahame; one *s* two *d*. *Educ:* King's School, Worcester; Exeter Univ. (LLB); Coll. of Law, Guildford. Articled Clerk and Asst Solicitor, Windeatt & Windeatt, 1965–68; Asst Solicitor, Lee Bolton & Lee, 1968–69. Jt Registrar, Dio. St Albans, 1969–78; Registrar, Woodard Corp., 1987–; Legal Advr, Nat. Soc. (C of E) for Promoting Religious Educn, 1975–; Secretary: Ecclesiastical Law Assoc., 1978–98 (Vice-Chm., 1998–2000; Chm., 2000–02); Ecclesiastical Law Soc., 1987–; Mem. Legal Adv. Commn, General Synod of C of E, 1992–; Pres., City of Westminster Law Soc., 1991–92. Mem., Glaziers' Trust, 1996– (Vice-Chm., 1998–2000; Chm., 2000–03). Liveryman, Glaziers' and Painters' of Glass Co., 1981 (Mem. Ct Assts, 1995–; Master, 2005–06). Trustee, Arbory Trust, 2000–; Bishopsland Educnl Trust, 2002–. Governor: Hampstead Parochial Sch., 1983–2003 (Chm., 1986–95); Sarum Hall Sch., 1997–. *Publications:* (contrib. jtly) Encyclopaedia of Forms and Precedents, Vol. 13, Ecclesiastical Law, 1987; Anglican Marriage in England and Wales, a Guide to the Law for Clergy, 1992. *Address:* (office) 1 The Sanctuary, Westminster, SW1P 3JT. *T:* (020) 7222 5381. *Clubs:* Athenæum, St Stephen's, MCC.

BEESON, Andrew Nigel Wendover; company director; *b* 30 March 1944; *s* of Nigel Wendover Beeson (killed in action 1944) and Anne Beeson (*née* Sutherland, now Hodges); *m* 1st, 1971, Susan Gerard (marr. diss. 1983); one *s* one *d*; 2nd, 1986, Carrie Martin; one *d*. *Educ:* Eton Coll. Partner, Capel Cure Myers, 1972–85; Director: ANZ Merchant Bank, 1985–87; ANZ McCaughan, 1987–89; Founder, Beeson Gregory Holdings Ltd, 1989; CEO, 1989–2001, Dep. Chm., 2001, Beeson Gregory Gp; Chm., Evolution Gp plc, 2002–03. Non-executive Director: IP2IPO Gp, 2001–04; Woolworths Gp, 2001–; NB Real Estate Gp (formerly Nelson Bakewell Hldgs), 2001–; Schroder Gp plc, 2004–; Datawind UK. Founding Chm., City Gp for Small Cos, 1992–95; Director: European Assoc. Securities Dealers, 1995–2002; European Assoc. Securities Dealers Automatic Quotations, 1996–2001; Assoc. of Private Client Investment Managers and Stockbrokers, 2002–03. Trustee, Tennis and Rackets Assoc., 1996. Achievement Award, Coopers & Lybrand, 1995. *Recreations:* Real tennis, shooting, collecting. *Address:* 21 Warwick Square, SW1V 2AB. *T:* (020) 7834 2903. *Clubs:* MCC (Mem. Cttee, 2004–), Pratt's, White's; Swinley Golf (Ascot); Royal West Norfolk Golf.

BEESON, Very Rev. Trevor Randall, OBE 1997; writer; Dean of Winchester, 1987–96, now Dean Emeritus; *b* 2 March 1926; *s* of late Arthur William and Matilda Beeson; *m* 1950, Josephine Grace Cope (*d* 1997); two *d*. *Educ:* King's Coll., London (AKC 1950; FKC 1987); St Boniface Coll., Warminster. RAF Met Office, 1944–47. Deacon, 1951; Priest, 1952; Curate, Leadgate, Co. Durham, 1951–54; Priest-in-charge and subseq. Vicar of St Chad, Stockton-on-Tees, 1954–65; Curate of St Martin-in-the-Fields, London, 1965–71; Vicar of Ware, Herts, 1971–76; Canon of Westminster, 1976–87; Treasurer, Westminster, 1978–82; Rector of St Margaret's, Westminster, 1982–87; Chaplain to Speaker of House of Commons, 1982–87. Chaplain of St Bride's, Fleet Street, 1967–84. Television and radio commentator and presenter, 1968–82; Religious Programmes Advr, LWT, 1970–86. Chm., Christian Action, 1988–96. Gen. Sec., Parish and People, 1962–64; Editor, New Christian, and Man. Dir, Prism Publications Ltd, 1965–70; European Corresp. of The Christian Century (Chicago), 1970–83; Chm., SCM Press Ltd, 1978–87. Select Preacher, Oxford, 1980, 1991. Mem. Council, WWF, 1987–94. MA (Lambeth) 1976; Hon. DLitt Southampton, 1999. *Publications:* New Area Mission, 1963; (jtly) Worship in a United Church, 1964; An Eye for an Ear, 1972; The Church of England in Crisis, 1973; Discretion and Valour: religious conditions in Russia and Eastern Europe, 1974; Britain Today and Tomorrow, 1978; Westminster Abbey, 1981; A Vision of Hope: the churches and change in Latin America, 1984; (contrib.) God's Truth, 1988; A Dean's Diary: Winchester 1987–1996, 1997; Window on Westminster, 1998; Rebels and Reformers, 1999; (contrib.) AD 2000 Years of Christianity, 1999; The Bishops, 2002; (ed) Priests and Prelates, Daily Telegraph Obituaries, 2002; The Deans, 2004; (contrib.) Christianity: a complete guide, 2005; The Canons, 2006; Round the Church in 50 Years: a personal journey, 2007; contrib. to DNB, Oxford Dictionary of the Church. *Recreation:* gardening. *Address:* 69 Greatbridge Road, Romsey, Hants SO51 8FE. *T:* (01794) 514627.

See also Very Rev. C. W. Taylor.

BEESTON, James, OBE 2004; Chairman, Invigour Ltd, since 2001; Director, Beeston Associates Ltd, since 2001; *b* 2 April 1947; *s* of Richard and Mary Beeston; *m* 1971, Christine, *d* of Barry and Enid Thomas; two *s*. *Educ:* King Edward's, Camp Hill; Birmingham Sch. of Planning. DipTP; MRTPI. Birmingham City Council: Public Works Dept, 1965–74; Central Area Planning Officer, 1974–80; Divl Planning Officer, 1980–85; Asst Dir of Develt, 1985–87; Project Controller, National Indoor Arena; Co-ordinator, first phase, Birmingham Olympics bid; Develt Manager and Dep. Chief Exec., Birmingham Heartlands Ltd, 1987–92; Chief Executive: Birmingham Heartlands Develt Corp., 1992–98; Millennium Point Trust Co., 1997–2001. Mem., Lunar Soc., Birmingham. Mem., Governing Body, Birmingham City Univ., 2007–. Governor: King Edward VI Camp Hill Sch. for Boys, Birmingham, 1996–; King Edward VI Foundn, 2003–. *Publication:* (jtly) Negotiating with Planning Authorities. *Recreations:* family, cricket, sport, gardening. *Address:* c/o Invigour Ltd, 2nd Floor, 23 Colmore Row, Birmingham B3 2BP.

BEESTON, Kevin Stanley; Chairman, Serco Group plc, since 2007 (Executive Chairman, 2002–07); *b* 18 Sept. 1962; *s* of Denis and Patricia Beeston; *m* 1991, Jayne Anne Knowles; two *s* one *d*. *Educ:* Gorleston Grammar Sch. ACMA 1986, FCMA 1990. Serco Group plc, 1985–: Finance Dir, 1996–99; Chief Exec., 1999–2002. Dir, Ipswich Town FC Co. Ltd, 2003–. Mem. Bd, CCMI, 2004–. FRSA. *T:* (020) 8334 4331, *Fax:* (020) 8334 4301; *e-mail:* heidi.ranger@serco.com.

BEESTON, Richard Nicholas; Foreign Editor, The Times, since 2008; *b* London, 18 Feb. 1963; *s* of William Richard Charles Beeston and Moyra Alice Beeston (*née* Salmon); *m* 1989, Natasha Fairweather; one *s* one *d*. *Educ:* Westminster Sch.; Nat. Council for Trng of Journalists. Reporter, Financial Mail, Johannesburg, 1983–84; freelance corresp., Beirut, 1984–86; The Times: foreign reporter, 1986–91; Jerusalem corresp., 1991–94; Moscow corresp., 1994–98; Foreign News Ed., 1998–2000; Diplomatic Ed., 2000–07. *Recreations:* fishing, poker. *Address:* c/o The Times, 1 Pennington Street, E98 1TT. *T:* (020) 7782 5234, *Fax:* (020) 7782 5140; *e-mail:* richard.beeston@thetimes.co.uk. *Club:* Frontline.

BEETHAM, Geoffrey Howard, CB 1992; Legal Adviser to Department of Transport, 1983–93; Principal Assistant Solicitor, Treasury Solicitor's Department, 1983–93; *b* 9 Jan. 1933; *s* of Reginald Percy Beetham and Hetty Lilian Beetham (*née* Redman); *m* 1st, 1956, Valerie Douglass (marr. diss. 1975); three *d*; 2nd, 1977, Carol Ann Dorrell; two step *s*. *Educ:* City of London Sch.; St John's Coll., Oxford (BA Jurisp.). Nat. Service, RAF, 1951–53. Solicitor, 1960; Assistant Solicitor: Metropolitan Borough of Battersea, 1960–65; London Borough of Wandsworth, 1965–70; Sen. Legal Assistant and Asst Solicitor, DoE, 1970–77; Asst Solicitor, Dept of Transport, 1977–83. Legal Mem., Mental Health Review Tribunal, 1994–2005. *Recreations:* throwing pots, music, countryside.

BEETHAM, Marshal of the Royal Air Force Sir Michael (James), GCB 1978 (KCB 1976); CBE 1967; DFC 1944; AFC 1960; DL; FRAeS; Chief of the Air Staff, 1977–82; Air ADC to the Queen, 1977–82; *b* 17 May 1923; *s* of Major G. C. Beetham, MC; *m* 1956, Patricia Elizabeth Lane; one *s* one *d*. *Educ:* St Marylebone Grammar School. Joined RAF, 1941; pilot trng, 1941–42; commnd 1942; Bomber Comd: 50, 57 and 35 Sqdns, 1943–46; HQ Staff, 1947–49; 82 (Recce) Sqdn, E Africa, 1949–51; psa 1952; Air Min. (Directorate Operational Requirements), 1953–56; CO 214 (Valiant) Sqdn Marham, 1958–60; Gp Captain Ops, HQ Bomber Comd, 1962–64; CO RAF Khormaksar, Aden, 1964–66; idc 1967; Dir Ops (RAF), MoD, 1968–70; Comdt, RAF Staff Coll., 1970–72; ACOS (Plans and Policy), SHAPE, 1972–75; Dep. C-in-C, Strike Command, 1975–76; C-in-C RAF Germany, and Comdr, 2nd Tactical Allied Air Force, 1976–77. Hon. Air Cdre, 2620 (Co. of Norfolk) Sqdn, RAuxAF Regt, 1983–2001; Pres., Bomber Comd

Assoc., 1986–. Chm., GEC Avionics Ltd, 1986–90 (Dir, 1984–91); Dir, Brixton Estate PLC, 1983–93. Chm. Trustees, 1983–99, Pres. Soc. of Friends, 1999–, RAF Museum; Pres., RAF Historical Soc., 1993–. Governor: Cheltenham Coll., 1983–89; Wymondham Coll., 1990–98. FRSA 1979; FRAeS 1982. DL Norfolk, 1989. Hon. Liveryman, GAPAN, 1983. Polish Order of Merit, 1998. *Recreations:* golf, tennis. *Clubs:* Royal Air Force (Pres., 1992–2002, Vice Patron, 2003–); Royal West Norfolk Golf.

See also Maj.-Gen. G. Risius.

BEETHAM, Roger Campbell, CMG 1993; LVO 1976; HM Diplomatic Service, retired; *b* 22 Nov. 1937; *s* of Henry Campbell and Mary Beetham; *m* 1st, 1965, Judith Rees (marr. diss. 1986); 2nd, 1986, Christine Marguerite Malerme. *Educ:* Peter Symonds Sch., Winchester; Brasenose Coll., Oxford (MA). Entered HM Diplomatic Service, 1960; FO, 1960–62; UK Delegation to Disarmament Conference, Geneva, 1962–65; Washington, 1965–68; News Dept, FCO, 1969–72; Head of Chancery, Helsinki, 1972–76; FCO, 1976; seconded to European Commission, Brussels, as Spokesman of the President, Rt Hon. Roy Jenkins, 1977–80; Counsellor (Econ. and Commercial), New Delhi, 1981–85; Head of Maritime, Aviation and Envmt Dept, FCO, 1985–90; Ambassador to Senegal and (non-resident) to Cape Verde, Guinea, Guinea-Bissau and Mali, 1990–93; UK Perm. Rep. (with personal rank of Ambassador) to Council of Europe, Strasbourg, 1993–97; European Manager, Surrey CC, 1998–2000. Trustee, Eur. Opera Centre, 2002– (Vice-Chm., 2005–). Order of the White Rose of Finland, 1976. *Publication:* (ed) The Euro Debate: persuading the people, 2001. *Recreations:* oenology, cooking, travel. *Clubs:* National Liberal; Cercle Royal Gaulois (Brussels).

BEETON, David Christopher, CBE 1998; Director General, British Casino Association, 2000–04; *b* 25 Aug. 1939; *s* of Ernest Beeton and Ethel Beeton; *m* 1968, Brenda Lomax; two *s*. *Educ:* Ipswich Sch.; King's Coll., London Univ. (LLB). Solicitor. Chief Exec., Bath CC, 1973–85; Sec., National Trust, 1985–89; Chief Exec., Historic Royal Palaces, 1989–99. Hon. MA Bath, 2003. *Recreations:* swimming, historic buildings, cooking, music. *Address:* 61 Lyncombe Hill, Bath BA2 4PH. *T:* (01225) 317026.

BEETON, Kenneth George; Director, Government Reporting, HM Treasury, since 2007; *b* 16 Dec. 1951; *s* of Laurence Owen Beeton and late Ruth Isobel Mary Beeton; *m* 2000, Amanda; two *d* and two step *s*. *Educ:* Deacons Grammar Sch. FCA 1976. Private sector posts in: accountancy, 1976–78; mfg, 1979–80; building socs, 1980–89; insce, 1989–94; Head of Financial Services and Accountancy, 1994–97, Head of Schs Capital and Bldgs, 1997–2003, DfEE, subseq. DfES; Dir of Finance, DfT, 2003–07. *Address: e-mail:* ken.beeton@ntlworld.com.

BEEVOR, Antony James, FRSL; author; *b* 14 Dec. 1946; *s* of John Grosvenor Beevor and Carinthia Jane Beevor (*née* Waterfield); *m* 1986, Hon. Artemis Cooper, *d* of Viscount Norwich, *qv*; one *s* one *d*. *Educ:* Winchester Coll.; RMA Sandhurst. Served 11th Hussars (PAO), 1967–70; posts in mktg and advertising, London and Paris, 1971–75; occasional journalism and literary criticism. Mem., Armed Forces into the 21st Century seminars, KCL, 1993–95; Vis. Prof., Sch. of Hist., Classics and Archaeology, Birkbeck Coll., London Univ., 2002–; Lees Knowles Lectr, Cambridge, 2002. Member: Exec. Council, French Theatre Season, 1996–97; Council, Soc. for Army Historical Res., 2000–03; Mgt Cttee, Soc. of Authors, 2001– (Chm. of Soc., 2003–05; Mem. Council, 2005–); Cttee, London Library, 2002–04. Dir, Ocito Ltd, 2003–. Judge: Shiva Naipaul Meml Prize, 2000; British Acad. Book Prize, 2004; David Cohen Prize, 2005; Mem., Steering Cttee, Samuel Johnson Prize, 2004–. Patron, Nat. Acad. of Writing, 2000–. FRSL 1999. Hon. DLitt Kent, 2004. Chevalier de l'Ordre des Arts et des Lettres (France), 1997. *Publications:* four novels; The Spanish Civil War, 1982; Inside the British Army, 1990; Crete: the battle and the resistance, 1991 (Runciman Prize); (with Artemis Cooper) Paris After the Liberation, 1994; Stalingrad, 1998 (Samuel Johnson Prize, Wolfson Prize for History, Hawthornden Prize, 1999); (contrib.) The British Army, Manpower and Society, 1999; Berlin: The Downfall 1945, 2002 (Longman-History Today Trustees' Award, 2003); The Mystery of Olga Chekhova, 2004; (ed with L. Vinogradova) A Writer At War: Vasily Grossman with the Red Army 1941–1945, 2005; (contrib.) Russia, War, Peace and Diplomacy: essays in honour of John Erickson, 2005; La Guerra Civil Española, 2005 (La Vanguardia Prize, 2005; UK edn as The Battle for Spain, 2006). *Address:* 54 St Maur Road, SW6 4DP; *web:* www.antonybeevor.com. *Club:* Brooks's.

BEEVOR, Antony Romer; Senior Advisor, SG Hambros, 2000–03 (Managing Director, 1998–2000); *b* 18 May 1940; *s* of late Miles Beevor and Sybil (*née* Gilliat); *m* 1970, Cecilia Hopton; one *s* one *d*. *Educ:* Winchester; New Coll., Oxford (BA). Admitted Solicitor, 1965. Ashurst Morris Crisp & Co., 1962–72 (on secondment as Sec., Panel on Takeovers and Mergers, 1969–71); joined Hambros Bank, 1972; Dir, 1974–98; Exec. Dir, 1985–98; on secondment, as Dir-Gen., Panel on Takeovers and Mergers, 1987–89 (Dep. Chm., 1999–); Director: Hambros plc, 1990–98; (non-exec.), Rugby Gp, 1993–2000; Gerrard Group, 1995–2000; Croda International, 1996–2005 (Chm., 2002–05); Helical Bar, 2000–; Nestor Healthcare Gp, 2000–03 (Chm., 2002–03). Mem. Council, 1970–, Chm., 1999–, Fairbridge; Chm., Croda Trustees Ltd, 2006–. *Recreations:* shooting, low level golf, the countryside. *Clubs:* Hurlingham, Brooks's.

BEEVOR, Sir Thomas Agnew, 7th Bt *cr* 1784; *b* 6 Jan. 1929; *s* of Comdr Sir Thomas Beevor, 6th Bt, and Edith Margaret Agnew (who *m* 2nd, 1944, Rear-Adm. R. A. Currie, CB, DSC; she *d* 1985); *S* father, 1943; *m* 1st, 1957, Barbara Clare (marr. diss., 1965), *y d* of Capt. R. L. B. Cunliffe, RN (retd); one *s* two *d*; 2nd, 1966, Carola (marr. diss. 1975), *d* of His Honour J. B. Herbert, MC; 3rd, 1976, Mrs Sally Bouwens, White Hall, Saham Toney, Norfolk. *Heir: s* Thomas Hugh Cunliffe Beevor [*b* 1 Oct. 1962; *m* 1988, Charlotte Louise, *e d* of Keith E. Harvey; two *s* one *d*]. *Address:* The Old Woodyard, Hargham, Norwich NR16 2JW.

BEFFA, Jean-Louis Guy Henri, Hon. CBE 2005; Commandeur de la Légion d'Honneur; Chairman and Chief Executive Officer, Compagnie de Saint-Gobain, since 1986; *b* 11 Aug. 1941; *m* 1967, Marie-Madeleine Brunel; two *s* one *d*. *Educ:* Ecole Polytechnique (Ing. au Corps des Mines); Dip. de l'Inst. d'Etudes Politiques de Paris. Compagnie de Saint-Gobain: Vice-Pres., Corporate Planning, 1974–77; Pres., Pipe Div., 1978–82; Chief Operating Officer, 1982–86. Vice Chm. Bd, BNP Paribas, 2000–. Comdr, Order of Merit (Germany); Order of Rio Branco (Brazil). *Recreations:* golf, classical music. *Address:* c/o Compagnie de Saint-Gobain, Les Miroirs, 18 avenue d'Alsace, 92096 Paris la Défense cedex, France. *T:* 147623310.

BEGENT, Prof. Richard Henry John, MD; FRCP, FRCR; FMedSci; Professor of Clinical Oncology, Royal Free and University College Medical School of University College London (formerly Royal Free Hospital Medical School), since 1990; *b* 14 Feb. 1945; *s* of Harry Hawley Begent and Doris Ena Begent; *m* 1969, Nicola Ann Thomerson; one *s* two *d*. *Educ:* Haileybury and Imperial Service Coll.; St Bartholomew's Hosp. Medical Coll. (MB BS; MD 1978). FRCP 1986; FRCR 1999. House Officer, Prince of Wales, St Leonard's, Southend and Royal Marsden Hosps, 1967–71; Registrar in Medicine, Royal Marsden, St George's and Chichester Hosps, 1971–75; Clin. Res. Fellow, ICRF, 1975–77; Charing Cross Hospital Medical School: Lectr in Medical Oncology, 1977–80; Sen. Lectr and Hon. Consultant Physician, 1980–86; Gibb Res. Fellow, CRC, 1986–90; Reader in Med. Oncology, Charing Cross and Westminster Med. Sch., 1986–90; Head, Department of Oncology: Royal Free Hosp. Med. Sch., 1990–97; UCL, 1997–; Hon. Consultant Physician, Royal Free Hosp., 1990–. Chm., Nat. Cancer Res. Inst. Informatics Task Force, 2004–. FMedSci 2000. *Publications:* contribs on antibody targeting of cancer and gastrointestinal oncology. *Recreations:* gardening, ski-ing. *Address:* 6 St Albans Road, NW5 1RD; *e-mail:* r.begent@ucl.ac.uk.

BEGG, Anne; *see* Begg, M. A.

BEGG, Prof. David; Chairman, Tube Lines, since 2006; *b* 12 June 1956. *Educ:* Portobello Secondary Sch.; Heriot-Watt Univ. Mgt trainee, British Rail, 1979–81; Lectr in Econs, Napier Poly., then Napier Univ., 1981–97; Prof. of Transport Policy and Dir, Centre for Transport Policy, Robert Gordon Univ., 1997. Chm., UK Commn for Integrated Transport, 1999–2005. Non-executive Director: BRB, 1997–99; Shadow SRA, 1999–2001; SRA, 2001–05; Manchester Passenger Transport Exec., 2003–; First Gp, 2005–; Mem. Bd, Transport for London, 2000–05. Chm., Northern Way Transport Compact, 2006–. Dir, Portobello Partnership, 2003–. Publisher, Transport Times, 2005–. Member (Lab): Lothian Regl Council (Chm., Finance Cttee, 1990–94); Edinburgh City Council (Chm., Transport Cttee, 1994–99). *Recreations:* golf, watching football (Hibs). *Address:* (office) Suite 21, 35–37 Grosvenor Gardens, SW1W 0BS.

BEGG, Prof. David Knox Houston, PhD; FRSE; Professor of Economics, and Principal, Tanaka Business School, Imperial College London, since 2003; *b* 25 June 1950; *s* of late Robert William Begg, CBE and of Sheena Margaret Begg (*née* Boyd); *m* 2002, Jenny Holland. *Educ:* St John's Coll., Cambridge (BA Econs 1972 (double 1st); Adam Smith Prize 1971); Nuffield Coll., Oxford (MPhil 1974); MIT (PhD 1977; Kennedy Schol.). Oxford University: Fellow in Econs, Worcester Coll., and Lectr, 1977–86; Tutor, 1980–82, Sen. Tutor, 1983–86, Business Summer Sch.; Birkbeck College, London: Prof. of Econs, 1987–2002 (Hd of Dept, 1987–90 and 1996–98); Actg Vice Master, 1997. Res. Dir, Centre for Econ. Forecasting, London Business Sch., 1981–83; Centre for Economic Policy Research: Res. Fellow, 1983–; Mem., Exec. Cttee, 2002–. Vis. Asst Prof., Princeton Univ., 1979; Visiting Professor: MIT, 1994; INSEAD, 1995; Visiting Fellow: IMF, 1999; Reserve Bank of Australia, 2000. Econ. Policy Advr, Bank of England, 1986. Chm., Begg Commn on future of UK outside the euro, 2002. Non-exec. Dir, Trace Gp plc, 2006–07. FRSE 2004; FCGI 2006. Founding Man. Ed., Econ. Policy, 1985–2000. *Publications:* The Rational Expectations Revolution in Macroeconomics, 1981; (jtly) Economics, 1984, 9th edn 2008 (trans. French, Spanish, Italian, Polish, Vietnamese, Chinese); Monetarism and Macroeconomics: contributions on the UK policy debate, 1987; (jtly) The Impact of Eastern Europe, 1990; (jtly) The Making of Monetary Union, 1991; (jtly) Making Sense of Subsidiarity, 1993; (jtly) EU Enlargement, 1993; (jtly) Independent and Accountable: a new mandate for the Bank of England, 1993; (jtly) EMU: getting the endgame right, 1997; (ed jtly) EMU: prospects and challenges for the Euro, 1998; (jtly) Monetary and Exchange Rate Policies, EMU, and Central and Eastern Europe, 1999; Safe at Any Speed?: monitoring the European Central Bank, 1999; (jtly) Foundations of Economics, 2000, 3rd edn 2006; Global Economics: contemporary issues for 2002, 2002; (jtly) Surviving the Slowdown: monitoring the European Central Bank, 2003; (with D. Ward) Economics for Business, 2003, 2nd edn 2007; (jtly) Sustainable Regimes of Capital Movements in Accession Countries, 2003; contribs to learned jls, esp. on exchange rates and monetary policy. *Recreations:* music, crosswords, gardening, all sport. *Address:* Tanaka Business School, Imperial College London, SW7 2AZ. *T:* (020) 7594 9100; *e-mail:* d.begg@imperial.ac.uk.

BEGG, Prof. Hugh MacKemmie, PhD; consultant in private practice; Member, Local Government Boundary Commission for Scotland, 1999–2007; *b* 25 Oct. 1941; *s* of Hugh Alexander Begg and Margaret Neil Begg; *m* 1968, Jane Elizabeth Harrison; two *d*. *Educ:* High Sch., Glasgow; Univ. of St Andrews (MA Hons 1964); Univ. of British Columbia (MA 1966); Univ. of Dundee (PhD 1979); Edinburgh Coll. of Art (DipTP 1981). FRTPI 1991. Lectr in Pol Econ., Univ. of St Andrews, 1966–67; Res. Fellow, Tayside Study, 1967–69; Lectr in Econs, Univ. of Dundee, 1969–76; Asst Dir of Planning and Develt, Tayside Regl Council, 1976–79; Prof. and Hd, Sch. of Town and Regl Planning, and Dean, Fac. of Envmtl Studies, Univ. of Dundee, 1979–93. Vis. Prof. of Econs, Abertay Univ., Dundee, 2000–. Consultant, UNDP, 1986–2000. Mem., Private Legislation Procedure (Scot.) Extra-Parly Panel, 1993–99; Reporter, Scottish Exec. Inq. Reporters Unit, 1995–; External Complaints Adjudicator, Scottish Enterprise, 1996–2002; Convenor, Standards Commn for Scotland, 2002–03; Assessor, Private Bills Unit, Scottish Parlt, 2006–07. Convenor, RTPI in Scotland, 1991. Mem., Dundee Bonnetmakers' Craft. *Publications:* numerous contribs to academic, professional and tech. jls relating mainly to econs, town and regl planning, and monitoring and evaluation of public policy. *Recreations:* hill walking, Guide Dogs for the Blind (puppy walker), watching Rugby. *Address:* 4 The Esplanade, Broughty Ferry, Dundee DD5 2EL. *T:* (01382) 779642; *e-mail:* HughBegg @blueyonder.co.uk. *Club:* Monifieth and District Rotary.

BEGG, (Margaret) Anne; MP (Lab) Aberdeen South, since 1997; *b* 6 Dec. 1955; *d* of David Begg, MBE and Margaret Catherine Begg (*née* Ross). *Educ:* Brechin High Sch.; Univ. of Aberdeen (MA); Aberdeen Coll. of Education. English and History Teacher, Webster's High Sch., Kirriemuir, 1978–88; Asst Principal English Teacher, 1988–91, Principal English Teacher, 1991–97, Arbroath Acad. Member: Scottish Affairs Select Cttee, 1998–2001; Work and Pensions Select Cttee, 2001–; Speaker's Panel of Chairmen, 2002–. Vice-Chm., Labour Party Nat. Policy Forum, 2006–. Mem., NEC, Lab Party, 1998–99. *Recreations:* reading, theatre, cinema, public speaking, meeting people. *Address:* House of Commons, SW1A 0AA. *T:* (020) 7219 2140.

BEGGS, Prof. Jean Duthie, CBE 2006; PhD; FRS 1998; FRSE; Professor of Molecular Biology, since 1999 (SHEFC Professor, 1999–2005), and Royal Society Darwin Trust Research Professor, since 2005, Wellcome Trust Centre for Cell Biology, Institute of Cell Biology, University of Edinburgh; *b* 16 April 1950; *d* of William Renfrew Lancaster and Jean Crawford Lancaster (*née* Duthie); *m* 1972, Dr Ian Beggs; two *s*. *Educ:* Glasgow High Sch. for Girls; Univ. of Glasgow (BSc Hons 1971; PhD 1974). FRSE 1995. Postdoctoral Fellow: Dept of Molecular Biol., Univ. of Edinburgh, 1974–77; Plant Breeding Inst., Cambridge, 1977–79; Beit Meml Fellow for Med. Res., 1976–79; Lectr, Dept of Biochem., ICSTM, 1979–85; University of Edinburgh: Royal Soc. Univ. Res. Fellow, Dept of Molecular Biol., 1985–89; Royal Soc. EPA Cephalosporin Fund Sen. Res. Fellow, 1989–99, Professorial Res. Fellow, 1994–99, Inst. Cell and Molecular Biol. Mem., EMBO, 1991; MAE 2000. Gabor Medal, Royal Soc., 2003; Novartis Medal, Biochemical Soc., 2004; Chancellor's Award, Univ. of Edinburgh, 2005. *Publications:* research papers and reviews on gene cloning in yeast and molecular biology of RNA splicing. *Recreations:* walking, ski-ing, scuba diving, classical music. *Address:* Wellcome Trust Centre for Cell Biology, Institute of Cell Biology, University of Edinburgh, King's Buildings, Mayfield Road, Edinburgh EH9 3JR. *T:* (0131) 650 5351.

BEGGS, John Robert, (Roy); Member (UU), Larne Borough Council, since 1973; *b* 20 Feb. 1936; *s* of John Beggs; *m* 1959, Wilma Lorimer; two *s* two *d*. *Educ:* Ballyclare High

Sch.; Stranmillis Trng Coll. (Certificate/Diploma in Educn). Teacher, 1957–78, Vice-Principal, 1978–83, Larne High Sch. Mem., 1973–, Vice-Chm., 1981–, NE Educn and Library Bd; Pres., Assoc. of Educn and Liby Bds, NI, 1984–85 (Vice-Pres., 1983–84). Mayor of Larne, 1978–83; Mem. for N Antrim, NI Assembly, 1982–86. MP (UU) East Antrim, 1983–2005 (resigned seat Dec. 1985 in protest against Anglo-Irish Agreement; re-elected Jan. 1986); contested (UU) same seat, 2005. Mem., H of C Public Accounts Commn, 1984–2005. Mem., NI Drainage Council, 2006–. Chm., N Eastern Educn and Liby Bd, 2007–. *Address:* 171 Carrickfergus Road, Larne, Co. Antrim BT40 3JZ. *T:* and *Fax:* (028) 2827 8976.

See also R. Beggs.

BEGGS, Roy; Member (UU) Antrim East, Northern Ireland Assembly, since 1998; *b* 3 July 1962; *s* of John Robert Beggs, *qv* and Elizabeth Wilhelmina Beggs (*née* Lorimer); *m* 1989, Sandra Maureen Gillespie; two *s* one *d. Educ:* Larne Grammar Sch.; Queen's Univ., Belfast (BEng Hons Industrial Engrg). Hon. Secretary: Ulster Young Unionist Council, 1986 and 1987; E Antrim UU Assoc., 1992–2002. Northern Ireland Assembly: Member: Higher and Further Educn, Trng & Employment Deptl Cttee, subseq. Employment and Learning Cttee, 1999–2002; Public Accounts Cttee, 1999–2003; Cttee of the Centre, 2000–03; Vice Chairman: Cttee on Standards and Privileges, 1999–2002; Finance and Personnel Cttee, 2002–03, 2007–; Public Accounts Cttee, 2007–; Chm., All Party Assembly Gp on Children and Young People, 2007–. Mem. (UU), Carrickfergus BC, 2001–. Vice-Chairman: Carrickfergus Community Safety Partnership, 2004–07; Mem., Carrickfergus Dist Policing Partnership, 2003–. Mem. Cttee, Raloo Presbyterian Church, 1999–. Gov., Glynn Primary Sch. *Recreations:* walking, cycling; Officer, 1st Raloo Boys' Brigade. *Address:* (office) 3 St Brides Street, Carrickfergus, Northern Ireland BT38 8AF. *T:* (028) 9336 2995, *Fax:* (028) 9336 8048; *e-mail:* roy.beggs@btopenworld.com.

BEGLEY, Kim Sean Robert; tenor; *b* 23 June 1952; *s* of late William Begley and of Elizabeth Begley (*née* Cooke); *m* 1986, Elizabeth Mary, *d* of Charles Collier; two *s. Educ:* Rock Ferry High Sch., Birkenhead; Wimbledon Sch. of Art (costume course); Guildhall Sch. of Music and Drama (theory, piano and voice); Nat. Opera Studio. Early career in theatre: Wardrobe Dept, Gateway Th., Chester; acted in Liverpool, Newbury, London and tours; with RSC, 1977–78; many rôles as principal tenor, Royal Opera House, 1983–89: operas included A Midsummer Night's Dream, King Priam, Florentine Tragedy, Otello, Das Rheingold, Tannhäuser, and Katya Kabanová; début: with Glyndebourne Touring Opera as Don Ottavio in Don Giovanni, 1986; with Glyndebourne Festival Opera as Gastone in La Traviata, 1988; subseq. rôles at Glyndebourne include: Graf Elemer in Arabella, 1989; Boris in Katya Kabanová, 1990; High Priest in Idomeneo, and Pellegrin in New Year, 1991; Laca in Jenůfa, 1992; Albert Gregor in The Makropulos Case, 1995 (also WNO, 1994, and Chicago Lyric Opera (US début), 1995); Florestan in Fidelio, 2001; other rôles include: Male Chorus in The Rape of Lucretia, ENO, 1993; Novagerio in Palestrina, 1997, Drum-Major in Wozzeck, 2002, Royal Opera House; also appearances at the Proms, at opera houses in Frankfurt, Geneva, Salzburg, Cologne, and at La Scala, Milan. *Address:* c/o IMG Artists, The Light Box, 111 Power Road, Chiswick, W4 5PY.

BEGOVIĆ, Elvira; General Manager, ONASA Independent News Agency, since 2006 (Executive Manager, 2005–06); *b* 28 Jan. 1961; *d* of Arif and Zejna Dizdarević; *m* 1983, Mirza Begović. *Educ:* Univ. Džemal Bijedić Mostar (BA Econs; postgrad. studies in Mgt and Inf. Technologies). Head Office Manager, Zoitours, Olympic Center, Sarajevo, 1983–95; Exec. Manager, 1995–97, Dir, 1997–98, Futura Media, Mktg and Publishing Agency; Exec. Manager of Internat. Mktg, OSSA Mktg Agency, 1998–99; Dep. Gen. Manager, ONASA Indep. News Agency, 1999–2001; Ambassador of Bosnia and Herzegovina to UK, 2001–05, and, non-resident, to Ireland, 2003–05. First Award, MIT Centre, Sarajevo, 1996; Special Recognition, Orgn of Women in Internat. Trade, USA, 1997. *Publication:* (jtly) Let's Buy Domestic Goods, 1998. *Recreations:* music, walking, reading, theatre, art. *Address:* Dženetića Čikma 10/IV, 71000 Sarajevo, Bosnia and Herzegovina.

BEHAR, Richard Victor Montague Edward; His Honour Judge Behar; a Circuit Judge, since 2000; *b* 14 Feb. 1941; *s* of Edward Behar and Eilleen Behar, *d* of Montague Evans; *m* 1982, Iwona Krystyna (*née* Grabowska); two *s* one *d. Educ:* Stowe Sch. (Schol.); St John's Coll., Oxford (MA). Called to the Bar, Middle Temple, 1965; in practice at the Bar, 1967–2000; SE Circuit; Asst Recorder, 1991–95; a Recorder, 1995–2000; part-time immigration and asylum adjudicator, 1998–2000. Chairman: Bar European Gp, 1988–90; British-Ukrainian Law Assoc., 1993–2000; Co-opted Mem., Internat. Relns Cttee, Gen. Council of Bar, 1988–2000. *Recreations:* foreign languages and travel, cinema, theatre, reading. *Address:* c/o Circuit Secretariat, Rose Court, 2 Southwark Bridge, SE1 9HS. *Clubs:* Oxford and Cambridge, Hurlingham.

BEHARRY, Johnson Gideon, VC 2005; Lance-Corporal, Princess of Wales's Royal Regiment, since 2006; *b* Grenada, 26 July 1979; *s* of Michael Bolah and Florette Beharry. *Educ:* Samaratin Presbyterian Sch., Grenada. Joined Princess of Wales's Royal Regt, 2001; Private, 2001–06. *Publication:* Barefoot Soldier, 2006. *Address:* c/o RHQ Princess of Wales's Royal Regiment, Howe Barracks, Canterbury, Kent CT1 1JY. *T:* (01227) 818095; *e-mail:* regt1-sec@pwrr.army.mod.uk.

BEHRENS, Clive Owen John; His Honour Judge Behrens; a Circuit Judge, since 1996; *b* 14 Sept. 1948; *s* of Col William Edward Behrens and Dulcie Bella Behrens; *m* 1974, Clemency Anne Susan Butler; one *s* one *d. Educ:* Eton Coll.; Trinity Coll., Cambridge (BA Hons). Called to the Bar, Gray's Inn, 1972; in practice at the Bar, 1974–96; specialised in Chancery and commercial work; a Recorder, 1992–96. *Recreations:* golf, bridge, tennis, walking. *Address:* Birstwith House, Harrogate HG3 2NG. *Club:* Alwoodley (Leeds).

BEHRENS-ABOUSEIF, Prof. Doris, PhD; Nasser D. Khalili Professor of Islamic Art and Architecture, School of Oriental and African Studies, University of London, since 2000; *b* 7 Jan. 1946; *d* of Mounir H. Abouseif and Mary Badawy; *m* 1964, Dr Gerhard Behrens; one *s. Educ:* American Univ. of Cairo (MA); Univ. of Hamburg (PhD 1972); Univ. of Freiburg (Habilitation 1992). Privatdozent: Univ. of Freiburg, 1993–95; Univ. of Munich, 1995–2000. Vis. prof. at univs incl. Freie Univ., Berlin, 1995–96, Harvard Univ., 1998, 1999. *Publications:* The Minarets of Cairo, 1985; Islamic Architecture in Cairo: an introduction, 1989; Egypt's Adjustment to Ottoman Rule: institutions, Waqf and architecture in Cairo (16th & 17th centuries), 1994; Beauty in Arabic Culture, 1999; Cairo of the Mamluks: a history of architecture and its culture, 2007; contrib. articles to Encyclopaedia of Islam, Encyclopaedia of the Quran, Annales Islamologiques, Der Islam, Mamluk Studies Rev., Muqarnas. *Recreation:* golf. *Address:* Department of Art and Archaeology, School of Oriental and African Studies, University of London, Thornhaugh Street, Russell Square, WC1H 0XG. *T:* (020) 7898 4455, *Fax:* (020) 7898 4477; *e-mail:* da30@soas.ac.uk.

BEIGHTON, Leonard John Hobhouse, CB 1992; Deputy Chairman, Board of Inland Revenue, 1992–94 (Director General, 1988–92); *b* 20 May 1934; *s* of John Durant Kennedy Beighton, OBE and Leonora Hobhouse; *m* 1962, Judith Valerie Bridge (decd); one *s* one *d. Educ:* Tonbridge Sch.; Corpus Christi College, Oxford (MA PPE). Inland Revenue, 1957; seconded HM Treasury, 1968–69 (Private Sec. to Chief Sec.), and 1977–79. Director: Shared Interest Soc. Ltd, 1994–2003 (Moderator, 1998–2001); World Vision UK, 1997–2007 (Vice Chm., 2002–04, Chm., 2004–07). Member: Council, Shaftesbury Soc., 1995–2007 (Treas., 1998–99); Council, Christians Aware, 2003– (Treas., 2004–09). Trustee, Grooms-Shaftesbury, 2007–. *Address:* 160 Tilt Road, Cobham, Surrey KT11 3HR.

BEITH, Rt Hon. Sir Alan (James), Kt 2008; PC 1992; MP, Berwick-upon-Tweed, since Nov. 1973 (L 1973–88, Lib Dem since 1988); Deputy Leader, Liberal Democrats, 1992–2003; *b* 20 April 1943; *o s* of James and Joan Beith, Poynton, Ches.; *m* 1st, 1965, Barbara Jean Ward (*d* 1998); one *d* (one *s* decd); 2nd, 2001, Baroness Maddock, *qv. Educ:* King's Sch., Macclesfield; Balliol and Nuffield Colls, Oxford (BLitt, MA). Lectr, Dept of Politics, Univ. of Newcastle upon Tyne, 1966–73. Vice-Chm., Northumberland Assoc. of Parish Councils, 1970–71 and 1972–73; Member: Gen. Adv. Council of BBC, 1974–84; Hexham RDC, 1969–74; Corbridge Parish Council, 1970–74; Tynedale District Council, 1973–74; NE Transport Users' Consultative Cttee, 1970–74. Mem., House of Commons Commn, 1979–97; UK Rep. to Council of Europe and WEU, 1976–84. Liberal Chief Whip, 1976–85; Dep. Leader, Liberal Party, 1985–88. Member: Select Cttee on Treasury affairs, 1987–94; Intelligence and Security Cttee, 1994–; Chm., Select Cttee on Constitutional Affairs (formerly LCD), 2003–; Dep. Chm., Speaker's Cttee on Electoral Commn, 2001–03. Trustee, Historic Chapels Trust, 1993– (Chm., 2002–). Hon. DCL Newcastle upon Tyne, 1998. Methodist Local Preacher. *Publications:* The Case for the Liberal Party and the Alliance, 1983; (jtly) Faith and Politics, 1987; chapter in The British General Election of 1964, ed Butler and King, 1965. *Recreations:* walking, music, boating, looking at old buildings. *Address:* House of Commons, SW1A 0AA. *T:* (020) 7219 3540. *Clubs:* Athenæum, National Liberal.

BEKER, Prof. Henry Joseph, PhD; FREng; Chairman, Bladerunner Ltd, since 2001; Visiting Professor of Information Technology, Royal Holloway (formerly Royal Holloway College, then Royal Holloway and Bedford New College), University of London, since 1984; *b* 22 Dec. 1951; *s* of Jozef and Mary Beker; *m* 1976, Mary Louise (*née* Keilthy); two *d. Educ:* Kilburn Grammar Sch.; Univ. of London (BSc Maths 1973, PhD 1976); Open Univ. (BA 1982). CEng, FIET (FIEE 1997; MIEE 1984); FIS (MIS 1977); CStat 1993; CMath, FIMA 1994 (AFIMA 1978). Sen. Res. Asst, Dept of Statistics, University Coll. of Swansea, 1976–77; Principal Mathematician, Racal-Comsec Ltd, 1977–80, Chief Mathematician, 1980–83; Dir of Research, Racal Research Ltd, 1983–85; Dir of Systems, Racal-Chubb Security Systems Ltd, 1985–86; Man. Dir, Racal-Guardata Ltd, 1986–88; Chm., Zergo Hldgs, then Baltimore Technologies plc, 1989–2000 (Chief Exec., 1988–99). Chm., Shopcreator plc, 2000–02; Director: i-NET VCT plc, 2000–02; Close Finsbury Eurotech Trust plc, 2000–02. Chm., e-Learning Foundn, 2000–03. Mem. Council, British Mycological Soc., 2001–03. Vis. Prof. of IT, Westfield Coll., Univ. of London, 1983–84. Pres., IMA, 1998–99 (Vice Pres., 1988–89). Hon. Fellow: RHBNC, 2000; Queen Mary, Univ. of London, 2004. FREng 2000. Freeman, Co. of Information Technologies, 1995. *Publications:* Cipher Systems, 1982; Secure Speech Communications, 1985; Cryptography and Coding, 1989. *Recreations:* mycology, natural history, travel. *Address:* Rue Père de Deken 19, 1040 Brussels, Belgium; *e-mail:* henry@hjbeker.com.

BEKKER, Althea Enid Philippa D.; *see* Dundas-Bekker.

BEKOE, Dr Daniel Adzei; Chairman, Council of State, Republic of Ghana, since 2005 (Member, since 2001); *b* 7 Dec. 1928; *s* of Aristocles Silvanus Adzete Bekoe and Jessie Nadu (*née* Awuletey); *m* 1958, Theresa Victoria Anyisaa Annan (marr. diss. 1983); three *s* (and one *s* decd); *m* 1988, Bertha Augustina Ashia Randolph. *Educ:* Achimota Sch.; University Coll. of Gold Coast (BSc London); Univ. of Oxford (DPhil). Jun. Res. Asst, Univ. of Calif, LA, 1957–58; Univ. of Ghana (formerly University Coll. of Ghana): Lectr, 1958–63; Sen. Lectr, 1963–65; Associate Prof., 1965–74; Prof. of Chemistry, 1974–83; Vice-Chancellor, 1976–83; Dir, UNESCO Regl Office for Sci. and Technol. for Africa, 1983–85; Regl Dir, Internat. Develt Res. Centre, Nairobi, 1986–92. Chm., Ghana Atomic Energy Commn, 2001–06; Mem., Bd of Govs, IAEA, 2004–06. Sabbatical year, Univ. of Calif, LA, 1962–63; Vis. Associate Prof., Univ. of Ibadan, 1966–67. Member: UN Univ. Council, 1980–83; UN Adv. Cttee on Science and Technology for Develt, 1980–82. Chm., Presbyterian Univ. Council, 2003–05. President: ICSU, 1980–83; Ghana Acad. of Arts and Scis, 1993–96; African Assoc. of Pure and Applied Chem., 1995–98. *Publications:* articles on molecular structures in crystallographic and chemical jls; gen. articles in Proc. Ghana Acad. of Arts and Sciences. *Recreation:* music. *Address:* PO Box CT 3383, Accra, Ghana. *T:* (21) 774020.

BELCHER, John William, CBE 2006; PhD; Chief Executive, Anchor Trust, since 1995; *b* 1 May 1947; *m* 1973, Norma Wolffberg; one *s* one *d. Educ:* Univ. of Western Ontario (BA); London Sch. of Econs and Pol Sci. (PhD 1998). Dept of Nat. Health and Welfare, Canada, 1973–78; Lewisham LBC, 1978; Hd, Prog. Planning Div., Social Services, Bexley LBC, 1979–84; Dir, Social Services Div., Scope, 1984–88; Dir, Social Services, Health, Housing, Envmtl Health, Trading Standards, Redbridge LBC, 1988–94. *Address:* Anchor Trust, 2nd Floor, 25 Bedford Street, WC2E 9ES.

BELCHER, Penelope Mary; Her Honour Judge Penelope Belcher; a Circuit Judge, since 2006; *b* 27 Aug. 1957; *d* of Arthur John Lucas and Margaret Elizabeth Lucas; *m* 1985, Simon James Belcher; one *s* one *d. Educ:* St Hugh's Coll., Oxford (BA, MA Jurisprudence). Called to the Bar, Middle Temple, 1980; barrister, 1980–90; attorney, State Bar of Calif, 1988–89; admitted solicitor, 1993; solicitor: Eversheds, 1993–99, Partner, 1995; Hammonds, 2000–06, Asst Dir for Advocacy. *Recreations:* sailing, racket sports, playing flute, classical music, theatre, reading. *Address:* Leeds Combined Court Centre, The Court House, 1 Oxford Row, Leeds LS1 3BG. *T:* (0113) 306 2800; *e-mail:* HHJudgePenelope.Belcher@judiciary.gsi.gov.uk.

BELCOURT, Norma Elizabeth, (Mrs Emile Belcourt); *see* Burrowes, N. E.

BELDAM, Rt Hon. Sir (Alexander) Roy (Asplin), Kt 1981; PC 1989; a Lord Justice of Appeal, 1989–2000; *b* 29 March 1925; *s* of George William Beldam and Margaret Frew Shettle (formerly Beldam, *née* Underwood); *m* 1st, 1953, Elisabeth Bryant Farr (*d* 2005); two *s* one *d*; 2nd, 2007, Elizabeth Mary Warren. *Educ:* Oundle Sch.; Brasenose Coll., Oxford. Sub-Lt, RNVR Air Branch, 1943–46. Called to Bar, Inner Temple, 1950; Bencher, 1977; QC 1969; a Recorder of the Crown Court, 1972–81; Presiding Judge, Wales and Chester Circuit, Jan.–Oct. 1985; a Judge of the High Court of Justice, QBD, 1981–89. Chm., Law Commn, 1985–89. *Recreations:* sailing, cricket, naval history. *Address:* 16 The Riverside, Graburn Way, East Molesey, Surrey KT8 9BF.

BELFALL, David John; Member, Scottish Criminal Cases Review Commission, since 2002; *b* 26 April 1947; *s* of Frederick Belfall and Ada Belfall (*née* Jacobs); *m* 1972, Lorna McLaughlan; one *s* one *d. Educ:* Colchester Royal Grammar Sch.; St John's Coll., Cambridge (BA Hons). Joined Home Office, 1969: Pvte Sec. to Perm. Sec., 1973–74; Sec.

to Lord Scarman's Red Lion Square Inquiry, 1974–75; Principal, Police and Prisons Depts, 1975–82; Asst Sec., Police and Immigration Depts, 1982–88; Under-Secretary, Scottish Office: Emergency Services, Home and Health Dept, 1988–91; Health Policy and Public Health Directorate, 1991–95; Head, Housing and Area Regeneration Gp, Scottish Office, then Scottish Exec., Develt Dept, 1995–2002; Chm., Glasgow Council for the Voluntary Sector, 2002–06. Mem., NHS Lothian Bd, 2004–. *Address:* Scottish Criminal Cases Review Commission, 17 Renfield Street, Glasgow G2 5AH.

BELFAST, Earl of; James Chichester; *b* 19 Nov. 1990; *s* and *heir* of Marquess of Donegall, *qv*.

BELFAST, Dean of; *see* McKelvey, Very Rev. R. S. J. H.

BELHAVEN and STENTON, 13th Lord *cr* 1647; **Robert Anthony Carmichael Hamilton;** *b* 27 Feb. 1927; *o s* of 12th Lord Belhaven and Stenton; *S* father, 1961; *m* 1st, 1952, Elizabeth Ann, *d* of late Col A. H. Moseley, Warrawee, NSW; one *s* one *d*; 2nd, 1973, Rosemary Lady Mactaggart (marr. diss. 1986), *o d* of Sir Herbert Williams, 1st Bt, MP; one *d* (adopted); 3rd, 1986, Malgorzata Maria, *d* of Tadeusz Hruzik-Mazurkiewicz, advocate, Krakow, Poland; one *d*. *Educ:* Eton. Commissioned, The Cameronians, 1947. Commander Cross, Order of Merit (Poland), 1995. *Recreation:* cooking. *Heir: s* Master of Belhaven, *qv*. *Address:* 710 Howard House, Dolphin Square, SW1V 3PQ. *Club:* Carlton.

BELHAVEN, Master of; Hon. Frederick Carmichael Arthur Hamilton; *b* 27 Sept. 1953; *s* of 13th Lord Belhaven and Stenton, *qv*; *m* 1st, 1981, Elizabeth Anne (marr. diss. 1988), *d* of S. V. Tredinnick, Wisborough Green, Sussex; two *s*; 2nd, 1991, Philippa Martha Gausel Whitehead, *d* of Sir Rowland Whitehead, 5th Bt; one *d*. *Educ:* Eton.

BELICH, Sir James, Kt 1990; Mayor of Wellington, New Zealand, 1986–92, retired; *b* 25 July 1927; *s* of Yakov Belich and Maria (*née* Batistich); *m* 1951, Valerie Frances Anzulovich; one *s* two *d*. *Educ:* Otahuhu Coll.; Auckland Univ.; Victoria Univ. of Wellington (BA Hons Econs); IBM Teaching Fellow, Massey Univ. Consular/Internat. Trade, Auckland, Sydney, Wellington, 1948–56; Economist, Market Res. Manager, Dir, Chief Exec. and Chm., Research, Marketing, Public Relns, Advertising, 1956–86. Member: Wellington Harbour Bd; Wellington Regional Council. Director: Air NZ, 1987–89; Lambton Harbour Overview Ltd (Chm.); Wellington Internat. Airport. Pres. and Exec., various orgns incl.: Pres., UNA, Wellington and NZ; Founder Pres., UNICEF, NZ. FInstD; Fellow, Inst. of Advertising. *Recreations:* reading, walking, bowls. *Address:* 4 Indus Street, Khandallah, Wellington 4, New Zealand. *T:* (4) 4793339. *Clubs:* Wellington, Wellington Central Rotary (Wellington).

BELL, family name of **Baron Bell**.

BELL, Baron *cr* 1998 (Life Peer), of Belgravia in the City of Westminster; **Timothy John Leigh Bell,** Kt 1990; Chairman: Bell Pottinger (formerly Lowe Bell) Communications, since 1987; Chime Communications plc, since 1994; *b* 18 Oct. 1941; *s* of Arthur Leigh Bell and Greta Mary Bell (*née* Findlay); *m* 1988, Virginia Wallis Hornbrook; one *s* one *d*. *Educ:* Queen Elizabeth's Grammar Sch., Barnet, Herts. FIPA. ABC Television, 1959–61; Colman Prentis & Varley, 1961–63; Hobson Bates, 1963–66; Geers Gross, 1966–70; Man. Dir, Saatchi & Saatchi, 1970–75; Chm. and Man. Dir, Saatchi & Saatchi Compton, 1975–85; Gp Chief Exec., Lowe Howard-Spink Campbell Ewald, 1985–87; Dep. Chm., Lowe Howard-Spink & Bell, 1987–89. Dir, Centre for Policy Studies, 1989–92. Special Adviser to: Chm., NCB, 1984–86; South Bank Bd, 1985–86. Chm., Charity Projects, 1984–93 (Pres., 1993–). Member: Industry Cttee, SCF; Public Affairs Cttee, WWF, 1985–88; Public Relations Cttee, Greater London Fund for the Blind, 1979–86; Council, Royal Opera House, 1982–85; Steering Cttee, Percent Club. Governor, BFI, 1983–86. Council Mem., Sch. of Communication Arts, 1985–87. *Address:* (office) 14 Curzon Street, W1J 5HN.

BELL, Alan Scott; library and literary consultant; *b* 8 May 1942; *m* 1966, Olivia Butt; one *s* one *d*. *Educ:* Ashville Coll.; Selwyn Coll., Cambridge (MA); MA Oxon 1981. FSA 1996. Asst Registrar, Royal Commn on Historical MSS, 1963–66; Asst Keeper, Nat. Library of Scotland, 1966–81; Librarian: Rhodes House Library, Univ. of Oxford, 1981–93; The London Library, 1993–2002. Vis. Fellow, All Souls Coll., Oxford, 1980. Adv. Editor, Oxford DNB, 1993–. Chm., Marc Fitch Fund, 2001–. *Publications:* (ed) Scott Bicentenary Essays, 1973; (ed) Sir Leslie Stephen's Mausoleum Book, 1978; (ed) Henry Cockburn, 1979; Sydney Smith, 1980; (contrib.) Illustrated History of Oxford University, 1993; (ed) Letters of Lord Cockburn, 2005. *Address:* 38 Danube Street, Edinburgh EH4 1NT; *e-mail:* alan.s.bell@btinternet.com. *Clubs:* Brooks's; New (Edinburgh).

BELL, Alexander Gilmour, CB 1991; Chief Reporter for Public Inquiries, Scottish Office, 1979–93; Inquiry Reporter (Consultant), 1993–2003; *b* 11 March 1933; *s* of Edward and Daisy Bell; *m* 1966, Mary Chisholm; four *s*. *Educ:* Hutchesons' Grammar Sch.; Glasgow Univ. (BL). Admitted Solicitor, 1954. After commercial experience in Far East and in private practice, entered Scottish Office, as Legal Officer, 1967; Dep. Chief Reporter, 1973. *Recreations:* casual outdoor pursuits, choral music.

BELL, His Honour Alistair Watson; a Circuit Judge, 1978–97; *b* Edinburgh, 31 March 1930; *s* of Albert William Bell and Alice Elizabeth Watson; *m* 1957, Patricia Margaret Seed; one *s* two *d*. *Educ:* Lanark Grammar Sch.; George Watson's Coll.; Univs of Edinburgh (MA) and Oxford (MA, BCL). 2nd Lieut RASC, 1955. Called to Bar, Middle Temple, 1955; Harmsworth Scholar, 1956; entered practice, Northern Circuit, 1957; a Recorder of the Crown Court, 1972–78. Hon. Recorder, Carlisle, 1990–98. Contested (L) Chorley, 1964 and Westmorland, 1966. *Recreations:* hill walking, with or without golf clubs, political history and economics. *Address:* c/o Courts of Justice, Carlisle.

BELL, Andrew Montgomery; Sheriff of Lothian and Borders, 1990–2004; *b* 21 Feb. 1940; *s* of James Montgomery Bell and Mary Bell (*née* Cavaye), Edinburgh; *m* 1969, Ann Margaret Robinson; one *s* one *d*. *Educ:* Royal High Sch., Edinburgh; Univ. of Edinburgh (BL). Solicitor, 1961–74; called to Bar, 1975; Sheriff of S Strathclyde, Dumfries and Galloway at Hamilton, 1979–84; Sheriff of Glasgow and Strathkelvin, 1984–90. *Publication:* (contrib.) Stair Memorial Encyclopaedia of Scots Law, 1995. *Recreations:* reading, listening to music. *Address:* 5 York Road, Trinity, Edinburgh EH5 3EJ. *T:* (0131) 552 3859. *Club:* New (Edinburgh).

BELL, Sir Brian (Ernest), KBE 1994 (OBE 1977); Chairman and Managing Director, Brian Bell & Co. Ltd, since 1956; *b* 3 July 1928; *s* of Ernest James Bell and Evelyn Ivy Alice Bell (*née* Zeller); *m* 1962, Jean Ann Clough (*d* 1992); one *s* one *d*. *Educ:* Chinchilla State Sch., Qld, Australia; Toowoomba Grammar Sch., Qld; Queensland Univ. (pharmaceutical chemist, 1949). Went to Papua New Guinea, 1954; Bulk Med. Store, Dept of Health, 1954–56; estabd first Appliance and Service Orgn, 1956. Mem., first Port Moresby CC, 1971–88 (Dep. Lord Mayor, 1973). Citizen of PNG, 1976. Hon. Consul for: Sweden, 1974–88 (Consul Gen., 1988–2005); Norway, 1984–88 (Consul Gen., 1988–2004). Chm., Port Moresby Gen. Hosp. Mem., Salvation Army Adv. Bd, PNG, 1987–. Chm., Univ. of PNG Foundn, 1985–. Independence Medal (PNG), 1975; Silver Jubilee Medal, 1977; Tenth Anniversary Medal (PNG), 1985. CStJ 2004. Comdr, Royal Order of Polar Star (Sweden), 1990; Comdr, Royal Order of Merit (Norway), 2004 (Kt 1st Cl. 1992); Companion, Star of Melanesia (PNG), 2005. *Recreation:* interest in community affairs. *Address:* Brian Bell and Co. Ltd, PO Box 1228, Boroko, Papua New Guinea. *T:* 3255411; *e-mail:* bbadmin@brianbell.com.pg. *Club:* Papua (Port Moresby).

BELL, Catherine Elisabeth Dorcas, (Mrs R. J. Weber), CB 2003; PhD; Acting Permanent Secretary, Department of Trade and Industry, 2005; *b* 26 April 1951; *d* of late Frank Douglas Howe and of Phyllis (*née* Walsh); *m* 1993, Richard John Weber; one *s*. *Educ:* Balshaw's Grammar Sch., Leyland, Lancs; Girton Coll., Cambridge (MA); Univ. of Kent (PhD). Joined Department of Trade and Industry, 1975; Pvte Sec. to Sec. of State for Trade and Industry, 1980–81; Principal, 1981; Asst Sec., 1986; Under Sec., 1991; Head of Competition Policy Div., 1991–93; maternity leave, 1993–94; Resident Chm., CSSB, 1994–95; Hd of Central Policy Unit, 1995–97; Dir, Utilities Review Team, 1997–99, and Competition Policy, 1998–99; Dir Gen., Corporate and Consumer Affairs, subseq. Competition and Markets Gp, 1999–2002; Dir Gen., Services Gp, 2002–05. Non-executive Director: Swiss Re (UK), 1999–; CAA, 2006–; Ensus Ltd, 2006–; United Utilities, 2007–. *Recreations:* opera, ski-ing, gardening.

BELL, (Charles) Trevor; General Secretary, Colliery Officials and Staffs Area of the National Union of Mineworkers, 1979–89; Member, National Executive Committee of the National Union of Mineworkers, 1979–89; *b* 22 Sept. 1927; *s* of Charles and Annie Bell; *m* 1974, Patricia Ann Tappin. *Educ:* state schools; Technical Coll. (City and Guilds Engrg); Coleg Harlech, N Wales (Trades Union scholarship, 1955). Craftsman in coal mining industry, 1941. Mem., Labour Party, 1946–. *Recreations:* gardening, reading, bowls. *Address:* Wakefield, West Yorks.

BELL, Cressida Iras; textile and interior designer; Director, Cressida Bell Ltd, since 1984; *b* 13 April 1959; *d* of late Prof. Quentin Bell, FRSL and of (Anne) Olivier Bell (*née* Popham). *Educ:* St Martin's Sch. of Art (BA Hons Fashion); Royal Coll. of Art (MA). Group exhibitions include: Duncan Grant & Cressida Bell, Sally Hunter Fine Art, 1984; Scarf Show, Liberty's, 1987; Arts & Crafts to Avant-Garde, RFH, 1992; Colour into Cloth, Crafts Council, 1994; Bloomsbury: 3 Generations, NY, 1996. Commissions include: scarf for BM, 1988; scarf for V&A, 1992; book jacket, Song of Love, 1991; interiors, Soho Studios, 1994–; carpet for British Consulate, Hong Kong, 1996. *Publication:* The Decorative Painter, 1996. *Recreations:* travel, cookery, dress-making.

BELL, Sir David (Charles Maurice), Kt 2004; Chairman, Financial Times Group, since 1996; Director for People, Pearson plc, since 1998; *b* 30 Sept. 1946; *s* of Roderick Martin Bell and Mary Frances Bell (*née* Wade); *m* 1972, Primrose Frances Moran; two *s* one *d*. *Educ:* Worth Sch.; Trinity Hall, Cambridge (BA 2nd Cl. Hons Hist.); Univ. of Pennsylvania (MA Econs and Pol Sci.). Oxford Mail and Times, 1970–72; Financial Times, 1972–: Washington Corresp., 1975–78; News Editor, Internat. Edn, 1978–80; Features Editor, 1980–85; Man. Editor, 1985–89; Advertisement Dir, 1989–93; Marketing Dir, 1992–93; Chief Exec., 1993–96. Dir, Pearson plc, 1996–. Pres., Les Echos, 2003–07. Trustee, Common Purpose, 1994–; Chairman: Millennium Bridge Trust, 1997–; Internat. Youth Foundn, 1998–2006; Crisis, 2001–; Sadler's Wells, 2005–; Internat. Inst. for War and Peace Reporting, 2006–; Acting Chm., Media Standards Trust, 2006–. *Recreations:* cycling, theatre, Victorian social history. *Address:* 35 Belitha Villas, N1 1PE. *T:* (020) 7609 4000. *Club:* Garrick.

BELL, David John, CB 1998; FRICS; Commissioner of Valuation for Northern Ireland, 1988–98; Chief Executive, Valuation and Lands Agency, 1993–98; *b* 17 March 1938; *s* of James Bell and Elizabeth Bell; *m* 1962, Agnes Mona Eileen; two *d*. *Educ:* Regent House GS. FRICS 1981. Sen. Valuation Asst, Valuer I, Valuation Office, 1963–70; Department of the Environment, Northern Ireland: Divl Estates Surveyor (Belfast), 1975–80; Superintending Estates Surveyor, 1980–82; Chief Lands Officer, Lands Service, 1982–84; Asst Comr, 1984–87, Dep. Comr, 1987–88, Valuation and Lands Office, Dept of Finance and Personnel, NI. Hon. Fellow, Irish Auctioneers and Valuers Inst., 1996. *Recreations:* reading, gardening, church work, golf. *Address:* 1 Rockmount, Dundonald, Belfast BT16 2BY. *T:* (028) 9048 4241.

BELL, David Mackintosh; HM Diplomatic Service, retired; *b* 2 Aug. 1939; *s* of late David Little Bell and Kathleen Bell (*née* McBurnie); *m* 1st, 1963, Ann Adair Wilson (marr. diss.); one *s* one *d*; 2nd, 1996, Dominique Van Hille; two *s*. *Educ:* Ayr Acad.; Glasgow Univ. (MA 1959). Commonwealth Relations Office, 1960; served Karachi, Enugu, Havana and Mexico City; FCO, 1968–71; Budapest, 1971–74; 2nd, later 1st Sec., FCO, 1974–77; Commercial Consul, NY, 1977–81; FCO, 1981–86; Press Sec., Bonn, 1986–90; Consul-General, Lille, 1990–95; Consul-Gen., Zürich, and Dir, British Export Promotion in Switzerland and Liechtenstein, 1995–97. Lectr in Internat. Business Studies, Institut Supérieur Européen de Gestion, Lille, 1997–2002. Chm., British Community Assoc., Lille, 2002–05. *Recreations:* reading, crosswords, cooking. *Address:* 6 rue de Wattignies, 59139 Noyelles-lez-Seclin, France. *T:* (3) 20327910; *e-mail:* david.bell59139@orange.fr.

BELL, David Robert; Permanent Secretary, Department for Children, Schools and Families (formerly Department for Education and Skills), since 2006; *b* 31 March 1959; *s* of Robert Bell and Marie Blackie Slater Bell; *m* 1981, Louise Caroline Poole; two *d*. *Educ:* Univ. of Glasgow (MA, MEd); Jordanhill Coll. of Educn (PGCE Primary). Teacher, Cuthbertson Primary Sch., Glasgow, 1982–85; Dep. Headteacher, Powers Hall Jun. Sch., Essex, 1985–88; Headteacher, Kingston Primary Sch., Essex, 1988–90; Asst Dir of Educn, Newcastle CC, 1990–93 and 1994–95; Harkness Fellow, Atlanta, Georgia, 1993–94; Chief Educn Officer, 1995–98, Dir of Educn and Libraries, 1998–2000, Newcastle CC; Chief Exec., Beds CC, 2000–02; HM Chief Inspector of Schs, 2002–05. DUniv Strathclyde, 2004. *Publications:* Parents' Guide to the National Curriculum (Primary), 1991; Parents' Guide to the National Curriculum (Secondary), 1991; Inspirations for History, 1992; Bright Ideas: maths projects, 1992. *Recreations:* reading, Rushden and Diamonds FC, keeping fit. *Address:* Department for Children, Schools and Families, Sanctuary Buildings, Great Smith Street, SW1P 3BT. *T:* (020) 7925 6938; *e-mail:* permanent.secretary@dcsf.gsi.gov.uk.

BELL, Dr Donald Atkinson, CEng; Technical Director, Marchland Consulting Ltd, 1991–2004; *b* 28 May 1941; *s* of late Robert Hamilton Bell and Gladys Mildred Bell; *m* 1967, Joyce Louisa Godber; two *s*. *Educ:* Royal Belfast Academical Instn; Queen's Univ., Belfast (BSc); Southampton Univ. (PhD); Glasgow Univ. (MSc). FIMechE; MIET; FBCS. National Physical Lab., 1966–77; Dept of Industry, 1978–82; Dir, Nat. Engrg Lab., 1983–90; Hd of R&D, Strathclyde Inst., 1990–91. *Address:* 32 Elmfield Avenue, Teddington, Middx TW11 8BS. *T:* (020) 8943 1326; *e-mail:* donald@marchland.org.

BELL, Donald L.; *see* Lynden-Bell.

BELL, Prof. Donald Munro; international concert and opera artist; freelance singer; Professor of Music, Calgary University, since 1982; *b* 19 June 1934; one *s*. *Educ:* South

Burnaby High Sch., BC, Canada. Made Wigmore Hall (recital) debut, 1958; since then has sung at Bayreuth Wagner Festival, 1958, 1959, 1960; Lucerne and Berlin Festivals, 1959; Philadelphia and New York debuts with Eugene Ormandy, 1959; Israel, 1962; Russia Recital Tour, 1963; Glyndebourne Festival, 1963, 1974, 1982; with Deutsche Oper am Rhein, Düsseldorf, 1964–67; Scottish National Opera, 1974; Scottish Opera, 1978; Basler Kammer Orchestre, 1978; Australian Tour (Musica Viva), 1980. Prof. and Head of Vocal Dept, Ottawa Univ., 1979–82. Directed Opera Workshop at Univ. of Calgary, 1982–89; Artistic Dir, Univ. of Calgary Celebrity Series, 2004–08. Member: Nat. Assoc. of Teachers of Singing, 1985–; Nat. Opera Assoc., 1985– (Dir, Alberta Br., 1986–90, for Canada, 1988–90). Has made recordings. Arnold Bax Medal, 1955. *Address:* University of Calgary, Faculty of Fine Arts, Department of Music, 2500 University Drive NW, Calgary, Alberta T2N 1N4, Canada; *e-mail:* dmbell@ucalgary.ca.

BELL, Edward; Chairman, Bell Lomax Literary and Sport Agency, since 2002; *b* 2 Aug. 1949; *s* of Eddie and Jean Bell; *m* 1969, Junette Bannatyne; one *s* two *d*. *Educ:* Airdrie High Sch. Cert. of Business Studies. With Hodder & Stoughton, 1970–85; Man. Dir, Collins General Div., 1985–89; launched Harper Paperbacks in USA, 1989; HarperCollins UK: Publisher, 1990–2000; Dep. Chief Exec., 1990–91; Chief Exec., 1991–92; Chm., 1992–2000; Chm., HarperCollins India, 1994–2000. Non-executive Director: beCogent Ltd, 2000–; Haynes Publishing Gp plc, 2000–; Management Diagnostics Ltd, 2000–. *Recreations:* reading, golf, supporting Arsenal, opera, collecting old books. *Address:* Bell Lomax Agency, James House, 1 Babmaes Street, SW1Y 6HF. *T:* (020) 7930 4447, *Fax:* (020) 7925 0118. *Clubs:* Royal Automobile; AutoWink (Epsom); Addington Golf (Croydon).

BELL, Emily Jane; Director of Digital Content, Guardian News and Media, since 2006; *b* 14 Sept. 1965; *d* of Peter Bell and Bridget Bell; *m* 1994, Edmund Hugh Crooks; three *s*. *Educ:* Christ Church, Oxford (BA Juris. 1987). Reporter: Big Farm Weekly, 1987–88; Campaign, 1988–90; The Observer: reporter, 1990–96; Dep. Business Ed., 1996–98; Business Ed., 1998–2000; Founder and Ed., MediaGuardian.co.uk, 2000; Ed.-in-Chief, Guardian Unlimited, 2001–06. *Publication:* (with Chris Alden) The Media Directory, 2004. *Recreations:* child rearing, cooking, season ticket holder Arsenal FC. *Address:* Guardian News and Media, Kings Place, 90 York Way, N1 9AG; *e-mail:* emily.bell@guardian.co.uk.

BELL, Geoffrey Lakin; President, Geoffrey Bell and Co., New York, since 1982; Chairman, Guinness Mahon Holdings, 1987–93; *b* 8 Nov. 1939; *s* of Walter Lakin Bell and Ann (*née* Barnes); *m* 1973, Joan Abel; one *d*. *Educ:* Grimsby Technical Sch.; London School of Economics and Political Science. Economic Asst, HM Treasury, 1961–63; Vis. Scholar, Fed. Reserve System, principally with Federal Reserve Bank of St Louis, 1963–64; HM Treasury, also Special Lectr at LSE, 1964–66; Economic Advr, British Embassy, Washington, 1966–69; 1969–82: Asst to Chm., J. Henry Schroder Wagg; Dir, Schroder Wagg; Exec. Vice Pres., Schroder Internat. and Sen. Advr, Schroder Bank and Trust Co., NY; Special Columnist on Econs and Finance, The Times, 1969–74; Exec. Sec. and Mem., Gp of Thirty, 1978–. Mem., Court of Govs, LSE, 1994–. Cons. Editor, International Reports, 1983–93. *Publications:* The Euro-Dollar Market and the International Financial System, 1973; numerous articles on internat. econs and finance in UK and USA. *Address:* 17 Abbotsbury House, Abbotsbury Road, W14 8EN. *T:* (020) 7603 9408; 455 East 57th Street, New York, NY, USA. *T:* (212) 8381193. *Club:* Reform.

BELL, Graham Andrew; television presenter; Presenter, BBC Ski Sunday, since 2001; *b* Akrotiri, Cyprus, 4 Jan. 1966; *s* of Rod and Jean Bell; *m* 1991, Sarah Edwards; one *s* one *d*. *Educ:* George Watson's Coll. British Alpine Ski Team, 1982–98; British Olympic Team, 1984, 1988, 1992, 1994, 1998; Performance Dir, Snowsport GB, 1999–2003; commentator, Eurosport, 1998–2001. *Recreations:* ski-ing, cycling, triathlon, dangerous stuff, science. *Address:* Cunningham Management, London House, 271 King Street, W6 9LZ. *T:* (020) 8233 2824; *e-mail:* info@cunningham-management.co.uk. *Club:* Kandahar Ski.

BELL, Griffin Boyette; Attorney-General, USA, 1977–79; Senior Counsel, King and Spalding, Atlanta, since 2004; *b* Americus, Georgia, 31 Oct. 1918; *s* of A. C. Bell and Thelma Pilcher; *m* 1st, 1943, Mary Foy Powell (*d* 2000); one *s*; 2nd, 2001, Nancy Duckworth Kinnebrew. *Educ:* Southwestern Coll., Ga; Mercer Univ. (LLB *cum laude* 1948, LLD 1967). Served AUS, 1941–46, reaching rank of Major. Admitted to Georgia Bar, 1947; practice in Savannah and Rome, 1947–53. Partner in King and Spalding, Atlanta, 1953–59, 1976–77, 1979–2004, Managing Partner, 1959–61; United States Judge, 5th Circuit, 1961–76. Chairman: Atlanta Commn on Crime and Delinquency, 1965–66; CSCE, 1980. Mem., Vis. Cttee, Law Sch., Vanderbilt Univ.; Trustee, Mercer Univ.; Member: Amer. Law Inst.; Amer. Coll. of Trial Lawyers (Pres., 1985–86). *Address:* King & Spalding, 1180 Peachtree Street, Atlanta, GA 30309, USA.

BELL, Guy Davies; Director, BAA plc, 1988–89; Managing Director, Gatwick Airport Ltd, 1985–89; *b* 19 May 1933; *s* of Percival and Margaret Bell; *m* 1958, Angela Mary Joan Bickersteth; two *s* one *d* (and one *s* decd). *Educ:* Sedbergh Sch. British Transport Docks Bd, 1963–68; British Airports Authority, 1968–86, Engrg Dir, 1977–85; BAA, 1986–89. *Recreations:* gardening, open air, music. *Club:* Royal Automobile.

BELL, Howard James; Chief Executive, Provident Financial plc, 1997–2001; *b* 28 March 1944; *m* 1969, Susan Vivienne Fell; one *s* (one *d* decd). *Educ:* Bradford Univ. (MBA). Yorkshire Imperial Metals Ltd, 1963–67; Provident Financial plc, 1967–2001: computer systems analyst, 1967–72; personnel and trng, 1972–80; Line Manager, 1980–89; Dir, 1989–2001. Chm., Invocas Gp plc, 2006–. Chm., Meningitis Res. Foundn, 1997–2005. *Recreations:* sport, travel.

BELL, Prof. Ian Frederick Andrew, PhD; Professor of American Literature, University of Keele, since 1992; *b* 31 Oct. 1947; *s* of Frederick George Bell and Cecilia Bell; *m* 1983, Elizabeth Mary Tagart (marr. diss. 1989); two *s*; one *s*. *Educ:* West Bridgford Grammar Sch.; Univ. of Reading (BA 1970; PhD 1978). Lectr, Sen. Lectr and Reader in Amer. Lit., Univ. of Keele, 1973–92. *Publications:* Critic as Scientist: the modernist poetics of Ezra Pound, 1981; (ed) Ezra Pound: tactics for reading, 1982; (ed) Henry James: fiction as history, 1984; (ed jtly) American Literary Landscapes: the fiction and the fact, 1988; Henry James and the Past: readings into time, 1991; (ed) The Best of O. Henry, 1993; Washington Square: styles of money, 1993. *Recreations:* visual arts, cinema, ferret wrangling. *Address:* Department of American Studies, University of Keele, Staffs ST5 5BG. *T:* (01782) 583012.

BELL, Rt Rev. James Harold; *see* Knaresborough, Bishop Suffragan of.

BELL, Janet; *see* Browne, E. J.

BELL, Prof. Jeanne Elisabeth, (Mrs D. Rutovitz), CBE 2007; MD; FRCPath, FMedSci; FRSE; Professor of Neuropathology, University of Edinburgh, 1999–2007, now Emeritus; Hon. Consultant in Neuropathology, Western General Hospital, Edinburgh, since 1999; *b* 10 Aug. 1942; *d* of Rhys and Joan Hall; *m* 1983, Dr Denis Rutovitz, MBE; two step *s* two step *d*, and one *s* from former marr. *Educ:* Univ. of Newcastle upon Tyne (BSc Hons Anatomy 1963; MD 1972); Univ. of Durham (MB BS 1966). FRCPath 1995. Lectr in Anatomy, Univ. of Newcastle upon Tyne, 1967–70; Res. Officer, MRC Human Genetics Unit, Edinburgh, 1974–79; Sen. Registrar in Paediatric Pathology, Royal Hosp. for Sick Children, Edinburgh, 1979–84; Sen. Lectr in Neuropathol., Univ. of Edinburgh, 1984–99. FRSE 1998; FMedSci 2002. *Publications:* (jtly) Colour Atlas of Neuropathology, 1995; contrib. chapters on develt and forensic, psychiatric and neurol medicine; scientific papers and reviews in neurosci. jls. *Recreations:* travel, handicrafts, films, looking after grandchildren, humanitarian aid work (founded Edinburgh Direct Aid with husband, 1992). *Address:* CJD Surveillance Unit, Bryan Matthews Building, Western General Hospital, Crewe Road, Edinburgh EH4 2XU. *T:* (0131) 537 2145, *Fax:* (0131) 343 1404; *e-mail:* Jeanne.Bell@ed.ac.uk.

BELL, Dame Jocelyn; *see* Bell Burnell, Dame S. J.

BELL, Sir John (Irving), Kt 2008; DM; FRCP; FRS 2008; Regius Professor of Medicine, University of Oxford, since 2002; Student of Christ Church, Oxford, since 2002; *b* 1 July 1952; *s* of Robert Edward Bell and Mary Agnes (*née* Wholey). *Educ:* Univ. of Alberta, Canada (BSc Medicine); Oxford Univ. (BA Hons Physiol Sci.; BM, BCh; DM 1990). FRCP 1992. Rhodes Scholar, Univ. of Alberta and Magdalen Coll., Oxford, 1975. Postgraduate training in medicine, 1979–82 (John Radcliffe Hosp., Hammersmith Hosp., Guy's Hosp., Nat. Hosp. for Neurol Disease); Clinical Fellow in Immunology, Stanford Univ., USA, 1982–87; University of Oxford: Wellcome Sen. Clin. Fellow, 1987–89; University Lectr, 1989–92; Nuffield Prof. of Clin. Medicine, 1992–2002; Fellow, Magdalen Coll., 1990–2002. Mem., MRC, 1996–2002. Chm., OSCHR, 2006–. Founder FMedSci 1998 (Pres., 2006–). Sen. Mem., OUBC, 1996–. *Publications:* scientific papers in immunology and genetics. *Recreations:* rowing, swimming, sailing. *Address:* Christ Church, Oxford OX1 1DP. *Clubs:* Leander (Henley-on-Thames); Vincent's (Oxford).

BELL, Sir John Lowthian, 5th Bt *cr* 1885; *b* 14 June 1960; *s* of Sir Hugh Francis Bell, 4th Bt and Lady Bell (*d* 1990) (Mary Howson, MB, ChB, *d* of late George Howson, The Hyde, Hambledon); *S* father, 1970; *m* 1985, Venetia, *d* of J. A. Perry, Taunton; one *s* one *d*. *Recreations:* shooting, fishing. *Heir:* *s* John Hugh Bell, *b* 29 July 1988.

BELL, Prof. (John) Nigel (Berridge), PhD; Professor of Environmental Pollution, Imperial College London, since 1989; *b* 26 April 1943; *s* of John Edward Donald Bell and Dorothy Elise Bell (*née* White); *m* 1st, 1970, Jennifer Margaret Pollard (marr. diss. 1977); 2nd, 1978, Carolyn Mary Davies (marr. diss. 1992); three *s*; 3rd, 2006, Elinor Margaret Lord. *Educ:* County Grammar Sch. of King Edward VII, Melton Mowbray; Univ. of Manchester (BSc Botany 1964; PhD Plant Ecol. 1969); Univ. of Waterloo, Ont. (MSc Biol. 1965; Science Alumnus of Honour 2007). Teaching Fellow, Univ. of Waterloo, 1964–65; Res. Asst, Bedford Coll., Univ. of London, 1968–70; Imperial College, University of London: Res. Asst, 1970–72; Lectr, 1972–83; Sen. Lectr, 1983–87; Reader in Envmtl Pollution, 1987–89; Dir, Centre for Envmtl Technology, 1986–94; Dir, MSc in Envtl Technol. (formerly MSc Studies), 1994–; Head, Agricl and Envmtl Mgt Sect., Dept of Biology, 1986–2001. Hon. DES Waterloo, 1998. *Publications:* (ed) Ecological Aspects of Radionuclide Releases, 1983; Air Pollution Injury to Vegetation, 1986; (ed) Acid Rain and Britain's Natural Ecosystems, 1988; Air Pollution and Forest Health in the European Community, 1990; (ed) Air Pollution and Plant Life, 2nd edn 2002; Biosphere Implications of Deep Disposal of Nuclear Waste, 2007; numerous papers in jls on air pollution and radioactive pollution. *Recreations:* classical music, travel, walking, railways. *Address:* Centre for Environmental Policy, Mechanical Engineering Building, Imperial College London, SW7 2AZ. *T:* (020) 7594 9288; 48 Western Elms Avenue, Reading, Berks RG30 2AN. *T:* (0118) 958 0653.

BELL, Prof. John Stephen, DPhil; FBA 1999; Professor of Law, University of Cambridge, since 2001; Fellow, Pembroke College, Cambridge, since 2001; *b* 5 May 1953; *s* of Harry Bell and Elsie Bell (*née* Walmsley); *m* 1983, Sheila Brookes; two *s*. *Educ:* Trinity Coll., Cambridge (BA 1974; MA 1977); Gregorian Univ., Rome (Baccalaureus in Philosophy 1976); Wadham Coll., Oxford (DPhil 1980). Asst, Inst de droit comparé, Paris II, 1974–75; Fellow and Tutor in Law, Wadham Coll., Oxford, 1979–89; Leeds University: Prof. of Public and Comparative Law, 1989–2001; Pro-Vice Chancellor for Teaching, 1992–94. Professeur associé: Univs of Paris I and Paris II, 1985–86; Univ. du Maine, 1995–96; Vis. Prof., Katholieke Univ., Brussels, 1993–. Mem., Res. Council, Eur. Univ. Inst., Florence, 1997–2003. Pres., SPTL, 1998–99. FRSA 1995. Hon. QC 2003. *Publications:* Policy Arguments in Judicial Decisions, 1983; French Constitutional Law, 1992; (with L. N. Brown) French Administrative Law, 4th edn 1993, 5th edn 1998; (with G. Engle) Cross on Statutory Interpretation, 3rd edn 1995; (jtly) Principles of French Law, 1998; (contrib.) New Directions in European Public Law, 1998; French Legal Cultures, 2001; Judiciaries within Europe, 2006; contribs to learned jls. *Recreation:* learning and speaking foreign languages. *Address:* Faculty of Law, University of Cambridge, 10 West Road, Cambridge CB3 9DZ.

BELL, Dr Jonathan Richard, CB 2006; CSci; CChem, FRSC; Director, Jon Bell Associates Ltd, since 2006; *b* 12 Nov. 1947; *s* of late Stanley and Marjorie Bell; *m* 1971, Lynne Trezise; one *s*. *Educ:* Cambridge Grammar Sch. for Boys; Univ. of Hull (BSc 1969; PhD 1972). CChem 1973, FRSC 1992; CSci 2005. Post doctoral researcher, Dyon Perrins Lab., Univ. of Oxford, 1973–74; Packaging Chemist, Metal Box Co., 1974–75; Ministry of Agriculture, Fisheries and Food, 1975–2000: Head: Food Sci. Div. I, 1989–92; Food Sci. Div. II, 1992–95; Additives and Novel Food Div., 1995–2000; Food Standards Agency: Dir, Food Safety Policy, Chief Scientific Advr and Dep. Chief Exec., 2000–03; Chief Exec. and Chief Scientific Advr, 2003–06. *T:* 0871 855 2988; *e-mail:* jon.bell@jonbellassociates.co.uk.

BELL, Joshua; violinist; *b* Indiana, 9 Dec. 1967; *s* of Alan and Shirley Bell. *Educ:* Sch. of Music, Univ. of Indiana (studied with Josef Gingold). Internat. début with Philadelphia Orch., 1981; performances with orchs in Europe, USA and Canada incl. Royal Philharmonic, London Philharmonic, BBC Symphony, Philharmonia, CBSO, Chicago Symphony, Boston Symphony, LA Philharmonic, NY Philharmonic and Cleveland Orch. Recitals in Europe and USA. Vis. Prof., Royal Acad. of Music, 1997–. Numerous recordings (Grammy Award, 2001). Mercury Music Prize, 2000. *Recreations:* golf, tennis, computers. *Address:* c/o IMG Artists, The Light Box, 111 Power Road, Chiswick, W4 5PY.

BELL, Leslie Gladstone, CEng, FRINA; RCNC; Director of Naval Ship Production, Ministry of Defence, 1977–79, retired; *b* 20 Oct. 1919; *s* of late John Gladstone Bell and Jessie Gray Bell (*née* Quigley); *m* 1963, Adriana Agatha Jacoba van den Berg; one *s* one *d*. *Educ:* Portsmouth Dockyard Tech. Coll.; Royal Naval Engineering Coll., Keyham; Royal Naval Coll., Greenwich. Staff Constructor Cdr, Home Fleet, 1953–56; Aircraft Carrier Design, 1956–59; Chief Constructor, Weapon Development, 1959–67; IDC, 1968; Asst Dir, Submarine Design, 1969–72; Director, Submarine Project Team, 1972–77. *Recreations:* gardening, golf, music. *Address:* Haytor, Old Midford Road, Bath, Avon BA2 7DH. *T:* (01225) 833357. *Club:* Bath Golf.

BELL, Lindsay Frances; Director, Local Government Finance, Department for Communities and Local Government (formerly Office of the Deputy Prime Minister), since 2004; *b* 29 April 1950; one *s* one *d*. *Educ:* University Coll. London (BA 1971); St Anne's Coll., Oxford (BPhil 1973). Department of the Environment, later Department of the Environment, Transport and the Regions, subseq. Office of the Deputy Prime Minister, 1975–: Head: Finance Deptl Services, 1987–89; Water Regulation Div., 1989–90; Local Govt Reorgn Div., 1990–94; Local Authy Grants, 1994–97; Dir, Regl Policy, 1997–2000; Dep. Hd, Domestic Affairs, Cabinet Office (on secondment), 2000–03; Dir, Strategy, Neighbourhood Renewal Unit, 2003–04. *Address:* Department for Communities and Local Government, 5/E2 Eland House, Bressenden Place, SW1E 5DU.

BELL, Marcus David John; Director of Workforce Strategy, Department for Children, Schools and Families, since 2008; *b* N Tarrytown, NY, 10 Nov. 1966; *s* of Colin James Bell and Kathleen Bell; *m* 1999, Deborah Parkin; twin *s*. *Educ:* Winchester Coll. (Schol.); Balliol Coll., Oxford (Markby Schol.; BA Hons Hist. and Mod. Langs). Admin trainee, DES, 1989–92; Private Sec., Chancellor of Duchy of Lancaster, 1992–93; Principal, DFE, 1993–96; Registrar, Bishop Grosseteste Coll., Lincoln, 1996–98; Principal, DFEE, 1998–2001; Deputy Director: Social Exclusion Unit, Cabinet Office, 2001–04; Young People at Risk Div., DFES, then DCSF, 2004–08. *Recreations:* cooking, cycling. *Address:* Department for Children, Schools and Families, Sanctuary Buildings, Great Smith Street, SW1P 3BT. *T:* (020) 7925 5000.

BELL, Marian Patricia, CBE 2005; economist; Member, Monetary Policy Committee, Bank of England, 2002–05; *b* 28 Oct. 1957; *d* of Joseph Denis Milburn Bell and Wilhelmenia Maxwell Bell (*née* Miller). *Educ:* Hertford Coll., Oxford (BA PPE); Birkbeck Coll., London (MSc Econs). Sen. Economist, Royal Bank of Scotland, 1985–89; Econ. Advr, HM Treasury, 1989–91; Sen. Treasury Economist, 1991–97; Hd of Res., Treasury and Capital Mkts, Royal Bank of Scotland, 1997–2000; Consultant, alpha economics, 2000–02, 2005–. Dep. Chm., Forum for Global Health Protection Community Interest Co., 2006–. Gov., Contemporary Dance Trust, The Place, 2005–.

BELL, Martin, OBE 1992; Ambassador (formerly Special Representative) for Humanitarian Emergencies, UNICEF, since 2001; *b* 31 Aug. 1938; *s* of late Adrian Hanbury Bell and Marjorie H. Bell; *m* 1st, 1971, Nelly Lucienne Gourdon (marr. diss.); two *d*; 2nd, 1985, Rebecca D. Sobel (marr. diss.); 3rd, 1998, Fiona Goddard. *Educ:* The Leys Sch., Cambridge; King's Coll., Cambridge (MA). BBC TV News: Reporter, 1965–77; Diplomatic Correspondent, 1977–78; Chief Washington Correspondent, 1978–89; Berlin Correspondent, 1989–93; E European Correspondent, 1993–94; Foreign Affairs Correspondent, 1994–96; Special Correspondent, BBC Nine O'Clock News, 1997. Pool TV Reporter, 7th Armoured Bde, Gulf War, 1991. MP (Ind.) Tatton, 1997–2001. Contested (Ind.) Brentwood and Ongar, 2001. Pres., Japanese Labour Camp Survivors' Assoc., 2001–. DUniv Derby, 1996; Hon. MA: East Anglia, 1997; N London, 1997; Hon. DLit Kingston, 2002. RTS Reporter of the Year, 1977, TV Journalist of the Year, 1992. *Publications:* In Harm's Way, 1995; An Accidental MP, 2000; Through Gates of Fire, 2003; The Truth that Sticks: New Labour's breach of trust, 2007. *Address:* 71 Denman Drive, NW11 6RA.

BELL, Martin George Henry; Senior Partner, Ashurst Morris Crisp, 1986–92; *b* 16 Jan. 1935; *s* of Leonard George Bell and Phyllis Bell (*née* Green); *m* 1965, Shirley Wrightson; two *s*. *Educ:* Charterhouse. Nat. Service, 1953–55. Articles, 1956–61, admitted Solicitor, 1961, Assistant, 1961, Partner, 1963, Ashurst Morris Crisp. Dir, Laird Gp, 1994–2002. *Recreation:* walking. *Address:* Mulberry, Woodbury Hill, Loughton, Essex IG10 1JB. *T:* (020) 8508 1188.

BELL, Mary Elizabeth; *see* Stacey, M. E.

BELL, Prof. Michael, PhD; FBA 2008; Professor of English, University of Warwick, 1994–2008, now Emeritus; *b* Chelmsford, 21 July 1941; *s* of Michael James Bell and Josephine Bell; *m* (marr. diss.); one *s* one *d*. *Educ:* University Coll. London (BA; PhD 1970). English asst, Lyons, France, 1962–63; teacher of English and French, St Stephen's Sch., Welling, 1963–64; English asst, Erlangen, Germany, 1964–65; Instructor, 1965–69, Lectr, 1969–70, Univ. of Western Ontario; Associate Prof., Ithaca Coll., NY, 1970–73; University of Warwick: Lectr, 1973–81; Sen. Lectr, 1981–92; Reader in English, 1992–94. *Publications:* Primitivism, 1972; (ed) Context of English Literature 1900–1930, 1982; The Sentiment of Reality: truth of feeling in the European novel, 1983; F. R. Leavis, 1988; D. H. Lawrence: language and being, 1992; Gabriel García Márquez: solitude and solidarity, 1993; Literature, Modernism and Myth: belief and responsibility in the Twentieth Century, 1997; Sentimentalism, Ethics and the Culture of Feeling, 2001; Open Secrets: literature and education and authority from J.-J. Rousseau to J. M. Coetzee, 2007. *Recreation:* walking. *Address:* 9 Clapham Street, Leamington Spa, Warks CV31 1JJ. *T:* (01926) 312719; *e-mail:* Bell.Michael@talktalk.net.

BELL, Michael John Vincent, CB 1992; Group Export Controls Consultant, BAE Systems, since 2004; *b* 9 Sept. 1941; *e s* of late C. R. V. Bell, OBE and Jane Bell, MBE; *m* 1983, Mary Shippen, *o d* of late J. W. and Margaret Shippen; one *s* two *d*. *Educ:* Winchester Coll.; Magdalen Coll., Oxford (BA Lit.Hum). Res. Associate, Inst. for Strategic Studies, 1964; Ministry of Defence: Asst Principal, 1965; Principal, 1969; Asst Sec., 1975; on loan to HM Treasury, 1977–79; Asst Under Sec. of State (Resources and Programmes), 1982–84; Dir Gen. of Management Audit, 1984–86; Asst Sec. Gen. for Defence Planning and Policy, NATO, 1986–88; Dep. Under-Sec. of State (Finance), 1988–92, (Defence Procurement), 1992–95; Dep. Chief of Defence Procurement (Support), 1995–96; Project Dir, European Consolidation, BAe (on secondment), 1996–99; Gp Hd of Strategic Analysis, BAe, subseq. BAE Systems, 1999–2003. *Recreation:* military history. *Address:* BAE Systems plc, Farnborough Aerospace Centre, Farnborough, Hants GU14 6YU.

BELL, Nigel; *see* Bell, J. N. B.

BELL, Nigel Christopher, CEng; Director and Principal Consultant, Ophis Ltd, since 2002; *b* 29 July 1959; *s* of Leonard Norman Bell and Marlene Bell (*née* Gould); *m* 1985, Colette Julia Stein; one *s* one *d*. *Educ:* Kendal Grammar Sch.; Loughborough Univ. (BSc Hons Computer Studies); Sheffield Hallam Univ. (MSc Managing Change). MBCS 1987; CEng 1990. Analyst Programmer, Comshare, 1981–85; Project Co-ordinator, Honeywell Bull, 1985–87; Project Manager, Boots, 1987–88; Mgt Consultant, Price Waterhouse, 1988–93; Div. Dir, Eur. Inf. Systems, Low & Bonar, 1993–96; Vice-Pres., Inf. Systems and Services, Astra Charnwood, 1996–98; Inf. Systems and Technol. Dir for Drug Develt, Astra AB, 1998–99; Chief Exec., NHS Information Authy, 1999–2001; Dir, Service Transformation, Office of e-Envoy, Cabinet Office, 2001–02. *Recreations:* fell-walking, tai chi, motor cycling.

BELL, Peter Robert; Emeritus Professor of Botany, University of London; *b* 18 Feb. 1920; *s* of Andrew and Mabel Bell; *m* 1952, Elizabeth Harrison; two *s*. *Educ:* Simon Langton School, Canterbury; Christ's Coll., Cambridge (MA 1949). University College London: Asst Lecturer in Botany, 1946; Lectr in Botany, 1949; Reader in Botany, 1967; Prof. of Botany, 1967; Quain Prof. of Botany and Head of Dept of Botany and Microbiol., 1978–85; Dean of Science, 1979–82; Mem. Council, 1979–85. Visiting Professor: Univ. of California, Berkeley, 1966–67; Univ. of Delhi, India, 1970. British Council Distinguished Visitor, NZ, 1976; many other visits overseas, including exploration of Ecuadorian Andes. Vice-Pres., Linnean Soc., 1962–65; Mem. Biological Sciences Cttee, 1974–79 (Chm. Panel 1, 1977–79), SRC. *Publications:* Darwin's Biological Work, Some Aspects Reconsidered, 1959; (with C. F. Woodcock) The Diversity of Green Plants, 1968, 3rd edn 1983; (trans., with D. E. Coombe) Strasburger's Textbook of Botany, 8th English edn, 1976; Green Plants: their origin and diversity, 1992, 2nd edn (with A. R. Hemsley) 2000; scientific papers on botanical topics, particularly reproductive cells of land plants, and on history of botany. *Recreation:* mountains. *Address:* 13 Granville Road, Barnet, Herts EN5 4DU. *T:* (020) 8449 9331.

BELL, Sir Peter (Robert Frank), Kt 2002; MD; FRCS, FRCSGlas; Professor and Head of Department of Surgery, University of Leicester, 1974–2003, now Emeritus; *b* 12 June 1938; *s* of Frank and Ruby Bell; *m* 1961, Anne Jennings; one *s* two *d*. *Educ:* Univ. of Sheffield (MB, ChB Hons 1961; MD 1969). FRCS 1965; FRCSGlas 1968. Postgrad. surg. career in Sheffield hosps, 1961–65; Lectr in Surgery, Univ. of Glasgow, 1965–68; Sir Henry Wellcome Travelling Fellow, Univ. of Colorado, 1968–69; Consultant Surgeon and Sen. Lectr, Western Infirm., Glasgow, 1969–74. President: Surgical Res. Soc., 1986–88; European Soc. of Vascular Surgery, 1994; Vascular Soc. of GB and Ireland, 1998–99; Internat. Soc. of Vascular Surgeons, 2003–; Mem. Council, RCS, 1992– (Vice Pres., 2001–04). Pres., Hope Foundn for Cancer Res.; Chm., Circulation Foundn. Founder FMedSci 1998. Hon. DSc Leicester, 2003. *Publications:* Surgical Aspects of Haemodialysis, 1974, 2nd edn 1983; Operative Arterial Surgery, 1982; Arterial Surgery of the Lower Limb, 1991; Surgical Management of Vascular Disease, 1992; pubns on vascular disease, transplantation and cancer in med. and surg. jls. *Recreations:* horticulture, oil painting, bowls.

BELL, Hon. Sir Rodger, Kt 1993; a Judge of the High Court of Justice, Queen's Bench Division, 1993–2006; a Presiding Judge, South Eastern Circuit, 2001–05; *b* 13 Sept. 1939; *s* of John Thornton Bell and Edith Bell; *m* 1969, (Sylvia) Claire Tatton Brown; one *s* three *d*. *Educ:* Moulsham Sch.; Brentwood Sch.; Brasenose Coll., Oxford (BA). Called to the Bar, Middle Temple, 1963, Bencher, 1989; QC 1982; a Recorder, 1980–93; Chm., NHS Tribunal, 1991–93; Legal Mem., Mental Health Review Tribunals, 1983–93; Mem., Parole Board, 1990–93. *Address:* The Mill House, Upton Hellions, Crediton, Devon EX17 4AE.

BELL, Prof. Ronald Leslie, CB 1988; FREng; FInstP; Director-General, Agricultural Development and Advisory Service and the Regional Organisation, and Chief Scientific Adviser, Ministry of Agriculture, Fisheries and Food, 1984–89; *b* 12 Sept. 1929; *s* of Thomas William Alexander Bell and Annie (*née* Mapleston); *m* 1954, Eleanor Joy (*née* Lancaster); one *s* one *d* (and one *d* decd). *Educ:* The City School, Lincoln; Univ. of Birmingham (BSc, PhD). Research Fellow, Royal Radar Estabt, Malvern, 1954–57; Imperial College, Univ. of London: Lectr in Metallurgy, 1957–62; Reader in Metallurgy, 1962–65; University of Southampton: Prof. of Engrg Materials, 1965–77; Head of Dept of Mech. Engrg, 1968; Dean of Faculty of Engrg and Applied Scis, 1970–72; Dep. Vice Chancellor, 1972–76; Dir, NIAE, 1977–84. Vis. Prof., Cranfield Inst. of Technology, 1979–89. Pres., British Crop Protection Council, 1985–89; Member: AFRC, 1984–89; Council, RASE, 1984–89. Sen. Treas., Methodist Church Div. of Ministries, 1992–96. FREng (FEng 1991). Hon. DSc Southampton, 1985. *Publications:* papers in learned jls dealing with twinning and brittle fracture of metals, grain boundary sliding and creep in metals, dislocations in semi-conductors, agricultural engineering. *Recreations:* the bassoon, musical acoustics, painting, Association football, gardening. *Address:* 3 Old Garden Court, Mount Pleasant, St Albans AL3 4RQ.

BELL, Prof. Stephen David, PhD; Professor of Microbiology, University of Oxford, since 2007; Fellow, Wadham College, Oxford, since 2007; *b* Glasgow, 10 July 1967; *s* of David and Jean Bell; *m* 2007, Rachel Yvonne Samson. *Educ:* Glasgow Univ. (BSc Hons Molecular Biol. 1989; PhD 1992). Post-doctoral res., Wellcome Centre for Molecular Parisitology, 1992–95, Gurdon Inst., Cambridge, 1996–2001; Gp Leader, MRC Cancer Cell Unit, Cambridge, 2001–07. Fellow, EMBO, 2006. Tenovus Medal, Tenovus Scotland, 2006. *Publications:* contrib. scientific jls in fields of transcription and DNA replication. *Recreations:* climbing, bird watching, sleeping. *Address:* Sir William Dunn School of Pathology, University of Oxford, South Parks Road, Oxford OX1 3RE.

BELL, Steve W. M.; freelance cartoonist and illustrator, since 1977; *b* 26 Feb. 1951; *m* 1977; four *c*. *Educ:* Slough Grammar Sch.; Teesside Coll. of Art; Univ. of Leeds (BA Fine Art 1974); Exeter Univ. (teaching cert.). Teacher of art, Aston Manor Sch., Birmingham, 1976–77. Contribs to Whoopee!, Cheeky, Jackpot, New Statesman, New Society, Social Work Today, NME, Journalist; Maggie's Farm series, Time Out, then City Limits, 1979; IF…series, Guardian, 1981–. Exhibns of cartoons at Barbican Gall. and Cartoon Gall. *Publications:* Maggie's Farm, 1981; Further Down on Maggie's Farm, 1982; The If Chronicle, 1983; (with B. Homer) Waiting for the Upturn, 1986; Maggie's Farm: the last round up, 1987; If…Bounces Back, 1987; If…Breezes In, 1988; (with R. Woddis) Funny Old World, 1991; If…Goes Down the John, 1992; If…Bottoms Out, 1993; Big If…, 1995; (with S. Hoggart) Live Briefs: a political sketchbook, 1996; If…Files, 1997; Bell's Eye, 1999; (with B. Homer) Chairman Blair's Little Red Book, 2001; Unstoppable If…, 2001; Unspeakable If…, 2003. *Address:* c/o The Guardian, Kings Place, 90 York Way, N1 9AG.

BELL, Sir Stuart, Kt 2004; MP (Lab) Middlesbrough, since 1983; Second Church Estates Commissioner, since 1997; barrister; *b* High Spen, Co. Durham, 16 May 1938; *s* of Ernest and Margaret Rose Bell; *m* 1st, 1960, Margaret, *d* of Mary Bruce; one *s* one *d*; 2nd, 1980, Margaret, *d* of Edward and Mary Allan; one *s*. *Educ:* Hookergate Grammar Sch. Formerly colliery clerk, newspaper reporter, typist and novelist. Called to the Bar, Gray's Inn, 1970. Conseil Juridique and Internat. Lawyer, Paris, 1970–77. Member: Newcastle City Council, 1980–83 (Mem., Finance, Health and Environment, Arts and Recreation Cttees; Chm., Youth and Community Cttee; Vice-Chm., Educn Cttee); Educn Cttee, AMA; Council of Local Educn Authorities; Newcastle AHA (T), 1980–83. Contested (Lab) Hexham, 1979. PPS to Dep. Leader of Opposition, Rt Hon. Roy Hattersley, 1983–84; Opposition front bench spokesman: on NI, 1984–87; on trade and industry, 1992–97. Chm., Finance and Services Select Cttee, 2000–; Mem., H of C Commn, 2000–. Founder Mem. and Vice Chm., British-Irish Inter Parly Body, 1990–93; Chm., Franco-British Parly Relns Gp, 2005–. Freeman, City of London, 2003. Member: Fabian Soc.; Soc. of Lab. Lawyers; GMB. Chevalier de la Légion d'Honneur (France), 2006. *Publications:* How to Abolish the Lords (Fabian Tract), 1981; Valuation for United States Customs Purposes, 1981; When Salem Came to the Boro: the true story of the Cleveland child abuse crisis, 1989; Annotation of The Children Act, 1989; Raising the Standard: the case for first past the post, 1998; Where Jenkins Went Wrong, 1999; Pathway to the Euro, 2002; An Ever

Closer Union—The Forward March, 2007; *autobiography:* Tony Really Loves Me, 2000; Lara's Theme, 2004; Softly in the Dusk, 2004; *fiction:* Paris 69, 1973; Days That Used To Be, 1975; Binkie's Revolution, 2002; The Honoured Society, 2002; The Ice Cream Man and Other Stories, 2007. *Recreation:* writing. *Address:* House of Commons, SW1A 0AA.

BELL, Trevor; *see* Bell, C. T.

BELL, William Bradshaw, OBE 2005; JP; Member (UU) Lagan Valley, Northern Ireland Assembly, 1998–2007; *b* 9 Oct. 1935; *s* of Robert Bell and Mary Ann Bell; *m* 1969, Leona Maxwell; one *s* three *d. Educ:* Fane Street Primary School, Belfast; Grosvenor High School, Belfast. Member: for N Belfast, NI Constitutional Convention, 1975–76; Belfast City Council, 1976–85 (Unionist spokesman on housing, 1976–79; Lord Mayor of Belfast, 1979–80); for S Antrim, NI Assembly, 1982–86 (Dep. Chm., Finance and Personnel Cttee, 1984–86); Lisburn CC (formerly BC), 1989–2005 (Chairman: Police Liaison Cttee, 1991; Finance Cttee, 1993–95; Economic Develt Cttee, 1996–98; Mayor of Lisburn, 2003–04). Chm., NI Public Accounts Cttee, 1999–2002. Contested (UU) Lagan Valley, NI Assembly, 2007. *Recreations:* music, motoring, writing.

BELL, William Edwin, CBE 1980; Deputy Chairman, Enterprise Oil plc, 1991–97 (Chairman, 1984–91); *b* 4 Aug. 1926; *s* of late Cuthbert Edwin Bell and Winifred Mary Bell (*née* Simpson); *m* 1952, Angela Josephine Vaughan; two *s* two *d. Educ:* Birmingham University (BSc Civil Eng.); Royal School of Mines, Imperial College. Joined Royal Dutch Shell Group, 1948; tech. and managerial appts, Venezuela, USA, Kuwait, Indonesia; Shell International Petroleum Co. (Middle East Coordination), 1965–73; Gen. Man., Shell UK Exploration and Production and Dir, Shell UK, 1973; Man. Dir, Shell UK, 1976–79; Middle East Regional Coordinator and Dir, Shell International Petroleum Co., 1980–84, retired; non-exec. Dir, Costain Group, 1982–92. Pres., UK Offshore Operators Assoc., 1975–76. *Publications:* contribs to internat. tech. jls, papers on offshore oil industry develts. *Recreations:* golf, sailing. *Address:* Fordcombe Manor, near Tunbridge Wells, Kent TN3 0SE. *Club:* Nevill Golf.

BELL, Sir William Hollin Dayrell M.; *see* Morrison-Bell.

BELL, William Lewis, CMG 1970; MBE (mil.) 1945; retired; Information Officer, University of Oxford, 1977–84; *b* 31 Dec. 1919; *s* of Frederick Robinson Bell and Kate Harper Bell (*née* Lewis); *m* 1943, Margaret Giles (*d* 2003); one *s* one *d. Educ:* Hymers Coll., Hull; Oriel Coll., Oxford. Served The Gloucestershire Regt (Major), 1940–46. Colonial Administrative Service, Uganda, 1946–63: Dep. Sec. to the Treasury, 1956–58; Perm. Sec., Min. of Social Services, 1958–63; Fellow, Economic Develt Inst., World Bank, 1958. Chm., Uganda National Parks, 1962; Pres., Uganda Sports Union, 1961–62. Director, Cox & Danks Ltd (Metal Industries Group), 1963–64. Sec. to the Governors, Westfield Coll., Univ. of London, 1964–65; Founding Head of British Develt Div. in the Caribbean, ODA, 1966–72; UK Dir, Caribbean Develt Bank, 1970–72; Founding Dir-Gen., Technical Educn and Training Org. for Overseas Countries, 1972–77. *Recreations:* cricket, Caribbeana. *Address:* Hungry Hatch, Fletching, E Sussex TN22 3SH. *Clubs:* MCC; Vincent's (Oxford).

BELL BURNELL, Dame (Susan) Jocelyn, DBE 2007 (CBE 1999); PhD; FRS 2003; FRSE, FRAS, FInstP; astronomer; Visiting Professor of Astrophysics, University of Oxford, since 2004; *b* 15 July 1943; *d* of G. Philip and M. Allison Bell; *m* 1968, Martin Burnell (separated 1989); one *s. Educ:* The Mount Sch., York; Glasgow Univ. (BSc); New Hall, Cambridge (PhD; Hon. Fellow, 1996). FRAS 1969; FRSE 2004. Res. Fellowships, Univ. of Southampton, 1968–73; Res. Asst, Mullard Space Science Lab., UCL, 1974–82; Sen. Res. Fellow, 1982–86, SSO, 1986–89, Grade 7, 1989–91, Royal Observatory, Edinburgh; Prof. of Physics, Open Univ., 1991–2001; Dean, Science Faculty, Univ. of Bath, 2001–04. An Editor, The Observatory, 1973–76. Vis. Fellow, 1999, Vis. Prof. for Distinguished Teaching, 1999–2000, Princeton Univ.; Sackler Vis. Prof., Univ. of Calif, Berkeley, 2000; Philips Visitor, Haverford Coll., Pa, 1999; Tuve Fellow, Carnegie Instn of Washington, 2000. Lectures: Marie Curie, Inst. of Physics, 1994; Appleton, Univ., Edinburgh, 1994; Jansky, Nat. Radio Astronomy Observatory, USA, 1995; Royal Instn, 1996; Maddison, Keele Univ., 1997; Flamsteed, Derby Univ., 1997; Royal Soc., 1997; Hamilton, Princeton Univ., 1997; Women in Physics, Aust. Inst. of Physics, 1999; Bishop, Columbia Univ., NY, 1999; Elizabeth Spreadbury, UCL, 2001; Flamsteed, Royal Observatory, Greenwich, 2003; Herschel, Bath, 2003; Robinson (and medal), Armagh, 2004; Nuffield, Assoc. of Sci. Educators, 2005; Inst. of Physics, Ireland, 2005; Campbell, Southampton, 2006; Gordon, Cornell, 2006; Athena, Keele, 2006; Kelvin (and Medal), Royal Philosophical Soc., Glasgow, 2007; Compton, Washington Univ., St Louis, Mo, 2008; Distinguished Lectr, Internat. Space Univ., 2000, 2002. Mem., IAU, 1979–; Chm., Physics Trng and Mobility of Researchers Fellowships Panel, EC, 1996–98 (Vice Chm., 1995); Pres., RAS, 2002–04 (Vice-Pres., 1995–97); Mem. Council, Royal Soc., 2004–06; Mem. Panel, Women for Sci., Inter Acad. Council, 2005–06. Mem. Council, Open Univ., 1997–99. Trustee, Nat. Maritime Mus., 2000–. Chm., Grand Jury, Eur. Commn Marie Curie Excellence Awards, 2005. Foreign Member: Onsala Telescope Bd, Sweden, 1996–2002; Nat. Acad. of Scis, USA, 2005. Hon. Mem., Sigma-Pi-Sigma, 2000. FRSA 1999; Hon. Fellow, BAAS, 2006. Hon. DSc: Heriot-Watt, 1993; Newcastle, Warwick, 1995; Cambridge, 1996; Glasgow, Sussex, 1997; St Andrews, London, 1999; Leeds, Haverford Coll., Penn, Williams Coll., Mass, 2000; Portsmouth, QUB, 2002; Edinburgh 2003; Keele, 2005; Harvard 2007; Durham 2007; DUniv York, 1994. Michelson Medal, Franklin Inst., Philadelphia (jtly with Prof. A. Hewish), 1973; J. Robert Oppenheimer Meml Prize, Univ. of Miami, 1978; Rennie Taylor Award, Amer. Tentative Soc., NY, 1978; (first) Beatrice M. Tinsley Prize, Amer. Astronomical Soc., 1987; Herschel Medal, RAS, 1989; Edinburgh Medal, City of Edinburgh, 1999; Targa Giuseppe Piazzi Award, Palermo, Sicily, 1999; Magellanic Premium, Amer. Philos. Soc., 2000; Joseph Priestly Award, Dickinson Coll., Penn, 2002. Discovered the first four pulsars (neutron stars), 1967–68. *Publications:* Broken for Life, 1989; (ed jtly) Next Generation Infrared Space Observatory, 1992; papers in Nature, Science, Astronomy and Astrophysics, Jl of Geophys. Res., Monthly Notices of RAS. *Recreations:* Quaker interests, walking. *Address:* University of Oxford, Department of Astrophysics, Keble Road, Oxford OX1 3RH.

BELL DAVIES, Vice-Adm. Sir Lancelot (Richard), KBE 1977; *b* 18 Feb. 1926; *s* of late Vice-Adm. R. Bell Davies, VC, CB, DSO, AFC, and Mrs Bell Davies, Lee on Solent, Hants; *m* 1949, Emmeline Joan (*née* Molengraaff), Wassenaar, Holland; one *s* two *d. Educ:* Boxgrove Preparatory Sch., Guildford; RN Coll., Dartmouth. War of 1939–45: Midshipman, HMS Norfolk, 1943 (Scharnhorst sunk); joined Submarines, 1944. First Command, HMS Subtle, 1953; subseq. commands: HMS Explorer, 1955; Comdr, HMS Leander, 1962; Captain: HMS Forth, also SM7, 1967, and HMS Bulwark, 1972; Rear-Adm., 1973. Ministry of Defence Posts: (Comdr) Naval Staff, 1960; (Captain) Naval Asst to Controller, 1964; Director of Naval Warfare, 1969; Comdr, British Naval Staff, Washington, and UK Rep. to Saclant, 1973–75; Supreme Allied Commander Atlantic's Rep. in Europe, 1975–78; Comdt, Nato Defence Coll., Rome, 1978–81. Chm., Sea Cadet Council, 1983–92; President: HMS Norfolk Assoc., 1987–; Portsmouth Sea Cadets, 1992–2005; Square Rigger Club, 1997–2005. Pres., Southampton MND Assoc., 1998–; Vice Pres., Trincomalee Trust, 1999–2008. CCMI (FBIM 1977). *Recreations:* sailing, gardening. *Address:* Wessex Bungalow, Satchell Lane, Hamble, Hampshire SO31 4HS. *T:* (023) 8045 7415. *Clubs:* Naval and Military; Royal Yacht Squadron, Royal Naval Sailing Association.

BELLAK, John George; Chairman, Severn Trent plc (formerly Severn-Trent Water Authority), 1983–94; *b* 19 Nov. 1930; *m* 1960, Mary Prudence Marshall; three *s* one *d. Educ:* Uppingham; Clare College, Cambridge. MA (Economics). Sales and Marketing Dir, Royal Doulton, 1968–80, Man. Dir, 1980–83; Chairman: Royal Crown Derby, 1972–83; Lawleys Ltd, 1972–83. President: British Ceramic Manufacturers' Fedn, 1982–83; Fedn of European Porcelain and Earthenware Manufacturers, 1982–83; European Waste Water Group, 1991–93; Dep. Chm., Water Services Assoc., 1992 (Vice-Chm., 1990–91; Chm., 1991). Chm., Aberdeen High Income Trust (formerly Abtrust High Income Investment Trust), 1994–2003; Dir, Ascot Holdings, 1993–96. Mem., Grand Council, CBI, 1984–94. Mem. Court, Keele Univ., 1984–96. *Recreations:* ornithology, field sports, reading. *Address:* 1 Council House Court, Shrewsbury SY1 2AU. *Clubs:* Carlton, Beefsteak.

BELLAMY, Rear-Adm. Albert John, CB 1968; OBE 1956; CMath, FIMA; first Deputy Director, Polytechnic of the South Bank, 1970–80; *b* Upton-on-Severn, 26 Feb. 1915; *s* of late A. E. Bellamy and late Mrs A. E. Bellamy; *m* 1942, Dorothy Joan Lawson; one *s* one *d. Educ:* Hanley Castle Grammar Sch.; Downing Coll., Cambridge (Buchanan Exhibitioner; 1st cl. hons Pts I and II, Math. tripos, MA 1939). FIMA 1960; CMath 1992. Asst master, Berkhamsted Sch., 1936–39. Joined RN, 1939, as Instructor Lieut; Fleet Instr and Meteorological Officer, America and WI, 1948–50 (HMS Glasgow); Instr Comdr, 1950; Headmaster, RN Schs, Malta, 1951–54; HMS Ark Royal, 1955–56; Dean of the College, RN Engineering Coll., Manadon, Plymouth, 1956–60; Instr Capt., 1958; staff of Dir, Naval Educn Service, 1960–63; Dir of Studies, RN Electrical, Weapons and Radio Engineering Sch., HMS Collingwood, 1963–65; Instr Rear-Adm., 1965; Dir, Naval Educn Service and Hd of Instructor Branch, MoD, 1965–70. Mem., Home Office Extended Interview non-Service Mems Panel, 1980–87. *Recreations:* gardening, show jumping, crosswords, parish council work, finance work with two charities, keeping old age at bay by being involved. *Address:* The Cottage, Kington Magna, Gillingham, Dorset SP8 5EG. *T:* (01747) 838668.

BELLAMY, Sir Christopher (William), Kt 2000; Senior Consultant, Linklaters, since 2007; President of the Competition Appeal Tribunal, 2003–07; *b* 25 April 1946; *s* of late William Albert Bellamy, TD, MRCS, LRCP and Vyvienne Hilda, *d* of Albert Meyrick, OBE; *m* 1989, Deirdre Patricia (*née* Turner); one *s* two *d. Educ:* Tonbridge Sch.; Brasenose Coll., Oxford (MA). Called to the Bar, Middle Temple, 1968; Bencher, 1994. Taught in Africa, 1968–69; in practice at Bar, 1970–92; QC 1986; Asst Recorder, 1989–92; Judge: Court of First Instance, EC, 1992–99; Employment Appeal Tribunal, 2000–07; a Recorder, 2000–07; a Deputy High Court Judge, 2000–; Pres., Appeal Tribunals, Competition Commn, 1999–2003. President: Assoc. of European Competition Law Judges, 2002–06 (Hon. Pres., 2008); UK Assoc. of European Law, 2004–; Mem., Selection Cttee for Judges of Eur. Civil Service Tribunal, 2004–. Mem., Council, 2000–06, Adv. Bd, 2007–, British Inst. of Internat. and Comparative Law. Gov., Ravensbourne Coll. of Design and Communication, 1988–92. *Publications:* (with G. Child) Common Market Law of Competition, 1973, 6th edn (ed P. Roth and V. Rose), 2007; public lectures, papers and articles on legal matters. *Recreations:* history, walking, family life. *Address:* Linklaters, 1 Silk Street, EC2Y 8HQ. *T:* (020) 7456 3457. *Clubs:* Athenæum, Garrick.

BELLAMY, Clifford William; His Honour Judge Bellamy; a Circuit Judge, since 2004; Designated Family Judge, Coventry County Court, since 2006; *b* 20 May 1952; *s* of late William Broughton Bellamy and Joan Ernestine Bellamy; *m* 1976, Christine Ann Hughes; two *s. Educ:* Burton upon Trent Grammar Sch.; University Coll. London (LLB); Coll. of Ripon and York St John (MA). Admitted solicitor, 1976; Dist Judge, 1995–2004. Ordained Methodist Minister, 2001. *Publications:* Complaints and Discipline in the Methodist Church, 2000; (contrib.) What is a Minister?, 2002. *Recreations:* reading, theatre. *Address:* Coventry Combined Court Centre, 140 Much Park Street, Coventry CV1 2SN. *T:* (024) 7653 6166, *Fax:* (024) 7652 0443.

BELLAMY, David Charles; Chief Executive Officer, St James's Place PLC, since 2007; *b* 15 April 1953; *s* of Percival Leonard Bellamy and Elizabeth Margaret Bellamy; *m* 1970, Janette Godfrey; two *s* one *d. Educ:* Sutton High Grammar Sch., Plymouth. Hambro Life Assce, subseq. Allied Dunbar Assce, 1973–91 (Divl Dir, Strategic Res. Unit, 1988–91); Sales Ops, J. Rothschild Assce Gp, 1991–97; Gp Ops Dir, 1997–2000, Man. Dir, 2000–07, St James's Place. Trustee, St James's Place Foundn (Charitable Trust), 1997–. *Recreations:* family, horse racing, horse racing ownership. *Address:* St James's Place House, Dollar Street, Cirencester, Glos GL7 2AQ. *T:* (01285) 878005; *e-mail:* david.bellamy@sjp.co.uk.

BELLAMY, David James, OBE 1994; PhD; FLS; CBiol, FIBiol; botanist; writer and broadcaster; *b* 18 Jan. 1933; *s* of Thomas Bellamy and Winifred (*née* Green); *m* 1959, Rosemary Froy; two *s* three *d. Educ:* London University: Chelsea Coll. of Science and Technology (BSc); Bedford Coll. (PhD). Lectr, then Sen. Lectr, Dept of Botany, Univ. of Durham, 1960–80; Hon. Prof. of Adult and Continuing Educn, 1980–82; Special Prof., then Special Prof. of Geog., Nottingham Univ., 1987–; Vis. Prof. of Natural Heritage Studies, Massey Univ., NZ, 1988–89; Hon. Prof., Univ. of Central Qld, 1999–. Dir, David Bellamy Associates, envmtl consultants, 1988–95; Associate Dir, P-E Internat., 1993–94; Chm., Greengro Produce Ltd, 2002–; Hon. Dir, Zander Corp., 2004–. Founder Dir, 1982, Pres., 1998, Conservation Foundn; Trustee: WWF, 1985–89; Living Landscape Trust, 1985–; President: WATCH, 1982–2005; YHA, 1983–2004; Population Concern, 1988–2003; Nat. Assoc. Envmtl Educn, 1989–; Assoc. of Master Thatchers, 1991–97; Council, Zool Soc. of London, 1991–94, 2002–; Plantlife, 1994–2005; Wildflower Soc., 1995–98; Wildlife Trust Partnership, 1996–2005; British Holiday and Home Parks Assoc., 2002–; Camping and Caravanning Club, 2002–; Vice-Pres., Wild Trout Trust, 2005–. Chair: Welsh Fest. of Countryside, 1999–2002; Abela Conservation Foundn, 2003; Cedrus Ltd, 2003–04; Chair of Govs, Mareeba Wetland Foundn, 2002. Governor, Repton Sch., 1983–89. Chief I Spy, 1983. Contested (Referendum) Huntingdon, 1997. Presenter and script writer for television and radio programmes, BBC and ITV; programmes include Longest Running Show on Earth, 1985; main series: Life in our Sea, 1970; Bellamy on Botany, 1973; Bellamy's Britain, 1975; Bellamy's Europe, 1977; Botanic Man, 1979; Up a Gum Tree, 1980; Backyard Safari, 1981; The Great Seasons, 1982; Bellamy's New World, 1983; You Can't See The Wood, 1984; Discovery, 1985; Seaside Safari, 1985; End of the Rainbow Show, 1985; Bellamy's Bugle, 1986; Turning the Tide, 1986; The End of the Rainbow Show, 1986; Bellamy's Bird's Eye View, 1988; Moa's Ark, 1990; Bellamy Rides Again, 1991, 1992; Wetlands, 1991; England's Last Wilderness, 1992; Blooming Bellamy, 1993; Routes of Wisdom, 1993; Bellamy's Border Raids: the Peak District, 1994; Westwatch, 1996; A Welsh Herbal, 1998; Making Tracks, 1998 and 1999; A Celtic Herbal, 1999; Kite Country, Bellamy and the Argonauts, 2000; The Challenge, 2000; Agrissentials. 2006. FCIWEM 1996; FRIN 2005. Hon. Fellow, BICSc 1997; Hon. FLS 1997. Hon. Fellow, Univ. of Lancaster, 1997.

DUniv Open, 1984; Hon. DSc: CNAA, 1990; Nottingham, 1993; Dunelm, 1995; Bournemouth, 1999; Kingston, 2000; Oxford Brookes, 2004. Frances Ritchie Meml Prize, Rambler's Assoc., 1989; UNEP Global 500 Award, 1990; Environmental Communicator of the Year, British Assoc. of Communicators in Business, 1996; Guild of Travel Writers Award, 1996; Busk Medal, RGS, 2001. Order of the Golden Ark (Netherlands), 1989. *Publications:* Peatlands, 1974; Bellamy on Botany, 1974; Bellamy's Britain, 1975; Bellamy's Europe, 1977; Life Giving Sea, 1977; Botanic Man, 1978; Half of Paradise, 1979; The Great Seasons, 1981; Backyard Safari, 1981; Discovering the Countryside with David Bellamy: vols I and II, 1982, vols III and IV, 1983; The Mouse Book, 1983; Bellamy's New World, 1983; The Queen's Hidden Garden, 1984; Turning the Tide, 1986; The Vanishing Bogs of Ireland, 1986; Bellamy's Changing Countryside, 4 vols, 1989; (with Brendan Quayle) England's Last Wilderness, 1989; England's Lost Wilderness, 1990; (with Jane Gifford) Wilderness in Britain, 1991; How Green Are You?, 1991; Tomorrow's Earth, 1991; (with Andrea Pfister) World Medicine, 1992; Blooming Bellamy, 1993; Poo, You and the Potoroo's Loo, 1997; (contrib.) The Blue UNESCO, 1999; The English Landscape, 2000; (consultant) The Countryside Detective, 2000; The Jolly Green Giant (autobiog.), 2002; (with Piers Browne) The Glorious Trees of Great Britain, 2002; The Bellamy Herbal, 2003; Conflicts in the Countryside, 2005. *Recreations:* children, ballet. *Address:* Mill House, Bedburn, Bishop Auckland, Co. Durham DL13 3NW. *Club:* Farmers.

BELLAMY, (Kenneth) Rex; Tennis Correspondent, The Times, 1967–89; *b* 15 Sept. 1928; *s* of Sampson Bellamy and Kathleen May Bellamy; *m* 1st, 1951, Hilda O'Shea (*d* 2000); one step *d*; 2nd, 2006, Wendy Elizabeth Matthews. *Educ:* Yeovil; Woodhouse Grammar Sch., Sheffield. National Service, RA and RASC, 1946–49. Sports and Feature Writer, Sheffield Telegraph, 1944–46 and 1949–53; Sports Writer: Birmingham Gazette, 1953–56; The Times, 1956–89. World Championship Tennis award for service to tennis, 1988; International Tennis-writing Awards: 5 from Assoc. of Tennis Professionals, 1975–79 (award discontinued); 2 from Women's Tennis Assoc., 1977–78. *Publications:* Teach Yourself Squash (jtly), 1968; The Tennis Set, 1972; The Story of Squash, 1978 rev. edn as Squash—A History, 1988; The Peak District Companion, 1981; Walking the Tops, 1984; Game, Set and Deadline, 1986; Love Thirty, 1990; The Four Peaks, 1992. *Recreations:* hill-walking, table tennis. *Address:* Ashfield Lodge, 68 Petersfield Road, Midhurst, W Sussex GU29 9JR.

BELLAMY, Prof. Richard Paul, PhD; Professor of Political Science, and Director, School of Public Policy, University College London, since 2005; *b* 15 June 1957; *s* of late Edmund Henry Bellamy and of Joan Bellamy (*née* Roberts); partner, Louise Regina Dominian; one *d*. *Educ:* Trinity Hall, Cambridge (BA 1979; PhD 1982). ESRC Post-doctoral Res. Fellow, Nuffield Coll., Oxford, 1983–86 (Jun. Dean, 1985–86); Lectr, House of Politics, Christ Church, Oxford, 1984–86; Fellow and Coll. Lectr in Hist., Jesus Coll., Cambridge, and Lector, Trinity Coll., Cambridge, 1986–88; Lectr in Politics, Univ. of Edinburgh, 1988–92; Professor: of Politics, UEA, 1992–96; of Politics and Internat. Relns, Univ. of Reading, 1996–2002; of Govt, Univ. of Essex, 2002–05. Acad. Dir, Eur. Consortium for Pol Res., 2002–06. Visiting Fellow: Nuffield Coll., Oxford, 1995; Nat. Europe Centre, ANU, 2005; Jean Monnet Fellow, Social and Pol Sci. Dept, European Univ. Inst., Florence, 2000–01. *Publications:* Modern Italian Social Theory: ideology and politics from Pareto to the present, 1987 (trans. Indonesian); Liberalism and Modern Society: an historical argument, 1992 (trans. Portuguese and Chinese); (with D. Schecter) Gramsci and the Italian State, 1993 (trans. Japanese); Liberalism and Pluralism: towards a politics of compromise, 1999; Rethinking Liberalism, 2000 (trans. Chinese); Political Constitutionalism: a Republican defence of the constitutionality of democracy, 2007; A Very Short Introduction to Citizenship, 2008; *editor:* Liberalism and Recent Legal and Social Philosophy, 1989; Victorian Liberalism: nineteenth century political thought and practice, 1990; Theories and Concepts of Politics: an introduction, 1993; (jtly) Democracy and Constitutional Culture in the Union of Europe, 1995; Constitutionalism, Democracy and Sovereignty: American and European perspectives, 1996; (with A. Ross) A Textual Introduction to Social and Political Thought, 1996; (with D. Castiglione) Constitutionalism in Transformation: European and theoretical perspectives, 1996; (with M. Hollis) Pluralism and Liberal Neutrality, 1999; (with A. Warleigh) Citizenship and Governance in the European Union, 2001; (with A. Mason) Political Concepts, 2003; (with T. Ball) The Cambridge History of Twentieth Century Political Thought, 2003 (trans. Arabic, Turkish and Chinese); (jtly) Lineages of European Citizenship: rights, belonging and participation in eleven nation states, 2004; The Rule of Law and the Separation of Powers, 2005; (jtly) Making European Citizens: civic inclusion in a transitional context, 2006; contrib. chapters in books and numerous articles to jls incl. Political Studies, British Jl Pol Sci., Philosophical Qly, Eur. Law Jl, Law and Philosophy, Eur. jl Pol Res., Govt and Opposition, Eur. Jl Pol Theory, Hist. of Pol Thought, Philosophical Forum, Jl Modern Italian Studies. *Recreations:* listening to and playing music of all kinds, reading and writing, walking, talking, eating and drinking. *Address:* Department of Political Science, School of Public Policy, University College London, 29/30 Tavistock Square, WC1H 9QH. *T:* (020) 7679 4999, *Fax:* (020) 7679 4969; *e-mail:* r.bellamy@ucl.ac.uk.

BELLAMY, Stephen Howard George Thompson; QC 1996; a Recorder, since 2000; *b* 27 Sept. 1950; *s* of George and Clarice Bellamy; *m* 1988, Rita James; one *d*. *Educ:* The Grammar Sch., Heckmondwike; Trinity Hall, Cambridge (MA Hons Law). ACIArb. Called to the Bar, Lincoln's Inn, 1974, Bencher, 2006; Asst Recorder, 1997–2000; Dep. High Court Judge, 2000–. Asst Parly Boundary Comr, 2000–. Family Mediator, 2007. Member: Cttee, Family Bar Assoc., 1989–96, 2001–02; General Council of the Bar, 1993–96. Chm., Bar Council Scholarship Trust, 2000–; Mem., Foreign Office (Consular Directorate) Pro Bono Panel, 2005–. Member: British Inst. of Internat. and Comparative Law, 1991–97; Family Mediators' Assoc. Fellow, Inst. of Advanced Legal Studies, 2000. *Recreations:* music, opera, ski-ing, gardening. *Address:* 1 King's Bench Walk, Temple, EC4Y 7DB. *T:* (020) 7936 1500, *Fax:* (020) 7936 1590.

BELLANY, Prof. Ian; Professor of Politics, University of Lancaster, 1979–2006, now Emeritus; *b* 21 Feb. 1941; *s* of James Bellany and Jemima Bellany (*née* Emlay); *m* 1965, Wendy Ivey, *d* of Glyndwr and Bronwen Thomas; one *s* one *d*. *Educ:* Preston Lodge, Prestonpans; Firth Park Grammar Sch., Sheffield; Balliol Coll., Oxford (State Scholar, MA, DPhil). Foreign and Commonwealth Office, 1965–68; Res. Fellow in Internat. Relations, ANU, 1968–70; University of Lancaster: Lectr. later Sen. Lectr in Politics, 1970–79; Dir, Centre for Study of Arms Control and Internat. Security, 1979–90; Head, Dept of Politics, 1985–86. Leverhulme Res. Fellow, 1982 and 2003; NATO Instl Fellow, 1989–90. Examr in Internat. Relations, LSE, 1985–88 and 1999–2002, in Internat. Studies, Birmingham Univ., 1990–93, in Internat. Relations, Aberdeen Univ., 1995–99. Founding Editor, Arms Control: Journal of Arms Control and Disarmament, 1980–91. Trench Gascoigne Essay Prize, RUSI, 2002. *Publications:* Australia in the Nuclear Age, 1972; A Basis for Arms Control, 1991; Reviewing Britain's Defence, 1994; The Environment in World Politics, 1997; Curbing the Spread of Nuclear Weapons, 2005; edited jointly: Antiballistic Missile Defences in the 1980s, 1983; The Verification of Arms Control Agreements, 1983; The Nuclear Non-Proliferation Treaty, 1985; New Conventional Weapons and Western Defence, 1987; Terrorism and Weapons of Mass Destruction, 2007; contribs to jls. *Recreations:* broadcasting, coarse carpentry, computing. *Address:* 11 Spruce Avenue, Lancaster LA1 5LB. *T:* (01524) 68157.

BELLANY, John, CBE 1994; RA 1991 (ARA 1986); artist (painter); *b* Scotland, 18 June 1942; *s* of Richard Weatherhead Bellany and Agnes Craig Bellany; *m* 1st, 1964, Helen Margaret Percy (marr. diss. 1974); two *s* one *d*; 2nd, 1980, Juliet Gray (*née* Lister) (*d* 1985); 3rd, 1986 (for 2nd time), Helen Margaret Bellany. *Educ:* Cockenzie Public Sch., Scotland; Preston Lodge Sch., Scotland; Edinburgh Coll. of Art (DA); Royal Coll. of Art (MA Fine Art; ARCA). Lectr in Fine Art in various art colls and univs in Gt Britain, incl. Winchester Coll. of Art, Goldsmiths' Coll., London Univ., RCA; Artist in Residence, Victorian Coll. of the Arts, Melb., 1982. *One man exhibitions:* Nat. Portrait Gall., 1986; Fischer Fine Art, London, 1988–89, 1991; Scottish Nat. Gall. of Modern Art, 1989; Raab Gall., Berlin and Ruth Siegel Gall., NY, 1990; Fitzwilliam Mus., Cambridge, 1991; Kelvingrove Art Gall. and Mus., Glasgow, 1992; Beaux Arts Gall., London, 1997, 1998, 2000, 2001, 2006; Galeria K, Mexico City, 1997; Elaine Baker Gall., Florida, 1999; Soloman Gall., London, 2000; many others in Britain, USA, Australia, Europe; *retrospective exhibitions:* Scottish Nat. Gall. of Modern Art, Edin., and Serpentine Gall., London, 1986; Kunsthalle, Hamburg, 1988. Works represented in major museums and private collections throughout the world, incl. Tate Gall., V&A Mus., Mus. of Modern Art, NY, Metropolitan Mus., NY, Nat. Gall. of NSW, Melbourne. Sen. Fellow, RCA, 1999. Hon. Fellow Commoner, Trinity Hall, Cambridge, 1988. Hon. RSA 1987. Dr (*hc*) Edinburgh, 1996; Hon. DLitt Heriot-Watt, 1998. *Relevant publications:* John Bellany, by Victor Musgrave and Philip Rawson, 1982; John Bellany, a Retrospective, by Douglas Hall, 1986; John Bellany (Portraits) (The Maxi Hudson Collection), by Robin Gibson, 1986; John Bellany, by Richard Cork, 1986; John Bellany, Retrospective, by Prof. D. Werner Hofmann and Keith Hartley, 1988; John Bellany, by John McEwen, 1994. *Recreation:* climbing to and fro across Hadrian's Wall. *Address:* 2 Windmill Drive, SW4 9DE. *T:* (020) 8675 7909, *Fax:* (01799) 542062; 19 Great Stuart Street, Edinburgh EH2 7TP. *T:* (0131) 226 5183; Beaux Arts Gallery, 22 Cork Street, W1X 1HB. *T:* (020) 7437 5799; Berkeley Square Gallery, 23A Bruton Street, W1X 7DA. *T:* (020) 7493 7939. *Clubs:* Chelsea Arts; Scottish Arts (Edinburgh).

BELLENGER, Rt Rev. Dr Dominic Terence Joseph, (Dom Aidan Bellenger), OSB; FSA; FRHistS; Abbot of Downside, since 2006; Parish Priest, St Benedict's, Stratton-on-the-Fosse, since 1999; *b* 21 July 1950; *s* of Gerald Bellenger and Kathleen Bellenger (*née* O'Donnell). *Educ:* Finchley Grammar Sch.; Jesus Coll., Cambridge (Scholar, MA, PhD); Angelicum Univ., Rome. Res. Student in History, 1972–78 and Lightfoot Schol. in Eccl. Hist., Cambridge, 1975–78; Assistant Master: St Mary's Sch., Cambridge, 1975–78; Downside Sch., 1978–82; Benedictine Monk, Downside Abbey, 1982; Priest, 1988; Housemaster, 1989–91, Head Master, 1991–95, Downside Sch.; Dir of Histl Res., Downside Abbey, 1995–; Parish Priest: Little Malvern, 1995–99; St Aldhelm's, Chilcompton, 2002–06; Prior, Downside Abbey, 2001–06. Member: Cttee, Eccl. Hist. Soc., 1982–85; Cttee, English Benedictine Hist. Commn, 1987–; Council, Catholic Record Soc., 1990–99, 2005–; Clifton Diocesan Educn Commn, 1995–2001; Delegate, Benedictine Gen. Chapter, 2001–. Trustee: Catholic Family Hist. Soc., 1990–99; Andrew C. Duncan Catholic History Trust, 1993–; Friends of Somerset Churches, 1996–; Somerset Record Soc., 1998–; Pres., English Catholic Hist. Assoc., 1991–. Governor: Moor Park Sch., Ludlow, 1991–99; St Antony's, Leweston, Sherborne, 1991–93; St Mary's Sch., Shaftesbury, 1992–96; Moreton Hall, Suffolk, 1995–2001; St Joseph's, Malvern, 1997–99; Downside Sch., 1999– (Chm.); St Gregory's, Bath, 2001–05; Ammerdown Centre, 2006–. Chaplain, Kts of Malta, 2004–. Vis. Scholar, Sarum Coll., 2004–. York Minster Lecture, 2001. Leverhulme Res. Award, 1986. FRSA. Editor, South Western Catholic History, 1982–; English correspondent, Rev. d'Hist. de l'Eglise de France, 1982–85. *Publications:* English and Welsh Priests 1558–1800, 1984; The French Exiled Clergy, 1986; (ed) Opening the Scrolls, 1987; (ed jtly) Les Archives du Nord, Calendar of 20 H, 1987; St Cuthbert, 1987; (ed jtly) Letters of Bede Jarrett, 1989; (ed) Fathers in Faith, 1991; (ed) The Great Return, 1994; (ed) Downside: a pictorial history, 1998; (jtly) Princes of the Church, 2001; (jtly) Medieval Worlds, 2003; (jtly) The Mitre and the Crown, 2005; (jtly) The Medieval Church, 2006; Downside: a history, 2007; contributor to many other books; articles in learned jls and periodicals. *Recreations:* books, church architecture, travel, visual arts, writing. *Address:* Downside Abbey, Stratton-on-the-Fosse, Bath BA3 4RJ. *T:* (01761) 235119.

BELLEW; *see* Grattan-Bellew.

BELLEW, family name of **Baron Bellew**.

BELLEW, 7th Baron *cr* 1848; **James Bryan Bellew;** Bt 1688; *b* 5 Jan. 1920; *s* of 6th Baron Bellew, MC, and Jeanie Ellen Agnes (*d* 1973), *d* of late James Ormsby Jameson; *S* father, 1981; *m* 1st, 1942, Mary Elizabeth (*d* 1978), *d* of Rev. Edward Eustace Hill; two *s* one *d*; 2nd, 1978, Gwendoline (*d* 2002), formerly wife of Major P. Hall and *d* of late Charles Redmond Clayton-Daubeny. Served War of 1939–45, Irish Guards (Captain). *Heir: s* Hon. Bryan Edward Bellew [*b* 19 March 1943; *m* 1968, Rosemary Sarah, *d* of Major Reginald Kilner Brasier Hitchcock; one *s* (and one *s* decd)]. *Address:* c/o Royal Bank of Scotland, 45 The Promenade, Cheltenham, Glos GL50 1PY.

BELLINGHAM, Prof. Alastair John, CBE 1997; FRCP, FRCPE, FRCPGlas, FRCPath; Professor of Haematology, King's College London, 1984–97; *b* 27 March 1938; *s* of Stanley Herbert Bellingham and Sybil Mary Milne; *m* 1st, 1963, Valerie Jill Morford (*d* 1997); three *s*; 2nd, 2002, Julia de Quetteville Willott. *Educ:* Tiffin Boys' Sch., Kingston upon Thames; University Coll. Hosp. (MB BS). Research Fellow, Univ. of Washington, 1969–71; Sen. Lectr, UCH, 1971–74; Prof. of Haematology, Univ. of Liverpool, 1974–84; Hon. Consultant Haematologist: Royal Liverpool Hosp., 1974–84; KCH, 1984–97. Transition Dir, Liverpool, Nat. Blood Service, 1997–99; Chairman: Confidentiality Adv. Gp, DoH, 1997–2001; NHS Inf. Authy, 1999–2005; Kennet and N Wilts PCT, 2005–06. Mem. Bd, Inst. of Cancer Res., 1997–2003. Chm. Govs, St Dunstan's Coll., Catford, 1999–2001. Vice-Pres., 1990–93, Pres., 1993–96, RCPath; Past Pres., British Soc. for Haematology; Vice-Pres., Eur. Div., Internat Soc. Haematology, 1992–98. FFPath, RCPI, 1996. Hon. Fellow, Hong Kong Coll. of Path., 1995. *Publications:* contribs to books and jls on haematol., esp. red cell physiol. and inherited red cell disorders, incl. enzyme deficiencies, sickle cell disorders and thalassaemia. *Recreations:* oenology, viticulture, cricket, photography. *Address:* Broadstones, The Street, Teffont Magna, Salisbury SP3 5QP. *T:* (01722) 716267. *Club:* Savage.

BELLINGHAM, Sir Anthony Edward Norman, 8th Bt (2nd creation) *cr* 1796, of Castle Bellingham, co. Louth; Managing Director, City Financial Executive Recruitment, since 1980; *b* 24 March 1947; *yr s* of Sir Roger Carroll Patrick Stephen Bellingham, 6th Bt and of Mary, *d* of William Norman; *S* brother, 1999; *m* 1991, Denise Marie Moity (marr. diss. 1998); one *s*; *m* 1998, Namfon Bellingham (marr. diss. 2001). *Educ:* Rossall. *Heir: s* William Alexander Noel Henry Bellingham, *b* 19 Aug. 1991.

BELLINGHAM, Henry Campbell; MP (C) Norfolk North West, 1983–97 and since 2001; director of and consultant to companies, since 1998; *b* 29 March 1955; *s* of late

Henry Bellingham; *m* 1993, Emma, *o d* of P. J. H. Whiteley and Lady Angela Whiteley. *Educ:* Eton; Magdalene Coll., Cambridge (BA 1977). Called to the Bar, Middle Temple, 1978. Contested (C) Norfolk North West, 1997. PPS to Sec. of State for Transport, 1990–92, for Defence, 1992–95, for Foreign and Commonwealth Affairs, 1995–97; Opposition spokesman on Trade and Industry, and Shadow Minister for Small Businesses and Employment, 2002–05; Opposition Whip, 2005–. Member: Select Cttee on the Environment, 1987–90; NI Select Cttee, 2001–02; Trade and Industry Select Cttee, 2003–04. Chm., Cons. Council on Eastern Europe, 1989–94; officer, Cons. back bench cttees, 1983–90. *Address:* c/o House of Commons, SW1A 0AA. *Club:* White's.

BELLINGHAM, Peter Gordon; Executive Director, Welsh National Opera, since 2002 (Director of Marketing, 1994–2002); *b* 23 Jan. 1956; *s* of Arthur Stanley and Kathleen Bellingham; *m* 1985, Julie Robinson (stage name, Julie Jensen); two *s* one *d*. *Educ:* Royal Northern Coll. of Music. Mgt Trainee, Fulcrum Centre, Slough, 1977–78; Publicity Officer, Torch Th., Milford Haven, 1978–80; PRO, Northern Ballet Th., 1980–81; Festivals Asst, Cheltenham Festivals, 1981–82; Mktg Manager, Northern Ballet Th., 1982–85; Music Officer, 1985–86, Theatres Manager, 1986–87, Bradford CC; Account Dir, sponsorship and events, PRC Communications, 1987–89; Hd, Sales and Mktg, 1989–92, Hd, Planning, 1992–93, Bradford Theatres; freelance arts consultant, 1993–94. *Recreations:* football, tennis, running. *Address:* Welsh National Opera, Wales Millennium Centre, Bute Place, Cardiff Bay CF10 5AL. *T:* (029) 2063 5006, *Fax:* (029) 2063 5098; *e-mail:* peter.bellingham@wno.org.uk.

BELLIS, Bertram Thomas; Headmaster, The Leys School, Cambridge, 1975–86; *b* 4 May 1927; *s* of Rev. Thomas J. Bellis and Mary A. Bellis; *m* 1952, Joan Healey; two *s*. *Educ:* Kingswood Sch., Bath; St John's Coll., Cambridge (Exhibr in Maths, MA). Rossall Sch., 1951–55; Highgate Sch., 1955–65; Headmaster, Daniel Stewart's Coll., 1965–72; Principal, Daniel Stewart's and Melville Coll., 1972–75. Founding Dir, Mathematics in Educn and Industry Schools Project, 1963–65. Chm., Scottish Educn Dept Cttee on Computers and the Schools (reports, 1969 and 1972); Member: Council, Inst. of Math., 1975–79; Educational Research Bd, SSRC, 1975–80. Governor: Queenswood Sch., 1980–92; St John's Coll. Sch., 1981–86. Pres., Mathematical Assoc., 1971–72. Schoolmaster Fellow, Balliol Coll., Oxford, 1963; FIMA 1964; FRSE 1972. *Address:* 13 Marlborough Court, Grange Road, Cambridge CB3 9BQ.

BELLOS, Linda Ann, OBE 2007; Founder and Director, Diversity Solutions Consultancy Ltd, since 2003; *b* 13 Dec. 1950; *d* of Emmanuel Adebowale and Renee Sackman; *m* 1970, Jonathan Bellos (marr. diss. 1983); one *s* one *d*; civil partnership 2005, Caroline Jones. *Educ:* Silverthorne Girls' Sec. Mod. Sch.; Dick Shephard Comp. Sch.; Univ. of Sussex (BA Hons 1981). HM Inspector of Taxes, Tax Office, 1972–77; finance worker/journalist, Spare Rib, 1981–83; Community Accountant, Lambeth Inner City Consultancy Gp, 1983–84; Team Leader, Women's Unit, GLC, 1984–86; Mem. (Lab), Lambeth LBC, 1985–88 (Leader, 1986–88); Hd, Women's Unit, 1988–90, Actg Asst Dir, Social Services, 1990–91, Hackney LBC; freelance journalist and consultant, 1992–99; Regl Manager, Focus Consultancy Ltd, 1999–2002; self-employed, 2002–03. Community activist: Queen's Park Community Assoc., Brighton, 1974–81; Women Against Violence Against Women, 1981–86. Vice-Chm., Black Sections, Labour Party, 1984–87; Treas., African Reparations Movt UK, 1994–97; Chairman: New Initiatives Youth and Community Assoc., 1998–2005; Southwark Anti-Homophobic Forum, 1998–2004; Southwark Action for Voluntary Orgns, 2001–07; Southwark Lesbian, Gay, Bisexual and Transgender network, 2002–06; Bronze Woman Proj., 2002–; Co-Chm., LGBT Community Adv. Gp, and Mem., Diversity Bd, Metropolitan Police Service, 2000–03. *Publications:* (contrib.) A Vision Back and Forth, 1995; (contrib.) Making Black Waves, 1995; (contrib.) IC3: the Penguin book of new Black writing in Britain, 2000; contrib. papers, essays and articles in books and magazines. *Recreations:* gardening, reading, music. *Address:* c/o Silverman Sherliker, 7 Bath Place, EC2A 3DR. *T:* (Diversity Solutions) 0845 260 0028.

BELLOTTI, David Frank; Member (Lib Dem), since 2003, and Chairman, since 2008, Bath and North East Somerset Council; *b* 13 Aug. 1943; *s* of Patrick Frank Bellotti and Elsie (*née* Venner); *m* 1st, 1965, Sheila (*née* Jones); one *s* one *d*; 2nd, 1973, Jennifer (*née* Compson); one *s*; 3rd, 1996, Josephine (*née* Brown); one *s* one *d*. *Educ:* Exeter Sch.; YMCA National Coll. (Diploma in Youth Service); Brighton Polytechnic (Diploma in Counselling); Univ. of Sussex (MA). Civil Service, 1961–64; Young Men's Christian Association: student, Nat. Coll., 1964–65; Sec., St Helens, Llanelli, Norwich and Lewes, 1965–76; Regional Sec., South-East, 1977–81; Dir, Hove, 1981–90. Dep. Chm. and Chief Exec., Brighton and Hove Albion FC, 1993–97. Mem. (L, then Lib Dem), E Sussex CC, 1981–97 (Chm., 1993–94). Chm., Sussex Police Authy, 1993–95. Mem., Cttee of the Regions, EU, 1994–98. MP (Lib Dem) Eastbourne, Oct. 1990–1992; contested same seat, 1992. Contested (Lib Dem), European Parliamentary elections: E Sussex and Kent S, 1994; SE Reg., 1999. *Recreations:* Association Football, politics. *Address:* 12 Kipling Avenue, Bath BA2 4RB. *Club:* National Liberal.

BELLOWS, James Gilbert; TV, newspaper, on-line executive; *b* 12 Nov. 1922; *s* of Lyman Hubbard Bellows and Dorothy Gilbert Bellows; *m* 1950, Marian Raines (decd); three *d*; *m* 1964, Maggie Savoy (decd); *m* 1971, Keven Ryan; one *d*. *Educ:* Kenyon Coll. (BA, LLB). Columbus (Ga) Ledger, 1947; News Editor Atlanta (Ga) Jl, 1950–57; Asst Editor, Detroit (Mich.) Free Press, 1957–58; Managing Editor Miami (Fla) News, 1958–61; Exec. Editor (News Ops), NY Herald Tribune, 1961–62; Editor, 1962–66; associate Editor, Los Angeles Times, 1966–75; Editor: Washington Star, 1975–78; Los Angeles Herald Examiner, 1979–82; Managing Editor, Entertainment Tonight (TV show), 1982–83; Exec. Editor, ABC-TV News, 1983–86; Dir of Editorial Devel t, Prodigy, 1986–88; Managing Editor, USA Today on TV, 1988–89; Vice Pres. Editorial, MediaNews Gp, 1990–91; Los Angeles Bureau Chief, TV Guide, 1992–94; Exec. Editor, Excite Inc. Software, 1995–96; Chm., Editl Adv. Bd, Excite, 1997; Consultant, LA Daily News, 1998–99. Member: Kenyon Review Adv. Bd; Amer. Soc. of Newspaper Editors. *Publication:* The Last Editor: how I saved the New York Times, the Washington Post and the Los Angeles Times (memoir), 2002. *Address:* 555 South Barrington Avenue, Los Angeles, CA 90049–4344, USA. *Club:* Bel-Air Country (Los Angeles).

BELMAHI, Mohammed; Ambassador of Morocco to the Court of St James's, since 1999; *b* 18 Aug. 1948; *s* of Redouane Belmahi and Aziza Filal Belmahi; *m* 1973, Åse Ask; one *d*. *Educ:* Ecole Nationale d'Architecture, Toulouse (Architect DPLG 1973); New York Univ. (Master of Urban Planning 1975; PhD Prog. in Public Admin 1976; MPhil 1985); Harvard Inst. for Internat. Devel t, 1981. London Business Sch. (Sen. Exec. Prog.), 1991. UN Center for Housing, Building and Planning, NY, 1975–76; Min. of Housing and Land Use Planning, and Dir, Land Use Planning, Rabat, 1977–79; Prime Minister's Office, Rabat (Mem., State Owned Enterprise Reform Task Force), 1979–82; Dir of Tourism, Min. of Tourism, 1982–86; Dir Gen., Moroccan Nat. Tourist Bd, 1987–88; Mem., Exec. Cttee, ONA Hldg Gp, Casablanca, 1988–96; Dir Gen. for Real Estate and Tourism, and Dir Gen., Casablanca World Trade Center; Ambassador to India and Nepal, 1996–99. Freeman, City of London, 2006. Indira Gandhi Meml Award, 1997. Officer, National Order of Merit (Portugal), 1991; Kt Comdr, Royal Order of Francis I, 2003. *Recreations:* golf, swimming, collecting miniature elephants, drawing portraits, calligraphy (Arabic). *Address:* Embassy of Morocco, 49 Queen's Gate Gardens, SW7 5NE. *T:* (020) 7581 5001; *e-mail:* mbelmahi@hotmail.com. *Clubs:* Athenæum, Travellers; Dar Es Salam Golf (Rabat).

BELMONT, Abbot of; *see* Stonham, Rt Rev. Dom P.

BELMORE, 8th Earl of, *cr* 1797; **John Armar Lowry-Corry;** Baron Belmore, 1781; Viscount Belmore, 1789; *b* 4 Sept. 1951; *s* of 7th Earl of Belmore and Gloria Anthea, *d* of late Herbert Bryant Harker, Melbourne, Australia; *S* father, 1960; *m* 1984, Lady Mary Meade, *d* of 6th Earl of Clanwilliam; two *s* one *d*. *Educ:* Lancing; Royal Agricultural Coll., Cirencester. Member: Adv. Bd, PRO, Belfast, 1996–2006; Bd of Govs and Guardians, Nat. Gall. of Ireland, 1998–2003. *Recreation:* fishing. *Heir:* *s* Viscount Corry, *qv*. *Address:* The Garden House, Castle Coole, Enniskillen, N Ireland BT74 6JY. *T:* (028) 6632 2463.

BELOFF, Hon. Michael Jacob, MA; QC 1981; barrister and writer; President, Trinity College, University of Oxford, 1996–2006; *b* 18 April 1942; *s* of Baron Beloff, FBA and of Helen Dobrin; *m* 1969, Judith Mary Arkinstall; one *s* one *d*. *Educ:* Dragon Sch., Oxford; Eton Coll. (King's Schol.; Captain of Sch. 1960); Magdalen Coll., Oxford (Demy; H. W. C. Davis Prizeman, 1962; BA Hist. (1st cl.) 1963, Law 1965; MA 1967). Pres., Oxford Union Soc., 1962 (Sen. Trustee, 1997–); Oxford Union tour of USA, 1964. Called to the Bar, Gray's Inn, 1967 (Gerald Moody Schol., 1963, Atkin Schol., 1967; Bencher, 1988; Treas., 2008); Jt Head of Chambers, 4–5 Gray's Inn Sq., 1993–2000; a Recorder, 1985–95; a Dep. High Court Judge, 1989–99; a Judge of the Courts of Appeal, Jersey and Guernsey, 1995–, Sen. Ordinary Appeal Judge, 2004–. Vice-Pres., Interception of Communications (Bailiwick of Guernsey) Tribunal, 1998–; Dep. Chm., Data Protection (Nat. Security) Tribunal, 2000–; Chm., Interception of Communications (Bailiwick of Jersey) Tribunal, 2003–; Pres., Investigatory Powers Tribunal, Guernsey, 2005–. Lectr in Law, Trinity Coll., Oxford, 1965–66. Legal Correspondent: New Society, 1969–79; The Observer, 1979–81; Columnist, San Diego Law Jl, 1999–. First Chm., Administrative Law Bar Assoc., 1986–90, now Chm. Emeritus. Member: Bingham Law Reform Cttee on Discovery of Documents and Disclosure, 1982–; Sen. Salary Review Bd, 1995–2002 (Chm., Judicial Sub-Cttee, 1998–2002); Court of Arbitration for Sport, 1996– (Mem., *ad hoc* Panel, Olympic Games, Atlanta, 1996, Sydney, 2000, Athens, 2004, Beijing, 2008, Commonwealth Games, Kuala Lumpur, 1998, Manchester, 2002, Football World Cup (Germany), 2006); Chm., ICC Code of Conduct Commn, 2002– (Mem., Dispute Resolution Panel, Cricket World Cup (Caribbean), 2007); Ethics Comr, London 2012, 2004–. Chm., Oxford Univ. Tribunal into Alleged Plagiarism, 1990. Gov., Dragon Sch., Oxford, 1995–2003; Mem. Council, Cheltenham Ladies' Coll., 1996–2002. Chm., Jardine Scholarship Foundn, 2000–06. For. Consultant, Law Counsel (Dacca), 1990–. Visiting Professor: Tulane Univ., 2001, 2003; Buckingham Univ., 2006–. Lectures: Statute Law Soc., 1994; Admin. Law Bar Assoc., 1995; John Kelly Meml, UC Dublin, 1997; Lasok, Univ. of Exeter, 1998; Atkin, Reform Club, 1999; K. Ramamani, Madras, 1999; Margaret Howard, Trinity Coll., Oxford, 2000; Bailiff's, Guernsey, 2002; Espeland, Oslo, 2002; Alexander Howard, RCP, 2003; David Hall Meml, Envmtl Law Foundn, Law Soc., 2004; Neill, All Souls Coll., Oxford, 2006; Ben Kingsley, Warwick Sch., 2008. Consultant Ed., Judicial Review Bulletin, 1996; Gen. Ed., Internat. Sports Law Review, 2000–; an Associate Ed., Oxford DNB. Hon. Mem., Internat. Athletes' Club. FRSA 1996. Hon. Fellow, Soc. for Advanced Legal Studies, 1997. Fellow, Inst. of Continuing Professional Devel t, 1998. AcSS 2003. Hon. DLitt Fairleigh Dickinson, 2003. Women's Legal Defence Award (first winner), 1991. *Publications:* A Short Walk on the Campus (ed with J. Aitken), 1966; The Plateglass Universities, 1968; The Sex Discrimination Act, 1976; (jtly) Sports Law, 1999; contributor to: Halsbury's Laws of England (contribution on Time), 1983, 2nd edn 1999; Judicial Safeguards in Administrative Proceedings, 1989; Judicial Review, 1991, 2nd edn 1998; Practitioner's Handbook of EC Law, 1998; Israel Among the Nations, 1998; The Human Rights Act, 1999; The University: international expectations, 2002; Blair's Britain, 1997–2007, 2007; Festschriften for: Lord Cooke of Thorndon, 1997; Sir William Wade, 1998; Sir Louis Blom-Cooper, 1999; Sir David Williams, 2000; Lord Slynn of Hadley, 2000; Rolf Ryssdal, 2001; H. M. Seervai, 2002; contrib. Encounter, Minerva, Irish Jurist, Political Qly, Current Legal Problems, Public Law, Statute Law Review, Modern Law Review, British Jl of Sport and Law, Denning Law Jl, Singapore Law Jl, NZ Law Jl, TLS, Spectator, etc. *Recreation:* running slowly. *Address:* Blackstone Chambers, Blackstone House, Temple, EC4Y 7BW. *T:* (020) 7583 1770. *Clubs:* Reform, Royal Automobile (Steward, 1999–); Vincent's, Gridiron (Oxford); Achilles.

BĚLOHLÁVEK, Jiří; Chief Conductor, BBC Symphony Orchestra, since 2006; *b* 24 Feb. 1946; *m* 1971, Anna Fejerova. *Educ:* Prague Conservatory and Acad. of Performing Arts. Chief Conductor, Prague SO, 1977–89; Conductor, 1981–92, Music Dir, 1990–92, Czech Philharmonic Orch.; Founder and Music Dir, Prague Philharmonia, 1994–2005, now Music Dir Laureate; Principal Conductor, Slovak Philharmonic Orch., 2003–04; Principal Guest Conductor, BBC SO, 1995–2000; conductor with major orchestras incl. Berlin Philharmonic, Vienna SO, LPO, Japanese Philharmonic and orchestras in N America. Numerous recordings. Prof. of Arts, 1997. State Award (Czech Republic) 2001. *Recreations:* gardening, hiking, nature. *Address:* c/o IMG Artists, The Light Box, 111 Power Road, W4 5PY.

BELPER, 5th Baron *cr* 1856, of Belper, co. Derby; **Richard Henry Strutt;** *b* 24 Oct. 1941; *o s* of 4th Baron Belper and of Zara Sophie Kathleen Mary, *y d* of Sir Harry Mainwaring, 5th Bt; *S* father, 1999; *m* 1st, 1966, Jennifer Vivian (marr. diss. 1979), *d* of late Capt. Peter Winser; one *s* one *d*; 2nd, 1980, Judith Mary de Jonge (*née* Twynam). *Educ:* Harrow; RAC Cirencester. *Heir:* *s* Hon. Michael Henry Strutt [*b* 5 Jan. 1969; *m* 2004, Vanessa Hoare; two *d*]. *Address:* The Park, Kingston on Soar, Nottingham NG11 0DH.

BELSKY, Prof. Jay, PhD; Professor of Psychology and Director, Institute for the Study of Children, Families and Social Issues, Birkbeck, University of London, since 1999; *b* 7 July 1952; *s* of Irving and Sylvia Belsky; two *s*. *Educ:* Vassar Coll. (BA Psychology 1974); Cornell Univ. (MS Child Devel t 1976; PhD Human Devel t and Family Studies 1978). Res. Associate, Prenatal/Early Infancy Proj., Elmira, NY, 1977–78; Asst Prof., 1978–83, Associate Prof., 1983–86, Prof., 1986–96, Distinguished Prof., 1996–2001, of Human Devel t, Dept of Human Devel t and Family Studies, Penn State Univ. *Publications:* (ed) In the Beginning: readings on infancy, 1982; (jtly) The Child in the Family, 1984; (ed jtly) Clinical Implications of Attachment, 1988; (with J. Kelly) The Transition to Parenthood, 1994; (jtly) Childhood, 1995; (ed jtly) Evaluating Sure Start: does area-based early intervention work?, 2007. *Recreations:* swimming, travelling. *Address:* Institute for the Study of Children, Families and Social Issues, Birkbeck, University of London, 7 Bedford Square, WC1B 3RA. *T:* (020) 7079 0835, 07507 640064, *Fax:* (020) 7323 4735; *e-mail:* j.belsky@bbk.ac.uk.

BELTON, Prof. Peter Stanley, PhD; Professor of Biomaterials Science, since 2001, and Associate Dean, Faculty of Science, since 2006, University of East Anglia (Head of

Chemistry, School of Chemical Sciences and Pharmacy, 2004–06); *b* 19 June 1947; *s* of Stanley Belton and Bertha (*née* Lawrence); *m* 1976, Teresa Stutz; three *s*. *Educ:* Cooper's Sch., Bow; Chelsea Coll., Univ. of London (BSc 1st Cl. Hons Chem. 1968; PhD 1972). University of East Anglia: Open Univ. Fellowship, 1971–72; ICI Fellowship, 1972–74; Res. Leader, Unilever Res., Port Sunlight, 1974–79; AFRC, later BBSRC, Institute of Food Research Norwich Laboratory: Hd, Molecular Spectroscopy Gp, 1979–87; Hd, Chem. Physics Dept, 1987–90; Hd, Food Structure & Biopolymer Technol. Dept, 1990–91; Hd, Food Colloid & Biopolymer Sci. Dept, 1991–92; Hd, Norwich Lab., 1992–99; Dep. Dir, Inst. of Food Res., AFRC, later BBSRC, 1994–99; Hd, Food Materials Div., Inst. of Food Res., BBSRC, 1999–2001. Visiting Professor: Univ. of São Paulo, 1976; Centre D'Etudes Nucléaire, 1989. FIFST 1994 (Vice-Pres., 2001–02; Pres., 2003–05). Series Editor, Monographs in Food Analysis, 1994–. *Publications:* (jtly) From Arms Race to World Peace, 1991; Food, Science and Society, 2002; contrib. books and jls. *Recreations:* coarse fishing, listening to music, making wine. *Address:* School of Chemical Sciences and Pharmacy, University of East Anglia, Norwich NR4 7TJ; 79 The Avenues, Norwich, Norfolk NR2 3QR. *T:* (01603) 465851.

BELTRAM, Geoffrey; Under-Secretary, Department of Health and Social Security, 1973–81; *b* 7 April 1921; *s* of George and Beatrice Dorothy Beltram; *m* 1945, Audrey Mary (*née* Harkett); one *s* one *d*. *Educ:* Dame Alice Owen's School. Tax Officer, Inland Revenue, 1938; served in RAF, 1941–46; Exec. Officer and Higher Exec. Officer, Min. of Town and Country Planning, 1947–51; Asst Principal, Nat. Assistance Bd, 1951–55; Principal 1955–63; Asst Sec. 1963–73 (NAB 1963–66, Min. of Social Security 1966–68, DHSS 1968–73). Vis. Res. Associate, LSE, 1981–84. Vis. social worker, Ind. Living Fund, 1988–93. *Publication:* Testing the Safety Net: a study of the Supplementary Benefit scheme, 1984. *Recreations:* literature, listening to music, opera, ballet, theatre, walking, swimming.

BELTRAMI, Adrian Joseph; QC 2008; *b* Glasgow, 8 Nov. 1964; *s* of Joseph Beltrami and Brigid Dolores Beltrami (*née* Fallon); *m* 1991, Charlotte Bentley; one *s* two *d*. *Educ:* Stonyhurst; Downing Coll., Cambridge (BA 1987); Harvard Law Sch. (LLM). Called to the Bar, Lincoln's Inn, 1989; in practice at the Bar, specialising in commercial litigation, banking and financial services, insolvency, professional negligence and civil fraud. *Publication:* (principal contributor) Banking Litigation, 1999, 2nd edn 2005. *Recreations:* family, tennis, Dickens, wine, Wiltshire. *Address:* 3 Verulam Buildings, Gray's Inn, WC1R 5NT; *e-mail:* abeltrami@3vb.com. *Club:* Riverside Raquet.

BEMIS, Michael Bruce; Chief Executive, London Electricity plc, 1997–99; President, Exelon Energy Delivery, 2003–04 (President, Exelon Power, 2002–03); *b* 24 March 1947; *m* 1981, Ann Elizabeth; one *d*. *Educ:* Univ. of Southern Mississippi (BS Accounting 1970); Harvard Business Sch. (Exec. Prog. 1989). Deloitte Haskins and Sells, 1970–82, Electricity Utility Specialist, and Partner; Sen. Vice Pres. and Chief Financial Officer, Entergy Arkansas Inc., 1982–89; President and Chief Operating Officer: Entergy Mississippi Inc., 1989–91; Entergy Louisiana, 1991–92; Exec. Vice Pres., Retail Services, Entergy Corp., 1992–97. FInstD 1997. *Recreation:* golf. *Clubs:* New Orleans Country (New Orleans); Wentworth Golf, Annandale Golf.

BEN AHMED, Mohamed, PhD; Minister of State for Scientific Research and Technology, Tunisia, 1998; *b* Tunis, 28 March 1941; *m* Prof. Zeinib Benoshan; one *d*. *Educ:* Faculté des Sciences de Paris (PhD 1966); Institut de Recherche en Informatique, Paris (Doctorat d'Etat 1978). Lectr, Faculté des Sciences, Tunis, 1967–72; Researcher, Institut de Recherche en Informatique, Paris, 1972–77; Faculté des Sciences, Tunis: Sen. Lectr, 1977–78; Asst Prof., 1978–82; Dir, Computer Dept, 1981–84; Univ. Full Prof., 1983; Ecole Nationale des Sciences de l'Informatique, Univ. of Tunis: Founder and Dir, 1984–90; Prof., 1991–93, 1996–97; Chm., Nat. Computer Centre, 1993–95; Minister of State for Computer Scis at Prime Ministry, 1995–96; Ambassador of Tunisia to UK, 1997–98.

BEN-TOVIM, Atarah, (Mrs Douglas Boyd), MBE 1980 (for services to children's music); Artistic Director, Children's Music Foundation, since 1995; Artistic Director, Children's Classic Concerts, since 1995; *b* 1 Oct. 1940; *d* of Tsvi Ben-Tovim and Gladys Ben-Tovim; *m*; one *d*; *m* 1976, Douglas Boyd. *Educ:* Royal Acad. of Music, London. ARAM 1967. Principal Flautist, Royal Liverpool Philharmonic Orchestra, 1962–75; children's concerts with Atarah's Band, 1973–88; Founder and Artistic Dir, Children's Concert Centre, 1975–95. Hon. DMus CNAA, 1991. *Publications:* Atarah's Book (autobiog.), 1976, 2nd edn 1979; Atarah's Band Kits (14 published), 1978–; Children and Music, 1979; (jtly) The Right Instrument For Your Child, 1985; You Can Make Music!, 1986; The Young Orchestral Flautist, Books 1–3, 1990; Queen Eleanor's Legacy, 1994; The Flute Book, 1997. *Recreations:* music, writing, France and the Mediterranean. *Address:* c/o Watson Little Ltd, Capo Di Monte, Windmill Hill, NW3 6RJ. *T:* (020) 7431 0770.

BENACERRAF, Prof. Baruj; Fabyan Professor of Comparative Pathology, Harvard Medical School, 1970–91, Professor Emeritus, since 1991; President: Dana-Farber, Inc., 1991–96; Dana-Farber Cancer Institute, Boston, 1980–91; *b* 29 Oct. 1920; *m* 1943, Annette Dreyfus; one *d*. *Educ:* Lycée Janson, Paris (BèsL 1940); Columbia Univ. (BS 1942); Medical Coll. of Virginia (MD 1945). Served US Army, 1946–48. Intern, Queens Gen. Hosp., NY, 1945–46; Res. Fellow, Dept of Micro-biol., Coll. of Physicians and Surgeons, Columbia Univ., 1948–49; Chargé de Recherches, CNRS, Hôpital Broussais, Paris, 1950–56; New York University School of Medicine: Asst Prof. of Pathol., 1956–58; Assoc. Prof. of Pathol., 1958–60; Prof. of Pathol., 1960–68; Chief, Lab. of Immunol., Nat. Inst. of Allergy and Infectious Diseases, NIH, Bethesda, 1968–70. Scientific Advr, WHO; Chm., Scientific Adv. Cttee, Centre d'Immunologie de Marseille, CNRS-INSERM; Member: Immunology A Study Sect., NIH, 1965–69; Adv. Council, National Inst. of Allergy and Infectious Disease, 1985–88; Scientific Adv. Cttee, Basel Inst. of Immunology, 1985–89; Member Scientific Advisory Board: Trudeau Foundn, 1970–76; Mass Gen. Hosp., 1971–74. President: Amer. Assoc. of Immunologists, 1973–74; Fedn of Amer. Socs for Exptl Biol., 1974–75; Internat. Union of Immunol Socs, 1980–83. Fellow, Amer. Acad. of Arts and Scis, 1972. Correspondent Emérite, Institut National de la Santé et de la Recherche Scientifique, 1988. Member: Nat. Acad. of Scis, 1973; Nat. Inst. of Med., 1981; Amer. Assoc. of Pathologists and Bacteriologists; Amer. Soc. for Exptl Pathol.; British Assoc. for Immunol.; French Soc. of Biol Chem.; Harvey Soc. Lectures: R. E. Dyer, NIH, 1969; Harvey, 1971, 1972; J. S. Blumenthal, Univ. of Minnesota, 1980. Hon. MD Geneva, 1980; Hon. DSc: Virginia Commonwealth Univ., 1981; NY Univ., 1981; Yeshiva Univ., 1982; Univ. Aix-Marseille, 1982; Columbia Univ., 1985; Adelphi Univ., 1988; Weizmann Inst., 1989; Harvard Univ., 1992; Univ. Bordeaux, 1993; Univ. Vienna, 1995. Rabbi Shai Shacknai Lectr and Prize, Hebrew Univ. of Jerusalem, 1974; T. Duckett Jones Meml Award, Helen Hay Whitney Foundn, 1976; Waterford Biomedical Science Award, 1980; (jtly) Nobel Prize for Physiology or Medicine, 1980; Rous-Whipple Award, Amer. Assoc. of Pathologists, 1985; Nat. Medal of Science, US, 1990. *Publications:* (with D. Katz) Immunological Tolerance, 1974; Immunogenetics and Immunodeficiency, 1975; (with D. Katz) The Role of Products of the Histocompatibility Gene Complex in Immune Responses, 1976; Textbook of Immunology, 1979; 650 articles in professional journals. *Recreations:* music, art collecting. *Address:* 111 Perkins Street, Boston, MA 02130–4313, USA.

BÉNARD, André Pierre Jacques, Hon. KBE 1991; French business executive; Hon. Chairman, Eurotunnel, 1996–2004 (Co-Chairman, 1986–90, Chairman, 1990–94; non-executive Director, 1994–96); *b* 19 Aug. 1922; *s* of Marcel Bénard and Lucie Thalmann; *m* 1946, Jacqueline Preiss; one *s*. *Educ:* Lycée Janson-de-Sailly; Lycée Georges Clémenceau, Nantes; Lycée Thiers, Marseilles; Ecole Polytechnique, Paris. Joined Royal Dutch Shell Group, 1946; with Société Anonyme des Pétroles Jupiter, 1946–49; Société des Pétroles Shell Berre, 1950–59; Shell Française: Pres. Man. Dir, 1967–70; Regional Co-ordinator Europe, 1970; Man. Dir, 1971–83, Mem. Supervisory Bd, 1983–93, Royal Dutch Shell Group. Director: La Radiotechnique SA, Paris, 1980–95; Barclays Bank SA, Paris, 1989–96. Senior Adviser, Lazard Frères, NY, 1983–90. Mem. Bd, INSEAD, Fontainebleau, 1983–99. Hon. Pres., French Chamber of Commerce and Industry, Netherlands, 1980–; Chm., Autumn Fest., Paris, 1995–2006. Médaille des Evadés; Médaille de la Résistance; Chevalier du Mérite Agricole; Chevalier de l'Ordre National du Mérite; Comdr, Légion d'Honneur; Comdr, Order of Orange Nassau. *Recreations:* music, golf. *Address:* 45 Paulton's Square, SW3 5DT.

BENARROCH, Heather Mary, (Mrs E. J. Benarroch); *see* Harper, Heather.

BENAUD, Richard, OBE 1961; international sports consultant, journalist and media representative; television commentator, Nine Network, Australia, since 1977; *b* 6 Oct. 1930; *s* of Louis Richard Benaud and Irene Benaud; *m* 1967, Daphne Elizabeth Surfleet; two *s* by previous marr. *Educ:* Parramatta High Sch. Captain, Australian Cricket Team, 28 Tests, played for Australia 63 Tests, Tours to England, 1953, 1956, 1961; first cricketer to achieve Test double, 2000 runs, 200 wickets, 1963. TV commentator: BBC, 1960–99; Channel 4, 1999–2005. *Publications:* Way of Cricket, 1960; Tale of Two Tests, 1962; Spin Me a Spinner, 1963; The New Champions, 1965; Willow Patterns, 1972; Benaud on Reflection, 1984; The Appeal of Cricket, 1995; Anything but… An Autobiography, 1998; My Spin on Cricket, 2005. *Recreation:* golf. *Address:* (office) 19/178 Beach Street, Coogee, NSW 2034, Australia. *T:* (2) 96641124.

BENDALL, David Vere, CMG 1967; MBE 1945; HM Diplomatic Service, retired; *b* 27 Feb. 1920; *s* of John Manley Bendall; *m* 1941, Eve Stephanie Merrilees Galpin; one *d*. *Educ:* Winchester; King's Coll., Cambridge (BA). Served Grenadier Guards, 1940–46. Third Sec., Allied Force HQ, Caserta, 1946; Rome, 1947; FO, 1949; First Sec., Santiago, 1952; FO, 1955; seconded to NATO Secretariat, Paris 1957; FO, 1960; NATO Secretariat, Paris as Dep. Head, Economic and Finance Div. and Special Advisor on Defence Policy, 1962; Counsellor, 1962; Counsellor, Washington, 1965–69; Asst Under-Sec. of State for Western Europe, 1969–71. Chairman: Banque Morgan Grenfell en Suisse (formerly Morgan Grenfell Switzerland), 1974–90; Morgan Grenfell Internat. Ltd, 1979–85; Morgan Grenfell Italia, 1982–93; Banca Nazionale del Lavoro Investment Bank, 1986–94. Director: Morgan Grenfell (Holdings) Ltd, 1971–85; Morgan Grenfell France, 1986–90; Dep. Chm., Avon Cosmetics, 1979–90; Member: Morgan Grenfell Internat. Adv. Council, 1986–87; Internat. and London Adv. Bds, Banque de l'Indochine et de Suez, 1974–87. Chm., BRCS, 1980–85 (Vice-Chm., 1979–80); Vice-Chm., Finance Cttee, League of Red Cross Socs, 1981–85. OStJ 1985. *Recreations:* golf, tennis, shooting, languages. *Address:* 3 Eaton Terrace Mews, SW1W 8EU; Ashbocking Hall, near Ipswich, Suffolk IP6 9LG. *T:* (01473) 890262. *Club:* Boodle's.

BENDALL, Dr Eve Rosemarie Duffield; Chief Executive Officer, English National Board for Nursing, Midwifery and Health Visiting, 1981–86; *b* 7 Aug. 1927; *d* of Col F. W. D. Bendall, CMG, MA, and Mrs M. L. Bendall, LRAM, ARCM. *Educ:* Malvern Girls' Coll.; London Univ. (MA, PhD); Royal Free Hosp. (SRN). Ward Sister, Dorset County Hosp., 1953–55; Night Supt, Manchester Babies' Hosp., 1955–56; Nurse Tutor: United Sheffield Hosps Sch. of Nursing, 1958–61; St George's Hosp., London, 1961–63; Principal, Sch. of Nursing, Hosp. for Sick Children, Gt Ormond Street, 1963–69. Registrar, GNC, 1973–77. *Publications:* (jtly) Basic Nursing, 1963, 3rd edn 1970; (jtly) A Guide to Medical and Surgical Nursing, 1965, 2nd edn 1970; (jtly) A History of the General Nursing Council, 1969; So You Passed, Nurse (research), 1975. *Recreation:* auspicious ageing. *Address: e-mail:* erdb.7827@tiscali.co.uk.

BENDALL, Vivian Walter Hough; chartered surveyor and valuer in private practice, since 1956; *b* 14 Dec. 1938; *s* of late Cecil Aubrey Bendall and Olive Alvina Bendall (*née* Hough); *m* 1969, Ann Rosalind Jarvis (marr. diss. 1992). *Educ:* Coombe Hill House, Croydon; Broad Green Coll., Croydon. IRRV; FNAEA 1984. Mem. Croydon Council, 1964–78; Mem. GLC, 1970–73; Chm., Greater London Young Conservatives, 1967–68. Contested (C): Hertford and Stevenage, Feb. and Oct. 1974; Ilford North, 1997 and 2001. MP (C) Ilford North, March 1978–1997. Backbench Committees: Vice-Chm., Transport Cttee, 1982–83; Sec., Foreign and Commonwealth Affairs Cttee, 1981–84; Vice-Chm., Employment Cttee, 1984–87 (Jt Sec. 1981–84). Former Member: Central Council for Care of the Elderly; South Eastern Area Reg. Assoc. for the Blind; Dr Barnardo's New Mossford Home Fund Raising Cttee. AMRSH 1991. Hon. FASI. *Recreations:* cricket, motor sport. *Address:* (office) 25A Brighton Road, South Croydon, Surrey CR2 6EA. *T:* (020) 8688 0341. *Club:* St Stephen's.

BENDER, Sir Brian (Geoffrey), KCB 2003 (CB 1998); PhD; Permanent Secretary, Department for Business, Enterprise and Regulatory Reform (formerly Department of Trade and Industry), since 2005; *b* 25 Feb. 1949; *s* of late Prof. Arnold Eric Bender; *m* 1974, Penelope Clark; one *s* one *d*. *Educ:* Greenford Grammar Sch.; Imperial Coll., London Univ. (BSc, PhD; FIC 2006). Joined DTI, 1973; Private Sec. to Sec. of State for Trade, 1976–77; First Sec. (Trade Policy), Office of UK Permanent Rep. to EC, 1977–82; Principal (responsible for internat. steel issues), DTI, 1982–84; Counsellor (Industry), Office of UK Permanent Rep. to EC, 1985–89; Under Sec. and Dep. Head of European Secretariat, Cabinet Office, 1990–93; Hd of Regl Develt Div., DTI, 1993–94; Dep. Sec. and Head of European Secretariat, Cabinet Office, 1994–98; Head of Public Service Delivery, Cabinet Office, 1998–99; Permanent Secretary: Cabinet Office, 1999–2000; MAFF, 2000–01; DEFRA, 2001–05. *Address:* Department for Business, Enterprise and Regulatory Reform, 1 Victoria Street, SW1H 0ET.

BENDERSKY, Pamela May H.; *see* Hudson-Bendersky.

BENDIGO, Bishop of, since 2003; **Rt Rev. Andrew William Curnow;** *b* 26 Feb. 1950; *s* of Thomas William Curnow and Esma Jean Curnow (*née* Cook); *m* 1978, Jan Christina Jenkins; two *s* one *d*. *Educ:* Univ. of Melbourne (BComm); Melbourne Coll. of Divinity (BD); Presbyterian Sch. of Christian Educn, Richmond, VA, USA, (MA). Asst Curate, St Alban's, West Coburg, 1973–75; Rector, Parish of Milloo, 1975–79; on leave, USA, dios New York and Virginia, 1979–80; Rector of Elmore, 1980–83; Dir, Council for Christian Educn in Schools, Prov. of Victoria, 1983–89; Vicar of St George's, Malvern, 1989–94; Archdeacon of Kew, 1991–94; Asst Bishop, 1994–2003, Registrar, 2001–03, Dio. Melbourne. Mem., Standing Cttee, Gen. Synod, 1998–. Chairman: Anglicare Australia, 1997–2001; Anglican Superannuation Australia, 2003–06; Dir, Benetas, 2006–;

Pres., Bd of St Luke's Anglicare, 2007–. Exec. Chm., Trinity Coll. Theol Sch., 1997– (Dir, 2003–; Mem. Bd, 2004–); Pres., Melbourne Coll. of Divinity, 2001–02. Life Mem., Oxford Business Alumni, 2002–. *Recreations:* reading, theatre, travel. *Address:* PO Box 2, Bendigo, Vic 3552, Australia. *T:* (3) 54434711, *Fax:* (3) 54412173. *Clubs:* Royal Automobile of Victoria (Melbourne); Sandhurst (Bendigo).

BENDJAMA, Amar; Ambassador of Algeria to Japan, since 2001; *b* Constantine, Algeria, 1 Jan. 1951; *m*; two *c. Educ:* Nat. Sch. of Admin., Algiers. Ministry of Foreign Affairs, Algeria: Hd of Official Visits Desk, Protocol Dept, 1975–79; Counsellor, Moscow, 1980–84; Dep. Dir, European Dept, 1984–89; First Counsellor, Perm. Mission to UN in NY, and Dep. Rep. to Security Council, 1989–90; Chargé d'Affaires, Perm. Mission to UN in NY, 1990–91; Ambassador: to Ethiopia, Djibouti and Eritrea, 1992–94; to UK, 1994–96; Sec. Gen., Min. of Foreign Affairs, Algeria, 1996–2001. Permanent Representative to OAU and UNECA, 1992–94; Chairman: Conf. Cttee, OAU, 1992–93; Adv. Cttee for Admin. and Budgetary Issues, OAU, 1993–94. *Address:* Algerian Embassy, 2–10–67 Mita, Meguro-ku, Tokyo 153–0062, Japan.

BENEDETTI, Renato Giovanni, RIBA; architect; Partner, McDowell+Benedetti, since 1996; Director, McDowell+Benedetti Ltd, since 1998; *b* 30 Nov. 1962; *s* of Giovanni Benedetti and Giulia (*née* Fugaccia). *Educ:* Cobourg Dist Collegiate Inst. East (Ontario Schol. 1981); Univ. of Waterloo Sch. of Architecture, Ontario (BES 1985; BArch 1988). RIBA 1996. Stonemason and bricklayer, 1976–81; Associate, David Chipperfield Architects, 1989–96; with Jonathan McDowell formed McDowell+Benedetti, 1996; main projects include: Smithfield Regeneration, Dublin, 1992; Oliver's Wharf Penthouse, Wapping, 1996; HQ Building, Options, London, 1997; (with YRM Architects) New Univ. of Commonwealth, Malaysia, 1998; Assoc. of Photographers, New Gall. and HQ, London, 1998; Suncourt House, Islington, 2002; Nursing Home for Merchant Taylors' Co., Lewisham, 2002; Kingston Univ. Faculty of Design, 2003. Dir, The Dance Movement, 1999–. Mem. Panel, Art for Architecture Award, RSA, 1999–. FRSA 1999. *Recreations:* travel, arts, sport. *Address:* (office) Karen House, 1–11 Baches Street, N1 6DL. *Clubs:* Architecture, Soho House.

BENEDICT XVI, His Holiness Pope, (Joseph Alois Ratzinger); *b* Marktl am Inn, Germany, 16 April 1927; *s* of Joseph Ratzinger and Maria Ratzinger (*née* Peintner). *Educ:* St Michael Seminary, Traunstein; Ludwig-Maximilian Univ., Munich. Military service, 1943–45. Ordained priest, 1951. Professor: Freising Coll., 1958; Univ. of Bonn, 1959; Univ. of Münster, 1963; Univ. of Tübingen, 1966; Univ. of Regensburg, 1969; Archbishop of Munich and Freising, 1977–82; Prefect, Congregation for the Doctrine of the Faith, 1981–2005. Cardinal Priest, 1977, Cardinal Bishop of Velletri-Segni, 1993; Vice-Dean, 1998–2002, Dean, 2002–05, Sacred Coll. of Cardinals; elected Pope, 19 April 2005. *Publications include:* God of Jesus Christ, 1978; The Ratzinger Report, 1985; Feast of Faith, 1986; Principles of Christian Morality, 1986; Principles of Catholic Theology, 1987; 'In the Beginning'...: a Catholic understanding of the story of the creation and the fall, 1990; To Look on Christ, 1991; The Meaning of Christian Brotherhood, 1993; A Turning Point for Europe?, 1994; The Nature and Mission of Theology, 1995; Called to Communion, 1996; Gospel, Catechesis, Catechism, 1997; *Ad Tuendam Fidem* - to Protect the Faith, 1998; Milestones: memoirs 1927–1977, 1998; Many Religions, One Covenant, 1999; The Spirit of the Liturgy, 2000; God is Near Us, 2003; Truth and Tolerance, 2004; The End of Time?, 2005; Pilgrim Fellowship of Faith, 2005; Values in a Time of Upheaval, 2006; Jesus of Nazareth, vol. 1, 2007. *Address:* Apostolic Palace, 00120 Vatican City.

BENEDICTUS, David Henry; writer and director for stage, television and radio; *b* 16 Sept. 1938; *s* of late Henry Jules Benedictus and Kathleen Constance (*née* Ricardo); *m* 1971, Yvonne Daphne Antrobus (marr. diss. 2002); one *s* one *d*; and one *s* one *d*. *Educ:* Stone House, Broadstairs; Eton College; Balliol College, Oxford (BA English); State Univ. of Iowa. News and current affairs, BBC Radio, 1961; Drama Director, BBC TV, 1962; Story Editor, Wednesday Play and various series, BBC, 1965; Thames TV Trainee Director, at Bristol Old Vic, 1968; Asst Dir, RSC, Aldwych, 1970; Judith E. Wilson Vis. Fellow, Cambridge, and Fellow Commoner, Churchill Coll., Cambridge, 1981–82; Commissioning Editor, Drama Series, Channel 4 TV, 1984–86 (commissions included: The Manageress, 1987; Porterhouse Blue (Internat. Emmy), 1987); BBC Radio: Readings Editor, 1989–91; Editor, Readings, 1991; Editor, Radio 3 Drama, 1992; Sen. Producer, Serial Readings, 1993 (incl. The Bible, 1992; Arcadia, 1993; Macbeth, 1995); also producer of radio series on Cole Porter, Rodgers and Hart, Glenn Miller, film music, etc. Writer in Residence: Sutton Library, Surrey, 1975; Kibbutz Gezer, Israel, 1978; Bitterne Library, Southampton, 1983–84; Snowsfields Sch., Bermondsey, 2001–02; Head of Drama, Putney High Sch., 2003–04; Royal Lit. Fund Fellow, Goldsmiths Coll., 2007; supply teacher variously. Antiques corresp., Standard, 1977–80; reviewer for books, stage, films, records, for major newspapers and magazines, principally The Economist. Dir, Kingston Books, 1988–90. Member: Amnesty International; Writers' Guild; Directors' Guild. Plays include: Betjemania, 1976, 1996; The Golden Key, 1982; What A Way To Run A Revolution!, 1985; You Say Potato, 1992. *Publications:* The Fourth of June, 1962; You're a Big Boy Now, 1963; This Animal is Mischievous, 1965; Hump, or Bone by Bone Alive, 1967; The Guru and the Golf Club, 1969; A World of Windows, 1971; The Rabbi's Wife, 1976; Junk, how and where to buy beautiful things at next to nothing prices, 1976; A Twentieth Century Man, 1978; The Antique Collector's Guide, 1980; Lloyd George (from Elaine Morgan's screenplay), 1981; Whose Life is it Anyway? (from Brian Clarke's screenplay), 1981; Who Killed the Prince Consort?, 1982; Local Hero (from Bill Forsyth's screenplay), 1983; The Essential London Guide, 1984; Floating Down to Camelot, 1985; The Streets of London, 1986; The Absolutely Essential London Guide, 1986; Uncle Ernie's System, 1988–; Little Sir Nicholas, 1990; (with Prof. Hans Kalmus) Odyssey of a Scientist, 1991; Sunny Intervals and Showers, 1992; The Stamp Collector, 1994; How to Cope When the Money Runs Out, 1998; Dropping Names (memoirs), 2005; The Hundred Acre Wood, 2009; numerous short stories for Radio 4 etc. *Recreations:* chess, tennis, cricket, auctions, table tennis, piano playing, horse racing, car boot sales, eating. *Address:* 95D Talfourd Road, SE15 5NN. *T:* (020) 7701 0989; *e-mail:* davidbenedictus@hotmail.com.

BENEDIKTSSON, Einar, MA; Knight Commander, Order of the Falcon, Iceland; Chairman, UNICEF Iceland, since 2003; Ambassador of Iceland, retired 2001; *b* Reykjavík, 30 April 1931; *s* of Stefan M. Benediktsson and Sigridur Oddsdóttir; *m* 1956, Elsa Petursdóttir; three *s* two *d*. *Educ:* Colgate Univ., NY; Fletcher Sch. of Law and Diplomacy, Mass; London Sch. of Econs and Pol. Science; Inst. des Etudes Européennes, Turin. With OEEC, 1956–60; Head of Section, Mins of Econ. Affairs and Commerce, 1961–64, and Min. of For. Affairs, 1964; Counsellor, Paris, 1964–68; Head of Section, Min. of For. Affairs, 1968–70; Perm. Rep. to Internat. Orgns, Geneva, 1970–76; Chm., EFTA Council, 1975; Ambassador to France, also accredited to Spain and Portugal, and Perm. Rep. to OECD and UNESCO, 1976–82; Ambassador to UK and concurrently to The Netherlands, Nigeria and Ireland, 1982–86; Perm. Rep. to N Atlantic Council, 1986–90, and Ambassador to Belgium and Luxembourg, 1986–91; Ambassador to Norway, also to Poland and Czechoslovakia, 1991–93; Ambassador to USA, also accredited to Canada, Mexico, Chile, Argentina, Uruguay, Venezuela and Costa Rica, 1993–97; Exec. Dir, Leifur Eiriksson Millennium Commn of Iceland, 1997–2001; Advr, Office of the Prime Minister and Ministry of Foreign Affairs, Reykjavík, 2001–02. Holds foreign decorations. *Publication:* Iceland and European Development—A Historical Account from a Personal Perspective, 2003. *Address:* Hvassaleiti 28, 103 Reykjavík, Iceland. *T:* 5681943; *e-mail:* mason@islandia.is.

BENETTON, Luciano; industrialist; *b* 13 May 1935. Established Fratelli Benetton (with brothers), 1965; founder and Pres., Benetton, 1978; Benetton Holdings, 1981; Vice-Pres. and Man. Dir, Benetton Group SpA; Mem. Board, Edizione Holding SpA; Pres., Benetton Foundn. Mem., Italian Senate, 1992–94. Awards: Civiltà Veneta, 1986; Premio Creatività, 1992. *Publications:* contribs to La Biblioteca di Harvard, economic and business strategies, 1988. *Address:* Benetton Group SpA, via Villa Minelli 1, 31050 Ponzano Veneto (TV), Italy. *T:* (422) 4491.

BENHAM, George Frederick; Headmaster, Cardinal Hinsley RC High School, 1999–2003; *b* 26 Oct. 1946; *m* 1996, Elizabeth Maria; two *s*. *Educ:* Queen Mary Coll., London (BA 1969; MPhil 1972); Inst. of Educn, London Univ. (DipEd 1978; MA 1980). Lectr, Univ. of Aberdeen, 1971–75; teacher at various schs in London, 1975–85; Educn Advr, 1985–87; London Borough of Brent: Dep. Dir of Educn, 1987–88, Dir, 1989–95; Chief Exec., 1995–98. FRSA 1978; FCMI (FBIM 1978). *Publications:* contribs on education to learned jls in USA, Holland, UK and Switzerland.

BENJAMIN, Floella, OBE 2001; actress, independent producer, writer and children's campaigner; Founder, 1987, Chief Executive, since 1998, Floella Benjamin Productions Ltd; *b* 23 Sept. 1949; *d* of Roy Benjamin and Veronica Benjamin (*née* Dryce); *m* 1980, Keith Taylor; one *s* one *d*. *Educ:* Penge Girls' Sch. Chief Accountants Office, Barclays Bank, 1967–69; Actress: *stage:* Hair, Shaftesbury Th., 1970–72; Jesus Christ Superstar, Palace, 1972–74; Black Mikado, Cambridge Th., 1974–75; The Husband-in-Law, Comedy, 1976; *television* includes: Within These Walls, 1973–75; Playschool, 1976–88; Playaway, 1976–82; Angels, 1978–80; Send in the Girls, Waterloo Sunset, 1980; Maybury, 1981; Kids, 1982; Fast Forward, 1983–85; Lay-on-Five, 1986–87; Line of Beauty, 2006; Mama Mirabelle's Home Movies, 2007; Sarah Jane Adventures, 2007–08; also produced and starred in: Treehouse, 1987; Playabout, 1990–92; Hullaballoo, 1994; Caribbean Light, 1998; Jamboree, 1998–2001; Caribbean Kitchen, 1999; Taste of Barbados, 2000; Taste of Cuba, 2001; Coming to England, 2003 (RTS Award 2004); *films:* Black Joy, 1977; Run Fatboy Run, 2007. Member: Royal Mail Stamp Adv. Cttee, 1994–2001; Video Consultative Council, 1996–2000, Children's Viewing Adv. Gp, 2000–04, BBFC; Foreign and Commonwealth Caribbean Adv. Gp, 1998–2002; Millennium Commn, 1999–2007; Chairman: Women of Year Lunch, 1996–2000; Pegasus Opera Co., 2007–08. Member: BAFTA, 1990–2001 (Vice-Chm., 1998–99; Chm., TV, 1999–2000); Content Bd, Ofcom, 2003–06. Chancellor, Univ. of Exeter, 2006–. Governor: Nat. Film and Television Sch., 1995–; Commonwealth Inst., 1998–2006; Dulwich Coll., 2001–. Pres., Ramblers' Assoc., 2008–. Hon. DLitt Exeter, 2005. Special Lifetime Achievement Award, BAFTA, 2004. *Publications:* Caribbean Cookery, 1986; *for children:* Floella's Fun Book, 1984; Why the Agouti Has No Tail, 1984; Floella's Funniest Jokes, 1985; Floella's Favourite Folk Tales, 1986; Fall About with Flo, 1986; Floella's Fabulous Bright Ideas, 1986; Floella's Floorboard Book, 1987; Flo and Aston's Books (series of six books), 1987; Snotty and the Rod of Power, 1987; Floella's Cardboard Box Book, 1987; Exploring Caribbean Food in Britain, 1988; For Goodness Sake, 1994; Skip Across the Ocean, 1995; Coming to England, 1995; My Two Grannies, 2007. *Recreations:* golf, cooking, running. *Address:* 73 Palace Road, SW2 3LB; *web:* www.floellabenjamin.com. *Club:* Royal Commonwealth Society (Vice-Pres.).

BENJAMIN, George William John; composer, conductor and pianist; Henry Purcell Professor of Composition, King's College, London University, since 2001; *b* 31 Jan. 1960; *s* of William Benjamin and Susan Benjamin (*née* Bendon). *Educ:* Westminster School (private tuition with Peter Gellhorn); Paris Conservatoire (Olivier Messiaen); King's College, Cambridge (Alexander Goehr). MA, MusB. First London orchestral performance, BBC Proms, 1980; research at Institut de Recherche et Coordination Acoustique/Musique, Paris, 1984–87; Prince Consort Prof. of Composition, RCM, 1994–2001 (Vis. Prof., 1987–94); Principal Guest Artist, Hallé Orch., 1993–96; operatic conducting début, Pelléas et Mélisande, La Monnaie, Brussels, 1999. Artistic Dir, contemp. music festivals, USA (San Francisco Symphony Orch.), France (Opéra Bastille), 1992, and London (South Bank), 1993. Artistic consultant, Sounding the Century, BBC R3, 1996–99. Featured composer: Salzburg Fest., 1995; Tanglewood Fest., 1999, 2002, 2003; LSO Fest,. 2002–03; Deutsches Symphonie Orch., Berlin, 2005; Strasbourg Musica, 2005; Carta Blanca, Madrid, 2005; Fest. d'Automne, Paris, 2006. Hon. FRCM 1993; Hon. RAM 2003. Mem., Bavarian Acad. of Arts, 2000. Lili Boulanger Award, USA, 1985; Koussevitzky Internat. Record Award, 1987; Gramophone Contemp. Music Award, 1990; Edison Award, Holland, 1998; Schönberg Prize, Berlin, 2002; Royal Philharmonic Soc. Awards, 2003, 2004. Chevalier, Ordre des Arts et des Lettres (France), 1996. *Publications: include: orchestral:* Altitude, 1977; Ringed by the Flat Horizon, 1980; A Mind of Winter, 1981; At First Light, 1982; Jubilation, 1985; Antara, 1987; Sudden Time, 1993; Three Inventions for Chamber Orchestra, 1995; Sometime Voices, 1996; Palimpsests I and II, 2000 and 2002; Olicantus, 2002; Dance Figures, 2004; *chamber music:* Violin Sonata, 1977; Piano Sonata, 1978; Octet, 1978; Flight, 1979; Sortilèges, 1981; Three Studies for Solo Piano, 1985; Upon Silence, 1990, 1991; Viola, Viola, 1997; Shadowlines, for solo piano, 2001; Three Miniatures for Violin, 2001; Piano Figures, 2004; *opera:* Into the Little Hill, 2006. *Address:* c/o Faber Music Ltd, 3 Queen Square, WC1N 3AU.

BENJAMIN, Jon; *see* Benjamin, M. J.

BENJAMIN, Leanne, OBE 2005; Principal, Royal Ballet Company, since 1993; *b* Australia, 1964. *Educ:* Royal Ballet Sch. (Adeline Genée Gold Medal). Joined Sadler's Wells Royal Ballet, 1983: Soloist, 1985–87; Principal, 1987–88; Principal: English Nat. Ballet, 1988–90; Deutsche Oper Ballet, Berlin, 1990–92; joined Royal Ballet Co., 1992. Numerous leading rôles; *created roles*: Greta in Metamorphosis; Earth in Homage to the Queen; Mr Worldly Wise; Two-Part Invention; Masquerade; Qualia; Tanglewood; Despite; DGV; Children of Adam. Prix de Lausanne, 1981. *Address:* c/o Royal Ballet, Royal Opera House, Covent Garden, WC2E 9DD.

BENJAMIN, Marc Jonathan, (Jon); Director General and Chief Executive, Board of Deputies of British Jews, since 2005; *b* 31 Oct. 1964; *s* of Alan and Barbara Benjamin; *m* 1990, Suzanne Nicola Taylor; one *s* one *d*. *Educ:* Dulwich Coll.; Univ. of Manchester (LLB Hons); Coll. of Law (Dist.). With Denton Hall, 1988–92; admitted solicitor, 1990; solicitor, Teacher Stern Selby, 1993–96; Hd, Business Div., United Jewish Israel Appeal, 1996–99; Chief Exec., British ORT, 1999–2004. *Recreations:* family, travel, cycling, reading (histories in particular), ski-ing, Crystal Palace FC, music. *Address:* Board of Deputies of British Jews, 6 Bloomsbury Square, WC1A 2LP. *T:* (020) 7543 5400, *Fax:* (020) 7543 0010; *e-mail:* info@bod.org.uk.

BENJAMIN, Dr Ralph, CB 1980; DSc(Eng), PhD, BSc, FCGI, FREng, FIET; Visiting Professor: University College, London, since 1988; University of Bristol, since 1993; *b* 17 Nov. 1922; *s* of Charles Benjamin and Claire Benjamin (*née* Stern); *m* 1951, Kathleen Ruth Bull, BA; one *s* (and one *s* decd). *Educ:* in Germany and Switzerland; St Oswald's Coll., Ellesmere; Imperial Coll. of Science and Technology, London. DSc(Eng) London, 1970; FREng (FEng 1983); FCGI 1982. Joined Royal Naval Scientific Service, 1944; Senior Scientific Officer, 1949; Principal Scientific Officer, 1952; Senior Principal Scientific Officer (Special Merit), 1955; Deputy Chief Scientific Officer (Special Merit), 1960; Head of Research and Deputy Chief Scientist, Admiralty Surface Weapons Establishment, 1961; Dir and Chief Scientist, Admiralty Underwater Weapons Estab., 1964–71, and Dir, Underwater Weapons R&D (Navy), 1965–71; Chief Scientist, GCHQ, 1971–82; Head of Communications Techniques and Networks, SHAPE (NATO) Technical Centre, The Hague, 1982–87. Hon. consultant: Univ. of Illinois; US Office of Naval Research, 1956. Mem. Council, IEE, 1994–97 (Chm., Bristol Area, 1992–93; Chm., Western Centre, 1995–96). Council Mem., Brit. Acoustical Soc., 1971. Visiting Professor: Dept of Electrical and Electronic Engineering, Univ. of Surrey, 1973–80; ICSTM, Univ. of London, 1988–2001; Cranfield Univ., 1991–95. Mem. Court, Brunel Univ., 1997–2003. FRSA 1984. Hon. DEng Bristol, 2000. IEE Marconi Premium, 1964; IERE Heinrich Hertz Premium, 1980, 1983; Clark Maxwell Premium, 1995; IET Award, 2006; Oliver Lodge Medal, 2007. *Publications:* Modulation, Resolution and Signal Processing for Radar Sonar and Related Systems, 1966; Five Lives in One (autobiog.), 1996; contribs to various advisory cttees, working parties, symposia, etc; articles in various professional jls. *Recreations:* work, hill-walking, swimming. *Address:* 13 Bellhouse Walk, Rockwell Park, Bristol BS11 0UE. *Club:* Athenæum.

BENN, Anthony, OBE 1945; *b* 7 Oct. 1912; *s* of late Francis Hamilton Benn and Arta Clara Benn (*née* Boal); *m* 1943, Maureen Lillian Kathleen Benn (*née* Denbigh) (*d* 1992); two *s* four *d*. *Educ:* Harrow; Christ Church, Oxford (Scholar). Oxford Univ. Cricket XI, 1935. Price & Pierce Ltd, 1935 (Director, 1947, Chm., 1956–72). Joined Surrey and Sussex Yeomanry, 1936. Served War of 1939–45 (OBE): Staff Coll., 1942; Instructor, Middle East Staff Coll., 1943. Comdr, Order of the Lion of Finland, 1958. *Recreation:* travel.

BENN, Edward, CMG 1981; Minister (Defence, Research and Development, later Defence Equipment), British Embassy, Washington, 1978–82, retired; *b* 8 May 1922; *s* of John Henry Benn and Alice (*née* Taylor); *m* 1947, Joan Taylor; one *d*. *Educ:* High Storrs Grammar Sch., Sheffield; Sheffield Univ. (BEng; 1st Cl. Hons Civil Engrg; Mappin Medal, 1943). Operational Research with Army, 1943–48; India and Burma, 1944–46 (Major); entered War Office, 1948; tank research, Supt Special Studies, and later Dep. Dir, Army Op. Res. Estabt, 1961; Asst Sci. Adviser to SACEUR, Paris, 1962–65; Dep. Chief Sci. Adviser, Home Office, 1966–68; Dir, Defence Policy, MoD, 1968–75; Under Sec. and Dep. Chief Scientist (RAF), MoD, 1975–78. *Recreation:* golf. *Address:* 7 Hiatt Road, Minchinhampton, Glos GL6 9DB. *T:* (01453) 883005. *Club:* Minchinhampton Golf.

BENN, Rt Hon. Hilary (James Wedgwood); PC 2003; MP (Lab) Leeds Central, since June 1999; Secretary of State for Environment, Food and Rural Affairs, since 2007; *b* 26 Nov. 1953; *s* of Rt Hon. Tony Benn, *qv*; *m* 1st, 1973, Rosalind Caroline Retey (*d* 1979); 2nd, 1982, Sally Christina Clark; three *s* one *d*. *Educ:* Holland Park Comprehensive Sch.; Sussex Univ. (BA Hons Russian and East European Studies). Res. Asst, Nat. Referendum Campaign, 1975; Res. Officer, 1975–93, Head of Res., 1993–96, Head of Policy and Communications, 1996–97, ASTMS, then MSF; Jt Sec., Finance Panel, Labour Party Commn of Inquiry, on secondment, 1980; Special Advr to Sec. of State for Educn and Employment, 1997–99. MSF Rep., Labour Party Nat. Policy Forum, 1994–97; Chair: Educn Cttee, ALA, 1988–90; Unions 21, 1995–99; Member: Educn Cttee, AMA, 1986–90; Envmt Policy Commn, Labour Party, 1994–97; Party into Power Task Force on Labour Party's Democracy, 1996–97. Parliamentary Under-Secretary of State: DFID, 2001–02; Home Office, 2002–03; Minister of State, DFID, 2003; Sec. of State for Internat. Develt, 2003–07. Mem., Envmt, Transport and the Regions Select Cttee, 1999–2001. Vice-Chair, PLP Educn and Employment Cttee, 2000–01; Pres., Acton CLP, 1979–82. Mem. (Lab) Ealing LBC, 1979–99 (Dep. Leader, 1986–90; Chair, Educn Cttee, 1986–90; Dep. Leader, Labour Gp, 1984–94). Vice-Chm., Commn for Africa, 2004–05. Contested (Lab) Ealing N, 1983, 1987. *Publications:* (contrib.) Beyond 2002: long-term policies for Labour, 1999; (contrib.) Men Who Made Labour, 2006. *Recreations:* watching sport, gardening. *Address:* House of Commons, SW1A 0AA.

BENN, Sir (James) Jonathan, 4th Bt *cr* 1914; Chairman, SCA Pension Trusts Ltd, 1988–98; *b* 27 July 1933; *s* of Sir John Andrews Benn, 3rd Bt, and Hon. Ursula Lady Benn, *o d* of 1st Baron Hankey, PC, GCB, GCMG, GCVO, FRS; *S* father, 1984; *m* 1960, Jennifer Mary, *e d* of late Dr Wilfred Howells, OBE; one *s* one *d*. *Educ:* Harrow; Clare College, Cambridge (MA). Various positions with Reed International PLC (formerly A. E. Reed & Co.), 1957–88; Dir, Reed Paper & Board (UK) Ltd, 1971, Man. Dir 1976; Dir, Reed Group Ltd, 1976; Chm. and Chief Exec., Reed Paper & Board (UK) Ltd, 1977–90; Chm., Reedpack Paper Gp, 1988–90; Dir, Reedpack Ltd, 1988–90. Pres., British Paper and Board Industries Fedn, 1985–87. Dir, Broomhill Trust, 1991–96. *Recreations:* golf, ski-ing, music. *Heir:* *s* Robert Ernest Benn [*b* 17 Oct. 1963; *m* 1985, Sheila Margaret, 2nd *d* of Dr Alastair Blain; one *s* one *d*]. *Address:* Fielden Lodge, Ightham, Kent TN15 9AN.

See also T. J. Benn.

BENN, Timothy John; Chairman, Timothy Benn Publishing Ltd, 1983–97, and other companies; *b* 27 Oct. 1936; *yr s* of Sir John Andrews Benn, 3rd Bt, and Hon. Ursula Helen Alers Hankey; *m* 1982, Christina Grace Townsend. *Educ:* Harrow; Clare Coll., Cambridge (MA); Princeton Univ., USA; Harvard Business Sch., USA (National Marketing Council Course; Scholarship Award). FInstM. 2nd Lieut Scots Guards, 1956–57. Benn Brothers Ltd: Board Member, 1961–82; Managing Director, 1972–82; Dep. Chm., 1976–81; Chm., Benn Brothers plc, 1981–82; Ernest Benn: Board Member, 1967–82; Managing Director, 1973–82; Chairman and Managing Director, 1974–82. Chairman: Bouverie Publishing Co., 1983–2003; Buckley Press, 1984–97; Henry Greenwood and Co., 1987–98; Dalesman Publishing Co., 1989–2004; The Countryman Publishing Co., 2000–04; Dir, Huveaux plc, 2001–06. Chairman: Council, PPA, 1970–73; Nat. Advertising Benevolent Soc., 1970–71; Member: Council, Advertising Assoc., 1962; Special Projects Cttee, Crafts Council, 1979–82. President: Thirty Club of London, 1979–82; Tonbridge Civic Soc., 1982–87. *Publication:* The (Almost) Compleat Angler, 1985. *Recreations:* writing, gardening, flyfishing, toymaking. *Address:* Chase Cottage, Chase Lane, Blackdown, Haslemere, Surrey GU8 6LG. *Club:* Flyfishers'.

See also Sir J. J. Benn.

BENN, Rt Hon. Tony; PC 1964; *b* 3 April 1925; *er* surv. *s* of 1st Viscount Stansgate, DSO, DFC, PC, former Labour MP and Cabinet Minister (*d* 1960); having unsuccessfully attempted to renounce his right of succession, 1955 and 1960, won a bye-election in May 1961 only to be prevented from taking seat; instigated Act to make disclaimer possible, and disclaimed title for life, 1963; *m* 1949, Caroline Middleton De Camp, MA (*d* 2000); three *s* one *d*. *Educ:* New Coll., Oxford (Hon. Fellow, 2005). Served: RAFVR, 1943–45; RNVR, 1945–46. Joined Labour Party, 1943; Mem., NEC, 1959–60, 1962–93 (Chm., 1971–72); candidate for leadership of Labour Party, 1976, 1988, and for dep. leadership, 1971, 1981. MP (Lab): Bristol SE, Nov. 1950–1960 and Aug. 1963–1983; Chesterfield, 1984–2001; Postmaster-Gen., 1964–66; Minister of Technology, 1966–70, assumed responsibility for Min. of Aviation, 1967 and Min. of Power, 1969; opposition spokesman on Trade and Industry, 1970–74; Sec. of State for Industry, 1974–75; Sec. of State for Energy, 1975–79. Pres., EEC Council of Energy Ministers, 1977. Pres., Campaign Gp, subseq. Socialist Campaign Gp of Lab. MPs, 1987–2001. Contested (Lab) Bristol East, 1983. Vis. Prof. of Govt, LSE, 2001–03. Pres., Stop the War Coalition, 2004–. Freedom of the City of Bristol, 2003. Awarded 10 hon. doctorates from univs in UK and USA. *Publications:* The Privy Council as a Second Chamber, 1957; The Regeneration of Britain, 1964; The New Politics, 1970; Speeches, 1974; Arguments for Socialism, 1979; Arguments for Democracy, 1981; (ed) Writings on the Wall: a radical and socialist anthology 1215–1984, 1984; Out of the Wilderness, Diaries 1963–1967, 1987; Fighting Back: speaking out for Socialism in the Eighties, 1988; Office Without Power, Diaries 1968–72, 1988; Against the Tide, Diaries 1973–76, 1989; Conflicts of Interest, Diaries 1977–80, 1990; A Future for Socialism, 1991; The End of an Era, Diaries 1980–1990, 1992; (jtly) Common Sense, 1993; Years of Hope: Diaries, Letters and Papers 1940–1962, 1994; The Benn Diaries 1940–1990, 1995; Free at Last!: Diaries 1990–2001, 2002; Free Radical, 2003; Dare to Be a Daniel, 2004; More Time for Politics: diaries 2001–2007, 2007; numerous pamphlets, videos and audio tapes. *Address:* 12 Holland Park Avenue, W11 3QU; *e-mail:* tony@tbenn.fsnet.co.uk.

See also Rt Hon. H. J. W. Benn.

BENN, Rt Rev. Wallace Parke; *see* Lewes, Bishop Suffragan of.

BENNATHAN, Joel Nathan; QC 2006; *b* 15 July 1961; *s* of Esra and Marion Bennathan; *m* 2004, Melanie Gingell; one *s* two *d*. *Educ:* Bristol Grammar Sch.; Queen Mary Coll., Univ. of London (LLB). Called to the Bar, Middle Temple, 1985; specialising in criminal law. Dep. Chm., Soc. of Labour Lawyers, 2003–. *Publications:* legal articles in The Times, Solicitors' Jl and New Statesman. *Recreations:* art, theatre, family, socialism. *Address:* Tooks Chambers, 8 Warner Yard, Warner Street, E1R 5EY.

BENNER, Patrick, CB 1975; Deputy Secretary, Department of Health and Social Security, 1976–84; *b* 26 May 1923; *s* of Henry Grey and Gwendolen Benner; *m* 1952, Joan Christabel Draper; two *d*. *Educ:* Ipswich Sch.; University Coll., Oxford. Entered Min. of Health as Asst Princ., 1949; Princ., 1951; Princ. Private Sec. to Minister, 1955; Asst Sec., 1958; Under-Sec., Min. of Health, 1967–68, DHSS 1968–72; Dep. Sec., Cabinet Office, 1972–76. Chm., Rural Dispensing Cttee, 1987–91; Member: Exec. Council, Hosp. Saving Assoc., 1984–99; Exec. Cttee, Musicians Benevolent Fund, 1985–99 (Dep. Chm., 1996–99). *Address:* 12 Manor Gardens, Hampton, Middx TW12 2TU. *T:* (020) 8783 0848. *Club:* National Liberal.

BENNET, family name of **Earl of Tankerville**.

BENNET, Dr Carey Louise; Director for Schools, Children and Families, Essex County Council, since 2007; *b* 10 Jan. 1958; *d* of Robin Bennet and Ann-Marie Bennet; *m* 1989, Peter James Cunningham; two *s*. *Educ:* Froebel Inst., Roehampton; Jesus Coll., Oxford; Linacre Coll., Oxford (DPhil). Education Officer: Leics CC, 1987–90; Cambs CC, 1990–2000; Asst Dir of Educn, Northants CC, 2000–03; Dir for Schs, Essex CC, 2003–06. *Publication:* (with P. J. Downes) Help Your Child Through Secondary School, 1997. *Recreation:* art, travel, cinema, theatre. *Address:* Essex County Council, County Hall, Chelmsford, Essex CM1 1LX. *T:* (01245) 431893; *e-mail:* carey.bennet@essexcc.gov.uk.

BENNETT, Alan; dramatist and actor; *b* 9 May 1934; *s* of Walter Bennett and Lilian Mary Peel; civil partnership 2006, Rupert Thomas. *Educ:* Leeds Modern Sch.; Exeter Coll., Oxford (BA Modern History, 1957; Hon. Fellow, 1987). Jun. Lectr, Modern History, Magdalen Coll., Oxford, 1960–62. Trustee, National Gall., 1993–98. Hon. FRA 2000. Hon. DLitt Leeds, 1990. Co-author and actor, Beyond the Fringe, Royal Lyceum, Edinburgh, 1960, Fortune, London, 1961 and Golden, NY, 1962; author and actor, On the Margin (TV series), 1966; *stage plays:* Forty Years On, Apollo, 1968; Getting On, Queen's, 1971; Habeas Corpus, Lyric, 1973; The Old Country, Queen's, 1977; Enjoy, Vaudeville, 1980; Kafka's Dick, Royal Court, 1986; Single Spies (double bill: A Question of Attribution; An Englishman Abroad (also dir)), NT, 1988; The Wind in the Willows (adapted), NT, 1990; The Madness of George III, NT, 1991; Talking Heads, Comedy, 1992 and 1996; The Lady in the Van, Queen's, 1999; The History Boys, NT, 2004, NY, 2006; *BBC TV films:* A Day Out, 1972; Sunset Across the Bay, 1975; *TV Plays for LWT,* 1978–79: Doris and Doreen; The Old Crowd; Me! I'm Afraid of Virginia Woolf; All Day on the Sands; Afternoon Off; One Fine Day; *BBC TV plays:* A Little Outing, A Visit from Miss Prothero, 1977; Intensive Care, Say Something Happened, Our Winnie, Marks, A Woman of No Importance, Rolling Home; An Englishman Abroad, 1983; The Insurance Man, 1986; Talking Heads (series), 1988 (adapted for stage comedy, 1992); 102 Boulevard Haussmann, 1991; A Question of Attribution, 1991; Talking Heads 2 (series), 1998; Telling Tales (series), 2000; *BBC TV documentaries:* Dinner at Noon, 1988; Portrait or Bust, 1994; The Abbey, 1995; *Channel 4:* Poetry in Motion, 1990; Poetry in Motion 2, 1992; *feature films:* A Private Function, 1984; Prick Up Your Ears, 1987; The Madness of King George, 1995; The History Boys, 2006. *Publications:* (with Cook, Miller and Moore) Beyond the Fringe, 1962; Forty Years On, 1969; Getting On, 1972; Habeas Corpus, 1973; The Old Country, 1978; Enjoy, 1980; Office Suite, 1981; Objects of Affection, 1982; A Private Function, 1984; The Writer in Disguise, 1985; Prick Up Your Ears (screenplay), 1987; Two Kafka Plays, 1987; Talking Heads, 1988 (Hawthornden Prize, 1989); Single Spies, 1989; The Lady in the Van, 1990; Poetry in Motion, 1990; The Wind in the Willows (adaptation), 1991; The Madness of George III, 1992; (jtly) Poetry in Motion 2, 1992; Writing Home, 1994 (collected articles); The Madness of King George (screenplay), 1995; The Clothes They Stood Up In, 1998; The Complete Talking Heads, 1998; The Lady in the Van, 2000; Father! Father! Burning Bright, 2000; Telling Tales (autobiog.), 2000; The Laying On of Hands, 2001; The History Boys, 2004, screenplay, 2006; Untold Stories, 2005; The Uncommon Reader, 2007. *Address:* c/o Chatto & Linnit, 123A King's Road, SW3 4PL. *T:* (020) 7352 7722.

BENNETT, (Albert) Edward; Director, G24 Nuclear Safety Assistance Co-ordination Centre, 1992–95, and Directorate of Nuclear Safety, Industry and the Environment, and Civil Protection (formerly of Nuclear Safety and Control of Chemical Pollution), 1987–95, European Commission; *b* 11 Sept. 1931; *s* of Albert Edward and Frances Ann Bennett; *m* 1957, Jean Louise Paston-Cooper; two *s*. *Educ:* University Coll. Sch., Hampstead; London Hosp. Med. Coll. MB BS London; FFCM 1972, FFOM 1984. Surgeon Lieut, RN, 1957–60; Senior Lectr, Dept of Clinical Epidemiology and Social Medicine, St. Thomas's Hosp. Med. Sch., 1964–70; Dir, Health Services Evaluation Gp, Univ. of Oxford, 1970–77; Prof. and Head of Dept of Clinical Epidemiology and Social Medicine, St George's Hosp. Med. Sch., Univ. of London, 1974–81; Director: Health and Safety Directorate, EEC, 1981–87. Hon. Editor, Internat. Jl of Epidemiology, 1977–81. *Publications:* Questionnaires in Medicine, 1975; (ed) Communications between Doctors and Patients, 1976; (ed) Recent Advances in Community Medicine, 1978; numerous sci. reports and contribs on epidemiology of chronic disease and evaluation of health services. *Recreations:* opera, gardening, browsing.

See also N. E. F. Bennett.

BENNETT, Andrew Francis; retired teacher; *b* Manchester, 9 March 1939; *m*; two *s* one *d*. *Educ:* Birmingham Univ. (BSocSc). Joined Labour Party, 1957; Member, Oldham Borough Council, 1964–74. Member, National Union of Teachers. Contested (Lab) Knutsford, 1970. MP (Lab) Stockport North, Feb. 1974–1983, Denton and Reddish, 1983–2005. An Opposition spokesperson on educn, 1983–88. Jt Chm., Select Cttee on Envmt, Transport and Regl Affairs, 1997–2005 (Chm., Envmt Sub-Cttee, 1997–2005). Interested especially in environment and education. *Recreations:* photography, walking, climbing. *Address:* 28 Brownsville Road, Stockport SK4 4PF.

BENNETT, Andrew John, CMG 1998; Director, Syngenta Foundation for Sustainable Agriculture, since 2002 (Executive Director, 2002–07); *b* 25 April 1942; *s* of Leonard Charles Bennett and Edna Mary Bennett (*née* Harding); *m* 1996, Yin Yin Jackson. *Educ:* St Edward's Sch., Oxford; University Coll. of N Wales (BSc Agr Scis 1965); Univ. of West Indies, Trinidad (DipTropAg 1967); Univ. of Reading (MSc Crop Protection 1970). VSO Kenya, 1965–66; Agricl Officer (Research), Govt of St Vincent, 1967–69; Maize Agronomist, Govt of Malawi, 1971–74; Crop Develt Manager, 1976–78, Chief Research Officer. 1978–79, S Region, Sudan; Asst Agricl Adviser, ODA, 1980–83; Natural Resources Adviser (ODA), SE Asia Develt Div., Bangkok, 1983–85; Head, British Develt Div. in Pacific (ODA), Fiji, 1985–87; Chief Natural Resources Advr, ODA, FCO, subseq. DFID, 1987–2002. Dir and Sec., Eynesbury Estates, 1990–. Pres., Tropical Agric. Assoc., 2003–. Chm., Bd of Trustees, Sci. Develt Network, 2008–; Member: Bd Trustees, Centre for Internat. Forestry Res., 2002– (Chm., 2006–); Council, ODI, 2003–; Interim Panel, Global Crop Diversity Trust, 2003–06; Dir, Doyle Foundn, 2002–. FRSA 2000. Hon. DSc Cranfield, 1999. *Recreations:* walking, gardening. *Address:* 65D Warwick Square, SW1V 2AL. *T:* (020) 7834 3093; *e-mail:* andrewj.bennett@btinternet.com.

BENNETT, Brian Maurice; HM Diplomatic Service, retired; Ambassador to Belarus, 2003–07; Administrator, Humphrey Richardson Taylor Charitable Trust, since 2008; *b* 1 April 1948; *s* of Valentine and Dorothy Bennett; *m* 1969, Lynne Skipsey; three *s*. *Educ:* Totton Grammar Sch.; Sheffield Univ. (BA Hons Russian). AIL 1988. Joined HM Diplomatic Service, 1971; Prague, 1973–76; Helsinki, 1977–79; Bridgetown, Barbados, 1983–86; Vienna, 1986–88; The Hague, 1988–92; Dep. Hd of Mission, Tunis, 1997–2000. *Recreations:* singing, walking, table tennis.

BENNETT, Clive Ronald Reath, CBE 2007; CEng; Managing Director, Imago Services Ltd, since 2008; *b* 20 Dec. 1947; *s* of Ron and Betty Bennett; *m* 1970, Pauline Weeks; two *d*. *Educ:* Hatfield Poly. (BSc). CEng 1971. Design Engr, Norton Abrasives Ltd, 1970–71; Industrial Engr, Radiomobile (Smiths Industries), 1971–73; Rank Xerox (UK) Ltd: Technical Service and Supply Dir, 1973–83; Gen. Manager, Supplies Distribn, 1983–84; Gen. Manager, Distribn, Polycell Products, 1984–87; Business Excellence Dir, Sara Lee Household and Personal Care, 1987–94; Gp Ops Dir, Norton Health Care, 1994–99; Chief Exec., DVLA, 2000–07. *Recreations:* music, swimming.

BENNETT, Corinne Gillian, MBE 1988; FSA; historic buildings consultant, 1996–98; Cathedrals Architect at English Heritage, 1992–96; *b* 3 March 1935; *d* of Gilbert Wilson and Lucile (*née* Terroux); *m* 1979, Keith Charles Hugh Bennett. *Educ:* University Coll. London (BA Hons Arch. 1957; Inst. of Archaeology, London Univ. (Dip. Conservation of Historic Monuments 1964). ARIBA 1959. FSA 1996. Assistant Architect: Powell & Moya, 1958–61; Manning & Clamp, 1961–62; Architect, Ancient Monuments Br., MPBW, 1963–68; joined Purcell Miller Tritton, Associate, 1968, Partner, 1972–92. Consulting Surveyor, Archdeacons of Rochester Dio., 1969–84; Architect, Dean and Chapter of Winchester, 1974–89; Consultant Architect, Brighton BC (for Royal Pavilion), 1981–92. Mem., Cathedrals Fabric Commn for England, 1996–2006. DHS 1979, DCHS 1988, DGCHS 2000. *Recreations:* opera, walking, gardening.

BENNETT, David John, FCA; Group Chief Executive (formerly Managing Director), Sanctuary Housing Group, since 1992; *b* 16 April 1951; *s* of Wing Comdr Donald Albert Bennett, MBE and Eva Mary Bennett; *m* 1987, Katrina Momcilovic; two *d*. *Educ:* De Aston Sch. FCA 1975. Payne Stone Fraser, Chartered Accountants, 1969–74; Management Accountant, Beecham Pharmaceuticals, 1974–76; Chief Accountant, Heurtey Petrochem, 1976–80; Financial Controller: Samuel Lewis Trust, 1980–82; Peabody Trust, 1982–85; Finance Dir, 1985–86, Chief Exec., 1986–89, Spiral Housing Assoc.; Dep. Chief Exec., Sanctuary Housing Assoc., 1989–92. Gov., Sutton Community Sch., 2003–. *Recreations:* music, photography, game fishing. *Address:* c/o Sanctuary House, Chamber Court, Castle Street, Worcester WR1 3ZQ. *T:* (01905) 338607, *Fax:* (01905) 338701; *e-mail:* davidbt@sanctuary-housing.co.uk.

BENNETT, David Jonathan; Group Chief Executive, Alliance & Leicester plc, since 2007; *b* 26 March 1962; *m* 1991, Sue Moss; two *s*. *Educ:* King's Coll. Sch., Wimbledon; Queens' Coll., Cambridge (BA Hons Econs 1983). Grindlays Bank, 1983–85; Money Market Dealer: Chemical Bank, 1985–86; Abbey Nat. Building Soc., 1986–88; Cheltenham & Gloucester plc: Gen. Mgr (Treasury and Investments), 1988–93; Head: of Strategic Planning, 1994; of Sales and Marketing, 1994–95; Finance Dir, 1995–96; Exec. Dir, NBNZ, 1996–98; CEO, Countrywide Bank, Lloyds TSB Gp, 1999; Alliance & Leicester plc: Gp Treas., 1999–2000; Exec. Dir, 2000–01; Gp Finance Dir, 2001–07. Non-exec. Dir, easyJet plc, 2005–. *Recreations:* travel, Rugby supporter. *Address:* c/o Alliance & Leicester plc, Carlton Park, Customer Service Centre, Narborough, Leicester LE19 0AL.

BENNETT, Douglas Simon; Chief Executive, North London Hospice, since 2002; *b* 18 Aug. 1958. *Educ:* Bristol Univ. (LLB); Brunel Univ. (MA Public Sector Mgt 1989). Trainee Solicitor, Slaughter & May, 1980–82; admitted Solicitor, 1982; Society of Voluntary Associations: Inner London Co-ordinator, 1982–84; Asst Dir, 1984–86; Dep. Dir, 1986–88; Dir, Age Concern, Brent, 1989; Head of Planning, British Red Cross, 1989–97; Chief Exec., Nat. Soc. for Epilepsy, 1997–2000; Univ. of Salamanca, 2000–01. *Recreations:* meals with friends, walking, swimming, reading, going to cinema and theatre. *Address:* North London Hospice, 47 Woodside Avenue, N12 8TF.

BENNETT, Dudley Paul; His Honour Judge Dudley Bennett; a Circuit Judge, since 1993; *b* 4 Aug. 1948; *s* of late Patrick James Bennett and of Mary Bennett (*née* Edmondson); *m*; two *d*. *Educ:* Bradfield Coll.; LSE (LLB). Called to the Bar, Inner Temple, 1972; Recorder of the Crown Court, 1988–93. *Recreations:* travel, gardening, Afghan Hounds. *Address:* The Crown Court, Canal Street, Nottingham NG1 7EJ. *Club:* United Services (Nottingham).

BENNETT, Edward; *see* Bennett, A. E.

BENNETT, Elizabeth Martin; *see* Allen, E. M.

BENNETT, Air Vice Marshal Sir Erik Peter, KBE 1990; CB 1984; retired from RAF, 1991; Commander, Sultan of Oman's Air Force (in the rank of Air Marshal), 1974–90; *s* of Robert Francis and Anne Myra Bennett. *Educ:* The King's Hospital, Dublin. Air Adviser to King Hussein, 1958–62; RAF Staff College, 1963; Jt Services Staff Coll., 1968; RAF Coll. of Air Warfare, 1971. Order of Istiqlal (Jordan), 1960; Order of Oman, 1980; Order of Merit (Oman), 1989; Order of Sultan Qaboos (Oman), 1985; Medal of Honour (Oman), 1989. *Recreations:* riding, sailing, big game fishing. *Address:* Al Hail Farm, Seeb-Hail Al Awahir, PO Box 1751, Postal Code 111, Sultanate of Oman. *Clubs:* Royal Air Force, Beefsteak, Pratt's.

BENNETT, His Honour Harry Graham; QC 1968; a Circuit Judge, 1972–91; Designated Circuit Judge, Leeds, 1988–91; *b* 19 Sept. 1921; *s* of Ernest and Alice Mary Bennett, Cleckheaton, Yorks; *m* 1987, Elizabeth, *widow* of Judge Allister Lonsdale. *Educ:* Whitcliffe Mount Grammar Sch., Cleckheaton; King's Coll., London. Royal Artillery, 1943–47. Called to Bar, Gray's Inn, 1948. Recorder: Doncaster, 1966–68; York, 1968–71 (Hon. Recorder, 1972–93); Crown Court, 1972; Dep. Chm., ER of Yorks QS, 1964–71. Chm., Agricl Land Tribunal (N Area), 1967–72; Chm., Cttee of Inquiry into Police Interrogation Procedures in NI, 1978–79.

BENNETT, Hon. Sir Hugh (Peter Derwyn), Kt 1995; **Hon. Mr Justice Bennett;** DL; a Judge of the High Court of Justice, Family Division, since 1995; Nominated Administrative Court Judge, since 2004; *b* 8 Sept. 1943; *s* of late Peter Ward Bennett, OBE, and Priscilla Ann Bennett; *m* 1969, Elizabeth (*née* Landon); one *s* three *d*. *Educ:* Haileybury and ISC; Churchill College, Cambridge (MA). Called to the Bar, Inner Temple, 1966, Bencher, 1993; an Assistant Recorder, 1987; QC 1988; a Recorder, 1990–95. Presiding Judge, NE Circuit, 1999–2002. Mem., Supreme Court Rule Cttee, 1988–92; Chm. (part-time), Betting Levy Appeal Tribunal, 1989–95. Hon. Legal Advr, Sussex County Playing Fields Assoc., 1988–95. Chm., Sussex Assoc. for Rehabilitation of Offenders, 1998–2004. Fellow of Woodard Corp., 1987–99; Mem. Council, Lancing Coll., 1981–95. DL W Sussex, 2003. *Recreations:* cricket, tennis, shooting, fishing. *Address:* Royal Courts of Justice, Strand, WC2A 2LL. *Clubs:* Garrick, Pilgrims, MCC; Sussex.

See also Sir H. J. F. S. Cholmeley, Bt.

BENNETT, Hywel Thomas; actor; director; *b* Wales, 8 April 1944; *s* of Gordon Bennett and Sarah Gwen Bennett (*née* Lewis); *m* 1st, 1967, Cathy McGowan (marr. diss. 1988); one *d*; 2nd, 1996, Sandra Elayne Fulford. *Educ:* Henry Thornton Grammar School, Clapham; RADA (scholarship). *Stage:* Nat. Youth Theatre for 5 years; repertory, Salisbury and Leatherhead; first major roles in The Screwtape Letters and A Smashing Day, Arts Th., 1966; Shakespeare at Mermaid, Young Vic, Shaw Theatres; repertory, 1972–77 (roles included Jimmy Porter, in Look Back in Anger, Belgrade, and Hamlet, S Africa); Otherwise Engaged, Comedy, 1977; Night Must Fall, Shaw Th., 1977; Levantine, Her Majesty's, 1979; Terra Nova, Chichester, 1980; Fly Away Home, Lyric, Hammersmith, 1983; She Stoops to Conquer, Nat. Theatre, 1985; Toad of Toad Hall; Three Sisters, Albery, 1987; Edinburgh Festival, 1967 and 1990 (Long John Silver, in Treasure Island); *directed:* plays at provincial theatres incl. Lincoln, Leatherhead, Birmingham, Coventry, Sheffield and Cardiff; *films:* The Family Way, 1966; Twisted Nerve, 1968; The Virgin Soldiers, 1969; Loot, 1970; The Buttercup Chain, 1971; Endless Night, 1971; Alice in Wonderland, 1972; Twilight Zone, 1987; Murder Elite, 1990; War Zone, 1990; Age Unknown, 1992; Deadly Advice, 1994; Married to Malcolm, 1997; Misery Harbour, 1998; Nasty Neighbours, 1998; Vatel, 1999; Mary of Nazareth, 1999; *TV plays and films include:* Romeo and Juliet; The Idiot; A Month in the Country; Trust Me; Artemis 81; Frankie and Johnnie; The Other Side of Paradise; Murder Most Horrid; The Quest; Lloyd and Hill; One for the Road; *TV series:* Malice Aforethought; Pennies from Heaven; Tinker, Tailor, Soldier, Spy; Shelley (10 series); Where the Buffalo Roam; Death of a Teddy Bear; The Consultant; Absent Friends; Myself a Mandarin; The Secret Agent; A Mind to Kill; Casualty; Virtual Murder; Neverwhere; Lock Stock; Frontiers; Karaoke; Last of the Summer Wine; Time Gentlemen Please; The Bill; Eastenders, 2002; The Quest 1–3, 2002–04; many radio plays, commercial voiceovers and film narrations. Hon. Fellow, Cardiff Univ., 1996. *Recreations:* fishing, golf, reading, walking. *Address:* c/o Gavin Barker Associates, 2D Wimpole Street, W1G 0EB. *T:* (020) 7499 4777. *Club:* Savile.

BENNETT, Dr James Arthur; Director, Museum of the History of Science, and Fellow of Linacre College, University of Oxford, since 1994; *b* 2 April 1947; *s* of James Hutchinson Bennett and Margaret Anna Bennett (*née* McCune); *m* 1st, 1971, France Annie Ramette (marr. diss. 2002); two *d*; 2nd, 2005, Sylvia Sumira. *Educ:* Grosvenor High Sch., Belfast; Clare Coll., Univ. of Cambridge (BA 1969; PhD 1974). FRAS 1976; FSA 1989. Lectr, Univ. of Aberdeen, 1973–74; Archivist, Royal Astronomical Soc., 1974–1976; Curator of Astronomy, Nat. Maritime Mus. 1977–79; Curator, Whipple Mus. of Hist. of Sci., Cambridge, 1979–94; Sen. Res. Fellow, 1984–94, Sen. Tutor, 1992–94, Churchill Coll., Cambridge. Mem. Cttee, Sci. Mus., 2004–. President: Scientific Instrument Commn, IUHPS, 1998–2002; British Soc. for History of Sci., 2000–02. Paul Bunge Prize, German Chemical Soc., 2001. Member, Editorial Board: Jl for History of Astronomy, 1990–; Notes and Records, Royal Soc., 2000–; Isis, 2001–03; Nuncius, 2001–. *Publications:* The Mathematical Science of Christopher Wren, 1982; The Divided Circle, 1987; Church, State and Astronomy in Ireland, 1990; (ed jtly) Making Instruments Count, 1993; (with S. Johnston) The Geometry of War, 1996; (with S. Mandelbrote) The Garden, the Ark, the Tower, the Temple, 1998; (jtly) London's Leonardo, 2003; (ed jtly) Oxford Companion to the History of Modern Science, 2003; articles in books and jls, and exhibition catalogues. *Recreations:* music, Rugby, cooking. *Address:* Museum of the History of Science, Broad Street, Oxford OX1 3AZ. *T:* (01865) 277280.

BENNETT, Jana Eve, OBE 2000; Director of Vision (formerly Television), BBC, since 2002; *b* 6 Nov. 1956; *d* of Gordon Willard Bennett and Elizabeth (*née* Cushing); *m* 1996, Richard Clemmow; one *s* one *d*. *Educ:* Bognor Regis Comprehensive Sch.; St Anne's Coll., Oxford (BA PPE); London Sch. of Econs (MSc with dist. Internat. Relns). Co-editor, Millennium, jl internat. relns; British Broadcasting Corporation: news trainee, 1978; news daily editor; series producer, then Ed., Antenna, 1987; Ed., Horizon, 1990; Head, BBC Science, 1994–97; Dir and Dep. Chief Exec., BBC Prodn, 1997–99; Exec. Vice-Pres., Learning Channel, US Discovery Communications Inc., 1999–2002; Member: Exec. Bd, BBC; Bd, BBC Worldwide; Bd, UKTV. Trustee, Natural Hist. Mus., 1999–2004 (American Friend, 2004–). Gov., RSC, 2005–. Gov., LSE, 2002–07. FRTS 1999. *Publication:* (jtly) The Disappeared: Argentina's dirty war, 1986. *Recreations:* ski-ing, family, travel, world music. *Address:* BBC TV Centre, Wood Lane, W12 7RJ.

BENNETT, Jeremy John Nelson; independent producer; Director, 3BM Television, 1995–2004 (Managing Director and Chairman, 1995–2001); *b* 1 Dec. 1939; *s* of Denis Pengelley Bennett and Jill (*née* Nelson); *m* 1963, Tine Langkilde; three *s*. *Educ:* Haileybury; Clare Coll., Cambridge (Open Schol. in Hist.; MA); Copenhagen Univ. (Churchill Fellow). With British Council, 1963–65; BBC European Service, 1966–68; Producer/Dir, BBC TV documentaries, 1968–89; Producer, Richard Dimbleby Lecture, 1983–87; Exec. Producer, Contemporary Hist. Unit, 1989–92; freelance, 1993–95. *Productions* include: Cry Hungary, 1986 and 1996 (Blue Ribbon Award, American Film Fest.); Juan Carlos, King of All the Spaniards, 1980 and 1986; Alphabet: the Story of Writing (Silver Award, NY Film and TV Fest., 1980; Times Newcomer Award); Monty: in Love and War, 1987 (Blue Ribbon Award, American Film Fest.); Churchill, 1992; The Cuban Missile Crisis, 1992 (US Nat. Emmy Award); Chairman Mao: The Last Emperor, 1993; Hiroshima, 1995; The Suez Crisis, 1996; The Berlin Airlift, 1998; The Illuminator, 2003; *TV histories of the BBC:* What Did You Do in the War, Auntie?, 1995; Auntie: The Inside Story, 1997. Associate Fellow, Centre for Cultural Policy Studies, Warwick Univ., 2003–. Chairman: Camberwell Soc., 1979–85 (Pres., 2007–); Southwark Envmt Trust, 1987–95; Groundwork Southwark and Lambeth (formerly Southwark), 1995–2007; Groundwork London, 2007–; Member: Bd, Cross River Partnership, 1995–2006; Bd, Groundwork Nat. Fedn, 1999–; Bd, Southwark Alliance, 2006–. Southwark Citizen of the Year, Southwark LBC, 2003. Cross of Merit, Order of Vitez (Hungary), 1987. *Publications:* British Broadcasting and the Danish Resistance Movement 1940–45, 1966; The Master-Builders, 2004. *Recreations:* fishing, walking in Powys, the urban environment. *Address:* 30 Grove Lane, Camberwell, SE5 8ST. *T:* (020) 7703 9971.

BENNETT, John, MBE 1945; HM Senior Chief Inspector of Schools for Scotland, 1969–73; *b* 14 Nov. 1912; *m* 1940, Johanne R. McAlpine, MA; two *s* one *d*. *Educ:* Edinburgh Univ. MA (first class hons) 1934. Schoolmaster until 1951. Served War of 1939–45: Capt. REME, 79 Armd Div., 1940–46. HM Inspector of Schools, 1951. *Recreations:* mathematics, golf, bridge.

BENNETT, Jonathan Simon; a District Judge (Magistrates' Courts), since 2003; *b* 13 July 1957; *s* of Leonard Arthur Covil Bennett and Edith Irene Bennett; *m* 1982, Sarah Jayne Blackmore; three *s* one *d*. *Educ:* City of London Sch.; Reading Univ. (LLB Hons). Admitted solicitor, 1982; Dep. Dist Judge, 1998–2003. Chm. (pt-time), Appeals Service, 1997–2003. *Recreations:* following Charlton Athletic, lay leader within St Thomas' Church, Philadelphia, Sheffield. *Address:* Wakefield Magistrates' Court, The Court House, Cliff Parade, Wakefield, W Yorks WF1 2TW; *e-mail:* jonathan@benno44.freeserve.co.uk.

BENNETT, Linda Kristin, OBE 2007; Chief Executive, L. K. Bennett, since 1990; *b* 8 Sept. 1962; *d* of Peter and Hafdis Bennett; *m* 2000, Philip W. Harley; one *d*. *Educ:* Haberdashers' Aske's Sch. for Girls; Univ. of Reading (BSc). Founded L. K. Bennett, 1990. Hon. Fellow, Univ. of Arts, London, 2004. Hon. LLD Reading, 2005. Veuve Clicquot Business Woman of Year Award, 2004. *Recreations:* architectural history, British 20th century art, walking, travel, cinema. *Address:* L. K. Bennett, 3 Cavendish Square, W1G 0LB. *T:* (020) 7637 6724, *Fax:* (020) 7637 6728; *e-mail:* linda.bennett@lkbennett.com.

BENNETT, Margaret Joan; Deputy Director, Further Education and Skills Directorate, Department for Innovation, Universities and Skills (formerly Manager, Lifelong Learning and Technologies Division, then Lifelong Learning Directorate, Department for Children, Schools and Families, later Department for Education and Skills), since 2001; *b* 22 Dec. 1960; *d* of Rev. Canon Ian Frederick Bennett and Dr Rachel Bennett; *m* 1987, David Hill (marr. diss. 1994); one *s*. *Educ:* St Anne's Coll., Oxford (BA Hons PPE 1983). Chartered Accountant, KPMG, 1983–87; Finance Officer, West Midlands Arts, 1987–89; Asst Dir, North West Arts, 1989–91; Central Services Dir, Nottingham Community Housing Assoc., 1992–96; Chief Exec., Nat. Liby for the Blind, 1996–2001. *Recreations:* the arts, reading, walking, music, cooking. *Address:* (home) 23 Endcliffe Rise Road, Sheffield S11 8RU. *T:* (0114) 268 3053; Department for Innovation, Universities and Skills, Moorfoot, Sheffield S1 4PQ.

BENNETT, Prof. Martin Arthur, FRS 1995; FRSC, FRACI, FAA; Professor, Research School of Chemistry, Australian National University, 1991–2000, Emeritus Professor, since 2001; *b* 11 Aug. 1935; *s* of late Arthur Edward Charles Bennett and Dorothy Ivy Bennett; *m* 1964, Rae Elizabeth Mathews; two *s*. *Educ:* Haberdashers' Aske's Hampstead Sch.; Imperial Coll. of Science and Technology, London (BSc 1957; PhD 1960; DSc 1974). FRACI 1977; FAA 1980; FRSC 1997. Postdoctoral Fellow, Univ. of S California, 1960–61; Turner and Newall Fellow, 1961–63, Lectr, 1963–67, UCL; Fellow, 1967–70, Sen. Fellow, 1970–79, Professorial Fellow, 1979–91, Res. Sch. of Chem., ANU. Adjunct Prof., RMIT, 2000–. Vis. Prof. and Vis. Fellow, univs in Canada, Germany, USA, Japan, China and NZ. Corresp. Mem., Bayerische Akademie der Wissenschaften, 2005. Numerous awards, Aust. learned instns; Nyholm Medal, RSC, 1991; Max Planck Soc. Res. Award, 1994. *Publications:* chapters on Ruthenium in Comprehensive Organometallic Chemistry; contribs to learned jls. *Recreations:* golf, reading, foreign languages, esp. German and Japanese. *Address:* Research School of Chemistry, Australian National University, Canberra, ACT 0200, Australia. *T:* (2) 61253639; 21 Black Street, Yarralumla, ACT 2600, Australia. *T:* (2) 62824154.

BENNETT, Neil Edward Francis; Managing Partner, Maitland, since 2004; *b* 15 May 1965; *s* of Albert Edward Bennett, *qv*; *m* 1992, Carole Kenyon; two *d*. *Educ:* Westminster Sch.; University Coll. London (BA Medieval Archaeol.); City Univ. (Dip. Journalism). Staff writer, Investors Chronicle, 1987–89; The Times: Banking Corresp., 1989–92; Ed., Tempus column, 1992–94; Dep. Business Editor, 1994–95; City Editor, Sunday Telegraph, 1995–2002; Chief Exec., Gavin Anderson & Co. Ltd, 2002–04. Principal financial columnist, jagnotes-euro.com, 1999–2000. Jun. Wincott Foundn Award, 1992; Business Journalist of the Year, British Press Awards, 1998, 1999. *Recreations:* running, antiquarian book collecting, Irish Terriers. *Address:* Maitland, Orion House, 5 Upper St Martin's Lane, WC2H 9EA. *Club:* Capital.

BENNETT, Nicholas Jerome; JP; Managing Director, Kent Refurbishment Ltd, since 2002; *b* 7 May 1949; *s* of late Peter Ramsden Bennett and Antonia Mary Flanagan; *m* 1995, Ruth, *er d* of late Andrew and Alma Whitelaw, Barnham Broom, Norfolk. *Educ:* Sedgehill Sch.; Polytechnic of North London (BA Hons Philosophy); Univ. of London Inst. of Educn (PGCE Distinction); Univ. of Sussex (MA). Educnl publishing, 1974; schoolmaster, 1976–85; educn officer, 1985–87; Advr on public affairs, Price Waterhouse, 1993–98; Chief Exec., ACE, 1998–2002. Member (C): Lewisham LBC, 1974–82 (Leader of the Opposition, 1979–81); co-opted Mem., ILEA Educn Cttee, 1978–81; Bromley LBC, 2006–. Mem., FEFCE, 1992–97. Contested (C): St Pancras N, 1973 and Greenwich, by-elec. 1974, GLC elections; Hackney Central, 1979. MP (C) Pembroke, 1987–92; contested (C): Pembroke, 1992; Reading W, 1997. PPS to Minister of State, Department of Transport, 1990; Parly Under-Sec. of State, Welsh Office, 1990–92. Member: Select Cttee on Welsh Affairs, 1987–90; Select Cttee on Procedure, 1988–90; Vice-Chm. (Wales), Cons. backbench Party Organisation Cttee, 1990. Chm., Beckenham Constituency Cons. Assoc., 2006–. Chm., Nat. Council for Civil Protection, 1990. Mem., Western Front Assoc. FRSA 1998. JP, SW Div., Greater (formerly Inner) London, 1998. *Publication:* (contrib.) Primary Headship in the 1990s, 1989. *Recreations:* swimming, history, transport, browsing in second-hand bookshops, cinema, small scale gardening, visiting battlefields of First and Second World War. *Address:* 18 Upper Park Road, Bromley, Kent BR1 3HT. *T:* and *Fax:* (020) 8466 1363; *e-mail:* md@kentrefurbishment.co.uk.

BENNETT, Nicholas John, CB 2008; CEng, FIET; Director General, Strategic Technologies, Ministry of Defence, since 2005; *b* 30 Sept. 1948; *s* of John Douglas Bennett and Betty Yvonne Bennett (*née* Harker); *m* 1st, 1971, Susan Mary Worthington (*d* 1997); one *s* one *d*; 2nd, 2000, Lesley Ann Davie (*née* Thorpe). *Educ:* Bishop Wordsworth Sch., Salisbury; Brunel Univ. (BTech Hons Electronic Engrg 1971). CEng 1973; FIET (FIEE 1986). Ministry of Defence: HQ No 90 (S) Gp, 1971–77; A&AEE, 1977–80; Hd, Engrg Design, RAF Signals Engrg Estabt, 1980–83; Principal D Air Radio, 1983–84; Asst Chief Design Engr, RAF Signals Engrg Estabt, 1984–86; Asst Dir, European Fighter Aircraft, 1986–89; rcds 1990; Hd, Civilian Mgt (Specialists) 2, 1991–92; Dir, Ops and Engrg, NATO European Fighter Aircraft Mgt Agency, 1992–96; Chief Exec., Specialist Procurement Services, 1996–99; Dir Gen., Human Resources, Defence Logistics Orgn, 1999–2001; Dir Gen., Scrutiny and Analysis, 2001–05. *Recreations:* cricket, ski-ing, practical study of wine. *Address:* Ministry of Defence, Main Building, Whitehall, SW1A 2HB.

BENNETT, Patrick; QC 1969; a Recorder of the Crown Court, 1972–97; *b* 12 Jan. 1924; *s* of Michael Bennett; *m* 1951, Lyle Reta Pope; two *d*. *Educ:* Bablake Sch., Coventry; Magdalen Coll., Oxford. State Scholar, 1941, MA, BCL 1949. Served RNVR, 1943–46, Sub Lt. Called to Bar, Gray's Inn, 1949, Bencher 1976, Master of Students, 1980; Asst Recorder, Coventry, 1969–71; Dep. Chm., Lindsey QS, 1970–71. Mem., Mental Health Act Commn, 1984–86. Fellow: Internat. Soc. of Barristers, 1984; Nat. Inst. of Advocacy, 1980. Pres., Thomas More Soc., 1990–93. Associate Mem., Guild of Sommeliers of Northern France, 2007. *Publications:* Assessment of Damages in Personal Injury and Fatal Accidents, 1980; The Common Jury, 1986; Trial Techniques, 1986. *Recreations:* food, flying, spoiling two granddaughters. *Address:* (home) 22 Wynnstay Gardens, W8 6UR. *T:* (020) 7937 2110; 233 rue Nationale, Boulogne sur Mer, France. *T:* 321913339. *Club:* Spartan Flying (Denham).

BENNETT, Penelope Anne; Commissioner for Health and Social Care, South West Region, Appointments Commission (formerly NHS Appointments Commission), since 2003; *b* 5 June 1956; *d* of late Peter Atherton Pettican-Runnicles and of Dorothy Isabel Pettican-Runnicles (*née* Grover); *m* 1982, John David Bennett; three *d*. *Educ:* West Hatch, Chigwell; Hatfield Poly. (BSc Hons); Open Univ. (MBA). Admitted as solicitor, 1982; solicitor in private practice, 1982–95; non-exec. Dir and Vice Chm., 1995–98, Chm., 1998–2002, E Glos NHS Trust; non-exec. Dir and Vice Chm., Avon, Glos and Wilts Strategic HA, 2002–04. Ind. Mem., Standards Cttee, Cotswold DC, 2001–. Gp Bd Dir, Chm., Audit Cttee and Trustee, Hanover Housing Assoc., 2004–. *Recreations:* family life, travel, walking, reading, gardening. *Address:* 11 St Peters Road, Cirencester, Glos GL7 1RE. *T:* (01285) 640691; *e-mail:* pennybennett@cotswold99.freeserve.co.uk.

BENNETT, Peter Gordon, FRICS; City Surveyor, City of London Corporation, since 2008; *m* 1973, Janetta Hall; two *s* one *d*. *Educ:* Fitzwilliam Coll., Cambridge (BA Geog. 1970). Chartered Surveyor, 1977. FRICS 1989. Res. Officer, Wool, Jute and Flax Trng Bd, 1970–72; Valuer, Valuation Office, Bd of Inland Revenue, 1972–76; Valuer, then Sen. Mgt Surveyor, Bradford CC, 1976–85; Dep. City Estate Agent, 1985–88, City Estate Agent and Valuer, 1988–90, Swansea CC; Dep. City Surveyor, Corp. of London, subseq. City of London Corp., 1990–2008. Perm. Mem., Bank of England Property Forum, 2002–. Mem., London Council, CBI, 2004–. First Chm., London Reg., RICS, 2001–04. Charity Trustee, Royal Grammar Sch., High Wycombe, 2003–. *Recreations:* Rugby, opera, gardening. *Address:* City of London Corporation, PO Box 270, Guildhall, EC2P 2EJ. *T:* (020) 7332 1502, *Fax:* (020) 7322 3955; *e-mail:* peter.bennett@cityoflondon.gov.uk.

BENNETT, Gen. Sir Phillip (Harvey), AC 1985 (AO 1981); KBE 1983; DSO 1969; Chairman, Australian War Memorial Foundation, 1996–2003; National President, Order of Australia Association, 1997–2000; *b* 27 Dec. 1928; *m* 1955, Margaret Heywood; two *s* one *d*. *Educ:* Perth Modern Sch.; Royal Mil. Coll.; jssc, rcds, psc (Aust.). Served, 1950–57: 3rd Bn RAR, Korea (despatches 1951), Sch. of Infantry (Instr), 25 Cdn Bde, Korea, 1952–53, Pacific Is Regt, PNG, and 16th Bn Cameron Highlanders of WA; Commando training, Royal Marines, England, Malta and Cyprus, 1957–58; OC 2 Commando Co., Melb., 1958–61; Aust. Staff Coll., 1961–62; Sen. Instr, then Chief Instr, Officer Cadet Sch., Portsea, 1962–65; AAG Directorate of Personal Services, AHQ, 1965–67; Co. 1 RAR, 1967–69 (served Vietnam; DSO); Exchange Instr, Jt Services Staff Coll., England, 1969–71; COL Directorate of Co-ordination and Organization, AHQ, 1971–73; COS HQ Fd Force Comd, 1974–75; RCDS, England, 1976; Comdr 1st Div., 1977–79; Asst Chief of Def. Force Staff, 1979–82; Chief of General Staff, 1982–84; Chief of Defence Force, Australia, 1984–87; Governor, Tasmania, 1987–95. Hon. Col, Royal Tasmania Regt, 1987–95. KStJ 1988. Hon. LLD: New South Wales, 1987; Tasmania, 1992. *Recreations:* reading, golf. *Address:* c/o Commonwealth Club, ACT 2600, Australia. *Clubs:* Commonwealth, University House (Canberra).

BENNETT, Ralph Featherstone; *b* 3 Dec. 1923; *o s* of late Mr and Mrs Ralph J. P. Bennett, Plymouth, Devon; *m* 1948, Delia Marie, *o d* of late Mr and Mrs J. E. Baxter, Franklyns, Plymouth; two *s* two *d*. *Educ:* Plympton Grammar Sch.; Plymouth Technical Coll. Articled pupil to City of Plymouth Transport Manager, 1940–43; Techn. Asst, Plymouth City Transp., 1943–54; Michelin Tyre Co., 1954–55; Dep. Gen. Man., City of Plymouth Transp. Dept, 1955–58; Gen. Manager: Gt Yarmouth Transp. Dept, 1958–60; Bolton Transp. Dept, 1960–65; Manchester City Transp., 1965–68; London Transport Executive (formerly London Transport Board): Mem., 1968–71; Dep. Chm., 1971–78; Chief Exec., 1975–78; Chairman: London Transport Executive, 1978–80; London Transport International, 1976–80. Pres., Confedn of Road Passenger Transport, 1977–78; Vice-President: Internat. Union of Public Transport, 1978–81; CIT, 1979–82. CEng; FIMechE; FCILT; FRSA. *Address:* 3 Old Kennels Close, Winchester, Hants SO22 4LB. *T:* (01962) 867362.

BENNETT, His Honour Raymond Clayton Watson; a Circuit Judge, 1989–2004; *b* 20 June 1939; *s* of Harold Watson and Doris Helena Bennett (previously Watson); *m* 1965, Elaine Margaret Haworth; one *s* one *d*. *Educ:* Bury Grammar Sch.; Manchester Univ. (LLB). Solicitor, 1964–72; called to the Bar, Middle Temple, 1972; practising barrister, 1972–89; an Asst Recorder, 1984; a Recorder, 1988. Hon. Recorder, Burnley, 1998–2004. *Recreations:* tennis, reading, painting, gardening, golf.

BENNETT, Richard Charles; Head of Ports Division, Department for Transport, since 2007; *b* 8 Sept. 1958; *s* of Ben and Cynthia Bennett. *Educ:* Bristol Grammar Sch.; Christ's Coll., Cambridge (MA). Joined Dept of Transport, 1983; various roles, incl. internat. aviation, streetworks and investigation into King's Cross fire; Private Sec. to Minister of State for Transport, 1984–85; Railways Div., 1993–96, Finance Div., 1996–99, Dept of Transport, later DETR; Divl Manager, 1999–2001, Dir, 2001–03, London Underground Task Gp, DTLR, later DfT; Corporate Dir, Highways Agency, 2003–05; Shared Services Prog. Manager, DfT, 2006–07. *Address:* Ports Division, Department for Transport, Great Minster House, 76 Marsham Street, SW1P 4DR; *e-mail:* richard.bennett@dft.gsi.gov.uk.

BENNETT, Richard Clement W.; *see* Wheeler-Bennett.

BENNETT, Sir Richard Rodney, Kt 1998; CBE 1977; composer; Visiting Professor of Composition, Royal Academy of Music, since 1995; *b* 29 March 1936; *s* of H. Rodney and Joan Esther Bennett. *Educ:* Leighton Park Sch., Reading; Royal Academy of Music. Works performed, 1953–, at many Festivals in Europe, S Africa, USA, Canada, Australia, etc. Has written music for numerous films including: Indiscreet; The Devil's Disciple; Only Two Can Play; The Wrong Arm of the Law; Heavens Above; Billy Liar; One Way Pendulum; The Nanny; Far from the Madding Crowd; Billion Dollar Brain; Secret Ceremony; The Buttercup Chain; Figures in a Landscape; Nicholas and Alexandra; Lady Caroline Lamb; Voices; Murder on the Orient Express (SFTA award; Academy Award Nomination; Ivor Novello award, PRS); Permission to Kill; Equus (BAFTA Nomination); The Brinks Job; Yanks (BAFTA Nomination); Return of the Soldier; Four Weddings and a Funeral; Swann; also the music for television series: The Christians; L. P. Hartley trilogy; The Ebony Tower; Tender is the Night; The Charmer; Poor Little Rich Girl; The Hiding Place; The Story of Anne Frank; Gormenghast. Commissioned to write 2 full-length operas for Sadler's Wells: The Mines of Sulphur, 1965, A Penny for a Song, 1968; commnd to write opera for Covent Garden: Victory, 1970; other compositions include: Symphony No 1, 1965; Symphony No 2, 1967; (children's opera) All the King's Men, 1969; Guitar Concerto, 1970; Spells (choral work), 1975; Sonnets to Orpheus, 1979; Symphony No 3, 1987; Concerto for Stan Getz, 1990; Concerto for Trumpet, 1993; Partita, 1995; Reflections on a 16th Century Tune, 1999; Rondel (for large jazz ensemble), 1999; On Christmas Day (choral work), 1999; Seven Country Dances (for oboe and strings), 2000; Songs Before Sleep, 2003; Reflections on a Scottish Folk Song, 2004. *Publications include:* chamber music, orchestral music, educational music, song cycles, etc; articles for periodicals, about music. *Recreations:* cinema, modern jazz, painting. *Address:* c/o Novello & Co., 14–15 Berners Street, W1T 3LJ.

BENNETT, Prof. Robert John, PhD; FBA 1991; Professor of Geography, and Fellow of St Catharine's College, University of Cambridge, since 1996; *b* 23 March 1948; *s* of Thomas Edward Bennett and Kathleen Elizabeth Robson; *m* 1971, Elizabeth Anne Allen; two *s*. *Educ:* Taunton's Sch., Southampton; St Catharine's Coll., Cambridge (BA 1970; PhD 1974). Lecturer: University Coll. London, 1973–78; Univ. of Cambridge, 1978–85; Fellow and Dir of Studies, 1978–85, Tutor, 1981–85, Fitzwilliam Coll., Cambridge; Prof. of Geography, LSE, 1985–96. Leverhulme Personal Res. Prof., 1996–2000. Vis. Prof., Univ. California at Berkeley, 1978; Guest Schol., Brookings Instn, Washington DC, 1978, 1979, 1981; Hubert Humphrey Inst. Fellow, Univ. Minnesota, 1985; Univ. Fellow, Macquarie, 1987; Snyder Lectr, Toronto, 1988. Treas., IBG, 1990–93; Vice Pres., RGS, 1993–95 and 1998–2001 (Mem. Council, 1990–2001); Chm., Council of British Geography, 1995–2000; Vice Pres. and Res. Chm., British Acad., 2001–08. Vice Pres., Inst. of Small Business and Entrepreneurship, 2004–07. Mem., Res. Awards Adv. Panel, Leverhulme Trust, 2000–07. MInstD. Murchison Award, 1982, Founder's Medal, 1998, RGS. Gen. Editor, Government and Policy, 1982–; European Co-Editor, Geographical Analysis, 1985–88. *Publications:* Environmental Systems (with R. J. Chorley), 1978; Spatial Time Series, 1979; Geography of Public Finance, 1980; (ed) European Progress in Spatial Analysis, 1981; (ed with N. Wrigley) Quantitative Geography, 1981; Central Grants to Local Government, 1982; (with K. C. Tan) Optimal Control of Spatial Systems, 1984; Intergovernmental Financial Relations in Austria, 1985; (with A. G. Wilson) Mathematical Methods in Human Geography and Planning, 1985; (ed with H. Zimmermann) Local Business Taxes in Britain and Germany, 1986; (with G. Krebs) Die Wirkung Kommunaler Steuern auf die Steuerliche Belastung der Kapitalbildung, 1987; (with G. Krebs) Local Business Taxes in Britain and Germany, 1988; (ed) Territory and Administration in Europe, 1989; (ed) Decentralisation, Local Governments and Markets, 1990; (with G. Krebs) Local Economic Development Initiatives in Britain and Germany, 1991; (ed with R. C. Estall) Global Change and Challenge, 1991; (with A. McCoshan) Enterprise and Human Resource Development, 1993; (jtly) Local Empowerment and Business Services, 1994; (with G. Krebs and H. Zimmermann) Chambers of Commerce in Britain and Germany, 1994; (ed) Trade Associations in Britain and Germany, 1997; (with D. Payne) Local and Regional Economic Development, 2000. *Recreations:* the family, genealogy. *Address:* Department of Geography, University of Cambridge, Downing Place, Cambridge CB2 3EN.

BENNETT, Robin; adult educator; *b* 6 Nov. 1934; *s* of James Arthur Bennett, Major RA, and Alice Edith Bennett, Ipswich; *m* 1st, 1962, Patricia Ann Lloyd (marr. diss. 1991); one *s* one *d*; 2nd, 1992, Margaret Jane Allen. *Educ:* Northgate Grammar School, Ipswich; St John's Coll., Univ. of Durham (BA 1958); Queen's Coll., and Univ. of Birmingham (Dip Th 1960); MEd Birmingham 1987. Ordained deacon, 1960, priest, 1961; curacies and incumbencies in Essex and E London, 1960–75; appts in C of E educn, incl. Principal, Aston Training Scheme, 1977–82; Archdeacon of Dudley, 1985–86; left C of E and joined Soc. of Friends, 1988; Vice-Principal, Clapham Battersea Adult Educn Inst., 1986–89; Dep. Principal, Wandsworth Adult Coll., 1989–95. Mem. (Lab), Ludlow Town Council, 1999–2003. Clerk, Quaker Cttee for Racial Equality, 1998–2004; Quaker Mem., Churches Commn for Racial Justice, 1998–2005. Governor: Fircroft Coll., 1983–99; Ludlow County Jun. Sch., 2001–. Trustee: Woodbrooke Quaker Study Centre, 1998–2000; Rockspring Trust, Ludlow, 1998–2004; Ludlow and Dist Community Assoc., 1999–2005 (Chm., 2001–05); Gallows Bank Millennium Green, Ludlow, 1999– (Chm., 2000–07). *Recreations:* travel, music, football. *Address:* 31 Poyner Road, Ludlow, Shropshire SY8 1QT. *T:* (01584) 874752; *e-mail:* robin@megandrobin.co.uk.

BENNETT, Sir Ronald (Wilfred Murdoch), 3rd Bt *cr* 1929; *b* 25 March 1930; *o s* of Sir Wilfred Bennett, 2nd Bt, and Marion Agnes, OBE (*d* 1985), *d* of late James Somervell, Sorn Castle, Ayrshire, and step *d* of late Edwin Sandys Dawes; *S* father, 1952; *m* 1st, 1953, Rose-Marie Audrey Patricia, *o d* of Major A. L. J. H. Aubépin, France and Co. Mayo, Ireland; two *d*; 2nd, 1968, Anne, *d* of late Leslie George Tooker; *m* 3rd. *Educ:* Wellington Coll.; Trinity Coll., Oxford. *Heir: cousin* Mark Edward Francis Bennett [*b* 5 April 1960; *m* 1995, Jayne M. Jensen (marr. diss. 1998)]. *Clubs:* Kampala, Uganda (Kampala).

BENNETT, Seton John, CBE 2006; PhD; Deputy Director, National Physical Laboratory, since 2002; *b* 10 July 1945; *s* of John and Joyce Bennett; *m* 1966, Lesley Downs; two *s*. *Educ:* Norfolk House Primary Sch., Barnet; Queen Elizabeth's Grammar Sch., Barnet; Oriel Coll., Oxford (BA 1967); Imperial Coll., London (PhD 1973). CPhys; FInstP 1982. Res. Scientist, Nat. Physical Lab., 1967–85; Dep. Dir, 1985–90, Chief Exec., 1990–2001, Nat. Weights and Measures Lab. Chairman: WELMEC, 1990–2001; EUROMET, 2004–06; Mem., Internat. Cttee for Weights and Measures, 2002–. Chm., Keychange Charity, 2008–. FRSA. *Recreations:* running, walking, sitting still. *Address:* National Physical Laboratory, Hampton Road, Teddington TW11 0LW; *e-mail:* seton.bennett@npl.co.uk.

BENNETT, Hon. William Richards; PC (Can.) 1982; Premier of British Columbia, 1975–86; *b* 14 April 1932; *y s* of late Hon. William Andrew Cecil Bennett, PC (Can.) and of Annie Elizabeth May Richards; *m* 1955, Audrey Lyne, *d* of late Jack James; four *s*. Began a business career. Elected MP for Okanagan South (succeeding to a constituency which had been held by his father), 1973; Leader of Social Credit Group in Provincial House, 1973; formed Social Credit Govt after election of Dec. 1975.

BENNETT-JONES, Peter; Chairman: Tiger Television, since 1988; PBJ Management, since 1988; Tiger Aspect Productions, since 1993; Tiger Aspect Pictures, since 1999; Comic Relief, since 1998; United Agents, since 2007; *b* 11 March 1955; *s* of late Dr Nicholas and of Ruth Bennett-Jones; *m* 1990, Alison E. Watts; two *s* one *d*. *Educ:* Winchester Coll.; Magdalene Coll., Cambridge (MA Law). Director: Oxford and Cambridge Shakespeare Co. Ltd, 1977–82; Pola Jones Assocs, 1977–82; Managing Director: Talkback, 1982–86; Corporate Communications Consultants Ltd, 1986–88. Production credits include: Mr Bean; The Vicar of Dibley; Harry Enfield; Billy Elliot; Our House (Olivier Award, 2003). Mem. Council, RADA, 2007–. Trustee, Arnold Foundn, 2007–. Hon. Golden Rose of Montreux, 1999. *Recreation:* simply messing about in boats. *Address:* (office) 7 Soho Street, W1D 3DQ; 8 Rawlinson Road, Oxford OX2 6UE. *T:* (01865) 515414. *Clubs:* Oxford and Cambridge, Groucho, Soho House.

BENNETTS, Rt Rev. Colin James; Bishop of Coventry, 1998–2008; *b* 9 Sept. 1940; *s* of James Thomas Bennetts and Winifred Florence Bennetts (*née* Couldrey); *m* 1965, Veronica Jane Leat; two *s* two *d*. *Educ:* Battersea Grammar Sch.; Jesus Coll., Cambridge (Exhibnr); Ridley Hall, Cambridge. MA (Cantab); MA (Oxon) by incorporation. Assistant Curate: St Stephen, Tonbridge, 1965–69; St Aldate, Oxford, 1969–73; Chaplain to Oxford Pastorate, 1969–73; Chaplain, Jesus Coll., Oxford, 1973–80; Vicar, St Andrew, Oxford, 1980–90; RD of Oxford, 1984–90; Canon Residentiary of Chester Cathedral, 1990–94; Canon Librarian and Diocesan Director of Ordinands, Chester, 1990–94; Area Bishop of Buckingham, 1994–98. Co-Chm., Springboard, 1995–2001; Vice-Chm., Liturgical Commn, 2001–. Chm., Bible Reading Fellowship, 1999–2001 (Vice-Chm., 1994–98). *Recreations:* mediaeval music, woodcutting. *Address:* 23 Brox Road, Ottershaw, Surrey KT16 0HG.

BENNETTS, Denise Margaret Mary; Co-Founder and Director, Bennetts Associates Architects, since 1987; *b* 26 Jan. 1953; *d* of James and Agnes Smith; *m* 1974, Robert John, (Rab), Bennetts, *qv*; one *s* one *d*. *Educ:* Heriot-Watt Univ./Edinburgh Coll. of Art (BArch Hons 1976; DipArch 1977). RIBA 1979. Casson Conder Partnership, 1978–88. Major projects include: Brighton Central Liby; Wessex Water Operations Centre, Bath; BT Headquarters, Edinburgh. Assessor: Civic Trust Awards, 1997–; RIBA Awards, 2005. *Address:* Bennetts Associates Architects, 1 Rawstorne Place, EC1V 7NL. *T:* (020) 7520 3300, *Fax:* (020) 7520 3333; *e-mail:* denise.bennetts@bennettsassociates.com.

BENNETTS, Robert John, (Rab), OBE 2003; Co-Founder and Director, Bennetts Associates Architects, since 1987; *b* 14 April 1953; *s* of Frank Vivian Bennetts and Frances Mary Bennetts; *m* 1974, Denise Margaret Mary Smith (*see* D. M. M. Bennetts); one *s* one *d*. *Educ:* Heriot-Watt Univ./Edinburgh Coll. of Art (BArch Hons 1976; DipArch 1977). RIBA 1979. Architect, Arup Associates, 1977–87. Major projects include: Powergen HQ, 1994; Wessex Water Offices, 2000; Hampstead Th., 2003; Brighton Central Liby, 2005; New Street Square, City of London, 2003; Royal Shakespeare Th., Stratford upon Avon, 2005. Member: Movt for Innovation Bd, DTI, 1999–2002; Planning Cttee, Islington LBC, 2000–03; Strategic Forum for Construction, Olympic Task Gp, 2005–; Bd, UK Green Bldgs Council, 2007–. Chm., Competitions Cttee, RIBA, 1995–98, 2004–. Dir, Sadler's Wells Th., 2006–. *Publications:* (contrib.) The Commercial Offices Handbook, 2003; Bennetts Associates - Four Commentaries, 2005. *Recreations:* travel (especially with family), drawings, arts generally, watching football (Arsenal) and attempting to play. *Address:* Bennetts Associates Architects, 1 Rawstorne Place, EC1V 7NL. *T:* (020) 7520 3300, *Fax:* (020) 7520 3333; *e-mail:* rab.bennetts@bennettsassociates.com. *Club:* Architecture.

BENNION, Francis Alan Roscoe; writer; *b* 2 Jan. 1923; *o s* of Thomas Roscoe Bennion, Liverpool; *m* 1st, 1951, Barbara Elisabeth Braendle (separated 1971, marr. diss. 1975); three *d*; 2nd, 1977, Mary Field. *Educ:* John Lyon's, Harrow; Balliol Coll., Oxford. Pilot, RAFVR, 1941–46. Gibbs Law Scholar, Oxford, 1948. Called to Bar, Middle Temple, 1951 (Harmsworth Scholar); practised at Bar, 1951–53, 1985–94. Lectr and Tutor in Law, St Edmund Hall, Oxford, 1951–53; Office of Parly Counsel, 1953–65, and 1973–75; Dep. Parly Counsel, 1964; Parly Counsel, 1973–75; seconded to Govt of Pakistan to advise on drafting of new Constitution, 1956; seconded to Govt of Ghana to advise on legislation and drafting Constitution converting the country into a Republic, 1959–61. Sec., RICS, 1965–68; Governor, College of Estate Management, 1965–68. Co-founder and first Chm., Professional Assoc. of Teachers, 1968–72; Founder: Statute Law Soc., 1968 (Chm., 1978–79); Freedom Under Law, 1971; Dicey Trust, 1973; Towards One World, 1979; Statute Law Trust, 1991; founder and first Chm., World of Property Housing Trust (later Sanctuary Housing Assoc.), 1968–72 (Vice-Pres., 1986–); Co-founder, Areopagitica Educnl Trust, 1979. *Publications:* Constitutional Law of Ghana, 1962; Professional Ethics: The Consultant Professions and their Code, 1969; Tangling with the Law, 1970; Consumer Credit Control, 1976–2001; Consumer Credit Act Manual, 1978, 3rd edn 1986; Statute Law, 1980, 3rd edn 1990; Statutory Interpretation, 1984, 5th edn 2008; Victorian Railway Days, 1989; The Sex Code: Morals for Moderns, 1991; Statutes, in Halsbury's Laws of England, 1996; Understanding Common Law Legislation, 2001; The Blight of Blairism, 2002; Poemotions: Bennion undraped (poems), 2002; Sexual Ethics and Criminal Law, 2003; articles and contribs to books on legal and other subjects. *Recreation:* maintaining my website (with the help of my webmaster). *Address:* 29 Pegasus Road, Oxford OX4 6DS. *T:* (01395) 442265; *e-mail:* f.bennion.1946@balliol.org. *Clubs:* Royal Commonwealth Soc., MCC.

BENSBERG, Mark; HM Diplomatic Service; High Commissioner, Namibia, since 2007; *b* 19 July 1962; *s* of Anthony Charles Bensberg and Ann Bensberg; *m* 1991, Jacqueline Margaret Campbell; one *d*. *Educ:* Tiffin Sch. Entered FCO, 1980; Paris, 1982–85; Africa/ME floater, 1985–88; Vice-Consul, Vienna, 1988–91; FCO, 1991–94; Accra, 1994–97; Second Sec., Brussels, 1997–2000; FCO, 2000–04; Dep. Hd of Mission, Kinshasa, 2004–06. *Recreations:* cooking, photography, shooting, ski-ing. *Address:* c/o Foreign and Commonwealth Office, King Charles Street, SW1A 2AH.

BENSON, Sir Christopher (John), Kt 1988; DL; FRICS; Chairman: Cross London Rail Links Ltd, 2001–04; Stratford (East London) Renaissance Partnership, since 2006; Director, Eredene Capital plc, since 2006; *b* 20 July 1933; *s* of Charles Woodburn Benson and Catherine Clara (*née* Bishton); *m* 1960, Margaret Josephine, OBE, JP, DL, *d* of Ernest Jefferies Bundy; two *s*. *Educ:* Worcester Cathedral King's Sch.; Thames Nautical Trng Coll., HMS Worcester. FRICS. Chartered surveyor and agricl auctioneer, Worcs, Herefords, Wilts, Dorset, Hants, 1953–64; Dir, Arndale Develts Ltd, 1965–69; Chm., Dolphin Develts Ltd, 1969–71; Man. Dir, 1976–88, Chm., 1988–93, MEPC; Chairman: The Boots Company, 1990–94 (Dir, 1989–94); Sun Alliance Gp, 1993–96 (Dir, 1988; Dep. Chm., 1992–93); Costain plc, 1993–96; Albright & Wilson, 1995–99; Dep. Chm., Thorn Lighting Gp, 1994–98. Dir, House of Fraser plc, 1982–86; Chairman: LDDC, 1984–88; Reedpack Ltd, 1989–90; Housing Corp., 1990–94; Funding Agency for Schs, 1994–97. Pres., British Property Fedn, 1981–83; Chm., Property Adv. Gp to DoE, 1988–90; Pres., London Chamber of Commerce and Industry, 2000–01; Mem. Council, CBI, 1990–97. Dir, Royal Opera House, 1984–92. Chm., Britain-Australia Soc., 2007–. Chm., Civic Trust, 1985–90; Trustee: Metropolitan Police Museum, 1986–; Hope,

2001–; Sea Cadets Assoc., 2002–05; Marine Soc. and Sea Cadets, 2005–; Vice President: Macmillan Cancer Relief (formerly Cancer Relief Macmillan Fund), 1991–2001; RSA, 1992–97; Pres., Nat. Deaf Children's Soc., 1995–; Patron, Changing Faces, 1993–; Chm., Coram (formerly Coram Family), 2005–08. Lay-Gov., London Hosp. Med. Coll., 1993–95; Mem. Council, Marlborough Coll., 1982–90; Gov., Inns of Court Sch. of Law, 1996–2001 (Principal, 2000–01). Freeman: City of London, 1975; Co. of Watermen and Lightermen, 1985 (Master, 2004–05); Liveryman: Co. of Gold and Silver Wyre Drawers, 1975; Guild of Air Pilots and Air Navigators, 1981; Co. of Chartered Surveyors, 1984. High Sheriff of Wilts, 2002. DL Greater London, 2005. Lay Canon, Salisbury Cathedral, 2000. Hon. FRCPath 1992; Hon. FCIOB 1992. Hon. Fellow, Wolfson Coll., Cambridge, 1990. Hon. Bencher, Middle Temple, 1984. Hon. DSc: City, 2000; Bradford, 2001. *Recreations:* farming, aviation, opera, ballet. *Address:* 2, 50 South Audley Street, W1K 2QE. *T:* (020) 7629 2398. *Clubs:* Garrick, Royal Automobile, MCC; Australian (Sydney).

BENSON, David Holford; Senior Adviser, Fleming Family & Partners, since 2002; *b* 26 Feb. 1938; *s* of Sir Rex Benson, DSO, MVO, MC, and Lady Leslie Foster Benson; *m* 1964, Lady Elizabeth Mary Charteris, *d* of 12th Earl of Wemyss and March, *qv*; one *s* two *d*. *Educ:* Eton Coll.; Madrid. CIGEM (CIGasE 1989). Shell Transport & Trading, 1957–63; Kleinwort Benson Gp, subseq. Dresdner Kleinwort Benson Gp, 1963–2004: Vice-Chm., 1989–92; non-exec. Dir, 1992–98; Chm., Charter European Trust, 1992–2003. Non-executive Director: Rouse Co., 1987–2004; BG Group plc (formerly British Gas), 1988–2004; Dover Corp., 1995–; Daniel Thwaites plc, 1998–2006; Murray Internat. Investment Trust, 2000–; Vice Chm., Leach Internat. (formerly Leach Relais), 1992–2004. Chairman: COIF Charities Funds (formerly Charities Official Investment Fund), 1984–2005; Trustees, Edward James Foundn, 2002– (Trustee, 1996–); Trustee, UK Historic Bldg Preservation Trust, 1996–2001. *Recreation:* painting. *Address:* Fleming Family & Partners, Ely House, 37 Dover Street, W1S 4NJ; Cucumber Farm, Singleton, Chichester, W Sussex PO18 0HG. *Clubs:* White's, English-Speaking Union.

BENSON, Prof. Frank Atkinson, OBE 1988; DL; BEng, MEng (Liverpool); PhD, DEng (Sheffield); FIET, FIEEE; Professor and Head of Department of Electronic and Electrical Engineering, University of Sheffield, 1967–87; Pro-Vice Chancellor, 1972–76; *b* 21 Nov. 1921; *s* of late John and Selina Benson; *m* 1950, Kathleen May Paskell (*d* 2006); two *s*. *Educ:* Ulverston Grammar Sch.; Univ. of Liverpool. Mem. research staff, Admty Signal Estab., Witley, 1943–46; Asst Lectr in Electrical Engrg, University of Liverpool, 1946–49; Lectr 1949–59, Sen. Lectr 1959–61, in Electrical Engrg, University of Sheffield; Reader in Electronics, University of Sheffield, 1961–67. DL South Yorks, 1979. *Publications:* Voltage Stabilizers, 1950; Electrical Engineering Problems with Solutions, 1954; Voltage Stabilized Supplies, 1957; Problems in Electronics with Solutions, 1958; Electric Circuit Theory, 1959; Voltage Stabilization, 1965; Electric Circuit Problems with Solutions, 1967; Millimetre and Submillimetre Waves, 1969; Fields, Waves and Transmission Lines, 1991; many papers on microwaves, gas discharges and voltage stabilization in learned jls. *Address:* 64 Grove Road, Sheffield S7 2GZ. *T:* (0114) 236 3493.

BENSON, Glenwyn; Creative Lead, BBC response to OFCOM review of Public Service Broadcasting, since 2007; *b* 23 Nov. 1947; *d* of late Tudor David, OBE and Nancy David; *m* 1973, Dr Ian Anthony Benson; one *s* one *d*. *Educ:* Nonsuch County Grammar Sch. for Girls, Cheam; Girton Coll., Cambridge (MA); Harvard Univ. (Frank Knox Fellow). Dep. Editor, Weekend World, LWT, 1986–88; BBC: Editor: On the Record, 1990–92; Panorama, 1992–95; Head: of Commng, Adult Educn, 1995–97; of Science, 1997–2000; Controller, Specialist Factual, 2000–01; Jt Dir, Factual and Learning, 2001–03; Mem., Exec. Cttee, 2001–03; Controller, BBC Knowledge (formerly Factual TV), 2003–07. Mem., RTS, 2005–. Gov., Nat. Film and Television Sch., 2001–. FRSA. Hon. FRTS 2008. *Recreations:* gardening, music. *Address:* BBC, 201 Wood Lane, W12 7TS. *T:* (020) 8752 6178.

BENSON, Gordon Mitchell, OBE 2000; RA 2000; FRIAS; Partner, Benson+Forsyth, architects, established 1978; *b* 5 Oct. 1946; *s* of William Benson and Gavina Dewar (*née* Mitchell); one *s* one *d*. *Educ:* Univ. of Strathclyde; Architectural Assoc. Sch. of Architecture (AA Dip). SADG; FRIAS; ARIBA. London housing projects, Camden Council, 1968–78. Prof. of Architecture, Strathclyde Univ., 1986–90; Vis. Prof., Edinburgh Univ., 1991–96. Mem., Royal Fine Art Commn for Scotland, 1993. *Built work:* Branch Hill Housing, 1974; Mansfield Rd Housing, 1975; Lambie St Housing, 1975; Maiden Lane, 1976; Marico Furniture Workshop and Residence, 1979; Boarbank Oratory, 1985; Physio Room, Cumbria, 1986; Pavilion, Glasgow Garden Fest., 1989; Machi Nakao: The Divided House, Jyohanna Mus., Japan, 1994; Gall. 22 Admin Bldg, Mus. of Scotland, 1997; Mus. of Scotland, 1998; extension, Nat. Gall. of Ireland, 2000. Has won numerous awards and competitions. *Publications:* contribs to Scotsman, Daily Telegraph, Sunday Times and professional jls incl. Architectural Rev., Architects Jl, Bldg Design, RIBA Jl, RSA Jl and overseas architectural jls. *Address:* (office) 37D Mildmay Grove North, N1 4RH. *T:* (020) 7359 0288.

BENSON, (Harry) Peter (Neville), CBE 1982; MC 1945; FCA; Chairman, Davy Corporation PLC, 1982–85; *b* 10 Feb. 1917; *s* of Harry Leedham Benson and Iolanthe Benson; *m* 1948, Margaret Young Brackenridge; two *s* one *d*. *Educ:* Cheltenham Coll. FCA 1946. Served War, S Staffs Regt, 1939–45 (Major; MC). Moore Stephens, 1946–48; John Mowlem, 1948–51; Dir, 1951–54, Man. Dir, 1954–57, Waring & Gillow; Dir, APV Co., 1957–66; Man. Dir, 1966–77, Chm., 1977–82, APV Holdings. Director: Rolls Royce Motors, 1971–80; Vickers Ltd, 1980–82. *Recreation:* golf. *Address:* The Gate House, Little Chesters, Nursery Road, Walton-on-the-Hill, Tadworth, Surrey KT20 7TX. *T:* (01737) 813767. *Club:* Walton Heath Golf.

BENSON, James, OBE 2003; President, James Benson Associates Inc., since 1987; *b* 17 July 1925; *s* of Henry Herbert Benson and Olive Benson (*née* Hutchinson); *m* 1950, Honoria Margaret Hurley; one *d*. *Educ:* Bromley Grammar Sch., Kent; Emmanuel Coll., Cambridge (MA). RN, 1943–46 (Midget Subs (X-craft) and Minesweepers). Manager, Res. and Promotion, Kemsley Newspapers, 1948–58; Dir, Mather & Crowther, 1959–65; Man. Dir, 1966–69, Chm., 1970–71 and 1975–78, Ogilvy & Mather Ltd; Vice-Chm., The Ogilvy Group (formerly Ogilvy & Mather Internat.) Inc., 1971–87. Chm. Emeritus, American Associates of the Royal Acad. Trust, 2001– (Chm., 1983–2001); Trustee, Royal Medical Benevolent Fund, 2001–. *Publications:* Above Us The Waves, 1953; The Admiralty Regrets, 1956; Will Not We Fear, 1961; The Broken Column, 1966; Silent Unseen, 1995. *Recreations:* swimming, walking, painting, reading. *Address:* 64 Harley House, Regent's Park, NW1 5HL.

BENSON, Jeremy Keith; QC 2001; a Recorder, since 1997; *b* 17 Jan. 1953; *s* of Jack Henry Benson and Renee Esther Benson; *m* 1985, Dr Karen Judith Silkoff; two *s* one *d*. *Educ:* City of London Sch.; Essex Univ. (BA Hons 1973); St Peter's Coll., Saltley, Birmingham (PGCE 1974). Hd of Econs Dept, King's Heath Boys' Sch., 1974–76; called to the Bar, Middle Temple, 1978, Bencher, 2002. Asst Recorder, 1993–97. Mem. Cttee, Criminal Bar Assoc., 1997–2003. Mem., Political Cartoon Soc. 2001–. *Recreations:* cricket, collecting political cartoons. *Address:* 2 Hare Court, Temple, EC4Y 7BH. *T:* (020) 7353 5324.

BENSON, John Trevor; QC 2001; a Recorder, since 1998; *b* 22 Jan. 1955; *s* of Trevor Benson and Ruth (*née* Oliver); *m* 1984, Sheila Patricia Riordan; one *s* two *d*. *Educ:* Liverpool Univ. (LLB Hons). Called to the Bar, Middle Temple, 1978. *Recreations:* cookery, Liverpool FC, music. *Address:* Atlantic Chambers, 4/6 Cook Street, Liverpool L2 9QU. *T:* (0151) 236 4421; 1 Mitre Court Chambers, Mitre Court, Temple, EC4Y 7BS.

BENSON, Hon. Michael D'Arcy; Chairman, Ashmore Group, since 2006; *b* Windsor, 23 May 1943; *s* of Baron Benson, GBE; *m* 1969, Rachel Woods; one *s* two *d*. *Educ:* Eton. Dir, Lazard Bros, 1979–85; CEO, Scimitar Asset Mgt, 1985–92; Dir, Capital House, 1992–94; CEO, Invesco Asia, 1994–97; CEO, 1997–2003, Chm., 2003–05, Invesco Global; Vice Chm., Amvescap, 2001–05. Director: Border Asset Mgt, 2006–; Morse plc, 2007–. Dir, York Minster Fund, 2007–. *Recreations:* sailing, shooting, gardening. *Address:* Grange Farm, Weston, York YO60 7NJ. *T:* (01653) 658296; *e-mail:* mdbenson@btinternet.com. *Clubs:* Brooks's; Newport Sailing (S Wales).

BENSON, Neil Winston, OBE 2004; FCA; Senior Partner, Lewis Golden & Co., Chartered Accountants, since 1980; *b* 17 Oct. 1937; *s* of late John William Benson and Rebecca (*née* Winston); *m* 1960, Ann Margery Licht; one *s* one *d*. *Educ:* Clifton Coll. FCA 1961. Articled clerk with Hartleys, Wilkins and Flew, 1955–60; qualified as chartered accountant, 1961; Lewis Golden & Co.: Sen. Clerk, 1961–63; Partner, 1963–. Director: Davis Service Gp Plc, 1981–2005 (Chm., 1989–2005); Shaftesbury Plc, 1986–2003; Moss Bros Gp Plc, 1989–2001 (Chm., 1990–2001); Business Post Gp Plc, 1993–2001 (Chm., 1995–2001). Royal Shakespeare Company: Gov. and Main Bd Dir, 1997–2008; Corp. of London Assessor, 1995–97. Hon. Treasurer and Trustee: Cystic Fibrosis Res. Trust, 1990–99; Foundn for Liver Res. (formerly Liver Res. Trust), 1991–2005. *Recreations:* Real tennis, golf, watching Rugby, theatre, my Alvis. *Address:* 40 Queen Anne Street, W1G 9EL. *T:* (020) 7580 7313. *Clubs:* Garrick, Royal Automobile, MCC, Saints and Sinners (Hon. Sec.; Chm., 1979); Highgate Golf, Lake Nona Golf (Orlando, Fla).

BENSON, Peter; *see* Benson, H. P. N.

BENSON, Peter Charles; His Honour Judge Peter Benson; a Circuit Judge, since 2001; *b* 16 June 1949; *s* of Robert Benson and Dorothy Benson (*née* Cartman). *Educ:* Bradford Grammar Sch.; Birmingham Univ. (BSocSc). Called to the Bar, Middle Temple, 1975; in practice at the Bar, Leeds, 1975–2001. A Recorder of the Crown Court, 1995–2001; Liaison Judge for Calderdale and Huddersfield Magistrates' Cts, 2003–. Mem., Parole Bd, 2003–. *Recreations:* golf, wine, travel. *Address:* c/o Bradford Crown Court, Exchange Square, Bradford BD1 1JA. *T:* (01274) 840274. *Clubs:* East India; Bradford; Ilkley Golf, Ganton Golf, Ilkley Bowling.

BENSON, Maj.-Gen. Peter Herbert, CBE 1974 (MBE 1954); Member, Lord Chancellor's Panel of Independent Inspectors, Planning Inspectorate, Departments of Environment and Transport, 1981–88; *b* 27 Oct. 1923; *s* of Herbert Kamerer Benson and Edith Doris Benson; *m* 1949, Diana Betty Ashmore; one *s* one *d*. Joined Army, 1944; commnd into S Wales Borderers, 1945; transf. to RASC, 1948, and Royal Corps of Transport, 1965; served, Palestine, Cyprus, Germany, Malaya and Singapore (three times), Borneo, Africa and Australia; Comdr, 15 Air Despatch Regt, 1966–68; GSO1 (DS) Staff Coll., Camberley, and Australian Staff Coll., 1968–70; Col Q (Movements), MoD (Army), 1971–72; Comdr, 2 Transport Gp RCT (Logistic Support Force), 1972–73; Comdr, ANZUK Support Gp Singapore, Sen. British Officer Singapore, and Leader, UK Jt Services Planning Team, 1973–74; Chief Transport and Movements Officer, BAOR, 1974–76; Dir Gen. of Transport and Movements (Army) (formerly Transport Officer in Chief (Army)), MoD, 1976–78. Chm., Grants Cttee, Army Benevolent Fund, 1980–92. Col Comdt, RCT, 1978–90. Chm., Abbeyfield Soc., Beaminster, 1982–92. Pres., Army Officers' Golfing Soc., 1993–96. Liveryman, Co. of Carmen, 1977. *Recreations:* golf, wood turning, photography. *Club:* Lyme Regis Golf (Captain, 1993).

BENSON, Richard Anthony; QC 1995; a Recorder, since 1995; *b* 20 Feb. 1946; *s* of Douglas Arthur Benson and Muriel Alice Benson (*née* Fairfield); *m* 1st, 1967, Katherine Anne Smith (marr. diss. 1997); one *s* two *d*; 2nd, 2000, Sarah Levina Gaunt (marr. diss. 2004); three *s* one *d*; *m* 3rd, 2006, Dr Alison Jane Simmons. *Educ:* Wrekin Coll.; Coll. of Law; Inns of Court Sch. of Law. Sailing and overland expedition to Africa, 1964–65; articled to Bircham & Co. (Solicitors), 1965–67; joined Inner Temple as student, 1968; adventuring in Sudan, 1969–70; called to the Bar, Inner Temple, 1974; in practice on Midland and Oxford Circuit, specialising in criminal law; Asst Recorder, 1991–95. *Recreations:* flying (flew Atlantic via Greenland 1983), off-shore cruising, drama, writing and performing in reviews, after-dinner speaking, the company of friends! *Address:* Citadel Chambers, 190 Corporation Street, Birmingham B4 6QD. *T:* (0121) 233 8500. *Club:* Bar Yacht.

BENSON, His Honour Richard Stuart Alistair; a Circuit Judge, 1993–2004; *b* 23 Nov. 1943; *s* of late Frank Benson and of Jean Benson; *m* 1980, Susan (marr. diss. 1998). *Educ:* Clapham Coll.; Univ. of Nottingham (BA Politics). Called to the Bar, Gray's Inn, 1968; in practice at the Bar, firstly Midland Circuit, later Midland and Oxford Circuit, Nottingham, 1968–92; a Recorder, 1991–93. Member, Court of Appeal: St Helena, 1997–; Falkland Is, 2000–; British Antarctic Territory, 2000–; British Indian Ocean Territories, 2002–. *Recreations:* steeplechasing, horses (Joint Master, Trent Valley Draghounds), books, France, whiskey and wine. *Address:* 1 High Pavement, Nottingham NG1 1HF. *T:* (0115) 941 8218. *Clubs:* Nottingham and Notts United Services; Darley Dale Fly Fishing, Beeston Fields Golf.

BENT, Margaret (Hilda), CBE 2008; PhD; FBA 1993; musicologist; Senior Research Fellow, All Souls College, Oxford, since 1992; *b* 23 Dec. 1940; *d* of late Horace Bassington and Miriam (*née* Simpson); *m*; one *s* one *d*; partner, Myles Fredric Burnyeat, *qv*. *Educ:* Haberdashers' Aske's Acton Sch.; Girton Coll., Cambridge (organ schol.; BA 1962; MusB 1963; MA; PhD 1969). FSA 2002. Lectr, then Sen. Lectr, Music Dept, Goldsmiths' Coll., London Univ., 1972–75; Vis. Prof., then full Prof. and Chm., Music Dept, Brandeis Univ., 1975–81; Prof., later Chm., Music Dept, Princeton Univ., 1981–92. Guggenheim Fellow, 1983–84. Pres., Amer. Musicological Soc., 1984–86 (Corresp. Mem., 1995). MAE 1995. For. Hon. Mem., Amer. Acad. of Arts and Scis, 1994; Corresp. Fellow, Medieval Acad. of America, 2004. FRHistS 1995. Hon. DMus Glasgow, 1997; Hon. DFA Notre Dame, 2002. F. Ll. Harrison Medal, Soc. for Musicol. in Ireland, 2007. *Publications:* (ed jtly) Old Hall Manuscript, vols I and II 1969, vol III 1973; (ed jtly) John Dunstable, Complete Works, 1970; (ed) Four Anonymous Masses, 1979; Dunstaple, 1981; (ed jtly) Ciconia, 1985; (ed) Rossini, Il Turco in Italia, 1988; Fauvel Studies, 1998; Counterpoint, Composition and Musica Ficta, 2002; (contrib.) New Grove Dictionary of Music and Musicians, 1980; contrib. Musica Disciplina, Jl of Amer. Musicol Soc., Early Music Hist. etc. *Address:* All Souls College, Oxford OX1 4AL. *T:* (01865) 279379.

BENTALL, Edward; *see* Bentall, L. E.

BENTALL, Hugh Henry, MB; FRCS; Professor of Cardiac Surgery, Royal Postgraduate Medical School, University of London, 1965–85, now Professor Emeritus at Imperial College School of Medicine at Hammersmith Hospital; *b* 28 April 1920; *s* of late Henry Bentall and Lilian Alice Greeno; *m* 1944, Jean, *d* of late Hugh Cameron Wilson, MD, FRCS; three *s* one *d*. *Educ:* Seaford Coll., Sussex; Medical Sch. of St Bartholomew's Hospital, London. RNVR, Surg. Lieut, 1945–47. Consultant Thoracic Surgeon, Hammersmith Hosp., 1955–85; Lecturer in Thoracic Surgery, Postgraduate Medical Sch., London, 1959; Reader, 1962–65. Order of Yugoslav Flag with Gold Leaves, 1984. *Publications:* books and papers on surgical subjects. *Recreations:* sailing, antique horology. *Address:* Imperial College School of Medicine at Department of Surgery, Hammersmith Hospital, Ducane Road, W12 0NN. *T:* (020) 8743 2030. *Club:* Royal Naval Sailing Association (Portsmouth).

BENTALL, (Leonard) Edward, FCA; DL; Chairman, Bentalls, 1982–2001; *b* 26 May 1939; *s* of late Leonard Edward Rowan Bentall and Adelia Elizabeth Bentall (*née* Hawes); *m* 1964, Wendy Ann Daniel; three *d*. *Educ:* Stowe School. Articled Clerk, Dixon Wilson Tubbs & Gillett, 1958–64. Bentalls, 1965–2001: Management Accountant, Merchandise Controller, Merchandise Dir, Man. Dir, Chm. and Man. Dir, Chm. and Chief Exec. Non-exec. Dir, Associated Independent Stores, 1979–82. Pres., Textile Benevolent Assoc., 1991–95. Non-exec. Director: Kingston Hosp. Trust, 1990–98 (Dep. Chm., 1998); Riverside Radio, 1996–99. Governor: Brooklands Tech. Coll., 1981–90; Kingston Coll., 1990–; Kingston Grammar Sch., 1992–2002; Patron, Bedelsford Sch. Assoc., 1997–2008. Trustee: Kingston and Dist Sea Cadet Corps TS Steadfast, 1966– (Chm., Unit Mgt Cttee, 1994–2004); Spirit of Normandy Trust, 2000–; Chm. Bd of Trustees, Shooting Star Trust Children's Hospice Appeal, 2000–03. Vice-Pres., Surrey PGA, 1995–. Steward, Nat. Greyhound Racing Club, 1998–2007 (Sen. Steward, 2005–07). Hon. Life Mem., Tamesis Sailing Club, 1997. FInstD. DL Greater London, 1999. *Address:* Heneage Farm, Windlesham Road, Chobham, Woking, Surrey GU24 8QR. *T:* (01276) 858256. *Clubs:* Naval, MCC, Saints and Sinners; Surrey Cricket.

BENTHALL, Jonathan Charles Mackenzie; social researcher; Director, Royal Anthropological Institute, 1974–2000; Editor, Anthropology Today, 1985–2000; *b* Calcutta, 12 Sept. 1941; *s* of Sir Arthur Paul Benthall, KBE and Mollie Pringle; *m* 1975, Zamira, *d* of Baron Menuhin, OM, KBE; two *s* and one step *s*. *Educ:* Eton (KS); King's Coll., Cambridge (MA). Sec., Inst. of Contemporary Arts, 1971–73. Member: UK Adv. Cttee, 1981–87, Overseas Adv. Cttee, 1985–86, 1990–96, Council, 1987–90, Assembly, 1990–98, SCF; Assoc. of Social Anthropologists, 1983; Trustee: Internat. NGO Trng and Res. Centre, 1997–2006 (Chm., 1998–2003); Alliance of Religions and Conservation, 1997–2004. Hon. Res. Fellow, Dept of Anthropology, UCL, 1994–. Advr on Islamic charities, Swiss Fed. Dept of Foreign Affairs, 2005–. Anthropology in Media Award, Amer. Anthropol Assoc., 1993; Patron's Medal, RAI, 2001. Chevalier de l'Ordre des Arts et des Lettres (France), 1973. *Publications:* Science and Technology in Art Today, 1972; (ed) Ecology: the Shaping Enquiry, 1972; (ed) The Limits of Human Nature, 1973; (ed jtly) The Body as a Medium of Expression, 1975; The Body Electric: patterns of western industrial culture, 1976; Disasters, Relief and the Media, 1993; (ed) The Best of Anthropology Today, 2002; (jtly) The Charitable Crescent: politics of aid in the Muslim world, 2003; Returning to Religion: why a secular age is haunted by faith, 2008. *Recreations:* listening to music, swimming, mountain walking, books, writing light verse. *Address:* Downingbury Farmhouse, Pembury, Tunbridge Wells, Kent TN2 4AD. *Club:* Athenæum.

BENTHAM, Howard Lownds; QC 1996; a Recorder, since 1988; *b* 26 Feb. 1948; *s* of William Foster Bentham and Elsie Bentham; *m* 1978, Elizabeth Anne Owen; one *s*. *Educ:* Malvern Coll.; Liverpool Univ. (LLB). Called to the Bar, Gray's Inn, 1970; Asst Recorder, 1985–88. *Recreations:* motor racing, scuba diving, watching wildlife. *Address:* Peel Court Chambers, First Floor, Sunlight House, Quay Street, Manchester M3 3JZ. *T:* (0161) 832 3791.

BENTHAM, Prof. Richard Walker; Professor of Petroleum and Mineral Law, and Director of the Centre for Petroleum and Mineral Law Studies, University of Dundee, 1983–90; Professor Emeritus, since 1991; *b* 26 June 1930; *s* of Richard Hardy Bentham and Ellen Walker (*née* Fisher); *m* 1956, Stella Winifred Matthews; one *d*. *Educ:* Campbell Coll., Belfast; Trinity Coll., Dublin (BA, LLB). Called to the Bar, Middle Temple, 1955. Lecturer in Law: Univ. of Tasmania, 1955–57; Univ. of Sydney, 1957–61; Legal Dept, The British Petroleum Co. PLC, 1961–83 (Dep. Legal Advisor, 1979–83). Founder Mem., Scottish Council for Internat. Arbitration (formerly Scottish Council for Arbitration), 1988–99; Mem. Council, Inst. of Internat. Business Law and Practice, ICC, 1988–94; British nominated Mem., Panel of Arbitrators, Dispute Settlement Centre, IEA, 1989–. Mem. and consultant, Russian Petroleum Legislation Project (sponsored by Univ. of Houston, World Bank and ODAS), 1991–96. FRSA 1986. *Publications:* articles in learned jls in UK and overseas. *Recreations:* cricket, military history, military modelling. *Address:* Earlham, 41 Trumlands Road, St Marychurch, Torquay, Devon TQ1 4RN. *T:* (01803) 314315.

BENTHAM-MacLEARY, Donald Whyte, OBE 2004; Guest Principal Répétiteur to the Principal Artists, Royal Ballet (Répétiteur, 1981–94; Senior Répétiteur, 1994–99; Principal Répétiteur, 1999–2002); *b* Glasgow, 22 Aug. 1937; *s* of Donald Herbert MacLeary, MPS, and Jean Spiers (*née* Leslie); adopted surname Bentham-MacLeary, 2006; civil partnership 2006, Trevor Bentham. *Educ:* Inverness Royal Academy; The Royal Ballet School. Principal male dancer, 1959–78, Ballet Master, 1978–81, Royal Ballet. *Classical Ballets:* (full length) Swan Lake, Giselle, 1958; Sleeping Beauty, Cinderella, Sylvia, 1959; Ondine, La Fille Mal Gardée, 1960; (centre male rôle) in Ashton's Symphonic Variations, 1962; Sonnet Pas de Trois, 1964; Romeo and Juliet, 1965; Eugene Onegin, Stuttgart, 1966; Apollo, 1966; Nutcracker, 1968; Swan Lake with N. Makarova, 1972. *Creations:* (1954–74): Solitaire, The Burrow, Danse Concertante, Antigone, Diversions, Le Baiser de la Fée, Jabez and the Devil, Raymonda Pas de Deux (for Frederick Ashton), two episodes in Images of Love; Song of the Earth; Lilac Garden (revival); Jazz Calendar; Raymonda (for Nureyev); The Man in Kenneth MacMillan's Checkpoint; leading rôle in Concerto no 2 (Balanchine's Ballet Imperial, renamed); Elite Syncopations, 1974; Kenneth MacMillan's Four Seasons Symphony; the Prince in Cinderella; Catalabutte in Sleeping Beauty, 2003. Toured Brazil with Royal Ballet, Spring 1973. Guest dancer, Scottish Ballet, 1979. *Recreations:* reading, theatre, records (all types); riding, swimming.
See also A. R. MacLeary.

BENTINCK, Timothy; *see* Portland, Earl of.

BENTINCK van SCHOONHETEN, Baron Willem Oswald; Ambassador of the Netherlands to the Court of St James's, 1999–2003 (and concurrently to Iceland, 1999–2002); *b* 9 March 1940; *s* of late Baron Oswald François Bentinck van Schoonheten and Meta Hendrica Bentinck van Schoonheten (*née* van der Slooten); *m* 1974, Corinne C. Elink Schuurman; two *s* one *d*. *Educ:* Univ. of Utrecht (Master of Law). Entered Netherlands Foreign Service, 1968; Buenos Aires, 1968–71; Rome, 1971–73; Internat. Relns Dept, Min. of Foreign Affairs, 1973–76; Perm. Rep., NY, 1976–79; Economic Counsellor, Moscow, 1979–81; Counsellor and Dep. Hd of Mission, Ottawa, 1981–84; Hd of Political Affairs Section and Dep. Dir, Atlantic Co-operation and Security Affairs Dept, Min. of Foreign Affairs, 1984–87; Minister and Deputy Head of Mission: Moscow, 1987–90; Washington, 1990–94; Ambassador to Madrid, 1994–98. Officer, Order of Orange Nassau (Netherlands), 1992; Kt, Order of Merit (Italy), 1972; Grand Cross, Order of Isabella la Católica (Spain), 1999. *Recreations:* shooting, golf. *Address:* Neuhuyskade 20, 2596 XL Den Haag, The Netherlands. *Clubs:* Beefsteak; Haagsche (Plaats Royaal); Royal Haagsche Golf and Country.

BENTLEY, (Anthony) Philip; QC 1991; Barrister, McDermott Will & Emery/Stanbrook (formerly Stanbrook & Hooper), Brussels, since 1980; *b* 5 Dec. 1948; *s* of late Kenneth Bentley and of Frances Elizabeth (*née* Scott); *m* 1980, Christine Anne-Marie Odile Bausier; two *s* two *d*. *Educ:* St George's Coll., Weybridge; St Catharine's Coll., Cambridge (MA); Faculté de droit d'Aix-en-Provence (Dip.). Called to the Bar, Lincoln's Inn, 1970. With ICI, 1973–77; Dilley & Custer, 1977–80. Dir, Bar Mutual Indemnity Fund, 1989–2003. Mem., Fondation Universitaire, Brussels. Oboist and Librarian, Orch. symphonique des étudiants, Catholic Univ. of Louvain. *Publications:* (with C. Stanbrook) Dumping and Subsidies, 2nd edn 1996; (with A. Silberston) Anti-Dumping and Countervailing Action: limits imposed by economic and legal theory, 2007. *Address:* (office) Rue Père Eudore Devroye 245, 1150 Brussels, Belgium. *T:* (2) 2305059.

BENTLEY, Rt Rev. David Edward; Bishop of Gloucester, 1993–2003; Hon. Assistant Bishop, Lichfield Diocese, since 2004; *b* 7 Aug. 1935; *s* of William Bentley and Florence (*née* Dalgleish); *m* 1962, Clarice Lahmers; two *s* two *d*. *Educ:* Gt Yarmouth Grammar School; Univ. of Leeds (BA English); Westcott House, Cambridge. Deacon 1960, priest 1961; Curate: St Ambrose, Bristol, 1960–62; Holy Trinity with St Mary, Guildford, 1962–66; Rector: Headley, Bordon, 1966–73; Esher, 1973–86; RD of Emly, 1977–82; Suffragan Bishop of Lynn, 1986–93; Warden, Community of All Hallows, Ditchingham, 1989–93. Hon. Canon of Guildford Cathedral, 1980. Chairman: Guildford dio. House of Clergy, 1977–86; Guildford dio. Council of Social Responsibility, 1980–86; ACCM Candidates Cttee, 1987–91; ABM Recruitment and Selection Cttee, 1991–93; ABM Ministry Develt and Deployment Cttee, 1995–98; Deployment, Remuneration and Conditions of Service Cttee, Ministry Div., Archbishops' Council, 1999–2002. Hon. PhD Gloucestershire, 2002. *Recreations:* music; sport, especially cricket; theatre, travel. *Address:* 19 Gable Croft, Lichfield WS14 9RY. *T:* (01543) 419376. *Clubs:* MCC; Warwickshire CC.

BENTLEY, David Jeffrey, CB 1993; Legal Counsellor, Foreign and Commonwealth Office, 1995–97; *b* 5 July 1935; *s* of late Harry Jeffrey Bentley and Katherine (*née* Barnett). *Educ:* Watford Grammar School; New College, Oxford (BCL, MA). Called to the Bar, Lincoln's Inn, 1963; University teaching, 1957–79; Asst Parly Counsel, 1965–67; Legal Adviser's Branch, Home Office, 1979–95, Principal Asst Legal Advr, 1988–95. Mem., Royal Patriotic Fund Corp., 2002–. *Recreations:* reading, listening to music, walking. *Address:* 192 Randolph Avenue, W9 1PE. *Club:* Oxford and Cambridge.

BENTLEY, His Honour David Ronald; QC 1984; a Circuit Judge, 1988–2005; Designated Civil Judge, South Yorkshire, 1998–2005; *b* 24 Feb. 1942; *s* of Edgar Norman and Hilda Bentley; *m* 1978, Christine Elizabeth Stewart; two *s*. *Educ:* King Edward VII Sch., Sheffield; University Coll. London (LLB (Hons) 1963); LLM and Brigid Cotter Prize, London Univ., 1979; PhD Sheffield, 1994. Called to the Bar, Gray's Inn, 1969 (Macaskie Scholar). In practice at the bar, 1969–88; a Recorder, 1985–88. *Publications:* Select Cases from The Twelve Judges' Notebooks, 1997; Criminal Justice in Nineteenth-Century England, 1998; Victorian Men of Law, 2000; The Sheffield Hanged 1750–1864, 2002; Sheffield Murders 1865–1965, 2003; Crimes and Misdemeanours, 2005. *Recreations:* legal history, watching Sheffield United.

BENTLEY, Ven. Frank William Henry; Archdeacon of Worcester and Canon Residentiary of Worcester Cathedral, 1984–99, now Emeritus; Chaplain to the Queen, 1994–2004; *b* 4 March 1934; *s* of Nowell and May Bentley; *m* 1st, 1957, Muriel Bland (*d* 1958); one *s*; 2nd, 1960, Yvonne Wilson (*d* 2000); two *s* one *d*; 3rd, 2006, Kathleen M. Gibbs. *Educ:* Yeovil School; King's College London (AKC). Deacon 1958, priest 1959; Curate at Shepton Mallet, 1958–62; Rector of Kingsdon with Podymore Milton and Curate-in-charge, Yeovilton, 1962–66; Rector of Babcary, 1964–66; Vicar of Wiveliscombe, 1966–76; Rural Dean of Tone, 1973–76; Vicar of St John-in-Bedwardine, Worcester, 1976–84; Rural Dean of Martley and Worcester West, 1979–84. Hon. Canon of Worcester Cathedral, 1981. *Recreations:* gardening, countryside. *Address:* Willow Cottage, Station Road, Fladbury, Pershore, Worcs WR10 2QW. *T:* (01386) 861847.

BENTLEY, Prof. George, DSc; FRCS, FRCSE; Professor of Orthopaedic Surgery, University of London, 1982–2002, now Emeritus Professor of Orthopaedics; Hon. Consultant Orthopaedic Surgeon, Royal National Orthopaedic Hospital, Stanmore, since 1982; *b* 19 Jan. 1936; *s* of George and Doris Bentley; *m* 1960, Ann Gillian Hutchings; two *s* one *d*. *Educ:* Rotherham Grammar Sch.; Sheffield Univ. (MB, ChB, ChM; DSc 2002). FRCS 1964; FRCSE 2000. House Surgeon, Sheffield Royal Infirmary, 1959–61; Lectr in Anatomy, Birmingham Univ., 1961–62; Surg. Registrar, Sheffield Royal Infirm., 1963–65; Sen. Registrar in Orthopaedics, Nuffield Orthopaedic Centre and Radcliffe Infirm., Oxford, 1967–69; Instructor in Orth., Univ. of Pittsburgh, USA, 1969–70; Lectr, 1970–71, Sen. Lectr and Reader in Orth., 1971–76, Univ. of Oxford; Prof. of Orth. and Accident Surgery, Univ. of Liverpool, 1976–82; Dir, Inst. of Orthopaedics, UC and Middx Sch. of Medicine, Univ. of London, 1982–2000. Hon. Consultant Orthopaedic Surgeon, Middlesex Hosp., 1984–2001. Eur. Ed.-in-Chief, Jl Arthroplasty, 2001–; Member, Editorial Board: Jl Bone and Jt Surgery, 1974–76, 2006–; The Knee, 1993–2004; Clinical Materials, 1993–98; Orthopaedics Internat., 1997–. Numerous lectures including: Hunterian Prof., RCS, 1972; Watson-Jones, 1996, Alan Apley Meml, 2006, Robert Jones, 2007, RCS and BOA. Chairman: Scientific Cttee, EFORT, 1995–2002; Intercollegiate Bd, Exam. in Orthopaedics UK, 1996–99. Vice-Pres., RCS, 2001–03 (Mem. Council); Mem. Council, British Orthopaedic Assoc. (Pres., 1992); Pres., British Orthopaedic Res. Assoc., 1985–87; Vice-Pres., 2002–03, Pres., 2004–05, European Fedn of Nat. Assocs of Orthopaedics and Traumatology; Member Council: Orthopaedic Association: Australia; NZ; SA; Eastern; Argentina; Amer. Orthopaedic and Res. Assoc.; Eur. Orthopaedic Res. Assoc.; SICOT; ESSKA; ISAKOS. Pres., Seddon Soc., 1996–. FMedSci 1999. Hon. Mem., French Soc. of Trauma and Orthopaedics, 1999; Hon. Fellow: British Orthopaedic Assoc., 2004; RSocMed, 2004; Czech Orthopaedic Assoc., 2004. *Publications:* (ed) 3rd edn vols I and II, Rob and Smith Operative Surgery—Orthopaedics, 1979, 4th edn 1991; (ed) Mercer's Orthopaedic Surgery, 8th edn, 1983, 9th edn 1996; papers on cell-engineered cartilage grafting of joints, arthritis, accident surgery and scoliosis in leading med. and surg. jls. *Recreations:* golf, tennis, music. *Address:* Institute of Orthopaedics, Royal National Orthopaedic Hospital, Stanmore, Middx HA7 4LP. *T:* (020) 8909 5532.

BENTLEY, John Ransome; Chairman, Prize Mobile Plc, since 2007; *b* 19 Feb. 1940; *m* 1st, 1960, Dorothy (marr. diss. 1969; decd); one *s* one *d*; two *d*; 2nd, 1982, Katherine Susan (marr. diss. 1986), *d* of Gerald Percy and the Marchioness of Bute; 3rd, 2002, Janet.

Educ: Harrow Sch. Chairman: Barclay Securities plc, 1969–73; Intervision Video (Holdings) plc, 1980–83; Viewcall America Inc., 1995–97; Electronic Game Card Inc., 2002–05. Inventor: of NET TV; of electronic gamecards, 2001; of mobile video reward games, 2005. *Recreation:* life. *Address: e-mail:* j.bentley2@btinternet.com; *web:* www.johnbentley.biz.

BENTLEY, Philip; *see* Bentley, A. P.

BENTLEY, Sarah Rosamund Irvine; *see* Foot, S. R. I.

BENTLY, Prof. Lionel Alexander Fiennes; Herchel Smith Professor of Intellectual Property Law, and Director, Centre of Intellectual Property and Information Law, University of Cambridge, since 2004; Professorial Fellow, Emmanuel College, Cambridge, since 2004; *b* 2 July 1964; *s* of Lionel Charles Warwick Bently and Helen Joy Bently (*née* Wright); partner, Clair Milligan. *Educ:* Pembroke Coll., Cambridge (BA Law). Prof. of Law, KCL, 2002–04. Door Tenant, Hogarth Chambers, Lincoln's Inn, 2004–. *Publications:* with Brad Sherman: The Making of Modern Intellectual Property Law, 1999; Intellectual Property Law, 2001, 2nd edn 2004. *Recreations:* football (Mem., Arsenal FC), punk rock, industrial and related music. *Address:* Centre of Intellectual Property and Information Law, Faculty of Law, University of Cambridge, 10 West Road, Cambridge CB3 9DZ. *T:* (01223) 330081, *Fax:* (01223) 330086; *e-mail:* lb329@cam.ac.uk.

BENTON, Joseph Edward; JP; MP (Lab) Bootle, since Nov. 1990; *b* 28 Sept. 1933; *s* of Thomas and Agnes Benton; *m* 1959, Doris Wynne; four *d. Educ:* St Monica's Primary and Secondary Sch.; Bootle Technical Coll. Nat. Service, RAF, 1955. Apprentice fitter and turner, 1949; former Personnel Manager, Pacific Steam Navigation Co.; Girobank, 1982–90. Councillor, Sefton Borough Council, 1970–90 (Leader, Labour Gp, 1985–90). An Opposition Whip, 1994–97. Mem., Speaker's Panel of Chairmen, 1992–94, 1997–. Mem., Select Cttee on Educn, 1997–98; Sec., All Party Parly Pro-Life Gp, 1992–; Member: British/Spanish Parly Gp, 1997–; British/Irish Parly Gp, 1997–. Mem., Bd Visitors, Liverpool Prison (Walton), 1974–81. Chm. of Govs, Hugh Baird Coll. of Technology, 1972–93. Assoc. Mem., IPM, 1965; MIL 1963. JP South Sefton, 1969. *Address:* c/o House of Commons, SW1A 0AA.

BENTON, Margaret Carole; Director, The Making, since 2003; *b* 14 April 1943; *d* of late Lawrence and Mary Benton; *m* Stephen Green. *Educ:* The Red Maids Sch., Bristol; Univ. of Wales (BA Hons French). British Broadcasting Corporation: Radio, 1966–67; News, Paris Office, 1967–69; Schools Television, 1969–70; Gen. Features Television, 1970–71; COI (Overseas Documentaries/Co-prodns), 1971–75; BBC Television, Bristol, 1975–85; Nat. Museum of Photography, Film and Television, 1985–90; Dir, Theatre Mus., V&A, 1990–2003. Member: Theatres Adv. Council, 1991–2002; Council of Management (British Centre), Internat. Theatre Inst.; Museums Assoc.; Pres., Société Internationale des Bibliothèques et des Musées des Arts du Spectacle, 1992–96. Prod and dir. numerous television documentaries and other progs for BBC. *Recreations:* rural "idylling", theatre, cinema, visual arts, gardens, historic buildings. *Address:* The Making, Civic Offices, London Road, Basingstoke RG21 4AH.

BENTON, Prof. Michael James, PhD; FGS, FLS; FRSE; Professor of Vertebrate Palaeontology, University of Bristol, since 1997; *b* 8 April 1956; *s* of Alexander Charles Benton and Elsie Christine Benton (*née* Taylor); *m* 1983, Mary Monro; one *s* one *d. Educ:* Univ. of Aberdeen (BSc Hons Zool. 1978); Univ. of Newcastle upon Tyne (PhD Geol. 1981). FLS 1983; FGS 1987. SO, NCC, 1981–82; Jun. Res. Fellow, Trinity Coll., Oxford, 1982–84; Lectr, QUB, 1984–89; University of Bristol: Lectr, Dept of Geol., 1989–92; Reader in Vertebrate Palaeontol., 1992–97; Hd, Dept of Earth Scis, 2001–08. Pres., Geologists' Assoc., 2006–08. FRSE 2008. Lyell Medal, Geol Soc. of London, 2005; T. Neville George Medal, Geol Soc. of Glasgow, 2006. *Publications:* The Phylogeny and Classification of the Tetrapods, 1988; Vertebrate Palaeontology, 1990, 3rd edn 2004; Fossil Record 2, 1993; Fossil Reptiles of Great Britain, 1995; The Penguin Historical Atlas of Dinosaurs, 1996; (with D. A. T. Harper) Basic Palaeontology, 1997; Walking with Dinosaurs: the facts, 2000; (jtly) The Age of Dinosaurs in Russia and Mongolia, 2001; (jtly) Permian and Triassic Red Beds and the Penarth Group of Great Britain, 2002; When Life Nearly Died: the greatest mass extinction of all time, 2003; Mesozoic and Tertiary Fossil Mammals and Birds of Great Britain, 2005; (with D. A. T. Harper) Introduction to Paleobiology and the Fossil Record, 2008; Very Short Introduction to the History of Life, 2008; The Seventy Great Mysteries of the Natural World, 2008; 43 popular books and over 200 scientific papers. *Recreations:* reading, travelling, swimming, crosswords. *Address:* Department of Earth Sciences, University of Bristol, Bristol BS8 1RJ. *T:* (0117) 954 5433, *Fax:* (0117) 925 3385; *e-mail:* mike.benton@bristol.ac.uk.

BENTON, Rev. Canon Michael John; Priest-in-charge, Kingsclere, 1996–2003; Chaplain to the Queen, 1998–2008; *b* 3 Nov. 1938; *s* of William James Benton and Violet May Benton (*née* Pearse); *m* 1960, Frances Elizabeth Margaret Joyce Harris; two *s* one *d. Educ:* Chichester High Sch. for Boys; University Coll. London (BSc Hons 1960); Fitzwilliam House, Cambridge (CertEd 1961). Asst Biology Master, Alleynes GS, Stevenage, 1961–63; Head of Biology, Perse Sch., Cambridge, 1963–69; Lectr and Sen. Lectr, Biol Scis, King Alfred's Coll., Winchester, 1969–76. Theol study, Salisbury Theol Coll. and St George's Coll., Jerusalem, 1972–74; ordained deacon and priest, 1974; Hon. Curate, Weeke, 1974–76; full time priest in C of E, 1976–2003; Curate, Bursledon, 1976–78; Rector, Over Wallop with Nether Wallop, 1978–83; Rector, St Lawrence and St Maurice with St Swithun, Winchester, 1983–90; Dir of Educn, Dio. of Winchester, 1979–95; Hon. Canon, Winchester Cathedral, 1989–2003, now Canon Emeritus. *Publications:* regular Christian comment column for Hampshire Chronicle, 1988–2002; occasional papers and articles. *Recreations:* reading, science and faith debate (Mem. SOSc), history, bird-watching, growing shrub roses, watching vintage aircraft (Mem. Spitfire Soc.), archaeology. *Address:* South Lodge, Auchterarder, Perthshire PH3 1ER.

BENTON, Peter Faulkner, MA; Director-General, British Institute of Management, 1987–92; *b* 6 Oct. 1934; *s* of late S. F. Benton and Mrs H. D. Benton; *m* 1959, Ruth, *d* of late R. S. Cobb, MC, FRIBA and Mrs J. P. Cobb; two *s* three *d. Educ:* Oundle; Queens' Coll., Cambridge (MA Nat. Sciences). 2nd Lieut RE, 1953–55. Unilever Ltd, 1958–60; Shell Chemicals Ltd, 1960–63; Berger Jenson and Nicholson Ltd, 1963–64; McKinsey & Co. Inc., London and Chicago, 1964–71 (led reorgn of British gas industry, 1967–71); Gallaher Ltd, 1971, Dir, 1973–77; Man. Dir, Post Office Telecommunications, 1978–81; Dep. Chm., British Telecom, 1981–83. Advr, Stern Stewart Inc., 1995–2002. Chairman: Saunders Valve Ltd, 1972–77; Mono Pumps Group, 1976–77; European Practice, Nolan, Norton & Co., 1984–87; Identica Ltd, 1992–93; Director: Singer and Friedlander, 1983–89; Woodside Communications, 1995–96; Mem., Supervisory Bd, Hiross Holdings AG, Austria, 1992–94. Dir, Turing Inst., 1985–94. Chairman: Enfield Dist HA, 1986–92; Enterprise Support Gp, 1993–96. Chm., Heating, Ventilating, Air Conditioning and Refrigerating Equipment Sector Working Party, NEDO, 1976–79; Member: Electronics Industry EDC, 1980–83; Econ. and Financial Policy Cttee, CBI, 1979–83; Special Adviser to EEC, 1983–84; Nat. Curriculum Science Wkg Gp, 1987–88; Indust. Develt Adv. Bd, DTI, 1988–94; Ind. Mem., British Liby Adv. Council, 1988–93; Internat. Adv. Bd for Science and Technology to Govt of Portugal, 1996–2003. Adviser, Arthur Andersen Société Coopérative, 1993–98. Vice-President: British Mech. Engrg Confedn, 1974–77; European Council of Management, 1989–93. Chairman: Ditchley Conf. on Inf. Technol., 1982; Financial Times Conf., World Electronics, 1983; World Bank Conf. on Catastrophe Avoidance, Washington, 1988, Karlstad, 1989; Vis. Gp, Inst. for Systems Engrg and Informatics, Italy, 1993; Inst. for Systems, Informatics and Safety, 1996; Euromoney Conf., New Delhi, 1998; Jt Chm., European Mgt Congress, Prague, 1990. Royal Signals Instn Lectr, London, 1980; ASLIB Lectr, 1988; Adam Smith Lectr, 1991. Pres., Highgate Literary and Scientific Instn, 1981–88. Chm., N London Hospice Gp, 1985–89. Governor, Molecule Club Theatre, 1985–91. CCMI. *Publications:* Riding the Whirlwind, 1990; articles on management, science and IT. *Recreations:* reading, baroque music, sailing, conversation, looking at buildings. *Address:* Northgate House, Highgate Hill, N6 5HD. *T:* (020) 8341 1122; Dolphins, Polruan, Cornwall PL23 1PP. *Clubs:* Athenæum, Oxford and Cambridge, The Pilgrims; Blythe Sappers; Royal Fowey Yacht.

BENTON JONES, Sir Simon Warley Frederick; *see* Jones.

BENYON, Richard Henry Ronald; MP (C) Newbury, since 2005; *b* 21 Oct. 1960; *s* of Sir William Richard Benyon, *qv*; *m* 2004, Zoe Robinson; two *s*, and three *s* from previous marriage. *Educ:* Bradfield Coll.; Royal Agricl Coll. MRICS. Served Army, 1980–84: commnd RGJ; served NI and Far East. Land Agent, 1987–90; farmer, Englefield, Berks, 1990–; Chm., Englefield Estate Trust Corp. Ltd (Rural and Urban Land Hldgs), 2001–. *Recreations:* walking, conservation, shooting, cooking. *Address:* House of Commons, SW1A 0AA. *Club:* Beefsteak.

BENYON, Thomas Yates; Founder and Director, ZANE: Zimbabwe A National Emergency, since 2000; Director of various companies; *b* 13 Aug. 1942; *s* of late Thomas Yates Benyon and Joan Ida Walters; *m* 1968, Olivia Jane (*née* Scott Plummer); two *s* two *d. Educ:* Wellington Sch., Somerset; RMA Sandhurst; Wycliffe Hall, Oxford (DBTS 2002). Lieut, Scots Guards, 1963–67. Insurance broking and banking, 1967–79. Chm., Milton Keynes HA, 1989–94; Dir, Bucks Purchasing Authy, 1994–96. Councillor, Aylesbury Vale DC, 1976–79. Contested (C): Huyton, Feb. 1974; Haringey (Wood Green), Oct. 1974; MP (C) Abingdon, 1979–83; Vice Chm., Health and Social Services Cttee, 1982–83; Mem., Social Services Select Cttee, 1980–83. Founder Chm., Assoc. of Lloyd's Members, 1982–87; Founder: Soc. of Names, 1990–; Insurance Insider Publishing plc, 1997–; Guild Acquisitions plc, 2006–. Mem., Gen. Synod of C of E, 2005–. *Recreations:* family, litigation. *Address:* Rectory Farm House, Bladon, Oxon OX20 1RS. *Clubs:* Royal Automobile, Pratt's; Third Guards.

BENYON, Sir William (Richard), Kt 1994; DL; landowner, since 1964; Vice Lord-Lieutenant, Berkshire, 1994–2005; *b* 17 Jan. 1930; *e s* of late Vice-Adm. R. Benyon, CB, CBE, and of Mrs Benyon, The Lambdens, Beenham, Berkshire; *m* Elizabeth Ann Hallifax; two *s* three *d. Educ:* Royal Naval Coll., Dartmouth. Royal Navy, 1947–56; Courtaulds Ltd, 1956–64. Mem., Berks CC, 1964–74. MP (C) Buckingham, 1970–83, Milton Keynes, 1983–92. PPS to Minister of Housing and Construction, 1972–74; Conservative Whip, 1974–76. Chairman: Peabody Trust, 1993–98; Ernest Cook Charitable Trust, 1993–2004. JP 1962–78, DL 1970, High Sheriff 1995, Berks. *Address:* Wimbletons Barn, Englefield, Reading, Berkshire RG7 5EH. *T:* (0118) 930 2221, *Fax:* (0118) 930 3226; *e-mail:* benyon@englefield.co.uk. *Clubs:* Boodle's, Pratt's, Beefsteak.
See also R. H. R. Benyon.

BERAL, Prof. Valerie, MD; FRCP; FRS 2006; Director, Cancer Research UK Cancer Epidemiology Unit (formerly ICRF Clinical Trials and Epidemiology, then Cancer Epidemiology, Unit), Oxford, since 1989; Fellow of Green Templeton College (formerly Green College), Oxford, since 1989; Professor of Epidemiology, University of Oxford, since 1996; *b* 28 July 1946; partner, Prof. Paul E. M. Fine; two *s. Educ:* Univ. of Sydney (MB BS 1969; MD 2001). MRCP 1971, FRCP 1992. Lectr, Sen. Lectr, then Reader in Epidemiol., LSHTM, 1970–88. Chm., DoH Adv. Cttee on Breast Cancer Screening, 2000–. Hon. FFPH (Hon. FFPHM 2000); Hon. FRCOG 2001. *Publications:* articles on causes of breast and other cancers in women. *Address:* 193 Morrell Avenue, Oxford OX4 1NF; Cancer Epidemiology Unit, Richard Doll Building, Roosevelt Drive, Oxford OX3 7LF.

BERASATEGUI, Vicente Ernesto; Ambassador of the Argentine Republic to the Court of St James's, 2000–03; *b* 13 May 1934; *s* of Miguel Bernardo Gabriel Berasategui and Maria Luisa Rivanera Carles; *m* 1960, Teresita Mazza. *Educ:* Univ. of Buenos Aires (degree in Law); American Univ., Washington (Master in Internat. Relns and Orgn). Joined Argentine Foreign Service, 1954: Attaché, 1954–59; Hd, OAS Div., Foreign Min., 1960–61; Third, later Second, Sec., USA, 1961–65; Sec., Policy Making Cttee, Minister for Foreign Affairs, 1967–69; Dep. to Dir Gen. for Political Affairs, Foreign Min., 1970–72; Dep. Perm. Rep. to UN, Geneva, 1972–76; Minister, 1973; Ambassador, 1985; Dir for Western Eur. Affairs, Foreign Min., 1994–96; Ambassador to Denmark, 1997–2000. Rep., and Hd of delegns, to internat. confs, 1959–76 (Hd, Delegn to Conf. of Cttee on Disarmament, 1974–76); Mem., and Hd for meeting of delegns with heads of state and political consultations, 1971–98. United Nations posts include: Consultant, Centre for Disarmament, 1977–78; Sec., First Cttee of Gen. Assembly and Dep. Sec., Cttee on Disarmament, 1980; Dir, Geneva Br., Dept for Disarmament Affairs, 1983; Dep. Sec.-Gen., 1984–92, Sec.-Gen., 1992–93, Conf. on Disarmament (also Personal Rep. of Sec.-Gen. of UN); Chm., Adv. Bd of Sec.-Gen. on disarmament, 2005. Dir, Sch. of Internat. Relns and Prof. of Theory of Internat. Relns and Contemp. Internat. Politics, Univ. of Salvador, 1967–70; Visiting Professor: of Foreign Policy, Sch. of Law, Univ. of Buenos Aires, 1971; Prog. of Diplomatic Studies, Grad. Inst. of Internat. Studies, Geneva, 1987–93; lectures on subjects concerning internat. relns, mainly disarmament, in Argentina, France and USA. Grand Cross, Order of Dannebrog (Denmark), 2000; Grand Officer: Order of Dist. Services (Peru), 1968; Order of Merit (Italy), 1995; Commander: Order Bernardo O'Higgins (Chile), 1971; Order of Condor of the Andes (Bolivia), 1971; Order of Civil Merit (Spain), 1995; Order of Merit (France), 1999. *Address:* Avenida Alvear 1494, 1014 Buenos Aires, Argentina. *T:* (11) 48159811.

BERCOW, John Simon; MP (C) Buckingham, since 1997; *b* 19 Jan. 1963; *s* of late Charles Bercow and of Brenda Bercow (*née* Bailey); *m* 2002, Sally Illman; two *s* one *d. Educ:* Finchley Manorhill Sch.; Univ. of Essex (BA 1st Cl. Hons Govt 1985). Nat. Chm., Fedn of Cons. Students, 1986–87; Credit Analyst, Hambros Bank, 1987–88; Public Affairs Consultant, Sallingbury Casey, later Rowland Sallingbury Casey, 1988–95; Dir, Rowland Co., 1994–95; Special Adviser to: Chief Sec. to Treasury, 1995; Sec. of State for Nat. Heritage, 1995–96; free-lance consultant, 1996–97. Councillor (C), Lambeth BC, 1986–90 (Dep. Leader, Opposition Gp, 1987–89). Vice-Chm., Cons. Collegiate Forum, 1987. Contested (C): Motherwell S, 1987; Bristol S, 1992. Opposition spokesman: on educn and employment, 1999–2000; on home affairs, 2000–01; Shadow Chief Sec. to HM Treasury, 2001–02; Shadow Minister for Work and Pensions, 2002; Shadow Sec. of State for Internat. Devolt, 2003–04. Member: Trade and Industry Select Cttee, 1998–99; Internat. Devolt Select Cttee, 2004–. Co-Dir, Advanced Speaking and Campaigning

Course, 1989–. *Recreations:* tennis, swimming, reading, cinema. *Address:* House of Commons, SW1A 0AA.

BERESFORD, family name of **Baron Decies** and **Marquess of Waterford**.

BERESFORD, Sir (Alexander) Paul, Kt 1990; dental surgeon; MP (C) Mole Valley, since 1997 (Croydon Central, 1992–97); *b* 6 April 1946; *s* of Raymond and Joan Beresford; *m* Julie Haynes; three *s* one *d*. *Educ:* Richmond Primary Sch., Richmond, Nelson, NZ; Waimea Coll., Richmond; Otago Univ., Dunedin. Mem. (C), Wandsworth BC, 1978–94 (Leader of Council, 1983–92). Mem., Audit Commn, 1991–92. Parly Under-Sec. of State, DoE, 1994–97. *Address:* c/o House of Commons, SW1A 0AA.

BERESFORD, Marcus de la Poer, CBE 2003; Chairman, Ricardo plc, since 2004; *b* 15 May 1942; *s* of late Anthony de la Poer Beresford and Mary (*née* Canning); *m* 1965, Jean Helen Kitchener; two *s*. *Educ:* Harrow Sch.; St John's Coll., Cambridge (MA Mech. Sci.). FIET (FIEE 1986). Man. Dir, Automotive Instrumentation Gp, Smiths Industries, 1978–83; Dir and Gen. Manager, Lucas Electronics Ltd, 1983–85; Man. Dir, Siemens Plessey Controls Ltd, 1985–92; Dir, Siemens plc, 1991–92; Man. Dir, GKN Industrial Services, 1992–2001; Dir, 1992–2002, Chief Exec., 2001–02, GKN plc. Non-executive Director: Camas, then Aggregate Industries, plc, 1994–2000; Spirent plc, 1999–2006; Cobham plc, 2004–. Non-exec. Dir, Engrg and Technol. Bd, 2002–05. Mem. Council, Open Univ., 1997–2000. Freeman, City of London, 1963; Liveryman, Skinners' Co., 1973. *Recreations:* golf, tennis, gardening. *Address:* Ricardo plc, Bridge Works, Shoreham by Sea, West Sussex BN43 5FG. *Club:* Royal Over-Seas League.

BERESFORD, Meg; Manager, Wiston Lodge (formerly YMCA Centre, Wiston Lodge), since 1997 (Assistant Director, 1994–97); *b* 5 Sept. 1937; *d* of late John Tristram Beresford and of Anne Stuart-Wortley; *m* 1959, William Tanner; two *s*. *Educ:* Sherborne School for Girls; Seale Hayne Agricultural Coll., Newton Abbot; Univ. of Warwick. Community worker, Leamington Spa; Organising Sec., European Nuclear Disarmament, 1981–83; Gen. Sec., CND, 1985–90; gardener, 1991–92, Staff Co-ordinator, 1992–94, Iona Community. *Publications:* Into the Twenty First Century, 1989; contributor to End Jl, Sanity. *Recreations:* walking, reading, camping, music. *Address:* Wiston Lodge, Wiston, Biggar ML12 6HT.

BERESFORD, Sir Paul; *see* Beresford, Sir A. P.

BERESFORD-PEIRSE, Sir Henry Grant de la Poer, 6th Bt *cr* 1814; *b* 7 Feb. 1933; *s* of Sir Henry Campbell de la Poer Beresford-Peirse, 5th Bt, CB, and Margaret (*d* 1995), *d* of Frank Morison Seafield Grant, Knockie, Inverness-shire; *S* father, 1972; *m* 1966, Jadranka, *d* of Ivan Njerš, Zagreb, Croatia; two *s*. *Heir: s* Henry Njerš de la Poer Beresford-Peirse [*b* 25 March 1969; *m* 2005, Joanna Tamlyn; one *s*].

BERG, Adrian, RA 1992; *b* 12 March 1929; *s* of Charles Berg, MD, DPM and Sarah (*née* Sorby). *Educ:* Charterhouse; Gonville and Caius Coll., Cambridge (MA); Trinity Coll., Dublin (HDipEd); St Martin's Sch. of Art (Intermediate Arts & Crafts); Chelsea Sch. of Art (NDD); Royal Coll. of Art (ARCA; Hon. FRCA 1994). Nat. Service, 1947–49. Taught at various art schools, esp. Central Sch. of Art and Design and Camberwell Sch. of Arts and Crafts, 1961–78; Sen. Tutor, RCA, 1987–88. One-man exhibitions include: Arthur Tooth & Sons Ltd, London, 1964, 1967, 1969, 1972 and 1975; Galleria Vaccarino, Florence, 1973; Galerie Burg Diesdonk, Düsseldorf, 1976; Waddington and Tooth Galls, London, 1978; Waddington Galls, Montreal and Toronto and Grace Hokin, Inc., Chicago, 1979; London: Waddington Galls, 1981 and 1983; Serpentine Gall., 1973, 1984 and 1986; Piccadilly Gall., 1985, 1988, 1989, 1991, 1993, 1999 and 2002; Concourse Gall., Barbican Centre, 1993; Friends' Room, RA, 1999; Walker Art Gall., Liverpool, 1986; Victoria Art Gall., Bath, 1993; Plymouth City Mus. and Art Gall., 1993; Newport Mus. and Art Gall., Gwent, 1993; Mappin Gall., Sheffield, 1993; Hatton Gall., Newcastle, 1994; Royal Botanic Gdn, Edinburgh, 1994; Rye Art Gall., 1994; (contrib.) Art of the Garden, Stourhead, 2004; Richmond Hill Gall., 2008. Lorne Scholarship, 1979–80. Gold Medal, Florence Biennale, 1973; minor and major prizes, John Moores Nat. Exhibns, 1980 and 1982; Major Prize, 3rd Tolly Cobbold, Eastern Arts Nat. Exhibn, 1981; Foundn for Art Award, NT, 1987; First Prize, RWS Open, 2001. *Recreations:* imaginative reading, criticism. *Address:* Royal Academy of Arts, Piccadilly, W1J 0BD.

BERG, Alan; District Judge (Magistrates' Courts) (formerly Stipendiary Magistrate), Greater Manchester, since 1994; *b* 17 Feb. 1943; *s* of Simon and Esther Berg; *m* 1967, Lorna Lewis; two *s*. *Educ:* King George V Grammar Sch., Southport; Law Coll., Liverpool. Solicitor in private practice, Liverpool, 1967–94; Sen. Partner, Canter Levin & Berg, 1980–93; Asst Stipendiary Magistrate, 1991–94. *Recreations:* grandchildren, reading, worrying. *Address:* Manchester City Magistrates' Court, Crown Square, Manchester M60 1PR. *T:* (0161) 832 7272.

BERG, Eddie; Artistic Director, BFI Southbank, since 2005; *b* 25 Aug. 1958; *s* of Francis and Edith Hollingsworth; *m* 1986, Karen Berg (marr. diss.); one *s*. *Educ:* Open Univ. House Manager, Everyman Th., Liverpool, 1984–87; Dir, Moviola, Liverpool, 1988–96; Chief Exec., Foundn for Art and Creative Technol., Liverpool, 1996–2005. FRSA. *Publications:* (contrib.) Empire, Ruins and Networks: the transcultural agenda in art, 2005; Factors: 1988–2005. *Recreations:* films, media art, music, cooking, eating out, discovering new ideas/places/people, football, travel, thinking, soaking up the sun, reading. *Address:* c/o BFI Southbank, Belvedere Road, SE1 8XT. *T:* (020) 7815 1300; *e-mail:* eddie.berg@bfi.org.uk.

BERG, Geoffrey, MVO 1976; HM Diplomatic Service, retired; *b* 5 July 1945; *s* of Bertram Lionel Berg and Irene Amelia Berg; *m* 1970, Sheila Maxine Brown; one *s*. *Educ:* Woking County Grammar Sch. for Boys. Joined CRO, 1963; Diplomatic Service Admin, 1965–68; Latin American floater duties, 1968–70; Third Sec. (Vice-Consul), Bucharest, 1970–72; FCO, 1972–75; Second, later First Sec. (Inf.), Helsinki, 1975–79; FCO, 1979–84; First Sec. (Commercial), Madrid, 1984–88; FCO, 1988–90; Counsellor on secondment to DTI, 1990–93; Dep. Head of Mission, Mexico City, 1993–96; Dep. Consul-Gen. and Dir of Trade, NY, 1997–2001; Consul-Gen., Toronto and Dir, Trade and Investment, Canada, 2002–05. Chevalier First Cl., Order of Lion (Finland), 1976; Official Cross, Order of Civil Merit (Spain), 1988. *Recreations:* travel, photography. *Club:* Royal Over-Seas League.

BERG, Rev. John J.; *see* Johansen-Berg.

BERG, Prof. Maxine Louise, DPhil; FBA 2004; FRHistS; Professor of History and Director, Warwick Eighteenth Century Centre, University of Warwick; *b* 22 Feb. 1950; *m* 1977, John Charles Robertson; three *d*. *Educ:* Simon Fraser Univ., BC (BA); Univ. of Sussex (MA); Univ. of Oxford (DPhil 1976). Sir Lewis Namier Jun. Res. Fellow in Hist., Balliol Coll., Oxford, 1974; University of Warwick, 1978–: Lectr, then Sen. Lectr, Dept of Econs; Sen. Lectr, then Reader, Dept of History. *Publications:* (ed) Technology and Toil in Nineteenth Century Britain, 1979; Machinery Question and the Making of Political Economy 1815–48, 1982; (ed jtly) Manufacture in Town and Country Before the Factory, 1983; The Age of Manufactures: industry, innovation and work in Britain 1700–1820, 1985, 2nd edn 1994; Political Economy in the Twentieth Century, 1989; A Woman in History: Eileen Power 1889–1940, 1996; (ed with Kristine Bruland) Technological Revolutions in Europe 1760–1860, 1997; (ed with Helen Clifford) Consumers and Luxury in Europe 1650–1850, 1999; (ed with Elizabeth Eger) Luxury in the Eighteenth Century: debates, desires and delectable goods, 2002; Luxury and Pleasure in Eighteenth-Century Britain, 2005; contrib. learned jls. *Address:* Department of History, University of Warwick, Coventry CV4 7AL.

BERG, Prof. Paul, PhD; Cahill Professor in Cancer Research (Biochemistry), 1994–2000, now Professor Emeritus, and Director, Beckman Center for Molecular and Genetic Medicine, 1985–2000, Stanford University School of Medicine; *b* New York, 30 June 1926; *m* Mildred Levy; one *s*. *Educ:* Pennsylvania State Univ. (BS); Western Reserve Univ. (PhD). Pre-doctoral and post-doctoral med. research, 1950–54; scholar in cancer research, American Cancer Soc., Washington Univ., 1954; Asst to Associate Prof. of Microbiology, Washington Univ., 1955–59; Stanford Univ. Sch. of Medicine: Associate Prof. of Biochem., 1959–60; Prof., Dept of Biochem., 1960, Chm. 1969–74; Willson Prof. of Biochem., 1970–93; Non-resident Fellow, Salk Inst., 1973–83. Editor, Biochemical and Biophysical Res. Communications, 1959–68; Member: NIH Study, Sect. on Physiol Chem.; Editorial Bd, Jl of Molecular Biology, 1966–69; Bd of Sci. Advisors, Jane Coffin Childs Foundn for Med. Res.; Adv. Bds to Nat. Insts of Health, Amer. Cancer Soc., Nat. Sci. Foundn, MIT and Harvard, 1970–80; Council, Nat. Acad. of Scis, 1979. Former Pres., Amer. Soc. of Biological Chemists; Foreign Member: Japan Biochem. Soc., 1978; French Acad. of Scis, 1981; Royal Soc., 1992; Pontifical Acad. of Scis, 1996. Lectures: Harvey, 1972; Lynen, 1977; Weizmann Inst., 1977; Univ. of Pittsburgh, 1978; Priestly, Pennsylvania State Univ., 1978; Shell, Univ. of California at Davis, 1978; Dreyfus, Northwestern Univ., 1979; Jesup, Columbia Univ., 1980; Karl-August-Förster, Univ. of Mainz, 1980; David Rivett Meml, CSIR, Melb., 1980. Hon. DSc: Rochester and Yale Univs, 1978; Washington Univ., St Louis, 1986; Pennsylvania State Univ., 1995; numerous awards include: Eli Lilly Award, 1959; Calif. Scientist of the Year, 1963; Nat. Acad. of Scis, 1966, 1974; Amer. Acad. of Arts and Scis, 1966; Henry J. Kaiser, Stanford Univ. Sch. of Med., 1969, 1972; V. D. Mattia Prize of Roche Inst. for Molec. Biol., 1972; Gairdner Foundn Award, Nobel Prize in Chemistry, New York Acad. of Scis and Albert Lasker Med. Res. awards, 1980; National Medal of Science, 1983. *Publications:* (jtly) Genes and Genomes: a changing perspective, 1990; (jtly) Dealing with Genes: the language of heredity, 1992; (jtly) George Beadle: an uncommon farmer, 2003; many scientific articles and reviews. *Address:* Beckman Center-BO62, Stanford University Medical Center, Stanford, CA 94305–5301, USA.

BERGANZA, Teresa; singer (mezzo-soprano); *b* Madrid, Spain; *d* of Guillermo and Maria Ascension Berganza; *m*; three *c*. Début in Aix-en-Provence, 1957; début in England, Glyndebourne, 1958; appeared at Glyndebourne, 1959; Royal Opera House, Covent Garden, 1959, 1960, 1963, 1964, 1976, 1977, 1979, 1981, 1984, 1985; Royal Festival Hall, 1960, 1961, 1962, 1967, 1971; appears regularly in Vienna, Milan, Aix-en-Provence, Holland, Japan, Edinburgh, Paris, Israel, America; Carmen, opening ceremonies, Expo 92, Seville; participated opening ceremonies, Barcelona Olympics, 1992. Mem. (first elected woman), Spanish Royal Acad. of Arts, 1994. Prizes: Lucretia Arana; Nacional Lírica, Spain; Lily Pons, 1976; Acad. Nat. du Disque Lyrique; USA record award; Harriet Cohen Internat. Music Award, 1974; Grand Prix Rossini; Médaille d'or, Ville Aix-en-Provence; International Critic Award, 1988. Charles Cross (6 times); Grand Cross, Isabel la Católica, Spain; Gran Cruz al Mérito en las Bellas Artes, Spain; Commandeur, l'Ordre des Arts et des Lettres, France. *Publication:* Flor de Soledad y Silencio, 1984. *Recreations:* music, books, the arts. *Address:* Avenida de Juan de Borbón y Battenberg 16, 28200 San Lorenzo del Escorial, Madrid, Spain.

BERGER, John; author and art critic; *b* London, 5 Nov. 1926; *s* of late S. J. D. Berger, OBE, MC, and Mrs Miriam Berger (*née* Branson). *Educ:* Central Sch. of Art; Chelsea Sch. of Art. Began career as a painter and teacher of drawing; exhibited at Wildenstein, Redfern and Leicester Galls, London. Art Critic: Tribune; New Statesman. Vis. Fellow, BFI, 1990–. Numerous TV appearances, incl.: Monitor; two series for Granada TV. Scenario: (with Alain Tanner) La Salamandre; Le Milieu du Monde; Jonas (New York Critics Prize for Best Scenario of Year, 1976); Play me Something (also principal rôle) (Europa Prize, Barcelona Film Fest., 1989). George Orwell Meml Prize, 1977; Lannan Foundn Lit. Award for Fiction, USA, 1989; State Prize for Artistic Achievement, Austria, 1990; Petrarca Award, Germany, 1991. *Publications: fiction:* A Painter of Our Time, 1958; The Foot of Clive, 1962; Corker's Freedom, 1964; G (Booker Prize, James Tait Black Meml Prize), 1972; Into their Labours (trilogy), 1992: Pig Earth, 1979; Once in Europa, 1989; Lilac and Flag, 1991; To The Wedding, 1995; Photocopies, 1996; King: a street story, 1999; Here is Where We Meet, 2005; From A to X: a story in letters, 2008; *theatre:* with Nella Bielski: Question of Geography, 1986 (staged Marseilles, 1984, Paris, 1986 and by RSC, Stratford, 1987); Francisco Goya's Last Portrait, 1989; *non-fiction:* Marcel Frishman, 1958; Permanent Red, 1960; The Success and Failure of Picasso, 1965; (with J. Mohr) A Fortunate Man: the story of a country doctor, 1967; Art and Revolution, Moments of Cubism and Other Essays, 1969; The Look of Things, Ways of Seeing, 1972; The Seventh Man, 1975 (Prize for Best Reportage, Union of Journalists and Writers, Paris, 1977); About Looking, 1980; (with J. Mohr) Another Way of Telling, 1982 (televised, 1989); And Our Faces, My Heart, Brief as Photos, 1984; The White Bird, 1985 (USA, as The Sense of Sight, 1985); Keeping a Rendezvous (essays and poems), 1992; Pages of the Wound (poems), 1994; (with K. Berger-Andreadakis) Titian: nymph and shepherd, 1996; (with J. Christie) I Send You This Cadmium Red, 2000; The Shape of a Pocket (essays), 2001; Selected Essays (ed G. Dyer), 2001; Hold Everything Dear: dispatches on survival and resistance, 2007; *translations:* (with A. Bostock): Poems on the Theatre, by B. Brecht, 1960; Return to My Native Land, by Aime Cesaire, 1969; (with Lisa Appignanesi): Oranges for the Son of Alexander Levy, by Nella Bielski, 1982; The Year is '42, by Nella Bielski, 2004. *Address:* Quincy, Mieussy, 74440 Taninges, France.

BERGERSEN, Dr Fraser John, AM 2000; FRS 1981; FAA 1985; Visiting Fellow, Division of Biochemistry and Molecular Biology, School of Life Sciences, 1994–2002, and University Fellow, 1996–98, Australian National University; *b* 26 May 1929; *s* of Victor E. and Arabel H. Bergersen; *m* 1952, Gladys Irene Heather; two *s* one *d*. *Educ:* Univ. of Otago, New Zealand (BSc, MSc (Hons)); Univ. of New Zealand (DSc 1962). Bacteriology Dept, Univ. of Otago, 1952–54; Div. of Plant Industry, CSIRO, Canberra, Aust., 1954–94, Chief Res. Scientist, 1972–94; formerly engaged in scientific research in microbiology, with special reference to symbiotic nitrogen fixation in legume root-nodules. Foreign Sec., Aust. Acad. of Science, 1989–93. David Rivett Medal, CSIRO Officers' Assoc., 1968. *Publications:* Methods for Evaluating Biological Nitrogen Fixation, 1980; Root Nodules of Legumes: structure and functions, 1982; over one hundred and sixty articles and chapters in scientific journals and books. *Recreations:* music, gardening. *Address:* PO Box 4287, Manuka, ACT 2603, Australia.

BERGHUSER, Sir Hugo (Erich), Kt 1989; MBE 1981; *b* Germany, 25 Oct. 1935; *m* Christa; one *s* one *d*. *Educ:* Volksschule, Stiepel; Trade School, Bochum. Cabinet-maker.

Embarked on ship to emigrate to Australia, 1958; ship (Skaubryn) caught fire and sank in the Indian Ocean; arrived in Papua New Guinea in 1959; active in the building industries, meat trade and timber sawmilling trade, employing over 700. MP, PNG, 1987–92; Minister for Civil Aviation, Tourism and Culture, 1987. Independence Medal, PNG, 1975; Silver Jubilee Medal, 1977; Service Medal, PNG, 1980; Long Service Medal, PNG, 1985. Distinctive Cross, 1st Cl. (Germany), 1986; Grand Cross (Germany), 1991; Hon. Consulate Gen. (Turkey). *Address:* PO Box 1785, Boroko, NCD, Papua New Guinea. *Club:* Papua.

BERGIN, Prof. Joseph, LittD; FBA 1996; Professor of History, University of Manchester, since 1996; *b* Kilkenny, 11 Feb. 1948; *s* of Cornelius Bergin and Brigid (*née* Phelan); *m* 1978, Sylvia Papazian; one *s* one *d. Educ:* Rockwell Coll., Co. Tipperary; University Coll., Dublin; Peterhouse, Cambridge; LittD Manchester 2004. Lectr in History, Maynooth Coll., 1976–78; Manchester University: Lectr in History, 1978–88; Sen. Lectr, 1988–92; Reader, 1992–96. Visiting Professor: Lyon Univ., 1991–92; Ecole des Chartes, Paris, 1995; Nancy Univ., 1999; Montpellier, 2004; Sorbonne, 2005. Leverhulme Major Res. Fellow, 2000–03; Fellow, Wissenschaftskolleg, Berlin, 2006–07. Prix Richelieu, Rueil-Malmaison, France, 1995. *Publications:* Cardinal Richelieu: power and the pursuit of wealth, 1985; Cardinal La Rochefoucauld, 1987; The Rise of Richelieu, 1991; The Making of the French Episcopate 1589–1661, 1996; Seventeenth Century Europe, 2000; Crown, Church and Episcopate under Louis XIV, 2004. *Recreations:* sports, book hunting, music. *Address:* 9 Sibley Road, Heaton Moor, Stockport, Cheshire SK4 4HH. *T:* (0161) 432 4650.

BERGONZI, Prof. Bernard, FRSL; Professor of English, University of Warwick, 1971–92, now Emeritus; *b* 13 April 1929; *s* of late Carlo and Louisa Bergonzi; *m* 1st, 1960, Gabriel Wall (*d* 1984); one *s* two *d*; 2nd, 1987, Anne Samson. *Educ:* Wadham Coll., Oxford (BLitt, MA). Asst Lectr in English, Manchester Univ., 1959–62; Lectr, 1962–66; Sen. Lectr, Univ. of Warwick, 1966–71, Pro-Vice-Chancellor, 1979–82. Vis. Lectr, Brandeis Univ., 1964–65; Visiting Professor: Stanford Univ., 1982; Univ. of Louisville, 1988; Nene Coll., 1994–2000; Vis. Fellow, New Coll., Oxford, 1987. FRSL 1984. *Publications:* Descartes and the Animals (verse), 1954; The Early H. G. Wells, 1961; Heroes' Twilight, 1965; The Situation of the Novel, 1970; Anthony Powell, 1971; T. S. Eliot, 1972; The Turn of a Century, 1973; Gerard Manley Hopkins, 1977; Reading the Thirties, 1978; Years (verse), 1979; The Roman Persuasion (novel), 1981; The Myth of Modernism and Twentieth Century Literature, 1986; Exploding English, 1990; Wartime and Aftermath, 1993; David Lodge, 1995; War Poets and Other Subjects, 1999; A Victorian Wanderer, 2003; A Study in Greene, 2006. *Recreations:* conversation, retrospection. *Address:* 19 St Mary's Crescent, Leamington Spa CV31 1JL. *T:* (01926) 883115.

BERGQUIST, Mats Fingal Thorwald, Hon. CMG 1983; PhD; Ambassador of Sweden to the Court of St James's, 1997–2004; *b* 5 Sept. 1938; *s* of Thorwald and Ingrid Bergquist; *m* 1st, 1968, Marianne Lübeck (*d* 1979); two *s*; 2nd, 1991, Agneta Lorichs; two *s. Educ:* Univ. of Lund (MA 1960; PhL 1964; PhD 1970). Joined Swedish Diplomatic Service, 1964: served: London, 1964–66; Perm. Mission to UN, NY, 1966–68; First Sec., subseq. Counsellor, Foreign Ministry, 1970–76; Counsellor, Washington, 1976–81; Asst Dep. Under Sec., 1981–85; Dep. Under Sec. for Political Affairs, 1985–87; Ambassador to: Israel, 1987–92; Finland, 1992–97. Chm., Swedish Inst. for Internat. Affairs, 2006–. Chancellor, Växjö Univ., 2005–. Commander: Légion d'Honneur (France), 1983; Order of Orange-Nassau (Netherlands), 1987; Grand Cross, Finnish Lion (Finland), 1994. *Publications:* Sweden and the EEC, 1970; War and Surrogate War, 1976; Balance of Power and Deterrence, 1988; Conflict Without End?, 1993; From Cold War to Lukewarm Peace, 1998; The Blair Experiment, 2007. *Recreations:* music, tennis. *Address:* Bergsgatan 16, 11223 Stockholm, Sweden.

BERGQUIST, Prof. Dame Patricia (Rose), DBE 1994; DSc; FRSNZ; Professor of Zoology, University of Auckland, 1981–2000, now Emeritus; *b* 10 March 1933; *d* of William Smyth and Bertha Ellen Smyth (*née* Penny); *m* 1958, Peter Leonard Bergquist; one *d. Educ:* Devonport Primary Sch.; Takapuna Grammar; Univ. of Auckland (BSc 1954; MSc Hons 1957; PhD 1961; DSc 1979). University of Auckland: Lectr, then Sen. Lectr in Zool., 1958–69; Associate Prof., 1970–80; Head of Zool., 1986–92; Asst Vice-Chancellor Academic, 1989–96; Dep. Vice-Chancellor, 1993; Special Asst to Vice-Chancellor, 1997–2000. Research Fellow: Yale 1962 and 1968; Marseille, 1973; Natural Hist. Mus., London, 1978; Amer. Mus. of Natural Hist., 1990; Sen. Queen's Fellow in Marine Sci., Australia, 1984. FRSNZ 1981 (Hector Medal and Prize, 1989). *Publications:* Sponges, 1978; numerous papers and monographs in learned jls. *Recreations:* music, stamp collecting, swimming, wind-surfing. *Address:* Department of Anatomy, School of Medicine, University of Auckland, Private Bag 92019, Auckland, New Zealand. *T:* (9) 373599.

BERINGER, Guy Gibson; Senior Partner, Allen & Overy, 2000–08; *b* 12 Aug. 1955; *s* of Lt Col Frederick Richard Beringer and Hazel Margaret Beringer (*née* Orr); *m* 1979, Margaret Catherine Powell; three *d. Educ:* Campbell Coll., Belfast; St Catharine's Coll., Cambridge (MA). Admitted Solicitor, 1980; joined Allen & Overy, 1980: Asst Solicitor, 1980–85; Partner, 1985–2008; Managing Partner, Corporate Dept, 1994–99. Non-exec. Dir, Fleming Family & Partners Ltd, 2008–. Non-exec. Mem. Bd, HM Courts Service, 2008–. Mem., Law Soc., 1980–. Adjunct Prof., Tanaka Business Sch., Imperial Coll., London, 2008–. Fellow Commoner, St Catharine's Coll., Cambridge, 2008. Hon. QC 2006. *Recreations:* choral singing, golf, boating. *Address:* The River House, Wey Road, Weybridge, Surrey KT13 8HR. *T:* (01932) 844868. *Clubs:* Athenæum; Hawks (Cambridge); Port Navas Yacht (Cornwall).

BERINGER, Prof. Sir John (Evelyn), Kt 2000; CBE 1993; Professor of Molecular Genetics, 1984–2005, now Professor Emeritus, and Pro-Vice-Chancellor, 2001–05, University of Bristol; *b* 14 Feb. 1944; *s* of late Group Captain William Beringer and of Evelyn Joan Beringer (*née* Buckley); *m* 1970, Sheila Murray (*née* Gillies); three *s. Educ:* Univ. of Edinburgh (Scottish Dip. in Agric. 1965; BSc 1970); Univ. of East Anglia (PhD 1973). Microbial Geneticist, John Innes Inst., 1970–80; Head, Dept of Microbiology, Rothamsted Exptl Station, Harpenden, 1980–84; University of Bristol: Dir, Molecular Genetics Unit, 1984–88; Head, Dept of Microbiology, 1986–90; Head, Dept of Botany, 1990–93; Dean of Science, 1996–2001. Chairman, advisory committees: Genetic Manipulation Planned Release Sub-Cttee, 1987–90; Releases to Envmt, 1990–99; Chm., Main Panel D, 2008 RAE. Member: NERC, 1996–2001; Council for Sci. and Technol., 2004–. Chairman: Governing Council, John Innes Centre, 2000–; Inst. of Garden and Landscape History, 2006–. Fleming Lectr, Soc. for Gen. Microbiology, 1979. Hon. DSc Exeter, 2006. *Publications:* sci. contribs to biological jls and proceedings. *Recreations:* gardening, reading, travel, classic cars. *Address:* 92 Church Lane, Backwell, Bristol BS48 3JW. *T:* (01275) 462880.

BERKELEY, 18th Baron *cr* 1421; **Anthony Fitzhardinge Gueterbock,** OBE 1989; Baron Gueterbock (Life Peer) 2000; Chairman, Rail Freight Group, since 1996; *b* 20 Sept. 1939; *o s* of Brig. E. A. L. Gueterbock (*d* 1984) and Hon. Cynthia Ella Gueterbock (*d*

1991), *sister* of Baroness Berkeley, 17th in line; *S* aunt, 1992; *m* 1st, 1965, Diane Christine (marr. diss. 1998), *e d* of Eric William John Townsend; two *s* one *d*; 2nd, 1999, Julia Rosalind, *d* of Michael Clarke. *Educ:* Eton; Trinity Coll., Cambridge (MA). CEng, MICE. Engineering, construction and planning, Sir Alexander Gibb & Partners, 1961–65; multi-disciplinary engineering and construction, planning and business develt, George Wimpey PLC, 1965–81; The Channel Tunnel Group/Eurotunnel, 1981–96. Chm., Piggyback Consortium, 1992–98. Chm., UK Marine Pilots' Assoc., 1998–; Mem. Bd, Eur. Rail Freight Assoc., 2007–. Harbour Comr, Port of Fowey, 2006–. Hon. DSc Brighton, 1996. *Recreations:* ski-ing, sailing. *Heir: s* Hon. Thomas Fitzhardinge Gueterbock [*b* 5 Jan. 1969; *m* 1995, Helen Ruth, *er d* of Lt-Comdr Brian Walsh, RN retd]. *Address:* c/o House of Lords, SW1A 0PW.

BERKELEY, Michael Fitzhardinge; composer and broadcaster; *b* 29 May 1948; *s* of late Sir Lennox Randal Berkeley and of Elizabeth Freda (*née* Bernstein); *m* 1979, Deborah Jane Coltman-Rogers; one *d. Educ:* Westminster Cathedral Choir Sch.; The Oratory Sch.; Royal Acad. of Music (ARAM 1984; FRAM 1996). FRWCMD 2003; FRNCM 2004. Studied privately with Richard Rodney Bennett; rock musician; phlebotomist, St Bartholomew's Hosp., 1969–71; Presentation Asst, LWT, 1973; Announcer, BBC Radio 3, 1974–79; regular presenter of arts programmes for BBC (Meridian, World Service, Private Passions, Radio 3); introduces proms, concerts and festivals for BBC2 and Radio 3, BBC television documentaries and Glyndebourne for C4. Associate Composer: to Scottish Chamber Orch., 1979; to BBC Nat. Orch. of Wales, 2001–08. Jt Artistic Dir, Spitalfields Fest., 1994–97; Artistic Dir, Cheltenham Fest., 1995–2004. Member: Exec. Cttee, Assoc. of Professional Composers, 1982–84; Central Music Adv. Cttee, BBC, 1986–90; Gen. Adv. Council, BBC, 1990–95; New Music Sub-Cttee, Arts Council of GB, 1984–86; Music Panel Adviser to Arts Council, 1986–90; Mem., Bd of Dirs, Royal Opera House, Covent Gdn, 1996–2001 (Mem., 1994–98, Chm., 1998–99, Opera Bd). Vis. Prof., Huddersfield Univ. (formerly Poly.), 1991–94. Governor: NYO, 1994–96; Royal Ballet, 2001– (Chm., 2003–); Dir, Britten-Pears Foundn, 1996–. Hon. DMus UEA, 2007. *Compositions: orchestral music:* Fanfare and National Anthem, 1979; Primavera, 1979; Flames, 1981; Gregorian Variations, 1982; Daybreak and a Candle End, 1985; Gethsemane Fragment, 1990; Secret Garden, 1998; The Garden of Earthly Delights, 1998; Tristessa, 2003; Concerto for Orchestra, 2005; Slow Down, 2008; *for chamber or small orchestra:* Meditations, 1977 (Guinness Prize for Composition); Fantasia Concertante, 1978; Uprising: Symphony in one movement, 1980; Suite: the Vision of Piers the Ploughman, 1981; The Romance of the Rose, 1982; Coronach, 1988; Entertaining Master Punch, 1991; Abstract Mirror, 2002; *concertos:* Concerto for Oboe and String Orch., 1977; Concerto for Cello and Small Orch., 1983; Concerto for Horn and String Orch., 1984; Organ Concerto, 1987; Clarinet Concerto, 1991; Viola Concerto, 1994; *chamber music:* String Trio, 1978; American Suite, 1980; Chamber Symphony, 1980; String Quartet No 1, 1981; Nocturne, 1982; Piano Trio, 1982; Music from Chaucer, 1983; Quintet for Clarinet and Strings, 1983; String Quartet No 2, 1984; The Mayfly, 1984; Pas de deux, 1985; For the Savage Messiah, 1985; Quartet Study, 1987; Catch Me if You Can, 1993; Torque and Velocity, 1997; *strings:* Etude de Fleurs, 1979; Sonata for Violin and Piano, 1979; Iberian Notebook, 1980; Variations on Greek Folk-Songs, 1981; Funerals and Fandangos, 1984; A Mosaic for Father Popieluszko, 1985; *guitar:* Lament, 1980; Worry Beads, 1981; Sonata in One Movement, 1982; Impromptu, 1985; Magnetic Field, 1995; *keyboard:* Passacaglia, 1978; Strange Meeting, 1978; Organ Sonata, 1979; Dark Sleep, 1994; *woodwind:* Three Moods, 1979; American Suite, 1980; Fierce Tears, 1984; Flighting, 1985; Keening, 1987; *vocal music for solo voice:* The Wild Winds, 1978; Rain, 1979; Wessex Graves, 1981; Songs of Awakening Love, 1986; Speaking Silence, 1986; *vocal/orchestral:* Love Cries, 1999 (adaptation from the Second Mrs Kong by Harrison Birtwistle); *choral music:* At the Round Earth's Imagin'd Corners, 1980; The Crocodile and Father William, 1982; Easter, 1982; As the Wind Doth Blow, 1983; Hereford Communion Service, 1985; Pasce Oves Meas, 1985; Verbum Caro Factum Est, 1987; The Red Macula, 1989; Night Song in the Jungle, 1990; Winter Fragments, 1996; Farewell, 1999; Torch Light, 2006; *oratorio:* Or Shall We Die?, 1983 (text by Ian McEwan; filmed for Channel 4); *opera:* libretti by David Malouf: Baa Baa Black Sheep, 1993; Jane Eyre, 2000; libretti by Ian McEwan: For You, 2008; *ballet:* Bastet, 1988; *film music:* Captive, 1986; Twenty-one, 1990. *Publications:* The Music Pack, 1994; musical compositions; articles in The Observer, The Guardian, The Listener, The Sunday Telegraph, and Vogue. *Recreations:* looking at paintings, reading, walking and hill farming in mid-Wales. *Address:* c/o Oxford University Press, 70 Baker Street, W1U 7DN. *T:* (020) 7616 5900, *Fax:* (020) 7616 5901.

BERKLEY, David Nahum; QC 1999; a Recorder, since 2001; *b* 3 Dec. 1955; *s* of Elchanan Berkovitz and Doreen Berkley (*née* Wacks); *m* 1978, Deborah Fay Haffner; one *s* four *d. Educ:* Manchester Jewish Grammar Sch.; Gateshead Yeshiva; Univ. of Manchester (LLB (Hons)). Litigation Asst, Halliwell Landau, 1978–79; called to the Bar, Middle Temple, 1979; Founding Head, Merchant Chambers, Northern Circuit, 1996. Dep. Dist Judge, 1998–2001. Chm., N Circuit Commercial Bar Assoc., 2003– (Sec. 1997–2003). *Recreation:* books. *Address:* St Johns Buildings, 24A–28 St John Street, Manchester M3 4DJ. *T:* (0161) 214 1500, *Fax:* (0161) 835 3929; *e-mail:* dberkley@stjohnsbuildings.co.uk; Tanfield Chambers, 2–5 Warwick Court, WC1R 5DJ. *T:* (020) 7421 5300.

BERKOFF, Steven; actor, director and writer; *b* 3 Aug. 1937; *s* of Polly and Al Berks (formerly Berkovitch); *m* (marr. diss.). *Educ:* Raines Foundation Grammar School, Stepney; Grocers' Co. Sch., Hackney. Plays acted, 1965–: Zoo Story; Arturo Ui; plays *directed/acted/wrote,* 1969–: Metamorphosis (also directed on Broadway, 1989, Japan, 1992); Macbeth (directed and acted); Agamemnon; The Trial; The Fall of the House of Usher; East; Kvetch (Evening Standard Comedy of the Year Award, 1991); season of 3 plays, NT; Hamlet (directed and acted); Decadence (filmed, 1993); Brighton Beach Scumbags; Greek; West; One Man; Shakespeare's Villains (one-man show), Haymarket, 1998; Messiah, Old Vic, 2003; *wrote and directed:* Sink the Belgrano, Mermaid, 1986, Acapulco, 1992; *directed:* Coriolanus, NY, 1988, Munich, 1991; Salomé, Edinburgh Festival, NT (and acted), 1989, Phoenix (and acted), 1990; The Trial, NT, 1991; Coriolanus, Mermaid (and acted), 1996; Massage, LA (and acted), 1997; East, Vaudeville, 1999; Messiah, 2000; The Secret Love Life of Ophelia, 2001; Sit and Shiver, New End, 2006; On the Waterfront, Nottingham Playhouse (and adapted), 2008; *films acted:* A Clockwork Orange; Barry Lyndon; The Passenger; McVicar; Outland; Octopussy; Beverly Hills Cop; Rambo; Underworld; Revolution; Sins; Under the Cherry Moon; Absolute Beginners; Prisoner of Rio; The Krays; War and Remembrance; Decadence; Fair Game; Another 9½ Weeks; Legionnaire; Rancid Aluminium. *Publications:* East, 1977; Gross Intrusion (short stories), 1979; Decadence, 1982; Greek, 1982; West, 1985; Lunch, 1985; Harry's Xmas, 1985; Kvetch, 1987; Acapulco, 1987; Sink the Belgrano, 1987; Massage, 1987; America, 1988; I Am Hamlet, 1989; A Prisoner in Rio, 1989; The Theatre of Steven Berkoff (photographic), 1992; Coriolanus in Deutschland, 1992; Meditations on Metamorphosis, 1995; Free Association (autobiog.), 1996; Graft: tales of an actor (short stories), 1998; Shopping in the Santa Monica Mall, Ritual in Blood, Messiah, Oedipus, 2000; The Secret Love Life of Ophelia, 2001; Tough Acts, 2003; *play adaptations:* The Fall of the House of Usher, 1977; Agamemnon, 1977; The Trial, 1981; Metamorphosis, 1981;

In the Penal Colony, 1988. *Recreations:* ping-pong, photography, travelling. *Address:* c/o Joanna Marston, 1 Clareville Grove Mews, SW7 5AH. *T:* (020) 7370 1080.

BERKOVIC, Prof. Samuel Frank, AM 2005; MD; FRS 2007; FRACP; FAA; neurologist and clinical researcher; Laureate Professor, Department of Medicine, since 2007, and Australia Fellow, since 2007, University of Melbourne; *b* Melbourne, 13 Oct. 1953; *s* of Alexander and Eva Clara Berkovic; *m* 1977, Helena Makowski; one *s* two *d*. *Educ:* Univ. of Melbourne (MB BS 1977; BMedSci 1977; MD 1985). FRACP 1985. Department of Medicine, University of Melbourne: Sen. Lectr, 1989–94; Associate Prof., 1995–98; Prof., 1998–2007; Scientific Dir, Brain Res. Inst., Melbourne, 2001–; Dir, Epilepsy Res. Centre, 1998–. Adjunct Prof., Dept of Neurol. and Neurosurgery, Faculty of Medicine, McGill Univ., Canada, 1989–. FAA 2005. Epilepsy Res. Recognition Award, Amer. Epilepsy Soc., 1995; Novartis Prize for Epilepsy Res., 2001; GlaxoSmithKline Australia Award for Res. Excellence, 2002; Zulch Prize for Basic Neurol Res., Max Planck Soc., Germany, 2005; Curtin Medal, ANU, 2005; Clive and Vera Ramaciotti Medal for Excellence in Biomed. Res., 2006. *Address:* Department of Medicine, University of Melbourne, Level 1, Neurosciences Building, Heidelberg Repatriation Hospital, Austin Health, 300 Waterdale Road, W Heidelberg, Vic 3081, Australia. *T:* (3) 94962330, *Fax:* (3) 94962291; *e-mail:* s.berkovic@unimelb.edu.au.

BERKSHIRE, Archdeacon of; *see* Russell, Ven. N. A.

BERLINS, Marcel Joseph; journalist and broadcaster; *b* 30 Oct. 1941; *s* of Jacques and Pearl Berlins; *m* 2005, Lisa Forrell. *Educ:* schools in France and South Africa; Univ. of Witwatersrand (BComm, LLB); LSE (LLM). Legal Asst, Lord Chancellor's Dept, 1969–71; Legal Corresp. and leader writer, The Times, 1971–82; freelance writer and TV presenter, 1982–86; Editor, Law Magazine, 1987–88; presenter, Radio 4 Law in Action, 1988–2004; columnist, The Guardian, 1988–. Visiting Professor: Queen Mary, London Univ. 2004–; UCL; City Univ., 2005–. *Publications:* Barrister behind Bars, 1974; (with Geoffrey Wansell) Caught in the Act, 1974; (with Clare Dyer) Living Together, 1982; (with Clare Dyer) The Law Machine, 1982, 5th edn 2000; (ed) The Law and You, 1986; numerous articles for newspapers, magazines and legal jls. *Recreations:* cinema, jazz. *Address:* 83 Bedford Court Mansions, Bedford Avenue, WC1B 3AE. *T:* (020) 7323 9981.

BERLUSCONI, Silvio; MP (Forza Italia) Italy, 1994 and since 1996; Prime Minister of Italy, 1994, 2001–06 and since 2008; *b* 29 Sept. 1936; *s* of late Luigi Berlusconi and Rosella Berlusconi (*née* Bossi); *m* 1st, 1965, Carla Elvira Dall'Oglio (marr. diss. 1985); one *s* one *d*; 2nd, 1990, Veronica Lario, actress; one *s* two *d*. *Educ:* Univ. of Milan (law degree 1961). Founder: Edilnord construction co., 1962; Telemilano, cable TV station, 1974; Fininvest, 1975–94, hldg co. with interests in commercial TV, printed media, publishing, advertising, insurance, financial services, retailing and football; companies created/acquired include: TV networks, Canale 5, 1980, Italia 1, 1982, Rete 4, 1984, La Cinq, 1986, Telefunf, 1987, Telecinco, 1989; cinema chain, Cinema 5, 1985; dept store chain, La Standa, 1988; publg co., Arnoldo Mondadori Editore, 1990; newspaper, Il Giornale; Chm., AC Milan FC, 1986–2004 and 2006–. Leader, Forza Italia, 1993–; Leader of the Opposition, Italy, 1996–2001; Minister of Foreign Affairs, 2002. *Address:* Palazzo Chigi, Piazza Colonna 370, 00186 Rome, Italy.

BERMAN, Edward David, (ED Berman), MBE 1979; social entrepreneur, playwright, theatre director and producer; educationalist; Founder, Chief Executive and Artistic Director, Inter-Action, since 1968; *b* 8 March 1941; 2nd *s* of Jack Berman and Ida (*née* Webber); naturalized British citizen, 1976. *Educ:* Harvard (BA Hons); Exeter Coll., Oxford (Rhodes Schol.); Dept of Educnl Studies, Oxford (1978–). *Plays:* 8 produced since 1966; *director: theatre:* (premières) *inter alia* Dirty Linen (London and Broadway), 1976, and The Dogg's Troupe (15 minute) Hamlet, (ed) by Tom Stoppard, 1976 (also filmed, 1976); The Irish Hebrew Lesson, 1976 and Samson and Delilah, 1978, by Wolf Mankowitz; Dogg's Hamlet, Cahoot's Macbeth, 1979, by Tom Stoppard; *producer: theatre:* 125 stage premières for adults and 170 new plays for children, London, 1967–89; *maker of films:* (educational) The Head, 1971; Two Weeler, 1972; Farm in the City, 1977; Marx for Beginners Cartoon (co-prod., voice dir), 1978; *actor:* over 1200 performances as Prof. Dogg, Otto Première Check, Super Santa. Editor: 18 community arts, action and constructive leisure handbooks, 1972–; 2 anthologies of plays, 1976–78. Trustee and Founder, Inter-Action Trust, 1968; Director and Founder: Ambiance Lunch-Hour Th. Club, 1968; Prof. Dogg's Troupe for Children, 1968; Labrys Trust, 1969; Inter-Action Advisory Service, 1970; Infilms, 1970; The Almost Free Th., 1971; Inprint Publishing Unit, 1972; City Farm 1, 1972; Alternative Education Project, 1973–84; Inter-Action Trust Ltd, 1974; Town and Country Inter-Action (Milton Keynes) Ltd, 1975; Ambiance Inter-Action Inc., 1976; Talacre Centre Ltd, 1977; Co-Founder: Inter-Action Housing Trust Ltd, 1970; NUBS, Neighbourhood Use of Bldgs and Space; Community Design Centre, 1974; Beginners Books Ltd, 1978; Inter-Action Housing Co-operative, 1978. Founder, Artistic Dir, BARC, British Amer. Rep. Co., 1978. Devised: Inter-Action Creative Game Method, 1967; Super Santa, Father Xmas Union, 1967–82; Chairman: Save Piccadilly Campaign, 1971–80; Talacre Action Gp, 1972; Nat. Assoc. of Arts Centres, 1975–79; Dir, Islington Bus Co., 1974–76; Treas., Fair Play for Children Campaign, 1975–77; Founder: City Farm Movement, 1976; WAC—Weekend Arts Coll., 1979; co-founder: Sport-Space, 1976; FUSION—London and Commonwealth Youth Ensemble, 1981. Founder and Co-Director: Internat. Inst. for Social Enterprise, 1980; Country Wings, 1981; OPS, Occupation Preparation Systems, 1982; Options Training Ltd, 1983; Social Enterprise Projects Ltd, 1984; Founder and Trustee: Inter-Action Social Enterprise Trust Ltd, Social Enterprise Foundn of Inter-Action, 1984; Inter-Action Trust, South Africa, 2001–04; Cdre, Ships-in-the-City, 1988; Pres., HMS President (1918), 1988–2004; Founder and Director: Network Inter-Action; Youth-Tech; Star Dome, 1989; Marketing and Business Services International Ltd, 1992. Special Adviser: on inner city matters to Sec. of State for the Environment, 1982–83; Ministry of Labour, Russia, 1992–94, Min. of Economy, 1993–95. As community artist: created 17 formats for participatory theatre, 1968–85; Community Media Van, 1983; Community Cameos, 1977–83; MIY—Make It Yourself, 1978; RIY—Raise It Yourself, 1981; IES—Instant Enterprise Systems, 1981; Learning Domes, 1993; Public Art Workshop, 1994. Freeman, City of London, 2003; Mem. Guild of Freemen, City of London. Pearly King of River Thames, 2002–. *Publications:* Prof. R. L. Dogg's Zoo's Who I and II, 1975; Selecting Business Software, 1984; Make a Real Job of It, Breaks for Young Bands, 1985; How to Set Up a Small Business, 1987; Healthy Learning Songs & Activities, 1989; New Game Songs & Activities, 1989; (research paper) The Democracy Handbook, 1999. *Recreations:* solitude, conversation, work, music. *Address:* Inter-Action, 55 Anchorage Point, Chandlers Mews, Isle of Dogs, E14 8NF. *T:* (020) 7515 4449, *Fax:* (020) 7515 4450.

BERMAN, Sir Franklin (Delow), KCMG 1994 (CMG 1986); HM Diplomatic Service, retired; barrister and international arbitrator; Visiting Professor of International Law: University of Oxford, since 2000; University of Cape Town, since 2000; King's College London, since 2001; *b* 23 Dec. 1939; *s* of Joshua Zelic Berman and Gertrude (*née* Levin); *m* 1964, Christine Mary Lawler; two *s* three *d* (triplets). *Educ:* Rondebosch Boys' High

Sch., Cape Town; Univ. of Cape Town; Wadham and Nuffield Colls, Oxford (Hon. Fellow, Wadham Coll., 1995). BA, BSc Cape Town; MA Oxford. Rhodes Scholar, 1961; Martin Wronker Prizeman, 1963; called to Bar, Middle Temple, 1966 (Hon. Bencher, 1997). HM Diplomatic Service, 1965–99: Asst Legal Adviser, FO, 1965; Legal Adviser: British Military Govt, Berlin, 1971; British Embassy, Bonn, 1972; Legal Counsellor, FCO, 1974; Counsellor and Legal Adviser, UK Mission to UN, NY, 1982; FCO, 1985, Dep. Legal Advr, 1988, Legal Advr, 1991–99. *Ad hoc* Judge, Internat. Court of Justice, 2003–05. Chairman: Diplomatic Service Assoc., 1979–82; Appeals Bd, Internat. Oil Pollution Compensation Fund, 1986–2004; Claims Cttee, General Settlement Fund, Austria, 2001–; Diplomatic Service Appeal Bd, 2002–06; Appeals Bd, WEU, 2002–05. Member: Council of Mgt, then Bd of Trustees, British Inst. of Internat. and Comparative Law, 1992–; Council, British Br., Internat. Law Assoc., 1993–; Adv. Council, Centre for Advanced Study of European and Comparative Law, Oxford, 1995–; Adv. Council, Oxford Univ. Law Foundn, 1998–2004; Gov., Inst. of Advanced Legal Studies, Univ. of London, 1992–98. J. C. Smith Vis. Fellow, Nottingham Univ., 1993. Hon. Fellow, Soc. of Advanced Legal Studies, 1997. Trustee: Greenwich Foundn for RNC, 1997–2005; Univ. of Cape Town Trust, 2001–. Hon. QC 1992. Mem. Editl Bd, British Yearbook of Internat. Law, 1994–. Grand Decoration of Honour in Gold with Star (Austria), 2007. *Recreations:* walking, reading, music, choral singing. *Address:* Essex Court Chambers, 24 Lincoln's Inn Fields, WC2A 3EG. *Club:* Oxford and Cambridge.

BERMAN, Lawrence Sam, CB 1975; retired; *b* 15 May 1928; *yr s* of late Jack and Violet Berman; *m* 1954, Kathleen D. Lewis (*d* 1996); one *s* one *d*. *Educ:* St Clement Danes Grammar Sch.; London Sch. of Economics. BSc (Econ) 1st cl. hons 1947; MSc (Econ) 1950. Res. Asst, LSE, 1947; Nuffield Coll., Oxford, 1948; Econ. Commn for Europe, 1949; Central Statistical Office: Asst Statistician 1952; Statistician 1955; Chief Statistician 1964; Asst Dir 1968; Dir of Statistics, Depts of Industry and Trade, 1972–83. Statistical Advr, Caribbean Tourism R&D Centre, Barbados, 1984–85. Editor, National Income Blue Book, 1954–60; Member: Council, Royal Statistical Soc., 1970–74 (Vice-Pres., 1973–74); Council, Internat. Assoc. for Research in Income and Wealth, 1980–85; ISI. *Publications:* Caribbean Tourism Statistical Reports; articles and papers in Jl of Royal Statistical Soc., Economica, Economic Trends, Statistical News, etc. *Recreations:* bridge, travel, theatre. *Address:* 10 Carlton Close, Edgware, Middx HA8 7PY. *T:* (020) 8958 6938.

BERMINGHAM, Gerald Edward; barrister; *b* Dublin, 20 Aug. 1940; *s* of late Patrick Xavier Bermingham and Eva Terescena Bermingham; *m* 1st, 1964, Joan (marr. diss.); two *s*; 2nd, 1978, Judith (marr. diss.); 3rd, 1998, Jilly; one *s*. *Educ:* Cotton College, N Staffs; Wellingborough Grammar School; Sheffield University (LLB Hons). Admitted Solicitor, 1967; called to the Bar, Gray's Inn, 1985. Councillor, Sheffield City Council, 1975–79, 1980–82. Contested (Lab) SE Derbyshire, 1979. MP (Lab) St Helens South, 1983–2001. *Recreations:* sport, reading, TV. *Address:* 5 Fountain Court, Steelhouse Lane, Birmingham B4 6DR.

BERNARD, Beverley Amari; *see* Blaize, B. A.

BERNARD, Sir Dallas (Edmund), 2nd Bt *cr* 1954; international financial consultant; Chairman: National & Foreign Securities Trust Ltd, 1981–86; Thames Trust Ltd, 1983–86; *b* 14 Dec. 1926; *o s* of Sir Dallas Gerald Mercer Bernard, 1st Bt, and Betty (*d* 1980), *e d* of late Sir Charles Addis, KCMG; *S* father, 1975; *m* 1st, 1959, Sheila Gordon Robey (marr. diss. 1979); two *d* (and one *d* decd); 2nd, 1979, Mrs Monica Montford (*née* Hudson) (marr. diss. 2003); one *d*; 3rd, 2003, Mrs Graciela Scorza de Jauregui, *d* of late Francisco Scorza Fúster and Celmira Legnizamón O'Higgins. *Educ:* Eton Coll.; Corpus Christi Coll., Oxford (MA). FCIS. Director: Dreyfus Intercontinental Investment Fund NV, 1970–91; Morgan Grenfell (Holdings) Ltd, 1972–79; Morgan Grenfell & Co. Ltd, 1964–77; Dominion Securities Ltd, Toronto, 1968–79; Italian Internat. Bank Plc, 1978–89; Dreyfus Dollar Internat. Fund Inc., 1982–91. Mem. Monopolies and Mergers Commn, 1973–79. Mem. Council, GPDST, 1988–93 (Finance Cttee, 1975–92). *Heir:* none. *Address:* Rycote Farm Cottage, Rycote Farm, Thame, Oxon OX9 2PF. *T:* (01844) 339203. *Club:* Army and Navy.

BERNARD, Daniel Camille; Deputy Chairman, Kingfisher plc, since 2007 (Joint Deputy Chairman, 2006–07); *b* 18 Feb. 1946; *s* of Paul Bernard and Simone (*née* Doise); *m* 1968, Chantal Leduc; one *s* two *d*. *Educ:* Lycée Camille Desmoulins, Cateau; Lycée Faidherbe, Lille; HEC Business Sch.; Univ. of Paris. Divl Manager, Mammouth, 1976–81; Chief Exec. Officer, Metro France, 1981–89; Mem. Bd, Metro Internat., 1990–92; Carrefour Group: CEO, 1992–98; Chm., 1998–2005. Pres., Provestis; non-executive Director: Alcatel-Lucent (formerly Alcatel), 2006–; Cap Gemini, 2005–. *Recreations:* mountains, ski-ing, opera. *Address:* c/o Kingfisher plc, 3 Sheldon Square, W2 6PX.

BERNARD, Joan Constance, MA, BD; FKC; Principal of Trevelyan College, University of Durham, and Honorary Lecturer in Theology, 1966–79; *b* 6 April 1918; *d* of late Adm. Vivian Henry Gerald Bernard, CB, and Eileen Mary Bernard. *Educ:* Ascham Sch., Sydney, NSW; St Anne's Coll., Oxford Univ. (BA Lit. Hum. 1940, MA 1943); King's Coll., London (BD 1961). War Service, ATS, 1940–46; AA Comd, 1940–44; SO Air Def. Div., SHAEF, 1944–45 (mentioned in despatches 1945); Special Projectile Ops Gp, July-Nov. 1945. Dep. Admin. Officer, NCB, 1946–50; Asst Sec., Educn, Music and Drama, NFWI, 1950–57; full-time student, 1957–61; Warden, Canterbury Hall, Univ. of London, and part-time Lectr, Dept of Theol., KCL, 1962–65; FKC 1976. Mem., Ordination Candidates' Cttee, ACCM, 1972–91; Examining Chaplain to Bishop of Southwark, 1984–94. Mem., Fabric Adv. Cttee, Southwark Cathedral, 1992–97. FRSA 1984. *Recreations:* music (assisted John Tobin in Handel research for many years); mountaineering, photography, travel. *Address:* 89 Rennie Court, Upper Ground, SE1 9NZ.

BERNARD, Ralph Mitchell, CBE 2002; Chairman, Classic FM plc, since 2007 (Director, since 1991; Chief Executive, 1997–2005); *b* 11 Feb. 1953; *s* of Reginald and Irene Bernard; *m* 1977, Lisa Anne Susan Kiené; four *d*. *Educ:* Caterham High Sch., Ilford. Copy boy, London News Service, 1970–71; Reporter: Express and Independent, Leytonstone, 1971–72; Stratford Express, 1972–73; Cambridge Evening News, 1973–75; radio journalist, 1975–78, Documentaries Ed., 1978–80, Radio Hallam, Sheffield; News Ed., Hereward Radio, Peterborough, 1980–82; Prog. Controller, 1982–83, Man. Dir, 1983–85, Wiltshire Radio; Pre-launch Manager, Classic FM, 1991; Exec. Chm., GWR Gp plc, 2001–05; Chief Exec., GCap Media plc, 2005–07. Chairman: London News Radio (LBC and News Direct), 1996–2001; Digital One Ltd, 1998–; Director: Ind. Radio News, 1994–; Watermill Th., Newbury, 2005–. Chm., Campaign Bd, Great Western Hosp., Swindon, 2000–02. Fellow, Radio Acad., 1999. Sony Gold Award, 2000. *Recreations:* music (most), walking, newspaper originals, cricket. *Address:* Classic FM plc, 30 Leicester Square, WC2H 7LA.

BERNAYS, Rosamund; *see* Horwood-Smart, R.

BERNBAUM, Prof. Gerald; Vice-Chancellor and Chief Executive, South Bank University, 1993–2001; *b* 25 March 1936; *s* of Benjamin Bernbaum and Betty (*née* Sack);

m 1959, Pamela Valerie Cohen (marr. diss. 1987); two *s*. *Educ:* Hackney Downs Grammar Sch.; LSE (BSc Econ 1957); London Inst. of Educn (PGCE 1958). Mitcham Grammar School for Boys: Asst Master, 1958–59; Head of Dept, 1959–62; Head of Dept, Rutherford Comprehensive Sch., 1962–64; University of Leicester School of Education: Lectr, 1964–70; Sen. Lectr, 1970–74; Prof. of Educn, 1974–93; Dir, 1976–85; Pro-Vice-Chancellor, 1985–87; Exec. Pro-Vice-Chancellor and Registrar, 1987–93. Chm. of Govs., Morley College, 2004–06. Hon. LLD Leicester, 2000; Hon. DLitt Assumption Univ., Bangkok, 1997; Hon. DEd: E London, 2002; South Bank, 2004. *Publications:* Social Change and the Schools, 1967; Knowledge and Ideology in the Sociology of Education, 1977; (ed) Schooling in Decline, 1978; (with H. Patrick and M. Galton) Educational Provision in Small Primary Schools, 1990; articles in Sociol Rev., Brit. Jl Educnl Studies. *Recreations:* public affairs, professional sport, music. *Address:* c/o London South Bank University, 103 Borough Road, SE1 0AA. *T:* (020) 7815 6004.

BERNERD, Elliott; Chairman, Chelsfield plc, 1987–2004; *b* 23 May 1945; *s* of late Geoffrey Bernerd and of Trudie Malawer (*née* Melzack); *m* 1st, 1968, Susan Elizabeth Lynton (marr. diss. 1989); two *d*; 2nd, 1992, Sonia Ramsay (*née* Ramalho). Chm. Wentworth Group Holdings Ltd, 1990. Chairman: London Philharmonic Trust, 1987–94; South Bank Foundn, 1996; South Bank Bd Ltd, 1998–2002. Chm. Trustees, Facial Surgery Res. Foundn. *Recreations:* tennis, ski-ing. *Clubs:* Savile, Cavalry and Guards, Royal Automobile; Wentworth.

BERNERS, Baroness (16th in line), *cr* 1455; **Pamela Vivien Kirkham;** *b* 30 Sept. 1929; *er d* of Harold Williams and Baroness Berners, 15th in line (*d* 1992); *S* to Barony of mother (called out of abeyance, 1995); *m* 1952, Michael Joseph Sperry Kirkham; two *s* one *d*. *Educ:* Bredenbury Court, Hereford; Stonar Sch., Wilts. Radcliffe Infirmary, Oxford (SRN 1951). *Recreations:* painting, drawing, gardening, reading. *Heir:* *s* Hon. Rupert William Tyrwhitt Kirkham [*b* 18 Feb. 1953; *m* 1994, Lisa Carol Judy Lipsey; one *s*].

BERNERS-LEE, Sir Timothy (John), OM 2007; KBE 2004 (OBE 1997); FRS 2001; FREng; 3Com Founders Professor, since 1999, Director, World Wide Web Consortium, and Senior Research Scientist, Computer Science and Artificial Intelligence Laboratory, Massachusetts Institute of Technology; *b* London, 8 June 1955. *Educ:* Emanuel Sch., London; Queen's Coll., Oxford (BA 1976; Hon. Fellow, 1999). Plessey Telecommunications Ltd, 1976–78; software engr, D. G. Nash Ltd, 1978; ind. consultant, 1978–80, incl. software consultancy, CERN, Geneva (wrote unpublished prog., Enquire, forerunner of World Wide Web); Founding Dir, responsible for tech. design, Image Computer Systems Ltd, 1981–84; Fellowship, CERN, 1984–94: global hypertext project, 1989, became World Wide Web, 1990 (available on Internet, 1991); designed URL (universal resource locator) and HTML (hypertext markup lang.); joined Lab. for Computer Sci., MIT, 1994. MacArthur Fellow, John D. and Catherine T. MacArthur Foundn, 1998. Distinguished FBCS; FREng 2001. Hon. DSc Oxon, 2001. *Publication:* Weaving the Web, 2000. *Address:* Computer Science and Artificial Intelligence Laboratory, 77 Massachusetts Avenue, Cambridge, MA 02139, USA.

BERNEY, Sir Julian (Reedham Stuart), 11th Bt *cr* 1620; Director of International Investment, Atis Real; *b* 26 Sept. 1952; *s* of Lieut John Reedham Erskine Berney (killed on active service in Korea, 1952), Royal Norfolk Regt, and Hon. Jean Davina, *d* of 1st Viscount Stuart of Findhorn, PC, CH, MVO, MC; *S* grandfather, 1975; *m* 1976, Sheena Mary, *yr d* of Ralph Day and late Ann Gordon Day; two *s* one *d*. *Educ:* Wellington Coll.; North East London Polytechnic. FRICS 1992. Formerly Internat. Dir, Jones Lang LaSalle. Freeman, Fishmongers' Co. *Recreation:* sailing. *Heir:* *s* William Reedham John Berney, *b* 29 June 1980. *Address:* Reeds House, 40 London Road, Maldon, Essex CM9 6HE. *T:* (01621) 853420. *Clubs:* Royal Ocean Racing; Royal Cruising; Royal Yacht Squadron.

BERNSTEIN, family name of **Baron Bernstein of Craigweil**.

BERNSTEIN OF CRAIGWEIL, Baron *cr* 2000 (Life Peer), of Craigweil, in the co. of West Sussex; **Alexander Bernstein;** Chairman, Granada Group plc, 1979–96 (Director, 1964–96); Director, Waddington Galleries, since 1966; *b* 15 March 1936; *s* of late Cecil Bernstein and of Myra Ella, *d* of Lesser and Rachel Lesser; *m* 1st, 1962, Vanessa Anne Mills (marr. diss. 1993; she *d* 2003); one *s* one *d*; 2nd, 1995, Angela Mary Serota (CBE 2008). *Educ:* Stowe Sch.; St John's Coll., Cambridge. Man. Dir, 1964–68, Chm., 1977–86, Granada TV Rental Ltd; Jt Man. Dir, Granada Television Ltd, 1971–75. Trustee: Civic Trust for the North-West, 1964–86; Granada Foundn, 1968–; Theatres Trust, 1996–2000; Trusthouse Charitable Foundn, 1996–; Chairman: Royal Exchange Theatre, 1983–94 (Dep. Chm., 1980–83); Old Vic Theatre Trust, 1998–2002. Mem., Nat. Theatre Develt Council, 1996–98. Member of Court: Univ. of Salford, 1976–87; Univ. of Manchester, 1983–98. Hon. DLitt Salford 1981; Hon. LLD Manchester, 1996. *Address:* c/o House of Lords, SW1A 0PW.

BERNSTEIN, Sir Howard, Kt 2003; Chief Executive, Manchester City Council, since 1998; *b* 9 April 1953; *s* of Maurice and Miriam Bernstein; *m* 1980, Yvonne Selwyn (marr. diss. 2004); one *s* one *d* (and one *s* decd); *m* 2004, Vanessa. *Educ:* Ducie High Sch., Manchester; London Univ. (ext.). Manchester City Council: Head of Urban Policy, 1980–86; Asst Chief Exec., 1986–90; Dep. Chief Exec., 1990–98; Dep. Clerk, 1986–98, Clerk, 1998–, Gtr Manchester PTA; Chief Exec., Manchester City Centre Task Force, 1996–. Sec., Commonwealth Games Organising Cttee, 1996–2002; Mem. Bd, Olympic Delivery Authy, 2006–08. Chm., ReBlackpool, 2008–. *Recreations:* sport, particularly football and cricket. *Address:* Manchester City Council, Town Hall, Manchester M60 2LA. *T:* (0161) 234 3006.

BERNSTEIN, Her Honour Ingeborg, (Inge); a Circuit Judge, 1991–2001; *b* 24 Feb. 1931; *d* of Sarah and Eli Bernstein; *m* 1967, Eric Geoffrey Goldrein; one *s* one *d*. *Educ:* Peterborough County School; St Edmund's College, Liverpool; Liverpool University. Called to the Bar, Inner Temple, 1952; practice on Northern Circuit; a Recorder, 1978–91. Chm., Mental Health Review Tribunal, 1968–91 and 1992–2007; Mem., Mental Health Act Commn, 1984–86. *Recreation:* the domestic arts.

BERNSTEIN, Ingrid Ann; *see* Simler, I. A.

BERRAGAN, Maj.-Gen. Gerald Brian, CB 1988; Chief Executive, Institute of Packaging, 1988–98; *b* 2 May 1933; *s* of William James and Marion Beatrice Berragan; *m* 1956, Anne Helen Kelly; three *s*. Commissioned REME 1954; attached 7th Hussars, Hong Kong, 1954–55; transf. RAOC 1956; served UK, Belgium, Germany and with 44 Para Bde (TA); Staff College, 1966; Nat. Defence Coll., 1972–73; Comdr RAOC 3 Div., 1973–76; AQMG HQ N Ireland, 1976–78; HQ DGOS, 1978–80; Comdt Central Ordnance Depot, Chilwell, 1980–82; Sen. Management Course, Henley, 1982; Comdt COD Bicester, 1982–83; Dir, Supply Ops (Army), 1983–85; Sen. Internat. Defence Management Course, USA, 1985; Dir Gen. of Ordnance Services, 1985–88. Col Comdt, RAOC, 1988–93, RLC 1993–98. UK Dir, World Packaging Orgn, 1988–98. FInstPkg. *Recreation:* tennis.

BERRIDGE, (Donald) Roy, CBE 1981; FREng; Chairman, South of Scotland Electricity Board, 1977–82 (Deputy Chairman, 1974–77); *b* 24 March 1922; *s* of Alfred Leonard Berridge and Pattie Annie Elizabeth (*née* Holloway); *m* 1945, Marie (*née* Kinder); one *d*. *Educ:* King's Sch., Peterborough; Leicester Coll. of Art and Technology. FREng (FEng 1979); FIMechE 1962. Taylor, Taylor & Hobson Ltd, Leicester, 1940; James Gordon & Co., 1946; British Electricity Authority, 1948; seconded to AERE, Harwell, 1952; Reactor Design Engr, CEGB, 1962; Chief Generation Design Engr, 1964–70; Dir-Gen., Gen. Develt Constr. Div., CEGB, 1970–72; Dir of Engrg, SSEB, 1972–74. Dir, Howden Gp, 1982–88. Member: N of Scotland Hydro-Electric Bd, 1977–82; Scottish Economic Council, 1977–83; CBI (Scottish Council), 1977–83. *Address:* East Gate, Chapel Square, Deddington, Oxon OX15 0SG.

BERRIDGE, Sir Michael (John), Kt 1998; PhD; FRS 1984; Fellow of Trinity College, Cambridge, since 1972; Head of Signalling Programme, Babraham Institute Laboratory of Molecular Signalling, 1996–2003, now Emeritus Babraham Fellow; *b* 22 Oct. 1938; *s* of George Kirton Berridge and Stella Elaine Hards; *m* 1965, Susan Graham Winter; one *s* one *d*. *Educ:* University Coll. of Rhodesia and Nyasaland (BSc); Univ. of Cambridge (PhD). Post-doctoral Fellow: Univ. of Virginia, 1965–66; Case Western Reserve Univ., Cleveland, Ohio, 1966–69; AFRC Lab. of Molecular Signalling (formerly Unit of Insect Neurophysiology and Pharmacology), Dept of Zoology, Univ. of Cambridge, 1969–90; Babraham Inst. Lab. of Molecular Signalling, 1990–2003. Founder FMedSci 1998. King Faisal Internat. Prize in Sci., 1986; Jeantet Prize in Medicine, 1986; Gairdner Foundn Internat. Award, 1988; Lasker Basic Med. Res. Award, 1989; Dr H. P. Heineken Prize for Biochemistry and Biophysics, 1994; Wolf Foundn Prize in Medicine, 1995; Shaw Prize in Life Sci. and Medicine, Shaw Prize Foundn, 2005. *Publications:* papers in Jl Exptl Biol., Biochem. Jl and Nature. *Recreations:* golf, gardening. *Address:* The Babraham Institute, Babraham Hall, Babraham, Cambridge CB2 4AT. *T:* (01223) 496621.

BERRIDGE, Roy; *see* Berridge, D. R.

BERRIEDALE, Lord; Alexander James Richard Sinclair; *b* 26 March 1981; *s* and *heir* of Earl of Caithness, *qv*. *Educ:* St David's Coll., Llandudno. Studying to be a commercial pilot. *Recreations:* outdoor pursuits.

BERRILL, Sir Kenneth, GBE 1988; KCB 1971; Chairman, Moneda Chile Fund, 1995–2007; *b* 28 Aug. 1920; *m* 1st, 1941, Brenda West (marr. diss.); one *s*; 2nd, 1950, June Phillips (marr. diss.; she *d* 2003); one *s* one *d*; 3rd, 1977, Jane Marris. *Educ:* London Sch. of Economics; Trinity Coll., Cambridge. BSc(Econ) London; MA Cantab, 1949. Served War, 1939–45, REME. Economic Adviser to Turkey, Guyana, Cameroons, OECD, and World Bank. Univ. Lectr in Economics, Cambridge, 1949–69; Rockefeller Fellowship Stanford and Harvard Univs, 1951–52; Fellow and Bursar, St Catharine's Coll., Cambridge, 1949–62, Hon. Fellow, 1974; Prof., MIT, 1962; Fellow and First Bursar, King's Coll., Cambridge, 1962–69, Hon. Fellow, 1973; HM Treasury Special Adviser (Public Expenditure), 1967–69; Chm., UGC, 1969–73; Head of Govt Econ. Service and Chief Economic Advr, HM Treasury, 1973–74; Head of Central Policy Review Staff, Cabinet Office, 1974–80; Chm., Vickers da Costa Ltd and Vickers da Costa & Co. Hong Kong Ltd, 1981–85; Chm., SIB, 1985–88; Dep. Chm., 1982–87, Chm., 1987–90, Robert Horne Gp; Chm., Commonwealth Equities Fund, 1990–95. Mem., Stock Exchange, London, 1981–85. Member: Council for Scientific Policy, 1969–72; Adv. Bd for Research Councils, 1972–77; Adv. Council for Applied R&D, 1977–80; Brit. Nat. Commn for UNESCO, 1967–70; UN Cttee for Develt Planning, 1984–87; Inter-Univ. Council, 1969–73; UGC, Univ. of S Pacific, 1972–85; Council, Royal Economic Soc., 1972– (Vice Pres., 1986–); Adv. Bd, RCDS, 1974–80; Review Bd for Govt Contracts, 1981–85; Chm. Exec. Cttee, NIESR, 1988–96; (Nominated), Governing Council, Lloyd's, 1983–88. Dir, UK-Japan 2000 Gp, 1986–90. Advr, Nippon Credit Internat. Ltd, 1989–99; Dep. Chm., General Funds Investment Trust, 1982–85; Member: Baring Private Equity Partners Adv. Council, 1996–2000; Baring Eur. Private Equity Fund Adv. Council, 1999–; Director: Investing in Success Investment Trust, 1965–67; Ionian Bank, 1969–73; Dep. Chm., Universities' Superannuation Scheme, 1981–85 (Chm., Jt Negotiating Cttee, 1990–2007). Trustee: London Philharmonic, 1987–2006; Newnham Coll. Develt Trust, 1989–95; Nat. Extension Coll., 1990–2006 (Vice-Chm. Trustees, 1997–2006); Res. Inst. for Consumer Affairs, 1990–96. Pro-Chancellor, and Chm. Council, Open Univ., 1983–96; Governor: Admin. Staff Coll., Henley, 1969–84; ODI, 1969–73; Mem. Council, Salford Univ., 1981–84. McDonnell Scholar, World Inst. for Develt Economic Res., 1988, 1990. Mem., Cambridge City Council, 1963–67. CCMI (CBIM 1987). FRSA 1988; Hon. Fellow: LSE, 1970; Chelsea Coll., London, 1973; Hon. FKC 1989; Fellow, Open Univ., 1997. Hon. LLD: Cambridge, 1974; Bath, 1974; East Anglia, 1975; Leicester, 1975; DUniv Open, 1974; Hon. DTech Loughborough, 1974; Hon DSc Aston, 1974. Jephcott Lectr and Medallist, 1978; Stamp Meml Lectr, 1980. *Recreations:* gardening, sailing, music. *Address:* Salt Hill, Bridle Way, Grantchester, Cambs CB3 9NY. *T:* (01223) 840335, *Fax:* (01223) 845939. *Clubs:* Climbers (Hon. Mem.); Himalayan; Cambridge Alpine.

BERRIMAN, Sir David, Kt 1990; FCIB; Chairman, Association of Lloyd's Members, 1994–98 (Committee Member, 1993–98); *b* 20 May 1928; *s* of late Algernon Edward Berriman, OBE and late Enid Kathleen Berriman (*née* Sutcliffe); *m* 1st, 1955, Margaret Lloyd (*née* Owen) (marr. diss. 1970; she *d* 1995); two *s*; 2nd, 1971, Shirley Elizabeth (*née* Wright) (*d* 1993); 3rd, 1995, Patricia Ann Salter (*née* Walker). *Educ:* Winchester; New Coll., Oxford (MA, Dip. Econ. and Pol. Sc.); Harvard Business Sch. PMD course, 1961. First National City Bank of New York, 1952–56; Ford Motor Co. Ltd, 1956–60; AEI Hotpoint, 1960–63; Gen. Manager, United Leasing Corporation Ltd, 1963–64; Morgan Grenfell & Co. Ltd: Manager, 1964; Exec. Dir, 1968–73; Dir, Guinness Mahon & Co. Ltd, 1973–87 (Exec. Dir, 1973–85). Chairman: Bunzl Textile Holdings Ltd, 1981–88 (Dep. Chm., 1980); Alban Communications Ltd, 1988–90 (Dir, 1983–; Dep. Chm., 1987–88); Privatised Public Service Pension Plan Trustees Ltd, 1994–97; Director (non-exec.): Cable and Wireless, 1975–88; Sky Television (formerly Satellite Television), 1981–89 (Chm., 1981–85); Bahrain Telecommunications Corp., 1982–88; Britannia Building Soc., 1983–93; Ashenden Enterprises Ltd, 1983–; Videotron Hldgs plc, 1989–97; KDB Bank (UK) Ltd, 1991–98. Chairman: Lewisham and N Southwark DHA, 1981–84; NE Thames RHA, 1984–90. Member: Govt review body on Harland and Wolff diversification, 1980; Corp. of Lloyd's Disciplinary Bd, 1996–2001; Bd of Trade's Interim Action Cttee for the Film Industry, 1977–85; British Screen Adv. Council, 1985–91. Director: British Screen Finance Ltd, 1985–91; Nat. Film Develt Fund, 1985–91. Dep. Chm., Nat. Film and Television School, 1988–92 (Gov., 1977–92). Chairman: MacIntyre Care, 1978–92 (Gov., 1977–92); MacIntyre Charitable Trust, 1986–92; MacIntyre Foundn, 1993–95; Member, Council: Internat. Hosp. Fedn, 1985–86; King Edward's Hosp. Fund for London, 1985–90. Trustee: New Coll., Oxford Development Fund, 1983–95; Kent Community Housing Trust, 1990– (Dep. Chm., 1998–). CCMI. *Recreations:* golf, lawn tennis. *Clubs:* Royal Automobile, International Lawn Tennis; Wildernesse Golf (Sevenoaks); Royal St George's Golf.

BERRY, family name of **Viscounts Camrose** and **Kemsley**.

BERRY, Anthony Arthur; Chairman, Berry Bros & Rudd Ltd, 1965–85; *b* 16 March 1915; *s* of Francis L. Berry and Amy Marie (*née* Freeman); *m* 1953, Sonia Alice, *d* of Sir Harold Graham-Hodgson, KCVO; one *s* one *d*. *Educ:* Charterhouse; Trinity Hall, Cambridge. Served War, RNVR, 1939–45, incl. 2¼ yrs in the Mediterranean. Joined the wine trade on leaving Cambridge, 1936; rejoined family firm of Berry Bros & Rudd on completion of war service; Dir, 1946–. Worshipful Co. of Vintners: Liveryman, 1946; Mem. Court, 1972–; Master, 1980–81. *Clubs:* Boodle's, MCC; Saintsbury; Royal Wimbledon Golf; Royal St George's Golf (Sandwich).

BERRY, Anthony Charles; QC 1994; *b* 4 Oct. 1950; *s* of Geoffrey Vernon Berry and Audrey Millicent Berry (*née* Farrar); *m* 1977, Susan Carmen Traversi; three *s* one *d*. *Educ:* Downside Sch.; Lincoln Coll., Oxford (BA Phil. and Psychol.). Called to the Bar, Gray's Inn, 1976, Bencher, 2002. Sec., Criminal Bar Assoc., 1991–93; Mem., Bar Council, 1993–95. *Recreations:* tennis, golf. *Address:* 9 Bedford Row, WC1R 4AZ. *T:* (020) 7489 2727.

BERRY, (Anthony) Scyld (Ivens); cricket correspondent, The Sunday Telegraph, since 1993; Editor, Wisden Cricketers' Almanack, since 2007; *b* 28 April 1954; *s* of late Prof. Francis Berry; *m* 1984, Sunita Ghosh; two *s* one *d*. *Educ:* Westbourne School, Sheffield; Ampleforth College; Christ's College, Cambridge (MA Oriental Studies). Cricket correspondent: The Observer, 1978–89; The Sunday Correspondent, 1989–90; The Independent on Sunday, 1991–93. *Publications:* Cricket Wallah, 1982; Train to Julia Creek, 1984; (ed) The Observer on Cricket, 1987; Cricket Odyssey, 1988; (with Phil Edmonds) 100 Great Bowlers, 1989; (with Rupert Peploe) Cricket's Burning Passion, 2006. *Recreations:* playing village cricket, being at home. *Address:* c/o The Sunday Telegraph, 111 Buckingham Palace Road, SW1W 0DT. *Club:* Hinton Charterhouse Cricket.

BERRY, Cicely Frances, (Mrs H. D. Moore), OBE 1985; Voice Director, Royal Shakespeare Co., since 1969; *b* 17 May 1926; *d* of Cecil and Frances Berry; *m* 1951, Harry Dent Moore (*d* 1978); two *s* one *d*. *Educ:* Eothen Sch., Caterham, Surrey; Central Sch. of Speech and Drama, London. Teacher, Central Sch. of Speech and Drama, 1948–68; 4-week Voice Workshops: Nat. Repertory Co. of Delhi, 1980; Directors and Actors in Australia (org. by Aust. Council), 1983; Directors, Actors, Teachers in China, Chinese Min. of Culture, 1984; text-based workshops: Theatre Voice, Stratford, 1992; Actors in Croatia, Poland, Bulgaria and the Netherlands, 1993; workshops: Writers in Stratford, 1993; Eur. League of Insts of Arts, Berlin, 1994; Theatre For A New Audience, NY, 1997 and 1998 (Artistic Associate, 1997); Theatre Lab., Sydney, 2001; work with Theatre for a New Audience, NY, 2001, and with Nos Do Morro theatre co., Vidigal, Rio, 2005 and 2006; has also taught and lectured in Brazil; taught in Colombia and Croatia, 1998. Hon. Prof., de Montfort Univ.; Vis. Fellow, Central Sch. of Speech and Drama, 1994–. Organised: Internat. Voice Conf., Stratford, 1995, 1998; debate, Theatre and Citizenship, Barbican, 1997. Plays directed: Hamlet, Educn Dept, NT, 1985; King Lear, The Other Place, Stratford and Almeida Theatre, 1989. Patron of Northumberland and Leicester Youth Theatres. FRSAMD 1987. Hon. Dr, Nat. Acad. of Theatre Studies, Bulgaria, 1997; Hon. DLitt Birmingham, 1999; DUniv Open, 2001. Sam Wanamaker Award, Globe Theatre, 2000; Samuel H. Scripps Award, Theatre for a New Audience, NY, 2007. *Publications:* Voice and the Actor, 1973, 7th edn 2000; Your Voice and How to Use it Successfully, 1975, 2nd edn as Your Voice and How to Use it, 1994, 3rd edn 2000; The Actor and the Text, 1987, 2nd edn 2000; Text in Action, 2001.

BERRY, Sir Colin (Leonard), Kt 1993; DSc; FRCPath; Professor of Morbid Anatomy, University of London, at The London Hospital Medical College, 1976–2002, now Emeritus; Warden of Joint Medical and Dental School, St Bartholomew's and Royal London Hospitals, and Vice-Principal for Medicine and Dentistry, Queen Mary and Westfield College, London University, 1995–96; *b* 28 Sept. 1937; *s* of Ronald Leonard Berry and Peggy-Caroline (*née* Benson); *m* 1960, Yvonne Waters; two *s*. *Educ:* privately, and Beckenham Grammar Sch.; Charing Cross Hosp. Med. Sch. (MB, BS; Governors' Clinical Gold Medal, Llewellyn Schol., Pierera Prize in Clinical Subjects, Steadman Prize in Path.); trained in Histopath., Charing Cross Hosp., 1962–64. MD 1968, PhD 1970, DSc 1993 (London). FRCPath 1979; FFPM 1991; FRCP 1993; FFOM 1995; FRCPE 1997. Lectr and Sen. Lectr, Inst. of Child Health, London, 1964–70; Reader in Pathology, Guy's Hosp. Med. Sch., 1970–76; Dean, London Hosp. Med. Coll., 1994–95. Gillson Scholar, Worshipful Soc. of Apothecaries, 1967–68 and 1970–72; Arris and Gail Lectr, RCS, 1973; Lectures: Bawden, BCPC, 1990; John Hull Grundy, Royal Army Med. Coll., 1992; Simonides, European Soc. of Pathology, 1993; Lucas, RCP, 1994. Chairman: Cttee on Dental and Surgical Materials, 1982–92 (Vice-Chm., 1979–82); Scientific Sub-Cttee on Pesticides, MAFF, 1984–87; Adv. Cttee on Pesticides, MAFF/DHSS, 1988–99 (Mem., 1982–87); Bd in Histology and Cytology, Union Européenne des Médecins Spécialistes, 1993–99; Member: Toxicology Review Panel, WHO, 1976–84, 1987–; Scientific Adv. Cttee on Pesticides, EEC, 1981–88; Cttee on Toxicity of Chemicals in Food, Consumer Products and the Environment, 1982–88; Cttee on Safety of Medicines, Dept of Health, 1990–92; Ownership Bd, Pesticides Safety Directorate, 1994–99; Steering Gp on Envmt and Health, ESF, 1995–; Radical Review of Coroner Service, Home Office, 2001–03; MRC, 1990–; GMC, 1993–96 and 1998–; Chm., Physiological Systems and Disorders Bd, MRC, 1990–92 (Mem., 1988–). Member, Advisory Board: Sci. and Policy, American Council on Sci. and Health, 2001–; Sense about Science, 2003–; Scientific Alliance, 2003–. President: Developmental Path. Soc., 1976–79; European Soc. of Pathology, 1989–91 (Pres. elect, 1987–89); British Acad. of Forensic Scis, 2003–05 (Pres. elect, 2001–02). Sec., Fedn of Assocs of Clinical Profs, 1987– (Hon. Fellow, 2007); Chm. Council, 1993–99, Hon. Vice-Pres., 2000–, Res. Defence Soc.; Hon. Sec., ACP, 1982–85 (Meetings Sec., 1979–82). Scientific Advr, BIBRA, 1987–90. Hon. Curator, Deutsches Mus., Munich, 2006–. Treasurer, RCPath, 1988–93 (Asst Registrar, 1981–84). Asst to Court, Apothecaries' Soc., 1990– (Master, 2003–04; Treas., 2004–). Mem. Council, Imp. Soc. of Knights Bachelor, 1997– (Treas., 2006–). Founder FMedSci 1998. Hon. Fellow, British Toxicol. Soc., 2006. Corresp. Mem., Deutsche Akad. der Naturforscher Leopoldina, 1993 (Hon. Mem., 2005). Hon. MD Ioannina, Greece, 2003. *Publications:* Teratology: trends and applications, 1975; Paediatric Pathology, 1981, 3rd edn 1995; Diseases of the Arterial Wall, 1988; contrib. to many texts; numerous publns in Jl of Path., Circulation Res. and other path. jls. *Recreations:* fishing, pond building. *Clubs:* Reform, Farmers'; Le Touquet Golf, Dulwich & Sydenham Golf.

BERRY, Rt Rev. Fraser; *see* Berry, Rt Rev. R. E. F.

BERRY, Graham; Director, Scottish Arts Council, 2002–07; *b* 12 Jan. 1945; *s* of Alexander and Émélie Berry; one *s* one *d*. *Educ:* Royal High Sch., Edinburgh. ICAS. Chartered accountant, Price Waterhouse, 1968–70; Divl Chief Accountant, Trust House Forte, 1970–74; Company Secretary, 1974–86: Scottish Film Council; Scottish Council for Educn and Technol.; Glasgow Film Th.; Filmhouse, Edinburgh; Scottish Film Prodn Fund; Finance Officer, Univ. of Stirling, 1986–89; Hd of Funding and Resources, Scottish Arts Council, 1989–2002. *Recreations:* mountaineering, photography.

BERRY, (Gwenda) Lynne, OBE 2006; Chief Executive, Women's Royal Voluntary Service, since 2007; *b* 27 Jan. 1953. Social Worker, Wandsworth LBC, 1976–79; Community Worker, Camden Council of Social Service, 1979–81; Lecturer: PCL, 1981–84; NISW, 1984–88; Social Services Inspector, DoH, 1988–90; Chief Exec., Family Welfare Assoc., 1990–96; Exec. Dir, Charity Commn, 1996–99; Chief Executive: EOC, 1999–2001; Gen. Social Care Council, 2001–07. Non-exec. Dir, Europe Div., DTI, 1998–2001. Chm., CPAG, 2001–05; Mem., Better Regulation Commn (formerly Better Regulation Task Force), 2005–. Trustee: Tomorrow Project, 2001–06; Nat. Centre for Social Res., 2002–. Former Member of Council: Inst. of Educn, London Univ.; Franco-British Council. FRSA. Merit Award, Social Care Assoc., 2006. *Publications:* contrib. books on Europe and social policy, complaints procedures and consumer rights, and jls on social policy and women's issues. *Address:* WRVS, Garden House, Milton Hill, Steventon, Abingdon OX13 6AD. *T:* (01235) 442903; *e-mail:* lynne.berry@wrvs.org.uk.

BERRY, Dr James William; Director General (formerly Director) of Scientific and Technical Intelligence, 1982–89; *b* 5 Oct. 1931; *s* of Arthur Harold Berry and Mary Margaret Berry; *m* 1960, Monica Joan Hill; three *d*. *Educ:* St Mary's Coll., Blackburn; Municipal Technical Coll., Blackburn; Manchester Univ. (BSc); Leeds Univ. (PhD). FIET. Royal Signals and Radar Estab., Malvern, 1956–60; Admiralty Surface Weapons Estab., Portsdown, 1960–76 (Head of Computer Div., 1972–76); Dir of Long Range Surveillance and Comd and Control Projs, MoD (PE), 1976–79; Dir Gen. Strategic Electronic Systems, MoD (PE), 1979–82. Organist, St Michael's RC Church, Leigh Park, Havant; 'cellist mem. of Petersfield Orch. *Recreations:* music (organ, 'cello, piano), walking, watching wild life, geriatric sport. *Club:* Civil Service.

BERRY, Janette Susan, QPM 2006; Chairman, Police Federation of England and Wales, since 2002; *b* Carshalton, 29 Aug. 1954; *d* of Ralph Cooke and Marian (*née* Hook); *m* 1980, Graham Berry; one *s* one *d*. *Educ:* Fosse Bank Girls' Sch., Tonbridge; Open Univ. (BA). Kent County Constabulary, 1971–: Cadet, 1971–73; Constable, 1973–75; Detective Constable, 1975–77; Sergeant, 1977–79; Sergeant (Instructor), 1979–81; Patrol Sergeant, 1981–84; Inspector, 1984–97; Force Crime Prevention Officer, 1986–2000; Chief Inspector, 1987–. Chm., Kent Police Fedn, 1991–97. Sec., Inspectors' Central Cttee, 1987–2001. FRSA. Police Long Service and Good Conduct Medal, 1996; Golden Jubilee Medal, 2002. *Recreations:* family, theatre, current affairs, travel, supporting Crystal Palace Football Club, armchair sports fan. *Address:* Police Federation of England and Wales, 15–17 Langley Road, Surbiton, Surrey KT6 6LP; *e-mail:* jberry@jcc.polfed.org.

BERRY, Lynne; *see* Berry, G. L.

BERRY, Mary Rosa Alleyne, (Mrs P. J. M. Hunnings); cookery writer and television cook, since 1966; *b* Bath, 24 March 1935; *d* of Alleyne and Margery Berry; *m* 1966, Paul John March Hunnings; one *s* one *d* (and one *s* decd). *Educ:* Bath High Sch.; Bath Coll. of Home Econs; C&G Teaching; Paris Cordon Bleu. Cookery Editor: Housewife mag., 1966–70; Ideal Home mag., 1970–73; TV series and appearances, 1978–, radio, 1980–. *Publications:* Cook Book, 1970; Popular Freezer Cookery, 1972; Popular French Cookery, 1972; Good Afternoon Cookery Book, 1976; One Pot Cooking, 1978; Family Recipes, 1979; Television Cook Book, 1979; Glorious Puds, 1980; Home Cooking, 1980; Cooking with Cheese, 1980; Day by Day Cooking, 1981; Mary Berry's Main Course, 1981; Recipes from Home and Abroad, 1981; New Book of Meat Cookery, 1981; Fruit Fare, 1982; County Cooking, 1982; The Perfect Sunday Lunch, 1982; Crockery Cookery, 1983; Cooking at Home, 1983; Complete Television Cook Book, 1983; Food as Presents, 1983; Fast Desserts, 1983; Family Cooking, 1984; Iceland Guide to Cooking from your Freezer, 1985; Kitchen Wisdom, 1985; Feed Your Family the Healthier Way, 1985; New Freezer Cook Book, 1985; Cooking for Celebrations, 1986; Chocolate Delights, 1987; Mary Berry's Favourite Microwave Recipes, 1988; Mary Berry's Favourite Recipes, 1990; Mary Berry's Desserts and Confections, 1991; Mary Berry's Food Processor Cookbook, 1992; Hamlyn All Colour Cookbook, 1992; Fast Cakes, 1992; Mary Berry's Cookery Course, 1993; Mary Berry's Quick and Easy Cakes, 1993; Mary Berry's Freezer Cookbook, 1994; More Fast Cakes, 1994; Fast Suppers, 1994; Ultimate Cakes, 1994, 2nd edn as Mary Berry's Ultimate Cake Book, 2003; Favourite French Recipes, 1995; Classic Home Cooking, 1995; Mary Berry's Complete Cookbook, 1995, 2nd edn 2003; Mary Berry's Perfect Sunday, 1996; The Aga Book, 1996; Mary Berry Cooks Puddings and Desserts, 1997; The New Cook, 1997; Favourite Cakes, 1997; Mary Berry Cooks Cakes, 1998; Mary Berry's New Aga Cookbook, 1999; Mary Berry at Home, 2001; Mary Berry's Cakes, Puddings and Breads, 2001; Mary Berry's Classic Meat Dishes, 2001; Mary Berry's Soups, Salads and Starters, 2001; Cook Now, Eat Later, 2002; Mary Berry's Foolproof Cakes, 2004; Real Food Fast, 2005; Mary Berry's Christmas Collection, 2006; One Step Ahead with Mary Berry, 2007. *Recreations:* gardening, tennis, walking. *Address:* *e-mail:* info@maryberry.co.uk; *web:* www.maryberry.co.uk.

BERRY, Sir Michael (Victor), Kt 1996; FRS 1982; Professor of Physics, Bristol University, 1978–88 and since 2006 (Royal Society Research Professor, 1988–2006); *b* 14 March 1941; *s* of Jack and Marie Berry; *m* 1st, 1961, Eveline Ethel Fitt (marr. diss. 1970); two *s*; 2nd, 1971, Lesley Jane Allen (marr. diss. 1984); two *d*; 3rd, 1984, Monica Suzi Saiovici; one *s* one *d*. *Educ:* Univ. of Exeter (BSc; Hon. PhD 1991); Univ. of St Andrews (PhD). Bristol University: Res. Fellow, 1965–67; Lectr, 1967–74; Reader, 1974–78. Bakerian Lectr, Royal Soc., 1987. Mem., Royal Scientific Soc., Uppsala, 1988; Foreign Member: US Nat. Acad. of Sci., 1995; Royal Netherlands Acad. of Arts and Scis, 2000. Hon. FInstP 1999. Maxwell Medal and Prize, Inst. of Physics, 1978; Dirac Medal and Prize, Inst. of Physics, 1990; Lilienfeld Prize, Amer. Physical Soc., 1990; Royal Medal, Royal Soc., 1990; Naylor Prize and Lectureship in Applied Maths, London Math. Soc., 1992; Science for Art Prize, LVMH, Paris, 1994; Hewlett Packard Europhysics Prize, 1995; Dirac Medal, Internat. Centre for Theoretical Physics, 1996; Kapitsa Medal, Russian Acad. of Scis, 1997; Wolf Prize for Physics, Wolf Foundn, Israel, 1998; Ig Nobel Prize for Physics, 2000; Onsager Medal, Norwegian Technical Univ., 2001; 1st and 3rd prizes, Visions of Sci., Novartis/Daily Telegraph, 2002. *Publications:* Diffraction of Light by Ultrasound, 1966; Principles of Cosmology and Gravitation, 1976; about 400 research papers, book reviews, etc, on physics. *Recreation:* anything but sport. *Address:* H. H. Wills Physics Laboratory, Tyndall Avenue, Bristol BS8 1TL. *T:* (0117) 928 8735.

BERRY, Nicholas (William); Chairman: Stancroft Trust Ltd, since 1972; Mintel International Ltd; Intersport PSC Holding AG; *b* 3 July 1942; *yr s* of Baron Hartwell, MBE, TD; *m* 1977, Evelyn Prouvost; two *s*. *Educ:* Eton; Christ Church, Oxford. Publisher and investor; former Chairman: Harrap Publg; Manchester Ship Canal; Director: Blackwells, 1997–2003; Sibir Energy, 2000–03; Daily Mail Gp, 2007–, and other cos. *Address:* Stancroft Trust, 20 Bride Lane, EC4Y 8JP. *T:* (020) 7583 3808. *Club:* White's.
See also Viscount Camrose.

BERRY, Paul L.; Member, Armagh City and District Council; *b* 3 June 1976. *Educ:* Craigavon Coll. of Further Educn. Sales person, hardware warehouse, 1994–96; examr, shoe firm, 1996–98. Northern Ireland Assembly: Mem. (DUP, 1998–2006, Ind., 2006–07) Newry and Armagh; contested (Ind.) same seat, 2007; Mem., Health Cttee and Standards and Privileges Cttee. Mem., Health Action Zone. Member: Loyal Orange Instn;

Royal Black Perceptory; Apprentice Boys of Derry. Contested (DUP) Newry and Armagh, 2005. *Recreation:* interest in football.

BERRY, Very Rev. Peter Austin; Provost of Birmingham, 1986–99, now Emeritus; *b* 27 April 1935; *s* of Austin James Berry and Phyllis Evelyn Berry. *Educ:* Solihull Sch.; Keble Coll., Oxford (BA English, BTh, MA); St Stephen's House, Oxford. Intelligence Corps, 1954–56. Ordained deacon, 1962, priest, 1963; Chaplain to Bishop of Coventry, 1963–70; Midlands Regl Officer, Community Relations Commn, 1970–73; Canon Residentiary, Coventry Cathedral, 1973–86, Canon Emeritus 1987; Vice-Provost of Coventry, 1977–85. Mem., Gen. Synod of C of E, 1990–99; Church Comr, 1994–99. Chaplain to High Sheriff of W Midlands, 2005–06 and 2006–07. Chairman: Standing Adv. Cttee for Religious Educn, Birmingham, 1987–93; Birmingham Internat. Council, 1987–99 (Vice Pres., 1999–); Birmingham/Pakistan Friendship Assoc., 1995–99 (Vice Pres., 1999–); Pre-Raphaelite Soc., 1986–2000 (Life Pres., 2000). Pres., Birmingham and Midland Inst., 2005–06. Vice-Chm., Iqbal Acad. Life Fellow, Coventry Univ. (Fellow, Lanchester Coll., Coventry, 1985). FRAS 2006. Hon. DD Birmingham, 1997. *Recreations:* music, theatre, architecture. *Address:* Reed Lodge, D5 Kenilworth Court, Hagley Road, Birmingham B16 9NU. *T:* (0121) 454 0021.

BERRY, Peter Fremantle, CMG 1999; Chairman, Crown Agents for Oversea Governments and Administrations, 1998–2007; President, Crown Agents Foundation, since 2003; *b* St Andrews, Fife, 17 May 1944; *s* of late John Berry, CBE and Hon. Bride Berry, *d* of 3rd Baron Cottesloe, CB; *m* 1972, Paola Padovani; one *s* two *d*. *Educ:* Eton Coll.; Lincoln Coll., Oxford (MA Hons Mod. History). Harrisons & Crosfield, London, 1966–73: Manager: Kuala Belait, Brunei, 1968; Indonesia, 1970; Anglo Indonesian Corp., London: Gen. Man., 1973; Dir, 1974–82; Crown Agents for Oversea Governments and Administrations, 1982–: Director: Asia and Pacific, based Singapore, 1982–84; ME, Asia and Pacific, based London, 1984–88; Man. Dir and Crown Agent, 1988–2002; Chm. of Crown Agents' banking and asset mgt subsidiaries. Director: Thomas Tapling Ltd, 1987–; Anglo-Eastern Plantations Plc, 1991–93; Henderson TR Pacific Investment Trust, 1994–; Scottish Eastern Investment Trust, 1995–98; Kier Group plc, 1997–; Martin Currie Portfolio Investment Trust plc, 1999– (Chm., 2000–); Martin Currie Capital Return Trust plc, 1999–2000. Member: Management Bd, Resource, 1989–92; Internat. Bd, Transparency Internat., 1993–; Pres., Transparency Internat. (UK), 2003–. Member: Rubber Growers Assoc., 1978–82; UK Task Force on Kuwait, 1991; UK-Japan 21st Century (formerly UK-Japan 2000) Gp, 1992– (Dir, 2000–03); Whitehall Export Promotion Cttee, 1992–98; Internat. Cttee, CBI, 1997–2003; British Trade Internat. Sectors and Projects, subseq. Business Adv., Gp, 1998–2004; Council: Malaysia, Singapore and Brunei Assoc., 1982–87; Indonesia Assoc., 1974–93 (Chm., 1986–89). Advr on econ. develt, Corp. of London, 2003–. Trustee, CAF, 2000– (Chm., Internat. Cttee, 2000–); Dir and Trustee, Charity Bank, 2003–. Governor, Scottish Crop Res. Inst., 2007–. FRSA. *Recreations:* wildlife and country pursuits in Britain and Italy, travel and international development. *Address:* St Nicholas House, St Nicholas Road, Sutton, Surrey SM1 1EL. *T:* (020) 8643 3311. *Club:* Royal Automobile.

BERRY, Prof. Peter Jeremy, FRCP, FRCPath, FRCPCH; Professor of Paediatric Pathology, University of Bristol, 1991–2001, now Emeritus; *b* 21 March 1950; *s* of Peter Berry and Marjorie Berry (*née* Lang). *Educ:* Epsom Coll.; Magdalene Coll., Cambridge (BA, MB, BChir). Kent and Canterbury Hosp., 1975–77; Sen. Registrar in Histopathology, Addenbrooke's Hosp., 1977–81; Research Fellow, Children's Hosp., Denver, 1981–83; Consultant Paediatric Pathologist, Bristol Royal Hosp. for Sick Children, 1983–2001. *Publications:* chapters and papers on cot death and children's tumours. *Recreations:* walking, fishing, music. *Clubs:* Athenæum, Royal Society of Medicine.

BERRY, Rt Rev. (Robert Edward) Fraser; Bishop of Kootenay, 1971–89; *b* Ottawa, Ont, 21 Jan. 1926; *s* of Samuel Berry and Claire Hartley; *m* 1951, Margaret Joan Trevorrow Baillie; one *s* one *d*. *Educ:* Sir George Williams Coll., Montreal; McGill Univ., Montreal; Montreal Diocesan Theological Coll. Assistant, Christ Church Cathedral, Victoria, BC, 1953–55; Rector: St Margaret's, Hamilton, Ont, 1955–61; St Mark's, Orangeville, Ont, 1961–63; St Luke's, Winnipeg, Manitoba, 1963–67; St Michael and All Angels, Kelowna, BC, 1967–71. Chaplain: RCAF Assoc. 883 (Kelowna) Wing, 1988–; Royal Canadian Legion 23 (Kelowna) Br., 1994–; Royal Canadian Mounted Police Okanagan Div., 1995–; (on call), Kelowna Gen. Hosp., 1992–, Asst (on call), St Andrew's, Okanagan Mission, Kelowna, 1992–. Hon. DD Montreal Diocesan Theol Coll., 1973. *Recreations:* reading, boating, angling, swimming, walking, computer communications. *Address:* 13–1101 Cameron Avenue, Kelowna, BC V1Y 8V6, Canada. *T:* (250) 7622923. *Clubs:* Vancouver (Vancouver); Kelowna Yacht.

BERRY, Prof. Robert James, FRSE 1981; FIBiol; Professor of Genetics in the University of London, 1974–2000, then Emeritus; *b* 26 Oct. 1934; *o s* of Albert Edward James Berry and Nellie (*née* Hodgson); *m* 1958, Anne Caroline Elliott, *d* of Charles Elliott and Evelyn Le Cornu; one *s* two *d*. *Educ:* Shrewsbury Sch.; Caius Coll., Cambridge (MA); University Coll. London (PhD; DSc 1976). Lectr, subseq. Reader, then Prof., in Genetics, at Royal Free Hospital Sch. of Medicine, 1962–78; Prof. of Genetics at University Coll. London, 1978–2000. Leverhulme Emeritus Fellow, 2001–04. Gifford Lectr, Glasgow Univ., 1997–98; Hooker Lectr, Linnean Soc. Mem., Human Fertilization and Embryology Authy, 1990–96. Member: Gen. Synod, 1970–90; Board of Social Responsibility of the General Synod, 1976–91; Natural Environment Research Council, 1981–87; Council, Zoological Soc. of London, 1986–90 (Vice-Pres., 1988–90); President: Linnean Soc., 1982–85; British Ecological Soc., 1987–89; Christians in Science (formerly Research Scientists' Christian Fellowship), 1993–95 (Chm., 1968–88); Mammal Soc., 1995–97; Chm., Environmental Issues Network, 1992–. Trustee, Nat. Museums and Galleries, Merseyside, 1986–94. Governor: Monkton Combe Sch., 1979–91; Walthamstow Hall Sch., 2001–05. Templeton UK Award, 1996; Marsh Award for Ecology, Marsh Trust, 2001. *Publications:* Teach Yourself Genetics, 1965, 3rd edn 1977; Adam and the Ape, 1975; Inheritance and Natural History, 1977; (jtly) Natural History of Shetland, 1980; (ed) Biology of the House Mouse, 1981; Neo-Darwinism, 1982; (ed) Evolution in the Galapagos, 1984; (jtly) Free to be Different, 1984; Natural History of Orkney, 1985; (ed jtly) The People of Orkney, 1986; (ed jtly) Nature, Natural History and Ecology, 1987; (ed jtly) Changing Attitudes to Nature Conservation, 1987; God and Evolution, 1988; (ed jtly) Evolution, Ecology and Environmental Stress, 1989; (ed) Real Science, Real Faith, 1991; (ed jtly) Genes in Ecology, 1992; (ed) Environmental Dilemmas, 1993; God and the Biologist, 1996; (jtly) Science, Life and Christian Belief, 1998; Orkney Nature, 2000; (ed) The Care of Creation, 2000; God's Book of Works, 2003; (ed) Environmental Stewardship, 2006; (ed) When Enough is Enough, 2007. *Recreation:* remembering hill-walking (especially Munros) and then dreaming. *Address:* Quarfseter, Sackville Close, Sevenoaks, Kent TN13 3QD. *T:* (01732) 451907.

BERRY, Dr Robert Langley Page, CBE 1979; Chairman, 1968–78, Deputy Chairman, 1978–79, Alcoa of Great Britain Ltd; *b* 22 Nov. 1918; *s* of Wilfred Arthur and Mabel Grace Berry; *m* 1946, Eleanor Joyce (*née* Cramp); one *s* one *d*. *Educ:* Sir Thomas Rich's Sch., Gloucester; Birmingham Univ. (BSc (Hons), PhD). Served war, Royal Engrs, 1939–45. ICI Metals Div., 1951–66, Director, 1960–66; Man. Dir, Impalco, 1966–68. Non-Exec. Dir, Royal Mint, 1981–86. Dir, Nat. Anti-Waste Prog., 1976–80. President: Inst. of Metals, 1973; Aluminium Fedn, 1974. Chm., Friends of Fairford Church, 1985–97. *Publications:* several, in scientific jls. *Recreations:* fly-fishing, gardening. *Address:* Waterloo Cottage, Waterloo Lane, Fairford, Glos GL7 4BP. *T:* (01285) 712038. *Club:* Army and Navy.

BERRY, Prof. Roger Julian, RD 1987; FRCP; FRCR; FFOM; Director, Westlakes Research Institute, Cumbria, 1992–95; Chairman, British Committee on Radiation Units and Measurements, 1995–2000 (Member, 1978–2000; Vice-Chairman, 1984–95); *b* 6 April 1935; *s* of Sidney Norton Berry and Beatrice (*née* Mendelson); *m* 1960, Joseline Valerie Joan (*née* Butler). *Educ:* Stuyvesant High Sch., New York; New York Univ. (BA); Duke Univ. (BSc, MD); Magdalen Coll., Oxford (MA, DPhil). MRC External Staff and Hd, Radiobiol. Lab., Churchill Hosp., Oxford, also Hon. Cons. Med. Radiobiologist, Oxford AHA, and Clin. Lectr, Univ. of Oxford, 1969–74; Hd, Neutrons and therapy-related effects gp, MRC Radiobiol. Unit, Harwell, 1974–76; Sir Brian Windeyer Prof. of Oncology, Middx Hosp. Med. Sch., 1976–87; Dir, Health, Safety and Environmental Protection, British Nuclear Fuels, 1987–92. Vis. Prof., Inst. of Envmtl and Natural Scis, Lancaster Univ., 1993–2003. Member: Internat. Commn on Radiological Protection, 1985–89; Nat. Radiological Protection Bd, 1982–87; MRC Cttee on Effects of Ionizing Radiation, and Chm., Radiobiol. Sub-Cttee, 1983–87; DoE Radioactive Waste Management Cttee, 1984–87; DHSS Cttee on Med. Aspects of Radiation in the Environment, 1985–87, Black Enquiry on Windscale; HSC Adv. Cttee on Safety of Nuclear Installations, 1992–96; CBI Health and Safety Policy Cttee, 1988–92; CIA Health, Safety and Envmt Council, 1990–92. President: BIR, 1986–87; Radiology Sect., RSM, 1985–86; Chm., Sci. Adv. Cttee, Thames Cancer Registry, 1985–87. Surg. Captain, RNR, 1986, and PMO (Reserves), 1987–89. QHP 1987–89. County Comdr, St John Ambulance, IoM, 2005–. Gov., King William's Coll., IOM and Trustee, Bishop Barrow's Charity, 2000–. Hon. Fellow, Amer. Coll. of Radiology, 1983. CStJ 2005. Editor, Cell and Tissue Kinetics, 1976–80. *Publications:* Manual on Radiation Dosimetry (jtly), 1970; contributor to Oxford Textbook of Medicine, Florey's Textbook of Pathology; over 190 sci. papers in Brit. Jl of Radiology, etc. *Recreations:* sailing, music, naval history. *Address:* 109 Fairways Drive, Mount Murray, Santon, Douglas, Isle of Man IM4 2JE. *T:* and *Fax:* (01624) 617959. *Clubs:* Royal Over-Seas League, Royal Naval Sailing Association.

BERRY, Dr Roger Leslie; MP (Lab) Kingswood, since 1992; *b* 4 July 1948; *s* of Mary Joyce Berry and Sydney Berry; *m* 1996, Alison Delyth. *Educ:* Dalton County Jun. Sch.; Huddersfield New Coll.; Univ. of Bristol (BSc); Univ. of Sussex (DPhil). Lectr in Econs and Associate Fellow, IDS, Univ. of Sussex, 1973–74; Lecturer in Economics: Univ. of Papua New Guinea, 1974–78; Univ. of Bristol, 1978–92. Avon County Council: Mem., 1981–93; Chm., Finance and Admin. Cttee, 1981–84; Dep. Leader of Council, 1985–86; Leader, Labour Group, 1986–92. Contested (Lab): Weston-super-Mare, 1983; Kingswood, 1987. Mem., Trade and Industry Select Cttee, 1995–; Sec., All-Party Disability Gp, 1994–. Vice-Chair, British Gp, IPU, 2004–. Chair, Full Employment Forum, 1994–99. Dir, Tribune Publications Ltd, 1997–2003. Vice Pres., Disabled Drivers Assoc., 1997–; Trustee: Disabled Law Service, 1997–99; Snowdon Award Scheme, 1997–2003; Patron, Circomedia, 1997–. *Publications:* contribs to learned jls; newspaper articles and pamphlets. *Recreations:* travel, cooking, reading, cinema, theatre. *Address:* 9 Manor Road, Bristol BS16 2JD. *T:* (0117) 965 4889. *Club:* Kingswood Labour.

BERRY, (Roger) Simon; QC 1990; a Recorder, 2000–05; a Deputy High Court Judge, 2001–05; *b* 9 Sept. 1948; *e s* of Kingsland Jutsum Berry and Kathleen Margaret Parker; *m* 1974, Jennifer Jane, *d* of Jonas Birtwistle Hall and Edith Emilé Vester; three *s*. *Educ:* St Brendan's Coll., Bristol; Manchester Univ. (LLB). Admitted Solicitor, 1973; Partner, Stanley, Wasbrough & Co., Solicitors, Bristol (later Veale Wasbrough), 1975–77; removed from Roll, 1977, at own request, in order to seek call to the Bar; called to the Bar, Middle Temple, 1977; Mem., Middle Temple and Lincoln's Inn; Harmsworth Benefactor's Law Schol.; Mem., Western Circuit, 1978–2005; in practice at Chancery Bar, 1978–2005; Asst Recorder, 1996–2000; Ordinary Bencher, Lincoln's Inn, 1998. Member: Bar Council, 1996–99 (Mem., Professional Conduct Cttee, 1996–99, and Practice Mgt and Develt Cttee, 1998–99); Chancery Bar Assoc., 1978–2005 (Mem. Cttee, 1984, 1985); Professional Negligence Bar Assoc., 1991–2005; Property Bar Assoc., 2001–05. Mem., Theatre Panel of Judges, Olivier Awards, 2000. *Publication:* (contrib.) Professional Negligence and Liability, 2000. *Recreations:* family, the performing arts, keeping fit, climbed Mt Kilimanjaro in Tanzania, walked Inca Trail in Peru. *Club:* Riverside.

BERRY, Scyld; *see* Berry, A. S. I.

BERRY, Simon; *see* Berry, Roger S.

BERRY, Thomas Henry Seager S.; *see* Seager Berry.

BERTHET, Dr Miguel Jorge; Ambassador of Uruguay to the Court of St James's, 2001–04; *b* Montevideo, 11 April 1934; *m* Maria Pilar Diaz (*d* 2004); three *d*. *Educ:* Univ. de la República, Uruguay (Dr in Law and Social Scis). Entered Foreign Service, Uruguay, 1962: Legal Asst, 1962; Asst Legal Counsellor and Dir, Diplomatic Legal Affairs Div.; Director: Internat. Econ. Orgns; Internat. Political Orgns; Hd, Uruguayan Delegn, Treaty of Asunción, 1991; Gen. Dir for Econ. Affairs and for Foreign Trade, Min. of Econ. and Finance; Sec. Gen.; Director General: for Tech.-Admin. Affairs; for Foreign Policy; Ambassador: to UN, GATT and internat. orgns, Geneva; to Belgium, Luxembourg and the EC; Minister, Brasilia; Minister Counsellor: London; Brussels, Luxembourg and the EC. Prof. of Air, Maritime and Commercial Law, Univ. de la República, Montevideo. Grand Cross: Order of Mayo (Argentina); Order Baron de Rio Branco (Brazil); Order of Merit (Peru). *Publications:* several books and papers. *Address:* c/o Embassy of Uruguay, 2nd Floor, 140 Brompton Road, SW3 1HY.

BERTHOIN, Georges Paul; Chevalier, Légion d'Honneur, 1990; Médaille militaire, Croix de Guerre, Médaille de la Résistance avec Rosette, France, 1945; Executive Member of the Trilateral Commission (Japan, N America, W Europe), 1973–75, and since 1993 (Chairman, 1975–92, Hon. European Chairman, since 1992); Honorary International Chairman, the European Movement, since 1981 (Chairman, 1978–81); *b* Nérac, France, 17 May 1925; *s* of Jean Berthoin and Germaine Mourgnot; *m* 1st, 1950, Ann White Whittlesey; four *d*; 2nd, 1965, Pamela Jenkins; two *s*. *Educ:* Grenoble Univ.; École Sciences Politiques, Paris; Harvard Univ. Licencié ès Lettres (Philosophie), Licencié en Droit, Laureate for Economics (Grenoble). Lectr, McGill Univ., Montreal, 1948; Private Sec. to French Minister of Finance, 1948–50; Head of Staff of Superprefect of Alsace-Lorraine-Champagne, 1950–52. Joined High Authority of European Coal and Steel Community, and then Principal Private Sec. to its Pres. (Jean Monnet), 1952–53–55. Dep. Chief Rep. of ECSC in UK, 1956–67; Chargé d'Affaires for Commission of the European Communities (ECSC Euratom-Common Market), 1968; Principal Adviser to the Commission, and its Dep. Chief Rep. in London, 1969–70, Chief Representative,

1971–73. Member: Nine Wise Men Gp on Africa, 1988–89; Bd, Aspen Inst., Berlin; Adv. Bd, Johns Hopkins Univ. Bologna Center Sch. of Advanced Studies. Hon. Chm., Jean Monnet Assoc., 2001–. Regular Lectr, RCDS, London. *Recreations:* art, theatre, walking, collecting objects. *Address:* 67 Avenue Niel, 75017 Paris, France.

BERTHOUD, Prof. Jacques Alexandre; Professor of English, Department of English and Related Literature, University of York, 1980–2002, now Emeritus (Head of Department, 1980–97; Deputy Vice-Chancellor, 1987–90); *b* 1 March 1935; *s* of Alexandre L. Berthoud and Madeleine (*née* Bourquin); *m* 1958, Astrid Irene (*née* Titlestad); one *s* two *d*. *Educ:* Univ. of the Witwatersrand, Johannesburg (BA and BA Hons). Lectr, English Dept, Univ. of Natal, Pietermaritzburg, 1960–67; Lectr, subseq. Sen. Lectr, English Dept, Univ. of Southampton, 1967–79. Vis. Fellow Commoner, Trinity College, Cambridge, 1990–91. British Chm., Amnesty Internat., 1978–80. *Publications:* (with Dr C. van Heyningen) Uys Krige, 1966; Joseph Conrad, the Major Phase, 1978; Joseph Conrad: au cœur de l'œuvre, 1992; (ed jtly) 'Twixt Land and Sea, 2007; (ed) books for OUP and Penguin Books; articles in jls. *Recreation:* music. *Address:* 30 New Walk Terrace, Fishergate, York YO10 4BG. *T:* (01904) 629212.

BERTHOUD, Sir Martin (Seymour), KCVO 1985; CMG 1985; HM Diplomatic Service, retired; *b* 20 Aug. 1931; *s* of Sir Eric Berthoud, KCMG and late Ruth Tilston, *d* of Sir Charles Bright, FRSE; *m* 1960, Marguerite Joan Richarda Phayre; three *s* one *d*. *Educ:* Rugby Sch.; Magdalen Coll., Oxford (MA). Served with British Embassies in: Tehran, 1956–58; Manila, 1961–64; Pretoria/Cape Town, 1967–71; Tehran, 1971–73; Counsellor, Helsinki, 1974–77; Inspector, HM Diplomatic Service, 1977–79; Head of N. American Dept, FCO, 1979–81; Consul-General, Sydney, 1982–85; High Comr, Trinidad and Tobago, 1985–91. EC Monitor, Croatia, 1991. Dir, The Wates Foundn, 1993–2001. Patron: Green Light Trust, 2001–; Prisoners Abroad, 2002–; Church Housing Trust, 2002–. EC Monitoring Mission Service Medal, 1994. Commander, Order of the Lion (Finland), 1976; Keys of City of San Fernando (Trinidad), 1991. *Recreations:* writing, golf, tennis, bird-watching, acting as under-gardener to wife, grandchildren. *Address:* Gillyflower Cottage, Stoke by Nayland, Suffolk CO6 4RD. *T:* (01206) 263237. *Club:* Oxford and Cambridge.

BERTIE, family name of **Earl of Lindsey and Abingdon**.

BERTRAM, Dr Brian Colin Ricardo; Special Projects Co-ordinator, Bristol Zoo Gardens, 1995–2003; *b* 14 April 1944; *s* of late Dr Colin Bertram and Dr (Cicely) Kate Bertram; *m* 1975, Katharine Jean Gillie; one *s* two *d*. *Educ:* Perse School, Cambridge; St John's Coll., Cambridge (BA 1965; MA 1968); PhD Cambridge, 1969. FIBiol 1981. Research Fellow, Serengeti Res. Inst., Tanzania, 1969–73; Sen. Res. Fellow, King's Coll., Cambridge, 1976–79; Curator of Mammals, 1980–87, and Curator of Aquarium and Invertebrates, 1982–87, Zoological Society of London; Dir-Gen., Wildfowl and Wetlands Trust, 1987–92. Vice-Pres., World Pheasant Assoc., 1990–97; Mem. Council, Zool Soc. of London, 1993–97, 1999–2002, 2004–07. *Publications:* Pride of Lions, 1978; The Ostrich Communal Nesting System, 1992; Lions, 1998. *Recreations:* family, friends, zoology, garden, travel. *Address:* Fieldhead, Amberley, Stroud, Glos GL5 5AG. *T:* (01453) 872796. *Club:* Zoological.

BERTRAM, (Charles) William, RIBA; Founder and Managing Director, William Bertram of Bath Ltd, since 2006; *b* 2 Oct. 1939; *s* of Lt Col Richard Bertram and Elizabeth Florence Oriana Bertram (*née* Bedwell); *m* 1963, Victoria Harriette Ingle; one *s* two *d*. *Educ:* Sherborne Sch.; AA Sch. of Architecture (AA Dip. Hons 1964). RIBA 1965. Founder: William Bertram Fell (architectural practice), 1970; William Bertram, Consulting Architect, 1996–2006. Architect to the Prince of Wales, 1987–; Consultant Architect: to Strangways Estate, 1972–; to Duchy of Cornwall Eastern Reg., 1987–; to RNLI, 2002–; Architect to Churchill Graves Trust, 1996–; Advr to Theatre Royal, Bath, 2005–. Major projects include: *conversions and restorations:* Nos 15 and 16 into Royal Crescent Hotel, Bath, 1979; Abbotsbury Village, Dorset, 1980 (UK Council EAHY Award, 1987); Dower House, Bath (Civic Trust Award for Conservation), 1986; Cliveden into hotel, 1986–89; farm buildings and visitor's extension, Highgrove, Glos, 1988; Perrystone Court, Herefordshire, 1996; Shooting Lodge, Easter Auchintoul, 1998 (Inverness Civic Trust Biennial Award, 1999); Dinmore Manor, 2000–05; Rockley Manor, Wilts, 2000–03; Parnham House, Dorset (re-ordering), 2005; Encombe House, Dorset, 2005 (Georgian Group Award, 2006); *new work:* Stradling House, Somerset, 1979; Angmering Park, Sussex, 1983–85; Cavendish Lodge, Bath, 1986–97 (Stone Fedn Award, 1997); tree house, Highgrove, 1988; Dunley Farmhouse, Hants, 1996; South Kenwood, Devon, 1997; Nos 25, 1997, and 57, 1999, Winnington Rd, Hampstead; *gardens:* Highgrove, Camerton Court, Dinmore Manor, Albemarle House, Va, USA. Trustee, Bath Preservation Trust, 1966–68. Chm., Compton Dando Ch Estate Trust, 1981–2005. Bath Conservation Area Adv. Cttee Envmntl Award for St Anne's Place, Bath, 1987. *Publication:* An Appreciation of Abbotsbury, 1973. *Recreations:* garden designing, tennis, golf (badly), walking, writing, upsetting planners. *Address:* Woodrising, Loves Hill, Timsbury, Bath BA2 0EU. *T:* (01761) 471100, *Fax:* (01761) 479102.

BERTRAM, Dr Christoph; Director, Stiftung Wissenschaft und Politik (Foundation Science and Policy), 1998–2005; Steven Müller Chair in German Studies, School of Advanced International Studies, Bologna Center, Johns Hopkins University, 2005–06; *b* 3 Sept. 1937; German national; *m* 1st, 1967, Renate Edith Bergemann (marr. diss. 1980); 2nd, 1980, Ragnhild Lindemann; two *s* two *d*. *Educ:* Free Univ. Berlin and Bonn Univ. (law); Institut d'Etudes Politiques, Paris (political science). Dr of Law 1967. Joined Internat. Inst. for Strategic Studies as Research Associate, 1967, Asst Dir, 1969–74, Dir, 1974–82; Mem. Planning Staff, West German Min. of Defence, 1969–70. Political and Foreign Editor, 1982–85, Diplomatic Correspondent, 1986–98, Die Zeit. *Publications:* (with Alastair Buchan *et al.*) Europe's Futures—Europe's Choices, 1969; Mutual Force Reductions in Europe: the political aspects, 1972; (ed, with Johan J. Holst) New Strategic Factors in the North Atlantic, 1977; Arms Control and Technological Change, 1979; Europe in the Balance, 1995. *Recreations:* clocks, sailing.

BERTRAM, George, CB 1999; Director, National Services, Board of Inland Revenue, 2000–01; *b* 19 Sept. 1944; *s* of late George Bertram and of Muriel Bertram; *m* 1969, Jean Swales. *Educ:* Houghton-le-Spring Grammar Sch. Nat. Assistance Bd, Sunderland, 1964–70; Department of Health and Social Security, then Department of Social Security: Staff Trng, Billingham, 1970–73; Sunderland, 1973–76; Regl Office, Newcastle upon Tyne, 1976–80; South Shields, 1980–83; Manager: Peterlee, 1983; Hartlepool, 1983–84; Middlesbrough, 1984–89; Sunderland, 1989; Contributions Agency: Head of Field Ops, 1989–92; Dep. Chief Exec., and Dir of Compliance and Educn, 1992–94; actg Chief Exec., 1994–95; Dep. Chief Exec., and Dir of Ops, 1995–97; Chief Exec., 1997–99; Dir., Nat. Insce Contribns, Bd of Inland Revenue, 1999–2000. Mem., CSAB, 2001–. *Recreations:* sport, especially golf, cricket, football, gardening. *Address:* 8 Holmewood Drive, Rowlands Gill, Tyne and Wear NE39 1EL. *Club:* Garesfield Golf.

BERTRAM, Robert David Darney; Member, Competition (formerly Monopolies and Mergers) Commission, 1998–2005; *b* 6 Oct. 1941; *s* of late D. N. S. Bertram; *m* 1967, Patricia Joan Laithwaite; two *s*. *Educ:* Edinburgh Academy; Oxford Univ. (MA); Edinburgh Univ. (LLB (Hons), Berriedale Keith Prize). An Assistant Solicitor, Linklaters & Paines, London, 1968–69; Partner: Dundas & Wilson, CS, 1969–92; Shepherd & Wedderburn, WS, 1992–98. Associate, Institute of Taxation, 1970 (Mem., Technical Cttee, 1986); Examiner (pt-time), Law Society of Scotland, 1972–75; Member: Scottish Law Commn, 1978–86; VAT Tribunal, Scotland, 1984–92; Council, UKCC (later Nurses' and Midwives' Council), 1988–2002 (Chm., Audit Cttee, 1998–2002; Lay Panellist, 2002–); Insolvency Practices' Council, 2000–; Audit Adv. Bd, Scottish Parlt Corporate Body, 2002–. Assessor, Edinburgh Univ. Ct, 2000–03. Vis. Prof., Edinburgh and Heriot-Watt Univs, 2000–. Non-exec. Dir, The Weir Group plc, 1983–2000. Trustee, David Hume Inst., 1998–. *Publications:* contribs to professional jls. *Recreations:* books, jazz, browsing. *Clubs:* Royal Over-Seas League; Scottish Arts (Edinburgh).

BERTRAM, William; *see* Bertram, C. W.

BESAG, Prof. Julian E., FRS 2004; Professor of Statistics, University of Washington, Seattle, 1991; *b* 26 March 1945; one *s* one *d*. *Educ:* Univ. of Birmingham (BSc Hons Mathematical Stats 1968). Res. Asst, Univ. of Oxford, 1968–69; Lectr in Stats, Univ. of Liverpool, 1969–75; Reader in Stats, 1975–85, Prof. of Stats, 1985–89, Univ. of Durham; Prof. of Stats, Univ. of Newcastle upon Tyne, 1990–91. Visiting Professor: Princeton Univ., 1975; Univ. of Newcastle upon Tyne, 1987–88; Univ. of Washington, Seattle, 1989–90. *Recreation:* sailing. *Address:* Department of Statistics, Box 354322, University of Washington, Seattle, WA 98195, USA. *T:* (206) 5433871, *Fax:* (206) 6857419; *e-mail:* julian@stat.washington.edu. *Clubs:* Northwest Riggers Yacht, Washington Yacht.

BESGROVE, Maj.-Gen. Peter Vincent Ronald, CBE 1992; CEng, FIET, FCMI; Chief Executive, Haig Homes, since 2002; *b* 23 Oct. 1948; *s* of Ronald Alfred Besgrove and Josephine Besgrove (*née* Buckley); *m* 1971, Eileen McEwan; two *d*. *Educ:* Magdalen Coll. Sch.; Welbeck Coll.; Royal Military Coll. of Sci. (BSc Eng Hons). CEng 1985; FIET (FIEE 1997). Commnd REME, 1968: served BAOR, NI and England, 1968–79; Staff Coll., 1980; Dep. COS, 6 Armd Bde, 1981–83; Comd, 5 Armd Workshop, BAOR, 1983–84; jsdc 1985; DS, Staff Coll., 1985–87; Comd Maintenance 3 Armd Div., BAOR, 1987–89; Asst COS, HQ NI, 1989–91; Comdt, Sch. of Electrical and Mechanical Engrg, 1991–92; Comd, REME Trng Gp, 1992–93; rcds 1994; Dir of Manning (Army), 1995–97; Dir Gen. Equipment Support (Army), 1997–99; Asst COS J1, HQ Allied Forces S, 1999–2001. Col Comdt, REME, 1999–2004. Non-exec. Dir, SCS Ltd, 2002–06. Mem. Bd of Trustees, Treloar Trust, 2002–; Chm. of Govs, Treloar Coll., 2003–. Dir, United Services Trustee, 2007–. FCMI (FIMgt 2001). *Recreations:* fishing, shooting, sailing, DIY. *Address:* c/o Regimental HQ REME, Isaac Newton Road, Arborfield, Reading, Berks RG2 9NJ. *T:* (0118) 976 3672. *Club:* Army and Navy.

BESLEY, Morrish Alexander, (Tim), AC 2002 (AO 1992); FTSE; Chairman: Australian Research Council, 2002–06; Co-operative Research Centre for greenhouse gas technology, since 2003; Wheat Export Authority, 2005–07; *b* New Plymouth, NZ, 14 March 1927; *s* of Hugh Morrish Besley and Isabel (*née* Alexander); *m* 1st, 1952, Nancy Cave (marr. diss. 2001); three *s*; 2nd, 2001, Sarah Harrington; one *s* one *d*. *Educ:* Univ. of New Zealand (BE Civil); Macquarie Univ. (BLegS). Hon. FIEAust 2005 (FIEAust 1982); FTSE (FTS 1985). Engr, Ministry of Works, NZ, 1950; Snowy Mts Hydro-Electric Authy, Australia, 1950–67; First Assistant Secretary: Dept of External Territories, Australia, 1967–73; Dept of Treasury, Australia, 1973–76 (Exec. Mem., Foreign Investment Rev. Bd, 1975–76); Sec., Commonwealth Dept of Business and Consumer Affairs, and Comptroller General of Customs, Australia, 1976–81; Monier Ltd: Man. Dir, 1982–87; Chm. and Chief Exec., 1987; Chairman: Monier Redland Ltd, 1988; Redland Australia, 1988–95; CIG Gp, 1988–93; Commonwealth Banking Corp., 1988–91; Leighton Hldgs Ltd, 1990–2001; Commonwealth Bank of Australia, 1991–99. Director: Amcor Ltd, 1985–97; Fujitsu Australia Ltd, 1988–97; O'Connell Street Associates Pty Ltd, 1990–; Clyde Industries Ltd, 1991–96. Mem., NSW Council and Nat. Exec., Metal Trades Industry Assoc. (Pres., 1991–92). Chancellor, Macquarie Univ., 1994–2001. Mem. Bd, Carrick Inst. for Teaching and Learning in Higher Educn, 2006–. Chm., Sydney Royal Botanic Gardens Trust, 1988–92; Trustee, Royal Botanic Gdns Sydney Foundn, 1992–99; Governor, Australian Nat. Gall. Foundn, 1992–; Chm., Centenary Inst. Med. Res. Foundn, 1992–96; Mem., Aust. Bd of Reference, World Vision, 1992–. Pres., AATSE, 1998–2002. Mem., Red Shield Appeal Cttee, 1988–99, Sydney Adv. Bd, 1994–99, Salvation Army. Hon. DSc Macquarie, 2002. *Recreations:* golf, fishing. *Address:* PO Box 304, Cammeray, NSW 2062, Australia. *Clubs:* Australian, Union (Sydney); National Press (Canberra); Elanora Country; Royal Sydney Yacht Squadron.

BESLEY, Prof. Timothy John, DPhil; FBA 2001; Kuwait Professor of Economics and Political Science, London School of Economics, since 2007 (Professor of Economics and Political Science, 1995–2007); Member, Monetary Policy Committee, Bank of England, 2006–Aug. 2009; *b* 14 Sept. 1960; *s* of John Besley and June Besley (*née* Turton); *m* 1993, Gillian Nicola Paull; two *s*. *Educ:* Keble Coll., Oxford (BA PPE 1983); All Souls Coll., Oxford (MPhil; DPhil 1988). Prize Fellow, All Souls Coll., Oxford, 1984–91 and 1995–2000; Asst Prof., Princeton Univ., 1988–95; Dir, Suntory Toyota Internat. Centres for Econs and Related Disciplines, LSE, 2001–. Res. Fellow, Inst. for Fiscal Studies, 1995–. Co-Ed., Amer. Econ. Rev., 1999–2004. Fellow, Econometric Soc., 2000. *Publications:* contribs to Amer. Econ. Rev., Jl Political Econ., Econometrica, Qly Jl Econs and other scholarly jls. *Recreations:* squash, playing violin. *Address:* London School of Economics, Houghton Street, WC2A 2AE. *T:* (020) 7955 6702.

BESSANT, Rev. Canon Simon David; Diocesan Director for Mission, Diocese of Blackburn, since 1998; *b* 16 Feb. 1956; *s* of Ernest and Joan Bessant; *m* 1978, Ruth Margaret Hadfield; three *d*. *Educ:* Sheffield Univ. (BMus 1977; MA 2000); Nottingham Univ. (DipTh 1979). Ordained deacon, 1981, priest, 1982; Curate, St John and St James, Liverpool, 1981–84; Vicar: Emmanuel Ch, Holloway, 1984–91; Ch of the Redeemer, Blackburn, 1991–98; RD, Blackburn, 1997–98. Member: Gen. Synod of C of E, 2001–; Archbishops' Council, 2006–. Hon. Canon, Blackburn Cathedral, 2006–. *Recreations:* listening to Schoenberg, reading counterfactuals, experimental fish cookery. *Address:* 1 Swallowfields, Blackburn BB1 8NR. *T:* and *Fax:* (01254) 580176; *e-mail:* simon.bessant@dsl.pipex.com.

BESSBOROUGH, 12th Earl of, cr 1739 (Ire.); **Myles Fitzhugh Longfield Ponsonby;** Baron Bessborough (Ire.) 1721; Viscount Duncannon (Ire.) 1722; Baron Ponsonby (GB) 1749; Baron Duncannon (UK) 1834; *b* 16 Feb. 1941; *e s* of 11th Earl of Bessborough and his 1st wife, Patricia, *d* of Col Fitzhugh Minnigerode; *S* father, 2002; *m* 1972, Alison, *d* of William Storey, OBE; two *s* one *d*. *Heir: s* Viscount Duncannon, *qv*. *Address:* Broadreed, Stansted Park, Rowlands Castle, Hants PO9 6DZ.

BESSER, Prof. (Gordon) Michael, MD, DSc; FRCP, FMedSci; Consultant Endocrinologist, The London Clinic Centre for Endocrinology, since 2001; Professor of Medicine and Head of Department of Endocrinology and the Medical Professorial Unit, St Bartholomew's and the Royal London School of Medicine and Dentistry, Queen Mary and Westfield College (formerly St Bartholomew's Hospital Medical College), London

University, at St Bartholomew's Hospital, 1992–2001, and at Royal London Hospital, 1994–2001, now Professor Emeritus, Queen Mary, University of London; Consultant and Lead Clinician, Department of Endocrinology, Bart's and the London (formerly Royal Hospitals) NHS Trust, 1994–2001, now Hon. Consultant Physician; *b* 22 Jan. 1936; *s* of Hyman Besser and Leah Besser (*née* Geller); *m* 1972; one *s* one *d*. *Educ:* Hove County Grammar Sch.; Bart's Med. Coll., Univ. of London (BSc, MB BS, MD, DSc). FRCP 1973. St Bartholomew's Hospital: Lectr in Medicine, 1966–70; Sen. Lectr and Hon. Consultant Physician, 1970–74; Prof. of Endocrinology, Med. Coll., 1974–92; Consultant and Physician i/c Dept of Endocrinology, 1974–2001; Dir of Medicine, 1989–93; Chief Exec., 1992–94. Consultant Endocrinologist to RN, 1989–2001. Vis. Prof., univs and med. estabts in Australasia, Canada, China, Hong Kong, Italy, Malta, S Africa, USA, Yugoslavia. Cttee work for RCP, RSocMed, Soc. for Endocrinology, Jt Cttee on Higher Med. Training; Medical Research Council: former Mem., Physiol. Systems Bd and Grants Cttee (Chm., 1984–86); Chm., Working Party on Hormone Replacement Therapy, 1992–95. Royal College of Physicians: Lectr, 1974, 1993, 1999; Censor, 1990–92; Sen. Vice-Pres. and Sen. Censor, 1995–97; Chm. Clinical Examng Bd, MRCP (UK), 1999–2003. Founder FMedSci 1998. Hon. MD Turin, 1985. Mem. Editl Bd, Clinics in Endocrinology and Metabolism, 1977–92; former Mem. Editl Bd, Jl of Endocrinol., Neuroendocrinol., and Clinical Endocrinol. Trustee: Barts Foundn for Res., 1985–; Barlow Collection of Chinese Ceramics, Univ. of Sussex, 2004–; William Harvey Res. Foundn, 2005–. *Publications:* Fundamentals of Clinical Endocrinology (with R. Hall and J. Anderson), 2nd edn 1978, 3rd edn 1980, (ed with R. Hall) 4th edn 1989; Clinical Neuroendocrinology, 1977; Recent Advances in Medicine, 3 edns, 1981–87; (ed jtly) Endocrinology, 2nd edn 1989, 3rd edn 1994; Clinical Endocrinology, 1986, 3rd edn 2002; Clinical Diabetes, 1988; contribs to learned jls. *Recreations:* early Chinese ceramics, modern European art, opera, ballet, theatre, keeping fit. *Address:* The London Clinic Centre for Endocrinology, 145 Harley Street, W1G 6SL. *Club:* Garrick.

BEST, family name of **Barons Best** and **Wynford**.

BEST, Baron *cr* 2001 (Life Peer), of Godmanstone in the County of Dorset; **Richard Stuart Best,** OBE 1988; President, Local Government Association, since 2005; *b* 22 June 1945; *s* of Walter Stuart Best, DL, JP and Frances Mary Chignell; *m* 1st, 1970, Ima Akpan (marr. diss. 1976); one *s* one *d*; 2nd, 1978, Belinda Janie Tremayne Stemp; one *s* one *d*. *Educ:* Shrewsbury School; University of Nottingham (BA). British Churches Housing Trust, 1968–73 (Dir, 1971–73); Director: Nat. Fedn of Housing Assocs, 1973–88; Joseph Rowntree Foundn, 1988–2006. Chairman: Hanover Housing Assoc., 2006–; Hull Partnership Liaison Bd, 2002–; Westminster Housing Commn, 2004–05; The Giving Forum, 2005–; Sec., Duke of Edinburgh's Inquiry into British Housing, 1984–91. Chm., UK Nat. Council for UN City Summit, 1995–96. Trustee: Sutton Housing Trust, 1971–84 (Dep. Chm., 1983–84); Internat. Year of Shelter for the Homeless 1987 Trust; RSA, 2006–; Committee Member: UK Housing Trust, 1976–88; Sutton Hastoe Housing Assoc., 1982–2000. Chm., H of L Audit Cttee, 2005–. Member: Social Policy Cttee, C of E Bd for Social Responsibility, 1986–91; BBC/IBA Central Appeals Cttee, 1989–91; Cttee, Assoc. of Charitable Foundns, 1989–92; Council for Charitable Support, 1995–2005; Housing Minister's Sounding Bd, DETR, 1999–2001; DTI Foresight Panel on Built Envmt, 1999–2001; Minister for Local Govt's Sounding Bd, DTLR/ODPM, 2001–05; NCVO Adv. Council, 2001–; Commn on Future of Birmingham's Council Housing, 2002; Comr, Rural Develt Commn, 1989–98. Mem. Council, Ombudsman for Estate Agents, 2007–. Vice Pres., TCPA, 2007–. Pres., Continuing Care Conf., 2002–. Patron: Nat. Family and Parenting Inst., 2001–; Housing Assocs Charitable Trust, 2007–; Vice-Patron, Servite Houses, 2001–. *Publications:* Rural Housing: problems and solutions, 1981; Housing Associations 1890–1990, 1991; Housing After 2000 AD, 1992; The Inclusive Homes of the Future, 1999. *Address:* House of Lords, SW1A 0PW. *Club:* Travellers.

See also J. L. S. Best.

BEST, Dr Anthony; Chief Executive, Sense, 2001–08; *b* 1 June 1947. *Educ:* Univ. of Leeds (Teacher's Cert.); Univ. of Newcastle upon Tyne (Dip. Special Ed.); Univ. of Birmingham (MEd; PhD 1993). Lectr in Special Educn, Univ. of Birmingham, 1978–90; Educn Develt Consultant, Hilton Perkins, USA, 1990–93; Principal, RNIB, 1993–2001. *Publications:* Steps to Independence, 1987; Teaching Children with Visual Impairment, 1992; The Management of Visually Impaired Children, 1993.

BEST, David William; Chairman, MMI Group plc, 1996–2008 (Chief Executive, 1995–96); *b* 1 Dec. 1949; *s* of William Robertson Best and Frances Best; *m* 1972, Margaret Smart Mitchell; one *s* one *d*. *Educ:* North Manchester Grammar Sch.; Univ. of Edinburgh. Mgt posts in pharmaceutical industry, 1973–88; Co-Founder, and Man. Dir, Medical Marketing Internat. Ltd (first private sector technology mgt co. in Europe), 1988–96; Founder and CEO, Bioscience Innovation Centre plc, 1996–; Chairman: BioStarter Initiative, 2001–; Oncosense Ltd, 2003–; Viratis Ltd, 2003–; Genvax Ltd, 2004–; Founder, Bioscience Venture Capital Trust plc, 2001. Mem., AIM Adv. Panel, London Stock Exchange, 2002–. Gold Friend, Duke of Edinburgh's Internat. Award, 2000–; Mem., Internat. Fundraising Cttee, British Red Cross, 2001–. Founder Mem., Global Scots, 2003. Ambassador, Med. Emergency Relief Internat., 2002–. *Recreations:* running, alpine climbing.

BEST, Dr Geoffrey Francis Andrew, FBA 2003; Member, St Antony's College, Oxford (Senior Associate Member, 1988–2004); *b* 20 Nov. 1928; *s* of Frederick Ebenezer Best and Catherine Sarah Vanderbrook (*née* Bultz); *m* 1955, Gwenllyan Marigold Davies; two *s* one *d*. *Educ:* St Paul's Sch.; Trinity Coll., Cambridge (MA, PhD). Army (RAEC), 1946–47; Choate Fellow, Harvard Univ., 1954–55; Fellow of Trinity Hall and Asst Lectr, Cambridge Univ., 1955–61; Lectr, Edinburgh Univ., 1961–66; Sir Richard Lodge Prof. of History, Edinburgh Univ., 1966–74; Prof. of History, Sch. of European Studies, 1974–85 (Hon. Prof., 1982–85), Dean, 1980–82, Univ. of Sussex; Academic Visitor, Dept of Internat. Relations, LSE, 1985–88. Visiting Professor: Chicago Univ., 1964; York Univ., Toronto, 1968; Visiting Fellow: All Souls Coll., Oxford, 1969–70; LSE, 1983–85; ANU, 1984; Fellow, Woodrow Wilson Internat. Center, Washington, DC, 1978–79. Lees Knowles Lectr, Cambridge, 1970; Joanne Goodman Lectr, Univ. of Western Ontario, 1981; Cyril Foster Lectr, Univ. of Oxford, 1999. Mem. Council, British Red Cross Soc., 1981–84, Hon. Consultant, 1985–91. Emery Reves Award, Churchill Centre, Washington, 2002. Editor, Cambridge Review, 1953–54; Jt Editor, Victorian Studies, 1958–68; Editor, War and Society Newsletter, 1973–82. Paul Reuter Prize, ICRC, 1997. *Publications:* Temporal Pillars, 1964; Shaftesbury, 1964; Bishop Westcott and the Miners, 1968; Mid-Victorian Britain, 1971; (ed) Church's Oxford Movement, 1971; (jt ed) War, Economy and the Military Mind, 1976; Humanity in Warfare, 1980; War and Society in Revolutionary Europe, 1982; Honour Among Men and Nations, 1982; Nuremberg and After: the continuing history of war crimes and crimes against humanity, 1984; (ed jtly) History, Society and the Churches, 1985; (ed) The Permanent Revolution: the French Revolution and its legacy, 1789–1989, 1988; War and Law since 1945, 1994; Churchill: a study in greatness, 2001; Churchill and War, 2005; contrib. various jls. *Address:* 19 Buckingham Street, Oxford OX1 4LH.

BEST, Harold; *b* 18 Dec. 1937; *s* of Fred and Marie Patricia Best; *m* 1960, Mary Glyn; two *s* two *d*. *Educ:* Meanwood County Sch.; Leeds Coll. of Technol. Electrical technician; worked for Co-op. Movt, in electrical contracting industry, and in educn (technical support). MP (Lab) Leeds North West, 1997–2005. *Address:* 19 Wynmore Avenue, Bramhope, Leeds LS16 9DD.

BEST, James Leigh Stuart; Director, DDB Worldwide, since 1991 (Chief Strategy and People Officer, 2002–07); *b* 1 April 1954; *s* of Walter Stuart Best, DL, JP and Frances Mary Best (*née* Chignell); *m* 1979, Priscilla Mary Rose McNeile; two *s* one *d*. *Educ:* Shrewsbury Sch.; New Coll., Oxford (BA, MA). Dir, Boase Massimi Pollitt plc, 1985–89; Chm., BMP DDB, 1989–2000; Gp Chm., DDB UK, 2000–05. Non-exec. Dir, Sustainable Forestry Mgt Ltd, 2007–. Chm., UK Advertising Assoc., 1997–2002; Mem. Council, ASA, 2007–. Pres., Eur. Assoc. Communications Agencies, 2003–05. FIPA 1996; FRSA 2007. *Publications:* (ed) Scottish Advertising Works, vol. 3 2003, vol. 4 2005. *Recreations:* countryside, wildlife, travelling, scuba. *Address:* Manor Farm House, Godmanstone, Dorset DT2 7AQ.

See also Baron Best.

BEST, Keith (Lander), TD; Chief Executive, Immigration Advisory Service, since 1993; *b* 10 June 1949; *s* of late Peter Edwin Wilson Best and Margaret Louisa Best; *m* 1990, Elizabeth Margaret Gibson; two *d*. *Educ:* Brighton Coll.; Keble Coll., Oxford (BA (Hons) Jurisprudence; MA). Assistant Master, Summerfields Sch., Oxford, 1967; called to the Bar, Inner Temple, 1971; Lectr in Law, 1973. Served: 289 Parachute Battery, RHA (V), 1970–76; with RM on HMS Bulwark, 1976; Naval Gunfire Liaison Officer with Commando Forces (Major). Councillor, Brighton Borough Council (Chm. Lands Cttee, Housing Cttee), 1976–80. Dir, Prisoners Abroad, 1989–93. MP (C): Anglesey, 1979–83; Ynys Môn, 1983–87. PPS to Sec. of State for Wales, 1981–84. Former Chm., All Party Alcohol Policy and Services Gp; former Mem., Select Cttee on Welsh Affairs. Chairman: Bow Gp Defence Cttee; British Cttee for Vietnamese Refugees; Internat. Council of Parliamentarians' Global Action; World Federalist Movement, 1987–; Conservative Action for Electoral Reform, 1992–; Vauxhall Conservative Assoc., 1997–99; Electronic Immigration Network, 1998–; Electoral Reform Soc., 1998–2003 (Mem. Council, 1996–; Chm., Mgt Cttee, 1997–2003); Assoc. of Regulated Immigration Advrs, 2003–; Chm., Electoral Reform Internat. Services, 2007– (Dir, 2004–). Member: Conservative Gtr London Area Exec. Cttee, 1997–99; UN Disarmament Cttee; Young Conservative Nat. Adv. Cttee, 1978. Mem. Cttee, Assoc. of Lloyd's Mems. Pres., Holyhead Leisure Fest. Ltd, 1981–. Trustee, Cranstoun Drug Services (formerly Odyssey Trust), 2003–. Founder Member: Two Piers Housing Co-operative, 1977; Brighton Housing Trust, 1976; school manager, Downs County First Sch. and Downs Middle Sch., 1976. *Publications:* Write Your Own Will, 1978 (paperback); The Right Way to Prove a Will, 1980 (paperback); contrib. District Councils Rev. *Recreations:* parachuting, walking, photography, travel. *Address:* 15 St Stephen's Terrace, SW8 1DJ; 7 Alderley Terrace, Holyhead, Anglesey LL65 1NL. *Clubs:* New Cavendish; Royal Artillery Mess (Woolwich); Holyhead Conservative.

BEST, Matthew Robert; Founder/Musical Director, Corydon Singers, since 1973, Corydon Orchestra, since 1991, Artistic Director, since 1996; *b* 6 Feb. 1957; *s* of late Peter Best and of Isabel Mary Best; *m* 1983, Rosalind Sandra Mayes; one *s* one *d*. *Educ:* Sevenoaks Sch.; King's Coll., Cambridge (Choral Schol.; MA Hons Music). Singer: Nat. Opera Studio, 1979–80; Principal bass, Royal Opera, 1980–86; Guest Artist, Royal Opera, Opera North, WNO, ENO, Scottish Opera, Netherlands Opera, Florida Grand Opera, Théâtre du Châtelet (Paris), Opéra de Nancy, Staatstheater Stuttgart, Théâtre de la Monnaie, Brussels, Opéra de Lyon, Santa Fé Opera, and others, 1982–; principal operatic rôles incl. Flying Dutchman, Scarpia, Pizarro, Wotan (complete Ring Cycle, Edinburgh Internat. Fest., 2003), Amfortas, Kurwenal, Orest, Jochanaan; has performed in concerts worldwide and at major European and American fests. Conductor: concert appearances at fests throughout UK and Europe, at South Bank and BBC Promenade concerts; Prin. Conductor, The Hanover Band, 1998–99; Guest Conductor with English Chamber Orch., London Mozart Players, City of London Sinfonia, Royal Seville SO, English Northern Philharmonia, New Queen's Hall Orch., Manchester Camerata, RTE Concert Orch., Northern Sinfonia and BBC Nat. Orch. of Wales; has made numerous recordings of choral/orchestral music and opera. *Recreations:* reading, hill-walking. *Address:* c/o Intermusica Artists' Management Ltd, 16 Duncan Terrace, N1 8BZ. *T:* (020) 7278 5455.

BEST, Sir Richard (Radford), KCVO 1990; CBE 1989 (MBE 1977); HM Diplomatic Service, retired; *b* 28 July 1933; *s* of Charles and Frances Best (*née* Raymond); *m* 1st, 1957, Elizabeth Vera Wait (*d* 1968); two *d*; 2nd, 1969, Mary Hill (*née* Wait); one *s*. *Educ:* Worthing High Sch.; University Coll. London (BA Hons). Home Office, 1957–66; HM Diplomatic Service, 1966–91: CO (formerly CRO), 1966–68; Lusaka, 1969–72; Stockholm, 1972–76; FCO, 1976–79; New Delhi, 1979–83; FCO, 1983–84; Dep. High Comr, Kaduna, 1984–88; Ambassador to Iceland, 1989–91; FCO, 1991. Mem., Patching Parish Council, 1993–2007. Chm., Friends of Clapham and Patching Churches, 1996–2006. BBC 'Brain of Britain', 1966. Life Mem., Kaduna Br., Nigeria-Britain Assoc. Grand Cross, Order of Icelandic Falcon, 1990. *Recreation:* gardening. *Address:* Holly Howe, The Street, Patching, near Worthing, West Sussex BN13 3XF.

BEST-SHAW, Sir John (Michael Robert), 10th Bt *cr* 1665; retired; *b* 28 Sept. 1924; *s* of Sir John James Kenward Best-Shaw, 9th Bt, Commander RN, and Elizabeth Mary Theodora (*d* 1986), *e d* of Sir Robert Hughes, 12th Bt; *S* father, 1984; *m* 1960, Jane Gordon, *d* of A. G. Guthrie; two *s* one *d* (and one *s* decd). *Educ:* Lancing; Hertford Coll., Oxford (MA); Avery Hill Coll., London (Teachers' Cert.). Captain Royal West Kent Regt, 1943–47. Royal Fedn of Malaya Police, 1950–58; church work, 1958–71; teaching, 1972–82. *Recreations:* bridge, writing. *Heir:* *s* Thomas Joshua Best-Shaw [*b* 7 March 1965; *m* 1992, Emily Susan, *d* of Vivian Rubin; two *s*]. *Address:* Belmont, 104 High Street, West Malling, Kent ME19 6NE. *T:* (01732) 843823. *Club:* Commonwealth.

BESTERMAN, Tristram Paul; consultant, museums and cultural studies; *b* 19 Sept. 1949; *s* of late Dr Edwin Melville Mack Besterman and of Audrey (*née* Heald); *m* 1977, Perry Garceau; two *s* one *d*. *Educ:* Stowe Sch.; Trinity Coll., Cambridge (BA 1971, MA 1979). FGS 1978; AMA 1979, FMA 1986. Studio Manager, BBC, 1971–73; Preparator's Asst, Geological and Mining Mus., Sydney, NSW, 1974; jackaroo, cattle station, Qld, 1974; Educn Asst, Sheffield City Museums, 1974–78; Dep. Curator and Keeper of Geology, Warwickshire Museums, 1978–85; City Curator, Plymouth City Museums and Art Gall., 1985–93; Dir, Manchester Mus., 1994–2005. Chm., Ethics Cttee, Museums Assoc., 1994–2001; Mem., Ministerial Working Gp on Human Remains, 2001–03. FRSA 2001. *Publications:* contribs to museological literature. *Recreations:* music, sampling antipodean wines and culture. *Address:* Hollywell House, Lodge Hill, Liskeard, Cornwall PL14 4EH. *T:* (01579) 349146.

BETHEL, Dr Keva Marie, CMG 1995; President, College of the Bahamas, 1995–98, President Emerita, 2005; *b* 18 Aug. 1935; *d* of late Sidney Alexander Eldon and Rowena Beatrice Eldon (*née* Hill); *m* 1962, E. Clement Bethel (*d* 1987); one *s* one *d*. *Educ:* Girton

Coll., Cambridge (BA, MA); Univ. of Alberta (PhD 1981). Government High School, Nassau, Bahamas: Asst Mistress, Spanish and French, 1959–66; Head, Mod. Langs Dept, 1966–72; Dep. Headmistress, 1972–75; College of the Bahamas: Chm., Div. of Humanities, 1975–77; Dean, Acad. Affairs, 1977–78; Vice Principal, 1979–81; Actg Principal, Jan.–June 1982; Principal, 1982–95. Hon. LLD Univ. of W Indies, 1998. *Publications:* (contrib.) Handbook of World Education, ed Walter Wickremasinghe, 1991; (contrib.) Educational Reform in the Commonwealth Caribbean, ed Errol Miller, 1999; (contrib.) Bahamas: independence and beyond, ed W K. Jones and D. G. Saunders, 2003. *Recreations:* reading, music. *Address:* PO Box N1232, Nassau, New Providence, Bahamas.

BETHEL, Martin; QC 1983; a Recorder of the Crown Court, since 1979; *b* 12 March 1943; *o s* of late Rev. Ralph Bethel and Enid Bethel; *m* 1974, Kathryn Denby; two *s* one *d.* *Educ:* Kingswood Sch.; Fitzwilliam Coll., Cambridge (MA, LLM). Called to the Bar, Inner Temple, 1965; North-Eastern Circuit (Circuit Junior, 1969); a Dep. High Court Judge, 1995–. Member: Criminal Injuries Compensation Bd, 1999–2000; Criminal Injuries Compensation Appeals Panel, 2000–. Governor, Ashville Coll., Harrogate, 1989–2001. Pres., Runswick Bay Rescue Boat, 2001–04. *Recreations:* family, boating, ski-ing, golf. *Address:* (chambers) St Pauls Chambers, 23 Park Square, Leeds LS1 2ND. *T:* (0113) 245 5866.

BETHELL, family name of **Barons Bethell** and **Westbury**.

BETHELL, 5th Baron *cr* 1922, of Romford, co. Essex; **James Nicholas Bethell;** Bt 1911; Managing Partner, Portland, since 2006; *b* 1 Oct. 1967; *e s* of 4th Baron Bethell and Cecilia Lothian Bethell (*née* Honeyman); *S* father, 2007; *m* 2004, Melissa, *d* of Douglas Wong, Newport Beach, Calif; one *s.* *Educ:* Harrow; Edinburgh Univ. (MA Hons History). Legislative aide, Office of Sec. of State, US Senate, 1985; Stagière, DG IV, EC, 1989; reporter, Sunday Times, 1990–93; correspondent, The Independent, 1993–94; Ministry of Sound, 1995–2001 (latterly Man. Dir); Capital Radio plc, 2001–05. Contested (C) Tooting, 2005. *Publications:* (ed) A Pub Guide to Edinburgh, 1989; (jtly) Blue Skies Ahead, 1997. *Recreations:* mountaineering, backgammon. *Heir:* *s* Hon. Jacob Nicholas Douglas Bethell, *b* 17 Oct. 2006. *Address:* 32 Bark Place, W2 4AT. *T:* (020) 7229 1850. *Club:* Soho House.

BETHELL, Prof. Leslie Michael; Director, Centre for Brazilian Studies, University of Oxford, 1997–2007; Fellow, St Antony's College, Oxford, 1997–2007, now Emeritus; *b* 12 Feb. 1937; *s* of late Stanley Bethell and Bessie Bethell (*née* Stoddart); *m* 1961 (marr. diss. 1983); two *s.* *Educ:* Cockburn High Sch., Leeds; University Coll. London (BA, PhD). Lectr in History, Univ. of Bristol, 1961–66; Lectr 1966–74, Reader 1974–86, in Hispanic Amer. and Brazilian History, UCL; Prof. of Latin Amer. Hist., 1986–92, now Emeritus, and Dir, Inst. of Latin Amer. Studies, 1987–92, London Univ.; Sen. Res. Fellow, St Antony's Coll., Oxford, 1993–97. Visiting Professor: Instituto Universitario de Pesquisas do Rio de Janeiro, 1979; Univ. of California at San Diego, 1985; Woodrow Wilson Internat. Center for Scholars, Washington, 1986, 1996–97 and 2008–March 2009; Univ. of Chicago, 1992–93; Centro de Pesquisa e Documentação de História, Fundação Getúlio Vargas, Rio de Janeiro, 2008–. Grand Officer, Nat. Order of the Southern Cross (Brazil), 1999 (Comdr, 1994). *Publications:* The Abolition of the Brazilian Slave Trade, 1970; (ed) The Cambridge History of Latin America: vols I and II, Colonial Latin America, 1984; vol. III, From Independence to *c* 1870, 1985; vols IV and V, From *c* 1870 to 1930, 1986; vol. VII, Mexico, Central America and the Caribbean since 1930, 1990; vol. VIII, Spanish South America since 1930, 1991; vol. VI, Economy, Society and Politics since 1930, Part 1, Economy and Society, Part 2, Politics and Society, 1994; vol XI, Bibliographical Essays, 1995; vol. X, Ideas, Culture and Society since 1930, 1995; vol. IX, Brazil since 1930, 2008; (jtly) Latin America between the Second World War and the Cold War 1944–48, 1992; (jtly) A Guerra do Paraguai, 1995; (ed) Brasil. Fardo do Passado, Promesa do Futuro: dez ensaios sobre politíca e sociedade brasileira, 2002; Brazil by British and Irish authors, 2003; (jtly) Joaquim Nabuco e os abolicionistas ingleses, 2008; articles and chapters on Latin American history, Brazilian history and politics, Britain and Latin America. *Address:* Rua Paul Redfern 24/301, Rio de Janeiro 22410–080, Brazil. *T:* (21) 25123467; (mobile) (21) 92855955; c/o St Antony's College, Oxford OX2 6JF.

BETT, Sir Michael, Kt 1995; CBE 1990; MA; Chairman, National Security Inspectorate, 2000–07; First Civil Service Commissioner, 1995–2000; *b* 18 Jan. 1935; *s* of Arthur Bett, OBE and Nina Daniells; *m* 1959, Christine Angela Reid; one *s* two *d.* *Educ:* Aldenham Sch.; Pembroke Coll., Cambridge (Hon. Fellow, 2004). Dir, Industrial Relations, Engrg Employers' Fedn, 1970–72; Personnel Dir, General Electric Co. Ltd, 1972–77; Dir of Personnel, BBC, 1977–81; British Telecom: Bd Mem. for Personnel, 1981–84; Corporate Dir, Personnel and Corporate Services, 1984–85; Man. Dir Local (Inland) Communications Services, 1985–87; Man. Dir, UK Communications, 1987–88; Man. Dir, British Telecom UK, 1988–91; Vice-Chm., 1990–91; Dep. Chm., 1991–94; non-exec. Dir, 1994–96. Chairman: Cellnet, 1991–99; Workhouse Ltd, 1992–95; J2C plc, 2000–02; Pace Micro Technology Plc, 2000–06; Director: Compel Gp plc, 1993–2005 (Chm., 2000–05); KMG Financial Services, 1994–99; Eyretel plc, 1996–2003; non-exec. Dir, Ordnance Survey, 2002–06. Chairman: Nurses Pay Rev. Body, 1990–95; Social Security Adv. Cttee, 1993–95; Armed Forces Indep. Review on Manpower, 1994–95; Nat. Council, TEC, 1994–95; Inspectorate of the Security Industry, 1994–2000; Pensions Protection and Investment Accreditation Bd, 2000–06; Indep. Review of Pay and Conditions of Service in Higher Educn; Co Chm., British N Amer. Cttee, 1997–99; Member: Pay Bd, 1973–74; Training Levy Exemption Referee, 1975–82; Civil Service Arbitration Tribunal, 1977–83; Cttee of Inquiry into UK Prison Services, 1978–79; Cttee of Inquiry into Water Service Dispute, 1983; NHS Management Inquiry, 1983; Armed Forces Pay Review Body, 1983–87; Civil Service Coll. Adv. Council, 1983–88; Trng Commn (formerly MSC), 1985–89. Member Council: St Christopher's Hospice, 1993–99; Royal Hosp. for Neurodisability, 1996–2005 (Chm., 1998–2005); Cranfield Inst. of Technology, 1982–87; Vice-Pres., Roffey Park Mgt Inst., 1999–; Chancellor, Aston Univ., 2004– (Pro-Chancellor, 1993–2003). Chairman: Bromley CABx, 1985–93; SCF, 1992–98. Chm. of Govs, Cranbrook Sch., 1992–2000. Dir, English Shakespeare Co., 1988–95; Chairman: One World Broadcasting Trust, 1996–2002; English Shakespeare Internat., 1997–2000. Chm., Sevenoaks Volunteer Develt Agency, 2005–07. CCIPD (Pres., 1992–98); CCMI; FRSA. Hon. Col, 81 Signal Sqn (Vols), RCS, 1990–96. DBA (*hc*): IMCB, 1986; CNAA/Liverpool Poly., 1991; Hon. DSc Aston, 1996. *Recreations:* television and radio, theatre, music, cooking, gardening. *Address:* Colets Well, The Green, Otford, Kent TN14 5PD.

BETTISON, Sir Norman (George), Kt 2006; QPM 2000; Chief Constable, West Yorkshire Police, since 2007; *b* 3 Jan. 1956; *s* of George and Betty Bettison; *m* 2004, Gillian. *Educ:* Queen's Coll., Oxford (MA Psychol. and Philosophy); Sheffield Hallam Univ. (MBA). Police officer, 1972–2004: S Yorks Police, 1972–93; W Yorks Police, 1993–98; Chief Constable, Merseyside Police, 1998–2004; Chief Exec., Centrex (nat. trng body to Police Service), 2004–06. Hon. Fellow, John Moores Univ., 2004. Independence Medal (Rhodesia), 1980. *Address:* West Yorkshire Police HQ, PO Box 9, Wakefield WF1 3QP. *T:* (01924) 292002.

BETTLEY-SMITH, Robert, FRICS; Chief Executive, Government Decontamination Service, Department for Environment, Food and Rural Affairs, since 2005; *b* 27 July 1953; *s* of late Dr Neville Smith and Joyce Bettley; *m* 1980, Judith, (Judy), Patricia Naylor, MA (Cantab); two *s* one *d.* *Educ:* Royal Wolverhampton Sch.; Royal Agricl Coll., Cirencester (Prizeman); Queens' Coll., Cambridge. Surveyor, 1980–83, Sen. Surveyor, 1983–85, ADAS; Principal, 1985–91, Regl Dir, 1992–98, MAFF; Chief Exec., FWAG (on secondment), 1998–2002; Dir, Project Team, DEFRA, 2003–05. Director: Mercian Mktg Ltd, 1997–2002; Peak Produce Ltd, 2001–05; Camley Estates Ltd, 2002–. Chm., Betley PC, 2007– (Vice Chm., 2005–07). Mem., British Pottery Manufrs Fedn Club, 1995–. FCMI. *Publications:* Capital Investment by Landowners 1972–1977; contribs to RASE Jl, Chartered Surveyor, NBC International and other professional jls. *Recreations:* Christian faith, village activities, Association Football (referee and spectator), our narrow boat, fruit growing, ski-ing, steam engines. *Address:* MoD Stafford, Beaconside, Stafford ST18 0AQ. *T:* (01785) 216333, *Fax:* (01785) 216363; *e-mail:* gds@defra.gsi.gov.uk. *Club:* Farmers.

BETTRIDGE, Brig. John Bryan, CBE 1983; Principal, Emergency Planning College (formerly Civil Defence College), 1984–93; *b* 16 Aug. 1932; *s* of Henry George Bettridge and Dorothy Bettridge; *m* 1959, one *s* one *d.* *Educ:* Eastbourne Grammar School. Commissioned RA, 1951; regimental duty, 4 RHA and 52 Locating Regt, 1952–59; Instructor, RMA Sandhurst, 1959–61; Student, Staff Coll., Camberley, 1962; War Office, 1964–66; Bty Comd, 1 RHA, 1968–70; Comd, 3 RHA, 1973–75, Hong Kong; Chief Instructor, Tactics, RSA, 1976; Comd RA 2 Div., 1977–78; RCDS 1979; Dep. Comdt, Staff Coll., 1980–82; Comdt, RSA Larkhill, 1983–84. *Recreations:* golf, carpentry. *Address:* Cherry Garth, Main Street, Bishopthorpe, York YO23 2RB. *T:* (01904) 704270.

BETTS, Charles Valentine, CB 1998; FREng, FRINA; Director General Submarines, and Deputy Controller of the Navy, Ministry of Defence, 1994–98; Head, Royal Corps of Naval Constructors, 1992–98; *b* 10 Jan. 1942; *s* of Harold Blair Betts and late Mary Ellis Betts (*née* France); *m* 1965, Rev. Patricia Joyce Bennett; two *s.* *Educ:* St Catharine's Coll., Cambridge (BA Hons, MA Mech. Scis); Royal Naval Coll., Greenwich (Prof. Cert., Naval Arch.); Univ. of London (MPhil Naval Arch.). CEng; FREng (FEng 1991). Asst Constructor, MoD, 1966–71; Lectr in Naval Arch., UCL, 1971–74; Constructor, HM Dockyard, Portsmouth, 1974–77; Constructor and Chief Constructor, MoD, Bath, 1977–83; Chief Constructor, MoD, London, 1983–85; Prof. of Naval Arch., UCL, 1985–89; Dir, Surface Ships B, MoD, Bath, 1989–92; Dir Gen., Surface Ships, MoD, 1992–94. Director (non-executive): BMT Group Ltd, 1999–2001; BMT Reliability Consultants Ltd, 2000–01; BMT Gp Ltd (formerly British Maritime Technology Ltd, later BMT Ltd), 2001–. Mem., Nat. Historic Ships Cttee, 2000–06. Mem. Council, RINA, 1985–2002, 2003– (Vice-Pres., 2003–). Trustee: Alpha Internat. Ministries, 1993–2001; The Coverdale Trust, 2001–04 (Vice-Chm.); BMT Gp Employee Benefit Trust, 2006–; Chm. Trustees, BMT Pension and Life Assurance Scheme, 2006–. Mem. Court, Univ. of Bath, 2007–. FRSA. *Publications:* (jtly) The Marine Technology Reference Book, 1990; papers in professional jls. *Recreations:* supporting my wife in her rôle as Church of England priest, cruising together under sail, listening to music. *Clubs:* Royal Naval Sailing Association; Royal Victoria Yacht (IoW).

BETTS, Clive James Charles; MP (Lab) Sheffield Attercliffe, since 1992; *b* 13 Jan. 1950; *s* of late Harold and Nellie Betts. *Educ:* Longley Sch., Sheffield; King Edward VII Sch., Sheffield; Pembroke Coll., Cambridge (BA Econ). Sheffield City Council: Councillor (Lab), 1976–92; Chm., Housing Cttee, 1980–86; Chm., Finance Cttee, 1986–88; Dep. Leader, 1986–87; Leader, 1987–92. Chm., S Yorks Pension Authority, 1989–92; Dep. Chm., AMA, 1988–91 (Chm., Housing Cttee, 1985–89). An Asst Government Whip, 1997–98; a Lord Comr of HM Treasury (Govt Whip), 1998–2001. Member, Select Committee on: HM Treasury, 1995–96; Selection, 1997–2001; Transport, Local Govt and the Regions, 2001–02; DCLG (formerly ODPM), 2002–; Finance and Services, 2005–. Member: Parly Contributory Pension Fund, 2005–; H of C Members' Fund, 2005–. Chm., 1995–96, Sec., 1995–97, Labour's Treasury Deptl Cttee; Labour Ldr's Campaign Team, 1995–96. *Recreations:* Sheffield Wednesday FC, football, squash, walking, real ale. *Address:* House of Commons, SW1A 0AA.

BETTS, Jane Margaret; *see* Mordue, J. M.

BETTS, Lily Edna Minerva, (Mrs John Betts); *see* Mackie, L. E. M.

BETTS, Peter George; Director, Fire and Resilience, Department for Communities and Local Government, since 2006; *b* 3 March 1959; *s* of George Frank Betts and Joyce Ann Betts (*née* Pedder); *m* 2006, Fiona Jane MacGregor. *Educ:* Emanuel Sch., Battersea; Mansfield Coll., Oxford (BA Hist. 1982); Ecole Nationale d'Administration, Paris. Joined Civil Service, 1984; First Sec. (Envmt), Office of UK Permt Rep. to EU, Brussels, 1994–98; Head: Global Atmosphere Div., DETR, 1998–2001; Work and Pensions Team, 2001–02, Pension and Savings Team, 2002–04, HM Treasury; Principal Private Sec. to Dep. Prime Minister, ODPM, 2004–05; Dir, Regl Policy, ODPM, subseq. DCLG, 2005–06. *Address:* Department for Communities and Local Government, Eland House, Bressenden Place, SW1E 5DU; *e-mail:* peter.betts@communities.gsi.gov.uk.

BEVAN, Anthony Richard Van, RA 2007; artist (painter); *b* Bradford, 22 July 1951; *s* of Adrian Van Christkarken Bevan and Margaret Betty Bevan (*née* Pemberton); *m* 1991, Glenys Johnson; one *d.* *Educ:* Bradford Sch. of Art; Goldsmith's Coll., London (DipAD); Slade Sch. of Fine Art (HDFA). *Solo exhibitions*: Tony Bevan: Paintings 1980–87, ICA, London, Orchard Gall., Derby, Kettle's Yard, Cambridge and Cartwright Hall, Bradford, 1987–88; Haus der Kunst, Munich, 1989; Whitechapel Art Gall., 1993; (retrospective) Inst. Valencia d'Art Modern, Valencia, 2005–06. *Relevant publication*: Tony Bevan, 2006. *Recreations:* food and wine. *Address:* 20 Blackheath Park, Blackheath, SE3 9RP. *T:* (020) 8852 0250, *Fax:* (020) 8469 0856; *e-mail:* glenys.johnson@btconnect.com.

BEVAN, Dianne; Deputy Clerk, since 2003, and Chief Operating Officer, since 2007, National Assembly for Wales; *b* 31 Oct. 1958; *d* of Alan and Brenda Roe; *m* 1986, Nigel Bevan; one *s* one *d.* *Educ:* Selby Grammar Sch., N Yorks; Univ. of Hull (LLB Hons); Chester Coll. of Law (Solicitors' Finals). Articled clerk, Surrey CC, 1981–83; admitted solicitor, 1983; Solicitor: W Sussex CC, 1983–85; S Glamorgan CC, 1985–88; Chief Solicitor, 1988–91, Asst Co. Sec., 1991–93, W Glamorgan CC; Director, Legal and Administrative Services: S Glamorgan CC, 1993–96; Cardiff CC, 1996–99; Corporate Manager, Cardiff CC, 1999–2003. *Recreations:* travel, theatre, cinema, visual arts. *Address:* National Assembly for Wales, Cardiff Bay, Cardiff CF99 1NA. *T:* (029) 2089 8802, *Fax:* (029) 2089 8686; *e-mail:* dianne.bevan@wales.gsi.gov.uk.

BEVAN, (Edward) Julian; QC 1991; *b* 23 Oct. 1940; *m* 1966, Bronwen Mary Windsor Lewis; two *s* two *d.* *Educ:* Eton. Called to the Bar, Gray's Inn, 1962, Bencher, 1989; Standing Counsel for the Inland Revenue, 1974; Jun. Treasury Counsel, 1977, Sen. Treasury Counsel, 1985, First Sen. Treasury Counsel, 1989–91, Central Criminal Court. *Address:* Cloth Fair Chambers, 39–40 Cloth Fair, EC1A 7NR. *Club:* Garrick.

BEVAN, Prof. Hugh Keith; JP; Professor of Law, University of Hull, 1969–89; *b* 8 Oct. 1922; *s* of Thomas Edward Bevan and Marjorie Avril Bevan (*née* Trick); *m* 1950, Mary Harris; one *d* (one *s* decd). *Educ:* Neath Grammar Sch.; University Coll. of Wales, Aberystwyth. LLB 1949, LLM 1966. Called to the Bar, Middle Temple, 1959. Served RA, 1943–46. University of Hull: Lectr in Law, 1950–61; Sen. Lectr in Law, 1961–69; Pro Vice-Chancellor, 1979–82; Wolfson College, Cambridge: Vis. Fellow, 1986 and 1989–90; Fellow, 1990–92; Hon. Fellow, 1992. Chm., Rent Assessment Cttees, 1982–92. Pres., Soc. of Public Teachers of Law, 1987–88. JP Kingston-upon-Hull, 1972 (Chm. of Bench, 1984–89). Hon. Fellow, Swansea Univ., 2007. Hon. LLD: Hull, 1990; Sheffield, 2000. *Publications:* Source Book of Family Law (with P. R. H. Webb), 1964; Law Relating to Children, 1973; (with M. L. Parry) The Children Act 1975, 1978; Child Law, 1988; numerous articles. *Recreations:* music, golf. *Address:* Wolfson College, Cambridge CB3 9BB. *T:* (01223) 335900.

BEVAN, James David, CMG 2006; HM Diplomatic Service; Director General, Change and Delivery, Foreign and Commonwealth Office, since 2007; *b* 13 July 1959; *s* of late Douglas Bevan and of Diana Bevan; *m* 1984, Janet Purdie; three *d*. *Educ:* Univ. of Sussex (BA Hons Social Anthropology). Joined FCO, 1982; Kinshasa, 1984–86; UK Delegn to NATO, Brussels, 1986–90; FCO, 1990–92; Paris, 1993; Washington, 1994–98; Hd, Africa Dept (Equatorial), FCO, 1998–2000; Hd, EU Dept (Internal), FCO, 2000–01; Director: SE Europe and Gibraltar, FCO, 2002; Africa, FCO, 2003–06. FCO Vis. Fellow, Harvard Univ., 2006. *Recreations:* music, not worrying. *Address:* c/o Foreign and Commonwealth Office, King Charles Street, SW1A 2AH.

BEVAN, John Penry Vaughan; QC 1997; **His Honour Judge Bevan;** a Circuit Judge, since 2004; *b* 7 Sept. 1947; *s* of late Llewellyn Vaughan Bevan and of Hilda Molly Bevan; *m* 1st, 1971, Dinah Nicholson; two *d*; 2nd, 1978, Veronica Aliaga-Kelly; one *s* one *d*. *Educ:* Radley Coll.; Magdalene Coll., Cambridge (BA). Called to the Bar, Middle Temple, 1970, Bencher, 2001. A Recorder, 1988–2004; Sen. Treasury Counsel, CCC, 1989–97. *Recreation:* sailing. *Clubs:* Leander (Henley-on-Thames); Aldeburgh Yacht; Orford Sailing.

BEVAN, John Stuart, OBE 1995; Further Education Funding Council for England Ombudsman, 1996–2001; *b* 19 Nov. 1935; *s* of Frank Oakland and Ruth Mary Bevan; *m* 1960, Patricia Vera Beatrice (*née* Joyce); two *s* two *d*. *Educ:* Eggar's Grammar Sch.; Jesus Coll., Oxford; S Bartholomew's Hosp. Med. Coll. MA, MSc; FInstP. Health Physicist, UK Atomic Energy Authority, 1960–62; Lectr, then Sen. Lectr in Physics, Polytechnic of the South Bank (previously Borough Polytechnic), 1962–73; Inner London Education Authority: Asst Educn Officer, then Sen. Asst Educn Officer, 1973–76; Dep. Educn Officer, 1977–79; Dir of Educn, 1979–82; Sec., NAB, 1982–88; Dir of Educn Services, London Residuary Body, 1989–92; Chief Exec., ACFHE, 1992–93; Sec., Assoc. for Colls, 1993–94. Former Member, National Executive Committees: Nat. Union of Teachers; Assoc. of Teachers in Technical Instns (Pres., 1972–73). Chm., Nat. Youth Agency, 1996–2002. Scout Association: Asst, later Dep. Comr, Kent, 1982–99; Chm., Nat. Activities Bd, 1988–93; Nat. Comr for Activities, 1994–95; Chm., Programme and Trng, 1995–96; Chm., Cttee of Council, 1996–2001; Skills Instructor, Eden Dist, 2000–. Mem., Adventure Activities Industry Adv. Cttee, CCPR (formerly HSC), 1997–2007 (Chm., 2004–07). Vice-Chm., Cumbria Local Access Forum, 2001–. Hon. Fellow: S Bank Univ. (formerly Poly of the S Bank), 1987; Westminster Coll., Oxford, 1990. DUniv Surrey, 1990; Hon. LLD CNAA, 1992. *Publications:* occasional papers in the educnl press. *Recreations:* scouting, mountaineering. *Address:* The Hollies, Great Asby, Appleby, Cumbria CA16 6HD. *T:* (01768) 353433.

BEVAN, Julian; *see* Bevan, E. J.

BEVAN, Sir Martyn Evan E.; *see* Evans-Bevan.

BEVAN, Prof. Michael John, PhD; FRS 1991; Investigator, Howard Hughes Medical Institute, and Professor, Department of Immunology, University of Washington, Seattle, since 1990; *b* 20 Sept. 1945; *s* of Thomas John Bevan and Doris Mary (*née* Prior); *m* 1985, Pamela Jean Fink; two *s*. *Educ:* Pontypridd Boys' Grammar Sch.; University Coll. London (BSc Zool. 1967; MSc Biochem. 1968); Nat. Inst. for Med. Research, London (PhD 1972). Postdoctoral Fellow, Salk Inst. for Biol Studies, La Jolla, Calif, 1973–76, Asst Res. Prof., 1976–77; Asst, then Associate, Prof., Dept of Biology, MIT, 1977–82; Associate, then Member, Dept of Immunology, Scripps Res. Inst., La Jolla, Calif, 1982–90. *Publications:* numerous original res. pubns in scientific jls incl. Nature, Science, Cell, Jl Exptl Medicine. *Recreation:* hiking. *Address:* Howard Hughes Medical Institute, Department of Immunology, University of Washington, Box 357370, Seattle, WA 98195–7370, USA. *T:* (206) 6853610.

BEVAN, Prof. Michael Webster; Head, Cell and Developmental Biology Department, John Innes Centre, Biotechnology and Biological Sciences Research Council; Professor, University of East Anglia, since 1997; *b* 5 June 1952; *s* of John Vernon Bevan and Sue (*née* Webster); *m* 1982, Jane Foster; two *s*. *Educ:* Univ. of Auckland (BSc 1973; MSc Hons 1974); Univ. of Cambridge (PhD 1979). Res. Fellow, Washington Univ., St Louis, Mo, 1980; Higher Scientific Officer, 1982–84, SSO, 1984–86, PSO, 1986–88, Plant Breeding Inst., Cambridge; Hd, Dept of Molecular Genetics, then Cell and Develtl Biol., Inst. of Plant Sci. Res., AFRC, subseq. John Innes Centre, BBSRC, 1988–. Rank Prize, Rank Foundn, 1986. *Publications:* contrib. numerous chapters in books and articles to learned jls. *Recreations:* reading modern literature, riding, ski-ing, walking. *Address:* 329 Unthank Road, Norwich NR4 7QA. *T:* (01603) 504181.

BEVAN, Sir Nicolas, Kt 2001; CB 1991; Speaker's Secretary, House of Commons, 1993–2003; *b* 8 March 1942; *s* of late Roger Bevan, BM, and Diana Mary Bevan (*née* Freeman); *m* 1982, Christine, *d* of N. A. Berry. *Educ:* Westminster Sch. (Hon. Fellow 2003); Corpus Christi Coll., Oxford (MA LitHum). Ministry of Defence: Asst Principal, 1964; Principal, 1969; Private Sec. to Chief of Air Staff, 1970–73; Cabinet Office, 1973–75; Asst Sec., 1976; RCDS 1981; Asst Under Sec. of State, 1985; Under Sec., Cabinet Office, 1992–93. *Recreations:* gardening, bridge. *Clubs:* National Liberal, Lansdowne.

BEVAN, Prof. Peter Gilroy, CBE 1983; MB, ChB; FRCS; Consultant Surgeon, Dudley Road Hospital, Birmingham, 1958–87; Professor of Surgery and Postgraduate Medical Education, University of Birmingham, 1981–87, now Emeritus Professor; *b* 13 Dec. 1922; *s* of Rev. Thomas John Bevan and Norah (*née* Gilroy); *m* 1st, 1949, Patricia Joan (*née* Laurie) (*d* 1985); one *s* one *d*; 2nd, 1990, Beryl Margaret (*née* Perry). *Educ:* King Edward VI High Sch., Birmingham; Univ. of Birmingham Medical Sch. (MB, ChB 1946; ChM 1958). LRCP MRCS 1946, FRCS 1952; Hon. FRCSI 1984; Hon. FBIDST 2002. Served RAMC, BAOR, 1947–49 (Captain). Demonstrator in Anatomy, Univ. of Birmingham, 1949–51; Resident Surgical Officer, Birmingham Children's Hosp., 1954–55; Lectr in Surgery and Sen. Surgical Registrar, Queen Elizabeth Hosp., Birmingham, 1954–58; WHO Vis. Prof. of Surgery to Burma, 1969; Director, Board of Graduate Clinical Studies, Univ. of Birmingham, 1978–87; Birmingham Medical Institute: Postgrad. Tutor, 1987–94; Organiser, GP Surg. Workshops, 1994–2004; Pres., 1994–2003. Royal College of Surgeons: Vice-Pres., 1980–82; Member: Council, 1971–83; Court of Patrons, 1988–; Bd of Hunterian Trustees, 1990–; Dir, Overseas Doctors Training Scheme Cttee, 1986–90. Founder Chm., W Midlands Oncology Assoc., 1974–79; Vice-Pres., Brit. Assoc. of Surgical Oncology, 1975–78; President: Pancreatic Soc. of GB, 1977; British Inst. of Surgical Technologists, 1980–95 (Hon. Fellow, British Inst. of Surgical and Dental Technologists, 1999); Assoc. of Surgeons of GB and Ireland, 1984–85 (Fellow, 1960–; Mem. Council, 1975–85); W Midlands Surgical Soc., 1986; Nat. Assoc. of Theatre Nurses, 1992–94. EEC: UK representative: on Monospecialist Section of Surgery, 1975–84; on Adv. Cttee on Medical Trng, 1980–85. Civil Consultant Advr in Gen. Surgery to RN, 1973–84; Med. Adviser, Midlands Div., Ileostomy Assoc., 1976–87. Chm., Adv. Cttee of Deans, 1986–88. Chairman: Steering Gp on Operating Theatres, Dept of Health, 1988–89; Jt Planning Adv. Cttee, Dept of Health, 1990–95; Medical Mem., Pensions Appeal Tribunals, 1987–89; Mem., Medical Appeals Tribunal, 1989–95. Former Member: Jt Planning Adv. Cttee; Central Manpower Cttee; Jt Consultants Cttee; Council for Postgraduate Med. Educn. Pres., Sands Cox Soc., 2003. Mem. Editl Bd, Health Trends, 1990–97. *Publications:* Reconstructive Procedures in Surgery, 1982; Handbook of General Surgery, 1992; various surgical papers in BMJ, Brit. Jl Surgery, Lancet, Annals of RCS; papers on illnesses of classical composers. *Recreations:* inland waterways, golf, photography, music, gardening. *Address:* 10 Russell Road, Moseley, Birmingham B13 8RD. *T:* (0121) 449 3055. *Clubs:* Royal Navy Medical; Edgbaston Golf (Birmingham).

BEVAN, Rev. Canon Richard Justin William, PhD; ThD; Chaplain to The Queen, 1986–92; Canon Emeritus, Carlisle Cathedral, since 1989 (Canon Residentiary, Carlisle Cathedral, 1982–89, Treasurer and Librarian, 1982–89, Vice-Dean, 1987–89); *b* 21 April 1922; *s* of Rev. Richard Bevan, Vicar of St Harmon, Radnorshire and Margaret Bevan; *m* 1948, Sheila Rosemary Barrow, Fazakerley, Liverpool; three *s* one *d* (and one *s* decd). *Educ:* St Edmund's Sch., Canterbury; St Augustine's Coll., Canterbury; Lichfield Theol Coll.; St Chad's Coll., Univ. of Durham (Theol. Prizeman; BA, LTh). ThD: Geneva Theol. Coll., 1972; Greenwich Univ., USA, 1990; PhD Columbia Pacific Univ., 1980. Ordained deacon, Lichfield Cathedral, 1945, priest, 1946; Asst Curate, Stoke-on-Trent, 1945–49; Chaplain, Aberlour Orphanage and licence to officiate, dio. of Moray, Ross and Caithness, 1949–51; Asst Master, Burnley Tech. High Sch., 1951–60; Asst Curate, Church Kirk, 1951–56, Whalley, 1956–60; Rector, St Mary-le-Bow, Durham and Chaplain to Durham Univ., 1960; Vicar, St Oswald's United Benefice, 1964–74; Convener of Chaplains, Univ. of Durham, 1964–74; Rector of Grasmere, 1974–82. Examg Chaplain to Bishop of Carlisle, 1970–; Chaplain, Durham Girls' High Sch., 1966–74; Vice-President: Friends of St Chad's Coll., 1990– (Governor, St Chad's Coll., 1969–89); Greenwich Sch. of Theology, 1977–2003 (Hon. Vice-Pres. and Hon. Governor, 2003–). First Pres., and Founder Mem., Grasmere Village Soc., 1976–78; Dove Cottage Local Cttee, 1974–82. Chancellor's medal, North-West Univ. (Potchefstroom campus), S Africa, 2004. *Publications:* (ed) Steps to Christian Understanding, 1959; (ed) The Churches and Christian Unity, 1964; (ed) Durham Sermons, 1964; Unfurl the Flame (poetry), 1980; A Twig of Evidence: does belief in God make sense?, 1986; (contrib.) John Cosin: from priest to prince bishop, 1997; articles on ethics and culture. *Recreations:* poetry reading, musical appreciation, train spotting. *Address:* Beck Cottage, West End, Burgh-by-Sands, Carlisle CA5 6BT. *T:* (01228) 576781. *Club:* Victory Services.

BEVAN, Robert, MBE 2004; after-dinner speaker (as Bob "the Cat" Bevan), writer, broadcaster, comedian, journalist; *b* 26 Feb. 1945; *s* of Eric and Iris Rose Bevan; partner, Laura Collins. *Educ:* Wilson's Grammar Sch., Camberwell. MCIPR 1974. Trainee sales rep., Nicholls & Clarke, 1961–62; Asst Chief Reporter, Lloyd's List and Shipping Gazette, 1962–66; PR Manager, Shorthorn Soc. of GB and Ireland, 1966; Dep. Ed., Travel Agency Mag., 1967–69; Hertford Public Relations Ltd: Account Exec., 1969–70; Dir, 1970–72; Man. Dir, 1972–74; Gp Dir of PR, European Ferries Plc, 1974–83; Chm., Bevan PR Ltd, 1983–92. Mem., Soc. of Authors. Hon. Barker, Variety Club of GB, 1990–; Mem., Grand Order of Water Rats, 2006. Pres., Old Wilsonians' Assoc., 1995; Vice President: Old Wilsonians' FC, 1970–; Crystal Palace FC, 1986–2006; Middlesex Wanderers FC, 1996–; Dulwich Hamlet FC, 2000–; Tonbridge Angels FC, 2002–. *Publication:* Nearly Famous, 2003. *Recreations:* football, cricket, reading, travel, food, drink. *Address:* Barelands Oast, Bells Yew Green, Kent TN3 9BD. *Fax:* (01892) 750089; *e-mail:* Bob@bobthecatbevan.co.uk. *Clubs:* Les Ambassadeurs, Lord's Taverners (Trustee, 1995–2004); Kent CC, Bells Yew Green Cricket (Pres., 1996–).

BEVAN, Tim, CBE 2005; film producer; Co-Founder and Co-Chairman, Working Title Films, since 1984; *m* 1992, Joely Richardson, *qv* (marr. diss. 2001); one *d*; partner, Amy Gadney; one *s* one *d*. Formerly runner, Video Arts; co-founder, Aldabra, 1984. Film producer (jointly): A World Apart, 1988; Fools of Fortune, 1990; Drop Dead Fred, 1991; Bob Roberts, 1992; with Sarah Radclyffe: My Beautiful Laundrette, 1986; Sammy and Rosie Get Laid, Personal Services, 1987; Paperhouse, For Queen and Country, 1989; Dark Obsession, The Tall Guy, Chicago Joe and the Showgirl, 1990; London Kills Me, Rubin and Ed, 1992; with Eric Fellner: Posse, Romeo is Bleeding, 1993; Four Weddings and a Funeral, The Hudsucker Proxy, 1994; Loch Ness, Panther, French Kiss, Moonlight & Valentino, Dead Man Walking, 1995; Fargo, 1996; Bean, The Matchmaker, The Borrowers, The Hi-Lo Country, 1997; Elizabeth, The Big Lebowski, What Rats Won't Do, 1998; Notting Hill, Plunkett & Macleane, 1999; O Brother, Where Art Thou?, Billy Elliot, 2000; Bridget Jones's Diary, Captain Corelli's Mandolin, The Man Who Wasn't There, Long Time Dead, 2001; 40 Days and 40 Nights, About a Boy, Ali G Indahouse, The Guru, My Little Eye, 2002; Love Actually, Calcium Kid, Ned Kelly, Shape of Things, Johnny English, Thirteen, 2003; Thunderbirds, Inside I'm Dancing, Wimbledon, Shaun of the Dead, Bridget Jones: The Edge of Reason, 2004; Mickybo and Me, Pride and Prejudice, Nanny McPhee, The Interpreter, 2005; United 93, Hot Stuff, 2006; The Golden Age, Atonement, Mr Bean's Holiday, Hot Fuzz, Gone, Smokin' Aces, 2007; sole producer, High Fidelity, 2000. Television includes: Tales of the City, 1993; The Borrowers, 1993; More Tales of the City, 1998. *Address:* Working Title Films, Oxford House, 76 Oxford Street, W1D 1BS.

BEVAN, Sir Timothy (Hugh), Kt 1984; Deputy Chairman, Foreign & Colonial Investment Trust plc, 1993–98 (Director, 1988–98); *b* 24 May 1927; *y s* of late Hugh Bevan and Pleasance (*née* Scrutton); *m* 1952, Pamela, *e d* of late Norman and Margaret Smith; two *s* two *d*. *Educ:* Eton. Lieut Welsh Guards. Called to Bar, 1950. Joined Barclays Bank Ltd, 1950; Dir, 1966–93; Vice-Chm., 1968–73; Dep. Chm., 1973–81; Chm., 1981–87. Dir, BET, 1987–92 (Chm., 1988–91). Chm., Cttee of London Clearing Bankers, 1983–85. Mem., NEDC, 1986–87. *Recreations:* sailing, gardening. *Address:* c/o Barclays Bank, 1 Churchill Place, E14 5HP. *Clubs:* Cavalry and Guards, Royal Ocean Racing; Royal Yacht Squadron.

BEVAN, Rear-Adm. Timothy Michael, CB 1986; Assistant Chief of Defence Staff (Intelligence), 1984–87; *b* 7 April 1931; *s* of Thomas Richard and Margaret Richmond Bevan; *m* 1970, Sarah Knight; three *s*. *Educ:* Eton College. psc(n), jssc. Entered RN, 1949; commanded: HMS Decoy, 1966; HMS Caprice, 1967–68; HMS Minerva, 1971–72; HMS Ariadne, 1976–78; HMS Ariadne, and Captain of 8th Frigate Sqdn, 1980–82;

Britannia Royal Naval Coll., 1982–84; retd 1987. Dep. Dir, ACRE, The Rural Communities Charity, 1990–95; Chm., SSAFA Glos, 1996–2000.

BEVAN, Dame Yasmin (Prodhan), DBE 2007; Headteacher, Denbigh High School, since 1991; *b* 3 Dec. 1953; *d* of Badiuzzaman and Selima Prodhan. *Educ:* London Sch. of Econs (BSc Hons Govt 1976); Roehampton Inst. (PGCE 1977); Open Univ. (BA 1983); Inst. of Educn, Univ. of London (MA 1990). Teacher of Maths, Greenford High Sch., Ealing, 1977–78; Hd of Sixth Form and Hd of Maths, Pen Park Girls' Sch., Bristol, 1979–86; Dep. Hd, Canons High Sch., Harrow, 1987–91. Member: Practitioners' Gp on Sch. Behaviour and Discipline, DfES, 2005; Sure Start Stakeholders' Gp, DfES, 2006–; Ministerial Task Force on Gifted and Talented Educn, 2007–. Mem., Governing Council, 2000–04, Adv. Gp on Nat. Leaders of Educn, 2006, Nat. Coll. for Sch. Leadership. *Recreations:* reading, keeping fit, cinema, opera, gardening, spending time with family and friends. *Address:* Denbigh High School, Alexandra Avenue, Luton, Beds LU3 1HA. *T:* (01582) 736611; *e-mail:* Denbigh.high.head@luton.gov.uk.

BEVERIDGE, Crawford William, CBE 1995; Executive Vice President, and Chairman of Sun Microsystems Europe, Sun Microsystems Inc., since 2006; *b* 3 Nov. 1945; *s* of William Wilson Beveridge and Catherine Crawford Beveridge; *m* 1977, Marguerite DeVoe; one *s* one *d*. *Educ:* Edinburgh Univ. (BSc); Bradford Univ. (MSc). Appts with Hewlett Packard in Scotland, Switzerland, USA, 1968–77; European Personnel Manager, Digital Equipment Corp., 1977–81; Vice-Pres., Human Resources, Analog Devices, 1982–85; Vice-Pres., Corporate Resources, Sun Microsystems, 1985–90; Chief Exec., Scottish Enterprise, 1991–2000; Exec. Vice-Pres., People and Places, and Chief Human Resources Officer, Sun Microsystems Inc., 2000–06. *Recreations:* music, cooking, paperweights. *Address:* Sun Microsystems Inc., 4150 Network Circle, Santa Clara, CA 95054, USA; *e-mail:* crawford.beveridge@sun.com.

BEVERIDGE, John Caldwell; QC 1979; Recorder, Western Circuit, 1975–96; *b* 26 Sept. 1937; *s* of late Prof. William Ian Beardmore Beveridge; *m* 1st, 1972, Frances Ann Clunes Grant Martineau (marr. diss. 1988); 2nd, 1989, Lilian Moira Weston Adamson (marr. diss. 2003); 3rd, 2005, Rebecca Boulos-Hanna. *Educ:* Jesus Coll., Cambridge (MA, LLB). Called to the Bar, Inner Temple, 1963, Bencher, 1985; Western Circuit; called to the Bar, NSW, 1975, QC (NSW), 1980. Mem. (C), Westminster City Council, 1968–72. Trustee: Dogs Trust (formerly Nat. Canine Defence League), 1998–; Manchester Dogs Home, 2003– (Vice-Pres., 2007–). Freeman, City of London. Jt Master, Westmeath Foxhounds, 1976–79. Comdr, Star of Honour (Ethiopia), 1992. *Recreations:* conversation, travelling. *Address:* 9 St James's Chambers, Ryder Street, SW1Y 6QA. *T:* (020) 7930 1118, *Fax:* (020) 7930 1119. *Clubs:* Beefsteak, Pratt's, Turf; Brook (New York).

BEVERLEY, Bishop Suffragan of, since 2000; **Rt Rev. Martyn William Jarrett;** Episcopal Visitor for the Northern Province, since 2000; *b* 25 Oct. 1944; *s* of Frederick and Ivy Jarrett, Bristol; *m* 1968, Betty, *d* of Frank and Mabel Wallis, Bristol; two *d*. *Educ:* Cotham GS, Bristol; King's Coll., London (BD 1967; AKC 1967); Hull Univ. (MPhil 1991); St Boniface, Warminster. Ordained deacon, 1968, priest, 1969; Curate: St George, Bristol, 1968–70; Swindon New Town, 1970–74; St Mary, Northolt, 1974–76; Vicar: St Joseph the Worker, Northolt West End, 1976–81; St Andrew, Hillingdon, 1981–83; Priest-in-charge, Uxbridge Moor, 1982–83; Vicar, St Andrew with St John, Uxbridge, 1983–85; Selection Sec., 1985–88, Sen. Selection Sec., 1989–91, ACCM; Vicar, Our Lady and All Saints, Chesterfield, 1991–94; Suffragan Bp of Burnley, 1994–2000; Hon. Assistant Bishop: Ripon and Leeds, Durham, Sheffield, 2000–; Manchester, Southwell and Wakefield, 2001–; Bradford, 2002–; Liverpool, 2003–. Member: Bishops' Urban Panel, 1998–; Gen. Synod, 2000–; Churches Commn for Inter-Faith Relations, 2000–06; Council for Christian Unity, 2001–; C of E and C of S Jt Study Gp, 2006–. Vice Chm., Internat. Bps' Conf. on Faith and Order, 1998–. Patron, Coll. of Readers, 2003–. *Recreations:* psephology, reading, bird watching. *Address:* 3 North Lane, Roundhay, Leeds LS8 2QJ. *T:* (0113) 265 4280, *Fax:* (0113) 265 4281.

BEVERLEY, Lt-Gen. Sir Henry (York La Roche), KCB 1991; OBE 1979; Commandant General Royal Marines, 1990–93; Director-General, Winston Churchill Memorial Trust, 1993–2002; *b* 25 Oct. 1935; *s* of Vice-Adm. Sir York Beverley, KBE, CB, and Lady Beverley; *m* 1963, Sally Anne Maclean; two *d*. *Educ:* Wellington College. DS Staff Coll., 1976–78; CO 42 Cdo RM, 1978–80; Comdt CTC RM, 1980–82; Director RM Personnel, MoD, 1983–84; Comd 3 Cdo Bde RM, 1984–86; Maj.-Gen. Trng and Reserve Forces RM, 1986–88; COS to CGRM, 1988–90. Chm. Trustees, Royal Marines Mus., 1997–2007. *Recreations:* golf, ski-ing. *Club:* Royal Thames Yacht.

BEVERLEY, Prof. Peter Charles Leonard, DSc; Scientific Head, Edward Jenner Institute for Vaccine Research, 1995–2005; Principal Research Fellow, University of Oxford, since 2005; *b* 7 March 1943; *s* of Samuel and Elinor Beverley; *m* 1967, Elisabeth A. Copleston (separated); two *s*; one *d* with Prof. Elizabeth Simpson, *qv*. *Educ:* University Coll. London (BSc, MB BS; DSc 1987). Research Fellow: NIMR, London, 1969–72; Sloan-Kettering Inst., NY, 1972–73; ICRF Tumour Immunology Unit, UCL, 1973–78; permanent staff mem., ICRF, 1978–95; Prof. of Tumour Immunology, UCL, 1988–95; Dep. Dir, 1988–92, Dir, 1992–95, Tumour Immunology Unit, UCL. *Publications:* contribs to immunological, biological and med. jls. *Recreations:* music, reading. *Address:* Edward Jenner Institute for Vaccine Research, Compton, Newbury, Berks RG20 7NN. *T:* (01635) 577902.

BEVINGTON, Christian Veronica; Her Honour Judge Bevington; a Circuit Judge, since 1998; *b* 1 Nov. 1939; *d* of late Michael Falkner Bevington and Dulcie Marian Bevington (*née* Gratton); *m* 1961, David Levitt, OBE (marr. diss. 1973); one *s* two *d*. *Educ:* St James's, W Malvern; London Sch. of Econs (LLB Hons). Called to the Bar: Inner Temple, 1961 (Bencher, 1994); Lincoln's Inn, *ad eundem* 1971. Co-Founder, Charitable Housing Trust, 1966: Company Sec. and Housing Manager, Circle 33 Housing Trust, 1966–76; joined Peat Marwick & Co., 1976; returned to full-time practice at the Bar, 1980; Head of Chambers, 1981–98; Recorder, 1994–98. Chm., Independent Inquiry for City and County of Cardiff, 1997. Mem., Mental Health Review Tribunals, 2002–03. *Publication:* The Bevington Report, 1997. *Recreations:* music, travel.

See also A. F. J. Levitt.

BEW, family name of **Baron Bew**.

BEW, Baron *cr* 2007 (Life Peer), of Donegore in the County of Antrim; **Paul Anthony Elliott Bew,** PhD; Professor of Irish Politics, Queen's University of Belfast, since 1991; *b* 22 Jan. 1950; *s* of Dr Kenneth Bew and Dr Mary Bew (*née* Leahy); *m* 1977, Prof. Greta Joyce Jones; one *s*. *Educ:* Brackenber House Sch.; Campbell Coll., Belfast; Pembroke Coll., Cambridge (MA; PhD 1974). Lectr, Sch. of Humanities, Ulster Coll., 1975–79; Queen's University, Belfast: Lectr in Eur. and American Hist., 1979–84; Lectr, 1984–87, Reader, 1987–91, Dept of Politics. Vis. Lectr, Univ. of Pennsylvania, 1982–83; Parnell Fellow, Magdalene Coll., Cambridge, 1996–97; Vis. Prof., Surrey Univ., 1997–; Burns Vis. Schol., Boston Coll., 1999–2000. Historical Advr to Bloody Sunday Tribunal. Pres., Irish Assoc. for Econs and Cultural Relns, 1990–92; Exec. Mem., British Irish Assoc., 1995–. MRIA 2004. *Publications:* Land and the National Question in Ireland 1858–82, 1978; (jtly) The State in Northern Ireland, 1979, 2nd edn 1996; C. S. Parnell, 1980, 2nd edn 1991; (jtly) Seán Lemass and the Making of Modern Ireland, 1983; (jtly) The British State and the Ulster Crisis, 1985; Conflict and Conciliation in Ireland 1890–1910, 1987; (jtly) The Dynamics of Irish Politics, 1989; (ed jtly) Passion and Prejudice, 1993; (jtly) Northern Ireland: a chronology of the Troubles, 1993, rev. edn 1999; Ideology and the Irish Question, 1994; John Redmond, 1996; (jtly) The Northern Ireland Peace Process 1993–96, 1996; (jtly) Between War and Peace, 1997; Ireland: the politics of enmity 1789–2006, 2007; The Making and Re-making of the Good Friday Agreement, 2007; contrib. numerous articles and reviews. *Recreations:* soccer, cinema, theatre. *Address:* Department of Politics, Queen's University of Belfast, 21 University Square, Belfast BT7 1NN. *T:* (028) 9024 5133.

BEWES, Rev. Preb. Richard Thomas, OBE 2005; Rector, All Souls Church, Langham Place, 1983–2004; Prebendary of St Paul's Cathedral, 1988–2005, now Prebendary Emeritus; *b* 1 Dec. 1934; *s* of late Rev. Canon Cecil and Sylvia Bewes; *m* 1964, Elisabeth Ingrid Jaques (*d* 2006); two *s* one *d*. *Educ:* Marlborough Sch.; Emmanuel Coll., Cambridge (MA); Ridley Hall, Cambridge. Deacon, 1959; priest, 1960; Curate of Christ Church, Beckenham, 1959–65; Vicar: St Peter's, Harold Wood, 1965–74; Emmanuel, Northwood, 1974–83. *Publications:* God in Ward 12, 1973; Advantage Mr Christian, 1975; Talking about Prayer, 1979; The Pocket Handbook of Christian Truth, 1981; John Wesley's England, 1981, 2nd edn as Wesley Country, 2003; The Church Reaches Out, 1981; The Church Overcomes, 1983; On The Way, 1984; Quest for Truth, 1985; Quest for Life, 1985; The Church Marches On, 1986; When God Surprises, 1986; The Resurrection, 1989; A New Beginning, 1989; Does God Reign?, 1995; Speaking in Public—Effectively, 1998; Great Quotations of the 20th Century, 1999, 2nd edn as Words that Circled the World, 2002; The Lord's Prayer, 2000; The Lamb Wins, 2000; The Bible Truth Treasury, 2000; The Stone that became a Mountain, 2001; The Top 100 Questions, 2002; Beginning the Christian Life, 2004; 150 Pocket Thoughts, 2004. *Recreations:* tennis, photography, hosting video and TV Bible studies. *Address:* 50 Curzon Road, W5 1NF; *web:* www.richardbewes.com.

BEWICKE-COPLEY, family name of **Baron Cromwell**.

BEWLEY, Dame Beulah (Rosemary), DBE 2000; MD; FRCP, FFPH, FRCPCH; Reader in Public Health Sciences, St George's Hospital Medical School, University of London, 1992–93, now Emeritus; *b* 2 Sept. 1929; *d* of John B. Knox and Ina E. (*née* Charles); *m* 1955, Thomas Henry Bewley, *qv*; one *s* three *d* (and one *d* decd). *Educ:* Alexandra Sch. and Coll., Dublin; Trinity Coll., Dublin (MA); LSHTM, Univ. of London (MSc Social Medicine 1971); MD 1974. FRCP 1992; FFPH (FFPHM 1980). Qualified TCD, 1953; trained at Queen Elizabeth Hosp. for Children, London, Maudsley Hosp., London and Children's Hosp., Cincinatti; postgrad. trng at LSHTM and St Thomas's Hosp. Med. Sch.; Consultant, St Thomas' Hosp., 1974–79; Senior Lecturer and Hon. Consultant: KCH Med. Sch., 1979–83; LSHTM, 1979–86; St George's Hosp. Med. Sch., 1987–93; Undergrad. and postgrad. teacher/examr, Univ. of London, 1973–93; Chm., Bd of Studies in Public Health Medicine, London Univ., 1987–89; Postgrad. Acad. Tutor, SW Thames Reg., 1987–93. Mem., GMC, 1979–99 (Treas., 1992–99). Pres., Med. Women's Fedn, 1986. Mem. and Mem. Exec. Cttee, Women's Nat. Commn, 1992–99. FRSocMed 1969 (Vice Pres. and Past Pres., Section of Epidemiology and Public Health); FRCPCH (Mem., BPA 1985). Hon. LLD TCD, 2002. *Publications:* Choice not Chance, 1975; contrib. numerous articles and papers on research on children's smoking, adolescence, med. educn, women doctors and women's health. *Recreations:* piano, opera, travel. *Address:* 4 Grosvenor Garden Mews North, SW1W 0JP. *T:* (020) 7730 9592. *Clubs:* Reform, London Chapter of Irish Georgian Society.

BEWLEY, Edward de Beauvoir; Judge of the High Court of Hong Kong, 1980–96; Commissioner, Supreme Court of Brunei, since 1996 (with desig. Hon. Mr Justice Bewley); *b* 12 March 1931; *s* of Harold de Beauvoir Bewley and Phyllis Frances Cowdy; *m* 1st, 1956, Sheelagh Alice Brown; one *s*; 2nd, 1968, Mary Gwenefer Jones; three *d*. *Educ:* Shrewsbury School; Trinity College, Dublin. BA, LLB. Called to the Bar, Gray's Inn, 1956. Administrative Officer, Northern Rhodesia, 1956–59; English Bar, 1960–61; Resident Magistrate, Nyasaland, 1961–64; Magistrate, Hong Kong, 1964–76, District Judge, 1976–80. *Recreations:* golf, ski-ing, reading, wine. *Address:* Ysgubor Fawr, Llanfairpwll, Ynys Môn LL61 6PX. *T:* and *Fax:* (01248) 430162. *Clubs:* Hong Kong; Royal Irish Yacht (Dun Laoghaire), Holyhead Golf, Hong Kong Golf.

BEWLEY, Thomas Henry, Hon. CBE 1988; MA; MD; FRCP, FRCPI, FRCPsych; Consultant Psychiatrist, Tooting Bec and St Thomas' Hospitals, 1961–88, now Emeritus Consultant, St Thomas' Hospital; *b* 8 July 1926; *s* of Geoffrey Bewley and Victoria Jane Wilson; *m* 1955, Beulah Rosemary Knox (*see* Dame B. R. Bewley); one *s* three *d* (and one *d* decd). *Educ:* St Columba's College, Dublin; Trinity College, Dublin University (MA; MD 1958). FRCPsych 1972, Hon. FRCPsych 1989. Hon. MD Dublin, 1987. Qualified TCD, 1950; trained St Patrick's Hosp., Dublin, Maudsley Hosp., Univ. of Cincinnati. Hon. Sen. Lectr, St George's Hosp. Med. Sch., 1968–96. Member: Standing Adv. Cttee on Drug Dependence, 1966–71; Adv. Council on Misuse of Drugs, 1972–84; Consultant Adviser on Drug Dependence to DHSS, 1972–81; Consultant, WHO, 1969–88. Pres., RCPsych, 1984–87 (Dean, 1977–82); Jt Co-founder and Mem. Council, Inst. for Study of Drug Dependence, 1967–96. *Publications:* Handbook for Inceptors and Trainees in Psychiatry, 1976, 2nd edn 1980; Madness to Mental Illness, 2008; papers on drug dependence, medical manpower and side effects of drugs. *Address:* 4 Grosvenor Gardens Mews North, SW1W 0JP. *T:* (020) 7730 9592. *Clubs:* Reform, London Chapter of Irish Georgian Society.

BEXON, Roger, CBE 1985; Chairman: Laporte plc, 1986–95; Goal Petroleum, 1990–96; Managing Director, British Petroleum Co., 1981–86, and Deputy Chairman, 1983–86; *b* 11 April 1926; *s* of late MacAlister Bexon, CBE, and Nora Hope Bexon (*née* Jenner); *m* 1951, Lois Loughran Walling; one *s* one *d*. *Educ:* Denstone Coll. (schol.); St John's Coll., Oxford (MA); Tulsa Univ. (MS). Geologist and petroleum engineer with Trinidad Petroleum Development Co. Ltd, 1946–57; management positions with British Petroleum Co., E Africa, 1958–59; Libya, 1959–60; Trinidad, 1961–64; London, 1964–66; Manager, North Sea Operations, 1966–68; General Manager, Libya, 1968–70; Regional Coordinator, Middle East, London, 1971–73; Gen. Manager, Exploration and Production, London, 1973–76; Managing Director, BP Exploration Co. Ltd, London, 1976–77; Dir and Sen. Vice Pres., 1977–80, and Dir, 1982–86, Standard Oil Co. of Ohio; Director: BP Canada Inc., 1983–87; BICC, 1985–92; Lazard Bros, 1986–91; Fenner plc, 1986–89; Cameron Iron Works, 1987–89; Astec (BSR) PLC, 1989–95. Mem. Council, British-N American Res. Assoc., 1986–95. *Publications:* general and technical contribs to internat. jls on oil and energy matters. *Recreations:* swimming, reading, crossword puzzles. *Address:* c/o 53 Davies Street, W1K 5JH. *T:* (020) 7496 5821.

BEYER, John Charles; HM Diplomatic Service; Ambassador to Moldova, since 2006; *b* 29 April 1950; *s* of William Herbert Beyer and Doris Irene Beyer (*née* Tomline); *m* 1971, Letty Marindin Minns; one *s* one *d*. *Educ:* Abingdon Sch.; Queens' Coll., Cambridge

(MA). Vis. Schol., Université de Paris VII, 1973–74; British Council Schol., Beijing Langs Inst., 1974–75; Lectr, Dept of Oriental Langs, Univ. of Calif, Berkeley, 1979–80; Researcher, Dept of Chinese Studies, Leeds Univ., 1980–82; Missions Exec., Sino-British Trade Council, 1983–85; Editor, China-Britain Trade Rev., 1985–90; Dir, Sino-British Trade Council, 1990–91; Dir, China-Britain Trade Gp, 1991–98; Head, Mediterranean Section, EU Dept, FCO, 1999–2002; Dep. Hd of Mission, Luxembourg, 2002–05. *Recreation:* family. *Address:* 44 South Hill Park, NW3 2SJ. *T:* (020) 7435 4795.

BEYFUS, Drusilla Norman; writer, editor, broadcaster; Tutor, Central St Martin's College of Art, 1989–2007; *d* of Norman Beyfus and Florence Noel Barker; *m* 1956, Milton Shulman (*d* 2004); one *s* two *d*. *Educ:* Royal Naval Sch.; Channing Sch. Woman's Editor, Sunday Express, 1950; columnist, Daily Express, 1952–55; Associate Editor, Queen magazine, 1956; Home Editor, The Observer, 1963; Associate Editor, Daily Telegraph magazine, 1966; Editor, Brides and Setting Up Home magazine, 1972–79; Associate Editor, 1979–87, Contributing Editor, 1987–88, Vogue magazine; Editor, Harrods Magazine, 1987–88; columnist, Sunday Telegraph, 1990–91; Contributing Editor, Telegraph Magazine, 1991–; columnist, You magazine (Mail on Sunday), 1994–2002. TV and radio appearances, incl. Call My Bluff, The Big Breakfast and talks programmes. Hon. MA London Inst., 2002. *Publications:* (with Anne Edwards) Lady Behave, 1956 (rev. edn 1969); The English Marriage, 1968; The Brides Book, 1981; The Art of Giving, 1987; Modern Manners, 1992; The Done Thing (series): Courtship, 1992; Parties, 1992; Business, 1993; Sex, 1993; The You Guide to Modern Dilemmas, 1997; contrib. to Sunday Times, Punch, New Statesman, Daily Telegraph, Daily Mail. *Recreations:* walking, modern art, cooking. *Address:* 51G Eaton Square, SW1W 9BE. *T:* (020) 7235 7162.

See also Marchioness of Normanby, A. Shulman.

BEYNON, Ann, OBE 2008; Director, Wales, BT, since 2004 (National Manager, 1998–2004); *b* 14 April 1953; *d* of Roger Talfryn Jones and Margaret Rose Beynon Jones; name changed to Beynon by deed poll, 1981; *m* 1st, 1976, John Trefor (marr. diss. 1983); 2nd, 1986, William Gwenlyn Parry (*d* 1991); one *s* one *d*; 3rd, 1996, Leighton Russell Andrews, *qv*. *Educ:* UCNW, Bangor (BA Hons). Pres., Students' Union, UCNW, 1974–75. Administrator, Yr Academi Gymreig (Welsh Acad.), 1977–81; S4C, 1981–95: Press Officer, 1981–83; Head of Press and PR, 1983–91; Head, Political and Internat. Affairs, 1991–95; Dir of Business Develt, Cardiff Bay Develt Corp., 1995–98. Mem. Bd, BITC UK, 2006–; Chm., BITC Wales Cttee, 2006–. Member: Royal Commn on H of L Reform, 1999; Welsh Lang. Bd, 1995–2000; Wales Cttee, EOC, 2000–07. Gov., Nat. Film and TV Sch., 1995–2002; Mem. Council, Univ. of Wales, Bangor, 2004–. Chm., Sgript Cymru Theatre Co., 1999–2007. *Recreations:* reading, languages, tapestry, managing my late husband's literary estate. *Address:* 11 Waungron Road, Llandaff, Cardiff CF5 2JJ. *T:* (029) 2055 5425.

BEYNON, Ernest Geoffrey; Joint General Secretary, Assistant Masters and Mistresses Association, 1979–87; *b* 4 Oct. 1926; *s* of late Frank William George and Frances Alice Pretoria Beynon; *m* 1956, Denise Gwendoline Rees; two *s* one *d*. *Educ:* Borden Grammar Sch., Kent; Univ. of Bristol, 1944–47, 1949–50 (BSc (Hons Maths) 1947, CertEd 1950). National Service, Royal Artillery, 1947–49. Mathematics Master, Thornbury Grammar Sch., Glos, 1950–56; Mathematics Master and Sixth Form Master, St George Grammar Sch., Bristol, 1956–64; Asst Sec., Assistant Masters Assoc., 1964–78. Last Chm., Teachers' Panel, Burnham Primary and Secondary Cttee, 1985–87. Mem., Univ. of Bristol Court, 1986–; Trustee and Manager, Muntham House Sch., 1979–97. Treasurer: Welwyn Garden City Soc., 1988–; Welwyn Garden Decorative and Fine Arts Soc., 1992–99. Former Tower Captain, St John's, Lemsford. Hon. FCP, 1985. *Publications:* many reports/pamphlets for AMA, incl. The Middle School System, Mixed Ability Teaching, Selection for Admission to a University. *Recreations:* family, campanology, puzzles, special interest tours abroad, books. *Address:* 3 Templewood, Welwyn Garden City, Herts AL8 7HT. *T:* (01707) 321380.

BEYNON, Prof. Huw, DSocSc; Professor, and Director, School of Social Sciences, Cardiff University, since 1999; *b* 10 Dec. 1942; *s* of Dewi and Megan Beynon; *m* 1994, Helen Anne Sampson; one *s* from previous *m*. *Educ:* University Coll. of Wales, Aberystwyth (BA 1964); Univ. of Liverpool (Dip. Industrial Admin); Univ. of Manchester (DSocSc 1999). Lectr, Univ. of Bristol, 1968–73; Simon Marks Res. Fellow, Univ. of Manchester, 1973–75; Lectr, then Reader, Durham Univ., 1975–87; Prof. and Res. Dean, Univ. of Manchester, 1987–99. AcSS 2000. *Publications:* (with R. M. Blackburn) Perceptions of Work: variations within a factory, 1972; Working for Ford, 1985; (with T. Nichols) Living with Capitalism: class relations in the modern factory, 1977; (with H. Wainwright) The Workers' Report on Vickers Ltd, 1978; (with N. Hedges) Born to Work, 1980; (ed) Digging Deeper: issues in the 1984 miners' strike, 1987; (jtly) A Tale of Two Industries: the decline of coal and steel in the North East of England, 1991; (jtly) A Place Called Teesside: a locality in a global economy, 1994; (with T. Austrin) Masters and Servants: class and patronage in the making of a labour organisation, 1994; (ed with P. Glavanis) Patterns of Social Inequality, 1999; (jtly) Digging Up Trouble: protest and the environment on the coal-fields, 2000; (jtly) Coalfield Regeneration: dealing with the consequences of industrial decline, 2000; (ed with S. Rowbotham) Looking at Class, 2002; (jtly) Managing Employment Change: the new reality of work, 2002; (jtly) Exploring the Tomato: transformations of nature, society and economy, 2002; (ed jtly) The Fordism of Ford and Modern Management: Fordism and post-Fordism, vols 1 and 2, 2006; (ed jtly) Patterns of Work in the post-Fordist Era: Fordism and post-Fordism, vols 1 and 2, 2006. *Recreations:* hill-walking, gardening. *Address:* Bryn Celyn, The Bryn, Abergavenny NP7 9AL. *T:* (029) 2087 4848; *e-mail:* beynonh@cardiff.ac.uk. *Club:* The Bryn Social.

BEYNON, Dr John David Emrys, FREng, FIET; Principal, King's College London, 1990–92; *b* 11 March 1939; *s* of John Emrys and Elvira Beynon; *m* 1964, Hazel Janet Hurley; two *s* one *d*. *Educ:* Univ. of Wales (BSc); Univ. of Southampton (MSc, PhD). FIERE 1977; FIET (FIEE 1978); FREng (FEng 1988). Scientific Officer, Radio Res. Station, Slough, 1962–64; Univ. of Southampton: Lectr, Sen. Lectr and Reader, 1964–77; Prof. of Electronics, UWIST, Cardiff, 1977–79; University of Surrey: Prof. of Elec. Engrg, 1979–90; Head of Dept of Electronic and Elec. Engrg, 1979–83; Pro-Vice-Chancellor, 1983–87; Sen. Pro-Vice-Chancellor, 1987–90. Vis. Prof., Carleton Univ., Ottawa, 1975; Cons. to various cos, Govt estabts and Adviser to British Council, 1964–. Member: Accreditation Cttee, IEE, 1983–89; Adv. Cttee on Engrg and Technology, British Council, 1983–92; Technology Sub-Cttee, UGC, 1984–89; Nat. Electronics Council, 1985–91; Cttee 1, 1990–92, Main Cttee, 1991–94, CICHE; Adv. Cttee, Erasmus, 1990–92; Standing Cttee on Educn and Trng, Royal Acad. of Engrg, 1992–95; Adv. Council, British Liby, 1994–99; ITC, 1995–2000. Engrg Professors' Conference: Hon. Sec., 1982–84; Vice-Chm., 1984–85 and 1987–88; Chm., 1985–87. Chm., Westminster Christian Council, 1998–2000; Sec., Bloomsbury Central Baptist Church, 2000–. FRSA 1982; FKC 1990. Hon. Fellow, UC Swansea, 1990. *Publications:* Charge-Coupled Devices and Their Applications (with D. R. Lamb), 1980; papers on plasma physics, semiconductor devices and integrated circuits, and engrg educn. *Recreations:* music, photography, travel. *Address:* 13 Great Quarry, Guildford, Surrey GU1 3XN.

BEYNON, Prof. John Herbert, DSc; FRS 1971; Professor Emeritus, University of Wales, since 1991; *b* 29 Dec. 1923; British; *m* 1947, Yvonne Lilian (*née* Fryer); no *c*. *Educ:* UC Swansea, Univ. of Wales (BSc (1st cl. hons Physics); DSc 1960). CPhys; FInstP; CChem; FRSC; CSci. Experimental Officer, Min. of Supply, Tank Armament Research, 1943–47; ICI Ltd (Organics Div.), 1947–74: Associate Research Man. i/c Physical Chemistry, 1962–70; Sen. Res. Associate, 1965–74; University College of Swansea, University of Wales, subseq. University of Wales Swansea, then Swansea University: first Hon. Professorial Fellow, and Lectr in Chemistry, 1967–74; Royal Soc. Res. Prof., 1974–86; Res. Prof., Depts of Physics and Chemistry, 1987–. Boomer Meml Fellow, Univ. of Minnesota, 1955; Prof. of Chemistry, Purdue Univ., Indiana, 1969–75; Associate Prof. of Molecular Sciences, Univ. of Warwick, 1972–74; Vis. Prof., Univ. of Essex, 1973–74, 1982–; Hon. Prof., Univ. of Warwick, 1977–; Associate, Institut Jožef Stefan, Ljubljana, 1980–. Chm., Schs Curriculum Develt Cttee, Cttee for Wales, 1983–88; Pres., Assoc. for Sci. Educn, Wales, 1985–86. Founder Chm., British Mass Spectrometry Soc., 1960 (Hon. Mem. 1988); Founder Pres., Europ. Mass Spectrometry Soc., 1993–97. Hon. Member, Mass Spectrometry Societies: Japan, 1967; Yugoslavia, 1977; China, 1986; Italy, 1990. Hon. Life Mem., Swansea Camera Club. Editor, Internat. Jl of Mass Spectrom. Ion Processes, 1983–85; Founder Editor-in-Chief, Rapid Communications in Mass Spectrom., 1987–97. Hon. DSc: Purdue, USA, 1995; Babeş-Bolyai, Romania, 1997. Sigma-Xi Res. Award, Purdue Univ., USA, 1973; Hasler Award of Applied Spectroscopy, USA, 1979; Medal, Serbian Chemical Soc., 1981; Techmart Trophy, British Technol. Gp, 1984; Jan Marc Marci Medal, Czechoslovak Spectrometry Soc., 1984; Field and Franklin Medal, Amer. Chem. Soc., 1987; Gold Medal: Internat. Mass Spectrometry Soc., 1985; British Mass Spectrometry Soc., 1987; Italian Mass Spectrometry Soc., 1992. *Publications:* Mass Spectrometry and its Applications in Organic Chemistry, 1960; Mass and Abundance Tables for use in Mass Spectrometry, 1963; The Mass Spectra of Organic Molecules, 1968; Table of Ion Energies for Metastable Transitions in Mass Spectrometry, 1970; Metastable Ions, 1973; An Introduction to Mass Spectrometry, 1981; Current Topics in Mass Spectrometry and Chemical Kinetics, 1982; Application of Transition State Theory to Unimolecular Reactions, 1983; papers in Proc. Royal Soc., Nature, Jl Sci. Inst., Jl Applied Physics, Chem. Soc., JACS, Trans Faraday Soc., Int. Jl Mass Spectrom. and Ion Physics, Org. Mass Spectrom., Anal. Chem., etc. *Recreations:* photography, golf. *Address:* 5 Willow Court, Clyne Common, Swansea SA3 3JB. *T:* (01792) 235205. *Clubs:* Swansea Cricket and Football (Bd Mem., 1990–92), Swansea Sports (Chm., 1988–93); Glamorgan County Cricket (Life Vice Pres.); Bristol Channel Yacht; Buxton and High Peak Golf (Captain, 1965).

BEYNON, Timothy George, MA; FRGS 1983; President, British Dragonfly Society, 2000–04; *b* 13 Jan. 1939; *s* of George Beynon and Fona I. Beynon; *m* 1973, Sally Jane Wilson; two *d*. *Educ:* Swansea Grammar Sch.; King's Coll., Cambridge (MA). City of London Sch., 1962–63; Merchant Taylors' Sch., 1963–78; Headmaster: Denstone Coll., 1978–86; The Leys Sch., Cambridge, 1986–90. Sen. Warden, Saltwells Local Nature Reserve, Dudley, 1992–99. *Recreations:* odonatology, ornithology, fishing, sport, music, expeditions. *Address:* 34 Church Lane, Checkley, Stoke-on-Trent ST10 4NJ.

BEZOS, Jeffrey Preston; Founder, and Chairman, since 1994, Chief Executive Officer, since 1996, Amazon.com Inc., internet bookseller, since 1994; founder, Blue Origin, Seattle, 2000; *b* 12 Jan. 1964; *m* 1993, MacKenzie Tuttle; four *c*. *Educ:* Princeton Univ. (degree in elec. engrg and computer sci., *summa cum laude*, 1986). Mem. staff, FITEL, NY, 1986–88; Bankers Trust Co., 1988–90 (Vice-Pres., 1990); D. E. Shaw & Co., 1990–94 (Sen. Vice-Pres., 1992–94). *Address:* Amazon.com Inc., 1200 12th Avenue South, Seattle, WA 98144, USA.

BHADESHIA, Prof. Harshad Kumar Dharamshi Hansraj, PhD; FRS 1998; FREng; Professor of Physical Metallurgy, since 1999, and Fellow of Darwin College, since 1993, University of Cambridge; *b* 27 Nov. 1953; *s* of Dharamshi Hansraj Bhadeshia and Narmda Dharamshi Bhadeshia; *m* 1978 (marr. diss. 1992); two *d*. *Educ:* City of London Poly. (BSc 1976); Univ. of Cambridge (PhD 1979). CEng. Technician: British Oxygen Co., 1970–72; Murex Welding Processes, 1972–73; University of Cambridge: engaged in res., 1976–79; SERC Res. Fellow, 1979–81; Demonstrator, 1981–85; Lectr in Physical Metallurgy, 1985–93; Reader in Physical Metallurgy, 1993–99. FREng 2002. *Publications:* Geometry of Crystals, 1987; Bainite in Steels, 1992; (with R. W. K. Honeycombe) Steels, 1995; more than 260 res. papers. *Recreation:* squash.

BHANJI, Abdul Fazal, FCA; Special Advisor to the Senior Partner, PricewaterhouseCoopers, since 2001; *b* 11 Sept. 1949; *s* of Fazal Bhanji Jessa and Jenabai Karmali Jinah; *m* 1980, Arzina Dhalla; three *s*. *Educ:* Kelly Coll., Tavistock; Univ. of Kent, Canterbury (BA Hons Accounting). FCA 1980. Coopers & Lybrand, then PriceWaterhouseCoopers, 1972–: work in audit, accountancy and adv. practice in London, Canada, India and Switzerland; estabd Business Develt practice in UK, 1986–2001; Partner, 1988; Partner-in-Charge, Business Develt in UK, 1988–2001; Chairman: India Desk, 1995–2001; Charity Focus Gp, 1995–2001. Chm. and owner, AFB Associates, 2001–; Deputy Chairman: Agenda Gp, 2001–03; SpS Infoquest, 2001–02; non-executive Director: Surgicraft Ltd, 2004–06; Whitehead Mann plc, 2005–06; Advisor: Leonard Hull Internat., 2001–05; Cubitt Consulting Ltd, 2004–06. Member: FEFC for Gtr London, 1993–99; City of London Early Years Develt and Childcare Partnership, 1999–2000. Mem., Europe Cttee, 2002–, London Reg. Council, 2006–, CBI. Mem. and Chm., Finance Cttee, Marshall Aid Commemoration Commn, 2001–. Member: Governing Body, SOAS, 2000–; Council, Open Univ., 2001–02. Mem., Develt Cttee, Asia House, 2000–02. Charter Mem., Indus Entrepreneurs (TiE), 2000–04. Chairman: Aga Khan Econ. Planning Bd, UK, 1990–93; Nat. Cttee, Aga Khan Foundn (UK), 1997–2006; Mem., HH Prince Aga Khan Shia Imami Ismaili Council, UK, 1990–93. FRSA. Freeman, City of London, 1987; Liveryman, Co. of Glaziers and Painters of Glass, 2003. *Recreations:* cricket, bridge, squash, golf, chess, ski-ing, backgammon. *Address:* PricewaterhouseCoopers LLP, Plumtree Court, EC4A 4HT. *Clubs:* Brooks's, Farmers, Mosimann's.

BHARDWAJA, Neelam; Corporate Director, Adult and Children's Social Services, Education and Lifelong Learning (formerly Corporate Director, Opportunities), Cardiff Council, since 2005; one *s*. *Educ:* Univ. of E Anglia (BSc Hons 1978; MA; CQSW 1982). Social worker, Birmingham CC, 1978–80 and 1982–83; various appts, Cambs CC, 1983–2001; Service Manager, Peterborough CC, 2001–03; Hd, Children's and Families, Bor. of Poole, 2003–05. Mem., Children and Families Cttee, ADSS, 2003–05; Vice Pres., 2008–April 2009, Pres., April 2009–, ADSS Cymru. *Publications:* various articles. *Recreations:* enjoying Welsh countryside and beaches, enjoying success and achievements to date. *Address:* Cardiff Council, County Hall, Cardiff CF10 4UW. *T:* (029) 2087 2461, *Fax:* (029) 2087 3653; *e-mail:* NBhardwaja@cardiff.gov.uk.

BHARUCHA, Chitra, FRCPath; Vice-Chairman, BBC, since 2007; Chairman, Advisory Committee on Animal Feeding Stuffs, Food Standards Agency, since 2002; Member, Council, Advertising Standards Authority, 2004–07; *b* 6 April 1945; *d* of late George Gnanadickam and Mangalam Gnanadickam (*née* Ramaiya); *m* 1967, Hoshang Bharucha;

two *d.* *Educ:* Ewart Sch., Madras; Christian Med. Coll., Vellore, India (MB BS); Queen's Univ. Belfast (Cert. Commercial Law 1993). Nuffield Schol., 1967; Council of Europe Fellow, 1980. Dep. Dir, NI Blood Transfusion Service, 1981–2000; Consultant Haematologist, Belfast City Hosp., 1981–2000. Non-exec. Dir, UK Transplant, 2000–01. Mem., Lab. Services Adv. Cttee, DHSS NI, 1995–2000. Mem., Partners' Council, NICE, 1999–2000. UK Blood Transfusion Service: Mem., Standing Adv. Cttee for Selection of Blood Donors, 1995–98; Chm., Standing Adv. Cttee for Transfusion Transmitted Infections, 1998–2000. Member: WHO Expert Adv. Panel for Blood Products, 1988–2000; Blood Safety Adv. Cttee, NI, 1998–2000; Standing Adv. Cttee for Pathology, NI, 1998–2000. Mem., Scientific Cttee, Eur. Sch. of Blood Transfusion, 1996–2000; Co-ordinator of Standardisation for Eur. Cord Blood Banking, 1996–2000. Mem., 1999–2003, Associate Mem., 2004–07, GMC. Royal College of Pathologists: Mem. Council, 1996–2000; Chm., NI Affairs Cttee, 1998–2000; Mem., Patient Liaison Gp, 1998–2001. Pres., Med. Women's Fedn, 1994–95. Mem. Council, Internat. Soc. of Blood Transfusion, 1996–2000. Vice-Chm., NI Council for Postgrad. Med. Educn, 1999–2000. Member: Council, BBC NI, 1996–99; ITC, 2001–03. Member: Adv. Forum (NI), Sargent Cancer Care for Children, 2000–03; Council, Leprosy Mission for NI, 1994–2003; Trustee, Marie Curie Cancer Care, 2007–. Chm., Encounter Conf., 2001. Gov., Methodist Coll., Belfast, 1990–93; Mem., Exec. Cttee, Assoc. of Governing Bodies of Voluntary Grammar Schs, 1990–95. FRSA 2002. *Recreations:* opera, theatre, classical music, hill walking, cycling. *Club:* Reform.

BHASKAR, Prof. Krishan Nath; Founder, 1983, Director, 1988–94, Motor Industry Research Unit Ltd, Norwich; *b* 9 Oct. 1945; *s* of late Dr Ragu Nath Bhaskar and Mrs Kamla Bhaskar (*née* Dora Skill); *m* 1977, Fenella Mary (*née* McCann); one *s* one *d.* *Educ:* St Paul's Sch., London; London Sch. of Econs and Pol. Science (BSc Econ 1st Cl. Hons, MSc Econ). Lectr, LSE, 1968–70; Lectr in Accounting, Univ. of Bristol, 1970–78; Prof. of Accountancy and Finance, UEA, 1978–88. Founder, Computer Industry Res. Unit, 1985. *Publications:* (with D. Murray) Macroeconomic Systems, 1976; Building Financial Models: a simulation approach, 1978; Manual to Building Financial Models, 1978; The Future of the UK Motor Industry, 1979; The Future of the World Motor Industry, 1980; (with M. J. R. Shave) Computer Science Applied to Business Systems, 1982; The UK and European Motor Industry: analysis and future prospects, 1983; (jtly) Financial Modelling with a Microcomputer, 1984; (with R. J. Housden) Management Information Systems and Data Processing for the Management Accountant, 1985, new edn, as Information Technology Management, 1990; (with B. C. Williams) The Impact of Microprocessors on the Small Practice, 1985; A Fireside Chat on Databases for Accountants, 1985; Computer Security—Threats and Countermeasures, 1993; *reports:* A Research Report on the Future of the UK and European Motor Industry, 1984; Jaguar: an investor's guide, 1984; Car Pricing in Europe, 1984; (with G. R. Kaye) Financial Planning with Personal Computers, Vol. 1, 1985, Vol. 2, 1986; State Aid to the European Motor Industry, 1985, updated edn 1987; Demand Growth: a boost for employment?, 1985; Japanese Automotive Strategies: a European and US perspective, 1986; Quality and the Japanese Motor Industry: lessons for the West?, 1986; The Future of Car Retailing in the UK, 1987; A Single European Market? an automotive perspective, 1988; Rover: profile, progress and prospects, 1988; Automotive Trade Restrictions in Western Europe, 1989; The Greek Vehicle Market: future opportunities, 1989; Into the 1990s: future strategies of the vehicle producers of South Korea and Malaysia, 1990; UK Local Content of UK and European Cars, 1993; 1993 European Production Forecast, 1993. *Recreations:* gardening, vegetarian cooking, travel, wine.

BHASKAR, Sanjeev, OBE 2006; actor and writer; *b* 31 Oct. 1963; *s* of Inderjit and Janak Bhaskar; *m* 2005, Meera Syal, *qv*; one *s*, and one step *d.* *Educ:* Springwell Primary Sch., Heston; Cranford Community Coll.; Univ. of Hertfordshire (BA Hons Business Studies (Mktg)). Mktg Exec., IBM, 1987–88; Tour Manager, Arts Council (GB) Project, 1990–92; Mktg Officer, Tom Allen Arts Centre, Stratford, London, 1993–95. Performer and writer: Goodness Gracious Me, Radio 4, 1996–98, BBC TV, 1998–2000; The Kumars at No 42, BBC TV, 2001–; actor: Life Isn't All Ha Ha Hee Hee, BBC TV, 2005; actor in films: Notting Hill, 1999; The Mystic Masseur, 2001; The Guru, 2002; Anita and Me, 2002. Presenter, India with Sanjeev Bhaskar, BBC TV series, 2007. Ambassador, Prince's Trust, 2000–. Hon. DLitt, 2004. *Publication:* India with Sanjeev Bhaskar, 2007. *Recreations:* dreaming, chatting, collecting and watching movies, staying in, anything relating to Elvis Presley/Beatles/film trivia/gadgets. *Address:* c/o Lou Coulson Publishing, 37 Berwick Street, W1V 3RF.

BHATIA, Baron *cr* 2001 (Life Peer), of Hampton in the London Borough of Richmond-upon-Thames; **Amirali Alibhai Bhatia,** OBE 1997; Chairman, Forbes Trust, since 1985; *b* 18 March 1932; *s* of Alibhai Bhatia and Fatma Alibhai Bhatia; *m* 1954, Nurbanu Amersi Kanji; three *d.* Career in manufacturing, Tanzania, 1960–72; Dir, Casley Finance Ltd and Forbes Campbell (Internat.) Ltd, 1973–2001. Chm., SITPRO, 1998–; Board Member: E London TEC, 1991–; Nat. Lottery Charities Bd, 1995–2000; Local Investment Fund, 1997–; Project Fullemploy, 1997– (Chm., 1994–97); Mem., Prime Minister's Adv. Cttee for Queen's Award, 1999–. Chairman: Council of Ethnic Minority Vol. Sector Orgns, 1999–; Ethnic Minority Foundn, 1999–; Hon. Treas., Mem. Bd and Exec. Cttee, Internat. Alert, 1994–2000; Trustee: Oxfam, 1985–99 (Chm., Trading Bd, 1986–92); Community Develt Foundn, 1988–97 (Mem., Budget and Finance Cttee); Charities Evaluation Services, 1989–90; Water Aid, 2000–03; St Christopher's Hospice, 1997–2003 (Mem., Audit Cttee); Bd, Diana, Princess of Wales Meml Fund, 2001–03. Trustee, High/Scope Educn Res. Foundn, Mich, 1985–97; Bd Mem., Tower Hamlets Coll., 1991–98. MInstD. Personality of the Year, UK Charity Awards, 2001; Beacon Prize for Leadership, Beacon Fellowship, 2003. *Recreations:* reading, cricket, voluntary work. *Address:* The Forbes Trust, 9 Artillery Lane, E1 7LP. *T:* (020) 7377 8484. *Club:* Royal Commonwealth Society.

BHATNAGAR, Sir Rajeshwar Sarup, (Sir Roger), KNZM 1998; Chief Executive, R. B. Investments; *b* 26 Oct. 1942; separated; one *s* one *d.* Man. Dir, Sound Plus, 1980–93; Chm., Noel Leeming/Pacific Retail Gp, 1990–98. *Recreation:* fishing. *Club:* Auckland.

BHATTACHARYA, Satyajit, FRCSE, FRCS; Consultant Surgeon, Royal London Hospital and St Bartholomew's Hospital, since 1999 (specialist in liver, biliary and pancreatic surgery); Surgeon to the Royal Household, since 2006; *b* Mumbai, 22 Nov. 1962; *s* of Durga Prasanna and Kalpana Bhattacharya; *m* 1988, Dr Shanti Vijayaraghavan; one *d.* *Educ:* Don Bosco Sch. and St Xavier's Coll., Mumbai; Grant Med. Coll., Mumbai (MB BS 1984, MS 1988); Royal Free Hosp. Sch. of Medicine (MPhil 1995). FRCSE 1991; FRCS 1998. Registrar and Lectr, Royal Free and University Coll. Hosps, 1989–95 and 1996–98. Mem., Ct of Examrs, RCS, 2005–. *Publications:* contrib. chapters to med. textbooks; papers in med. jls incl. Nature Clin. Practice, Hepatology, British Jl Surgery, British Jl Cancer. *Recreations:* reading, walking on Hampstead Heath, watching cricket. *Address:* HPB Surgery Unit, Royal London Hospital, Whitechapel, E1 1BB. *T:* and *Fax:* (020) 7377 7439; *e-mail:* s.bhattacharya@bartsandthelondon.nhs.uk.

BHATTACHARYA, Prof. Shoumo, MD; FRCP, FMedSci; Professor of Cardiovascular Medicine, University of Oxford, since 2004; Fellow, Green Templeton College (formerly Green College), Oxford, since 2004; *b* 24 Feb. 1960; *s* of Cdre Asoke Kumar Bhattacharya and Jayashri Bhattacharya; *m* 1989, Dr Jane Caldwell; two *s.* *Educ:* All India Inst. of Med. Sci., New Delhi (MD 1985); King's Coll. London (MSc). FRCP 2003. Jun. Resident in Medicine, All India Inst. of Med. Scis, New Delhi, 1983–85; Registrar in Cardiology and Medicine, Northwick Park Hosp., Harrow, 1987–90; MRC Trng Fellow and Hon. Sen. Registrar, Northwick Park Hosp., Harrow and Hammersmith Hosp., London, 1990–94; BHF Internat. Res. Fellow, 1994–96, Instructor in Medicine, 1996–98, Dana-Farber Cancer Inst. and Harvard Med. Sch., Boston, Mass; Wellcome Trust Sen. Fellow in Clinical Sci. and Hon. Consultant Cardiologist, Dept of Cardiovascular Medicine and Wellcome Trust Centre for Human Genetics, Univ. of Oxford, 1998–. FMedSci 2006. *Publications:* articles in Nature, Nature Genetics, Cell, Genes & Develt, Jl Biol Chem. *Recreations:* science, history, theory and practice of the culinary arts. *Address:* Wellcome Trust Centre for Human Genetics, Roosevelt Drive, Oxford OX3 7BN. *T:* (01865) 287771; *e-mail:* sbhattac@well.ox.ac.uk.

BHATTACHARYYA, family name of **Baron Bhattacharyya**.

BHATTACHARYYA, Baron *cr* 2004 (Life Peer), of Moseley in the County of West Midlands; **Sushantha Kumar Bhattacharyya,** Kt 2003; CBE 1997; FREng, FIMechE; Professor of Manufacturing (formerly of Manufacturing Systems Engineering), since 1980, Director, Warwick Manufacturing Group, since 1980, University of Warwick; *b* 6 June 1940; *s* of Sudhir Bhattacharyya and Hemanalini (*née* Chakraborty); *m* 1981, Bridie Rabbitt; three *d.* *Educ:* IIT, Kharagpur (BTech); Univ. of Birmingham (MSc, PhD). MIMechE, FIMechE 2005; FIET; FREng (FEng 1991). CAV Ltd, 1960–63; Prodn Engr, Joseph Lucas Ltd, 1964–68; Lectr, Dept of Engrg Prodn, Univ. of Birmingham, 1970. Advr, nat. and multinat. cos, UK and abroad. Non-exec. Dir, Technology Rover Gp, 1986–92; Mem. Bd, Transnet Ltd, S Africa, 2003–04. Member: Nat. Consumer Council, 1990–93; Council for Sci. and Technology, 1993–2003; UK Technol. Foresight Panel on Manufg, 1994–97; Indo-British Partnership Area Adv. Gp, 1994–2000; W Midlands Regl Develt Agency, 1999–2003; Competitiveness Council, 1999–2000; Rover Task Force, 2000; Trade Partners UK: India Advisors, 2000–03. Mem., Scientific Adv. Bd, Singapore Inst. of Manufg Technol., 2002–. Trustee, IPPR, 1998–. Hon. Professor: Hong Kong Poly. Univ., 1992; Univ. of Technol., Malaysia, 1993; Min. of Machinery, Beijing, 1994. Mem. Council, Edgbaston High Sch. for Girls, Birmingham. Fellow: World Acad. of Productivity, 1999; NAE, India, 1999. CCMI (CIMgt 1996). Hon. FILog 1996. DUniv Surrey, 1992; Hon. DEng Univ. of Technol., Malaysia; Hon. DBA Hong Kong Poly., 2003; Hon. DSc Birmingham, 2004. Dist. Alumnus Award, IIT, Kharagpur, 2005. Mensforth Internat. Gold Medal, IEE, 1998; Sir Robert Lawrence Award, Inst. of Logistics and Transport, 2000. Padma Bhushan (India), 2002. *Publications:* numerous, on operational and technological change in manufacturing industry. *Recreations:* family, flying, cricket. *Address:* International Manufacturing Centre, University of Warwick, Coventry CV4 7AL. *T:* (024) 7652 3155. *Club:* Athenæum.

BHOGAL, Rev. Inderjit Singh, OBE 2005; Director, Yorkshire and Humber Faiths Forum, since 2005; President, Methodist Conference, 2000–01; *b* Nairobi, 17 Jan. 1953; *m* 1986, Kathryn Anne; one *s* one *d.* *Educ:* Khalsa Sikh Sch., Nairobi; Blue Coat C of E Sch., Dudley; Dudley Tech. Coll.; Hartley Victoria Coll., Manchester (BA Manchester Univ. 1979); Westminster Coll., Oxford (MA 1991). Minister: Darlington Street Circuit, 1979–87; Carver Street Circuit, Sheffield, 1987–94; Sheffield Inner City Ecumenical Mission, 1994–2004. Co-ordinator, Wolverhampton Inter-Faith Gp, 1984–87; Mem., Sheffield Chaplaincy to Higher Educn, 1987–94 (Chm., 1990–94); Dir of Studies, 1994–97, Dir, 1997–2004, Urban Theol. Unit, Sheffield; Consultant Theologian, Christian Aid, 2004–05. Mem., Home Office Race Equality Adv. Panel, 2003–. Patron, Race Equality in Employment Prog., 2003–. DUniv: Oxford Brookes, 2001; Sheffield Hallam, 2002. *Publications:* A Table for All, 2000; On the Hoof: theology in transit, 2001; Unlocking the Doors, 2002. *Recreations:* walking, cooking, sport.

BHOWMICK, Prof. Bimal Kanti, OBE 2001; MD; FRCP; Professor (personal chair), Cardiff University, 2004; Consultant Physician, now Emeritus, Care of the Elderly, 1976–2005, Intermediate Care, since 2006, Glan Clwyd Hospital, Rhyl; *b* 13 Feb. 1940; *s* of late Jamini Mohan Bhowmick and of Ashalata Bhowmick; *m* 1969, Dr Aparna Banerjee; two *s* one *d.* *Educ:* Calcutta Univ. (MB BS; MD 1968). FRCP 1987. SHO, Victoria Hosp., Blackpool, 1969–71; SHO, 1971–72, Registrar, 1972–74, Burton Rd Hosp., Dudley; Sen. Registrar, H. M. Stanley Hosp., St Asaph, 1974–76; Clin. Dir, 1993–2004, Clin. Dir of Integrated Medicine, 2001–02, Care of the Elderly, Glan Clwyd Hosp., Rhyl. Associate Dean for Overseas Doctors in Wales, Sch. of Postgrad. Med. and Dental Educn, Univ. of Wales Coll. of Med., 1997–2006; Hon. Sen. Lectr, Inst. of Res., Univ. of Wales, Bangor, 1998–. Mem. Council, 1998–2001, Censor, 2001–03, RCP. Fellow, UWCM, 2003. *Publications:* (contrib.) Parkinson's Disease and Parkinsonism in the Elderly, 2000; numerous contribs to learned jls. *Recreations:* reading, gardening, cinema. *Address:* Glan Clwd Hospital, Rhyl, Denbighshire, LL18 5UJ. *T:* (01745) 583910; Jamini Allt Goch, St Asaph, Denbighshire LL17 0BP.

BHUGRA, Prof. Dinesh Kumar Makhan Lal, PhD; Professor of Mental Health and Cultural Diversity, Institute of Psychiatry, King's College London, since 2004; President, Royal College of Psychiatrists, since 2008 (Dean, 2003–08); *b* Yamuna Nagar, India, 8 July 1952; *s* of Makhan Lal and Shanta Bhugra; partner, Michael Bryn Thacker. *Educ:* Univ. of Poona (MB BS 1976); Univ. of Leicester (MPhil Psychiatry 1990); S Bank Univ. (MSc Sociol. 1991); Univ. of London (MA Social Anthropol. 1996; PhD Psychiatry 1999). LMSSA 1980; MRCPsych 1985. Registrar, then SHO, Leics Rotation Scheme, 1981–86; Sen. Registrar, Maudsley Trng Scheme, 1986–89; Lectr, MRC Social Psychiatry Unit, 1989–92; Sen. Lectr, Maudsley Hosp., 1992–2002; Reader, S London and Maudsley NHS Trust, 2002–04; Hon. Consultant, S London and Maudsley Foundn NHS Trust (formerly Maudsley Hosp., then S London and Maudlsey NHS Trust), 2004–. *Publications:* Mad Tales from Bollywood: portrayal of mental illness in conventional Hindi cinema, 2006; (ed with K. Bhui) Culture and Mental Health: a comprehensive textbook, 2007; (ed with K. Bhui) Textbook of Cultural Psychiatry, 2007; (ed jtly) A Selected Annotated Bibliography of Public Attitudes to Mental Health, 1975–2005, 2007; (ed jtly) Workplace-based Assessments in Psychiatry, 2007; (ed jtly) Management for Psychiatrists, 3rd edn 2007; (ed with O. Howes) Handbook for Psychiatric Trainees, 2007. *Recreations:* reading crime novels and fiction by Indian authors, cinema (Hitchcock and Billy Wilder), theatre, Hindi film music. *Address:* PO 25, HSPRD, Institute of Psychiatry, King's College London, De Crespigny Park, SE5 8AF. *T:* (020) 7848 0500, *Fax:* (020) 7848 0333; *e-mail:* d.bhugra@iop.kcl.ac.uk. *Club:* Reform.

BIANCHERI, Boris, Hon. GCVO 1990; Chairman, Agenzia Nazionale Stampa Associata, since 1997; President: Institute for International Political Studies, Milan, since 1998; Italian Federation of Newspaper Publishers, Rome, since 2004; *b* 3 Nov. 1930; *s* of Augusto and Olga Wolff von Stomersee; *m* 1979, Flavia Arzeni; one *s* one *d.* *Educ:* Univ. of Rome (Law Degree). Joined Min. of Foreign Affairs, 1956; served Athens, 1959;

Economic Dept, Min. of Foreign Affairs, 1964–67; Sec.-Gen., Commn for 1970 Osaka Exhibn, 1968; First Counsellor, Cultural Relations, Min. of Foreign Affairs, 1971; Political Counsellor, London, 1972–75; Chef de Cabinet, Sec. of State for Foreign Affairs, 1978; Minister, 1979; Ambassador, Tokyo, 1980–84; Dir Gen., Political Affairs, Min. of Foreign Affairs, 1985; Ambassador: UK, 1987–91; USA, 1991–95; Sec.-Gen., Min. of Foreign Affairs, 1995–97. Gran Croce, Ordine al Merito della Repubblica Italiana; numerous foreign orders. *Recreations:* gardening, boating, swimming, horse-riding. *Address:* Agenzia Nazionale Stampa Associata, Via delle Dataria 94, 00187 Rome, Italy. *Club:* Circolo Della Caccia (Rome).

BIANCHI, Adrian Max, MOM 1995; MD; FRCS, FRCSE; Consultant Specialist Paediatric and Neonatal Surgeon, Manchester and North Western Region, since 1984; *b* 19 Jan. 1948; *s* of Loris and Yvonne Bianchi (*née* Ganado); *m* 1970, Claire (*née* Sammut); two *s* one *d*. *Educ:* Medical Sch., Royal Univ. of Malta (MD 1969). FRCS 1975; FRCSE 1975. Specialised in paediatric and neonatal surgery through surgical progs, Liverpool and Manchester; Dir, Neonatal Surgery, and Mem., Bd of Mgt, St Mary's Hosp., Manchester, 1987–2002; Paediatric Surgical Rep., Mgt Bd, Royal Manchester Children's Hosp., 1984–90; has developed orig. surgical techniques and new surgical approaches incl. surgical mgt of children with short bowel. *Publications:* contrib. chapters in paediatric surgical operative and gen. surgical textbooks; 65 articles in medical jls. *Recreations:* reproduction of antique furniture, marquetry, ancient civilizations, swimming, gardening (bonsai, carnations). *Address:* Royal Manchester Children's Hospital, Hospital Road, Pendlebury, Manchester M27 4HA. *T:* (0161) 922 2193; *e-mail:* adrian.bianchi@cmmc.nhs.uk.

BIBBY, Benjamin; *see* Bibby, J. B.

BIBBY, Dame Enid, DBE 2004; Headteacher, Wood Green High School College of Sport, Maths and Computing, Wednesbury, 1998–2006; *b* 8 Feb. 1951; *d* of Fred and Ivy Kemp; *m* 1999, Dr Bob Bibby; two step *d*. *Educ:* Lancaster Univ. (BA Hons English); Liverpool Univ. (PGCE); Univ. of Cambridge (AdvDip. Ed). Deputy Headteacher: Lealands Community Sch., Luton, 1986–89; Leon Community Sch., Bletchley, 1989–95; Headteacher, Silverdale Sch., Sheffield, 1995–98. Mem. Council, Specialist Schs and Acads (formerly Special Schs) Trust, 2002–05; Mem. Bd, British Educnl Communications and Technol. Agency, 2004–05. Gov., Ofsted, 2007–08. Man. Dir, DEB Consulting Ltd, 2006–. Unilever Fellow, London Leadership Centre, 2002. FRSA 1997; FCMI (FIMgt 1998). JP Milton Keynes, 1989–94. *Recreations:* sailing (ocean and dinghy), fell walking, modern literature, Bridgnorth's Theatre on the Steps (mem.), Van Morrison. *Address:* Sabrina House, 2 Southwell Riverside, Bridgnorth, Shropshire WV16 4AS. *T:* (01746) 768956; *e-mail:* dameenid@btinternet.com. *Club:* Chelmarsh Sailing.

BIBBY, (John) Benjamin; Director, 1961–94, Chairman, 1970–78, J. Bibby & Sons PLC; *b* 19 April 1929; *s* of late J. P. and D. D. Bibby; *m* 1956, Susan Lindsay Paterson; two *s* one *d*. *Educ:* Oundle Sch.; St Catharine's Coll., Cambridge (MA). Nat. Service, 2nd Lieut, King's Regt, 1948–49. Called to the Bar, Gray's Inn, 1981. Held various positions in J. Bibby & Sons PLC, 1953–94. Mem. Council, Univ. of Liverpool, 1978–81; Mem. Exec. Cttee, West Kirby Residential Sch., 1978–87. Mem. Cttee, 1982–2001, Chm., 1983–87, Hon. Treas., 1987–2001, Hon. Membership Sec., 2002–04, Nat. Squib Owners' Assoc.; Pres., Merseyside and Deeside Br., STA (formerly STA Schooners), 1992–2003. Fellow Commoner, St Catharine's Coll., Cambridge, 1996–. JP Liverpool 1975–81. *Publications:* (with C. L. Bibby) A Miller's Tale, 1978; A Birthday Ode and Other Verse, 1994; A Letter to a Grandson and Other Verse, 1994. *Recreations:* sailing, gardening. *Address:* Kirby Mount House, 1 Kirby Mount, West Kirby, Wirral, CH48 2HU. *T:* (0151) 625 8071. *Clubs:* Royal Thames Yacht; West Kirby Sailing; Royal Mersey Yacht; Royal Anglesey Yacht.

BIBBY, Sir Michael (James), 3rd Bt *cr* 1959, of Tarporley, Co. Palatine of Chester; Managing Director, Bibby Line Group Ltd, since 2000; *b* 2 Aug. 1963; *e s* of Sir Derek Bibby, 2nd Bt and Christine Maud, *d* of Rt Rev. F. J. Okell, Bishop Suffragan of Stockport; *S* father, 2002; *m* 1994, Beverley, *o d* of Donald Graham; two *s* (twins). *Educ:* Rugby; Trinity Coll., Oxford Univ. *Heir: s* Alexander James Bibby, *b* 24 Aug. 1997. *Address:* Bibby Line Group Ltd, 105 Duke Street, Liverpool L1 5JQ.

BIĆANIĆ, Prof. Nenad Josip Nikola, PhD; FICE, FIACM; Regius Professor of Civil Engineering, University of Glasgow, since 1994 (Head of Department of Civil Engineering, 1997–2001); *b* Zagreb, Croatia, 6 Sept. 1945; *s* of Vladimir Bićanić and Elizabeta (*née* Kostial-Živanović); *m* 1969, Jasna Babić; one *s* one *d*. *Educ:* Zagreb Univ., Croatia (Dip. Ing 1968); Univ. of Wales, Swansea (PhD 1978). Structural Engr, Zagreb, 1968–69; Consulting Engr, Arnhem, Netherlands, 1969–72; Zagreb University: Lectr and Researcher, 1972–76; Docent, Prof., 1978–83; Prof., 1984–85; Lectr, Sen. Lectr, then Reader, Univ. of Wales, Swansea, 1985–94. Vis. Prof., Univ. of Colo, Boulder, 1983–84. FICE 1998; FIACM 1998. *Publications:* Computer Aided Analysis and Design of Concrete Structures, 1990; (ed) Computational Modelling of Concrete Structures, 1994, revd edn 1998, 2003; papers in learned and professional jls. *Recreations:* international folk-dancing, ski-ing, tennis. *Address:* 20 Ledcameroch Road, Bearsden, Glasgow G61 4AE. *T:* (0141) 942 0711. *Club:* College (Glasgow).

BICESTER, 3rd Baron *cr* 1938, of Tusmore; **Angus Edward Vivian Smith;** *b* 20 Feb. 1932; *s* of Lt-Col Hon. Stephen Edward Vivian Smith (*d* 1952) (2nd *s* of 1st Baron) and Elenor Anderson, *d* of Edward S. Hewitt, New York City; *S* uncle, 1968. *Educ:* Eton. *Heir: b* Hugh Charles Vivian Smith, *b* 8 Nov. 1934.

BICHARD, Sir Michael (George), KCB 1999; Chairman, Design Council, since 2008; Director, Institute for Government, since 2008; *b* 31 Jan. 1947. *Educ:* Manchester Univ. (LLB); Birmingham Univ. (MSocSci). Chief Executive: Brent BC, 1980–86; Gloucestershire CC, 1986–90; Social Security Benefits Agency, 1990–95; Perm. Sec., Employment Dept Gp, April–July 1995; Jt Perm. Sec., July–Dec. 1995, Perm. Sec., 1996–2001, DfEE. Rector, London Inst., subseq. Univ. of the Arts London, 2001–08. Chm., Soham Murders Inquiry, 2004. Chm., Legal Services Commn, 2005–08. Chairman: Rathbone Training Ltd, 2001–08; RSe Consulting, 2003–; non-exec. Dir, Reed Exec. plc, 2002–04. Mem., ESRC, 1989–92. Chm. Bd Dirs, ARTIS, 2003–06. Dir, River and Rowing Mus. Foundn, 2002–. Governor: Henley Mgt Coll., 2002–; Council, Dyslexia Inst., 2003–06. Hon. Fellow, Inst. of Local Govt Studies, Birmingham Univ. FIPD; CCMI; FRSA. DUniv: Leeds Metropolitan, 1992; Middlesex, 2001; Southampton Inst., 2002; Hon. LLD: Birmingham, 1999; Bradford, 2004. *Address:* Design Council, 34 Bow Street, WC2E 7DL. *T:* (020) 7420 5200, *Fax:* (020) 7420 5300.

BICK; *see* Moore-Bick.

BICKERSTETH, Rt Rev. John Monier, KCVO 1989; Clerk of the Closet to The Queen, 1979–89; *b* 6 Sept. 1921; *yr s* of late Rev. Canon Edward Monier, OBE and Inez Katharine Bickersteth; *m* 1955, Rosemary, *yr d* of late Edward and Muriel Cleveland-Stevens, Gaines, Oxted; three *s* one *d*. *Educ:* Rugby; Christ Church, Oxford (MA 1953); Wells Theol College; Open Univ. 1997. Captain, Buffs and Royal Artillery, 1941–46. Priest, 1951; Curate, St Matthew, Moorfields, Bristol, 1950–54; Vicar, St John's, Hurst Green, Oxted, 1954–62; St Stephen's, Chatham, 1962–70; Hon. Canon of Rochester, 1968–70; Bishop Suffragan of Warrington, 1970–75; Bishop of Bath and Wells, 1975–87. A C of E delegate to 4th Assembly, WCC, 1968. Chaplain and Sub-Prelate, OStJ, 1977–96. Chairman: Royal Sch. of Church Music, 1977–88; Bible Reading Fellowship, 1978–90; Vice Chm., Central Bd of Finance of Church of England, 1981–84. Member: Marlborough Coll. Council, 1980–91; Wilts Wildlife Trust Council, 1989–95. Freeman of the City of London, 1979. *Publications:* (jtly) Clerks of the Closet in the Royal Household, 1991; (ed) The Bickersteth Diaries 1914–1918, 1995, 3rd edn 1998; Run o' the Mill Bishop (autobiog.), 2005. *Address:* Beckfords, Newtown, Tisbury, Wilts SP3 6NY. *T:* (01747) 870479. *Club:* Royal Commonwealth Society.

BICKFORD, James David Prydeaux, CB 1995; Chairman, Bickford Associates; author; *b* 28 July 1940; *s* of late William A. J. P. Bickford and Muriel Bickford (*née* Smythe); *m* 1965, Carolyn Jane, *d* of late Major W. A. R. Sumner, RHA; three *s*. *Educ:* Downside; Law Society's College of Law, London. Admitted to Roll of Solicitors, 1963; Solicitor of the Supreme Court. In practice, J. J. Newcombe, Solicitors, Okehampton, 1963–69; Crown Counsel and Legal Advr to Govt of Turks and Caicos Islands, BWI, 1969–71; Asst Legal Advr, FCO, 1971–79 and 1982–84; Legal Advr, British Mil. Govt, Berlin, 1979–82; Legal Counsellor, FCO, 1984–87; Under Sec., MoD, and Legal Advr to Security and Intelligence Services, 1987–95. Judge Ben C. Green Lectr in Law, Case Western Reserve Univ., USA; Vis. Prof. of Law, Cleveland State Univ., USA. Mem., Panel of Legal Experts, Internat. Telecommunications Satellite Orgn, 1985–87; Chm., Assembly of Internat. Maritime Satellite Orgn, 1985–87. Mem., Law Soc. Hon. Mem., Nat. Security Cttee, Amer. Bar Assoc. *Publications:* Land Dealings Simplified in the Turks and Caicos Islands, 1971; *fiction:* The Face of Tomorrow, 2004; contribs on intelligence, organised crime and money-laundering issues to symposia, jls, media and internet. *Recreations:* the family, sailing, fishing. *Address:* c/o National Westminster Bank, Torrington, Devon EX38 8HP.

BICKFORD-SMITH, Margaret Osborne; QC 2003; a Recorder, since 1997; *b* 4 June 1950; *d* of James Maclean Todd and Janet Gillespie Todd (*née* Holmes); *m* 1970, Stephen William Bickford-Smith; one *s*. *Educ:* Headington Sch.; Lady Margaret Hall, Oxford (MA). Called to the Bar, Inner Temple, 1973, Bencher, 1993 (Master of Debates, 1993–2000). Mem., Hounslow LBC, 1974–82. *Recreations:* Italy, art, music. *Address:* Crown Office Chambers, 2 Crown Office Row, Temple, EC4Y 7HJ. *T:* (020) 7797 8100, *Fax:* (020) 7797 8101. *Club:* Royal Automobile.

BICKLE, Prof. Michael James, DPhil; FRS 2007; Professor, Department of Earth Sciences, University of Cambridge, since 2000; *b* 26 Feb. 1948; *s* of Ronald Stancliffe Bickle and René Florence Bickle; *m* 1978, Hazel Joan Chapman; two *d*. *Educ:* Queens' Coll., Cambridge (BA 1970); DPhil Oxon. Lectr, then Sen. Lectr, Univ. of Western Australia, 1978–83; Lectr, 1983–95, Reader, 1995–2000, in Earth Scis, Univ. of Cambridge. *Recreations:* orienteering, sailing. *Address:* Department of Earth Sciences, Downing Street, Cambridge CB2 3EQ. *T:* (01223) 333400, *Fax:* (01223) 333450; *e-mail:* mb72@esc.com.ac.uk.

BIDDER, Neil; QC 1998; **His Honour Judge Bidder;** a Circuit Judge, since 2004; *b* 22 July 1953; *s* of Glyn Turner Bidder and Constance Mabel Bidder; *m* 1978, Madeleine Thomas; two *s*. *Educ:* Ogmore Grammar Sch.; Queens' Coll., Cambridge (BA 1974; MA 1977); Dalhousie Univ., Canada (LLM 1977). Called to the Bar, Lincoln's Inn, 1976, Additional Bencher, 2008; in practice at the Bar, 1976–; an Asst Recorder, 1991–94; a Recorder, 1994–2004; Hd of Chambers, 2001–04. Founder Chm., Welsh Personal Injury Lawyers Assoc., 1999–2002; Legal Chm., Six Nations Rugby Disciplinary Cttee, 1999–. *Recreations:* choral singing, opera, gardening, sport. *Address:* Cardiff Crown Court, Cathays Park, Cardiff CF10 3PG.

BIDDLE, Prof. Martin, OBE 1997; FBA 1985; FSA; Professor of Medieval Archaeology, University of Oxford, 1997–2002, now Emeritus; Astor Senior Research Fellow in Medieval Archaeology, Hertford College, Oxford, 1989–2002, now Emeritus; Director, Winchester Research Unit, since 1968; *b* 4 June 1937; *s* of Reginald Samuel Biddle and Gwladys Florence Biddle (*née* Baker); *m* 1966, Birthe, *d* of Landsretssagfører Axel Th. and Anni Kjølbye of Sønderborg, Denmark; two *d*, and two *d* by previous marriage. *Educ:* Merchant Taylors' Sch., Northwood; Pembroke Coll., Cambridge (MA 1965); MA Oxon 1967; MA Pennsylvania 1977. FSA 1964. Second Lieut, 4 RTR, 1956; 1 Indep. Sqn, RTR, Berlin, 1956–57. Asst Inspector of Ancient Monuments, MPBW, 1961–63; Lectr in Medieval Archaeology, Univ. of Exeter, 1963–67; Vis. Fellow, All Souls Coll., Oxford, 1967–68; Dir, University Museum, and Prof. of Anthropology and of History of Art, Univ. of Pennsylvania, 1977–81; Lectr of The House, Christ Church, Oxford, 1983–86. Directed excavations and investigations: Nonsuch Palace, 1959–60; Winchester, 1961–71; (with Birthe Biddle): Repton, 1974–88, 1993; St Alban's Abbey, 1978, 1982–84, 1991, 1994–95, 2003, 2006; Holy Sepulchre, Jerusalem, 1989–90, 1992, 1993, 1998; Qasr Ibrim, Egypt, 1990, 1992, 1995, 2000. Archaeological Consultant: Canterbury Cathedral; St Alban's Abbey and Cathedral Church; Eurotunnel, etc. Chm., Rescue, Trust for British Archaeology, 1971–75. Mem., Royal Commn on Historical Monuments of England, 1984–95. Chm., Historic Towns Atlas Cttee, 1994–; Pres., Soc. for Medieval Archaeology, 1995–98; Vice-Pres., Soc. of Antiquaries, 2006–. General Editor, Winchester Studies, 1976–. Hon. DLitt Southampton, 2003. (With Birthe Biddle) Frend Medal, Soc. of Antiquaries, 1986. *Publications:* (with C. Heighway) The Future of London's Past, 1973; (with F. Barlow and others) Winchester in the Early Middle Ages, 1976; (with H.M. Colvin, J. Summerson and others) The History of the King's Works, vol. iv, pt 2, 1982; Object and Economy in Medieval Winchester, 1990; The Tomb of Christ, 1999 (German edn, 1998; Italian edn, 2002); King Arthur's Round Table, 2000; (jtly) Henry VIII's Coastal Artillery Fort at Camber Castle, Rye, Sussex, 2001; Nonsuch Palace: the material culture of a noble restoration household, 2005; papers on archaeological, historical and art-historical subjects in learned jls. *Recreations:* travel, esp. Hellenic travel, reading. *Address:* 19 Hamilton Road, Oxford OX2 7PY. *T:* and *Fax:* (01865) 559017. *Club:* Athenæum.

BIDDLECOMBE, Henrietta Catherine; *see* Knight, H. C.

BIDDLESTONE, Prof. Anthony Joseph, (Joe), PhD; CEng, FIChemE; Professor of Chemical Engineering, 1993–2004, now Professor Emeritus, and University Foundation Fellow, since 2005, University of Birmingham; *b* 8 Aug. 1937; *s* of William Albert and Ivy Evelyn Biddlestone; *m* 1973, Marion Summers; two *s*. *Educ:* George Dixon Grammar Sch., Birmingham; Univ. of Birmingham (BSc 1958; PhD 1961). CEng 1964; FIChemE 1973. University of Birmingham: Lectr, 1965–85; Sen Lectr, 1985–93; Hd, Sch. of Chem. Engrg, 1993–98; Dean of Engrg, 1998–2002. Chm., Accreditation Bd, IChemE, 1992–99. FRSA 1999. *Publications:* numerous contribs to refereed learned jls on aerobic biodegradation of organic wastes. *Recreations:* church music, organist, conductor. *Address:* School of Chemical Engineering, University of Birmingham, Edgbaston, Birmingham B15 2TT. *T:* (0121) 414 7452.

BIDDULPH, family name of **Baron Biddulph**.

BIDDULPH, 5th Baron *cr* 1903; **Anthony Nicholas Colin Maitland Biddulph;** interior designer; sporting manager; *b* 8 April 1959; *s* of 4th Baron Biddulph and of Lady Mary, *d* of Viscount Maitland (killed in action, 1943) and *g d* of 15th Earl of Lauderdale; *S* father, 1988; *m* 1993, Hon. Sian Diana (marr. diss. 2001), *y d* of Baron Gibson-Watt, MC; two *s. Educ:* Cheltenham; RAC, Cirencester. Liveryman, Amourers' and Brasiers' Co., 1995. *Recreations:* shooting, fishing, painting. *Heir: s* Hon. Robert Julian Maitland Biddulph, *b* 8 July 1994. *Address:* 8 Orbel Street, SW11 3NZ; Makerstoun House, Kelso TD5 7PA. *Clubs:* Cavalry and Guards, Raffles, White's.

BIDDULPH, Constance; see Holt, C.

BIDDULPH, Sir Ian D'Olier, (Jack), 11th Bt *cr* 1664, of Westcombe, Kent; *b* 28 Feb. 1940; *s* of Sir Stuart Royden Biddulph, 10th Bt and Muriel Margaret (*d* 1995), *d* of Angus Harkness, Hamley Bridge, S Australia; *S* father, 1986; *m* 1967, Margaret Eleanor, *o d* of late John Gablonski, Oxley, Brisbane; one *s* two *d. Heir: s* Paul William Biddulph [*b* 30 Oct. 1967; *m* 2000, Susan, *d* of late James Adkins; two *d*]. *Address:* 17 Kendall Street, Oxley, Qld 4075, Australia.

BIDSTRUP, (Patricia) Lesley, MD, FRCP, FRACP; Member, Medical Appeals Tribunal, 1970–88; private consulting concerned mainly with industrial medicine, since 1958; *b* 24 Oct. 1916; *d* of Clarence Leslie Bidstrup, Chemical Works Manager, South Australia, and Kathleen Helena Bidstrup (*née* O'Brien); *m* 1952, Ronald Frank Guymer, TD, MD, FRCP, FRCS, DPH, DIH; one step *s* one step *d. Educ:* Kadina High Sch. and Walford House, Adelaide, SA. MB, BS (Adel.) 1939; MD (Adel.) 1958; FRACP 1954; FRCP (Lond.) 1964. Resident Ho. Phys. and Registrar, Royal Adelaide Hosp., SA, 1939–41. Hon. Capt., AAMC, 1942–45. MO, UNRRA, Glyn-Hughes Hosp., Belsen, 1945–46. General practice: Acting Hon. Asst Phys., Royal Adelaide Hosp.; Tutor in Med., St Mark's Coll., Adelaide, and in Univ. of Adelaide Med. Sch.; Lectr in Med., Univ. of Adelaide Dental Faculty, 1942–45; Asst, Dept for Research in Industrial Medicine, MRC, 1947–58; Clinical Asst (Hon.), Chest Dept, St Thomas' Hosp., 1958–78. Member: Scientific Sub-Cttee on Poisonous Substances used in Agriculture and Food Storage, 1956–58; Industrial Injuries Adv. Council, 1970–83. Visiting Lectr, TUC Centenary Inst. of Occupational Health; Examiner for Diploma in Industrial Health: Conjoint Bd, 1965–71, 1980–82; Society of Apothecaries, 1970–76; External Examiner for Diploma in Industrial Health, Dundee, 1980–82. Fellow, Amer. Coll. of Occupational Medicine. William P. Yant Award, Amer. Industrial Hygiene Assoc., 1989. Mayoress, Royal Borough of Kingston-upon-Thames, 1959, 1960. *Publications:* The Toxicity of Mercury and its Compounds, 1964; chapters in: Cancer Progress, 1960; The Prevention of Cancer, 1967; Clinical Aspects of Inhaled Particles, 1972; contribs to Brit. Jl Indust. Med., Lancet, BMJ, Proc. Royal Soc. Med., ILO Encyclopaedia on Industrial Diseases. *Recreations:* people, theatre, music. *Address:* 11 Sloane Terrace Mansions, Sloane Terrace, SW1X 9DG. *T:* (020) 7730 8720.

BIDWELL, Sir Hugh (Charles Philip), GBE 1989; Deputy Chairman, ITE Group plc (formerly International Trade & Exhibitions J/V Ltd), 1996–2003; Lord Mayor of London, 1989–90; *b* 1 Nov. 1934; *s* of late Edward and Elisabeth Bidwell; *m* 1st, 1962, Jenifer Celia Webb (*d* 2001); two *s* one *d*; 2nd, 2003, Priscilla Pode (*née* Hunter). *Educ:* Stonyhurst College. Nat. Service, 1953–55; commissioned E Surrey Regt, seconded to 1st Bn KAR, based Nyasaland. Viota Foods, 1956–70 (Dir, 1962–70); Dir, Robertson Foods, 1969–70; Chairman: Pearce Duff & Co. Ltd, 1970–84; Gill & Duffus Foods Ltd, 1984–85; British Invisibles, 1991–94; Chief Exec., Allied Lyons Eastern, 1985–91; non-executive Chairman: Riggs AP Bank Ltd, 1989–92; Julius Gp Ltd (formerly Octavian Gp Ltd), 1993–97; non-exec. Dep. Chm., London Forum, 1992–93; non-executive Director: Argyll Group plc, 1990–95; Rothschild Asset Mgt Ltd, 1992–98; Fleming Geared Income and Assets Investment Trust plc, 1993–97; Alpha Airports Gp plc, 1994–2003. Chm., London Tourist Bd, 1992–93; Member: Exec. Cttee, London Chamber of Commerce and Industry, 1976–85; Food from Britain Council, 1983–89 (Chm., Export Bd, 1983–86); European Trade Cttee, 1989–91; British-Soviet Chamber of Commerce, 1989–92; China-Britain (formerly Sino-British) Trade Gp, 1989–94; E European Trade Gp, 1991–92; BOTB, 1992–94. Pres., British Food Export Council, 1980–87; Dep. Pres., Food and Drink Fedn, 1985–86. Alderman, Billingsgate Ward, 1979–96; Sheriff of the City of London, 1986–87. Master, Grocers' Co., 1984–85. President: Billingsgate Ward Club; Fishmongers' & Poulterers' Instn, 1980–98. *Recreations:* golf, fishing, tennis, cricket, shooting. *Clubs:* White's, City of London, MCC; Royal & Ancient; Denham Golf; Royal St George's.

See also J. R. P. Bidwell.

BIDWELL, James Richard Philip; Chief Executive Officer: Visit London, since 2005; London Unlimited, since 2005; *b* 19 Jan. 1965; *s* of Sir Hugh Charles Philip Bidwell, *qv*; *m* 1995, Rebecca Mathiesen; three *d. Educ:* Eton Coll.; Univ. of Bristol (BA Hons French). Account Mgr, Lowe Howard-Spink Advertising, 1987–92; Marketing Mgr, Walt Disney Attractions, 1992–97; Head of Marketing, Seaworld, 1997–98; Marketing Dir, Carland LP, 1998–99; Marketing Director: eToys Inc., 1999–2001; Selfridges plc, 2001–05. Liveryman, Co. of Grocers, 1999–. *Recreations:* mountain biking, fly fishing, skiing. *Address:* Visit London, 2 More London Riverside, SE1 2RR. *T:* (020) 7234 5801; *e-mail:* jbidwell@visitlondon.com. *Clubs:* Home House; Frensham Flyfishers.

BIDWELL, Robin O'Neill, CBE 1999; PhD; Executive Chairman, ERM, since 1993; *b* 15 Sept. 1944; *s* of late Philip John Bidwell and Ellen O'Neill Bidwell; *m* 1st, 1970, Caroline Margaret Budd (marr. diss. 1993); one *s* one *d*; 2nd, 1995, Veronica Rosemary Lucia Verey. *Educ:* Charterhouse; Christ Church, Oxford (BA 1966; MA 1970); Bradford Mgt Centre (PhD 1974). Joined ERL, now ERM, 1973: Dir, 1974–; Man. Dir, 1977–93. Non-exec. Dir, CU Envmtl Trust plc, 1992–2002. Non-exec. Mem., Ofgem, 2003–. Advr, Prince of Wales Business Leaders Forum, 1993–; Trustee, Heritage Trust, 1987–96; Member: Task Force on envmtl implications of 1992, EC, 1989–90; Bd, Sustainability Challenge Foundn, Netherlands, 1993–2003; NERC, 1996–2002; Adv. Cttee on Business and the Envmt, 1999–2003; Member Council: World Business Council for Sustainable Develt, 1997–; UK Roundtable on Sustainable Develt, 1998–2000. Mem. Exec. Cttee, Green Alliance, 1995–. *Recreations:* reshaping landscapes, ski-ing, reading. *Address:* Woodchester Park House, Nympsfield, Glos GL10 3UN. *T:* (office) (020) 7465 7331.

BIENZ, Dr Mariann, (Mrs H. R. B. Pelham), FRS 2003; Senior Scientific Staff Member, since 1991, and Joint Head of Cell Biology, since 2007, MRC Laboratory of Molecular Biology; *b* 21 Dec. 1953; *d* of Jürg Bienz and Lilly Bienz (*née* Gubler); *m* 1996, Hugh Reginald Brentnall Pelham, *qv*; one *s* one *d. Educ:* Gymnasium Winterthur; Univ. of Zürich (Dip. Zool. and Molecular Biol.; PhD 1981). Postdoctoral res. at MRC Lab. of Molecular Biol., Cambridge; Asst Prof., 1986–90, Associate Prof., 1990–91, Univ. of Zürich. Mem., EMBO, 1989. FMedSci 2006. Friedrich Miescher Prize, Swiss Biochemical Soc., 1990. *Publications:* contribs on cell and molecular biol. to various internat. jls. *Recreations:* music, mountain walking. *Address:* MRC Laboratory of Molecular Biology, Hills Road, Cambridge CB2 0QH.

BIGG, Sally; see Gunnell, S.

BIGGAM, Sir Robin (Adair), Kt 1993; Chairman, Independent Television Commission, 1997–2003; *b* 8 July 1938; *s* of Thomas and Eileen Biggam; *m* 1962, Elizabeth McArthur McDougall; one *s* two *d. Educ:* Lanark Grammar Sch. Chartered accountant. Peat Marwick Mitchell, 1960–63; ICI, 1964–81; Director: ICL, 1981–84; Dunlop Holdings plc, 1984–85; Man. Dir, 1986–87, Chief Exec., 1987–91, Chm., 1992–96, BICC plc; Chm., Spectris (formerly Fairey Gp), 1996–2001. Non Executive Director: Chloride Group plc, 1985–87; Lloyds Abbey Life plc (formerly Abbey Life Gp), 1985–90; Redland Gp plc, 1991–97; BAE Systems (formerly British Aerospace) plc, 1994–2003; Foreign & Colonial German Investment Trust plc, 1995–98; British Energy plc, 1996–2002. Pres., German-British Chamber of Commerce, 1995–97. *Recreations:* golf, fishing, gardening, watching television.

BIGGAR, Rev. Canon Prof. Nigel John, PhD; Regius Professor of Moral and Pastoral Theology, University of Oxford, since 2007; Canon of Christ Church, Oxford, since 2007; *b* 14 March 1955; *s* of Francis and Jeanne Biggar; *m* 1982, Virginia Dunn. *Educ:* St Mary's Primary Sch., Castle-Douglas; Drumley House, Ayr; Monkton Combe Sen. Sch., Bath; Worcester Coll., Oxford (BA Modern Hist. 1976; MA 1988); Regent Coll., Vancouver (Master of Christian Studies 1981); Univ. of Chicago (AM Religious Studies 1980; PhD Christian Theol. 1986). Librarian, Latimer Hse, Oxford, 1985–91; Lectr in Christian Ethics, Wycliffe Hall, Oxford, 1987–94; ordained deacon, 1990, priest, 1991; Fellow and Chaplain, Oriel Coll., Oxford, 1990–99; Prof. of Theol., Dept of Theol. and Religious Studies, Univ. of Leeds, 1999–2004; Prof. of Theol., Sch. of Religions and Theol., 2004–07, Fellow, 2005–07, TCD; Canon, Christ Ch Cathedral, Dublin, 2004–07. Lectr, Leeds Parish Ch, 1999–2003. Mem., Cttee on Ethical Issues in Medicine, RCP, 2000–. Pres., Soc. for Study of Christian Ethics, 2003–06. *Publications:* (ed jtly) Cities of Gods: faith, politics and pluralism in Judaism, Christianity and Islam, 1986; (ed) Reckoning with Barth: essays in commemoration of the 100th anniversary of the birth of Karl Barth, 1988; Theological Politics: a critique of Faith in the City, the report of the Archbishop of Canterbury's Commission on Urban Priority Areas (1985), 1988; The Hastening that Waits: Karl Barth's Ethics, 1993, rev. edn 1995; Good Life: reflections on what we value today, 1997; (ed with Rufus Black) The Revival of Natural Law: philosophical, theological and ethical responses to the Finnis-Grisez School, 2000; (ed) Burying the Past: making peace and doing justice after civil conflict, 2001, rev. edn 2003; Aiming to Kill: the ethics of suicide and euthanasia, 2004. *Recreations:* reading history, walking battlefields, visiting historic cemeteries, playing cards. *Address:* Christ Church, Oxford OX1 1DP.

BIGGAR, (Walter) Andrew, CBE 1980 (OBE 1967); MC 1945; TD 1995; FRAgS; farming since 1956; *b* 6 March 1915; *s* of Walter Biggar and Margaret Sproat; *m* 1945, Patricia Mary Irving Elliot (*d* 2007); one *s* one *d. Educ:* Sedbergh Sch., Cumbria; Edinburgh Univ. (BScAgric). FRAgS 1969. Commnd Royal Signals, 1938; War Service, 51st Highland Div., 1939–46; POW, Germany, 1940–45. Rowett Res. Inst., 1935–54. Director and Trustee: Scottish Soc. for Research in Plant Breeding, 1958–88; Animal Diseases Res. Assoc., 1966–96. Member: Farm Animals Welfare Adv. Cttee, 1967–77; ARC, 1969–80; Scottish Agricultural Develt Council, 1971–82; JCO Consultative Bd, 1980–84; Chm., Animals Bd, JCO, 1973–80. Chm., Moredun Animal Health Trust, 1988–94; Dir, Moredun Foundn, 1996–98. Governor: St Margaret's Sch., Edinburgh, 1960–81; Grassland Res. Inst., 1962–81 (Hon. Fellow, 1981); Scottish Crop Res. Inst., 1980–83. *Recreation:* photography. *Address:* Magdalenehall, St Boswells, Roxburghshire TD6 0EB. *T:* (01835) 823741.

BIGGART, (Thomas) Norman, CBE 1984; WS; Partner, Biggart Baillie & Gifford, WS, Solicitors, Glasgow and Edinburgh, 1959–95; *b* 24 Jan. 1930; *o s* of Andrew Stevenson Biggart, JP and Marjorie Scott Biggart; *m* 1956, Eileen Jean Anne Gemmell; one *s* one *d. Educ:* Morrisons Acad., Crieff; Glasgow Univ. (MA 1951, LLB 1954). Served RN, 1954–56 (Sub-Lt RNVR). Law Society of Scotland: Mem. Council, 1977–86; Vice-Pres., 1981–82; Pres., 1982–83. Mem., Council on Tribunals, and Chm., Scottish Cttee, 1990–98. Pres., Business Archives Council, Scotland, 1977–86. Member: Exec. Cttee, Scottish Council (Development and Industry), 1984–93; Scottish Tertiary Educn Adv. Council, 1984–87; Scottish Records Adv. Council, 1985–91. Director: Clydesdale Bank, 1985–97; Independent (formerly New Scotland) Insurance Gp, 1986–2000 (Chm., 1989–93); Beechwood Glasgow, 1989–97 (Chm., 1989–97). Trustee, Scottish Civic Trust, 1989–97. Hon. Mem., American Bar Assoc., 1982. OStJ 1968. *Recreations:* golf, hill walking. *Address:* Gailes, Kilmacolm, Renfrewshire PA13 4LZ. *T:* (01505) 872645. *Club:* The Western (Glasgow).

BIGGS, Dr John, FRSC; Chairman, Free Church Federal Council, 1993–97 (Moderator, 1992–93); *b* 3 Jan. 1933; *s* of Horace James Biggs and Elsie Alice Biggs, Leicester; *m* 1965, Brenda Muriel Hicklenton. *Educ:* Wyggeston Grammar Sch. for Boys, Leicester; Downing Coll., Cambridge (Graystone Scholar). MA, PhD (Cantab). CChem; FRSC (FCS 1958). DSIR Res. Fellow, Cambridge, 1958–60; Lectr in Chemistry, Univ. of Hull, 1960–87. President: Baptist Students' Fedn, 1955–56; Yorkshire Baptist Assoc., 1973–74; Vice-Pres., Baptist Men's Movement, 1995–97, Pres., 1997–98; Baptist Union of GB: Chm., Home Mission Working Gp, 1981–88; Mem. Council, 1978–, Chm., 1990–94; Pres., 1989–90; Mem., Scholarships and Ministerial Trng Bursary Cttee, 1978–2001 (Chm., 1995–2001). Governor, Northern Baptist Coll., Manchester, 1989–2000; Chm., Relocation Steering Cttee, Baptist Theol Seminary, Prague, 1994–96 (Mem. Bd of Trustees, Rüschlikon, Zürich, 1989–94, Vice-Chm., 1992–94). Member: Envmtl Issues Network, CTBI (formerly CCBI), 1990–2007 (Mem. Steering Cttee and Adv. Panel, Eco-Congregation Prog., 1999–2004); Envmt Gp, Churches Together in Cumbria, 1997–; Chm., Sustainable Communities (Cumbria), 2004–. *Publication:* (contrib.) Energy, 2003. *Recreations:* fell-walking, opera, photography. *Address:* Fellcroft, Easedale Road, Grasmere, Ambleside, Cumbria LA22 9QR.

BIGGS, John; Member (Lab) City and East, London Assembly, Greater London Authority, since 2000; *b* 19 Nov. 1957; *s* of late Robert Edmund Biggs and of Mary Jeanette Biggs (*née* Phillips); *m* 1993, Christine Sibley; one *d. Educ:* Queen Elizabeth's Boys' Sch., Barnet; Bristol Univ. (BSc Hons Chem. 1979); Birkbeck Coll., London Univ. (Postgrad. Dip. Computer Sci. 1984); Westminster Univ. (Postgrad. Dip. Law 1996, Legal Practice Course 1998). Operating theatre orderly, 1979–80; lab. technician, 1980–83; systems analyst, 1984–91; self-employed computer consultant, 1991–92. Mem. (Lab), Tower Hamlets BC, 1988–2002 (Leader of Opposition, 1991–94; Leader, 1994–95). Non-exec. Dir, Tower Hamlets HAT, 1996–2004 (Vice-Chm., 1999–2004); Vice Chm., London Develt Agency, 2004–; Dep. Chm., London Thames Gateway Develt Corp., 2004–. Dir, Socialist Health Assoc., 1997–2000. *Recreations:* reading, walking, travel. *Address:* Greater London Authority, City Hall, Queen's Walk, SE1 2AA. *T:* (020) 7983 4356; 7 Louisa Gardens, Stepney Green, E1 4NG. *T:* (020) 7790 9710.

BIGGS, John Sydney Grainge, MD; FRCOG, FRACOG; Postgraduate Medical Dean, University of Cambridge, and Eastern Region, NHS Executive, 1991–2001; *b* 16 Dec. 1935; *s* of Charles V. G. Biggs and Leah M. Biggs (*née* Price); *m* 1960, T. Glyndon Daley;

three *s* two *d*. *Educ:* Carey Grammar Sch., Melbourne; Univ. of Melbourne (MB BS 1960); MD Aberdeen 1973; MA Cantab 1994. MRCOG 1966, FRCOG 1980; FRACOG 1979; DHMSA 1993. House Officer, Royal Melbourne Hosp., 1961; RMO, Royal Children's Hosp., Melbourne, 1962; RMO and Registrar, Royal Women's Hosp., Melbourne, 1963–64; Lecturer in Obstetrics and Gynaecology: Univ. of Qld, 1965; Univ. of Aberdeen, 1966–69; University of Queensland: Sen. Lectr, 1969–72; Reader, 1973–82; Dean of Medicine and Prof., 1983–91. Chm. Bd, Coast City Country Trng, 2006–. Conducted evaluation of postgrad. med. trng for Higher Educn Commn, Pakistan, 2006–07. Hon. Prof., UEA, 1997–2001. Pres., ASME, 1999–2002 (Chm., 1996–99). *Publications:* contrib. to learned jls on ovarian structure and function, 1996–82, and medical educn, 1983–2001. *Recreations:* gardening, walking, reading. *Address:* 21 Conyers Street, Hughes, ACT 2605, Australia. *T:* (2) 61616643. *Club:* Royal Society of Medicine.

BIGGS, Lewis; Director/Chief Executive, Liverpool Biennial of Contemporary Art, since 2000; *b* 22 April 1952; *s* of Lewis Ian Biggs and Penelope Torre Biggs (*née* Torr); *m* 1983, Ann Margaret Compton (marr. diss. 2002); one *s* one *d*; partner, Lisa Katharine Milroy, *qv*. *Educ:* New Coll., Oxford (MA Mod. Hist. 1974); Courtauld Inst., Univ. of London (MA Hist. of Art 1979). Gallery Co-ordinator, Arnolfini Gall., Bristol, 1979–84; Exhibns Officer, British Council, 1984–87; Curator of Exhibns, Tate Gall., Liverpool, 1987–90; Curator, then Dir, Tate Gall., Liverpool, 1990–2000. Director: Oriel Mostyn Gall., Llandudno, 1991–98; Art Transpennine Ltd, 1996–2002; Culture Campus Ltd, 2005–; Another Place Ltd, 2006–. Member: Visual Arts Adv. Cttee, British Council, 1991–2007; Visual Arts Panel, Arts Council of England, 1996–99; NW Arts Bd, 1997–2002; Liverpool Cath. Fabric Adv. Cttee, 1995–98; Liverpool Urban Design and Conservation Panel, 2003–. Trustee, Liverpool Architecture and Design Trust, 1997–99; Dir, Liverpool Biennial Trust, 1998–2000. Vis. Prof. of Contemporary Art, Liverpool Art Sch., 2001–04. Associate Fellow, Univ. of Liverpool, 1992; Hon. Fellow, Liverpool John Moores Univ., 1998. Gen. series Ed., Tate Modern Artists, 2001–. *Address:* PO Box 1200, Liverpool L69 1XB. *T:* (0151) 709 7444, *Fax:* (0151) 709 7377.

BIGGS, Michael Nicholas; Group Chief Executive, Resolution plc, 2007–08; *b* 14 Aug. 1952; *s* of Eric Peter and Hilda May Biggs; two *s*. *Educ:* Alleyne's Grammar Sch.; Worcester Coll., Oxford (MA 1974). ACA 1979. Arthur Andersen & Co., 1976–84; HSBC, 1984–87; Gp Financial Controller, Morgan Grenfell & Co., 1987–91; Norwich Union: Gp Financial Controller, 1991–95; Gen. Manager Internat., 1995–97; Gp Finance Dir, 1997–2000; Gp Exec. Dir, 2000–01, Gp Finance Dir, 2001–03, CGNU, subseq. Aviva; Gp Finance Dir, Resolution plc, 2005–07. *Recreations:* gardening, history, antiques.

BIGGS, Sir Norman (Parris), Kt 1977; Director, Banco de Bilbao, 1981–87; *b* 23 Dec. 1907; *s* of John Gordon Biggs and Mary Sharpe Dickson; *m* 1936, Peggy Helena Stammwitz (*d* 1990); two *s* one *d*. *Educ:* John Watson's Sch., Edinburgh. Bank of England, 1927–46; Dir, Kleinwort Sons & Co. Ltd, 1946–52; Esso Petroleum Company, Ltd: Dir, 1952–66, Chm., 1968–72; Chairman: Williams & Glyn's Bank Ltd, 1972–76; United International Bank Ltd, 1970–79; Deputy Chairman: National and Commercial Banking Gp Ltd, 1974–76; Privatbanken Ltd, 1980–83; Director: Royal Bank of Scotland, 1974–76; Gillett Bros Discount Co. Ltd, 1963–77. Mem., Bullock Cttee on Industrial Democracy, 1976. *Address:* Northbrooks, Danworth Lane, Hurstpierpoint, Sussex BN6 9LW. *T:* (01273) 832022.

BIGGS, Prof. Peter Martin, CBE 1987; PhD, DSc; FRS 1976; Director of Animal Health (formerly Animal Disease Research), Agricultural and Food Research Council, 1986–88, retired; Visiting Professor of Veterinary Microbiology, Royal Veterinary College, University of London, since 1982; *b* 13 Aug. 1926; *s* of Ronald Biggs and Cécile Biggs (*née* Player); *m* 1950, Alison Janet Molteno; two *s* one *d*. *Educ:* Bedales Sch.; Cambridge Sch., USA; Queen's Univ., Belfast; Royal Veterinary Coll., Univ. of London (BSc 1953, DSc 1975); Univ. of Bristol (PhD 1958). FRCVS, FRCPath, FIBiol, CBiol. Served RAF, 1944–48; Research Asst, Univ. of Bristol, 1953–55, Lectr, 1955–59; Houghton Poultry Research Station: Head of Leukosis Experimental Unit, 1959–74; Dep. Dir, 1971–74; Dir, 1974–86. Andrew D. White Prof.-at-Large, Cornell Univ., 1988–94. Sir William Dick Meml Lectr, Univ. of Edinburgh, 1974 and 1987; E. H. W. Wilmott Guest Lectr, Univ. of Bristol, 1977; Leeuwenhoek Prize Lectr, Royal Soc., 1997. Member: Veterinary Products Cttee, 1973–98; Management Bd, AFRC, 1986–88. President: BVPA, 1974–75; World Vet. Poultry Assoc., 1981–85 (Hon. Life Pres., 1985); Internat. Assoc. for Comparative Res. on Leukemia and Related Diseases, 1981–83; Inst. of Biol., 1990–92; Vice Pres., BVA, 1996–98. Founder FMedSci 1998. Hon. FRASE 1986. Hon. DVM Ludwig-Maximilians Univ., 1976; Dr *hc* Liège, 1991. Tom Newman Meml Award, 1964; Poultry Science Award, British Oil and Cake Mills, 1968; J. T. Edwards Meml Medal, 1969; Dalrymple-Champneys Cup and Medal, 1973; Bledisloe Veterinary Award, 1977; Wooldridge Meml Medal and Lecture, 1978; Joszef Marek Meml Medal, Vet. Univ. of Budapest, 1979; Victory Medal, Central Vet. Soc., 1980; Gordon Meml Medal and Lecture, Robert Fraser Gordon Meml Trust, 1989; Wolf Foundn Prize in Agric., 1989; Chiron Award, BVA, 1999. *Publications:* scientific papers on viruses and infectious disease. *Recreations:* music making, natural history. *Address:* Willows, London Road, St Ives, PE27 5ES. *T:* and *Fax:* (01480) 463471. *Clubs:* Athenæum, Farmers'.

BIGHAM, family name of **Viscount Mersey**.

BIGLAND, Brenda, CBE 2006; Headteacher, Lent Rise School, Burnham, since 1993; *b* 6 June 1951; *d* of Edwin and Sylvia Francis; *m* 1972, Paul Bigland; one *s*. *Educ:* Calcot Primary Sch., Reading; St Joseph's Convent, Reading; St Osyth's Coll., Essex; British Dyslexia Inst. (Associate Mem.); Bulmershe Coll. (BEd Hons 1989); Reading Univ. (MA Instnl Mgt and Educnl Admin 1993). Teacher: Garland Primary Sch., Berks, 1972–74; Aldermaston Sch., Berks, 1974–75; Francis Bailey Sch., Berks, 1975; Dep. Hd, St John Bosco (Indep.) Sch., Reading, 1978–80; Hd, Prep. Sch., Presentation Coll. (Indep.), Reading, 1980–88; Dep. Hd, Marish Sch., Berks, 1988–92. Consultant/Adviser, 2002–: DES; Nat. Coll. of Sch. Leadership; Specialist Schs and Academies Trust. Member: Bd, Trng and Develt Agency, 2002–; Nat. Educn Leadership Gp for Business in the Community, 2002–; Implementation Rev. Gp (Educn), 2006–. Work with British Council to promote educnl collaboration across nations. Fellow, Teaching Awards Trust, 2006. Trustee, Bentley Priory Battle of Britain Trust, 2008–. *Publications:* articles on educn subjects. *Recreations:* travel, theatre, music, reading, spending time with family and friends. *Address:* Lent Rise School, Coulson Way, Burnham, Bucks SL1 7NP. *T:* (01628) 662913; *e-mail:* b.bigland@lentrise.bucks.sch.uk.

BIGNELL, (Francis) Geoffrey; Principal, Just Employment, Solicitors, since 1999; *b* 7 March 1949; *s* of Ernest Francis John Bignell and Olive Ethel Bignell (*née* Peatson); *m* 1978, Susan Rachel Harrison; two *s* one *d*. *Educ:* Isleworth Grammar Sch.; Trinity Hall, Cambridge (MA); Coll. of Law. Social work in Basildon and Worksop, 1971–74; articled to Notts CC, 1975–78; admitted Solicitor, 1977; Prosecuting Solicitor, Notts Police Authy, 1978–80; Asst and Sen. Asst Solicitor, Leics CC, 1980–83; Prin. Solicitor, Warwicks CC, 1983–87; Asst Sec.-Gen. (Management), Law Soc., 1987–95; Chief Executive: Law Soc. Services Ltd, 1995–97; Solicitors Property Centres Ltd, 1997–98. Non-executive Director: Cheviot Financial Services (formerly Cheviot Personal Pensions) Ltd, 1992–2005; Ambersham Holdings Ltd, 1998–2001; Lawyers Defence Union Ltd, 1999–2002; Peter Honey Publications Ltd, 2000–02. Member: Rail Passengers' (formerly Rail Users') Consultative Cttee for Southern England, 1997–2005 (Vice-Chm., 2002–05); SW Trains Passenger Panel, 2002–. Gov., George Abbot Sch., 1995–2001 (Vice-Chm., 1998–2001); Mem., Corp. of Guildford Coll., 1997–2001 (Vice-Chm., 1998–2001). *Publications:* contribs to learned jls. *Recreations:* photography, shares, railways. *Address:* (office) St Mary's Chambers, 59 Quarry Street, Guildford, Surrey GU1 3UA. *T:* (01483) 303636.

BIJUR, Peter Isaac; Chairman of the Board and Chief Executive Officer, Texaco Inc., 1996–2001; *b* 14 Oct. 1942; *m* 2000, Kjestine M. Anderson; two *s* one *d* from former marriage. *Educ:* Univ. of Pittsburgh (BA Pol. Sci. 1964); Columbia Univ. (MBA 1966). Texaco, 1966–2001: Manager, Buffalo sales dist, 1971–73; Asst Manager to Vice-Pres. for public affairs, 1973–75; Staff Co-ordinator, dept of strategic planning, 1975–77; Asst to Exec. Vice-Pres., 1977–80; Manager, Rocky Mountain Refining and Marketing, 1980–81; Asst to Chm. of Bd, 1981–83; Pres., Texaco Oil Trading & Supply Co., 1984; Vice-Pres., special projects, 1984–86; Pres. and Chief Exec., Texaco Canada, 1987–89; Chm., Pres. and Chief Exec., Texaco Canada Resources, Calgary, 1988–89; Chm., Texaco Ltd, 1989–91; Pres., Texaco Europe, 1990–92; Sen. Vice Pres., 1992–96, Vice Chm. Bd, 1996, Texaco Inc. Director: GulfMark Offshore, Inc., 2003–; AB Volvo, 2006–.

BILBY, Prof. Bruce Alexander, BA, PhD; FRS 1977; consultant; Professor of the Theory of Materials, University of Sheffield, 1966–84, now Emeritus; *b* 3 Sept. 1922; *e s* of late George Alexander Bilby and Dorothy Jean (*née* Telfer); *m* 1st, 1946, Hazel Joyce (*née* Casken); two *s* one *d*; 2nd, 1966, Lorette Wendela (*née* Thomas); two *s*. *Educ:* Dover Grammar Sch.; Peterhouse, Cambridge (BA); Univ. of Birmingham (PhD). Admiralty, 1943–46. Research, Birmingham, 1946–51; Univ. of Sheffield: Royal Soc. Sorby Res. Fellow, 1951–57; J. H. Andrew Res. Fellow, 1957–58; Reader in Theoretical Metallurgy, 1958–62, Prof., 1962–66. Has made contributions to theory of dislocations and its application to the deformation, transformation and fracture of metallic crystals. Rosenhain Medal, Inst. of Metals, 1963; Griffith Medal, European Structural Integrity Soc., 1994. *Publications:* contribs to learned jls. *Recreation:* sailing. *Address:* 32 Devonshire Road, Sheffield S17 3NT. *T:* (0114) 236 1086; Department of Mechanical Engineering, The University, Mappin Street, Sheffield S1 3JD. *T:* (0114) 222 7713.

BILDT, Carl, Hon. KCMG; Minister of Foreign Affairs, Sweden, since 2006; *b* Halmstad, 15 July 1949; *s* of Daniel B. Bildt and Kerstin Bildt (*née* Andersson); *m* 1984, Mia Bohman; one *s* one *d*; *m* 1998, Anna Maria Corazza. *Educ:* Stockholm Univ. Mem., Stockholm CC, 1974–77; MP (Moderate Party), Sweden, 1979–2001; Under-Sec. of State for Co-ordination and Planning, Cabinet Office, 1979–81; Member: Parly Standing Cttee in Foreign Affairs, 1982–86; Adv. Council on Foreign Affairs, 1982–99; Submarine Defence Commn, 1982–83; 1984 Defence Cttee, 1984–87; Prime Minister of Sweden, 1991–94; EU Special Rep. to Conflict in Former Yugoslavia, and Co-Chm., Internat. Conf. on Former Yugoslavia, 1995; High Rep. for Peace Implementation in Bosnia and Herzegovina, 1996–97; Special Envoy of UN Sec. Gen., Balkans, 1999–2001. Chm., Moderate Party, 1986–99. Chm., Kreab Gp, Sweden; Sen. Advr, IT Provider, Stockholm; Director: Legg Mason Inc.; HiQ; Lundin Petroleum; Vostok Nafta; Öhmans. Trustee, RAND Corp. Mem., IISS, 1981–. Mem., Nordic Council, 1986– (Chm., Conservative Gp, 1988–91). Chm., Nordic Venture Network. Chm., Internat. Democratic Union, 1992–99. *Publications:* Landet Som Steg ut i Kylan, 1972; Framtid i Frihet, 1976; Hallänning, Svensk, Europé, 1991; Peace Journey, 1998. *Address:* Ministry of Foreign Affairs, Gustav Adolfs torg 1, 10339 Stockholm, Sweden.

BILGER, Pierre; Chairman of the Board, Alstom, 2003 (Chairman and Chief Executive Officer, 1998–2003); *b* Colmar, 27 May 1940; *s* of Joseph Bilger and Suzanne Gillet; *m* 1966, Eliane Oyon; two *s* three *d*. *Educ:* Institut d'Etudes Politiques; Ecole Nationale d'Admin, Paris. Sen. posts at French Min. of Econ. and Finance (Inspection Générale des Finances and Budget Dept), 1967–82; sen. posts with Cie Générale d'Electricité, subseq. Alcatel Alsthom, then Alcatel, 1982–87 (Dep. Man. Dir, 1987); joined Alsthom, 1987; Pres. and CEO, Gec Alsthom, 1991–98. *Address:* 7 rue de l'Assomption, 75016 Paris, France.

BILIMORIA, family name of **Baron Bilimoria**.

BILIMORIA, Baron *cr* 2006 (Life Peer), of Chelsea in the Royal Borough of Kensington and Chelsea; **Karan Faridoon Bilimoria,** CBE 2004; FCA; DL; Founder, 1989, and Chairman, since 2007, Cobra Beer (Chief Executive, 1989–2007); *b* 26 Nov. 1961; *s* of late Lt Gen. Faridoon Noshir Bilimoria, PVSM, ADC and of Yasmin Bilimoria; *m* 1993, Heather Walker; two *s* two *d*. *Educ:* Indian Inst. of Mgt and Commerce, Osmania Univ., Hyderabad (BCom Hons); City of London Poly. (Dip. Acctg 1982); Sidney Sussex Coll., Cambridge (BA Law 1988; half blue polo; MA; Hon. Fellow 2007); Cranfield Univ. (Business Growth Prog. 1998). ACA 1986, FCA 2002. Trainee articled chartered accountant, Ernst & Young, 1982–86, qualified chartered accountant, 1987; Consulting Accountant, Cresvale Ltd, London, 1988–89; Sales and Mktg Dir, Eur. Accounting Focus Mag., 1989; Founder, Gen. Bilimoria Wines, 1989. Non-executive Director: Brake Bros Ltd, 2004–07; Booker Gp plc, 2007–. Vis. Entrepreneur, Centre for Entrepreneurial Learning, Cambridge Univ., 2004–; Guest Lecturer: Judge Business Sch., Cambridge; Cranfield Univ. Sch. of Mgt; London Business Sch. UK Chm., Indo-British Partnership, UK Trade and Investment, DTI and FCO, 2003–; Chairman: Indo-British Partnership Network, 2005–07; UK India Business Council, 2007–; Mem., UK India Consultative Gp, FCO, 2002–03; Member: Nat. Employment Panel, DWP, 2001–07 (Chm., Small and Med. Size Enterprise Bd, 2001–05); New Deal Task Force, DfEE, 1999–2001; Neighbourhood Renewal Private Sector Panel, ODPM, 2003–05. Mentor, Metropolitan Police Jt Mentoring Initiative, 2002–04. Vice-Chm., Asian Business Assoc., LCCI, 2003–08; Mem., LCCI/Asian Business Assoc. Panel, Bank of England, 2000–03; Charter Mem., Indus Entrepreneurs, 2002–; Mem. Bd, Indus Entrepreneurs, UK, 2003–06; Founding Pres., UK Zoroastrian Chamber of Commerce, 2003–06. Member: Young Presidents' Orgn, 2000– (Chm., London Chapter, 2004–05); Birmingham Business Sch. Adv. Bd, 2005–; Adv. Council, CIDA Foundn UK, 2006–; Duke of York's Business Adv. Council, 2006–; Enterprise Leader, Prince's Trust, 2008–. Chm., Meml Gates Cttee, 2003– (Vice Patron, Meml Gates Trust, 1999–2004). Mem., Pres.'s Cttee, London First, 2002–06; Ambassador: London 2012 Olympic Bid, 2005; Interactive Univ., UK, 2005–. Nat. Champion, Nat. Council for Grad. Entrepreneurship, 2004–. Chancellor, Thames Valley Univ., 2005– (Gov., 2001–04); Mem., Adv. Bd, Judge Business Sch., Univ. of Cambridge, 2008–. Comr, Royal Hosp. Chelsea, 2006–. Gov., Ditchley Foundn, 2004–. Trustee, British Cardiovascular Res. Trust, 2006–. Patron: Rethink severe mental illness, 2003–; Children in Need Inst. UK, 2008–; founding Patron, Oxford Entrepreneurs, 2004–; Member, Advisory Board: Adab Trust, 2007–; Roundhouse Trust, 2008–. Vice-Pres., Cambridge Union. FInstD 2005; CCMI 2005. Hon. Life FRSA 2004 (Council Mem., 2004–07). Freeman, City of London; Mem., Drapers' Co., 2005. Rep. DL

Hounslow, 2001. Hon. DBus Brunel, 2005; Hon. DLitt Heriot-Watt, 2005; DUniv Staffs, 2006. Numerous awards, including: Outstanding Achievement Award: Execs Assoc. of GB, 2002; ICAEW, 2005; Asian of the Year, Asian Who's Who, 2002; Entrepreneur of the Year: Asian Achievers Awards, 2003; LCCI, 2003; Nat. Business Awards, London and SE England, 2004; Business Person of the Year, LCCI, 2004; Albert Medal, RSA, 2004; Leadership Award, Dir Mag., IoD, 2008; Special Recognition Award, UK Trade and Investment India. Pravasi Bharti Samman (India), 2008. *Publication:* (jtly) Bottled for Business: the less gassy guide to entrepreneurship, 2007. *Recreations:* reading, current affairs, travel, art, music, theatre, tennis, horse riding, golf, scuba diving, sailing. *Address:* Cobra Beer Ltd, Alexander House, 14–16 Peterborough Road, SW6 3BN. *T:* (020) 7731 6200; *e-mail:* bilimoria@parliament.uk. *Clubs:* Carlton, Royal Commonwealth Society; Hawks', University Pitt (Cambridge); Guards' Polo; Delhi Gymkhana, Delhi Golf; Secunderabad; FRIMA Golf (Dehra Dun); Kelvin Grove (Cape Town).

BILK, Bernard Stanley, (Acker), MBE 2001; musician (jazz clarinettist) and composer; band leader, since 1951; *b* 28 Jan. 1929; *s* of William and Lillian Bilk; *m* 1954, Jean Hawkins; one *s* one *d*. *Educ:* Pensford Sch., Somerset. Nat. Service, RE, 1948. Founder, Bristol Paramount Jazz Band, 1951; with Ken Colyer's Band, London, as clarinettist, 1952–53; has made numerous recordings; singles include: Summer Set, 1960; Stranger on the Shore, 1961 (first No 1 simultaneously in UK and USA; BMI award for over 4 million broadcasts, 2004); A Taste of Honey, 1963; Aria, 1976; albums include: Blue Acker, with the Stan Tracey Big Brass, 2005; has toured worldwide, incl. Europe, Scandinavia, Australia, NZ, Far East, ME, USA, Canada and Ireland. Hon. MA Bristol, 2005. *Recreation:* oil painting. *Address:* c/o Acker's Agency, 53 Cambridge Mansions, Cambridge Road, SW11 4RX.

BILL, Lt Gen. David Robert, CB 2006; UK Military Representative to NATO, since 2008; *b* 17 Nov. 1954; *s* of late Robert Bill, DSO, RN and Wendy Jean Bill (*née* Booth); *m* 1981, Gabrielle Catherine Thunder; two *s* one *d*. *Educ:* Charterhouse; Welbeck Coll.; RMA Sandhurst; RMCS (BA Hons Eng 1978). Maj., Dir Mil. Ops, 1987–88; 33 Ind. Field Sqn, RE, 1989–90; DS Staff Coll., 1991–92; in Comd, 39 Engr Regt, 1992–94; Col, Army Staff Duties, 1994–97; Comdr Engr, 1997–99, BGS, 1999–2001, HQ Land Comd; rcds, 2002; GOC UK Support Comd (Germany), 2003–06; Dep. Comdr, NATO Rapid Deployable Corps, Italy, 2006–08. Col, Queen's Gurkha Engrs, 2006–. Pres., RE Rugby League, 2001. *Recreations:* alpine ski-ing, golf, hockey, bridge. *Address:* UKMILREP, HQ NATO, BFPO 49; *e-mail:* the.bills@talk21.com. *Club:* MCC.

BILL, Peter Anthony; Editor, Estates Gazette, since 1998; *b* 14 March 1947; *s* of John Samuel Bill and Margaret Mary Bill; *m* 1969, Elizabeth Allen; one *s* one *d*. *Educ:* St Bartholomew's Grammar Sch., Newbury; Oxford Poly. (HNC Building). Surveyor, construction industry: Bance & Sons, Newbury, 1962–64; Kingerlee of Oxford, 1964–69; George Wimpey, Bristol, 1969–75, and Kent, 1977–83; Anglo-American (Zambia), 1975–77; journalist: Contract Jl, 1983–85; Building mag., 1985–96 (Ed., 1990–96); Hd of Pubns, Fleming Securities, 1996–97. Columnist, Evening Standard, 2007–. Pres., Internat. Bldg Press, 1991–95 and 1997–2000. *Publications:* monographs for Smith Institute on housing, building sustainable communities, and environmental policies. *Recreations:* reading, writing. *Address:* Flat 29, 43 Bartholomew Close, EC1A 7HN. *T:* (020) 7911 1805, *Fax:* (020) 7911 1900; *e-mail:* peter.bill@rbi.co.uk. *Club:* Reform.

BILLETT, Paul Rodney, CB 1981; *b* 19 Feb. 1921; *s* of late Arthur William and Grace Hilda Billett; *m* 1st, 1945, Muriel Gwendoline Marsh (*d* 1977); one *s*; 2nd, 1985, Eileen May Nourse. *Educ:* Commonweal and College Grammar Schools, Swindon. Entered Exchequer and Audit Dept, 1939. Served RASC, 1941–46. Deputy Secretary, Exchequer and Audit Dept, 1975–81 (retired). *Address:* Wynthorpe, Cornsland, Brentwood, Essex CM14 4JL. *T:* (01277) 224830.

BILLINGHAM, family name of **Baroness Billingham**.

BILLINGHAM, Baroness *cr* 2000 (Life Peer), of Banbury in the co. of Oxfordshire; **Angela Theodora Billingham;** JP; *b* 31 July 1939; *d* of late Theodore Vincent Case and Eva Case (*née* Saxby); *m* 1962, Anthony Peter Billingham (*d* 1992); two *d*. *Educ:* Aylesbury GS; London Univ. Teacher, 1960–90; Examiner, 1990–95. Mayor of Banbury, 1976; Member (Lab): Banbury BC, 1970–74; Cherwell DC, 1974–84; Oxfordshire CC, 1993–94. Contested (Lab) Banbury, 1992. MEP (Lab) Northants and Blaby, 1994–99; contested (Lab) E Midlands Reg., 1999. Chief Whip, Party of European Socialists, EP, 1995–99. Chm., Corby Urban Regeneration Bd, 2001–. JP N Oxfordshire and Bicester, 1976. *Recreations:* tennis, gardening, bridge, cinema, grandchildren. *Address:* 6 Crediton Hill, NW6 1HP; c/o House of Lords, SW1A 0PW. *Club:* Cumberland Lawn Tennis (W Hampstead).

See also S. A. Jones.

BILLINGHAM, Mark Philip David; writer and comedian; *b* Birmingham, 2 July 1961; *s* of Jeff Billingham and Patricia Billingham (*née* Grice, now Thompson); *m* 1994, Claire Winyard; one *s* one *d*. *Educ:* King Edward VI Camp Hill Grammar Sch. for Boys; Birmingham Univ. (BA Hons Drama and Th. Arts). Stand-up comedian, 1987–; television actor: Boon, 1984; Dempsey and Makepeace, 1985; Juliet Bravo, 1985; Maid Marian and Her Merry Men, 1989–92 (also writer, 1992); Harry's Mad, 1993–96 (also writer, 1993); Knight School (also writer), 1997–98; writer for television, The Cramp Twins, 1998–2001. *Publications:* Knight School, 1998; Sleepyhead, 2001; Scaredy Cat, 2002; Lazybones, 2003; The Burning Girl, 2004; Lifeless, 2005; Buried, 2006; Death Message, 2007; In the Dark, 2008; The Life Thief, 2009; *as Will Peterson:* Triskellion, 2008; Triskellion 2: The Burning, 2009. *Recreations:* music, especially country (alt and cheesy), movies, poker, tennis, food, embarrassing my children, supporting Wolverhampton Wanderers in spite of everything, trying to smuggle examples of Victorian taxidermy into the house. *Address:* c/o Lutyens & Rubinstein, 231 Westbourne Park Road, W11 1EB. *T:* (020) 7792 4855; *e-mail:* mail@markbillingham.com. *Club:* One Alfred Place.

BILLINGTON, Brenda May, FRCS, FRCOphth; Consultant Ophthalmic Surgeon, Royal Berkshire Hospital, Reading, since 1985; President, Royal College of Ophthalmologists, 2006–May 2009; *b* 19 Jan. 1951; *d* of Gwynn and Leslie Billington; *m* 1987, James (marr. diss. 1997); one *s*. *Educ:* Queen Anne's Sch., Caversham; Univ. of Birmingham (MB ChB 1974). FRCS 1980; FRCOphth 1989. Resident Surgical Officer, Moorfields Eye Hosp., 1978–81; Sen. Registrar in Ophthalmology, St Thomas' Hosp. and Moorfields Eye Hosp., 1982–85. Liveryman, Soc. of Apothecaries, 1989–. Fellow, European Bd of Ophthalmology, 2003. *Publications:* contribs to ophthalmic scientific jls, mainly clinical studies of treatment for patients with retinal detachment. *Recreation:* returning purchases to clothes shops. *Address:* 72 Berkeley Avenue, Reading RG1 6HY. *T:* (0118) 955 3452, *Fax:* (0118) 955 3478. *Club:* Royal Society of Medicine.

BILLINGTON, Brian John, (Bill); consultant on roads and transport, since 1998; *b* 25 Feb. 1939; *s* of late Kenneth Jack Billington and Doris Violet Billington; *m* 1965, Gillian Elizabeth Annis; two *d*. *Educ:* Slough Grammar Sch.; The Polytechnic, Regent Street (BSc(Econ)); LSE (MSc). Lectr, The Polytechnic, Regent Street, 1966–68; Min. of Power, later Dept of Energy, 1969–74; Dept of Transport, later Dept of Envmt, Transport and the Regions, 1974–98; Highways Agency, 1994–98; Under Sec., 1991–98. *Address:* 100 Fox Lane, N13 4AX. *T:* (020) 8886 0898.

BILLINGTON, Dr James Hadley; Librarian of Congress, USA, since 1987; *b* 1 June 1929; *s* of Nelson Billington and Jane Coolbaugh; *m* 1957, Marjorie Anne Brennan; two *s* two *d*. *Educ:* Princeton Univ.; Balliol College, Oxford (Rhodes Scholar; DPhil 1953). Served US Army, 1953–56. Harvard University: Instructor in History, 1957–58; Asst Prof. of History and Res. Fellow, Russian Res. Center, 1958–59; Asst Prof. of History, 1958–61; Associate Prof. of History, 1962–64, Prof., 1964–73, Princeton; Dir, Woodrow Wilson Internat. Center for Scholars, Washington, 1973–87. Chm., Bd of Foreign Scholarships, 1971–73. Visiting Research Professor: Inst. of History, Acad. of Scis, USSR, 1966–67; Univ. of Helsinki, 1960–61; Ecole des Hautes Etudes en Scis Sociales, Paris, 1985, 1988; Vis. Lectr, USA, Europe, Asia; Guggenheim Fellow, 1960–61. Writer and host, The Face of Russia, TV series, 1998. Member: Amer. Acad. of Arts and Scis; Amer. Philosophical Soc.; Russian Acad. of Scis; numerous hon. degrees; Hon. DLitt Oxon, 2002. Chevalier and Comdr, Ordre des Arts et des Lettres. *Publications:* Mikhailovsky and Russian Populism, 1958; The Icon and the Axe: an interpretive history of Russian culture, 1966; The Arts of Russia, 1970; Fire in the Minds of Men: origins of the Revolutionary Faith, 1980; Russia Transformed: breakthrough to hope, Moscow, August 1991, 1992; The Face of Russia, 1998; Russia in Search of Itself, 2004; contribs to learned jls. *Address:* Office of the Librarian, Library of Congress, 101 Independence Avenue, Washington, DC 20540–1000, USA. *T:* (202) 7075205.

BILLINGTON, Kevin; film, theatre and television director; *b* 12 June 1934; *s* of Richard and Margaret Billington; *m* 1967, Lady Rachel Mary Pakenham (*see* Lady Rachel Billington); two *s* two *d*. *Educ:* Bryanston Sch.; Queens' Coll., Cambridge (BA); Open Univ. (MusDip 1999; BA Hons 2002; MA (Mus) 2007). Film dir, BBC prog., Tonight, 1960–63; documentary film dir, BBC, 1963–67; films include: A Sort of Paradise; Many Mexicos; The Mexican Attitude; Twilight of Empire; Mary McCarthy's Paris; These Humble Shores; Matador; A Few Castles in Spain; The English Cardinal; A Socialist Childhood; Madison Avenue, USA; ATV documentary, All The Queen's Men. *Feature Film Director:* Interlude, 1967; The Rise and Rise of Michael Rimmer, 1969; The Light at the Edge of the World, 1970; Voices, 1974; Reflections, 1984. *Television Director:* And No One Can Save Her, 1973; Once Upon a Time is Now (documentary), 1978; The Music Will Never Stop (documentary), 1979; Henry VIII, 1979; The Jail Diary of Albie Sachs, 1980; The Good Soldier, 1981; Outside Edge, 1982; The Sonnets of William Shakespeare, 1984; Heartland, 1989; Small Doses, 1990; A Time to Dance, 1992. *Theatre Director:* Find Your Way Home, 1970; Me, 1973; The Birthday Party, 1974; The Caretaker, 1975; Bloody Neighbours, 1975; Emigrés, 1976; The Homecoming, 1978; Quartermaine's Terms, 1982; The Deliberate Death of a Polish Priest, 1985 (Channel Four, 1986); The Philanthropist, 1986; The Lover, and A Slight Ache (double bill), 1987; The Breadwinner, 1989; Veterans Day, 1989; Quartermaine's Terms, 1993; Old Times, 1994; Six Characters in Search of an Author, 1999; Our Country's Good, 1999; Victory, 2001; Wild Honey, 2002. *Screenplays:* Bodily Harm, 2000; Loving Attitudes, 2001. Chm., BAFTA, 1989–90 and 1990–91. Screenwriters' Guild Award, 1966 and 1967; Guild of TV Producers and Directors Award, 1966 and 1967. *Recreation:* swimming. *Address:* The Court House, Poyntington, Sherborne, Dorset DT9 4LF. *Club:* Garrick.

BILLINGTON, Michael; Drama Critic of The Guardian, since 1971; *b* 16 Nov. 1939; *s* of Alfred Billington and Patricia (*née* Bradshaw); *m* 1978, Jeanine Bradlaugh. *Educ:* Warwick Sch.; St Catherine's Coll., Oxford (BA; Hon. Fellow 2005). Trained as journalist with Liverpool Daily Post and Echo, 1961–62; Public Liaison Officer and Director for Lincoln Theatre Co., 1962–64; reviewed plays, films and television for The Times, 1965–71. Film Critic: Birmingham Post, 1968–78; Illustrated London News, 1968–81; London Arts Correspondent, New York Times, 1978–; Drama Critic, Country Life, 1987–. Contributor to numerous radio and television Arts programmes, incl. Kaleidoscope, Critics' Forum, The Book Programme, Arena. Presenter, The Billington Interview and Theatre Call, BBC World Service. Writer and Presenter, television profiles of Peggy Ashcroft, Peter Hall and Alan Ayckbourn. Prof. of Drama, Colorado Coll., 1981; Vis. Prof., KCL, 2002–. IPC Critic of the Year, 1974. *Publications:* The Modern Actor, 1974; How Tickled I Am, 1977; (ed) The Performing Arts, 1980; The Guinness Book of Theatre Facts and Feats, 1982; Alan Ayckbourn, 1983; Tom Stoppard, 1987; Peggy Ashcroft, 1988; (ed) Twelfth Night, 1990; One Night Stands, 1993; The Life and Work of Harold Pinter, 1996; (ed) Stage and Screen Lives, 2001; State of the Nation, 2007. *Recreations:* work, travel, cricket. *Address:* 15 Hearne Road, W4 3NJ. *T:* (020) 8995 0455.

BILLINGTON, Lady Rachel (Mary); writer; *b* 11 May 1942; *d* of 7th Earl of Longford, KG, PC, and Elizabeth, Countess of Longford, CBE; *m* 1967, Kevin Billington, *qv*; two *s* two *d*. *Educ:* London Univ. (BA English). Work includes: short stories; four BBC radio plays; two BBC TV plays, Don't be Silly, 1979, Life After Death, 1981. Reviewer and feature writer. *Publications:* All Things Nice, 1969; The Big Dipper, 1970; Lilacs out of the Dead Land, 1971; Cock Robin, 1973; Beautiful, 1974; A Painted Devil, 1975; A Woman's Age, 1979; Occasion of Sin, 1982; The Garish Day, 1985; Loving Attitudes, 1988; Theo and Matilda, 1990; Bodily Harm, 1992; The Family Year, 1992; The Great Umbilical: mother, daughter, mother, 1994; Magic and Fate, 1996; Perfect Happiness: the sequel to Emma, 1996; Tiger Sky, 1998; A Woman's Life, 2002; The Space Between, 2004; One Summer, 2006; Lies and Loyalties, 2008; *for children:* Rosanna and the Wizard-Robot, 1981; The First Christmas, 1983; Star-Time, 1984; The First Easter, 1987; The First Miracles, 1990; Life of Jesus, 1996; Life of St Francis, 1999; Far-out, 2002; There's More to Life, 2006. *Recreation:* nature. *Address:* The Court House, Poyntington, near Sherborne, Dorset DT9 4LF. *Clubs:* Society of Authors, PEN (Pres., 1997–2000).

BILLOT, Barbara Kathleen; Deputy Director (Under-Secretary), Department for National Savings, 1974–80; *b* 26 May 1920; *d* of Alfred Billot and Agnes Billot (*née* Hiner). *Educ:* Petersfield County High Sch. for Girls. Post Office Savings Bank: Clerical Officer 1938; Exec. Off. 1939; Higher Exec. Off. 1946; Sen. Exec. Off. 1953; Chief Exec. Off. 1957; Principal, Post Office Headquarters, 1960; Sen. Chief Exec. Off., PO Savings Dept, 1961; Principal Exec. Off. (Estabt Off.), 1969; Asst Sec., Dept for Nat. Savings, 1971. *Recreations:* reading, theatre-going. *Address:* 6 Springbank, Chichester, W Sussex PO19 6BX. *T:* (01243) 776295.

BILLS, David James, CBE 2001; Director General, Forestry Commission, 1995–2004; *b* 9 Feb. 1948; *s* of Nigel Bills and Sue Bills; *m* 1970, Michele Clutha Ellis; one *s* two *d*. *Educ:* Australian Nat. Univ. (BSc Forestry); MIT (SMP 1991). FICFor. Research Scientist, Australian Forest Res. Inst., 1970–74; Officer, Dept of Primary Industry, Australian Govt, 1974–77; various posts with Associated Pulp & Paper Mills and North Broken Hill Ltd, 1977–95 (Gen. Manager, Forest Products and Dir, 1986–95). Vice Pres., Australian Forest Develt Inst., 1982–86; Pres., Nat. Assoc. Forest Industries, 1992–95. Warden, Hobart Marine Bd, 1992–95. *Publications:* contribs to various scientific jls and to Australian Forestry Conf. Proc. *Recreations:* sailing, classic cars, ski-ing. *Club:* Edinburgh Sports (Edinburgh).

BILSLAND, Christopher Nigel; Chamberlain, City of London Corporation, since 2007; *b* 5 May 1954; *s* of John Bilsland and Dallas Aileen Bilsland; *m* 1980, Gillian Smith; one *s* one *d*. *Educ*: Doncaster Grammar Sch.; Chesterfield Coll. of Technol. CPFA 1976. Accountant, Doncaster MBC, 1972–79; Chief Auditor, Derby CC, 1979–82; Sen. Manager, Deloitte Haskins & Sells, 1982–87; Asst County Treas., Hampshire CC, 1987–91; County Treas., Somerset CC, 1991–2006. Mem. Council, CIPFA, 1998–2007. *Recreations*: high handicap golfer, horseracing, taking credit for children's achievements. *Address*: City of London, PO Box 270, Guildhall, EC2P 2EJ; *e-mail*: chris.bilsland@cityoflondon.gov.uk.

BILSTON, Baron *cr* 2005 (Life Peer), of Bilston in the county of West Midlands; **Dennis Turner**; *b* 26 Aug. 1942; *s* of Mary Elizabeth Peasley and Thomas Herbert Turner; *m* 1976, Patricia Mary Narroway; one *s* one *d*. *Educ*: Stonefield Secondary Modern School, Bilston; Bilston College of Further Education; Bilston Black Country. Office boy, salesman, market trader, steel worker, partner in worker co-operative. Mem. (Lab), Wolverhampton BC, 1966–86 (Chairman of Committees: Social Services, 1972–79; Educn, 1979–86; Econ. Develt, 1982–85; Housing, 1985–86). MP (Lab and Co-op) Wolverhampton SE, 1987–2005. An Opposition Whip, 1993–97; PPS to Sec. of State for Internat. Develt, 1997–2001. Mem., Educn Select Cttee, 1989–94; Chairman: All Party Gp on Further Educn, 1988–2005; H of C Catering Cttee, 1997–2005; W Midlands Gp Parly Lab MPs, 2001–05. Vice Pres., LGA. Chm., Wolverhampton Fair Trade Partnership. Patron, Wolverhampton Interfaith. Freedom, City of Wolverhampton, 2007. Hon. DLitt Wolverhampton, 2006. *Address*: House of Lords, SW1A 0PW; Ambleside, King Street, Bradley, Bilston, W Midlands WV14 8PQ. *Club*: Springvale Sports and Social (Bilston).

BINCHY, Maeve, (Mrs Gordon Snell); writer; *b* Dublin, 28 May 1940; *d* of William Binchy and Maureen Blackmore; *m* 1977, Gordon Snell, writer and broadcaster. *Educ*: Holy Child Convent, Killiney, Dublin; University College, Dublin. History teacher in girls' schs, 1960–68; columnist, Irish Times, 1968–. *Publications*: novels: Light a Penny Candle, 1982; Echoes, 1985; Firefly Summer, 1987; Circle of Friends, 1990 (filmed, 1995); Copper Beech, 1992; The Glass Lake, 1994; Evening Class, 1996; Tara Road, 1998; Scarlet Feather, 2000; Quentins, 2002; Nights of Rain and Stars, 2004; Whitethorn Woods, 2006; *novella*: Star Sullivan, 2006; *short stories*: Central Line, 1978; Victoria Line, 1980; Dublin 4, 1982; The Lilac Bus, 1984; Silver Wedding, 1988; This Year It Will Be Different, 2007. *Recreations*: reading, theatre, very bad bridge, gardening. *Address*: Dalkey, Co. Dublin, Ireland.

BINDMAN, Sir Geoffrey (Lionel), Kt 2007; Consultant, Bindman & Partners, Solicitors, since 2004 (Senior Partner, 1974–2004); *b* 3 Jan. 1933; *s* of Dr Gerald and Lena Bindman; *m* 1961, Lynn Janice Winton; two *s* one *d*. *Educ*: Newcastle upon Tyne Royal Grammar Sch.; Oriel Coll., Oxford (BCL 1956; MA 1959). Admitted Solicitor, 1959; Teaching Fellow, Northwestern Univ., Ill, 1959–60; Partner, Lawford & Co., 1965–74. Legal adviser: Race Relations Bd, 1966–76; CRE, 1976–83. Visiting Professor of Law: UCLA, 1982; UCL, 1990–; London South Bank Univ., 2003–. Hon. Pres., Discrimination Law Assoc., 1999–; Chm., Soc. of Labour Lawyers, 1999–2001. Chm., British Inst. of Human Rights, 2005–. Pres., Client Interviewing Comp. for England and Wales, 1990–. Trustee: Wordsworth Trust; One World Trust; Helen Bamber Foundn. Hon. LLD: De Montfort, 2000; Kingston, 2006. Liberty Award for Lifetime Human Rights Achievement, 1999; Centenary Award for Human Rights, Law Soc. Gazette, 2003. *Publications*: (jtly) Race and Law, 1972; (ed) South Africa: human rights and the rule of law, 1988. *Recreations*: walking, music, book collecting. *Address*: (office) 275 Gray's Inn Road, WC1X 8QB. *T*: (020) 7833 4433.

BING, Inigo Geoffrey; His Honour Judge Bing; a Circuit Judge, since 2000; *b* 1 April 1944; *s* of late Geoffrey Henry Cecil Bing, QC and Crystal Frances Bing; *m* 1st, 1980, Shirley-Anne Holmes (*née* Benka) (*d* 2003); three step *c*; 2nd, 2004, Judith Caroline Anne Hughes, *qv*. *Educ*: St Olave's Grammar Sch., Southwark; Birmingham Univ. (LLB). Called to the Bar, Inner Temple, 1967; practised London and SE Circuit; a District Judge (Magistrates' Courts) (formerly a Metropolitan Stipendiary Magistrate), 1989–2000; a Recorder, 1996–2000. Mem., Parole Bd, 2002–08. Mem. (Lab) London Borough of Lambeth, 1971–78 (Chm., F and GP Cttee, 1974–78); Co-founder, Lambeth Community Law Centre. Contested Braintree: (SDP) 1983; (SDP/Alliance) 1987. *Publication*: Criminal Procedure and Sentencing in the Magistrates' Court, 1990, 5th edn 1999. *Recreations*: music, travel. *Address*: Snaresbrook Crown Court, Hollybush Hill, E11 1QW. *Club*: Reform.

BING, Judith Caroline Anne; see Hughes, J. C. A.

BINGHAM, family name of **Barons Bingham of Cornhill** and **Clanmorris** and of **Earl of Lucan**.

BINGHAM OF CORNHILL, Baron *cr* 1996 (Life Peer); **Thomas Henry Bingham**; KG 2005; Kt 1980; PC 1986; Senior Lord of Appeal in Ordinary, 2000–08; *b* 13 Oct. 1933; *o s* of late Dr T. H. Bingham and Dr C. Bingham, Reigate; *m* 1963, Elizabeth, *o d* of late Peter Loxley; two *s* one *d*. *Educ*: Sedbergh; Balliol Coll., Oxford (MA; Hon. Fellow, 1989). Royal Ulster Rifles, 1952–54 (2nd Lt); London Irish Rifles (TA) 1954–59. Univ. of Oxford: Gibbs Schol. in Mod. Hist., 1956; 1st cl. Hons, Mod. Hist., 1957. Eldon Law Schol., 1957; Arden Schol., Gray's Inn, 1959; Cert. of Honour, Bar Finals, 1959; called to Bar, Gray's Inn, 1959; Bencher, 1979. Standing Jun. Counsel to Dept of Employment, 1968–72; QC 1972; a Recorder of the Crown Court, 1975–80; Judge of the High Court of Justice, Queen's Bench Div., and Judge of the Commercial Court, 1980–86; a Lord Justice of Appeal, 1986–92; Master of the Rolls, 1992–96; Lord Chief Justice, 1996–2000. Leader, Investigation into the supply of petroleum and petroleum products to Rhodesia, 1977–78; Chm., King's Fund Working Parties into Statutory Registration of Osteopaths and Chiropractors, 1989–93; Inquiry into the Supervision of BCCI, 1991–92; Comr, Interception of Communications Act 1985, 1992–94. Chairman: Council of Legal Educn, 1982–86; Adv. Council, Centre for Commercial Law Studies, Queen Mary and Westfield Coll., London Univ., 1989–92; Adv. Council on Public Records, 1992–96; Magna Carta Trust, 1992–96; Royal Commn on Historical Manuscripts, 1994–2003; Council of Mgt, British Inst. of Internat. and Comparative Law, 2001–. President: CIArb, 1991–95; British Records Assoc., 1992–96. Visitor: Balliol Coll., Oxford, 1986–; RPMS, 1989–96; UCL, 1992–96; Nuffield Coll., Oxford, 1992–96; London Business Sch., 1992–96; Templeton Coll., subseq. Green Templeton Coll., Oxford, 1996–; Darwin Coll., Cambridge, 1996; University Coll., Oxford, 2006–; High Steward, Oxford Univ., 2001–08. Governor: Sedbergh, 1978–88; Atlantic Coll., 1984–89. Special Trustee, St Mary's Hosp., 1985–92 (Chm., 1988–92); Member: St Mary's Med. Sch. Delegacy, 1988–92; Council, KCL, 1989–93. Trustee, Pilgrim Trust, 1991–2006; Chm., Butler Trust, 2001–04. President: Seckford Foundn, 1994–; Hay Fest., 2000–. Fellow, Winchester, 1983–93; Presentation Fellow, KCL, 1992; Fellow, QMW, 1993; Hon. Fellow: Amer. Coll. of Trial Lawyers, 1994; Coll. of Estate Mgt, 1996; UCL, 1997; Acad. of Athens. Hon. FBA 2003. Hon. Bencher: Inn of Court of NI, 1993; Inner Temple, 1999; Middle Temple, 2002. Hon. LLD: Birmingham, 1993; Wales, London,

1998; Glamorgan, 1999; Dickinson Sch. of Law (Pennsylvania State Univ.), 2000; City, 2005; Roma Tre, 2008; Hon. DCL Oxford, 1994; DU Essex, 1997. *Publications*: Chitty on Contracts, (Asst Editor) 22nd edn, 1961; The Business of Judging, 2000. *Address*: House of Lords, SW1A 0PW.

BINGHAM, Lord; George Charles Bingham; *b* 21 Sept. 1967; *s* and heir of 7th Earl of Lucan, *qv*. *Educ*: Eton; Trinity Hall, Cambridge. *Clubs*: Turf, White's, Pratt's.

BINGHAM, Hon. Charlotte Mary Thérèse; playwright and novelist; *b* 29 June 1942; *d* of 7th Baron Clanmorris (John Bingham) and of Madeleine Mary, *d* of late Clement Ebel; *m* 1964, Terence Brady, *qv*; one *s* one *d*. *Educ*: The Priory, Haywards Heath; Sorbonne. *TV series* with Terence Brady: Boy Meets Girl; Take Three Girls; Upstairs Downstairs; Away From It All; Play for Today; No—Honestly; Yes—Honestly; Pig in the Middle; Thomas and Sarah; The Complete Lack of Charm of the Bourgeoisie; Nanny; Oh Madeline! (USA TV); Father Matthew's Daughter; Forever Green; The Upper Hand; *TV films*: Love With a Perfect Stranger, 1986; Losing Control, 1987; The Seventh Raven, 1987; This Magic Moment, 1988; screenwriter with Terence Brady, Riders, 1993; *stage*: with Terence Brady: (contrib.) The Sloane Ranger Revue, 1985; I Wish, I Wish, 1989; (adaptation) The Shell Seekers, 1999. *Publications*: Coronet among the Weeds, 1963; Lucinda, 1965; Coronet among the Grass, 1972; Belgravia, 1983; Country Life, 1984; At Home, 1986; To Hear A Nightingale, 1988; The Business, 1989; In Sunshine or In Shadow, 1991; Stardust, 1992; By Invitation, 1993; Nanny, 1993; Change of Heart, 1994 (Romantic Novel of the Year Award, 1995, Romantic Novelists' Assoc.); Debutantes, 1995; The Nightingale Sings, 1996; Grand Affair, 1997; Love Song, 1998; The Kissing Garden, 1999; The Love Knot, 2000; The Blue Note, 2000; The Season, 2001; Summertime, 2001; Distant Music, 2002; The Chestnut Tree, 2002; The Wind off the Sea, 2003; The Moon at Midnight, 2003; Daughters of Eden, 2004; House of Flowers, 2004; The Magic Hour, 2005; Friday's Girl, 2005; Out of the Blue, 2006; In Distant Fields, 2006; The White Marriage, 2007; Goodnight Sweetheart, 2007; The Enchanted, 2008; The Land of Summer, 2008; with Terence Brady: Victoria, 1972; Rose's Story, 1973; Victoria and Company, 1974; Yes—Honestly, 1977. *Recreations*: horses, watching other people garden, shouting back at the television. *Address*: c/o United Authors, Garden Studios, 11–15 Betterton Street, WC2H 9BP. *Club*: Society of Authors.

BINGHAM, Sir (Eardley) Max, Kt 1988; QC (Tas.) 1974; Chairman, Queensland Criminal Justice Commission, 1989–92; *b* 18 March 1927; *s* of Thomas Eardley and Olive Bingham; *m* 1952, Margaret Garrett Jesson; three *s* one *d*. *Educ*: Univ. of Tasmania (LLB (Hons)); Lincoln Coll., Oxford (BCL; Rhodes Schol., 1950); Univ. of California at Berkley (Harkness Commonwealth Fund Fellow, 1963). RANR, 1945–46. Legal practice, and teaching, Univ. of Tasmania, 1953–69. MHA Tasmania, 1969–84; Attorney-General, 1969–72; Leader of the Opposition, 1972–79, Dep. Leader of the Opposition, 1982; Dep. Premier of Tas., 1982–84. Mem., Nat. Crime Authority, 1984–87. Hon. LLD Tasmania, 1998. *Publications*: contribs to jls. *Recreations*: reading, sailing. *Address*: 14 Musgrove Road, Geilston Bay, Tas 7015, Australia. *Clubs*: Tasmanian, Royal Yacht of Tasmania (Hobart).

BINGHAM, James Stewart, TD 1982; FRCP, FRCPE, FRCOG; Consultant Physician in Genitourinary and HIV Medicine, Guy's and St Thomas' NHS Foundation Trust, since 1992; *b* 31 July 1945; *s* of Dr William Bingham and Nora Mary Bingham (*née* Beckett); *m* 1974, Elizabeth Eleanor Stewart; one *s*. *Educ*: Campbell Coll., Belfast; Queen's Univ., Belfast (MB BCh BAO 1969). MRCOG 1974, FRCOG 1989; FRCPE 1994; FRCP 1999. Initial career in obstetrics and gynaecology in NI, Rhodesia and Canada, 1970–75; Middlesex Hospital: Sen. Registrar in Venereology, 1975–77; Consultant in Genitourinary Med., 1977–92; Consultant Physician in Genitourinary Med., Bromley Hosps, 1992–94. Hon. Consultant in Genitourinary Medicine to the Army, 2000–. Pres. Exec. Cttee, Internat. Union against Sexually Transmitted Infections, 2001–03 (Mem., 1995–; Hon. Treas., 1995–99; Mem. jt initiative with WHO Europe and Open Soc. Inst. to introduce protocols to Central Asia, 2004–06; Sen. Counsellor, 2005–); Member: Council, Med. Soc. for Study of Venereal Diseases, 1979–82, 1983–97, 1999–2001 (Hon. Treas., 1986–93; Pres., 1993–95; Hon. Life Fellow, 2007); Cttee, Assoc. for Genitourinary Medicine, 1993–2003 (Chm., 1999–2001); Specialist Adv. Cttee in Genitourinary Medicine, Jt Cttee for Higher Med. Trng, 1988–95, 2003– (Sec., 1989–93; Chm., 1993–95); Working Party on Med. Audit in Genitourinary Medicine, 1989–94; Dermatology and Venereology subcttee, Central Consultants' and Specialists' Cttee, BMA, 1992–2008 (Chm., 1998–2000); Working Gp on Read Codes (Genitourinary Medicine), 1993–94; Exec. Cttee, British HIV Assoc., 1996–2000 (Founding Hon. Treas., 1996–2000; Hon. Fellow, 2002). Examiner in Genitourinary Medicine: Soc. of Apothecaries, 1982– (Convenor, 1992–95); Univ. of Liverpool, 1996–98; Prince of Songkla Univ., Thailand, 2000–02; UCL, 2005–07. WHO: Consultant, Bulgaria, 1993; Advr, STD interventions for preventing HIV infection, Geneva, 1998; UK rep., Dermatovenereology cttee, Union of European Monospecialties, 2003– (Treas., 2005–). Mem., Editl Bd, Eur. S&D Guidelines. Trustee: BMA Foundn for AIDS, subseq. Med. Foundn for AIDS and Sexual Health, 2000–06; River House, 1996–2002. 257 (NI) Field Ambulance and 217 General Hosp. RAMC(V), TA, 1969–83. Silver Medal Oration, Inst. of Venereology, India, 2000. *Publications*: Sexually Transmitted Diseases: a pocket picture guide, 1984, 2nd edn 1989; articles and chapters on aspects of genital tract and HIV infections. *Recreations*: military and medical history, gardening. *Address*: Lydia Department, St Thomas' Hospital, Lambeth Palace Road, SE1 7EH. *T*: (020) 7188 2660, *Fax*: (020) 7188 7706; *e-mail*: james.bingham@gstt.nhs.uk. *Clubs*: Army and Navy, City Volunteer Officers.

BINGHAM, Col Jeremy David S.; see Smith-Bingham.

BINGHAM, John, CBE 1991; FRS 1977; Plant Breeding International, Cambridge, 1981–91; *b* 19 June 1930; *s* of Thomas Frederick Bingham and Emma Maud Lusher; *m* 1983, Jadwiga Anna Siedlecka; one *s*. Mem. of staff, Plant Breeding Inst. of Cambridge, subseq. Plant Breeding Internat. Cambridge Ltd, 1954–91. Has researched in plant breeding, culminating in production of improved winter wheat varieties for British agriculture. Pres., Royal Norfolk Agricl Assoc., 1991. Hon. FRASE, 1983. Hon. ScD UEA, 1992. Res. Medal, RASE, 1975; Mullard Medal of Royal Society, 1975; Massey Ferguson Nat. Award for Services to UK Agric., 1984. *Recreations*: farming, conservation of wild life. *Address*: Hereward Barn, Church Lane, Mattishall Burgh, Dereham, Norfolk NR20 3QZ. *T*: (01362) 858354.

BINGHAM, Judith Caroline; composer; *b* 21 June 1952; *d* of Jack Bingham and Peggy (*née* MacGowan); *m* 1985, Andrew Petrow. *Educ*: High Storrs Grammar Sch., Sheffield; Royal Acad. of Music (Principal's Prize for Music, 1972; ARAM 1997). Mem., BBC Singers, 1983–95. *Major works*: The Divine Image, 1976; Cocaine Lil, 1977; Flynn, 1979; Chamouni, 1982; Cradle Song of the Blessed Virgin, Scenes From Nature, 1983; Just Before Dawn, 1985; A Cold Spell, 1987; Christmas Past, Christmas Present, 1988; Chartres, 1988; Dove Cottage by Moonlight, 1989; Four Minute Mile, 1991; The Stars Above, The Earth Below, 1991; Unpredictable But Providential, 1991; Irish Tenebrae, The Uttermost, 1992; O Magnum Mysterium, Santa Casa, Beyond Redemption, 1994;

Evening Canticles, Epiphany, Salt in the Blood, The Red Hot Nail, 1995; The Mysteries of Adad, The Temple at Karnak, No Discord, 1996; Gleams of a Remoter World, The Waning Moon, Below the Surface Stream, Chapman's Pool, 1997; Missa Brevis, The Clouded Heaven, Bassoon Concerto, Unheimlich, Vorarlberg, Shelley Dreams, 1998; The Shooting Star, Walzerspiele, The Cathedral of Trees, Water Lilies, Otherworld, 1999; Necklace of Light, Annunciation, The Shepherd's Gift, St Bride, Assisted by Angels, These are Our Footsteps, 2000; 50 Shades of Green; The Shadow Side of Joy Finzi, 2001; Beneath these alien stars, 2001; Bright Spirit, 2001; My Father's Arms, 2002; Ave Verum Corpus, enter GHOST, The Mystery of Boranup, Aquileia, Uppon the First Sight of New England, Incarnation with Shepherds Dancing, 2002; Missa Brevis No 2, The Road to Emmaeus, The Moon over Westminster Cathedral, Ancient Sunlight, The Christmas Truce, Bach's Tomb, O Clap Your Hands, 2003; The Ivory Tree, The Secret Garden, The Yearning Strong, Limehouse Nocturne, Lo in the Silent Night, Our Faith is a Light, Margaret Forsaken, Down and Out, Touch'd by Heavenly Fire, In Nomine, 2004; Ghost Towns of the American West, A Formal Order, Down and Out, We Two, Edington Canticles, The Shepheardes Calender, 2005; Hidden City, La Boiteuse, An Ancient Music, Winter's Pilgrimage, My Heart Strangely Warm'd, The Cruelty of the Gods, The Flying Hours, The Morning-Watch, Capriccio, 2006; Missa Brevis, Awake My Soul, The Hired Hand, Ziggurat, Jacob's Ladder, Fantasia, Shakespeare Requiem, 2007; She Walks in Beauty, Byron, violent progress, 2008. BBC Young Composer, 1977; Barlow Prize for choral music, 2004; British Composer Awards for liturgical music, 2004, and for choral music, 2004, 2006. FRNCM; FRSCM. *Recreations:* art, books, friends. *Address:* c/o Peters Edition, 10–12 Baches Street, N1 6DN. *T:* (020) 8660 4766.

BINGHAM, Sir Max; *see* Bingham, Sir E. M.

BINGHAM, Dr Sheila Anne, (Mrs S. H. Rodwell); Director, MRC Centre for Nutrition and Cancer, and Hon. Professor, University of Cambridge, since 2006; Head of Group, Dunn Human Nutrition Unit, MRC, since 1998; *b* 7 March 1947; *d* of Bernard Walter Harrison and Audrey Jean Harrison (*née* Wootton); *m* 1st, 1970, Roger Bingham (marr. diss. 1979); 2nd, 2000, Simon Hunter Rodwell. *Educ:* Loughborough High Sch.; King's Coll., London (BSc 1968; PhD 1983); MA Cantab 1996. Dietitian, University Coll. and St Phillip's Hosps, London, 1969–74; Dunn Human Nutrition Unit, 1976–: MRC Res Officer, 1976–88; MRC Scientific Staff, 1988–95; MRC Special Appt, 1995; Dep. Dir, 1998–2005. Associate Lectr, Faculty of Clinical Medicine, Univ. of Cambridge, 1992–. Vis. Prof., Univ. of Ulster, 1994–. Member: Cttee on Med. Aspects of Food Policy, 1991–2000; Scientific Adv. Cttee on Nutrition, 2000. FRSocMed 1993; FMedSci 2001. *Publications:* Dictionary of Nutrition, 1977; Everyman Companion to Food and Nutrition, 1987; numerous articles in learned jls. *Address:* High Hall, Norton Little Green, Bury St Edmunds, Suffolk IP31 3NN.

BINI SMAGHI, Lorenzo, PhD; Member, Executive Board, European Central Bank, since 2005; *b* Florence, 29 Nov. 1956. *Educ:* Univ. Catholique de Louvain (Lic. Scis Econs 1978); Univ. of Southern Calif (MA Econs 1980); Univ. of Chicago (PhD Econs 1988). Research Department, Banca d'Italia: Economist, Internat. Section, 1983–88; Hd of Exchange Rate and Internat. Trade Div., 1988–94; Hd of Policy Div., EMI, Frankfurt, 1994–98; Dep. Dir Gen. for Res., ECB, Frankfurt, 1998; Dir Gen. for Internat. Financial Relns, Min. of the Economy and Finance, Italy, 1998–2005. Vice Pres., Econ. and Financial Cttee, EU, 2003–05. Pres., Fondazione Palazzo Strozzi, Florence. Grande Ufficiale al Merito della Repubblica Italiana, 2006. *Publications:* L'Euro, 1998, 3rd edn 2001; (with D. Gros) Open Issues in European Central Banking, 2000; Chi Ci Salva dalla Prossima Crisi Finanziaria?, 2000. *Address:* European Central Bank, Kaiserstrasse 29, 60311 Frankfurt am Main, Germany. *T:* (69) 13447170, *Fax:* (69) 13447163; *e-mail:* office.binismaghi@ecb.int.

BINLEY, Brian Arthur Roland; MP (C) Northampton South, since 2005; *b* 1 April 1942; *s* of Frank Binley and Phyllis Binley (*née* Underwood); *m* 1985, Jacqueline Denise Gibbs; two *s*. *Educ:* Finedon Mulso (C of E) Sch. Chairman and Founder: BCC Mktg Services Ltd, 1989–; Beechwood House Publishing Ltd, 1993–2001 (publishers of Binley's Directories). Mem. (C) Northants CC, 1997–. FRSA 1996. *Recreations:* golf, Association football, cricket, opera. *Address:* House of Commons, SW1A 0AA; 1 Berry Close, Hackleton, Northampton NN7 2BS. *T:* (01604) 250252; *e-mail:* brian-binley@bccmarketing.co.uk. *Clubs:* Carlton; Northampton Town and County.

BINMORE, Prof. Kenneth George, CBE 2001; PhD; FBA 1995; Professor of Economics, University College London, 1991–2003, now Emeritus; *b* 27 Sept. 1940; *s* of Ernest George Binmore and Maud Alice (*née* Holland); *m* 1968, Josephine Ann Lee; two *s* two *d*. *Educ:* Imperial Coll., London (BSc; PhD 1964). Lectr, Reader and Prof. of Maths, LSE, 1969–88; Prof. of Econs, LSE and Univ. of Michigan, 1988–93; Dir, ESRC Centre for Econ. Learning and Social Evolution, 1994–2002. *Publications:* Mathematical Analysis, 1977, 2nd edn 1982; Logic, Sets and Numbers, 1980; Topological Ideas, 1981; Calculus, 1982; Economic Organizations as Games, 1986; Economics of Bargaining, 1986; Essays on the Foundations of Game Theory, 1991; Fun and Games, 1992; Frontiers of Game Theory, 1993; Game Theory and the Social Contract: vol. I, Playing Fair, 1994; vol. II, Just Playing, 1998; Natural Justice, 2005; Playing for Real, 2007; Does Game Theory Work?, 2007; Very Short Introduction to Game Theory, 2007; Rational Decisions, 2008; papers. *Recreation:* philosophy. *Address:* Newmills, Whitebrook, Monmouth, NP25 4TY. *T:* (01600) 860691.

BINNEY, Prof. James Jeffrey, DPhil; FRS 2000; FRAS, FInstP; Professor of Physics, University of Oxford, since 1996; Fellow, Merton College, Oxford, since 1981; *b* 12 April 1950; *s* of Harry Augustus Roy Binney and Barbara Binney (*née* Poole); *m* 1993, Lucy Elliot Buckingham; one *s* one *d*. *Educ:* King's Coll. Sch., Wimbledon; Churchill Coll., Cambridge (BA 1971, MA 1975); Albert Ludwigs Univ., Freiburg im Breisgau; Christ Church and Magdalen Coll., Oxford (DPhil 1976). Fellow, Magdalen Coll., Oxford, 1975–79; Vis. Asst Prof., Princeton Univ., 1979–81; Lectr in Theoretical Physics, 1981–90, Reader, 1990–96, Oxford Univ. Lindemann Fellow, Princeton Univ., 1975–76; Fairchild Dist. Schol., CIT, 1983–84; Visiting Fellow: Univ. of Arizona, 1989; Princeton Univ., 1992; ANU, 1995. FRAS 1973; FInstP 2000. Maxwell Medal and Prize, Inst. Physics, 1986; Brouwer Award, American Astronomy Soc., 2003. *Publications:* jointly: Galactic Astronomy: structure and kinematics, 1981; Galactic Dynamics, 1987; PICK for Humans, 1990; The Theory of Critical Phenomena, 1992; Galactic Astronomy, 1998. *Recreations:* carpentry, stone and metalwork, walking. *Address:* Rudolf Peierls Centre for Theoretical Physics, Keble Road, Oxford OX1 3NP. *T:* (01865) 273979.

BINNEY, Marcus Hugh Crofton, CBE 2006 (OBE 1983); FSA; writer, journalist, conservationist; Founder, 1975, and President, since 1984, Save Britain's Heritage (Chairman, 1975–84); *b* 21 Sept. 1944; *s* of late Lt-Col Francis Crofton Simms, MC and of Sonia, *d* of Rear-Adm. Sir William Marcus Charles Beresford-Whyte, KCB, CMG (she *m* 2nd, Sir George Binney, DSO); *m* 1st, 1966, Hon. Sara Anne Vanneck (marr. diss. 1976), *e d* of 6th Baron Huntingfield; 2nd, 1981, Anne Carolyn, *d* of Dr T. H. Hills, Merstham, Surrey; two *s*. *Educ:* Magdalene Coll., Cambridge (BA 1966). Architectural writer, 1968–77, Architectural Editor, 1977–84, Editor, 1984–86, Country Life; Ed., Landscape, 1987–88; envmt correspondent, Harpers & Queen, 1989–90; architecture correspondent, The Times, 1991–. Sec., UK Cttee, Internat. Council on Monuments and Sites, 1972–81; Mem., Montagu Cttee (report, Britain's Historic Buildings, published 1980); Director: Rly Heritage Trust, 1985–; HMS Warrior; Chm., Save Europe's Heritage, 1995–; President: Friends of City Churches, 1998– (Chm., 1995–98); Save Jersey's Heritage, 1990–. Television series: Co-Presenter, Great Houses of Europe, 1993, 1996, 1997. Exhibitions: (joint organizer) The Destruction of the Country House, V&A Mus., 1974; Change and Decay: the future of our churches, V&A Mus., 1977. FSA 1989. Hon. FRIBA 2004. London Conservation Medal, 1985. *Publications:* (with Peter Burman): Change and Decay: the future of our churches, 1977; Chapels and Churches: who cares?, 1977; (with Max Hanna) Preservation Pays, 1978; (ed jtly) Railway Architecture, 1979; (ed jtly) Satanic Mills, 1979; (ed jtly) Our Past Before Us, 1981; (with Kit Martin) The Country House: to be or not to be, 1982; (with Max Hanna) Preserve and Prosper, 1983; The Architecture of Sir Robert Taylor, 1984; Our Vanishing Heritage, 1984; Country Manors of Portugal, 1987; (jtly) Bright Futures: the reuse of industrial buildings, 1990; Palace on the River, 1991; (with M. Watson-Smyth) The Save Action Guide, 1991; Châteaux of the Loire, 1992; (with R. Runciman) Glyndebourne: building a vision, 1994; The Châteaux of France: photographs by Frederick Evans 1906–7, 1994; Railway Architecture: the way ahead, 1995; (with Patrick Bowe) Houses and Gardens of Portugal, 1998; Town Houses: 800 years of evolution and innovation in urban design, 1998; Airport Builders, 1999; The Ritz Hotel, London, 1999, Centenary edn 2006; (with Graham Byfield) London Sketchbook: a city observed, 2001; Women Who Lived for Danger, 2002; Great Houses of Europe, 2003; Secret War Heroes, 2005; Save Britain's Heritage 1975–2005: thirty years of campaigning, 2005. *Address:* Domaine des Vaux, St Lawrence, Jersey JE3 1JG. *T:* (01534) 864424, *Fax:* (01534) 862612; *e-mail:* mbinney@msn.com.

BINNIE, David Stark, OBE 1979; General Manager, British Rail, London Midland Region, 1977–80; *b* 2 June 1922; *s* of Walter Archibald Binnie and Helen (*née* Baxter), Bonkle, Lanarkshire; *m* 1947, Leslie Archibald; one *s* one *d*. *Educ:* Wishaw High School. British Railways: Gen. and Signalling Asst to Gen. Manager Scottish Region, 1955; Asst District Operating Supt 1961, District Operating Supt 1963, Glasgow North; Divisional Movements Manager, Glasgow Div., 1965; Movements Manager, Scottish Region, 1967; Divisional Manager, SE Div., Southern Region, 1969; Asst Gen. Manager, Southern Region, 1970, Gen. Manager, 1972; Exec. Dir, Freight, BR Board, 1974–76. Lt-Col Engineer and Railway Staff Corps, RE (T&AVR). OStJ. *Recreation:* Dartmoor and Highland life. *Address:* Above Ways, Lower Knowle Road, Lustleigh, Devon TQ13 9TR. *T:* (01647) 277386.

BINNIE, Frank Hugh, FCSD; Chairman and Chief Executive, Binnie International, since 1998; *b* 1 March 1950; *s* of Dr Hugh Lawson Binnie and Isobel May Van Dijk (*née* Nairn); *m* 1996, Fiona Margaret Maclean Nicolson (*née* Hart); one *s* one *d*; and three *s* by previous marriage. *Educ:* Loughborough GS. FCSD 1992. Mgt trainee, Corah Textiles, Leicester, 1970–73; Ops Manager, Floreal Knitwear, Mauritius, 1973–76; Sales Manager, Kemptons Knitwear, Leicester, 1976–79; Gen. Manager, Texport Unilever, 1979–82; Manager, Kilspindie Knitwear, Haddington, 1982–85; Dir and Co. Sec., Midlothian Enterprise, 1985–88; Man. Dir, Perkins, Hodgkinson & Gillibrand, 1988–90; Chief Exec., Design Council, Scotland, then Scottish Design, 1990–96. Chief Exec., Caledonian Foundn, 1996–97; Chief Executive Officer: Internet Soc. Scotland, 1998–2003; ScotlandIS, 2000–03; Executive Chairman: Scottish Internet Exchange, 1999–2003; Scotnom Ltd, 2000–05; Internat. Soc. Foundn, 2001–04; Broadband Scotland Ltd, 2001–04; Chm., EBusiness Scotland Ltd, 1999–2004; Co-Founder, Ecommerce Exchange (Scotland) Ltd, 1999–2004; Sen. Consultant, Career Associates, 1998–. Vis. Prof., Strathclyde Univ., 1990–96; External Assessor: MBA, Westminster Univ., 1995–97; Design Mgt, De Montfort Univ., 1996–99. Chm., Sector Gp for Design, Scotvec, 1995–96. Mem. Exec. Council, Scottish Council of Develt and Industry, 2001–. Gen. Manager (pt-time), Kenilworth Court Assoc., 2005–. Formerly Mem. Bd, 1996 UK City of Architecture and Design. Mem. Cttee, Hurlingham Yacht Club, 2005–. FRSA 1992; MInstD. *Recreations:* sailing, chess, classic cars, scriptwriter. *T:* (020) 8789 1473.

BINNIG, Prof. Dr Gerd Karl; IBM Fellow, since 1986; Honorary Professor of Physics, University of Munich, since 1987; Consultant, Definiens AG, since 1994; *b* 20 July 1947; *m* 2003, Renate; one *s* one *d* by former marriage. *Educ:* J. W. Goethe Univ., Frankfurt/M (DipPhys; PhD). Research staff mem., IBM Zurich Res. Lab., in fields of superconductivity of semiconductors and scanning tunneling microscopy, 1978–, Gp Leader 1984–; IBM Almaden Res. Center, San José, and collab. with Stanford Univ., 1985–86; Vis. Prof., Stanford Univ., 1985–86. Member: Technology Council, IBM Acad., 1989–92; Supervisory Bd, Mercedes Automobil Holding AG, 1989–95. For. Associate Mem., Acad. of Scis, Washington, 1987. Hon. FRMS 1988. Scanning Tunneling Microscopy awards: Physics Prize, German Phys. Soc., 1982; Otto Klung Prize, 1983; (jtly) King Faisal Internat. Prize for Science and Hewlett Packard Europhysics Prize, 1984; (jtly) Nobel Prize in Physics, 1986; Elliot Cresson Medal, Franklin Inst., Philadelphia, 1987; Minnie Rosen Award, Ross Univ., NY, 1988. Grosses Verdienstkreuz mit Stern und Schulterband des Verdienstordens (FRG), 1987; Bayerischer Verdienstorden, 1992. *Recreations:* music, tennis, soccer, golf. *Address:* Definiens AG, Trappentreu Strasse 1, 80339 Munich, Germany.

BINNING, Lord; George Edmund Baldred Baillie-Hamilton; *b* 27 Dec. 1985; *s* and *heir* of Earl of Haddington, *qv*.

BINNING, Kenneth George Henry, CMG 1976; consultant, public policy and international regulation, since 1992; *b* 5 Jan. 1928; *o s* of late Henry and Hilda Binning; *m* 1953, Pamela Dorothy, *o d* of A. E. and D. G. Pronger; three *s* one *d*. *Educ:* Bristol Grammar Sch.; Balliol Coll., Oxford. Joined Home Civil Service, 1950; Nat. Service, 1950–52; HM Treasury, 1952–58; Private Sec. to Financial Sec., 1956–57; AEA, 1958–65; seconded to Min. of Technology, 1965; rejoined Civil Service, 1968; Dir-Gen. Concorde, 1972–76 and Under-Sec., DTI later Dept of Industry, 1972–83. Mem., BSC, 1980–83; Director of Government Relations: NEI Internat. subseq. NEI plc, 1983–90; Rolls Royce plc, 1991–93. Consultant on regulatory policy to govts of Hungary, Poland, Slovakia and Lithuania, 1993–2000. *Recreations:* music, appreciation of other people's gardens. *Address:* Flat 11, Oakbrook, 8 Court Downs Road, Beckenham, Kent BR3 6LR. *T:* (020) 8650 0273.

BINNS, David John, CBE 1989; Trust Board Secretary, Halton General Hospital NHS Trust, 1995–99 (non-executive Director, 1992–94); *b* 12 April 1929; *s* of Henry Norman Binns, OBE and Ivy Mary Binns; *m* 1957, Jean Margaret Evans; one *s* (one *d* decd). *Educ:* Fleetwood Grammar Sch.; Rossall Sch.; Sheffield Univ. LLB 1951. Solicitor 1954. Articled Clerk, Sheffield City Council, 1949; Asst Solicitor, Warrington County Borough Council, 1954; Dep. Town Clerk, Warrington County Borough Council, 1958; General Manager: Warrington Develt Corp., 1969–81; Warrington and Runcorn Develt Corp., 1981–89. Mem., Warrington DHA, 1990–92. *Recreations:* walking, gardening, music. *Address:* 4 Cedarways, Appleton, Warrington, Cheshire WA4 5EW.

BINNS, Gareth Ian; Director of Operations, Personal Finance Education Group, since 2006; *b* 6 Feb. 1958; *s* of Ian Binns and Mavis Eleanor Binns (*née* Jones); partner, Sally Bacon; one *s*. *Educ:* Southampton Univ. (BA Hons Archaeol. and Geog.); Durham Univ. (MA Anglo-Saxon and Viking Archaeol.); Nottingham Univ. (PGCE Geog. and Hist.); Birkbeck Coll., London (Dip. Multimedia Mgt). Actg Hd of Dept, and Div. Leader, Bilborough Sixth Form Coll., 1984–88; Educn Officer, Council for British Archaeol., 1988–91; Countryside and Envmtl Educn Officer, 1991–98, Hd of Educn and Interpretation, 1998–2000, NT; Educn Dir, NESTA, 2000–03; Keeper of Learning and Inf., BM, 2003–06. *Recreations:* museums and galleries, hill-walking, art appreciation and collecting, historic buildings, landscape history, running. *Address:* Personal Finance Education Group, Fifth Floor, 14 Bonhill Street, EC2A 4BX. *T:* (020) 7330 9470.

BINNS, Jacqueline Sukie, (Mrs W. A. T. Hills); artist, embroiderer and sculptor, since 1986; *b* 24 May 1963; *d* of Dennis Binns and Eileen (*née* Andrews); *m* 1986, Warwick Alan Theodore Hills. *Educ:* Goldsmiths' Coll., London (BA Textiles 1986). Exhibitions include: Southwark Cathedral, Leicester Mus., Salisbury Cathedral, 1987 and 2007; Gawthorpe Hall, Peterborough Cathedral, 1988; St Alban's Abbey, 1989, 1992; St Paul's Cathedral, 1990; Royal Sch. of Needlework, 1993; Sheffield Cath., Goldsmiths' Coll., 1997; Shrewsbury Abbey, 1998; Wimpole Hall, Cambridge, Winchester Cath., 1999; Guildford Cath., Portsmouth Cath., Alexandra Palace, 2000; De Morgan Centre, 2003; Guildford Cathedral, 2008; works of art in private collections and cathedrals and churches in America, Australia, Europe and UK; works include: St Alban Cope, the Anniversary Cope for St Paul's Cathedral; lifesize Crucifixion sculpture for St Peter's Ch, Plymouth. *Recreations:* walking, the arts, costume. *Address:* 1 Cargill Road, Earlsfield, SW18 3EF. *T:* (020) 8874 0895; *e-mail:* jb@jacquiebinns.com.

BINNS, James Wallace, PhD, DLitt; FBA 2004; Lecturer, 1984–91, Reader, 1991–2002, in Latin Literature, Honorary Fellow, since 2002, University of York; *b* 1 Sept. 1940; *s* of Wallace William and Madge Binns. *Educ:* Univ. of Birmingham (BA 1964; MA 1965; PhD 1969; DLitt 1992). Exec. Officer, War Office, 1958–61; Lectr in Later Latin, Univ. of Birmingham, 1965–84. Hon. Lectr, Univ. of Leeds, 1987–. *Publications:* Intellectual Culture in Elizabethan and Jacobean England, 1990; (ed with S. E. Banks) Gervase of Tilbury: Otia Imperialia, 2002. *Recreations:* travel, films, military history. *Address:* Centre for Medieval Studies, University of York, King's Manor, York YO1 7EP. *T:* (01904) 433910, *Fax:* (01904) 433918.

BINNS, Rev. John Richard, PhD; Vicar, St Mary the Great with St Michael, Cambridge, since 1994; Rural Dean of North Cambridge, since 2007; *b* 10 Jan. 1951. *Educ:* St John's Coll., Cambridge (MA 1976); King's Coll., London (PhD 1989); Coll. of the Resurrection, Mirfield. Ordained deacon, 1976, priest, 1977; Assistant Curate: Holy Trinity, Clapham, 1976–78; Clapham Old Town, 1978–80; Team Vicar, Mortlake with E Sheen, 1980–87; Vicar, Holy Trinity, Upper Tooting, 1987–94. Hon. Canon, Ely Cathedral, 2007–. *Publications:* Cyril of Scythopolis: lives of the Monks of Palestine, 1991; Ascetics and Ambassadors of Christ, 1994; Great St Mary's, Cambridge's University Church, 2000; An Introduction to the Christian Orthodox Churches, 2002. *Address:* Great St Mary's Vicarage, 39 Madingley Road, Cambridge CB3 0EL. *T:* (01223) 355285.

BINNS, Malcolm; concert pianist; *b* 29 Jan. 1936; *s* of Douglas and May Binns. *Educ:* Bradford Grammar Sch.; Royal Coll. of Music (ARCM, Chappell Gold Medal, Medal of Worshipful Co. of Musicians). London début, 1957; Henry Wood Proms début, 1960; Royal Festival Hall début, 1961; Festival Hall appearances in London Philharmonic Orchestra International series, 1969–; toured with Scottish Nat. Orch., 1989; concerts at Aldeburgh, Leeds, Three Choirs (1975), Bath and Canterbury Festivals; regular appearances at Promenade concerts and broadcasts for BBC Radio; celebrated 60th birthday with series of concerts, 1996; series of recitals for BBC linking Clementi and Beethoven, 1997. First complete recording of Beethoven piano sonatas on original instruments, 1980; première recordings of Sir William Sterndale Bennett's piano concertos with London Philharmonic and Philharmonia Orchs, 1990; première recording of Stanford's re-discovered Third Piano Concerto, with RPO, 1996. *Recreation:* collecting antique gramophone records. *Address:* 233 Court Road, Orpington, Kent BR6 9BY. *T:* (01689) 831056.

BINNS, Hon. Patrick George; Ambassador of Canada to Ireland, since 2007; *b* Saskatchewan, 8 Oct. 1948; *s* of Stan and Phyllis Binns; *m* 1971, Carol MacMillan; three *s* one *d*. *Educ:* Univ. of Alberta (BA, MA 1971). Rural Develt Council, PEI, 1974–78; MLA (PC) 4th Kings, PEI, 1978–84; Minister: of Municipal Affairs, Labour, and Envmt, 1979–80; of Community Affairs, 1980–82; of Fisheries and of Industry, 1982–84; MP (PC) Cardigan, 1984–88; Parly Sec. to Minister of Fisheries and Oceans, 1984–88; MLA (PC) Dist 5, Murray River-Gaspereaux, PEI, 1996–2007; Premier and Pres. of Exec. Council, PEI, 1996–2007; Leader, PC Party, PEI, 1996–2007; Minister responsible for Intergovtl Affairs, 1996–2007; Minister of Agriculture, Fisheries and Aquaculture, 2006–07. President: Island Bean Ltd, 1988–96; Pat Binns & Associates, 1988–96. Silver Jubilee Medal, 1977; Golden Jubilee Medal, 2002. *Recreations:* hockey, ski-ing. *Address:* Canadian Embassy, 7–8 Wilton Terrace, Dublin 2, Ireland; (home) Hopefield, Murray River RR#4, PE C0A 1W0, Canada. *T:* (902) 9622196.

BINNS, Susan May; Director, Information Society and Media, European Commission, since 2005; *b* 22 April 1948; *d* of Jack and Mollie Binns. *Educ:* Harrogate Coll.; LSE (BSc Econ Internat. Relations). HM Diplomatic Service, 1968–80: served FCO and Brussels; New Delhi, 1978–80; Cabinet of Ivor Richard, EC Member, Brussels, 1981–84; Counsellor, EC Delegations: Washington, 1985–88; Belgrade, 1988; Dep. Chef de Cabinet of Bruce Millan, EC Mem. resp. for regl policies, 1989–91, Chef de Cabinet, 1991–95; Dir, Internal Market, EC, 1995–2004. *Recreation:* gardening. *Address:* European Commission, 1049 Brussels, Belgium. *T:* (2) 2963285.

BINSKI, Prof. Paul, PhD; FSA; FBA 2007; Professor of the History of Medieval Art, University of Cambridge, since 2006; Fellow, Gonville and Caius College, Cambridge, 1983–87 and since 1996; *b* 9 Nov. 1956; *s* of late Eugene and Pamela Binski. *Educ:* Harrow Sch.; Gonville and Caius Coll., Cambridge (BA 1979, MA); PhD 1984. Asst Prof., Dept of History of Art, Yale Univ., and Fellow, Saybrook Coll., 1988–91; Lecturer, Department of History of Art: Univ. of Manchester, 1991–95; Cambridge Univ., 1996–2002 (Hd of Dept, 1999–2001); Reader in Hist. of Medieval Art, Cambridge Univ., 2002–06. Slade Prof. of Fine Art, Univ. of Oxford, 2007. Vis. Mem., IAS, Princeton, 1987–88; Getty Postdoctoral Fellow, Dept of Art and Archaeol., Princeton Univ., 1987–88; Ailsa Mellon Bruce Vis. Sen. Fellow, Center for Advanced Study in Visual Arts, Nat. Gall. of Art, Washington, 1992; British Acad./Leverhulme Trust Sen. Res. Fellow, 2003–04. Associate Ed., Art History, 1992–97; Mem., Res. and Pubn Cttee, British Acad. *Corpus Vitrearum Medii Aevi*, 1995–; Mem., Editl Bd, British Art Jl, 1999–. Member: Peterborough Cathedral Fabric Adv. Cttee, 1996–2006; Westminster Abbey Fabric Commn, 1998–. Mem., Exec. Cttee, Walpole Soc., 1999–2003. Foreign Advr, Internat. Center of Medieval Art, The Cloisters, NY, 2004–. Presenter, Divine Designs, Channel 5, 2002–04. FSA 1998. *Publications:* The Painted Chamber at Westminster, 1986; (jtly) Dominican Painting in East Anglia: the Thornham Parva Retable and the Musée de Cluny Frontal, 1987; (ed with J. Alexander) Age of Chivalry: art in Plantagenet England 1200–1400, 1987; Westminster Abbey and the Plantagenets: kingship and the representation of power 1200–1400, 1995; Medieval Death: ritual and representation, 1996; (ed with W. Noel) New Offerings, Ancient Treasures: essays in medieval art in honour of George Henderson, 2001; Becket's Crown: art and imagination in Gothic England 1170–1300, 2004; (ed with S. Panayotova) The Cambridge Illuminations: ten centuries of book production in the Medieval West, 2005; contrib. articles to learned jls. *Recreations:* organ music, old churches and houses, conversation. *Address:* Gonville and Caius College, Cambridge CB2 1TA. *Club:* Athenæum.

BINTLEY, David Julian, CBE 2001; choreographer; Director, Birmingham Royal Ballet, since 1995; *b* 17 Sept. 1957; *s* of David Bintley and Glenys Bintley (*née* Ellinthorpe); *m* 1981, Jennifer Catherine Ursula Mills; two *s*. *Educ:* Holme Valley Grammar School. Royal Ballet School, 1974; Sadler's Wells Royal Ballet, 1976; first professional choreography, The Outsider, 1978; first three act ballet, The Swan of Tuonela, 1982; Company Choreographer, 1983–85, Resident Choreographer, 1985–86, Sadler's Wells Royal Ballet; Resident Choreographer and Principal Dancer, Royal Ballet, 1986–93. Ballets created include: Carmina Burana, 1995; Far From the Madding Crowd, 1996; The Nutcracker Sweeties; The Protecting Veil, 1998; The Shakespeare Suite; Arthur, Part One, 2000; Arthur, Part Two, 2001; Beauty and the Beast, 2003; Take Five, 2007. Evening Standard Award for Ballet, for Choros and Consort Lessons, both 1983; Laurence Olivier Award for Petrushka, 1984; Manchester Evening News Award for Dance, for Still Life at the Penguin Café, 1987, for Edward II, 1998. *Address:* Birmingham Royal Ballet, Birmingham Hippodrome, Thorp Street, Birmingham B5 4AU.

bin YEOP, Tan Sri Abdul Aziz, Al-Haj; PSM (Malaysia); Hon. GCVO 1972; Partner in legal firm, Aziz and Mazlan, Advocates and Solicitors, Kuala Lumpur, 1966–71, and since 1973; *b* 5 Oct. 1916; *m* 1942, Puan Sri Hamidah Aziz; seven *s* three *d*. *Educ:* King Edward VII Sch., Perak, Malaysia. Malay Administrative Service, 1937; called to Bar, Lincoln's Inn, 1950; Malayan Civil Service, 1951; First Asst State Sec., Perak 1954; London Univ. (course in Community Development), 1955. Permanent Sec., Min. of Agriculture, 1958–62; Dep. Sec., Malaysian Affairs Div., Prime Minister's Dept, 1962–64; Permanent Sec., Min. of Education, 1964–66. Chm. and Dir of firms in Malaysia, 1966–71. High Comr for Malaysia in London, 1971–73. First Chm., Bd of Governors of BERNAMA (Malaysia's National News Agency), 1967–71; Chairman: Council, Universiti Teknologi, Malaysia, 1974– (Pro-Chancellor, 1977–80); Majlis Amanah Raayat, Malaysia, 1975–. *Recreations:* walking, reading, fishing. *Address:* c/o Aziz and Mazlan, Advocates and Solicitors, B-3-3 & B-3-4, 3rd Floor, Megan Phileo Promenade 189, Jalan Tun Razak, 50400 Kuala Lumpur, Malaysia. *T:* (3) 21617967, *Fax:* (3) 21633525; *e-mail:* azizmazlan@hotmail.com.

BIRAN, Yoav; Ambassador; Director General, Ministry of Foreign Affairs, Jerusalem, 2002–04 (Deputy Director General, 1993–98, Senior Deputy Director General, 1998–2002, with special responsibility for the Middle East and the peace process); *b* 17 July 1939; *s* of Michael and Rachel Barsky; *m* (marr. diss.); one *s* two *d*; *m* 1991, Mrs Jane Moonman. *Educ:* Hebrew University of Jerusalem (post grad. studies, history, internat. relns). Joined Min. of For. Affairs, Jerusalem, 1963; ME and Afr. Depts, 1963–65; Second Sec., Ethiopia, 1965–67; First Sec., Uganda, 1967–70; Prin. Asst to Asst Dir-Gen. in charge of World Jewry and Inf., 1970–72, Dep. Dir of Dir-Gen.'s Cabinet, 1972–74, Min. of For. Affairs; Mem., Israel Delegn to Geneva Peace Conf., Dec. 1973; Dir of Dept, Center for Res. and Policy Planning, Min. of For. Affairs, 1975–77; Minister Plenipotentiary, 1977–82, Chargé d'Affaires, 1982–83, London; elected Distinguished Mem., Israel For. Service and of Israel Civil Service, 1983; Asst Dir Gen., Admin, 1984–87, N Amer. and Disarmament Affairs, 1987–88, FO, Jerusalem; Ambassador to UK, 1988–93; Dep. Nat. Security Advr (Foreign Policy), Prime Minister's Office, 1999–2001. *Recreations:* theatre, collecting antiquarian maps and books. *Address:* c/o Ministry of Foreign Affairs, Hakirya, Romema, Jerusalem 91950, Israel.

BIRCH, family name of **Baroness Young of Hornsey**.

BIRCH, Prof. Anthony Harold, PhD; FRSC 1988; Professor of Political Science, University of Victoria, British Columbia, 1977–89, now Emeritus; *b* 17 Feb. 1924; *o s* of late Frederick Harold Birch and Rosalind Dorothy Birch; *m* 1953, Dorothy Madeleine Overton, Bayport, New York; one *s* one *d*. *Educ:* The William Ellis Sch.; University Coll., Nottingham; London Sch. of Economics. BSc (Econ) London, with 1st cl. hons, 1945; PhD London, 1951. Asst Principal, Board of Trade, 1945–47; University of Manchester: Asst Lectr in Govt, 1947–51; Lectr, 1951–58; Senior Lectr in Government, 1958–61; Prof. of Political Studies, Univ. of Hull, 1961–70; Prof. of Political Sci., Exeter Univ., 1970–77. Commonwealth Fund Fellow at Harvard Univ. and University of Chicago, 1951–52. Consultant to Government of Western Region of Nigeria, 1956–58. Vis. Prof. Tufts Univ., 1968; Vis. Fellow, ANU, 1987. Vice-Pres., Internat. Political Sci. Assoc., 1976–79. Sir Isaiah Berlin Prize, Political Studies Assoc., 2002. *Publications:* Federalism, Finance and Social Legislation, 1955; Small-Town Politics, 1959; Representative and Responsible Government, 1964; The British System of Government, 1967, 10th edn 1998; Representation, 1971; Political Integration and Disintegration in the British Isles, 1977; Nationalism and National Integration, 1989; The Concepts and Theories of Modern Democracy, 1993, 3rd edn 2007; articles in various journals. *Recreations:* reading, music, bridge. *Address:* 1901 Fairfield Road, Victoria, BC V8S 1H2, Canada.

BIRCH, Prof. Bryan John, FRS 1972; Professor of Arithmetic, University of Oxford, 1985–98, now Emeritus; Fellow of Brasenose College, Oxford, 1966–98, now Emeritus; *b* 25 Sept. 1931; *s* of Arthur Jack and Mary Edith Birch; *m* 1961, Gina Margaret Christ (*d* 2005); two *s* one *d*. *Educ:* Shrewsbury Sch.; Trinity Coll., Cambridge (MA, PhD). Harkness Fellow, Princeton, 1957–58; Fellow: Trinity Coll., Cambridge, 1956–60; Churchill Coll., Cambridge, 1960–62; Sen. Lectr, later Reader, Univ. of Manchester, 1962–65; Reader in Mathematics, Univ. of Oxford, 1966–85. Deleg., OUP, 1988–98. Ed., Proc. London Math. Soc., 2001–03. Sen. Whitehead Prize, 1993; De Morgan Medal, 2007. *Publications:* articles in learned jls, mainly on number theory; various editorships. *Recreations:* gardening (theoretical), opera, hunting wild flowers and watching marmots. *Address:* Green Cottage, Boars Hill, Oxford OX1 5DQ. *T:* (01865) 735367, *Fax:* (01865) 730687; Mathematical Institute, 24–29 St Giles, Oxford OX1 3LB; *e-mail:* birch@maths.ox.ac.uk.

BIRCH, Dennis Arthur, CBE 1977; DL; Councillor, West Midlands County Council, 1974–77; *b* 11 Feb. 1925; *s* of George Howard and Leah Birch; *m* 1948, Mary Therese Lyons; one *d*. *Educ:* Wolverhampton Municipal Grammar Sch. Wolverhampton County Borough Council: elected, 1952; served, 1952–74; Alderman, 1970–73; Mayor, 1973–74; Leader, 1967–73. Elected (following Local Govt reorganisation) Chm. West Midlands CC, 1974–76. DL West Midlands, 1979. *Address:* 3 Tern Close, Wolverhampton Road East, Wolverhampton WV4 6AU. *T:* (01902) 883837.

BIRCH, Frank Stanley Heath; public sector consultant; Commander, London District, St John Ambulance, 1992–2002 (Deputy Commander, 1990–92); *b* 8 Feb. 1939; *s* of late

John Stanley Birch, CEng and Phyllis Edna Birch (*née* Heath), BA; *m* 1963, Diana Jacqueline Dine Davies, BA; one *d. Educ:* Weston-super-Mare Grammar Sch. for Boys; Univ. of Wales (BA); Univ. of Birmingham (Inst. of Local Govt Studies). IPFA; MBIM. Entered local govt service, 1962; various appts, City Treasurer and Controller's Dept, Cardiff, 1962–69; Chief Internal Auditor, Dudley, 1969–73; Asst County Treasurer, 1973–74, Asst Chief Exec., 1974–76, W Midlands CC; Chief Exec., Lewisham, 1976–82; Town Clerk and Chief Exec., Croydon, 1982–90. Hon. Clerk, Gen. Purposes Cttee, 1982–90, Principal Grants Advr, 1983–86, London Boroughs Assoc.; Sec., London Co-ordinating Cttee, 1985–86. Dir, Croydon Business Venture Ltd, 1983–92. Chm., Lifecare NHS Trust, 1994–98. Freeman, City of London, 1980. FRSA 1980. KStJ 1997 (OStJ 1988; CStJ 1992); Mem. Council, Order of St John, London, 1986–2006; Vice-Pres., London SJAB, 1988–90. *Publications:* various articles on public admin and local govt management. *Recreations:* music, walking, the countryside, France and all things French. *Address:* The Old Liberal Club, 5 Lower Lane, Chinley, Derbys SK23 6BE.

BIRCH, Sir John (Allan), KCVO 1993; CMG 1987; HM Diplomatic Service, retired; Ambassador to Hungary, 1989–95; *b* 24 May 1935; *s* of late C. Allan Birch, MD, FRCP and Marjorie (*née* Bold); *m* 1960, Primula Haselden; three *s* one *d. Educ:* Leighton Park Sch.; Corpus Christi Coll., Cambridge (MA). Served HM Forces, Middlesex Regt, 1954–56. Joined HM Foreign Service, 1959; served: Paris, 1960–63; Singapore, 1963–64; Bucharest, 1965–68; Geneva, 1968–70; Kabul, 1973–76; Royal Coll. of Defence Studies, 1977; Comprehensive Test Ban Treaty Negotiations, Geneva, 1977–80; Counsellor, Budapest, 1980–83; Hd of East European Dept, FCO, 1983–86; Ambassador and Dep. Perm. Rep. to UN, NY, 1986–89. Dir and Chief Exec., British Assoc. for Central and Eastern Europe, 1995–2004. Dir, Schroder Emerging Countries Fund plc, 1996–2004. Chm., Adv. Bd, SSEES, 2006– (Mem. Council, 1995–99); Member Council: RIIA, 1997–2003; UCL, 1999–2008 (Vice-Chm., 2005–08). Trustee, Wytham Hall, 1999–. Comdr, Order of Merit (Hungary), 2004. *Recreations:* tennis, ski-ing, shooting, carpentry. *Address:* 185 Emery Hill Street, SW1P 1PD. *Club:* Athenæum.

BIRCH, John Anthony, MA, DMus; FRCM, FRCO(CHM), LRAM; Curator-Organist, Royal Albert Hall, since 1984; Professor, Royal College of Music, 1959–97, now Consultant; Organist: to the Royal Choral Society, since 1966; of the Royal Philharmonic Orchestra, since 1983; *b* 9 July 1929; *s* of late Charles Aylmer Birch and Mabel (*née* Greenwood), Leek, Staffs; unmarried. *Educ:* Trent Coll.; Royal Coll. of Music (ARCM; Pitcher Schol. of RCO). Nat. Service, Royal Corps of Signals, 1949–50. Organist and Choirmaster, St Thomas's Church, Regent Street, London, 1950–53; Accompanist to St Michael's Singers, 1952–58; Organist and Choirmaster, All Saints Church, Margaret Street, London, 1953–58; Sub-Organist, HM Chapels Royal, 1957–58; Organist and Master of the Choristers, Chichester Cathedral, 1958–80; Organist and Dir of Choir, Temple Church, 1982–97. With the Cathedral Organists of Salisbury and Winchester re-established the Southern Cathedrals Festival, 1960; Musical Advr, Chichester Festival Theatre, 1962–80; Choirmaster, Bishop Otter Coll., Chichester, 1963–69. Rep., 1950–66, and Man. Dir, 1966–73, C. A. Birch Ltd, Staffs. Accompanist, Royal Choral Soc., 1965–70; Examr to Associated Bd, Royal Schs of Music, 1958–77; a Gen. Ed., Novello & Co., 1967–77. Univ. Organist, 1967–94 and Vis. Lectr in Music, 1971–83, Univ. of Sussex. Special Comr, Royal Sch. of Church Music; Royal College of Organists: Mem. Council, 1964–2003, 2005–; Pres., 1984–86; Vice-Pres., 1986–; Hon. Treas., 1997–2002. Pres., Burgon Soc., 2001– (Fellow, 2001). Fellow, Corp. of SS Mary and Nicolas (Woodard Schs), 1973–99; Governor: Hurstpierpoint Coll., 1974–93; St Catherine's, Bramley, 1981–89; Mem. Council, Corp. of Cranleigh and Bramley Schs, 1981–90. Trustee, Ouseley Trust, 1989–. Waywarden, Liberty of the Close, Salisbury Cathedral, 1997–2004. Has made concert appearances in France, Belgium, Italy, Austria, Germany, Poland, Roumania, Switzerland, Netherlands, Spain, Portugal, Scandinavia, Japan, USA, Mexico and Far East; recital tours: Canada and US, 1966 and 1967, Australia and NZ, 1969, S Africa, 1978. Underwriting Mem., Lloyds, 1976–2002. Hon. Bencher, Middle Temple, 1998. Freeman: City of London, 1991; Co. of Glaziers and Painters of Glass, 2006. DMus Lambeth, 1989; Hon. MA Sussex, 1971. *Address:* 2 The Chantry, Canon Lane, Chichester, W Sussex PO19 1PZ. *T:* (01243) 537333, *Fax:* (01243) 537377; *e-mail:* DrJohnBirch@aol.com. *Clubs:* Garrick; New (Edinburgh).

BIRCH, Peter Gibbs, CBE 1992; Chairman, Land Securities PLC, 1998–2007; Chairman, Legal Services Commission, 2000–03; *b* 4 Dec. 1937; *m* 1962, Gillian (*née* Benge); three *s* one *d. Educ:* Allhallows Sch., Devon. Royal West Kent Regt, seconded to Jamaica Regt, 1957–58 (2nd Lieut). Nestlé Co., UK, Singapore and Malaysia, 1958–65; Sales and Mkting Manager, Gillette, 1965; Gen. Sales Manager, Gillette Australia, 1969; Man. Dir, Gillette, NZ, 1971; Gen. Manager, Gillette, SE Asia (based Singapore), 1973; Gp Gen. Manager, Gillette, Africa, ME, Eastern Europe, 1975; Man. Dir, Gillette UK, 1981; Dir and Chief Exec., Abbey Nat. Building Soc., then Abbey Nat. plc, 1984–98. Chairman: Trinity plc, 1998–99; UCTX, 2000–01; Kensington Gp, 2000–07; Trigold plc, 2007–; Sen. non-exec. Dir, Trinity Mirror plc, 1999–2007; non-executive Director: Hoskyns Gp, 1988–93; Argos, 1990–98; Scottish Mutual Assurance, 1992–98; N. M. Rothschild & Sons, 1998–2004 (Advr, 2004–); Dalgety, 1993–98; PIC, 1998–2000; Coca-Cola Beverages, 1998–2000; Travelex plc, 1999–; Sainsbury's Bank plc, 2002–06; Lamprell Energy Ltd, 2006– (Chm., 2007–); Banco Finantia, 2007–; Advr, Cambridge Place Investment Mgt LLP, 2004–. Chm., Council of Mortgage Lenders, 1991–92. FCBSI. Pres., Middlesex Young People's (formerly Middlesex Assoc. of Boys') Clubs, 1988–. *Recreations:* active holidays, swimming. *Address:* N. M. Rothschild & Sons, New Court, St Swithin's Lane, EC4P 4DU. *T:* (020) 7280 5000.

BIRCH, Robin Arthur, CB 1995; DL; voluntary worker; civil servant, retired; *b* 12 Oct. 1939; *s* of late Arthur and Olive Birch; *m* 1962, Jane Marion Irvine Sturdy; two *s. Educ:* King Henry VIII Sch., Coventry; Christ Church, Oxford (MA). Entered Min. of Health as Asst Principal, 1961; Private Sec. to Charles Loughlin, MP (Parly Sec.), 1965–66; Principal, 1966; seconded to: Interdeptl Social Work Gp, 1969–70; Home Office (Community Develt Project), 1970–72; Asst Sec., DHSS, 1973; Chm., Working Party on Manpower and Trng for Social Services, 1974–76 (HMSO Report, 1976); Principal Private Sec. to Leader of the House of Commons, 1980–81; Under Sec., DHSS, 1982; Asst Auditor Gen., Nat. Audit Office, 1984–86, on secondment; Dir, Regl Orgn, 1988–90; Dep. Sec. (Policy), 1990–95, DSS. Hon. Sec., Friends of Christ Church Cathedral, Oxford, 1978–2006. Vice-Pres., Age Concern England, 1998– (Chm., 1995–98). Chairman: Response Organisation (formerly Oxfordshire Gp Homes), 1995–; Low Vision Services Implementation Gp for England, 1999–2005 (Chm. Working Gp, 1998–99; Report, 1999); City of Oxford Charity, 2004–; Oxford Credit Union, 2005–. Trustee: Oxford CAB, 1996–2004 (Chm., 1997–2002); Oxfordshire Community Foundn, 1996–2002; Age Concern Oxfordshire, 1998–2005; Wyndham Housing Assoc., 2001–; Roman Research Trust, 2002–; Lady Nuffield Home (Oxford), 1996–. DL Oxfordshire, 1996. *Recreations:* family and friends, travel, music, byways of classical antiquity, garden railway. *Address:* The Cathedral, Christ Church, Oxford OX1 1DP. *Clubs:* Oxford Rotary (Pres., 2008–09), Royal Green Jackets (Hon.) (Oxford); Warwickshire CC.

BIRCH, Sir Roger, Kt 1992; CBE 1987; QPM 1980; Chief Constable, Sussex Police, 1983–93; *b* 27 Sept. 1930; *s* of John Edward Lawrence Birch and Ruby Birch; *m* 1954, Jeanne Margaret Head (*d* 2006); one *s. Educ:* King's Coll., Taunton. Cadet, Royal Naval Coll., Dartmouth, 1949–50; Pilot Officer, RAF, 1950–52. Devon Constabulary, 1954–72: Constable, uniform and CID; then through ranks to Chief Supt; Asst Chief Constable, Mid-Anglia Constab., 1972–74; Dep. Chief Constable, Kent Constab., 1974–78; Chief Constable, Warwickshire Constab., 1978–83. Dir, Police Extended Interviews, 1983–91; Pres., Assoc. of Chief Police Officers, 1987–88 (Vice-Pres., 1986–87; Chm., Traffic Cttee, 1983–86; Chm., Internat. Affairs Adv. Cttee, 1988–92); Vice Chm., Internat. Cttee, Internat. Assoc. of Chiefs of Police, 1989–93; Trustee: Police Dependants' Trust, 1981–93; Police Gurney Fund, 1983–91. Mem., St John Ambulance Council, Sussex, 1986–93. UK Vice-Pres., Royal Life Saving Soc., 1985–93 (Chm., SE Region, 1983–93). Mem. Council, IAM, 1984–93. Hon. Fellow, Centre for Legal Studies, 1993. Hon. LLD Sussex, 1991. *Publications:* articles on criminal intelligence, breath measuring instruments and on the urban environment, in learned jls. *Recreations:* walking, music. *Club:* Royal Air Force.

BIRCH, Prof. William; *b* 24 Nov. 1925; *s* of Frederick Arthur and Maude Olive Birch; *m* 1950, Mary Vine Stammers; one *s* one *d. Educ:* Ranelagh Sch.; Univ. of Reading. BA 1949, PhD 1957. Royal Navy, 1943–46, Sub-Lt RNVR. Lectr, Univ. of Bristol, 1950–60; Prof. of Geography, Grad. Sch. of Geog., Clark Univ., Worcester, Mass, USA, 1960–63; Prof., and Chm. of Dept of Geog., Univ. of Toronto, Canada, 1963–67; Prof., and Head of Dept of Geog., Univ. of Leeds, 1967–75; Dir, Bristol Polytechnic, 1975–86. Visiting Professor: Inst. of Educn, London Univ., 1986–88; Univ. of Bristol, 1990–94. Pres., Inst. of British Geographers, 1976–77; Chm., Cttee of Directors of Polytechnics, 1982–84. Mem., ESRC, 1985–88. Hon. DLitt CNAA, 1989. *Publications:* The Isle of Man: a study in economic geography, 1964; The Challenge to Higher Education: reconciling responsibilities to scholarship and society, 1988; contribs on higher educn policy and on geography and planning, Trans Inst. Brit. Geographers, Geog. Jl, Economic Geog., Annals Assoc. Amer. Geographers, Jl Environmental Management, Studies in Higher Educn, etc. *Recreations:* yachting, travel, gardening, pottery. *Address:* 3 Rodney Place, Clifton, Bristol BS8 4HY. *T:* (0117) 973 9719.

BIRCH, Rt Hon. Sir William (Francis), GNZM 1999; PC 1992; consultant in public policy and affairs; company director; Minister of Finance, 1993–99, Treasurer, 1998–99, New Zealand; *b* 9 April 1934; *s* of Charles William Birch and Elizabeth Alicia (*née* Wells); *m* 1953, Rosa Mitchell; three *s* one *d.* Surveyor. Borough Councillor 1965–74, Dep. Mayor 1968–74, Pukekohe. MP (Nat.) Pukekohe, NZ, 1972–99; Jun. Opposition Whip, 1973–75; Sen. Govt Whip, 1975–78; Minister of: Energy, Science and Technol. and Nat. Develt, 1978–81; Energy, Regl Develt and Nat. Develt, 1981–84; Labour, Immigration and State Services, 1990–93; Employment, 1991–93; Health, 1993; Minister for Pacific Island Affairs, 1990–91. Chm., Internat. Energy Agency, 1983. *Recreation:* fishing. *Address:* 420 Bremner Road, RD2, Drury, New Zealand. *Clubs:* Rotary; Jaycee International.

BIRCHENOUGH, (John) Michael, BSc, PhD; Visiting Professor, School of Education, Open University, 1986–89; *b* 17 Jan. 1923; *s* of John Buckley Birchenough and Elsie Birchenough; *m* 1945, Enid Humphries; two *s. Educ:* Ashford Grammar Sch., Kent; Chiswick County Sch.; London Univ. Chemist, May & Baker Ltd, 1943–45; teaching posts, 1946–60; HM Inspector of Schools, 1960; Staff Inspector, 1966; Chief Inspector, 1968–72; Chief Inspector, ILEA, 1973–83; Res. Fellow, Sch. of Educn, Univ. of Bristol, 1983–86. Pres., Educn Section, BAAS Annual Meeting, Stirling, 1974. *Publications:* contribs to Jl of Chem. Soc. and other scientific jls. *Address:* 46B Sandfield Road, Arnold, Nottingham NG5 6QB.

BIRD, Prof. Adrian Peter, CBE 2005; PhD; FRS 1989; Buchanan Professor of Genetics, Edinburgh University, since 1990; Director, Wellcome Trust Centre for Cell Biology, since 1999; *b* 3 July 1947; *s* of Kenneth George Bird and Aileen Mary Bird; *m* 1st, 1976; one *s* one *d*; 2nd, 1993, Dr Catherine Mary Abbott; one *s* one *d. Educ:* Queen Elizabeth's Grammar School, Hartlebury; Univ. of Sussex (BSc(Hons)); Univ. of Edinburgh (PhD 1971). Damon Runyan Fellow, Yale, 1972–73; postdoctoral fellowship, Univ. of Zurich, 1974–75; Medical Research Council, Edinburgh: scientific staff, Mammalian Genome Unit, 1975–87; Hd of Structural Studies Sect., Clin. and Population Cytogenetics Unit, 1987; Sen. Scientist, Inst. for Molecular Pathol., Vienna, 1988–90. Mem. Bd of Govs, Wellcome Trust, 2000–. Louis Jeantet Prize for Med. Res., 1999; Gabor Medal, Royal Soc., 1999. *Publications:* articles in Nature, Cell and other jls. *Recreations:* running, music, food. *Address:* Wellcome Trust Centre for Cell Biology, University of Edinburgh, King's Buildings, Mayfield Road, Edinburgh EH9 3JR. *T:* (0131) 650 5670.

BIRD, Anthony Patrick Michael, OBE 1991; Chairman, Bird Group of Companies Ltd, since 2002 (Director, since 1958); *b* 28 Dec. 1935; *s* of William Thomas Bird and May Frances Bird; *m* 1985, Janet Eleanor Burns; one *s* six *d. Educ:* Ratcliffe Coll., Leics. Served 4th RTR. Jt Man. Dir, Bird Gp of Cos, 1973–2002. Chm., Nuclear Services Gp Ltd, 1982–91. Member: Minerals, Metals, Materials and Chemicals Requirements Cttee, 1983–85, Industrial Materials and Vehicles Mkt Adv. Cttee, 1985–86, DTI; Lead Waste Cttee, DoE, 1984–85; Adv. Gp on Decommng of North Sea Oil Platforms, 1985–90 (Chm.); Adv. Cttee on Business and the Envmt, 1990–93; Bd, Envmtl Mgt Agency, Welsh Office, 1991–93. Mem. Bd, Warwickshire Police Authy, 1995–2003. Bureau International de la Récupération: Pres., Ferrous Div., 1976–95; Pres., 1995–99 (Pres. of Honour, 1999); Treas., 2000–. President: Midwest Metals Assoc., 1975–76; British Metals Fedn, 1979–80 (Life Pres., 1992); Fedn of Eur. Recycling Industry, 1981–89 and 2001–03 (Pres. of Honour, 2003). Gov., 2002–, Chm. Trustees, 2004–, King Edward VI GS, Stratford-upon-Avon. Prince of Wales Award for Prodn and Innovation, 1986. *Recreations:* field sports, Rugby football, agriculture, architecture, fine arts. *Address:* c/o Bird Group of Companies Ltd, The Hunting Lodge, Billesley Road, Stratford-upon-Avon, Warwicks CV37 9RA. *Club:* Carlton.

BIRD, Rev. Dr Anthony Peter; General Medical Practitioner, since 1979; Principal of The Queen's College, Edgbaston, Birmingham, 1974–79; *b* 2 March 1931; *s* of late Albert Harry Bird and Noel Whitehouse Bird; *m* 1962, Sabine Boehmig; two *s* one *d. Educ:* St John's Coll., Oxford (BA LitHum, BA Theol, MA); Birmingham Univ. (MB, ChB, 1970; DipMus 2001). Deacon, 1957; Priest, 1958; Curate of St Mary's, Stafford, 1957–60; Chaplain, then Vice-Principal of Cuddesdon Theological Coll., 1960–64. General Medical Practitioner, 1972–73. Member: Home Office Policy Adv. Cttee on Sexual Offences, 1976–80; Parole Board, 1977–80. Freedom of Information Campaign Award, 1986. *Publication:* The Search for Health: a response from the inner city, 1981. *Recreations:* sailing, walking, music—J. S. Bach, innovation in primary health care, Wolverhampton Wanderers FC.

BIRD, Prof. Colin Carmichael, CBE 2000; PhD; FRCPath, FRCPE, FRCSE, FMedSci; FRSE; Dean, Faculty of Medicine and Provost, Faculty Group of Medicine and Veterinary Medicine, University of Edinburgh, 1995–2002; *b* 5 March 1938; *s* of John and Sarah Bird; *m* 1964, Ailsa M. Ross; two *s* one *d. Educ:* Lenzie Acad.; Glasgow Univ. (MB ChB 1961; PhD 1967). FRCPath 1978 (MRCPath 1968); FRCPE 1989; FRCSE 1995;

FRSE 1992. Research Fellow and Lectr in Pathology, Univ. of Glasgow, 1962–67; Lectr in Pathology, Univ. of Aberdeen, 1967–72; Sen. Lectr in Pathology, Univ. of Edinburgh, 1972–75; Professor of Pathology: Univ. of Leeds, 1975–86; Univ. of Edinburgh, 1986–95. Founder FMedSci 1998. Dr *hc* Edinburgh, 2004. *Publications:* contribs to various scientific jls on cancer and cancer genetics. *Recreations:* golf, walking, music, reading. *Address:* 45 Ann Street, Edinburgh EH4 1PL. *T:* (0131) 332 5568. *Club:* New (Edinburgh).

BIRD, Ven. (Colin) Richard (Bateman); Minister Provincial, Third Order of the Society of St Francis (European Province), since 2002; *b* 31 March 1933; *s* of Paul James Bird and Marjorie Bird (*née* Bateman); *m* 1963, Valerie Wroughton van der Bijl; two *d* one *s*. *Educ:* privately; County Technical Coll., Guildford; Selwyn Coll., Cambridge (MA); Cuddesdon Theol Coll. Curate: St Mark's Cathedral, George, S Africa, 1958–61; St Saviour's Claremont, Cape Town, 1961–64; Rector, Parish of Northern Suburbs, Pretoria, 1964–66; Rector, Tzaneen with Duiwelskloof and Phalaborwa, N Transvaal, 1966–70; Curate, Limpsfield, Surrey, 1970–75; Vicar of St Catherine, Hatcham, 1975–88; RD, Deptford, 1980–85; Hon. Canon of Southwark, 1982–88; Archdeacon of Lambeth, 1988–99; Priest-in-Charge, St Saviour's, Brixton Hill, 1989–94. *Recreations:* theatre and concert going, walking, bird-watching, cooking. *Address:* 32 Bristol Road, Bury St Edmunds, Suffolk IP33 2DL. *T:* (01284) 723810; *e-mail:* dickbird@btopenworld.com.

BIRD, Dickie; *see* Bird, H. D.

BIRD, Drayton Charles Colston; Founder, 1991, Chairman, since 1992, Drayton Bird Associates (formerly Partnership); *b* 22 Aug. 1936; *s* of George Freeman Bird and Marjorie Louise Bird; *m* 1st, 1957, Pamela Bland (marr. diss.); two *s* one *d*; 2nd, 1971, Anna Te Paora (marr. diss.); 3rd, 1982, Cece Topley. *Educ:* Trent Coll.; Manchester Univ. Asst. Sec., Manchester Cotton Assoc., 1955–57; with sundry advertising agencies, 1957–68; Founder, Small Business Inst., 1968; publisher, Business Ideas newsletter, 1968–70; Co-Founder, then Man. Dir, Trenear-Harvey, Bird & Watson, 1977–85; Vice Chm., Ogilvy & Mather Direct Worldwide, 1985–91. Inaugural Fellow, Inst. Direct Mktng, 1996. *Publications:* Some Rats Run Faster, 1964; Commonsense Direct Marketing: the printed shop, 1982, 5th edn 2007; How To Write Sales Letters That Sell, 1994, 2nd edn 2002; Marketing Insights and Outrages, 1999. *Recreations:* music, reading, wine, writing. *Address:* Drayton Bird Associates, 32 Newman Street, W1T 1PU. *T:* (020) 7323 6881.

BIRD, Harold Dennis, (Dickie), MBE 1986; umpire of first-class cricket, 1970–98, and of Test cricket, 1970–96; foundation Member, Independent International Panel of Umpires, 1993; Founder and Trustee, Dickie Bird Foundation, since 2004; *b* 19 April 1933; *s* of James Harold Bird and Ethel Bird; unmarried. *Educ:* Burton Road Primary Sch.; Raley Sch., Barnsley. Played county cricket for Yorkshire, 1956–60 (highest first-class score, 181 not out *v* Glamorgan, 1959), and Leicestershire, 1960–66; qualified MCC Advanced Cricket Coach, 1966; umpired 159 international matches (world record in 1996): 67 Tests (world record in 1994), incl. Queen's Silver Jubilee Test, Lord's, 1977, Centenary Test, Lord's, 1980, Bi-Centenary Test, Lord's, 1987, 3 in Zimbabwe, and WI *v* Pakistan series, 1993, in NZ, Pakistan and India, 1994, and Australia *v* Pakistan series, 1995; 92 one-day internationals, 1973–96 (world record in 1994); 4 World Cup tournaments, 1975–87, and Final at Lord's, 1975, 1979, 1983; Women's World Cup, and Final, NZ, 1982; finals of Gillette, NatWest, and Benson & Hedges competitions, Lord's, 1974–98; Rest of the World XI *v* World XI, Wembley Stadium, 1983; Centenary of Test Cricket, England *v* WI, Old Trafford, 1984; Rothmans Cup, 1983, 1985, Asia Cup, 1984, 1985, Champion's Cup, 1986, and Sharjah Tournament, 1993, UAE. Has travelled worldwide. Guest appearances on TV and radio progs include Down Your Way, Question of Sport, This is Your Life, Breakfast with Frost and Desert Island Discs; subject of BBC2 documentary, 1996. Freeman of Barnsley, 2000. DUniv Sheffield Hallam, 1996; Hon. LLD Leeds, 1997. Yorkshire Personality of the Year, 1977; Yorkshire Man of the Year, 1996; People of the Year Award, RADAR/Abbey Nat., 1996; Special Sporting Award, Variety Club of GB, 1997; Cricket Writer's Award, 1997; English Sports Council (Yorks Reg.) Award, 1998; Special Merit Award, Professional Cricketers' Assoc., 1998; Barnsley Millennium of Merit Award, 2000; Yorkshire Hall of Fame, BBC Yorkshire Sports Awards, 2006. *Publications:* Not Out, 1978; That's Out, 1985; From the Pavilion End, 1988; Dickie Bird, My Autobiography, 1997; White Cap and Bails, 1999; Dickie Bird's Britain, 2002. *Recreations:* watching football, listening to Barbra Streisand, Nat King Cole, Diana Ross and Shirley Bassey records. *Address:* White Rose Cottage, 40 Paddock Road, Staincross, Barnsley, Yorks S75 6LE. *T:* (01226) 384491. *Clubs:* MCC (Hon. Life Mem., 1996), Lord's Taverners; Yorkshire CC (Hon. Life Mem., 1994); Leicestershire CC (Hon. Life Mem., 1996); Cambridge University Cricket (Hon. Life Mem., 1996); Barnsley Football (Hon. Life Mem., 2003).

BIRD, John Anthony, MBE 1995; Founder, and Editor-in-Chief: The Big Issue, since 1991; ITTIA, since 2004; Wedge Card, since 2007; *b* 30 Jan. 1946; *s* of Alfred Ernest Bird and Eileen Mary (*née* Dunne); *m* 1st, 1965, Linda Stuart Haston (marr. diss.); one *d*; 2nd, 1973, Isobel Theresa (marr. diss.), *d* of Sir Robert Ricketts, 7th Bt; one *s* one *d*; 3rd, 2004, Parveen Sodhi; one *s* one *d*. *Educ:* St Thomas Moores Secondary Mod. Sch.; Ealing Coll. (BA Hons Hum.). Gardening asst, Royal Borough of Kensington and Chelsea, 1963–64; printer, Acrow Engrg, 1964–73; bean canner, H. J. Heinz, 1973–74; printer: Pictorial Charts Educnl Trust, 1974–75; Broadoak Press, 1978–83; print and publishing consultant, 1983–91. Contested Mayor of London, 2008. Hon. Fellow, Liverpool John Moores Univ., 2000. Hon. Dr Oxford Brookes, 2001. *Publications:* Some Luck (autobiog.), 2003; How to Change Your Life in 7 Steps, 2006. *Recreations:* swimming, cycling, running, drawing, talking. *Address:* c/o The Big Issue, 1–5 Wandsworth Road, SW8 2LN.

BIRD, John Michael; actor and writer; *b* 22 Nov. 1936; *s* of Horace George Bird and Dorothy May Bird (*née* Haubitz); *m* Libby Crandon, musician. *Educ:* High Pavement Grammar Sch., Nottingham; King's Coll., Cambridge (BA 1958). Asst Artistic Dir, 1959–61, Associate Artistic Dir, 1961–63, Royal Court Theatre; writer and performer, The Establishment, 1961–64; Joint Founder: New York Establishment, 1963; New Theatre, NY, 1963. *Stage* includes: Luv, tour, 1971; Who's Who?, Arnaud, Guildford, 1972; Habeas Corpus, Lyric, 1973; The Ball Game, Open Space, 1978; Bremner, Bird and Fortune, Albery, 2002; *films:* Take a Girl Like You; The Seven Per Cent Solution; Yellow Pages; A Dandy in Aspic; *television* includes: Not so much a Programme, 1965–66; The Late Show, 1966; BBC3; A Series of Birds; With Bird Will Travel; John Bird/John Wells; Blue Remembered Hills; A Very Peculiar Practice; Travelling Man; El C.I.D., 1990, 1991, 1992; Rory Bremner—Who Else?, 1992–99 ((jtly) BAFTA Award for best light entertainment performance, 1997); The Long Johns, 1996–99; In the Red, 1998; Bremner, Bird and Fortune, 1999–; Chambers, 2000, 2001; Absolute Power, 2003, 2005. Hon. DLitt Nottingham, 2002. *Publications:* (with John Fortune) The Long Johns, 1996; (with Rory Bremner and John Fortune) You Are Here, 2004. *Address:* c/o Chatto & Linnit Ltd, 123A King's Road, SW3 4PL. *T:* (020) 7352 7722.

BIRD, Judith Pamela; *see* Kelly, J. P.

BIRD, Michael George, OBE 2000; Director, Germany, British Council, since 2005; *b* 5 Jan. 1960; *s* of George Bird and Margaret Bird; *m* 2003, Simone Lees. *Educ:* Bedales Sch.; Emmanuel Coll., Cambridge (BA 1982); Voronezh Univ. (Dip. Russian Studies). Kennedy Schol., Harvard Univ., 1982–83. Teacher, Vienna, 1983–85; British Council: London, 1985–87; Asst Dir, Moscow, 1987–91; Europ. Liaison Officer, Brussels, 1991–93; Director: St Petersburg, 1993–97; Ukraine, 1997–2001; Scotland, 2001–05. *Recreations:* music, travel, mountaineering. *Address:* British Council, Alexanderplatz 1, 10178 Berlin, Germany. *T:* (30) 31109924, *Fax:* (30) 31109932; *e-mail:* Michael.Bird@britishcouncil.de.

BIRD, Michael James; Regional Employment Judge (formerly Chairman of Industrial, later Employment Tribunals) for Wales, since 1992; *b* 11 Nov. 1935; *s* of Walter Garfield and Ireen Bird; *m* 1963, Susan Harris; three *d*. *Educ:* Lewis Sch., Pengam; King's Coll., Univ. of London (LLB Hons). Solicitor (Hons) 1961. Assistant solicitor, 1961–62; Partner, T. S. Edwards & Son, 1962–67, Sen. Partner, 1967–84. Deputy Registrar of County and High Court, 1976–77; Chairman of Industrial Tribunal, Cardiff (part-time), 1977–83; Chm. of Industrial Tribunal, Bristol, 1984–87, Cardiff, 1987–92. Chm., Gwent Italian Soc., 1978–86 (Sec., 1976–78); Member: Royal Life Saving Soc., 1976– (President's Commendation, 1984); Amateur Swimming Assoc. (Advanced Teacher, 1981–); Newport and Maindee ASC; Crawshays Welsh RFC. *Recreations:* water sports, opera. *Address:* 17 Allt-yr-yn Avenue, Newport, Gwent NP20 5DA. *T:* (01633) 252000.

BIRD, Peter Frederick, RIBA; FSA; Caroe & Partners Architects, since 1979 (Partner, since 1983); *b* 20 March 1947; *s* of W. J. and S. M. Bird; *m* 1971, Charlotte Maclagan; two *s*. *Educ:* Birmingham Sch. of Architecture; King Edward's Five Ways Sch., Birmingham; Univ. of Aston, Birmingham (BSc Hons; DipArch; SPAB Lethaby Schol. 1970). RIBA 1972; AABC 2000. Asst Architect, then Associate, Twist & Whitley, Cambridge, 1970–76; Conservation Architect, Bath CC, 1976–79. Cathedral Architect to St Davids, 1984–, Winchester, 1989–, Exeter, 1989– and Wells, 1994–. FSA 1994. *Publication:* (contrib.) Historic Floors: their care and conservation, ed J. Fawcett, 1998. *Recreations:* archaeology, history, engineering history, railways, canals. *Address:* Caroe & Partners, Penniless Porch, Market Place, Wells BA5 2RB. *T:* (01749) 677561; *e-mail:* wells@caroe.co.uk.

BIRD, Ven. Richard; *see* Bird, Ven. C. R. B.

BIRD, Richard; Executive Director, UK Major Ports Group, since 2007; *b* 12 Feb. 1950; *s* of late Desmond and Betty Bird; *m* 1973, Penelope Anne Frudd; one *s* one *d*. *Educ:* King's Sch., Canterbury; Magdalen Coll., Oxford. Admin Trainee, DoE, 1971–73; Asst Private Sec. to Minister for Planning and Local Govt, 1974–75; Principal, Dept of Transport, 1975–78; First Sec., UK Rep. to EC, Brussels, 1978–82; Principal Private Sec. to Sec. of State for Transport, 1982–83; Asst Sec., 1983, Under Sec., 1990, Dept of Transport; Cabinet Office, 1992–94; Dir of Personnel, Dept of Transport, 1994–97; Dir, Urban, then Integrated, and Local Transport, DETR, 1997–2001; Dir of Energy, Envmt and Waste, 2001–03, of Water, 2003–07, DEFRA. Mem., Oxford Univ. Fencing Club, 1969–71 (represented Britain at World Youth Fencing Championship, 1970). *Recreations:* choral singing, summer sports. *Address:* UK Major Ports Group, 2nd Floor, Africa House, 64–78 Kingsway, WC2B 6AH. *T:* (020) 7430 7460.

BIRD, Sir Richard (Geoffrey Chapman), 4th Bt *cr* 1922; *b* 3 Nov. 1935; *er* surv. *s* of Sir Donald Bird, 3rd Bt, and of Anne Rowena (*d* 1969), *d* of late Charles Chapman; *S* father, 1963; *m* 1st, 1957, Gillian Frances (*d* 1966), *d* of Bernard Haggett, Solihull; two *s* four *d*; 2nd, 1968, Helen Patricia, *d* of Frank Beaumont, Pontefract; two *d*. *Educ:* Beaumont. *Heir: s* John Andrew Bird, *b* 19 Jan. 1964. *Address:* 20 Milcote Road, Solihull, W Midlands B91 1JN.

BIRD, Richard Herries, CB 1983; Deputy Secretary, Department of Education and Science, 1980–90; *b* 8 June 1932; *s* of late Edgar Bird and Armorel (*née* Dudley-Scott); *m* 1963, Valerie, *d* of Edward and Mary Sanderson; two *d*. *Educ:* Winchester Coll.; Clare Coll., Cambridge. Min. of Transport and Civil Aviation, 1955; Principal Private Sec. to Minister of Transport, 1966–67; CSD 1969; DoE 1971; DES 1973. *Address:* 15 Pinehurst, Sevenoaks, Kent TN14 5AQ.

BIRD, Prof. Richard Simpson, PhD; Professor of Computation, University of Oxford, 1996–2008; Fellow, Lincoln College, Oxford, since 1988; *b* 13 Feb. 1943; *s* of John William Bird and Martha (*née* Solar); *m* 1967, Norma Christine Lapworth. *Educ:* St Olave's Grammar Sch.; Gonville and Caius Coll., Cambridge (MA); Inst. of Computer Sci., Univ. of London (MSc; PhD 1973). Lecturer: in Computer Sci., Reading Univ., 1972–83; Oxford Univ., 1983–88; Dir, Computing Lab., Oxford Univ., 1998–2003. *Publications:* Programs and Machines, 1977; Introduction to Functional Programming, 1988, 2nd edn 1998; Algebra of Programming, 1996. *Recreations:* jogging, bridge. *Address:* Stocks, Chapel Lane, Blewbury, Oxon OX11 9PQ. *T:* (01235) 850258; Lincoln College, Oxford OX1 3DR.

BIRD, Roger Charles; District Judge, Bristol County Court and District Registry of High Court, 1987–2005; *b* 28 April 1939; *s* of late Bertram Charles Bird and Olive Mary Bird; *m* 1964, Marie-Christine Snow; two *s*. *Educ:* Millfield Sch.; Univ. of Bristol (LLB Hons). Admitted solicitor, 1965; asst solicitor with various firms, 1965–69; Partner, Wilmot Thompson and Bird, Bristol, 1969–79; Registrar, Yeovil County Court, 1979–86. Member: Matrimonial Causes Rule Cttee, 1986–90; President's Adoption Cttee, Family Div., 1990–2002; Children Act Adv. Cttee, 1993–97; Lord Chancellor's Adv. Gp on Ancillary Relief, 1993–2004; Judicial Adv. Gp, Children and Family Court Adv. Support Service, 2000–01. Chm., Child Protection Commn, dio. of Clifton, 2002–. Pres., Assoc. of Dist Judges, 1995–96. *Publications:* (with C. F. Turner) Bird and Turner's Forms and Precedents, 1985, 3rd edn 1992; (editor-in-chief) Sweet and Maxwell's Family Law Manual, 1985–96; Child Maintenance: the new law, 1992, 6th edn 2008; Domestic Violence, 1996, 5th edn 2005; (with S. M. Cretney) Divorce: the new law, 1996; Ancillary Relief Handbook, 1998, 6th edn 2007; Pension Sharing: the new law, 2000; (editor-in-chief) Emergency Remedies in the Family Courts, 2000; (editor-in-chief) Jordan's Precedents Service, 2002; numerous articles in legal jls. *Recreations:* wine, listening to music, gardens and gardening, rural walks. *Address:* West Villa Lodge, South Horrington, Wells, Somerset BA5 3DQ.

BIRDS, Prof. John Richard; Professor of Commercial Law, University of Manchester, since 2006; *b* 20 June 1948; *s* of John Sidney Birds and Katharine Charlotte Birds; *m* 1973, Margaret Rhona Richardson (marr. diss. 2008); two *s* one *d*. *Educ:* Chesterfield Grammar Sch.; University College London (LLB, LLM). Lectr in Law: Newcastle Polytechnic, 1970; QMC, Univ. of London, 1972; University of Sheffield: Lectr in Law, 1978–82; Sen. Lectr, 1982–85; Reader, 1985–89; Hd, Dept of Law, 1987–99 and 2002–05; Prof. of Commercial Law, 1989–2006. FRSA. Pres., Soc. of Legal Scholars, 2003–04. *Publications:* Modern Insurance Law, 1982, 7th edn 2007; (with A. J. Boyle) Company Law, 1983, 7th edn 2007; (jtly) Secretarial Administration, 1984; (ed jtly) MacGillivray and Parkington on Insurance Law, 8th edn 1988, 9th edn (as MacGillivray on Insurance Law) 1997, 10th edn 2002; General Editor: Encyclopedia of Insurance Law, 2006; Annotated Companies Acts, 2007; articles in learned jls. *Recreations:* music, gardening, walking.

BIRDSALL, Derek Walter, RDI; freelance graphic designer; *b* 1 Aug. 1934; *s* of Frederick Birdsall and Hilda Birdsall (*née* Smith); *m* 1954, Shirley Thompson; three *s* one *d. Educ:* King's Sch., Pontefract, Yorks; Wakefield Coll. of Art, Yorks; Central Sch. of Arts and Crafts, London (NDD). National Service, RAOC Printing Unit, Cyprus, 1955–57. Lectr in Typographical Design, London Coll. of Printing, 1959–61; freelance graphic designer, working from his studio in Covent Garden, later Islington, 1961–; Founding Partner, Omnific Studios Partnership, 1983. Vis. Prof. of Graphic Art and Design, RCA, 1987–88. Consultant designer, The Independent Magazine, 1989–93; Tutor and designer of house-style for Prince of Wales's Inst. of Arch., 1991; Design Consultant, NACF, 1992–97; Consultant Designer to C of E, 1999–. Has broadcast on TV and radio on design subjects and his work; catalogue designs for major museums throughout the world have won many awards, incl. Gold Medal, New York Art Directors' Club, 1987. Mem., AGI, 1968–96; FCSD (FSIAD 1964); RDI 1982; FRSA; Hon. FRCA 1988; Hon. FISTD 2005. Prince Philip Designers Prize, 2005. *Publications:* (with C. H. O'D. Alexander) Fischer *v* Spassky, 1972; (with C. H. O'D. Alexander) A Book of Chess, 1974; (with Carlo M. Cippola) The Technology of Man—a visual history, 1978; (with Bruce Bernard) Lucian Freud, 1996; Notes on Book Design, 2004. *Recreations:* chess, poker. *Address:* 8 Compton Terrace, Islington, N1 2UN. *T:* (020) 7359 1201. *Club:* Chelsea Arts.

BIRDWOOD, family name of **Baron Birdwood**.

BIRDWOOD, 3rd Baron *cr* 1938, of Anzac and of Totnes; **Mark William Ogilvie Birdwood;** Bt 1919; Chairman, Martlet Ltd, since 1986; *b* 23 Nov. 1938; *s* of 2nd Baron Birdwood, MVO, and Vere Lady Birdwood, CVO (*d* 1997); *S* father, 1962; *m* 1963, Judith Helen, *e d* of late R. G. Seymour Roberts; one *d. Educ:* Radley Coll.; Trinity Coll., Cambridge. Commnd RHG. Director: Wrightson Wood Ltd, 1979–86; Du Pont Pixel Systems (formerly Benchmark Technology); Comac plc, 1988–92; Scientific Generics, 1989–97; Terra Firma, 1990–95; Fiortho plc, 1995–2001 (Chm.); The Character Gp (formerly Toy Options) plc, 1995–; IMS plc, 1997–2000; Steeltower Ltd, 2001–. Mem., Select Cttee on Science and Technol., H of L, 1998–99. Associate, LSE Centre for Philosophy of Nat. and Social Sci., 2001–. Trustee of charities. Liveryman, Glaziers' Co. *Address:* 5 Holbein Mews, SW1W 8NW; Russell House, Broadway, Worcs WR12 7BU. *Club:* Brooks's.

See also D. J. Montgomery, Earl of Woolton.

BIREEDO, Omer Yousif; Director, Political Department, Palace of the President of Sudan, Khartoum, since 1999; *b* 1 Jan. 1939; *s* of Yousif Bireedo and Fatima Hasan; *m* 1978, Kalthoum M. E. Barakat; one *s* two *d. Educ:* Univ. of Khartoum (BA); Delhi Univ. (MA). Sudanese Diplomatic Service: Third Sec., New Delhi, 1963–66; London, 1966–69; Dep. Dir, Consular Dept, Min. of Foreign Affairs, Khartoum, 1969–71; Uganda, 1971–73; Mission to UN, NY, 1973–76; Dir, Dept of Internat. Orgns, Min. of Foreign Affairs, Khartoum, 1976–78 and 1986–89; Ambassador and Perm. Rep. to UN and Internat. Orgns, Geneva and Vienna, 1978–83, NY, 1983–86; Ambassador to Saudi Arabia, 1989–92; 1st Undersec., Min. of Foreign Affairs, Khartoum, 1992–95; Ambassador to UK, 1995–99. Mem., UN Admin. Tribunal, 2001–04. Republican Order (Sudan), 1972. *Recreations:* walking, reading. *Address:* c/o Ministry of Foreign Affairs, Khartoum, Sudan.

BIRGENEAU, Dr Robert Joseph, FRS 2001; FRSC 2002; Chancellor, University of California, Berkeley, since 2004; *b* Toronto, 25 March 1942; *m* 1964, Mary Catherine Ware; one *s* three *d. Educ:* Univ. of Toronto (BSc 1963); Yale Univ. (PhD 1966). Grad. Student, 1963–66, Instructor, 1966–67, Dept of Engrg and Applied Sci., Yale Univ.; Nat. Res. Council of Canada Postdoctoral Fellow, Oxford Univ., 1967–68; Bell Laboratories, Murray Hill, NJ: Mem., Tech. Staff, Physical Res. Lab., 1968–74; Res. Hd, Scattering and Low Energy Physics Dept, 1975; Consultant, 1977–80; Massachusetts Institute of Technology: Prof. of Physics, 1975–2000; Cecil and Ida Green Prof. of Physics, 1982–2000; Associate Dir, Res. Lab. of Electronics, 1983–86; Head: Solid State, Atomic and Plasma Physics, 1987–88; Dept of Physics, 1988–91; Dean, Sch. of Sci., 1991–2000; Pres. and Prof. of Physics, Univ. of Toronto, 2000–04. Consultant: IBM Res. Labs, NY, 1980–83; Sandia Nat. Labs, Albuquerque, 1985–90. Guest Sen. Physicist, Brookhaven Nat. Lab., NY, 1968–; Vis. Scientist, Riso Nat. Lab., Roskilde, Denmark, 1971, 1979. Numerous lectures at univs in USA, Canada, UK and Israel, incl. A. W. Scott Lecture, Cambridge Univ., 2000. Co-Chm., Polaroid Sci. and Technol. Bd, 1998–2002. Mem., Ext. Adv. Cttee, Physics Dept, Oxford Univ., 2000. FAAAS 1982; Fellow: APS, 1980; Amer. Acad. Arts and Scis, 1987. Trustee, Boston Mus. of Sci., 1992–2001; Gov., Argonne Nat. Lab., 1992–2001; Mem., Adv. Council, Nippon Electric Co. Res. Inst., 1995–2000. Holds numerous awards and prizes. *Publications:* numerous contribs to learned jls on phases and phase transition behaviour of novel states of matter. *Address:* University of California, Berkeley, 200 California Hall, Berkeley, CA 94720–1500, USA.

BIRKENHEAD, Bishop Suffragan of, since 2007; **Rt Rev. (Gordon) Keith Sinclair;** *b* 3 Dec. 1952; *s* of Donald and Joyce Sinclair; *m* 1989, Rosemary Jones; two *s* one *d. Educ:* Christ Church, Oxford (BA, MA 1975); Cranmer Hall, Durham (BA 1984). Ordained deacon, 1984, priest, 1985; Asst Curate, Christ Church, Summerfield, 1984–88; Vicar, St Peter and St Paul, Aston, 1988–2001; Area Dean, Aston, 2000–01; Vicar, Holy Trinity, Coventry, 2001–07. Hon. Canon, Birmingham Cathedral, 2000–01. *Recreations:* walking, cinema, theatre. *Address:* Bishop's Lodge, 67 Bidston Road, Prenton CH43 6TR. *T:* (0151) 652 2741, *Fax:* (0151) 651 2330; *e-mail:* bpbirkenhead@chester.anglican.org.

BIRKETT, family name of **Baron Birkett**.

BIRKETT, 2nd Baron *cr* 1958, of Ulverston; **Michael Birkett;** Chairman, Donatella Flick Conducting Competition, 1990–2008; *b* 22 Oct. 1929; *s* of 1st Baron Birkett, PC and Ruth Birkett (*née* Nilsson, she *d* 1969); *S* father, 1962; *m* 1st, 1960, Junia Crawford (*d* 1973); 2nd, 1978, Gloria Taylor (*d* 2001); one *s. Educ:* Stowe; Trinity Coll., Cambridge. Asst Dir at Ealing Studios and Ealing Films, 1953–59; Asst Dir, 1959–61, on films including: The Mark; The Innocents; Billy Budd; Associate Producer: Some People, 1961–62; Modesty Blaise, 1965; Producer: The Caretaker, 1962; Marat/Sade, 1966; A Midsummer Night's Dream, 1967; King Lear, 1968–69; Director: The Launching and The Soldier's Tale, 1963; Overture and Beginners, the More Man Understands, 1964; Outward Bound, 1971. Vice Pres., British Bd of Film Classification, 1985–97. Dep. Dir, National Theatre, 1975–77; Consultant to Nat. Theatre on films, TV and sponsorship, 1977–79; Dir for Recreation and Arts, GLC, 1979–86; Adviser to South Bank Bd, 1986–89; Exec. Dir, Royal Philharmonic Soc., 1989–90; Dir, Olympic Festival 1990, Manchester, 1990. Chairman: Children's Film & TV Foundn, 1981–99; Theatres Adv. Council, 1986–2002; Adv. Cttee, Nat. Sound Archive, 1993–2003; Music Adv. Cttee, British Council, 1994–2001. Chm., Management Cttee, Park Lane Gp, 1991–2005. Chm. Governors, BRIT Sch. for Performing Arts and Technology, 1990–2001. Master, Curriers' Co., 1975–76. *Recreations:* music, printing, horticulture. *Heir: s* Hon. Thomas Birkett, *b* 25 July 1982. *Address:* Great Allfields, Balls Cross, Petworth GU28 9JU.

BIRKETT, Peter Vidler; QC 1989; a Recorder, since 1989; *b* 13 July 1948; *s* of Neville Lawn Birkett, MA, MB BCh, FRES and late Marjorie Joy Birkett; *m* 1976, Jane Elizabeth Fell; two *s. Educ:* Sedbergh School; Univ. of Leicester. Called to the Bar, Inner Temple, 1972, Bencher, 1996; practice on SE Circuit, 1973–77, on N Circuit, 1977– (Leader, 1999–2001). Asst Recorder, 1986–89; Acting Deemster, High Ct, IOM, 2000. Mem., General Council of the Bar, 1999–2001. Vice-Chm., Advocacy Trng Council of Eng. and Wales, 2004–. Hon. Fellow, Manchester Metropolitan Univ., 2007. *Recreations:* golf, conversation, playing the piano. *Address:* 18 St John Street, Manchester M3 4EA. *T:* (0161) 834 9843; 23 Essex Street, WC2R 3AA. *Club:* Wilmslow Golf.

BIRKHEAD, Prof. Timothy Robert, DPhil, DSc; FRS 2004; Professor of Zoology, Department of Animal and Plant Sciences, University of Sheffield, since 1992; *b* 28 Feb. 1950; *s* of Robert Harold and Nancy Olga Birkhead; *m* 1976, Miriam Enid Appleton; one *s* two *d. Educ:* Univ. of Newcastle upon Tyne (BSc; DSc 1989); Wolfson Coll., Oxford (DPhil 1976). Department of Animal and Plant Sciences, University of Sheffield: Lectr, 1976–86; Sen. Lectr, 1986–89; Reader, 1989–92. Nuffield Res. Fellow, 1990–91; Leverhulme Res. Fellow, 1995–96. *Publications:* (with C. M. Perrins) Avian Ecology, 1983; (with M. E. Birkhead) The Survival Factor, 1989; The Magpies: the ecology and behaviour of black-billed and yellow-billed magpies, 1991; (with A. P. Møller) Sperm Competition in Birds: evolutionary causes and consequences, 1992; Great Auk Islands, 1993; (with A. P. Møller) Sperm Competition and Sexual Selection, 1998; Promiscuity, 2000; The Red Canary, 2003; The Wisdom of Birds, 2008. *Recreations:* art, music, walking. *Address:* 47 Whiteley Wood Road, Sheffield S11 7FF. *T:* (0114) 222 4622, *Fax:* (0114) 222 0002; *e-mail:* t.r.birkhead@sheffield.ac.uk.

BIRKIN, Sir Derek; *see* Birkin, Sir J. D.

BIRKIN, Sir John (Christian William), 6th Bt *cr* 1905, of Ruddington Grange, Notts; *b* 2 July 1953; *s* of Sir Charles Lloyd Birkin, 5th Bt and Janet (*d* 1983), *d* of Peter Johnson; *S* father, 1985; *m* 1994, Emma Gage; one *s* one *d. Educ:* Eton; Trinity Coll., Dublin; London Film School. *Heir: s* Benjamin Charles Birkin, *b* 4 Nov. 1995. *Address:* Place Barton, Ashton, Exeter, Devon EX6 7QP.

BIRKIN, Sir (John) Derek, Kt 1990; TD 1965; Chairman, The RTZ Corporation PLC (formerly Rio Tinto-Zinc Corporation), 1991–96 (Chief Executive and Deputy Chairman, 1985–91); *b* 30 Sept. 1929; *s* of Noah and Rebecca Birkin; *m* 1952, Sadie Smith; one *s* one *d. Educ:* Hemsworth Grammar Sch. Managing Director: Velmar Ltd, 1966–67; Nairn Williamson Ltd, 1967–70; Dep. Chm. and Man. Dir, Tunnel Holdings Ltd, 1970–75; Chm. and Man. Dir, Tunnel Holdings, 1975–82; Dir, Rio Tinto-Zinc, then RTZ, Corp., 1982–96, Dep. Chief Exec., 1983–85. Director: Smiths Industries, 1977–84; British Gas Corp., 1982–85; George Wimpey, 1984–92; CRA Ltd (Australia), 1985–94; Rio Algom Ltd (Canada), 1985–92; The Merchants Trust PLC, 1986–99; British Steel plc (formerly BSC), 1986–92; Barclays PLC, 1990–95; Merck & Co. Inc. (USA), 1992–2000; Carlton Communications Plc, 1992–2001; Unilever PLC, 1993–2000; Chm., Watmoughs (Holdings) PLC, 1996–98. Member: Review Body on Top Salaries, 1986–89; Council, Industrial Soc., 1985–97. Dir, Royal Opera House, 1993–97 (Trustee, 1990–93). CCMI (CBIM 1980); FRSA 1988. Hon. LLD Bath, 1998. *Recreations:* opera, Rugby, cricket.

BIRKMYRE, Sir James, 4th Bt *cr* 1921, of Dalmunzie, County of Perth; Director of Championship Management, PGA European Tour, since 1994; *b* 29 Feb. 1956; *s* of Sir Archibald Birkmyre, 3rd Bt and of Gillian Mary (*née* Downes); *S* father, 2001; *m* 1990, Leslie Amanda, *d* of Dr Richard Lyon, Seal Beach, Calif; one *s. Educ:* Radley Coll.; Ecole Supérieure de Commerce, Neuchâtel; Ealing Tech. Coll. (BA Hons). Account Mgr, Collet Dickenson & Pearce Advertising, 1978–82; Account Dir, TBWA Advertising, 1982–87; Sponsorship Dir, The Wight Co., 1987–93; Man. Dir, Birchgrey, 1993–94. *Recreations:* tennis, fly-fishing, golf, ski-ing. *Heir: s* Alexander Birkmyre, *b* 24 May 1991. *Address:* Ashmore Green Cottage, Ashmore Green, near Newbury, Berks RG18 9EY. *T:* (01635) 862756. *Clubs:* MCC, Lord's Taverners; Sunningdale Golf.

BIRLEY, James Leatham Tennant, CBE 1990; FRCP, FRCPsych, DPM; Consultant Psychiatrist, Bethlem Royal and Maudsley Hospitals, 1969–90, Emeritus Psychiatrist, 1990; President, British Medical Association, 1993–94; *b* 31 May 1928; *s* of late Dr James Leatham Birley and Margaret Edith (*née* Tennant); *m* 1954, Julia Davies; one *s* three *d. Educ:* Winchester Coll.; University Coll., Oxford; St Thomas' Hosp., London. Maudsley Hospital: Registrar, 1960; Sen. Registrar, 1963; Mem. Scientific Staff, MRC Social Psychiatry Research Unit, 1965; Dean, Inst. of Psychiatry, 1971–82. Dean, 1982–87, Pres., 1987–90, RCPsych. *Publications:* contribs to scientific jls. *Recreations:* music, gardening. *Address:* Upper Bryn, Longtown, Hereford HR2 0NA.

BIRLEY, Michael Pellew, MA (Oxon); Housemaster, 1970–80, Assistant Master, 1980–84, Marlborough College; *b* 7 Nov. 1920; *s* of late Norman Pellew Birley, DSO, MC, and Eileen Alice Morgan; *m* 1949, Ann Grover (*née* Street); two *s* two *d. Educ:* Marlborough Coll.; Wadham Coll., Oxford. 1st class Classical Honour Moderations, 1940; 1st class *Litterae Humaniores*, 1947; MA 1946. Served War of 1939–45 with the Royal Fusiliers; joined up, Sept. 1940; commissioned, April 1941; abroad, 1942–45 (despatches); demobilised, Jan. 1946. Taught Classics: Shrewsbury Sch., 1948–50; Eton Coll., 1950–56; Headmaster, Eastbourne College, 1956–70. Member Council: Ardingly Coll., 1981–90; Marlborough Coll., 1985–90. Fellow, Woodard Corp., 1983–90. *Recreations:* gardening, wine-making. *Address:* Long Summers, Cross Lane, Marlborough, Wilts SN8 1LA. *T:* (01672) 512830.

BIRLEY, Prof. Susan Joyce, (Mrs David Norburn); Professor of Entrepreneurship, The Business School (formerly Professor of Management), Imperial College, London, 1990–2003; Director, Entrepreneurship Centre, 2000–03; *m* 1st, 1964, Arwyn Hopkins (marr. diss. 1970); 2nd, 1975, Prof. David Norburn, *qv. Educ:* Nelson Grammar Sch.; University College London (BSc 1964; Fellow, 2004); PhD London 1974. FSS. Teacher, Dunsmore Sch., 1964–66; Lectr, Lanchester Polytechnic, 1966–68; Lectr and Sen. Lectr, Poly. of Central London, 1968–72; Sen. Res. Fellow, City Univ., 1972–74; London Business School: Sen. Res. Fellow, 1974–79; Lectr in Small Business, 1979–82; University of Notre Dame, USA: Adjunct Associate Prof., 1978–82; Associate Prof. of Strategy and Entrepreneurship, 1982–85; Philip and Pauline Harris Prof. of Entrepreneurship, Cranfield Inst. of Technol., 1985–90. Academic Dir, European Foundn for Entrepreneurship Res., 1988–91. Member: CNAA, 1987–90; NI Economic Council, 1988–94; PCFC, 1988–92; Adv. Panel on Deregulation, DTI, 1989–91; Bd, LEDU, NI, 1992–93. Founder Director and Shareholder: Guidehouse Group, 1980–85; Greyfriars Ltd, 1982–85; Newchurch & Co., 1986–97 (Chm.); Director: NatWest Bank, 1996–2000; Process Systems Enterprise Ltd, 1997–2003; IC Innovations Ltd, 1997–2003; BAE Systems, 2000–07. Mem. Panel, Foresight Steering Gp, 1997–2001. Governor, Harris City Technol. Coll., 1990–92. FCGI 2001; Fellow, British Acad. of Mgt, 1996. Freeman, City of London, 1964. Mem. Editl Bds, various business jls. *Publications:* From Private to Public (jtly), 1977; The Small Business Casebook, 1979; The Small Business Casebook: teaching manual, 1980; New Enterprises, 1982; (contrib.) Small Business and Entrepreneurship, ed Burns and Dewhurst, 1989; (jtly) Exit Routes, 1989; (jtly) The British Entrepreneur, 1989; (ed) European Entrepreneurship: emerging growth companies, 1989; (ed jtly) International Perspectives on Entrepreneurship, 1992; Entrepreneurship Research: global perspectives, 1993; Mastering Enterprise, 1997; Mastering Entrepreneurship, 2000; Franchising: pathway to wealth creation, 2004; numerous contribs to learned jls. *Recreation:* gardening.

BIRMINGHAM, Archbishop of, (RC), since 2000; **Most Rev. Vincent Gerard Nichols;** Titular Bishop of Othona; *b* 8 Nov. 1945; *s* of Henry Joseph Nichols and Mary Nichols (*née* Russell). *Educ:* St Mary's College, Crosby; Gregorian Univ., Rome (STL PhL); Manchester Univ. (MA Theol); Loyola Univ., Chicago (MEd). Chaplain, St John Rigby VI Form College, Wigan, 1972–77; Priest, inner city of Liverpool, 1978–81; Director, Upholland Northern Inst., with responsibility for in service training of clergy and for adult Christian educn, 1981–84; Gen. Sec., RC Bishops' Conf. of England and Wales, 1984–91; Auxiliary Bp of Westminster (Bp in N London), 1992–2000. Chairman: Catholic Educn Service, 1998–; Dept of Catholic Educn and Formation, RC Bishops' Conf. of Eng. and Wales, 1998–. Advr to Cardinal Hume and Archbishop Worlock, Internat. Synods of Bishops, 1980, 1983, 1985, 1987. Deleg. of Bishops' Conf. to Synod of Bishops, 1994; Mem., Synod of Bishops for Oceania, 1998, for Europe, 1999. *Publications:* Promise of Future Glory, 1997; Missioners, 2007; articles in Priests and People, Business Economist. *Address:* Archbishop's House, 8 Shadwell Street, Birmingham B4 6EY. *T:* (0121) 236 9090.

BIRMINGHAM, Bishop of, since 2006; **Rt Rev. David Andrew Urquhart;** Prelate of the Most Distinguished Order of St Michael and St George, since 2005; *b* 14 April 1952; *s* of late Hector Maconochie Urquhart, FRCSE and of Elizabeth Mary Florence Urquhart (*née* Jones). *Educ:* Croftinloan; Rugby Sch.; Ealing Business Sch. (BA Hons); Wycliffe Hall, Oxford. Volunteer in Uganda, 1971; BP plc, 1972–82; ordained deacon, 1984, priest, 1985; Curate, St Nicholas, Kingston upon Hull, 1984–87; Team Vicar, Drypool, 1987–92; Vicar, Holy Trinity, Coventry, 1992–2000; Bp Suffragan of Birkenhead, 2000–06. Hon. Canon, Coventry Cathedral, 1999–2000. Archbp of Canterbury's Episcopal Link with China, 2006–. Chairman: Hull and E Yorks Faith in the City Gp, 1985–90; Chester Dio. Bd of Educn, 2001–06; CMS, 1994–2007; Wirral Local Strategic Partnership, 2002–06. Dir, Coventry City Centre Co., 1997–2000. Chm. Governors, Craven (LEA) Primary Sch., 1988–92; Gov., Rugby Sch., 1999–. Hon. Freeman, Metropolitan Borough of Wirral, 2006. Tallow Chandlers Medal, BP, 1977. *Recreations:* squash, fives (half blue, Rugby fives, 1984), watching films, collecting books on red deer. *Address:* Bishop's Croft, Old Church Road, Harborne, Birmingham B17 0BG. *T:* (0121) 427 1163; *e-mail:* bishop@birmingham.anglican.org.

BIRMINGHAM, Auxiliary Bishops of, (RC); *see* Kenney, Rt Rev. W.; McGough, Rt Rev. D.; Pargeter, Rt Rev. P.

BIRMINGHAM, Dean of; *see* Wilkes, Very Rev. R. A.

BIRMINGHAM, Archdeacon of; *see* Osborne, Ven. H. J.

BIRNBAUM, Michael Ian; QC 1992; a Recorder, since 1995; *b* 26 Feb. 1947; *s* of Samuel Birnbaum and Anne (*née* Zucker); *m* 1984, Aimee Dara Schachter. *Educ:* Southgate County Grammar Sch.; Christ Church, Oxford (BA Jurisp.). Called to the Bar, Middle Temple, 1969; practice mainly in criminal law, extradition and human rights; Asst Recorder, 1990–95. Chm., W Africa Sub-Cttee, Bar Human Rights Cttee, 2002–; Mem., Bar Internat. Relns Cttee, 2001–. *Publications:* two reports on the case in Nigeria of Ken Saro-Wiwa and others. *Recreations:* singing, opera, reading. *Address:* 9–12 Bell Yard, WC2A 2LF. *T:* (020) 7400 1800.

BIRNIE, Dr Esmond; Ministerial Special Advisor, Department for Employment and Learning, Northern Ireland, since 2007; *b* 6 Jan. 1965; *s* of Dr James Whyte Birnie and Ruth Alexandra Birnie (*née* Bell). *Educ:* Gonville and Caius Coll., Cambridge (BA 1st Cl. Hons Econs 1986); Queen's Univ., Belfast (PhD Econs 1994). Res. Asst, NI Econ. Res. Centre, 1986–89; Lectr in Econs, 1989–2000, Sen. Lectr in Econs and Mgt, 2000–07, QUB. Northern Ireland Assembly: Mem. (UU) Belfast S, 1998–2007; contested same seat, 2007; Chm., Cttee for Higher and Further Educn, Trng and Employment, then for Employment and Learning, 1999–2002. UU Party spokesman: on North-South affairs and British-Irish Council, 1999–2003; on Dept of Finance and Family, 2006–07; Talks negotiator, 2006–07. *Publications:* Without Profit or Prophets, 1997; *jointly:* Closing the Productivity Gap, 1990; East German Productivity, 1993; The Competitiveness of Industry in Ireland, 1994; Competitiveness of Industry in the Czech Republic and Hungary, 1995; An Economics Lesson for Irish Nationalists and Republicans, 1995; Environmental Regulation, the Firm and Competitiveness, 1998; The Northern Ireland Economy, 1999; Environmental Regulation and Competitive Advantage, 2000; Can the Celtic Tiger Cross the Border?, 2001; A Brighter Future for Northern Ireland: the case against the Euro, 2002. *Recreations:* cycling, jogging, art, architecture, music, church choir, active church member and Elder. *Address:* 32 Finaghy Road South, Finaghy, Belfast BT10 0DR.

BIRO, Bálint Stephen, (Val); illustrator, painter, and author of children's books; *b* Budapest, 6 Oct. 1921; *s* of late Dr Bálint Biro and Margaret Biro (*née* Gyulaházi); *m* 1st, 1945, Vivien Woolley (marr. diss. 1970; she *d* 1991); one *d*; 2nd, 1970, Marie-Louise Ellaway; one step *s* one step *d*. *Educ:* Cistercian Sch., Budapest; Central Sch. of Art, London. Nat. Fire Service, London, 1942–45; Studio Manager, Sylvan Press, 1944–46; Production Manager, C. & J. Temple, 1946–48; Art Dir, John Lehmann, 1948–53; weekly illustrations for Radio Times, 1951–72; freelance illustrator and designer of book covers, 1953–. Mem., Chesham UDC, 1966–70. Vice Chm., Bosham Assoc., 1989–91; Member: Soc. of Authors, 1970; Vintage Austin Register, 1961. Chm. of Govs, Amersham Coll. of Art and Design, 1974–84. *Publications:* author and illustrator of over ninety books, including: Bumpy's Holiday, 1943; 36 Gumdrop titles, incl. Gumdrop: the adventures of a vintage car, 1966, Gumdrop's School Adventure, 2001; Hungarian Folk Tales, 1981 (trans. Spanish 1991); The Magic Doctor, 1982; The Hobyahs, 1985; Tobias and the Dragon, 1989; Peter Cheater, 1989; Look and Find ABC, 1990; Miranda's Umbrella, 1990; Rub-a-Dub-Dub Nursery Rhymes, 1991; Three Billy Goats Gruff, 1993; Lazy Jack, 1995; Jasper's Jungle Journey, 1995; Bears Can't Fly, 1996; Hansel and Gretel, 1996; Goldilocks and the Three Bears, 1998; Little Red Riding Hood, 2000; The Joking Wolf, 2001; Aesop's Fables (18 titles), 2002; Hans Christian Andersen Fairy Tales, 2005; Grimm's Fairy Tales, 2008; illustrator of numerous books, including: Denys Val Baker, Worlds Without End, 1945; H. E. Todd, children's picture books, 1954–88; Jean Plaidy, historical novels, 1960–74; Anthony Hope, The Prisoner of Zenda, 1961; L. Frank Baum, Wizard of Oz books, 1965, 1967; Lord Tweedsmuir, One Man's Happiness, 1968; Eric Shipton, That Untravelled World, 1969; J. H. B. Peel, Country Talk books, 1970–81; The Good Food Guide, 1971; The Robert Carrier Cookery Course, 1974; Kenneth Grahame, Wind in the Willows, 1983; Margaret Mahy, The King's Jokes, 1987; My Oxford Picture Word Book, 1994; Ted Wragg, The Flying Boot reading scheme, 1994–95; Christina Butler, The Dinosaur's Egg, 1994; Anthony Trollope, The Landleaguers, 1995; Golden Lion of Grandpere, 1997; G. K. Chesterton, Father Brown Stories, 1996; Michael Hardcastle, Carole's Camel, 1997; Anthony Buckeridge: Jennings Sounds the Alarm, 1999; Jennings Breaks the Record, 2000; Jennings Joins the Search Party, 2001; Jennings and the Old Rattletrap, 2003; 100 Bible Stories for Children, 2002; 100 New Testament Stories for Children, 2003; Enid Blyton, Secret of the Lost Necklace, 2003; Dot Meharry, The Dinosaur Dance, 2005; Macmillan Primary Integrated Studies (Jamaica), 3 pts, 2005–06. *Recreations:* vintage car rallies, painting, photography. *Address:* Bridge Cottage, Brook Avenue, Bosham, West Sussex PO18 8LQ. *T:* (01243) 574195. *Club:* Vintage Sports-Car (Chipping Norton).

BIRRELL, Sir James (Drake), Kt 1993; FCA; FCBSI; Chief Executive, Halifax Building Society, 1988–93; *b* 18 Aug. 1933; *s* of James Russell Birrell, MA and Edith Marion Birrell, BSc (*née* Drake); *m* 1958, Margaret Anne Pattison; two *d*. *Educ:* Belle Vue Grammar School, Bradford. FCA 1955; FCBSI 1989. Boyce Welch & Co. (articled clerk), 1949–55; Pilot Officer, RAF, 1955–57; chartered accountant, Price Waterhouse, 1957–60; Accountant, ADA Halifax, 1960–61; Management Accountant, Empire Stores, 1961–64; Dir and Co. Sec., John Gladstone & Co., 1964–68; Halifax Building Society, 1968–93. Non-executive Director: Securicor, 1993–2003; Wesleyan Gen. Assce Soc., 1993–2004. Mem., Building Societies Commn, 1994–2001. *Recreations:* golf, gardening, archaeology, local history. *Address:* 4 Marlin End, Berkhamsted, Herts HP4 3GB.

BIRSE, Peter Malcolm; Chairman, Birse Group, 1999–2001 (Chairman and Chief Executive, 1970–99); *b* 24 Nov. 1942; *s* of Peter A. M. Birse and Margaret C. Birse; *m* 1969, Helen Searle; two *s* one *d*. *Educ:* Arbroath High Sch.; St Andrews Univ. (BScEng). MICE. Engineer, John Mowlem, 1963–66; Site Manager: Cammon (Ghana), 1966–68; Cammon (UK), 1968–69; Engineer, Foster Wheeler, 1969–70; founded Birse Group, 1970. *Recreations:* sailing, ski-ing. *Address:* c/o Birse Group, Humber Road, Barton-on-Humber, N Lincs DN18 5BW. *Club:* Royal Ocean Racing.

BIRSS, Colin Ian; QC 2008; *b* Thurso, 28 Dec. 1964; *s* of Ian and Davina Birss; *m* 1987, Kathryn Squibbs; two *s* one *d*. *Educ:* Downing Coll., Cambridge (BA Natural Sci. 1986); City Univ. (Dip. Law 1989). Called to the Bar, Middle Temple, 1990; in practice at the Bar, 1990–; Standing Counsel to Comptroller-Gen. of Patents, 2003–08. *Publication:* Terrell on the Law of Patents, 16th edn, 2006. *Recreation:* beekeeping. *Address:* 3 New Square, Lincoln's Inn, WC2A 3RS. *T:* (020) 7405 1111; *e-mail:* birss@3newsquare.co.uk.

BIRT, family name of **Baron Birt**.

BIRT, Baron *cr* 2000 (Life Peer), of Liverpool in the County of Merseyside; **John Birt,** Kt 1998; Prime Minister's Strategy Adviser, 2001–05; *b* 10 Dec. 1944; *s* of Leo Vincent Birt and Ida Birt; *m* 1965, Jane Frances (*née* Lake) (marr. diss. 2006); one *s* one *d*; *m* 2006, Eithne Victoria Wallis, *qv*. *Educ:* St Mary's Coll., Liverpool; St Catherine's Coll., Oxford (MA; Hon. Fellow 1992). Producer, Nice Time, 1968–69; Joint Editor, World in Action, 1969–70; Producer, The Frost Programme, 1971–72; Executive Producer, Weekend World, 1972–74; Head of Current Affairs, LWT, 1974–77; Co-Producer, The Nixon Interviews, 1977; Controller of Features and Current Affairs, LWT, 1977–81; Dir of Programmes, LWT, 1982–87; Dep. Dir-Gen., 1987–92, Dir-Gen., 1992–2000, BBC. Adviser: McKinsey & Co., 2000–05; Terra Firma, 2005–; Capgemini, 2006–. Chairman: Lynx New Media, subseq. Lynx Capital Ventures, 2000–04; Waste Recycling Gp, 2006; Infinis, 2006–07; non-executive Director: PayPal (Europe) Ltd, 2004–; Eutelsat, 2006–; Maltby Capital Ltd, 2007–. Advr to Prime Minister on Criminal Justice, 2000–01; Mem., Cabinet Office Strategy Bd, 2003–05. Vis. Fellow, Nuffield Coll., Oxford, 1991–99. Member: Wilton Park Academic Council, 1980–83; Media Law Gp, 1983–94; Opportunity 2000 (formerly Women's Economic) Target Team, BITC, 1991–98; Internat. Council, Mus. of TV and Radio, NY, 1994–2000; Broadcasting Research Unit: Mem., Working Party on the new Technologies, 1981–83; Mem., Exec. Cttee, 1983–87. Vice-Pres., RTS, 1994–2000 (Fellow, 1989). FIET (CompIEE 1998). Hon. Fellow, Univ. of Wales Cardiff, 1997. Hon. DLitt: Liverpool John Moores, 1992; City, 1998; Hon. DLitt Bradford, 1999. Emmy Award, US Nat. Acad. of Television, Arts and Scis, 1995. *Publications:* The Harder Path (autobiog.), 2002; various articles in newspapers and journals. *Recreation:* football, walking, cinema. *Address:* c/o House of Lords, SW1A 0PW.

BIRT, Michael Cameron St John; QC 1995; Deputy Bailiff, Jersey, since 2000; *b* 25 Aug. 1948; *s* of St John Michael Clive Birt and Mairi Araminta Birt (*née* Cameron); *m* 1973, Joan Frances Miller; two *s* one *d*. *Educ:* Marlborough Coll.; Magdalene Coll., Cambridge (MA Law). Called to the Bar, Middle Temple, 1970, to Jersey Bar, 1977; in practice: London, 1971–75; as Jersey advocate, with Ogier & Le Cornu, St Helier, 1976–93; Crown Advocate of Jersey, 1987–93; HM Attorney General, Jersey, 1994–2000. *Recreations:* ski-ing, yachting, golf. *Address:* Bailiff's Chambers, Royal Court House, St Helier, Jersey JE1 1BA. *T:* (01534) 441100, *Fax:* (01534) 441137. *Clubs:* Royal Channel Islands Yacht; Royal Jersey Golf.

BIRTLES, William Jack; His Honour Judge Birtles; a Circuit Judge, since 2002; *b* 27 Oct. 1944; *s* of William George Birtles and Dorothy Louisa Birtles (*née* Martin); *m* 1981, Rt Hon. Patricia Hope Hewitt, *qv*; one *s* one *d*. *Educ:* King's Coll. London (LLB, AKC 1967; LLM 1968); Harvard Law Sch. (Kennedy Schol.; LLM 1971); New York Univ. Law Sch. (Robert Marshall Fellow). Called to the Bar: Gray's Inn, 1970, Bencher, 2008; Lincoln's Inn, 1986; NI, 1998; Lecturer in Law: KCL, 1968–70; UCL, 1972–74; in practice as barrister, 1974–2002. Vis. Fellow, 1993–94, Sen. Associate Mem., 1996–, St Antony's Coll., Oxford. *Publications:* (with R. Stein) Planning and Environmental Law, 1994; (with A. Forge) Local Government Finance Law, 2000; (jtly) Environmental Liability, 2004; contrib. legal jls. *Recreations:* listening to opera and classical music, reading fiction and poetry, collecting European travel books, international relations. *Address:* Snaresbrook Crown Court, 75 Hollybush Hill, Snaresbrook, E11 1QW. *T:* (020) 8530 0044, *Fax:* (020) 8530 0072.

BIRTS, Peter William; His Honour Judge Birts; QC 1990; QC (NI) 1996; a Circuit Judge, since 2005; *b* 9 Feb. 1946; *s* of John Claude Birts and Audrey Lavinia Birts; *m* 1st, 1971, Penelope Ann Eyre (marr. diss. 1997); two *d* one *s*; 2nd, 1997, Mrs Angela Forcer-Evans. *Educ:* Lancing College; St John's College, Cambridge (choral scholarship; MA). Called to the Bar, Gray's Inn, 1968, Bencher 1998; a Recorder, 1989–2005; a Dep. High Ct Judge, 2000–05; Mem., Gen. Council of the Bar, 1989–95 (Chm., Legal Aid and Fees Cttee, 1994–95). Member: Judicial Studies Bd (Main Bd and Civil and Family Cttee), 1991–96; County Court Rules Cttee, 1991–99; Legal Member: Mental Health Review Tribunals, 1994–; Parole Bd, 2006–. Asst Parly Boundary Comr, 1992–95. Freeman, City of London, 1967; Liveryman, Carpenters' Co., 1967–. *Publications:* Trespass: summary procedure for possession of land (with Alan Willis), 1987; Remedies for Trespass, 1990; (ed and contrib.) Butterworths Costs Service, 1999–. *Recreations:* music, shooting, fishing, walking, tennis. *Address:* Snaresbrook Crown Court, 75 Hollybush Hill, E11 1QW. *T:* (020) 8530 0000. *Club:* Hurlingham.

BIRTWISTLE, Maj.-Gen. Archibald Cull, CB 1983; CBE 1976 (OBE 1971); DL; Signal Officer in Chief (Army), 1980–83, retired; Master of Signals, 1990–97; *b* 19 Aug. 1927; *s* of Walter Edwin Birtwistle and Eila Louise Cull; *m* 1956, Sylvia Elleray; two *s* one *d*. *Educ:* Sir John Deane's Grammar School, Northwich; St John's Coll., Cambridge (MA

Mech. Sciences). CEng, MIEE. Commissioned, Royal Signals, 1949; served: Korea (despatches, 1952); UK; BAOR; CCR Sigs 1 (Br) Corps, 1973–75; Dep. Comdt, RMCS, 1975–79; Chief Signal Officer, BAOR, 1979–80. Col Comdt, Royal Corps of Signals, 1983–89, and 1990–97; Hon. Colonel: Durham and South Tyne ACF, 1983–88; 34 (Northern) Signal Regt (Vol.), TA, 1988–90. Pres., British Korean Veterans Assoc., 1997–2006. DL N Yorks, 1991. *Recreations:* all sports, especially Rugby (former Chairman, Army Rugby Union), soccer and cricket; gardening. *Address:* c/o National Westminster Bank PLC, 97 High Street, Northallerton, North Yorks DL7 8PS.

BIRTWISTLE, Sir Harrison, CH 2001; Kt 1988; composer; Henry Purcell Professor of Composition, King's College London, 1994–2001; *b* 1934; *m* Sheila; three *s*. *Educ:* Royal Manchester Coll. of Music; RAM (Hon. FRAM). Dir of Music, Cranborne Chase Sch., 1962–65. Composer-in-residence, London Philharmonic Orch., 1993–. Vis. Fellow, Princeton Univ., 1966–68; Cornell Vis. Prof. of Music, Swarthmore Coll., 1973; Vis. Slee Prof., State Univ. of NY at Buffalo, 1974–75. An Associate Dir, NT, 1975–88. Mem., Akademie der Kunst, Berlin. FKC 1998. Hon. DMus Sussex; Hon. DLitt Salford. Evening Standard Award for Opera, 1987, 1991; Ernst von Siemens Foundn Prize, 1995. Chevalier des Arts et des Lettres (France), 1986. *Publications:* Refrains and Choruses, 1957; Monody for Corpus Christi, 1959; Précis, 1959; The World is Discovered, 1960; Chorales, 1962, 1963; Entr'actes and Sappho Fragments, 1964; Three Movements with Fanfares, 1964; Tragoedia, 1965; Ring a Dumb Carillon, 1965; Carmen Paschale, 1965; The Mark of the Goat, 1965, 1966; The Visions of Francesco Petrarca, 1966; Verses, 1966; Punch and Judy, 1966–67 (opera); Three Lessons in a Frame, 1967; Linoii, 1968; Nomos, 1968; Verses for Ensembles, 1969; Down by the Greenwood Side, 1969; Hoquetus David (arr. of Machaut), 1969; Cantata, 1969; Ut Hermita Solvs, 1969; Medusa, 1969–70; Prologue, 1970; Nenia on the Death of Orpheus, 1970; An Imaginary Landscape, 1971; Meridian, 1971; The Fields of Sorrow, 1971; Chronometer, 1971; Epilogue—Full Fathom Five, 1972; Tombeau, 1972; The Triumph of Time, 1972; La Plage: eight arias of remembrance, 1972; Dinah and Nick's Love Song, 1972; Chanson de Geste, 1973; The World is Discovered, 1973; Grimethorpe Aria, 1973; 5 Chorale Preludes from Bach, 1973; Chorales from a Toyshop, 1973; Interludes from a Tragedy, 1973; The Mask of Orpheus, 1973–84 (opera) (Grawemeyer Award, Univ. of Louisville, 1987); Melencolia I, 1975; Pulse Field, Bow Down, Silbury Air, 1977; For O, for O, the Hobby-horse is forgot, 1977; Carmen Arcardiae Mechanicae Perpetuum, 1978; agm, 1979; On the Sheer Threshold of the Night, 1980; Quintet, 1981; Pulse Sampler, 1981; Deowa, 1983; Yan Tan Tethera, 1984; Still Movement, 1984; Secret Theatre, 1984; Songs by Myself, 1984; Earth Dances, 1986; Fanfare for Will, 1987; Endless Parade, 1987; Gawain, 1990 (opera); Four Poems by Jaan Kaplinski, 1991; Gawain's Journey, 1991; Antiphonies, 1992; The Second Mrs Kong, 1994 (opera); Cry of Anubis, 1995; Panic, 1995; Pulse Shadows, 1996; Slow Frieze, 1997; Exody, 1997; Harrison's Clocks, 1998; The Silk House Antiphonies, 1999; The Woman and the Hare, 1999; The Last Supper (opera), 2000; The Axe Manual, 2001; The Shadow of Night, 2002; Theseus Game, 2003; 26 Orpheus Elegies, 2003; Ring Dance of the Nazarene, 2003; The Gleam, 2003; The Io Passion, 2004; Night's Black Bird, 2004; Neruda Madrigales, 2005; The Minotaur, 2008; The Tree of Strings, 2008. *Address:* c/o Allied Artists Agency, 42 Montpelier Square, SW7 1JZ.

BIRTWISTLE, Susan Elizabeth, (Lady Eyre); film and television producer; *d* of late Frank Edgar Birtwistle and Brenda Mary Birtwistle (*née* Higham); *m* 1973, Richard Charles Hastings Eyre (*see* Sir Richard Eyre); one *d*. Theatre director: Royal Lyceum Th. in Educn Co., 1970–72; Nottingham Playhouse Roundabout Co., 1973–78; freelance TV producer, 1980–: work includes: Hotel du Lac, 1986 (BAFTA Award; Cable/Ace Award); Scoop; 'v' (RTS Award); Or Shall We Die?; Dutch Girls; Ball Trap on the Côte Sauvage; Anna Lee, 1993; Pride and Prejudice, 1995 (TRIC Award, TV Critics of Britain Award, 1995; TV Critics of America Award, Peabody Award, Voice of the Listener and Viewer Award, 1996; BVA Award, English Heritage Award, Banff Award, Banff Victor Ludorum Award); Emma, 1996; King Lear, 1998; Wives and Daughters, 1999; Armadillo, 2001; Cranford, 2007. Mem., Arts Council Drama Panel, 1975–77. *Publications:* The Making of Pride and Prejudice, 1995; The Making of Jane Austen's Emma, 1996. *Recreations:* gardening, theatre, music, books, croquet. *Address:* c/o Nick Marston, Curtis Brown, 4th Floor, Haymarket House, 28–29 Haymarket, SW1Y 4SP. *T:* (020) 7396 6600.

BISCHOFF, Dr Manfred; Chairman, Supervisory Board, DaimlerChrysler AG, since 2007; *b* Calw, Germany, 22 April 1942. *Educ:* Univ. of Tubingen; Univ. of Heidelberg (MEc; Dr rer. pol. 1973). Asst Prof. for Econ. Politics and Internat. Trade, Alfred Weber Inst., Univ. of Heidelberg, 1968–76; joined Daimler-Benz AG, 1976; Project Co-ordinator for Mercedes Benz Cross Country Cars, Corporate Subsids, M & A Dept, 1976–81; Internat. Projects, M & A, Finance Dept, 1981–88 (Vice-Pres., Finance Cos and Corporate Subsids); Member, Board of Management: and Chief Financial Officer, Mercedes do Brasil, 1988–89; and Chief Financial Officer, Deutsche Aerospace AG, later Daimler-Benz Aerospace AG, 1989–95; Daimler-Benz AG, later Daimler Chrysler AG, 1995–2003; and Pres. and CEO, DASA, 1995–2000; Mitsubishi Motors Corp., 2000–03; Chm. Supervisory Bd, MTU Aero Engines, 2000–03; Chm., EADS (European Aeronautic Defence and Space Co.), 2000–07; Mem. several supervisory bds. President: Eur. Assoc. Aerospace Industries, 1995–96; Fedn of German Aerospace Industries, 1996–2000. *Address:* DaimlerChrysler AG, 70546 Stuttgart, Germany.

BISCHOFF, Sir Winfried Franz Wilhelm, (Sir Win), Kt 2000; Chairman, Citigroup Inc., since 2007; Director, J. Henry Schroder & Co. Ltd, since 1978 (Chairman, 1983–94); *b* 10 May 1941; *s* of late Paul Helmut Bischoff and Hildegard (*née* Kühne); *m* 1972, Rosemary Elizabeth, *d* of Hon. Leslie Leathers; two *s*. *Educ:* Marist Brothers, Inanda, Johannesburg, S Africa; Univ. of the Witwatersrand, Johannesburg (BCom). Man. Dir, Schroders Asia Ltd, Hong Kong, 1971–82; Dir, 1983–2000, Gp Chief Exec., 1984–95, Chm., 1995–2000, Schroders plc. Dep. Chm., Cable and Wireless, 1995–2003 (non-exec. Dir, 1991–2003); Chm., Citigroup Europe, 2000–07; non-executive Director: Land Securities, 1999–2008; McGraw-Hill Cos, Inc., 1999–; IFIL, Finanziaria di Partecipazioni SpA, 2000–04; Eli Lilly & Co., 2000–; Siemens Hldgs plc, 2001–03; Prudential plc, 2007–; Akbank, 2007–. *Recreations:* opera, music, golf. *Address:* Citigroup Centre, 33 Canada Square, E14 5LB. *T:* (020) 7986 2601. *Clubs:* Woking Golf, Swinley Forest Golf, Frilford Heath Golf.

BISCOE, Prof. Timothy John; Visiting Professor, University of Bristol, since 2006; Pro-Provost, China, University College London, 1996–99; *b* 28 April 1932; *s* of late Rev. W. H. Biscoe and Mrs M. G. Biscoe; *m* 1955, Daphne Miriam (*née* Gurton) (decd); one *s* two *d*. *Educ:* Latymer Upper School; The London Hospital Medical College. BSc (Hons) Physiology, 1953; MB, BS 1957; DSc London, 1993; FRCP 1983. London Hospital, 1957–58; RAMC Short Service Commission, 1958–62; Physiologist, CDEE, Porton Down, 1959–62; ARC Inst. of Animal Physiology, Babraham, 1962–65; Res. Fellow in Physiology, John Curtin Sch. of Med. Res., Canberra, 1965–66; Associate Res. Physiologist, Cardiovascular Res. Inst., UC Medical Center, San Francisco, 1966–68; University of Bristol: Res. Associate, Dept of Physiology, 1968–70; 2nd Chair of Physiology, 1970–79; Head of Dept of Physiology, 1975–79. University College London: Jodrell Prof. of Physiology, 1979–92; Vice Provost, 1990–92; Hon. Fellow, 1996; Dep. Vice-Chancellor, Univ. of Hong Kong, 1992–95. McLaughlin Vis. Prof., McMaster Univ., Ont, 1986; Hooker Distinguished Vis. Prof., McMaster Univ., 1990. Hon. Sec., Physiological Soc., 1977–82; Member Council: Harveian Soc., 1983–86; Research Defence Soc., 1983–90 (Hon. Sec., 1983–86). Mem., Academia Europaea, 1991. *Publications:* papers on neurophysiology in Journal of Physiology, etc. *Recreations:* looking, listening, reading. *Address:* c/o Physiology Department, University of Bristol, Bristol BS8 1TD. *Club:* Garrick.

BISH-JONES, Trevor Charles; Chief Executive Officer, Woolworths Group plc, 2002–08; *b* 23 April 1960; *m* 1990, Amanda Zeil; two *d*. *Educ:* Varndean Grammar Sch., Brighton; Portsmouth Sch. of Pharmacy (BSc Hons Pharmacy). Res. Chemist, Tosco Corporate, Colorado, 1980–81; Boots plc: Store Manager, 1981–84; EPOS Project Manager, 1984–86; Buying and Marketing Controller for Photo/Sound/Vision/Home, 1987–94; Dixons Group: Marketing Dir, PC World and Dixons, 1994–97; Man. Dir, The Link, then Dixons, then Currys, 1997–2002. *Recreation:* horse riding. *Address:* c/o Woolworths Group plc, 242 Marylebone Road, NW1 6JL.

BISHKO, Roy Colin; Founder, and Co-Chairman, Tie Rack Ltd, since 1999 (Chairman, 1981–99); *b* 2 March 1944; *s* of Isidore Bishko and Rae Bishko; *m* 1969, Barbara Eileen (*née* Hirsch); one *s* one *d*. *Educ:* Grey Coll., Bloemfontein, SA; Univ. of S Africa (Attorney's Admission 1967). With Schlesinger Orgn, 1969–74; Dir, Dorrington Investment Co. Ltd, 1974–76; Man. Dir, Chaddesley Investments, London, 1976–78. FRSA 1992. *Recreations:* golf, history.

BISHOP, family name of **Baroness O'Cathain**.

BISHOP, Alan Henry, CB 1989; HM Chief Inspector of Prisons for Scotland, 1989–94; *b* 12 Sept. 1929; *s* of Robert Bishop and May Watson; *m* 1959, Marjorie Anne Conlan; one *s* one *d*. *Educ:* George Heriot's Sch., Edinburgh; Edinburgh Univ. (MA Hons Econ. Sci., 1951, History, 1952). Served RAF Educn Br., 1952–54. Asst Principal, Dept of Agric. for Scotland, 1954; Private Sec. to Parly Under-Secs of State, 1958–59; Principal, 1959; First Sec., Agric. and Food, Copenhagen and The Hague, 1963–66; Asst Sec., Commn on the Constitution, 1969–73; Asst Under-Sec. of State, 1980–84, Principal Establishment Officer, 1984–89, Scottish Office. *Recreations:* contract bridge (Pres., Scottish Bridge Union, 1979–80), theatre, golf. *Address:* Beaumont Court, 19/8 Wester Coates Gardens, Edinburgh EH12 5LT. *T:* (0131) 346 4641. *Clubs:* New (Edinburgh); Melville Bridge, Murrayfield Golf.

BISHOP, Alan John; Chief Executive, Central Office of Information, since 2003; *b* 2 Aug. 1953; *s* of Ronald and Betty Bishop. *Educ:* Queen's Coll., Oxford (BA Hons). With various advertising agencies, incl. Bates & FCB, 1974–85; joined Saatchi & Saatchi, 1985; Chairman: N America, 1994–97; UK, 1997–98; International, 1998–2002. *Recreations:* bridge, cricket. *Address:* Central Office of Information, Hercules House, Hercules Road, SE1 7DU. *T:* (020) 7928 2345. *Club:* Soho House.

BISHOP, Anthony; *see* Bishop, K. A.

BISHOP, Ven. (Anthony) Peter, CB 2001; Associate Priest, Tewkesbury with Walton Cardiff and Twyning, 2001–06; *b* 24 May 1946; *s* of Geoffrey Richard Bishop and Dora Annie Bishop; *m* 1970, Ruth Isabel Jordan; two *s*. *Educ:* London Coll. of Divinity; St John's Coll., Nottingham (LTh 1971; MPhil 1983). Civil Servant, MoT, 1963–67; ordained deacon 1971, priest 1972; Curate, Beckenham, 1971–75; RAF Chaplain, 1975–2001: Asst Chaplain-in-Chief, 1991–98; Chaplain-in-Chief, and Archdeacon, RAF, 1998–2001. QHC 1996–2001. Canon of Lincoln, 1998–2001. Mem., Gen. Synod of C of E, 1998–2001. Mem. Council, RAF Benevolent Fund, 1998–2001; Vice-Pres., RAFA, 1998–. Vice-Pres., Friends of St Clement Danes, 1998–. FRSA 1983; FRAeS 1999. *Recreations:* walking, history, biography, cookery, living in France. *Address:* La Croix Blanche, 50810 St Germain d'Elle, France.

BISHOP, Dr Arthur Clive; Deputy Director, British Museum (Natural History), 1982–89, and Keeper of Mineralogy, 1975–89; *b* 9 July 1930; *s* of late Charles Henry Bishop and Hilda (*née* Clowes); *m* 1962, Helen (*née* Bennison) (*d* 2005); one *d*. *Educ:* Wolstanton County Grammar Sch., Newcastle, Staffs; King's Coll., Univ. of London (Shell Scholar; FKC 1985). BSc 1951, PhD 1954. Geologist, HM Geological Survey, 1954; served RAF Educn Br., 1955–57; Lectr in Geology, Queen Mary Coll., Univ. of London, 1958; Principal Sci. Officer, British Museum (Natural History), 1969, Deputy Keeper 1972. Geological Society: Daniel Pidgeon Fund, 1958; Murchison Fund, 1970; Vice-Pres., 1977–78; Mineralogical Society: Gen. Sec., 1965–72; Vice-Pres., 1973–74; Pres., 1986–87; Pres., Geologists' Assoc., 1978–80 (Halstead Medallist, 1999); Vice-Pres., Inst. of Science Technology, 1973–82. Mem. d'honneur, La Société Jersiaise, 1983. *Publications:* An Outline of Crystal Morphology, 1967; (with W. R. Hamilton and A. R. Woolley) Hamlyn Guide to Minerals, Rocks and Fossils, 1974, rev. edn as Philip's Minerals, Rocks and Fossils, 1999; papers in various jls, mainly on geology of Channel Is and Brittany, and on dioritic rocks. *Recreations:* drawing and painting.

BISHOP, Prof. David Hugh Langler, PhD, DSc; FIBiol; Fellow, St Cross College, Oxford, 1984–98, now Emeritus; Director, Natural Environment Research Council Institute of Virology and Environmental Microbiology (formerly Institute of Virology), 1984–95; *b* 31 Dec. 1937; *s* of late Reginald Samuel Harold Bishop and of Violet Rosina May Langler; *m* 1st, 1963, Margaret Duthie (marr. diss.); one *s* one *d*; 2nd, 1971, Polly Roy (marr. diss.); one *s*; 3rd, 1999, Margreta Buijs; one *s* two *d*. *Educ:* Liverpool Univ. (BSc 1959, PhD 1962); MA 1984, DSc 1988, Oxon. FIBiol 1989. Postdoctoral Fellow, CNRS, Gif-sur-Yvette, 1962–63; Research Associate, Univ. of Edinburgh, 1963–66, Univ. of Illinois, 1966–69; Asst Prof., 1969–70, Associate Prof., 1970–71, Columbia Univ.; Associate Prof., 1971–75, Prof., 1975, Rutgers Univ.; University of Alabama at Birmingham: Prof., 1975–84; Sen. Scientist, Comprehensive Cancer Center, 1975–84; Chm., Dept of Microbiology, 1983–84; Adjunct Prof., Dept of Internat. Health, 1996–99. Vis. Fellow, Lincoln Coll., Oxford, 1981–82; Vis. Prof. of Virology, Oxford Univ., 1984–97; Hon. Prof., Dept of Microbiol., Univ. of Qld, 1997–2000. Nathaniel A. Young Award in Virology, 1981. *Publications:* Rhabdoviruses, 1979; numerous contribs to books and jls. *Recreation:* hill walking. *Address:* 12 Chemin du Haut Morier, 41000 Blois Les Grouets, Loir et Cher, France.

BISHOP, Prof. Dorothy Vera Margaret, DPhil; FBA 2006; FMedSci; Professor of Developmental Neuropsychology, since 1999, and Wellcome Principal Research Fellow, since 1998, University of Oxford; *b* 14 Feb. 1952; *d* of Aubrey Francis Bishop and Annemarie Sofia Bishop (*née* Eucken); *m* 1976, Patrick Michael Anthony Rabbitt, *qv*. *Educ:* St Hugh's Coll., Oxford (BA Hons 1973; MA; DPhil 1978); Inst. of Psychiatry, Univ. of London (MPhil 1975). Res. Officer, Neuropsychology Unit, Dept of Clinical Neurology, Univ. of Oxford, 1975–82; Sen. Res. Fellow, MRC, at Univs of Newcastle upon Tyne and Manchester, 1982–91; Sen. Res. Scientist, MRC Applied Psychology Unit, Cambridge, 1991–98. Adjunct Prof., Univ. of Western Australia, 1998. Mem., ESRC, 1996–2000. FMedSci 2000. Hon. DM Lund, 2004. *Publications:* (ed with K.

Mogford) Language Development in Exceptional Circumstances, 1988; Handedness and Developmental Disorders, 1990; Uncommon Understanding: development and disorders of language comprehension in children, 1997; (ed with L. B. Leonard) Speech and Language Impairments in Children, 2000. *Recreations:* Victorian novels, pre-1945 films. *Address:* Department of Experimental Psychology, South Parks Road, Oxford OX1 3UD. *T:* (01865) 271386.

BISHOP, George Robert, CBE 1993; DPhil; FRSE; CPhys, FInstP; Director General, Ispra Establishment, Joint Research Centre, European Commission, Ispra, Italy, 1983–92, retired (Director, 1982–83); *b* 16 Jan. 1927; *s* of George William Bishop and Lilian Elizabeth Garrod; *m* 1952, Adriana Giuseppina, *d* of Luigi Caberlotto and Giselda Mazzariol; two *s* one *d*. *Educ:* Christ Church, Oxford (MA, DPhil). ICI Research Fellow, Univ. of Oxford, 1951; Research Fellow, St Antony's Coll., Oxford, 1952; Chercheur, Ecole Normale Supérieure, Paris, 1954; Ingénieur-Physicien, Laboratoire de l'Accelerateur Linéaire, ENS, Orsay, 1958; Prof., Faculté des Sciences, Univ. de Paris, 1962; Kelvin Prof. of Natural Philosophy, Univ. of Glasgow, 1964–76; Dir, Dept of Natural and Physical Sciences, JRC, Ispra, 1974–82. Hon. DSc, Strathclyde, 1979. *Publications:* Handbuch der Physik, Band XLII, 1957; β and X-Ray Spectroscopy, 1960; Nuclear Structure and Electromagnetic Interactions, 1965; numerous papers in learned jls on nuclear and high energy physics. *Recreations:* literature, music, swimming, tennis, gardening, travel. *Address:* via Favretti 23/A, Mogliano Veneto, 31021 (TV), Italy. *T:* (41) 455813.

BISHOP, James Drew; writer and editor; Chairman, National Heritage, since 1998 (Trustee, since 1995); *b* 18 June 1929; *s* of late Sir Patrick Bishop, MBE, MP, and Vera Drew; *m* 1959, Brenda Pearson; two *s*. *Educ:* Haileybury; Corpus Christi Coll., Cambridge. Reporter, Northampton Chronicle & Echo, 1953; joined editorial staff of The Times, 1954; Foreign Correspondent, 1957–64; Foreign News Editor, 1964–66; Features Editor, 1966–70; Editor, Illustrated London News, 1971–87; Editor-in-Chief, Illustrated London News Publications, 1987–94. Director: Illustrated London News & Sketch Ltd, 1973–94; International Thomson Publishing Ltd, 1980–85. Chm., Assoc. of British Editors, 1987–96. Mem., 1970–, Chm., 2000–, Adv. Bd, Annual Register (contributor, Amer. sect., 1960–88); Chm. Editl Bd, Natural World, 1981–97. *Publications:* A Social History of Edwardian Britain, 1977; Social History of the First World War, 1982; (with Oliver Woods) The Story of The Times, 1983; (ed) The Illustrated Counties of England, 1985; The Sedgwick Story, 1998. *Recreations:* reading, walking, looking and listening. *Address:* Black Fen, Scotland Street, Stoke by Nayland, Suffolk CO6 4QD. *T:* (01206) 262315, *Fax:* (01206) 262876. *Clubs:* Oxford and Cambridge, MCC.

BISHOP, His Honour John Edward; a Circuit Judge, 1993–2004; *b* 9 Feb. 1943; *s* of Albert George Bishop and Frances Marion Bishop; *m* 1968, Elizabeth Ann Grover; two *d*. *Educ:* St Edward's Sch., Oxford. Articled to P. F. Carter-Ruck at Messrs Oswald Hickson Collier & Co., WC2, 1962–66; admitted solicitor, 1966; Partner: Messrs Copley Clark & Co., Sutton, 1969–81; Messrs Tuck & Mann, Epsom, 1981–85; Registrar: Woolwich County Court, 1985–88; Croydon County Court, 1988–93 (District Judge, 1992–93); an Asst Recorder, 1987–90; a Recorder, 1990–93. Pres., Mid-Surrey Law Soc., 1980–81. *Recreations:* golf, walking, music, reading, garden, family. *Club:* Walton Heath Golf.

BISHOP, Dr John Edward Lucas; freelance musician; *b* 23 Feb. 1935; *s* of late Reginald John Bishop and of Eva Bishop (*née* Lucas). *Educ:* Cotham Sch., Bristol; St John's Coll., Cambridge (Exhibnr; MA, MusB); Reading Univ. (DipEd (Dist.)); Edinburgh Univ. (DMus). FRCO (CHM); ADCM; Hon. FBC. John Stewart of Rannoch Schol. (Univ. prize) 1954. Organist and Asst Dir of Music, Worksop Coll., Notts, 1958–69; Dir of Music, Worksop Coll., 1969–73; Birmingham School of Music: Dir of Studies, 1973–74; Sen. Lectr, 1974–79; Principal Lectr, Head of Organ Studies and Head of Admissions, 1979–87. Dir of Music, Cotham Parish Church, Bristol, 1976–90; Hon. Dir of Music, St Paul's Church, Birmingham, 1986; Dir, Bristol Highbury Singers, 1978–90; Consultant, Wells Cathedral Sch., 1986–93; Organist, St Augustine's Chapel, 2004– and Hon. Dir of Music, 2006–, St Monica Trust. Organ recitalist (incl. many broadcasts) and choral conductor (Conductor, 1997–2000, Pres., 2000–05, Portishead Choral Soc.), pianist, coach and adjudicator, 1960–. Former Pres., Sheffield, Birmingham and Bristol Organists' Assocs; Member: Council, ISM, 1991–97; Music Adv. Panel, Henleaze Concert Soc., 1995–2002; Bd of Mgt, Emerald Chamber Players, 1997–2002. *Publications:* various articles on history and practice of church music and 19th century organ design. *Recreations:* food and friends, walking, ecclesiology, savouring the countryside, cities and towns, railways, architecture. *Address:* 38 Westfield House, Cote Lane, Westbury-on-Trym, Bristol BS9 3TJ. *T:* (0117) 949 4838.

BISHOP, Prof. (John) Michael, MD; Professor of Microbiology and Immunology, since 1972, and of Biochemistry and Biophysics, since 1982, University Professor, since 1994, Director, G. W. Hooper Research Foundation, since 1981, and Chancellor, since 1998, University of California, San Francisco; *b* 22 Feb. 1936; *s* of John and Carrie Bishop; *m* 1959, Kathryn Putman; two *s*. *Educ:* Gettysburg Coll., Gettysburg (AB); Harvard Univ., Boston (MD). Intern/Asst Resident in Internal Med., Mass. Gen. Hosp., 1962–64; Res. Associate, NIAID, NIH, 1964–67; Vis. Scientist, Heinrich-Pette Inst., Hamburg, 1967–68; Asst Prof., Microbiology, 1968–70, Associate Prof., Microbiology, 1970–72, Univ. of California. Member: Nat. Acad. of Scis, 1980–; Amer. Acad. of Arts and Scis, 1984–. Hon. DSc Gettysburg, 1983. Albert Lasker Award for Basic Med. Res., 1982; Passano Foundn Award, 1983; Warren Triennial Prize, 1983; Armand Hammer Cancer Res. Award, 1984; Gen. Motors Cancer Res. Award, 1984; Gairdner Foundn Internat. Award, 1984; ACS Medal of Honor, 1985; (jtly) Nobel Prize in Physiology or Medicine, 1989. *Publications:* The Rise of the Genetic Paradigm, 1995; Proto-oncogenes and Plasticity in Cell Signaling, 1995; How to Win the Nobel Prize: an unexpected life in science, 2003; over 400 pubns in refereed sci. jls. *Recreations:* music, reading, theatre. *Address:* 1542 HSW, University of California, San Francisco, CA 94143–0552, USA. *T:* (415) 4763211.

BISHOP, (Kenneth) Anthony, CMG 1998; OBE 1973; HM Diplomatic Service, retired; *b* 22 Jan. 1938; *s* of Charles William Bishop and Mary Ann Bishop (*née* Bell); *m* 1962, Christine Mary Pennell; one *s* one *d*. *Educ:* Wade Deacon GS, Widnes; Emmanuel Coll., Cambridge (BA Hons Mod. Langs 1961). Nat. Service, RAF, 1956–58. Joined Foreign Office, 1961; Principal Conf. Interpreter, 1968–98, Res. Counsellor, 1981–98, FCO Research Department: Moscow, 1963–65; Berlin Four-Power Negotiations, 1970–71; Bonn, 1971–72; Geneva Comprehensive Test Ban Talks, 1978–81; Royal Visit to Russia, 1994; Russian State Visit, 2003; Anglo-Soviet/Russian summits, 1961–2004. Medal for Outstanding Contribution to the UK/USA Intelligence Relationship, CIA, 1997. *Recreations:* church-based charity work in Russia, hill walking, choral singing. *Address:* 33 Lansdowne Road, Sevenoaks, Kent TN13 3XU. *T:* (01732) 452718.

BISHOP, Malcolm Leslie; QC 1993; a Recorder, since 2000; *b* 9 Oct. 1944; *s* of late John Bishop and Irene Bishop (*née* Dunn). *Educ:* Ruabon Grammar Sch.; Regent's Park Coll., Oxford Univ. (Samuel Davies Prizeman; Hon. Mods in Theology, BA Jurisprudence, MA). Chm., OU Dem. Lab. Club, 1966. Called to the Bar, Inner Temple, 1968, Bencher, 2003; in practice on Wales and Chester Circuit. A Dep. High Court Judge, Family Div., 1997; an Asst Recorder, 1998–2000. Chm., I of M Legal Services Commn, 2002. Circuit Rep., Bar Council, 1987–92; Mem., Exec. Cttee, Family Law Bar Assoc., 1985–. Contested (Lab), Bath, Feb. and Oct. 1974. *Recreations:* politics, wine. *Address:* 30 Park Place, Cardiff CF10 3BS. *T:* (029) 2039 8421; 2 Paper Buildings, Temple, EC4Y 7ET. *T:* (020) 7556 5500. *Clubs:* Oxford and Cambridge; Cardiff and County (Cardiff).

BISHOP, Michael; *see* Bishop, J. M.

BISHOP, Sir Michael (David), Kt 1991; CBE 1986; Chairman: British Midland Plc (formerly Airlines of Britain Holdings Plc), since 1978; British Regional Air Lines Group Plc, and Manx Airlines, 1982–2001; *b* 10 Feb. 1942; *s* of Clive Leonard Bishop. *Educ:* Mill Hill School. Joined: Mercury Airlines, Manchester, 1963; British Midland Airways, 1964; Director: Airtours plc, 1987–2001 (Dep. Chm., 1996–2001); Williams Plc, 1993–2000. Member: E Midlands Electricity Bd, 1980–83; E Midlands Reg. Bd, Central Television, 1981–89; Dep. Chm., 1991–93, Chm., 1993–97, Channel 4 Television Corp. Non-exec. Dir, Kidde plc, 2000–02. Chm., D'Oyly Carte Opera Trust Ltd, 1989–. Trustee and Dir, Friends in the UK, Royal Flying Doctor Service of Australia, 2005–. Hon. Mem., Royal Soc. of Musicians of GB, 1989. *Address:* Donington Hall, Castle Donington, near Derby DE74 2SB. *T:* (01332) 854000. *Clubs:* Brooks's; St James's (Manchester).

BISHOP, Michael William; JP; Chairman, Heritage Care Ltd, 2001; *b* 22 Oct. 1941; *s* of Ronald Lewis William and Gwendoline Mary Bishop; *m* Loraine Helen Jones; two *s* one *d*. *Educ:* Manchester Univ. (BA (Econs) IIi Hons); Leicester Univ. (CertAppSocStudies). Director of Social Services: Cleveland CC, 1981–89; Manchester City Council, 1989–95. Mem., Derbys Probation Bd, 2004–. Non-exec. Dir, Derbys NHS PCT, 2007–. Chm., Derbys Assoc. for Blind People, 2004; Trustee, RNID, 1996–2004 (Dep. Chm., 2002–04); Mem., Hearing Aid Council, 2004–. JP Manchester City, 1996–2000, High Peak, 2000. *Address:* Cowley Croft, Cowley Lane, Holmesfield, Dronfield, Derbys S18 7SD.

BISHOP, Ven. Peter; *see* Bishop, A. P.

BISHOP, Peter Antony; Director, Design for London, since 2007; *b* 15 Sept. 1953; *s* of Jack and Audrey Bishop; *m* 1998, Lesley Williams; one *s* one *d*. *Educ:* Trinity Sch. of John Whitgift; Univ. of Manchester (BA 1st Cl. Hons). Hd of Planning, London Bor. of Tower Hamlets, 1985–87; Dir, Engrg and Property, London Bor. of Haringey, 1987–97; Director of Environment: London Bor. of Hammersmith & Fulham, 1997–2001 (projects included: develt of White City, the BBC, Fulham FC); London Bor. of Camden, with resp. for redevelt of King's Cross, 2001–06. Mem., London Adv. Cttee, English Heritage, 2007–. Has lectured and taught extensively. Hon. Fellow, UCL, 2008. *Recreations:* rock climbing, squash, collecting antiquarian books, European cinema. *Address:* Design for London, Palestra, 197 Blackfriars Road, SE1 8AA. *T:* (020) 7593 8328; *e-mail:* peter.bishop@designforlondon.gov.uk.

BISHOP, Prof. Peter Orlebar, AO 1986; DSc; FRS 1977; FAA; Professor Emeritus, Australian National University, since 1983; Hon. Research Associate, Department of Anatomy and Histology, University of Sydney, since 1987; *b* 14 June 1917; *s* of Ernest John Hunter Bishop and Mildred Alice Havelock Bishop (*née* Vidal); *m* 1942, Hilare Louise Holmes; one *s* two *d*. *Educ:* Barker Coll., Hornsby; Univ. of Sydney (MB, BS, DSc). Neurol Registrar, Royal Prince Alfred Hosp., Sydney, 1941–42; Surgeon Lieut, RANR, 1942–46; Fellow, Postgrad. Cttee in Medicine (Sydney Univ.) at Nat. Hosp., Queen Square, London, 1946–47 and Dept Anatomy, UCL, 1947–50; Sydney University: Res. Fellow, Dept Surgery, 1950–51; Sen. Lectr, 1951–54, Reader, 1954–55, Prof. and Head, Dept Physiology, 1955–67; Prof. and Head of Dept of Physiology, John Curtin School of Medical Res., ANU, 1967–82; Vis. Fellow, ANU, 1983–87. Visiting Professor: Japan Soc. for Promotion of Science, 1974, 1982; Katholieke Universiteit Leuven, Belgium, 1984–85; Guest Prof., Zürich Univ., 1985; Vis. Fellow, St John's Coll., Cambridge, Jan.–Oct. 1986. FAA 1967; Fellow: Aust. Postgrad. Fedn in Medicine, 1969; Nat. Vision Res. Inst. of Australia, 1983. Hon. Member: Neurosurgical Soc. of Aust., 1970; Ophthalmol Soc. of NZ, 1973; Aust. Assoc. of Neurologists, 1977; Australian Neuroscience Soc., 1986; Aust. Physiol and Pharmacol Soc., 1987. Hon. MD Sydney, 1983. (Jtly) Australia Prize, 1993; Centenary Medal, Australia, 2003. *Publications:* contribs on physiological optics and visual neurophysiology. *Recreation:* bushwalking. *Address:* Department of Anatomy and Histology, University of Sydney, NSW 2006, Australia.

BISHOP, Stephen; *see* Kovacevich, S.

BISHOP-KOVACEVICH, Stephen; *see* Kovacevich, S.

BISHOPP, Colin Philip; Special Commissioner of Income Tax, since 2001; Chairman: VAT and Duties Tribunal, since 2001 (part-time Chairman, 1990–2001); Financial Services and Markets Tribunal, since 2001; Pensions Regulator Tribunal, since 2005; Claims Management Services Tribunal, since 2007; *b* 10 Oct. 1947; *s* of Clement Walter Bishopp and Alison Moray Bishopp (*née* Stewart); *m* 1st, 1970, Margaret Bullock (marr. diss. 1987); one *s* one *d*; 2nd, 1988, Anne-Marie Jeanne Baissac; three *s*. *Educ:* Manchester Grammar Sch.; St Catharine's Coll., Cambridge (BA 1968, MA 1971). Admitted solicitor, 1971; Partner: A. W. Mawer & Co., Solicitors, 1973–88; Lace Mawer, Solicitors, 1988–97; Berrymans Lace Mawer, Solicitors, 1997–2001. *Recreations:* ski-ing, walking, classical music, providing taxi service for children. *Address:* VAT and Duties Tribunal, Alexandra House, 18–22 The Parsonage, Manchester M3 2JA. *T:* (0161) 833 5110, *Fax:* (0161) 833 5151; *e-mail:* colin.bishopp@judiciary.gsi.gov.uk.

BISIGNANI, Giovanni; Director General and Chief Executive Officer, International Air Transport Association, since 2002 (Member, Executive Committee, 1991–94); *b* 10 Dec. 1946; *s* of Renato Bisignani and Vincenza Carpano; *m* 1975, Elena Pasanisi; one *d*. *Educ:* Rome Univ. (Master of Law); Harvard Business Sch. First National City Bank, NY, 1970; Asst to Pres., ENI, Rome, 1976–79; Istituto Ricostruzione Industriale, Rome: Asst to Pres. and Rep. on Bds of Finsider, Italstat, SME and Fincantieri, 1979–89; Corporate Exec. Vice Pres., Head of Foreign Affairs, 1989; Man. Dir and CEO, Alitalia, Rome, 1989–94; Chm., Galileo Internat., Chicago, 1993–94; Pres., Tirrenia di Navigazione SpA, Rome, 1994–98; SM Logistics-Gruppo Serra Merzario SpA, 1998–2000: Man. Dir and CEO, Milan; Chm., Merzario USA, Inc., NY; Bd Mem., Merzario UK, London; Opodo, 2001–02: CEO, London; Man. Dir, Berlin; Man. Dir, Paris. Chm., AEA, 1992; Member: Bd, Assolombarda, Milan, 1998–2000; European Adv. Bd, Pratt & Whitney, United Technologies, 1998–2001; Bd, UK NATS Ltd, 2002–. *Recreations:* golf, tennis, riding. *Address:* International Air Transport Association, Route de l'Aéroport 33, PO Box 416, 1215 Geneva 15 Airport, Switzerland. *T:* (22) 7702903, *Fax:* (22) 7702680; *e-mail:* iata.dg.ceo@iata.org.

BISS, Adele, (Mrs R. O. Davies); Chairman, A. S. Biss & Co., 1996–2007; *b* 18 Oct. 1944; *d* of Robert and Bronia Biss; *m* 1973, Roger Oliver Davies, *qv*; one *s*. *Educ:* Cheltenham Ladies' Coll.; University Coll. London (BSc Econ). Unilever, 1968;

Thomson Holidays, 1970; Chief Exec., Biss Lancaster, 1978–88; Chm., BTA and English Tourist Bd, 1993–96. Director: Aegis plc, 1985–90; BR, 1987–92; European Passenger Services, subseq. Eurostar (UK) Ltd, 1990–; Bowthorpe plc, 1993–97; Harry Ramsden's, 1995–99; Engine Gp, 2005–. Gov., Middx Univ., 1995–2007; Member Council: GDST (formerly GPDST), 1996–2003; UCL, 1997–2007. Fellow, UCL, 2008. Hon. DBA Lincoln, 2002. *Recreations:* piano, hiking, ski-ing. *Address:* Engine Group, 60 Great Portland Street, W1W 7RT; *e-mail:* adele.biss@dial.pipex.com.

BISSELL, Frances Mary; freelance writer; *b* 19 Aug. 1946; *d* of Robert Maloney and Mary Maloney (*née* Kelly); *m* 1970, Thomas Emery Bissell; one step *d*. *Educ:* Univ. of Leeds (BA Hons French). VSO Nigeria, 1965–66; Assistante, Ecole Normale, Albi, 1968–69; British Council, 1970–87; The Times Cook, 1987–2000; food and cookery writer, cook and consultant, 1983–, TV presenter, 1995–. Guest cook: Mandarin Oriental, Hong Kong, 1987, 1990, 1995; London Intercontinental, 1987, 1988 and 1996; Manila Peninsula, 1989; Colombo Hilton, Sri Lanka, 1991; The Dusit Thani, Bangkok, 1992; George V, Paris, 1994; The Mark, NY, 1997, 1999 and 2000; Rio Suites Hotel, Las Vegas, 1997; guest teacher: Bogotá Hilton, Colombia, 1988; Ballymaloe Cooking Sch., Ireland, 1990; The Times cookery evenings at Leith's Sch. of Food and Wine, 1991; Learning for Pleasure, Spain, 1995 and 1996; Consultant: Ta' Frenc, Gozo, 2004–; Sloane Club, 2006–; Guest Lectr, Hebridean Internat. Cruises, 2005–. Member judging panel: THF Hotels Chef of the Year, 1988 and 1990; Annual Catey Award Function Menu, 1989–94; A Fresh Taste of Britain, Women's Farming Union, 1989; UK Finals, Prix Taittinger, 1993, 1994; Roux Diners Club Scholarship, 1995–98; Roux Scholarship, 2000–02; Slow Food, 2003–; Gourmet Voice, 2006–; Shackleton Fund Fellowship, 2001. Founder Mem., Guild of Food Writers, 1985. Chef Mem., Acad. of Culinary Arts (formerly Académie Culinaire de France), 1997. Columnist: Caterer & Hotelkeeper, 1988–94; Hampstead and Highgate Express, 1999–; Sunday Times of Malta, 2003–; Malta Taste, 2005–. FRSA. Glenfiddich Cookery Writer of the Year, 1994; James Beard Foundn Award, USA, 1995. *Television:* Frances Bissell's Westcountry Kitchen, 1995; Frances Bissell's Christmas Cooking, 1996. *Publications:* A Cook's Calendar, 1985; The Pleasures of Cookery, 1986; Ten Dinner Parties for Two, 1988; Sainsbury's Book of Food, 1989 (US edn, as The Book of Food, 1994); Oriental Flavours, 1990; The Real Meat Cookbook, 1992; The Times Cookbook, 1993; Frances Bissell's West Country Kitchen, 1996; (with Tom Bissell) An A–Z of Food and Wine in Plain English, 1999; The Organic Meat Cookbook, 1999; Modern Classics, 2000; Entertaining, 2002; Preserving Nature's Bounty, 2006; The Scented Kitchen, 2007; contrib. to Caterer and Hotelkeeper, Sunday Times Mag., Homes and Gardens, House & Garden, Country Living, Decanter, Country Life. *Recreations:* travelling and reading. *Address:* 2 Carlingford Road, Hampstead, NW3 1RX.

BISSON, Hon. Claude, OC 1999; Counsel, McCarthy Tétrault, Montreal, since 1996; a Judge of the Court of Appeal, Quebec, 1980–96; Chief Justice of Quebec, 1988–94; *b* 9 May 1931; *m* 1957, Louisette Lanneville; two *s* one *d*. *Educ:* Univ. de Laval, Quebec (BA 1950; LLL 1953). Called to Bar, Quebec, 1954. Superior Court Judge, Montreal, 1969–80. *Address:* (office) 1000 de La Gauchetière Street West, Montreal, QC H3B 0A2, Canada.

BISSON, Rt Hon. Sir Gordon (Ellis), Kt 1991; PC 1987; Judge of the Court of Appeal: New Zealand, 1986–91; Samoa, 1994–2004; Kiribati, 1999–2002; Chairman, New Zealand Banking Ombudsman Commission, 1992–97; *b* 23 Nov. 1918; *s* of Clarence Henry Bisson and Ada Ellis; *m* 1948, Myra Patricia Kemp; three *d*. *Educ:* Napier Boys High Sch.; Victoria Coll., Wellington; Univ. of NZ. LLB. Served War of 1939–45, RN and RNZN, 1940–45 (mentioned in despatches); Lt Comdr RNZNVR. Partner, Bisson Moss Robertshawe & Co., Barristers and Solicitors, Napier, NZ, 1946–78; Crown Solicitor, Napier, 1961; Judge, Courts Martial Appeal Ct, 1976; Judge of Supreme Ct, 1978. Vice-Pres., NZ Law Soc., 1974–77; Chm., NZ Sect., Internat. Commn of Jurists, 1979–92. Chairman: Indep. Tribunal for Allocation of Meat Export Quotas, 1995–97; New Entrants Allocation Cttee, NZ Meat Bd, 1998–2005. Order of Samoa, 2005. *Publication:* (jtly) Criminal Law and Practice in New Zealand, 1961. *Recreations:* tennis, fly-fishing, golf. *Address:* 341/4 Fergusson Drive, Heretaunga, Wellington 5018, New Zealand. *Clubs:* Wellington, Royal Wellington Golf (Wellington, NZ).

BISZTYGA, Jan; Officer's Cross of the Order of Polonia Restituta 1970; Order of Merit 1973; Senior Advisor to President, Bartimpex; *b* 19 Jan. 1933; *s* of Kazimierz Biszytyga; *m* 1956, Otylia; one *s*. *Educ:* Jagiellonian Univ. (MSc Biochemistry). Asst Professor, Jagiellonian Univ., Cracow, 1954–57; political youth movement, 1956–59; Min. for Foreign Affairs, 1959–63; Attaché, New Delhi, 1963–64; Min. for Foreign Affairs, 1964–69; Head of Planning Dept, Min. for Foreign Affairs, 1969–71; Dep. Foreign Minister, 1972–75; Ambassador in Athens, 1975–78, to UK, 1978–81; Ideology Dept, Polish United Workers' Party; expert in Office of Pres. of Polish Republic, 1990–91; Advr on Foreign Trade Enterprise, Euroamer, 1991–94; Advr to PM's Office, 1994–97; Pol Advr to Minister of Interior and Admin, 1997–2001; Advisor: to PM of Poland, 2001–03; The Foreign Trade Enterprise Bartimpex, 2003–06. *Recreations:* game shooting, fishing, history. *Address:* (home) Jaworzyńska 11–18, Warsaw, Poland; (office) Bartimpex, Al. Szucho 9, Warsaw, Poland. *T:* (622) 2757, 0604 787878, *Fax:* (621) 0943; *e-mail:* biuro@bartimpex.com.pl.

BITEL, Nicholas Andrew; Partner, Max Bitel Greene, since 1983; Chief Executive, London Marathon, since 1995; *b* 31 Aug. 1959; *s* of Max and Cecilia Bitel; *m* 1982, Sharon Levan; three *s*. *Educ:* St Paul's Sch., London; Davidson Coll., NC (Dean Rusk Schol.); Manchester Univ. (LLB). Admitted solicitor, 1983. Mem., Council, UK Sport, 2003–. Vice-Chm., Wigan Athletic, 1991–95. *Publications:* contribs to Sport and the Law Jl. *Recreations:* sports, theatre. *Address:* One Canonbury Place, N1 2NG. *T:* (020) 7354 2767, *Fax:* (020) 7226 1210. *Club:* MCC.

BJERREGAARD, Ritt Jytte; Lord Mayor, City of Copenhagen, since 2006; *b* Copenhagan, 19 May 1941; *d* of Gudmund Bjerregaard and Rita (*née* Hærslev); *m* 1966, Prof. Søren Mørch. Qualified as teacher, 1964. MP (Social Dem.), Denmark: Otterup (Fyn), 1971–95; Lejre, 1999–2005; Minister for: Educn, 1973 and 1975–78; Social Affairs, 1979–81; Mem., EC, 1995–99; Minister for Food, Agric. and Fisheries, 2000–01. Chm., Social Dem. Parly Gp, 1981–82 and 1987–92 (Dep. Chm., 1982–87). Pres., Danish European Movt, 1992–94. Mem., Trilateral Commn, 1982–2001. Vice-Pres., Danish delgn, CSCE, 1992–94. Vice-Pres., Socialist Internat. Women, 1992–94. *Publications:* books on educn and politics in Denmark, including: Strid, 1979; Til venner og fjender, 1982; I opposition, 1987; (with S. Mørch) Fyn med omliggende oor, 1989; Verden er saa stor, saa stor, 1990; Mine Æbler, 2003; Mit København, 2005; articles in Danish jls. *Recreation:* growing apples. *Address:* Rådhuset, 1599 København V, Denmark; Stestrup Old 17, 4360 Kirke Eskilstrup, Denmark.

BLACH, Rolf Karl, MD; FRCS, FRCOphth; Ophthalmologist, St Dunstan's, 1967–2004; Consultant Surgeon, Moorfields Eye Hospital, 1970–95; Dean, Institute of Ophthalmology, London University, 1985–91; *b* 21 Jan. 1930; *s* of Paul Samuel Blach and Hedwig Jeanette Blach; *m* 1960, Lynette Cecilia Sceales; two *s* one d. *Educ:* Berkhamsted Sch.; Trinity Coll., Cambridge (Sen. Schol.; MA); St Thomas' Hosp. MD 1965; FRCS

1962; FRCOphth (FCOphth 1989). Capt. RAMC, 1957–58. Jun. medical appts, St Thomas' Hosp. and Moorfields Eye Hosp., 1955–62; Sen. Registrar, Middlesex Hosp., 1962–63; Consultant Ophthalmic Surgeon, St Mary's Hosp., 1963–70; Hon. Consultant Ophthalmologist, RPMS, Hammersmith, 1967–70. Dep. Master, Oxford Ophthal. Congress, 1985. Vice Chm., British Council for Prevention of Blindness, 1996–2004; Mem. Cttee, W Berks Div., BMA, 2002–. Vice-Chm., Harpsden Parish Council (Mem., 2003–). Trustee, Harpsden Hall Trust, 2004–. Liveryman, Soc. of Apothecaries, 1970. *Publications:* articles on ophthalmology, esp. medical and surgical retina. *Recreations:* my family, aspects of history and PPE. *Address:* Summers, Northfield Avenue, Lower Shiplake, Henley-on-Thames, Oxon RG9 3PB. *T:* (0118) 940 4549, *Fax:* (0118) 940 2848; *e-mail:* rblach@waitrose.com. *Club:* Phyllis Court (Henley-on-Thames).

BLACK OF CROSSHARBOUR, Baron *cr* 2001 (Life Peer), of Crossharbour in the London Borough of Tower Hamlets; **Conrad Moffat Black,** OC 1990; PC (Can.) 1992; Chairman and Chief Executive Officer, Hollinger International Inc., 1990–2003; *b* 25 Aug. 1944; *m* 1st, 1978, Joanna Catherine Louise Hishon (name changed by deed poll in 1990 from Shirley Gail Hishon) (marr. diss., 1992); two *s* one *d*; 2nd, 1992, Barbara Amiel. *Educ:* Carleton Univ. (BA); Laval Univ. (LLL); MA History McGill, 1973. Chm. and Chief Exec., Ravelston Corp., 1979–2005; Chm., 1979, Chief Exec., 1985–2005, Argus Corp.; Chm., The Telegraph Gp Ltd, 1987–2005 (Dir, 1985–2005). Member: Editl Bd, Nat. Interest, Washington, 1997; Bd, Hudson Inst., USA, 2001. Hon. LLD: St Francis Xavier, 1979; McMaster, 1979; Carleton, 1989; Hon. LittD Univ. of Windsor, 1979. KLJ; KCSG 2001. *Publications:* Duplessis, 1977, rev. edn as Render Unto Caesar, 1998; A Life in Progress (autobiog.), 1993; Franklin Delano Roosevelt: champion of freedom, 2003; The Invincible Quest: the life of Richard Milhous Nixon, 2007.

BLACK, Alastair Kenneth Lamond, CBE 1989; DL; Under Sheriff of Greater London, 1974–94; Clerk, Bowyers' Company, 1985–94; *b* 14 Dec. 1929; *s* of Kenneth Black and Althea Joan Black; *m* 1st, 1955, Elizabeth Jane (*d* 1995), *d* of Sir Henry Darlington, KCB, CMG, TD; one *s* two *d*; 2nd, 1997, Mrs Susan Mary Miller. *Educ:* Sherborne Sch.; Law Soc. Coll. of Law. Admitted solicitor, 1953. Nat. Service, Intelligence Corps, 1953–55, Lieut. Partner in Messrs Burchell & Ruston, Solicitors, 1953–94. Dep. Sheriff, Co. of London, then Greater London, 1953–74; DL Greater London, 1978. Mem. Council, Shrievalty Assoc., 1985–91; Vice-Pres., Under Sheriffs Assoc., 1985–87, Pres., 1987–93. Member: House of Laity, Gen. Synod, 1982–97; (a Chm., Gen. Synod, 1991); Dioceses Commn, 1986–91; Ecclesiastical Fees Adv. Commn, 1986–96; Bd of Social Responsibility, 1992–96. Lay Reader, 1983–97. Governor, St Matthew's C of E Infant Sch., Cobham, 1995–97. *Publications:* contributions to: Halsbury's Laws of England, 4th edn, vols 25, 1978 (rev. edn 1994), and 42, 1983 (rev. edn 1999); Atkin's Court Forms, 3rd edn, vols 19, 1972 (rev. edn 1985), 22, 1968, and 36, 1977 (rev. edn 1988); Enforcement of a Judgement, 8th edn, 1993. *Recreations:* horseracing, gardening, travel. *Address:* Ashdene Farm, Priors Dean, Petersfield, Hants GU32 1BP. *T:* (01730) 827535.

BLACK, Dr Aline Mary; Headteacher, Colchester County High School for Girls, 1987–98; *b* 2 July 1936; *d* of Maurice and Harriet Rose; *m* 1972, David Black. *Educ:* Manchester Univ.; Birkbeck and King's Colls, London (BSc Hons Physics 1957; PGCE 1959; BSc Hons Chemistry 1970; PhD 1973). Res. Physicist, Richard, Thomas & Baldwins, 1957–58; Physics Teacher, Sir William Perkins' Sch., 1959–61; Head of Physics, City of London Sch. for Girls, 1961–71; Science Advr, Waltham Forest LBC, 1973–75; Science and Maths Advr, Bexley LBC, 1975–77; Headteacher: Leyton Sen. High Sch. for Girls, 1977–82; Gravesend Grammar Sch. for Girls, 1982–87. *Recreations:* archaeology, flying, sailing. *Address:* 11 Winchester Road, Frinton on Sea, Essex CO13 9JB. *T:* (01255) 852794.

BLACK, Col Anthony Edward Norman, OBE 1981; Chief Executive Commissioner, Scout Association, 1987–95; *b* 20 Jan. 1938; *s* of late Arthur Norman Black and Phyllis Margaret Ranicar; *m* 1963, Susan Frances Copeland; two *s*. *Educ:* Brighton College; RMA Sandhurst. Commissioned RE, 1957; served Kenya, Aden, Germany, Cyprus; Army Staff Course, Camberley, 1970; GSO1 Ghana Armed Forces Staff Coll., 1976–78; CO 36 Engr Regt, 1978–80; Col GS MGO Secretariat, 1980–82; Comd Engrs Falkland Islands, 1983; Comdt, Army Apprentices Coll., Chepstow, 1983–86; retired 1987. *Recreations:* gardening, bird watching. *Address:* National Westminster Bank, 50 High Street, Egham, Surrey TW20 9EU.

BLACK, His Honour Barrington (Malcolm); a Circuit Judge, 1993–2005; a Deputy Circuit Judge, since 2005; *b* 16 Aug. 1932; *s* of Louis and Millicent Black; *m* 1962, Diana Heller, JP; two *s* two *d*. *Educ:* Roundhay Sch.; Leeds Univ. (Pres. of Union, 1952; Vice-Pres., NUS, 1953–54; LLB). Admitted Solicitor, 1956. Served Army, 1956–58, commnd RASC. Partner, Walker, Morris & Coles, 1958–69; Sen. Partner, Barrington Black, Austin & Co., 1969–84. An Asst Recorder, 1987–91, a Recorder, 1991–93; a Metropolitan Stipendiary Magistrate, 1984–93. Chairman: Inner London Juvenile Court, 1985–93; Family Court, 1991–93. Mem. Court and Council, Leeds Univ., 1979–84. Councillor, Harrogate Bor. Council, 1964–67; contested (L) Harrogate, 1964. *Recreations:* ski-bobbing, opera, music. *Address:* c/o Harrow Crown Court, Harrow HA1 4TU.

BLACK, Benjamin; *see* Banville, J.

BLACK, Dame Carol (Mary), DBE 2005 (CBE 2002); FRCP, FMedSci; National Director for Health and Work, Department of Health and Department of Work and Pensions, since 2006; Chair, Academy of Medical Royal Colleges, since 2006; *b* 26 Dec. 1939; *d* of Edgar and Annie Herbert; *m* 1st, 1973, James Black (marr. diss. 1983); 2nd, 2002, Christopher Morley. *Educ:* Univ. of Bristol (BA Hist. 1962; Dip. Med. Social Studies 1963; MB ChB 1970; MD 1974). FRCP 1988; FRCSGlas 2003; FRCPI 2003; FRCPE 2003; FRCPCH 2003; FRACP 2003. Res. Fellow, Univ. of Bristol Sch. of Medicine, 1971–73; Consultant Rheumatologist: W Middx Univ. Hosp., 1981–89; Royal Free Hampstead NHS Trust, 1989–94; Prof. of Rheumatol., Royal Free and University Coll. Med. Sch., Univ. of London, 1994–2006 (Hon. Prof., 2006–); Med. Dir, Royal Free Hampstead NHS Trust, 2000–02. Member: Nat. Specialist Commng Adv. Gp, DoH, 2000–06; Appraisal Cttee, NICE, 1999–2002; NHS Modernisation Bd, DoH, 2002–04. Chm., Nuffield Trust, 2006–; Mem., Clin. Interest Gp, Wellcome Trust, 1996–2003 (Vice-Chm., 1997). Mem., Scientific Co-ordinating Cttee, Arthritis Res. Campaign, 1999–2004; Founder Member and Chairman: UK Scleroderma Gp, 1985–; Eur. Scleroderma Club, 1989–2003. Member Council: Section of Clin. Immunol. and Allergy, RSocMed, 1998–2000 (Pres., 1997–99); Acad. Med. Sci. Vice-Pres., 1998–2002, Pres., 2002–06, RCP; Vice-Chm., Acad. of Med. Royal Colls, 2003–05. FMedSci 1999; FACP 2002; FAMM 2003; FAMS 2003; Mem., Assoc. Physicians, 1997; CCMI 2002. Hon. Member: Italian Soc. Rheumatol., 1995; Turkish Soc. Rheumatol., 1995–. Hon. Fellow: UCL, 2003; Lucy Cavendish Coll., Cambridge, 2004. Hon. DSc Bristol, 2003. Mem., editl bds, various scientific jls. *Publications:* (with A. R. Myers) Systemic Sclerosis, 1985; (with J. Jayson) Scleroderma, 1988; contrib. scientific and med. papers in learned jls. *Recreations:* music, walking, travel, theatre. *Address:* Academy of Medical Royal Colleges, 1 Wimpole Street, W1G 0AE.

BLACK, Charles Stewart Forbes; a District Judge (Magistrates' Courts) (formerly a Metropolitan Stipendiary Magistrate), since 1993 (Chairman, Youth Courts, since 1994); *b* 6 Feb. 1947; *s* of Roger Bernard Black and Mary Agnes (*née* Murray); *m* 1976, Mhairi Shuna Elspeth McNab; one *d. Educ:* Kent Coll., Canterbury; Council of Legal Educn. Called to the Bar, Inner Temple, 1970; *ad eundem* Gray's Inn, 1973; Head of Chambers, 1981–93. *Recreations:* reading, playing with computers. *Address:* c/o Tower Bridge Magistrates' Court, 211 Tooley Street, SE1 2JY.

BLACK, Cilla, OBE 1997; entertainer; *b* 27 May 1943; *née* Priscilla Maria Veronica White; *m* 1969, Bobby Willis (*d* 1999); three *s. Television series include:* Cilla (8 series), 1968–76; Cilla's World of Comedy, 1976; Surprise, Surprise, 1984–99; Blind Date, 1985–2003; The Moment of Truth, 1998–2001; Soapstar Superstar, 2005; *films:* Ferry Cross the Mersey, 1964; Work is a Four-Letter Word, 1968; *recordings include:* (singles): Anyone Who Had a Heart, 1964; You're My World, 1964; It's For You, 1964; You've Lost that Lovin' Feeling, 1965; Love's Just a Broken Heart, 1966; Alfie, 1966; Don't Answer Me, 1966; Step Inside Love, 1968; Surround Yourself With Sorrow, 1969; Conversations, 1969; Something Tells Me, 1971; (albums): Cilla, 1965; Cilla Sings a Rainbow, 1966; Sher-oo!, 1968; Beginnings, 2003. Top TV Female Personality, Sun Awards, 1970, 1971, 1972, 1973 and 1974 (including a Gold Award); Favourite Female Personality on TV Awards, TV Times, 1986, 1988, 1989 and 1990; Top Female Comedy Star, Writers' Guild of GB, 1975; Variety Club Showbusiness Personality, 1991; Lew Grade Award, BAFTA, 1995. *Publications:* Step Inside, 1985; Through the Years: my Life in Pictures, 1993; What's It All About?, 2003.

BLACK, Colin Hyndmarsh; Chairman: Kleinwort Benson Investment Management Ltd, 1988–95; Merchants Trust, 1993–2000 (Director, 1992–2000); *b* 4 Feb. 1930; *s* of Daisy Louise (*née* Morris) and Robert Black; *m* 1955, Christine Fleurette Browne; one *s* one *d. Educ:* Ayr Acad.; Fettes Coll.; St Andrews Univ. (MA); Edinburgh Univ. (LLB). Brander and Cruickshank, Aberdeen, 1957–71 (Partner in charge of investment management); Globe Investment Trust, 1971–90, Dep. Chm., 1983–90. Chairman: Scottish Widows' Fund and Life Assurance Soc., 1987–95; Assoc. of Investment Trust Cos, 1987–89; non-executive Director: Temple Bar Investment Trust, 1963–2000; Clyde Petroleum, 1976–96; Electra Investment Trust, 1975–94; Kleinwort Benson Gp plc, 1988–95; Scottish Power plc, 1990–95; East German Investment Trust, 1990–96; Govett Asian Smaller Cos Investment Trust, 1994–2000 (Chm., 1994–2000); Postern Fund Management Ltd, 1996–99; PFM Carried Interest Ltd, 1996–2000. *Recreations:* travel, watching cricket, walking Labradors. *Address:* Patney House, Bath Road, Fyfield, Wilts SN8 1PU. *T:* (01672) 861451.

BLACK, Sir David; *see* Black, Sir R. D.

BLACK, Don, OBE 1999; lyric writer; *b* 21 June 1938; *s* of Betsy and Morris Blackstone; *m* 1958, Shirley Berg; two *s. Educ:* Hackney Central Sch. Professional lyric writer, 1960–; collaborates with Andrew Lloyd Webber, John Barry, Jule Styne, Elmer Bernstein and other leading composers; musicals include: Billy, 1974; Tell Me on a Sunday, 1979; Song and Dance, 1982; Aspects of Love, 1989; Sunset Boulevard, 1993; The Goodbye Girl, 1997; Bombay Dreams, 2002; Dracula, 2002; Romeo and Juliet: The Musical, 2002; Brighton Rock, 2004; films include: Thunderball, 1965; Diamonds Are Forever, 1971; The Man with the Golden Gun, 1974; Tomorrow Never Dies, 1997; The World is Not Enough, 1999. Numerous awards, UK and USA, including: Academy Award, 1966, for song Born Free; Tony Award, 1995, for Sunset Boulevard (Best Book for a musical, and Best Score, lyrics). Hon. DArts City, 2005. *Recreations:* snooker, swimming. *Address:* c/o John Cohen, Clintons, 55 Drury Lane, WC2B 5SQ. *T:* (020) 7379 6080. *Clubs:* Royal Automobile, Groucho.

BLACK, Air Vice-Marshal George Philip, CB 1987; OBE 1967; AFC 1962 (Bar 1971); FRAeS; Royal Air Force, retired 1987; Defence Consultant: BAE SYSTEMS, 2001–05; SELEX (Sensors and Airborne Systems), since 2005; *b* 10 July 1932; *s* of William and Elizabeth Black; *m* 1954, Ella Ruddiman (*née* Walker); two *s. Educ:* Hilton Acad., Aberdeen. Joined RAF, 1950; flying trng in Canada, 1951; served, 1952–64: fighter pilot; carrier pilot (on exchange to FAA); Flying Instr; HQ Fighter Comd; commanded No 111 (Fighter) Sqdn, 1964–66; Mem., Lightning Aerobatic Team, 1965; commanded Lightning Operational Conversion Unit, 1967–69; commanded No 5 (Fighter) Sqdn, 1969–70 (Huddleston Trophy); JSSC, 1970; Air Plans, MoD, 1971–72; Stn Comdr, RAF Wildenwrath, and Harrier Field Force Comdr, RAF Germany, 1972–74; Gp Captain Ops HQ 38 Gp, 1974–76; RCDS, 1977; Gp Captain Ops HQ 11 (Fighter) Gp, 1978–80; Comdr Allied Air Defence Sector One, 1980–83; Comdt ROC, 1983–84; DCS (Ops), HQ AAFCE, 1984–87. Air ADC to the Queen, 1981–83. Sen. Defence Advr, subseq. Dir, Mil. Marketing, GEC-Ferranti, 1987–93; Dir, Mil. Business Develt, Marconi Electronic Systems, subseq. BAE SYSTEMS, 1993–2000. FCMI (FBIM 1977). FRAeS 2001. *Recreations:* military aviation history, railways. *Address:* (office) 300 Capability Green, Luton, Beds LU1 3PG. *Club:* Royal Air Force.

BLACK, Guy Vaughan; Corporate Affairs Director, Telegraph Media Group, since 2005; *b* 6 Aug. 1964; *s* of Thomas Black and Monica Black (*née* Drew); civil partnership 2006, Mark William Bolland, *qv. Educ:* Brentwood Sch., Essex; Peterhouse, Cambridge (John Cosin Schol.; Sir Herbert Butterfield Prize for History, 1985; MA). Graduate Trainee, Corporate Banking Div., BZW, 1985–86; Desk Officer, Conservative Res. Dept, 1986–89; Special Advr to Sec. of State for Energy, 1989–92; Account Dir, Westminster Strategy, 1992–94; Associate Dir, Lowe Bell Good Relns, 1994–96; Dir, Press Complaints Commn, 1996–2003; Press Sec. to Leader of the Opposition, and Dir of Media, Conservative Central Office, 2004–05. Director: Advertising Standards Bd of Finance, 2005–; Press Standards Bd of Finance, 2006–. Mem. (C), Brentwood DC, 1988–92. Patron, Peterhouse Politics Soc., 2004–. Trustee: Sir Edward Heath's Charitable Foundn, 2006–; Imperial War Museum, 2007–. FRSA 1997; MCIPR 2007. *Recreations:* music, cats, reading. *Address:* (home) 34 Cannon Court, 5 Brewhouse Yard, EC1V 4JQ. *T:* (office) (020) 7931 3806. *Clubs:* Athenæum, London Press (Hon. Mem.).

BLACK, Helen Mary; Her Honour Judge Black; a Circuit Judge, since 2007; *b* 14 June 1959; *d* of Dennis and Carole Clifford; *m* 1981, Jonathan Black; two *s. Educ:* Ashburton High Sch.; Coll. of Law, Chester. Admitted solicitor, 1982; Partner, Addison Madden, Portsmouth, 1982–2000; Dep. Dist Judge, 1995–2000, Dist Judge, 2000–07, Principal Registry of Family Div.; Recorder, 2005–07. Family Tutor Team Mem., Judicial Studies Bd, 2004–. *Publication:* (ed) Butterworth's Family Law Service: vol. 21, Atkins Court Forms: Husband and Wife and Cohabitation, and civil partnerships, 2004–. *Recreations:* marathon running, ski-ing, mountain biking, having fun, Crystal Palace FC. *Address:* Portsmouth Combined Court Centre, The Courts of Justice, Winston Churchill Avenue, Portsmouth, Hants PO1 2EB. *Club:* Ladies' Ski (Chichester).

BLACK, James Walter; QC 1979; **His Honour Judge Black;** Judge, District Court of New South Wales, since 2000; *b* 8 Feb. 1941; *s* of Dr James Black and Mrs Clementine M. Black (*née* Robb); *m* 1st, 1964, Jane Marie Keyden; two *s* one *d*; 2nd, 1985, Diana Marjorie Day (*née* Harris); one *d. Educ:* Harecroft Hall, Gosforth, Cumbria; Trinity Coll., Glenalmond, Perthshire; St Catharine's Coll., Cambridge (MA). Called to the Bar, Middle Temple, 1964, NSW Bar, 1986; a Recorder, 1976–87. *Recreations:* fishing, sailing, golf. *Address:* PO Box 18, Lismore, NSW 2480, Australia.

BLACK, Sir James (Whyte), Kt 1981; OM 2000; FRCP; FRS 1976; Professor of Analytical Pharmacology, King's College Hospital Medical School, University of London, 1984–93, now Emeritus; Chancellor, Dundee University, 1992–2006; *b* 14 June 1924; *m* 1994, Rona McLeod MacKie, *qv. Educ:* Beath High Sch., Cowdenbeath; Univ. of St Andrews (MB, ChB). Asst Lectr in Physiology, Univ. of St Andrews, 1946; Lectr in Physiology, Univ. of Malaya, 1947–50; Sen. Lectr, Univ. of Glasgow Vet. Sch., 1950–58; ICI Pharmaceuticals Ltd, 1958–64; Head of Biological Res. and Dep. Res. Dir, Smith, Kline & French, Welwyn Garden City, 1964–73; Prof. and Head of Dept of Pharmacology, University College, London, 1973–77; Dir of Therapeutic Research, Wellcome Res. Labs, 1978–84. Mem., British Pharmacological Soc., 1961–. Hon. FRSE 1986. Hon. Fellow, London Univ., 1990. Mullard Award, Royal Soc., 1978; (jtly) Nobel Prize for Physiology or Medicine, 1988. *Address:* James Black Centre, King's College School of Medicine, SE5 9NU.

BLACK, Prof. Jeremy Martin, MBE 1999; PhD; Professor of History, University of Exeter, since 1996; *b* 30 Oct. 1955; *s* of Cyril Alfred Black and Doreen Black (*née* Ellis); *m* 1981, Sarah Elizabeth Hollis; one *s* one *d. Educ:* Haberdashers' Aske's Sch.; Queens' Coll., Cambridge (Entrance Schol.; Foundn Schol.; BA Starred First 1978; MA); St John's Coll., Oxford; Merton Coll., Oxford (Harmsworth Schol.; MA); PhD Dunelm 1983. University of Durham: Lectr, 1980–90; Sen. Lectr, 1990–91; Reader, 1991–94; Prof., 1994–95; Dir, Res. Foundn and Soc. of Fellows, 1990–95. Sen. Fellow, Foreign Policy Res. Inst., 2002–. Trustee, Agora. Mem., Council, Univ. of Exeter, 1999–2003. Ed., Archives, 1989–2005. FRSA 2005. *Publications:* The British and the Grand Tour, 1985; British Foreign Policy in the Age of Walpole, 1985; Natural and Necessary Enemies: Anglo-French relations in the eighteenth century, 1986; The English Press in the Eighteenth Century, 1987; The Collapse of the Anglo-French Alliance 1727–31, 1987; Culloden and the '45, 1990; The Rise of the European Powers 1679–1793, 1990; Robert Walpole and the Nature of Politics in Early-Eighteenth Century Britain, 1990; Europe in the Eighteenth Century, 1990, 2nd edn 2000; A System of Ambition?: British foreign policy 1660–1793, 1991; A Military Revolution?: military change and European society 1550–1800, 1991; War for America: the fight for independence 1775–1783, 1991; The British Abroad: the Grand Tour in the eighteenth century, 1992; Pitt the Elder, 1992; The Politics of Britain 1688–1800, 1993; History of England, 1993; British Foreign Policy in an Age of Revolution, 1994; European Warfare 1660–1815, 1994; Convergence or Divergence? Britain and the Continent, 1994; A History of the British Isles, 1996, 2nd edn 2003; Illustrated History of Eighteenth Century Britain, 1996; Warfare Renaissance to Revolution 1492–1792, 1996; America or Europe: British foreign policy 1739–63, 1997; Maps and History, 1997; Maps and Politics, 1997; War and the World: military power and the fate of continents 1450–2000, 1998; Why Wars Happen, 1998; From Louis XIV to Napoleon: the fate of a great power, 1999; Britain as a Military Power 1688–1815, 1999; A New History of England, 2000; Historical Atlas of Britain: the end of the Middle Ages to the Georgian era, 2000; War: past, present and future, 2000; Modern British History, 2000; A New History of Wales, 2000; British Diplomats and Diplomacy 1688–1800, 2001; The Politics of James Bond, 2001; War in the New Century, 2001; Eighteenth Century Britain, 2001; The English Press 1621–1861, 2001; Western Warfare 1775–1882, 2001; Western Warfare 1882–1975, 2001; Walpole in Power, 2001; The Making of Modern Britain. The Age of Edinburgh to the New Millennium, 2001; Europe and the World 1650–1830, 2001; European Warfare 1494–1660, 2002; The World in the Twentieth Century, 2002; America as a Military Power 1775–1882, 2002; France and the Grand Tour, 2003; Italy and the Grand Tour, 2003; World War Two: a military history, 2003; Visions of the World: a history of maps, 2003; Britain Since the Seventies: politics and society in the consumer age, 2003; Georgian Devon, 2003; The Hanoverians, 2004; The British Seaborne Empire, 2004; Parliament and Foreign Policy in the Eighteenth Century, 2004; Kings, Nobles and Commoners: states and societies in early modern Europe, 2004; War and the New Disorder in the 21st Century, 2004; Rethinking Military History, 2004; War since 1945, 2004; Using History, 2005; Introduction to Global Military History, 2005; A Subject for Taste: culture in eighteenth century England, 2005; The Continental Commitment: Britain, Hanover and interventionism 1714–1793, 2005; The European Question and the National Interest, 2006; George III, 2006; The Age of Total War 1860–1945, 2006; The Dotted Red Line: Britain's defence policy in the modern world, 2006; A Military History of Britain, 2006; The Slave Trade, 2006; Altered States: America since the Sixties, 2006; War in European History 1494–1660, 2006; Trade, Empire and British Foreign Policy 1689–1815, 2007; European Warfare in a Global Context 1660–1815, 2007; George II, 2007; A Short History of Britain, 2007; The Holocaust, 2008; The Curse of History, 2008; Great Powers and the Quest for Hegemony: the world order since 1500, 2008. *Recreations:* pub lunches, country walks, reading detective novels in a hot bath, talking, family and friends, travel to the USA. *Address:* Department of History, University of Exeter, Amory Building, Rennes Drive, Exeter EX4 4RJ. *T:* and *Fax:* (01392) 254567. *Club:* Athenæum.

BLACK, Hon. Dame Jill (Margaret), DBE 1999; **Hon. Mrs Justice Black;** a Judge of the High Court of Justice, Family Division, since 1999; *b* 1 June 1954; *d* of Dr James Irvine Currie and late Dr Margaret Yvonne Currie; *m* 1978, David Charles Black; one *s* one *d. Educ:* Penrhos Coll., Colwyn Bay; Durham Univ. (BA Hons Law). Called to the Bar, Inner Temple, 1976; QC 1994; a Recorder, 1999. *Publications:* Divorce: the things you thought you'd never need to know, 1982, 6th edn 2002; A Practical Approach to Family Law, 1986, 7th edn 2004; (with J. Bridge and T. Bond) The Working Mother's Survival Guide, 1988; (jtly) The Family Court Practice, annually, 1993–. *Address:* Royal Courts of Justice, Strand, WC2A 2LL.

BLACK, John Alexander; QC 1998; *b* 23 April 1951; *s* of late John Alexander Black and Grace Gardiner Black (*née* Cornock); *m* 1977, Penelope Anne Willdig (marr. diss. 2007); one *s* two *d. Educ:* St James' Choir Sch., Grimsby; Hull Univ. (LLB 1974). Called to the Bar, Inner Temple, 1975. *Recreations:* classical music, motor cars, political history. *Address:* 18 Red Lion Court, EC4 3EB.

BLACK, Adm. Sir (John) Jeremy, GBE 1991 (MBE 1963); KCB 1987; DSO 1982; Stia Negara Brunei 1963; Vice Admiral of the United Kingdom and Lieutenant of the Admiralty, 2001–03 (Rear Admiral of the United Kingdom, 1997–2001); *b* 17 Nov. 1932; *s* of Alan H. Black and G. Black; *m* 1958, Alison Pamela Barber; two *s* one *d. Educ:* Royal Naval College, Dartmouth (entered 1946). Korean War and Malayan Emergency, 1951–52; qualified in gunnery, 1958; commanded HM Ships: Fiskerton, 1960–62 (Brunei Rebellion, 1962); Decoy, 1969 (Comdr 1969, Captain 1974); Fife, 1977; RCDS 1979; Director of Naval Operational Requirements, Naval Staff, 1980–81; commanded HMS Invincible (Falklands), 1982–83; Flag Officer, First Flotilla, 1983–84; ACNS (Policy), Oct.-Dec. 1984; ACNS, 1985–86; Dep. CDS (Systems), 1986–89; C-in-C Naval Home Comd, 1989–91; Flag ADC, 1989–91. Chairman: Remy and Associates (UK) Ltd, 1992–96; Applied Visuals Ltd, 1998–2000; Berry Birch & Noble, 1999–2002; Director:

Devonport Management Ltd, 1992–97; Macallan-Glenlivet plc, 1993–96; Global Emerging Markets Europe Ltd, 1993–96; St Davids Investment Trust, 1996–98; Gosport Seaport Ltd, 1993–96; Consultant: Shorts, 1992–98; British Aerospace, 1993–97; Krug Champagne, 1996–99. Trustee, Imperial War Mus., 1991–97; Chm., Britain at War Mus., 1999–; Dir, Nat. Army Mus., 2004–. Mem. Council, RUSI, 1987–89. Gov., Wellington Coll., 1992–2003; Chm. Govs, Eagle House, 1998–2003. Chairman: Whitbread Round the World Race Cttee, 1990–94; Royal Navy Club of 1765 and 1785, 1992–95; Governor, Ocean Youth Club, 1991–95 (Chm., World Voyage, 1994–97). Life Vice Cdre, RNSA, 1991 (Cdre, 1989–91). *Recreations:* sailing, history. *Clubs:* Boodle's; Royal Yacht Squadron.

BLACK, John Newman, CEng, FICE, FIMarEST; FRGS; Partner, Robert West and Partners, Chartered Consulting Engineers, 1988–90; *b* 29 Sept. 1925; *s* of late John Black and late Janet Black (*née* Hamilton); *m* 1952, Euphemia Isabella Elizabeth Thomson; two *d*. *Educ:* Cumberland and Medway Technical Colls. Civil and marine engrg naval stations and dockyards, UK and abroad, incl. Singapore, Hong Kong, Colombo, Gibraltar and Orkney Isles, 1941–64; joined PLA as Civil Engr, 1964; Planning and Construction, Tilbury Docks, 1964–66; Planning Manager, 1967; seconded to Thames Estuary Develt Co. Ltd, for work on Maplin Airport/Seaport Scheme, 1969; Asst Dir Planning, PLA, 1970; Director: Maplin, 1972; Tilbury Docks, 1974; all London Docks, 1977; Man. Dir, 1978–81; Bd Mem., 1978–86, Chief Exec., 1982–86, and Dep. Chm., 1985–86, PLA. Dep. Chm., PLA (Met. Terminals) Ltd, 1974; Director: PLACON Ltd (PLA's cons. subsid. co.), 1972; Orsett Depot Ltd, 1974; Port Documentation Services Ltd (Chm.), 1978; Chairman: Thames Riparian Housing Assoc., 1974; PLA Group Property Holdings, 1984. Member: Exec. Council, British Ports Assoc., 1982–86; Exec. Cttee, Nat. Assoc. of Port Employers, 1982–86 (Vice-Chm., 1984–86); British Nat. Cttee, Permt Internat. Assoc. of Navigation Congresses, 1981–; London Maritime Assoc., 1975; Council, ICHCA Internat., 1985–86; Nat. Exec. Cttee, ICHCA (UK), 1985–88. Co-Adviser to Indian Govt on port ops and potential, 1968; lectures: for UN, Alexandria, 1975; for ESCAP (UN), Bangkok, 1983. Freeman: City of London, 1977; Watermen and Lightermen of River Thames, 1977. *Publications:* numerous articles and papers in Geographical Jl, Civil Engr and other learned jls. *Recreations:* shooting, fishing. *Address:* Westdene Cottage, Tanyard Hill, Shorne, near Gravesend, Kent DA12 3EN.

BLACK, John Nicholson, MA, DPhil, DSc; FRSE; Principal, Bedford College, University of London, 1971–81; *b* 28 June 1922; *e s* of Harold Black, MD, FRCP, and Margaret Frances Black (*née* Nicholson); *m* 1st, 1952, Mary Denise Webb (*d* 1966); one *s* one *d*; 2nd, 1967, Wendy Marjorie Waterston; two *s*. *Educ:* Rugby Sch.; Exeter Coll., Oxford. MA 1952, DPhil 1952, Oxford; DSc 1965, Adelaide; FRSE 1965. Served War, RAF, 1942–46. Oxford Univ., 1946–49; BA Hons Cl. 1 (Agric.) 1949; Agricl Research Council Studentship, 1949–52; Lectr, Sen. Lectr, Reader, Univ. of Adelaide (Waite Agricl Research Inst.), 1952–63; André Mayer Fellowship (FAO), 1958; Prof. of Forestry and Natural Resources, Univ. of Edinburgh, 1963–71. Dir and Sec., The Wolfson Foundn, 1981–87; Dir, The Wolfson Family Charitable Trust, 1987–89. Tutor in Ceramic Restoration, Missenden Abbey, 1993–98. Mem., NERC, 1968–74; Mem. Council and Finance Cttee, RAF Benevolent Fund, 1989–97. Conductor, City of Burnside Symphony Orch., SA, 1956–63; Chm., Donizetti Soc., 1984–87. Hon. Pres., Oxford Ceramic Gp, 2007–. *Publications:* The Dominion of Man, 1970; Donizetti's Operas in Naples, 1983; The Italian Romantic Libretto, 1984; (contrib. entries (26) on Italian librettists) The New Grove Dictionary of Opera, 1992; British Tinglazed Earthenware, 2001; papers on: ecological subjects in scientific jls (60); Italian opera libretti (25); history of ceramics (7). *Recreations:* music, repair and restoration of porcelain and pottery, lecturing on English delftware. *Address:* Paddock House, Pyrton, Watlington, Oxford OX49 5AP. *T:* (01491) 612600.

BLACK, Very Rev. Leonard Albert, SSC; Dean of Moray, Ross and Caithness, since 2003; Rector, St Michael and All Angels, Inverness, since 1980; *b* 19 March 1949; *s* of James Morrison Black and Mary Cruickshanks Black (*née* Walker); *m* 1975, Ruth Catherine (*née* Morrison); two *s* one *d*. *Educ:* Bernard Gilpin Soc., Durham; Edinburgh Theol Coll. (Luscombe Schol. 1972). Ordained deacon, 1972, priest, 1973; Curate, St Margaret of Scotland, Aberdeen, 1972–75; Chaplain, St Paul's Cathedral, and St Martin's, Dundee, with All Souls, Invergowrie, 1975–77; Priest i/c, St Ninian's, Aberdeen, 1977–80; Rector, St John the Evangelist, Inverness, and Priest i/c, Culloden Mission, 1980–87. Canon, St Andrew's Cathedral, Inverness, 1992–. Area Chaplain (Scotland), Actors' Church Union, 1987–2003; Northern Area Regional Chaplain, Missions to Seamen (Scotland), 1991–2002; Synod Clerk, Dio. of Moray, Ross and Caithness, 1992–2003. Mem., SSC, 1979–. Regional Dean (Scotland), Forward in Faith, 2001–. Commissary to Bishop of the Murray, Anglican Church of Australia, 2006; permission to officiate, dio. of the Murray, 2006. Religious Affairs and Community Progs Producer, Moray Firth Radio, Inverness, 1987–2004. Ed., Diocese of Moray, Ross and Caithness Diocesan Directory, 1985–2003. *Publications:* Churches of Diocese of Moray, Ross and Caithness, 1992, 2004; Sir Ninian Comper - Liturgical Architect, 1999; The Church that Moved Across the Water, 2003. *Recreations:* visiting Baroque churches and ancient archaeological sites, music, theatre, meeting people, reading. *Address:* St Michael's Rectory, Abban Street, Inverness IV3 8HH. *T:* (01463) 233797; *e-mail:* fr.len@angelforce.co.uk.

BLACK, Hon. Michael Eric John, AC 1998; **Hon. Chief Justice Black;** Chief Justice, Federal Court of Australia, since 1991; *b* 22 March 1940; *s* of Col E. R. E. Black, OBE; *m* 1963, Margaret Dungan; one *s* one *d*. *Educ:* St John's on the Hill, Chepstow; Wesley Coll., Melbourne; Univ. of Melbourne (LLB). Practice, Victorian Bar, 1964–90, ACT Bar, 1974–90; QC Victoria 1980, QC Tasmania 1984. Mem. Board, Royal Melbourne Hosp., 1986–90 (Chm., Ethics Cttee); The Defence Force Advocate, 1987–90. Co-Pres., Internat. Assoc. of Supreme Admin. Jurisdictions, 2007–. *Address:* Chief Justice's Chambers, Federal Court of Australia, 305 William Street, Melbourne, Vic 3000, Australia.

BLACK, Michael Jonathan; QC 1995; a Recorder, since 1999; *b* 31 March 1954; *s* of Samuel and Lillian Black; *m* 1984, Ann, *e d* of Keith and Rosa Pentol; two *s*. *Educ:* Stand Grammar Sch.; University College London (LLB). FCIArb 1991. Called to the Bar, Middle Temple, 1978, Bencher, 2006; an Asst Recorder, 1995–99; a Dep. Judge, Technology and Construction Court, 1999–. Asst Comr, Parly Boundary Commn for England, 2000–. Admitted to Bar: of Dubai Internat. Financial Centre Court, 2006; of Eastern Caribbean Supreme Court, 2007. Member: Civil Procedure Cttee, 2000–04; Panel of Mediators, Court of Appeal, 2001–03; Civil Justice Council, 2005–. Vis. Res. Fellow, UMIST, 1996–2002; Vis. Prof. of Construction and Engrg Law, Sch. of Mech., Aerospace and Civil Engrg, Manchester Univ. (formerly Manchester Centre for Civil and Construction Engrg), 2002–. FInstCES 2001. Liveryman, Arbitrators' Co., 2002 (Freeman, 2000). *Publications:* (contrib.) New Horizons in Construction Law, 1998; (contrib.) The Law and Practice of Compromise, 5th edn 2002, 6th edn 2005; (contrib.) Discovery Deskbook for Construction Disputes, 2006. *Address:* 2 Temple Gardens, Temple, EC4Y 9AY. *T:* (020) 7822 1200, *Fax:* (020) 7822 1300; Byrom Street Chambers, 12 Byrom Street, Manchester M3 4PP. *T:* (0161) 829 2100, *Fax:* (0161) 829 2101; *e-mail:* mbqc@2tg.co.uk. *Club:* Athenæum.

BLACK, Neil Cathcart, OBE 1989; Principal Oboist, English Chamber Orchestra, 1970–98; *b* 28 May 1932; *s* of Harold Black and Margaret Frances Black; *m* 1st, 1960, Jill (*née* Hemingsley); one *s* two *d*; 2nd, 1984, Janice Mary (*née* Knight). *Educ:* Rugby; Exeter College, Oxford (BA History). Entered musical profession, 1956; Principal Oboist: London Philharmonic Orch., 1959–61; in various chamber orchs, incl. London Mozart Players, Acad. of St Martin-in-the-Fields, 1965–72; Musical Dir, Kirckman Concert Soc., 1997–; oboe soloist internationally. Hon. RAM 1969. *Recreations:* wine, travel.

BLACK, Prof. Paul Joseph, OBE 1983; PhD; FInstP; Professor of Science Education, University of London, 1976–95 (in School of Education, King's College, 1985–95), now Emeritus Professor; Visiting Professor, Stanford University, California, 1999–2002; *b* 10 Sept. 1930; *s* of Walter and Susie Black; *m* 1957, Mary Elaine Weston; four *s* one *d*. *Educ:* Rhyl Grammar Sch.; Univ. of Manchester (BSc); Univ. of Cambridge (PhD). FInstP 1986. Royal Society John Jaffé Studentship, 1953–56. Univ. of Birmingham: Lectr in Physics, 1956–66; Reader in Crystal Physics, 1966–74; Prof. of Physics (Science Education), 1974–76; Dir, Centre for Science and Maths Educn, Chelsea Coll., Univ. of London, 1976–85; subseq., following merger of colls, Head, Centre for Educnl Studies, KCL, 1985–89 (FKC 1990); Dean, Faculty of Educn, Univ. of London, 1978–82. Educnl Consultant: to Nuffield Chelsea Curriculum Trust, 1978–93 (Chm., 1992–93); to OECD, 1988–96; Consultant to: World Bank, 1991; US Nat. Sci. Foundn, 1992. Vice-Pres., Royal Instn of Great Britain, 1983–85; Chairman: National Curriculum Task Gp on Assessment and Testing, DES, 1987–88; Internat. Commn on Physics Educn, 1993–99 (Mem., 1987–93); S London Cttee, RC Archdio. of Southwark Schs' Commn, 1996–2006; Dep. Chm., Grubb Inst. for Behavioural Studies, 1990–2002 (Mem. Council, 1983–2002; Chm., 1985–90; Hon. Vice-Pres., 1997); Member: School Curriculum Develt Cttee, 1984–88; Nat. Curriculum Council, 1988–91 (Dep. Chm., 1989–91); Exec., Univs Council for Educn of Teachers, 1982–86; Res. Grants Bd, ESRC, 1987–90; Exec., Editl Cttee for Nat. Sci. Educn Standards, Nat. Res. Council, USA, 1994–95; US Nat. Acad. of Scis Bd on Testing and Assessment, 1995–99. President: Groupe Internat. de la Recherche sur l'Enseignement de la Physique, 1984–91; Educn Section, British Assoc., 1992–93; Vice Pres. and Mem. Council, IUPAP, 1997–99; Hon. Pres., Assoc. for Science Educn, 1986 (Hon. Life Mem., 1986); Hon. Mem., Standing Conf. on Sch. Science and Technol., 1989. Trustee: Nat. Energy Foundn, 1992–2000; One Plus One Marriage and Partnership Research, 1996– (Chair of Trustees, 1997–). Hon. Mem., CGLI, 1989. FRSA 1990; Osher Fellow, San Francisco Exploratorium, 1993. DUniv: Surrey, 1991; Open, 2002; Hon. DEd Kingston, 2003. Bragg Medal, Inst. of Physics, 1973; Medal, Internat. Commn on Physics Educn, 2000; Dist. Contribs to Sci. Educn Res. Award, Nat. Assoc. for Res. in Sci. Teaching, USA, 2004; Lifetime Achievement Award, Assoc. for Sci. Educn, 2005. Kt of St Gregory, 1973. *Publications:* (jtly) Nuffield Advanced Physics Project, 1972; (contrib.) Higher Education Learning Project Books, 1977; (jtly) Open Work in Science, 1992; Nuffield Primary Science books (for Key Stages 1 and 2), 1993; (ed jtly) Children's Informal Ideas in Science, 1993; (ed jtly) Teachers Assessing Pupils: lessons from science classrooms, 1995; (jtly) Primary SPACE Project Research Reports: Light, 1990, Electricity, 1991, Processes of Life, 1992, The Earth in Space, 1994; (ed jtly) Changing the Subject, 1996; Testing: friend or foe, 1998; (jtly) Inside the Black Box, 1998; (ed jtly) Classroom Assessment and the National Science Education Standards, 2001; (jtly) Working Inside the Black Box, 2002; (jtly) Standards in Public Examinations, 2002; (jtly) Inside Science Education Reform, 2003; (jtly) Assessment for Learning, 2003; (jtly) Science Inside the Black Box, 2004; papers on crystallography, physics and science, technology education, and assessment in education. *Address:* 16 Wilton Crescent, SW19 3QZ. *T:* (020) 8542 4178.

BLACK, Peter Malcolm; Member (Lib Dem) South Wales West, National Assembly for Wales, since 1999; *b* 30 Jan. 1960; *s* of John Malcolm and Joan Arlene Black; *m* 1st, 1984, Patricia Mary Hopkin (marr. diss. 1995); 2nd, 2000, Angela Lynette Jones. *Educ:* Wirral Grammar Sch. for Boys; University Coll. of Swansea (BA Hons English and History). Exec. Officer, Land Registry for Wales, 1983–99. Member: (L) Swansea City Council, 1984–96; (Lib Dem) City and County of Swansea Unitary Council, 1996–. Chm., Lib Dem Wales, 1995–97 (Sec., Finance and Admin. Cttee, 1996–99). *Recreations:* theatre, poetry, films. *Address:* 115 Cecil Street, Manselton, Swansea SA5 8QL.

BLACK, Prof. Robert; QC (Scot.) 1987; FRSE; Professor of Scots Law, University of Edinburgh, 1981–2004, now Emeritus; *b* 12 June 1947; *s* of James Little Black and Jeannie Findlay Lyon. *Educ:* Lockerbie Acad.; Dumfries Acad.; Edinburgh Univ. (LLB); McGill Univ., Montreal (LLM); Lord Pres. Cooper Meml Prize, Univ. of Edinburgh, 1968; Vans Dunlop Scholarship, Univ. of Edinburgh, 1968; Commonwealth Scholarship, Commonwealth Scholarship Commn, 1968. Advocate, 1972; Lectr in Scots Law, Univ. of Edinburgh, 1972–75; Sen. Legal Officer, Scottish Law Commn, 1975–78; in practice at Scottish Bar, 1978–81; Temp. Sheriff, 1981–95. Chm., Inquiry into operations of Monklands DC, 1994–95. Gen. Editor, The Laws of Scotland: Stair Memorial Encyclopaedia, 1988–96 (Dep., then Jt, Gen. Editor, 1981–88). FRSA 1991; FRSE 1992; Founding Fellow, Inst. of Contemporary Scotland, 2000. *Publications:* An Introduction to Written Pleading, 1982; Civil Jurisdiction: the new rules, 1983; articles in UK, US and S African legal jls. *Recreation:* seeking to overturn the Lockerbie conviction. *Address:* 6/4 Glenogle Road, Edinburgh EH3 5HW. *T:* (0131) 557 3571; *e-mail:* rblackqc@gmail.com. *Club:* Royal Over-Seas League.

BLACK, Sir (Robert) David, 3rd Bt *cr* 1922; *b* 29 March 1929; *s* of Sir Robert Andrew Stransham Black, 2nd Bt, ED, and Ivy (*d* 1980), *d* of late Brig.-Gen. Sir Samuel Wilson, GCMG, KCB, KBE; *S* father, 1979; *m* 1st, 1953, Rosemary Diana (marr. diss. 1972), *d* of Sir Rupert John Hardy, 4th Bt; two *d* (and one *d* decd); 2nd, 1973, Dorothy Maureen, *d* of Major Charles R. Eustace Radclyffe and *widow* of A. R. D. Pilkington. *Educ:* Eton. Lieut, Royal Horse Guards, 1949; Captain 1953; Major 1960; retired, 1961. Served with Berkshire and Westminster Dragoons, TA, 1964–67, and Berkshire Territorials, TAVR III, 1967–69; Vice-Chm., Berkshire, Eastern Wessex TAVRA, 1985–92. Joint Master, Garth and South Berks Foxhounds, 1965–73. Hon. Col, 94 (Berks Yeo.) Signal Sqn (TA), 1988–98. DL Caithness, 1991–2004; High Sheriff, Oxfordshire, 1993. *Recreations:* shooting, gardening, fishing. *Heir:* none. *Address:* Beech Farm House, Woodcote, near Reading, Berks RG8 0PX. *T:* (01491) 682234. *Clubs:* Flyfishers', Cavalry and Guards.

BLACK, Prof. Robert Denis Collison, FBA 1974; Professor of Economics, and Head of Department of Economics, Queen's University Belfast, 1962–85, now Emeritus; *b* 11 June 1922; *s* of William Robert Black and Rose Anna Mary (*née* Reid), Dublin; *m* 1953, Frances Mary, *o d* of William F. and Mary Weatherup, Belfast; one *s* one *d*. *Educ:* Sandford Park Sch.; Trinity Coll., Dublin (Hon. Fellow, 1982). BA 1941, BComm 1941, PhD 1943, MA 1945. Dep. for Prof. of Polit. Economy, Trinity Coll., Dublin, 1943–45; Asst Lectr in Economics, Queen's Univ., Belfast, 1945–46, Lectr, 1946–58, Sen. Lectr, 1958–61, Reader, 1961–62. Rockefeller Post-doctoral Fellow, Princeton Univ., 1950–51; Visiting Prof. of Economics, Yale Univ., 1964–65; Dean of Faculty of

Economics and Social Sciences, QUB, 1967–70; Pro-Vice-Chancellor, 1971–75. President: Statistical & Social Inquiry Soc. of Ireland, 1983–86; Section F, BAAS, 1984–85. Distinguished Fellow, History of Economics Soc., USA, 1987. MRIA 1974. Hon. DSc(Econ) QUB, 1988. *Publications:* Centenary History of the Statistical Society of Ireland, 1947; Economic Thought and the Irish Question 1817–1870, 1960; Catalogue of Economic Pamphlets 1750–1900, 1969; Papers and Correspondence of William Stanley Jevons, Vol. I, 1972, Vol. II, 1973, Vols III-VI, 1977, Vol. VII, 1981; Ideas in Economics, 1986; Economic Theory and Policy in Context, 1995; articles in Economic Jl, Economica, Oxford Econ. Papers, Econ. History Review, Oxford DNB, etc. *Recreations:* travel, music. *Address:* Queen's University, Belfast, Northern Ireland BT7 1NN. *T:* (028) 9024 5133.

BLACK, Robert William, FSS; FRSE; Auditor General for Scotland, since 2000; *b* 6 Nov. 1946; *s* of Robert G. Black and Nell Black (*née* Gray); *m* 1970, Doreen Mary Riach, MBE; three *s* one *d.* *Educ:* Univ. of Aberdeen (MA Hons Econs); Heriot-Watt Univ. (MSc Town Planning); Univ. of Strathclyde (MSc Public Policy). Planner, Notts CC, 1971–73; Supervisory Planner, Glasgow CC, 1973–75; Gp Leader, Res. and Intelligence, 1975–80, Sen. Exec., Chief Exec.'s Dept, 1980–85, Strathclyde Regl Council; Chief Executive: Stirling DC, 1985–90; Tayside Regl Council, 1990–95; Controller of Audit, Accounts Commn for Scotland, 1995–2000. FSS 1984; FRSE 2006. Hon. LLD Aberdeen, 2004; Hon. DBA Queen Margaret UC, Edinburgh, 2006. *Recreations:* the outdoors, the arts. *Address:* Audit Scotland, 110 George Street, Edinburgh EH2 4LH. *T:* 0845 1461010, *Fax:* 0845 1461009. *Club:* New (Edinburgh).

BLACK, Roger Anthony, MBE 1992; former athlete; presenter, BBC Television, since 1998; corporate motivational speaker; *b* 31 March 1966; *s* of late David Black and of Thelma Black; one *d*; *m* 2002, Julia Burgess; twin *s.* *Educ:* Portsmouth Grammar Sch. Commonwealth Games: gold medal for 400m and 4 × 400m, 1986; European Championships: gold medal for 400m and 4 × 400m, 1986, 1990; silver medal for 400m, 1994; World Championships: gold medal for 4 × 400m, silver medal for 400m, 1991; Olympic Games: bronze medal for 4 × 400m, 1992; silver medal for 400m and 4 × 400m, 1996. Hon. MA Southampton, 1992. *Publication:* How Long's the Course? (autobiog.), 1998. *Recreations:* guitar, football, dog. *Address:* (office) 7 Stratfield Park, Elettra Avenue, Waterlooville, Hants PO7 7XN. *T:* (02392) 268866, *Fax:* (02392) 268777; *e-mail:* roger@rogerblack.co.uk.

BLACK, Rona McLeod, (Lady Black); *see* MacKie, R. M.

BLACK, Stewart; *see* Black, C. S. F.

BLACK, Prof. Susan Margaret, (Sue), OBE 2001; PhD; FRSE; Professor of Anatomy and Forensic Anthropology, University of Dundee, since 2003; *b* 7 May 1961; *d* of Alasdair John Gunn and Isabel Ann Gunn (*née* Bailey); *m* 1993, Thomas William Black; three *d.* *Educ:* Univ. of Aberdeen (BSc Hons 1982; PhD 1987). Lectr in Anatomy, UMDS, 1987–92; Consultant Forensic Anthropologist, Univ. of Glasgow, 1995–2001. Hd, Forensic Anthropol., Kosovo Mission, FCO, 1999–2000. Founder, 2001, and Sen. Ed., British Assoc. for Human Identification. Director: Centre for Internat. Forensic Assistance, 2001–; Nat. Advanced Training in Disaster Victim Identification, 2007–. FRSE 2005; Hon. FRCPSGlas 2007. Hon. DSc Robert Gordon, 2003. *Publications:* Developmental Juvenile Osteology, 2000; The Juvenile Skeleton, 2004. *Recreations:* writing, family. *Address:* Department of Anatomy and Forensic Anthropology, Faculty of Life Sciences, University of Dundee, Dundee DD1 5EH. *T:* (01382) 385776, *Fax:* (01382) 385893; *e-mail:* s.m.black@dundee.ac.uk.

BLACK, Timothy Reuben Ladbroke, CBE 1994; Founder, 1975 and Chief Executive, 1975–2006, Marie Stopes International; *b* 7 Jan. 1937; *s* of Stephen Joscelyn Ladbroke Black and Dorothy Joyce (*née* Bedford, now Mrs Paul Fletcher); *m* 1962, Jean Carter; two *d.* *Educ:* Dartington Hall Sch., Devon; Brighton Tech. Coll.; St George's Hosp., London Univ. (MB BS); Univ. of Northern Carolina (MPH 1970). MRCS 1962; LRCP 1962, MRCP 1966; DTM&H 1968; CDipAF 1989. Jun. House Officer, Harare Hosp., Salisbury, Rhodesia, 1962–63; Sen. House Officer, Croydon General and Mayday Hosps, 1963–64; Medical Registrar, Harefield Hosp., 1964–65; Consultant Physician, Rabaul and E Sepik Reg., New Guinea Med. Service, 1967; GP, NZ, 1968; Population Studies Fellow, Population Council and Ford Foundn, Univ. of N Carolina, 1969–70; Population Services International: Co-founder, 1970; Vice-Pres., 1970–75; Africa Regl Dir, Nairobi, Kenya, 1972–74. Chm., Options Consultancy Services Ltd, 1992–; Vice Pres., DKT Internat., 1985–. FRSTM&H 1970; FCMI (FIMgt 1985); FCIM 1989; FFSRH (FFFP 2006). *Publications:* numerous articles in population/family planning jls covering service delivery, contraceptive social marketing and mgt issues. *Recreations:* gardening, geese, hill-walking, trees, reading. *Address:* Gorsedene, Lower Beeding, Sussex RH13 6PX. *Club:* Royal Society of Medicine.

BLACKADDER, Dame Elizabeth (Violet), DBE 2003 (OBE 1982); RA 1976; RSA 1972; artist; Her Majesty's Painter and Limner in Scotland, since 2000; *b* 24 Sept. 1931; *m* 1956, John Houston. *Educ:* Falkirk High Sch.; Univ. of Edinburgh; Edinburgh Coll. of Art. Lectr, Sch. of Drawing and Painting, Edinburgh Coll. of Art, 1962–86. Exhibns, Mercury Gall., London, 1965–; retrospective exhibitions: Scottish Arts Council, 1981; Aberystwyth Arts Centre, 1989; Talbot Rice Gall., Edinburgh, 2000. Work in collections including: Scottish Nat. Gall. of Modern Art; Scottish Nat. Portrait Gall.; Nat. Portrait Gall.; Government Art Collection; Kettle's Yard, Cambridge; Hunterian Art Gall., Glasgow. Hon. FRIAS 1986; Hon. FRSE 1994. Hon. DLitt: Heriot-Watt, 1989; Strathclyde, 1998; Glasgow, 2001; St Andrews, 2003; Dr (*hc*): Edinburgh, 1990; London, 2004; Hon. LLD Aberdeen, 1997; Hon. Dr Stirling, 2002. *Relevant publications:* Elizabeth Blackadder, by Judith Bumpus, 1988; Elizabeth Blackadder, by Duncan Macmillan, 1999; Elizabeth Blackadder Prints, by Christopher Allan, 2003. *Address:* c/o Royal Scottish Academy, The Mound, Edinburgh EH2 2EL.

BLACKBEARD, Roy Warren; High Commissioner for Botswana in the United Kingdom, since 1998; *b* 16 April 1953. *Educ:* Kimberley Boys' High Sch. Official Learner, Metallurgy, De Beers, 1972–79; Audit Clerk, Price Waterhouse, 1973–74; CEO, Blackbeard & Co. (Pty) Ltd, 1974–89; ranch manager, 1974–96. MP, Serowe N, 1989–98; Asst Minister, 1992–94, Minister, 1994–97, of Agriculture, Botswana. Mem., Central DC, 1979–89 (Member: Gen. Purposes and Finance Cttee, 1979–89; Livestock Industry Adv. Cttee, 1979–89). Treas., Youth Wing, Botswana Democratic Party, 1980–96. Dir, Air Botswana, 1979–89. *Recreations:* sporting, skeet shooting, theatre, cinema, tennis. *Address:* Botswana High Commission, 6 Stratford Place, W1N 9AE. *T:* (020) 7499 0031, *Fax:* (020) 7495 8595; 34 Winnington Road, Hampstead, N2 0UB.

BLACKBOURN, Prof. David Gordon, PhD; FRHistS; Professor of History, since 1992, Coolidge Professor of History, since 1997, Harvard University; Director, Center for European Studies, Harvard, since 2007; *b* 1 Nov. 1949; *s* of Harry Blackbourn and Pamela Jean (*née* Youngman); *m* 1985, Deborah Frances Langton; one *s* one *d.* *Educ:* Leeds Modern Grammar Sch.; Christ's Coll., Cambridge (BA Hons Hist. 1970); MA 1974, PhD 1976, Cambridge. Res. Fellow, Jesus Coll., Cambridge, 1973–76; Lectr in History, QMC, Univ. of London, 1976–79; Birkbeck College, University of London: Lectr, 1979–85; Reader, 1985–89; Prof. of Mod. European History, 1989–92. Research Fellow: Inst. of European Hist., Mainz, 1974–75; Alexander von Humboldt Foundn, Bonn-Bad Godesberg, 1984–85; John Simon Guggenheim Meml Foundn, NY, 1994–95; Vis. Kratter Prof. of European Hist., Stanford Univ., 1989–90; Walter Channing Cabot Fellow, Harvard Univ., 2003–04. Lectures: Annual, German Histl Inst., London, 1998; Malcolm Wynn, Stetson Univ., Fla, 2002; George C. Windell Meml, Univ. of New Orleans, 2006; Crayenborgh, Leiden, Netherlands, 2007. Mem., Editl Bd, Past and Present, 1988–. Sec. 1979–81, Mem. Cttee 1981–86, German Hist. Soc.; Member, Academic Advisory Board: German Hist. Inst., London, 1983–92; Inst. for European Hist., Mainz, 1995–2006; Vice-Pres., 2002, Pres., 2003, Conference Gp on Central European Hist., American Hist. Assoc. Mem. Adv. Bd, Edmund Spevack Meml Foundn, 2003–. Pres., Bd of Friends, German Histl Inst., Washington, 2007– (Mem. 2004–). FRHistS 1987; Fellow, American Acad. of Arts and Scis, 2007. *Publications:* Class, Religion and Local Politics in Wilhelmine Germany, 1980; (with Geoff Eley) Mythen Deutscher Geschichtsschreibung, 1980 (Japanese edn 1983); (with Geoff Eley) The Peculiarities of German History, 1984; Populists and Patricians, 1987; (ed with Richard J. Evans) The German Bourgeoisie, 1991; Marpingen: apparitions of the Virgin Mary in Bismarckian Germany, 1993 (Amer. Historical Assoc. prize for best book in German history); The Fontana History of Germany: the long nineteenth century 1780–1918, 1997, 2nd edn as A History of Germany 1780–1918: the long nineteenth century, 2003; The Conquest of Nature: water, landscape and the making of modern Germany, 2006 (George L. Mosse Prize, Weyerhaeuser Prize, H-Soz-u-Kult Prize); (ed with James Retallack) Localism, Landscape and the Ambiguities of Place, 2007. *Recreations:* reading, jazz and classical music, sport, family. *Address:* Minda de Gunzburg Center for European Studies, Harvard University, 27 Kirkland Street, Cambridge, MA 02138, USA. *T:* (617) 4954303, *Fax:* (617) 4958509.

BLACKBURN, Bishop of, since 2004; **Rt Rev. Nicholas Stewart Reade;** *b* 9 Dec. 1946; *s* of late Sqdn Ldr Charles Sturrock Reade and Eileen Vandermere (*née* Fleming); *m* 1971, Christine Jasper, *d* of late Very Rev. R. C. D. Jasper, CBE, DD and of Ethel Jasper; one *d.* *Educ:* Elizabeth Coll., Guernsey; Univ. of Leeds (BA, DipTh); Coll. of the Resurrection, Mirfield. Ordained deacon, 1973, priest, 1974; Assistant Curate: St Chad's, Coseley, 1973–75; St Nicholas, Codsall, and Priest-in-charge of Holy Cross, Bilbrook, 1975–78; Vicar, St Peter's, Upper Gornal and Chaplain, Burton Road Hosp., Dudley, 1978–82; Vicar: St Dunstan's, Mayfield, 1982–88; St Mary's, Eastbourne, 1988–97; Archdeacon of Lewes and Hastings, 1997–2004. Rural Dean: Dallington, 1982–88; Eastbourne, 1988–97; Canon of Chichester Cathedral, 1990–2004 (Prebendary, 1990–97). Member: Gen. Synod of C of E, 1995–2000, 2002–; Dioceses Commn, 2001–05; Chm., Chichester Dio. Liturgical Cttee, 1989–97. President: Eastbourne and Dist Police Court Mission, 1994–; Crowhurst Christian Healing Centre, 2001–. Trustee: St Wilfrid's Hospice, Eastbourne, 1995–98; UC, Chichester, 2000–03; House of Bishops Healing Group, 2005–. Patron: Rosemere Cancer Foundn, 2005–; Derian House Children's Hospice, Chorley, 2006–; Skipton-East Lancs Rail Action Partnership, 2006–. *Recreations:* cycling, steam trains, modern ecclesiastical and political biographies. *Address:* Bishop's House, Ribchester Road, Clayton-le-Dale, Blackburn, Lancs BB1 9EF. *T:* (01254) 248234, *Fax:* (01254) 246668; *e-mail:* bishop@bishopofblackburn.org.uk. *Club:* National Liberal.

BLACKBURN, Dean of; *see* Armstrong, Very Rev. C. J.

BLACKBURN, Archdeacon of; *see* Hawley, Ven. J. A.

BLACKBURN, Dr Bonnie Jean, FBA 2005; freelance editor, since 1990; *b* 15 July 1939; *d* of John Hall Blackburn and Ruth Blackburn; *m* 1st, 1971, Edward E. Lowinsky (*d* 1985); one *d*; 2nd, 1990, Leofranc Holford-Strevens. *Educ:* Wellesley Coll., Mass (BA 1961); Univ. of Chicago (MA 1963, PhD 1970). Vis. Associate Prof., Univ. of Chicago, 1986; Lectr, Sch. of Music, Northwestern Univ., 1987; Vis. Associate Prof., State Univ. of NY, Buffalo, 1989–90; Mem., Common Room, Wolfson Coll., Oxford, 1993–. Hon. Mem., Faculty of Music, Oxford Univ., 1999–. *Publications:* (ed) Johannis Lupi Opera omnia, 3 vols, 1980–89; (ed jtly) A Correspondence of Renaissance Musicians, 1991; (with L. Holford-Strevens) The Oxford Companion to the Year, 1999; Composition, Printing and Performance: studies in Renaissance music, 2000; (with L. Holford-Strevens) The Oxford Book of Days, 2000; (ed) New Josquin Edition, 21–22: Motets on Non-biblical Texts De Domino Jesu Christo, 2003–07; contrib. articles to Basler Jahrbuch für historische Musikpraxis, Early Music Hist., Jl Musicol., Jl Amer. Musicol. Soc., Musica disciplina, Musical Qly, Studi musicali, Tijdschrift van de Koninklijke Vereniging voor Nederlandse Muziekgeschiedenis. *Recreation:* travel. *Address:* 67 St Bernard's Road, Oxford OX2 6EJ. *T:* (01865) 552808, *Fax:* (01865) 512237; *e-mail:* bonnie.blackburn@wolfson.ox.ac.uk.

BLACKBURN, Vice Adm. Sir David Anthony James, (Sir Tom), KCVO 2004 (LVO 1978); CB 1999; Master of HM Household, 2000–05; an Extra Equerry to the Queen, since 2000; *b* 18 Jan. 1945; *s* of late Lieut J. Blackburn, DSC, RN, and late Mrs M. J. G. Pickering-Pick; *m* 1973, Elizabeth Barstow; three *d.* *Educ:* Taunton Sch. RNC Dartmouth, 1963; HMS Kirkliston (in comd), 1972–73; Equerry-in-Waiting to the Duke of Edinburgh, 1976–78; Exec. Officer, HMS Antrim, 1978–81; MoD (Navy), 1981–83; Comdr, HMS Birmingham, 1983–84; MoD (Navy), 1984–86; HMS York (in comd) and Captain Third Destroyer Sqn, 1987–88; Dir, Naval Manpower and Trng (Seamen), MoD, 1988–90; Cdre, Clyde, and Naval Base Comdr, Clyde, 1990–92; HMS Cornwall (in comd) and Captain, Second Frigate Sqn, 1992–93; Defence Attaché and Hd of British Defence Staff, Washington, 1994–97; COS to Comdr Allied Naval Forces Southern Europe, 1997–99. Mem., Pensions Appeal Tribunal, 2005–. Chairman: St John Ambulance (London Dist), 2006–; Marine Soc. & Sea Cadets, 2006–; Dep. Chm., RYA, 2007–. *Clubs:* Army and Navy; Royal Cruising.

BLACKBURN, Elizabeth; QC 1998; *b* 5 Oct. 1954; *d* of Robert Arnold Parker and Edna Parker (*née* Baines); *m* 1979, John Blackburn, *qv*; two *s.* *Educ:* City of London Sch. for Girls; Manchester Univ. (BA Hons English 1976). Called to the Bar, Middle Temple, 1978 (Harmsworth Schol.); in practice at the Bar, 1978–, specialising in commercial and admiralty law, 1980–; Examr, High Court, 1987–90. Mem., Exec. Cttee, British Maritime Law Assoc., 2003–. Mem., UK delegn, Internat. Oil Pollution Compensation Supplementary Fund Protocol Diplomatic Conf., 2003; Legal Mem., DCMS Adv. Cttee on Historic Wreck Sites, 2004–. *Recreations:* family life, gardening, France. *Address:* Stone Chambers, 4 Field Court, Gray's Inn, WC1R 5EF. *T:* (020) 7440 6900.
See also R. S. Parker.

BLACKBURN, Prof. Elizabeth Helen, (Mrs J. W. Sedat), PhD; FRS 1992; Professor of Biochemistry and Biophysics, University of California, San Francisco, since 1990 (Chair, Department of Microbiology and Immunology, 1993–99); *b* 26 Nov. 1948; *d* of Harold Stewart Blackburn and Marcia Constance (*née* Jack); *m* 1975, John William Sedat; one *s.* *Educ:* Univ. of Melbourne (BSc Hons 1970; MSc 1972); Cambridge Univ. (PhD 1975). University of California, Berkeley: Asst Prof., Dept of Molecular Biol., 1978–83; Associate Prof., 1983–86; Prof. of Molecular Biology, 1986–90. Pres., Amer. Soc. for Cell

Biol., 1998. Mem., Amer. Acad. Arts and Scis; For. Associate, Nat. Acad. of Scis, USA, 1993. Hon. DSc Yale, 1991. Award for Molecular Biol., Nat. Acad. Scis, USA, 1990; Australia Prize, 1998; Gairdner Prize, Gairdner Foundn, 1998; General Motors Sloan Prize, 2001; Lasker Prize, 2006. *Publications:* research and review articles in Nature, Science, Cell. *Recreation:* music. *Address:* Department of Biochemistry and Biophysics, University of California, 600 16th Street, Box 2200, San Francisco, CA 94143–2200, USA. *T:* (415) 4764912.

BLACKBURN, (Jeffrey) Michael; Chief Executive, Halifax Building Society, then Halifax plc, 1993–98; *b* 16 Dec. 1941; *s* of Jeffrey and Renee Blackburn; *m* 1987, Louise Clair Jouny; two *s*, and one *s* one *d* from a previous marriage. *Educ:* Northgate Grammar Sch., Ipswich. FCIB. Chief Manager, Lloyds Bank Business Adv. Service, 1979–83; Dir and Chief Exec., Joint Credit Card Co. Ltd, 1983–87; Dir and Chief Exec., Leeds Permanent Building Soc., 1987–93. Director: DFS Furniture plc, 1999–2004; George Wimpey PLC, 1999–2005; Town Centre Securities plc, 1999–2002; In Kind Direct, 1999– (Dep. Chm., 2001–); Freeport plc, 2003–07; Chm., Fairpoint (formerly Debt Free Direct) Gp plc, 2005–. Pres., CIB, 1998–99. Mem. Court, Leeds Univ., 2001–07. Gov., NYO, 1999–2007; Trustee, Duke of Edinburgh's Award, 1998–. CCMI; FRSA. DUniv Leeds Metropolitan, 1998; Hon. DLitt Huddersfield, 1998. *Recreations:* music, theatre. *Address:* c/o Fairpoint Group plc, Fairclough House, Church Street, Adlington, Chorley, PR7 4EX. *Club:* Oriental.

BLACKBURN, John; QC 1984; barrister; *b* 13 Nov. 1945; *s* of Harry and Violet Blackburn; *m* 1st, 1970, Alison Nield (marr. diss. 1978); 2nd, 1979, Elizabeth Parker (*see* E. Blackburn); two *s*. *Educ:* Rugby Sch.; Worcester Coll., Oxford (Scholar, 1967; Gibbs Prize in Law, 1967). Called to the Bar, Middle Temple, 1969 (Astbury Law Scholar), Bencher, 1993. Practising barrister, 1970–. *Recreations:* cricket, golf, paintings, wine. *Address:* 1 Atkin Building, Gray's Inn, WC1R 5AT.

BLACKBURN, Ven. John, CB 2004; Vicar of Risca, Gwent, since 2004; *b* 3 Dec. 1947; *m* 1970, Anne Elisabeth Woodcock; two *d*. *Educ:* University Coll., Cardiff (DipTh); St Michael's Coll., Llandaff (DPS 1971); Open Univ. (BA Hons 1988; AdvDipEd; BSc 2004). Deacon 1971, priest 1972; Curate, Risca, 1971–76; Chaplain, HM Forces, 1976–2004: Dep. Chaplain-Gen., 1999–2000, Chaplain-Gen., 2000–04; Archdeacon of HM Land Forces, 1999–2004, now Emeritus. QHC 1996–2004. Hon. Canon, Ripon Cathedral, 2001–04, now Canon Emeritus. Chm., Gwent Br., SSAFA, 2006–. FRSA 1999. *Recreations:* travelling, game shooting, reading, English watercolours. *Address:* The Vicarage, 1 Gelli Crescent, Risca, Newport, Gwent NP1 6QG. *Club:* National.

BLACKBURN, Mark Alistair Sinclair, PhD; FSA; Keeper of Coins and Medals, Fitzwilliam Museum, since 1991, and Reader in Numismatics and Monetary History, since 2004, University of Cambridge; Fellow, Gonville and Caius College, Cambridge, since 2005; *b* 5 Jan. 1953; *y s* of late Neil Blackburn and Joan Wallace Blackburn; *m* 1980, Fiona Anne Haigh; two *s* one *d*. *Educ:* Skinners' Sch.; St Edmund Hall, Oxford (BA Juris. 1975); Gonville and Caius Coll., Cambridge (PhD 1994). Called to the Bar, Middle Temple, 1976; in practice, 1976–78; Kleinwort Benson Ltd, 1978–82; Res. Associate, 1982–86, Sen. Res. Associate, 1986–91, Fac. of Hist., Univ. of Cambridge; Bye-Fellow, Gonville and Caius Coll., Cambridge, 1990–91. Mem. British Acad. Cttee, Sylloge of Coins of the British Isles, 1980– (Jt Editor, 1980–87; Gen. Editor and Sec., 1987–); Dir, Corpus of Early Medieval Coin Finds from British Isles proj., 1996–. Pres., British Numismatic Soc., 2003– (Ed., British Numismatic Jl, 1983–87); FRNS 1976 (Editor, Numismatic Chronicle, 1992–98); FSA 1983; FRHistS 1989. Member Editorial Board: Studies in Anglo-Saxon History, 1985–98; Anglo-Saxon England, 1991–; Revue Belge de Numismatique, 2007–. Gov., Skinners' Sch., 2007–. Liveryman, Skinners' Co., 2008. Société Française de Numismatique Medal, 1991; Royal Numismatic Soc. Medal, 2008. *Publications:* (ed jtly) Viking-Age Coinage in the Northern Lands, 1981; (jtly) Early Medieval Coins from Lincoln and its Shire c.770–1100, 1983; (jtly) Medieval European Coinage 1: the Early Middle Ages (5th–10th Century), 1986; (ed) Anglo-Saxon Monetary History, 1986; (ed jtly) Kings, Currency and Alliances, 1996; contrib. books and learned jls. *Recreation:* travelling off the beaten track. *Address:* Fitzwilliam Museum, Trumpington Street, Cambridge CB2 1RB. *T:* (01223) 332900; *e-mail:* mab1001@cam.ac.uk.

BLACKBURN, Michael; *see* Blackburn, J. M.

BLACKBURN, Michael John, FCA; Chairman, Touche Ross & Co., 1990–92 (Managing Partner, 1984–90); *b* 25 Oct. 1930; *s* of Francis and Ann Blackburn; *m* 1955, Maureen (*née* Dale); one *s* two *d*. *Educ:* Kingston Grammar Sch. Joined Touche Ross, 1954; Partner, 1960. Chm., GEI International, 1990–95; Deputy Chairman: Aerostructures Hamble Hldgs, 1992–95; Blue Arrow Hldgs, 1992–96; Director: Chubb Security, 1992–97; William Hill Gp, 1992–99; Steel, Burrill Jones, 1992–99; Wolverhampton Wanderers FC, 1995–97. Chm., Voices for Hospices, 1990–2001. *Recreations:* horse racing, the garden.

BLACKBURN, Peter Hugh, CBE 2003; FCA; Chairman, Northern Foods, 2002–05; *b* 17 Dec. 1940; *s* of Hugh Edward Blackburn and Sarah Blackburn (*née* Moffatt); *m* 1967, Gillian Mary Popple; three *d*. *Educ:* Douai Sch., Reading; Leeds Univ. (BA Hons Philosophy and French); Poitiers Univ. (Dipl. French); Inst. of Chartered Accts; AMP, Harvard Business Sch., 1976. R. S. Dawson & Co., Bradford (articles), 1962–66; various positions within John Mackintosh and Rowntree Mackintosh, 1966–91; Chm., Rowntree UK, 1985–91; Head, Nestlé Chocolate, Confectionery and Biscuit Strategy Group, 1989–90; Chm. and Chief Exec., Nestlé UK, 1991–96 and 1997–2001; Pres. and Dir Gen., Nestlé France, 1996–97. Non-executive Director: SIG, 2001–; Compass Gp, 2002–07. President: ISBA, 1998–2000; FDF, 2000–02. Nat. Pres., Modern Languages Assoc., 1987–89; Chm., Council, Festival of Languages Young Linguist Competition, 1985–89; Chm., Harrogate Internat. Fest., 2004–. Mem., Council of Industry and Higher Educn, 1990–92. Mem. Council, York Univ., 1989–92, 2001–03. York Merchant Adventurers, 1989–2006. FIGD 1991. Hon. FCIL (Hon. FIL 1989). Hon. DLitt Bradford, 1991; Hon. DBA Leeds Metropolitan, 2005. Chevalier du Tastevin, 1984. *Recreations:* fell walking, swimming, photography.

BLACKBURN, Ven. Richard Finn; Archdeacon of Sheffield and Rotherham (formerly Archdeacon of Sheffield), since 1999; *b* 22 Jan. 1952; *s* of William Brow Blackburn and Ingeborg Blackburn (*née* Lerche-Thomsen); *m* 1980, Helen Claire Davies; one *s* three *d*. *Educ:* Aysgarth Sch.; Eastbourne Coll.; St John's Coll., Durham Univ. (BA); Hull Univ. (MA); Westcott House, Cambridge. National Westminster Bank, 1976–81; deacon 1983, priest 1984; Curate, St Dunstan and All Saints, Stepney, 1983–87; Priest-in-charge, St John the Baptist, Isleworth, 1987–92; Vicar of Mosborough, 1992–99; RD of Attercliffe, 1996–99; Hon. Canon, 1998–99, Residentiary Canon, 1999–2005, Sheffield Cathedral. Dignitary in Convocation, 2000–05. Mem., C of E Pensions Bd, 2003– (Vice Chm., 2006–); Chair, Churches Regl Commn for Yorks and the Humber, 2005–. Member, School Council: Worksop Coll., 2000–; Ranby House Sch., 2000–. *Recreations:* rowing, walking, gardening, music. *Address:* Sheffield Diocesan Church House, 95–99 Effingham Street, Rotherham, South Yorks S65 1BL. *T:* (01709) 309110; *e-mail:* archdeacons.office@sheffield.anglican.org; (home) 34 Wilson Road, Sheffield S11 8RN.

BLACKBURN, Prof. Simon Walter, PhD; FBA 2002; Professor of Philosophy, University of Cambridge, since 2001; *b* 12 July 1944; *s* of Cuthbert and Edna Blackburn; *m* 1968, Angela Bowles; one *s* one *d*. *Educ:* Trinity Coll., Cambridge (BA 1965; PhD 1970). Research Fellow, Churchill Coll., Cambridge, 1967–70; Fellow and Tutor in Philosophy, Pembroke Coll., Oxford, 1970–90; Edna J. Koury Dist. Prof. of Philosophy, Univ. of N Carolina, 1990–2000. Visiting Professor: Princeton Univ., 1987; Ohio State Univ., 1988; Adjunct Prof., ANU, 1993–. Fellow, Amer. Acad. of Arts and Scis, 2008. Editor, Mind, 1984–90. *Publications:* Reason and Prediction, 1973; Spreading the Word, 1984; Essays in Quasi Realism, 1993; Oxford Dictionary of Philosophy, 1994; Ruling Passions, 1998; Think, 1999; Being Good, 2001; Lust, 2004; Truth: a guide for the perplexed, 2005; Plato's Republic, 2006; How to Read Hume, 2008. *Recreations:* hill-walking, sailing, photography. *Address:* 141 Thornton Road, Cambridge CB3 0NE. *T:* (01223) 528278.

BLACKBURN, Vice Adm. Sir Tom; *see* Blackburn, Vice Adm. Sir D. A. J.

BLACKBURNE, Alison; HM Diplomatic Service; Counsellor and Deputy Head of Mission, Harare, since 2003; *b* 20 June 1964. *Educ:* Leeds Univ. (BA Hons French/Russian). Entered FCO, 1987; Third, later Second, Sec. (Chancery), Warsaw, 1989–92; First Secretary: FCO, 1992–96; UKMIS, NY, 1996–2000; (Political), Stockholm, 2000–03. *Address:* c/o Foreign and Commonwealth Office, King Charles Street, SW1A 2AH.

BLACKBURNE, Hon. Sir William (Anthony), Kt 1993; **Hon. Mr Justice Blackburne;** Judge of the High Court of Justice, Chancery Division, since 1993; *b* 24 Feb. 1944; *m* 1996, Vivien, *d* of A. C. Webber. Vice-Chancellor of the County Palatine of Lancaster, 1998–2002. *Address:* Royal Courts of Justice, Strand, WC2A 2LL.

BLACKER, Dr Carmen Elizabeth, OBE 2004; FBA 1989; FSA; Lecturer in Japanese, 1958–91, and Fellow of Clare Hall, 1965–91, now Fellow Emeritus, Cambridge University; Professor, Ueno Gakuen University, Tokyo, since 1996; *b* 13 July 1924; *d* of Carlos Paton Blacker, MC, GM, MA, MD, FRCP and Helen Maud Blacker (*née* Pilkington). *Educ:* Benenden School; School of Oriental Studies, London University; Somerville Coll., Oxford (Hon. Fellow, 1991). PhD London Univ., 1957. Visiting Professor: Columbia Univ., 1965; Princeton Univ., 1979; Ueno Gakuen Univ., Tokyo, 1991; Toronto Univ., 1992; Vis. Fellow, Kyoto Univ., 1986. Pres., Folklore Soc., 1982–84 (Hon. Mem., 1988). Minakata Kumagusu Prize, 1997. FSA 2004. Order of the Precious Crown (Japan), 1988. *Publications:* The Japanese Enlightenment: a study of the writing of Fukuzawa Yukichi, 1964; The Catalpa Bow: a study of Shamanistic practices in Japan, 1975, rev. edn 1986; Collected Papers, 2000; The Straw Sandal or The Scroll of the Hundred Crabs, 2008; articles in Monumenta Nipponica, Folklore, Trans of Asiatic Soc. of Japan, Asian Folklore Studies, etc. *Recreations:* walking, comparative mythology. *Address:* Willow House, Grantchester, Cambridge CB3 9NF. *T:* (01223) 840196. *Club:* University Women's.

BLACKER, Captain Derek Charles, RN; Director of Personnel, Orion Royal Bank Ltd, 1984–88; *b* 19 May 1929; *s* of Charles Edward Blacker and Alexandra May Farrant; *m* 1952, Brenda Mary Getgood (*d* 2001); one *s* one *d*. *Educ:* County Sch., Isleworth; King's Coll., Univ. of London (BSc Hons 1950). Entered RN, 1950; specialisations: navigation, meteorology, oceanography; HMS Birmingham, HMS Albion, BRNC Dartmouth, HMS Hermes, 1956–69; Comdr 1965; NATO Commands: SACLANT, 1969; CINCHAN, 1972; SACEUR, 1974; Captain 1975; Dir of Public Relations (RN), 1977–79; Bd Pres., Admiralty Interview Bd, 1980; staff of C-in-C, Naval Home Comd, 1980–81; Dir of Naval Oceanography and Meteorology, MoD, 1981–84. Naval ADC to the Queen, 1983–84. Chm., Teignbridge DFAS, 2006– (Visits Sec., 1997–2003; Hon. Treas., 2003–06). Hon. Treas., Exeter Br., ESU, 2005–. *Recreations:* music, golf, country pursuits. *Address:* Frenchacre, 16 Coach Road, Newton Abbot, Devon TQ12 1EW. *Club:* Army and Navy.

BLACKER, Norman; Executive Director, British Gas, 1989–95; *b* 22 May 1938; *m* 1st, 1961, Jennifer Mary Anderson (*d* 1992); 2nd, 1994, Carol Anderson. *Educ:* Wolverton Grammar School. CPFA. British Gas: Dir of Finance, Northern Reg., 1976–80; Dir of Finance, 1980–84; Chm., N Eastern Region, then British Gas N Eastern, 1985–89; Managing Director: Eastern Regions, 1989–91; Regl Services, 1991–92; Gas Business, 1992–94. Chm., Nat. Council for Hospice and Specialist Palliative Care Services, 1994–2000. *Address:* 4 White Heather Court, Hythe Marina Village, Hythe SO45 6DT.

BLACKETT, Sir Hugh Francis, 12th Bt *cr* 1673, of Newcastle, Northumberland; *b* 11 Feb. 1955; *e s* of Major Sir Francis Hugh Blackett, 11th Bt and his 1st wife, Elizabeth Eily Barrie (*née* Dennison) (*d* 1982); *S* father, 1995; *m* 1982, Anna, *yr d* of J. St G. Coldwell; one *s* three *d*. *Educ:* Eton. High Sheriff, Northumberland, 2007–08. *Heir:* *s* Henry Douglas Blackett, *b* 2 Feb. 1992.

BLACKETT, Jeffrey; His Honour Judge Cdre Blackett; a Circuit Judge and Judge Advocate General of the Armed Forces, since 2004; *b* 20 May 1955; *s* of Lt Comdr William Blackett and Gwendoline Blackett; *m* 1981, Sally Anne Fulford; one *s* one *d*. *Educ:* Portsmouth Grammar Sch.; University Coll. London (LLB 1976); Council of Legal Educn; St Antony's Coll., Oxford (MSt 2000). Called to the Bar, Gray's Inn, 1983. Served RN, Supply and Secretariat Br., 1973–2004; Comdr, HMS Collingwood, 1995–97; Dir, Pay and Pensions, 1997–99; Chief Naval Judge Advocate, 2000–04. Actg Metropolitan Stipendiary Magistrate, 1995–99; a Recorder, 2000–04. *Publication:* (with J. W. Rant) Courts-Martial, Discipline and the Criminal Process in the Armed Services, 2003. *Recreations:* Rugby (Hon. Discipline Officer, RFU), squash, golf. *Address:* Office of the Judge Advocate General, 81 Chancery Lane, WC2A 1BQ. *T:* (020) 7218 8075, *Fax:* (020) 7218 8090; *e-mail:* jeff.blackett@justice.gsi.gov.uk.

BLACKETT-ORD, His Honour Andrew James, CVO 1988; a Circuit Judge, 1972–87; Vice-Chancellor, County Palatine of Lancaster, 1973–87; *b* 21 Aug. 1921; 2nd *s* of late John Reginald Blackett-Ord, Whitfield, Northumberland; *m* 1945, Rosemary Bovill; three *s* one *d*. *Educ:* Eton; New Coll., Oxford (MA). Scots Guards, 1943–46; called to Bar, 1947, Bencher, Lincoln's Inn, 1985; County Court Judge, 1971. Mem. Council, Duchy of Lancaster, 1973–87. Chancellor, dio. of Newcastle-upon-Tyne, 1971–98. *Recreations:* reading, art, shooting, country life, travel. *Address:* Helbeck Hall, Brough, Kirkby Stephen, Cumbria CA17 4DD. *T:* (017683) 41323. *Clubs:* Garrick, Lansdowne.

BLACKHAM, Vice-Adm. Sir Jeremy (Joe), KCB 1999; Chairman: Atmaana Ltd, 2005–08 (Director, since 2002); Sarnmere, since 2006; *b* 10 Sept. 1943; *s* of Rear-Adm. Joseph Leslie Blackham, CB; *m* 1971, Candy Carter. *Educ:* Bradfield Coll., Berks; Open Univ. (BA 1st Cl. Hons 1979); RN Staff Course, 1974. Joined RN, 1961; Spanish Interpreter, 1966; commanded HM Ships Beachampton, 1969–70, Ashanti, 1977–79, Nottingham, 1984–85; RCDS 1986; Commandant, RN Staff Coll., Greenwich,

1987–89; Dir of Naval Plans, 1989–92; Captain, HMS Ark Royal, 1992–93 (Comdr RN Task Group, Adriatic); DG, Naval Personnel Strategy and Plans, 1993–95; ACNS and Adm. Pres., RNC, Greenwich, 1995–97; Dep. Comdr, Fleet, 1997–99; DCDS (Progs and Personnel), 1999; DCDS (Equipment Capability), MoD, 1999–2002. Lectr, RUSI and defence orgns. UK Pres., EADS, 2003–06; Chm., EADS Defence Systems UK, 2004–06. Director: Condor PM, 2006–; Eurocopter, 2007–. Chm., Academic Adv. Bd, Aeronautical Engrg Faculty, City Univ., 2004–07; Member: Council, RUSI (Vice Pres., 2003–); RIIA; MInstD. Chm., Blackheath Conservatoire of Music and Arts, 2000–07. Liveryman, Shipwrights' Co., 1999–. Ed., Naval Review, 2002–; Mem., Editorial Adv. Bd, Defence Procurement Analysis, 2004–06. Mem., Adv. Bd, City Forum, 2005–. *Publications:* numerous articles on defence, strategic affairs and walking. *Recreations:* cricket, music, theatre, language, travel, walking. *Address:* c/o Lloyds TSB, 15 The Village, Blackheath, SE3 9LH. *Club:* MCC.

BLACKHURST, Christopher Charles; City Editor, Evening Standard, since 2002; *b* Barrow-in-Furness, 24 Dec. 1959; *s* of Donald Blackhurst and Rose Bestwick Blackhurst (*née* Wood); *m* 1st, 1986, Lynette Dorothy Wood Grice (marr. diss. 2003); two *s* one *d*; 2nd, 2004, Annabelle Sara Fisher; one *s* one *d*. *Educ:* Barrow-in-Furness Grammar Sch. for Boys; Trinity Hall, Cambridge (BA Hons Law 1982). With Cameron Markby Solicitors, 1983–84; Asst Ed., 1984–85, Dep. Ed., 1985–86, Internat. Financial Law Rev.; Sen. Writer, Business Mag., 1986–89; Business Feature Writer and Dep. Insight Ed., Sunday Times, 1989–90; City Ed., Sunday Express, 1990–92; Sen. Business Writer, Independent on Sunday, 1992–93; Westminster corresp., Independent, 1993–96; Asst Ed., Independent on Sunday, 1996–97; Deputy Editor: Independent and Independent on Sunday, 1997–98; Daily Express and Sunday Express, 1998–2001. Trustee and Dir, Kingston Th. Trust, 2004–. Mem., Fund Raising Bd, Maggie's Cancer Care Charity, 2005–07. *Recreations:* golf, tennis, theatre. *Address:* Evening Standard, Northcliffe House, 2 Derry Street, Kensington, W8 5EE. *T:* (020) 7938 6902, *Fax:* (020) 7938 6916; *e-mail:* chris.blackhurst@standard.co.uk. *Clubs:* Reform, Roehampton.

BLACKIE, Jonathan Adam; Regional Director, Government Office for the North East, since 2002; *b* 29 April 1953; *s* of late James Blackie and of Nansie Blackie; *m* 1983, Julie; four *d*. *Educ:* Heriot-Watt Univ./Edinburgh Coll. of Art (BSc Hons Town and Country Planning 1976). Res. Associate, Univ. of Edinburgh, 1976–81; Sen. Policy Officer, Newcastle CC, 1981–87; Principal Policy Officer, Kirklees MDC, 1987–89; Regl Projects Manager, Audit Commn, 1989–92; Dir, Newcastle City Challenge, 1992–96; Regl Dir, English Partnerships (NE), 1996–99; Dir, One NorthEast RDA, 1999–2002. *Recreations:* arts, golf, tennis. *Address:* Government Office for the North East, Citygate, Gallowgate, Newcastle upon Tyne NE1 4WH. *T:* (0191) 202 3801, *Fax:* (0191) 202 3906; *e-mail:* jonathan.blackie@gone.gsi.gov.uk.

BLACKLEY, Air Vice-Marshal Allan Baillie, CBE 1983; AFC; BSc; Principal, Emergency Planning College, 1993–97; *b* 28 Sept. 1937. Flight Lieut, 1961; Sqn Leader, 1968; Wing Comdr, 1974; Directorate of Air Staff Plans, Dept of CAS, Air Force Dept, 1977; Gp Capt., 1980; OC RAF Valley and ADC to the Queen, 1980–82; Gp Capt. (Air Defence) RAF Strike Comd, 1982–83; Dir (Air Defence), MoD, 1984–85; Air Cdre, 1985; Comdt, RAF CFS, Scampton, 1985–87; SASO, No 11 Gp, 1987–89; Dep. COS (Ops), HQ AFCENT, 1989–91; AO Scotland and NI, 1991–93. Chm., Lincs and Notts Air Ambulance Charitable Trust, 1998–2001. *Address:* Robin Lodge, 40 Horncastle Road, Woodhall Spa, Lincs LN10 6UZ.

BLACKLEY, Ian Lorimer; HM Diplomatic Service, retired; *b* 14 Dec. 1946; *s* of late John Lorimer Blackley and Christina Ferrier (*née* Aitken); *m* 1981, Pamela Ann Helena Belt; one *s*. *Educ:* Sedbergh Sch.; St Catharine's Coll., Cambridge (MA). Joined Diplomatic Service, 1969; MECAS, Lebanon, 1971–72; Third Sec., Tripoli, 1972–73; Second Sec., Berlin, 1973–74; First Sec., Damascus, 1974–77; FCO, 1977–80; Head of Chancery and HM Consul, Beirut, 1980–82; First Sec. (Agric.), The Hague, 1982–86; Asst Head, ME Dept, FCO, 1986–88; Counsellor, Kuwait, 1988–90; British Rep. to Govt of Occupied Kuwait in Exile, Aug. 1990–March 1991; Counsellor, Damascus, 1991–93; Spokesman, EU Electoral Mission, Palestinian Elections, 1995–96; Sen. Observer, British Mission to Yemeni Elections, 1997. *Recreations:* fly fishing, Islamic art. *Address:* 63 Northumberland Street, Edinburgh EH3 6JQ.

BLACKMAN, Elizabeth Marion; MP (Lab) Erewash, since 1997; *b* 26 Sept. 1949; *m* Derek Blackman (marr. diss.); one *s* one *d*. *Educ:* Carlisle County Sch. for Girls; Prince Henry's Grammar Sch., Otley; Clifton Coll., Nottingham (BEd Hons). Teacher, 1972–93, Hd, 1993–97, Upper Sch., Bramcote Park Comp., Nottingham. Mem. (Lab) Broxtowe BC, 1991–98 (Dep. Leader, 1995–97). PPS to Sec. of State for Defence, 2000–05, to Leader of the H of C, 2005–06; an Asst Govt Whip, 2006–07; Vice-Chamberlain of HM Household, 2007–08. Mem., Treasury Select Cttee, 1997–2000. Chm., All-Pty Parly Gp on Autism, 2004–06. *Address:* House of Commons, SW1A 0AA.

BLACKMAN, Sir Frank (Milton), KA 1985; KCVO 1985 (CVO 1975); OBE 1969 (MBE 1964); Ombudsman for Barbados, 1987–93; *b* 31 July 1926; *s* of late A. Milton Blackman and Winnifred Blackman (*née* Pile); *m* 1st, 1958, Edith Mary Knight (*d* 1994); one *s*; 2nd, 1995, Norma Cox Astwood. *Educ:* Wesley Hall Boys' Sch., Barbados; Harrison Coll., Barbados. Clerical Officer, Colonial Secretary's Office, 1944–56; Sec., Public Service Commn, 1956–57; Asst. Sec., Colonial Sec.'s Office, 1957; Cabinet Office/Premier's Office, 1958–66: Clerk of the Legislative Council, 1958–64; Perm. Sec./Cabinet Sec., 1966–86; Head of CS, 1981–86. *Address:* Lausanne, Rendezvous Hill, Christ Church, BB 15115 Barbados. *T:* 4273463.

BLACKMAN, Gilbert Albert Waller, CBE 1978 (OBE 1973); FREng, CEng, FIMechE; Chairman, Central Electricity Generating Board, Jan.–March 1990, retired; *b* 28 July 1925; *s* of Ernest Albert Cecil Blackman and Amy Blackman; *m* 1948, Lilian Rosay. *Educ:* Wanstead County High Sch.; Wandsworth Tech. Coll. CEng, FIMechE 1967; Hon. FInstE (FInstF 1964). Commnd RE, 1945–48. Trainee Engr, London Div., Brit. Electricity Authority, 1948–50; various appts in power stns, 1950–63; Central Electricity Generating Board: Stn Supt, Belvedere, 1963–64; Asst Reg. Dir, E Midlands Div., 1964–67; Asst Reg. Dir, Midlands Reg., 1967–70; Dir of Generation, Midlands Reg., 1970–75; Dir Gen., N Eastern Reg., 1975–77; Mem., 1977–90; Dep. Chm. and Prodn Man. Dir, 1986–89; Chm., British Electricity Internat. Ltd, 1988–90; Dir, Nat. Power, 1990–94. *Recreations:* music, photography, art.

See also L. C. F. Blackman.

BLACKMAN, Dr Lionel Cyril Francis; Director, British American Tobacco Co. Ltd, 1980–84 (General Manager, Group Research and Development, 1978–80); *b* 12 Sept. 1930; *s* of Mr and Mrs Ernest Albert Cecil Blackman; *m* 1955, Susan Hazel Peachey (marr. diss. 1983); one *s* one *d*. *Educ:* Wanstead High Sch.; Queen Mary Coll., London. BSc 1952; PhD 1955. Scientific Officer, then Senior Research Fellow, RN Scientific Service, 1954–57; ICI Research Fellow, then Lectr in Chemical Physics of Solids, Imperial Coll., London, 1957–60; Asst Dir (London), then Dir, Chemical Research Div., BR, 1961–64; Dir of Basic Research, then Dir Gen., British Coal Utilisation Research Assoc., 1964–71; Director: Fibreglass Ltd (subsid. of Pilkington Bros Ltd), 1971–78; Compocem Ltd, 1975–78; Cemfil Corp. (US), 1975–78; Vice-Pres., Cementos y Fibras SA (Spain), 1976–78. Chm., Hockering Residents Assoc., 1995–2003. CEng; CChem; FRSC; DIC; Sen. FEI. *Publications:* (ed) Modern Aspects of Graphite Technology, 1970; Athletics World Records in the 20th Century, 1988; History of the Early Development of the Hockering Estate, Woking, 2007; papers in various scientific and technical jls on dropwise condensation of steam, ferrites, sintering of oxides, graphite and its crystal compounds, glass surface coatings, glass reinforced cement. *Recreations:* gardening, music, wine. *Address:* Griffin House, Knowl Hill, The Hockering, Woking, Surrey GU22 7HL. *T:* (01483) 766328.

See also G. A. W. Blackman.

BLACKMAN, Robert; Member (C) Brent and Harrow, London Assembly, Greater London Authority, 2004–08; *b* 26 April 1956; *m* 1988, Nicola Jennings. *Educ:* Univ. of Liverpool (BSc). Sales trng, 1991–98, Regulatory Compliance Manager, 1998–, BT. Mem. (C) Brent BC, 1986–: Leader, 1991–96; Dep. Leader, 2006–. Contested (C): Brent S, 1992; Bedford, 1997; Brent N, 2005. *Address:* 48 Forty Avenue, Wembley HA9 8LQ.

BLACKMAN-WOODS, Roberta C., PhD; MP (Lab) City of Durham, since 2005; *b* 16 Aug. 1957; *d* of Charles and Eleanor Woods; *m* Prof. Timothy J. Blackman; one *d*. *Educ:* Univ. of Ulster (BSc Combined Soc. Scis 1979; PhD 1989). Welfare Rights Officer, Newcastle CC, 1982–85; Lectr in Social Policy, Univ. of Ulster, then Univ. of Newcastle upon Tyne, 1985–95; Dean of Social and Labour Studies, Ruskin Coll., Oxford, 1995–2000; Prof. of Social Policy and Dep. Dean, Sch. of Arts and Social Scis, Univ. of Northumbria, 2000–05. Mem., Child Poverty Action Gp. *Recreation:* music. *Address:* (office) The Miners' Hall, Redhills, Durham DH1 4BD. *T:* (0191) 374 1915, *Fax:* (0191) 374 1916; *e-mail:* mail@roberta.org.uk; House of Commons, SW1A 0AA.

BLACKMORE, Prof. Stephen, PhD; FRSE; CBiol, FIBiol; FLS; Regius Keeper, Royal Botanic Garden Edinburgh, since 1999; *b* 30 July 1952; *s* of Edwin Arthur and Josephine Blackmore; *m* 1973, Patricia Jane Melrose Hawley; one *s* one *d*. *Educ:* Univ. of Reading (BSc 1973; PhD 1976). CBiol, FBiol, 1993; FLS 1976. Botanist and Administrator, Royal Society Aldabra Research Station, Indian Ocean, 1976–77; Head of Nat. Herbarium and Lectr in Botany, Univ. of Malaŵi, 1977–80; Head of Palynology Section, Dept of Botany, BM (Natural Hist.), 1980–90; Keeper of Botany, 1990–99, Associate Dir, 1992–95, Natural Hist. Mus. Visiting Professor: Reading Univ., 1995–; Glasgow Univ., 1999–; Kunming Inst. of Botany, 2004–; Hon. Prof., Univ. of Edinburgh, 2004–. Pres., Systematics Assoc., 1994–97; Chm., UK Systematics Forum, 1993–99. Trustee: Little Sparta Trust, 2001–; Botanic Gardens Conservation Internat., 2000–; Seychelles Islands Foundn, 2007–; Mem., Bd of Govs, Edinburgh Coll. of Art, 2004–. FRSE 2000. Hon. Fellow, 48 Gp Club 'The Icebreakers', 2005. *Publications:* Bee Orchids, 1985; Buttercups, 1985; (ed jtly) Pollen and Spores: form and function, 1986; (ed jtly) Evolution, Systematics and Fossil History of the Hamamelidae, 2 vols, 1989; (ed jtly) Microspores: evolution and ontogeny, 1990; (ed jtly) Pollen and Spores: patterns of diversification, 1991; (ed jtly) An Atlas of Plant Sexual Reproduction, 1992; (ed jtly) Systematics Agenda 2000: The Challenge For Europe, 1996; Pollen and Spores: morphology and biology, 2000; contribs to professional jls. *Recreations:* hill walking, photography, blues guitar music. *Address:* (office) 20A Inverleith Row, Edinburgh EH3 5LR. *T:* (0131) 248 2930. *Club:* New (Edinburgh).

BLACKSELL, Henry Oliver; QC 1994; **His Honour Judge Blacksell;** a Circuit Judge, since 1996; *b* 28 Nov. 1948; *s* of James Edward Blacksell, MBE and Joan Simmons Yates Blacksell (*née* Yates); *m* 1st, 1971, Diana Frances Mary Burton (marr. diss. 1985; she *d* 2005); 2nd, 1986, Miranda Jane, *d* of His Honour W. A. L. Allardice; one *s* one *d*. *Educ:* Barnstaple Grammar Sch.; Exeter Univ. (LLB). Called to the Bar, Inner Temple, 1972; a Recorder, 1993–96. *Recreations:* family, theatre, ancient humour. *Address:* Blackfriars Crown Court, 1–15 Pocock Street, SE1 0BJ. *Club:* Harlequin Rugby Football.

BLACKSHAW, Alan, OBE 1992; VRD 1970; business consultant; President, Union Internationale des Associations d'Alpinisme, 2005; *b* 7 April 1933; *s* of late Frederick William Blackshaw and Elsie (*née* MacDougall); *m* 1st, 1956, Jane Elizabeth Turner (marr. diss. 1983); one *d*; 2nd, 1984, Dr Elspeth Paterson Martin, *d* of late Rev. Gavin C. Martin and Agnes Martin; one *s* two *d*. *Educ:* Merchant Taylors' Sch., Crosby; Wadham Coll., Oxford (MA). Royal Marines (commnd), 1954–56, and RM Reserve, 1956–76. Entered Home Civil Service, Min. of Power, 1956; 1st Sec., UK Delegn to OECD, Paris, 1965–66; Principal Private Sec. to Minister of Power, 1967–69; with Charterhouse Gp on loan, 1972–73; Dept of Energy: Under Sec., 1974; Offshore Supplies Office, 1974–78 (Dir-Gen., 1977–78); Coal Div., 1978–79; Consultant, NCB, 1979–86. Consultant Dir, Strategy Internat., 1980–91; Director: Paths for All Partnership, 1996–97; Badenoch, Moray and Strathspey Enterprise, 1998–2000. Member: Scottish Council for Develt and Industry, 1974–78; Offshore Energy Technol. Bd, 1977–78; Ship and Marine Technol. Requirements Bd, 1977–78; Scottish Sports Council, 1990–95; Scottish Natural Heritage, 1992–97 (Chairman: Task Force on Access, 1992–94; Audit Cttee, 1994–97); Adventure Activities Licensing Authy, 1996–; Bd, Cairngorms Partnership, 1998–2003 (Chm., Recreational Forum, 1998–2003); Rights of Way Survey Steering Gp, Countryside Agency, 2000–02. University of Highlands and Islands Project: Academic Advr, 1997–2001; Chm., Working Gp on Tourism and Leisure, 1998–99; Mem., Scis and Envmt Faculty Bd, 1999–2004. Libel damages against Daily Telegraph (upheld in Ct of Appeal, 1983) and Daily Mail, 1981. Pres., Oxford Univ. Mountaineering Club, 1953–54; Climbers' Club: Sec., 1956–61; Vice-Pres., 1973–75; Hon. Mem., 1998; Alpine Club: Editor, Alpine Jl, 1968–70; Vice-Pres., 1979–81; Trustee, 1980–90; Hon. Mem., 1998; Pres., 2001–04; British Mountaineering Council: Pres., 1973–76; Patron, 1979–; Chairman: Standing Adv. Cttee on Mountain Trng Policy, 1980–86 and 1990–93; Ski Touring and Mountaineering Cttee, 1981–91. Chairman: Sports Council's Nat. Mountain Centre (formerly Nat. Centre for Mountain Activities), Plas y Brenin, 1986–95; Mountaineering Cttee, UIAA, 1990–2000 (Mem., 1985–89; Dep. Chm., 1989–90); UIAA Gp on competitions in mountain areas, 1993–96, on mountain access, 1995–99; UK Mountain Trng Bd, 1991–94; Scottish Adventure Activities Forum, 1999–; Interim Wkg Gp on Leadership in Outdoor Activities, Sports Council, 1990–91; Leader, British Alpine Ski Traverse, 1972; UIAA Special Representative: UN Inter-Agency Gp on Mountains, 1996–2005; UN Year of Mountains 2002, 2000–03; Adviser on public access to land: Scottish Envmt Link, 1994–; CCPR, 1997–2003; Hon. Advr, Mountaineering Council of Scotland, 1994–. Pres., Snowsport Scotland (formerly Scottish Nat. Ski Council), 1994–2000 (Chm., 1991–94); Ski Club of Great Britain: Vice-Pres., 1977–80, 1983–85; Pres., 1997–2003; Pery Medal, 1977; Hon. Mem., 1992; Pres., Eagle Ski Club, 1979–81 (Hon. Mem., 1982); British Ski Federation: Vice-Pres., 1983–84; Chm., 1984–86. Sec., Edinburgh Br., Oxford Soc., 1989–98. Hon. Advr, Venture Scotland, 1995–2004. Freeman, City of London. FRGS; FEI. Award for voluntary service to sport and Olympism, IOC, 2001. *Publication:* Mountaineering, 1965, 3rd revision 1975. *Recreations:* mountaineering, ski-ing, sailing. *Address:* Rhu Grianach, Kingussie Road, Newtonmore, Inverness-shire PH20 1AY. *T:* (01540) 673239; Les Autannes, Le Tour, Argentière, 74440, France. *T:* 450541220.

BLACKSHAW, William Simon; Headmaster of Brighton College, 1971–87; *b* 28 Oct. 1930; *s* of late C. B. Blackshaw, sometime Housemaster, Cranleigh School and Kathleen Mary (who *m* 1965, Sir Thomas McAlpine, 4th Bt); *m* 1956, Elizabeth Anne Evans; one *s* one *d* (and one *s* decd). *Educ:* Sherborne Sch.; Hertford Coll., Oxford. 2nd cl. hons Mod. Langs. Repton School: Asst Master, 1955–71; Head of Modern Languages Dept, 1961–66; Housemaster, 1966–71. Chm., Bankside Gall., 1994–2000. Chm., Sussex Schs Cricket Assoc., 1994–96. Hon. RWS 2000. *Publications:* Regardez! Racontez!, 1971; A History of Bilton Grange School, 1997. *Recreations:* painting, cricket, golf. *Address:* Squash Court, The Green, Rottingdean, East Sussex BN2 7HA.

BLACKSTONE, Baroness *cr* 1987 (Life Peer), of Stoke Newington in Greater London; **Tessa Ann Vosper Blackstone;** PC 2001; PhD; Vice-Chancellor, University of Greenwich, since 2004; *b* 27 Sept. 1942; *d* of late Geoffrey Vaughan Blackstone, CBE, GM, QFSM, and of Joanna Blackstone; *m* 1963, Tom Evans (marr. diss.; he *d* 1985); one *s* one *d. Educ:* Ware Grammar Sch.; London School of Economics (BScSoc, PhD; Fellow, 1995). Associate Lectr, Enfield Coll., 1965–66; Asst Lectr, then Lectr, Dept of Social Administration, LSE, 1966–75; Adviser, Central Policy Review Staff, Cabinet Office, 1975–78; Prof. of Educnl Admin, Univ. of London Inst. of Educn, 1978–83; Dep. Educn Officer (Resources), then Clerk and Dir of Education, ILEA, 1983–87; Master, Birkbeck Coll., London Univ., 1987–97 (Fellow, 1998). Fellow, Centre for Studies in Social Policy, 1972–74; Special Rowntree Visiting Fellow, Policy Studies Inst., 1987. Vis. Prof., LSE, 2003–. Chm., Gen. Adv. Council of BBC, 1987–91; First Chm., Inst. for Public Policy Research, 1988–97. Non-executive Director: Project Fullemploy, 1984–91; Royal Opera House, 1987–97; Thames Television, 1991–92; Granada Learning, 2003–06; VT Gp plc, 2004–; Mott McDonald, 2005–07. Chm. Ballet Bd, 1991–97; Member: Planning Bd, Arts Council of GB, 1986–90; Management Cttee, King Edward's Hosp. Fund for London, 1990–95; Marshall Aid Commemoration Commn, 2005–; Gov. and Mem. of Council, Ditchley Foundn, 1990–97; Gov., Royal Ballet, 1991–2001. Vice Pres., VSO, 1992–. Chm., RIBA Trust, 2003–. Opposition spokesman, House of Lords: on educn and science, 1988–92; on foreign affairs, 1992–97; Minister of State, DfEE, 1997–2001; Minister of State (Minister for Arts), DCMS, 2001–03. Trustee: Architecture Foundn, 1991–97; Nat. Hist. Mus., 1992–97. Hon. DLitt: Bradford, 1990; Bristol Poly., 1991; DUniv: Middlesex, 1993; Strathclyde, Leeds Metropolitan, 1996; QUB, 2007; Hon. LLD: Aberdeen, 1994; St Andrews, 1995; Hon DR Sorbonne, 1998; Rome, 2004; Hon. FRIBA 2005. *Publications:* Students in Conflict (jtly), 1970; A Fair Start, 1971; Education and Day Care for Young Children in Need, 1973; The Academic Labour Market (jtly), 1974; Social Policy and Administration in Britain, 1975; Disadvantage and Education (jtly), 1982; Educational Policy and Educational Inequality (jtly), 1982; Response to Adversity (jtly), 1983; Testing Children (jtly), 1983; Inside the Think Tank (jtly), 1988; Prisons and Penal Reform, 1990; Race Relations in Britain, 1997. *Address:* House of Lords, SW1A 0PW; University of Greenwich, Old Royal Naval College, Park Row, SE10 9LS.

BLACKWELL, family name of **Baron Blackwell.**

BLACKWELL, Baron *cr* 1997 (Life Peer), of Woodcote in the co. of Surrey; **Norman Roy Blackwell;** Chairman, Centre for Policy Studies, since 2000; *b* 29 July 1952; *s* of Albert Blackwell and Frances Blackwell (*née* Lutman); *m* 1974, Brenda Clucas; three *s* two *d. Educ:* RAM (Jun. Exhibnr); Trinity Coll., Cambridge (MA); Wharton Business Sch., Univ. of Pennsylvania (AM, MBA; PhD 1976). With Plessey Co., 1976–78; Partner, McKinsey & Co., 1978–95, elected Partner, 1984; Special Advr, Prime Minister's Policy Unit, 1986–87 (on leave of absence); Head, Prime Minister's Policy Unit, 1995–97; Dir, Gp Develt, NatWest Gp, 1997–2000; Special Advr, KPMG Corp. Finance, 2000–. Non-executive Director: Dixons Gp, 2000–03; Corporate Services Gp, 2000–06; Segro (formerly Slough Estates), 2001–; SmartStream Technologies Ltd, 2001–06; Standard Life Assurance, 2003–; OFT, 2003–; Chm., Interserve plc, 2006–. *Recreations:* classical music, walking. *Address:* c/o House of Lords, SW1A 0PW; *e-mail:* blackwelln@parliament.uk. *Clubs:* Carlton, Royal Automobile.

BLACKWELL, Prof. Donald Eustace, MA, PhD; Savilian Professor of Astronomy, University of Oxford, 1960–88, now Emeritus; Fellow of New College, Oxford, 1960–88, now Emeritus; *b* 27 May 1921; *s* of John Blackwell and Ethel Bowe; *m* 1951, Nora Louise Carlton; two *s* two *d. Educ:* Merchant Taylors' Sch.; Sandy Lodge; Sidney Sussex Coll., Cambridge. Isaac Newton Student, University of Cambridge, 1947; Stokes Student, Pembroke Coll., Cambridge, 1948; Asst Director, Solar Physics Observatory, Cambridge, 1950–60. Various Astronomical Expeditions: Sudan, 1952; Fiji, 1955; Bolivia, 1958 and 1961; Canada, 1963; Manuae Island, 1965. Pres., RAS, 1973–75. *Publications:* papers in astronomical journals. *Address:* 4 Pullens Field, Headington, Oxford OX3 0BU.

BLACKWELL, Rt Rev. Douglas Charles; an Area (formerly Suffragan) Bishop of Toronto (Area Bishop of Trent-Durham), 1988–2003; *b* 3 June 1938; *s* of late William John Blackwell and Ethel N. Blackwell (*née* Keates); *m* 1963, Sandra Dianne Griffiths; one *s* two *d. Educ:* Wycliffe Coll., Univ. of Toronto (DipTh, LTh). Deacon 1963, priest 1964; Asst Curate, St Stephen's, Calgary, 1964; Vicar, Cochrane Mission, Diocese of Calgary, 1966; Rector, St Paul's, North Battleford, Diocese of Saskatoon, 1969; Regional Dean of Battleford, 1970; Archdeacon of Battlefords-Lloydminster, 1973; Asst Director, Aurora Conf. Centre, Diocese of Toronto, 1974; Executive Asst to Archbishop of Toronto, 1977; Canon of St James's Cathedral, Toronto, 1978; Archdeacon of York, 1986. Hon. DD Wycliffe Coll., Toronto, 1990. *Address:* 63 Glen Dhu Drive, Whitby, ON L1R 1K3, Canada. *T:* (905) 4308460.

BLACKWELL, Prof. Jenefer Mary; Professor of Genetics and Health, Telethon Institute for Child Health Research, University of Western Australia, since 2007; Affiliated Principal Investigator, Cambridge Institute for Medical Research, since 2007; Professorial Fellow, Newnham College, Cambridge, since 1993; *b* 8 Dec. 1948; *d* of Frank Blackwell and Elsie Winifred Broadhurst; *m* 1973, Simon John Miles; one *s* one *d. Educ:* Univ. of Western Australia (BSc 1969 (1st Cl. Hons Zoology); PhD 1974 (Population Genetics)). Cons. Biologist and Res. Officer, WA Govt Depts, 1973–74; Lectr in Biol., Avery Hill Coll. of Educn, London, 1975–76; London School of Hygiene and Tropical Medicine: Res. Fellow, Ross Inst. of Tropical Hygiene, 1976–82; Wellcome Trust Sen. Lectr, Dept of Trop. Hygiene, 1982–88; Dept of Med. Parasitology, 1988–91 (and Head, Immunobiol. of Parasitic Diseases Unit); Reader, Univ. of London, 1989–91; Glaxo Prof. of Molecular Parasitology, Univ. of Cambridge, 1991–2007; Dir, Cambridge Inst. for Med. Res., 1998–2001. Faculty Mem., Molecular Biol. of Parasitism Course, Marine Biol. Labs, Wood's Hole, Mass, 1988. *Publication:* (with D. Wakelin) Genetics of Resistance to Bacterial and Parasitic Infection, 1988. *Recreations:* music, walking. *Address:* Division of Genetics and Health, Telethon Institute for Child Health Research, PO Box 855, West Perth, WA 6872, Australia. *T:* (8) 94897910.

BLACKWELL, Julian, (Toby); DL; President, since 1995, and Chairman, 1996–99, Blackwell Ltd; Chairman, The Blackwell Group Ltd, 1980–94; *b* 10 Jan. 1929; *s* of Sir Basil Henry Blackwell and late Marion Christine, *d* of John Soans; *m* 1953, Jennifer Jocelyn Darley Wykeham; two *s* one *d. Educ:* Winchester; Trinity Coll., Oxford. Served 5th RTR, 1947–49; 21st SAS (TA), 1950–59. Dir and Chm., various Blackwell

companies, 1956–2003. Chm. Council, ASLIB, 1966–68 (Vice-Pres., 1982); Co-founder and Chm., Mail Users' Assoc., 1975–78 and 1987–90; Pres., Booksellers' Assoc., 1980–82; Chairman: Thames Business Advice Centre, 1986–97; Heart of England TEC, 1989–94; Fox FM, 1989–98. Chm., Son White Meml Trust, 1991–. DL Oxon 1987, High Sheriff, 1991–92. Hon. DLitt Robert Gordon, 1997; DUniv Sheffield Hallam, 1998; Hon. DBA Oxford Brookes, 1999. *Recreations:* fighting the Eurocrats, sawing firewood. *Address:* c/o 50 Broad Street, Oxford OX1 3BQ. *T:* (01865) 792111. *Clubs:* Special Forces; Royal Yacht Squadron; Leander (Henley); Royal Southern Yacht (Southampton); Rock and District Sports.

BLACKWELL, Nigel Stirling; Chairman, Blackwell Publishing Ltd, 2001–07; *b* 18 March 1947; *s* of late Richard Blackwell, DSC and of Marguerite Brook Blackwell (*née* Holliday); *m* 1st, 1984, Eliza Pumpelly Mauran (*d* 1995), *d* of Frank Mauran III; one *s* one *d;* 2nd, 2005, Christina Lowry, *d* of Rolf Pasold. *Educ:* Dragon Sch., Oxford; Winchester; St Edmund Hall, Oxford (MA). Dep. Chm. and CEO, Blackwell N America, 1979–86; Jt Man. Dir, B. H. Blackwell Ltd, 1980–83 (Dir, 1974–89); Man. Dir, Blackwell Gp, 1983–89; Chm. and Man. Dir, Blackwell Retail Gp, 1983–89; Chairman: Basil Blackwell Ltd, subseq. Blackwell Publishers, 1985–2001; Blackwell Scientific, subseq. Blackwell Science, 1990–2001; Munksgaard Publishers, Copenhagen, 1992–2001. Dir, 1990–2004, Vice Pres., 2003–, Western Provident Assoc.; Chm., Richard Blackwell Scholarship Trust, 1984–2001; Sen. Trustee, Pharsalia Charitable Trust, 2007–. Mem., York Harbor Volunteer Veteran Firemans' Assoc., Maine, 2001. *Recreations:* country pursuits, swimming, sailing, collecting. *Address: e-mail:* nsb@shakespeareheadpress.com. *Clubs:* White's; Vincent's (Oxford); Leander; York Harbor Reading Room (Maine); Dunes (Narragansett, RI).

BLACKWOOD, family name of **Baron Dufferin and Clandeboye.**

BLAHNIK, Manolo, Hon. CBE 2007; designer of shoes and furniture, since 1973; Director, Manolo Blahnik International Ltd, since 1973; *b* Canary Is, 28 Nov. 1942; *s* of late E. Blahnik and of Manuela Blahnik. *Educ:* Univ. of Geneva; Louvre Art Sch., Paris. Hon. RDI 2001. Hon. DArts RCA, 2001. Retrospective exhibn, Design Mus., London, 2003. Fashion Council of America Award, 1987, 1990, 1997; Balenciaga Award, 1989; Antonio Lopez Award, Hispanic Inst., Washington, 1990; British Fashion Council Award, 1990, 1999; American Leather New York Award, 1991; Silver Slipper Award, Houston Mus. of Fine Art, 1999 (first awarded to a shoe designer); Neiman Marcus Award, USA, 2000; Golden Needle Award, Spain, 2001; Medalla de Oro al Mérito en las Bellas Artes, Spain, 2002; Medalla de Oro de Canarias, Spain, 2003; Shoe Designer of the Year, Footwear News, 2003; Accessory Designer of the Year, Lycra British Style Awards, 2003; Pinnacle in Art and Design Award, Pratt Inst., NY, 2005. *Publication:* Manolo Blahnik: Drawings, 2003; *relevant publications:* Manolo Blahnik, by Colin McDowell, 2000; Blahnik by Boman: a photographic conversation, by Eric Boman, 2005. *Recreations:* travel, painting. *Address:* (office) 49–51 Old Church Street, SW3 5BS. *T:* (020) 7352 8622.

BLAIN, Prof. Peter George, CBE 2002; PhD; FRCP, FRCPE, FFOM; CBiol, FIBiol; Professor of Environmental Medicine, University of Newcastle upon Tyne, since 1986; Head of Medical Toxicology, Health Protection Agency, since 2004; Director, Medical Toxicology Research Centre, since 2006; *b* 15 March 1951; *s* of Reginald Blain and Margaret (*née* Graham); *m* 1977, Patricia Anne Crawford; two *s* one *d. Educ:* Univ. of Newcastle upon Tyne (BMedSci; MB, BS; PhD 1988). MFOM 1990, FFOM 1997; FRCP 1990; FRCPE 1991; CBiol 1986; FIBiol 1989. Jun. hosp. doctor, Royal Victoria Infirmary, Newcastle upon Tyne, 1975–79; University of Newcastle upon Tyne: Lectr in Clinical Pharmacol., 1979–80; Wellcome Res. Fellow in Clinical Pharmacol. and Neurology, 1980–81; First Asst in Clinical Pharmacol., 1981–85; Hd, Biomed. Scis and Human Toxicol. Res., ICI plc, 1985–86. Consultant Physician: Freeman Gp of Hosps NHS Trust (formerly Freeman Hosp.), 1988–; Royal Victoria Infirmary NHS Trust (formerly Royal Victoria Inf.), 1988–; Newcastle Hosps NHS Trust, 1998–; Consultant in Envmtl Medicine and Toxicol., Northern and Yorks RHA, 1992–. Chairman: Chem., Biol, Radiol or Nuclear Defence and Human Scis Bd (formerly Chem., Biol and Human Technologies Bd), MoD, 1994–; Adv. Gp on Med. Countermeasures, MoD, 1998–; Mem., Defence Scientific Adv. Council, MoD, 1994–. FBTS 2007. *Publications:* contrib. to textbooks in toxicol. and medicine; res. papers in acad. jls in toxicol. *Recreation:* hill walking. *Address:* Department of Environmental Medicine, Medical School, Newcastle upon Tyne NE2 4HH. *T:* (0191) 222 7195, *Fax:* (0191) 222 6442; *e-mail:* p.g.blain@ncl.ac.uk.

BLAIN, Sophie Clodagh Mary; see Andreae, S. C. M.

BLAIR, Rt Hon. Anthony Charles Lynton, (Tony); PC 1994; Quartet Representative, since 2007; Senior Advisor, JPMorgan Chase, since 2008; *b* 6 May 1953; *s* of Leo Charles Lynton Blair and late Hazel Blair; *m* 1980, Cherie Booth, *qv*; three *s* one *d. Educ:* Durham Choristers School; Fettes College, Edinburgh; St John's College, Oxford. Called to the Bar, Lincoln's Inn, 1976; Hon. Bencher, 1994. MP (Lab) Sedgefield, 1983–June 2007. Leader of the Opposition, 1994–97; Prime Minister and First Lord of the Treasury, 1997–2007. Leader of the Labour Party, 1994–2007. *Publications:* New Britain: my vision of a young country, 1996; The Third Way, 1998. *Address:* PO Box 60519, London W2 7JU. *Clubs:* Trimdon Colliery and Deaf Hill Working Men's, Constituency Labour (Trimdon); Fishburn Working Men's.
See also Hon. Sir W. Blair.

BLAIR, Bruce Graeme Donald; QC 1989; a Recorder, since 1995; *b* 12 April 1946; *s* of late Dr Donald Alexander Sangster Blair, MA, MD, DPM and Eleanor Violet Blair (*née* Van Ryneveld); *m* 1970, Susanne Blair (*née* Hartung); three *d* (and one *s* decd). *Educ:* Harrow School; Magdalene College, Cambridge. Called to the Bar, Middle Temple, 1969, Bencher, 1997. *Publication:* Practical Matrimonial Precedents (jtly), 1989. *Recreations:* bridge, golf, turf. *Address:* 1 Hare Court, Temple, EC4Y 7BE. *T:* (020) 7797 7070. *Clubs:* MCC.

BLAIR, Lt-Gen. Sir Chandos, KCVO 1972; OBE 1962; MC 1941 and bar, 1944; GOC Scotland and Governor of Edinburgh Castle, 1972–76; *b* 25 Feb. 1919; *s* of Brig.-Gen. Arthur Blair and Elizabeth Mary (*née* Hoskyns); *m* 1947, Audrey Mary Travers (*d* 1997); one *s* one *d. Educ:* Harrow; Sandhurst. Commnd into Seaforth Highlanders, 1939; comd 4 KAR, Uganda, 1959–61; comd 39 Bde, Radfan and N. Ireland. GOC 2nd Division, BAOR, 1968–70; Defence Services Secretary, MoD, 1970–72. Col Comdt, Scottish Div., 1972–76; Col, Queen's Own Highlanders, 1975–83. *Recreations:* golf, fishing, shooting.

BLAIR, Cherie; see Booth, C.

BLAIR, Claude, CVO 2005; OBE 1994; FSA 1956; Keeper, Department of Metalwork, Victoria and Albert Museum, 1972–82; *b* 30 Nov. 1922; *s* of William Henry Murray Blair and Lilian Wearing; *m* 1952, Joan Mary Greville Drinkwater (*d* 1996); one *s. Educ:* William Hulme's Grammar Sch., Manchester; Manchester Univ. (MA). Served War, Army (Captain RA), 1942–46. Manchester Univ., 1946–51; Asst, Tower of London

Armouries, 1951–56; Asst Keeper of Metalwork, V&A, 1956–66; Dep. Keeper, 1966–72. Hon. Editor, Jl of the Arms and Armour Soc., 1953–77. Consultant to Christie's, 1983–84; Member: Arch. Adv. Panel, Westminster Abbey, 1979–98; Council for the Care of Churches, 1991–96 (Mem. Exec. Cttee, 1983–91); Trustee, Churches Conservation Trust (formerly Redundant Churches Fund), 1982–97. Vice-Pres., Soc. of Antiquaries, 1990–93; Hon. Pres., Meyrick Soc., 1979–94; Hon. Vice-President: Soc. for Study of Church Monuments, 1984– (Hon. Pres., 1978–84); Monumental Brass Soc. Hon. Mem., Accademia di San Marciano, Turin, 2002. Hon. Liveryman, Cutlers' Co. Liveryman: Goldsmiths' Co.; Armourers and Brasiers' Co. Hon. LittD Manchester, 2004. Medal of Museo Militar, Barcelona, 1969; Medal of Arms and Armour Soc., 1986; Gold Medal, Soc. of Antiquaries, 1998. *Publications:* European Armour, 1958 (2nd edn, 1972); European and American Arms, 1962; The Silvered Armour of Henry VIII, 1965; Pistols of the World, 1968; Three Presentation Swords in the Victoria and Albert Museum, 1972; The James A. de Rothschild Collection: Arms, Armour and Miscellaneous Metalwork, 1974; (gen. editor and contrib.) Pollard's History of Firearms, 1983; (ed) The History of Silver, 1987; (gen. editor and contrib.) The Crown Jewels, 1998; numerous articles and reviews in Archaeological Jl, Jl of Arms and Armour Soc., Connoisseur, Waffen und Kostümkunde, etc. *Recreations:* travel, looking at churches, listening to music. *Address:* 90 Links Road, Ashtead, Surrey KT21 2HW. *T:* (01372) 275532. *Clubs:* Civil Service, Royal Over-Seas League.
See also W. J. Blair.

BLAIR, Prof. Gordon Purves, CBE 1995; PhD, DSc; FREng, FIMechE, FSAE; Professor of Mechanical Engineering, Queen's University of Belfast, 1976–96, now Emeritus; Senior Associate, Professor Blair and Associates, since 2002; *b* 29 April 1937; *s* of Gordon Blair and Mary Helen Jones Blair; *m* 1964, Norma Margaret Millar; two *d*. *Educ:* Queen's Univ. of Belfast (BSc; PhD 1962; DSc 1978). CEng, FIMechE 1977; FSAE 1979; FREng (FEng 1982). Asst Prof., New Mexico State Univ., 1962–64; Queen's University of Belfast: Lectr, 1964–71; Sen. Lectr, 1971–73; Reader, 1973–76; Head of Dept of Mechl and Industrial Engrg, 1982–89, and of Dept of Mechl and Manufacturing, Aeronautical and Chemical Engrg, 1987–89; Dean, Faculty of Engrg, 1985–88; Pro-Vice-Chancellor, 1989–94. Chm., Automobile Div., IMechE, 1991. *Publications:* The Basic Design of Two-Stroke Engines, USA, 1990; Design and Simulation of Two-Stroke Engines, 1996; Design and Simulation of Four-Stroke Engines, 1999; wide pubn in IMechE and SAE Jls on design and develt of internal combustion engines. *Recreations:* golf, fishing, motorcycles. *Address:* 9 Ben Madigan Park South, Newtownabbey, N Ireland BT36 7PX. *T:* (028) 9037 0368. *Clubs:* Cairndhu Golf; Royal Portrush Golf.

BLAIR, Ian Charles; public finance consultant; *b* 31 Aug. 1947; *s* of John Blair and Robina Poppy Blair (*née* Carr); *m* 1974, Jennifer Mary Hodgson (*d* 2007); one *s* one *d*. *Educ:* Liberton Sch., Edinburgh; Open Univ. (BA 1995). CPFA (IPFA 1969). Accountant, Midlothian CC, 1964–72; Sen. Accountant, Scottish Special Housing Assoc., 1972–75; Sen. Asst Treas., Lothian Health Bd, 1975–81; City Treasurer: Bath CC, 1981–91; Nottingham CC, 1991–2002; Treas., Derbys Probation Bd. Advr, ADC, 1992–97. Chm., S Wales and West, CIPFA, 1991; Pres., Audit Cttee, Eurocities, 1999–2002; Mem., Exec., Soc. Municipal Treasurers, 1999–2002. Sen. Res. Associate, Warwick Business Sch., 2007. *Publications:* contribs to prof. jls, govt research papers. *Recreations:* family, sports (Hearts FC and Bath RFC), theatre. *Address:* 24 Purbeck Drive, West Bridgford, Notts NG2 7UA. *T:* (0115) 982 2802.

BLAIR, Sir Ian (Warwick), Kt 2003; QPM 1999; Commissioner, Metropolitan Police, 2005–08 (Deputy Commissioner, 2000–05); *b* 19 March 1953; *yr s* of late Francis James Blair and Sheila Kathleen Blair; *m* 1980, Felicity Jane White; one *s* one *d*. *Educ:* Wrekin Coll.; Harvard High Sch., LA; Christ Church, Oxford (MA; Hon. Student, 2005). Joined Metropolitan Police, 1974; uniform and CID posts, 1974–91; Chief Supt, SO to HM Chief Inspector of Constabulary, 1991–93; Asst Chief Constable, 1994–97, des. Dep. to Chief Constable, 1997, Thames Valley Police; Chief Constable, Surrey Police, 1998–2000. Visiting Fellow: Internat. Centre for Advanced Studies, NY Univ., 1998; Nuffield Coll., Oxford, 2001. *Publication:* Investigating Rape: a new approach for police, 1985. *Recreations:* ski-ing, tennis, golf, theatre.

BLAIR, John; *see* Blair, W. J.

BLAIR, Michael Campbell; barrister in independent practice; *b* 26 Aug. 1941; *s* of Sir Alastair Campbell Blair, KCVO and Catriona Hatchard Blair (*née* Orr); *m* 1966, Halldóra Isabel (*née* Tunnard); one *s*. *Educ:* Rugby Sch.; Clare Coll., Cambridge (MA, LLM); Yale Univ., USA (Mellon Fellow; MA). Called to the Bar, Middle Temple, 1965 (Harmsworth Law Scholar); Bencher, 1995, Dep. Treas., 2007, Treas., 2008. Lord Chancellor's Dept, 1966–87: Private Sec. to the Lord Chancellor, 1968–71; Sec., Law Reform Cttee, 1977–79; Under Sec., 1982–87; Circuit Administrator, Midland and Oxford Circuit, 1982–86; Hd, Courts and Legal Services Gp, 1986–87. Securities and Investments Board: Dir of Legal Services, 1987–91; General Counsel, 1991–93; Head of Policy and Legal Affairs, 1993–95; Dep. Chief Exec. and Gen. Counsel, 1996–98; Gen. Counsel to Bd, FSA, 1998–2000; Chairman: PIA, 2000–02; IMRO, 2000–02; SFA, 2001–02. Dep. Chm., 2007–08, Chm., 2008–, SWX Swiss Exchange Europe Ltd. Dir, Financial Services Compensation Scheme Ltd, 2000–05. Mem., Competition Appeal Tribunal, 2000–; Chm., Review Body on Doctors' and Dentists' Remuneration, 2001–07; Pres., Guernsey Financial Services Tribunal, 2002–; Mem. Bd, Dubai FSA, 2003–. Chairman: Bar Assoc. for Commerce, Finance and Industry, 1990–91; Bar Conf., 1993; Member: Gen. Council of the Bar, 1989–98 (Chm., Professional Standards Cttee, 1994; Treas., 1995–98); Council of Legal Educn, 1992–97. Hon. QC 1996. FRSA 1992. *Publications:* Sale of Goods Act 1979, 1980; Financial Services: the new core rules, 1991; (ed) Blackstone's Guide to the Bank of England Act 1998, 1998; (ed) Blackstone's Guide to the Financial Services and Markets Act 2000, 2001; (ed) Butterworths Financial Regulation Service, 2002–07; (ed) Financial Services, Halsbury's Laws of England, vol. 18(i), 4th edn, 2003; (ed jtly) Financial Services Law, 2006; (ed jtly) Financial Markets and Exchanges Law, 2007; legal articles in jls. *Address:* 3 Burbage Road, SE24 9HJ. *T:* (020) 7274 7614. *Club:* Athenæum.
See also R. O. Blair.

BLAIR, Capt. Neil; *see* Blair, Capt. R. N.

BLAIR, Sir Patrick David H.; *see* Hunter Blair.

BLAIR, Peter Michael; QC 2006; a Recorder, since 1999; *b* 24 Aug. 1961; *s* of Michael Blair and Joan (*née* Goodwin); *m* 1984, Sharon Atherton; one *s* two *d*. *Educ:* Princess Sophie Primary Sch., Addis Ababa; Brocksford Hall; Monkton Combe Sch.; Univ. of Oxford (BA Juris.). Called to the Bar, Inner Temple, 1983; in practice as barrister, Guildhall Chambers, Bristol, 1984–; Hd of Chambers, 2006–. Asst Recorder, 1997–99. Mem., Western Circuit Cttee, 1991–97. Mem., Bath CC, 1988–92. *Recreations:* landscape oil painting, poultry and pig keeping, gadgets. *Address:* Guildhall Chambers, 23 Broad Street, Bristol BS1 2HG. *T:* (0117) 930 9000, *Fax:* (0117) 930 3840; *e-mail:* peter.blair@guildhallchambers.co.uk.

BLAIR, Capt. (Robert) Neil, RN; CVO 2001 (LVO 1997); Private Secretary, Treasurer and Extra Equerry to the Duke of York, 1990–2001; Private Secretary to Princess Alexandra, the Hon. Lady Ogilvy, 1995–2001; *b* 14 July 1936; *s* of Harley Blair and Jane Blair (*née* Tarr); *m* 1960, Barbara Jane, *d* of Ian and Monica Rankin; two *s* one *d*. *Educ:* St John's Coll., Johannesburg; RNC, Dartmouth. Joined RN, 1954: served HMY Britannia, 1958–59 and 1970–71; FAA, 1961–70; in command: HMS Shavington, 1965–67; HMS Ashanti, 1972–74; HMS Royal Arthur, 1978; Comdr, BRNC, Dartmouth, 1979–80; Naval and Air Attaché, Athens, 1982–85; Defence and Naval Attaché, The Hague, 1986–89. Younger Brother, Trinity House, 1991. *Recreations:* photography, cricket, hill-walking. *Clubs:* Army and Navy, MCC.

BLAIR, Robin Orr, CVO 2008 (LVO 1999); Lord Lyon King of Arms and Secretary of the Order of the Thistle, 2001–08; *b* 1 Jan. 1940; *s* of Sir Alastair Campbell Blair, KCVO and Catriona Hatchard Blair (*née* Orr); *m* 1st, 1972, Elizabeth Caroline McCallum Webster (*d* 2000); two *s* one *d*; 2nd, 2005, Lel Simpson. *Educ:* Cargilfield; Rugby; St Andrews Univ. (MA); Edinburgh Univ. (LLB). WS 1965. Partner: Davidson & Syme WS, 1967–72; Dundas & Wilson CS, 1972–97 (Managing Partner, 1976–83, 1988–91); Turcan Connell WS, 1997–2000. Chm., Top Flight Leisure Gp, 1987–98 (non-exec. Dir, 1977–98); non-exec. Dir, Tullis Russell & Co. Ltd, 1977–98. Chm., Scottish Solicitors' Staff Pension Scheme, 1985–91. Hon. Sec., Assoc. of Edinburgh Royal Tradesmen, 1966–91. Purse Bearer to Lord High Comr to Gen. Assembly, C of S, 1988–2002. Chm., Scotland's Churches Scheme, 1997–. Gen. Council Assessor, Ct of Edinburgh Univ., 2003–07. Mem., Royal Co. of Archers. *Address:* 2 Blacket Place, Edinburgh EH9 1RL. *T:* (0131) 667 2906. *Clubs:* New (Edinburgh); Hon. Company of Edinburgh Golfers.
See also M. C. Blair.

BLAIR, Rt Hon. Tony; *see* Blair, Rt Hon. A. C. L.

BLAIR, Hon. Sir William James Lynton, Kt 2008; **Hon. Mr Justice Blair;** a Judge of the High Court of Justice, Queen's Bench Division, since 2008; *b* 31 March 1950; *s* of Leo Charles Lynton Blair and late Hazel Elizabeth (*née* Corscadden); *m* 1982, Katy Tse. *Educ:* Fettes Coll., Edinburgh; Balliol Coll., Oxford (BA 1971). Called to the Bar, Lincoln's Inn, 1972, Bencher, 2003; QC 1994; Asst Recorder, 1996–98; Recorder, 1998–2008; Dep. High Court Judge, 2003–08. Visiting Professor of Law: LSE, 1994–; Centre for Commercial Law Studies, QMW, 1999–. Part-time Chm., Financial Services and Markets Tribunal, 2001–. Member: Internat. Monetary Law Cttee, 1996– (Chm., 2004–), Council, British Br., 2000–, Internat. Law Assoc. Hon. Fellow, Soc. for Advanced Legal Studies, 1997. *Publications:* (ed) Encyclopaedia of Banking Law, 1982; (jtly) Banking and the Financial Services Act, 1993, 3rd edn, as Banking and Financial Services Regulation, 2002; (ed) Bullen, Leake and Jacob's Precedents of Pleading, 15th edn, 2004; contrib. other legal books and jls. *Recreations:* travel, walking. *Club:* Athenæum.
See also Rt Hon. A. C. L. Blair.

BLAIR, Prof. (William) John, DPhil; FBA 2008; FSA; historian and archaeologist; Fellow and Praelector in History, Queen's College, Oxford, since 1981; Professor of Medieval History and Archaeology, University of Oxford, since 2006; *b* Woking, 4 March 1955; *s* of Claude Blair, *qv*; *m* 2005, (Terttu) Kanerva Heikkinen; one *s*. *Educ:* St John's Sch., Leatherhead; Brasenose Coll., Oxford (BA 1st Cl. 1976; DPhil 1983). FSA 1983. Freeman, Cutlers' Co., 2004. *Publications:* (ed) Minsters and Parish Churches, 1988; (ed with N. Ramsay) English Medieval Industries, 1991; Early Medieval Surrey, 1991; (ed with R. Sharpe) Pastoral Care before the Parish, 1992; Anglo-Saxon Oxfordshire, 1994; (ed with B. Golding) The Cloister and the World, 1996; (ed jtly) The Blackwell Encyclopaedia of Anglo-Saxon England, 1999; The Church in Anglo-Saxon Society, 2005; (ed) Waterways and Canal-Building in Medieval England, 2007; contribs to books and jls. *Recreations:* travel, landscape and architecture, reading, listening to music. *Address:* Queen's College, Oxford OX1 4AW. *T:* (01865) 279120; *e-mail:* john.blair@queens.ox.ac.uk.

BLAIS, Hon. Jean Jacques; PC (Can.) 1976; QC (Can.) 1978; Counsel, Marusyk, Miller & Swain, Ottawa, since 1999; *b* 27 June 1940; *m* 1968, Maureen Ahearn; two *s* one *d*. *Educ:* Secondary Sch., Sturgeon Falls; Univ. of Ottawa (BA, LLB, LLM). Professional lawyer. MP (L) Nipissing, Ontario, 1972, re-elected 1974, 1979, 1980; defeated Sept. 1984; Parliamentary Sec. to Pres. of Privy Council, 1975; Post Master General, 1976; Solicitor General, 1978; Minister of Supply and Services, and Receiver General, 1980; Minister of Nat. Defence, 1983–84. Lectr in Private Internat. Law, Ottawa Univ., 1986–88. Dir, Canada Israel Industrial R & D Foundn, 1994–. Mem., Security and Intelligence Review Cttee, 1984–91; Dep. Chm., Provisional Election Commn, Bosnia and Herzegovina, 1998; Head of Mission: Elections Canada/Internat. Foundn of Election Systems mission to Afghanistan, 2003; Internat. Foundn for Electoral Systems, Iraq, 2003. Chm., Canadian Inst. of Strategic Studies, 1993–2003, 2004–05; Chm. Emeritus, Pearson Internat. Peacekeeping Center, 2003– (Chm., 1994–2003); Dir, Canadian Parly Center, 2005–. Chm., Heart Inst., Univ. of Ottawa, 2005– (Dir, 1995–2003). Hon DLitt Nipissing, 2007. *Recreations:* squash, ski-ing, swimming. *Address:* (office) 270 Albert Street, 14th Floor, Ottawa, ON K1P 5G8, Canada. *T:* (613) 5679348, *Fax:* (613) 5637671; *e-mail:* jjblais@mbm.com.

BLAIZE, Beverley; health practitioner; Deputy Chair, Commission for Racial Equality, 2000–03; *b* 9 Aug. 1949; *d* of Edmund Blaize and Jane John Baptist; *m* 1974, Leslie Bernard; one *d*. *Educ:* Univ. of Westminster (BA Hons); De Montfort Univ. (MA). Founder Trustee and CEO, Windsor Fellowship, 1985–95; Advr to Kagiso Trust, 1995–96, Man. Trustee, Nations Trust, 1995–98, RSA. Trustee, Esmée Fairbairn Foundn, 2003–06. *Publication:* The Homecoming: journey of the orphan child, 2006. *Recreations:* movie buff, rough cooking, dreaming. *Address:* 27 Ford Square, E1 2HS. *Club:* Bougainvillea (Barbados).

BLAKE, Sir Alfred (Lapthorn), KCVO 1979 (CVO 1975); MC 1945; DL; Director, The Duke of Edinburgh's Award Scheme, 1967–78; Consultant with Blake Lapthorn, Solicitors, Portsmouth and area, 1985–2000 (Partner, 1949–85, Senior Partner, 1983–85); *b* 6 Oct. 1915; *s* of late Leonard Nicholson Blake and Nora Woodfall Blake (*née* Lapthorn); *m* 1st, 1940, Beatrice Grace Nellthorp (*d* 1967); two *s*; 2nd, 1969, Alison Kelsey Dick, Boston, Mass, USA. *Educ:* Dauntsey's Sch. LLB (London), 1938. Qual. Solicitor and Notary Public, 1938. Royal Marines Officer, 1939–45: Bde Major 2 Commando Bde, 1944; Lieut-Col comdg 45 (RM) Commando and Holding Operational Commando, 1945 (despatches). Mem., Portsmouth CC, 1950–67 (Past Chm., Portsmouth Educn Cttee); Lord Mayor of Portsmouth, 1958–59. Mem., Youth Service Development Coun., 1960–66; Pres., Portsmouth Youth Activities Cttee, 1976–2007; Patron: Elizabeth Foundn, 1984–; Portsmouth Family Welfare, 1987–. Lay Canon, Portsmouth Cathedral, 1962–72. DL Hants, 1991. Hon. Fellow, Portsmouth Univ. (formerly Poly.), 1981. Hon. Freeman, City of Portsmouth, 2003. *Recreation:* golf. *Address:* 52 Arethusa House, Gunwharf Quays, Portsmouth PO1 3TQ. *T:* (023) 9275 0780.

BLAKE, Prof. Andrew, PhD; FRS 2005; FREng, FIET, FIEEE; Principal Research Scientist (formerly Senior Research Scientist), Microsoft Research Ltd, since 1999;

Partner, Microsoft Corp, since 2005; Fellow Clare Hall, Cambridge, since 2000; *b* 12 March 1956; *s* of Alan Geoffrey Blake and Judith Anne Blake (*née* Hart); *m* 1982, Fiona Anne-Marie Hewitt; one *s* one *d*. *Educ:* Rugby Sch.; Trinity Coll., Cambridge (MA); Univ. of Edinburgh (PhD 1983). FIET (FIEE 1994); FREng (FEng 1998); FIEEE 2008. Kennedy Meml Fellow, MIT, 1977–78; Research Scientist, Ferranti Edinburgh, 1978–80; University of Edinburgh: Res. Associate, 1980–83; Lectr in Computer Sci., 1983–87; Royal Soc. Res. Fellow, 1984–87; University of Oxford: Lectr in Image Processing, 1987–96; Fellow, Exeter Coll., 1987–99; Prof. of Engrg Sci., 1996–99; Royal Soc. Sen. Res. Fellow, 1998–99; Vis. Prof. of Engrg, 1999–. Honorary Professor: of Informatics, Univ. of Edinburgh, 2006–; of Machine Intelligence, Univ. of Cambridge, 2007–. Marr Prize, IEEE, 2001; Silver Medal, RAEng, 2006; Mountbatten Medal, IET, 2007. *Publications:* (with A. Zisserman) Visual Reconstruction, 1987; (with T. Troscianko) AI and the Eye, 1990; (with A. Yuille) Active Vision, 1992; (with M. Isard) Active Contours, 1998; articles on machine vision, robotics, visual psychology. *Address:* Microsoft Research Ltd, 7 J. J. Thomson Avenue, Cambridge CB3 0FB.

BLAKE, Andrew Nicholas Hubert; His Honour Judge Blake; a Circuit Judge, since 1999; *b* 18 Aug. 1946; *s* of late John Berchmans Blake and of Beryl Mary Blake; *m* 1978, Joy Ruth Shevloff; one *s*. *Educ:* Ampleforth Coll.; Hertford Coll., Oxford (MA Hist.). Called to the Bar, Inner Temple, 1971; in practice in Manchester, 1972–99. Mem. Cttee, Council of Circuit Judges, 2004–. *Recreations:* ski-ing, fishing, cycling, the Turf. *Address:* Manchester Crown Court, Crown Square, Manchester M3 3FL. *Club:* Norbury Fishing.

BLAKE, Sir Anthony Teilo Bruce, 18th Bt *cr* 1622, of Menlough; *b* 5 May 1951; *s* of Major Charles Anthony Howell Bruce Blake (killed in action, Korea, 1951) and Elspeth, *d* of late Lt-Col A. M. Arnott; *S* kinsman, 2008; *m* 1988, Geraldine, *d* of Cecil Shnaps; one *s* two *d*. *Educ:* Wellington Coll. *Heir:* *s* Charles Valentine Bruce Blake, *b* 1994.

BLAKE, Carole Rae; Joint Managing Director, Blake Friedmann Literary Agency Ltd, since 1983; *b* 29 Sept. 1946; *née* Blake; *d* of Maisie Lock and step *d* of Gilbert Lock; *m* 1st, 1970, David Urbani (marr. diss. 1982); 2nd, 1983, Julian Friedmann (marr. diss. 1996). *Educ:* Pollards Hill Co. Secondary Sch. Rights Manager, George Rainbird Ltd, 1963–70; Rights and Contracts Manager: Michael Joseph Ltd, 1970–74; W. H. Allen Ltd, 1974–75; Marketing Dir, Sphere Books Ltd, 1975–76; founded Carole Blake Literary Agency Ltd, subseq. Blake Friedmann Literary Agency Ltd, 1976. Pres., Assoc. of Authors' Agents, 1991–93. Mem., Soc. of Bookmen, 1991– (Chm., 1997–98); Dir, Book Trade Benevolent Soc., 1999–2007 (Chm., 2004–07). Member, Advisory Board: Publishing Studies, City Univ., 2000–; UCL Centre for Publishing, 2006–. *Publication:* From Pitch to Publication, 1999. *Recreations:* reading, classical music, wildlife, Medieval and Ancient Egyptian history. *Address:* (office) 122 Arlington Road, NW1 7HP. *T:* (020) 7284 0408, *Fax:* (020) 7284 0442; *e-mail:* carole@blakefriedmann.co.uk.

BLAKE, Prof. Christopher, CBE 1991; FRSE; Chairman, Glenrothes Development Corporation, 1987–96; *b* 28 April 1926; *s* of George Blake and Eliza Blake; *m* 1951, Elizabeth McIntyre; two *s* two *d*. *Educ:* Dollar Academy; St Andrews Univ. (MA 1950; PhD 1965). Served in Royal Navy, 1944–47. Teaching posts, Bowdoin Coll., Maine, and Princeton Univ., 1951–53; Asst, Edinburgh Univ., 1953–55; Stewarts & Lloyds Ltd, 1955–60; Lectr and Sen. Lectr, Univ. of St Andrews, 1960–67; Sen. Lectr and Prof. of Economics, 1967–74, Bonar Prof. of Applied Econs, 1974–88, Univ. of Dundee. Dir, Alliance Trust plc, 1974–94; Chm., William Low & Co. plc, 1985–90 (Dir, 1980–90). Member: Council for Applied Science in Scotland, 1978–86; Royal Commn on Envtl Pollution, 1980–86. Treasurer, RSE, 1986–89. *Publications:* articles in economic and other jls. *Recreation:* golf. *Address:* Westlea, 14 Wardlaw Gardens, St Andrews, Fife KY16 9DW. *T:* (01334) 473840. *Clubs:* New (Edinburgh); Royal and Ancient (St Andrews).

BLAKE, Clifford Douglas, AO 2002 (AM 1988); PhD; Vice-Chancellor, University of Adelaide, 2001–02; *b* 27 Aug. 1937; *s* of William Oscar Blake and Isobel Florence Blake (*née* Keown). *Educ:* Muswellbrook High Sch.; Univ. of Sydney (BScAgr); Univ. of London (PhD). FAIAS. Lectr and Sen. Lectr in Plant Pathology, Univ. of Sydney, 1963–70; foundation Principal, Riverina College of Advanced Educn, subseq. renamed Riverina-Murray Inst. of Higher Educn, 1971–90; Vice-Chancellor, Charles Sturt Univ., 1990–2001. Pres., Aust. Higher Educn Industrial Assoc., 1992–99; Member, Board of Directors: Open Learning Agency of Australia Pty, 1993–96; Australian Vice Chancellors' Cttee, 1994–99; Convenor, NSW Vice Chancellors' Cttee, 1996–98. Member: NSW Bd, Vocational and Tech. Educn, 2001–02; NSW Admin. Appeals Tribunal, 2002–. Gov., Commonwealth of Learning, 1992–2000; Chm., Nat. Cttee on Distance Educn, 1994–95. Freeman, City of Wagga Wagga, 1996; Hon. Citizen, City of Bathurst, 1998. Hon. Fellow, Commonwealth Learning, 2002. Hon. DEd Admin, Sydney, 2001; DUniv Charles Sturt, 2001. Farrer Medallist for contribn to Aust. agriculture, 1996; Paul Harris Fellow, Rotary Club, 2001. *Publication:* (ed) Fundamentals of Modern Agriculture, 1967, 3rd edn 1971. *Recreation:* travel. *Address:* 55 Waratah Road, Wentworth Falls, NSW 2782, Australia. *Club:* Union, University and Schools (Sydney).

BLAKE, David Charles, Eur Ing, CEng, FIMechE; Partner, Bee Services, since 1996; *b* 23 Sept. 1936; *s* of Walter David John Blake and Ellen Charlotte Blake; *m* 1st, 1959, Della Victoria Stevenson (marr. diss. 1996); two *s*; 2nd, 1996, Christine Emmett; one *d*. *Educ:* South East Essex Technical Sch.; South East Essex Technical Coll. British Transport Commn, later British Railways Board, 1953–96: Engrg apprentice, Stratford Locomotive Works, 1953–57; Technical Management, BR Eastern Reg., 1957–69; Construction Engr, W Coast Main Line Electrification, 1969–74; Area Maintenance Engineer: Motherwell Scottish Reg., 1974–75; Shields Scottish Reg., 1975–76; Rolling Stock Engr, Scottish Reg., 1976–78; Electrical Engr, E Reg., 1978–80; Chief Mechanical and Electrical Engr, Southern Reg., 1980–82; Director: Manufacturing and Maintenance Policy, BRB, 1983–87; Mech. and Elec. Engrg, BRB, 1987–90; Man. Dir, King's Cross Projects Gp, BRB, 1990–93; Man. Dir, Vendor Unit, BRB, 1993–96. Non-exec. Director: Engineering Link Ltd, 1999–2003; Leics County and Rutland PCT, 2006–. Gov., St Mary & St John C of E Voluntary Aided Primary Sch., North Luffenham, 2004–. *Recreations:* gardening, hill walking. *Address:* The Windmill, Morcott, Rutland LE15 9DQ. *T:* (01572) 747000, *Fax:* (01572) 747373.

BLAKE, Prof. David Leonard; Professor of Music, University of York, 1976–2001, now Emeritus; *b* 2 Sept. 1936; *s* of Leonard Blake and Dorothy Blake; *m* 1960, Rita Muir; two *s* one *d*. *Educ:* Latymer Upper School; Gonville and Caius College, Cambridge (BA 1960, MA 1963); Deutsche Akademie der Künste, Berlin, GDR. School teacher: Ealing Grammar Sch., 1961–62; Northwood Secondary Sch., 1962–63; University of York: Granada Arts Fellow, 1963–64; Lectr in Music, 1964; Sen. Lectr, 1971–76. *Recordings* (own compositions): Violin concerto: In Praise of Krishna; Variations for Piano; The Almanack. *Compositions* include: String Quartet No 1, 1962; It's a Small War (musical for schools), 1962; Chamber Symphony, 1966; Lumina (text from Ezra Pound's Cantos) (cantata for soprano, baritone, chorus and orch.), 1969; Metamorphoses, for large orch., 1971; Nonet, for wind, 1971; The Bones of Chuang Tzu (cantata for baritone and piano), 1972; In Praise of Krishna: Bengali lyrics, 1973; String Quartet No 2, 1973; Violin Concerto, 1976; Toussaint (opera), 1974–77; From the Mattress Grave (song cycle), 1978; Nine Songs of Heine, 1978; Clarinet Quintet, 1980; String Quartet No 3, 1982; Rise Dove, for bass and orch., 1983; The Plumber's Gift (opera), 1985–88; Cello Concerto, 1992; Three Ritsos Choruses, 1992; The Griffin's Tale, for baritone and orch., 1994; Diversions on Themes of Hanns Eisler, for alto sax. and piano, 1995; The Fabulous Adventures of Alexander the Great, for chorus and orch. of young people, 1996; Scoring a Century (entertainment), 1999; The Shades of Love, for bass and small orch., 2000; The Lonely Wife I and II (poems from the Chinese for soprano and mezzo), 2003; String Quartet No 4, 2004; Rings of Jade (poems by Ho Chi Minh), for medium voice and orch., 2005. *Publication:* (ed) Hanns Eisler: a miscellany, 1995. *Recreation:* land management. *Address:* Mill Gill, Askrigg, Leyburn, North Yorks DL8 3HR. *T:* (01969) 650364; *e-mail:* dl.blake@tiscali.co.uk.

BLAKE, Sir Francis Michael, 3rd Bt *cr* 1907; *b* 11 July 1943; *o s* of Sir F. Edward C. Blake, 2nd Bt and Olive Mary (*d* 1946) *d* of Charles Liddell Simpson; *S* father, 1950; *m* 1968, Joan Ashbridge, *d* of F. C. A. Miller; two *s*. *Educ:* Rugby. High Sheriff, Northumberland, 2002. *Heir:* *s* Francis Julian Blake [*b* 17 Feb. 1971; *m* 2000, Dr Jennifer Armstrong (marr. diss. 2007), *o d* of Peter Armstrong]. *Address:* The Dower House, Tillmouth Park, Cornhill-on-Tweed, Northumberland TD12 4UR. *T:* (01890) 882443.

BLAKE, Howard David, OBE 1994; FRAM; composer; *b* 28 Oct. 1938; *s* of Horace C. Blake and Grace B. Blake (*née* Benson). FRAM 1989. Dir, PRS, 1978–87; Co-founder, Assoc. of Professional Composers, 1980. *Compositions: concert works:* The Song of Francis, 1976; Benedictus, 1979; Sinfonietta for brass ensemble, 1981; Clarinet Concerto, 1984; Shakespeare Songs, 1987; Festival Mass, 1987; Diversions for Cello and Orchestra, 1989; Four Songs of the Nativity, 1990; Piano Concerto for Princess of Wales, 1990; Violin Concerto for City of Leeds, 1993; The Land of Counterpane, 1995; Charter for Peace (commissioned by FCO for 50th anniv. of UN), 1995; All God's Creatures, 1995; Lifecycle for solo piano, 1996; Flute Concerto, 1996; Still Falls the Rain, 1998; The Passion of Mary, 2002; The Rise of the House of Usher, 2003; Songs of Truth and Glory, 2005; Winterdream, 2006; *stage works:* Henry V, 1984, As You Like It, 1985, RSC; The Snowman (ballet), 1993; Eva (ballet), Gothenburg Opera House, 1996; *film and television scores include:* The Duellists, 1977; The Snowman (TV), 1982; A Month in the Country, 1986 (BFI Anthony Asquith Award); Granpa (TV), 1987; A Midsummer Night's Dream (RSC and Channel 4), 1996; The Bear (TV), 1998; My Life So Far, 1999. *Recreations:* reading, walking, swimming. *Address:* Studio 6, 18 Kensington Court Place, W8 5BJ. *T:* and *Fax:* (020) 7938 1969; *e-mail:* howardblake.obe@virgin.net. *Clubs:* Groucho, Chelsea Arts.

BLAKE, John Michael; Managing Director: Blake Publishing, since 1991; John Blake Publishing, since 2000; Metro Publishing, since 2001; *b* 6 Nov. 1948; *s* of late Major Edwin Blake, MBE, and of Joyce Blake; *m* 1968, Diane Sutherland Campbell; one *s* two *d*. *Educ:* Westminster City Grammar Sch.; North-West London Polytechnic. Reporter: Hackney Gazette, 1966; Evening Post, Luton, 1969; Fleet Street News Agency, 1970; Columnist: London Evening News, 1971; London Evening Standard, 1980; The Sun, 1982; Asst Editor, Daily Mirror, 1985; Editor, The People, 1988–89; Pres., Mirror Group Newspapers (USA), 1989; Exec. Producer, Sky Television, 1990. *Publications:* Up and Down with The Rolling Stones, 1978; All You Needed Was Love, 1981. *Recreation:* messing about in boats. *Address:* John Blake Publishing Ltd, 3 Bramber Court, 2 Bramber Road, W14 9PB. *Clubs:* Groucho, Chelsea Arts.

BLAKE, Jonathan Elazar; Senior Partner, SJ Berwin LLP, since 2006; *b* 7 July 1954; *s* of late Asher Blake and Nomi Blake; *m* Isabel Horovitz; three *s* one *d*. *Educ:* Haberdashers' Aske's Sch.; Queens' Coll., Cambridge (BA 1975; LLB 1976). Stephenson Harwood, 1977–82; Partner, SJ Berwin, 1982–. Former Mem. Council, British Venture Capital Assoc.; former Chm., Tax and Legal Cttee, European Private Equity and Venture Capital Assoc. *Recreations:* ski-ing, walking, theatre, travel, family. *Address:* SJ Berwin LLP, 10 Queen Street Place, EC4R 1BE. *T:* (020) 7111 2317, *Fax:* (020) 7111 2000; *e-mail:* jonathan.blake@sjberwin.com.

BLAKE, Mary Netterville, MA; Headmistress, Manchester High School for Girls, 1975–83; *b* 12 Sept. 1922; *d* of John Netterville Blake and Agnes Barr Blake. *Educ:* Howell's Sch., Denbigh; St Anne's Coll., Oxford (MA). Asst Mistress, The Mount Sch., York, 1945–48; Head of Geography Dept, King's High Sch., Warwick, 1948–56; Associate Gen. Sec., Student Christian Movement in Schools, 1956–60; Head Mistress, Selby Grammar Sch., 1960–75. Pres., Assoc. of Headmistresses, 1976–77; first Pres., Secondary Heads Assoc., 1978. *Address:* 11 Baldenhall, Hall Green, Malvern, Worcs WR14 3RZ. *T:* (01684) 564359.

BLAKE, Hon. Sir Nicholas (John Gorrod), Kt 2007; **Hon. Mr Justice Blake;** a Judge of the High Court of Justice, Queen's Bench Division, since 2007; *b* 21 June 1949; *s* of Leslie Gorrod Blake and Jean Margaret (*née* Ballinger); *m* 1986, Clio Whittaker; one *s* two *d* (and one *s* decd). *Educ:* Cranleigh Sch.; Magdalene Coll., Cambridge (BA Hons Hist.); Inns of Court Sch. of Law. Called to the Bar, Middle Temple, 1974, Bencher, 2002. QC 1994; Asst Recorder, 1999–2000; Recorder, 2000–07; Dep. Judge of the High Court, 2003–07. Chm., Immigration Lawyers Practitioners Assoc., 1994–97. Mem. Council, Justice, 1995–2007. Trustee, NPG, 2005–. FRSA. *Publications:* Police Law and the People, 1974; (jtly) Wigs and Workers, 1980; (jtly) New Nationality Law, 1983; (ed jtly) Immigration Law and Practice, 3rd edn 1991, 4th edn 1995; Immigration Asylum and Human Rights, 2002. *Recreation:* the visual arts. *Address:* Royal Courts of Justice, Strand, WC2A 2LL.

BLAKE, Sir Peter (Thomas), Kt 2002; CBE 1983; RDI 1987; ARCA; painter; *b* 25 June 1932; *s* of Kenneth William Blake; *m* 1963, Jann Haworth (marr. diss. 1982); two *d*; *m* 1987, Chrissy Wilson; one *d*. *Educ:* Gravesend Tech. Coll.; Gravesend Sch. of Art; RCA. ARA 1974; RA 1980, resigned 2005; Prof. of Drawing, Royal Acad., 2002–04. Works exhibited: ICA, 1958, 1960; Guggenheim Competition, 1958; Cambridge, 1959; RA, 1960; Musée d'Art Moderne, Paris, 1968; Waddington Galls, 1970, 1972, 1977 and 1990; Stedelijk Mus., Amsterdam, 1973; Kunstverein, Hamburg, 1973; Gemeentemuseum, Arnhem, 1974; Palais des Beaux-Arts, Brussels, 1974; Galleria Documenta, Turin, 1982; retrospective exhibitions: Tate Gall., 1983; Gal. Claude Bernard, Paris, 1984; Nishimura Gall., Tokyo, 1988; Nat. Gall., 1996; London Inst. Gall., 2003; Tate Liverpool, 2007; works in public collections: Trinity Coll., Cambridge; Carlisle City Gall.; Tate Gall.; Arts Council of GB; Mus. of Modern Art, NY; V & A Mus.; Mus. Boymans-van Beuningen, Rotterdam; Calouste Gulbenkian Foundn, London; RCA; Whitworth Art Gall., Univ. of Manchester; Baltimore Mus. of Art, Md. Third Associate Artist, Nat. Gall., 1994. *Publications:* illustrations for: Oxford Illustrated Old Testament, 1968; Roger McGough, Summer with Monica, 1978; cover illustration, Arden Shakespeare: Othello, 1980; Anthony and Cleopatra, 1980; Timon of Athens, 1980; contribs to: Times Educnl Supp.; Ark; Graphis 70; World of Art; Architectural Rev.; House and Garden; Painter and Sculptor. *Recreations:* sculpture, wining and dining, going to rock and roll concerts, boxing and wrestling matches; living well is the best revenge. *Address:* c/o Waddington Galleries Ltd, 11 Cork Street, W1X 2LT.

BLAKE, Quentin Saxby, CBE 2005 (OBE 1988); RDI 1981; freelance artist and illustrator, since 1957; Visiting Professor, Royal College of Art, since 1989; first Children's Laureate, 1999–2001; *b* 16 Dec. 1932; *s* of William Blake and Evelyn Blake. *Educ:* Chislehurst and Sidcup Grammar Sch.; Downing Coll., Cambridge (MA; Hon. Fellow, 2000); Inst. of Education, Univ. of London (PGCE). Royal College of Art: Tutor, 1965–77; Head, Dept of Illustration, 1978–86; Vis. Tutor, 1986–89; Sen. Fellow, 1988. Exhibitions of watercolour drawings, Workshop Gallery: Invitation to the Dance, 1972; Runners and Riders, 1973; Creature Comforts, 1974; Water Music, 1976; exhibitions of illustration work: Chris Beetles Gall., 1993, 1996, 2004, 2007; Dulwich Picture Gall., 2004; South Kensington and Chelsea Mental Health Care Centre: The Kershaw Pictures, 2006; Sixty New Drawings, 2006; retrospective: Nat. Theatre, 1984; Paris, 1995, 1999; Somerset House, 2003. Curator: Tell Me A Picture, Nat. Gall., 2001; A Baker's Dozen, Bury St Edmunds, 2001; Magic Pencil, British Council, 2001; In All Directions, Arts Council, 2005; Quentin Blake et les Demoiselles des Bords de Seine, Paris, 2005. Hon. Fellow, Brighton Univ. Hon. FRA 2001. Hon. Dr: London Inst., 2000; RCA, Northumbria, 2001; Anglia Ruskin, 2007; Inst. of Educn, London, 2008; Hon. LittD Cambridge, 2004; DUniv Open, 2006; Hon. DLitt Loughborough, 2007. Hans Christian Andersen Award, 2002. Officier, l'Ordre des Arts et des Lettres (France), 2007. *Publications:* (author and illustrator) for children: Patrick, 1968; Jack and Nancy, 1969; Angelo, 1970; Snuff, 1973; The Adventures of Lester, 1977; Mr Magnolia, 1980 (Fedn of Children's Bk Gps Award; Kate Greenaway Medal, 1981); Quentin Blake's Nursery Rhyme Book, 1983; The Story of the Dancing Frog, 1984; Mrs Armitage on Wheels, 1987; Quentin Blake's ABC, 1989; All Join In, 1990; Cockatoos, 1991; Simpkin, 1993; Clown, 1995 (Bologna Ragazzi Prize, 1996); Mrs Armitage and the Big Wave, 1997; Dix Grenouilles, 1997; The Green Ship, 1998; Zagazoo, 1998; Fantastic Daisy Artichoke, 1999; Un Bateau dans le Ciel, 2000; Loveykins, 2002; Mrs Armitage Queen of the Road, 2003; Angel Pavement, 2004; (editor and illustrator) for children: Custard and Company, by Ogden Nash, 1979; The Quentin Blake Book of Nonsense Verse, 1994; The Quentin Blake Book of Nonsense Stories, 1996; Promenade de Quentin Blake au Pays de la Poésie Française, 2003; (illustrator) for children: Russell Hoban: How Tom Beat Captain Najork and his Hired Sportsmen, 1974 (Whitbread Lit. Award, 1975; Hans Andersen Honour Book, 1975); A Near Thing for Captain Najork, 1976; The Rain Door, 1986; Hilaire Belloc: Algernon and Other Cautionary Tales, 1991; Michael Rosen: Mind Your Own Business, 1974; Wouldn't You Like to Know, 1977; You Can't Catch Me, 1981; Quick Let's Get Out of Here, 1982; Don't Put Mustard in the Custard, 1985; Michael Rosen's Sad Book, 2005; Roald Dahl: The Enormous Crocodile, 1978; The Twits, 1980; George's Marvellous Medicine, 1981; Revolting Rhymes, 1982; The BFG, 1982; The Witches, 1983; Dirty Beasts, 1984; The Giraffe and the Pelly and Me, 1985; Matilda, 1988; Rhyme Stew, 1989; Esio Trot, 1990; Dahl Diary, 1991; My Year, 1993; Danny Champion of the World, 1994; Roald Dahl's Revolting Recipes, 1994; Charlie and the Chocolate Factory, 1995; Charlie and the Great Glass Elevator, 1995; James and the Giant Peach, 1995; The Magic Finger, 1995; Fantastic Mr Fox, 1996; Even More Revolting Recipes, 2001; John Yeoman: Featherbrains, 1993; The Singing Tortoise, 1993; The Family Album, 1993; The Do-It-Yourself House that Jack Built, 1994; Mr Nodd's Ark, 1995; Up with Birds!, 1997; The Princes' Gifts, 1997; The Heron and the Crane, 1999; Joan Aiken, The Winter Sleepwalker, 1994; books by Clement Freud, Sid Fleischman, Sylvia Plath, Margaret Mahy, Dr Seuss and Michael Morpurgo; (illustrator) for adults: Aristophanes, The Birds, 1971; Lewis Caroll, The Hunting of the Snark, 1976; Stella Gibbons, Cold Comfort Farm, 1977; Evelyn Waugh, Black Mischief, 1980, Scoop, 1981; George Orwell, Animal Farm, 1984; Cyrano de Bergerac, Voyages to the Sun and Moon, 1991; Cervantes, Don Quixote, 1995; Charles Dickens, A Christmas Carol, 1995; Victor Hugo, The Hunchback of Notre Dame, 1998; *non-fiction:* (author) La Vie de la Page, 1995; (jtly) Drawing for the Artistically Undiscovered, 2000; Words and Pictures, 2000; Woman with a Book (drawings), 2000; The Laureate's Party, 2000; Tell me a Picture, 2001; Laureate's Progress, 2002; In All Directions, 2005; Quentin Blake et les Demoiselles des Bords de Seine, 2005; The Life of Birds (drawings), 2005; Vive Nos Vieux Jours!, 2007. *Address:* 30 Bramham Gardens, SW5 0HF. *T:* (020) 7373 7464.

BLAKE, Richard Andrew; a District Judge (Magistrates' Courts), since 2006; *b* 14 March 1955; *s* of late Lionel Henry Blake and of Betty Blake; civil partnership 2006, Jonathan Neil Langston. *Educ:* Magistrates Law Dip. 1980; Poly. of Central London (Dip. Law 1981); Inns of Court Sch.of Law (Bar. Dip. 1982). Magistrates' Courts Service, 1974–83, Sen. Ct Clerk, Willesden Magistrates' Ct, 1982–83; called to the Bar, Gray's Inn, 1982; Avon and Somerset Prosecuting Solicitor's Office, 1983–86; Sen. Crown Prosecutor, Kingston, 1986–89, Principal Crown Prosecutor, 1989–90, CPS; in private practice as a barrister, One Inner Temple Lane, 1990–2006; apptd Dep. Stipendiary Magistrate, later Dist Judge, 1999. *Recreations:* boating, Jaguar motor cars, Isle of Wight. *Address:* The Court House, 358 High Street, Lincoln LN5 7QA. *T:* (01522) 582847, *Fax:* (01522) 525832. *Club:* Island Sailing (Cowes).

BLAKE, Richard Frederick William; Editor, Whitaker's Almanack, 1981–86; *b* 9 April 1948; *s* of late Frederick William Blake and Doris Margaret Blake; *m* 1973, Christine Vaughan; one *d*. *Educ:* Archbishop Tenison's Grammar School. Joined J. Whitaker & Sons, Ltd (Whitaker's Almanack Dept), 1966; apptd Asst Editor of Whitaker's Almanack, 1974. *Recreation:* listening to music. *Address:* 118 Warren Drive, Elm Park, Hornchurch, Essex RM12 4QX.

BLAKE, Simon Anthony; Chief Executive, Brook, since 2006; *b* 28 Jan. 1974; *s* of John and Margaret Blake; partner, Dr John Swift. *Educ:* Univ. of Wales Coll. of Cardiff (BA Psychol.); Univ. of Wales Coll., Newport (Postgrad. Cert. Counselling); London South Bank Univ. (Postgrad. Dip. Social Res. Methods). Develt Officer, FPA, 1996–99; Dir, Sex Educn Forum, 1999–2002; Asst Dir, Nat. Children's Bureau, 2002–06; on secondment to DoH as Children's Policy Advr, 2004. Chm., Compact Voice, 2008–. *Publications:* (with J. Laxton) Strides: a practical guide to sex and relationships education with young men, 1998; A Whole School Approach to PSHE and Citizenship, 2000, 2nd edn 2006; (with G. Frances) Just Say No to Abstinence Education!, 2001; (with M. Biddulph) Moving Goalposts: setting a training agenda for sexual health work with boys and young men, 2001; (with Z. Katrak) Faith, Values and Sex and Relationships Education, 2002; Sex and Relationships Education: a step-by-step guide for teachers, 2002; (with P. Power) Teaching and Learning About HIV: a resource for Key Stages 1 to 4, 2003; (with J. Lynch) Sex, Alcohol and Other Drugs: exploring the links in young people's lives, 2004; (with A. Shutt) Be Aware: young people, alcohol and other drugs, 2004; Cards for Life: promoting emotional and social development, 2005; (with S. Plant) Addressing Inequalities and Inclusion through Personal, Social, Health Education and Citizenship, 2005; (with S. Muttock) Assessment and Evaluation in Sex and Relationships Education, 2005; (jtly) Promoting Emotional and Social Development in Schools: a practical guide, 2007. *Recreations:* swimming, running, horseriding. *Address:* Brook, 421 Highgate Studios, 53–79 Highgate Road, NW5 1TL. *T:* (020) 7284 6065, *Fax:* (020) 7284 6050; *e-mail:* simonb@brookcentres.org.uk.

BLAKE-JAMES, Linda Elizabeth; *see* Sullivan, L. E.

BLAKELEY, Trevor, CEng; FRINA; FIMarEST; FIMechE; Chief Executive, Royal Institution of Naval Architects, since 1997; *b* 22 Nov. 1943; *m* 1965, Patricia Challenger; one *s* one *d*. *Educ:* Goole Grammar Sch.; BRNC Dartmouth; RNEC Manadon (BSc 1968); BA Open Univ. 1995. CEng 1973; FIMarEST (FIMarE 1996); FIMechE 1996; FRINA 1997. Joined RN, 1963; served as engineering specialist; retired 1996. Mem. Ct, Cranfield Univ., 1999–; Gov., Horndean Technol. Coll., 2002–. Mem., Shipwrights' Co., 1999–. *Recreations:* theatre, music, horse riding. *Address:* Royal Institution of Naval Architects, 10 Upper Belgrave Street, SW1X 8BQ. *T:* (020) 7235 4622.

BLAKEMORE, Prof. Colin (Brian), FRS 1992; Professor of Neuroscience, Oxford University, since 2007; Fellow of Magdalen College, Oxford, since 1979; Professor of Neuroscience, University of Warwick, since 2007; *b* 1 June 1944; *s* of Cedric Norman Blakemore and Beryl Ann Smith; *m* 1965, Andrée Elizabeth Washbourne; three *d*. *Educ:* King Henry VIII Sch., Coventry; Corpus Christi Coll., Cambridge (Smyth Scholar; BA 1965; MA 1969; ScD 1988; Hon. Fellow, 1994); Univ. of Calif, Berkeley (PhD 1968); Magdalen Coll., Oxford (MA 1979; DSc 1989). FIBiol, CBiol 1996 (Hon. FIBiol 2004). Harkness Fellow, Neurosensory Lab., Univ. of Calif, Berkeley, 1965–68; Cambridge University: Fellow and Dir of Medical Studies, Downing Coll., 1971–79; Univ. Demonstr in Physiol., 1968–72; Univ. Lectr in Physiol., 1972–79; Leverhulme Fellow, 1974–75; Royal Soc. Locke Res. Fellow, 1976–79; Oxford University: Waynflete Prof. of Physiology, 1979–2007 (on leave of absence, 2003–07); Director: McDonnell-Pew Centre for Cognitive Neuroscience, 1990–2003; MRC IRC for Cognitive Neurosci., 1996–2003. Chief Exec., MRC, 2003–07 (Chm., Neurobiology and Mental Health Bd Grants Cttee, 1977–79). Non-exec. Dir, BTG plc, 2007–. Agency for Science, Technology and Research, Singapore: Mem., Biomed. Scis Internat. Adv. Cttee, 2005–; Chairman: Neurosci. Adv. Cttee, 2006–; Duke-Nat. Univ. of Singapore Grad. Med. Sch. Partnership in Neurosci., 2007–. Vis. Professor: NY Univ., 1970; MIT, 1971; Royal Soc. Study Visit, Keio Univ., Tokyo, 1974; Lethaby Prof., RCA, 1978–79; Storer Vis. Lectr, Univ. of Calif, Davis, 1980; Vis. Scientist, Salk Inst., 1982, 1983, 1992; Macallum Vis. Lectr, Univ. of Toronto, 1984; McLaughlin Vis. Prof., McMaster Univ., Ont, 1992; Regents' Prof. and Vis. Prof., Univ. of Calif, Davis, 1995–97; Spinoza Prof., Univ. of Amsterdam, 1996; Dist. Visitor, BioMed. Res. Council, Singapore, 2005. Chm. Council, BAAS, 2001–04 (Pres., Gen. Section, 1989; Pres., 1997–98, Vice-Pres., 1990–97, 1998–2001; Hon. Fellow, 2001); President: British Neurosci. Assoc., 1997–2000; Physiological Soc., 2001–03; Bioscis Fedn, 2002–04. Hon. Pres., World Cultural Council, 1983–. Mem., World Fedn of Scientists, 1988–; Fellow: World Econ. Forum, 1994–98; World Innovation Foundn, 2002–. Founder Mem., Bd of Govs, Internat. Brain Injury Assoc. (Nat. Head Injury Foundn Inc., Washington), 1993–; Mem. Professional Adv. Panel, and Patron, Headway (Nat. Head Injuries Assoc.), 1997–; Member: Council, Internat. Brain Res. Org., 1973–2001; BBC Science Consultative Group, 1975–79; British Nat. Cttee for Physiol. Scis, 1985–86; Professional Adv. Cttee, Schizophrenia: A National Emergency, 1989–95 (Trustee, 2001–03; Vice-Patron, 2003–); Adv. Gp on Non-Ionising Radiation, NRPB, 1992–2003; Council, Fedn of European Neuroscience Socs, 1998–2000; Nat. Cttee for 2000 Forum for European Neurosci., Brighton, 1998–2000; Ind. Expert Gp on Mobile Phones, DoH, 1999–2000; Prog. Mgt Cttee, UK Telecoms Health Res. Prog., 2000–03; UK Drug Policy Commn, 2006–. Mem. Exec. Cttee, Dana Alliance for Brain Initiatives, NY, 1996–; Vice-Chm., European Dana Alliance for the Brain, 1996–. Royal Society: Chairman: Wkg Gp, Public Prog., 2001–03; Partnership Grants Cttee, 2001–03; Member: Council, COPUS, 2001–02; Sci. in Soc. Cttee, 2001–04; Michael Faraday Prize Cttee, 2001–05; Jt Acad. Med. Scis Wkg Gp on Sci. of Transmissible Spongiform Encephalopathies, 2000; Member: Adv. Gp, Sense about Science, 2002–; Exec. Council, Novartis Foundn, 2002–; Sci., Engrg and Envmt Adv. Cttee, British Council, 2003–; Bd, Coalition for Med. Progress, 2003– (Chm., 2005–; Trustee, 2005–); Council, Med. Genetics Sect., RSocMed, 2007–; Adv. Council, ABPI, 2007–; Pres., British Biol. Olympiad, 2005–. Hon. Associate: Rationalist Press Assoc., 1986–; Rationalist Internat., 2000–; Cheltenham Fest. of Sci., 2001–; Founder Mem. Cttee, Harkness Fellowships Assoc., 1997–; Patron: Assoc. for Art, Sci., Engrg and Technol., 1997–; Clifton Scientific Trust, Bristol, 1999–; Patron, 1996–, and Scientific Advr, At-Bristol Science Centre; Pres., Assoc. of British Sci. Writers, 2004–. Pres., Oxon Motor Neurone Disease Assoc., 2004– (Hon. Mem., Motor Neurone Disease Assoc., 2005–); Vice-Pres., Progressive Supranuclear Palsy Assoc., 2004–; Trustee: Brain Child, 1991–; Bhopal Med. Appeal, 2003–; Patron: Corpal, 1989–; Saferworld, 1991–; Member: Med. Panel, Patients' Voice for Med. Advance (formerly Seriously Ill for Med. Res.), 2002–; Internat. Adv. Council, Louise T. Blouin Foundn, 2005–; Scientific Adv. Bd, Lifeboat Foundn, 2006–; Neurosci. Adv. Bd, Peter and Patricia Gruber Foundn, 2006–; Scientific Advr, Beckley Foundn, 2001–; Consultant, Thriving Child Project, Jabadao (Centre for Study of Movt, Learning and Health), 2002–. BBC Reith Lectr, 1976; Presenter, BBC TV series: The Mind Machine, 1988; The Next Big Thing, 2000, 2001; Lectures include: Aubrey Lewis, Inst. of Psych., 1979; Lord Charnwood, Amer. Acad. of Optometry, 1980; Vickers, Neonatal Soc., 1981; Harveian, Harveian Soc. of London, 1982; Christmas, Royal Instn, 1982; George Frederic Still, BPA, 1983, RCPCH, 2005; Edridge-Green, RCS, 1984; Halliburton, KCL, 1986; Cairns Meml (also Medal), Cambridge Univ., 1986; Bertram Louis Abrahams, RCP, 1986; Norman McAlister Gregg (also Medal), RACO, 1988; Dietrich Bodenstein, Univ. of Va, 1989; Charnock Bradley, Univ. of Edinburgh, 1989; Doyne, Oxford Ophthalmol Congress, 1989 (also Medal); G. L. Brown, Physiol Soc., 1990; Sir Douglas Robb, Univ. of Auckland, 1991; James Law, Cornell, 1994; Newton, Cos of Spectacle Makers, and Clockmakers and Scientific Instrument Makers, 1997; Cockcroft, UMIST, 1997; David Oppenheimer Meml, Oxford, 2000; Alfred Meyer Meml (also Medal), British Neuropathol Soc., 2001; Dorothy J. Killam, Dalhousie Univ., 2001; Menzies Foundn (and Medal), 2002; Miller Com, Univ. of Illinois, 2003; Gordon Holmes, Cambridge Univ., 2004; Lord David Sainsbury, Bristol Univ., 2005; Harveian Oration, RCP, 2006; Kenneth Myer, Howard Florey Inst., Univ. of Melbourne, 2006 (also Medal); IBM Hursley, Southampton Univ., 2006. Hon. Professor: China Acad. of Mgt Sci., 1990–; Peking Union Med. Coll., 2005. Mem., Academia Rodinensis Pro Remediatione, 1988; MAE 1995; Founder FMedSci 1998; FRSocMed 2003. Hon. FRCP 2004. Foreign Mem., Royal Netherlands Acad. of Arts and Scis, 1993. Hon. Member: Alpha Omega Alpha Honor Med. Soc., USA, 1996; Physiol Soc., 1998. Freeman, City of London, 1998; Mem., Co. of Spectacle Makers, 1997, Liveryman, 1998–. Hon. Fellow: Cardiff Univ., 1998; Downing Coll., Cambridge, 1999. Hon. DSc: Aston, 1992; Salford, 1994; Manchester, 2005; Aberdeen, 2005; London, 2007. Robert Bing Prize, Swiss Acad. of Med. Sciences, 1975; Richardson Cross Medal, S Western Ophthalmol Soc., 1978; Copeman Medal, Corpus Christi Coll., Cambridge, 1977; Man of the Year, Royal Assoc. for Disability and Rehabilitation, 1978; Phi Beta Kappa Award in Sci., 1978; John Locke Medal, Apothecaries' Soc., 1983; Prix du Docteur Robert Netter, Acad. Nat. de Médecine, Paris, 1984; Michael Faraday Prize, Royal Soc., 1989; John P. McGovern Science and Soc. Medal, Sigma Xi, USA, 1990; Montgomery Medal, RCSI and Irish Ophthalmol Soc., 1991; Osler Medal, RCP, 1993; Ellison-Cliffe Medal, RSM, 1993; Annual Review Prize, Physiol Soc., 1994; Charles F. Prentice Award, Amer. Acad. of Optometry, 1994; Alcon Prize, Alcon Res. Inst., 1996; Meml Medal, Charles Univ., Prague, 1998; Charter Award, IBiol, 2001; Baly Medal, RCP, 2001; Outstanding Contribn to Neurosci. Award, British Neurosci. Assoc., 2001;

BioIndustry Assoc. Award, 2004; Lord Crook Gold Medal, Spectacle Makers' Co., 2004; Edinburgh Medal, City of Edinburgh, 2005; Sci. Educator Award, Soc. for Neurosci., 2005. *Publications:* Handbook of Psychobiology (with M. S. Gazzaniga), 1975; Mechanics of the Mind, 1977; (with S. A. Greenfield) Mindwaves, 1987; The Mind Machine, 1988, 2nd edn 1994; (with H. B. Barlow and M. Weston-Smith) Images and Understanding, 1990; Vision: coding and efficiency, 1990; (with S. D. Iversen) Gender and Society, 2000; (with S. Jennett) Oxford Companion to the Body, 2001; (with A. Parker and A. Derrington) The Physiology of Cognitive Processes, 2003; (with C. A. Heywood and A. D. Milner) The Roots of Visual Awareness, 2003; res. reports in Jl of Physiol., Jl of Neuroscience, Nature, Lancet, etc. *Recreation:* wasting time. *Address:* Magdalen College, Oxford OX1 4AU. *Club:* Chelsea Arts (Hon. Mem., 1992).

BLAKEMORE, Michael Howell, AO 2003; OBE 2003; freelance director; *b* Sydney, NSW, 18 June 1928; *s* of late Conrad Blakemore and Una Mary Blakemore (*née* Litchfield); *m* 1st, 1960, Shirley (*née* Bush); one *s*; 2nd, 1986, Tanya McCallin; two *d*. *Educ:* The King's Sch., NSW; Sydney Univ.; Royal Academy of Dramatic Art. Actor with Birmingham Rep. Theatre, Shakespeare Memorial Theatre, etc, 1952–66; Co-dir, Glasgow Citizens Theatre (1st prod., The Investigation), 1966–68; Associate Artistic Dir, Nat. Theatre, 1971–76. Dir, Players, NY, 1978. Resident Dir, Lyric Theatre, Hammersmith, 1980. Best Dir, London Critics, 1972. *Productions include:* A Day in the Death of Joe Egg, Comedy, 1967, Broadway 1968; Arturo Ui, Saville, 1969, Israel, 1969; Forget-me-not Lane, Apollo, 1971; Design for Living, Phoenix, 1973; Knuckle, Comedy, 1974; Separate Tables, Apollo, 1976; Privates on Parade, Aldwych (RSC), transf. Piccadilly, 1977; Candida, Albery, 1977; All My Sons, Wyndham's, 1981; Benefactors, Vaudeville, 1984, NY, 1986; Made in Bangkok, Aldwych, 1986; Lettice and Lovage, Globe, 1987, NY, 1990 (Outer Critics Circle Award, NY, 1990); Uncle Vanya, Vaudeville, 1988; City of Angels, Broadway, 1989 (Outer Critics Circle Award, NY, 1990), Prince of Wales Th., 1993; Tosca, WNO, 1992; Here, Donmar Warehouse, 1993; The Sisters Rosensweig, Old Vic, 1994; Now You Know, Hampstead, 1995; Sylvia, Apollo, 1996; Alarms and Excursions, Gielgud, 1998; Mr Peter's Connections, Almeida, 2000; Life After George, Duchess, 2002; The Three Sisters, Playhouse, 2003; Embers, Duke of York, 2006; *National Theatre:* The National Health, 1969; Long Day's Journey Into Night, 1971; The Front Page, Macbeth, 1972; The Cherry Orchard, 1973; Plunder, 1976; After the Fall, 1990; Copenhagen, 1998, transf. Duchess then Montparnasse, Paris, 1999 (Molière Award, Tony Award, Drama Desk Award, 2000); Democracy, 2004, transf. Wyndham's, then NY, 2005; Afterlife, 2008; *Royal Court Theatre:* Widowers' Houses, 1970; Don's Party, 1975; *Lyric Theatre, Hammersmith:* Make and Break, 1980, transf. Haymarket, 1980; Travelling North, 1980; The Wild Duck, 1980; Noises Off, 1982 (transf. to Savoy, 1982, NY, 1983 (Drama Desk Award, NY, 1983–84; Outer Critics Circle Award, NY, 1983; Hollywood Drama-League Award, LA, 1984)); *foreign productions include:* The White Devil, Minneapolis, 1976; Hay Fever, 1976, The Seagull, 1979, Aarhus; Mourning Becomes Electra, Melbourne, 1980; Death Defying Acts, NY, 1995; The Life (musical), Broadway, NY, 1997; Kiss Me Kate, Broadway, NY, 1999 (Tony Award, Drama Desk Award, 2000), transf. Victoria Palace, 2001; Deuce, Is He Dead?, Broadway, NY, 2007. *Films:* A Personal History of the Australian Surf, 1981 (Standard film award, 1982); Privates on Parade, 1983; Country Life, 1995 (Film Critics Circle of Australia Award, 1994). *Publications:* Next Season (novel), 1969; Arguments with England (memoir), 2005; contrib. The New Yorker. *Recreation:* surfing. *Fax:* (020) 7209 0141.

BLAKENEY, Hon. Allan Emrys, OC 1992; SOM 2000; PC (Can.) 1982; FRSC; Visiting Scholar, University of Saskatchewan, Saskatoon, since 1990; *b* Bridgewater, NS, 7 Sept. 1925; *m* 1st, 1950, Mary Elizabeth (Molly) Schwartz (*d* 1957), Halifax, NS; one *s* one *d*; 2nd, 1959, Anne Gorham, Halifax; one *s* one *d*. *Educ:* Dalhousie Univ. (BA, LLB); Queen's Coll., Oxford (MA). FRSC 2001. Univ. Medal for Achievement in Coll. of Law, Dalhousie; Rhodes Schol. Sec. and Legal Adviser, Saskatchewan Crown Corps, 1950; Chm., Saskatchewan Securities Commn, 1955–58; private law practice, 1958–60 and 1964–70. MLA, Saskatchewan, 1960–88; formerly Minister of Educn, Provincial Treas. and Health Minister; Chm., Wascana Centre Authority, 1962–64; Opposition Financial Critic, 1964–70; Dep. Leader, 1967–70; Federal New Democratic Party President, 1969–71; Saskatchewan NDP Leader and Leader of Opposition, 1970; Premier, 1971–82; Leader of Opposition, Sask, 1982–87. Prof. of Public Law, Osgoode Hall Law Sch., York Univ., Toronto, 1988–90. Hon. DCL Mount Allison; Hon. LLD: Dalhousie; York; Western Ontario; Regina; Saskatchewan. *Recreations:* reading, swimming, formerly ice hockey and badminton. *Address:* 1752 Prince of Wales Avenue, Saskatoon, SK S7K 3E5, Canada; College of Law, 15 Campus Drive, University of Saskatchewan, Saskatoon, SK S7N 5A6, Canada.

BLAKENHAM, 2nd Viscount *cr* 1963, of Little Blakenham; **Michael John Hare**; Chairman, Board of Trustees, Royal Botanic Gardens, Kew, 1997–2003; *b* 25 Jan. 1938; *s* of 1st Viscount Blakenham, PC, OBE, VMH, and Hon. Beryl Nancy Pearson (*d* 1994), *d* of 2nd Viscount Cowdray; *S* father, 1982; *m* 1965, Marcia Persephone, *d* of late Hon. Alan Hare, MC; one *s* two *d*. *Educ:* Eton College; Harvard Univ. (AB Econ.). National Service, 1956–57. English Electric, 1958; Harvard, 1959–61; Lazard Brothers, 1961–63; Standard Industrial Group, 1963–71; Royal Doulton, 1972–77; Pearson, 1977–97 (Chief Exec., 1978–90; Chm., 1983–97). Chairman: The Financial Times, 1983–93; MEPC plc, 1993–98; UK Chm., Japan 2001, 1999–2002; Partner, Lazard Partners, 1984–97; Director: Lazard Bros, 1975–97; Sotheby's Holdings Inc., 1987–; Lafarge, 1997–; Mem., Internat. Adv. Gp, Toshiba, 1997–2002. Member, House of Lords Select Committee: on Science and Technol., 1985–88; on Sustainable Develt, 1994–95. Chm., RSPB, 1981–86; Mem., Nature Conservancy Council, 1986–90; President: Sussex Wildlife Trust, 1983–2003; British Trust for Ornithology, 2001–05; Vice Pres., Suffolk Wildlife Trust, 2006–. Order of Merit of Republic of Italy, 1988; Gold and Silver Star, Order of Rising Sun (Japan), 2002. *Address:* 1 St Leonard's Studios, SW3 4EN.

BLAKER, family name of **Baron Blaker**.

BLAKER, Baron *cr* 1994 (Life Peer), of Blackpool in the County of Lancashire, and of Lindfield in the County of West Sussex; **Peter Allan Renshaw Blaker**, KCMG 1983; PC 1983; MA; *b* Hong Kong, 4 Oct. 1922; *s* of late Cedric Blaker, CBE, MC and Louisa Douglas Blaker (*née* Chapple); *m* 1953, Jennifer, *d* of late Sir Pierson Dixon, GCMG, CB; one *s* two *d*. *Educ:* Shrewsbury; Trinity Coll., Toronto (BA, 1st class, Classics); New Coll., Oxford (MA). Served 1942–46: Argyll and Sutherland Highlanders of Canada (Capt., severely wounded). Admitted a Solicitor, 1948. New Coll., Oxford, 1949–52; 1st Class, Jurisprudence, Pass degree in PPE. Pres. Oxford Union. Called to Bar, Lincoln's Inn, 1952. Admitted to HM Foreign Service, 1953; Western Orgns, FO, 1953–55; HM Embassy, Phnom Penh, 1955–57 (Chargé d'Affaires, 1956); UK High Commn, Ottawa, 1957–60; Levant Dept, FO, 1960–62; Private Sec. to Minister of State for Foreign Affairs, 1962–64. Attended Cuba missile crisis, UN and Disarmament Conf., Geneva; UN Gen. Assembly, 1962 and 1963; signing of Nuclear Test Ban Treaty, Moscow, 1963. MP (C) Blackpool South, 1964–92; an Opposition Whip, 1966–67; PPS to Chancellor of Exchequer, 1970–72; Parliamentary Under-Secretary of State: (Army), MoD, 1972–74;

FCO, 1974; Minister of State: FCO, 1979–81; for the Armed Forces, MoD, 1981–83. Joint Secretary: Conservative Parly Foreign Affairs Cttee, 1965–66; Trade Cttee, 1967–70; Exec. Cttee of 1922 Cttee, 1967–70; Vice-Chm., All-Party Tourism Cttee, 1974–79; Member: Select Cttee on Conduct of Members, 1976–77; Public Accounts Commn, 1987–92; Intelligence and Security Cttee, 1996–97; Chairman: Hong Kong Parly Gp, 1970–72, 1983–92; Cons. For. and Commonwealth Affairs Cttee, 1983–92 (Vice-Chm., 1974–79); Mem. Exec. Cttee, British-American Parly Gp, 1975–79; Hon. Sec., Franco-British Parly Relations Cttee, 1975–79. Chm., Bd, Royal Ordnance Factories, 1972–74; Chm. Governors, Welbeck Coll., 1972–74; Mem. Council: Chatham House, 1977–79, 1986–90; Council for Arms Control, 1983–99; Freedom Assoc., 1984–97; Vice-Chm., Peace Through NATO, 1983–93; Vice-Pres., 1983–92, Patron, 1993–, Cons. Foreign and Commonwealth Council; Mem. Council, Britain-Russia Centre (formerly GB-USSR Assoc.), 1974–79, and 1992–2000 (Vice-Chm., 1983–92); Governor, Atlantic Inst., 1978–79; Trustee, Inst. for Negotiation and Conciliation, 1984–92. Chm., Maclean Hunter Cablevision Ltd, 1989–94; farmer. *Publications:* Coping with the Soviet Union, 1977; Small is Dangerous: micro states in a macro world, 1984. *Recreations:* sailing, opera, shooting. *Address:* House of Lords, SW1A 0PW.

BLAKER, Sir John, 3rd Bt *cr* 1919; *b* 22 March 1935; *s* of Sir Reginald Blaker, 2nd Bt, TD, and Sheila Kellas, *d* of Dr Alexander Cran; *S* father, 1975; *m* 1st, 1960, Catherine Ann (marr. diss. 1965), *d* of late F. J. Thorold; 2nd, 1968, Elizabeth Katherine, *d* of late Col John Tinsley Russell, DSO. *Address:* Stantons Farm, East Chiltington, near Lewes, East Sussex BN7 3BB.

BLAKEY, David Cecil, CBE 1998; QPM 1993; DL; HM Inspector of Constabulary, 1999–2004; *b* 1943; *s* of Cecil and Elsie Jane Blakey; *m* 1966, Wendy Margaret Cartwright; one *s* one *d*. *Educ:* Jarrow Grammar Sch.; Univ. of Newcastle upon Tyne (MBA). VSO, Sarawak, 1962; Constable, Durham Constabulary, 1963; Police National Computer, 1972–76; Supt, Durham, 1979; Chief Supt, Northumbria, 1984; Asst Chief Constable, West Mercia, 1986; RCDS, 1989; Deputy Chief Constable: Leics, 1989–90; West Mercia, 1990–91; Chief Constable, W Mercia, 1991–99. Pres., ACPO, 1997–98. DL Worcs 1999. *Recreations:* books, history. *Address:* c/o HM Inspectorate of Constabulary, Bartleet House, 165a Birmingham Road, Bromsgrove, Worcs B61 0DJ.

BLAKEY, (Diana) Kristin; *see* Henry, D. K.

BLAKISTON, Sir Ferguson Arthur James, 9th Bt *cr* 1763; entrepreneur and writer; *b* 19 Feb. 1963; *er s* of Sir Arthur Norman Hunter Blakiston, 8th Bt, and Mary Ferguson (*d* 1982), *d* of late Alfred Ernest Gillingham, Cave, S Canterbury, NZ; *S* father, 1977; *m* 1993, Linda Jane, *d* of late Robert John Key, Queenstown, NZ; two *d*. *Educ:* Lincoln Coll., NZ (Diploma in Agriculture 1983); Auckland Inst. of Technology (Cert. in Marketing, 1993); NZ Inst. of Business Studies (Diploma in Travel Writing). *Heir:* *b* Norman John Balfour Blakiston, Executive Officer [*b* 7 April 1964; *m* 1994, Rhonda Maree Hart; two *s* one *d*]. *Address:* Cortington, 8 Waihi Terrace, Geraldine, S Canterbury, New Zealand.

BLAKSTAD, Michael Björn; External Professor of Digital Media, University of Glamorgan, since 2002; Director, michaelblakstad ltd, since 2002; *b* 18 April 1940; *s* of late Clifford and Alice Blakstad; *m* 1965, Patricia Marilyn Wotherspoon; one *s* twin *d*. *Educ:* Ampleforth Coll.; Oriel Coll., Oxford (MA Lit. Hum.). General trainee, BBC, 1962–68; Producer, Yorkshire Television, 1968–71; freelance TV producer, 1971–74; Programme Editor, BBC, 1974–80; Dir of Programmes, TV South, 1980–84. Founder and Managing Director, Blackrod, 1980 (Chm., 1981–84); Chairman and Chief Executive: Workhouse Productions, 1984–88; Chrysalis Television Ltd, 1988–90; Chm., 1990–2003, Chief Exec., 1990–94, Workhouse Ltd; Chairman: Filmscreen Internat. Ltd, 1984–86; Friday Productions, 1984–88; Blackrod Interactive Services, 1988–90; Winchester Independent Radio Ltd, 1995–98; Jt Chief Exec., Videodisc Co., 1984–88; Dir, Chrysalis Gp, 1988–90. Director: IPPA, 1986–90; Internat. Video Communications Assoc., 1988–90, 1999–2001; Winchester Theatre Royal, 1988–95 (Chm., 1990–95). Chairman: Southern Screen, 1998–2004; Exec. Steering Gp, broadbandshow, 2002–04. Chm. Govs, Bedales Schs, 2001–05. Hampshire Ambassador, 2005–. Awards include: Radio Industries Club, 1975, 1977, 1979; RTS, 1976; BAFTA/Shell Prize, 1976; BIM/John Player, 1976; Nyon, 1978. Hon. MSc Salford, 1983; FRSA; MRI. *Publications:* The Risk Business, 1979; Tomorrow's World looks to the Eighties, 1979; (with Aldwyn Cooper) The Communicating Organisation, 1995; The Liphook Story, 2004. *Recreations:* golf, writing. *Address:* The Tudor House, Workhouse Lane, East Meon, Hants GU32 1PD. *Club:* Reform.

BLAMEY, Marjorie Netta, MBE 2007; botanical illustrator and wildlife artist, since 1970; *b* 13 March 1918; *d* of Dr Arthur Percival Day and Janetta Day; *m* 1941, Philip Bernard Blamey; two *s* two *d*. *Educ:* private schools; Italia Conti Stage Sch.; RADA. Actress and part-time photographer, prior to 1939; farmer, Cornwall, 1948–70. *Publications:* include: wrote and illustrated: Learn to Paint Flowers in Watercolour, 1986; Painting Flowers, 1997; illustrated: R. Mabey, Food for Free, 1972; R. Fitter: Handguide to Wild Flowers, 1979; Collins Gem Guide to Wild Flowers, 1980; R. and A. Fitter: Wild Flowers of Britain and Northern Europe, 1974, 5th edn 1996 (trans. 8 langs); Wild Flowers of Britain and Ireland, 2003 (Botanical Soc. and Wild Flower Soc. Prize, 2003); C. Grey-Wilson: Alpine Flowers of Europe, 1979, 2nd edn 1995; The Illustrated Flora of Britain and Northern Europe, 1989; Mediterranean Wild Flowers, 1993; Cassell's Wild Flowers of Britain and Europe, 2003; P. Blamey: Collins Gem Guide to Fruits, Nuts and Berries, 1984; Wild Flowers by Colour, 1997. *Recreations:* bird watching, gardening, travel, walking, cooking, my family, painting!

BLANC, Christian; Deputy (Allied UDF) for Yvelines, French National Assembly, since 2002; *b* Talence, Gironde, 17 May 1942; *s* of Marcel Blanc and Encarna (*née* Miranda); *m* 1st, 1973, Asa Birgitta Hagglund (marr. diss.); two *d*; 2nd, 2003, Ingrid Arion. *Educ:* Institut d'Etudes Politiques, Bordeaux (Dip.). Asst Dir, Sopexa Scandinave, 1969; Dep. to Controller, Mission for Territorial Equipment, 1970–74; Hd of Bureau, Sec. of State for Youth and Sports, 1974–76; Asst Gen. Delegate, Tech. Interministerial Agency for Leisure and Fresh Air, 1976–80; Dir of Cabinet, Commn of EC, Brussels, 1981–83; Prefect: Commune of Haute-Pyrénées, 1983–84; Govt of New Caledonia, 1985; Seine and Marne, 1985–89; without portfolio, 1989. Pres. and Dir-Gen., Régie Autonome des Transports Parisiens, 1989–92; Pres., Air France, 1993–97; Vice-Chm., Merrill Lynch Europe, 2000–02; Chm., Merrill Lynch France SA, 2000–02. Director: Middle East Airlines, 1998–99; Carrefour; Cap Gemini. Dir, Chancery, Univs of Paris, 1991–2001. Pres. External Selection Cttee for Recruitment of Sen. Treasury Officials, 2000–. Officer, Légion d'Honneur (France), 1988; Officier, Ordre National du Merite (France), 1994. *Publications:* Le Lièvre et la Tortue, 1994; La Croissance ou le Chaos, 2006. *Address:* Assemblée Nationale, 126 rue de l'Université, 75355 Paris, France; 18 avenue de Bellevue, 78150 Le Chesnay, France. *T:* (1) 39544600.

BLANC, Raymond René, Hon. OBE 2007; chef; Patron and Chairman, Blanc Restaurants Ltd, since 1984; *b* 19 Nov. 1949; *m*; two *s*. *Educ:* CEG de Valdahon; Lycée technique de horlogerie, Besançon. Chef de rang, 1971; Manager and chef de cuisine, 1976; proprietor and chef, Les Quat' Saisons, Summertown, 1977; Dir and Chm., Maison Blanc, 1978–88; proprietor, Le Petit Blanc, 1984–88; Chef/patron and Chairman, Le Manoir aux Quat' Saisons, 1984–; co-owner: Brasserie Blanc (formerly Le Petit Blanc) restaurants: Oxford, 1996–; Cheltenham, 1998–; Birmingham, 1999–; Manchester, 2000–; Tunbridge Wells, 2004–. TV series: Blanc Mange, 1994; The Restaurant, 2007. Academicien Mentor, Academie Culinaire de France. Master Chef Great Britain. Hon. DBA Oxford Brookes Univ., 1999. Personalité de l'année, 1990. Commandeur de l'Assoc. Internat. des Maîtres Conseils en Gastronomie Française. *Publications:* Recipes from Le Manoir aux Quat' Saisons, 1988; Cooking for Friends, 1991; Blanc Mange, 1994; A Blanc Christmas, 1996; Blanc Vite, 1998; Foolproof French Cookery, 2002. *Recreations:* reading, tennis, riding, classical and rock music. *Address:* Le Manoir aux Quat' Saisons, Church Road, Great Milton, Oxford OX44 7PD.

BLANCH, Sir Malcolm, KCVO 1998 (CVO 1992; LVO 1981; MVO 1968); Clerk Comptroller to Queen Elizabeth the Queen Mother, 1967–98; *b* 27 May 1932; *s* of late John and Louie Blanch; *m* 1957, Jean Harding Richardson (*d* 2007); two *s*. *Educ:* Dinnington Sch., Yorks. Served RN, 1949–56. Asst Keeper and Steward in Royal Yachts, Victoria & Albert, 1953, Britannia, 1954–56; Queen Elizabeth the Queen Mother's Household, 1957–98: Clerk Accountant, 1960–67. Freeman, City of London, 1989. *Recreations:* gardening, music. *Address:* 12 Bishop's Drive, East Harnham, Salisbury, Wilts SP2 8NZ. *T:* (01722) 329862.

BLANCH, Dr Michael Dennis, TD and bar 1990; public sector management consultant, since 2003; *b* 22 Oct. 1946; *s* of Harold Clement Blanch and Jane Emily Blanch; *m* 1973, Penelope Ann Worthington; two *s*. *Educ:* William Ellis Sch.; Univ. of Birmingham (BScSoc 1969; DipEd 1970; PhD 1975). AMA 1979. Keeper of Education, Nat. Army Mus., 1973–77; Sen. Museums Keeper, Rotherham MBC, 1977–79; Asst Dir, Libraries, Oldham MBC, 1979–81; Dir of Museums, 1981–84, Dir of Leisure Services, 1984–88, Calderdale MBC; County Leisure Services Officer, Shropshire CC, 1988–91; Chief Executive: Eastbourne BC, 1991–95; London Borough of Bromley, 1995–2000; Falkland Is Govt, 2000–03 and 2007. FCMI (FIMgt 1985). *Publications:* War and Weapons, 1976; Soldiers, 1980. *Recreations:* mountain biking, hill walking, sailing, previously Territorial Army. *Address:* Strands, Simonstone, Hawes, N Yorks DL8 3LY. *T:* (01969) 667573.

BLANCHARD, Francis; Commandeur de la Légion d'Honneur; Member, French Economic and Social Council, since 1989; *b* Paris, 21 July 1916; *m* 1940, Marie-Claire Boué; two *s*. *Educ:* Univ. of Paris. French Home Office; Internat. Organisation for Refugees, Geneva, 1947–51; Internat. Labour Office, Geneva, 1951–89: Asst Dir-Gen., 1956–68; Dep. Dir-Gen., 1968–74; Dir-Gen., 1974–89. Dr *hc* Brussels, Cairo and Manila. *Recreations:* ski-ing, hunting, riding. *Address:* Prébailly, 01170 Gex, France. *T:* 450415170.

BLANCHARD, Rt Hon. Peter, DCNZM 2005; PC 1998; **Rt Hon. Justice Blanchard;** a Judge of the Supreme Court, New Zealand, since 2004; *b* 2 Aug. 1942; *s* of Cyril Francis Blanchard and Zora Louis Blanchard (now Parkinson); *m* 1968, Judith Isabel Watts; one *s* one *d*. *Educ:* King's Coll., Auckland; Univ. of Auckland (LLM 1968); Harvard Univ. (Frank Knox Fellow, 1968; Fulbright Fellow, 1968; LLM 1969). Admitted barrister and solicitor, Supreme Court of NZ, 1966; Partner: Grierson Jackson & Partners, 1968–83; Simpson Grierson, 1983–92; Judge: High Court of NZ, 1992–96; Court of Appeal of NZ, 1996–2003. Comr, Law Commn, 1990–94. *Publications:* Handbook on Agreements for Sale and Purchase of Land, 1978, 4th edn 1987; Company Receiverships in Australia and New Zealand, 1982, 2nd edn (jtly) 1994; (jtly) Private Receivers of Companies in New Zealand, 2008. *Recreations:* reading, music, theatre, walking. *Address:* Supreme Court of New Zealand, PO Box 61, Wellington, New Zealand. *T:* (4) 9188234.

BLANCHETT, Catherine Elise, (Cate); actress; Joint Artistic Director, Sydney Theatre Company, since 2008; *b* 1969; *d* of late Bob Blanchett and of June Blanchett; *m* 1997, Andrew Upton; three *s*. *Educ:* Methodist Ladies' Coll., Melbourne; Melbourne Univ.; Nat. Inst. of Dramatic Art, Sydney. *Theatre includes:* Top Girls, Sydney Th. Co., 1992; Kafka Dances (Newcomer Award, Sydney Th. Critics Circle, 1993); Oleanna, Sydney Th. Co. (Rosemont Best Actress Award); Hamlet, Belvoir Th. Co., 1995; Sweet Phoebe, Sydney Th. Co.; The Tempest, The Blind Giant is Dancing, Belvoir Street Th. Co.; The Seagull, 1996; Plenty, Almeida, 1999. *Television includes:* Heartland, GP, Police Rescue, 1994; Bordertown, 1995. *Films include:* Parkland, 1996; Paradise Road, Thank God He Met Lizzie, Oscar and Lucinda, 1997; Elizabeth, 1998 (Best Actress, BAFTA, and Best Actress in a Drama, Golden Globe Awards, 1999); An Ideal Husband, Pushing Tin, 1999; Dreamtime Alice (also co-prod.), The Talented Mr Ripley, The Man Who Cried, 2000; The Fellowship of the Ring, The Gift, Bandits, 2001; Heaven, The Shipping News, Charlotte Gray, Chasing the Dragon, The Two Towers, 2002; Veronica Guerin, The Return of the King, 2003; The Missing, Coffee & Cigarettes, 2004; The Aviator (Academy Award for Best Supporting Actress), The Life Aquatic with Steve Zissou, 2005; Little Fish, Babel, 2006; Notes on a Scandal, The Good German, I'm Not There, The Golden Age, 2007; Indiana Jones and the Kingdom of the Crystal Skull, 2008. *Address:* c/o Robyn Gardiner Management, PO Box 128, Surry Hills, NSW 2010, Australia.

BLANCKENHAGEN, Jane Maureen; *see* Kelly, J. M.

BLAND, Christopher Donald Jack; Lord-Lieutenant of the Isle of Wight, 1995–2006; Chairman, Hovertravel Ltd, since 1965; *b* 8 Oct. 1936; *s* of Christopher Donald James Bland and Iris Raynor Bland; *m* 1962, Judith Anne Louise Maynard; one *s* three *d*. *Educ:* Sandroyd Prep. Sch.; Clayesmore Public Sch. Nat. Service, Gordon Highlanders, later Lieut RE, 1955–57. Rolls Royce Ltd, 1957–61; Britten Norman Aircraft Co., 1961–65; Hovertravel Ltd (world's first hovercraft operator), 1965; Sen. Partner, Norwood, 1981–; Dir, Red Funnel Gp PLC, 1986–2006; Chm., Vectis Transport PLC, 1988–. Mem., Albany Prison Bd, 1978–88; Chm., IoW HA, 1988–90. High Sheriff, IoW, 1989–90. *Recreations:* flying vintage aircraft, vintage sports cars, tinkering with water mills. *Address:* Yafford House, Shorwell, Isle of Wight PO30 3LH. *T:* (home) (01983) 740428, (office) (01983) 565181. *Club:* Isle of Wight County.

BLAND, Sir (Francis) Christopher (Buchan), Kt 1993; Chairman, British Telecommunications plc, 2001–07; *b* 29 May 1938; *e s* of James Franklin MacMahon Bland and Jess Buchan Bland (*née* Brodie); *m* 1981, Jennifer Mary, Viscountess Enfield, *er d* of late Rt Hon. W. M. May, PC, FCA, MP, and of Mrs May, Mertoun Hall, Holywood, Co. Down; one *s*, and two step *s* two step *d*. *Educ:* Sedbergh; The Queen's Coll., Oxford (Hastings Exhibnr; Hon. Fellow, 2001). 2nd Lieut, 5th Royal Inniskilling Dragoon Guards, 1956–58; Lieut, North Irish Horse (TA), 1958–69. Dir, NI Finance Corp., 1972–76; Dep. Chm., IBA, 1972–80; Chairman: Sir Joseph Causton & Sons, 1977–85; LWT (Hldgs), 1984–94; Century Hutchinson Group, 1984–89; Phicom, subseq. Life Sciences Internat., 1987–97; NFC, 1994–2000; Director: Nat. Provident Instn, 1978–88; Storehouse plc, 1988–93. Chairman: Bd of Govs, BBC, 1996–2001; RSC, 2004–. Mem. GLC, for Lewisham, 1967–70; Chm., ILEA Schs Sub-Cttee, 1970; Mem. Burnham Cttee, 1970; Chm., Bow Group, 1969–70; Editor, Crossbow, 1971–72; Mem., Prime Minister's Adv. Panel on Citizen's Charter, 1991–94; Chm., Chancellor's Private Finance Panel, 1995–96 (Mem., 1994–96). Chairman: NHS Rev. Gp on Nat. Trng Council and Nat. Staff Cttees, 1982; Hammersmith and Queen Charlotte's Hosps (formerly Hammersmith) SHA, 1982–94; Hammersmith Hosps NHS Trust, 1994–96. Vis. Fellow, Nuffield Coll., Oxford, 2000. William Pitt Fellow, Pembroke Coll., Cambridge, 2005. Governor, Prendergast Girls Grammar Sch. and Woolwich Polytechnic, 1968–70; Mem. Council: RPMS, 1982–96 (Hon. Fellow, 1997); St Mary's Med Sch., 1984–88. Hon. LLD South Bank, 1994. *Publications:* Bow Group pamphlet on Commonwealth Immigration; (with Linda Kelly) Feasts, 1987. *Recreations:* fishing, ski-ing; formerly: Captain, OU Fencing Team, 1961; Captain, OU Modern Pentathlon Team, 1959–60; Mem. Irish Olympic Fencing Team, 1960. *Address:* Blissamore Hall, Clanville, Andover, Hants SP11 9HL. *T:* (01264) 772274; 10 Catherine Place, SW1E 6HF. *T:* (020) 7834 0021. *Club:* Beefsteak.

BLAND, Lt-Col Sir Simon (Claud Michael), KCVO 1982 (CVO 1973; MVO 1967); Extra Equerry to the Duke and Duchess of Gloucester, since 1989 (Comptroller, Private Secretary and Equerry, 1972–89); Extra Equerry to Princess Alice Duchess of Gloucester, 1989–2004; *b* 4 Dec. 1923; *s* of late Sir Nevile Bland, KCMG, KCVO, and Portia (*née* Ottley); *m* 1954, Olivia (DStJ 1999), *d* of late Major William Blackett, Arbigland, Dumfries; one *s* three *d*. *Educ:* Eton College. Served War of 1939–45, Scots Guards, in Italy; BJSM, Washington, 1948–49; 2nd Bn, Scots Guards, Malaya, 1949–51; Asst Mil. Adviser at UK High Commn, Karachi, 1959–60; Comptroller and Asst Private Sec. to late Duke of Gloucester, 1961–74 and Private Sec. to late Prince William, 1968–72. Dir, West End Bd, Commercial Union, 1964–95; Vice-Pres., Raleigh Internat. (formerly Operation Raleigh), 1989–96. Chm., Coll. of St Barnabas, 1993–97; Member Council: Pestalozzi Children's Village Trust, 1989–2006, Vice-Pres., 2006–; Elizabeth Finn Trust (formerly DGAA Homelife), 1990–; Order of St John for Kent, 1990–; President: Friends of Edenbridge Hosp., 1990–; Lingfield Br., Riding for the Disabled, 1990–. Freeman, City of London, 1988. KStJ 1988. *Address:* Totties, Mill Hill, Edenbridge, Kent TN8 5DB. *T:* (01732) 862340. *Club:* Buck's.

BLANDFORD, Marquess of; Charles James Spencer-Churchill; *b* 24 Nov. 1955; *e s* and *heir* of 11th Duke of Marlborough, *qv*; *m* 1st, 1990, Rebecca Mary (marr. diss. 2001), *d* of Peter Few Brown; one *s*; 2nd, 2002, Edla, *o d* of Alun Griffiths; one *d*. *Educ:* Pinewood; Harrow; RAC, Cirencester; Royal Berks Coll. of Agric. *Heir:* *s* Earl of Sunderland, *qv*. *Address:* Blenheim Palace, Woodstock, Oxon; 16 Lawrence Street, SW3 5NE; *e-mail:* lordblandford@aol.com. *Clubs:* Turf, Tramp's, Annabel's; Racquet and Tennis (New York).

BLANDFORD, Prof. Roger David, FRS 1989; Pehong and Adele Chen Professor of Particle Astrophysics and Cosmology, and Director, Kavli Institute for Astrophysics and Cosmology, Stanford University, since 2003; *b* 28 Aug. 1949; *s* of Jack George and Janet Margaret Blandford; *m* 1972, Elizabeth Denise Kellett; two *s*. *Educ:* King Edward's Sch., Birmingham; Magdalene Coll., Cambridge Univ. (BA, MA, PhD; Bye Fellow 1973). Res. Fellow, St John's Coll., Cambridge, 1973–76; Inst. for Advanced Study, Princeton, 1974–75; CIT, 1976–2003, Richard Chace Tolman Prof. of Theoretical Astrophysics, 1989–2003. Fellow, Amer. Acad. of Arts and Scis, 1993. *Address:* Department of Physics, Stanford University, 382 Via Pueblo Mall, Stanford, CA 94305–4060, USA. *T:* (650) 7234233; *e-mail:* rdb3@stanford.edu.

BLANDINO, Elizabeth Assunta, (Betty), (Mrs E. A. Jones); studio potter (self employed) and writer, since 1973; *b* 12 Sept. 1927; *d* of Pietro Pierino Blandino and Marie Bradlaugh; *m* 1973, Gwyn Owain Jones, CBE (*d* 2006); two step *d*. *Educ:* St Aloysius Convent Sch., London NW1; Univ. of Reading (Teacher's Cert. 1947); Goldsmith Coll. of Art, London Univ. (Painting and Ceramics 1958); Postgrad. Dip Art Educn, London Univ., 1973. Teacher, all levels, 1947–58; Asst Dir, 1958–61, Dir, 1961–67, Upper Gall., Whitechapel (ILEA); County Art Advr, E Sussex Educn Authy, 1967–71. Pres., Oxfordshire Craft Guild, 1990–93; Mem., Oxford Art Soc. *Exhibitions include:* solo/sole potter: Commonwealth Inst., London, 1975; Oriel, Welsh Arts Council Gall., Cardiff, 1976; Oxford Gall., 1978; Peter Dingley Gall., Stratford-upon-Avon, 1980; Beaux Arts, Bath, 1982; Prescote Gall., Cropredy, 1983; Primavera, Cambridge, 1986; Galerie L, Hamburg, 1988; Sheila Harrison Fine Art, London, 1991; Blue Gall., London, 1995; Manor House Gall., Chipping Norton, 1999; Abingdon Mus., 2008; group: New Faces, British Crafts Centre, London, 1977; Handbuilt Ceramics, Casson Gall., London, 1981; Keramic aus England, Marianne Heller Galerie, Heidelberg and Galerie Handwerk, Munich, 1989; Gall. North, Kirkby Lonsdale, 1990; Crafts in the City, Bluecoat Display Centre, Liverpool, 1992; South Bank Centre, RFH, London, 1993; Focus, V&A Mus., 1998; Spring Fever, Focus, Contemp. Applied Arts, London, 2000; Internat. Clay Works, Carlin Gall., Paris, 2000; work in public and private collections including: Bristol Mus. and Art Gall.; Buckinghamshire Co. Mus.; Cheltenham Art Gall. and Mus.; Cleveland Crafts Centre, Middlesbrough; Fitzwilliam Mus., Cambridge; Hereford City Mus. and Art Gall.; Merseyside Co. Mus, Liverpool; Nat. Mus. and Art Gall. of Wales, Cardiff; Southampton City Art Gall.; V&A Mus., London; York City Art Gall., Yorkshire Mus, York; Mus, Bellerive, Zurich; Mus. of Applied Arts, Cologne; Mus. für Kunst und Gewerbe, Hamburg. *Publications:* Coiled Pottery, 1984, revd edn 2003; The Figure in Fired Clay, 2001. *Recreations:* essentially sober cultural activities, life drawing and painting, gardening, food. *Address:* 12 Squitchey Lane, Oxford OX2 7LB. *T:* (01865) 510363; *e-mail:* Bettyablandino@onetel.com.

BLANDY, Prof. John Peter, CBE 1995; MA, DM, MCh, FRCS, FACS; Consultant Surgeon: The Royal London (formerly London) Hospital, 1964–92; St Peter's Hospital for the Stone, 1969–92; Professor of Urology, University of London, 1969–92, now Emeritus; *b* 11 Sept. 1927; *s* of late Sir E. Nicolas Blandy, KCIE, CSI, ICS and Dorothy Kathleen (*née* Marshall); *m* 1953, Anne, *d* of Hugh Mathias, FRCS, Tenby; four *d*. *Educ:* Clifton Coll.; Balliol Coll., Oxford (Hon. Fellow, 1992); London Hosp. Med. Coll. BM, BCh 1951; MA 1953; FRCS 1956; DM 1963; MCh 1963; FACS 1980. House Phys. and House Surg., London Hosp., 1952; RAMC, 1953–55; Surgical Registrar and Lectr in Surgery, London Hosp., 1956–60; exchange Fellow, Presbyterian St Luke's Hosp., Chicago, 1960–61; Sen. Lectr, London Hosp., 1961; Resident Surgical Officer, St Paul's Hosp., 1963–64. McLaughlin-Gallie Vis. Prof., Royal Coll. of Physicians and Surgeons of Canada, 1988. Member: BMA; RSM (Hon. FRSocMed 1995); Council, RCS, 1982–94 (Hunterian Prof., 1964; Hunterian Orator, 1991; a Vice-Pres., 1992–94); GMC, 1992–96; Internat. Soc. Pædiatric Urol. Surg.; Internat. Soc. of Urological Surgeons; British Assoc. Urological Surgeons (Pres., 1984); President: European Assoc. of Urology, 1986–88; European Bd of Urology, 1991–92. Chm., Nat. Confidential Enquiry into Perioperative Deaths, 1992–97. Fellow, Assoc. of Surgeons; Hon. FRCSI 1992; Hon. Fellow, Urological Society: of Australasia, 1973; of Canada, 1986; of Denmark, 1986; of Germany, 1987; of The Netherlands, 1990; of Romania, 1991; of Japan, 1991; Hon. Fellow: Mexican Coll. of Urology, 1974; Amer. Urol Assoc., 1989. Maurice Davidson Award, Fellowship of Postgrad. Med., 1980; St Peter's Medal, British Assoc. of Urol Surgs, 1982; Francisco Diaz Medal, Spanish Urol Assoc., 1988; Grégoir Medal, Eur. Assoc. of Urology, 2001. *Publications:* (with A. D. Dayan and H. F. Hope-Stone) Tumours of the Testicle, 1970; Transurethral Resection, 1971, 5th edn (with R. G. Notley and J. M. Reynard) 2004; (ed) Urology, 1976, 2nd edn (with C. G. Fowler) 1995; Lecture Notes on Urology,

1976; Operative Urology, 1978; (ed with B. Lytton) The Prostate, 1986; (with J. Moors) Urology for Nurses, 1989; (ed with R. T. D. Oliver and H. F. Hope-Stone) Urological and Genital Cancer, 1989; (ed with J. S. P. Lumley) History of the Royal College of Surgeons, 2000; papers in surgical and urological jls. *Recreation:* painting. *Address:* 362 Shakespeare Tower, Barbican, EC2Y 8NJ. *T:* (020) 7638 4095.

BLANK, Sir (Maurice) Victor, Kt 1999; Chairman, Lloyds TSB, since 2006; *b* 9 Nov. 1942; *s* of Joseph Blank and Ruth Blank (*née* Levey); *m* 1977, Sylvia Helen (*née* Richford); two *s* one *d*. *Educ:* Stockport Grammar Sch.; St Catherine's Coll., Oxford (MA; Domus Fellow, 1998; Hon. Fellow 2002). Solicitor of the Supreme Court. Joined Clifford-Turner as articled clerk, 1964: Solicitor, 1966; Partner, 1969; Charterhouse Bank: Dir, and Head of Corporate Finance, 1981; Chief Exec., 1985–96; Chm., 1985–97; Chief Exec., 1985–96, Chm., 1991–97, Charterhouse plc; Dir, Charterhouse Eur. Hldg, 1993– (Chm., 1993–97); Chairman: Mirror Group plc, 1998–99; Trinity Mirror PLC, 1999–2006; GUS (formerly The Great Universal Stores) plc, 2000–06 (Dir, 1993–2006; Dep. Chm., 1996–2000). Non-executive Director: Coats Viyella, subseq. Coats, plc, 1989– (Dep. Chm., 1999–2003); Williams (formerly Williams Hldgs) plc, 1995–2000; Sen. Ind. Dir, Chubb plc, 2000–03. Mem., 1998–2004, Chm., 1998–2004, Industrial Develt Adv. Bd; Mem., Financial Reporting Council, 2003–. Chm., Wellbeing, subseq. Wellbeing of Women, 1989–. Member: Council, Oxford Univ., 2000–07; Business Adv. Forum, Saïd Business Sch., Univ. of Oxford, 2005–. Mem., RSA. CCMI (CIMgt 2000). Hon. FRCOG 1998. *Publication:* (jtly) Weinberg and Blank on Take-Overs and Mergers, 3rd edn 1971 to 5th edn 1989. *Recreations:* family, cricket, tennis, theatre. *Address:* Lloyds TSB plc, 25 Gresham Street, EC2V 7HN. *T:* (020) 7626 1500, *Fax:* (020) 7356 2050.

BLANNING, Prof. Timothy Charles William, LittD; FBA 1990; Professor of Modern European History, University of Cambridge, since 1992; Fellow, Sidney Sussex College, Cambridge, since 1965; *b* 21 April 1942; *s* of Thomas Walter Blanning and Gwendolyn Marchant (*née* Jones); *m* 1988, Nicky Jones; one *s* one *d*. *Educ:* King's Sch., Bruton, Somerset; Sidney Sussex Coll., Cambridge (BA, MA; PhD 1967; LittD 1998). University of Cambridge: Res. Fellow, Sidney Sussex Coll., 1965–68; Asst Lectr in History, 1972–76; Lectr in History, 1976–87; Reader in Modern European History, 1987–92. *Publications:* Joseph II and Enlightened Despotism, 1970; Reform and Revolution in Mainz 1740–1803, 1974; The French Revolution in Germany, 1983; The Origins of the French Revolutionary Wars, 1986; The French Revolution: aristocrats versus bourgeois?, 1987; Joseph II, 1994; The French Revolutionary Wars 1787–1802, 1996; (ed) The Oxford Illustrated History of Modern Europe, 1996; (ed) The Rise and Fall of the French Revolution, 1996; (ed) History and Biography: essays in honour of Derek Beales, 1996; The French Revolution: class war or culture clash?, 1998; (ed) Reform in Great Britain and Germany 1750–1850, 1999; (ed) The Short Oxford History of Europe: the eighteenth century, 2000; (ed) The Short Oxford History of Europe: the nineteenth century, 2000; The Culture of Power and the Power of Culture: old regime Europe 1660–1789, 2002; (ed) Unity and Diversity in European Culture *c* 1800, 2006; The Pursuit of Glory: Europe 1648–1815, 2007. *Recreations:* music, gardening, dog-walking. *Address:* Faculty of History, West Road, Cambridge CB3 9EF. *T:* (01223) 335308. *Club:* Athenæum.

BLASHFORD-SNELL, Col John Nicholas, OBE 1996 (MBE 1969); Ministry of Defence consultant (on staff, 1983–91); *b* 22 Oct. 1936; *s* of late Rev. Prebendary Leland John Blashford Snell and Gwendolen Ives Sadler; *m* 1960, Judith Frances (*née* Sherman); two *d*. *Educ:* Victoria Coll., Jersey, CI; RMA, Sandhurst. Commissioned Royal Engineers, 1957; 33 Indep. Fd Sqdn RE Cyprus, 1958–61; comd Operation Aphrodite (Expedition) Cyprus, 1959–61; Instructor: Junior Leaders Regt RE, 1962–63; RMA Sandhurst, 1963–66; Adjt 3rd Div. Engineers, 1966–67; comd Great Abbai Expedn (Blue Nile), 1968; sc RMCS Shrivenham and Camberley, 1968–69; comd Dahlak Quest Expedn, 1969–70; GSO2 MoD, 1970–72; comd British Trans-Americas Expedn, 1971–72; OC 48 Fd Sqdn RE, service in Belize, Oman, Ulster, 1972–74; comd Zaire River Expedn, 1974–75; CO Junior Leaders Regt RE, 1976–78; Dir of Operations, Operation Drake, 1977–81; on staff (GSO1), MoD, 1978–82; in command, The Fort George Volunteers, 1982–83. Operation Raleigh: Operations Dir, 1982–88; Dir Gen., 1989–91; Leader, Kota Mama expedn, 1995–, and numerous other expedns. Hon. Chm., 1969–2008, Pres. 2008–, Scientific Exploration Soc.; Pres., Just A Drop, 2004– (Hon. Chm., 2001–04); Appeal Dir, Trinity Sailing Trust, 2004–; Trustee, Operation New World, 1995–. Hon. Pres., The Vole Club, 1996–; Hon. Life Pres., Centre for Fortean Zoology, 2003–. Chm., Liverpool Construction Crafts Guild, 2003–05 (Pres., 2005–). Freeman, City of Hereford, 1984. Hon. DSc Durham, 1986; Hon. DEng Bournemouth, 1997. Darien Medal (Colombia), 1972; Segrave Trophy, 1974; Livingstone Medal, RSGS, 1975; Paul Harris Fellow, Rotary Internat., 1981; Patron's Medal, RGS, 1993; Gold Medal, Instn of RE, 1994; La Paz Medal (Bolivia), 2000. *Publications:* Weapons and Tactics (with Tom Wintringham), 1970; (with Richard Snailham) The Expedition Organiser's Guide, 1970, 2nd edn 1976; Where the Trails Run Out, 1974; In the Steps of Stanley, 1975, 2nd edn 1975; (with A. Ballantine) Expeditions the Experts' Way, 1977, 2nd edn 1978; A Taste for Adventure, 1978; (with Michael Cable) Operation Drake, 1981; Mysteries: encounters with the unexplained, 1983; Operation Raleigh, the Start of an Adventure, 1987; (with Ann Tweedy) Operation Raleigh, Adventure Challenge, 1988; (with Ann Tweedy) Operation Raleigh, Adventure Unlimited, 1990; Something lost behind the Ranges, 1994; (with Rula Lenska) Mammoth Hunt, 1996; (with Richard Snailham) Kota Mama, 2000; (with Richard Snailham) East to the Amazon, 2002. *Recreations:* motoring, shooting, food, wine. *Clubs:* Buck's, Travellers; Artists' (Liverpool); Galley Hill Shooting (Hon. Pres.); Explorers' (New York); Jersey Pistol.

BLATCHLEY, Geraldine; *see* James, G.

BLATCHLY, John Marcus, MBE 2007; MA, PhD; FSA 1975; Headmaster, Ipswich School, 1972–93; *b* 7 Oct. 1932; *s* of late Alfred Ernest Blatchly and Edith Selina Blatchly (*née* Giddings); *m* 1955, Pamela Winifred, JP, *d* of late Major and Mrs L. J. Smith; one *s* one *d*. *Educ:* Sutton Grammar Sch., Surrey; Christ's Coll., Cambridge (Natural Scis Triposes; BA, MA, PhD). Instr Lieut RN, 1954–57. Asst Master and Head of Science Dept: King's Sch., Bruton, 1957–62; Eastbourne Coll., 1962–66; Charterhouse, 1966–72 (PhD awarded 1967 publication of work carried out with Royal Society grants at these three schools). Pres., Suffolk Inst. of Archaeology and History, 1975–2001; Chm., Suffolk Records Soc., 1988–. Editor, Conference and Common Room (Journal of HMC Schools), 1987–92; Hon. Treas., 1990–92, Hon. Associate Mem., 1993, HMC; lead inspector to HMC schs, 1994–2000. Co-ed., Bookplate Jl, 1994–98. Hon. Res. Associate, Oxford DNB, 2001. Gov. of several schs, 1993–2005. Hon. LittD UEA, 1993. *Publications:* Organic Reactions, vol. 19, 1972 (jtly, with J. F. W. McOmie); The Topographers of Suffolk, 1976, 5th edn 1988; (with Peter Eden) Isaac Johnson of Woodbridge, 1979; Eighty Ipswich Portraits, 1980; (ed) Davy's Suffolk Journal, 1983; The Town Library of Ipswich: a history and catalogue, 1989; The Bookplates of Edward Gordon Craig, 1997; Some Suffolk and Norfolk Ex-Libris, 2000; (jtly) The Journal of William Dowsing, 2001; The Bookplates of George Wolfe Plank, 2002; A Famous Antient Seed-Plot of Learning: a history of Ipswich School, 2003; John Kirby's Suffolk: his maps and roadbooks, 2004; (with Peter Northeast) Decoding Flint Flushwork on

Suffolk and Norfolk Churches, 2005; East Anglian Ex-Libris, 2008; many papers in chemical, educnl, archaeological and antiquarian jls. *Recreations:* East Anglian history, music, books. *Address:* 11 Burlington Road, Ipswich, Suffolk IP1 2HS.

BLATHERWICK, Sir David (Elliott Spiby), KCMG 1997 (CMG 1990); OBE 1973; HM Diplomatic Service, retired; Chairman, British Egyptian Chamber of Commerce, since 1999; *b* 13 July 1941; *s* of Edward S. Blatherwick; *m* 1964, (Margaret) Clare Crompton; one *s* one *d*. *Educ:* Lincoln Sch.; Wadham Coll., Oxford. Entered FO, 1964; Second Sec., Kuwait, 1968; First Sec., Dublin, 1970; FCO, 1973; Head of Chancery, Cairo, 1977; Head, Pol Affairs Dept, NI Office (Belfast), 1981; Hd, Energy, Science and Space Dept, FCO, 1983; sabbatical leave at Stanford Univ., Calif, 1985–86; Counsellor and Hd of Chancery, UK Mission to UN, NY, 1986–89; Prin. Finance Officer and Chief Inspector, FCO, 1989–91; Ambassador to: Republic of Ireland, 1991–95; Egypt, 1995–99. *Publication:* The International Politics of Telecommunications, 1987. *Recreations:* music, sailing, walking. *Club:* Athenæum.

BLATT, Prof. Michael Robert, PhD; FRSE; Regius Professor of Botany, University of Glasgow, since 2001; *b* 9 Sept. 1953; *s* of Frank Blatt and Gloria Blatt (*née* Freeman); *m* 1980, Jane Stroh; one *s* one *d*. *Educ:* Univ. of Wisconsin-Madison (BSc Biochem. and Botany 1975); Univ. Erlangen-Nürnberg (Matricula Natural Scis 1979); Stanford Univ. (PhD Biol Scis 1981). NRSA Res. Fellow, Dept of Physiol., Yale Univ. Sch. of Medicine, 1980–83; NATO Fellow and Sen. Res. Associate, Botany Sch., Univ. of Cambridge, 1983–90; Lectr and Reader in Plant Cell and Membrane Biol., 1990–97, Prof. of Plant Membrane Biol., 1997–2000, Wye Coll., Univ. of London; Prof. of Plant Physiol. and Biophysics, Imperial Coll., London, 2000–01. FRSE 2003. *Publications:* numerous res. articles in fields of biol membrane transport, plant and fungal cell biol. and sensory physiol. *Recreations:* ski-ing, mountaineering, sailing, music. *Address:* Institute of Biomedical and Life Sciences, Bower Building, University of Glasgow, Glasgow G12 8QQ. *T:* (0141) 330 4451, *Fax:* (0141) 330 4447; *e-mail:* m.blatt@bio.gla.ac.uk.

BLATTER, Joseph Sepp; President, Fédération Internationale de Football Association, since 1998; *b* 10 March 1936; *s* of Joseph and Berta Blatter-Nellen; *m* (marr. diss.); one *d*. *Educ:* Univ. of Lausanne (BA Business Admin and Econs). Gen. Sec., Swiss Ice-Hockey Fedn, 1964–66; Press Officer, Swiss Sports Orgn, 1966–68; Dir, Sports Timing and PR, Longines SA, 1968–75; Technical Dir, 1975–81, Gen. Sec. and CEO, 1981–98, FIFA. Mem., IOC, 1999–. Hon. Mem., Swiss FA. Hon. PhD Nelson Mandela Metropolitan, SA, 2006. Olympic Order, 1994; American Global Peace Award, 2003. Kt, Sultanate of Pahang, 1990; Order of Good Hope (S Africa), 1998; Chevalier, Légion d'Honneur (France); Grosse Verdienstkreuz (Germany), 2006. *Recreations:* crosswords, tennis, books (detective stories). *Address:* FIFA, FIFA Strasse 20, PO Box, 8044 Zurich, Switzerland. *T:* (43) 2227777.

BLAUG, Prof. Mark, PhD; FBA 1989; Professor of the Economics of Education, University of London Institute of Education, 1967–84, now Professor Emeritus; *b* 3 April 1927; *s* of Bernard Blaug and Sarah (*née* Toeman); *m* 1st, 1946, Rose Lapone (marr. diss.); 2nd, 1954, Brenda Ellis (marr. diss.); one *s*; 3rd, 1969, Ruth M. Towse; one *s*. *Educ:* Queen's Coll., NY (BA); Columbia Univ. (MA, PhD). Asst Prof., Yale Univ., 1954–62; Sen. Lectr, then Reader, Univ. of London Inst. of Educn, 1963–67; Lectr, LSE, 1963–78. Consultant Prof., Univ. of Buckingham, 1984–92, now Prof. Emeritus; Visiting Professor: Exeter Univ., 1989–2001; Univ. of Amsterdam, 1999–2008; Erasmus Univ., Rotterdam, 2000–07. Guggenheim Foundn Fellow, 1958–59. Dist. Fellow, Hist. of Econs Soc., 1988. Editl Consultant, Edward Elgar Publishing, 1986–. Foreign Hon. Mem., Royal Netherlands Acad. of Arts and Scis, 1984. Hon. DSc Buckingham, 1993. *Publications:* Ricardian Economics, 1958; Economic Theory in Retrospect, 1962, 5th edn 1996; (jtly) The Causes of Graduate Unemployment in India, 1969; Introduction to the Economics of Education, 1970; Education and the Employment Problem in Developing Countries, 1973; (jtly) The Practice of Manpower Forecasting, 1973; The Cambridge Revolution?, 1974; The Methodology of Economics, 1980, 2nd edn 1992; Who's Who in Economics, 1983, 4th edn (jtly) 2003; Great Economists Since Keynes, 1984, 2nd edn 1998; Great Economists Before Keynes, 1986; Economic History and the History of Economics, 1986; The Economics of Education and the Education of an Economist, 1987; Economic Theories: True or False?, 1990; Keynes: Life, Ideas and Legacy, 1990; (jtly) Appraising Economic Theories, 1991; (jtly) Quantity Theory of Money, 1995; Not Only an Economist, 1997. *Recreations:* talking, walking, sailing. *Address:* 5e Binnenvestgracht 9, 2311 VH Leiden, Netherlands. *T:* (71) 5663222; Langsford Barn, Peter Tavy, Tavistock, Devon PL9 9LY. *T:* (01822) 810562.

BLAYNEY, Elizabeth Carmel, (Eily); Head of Library and Records Department and Departmental Record Officer (Assistant Secretary), Foreign and Commonwealth Office, 1977–85, retired; *b* 19 July 1925; *d* of William Blayney, MRCS, LRCP, Medical Practitioner (previously County Inspector, RIC) of Harrold, Beds, and Mary Henrietta *d* of John Beveridge, sometime Town Clerk of Dublin. *Educ:* St Mary's Convent, Shaftesbury; The Triangle, S Molton Street. Chartered Librarian. Served War, WTS(FANY) in UK, India and Ceylon (Force 136), 1944–46. Library Asst, Hampstead Borough Libraries, 1947–50; Assistant Librarian: RSA, 1950–52; CO/CRO Jt Library, CRO, 1953; Head of Printed Library, FO, 1959–68; Librarian i/c, ODM, 1968–69; Librarian, FCO, 1969–77. *Address:* 6 Bamville Wood, East Common, Harpenden, Herts AL5 1AP. *T:* (01582) 715067.

BLAZE, Robin Peter; countertenor; Professor, Royal College of Music, since 1999; *b* 11 Jan. 1971; *s* of Peter Michael and Christine Margaret Blaze; *m* 1999, Lisa Jane Beckley; one *s*. *Educ:* Magdalen Coll., Oxford (MA Hons); Royal Coll. of Music (Postgrad. Dip.). First professional engagements, 1995; recital broadcasts BBC Radio 3, 1999–2002; Proms solo début, 2000; début recital Wigmore Hall, 2001; opera débuts: Glyndebourne Touring Opera, 2001 (Bertarido, in Rodelinda); ENO, 2002 (Arsemene, in Xerxes); Glyndebourne Fest. Opera (Didymus, in Theodora), and Royal Opera, Covent Gdn (Athamus, in Semele), 2003; concert appearances in Australia (Sydney Opera House), Japan (Tokyo Opera City), Argentina, Brazil, USA (Kennedy Centre) and across Europe. Solo recital recordings, 1999– incl. complete Bach series with Bach Collegium Japan. *Recreations:* golf, reading, cricket. *Address: e-mail:* blaze@blaze.aflex.net.

BLAZWICK, Iwona Maria Anna, OBE 2008; Director, Whitechapel Art Gallery, since 2001; *b* 14 Oct. 1955; *d* of Wojciech Blaszczyk and Danuta Mondry-Blaszczyk; one *d* by Dr Richard Noble. *Educ:* Exeter Univ. (BA 1977). Curator, 1980–85, Dir of Exhibns, 1987–93, Inst. of Contemporary Arts, London; Dir, A.I.R. Gall., 1985–87; Commng Editor, Phaidon Press, 1993–97; Curator, then Hd of Exhibns, Tate Gall. of Modern Art, subseq. Tate Modern, 1997–2001. Art critic, lectr and broadcaster on contemporary art, 1985–; Vis. Lectr, RCA, 1993–97. Curator: Ha-Ha: Contemporary British Artists in an 18th Century Park, Univ. of Plymouth and Nat. Trust, 1993; (jtly) On Taking a Normal Situation, Mus. of Contemporary Art, Antwerp, 1993; Now Here, Louisiana Mus., Denmark, 1996; New Tendencies in British and Japanese Art, Toyama Mus. of Modern Art, Japan, 1996. FRCA. Hon. MA London Metropolitan, 2003; Hon. DPhil Plymouth, 2006. *Publications:* An Endless Feast: on British situationism, 1988; Lawrence Weiner,

1993; Ilya Kabakov, 1998; (ed jtly) Tate Modern: the handbook, 2000; (ed) Century City, 2001; Faces in the Crowd, 2004; Alex Katz, 2006; Revolutions: forms that turn, 2008; exhibn catalogues; contribs to jls. *Recreations:* cinema, dancing, travel, photography. *Address:* 80–82 Whitechapel High Street, E1 7QX. *Club:* Blacks.

BLEAKLEY, Rt Hon. David Wylie, CBE 1984; PC (NI) 1971; President, Church Mission (formerly Church Missionary) Society, 1983–97; *b* 11 Jan. 1925; *s* of John Wesley Bleakley and Sarah Bleakley (*née* Wylie); *m* 1949, Winifred Wason; three *s. Educ:* Ruskin Coll., Oxford; Queen's Univ., Belfast. MA, DipEconPolSci (Oxon). Belfast Shipyard, 1940–46; Oxford and Queen's Univ., 1946–51; Tutor in Social Studies, 1951–55; Principal, Belfast Further Educn Centre, 1955–58; Lectr in Industrial Relations, Kivukoni Coll., Dar-es-Salaam, 1967–69; Head of Dept of Economics and Political Studies, Methodist Coll., Belfast, 1969–79; Chief Exec., Irish Council of Churches, 1980–92. MP (Lab) Victoria, Belfast, Parliament of N Ireland, 1958–65; contested: (Lab) East Belfast, General Elections, 1970, Feb. and Oct. 1974. Minister of Community Relations, Govt of NI, March–Sept. 1971; Member (NILP), E Belfast: NI Assembly, 1973–75; NI Constitutional Convention, 1975–76. Contested (Lab) Belfast E, NI Assembly, 1998. Mem., Cttee of Inquiry on Police, 1978. Chm., NI Standing Adv. Commn on Human Rights, 1980–84. Mem., Labour Delegn, NI Peace Talks, 1996–. Irish Deleg. to ACC, 1976; Delegate to WCC, to Conf. of European Churches. WEA and Open Univ. tutor; Vis. Sen. Lectr in Peace Studies, Univ. of Bradford, 1974–. Mem., Press Council, 1987–90. Hon. MA Open, 1975. *Publications:* Ulster since 1800: regional history symposium, 1958; Young Ulster and Religion in the Sixties, 1964; Peace in Ulster, 1972; Faulkner: a biography, 1974; Saidie Patterson, Irish Peacemaker, 1980; In Place of Work, 1981; The Shadow and Substance, 1983; Beyond Work—Free to Be, 1985; Will the Future Work, 1986; Europe: a Christian vision, 1992; Ageing and Ageism in a Technological Society, 1994; Peace in Ireland: two states, one people, 1995; Europe: obligations and opportunities for Christians, 1997; C. S. Lewis: at home in Ireland, 1998; regular contribs to BBC and to press on community relations and industrial studies. *Address:* 8 Thornhill, Bangor, Co. Down, Northern Ireland BT19 1RD. *T:* (028) 9145 4898, *Fax:* (028) 9127 4274.

BLEARS, Rt Hon. Hazel Anne; PC 2005; MP (Lab) Salford, since 1997; Secretary of State for Communities and Local Government, since 2007; *b* 14 May 1956; *d* of Arthur and Dorothy Blears; *m* 1989, Michael Halsall. *Educ:* Wardley Grammar Sch.; Trent Poly. (BA Hons Law). Trainee Solicitor, Salford Council, 1978–80; in private practice, 1980–81; Solicitor: Rossendale Council, 1981–83; Wigan Council, 1983–85; Principal Solicitor, Manchester City Council, 1985–97. Mem. (Lab) Salford City Council, 1984–92. Parly Under-Sec. of State, DoH, 2001–03; Minister of State, Home Office, 2003–06; Minister without Portfolio and Chair, Labour Party, 2006–07. Contested (Lab): Tatton, 1987; Bury S, 1992. *Recreations:* dance, motorcycling. *Address:* House of Commons, SW1A 0AA. *T:* (020) 7219 6595.

BLEASDALE, Alan; writer and producer; *b* 23 March 1946; *s* of George and Margaret Bleasdale; *m* 1970, Julia Moses; two *s* one *d. Educ:* St Aloysius RC Jun. Sch., Huyton; Wade Deacon Grammar Sch., Widnes; Padgate Teachers Trng Coll. (Teacher's Cert.). Schoolteacher, 1967–75. *TV series: writer:* Boys from the Blackstuff, 1982 (BPG TV Award for Best Series, 1982; Best British TV Drama of the Decade, ITV Achievement of the Decade Awards, 1989); Scully, 1984; The Monocled Mutineer, 1986; (also prod) GBH, 1991 (BPG TV Award for Best Drama Series, 1992); (also prod) Jake's Progress, 1995 (Best Writer Award, Monte Carlo Internat. TV Fest., 1996); (also prod) Melissa, 1997; (adapt.) Oliver Twist, 1999 (Best TV Drama Series, TRIC Award, 2000); *producer:* Alan Bleasdale Presents, 1994; Soft Sand, Blue Sea, 1997. Hon. DLitt Liverpool Poly., 1991. BAFTA Writers Award, 1982; RTS Writer of the Year, 1982. *Publications: novels:* Scully, 1975; Who's been sleeping in my bed, 1977; *play scripts:* No more sitting on the Old School Bench, 1979; Boys from the Blackstuff, 1982; Are you lonesome tonight?, 1985 (Best Musical, London Standard Drama Awards, 1985); Having a Ball, 1986; It's a Madhouse, 1986; The Monocled Mutineer, 1986; On the Ledge, 1993; *film script:* No Surrender, 1986. *Recreation:* rowing. *Address:* c/o The Agency, 24 Pottery Lane, Holland Park, W11 4LZ. *T:* (020) 7727 1346.

BLEASDALE, Cyril, OBE 1988; FCILT; Managing Director, Railnews Ltd, since 1996; *b* 8 July 1934; *s* of Frederick and Alice Bleasdale; *m* 1970, Catherine; two *d. Educ:* Evered High Sch., Liverpool; Stanford Univ., Calif (Sen. Exec. Program). Man. Dir, Freightliner Ltd, 1975–82; Dir, Inter City British Rail, 1982–86; Gen. Manager, BR London Midland Region, 1986–90; Dir, Scotrail, 1990–94. Dir, 1997–, Chm., 2003–, Hertfordshire Business Incubation Centre Ltd. Dir Gen., Internat. Council, Chartered Inst. (formerly Inst.) of Logistics and Transport, 1999–. FCMI. *Recreations:* music, fitness. *Address:* 22 Trafalgar Street, Cheltenham GL50 1UH. *Club:* Royal Automobile.

BLEASDALE, Paul Edward; QC 2001; a Recorder of the Crown Court, since 1996; *b* 18 Dec. 1955; *s* of late William Arthur Bleasdale and of Dorothy Elizabeth Bleasdale; *m* 1991, Dr Sarah Alexandra Nicholson; one *s* one *d. Educ:* Langley Park Sch. for Boys, Beckenham; Queen Mary Coll., London (LLB 1977). Called to the Bar, Inner Temple, 1978; Asst Recorder, 1992–96. Dep. Chm., Agricl Lands Tribunal, 1994–. *Recreations:* family holidays, outdoor sports. *Address:* 5 Fountain Court, Steelhouse Lane, Birmingham B4 6DR.

BLEDISLOE, 3rd Viscount *cr* 1935; **Christopher Hiley Ludlow Bathurst;** QC 1978; *b* 24 June 1934; *s* of 2nd Viscount Bledisloe, QC, and Joan Isobel Krishaber (*d* 1999); *S* father, 1979; *m* (marr. diss. 1986); two *s* one *d. Educ:* Eton; Trinity Coll., Oxford. Called to the Bar, Gray's Inn, 1959; Bencher, 1986. Elected Mem., H of L, 1999. *Heir: s* Hon. Rupert Edward Ludlow Bathurst [*b* 13 March 1964; *m* 2001, Shera, *d* of Rohinton and Irma Sarosh; one *s* two *d*]. *Address:* Lydney Park, Glos GL15 6BT. *T:* (01594) 842566; Fountain Court, Temple, EC4Y 9DH. *T:* (020) 7583 3335.

BLELLOCH, Sir John (Niall Henderson), KCB 1987 (CB 1983); Permanent Under-Secretary of State, Northern Ireland Office, 1988–90; *b* 24 Oct. 1930; *s* of late Ian William Blelloch, CMG and Leila Mary Henderson; *m* 1958, Pamela, *d* of late James B. and E. M. Blair; one *s* (and one *s* decd). *Educ:* Fettes Coll.; Gonville and Caius Coll., Cambridge (MA). Nat. Service, RA, 1949–51 (commnd 1950). Asst Principal, War Office, 1954; Private Sec. to successive Parly Under Secs of State, 1956–58; Principal, 1958; MoD, 1964–80; London Business Sch. (EDP 3), 1967; Asst Sec., 1968; RCDS, 1974; Asst Under-Sec. of State, 1976; Dep. Sec., NI Office, 1980–82; Dep. Under-Sec. of State (Policy and Programmes), MoD, 1982–84; Second Permanent Under-Sec. of State, MoD, 1984–88. Mem., Security Commn, 1991–2001; Jt Chm., Sentence Review Commn, NI, 1998–. Comr, Royal Hosp. Chelsea, 1988–94. Mem. Cttee, 1993–99, Vice-Chm., 1995–99, Automobile Assoc.; Pres., Emergency Planning Soc., 1993–2005. Trustee: RAF Mus., 1993–2002; Cheshire Foundn, 1996–2005; Gov., Fettes Coll., 1992–2002. *Recreations:* golf, music, books. *Address:* c/o Bank of Scotland, St James's Gate, 14–16 Cockspur Street, SW1 5BL. *Club:* Sherborne Golf.

BLENKINSOP, Dorothy, CBE 1990; Regional Nursing Officer, Northern Regional Health Authority, 1973–89, retired; *b* 15 Nov. 1931; *d* of late Joseph Henry Blenkinsop, BEM, and Thelma Irene (*née* Bishop). *Educ:* South Shields Grammar Sch. for Girls. MA (Dunelm) 1978. SRN 1953; SCM 1954; Health Visitors Cert. 1962. Ward Sister, Royal Victoria Infirmary, Newcastle upon Tyne, 1955–61; Health Visitor, S Shields, 1962–64; Dep. Matron, Gen. Hosp., S Shields, 1964–67; Durham Hospital Management Committee: Prin. Nurse, Durham City Hosps, 1967–69; Prin. Nursing Officer (Top), 1969–71; Chief Nursing Officer, 1971–73. Chm., S Tyneside Health Care Trust, 1992–96. Local Preacher, Methodist Church. Hon. MSc CNAA, 1990. *Publications:* (with E. G. Nelson): Changing the System, 1972; Managing the System, 1976; articles in nursing press. *Recreation:* gardening. *Address:* 143 Temple Park Road, South Shields, Tyne and Wear NE34 0EN. *T:* (0191) 456 1429.

BLENKINSOPP, Prof. Alison, PhD; Professor of the Practice of Pharmacy, Department of Medicines Management, Keele University, since 1999; *b* 22 June 1959; *d* of Ron and Margaret Morley; *m* 1988, John Blenkinsopp. *Educ:* Bradford Univ. (BPharm 1st Cl. Hons); Aston Univ. (PhD 1988). Lecturer in Pharmacy Practice: Aston Univ., 1982–88; Univ. of Bradford, 1988–91; Dir, NHS Centre for Pharmacy Postgrad. Educn, 1991–95; Sen. Lectr, Health Services Res., Keele Univ., 1995–99. Ed., Internat. Jl Pharmacy Practice, 1998–2005. Member: Cttee on Safety of Medicines, 1999–2005; NHS Access Taskforce, 2001–. Mem., Jt Nat. Formulary Cttee, 1989–. Charter Gold Medal, RPSGB, 2001. *Publications:* Symptoms in the Pharmacy, 1989, 6th edn 2008; Health Promotion for Community Pharmacists, 1991, 2nd edn 2000; Over the Counter Medication, 2005; Supporting Self Care in Primary Care, 2006. *Recreations:* travel, reading, contemporary music, Chicago Cubs supporter. *Address:* Department of Medicines Management, Keele University, Staffs ST5 5BG. *T:* (01782) 583474, *Fax:* (01782) 713586; *e-mail:* a.blenkinsopp@virgin.net.

BLENNERHASSETT, Sir (Marmaduke) Adrian (Francis William), 7th Bt, *cr* 1809; *b* 25 May 1940; *s* of Lieut Sir Marmaduke Blennerhassett, 6th Bt, RNVR (killed in action, 1940), and Gwenfra (*d* 1956), *d* of Judge Harrington-Morgan, Churchtown, Co. Kerry, and of Mrs Douglas Campbell; *S* father 1940; *m* 1972, Carolyn Margaret, *yr d* of late Gilbert Brown; one *s* one *d. Educ:* Michael Hall, Forest Row; McGill Univ.; Imperial Coll., Univ. of London (MSc); Cranfield Business Sch. (MBA). FRGS 2000. *Recreations:* sailing, ski-ing, adventure travelling. *Heir: s* Charles Henry Marmaduke Blennerhassett, *b* 18 July 1975. *Address:* 15D Farm Lane Trading Estate, 101 Farm Lane, SW6 1QJ. *Club:* Travellers.

BLESSED, Brian; actor, author and climber; *b* 9 Oct. 1936; *s* of William Blessed and Hilda Blessed (*née* Wall); *m* 1st, Anne Bomann (marr. diss.); one *d*; 2nd, 1978, Hildegard Neil (*née* Zimmermann); one *d. Educ:* Bolton-on-Dearne Sch.; Bristol Old Vic Theatre Sch. *Stage:* worked in rep., Nottingham, Birmingham, etc; Incident at Vichy, Phoenix, 1966; The Exorcism, Comedy, 1967; State of Revolution, NT, 1977; The Devil's Disciple, 1979 and The Eagle has Two Heads, Chichester; Hamlet, Richard III, and Henry V, RSC, 1984–85; The Relapse, RNT, 2001; dir, The Glass Menagerie, tour 1998; one-man show, An Evening with Brian Blessed, tours 1992–93, 1995–96; musicals: Old Deuteronomy, in Cats, New London, 1981; Metropolis, Piccadilly, 1989; Hard Times, Haymarket, 2000; Chitty Chitty Bang Bang, Palladium, 2002; narrator, Morning Heroes (Arthur Bliss), with LSO, 1991, and other works; *films include:* The Trojan Women, 1971; Man of La Mancha, 1972; Flash Gordon, 1980; Henry V, 1989; Robin Hood, Prince of Thieves, 1991; Much Ado About Nothing, 1993; Hamlet, 1997; Star Wars—The Phantom Menace, 1998; Walt Disney's Tarzan, 1999; Mumbo Jumbo, 2000; Alexander, 2004; As You Like It, The Conclave, The Day of Wrath, 2006; Back in Business, 2007; *television includes:* series: Fancy Smith, in Z Cars, 1962–78; The Little World of Don Camillo, 1980; The Black Adder, 1983; My Family and Other Animals, 1987; serials: The Three Musketeers, 1966; I, Claudius, 1976; Return to Treasure Island, 1986; War and Remembrance, 1988; Catherine the Great, 1995; Tom Jones, 1997; documentary, Ascent of Mars Mountain, 2005. Has made expeditions to: Mt Everest, 1991 (film, Galahad of Everest, won Canadian Grand Prix, Banff Fest., 1992), 1993, 1996; N Pole, Mt Aconcagua, 2002; Chile, 1993; Mt Ararat, Turkey, 2004; Mt Kuiten and Malkin, Mongolia; Mt Kilimanjaro, Africa. *Publications:* The Turquoise Mountain, 1991; The Dynamite Kid, 1992; Nothing's Impossible, 1994; Quest for the Lost World, 1999. *Address:* c/o AIM, 1 Blythe Road, W14 0HG.

BLESSLEY, Andrew Charles; Clerk to the Clothworkers' Co. of the City of London and Chief Executive, Clothworkers' Foundation, since 2001; *b* 20 May 1951; *s* of Kenneth Harry Blessley, *qv; m* 1979, Linda Kristine Marr; one *s* one *d. Educ:* Haberdashers' Aske's Sch., Elstree; St John's Coll., Cambridge (MA); Harvard Business Sch. (AMP). Joined National Westminster Bank, 1972: appointments in UK and USA, including: Dir, Energy and Natural Resources Gp, 1989–90; COS to Gp Chief Exec., 1990–92; Regl Dir, Central London, 1992–94; Dir, Gp Strategy, 1994–95; Vice-Chm. and Chief Operating Officer, NatWest Bancorp USA, 1995–96; Dir, Retail Mktg and Distribution, 1996–2001. Director: Fleet Bank NA, 1996–97; Lombard NatWest Commercial Services, 1996–98. Dir, Banking Ombudsman Bd, 1996–2000. Member: Regeneration Leadership Team, BITC, 1997–2001; HM Treasury Credit Union Taskforce, 1999–2000. Trustee, NatWest Gp Charitable Trust, 1996–2001. Dir, Prostate Centre, 2004–; Trustee, Prostate Cancer Charity, 2006–. Director: Brooklyn Acad. of Music, 1995–96; Corporate Culture, 2006–07. Member: Court, Univ. of Leeds, 2001–; Council, Metropolitan Soc. for the Blind, 2001–. FRSA 1993. *Recreations:* art, theatre, cinema, jazz, family, walking. *Address:* Clothworkers' Hall, Dunster Court, Mincing Lane, EC3R 7AH. *T:* (020) 7623 7041, *Fax:* (020) 7397 0107; *e-mail:* clerk@clothworkers.co.uk.

BLESSLEY, Kenneth Harry, CBE 1974 (MBE 1945); ED; Valuer and Estates Surveyor, Greater London Council, 1964–77; *b* 28 Feb. 1914; *s* of Victor Henry le Blond Blessley and Ellen Mary Blessley; *m* 1946, Gwendeline MacRae (*d* 2005); two *s. Educ:* Haberdashers' Aske's Hampstead Sch.; St Catharine's Coll., Cambridge (MA); Coll. of Estate Management. FRICS. Private practice, West End and London suburbs. Served War of 1939–45, TA Royal Engrs, Persia, Middle East, Sicily, Italy (despatches 1942 and 1944). Sen. Property Adviser, Public Trustee, 1946–50; Dep. County Valuer, Middx CC, 1950–53; County Valuer, Middx CC, 1953–65. Mem. Urban Motorways Cttee, 1970–72; Chm., Covent Garden Officers' Steering Gp, 1970–77; Chm., Thamesmead Officers' Steering Gp, 1971–76; Pres., Assoc. of Local Authority Valuers and Estate Surveyors, 1962 and 1972; Mem. Gen. Council, RICS, 1972–78, Pres., Gen. Practice Div., 1976–77. Pres., Old Haberdashers' Assoc., 1963 (Pres. RFC, 1966–68); Vice-Pres., Cambridge Univ. Land Soc., 1985–86. *Publications:* numerous articles and papers on compensation, property valuation and development. *Recreations:* music, drama, sport, motoring. *Address:* Sun Rise, Christchurch Road, Virginia Water, Surrey GU25 4BE.
See also A. C. Blessley.

BLETHYN, Brenda Anne, OBE 2003; actress; *b* 20 Feb. 1946; *d* of William Charles Bottle and Louisa Kathleen Bottle; partner, 1977, Michael Mayhew. *Educ:* St Augustine's RC Sch., Ramsgate; Thanet Tech. Coll., Ramsgate; Guildford Sch. of Acting. *Theatre* includes: work with NT, 1975–90, incl. Mysteries, 1979, Double Dealer, 1982, Dalliance, 1987, Beaux' Stratagem, 1989, Bedroom Farce; A Doll's House, 1987, Born Yesterday, 1988, An Ideal Husband, 1992, Royal Exchange, Manchester; Steaming, Comedy, 1981; Benefactors, Vaudeville, 1984; Wildest Dreams, RSC, 1993; The Bed Before Yesterday, Almeida, 1994; Habeas Corpus, Donmar Warehouse, 1996; Absent Friends, NY; Mrs Warren's Profession, Strand, 2002; *films* include: The Witches; A River Runs Through It, 1992; Secrets and Lies, 1996; Remember Me, 1996; Music From Another Room, 1997; Girls' Night, In the Winter Dark, 1998; Little Voice, Daddy and Them, 1999; Night Train, Saving Grace, 2000; Anne Frank - The Whole Story, 2001; Lovely and Amazing, 2002; Pumpkin, Yellow Bird, Plots with a View, Blizzard, Sonny, A Way of Life, 2003; Piccadilly Jim, Beyond the Sea, 2004; On a Clear Day, Pride and Prejudice, 2005; Atonement, Clubland, 2007; *television* includes: Henry VI Part I, 1981; King Lear, 1983; Chance in a Million (3 series), 1983–85; The Labours of Erica, 1987; The Bullion Boys, 1993; The Buddha of Suburbia, 1993; Sleeping with Mickey, 1993; Outside Edge (3 series), 1994–96; First Signs of Madness (Mona), 1996; Between the Sheets (series), 2003; Belonging, 2004; Mysterious Creatures, 2006; War and Peace, 2007. Hon. DLitt Kent, 1999. Numerous awards incl. Best Actress Awards for Secrets and Lies: Cannes Film Fest., 1996; Boston Film Critics, 1997; LA Film Critics, 1997; Golden Globe, 1997; London Film Critics, 1997; BAFTA, 1997. *Publication:* Mixed Fancies (memoir), 2006. *Recreations:* reading, swimming, cryptic crosswords. *Address:* c/o Independent Talent Group Ltd, Oxford House, 76 Oxford Street, W1D 1BS. *T:* (020) 7636 6565.

BLEWETT, Hon. Neal, AC 1995; DPhil; FRHistS; FASSA; High Commissioner for Australia in the United Kingdom, 1994–98; *b* 24 Oct. 1933; *s* of James and Phyllis Blewett; *m* 1962, Jill Myford (*d* 1988); one *s* one *d. Educ:* Launceston High Sch.; Univ. of Tasmania (Dip Ed, MA); Jesus Coll., Oxford (MA; Hon. Fellow, 1998); St Antony's Coll., Oxford (DPhil). FRHistS 1975. Oxford University: Sen. Schol., St Antony's Coll., 1959–61; Lectr, St Edmund Hall, 1961–63; Lectr in Politics, Univ. of Adelaide, 1964–69; Flinders University, S Australia: Reader, 1970–74; Prof., Dept of Pol Theory and Instns, 1974–77. MP (Lab) Bonython, SA, 1977–94; Mem., Jt Hse Cttee on Foreign Affairs and Defence, 1977–80; Deleg. to Australian Constitutional Convention, 1978; Opposition Spokesman on health and Tasmanian affairs, 1980–83; Minister for: Health, 1983–87; Community Services and Health, 1987–90; Trade and Overseas Develt, 1990–91; Social Security, 1991–93. Vis. Prof., Faculty of Medicine, Univ. of Sydney, 1998–2002. Member Council: Univ. of Adelaide, 1972–74; Torrens Coll. of Advanced Educn, 1972–78. Exec. Bd Mem., WHO, 1995–98. Nat. Pres., Australian Inst. of Internat. Affairs, 1998–2005; Pres., Alcohol and other Drugs Council of Australia, 2002–06. Chm., NSW Film and Television Office, 2006–. Hon. LLD: Tasmania, 1998; ANU, 2003; Hon. DLitt Hull, 1999. *Publications:* The Peers, the Parties and the People, 1972; (jtly) Playford to Dunstan: the politics of transition, 1971; A Cabinet Diary, 1999. *Recreations:* bush-walking, reading, cinema. *Address:* 32 Fitzroy Street, Leura, NSW 2780, Australia.

BLEWITT, Major Sir Shane (Gabriel Basil), GCVO 1996 (KCVO 1989; CVO 1987; LVO 1981); Keeper of the Privy Purse and Treasurer to the Queen, 1988–96; an Extra Equerry to the Queen, since 1996; *b* 25 March 1935; *s* of late Col Basil Blewitt; *m* 1969, Julia Morrogh-Bernard, *widow* of Major John Morrogh-Bernard, Irish Guards, and *d* of late Mr Robert Calvert; one *s* one *d* (and one step *s* one step *d*). *Educ:* Ampleforth Coll.; Christ Church, Oxford (MA Hons Mod. Languages). Served Irish Guards, 1956–74 (BAOR, NI, Aden, HK); Antony Gibbs and Sons, 1974; Asst Keeper, 1975–85, Dep. Keeper, 1985–88, of the Privy Purse; Receiver-General, Duchy of Lancaster, 1988–96. Gov., King Edward VII Hosp. Sister Agnes, 1988–; Mem. Gen. Council, King's Hosp. Fund, 1988–. *Address:* South Corner House, Duncton, Petworth, W Sussex GU28 0LT. *T:* (01798) 342143; *e-mail:* blewittshane@aol.com. *Clubs:* Army and Navy, White's.

BLIGH, family name of **Earl of Darnley**.

BLIGH, Stephen Ernest; Principal Consultant, Det Norske Veritas, since 2006; *b* 13 May 1953; *s* of George and Doreen Bligh; *m* 1977, Susan Jane Duncan; two *d. Educ:* Fullbrook Co. Secondary Sch.; Hull Nautical Coll. Master Mariner 1987. Served at sea with various cos, 1970–85; joined P&O, 1985; Fleet Ops Manager, P&O Containers Ltd, 1989–97; Fleet Marine Manager, P&O NedLloyd, 1997–2003; Chief Exec., Maritime and Coastguard Agency, 2003–06. *Recreations:* Rugby, sailing, flying. *Address:* Det Norske Veritas, Palace House, 3 Cathedral Street, SE1 9DE; *e-mail:* stephen.bligh@dnv.com.

BLIGHT, Denis Geoffrey, AO 2004; PhD; Chairman, LIS Pty Ltd, since 2006; Executive Director, Crawford Fund, since 2008; *b* 20 Feb. 1945; *s* of Geoffrey Ivan Blight and Bernice Ethel Janet Blight; *m* 1970, Sharon Hill; one *s* one *d. Educ:* Univ. of Western Australia (BSC Hons; PhD). Third, then Second Sec., Australian Embassy, Ankara, 1972–73; First Sec., Australian High Commn, Nairobi, 1976–78; First Sec., Australian High Commn, London, 1980–82; Centre Sec., Australian Centre for Internat. Agricultural Res., 1982–84; Asst Dir Gen., AusAID, 1984–86; Dep. Chief Exec., 1986–91, Chief Exec., 1991–2000, IDP Education Australia; Dir Gen., CAB Internat., 2000–05. Mem., Commonwealth Scholarship Commn, 2006–. FRSA. *Recreations:* golf, genealogy, writing. *Club:* Union (Sydney).

BLISHEN, Anthony Owen, OBE 1968; HM Diplomatic Service, retired; Counsellor, Foreign and Commonwealth Office, 1981–92; *b* 16 April 1932; *s* of Henry Charles Adolphus Blishen, MBE and Joan Cecile Blishen (*née* Blakeney); *m* 1st, 1963, Sarah Anne Joscelyne (marr. diss. 1994); three *s* one *d*; 2nd, 1994, Elizabeth Appleyard (*née* West). *Educ:* Clayesmore Sch., Dorset; SOAS, London Univ. Commnd Royal Hampshire Regt, 1951; Lt 1st Bn: BAOR, 1953; Malaya, 1953–55; Captain, GSO3 HQ 18 Inf. Bde, Malaya, 1955–56; attached HQ Land Forces, Hong Kong (language trng), 1957–59; GSO3 HQ Far East Land Forces, Singapore, 1960–62; FO, 1963–65; First Sec. and Consul, Peking, 1965–67; First Sec., FCO, 1968–70; Chargé d'Affaires (ad interim), Ulan Bator, 1970; Trade Comr (China trade), Hong Kong, 1971–73; First Sec., FCO, 1973–77; First Sec., 1977–78, Counsellor, 1978–81, Tokyo. *Publication:* contrib. Oxford DNB. *Recreations:* Renaissance music (founded Aragon Consort, 1990), oriental languages. *Address:* 5 Beechrow, Ham Common, Richmond, Surrey TW10 5HE.

BLISS, Prof. Christopher John Emile, PhD; FBA 1988; Nuffield Professor of International Economics, Oxford University, 1992–2007; Fellow of Nuffield College, Oxford, 1977–2007, now Emeritus; *b* 17 Feb. 1940; *s* of John Llewlyn Bliss and Patricia Paula (*née* Dubern); *m* 1983, Ghada (*née* Saqf El Hait); one *s*, and one *s* two *d* by previous marr. *Educ:* Finchley Catholic Grammar Sch.; King's Coll., Cambridge (BA 1962, MA 1964, PhD 1966). Fellow of Christ's Coll., Cambridge, 1965–71; Asst Lectr, 1965–67, and Lectr, 1967–71, Cambridge Univ.; Prof. of Econs, Univ. of Essex, 1971–77; Nuffield Reader in Internat. Econs, Oxford Univ., 1977–92. Dir, General Funds Investment Trust Ltd, 1980–87. Fellow, Econometric Soc., 1978–96. Editor or Asst Editor, Rev. of Econ. Studies, 1967–71; Managing Editor: Oxford Economic Papers, 1989–96; Economic Jl, 1996–2000. *Publications:* Capital Theory and the Distribution of Income, 1975; (with N. H. Stern) Palanpur: the economy of an Indian village, 1982; Economic Theory and Policy for Trading Blocks, 1994; Trade, Growth, and Inequality, 2007; papers and reviews in learned jls. *Recreation:* music. *Address:* Nuffield College, Oxford OX1 1NF. *T:* (01865) 278539.

BLISS, Dr Timothy Vivian Pelham, FRS 1994; Head, Division of Neurophysiology, National Institute for Medical Research, 1988–2006; *b* 27 July 1940; *s* of Pelham Marryat Bliss and Elizabeth Cotton Bliss (*née* Sproule); *m* 1st, 1975, Virginia Catherine Morton-Evans (*née* O'Rorke); one step *s* two step *d*; one *d* by Katherine Sarah Clough; 2nd, 1994, Isabel Frances Vasseur (*née* Wardrop); two step *s. Educ:* Dean Close Sch.; McGill Univ. (BSc 1963; PhD 1967). Mem., scientific staff, MRC, 1967–2006. Vis. Prof., Dept of Physiology, UCL, 1993–. Trustee, Sir John Soane Mus., 2005–. Founder FMedSci 1998. Bristol Myers Squibb Award for Neuroscience, 1991; Feldberg Prize, 1994; British Neurosci. Assoc. Award for outstanding services to British neurosci., 2003. *Publications:* (ed jtly) Long-term Potentiation, 2004; The Hippocampus Book, 2006; numerous papers on the neural basis of memory and other aspects of the neurophysiology of the brain. *Recreations:* naval history, wine. *Address:* 15 Highgate West Hill, N6 6NP. *T:* (020) 8341 1215; *e-mail:* tbliss@nimr.mrc.ac.uk. *Club:* Academy.

BLIX, Hans, PhD, LLD; Chairman, Weapons of Mass Destruction Commission, since 2004; Executive Chairman, UN Monitoring, Verification and Inspection Commission for Iraq, 2000–03; *b* 28 June 1928; *s* of Gunnar Blix and Hertha Blix (*née* Wiberg); *m* 1962, Eva Margareta Kettis; two *s. Educ:* Univ. of Uppsala; Columbia Univ.; Univ. of Cambridge (PhD); Stockholm Univ. (LLD). Associate Prof. in International Law, 1960; Ministry of Foreign Affairs, Stockholm: Legal Adviser, 1963–76; Under-Secretary of State, in charge of internat. development co-operation, 1976; Minister for Foreign Affairs, 1978; Under-Secretary of State, in charge of internat. development co-operation, 1979. Dir Gen., IAEA, 1981–97, now Dir Gen. Emeritus. Member: Sweden's delegn to UN General Assembly, 1961–81; Swedish delegn to Conference on Disarmament in Geneva, 1962–78. Hon. doctorates: Moscow State Univ., 1987; Bucharest Univ., 1994; Univ. of Managua, 1996; Vrije Univ. Brussel, 2003; Padova Univ., 2004; Gothenburg Univ., 2004; Cambridge, 2007. Foratom Award, 1994. *Publications:* Treaty Making Power, 1959; Statsmyndigheternas Internationella Förbindelser, 1964; Sovereignty, Aggression and Neutrality, 1970; The Treaty-Maker's Handbook, 1974; Disarming Iraq, 2004. *Recreation:* hiking.

BLIZZARD, Robert John; MP (Lab) Waveney, since 1997; a Lord Commissioner of HM Treasury (Government Whip), since 2008; *b* 31 May 1950; *s* of late Arthur Blizzard and Joan Blizzard; *m* 1978, Lyn Chance; one *s* one *d. Educ:* Univ. of Birmingham (BA Hons 1971). Head of English: Crayford Sch., Bexley, 1976–86; Lynn Grove High Sch., Gorleston, 1986–97. Mem. (Lab), Waveney DC, 1987–97 (Leader, 1991–97). PPS to Minister of State, MAFF, 1999–2001, to Minister of State for Work, DWP, 2001–03, to Minister of State for Europe, FCO, 2005–06, to Sec. of State for Transport, 2006–07; an Asst Govt Whip, 2007–08. Mem., Envmtl Audit Select Cttee, 1997–99; Chairman: British-Brazilian All Pty Gp, 1997–2007; British Offshore Oil and Gas Industry All Pty Gp, 1999–2007; British-Latin America All Pty Gp, 2004–07; British-Chile All Pty Gp, 2005–07; Sec., Jazz Appreciation All Pty Gp, 2004–07. *Recreations:* walking, ski-ing, travel, listening to jazz. *Address:* House of Commons, SW1A 0AA. *T:* (020) 7219 3000. *Clubs:* 606 Jazz; Royal Norfolk and Suffolk Yacht (Lowestoft).

BLOBEL, Prof. Günter, MD, PhD; John D. Rockefeller Jr Professor, since 1992, and Head of Laboratory of Cell Biology, since 1976, Rockefeller University, New York; Investigator, Howard Hughes Medical Institute, since 1986; *b* Waltersdorf, Germany (now Poland), 21 May 1936; US citizen 1982; *m* 1978, Laura Maioglio. *Educ:* Univ. of Tübingen (MD 1960); Univ. of Wisconsin (PhD 1967). Intern, German hosps, 1960–62; Laboratory of Cell Biology, Rockefeller University, New York: Fellow, 1967–69; Asst Prof., 1969–73; Associate Prof., 1973–76; Prof., 1976–92. Member: US Nat. Acad. of Scis, 1983; Amer. Acad. of Arts and Scis. Founder and Pres. Bd of Dirs, Friends of Dresden Inc. Nobel Prize for Physiology or Medicine, 1999. *Publications:* contribs to books and jls. *Address:* Laboratory of Cell Biology, Rockefeller University, 1230 York Avenue, New York, NY 10021–6399, USA; Apt 10D, 1100 Park Avenue, New York, NY 10128, USA.

BLOCH, Prof. Maurice Émile Félix, PhD; FBA 1990; Professor of Anthropology, University of London at London School of Economics, 1984–2005, now Emeritus; *b* 21 Oct. 1939; *s* of late Pierre Bloch and of Claude Kennedy; step *s* of John Stodart Kennedy, FRS; *m*; one *s* one *d. Educ:* Lycée Carnot, Paris; Perse Sch., Cambridge; LSE (BA 1962); Fitzwilliam Coll., Cambridge (PhD 1968). Asst Lectr, Univ. of Wales, Swansea, 1968; Lectr, LSE, 1969; Reader, London Univ., 1977. Prof., Collège de France, 2005–06. Corresp. Mem., Académie Malgache, Madagascar, 1965. *Publications:* Placing the Dead, 1971; Marxism and Anthropology, 1983; From Blessing to Violence, 1986; Ritual, History and Power, 1989; Prey into Hunter, 1992; How We Think They Think, 1998. *Recreation:* book binding. *Address:* Department of Anthropology, London School of Economics, Houghton Street, WC2A 2AE.

BLOCH, Dame Merle Florence; *see* Park, Dame M. F.

BLOCH, Michael Gordon; QC 1998; *b* 18 Oct. 1951; *s* of John and Thelma Bloch; *m* Caroline Williams (marr. diss.); two *d*; *m* 1998, Lady Camilla Bingham, *yr d* of 7th Earl of Lucan and of Veronica Mary (*née* Duncan); three *s. Educ:* Bedales Sch.; Corpus Christi Coll., Cambridge (MA); UEA (MPhil). Called to the Bar, Lincoln's Inn, 1979; in practice as a barrister, 1979–. Trustee, Childline. *Recreations:* squash, cinema. *Address:* Wilberforce Chambers, 8 New Square, Lincoln's Inn, WC2A 3QP. *Club:* Royal Automobile.

BLOCH, Selwyn Irving; QC 2000; *b* 23 Feb. 1952; *s* of Rev. Cecil Maurice Bloch and Esther Bloch; *m* 1983, Brenda Igra; three *d. Educ:* Potchefstroom Boys' High Sch.; Witwatersrand Univ. (BA); Stellenbosch Univ. (LLB). Attorney, S Africa, 1977–; called to the Bar, Middle Temple, 1982; in practice at the Bar, 1983–. *Publication:* (jtly) Employment Covenants and Confidential Information, 1993, 2nd edn 1999. *Recreations:* listening to music, walking, reading, theatre. *Address:* Littleton Chambers, 3 King's Bench Walk North, EC4Y 7HR. *T:* (020) 7797 8699.

BLOCK, David Greenberg, AC 1988 (AO 1983); *b* 21 March 1936; *s* of Emanuel Block and Hannah Greenberg; *m* 1959, Naomi Denfield; one *s* three *d. Educ:* King Edward VII Sch., Johannesburg; Univ. of Witwatersrand (BJuris cum laude). Joined Schroder-Darling & Co., 1964, Dir, 1967–72; Chairman: David Block & Associates, 1972–81; Trinity Properties, 1984–90; George Ward Group, 1986–89; Dep. Chm., Concrete Constructions, 1990; Director: CSR, 1977–88; Kalamazoo Holdings, 1986–94; Dep. Chm., Pacific Magazines & Publishing, 1991–95; Dir, Lloyds Bank NZA, Chm., Lloyds Internat., Dir, Lloyds Merchant Bank (UK) and Adviser, Lloyds Merchant Bank Holdings, 1981–86; Consultant, Coudert Brothers, 1986–91; Adviser: Coopers & Lybrand, 1986–93; S. G. Warburg Group, 1987–95. Consultant: to Prime Minister and Cabinet, 1986–89; to govts, cos and instns, 1986–96; to Premier's Dept, NSW, 1987–88; Mem., Cttee of Enquiry into inflation and taxation, 1975; Chm., Efficiency Scrutiny Unit and Admin. Reform Unit, 1986–88. Comr, Aust. Film Commn, 1978–81; Chm., Sydney Opera House Trust, 1981–89; Trustee, Japanese Friends of Sydney Opera House Foundn,

1992–96; Councillor: Asia-Australian Inst., 1991–96; Nat. Heart Foundn, 1994–96; Gov., Aust. Nat. Gall. Foundn, 1992–96. Dir, Univ. of NSW Foundn, 1989–96. Fellow, Senate of Univ. of Sydney, 1983–87. FAICD; FAIM; FSIA. Hon. LLD New South Wales, 1992. *Recreations:* swimming, squash, music, theatre. *Address:* 30 Clarke Street, Vaucluse, NSW 2030, Australia. *T:* (2) 93376211. *Club:* University (Sydney).

BLOCK, Neil Selwyn; QC 2002; *b* 24 May 1957; *s* of Ronald Sydney Block and Barbara Block; *m* 1988, Amanda Jane Hatton; four *s. Educ:* E Barnet Grammar Sch.; City of London Poly. (BA Hons Law); Exeter Univ. (LLM); Inns of Court Sch. of Law. Called to the Bar, Gray's Inn, 1980; in practice, specialising in law of professional negligence (incl. clinical negligence), personal injury, product liability, material loss claims, insurance related disputes and contract/commercial litigation. Accredited mediator, 2006. *Recreations:* tennis, golf, family, friends. *Address:* The Grange, Great Kimble, Bucks HP17 0XS; (chambers) 39 Essex Street, WC2R 3AT.

BLOCK, Simon Jonathan; General Secretary, British Boxing Board of Control, since 2000; *b* 13 Feb. 1950; *s* of Michael Abraham Hyman Block and Winifred Joy Block (*née* Harris); *m* 1998, Annette Mary Clements (*née* Dunphy); one *s*, and one step *d. Educ:* Sunbury Grammar Sch.; East Grinstead Grammar Sch.; Crawley Coll. of Further Educn. Boxed, Crawley Amateur Boxing Club, 1965–68; British Boxing Board of Control: joined, 1979; Sec., S Area Council, 1981–96; Asst Gen. Sec., 1986–99. Hon. Sec., Commonwealth Boxing Council, 1980–; Company Sec., European Boxing Union, 2000–; Mem. Bd Governors, World Boxing Council, 2000–03. Vice Pres., Kent and Sussex Ex-Boxers' Assoc.; Hon. Mem., London Ex-Boxers' Assoc.; Member: St George's Day Club; Soc. of Friends of Ashdown Forest. *Recreations:* walking, running (London Marathon, 1987, 1995), horse riding, songwriting (record 'He's the Guy' released 1975). *Address:* British Boxing Board of Control, The Old Library, Trinity Street, Cardiff CF10 1BH. *T:* (029) 2036 7000, *Fax:* (029) 2036 7019; *e-mail:* block@bbbofc.com.

BLOEMBERGEN, Prof. Nicolaas; Gerhard Gade University Professor, Harvard University, 1980–90, now Emeritus; *b* 11 March 1920; *m* 1950, Huberta Deliana Brink; one *s* two *d. Educ:* Univ. of Utrecht (BA, MA); Univ. of Leiden (PhD). Research Associate, Leiden, 1947–48; Harvard University: Associate Prof., 1951; Gordon McKay Prof. of Applied Physics, 1957; Rumford Prof. of Physics, 1974. Hon. Prof. of Optical Scis, Univ. of Arizona, 2001–. Hon. DSc: Laval Univ., 1987; Connecticut Univ., 1988; Univ. of Hartford, 1990; Univ. of Massachusetts at Lowell, 1994; Moscow State Univ., 1997; N Carolina State Univ., 1998; Harvard Univ., 2000. Stuart Ballantine Medal, Franklin Inst., 1961; Nat. Medal of Science, 1974; Lorentz Medal, Royal Dutch Acad. of Science, 1978; Alexander von Humboldt Senior US Scientist Award, Munich, 1980; (jtly) Nobel Prize in Physics, 1981; IEEE Medal of Honor, 1983; Dirac Medal, Univ. of NSW, 1983; Byvoet Medal, Univ. of Utrecht, 2001. Commander, Order of Orange Nassau (Netherlands), 1983. *Publications:* Nuclear Magnetic Relaxation, 1948 (New York 1961); Nonlinear Optics, 1965, reprinted 1996; Encounters in Magnetic Resonance, 1996; Encounters in Nonlinear Optics, 1996; over 370 papers in scientific jls. *Address:* Optical Sciences Center, University of Arizona, Tucson, AZ 85721, USA. *T:* (520) 6263479; *e-mail:* nbloembergen@optics.arizona.edu.

BLOEMFONTEIN, Bishop of; *see* Free State, Bishop of the Diocese of the.

BLOFELD, Sir John (Christopher Calthorpe), Kt 1991; DL; a Judge of the High Court of Justice, Queen's Bench Division, 1990–2001; *b* 11 July 1932; *s* of late T. R. C. Blofeld, CBE; *m* 1961, Judith Anne, *er d* of Alan Mohun and Mrs James Mitchell; two *s* one *d. Educ:* Eton; King's Coll., Cambridge. Called to Bar, Lincoln's Inn, 1956, Bencher, 1990; QC 1975; a Recorder of the Crown Court, 1975–82; a Circuit Judge, 1982–90; Presiding Judge, SE Circuit, 1993–96. Inspector, Dept of Trade, 1979–81. Chancellor: Dio. St Edmundsbury and Ipswich, 1973–; Dio. of Norwich, 1998–2007. DL Norfolk, 1991. *Recreations:* cricket, gardening.

BLOHM, Leslie Adrian; QC 2006; a Recorder, since 2003; *b* 27 Feb. 1959; *s* of Albert Blohm and Ann Blohm; *m* 1986, Helen Mifflin; two *d. Educ:* Christ's Hospital, Horsham; Keble Coll., Oxford (MA 1981). Called to the Bar, Lincoln's Inn, 1982 (Hardwicke and Jenkins Scholar, 1982); barrister, St John's Chambers, Bristol, 1984–; in practice, specialising in Chancery, esp. Real Property law. *Recreations:* cycling, restoring British motor cars of the sixties. *Address:* St John's Chambers, 101 Victoria Street, Bristol BS1 6PU. *T:* (0117) 921 3456, *Fax:* (0117) 921 4821; *e-mail:* leslie.blohm@ stjohnschambers.co.uk.

BLOIS, Sir Charles (Nicholas Gervase), 11th Bt *cr* 1686; farming since 1965; *b* 25 Dec. 1939; *s* of Sir Gervase Ralph Edmund Blois, 10th Bt and Mrs Audrey Winifred Blois (*née* Johnson) (*d* 1997); *S* father, 1968; *m* 1967, Celia Helen Mary Pritchett (marr. diss. 2004); one *s* one *d. Educ:* Harrow; Trinity Coll., Dublin; Royal Agricultural Coll., Cirencester. Australia, 1963–65. FRGS 1992. *Recreations:* yachting, shooting, travel. *Heir:* *s* Andrew Charles David Blois [*b* 7 Feb. 1971; *m* 2002, Judith, *d* of John Hardy]. *Address:* Benacre Hall, Benacre, Beccles, Suffolk NR34 7LT. *T:* (01728) 648200. *Clubs:* Cruising Association; Ocean Cruising.

BLOKH, Alexandre, PhD, (pen-name **Jean Blot**); writer, since 1956; Vice President, PEN Club, since 1998 (International Secretary, 1982–98); *b* Moscow, 31 March 1923; *s* of Arnold Blokh, man of letters, and Anne (*née* Berlinrote); *m* 1956, Nadia Ermolaiev. *Educ:* Bromsgrove Public Sch., Worcester; Univ. of Paris (PhD Law, PhD Letters). International Civil Servant, United Nations, 1947–62: New York, until 1956; Geneva, 1958–62; Director, Arts and Letters, UNESCO, Paris, 1962–81. Critic, arts and letters, in reviews: Arche, Preuves, NRF. Prix des Critiques, 1972; Prix Valéry Larbaud, 1977; Prix Cazes, 1982; Grand Prix de la Critique, 1986; Prix International de la Paix, 1990. Officier, Ordre des Arts et des Lettres, 1997. *Publications: novels:* Le Soleil de Cavouri, 1956; Les Enfants de New York, 1959; Obscur Ennemi, 1961; Les Illusions Nocturnes, 1964; La Jeune Géante, 1969; La Difficulté d'aimer, 1971; Les Cosmopolites, 1976; Gris du Ciel, 1981; Tout l'été, 1985; Sainte Imposture, 1988; Le Juif Margolin, 1998; Roses d'Amérique, 2003; *essays:* Marguerite Yourcenar; Ossip Mandelstam; Là où tu iras; Sporade; Ivan Gontcharov; La Montagne Sainte; Albert Cohen; Si loin de Dieu et autres voyages; Bloomsbury; Retour en Asie; Vladimir Nabokov; Moïse, notre contemporain; Le Soleil se couche a l'Est, 2005; Alexandre Blok: poète de la perspective Nevski, 2007. *Address:* 34 Square Montsouris, 75014 Paris, France. *T:* (1) 45893416.

BLOM-COOPER, Sir Louis (Jacques), Kt 1992; QC 1970; Independent Commissioner for the Holding Centres, Northern Ireland, 1993–2000; a Judge of the Courts of Appeal, Jersey and Guernsey, 1989–96; *b* 27 March 1926; *s* of Alfred Blom-Cooper and Ella Flesseman, Rotterdam; *m* 1952 (marr. diss. 1970); two *s* one *d; m* 1970, Jane Elizabeth, *e d* of Maurice and Helen Smither, Woodbridge, Suffolk; one *s* two *d. Educ:* Port Regis Prep. Sch.; Seaford Coll.; King's Coll., London (FKC 1994); Municipal Univ. of Amsterdam; Fitzwilliam Coll., Cambridge. LLB London, 1952; Dr Juris Amsterdam, 1954. HM Army, 1944–47: Capt., E Yorks Regt. Called to Bar, Middle Temple, 1952, Bencher, 1978, Reader, 1998. Mem., Home Secretary's Adv. Council on the Penal

System, 1966–78. Chairman: Panel of Inquiry into circumstances surrounding the death of Jasmine Beckford, 1985; Cttee of Inquiry into complaints about Ashworth Hosp., 1991–92; Commissioner of Inquiry: into allegations of arson and political corruption in the Turks and Caicos Is, 1986 (report published, 1986); into the N Creek Develt Project, Turks and Caicos Is, 1986–87. Chairman: Indep. Cttee for the Supervision of Standards of Telephone Information Services, 1986–93; Mental Health Act Commn, 1987–94; Commn on the future of Occupational Therapy, 1988–89; Press Council, 1989–90; Review of Mental Health Services in S Devon, 1994; Georgina Robinson Inquiry Cttee, 1994; Jason Mitchell Inquiry Panel, 1996. Vice-Pres., Howard League for Penal Reform, 1984– (Chm., 1973–84); Mem., Prison Reform Trust, 1982–2003; Chm., Expert Witness Inst., 1998–2004. Chm., BBC London Local Radio Adv. Council, 1970–73. Jt Dir, Legal Res. Unit, Bedford Coll., Univ. of London, 1967–82; Vis. Prof., QMC, London Univ., 1983–88. Trustee, Scott Trust (The Guardian Newspaper), 1982–88. Joint Editor, Common Market Law Reports. JP Inner London, 1966–79 (transf. City of London, 1969). FRSA 1984. Hon. DLitt: Loughborough, 1991; Ulster, 1994; UEA, 1998. *Publications:* Bankruptcy in Private International Law, 1954; The Law as Literature, 1962; The A6 Murder (A Semblance of Truth), 1963; (with T. P. Morris) A Calendar of Murder, 1964; Language of the Law, 1965; (with O. R. McGregor and Colin Gibson) Separated Spouses, 1970; (with G. Drewry) Final Appeal: a study of the House of Lords in its judicial capacity, 1972; (ed) Progress in Penal Reform, 1975; (ed with G. Drewry) Law and Morality, 1976; The Birmingham Six and Other Cases, 1997; (with T. P. Morris) With Malice Aforethought, 2004; contrib. to Modern Law Review, Criminal Law Review, Public Law, Brit. Jl of Criminology, Brit. Jl of Sociology. *Recreations:* watching and reporting on Association football, reading, music, writing, broadcasting. *Address:* 1 Southgate Road, N1 3JP. *T:* (020) 7704 1514, *Fax:* (020) 7226 5457; Southminster Hall, Southminster, Essex CM0 7EH. *T:* (01621) 772416. *Clubs:* Athenæum, MCC.

BLOMEFIELD, Sir (Thomas) Charles (Peregrine), 6th Bt *cr* 1807; fine art and philatelic consultant; *b* 24 July 1948; *s* of Sir Thomas Edward Peregrine Blomefield, 5th Bt, and of Ginette, Lady Blomefield; *S* father, 1984; *m* 1975, Georgina Geraldine, *d* of late Commander C. E. Over, Lugger End, Portscatho, Cornwall; one *s* two *d. Educ:* Wellington Coll., Berks; Mansfield Coll., Oxford. Christie's, 1970–75; Wildenstein and Co., 1975–76; Director: Lidchi Art Gallery, Johannesburg, 1976–78; Direct Import Ltd, 1985–; Man. Dir, Charles Blomefield and Co., 1980–. *Heir:* *s* Thomas William Peregrine Blomefield, *b* 16 July 1983. *Address:* Attlepin Farm, Chipping Campden, Glos GL55 6PP.

BLOMQVIST, Leif; Hon. GCVO 1995; Knight Commander, Order of the Lion of Finland, 1995; Knight, 1st Class, Order of White Rose of Finland, 1975; Ambassador of Finland: to Belgium, 1996; to NATO, 1997; *b* 20 March 1937; *s* of Viktor Hardy Blomqvist and Harriet Ellinor Knowles; *m* 1965, Marianne Sand, PhD. *Educ:* Univ. of Helsinki (LLM). Entered Finnish diplomatic service, 1965; Attaché, Addis Ababa, 1967–70; 2nd Sec., Tel Aviv, 1970–71; Dept of External Econ. Relns, Foreign Ministry, 1971–73; 1st Sec., Finnish Mission to CSCE, Geneva, 1973–75; Counsellor, Finnish Permanent Mission, Geneva, 1975–77; Vice-Chm., Finnish Delegn to CSCE follow-up meeting, Belgrade, 1977–78; Counsellor, Min. for Foreign Affairs, 1978–80; Dir and Dep. Dir Gen., External Econ. Relations, 1980–85; Ambassador to European Communities, Brussels, 1985–90; Ambassador, Min. for Foreign Affairs, 1990–91; Ambassador to UK, 1991–96. Comdr, Order of North Star (Sweden); Grosses Verdienstkreutz (Germany); Kt Comdr, Order of White Falcon (Iceland). *Recreations:* oriental rugs, English furniture. *Address:* c/o Embassy of Finland, avenue des Arts 58, 1000 Brussels, Belgium.

BLONDEL, Prof. Jean Fernand Pierre; Professor of Political Science, European University Institute, Florence, 1985–94; *b* Toulon, France, 26 Oct. 1929; *s* of Fernand Blondel and Marie Blondel (*née* Santelli); *m* 1st, 1954, Michèle (*née* Hadet) (marr. diss. 1979); two *d*; 2nd, 1982, Mrs Theresa Martineau. *Educ:* Collège Saint Louis de Gonzague and Lycée Henri IV, Paris; Institut d'Etudes Politiques and Faculté de Droit, Paris; St Antony's Coll., Oxford. Asst Lectr, then Lectr in Govt, Univ. of Keele, 1958–63; Vis. ACLS Fellow, Yale Univ., 1963–64; Prof. of Government, 1964–84, and Dean, Sch. of Comparative Studies, 1967–69, Univ. of Essex. Visiting Professor: Carleton Univ., Canada, 1969–70; Univ. of Siena, 1995–; Vis. Schol., Russell Sage Foundn, NY, 1984–85. Exec. Dir, European Consortium for Political Res., 1970–79. Member: Royal Swedish Acad. of Scis, 1990; Academia Europaea, 1993; Amer. Acad. of Scis, 2005. Hon. DLitt Salford, 1990; Dr *hc*: Essex, 1992; Univ. Catholique de Louvain, 1992; Turku, 1995; Macerata, 2007. Johan Skytte Prize, Johan Skytte Foundn, 2004. *Publications:* Voters, Parties and Leaders, 1963; (jtly) Constituency Politics, 1964; (jtly) Public Administration in France, 1965; An Introduction to Comparative Government, 1969; (jtly) Workbook for Comparative Government, 1972; Comparing Political Systems, 1972; Comparative Legislatures, 1973; The Government of France, 1974; Thinking Politically, 1976; Political Parties, 1978; World Leaders, 1980; The Discipline of Politics, 1981; The Organisation of Governments, 1982; (jtly) Comparative Politics, 1984; Government Ministers in the Contemporary World, 1985; Political Leadership, 1987; (ed jtly) Western European Cabinets, 1988; Comparative Government, 1990, 2nd edn 1995; (ed jtly) The Profession of Cabinet Minister in Western Europe, 1991; (ed jtly) Governing Together, 1993; (ed jtly) Party and Government, 1996; (jtly) People and Parliament in the European Union, 1998; (ed jtly) Democracy, Governance and Economic Performance, 1999; (ed jtly) The Nature of Party Government, 2000; (jtly) Cabinets in Eastern Europe, 2001; (jtly) Political Cultures, 2006; (jtly) Governing New Democracies, 2007; (jtly) Citizens and the State, 2007; articles in: Political Studies, Parliamentary Affairs, Public Administration, Revue Française de Science Politique, European Jl of Political Research, etc. *Recreation:* holidays in Provence. *Address:* 15 Marloes Road, W8 6LQ. *T:* (020) 7370 6008; 5 Via Sant'Agostino, 50125 Florence, Italy.

BLOOD, Baroness *cr* 1999 (Life Peer), of Blackwatertown in the county of Armagh; **May Blood,** MBE 1995; Information Officer, Great Shankhill Partnership Co. Ltd, since 1994; Founding Member, Northern Ireland Women's Coalition, since 1996; *b* 26 May 1938; *d* of William and Mary Blood. *Educ:* Donegall Road Primary Sch.; Linfield Secondary Sch. Cutter/Supervisor, Blackstaff Linen Mill Co. Ltd, 1952–90; Manager, Cairn Martin Wood Products, 1991–94. DUniv: Ulster, 1998; QUB, 2000; Open, 2001. *Recreations:* home decorating, reading, gardening. *Address:* 7 Black Mountain Place, Belfast BT13 3TT. *T:* (028) 9032 6514.

BLOOM, Anthony Herbert; Director: Rio Narcea Gold Mines Ltd, since 1995; Orthoworld plc, since 1999; *b* 15 Feb. 1939; *s* of Joseph Bloom and Margaret Roslyn Bloom; *m* 1973, Gisela von Mellenthin; two *s* two *d. Educ:* Univ. of Witwatersrand (BCom, LLB); Harvard Law Sch. (LLM); Stanford Graduate Sch. of Business (Sloan Fellow, 1970). Hayman Godfrey and Sanderson, S Africa, 1960–64; joined Premier Gp Ltd, S Africa, 1966, Dir, 1969; Dep. Chm., 1975–79, Chm., 1979–88; Director: Barclays Nat. Bank, later First Nat. Bank of Southern Africa Ltd, 1980–88; Liberty Life Assoc., 1982–88; South African Breweries Ltd, 1983–89; CNA Gallo Ltd, 1983–88; RIT Capital Partners plc, 1988–1997; Dir and Dep. Chm., Sketchley, 1990–95; Chm., Cineworld (formerly CINE-UK Ltd), 1995–. Dir, Ballet Rambert, 1995–2001; Mem., British Library

Bd, 1995–2000. Hon. LLD Witwatersrand, 2002. *Recreations:* opera, ballet, theatre, music. *Address:* 8 Hanover Terrace, NW1 4RJ. *T:* (020) 7723 3422.

BLOOM, Charles; QC 1987; **His Honour Judge Bloom;** a Circuit Judge, since 1997; *b* 6 Nov. 1940; *s* of Abraham Barnett Bloom and Freda Bloom (*née* Craft); *m* 1967, Janice Rachelle Goldberg; one *s* one *d*. *Educ:* Manchester Central Grammar School; Manchester University. LLB Hons 1962. Called to the Bar, Gray's Inn, 1963; practised on Northern Circuit, 1963–97; a Recorder, 1983–97. Chm., Medical Appeal Tribunals, 1979–97. Member: Larner Vinifloral Soc., 1996–; Rhodes Sabbatical Debating Soc., 2007. *Recreations:* tennis, horticulture. *Address:* c/o Circuit Administrator's Office, Northern Circuit, Young Street Chambers, 76 Quay Street, Manchester M3 4PR. *Club:* Friedland Postmusaf Tennis (Cheadle).

BLOOM, Claire; *b* London, 15 Feb. 1931; *d* of late Edward Bloom and Elizabeth Bloom; *m* 1st, 1959, Rod Steiger (marr. diss. 1969; he *d* 2002); one *d*; 2nd, 1969; 3rd, 1990, Philip Roth (marr. diss. 1995). *Educ:* Badminton, Bristol; America and privately. First work in England, BBC, 1946. Stratford: Ophelia, Lady Blanche (King John), Perdita, 1948; The Damask Cheek, Lyric, Hammersmith, 1949; The Lady's Not For Burning, Globe, 1949; Ring Round the Moon, Globe, 1949–50. Old Vic: 1952–53: Romeo and Juliet; 1953: Merchant of Venice; 1954: Hamlet, All's Well, Coriolanus, Twelfth Night, Tempest; 1956: Romeo and Juliet (London, and N American tour). Cordelia, in Stratford Festival Company, 1955 (London, provinces and continental tour); Duel of Angels, Apollo, 1958; Rashomon, NY, 1959; Altona, Royal Court, 1961; The Trojan Women, Spoleto Festival, 1963; Ivanov, Phoenix, 1965; A Doll's House, NY, 1971; Hedda Gabler, 1971; Vivat! Vivat Regina!, NY, 1971; A Doll's House, Criterion, 1973 (filmed 1973); A Streetcar Named Desire, Piccadilly, 1974; Rosmersholm, Haymarket, 1977; The Cherry Orchard, Chichester Fest., 1981, Cambridge, Mass, 1994; When We Dead Waken, Almeida, 1990; A Long Day's Journey into Night, ART, Cambridge, Mass, 1996; Electra, McCarter Th., Princeton, NJ, 1998, transf. NY, 1999; Conversations After a Burial, Almeida, 2000; A Little Night Music, Seattle, 2001, NY, 2003; Whistling Psyche, Almeida, 2004; Six Dance Lessons in Six Weeks, Haymarket, 2006. One-woman performances: These Are Women, 1981– (US tour, 1981–82); Enter the Actress, 1998–. First film, Blind Goddess, 1947; *films include:* Limelight; The Man Between; Richard III; Alexander the Great; The Brothers Karamazov; The Buccaneers; Look Back in Anger; Three Moves to Freedom; The Brothers Grimm; The Chapman Report; The Haunting; 80,000 Suspects; Alta Infedelta; Il Maestro di Vigevano; The Outrage; The Spy Who Came in From The Cold; Charly; Three into Two won't go; A Severed Head; Red Sky at Morning; Islands In The Stream; The Clash of the Titans, 1979; Always, 1984; Sammy and Rosie Get Laid, 1987; Crimes and Misdemeanors, 1989; Daylight, 1997; The Book of Eve, 2001; Imagining Argentina, 2002; Daniel and the Superdogs, 2003. *Television:* first appearance on television programmes, 1952, since when she has had frequent successes on TV in the US: In Praise of Love, 1975; Anastasia, 1986; Queenie, 1986; BBC: A Legacy, 1975; The Ghost Writer, 1983; Shadowlands, 1985 (BAFTA award Best TV Actress); Time and the Conways, 1985; Oedipus the King, 1986; What the Deaf Man Heard, 1997; BBC Shakespeare: Katharine in Henry VIII, 1979; Gertrude in Hamlet, 1980; the Queen in Cymbeline, Lady Constance in King John, 1983; ITV: series: Brideshead Revisited, 1981; Intimate Contact, 1987; Shadow on the Sun, 1988; play, The Belle of Amherst, 1986; Channel Four: series, The Camomile Lawn, 1992; The Mirror Crack'd, 1992; Remember, 1993; A Village Affair, 1994; Family Money, 1996; series, Imogen's Face, 1998; The Lady in Question, 1999; Law and Order, 2003. Many appearances as narrator in both contemporary and classic repertoire. Distinguished Vis. Prof., Hunter Coll., NY, 1989. *Publications:* Limelight and After (autobiog.), 1982; Leaving a Doll's House (autobiog.), 1996. *Recreations:* opera, music. *Address:* c/o Jeremy Conway, 18–21 Jermyn Street, SW1Y 6HB.

BLOOM, Godfrey, TD and bar 1988; Member (UK Ind) Yorkshire and North Lincolnshire, European Parliament, since 2004; *b* 22 Nov. 1949; *s* of Alan Bloom and Phylis Bloom; *m* 1986, Katryna Skowronek. *Educ:* St Olave's Sch. Fund Manager, Mercury Asset Mgt, 1988–93; Econ. Res. Dir, TBO Gp of Cos, 1993–2004. Econ. Advr, Educational Research Associates, 2008–. Member: IEA, 1995–2007; Campaign against Political Correctness, 2005–; British Charolais Cattle Soc. Life Mem., War Memls Trust, 2001. Hon. Life Mem., Cambridge Univ. Women's RFC, 2003. Micropal Award for Fund Mgt, 1992. Graduate, Armed Forces Parly Scheme, 2005. *Publications:* Beyond the Fridge, 2007; contribs to Financial Times pubns, Army Review and The Sprout. *Recreations:* hunting and shooting, cricket, military history. *Address:* Devlin House, 36 St George Street, Mayfair, W1S 2FW. *Clubs:* East India; Bentley Drivers; Royal Cornish (Hawkedon); Pocklington Rugby; Horsehouse Formals Cricket (Londesborough Park); Gadflys (Strasbourg).

BLOOM, Louise Anne; Member (Lib Dem) Eastleigh Borough Council, since 2002 (Cabinet Member for Environment); Vice Chair, South East England Regional Assembly, since 2006 (Executive Member, since 2002); *b* 7 April 1964; *d* of Christopher George Harris and Patricia Rose Harris (*née* Fray, now Lindsley); *m* 1987, Charles Neil Bloom (marr. diss.); two *d*. *Educ:* Kingston Poly. (BA Hons Applied Soc. Sci. 1985). Worked for various advertising agencies, 1985–90; freelance orgn mgt of press and publicity events, 1991–97; res. and admin assistant to Lib Dem councillors, Royal Bor. of Kingston upon Thames, 1991–93; Asst to Co-ordinator of Ind. Living Scheme, Kingston Assoc. of Disabled People, 1997; Inf. and Volunteer Develt Officer, Richmond Advice and Inf. on Disability, 1998–2000. Mem. (Lib Dem), London Assembly, GLA, 2000–02. Mem., Standards Bd for England, 2004–06. *Recreations:* theatre, music, reading, travelling, history, thinking up ways to keep my children entertained and away from the television. *Address:* 25 Mescott Meadows, Hedge End, Southampton SO30 2JT.

BLOOM, Margaret Janet, CBE 2003; Visiting Professor, School of Law, King's College London, since 2003; Senior Consultant, Freshfields Bruckhaus Deringer, since 2003; *b* 28 July 1943; *d* of John Sturrock and Jean Elizabeth Sturrock (*née* Ranken); *m* 1965, Prof. Stephen Robert Bloom, *qv*; two *s* two *d*. *Educ:* Sherborne Sch. for Girls; Girton Coll., Cambridge (MA). Economist, then Dep. Gp Economist, John Laing and Son, 1965–69; Gp Economist, Tarmac, 1969–70; Sen. Project Manager, NEDO, 1970–86; Sci. and Technol. Secretariat, Cabinet Office, 1986–89; Res. and Technol. Policy Div., 1989–91, Competition Policy Div., 1991–93, Finance and Resource Mgt Div., 1993–95, DTI; Head, Agencies Privatisation Team, 1995–96, Dir, Agencies Gp B, 1996, Cabinet Office; Dir of Competition Policy, subseq. Competition Enforcement, OFT, 1997–2003. Pt-time Lectr, 1977–80, Ext. Examr, 1985–88, for MSc in Architecture, UCL. Trustee, Money Advice Trust, 2003–. *Recreations:* family, foreign travel, eating out, rambling. *Address:* School of Law, King's College London, Strand, WC2R 2LS. *T:* (020) 7848 2324, *Fax:* (020) 7848 2443; *e-mail:* margaret.bloom@kcl.ac.uk.

BLOOM, Prof. Stephen Robert, MD, DSc; FRCP, FRCPath, FMedSci; Professor of Medicine, since 1982, Director of Metabolic Medicine, and Chief of Service for Chemical Pathology, since 1994, Imperial College Faculty of Medicine (formerly Royal Postgraduate Medical School), London University, since 1994; Consultant Physician, Hammersmith Hospital, since 1982; *b* 24 Oct. 1942; *s* of Arnold and Edith Bloom; *m* 1965, Margaret Janet Sturrock (*see* M. J. Bloom); two *s* two *d*. *Educ:* Queens' Coll., Cambridge (MA 1968; MD 1979); Middlesex Hosp. Med. Sch.; DSc London 1982. FRCP 1978; FRCPath 1993. Middlesex Hospital: Gastro House Physician, 1967–68; Cardiology House Physician, 1968; Casualty Med. Officer, 1969; Leverhulme Res. Schol., Inst. of Clin. Res., 1970; Med. Unit Registrar, 1970–72; MRC Clin. Res. Fellow, 1972–74; House Surgeon, Mount Vernon Hosp., 1968–69; Endocrinology House Physician, Hammersmith Hosp., 1969–70; Sen. Lectr, 1974–78, Reader in Medicine, 1978–82, RPMS, Hammersmith Hosp.; Dir, Endocrinol. Clin. Service, 1982–, and Head of Div. of Investigative Sci., 1997–2007, Imperial Coll., London (formerly RPMS). CSO, Thiakis, 2006–. Lectures: Copp, Amer. Diabetes Assoc.; Goulstonian, and Lumleian, RCP; Amer. Endocrine Soc. Transatlantic; Lawrence, and Arnold Bloom, British Diabetic Assoc.; Wellcome, RSM. Sen. Censor, RCP, 1999–2001. Chm., Soc. for Endocrinology, 2002–06 (Sec., 1999–2002). Founder FMedSci, 1998. Dale Medal, Soc. for Endocrinology, 2003. *Publications:* Toohey's Medicine, 15th edn, 1994; (with J. Lynn) Surgical Endocrinology, 1993. *Recreations:* walking, jogging, travelling, opera. *Address:* Department of Investigative Medicine, Imperial College Faculty of Medicine, 6th Floor Commonwealth Building, Hammersmith Campus, Du Cane Road, W12 0NN. *T:* (020) 8383 3242.

BLOOMER, Jonathan William, FCA; Managing Director, Cerberus UK Advisors LLP, since 2006; Executive Chairman, Lucida plc, since 2006; *b* 23 March 1954; *s* of Derick William Bloomer and Audrey Alexandra Bloomer; *m* 1977, Anne Elizabeth Judith May; one *s* two *d*. *Educ:* Halesowen Grammar Sch.; Imperial Coll., London (BSc, ARCS 1974). FCA 1982. Partner, Arthur Andersen, 1987–94; Gp Finance Dir, Prudential Corp. plc, 1995–99; Prudential plc: Dep. Gp Chief Exec., 1999–2000; Chief Exec., 2000–05. Non-exec. Dir, Hargreaves Lansdown plc, 2006–. Bd Mem., ABI, 2001–05; Chm., Financial Services Practitioner Panel, 2003–05 (Dep. Chm., 2001–03). CCMI (CIMgt 1996). *Recreations:* sailing, watching Rugby, gardening.

BLOOMFIELD, Keith George, CMG 2007; HM Diplomatic Service, retired; Ambassador to Nepal, 2002–06; *b* 2 June 1947; *s* of George William Bloomfield and Edith Joan Bloomfield; *m* 1976, Genevieve Charbonneau; three *d*. *Educ:* Kilburn Grammar Sch.; Lincoln Coll., Oxford (MA). Home Civil Service, 1969–80; Office of UK Rep. to EC, Brussels, 1980–85; FCO, 1985–87; Head of Chancery, Cairo, 1987–90; Dep. Head of Mission, Algiers, 1990–94; Counsellor (Political and Mgt), Rome, 1994–96; Minister and Dep. Head of Mission, Rome, 1997–98; Hd, Counter Terrorism Policy Dept, FCO, 1998–2002. *Recreations:* music, tennis, reading.

BLOOMFIELD, Sir Kenneth Percy, KCB 1987 (CB 1982); Joint International Commissioner, Commission for Location of Victims Remains, since 1999; Chairman, Board of Governors, Royal Belfast Academical Institution, since 2004 (Governor, since 1984); *b* 15 April 1931; *o c* of late Harry Percy Bloomfield and Doris Bloomfield, Belfast; *m* 1960, Mary Elizabeth Ramsey; one *s* one *d*. *Educ:* Royal Belfast Academical Instn; St Peter's Coll., Oxford (MA; Hon. Fellow, 1991). Min. of Finance, N Ireland, 1952–56; Private Sec. to Ministers of Finance, 1956–60; Dep. Dir, British Industrial Develt Office, NY, 1960–63; Asst and later Dep. Sec. to Cabinet, NI, 1963–72; Under-Sec., Northern Ireland Office, 1972–73; Sec. to Northern Ireland Executive, Jan.–May 1974; Permanent Secretary: Office of the Executive, NI, 1974–75; Dept of Housing, Local Govt and Planning, NI, 1975–76; Dept of the Environment, NI, 1976–81; Dept of Commerce, NI, 1981–82; Dept of Economic Develt, 1982–84; Head, NICS, and Second Perm. Under Sec. of State, NI Office, 1984–91. Nat. Gov. and Chm. of Broadcasting Council for NI, BBC, 1991–99. Review of Dental Remuneration, 1992; Consultant, Crown Appts Review Gp, 1999–2001. Comr, NI Victims Commn, 1997–98 (report published 1998). Chairman: Chief Executives' Forum for NI Public Services, 1991–97; NI Higher Educn Council, 1993–2001; Review of Criminal Injuries Compensation in NI, 1998–99; Bangor and Holywood Town Centre Mgt Ltd, 2000–06; Legal Services Commn for NI, 2003–04; Vice-Chm., Mus and Galls of NI, 2002–06. Pres., NI Council, Stationery Office, 1998–2000. Mem., NI Adv. Bd, Bank of Ireland, 1991–; Member of Board: Co-operation North, 1991–93; Opera, NI, 1992–97. Member: Statute Law Adv. Cttee, 1993–97; Nat. Steering Cttee, Give as You Earn, 1992–93; Adv. Cttee, Constitution Unit, 1997; Jersey Review of Machinery of Govt, 1999–2000. Chm., Children in Need Trust, 1992–98; Mem. Bd, Green Park Hosp. Trust, 1993–2001; Patron: Belfast Improved Houses, 1992–; NI Council for Integrated Educn, 1998–. Senator (Crown nominee), QUB, 1991–93; Pres., Ulster People's Coll., 1996–. Bass Ireland Lectr, Univ. of Ulster, 1991. Hon. LLD QUB, 1991; DUniv Open, 2000; Hon. DLitt Ulster, 2002. Dr Ben Wilson Trophy for Individual or Corporate Excellence, NI Chamber of Commerce and Industry, 1990. *Publications:* Stormont in Crisis (a memoir), 1994; A Tragedy of Errors, 2007; *contributions to:* Hope and History, 1996; Broadcasting in a Divided Community, 1996; People and Government: questions for Northern Ireland, 1997; Cool Britannia, 1998; various jls and periodicals. *Recreations:* history, travel, swimming. *Address:* 16 Larch Hill, Holywood, Co. Down BT18 0JN. *T:* (028) 9042 8340.

BLOOR, Prof. David; Scientific Adviser, Peratech Ltd, since 2003; Professor of Applied Physics, University of Durham, 1989–2002, now Emeritus (Chairman, Department of Physics, 1993–96); *b* 25 July 1937; *s* of Alfred Edwin Bloor and Gladys Ellen Bloor (*née* Collins); *m* 1960, Margaret E. A. Avery; four *s* (and one *s* decd). *Educ:* Queen Mary College London (BSc, PhD). CPhys, FInstP. Lectr, Dept of Physics, Univ. of Canterbury, NZ, 1961–64; Queen Mary College London: Lectr, Dept of Physics, 1964; Reader, 1980–84; Prof. of Polymer Physics, 1984–89. Humboldt Fellow: Univ. of Stuttgart, 1975–76; Univ. of Bayreuth, 1997–98; Erskine Fellow, Univ. of Canterbury, NZ, 1983; Royal Society SERC Indust. Fellow, GEC Marconi Res. Centre, 1985–86; Sir Derman Christopherson Foundn Fellow, Univ. of Durham, 1996–97. Co-ordinator, DTI/SERC Molecular Electronics Initiative, 1987–93. Mem., Exec. Cttee, Canon Foundn in Europe, 2000– (Chm., Selection Cttee, 2005–). *Publications:* contribs to professional jls. *Recreations:* cycling, gardening. *Address:* Department of Physics, Durham University, South Road, Durham DH1 3LE. *T:* (0191) 374 2391.

BLOSSE, Sir Richard Hely L.; *see* Lynch-Blosse.

BLOT, Jean; *see* Blokh, A.

BLOW, Bridget Penelope; Chairman (non-executive): Trustmarque Solutions, since 2006; Alba plc, since 2007 (Director, since 2005); *b* 2 June 1949; *m* Rod Blow (marr. diss.); one *d*. *Educ:* Caistor Grammar Sch. Systems Develt, Grimsby BC, 1968–79; Human Resources Dir, Divl Dir, Dir of Technol., then Exec. Dir, FI Gp, 1979–92; Systems Dir, 1992–94, Chief Exec., 1994–2005, ITNET; Gp Technol. Dir, Serco Gp plc, 2005–06. Dir, Bank of England, 2000–05. Non-exec. Dir, Coventry Bldg Soc., 2007–. CCMI. NatWest Midlands Business Woman of the Year, 1996. *Recreations:* golf, gym, tennis.

BLOW, Joyce; *see* Blow Darlington, J.

BLOW DARLINGTON, Joyce, OBE 1994; Chairman, Child Accident Prevention Trust, 1996–2002; *b* 4 May 1929; *d* of late Walter Blow and Phyllis (*née* Grainger); *m* 1974,

Lt-Col J. A. B. Darlington, RE retd. *Educ:* Bell Baxter Sch., Cupar, Fife; Edinburgh Univ. (MA Hons). John Lewis Partnership, 1951–52; FBI, 1952–53; Press Officer, Council of Indust. Design, 1953–63; Publicity and Advertising Manager, Heal & Son Ltd, 1963–65; entered Civil Service on first regular recruitment of direct entry Principals from business and industry: BoT, 1965–67; Monopolies Commn (gen. enquiry into restrictive practices in supply of prof. services), 1967–70; DTI, 1970, Asst Sec. 1972; Dept of Prices and Consumer Protection, 1974–77; Under-Secretary: OFT, 1977–80; DTI, 1980–84; Chairman: Mail Order Publishers' Authy, 1985–92; Direct Marketing Assoc. Authy, 1992–97. Chm., E Sussex FHSA, 1990–96. Pres., Assoc. for Quality in Healthcare, 1991–94; Vice-Pres., Trading Standards Inst. 1985–; Bd Mem., BSI, 1987–97 (Chm., Consumer Policy Cttee, 1987–93). Founder Mem. and Past Pres., Women in Public Relations. Trustee, Univ. of Edinburgh Develt Trust, 1990–94; Chm., PR Educn Trust, 1992–97. Freeman, City of London. Hon. FCIPR (FIPR 1964); FCMI; FRSA. *Publication:* Consumers and International Trade: a handbook, 1987. *Recreations:* music, art, architecture, travel, France. *Address:* 17 Fentiman Road, SW8 1LD. *T:* (020) 7735 4023; 9 Crouchfield Close, Seaford, E Sussex. *Clubs:* Arts, Reform.

BLOWERS, Dr Anthony John, CBE 1985; JP, DL; CBiol; FIBMS; Commissioner, Mental Health Act Commission, 1987–95; Director, Ogilvy Public Relations Worldwide, since 1999; *b* 11 Aug. 1926; *e s* of late Geoffrey Hathaway and Louise Blowers; *m* 1948, Yvonne Boiteux-Buchanan; two *s* one *d*. *Educ:* Sloane Sch., Chelsea; Sir John Cass Coll.; Univ. of London; Univ. of Surrey (PhD 1982). FIMLS 1983; CBiol 1984. Served War, RCS, 1944–45; served: RAMC, 1945–46; RWAFF, 1946–48. Min. of Agriculture, 1948–59, Exptl Officer, 1953–59; Sandoz Pharmaceuticals, 1959–91; Sen. Res. Officer, 1973–87; Psychopharmacology Consultant, 1987–91; Consultant in Bacteriology, Mansi Labs, 1973–90. Dir, Corporate Affairs, Magellan Medical Communications, 1990–99. Vis. Res. Fellow, Roehampton Inst., 1998–; Vis. Lectr, Dept of Psychiatry of Addictive Behaviour, St George's Hosp. Med. Sch., 1999–. Chairman: W Surrey and NE Hants HA, 1981–86; Mental Health and Learning Disabilities Monitoring Gp, SW Surrey HA, 1991–95; Member: Surrey AHA, 1973–80 (Vice Chm., 1976–77); SW Thames RHA, 1980–81; Mental Health Review Tribunal, 1975–99; Nat. Standing Cttees on Consent to Treatment and Community Care, 1992–95. Admin. Sec., All-Party Parly Gp on R & D in Fertility and Contraception, 1994–. Member: Chertsey UDC, 1964–74 (Chm., 1969–70, 1973–74); Runnymede BC, 1973–84 (Chm., 1973–74); Surrey CC, 1970–85 (Vice Chm., Social Services Cttee, 1973–77); Surrey Police Authority, 1973–90 (Chm., 1981–85); Chairman: Runnymede and Elmbridge Police Community Liaison Cttee, 1983–94; Surrey Drug Action Team, 1995–2001. Chm. SE Region, and Mem. Nat. Adv. Council, Duke of Edinburgh's Award, 1990–98; Chm., Surrey Magistrates' Soc., 1988–94; Member: Council, Magistrates' Assoc., 1986–91; Bd of Visitors, Coldingley Prison, 1978–93; Court, Surrey Univ., 1986–; Surrey Scout Council, 1991–; Pres., Runnymede Scout Council, 1970–84. Vice-President: Hosp. Saving Assoc., 1994–; Parkinson's Disease Soc., 1995– (Actg Chief Exec., 1995); Mem. Council, 1986–, Trustee, 1995–, Psychiatry Res. Trust; Chm., Knight Foundn for Cystic Fibrosis Appeal, 1997–. Mem., CGA, 2000–. Governor: Fullbrook Sch., 1967–85 (Chm., 1981–85); Ottershaw Sch., 1975–81 (Chm., 1979–81). Liveryman, Worshipful Soc. of Apothecaries, 1988– (Yeoman, 1983–88); Freeman, City of London, 1983; Hon. Freeman, Bor. of Runnymede, 1985. JP 1970, DL 1986, High Sheriff, 1990–91, Surrey. St John Ambulance: Asst Dir Gen., 1985–91; Dir Gen., 1991–94; Actg Chief Comdr, 1991–92; Comdr, Surrey, 1987–91; Chm., 1995–2001, Vice-Pres., 2001–, St John Fellowship. KStJ 1991 (Mem., Chapter-Gen., 1991–99; Mem. Priory, England and the Islands, 1999–2001). *Publications:* The Isolation of Salmonellae, 1978; Tardive Dyskinesia, 1982; Certificate in Drugs: prevention and education, 2002; contribs to med. and scientific books and jls. *Recreations:* tackling drug misuse; fund-raising, gardening. *Address:* Westward, 12 Birch Close, Boundstone, Farnham, Surrey GU10 4TJ. *T:* (01252) 792769.

BLOXHAM, Prof. Jeremy, PhD; FRS 2007; Mallinckrodt Professor of Geophysics, since 2004, Professor of Computational Science, since 2006, and Dean for Physical Sciences, since 2006, Harvard University; *b* 29 April 1960; *s* of Lawrence Bloxham and Christine Bloxham; *m* 1985, Katharine Jane Everist; two *s*. *Educ:* Portsmouth Grammar Sch.; Pembroke Coll., Cambridge (BA 1982; PhD 1985). Harvard University: Asst Prof. of Geophysics, 1987–90; John L. Loeb Associate Prof. of Natural Scis, 1990–93; Prof. of Geophysics, 1993–2004; Chair, Dept of Earth and Planetary Scis, 2000–06. *Publications:* over 60 articles in learned jls. *Recreations:* sailing, ski-ing, flying. *Address:* 14 Washington Square, Marblehead, MA 01945, USA. *T:* (office) (617) 4959517, *Fax:* (617) 4957660; *e-mail:* jeremy_bloxham@harvard.edu. *Club:* Eastern Yacht (Marblehead, Mass).

BLOXHAM, Thomas Paul Richard, MBE 1999; Chairman and Co-Founder, Urban Splash Group, since 1993; *b* 20 Dec. 1963; *m* 1987, Jo Speakman; two *s*. *Educ:* Manchester Univ. (BA Hons Politics and Mod. History). Founder, Urban Splash (Properties), 1992; Baa Bar Ltd, 1991–2006 (Chm.). Mem., Property Adv. Gp., DTLR. Chm., Arts Council England (North West) (formerly NW Arts Bd), 1999–; Mem., Arts Council England, 2003–. Dir, Liverpool Cultural Co. Ltd, 2001–; Chairman: Manchester Internat. Arts Fest., 2005–; IPPR Centre for Cities Think Tank, 2005–. Hon. RIBA; FRSA. Hon. Fellow: Liverpool John Moores Univ., 2001; Univ. of Central Lancashire, 2003. Hon. DDes: Oxford Brookes, 2004; Bristol, 2007; Hon. Dr Manchester, 2007. UK Property Entrepreneur of the Year, 1998; Nat. Young Entrepreneur of the Year, 1999; North Region Young Entrepreneur of the Year, 1999; Northwest Young Entrepreneur of the Year, IoD, 1999. *Address:* (office) Timber Wharf, 16–24 Worsley Street, Castlefield, Manchester M15 4LD; *e-mail:* tombloxham@urbansplash.co.uk.

BLUCK, Duncan Robert Yorke, CBE 1990 (OBE 1984); Chairman: British Tourist Authority, 1984–90; English Tourist Board, 1984–90; Director, John Swire & Sons, 1984–99; *b* 19 March 1927; *s* of Thomas Edward Bluck and Ida Bluck; *m* 1952, Stella Wardlaw Murdoch; one *s* three *d*. *Educ:* Taunton Sch. RNVR, 1944–47. Joined John Swire & Sons, 1948; Dir, 1964–99, Chief Exec., 1971–84, Chm., 1980–84, Cathay Pacific Airways; Chairman: John Swire & Sons (HK) Ltd, 1980–84; Swire Pacific Ltd, 1980–84; Swire Properties Ltd, 1980–84. Dir, Hongkong and Shanghai Banking Corp., 1981–84. Chairman: English Schools Foundn (Hongkong), 1978–84; Hongkong Tourist Assoc., 1981–84; Kent Economic Develt Bd, 1986–91; Cystic Fibrosis Trust, 1996–2003 (Pres., 2003–). Governor, Marlborough House Sch., 1986–2007; Mem. Ct, Univ. of Kent, 1991–2001. JP Hong Kong, 1981–84. *Recreation:* sailing. *Address:* West Cross House, Tenterden, Kent TN30 6JL. *T:* (01580) 766729. *Clubs:* Hongkong, Sheko (Hongkong); Rye Golf.

BLUCK, Rt Rev. John William; Bishop of Waiapu, 2002–08; *b* 22 July 1943; *m* 1969, Elizabeth Anne Frost; one *s* one *d*. *Educ:* Univ. of Canterbury, NZ (MA 1966); Episcopal Theol Sch., Cambridge, Mass, USA (BD *cum laude* 1969). Ordained deacon, 1970, priest, 1971; served Holy Trinity parish, Gisborne, 1970–72; Editor: NZ Methodist, 1972–77; One World, WCC, 1977–80; Dir of Communications, WCC, 1980–84; Prof. of Pastoral Theol. and Communication, Knox Theol Hall, 1984–90; Dean of Christchurch Cathedral, NZ, 1990–2002. *Publications:* Everyday Ecumenism, 1987; Christian Communication Reconsidered, 1989; Canberra Takeaways, 1991; Long, White and Cloudy, 1998; Waking Up in Strange Places, 1999; Killing Us Softly, 2001; The Giveaway God, 2001. *Recreations:* hunting, fishing, scuba diving, motorcycling. *Address:* 539 Apley Road, RD4, Napier, New Zealand. *T:* (6) 835 8230.

BLUE, Rabbi Lionel, OBE 1994; Lecturer, Leo Baeck College, since 1967; Convener of the Beth Din (Ecclesiastical Court) of the Reform Synagogues of Great Britain, 1971–88; *b* 6 Feb. 1930; *s* of late Harry and Hetty Blue. *Educ:* Balliol Coll., Oxford (MA History); University Coll. London (BA Semitics); Leo Baeck Coll., London (Rabbinical Dip). Ordained Rabbi, 1960; Minister to Settlement Synagogue and Middlesex New Synagogue, 1960–63; European Dir, World Union for Progressive Judaism, 1963–66; Co-Editor, Forms of Prayer, 1967–; broadcaster, 1967–; Feature Writer: The Universe, 1979–; The Standard, 1985–86; The Tablet, 1994–. Scriptwriter and presenter, TV series, In Search of Holy England, 1989. Templeton (UK) Prize, 1993. DUniv Open; Hon. DD Durham, 2007. *Publications:* To Heaven with Scribes and Pharisees, 1975; (jtly) A Taste of Heaven, 1977; (ed jtly) Forms of Prayer (Sabbath and Daily), 1977; A Backdoor to Heaven, 1979, revd edn 1985; (ed jtly) Forms of Prayer (Days of Awe), 1985; Bright Blue, 1985; (jtly) Simply Divine, 1985; Kitchen Blues, 1985; Bolts from the Blue, 1986; Blue Heaven, 1987; (jtly) Daytrips to Eternity, 1987; (jtly) The Guide to the Here and Hereafter, 1988; Blue Horizons, 1989; Bedside Manna, 1991; (jtly) How to Get Up When Life Gets You Down, 1992; (jtly) The Little Blue Book of Prayer, 1993; Tales of Body and Soul, 1994; (jtly) Kindred Spirits: a year of readings, 1995; My Affair with Christianity (autobiog.), 1998; (jtly) Sun, Sand and Soul, 1999; Blue's Jokes, 2001; A Little Book of Blue Thoughts, 2001; Hitchhiking to Heaven (autobiog.), 2004; The Best of Blue, 2006. *Recreations:* window shopping, package holidays, monasteries, cooking. *Address:* Leo Baeck College, 80 East End Road, N3 2SY. *T:* (020) 8349 4525.

BLUGLASS, Prof. Robert Saul, CBE 1995; MD; FRCP, FRCPsych; Professor of Forensic Psychiatry, University of Birmingham, 1979–96, now Emeritus; Hon. Consultant, Reaside Clinic, Birmingham, since 1995; *b* 22 Sept. 1930; *s* of Henry Bluglass and Fay (*née* Griew); *m* 1962, Jean Margaret Kerry (*née* Montgomery); one *s* one *d*. *Educ:* Warwick Sch., Warwick; Univ. of St Andrews (MB, ChB 1957, MD 1967). DPM 1962; MRCPsych 1971, FRCPsych 1976; MRCP 1994, FRCP 1997. Formerly, Sen. Registrar in Psych., Royal Dundee Liff Hosp. and Maryfield Hosp., Dundee; Consultant in Forensic Psychiatry: W Midlands RHA and the Home Office, 1967–94; S Birmingham Mental Health NHS Trust, 1994–95 (Med. Dir, 1995–96); Consultant i/c Midland Centre for For. Psych., All Saints Hosp., Birmingham, 1967–93; Clinical Dir, Reaside Clinic, Birmingham, 1986–95. Birmingham University: Hon. Lectr, 1968–75, Sen. Clin. Lectr in For. Psych., 1975–79; Regl Postgrad. Tutor in Forensic Psych., 1967–95; Jt Dir, Midland Inst. of For. Medicine, 1975–87. Dep. Regional Advr in Psychiatry, W Midlands RHA, 1985–87, Regional Advr, 1987–92; Specialist Advr, H of C Select Cttee on Social Services, 1985–87, on Health, 2000–01; Consultant Advr in Psych., RAF, 1992–2001, now Hon. Consultant; Advr in For. Psych., Bd of Corrections, Health Service, NSW, 1996–97. Member: Adv. Cttee on Alcoholism, DHSS, 1975–80; Adv. Council on Probation, Home Office, 1974–77; Mental Health Review Tribunal, 1979–2004; Mental Health Act Commn, 1983–85; Forensic Psych. Res. Liaison Gp, DHSS; Rev. of Services for Mentally Disordered Offenders (Reed Cttee), DoH, 1991–94; Inquiry into care and mgt of Christopher Edwards and Richard Linford, 1996–98; Judicial Inquiry into Personality Disorder Unit at Ashworth Special Hosp., 1997–99. Royal College of Psychiatrists: Mem., Ct of Electors, 1976–79; Mem. Council, Exec. and Finance Cttees, 1973–76, 1976–78, 1980–86, 1986–91; Vice-Pres., 1983–85; Chm., For. Psych. Specialist Section, 1978–82; Chm., Midlands Div., 1986–91; Chm., Midlands Soc. of Criminology, 1981–95 (Sec., 1970–81); Past Pres., Sect. of Psych., Birmingham Med. Inst.; Vice-Pres., RAF Psych. Soc.; Mem., Brit. Acad. of For. Sciences. FRSocMed 1975. Baron ver Heyden de Lancey Law Prize, RSocMed, 1983. *Publications:* Psychiatry, The Law and The Offender, 1980; A Guide to the Mental Health Act 1983, 1983; (ed with Prof. Sir Martin Roth) Psychiatry, Human Rights and the Law, 1985; (ed with Dr Paul Bowden) The Principles and Practice of Forensic Psychiatry, 1990; articles in Brit. Jl of Hosp. Med., BMJ, Brit. Jl of Psych., and Med., Science and the Law. *Recreations:* water-colour painting, cooking, gardening, swimming. *Address:* c/o Reaside Clinic, Birmingham Great Park, Bristol Road South, Rubery, Rednal, Birmingham B45 9BE.

BLUM, Heather Anne Elise Lilian M.; *see* Munroe-Blum.

BLUMBERG, Prof. Baruch Samuel, MD, PhD; Distinguished Scientist, and Senior Advisor to the President, Fox Chase Cancer Center, since 1989; Director, Astrobiology Institute, NASA, Ames Research Center, California, 1999–2002; *b* 28 July 1925; *s* of Meyer Blumberg and Ida Blumberg; *m* 1954, Jean Liebesman Blumberg; two *s* two *d*. *Educ:* Union Coll. (BS Physics, 1946); Columbia University Coll. of Physicians and Surgeons (MD 1951); Balliol Coll., Oxford (PhD Biochemistry, 1957; Hon. Fellow, 1977). FRCP 1984. US Navy, 1943–46 (Lieut JG). US Public Health Service (rank of med. dir, Capt.), and Chief, Geographic Medicine and Genetics Sect., Nat. Insts. of Health, Bethesda, Md, 1957–64; Associate Dir for Clinical Res., then Vice-Pres. for Population Oncology, Fox Chase Cancer Center, 1964–89; Univ. Prof. of Medicine and Anthropol., Univ. of Pennsylvania, 1977–; Clin. Prof., Dept of Epidemiology, Univ. of Washington Sch. of Public Health, 1983–89; Master of Balliol Coll., Oxford, 1989–94. Sen. Advr to Adminr, NASA, Washington, 2000–01. George Eastman Vis. Prof., Oxford Univ., 1983–84; Lokey Vis. Prof., Program in Human Biology, Stanford Univ., 1997–98; Fellow, Center for Advanced Study in Behavioural Scis, Stanford Univ. Mem. Nat. Acad. of Sciences, Washington. Pres., Amer. Philosophical Soc., 2005–. Hon. DSc: Univ. of Pittsburgh, 1977; Union Coll., Schenectady, NY, 1977; Med. Coll. of Pa, 1977; Dickinson Coll., Carlisle, Pa, 1977; Hahnemann Med. Coll., Philadelphia, Pa, 1977; Indian Acad. of Scis, 1977; Elizabethtown Coll., Pa, 1988; Ball State Univ., Muncie, 1989; Dr *hc* Univ. of Paris VII, 1978. (Jt) Nobel Prize in Physiology or Medicine, 1976. *Publications:* (ed) Genetic Polymorphisms and Geographic Variations in Disease, 1961; (ed jtly) Medical Clinics of North America: new developments in medicine, 1970; (ed jtly) Hepatitis B: the virus, the disease and the vaccine, 1984; Hepatitis B: the hunt for a killer virus, 2002; *chapters in:* McGraw-Hill Encyclopedia of Science and Technology Yearbook, 1962; The Genetics of Migrant and Isolate Populations, ed E. Goldschmidt, 1963; Hemoglobin: its precursors and metabolites, ed F. W. Sunderman and F. W. Sunderman, Jr, 1964; McGraw-Hill Yearbook of Science and Technology, 1970; (also co-author chapter) Viral Hepatitis and Blood Transfusion, ed G. N. Vyas and others, 1972; Hematology, ed W. J. Williams and others, 1972; Progress in Liver Disease, Vol. IV, ed H. Popper and F. Schaffner, 1972; Australia Antigen, ed J. E. Prier and H. Friedman, 1973; Drugs and the Liver, ed. W. Gerok and K. Sickinger, 1975 (Germany); (*jtly*) *chapters in:* Progress in Medical Genetics, ed A. G. Steinberg and A. G. Bearn, 1965 (also London); Viruses Affecting Man and Animals, ed M. Sanders and M. Schaeffer, 1971; Perspectives in Virology, 1971; Transmissible Disease and Blood Transfusion, ed T. J. Greenwalt and G. A. Jamieson, 1975; Physiological Anthropology, ed A. Damon, 1975; Hepatite a Virus B et Hemodialyse, 1975 (Paris); Onco-Developmental Gene Expression, 1976; contrib. symposia; over 460 articles in scientific jls. *Recreations:* cycling, canoeing, cattle raising. *Clubs:* Athenæum; Explorers (NY).

BLUME, Dame Hilary Sharon Braverman, (Dame Hilary Norton), DBE 2008; Founder and Director, Charities Advisory Trust (formerly Charity Trading Advisory Group), since 1979; *b* 9 Jan. 1945; *d* of Henry and Muriel Braverman; *m* 1st, 1965, Prof. Stuart Blume (marr. diss. 1977); two *s*; 2nd, 1977, Michael Aslan Norton, OBE; one *d*. *Educ:* London Sch. of Econs (BSc Econ.); Univ. of Sussex (MPhil). Fund raiser: War on Want, 1971–74; SHAC, 1975–79. Dir, Card Aid, 1984–. Comr, Nat. Lottery Commn, 1999–2000. Creator, Good Gifts Catalogue, 2003. Co-Chm., Finnart House Trust, 2007– (Vice-Chm., 1996–2007). Patron, Trees for London, 2000–. FRSA 2002 (Mem. Council, 2004–07). Creator, Peace Oil, 2006. *Publications:* Fund-raising: a comprehensive handbook, 1977; (jtly) Accounting and Financial Management for Charities, 1979, 2nd edn 1985; Charity Trading Handbook, 1981; Charity Christmas Cards, 1984; Museum Trading Handbook, 1987; Charity Shops Handbook, 1995. *Address:* Charities Advisory Trust, Radius Works, Back Lane, Hampstead, NW3 1HL.

BLUMENTHAL, Heston, OBE 2006; Chef Proprietor, The Fat Duck, Bray, since 1995; *b* 27 May 1966; *s* of Stephen Jeffrey Blumenthal and Celia Blumenthal; *m* 1991, Susanna Gage; one *s* two *d*. Credit controller, Team Leasing, 1987–95. Chef of the Year: Good Food Guide, 2001; AA Guide, 2002; GQ Mag., 2004; Catey Awards, Caterer & Hotelkeeper Magazine: Restaurateur of the Year, 2003; Chef of the Year, 2004; Food and Wine Personality of Year Award, GQ/Glenfiddich Awards, 2004; the restaurant has also received numerous best restaurant awards, incl. 3rd Michelin Star, 2004. *Publications:* Family Food, 2002, 2nd edn 2004; Perfection, 2006. *Recreations:* the study of historical food, nutrition and exercise, sport. *Address:* The Fat Duck, High Street, Bray, Berks SL6 2AQ. *T:* (01628) 580333, *Fax:* (01628) 776188; *e-mail:* heston@thefatduck.co.uk.

BLUMENTHAL, W(erner) Michael, PhD; US Secretary of the Treasury, 1977–79; Director, Jewish Museum Berlin, since 1997; *b* Germany, 3 Jan. 1926. *Educ:* Univ. of California at Berkeley; Princeton Univ. Research Associate, Princeton Univ., 1954–57; Vice-Pres., Dir, Crown Cork Internat. Corp., 1957–61; Dep. Asst Sec. of State for Econ. Affairs, Dept of State, 1961–63; Dep. Special Rep. of the President (with rank Ambassador) for Trade Negotiations, 1963–67; Pres., Bendix Internat., 1967–70; Bendix Corp.: Dir, 1967–77; Vice-Chm., 1970–71; Pres. and Chief Operating Officer, 1971–72; Chm. and Chief Exec. Officer, 1972–77; Burroughs Corp. subseq. Unisys: Chief Exec. Officer, 1980–90; Vice-Chm., 1980; Chm., 1981–90; Lazard Frères & Co. LLC, 1990–96. Director: Tenneco, Inc.; Daimler-Benz InterServices; Evercore Partners, NY; Debis AG; Internat. Adv. Bd, Chase Manhattan Corp. Mem., Business Council. *Publication:* The Invisible Wall: three hundred years of a German Jewish family, 1998. *Address:* 227 Ridgeview Road, Princeton, NJ 08540, USA; Jewish Museum Berlin, Lindenstrasse 9–14, 10969 Berlin, Germany.

BLUMER, Rodney Milnes, (Rodney Milnes), OBE 2002; Chief Opera Critic, The Times, 1992–2002; *b* 26 July 1936; *s* of Charles Eric Milnes Blumer and Kathleen Bertha Croft. *Educ:* Rugby School; Christ Church, Oxford (BA Hons Hist.). Editorial Dir, Rupert Hart-Davis Ltd, 1966–68; Music Critic, Queen magazine, later Harpers and Queen, 1968–87; Opera Critic: The Spectator, 1970–90; Evening Standard, 1990–92; Opera magazine: contribs, 1971–; Editl Bd, 1973; Associate Editor, 1976; Editor, 1986–99. Pres., Critics' Circle, 1988–90. Hon. RAM 2002. Kt, Order of White Rose (Finland). *Publications:* numerous opera translations. *Recreation:* travel. *Address:* c/o Opera Magazine, 36 Black Lion Lane, W6 9BE.

BLUMGART, Prof. Leslie Harold, MD; FRCS, FRCSE, FRCSGlas, FACS; Enid A. Haupt Professor of Surgery, Memorial Sloan-Kettering Cancer Center, New York, since 1991 (Chief, Section of Hepato-Biliary Surgery, 1995–2006; Director, Programme on Hepato-Biliary Diseases, since 1995); Professor of Surgery, Cornell University Medical Center, since 1992; *b* 7 Dec. 1931, of S African parentage; *m* 1955, Pearl Marie Navias (decd); *m* 1968, Sarah Raybould Bowen; two *s* two *d*. *Educ:* Jeppe High Sch., Johannesburg, SA; Univ. of Witwatersrand (BDS); Univ. of Sheffield (MB, ChB Hons; MD 1969). Prize Medal, Clin. Med. and Surg.; Ashby-de-la-Zouche Prize, Surg., Med., Obst. and Gynaecol. FRCS 1966; FRCSGlas 1973 (Hon. FRCSGlas 2001); FRCSE 1976. General dental practice, Durban, SA, 1954–59; Sen. Surgical Registrar, Nottingham Gen. Hosp. and Sheffield Royal Infirmary, 1966–70; Sen. Lectr and Dep. Dir, Dept of Surgery, Welsh Nat. Sch. of Med., also Hon. Cons. Surg., Cardiff Royal Inf., 1970–72; St Mungo Prof. of Surgery, Univ. of Glasgow, and Hon. Cons. Surg., Glasgow Royal Inf., 1972–79; Prof. of Surgery, Royal Postgrad. Sch. of London and Dir of Surgery, Hammersmith Hosp., 1979–86; Prof. of Surgery, Univ. of Bern, 1986–91. Moynihan Fellow, Assoc. of Surgs of Gt Brit. and Ire., 1972; Mayne Vis. Prof., Univ. of Queensland, Brisbane, 1976; Vis. Prof., Univ. of Lund, Sweden, 1977; Nimmo Vis. Prof., Adelaide Univ., 1982; Oliver Beahrs Vis. Prof., Mayo Clinic, 2002; Purvis Oration, 1974; President's Oration, Soc. for Surgery of Aliment. Tract, Toronto, 1977; Lectures: Honyman Gillespie, Univ. of Edinburgh, 1978; Walton, RCPGlas, 1984; Monsarrat, Univ. of Liverpool, 1985; Legg Meml, KCH, 1985; Philip Sandblom, Lund Univ., Sweden, 1986; T. E. Jones Meml, Cleveland Clinic, USA, 1986; L. W. Edwards, Vanderbilt Univ., USA, 1987; Ernest Miles, British Assoc. Surg. Oncology, 1995; DeQuervain, Insespital Bern, Switzerland, 2006; Dallas B. Phemister, Univ. of Chicago, 2007; Sabiston, Univ. Hosp., Zurich, 2007; Davis Foundn, RCPSG, 2007. Pres., Internat. Biliary Assoc., 1987. Member: BMA, 1963–; Assoc. of Surgs of GB and Ire., 1971–; Surgical Research Soc., 1971–; Brit. Soc. of Gastroenterology, 1972–; Swiss Surg. Soc., 1987–; Internat. Hepato-Biliar Pancreatic Assoc., 1992–; Amer. Surgical Assoc., 1993–; Soc. Surgical Oncology, 1994–. Hon. Member: Soc. for Surgery of Aliment. Tract, USA, 1977; Soc. Amer. Endoscopic Surgs, 1986–; Danish Surg. Soc., 1988; Yugoslavian Surg. Soc., 1988; French Surg. Soc., 1990; Austrian Surg. Soc., 2007; Hon. Fellow: Italian Surg. Soc., 2002; French Acad. of Surgery, 2008. Hon. FRCSI 2002. Hon. DSc Sheffield, 1998. Acral Medal, Swedish Soc. Surgery, 1990. Order of Prasidda, Prabala-Gorkha-Dakshin Bahu, Nepal, 1984. *Publications:* (ed with A. C. Kennedy), Essentials of Medicine and Surgery for Dental Students, 3rd edn 1977, 4th edn 1982; (ed) The Biliary Tract, 1982; (ed) Surgery of the Liver and Biliary Tract, vols 1 and 2, 1988, 4th edn as Surgery of the Liver, Biliary Tract and Pancreas, 2006; (ed) Surgical Management of Hepatobiliary and Pancreatic Disorders, 2003; chapters in books; numerous publications concerned with medical educn, gastrointestinal surgery and aspects of oncology with particular interests in surgery of the liver, pancreas and biliary tract and hepatic pathophysiology in med. and surgical jls. *Recreations:* water colour painting, wood carving. *Address:* Memorial Sloan-Kettering Cancer Center, 1275 York Avenue, New York, NY 10021, USA. *T:* (212) 6395526; 447 E 57th Street #3E, New York, NY 10022, USA.

BLUNDELL, Prof. Derek John; Professor of Environmental Geology, University of London, 1975–98, now Emeritus Professor of Geophysics; Dean of Research and Enterprise, Royal Holloway, University of London, 1995–98; *b* 30 June 1933; *s* of Frank and Mollie Blundell; *m* 1960, Mary Patricia, *d* of Archibald and Mildred Leonard. *Educ:* Univ. of Birmingham (BSc); Imperial Coll., London (DIC, PhD). Res. Fellow 1957, Lectr 1959, in Geology, Univ. of Birmingham; Sen. Lectr 1970, Reader 1972, in Geophysics, Univ. of Lancaster; Royal Soc. Vis. Prof., Univ. of Ghana, 1974; Prof. of Environmental Geol., Univ. of London, first at Chelsea Coll. (Hd of Geol. Dept), 1975, then at Royal Holloway and Bedford New Coll., 1985–98; Hd of Geol. Dept, 1992–97; Hon. Fellow, Royal Holloway, 2004. Leverhulme Emeritus Fellow, 1998–2000. Pres., Geological Soc., 1988–90. Mem., Academia Europaea, 1990. Coke Medal, Geological Soc., 1993. *Publications:* (jtly) A Continent Revealed: the European geotraverse, 1992; Lyell: the past is the key to the present, 1998; The Timing and Location of Major Ore Deposits in an Evolving Orogen, 2002; Geodynamics and Ore Deposit Evolution in Europe, 2005; contribs to learned jls mainly relating to seismic exploration of the earth's crust, to earthquake hazards and, early on, to palæomagnetism. *Recreations:* travel, golf. *Address:* Springwood, Tite Hill, Englefield Green, Surrey TW20 0NF. *T:* (01784) 433170. *Club:* Athenæum.

BLUNDELL, John; Director General (formerly General Director) and Ralph Harris Fellow, Institute of Economic Affairs, since 1993; *b* 9 Oct. 1952; *s* of James Blundell and Alice Margaret Blundell (*née* Taylor); *m* 1977, Christine Violet Lowry; two *s*. *Educ:* King's Sch., Macclesfield; London Sch. of Econs, Univ. of London. Head of Press, Parly Liaison and Res. Office, Fedn of Small Businesses, 1976–82; Councillor (C), Lambeth BC, 1978–82; Institute for Humane Studies, George Mason University: Dir, Public Affairs, 1982–85; Exec. Vice-Pres., 1985–88; Pres., 1988–91; Trustee, 1991–; Atlas Economic Research Foundation, Fairfax, Virginia: Pres., 1987–91; Chm., Exec. Cttee, 1991–2005; Chm., Inst. Develt & Rels Bd Cttee, 2005–; Director: Inst. for Economic Studies, Europe (formerly Inst. for Humane Studies Europe), Paris, 1988–2002; Fraser Inst., Vancouver, 1987–92; Humane Studies Foundn, 1988–91; Atlas Economic Res. Foundn (UK), 1993–2001; Centre for the New Europe, Brussels, 1998–2003; Internat. Policy Network (UK), 2001–; Founder Director: Inst. for Justice, Washington, 1991–93; Athens Inst., Alexandria, Va, 1992–2000; Founder Trustee, Buckeye Inst. for Public Policy Solutions, Dayton, Ohio, 1989–; Pres., Charles G. Koch and Claude R. Lambe Charitable Foundns, Washington DC, 1991–93. Co-founder and Chm., Inst. for Children, Cambridge, Mass, 1993–98. Advr, Business Wise, 1993–98; Member: Adv. Bd, Inst. de Libre Empresa, Peru, 2000–; Adv. Council, TaxPayers' Alliance, 2003–; Council of Reference, OPLAN Foundn, 2005–. Mem. Council, 1998–2006, Mem., Adv. Bd, 2006–, Fairbridge. Member: Mont Pélerin Soc., 1990– (Mem. Bd, 1998–2004; Vice Pres., 2002–04; Chm., Host Cttee, 2002); Philadelphia Soc., 1994– (Bd Mem., 2006–); Scientific Cttee, Adam Smith Soc., Milan, 2003–. Hon. Mem., Hayek Soc., LSE. Pres., Bd of Regents, Congressional Schs of Virginia, 1988–92. Associate Ed. for Internat. Business, Mid-Atlantic Jl of Business, 1996–. Member: Bd of Scholars, Centre for Civil Soc., New Delhi, 2001–; Selection Cttee, Milton Friedman Prize for Advancing Liberty, Cato Inst., 2002–08; Bd, Center for Freedom and Prosperity, Washington, 2005–; Bd, F. A. Hayek Inst., Vienna, 2005–; Judge, Sir Antony Fisher Meml Awards, 1990–93. CCMI 2003. Nat. Free Enterprise Award, Aims of Industry, 2000. Hon. Mem., Templeton World Charity Foundn (formerly John Templeton Foundn), 2001–. *Publications:* (with Brian Gosschalk) Beyond Left and Right, the New Politics of Britain, 1998; (with Colin Robinson) Regulation Without the State, 1999; (with Colin Robinson) Regulation Without the State...The Debate Continues, 2000; Waging the War of Ideas, 2001, 3rd edn 2007; (jtly) A Tribute to Peter Bauer, 2002; (with Gerald Frost) Friend or Foe?: what Americans should know about the European Union, 2004; papers, contribs to jls, forewords, introductions, newspaper columns and magazine articles. *Recreations:* cricket, golf, genealogy, Morgan sports cars, minimising the role of the state and maximising individual liberty. *Address:* 43 Ponsonby Place, SW1P 4PS; (office) 2 Lord North Street, SW1P 3LB. *T:* (020) 7799 8900, *Fax:* (020) 7799 2137; *e-mail:* jblundell@iea.org.uk; Alpine Lake, Terra Alta, WV 26764, USA. *T:* (304) 789 2115. *Clubs:* Political Economy; Marin Cricket (Calif, USA).

BLUNDELL, Prof. Richard William, CBE 2006; FBA 1997; Professor of Economics, University College London, since 1984; Leverhulme Personal Research Professor, since 1999; Director of Research, Institute for Fiscal Studies, since 1987; *b* 1 May 1952; *s* of Horace Leon and Marjorie Blundell; *m* 1984, Anne Gaynor Aberdeen; one *s* one *d*. *Educ:* Univ. of Bristol (BSc 1st cl. Hons Econs with Stats); LSE (MSc Econometrics). Lectr in Econometrics, Univ. of Manchester, 1975–85; Head, Dept of Economics, UCL, 1988–92; Dir, ESRC Centre for Microecon. Analysis of Public Policy, Inst. Fiscal Studies, 1991–. Visiting Professor: Univ. of BC, 1980–81; MIT, 1993; Univ. of Calif at Berkeley, 1994, 1999. Member, Council: Econometric Soc., 1991– (Fellow, 1991; Yrjö Jahnsson Prize, 1995; Frisch Medal, 2000; Mem. Exec. Cttee, 2001–; Pres., 2006); European Econ. Assoc., 1997– (Pres., 2004; Fellow 2004); NRC Panel Mem., Nat. Acad. of Sci., 1999–2000. Associate Editor: Rev. Econ. Studies, 1984–88; Jl of Human Resources, 1995–97; Co-Editor: Jl of Econometrics, 1991–97 (Mem., Exec. Council, 1997–); Econometrica, 1997–2001. Hon. For. Mem., Amer. Acad. of Arts and Science, 2002; Hon. Mem., AEA, 2001; Hon. FIA 2003. Hon. Dr, St Gallen, Switzerland, 2003. *Publications:* Unemployment, Search and Labour Supply, 1986; The Measurement of Household Welfare, 1994; contrib. Econometrica, Rev. Econ. Studies, Econ. Jl, Jl Econometrics. *Recreations:* saxophone, guitar, jazz music, travel. *Address:* Department of Economics, University College London, Gower Street, WC1E 6BT. *T:* (020) 7679 5863; *e-mail:* r.blundell@ucl.ac.uk.

See also Sir T. L. Blundell.

BLUNDELL, Sir Thomas Leon, (Sir Tom), Kt 1997; FRS 1984; FRSC; Sir William Dunn Professor of Biochemistry, 1995–Sept. 2009, Head of Department of Biochemistry, 1996–Sept. 2009, Chairman, School of Biological Sciences, 2003–Sept. 2009, and Professor, from Sept. 2009, Cambridge University; Fellow of Sidney Sussex College, Cambridge, since 1995; *b* 7 July 1942; *s* of Horace Leon Blundell and Marjorie Blundell; one *s*; *m* 1987, Bancinyane Lynn Sibanda; two *d*. *Educ:* Steyning Grammar Sch.; Brasenose Coll., Oxford (BA, DPhil; Hon. Fellow, 1989). FRSC 2006. Postdoctoral Res. Fellow, Laboratory of Molecular Biophysics, Oxford Univ., 1967–72; Jun. Res. Fellow, Linacre Coll., Oxford, 1968–70; Lectr, Biological Scis, Sussex Univ., 1973–76; Prof. of Crystallography, Birkbeck Coll., Univ. of London, 1976–90; Dep. Chm. and Dir Gen., AFRC, 1991–94; Chief Exec. and Dep. Chm., BBSRC, 1994–96 (on secondment). Director: International Sch. of Crystallography, 1981–; Babraham Inst., Cambridge, 1997–2002. Founder and non-exec. Dir, Astex Therapeutics, 1999–. Chm., Royal Commn on Envmtl Pollution, 1998–2005. Member: Council, AFRC, 1985–90; MRC AIDS Res. Steering Cttee, 1987–90; ACOST, 1988–90; Council, SERC, 1989–90 (Mem., 1979–82, Chm., 1983–87, Biological Scis Cttee; Mem., Science Bd, 1983–87); ABRC, 1991–94; Council, Royal Soc., 1997–99; R&D Bd, SmithKline Beecham, 1997–2000; Bd, Parly OST, 1998–2007. Hon. Dir, ICRF Unit of Structural Molecular Biology, 1989–96. Councillor, Oxford CBC, 1970–73 (Chm. Planning Cttee, 1972–73). Scientific Consultant, Oxford Molecular Ltd, 1996–99; Chm., Scientific Adv. Bd, Bioprocessing Ltd, 1997–2000; Member: UCB Sci. Adv. Bd, 2005–; Utek Sci. Adv. Bd, 2005–; Industrial Consultant: Celltech, 1981–86 (non-exec. Dir, 1997–2004; Chm., Scientific Adv. Bd, 1998–2004); Pfizer Central Res., Groton, USA and Sandwich, UK, 1984–90; Abingworth Management Ltd, 1988–90, 1996–. Pres., UK Bioscis Fedn, 2004–08. Dir, Lawes Agricl Trust, 1998–; Trustee, Daphne Jackson Trust, 1996–. Governor, Birkbeck Coll., 1985–89. Founder FMedSci 1998. Hon. Fellow, Linacre Coll., Oxford, 1991. Hon. FRASE 1993; Hon. FIChemE 1995. Hon. Mem., British Biophysics

Soc., 2006. Hon. DSc: Edinburgh, East Anglia, 1993; Sheffield, Strathclyde, 1994; Warwick, Antwerp, 1995; Nottingham, 1996; UWE, 1997; Stirling, 2000; Sussex, Pavia, 2002; St Andrews, 2002; London, 2003. Alcon Award for Dist. Work in Vision Research, 1985; Gold Medal, Inst. of Biotechnological Studies, 1987; Sir Hans Krebs Medal, Fedn of European Biochemical Socs, 1987; Ciba Medal, UK Biochemical Soc., 1988; Feldberg Prize for Biology and Medicine, 1988; Gold Medal, SCI, 1995; Pfizer Eur. Award for Innovation, 1998; Bernal Medal, Royal Soc., 1998. Joint Editor: Progress in Biophysics and Molecular Biology, 1979–; Current Opinion in Structural Biology, 1996–; Member Editorial Advisory Board: Biochemistry, 1986–89; Protein Engineering, 1986–2003; Protein Science, 1992–98; Structure, 1993–. *Publications:* Protein Crystallography, 1976; papers in Jl of Molecular Biology, Nature, European Jl of Biochemistry, etc. *Recreations:* playing jazz, listening to opera, walking, international travel. *Address:* Department of Biochemistry, Tennis Court Road, Cambridge CB2 1GA.

See also R. W. Blundell.

BLUNDEN, Sir George, Kt 1987; Deputy Governor, Bank of England, 1986–90 (Executive Director, 1976–84, Non-Executive Director, 1984–85); Joint Deputy Chairman, Leopold Joseph Holdings, 1984–85 and 1990–94; *b* 31 Dec. 1922; *s* of late George Blunden and Florence Holder; *m* 1949, Anne, *d* of late G. J. E. and Phyllis Bulford; two *s* one *d*. *Educ:* City of London Sch.; University Coll., Oxford (MA). Royal Sussex Regt, 1941–45. Bank of England, 1947–55; IMF, 1955–58; Bank of England: rejoined 1958; Dep. Chief Cashier, 1968–73; Chief of Management Services, 1973–74; Head of Banking Supervision, 1974–76. Director: Eagle Star Hldgs, 1984–85; Portals Hldgs, 1984–86; Grindlays Hldgs, 1984–85. Advr, Union Bank of Switzerland in London, 1990–94. Chairman: Group of Ten Cttees, BIS, Basle, on Banking Regulations and Supervisory Practices, 1974–77, on Payments Systems, 1981–83; cttee to oversee estabt and operation of Code of Banking Practice, 1990–94; London Pensions Fund Authy, 1989–92. Chm. Governors, St Peter's Gp of Hosps, 1978–82; Chm., St Peter's Hosps Special Trustees, 1982–96; Chm., Inst. of Urology, 1982–88 (Hon. Treasurer, 1975–78); Mem. Council, Imperial Cancer Res. Fund, 1981–94 (Treas., 1988–91; Chm., 1991–94). Chairman: Samuel Lewis Housing Trust, 1985 (Trustee, 1980–85); Centre for Study of Financial Innovation, 1995–98. President: Inst. of Business Ethics, 1994–96; British-Malaysia Soc., 1989–94. Member: Court, Mermaid Theatre Trust, 1979–84; Council, RCM, 1983–89 (Dep. Chm., 1990–97; Hon. FRCM 1987). Mem., Livery, Goldsmiths' Co., 1987. Hon. Fellow, UEA, 1997. *Address:* Ashdale, Gunthorpe, Melton Constable, Norfolk NR24 2NS. *T:* (01263) 860359. *Clubs:* Reform; Norfolk (Norwich).

BLUNDEN, Sir Philip (Overington), 7th Bt *cr* 1766, of Castle Blunden, Kilkenny; artist and art restorer; *b* 27 Jan. 1922; *s* of Sir John Blunden, 5th Bt and Phyllis Dorothy (*d* 1967), *d* of Philip Crampton Creaghe; *S* brother, 1985; *m* 1945, Jeannette Francesca Alexandra (*d* 1999), *e d* of Captain D. Macdonald, RNR; two *s* one *d*. *Educ:* Repton. Served RN, 1941–46 (1939–45 Star, Atlantic Star, Defence Medal). Estate Manager, Castle Blunden, 1947–60; engaged in marketing of industrial protective coatings, 1962–83; in art and art restoration, 1976–. Solo exhibns bi-annually, Dublin, Celbridge and Galway. *Recreations:* fishing, field sports, reading. *Heir: s* Hubert Chisholm Blunden [*b* 9 Aug. 1948; *m* 1975, Ellish O'Brien; one *s* one *d*]. *Club:* Royal Dublin Society (Life Mem.).

BLUNDY, Prof. Jonathan David, PhD; FRS 2008; Professor of Petrology, University of Bristol, since 2004; *b* Wallingford, 7 Aug. 1961; *s* of Peter Desmond Blundy and Jean Dorothy Blundy; *m* 1992, Katharine Melanie Fawcett (separated 2003); one *s* one *d*, and one step *d*. *Educ:* St Paul's Sch., São Paulo; Giggleswick Sch.; Leeds Grammar Sch.; University Coll., Oxford (BA Hons 1983); Trinity Hall, Cambridge (PhD 1989). Jun. Res. Fellow, Hertford Coll., Oxford, 1990–91; University of Bristol: NERC Res. Fellow, 1991–95; Royal Soc. Univ. Res. Fellow, 1995–2002; NERC Sen. Res. Fellow, 2002–07. *Publications:* over 80 articles in scientific jls. *Recreations:* rambling, cooking, public transport, Leeds United FC. *Address:* c/o Department of Earth Sciences, Wills Memorial Building, University of Bristol, Queens Road, Bristol BS8 1RJ.

BLUNKETT, Rt Hon. David; PC 1997; MP (Lab) Sheffield, Brightside, since 1987; *b* 6 June 1947; *m* (marr. diss.); three *s*; one *s*. *Educ:* night sch. and day release, Shrewsbury Coll. of Technol. and Richmond Coll. of Further Educn, Sheffield; Nat. Cert. in Business Studies, E Midlands Gas Bd; Sheffield Univ. (BA Hons Pol Theory and Instns); Huddersfield Holly Bank Coll. of Educn (Tech.) (PGCFE). Tutor in Industrial Relns, Barnsley Coll. of Technol., 1974–87. Elected to Sheffield City Council (at age of 22), 1970; Chm., Family and Community Services Cttee, 1976–80; Leader, 1980–87; Dep. Chm., AMA, 1984–87. Joined Labour Party at age of 16; Chm., Labour Party NEC, 1993–94 (Dep. Chm., 1992–93; Mem., 1983–98); Chm., Labour Party Cttee on Local govt, 1984–92. Front bench spokesman on the environment, with special responsibility for local govt and poll tax, 1988–92, on health, 1992–94, on educn, 1994–95, on educn and employment, 1995–97 (Mem., Shadow Cabinet, 1992–97); Secretary of State: for Educn and Employment, 1997–2001; for Home Dept, 2001–04; for Work and Pensions, 2005. *Publications:* (jtly) Local Enterprise and Workers' Plans, 1981; (jtly) Building from the Bottom: the Sheffield Experience, 1983; (jtly) Democracy in Crisis: the town halls respond, 1987; On a Clear Day, 1995; Politics and Progress, 2001; The Blunkett Tapes: my life in the bear pit, 2006. *Address:* House of Commons, SW1A 0AA.

BLUNT, Charles William; Chief Executive Officer, American Chamber of Commerce in Australia, since 1990. *Educ:* Sydney Univ. (BEcon). AASA; CPA. Exec. appts in mining, finance and agricultural industries. MP (Nat. Party) Richmond, NSW, 1984–90; Leader, Parly Nat. Party, 1989–90; opposition Minister, 1984–90, variously for: Sport, Recreation and Tourism; Social Security; Transport and Communications; Community Services and Aged Care; Trade and Resources. Former Mem., parly cttees and official delegns. Chairman: Permo-Drive Technologies Ltd; Man. Dir, American Business Services Pty Ltd. *Recreations:* tennis, reading. *Address:* PO Box 66, Wahroonga, NSW 2076, Australia. *Clubs:* Union, American (Sydney).

BLUNT, Crispin Jeremy Rupert; MP (C) Reigate, since 1997; *b* 15 July 1960; *s* of Maj. Gen. Peter Blunt, CB, MBE, GM and Adrienne (*née* Richardson); *m* 1990, Victoria Ainsley Jenkins; one *s* one *d*. *Educ:* Wellington Coll.; RMA, Sandhurst; Durham Univ. (BA 1984); Cranfield Inst. of Technology (MBA 1991). Commnd, 13th/18th Royal Hussars (QMO), 1980; Troop Leader: UK and Cyprus, 1980–81; BAOR, 1984–85; Regtl Signals Officer/Ops Officer, BAOR/UK, 1985–87; Sqn Leader, 2IC UK, 1987–89; resigned commn, 1990; Rep., Forum of Private Business, 1991–92; Consultant, Politics Internat., 1993; Special Advr to Sec. of State for Defence, 1993–95, to Foreign Sec., 1995–97. Opposition spokesman on NI, 2001–02, on trade, energy and science, 2002–03; Opposition Whip, 2004–. Member: Select Cttee on Defence, 1997–2000, 2003–04; Select Cttee on Envmt, Transport and the Regions, 2000–01. Sec., Cons. Foreign and Commonwealth Affairs Cttee, 1997–2001; Chm., Cons. Middle East Council, 2004–. Co-Chm., Council for Advancement of Arab-British Understanding, 2004–. *Recreations:* cricket, sport, travel, bridge, food and wine. *Address:* House of Commons, SW1A 0AA. *T:* (020) 7219 2254. *Clubs:* Royal Automobile, MCC; Reigate Priory Cricket.

See also O. S. P Blunt.

BLUNT, David Graeme, CVO 2001 (LVO 1986); HM Diplomatic Service; Ambassador to Croatia, since 2008; *b* 19 Jan. 1953; *s* of Daryl and Deidre Blunt; *m* 1975, Geirid Bakkeli; three *s*. *Educ:* Cranleigh Sch.; Manchester Univ. (BA Hons). Teacher, Blairmore Sch., Aberdeenshire, 1976–78; joined HM Diplomatic Service, 1978; FCO, 1978–79; Second, later First, Sec., Vienna, 1979–83; First Secretary: Peking, 1983–87; FCO, 1987–89; Canberra, 1989–94; Counsellor, FCO, 1994–97; Dep. Hd of Mission and Consul-Gen., Oslo, 1997–2001; Dep. Gov., Gibraltar, 2002–05; Hd of Office, then Ambassador, Pristina, Kosovo, 2006–08. *Recreations:* choral music, sailing, ski-ing, battling rabbits and weather at our Aberdeenshire property. *Address:* c/o Foreign and Commonwealth Office, King Charles Street, SW1A 2AH.

BLUNT, David John; QC 1991; a Recorder of the Crown Court, since 1990; writer; *b* 25 Oct. 1944; *s* of late Vernon Egerton Rowland Blunt and of Catherine Vera Blunt; *m* 1976, Zaibonessa Ebrahim; one *s* one *d*. *Educ:* Farnham Grammar Sch.; Trinity Hall, Cambridge (MA Hons). Called to the Bar, Middle Temple, 1967, Bencher, 2001. Asst Recorder, 1985–90. Contested (L): Lambeth Central, 1978, 1979; Cornwall SE, 1983. First TV play broadcast, 1976. *Recreations:* walking, running, cycling, reading, writing, old cars. *Address:* 4 Pump Court, Temple, EC4Y 7AN. *T:* (020) 7842 5555.

BLUNT, Sir David Richard Reginald Harvey, 12th Bt *cr* 1720; *b* 8 Nov. 1938; *s* of Sir Richard David Harvey Blunt, 11th Bt and Elisabeth Malvine Ernestine, *d* of Comdr F. M. Fransen Van de Putte, Royal Netherlands Navy (retd); *S* father, 1975; *m* 1969, Sonia Tudor Rosemary (*née* Day); one *d*. *Heir: kinsman* Robin Anthony Blunt, CEng, MIMechE [*b* 23 Nov. 1926; *m* 1st, 1949, Sheila Stuart (marr. diss. 1962), *d* of C. Stuart Brindley; one *s*; 2nd, 1962, June Elizabeth, *d* of Charles Wigginton; one *s*].

BLUNT, Oliver Simon Peter; QC 1994; a Recorder, since 1995; *b* 8 March 1951; *s* of Maj.-Gen. Peter Blunt, CB, MBE, GM and Adrienne (*née* Richardson); *m* 1979, Joanna Margaret Dixon; one *s* three *d*. *Educ:* Bedford Sch.; Southampton Univ. (LLB 1973). Called to the Bar, Middle Temple, 1974; Asst Recorder, SE Circuit, 1991–95. *Recreations:* cricket, golf, ski-ing, swimming, mini-rugby coach. *Address:* Furnival Chambers, 32 Furnival Street, EC4A 1JQ. *T:* (020) 7405 3232. *Clubs:* Roehampton; Bank of England Sports; Barnes Cricket; Rosslyn Park Rugby.

See also C. J. R. Blunt.

BLYE, Douglas William Alfred, CMG 1979; OBE 1973; Secretary for Monetary Affairs, Hong Kong Government, 1977–85; *b* 15 Dec. 1924; *s* of William Blye and Ethel Attwood; *m* 1955, Juanita, (June), Buckley. *Educ:* King's Road Sch., Herne Bay; Maidstone Polytechnic. ACMA. Served War, RAF, 1941–46. Various commercial and industrial appts in UK, 1947–55; Govt of Fedn of Malaya, 1955–58; Hong Kong Govt, 1958–85; Econ. and Financial Advr, Govt of Dubai, 1986–87. *Recreations:* squash, walking. *Address:* Middlefield, The Street, Goodnestone, Canterbury, Kent CT3 1PG. *T:* (01304) 842196. *Club:* Royal Automobile.

BLYTH, family name of **Barons Blyth** and **Blyth of Rowington**.

BLYTH, 4th Baron *cr* 1907; **Anthony Audley Rupert Blyth;** Bt 1895; *b* 3 June 1931; *er s* of 3rd Baron Blyth and Edna Myrtle (*d* 1952), *d* of Ernest Lewis, Wellington, NZ; *S* father, 1977; *m* 1st, 1954, Elizabeth Dorothea (marr. diss. 1962), *d* of R. T. Sparrow, Vancouver, BC; two *d* (one *s* decd); 2nd, 1963, Oonagh Elizabeth Ann, *yr d* of late William Henry Conway, Dublin; one *s* one *d*. *Educ:* St Columba's College, Dublin. *Heir: s* Hon. James Audley Ian Blyth [*b* 13 Nov. 1970; *m* 2003, Elodie Bernadette Andrée Odette, *d* of Jean-Georges Cadet de Fontenay; one *s* one *d*]. *Address:* Blythwood Estate, Athenry, Co. Galway, Ireland.

BLYTH OF ROWINGTON, Baron *cr* 1995 (Life Peer), of Rowington in the County of Warwickshire; **James Blyth,** Kt 1985; Chairman, Diageo plc, 2000–08 (Director, 1998–2008); Vice Chairman, Greenhill & Co., since 2004 (Senior Advisor, 2000–02; Partner, 2002–04); *b* 8 May 1940; *s* of Daniel Blyth and Jane Power Carlton; *m* 1967, Pamela Anne Campbell Dixon; one *d* (one *s* decd). *Educ:* Spiers Sch.; Glasgow Univ. Mobil Oil Co., 1963–69; General Foods Ltd, 1969–71; Mars Ltd, 1971–74; General Manager: Lucas Batteries Ltd, 1974–77; Lucas Aerospace Ltd, 1977–81; Head of Defence Sales, MoD, 1981–85; Man. Dir, Plessey Electronic Systems, 1985–86; Chief Exec., The Plessey Co. plc, 1986–87; The Boots Co.: Chief Exec., 1987–98; Dep. Chm., 1994–98; Chm., 1998–2000. Non-executive Director: Imperial Gp PLC, 1984–86; Cadbury-Schweppes PLC, 1986–90; British Aerospace, 1990–94; Anixter Internat. Inc., 1995–; NatWest Gp, 1998–2000. Chm., Adv. Panel on Citizen's Charter, 1991–97. Pres., ME Assoc., 1988–93; Patron, Combined Services Winter Sports Assoc., 1997–2002. Gov., London Business Sch., 1987–96 (Hon. Fellow, 1997). Liveryman, Coachmakers' and Coach Harness Makers' Co. Hon. LLD Nottingham, 1992. *Recreations:* ski-ing, tennis, paintings, theatre. *Address:* Greenhill & Co. International LLP, Lansdowne House, 57 Berkeley Square, W1J 6ER. *T:* (020) 7198 7400. *Clubs:* East India, Queen's.

BLYTH, Sir Charles, (Sir Chay), Kt 1997; CBE 1972; BEM 1967; Managing Director, The Challenge Business Ltd (formerly Crownfields Ltd), since 1989; *b* 14 May 1940; *s* of Robert and Jessie Blyth; *m* 1st, 1962, Maureen Margaret Morris (marr. diss. 1992); one *d*; 2nd, 1995, Felicity Rayson. *Educ:* Hawick High School. HM Forces, Para. Regt, 1958–67. Cadbury Schweppes, 1968–69; Dir, Sailing Ventures (Hampshire) Ltd, 1969–73. Organiser: British Steel Challenge Round World Yacht Race 1992–93, 1989–93; BT Global Challenge Round the World Yacht Race 1996–97, 1994–97. Rowed North Atlantic with Captain John Ridgway, June–Sept. 1966; circumnavigated the world westwards solo in yacht British Steel, 1970–71; circumnavigated the world eastwards with crew of paratroopers in yacht Great Britain II, and Winner, Elapsed Time Prize Whitbread Round the World Yacht Race, 1973–74; Atlantic sailing record, Cape Verde to Antigua, 1977; won Round Britain Race in yacht Great Britain IV, 1978 (crew Robert James); won The Observer/Europe 1 doublehanded transatlantic race in record time, 1981 (crew Robert James); Number One to Virgin Atlantic Challenge II successful attempt on the Blue Riband, 1986. Pres., Inst. of Professional Sales, 1998. Yachtsman of the Year, 1971, Special Award for outstanding services to yachting, Yachting Journalists Assoc., 1994; Chichester Trophy, RYS, 1971. Freeman of Hawick, 1972. *Publications:* A Fighting Chance, 1966; Innocent Aboard, 1968; The Impossible Voyage, 1971; Theirs is the Glory, 1974; The Challenge, 1993. *Recreations:* sailing, horse-riding, hunting. *Address:* (office) The Box Office, Box Lane, Minchinhampton, Glos GL6 9HA. *Clubs:* Special Forces, Royal Ocean Racing; Royal Southern Yacht, Royal Western Yacht.

BLYTH, John Douglas Morrison, CMG 1981; HM Diplomatic Service, retired; *b* 23 July 1924; *s* of late William Naismith Blyth and Jean (*née* Morrison); *m* 1st, 1949, Gabrielle Elodie (*née* Belloc) (*d* 1971); three *s* two *d*; 2nd, 1973, Lucy Anne (*née* Alcock), JP; one *s* one *d*. *Educ:* Christ's Coll.; Lincoln Coll., Oxford (MA); Downing Coll., Cambridge (MA). Served War, RNVR, 1942–46. Editor, The Polar Record (publd by Scott Polar Res. Inst., Cambridge), 1949–54; joined FO, 1954; served: Geneva, 1955; Athens, 1959; Leopoldville, 1963; Accra, 1964; FO, 1966; Athens, 1968; FCO, 1972; Vienna, 1974; FCO, 1977. Pres., Hélène Heroys Literary Foundn, 1975–2004. Hon. Sec., Suffolk

Preservation Soc., 1985–94. *Publications:* articles in The Polar Record. *Recreations:* gardening, military history, enjoying wine. *Address:* Crownland Hall, Walsham-le-Willows, Suffolk IP31 3BU. *T:* (01359) 259369. *Club:* Naval and Military.

BLYTHE, His Honour James Forbes, TD 1946; a Circuit Judge, 1978–92; solicitor; *b* Coventry, 11 July 1917; *s* of J. F. Blythe and Dorothy Alice (*née* Hazlewood); *m* 1949, Margaret, *d* of P. D. Kinsey; two *d. Educ:* Wrekin Coll.; Birmingham Univ. (LLB). Commissioned TA, Royal Warwickshire Regt, 1936–53 (Major); served War of 1939–45 with BEF in France (Dunkirk), 1939–40; Central Mediterranean Force (Tunisia, Sicily, Italy, Corsica, S France and Austria), 1942–45; Air Liaison Officer GSO II (Ops) with RAF (despatches); GSO II (Ops) 10 Corps, 1945; GSO II (Ops) HQ Polish Repatriation Gp, 1945–46. Admitted solicitor, 1947; private practitioner in partnership in Coventry and Leamington Spa, 1948. HM Deputy Coroner for City of Coventry and Northern Dist of Warwickshire, 1954–64; HM Coroner for City of Coventry, 1964–78; a Recorder of the Crown Court, 1972–78. Pres., Warwicks Law Soc., 1978–79. *Recreations:* shooting, sailing. *Address:* Hazlewood, Upper Ladyes' Hill, Kenilworth, Warwickshire CV8 2FB. *Clubs:* Army and Navy; Leamington Tennis Court.

BLYTHE, Mark Andrew, CB 1999; Principal Assistant Solicitor, Treasury Solicitor's Department, 1989–2003, and Legal Adviser, HM Treasury, 1993–2003; *b* 4 Sept. 1943; *s* of John Jarratt Blythe and Dorothy Kathleen Blythe; *m* 1972, Brigid Helen Frazer (*née* Skemp); two *s* one *d. Educ:* King Edward VII Grammar Sch., Sheffield; University Coll., Oxford (BCL, MA; Open Schol. in Classics, 1961; Gibbs Prize in Law, 1963). Called to the Bar, Inner Temple, 1966; Attorney, NY Bar, 1980. Teaching Associate, Univ. of Pennsylvania Law Sch., 1965–66; Chancery Bar, 1967–77; Legal Consultant, NY, 1978–80; Treasury Solicitor's Dept, 1981–2003: Assistant Solicitor, European Div., 1986–89; Hd, Central Adv. Div., 1989–93.

BLYTHE, Moira; *see* Gibb, M.

BLYTHE, Rex Arnold; Under-Secretary, Board of Inland Revenue, 1981–86, retired; *b* 11 Nov. 1928; *s* of late Sydney Arnold Blythe and Florence Blythe (*née* Jones); *m* 1953, Rachel Ann Best; one *s* two *d. Educ:* Bradford Grammar Sch.; Trinity Coll., Cambridge (MA Classics). Entered Inland Revenue as Inspector of Taxes, 1953; Sen. Inspector, 1962; Principal Inspector, 1968; Asst Sec., 1974. *Recreations:* golf, photography, walking, travel. *Address:* 18A Kirkwick Avenue, Harpenden, Herts AL5 2QX. *T:* (01582) 715833. *Club:* MCC.

BLYTHE, Ronald George; writer, since 1953; *b* 6 Nov. 1922; *s* of Albert George Blythe and Matilda Elizabeth (*née* Elkins). *Educ:* St Peter's and St Gregory's Sch., Sudbury, Suffolk. Librarian, 1943–54. Soc. of Authors' Travel Scholarship, 1969. Editor, Penguin Classics, 1966–87. Assistant, Aldeburgh Fest., 1955–57; Member: Eastern Arts Lit. Panel, 1975–85; Cttee, Centre of E Anglian Studies, UEA, 1975–80; Soc. of Authors' Management Cttee, 1980–85; Chm., Essex Fest., 1981–84. President: John Clare Soc., 1981–; Robert Bloomfield Soc., 2001–; Kilvert Soc., 2006–. Reader, C of E, 1984–; Lay Canon, St Edmundsbury Cathedral, 2003–. FRSL 1969. Hon. MA UEA, 1990; Hon. DLitt: Anglia Poly. Univ., 2001; Essex, 2002; MLitt Lambeth, 2001. Benson Medal for Literature, RSL, 2006. *Publications:* A Treasonable Growth, 1960; Immediate Possession, 1961; The Age of Illusion, 1963; William Hazlitt: selected writings, 1970; Akenfield (Heinemann Award), 1969; Aldeburgh Anthology, 1972; (ed jtly) Works of Thomas Hardy, 1978; The View in Winter, 1979, 2nd edn 2005; (ed) Writing in a War: stories, essays and poems of 1939–45, 1982; Places, 1982; From the Headlands, 1982; The Stories of Ronald Blythe (Angel Prize for Literature), 1985; Divine Landscapes, 1986; Each Returning Day: the pleasure of diaries, 1989; Private Words: letters and diaries of the Second World War, 1991; First Friends, 1998; Going to Meet George and other outings, 1999; Talking About John Clare, 1999; The Circling Year, 2001; Talking to the Neighbours, 2002; (ed) George Herbert, A Priest to the Temple or The Country Parson, 2003; Eight Poems, 2004; A Country Boy, 2004; The Assassin, 2004; A Writer's Day-Book, 2006; A Year At Bottengoms Farm, 2006; Field Work: selected essays, 2007; Wormingford Trilogy: Word from Wormingford, 1997; Out of the Valley, 2000; Borderland, 2005. *Recreations:* walking, looking, listening. *Address:* Bottengoms Farm, Wormingford, Colchester, Essex CO6 3AP. *T:* (01206) 271308.

BOA, Prof. Elizabeth Janet, PhD; FBA 2003; Professor of German and Head of Department of German, University of Nottingham, 1996–2001, now Emeritus Professor; *b* 20 March 1939. *Educ:* Univ. of Glasgow (MA 1961); Univ. of Nottingham (PhD). Lectr, Sen. Lectr, then Reader in German, Univ. of Nottingham, 1965–94; Prof. of Modern German Literature, Univ. of Manchester, 1994. *Publications:* (with James H. Reid) Critical Strategies: German fiction in the twentieth century, 1972; Sexual Circus: Wedekind's theatre of subversion, 1987; Kafka: gender, class and race in the letters and fictions, 1996; (with Rachel Palfreyman) Heimat—A German Dream: regional loyalties and national identity in German culture 1890–1990, 2000. *Address:* c/o Department of German, University of Nottingham, University Park, Nottingham NG7 2RD.

BOADEN, Helen; Director, BBC News, since 2004; *b* 1 March 1956; *d* of William John Boaden and Barbara Mary Boaden; *m* 1994, Stephen Burley. *Educ:* Univ. of Sussex (BA Hons English 1978). Care Asst, Hackney Social Services, 1978; Reporter: Radio WBAI, NY, 1979; Radio Tees and Radio Aire, 1980–83; Producer, BBC Radio Leeds, 1983–85; Reporter: File on 4, Radio 4, 1985–91; Brass Tacks, BBC 2, 1985–91; Presenter: Woman's Hour, Radio 4, 1985–91; Verdict, Channel 4, 1991–; Editor, File on 4, Radio 4, 1991–94; Head: Network Current Affairs, BBC Manchester, 1994–97; Business Progs, BBC News, 1997; Current Affairs and Business Progs, BBC, 1998–2000; Controller: BBC Radio 4, 2000–04; BBC7, 2002–04. Chm., Radio Acad., 2003–. Hon. Dr: UEA (Suffolk Coll.); Sussex, 2003; York, 2004. *Recreations:* walking, food, travel. *Address:* c/o BBC, Television Centre, Wood Lane, W12 7RJ. *T:* (020) 8743 8000.

BOAG, Shirley Ann; *see* Robertson, S. A.

BOAL, His Honour (John) Graham; QC 1993; a Senior Circuit Judge, and Permanent Judge at Central Criminal Court, 1996–2005; *b* 24 Oct. 1943; *s* of late Surg. Captain Jackson Graham Boal, RN, and late Dorothy Kenley Boal; *m* 1978, Elizabeth Mary East; one *s. Educ:* Eastbourne Coll.; King's Coll. London (LLB). Called to the Bar, Gray's Inn, 1966, Bencher, 1991; Junior Treasury Counsel, 1977–85; Sen. Prosecuting Counsel to the Crown, 1985–91; First Sen. Counsel to the Crown at CCC, 1991–93; a Recorder, 1985–96. Vice Chm., Criminal Bar Assoc., 1991–93. Judicial Mem., Parole Bd, 2001–05. Chm., Orchid Cancer Appeal, 1999–2005. *Recreations:* theatre, golf, walking, watching cricket. *Clubs:* Garrick, MCC; Royal West Norfolk Golf; New Zealand Golf.

BOAM, Maj.-Gen. Thomas Anthony, CB 1987; CBE 1978 (OBE 1973); Vice President, Leonard Cheshire, since 2003 (Trustee and Chairman, South Region, 1997–2003); *b* 14 Feb. 1932; *s* of late Lt-Col T. S. Boam, OBE, and of Mrs Boam; *m* 1961, Penelope Christine Mary Roberts; one *s* two *d. Educ:* Bradfield Coll.; RMA Sandhurst. Commissioned Scots Guards, 1952; Canal Zone, Egypt (with 1SG), 1952–54; GSO3, MO4 War Office, 1959–61; psc 1962; Kenya (with 2 Scots Guards), 1963–64; DAA&QMG 4 Guards Bde, 1964–65; Malaysia (with 1SG), 1966–67; BM 4 Guards Bde, 1967–69; GSO1 (DS) Staff Coll., Camberley, 1970–71; CO 2SG, 1972–74; RCDS 1974–75; Comd BAAT Nigeria, 1976–78; BGS (Trg) HQ UKLF, 1978; Dep. Comdr and COS Hong Kong, 1979–81; Hd of British Defence Staff Washington, and Defence Attaché, 1981–84, Mil. Attaché, 1981–83; Comdr, British Forces Hong Kong, and Maj.-Gen., Brigade of Gurkhas, 1985–87. MEC, Hong Kong, 1985–87. Dir, British Consultants Bureau, 1988–95. Chm., 4Sight, W Sussex Assoc. for the Blind, 2003–06. Gov., Hayes Dashwood Foundn, 1992–2006. Vice-Patron, Queen Alexandra Hosp. Home, 2006– (Gov., 1996–2006; Vice-Chm., 1998–2006). *Recreations:* shooting, gardening, sport. *Address:* Bury Gate House, Pulborough, W Sussex RH20 1HA. *Clubs:* Army and Navy, MCC; Sussex.

BOARD, Kathryn Margaret, OBE 1998; Geographical Director, Europe, Americas, Middle East and North Africa, British Council, since 2005; *b* 24 Dec. 1952; *d* of Nicholas Llewellyn Board and Eileen Gleeson; *m* (marr. diss.); one *s* one *d. Educ:* RHC, London (BA Hons (German/English) 1975; MA Dist. (Linguistics/Phonetics) 1979). Admin. Asst, ME Dept, 1975–77, Teacher, Afghanistan, 1977–79, British Council; Lectr, Applied Linguistics and Phonetics, Dept of English, Univ. of Ghent, Belgium, 1980–84; British Council: Consultant in ELT, UK, 1984–86; English Lang. Officer, Peru, 1986–89; Dir, Basque Country, 1989–92; Asst Dir, Ecuador, 1992–96; Director: Colombia, 1996–99; Argentina, 1999–2000; Policy Dir, Americas, 2000–02; Dir, Germany, 2002–05. *Address:* British Council, 10 Spring Gardens, SW1A 2BN. *T:* (020) 7389 4196; *e-mail:* kathryn.board@britishcouncil.org.

BOARDMAN, Christopher Miles, MBE 1993; professional cyclist, retired 2000; Director, Beyond Level Four Ltd, NWV Racing Team (GB); *b* 26 Aug. 1968; *s* of Keith and Carole Boardman; *m* 1988, Sally-Ann Edwards; four *s* two *d.* Gold Medal, Individual Pursuit, Olympic Games, Barcelona, 1992; World Champion: Pursuit, 1994; Time Trial, 1994; Yellow Jersey Holder, Tour de France, 1994, 1997, 1998; Silver Medal, Time Trial, World Championship, 1996; Bronze Medal, Time Trial, Olympic Games, Atlanta, 1996; World Champion, 4,000 Pursuit, 1996; World One Hour Record Holder: 52.270 km, 1993; 56.375 km, 1996; (under new regulations) 49.441 km, 2000. Mem., Sports Council for England, 1995–96, English Sports Council, 1996. Hon. DSc Brighton, 1997; Hon. MSc Liverpool, 1995. Man of Year Award, Cheshire Life mag., 1997. *Publication:* (with Andrew Longmore) The Complete Book of Cycling, 2000. *Address:* Beyond Level Four Ltd, Wirral Point, Hoylake, Wirral CH47 1HN.

BOARDMAN, Faith Rosemary; Chief Executive, London Borough of Lambeth, 2000–05; *b* 21 Aug. 1950; *d* of Kenneth Mills and Vera Mills (*née* Waterson); *m* 1974, David Boardman; one *s* one *d. Educ:* Lady Margaret Hall, Oxford (MA Modern Hist.). Fast-stream grad. trainee, 1972–77, Grade 7, VAT Policy, 1977–79, HM Customs and Excise; Fiscal Policy, HM Treasury, 1979–83; HM Customs and Excise: Tobacco Taxation, 1983–86; Personnel Policy, 1986–89, Grade 5, 1988; Chief Exec. (Collector), London Central, 1989–95; Chief Exec. (Grade 3), Contributions Agency, DSS, 1995–97; Grade 2, 1997; Chief Exec., CSA, 1997–2000. Mem., Metropolitan Police Authy, 2007–. Financial Services Woman of Year Award, 1990. *Recreations:* family, friends, music, hill-walking.

BOARDMAN, Sir John, Kt 1989; FSA 1957; FBA 1969; Lincoln Professor of Classical Archaeology and Art, and Fellow of Lincoln College, University of Oxford, 1978–94 (Hon. Fellow, 1995); *b* 20 Aug. 1927; *s* of Frederick Archibald Boardman; *m* 1952, Sheila Joan Lyndon Stanford (*d* 2005); one *s* one *d. Educ:* Chigwell Sch.; Magdalene Coll., Cambridge (BA 1948, MA 1951, Walston Student, 1948–50; Hon. Fellow 1984). 2nd Lt, Intell. Corps, 1950–52. Asst Dir, British Sch. at Athens, 1952–55; Asst Keeper, Ashmolean Museum, Oxford, 1955–59; Reader in Classical Archaeology, Univ. of Oxford, 1959–78; Fellow of Merton Coll., Oxford, 1963–78, Hon. Fellow, 1978. Geddes-Harrower Prof., Aberdeen Univ., 1974; Vis. Prof., Australian Inst. of Archaeology, 1987; Prof. of Ancient History, Royal Acad., 1989–; Lectures: Andrew W. Mellon, Washington, 1993; Myres Meml, Oxford, 1993. Editor: Journal of Hellenic Studies, 1958–65; Lexicon Iconographicum, 1972–99; Cambridge Ancient History, 1978–94. Conducted excavations on Chios, 1953–55, and at Tocra in Libya, 1964–65. Delegate, OUP, 1979–89. Pres. Fédn Internat. des Assocs d'Etudes Classiques, 1994–97. Corresponding Fellow: Bavarian Acad. of Scis, 1969; Athens Acad., 1997; Fellow, Inst. of Etruscan Studies, Florence, 1983; Hon. Fellow, Archaeol Soc. of Athens, 1989 (Vice Pres., 1998–); Member: Amer. Philosophical Soc., 1999; Accad. dei Lincei, Rome, 1999; Foreign Member: Royal Danish Acad., 1979; Russian Acad. of Scis, 2003; Mem. associé, Acad. des Inscriptions et Belles Lettres, Institut de France, 1991 (Correspondant, 1985); Hon. Mem., Archaeol Inst. of America, 1993. Hon. MRIA, 1986. Hon. Dr: Dept of Archaeology and History, Univ. of Athens, 1991; Sorbonne, 1994. Cromer Greek Prize, 1959, Kenyon Medal, 1995, British Acad. *Publications:* Cretan Collection in Oxford, 1961; Date of the Knossos Tablets, 1963; Island Gems, 1963; Greeks Overseas, 1964, rev. edn 1999; Greek Art, 1964, rev. edns 1973, 1984, 1996; Excavations at Tocra, vol. I 1966, vol. II 1973; Pre-Classical, 1967, repr. 1978; Greek Emporio, 1967; Engraved Gems, 1968; Archaic Greek Gems, 1968; Greek Gems and Finger Rings, 1970, repr. 2001; (with D. Kurtz) Greek Burial Customs, 1971; Athenian Black Figure Vases, 1974; Athenian Red Figure Vases, Archaic Period, 1975; Intaglios and Rings, 1975; Corpus Vasorum, Oxford, vol. 3, 1975; Greek Sculpture, Archaic Period, 1978; (with M. Robertson) Corpus Vasorum, Castle Ashby, 1978; (with M. L. Vollenweider) Catalogue of Engraved Gems, Ashmolean Museum, 1978; (with D. Scarisbrick) Harari Collection of Finger Rings, 1978; (with E. La Rocca) Eros in Greece, 1978; Escarabeos de Piedra de Ibiza, 1984; La Ceramica Antica, 1984; Greek Sculpture, Classical Period, 1985; (with D. Finn) The Parthenon and its Sculptures, 1985; (jtly) The Oxford History of the Classical World, 1986; Athenian Red Figure Vases, Classical Period, 1989; (jtly) The Oxford History of Classical Art, 1993; The Diffusion of Classical Art in Antiquity, 1994 (Runciman Prize, 1995); Greek Sculpture, Later Classical, 1995; Early Greek Vase Painting, 1998; Persia and the West, 2000; Greek Vases, 2001; Archaeology of Nostalgia, 2002 (Runciman Prize, 2003); Classical Phoenician Scarabs, 2003; A Collection of Classical and Eastern Intaglios, 2003; The World of Ancient Art, 2006; articles in jls. *Address:* 11 Park Street, Woodstock, Oxford OX20 1SJ. *T:* (01993) 811259. *Club:* Athenæum.

BOARDMAN, Hon. Nigel Patrick Gray; Partner, Slaughter and May, since 1982; *b* Northampton, 19 Oct. 1950; *s* of Baron Boardman, MC, TD; one *s* five *d. Educ:* Ampleforth Coll.; Bristol Univ. (BA Hons). Joined Slaughter and May, 1973. *Recreations:* my children, grandchild, dog, watching sport and digging up golf courses. *Address:* Slaughter and May, 1 Bunhill Row, EC1Y 8YY. *T:* (020) 7090 3418, *Fax:* (020) 7090 5000; *e-mail:* nigel.boardman@slaughterandmay.com.

BOARDMAN, Norman Keith, AO 1993; PhD, ScD; FRS 1978; FAA; FTSE; Chief Executive, Commonwealth Scientific and Industrial Research Organization, 1986–90 (post-retirement Fellow, 1990–99); *b* 16 Aug. 1926; *s* of William Robert Boardman and Margaret Boardman; *m* 1952, Mary Clayton Shepherd; two *s* five *d. Educ:* Melbourne

Univ. (BSc 1946, MSc 1949); St John's Coll., Cambridge (PhD 1954, ScD 1974). FAA 1972; FTSE (FTS 1986). ICI Fellow, Cambridge, 1953–55; Fulbright Scholar, Univ. of Calif, LA, 1964–66. Res. Officer, Wool Res. Section, CSIRO, 1949–51; CSIRO Div. of Plant Industry: Sen. Res. Scientist, 1956; Principal Res. Scientist, 1961; Sen. Prin. Res. Scientist, 1966; Chief Res. Scientist, 1968; Mem. Exec., 1977–85, Chm. and Chief Exec., 1985–86, CSIRO. Member: Aust. Res. Grants Cttee, 1971–75; Council, ANU, 1979–89 and 1990–91; Bd, Aust. Centre for Internat. Agricl Research, 1982–88; Nat. Water Research Council, 1982–85; Prime Minister's Science Council, 1989–90. Director: Sirotech Ltd, 1986–90; Landcare Aust. Ltd, 1990–98. Pres., Aust. Biochem. Soc., 1976–78; Sec. of Sci. Policy, Aust. Acad. of Sci., 1993–97 (Treas., 1978–81). Corresp. Mem., Amer. Soc. of Plant Physiologists; Foreign Mem., Korean Acad. of Sci. and Technology. Hon. DSc Newcastle, NSW, 1988. David Syme Res. Prize, Melbourne Univ., 1967; Lemberg Medal, Aust. Biochem. Soc., 1969. *Publications:* scientific papers on plant biochemistry, partic. photosynthesis and structure, function and biogenesis of chloroplasts; papers on science and technology policy. *Recreations:* reading, tennis, listening to music. *Address:* 6 Somers Crescent, Forrest, ACT 2603, Australia. *T:* (2) 62951746. *Club:* Commonwealth (Canberra).

BOAS, John Robert Sotheby, (Bob); Chairman, Federation of British Artists (Mall Galleries), 2001–07; *b* 28 Feb. 1937; *s* of Edgar Henry Boas and Mary Katherine Boas; *m* 1965, Elisabeth Gersted; one *s* one *d* (and one *s* decd). *Educ:* Corpus Christi Coll., Cambridge (BA Maths (Sen. Optimes)). FCA 1964. Price Waterhouse, 1960–65; ICI, 1965–66; S. G. Warburg, 1966–95; Dir, 1971–95; Vice Chm., 1990–95; Man. Dir, SBC Warburg, 1995–97. Non-executive Director: Chesterfield Properties, 1978–99; ENO, 1990–99; Norwich Union, 1998–2000; Invesco Continental Smaller Cos Trust, 1998–2004; Trident Safeguards Ltd, 1998–2003; Land Command Mgt Bd, 1998–2001; Prospect Publishing Co. Ltd, 2000–; Telecom Italia, 2004–07. Dir, SFA, 1988–96. Trustee: Nat. Heritage Meml Fund and Heritage Lottery Fund, 1998–2002; Guildhall Sch. Trust, 2000–; Paul Hamlyn Foundn, 2002–; Architectural Heritage Fund, 2003–; London String Quartet Foundn, 2006–. *Recreations:* music, art, theatre, reading, travelling. *Address:* 22 Mansfield Street, W1G 9NR. *Club:* Arts.

BOASE, Martin; Chairman, Omnicom UK plc, 1989–95; *b* 14 July 1932; *s* of Prof. Alan Martin Boase and Elizabeth Grizelle Boase; *m* 1st, 1960, Terry Ann Moir (marr. diss. 1971); one *s* one *d*; 2nd, 1974, Pauline Valerie Brownrigg; one *s* one *d*. *Educ:* Bedales Sch.; Rendcomb Coll.; New Coll., Oxford. MA; FIPA 1976. Executive, The London Press Exchange, Ltd, 1958–60; Pritchard Wood and Partners, Ltd: Manager, 1961–65; Dir, then Dep. Man. Dir, 1965–68; Founding Partner, The Boase Massimi Pollitt Partnership, Ltd, 1968; Chm., Boase Massimi Pollitt plc, 1977–89 (Jt Chm., 1977–79). Chairman: Maiden Outdoor, 1993–2006; Kiss 100 FM, 1993–2000; Herald Investment Trust, 1994–; Investment Trust of Investment Trusts, 1995–2005; Heal's, 1997–2000; Global Professional Media plc, 1999–2005; Jupiter Dividend & Growth Investment Trust, 1999–; Director: Omnicom Gp Inc., 1989–93; EMAP plc, 1991–2000; Matthew Clark plc, 1995–98; New Star Investment Trust, 2000–06. Chairman: Advertising Assoc., 1987–92; British Television Advertising Awards Ltd, 1993–2000. Dir, Oxford Playhouse Trust, 1991–97. *Recreation:* the Turf. *Address:* (office) 12 Bishop's Bridge Road, W2 6AA.

BOATENG, Rt Hon. Paul (Yaw); PC 1999; British High Commissioner in South Africa, since 2005; barrister-at-law; *b* 14 June 1951; *s* of Eleanor and Kwaku Boateng; *m* 1980, Janet Alleyne; two *s* three *d*. *Educ:* Ghana Internat. Sch.; Accra Acad.; Apsley Grammar Sch.; Bristol Univ. (LLB Hons); Coll. of Law. Admitted Solicitor, 1976; Solicitor, Paddington Law Centre, 1976–79; Solicitor and Partner, B. M. Birnberg and Co., 1979–87; called to the Bar, Gray's Inn, 1989. Legal Advr, Scrap Sus Campaign, 1977–81. Greater London Council: Mem. (Lab) for Walthamstow, 1981–86; Chm., Police Cttee, 1981–86; Vice-Chm., Ethnic Minorities Cttee, GLC, 1981–86. Chairman: Afro-Caribbean Educn Resource Project, 1978–86; Westminster CRC, 1979–81. Contested (Lab) Herts W, 1983. MP (Lab) Brent South, 1987–2005. Opposition frontbench spokesman: on treasury and economic affairs, 1989–92; on legal affairs, LCD, 1992–97; Parly Under-Sec. of State, DoH, 1997–98; Minister of State, 1998–2001, and Dep. Home Sec., 1999–2001, Home Office; Financial Sec., 2001–02, Chief Sec., 2002–05, HM Treasury. Mem., H of C Environment Cttee, 1987–89. Member: Home Sec.'s Adv. Council on Race Relations, 1981–86; WCC Commn on prog. to combat racism, 1984–91; Police Training Council, 1981–85; Exec., NCCL, 1980–86. Chm. Governors, Priory Park Sch., 1978–84; Governor, Police Staff Coll., Bramshill, 1981–84; Mem. Ct, Bristol Univ., 1994–. Mem. Bd, ENO, 1984–97. Broadcaster. Hon. LLD Bristol, 2007. *Publication:* (contrib.) Reclaiming the Ground, 1993. *Recreations:* opera, swimming. *Address:* British High Commission, 255 Hill Street, Arcadia, Pretoria, South Africa. *Clubs:* none.

BOBROW, Prof. Martin, CBE 1995; FRS 2004; FRCP, FRCPath, FMedSci; Professor of Medical Genetics, Cambridge University, 1995–2005, now Emeritus; *b* 6 Feb. 1938; *s* of Joe and Bessie Bobrow; *m* 1963, Lynda Geraldine Strauss; three *d*. *Educ:* Univ. of the Witwatersrand (BSc Hons 1958; MB BCh 1963; DSc Med 1979). MRCPath 1978, FRCPath 1990; FRCP 1986. Consultant in Clin. Genetics, Oxford, and Mem., MRC Ext. Sci. Staff, Genetics Lab., Oxford Univ., 1974–81; Prof. of Human Genetics, Univ. of Amsterdam, 1981–82; Prince Philip Prof. of Paediatric Res., UMDS of Guy's and St Thomas' Hosps, London Univ., 1982–95. Mem. Council, 1988–92, 1993–94, Chm., Molecular and Cellular Medicine Bd, 1992–95, MRC; Chairman: Cttee on Med. Aspects of Radiation in the Envt, 1985–92; Unrelated Live Donor Transplant Regulatory Authy, 1990–99; Nat. Council, Muscular Dystrophy Gp, 1995–; Member: Black Adv. Gp on Possible Increased Incidence of Cancer in West Cumbria, 1983–84; Cttee to examine the ethical implications of gene therapy, 1989–93; NHS Central R&D Cttee, DoH, 1991–97; Nuffield Council on Bioethics, 1996–2003; Human Genetics Adv. Commn, 1997–99. Non-exec. Dir, Cambridge Univ. NHS Foundn Trust, 2004–. Governor, Wellcome Trust, 1996–2007 (Dep. Chm., 2004–07). *Publications:* papers in sci. books and jls. *Address:* Department of Medical Genetics, Wellcome/MRC Building, Addenbrooke's Hospital, Cambridge CB2 2XY.

BODDINGTON, Caroline Elizabeth; Archbishops' Secretary for Appointments, since 2004; *b* 23 Feb. 1964; *d* of David Gamgee Boddington and Marianne Boddington; *m* 2006, Rt Rev. Dr Alastair Llewellyn John Redfern (*see* Bishop of Derby). *Educ:* Malvern Girls' Coll.; Keble Coll., Oxford (MA). MCIPD 1989. BG Gp plc, 1986–2003: Human Resources Manager, Learning and Develt, 1997–99; Business Analyst, Mediterranean Region, 2000; Head: Learning and Develt, 2000–01; Human Resources Ops, 2002–03. Mem., Adv. Council, Farnham Castle, 2004. *Recreations:* music, travel. *Address:* Cowley House, 9 Little College Street, SW1P 3SH. *T:* (020) 7898 1876, *Fax:* (020) 7898 1867; *e-mail:* caroline.boddington@c-of-e.org.uk.

BODDINGTON, Ewart Agnew; JP; DL; Chairman, The Boddington Group PLC (formerly Boddingtons' Breweries), 1970–88 (President, 1989–95); *b* 7 April 1927; *m* 1954, Vine Anne Clayton (*d* 1989); two *s* one *d*. *Educ:* Stowe Sch., Buckingham; Trinity Coll., Cambridge (MA). Jt Man. Dir, Boddingtons', 1957. Dir, Northern Bd, National Westminster Bank, 1977–92. Pres., Inst. of Brewing, 1972–74; Chm., Brewers' Soc., 1984–85; Mem., Brewers' Co., 1980–. JP Macclesfield, 1959; High Sheriff of Cheshire, 1978–79; DL Cheshire 1993. Chetham's School of Music: Feoffee, 1953– (Chm., 1969–92); Gov., 1953–99 (Chm., 1969–83). Trustee, NSPCC, 1993–2002. Hon. MA Manchester, 1977. *Recreations:* shooting, fishing, music. *Address:* Fanshawe Brook Barn, Henbury, Macclesfield, Cheshire SK11 9PP. *T:* (01260) 224387.

BODDY, Prof. Keith, CBE 1998 (OBE 1989); PhD, DSc; FRSE; Professor of Medical Physics, University of Newcastle upon Tyne, and Head of Regional Medical Physics Department, Northern Regional Health Authority, 1978–98; *b* 1 Nov. 1937; *s* of late Ernest Boddy and Edith Mary Boddy; *m* 1960, Sylvia Mary (*née* Goodier); two *s*. *Educ:* Liverpool Univ. (BSc 1959); St Bartholomew's Hosp. Med. Coll. (MSc 1961); Glasgow Univ. (PhD 1971); Strathclyde Univ. (DSc 1976). FRSE 1980; FInstP 1969; FIPEM (FIPSM 1988). Head of Health Physics, AEI Res. Lab., Aldermaston Court, 1959–63; Lectr, 1963–67, Sen. Lectr, 1967–78, and Head of Health Physics and Nuclear Medicine Unit, Scottish Univs Res. and Reactor Centre. Numerous eponymous lectures. Member: Radioactive Waste Mgt Adv. Cttee, 1989–2003; Cttee on Med. Aspects of Radiation in the Envmt, 1991–2000; Ionising Radiations Adv. Cttee, 1995–2001; Chm., Dounreay Particles Adv. Gp, SEPA, 2003–. President: Hosp. Physicists Assoc., 1986–88; Inst. of Physical Scis in Medicine, 1986–88; Internat. Orgn for Med. Physics, 1994–97; Internat. Union for Physical and Engrg Scis in Medicine, 1997–2000; Hon. Member: British Nuclear Medicine Soc., 1980; RCR, 1981; BIR, 1997; European Fedn of Med. Physics, 2002. Hon. FIPEM 1998; Hon. FSRP 1999. Hon. DSc De Montfort, 1997. Glazebrook Medal and Prize, Inst. of Physics, 1991; Hon. Distinction Medal, Univ. of Ioannina, Greece, 1997; Skinner Medal, RCR, 1999; Merit Award, Internat. Union for Phys. and Engrg Scis in Medicine, 2000. *Publications:* numerous papers, lectures, contribs to books; contribs to reports of nat. cttees. *Recreations:* walking, gardening, crosswords, logic puzzles, music, family activities, stray animals. *Address:* 2 Eppleton Hall, Colliery Lane, Hetton-le-Hole, Tyne and Wear DH5 0QZ. *T:* and *Fax:* (0191) 526 4315.

BODEN, Prof. Margaret Ann, OBE 2002; ScD, PhD; FBA 1983; Research Professor in Cognitive Science, University of Sussex, since 2002 (Professor of Philosophy and Psychology, 1980–2002); *b* 26 Nov. 1936; *d* of late Leonard Forbes Boden, OBE, LLB and Violet Dorothy Dawson; *m* 1967, John Raymond Spiers, *qv* (marr. diss. 1981); one *s* one *d*. *Educ:* City of London Sch. for Girls; Newnham Coll., Cambridge (Major schol. in Med. Scis; Sarah Smithson Scholar in Moral Scis; MA; Associate, 1981–93; ScD 1990); Harvard Grad. Sch. (Harkness Fellow; AM; PhD in Cognitive and Social Psychology). Asst Lectr, then Lectr, in Philosophy, Birmingham Univ., 1959–65; Sussex University: Lectr, 1965–72; Reader, 1972–80; Founding Dean, Sch. of Cognitive Sciences, later Cognitive and Computing Sciences, 1987. Vis. Scientist, Yale Univ., 1979. Co-founder, Dir, 1968–85, Sec., 1968–79, Harvester Press. Founding Chm., Hist. and Philosophy of Psychology Sect., BPsS, 1983; Pres., Sect. X, BAAS, 1993; Vice-Pres., and Chm. of Council, Royal Instn of GB, 1993–95 (Mem. Council, 1992–95). Member: Council for Science and Society, 1986–91 (Trustee, 1990–91); ABRC, 1989–90 (Chm., Working Gp on Peer-Review, 1989–90); Animal Procedures Cttee, Home Office, 1994–98; Council, Royal Inst. of Philosophy, 1987–; Council, British Acad., 1988–91 (Vice-Pres., 1989–91). Mem., Bd of Curators, Sch. of Advanced Study, Univ. of London, 1995–99. Mem., Soc. of Authors, 1982–98. Trustee, Eric Gill Trust, 1993–. Mem., Academia Europaea, 1993; Fellow, Amer. Assoc. for Artificial Intelligence, 1993; Life Fellow, Assoc. for Study of Artificial Intelligence and Simulation of Behaviour, 1997; Fellow, European Co-ord. Cttee for Artificial Intelligence, 1999. FRSA 1992. Hon. DSc: Sussex, 2001; Bristol, 2002; Open, 2004. Leslie McMichael Premium, IERE, 1977. *Publications:* Purposive Explanation in Psychology, 1972; Artificial Intelligence and Natural Man, 1977; Piaget, 1979; Minds and Mechanisms, 1981; Computer Models of Mind, 1988; Artificial Intelligence in Psychology, 1989; (ed) The Philosophy of Artificial Intelligence, 1990; The Creative Mind: myths and mechanisms, 1990, 2nd edn 2004; (ed) Dimensions of Creativity, 1994; (ed) The Philosophy of Artificial Life, 1996; (ed) Artificial Intelligence, 1996; Mind as Machine, 2006; General Editor: Explorations in Cognitive Science; Harvester Studies in Cognitive Science; Harvester Studies in Philosophy; contribs to philosophical and psychological jls. *Recreations:* dress-making, dreaming about the South Pacific. *Address:* Centre for Cognitive Science, University of Sussex, Brighton BN1 9QH. *T:* (01273) 678386. *Club:* Reform.

BODEY, Hon. Sir David (Roderick Lessiter), Kt 1999; **Hon. Mr Justice Bodey;** a Judge of the High Court of Justice, Family Division, since 1999; *b* 14 Oct. 1947; *s* of late Reginald Augustus Bodey, FIA and Betty Francis Bodey; *m* 1976, Ruth (*née* MacAdorey); one *s* one *d*. *Educ:* King's Sch., Canterbury; Univ. of Bristol (LLB Hons 1969). Called to the Bar, Middle Temple, 1970 (Harmsworth Scholar, 1970), Bencher, 1998; QC 1991; an Asst Recorder, 1989; a Recorder, 1993–98; a Dep. High Court Judge, 1994–98; Family Div. Liaison Judge for London, 1999–2001, for N Eastern Circuit, 2001–07. Mem., Family Justice Council, 2008–. Legal Assessor, 1983–94, Sen. Legal Assessor, 1994–98, UKCC. Mem., Supreme Court Procedure Cttee, 1995–97. Chm., Family Law Bar Assoc., 1997–98 (Sec., 1995–97); Mem., Family Cttee, Justice, 1995–98. Fellow, Internat. Acad. of Matrimonial Lawyers, 1995. *Recreations:* music, sometime marathon running, attempting to keep on road Triumph TR3. *Address:* Royal Courts of Justice, Strand, WC2A 2LL. *Club:* Lansdowne.

BODGER; *see* Steele-Bodger.

BODINETZ, Gemma, (Mrs R. Reddrop); Artistic Director, Liverpool Everyman and Playhouse Theatres, since 2003; *b* 4 Oct. 1966; *d* of Shirley McCarthy and Tony Bodinetz and adopted *d* of Terry Brown; *m* 1995, Richard Reddrop; one *s*. *Educ:* Trinity Coll., Dublin (BA Hons). Assistant Director: Royal Court Th., 1991–92; NT, 1992–93; freelance director, 1993–: major productions include: Chimps, Hampstead Th., 1997; Caravan, Bush Th., 1997; Guiding Star, Liverpool, transf. NT, 1998; Hamlet, Bristol Old Vic; Yard Girl, Royal Court; Shopping and Fucking, NYT Workshop; Luminosity, RSC, 2001; at Liverpool Everyman and Playhouse: Mayor of Zalamea, The Kindness of Strangers, 2004; Ma Rainey's Black Bottom; Yellowman, 2004; Who's Afraid of Virginia Woolf?, 2005; The Lady of Leisure, 2006; also at W Yorks Playhouse, Plymouth Th. Royal, and other theatres. Merseyside Woman of the Year, 2004. *Recreations:* lover of pop music, West Ham United, reading in bed, good coffee, running, people watching. *Address:* 40 Alderley Road, Hoylake, Wirral CH47 2BA. *T:* (0151) 632 4990; *e-mail:* g.bodinetz@everymanplayhouse.com.

BODINHAM, Susan; *see* Sowden, S.

BODMER, Sir Walter (Fred), Kt 1986; FRCPath; FRS 1974; FIBiol; Principal, Hertford College, Oxford, 1996–2005; *b* 10 Jan. 1936; *s* of late Dr Ernest Julius and Sylvia Emily Bodmer; *m* 1956, Julia Gwynaeth Pilkington, FMedSci (*d* 2001); two *s* one *d*. *Educ:* Manchester Grammar Sch.; Clare Coll., Cambridge (BA 1956; MA, PhD 1959). FRCPath 1984; FIBiol 1990. Research Fellow 1958–61, Official Fellow 1961, Hon. Fellow 1989, Clare Coll., Cambridge; Demonstrator in Genetics, Univ. of Cambridge, 1960–61; Asst Prof. 1962–66, Associate Prof. 1966–68, Prof. 1968–70, Dept of Genetics,

Stanford Univ.; Prof. of Genetics, Univ. of Oxford, 1970–79; Dir of Res., 1979–91, Dir Gen., 1991–96, ICRF. Non-exec. Dir, Fisons plc, 1990–96. Chm., BBC Sci. Consultative Gp, 1981–87; Member: BBC Gen. Adv. Council, 1981–91 (Chm., 1987); Council, Internat. Union Against Cancer, 1982–90; Adv. Bd for Res. Councils, 1983–88; Council, Found for Sci. and Technol., 1995–; Chairman: COPUS, 1990–93; Orgn of European Cancer Insts, 1990–93; NRPB, 1998–2003; Med. and Scientific Adv. Panel, Leukaemia Res. Fund, 2003–; President: Royal Statistical Soc., 1984–85 (Vice-Pres., 1983–84; Hon. Fellow, 1997); BAAS, 1987–88 (Vice-Pres., 1989–2001; Chm., Council, 1996–2001; Hon. Fellow, 2001); ASE, 1989–90; Human Genome Orgn, 1990–92; British Soc. for Histocompatibility and Immunogenetics, 1990–91 (Hon. Mem. 1992); EACR, 1994–96; British Assoc. for Cancer Res., 1998–2002; first Pres., Internat. Fedn of Assocs for Advancement of Sci. and Technol., 1992–94; Vice-President: Royal Instn, 1981–82; Parly and Scientific Cttee, 1990–93; Hon. Vice-Pres., Res. Defence Soc., 1990–. Trustee: BM (Natural History), 1983–93 (Chm., Bd of Trustees, 1989–93); Sir John Soane's Mus., 1982–2003; Foulkes Foundn, 2002–; Porter Foundn, 2006–. Chancellor, Salford Univ., 1995–2005. Chm. Bd of Dirs, Laban Centre, 1998–2005; Mem. Bd, Trinity Laban, 2005–08; Mem. Bd of Patrons, St Mark's Hosp. and Academic Inst., 1996. Founder FMedSci 1998. Hon. MRIA 1998; Hon. Member: British Soc. of Gastroenterology, 1989; Amer. Assoc. of Immunologists, 1985; St Mark's Assoc., 1995; British Transplantation Soc., 2002; For. Associate, US Nat. Acad. of Scis, 1981; For. Mem., Amer. Philosophical Soc., 1989; For. Hon. Mem., Amer. Acad. Arts and Scis, 1972; Fellow, Internat. Inst. of Biotechnology, 1989; Hon. Fellow: Keble Coll., Oxford, 1982; Green Coll., Oxford, 1993; Hon. FRCP 1985; Hon. FRCS 1986; Hon. FRSE 1992; Hon. FRSocMed 1994. Hon. DSc: Bath, Oxford, 1988; Hull, Edinburgh, 1990; Bristol, 1991; Loughborough, 1993; Lancaster, Aberdeen, 1994; Plymouth, 1995; London, Salford, 1996; UMIST, 1997; Witwatersrand, 1998; DUniv Surrey, 1990; Laurea *hc* in Medicine and Surgery, Univ. of Bologna, 1987; Dr *hc*: Leuven, 1992; Masaryk, 1994; Haifa, 1998; Hon. MD Birmingham, 1992; Hon. LLD Dundee, 1993. William Allan Meml Award, Amer. Soc. Human Genetics, 1980; Conway Evans Prize, RCP/Royal Soc., 1982; Rabbi Shai Shacknai Meml Prize Lectr, 1983; John Alexander Meml Prize and Lectureship, Univ. of Pennsylvania Med. Sch., 1984; Rose Payne Dist. Scientists Lectureship, Amer. Soc. for Histocompatibility and Immunogenetics, 1985; Bernal Lectr, Royal Soc., 1986; Neil Hamilton-Fairley Medal, RCP, 1990; Faraday Award, Royal Soc., 1994; Romanes Lectr, Univ. of Oxford, 1995; Harveian Orator, RCP, 1996; Dalton Medal, Manchester Lit. and Philos. Soc., 2002; D. K. Ludwig Award, 2002; Seroussi Foundn Res. Award, 2003. *Publications:* The Genetics of Human Populations (with L. L. Cavalli-Sforza), 1971; (with A. Jones) Our Future Inheritance: choice or chance?, 1974; (with L. L. Cavalli-Sforza) Genetics, Evolution and Man, 1976; (with Robin McKie) The Book of Man, 1994; research papers in genetical, statistical and mathematical jls, etc. *Recreations:* playing the piano, riding, swimming, scuba diving. *Address:* Cancer and Immunogenetics Laboratory, Weatherall Institute of Molecular Medicine, John Radcliffe Hospital, Oxford OX3 9DS. *T:* (01865) 222356. *Clubs:* Athenæum, Oxford and Cambridge.

BODMIN, Archdeacon of; *see* Cohen, Ven. C. R. F.

BODY, Sir Richard (Bernard Frank Stewart), Kt 1986; *b* 18 May 1927; *s* of Lieut-Col Bernard Richard Body, formerly of Hyde End, Shinfield, Berks; *m* 1959, Marion, *d* of late Major H. Graham, OBE; one *s* one *d*. *Educ:* Reading Sch.; Inns of Court Sch. of Law. RAF (India Comd), 1945–48. Called to the Bar, Middle Temple, 1949; Chm., E London Poor Man's Lawyer Assoc., 1952–59. Contested (C) Rotherham, 1950; Abertillery bye-election, 1950; Leek, 1951; MP (C): Billericay Div., Essex, 1955–Sept. 1959: Holland with Boston, 1966–97, Boston and Skegness, 1997–2001. Member: Jt Select Cttee on Consolidation of Law, 1975–91; Commons Select Cttee on Agric., 1979–87 (Chm., 1986–87). Jt Chm., Council, Get Britain Out referendum campaign, 1975. Chm. Trustees, Centre for European Studies, 1991–2003; Trustee, Leopold Kohr Inst., 2004–. President: William Cobbett Soc., 1996–; Ruskin Soc., 2002– (Chm., 1997–2002). Chm., Internat. Assoc. of Masters of Bloodhounds, 1997–2003. Director: New European Publications Ltd, 1986–; Salisbury Review Ltd, 2002–. Editor, World Review, 1996–. *Publications:* The Architect and the Law, 1954; (contrib.) Destiny or Delusion, 1971; (ed jtly) Freedom and Stability in the World Economy, 1976; Agriculture: The Triumph and the Shame, 1982; Farming in the Clouds, 1984; Red or Green for Farmers, 1987; Europe of Many Circles, 1990; Our Food, Our Land, 1991; The Breakdown of Europe, 1998; England for the English, 2001; A Democratic Europe: the alternative to the European Union, 2006. *Recreation:* trying to catch trout. *Address:* Jewell's Farm, Stanford Dingley, near Reading, Berks RG7 6LX. *T:* (0118) 9744295. *Clubs:* Athenæum, Carlton, Pratt's.

BOE, Norman Wallace; Deputy Solicitor to Secretary of State for Scotland, 1987–96; *b* 30 Aug. 1943; *s* of late Alexander Thomson Boe and Margaret Wallace Revans; *m* 1968, Margaret Irene McKenzie; one *s* one *d*. *Educ:* George Heriot's Sch., Edinburgh; Edinburgh Univ. LLB Hons 1965. Admitted Solicitor, 1967. Legal apprentice, Lindsays, WS, 1965–67; Legal Asst, Menzies & White, WS, 1967–70; Office of Solicitor to Sec. of State for Scotland, 1970–96. Volunteer with Volunteer Stroke Service, Chest, Heart and Stroke, Scotland, 1996–. *Recreations:* golf, gardening, travelling.

BOEGNER, Jean-Marc; Grand Officier, Légion d'Honneur; Commandeur, Ordre National du Mérite; Ambassadeur de France, 1973; *b* 3 July 1913; *s* of Marc and Jeanne Boegner; *m* 1945, Odilie de Moustier; three *d*. *Educ:* Lycée Janson-de-Sailly; Ecole Libre des Sciences Politiques; Paris University (LèsL); Concours des Affaires Etrangères. Joined French diplomatic service, 1939; Attaché: Berlin, 1939; Ankara, 1940; Beirut, 1941; Counsellor: Stockholm, 1945; The Hague, 1947; Ministry of Foreign Affairs, Paris, 1952–58; Counsellor to Charles de Gaulle, 1958–59; Ambassador to Tunisia, 1959–60; Permanent Representative of France: to EEC, 1961–72; to OECD, 1975–78. *Publication:* Le Marché commun de Six à Neuf, 1974.

BOEL, (Else) Mariann Fischer; *see* Fischer Boel.

BOEVEY, Sir Thomas (Michael Blake) C.; *see* Crawley-Boevey.

BOGDANOR, Prof. Vernon Bernard, CBE 1998; FBA 1997; Professor of Government, Oxford University, since 1996, and Fellow, Brasenose College, Oxford, since 1966; *b* 16 July 1943; *s* of Harry Bogdanor and Rosa (*née* Weinger); *m* 1972, Judith Evelyn Beckett (marr. diss. 2000); two *s*. *Educ:* Bishopshalt Sch.; The Queen's College, Oxford (BA 1st Cl. PPE 1964; MA 1968). Brasenose College, Oxford: Sen. Tutor, 1979–85, 1996–97; Vice-Principal, 2001–02; Reader in Government, Oxford Univ., 1990–96. Gresham Prof. of Law, 2004–07. Special Advr, H of L Select Cttee on European Communities, 1982–83; Advr on Constitutional and Electoral Matters to Czechoslovak, Hungarian, and Israeli Govts, 1988–; Special Advr, H of C Public Service Cttee, 1996; Mem., UK Delegn to CSCE Conf., Oslo, 1991. Mem. Council, Hansard Soc. for Parly Govt, 1981–97. Hon. Fellow, Soc. for Advanced Legal Studies, 1997. FRSA 1992. Sir Isaiah Berlin Prize for Lifetime Contribn to Pol Studies, Pol Studies Assoc., 2008. *Publications:* (ed) Disraeli: Lothair, 1975; Devolution, 1979; The People and the Party System, 1981; Multi-Party Politics and the Constitution, 1983; (ed) Democracy and Elections, 1983; (ed) Coalition Government in Western Europe, 1983; What is Proportional Representation?, 1984; (ed) Parties and Democracy in Britain and America, 1984; (ed) Constitutions in Democratic Politics, 1988; (ed) The Blackwell Encyclopaedia of Political Science, 1992; (jtly) Comparing Constitutions, 1995; The Monarchy and the Constitution, 1995; Politics and the Constitution: essays on British Government, 1996; Power and the People: a guide to constitutional reform, 1997; Devolution in the United Kingdom, 1999; (ed) The British Constitution in the 20th century, 2003; (ed) Joined-up Government, 2005; contribs to learned jls. *Recreations:* music, walking, talking. *Address:* Brasenose College, Oxford OX1 4AJ. *T:* (01865) 277830.

BOGDANOV, Michael; Founder and Artistic Director, Wales Theatre Company, since 2003; *b* 15 Dec. 1938; *s* of Francis Benzion Bogdin and Rhoda Rees Bogdin; *m* 1st, 1966, Patsy Ann Warwick (marr. diss. 2000); two *s* one *d*; 2nd, 2000, Ulrike Engelbrecht; one *s* one *d*. *Educ:* Lower School of John Lyon, Harrow; Univ. of Dublin Trinity Coll. (MA); Univs of the Sorbonne, and Munich. Writer, with Terence Brady, ATV series, Broad and Narrow, 1965; Producer/Director with Telefis Eireann, 1966–68; opening production of Theatre Upstairs, Royal Court, A Comedy of the Changing Years, 1969; The Bourgeois Gentilhomme, Oxford Playhouse, 1969; Asst Dir, Royal Shakespeare Theatre Co., 1970–71; Associate Dir, Peter Brook's A Midsummer Night's Dream, Stratford 1970, New York 1971, World Tour 1972; Dir, Two Gentlemen of Verona, São Paulo, Brazil, 1971; Associate to Jean Louis Barrault, Rabelais, 1971; Associate Director: Tyneside Th. Co., 1971–73; Haymarket Th., Leicester; Director: Phoenix Th., Leicester, 1973–77; Young Vic Th., London, 1978–80; an Associate Dir, Nat. Theatre, 1980–88; Artistic Dir, English Shakespeare Co., 1986–98; Intendant (Chief Exec.), Deutsches Schauspielhaus, Hamburg, 1989–92. National Theatre productions: Sir Gawain and the Green Knight, The Hunchback of Notre Dame, 1977–78; The Romans in Britain, Hiawatha, 1980; One Woman Plays, The Mayor of Zalamea, The Hypochondriac, 1981; Uncle Vanya, The Spanish Tragedy, 1982; Lorenzaccio, 1983; You Can't Take it With You, 1983; Strider, 1984; Royal Shakespeare Co. productions: The Taming of the Shrew, 1978 (SWET Dir of the Year award, 1979); Shadow of a Gunman, 1980; The Knight of the Burning Pestle, 1981; The Venetian Twins, 1993; The Hostage, 1994; Faust Parts I and II, 1995; English Shakespeare Co. productions: Henry IV (Parts I and II), Henry V, UK tour, European tour, Old Vic, and Canada, 1986–87; The Wars of the Roses (7 play history cycle), UK, Europe and world tour, 1987–89 (Laurence Olivier Award, Dir of the Year, 1989); Coriolanus, The Winter's Tale, UK and world tour, 1990–91; Macbeth, UK tour, 1992; The Tempest, 1992; Beowulf, 1997; As You Like It, 1998; Antony and Cleopatra, 1998; Wales Theatre Co. productions: Under Milk Wood, 2003; Twelfth Night, Cymbeline, The Merchant of Venice, 2004; Amazing Grace The Musical, Hamlet (Welsh/English), 2005; Contender, The Musical, 2007; The Servant of Two Masters, 2007; also directed: The Seagull, Toho Th. Co., Tokyo, 1980; Hamlet, Dublin, 1983; Romeo and Juliet, Tokyo, 1983, RSC, 1986, Lyric, Hammersmith, 1993; The Mayor of Zalamea, Washington, 1984; Measure for Measure, Stratford, Ont, 1985; Mutiny (musical), 1985; Donnerstag aus Licht, Royal Opera House, 1985; Julius Caesar, 1986 (also filmed by ZDF TV), Reineke Fuchs, 1987, Hamlet, 1989, Schauspielhaus, Hamburg; The Canterbury Tales, Prince of Wales, 1987; Montag, Stockhausen Opera, La Scala, Milan, 1988 (world première); Hair, Old Vic, 1993; Peer Gynt, Munich, 1995; Timon of Athens, Chicago, 1997; Troilus and Cressida, Olympic Arts Fest., Sydney Opera House, 2000; Lone Star Love, NY, 2001; The Winter's Tale, Chicago, 2003; The Servant of Two Masters, Hamburg, 2004; The Dresser, Hamburg, 2005; Waiting for Godot, Hamburg, 2007; UK Holocaust Meml Day Event, Wales Millennium Centre, 2006; Abolition of Slave Trade Bicentennial Event, St David's Hall, Cardiff, 2007; Ludlow Festival: Merry Wives of Windsor, 2002; The Winter's Tale, The Merchant of Venice, 2003; Twelfth Night, Cymbeline, 2004. *Television:* deviser and presenter, Shakespeare Lives, series, 1983; director: Shakespeare on the Estate (documentary), Bard on the Box series, 1995 (BAFTA, RTS, and Banff Film Fest. Awards); films: The Tempest in Butetown, 1996; Macbeth, 1997; Light in the Valley, 1998 (RTS Award); Light on the Hill, 1999; A Light in the City, 2001; The Welsh in Shakespeare, 2003. Co-author, plays, adaptations and children's theatre pieces. Hon. Prof., Univ. of Wales, 1993; Sen. Fellow, De Montfort Univ., 1992; Fellow, Sunderland Univ., 1997; Hon. FRWCMD (Hon. FWCMD 1994); Hon. Fellow in Drama, TCD, 1997; Hon. DLitt TCD, 2005. *Publications:* (jtly) The English Shakespeare Company, 1990; Shakespeare The Director's Cut, vol. 1, 2003, vol. 2, 2004. *Recreations:* cricket, wine, music. *Address:* Wales Theatre Company, 21 Dogo Street, Cardiff CF11 9JJ; *e-mail:* michael@walestheatrecompany.com.

BOGDANOVICH, Peter; American film director, writer, producer, actor; *b* Kingston, NY, 30 July 1939; *s* of Borislav Bogdanovich and Herma (*née* Robinson); *m* 1962, Polly Platt (marr. diss. 1970); two *d*; *m* 1988, L. B. Straten. Owner: Crescent Moon Productions, Inc., LA, 1986; Holly Moon Co. Inc., LA, 1992. Member: Dirs Guild of America; Writers' Guild of America; Acad. of Motion Picture Arts and Sciences. *Theatre:* Actor, Amer. Shakespeare Fest., Stratford, Conn, 1956, NY Shakespeare Fest., 1958; Dir and producer, off-Broadway: The Big Knife, 1959; Camino Real, Ten Little Indians, Rocket to the Moon, 1961; Once in a Lifetime, 1964. *Films include:* The Wild Angels (2nd-Unit Dir, co-writer, actor), 1966; Targets (dir, co-writer, prod., actor), 1968; The Last Picture Show (dir, co-writer), 1971 (NY Film Critics' Award for Best Screenplay, British Acad. Award for Best Screenplay); Directed by John Ford (dir, writer, interviewer), 1971; What's Up, Doc? (dir, co-writer, prod.), 1972 (Writers' Guild of America Award for Best Screenplay); Paper Moon (dir, prod.), 1973 (Silver Shell Award, Spain); Daisy Miller (dir, prod.), 1974 (Brussels Festival Award for Best Director); At Long Last Love (dir, writer, prod.), 1975; Nickelodeon (dir, co-writer), 1976; Saint Jack (dir, co-writer, actor), 1979 (Pasinetti Award, Critics' Prize, Venice Festival); They All Laughed (dir, writer), 1981; Mask (dir), 1985; Illegally Yours (dir, prod.), 1988; Texasville (dir, prod., writer), 1990; Noises Off (dir, exec. prod.), 1992; The Thing Called Love (dir), 1993; The Cat's Meow (dir), 2004. *Television:* The Great Professional: Howard Hawks, BBC, 1967; CBS This Morning (weekly commentary), 1987–89; Prowler, CBS, 1995; Blessed Assurance, To Sir With Love II, CBS-MOW, 1996. *Publications:* The Cinema of Orson Welles, 1961; The Cinema of Howard Hawks, 1962; The Cinema of Alfred Hitchcock, 1963; John Ford, 1968; Fritz Lang in America, 1969; Allan Dwan: the last pioneer, 1971; Pieces of Time: Peter Bogdanovich on the Movies 1961–85, 1973, enlarged 1985; The Killing of the Unicorn: Dorothy Stratten, 1960–1980, a Memoir, 1984; (ed with introd.) A Year and a Day Engagement Calendar, annually, 1991–; This is Orson Welles, 1992; Who The Devil Made It, 1997; Who the Hell's in It?, 2004; features on films in Esquire, New York Times, Village Voice, Cahiers du Cinema, Los Angeles Times, New York Magazine, Vogue, Variety etc, 1961–. *Address:* c/o William Peiffer, 30 Lane of Acres, Haddonfield, NJ 08033, USA.

BOGER, Prof. David Vernon, PhD; FRS 2007; FAA, FTSE; Professor of Chemical Engineering, since 1982, and Laureate Professor, since 2008, University of Melbourne; *b* Kutztown, Penn, 13 Nov. 1939; *s* of Charles and Edna Boger; *m* 2003, Reba Angstadt; one *s* two *d*. *Educ:* Bucknell Univ. (BSc 1961; MSc 1964); Univ. of Illinois (PhD 1965). Monash University: Lectr, 1965–71; Sen. Lectr, 1971–80; Reader, 1980–82; University of Melbourne: Dep. Dean Engrg, 1988–90; Associate Dean (Res.) Engrg, 1990–92; Hd,

Dept of Chemical Engrg, 1997–99; Dir, Particulate Fluids Res. Centre, 2000–04. Member: Australian Soc. of Rheology; British Soc. of Rheology; Amer. Soc. of Rheology; Inst. of Non-Newtonian Fluid Mechanics, Univ. of Wales. FTSE 1989; FAA 1993. *Publications:* Thermodynamics: an introduction, 1976, rev. edn 1987; Rheology and Flow of Non-Newtonian Systems, 1976; An Introduction to the Flow Properties of Polymers, 1980; Rheology and Non-Newtonian Fluid Mechanics, 1983; Rheological Phenomena in Focus, 1993; over 300 articles. *Recreations:* fly fishing, farming. *Address:* Department of Chemical and Biomolecular Engineering, University of Melbourne, Parkville, 3010 Vic, Australia. *T:* (3) 83447440, *Fax:* (3) 83446233; *e-mail:* dvboger@unimelb.edu.au.

BOGGIS, Andrew Gurdon, MA; Warden of Forest School, since 1992; *b* 1 April 1954; *s* of Lt-Col (Edmund) Allan (Theodore) Boggis and Myrtle (Eirene) Boggis (*née* Donald); *m* 1983, Fiona Mary Cocke; two *d* one *s. Educ:* Marlborough Coll.; New Coll., Oxford (MA); King's Coll., Cambridge (PGCE). Asst Master, Hitchin Boys' Sch., 1978–79; Eton College: Asst Master, 1979–92; Master-in-College, 1984–92. Chm., HMC, 2006 (Mem., Cttee, 2001–07); Member: Ind. Schs Exam. Bd, 1992–2001 (Chm., Langs Cttee, 1997–2001); Educn Cttee, ESU, 2004–. Liveryman, Skinners' Co., 1990– (Extra Mem. Ct, 2004–06). Governor: King's Coll. Sch., Cambridge, 1994–99; Skinners' Co.'s Sch. for Girls, 1997–; Mem. Ct, Essex Univ., 1997–2004. *Publications:* articles and reviews. *Recreations:* music, cookery, reading, Austria. *Address:* Forest School, College Place, Snaresbrook, E17 3PY. *T:* (020) 8520 1744. *Club:* East India.

BOGGIS, John Graham; QC 1993; **His Honour Judge Boggis;** a Circuit Judge, since 1996; *b* 2 April 1949; *s* of Robert Boggis and Joyce (*née* Meek). *Educ:* Whitgift Sch.; Univ. of London (LLB); Univ. of Keele (MA). Called to the Bar, Lincoln's Inn, 1972; a Recorder, 1994–96; a Chancery Circuit Judge, 1997–2001. Asst Boundary Comr, 1993–95. Member: Chancery Bar Assoc., 1982–84; Senate of the Inns of Court and Bar, 1984–85. Staff Rep. Gov., Sherborne Sch., 1993–98. *Recreation:* boating (Cdre, Fairey Owners' Club, 2006–08). *Address:* Southampton Combined Court Centre, London Road, Southampton SO15 2XQ.

BOGLE, Ellen Gray, CD 1987; consultant on international trade matters, Lascelles de Mercado Co. Ltd, since 2002; *d* of late Victor Gray Williams and Eileen Avril Williams; *m* (marr. diss.); one *s* one *d. Educ:* St Andrew High Sch., Jamaica; Univ. of the West Indies, Jamaica (BA). Dir of For. Trade, Min. of For. Affairs, Jamaica, 1978–81; Dir, Jamaica Nat. Export Corp., 1978–81; High Comr to Trinidad and Tobago, Barbados, E Caribbean and Guyana, and Ambassador to Suriname, 1982–89; High Comr, UK, 1989–93, and Ambassador to Denmark, Norway, Sweden, Spain and Portugal, 1990–93; Perm. Sec., Min. of Industry, Tourism and Commerce, subseq. Industry, Investment and Commerce, Jamaica, 1993–96; Min. of Foreign Affairs and Foreign Trade, 1996–2002. Special Envoy of Jamaica to Assoc. of Caribbean States and CARICOM, 1997–2001. *Recreations:* gardening, reading, cooking, table tennis.

BOGLE, Dr Ian Gibb, CBE 2003; FRCGP; Chairman of Council, British Medical Association, 1998–2003; general practitioner, Priory Medical Centre, Liverpool, 1962–2000; *b* 11 Dec. 1938; *s* of Dr John G. Bogle and Muriel Bogle (*née* Stoll); *m*; two *d*; *m* 2001, Julie Coulson. *Educ:* Liverpool Coll.; Liverpool Univ. (MB ChB 1961). FRCGP 1997. Member: Liverpool Exec. Health Council, 1972–74; Liverpool FPC, 1974–90 (Vice Chm., 1987–88); Liverpool AHA, 1978–90; Section 63 Wkg Party, DHSS, 1985; Standing Med. Adv. Cttee, DoH, 1991–2003; NHS Modernisation Bd, 2000–03. Secretary: Liverpool Div., BMA, 1978–82 (Pres., 1977); Jt Cttee on Post Graduate Trng for Gen. Practice, 1985–90; Chairman: Anfield CAB, 1970–74; Gen. Med. Services Cttee, 1990–97. Chm., Anfield Youth Club, 1968–74. Chm. Govs, Pinehurst Jun. Sch., 1968–73. Hon. MD Liverpool, 1999. Gold Medal, BMA, 2004. *Recreations:* football, golf, photography, travel, music. *Address:* Peach Cottage, Burnt Oak Corner, East Bergholt, Suffolk CO7 6TJ. *T:* (01206) 298073.

BOGORODSK, Bishop of; *see* Sourozh, Bishop of, (Russian Orthodox).

BOHAN, William Joseph, CB 1988; Assistant Under Secretary of State, Home Office, 1979–89, retired; *b* 10 April 1929; *s* of John and Josephine Bohan; *m* 1955, Brenda Skevington (*d* 1995); one *s* (one *d* decd). *Educ:* Finchley Catholic Grammar Sch.; Cardinal Vaughan Sch., Kensington; King's Coll., Cambridge (Chancellor's Classical Medallist, 1952). Home Office: Asst Principal, 1952; Principal, 1958; Sec., Cttee on Immigration Appeals, 1966–67; Asst Sec., 1967. Chm., European Cttee on Crime Problems, 1987–89. *Recreations:* languages and literature, walking. *Address:* 16 Mostyn Road, SW19 3LJ. *T:* (020) 8542 1127.

BOHR, Prof. Aage Niels, DSc, DrPhil; physicist, Denmark; Professor of Physics, University of Copenhagen, 1956–92; *b* Copenhagen, 19 June 1922; *s* of late Prof. Niels Bohr and Margrethe Nørlund; *m* 1st, Marietta Bettina (*née* Soffer) (*d* 1978); two *s* one *d*; 2nd, 1981, Bente, *d* of late Chief Physician Johannes Meyer and Lone (*née* Rubow) and *widow* of Morten Scharff. *Educ:* Univ. of Copenhagen. Jun. Scientific Officer, Dept of Scientific and Industrial Research, London, 1943–45; Research Asst, Inst. for Theoretical Physics, Univ. of Copenhagen, 1946; Dir, Niels Bohr Inst. (formerly Inst. for Theoretical Physics), 1963–70. Bd Mem., Nordita, 1958–74, Dir, 1975–81. Member: Royal Danish Acad. of Science, 1955–; Royal Physiolog. Soc., Sweden, 1959–; Royal Norwegian Acad. of Sciences, 1962–; Acad. of Tech. Sciences, Copenhagen, 1963–; Amer. Phil. Soc., 1965–; Amer. Acad. of Arts and Sciences, 1965–; Nat. Acad. of Sciences, USA, 1971–; Royal Swedish Acad. of Sciences, 1974–; Yugoslavia Acad. of Sciences, 1976–; Pontificia Academia Scientiarum, 1978–; Norwegian Acad. of Sciences, 1979–; Polish Acad. of Sciences, 1980–; Finska Vetenskaps-Societeten, 1980–; Deutsche Akademie der Naturforscher Leopoldina, 1981–. Awards: Dannie Heineman Prize, 1960; Pius XI Medal, 1963; Atoms for Peace Award, 1969; H. C. Ørsted Medal, 1970; Rutherford Medal, 1972; John Price Wetherill Medal, 1974; (jointly) Nobel Prize for Physics, 1975; Ole Rømer Medal, 1976. Dr *hc:* Manchester, 1961; Oslo, 1969; Heidelberg, 1971; Trondheim, 1972; Uppsala, 1975. *Publications:* Rotational States of Atomic Nuclei, 1954; (with Ben R. Mottelson) Nuclear Structure, vol. I, 1969, vol. II 1975; (with Ben R. Mottelson and O. Ulfbeck) The Principle Behind Quantum Mechanics, 2004; contrib. learned jls. *Address:* Strandgade 34, 1st Floor, 1401 Copenhagen K, Denmark.

BOILEAU, Sir Guy (Francis), 8th Bt *cr* 1838; antique dealer; *b* 23 Feb. 1935; *s* of Sir Edmond Charles Boileau, 7th Bt, and of Marjorie Lyle, *d* of Claude Monteath D'Arcy; *S* father, 1980; *m* 1962, Judith Frances, *d* of George Conrad Hannan; two *s* three *d. Educ:* Xavier College, Melbourne; Royal Military Coll., Duntroon, Australia. Lieut, Aust. Staff Corps, 1956; Platoon Comdr, 3rd Bn, Royal Aust. Regt, Malaysia, 1957–58; Observer, UN Mil. Observer Gp in India and Pakistan, 1959–60; Instructor, Aust. Army Training Team, Vietnam, 1963–64; attached US Dept of Defence, Washington, DC, 1966–68; Security Adviser, Dept of the Administrator, Territory of Papua-New Guinea, 1970–71; CO, Army Intelligence Centre, 1972–74; Directing Staff (Instructor), Aust. Staff Coll., 1975–76; SO1 Personnel, HQ Third Mil. Dist, 1979. *Recreations:* boating, fishing. *Heir: s* Nicolas Edmond George Boileau, *b* 17 Nov. 1964. *Club:* The Heroes (Toorak, Victoria).

BOISSIER, Martin Scobell; Vice Lord-Lieutenant of Derbyshire, 1992–2001; *b* 14 May 1926; *s* of Ernest Gabriel Boissier, DSC and Doris Mary Boissier (*née* Bingham); *m* 1955, Margaret Jean Blair, JP; one *s* one *d. Educ:* Bramcote Prep. Sch., Scarborough; RN Naval Coll., Dartmouth. Service in RN, 1943–58; qualified as Pilot, 1947; Lt-Comdr, retired 1958. Aiton & Co., Derby, 1958, Dir, 1976, retired 1988; Gp Personnel Controller and local Dir, Whessoe, 1980–88; former Director: Silkolene; ATV (Midlands). Mem., East Reg. Bd, Central ITV, 1982–92. Chm., Derbys FHSA, 1990–97. President: Royal Sch. for the Deaf, Derby, 1977–; Arkwright Soc., Cromford, 2002–. Freeman, City of London, 1978; Liveryman, Tinplate Workers alias Wire-workers' Co., 1978 (Mem., Ct of Assts, 1994–2005). DL 1977, High Sheriff, 1978–79, Derbys. *Recreations:* gardening; appreciation of art, music and wine; needlework, charity work. *Address:* Ithersay Cottage, Idridgehay, Belper, Derbyshire DE56 2SB. *T:* (01773) 550210. *Clubs:* Army and Navy, MCC; County (Derby).

See also R. H. Boissier.

BOISSIER, Vice Adm. Robin Paul, CB 2007; Deputy Commander-in-Chief Fleet and Chief Naval Warfare Officer, 2006–April 2009; *b* 14 Oct. 1953; *s* of late Peter Clement Boissier and Joan Rosemary Boissier; *m* 1980, Susan Jane Roxanna Stocker. *Educ:* Harrow Sch.; Emmanuel Coll., Cambridge (MA); London Business Sch. (MSc). Joined RN, 1974; in command: HMS Onyx, 1985; HMS Trafalgar, 1989; HMS Chatham, 1994; Asst Dir, Navy Staff Duties, 1996–97; Dir, Navy Plans and Progs, MOD, 1998–99; Portsmouth Naval Base, 2000–02; ADC to the Queen, 2000–02; Dep. Comdr, NATO Striking Forces, Southern Reg., 2002–04; Dep. Chief Exec., Warship Support Agency, 2004–05; Dir Gen. Logistics (Fleet), MoD, 2005–06. Younger Brother, Trinity House, 2007. *Publication:* Understanding the Rule of the Road, 2003. *Recreations:* sailing, gardening. *Clubs:* MCC; Royal Yacht Squadron (Cowes).

BOISSIER, Roger Humphrey, CBE 1992; non-executive Director, Royal Crown Derby Porcelain Co. Ltd, since 2007 (Chairman, 2000–07); *b* 30 June 1930; *y s* of late Ernest Boissier, DSC, CEng, FIEE and Doris Boissier (*née* Bingham), of Bingham's Melcombe; *m* 1965, (Elizabeth) Bridget (Rhoda), *e d* of Sir Gerald Ley, Bt, TD and Rosemary, Lady Ley; one *s* one *d. Educ:* Harrow. International Combustion Ltd, 1950–52; Cooper-Parry, Hall, Doughty & Co. 1952–53; Merz & McLellan, 1953–55; Aiton & Co., 1955–83, Man. Dir, 1975–83; Exec. Dir, Whessoe plc, 1975–83. Chm., Pressac Hldgs PLC, then Pressac plc, 1990–2002 (non-exec. Dir, 1984); non-executive Director: Derbyshire BS, 1972–81; Simmonds Precision NV, 1976–82; Ley's Foundries & Engrg, 1977–82; Allott & Lomax (Holdings) Ltd, 1984–2000; Severn Trent Water Authy, then Severn Trent plc, 1986–98; British Gas plc, 1986–96 (pt-time Mem., British Gas Corp., 1981–86); T & N plc, 1987–98; Edward Lumley Hldgs, 1988–2004; Kalon Gp plc, 1992–99 (Chm., 1992–95; Chm., Kalon Pension Trustees Ltd, 1992–2003); AMEC Power, 1992–96. Mem. Exec., British Energy Assoc. (formerly Brit. Nat. Cttee, World Energy Council), 1975–2005 (Chm., 1977–80); Mem. Council, 1991–2007, Mem. Court, 1991–, a Pro-Chancellor and Dep. Chm. Council, 2000–07, Loughborough Univ.; Mem. Court, Univ. of Derby, 1998–; Governor: Harrow Sch., 1976–96 (Dep. Chm., 1988–96); Landau Forte Coll., Derby, 1995–. Pres., Harrow Assoc., 2006–. High Sheriff of Derbyshire, 1987–88. Freeman, City of London, 1971; Master, Co. of Tin Plate Workers alias Wire Workers, 1988–89. CIGEM (CIGasE 1983); FRSA 1987; Hon. FEI 1991. Hon. DTech Loughborough, 2001. *Recreations:* cars, foreign travel, reading, meeting people. *Address:* Low Baronwood, Armathwaite, Carlisle, Cumbria CA4 9TW. *T:* (01697) 472347; *e-mail:* rogerboissier@btinternet.com. *Clubs:* Brooks's, MCC.

See also M. S. Boissier.

BOIZOT, Peter James, MBE 1986; DL; founded PizzaExpress Ltd, 1965; President, PizzaExpress Plc, since 1996 (Chairman, 1993–96); *b* 16 Nov. 1929; *s* of late Gaston Charles and Susannah Boizot. *Educ:* King's Sch., Peterborough (chorister, Peterborough Cathedral); St Catharine's Coll., Cambridge. MA (BA (Hons) History). Captain, MV Yarvic, 1951. Various jobs, predominantly in sales field, 1953–64; Chm. and Man. Dir, PizzaExpress Ltd, 1965–93; Dir, Connoisseur Casino, 1970–82. Publisher, monthly magazines: BOZ (formerly Jazz Express), 1983–; Hockey Sport (formerly Hockey Digest), 1995–; World Hockey, 1995. Proprietor: Pizza on the Park, 1976–2005; Kettners Restaurant, Soho, 1980–2002; Great Northern Hotel, Peterborough, 1993–. Founder and Chm., Soho Restaurateurs Assoc., 1980–. Founder and Dir, Soho Jazz Fest., 1986–. Dir, CENTEC, 1990–93. Chm., Westminster Chamber of Commerce, 1992–95. Mem., Royal Acad. Adv. Bd, 1988–91. Fellow Commoner, St Catharine's Coll., Cambridge, 1996. Contested (L) Peterborough, Feb. and Oct. 1974. Founder Mem., Soho Soc., 1972. Pres., Hampstead and Westminster Hockey Club, 1986–; a Vice-Pres., Hockey Assoc., 1990–; Chm., Peterborough United FC, 1997–. DL Cambs, 1998. FIH (FHCIMA 1989). Hon. LLD Westminster, 1995. Bolla Award, 1983; Hotel and Caterer Food Service Award, 1989. Commendatore, Al Merito della Repubblica Italiana, 1996 (Cavaliere Ufficiale, 1983). *Publication:* PizzaExpress Cook Book, 1976, rev. edn 1991. *Recreations:* hockey, presenting jazz, cabaret, dining out. *Address:* 10 Lowndes Square, SW1X 9HA. *T:* (020) 7235 9100. *Clubs:* National Liberal, Royal Automobile; Hawks (Cambridge); Vincent's (Oxford).

BOK, Derek; Professor of Law, since 1961, 300th Anniversary University Professor, since 1991, President, 1971–91, now President Emeritus, and Interim President, 2006–07, Harvard University; *b* Bryn Mawr, Pa, 22 March 1930; *s* of late Curtis and Margaret Plummer Bok (later Mrs William S. Kiskadden); *m* 1955, Sissela Ann Myrdal, *d* of late Prof. Karl Gunnar Myrdal and Alva Myrdal; one *s* two *d. Educ:* Stanford Univ. (BA); Harvard Univ. (JD); Inst. of Political Science, Univ. of Paris (Fulbright Scholar); George Washington Univ. (MA Economics). Served AUS, 1956–58. Asst Prof. of Law, Harvard Univ., 1958–61, Dean of Law Sch., 1968–71. Chairman: Common Cause, 1998–; Bd, Spencer Foundn, 2002–. *Publications:* The First Three Years of the Schuman Plan, 1955; (ed with Archibald Cox) Cases and Materials on Labor Law, 5th edn 1962, 6th edn 1965, 7th edn 1969, 8th edn 1977; (with John Dunlop) Labor and the American Community, 1970; Beyond the Ivory Tower, 1982; Higher Learning, 1986; Universities and the future of America, 1990; The Cost of Talent, 1993; The State of the Nation, 1996; The Shape of the River, 1998; The Trouble with Government, 2001; Universities in the Marketplace, 2003; Our Underachieving Colleges, 2006. *Recreations:* gardening, tennis, ski-ing. *Address:* c/o Kennedy School of Government, Harvard University, Mailbox 50, 79 JFK Street, Cambridge, MA 02138–5801, USA.

BOKHARY, Syed Kemal Shah; Hon. Mr Justice Bokhary; a Permanent Judge, Hong Kong Court of Final Appeal, since 1997; *b* 25 Oct. 1947; *s* of Syed Daud Shah Bokhary and Halima Bokhary (*née* Arculli); *m* 1977, Verina Saeeda Chung (*see* V. S. Bokhary); three *d. Educ:* King George V Sch., Hong Kong. Called to the Bar, Middle Temple, 1970 (Hon. Bencher, 2001); QC (Hong Kong) 1983; practised in Hong Kong and before the Judicial Cttee of the Privy Council, London, 1971–89; Judge of High Court, Hong Kong, 1989–93; Justice of Appeal, Supreme Court of Hong Kong, 1993–97. Mem., Law Reform Commn of Hong Kong, 2000–. Mem. Bd, Law Faculty, 1994–, and Chm., Law and Professional Legal Educn Depts Adv. Cttee, 1997–, City Univ., Hong Kong; Chm., Adv. Bd, Centre for Criminology, Dept. of Sociology, Univ. of Hong Kong, 1999–; Chm.

Academic Bd, Sch. of Law, Chinese Univ. of Hong Kong, 2006–. Hon. Lectr, Dept of Professional Legal Educn, Univ. of Hong Kong, 2000–; Affiliate, Centre of Near and Middle Eastern Studies, SOAS, 2001–. Mem., Acad. of Experts' Judicial Cttee, 2003–. Mem., RSAA, 1988–. FRAI 1998. Patron, Advocacy and Mooting Soc., Univ. of Hong Kong, 2003–. Mem., Welsh and W of England Bullmastiff Soc.; Life Mem., Southern Bullmastiff Soc. Mem. Editl Adv. Bd, Halsbury's Laws of Hong Kong, 1993–; Editor-in-Chief: Tort Law and Practice in Hong Kong, 2005–; Archbold Hong Kong, 2008–. *Publications:* articles in Hong Kong Law Jl and other learned jls. *Recreations:* dogs, opera, anthropology, reading, walking, travel, shooting. *Address:* Court of Final Appeal, 1 Battery Path, Hong Kong. *Clubs:* Hong Kong Jockey, Hong Kong Country, Aberdeen Marina, Hong Kong Clay Target Shooting Association, Hong Kong Rifle Association, Hong Kong Kennel (President).

BOKHARY, Verina Saeeda; Hon. Mrs Justice Bokhary; a Judge of the Court of First Instance of the High Court (formerly Judge of the High Court), Hong Kong, since 1996; *b* 5 Feb. 1950; *d* of Chung Hon-Wing and Hung Shui-Chan; *m* 1977, Syed Kemal Shah Bokhary, *qv*; three *d*. Called to the Bar, Lincoln's Inn, 1971; Temp. Asst Registrar, Royal Courts of Justice, Chancery Div., 1972; Legal Asst, HM Customs & Excise, 1972–76; Legal Officer, Unofficial Mems of the Exec. and Legislative Council Office, Hong Kong, 1976–78; in private practice, Hong Kong, 1978–85; Hong Kong Judiciary: Magistrate, 1985–87; Adjudicator, 1987–89; Dist Court Judge, 1989–95. Chm., Release under Supervision Bd, 1998–2003; Dep. Pres., Long-term Prison Sentences Rev. Bd, 1997–2003. Mem., Updating Gp, High Court Criminal Manual Specimen Directions, 1998–2004. Adv. Ed. and reviewer, Archbold HK, 2003–05. *Recreations:* homelife, antiques, reading. *Address:* High Court, 38 Queensway, Hong Kong. *T:* 28254312.

BOKSENBERG, Prof. Alexander, CBE 1996; PhD; FRS 1978; FInstP; FRAS; Research Professor, Institute of Astronomy, University of Cambridge and PPARC Senior Research Fellow, Universities of Cambridge and London, 1996–99; Extraordinary Fellow, Churchill College, Cambridge, since 1996; Director, Royal Observatories, 1993–96: Royal Greenwich Observatory, Cambridge; Royal Observatory, Edinburgh; Isaac Newton Group of optical telescopes, Canary Islands; Joint Astronomy Centre, Hawaii; *b* 18 March 1936; *s* of Julius Boksenberg and Ernestina Steinberg; *m* 1960, Adella Coren; one *s* one *d*. *Educ:* Stationers' Co.'s Sch.; Univ. of London (BSc, PhD); MA Cantab. Dept of Physics and Astronomy, University Coll. London: SRC Res. Asst, 1960–65; Lectr in Physics, 1965–75; Head of Optical and Ultraviolet Astronomy Res. Group, 1969–81; Reader in Physics, 1975–78; SRC Sen. Fellow, 1976–81; Prof. of Physics and Astronomy, 1978–81; Dir, Royal Greenwich Observatory, 1981–93. Sherman Fairchild Dist. Schol., CIT, 1981–82; Visiting Professor: Dept of Physics and Astronomy, UCL, 1981–; Astronomy Centre, Univ. of Sussex, 1981–89; Hon. Prof. of Experimental Astronomy, Univ. of Cambridge, 1991–. Chm., New Industrial Concepts Ltd, 1969–81. Chairman: SRC Astronomy II Cttee, 1980–81; Gemini Telescopes Project Expert Cttee, 1992 (Chm., UK Steering Cttee, 1992–93; Mem., USA Oversight Cttee, 1993–94); Mem. and Pres., Internat. Scientific Cttee, Canary Is Observatories, 1981–95; Member: ESA Hubble Space Telescope Instrument Definition Team, 1973–95; S African Astronomical Observatory Adv. Cttee, 1978–85; British Council Science Adv. Cttee, 1987–91; Anglo-Australian Telescope Bd, 1989–91 (Dep. Chm., 1991–92); Hubble Space Telescope Users Cttee, 1990–91; Fachbeirat, Max Planck Inst. für Astronomie, 1991–95; European Southern Observatory Vis. Cttee, 1993–95; Finance Cttee, IAU, 1997–2000; UK-Japan N+N Bd on Co-operation in Astronomy, 1997–; PPARC VISTA Review Bd, 1999–2000; formerly mem. or chm. of more than 40 other councils, boards, cttees, panels or courts, 1970–. Exec. Ed., Experimental Astronomy, 1995–. Mem. Council and Trustee, Royal Soc., 1995–97 (Mem., Technical Support Steering Gp, 1997–98; Chm., Internat. Exchanges Far East Panel, 2000–; Hughes Medal, 1999); Mem. Council, Trustee and Vice-Pres., Royal Astronomical Soc., 2000–03 (Chm., Awards Cttee A, 2002–03; Hannah Jackson Medal, 1998); Mem. Council, Inst. of Physics, 2001–03 (Mem., Women in Physics Cttee, 2002–03; Chm., Ethics Cttee, 2004–; Glazebrook Medal and Prize, 2000). Mem., Wkg Gp on Basic Scis and Basic Res., ICSU, 2004; UNESCO: Mem., Sci. Sector Cttee of Experts on Internat. Basic Scis Prog., 2002–; Mem., World Heritage Centre Cttee of Internat. Experts on Archaeo-Astronomical Sites and Observatories, 2004–; UK National Commission for UNESCO: Mem., Foundn Cttee, 1999–2000; Mem. Council, 2000–03; Chm., Sci. Cttee, 2000–03; Chm., Steering Cttee, Campaign Gp, 2003–04; UNESCO Regional Bureau for Science in Europe: Mem., Scientific Council, 2000; Mem., Task Force for Reconstruction of Scientific Co-operation in SE Europe, 2000–03; Chm., Wkg Gp on Restoring Human Potential in SE Europe, 2002–03. Pres., W London Astronomical Soc., 1978–; Hon. Pres., Astronomical Soc. of Glasgow, 1995–. Pres., British Horological Inst., 2000–01. Royal Soc. lecture tours: Russia, 1989; China, 1995; Japan, 1999; British Council lect. tour, India, 1999. Founding Member: Academia Europaea, 1989; European Astronomical Soc., 1990; Mem., Cambridge Philosophical Soc., 1996–. Member: Council, Churchill Coll., Cambridge, 1998–2003; Mgt Cttee, Language Centre, Univ. of Cambridge, 2003–. Fellow, UCL, 1991. FRAS 1965 (Hannah Jackson Medal, 1998); FInstP 1998; FRSA 1984. Clockmakers' Co.: Freeman, 1984; Liveryman, 1989; Mem., Court of Assts, 1994–; Master, 2000. Asteroid (3205) Boksenberg, named 1988. Dr *hc* l'Observatoire de Paris, 1982; DSc *hc* Sussex, 1991. *Publications:* (ed jtly) Modern Technology and its Influence on Astronomy, 1990; over 240 contribs to learned jls. *Recreation:* ski-ing. *Address:* University of Cambridge, Institute of Astronomy, The Observatories, Madingley Road, Cambridge CB3 0HA. *T:* (01223) 339909. *Club:* Athenæum.

BOLADUADUA, Emitai Lausiki; High Commissioner of Fiji in the United Kingdom, also accredited to the Republic of Ireland, Denmark, Germany, the Holy See, Israel and Arab Republic of Egypt, 2002–06; *b* 13 April 1944; *s* of Naibuka Lausiki and Mere Turavono; *m* 1973, Asinate U. Taleaua; four *d*. *Educ:* Queen Victoria Sch., Fiji; Suva Grammar Sch., Fiji; Univ. of New England, Armidale, NSW (BSc, DipEd); Univ. of Reading. Ratu Kadavulevu School: asst teacher, 1968–73; Vice Principal, 1973–81; Principal, 1981–84; Principal: Labasa Coll., 1984–87; Fiji Inst. of Technol., 1988–90; Deputy Secretary: for Educn, Youth and Sport, 1990–93; for Foreign Affairs and Civil Aviation, 1993–97; Permanent Secretary: for Inf., Broadcasting, TV and Telecommunications, 1997; for Home Affairs and Immigration, 1997–99; for Educn, 1999; for Foreign Affairs and External Trade, 1999–2000. Mem., Land Transport Authy, Fiji, 2002. Chm. Council, Fiji Inst. of Technol., 1999; Mem. Council, Univ. of S Pacific, 1990–92 and 1999. CS Medal (Fiji), 1995. *Recreations:* watching cricket, tennis, Rugby Union, reading. *Address:* PO Box 4528, Samabula, Fiji Islands.

BOLAM, James; actor; *b* Sunderland, 16 June 1938; *s* of Robert Alfred Bolam and Marion Alice Bolam (*née* Drury). *Educ:* Bede Grammar Sch., Sunderland; Bemrose Sch., Derby. First stage appearance, The Kitchen, Royal Court, 1959; later plays include: Events While Guarding the Bofors Gun, Hampstead, 1966; In Celebration, Royal Court, 1969; Veterans, Royal Court, 1972; Treats, Royal Court, 1976; Who Killed 'Agatha' Christie?, Ambassadors, 1978; King Lear (title rôle), Young Vic, 1981; Run for Your Wife!, Criterion, 1983; Arms and the Man, Cambridge; Who's Afraid of Virginia Woolf?, Birmingham, 1989; Victory, Chichester, 1989; Jeffrey Bernard is Unwell, Apollo, 1990; Glengarry Glen Ross, Donmar Warehouse, 1994; Wild Oats, National, 1995; Endgame, Nottingham Playhouse, 1999; Semi-Detached, 1999, How to Succeed in Business Without Really Trying, 2005, Chichester. *Films:* A Kind of Loving, 1962; The Loneliness of the Long Distance Runner, 1962; Half a Sixpence, 1967; Otley, 1969; Crucible of Terror, 1971; Straight on till Morning, 1972; In Celebration, 1974; Murder Most Foul; The Likely Lads, 1976; The Great Question; Seaview Knights; Clockwork Mice; Stella Does Tricks; Island on Bird Street; End of the Affair, 1999; It Was an Accident, 2000. *Television series:* The Likely Lads, 1965–69; Whatever Happened to the Likely Lads?, 1973; When the Boat Comes In, 1975–77; The Limbo Connection (Armchair Thriller Series); Only When I Laugh; The Beiderbecke Affair; Room at the Bottom; Andy Capp; The Beiderbecke Tapes; The Beiderbecke Connection; Second Thoughts; Eleven Men Against Eleven; Have your Cake, The Missing Postman, 1997; Pay and Display, Dirty Tricks, Close and True, 2000; Born and Bred, Shipman, 2002; New Tricks, 2003, 2004, 2005, 2006, 2007, 2008; The Plot Against Harold Wilson, 2006; also As You Like It, Macbeth, in BBC Shakespeare. *Address:* c/o Jane Brand, Independent Talent Group Ltd, Oxford House, 76 Oxford Street, W1D 1BS.

BOLAND, Leo; Chief Executive, London Borough of Barnet, since 2001; *b* 1 Aug. 1952; *s* of Stephen and Ellen Boland; *m* 1981, Margaret Gibbons; one *s*. *Educ:* Ushaw Coll., Durham; Bristol Univ. (BSc Hons Social Scis); Open Univ. Business Sch. (MBA). Grad. trainee, Ealing BC, 1974–75; Community Worker, Newham Rights Centre, 1975–79; Improvement Officer, Housing Dept, Islington BC, 1979–89; Newham Borough Council: Capital Prog. Manager, 1989–91; Asst Dir of Social Services, 1991–98; Asst Chief Exec., 1998–2001. *Recreations:* walking, reading, film, eating out. *Address:* London Borough of Barnet, North London Business Park, Oakleigh Road South, N11 1NP.

BOLEAT, Mark John; company director and consultant; *b* 21 Jan. 1949; *s* of Paul Boleat and Peggy Boleat (*née* Still); *m* 1991, Elizabeth Ann Baker (*née* Barker). *Educ:* Victoria College, Jersey; Lanchester Polytechnic and Univ. of Reading (BA Econ, MA Contemp. European Studies). FCIB. Asst Master, Dulwich College, 1972; Economist, Indust. Policy Group, 1973; The Building Societies Association: Asst Sec., 1974; Under Sec., 1976; Dep. Sec., 1979; Dep. Sec.-Gen., 1981; Sec.-Gen., 1986; Dir-Gen., 1987. Sec.-Gen., Internat. Union of Housing Finance Instns (formerly Internat. Union of Building Socs and Savings Assocs), 1986–89; Mem. Bd, Housing Corp., 1988–93; Chm., Circle 33 Housing Trust, 1990–93; Dir-Gen., ABI, 1993–99; Director: Comino Gp, 2000–06; Countryside Properties, 2001–05. Chm., Hillingdon Community Trust, 2003–. Member: NCC, 2000–05; Gibraltar Financial Services Commn, 2000–; Chm., Retail Motor Industry Code of Practice Scrutiny Cttee, 2003–05. Chm., Assoc. of Labour Providers, 2004–. Mem., Ct of Common Council, City of London, 2002–. *Publications:* The Building Society Industry, 1982; National Housing Finance Systems: a comparative study, 1985; Housing in Britain, 1986; (with Adrian Coles) The Mortgage Market, 1987; Building Societies: the regulatory framework, 1988, 3rd edn 1992; Trade Association Strategy and Management, 1996; Models of Trade Association Co-operation, 2000; Good Practice in Trade Association Governance, 2001; Managing Trade Associations, 2003; Housing Development and Housing Finance in Britain, 2008; articles on housing, insurance and finance. *Recreation:* golf. *Address:* 26 Westbury Road, Northwood, Middx HA6 3BU. *Clubs:* Moor Park Golf, La Moye Golf.

BOLES, Sir Jeremy John Fortescue, 3rd Bt *cr* 1922; *b* 9 Jan. 1932; *s* of Sir Gerald Fortescue Boles, 2nd Bt, and Violet Blanche (*d* 1974), *er d* of late Major Hall Parlby, Manadon, Crown Hill, S Devon, *S* father, 1945; *m* 1st, 1955, Dorothy Jane (marr. diss. 1970), *yr d* of James Alexander Worswick; two *s* one *d*; 2nd, 1970, Elisabeth Gildroy Willis Fleming (marr. diss. 1981), *yr d* of Edward Phillip Shaw; one *d*; 3rd, 1982, Marigold Aspey, *e d* of Donald Frank Seckington. *Heir: s* Richard Fortescue Boles [*b* 12 Dec. 1958; *m* 1990, Allison Beverley, *d* of Brian MacDonald; one *s* one *d*]. *Address:* Heriots, Brendon Close, Roadwater, Watchet TA23 0RG.

BOLES, Sir John Dennis, (Sir Jack), Kt 1983; MBE 1960; DL; Director General of the National Trust, 1975–83; *b* 25 June 1925; *s* of late Comdr Geoffrey Coleridge Boles and Hilda Frances (*née* Crofton); *m* 1st, 1953, Benita (*née* Wormald) (*d* 1969); two *s* three *d*; 2nd, 1971, Lady Anne Hermione, DL, *d* of 12th Earl Waldegrave, KG, GCVO. *Educ:* Winchester Coll. Rifle Brigade, 1943–46. Colonial Administrative Service (later Overseas Civil Service), North Borneo (now Sabah), 1948–64; Asst Sec., National Trust, 1965, Sec., 1968; Mem., Devon and Cornwall Regl Cttee, Nat. Trust, 1985–95. Dir, SW Region Bd, Lloyds Bank plc, 1984–91. Devon: DL 1991; High Sheriff 1993–94. *Address:* Rydon House, Talaton, near Exeter, Devon EX5 2RP. *Club:* Army and Navy.

See also J. D. Fishburn.

BOLGER, Rt Hon. James Brendan, (Jim), ONZ 1997; PC 1991; Chairman: Kiwibank Ltd, since 2001; New Zealand Post Ltd, since 2002; *b* 31 May 1935; *s* of Daniel Bolger and Cecilia (*née* Doyle); *m* 1963, Joan Maureen Riddell; six *s* three *d*. *Educ:* Opunake High Sch. Sheep and cattle farmer, Te Kuiti, 1965–72. Federated Farmers: Br. Chm., 1967–72; sub-provincial Chm., 1970–72; Vice-Pres., Waikato, 1971–72; Mem., Dominion Exec., 1971–72. MP (Nat. Party) King Country, 1972–98; Parly Under-Sec., Min. of Agric. and Fisheries, Min. of Maori Affairs, then Minister i/c of Rural Banking Finance Corp., 1975–77; Minister of Fisheries and Associate Minister of Agric., 1977–78; Minister of Labour, 1978–84; Minister of Immigration, 1978–81; Leader of Nat. Party, 1986–97; Leader of the Opposition, 1986–90; Prime Minister of NZ, 1990–97; NZ Ambassador to USA, 1998–2002. Chairman: Adv. Bd, World Agricl Forum, 2002–; Ian Axford (NZ) Fellowship in Public Policy, 2002–; Gas Industry Co., 2004–; Express Couriers Ltd, 2004–; Trustees Executors Ltd, 2006–. Chancellor, Waikato Univ., 2007–. Pres., ILO, 1983. Hon. Dr Agricl Econs Khon Kaen, 1994; Hon. DLitt Massey, 2002. Silver Jubilee Medal, 1977; NZ Commemoration Medal, 1990; NZ Suffrage Centennial Medal, 1993. *Recreations:* hiking, fishing, reading, Rugby, cricket. *Address:* New Zealand Post Ltd, Private Bag 39–990, Wellington, New Zealand; Sommeville Road, PO Box 406, Te Kuiti, New Zealand.

BOLINGBROKE, 7th Viscount *cr* 1712, **AND ST JOHN,** 8th Viscount *cr* 1716; **Kenneth Oliver Musgrave St John;** Bt 1611; Baron St John of Lydiard Tregoze, 1712; Baron St John of Battersea, 1716; Founder, 1956, Chairman, 1958–75, Atlantic and Pacific Travel Ltd; *b* 22 March 1927; *s* of Geoffrey Robert St John, MC (*d* 1972) and Katherine Mary (*d* 1958), *d* of late A. S. J. Musgrave; *S* cousin, 1974; *m* 1st, 1953, Patricia Mary McKenna (marr. diss. 1972); one *s*; 2nd, 1972, Jainey Anne McRae (marr. diss. 1987); two *s*. *Educ:* Eton; Geneva Univ. Director: Shaw Savill Holidays Pty Ltd; Bolingbroke and Partners Ltd; Wata Investment Inc., Panama. Pres., Travel Agents Assoc. of NZ, 1965–67; Dir, World Assoc. of Travel Agencies, 1966–75; Chm., Aust. Council of Tour Wholesalers, 1972–75. Fellow, Aust. Inst. of Travel; Mem., NZ Inst. of Travel. *Recreations:* golf, cricket, tennis, history. *Heir: s* Hon. Henry Fitzroy St John, *b* 18 May 1957.

BOLKESTEIN, Frederik, (Frits); Member, European Commission, 1999–2004; *b* 4 April 1933; *m* 1988, Femke Boersma; two *s* one *d*. *Educ:* Oregon State Coll., USA; Gemeentelijke Univ., Amsterdam; Univ. of Leiden (Master of Law). Shell Group,

1960–76: posts in E Africa, Honduras, El Salvador, UK, Indonesia and France; Dir, Shell Chimie, Paris, 1973–76. Mem. Parliament (VVD), Netherlands, 1978–82, 1986–88 and 1989–99; Minister for Foreign Trade, 1982–86; Minister of Defence, 1988–89; Chm., VVD Parly Gp, 1990–98. Pres., Liberal Internat., 1996–99. Visiting Professor: Univ. of Leiden, 2005–; Univ. of Delft, 2005–. Member Supervisory Board: Central Bank of the Netherlands, 2005–; AF/KLM, 2005–. MRIIA. *Publications:* The Limits of Europe, 2004; (with Michel Rocard) Peut-on réformer la France?, 2006. *Web:* www.fritsbolkestein.com.

BOLLAND, Alexander; QC (Scot.) 1992; *b* 21 Nov. 1950; *s* of James Bolland and Elizabeth Agnes (*née* Anderson); *m* 1973, Agnes Hunter, *d* of Dr George Pate Moffat, Crookedholm; one *s* two *d*. *Educ:* Kilmarnock Acad.; Univ. of St Andrews (BD 1973); Glasgow Univ. (LLB 1976). Admitted to Faculty of Advocates, 1978; Capt., Directorate of Army Legal Services, later Army Legal Corps, 1978–80; Standing Jun. Counsel to Dept of Employment in Scotland, 1988–92; Temp. Sheriff, 1988–99; part-time Chm., Employment (formerly Industrial) Tribunals, 1993–. *Recreations:* Hellenistics, walking, reading. *Address:* The Old Dairy, 60 North Street, St Andrews, Fife KY16 9AH. *T:* (01334) 474599. *Clubs:* Naval and Military; New (Edinburgh).

BOLLAND, (David) Michael; broadcast consultant, since 2007; *b* 27 Feb. 1947; *s* of Allan Bolland and Eileen Lindsay; *m* 1987, Katie Lander; one *s* one *d*, and one *s* two *d* by former marrs. *Educ:* Hillhead High School, Glasgow. Film editor, BBC Scotland, 1965–73; TV Producer, BBC TV, 1973–81; Channel Four Television: Commissioning Editor, Youth, 1981–83; Senior Commissioning Editor, Entertainment, 1983–87; Asst Dir of Programmes, and Head of Art and Entertainment Gp, 1987–88; Controller Arts and Entertainment, and Dep. Dir of Progs, 1988–90; Man. Dir, Initial Films and Television, 1990; Man. Dir, Channel X Ltd, 1990–96; Project Dir, Channel X Broadcasting (Scotland) Ltd, 1991–95; BBC Scotland: Hd of Arts and Entertainment, 1996–2001; Hd of Comedy and Entertainment, 2001–04; Dir of Television, 2004–07, Creative Dir, 2006–07, Nat. Film and Television Sch. Chairman: Edinburgh Internat. TV Fest., 1990; Producers' Alliance for Film and Television, 1995. Member: RTS; BAFTA. *Recreation:* catching up with the world. *Address:* 1 Westbourne Gardens, Glasgow G12 9XE.

BOLLAND, Sir Edwin, KCMG 1981 (CMG 1971); HM Diplomatic Service, retired; Ambassador to Yugoslavia, 1980–82; *b* 20 Oct. 1922; *m* 1948, Winifred Mellor; one *s* three *d* (and one *s* decd). *Educ:* Morley Grammar Sch.; University Coll., Oxford. Served in Armed Forces, 1942–45. Foreign Office, 1947; Head of Far Eastern Dept, FO, 1965–67; Counsellor, Washington, 1967–71; St Antony's Coll., Oxford, 1971–72; Ambassador to Bulgaria, 1973–76; Head of British delegn to Negotiations on MBFR, 1976–80. *Recreations:* walking, gardening. *Address:* 2A Dukes Meadow, Stapleford, Cambridge CB22 5BH. *T:* (01223) 847139.

BOLLAND, Hugh Westrope; Vice Chairman, Schroder Investment Management Ltd, 1999–2000; *b* 14 May 1946; *s* of late Gp Capt. Guy Alfred Bolland, CBE; *m* 1972, Marian Wendy Elton; two *s* one *d*. *Educ:* St Edward's Sch., Oxford; Univ. of Exeter (BA (Hons) Econs). Joined Schroders, 1970; Man. Dir, Schroders Asia Ltd, Hong Kong, 1984–87; Chief Exec., Schroders Australia Ltd, 1987–90; Chm., Schroder Unit Trusts Ltd, 1990–92; Jt Chief Exec., 1995–96, Chief Exec., 1997–99, Schroder Investment Management Ltd (Dir, 1990–2000); Director: Schroder Split Fund plc, 1993–2002; Fidelity Asian Values plc, 2004–; JP Morgan Indian Investment Trust, 2004–; Alliance Trust plc, 2007–. Mem. Supervisory Bd, Eurocommercial Properties NV, 1998–. Gov., St Edward's Sch., Oxford, 1999–. *Recreations:* sailing, golf, music. *Clubs:* Hong Kong, Hong Kong Jockey (Hong Kong); Woking Golf, Royal Motor Yacht.

BOLLAND, Mark William; communications consultant, since 2002; *b* 10 April 1966; *s* of late Robert Arthur Bolland and of Joan Bolland (*née* Barker); civil partnership 2006, Guy Vaughan Black, *qv*. *Educ:* Kings Manor Sch., Middlesbrough; Univ. of York (BSc). Res. Manager, and Advr to Dir Gen., Advertising Standards Authy, 1988–91; Exec. Asst to Chm., 1991–92, Dir, 1992–96, Press Complaints Commn; Asst Private Sec., 1996–97, Dep. Private Sec., 1997–2002, to HRH the Prince of Wales. Columnist: News of the World, 2003–05; London Evening Standard, 2006–. Vice Pres., Journalists' Charity, 2007–. *Address:* 34 Cannon Court, 5 Brewhouse Yard, EC1V 4JQ. *T:* (020) 7847 5700; *e-mail:* mark@markbolland.com. *Club:* Garrick.

BOLLAND, Michael; *see* Bolland, D. M.

BOLLOBÁS, Prof. Béla, PhD, DSc; Fellow of Trinity College, Cambridge, since 1971; Distinguished Professor of Excellence in Combinatorics, University of Memphis, Tennessee, since 1995; *b* 3 Aug. 1943; *s* of Béla Bollobás and Emma Varga; *m* 1969, Gabriella Farkas; one *s*. *Educ:* Univ. of Budapest (BA 1966; Dr rer nat 1967); Univ. of Cambridge (PhD 1972; DSc 1984). Res. Scientist, Hungarian Acad. of Scis, 1966–69; Vis. Scientist, Soviet Acad. of Scis, 1967–68; Vis. Fellow, Oxford, 1969; Cambridge University: Res. Fellow, 1970–72, Dir of Studies in Maths, 1972–96, Trinity Coll.; Asst Lectr, 1971–74, Lectr in Maths, 1974–85; Reader in Pure Maths, 1985–96. Foreign Mem., Hungarian Acad. of Scis, 1990. *Publications:* Extremal Graph Theory, 1978; Graph Theory, 1979; Random Graphs, 1985, 2nd edn 2001; Combinatorics, 1986; Linear Analysis, 1990; Modern Graph Theory, 1998; (with O. M. O'Riordan) Percolation Theory, 2006; The Art of Mathematics, 2006; over 350 papers in learned jls. *Recreations:* books, opera, theatre, tennis, swimming, jogging, windsurfing, riding, ski-ing. *Address:* Trinity College, Cambridge CB2 1TQ; 5 Selwyn Gardens, Cambridge CB3 9AX. *T:* (01223) 354872; 1644 Neshoba Trace Cove, Germantown, TN 38138, USA. *T:* (901) 7514162.

BOLSOVER, John Derrick; Chairman and Chief Executive, Baring Asset Management Holdings Ltd, 1995–2002; *b* 21 June 1947; *m* 1st, 1971, Susan Elizabeth Peacock; two *s* one *d*; 2nd, 1994, Kate Woollett. *Educ:* Repton Sch.; McGill Univ., Canada (BA). Director: Baring Internat. Investment Mgt Ltd (Hong Kong), 1973–85; Baring Asset Mgt (Japan) Ltd, 1986–2002; Baring Asset Mgt Ltd, 1994–2002; Dep. Chm., Baring Hldgs Ltd, 1995–97; Dir, Baring Asset Mgt Hldgs Inc., 1996–98. *Recreation:* sport. *Clubs:* Boodle's, City; Sunningdale Golf, Valderrama Golf.

BOLT, (Mohan) Paul; Director, Sport and Leisure, Department for Culture, Media and Sport, since 2008; *b* 8 Feb. 1954; *s* of Sydney Bolt and Jaya Bolt (*née* Chandran); *m* 1991, Carol Spekes. *Educ:* Trinity Coll., Cambridge (BA 1975); Open Univ. (MBA 1995). Joined Home Office as admin trainee, 1975: Principal, 1980–89; Hd, Mgt Div., 1989–92; Department of National Heritage, then Department for Culture, Media and Sport, 1992–2001: Head: Libraries Div., 1992–94; Fundamental Expenditure Rev., 1994–95; Broadcasting Bill Team, 1995–96; Broadcasting Policy Div., 1996–98; Dir, Strategy and Communications, 1998–2001; Dir, Broadcasting Standards Commn, 2001–03; Dir, Olympic Games Unit, DCMS, 2003–05; Interim Dir, Olympic Bd Secretariat, 2005–06; Dir, Capability Reviews Team, Cabinet Office, 2006–07. *Recreations:* cricket, theatre, reading, bridge. *Address:* Department for Culture, Media and Sport, 2–4 Cockspur Street, SW1Y 5DH. *Clubs:* Reform; Lancashire County Cricket.

BOLT, Ranjit Ralph, OBE 2003; writer and translator, since 1988; *b* Manchester, 10 Jan. 1959; *s* of Sydney Bolt and Jaya Bolt (*née* Chandran). *Educ:* Perse Sch., Cambridge; Balliol Coll., Oxford (BA Lit. Hum. 1982). Fund Manager: S. G. Warburg, 1982–88; Smith & Williamson, 1988–90; writer and translator, mainly of French verse plays, including: The Liar, 1989, The Illusion, 1990, Old Vic; Arturo Ui, NT 1991; Tartuffe, Playhouse Th., 1991; The Sisterhood, Chichester, 1991; The Venetian Twins, RSC, 1993; Lysistrata, Old Vic, 1993; Le Cid, NT, 1994; The School for Wives, Piccadilly Th., 1996; co-writer, Hard Times (musical), 2002; lyricist, Merry Wives, The Musical, RSC, 2006. *Publications:* Losing It (novel in verse), 2002; (trans.) La Fontaine, The Hare and the Tortoise, 2006. *Recreations:* fishing, poker. *Address:* *e-mail:* ranjitbolt72@hotmail.com.

See also M. P. Bolt.

BOLT, Air Marshal Sir Richard (Bruce), KBE 1979 (CBE 1973); CB 1977; DFC 1945; AFC 1959; Chairman, Pacific Aerospace Corp. of New Zealand, 1982–95; *b* 16 July 1923; *s* of George Bruce Bolt and Mary (*née* Best); *m* 1st, 1946, June Catherine South (*d* 1984); one *s* one *d*; 2nd, 1987, Janice Caroline Tucker. *Educ:* Nelson Coll., NZ. Began service with RNZAF in mid 1942; served during 2nd World War in RAF Bomber Command (Pathfinder Force); Chief of Air Staff, NZ, 1974–76; Chief of Defence Staff, NZ, 1976–80. *Recreations:* fly fishing, golf, horse racing. *Club:* Wellington (Wellington, NZ).

BOLTON, 8th Baron *cr* 1797, of Bolton Castle, co. York; **Harry Algar Nigel Orde-Powlett;** *b* 14 Feb. 1954; *s* of 7th Baron Bolton and of Hon. Christine, *e d* of 7th Baron Forester; *S* father, 2001; *m* 1977, Philippa, *d* of Major Peter Tapply; three *s*. *Educ:* Eton. *Heir:* *s* Hon. Thomas Peter Algar Orde-Powlett, MC, *b* 16 July 1979. *Address:* Bolton Hall, Wensley, Leyburn, N Yorks DL8 4UF. *T:* (01969) 623674.

BOLTON, Bishop Suffragan of, since 2008; **Rt Rev. Christopher Paul Edmondson;** *b* Carlisle, 25 June 1950; *s* of Jack and Margaret Edmondson; *m* 1973, Susan Heap; two *s*. *Educ:* St John's Coll., Durham Univ. (BA 1971, MA 1981); Cranmer Hall, Durham (DipTh 1972). Ordained deacon, 1973, priest, 1974; Asst Curate, Kirkheaton, Huddersfield, 1973–79; Vicar, St George's, Halifax, 1979–86; Diocesan Officer for Evangelism, Dio. of Carlisle, 1986–92; Vicar, St Peter's, Shipley, 1992–2002; Warden, Lee Abbey, Devon, 2002–08. Occasional Lecturer: Trinity Coll., Bristol; Cliff Coll., Derbyshire. *Publications:* How Shall They Hear?, 1994; Minister, Love Thyself, 2000; Fit to Lead, 2002, 2nd edn 2007; (contrib.) Vicar's Guide, 2004; (jtly) Celebrating Community, 2006; Leaders Learning to Listen, 2009. *Recreations:* cricket, football, playing piano, guitar and organ (former organ scholar), walking, MG Midget owner. *Address:* Bishop's Lodge, Walkden Road, Worsley, Manchester M28 2WH. *T:* (0161) 790 8289, *Fax:* (0161) 703 9157; *e-mail:* BishopChris@manchester.anglican.org.

BOLTON, Archdeacon of; *no new appointment at time of going to press.*

BOLTON, Beatrice Maud; Her Honour Judge Bolton; a Circuit Judge, since 2001; *b* 26 July 1953; *d* of late Arthur Henry Bolton and of Freda Bolton; divorced; one *s*. *Educ:* Newcastle upon Tyne Church High Sch.; Sheffield Univ. (LLB Hons). Called to the Bar, Gray's Inn, 1975; Asst Recorder, 1994–98; a Recorder, 1998–2001. *Recreations:* playing tennis, gardening, football, in particular Newcastle United FC. *Address:* Newcastle upon Tyne Combined Court Centre, Quayside, Newcastle upon Tyne NE1 3LA.

BOLTON, Catriona; *see* Jarvis, C.

BOLTON, Group Captain David; Director, Royal United Services Institute, 1981–94 (Deputy Director, 1980–81); *b* 15 April 1932; *o s* of late George Edward and Florence May Bolton; *m* 1955, Betty Patricia Simmonds; three *d*. *Educ:* Bede Sch., Co. Durham. Commnd RAF Regt, 1953; subsequent service in Egypt, Jordan, Singapore, Aden, Cyprus, Malta and Germany; RAF Staff Coll., 1969; National Def. Coll., 1972; Central Planning Staff, MoD, 1973–75; OC 33 Wing RAF Regt, 1975–77; Comdt RAF Regt Depot, Catterick, 1977–80; retd 1980. Chm., Macbeth Associates, 1994–2000; Vice-Chm., TASC Eur., 1994–97. Member: RUSI Council, 1973–79; IISS, 1964–90; RIIA, 1975; Council, British Atlantic Cttee, 1981–91; Bd of War Studies, Univ. of London, 1984–92; a founding Mem., Adv. Bd, British-American Project, 1985–99. Hon. Steward, Westminster Abbey, 1981–. Trench Gascoigne Essay Prize, RUSI, 1972. Editor: Brassey's Defence Year Bk, 1982–92; MacMillan-RUSI Defence Studies, 1982–94; RUSI Internat. Security Review, 1992–94. *Publications:* contrib. learned jls. *Recreations:* choral music, international affairs, gardening. *Address:* Churchfield House, Churchfield Lane, Benson, Wallingford, Oxon OX10 6SH. *Club:* Royal Air Force.

BOLTON, David Michael William; education consultant; Head Master, Dame Alice Owen's School, 1982–94; *b* 29 Feb. 1936; *s* of William Benedict Bolton and Edith Phyllis Bolton; *m* 1961, Janet Christine Fleming; two *s* one *d*. *Educ:* St Francis Xavier's Coll., Liverpool; St Edmund Hall, Oxford (BA 1960; MA 1964); DipEd London 1971. Nat. Service, RAF (Coastal Command), 1955–57. Reckitt & Colman Ltd, 1960–62; Alleyn's Sch., Dulwich, 1962–63; Housemaster, Highgate Sch., 1963–72; Dep. Head, Chancellor's Sch., Herts, 1972–74; Headmaster, Davenant Foundn Grammar Sch., 1974–82. OFSTED Inspector, 1995–. Mem. Council, Secondary Heads Assoc., 1991–94 (Chm., Area Five). Governor, St Albans High School for Girls, 1997–. FRSA 1993. Freeman, City of London, 1994. *Publications:* articles and reviews in TES. *Recreations:* reading, music, jazz especially, travel, walking, sport. *Address:* Mayfield, 8 Wykeham Gate, Haddenham, Bucks HP17 8DF.

BOLTON, Eric James, CB 1987; Deputy Chairman, New Opportunities Fund, 2001–04 (Member Board, 1998–2004); *b* 11 Jan. 1935; *s* of late James and Lilian Bolton; *m* 1960, Ann Gregory; one *s* twin *d*. *Educ:* Wigan Grammar Sch.; Chester Coll.; Lancaster Univ. MA. English teacher at secondary schs, 1957–68; Lectr, Chorley Teacher Training Coll., 1968–70; Inspector of Schs, Croydon, 1970–73; HM Inspector of Schs, 1973–79; Staff Inspector (Educnl Disadvantage), 1979–81; Chief Inspector of Schools, DES, 1981–83, Sen. Chief Inspector of Schools, 1983–91; Prof. of Teacher Educn, Inst. of Educn, London Univ., 1991–96. Chairman: Book Trust, 1997–2000 (Vice Chm., 1996–97); ITC Schs Adv. Cttee, 1997–2000; Member: Educn Adv. Cttee, LSO, 1997–; Educn Cttee, NESTA, 1999–2002; Trustee, Foundn of Young Musicians, 1992–. *Publications:* Verse Writing in Schools, 1964; various articles in educnl jls. *Recreations:* reading, music and opera, fly fishing. *Address:* 50 Addington Road, Sanderstead, South Croydon, Surrey CR2 8RB.

BOLTON, Erica Jane; Director, Bolton & Quinn Ltd, since 1981; *b* 29 June 1953; *d* of Alwyn Bolton and Betty Bolton (*née* Pile); *m* 1986, Robert Alwyn Petrie Hewison, *qv*; two *d*. *Educ:* Westonbirt Sch.; Westfield Coll., Univ. of London (BA Hist. and Hist. of Art 1974). Established Erica Bolton and Jane Quinn Ltd, 1981. Trustee: Architecture Foundn; Kids Company; Thames Fest. *Recreations:* walking, going to museums. *Address:* c/o Bolton & Quinn Ltd, 10 Pottery Lane, W11 4LZ. *T:* (020) 7221 5000.

BOLTON, Prof. Geoffrey Curgenven, AO 1984; DPhil; Chancellor, Murdoch University, 2002–06 (Pro-Chancellor, 2000–02); Professor of History, Edith Cowan University, 1993–96, now Emeritus; *b* 5 Nov. 1931; *s* of Frank and Winifred Bolton,

Perth, W Australia; *m* 1958, (Ann) Carol Grattan; two *s*. *Educ:* North Perth State Sch.; Wesley Coll., Perth; Univ. of Western Australia; Balliol Coll., Oxford, (DPhil). FRHistS 1967; FAHA 1974; FASSA 1976. Res. Fellow, ANU, 1957–62; Sen. Lectr, Monash Univ., 1962–65; Prof. of Modern Hist., Univ. of Western Australia, 1966–73; Prof. of History, 1973–82 and 1985–89, and Pro-Vice-Chancellor, 1973–76, Murdoch Univ.; Prof. of Australian Studies, Univ. of London, 1982–85; Prof. of Australian Hist., Univ., of Queensland, 1989–93. Vis. Fellow, All Souls Coll., Oxford, 1995; Sen. Scholar in Residence, Murdoch Univ., 1997–. Mem. Council, Australian Nat. Maritime Museum, Sydney, 1985–91. Boyer Lectr, Australian Broadcasting Corp., 1992. FRSA. General Editor, Oxford History of Australia, 1987–91. DUniv Murdoch, 1995. *Publications:* Alexander Forrest, 1958; A Thousand Miles Away, 1963; The Passing of the Irish Act of Union, 1966; Dick Boyer, 1967; A Fine Country to Starve In, 1972; Spoils and Spoilers: Australians Make Their Environment, 1981; Oxford History of Australia, vol. 5, 1990; Daphne Street, 1997; Claremont: a history, 1999; Edmund Barton, 2000; May It Please Your Honour, 2005; Land of Vision and Mirage: Western Australia since 1826, 2008; articles in learned jls. *Recreation:* sleep. *Address:* PO Box 792, Claremont, WA 6910, Australia. *Club:* Athenæum.

BOLTON, Ivor; conductor; Music Director, Salzburg Mozarteum Orchestra, since 2004; *b* 17 May 1958; *s* of Cyril John Bolton and Elsie Bolton (*née* Worthington); *m* 1984, Tessa Wendy Knighton, *qv*; one *s*. *Educ:* Queen Elizabeth's GS, Blackburn; Clare Coll., Cambridge (MusB, MA); Royal Coll. of Music (schol.); Nat. Opera Studio. FRCO (CHM) 1976; LRAM 1976. Conductor, Schola Cantorum of Oxford, 1981–82; Music Dir, St James's, Piccadilly, 1982–90; Chorus Master, Glyndebourne, 1985–88; Music Director: English Touring Opera, 1990–93; Glyndebourne Touring Opera, 1992–97; Chief Conductor, Scottish Chamber Orchestra, 1993–96. Founder Dir, St James's Baroque Players, 1984–; Founder and Music Dir, Lufthansa Fest. of Baroque Music, 1985–. Bayerische Staatsoper début, 1994; Royal Opera début, world première of Goehr's Arianna, 1995; Salzburg Fest. début, 2000. Has made several recordings. Bayerische Theaterpreis, Bavarian Govt, 1998. *Recreation:* football (keen follower of Arsenal and Blackburn Rovers). *Address:* 171 Goldhurst Terrace, NW6.

BOLTON, John Robert, JD; Senior Fellow, American Enterprise Institute, since 2007; *b* 20 Nov. 1948; *s* of Edward and Virginia Bolton; *m* 1986, Gretchen Brainard; one *d*. *Educ:* Yale Coll. (BA 1970); Yale Law Sch. (JD 1974). Associate, 1974–81, Partner, 1983–85, Covington & Burling, Washington; Gen. Counsel, 1981–82, Asst Adminr, 1982–83, US Agency for Internat. Devclt; Asst Attorney Gen., Legislative Affairs, 1985–88, Civil Div., 1988–89, US Dept of Justice; Asst Sec. of State, Internat. Orgn, 1989–93; Partner, Lerner, Reed Bolton & McManus, Washington, 1993–99; Of Counsel, Kutak Rock LLP, 1999–2001; Under Sec. of State, Arms Control and Internat. Security, 2001–05; US Perm. Rep. to UN, 2005–06. Sen. Vice Pres., American Enterprise Inst., 1997–2001. *Publications:* contributor: The Bush Presidency, 1997; Delusions of Grandeur: the United Nations and global intervention, 1997; US International Leadership in the 21st Century, 2000; The Oxford Companion to Politics of the World, 2nd edn 2001; contrib. numerous articles to jls incl. Foreign Policy, Foreign Affairs, Eur. Jl, National Interest, Legal Times, etc. *Address:* American Enterprise Institute, 1150 Seventeenth Street NW, Washington, DC 20036, USA.

BOLTON, Tessa Wendy; *see* Knighton, T. W.

BOMBAY, Archbishop of, (RC), since 2006; **His Eminence Cardinal Oswald Gracias;** *b* 24 Dec. 1944; *s* of Jervis and Aduzinda Gracias. *Educ:* St Xavier's Coll., Ranchi (BA 1976); Urban Univ., Rome (DCL 1982); Gregorian Univ., Rome (Dip. Jurisprudence 1982). Ordained priest, 1970; Sec. and Chancellor, Dio. of Jamshedpur, 1971–76; Sec. to Archbp of Bombay, 1982–86; Chancellor, Archdio. of Bombay, 1982–97; Aux. Bishop of Bombay, 1997–2000; Archbishop of Agra, 2000–06. Cardinal, 2007. Judicial Vicar, 1988–98, Vicar Gen., 1998–2000, Archdio. of Bombay. President: Canon Law Soc. of India, 1987–91 and 1993–97; Catholic Bishops' Conf. of India, 2005– (Sec. Gen., 1998–2002). *Address:* Archbishop's House, 21 Nathalal Parekh Marg, Mumbai 400 001, India.

BOMFORD, David Robert Lee; Associate Director for Collections, J. Paul Getty Museum, Los Angeles, since 2007; Secretary-General, International Institute for Conservation, 1994–2003; *b* 31 March 1946; *s* of Donald James Bomford and Margaret Vanstone Bomford (*née* Spalding); *m* 1st, 1969, Helen Graham (marr. diss. 1989); one *s* two *d*; 2nd, 1990, Zahira Véliz; one *s* one *d*. *Educ:* Merchant Taylors' Sch.; Univ. of Sussex (BSc 1967; MSc 1968). Asst Restorer, 1968–74, Sen. Restorer of Paintings, 1974–2007, National Gall. Editor, Studies in Conservation, 1981–91. Vis. Prof., Churubusco Nat. Inst. of Conservation, Mexico City, 1987; Slade Prof. of Fine Art, Univ. of Oxford, 1996–97; Guest Schol., J. Paul Getty Mus., LA, 2005. FIIC 1979. *Publications:* Art in the Making: Rembrandt, 1988; Art in the Making: Italian painting before 1400, 1989; Art in the Making: Impressionism, 1990; Conservation of Paintings, 1997; Venice through Canaletto's Eyes, 1998; Colour, 2000; Art in the Making: underdrawings in Renaissance paintings, 2002; Art in the Making: Degas, 2004; Readings in Conservation, 2004. *Recreations:* walking, travel, theatre. *Address:* J. Paul Getty Museum, 1200 Getty Center Drive, Los Angeles, CA 90049–1687, USA; *e-mail:* dbomford@getty.edu.

BOMFORD, Nicholas Raymond, MA; Head Master of Harrow, 1991–99; *b* 27 Jan. 1939; *s* of late Ernest Raymond Bomford and of Patricia Clive Bomford (*née* Brooke), JP; *m* 1966, Gillian Mary Reynolds; two *d*. *Educ:* Kelly Coll.; Trinity Coll., Oxford (MA, Mod. History). Teaching appts, 1960–64; Lectr in History and Contemp. Affairs, BRNC, Dartmouth, 1964–66, Sen. Lectr, 1966–68; Wellington Coll., 1968–76 (Housemaster, 1973–76); Headmaster: Monmouth Sch., 1977–82; Uppingham Sch., 1982–91. Chm., Jt Standing Cttee, HMC/IAPS, 1986–89; Nat. Rep., HMC Cttee, 1990–91; Mem., Exec. Cttee, Assoc. Governing Bodies of Indep. Schs, 2003–08. Mem. Navy Records Soc. (Councillor, 1967–70, 1973–76, 1984–88). Governor: Sherborne Sch. for Girls, 1994–2007 (Chm., 2000–07); Elstree Prep. Sch., 1996– (Chm., 2001–); Lord Wandsworth Coll., 1999–2006; Kelly Coll., 1999–; Malvern Coll., 2000–06. Chm., Usk Rural Life Mus., Monmouthshire, 2002–. Freeman, Haberdashers' Co., 1992. *Publications:* Documents in World History, 1914–70, 1973; (contrib.) Dictionary of World History, 1973. *Recreations:* shooting (Captain OURC, 1959–60; England VIII (Elcho match), 1960), fishing, gardening, music, enjoying Welsh border country and travel in the USA. *Address:* Long Meadow House, Millend, Newland, Glos GL16 8NF.

BOMPAS, (Anthony) George; QC 1994; *b* 6 Nov. 1951; *s* of Donald George Bompas, *qv*; *m* 1981, Donna Linda, *d* of J. O. Schmidt; two *s* one *d*. *Educ:* Merchant Taylors' Sch., Northwood; Oriel Coll., Oxford (Schol., MA). Called to the Bar, Middle Temple, 1975; Bencher, Lincoln's Inn, 2001. Junior Counsel (Chancery), DTI, 1989–94. Liveryman, Merchant Taylors' Co., 1982–. *Address:* 4 Stone Buildings, Lincoln's Inn, WC2A 3XT. *T:* (020) 7242 5524.

BOMPAS, Donald George, CMG 1966; Secretary, United Medical and Dental Schools of Guy's and St Thomas's Hospitals, 1984–86; *b* 20 Nov. 1920; *yr s* of Rev. E. Anstie Bompas; *m* 1946, Freda Vice, *y d* of F. M. Smithyman, Malawi; one *s* one *d*. *Educ:* Merchant Taylors' Sch., Northwood; Oriel Coll., Oxford (MA Oxon 1947). Overseas Audit Service, 1942–66, retired; Nyasaland, 1942–47; Singapore, 1947–48; Malaya, then Malaysia, 1948–66; Deputy Auditor-General, 1957–60; Auditor-General, Malaya, then Malaysia, 1960–66. Dep. Sec., Guy's Hosp. Med. and Dental Schools, 1966–69, Sec., 1969–82; Dep. Sec., UMDS of Guy's and St Thomas's Hosps, 1982–83 (Hon. Fellow, 1996). Chm., Univ. of London Purchasing Gp, 1976–82. Mem. Exec., Federated Pension Schemes, 1979–86. Man. Exec., Philip and Pauline Harris Charitable Trust, 1986–2005. Mem. Council and Exec. Cttee, Technology (formerly City Technology) Colls Trust, 1990–2000; Trustee, Bacon's Coll., 1991–2005; Gov., St Olave's and St Saviour's Grammar Sch. Foundn, 1992–2001. FKC 1998. Liveryman, Merchant Taylors' Co., 1951. JMN (Hon.) Malaya, 1961. *Address:* 3 Chesil House, St Paul's Cray Road, Chislehurst, Kent BR7 6QF. *T:* (01689) 821661; *e-mail:* dbompas@btinternet.com. *Club:* Royal Commonwealth Society.

See also A. G. Bompas.

BOMPAS, George; *see* Bompas, A. G.

BON, Michel Marie; Chairman: Editions du Cerf, since 1997; Devoteam, since 2006; *b* 5 July 1943; *s* of Emmanuel Bon and Mathilde (*née* Aussedat); *m* 1971, Catherine de Sairigné; one *s* three *d*. *Educ:* Lycée Champollion, Grenoble; Ecole supérieure des scis économiques et commerciales, Paris; Inst. d'Etudes Politiques, Paris; Ecole Nat. d'Administration, Paris. Insp. of Finance, Min. of Finance, 1971–75; Crédit National, 1975–78; Caisse Nat. de Crédit Agricole, 1978–85; Carrefour, 1985–93 (Chm. and CEO, 1990–93); Dir, Agence Nationale pour l'Emploi, France, 1993–95; Chm. and CEO, France Telecom, 1995–2002; Chm., Institut Pasteur, 2003–05. *Address:* 4 avenue de Camoëns, 75116 Paris, France.

BONA, Sir Kina, KBE 1993; Deputy Registrar, Integrity of Political Parties and Candidates Commission, Papua New Guinea; *b* 14 Feb. 1954; *m* 1990, Judith Lilian Sharples; one *d*. *Educ:* Univ. of Papua New Guinea (LLB 1976). Legal Officer, PNG, 1976–78; Teaching Fellow, Univ. of PNG, 1979; Sen. Legal Officer, 1980–82; Asst Sec., Dept of Justice, 1985–87; Public Prosecutor, PNG, 1988–94; High Comr for PNG in the UK, 1996–2002; lawyer in private practice, 2002–07. *Address:* PO Box 58, Waigani, National Capital District, Papua New Guinea.

BONALLACK, Sir Michael (Francis), Kt 1998; OBE 1971; Director: The Old Course Ltd (St Andrews), since 1990; Sea Island Co. (USA), since 2000; *b* 31 Dec. 1934; *s* of Sir Richard (Frank) Bonallack, CBE; *m* 1958, Angela Ward; one *s* three *d*. *Educ:* Chigwell; Haileybury. National Service, 1953–55 (1st Lieut, RASC). Joined family business, Bonallack and Sons Ltd, later Freight Bonallack Ltd, 1955, Dir, 1962–74; Dir, Buckley Investments, 1976–84. Sec., 1983–99, Captain, 1999, Royal and Ancient Golf Club of St Andrews. Non-exec. Dir, PGA European Tour, 2000–. Chairman: Golf Foundn, 1977–83 (Pres., 2000–); Professional Golfers' Assoc., 1976–82; President: English Golf Union, 1982; PGA of Europe, 2003–04. Hon. Fellow, Myerscough Coll., 2000. DUniv Stirling, 1994; Hon. LLD: Abertay, Dundee, 2000; St Andrews, 2003. *Recreation:* golf (British Amateur Champion, 1961, 1965, 1968, 1969, 1970; English Amateur Champion, 1962–63, 1965–67 and 1968; Captain, British Walker Cup Team, 1971; Bobby Jones Award for distinguished sportsmanship in golf, 1972). *Address:* Clatto Lodge, Blebo Craigs, Cupar, Fife KY15 5UF. *T:* (01334) 850600. *Clubs:* Royal and Ancient Golf (St Andrews); Golf House (Elie); Pine Valley, Augusta National, Ocean Forest (USA); Hermanus (RSA).

BOND, Alan; *b* 22 April 1938; *s* of Frank and Kathleen Bond; *m* 1st, 1956, Eileen Teresa Hughes (marr. diss. 1992); two *s* one *d* (and one *d* decd); 2nd, 1995, Diana Bliss. *Educ:* Perivale Sch., Ealing, UK; Fremantle Boys' Sch., W Australia. Chairman, Bond Corporation Holdings Ltd, 1969–90 (interests in property, brewing, electronic media, oil and gas, minerals, airships); Chairman: North Kalgurli Mines Ltd, 1985–89; Gold Mines of Kalgoorlie Ltd, 1987–89; Dallhold Investments Pty, 1987. Founder, Bond Univ., Qld, 1991. Syndicate Head, America's Cup Challenge 1983 Ltd; Australia II Winners of 1983 America's Cup Challenge, following three previous attempts: 1974 Southern Cross, 1977 Australia, 1980 Australia. Australian of the Year, 1977. AO 1984. *Publication:* (with Rob Mundle) Bond (autobiog.), 2004. *Recreation:* yachting. *Address:* GPO Box H555, Perth, WA 6001, Australia. *Clubs:* Royal Ocean Racing; Young Presidents Organisation, Royal Perth Yacht, Cruising Yacht, Western Australian Turf (WA).

BOND, Andrew, CEng; President and Chief Executive Officer, Asda Stores, since 2005; *b* Grantham, 16 March 1965; *s* of Terence and Christine Bond; *m* 1997, Susan Stringfellow; one *s* one *d*. *Educ:* King's Grammar Sch., Grantham; Salford Univ. (BSc 1st Cl. Hons 1987); Cranfield Sch. of Mgt (MBA 1993); CEng 1992. Grad. prog., British Gas, 1987–88; Product Dir and Mktg Manager, Hopkinsons Plc, 1988–92; Mktg Manager, 1994–97, Corporate Mktg Dir, 1997–99, Asda; Eur. Own Label Dir, Asda and Wal-Mart Germany, 1999–2000; Man. Dir, George at Asda, 2000–04; Chief Operating Officer, Asda, and Man. Dir, Global George, 2004–05. *Recreations:* running, cycling. *Address:* Asda House, Southbank, Great Wilson Street, Leeds LS11 5AD. *T:* (0113) 241 7007, *Fax:* (0113) 241 7654.

BOND, Prof. Brian James, FRHistS; Professor of Military History, King's College, University of London, 1986–2001, now Emeritus; *b* 17 April 1936; *s* of Edward Herbert Bond and Olive Bessie Bond (*née* Sartin); *m* 1962, Madeleine Joyce Carr. *Educ:* Sir William Borlase's Sch., Marlow; Worcester Coll., Oxford (BA Hist. 1959); King's Coll. London (MA Hist. 1962; FKC 1996). FRHistS 1978. Nat. Service, 1954–56, commnd RA. Tutor in Mod. Hist., Univ. of Exeter, 1961–62; Lectr, Univ. of Liverpool, 1962–66; King's College London: Lectr in War Studies, 1966–78; Reader, 1978–86. Vis. Prof., Univ. of Western Ontario, 1972–73; Visiting Fellow: Brasenose Coll., Oxford, 1992–93; All Souls Coll., Oxford, 2000. Liddell Hart Lectr, KCL, 1997; Lees Knowles Lectr, Cambridge Univ., 2000; War Studies Lectr, KCL, 2001. Mem. Council, RUSI, 1972–84. Pres., British Commn for Mil. Hist., 1986–2006. Member Editorial Board: Jl Contemp. Hist., 1988–2004; Jl Strategic Studies, 1978–2005; Jl Mil. Hist. (USA), 1992–96; War in Hist., 1994–; an Associate Editor, Oxford DNB, 1996–2002. *Publications:* (ed) Victorian Military Campaigns, 1967, 2nd edn 1994; The Victorian Army and the Staff College, 1972; (ed) Chief of Staff: the diaries of Lt-Gen. Sir Henry Pownall 1933–1944, vol. 1, 1972, vol. 2, 1974; Britain, France and Belgium, 1939–1940, 1975, 2nd edn 1990; Liddell Hart: a study of his military thought, 1977, 2nd edn 1991; British Military Policy between the Two World Wars, 1980; War and Society in Europe 1870–1970, 1984; (ed with S. Robbins) Staff Officer: the diaries of Lord Moyne 1914–1918, 1987; (ed) The First World War and British Military History, 1991; (ed) Fallen Stars: eleven studies of twentieth century military disasters, 1991; The Pursuit of Victory: from Napoleon to Saddam Hussein, 1996; (ed with N. Cave) Haig: a reappraisal 70 years on, 1999; The Unquiet Western Front: Britain's role in literature and history, 2002; (ed) War Memoirs of Earl Stanhope 1914–1918, 2006; Survivors of a Kind: memoirs of the Western Front, 2008. *Recreations:* gardening, visiting country houses, observing and protecting wild animals (especially foxes). *Address:* Olmeda, Ferry Lane, Medmenham, Marlow, Bucks SL7 2EZ. *T:* (01491) 571293. *Club:* Royal Over-Seas League.

BOND, Rt Rev. (Charles) Derek; appointed Bishop Suffragan of Bradwell, 1976, Area Bishop, 1984–92; Hon. Assistant Bishop, dioceses of Gloucester and Worcester, since 1992; *b* 4 July 1927; *s* of Charles Norman Bond and Doris Bond; *m* 1951, Joan Valerie Meikle; two *s* two *d*. *Educ*: Bournemouth Sch.; King's Coll., London. AKC (2nd hons). Curate of Friern Barnet, 1952; Midlands Area Sec. of SCM in Schools and Public Preacher, dio. Birmingham, 1956; Vicar: of Harringay, 1958; of Harrow Weald, 1962; Archdeacon of Colchester, 1972–76. Nat. Chm., CEMS, 1983–86; Chm., Retired Clergy Assoc., 1998–2003. *Recreation*: travel. *Address*: 52 Horn Book, Saffron Walden, Essex CB11 3JW. *T*: (01799) 521308; *e-mail*: BondD46@aol.com.

BOND, Edward; playwright and director; *b* 18 July 1934; *m* 1971, Elisabeth Pablé. Northern Arts Literary Fellow, 1977–79. Hon. DLitt Yale, 1977. George Devine Award, 1968; John Whiting Award, 1968; Obie Award, 1976; City of Lyon Medal, 2007. *Opera Libretti*: We Come to the River (music by Hans Werner Henze), 1976; The English Cat (music by Hans Werner Henze), 1982; *ballet libretto*: Orpheus, 1982; *translations*: Chekhov, The Three Sisters, 1967; Wedekind, Spring Awakening, 1974; Wedekind, Lulu—a monster tragedy, 1992. *Publications*: Theatre Poems and Songs, 1978; Collected Poems 1978–1985, 1987; Notes on Post-Modernism, 1990; Notes on Imagination, 1995; Selected Letters (5 vols), 1994–2004; Selected Notebooks, vol. 1, 2000, vol. 2, 2001; The Hidden Plot: notes on theatre and the state, 2000; My Day, a song cycle for young people, 2005; *plays*: The Pope's Wedding, 1962; Saved, 1965; Narrow Road to the Deep North, 1968; Early Morning, 1968; Passion, 1971; Black Mass, 1971; Lear, 1972; The Sea, 1973; Bingo, 1974; The Fool, 1976; A-A-America! (Grandma Faust, and The Swing), 1976; Stone, 1976; The Woman, 1978; The Bundle, 1978; The Worlds with The Activist Papers, 1980; Restoration, 1981; Summer: a play for Europe, and Fables (short stories), 1982; Derek, 1983; Human Cannon, 1984; The War Plays (part 1, Red Black and Ignorant; part 2, The Tin Can People; part 3, Great Peace), 1985; Jackets, 1989; In The Company of Men, 1990; September, 1990; Olly's Prison, 1993; Tuesday, 1993; Coffee: a tragedy, 1995; At the Inland Sea: a play for young people, 1996; Eleven Vests, 1997; The Crime of the Twenty-first Century, 1998; The Children: a play for two adults and sixteen children, 2000; Chair, 2000; Have I None, 2000; Existence, 2002; The Balancing Act, 2003; The Short Elektra, 2004; The Under Room, 2005; Born, 2006; People, 2006; Arcade, 2006; Tune, 2007; Collected Plays (8 vols), 1977–2007. *Address*: c/o Casarotto Ramsay, Waverley House, 7–12 Noel Street, W1F 8GQ.

BOND, Geoffrey Charles, OBE 2008; FSA; DL; heritage consultant; Chairman, Geoffrey Bond Consultancy, since 1996; *b* 14 Oct. 1939; *s* of Frederick Richard Bond and Dorothy Bond (*née* Gardner); *m* 1963, Dianora Dunnet; one *s* one *d*. *Educ*: Becket Sch., Nottingham; Univ. of Hull (BSc Econ Hons 1963). FSA 2008. Baring Bros, London, 1963–64; admitted solicitor, 1969; articled to Ashton Hill & Co., Nottingham, later Ashton Bond Gigg, 1964–68, Partner, 1970–85, Sen. Partner, 1985–96. Chairman: Linpack Packaging plc, 1982–89; Old Market Square Securities, 1984–99; non-executive Director: Charles Lawrence Gp plc, 1973–; Hooley Gp of Cos, 1976–; Regl Bd, Central Indep. TV plc, 1982–92. Hon. Solicitor to: British Sporting Art Trust, London, 1977–2008; Derby Internat. Porcelain Soc., 1985–. Dep. Chm., Nat. Mus. of Law and Nat. Centre for Citizenship and the Law, 1993–; Chairman: Arts & Business Midlands, 1999–2003; Gp for Educn in Museums, 2001–07; Mem. Council, MLA, 2006– (Mem., Acceptance in Lieu Panel, 2006–; Chm., MLA London, 2002–). Mem., Editl Bd, Byron Jl (Chm., 1996–2003); Chairman: London Byron Soc., 1996–2003 (Vice Pres., 2004–); Scottish Byron Soc., 2008–. Founder Trustee, Papplewick Pumping Stn Trust, 1976– (Chm., 1999–); Chm., Water Educn Trust; Patron, Notts Historic Gdns Trust, 1990–. Mem., City of London Cttee, St John Ambulance (Prince of Wales') Dist, 2003–. Hon. Consul for Norway in Midlands, 1981–2007; Chm., Assoc. of Hon. Norwegian Consuls in British Isles and Ireland, 1997–99. *Radio*: presenter, The Antiques Shop, Radio Nottingham, 1973–80; *television*: Mem., team of experts, Antiques Roadshow, 1979–84; presenter, Something to Treasure (series), 1985–91; *television films*: producer, Byron's Mine, 1994; assistant producer: The Heart of Shelley, 1992; The Sweet Life, 1997. Sheriff, City of London, 2003–04; Chm., Livery Cttee, 2007–; Liveryman, Co. of Glaziers and Painters of Glass, 1973 (Mem., Ct of Assts, 1992; Master, 1997); Mem., Guild of Educators, 2002–; Master, Guild of Arts Scholars, Dealers & Collectors, 2006–08; Mem. Court, City of London Solicitors' Co., 2006–. DL Notts, 1998. OStJ 2004. Kt First Class, Royal Norwegian Order of Merit, 1989. *Publications*: (contrib.) Byron: the image of the poet, 2008; articles for learned jls incl. Byron Jl, Newstead Byron Soc. Rev., Studies in Romanticism, Sir Walter Scott Club Rev., Keats-Shelley Jl, Collectors Guide. *Recreations*: antiquarian book collecting, gardening, golf, entertaining, music, giving lectures. *Address*: Burgage Manor, Southwell, Notts NG25 0EP. *T*: (01636) 816855, *Fax*: (01636) 816844; *e-mail*: consultancy@gbond.demon.co.uk. *Clubs*: Garrick, Athenæum.
See also Sir M. R. Bond.

BOND, Maj.-Gen. Henry Mark Garneys, OBE 1993; JP; Vice Lord-Lieutenant of Dorset, 1984–99; *b* 1 June 1922; *s* of W. R. G. Bond, Tyneham, Dorset; unmarried. *Educ*: Eton. Enlisted as Rifleman, 1940; commnd in Rifle Bde, 1941; served Middle East and Italy; seconded to Parachute Regt, 1947–50; ADC to Field Marshal Viscount Montgomery of Alamein, 1950–52; psc 1953; served in Kenya, Malaya, Cyprus and Borneo; Comd Rifle Bde in Cyprus and Borneo, 1964–66; Comd 12th Inf. Bde, 1967–68; idc 1969; Dir of Defence Operational Plans and Asst Chief of Defence Staff (Ops), 1970–72; retd 1972. President: Dorset Natural History and Archaeological Soc., 1972–75; Dorset Br., CPRE, 1990–95; Dorset Community Council, 1988–97; Dorset Assoc. of Parish Councils, 1990–97; Chm., Dorset Police Authy, 1980–92. Mem., Dorset CC, 1973–85 (Vice-Chm., 1981–85). JP Dorset, 1972 (Chm., Wareham Bench, 1984–89). High Sheriff of Dorset, 1977, DL Dorset, 1977. Chm., Governors of Milton Abbey Sch., 1982–94 (Visitor, 1994–98). *Recreations*: forestry, reading. *Address*: Moigne Combe, Dorchester, Dorset DT2 8JA. *T*: (01305) 852265. *Club*: Boodle's.

BOND, Ian Andrew Minton, CVO 2006; HM Diplomatic Service; Counsellor, Washington, since 2007; *b* 19 April 1962; *s* of Roy and Joan Bond; *m* 1987, Kathryn Joan Ingamells; two *s* one *d*. *Educ*: King Edward VI Sch., Birmingham; Phillips Acad., Andover, Mass; Balliol Coll., Oxford (BA Hons). Joined Diplomatic Service, 1984; FCO, 1984–87; Mem., UK Delegn to NATO, 1987–90; FCO, 1990–93; First Secretary: Moscow, 1993–96; FCO, 1996–2000; Counsellor and Dep. Hd of Mission, UK Delegn to OSCE, Vienna, 2000–04; Ambassador to Latvia, 2005–07. *Recreations*: music, opera, choral singing, travel, reading, cross-country ski-ing. *Address*: c/o Foreign and Commonwealth Office, King Charles Street, SW1A 2AH.

BOND, Jennie, (Mrs James Keltz); broadcaster and professional speaker; Court Correspondent, BBC News, 1989–2003; *b* 19 Aug. 1950; *d* of late Kenneth Bond and of Pamela Bond; *m* 1982, James Keltz; one *d*, and one step *s* one step *d*. *Educ*: St Francis Coll., Letchworth; Univ. of Warwick. Reporter: Richmond Herald, 1972–75; Evening Mail, Uxbridge, 1975–77; News Producer, BBC, 1977–86; News Correspondent, BBC, 1986–89. *Publications*: Reporting Royalty (autobiog.), 2001; Elizabeth, Fifty Glorious Years, 2002; Elizabeth, 80 Glorious Years, 2006. *Recreations*: family, walking by the sea. *Address*: c/o Knight Ayton, 114 St Martin's Lane, WC2N 4BE.

BOND, Sir John (Reginald Hartnell), Kt 1999; Chairman, Vodafone, since 2006 (non-executive Director, since 2005); *b* 24 July 1941; *s* of late Capt. R. H. A. Bond, OBE and of E. C. A. Bond; *m* 1968, Elizabeth Caroline Parker; one *s* two *d*. *Educ*: Tonbridge Sch., Kent; Cate Sch., Calif, USA (E-SU Scholar). Joined Hongkong & Shanghai Banking Corp., 1961; worked in Hong Kong, Thailand, Singapore, Indonesia and USA; Chief Exec., Wardley Ltd (Merchant Banking), 1984–87; Hongkong & Shanghai Banking Corporation: Exec. Dir, 1988–91; responsible for: Americas, 1988–89; commercial banking, based in Hong Kong, 1990–91; Pres. and Chief Exec., Marine Midland Banks Inc., Buffalo, USA, 1991–92. Chairman: Hongkong Bank of Canada, 1987–98; HSBC Americas Inc., 1997–2003; Marine Midland Bank, then HSBC Bank USA, 1997–2003; British Bank of the Middle East, then HSBC Bank Middle East, 1998–2004; Midland Bank, then HSBC Bank Plc, 1998–2004; Gp Chief Exec., 1993–98, Gp Chm., 1998–2006, HSBC Hldgs plc; Director: Hang Seng Bank Ltd, 1990–96; HSBC Hldgs, 1990–2006; HSBC Bank plc (formerly Midland Bank), 1993–2004 (Dep. Chm., 1996–98); Bank of England, 2001–04; HSBC N Amer. Hldgs Inc., 2005–06; non-executive Director: London Stock Exchange, 1994–99; British Steel, 1994–98; Orange plc, 1996–99; Ford Motor Co., 2000–; Shui On Land Ltd, Hong Kong, 2006–. Member: Mayor of Shanghai's Internat. Business Leaders' Adv. Council, 1999– (Chm., 2006–07); China Develt Forum, Beijing, 2001–. Chm., Inst. of Internat. Finance, Washington, 1998–2003. FCIB (FIB 1982). Hon. Fellow, London Business Sch., 2003. Hon. DEc Richmond, American Univ. in London, 1998; Hon. DLitt: Loughborough, 2000; Sheffield, 2002; Hon. DCL South Bank, 2000; Hon. DSc City, 2004; Hon. DBA London Metropolitan, 2004; Hon. LLD: Nottingham, 2005; Bristol, 2005. Foreign Policy Assoc. Medal, NY, 2003; Magnolia Gold Award, Shanghai Municipal People's Govt, 2003. *Recreations*: golf, ski-ing, reading biography. *Address*: Vodafone House, The Connection, Newbury, Berks RG14 2FN. *Clubs*: MCC; Royal Ashdown Forest Golf; Hong Kong (Hong Kong); John's Island (Florida).

BOND, Prof. (John) Richard, OC 2004; OOnt 2008; PhD; FRS 2001; FRSC; Professor, since 1987, and University Professor, since 1999, Canadian Institute for Theoretical Astrophysics (Director, 1996–2006); *b* 15 May 1950; *s* of Jack Parry Bond and Margaret Bond. *Educ*: Univ. of Toronto (BSc); Calif Inst. of Technol. (MS, PhD 1979). FRSC 1996. Res. Asst, Kellogg Lab., CIT, 1973–78; Postdoctoral Fellow, Univ. of Calif, Berkeley, 1978–81; Res. Fellow, Inst. of Astronomy, Cambridge, 1982–83; Asst Prof., 1981–85, Associate Prof., 1985–87, Stanford Univ.; Associate Prof., 1985–87, Actg Dir, 1990–91, Canadian Inst. for Theoretical Astrophysics. Fellow, 1988–, Dir, 2002–, Cosmology and Gravity Prog., Canadian Inst. for Advanced Research. Fellow, APS, 1998. Foreign Hon. Mem., American Acad. of Arts and Scis, 2003. *Address*: Canadian Institute for Theoretical Astrophysics, University of Toronto, 60 St George Street, Toronto, ON M5S 3H8, Canada. *T*: (416) 9786874.

BOND, Dr Martyn Arthur; Deputy Chairman, London Press Club, since 2005 (Director, 2000–05); *b* 10 Oct. 1942; *s* of Jack Bond and Muriel Caroline Janet (*née* Webb); *m* 1965, Dinah Macfarlane; two *s* one *d*. *Educ*: Portsmouth Grammar Sch.; Peter Symonds Sch.; Winchester Coll.; Queens' Coll., Cambridge (MA); Univ. of Sussex (DPhil 1971); Univ. of Hamburg. Producer, BBC, 1966–70; Lectr in W European Studies, NUU, 1970–73; Press Officer, Gen. Secretariat, Council of Ministers of EC, 1974–81; BBC Rep., Berlin, 1981–83; Principal Adminr, Gen. Secretariat, Council of Ministers of EC, 1983–88; Dir, UK Office of EP, 1989–99; Dir, Federal Trust, 1999–2002; Dir, Information Europe Ltd, 1999–. Mem. Bd, Europe-China Assoc., 1976–82; Founder Mem., Quaker Council for European Affairs, 1979–. Contested (SDP/Alliance) Hull W, 1987. Chm., Internat. Adv. Council, 1987–94, Sen. Fellow, 1995–; Salzburg Seminar in American Studies. Vis. Prof. of European Politics, RHBNC, 1999–. Dir, English Coll. Foundn, 1993–; Gov., English Coll. in Prague, 1995–. FRSA 1992. *Publications*: A Tale of Two Germanies, 1991; (ed) Eminent Europeans, 1996; (ed) The Treaty of Nice Explained, 2001; (ed) Europe, Parliaments and the Media, 2003; contrib. to Jl Legislative Studies, German Life and Letters, Parliament Mag., House Mag. *Recreation*: Europe.

BOND, Michael, OBE 1997; author; *b* 13 Jan. 1926; *s* of Norman Robert and Frances Mary Bond; *m* 1950, Brenda Mary Johnson (marr. diss. 1981); one *s* one *d*; *m* 1981, Susan Marfrey Rogers. *Educ*: Presentation College, Reading. RAF and Army, 1943–47; BBC Cameraman, 1947–66; full-time author from 1966. Paddington TV series, 1976. Hon. DLitt Reading, 2007. *Publications*: *for children*: A Bear Called Paddington, 1958; More About Paddington, 1959; Paddington Helps Out, 1960; Paddington Abroad, 1961; Paddington at Large, 1962; Paddington Marches On, 1964; Paddington at Work, 1966; Here Comes Thursday, 1966; Thursday Rides Again, 1968; Paddington Goes to Town, 1968; Thursday Ahoy, 1969; Parsley's Tail, 1969; Parsley's Good Deed, 1969; Parsley's Problem Present, 1970; Parsley's Last Stand, 1970; Paddington Takes the Air, 1970; Thursday in Paris, 1970; Michael Bond's Book of Bears, 1971, 1992; Michael Bond's Book of Mice, 1972; The Day the Animals Went on Strike, 1972; Paddington Bear, 1972; Paddington's Garden, 1972; Parsley the Lion, 1972; Parsley Parade, 1972; The Tales of Olga da Polga, 1972; Olga Meets her Match, 1973; Paddington's Blue Peter Story Book, 1973; Paddington at the Circus, 1973; Paddington Goes Shopping, 1973; Paddington at the Sea-side, 1974; Paddington at the Tower, 1974; Paddington on Top, 1974; Windmill, 1975; How to make Flying Things, 1975; Eight Olga Readers, 1975; Paddington's Loose End Book, 1976; Paddington's Party Book, 1976; Olga Carries On, 1976; Paddington's Pop-up Book, 1977; Paddington Takes the Test, 1979; Paddington's Cartoon Book, 1979; J. D. Polson and the Liberty-Head Dime, 1980; J. D. Polson and the Dillogate Affair, 1981; Paddington on Screen, 1981; Olga Takes Charge, 1982; The Caravan Puppets, 1983; Paddington at the Zoo, 1984; Paddington and the Knickerbocker Rainbow, 1984; Paddington's Painting Exhibition, 1985; Paddington at the Fair, 1985; Oliver the Greedy Elephant, 1985; Paddington at the Palace, 1986; Paddington Minds the House, 1986; Paddington's Busy Day, 1987; Paddington and the Marmalade Maze, 1987; Paddington's Magical Christmas, 1988; Paddington and the Christmas Surprise, 1997; Paddington at the Carnival, 1998; Paddington's Scrap Book, 1999; Paddington in Hot Water, 2000; Paddington's Party Tricks, 2000; Olga Moves House, 2001; Olga Follows Her Nose, 2002; Paddington's Grand Tour, 2003; with Karen Bond: Paddington Posts a Letter, 1986; Paddington at the Airport, 1986; Paddington's London, 1986; Paddington Goes to Hospital, 2001; Paddington Rules the Waves, 2008; Paddington Here and Now, 2008; Paddington: my book of marmalade, 2008; *for adults*: Monsieur Pamplemousse, 1983; Monsieur Pamplemousse and the Secret Mission, 1984; Monsieur Pamplemousse on the Spot, 1986; Monsieur Pamplemousse Takes the Cure, 1987; The Pleasures of Paris, 1987; Monsieur Pamplemousse Aloft, 1989; Monsieur Pamplemousse Investigates, 1990; Monsieur Pamplemousse Rests His Case, 1991; Monsieur Pamplemousse Stands Firm, 1992; Monsieur Pamplemousse on Location, 1992; Monsieur Pamplemousse takes the Train, 1993; Monsieur Pamplemousse Afloat, 1998; Monsieur Pamplemousse on Probation, 2000; Monsieur Pamplemousse on Vacation, 2002; Monsieur Pamplemousse Hits the Headlines, 2003; Monsieur Pamplemousse and the Militant Midwives, 2006; Monsieur Pamplemousse and the French Solution, 2007; *autobiography*: Bears and Forebears: a life so far, 1996. *Recreations*: photography, travel, food and wine. *Address*: The Agency, 24 Pottery Lane, W11 4LZ. *T*: (020) 7727 1346.

BOND, Sir Michael (Richard), Kt 1995; FRCPsych, FRCPGlas, FRCSE; Professor of Psychological Medicine, University of Glasgow, 1973–98 (Vice Principal, 1986–97; Administrative Dean, Faculty of Medicine, 1991–97); *b* 15 April 1936; *s* of Frederick Richard Bond and Dorothy Bond (*née* Gardner); *m* 1961, Jane Issitt; one *s* one *d*. *Educ:* Magnus Grammar Sch., Newark, Notts; Univ. of Sheffield (MD, PhD). FRSE 1998. Ho. Surg./Ho. Phys., Royal Inf., Sheffield, 1961–62; Asst Lectr/Res. Registrar, Univ. Dept of Surgery, Sheffield, 1962–64; Res. Registrar/Lectr, Univ. Dept of Psychiatry, Sheffield, 1964–67; Sen. Ho. Officer/Res. Registrar, Registrar/Sen. Registrar, Inst. of Neurological Scis, Glasgow, 1968–71; Lectr in Neurosurgery, Univ. Dept of Neurosurgery, Glasgow, 1971–73. Locum Cons. Neurosurgeon, Oxford, 1972; Hon. Cons. Psychiatrist, Greater Glasgow Health Bd, 1973–98. Member: UGC, 1982–91; UFC, 1991–93; SHEFC, 1992–96; Chm., Jt Med. Adv. Cttee, 1992–95. Pres., Pain Soc., 1999–2001; Member Council: Internat. Assoc. for Study of Pain, 1981–93, 1996– (Pres. 2002–05); St Andrews Ambulance Assoc., 1995–2000. Dir, Prince and Princess of Wales Hospice, Glasgow, 1997–2002. Chm., Head Injuries Trust for Scotland, 1989–99; Mem., The London Inquiry, 1991–92. Trustee, Lloyds TSB Foundn, 1999–2005. Gov., High Sch., Glasgow, 1990– (Chm., 2001–06). FRSA 1992. Hon. DSc Leicester, 1996; DUniv Glasgow, 2001. *Publications:* Pain, its nature, analysis and treatment, 1979, 2nd edn 1984; (co-ed) Rehabilitation of the Head Injured Adult, 1983, 2nd edn 1989; (with K. H. Simpson) Pain: its nature and treatment, 2006; papers on psychological and social consequences of severe brain injury, psychological aspects of chronic pain and cancer pain, 1963–, and others on similar topics. *Recreations:* painting, collecting antique books, forest walking, ornithology, gardening. *Address:* 33 Ralston Road, Bearsden, Glasgow G61 3BA. *T:* (home) (0141) 942 4391; (work) (0141) 330 3692; *e-mail:* m.bond@admin.gla.ac.uk. *Club:* Athenæum.

See also G. C. Bond.

BOND, Richard; *see* Bond, J. R.

BOND, Richard Douglas; Senior Partner, Herbert Smith, 2000–05; *b* 23 July 1946; *s* of Douglas Charles Bond and Vera Eileen Bond; *m* 1973, Anthea Mary Charrington (*d* 1996); two *d*; *m* 2007, Julie Ann Nicholls. *Educ:* Berkhamsted Sch. Articled Clerk, Halsey, Lightly & Hemsley, 1964–69; joined Herbert Smith, 1969; seconded to BNOC, 1976–78; Partner, 1977; Head of Corporate, 1993–2000. *Recreations:* golf, cricket, theatre. *Club:* MCC.

BOND, Richard Henry; His Honour Judge Bond; a Circuit Judge, since 1997; *b* 15 April 1947; *s* of Ashley Raymond Bond and Hester Mary Bond (*née* Bowles); *m* 1987, Annabel Susan Curtis; one *s* one *d*. *Educ:* Sherborne Sch. Called to the Bar, Inner Temple, 1970. *Recreations:* architecture, walking, gardening. *Address:* Combined Court Centre, Deansleigh Road, Bournemouth BH7 7DS.

BOND, Samantha; actress; *b* 27 Nov. 1961; *d* of Philip Bond and late Pat Bond (then Sandys); *m* 1989, Alexander Hanson; one *s* one *d*. *Educ:* Godolphin and Latymer Sch.; Bristol Old Vic Theatre Sch. *Theatre* includes: Juliet in Romeo and Juliet, Lyric, Hammersmith, 1986; Beatrice in Much Ado About Nothing, Phoenix, 1988; Hermione in The Winter's Tale, 1992–93, Rosalind in As You Like It, 1992–93, RSC; C in Three Tall Women, Wyndham's, 1995; Amy in Amy's View, RNT, transf. Aldwych, then NY, 1997; Mary in Memory of Water, Vaudeville, 1998; Lady Macbeth in Macbeth, Albery, 2002; title rôle in A Woman of No Importance, Th. Royal, Haymarket, 2003; Lady Driver in Donkey's Years, Comedy, 2006; *television* includes: The Ginger Tree, Emma, Family Money, Tears Before Bedtime, Morse, Manhunt, The Hunt, Donovan, Distant Shores, Clapham Junction, Wolfenden, Fanny Hill, Midsomer Murders; *films* include: Eric The Viking, 1989; What Rats Won't Do, 1998; Blinded, 2005; Yes, 2005; rôle of Moneypenny in: Goldeneye, 1995; Tomorrow Never Dies, 1997; The World is Not Enough, 1999; Die Another Day, 2002. Ambassador: The Prince's Trust, 1997–; Macmillan Cancer Support, 2006–; Patron, Shooting Star Children's Hospice, 2006–. *Recreations:* Scrabble, crosswords, gardening, dancing, watching cricket. *Address:* c/o Conway Van Gelder Grant Ltd, 18–21 Jermyn Street, SW1Y 6HP. *T:* (020) 7287 0077, *Fax:* (020) 7287 1940.

BONDEVIK, Rev. Kjell Magne; President, Oslo Center for Peace and Human Rights, since 2006; *b* Molde, Norway, 3 Sept. 1947; *s* of Johannes and Margit Bondevik; *m* 1970, Bjørg Rasmussen; two *s* one *d*. *Educ:* Free Faculty of Theology, Oslo (*Candidatus Theologiae* 1975). Ordained priest, Lutheran Church of Norway, 1979. State Sec., Prime Minister's Office, 1972–73; MP (KrF) Møre og Romsdal, Norway, 1973–2005; Minister of Church and Educn, 1983–86; Minister of Foreign Affairs, 1989–90; Prime Minister of Norway, 1997–2000 and 2001–05. UN Special Humanitarian Envoy for the Horn of Africa, 2006–07. *Publication:* Et liv i spenning (memoir), 2006. *Address:* c/o Oslo Center for Peace and Human Rights, PO Box 2753 Solli, 0204 Oslo, Norway.

BONE, Charles, PPRI, ARCA; President, Royal Institute of Painters in Water Colours, 1979–89; Governor, Federation of British Artists, 1976–81 and since 1983 (Member, Executive Council, 1983–84 and 1986–88); *b* 15 Sept. 1926; *s* of William Stanley and Elizabeth Bone; *m* Sheila Mitchell, FRBS, ARCA, sculptor; two *s*. *Educ:* Farnham Coll. of Art; Royal Coll. of Art (ARCA). FBI Award for Design. Consultant, COSIRA, 1952–70; Craft Adviser, Malta Inds Assoc., Malta, 1952–78; Lecturer, Brighton Coll. of Art, 1950–86; Director, RI Galleries, Piccadilly, 1965–70. Many mural paintings completed, including those in Eaton Square and Meretea, Italy; oils and water colours in exhibns of RA, London Group, NEAC and RBA, 1950–; 50 one-man shows, 1950–; works in private collections in France, Italy, Malta, America, Canada, Japan, Australia, Norway, Sweden, Germany. Designer of Stourhead Ball, 1959–69; produced Ceramic Mural on the History of Aerial Photography. Critic for Arts Review. Mem. Council, RI, 1964– (Vice-Pres. 1974). Hon. Member: Medical Art Soc.; Soc. Botanical Artists. Hon. FCA (Can.). Hunting Gp Prize for a British Watercolour, 1984. *Film:* Watercolour Painting: a practical guide, 1990. *Publications:* author and illustrator: Waverley, 1991; Authors Circle, 1998; Cathedrals, 2000. *Address:* Winters Farm, Puttenham, Guildford, Surrey GU3 1AR. *T:* (01483) 810226.

BONE, Sir (James) Drummond, Kt 2008; Vice-Chancellor, University of Liverpool, 2002–08; *b* 11 July 1947; *s* of William Drummond Bone, ARSA, RSW and Helen Bone (*née* Yuill); *m* 1970, Vivian Clare Kindon. *Educ:* Ayr Acad.; Univ. of Glasgow (MA); Balliol Coll., Oxford (Snell Exhibnr, 1968–72). Lectr, English and Comparative Literature, Univ. of Warwick, 1972–80; University of Glasgow: Lectr, 1980–89, Sen. Lectr, 1989–95, in English Literature; Dean, Faculty of Arts, 1991–95; Vice-Principal, 1995–99; Prof. of English Literature, 1995–2000; Principal, RHBNC, London Univ., 2000–02 (Hon. Fellow, 2004); Pro-Vice-Chancellor, London Univ., 2001–02. Pres., UUK, 2005–07. Chairman: Foundn for Art and Creative Technol., 2004–; Liverpool Capital of Culture Bd, 2005–; Vice Chm., The Northern Way, 2004–. Jt Editor, Romanticism jl, 1993–. FRSA 1995; FRSE 2008. Freeman, Coachmakers' Co., 2007. Hon. DLitt Chester, 2008. *Publications:* Writers and their Work: Byron, 2000; Cambridge Companion to Byron, 2004. *Recreations:* music, ski-ing, Maseratis. *Club:* Athenæum.

BONE, Rt Rev. John Frank Ewan; Area Bishop of Reading, 1989–96; *b* 28 Aug. 1930; *s* of Jack and Herberta Blanche Bone; *m* 1954, Ruth Margaret Crudgington; two *s* two *d* and one adopted *s*. *Educ:* Monkton Combe School, Bath; St Peter's Coll., Oxford (MA); Ely Theological Coll.; Whitelands Coll. of Education (Grad. Cert. in Education). Ordained, 1956; Assistant Curate: St Gabriel's, Warwick Square, 1956–60; St Mary's, Henley on Thames, 1960–63; Vicar of Datchet, 1963–76; Rector of Slough, 1976–78; Rural Dean of Burnham, 1974–77; Archdeacon of Buckingham, 1978–89. Mem. of General Synod, 1980–85. Hon. Asst Bishop, Dio. of Oxford, 1996–. *Recreations:* collecting maps, topographical books and prints, classical music, walking. *Address:* 4 Grove Road, Henley-on-Thames, Oxon RG9 1DH.

BONE, Peter William, FCA; MP (C) Wellingborough, since 2005; *b* 19 Oct. 1952; *m* 1981, Jeanette Sweeney; two *s* one *d*. *Educ:* Westcliff-on-Sea Grammar Sch. FCA 1976. Financial Dir, Essex Electronics and Precision Engrg Gp, 1977–83; Chief Exec., High Tech Electronics Co., 1983–90; Man. Dir, Palm Travel (West) Ltd, 1990–2002. Mem. (C), Southend-on-Sea BC, 1977–86. Contested (C): Islwyn, 1992; Pudsey, 1997; Wellingborough, 2001. *Address:* House of Commons, SW1A 0AA; (office) 21 High Street, Wellingborough, Northants NN8 4JZ.

BONE, Quentin, MA, DPhil; FRS 1984; zoologist; Hon. Research Fellow, Marine Biological Association UK; *b* 17 Aug. 1931; *s* of late Stephen Bone (landscape painter) and Mary Adshead (mural painter); *m* 1958, Susan Elizabeth Smith; four *s*. *Educ:* Warwick Sch.; St John's Coll., Oxon (Hon. Fellow, 1998). Naples Scholarship, 1954; Fellow by examination, Magdalen Coll., Oxford, 1956. Zoologist at Plymouth Laboratory, Marine Biol Assoc., 1959–91. *Publications:* Biology of Fishes (with N. B. Marshall), 1983, 2nd edn (with J. S. Blaxter also), 1994, 3rd edn (with R. Moore), 2008; (ed) Biology of Pelagic Tunicates, 1998; papers on fish and invertebrates, mainly in Jl of Mar. Biol Assoc. UK. *Address:* Marchant House, 98 Church Road, Plymstock, Plymouth PL9 9BG.

BONE, Sir Roger (Bridgland), KCMG 2002 (CMG 1996); HM Diplomatic Service, retired; President, Boeing UK, since 2005; *b* 29 July 1944; *s* of late Horace Bridgland Bone and Dora R. Bone (*née* Tring); *m* 1970, Lena M. Bergman; one *s* one *d*. *Educ:* William Palmer's Sch., Grays; St Peter's Coll., Oxford (MA). Entered HM Diplomatic Service, 1966; UK Mission to UN, 1966; FCO, 1967; 3rd Sec., Stockholm, 1968–70; 2nd Sec., FCO, 1970–73; 1st Secretary: Moscow, 1973–75; FCO, 1975–78; 1st Sec., UK Perm. Representation to European Communities, Brussels, 1978–82; Asst Private Sec. to Sec. of State for Foreign and Commonwealth Affairs, 1982–84; Vis. Fellow, Harvard Univ. Center for Internat. Affairs, 1984–85; Counsellor, 1985–89, and Head of Chancery, 1987–89, Washington; Counsellor, FCO, 1989–91; Asst Under Sec. of State, FCO, 1991–95; Ambassador to Sweden, 1995–99; Ambassador to Brazil, 1999–2004. Non-exec. Dir, Foreign and Colonial Investment Trust plc, 2008–. Mem. Council, Brazilian Chamber of Commerce, 2005–. Mem., Exec. Council, RUSI, 2007–. Chm., Anglo-Latin America Foundn, 2005–; Trustee, Nobrega Foundn, 2005–; Mem. Council, Air League, 2007–. *Recreations:* music, wine. *Address:* The Boeing Company, 16 St James's Street, SW1A 1ER. *T:* (020) 7930 5000. *Club:* Oxford and Cambridge.

BONE, Prof. Thomas Renfrew, CBE 1987; Deputy Principal, University of Strathclyde, 1992–96; *b* 2 Jan. 1935; *s* of James Renfrew Bone and Mary Williams; *m* 1959, Elizabeth Stewart; one *s* one *d*. *Educ:* Greenock High Sch.; Glasgow Univ. MA 1st cl. English 1956, MEd 1st cl. 1962, PhD 1967. Teacher, Paisley Grammar Sch., 1957–62; Lecturer: Jordanhill Coll. of Educn, 1962–63; Glasgow Univ., 1963–67; Jordanhill College of Education: Hd of Educn Dept, 1967–71; Principal, 1972–92. FCCEA 1984; FRSGS 1997. *Publications:* Studies in History of Scottish Education, 1967; School Inspection in Scotland, 1968; *chapters in:* Whither Scotland, 1971; Education Administration in Australia and Abroad, 1975; Administering Education: international challenge, 1975; European Perspectives in Teacher Education, 1976; Education for Development, 1977; Practice of Teaching, 1978; World Yearbook of Education, 1980; The Management of Educational Institutions, 1982; The Effective Teacher, 1983; Strathclyde: changing horizons, 1985; The Changing Role of the Teacher, 1987; Teacher Education in Europe, 1990; Educational Leadership: challenge and change, 1992. *Recreations:* golf, bridge. *Address:* 7 Marchbank Gardens, Paisley PA1 3JD. *Clubs:* Western Gailes Golf, Buchanan Bridge; Paisley Burns.

BONELL, Carlos Antonio; guitarist; concert artist since 1969; *b* London, 23 July 1949; *s* of Carlos Bonell and Ana Bravo; *m* 1975, Pinuccia Rossetti; two *s*. *Educ:* William Ellis Sch., Highgate; Royal Coll. of Music (Hon. RCM 1973). Lectr, City Lit, 1970; Prof., RCM 1972. Début as solo guitarist, Purcell Room, 1971; GLAA Young Musician, 1973; resident guitarist, London Contemp. Dance Theatre, 1974; concert tours and recording with John Williams & Friends, 1975; first solo album, 1975; concerto début, RFH, 1977; NY début, 1978; Carlos Bonell Ensemble début, QEH, 1983, and tours in Europe and Far East; soloist with all major UK orchestras; commissioned and first performed Sonata by Stephen Oliver, 1981; first performance of: guitar concertos by Bryan Kelly, 1979, Barrington Pheloung, 1994, Armand Coeck, 1997; recorded Rodrigo's Concierto de Aranjuez, 1981; first recording of Carlos Bonell Ensemble, The Sea in Spring, 1997; numerous other solo records and awards. *Publications:* Spanish folk songs and dances, 1975; Gaspar Sanz airs and dances, 1977; A Tarrega collection, 1980; First Pieces for solo guitar, 1980; The romantic collection, 1983; The classical collection, 1983; Spanish folk songs for 3 guitars, 1984; Purcell: 3 pieces, 1984; Tarrega Fantasia, 1984; Technique Builder, 1998; Carlos Bonell Guitar Series, 1998. *Recreations:* cinema, reading, history, playing the guitar, listening to music. *Address: e-mail:* carlos@carlosbonell.com; *web:* www.carlosbonell.com.

BONELLO DU PUIS, George, KOM 1995; LLD; High Commissioner for Malta in London, 1999–2005; *b* 24 Jan. 1928; *s* of Joseph Bonello and Josephine (*née* Du Puis); *m* 1957, Mary Iris sive Iris Gauci Maistre'; two *s* one *d*. *Educ:* St Catherine's High Sch., Malta; The Lyceum, Malta; Royal Univ. of Malta (LLD 1952). Law Practice, 1953–87 and 1995–98. MP, Malta, 1971–96; Minister of Finance, 1987–92; Minister for Econ. Services, 1992–95. Chm., Sliema Wanderers FC, 1961–87. *Recreations:* billiards and sports in general, football in particular. *Address:* The Park, Antonio Nani Street, Ta'Xbiex, Malta. *T:* 335415. *Clubs:* Royal Over-Seas League; Casino Maltese (Valletta, Malta).

BONES, Christopher John; Principal, Henley Business School (formerly Management College), since 2005; *b* 12 June 1958; *s* of James C. E. and Sydness M. Bones; *m* 1984, Pamela Gail Fawcett; one *s* one *d*. *Educ:* Dulwich Coll.; Aberdeen Univ. (MA Hons). Advr, Employee Relns, 1982–84, Industrial Relns, 1985–87, Shell; Group Management Development Manager: Grand Met Brewing, 1987–89; Grand Met Retailing, 1989; Personnel and Admin Dir, GME, 1990–92; United Distillers: Orgn Develt Manager, 1992–95; HR Dir, Internat., 1995–97; HR Dir, Europe, 1997–99; Gp Compensation and Benefits Dir, 1999; Gp Orgn Effectiveness and Develt Dir, Cadbury Schweppes plc, 1999–2004. Mem. Bd, Govt Skills, 2005–; non-exec. Ind. Dir, Agric. and Horticulture Develt Bd UK, 2007–. Chm., Lib Dem Party Reform Commn, 2008. CCMI 2007; FCIPD 2002; FRSA 2001. *Publications:* The Self-Reliant Manager, 1993; regular contribs to Human Resources mag. *Recreations:* gardening, theatre, eradicating bullshit. *Address:*

Henley Business School, Greenlands, Henley-on-Thames, Oxon RG9 3AU. *T:* (01491) 418831, *Fax:* (01491) 418862; *e-mail:* chris.bones@henleymc.ac.uk.

BONEY, Guy Thomas Knowles; QC 1990; **His Honour Judge Boney;** a Circuit Judge, since 2003; *b* 28 Dec. 1944; *o c* of Thomas Knowles Boney, MD and Muriel Hilary Eileen Long, FRCS; *m* 1976, Jean Harris Ritchie, *qv*; two *s. Educ:* Winchester College; New College, Oxford (BA 1966; MA 1987). Called to the Bar, Middle Temple, 1968 (Harmsworth Scholar), Bencher, 1997; in practice on Western Circuit, 1969–2003; Head of Pump Court Chambers, 1992–2001; a Recorder, 1985–2003; a Dep. High Court Judge, 1994–2003. Chm., Friends of Winchester Coll., 2001–. Lord of the Manor, Stockbridge, 2003–. *Publications:* The Road Safety Act 1967, 1971; contribs to: Halsbury's Laws of England, 4th edn (Road Traffic); horological jls. *Recreations:* horology, music (Organist, King's Somborne Parish Church, 1980–), amateur theatre. *Address:* Winchester Combined Court Centre, Winchester SO23 9EL. *Club:* Garrick.

BONEY, Jean Harris, (Mrs G. T. K. Boney); *see* Ritchie, J. H.

BONFIELD, Sir Peter (Leahy), Kt 1996; CBE 1989; FREng; international business executive; *b* 3 June 1944; *s* of George and Patricia Bonfield; *m* 1968, Josephine Houghton. *Educ:* Hitchin Boys' Grammar School; Loughborough Univ. (BTech Hons; Hon. DTech, 1988). FIET (FIEE 1990), FBCS 1990, FCIM 1990; FREng (FEng 1993). Texas Instruments Inc., Dallas, USA, 1966–81; Group Exec. Dir, ICL, 1981–84; Chm. and Man. Dir, STC Internat. Computers Ltd, 1984–90; Chm. and Chief Exec., 1985–96, Dep. Chm., 1997–2000, ICL plc; Dep. Chief Exec., STC plc, 1987–90; Chief Exec., BT plc, 1996–2002. Director: BICC PLC, 1992–96; Ericsson, 2002–; Mentor Graphics Corp., 2002–; Taiwan Semiconductor Manufacturing, 2002–; Sony Corp., Japan, 2005–; Member: Internat. Adv. Bd, Citigroup (formerly Salomon Smith Barney), 1999–; Adv. Bd, Sony Corp., 2004–; New Venture Partners LLP, 2006–; Chm. Supervisory Bd, NXP Semiconductors, 2006–; non-exec. Mem., Supervisory Bd, Actis LLP, 2005–; non-exec. Dir, Dubai Internat. Capital, 2007–. Member: European Round Table, 1996–2002; EU-Japan Business Dialogue Round Table, 1999–2002; Ambassador for British Business. Mem., British Quality Foundn, 1993– (Vice-Pres.). Mem., CS Coll. Adv. Council, 1993–97. FRSA 1992. Freeman, City of London, 1990; Liveryman, Information Technologists' Co., 1992. Hon. Citizen, Dallas, Texas, 1994. Hon. doctorates from univs of Loughborough, Surrey, Mid Glamorgan, Nottingham Trent, Brunel, Open, Northumbria at Newcastle, Kingston, Cranfield, Essex and London. Mountbatten Medal, Nat. Electronics Council, 1995; Gold Medal, Inst. of Mgt, 1996. Comdr, Order of the Lion (Finland), 1995. *Recreations:* music, sailing, ski-ing. *Address:* PO Box 129, Shepperton, Middx TW17 9WL. *Club:* Royal Automobile, Royal Thames Yacht.

BONFIELD, Prof. William, CBE 1998; PhD; FRS 2003; FREng; Professor of Medical Materials, University of Cambridge, 2000–05, now Professor Emeritus; Director, Pfizer Institute for Pharmaceutical Materials Science, 2002–05; *b* 6 March 1937; *s* of Cecil William Bonfield and Ellen Gertrude Bonfield; *m* 1960, Gillian Winifred Edith Cross; one *s* two *d. Educ:* Letchworth GS; Imperial College, London (Perry Meml and Bessemer Medals; BScEng, PhD, DIC, ARSM). CEng, FIMMM; FREng (FEng 1993); CPhys 2003; FInstP 2003; FRSC 2005. Honeywell Res. Center, Hopkins, Minn, USA, 1961–68; Queen Mary, later Queen Mary and Westfield College, London: Reader in Materials Science, 1968; Prof. of Materials, 1974–99; Head, Dept of Materials, 1980–90; Chm., Sch. of Engineering, 1981–88; Dean of Engineering, 1985–89; Dir, Univ. of London IRC in Biomedical Materials, 1991–99. Visiting Professor: Chulalongkorn Univ., Bangkok, 1988–98; Henry Ford Hosp., Detroit, 1992; Nat. Univ. of Singapore, 2007; OCMR Dist. Vis. Prof., Univ. of Toronto, 1990; Honorary Professor: Univ. of Sichuan, 1992–; UCL, 2007–. Lectures: Royal Microscopical Soc., 1992; Mellor Meml, Inst. of Materials, 1993; Prof. Moore Meml, Univ. of Bradford, 1994; Dist. Scholar, QUB, 1994; C. W. Hall Meml, SW Res. Inst., San Antonio, Texas, 1996; Hatfield Meml, Univ. of Sheffield, 1996; CSE Internat., Royal Acad. of Engrg, 1998; Hawksley Meml, IMechE, 1999; William Mong Dist., Univ. of Hong Kong, 2002; Robert Warner, Founders' Co., 2005. Project Leader, EEC Concerted Action in Skeletal Implants, 1989–96. Chm., Med Engrg Cttee, 1989, Mem., Materials Cttee, later Materials Commn, 1983–88, SERC; Institute of Materials: Chairman: Biomaterials Cttee, 1989–96; Biomedical Applications Div., 1996–2005; Vice-Pres., 1998–2002; Member: Materials Sci. Bd, 1989–95; Council, 1996–2005; Member: Jt Dental Cttee, 1984–89; DoH Cttee on Dental and Surgical Materials, 1986–90; Directive Council, Internat. Soc. for Bio-analoging Skeletal Implants, 1988–95; Jl Cttee, Internat. Fedn for Med. and Biol Engrg, 1989–2001; Techl Cttee, BSI, 1992–; Metallurgy and Materials Res. Assessment Panel, HEFC, 1995–96 and 2001–02; Materials Foresight Panel, OST, 1995–98; Chm., UK Focus on Med. Engrg, Royal Acad. of Engrg, 1998–2001. Chm., London Metallurgical Soc., 1991; Sec. Gen., Internat. Soc. for Ceramics in Medicine, 1998–2005. Director: Abonetics Ltd, 1996–; Biocompatibles plc, 2000–02; Apatech Ltd, 2001–; OrthoMimetics, 2007–. Chm., Editl Bd, Materials in Electronics, 1990–; Mem., Editl Bd, Jl of Applied Polymer Sci., 1992–; Editor: Jl of Materials Science, 1973–2002; Jl Royal Soc.: Interface, 2004–; Founding Editor: Jl of Materials Science Letters, 1981–2002; Materials in Medicine, 1990–2006. Freeman: Armourers' and Brasiers' Co., 1994 (Liveryman, 1999; Mem., Ct of Assts, 2001–; Master, 2007–08); City of London, 1998. Hon. Member: Canadian Ortho. Res. Soc., 1983; Materials Res. Soc. of India, 1993. Hon. FIPEM 2003; Hon. Fellow, Queen Mary, Univ. of London, 2007. Hon. DSc Aberdeen, 2002. Griffith Medal, Inst. of Metals, 1991; Royal Soc. Armourers' and Brasiers' Co. Medal, 1991; George Winter Award, Eur. Soc. for Biomaterials, 1994; Kelvin Medal, ICE, 1995; Acta Metallurgica J. Herbert Holloman Award, 2000; Chapman Medal, Inst. of Materials, Minerals, and Mining, 2003; Japanese Soc. for Biomaterials Medal, 2003; Prince Philip Gold Medal, Royal Acad. Engrg, 2004; President's Prize, UK Soc. for Biomaterials, 2004. *Publications:* Bioceramics, 1991; over 400 research papers on biomaterials, biomechanics and physical metallurgy in sci. jls. *Recreation:* cycling. *Address:* Department of Materials Science and Metallurgy, University of Cambridge, New Museums Site, Pembroke Street, Cambridge CB2 3QZ. *Clubs:* Athenæum; North Road Cycling.

BONGERS de RATH, Paul Nicholas; international relations consultant in urban affairs, 1996–2002; *b* 25 Oct. 1943; *s* of late Henry Bongers and Marjorie Bongers (*née* Luxton); *m* 1968, Margaret Rennie Huddleston Collins; one *s* two *d. Educ:* Bradfield Coll.; New Coll., Oxford (MA); DPA Univ. of London (external), 1968. Administrative Trainee, City of Southampton, 1965–68; Personal Asst to Chief Exec., City of Nottingham, 1968–69; Administrator, Council of Europe, 1969–71; Assistant Secretary: AMC, 1971–74; AMA, 1974–78; Exec. Sec., British Sections, IULA/CEMR, 1978–88; Dir, Local Govt Internat. Bureau, 1988–95. Special Advr, CEMR, 1996–2001; Consultant: World Assocs of Cities and Local Authorities Co-ordination, 1996–99; UN Human Settlements Prog., 2001–02; Special Rep., Bremen Initiative, 1999–2001. Hon. Sec. and Dist Officer, Local Govt Gp for Europe, 1999–2005; Mem., Exec. Cttee, European Movt, 2005–07. *Publications:* Local Government and 1992, 1990, 2nd edn as Local Government and the European Single Market, 1992; articles in local govt jls. *Recreations:* family, music, countryside, travel, the arts. *Address:* Old Lawn Place, Cosmore, Dorset DT2 7TW. *Club:* Reform.

BONHAM, Major Sir Antony Lionel Thomas, 4th Bt *cr* 1852; DL; late Royal Scots Greys; *b* 21 Oct. 1916; *o s* of Maj. Sir Eric H. Bonham, 3rd Bt, and Ethel (*d* 1962), *y d* of Col Leopold Seymour; *S* father, 1937; *m* 1944, Felicity (*d* 2003), *o d* of late Col. Frank L. Pardoe, DSO, Bartonbury, Cirencester; three *s. Educ:* Eton; RMC. Served Royal Scots Greys, 1937–49; retired with rank of Major, 1949. DL Glos 1983. *Heir: s* (George) Martin (Antony) Bonham [*b* 18 Feb. 1945; *m* 1979, Nenon Baillieu (marr. diss. 1992), *e d* of R. R. Wilson and Hon. Mrs Wilson, Durford Knoll, Upper Durford Wood, Petersfield, Hants; one *s* three *d*]. *Address:* Greystones, The Croft, Fairford, Glos GL7 4BB. *T:* (01285) 712258.

BONHAM, Nicholas; Chairman: Noble Investments (UK) plc, since 2004; Corporate Communication Ltd, since 2006; Sugar Collection Ltd, since 2006; *b* 7 Sept. 1948; *s* of late Leonard Charles Bonham and Diana Maureen (*née* Magwood); *m* 1st, 1977, Kaye Eleanor (*née* Ivett) (marr. diss. 1999); two *d*; 2nd, 2003, Susan Angela Chester. *Educ:* Trent College. Joined W. & F. C. Bonham & Sons Ltd, Fine Art Auctioneers, 1966; Dir, 1970; Man. Dir, 1975–87; Dep. Chm., W. & F. C. Bonham & Sons Ltd, subseq. Bonhams & Brooks, then Bonhams, 1987–2004. Director: Montpelier Properties, 1970–95; Bonhams Gp, 1995–2001; Hodie Ltd, 2001–. *Recreations:* sailing, tobogganing, ski-ing, swimming, golf. *Clubs:* Kennel; Royal Thames Yacht, South West Shingles Yacht, Seaview Yacht; Berkshire Golf; St Moritz Tobogganing, St Moritz Sporting.

BONHAM-CARTER OF YARNBURY, Baroness *cr* 2004 (Life Peer), of Yarnbury in the County of Wiltshire; **Jane Mary Bonham Carter;** Associate, Brook Lapping Productions, Ten Alps plc, since 2004; *b* 20 Oct. 1957; *d* of Baron Bonham-Carter and Leslie Adrienne, *d* of Condé Nast. *Educ:* St Paul's Girls' Sch.; University Coll. London (BA Philosophy). Producer, Panorama and Newsnight, BBC, 1988–93; Ed., A Week in Politics, Channel 4, 1993–96; Dir of Communications, Lib Dem Party, 1996–98; Ind. producer, Brook Lapping Productions, 1998–2004. Member: Lib Dem Campaigns and Communications Cttee, 1998–2006; Council, Britain in Europe, 1998–2005; Referendum Campaign Team, 2004–05. Member: Adv. Cttee, Centre Forum (formerly Centre for Reform), 1998–; RAPt (Rehabilitation for Addicted Prisoners Trust), 1999–. Member: H of L sub-cttee on Home Affairs, 2004–07; H of L Select Cttee on BBC Charter Review, 2005–06. *Address:* House of Lords, SW1A 0PW. *Clubs:* Groucho, Electric House.

BONHAM CARTER, Helena; actress; *b* 26 May 1966; *d* of late Hon. Raymond Bonham Carter and of Elena Bonham Carter (*née* Propper de Callejón); partner, Tim Burton, *qv*; one *s* one *d. Educ:* Hampstead High Sch. for Girls; Westminster Sch. *Films include:* Lady Jane, 1985; A Room with a View, 1986; A Hazard of Hearts, The Mask, 1988; St Francis of Assisi, Getting it Right, 1989; Hamlet, Where Angels Fear to Tread, 1990; Howard's End, 1992; Fatal Deception, 1993; Mary Shelley's Frankenstein, 1994; Mighty Aphrodite, Twelfth Night, 1996; Margaret's Museum, Portraits Chinois, Keep the Aspidistra Flying, 1997; The Wings of the Dove, The Theory of Flight, 1998; The Revengers' Comedies, Fight Club, 1999; Planet of the Apes, Women Talking Dirty, 2001; Novocaine, 2002; Til Human Voices Wake Us, Heart of Me, Big Fish, 2003; Charlie and the Chocolate Factory, 2005; Sixty Six, 2006; Conversations With Other Women, Harry Potter and the Order of the Phoenix, 2007; Sweeney Todd: The Demon Barber of Fleet Street, 2008; *television includes:* Miami Vice, 1987; The Vision, 1988; Arms and the Man, 1988; Dancing Queen, 1993; A Dark Adapted Eye, 1994; Live from Baghdad, 2002; Henry VIII, 2003; *theatre includes:* Woman in White, Greenwich, 1988; The Chalk Garden, Windsor, 1989; House of Bernarda Alba, Nottingham Playhouse, 1991; The Barber of Seville, Palace, Watford, 1992; Trelawney of the Wells, Comedy, 1992; *radio:* The Reluctant Debutante; Marie Antoinette; The Seagull. *Recreation:* reading. *Address:* c/o Conway van Gelder Grant Ltd, 18/21 Jermyn Street, SW1Y 6HP. *T:* (020) 7287 0077.

BONINGTON, Sir Christian (John Storey), Kt 1996; CBE 1976; DL; mountaineer, writer and photographer; *b* 6 Aug. 1934; *s* of Charles Bonington, journalist, and Helen Anne Bonington (*née* Storey); *m* 1962, Muriel Wendy Marchant; two *s* (and one *s* decd). *Educ:* University Coll. Sch., London. RMA Sandhurst, 1955–56; commnd Royal Tank Regt, 1956–61. Unilever Management Trainee, 1961–62; writer and photographer, 1962–. Climbs: Annapurna II, 26,041 ft (1st ascent) 1960; Central Pillar Freney, Mont Blanc (1st ascent), 1961; Nuptse, 25,850 ft (1st ascent), 1961; North Wall of Eiger (1st British ascent), 1962; Central Tower of Paine, Patagonia (1st ascent), 1963; Mem. of team, first descent of Blue Nile, 1968; Leader: successful Annapurna South Face Expedition, 1970; British Everest Expedition, 1972; Brammah, Himalayas (1st ascent), 1973; co-leader, Changabang, Himalayas (1st ascent), 1974; British Everest Expedition (1st ascent SW face), 1975; Ogre (1st ascent), 1977; jt leader, Kongur, NW China (1st ascent), 1981; Shivling West (1st ascent), 1983; Mt Vinson, highest point of Antarctica (1st British ascent), 1983; reached Everest summit, 1985; Panch Chuli II (W Ridge), Kumaon, Himalayas (1st ascent), 1992; Mejslen, Greenland (1st ascent), 1993; Rang Rik Rang, Kinnaur, Himalayas (1st ascent), 1994; Drangnag Ri (1st ascent), 1995; Danga II (1st ascent), 2000. President: British Mountaineering Council, 1988–91 (Vice-Pres., 1976–79, 1985–88); British Orienteering Fedn, 1985–; NT Lake Dist Appeal, 1989–; Council for National Parks, 1992–2000 (Life Vice-Pres., 2000); Vice-President: Army Mountaineering Assoc., 1980–; YHA, 1990–. Non-exec. Chm., Berghaus Ltd, 1998–. Chm., Mountain Heritage Trust, 2000–04; Trustee, Outward Bound, 1998– (Chm., Risk Mgt Cttee, 1998–2007). Chancellor, Lancaster Univ., 2005–. Pres., LEPRA, 1983. DL Cumbria, 2004. MInstD 1992. FRGS (Founders' Medal, 1974); FRPS 1991; FRSA 1996. Hon. Fellow: UMIST, 1976; Lancashire Polytechnic, 1991. Hon. MA Salford, 1973; Hon. DSc: Sheffield, 1976; Lancaster, 1983; Hon. DCL Northumbria, 1996; Hon. Dr Sheffield Hallam, 1998; Hon. DLitt Bradford, 2002. Lawrence of Arabia Medal, RSAA, 1986; Livingstone Medal, RSGS, 1991. *Publications:* I Chose to Climb (autobiog.), 1966; Annapurna South Face, 1971; The Next Horizon (autobiog.), 1973; Everest, South West Face, 1973; Everest the Hard Way, 1976; Quest for Adventure, 1981; Kongur: China's elusive summit, 1982; (jtly) Everest: the unclimbed ridge, 1983; The Everest Years, 1986; Mountaineer (autobiog.), 1989; The Climbers, 1992; (with Robin Knox-Johnston) Sea, Ice and Rock, 1992; Chris Bonington's Lake District, 1997; (with Charles Clarke) Tibet's Secret Mountain, 1999; Boundless Horizons (autobiog.), 2000; Quest for Adventure, 2000; Chris Bonington's Everest, 2002. *Recreations:* mountaineering, ski-ing, orienteering. *Address:* Badger Hill, Nether Row, Hesket Newmarket, Wigton, Cumbria CA7 8LA. *T:* (01697) 478286; *e-mail:* chris@bonington.com. *Clubs:* Travellers, Alpine (Pres., 1996–99), Alpine Ski, Army and Navy; Climbers, Fell and Rock Climbing, Border Liners, Carlisle Mountaineering, Keswick Mountaineering; American Alpine, Himalayan.

BONINO, Emma; Vice-President of Italian Senate, since 2008; *b* 9 March 1948. *Educ:* Bocconi Univ., Milan (BA 1972). Mem., Italian Chamber of Deputies, 1976–94; posts include: Chm., Radical Party Gp, 1979–81; Mem., Bureau of Parlt, 1992–94; MEP, 1979–94 and 1999–2006; Mem., European Commn, 1994–99. Transnational Radical Party: Pres., 1991–93; Sec., 1993–95. *Recreations:* snorkling, scuba-diving. *Address:* Senato della Repubblica, Palazzo Giustiniani, Via della Dogana Vecchia 29, 00186 Rome, Italy.

BONNER, Mark; Founder and Creative Director, GBH Design, since 1999; *b* 24 June 1970; *s* of John and Joan Bonner; partner, Janice Davison; one *s* one *d*. *Educ:* Hounslow Coll. (Nat. Dip. BTEC (Dist.)); Kingston Univ. (BA 1st Cl. Hons 1991); Royal Coll. of Art (MA 1993). The Partners, 1993–95; Carter Wong & Partners, 1995–96; SAS Design, 1997–99. Tutor in Graphic Design: W Bucks Coll., 1995–97; Kingston Univ., 1999–. Chm., Consort Royal Awards, 2004. Mem., D&AD, 2000–. Mem., Club 24 (Le Mans Auto. Club de l'Ouest). D&AD Annual Award, 1991, 1993, 1994, 1995, 1996, 1997, 1998, 1999, 2001, 2002, 2003, 2004, 2005, 2007, Silver Award, 2005; Silver Award, NY Art Dirs Club, 2003; Design Week Award, 2003, 2005, 2007, and Best of Show, 2003; Benchmark Award, 2007. *Address:* GBH Design, Chiswick Station House, Burlington Lane, Chiswick, W4 3HB. *T:* (020) 8742 2277, *Fax:* (020) 8995 8467; *e-mail:* mark@gregorybonnerhale.com.

BONNER, Paul Max, OBE 1999; writer; Director, Secretariat, ITV Network Centre, 1993–94; *b* 30 Nov. 1934; *s* of late Jill and Frank Bonner; *m* 1956, Jenifer Hubbard; two *s* one *d*. *Educ:* Felsted Sch., Essex. National Service commission, 1953–55. Local journalism, 1955; Radio production, BBC Bristol, 1955–57; Television production, BBC Bristol, 1957–59; BBC Lime Grove, 1959–62; Television Documentary prodn and direction, BBC Lime Grove and Kensington House, 1962–74; Editor, Community Programmes for BBC, 1974–77; Head of Science and Features Programmes for BBC, 1977–80; Channel Controller, Channel Four TV, 1980–83; Exec. Dir and Programme Controller, Channel Four TV, 1983–87; Dir, Programme Planning Secretariat, ITVA, 1987–93. A Manager, Royal Instn, 1982–85; Governor, Nat. Film and TV School, 1983–88; Director: Broadcasting Support Services, 1982–93; House of Commons Broadcasting Unit Ltd, 1989–91; Parly Broadcasting Unit, 1991–94; Chm., Sponsorship and Advertising Cttee, EBU, 1991–94; Member: Bd, Children's Film Unit, 1989–97; COPUS, 1986–92 (Chm., Broadcast Trust, 1995–98). FRTS 1989. *Publications:* Independent Television in Britain: Vol. 5, ITV and the IBA 1981–1992, 1998, Vol. 6, New Developments in Independent Television 1981–92: Channel Four, TV-am, cable and satellite, 2002; *documentaries include:* Strange Excellency, 1964; Climb up to Hell, 1967; Lost: Four H Bombs, 1967; Search for the Real Che Guevara, 1971; Who Sank the Lusitania?, 1972. *Recreations:* photography, the theatre, listening to good conversation. *Address:* North View, Wimbledon Common, SW19 4UJ. *Clubs:* Reform, Chelsea Arts.

BONNET, Maj.-Gen. Peter Robert Frank, CB 1991; MBE 1975; Colonel Commandant, Royal Regiment of Artillery, 1990–2000; *b* 12 Dec. 1936; *s* of James Robert and Phyllis Elsie Bonnet; *m* 1961, Sylvia Mary Coy; two *s*. *Educ:* Royal Military Coll. of Science, Shrivenham. BSc (Engrg). Commnd from RMA Sandhurst, 1958; RMCS Shrivenham, 1959–62; apptd to RHA, 1962; Staff trng, RMCS and Staff Coll., Camberley, 1969–70; Comd (Lt-Col), 26 Field Regt, RA, 1978–81; Comd RA (Brig.) 2nd Div., 1982–84; attendance at Indian Nat. Defence Coll., New Delhi, 1985; Dir RA, 1986–89 (Maj.-Gen. 1986); GOC Western Dist, 1989–91, retd 1992. Mem., Exec. Cttee, ABF, 1993–99; Gen. Sec., Officers' Pensions Soc., 1995–2000; Dir, OPS Investment Co. Ltd, 1995–2000; Man. Trustee, OPS Widows' Fund, 1995–2000; Vice Patron, Council Officers' Assoc., 1995–. Hon. Col, 26 Field Regt RA, 1992–99. Vice-Pres., Nat. Artillery Assoc., 1989–99. Trustee: Kelly Holdsworth Meml Trust, 1996–2004; Council, Age Concern, 1998–99. *Publications:* International Terrorism, 1985; A Short History of the Royal Regiment of Artillery, 1994. *Recreations:* tennis, sculpture, painting. *T:* (01398) 341324. *Club:* Army and Navy.

BONNETT, Prof. Raymond, CChem, FRSC; Professor of Organic Chemistry, Queen Mary, then Queen Mary and Westfield, College, University of London, 1974–94, now Professor Emeritus; *b* 13 July 1931; *s* of Harry and Maud Bonnett; *m* 1956, Shirley Rowe; two *s* one *d*. *Educ:* County Grammar Sch., Bury St Edmunds; Imperial Coll. (BSc, ARCS); Cambridge Univ. (PhD); DSc London 1972. Salters' Fellow, Cambridge, 1957–58; Res. Fellow, Harvard, 1958–59; Asst Prof., Dept of Chemistry, Univ. of British Columbia, 1959–61; Queen Mary, subseq. Queen Mary and Westfield, College, London: Lectr in Organic Chem., 1961–66; Reader in Organic Chem., 1966–74; Hd of Dept of Chemistry, 1982–87; Scotia Res. Prof., 1994–2000. *Publications:* sci. papers, esp. in Jls of Royal Soc. of Chemistry and Biochemical Soc. *Recreations:* theatre, bookbinding, gardening. *Address:* Elmbank, 19 Station Road, Epping, Essex CM16 4HG. *T:* (01992) 573203.

BONNEY, Barbara; soprano; *b* Montclair, NJ, 14 April 1956; *d* of Alfred Bonney III and Janet Gates; *m* 1989, Håkan Hagegård; *m* Maurice Whitaker. *Educ:* Univ. of New Hampshire; Mozarteum, Salzburg. Performances include: Der Rosenkavalier, Royal Opera, Covent Garden, 1984; Die Zauberflöte, La Scala, Milan, 1985; Ariadne auf Naxos, Falstaff, 1990, Metropolitan Opera, NY; The Marriage of Figaro, Royal Opera, 1995; Les Boréades, Salzburg Fest., 1999; Idomeneo, San Francisco, 1999; Orlando, Royal Opera, 2003. Regular recitals; numerous recordings.

BONNICI; *see* Mifsud Bonnici.

BONO; *see* Hewson, P. D.

BONOMY, Hon. Lord; Iain Bonomy; a Senator of the College of Justice in Scotland, since 1997; a Judge of the International Criminal Tribunal for the former Yugoslavia, since 2004; *b* 15 Jan. 1946; *s* of late John Bonomy and of Mary Gray Bonomy (*née* Richardson); *m* 1969, Janet (*née* Gray); two *d*. *Educ:* Dalziel High Sch., Motherwell; Univ. of Glasgow (LLB Hons). Apprentice solicitor, East Kilbride Town Council, 1968–70; Asst solicitor, then Partner, Ballantyne & Copland, solicitors, Motherwell, 1970–83; admitted Faculty of Advocates, 1984; Advocate Depute, then Home Advocate Depute, 1990–96; QC (Scot.) 1993. Surveillance Comr, under Pt III Police Act 1997 and Pt II Regulation of Investigatory Powers Act 2000, 1998–2004. Hon. LLD Strathclyde, 2006. *Recreations:* golf, gardening, travel, football terraces (now stands). *Address:* Parliament House, Parliament Square, Edinburgh EH1 1RQ; International Criminal Tribunal for the former Yugoslavia, Churchillplein 1, 2517 JW The Hague, The Netherlands. *Clubs:* Glasgow Art (Glasgow); Torrance House Golf, East Kilbride Golf, Motherwell Football and Athletic.

BONOMY, Iain; *see* Bonomy, Hon. Lord.

BONSALL, Sir Arthur (Wilfred), KCMG 1977; CBE 1957; *b* 25 June 1917; *s* of late Wilfred Bonsall and Sarah Bonsall; *m* 1941, Joan Isabel Wingfield (*d* 1990); four *s* three *d*. *Educ:* Bishop's Stortford Coll.; St Catharine's Coll., Cambridge. 2nd Cl. Hons Mod. Langs. Joined Air Ministry, 1940; transf. to FO 1942; IDC, 1962; Dir, Govt Communications HQ, 1975–78. *Recreation:* balcony gardening. *Address:* 17 Park Gate, Park Place, Cheltenham, Glos GL50 2QE.
　　See also F. F. Bonsall.

BONSALL, Prof. Frank Featherstone, FRS 1970; Professor of Mathematics, University of Edinburgh, 1965–84, now Emeritus; *b* 1920; *s* of late Wilfred Bonsall and Sarah Bonsall; *m* 1947, Gillian Patrick. *Educ:* Bishop's Stortford Coll.; Merton Coll., Oxford. *Publications:* (all with J. Duncan): Numerical Ranges of Operators on Normed Spaces and of Elements of Normed Algebras, 1971; Numerical Ranges II, 1973; Complete Normed Algebras, 1973. *Recreation:* walking.
　　See also Sir A. W. Bonsall.

BONSEY, Martin Charles Brian, AO 2005; CVO 2003 (LVO 2000); Official Secretary to the Governor-General of Australia, 1998–2003; *b* 2 May 1948; *s* of late Thory Richmond Bonsey and of Frances Mary Bonsey; *m* 1971, Joan Hair. *Educ:* Univ. of Melbourne (BA Hons Hist. and Pol Sci.); Australian Nat. Univ. (LLB). Public servant, Australia, 1974–2003. Secretary: Order of Australia, 1998–2003; Australian Bravery Decorations Council, 1998–2003. CStJ 1999.

BONSOR, Sir Nicholas (Cosmo), 4th Bt *cr* 1925; DL; barrister; *b* 9 Dec. 1942; *s* of Sir Bryan Cosmo Bonsor, 3rd Bt, MC, TD, and of Elizabeth, *d* of late Captain Angus Valdimar Hambro; *S* father, 1977; *m* 1969, Hon. Nadine Marisa Lampson, *d* of 2nd Baron Killearn; two *s* three *d* (including twin *d*). *Educ:* Eton; Keble College, Oxford (MA). Served Royal Buckinghamshire Yeomanry, 1964–69. Called to the Bar, Inner Temple, 1967; in practice at the Bar, 1967–75, 2003–. Mem., CLA Legal and Parly Sub-Cttee, 1978–82. MP (C) Nantwich, 1979–83, Upminster, 1983–97; contested (C) Upminster, 1997. Minister of State, FCO, 1995–97. Chm., Select Cttee on Defence, 1992–95; Sec., Cons. Tourism Sub-Cttee, 1979–80; Vice-Chairman: Cons. Foreign Affairs Cttee, 1981–83; Cons. Defence Cttee, 1987–90. Mem. Council, RUSI, 1992–95, 1997–2000. Chm., Food Hygiene Bureau, later Checkmate Plc, 1986–95; Pres. and non-exec. Dir, Liscombe Hldgs, 1997–2000; Director: London Mining plc, 2007–; Blue Note Mining Inc., 2007–. Chairman: Cyclotron Trust for Cancer Treatment, 1984–92 (Pres., 1992–); British Field Sports Soc., 1987–93; Standing Council of the Baronetage, 1990–93 (Vice-Chm., 1987–90); Baronets' Trust, 1993–95 (Trustee, 1986–95); Verdin Home for Mentally Handicapped, 1981–85. Mem., Council of Lloyd's, 1987–92. Hon. Col, 60 Signals Sqdn (V), 2000–06; Vice Chm., SE RFCA, 2000–. FRSA 1970. Freeman, City of London, 1988. DL Bucks, 2007. *Publications:* political pamphlets on law and trades unions and defence. *Recreations:* sailing, shooting, military history. *Heir: s* Alexander Cosmo Walrond Bonsor [*b* 8 Sept. 1976; *m* 2006, Jane, *d* of James Troughton; one *s*]. *Address:* c/o Brunswick Chambers, 2 Middle Temple Lane, EC4Y 7AA. *Clubs:* White's, Pratt's; Royal Yacht Squadron.

BONVIN, Her Honour Jane Anne Marie, (Mrs S. M. Poulter); DL; a Circuit Judge, 1995–2008; *b* 15 Dec. 1946; *d* of Jean Albert Bonvin and Phyllis Margaret (*née* Boyd); *m* 1972, Sebastian Murray Poulter (*d* 1998). *Educ:* Putney High Sch.; Bristol Univ. (LLB Hons). Law Lectr, IVS, Lesotho, 1969–71; called to the Bar, Gray's Inn, 1971; barrister, Western Circuit, 1972–77 and 1979–95. Editor, Lesotho Law Reports, 1977–79. DL Hampshire, 2003. *Recreations:* gardening, walking, travel.

BONYNGE, Dame Joan; *see* Sutherland, Dame Joan.

BONYNGE, Richard, AO 1983; CBE 1977; opera conductor; *b* Sydney, 29 Sept. 1930; *s* of C. A. Bonynge, Epping, NSW; *m* 1954, Dame Joan Sutherland, *qv*; one *s*. *Educ:* Sydney Conservatorium (pianist). Official debut, as Conductor, with Santa Cecilia Orch. in Rome, 1962; conducted first opera, Faust, Vancouver, 1963. Has conducted in most leading opera houses in world, and in Edinburgh, Vienna and Florence Fests. Has been Princ. Conductor and Artistic/Musical Dir of cos, incl. Sutherland/Williamson Internat. Grand Opera Co., Aust., 1965; Vancouver Opera, 1974–77; Australian Opera, 1976–85. Many opera and ballet recordings; also recital discs with Sutherland, Tebaldi, Tourangeau and Pavarotti, and many orchestral and ballet anthologies. Comdr, Ordre des Arts et des Lettres (France), 1989. *Publication:* (with Dame Joan Sutherland) The Joan Sutherland Album, 1986. *Address:* c/o Ingpen & Williams, 7 St George's Court, 131 Putney Bridge Road, SW15 2PA.

BOOKBINDER, Alan Peter; Director, Sainsbury Family Charitable Trusts, since 2006; *b* 16 March 1956; *s* of Geoffrey Ellis Bookbinder and Bridget Mary Bookbinder (*née* Doran); *m* 2005, Vicki Ambery-Smith; one *s* one *d*. *Educ:* Manchester Grammar Sch.; St Catherine's Coll., Oxford (BA Modern Hist. and Modern Langs); Harvard Univ. (MA Regl Studies). Producer, 1986–92, Exec. Producer, 1992–2001, BBC Television; Head of Religion and Ethics, BBC, 2001–06. *Publications:* Comrades, 1985; contribs to Spectator, Listener, The Tablet. *Address:* 34 Collingwood Avenue, N10 3ED. *T:* (020) 8883 4078.

BOOKER, Christopher John Penrice; journalist and author; *b* 7 Oct. 1937; *s* of late John Booker and Margaret Booker; *m* 1979, Valerie, *d* of late Dr M. S. Patrick, OBE and Alla Petrovna Patrick; two *s*. *Educ:* Dragon Sch., Oxford; Shrewsbury Sch.; Corpus Christi Coll., Cambridge (History scholar). Liberal News, 1960; jazz critic, Sunday Telegraph, 1961; Editor, Private Eye, 1961–63, and regular contributor, 1965–; resident scriptwriter, That Was The Week That Was, 1962–63, and Not So Much A Programme, 1963–64; contributor to Spectator, 1962–, Daily Telegraph, 1972– (Way of the World column, as Peter Simple II, 1987–90), and to many other newspapers and jls; columnist, Sunday Telegraph, 1990–. Wrote extensively on property develt, planning and housing, 1972–77 (with Bennie Gray, Campaigning Journalist of the Year, 1973); City of Towers—the Rise and Fall of a Twentieth Century Dream (TV prog.), 1979. Mem., Cowgill enquiry into post-war repatriations from Austria, 1986–90. *Publications:* The Neophiliacs: a study of the revolution in English life in the 50s and 60s, 1969; (with Candida Lycett-Green) Goodbye London, 1973; The Booker Quiz, 1976; The Seventies, 1980; The Games War: a Moscow journal, 1981; (with Lord Brimelow and Brig. A. Cowgill) The Repatriations from Austria in 1945, 1990; (with Richard North) The Mad Officials: how the bureaucrats are strangling Britain, 1993; (with Richard North) The Castle of Lies: why Britain must leave the European Union, 1996; A Looking Glass Tragedy: the controversy over the repatriations from Austria in 1945, 1997; Nice and Beyond, 2000; Britain and Europe: the culture of deceit, 2001; (with Richard North) The Great Deception: a secret history of the European Union, 2003; The Seven Basic Plots: why we tell stories, 2004; (with Richard North) Scared to Death: from BSE to global warming, why scares are costing us the Earth, 2007; contrib. Private Eye anthologies, 1962–, incl. The Secret Diary of John Major, 1992–95, St Albion Parish News, 1998–, Not the Foot and Mouth Report, 2001. *Recreations:* the psychology of storytelling, nature, music, playing village cricket, teasing global warmists. *Address:* The Old Rectory, Litton, Bath BA3 4PW. *T:* (01761) 241263; *e-mail:* cblitton@aol.com.

BOOKER, Gordon Alan, FIWEM; utility adviser; Deputy Director General of Water Services, 1990–98; *b* 17 Feb. 1938; *s* of Frederick William Booker and Beryl Booker; *m* 1957, Anne Christine Pike; two *s* one *d*. *Educ:* Dronfield Grammar Sch.; Sheffield Univ. (BEng (Hons) 1960). MICE 1963; FIWEM 1966. Sheffield Water, 1960–65; Birmingham Water, 1965–70; W Glam Water, 1970–74; Welsh Water, 1974–80; Chief Exec., E Worcester Water, 1980–89; Managing Director: Biwater Supply, 1987–90; Bournemouth and W Hants Water Cos, 1989–90. Mem., Council, Water Res. Centre, 1985–90; mem. and chm. of several water industry cttees on automation and leakage control. *Publications:* Water Distribution Systems, 1984; Telemetry and Control, 1986; contrib. Procs of ICE and of IWSA, reports for DoE and NWC, and Jls of IWEM and IAWPRC. *Recreations:*

walking, painting. *Address:* 106 The Holloway, Droitwich, Worcs WR9 7AH. *T:* (01905) 772432; Sheplegh Court, Blackawton, Devon TQ9 7AH.

BOOKER, Pamela Elizabeth; *see* Alexander, P. E.

BOOKER-MILBURN, Donald; Sheriff of Grampian, Highland and Islands, 1983–2005; *b* Dornoch, 20 May 1940; *s* of late Captain Booker Milburn, DSO, MC, Coldstream Guards, and late Betty Calthrop Calthrop; *m* 1963, Marjorie Lilian Elizabeth Burns; one *s* one *d*. *Educ:* Trinity College, Glenalmond; Grenoble Univ.; Jesus Coll., Cambridge (BA); Edinburgh Univ. (LLB). Admitted to Faculty of Advocates, 1968; Standing Junior Counsel to RAF, 1977–80; Sheriff of Lothian and Borders, 1980–83. *Recreations:* golf, skiing. *Clubs:* Royal & Ancient Golf (St Andrews); Royal Dornoch Golf.

BOON, (George) Peter (Richard); HM Diplomatic Service, retired; High Commissioner to Cameroon and non-resident Ambassador to Chad, Central African Republic, Gabon and Equatorial Guinea, 1998–2002; *b* 2 Nov. 1942; *s* of late George Alan James Boon and Enid Monica Boon (*née* Smith); *m* 1971, Marie Paule Calicis; one *s*. *Educ:* Repton Sch., Derbys. Joined CRO, later FCO, 1963; Bombay, 1966–69; Brussels, 1969–71; Vienna, 1971–74; on secondment to DTI, 1974–75; FCO, 1975–78; The Hague, 1978–81; Spokesman, BMG, Berlin, 1981–86; FCO, 1986–90; First Sec. (Political), Dhaka, 1990–93; FCO, 1994–97. *Address:* Barn End, London Road, Blewbury, Didcot, Oxon OX11 9PB.

BOORD, Sir Nicolas (John Charles), 4th Bt *cr* 1896; scientific translator; English training specialist; *b* 10 June 1936; *s* of Sir Richard William Boord, 3rd Bt, and of Yvonne, Lady Boord, *d* of late J. A. Hubert Bird; *S* father, 1975; *m* 1965, Françoise Renée Louise Mouret. *Educ:* Eton (Harmsworth Lit. Prize, 1952); Sorbonne, France; Societa Dante Alighieri, Italy; Univ. of Santander, Spain. *Publications:* (trans. jtly) The History of Physics and the Philosophy of Science—Selected Essays (Armin Teske), 1972; numerous translations of scientific papers for English and American scientific and technical jls. *Recreations:* English and French literature and linguistics. *Heir: b* Antony Andrew Boord [*b* 21 May 1938; *m* 1960, Anna Christina von Krogh; one *s* one *d*]. *Address:* 61 Traverse Le Mée, 13009 Marseille, France. *T:* (4) 91731395.

BOORMAN, Anthony John; Principal Ombudsman and Decisions Director, Financial Ombudsman Service, since 2000; *b* 14 Nov. 1958; *s* of William Harry and Margaret Boorman; *m* 1984, Alison Drury; two *s*. *Educ:* Kent Coll., Canterbury; New Coll., Oxford (BA). Various posts, Electricity Consumers' Council, 1985–90, Dir, 1989–90; Dir, Office of Electricity Regulation, 1990–98; Dep. Dir Gen., Office of Gas and Electricity Mkts, 1998–2000. Mem., Commn for Judicial Appts, 2001–06. *Address:* Financial Ombudsman Service, South Quay Plaza, 183 Marsh Wall, E14 9SR.

BOORMAN, Lt-Gen. Sir Derek, KCB 1986 (CB 1982); Chairman, Health Care Projects Ltd, since 1998; *b* 13 Sept. 1930; *s* of late N. R. Boorman, MBE, and Mrs A. L. Boorman (*née* Patman); *m* 1st, 1956, Jennifer Jane Skinner (*d* 1991); two *d* (one *s* decd); 2nd, 1992, Mrs Nicola Cox. *Educ:* Wolstanton Grammar Sch.; RMA Sandhurst. Commnd N Staffords, 1950; Adjt 1 Staffords, 1958–59; Staff Coll., 1961; HQ 48 Gurkha Inf. Bde, 1962–64; Jt Services Staff Coll., 1968; CO 1 Staffords, 1969–71; Instr, Staff Coll., 1972–73; Comdr 51 Inf. Bde, 1975–76; RCDS, 1977; Dir, Public Relations (Army), 1978–79; Director of Military Operations, 1980–82; Comdr, British Forces Hong Kong, and Maj.-Gen. Bde of Gurkhas, 1982–85; Chief of Defence Intelligence, 1985–88. Lieut, Tower of London, 1989–92. Colonel: 6th Queen Elizabeth's Own Gurkha Rifles, 1983–88; Staffordshire Regt (Prince of Wales's), 1985–90. Director: Tarmac Construction, 1988–95. Chairman: KCH Trust, 1992–93; Royal Hosps NHS Trust, 1994–97. Mem., Security Commn, 1991–96. Dep. Pro-Chancellor, Univ. of Kent, 2000–. *Recreations:* gardening, music, taking wife out to dinner.

BOORMAN, Edwin Roy Pratt, OBE 2002; DL; President, Kent Messenger Group, since 2006 (Managing Director, 1965–86; Chief Executive, 1986–2002; Chairman, 1986–2005); *b* 7 Nov. 1935; *s* of late H. R. P. Boorman, CBE and Enid (*née* Starke); *m* 1st, Merrilyn Ruth Pettit (marr. diss. 1982); four *d*; 2nd, 1983, Janine Craske; one *s*. *Educ:* Rydal; Queens' Coll., Cambridge (MA Econ. History). National Service, 1954–56. Cambridge Univ., 1956–59; Kent Messenger, 1959; Editor: South Eastern Gazette, 1960–62; Kent Messenger, 1962–65. Pres., Newspaper Soc., 2001–02 (Vice-Pres., 2000–01). Chm., Royal British Legion Industries, 2001– (Pres., RBL, Kent, 1998–2003). Chairman: N Kent Success, 1993–96; Kent River Walk, 1998–. Dep. Pres., Kent Youth and Kent Youth Trust, 2001–; Pres., Maidstone Sen. Cadets, 2004–. Trustee: Chatham Historic Dockyard, 1992–97; Kent Air Ambulance, 1993–2005. Chm., Kent Council, Order of St John, 1997–2004. Patron, Kent Child Witness Service, 1999–. Governor: Sutton Valence Sch., 1976–2002; Canterbury Christ Church Coll., 1996–2005; Mid Kent Coll., 2005–. Tax Comr, Maidstone District 2. Stationers' and Newspapermakers' Co.: Liveryman, 1960–86; Mem., Ct of Assts, 1987–2000 (Ct Emeritus list, 2000–). High Sheriff, Kent, 1997; DL Kent, 2001. Hon. DCL Kent, 2004. *Recreation:* sailing. *Address:* Messenger House, New Hythe Lane, Larkfield, Kent ME20 6SG. *Clubs:* Carlton; Maidstone, Kent CC; Veteran Car (Ashwell, Herts); Royal Yachting Association, Medway Yacht, Ocean Cruising.

BOORMAN, John, CBE 1994; film director; *b* 18 Jan. 1933; *m* 1st, 1956, Christel Kruse; one *s* three *d* ; 2nd, 1997, Isabella Weibrecht; one *s* two *d*. *Educ:* Salesian Coll., Chertsey. Film Editor, ITN, 1955–58; Dir and Producer, Southern TV, 1958–60; Head of Documentaries, BBC Bristol. *Films include:* Catch us if you Can, 1965; Point Blank, 1967; Hell in the Pacific, 1968; Leo the Last, 1969; Deliverance, 1972; Zardoz, 1973; The Heretic, 1976; Excalibur, 1981; The Emerald Forest, 1985; Hope and Glory, 1987; Where the Heart Is, 1989; I Dreamt I Woke Up, 1991; Beyond Rangoon, 1995; Two Nudes Bathing, 1995; The General, 1998; The Tailor of Panama, 2001; The Tiger's Tail, 2007. Gov., BFI, 1983–94. *Publications:* The Legend of Zardoz, 1973; Money into Light, 1985; Hope and Glory, 1987; Projections: (ed) no 1, 1992; (joint editor): no 2, 1993; no 3, 1994; nos 4 and 4½, 1995; nos 5 and 6, 1996; no 7, 1997; no 8, 1998; nos 9–12; no 13, 2004; Adventures of a Suburban Boy, 2003. *Address:* Merlin Films International, 16 Upper Pembroke Street, Dublin 2, Ireland.

BOOTE, Robert Edward, CVO 1971; first Director General, Nature Conservancy Council, 1973–80; *b* 6 Feb. 1920; *s* of Ernest Haydn Boote and Helen Rose Boote; *m* 1948, Vera (*née* Badian); one *s* one *d*. *Educ:* London Univ. (BSc Econ Hons). DPA; FREconS 1953–61; AIPR 1957–61; FCIS 1960–81. War service, 1939–46, Actg Lt-Col, Hon. Major. Admin. Officer, City of Stoke-on-Trent, 1946–48; Chief Admin. Officer, Staffs County Planning and Develt Dept, 1948–54; Principal, 1954–64, Dep. Dir, 1964–73, Nature Conservancy. Sec. 1965–71, formerly Dep. Sec., Countryside in 1970 Confs, 1963, 1965, 1970 and numerous study groups; a Chief Marshal to the Queen, 1970. Mem., Pesticides Cttee, 1958–73; Chm., Broadland Report, 1963–65; UK Deleg. to Council of Europe Cttee for Conservation of Nature and Natural Resources, 1963–71; Mem., Countryside Review Cttee, 1977–79; Various posts in meetings of UN, UNESCO, EEC and OECD, 1968–81; Member, UK Delegations: USA, 1978; USSR, 1978; China, 1982; Chm. Preparatory Gp for Eur. Conservation Year 1970; Chm. Organising Cttee for European Conservation Conf. 1970 (Conf. Vice-Pres.); Chm. European Cttee, 1969–71; Consultant for European Architectural Heritage Year 1975; Advr, H of L Select Cttee on Europ. Communities, 1980–81. A Vice-Pres. and Chm., Euro Fedn of Nature and Nat. Parks, 1980–81; International Union for Conservation of Nature and Natural Resources: Treas., 1975–78; Mem., Governing Council and Bureau, 1975–81; a Vice-Pres., 1978–81; Rep., Internat. Conf. on Antarctic Marine Living Resources, 1980; Chm., Antarctica Resolution, 1981; Election Officer, 1984; Founder and Chm., 1974–80, Mem., 1980–85, UK Cttee. Council Member: FFPS, 1979–83; RGS, 1983–86; BTCV (Vice-Pres.) 1980–; RSNC (Vice-Pres.) 1980–99; RSNC Wildlife Appeal, 1983–87; WWF, 1980–86; Ecological Parks Trust, 1980–85; YPTES (Chm.), 1982–87; Friends of ENO, 1980–87; Common Ground Internat., 1981–85; Cttees for UK Conservation and Develt Prog., 1980–83; HGTAC, Forestry Commn, 1981–87; Conservator, Wimbledon and Putney Commons, 1981–97; Patron, CSV, 1978–85; Chairman: Instn of Environmental Sciences, 1981–84; Seychelles Appeal Cttee, Royal Soc., 1980–87; Chm., Gp A, Ditchley Foundn Anglo/Amer. Conf. on Environment, 1970; Lead Speaker, Eurogespracht, Vienna, 1970; Mem., Entretiens Ecologiques de Dijon, 1981; UK Officer Rep., Eur. Environment Ministers Conf., 1976; Judge, Berlin world agro/environ films and TV competitions, 1970, 1972, 1974 and 1980. Initiator and Chm., Age Resource, 1988–98, now Chm. Emeritus; a Vice-Pres., Age Concern, 1990–. Trustee and Hon. Treas., New Renaissance Gp, 1995–2002. FRSA 1971. Hon. Associate, Landscape Inst., 1971; Hon. MRTPI, 1978. Greek Distinguished Service Medal, 1946; van Tienhoven European Prize, 1980; Merit Award, IUCN, 1984; Alfred Toepfer Prize for European nature protection, Goethe Foundn, 1995. Adviser: Macmillan Guide to Britain's Nature Reserves, 1980–94; Shell Better Britain Campaign, 1980–91. Member Editorial Boards: Internat. Jl of Environmental Studies, 1975–2002; Town Planning Review, 1979–85; Internat. Jl Environmental Educn and Information, 1981–83. Helped to prepare: Pacemaker (film), 1970 (also appeared in); Man of Action, BBC Radio, 1977. *Publications:* (as Robert Arvill) Man and Environment, 1967 (5th edn 1983); numerous papers, articles, addresses, TV and radio broadcasts, over 4 decades in UK and internat. professional confs in 50 countries. *Recreations:* travel, theatre, music, dancing. *Address:* 3 Leeward Gardens, Wimbledon, SW19 7QR. *T:* (020) 8946 1551.

BOOTE, Sarah Joan; *see* Thomas, S. J.

BOOTH; *see* Sclater-Booth, family name of Baron Basing.

BOOTH, Rt Hon. Albert Edward; PC 1976; *b* 28 May 1928; *e s* of Albert Henry Booth and Janet Mathieson; *m* 1957, Joan Amis; three *s*. *Educ:* St Thomas's Sch., Winchester; S Shields Marine Sch.; Rutherford Coll. of Technology. Engineering Draughtsman. Election Agent, 1951 and 1955. County Borough Councillor, 1962–65. Exec. Dir, S Yorks Passenger Transport Exec., 1983–87. MP (Lab) Barrow-in-Furness, 1966–83; Minister of State, Dept of Employment, 1974–76; Sec. of State for Employment, 1976–79; Opposition spokesman on transport, 1979–83. Chm., Select Cttee on Statutory Instruments, 1970–74. Treasurer, Labour Party, 1984. Contested (Lab): Tynemouth, 1964; Barrow and Furness, 1983; Warrington South, 1987. CompIMechE 1985. *T:* (020) 8650 5982.

BOOTH, Anthony John, CBE 1993; CEng, FIET; Director, RB Phusion Ltd, since 2001; *b* 18 March 1939; *s* of Benjamin and Una Lavinia Booth; *m* 1965, Elspeth Marjorie (*née* Fraser); one *s* one *d*. *Educ:* Bungay Grammar Sch.; London Univ. (BScEng, DMS). Joined Post Office Res. Dept, 1957; Exec. Engr and Sen. Exec. Engr, Telecom HQ, 1965–71; Asst Staff Engr, Central HQ Appointments, 1971–74; Head of Section and Div., External Telecom Exec., 1974–78; Head of Div., THQ, 1978–79; Dir, Internat. Networks, 1979–80; Regional Dir, London Region, 1980–83; Corporate Dir, British Telecommunications PLC, 1984–94; Managing Director: BT International, 1983–91; Business Communications, 1991–92; Special Businesses and Internat. Affairs Div., 1992–94; Chm., Ericsson Ltd, 1994–2002. Dir, Protek Network Mgt Ltd, 2001–04; Dir and Trustee, AQA (Assessment and Qualifs Alliance Ltd), 2000–06 (Vice-Chm., 2003–06); Trustee, AQA Pension Scheme, 2006–. Mem., HEFCE, 1996–2001. Gov., and Chm. Finance Cttee, Polytechnic of W London, 1991–92; Chm. of Govs, Thames Valley Univ., 1993–96; Mem. Council, Univ. of Surrey, 1998–2004. Member, Guild of Freemen of City of London, 1982–. Chm., SE Reg., RLSS, 1997–2001. FInstD 1997 (Chm., 1999–2002, Pres., 2002–, W Surrey); CCMI (CBIM 1986; Mem. Bd of Companions, 1999–2006); FRSA 1991. Hon. DPhil Thames Valley, 1998. *Recreations:* opera, golf. *Club:* Caledonian.

BOOTH, Brian George, OBE 2004; JP; DL; Chairman, Lancashire Teaching Hospitals (formerly Preston Acute Hospitals) NHS Trust, 1997–2005; Vice-Chancellor, University of Central Lancashire (formerly Rector and Chief Executive, Lancashire Polytechnic), 1989–98; *b* 6 Sept. 1942; *s* of George and Ada Booth; *m* 1965, Barbara Ann (*née* Wright); two *d*. *Educ:* Univ. of Manchester (BA Econ 1964); Brunel Univ. (MTech 1972). FSS 1968–2000. Asst Lectr in Statistics, High Wycombe Coll. of Technology, 1965–68; Lectr, Sen. Lectr, and Principal Lectr, Kingston Polytechnic, 1968–73; Head, Dept of Business and Admin, 1974–78, Dean, Faculty of Business and Management, 1978–82, Preston Polytechnic; Dep. Dir, Preston Polytechnic, later Lancashire Polytechnic, 1982–89. Chair of Bd, Preston Business Venture, 1983–92; Chair of Trustees, Preston Postgrad. Med. Centre, 1990–96; Director: Lancs Partnership Against Crime, 1997–; Central Lancs Develt Agency, 1998–2000; (non-exec.), Student Loans Co. Ltd, 1998–. Trustee, Nat. Football Museum, 1996– (Chm., 2001–). JP Preston, 1987; DL Lancs, 2002. CCMI (CIMgt 1992). DUniv Central Lancashire, 1998. *Recreations:* golf, watching Preston North End. *Address:* 9 Moorfield Close, Fulwood, Preston, Lancs PR2 9SW. *T:* (01772) 864243, *Fax:* (01772) 865636.

BOOTH, Cherie, (Mrs A. C. L. Blair); QC 1995; a Recorder, since 1999; *b* 23 Sept. 1954; *d* of Anthony and Gale Booth; *m* 1980, Rt Hon. Anthony Charles Lynton Blair, *qv*; three *s* one *d*. *Educ:* St Edmund's RC Primary Sch., Liverpool; Seafield Grammar Sch., Crosby; London Sch. of Economics (LLB; Hon. Fellow, 1999). Called to the Bar, Lincoln's Inn, 1976, Bencher, 1999; an Asst Recorder, 1996–99; barrister specialising in public, employment and EC law. Contested (Lab) Thanet North, 1983. Hon. Vice Pres., Barnardo's, 2001–; Vice Pres., 4children (formerly Kids Club Network), 1998–; Patron: Refuge, 1995–; Home Start, Islington, 1997–; Sargent Cancer Care for Children, subseq. CLIC Sargent, 1998–; Breast Cancer Care, 1998–; Islington Music Centre, 1999–; Victim Support, London, 1999–; Patron for Educn, SCOPE, 2002–. Trustee, Citizenship Foundn, 1995–. Fellow: Inst. of Advanced Legal Studies, 1998; Internat. Soc. of Lawyers for Public Service, 1999; FRSA. Chancellor Emeritus, Liverpool John Moores Univ. (Fellow, 1997; Chancellor, 1999–2006). Hon. Bencher, King's Inns, Dublin, 2002. DUniv Open, 1999; Hon. LLD: Westminster, 1999; Liverpool, 2003; Hon. DLitt UMIST, 2003. *Publications:* (with Cate Haste) The Goldfish Bowl: married to the Prime Minister, 2004; (contrib.) Evidence, 2004; The Negligence Liability of Public Authorities, 2006; Speaking for Myself (autobiog.), 2008. *Recreations:* theatre, the arts, keeping fit, enjoying my children. *Address:* Matrix Chambers, Gray's Inn, WC1R 5LN. *T:* (020) 7404 3447.

BOOTH, Sir Christopher (Charles), Kt 1983; Harveian Librarian, Royal College of Physicians, 1989–97; *b* 22 June 1924; *s* of Lionel Barton Booth and Phyllis Petley Duncan; *m* 1st, 1959, Lavinia Loughridge, Belfast; one *s* one *d*; 2nd, 1970, Soad Tabaqchali; one *d*; 3rd, 2001, Joyce Singleton. *Educ:* Sedbergh Sch., Yorks; University of St Andrews; MB 1951, MD 1958 (Rutherford Gold Medal). Junior appointments at Dundee Royal Infirmary, Hammersmith Hosp. and Addenbrooke's Hosp., Cambridge; successively Medical Tutor, Lecturer in Medicine and Senior Lecturer, Postgraduate Medical School of London; Prof. and Dir of Dept of Medicine, RPMS, London Univ., 1966–77; Dir, Clin. Res. Centre, MRC, 1978–88. Member: Adv. Bd to Res. Councils, 1976–78; MRC, 1981–84; Chm., Medical Adv. Cttee, British Council, 1979–85; President: British Soc. of Gastroenterology, 1978–79; BMA, 1986–87; RSocMed, 1988; Johnson Soc., 1987–88; Soc. Social History of Medicine, 1990. Hon. Prof., UCL, 2001. Chm., Royal Naval Personnel Cttee, 1985–91. Trustee, Coeliac Soc., 1968–93 (Chm., 1968–83). FRCP 1964; FRCPEd 1967; Hon. FACP 1973; Hon. FRSocMed 1991; Hon. FMedSci 2002. For. Mem., Amer. Philosophical Soc., 1981. Docteur (*hc*): Paris, 1975; Poitiers, 1981; Hon. LLD Dundee, 1982; Laurea (*hc*) Bologna, 1991. Dicke Gold Medal, Dutch Soc. of Gastroenterology, 1973; Ludwig Heilmeyer Gold Medal, German Soc. for Advances in Internal Medicine, 1982; Gold Medal, BMA, 1992; Fothergillian Medal, Med. Soc. of London, 2007. Chevalier de l'Ordre National du Mérite (France), 1977. *Publications:* (with Betsy C. Corner) Chain of Friendship: Letters of Dr John Fothergill of London, 1735–1780, 1971; (with G. Neale) Disorders of the Small Intestine, 1985; Doctors in Science and Society, 1987; A Physician Reflects, 2003; John Haygarth, FRS, 1740–1827, 2005; papers in med. jls on relationship of nutritional disorders to disease of the alimentary tract, and on medical history. *Recreations:* fishing, history. *Address:* Swakeley's Cottage, 2 The Avenue, Ickenham, Middx UB10 8NP. *T:* (01895) 677811.

BOOTH, Sir Clive, Kt 2003; PhD; Chairman, Big Lottery Fund, since 2004; *b* 18 April 1943; *s* of Henry Booth and Freda Frankland; *m* 1969, Margaret Sardeson. *Educ:* King's Sch., Macclesfield; Trinity Coll., Cambridge (1st cl. Hons Nat Scis Tripos; MA 1969); Univ. of California, Berkeley (Harkness Fellow, 1973; MA 1974; PhD 1976). Joined DES, 1965; Prin. Pvte Sec. to Sec. of State for Educn and Science, 1975–77; Asst Sec., 1977–81; Dep. Dir, Plymouth Polytechnic, 1981–84; Mem., HM Inspectorate, DES, 1984–86; Dir, Oxford Poly., 1986–92; Vice-Chancellor, 1992–97, Prof. Emeritus, 1997, Oxford Brookes Univ. Asst Comr, Nat. Commn on Educn, 1992–94; Chm., TTA, 1997–2003; Dep. Chm., SEEDA, 1999–2004; Chairman: Central Police Trng and Develt Authy, 2002–07; SE Reg. Bd for Reducing Reoffending, 2005–. Member: Governing Council, SRHE, 1981–90; Adv. Cttee, Brunel Univ. Educn Policy Centre, 1986–91; Computer Bd for Univs and Res. Councils, 1987–92; CNAA Cttee for Information and Develt Services, 1987–92; Fulbright Academic Administrators Selection Cttee, 1988–97; British Council Cttee for Internat. Co-operation in Higher Educn, 1988–96 (Chm., 1994–); Council for Industry and Higher Educn, 1990–97; Fulbright Commn, 1992–97; Royal Soc. Study Gp on Higher Educn, 1991–97; UFC Inf. Systems Cttee, 1991–93; Oxford Science Park Adv. Cttee, 1990–97; Oxford Inst. of Nursing Bd, 1991–95; Commonwealth Scholarships Commn, 1992–96; UK ERASMUS Council, 1992–97 (Chm., 1993–97); Oxford Trust Adv. Council, 1992–; Bd, British Inst., Paris, 1997–2005; Know How Fund Mgt Cttee, DFID, 1998–2000. Chairman: PCFC Steering Gp on Statistical Information, 1989–93; Heart of England Educn Forum, 1997–2002; Review Body for Nurses, Midwives and Professions Allied to Medicine, 1998–2005; Vice-Chm., CVCP, 1992–97. Chairman: Oxfordshire Learning Partnership, 1999–2004; Mgt Cttee, Oxfordshire Connexions, 2000–03; Director: Thames Action Resource Gp for Educn and Trng, 1986–2000; Thames Valley Technology Centre, 1989–93; British Council, 1995–97 (Sen. Advr, 1997–2005). Leverhulme Res. Fellow, 1983. Governor: Headington and Wheatley Park Schs; Westminster Coll., Oxford, 1997–2000. Jt Ed., Higher Educn Qly, 1986–97; Mem., Editorial Bd, Oxford Review of Educn, 1990–. DUniv Oxford Brookes, 2000; Hon. DEd Sunderland, 2002. *Recreations:* cycling, walking, bridge, opera. *Address:* 43 St John Street, Oxford OX1 2LH. *T:* (01865) 557762, *Fax:* (01865) 558886; *e-mail:* clive.booth@biglotteryfund.org.uk.

BOOTH, Sir Douglas Allen, 3rd Bt *cr* 1916; writer and producer for television, writer for films; Director, Barak Realty, New York City; *b* 2 Dec. 1949; *s* of Sir Philip Booth, 2nd Bt, and Ethel, *d* of Joseph Greenfield, NY, USA; *S* father 1960; *m* 1991, Yolanda Marcela (*née* Scantlebury); two *d*. *Educ:* Beverly Hills High Sch.; Harvard Univ. (Harvard Nat. Scholarship, Nat. Merit Scholarship, 1967); BA (*magna cum laude*) 1975. *Recreations:* music, back-packing. *Heir:* *b* Derek Blake Booth [*b* 7 April 1953; *m* 1st, 1981, Elizabeth Dreisbach (marr. diss. 2000); one *s* one *d*; 2nd, 2006, Stephanie Louise Moret, MS, PhD]. *Address:* 2576 Broadway, Apt 146, New York, NY 10025, USA.

BOOTH, Sir Gordon, KCMG 1980 (CMG 1969); CVO 1976; HM Diplomatic Service, retired; *b* 22 Nov. 1921; *s* of Walter and Grace Booth, Bolton, Lancs; *m* 1944, Jeanne Mary Kirkham; one *s* one *d*. *Educ:* Canon Slade Sch.; London Univ. (BCom). Served War of 1939–45: Capt. RAC and 13/18th Royal Hussars, 1941–46. Min. of Labour and Bd of Trade, 1946–55; Trade Comr, Canada and West Indies, 1955–65; Mem. HM Diplomatic Service, 1965–80; Counsellor (Commercial), British Embassy in Copenhagen, 1966–69; Dir, Coordination of Export Services, DTI, 1969–71; Consul-General, Sydney, 1971–74; HBM Consul-Gen., NY, and Dir-Gen. of Trade Develt in USA, 1975–80; Chm., SITPRO Bd, 1980–86. Chairman: London Clubs Internat. plc, 1992–95; Ritz Hotel Casino Ltd, 1998–2002. Director: Hanson PLC (formerly Hanson Trust), 1981–89; Bechtel Ltd, 1983–92; Allders Internat. Ltd, 1992–96. *Recreations:* golf, bridge. *Address:* Rivington, Hethfelton, Wareham, Dorset BH20 6HS. *T:* (01929) 401548.

BOOTH, Graham Harry; Member (UK Ind) South West Region, England, European Parliament, since Dec. 2002; *b* 29 March 1940; *s* of Harry Booth and Dinx Booth; *m* 1st, 1961 (marr. diss. 1969); two *s*; *m* 2nd, 1982, Pamela Jones; one step *s* two step *d*. *Educ:* Torquay Boys' Grammar Sch. Lloyds Bank, 1956–60; family holiday business, 1960–. Mem. NEC, UK Independence Party, 1997–. *Recreations:* golf, poetry, astronomy, coin collecting. *Address:* 41 Oyster Bend, Paignton, Devon TQ4 6NL. *T:* and *Fax:* (01803) 557433; *e-mail:* mrgrahambooth@aol.com. *Club:* Farmers.

BOOTH, Hartley; Chairman, Uzbek British Trade and Industry Council, British Trade International, since 1999; *b* 17 July 1946; *s* of late V. W. H. Booth and Eilish (*née* Morrow); *m* 1977, Adrianne Claire Cranefield; two *s* one *d*. *Educ:* Queen's Coll., Taunton; Bristol Univ. (LLB); Downing Coll., Cambridge (LLM, PhD). Called to the Bar, Inner Temple, 1970 (Scholar); in practice, 1970–84; Special Advr to Prime Minister and Mem., 10 Downing Street Policy Unit, 1984–88; Chief Exec., British Urban Develt, 1988–90; Consultant: Berwin Leighton (Solicitors), 1991–99; Maclay Murray Spens (Solicitors), 2003–06; Pinsent Masons, 2006–. Director: Canford Gp plc, 1978–; Edexcel, 1999–2001. MP (C) Finchley, 1992–97. PPS to Minister of State, FCO, 1992–94. Mem. Select Committees: Home Affairs, 1992; European Legislation, 1992; Public Service, 1995–97; Chm., Urban Affairs Select Cttee, 1994–97. Chm., British Uzbek Soc., 2001–. Vice President: Royal Life Saving Soc., 1990–; British Urban Regeneration Assoc., 1991–94 (Chm., 1990–91); AMA, 1992. Pres., Resources for Autism, 2004– (Chm., 1996–2004). European Editor, Current Law Year Books, 1974–84. *Publications:* British Extradition Law and Procedure, vol. I 1979, vol. II 1980; Return Ticket, 1994. *Recreations:* writing, swimming, delving into history, poetry. *Address:* c/o Pinsent Masons, 30 Aylesbury Street, EC1R 0ER.

BOOTH, Prof. Ian Westerby, MD; FRCP, FRCPCH; Director, Institute of Child Health, since 1993, Sir Leonard Parsons Professor of Paediatrics and Child Health, since 1996, and Dean, Medical School, since 2007, University of Birmingham; *b* 15 Aug. 1948; *s* of William Westerby Booth and Audrey Iris (*née* Corless). *Educ:* Sir George Monoux Grammar Sch., London; King's Coll. Hosp. Med. Sch., Univ. of London (BSc Hons Physiol. 1969; MB BS 1972; MSc with Dist. Biochem. 1982; MD 1987). DRCOG 1974; DCH 1975; MRCP 1977, FRCP 1991; Founder FRCPCH 1997. Eden Res. Fellow, RCP, 1980–83; Lectr, Inst. Child Health, London, 1983–85; University of Birmingham: Sen. Lectr in Paediatrics and Child Health, 1985–92; Prof. of Paediatric Gastroenterology and Nutrition, 1992–96; Associate Dean, Medical Sch., 2000–06; Hon. Consultant Paediatric Gastroenterologist, 1985–, Dir of Educn, 1998–2002, Mem. Exec. Bd, 1995–2002, Children's Hosp., Birmingham. Department of Health: Vice-Chm., Adv. Cttee on Borderline Substances, 1990–97; Member: Panel on Novel Foods, 1992–98; Wkg Gp on Nutritional Adequacy of Infant Formulas, 1994–96. Member: Med. and Res. Adv. Gp, HEA, 1994–99; Specialised Health Services Commn for Wales Wkg Gp on Tertiary Services for Children, 2000–02; Food Standards Agency Expert Gp on Choking Hazards, 2002–. Pres., British Soc. Paediatric Gastroenterology and Nutrition, 1995–98 (Sec., 1985–89); Royal College of Paediatrics and Child Health: Chairman: Standing Cttee on Nutrition, 1996–2002; Academic Bd, 1998–2003; Wkg Gp on Intestinal Failure, 1998–2002; Mem., Safety and Efficiency Register of New Interventional Procedures, Acad. of Med. Royal Colls, 1996–2001. GMC Visitor for Quality Assuring Basic Med. Educn, 2004–. Non-exec. Dir, Birmingham Women's Healthcare Foundn Trust Bd, 2005–. Associate Ed., Archives of Diseases of Childhood, 1993–96; Member, Editorial Board: Gut, 1996–2000; Internat. Jl of Gastroenterology, 1996–. *Publications:* (with E. Wozniak) Pocket Picture Guides in Clinical Medicine: Paediatrics, 1984; (with D. A. Kelly) An Atlas of Paediatric Gastroenterology and Hepatology, 1996; contribs to learned jls on paediatric gastroenterology and nutrition. *Recreation:* walking to restaurants. *Address:* The Medical School, University of Birmingham, Edgbaston, Birmingham B15 2TT. *T:* (0121) 414 4059, *Fax:* (0121) 414 7149; *e-mail:* i.w.booth@bham.ac.uk.

BOOTH, Sir Josslyn Henry Robert G.; *see* Gore-Booth.

BOOTH, Prof. Ken, PhD; FBA 2006; E. H. Carr Professor of International Politics, Aberystwyth University (formerly University of Wales, Aberystwyth), since 1999; *b* 29 Jan. 1943; *s* of Fred and Phyllis Booth; *m* 1967, Eurwen Jones; two *s*. *Educ:* King's Sch., Pontefract; University Coll. of Wales, Aberystwyth (BA 1st Cl. Hons; PhD 1982). Lectr, Sen. Lectr, then Reader, 1967–99, Hd of Dept, 1999–2005, Dept of Internat. Politics, UC of Wales, Aberystwyth, then Univ. of Wales, Aberystwyth. Scholar-in-Residence, US Naval War Coll., Newport, RI, 1977; Sen. Res. Fellow, Dalhousie Univ., Canada, 1979–81; Vis. Fellow, Cambridge Univ., 1992–93. Ed., Internat. Relns, 2003–. Chm., British Internat. Studies Assoc., 1995–96. AcSS 2002. FRSA 2006. Susan Strange Award, Internat. Studies Assoc., 2004. *Publications:* (ed jtly and contrib.) Soviet Naval Policy, 1975; (jtly) Contemporary Strategy: Vol. I: Theories and Concepts, 1975, 2nd edn 1987, Vol. II: The Nuclear Powers, 1987; Navies and Foreign Policy, 1977; (ed jtly and contrib.) American Thinking About Peace and War, 1978; Strategy and Ethnocentrism, 1979; Law, Force and Diplomacy at Sea, 1985; (with J. Baylis) Britain, NATO and Nuclear Weapons, 1989; (ed and contrib.) Strategic Power: USA/USSR, 1990; (ed and contrib.) New Thinking About Strategy and International Security, 1991; (with E. Herring) Strategic Studies: keyguide to information sources, 1994; (ed jtly and contrib.) International Relations Theory Today, 1995; (ed jtly and contrib.) International Theory: positivism and beyond, 1996; (ed and contrib.) Statecraft and Security: the Cold War and beyond, 1998; (ed jtly) The Eighty Years' Crisis, 1998; (ed jtly and contrib.) Strategic Cultures in the Asia-Pacific Region, 1999; (ed jtly) The Interregnum: controversies in world politics 1989–1999, 1999; (ed and contrib.) The Kosovo Tragedy, 2001; (ed jtly) How Might We Live?, 2001; (ed jtly) Great Transformations, 2001; (ed jtly and contrib.) Worlds in Collision, 2002; (ed and contrib.) Critical Security Studies in World Politics, 2005; Theory of World Security, 2007; (with N. J. Wheeler) The Security Dilemma, 2008; contrib. articles to Internat. Affairs, Rev. Internat. Studies, Political Qly, etc. *Recreations:* watching sport, and thinking of what might have been, reading obituaries, and thinking of what will be, hand-thrown pottery, hill-walking, Ceredigion mental health lobby. *Address:* Department of International Politics, Aberystwyth University, Penglais, Aberystwyth SY23 3FE. *T:* (01970) 622694, *Fax:* (01970) 621588; *e-mail:* kob@aber.ac.uk.

BOOTH, Dame Margaret (Myfanwy Wood), DBE 1979; President, National Family and Parenting Institute, since 2004 (Chairman, 1999–2004); a Judge of the High Court, Family Division, 1979–94; *b* 11 Sept. 1933; *d* of late Alec Wood Booth and Lilian May Booth; *m* 1st, 1982, Joseph Jackson, QC (*d* 1987); 2nd, 1993, Peter Glucksmann (*d* 2002). *Educ:* Northwood Coll.; University Coll., London (LLM; Fellow, 1982). Called to the Bar, Middle Temple, 1956; Bencher, 1979. QC 1976. Chairman: Family Law Bar Assoc., 1976–78; Matrimonial Causes Procedure Cttee, 1982–85; Inner London Adv. Cttee on Justices of the Peace, 1990–93; Children Act Procedure Adv. Cttee, 1990; Children Act 1989 Adv. Cttee, 1991–93 (report published, 1996); Bar Central Selection Bd, 1993–96; Family Law Cttee, Justice, 1993–98. Pres., Family Mediators Assoc., 1994–95; Chm. Govs, UK Coll. of Family Mediators, 1996–99. Vis. Prof. of Law, Liverpool Univ., 1994–99. Trustee: Rowntree Foundn, 1996–2003; Apex Charitable Trust Ltd, 1996–2003 (Chm., 1997–2003; Pres., 2003–06); Trustee and Chm., Communities That Care (UK), 1997–2003 (Pres., 2003–). Pres., Alone in London, 1998–; Vice-Pres., Rainer, 2007–; Patron, The Place to Be, 1999–; Governor, Northwood Coll., 1975–96; Member, Council: UCL, 1980–84; Liverpool Univ., 1994–99 (Vice-Pres., 1996–99). Hon. LLD Liverpool, 1992; DUniv 2007. *Publications:* (co-ed) Rayden on Divorce, 10th edn 1967, (cons. ed.) 17th edn 1997; (co-ed) Clarke Hall and Morrison on Children, 9th edn 1977, (cons. ed.) 10th edn 1985. *Address:* 15 Wellington House, Eton Road, NW3 4SY. *Club:* Reform.

BOOTH, Sir Michael Addison John W.; *see* Wheeler-Booth.

BOOTH, Michael John; QC 1999; *b* Salford, 24 May 1958; *s* of Eric Charles Booth and Iris Booth (*née* Race); *m* 1987, Sarah Jane Marchington; two *s* one *d*. *Educ:* Manchester Grammar Sch. (Schol.); Trinity Coll., Cambridge (Open Schol.; MA Hons Law). Pres., Cambridge Union Soc., Michaelmas, 1979. Called to the Bar, Lincoln's Inn, 1981, Bencher, 2008. Mem., Manchester GS's winning team, ESU Nat. Schools Public Speaking Comp., 1975. *Recreations:* walking, swimming, reading, watching football, wine. *Address:* King Chambers, 36 Young Street, Manchester M3 3FT.

BOOTH, Peter John Richard; National Organiser, Manufacturing, since 1999, and Textile National Trade Group Secretary, since 1986, T&G Section of Unite (formerly Transport and General Workers' Union); *b* 27 March 1949; *s* of Eric Albert and Edith Booth; *m* 1970, Edwina Ivy; three *s*. *Educ:* Little London Infant Sch.; Rawdon Littlemore Junior Sch., Rawdon; Benton Park Secondary Modern School. Dyers' Operative, 1964; National Union of Dyers, Bleachers and Textile Workers: District Officer, 1973; Nat. Research Officer, 1975; Nat. Organiser, 1980; transf. to TGWU, 1982; Nat. Trade Group Organiser, 1982. Member: Yorks and Humberside Regl Innovation Strategy, 1998–2000; Manufg Forum, DTI, 2005–; Manufg Task Gp, TUC, 2005–; Exec., Gen. Fedn of Trade Unions. Director: Man-Made Fibres Industry Trng Adv. Bd, 1986–98; Apparel, Knitting & Textiles Alliance, 1989–96; Nat. Textile Trading Orgn, 1998–2000; Skill-Fast UK, 2002–; Member: Internat. Textile, Garment and Leather Workers Fedn, 1986– (Pres., 1996–2004); Confedn of British Wool Textiles Trng Bd, 1986–98; Carpet Industry Trng Council, 1986–95 (Chm.); Nat. Textile Trng Gp, 1989–2000 (Vice Pres.); Textile, Clothing and Strategy Gp; Presidium, European TU Cttee, 1990–; Textiles Industry Adv. Cttee, 1994–; Cotton & Allied Textiles Industry Adv. Cttee, 1986–94; Chm., Wool Textile and Clothing Industry Action Cttee, 1996–98. FRSA; CCMI 2006. *Publication:* The Old Dog Strike, 1985. *Recreations:* walking, gardening, dominoes, chess. *Address:* Unite the Union (T&G Section), Transport House, 128 Theobalds Road, Holborn, WC1X 8TN.

BOOTH, Richard George William Pitt, MBE 2004; bookseller, since 1961; Chairman, Welsh Booksellers Association, since 1987; *b* 12 Sept. 1938; *m* 1987, Hope Estcourt Stuart (*née* Barrie). *Educ:* Rugby; Univ. of Oxford. Founding father of following towns as centres of bookselling: Hay-on-Wye, 1961; Redu, 1984; Becherel, 1988; Montolieu, 1989; Bredevoort, 1992; Fjaerland, 1996; Dalmellington, 1997. Life Pres., Internat. Book Town Movt, 2000. *Publications:* Country Life Book of Book Collecting, 1976; Independence for Hay, 1977. *Recreations:* creating a monarchy in Hay to promote tourism from books, gardening. *Address:* Hay Castle, Hay-on-Wye, via Hereford HR3 5DG.

BOOTH, Roger Hignett, CEng; Royal Academy of Engineering Visiting Professor, Department of Engineering Science, University of Oxford, 1998–2006; *b* 3 May 1940; *s* of David and Elsie Booth; *m* 1st, 1968, Maureen (*née* Howell) (marr. diss. 1996); two *s*; 2nd, 1997, Thelly (*née* Price). *Educ:* Bentham Grammar Sch.; Birmingham Univ. (BSc Chem. Engrg). MIChemE 1966; CEng 1973. Royal Dutch/Shell Gp (posts in UK, Indonesia, USA, Netherlands, Pakistan), 1961–96; Dir, Solar Century Hldgs Ltd, 1999–2003. Mem., Newnham Parish Council, 2004–. *Publications:* articles on renewable energy and sustainable develt. *Recreations:* golf, walking, dining with friends, listening to music. *Address:* Firtree Cottage, Newnham Road, Newnham, Hook RG27 9AE. *T:* (01256) 762456. *Club:* Tylney Park Golf.

BOOTH, Sarah Ann; *see* Hinkley, S. A.

BOOTH, Vernon Edward Hartley; *see* Booth, H.

BOOTH, Rev. Preb. William James, CVO 2007 (LVO 1999); Sub-Dean of Her Majesty's Chapels Royal, Deputy Clerk of the Closet, Sub-Almoner and Domestic Chaplain to The Queen, 1991–2007; Prebendary, St Paul's Cathedral, 2000–07; *b* 3 Feb. 1939; *s* of William James Booth and Elizabeth Ethel Booth. *Educ:* Ballymena Acad., Co. Antrim; TCD (MA). Curate, St Luke's Parish, Belfast, 1962–64; Chaplain, Cranleigh Sch., Surrey, 1965–74. Priest-in-Ordinary to The Queen, 1976–91; Priest-Vicar of Westminster Abbey, 1987–91. Chaplain, Westminster School, London, 1974–91 (Hon. Fellow 2006). Organiser, PHAB annual residential courses at Westminster (and formerly at Cranleigh). *Recreations:* music, hi-fi, cooking. *Address:* 48 South Everard Street, King's Lynn, Norfolk PE30 5HJ.

BOOTHBY, Sir Brooke (Charles), 16th Bt *cr* 1660, of Broadlow Ash, Derbyshire; Chairman, Adventure Activity Licensing Authority, since 1996; *b* 6 April 1949; *s* of Sir Hugo Robert Brooke Boothby, 15th Bt and (Evelyn) Ann (*d* 1993), *d* of late H. C. R. Homfray; *S* father, 1986; *m* 1976, Georgiana Alexandra, *o d* of late Sir John Wriothesley Russell, GCVO, CMG; two *d*. *Educ:* Eton; Trinity Coll., Cambridge (BA Econs). Chm., Associated Quality Services, 1994–; Man. Dir, 1979–95, Vice Chm., 1995–2003, Chm., 2004–, Fontygary Parks Ltd (formerly Fontygary Leisure); Dir, Bradford Rural Estates Ltd, 2001–. Chm., Capital Region Tourism, 2002–03; Dir, Wales Tourism Alliance, 2002–. Chairman: Historic Houses Assoc. Inheritance Cttee, 1984–86; Nat. Caravan Council Parks Div., 1987–90. President: Glamorgan Br., CLA, 1992–94; Vale of Glamorgan Nat. Trust, 1998–. Hon. Consul of Malta for Wales, 2007–. High Sheriff, South Glamorgan, 1986–87. Gov., United World Coll. of the Atlantic, 2003–06. *Recreation:* gardening. *Heir: kinsman* George William Boothby [*b* 18 June 1948; *m* 1977, Sally Louisa Thomas; three *d*]. *Address:* Fonmon Castle, Barry, Vale of Glamorgan CF62 3ZN. *T:* (01446) 710206, *Fax:* (01446) 711687; *e-mail:* Fonmon_Castle@msn.com.

BOOTHMAN, His Honour Campbell Lester; a Circuit Judge, 1988–2003; *b* 3 Sept. 1942; *s* of Gerald and Ann Boothman; *m* 1966, Penelope Evelyn Pepe; three *s*. *Educ:* Oundle; King's College, London. Called to the Bar, Inner Temple, 1965. A Recorder, 1985–88. *Recreations:* ski-ing, squash. *Address:* 13 The Keg Store, Bath Street, Bristol BS1 6HL.

BOOTHMAN, Derek Arnold, CBE 2003; FCA; non-executive Director, Remploy Ltd, 1987–2004; *b* 5 June 1932; *s* of Eric Randolph Boothman and Doris Mary Boothman; *m* 1958, Brenda Margaret; one *s* one *d*. *Educ:* William Hulme's Grammar Sch., Manchester. Mem., ICA, subseq. ICAEW, 1954. Articled to J. Needham & Co., 1948; National Service, RAF, 1954–56; Partner: J. Needham & Co., and successor cos (later part of Binder Hamlyn), 1957–74; Binder Hamlyn, Chartered Accts, 1974–88. Dep. Chm., Central Manchester Develt Corp., 1988–96. President: Manchester Chartered Accountants Students Soc., 1967–68; Manchester Soc. of Chartered Accountants, 1968–69; Institute of Chartered Accountants in England and Wales: Council Member, 1969–91; Treasurer, 1981–83; Vice-Pres., 1983–85; Dep. Pres., 1985–86; Pres., 1986–87. Member, Accounting Standards Cttee, 1974–82. Gov., William Hulme's Grammar Sch., 1982–2002 (Chm., 1988–99); Mem. Ct, Univ. of Manchester, 1990–99. Chm., Prestbury Probus, 2006–07. Liveryman, Worshipful Company of Chartered Accountants, 1976–. *Publications:* contribs to professional press and lectures on professional topics, internationally. *Recreations:* cricket, gardening, travel. *Address:* Ashworth Dene, Wilmslow Road, Mottram St Andrew, Cheshire SK10 4QH. *T:* (01625) 829101. *Clubs:* St James's (Manchester); Withington Golf (Manchester) (past Captain).

BOOTHMAN, Nicholas, CEng; Director of Technology, Metropolitan Police Service, 1992–2000; *b* 16 Dec. 1941; *s* of late Frederick Boothman and Sarah Ellen (*née* Kirk); *m* 1964, Ernestine Carole Jane Billings; one *d*. *Educ:* Threshfield Sch.; Ermysteds Grammar Sch., Skipton; Univ. of Birmingham (BSc Physics). CEng, MIET (MIEE 1972). Research at GEC Hirst Res. Centre, Wembley, 1963–72; project management of communication systems for RAF, MoD (PE), 1972–77; Project Manager, Metropolitan Police Office, 1977–88; Chief Engr, Metropolitan Police, 1988–92. *Recreations:* amateur musician, watching cricket, railways, unavoidable gardening. *Address:* 57A Wensleydale Road, Hampton, Middx TW12 2LP.

BOOTHROYD, Baroness *cr* 2000 (Life Peer), of Sandwell in the co. of West Midlands; **Betty Boothroyd,** OM 2005; PC 1992; Speaker of the House of Commons, 1992–2000; *b* Yorkshire, 8 Oct. 1929; *d* of Archibald and Mary Boothroyd. *Educ:* Dewsbury Coll. of Commerce and Art. Personal/Political Asst to Labour Ministers. Delegate to N Atlantic Assembly, 1974. MP (Lab) West Bromwich, May 1973–1974, West Bromwich West, 1974–92 (when elected Speaker); MP West Bromwich West, 1992–2000. An Asst Govt Whip, Oct. 1974–Nov. 1975; Dep. Chm. of Ways and Means, and Dep. Speaker, 1987–92. Member: Select Cttee on Foreign Affairs, 1979–81; Speaker's Panel of Chairmen, 1979–87; House of Commons Commn, 1983–87. Mem., European Parlt, 1975–77. Mem., Labour Party NEC, 1981–87. Contested (Lab): SE Leicester (by-elec.), 1957; Peterborough (gen. elec.), 1959; Nelson and Colne (by-elec.), 1968; Rossendale (gen. elec.), 1970. Chancellor, Open Univ., 1994–2007. Hon. FCOptom 2005. Freeman: Borough of Sandwell, 1992; Borough of Kirklees, 1992; City of London, 1993; Hon. Freeman: Lightmongers' Co., 2003; Grocers' Co., 2005; Hon. Liveryman: Feltmakers' Co., 1993; Glovers' Co., 1997. Hon. LLD: Birmingham, 1992; South Bank, 1992; Leicester, 1993; Cambridge, 1994; St Andrews, 2001; Hon. DLitt Bradford, 1993; DUniv: Leeds Metropolitan, 1993; North London, 1993; Hon. DCL Oxford, 1995. *Publication:* Betty Boothroyd: the autobiography, 2001. *Address:* House of Lords, SW1A 0PW.

BOOTLE, Roger Paul; Managing Director, Capital Economics Ltd, since 1999; *b* 22 June 1952; *s* of David Bootle and Florence (*née* Denman); *m* 1993, Sally Broomfield (marr. diss. 2007); one *s* two *d*. *Educ:* Merton Coll., Oxford (BA PPE 1973); Nuffield Coll., Oxford (MPhil Econs 1975). Chief Economist: Capel-Cure Myers, 1982–86; Lloyds Merchant Bank, 1986–89; Greenwell Montagu, 1989–92; HSBC Markets, 1992–96; Gp Chief Economist, HSBC, 1996–98. Vis. Prof., Manchester Business Sch., 1995–. Mem., Chancellor of the Exchequer's Panel of Indep. Econ. Advrs, 1997; Specialist Advr, H of C Treasury Cttee, 1998–. Econ. Advr, Deloitte, 1999–. Columnist: The Times, 1997–99; Sunday Telegraph, 1999–2006; Daily Telegraph, 2006–. *Publications:* (with W. T. Newlyn) Theory of Money, 1978; Index-Linked Gilts, 1985; The Death of Inflation, 1996; Money for Nothing, 2003. *Recreations:* squash, horse-racing, classical music, bridge. *Address:* 150 Buckingham Palace Road, SW1W 9TR. *T:* (020) 7823 5000.

BOOTLE-WILBRAHAM, family name of **Baron Skelmersdale.**

BOPA RAI, Aprampar Apar Jot Kaur, (Joti), (Mrs W. F. Casey); a District Judge (Magistrates' Courts), since 2004; *b* 18 Feb. 1957; *d* of Manjit Singh Bopa Rai and Swaran Kaur Bopa Rai; *m* 1993, William Francis Casey. *Educ:* Wolverhampton Polytech. (LLB (Law) 1980); Coll. of Law, Guildford. Admitted solicitor, 1984; Asst Solicitor, Partner, Elgoods, Cheltenham, 1984–89; Partner, Tarlings, Cheltenham, 1989–93; sole practitioner, 1993–2004; Dep. Dist Judge, 2000–04. *Recreations:* walking, ski–ing, reading, visiting historic sites. *Address:* Birmingham Magistrates' Court, Victoria Law Courts, Corporation Street, Birmingham B4 6QE. *T:* (0121) 212 6706.

BORBIDGE, Hon. Robert Edward, AO 2006; Chairman: Rotec Design Ltd; Asset Loan Co., since 2004; CEC Group, since 2004; Early Learning Services, since 2007; *b* Ararat, Vic, 12 Aug. 1954; *s* of Edward A. Borbidge and Jean Borbidge; *m* 1984, Jennifer Gooding; one *s* one *d*. *Educ:* Ararat High Sch., Vic; Overberg High Sch., S Africa. Mem. Bd, Gold Coast Visitors' Bureau, 1980. MLA (Nat.) Surfers Paradise, Qld, 1980–2001; formerly Mem., Qld Parly Delegn, Qld Govt Cttees on Transport, Tourism, Nat. Parks, Sport and Arts, Ind. and Commerce, Local Govt, Main Roads and Police; Minister: for Industry, Small Business, Communications and Technol., 1987–89; for Ind., Small Business, Technol. and Tourism, then for Police, Emergency Services and Corrective Services, and subseq. for Tourism and for Envmt, Conservation and Forestry, 1989; Opposition spokesman on Small Business, Manufg and Regl Develt and Assisting Leader on Econ. and Trade Develt, 1990–91; Dep. Leader of Opposition, 1989–91, Leader, 1991–96 and 1998–2001; Premier of Qld and Minister responsible for Ethnic Affairs, 1996–98; Leader, Qld Nat. Party-Lib. Party Coalition, 1992–2001. Griffith University: Chm., Exec. Task Force, Inst. for Glycomics, 2003–; Mem. Univ. Council, 2006–; Vice Chm., Univ. Foundn, 2006–; Trustee, Friends of Griffith Univ., 2004–. DUniv Griffith, 2004. *Recreations:* travel, reading, tourism, swimming. *Address:* 3 Tincurrin Court, Robina, Qld 4226, Australia.

BORCHERDS, Prof. Richard Ewen, FRS 1994; Professor of Mathematics, University of California at Berkeley, 1993–96 and since 1999; *b* 29 Nov. 1959; *s* of Dr Peter Howard Borcherds and Margaret Elizabeth Borcherds; *m* Ursula Gritsch. *Educ:* Trinity Coll., Cambridge (BA, MA; PhD 1985). Research Fellow, Trinity Coll., Cambridge, 1983–87; Morrey Asst Prof., Univ. of California, Berkeley, 1987–88; Cambridge University: Royal Soc. Univ. Res. Fellow, 1988–92; Lectr, 1992–93; Royal Soc. Prof., Dept of Maths, 1996–99. Fields Medal, Internat. Mathematical Union, 1998. *Publications:* papers in math. jls. *Address:* Department of Mathematics, University of California, 927 Evans Hall # 3840, Berkeley, CA 94720–3840, USA.

BORDEN, Prof. Iain Michael, PhD; Professor of Architecture and Urban Culture, since 2002, and Head, since 2005, Bartlett School of Architecture, University College London; *b* 9 Nov. 1962; *s* of Anthony Ian Borden and Shelagh Mary Borden; *m* 2001, Claire Haywood; one *s*. *Educ:* Univ. of Newcastle upon Tyne (BA Hist. of Art, Arch. and Ancient Hist. 1985); Bartlett Sch., University Coll. London (MSc Hist. of Modern Arch. 1986); Univ. of Calif, LA (MA Hist. of Arch. and Planning 1989); PhD London 1998. Bartlett School of Architecture, University College London: Lectr, 1989–97, Sen. Lectr, 1997–99, in Architectural Hist.; Reader in Arch. and Urban Culture, 1999–2002; Dir, 2001–05; Sub-Dean and Vice-Dean, Faculty of Built Envmt, UCL, 1996–2001. Hon. FRIBA 2003. FRSA 2003. *Publications:* (ed with D. Dunster) Architecture and the Sites of History: interpretations of buildings and cities, 1995; (ed jtly) Strangely Familiar: narratives of architecture in the city, 1996; (ed jtly) Gender Space Architecture: an interdisciplinary introduction, 1999; (ed jtly) The City Cultures Reader, 2000, 2nd edn 2003; (ed with J. Rendell) InterSections: architectural histories and critical theories, 2000; (with K. Rüedi) The Dissertation: an architecture student's handbook, 2000, 2nd edn 2005; (ed jtly) The Unknown City: contesting architecture and social space, 2001; Skateboarding, Space and the City: architecture and the body, 2001; Manual: the architecture and office of Alford Hall Monaghan Morris, 2003; (ed jtly) Bartlett Works, 2004; (ed jtly) Transculturation: cities, spaces and architectures in Latin America, 2005. *Recreations:* driving, photography, skateboarding, wandering around cities. *Address:* Bartlett School of Architecture, University College London, Wates House, 22 Gordon Street, WC1H 0QB. *T:* (020) 7679 4851, *Fax:* (020) 7679 4831; *e-mail:* i.borden@ucl.ac.uk.

BORDER, Allan Robert, AO 1989 (AM 1986); journalist and sports commentator; Director: Queensland Cricket, since 2001; Cricket Australia, since 2002; *b* 27 July 1955; *s* of John and Sheila Border; *m* 1980, Jane, *d* of John and Eve Hiscox; two *s* two *d*. *Educ:* N Sydney Tech. Sch.; N Sydney High Sch. First class cricket début, for NSW, 1976; professional cricketer, Queensland State, 1977–96 (Captain, 1983–84); Test début, 1978;

Captain, Australian cricket team, 1984–94; played 156 Test matches for Australia, with record of 93 as Captain, scored 27 centuries and 2 double centuries, record total of 11,174 Test runs, also took 39 wickets and record 156 catches; in all first-class cricket matches to 1994, had scored 25,551 runs incl. 68 centuries, and taken 102 wickets and 345 catches. Mem., Nat. Cricket Selection Panel, Aust., 1998–2005 and 2006. With Ronald McConnell Hldgs, 1980–84; with Castlemaine Perkins, 1984–98. Columnist, Courier Mail; commentator, Fox Sports TV. *Publication:* Beyond Ten Thousand: my life story, 1994. *Address:* c/o Cricket Australia, 60 Jolimont Street, Jolimont, Vic 3002, Australia.

BORE, Sir Albert, Kt 2002; Member (Lab), Birmingham City Council, since 1980 (Leader, 1999–2004); Chairman, University Hospital Birmingham NHS Foundation Trust, since 2006. Former Lectr in Physics, Aston Univ. Chairman: Birmingham Econ. Develt Cttee, 1984–93; Member: Bd, Advantage West Midlands, 1999–2002; Birmingham Marketing Partnership. Director: Aston Sci. Park; Nat. Exhibition Centre Ltd; Birmingham Technol. Ltd; NEC Finance plc; Optima Community Assoc.; non-exec. Dir, Colliers CRE, 2005–. Pres., EU Cttee of the Regions, 2002–04 (Mem., 1994–). *Address:* c/o Birmingham City Council, Council House, Victoria Square, Birmingham B1 1BB.

BOREEL, Sir Stephan Gerard, 14th Bt *cr* 1645, of Amsterdam; *b* 9 Feb. 1945; *s* of Gerard Lucas Boreel and Virginia Rae Bright; *S* kinsman, Sir Francis Boreel, 13th Bt, 2001; *m* 1972, Francien P. Kooijman; one *s*. *Heir: s* Jacob Lucas Cornelus Boreel, *b* 29 Sept. 1974.

BORELAND-KELLY, Dame Lorna (May), DBE 1998; JP; Mayday and Permanence Manager, Department of Children, Young People and Learners, Mayday NHS Trust, Croydon, since 2008; *b* 9 Aug. 1952; *d* of James Boreland and Hortence Boreland (*née* Boyd); *m* Anthony Owen Kelly; three *s* three *d*. *Educ:* North London Univ. (CQSW 1991). Sen. Practitioner, Social Work Children and Families, St Thomas' Hosp., 1997–2000; Team Manager, 2001–01, Hospital Manager, Children and Families, 2001–07, Mayday Hosp., Croydon. Mem., Judicial Appts Commn, 2006–. Chair of Govs, Lambeth Coll., 1992–. Mem., Union of Catholic Mothers. FRSA 2000. JP S Westminster, 1991. *Recreations:* reading, writing short stories (never to be published), watching my sons swim. *Address:* c/o Lambeth College, 45 Clapham Common, Southside, SW4 9BL. *T:* (020) 7501 5602.

BORG, Alan Charles Nelson, CBE 1991; PhD; FSA; Director, Victoria and Albert Museum, 1995–2001; *b* 21 Jan. 1942; *s* of late Charles John Nelson Borg and Frances Mary Olive Hughes; *m* 1st, 1964, Anne (marr. diss.), *d* of late Dr William Blackmore; one *s* one *d*; 2nd, 1976, Lady Caroline, *d* of late Captain Lord Francis Hill, *yr s* of 6th Marquess of Downshire; two *d*. *Educ:* Westminster Sch.; Brasenose Coll., Oxford (MA); Courtauld Inst. of Art (PhD). Lecteur d'anglais, Université d'Aix-Marseille, 1964–65; Lectr, History of Art, Indiana Univ., 1967–69; Asst Prof. of History of Art, Princeton Univ., 1969–70; Asst Keeper of the Royal Armouries, HM Tower of London, 1970–78; Keeper, Sainsbury Centre for Visual Arts, Univ. of E Anglia, 1978–82; Dir Gen., Imperial War Mus., 1982–95. Member: British Nat. Cttee for Hist. of Second World War, 1982–95; Bd of War Studies, KCL, 1982–95; COPUS, 1992–95; Council, Museums Assoc., 1992–95; Adv. Cttee on Public Records, 1993–99; Court of Advisers, St Paul's Cathedral, 1996–2000; Bd of Mgt, Courtauld Inst. of Art, 1998–2002; Chm., Nat. Inventory of War Memls, 1988–95; Admin. Council, Louvre Mus., 1999–2001. Chm., Nat. Mus. Dirs' Conf., 1998–2000. President: Elizabethan Club, 1994–2000; Meyrick Soc., 1994–. Trustee: Foundling Museum, 1998– (Chm. Trustees, 2006–); Handel House, 2002–06; St Paul's Cathedral Foundn, 2002–05; Topolski Memoir, 2007–. Governor: Thomas Coram Foundn for Children, 1995–2005; Westminster Sch., 1998–. Freeman, City of London, 1997; Hon. Liveryman, Painter Stainers' Co., 1997. Librarian, Priory of England and the Islands, Order of St John, 2007–. Hon. FRCA 1991; Hon. FRIBA 2001. DUniv Sheffield Hallam, 2000. *Publications:* Architectural Sculpture in Romanesque Provence, 1972; European Swords and Daggers in the Tower of London, 1974; Torture and Punishment, 1975; Heads and Horses, 1976; Arms and Armour in Britain, 1979; (ed with A. R. Martindale) The Vanishing Past: studies presented to Christopher Hohler, 1981; War Memorials, 1991; The History of the Worshipful Company of Painter-Stainers, 2005; articles in learned jls. *Recreations:* fencing (Oxford blue, 1962, 1963), music, travel. *Address:* Telegraph House, 36 West Square, SE11 4SP. *Clubs:* Beefsteak, Special Forces.

BORG, Björn Rune; professional tennis player, 1972–2000; *b* 6 June 1956; *s* of Rune and Margaretha Borg; *m* 1st, 1980, Mariana Simionescu (marr. diss. 1984); one *s* by Jannike Björling; 2nd, 1989, Loredana Berte (marr. diss. 1992); 3rd, 2002, Patricia Östfeldt; one *s*. *Educ:* Blombacka Sch., Södertälje. Started to play tennis at age of 9; won Wimbledon junior title, 1972; became professional player in 1972. Mem., Swedish Davis Cup team, annually 1972–80 (youngest player ever in a winning Davis Cup team, 1975). Championship titles: Italian, 1974, 1978; French, 1974, 1975, 1978, 1979, 1980, 1981; Wimbledon, record of 5 consecutive singles titles, 1976–80; World Champion, 1978, 1979, 1980; Masters, 1980, 1981. *Publication:* (with Eugene Scott) Björn Borg: my life and game, 1980. *Address:* c/o IMG, McCormack House, Hogarth Business Park, Chiswick, W4 2TH.

BORG, Joseph, LLD; Member, European Commission, since 2004; *b* 19 March 1952; *m* Isabelle Agius; one *s* one *d*. *Educ:* Univ. of Malta (NP 1974; LLD 1975). Legal advr to cos and corporate bodies, Malta and abroad, 1976–88; Lectr in Law, 1979–88, Sen. Lectr., 1988–2004, Univ. of Malta. Dir, Central Bank of Malta, 1992–95. MP (Nationalist), Malta, 1995–2004; Parly Sec., Min. of Foreign Affairs, 1998–99; Minister of Foreign Affairs, 1999–2004. *Address:* European Commission, Rue de la Loi 200, 1049 Brussels, Belgium.

BORG COSTANZI, Prof. Edwin J., MOM 1999; Rector, University of Malta, 1964–80 and 1988–91; *b* 8 Sept. 1925; 2nd *s* of late Michael Borg Costanzi and M. Stella (*née* Camilleri); *m* 1948, Lucy Valentino; two *s* one *d*. *Educ:* Lyceum, Malta; Royal University of Malta (BSc, BE&A); Balliol College, Oxford (BA 1946, MA 1952); Malta Rhodes Scholar, 1945. Professor of Mathematics, Royal University of Malta, 1950–64; Vis. Fellow, Univ. of Southampton, 1980–82; Professorial Res. Fellow, 1982–85, Hd of Dept of Computer Sci., 1985–87, Brunel Univ. Chm., 1976–77, Mem., 1965–66, 1968–69, 1972–74, 1977–78, Council of ACU. Chairman: Public Service Reform Commn, 1988–89; Public Service Commn, Malta, 1991–95. Hon. DLitt Malta, 1993. *Address:* 35 Don M. Rua Street, Sliema, SLM 1883, Malta. *Club:* Casino Maltese (Valletta, Malta).

BORINGDON, Viscount; Mark Lionel Parker; *b* 22 Aug. 1956; *s* and *heir* of 6th Earl of Morley, *qv*; *m* 1983, Carolyn Jill, *d* of Donald McVicar, Meols, Wirral, Cheshire; three *d*. *Educ:* Eton. Commissioned, Royal Green Jackets, 1976. *Address:* Pound House, Yelverton, Devon PL20 7LJ.

BÖRJESSON, Rolf Libert; Chairman: Rexam PLC, 2004–08 (Chief Executive, 1996–2004); Ahlsell AB, since 2006; *b* 27 Sept. 1942; *s* of Stig Allan Börjesson and Brita Ahlström; *m* 1969, Kristina Ivarsson; two *d*. *Educ:* Chalmers Univ., Gothenburg (MSc Chem. Engrg). With Steenberg & Flygt, 1968–71; ITT Europe, Brussels, 1971–74; President: Sund Akesson/Sundpacma, 1974–77; AB Securitas Industrier, 1977–81; Wayne Europe, 1981–87; PLM AB: Exec. Vice Pres., 1987–88; Chief Operating Officer, 1988–90; Pres. and CEO, 1990–96. Non-executive Director: SCA, 2003–; Avery Dennison, 2005–. *Recreations:* shooting, ski-ing, riding. *Address:* c/o Ahlsell AB, 117 98 Stockholm, Sweden.

BORLAUG, Norman Ernest, PhD; Consultant, International Center for Maize and Wheat Improvement, since 1979; Distinguished Professor of International Agriculture, Texas A & M University, since 1984; *b* 25 March 1914; *s* of Henry O. and Clara Vaala Borlaug; *m* 1937, Margaret Gibson (*d* 2007); one *s* one *d*. *Educ:* Univ. of Minnesota (BS 1937; MS 1940; PhD 1942). US Forest Service (USDA), 1935, 1937, 1938; Biologist, Dupont de Nemours & Co., 1942–44; Rockefeller Foundation: Plant Pathologist and Geneticist, Wheat Improvement, 1944–60; Associate Dir, Inter-American Food Crop Program, 1960–63; Dir of Wheat Res. and Production Program, International Center for Maize and Wheat Improvement (CIMMYT), 1964–79. Dir, Population Crisis Cttee, 1971–; Asesor Especial, Fundación para Estudios de la Población (Mexico), 1971; Member: Adv. Council, Renewable Natural Resources Foundn, 1973; Citizens' Commn on Science, Law and Food Supply, 1973–74; Council for Agricl Science and Tech., 1973–; Commn on Critical Choices for Americans 1973–74. Mem., Nat. Acad. of Scis (USA), 1968; Foreign Mem., Royal Soc., 1987. Outstanding Achievement Award, Univ. of Minnesota, 1959; Sitara-Imtiaz (Star of Distinction) (Pakistan), 1968, Hilal-I-Imtiaz 1978. Nobel Peace Prize, 1970. Holds numerous hon. doctorates in Science, both from USA and abroad; and more than 30 Service Awards by govts and organizations, including US Medal of Freedom, 1977, Congressional Gold Medal, 2007. *Publications:* more than 70 scientific and semi-popular articles. *Recreations:* hunting, fishing, baseball, wrestling, football, golf. *Address:* c/o International Center for Maize and Wheat Improvement (CIMMYT), Apartado Postal 6–641, 06600 Mexico DF, Mexico; Texas A & M University, Department of Crop Sciences, College Station, TX 77843–2474, USA.

BORLEY, Lester, CBE 1993; Secretary General, 1993–96, Member Council, since 1990, Europa Nostra, The Hague; *b* 7 April 1931; *er s* of Edwin Richard Borley and Mary Dorena Davies; *m* Mary Alison, *e d* of Edward John Pearce and Kathleen Florence Barratt; three *d*. *Educ:* Dover Grammar Sch.; Queen Mary Coll. and Birkbeck Coll., London Univ. Pres. of Union, QMC, 1953; Dep. Pres., Univ. of London Union, 1954; ESU debating team tour of USA, 1955. Joined British Travel Assoc., 1955; Asst to Gen. Manager, USA, 1957–61; Manager: Chicago Office, 1961–64; Australia, 1964–67; West Germany, 1967–69; Chief Executive: Scottish Tourist Bd, 1970–75; English Tourist Bd, 1975–83; Dir, Nat. Trust for Scotland, 1983–93 (Mem. Council, 2002–07). Member: Exec. Cttee, Scotland's Garden Scheme, 1970–75, 1983–93; Council, Nat. Gardens Scheme, 1975–83; Park and Gardens Cttee, Zool Soc. of London, 1979–83; Internat. Cultural Tourism Cttee, ICOMOS, 1990–; Chm., Cultural Tourism Cttee, ICOMOS (UK), 1993–2003. Adviser: World Monuments Fund, NY, 1995–; UNESCO World Heritage Centre, Paris, 2002–. Governor, Edinburgh Film House, 1987–96 (Hon. Vice Pres., 1996–); Trustee: Cromarty Arts Trust, 1995–2006; Hopetoun House Preservation Trust, 1998–2002. Visiting Lecturer: Acad. Istropolitana Nova, Bratislava, 1993–; Coll. of New Europe, Krakow, 1998–; Faculty Mem., Salzburg Seminar, 1996. Organiser of and speaker at many internat. confs on conservation and cultural heritage. Founder Fellow, Tourism Soc., 1978. FRSA 1982. Hon. FRSGS 1989. DLitt *hc* Robert Gordon Inst. of Technology, Aberdeen, 1991. Honorable Kentucky Col, 1963. *Publications:* English Cathedrals and Tourism, 1979; Historic Cities and Sustainable Tourism, 1995; Sustaining the Cultural Heritage of Europe, 1998; (ed) Dear Maurice: Culture and Identity in late 20th Century Scotland, 1998; (ed) To be a Pilgrim: meeting the needs of visitors to cathedrals and great churches in the UK, 2001; (ed) Hugh Miller in Context, 2002; (ed) Celebrating The Life and Times of Hugh Miller: Scotland in the early 19th century, 2003; contributor to: Patronage of the Arts by Foundations and NGOs in Europe, 1991; Universal Tourism, 1992; Cultural Tourism, 1994; Manual of Heritage Management, 1994; Tourism and Culture, 1996; Il Paesaggio Culturale nelle strategia europea, 1996; Preserving the Built Heritage, 1997. *Recreations:* reading, listening to music, visiting exhibitions, collecting glass and ceramics, gardening. *Address:* 4 Belford Place, Edinburgh EH4 3DH. *Club:* New (Edinburgh).

BORN, Prof. Gustav Victor Rudolf, FRCP 1976; FRS 1972; FKC; Professor of Pharmacology, King's College, University of London, 1978–86, now Emeritus; Research Professor, The William Harvey Research Institute, St Bartholomew's Hospital Medical College, since 1989; *b* 29 July 1921; *s* of late Prof. Max Born, FRS; *m* 1st, 1950, Wilfrida Ann Plowden-Wardlaw (marr. diss., 1961); two *s* one *d*; 2nd, 1962, Dr Faith Elizabeth Maurice-Williams; one *s* one *d*. *Educ:* Oberrealschule, Göttingen; Perse Sch., Cambridge; Edinburgh Academy; University of Edinburgh. Vans Dunlop Scholar; MB, ChB, 1943; DPhil (Oxford), 1951, MA 1956. Med. Officer, RAMC, 1943–47; Mem. Scientific Staff, MRC, 1952–53; Research Officer, Nuffield Inst. for Med. Research, 1953–60 and Deptl Demonstrator in Pharmacology, 1956–60, University of Oxford; Vandervell Prof. of Pharmacology, RCS and Univ. of London, 1960–73; Sheild Prof. of Pharmacology, Univ. of Cambridge, and Fellow, Gonville and Caius Coll., Cambridge, 1973–78. Vis. Prof. in Chem., NW Univ., Illinois, 1970; William S. Creasy Vis. Prof. in Clin. Pharmacol., Brown Univ., 1977; Prof. of Fondation de France, Paris, 1982–84. Hon. Dir, MRC Thrombosis Res. Gp, 1964–73. Scientific Advr, Vandervell Foundn, 1967–2001; Pres., Internat. Soc. on Thrombosis and Haemostasis, 1977–79; Adviser, Heineman Med. Res. Center, Charlotte, NC, 1981–; Vice-Pres., Alzheimer Res. Trust, 1997–. Member: Editl Board, Handbook of Experimental Pharmacology; Cttee of Enquiry into Relationship of Pharmaceut. Industry with Nat. Health Service (Sainsbury Cttee), 1965–67; Kuratorium, Lipid Liga, Munich; Kuratorium, Ernst Jung Foundn, Hamburg, 1983–91; Kuratorium, Shakespeare Prize, Hamburg, 1991–98; Forensic Science Adv. Gp, Home Office. Hon. Life Mem., New York Acad. of Scis. Lectures: Beyer, Wisconsin Univ., 1969; Sharpey-Schäfer, Edinburgh Univ., 1973; Cross, RCS, 1974; Wander, Bern Univ., 1974; Johnson Meml, Paris, 1975; Lo Yuk Tong Foundn, Hong Kong Univ., and Heineman Meml, Charlotte, NC, 1978; Carlo Erba Foundn, Milan, 1979; Sir Henry Dale, RCS, 1981; Rokitansky, Vienna, and Oration to Med. Soc., London, 1983. Mem., Akad. Leopoldina; Hon. Mem., German Physiological Soc.; Corresp. Member: German Pharmacological Soc.; Royal Belgian Acad. of Medicine; Rheinisch-Westfälische Akad. der Wissenschaften, Düsseldorf. Hon. Fellow, St Peter's Coll., Oxford, 1972; FKC 1988. Hon. FRCS 2002. Hon. D de l'Univ.: Bordeaux, 1978; Paris, 1987; Hon. MD: Münster, 1980; Leuven, 1981; Edinburgh, 1982; Munich, 1989; Düsseldorf, 2001; Hon. DSc: Brown, 1987; Loyola, 1995; London, 2006. Albrecht von Haller Medal, Göttingen Univ., 1979; Ratschow Medal, Internat. Kur. of Angiology, 1980; Auenbrugger Medal, Graz Univ., 1984; Royal Medal, Royal Soc., 1987; Morawitz Prize, German Soc. for Cardiovascular Res., 1990; Pfleger Prize, Robert Pfleger Foundn, Bamberg, 1990; Alexander von Humboldt Award, 1995; Internat. Sen. Aspirin Prize, 1995; Gold Medal for Medicine, Ernst Jung Foundn, Hamburg, 2001. Chevalier de l'Ordre National de Mérite, France, 1980. *Publications:* articles in scientific jls and books. *Recreations:* music, history past and future, being in the country. *Address:* William Harvey Research Institute,

Charterhouse Square, EC1M 6BQ. *T:* (020) 7882 6070; 5 Walden Lodge, 48 Wood Lane, N6 5UU.

BORODALE, Viscount; Sean David Beatty; *b* 12 June 1973; *s* and *heir* of 3rd Earl Beatty, *qv*; *m* 2002, Susan Jane Hill; two *s*. *Heir: s* Hon. Orlando Thomas Beatty, *b* 17 Nov. 2003.

BORRELL, Roger; Editor-in-Chief, Archant Life magazines (North West) and Editor, Lancashire Life magazine, since 2006; *b* 26 May 1954; *s* of Henry and Joy Borrell; *m* Anne Youngman (marr. diss.); one *s* one *d*; partner, Barbara Waite. *Educ:* Falmouth Grammar Sch. Dep. Ed., Newcastle Evening Chronicle, 1995–99; Editor: Lancs Evening Post, 1999–2001; Birmingham Evening Mail, 2001–05; Ed.-in-Chief, Trinity Mirror Midlands, 2003–05. *Recreations:* fly-fishing, hill-walking. *Address:* 3 Tustin Court, Port Way, Preston, Lancs PR2 2YC. *T:* (01772) 722022; *e-mail:* roger.borrell@lancashirelife.co.uk.

BORRELL FONTELLES, Josep; Member (PSOE), European Parliament, since 2004 (President, 2004–07); *b* 24 April 1947. *Educ:* Univ. Politécnica, Madrid; Complutense Univ., Madrid (DEconSci); Inst. français du Pétrole, Paris; Stanford Univ. Engr and Dir, Dept of Systems, Compañía Española de Petróleos, 1972–81. Councillor, Madrid, 1979–82; Hd of Finance, Madrid Regl Govt. 1979–82; Under Sec., Budget and Public Spending, 1982–84; Treasury Minister, 1984–91; Mem. (PSOE) for Barcelona, Congress of Deputies, 1986–2004; Minister of Public Works and Transport, 1991–96, of the Envmt, 1993–96. *Address:* European Parliament, Rue Wiertz 60, 1047 Brussels, Belgium.

BORRETT, Neil Edgar; non-executive Chairman, Forentech Ltd, since 2004; *b* 10 March 1940; *m* 1965; two *d*. *Educ:* Coll. of Estate Management. FRICS 1969. Dir of property cos, 1963–90; Dir, Property Hldgs, DoE, 1990–96; Chief Exec., Property Advisers to the Civil Estate, 1996–97; Dir, Urban Estate, Crown Estate, 1997–2000. Chm., Matek Business Media, 1994–2004. Governor: London South Bank (formerly S Bank) Univ., 1996–2004; Hillcroft Coll., Surbiton, 2005–. *Address:* 23 Glenmore Business Park, Colebrook Way, Andover SP10 3EZ.

BORRIE, Baron *cr* 1995 (Life Peer), of Abbots Morton in the County of Hereford and Worcester; **Gordon Johnson Borrie,** Kt 1982; QC 1986; Chairman of the Council, Ombudsman for Estate Agents, since 2007; *b* 13 March 1931; *s* of Stanley Borrie, Solicitor; *m* 1960, Dorene, *d* of Herbert Toland, Toronto, Canada; no *c*. *Educ:* John Bright Grammar Sch., Llandudno; Univ. of Manchester (LLB, LLM). Barrister-at-Law and Harmsworth Scholar of the Middle Temple; called to Bar, Middle Temple, 1952; Bencher, 1980. Nat. Service: Army Legal Services, HQ Brit. Commonwealth Forces in Korea, 1952–54. Practice as a barrister, London, 1954–57; Lectr and later Sen. Lectr, Coll. of Law, 1957–64; University of Birmingham: Sen. Lectr in Law, 1965–68; Prof. of English Law and Dir, Inst. of Judicial Admin, 1969–76; Dean of Faculty of Law, 1974–76; Hon. Prof. of Law, 1989–; Dir Gen. of Fair Trading, 1976–92. Chm., Advertising Standards Authy, 2001–07. Member: Parole Bd for England and Wales, 1971–74; CNAA Legal Studies Bd, 1971–76; Circuit Adv. Cttee, Birmingham Gp of Courts, 1972–74; Council, Consumers' Assoc., 1972–75; Consumer Protection Adv. Cttee, 1973–76; Equal Opportunities Commn, 1975–76; Chm., Commn on Social Justice, 1992–94. Director: Woolwich plc (formerly Woolwich Building Soc.), 1992–2000; Three Valleys Water, 1992–2003; Mirror Group, 1993–99; UAPT/Infolink, 1993–94; TeleWest Communications Group, 1994–2001; General Utilities, 1998–2003. Chm., Accountancy Foundn, 2000–03. Mem., H of L Select Cttee on the EC, 1996–2000, 2004–07. Pres., Inst. of Trading Standards Admin, 1992–96 (Vice-Pres., 1985–92, and 1996–). Sen. Treasurer, Nat. Union of Students, 1955–58. Hon. Mem., SPTL, 1989. Contested (Lab): Croydon, NE, 1955; Ilford, S, 1959. Gov., Birmingham Coll. of Commerce, 1966–70. FRSA 1982. Hon. LLD: City of London Poly., 1989; Manchester, 1990; Hull, 1991; Dundee, 1993; W of England, 1997; Nottingham, 2005; DUniv Nottingham Trent, 1996. *Publications:* Commercial Law, 1962, 6th edn 1988; The Consumer, Society and the Law (with Prof. A. L. Diamond), 1963, 4th edn 1981; Law of Contempt (with N. V. Lowe), 1973, 3rd edn 1995; The Development of Consumer Law and Policy (Hamlyn Lectures), 1984. *Recreations:* gastronomy, piano playing, travel. *Address:* Manor Farm, Abbots Morton, Worcestershire WR7 4NA. *T:* (01386) 792330; 4 Brick Court, Temple, EC4Y 9AD. *T:* (020) 7353 4434. *Clubs:* Garrick, Pratt's, Reform (Chm., 1990–91).

BORRIELLO, Prof. (Saverio) Peter, PhD; Director: Centre for Infections, Health Protection Agency, since 2006; Specialist and Reference Microbiology Division, and Research and Development, Health Protection Agency, since 2003; *b* 29 Oct. 1953; *s* of Pasquale Borriello and Margaret Rose (*née* Taylor); partner, Helen Georgina Archer; one *s* one *d*. *Educ:* Oldbury Grammar Sch., W Midlands; University Coll. London (BSc; Fellow 1998); Central Public Health Lab. and St Thomas's Hosp. Med. Sch. (PhD 1981). MRCPath 1987, FRCPath 1998; FFPH 2004. MRC Clinical Research Centre: Upjohn Res. Fellow, 1979–82; Res. Scientist, 1982–86; Head of Gp, 1986–92; University of Nottingham: Head of Gp, Dept of Microbiol., 1992–93; personal chair, 1993; Founding Dir, Inst. of Infections and Immunity, 1993–95; Special Prof., 1996–2004; Dir, Central Public Health Lab., 1995–2006, when it was integrated with Communicable Diseases Surveillance Centre to form Centre for Infections, HPA. Vis. Prof., LSHTM, 1997–2004. Oakley Lectr, Pathol Soc. of GB and Ireland, 1990. *Publications:* Antibiotic Associated Diarrhoea and Colitis, 1984; Clostridia in Gastro-intestinal Disease, 1985; Clinical and Molecular Aspects of Anaerobes, 1990; (ed) Topley & Wilson's Microbiology and Microbial Infections, 10th edition, 2005; papers in scientific jls. *Recreations:* antiques and bric a brac, interesting facts, questioning. *Address:* Health Protection Agency, Centre for Infections, 61 Colindale Avenue, Colindale, NW9 5EQ. *T:* (020) 8327 6838.

BORROW, David Stanley; MP (Lab) South Ribble, since 1997; *b* 2 Aug. 1952; *s* of James Borrow and Nancy (*née* Crawshaw). *Educ:* Mirfield Grammar Sch., W Yorks; Lanchester Poly. (BA Hons Econs). Trainee, Yorkshire Bank, 1973–75; Lancashire Valuation Tribunal: Asst Clerk, 1975–78; Dep. Clerk, 1978–81; Dep. Clerk, Manchester S Valuation Tribunal, 1981–83; Clerk to Tribunal, Merseyside Valuation Tribunal, 1983–97. Pres., Soc. of Clerks of Valuation Tribunals, 1990–92 and 1996–97. Mem. (Lab) Preston BC, 1987–98 (Leader, 1992–94, 1995–97). *Address:* House of Commons, SW1A 0AA; (constituency office) Crescent House, 2–6 Sandy Lane, Leyland, Lancs PR25 2EB. *T:* (01772) 454727.

BORTHWICK, family name of **Baron Borthwick**.

BORTHWICK, 24th Lord *cr* 1450 (Scot.); **John Hugh Borthwick of That Ilk;** DL; Baron of Heriotmuir and Laird of Crookston, Midlothian; Hereditary Falconer of Scotland to the Queen; landowner; *b* 14 Nov. 1940; *er twin s* of 23rd Lord Borthwick and Margaret Frances (*d* 1976), *d* of Alexander Campbell Cormack; *S* father, 1996; *m* 1974, Adelaide, *d* of A. Birkmyre; two *d*. *Educ:* Gordonstoun; Edinburgh School of Agriculture (SDA, NDA). DL Midlothian, 2001. *Recreations:* wild trout fishing, stalking, stamp and cigarette card collecting. *Heir: twin b* Hon. James Henry Alexander Borthwick, Master of Borthwick [*b* 14 Nov. 1940; *m* 1972, Elspeth, *d* of Lt-Col A. D. MacConachie; one *s*]. *Address:* Crookston, Heriot, Midlothian EH38 5YS. *T:* (01875) 835236. *Club:* New (Edinburgh).

BORTHWICK, Sir Antony Thomas, 4th Bt *cr* 1908, of Whitburgh, Humbie, Co. Haddington; *b* 12 Feb. 1941; *e s* of Sir John Borthwick, 3rd Bt and his 1st wife, Irene Sophie (*née* Heller); *S* father, 2002; *m* 1966, Gillian Deirdre Broke Thurston (marr. diss.); one *s* two *d*; *m* 2002, Martha Wheeler Donner. *Educ:* Eton. *Heir: s* Matthew Thomas Thurston Borthwick, *b* 2 July 1968.

BORTHWICK, Kenneth W., CBE 1980; JP; DL; Rt Hon. Lord Provost of the City of Edinburgh, 1977–80; Lord Lieutenant of the City and County of Edinburgh, 1977–80; *b* 4 Nov. 1915; *s* of Andrew Graham Borthwick; *m* 1942, Irene Margaret Wilson, *d* of John Graham Wilson, Aberdeen; two *s* one *d*. *Educ:* George Heriot Sch., Edinburgh. Served War of 1939–45: Flying Officer, RAF. Elected Edinburgh Town Council, 1963; Lothian Regional Council, 1974–77; Edinburgh District Council, 1976. Judge of Police, 1972–75. Member: Lothians River Bd, 1969–73; Organising Cttee, Commonwealth Games, Edinburgh, 1970; Edinburgh and Lothian Theatre Trust, 1975–76; Lothian and Borders Police Bd, 1975–77; British Airports Authorities Consultative Cttee, 1977–80; Convention of Scottish Local Authorities, 1977; Scottish Council Develt and Industry, 1977; Chairman: Edinburgh Dist. Licensing Court, 1975–77; Edinburgh Internat. Festival Soc., 1977–80; Edinburgh Military Tattoo Policy Cttee, 1977–80; Queen's Silver Jubilee Edinburgh Appeal Fund, 1977; Organising Cttee, XIII Commonwealth Games, Scotland 1986, 1983–86. Dean, Consular Corps, Edinburgh and Leith, 1991–92. Curator of Patronage, Univ. of Edinburgh, 1977–80. Governor, George Heriot Sch., 1965–73. Vice-President (ex officio): RZS of Scotland, 1977–80; Lowland TA&VRA, 1977–80. DL City of Edinburgh, 1980. Hon. Consul for Malaŵi, 1982, Hon. Consul Gen., 1993–94. OStJ. Commander, Order of the Lion (Malaŵi), 1993. *Recreations:* golf, gardening. *Address:* 17 York Road, Edinburgh EH5 3EJ.

BORWICK, family name of **Baron Borwick**.

BORWICK, 5th Baron *cr* 1922, of Hawkshead, co. Lancaster; **Geoffrey Robert James, (Jamie), Borwick;** Bt 1916; Chairman, Modec Ltd, since 2004; *b* 7 March 1955; *s* of Hon. Robin Sandbach Borwick (*d* 2003), 3rd *s* of 3rd Baron Borwick, and of Hon. Patricia Garnett Borwick, *d* of Baron McAlpine of Moffat (Life Peer); *S* uncle, 2007; *m* 1981, Victoria Lorne Peta (*née* Poore) (*see* V. L. P. Borwick); three *s* one *d*. *Educ:* Eton Coll. Sir Robert McAlpine & Sons Ltd, 1972–81; Manganese Bronze Holdings plc, 1981–2003 (CEO, 1987–2001; Chm., 2001–03); Chm., Federated Trust Corp. Ltd, 1981–; non-exec. Dir, Hansa Trust plc, 1984–. Trustee: Federated Foundn, 1985–; British Lung Foundn, 2001– (Dep. Chm.). *Recreations:* travel, swimming, walking. *Heir: s* Hon. Edwin Dennis William Borwick, *b* 14 April 1984. *Address:* 33 Phillimore Gardens, W8 7QG. *T:* (020) 7776 9000, *Fax:* (020) 7776 9001; 1 Love Lane, EC2V 7JN; *e-mail:* jamie@borwick.com. *Clubs:* Garrick; Bohemian (San Francisco).

BORWICK, Lady; Victoria Lorne Peta Borwick; Member (C), London Assembly, Greater London Authority, since 2008; *b* London, 26 April 1956; *d* of R. Dennis and Peta Poore; *m* 1981, Geoffrey Robert James Borwick (*see* Baron Borwick); three *s* one *d*. *Educ:* Wispers Sch. Dir, Clarion Events, 1976–2002; Dir, Treasurer's Dept, Conservative Central Office, 2002–04; Commercial Dir, ACI, 2004–06; Mem., Adv. Council, Open Europe, 2007–08. Mem. (C), RBK&C Council, 2002–. Gov., Golborne Children's Centre (formerly Ainsworth Nursery Sch.), 1990–. Trustee, Federated Foundn, 1985. FRSA. Freeman, City of London, 1999; Liveryman, Clockmakers' Co., 2000. *Publication:* The Cost of the London Mayor, 2007. *Recreations:* making fudge, ski-ing, tennis. *Address:* 33 Phillimore Gardens, W8 7QG. *T:* (020) 7376 9262, *Fax:* (020) 7937 2656; *e-mail:* cllr.borwick@rbkc.gov.uk.

BORYSIEWICZ, Sir Leszek (Krzysztof), Kt 2001; PhD; FRCP, FRCPath, FMedSci; FRS 2008; Chief Executive, Medical Research Council, since 2007 (Member, Technology Board, since 2007); *b* 13 April 1951; *s* of Jan Borysiewicz and Zofia Helena Woloszyn; *m* 1976, Gwenllian Sian Jones; two *d*. *Educ:* Cardiff High Sch.; Welsh Nat. Sch. of Medicine (BSc, MB BCh 1975); Univ. of London (PhD 1986). MRCP 1979, FRCP 1989; FRCPath 2002. Hosp. appts at University Hosp. of Wales, Hammersmith Hosp., Nat. Hosp. for Nervous Diseases and Ealing Hosp., 1975–79; Registrar, Dept of Medicine, Hammersmith Hosp., 1979–80; Royal Postgraduate Medical School: MRC Clinical Trng Fellow, 1980–82; Lister Res. Fellow and Sen. Lectr, 1982–86; Wellcome Trust Sen. Lectr in Infectious Diseases, Addenbrooke's Hosp., Cambridge, 1987–88; Lectr in Medicine, Univ. of Cambridge, 1988–91; Prof. of Medicine, Univ. of Wales Coll. of Medicine, 1991–2001; Principal, Faculty of Medicine, 2001–04, Dep. Rector, 2004–07, Imperial Coll. Chm., R&D Grants Cttee, NHS (Wales), 1994–98. Non-exec. Dir, NW London Strategic HA, 2003–05. Member: MRC, 1995–2000 (Chm., Molecular and Cell Bd, 1996–2000; Chm., Jt MRC/DoH Spongiform Encephalopathies Cttee, 1996–2002); Cancer Res. UK, 2004– (Mem. Council and Trustee, 2002–05; Chm., Sci. Cttee, 2002–04); Lister Inst., 2004–; Health Innovation Council, 2008–; Global Sci. and Innovation Forum, 2008–; Singapore Biomed. Scis Internat. Adv. Council, 2008–; Chairman: Sci. Council, Internat. Agency for Res. on Cancer, WHO, 2002–04; UK Stem Cell Funders' Forum, 2007–; Hds of Internat. (Biomed.) Res. Orgns, 2007–. Gov., Wellcome Trust, 2006–; Trustee, Nuffield Trust, 2002–07. Founder FMedSci 1998 (Mem. Council, 1997–2002); FCGI 2004. Mem., Polish Acad. Arts and Scis, 1996. Hon. Fellow, Wolfson Coll., Cambridge, 2002; Fellow, Cardiff Univ., 2006. Jephcott Medal, RSM, 2007. *Publications:* papers on immunology and pathogenesis of virus infection and viral induced cancer. *Recreations:* Rugby football, cricket, painting. *Address:* Medical Research Council, 20 Park Crescent, W1B 1AL. *T:* (020) 7636 5422, *Fax:* (020) 7580 4369. *Club:* Athenæum.

BOSANQUET, Prof. Nicholas; Professor of Health Policy, Imperial College, University of London, since 1993; *b* 17 Jan. 1942; *s* of late Lt Col Neville Richard Gustavus Bosanquet and Nancy Bosanquet; *m* 1st, 1974, Anne Connolly (marr. diss. 1993); two *d*; 2nd, 1996, Anna Zarzecka. *Educ:* Winchester Coll.; Clare Coll., Cambridge (BA Hist.); Yale Univ. (Mellon Fellow); London Sch. of Econs (MSc Econs). Econ. Advr, NBPI, 1967–69; Lecturer in Economics: LSE, 1969–72; King's Fund Coll., 1973–86; City Univ., 1977–84; Sen. Research Fellow, Centre for Health Econs, Univ. of York, 1984–88; Prof. of Health Policy, RHBNC, Univ. of London, 1988–93. Special Advr, Health Cttee, H of C, 1988–90, 2000–. Consultant: WHO, 1989; World Bank, 1993. Arbitrator, ACAS, 1983–90. Non-executive Director: Abbey Health, 1998–2000; Richmond and Twickenham Primary Care Trust, 2001–07. Health Policy Adviser: Care UK plc, 1995–2003; Sussex Health Care, 2003–; Advr on NHS Business Relns, Hosp. Corp. of America, 2002–04. Consultant Dir, Reform, 2005–; Chm., TBS (GB), 2006–. Chm., Health Service Rev. for Cornwall, 2007–08; Mem. Adv. Bd, Cancer Reform Strategy, 2007. MInstD. *Publications:* Industrial Relations in the NHS: the search for a system, 1980; After the New Right, 1983; Family Doctors and Economic Incentives, 1989; (with K. Sikora) The Economics of Cancer Care, 2006; contrib. to econ. and med. jls. *Recreations:* visiting battlefields, brainstorming with Americans and others about military history. *Address:* 231 High Street, Hampton Hill, Middx TW12 1NP.

BOSCAWEN, family name of **Viscount Falmouth**.

BOSCAWEN, Rt Hon. Robert Thomas, MC 1944; PC 1992; *b* 17 March 1923; 4th *s* of 8th Viscount Falmouth and Dowager Viscountess Falmouth, CBE; *m* 1949, Mary Alice, JP London 1961, *e d* of Col Sir Geoffrey Ronald Codrington, KCVO, CB, CMG, DSO, OBE, TD; one *s* two *d*. *Educ:* Eton; Trinity College, Cambridge. Served Coldstream Guards, 1941–50 (with 1st (armoured) Bn Coldstream Guards, Normandy to N Germany, wounded 1945); NW Europe, 1944–45; attached to British Red Cross Civilian Relief Orgn in occupied Europe, 1946–47. Mem., London Exec. Council, Nat. Health Service, 1954–65; Underwriting Mem. of Lloyd's, 1952–99. Contested Falmouth and Camborne (C), 1964, 1966; MP (C) Wells, 1970–83, Somerton and Frome, 1983–92. An Asst Govt Whip, 1979–81; a Lord Comr of HM Treasury, 1981–83; Vice-Chamberlain of HM Household, 1983–86, Comptroller, 1986–88. Mem., Select Cttee on Expenditure, 1974; Vice-Chm., Conservative Parly Health and Social Security Cttee, 1974–79. Mem. Parly Delegns, USSR 1977, Nepal 1981; led Parly Delegn to UN Assembly, 1987, to Canada, 1991. *Publication:* Armoured Guardsmen: a war diary, 2001. *Recreations:* sailing, shooting. *Address:* Ivythorn Manor, Street, Somerset BA16 0TZ. *Clubs:* Pratt's; Royal Yacht Squadron.

BOSE, Mihir, FICA; Sports Editor, BBC News, since 2007; *b* 12 Jan. 1947; *s* of Kiran Chandra Bose and Sova Rani Bose; *m* 1st, 1986, Kalpana (marr. diss. 1999); one *d*; 2nd, 2002, Caroline Alison Gascoyne-Cecil. *Educ:* St Xavier's High Sch.; St Xavier's Coll., Bombay (BSc Physics and Maths). Cricket Corresp., LBC, 1974–75; For. Corresp., Sunday Times, Spectator, New Society, 1975–78; freelance writer, 1979; Editor: Property Guide, 1980–81; International Fund Guide, 1980–81; Pensions, 1981–83; Financial Planning Ed. 1983–84, City Ed. 1984–86, Dep. Ed. 1985–86, Financial Weekly; City Features Ed., London Daily News, 1986–87; freelance writer, mainly on regular contract basis, specialising in finance, sports and feature writing for Sunday Times, Spectator, Mail on Sunday, Daily Telegraph, Independent, The Times, Guardian, 1987–2006. Mem., Gambling Review Body, Home Office, 2000–01. *Publications:* Keith Miller, 1979, 2nd edn 1980; The Lost Hero, 1982; All in a Day's Work, 1983; The Aga Khan, 1984; A Maidan View, 1986; The Crash, 1988, 3rd edn 1989, incl. Jap. edn; Insurance: are you covered?, 1988, 2nd edn 1991; Crash – a new money crisis, 1989; (jtly) Fraud, 1989; Cricket Voices, 1990; How to Invest in a Bear Market, 1990; History of Indian Cricket, 1990, 2nd edn 2002; Michael Grade: screening the image, 1992; (jtly) Behind Closed Doors, 1992; Sporting Colours, 1994; False Messiah: the life and times of Terry Venables, 1996; Sporting Alien, 1996; Sporting Babylon, 1999; Manchester Unlimited: the rise and rise of the world's premier football club, 1999; Raj, Spies, Rebellion, 2004; The Magic of Indian Cricket, 2006; Bollywood - a history, 2006; Manchester Disunited: trouble and takeover at the world's richest football club, 2007. *Recreations:* running his own cricket team, walking, reading, films, travelling. *Clubs:* Reform, MCC.

BOSHOFF, Prof. Christoffer, PhD; Professor of Cancer Medicine, since 2001, and Director, Cancer Institute, since 2006, University College London; Consultant Physician, Department of Oncology, University College London and University College London Hospitals, since 2000; *b* 22 June 1965. *Educ:* Pretoria Univ. (MB ChB 1987); PhD London 1998. MRCP 1991. Glaxo Wellcome Res. Fellow, UCL, 1998–2004. FMedSci 2005. *Address:* Wolfson Institute for Biomedical Research, University College London, Gower Street, WC1E 6BT. *T:* (020) 7679 6292, *Fax:* 08717 143543; *e-mail:* c.boshoff@ucl.ac.uk.

BOSNICH, Prof. Brice, PhD; FRS 2000; Gustavus F. and Ann M. Swift Distinguished Service Professor in Chemistry, University of Chicago, since 2004 (Professor of Chemistry, 1987–2004); *b* 3 June 1936; *s* of Frank Bosnich and Zorka (*née* Setimo); *m* 1992, Jayne Seberling. *Educ:* St Gregory's Coll., Australia; Univ. of Sydney (BSc); ANU (PhD 1962). DSIR Fellow, 1962–63, ICI Fellow, 1963–66, Lectr, 1966–69, UCL; University of Toronto: Associate Prof., 1969–75; Prof., 1975–87; Killam Fellow, 1979–81. Noranda Award in Inorganic Chem., CIC, 1978; Organometallic Award, 1994, Nyholm Award Medal, 1995, RSC; Award in Inorganic Chem., ACS, 1998. *Publications:* Asymmetric Catalysis, 1993; contrib. numerous papers to learned scientific jls. *Recreations:* art, Asian collection. *Address:* Department of Chemistry, University of Chicago, 5735 South Ellis Avenue, Chicago, IL 60637, USA. *T:* (773) 7020287.

BOSONNET, Paul Graham, CBE 1995; Deputy Chairman, BOC Group, 1985–92; *b* 12 Sept. 1932; *s* of Edgar Raymond Bosonnet and Sylvia Gladys Cradock; *m* 1958, Joan Colet Cunningham; one *s* two *d*. *Educ:* St John's College, Southsea. FCA. Accountant, British Oxygen Co., 1957; Dir, BOC International, 1976; Dep. Chm., British Telecommunications plc, 1991–95. Chairman: Logica, 1990–95; G. A. Day, 1996–2001; Director: MAM Gp, 1991–98; Lucas Varity (formerly Lucas Industries), 1993–97. Vice Chm., Council, Royal Holloway (formerly RHBNC), Univ. of London, 1986–95 (Hon. Fellow, 2003). *Recreations:* genealogy, walking. *Address:* The Old House Cottage, Pyrford Road, Pyrford, Surrey GU22 8UE. *T:* (01932) 342991.

BOSSANO, Hon. Joseph John; MP (Gibraltar Socialist Labour Party); Leader of the Opposition, Gibraltar, 1984–88 and since 1996; *b* 10 June 1939; *s* of Maria Teresa and Oscar Bossano; *m* (marr. diss.); three *s* one *d*; *m* 1988, Rose Torrilla. *Educ:* Gibraltar Grammar School; Univ. of London (BScEcon); Univ. of Birmingham (BA). Factory worker, 1958–60; Seaman, 1960–64; Health Inspector, 1964–68; student, 1968–72; building worker, 1972–74; Union leader, 1974–88; MP, Gibraltar, 1972–; Chief Minister, 1988–96. *Recreations:* thinking, cooking, gardening. *Address:* 2 Gowlands Ramp, Gibraltar.

BOSSOM, Hon. Sir Clive, 2nd Bt *cr* 1953; *b* 4 Feb. 1918; *s* of late Baron Bossom (Life Peer); *S* to father's Baronetcy, 1965; *m* 1951, Lady Barbara North, *sister* of 9th Earl of Guilford; three *s* one *d*. *Educ:* Eton. Regular Army, The Buffs, 1939–48; served Europe and Far East. Kent County Council, 1949–52; Chm. Council Order of St John for Kent, 1951–56; Mem. Chapter General, Order of St John (Mem., Jt Cttee, 1961–93; Chm., Ex-Services War Disabled Help and Homes Dept, 1973–87; Almoner, 1987–93). Contested (C) Faversham Div., 1951 and 1955. MP (C) Leominster Div., Herefordshire, 1959–Feb. 1974; Parliamentary Private Secretary: to Jt Parly Secs, Min. of Pensions and Nat. Insce, 1960–62; to Sec. of State for Air, 1962–64; to Minister of Defence for RAF, 1964; to Home Secretary, 1970–72. Chm., Europ Assistance Ltd, 1973–88. President: Anglo-Belgian Union, 1970–73, 1983–85 (Vice-Pres., 1974–82); Anglo-Netherlands Soc., 1978–89 (Vice Pres., 1989–); BARC, 1985–91; Vice-President: Industrial Fire Protection Assoc., 1981–88; Fédération Internationale de L'Automobile, 1975–81 (Vice-Pres. d'Honneur, 1982–); Internat. Social Service, 1989– (Internat. Pres., 1984–89); Chairman: RAC, 1975–78 (Vice Pres., 1998–); RAC Motor Sports Council, 1975–81; RAC Motor Sports Assoc. Ltd, 1979–82; Iran Soc. 1973–76; Mem. Council, RGS, 1982–86. Trustee, Brooklands Museum Trust, 1987–95; Vice-Pres., First Gear Foundn, 1996–2006. Pres., Ends of the Earth, 2004–. Liveryman of Worshipful Company of Grocers (Master, 1979). FRSA (Mem. Council, 1971–77). KStJ 1961. Badge of Honour, British Red Cross, 1993. Comdr, Order of Leopold II; Order of Homayoun III (Iran), 1977; Comdr, Order of the Crown (Belgium), 1977; Kt Comdr, Order of Orange Nassau (Netherlands), 1980. *Recreation:* travel. *Heir:* *s* Bruce Charles Bossom [*b* 22 Aug. 1952; *m* 1985, Penelope Jane, *d* of late Edward Holland-Martin and of Mrs Holland-Martin, Overbury Court, Glos; one *s* two *d*]. *Address:* 97 Cadogan Lane, SW1X 9DU. *T:* (020) 7245 6531; Rotherdown, Grove Lane, Petworth, Sussex GU28 0BT. *T:* (01798) 342329. *Clubs:* Royal Automobile (Vice Pres., 2000–), Carlton.

BOSSY, Prof. John Antony, PhD; FRHistS; FBA 1993; Professor of History, University of York, 1979–2000, now Emeritus; *b* 30 April 1933; *s* of Frederick James Bossy and Kate Louise Fanny Bossy (*née* White). *Educ:* St Ignatius' Coll., London; Queens' Coll., Cambridge (BA 1954; PhD 1961). FRHistS 1975. Res. Fellow, Queens' Coll., Cambridge, 1959–62; Lectr in Hist., Goldsmiths' Coll., London, 1962–66; Lectr, then Reader, in Mod. Hist., QUB, 1966–78. Mem., Editl Bd, Past and Present, 1972–2003. *Publications:* The English Catholic Community 1570–1850, 1976; Christianity in the West 1400–1700, 1984; Giordano Bruno and the Embassy Affair, 1991; Peace in the Post-Reformation, 1998; Under the Molehill, 2001. *Recreations:* chess, piano. *Address:* 80 Stockton Lane, York YO31 1BS. *T:* (01904) 424801.

See also Rev. M. J. F. Bossy.

BOSSY, Rev. Michael Joseph Frederick, SJ; Assistant Priest, St Ignatius Church, South Tottenham, since 2005; Rector, Stonyhurst College, 1993–97 (Headmaster, 1972–85); *b* 22 Nov. 1929; *s* of F. J. Bossy and K. Bossy (*née* White). *Educ:* St Ignatius Coll., Stamford Hill; Heythrop Coll., Oxon (STL); Oxford Univ. (MA). Taught at: St Ignatius Coll., Stamford Hill, 1956–59; St Francis Xavier's Coll., Liverpool, 1963–64; Stonyhurst Coll., 1965–85; Asst Priest, 1986–88, Rector and Parish Priest, 1988–92, Parish of St Aloysius, Glasgow; Actg Parish Priest, St Mary of the Angels, Liverpool, 1998; Asst Priest, Corpus Christi Church, Brixton, 1998–2005. *Recreation:* watching games. *Address:* St Ignatius Church, 27 High Road, N15 6ND.

See also J. A. Bossy.

BOSTOCK, Prof. Christopher John, PhD; Director, BBSRC Institute for Animal Health, 1997–2002; *b* 29 May 1942; *s* of John Major Leslie Bostock and Mildred Lilian Bostock; *m* 1st, 1963, Yvonne Pauline Kendrick (marr. diss. 1990); one *s* two *d*; 2nd, 1992, Patricia Roberts. *Educ:* Univ. of Edinburgh (BSc Hons; Sir Ramsay Wright Post-Grad. Schol., 1965; PhD 1968). Univ. Demonstr., Univ. of Edinburgh, 1965–69; Vis. Fellow, Univ. of Colorado, 1969–71; Res. Fellow, Univ. of St Andrews, 1971–72; Res. Scientist, MRC Clin. and Population Cytogenetics Unit, Edinburgh, 1972–77; Res. Scientist, 1977–83, Asst Dir, 1983–85, MRC Mammalian Genome Unit; Head of Molecular Biology: Animal Virus Res. Inst., AFRC, 1985–89; Inst. for Animal Health, AFRC, then BBSRC, 1989–97. Visiting Professor: Univ. of Wisconsin, 1985; Dept of Clin. Veterinary Sci., Univ. of Bristol, 1998–; Sch. of Animal and Microbial Scis, Univ. of Reading, 2000–. *Publications:* (with Adrian Sumner) The Eukaryotic Chromosome, 1978; scientific res. papers on chromosomes, tumour cell drug resistance, infectious disease agents. *Recreations:* French country life, walking, building.

BOSTOCK, David John, CMG 1998; Member, European Union Court of Auditors, since 2002; *b* 11 April 1948; *s* of John C. Bostock and Gwendoline G. (*née* Lee); *m* 1975, Beth Ann O'Byrne; one *s* one *d*. *Educ:* Cheltenham Grammar Sch.; Balliol Coll., Oxford (BA Mod. Hist. 1969); University Coll. London (MSc Econs of Public Policy 1978). VSO, Indonesia, 1970. Joined HM Treasury, 1971; Second Sec., Office of UK Permanent Rep. to EC, 1973–75; Principal: HM Treasury, 1975–81; Cabinet Office (Economic Secretariat), 1981–83; Asst Sec., HM Treasury, 1983–85; Financial and Econ. Counsellor, Office of UK Permanent Rep. to EC, 1985–89; Under Sec. and Head of EC Gp, HM Treasury, 1990–94; UK Dep. Perm. Rep. to EU, 1995–98; Head of European Secretariat, Cabinet Office, 1999–2000; Vis. Fellow, LSE, 2000–01; Practitioner Fellow, European Inst., Univ. of Sussex, 2001–. *Recreations:* choral singing, walking, looking at old buildings, reading.

BOSTOCK, Prof. Hugh, PhD; FRS 2001; Professor of Neurophysiology, Institute of Neurology, University College London, since 1996; *b* 25 Aug. 1944; *s* of Edward and Alice Bostock; *m* 1975, Kate Shaw; two *s* one *d*. *Educ:* Merton Coll., Oxford (BA); University Coll. London (MSc, PhD 1974). Institute of Neurology, London University, 1974–: Lectr, 1976–87; Sen. Lectr, 1987–92; Reader, 1992–96. *Publications:* contrib. papers to Jl Physiol., Brain and similar jls. *Address:* Newton House, Bridge Street, Olney, Bucks MK46 4AB.

BOSTOCK, Kate Margaret; Executive Director, Clothing, Marks & Spencer, since 2008; *b* Burton-on-Trent, 8 Sept. 1956; *d* of George and Ruth Parker; *m* 1991, Neil Andrew Bostock; two *s*. *Educ:* Ashby Grammar Sch. Work in design, 1982–92; Dir, Buying to Buying, 1992–95; Product Dir, Next, 1995–2001; Clothing Dir, George @ Asda, 2001–04; Womenswear Dir, Marks & Spencer, 2004–08. Hon. DA; Hon. Dr Business Studies. *Recreations:* music, art, theatre, travel, shopping!

BOSTON, family name of **Baron Boston of Faversham**.

BOSTON, 11th Baron *cr* 1761; **George William Eustace Boteler Irby;** Bt 1704; derivatives broker, since 1993; *b* 1 Aug. 1971; *s* of 10th Baron Boston and Rhonda Anne (*née* Bate); *S* father, 2007; *m* 1998, Nicola Sydney Mary (*née* Reid); two *s* two *d*. *Educ:* Eton; Bristol Univ. (BSc Hons Psychology). *Heir:* *s* Hon. Thomas William George Boteler Irby, *b* 9 Dec. 1999. *Address:* Hookers Farm, Hartley Wespall, Hook, Hants RG27 0AP.

BOSTON OF FAVERSHAM, Baron *cr* 1976 (Life Peer), of Faversham, Kent; **Terence George Boston;** QC 1981; barrister; a Deputy Speaker, House of Lords, since 1991; *b* 21 March 1930; *yr surv. s* of late George T. Boston and Kate (*née* Bellati); *m* 1962, Margaret Joyce (Member: SE Metropolitan Regional Hospital Board, 1970–74; Mental Health Review Appeals Tribunal (SE Metropolitan area), 1970–74; market research consultant), *er d* of late R. H. J. Head and Mrs E. M. Winters, and step *d* of late H. F. Winters, Melbourne, Australia. *Educ:* Woolwich Polytechnic Sch.; King's Coll., University of London. Dep. President, University of London Union, 1955–56. Commnd in RAF during Nat. Service, 1950–52; later trained as pilot with University of London Air Sqdn. Called to the Bar, Inner Temple, 1960. BBC News Sub-Editor, External Services, 1957–60; Senior BBC Producer (Current Affairs), 1960–64; also Producer of Law in Action series (Third Programme), 1962–64. Chm., TVS Entertainment, 1980–90. Joined Labour Party, 1946; contested (Lab) Wokingham, 1955 and 1959; MP (Lab) Faversham, Kent, June 1964–70; PPS to: Minister of Public Building and Works, 1964–66; Minister of Power, 1966–68; Minister of Transport, 1968–69; Asst Govt Whip, 1969–70; Minister of State, Home Office, 1979; opp. front bench spokesman on home affairs, 1979–84, on defence, 1984–86; Prin. Dep. Chm. of Cttees, 1992–94, Chm. of Cttees, 1994–2000, H of L. UK Deleg. to UN Gen. Assembly, XXXIst, XXXIInd and XXXIIIrd Sessions, 1976–78. Member: Executive Cttee, International Union of Socialist Youth, 1950; Select Cttee on Broadcasting Proceedings of Parliament, 1966; Speaker's Conference on Electoral Law, 1965–68. Trustee, Parly Lab. Party Benevolent Fund, 1967–70. Founder Vice-Chm., Great Britain-East Europe Centre, 1967–69; Chm., The Sheppey Gp, 1967–. Trustee, Leeds Castle Foundn, 1991–; Chm., Leeds Castle Enterprises Ltd, 2005–. *Recreations:* opera (going, not singing), fell-walking. *Address:* House of Lords, SW1A 0PW.

BOSTON, David Merrick, OBE 1976; MA; Director (formerly Curator), Horniman Public Museum and Public Park Trust (formerly Horniman Museum and Library), London, 1965–93; Hon. Curator, and tenant, 1996–2006, Hon. Archivist and Librarian, since 2006, Quebec House, National Trust; *b* 15 May 1931; *s* of late Dr H. M. Boston, Salisbury, Wilts; *m* 1961, Catharine, *d* of late Rev. Prof. (Edward) Geoffrey (Simons) Parrinder; one *s* two *d. Educ:* Rondebosch, Cape Town; Bishop Wordsworth's, Salisbury; Selwyn Coll., Cambridge; Univ. of Cape Town. BA History Cantab 1954; MA 1958. RAF, 1950–51; Adjt, Marine Craft Trng School. Field survey, S African Inst. of Race Relations, 1955; Keeper of Ethnology, Liverpool Museums, 1956–62; Asst Keeper, British Museum, New World archaeology and ethnography, 1962–65. Chm., British Nat. Cttee of Internat. Council of Museums, 1976–80; Vice-Chm., Internat. Cttee for Museums of Ethnography, 1989–95; Member, Council: Museums Assoc., 1969–70; Royal Anthropological Inst., 1969 and 1998–2001 (Vice-Pres., 1972–75, 1977–80, 1995–98, Hon. Sec., 1985–88, Hon. Librarian, 1992–2001). Visiting Scientist: National Museum of Man, Ottawa, 1970; Japan Foundation, Tokyo, 1986. Consultant, Prog. for Belize, 1994–. Gov., Dolmetsch Foundn, 1983–. Vice President: Dulwich Decorative & Fine Arts Soc., 1987–2001; Friends of the Horniman, 1995–2002; Mem. Cttee, Wolfe Soc., 1999–. Trustee, Haslemere Museum, 1996–. FMA; FRAI; FRGS; FRSA. Ordenom Jugoslavenske Zastave sa zlatnom zvezdom na ogrlici (Yugoslavia), 1981. *Publications:* Pre-Columbian Pottery of the Americas, 1980; contribs to learned jls and encyclopaedias and on Pre-European America, in World Ceramics (ed R. J. Charleston). *Address:* 14 The Green, Westerham, Kent TN16 1AS. *T:* (01959) 565812.

BOSTON, Kenneth George, AO 2001; PhD; Chief Executive, Qualifications and Curriculum Authority, since 2002; *b* 9 Sept. 1942; *s* of Kenneth Frances and Enid Beatrice Boston; *m* 1978, Yvonne Roep; one *d. Educ:* Univ. of Melbourne (MA; PhD 1981). Director-General: of Educn, SA, 1988–91; of Educn and Trng, NSW, 1991–2002. Pres., Australian Coll. of Educn, 2001–02. *Address:* Qualifications and Curriculum Authority, 83 Piccadilly, W1J 8QA. *T:* (020) 7509 5250, *Fax:* (020) 7509 6975; *e-mail:* bostonk@qca.org.uk. *Clubs:* Royal Sydney Yacht Squadron; Sydney Cricket.

BOSTRIDGE, Dr Ian Charles, CBE 2004; concert and operatic tenor; *b* 25 Dec. 1964; *s* of late Leslie John Bostridge and of Lilian Winifred (*née* Clark); *m* 1992, Lucasta Miller; one *s* one *d. Educ:* Dulwich Coll. Prep. Sch.; Westminster Sch. (Queen's Schol.); St John's Coll., Oxford (MA, DPhil Hist. 1990); St John's Coll., Cambridge (MPhil Hist. and Philosophy of Sci.). North Sen. Schol., St John's Coll., Oxford, 1988–90; Jun. Res. Fellow, and British Acad. Postdoctoral Res. Fellow, Corpus Christi Coll., Oxford, 1992–95 (Hon. Fellow, 2001). Professional début as Young Sailor in Tristan, RFH/LPO, 1993; operatic stage début as Lysander, Midsummer Night's Dream, Australian Opera at Edinburgh Fest., 1994; Royal Opera House début, in Salome, 1995; début: with ENO, as Tamino, 1996; with Munich State Opera, as Nerone in Poppaea, 1998; Vienna State Opera, as Ottavio, 2006; other rôles include: Belmonte, Die Entführung aus dem Serail; Vasek, The Bartered Bride; Quint, The Turn of the Screw; title rôle, Orfeo (Monteverdi); Sechs Gesänge aus dem Arabische (H. W. Henze); Caliban, The Tempest (world première, 2004); Jupiter, Semele; Vere, Billy Budd; Aschenbach, Death in Venice. Wigmore Hall recital début, 1995; Carnegie Hall début, 1999; recitals include: Edinburgh Fest., Aldeburgh Fest., Munich, Salzburg, Schubertiade Fests; Vienna Konzerthaus and Musikverein; Châtelet; Champs Elysées; Lincoln Center; Carnegie Hall; own Carte Blanche series, Concertgebouw, 2005; own Perspectives series, Carnegie Hall, 2006 and Barbican Centre, 2007–08; programmed own series at Schubertiade and Vienna Konzerthaus; première (Cologne) and dedicatee, Hans Werner Henze, Sechs Gesänge aus dem Arabischen. television includes: Schubert's Winterreise, Channel 4, 1997 (Prague TV Award); Britten Serenade, and as presenter, Janacek documentary, BBC; subject of S Bank Show profile. Has made numerous recordings. Edinburgh Fest. Univ. Lecture, 2000. Hon. RAM 2002. Hon. DMus St Andrews, 2003. NFMS award, 1990; Young Concert Artists' Trust award, 1992; Début Award, Royal Philharmonic Soc., 1995; Solo Vocal Award, Gramophone, 1996, 1998; Classical Music Award, South Bank Show, 1996; Munich Fest. Prize, 1998; Choc de l'Année Award, 1998, 2004; Edison Award, 1999, 2002; Grammy Award (opera), 1999; Brit Critics Award, 2000; Preis der Deutschen Schallplattenkritik, 2001, 2006; Acad. Charles Cros, Grand Prix du Disque, 2001; Japanese Recording Acad. Prize, 2004, 2007. *Publications:* Witchcraft and its Transformations c1650–c1750, 1997; (contrib.) Civil Histories: essays presented to Sir Keith Thomas, 2000; reviews and articles in The Times, TLS, Wall St Jl, Guardian, etc. *Recreations:* reading, cooking, looking at pictures. *Address:* c/o Askonas Holt Ltd, Lincoln House, 300 High Holborn, WC1V 7JH. *T:* (020) 7400 1700, *Fax:* (020) 7400 1799.

BOSVILLE MACDONALD OF SLEAT, Sir Ian Godfrey, 17th Bt *cr* 1625; Premier Baronet of Nova Scotia; DL; FRICS, MRSH; 25th Chief of Sleat; *b* 18 July 1947; *er s* of Sir (Alexander) Somerled Angus Bosville Macdonald of Sleat, 16th Bt, MC, 24th Chief of Sleat and Mary, Lady Bosville Macdonald of Sleat; *S* father 1958; *m* 1970, Juliet Fleury, *o d* of late Maj.-Gen. J. M. D. Ward-Harrison, OBE, MC; one *s* two *d. Educ:* Pinewood Sch.; Eton Coll.; Royal Agricultural Coll. ARICS 1972; FRICS 1986. Member (for Bridlington South), Humberside CC, 1981–84. MRSH 1972; Mem., Econ. Res. Council, 1979–. Chairman: Rural Devlt Commn, Humberside, 1988–95; Rural Partnership ER of Yorks Council, 2000–; President: Humber and Wolds Rural Community Council, 1996–; British Food and Farming in Humberside, 1989; Humberside Young Farmers, 1989–96; British Red Cross: Mem. Council and Trustee, 1995–97; Nat. Trustee, 2001–06; Chairman: N of England Reg., 2000–04; Nat. Assembly, 2002–07; President: Humberside Br., 1988–96; Hull and ER Br., 1996–2003. High Sheriff, Humberside, 1988–89; DL ER of Yorks, 1997. *Recreation:* ornithology. *Heir: s* Somerled Alexander Bosville Macdonald, younger of Sleat [*b* 30 Jan. 1976; *m* 2003, Charlotte, *yr d* of Richard Perkins; two *s*]. *Address:* Thorpe Hall, Rudston, Driffield, East Yorkshire YO25 4JE. *T:* (01262) 420239. *Clubs:* Lansdowne, White's; New, Puffin's (Edinburgh).

BOSWALL, Sir (Thomas) Alford H.; *see* Houstoun-Boswall.

BOSWELL, Lt-Gen. Sir Alexander (Crawford Simpson), KCB 1982; CBE 1974 (OBE 1971; MBE 1962); DL; Lieutenant-Governor and Commander-in-Chief, Guernsey, 1985–90; *b* 3 Aug. 1928; *s* of Alexander Boswell Simpson Boswell and Elizabeth Burns Simpson Boswell (*née* Park); *m* 1956, Jocelyn Leslie Blundstone Pomfret, *d* of Surg. Rear-Adm. A. A. Pomfret, CB, OBE; five *s. Educ:* Merchiston Castle Sch.; RMA, Sandhurst. Enlisted in Army, 1947; Commnd, Argyll and Sutherland Highlanders, Dec. 1948; regimental appts, Hong Kong, Korea, UK, Suez, Guyana, 1949–58; sc Camberley, 1959; Mil. Asst (GSO2) to GOC Berlin, 1960–62; Co. Comdr, then Second in Comd, 1 A and SH, Malaya and Borneo, 1963–65 (despatches 1965); Directing Staff, Staff Coll., Camberley, 1965–68; CO, 1 A and SH, 1968–71; Col GS Trng Army Strategic Comd, 1971; Brig. Comdg 39 Inf. Bde, 1972–74; COS, 1st British Corps, 1974–76; NDC (Canada), 1976–77; GOC 2nd Armd Div., 1978–80; Dir, TA and Cadets, 1980–82; GOC Scotland and Governor of Edinburgh Castle, 1982–85. Chairman: Scottish Veterans' Residences, 1991–2001; Officers Assoc. (Scottish Br.), 1991–98. Col, Argyll and Sutherland Highlanders, 1972–82; Hon. Col, Tayforth Univs OTC, 1982–86; Col Comdt, Scottish Div., 1982–86; Hon. Col, Scottish Transport Regt RLC(V), 1993–96. Captain of Tarbet, 1974–82. Pres., Friends of St Mary's Haddington, 1992–2003. KStJ 1985. DL East Lothian, 1993. *Address:* c/o Bank of Scotland, 44 Court Street, Haddington EH41 3NP.

BOSWELL, Lindsay Alice; QC 1997; *b* Nairobi, 22 Nov. 1958; *d* of Graham Leonard William Boswell and Erica Boswell (*née* Mayers); *m* 1987, Jonathan James Acton Davis, *qv*; one *s. Educ:* St Mary's, Ascot; Brooke House; University Coll. London (BSc Econ Hons); City Univ. (Dip. Law). Called to the Bar, Gray's Inn, 1982, Bencher, 2004. *Recreation:* houses and gardens. *Address:* Quadrant Chambers, 10 Fleet Street, Temple, EC4Y 1AU.

BOSWELL, Timothy Eric; MP (C) Daventry, since 1987; *b* 2 Dec. 1942; *s* of late Eric New Boswell and of Joan Winifred Caroline Boswell; *m* 1969, Helen Delahay, *d* of Rev. Arthur Rees; three *d. Educ:* Marlborough Coll.; New Coll., Oxford (MA; Dip. Agricl Econs). Conservative Res. Dept, 1966–73 (Head of Econ. Section, 1970–73); managed family farming business, 1974–87; part-time Special Adviser to Minister of Agriculture, Fisheries and Food, 1984–86. Chm., Leics, Northants and Rutland Counties Br., NFU, 1983; Mem. Council, 1966–90, Pres., 1984–90, Perry Foundn (for Agricl Res.); Mem., AFRC, 1988–90. PPS to Financial Sec. to the Treasury, 1989–90; an Asst Govt Whip, 1990–92; a Lord Comr of HM Treasury (a Govt Whip), 1992; Parly Under-Sec. of State, DFE, 1992–95; Parly Sec., MAFF, 1995–97; Opposition frontbench spokesman on Treasury matters, 1997, on trade and industry, 1997–99, on further and higher educn and disabilities, 1999–2001, 2002–03, on pensions and disabilities, 2001–02, on home, constitutional and legal affairs, 2003–04; Shadow Minister for Work, 2004–07; PPS to Chm., Cons. Party, 2005–07. Member Select Cttee for: Agriculture, 1987–89; Innovation, Univs and Skills, 2007–; Sec., Cons. Backbench Cttee on Agriculture, 1987–89; Chm., All-Party Charity Law Review Panel, 1988–90. Treas., 1976–79, Chm., 1979–83, Daventry Constituency Cons. Assoc. Contested (C) Rugby, Feb. 1974. Gov., Univ. of Wales Inst., 2007–. *Recreations:* the countryside, shooting, snooker, poetry. *Address:* House of Commons, SW1A 0AA. *T:* (020) 7219 3520. *Club:* Farmers'.

BOSWOOD, Anthony Richard; QC 1986; *b* 1 Oct. 1947; *s* of late Noel Gordon Paul Boswood and of Cicily Ann Watson; *m* 1973, Sarah Bridget Alexander; three *d. Educ:* St Paul's Sch.; New Coll., Oxford (BCL, MA). Called to Bar, Middle Temple, 1970, Bencher, 1995. *Recreations:* opera, riding, gardening, National Hunt racing. *Address:* Fountain Court, Temple, EC4Y 9DH. *T:* (020) 7583 3335; Podere Casanuova, Pievasciata, Castelnuovo Berardenga (SI), Italy; South Hay House, Binsted, Alton, Hants GU35 9NR; *e-mail:* a.boswood@dial.pipex.com. *Club:* Athenæum.

BOSWORTH, Prof. Clifford Edmund, FBA 1992; Professor of Arabic Studies, Manchester University, 1967–90, now Emeritus; *b* 29 Dec. 1928; *s* of Clifford Bosworth and Gladys Constance Gregory; *m* 1957, Annette Ellen Todd; three *d. Educ:* St John's College, Oxford (MA Mod. Hist.); Edinburgh Univ. (MA Arabic, Persian, Turkish; PhD). Dept of Agriculture for Scotland, 1952–54; Lectr in Arabic, St Andrews Univ., 1956–67. Vis. Associate Prof., Univ. of Toronto, 1965–66; Vis. Prof., UCLA, 1969; Center for Humanities Fellow, Princeton, 1984; Vis. Prof., Inst. of Arabic and Islamic Studies, Exeter Univ., 2004–Nov. 2009. Pres., British Soc. for Middle Eastern Studies, 1983–85. Hon. Mem., Hungarian Acad. of Scis, 2004. Avicenna Silver Medal, UNESCO, 1998; Dr Mahmud Afshar Foundn Award, Tehran, 2001; Royal Asiatic Soc. Award, 2004. *Publications:* The Ghaznavids, 1963; The Islamic Dynasties, 1967, 2nd edn as The New Islamic Dynasties, 1996; Sistan under the Arabs, 1968; The Book of Curious and Entertaining Information, 1968; The Medieval Islamic Underworld, 1976; The Later Ghaznavids, 1977; Al-Maqrizi's Book of contention and strife, 1981; Medieval Arabic Culture and Administration, 1982; The History of al-Tabari (annotated trans.), vols 5, 30, 32–3, 1987–99; The History of the Saffarids of Sistan and the Maliks of Nimruz, 1994; The Arabs, Byzantium and Iran, 1996; (ed) A Century of British Orientalists 1902–2001, 2001; An Intrepid Scot: the travels of William Lithgow 1609–21, 2006; (ed) The Turks in the Early Islamic World, 2007; (ed) Historic Cities of the Islamic World, 2007. *Recreations:* walking, listening to music, collecting detective fiction. *Address:* 1 Parsons Gate, Castle Cary, Som BA7 7JS. *T:* (01963) 350621.

BOSWORTH, Sir Neville (Bruce Alfred), Kt 1987; CBE 1982; Consultant, Grove Tompkins Bosworth, Solicitors, Birmingham, since 1989; *b* 18 April 1918; *s* of W. C. N. Bosworth; *m* 1945, Charlotte Marian Davis (*d* 2003); one *s* two *d. Educ:* King Edward's Sch., Birmingham; Birmingham Univ. LLB. Admitted Solicitor, 1941; Sen. Partner, Bosworth, Bailey Cox & Co., Birmingham, 1941–89. Birmingham City Council, 1950–96; County Bor. Councillor (Erdington Ward), 1950–61; Alderman, 1961–74; Dist Councillor (Edgbaston Ward), 1973–96; Hon. Alderman, 1996; Lord Mayor of Birmingham, 1969–70; Dep. Mayor, 1970–71; Leader of Birmingham City Council, 1976–80, 1982–84; Leader of Opposition, 1972–76, 1980–82 and 1984–87; Cons. Gp Leader, 1972–87 (Dep. Gp Leader, 1971–72); Chairman: Gen. Purposes Cttee, 1966–69; Finance Cttee, 1976–80, 1982–84; National Exhibn Centre Cttee, 1976–80. Chm., W Midlands Police Bd, 1985–86. County Councillor (Edgbaston Ward), W Midlands CC, 1973–86; Chm., Legal and Property Cttee, 1977–79; Vice-Chm., Finance Cttee, 1980–81. Chm., Sutton Coldfield Cons. Assoc., 1963–66; Vice-Chm., Birmingham Cons. Assoc., 1972–87; Mem., Local Govt Adv. Cttee, National Union of Cons. and Unionist Assocs, 1973–87; Pres., Edgbaston Constituency Cons. Assoc., 1992–. Vice Chm., Assoc. of Metropolitan Authorities, 1978–80, and Mem. Policy Cttee, 1976–80; Vice-Pres., Birmingham and Dist Property Owners Assoc.; Dir, Nat. Exhibn Centre Ltd, 1970–72, 1974–96; Mem., W Midlands Econ. Council, 1978–79. Trustee, several charitable trusts; Mem. Council, Birmingham Univ., 1962–91; Governor, King Edward VI Schs, Birmingham, 1970–87 (Dep. Bailiff, 1979–80). Hon. Freeman, City of Birmingham, 1982. *Recreations:* politics, football, bridge. *Address:* Hollington, Luttrell Road, Four Oaks, Sutton Coldfield, Birmingham B74 2SR. *T:* (0121) 308 0647; 54 Newhall Street, Birmingham B3 3QG. *T:* (0121) 236 9341.

BOTHA, Roelof Frederik, (Pik), DMS 1981; MP (National Party), 1977–96; Minister of Energy, South Africa, 1994–96; Leader, Transvaal National Party, 1992–96; *b* 27 April 1932; *m* 1953, Helena Susanna Bosman; two *s* two *d*; *m* 1998, Ina Joubert. *Educ:* Volkskool, Potchefstroom; Univ. of Pretoria (BA, LLB). Dept of Foreign Affairs, 1953; diplomatic missions, Europe, 1956–62; Mem. team from S Africa, in SW Africa case, Internat. Court of Justice, The Hague, 1963–66, 1970–71; Agent for S African Govt, Internat. Court of Justice, 1965–66; Legal Adviser, Dept of Foreign Affairs, 1966–68; Under-Sec. and Head of SW Africa and UN Sections, 1968–70. National Party, MP for Wonderboom, 1970–74. Mem., SA Delegn to UN Gen. Assembly, 1967–69, 1971, 1973–74. Served on select Parly Cttees, 1970–74. South African Permanent Representative to the UN, NY, 1974–77; South African Ambassador to the USA, 1975–77. Minister of Foreign Affairs, 1977–94; Minister of Information, 1978–86. Grand Cross, Order of Good Hope, 1980; Order of the Brilliant Star with Grand Cordon, 1980. *Address:* PO Box 16176, Pretoria North 0116, South Africa.

BOTHAM, Sir Ian (Terence), Kt 2007; OBE 1992; broadcaster, commentator and writer; Chairman, Mission Sports Management (formerly Mission Logistics) Ltd, since

2000; *b* 24 Nov. 1955; *s* of Leslie and Marie Botham; *m* 1976, Kathryn Waller; one *s* two *d*. *Educ:* Milford Junior Sch.; Buckler's Mead Secondary Sch., Yeovil. Bowler and batsman for County Cricket Clubs: Somerset, 1974–87 (Captain, 1983–85; Hon. Life Mem., 1993); Worcestershire, 1987–91; Durham, 1992–93 (Hon. Life Mem.); England Test cricketer, 1977–92 (Captain, 1980–81); scored 1,000 runs and took 100 wickets in 21 Tests at age 23, 1979; scored 3,000 runs and took 300 wickets in Tests to 1982; first player to score a century and take 10 wickets in a Test match, Bombay, 1979; made 100 runs and took 8 wickets in 3 Tests, 1978, 1980, 1984; made 5,200 runs, took 383 wickets and 120 catches in 102 Tests; played cricket for Queensland, football for Scunthorpe and Yeovil. Marathon walks for leukaemia research incl. Land's End to John o'Groats and Alps; Pres., Leukaemia Res. Fund, 2003–. Columnist, Daily Mirror. Team captain, A Question of Sport, BBC, 1989–96. Mem., Sky cricket commentary team, 1995–. *Publications:* Ian Botham on Cricket, 1980; (with Ian Jarrett) Botham Down Under, 1983; (with Kenneth Gregory) Botham's Bedside Cricket Book, 1983; (with Peter Roebuck) It Sort of Clicks, 1986, rev. edn 1987; (with Jack Bannister) Cricket My Way, 1989; Botham: my autobiography, 1994; (with Peter Hayter) The Botham Report, 1997; Botham's Century, 2001; My Illustrated Life, 2007; Head On: the autobiography, 2007. *Address:* North Yorkshire. *Club:* MCC (Hon. Mem. 1994).

BOTHROYD, Shirley Ann; barrister; *b* 23 July 1958. Called to the Bar, Middle Temple, 1982; Second Prosecuting Counsel, 1989–91, First Prosecuting Counsel, 1991–93, to Inland Revenue at CCC and Inner London Crown Ct. *Recreations:* ski-ing, scuba diving, wine, organizing others. *Address:* Littleton Chambers, 3 King's Bench Walk North, Temple, EC4Y 7HR. *T:* (020) 7797 8600.

BOTHWELL, Rt Rev. John Charles, DD; Archbishop of Niagara and Metropolitan of Ontario, 1985–91; *b* 29 June 1926; *s* of William Alexander Bothwell and Anne Bothwell (*née* Campbell); *m* 1951, Joan Cowan; three *s* two *d*. *Educ:* Runnymede Public School; Humberside Coll. Inst., Toronto; Trinity Coll., Univ. of Toronto (BA 1948, LTh 1951, BD 1952; DD 1972). Asst Priest, St James' Cathedral, Toronto, 1951–53; Sen. Assistant at Christ Church Cathedral, Vancouver, 1953–56; Rector: St Aidan's, Oakville, Ont, 1956–60; St James' Church, Dundas, Ont, 1960–65; Canon of Christ Church Cathedral, Hamilton, Ont, 1963; Dir of Programs for Niagara Diocese, 1965–69; Exec. Dir of Program, Nat. HQ of Anglican Church of Canada, Toronto, 1969–71; Bishop Coadjutor of Niagara, 1971–73; Bishop of Niagara, 1973–85. Chancellor, Trinity Coll., Univ. of Toronto, 1991–2003. Hon. Sen. Fellow, Renison Coll., Univ. of Waterloo, 1988. Hon. DD: Huron Coll., Univ. of Western Ont, 1989; Wycliffe Coll., Univ. of Toronto, 1989. *Publications:* Taking Risks and Keeping Faith, 1985; An Open View: keeping faith day by day, 1990; Old Time Religion or Risky Faith: the challenge and the vision, 1993. *Recreations:* golf, cross-country ski-ing, swimming. *Address:* #406–1237 North Shore Boulevard E, Burlington, ON L7S 2H8, Canada. *T:* (905) 6348649, *Fax:* (905) 6341049.

BOTT, Catherine Jane; singer and broadcaster; *b* 11 Sept. 1952; *d* of Maurice Bott and Patricia Bott (*née* Sherlock). *Educ:* King's High Sch. for Girls, Warwick; Guildhall Sch. of Music and Drama (GGSM). Concert, oratorio and recital singer; worldwide concert engagements, incl. world premières of Francis Grier's Five Joyful Mysteries, 2000, Joe Duddell's Not Waving but Drowning, 2002; first public performance of Jonathan Dove's Five Am'rous Sighs, 2002; radio broadcasts; numerous recordings with leading ensembles and orchestras, recital recordings and recordings of operatic roles, incl. Purcell's Dido, Messaggiera (l'Orfeo), Drusilla (l'Incoronazione di Poppaea), and Mandane (Artaxerxes). Co-Presenter, The Early Music Show, BBC Radio 3, 2003–; regular contribs to music and arts progs on Radio 3 and Radio 4. *Recreations:* exploring London, going to the ballet, learning Spanish. *Address:* c/o MAS, Masters Yard, 180A South Street, Dorking, Surrey RH4 2ES.

BOTT, Ian Bernard, FREng; Director, Admiralty Research Establishment, Ministry of Defence, 1984–88, retired; consultant engineer, since 1988; *b* 1 April 1932; *s* of late Edwin Bernard and Agnes Bott; *m* 1955, Kathleen Mary (*née* Broadbent); one *s* one *d*. *Educ:* Nottingham High Sch.; Southwell Minster Grammar Sch.; Stafford Technical Coll.; Manchester Univ. BSc Hons Physics. FIEE, FInstP; FREng (FEng 1985). Nottingham Lace Industry, 1949–53. Royal Air Force, 1953–55. English Electric, Stafford, 1955–57; Royal Radar Estabt, 1960–75 (Head of Electronics Group, 1973–75); Counsellor and Dep. Hd of Defence Research and Development Staff, British Embassy, Washington DC, 1975–77; Ministry of Defence: Dep. Dir Underwater Weapons Projects (S/M), 1977–79; Asst Chief Scientific Advr (Projects), 1979–81; Dir Gen., Guided Weapons and Electronics, 1981–82; Principal Dep. Dir, AWRE, MoD, 1982–84. Mem. Council, Fellowship of Engrg, 1987–90. Hon. Chm., Portsmouth Area Hospice, 1989–94 (Hon. Life Vice Pres., 1998). Trustee, Panasonic Trust, 1993–96. Freeman, City of London, 1985; Liveryman, Co. of Engineers, 1985. *Publications:* papers on physics and electronics subjects in jls of learned socs. *Recreations:* golf, horology, music. *Address:* The Lodge, Brand Lane, Ludlow, Shropshire SY8 1NN; *e-mail:* ianbbott@tiscali.co.uk. *Club:* Royal Automobile.

BOTT, Prof. Martin Harold Phillips, FRS 1977; Professor, 1966–88, Research Professor, 1988–91, in Geophysics, University of Durham, now Professor Emeritus; *b* 12 July 1926; *s* of Harold Bott and Dorothy (*née* Phillips); *m* 1961, Joyce Cynthia Hughes; two *s* one *d*. *Educ:* Clayesmore Sch. Dorset; Magdalene Coll., Cambridge (Scholar). MA, PhD. Nat. Service, 1945–48 (Lieut, Royal Signals). Durham University: Turner and Newall Fellow, 1954–56; Lectr, 1956–63; Reader, 1963–66. Anglican Reader Emeritus. Mem. Council, Royal Soc., 1982–84. Murchison Medallist, Geological Soc. of London, 1977; Clough Medal, Geol Soc. of Edinburgh, 1979; Sorby Medal, Yorkshire Geol Soc., 1981; Wollaston Medal, Geol Soc. of London, 1992. *Publications:* The Interior of the Earth, 1971, 2nd edn 1982; papers in learned jls. *Recreations:* walking, mountains (Scottish Munros completed in 2002), garden slavery.

BOTTAI, Bruno; President: Società Dante Alighieri, since 1996; Fondazione Premio Balzan, since 1999; *b* 10 July 1930; *s* of Giuseppe Bottai and Cornelia Ciocca. *Educ:* Univ. of Rome (law degree). Joined Min. for For. Affairs, 1954; Vice Consul, Tunis, 1956; Second Sec., Perm. Representation to EC, Brussels, 1958; Gen. Secretariat, Co-ord. Service, Min. for For. Affairs, 1961; Counsellor, London, 1966; Dep. Chef de Cabinet, Min. for For. Affairs, 1968; Minister-Counsellor, Holy See, 1969; Diplomatic Advr to Pres., Council of Ministers, 1970; Hd of Press and Inf. Dept 1972, Dep. Dir-Gen. of Political Affairs 1976, Min. for For. Affairs; Ambassador to Holy See and Sovereign Mil. Order of Malta, 1979; Dir-Gen. Pol. Affairs, Min. for For. Affairs, 1981; Ambassador to UK, 1985–87; Sec. Gen., Min. of Foreign Affairs, Italy, 1987–94; Ambassador of Italy to the Holy See, 1994–97. Numerous decorations from Europe, Africa, Latin Amer. countries, Holy See, Malta. *Publications:* political essays and articles. *Recreations:* modern paintings and modern sculpture, theatre, reading, walking. *Address:* Società Dante Alighieri, Piazza Firenze 27, 00186 Rome, Italy.

BOTTING, Maj.-Gen. David Francis Edmund, CB 1992; CBE 1986; Director General of Ordnance Services, Ministry of Defence, 1990–93; *b* 15 Dec. 1937; *s* of Leonard Edmund Botting and Elizabeth Mildred Botting (*née* Stacey); *m* 1962, Anne Outhwaite; two *s*. *Educ:* St Paul's School, London. National Service, RAOC, 1956; commissioned Eaton Hall, 1957; Regular Commission, 1958; regtl appts, Kineton, Deepcut, Borneo, Singapore and Malaya, 1957–67; sc 1968; BAOR, 1972–74; 1 Div., 1974–75; 3rd Div., 1981–82; Col AQ 1 Div., 1982–85; Comd Sup. 1 (BR) Corps, 1987; ACOS HQ UKLF, 1987–90. Rep. Col Comdt, RAOC, 1993; Col Comdt, RLC, 1993–2002. Trustee, Army Benevolent Fund, 1997–2007; Chm., RLC Mus. Trust, 2000–04; Pres., RAOC Charitable Trust, 2002–07. FILDM 1991; MInstPS 1991. Freeman, City of London, 1990; Liveryman, Co. of Gold and Silver Wyre Drawers, 1991. *Recreations:* golf, philately, furniture restoration. *Clubs:* Army and Navy; Tidworth Golf.

BOTTING, (Elizabeth) Louise, CBE 1993; Chairman, Douglas Deakin Young, since 1988 (Managing Director, 1982–88); *b* 19 Sept. 1939; *d* of Robert and Edith Young; marr. diss.; two *d*; *m* 1989, Leslie Arthur Carpenter, *qv*. *Educ:* Sutton Coldfield High School; London Sch. of Economics (BSc Econ.). Kleinwort Benson, 1961–65; Daily Mail, 1970–75; British Forces Broadcasting, 1971–83; Douglas Deakin Young, financial consultancy, 1975–. Director: Trinity International, 1991–99; CGU (formerly General Accident), 1992–2000; London Weekend Television, 1992–94; 102, Stratford-upon-Avon Radio Station, 1996–2001; Camelot plc, 1999–. Presenter, BBC Moneybox, 1977–92. Mem. Top Salaries Review Body, 1987–94. *Address:* Douglas Deakin Young Ltd, 1 Hobart Place, SW1W 0HU. *T:* (020) 7201 3030.

See also J. R. C. Young.

BOTTO DE BARROS, Adwaldo Cardoso; Director-General, International Bureau of Universal Postal Union, 1985–94; *b* 19 Jan. 1925; *s* of Julio Botto de Barros and Maria Cardoso Botto de Barros; *m* 1951, Neida de Moura; one *s* two *d*. *Educ:* Military Coll., Military Engineering Inst. and Higher Military Engineering Inst., Brazil. Railway construction, 1952–54; Dir, industries in São Paulo and Curitiba, 1955–64; Dir, Handling Sector, São Paulo Prefecture, Financial Adviser to São Paulo Engrg Faculty and Adviser to Suzano Prefecture, 1965–71; Regional Dir, São Paulo, 1972–74; Pres., Brazilian Telegraph and Post Office, Brasília-DF, 1974–84. Mem. and Head, numerous delegns to UPU and other postal assocs overseas, 1976–84. Numerous Brazilian and foreign hons and decorations. *Recreations:* philately, sports.

BOTTOMLEY, family name of **Baroness Bottomley of Nettlestone**.

BOTTOMLEY OF NETTLESTONE, Baroness *cr* 2005 (Life Peer), of St Helens, in the county of Isle of Wight; **Virginia Hilda Brunette Maxwell Bottomley;** PC 1992; JP; DL; *b* 12 March 1948; *d* of late W. John Garnett, CBE and of Barbara (*née* Rutherford-Smith); *m* Peter Bottomley, *qv*; one *s* two *d*. *Educ:* London Sch. of Econs and Pol Science (MSc). Research for Child Poverty Action Gp, 1971–73; behavioural scientist, 1973–84. Partner, Odgers, Ray and Berndtson Exec. Search, 2000–; Mem., Supervisory Bd, Akzo Nobel NV, 2000–. Non-exec. Dir, BUPA, 2007–. Mem., MRC, 1987–88. Contested (C) IoW, 1983. MP (C) Surrey SW, May 1984–2005. PPS: to Minister of State for Educn and Science, 1985–86; to Minister for Overseas Develt, 1986–87; to Sec. of State for Foreign and Commonwealth Affairs, 1987–88; Parly Under-Sec. of State, DoE, 1988–89; Minister for Health, 1989–92; Secretary of State: for Health, 1992–95; for Nat. Heritage, 1995–97. Mem., Select Cttee on Foreign Affairs, 1997–99. Fellow, Industry Parlt Trust, 1987 (Trustee, 2002–05); Indep. Trustee, Economist newspaper, 2005–. Vice-Chm., British Council, 1998–2001. Pro-Chancellor, Univ. of Surrey, 2005–; Chancellor, Univ. of Hull, 2006–. Mem. Bd, Prince of Wales Internat. Business Leaders Forum, 2002–; Pres., Farnham Castle, Centre for Internat. Briefing, 2003–. UK Adv. Bd, ICC, 2005–. Nat. Pres., Abbeyfield Soc., 2003–. Mem., Court of Govs, LSE, 1985–; Mem. Council, Ditchley Foundn, 2005– (Gov., 1991–2005); Gov., Univ. of the Arts (formerly London Inst.), 2000–06. JP Inner London, 1975 (Chm., Lambeth Juvenile Court, 1981–84). DL Surrey, 2006. Freeman, City of London, 1988. Lay Canon, Guildford Cathedral, 2002–. *Recreation:* grandchildren. *Address:* House of Lords, SW1A 0PW. *Clubs:* Athenæum; Seaview Yacht.

BOTTOMLEY, Sir James (Reginald Alfred), KCMG 1973 (CMG 1965); HM Diplomatic Service, retired; *b* 12 Jan. 1920; *s* of Sir (William) Cecil Bottomley, KCMG, and Alice Thistle Bottomley (*née* Robinson), JP; *m* 1941, Barbara Evelyn Vardon (*d* 1994); two *s* two *d* (and one *s* decd). *Educ:* King's College Sch., Wimbledon; Trinity Coll., Cambridge. Served with Inns of Court Regt, RAC, 1940–46. Dominions Office, 1946; Pretoria, 1948–50; Karachi, 1953–55; Washington, 1955–59; UK Mission to United Nations, 1959; Dep. High Commissioner, Kuala Lumpur 1963–67; Asst Under-Sec. of State, Commonwealth Office (later FCO), 1967–70; Dep. Under-Sec. of State, FCO, 1970–72; Ambassador to South Africa, 1973–76; Perm. UK Rep. to UN and other Internat. Organisations at Geneva, 1976–78; Dir, Johnson Matthey plc, 1979–85. Mem., British Overseas Trade Bd, 1972. *Recreation:* golf. *Address:* 22 Beaufort Place, Thompson's Lane, Cambridge CB5 8AG. *T:* (01223) 328760.

See also P. J. Bottomley.

BOTTOMLEY, Peter James; MP (C) Worthing West, since 1997 (Greenwich, Woolwich West, June 1975–1983, Eltham, 1983–97); *b* 30 July 1944; *er s* of Sir James Bottomley, *qv*; *m* 1967, Virginia Garnett (*see* Baroness Bottomley of Nettlestone); one *s* two *d*. *Educ:* comprehensive sch.; Westminster Sch.; Trinity Coll., Cambridge (MA). Driving, industrial sales, industrial relations, industrial economics. Contested (C) GLC elect., Vauxhall, 1973; (C) Woolwich West, gen. elecs, 1974. PPS to Minister of State, FCO, 1982–83, to Sec. of State for Social Services, 1983–84, to Sec. of State for NI, 1990; Parly Under Sec. of State, Dept of Employment, 1984–86, Dept of Transport, 1986–89, NI Office, 1989–90. Sec., Cons. Parly For. and Commonwealth Cttee, 1979–81. Pres., Cons. Trade Unionists, 1978–80; Vice-Pres., Fedn of Cons. Students, 1980–82. Chairman: British Union of Family Orgns, 1973–80; Family Forum, 1980–82; Church of England Children's Soc., 1983–84. Member Council: MIND, 1981–82; NACRO, 1997–2004; Trustee, Christian Aid, 1978–84. Parly Swimming Champion, 1980–81, 1984–86; Captain, Parly Football Team; occasional Parly Dinghy Sailing Champion. Mem., Ct of Assts, Drapers' Co. Castrol/Inst. of Motor Industry Road Safety Gold Medal, 1988. *Recreations:* children, book reviewing. *Address:* House of Commons, SW1A 0AA.

BOTTOMS, Sir Anthony Edward, Kt 2001; FBA 1997; Wolfson Professor of Criminology, 1984–2006, now Emeritus, and Director of the Institute of Criminology, 1984–98, University of Cambridge; Fellow of Fitzwilliam College, Cambridge, 1984–2006, now Life Fellow (President, 1994–98); Professorial Fellow in Criminology, University of Sheffield, 2002–07, now Honorary Professor; *b* 29 Aug. 1939; *yr s* of James William Bottoms, medical missionary, and Dorothy Ethel Bottoms (*née* Barnes); *m* 1962, Janet Freda Wenger; one *s* two *d*. *Educ:* Eltham Coll.; Corpus Christi Coll., Oxford (MA); Corpus Christi Coll., Cambridge (MA); Univ. of Sheffield (PhD). Probation Officer, 1962–64; Research Officer, Inst. of Criminology, Univ. of Cambridge, 1964–68; Univ. of Sheffield: Lecturer, 1968–72; Sen. Lectr, 1972–76; Prof. of Criminology, 1976–84; Dean of Faculty of Law, 1981–84. Canadian Commonwealth Vis. Fellow, Simon Fraser Univ., BC, 1982; Vis. Prof., QUB, 1999–2000. Member: Parole Bd for England and Wales, 1974–76; Home Office Res. and Adv. Gp on Long-Term Prison System, 1984–90. Editor, Howard Journal of Penology and Crime Prevention, 1975–81. Hon. LLD QUB,

2003. Sellin-Glueck Award, Amer. Soc. of Criminology, 1996; Eur. Criminology Award, Eur. Soc. of Criminology, 2007. *Publications:* (jtly) Criminals Coming of Age, 1973; (jtly) The Urban Criminal, 1976; (jtly) Defendants in the Criminal Process, 1976; The Suspended Sentence after Ten Years (Frank Dawtry Lecture), 1980; (ed jtly) The Coming Penal Crisis, 1980; (ed jtly) Problems of Long-Term Imprisonment, 1987; (jtly) Social Inquiry Reports, 1988; (jtly) Intermediate Treatment and Juvenile Justice, 1990; Crime Prevention facing the 1990s (James Smart Lecture), 1990; Intensive Community Supervision for Young Offenders, 1995; (jtly) Prisons and the Problem of Order, 1996; (jtly) Criminal Deterrence and Sentence Severity, 1999; (ed jtly) Community Penalties, 2001; (ed jtly) Ideology, Crime and Criminal Justice, 2002; (ed jtly) Alternatives to Prison, 2004; various articles and reviews. *Address:* Institute of Criminology, Sidgwick Avenue, Cambridge CB3 9DA. *T:* (01223) 335360; School of Law, Bartolomé House, Winter Street, Sheffield S3 7ND. *T:* (0114) 222 6839.

BOTTONE, Bonaventura; tenor; *b* 19 Sept. 1950; *s* of Bonaventura Bottone and Kathleen (*née* Barnes); *m* 1973, Jennifer Dakin; two *s* two *d*. *Educ:* Lascelles Secondary Mod. Sch., Harrow; Royal Acad. Music (ARAM 1984; FRAM 1998). Has appeared at numerous international venues, including: Nice Opera (début 1982); Houston Opera (début 1987); Royal Opera House, Covent Garden (début 1987); London Coliseum; Glyndebourne Fest. (début 1990); Bavarian State Opera, Munich (début 1991); Fundação de São Carlos, Lisbon (début 1994); Chicago Lyric Opera (début 1994); New Israeli Opera, Tel Aviv (début 1995); Metropolitan Opera, NY (début 1998); Opera del Teatro Municipal, Santiago (début 1998); Paris Opéra Bastille (début 2000); Atlanta Opera (début 2001); Brisbane SO (début 2002); Deutsches SO Berlin (début 2002); Philharmonia Orch; La Scala, Milan (début 2007); Los Angeles Opera (début 2008). Has performed with ENO, Royal Opera Co., Scottish Opera, Opera North and Welsh Opera; rôles include: Alfredo in La Traviata, Italian Tenor in Der Rosenkavalier, Governor General in Candide, Nanki-Poo in Mikado, Lenski in Eugene Onegin, Alfred in Die Fledermaus, Narraboth in Salome, Duke of Mantua in Rigoletto, Pinkerton in Madam Butterfly, Turridù in Cavalleria Rusticana, title rôle, Damnation of Faust, title rôle, Doctor Ox's Experiment (world première), Rodolfo in La Bohème, Riccardo in Un Ballo in Maschera, Troilus in Troilus and Cressida. Has made numerous recordings. *Recreations:* gardening, boating. *Address:* c/o Stafford Law Associates, Candle Way, Broad Street, Sutton Valence, Kent ME17 3AT; *web:* www.bonaventurabottone.com.

BOTWOOD, Richard Price; Director-General, Chartered Institute of Transport, 1989–98; *b* 1 June 1932; *s* of Allan Bertram and Hilda Amelia Botwood; *m* 1964, Victoria Sanderson; one *s* one *d*. *Educ:* Oundle School. Sec., Tozer Kemsley & Millbourn, 1952–56; Dir, International Factors, 1956–61; Asst Man. Dir, Melbray Group, 1961–73; Chm. and Man. Dir, W. S. Sanderson (Morpeth), wine and spirit merchants, 1973–85; Dir-Gen., Air Transport Users' Cttee, 1986–89. *Recreations:* opera, gardening, embroidery, golf. *Address:* 54 Bute Gardens, W6 7DX. *T:* (020) 8748 8875.

BOUCHARD, Hon. Lucien; PC (Can.) 1988; Senior Partner, Davies Ward Phillips & Vineberg LLP, since 2001; *b* 22 Dec. 1938; *m* Audrey Best; two *s*. *Educ:* Collège de Jonquière; Université Laval (BA, BSocSc, LLB 1964). Called to the Bar, Quebec, 1964; in private practice, Chicoutimi, 1964–85. Pres., Saguenay Bar, 1978; Mem., Admin. Cttee and Chm., Specialisation Cttee, Quebec Bar. Ambassador to France, 1985–88; MP (C), 1988–90, (Ind), 1990–91, (Bloc Québécois), 1991–96, Lac-St-Jean; Secretary of State, 1988–89; Minister of the Envmt, 1989–90; Chm. and Leader, Bloc Québécois, 1991–96; Leader of Federal Opposition, 1993–96; Mem. for Jonquière, Quebec Nat. Assembly, 1996–2001; Prime Minister of Quebec, 1996–2001; Leader, Parti Québécois, 1996–2001. *Publications:* (jtly) Martin-Bouchard Report, 1978; A visage découvert, 1992 (trans. English 1994); specialised articles in legal and labour relns jls. *Address:* (office) 1501 McGill College Avenue, 26th Floor, Montreal, QC H3A 3N9, Canada.

BOUCHER, Prof. Robert Francis, CBE 2000; PhD; FREng, FIMechE, FASME; DL; Vice-Chancellor, University of Sheffield, 2001–07; *b* 25 April 1940; *s* of Robert Boucher and Johanna (*née* Fox); *m* 1965, Rosemary Ellen Maskell; two *s* one *d* (and one *s* decd). *Educ:* St Ignatius Coll.; Borough Poly.; Nottingham Univ. (PhD 1966). FIMechE 1992; FREng (FEng 1994); FASME 1997. ICI Post-doctoral Fellow, Nottingham Univ., 1966; Queen's University, Belfast: Res. Fellow, 1966–68; Lectr, 1968–70; University of Sheffield: Lectr, 1970–76; Sen. Lectr, 1976–85; Prof. of Mech. Engrg, 1985–95; Pro-Vice-Chancellor, 1992–95; Principal and Vice-Chancellor, UMIST, 1995–2000. Chm., Engrg Profs' Council, 1993–95; Senator, Engrg Council, 1995–99; Member: Council, Royal Acad. of Engrg, 1996–99; Bd, British Council, 1996–2003 (Mem., 1996–2003, Chm., 1997–2003, CICHE); Council, ACU, 1997– (Treas., 2004–); User Panel, EPSRC, 1997–2001; Internat. Sector Gp, UUK (formerly CVCP), 1995–2006 (Chm., 1997–2006); Bd, UUK, 2002–; Bd, UCEA, 2004–; Chair, White Rose Univs Consortium, 2003–. Trustee, NPG, 2003–. Chairman: CSU Ltd, later Graduate Prospects, 1998–2004; Marketing Manchester, 1999–2000; Member: Bd of Patrons, Alliance Française de Manchester, 1997–2000; Bd, Yorkshire Forward, 2003–06. DL S Yorks, 2007. FCGI 2006. Hon. Mem., RNCM, 1999. Hon. DHL SUNY, 1998. *Publications:* in engrg jls and confs incl. Proc. IMechE, Trans ASME, Trans IEEE, Inst. of Physics jls. *Recreations:* hill-walking, music, exercise. *Address:* c/o University of Sheffield, Firth Court, Western Bank, Sheffield S10 2TN. *Club:* Athenæum.

BOUCHIER, Prof. Ian Arthur Dennis, CBE 1990; Professor of Medicine, University of Edinburgh, 1986–97; Chief Scientist, Scottish Office Department of Health (formerly Home and Health Department), 1992–97; *b* 7 Sept. 1932; *s* of E. A. and M. Bouchier; *m* 1959, Patricia Norma Henshilwood; two *s*. *Educ:* Rondebosch Boys' High Sch., Cape Town; Univ. of Cape Town. MB, ChB, MD, FRCP, FRCPE, FFPH; FRSE, FIBiol. Groote Schuur Hospital: House Officer, 1955–58; Registrar, 1958–61; Asst Lectr, Royal Free Hosp., 1962–63; Instructor in Medicine, Boston Univ. Sch. of Medicine, 1964–65; Sen. Lectr 1965–70, Reader in Medicine 1970–73, Univ. of London; Prof. of Medicine, 1973–86, and Dean, Faculty of Medicine and Dentistry, 1982–86, Univ. of Dundee. Pres., World Organisation of Gastroenterology, 1990–98 (Sec. Gen., 1982–90); British Society of Gastroenterology: Mem. Council, 1987–90; Chm. Educn Cttee, 1987–90; Pres., 1994–95. Member: Chief Scientist Cttee, Scotland, 1980–97; MRC, 1982–86; Council, RCPE, 1984–90. Goulstonian Lectr, RCP, 1971; Sydney Watson Smith Lectr, RCPE, 1991. Visiting Professor of Medicine: Michigan Univ., 1979; McGill Univ., 1983; RPMS, 1984; Shenyang Univ., Hong Kong Univ., 1988. FRSA. Hon. FCP (SoAf); Founder FMedSci 1998. Hon. Mem., Japanese Soc. Gastroenterology; Corresp. Member: Soc. Italiana di Gastroenterologia; Royal Catalonian Acad. of Medicine. Chm., Editl Bd, Current Opinion in Gastroenterology, 1987–91; Member, Editorial Board: Baillière's Clinical Gastroenterology, 1987–98; Hellenic Jl of Gastroenterology, 1988–98; Internat. Gastroenterology, 1988–98. Hon. MD Iasi, 2001. *Publications:* (ed jtly) Bilirubin Metabolism, 1967; (ed) Clinical Investigation of Gastrointestinal Function, 1969, 2nd edn 1981; (ed) Seventh Symposium on Advanced Medicine, 1971; (ed) Diseases of the Biliary Tract, vol. 2, 1973; Gastroenterology, 1973, 3rd edn 1982; (jtly) Aspects of Clinical Gastroenterology, 1975; (ed jtly) Clinical Skills, 1976, 2nd edn 1982; (ed) Recent Advances in Gastroenterology 3, 1976, 4, 1980, 5, 1983; (ed jtly) Textbook of Gastroenterology, 1984; (ed jtly) Inflammatory Bowel Disease, 1986, 2nd edn 1993; (ed jtly) Davidson's Principles and Practice of Medicine, 15th edn 1987 to 17th edn 1995; (ed jtly) Clinical Investigations in Gastroenterology, 1988; (ed) Jaundice, 1989; (ed jtly) Infectious Diarrhoea, 1993; (ed jtly) Gastroenterology Clinical Science and Practice, vols 1 and 2, 2nd edn 1993; (ed jtly) Quality Assurance in Medical Care, 1993; (ed jtly) French's Index of Differential Diagnosis, 13th edn 1996; 600 scientific papers and communications. *Recreations:* history of whaling, music of Berlioz, cooking.

BOUGH, Francis Joseph; broadcaster; Presenter, London News Radio, 1994–97; *b* 15 Jan. 1933; *m*; three *s*. *Educ:* Oswestry; Merton College, Oxford (MA). With ICI, 1957–62; BBC, 1962–89; presenter of Sportsview, 1964–67, of Grandstand, 1967–82, of Nationwide, 1972–83, of breakfast television, 1983–87, of Holiday, 1987–88; presenter: 6 o'clock Live, LWT, 1989–92; Sky TV, 1989–90; LBC Radio, 1992–96; Travel Live, on Travel TV (cable and satellite), 1996–. Former Oxford soccer blue, Shropshire sprint champion. *Publications:* Cue Frank! (autobiog.), 1980; Frank Bough's Breakfast Book, 1984. *Address:* c/o The Roseman Organisation, 51 Queen Anne Street, W1G 9HS.

BOUGHEY, Sir John (George Fletcher), 11th Bt *cr* 1798; medical practitioner; *b* 12 Aug. 1959; *s* of Sir Richard James Boughey, 10th Bt, and of Davina Julia (now Lady Loch), *d* of FitzHerbert Wright; *S* father, 1978; *m* 2004, Hebote Bishaw. *Educ:* Eton; Univ. of Zimbabwe (MB ChB 1984); LRCPE; LRCSE; LRCPSGlas 1990; MRCPI 1994. *Heir: b* James Richard Boughey [*b* 29 Aug. 1960; *m* 1989, Katy Fenwicke-Clennell; two *s* two *d*].

BOULDING, Hilary; Principal, Royal Welsh College of Music & Drama, since 2007; *b* 25 Jan. 1957; *d* of James Frederick Boulding and Dorothy Boulding (*née* Watson). *Educ:* Heaton Sch., Newcastle upon Tyne; St Hilda's Coll., Oxford (BA Hons Music). TV Dir, 1981–85, TV Producer, 1985–92, BBC Scotland; Head of Arts and Music, BBC Wales, 1992–97; Commissioning Editor, Music (Policy), BBC Radio 3, 1997–99; Dir of Music, Arts Council of England, subseq. Arts Council England, 1999–2007. *Recreations:* music, gardening. *Address:* Royal Welsh College of Music & Drama, Castle Grounds, Cathays Park, Cardiff CF10 3ER. *T:* (029) 2039 1333.

BOULDING, Philip Vincent; QC 1996; *b* 1 Feb. 1954; *s* of Vincent Fergusson Boulding and Sylvia Boulding; *m* 1988, Helen Elizabeth Richardson; one *s* one *d*. *Educ:* Downing Coll., Cambridge (Scholar; BA Law 1st Cl. Hons 1976; LLM 1977; MA 1979; Rugby Blue). Called to the Bar, Gray's Inn, 1979, Bencher, 2004; practice in London and South East, internat. arbitration practice in FE (esp. Hong Kong), regular arbitrator, adjudicator and mediator in commercial contract disputes, esp. in engrg and construction law; admitted to Hong Kong Bar, 1997. Pres., Cambridge Univ. Amateur Boxing Club, 1990–94 (Vice-Pres., 1994–2000); Sen. Pres., Downing Coll. Griffins' Club, Cambridge, 2004–. Gov., Hills Road VI Form Coll., Cambridge, 1997–2000. Consultant Ed., Construction Law Reports. *Recreations:* Rugby, tennis, swimming, shooting. *Address:* Keating Chambers, 15 Essex Street, WC2R 3AA. *Clubs:* Royal Automobile; Hawks (Cambridge).

BOULEZ, Pierre; Hon. CBE 1979; composer, conductor; Director, Institut de Recherche et de Coordination Acoustique/Musique, 1976–91; *b* Montbrison, Loire, France, 26 March 1925. *Educ:* Saint-Etienne and Lyon (music and higher mathematics); Paris Conservatoire. Studied with Messiaen and René Leibowitz. Theatre conductor, Jean-Louis Barrault Company, Paris, 1948; visited USA with French Ballet Company, 1952. Has conducted major orchestras in his own and standard classical works in Great Britain, Europe, USA, S America and Asia; also conducted Wozzeck in Paris and Frankfurt; Parsifal at Bayreuth, 1966–70; The Ring, at Bayreuth, 1976–80; Chief Conductor, BBC Symphony Orchestra, 1971–75; Music Dir, NY Philharmonic, 1971–77. Hon. DMus: Cantab, 1980; Oxon, 1987, etc. Charles Heidsieck Award for Outstanding Contribution to Franco-British Music, 1989. Interested in poetry and aesthetics of Baudelaire, Mallarmé and René Char. *Compositions include:* Sonata No 1 (piano), 1946; Sonatine for flute and piano, 1946; Sonata No 2 (piano), 1948; Polyphonie X for 18 solo instruments, 1951; Visage nuptial (2nd version), 1951, rev. version, 1989; Structures for 2 pianos, 1952; Le Marteau sans Maître (voice and 6 instruments), 1954; Sonata No 3 (piano), 1956; Deux Improvisations sur Mallarmé for voice and 9 instruments, 1957; Doubles for orchestra, 1958; Poésie pour Pouvoir for voices and orchestra, 1958; Soleil des Eaux (text by René Char) for chorus and orchestra, 1958; Pli selon Pli: Hommage à Mallarmé, for voice and orchestra, 1960; Eclat, 1965; Domaines for solo clarinet, 1968; Cummings ist der Dichter (16 solo voices and instruments), 1970; Eclat/Multiples, 1970; Explosante Fixe (8 solo instruments), 1972; Rituel, for orchestra, 1975; Messagesquisses (7 celli), 1977; Notations, for orch., 1980; Répons, for orch. and live electronics, 1981–86; Mémoriale, 1984; Dérive, 1985; Dialogue de l'Ombre Double, 1986; Anthèmes, for violin solo, 1991; … explosante/fixe …, for 3 flutes, large ensemble and electronics, 1993; Sur Incises, 1998; Dérive 2, 2007. *Publications:* Penser la musique d'aujourd'hui, 1966 (Boulez on Music Today, 1971); Relevés d'apprenti, 1967; Par volonté et par hasard, 1976; Points de Repère, 1981; Orientations, 1986; Jalons, 1989; Le pays fertile—Paul Klee, 1989. *Address:* IRCAM, 1 place Igor Stravinsky, 75004 Paris, France. *Fax:* (1) 44781540.

BOULT, Geoffrey Pattisson; Headmaster, Giggleswick School, since 2001; *b* 6 June 1957; *s* of late Peter and Jane Boult; *m* 1984, Katharine Goddard; four *d*. *Educ:* Durham Univ. (BA Hons; PGCE). Teacher, Canford Sch., Dorset, 1980–87; Hd of Humanities, Geelong GS, 1984–85; Hd of Geog., Cranleigh Sch., 1987–92; Housemaster, St Edward's Sch., Oxford, 1992–2001. Sec., Oxford Conf. in Educn, 1982–86; Dir, Boarding Schs Assoc., 2003– (Chm., 2007–08). *Recreations:* golf, fireworks, reading, visiting Southwold. *Address:* Holywell Toft, Giggleswick, Settle, N Yorks BD24 0DE. *T:* (01729) 893005, *Fax:* (01729) 893150; *e-mail:* gpboult@giggleswick.org.uk.

BOULTER, Prof. Donald, CBE 1991; FIBiol; Head of Department of Biological Sciences, University of Durham, 1988–91 (Professor of Botany and Head of Department of Botany, 1966–88); Director of Durham University Botanic Garden, 1966–91; *b* 25 Aug. 1926; *s* of late George Boulter and Vera Boulter; *m* 1956, Margaret Eileen Kennedy; four *d*. *Educ:* Portsmouth Grammar Sch.; Christ Church, Oxford (BA, MA, DPhil). FIBiol 1970. Served RAF, 1945–48. Sessel Fellow, Yale Univ., 1953–54; Asst Lectr in Botany, King's Coll., London, 1955–57; Lectr 1957–64, Sen. Lectr 1964–66, Liverpool Univ. Vis. Prof., Univ. of Texas, Austin, 1967. Chm., Plant Science Res. Ltd, Cambridge Lab., John Innes Centre, 1992–94. Member: AFRC, 1985–89; Biological Scis Sub-Cttee, UFC (formerly UGC), 1988–89; Chm., Plants & Soils Res. Grant Bd, 1986–89; Pres., Sect. K, BAAS, 1981. Dep. Chm. Governing Body, AFRC Inst. of Horticultural Res., 1987–90; Member, Governing Body: Scottish Crop Res. Inst., 1986–92; AFRC Inst. of Plant Sci. Res., 1989–92; Trustee, John Innes Foundn, 1994–97. Mem., Exec. Cttee, Horticultural Res. Internat., 1990–97. FRSA 1972. Tate & Lyle Award for Phytochem., 1975. *Publications:* (ed) Chemotaxonomy of the Leguminosae, 1971; (ed) Encyclopedia of Plant Physiology, vol. 14B: Nucleic Acids and Proteins, 1982; papers in sci. jls on molecular evolution, genetic engrg of crops, biochem. and molecular biol. of seed develt. *Recreation:* travel. *Address:* 5 Crossgate, Durham DH1 4PS. *T:* (0191) 386 1199.

BOULTER, Prof. Patrick Stewart, FRCSE, FRCS, FRCP; Consultant Surgeon Emeritus, Royal Surrey County Hospital and Regional Radiotherapy Centre, since 1991; President, Royal College of Surgeons of Edinburgh, 1991–94; *b* 28 May 1927; *s* of Frederick Charles Boulter, MC and Flora Victoria Boulter of Annan, Dumfriesshire; *m* 1946, Patricia Mary Eckersley Barlow, *d* of S. G. Barlow of Lowton, Lancs; two *d*. *Educ:* King's Coll. Sch.; Carlisle GS; Guy's Hosp. Med. Sch., Univ. of London (Sands Cox Schol. in Physiology, 1952; MB BS Hons and Gold Medal, 1955). FRCS 1958; FRCSE 1958; FRCPE 1993; FRCPSGlas 1993; FRCP 1997. Guy's Hospital and Medical School, University of London: House Surgeon, 1955–56; Res. Fellow, Dept of Surgery, 1956–57; Lectr in Anatomy, 1956–57; Sen. Surgical Registrar, 1959–62; Hon. Consultant Surgeon, 1963; Surgical Registrar, Middlesex Hosp., 1957–59; Consultant Surgeon, Royal Surrey County and St Luke's Hosps, Guildford, 1962–91; Vis. Surgeon, Cranleigh and Cobham Hosps, 1962–91; Surgical Dir, Jarvis Breast Screening Centre, DHSS, 1978–91. Sen. Mem., British Breast Gp (Mem., 1962–). Prof. Surrey Univ., 1986– (Hon. Reader, 1968–80); Vis. Prof., univs in USA, Australia, NZ, Pakistan and India; Wilson Wang Prof. in Surgery, Chinese Univ. of HK, 1993. Examnr, RCSGlas, and Univs of Edinburgh, London, Nottingham, Newcastle, Singapore and Malaya; Overseas Advr for sen. acad. appts in surgical specialities, Univ. of Malaya, 1993–; Ext. Advr for sen. surg. posts, King Saud Univ., Riyadh, 1993–; Advr, Anti-Cancer Council of Vic, Aust., 1992–. Mem. Clin. Adv. Gp, Health Risk Resources Internat., 1995–; Trustee and Mem., Health and Welfare Cttee, Thalidomide Trust, 1995–; Overseas Mem., Australian and NZ Breast Cancer Study Gp, 1989–. Chm., Conf. of Colls and Faculties (Scotland), 1992–94; Mem., Senate of Surgery of UK and Ire., 1992–95; Fellow, Assoc. of Surgeons of GB and Ire., 1962 (Mem. Council, and Chm., Educn Adv. Cttee, 1986–90); Royal College of Surgeons: Handcock Prize, 1955; Surgical Tutor, 1964; Regl Advr, 1975; Penrose May teacher, 1985–; Royal College of Surgeons of Edinburgh: Examnr, 1979; Mem. Council, 1984–; Vice-Pres., 1989–91; Regent, 1995. Hon. FRACS 1985; Hon. FCS(SA) 1992; Hon. FCSSL 1992; Hon. FRCSI 1993; Hon. FCSHK 1993; Hon. FCEM (Hon. FFAEM 1997); Mem., Acad. of Medicine of Malaysia, 1993; Hon. Member: N Pacific Surgical Assoc., USA, 1991; Assoc. of Surgeons of India, 1993; Soc. of Surgeons of Nepal, 1994; Surgical Res. Soc., 1995; Fellow, Acad. of Medicine of Singapore, 1994. Internat. Master Surgeon, Internat. Coll. of Surgeons, 1994. DUniv Surrey, 1996. Hon. Citizen, State of Nebraska, USA, 1967. *Publications:* articles and book chapters on surgical subjects, esp. breast disease, surgical oncology and endocrine surgery. *Recreations:* mountaineering, ski-ing, fly-fishing. *Address:* Quarry Cottage, Salkeld Dykes, Penrith, Cumbria CA11 9LL. *T:* (01768) 898822. *Clubs:* Alpine, Caledonian; New (Edinburgh); Yorkshire Fly Fishers; Swiss Alpine (Pres., Assoc. of British Members, 1978–80).

BOULTON, Adam; *see* Boulton, T. A. B.

BOULTON, Sir Clifford (John), GCB 1994 (KCB 1990; CB 1985); DL; Clerk of the House of Commons, 1987–94; *b* 25 July 1930; *s* of Stanley Boulton and Evelyn (*née* Hey), Cocknage, Staffs; *m* 1955, Anne, *d* of Rev. E. E. Raven, Cambridge; one adopted *s* one adopted *d*. *Educ:* Newcastle-under-Lyme High School; St John's Coll., Oxford (exhibnr). MA (Modern History). National Service, RAC, 1949–50; Lt Staffs Yeomanry (TA). A Clerk in the House of Commons, 1953–94: Clerk of Select Cttees on Procedure, 1964–68 and 1976–77; Public Accounts, 1968–70; Parliamentary Questions, 1971–72; Privileges, 1972–77; Clerk of the Overseas Office, 1977–79; Principal Clerk, Table Office, 1979–83; Clerk Asst, 1983–87. A school Governor and subsequently board mem., Church Schools Company, 1965–79; Trustee, Oakham Sch., 1998–. Trustee, Industry and Parliament Trust, 1991–95. Mem., Standing Cttee on Standards in Public Life, 1994–2000. Chairman: Standards Cttee, Rutland CC, 2000–05; Rutland Historic Churches Preservation Trust, 2004–. DL Rutland, 1997. Hon. LLD Keele, 1993. *Publications:* (ed) Erskine May's Parliamentary Practice, 21st edn, 1989; contribs to Halsbury's Laws of England, 4th edn, and Parliamentary journals. *Recreations:* visual arts, the countryside. *Address:* 2 Main Street, Lyddington, Oakham LE15 9LT. *T:* (01572) 823487.
See also F. J. Boulton.

BOULTON, David John; His Honour Judge Boulton; a Circuit Judge, since 2001; Liaison Judge, St Helens Justices, since 2004; *b* 2 July 1945; *s* of late John Ellis and Hilda May Boulton; *m* 1971, Suzanne Proudlove. *Educ:* Quarry Bank High Sch., Liverpool; Liverpool Univ. (LLB). Called to the Bar, Middle Temple, 1970; specialised in crime; Standing Counsel for DTI, 1989–99, Customs and Excise, 1993–99, Inland Revenue, 1997–99; a Recorder, 1989–2001. Mem., Bar Council, 1995–2001. Tutor Judge, Judicial Studies Bd, 2007–. *Recreations:* wine, gardens, travel. *Address:* c/o Queen Elizabeth II Law Courts, Derby Square, Liverpool L2 1XA. *Clubs:* Athenæum (Liverpool); Lancashire CC.

BOULTON, Fiona Jane; Headmistress, Guildford High School, since 2002; *b* 11 April 1964; *d* of Michael Harry Lockton and (Elizabeth) Iona Lockton; *m* 1994, Richard Edward Stanley Boulton, *s* of Sir Clifford (John) Boulton, *qv*; one *s* two *d*. *Educ:* University Coll., Cardiff (BSc Hons); Exeter Coll., Oxford (PGCE); Inst. of Educn, Univ. of London (MA; NPQH). Housemistress: Stowe Sch., 1989–91; Marlborough Coll., 1991–95; Dep. Head, Guildford High Sch., 1996–2002. *Recreations:* family, cooking, walking, music and art. *Address:* Waterton, Cleardown, The Hockering, Woking, Surrey GU22 7HH; *e-mail:* fiona.boulton@church-schools.com.

BOULTON, Prof. Geoffrey Stewart, OBE 2000; FRS 1992; FRSE; Regius Professor of Geology and Mineralogy, since 1986, Vice-Principal, since 1999, University of Edinburgh; *b* 28 Nov. 1940; *s* of George Stewart and Rose Boulton; *m* 1964, Denise Bryers Lawns; two *d*. *Educ:* Longton High Sch.; Birmingham Univ. BSc, PhD, DSc. FGS 1961; FRSE 1989. British Geol Survey, 1962–64; Demonstrator, Univ. of Keele, 1964–65; Fellow, Univ. of Birmingham, 1965–68; Hydrogeologist, Kenya, 1968; Lectr, then Reader, Univ. of E Anglia, 1968–86; Provost and Dean, Faculty of Sci. and Engrg, Univ. of Edinburgh, 1994–99. Prof., Amsterdam Univ., 1980–86. Mem., Royal Commn on Envmtl Pollution, 1994–2000. NERC: Chairman: Polar Sci. Bd, 1992–95; Earth Sci. and Technol. Bd, 1994–98; Mem. Council, 1993–98; Royal Society: Chm., Sect. Cttee 5 for Earth Sci. and Astronomy, 1993–95; Mem., Council, 1997–99; Gen. Sec., RSE, 2007–. Member: NCC Scotland, 1991–92; SHEFC, 1997–2003 (Chm., Res. Policy Cttee, 2000–03); Council, Scottish Assoc. for Marine Sci., 1997–2003; Scottish Sci. Adv. Cttee, 2003–; Council for Sci. and Technol., 2004–. UK Deleg. to IUGS, 1996–99. President: Geol Soc. of Edinburgh, 1991–93; Quaternary Res. Assoc., 1991–94; Council, Univ. of Heidelberg, 2007–. Hon. DTech Chalmers, Sweden, 2002; Hon. DSc: Birmingham, 2007; Keele, 2007. Kirk Bryan Medal, Geol Soc. of America, 1976; Seligman Crystal, Internat. Glaciol. Soc., 2001; Lyell Medal, Geol Soc., 2006; Tedford Sci. Medal, Inst. for Contemp. Scotland, 2006. *Publications:* numerous articles in learned jls on glaciology, quaternary, marine and polar geology. *Recreations:* violin, mountaineering, sailing. *Address:* 19 Lygon Road, Edinburgh EH16 5QD.

BOULTON, Prof. James Thompson, FBA 1994; Director, 1987–99, Deputy Director, 1999–2006, now Director Emeritus, Institute for Advanced Research in Arts and Social Sciences (formerly Institute for Advanced Research in the Humanities), University of Birmingham (Fellow, 1984); *b* 17 Feb. 1924; *e s* of Harry and Annie M. P. Boulton; *m* 1949, Margaret Helen Leary; one *s* one *d*. *Educ:* University College, Univ. of Durham; Lincoln Coll., Oxford. BA Dunelm 1948; BLitt Oxon 1952; PhD Nottingham 1960. FRSL 1968. Served as pilot in RAF, 1943–46 (Flt-Lt). Lectr, subseq. Sen. Lectr and Reader in English, Univ. of Nottingham, 1951–64; John Cranford Adams Prof. of English, Hofstra Univ., NY, 1967; Prof. of English Lit., Univ. of Nottingham, 1964–75, Dean, Faculty of Arts, 1970–73; University of Birmingham: Prof. of English Studies and Head of Dept of English Lang. and Lit., 1975–88, Prof. Emeritus, 1989; Dean of Faculty of Arts, 1981–84; Public Orator, 1984–88. Hon. Prof., Bangor Univ., 2007–. Chm. of Govs, Fircroft Coll., Selly Oak, 1985–92. Editor, Renaissance and Modern Studies, 1969–75, 1985. General Editor: The Letters of D. H. Lawrence, 1973–2001; The Works of D. H. Lawrence, 1975–. Hon. DLitt: Dunelm, 1991; Nottingham, 1993. *Publications:* (ed) Edmund Burke: A Philosophical Enquiry into…the Sublime and Beautiful, 1958, rev. edn 1987, 2008; (ed) C. F. G. Masterman: The Condition of England, 1960; The Language of Politics in the Age of Wilkes and Burke, 1963, 2nd edn 1975; (ed) Dryden: Of Dramatick Poesy etc., 1964; (ed) Defoe: Prose and Verse, 1965, 2nd edn 1975; (with James Kinsley) English Satiric Poetry: Dryden to Byron, 1966; (ed) Lawrence in Love: Letters from D. H. Lawrence to Louie Burrows, 1968; (ed) Samuel Johnson: The Critical Heritage, 1971; (with S. T. Bindoff) Research in Progress in English and Historical Studies in the Universities of the British Isles, vol. 1, 1971, vol. 2, 1976; (ed) Defoe: Memoirs of a Cavalier, 1972, rev. edn 1991; (ed) The Letters of D. H. Lawrence, vol. 1, 1979, vol. 2 (jtly), 1982, vol. 3 (jtly), 1984, vol. 4 (jtly), 1987, vol. 5 (jtly), 1989, vol. 6 (jtly), 1991, vol. 7 (jtly), 1993, vol. 8, 2000, Selected Letters, 1997, Further Letters, 2006, 2007; (ed) The Writings and Speeches of Edmund Burke, vol. 1, The Early Writings, 1997; D. H. Lawrence: man of learning, 2000; D. H. Lawrence, Philip Heseltine and Three Unpublished Letters, 2001; (ed) D. H. Lawrence: Late Essays and Articles, 2004; (ed jtly) James Boswell: An Account of Corsica, 2006; *contributed to:* The Familiar Letter in the 18th Century, 1966; Renaissance and Modern Essays, 1966; D. H. Lawrence, 1980; Renaissance and Modern Studies, 1985; D. H. Lawrence in Italy and England, 1999; papers in Durham Univ. Jl, Essays in Criticism, Renaissance and Modern Studies, Modern Drama, Jl of D. H. Lawrence Soc., etc. *Recreation:* gardening. *Address:* Ty'n y Ffynnon, Nant Peris, Caernarfon, Gwynedd LL55 4UH. *Club:* Royal Air Force.

BOULTON, (Thomas) Adam (Babington); Political Editor and Presenter, Sky News, since 1989; *b* 15 Feb. 1959; *s* of Dr Thomas B. Boulton and Helen C. Boulton; *m* 1st, 1985, Kerena Mond (marr. diss. 2004); three *d*; 2nd, 2006, Angela Jane Hunter, *qv*. *Educ:* St Andrew's Sch., Pangbourne; Westminster Sch.; Christ Church, Oxford (MA); Sch. of Advanced Internat. Studies, Johns Hopkins Univ. (MA). Stringer, Inter Press, Washington, 1981–82; Talks Writer, BBC External Services, 1982; TV Journalist, 1982–84, Political Editor, 1984–89, TV-am. Chm., Parly Lobby, 2007. Mem. Council, KCL, 2004–. *Publications:* (contrib.) Political Communications: why Labour won the general election of 1997, 2000; (contrib.) Political Communications: the general election campaign of 2005, 2007; Memories of the Blair Administration, 2008. *Recreations:* arts, gardening. *Address:* c/o Sky News, 2nd Floor, 4 Millbank, SW1P 3JA. *T:* (020) 7705 5500, *Fax:* (020) 7705 5501; *e-mail:* adam.boulton@bskyb.com.

BOULTON, Sir William (Whytehead), 3rd Bt *cr* 1944; Kt 1975; CBE 1958; TD 1949; Secretary, Senate of the Inns of Court and the Bar, 1974–75; *b* 21 June 1912; *s* of Sir William Boulton, 1st Bt, and Rosalind Mary (*d* 1969), *d* of Sir John Davison Milburn, 1st Bt, of Guyzance, Northumberland; *S* brother, 1982; *m* 1944, Margaret Elizabeth, *o d* of late Brig. H. N. A. Hunter, DSO; one *s* two *d*. *Educ:* Eton (Captain of Oppidans, 1931); Trinity Coll., Cambridge. Called to Bar, Inner Temple, 1936; practised at the Bar, 1937–39. Secretary, General Council of the Bar, 1950–74. Gazetted 2nd Lieut TA (Essex Yeo.), 1934; retired with rank of Hon. Lieut-Col, 1949; served War of 1939–45: with 104th Regt RHA (Essex Yeo.) and 14th Regt RHA, in the Middle East, 1940–44; Staff Coll., Camberley, 1944. Control Commission for Germany (Legal Div.), 1945–50. *Publications:* A Guide to Conduct and Etiquette at the Bar of England and Wales, 1st edn 1953, 6th edn, 1975. *Heir:* *s* John Gibson Boulton, *b* 18 Dec. 1946. *Address:* The Quarters House, Alresford, near Colchester, Essex CO7 8AY. *T:* (01206) 822450.

BOUNDS, (Kenneth) Peter; Chief Executive, Liverpool City Council, 1991–99; *b* 7 Nov. 1943; *s* of Rev. Kenneth Bounds and Doris Bounds; *m* 1965, Geraldine Amy Slee; two *s*. *Educ:* Ashville College, Harrogate. Admitted Solicitor, 1971. Dir of Admin, Stockport MBC, 1973–82; Chief Exec., Bolton MBC, 1982–91. A Civil Service Comr, 2001–07. Pres., Assoc. of Dist Secs, 1980–81; Chm., Soc. of Metropolitan Chief Execs, 1997; Company Secretary: Greater Manchester Econ. Develt Ltd, 1986–91; NW Tourist Bd, 1986–91; Royal Liverpool Philharmonic Soc., 2000–07, 2008– (Dir, 1993–2000; Dep. Chm., 1997–2000; Chm., 2007–08). Chairman: Liverpool City Challenge, 1991–95; Liverpool City of Learning, 1994–97; Liverpool Partnership Gp, 1994–99; Renew N Staffs (Housing Market Renewal Partnership), 2002–; Liverpool Cathedral Council, 2004–. Member: President's Council, Methodist Church, 1981–84; Bd of Trustees for Methodist Church Purposes, 1983–2008. Patron, Centre for Tomorrow's Company, 1997–. Hon. Fellow, Bolton Inst. of Higher Educn, 1991. FRSA 1994. *Recreations:* music, theatre. *Address:* The Coach House, 42 Church Road, Woolton, Liverpool L25 6DD.

BOURAGA, Sir Philip, KBE 2005 (CBE 1974); High Commissioner for Papua New Guinea in UK, 1989–91; *b* 10 Sept. 1939; *s* of Taunakekei Bouraga and Henao Ariavogo; *m* 1972, Hitolo Nouairi; three *s* one *d*. *Educ:* Thornburgh Coll., Qld; Inst. of Public Admin, Port Moresby, PNG (Dip. Public Admin). Perm. Sec., Dept of Prime Minister, PNG, 1974–79; Comr of Police, Royal PNG Constabulary, 1979–81; MP Nat. Capital Dist, 1982–87; State Minister for Finance, 1982–85; Consultant: to local level govts, 1987–89; to local and central provincial govts, 1991–2002. Chm., St John's Ambulance, PNG, 1975–77. Independence Medal (PNG), 1975. *Recreations:* reading, gardening, fishing. *Address:* PO Box 7386, Boroko, NCD, Papua New Guinea. *T:* (675) 3233589.

BOURDEAUX, Rev. Canon Michael Alan; Director, 1969–99, President, since 2003, Keston Institute, Oxford (formerly Keston College, Kent); *b* 19 March 1934; *s* of Richard Edward and Lillian Myra Bourdeaux; *m* 1st, 1960, Gillian Mary Davies (*d* 1978); one *s* one *d*; 2nd, 1979, Lorna Elizabeth Waterton; one *s* one *d*. *Educ:* Truro Sch.; St Edmund Hall, Oxford (MA Hons Mod. Langs); Wycliffe Hall, Oxford (Hons Theology); BD Oxon 1969. Moscow State Univ., 1959–60; Deacon, 1960; Asst Curate, Enfield Parish Church, Middx, 1960–64; researching at Chislehurst, Kent, on the Church in the Soviet Union, with grant from Centre de Recherches, Geneva, 1965–68. Vis. Prof., St Bernard's Seminary, Rochester, NY, 1969; Vis. Fellow, LSE, 1969–71; Research Fellow, RIIA, Chatham House, 1971–73; Dawson Lectr on Church and State, Baylor Univ., Waco, Texas, 1972; Chavasse Meml Lectr, Oxford Univ., 1976; Kathryn W. Davis Prof. in Slavic Studies, Wellesley Coll., Wellesley, Mass, 1981; Moorhouse Lectr, Melbourne, 1987; Vis. Fellow, St Edmund Hall, Oxford, 1989–90; Vis. Prof., Inst. for Econ., Political and Cultural Develt, Notre Dame Univ., Ind., 1993; Croall Lectr, Univ. of Edinburgh, 2002. Mem., High-Level Experts' Gp on For. Policy and Common Security, EC, 1993–94. Hon. Canon, Rochester Cathedral, 1990–99, now Canon Emeritus; Hon. Dir, Iffley Fest., 1996. Founded Keston College, a research centre on religion in the Communist countries, 1969. Founder of journal, Religion in Communist Lands, 1973, retitled Religion, State and Society: the Keston Jl, 1992. Mem. Council, Britain-Russia Centre, 1991–2000. DD Lambeth, 1996. Templeton Prize for Progress in Religion, 1984. Order of Grand Duke Gediminas, 1999, Order of Vytautas the Great, 2005 (Lithuania). *Publications:* Opium of the People, 1965, 2nd edn 1977; Religious Ferment in Russia, 1968; Patriarch and Prophets, 1970, 2nd edn 1975; Faith on Trial in Russia, 1971; Land of Crosses, 1979; Risen Indeed, 1983; (with Lorna Bourdeaux) Ten Growing Soviet Churches, 1987; Gorbachev, Glasnost and the Gospel, 1990, rev. US edn, The Gospel's Triumph over Communism, 1991; (ed) The Politics of Religion in Russia and the New States of Eurasia, 1995; (ed jtly) Proselytism and Orthodoxy in Russia, 1999; Religion and Society: essays on religious life in Russia today, 2002; (ed jtly) Contemporary Religious Life in Russia, vol. 1, 2003, vol. 2, 2003, vol. 3, 2005; (ed jtly) Atlas of Contemporary Religious Life in Russia, vol. 1, 2005, vol. 2, 2006, vol. 3, 2008. *Recreations:* choral singing, Member, Assoc. of British Tennis Officials. *Address:* 101 Church Way, Iffley, Oxford OX4 4EG. *T:* (01865) 777276. *Club:* Athenæum.

BOURDILLON, Peter John, FRCP; Consultant in Clinical Physiology (Cardiology), subsequently in Cardiovascular Disease, Hammersmith Hospital, 1975–2006; on secondment to Academy of Medical Royal Colleges, from Department of Health, 1997–2001; *b* 10 July 1941; *s* of John Francis Bourdillon and Pamela Maud Bourdillon (*née* Chetham); *m* 1964, Catriona Glencairn-Campbell, FGA, *d* of Brig. W. Glencairn-Campbell, OBE and Lady Muir-Mackenzie; one *s* two *d*. *Educ:* Rugby Sch.; Middlesex Hosp. Med. Sch. (MB BS 1965). MRCP 1968, FRCP 1983. House physician and surgeon posts in London, 1965–68; Medical Registrar: Middlesex Hosp., 1969–70; Hammersmith Hosp., 1970–72; Sen. Registrar in Cardiol., Hammersmith Hosp., 1972–74; part-time MO, 1975–81, part-time SMO, 1981–91, Hd of Med. Manpower and Educn Div., 1991–93, DHSS, then DoH; Head (Grade 3), Health Care (Med.), then Specialist Clin. Services, Div., DoH, 1993–97. Cardiologist (part-time), Hertford Cardiology (formerly Quantum Res.) Ltd, 2002–. Medical Awards Administrator, ACU, 2001–. Hon. Sen. Lectr, RPMS, later ICSM, London Univ., 1979–. QHP 1996–99. *Publications:* contrib. to med. jls. *Recreations:* writing software, golf, ski-ing. *Address:* 13 Grove Terrace, NW5 1PH. *T:* (020) 7485 6839; *e-mail:* pbourdillon@msn.com. *Club:* Highgate Golf.

BOURDON, Derek Conway, FIA; Director, 1981–84, and General Manager, 1979–84, Prudential Assurance Co. Ltd; Director, London and Manchester Group PLC, 1986–94; *b* 3 Nov. 1932; *s* of late Walter Alphonse Bourdon and Winifred Gladys Vera Bourdon; *m* Uta Margrit Bourdon. *Educ:* Bancroft's School. FIA 1957. RAF Operations Research (Pilot Officer), 1956–58. Joined Prudential, 1950; South Africa, 1962–65; Dep. General Manager, 1976–79. Chairman, Vanbrugh Life, 1974–79. Member, Policyholders Protection Board, 1980–84; Chm., Industrial Life Offices Assoc., 1982–84 (Vice-Chm., 1980–82). *Recreations:* golf, bridge. *Club:* Barton-on-Sea Golf.

BOURKE, family name of **Earl of Mayo**.

BOURKE, Christopher John; Metropolitan Stipendiary Magistrate, 1974–96; *b* 31 March 1926; *e s* of late John Francis Bourke of the Oxford Circuit and late Eileen Winifred Bourke (*née* Beddoes); *m* 1956, Maureen, *y d* of late G. A. Barron-Boshell; two *s* one *d*. *Educ:* Stonyhurst; Oriel Coll., Oxford. Served Army, 1944–48: commnd Glos Regt; served BAOR and Jamaica (ADC to Governor). Called to Bar, Gray's Inn, 1953; Oxford Circuit, 1954–55; Dir of Public Prosecutions Dept, 1955–74. *Recreations:* landscape painting, ballet. *Address:* 61 Kingsmead Road, SW2 3HY. *T:* (020) 8671 3977.
See also Baron Derwent.

BOURKE, (Elizabeth) Shân (Josephine) L.; *see* Legge-Bourke, E. S. J.

BOURKE, Martin; HM Diplomatic Service, retired; Deputy High Commissioner, New Zealand, 2000–04; *b* 12 March 1947; *s* of Robert Martin Bourke and Enid Millicent Bourke (*née* Love); *m* 1973, Anne Marie Marguerite Hottelet; four *s*. *Educ:* Stockport Grammar Sch.; University Coll. London (BA Hons 1969); King's Coll. London (MA 1970). Joined FCO, 1970; Brussels, 1971–73; Singapore, 1974–76; Lagos, 1978–80; on loan to DTI, 1980–84; Consul (Commercial), Johannesburg, 1984–88; Asst Head, Envmt, Sci. and Energy Dept, FCO, 1990–93; Gov., Turks and Caicos Islands, 1993–96; Area Manager, Prince's Trust (on secondment), 1996–99. *Recreations:* walking, reading, theatre, amateur dramatics.

BOURKE, Rt Rev. Michael Gay; Bishop Suffragan of Wolverhampton, 1993–2006; *b* 28 Nov. 1941; *s* of Gordon and Hilda Bourke; *m* 1968, Elizabeth Bieler; one *s* one *d*. *Educ:* Hamond's Grammar Sch., Swaffham, Norfolk; Corpus Christi Coll., Cambridge (Mod. Langs, MA); Univ. of Tübingen (Theology); Cuddesdon Theological Coll. Curate, St James', Grimsby, 1967–71; Priest-in-charge, Panshanger Conventional Dist (Local Ecumenical Project), Welwyn Garden City, 1971–78; Vicar, All Saints', Southill, Beds, 1978–86; Archdeacon of Bedford, 1986–93. Course Dir, St Albans Diocese Ministerial Trng Scheme, 1975–87. Hon. Canon, Lichfield Cathedral, 1993–2006. *Recreations:* astronomy, railways, European history. *Address:* The Maltings, Little Stretton, Church Stretton SY6 6AP.

BOURKE, Patrick Francis John O'D.; *see* O'Donnell Bourke.

BOURN, James; HM Diplomatic Service, retired; *b* 30 Aug. 1917; *s* of James and Sarah Gertrude Bourn; *m* 1st, 1944, Isobel Mackenzie (*d* 1977); one *s*; 2nd, 1981, Moya Livesey (*d* 1993). *Educ:* Queen Elizabeth's Grammar Sch., Darlington; Univ. of Edinburgh (MA Hons 1979). Executive Officer, Ministry of Health, 1936. War of 1939–45; served (Royal Signals), in India, North Africa and Italy; POW; Captain. Higher Exec. Officer, Ministry of National Insurance, 1947; Asst Principal, Colonial Office, 1947; Principal, 1949; Secretary to the Salaries Commission, Bahamas, 1948–49; Private Sec. to Perm. Under-Sec., 1949; seconded to Tanganyika, 1953–55; UK Liaison Officer to Commn for Technical Co-operation in Africa (CCTA), 1955–57; Commonwealth Relations Office, 1961; seconded to Central African Office, 1962; Dar es Salaam, 1963; Deputy High Commissioner in Zanzibar, Tanzania, 1964–65; Counsellor and Dep. High Comr, Malawi, 1966–70; Ambassador to Somalia, 1970–73; Consul-General, Istanbul, 1973–75. *Address:* c/o National Westminster Bank, 20 Market Place, Richmond, North Yorks DL10 4QF. *Club:* Royal Commonwealth Society.

BOURN, Sir John (Bryant), KCB 1991 (CB 1986); Comptroller and Auditor General, 1988–2008; Independent Adviser on Ministers' Interests, 2006–08; *b* 21 Feb. 1934; *s* of late Henry Thomas Bryant Bourn and Beatrice Grace Bourn; *m* 1959, Ardita Ann Fleming; one *s* one *d*. *Educ:* Southgate County Grammar Sch.; LSE. 1st cl. hons BScEcon 1954, PhD 1958. Air Min. 1956–63; HM Treasury, 1963–64; Private Sec. to Perm. Under-Sec., MoD, 1964–69; Asst Sec. and Dir of Programmes, Civil Service Coll., 1969–72; Asst Sec., MoD, 1972–74; Under-Sec., Northern Ireland Office, 1974–77; Asst Under-Sec. of State, MoD, 1977–82; Dep. Sec., Northern Ireland Office, 1982–84; Dep. Under Sec. of State (Defence Procurement), MoD, 1985–88; Auditor General for Wales, 1999–2005. Vis. Prof., LSE, 1983–. Chairman: Accountancy Foundn Review Bd, 2000–03; Professional Oversight Bd (formerly Professional Oversight Bd for Accountancy), 2003–. Chm., Multi-Lateral Audit Adv. Gp, World Bank, 1999–2008; Member: Financial Reporting Council, 1990–; Financial Reporting Review Panel, 1991–2008. FCIPS 1995; CCMI (CIMgt 1994). Hon. Fellow: Brighton Univ., 1989; LSE, 1995. Hon. LLD Brunel, 1995; DUniv Open, 1998. *Publications:* Public Sector Audit: is it value for money, 2007; articles and reviews in professional jls. *Recreations:* swimming, tennis.

BOURNE, Prof. (Frederick) John, CBE 1995; Professor of Animal Health, University of Bristol, since 1988; *b* 3 Jan. 1937; *s* of Sidney John Bourne and Florence Beatrice Bourne; *m* 1959, Mary Angela Minter; two *s*. *Educ:* Univ. of London (BVetMed); Univ. of Bristol (PhD). MRCVS 1961. Gen. vet. practice, 1961–67; University of Bristol: Lectr in Animal Husbandry, 1967–76; Reader in Animal Husbandry, 1976–80; Prof. and Hd of Dept of Veterinary Medicine, 1980–88; Dir, AFRC, subseq. BBSRC, Inst. for Animal Health, 1988–97. Vis. Prof., Univ. of Reading, 1990–97. Chm., Govt Ind. Scientific Gp for Control of Cattle TB, 1998–2007. For. Mem., Polish Acad. of Sci., 1994. Hon. Fellow, Edward Jenner Inst. for Vaccine Res., 2001. *Publications:* over 250 contribs to variety of jls, incl. Immunology, Vet. Immunology and Immunopath., Res. in Vet. Sci., Infection and Immunity. *Recreations:* gardening, fishing, golf, cricket, music. *Address:* Westlands, Jubilee Lane, Langford, Bristol BS40 5EJ. *T:* (01934) 852 464.

BOURNE, Gordon Lionel, FRCS, FRCOG; Hon. Consultant, Department of Obstetrics and Gynæcology, St Bartholomew's Hospital, London; Hon. Consultant Gynæcologist to Royal Masonic Hospital, since 1986 (Consultant, 1972–86); *b* 3 June 1921; *s* of Thomas Holland Bourne and Lily Anne (*née* Clewlow); *m* 1948, Barbara Eileen Anderson; three *s* one *d*. *Educ:* Queen Elizabeth Grammar Sch., Ashbourne; St Bartholomew's Hosp.; Harvard Univ. MRCS, LRCP 1945, FRCS 1954; MRCOG 1956, FRCOG 1962; FRSocMed. Highlands Hosp., 1948; Derbs Royal Infirm., 1949; City of London Mat. Hosp., 1952; Hosp. for Women, Soho, 1954; Gynæcol Registrar, Middlesex Hosp., 1956; Sen. Registrar, Obsts and Gynae., St Bartholomew's Hosp., 1958; Nuffield Trav. Fellow, 1959; Res. Fellow, Harvard, 1959; Cons. Gynæcol., St Luke's Hosp., 1963. Arris and Gale Lectr, RCS, 1964; Mem. Bd of Professions Suppl. to Medicine, 1964; Regional Assessor in Maternal Deaths, 1974; Examr in Obsts and Gynae., Univs of London, Oxford and Riyadh, Jt Conjt Bd and RCOG, Central Midwives Bd; Mem. Ct of Assts, Haberdashers' Co., 1968, Master, 1984; Mem. Bd of Governors, 1971–83, Chm., 1980–83, Haberdashers' Aske's Schs, Hatcham; Mem., 1983–95, Chm., 1987–95, Bd of Governors, Haberdashers' Aske's Schs, Elstree. *Publications:* The Human Amnion and Chorion, 1962; Shaw's Textbook of Gynæcology, 9th edn, 1970; Recent Advances in Obstetrics and Gynæcology, 11th edn, 1966 to 13th edn, 1979; Modern Gynæcology with Obstetrics for Nurses, 4th edn, 1969 and 5th edn, 1973; Pregnancy, 1972, 8th edn 2006; Bourne - The History of a Family 1647–2001, 2002; numerous articles in sci. and professional jls. *Recreations:* ski-ing, fishing, shooting, swimming, writing, golf. *Address:* Little Reuters, Common Road, Ightham, Kent TN15 9AY. *T:* (01732) 885746. *Club:* Carlton.

BOURNE, Ian Maclean; QC 2006; a Recorder, since 2000; *b* 19 Jan. 1954; *s* of late Ian Bourne and of Jean Talbot (*née* Scarrott); *m* 1993, Lucy Pollock; one *s* three *d*. *Educ:* Marlborough; Exeter Univ. (LLB). Called to the Bar, Inner Temple, 1977; in practice, S Eastern Circuit. Member: Criminal Bar Assoc., 1983–; CCC Bar Mess, 1985–. *Recreations:* cricket, gardening, photography. *Address:* Charter Chambers, 33 John Street, WC1N 2AT. *T:* (020) 7618 4400; *e-mail:* ian.bourne@charterchambers.com. *Club:* Hurlingham.

BOURNE, John; *see* Bourne, F. J.

BOURNE, Margaret Janet, OBE 1982; Chairman, CORDA Ltd, 1992–2001; *b* 18 Aug. 1931; *d* of Thomas William Southcott and Nora Annie Southcott (*née* Pelling); *m* 1960, George Brian Bourne. *Educ:* Twickenham Grammar Sch.; Royal Holloway Coll. (BSc). MRAeS 1962; CEng, FIET (FIEE 1997). Fairey Engineering, 1953–62; Army Operational Res. Estabt, 1962–65; Defence Operational Analysis Estabt, 1965–76; Asst Dir, Scientific Adv. Gp Army, 1976–80; Hd of Assessments Div., ASWE, 1980–82; Hd of Weapon Dept, ASWE, 1982–84; Dep. Dir, Admiralty Res. Estabt, 1984–87; Asst Chief Scientific Advr (Capabilities), MoD, 1987–91. *Recreations:* playing early music, gardening, natural history. *T:* (01428) 714329.

BOURNE, Matthew Christopher, OBE 2001; director and choreographer; Founder Director, New Adventures, since 2002; *b* 13 Jan. 1960; *s* of Harold Jeffrey, (Jim), Bourne and June Lillian Bourne (*née* Handley). *Educ:* Laban Centre for Movement and Dance (BA Hons Dance and Theatre 1986; Hon. Fellow 1997). Artistic Dir and Jt Founder Mem., Adventures in Motion Pictures, 1987–2002. Dir, Spitfire Trust, 1996–; Mem. Bd, Laban Centre for Movt and Dance, 1999–; Mem., Hon. Cttee, Dance Cares, 1995–. *Works include: for Adventures in Motion Pictures*, created and directed: Overlap Lovers, 1987; Spitfire, 1988; The Infernal Galop, 1989; Green Fingers, 1990; Town and Country, 1991; Deadly Serious, 1992; Nutcracker, 1992 (revised 2002); The Percys of Fitzrovia, 1992; Highland Fling, 1994 (revised 2005); Swan Lake, 1995 (Olivier Award, 1996; LA Drama Critics Award, 1997; 2 Tony Awards, 1999; 3 Drama Desk Awards, 1999; 2 Outer Critics' Circle Awards, 1999; Astaire Award, 1999); Cinderella, 1997; The Car Man (Evening Standard Award), 2000; *for other companies*, choreographed: As You Like It, RSC, 1989; Leonce and Lena, Crucible, Sheffield, 1989; Children of Eden, Prince Edward Theatre, 1991; A Midsummer Night's Dream, Aix-en-Provence Fest., 1991; The Tempest, NYT, 1991; Show Boat, Malmö Stadsteater, 1991; Peer Gynt, Ninagawa Co., Oslo, Barbican, 1994; Watch with Mother, Nat. Youth Dance Co., 1994; Oliver!, London Palladium, 1994; My Fair Lady, South Pacific, RNT, 2001; dir, Play Without Words, NT, 2002; co-dir and choreographer, Mary Poppins, Prince Edward Th., 2004; dir and choreographer, Edward Scissorhands, Sadler's Wells, 2005; as performer, created numerous rôles in AMP prodns on stage and in films; *films choreographed* include: Late Flowering Lust, 1993; Drip: a narcissistic love story, 1993. *Recreations:* old movies, theatre and music, reading obituaries. *Address:* c/o Jessica Sykes, Independent Talent Group Ltd, Oxford House, 76 Oxford Street, W1N 0AX. *T:* (020) 7636 6565; New Adventures, Sadler's Wells, Rosebery Avenue, EC1R 4TN. *Club:* Soho House.

BOURNE, Nicholas; Member (C) Mid & West Wales, and Leader of Conservatives, National Assembly for Wales, since 1999; *b* 1 Jan. 1952; *s* of late John Morgan Bourne and Joan Edith Mary Bourne. *Educ:* King Edward VI Sch., Chelmsford; UCW, Aberystwyth (LLB 1st Cl. Hons; LLM 1976); Trinity Coll., Cambridge (LLM). Called to the Bar, Gray's Inn, 1976. Supervisor in Law: Corpus Christi Coll., Cambridge, 1974–80; St Catharine's Coll., Cambridge, 1974–82; LSE, 1975–77; Principal, Chart Univ. Tutors Ltd, 1979–88; Co. Sec. and Dir, Chart Foulks Lynch plc, 1984–88; Dir, Holborn Gp Ltd, 1988–91; Swansea Institute: Prof. of Law, 1991–96; Dean of Law, 1992–96; Asst Principal, 1996–98. Lectr in Co. Law, Univ. of London Ext. Degree Prog. at UCL, 1991–96; Sen. Lectr in Law, South Bank Univ., 1991–92; Vis. Lectr, Hong Kong Univ., 1996–. Member: Editl Bd, Malaysian Law News, 1991–; Editl Adv. Bd, Business Law Rev., 1991–. Member: NE Thames RHA, 1990–92; W Glamorgan HA, 1994–97; Doctors' and Dentists' Review Body, 1998–99. MInstD 1984. *Publications:* Duties and Responsibilities of British Company Directors, 1982; British Company Law and Practice, 1983; Business Law for Accountants, 1987; Lecture Notes for Company Law, 1993, 3rd edn 1998; Essential Company Law, 1994, 2nd edn 1997; Business Law and Practice, 1994; (with B. Pillans) Scottish Company Law, 1996, 2nd edn 1999; Bourne on Company Law, 4th edn 2008; contrib. to business and co. law jls. *Recreations:* walking, tennis, badminton, squash, theatre, cricket, travel, cinema. *Address:* National Assembly for Wales, Cardiff Bay, Cardiff CF99 1NA. *T:* (029) 2089 8351. *Club:* Oxford and Cambridge.

BOURNE, (Rowland) Richard, OBE 2002; Head, Commonwealth Policy Studies Unit, Institute of Commonwealth Studies, London University, 1999–2005; *b* 27 July 1940; *s* of late Arthur Brittan and Edith Mary Bourne; *m* 1966, Juliet Mary, *d* of John Attenborough, CBE; two *s* one *d*. *Educ:* Uppingham Sch., Rutland; Brasenose Coll., Oxford (BA Mod. Hist.). Journalist, The Guardian, 1962–72 (Education correspondent, 1968–72); Asst Editor, New Society, 1972–77; Evening Standard: Dep. Editor, 1977–78; London Columnist, 1978–79; Founder Editor, Learn Magazine, 1979; Dep. Dir, Commonwealth Inst., 1983–89; Dir, Commonwealth Human Rights Initiative, 1990–92 (Chm., Trustee Cttee, 1994–2003); consultant, 1993–94; Co-Dir, Commonwealth Values in Educn Project, Inst. of Educn, London Univ., 1995–98; Dir, Commonwealth Non-Govtl Office for S Africa and Mozambique, 1995–97. Chm., Editl Bd, Round Table, 2005–. Consultant: Internat. Broadcasting Trust, 1980–81; Adv. Council for Adult and Continuing Educn, 1982. Chm., Survival Internat., 1983–98. Chm., Brazilian Contemporary Arts, 1995–98. Treas., Anglo-Portuguese Foundn, 1985–87. *Publications:* Political Leaders of Latin America, 1969; (with Brian MacArthur) The Struggle for Education, 1970; Getulio Vargas of Brazil, 1974; Assault on the Amazon, 1978; Londoners, 1981; (with Jessica Gould) Self-Sufficiency, 16–25, 1983; Lords of Fleet Street, 1990; News on a Knife-Edge, 1995; Britain in the Commonwealth, 1997; (ed) Universities and Development, 2000; (ed) Where Next for the Group of 54?, 2001; Invisible Lives, 2003; Lula of Brazil: the story so far, 2008; (ed) Sonny Ramphal: Commonwealth statesman, 2008. *Recreations:* theatre, fishing, supporting Charlton Athletic. *Address:* 26 Bennett Park, SE3 9RB. *T:* (020) 8297 4182. *Clubs:* Royal Automobile, Royal Commonwealth Society (Dep. Chm., 2001–07).

BOURNE, Stephen Robert Richard, FCA; University Printer and Chief Executive, Cambridge University Press, since 2002; Fellow, Clare Hall, Cambridge, since 2001; *b* 20 March 1952; *s* of Colyn M. Bourne and Kathleen Bourne (*née* Turner); *m* 1978, Stephanie Ann Bickford; one *s* one *d*. *Educ:* Berkhamsted Sch.; Univ. of Edinburgh (MA 1974); MA Cantab 2001. FCA 1977. Deloitte Haskins and Sells, London and Hong Kong, 1974–80; Exxon Chemical Asia-Pacific, Hong Kong, 1980–86; Dow Jones Telerate, Hong Kong and London: Financial Dir Asia, 1986–89; Gen. Manager, N Europe, 1989–94; Man. Dir, Financial Printing Div., St Ives plc, 1994–96; Cambridge University Press: Development Dir, 1997–2000; Chm., Printing, 2000–02. Director: Britten Sinfonia, 2003–; Wine Soc., 2004–. Council, CBI East, 2007–. Gov., Perse Sch. for Girls, 1998–2004. Treas. and Vice-Chm., RSPCA Hong Kong, 1981–86. Chm., Hong Kong Water Ski Assoc., 1980–85. Hon. Vice-President: Cambridge Univ. Lawn Tennis Club, 2005–; Exning Cricket Club, 2006–. Mem., Old Berkhamstedians Cttee, 1993– (Dep. Pres., 2008–). Liveryman, Stationers' Co. (Mem., Ct of Assts; Chm., Trade and Industry Forum). FRSA 2002. *Recreations:* performing arts, ski-ing, cricket-watching, fine wines. *Address:* Falmouth Lodge, Snailwell Road, Newmarket CB8 7DN. *T:* (01223) 312393, *Fax:* (01223) 325701; *e-mail:* sbourne@cambridge.org. *Clubs:* Athenæum, Royal Commonwealth Society; Middlesex CC, Kent CC, Cambridge University Cricket; Hong Kong, Aberdeen Boat (Treas., 1983–88) (Hong Kong).

BOURNE-ARTON, Simon Nicholas; QC 1994; a Recorder, since 1993; *b* 5 Sept. 1949; *s* of late Major Anthony Temple Bourne-Arton, MBE; *m* 1974, Diana Carr-Walker; two *s* one *d*. *Educ:* Aysgarth Prep. Sch.; Harrow; Teesside Poly. (HND Bus. Studies); Leeds Univ. (LLB Hons). Called to the Bar, Inner Temple, 1975, Bencher, 2003. Leader, North Eastern Circuit, 2006. *Recreations:* living in the country, golf, tennis, being with family and friends, drinking wine. *Address:* Park Court Chambers, 16 Park Place, Leeds LS1 1SJ.

BOURNEMOUTH, Archdeacon of; *see* Harbidge, Ven. A. G.

BOURNS, Prof. Arthur Newcombe, OC 1982; FRSC 1964; President and Vice-Chancellor, 1972–80, Professor of Chemistry 1953–81, now Emeritus, McMaster University; *b* 8 Dec. 1919; *s* of Evans Clement Bourns and Kathleen Jones; *m* 1943, Marion Harriet Blakney; two *s* two *d*. *Educ:* schs in Petitcodiac, NB; Acadia Univ. (BSc); McGill Univ. (PhD). Research Chemist, Dominion Rubber Co., 1944–45; Lectr, Acadia Univ., 1945–46; Asst Prof. of Chemistry, Saskatchewan Univ., 1946–47; McMaster University: Asst Prof., 1947–49; Associate Prof., 1949–53; Dean, Faculty of Grad. Studies, 1957–61; Chm., Chemistry Dept, 1965–67; Vice-Pres., Science and Engrg Div., 1967–72; Actg Pres., 1970. Nuffield Trav. Fellow in Science, University Coll., London, 1955–56. Chm., Gordon Res. Conf. on Chem. and Physics of Isotopes (Vice-Chm. 1959–60; Chm., 1961–62); Nat. Res. Council of Canada: Mem. Chem. Grant Selection Cttee, 1966–69 (Chm. 1968–69); Mem. Council, 1969–75; Mem. Exec. Cttee, 1969–75; Mem. or Chm. various other cttees; Natural Scis and Engrg Res. Council: Member: Council, 1978–85; Exec. Cttee, 1978–85; Allocations Cttee, 1978–86; Cttee on Strategic Grants, 1978–83; Chm., Grants and Scholarships Cttee, 1978–83; Mem., Adv. Cttee on University/Industry Interface, 1979–83; Vis. Res. Officer, 1983–84. Member: Ancaster Public Sch. Bd, 1963–64; Bd, Royal Botanic Gdns, 1972–80 (Vice-Chm.); Cttee on Univ. Affairs, Prov. Ontario; Canadian Cttee for Financing Univ. Res., 1978–80; Council of Ontario Univs, 1972–80; Bd of Dirs and Exec. Cttee, Assoc. of Univs and Colleges of Canada, 1974–77; Mohawk Coll. Bd of Dirs, 1975–82; Council, Canadian Inst. for Advanced Research, 1983–89; Chm., Internat. Adv. Cttee, Chinese Univ. Develt Project, 1985–92; Pres. and Chm. Exec. Cttee, Canadian Bureau for Internat. Educn, 1973–76. McMaster Univ. Med. Centre: Member: Bd of Trustees, 1972–80; Exec. Cttee, 1972–80. Director: Nuclear Activation Services, 1978–80; Slater Steel Industries Ltd, 1975–79. British Council Lectr, 1963. Assoc. Editor, Canadian Jl Chemistry, 1966–69; Mem. Editorial Bd, Science Forum, 1967–73. FCIC 1954 (Chm. Hamilton Section, 1952–53; Mem. Educn Cttee, 1953–59; Mem. Council, 1966–69; Montreal Medal, 1976). Hon. Prof., Jiangxi Univ., China, 1989. Hon. DSc: Acadia, 1968; McGill, 1977; New Brunswick, McMaster, 1981; Hon. LLD Brock, 1980. *Address:* No 1411, 100 Burloak Drive, Burlington, ON L7L 6P6, Canada. *T:* (905) 6396964.

BOUSHER, Stephen; Principal Assistant Solicitor, HM Revenue and Customs (formerly Board of Inland Revenue), since 2000; *b* 13 Feb. 1952; *s* of Leslie Arthur and Clare Bousher; *m* 1974, Jan Townsend; one *s* one *d*. *Educ:* Bec Grammar Sch., Tooting; Southampton Univ. (LLB). Called to the Bar, Gray's Inn, 1975; Board of Inland Revenue, 1976–: Asst Solicitor, 1988–2000; Team Leader, Tax Simplification, then Tax Law Rewrite, Project, 1996–2000. *Recreations:* cinema, watching sport, arguing with Holden, listening to The Grateful Dead, travelling. *Address:* c/o Solicitor's Office, HM Revenue and Customs, 100 Parliament Street, SW1A 2BQ.

BOUSTED, Dr Mary Winefride; General Secretary, Association of Teachers and Lecturers, since 2003; *b* 15 Sept. 1959; *d* of Edward and Winefride Bleasdale; *m* 1983, Donald Bousted; one *d*. *Educ:* Hull Univ. (BA Hons); Inst. of Educn, London Univ. (MA Dist.); York Univ. (PhD 1999). English teacher, Bentley Wood High Sch., Harrow, 1982–87; Hd of English, Whitmore High Sch., Harrow, 1988–91; Lectr, 1991–95, Dir, Initial Teacher Trng, 1995–97, Univ. of York; Head: Secondary Educn, Edge Hill Coll., 1997–99; Sch. of Educn, Kingston Univ., 1999–2003. *Publications:* contrib. English in Educn, Changing English, Educnl Rev. *Recreations:* walking, reading, film, music. *Address:* Association of Teachers and Lecturers, 7 Northumberland Street, WC2N 5RD. *T:* (020) 7930 6441, *Fax:* (020) 7930 1359. *Club:* Royal Commonwealth Society.

BOUTROS-GHALI, Boutros, PhD; President, Egyptian Human Rights Commission, since 2004; Secretary-General, United Nations, 1992–96; *b* Cairo, 14 Nov. 1922; *m* Maria Leia Nadler. *Educ:* Cairo Univ. (LLB 1946); Paris Univ. (PhD 1949). Prof. of Internat. Law and Internat. Relns, and Head, Dept of Political Scis, Cairo Univ., 1949–77; Minister of State for Foreign Affairs, Egypt, 1977–91; Dep. Prime Minister for Foreign Affairs, 1991–92. Mem., Secretariat, Nat. Democratic Party, 1980–92; MP 1987–92. Sec.-Gen., Orgn Internat. de la Francophonie, 1997–2002. Mem., UN Commn of Internat. Law, 1979–92. Founder and Editor: Al Ahram Iktisadi, 1960–75; Al-Siyassa Dawlya, 1965–91. *Publications:* Contribution à l'étude des ententes régionales, 1949; Cours de diplomatie et de droit diplomatique et consulaire, 1951; (jtly) Le problème du Canal de Suez, 1957; (jtly) Egypt and the United Nations, 1957; Le principe d'égalité des états et les organisations internationales, 1961; Contribution à une théorie générale des Alliances, 1963; Foreign Policies in a World of Change, 1963; L'Organisation de l'unité africaine, 1969; Le mouvement Afro-Asiatique, 1969; Les difficultés institutionelles du panafricanisme, 1971; La ligue des états arabes, 1972; Les Conflits de frontières en Afrique, 1973; Unvanquished: a US-UN saga, 1999; also many books in Arabic and numerous contribs to periodicals and learned jls. *Address:* 2 Avenue El Nil, Giza, Cairo, Egypt.

BOUVERIE; *see* Pleydell-Bouverie, family name of Earl of Radnor.

BOVEY, Kathleen Margaret; *see* Wales, K. M.

BOVEY, Dr Leonard; Editor, Materials & Design, 1985–2000; Head of Technological Requirements Branch, Department of Industry, 1977–84; *b* 9 May 1924; *s* of late Alfred and Gladys Bovey; *m* 1944, Constance Hudson (*d* 1987); one *s* one *d*. *Educ:* Hele's Sch., Exeter; Emmanuel Coll., Cambridge (BA, PhD). FInstP; CPhys. Dunlop Rubber, 1943–46; Post-doctoral Fellow, Nat. Res. Council, Ottawa, 1950–52; AERE Harwell, 1952–65; Head W Mids Regional Office, Birmingham, Min. of Technology, 1966–70; Regional Dir, Yorks and Humberside, DTI, 1970–73; Counsellor (Scientific and Technological Affairs), High Commn, Ottawa, 1974–77. Foreign correspondent, Soc. for Advancement of Materials and Processes Engineering (USA) Jl, 1987–. Mem., London Diplomatic Sci. Club. *Publications:* Spectroscopy in the Metallurgical Industry, 1963; papers on spectroscopy in Jl Optical Soc. Amer., Spectrochimica Acta, Jl Phys. Soc. London. *Recreations:* repairing neglected household equipment, work, reading (particularly crime novels), walking, theatre, music. *Address:* 32 Radnor Walk, Chelsea SW3 4BN. *T:* (020) 7352 4142. *Club:* Civil Service.

BOVEY, Philip Henry; Director, Company Law Reform Project, Department of Trade and Industry, 2004–07; *b* 11 July 1948; *s* of late Norman Henry Bovey and Dorothy Yvonne Kent Bovey; *m* 1974, Jenet Alison, *d* of late Rev. Canon J. M. McTear and Margaret McTear; one *s* one *d*. *Educ:* Rugby; Peterhouse, Cambridge (schol.; MA). Solicitor. 3rd Sec., FCO, 1970–71; with Slaughter and May, 1972–75; Legal Assistant, 1976; Sen. Legal Assistant, 1976; Depts of Trade and Industry, 1976–77; Cabinet Office, 1977–78; Depts of Trade, Industry, Prices and Consumer Protection, later DTI, 1978–2007; Asst Solicitor, 1982; Under-Sec., 1985; Dir, Legal Services, 1996–2004. Companies Act Inspector, 1984–88 (report published 1988); Legal Advr to Deregulation, subseq. Better Regulation, then Regulatory Impact Unit, Cabinet Office, 1995–2002. *Recreation:* photography. *Address:* 102 Cleveland Gardens, Barnes, SW13 0AH. *T:* (020) 8876 3710.

BOWATER, Sir Euan David Vansittart, 3rd Bt *cr* 1939, of Friston, Suffolk; *b* 9 Sept. 1935; *s* of Sir Noël Vansittart Bowater, 2nd Bt, GBE, MC, and Constance Heiton, *d* of David Gordon Bett; *S* father, 1984; *m* 1964, Susan Mary Humphrey, *d* of late A. R. O. Slater, FCA; two *s* two *d*. *Educ:* Eton; Trinity Coll., Cambridge (BA). *Recreations:* travel, golf, music. *Heir:* *s* Moray David Vansittart Bowater [*b* 24 April 1967; *m* 1993, Mandana Firoozan; two *d*].

BOWATER, Sir Michael Patrick, 5th Bt *cr* 1914, of Hill Crest, Croydon; *b* 18 July 1949; *s* of Sir J(ohn) Vansittart Bowater, 4th Bt, and Joan Kathleen Bowater (*née* Scullard); *S* father, 2008; *m* 1968, Alison, *d* of Edward Wall; four *d*. *Heir:* none.

BOWCOCK, John Brown, FICE; consulting engineer; Senior Consultant, Sir Alexander Gibb & Partners Ltd, 1996–99 (Director, 1989–96; Chairman, 1993–95); *b* 25 Oct. 1931; *s* of John Brown Bowcock and Mabel Bowcock; *m* 1955, Pauline Mary Elizabeth Dalton; three *d*. *Educ:* Hastings Grammar Sch.; St Catherine's Coll., Oxford (MA). FICE 1971. Nat. service, RAF, 1954–56. Joined Sir Alexander Gibb & Partners, 1957: worked on water resource projects overseas incl. Kariba (Zimbabwe), Roseires (Sudan) and Latiyan (Iran), 1957–70; responsible for major dam projects and Drakensberg pumped storage project, SA, 1970–78; Partner, 1978–89; Chief Exec., 1989–93. Chairman: British Dam Soc., 1992–93; British Consultants Bureau, 1991–92; ACE, 1995–96. *Recreations:* golf, music, reading. *Address:* Lothlorien, Crowsley Road, Shiplake, Oxon RG9 3JU. *T:* (0118) 940 4443. *Clubs:* Royal Air Force; Huntercombe Golf (Henley).

BOWDEN, Rev. Canon Andrew; *see* Bowden, Rev. Canon R. A.

BOWDEN, Sir Andrew, Kt 1994; MBE 1961; International Consultant, Global Equities Corp., since 2004; *b* 8 April 1930; *s* of William Victor Bowden, Solicitor, and Francesca Wilson; *m* 1970, Benita Napier; one *s* one *d*. *Educ:* Ardingly College. Paint industry, 1955–68; Man. Dir, Personnel Assessments Ltd, 1969–71; Man. Dir, Haymarket Personnel Selection Ltd, 1970–71; Director: Sales Education & Leadership Ltd, 1970–71; Jenkin and Purser (Holdings) Ltd, 1973–77. Mem., Wandsworth Borough Council, 1956–62. Contested (C): N Hammersmith, 1955; N Kensington, 1964; Kemp Town, Brighton, 1966. MP (C) Brighton, Kemptown, 1970–97; contested (C) same seat, 1997. Jt Chm., All Party Old Age Pensioners Parly Gp, 1972–97; Chm., All Party BLESMA Gp, 1975–97; Mem. Select Cttee on Expenditure, 1973–74, on Abortion, 1975, on Employment, 1979–83. Mem., Council of Europe, 1987–97. Nat. Chm., Young Conservatives, 1960–61. Internat. Chm., People to People, 1981–83. Nat. Pres., Captive Animals Protection Soc., 1978–98. Mem., Chichester Dio. Synod, 1998–2003. Mem. School Council, Ardingly Coll., 1982–97. *Publication:* (jtly) Dare We Trust Them? - a new vision for Europe, 2005. *Recreations:* birdwatching, chess, poker. *Address:* 4 Carden Avenue, Brighton BN1 8NA. *Club:* Carlton.

BOWDEN, Gerald Francis, TD 1971; barrister, chartered surveyor and university lecturer; *b* 26 Aug. 1935; *s* of Frank Albert Bowden and Elsie Bowden (*née* Burrill); *m* 1967, Heather Elizabeth Hill (*née* Hall) (*d* 1984); two *d*, and one step *s* one step *d*. *Educ:* Battersea Grammar School; Magdalen College, Oxford (MA); Coll. of Estate Mgt, London. FRICS 1984. Called to the Bar, Gray's Inn, 1962. Worked in advertising industry, 1964–68; property marketing and investment, 1968–72; Principal Lecturer in Law, Dept of Estate Management, Polytechnic of the South Bank, 1972–83; Vis. Lectr, Kingston Univ., 1993–2004. Chm. Panel, Examination in Public of Suffolk Co. Structure Plan, 1993. Mem. of Delegacy, KCL, 1978–84. Mem. GLC for Dulwich, 1977–81; a co-opted Mem., ILEA, 1981–84. MP (C) Dulwich, 1983–92; contested (C) Dulwich, 1992. PPS to Minister for Arts, 1990–92. Mem., Select Cttee on Educn, Sci. and Arts, 1990–92. Vice-Chairman: Cons. Backbench Educn Cttee, 1987–89; Cons. Backbench Arts and Heritage Cttee, 1987–92. Pres., Greater London Conservative Trade Unionists, 1985–88. Pres., Southwark Chamber of Commerce, 1986–89. Chairman: Walcot Educn Foundn, 1978–2001; Lambeth and Southwark Housing Assoc. (formerly Soc.), 1973–84; London Rent Assessment Panel, 1994–2006; Leasehold Valuation Tribunal, 1994–2006; Pres., Appeal Tribunal on Building Regulation, 1995–. Chm., Magdalen Soc., 1991–2001; Trustee, Magdalen Develt Trust, 1991–. Mem. Council, Royal Albert Hall, 1994–. Estates Gov., Alleyn's Coll. of God's Gift, Dulwich, 1992–2003 (Chm.). After Nat. Service, continued to serve in TA until 1984 (Lt-Col). *Publications:* An Introduction to the Law of Contract and Tort, 1977; The Housing Act, 1988. *Recreations:* gardening, books, pictures, renovating old houses. *Address:* 130 Kennington Park Road, SE11 4DJ. *T:* (020) 7582 7361. *Clubs:* Oxford and Cambridge (Trustee, 2002–), Chelsea Arts, Garrick.

BOWDEN, James Nicholas Geoffrey, OBE 2002; HM Diplomatic Service; Ambassador to Bahrain, since 2006; *b* 27 May 1960; *s* of Geoffrey Bowden and Gillian (*née* Mathieson); *m* 1st, 1986, Alison Hulme (marr. diss. 1999); one *s* one *d*; 2nd, 1999, Sarah Peaslee; twin *s* one *d*. *Educ:* Eton. Served RGJ, 1980–86. Entered HM Diplomatic Service, 1986; Second Sec., FCO, 1986–90; Dep. Consul Gen., Aden, 1990–91; Second Sec., Khartoum, 1991–93; First Secretary: FCO, 1993–96; Washington, 1996–99; Riyadh, 1999–2000; FCO, 2000–03; Deputy Head of Mission: Kuwait, 2003–04; Baghdad, 2004–05; Kuwait, 2005–06. *Recreations:* hunting, walking. *Address:* c/o Foreign and Commonwealth Office, King Charles Street, SW1A 2AH.

BOWDEN, Logan S.; *see* Scott-Bowden.

BOWDEN, Sir Nicholas Richard, 4th Bt *cr* 1915, of City of Nottingham; farmer, now retired; *b* 13 Aug. 1935; *s* of Sir Frank Bowden, 3rd Bt and his 1st wife, Marie-José Stiénon De Messey; *S* father, 2001. *Educ:* Millfield Sch. Asst to horse-trainer; farmer. *Recreation:* riding. *Heir: half-nephew* Alexander Gordan Bowden, *b* 14 May 1972. *Address:* 4 Hensting Farm Cottages, Fishers Pond, Eastleigh, Hants SO50 7HH. *Club:* Lansdowne.

BOWDEN, Rev. Canon (Robert) Andrew; Chaplain to the Queen, 1992–2008; Associate Priest, Thameshead benefice, diocese of Gloucester, 2004–08; *b* 13 Nov. 1938; *s* of Charles Bowden and Miriam (*née* Howard-Tripp); *m* 1966, Susan (*née* Humpidge); three *d*. *Educ:* Clifton Coll., Bristol; Worcester Coll., Oxford (Scholar; BA 1962; DipTh 1963; MA 1967; BDQ 1968); Cuddesdon Coll., Oxford. Ordained deacon, 1965, priest, 1966. Curate: St George, Wolverhampton, 1965–69; St Luke's, Duston, 1969–72; Rector: Byfield, 1972–79; Coates, Rodmarton and Sapperton with Frampton Mansell, 1979–2004. Chaplain, Royal Agricl Coll., Cirencester, 1979–93; Rural Advr, 1981–93, Local Ministry Officer, 1993–2004, dio. of Gloucester; Mem., Archbp's Commn on Rural Areas, 1988–90; Chm., Churches Rural Gp, 2004–07. Hon. Canon, Gloucester Cathedral, 1990–. *Publications:* Ministry in the Countryside, 1994; (with M. West) Dynamic Local Ministry, 2000. *Recreations:* breeding old breeds of poultry, Riding for the Disabled.

BOWDERY, Martin Howard; QC 2000; a Recorder, since 2004; *b* 2 July 1956; *s* of Ray Bowdery and Beryl Bowdery (*née* Porter); *m* 1st, 1982 (marr. diss. 1999); two *s* four *d*; 2nd, 2002, Lindsay Moffat, *d* of Ted and Joan Moffat. *Educ:* Trinity Sch. of John Whitgift; Pembroke Coll., Oxford (BA PPE 1978). Called to the Bar, Inner Temple, 1980; practising Barrister, 1982–. Ed., Internat. Construction Law Rev., 1983–87. *Publications:* contributor to: Construction Contract Reform: a plea for sanity, 1999; Construction Law Handbook, 2000. *Address:* 1 Atkin Building, Gray's Inn, WC1R 5AT. *T:* (020) 7404 0102. *Clubs:* Garrick; Isle of Purbeck Golf.

BOWDLER, (Anne) Caroline; Regional Director, Government Office for the East of England (GO-East), 2002–06; *b* 21 Dec. 1946; *d* of William James Gordon Darling and Edith Mary Darling (*née* Colhoun); *m* 1970, Keith Bowdler. *Educ:* Tonbridge Girls' Grammar Sch.; Lady Margaret Hall, Oxford (BA Hons). Various posts, DoE and Dept of Transport, 1973–94; Government Office for the East of England: Dep. Dir, Planning, 1994–97; Dir, Planning and Transport, 1997–2002. *Recreations:* reading, choral singing.

BOWDLER, Timothy John, CBE 2006; Chief Executive, Johnston Press plc, since 1997 (Group Managing Director, 1994–97); *b* 16 May 1947; *s* of Henry Neville Bowdler and Barbara Mary Bowdler (*née* Richardson); *m* 1976, Brita Margaretha Eklund; two *d*. *Educ:* Wrekin Coll.; Birmingham Univ. (BSc Engrg Prodn 1969); London Business Sch. (MBA 1975). Graduate mgt trainee, subseq. branch admin. manager, GKN Sankey Ltd, 1969–73; General Bearings Division, RHP Bearings Ltd: Commercial Manager, 1975–77; Gen. Manager, Business Ops, 1977–81; Sandvik Ltd: Dir and Gen. Manager, Sandvik Steel, 1981–84; Man. Dir, Spooner Industries Ltd, 1984–87; Man. Dir, Chloride Motive Power, Chloride Gp plc, 1987–88; Dir N Div., Tyzack & Partners Ltd, 1989–90; Divl Man. Dir, Cape Architectural Products, 1990–92, Cape Building and Architectural Products, 1992–94, Cape plc. Chm., Press Standards Bd of Finance Ltd, 2005– (Dir, 2000–); non-executive Director: ABP Hldgs plc, 2001–06; Press Assoc., 2001–; Miller Gp, 2004–. Council Mem., Newspaper Soc. (Pres., 2002–03). *Recreations:* golf, ski-ing. *Address:* Johnston Press plc, 53 Manor Place, Edinburgh EH3 7EG. *T:* (0131) 225 3361, *Fax:* (0131) 226 7230; *e-mail:* tbowdler@johnstonpress.co.uk. *Clubs:* New (Edinburgh); Bruntsfield Links Golfing Society.

BOWDON, Humphrey Anthony Erdeswick B.; *see* Butler-Bowdon.

BOWE, Colette, PhD; non-executive Director, Office of Communications, since 2008 (Chairman, Consumer Panel, 2003–07); *b* 27 Nov. 1946; *d* of Philip Bowe and Norah (*née* Hughes). *Educ:* Notre Dame High Sch., Liverpool; Queen Mary Coll., Univ. of London (BSc Econs, PhD); LSE (MSc Econs). Research Officer, LSE, 1969–70; Econ. Advr, Nat. Ports Council, 1971–73; Department of Industry: Econ. Advr, 1975–78; Principal, 1979–81; Department of Trade and Industry: Asst Sec., 1981–84; Dir of Information, 1984–87; Controller of Public Affairs, IBA, 1987–89; Dir, SIB, 1989–93; Chief Exec., PIA, 1994–97; Exec. Chm., Save & Prosper and Fleming Fund Mgt (Luxembourg), 1998–2001; Chm., Telecoms Ombudsman Service Council, 2002–03. Non-executive Director: Thames Water Utilities Ltd, 2001–06 (Dep. Chm., 2002–06); LCR, 2008–; Board Member: Yorkshire Building Soc., 2003–06; Framlington Gp, 2003–05; Axa Framlington, 2005–; Morgan Stanley Bank Internat., 2005–; Goldfish Bank, 2007–08; Electra Private Equity plc, 2007–. Mem., Statistics Commn, 2000–08. Chm., Alcohol Concern, 2002–06. Chm. Council, Queen Mary, Univ. of London, 2003–; Gov. and Mem. Council of Mgt, NIESR, 2002–. Trustee: Camden People's Theatre, 2002–; Wincott Foundn, 2004–. Hon. Fellow, Liverpool John Moores Univ., 1995. *Recreations:* music, London, watching football. *Address:* 18 Elia Street, N1 8DE. *T:* (020) 7713 8040.

BOWE, David Robert; Member (Lab) Yorkshire and the Humber Region, European Parliament, 1999–2004 (Cleveland and Yorkshire North, 1989–94; Cleveland and Richmond, 1994–99); *b* Gateshead, 19 July 1955; *m* 1978, Helena Scattergood; one *s* one *d*. *Educ:* Sunderland Polytechnic; Bath Univ. BSc; PGCE. Former science teacher. Mem., Middlesbrough Borough Council, 1983–89 (Chm., Monitoring and Review Cttee). European Parliament: Mem., Cttee on Envmt, Public Health and Consumer Protection, 1989–2004; substitute Member: Cttee on Econ. and Monetary Affairs, 1994–99; Industry Cttee, 1999–2004. Mem., UNISON. *Address:* 4 Silverdale Mount, Guiseley, Leeds LS20 8PY; *e-mail:* mail@davidbowe.demon.co.uk.

BOWEN, Anthony John; Lector, Faculty of Classics, 1990–2003, and Orator, 1993–2007, University of Cambridge; Fellow, Jesus College, Cambridge, 1995–2007, now Emeritus Fellow (President, 2003–05); *b* 17 May 1940; *s* of Dr Reginald Bowen and Dorothy Bowen (*née* Jinks). *Educ:* Bradfield Coll., Berks; St John's Coll., Cambridge. Teacher: Bradfield Coll., 1963–67 (producer of Greek play, 1961, 1964, 1967); Shrewsbury Sch., 1967–90. Contested (L/Alliance) Shrewsbury and Atcham, 1983. Member: (L, then Lib Dem) Shropshire CC, 1981–89; (Lib Dem) Cambridgeshire CC, 1997–2005. *Publications:* Aeschylus, Cheophori, 1986; The Story of Lucretia, 1987; Plutarch, the Malice of Herodotus, 1992; Xenophon, Symposium, 1998; (with Peter Garnsey) Lactantius, Divine Institutes, 2003. *Recreations:* travel, politics, music. *Address:* Jesus College, Cambridge CB5 8BL. *T:* (01223) 339309. *Clubs:* National Liberal; Royal St David's Golf.

BOWEN, Maj.-Gen. Bryan Morris, CB 1988; Paymaster-in-Chief and Inspector of Army Pay Services, 1986–89, retired; *b* 8 March 1932; *s* of Frederick Bowen and Gwendoline Bowen (*née* Morris); *m* 1955, Suzanne Rowena (*née* Howell); two *d*. *Educ:* Newport High Sch.; Exeter Univ. FCMA; ndc, psc†, sq, pfc. Joined RE, 1953, served UK and BAOR; transf. RAPC, 1958; Paymaster 1/6 QEO Gurkha Rifles, Malaya and UK, 1960–63; Army Cost and Management Accounting Services, 1963–68; DAAG, MoD, 1968–70; Exchange Officer, US Army, Washington, DC, 1970–72; Nat. Defence Coll., 1972–73; DS, RMCS Shrivenham, 1973–76; AAG, MOD, 1976–79; Col (Principal), MoD F4(AD), 1979–81; Chief Paymaster, Army Pay Office (Officers Accounts), 1981–82; Dep. Paymaster-in-Chief, 1982–85. Col Comdt, RAPC, 1990–92; Dep. Col Comdt, AGC, 1992–93. Mem. Council, CIMA, 1990–94; Chm., Oxfordshire Cttee, Army Benevolent Fund, 1990–92; Special Comr, Duke of York's Royal Mil. Sch., Dover, 1990–2000 (Chm., 1992–2000); Dir, United Services Trustee, 1990–2000; Pres., Nat. Service Veterans' Assoc., 2003–. Freeman, City of London, 1987. *Recreations:* golf, church affairs. *Address:* Foxlea, Yew Tree Farm, Goodworth Clatford, Andover, Hants SP11 7QY.

BOWEN, Carolyn Elizabeth Cunningham, (Mrs S. J. Bowen); *see* Sinclair, C. E. C.

BOWEN, Charles John; Chief Executive, Booker, 1993–98; *b* 11 Dec. 1941; *s* of John and late Millicent Bowen; *m* 1965, Naomi Stevens; one *s* one *d*. *Educ:* Exeter Univ. (BA Econs and Stats). Fellow, Royal Statistical Soc. Market Research Manager, ICI Paints Div., 1965–67; Product Manager, Unilever, 1967–73; Marketing Manager and Dir, General Foods UK, 1973–78; Gen. Manager, General Foods, Puerto Rico, 1978–82; Vice-Pres., General Foods Corp., USA, 1982–88; Exec. Dir, Hillsdown Holdings, 1988–93. Non-exec. Dir, Legal & General Gp, 1996–99. *Club:* Travellers.

BOWEN, Prof. David Aubrey Llewellyn, FRCP, FRCPE, FRCPath; Professor of Forensic Medicine, University of London, 1977–89, now Emeritus; Head of Department of Forensic Medicine and Toxicology, Charing Cross Hospital Medical School, 1973–89 (Charing Cross and Westminster Medical School, 1985–89); Hon. Consultant Pathologist, Charing Cross Hospital, 1973–89; *b* 31 Jan. 1924; *s* of late Dr Thomas Rufus Bowen and Catherine (*née* Llewellyn); *m* 1st, 1950, Joan Rosemary Davis (*d* 1973); two *s* one *d*; 2nd, 1975, Helen Rosamund Landcastle. *Educ:* Caterham Sch.; Garw Secondary Sch., Pontycymmer; University College of Wales, Cardiff; Corpus Christi Coll., Cambridge (MA); Middlesex Hosp. Med. Sch. (MB BChir 1947); DipPath 1955; DMJ Soc. of Apoth. of London 1962. FRCPE 1971; FRCPath 1975; FRCP 1982. Ho. posts at W Middlesex Hosp. and London Chest Hosp., 1947 and 1950; RAMC, 1947–49; Jun. Resident Pathologist, Bristol Royal Inf., 1950–51; Registrar in Path., London Chest Hosp., 1951–52; Registrar and Sen. Registrar in Clin. Path., National Hosp. for Nervous Diseases, 1952–56; Asst Pathologist and Sen. Registrar, Royal Marsden Hosp., 1956–57; Demonstr 1957–63, Lectr 1963–66, in Forensic Medicine, St George's Hosp. Med. Sch.; Sen. Lectr 1966–73, Reader 1973–77, in Forensic Medicine, Vice-Dean 1974–78, Charing Cross Hosp. Med. Sch.; Lectr in Forensic Medicine, Oxford Univ., 1974–89. Chairman: Div. of Pathology, Charing Cross Hosp., 1976–78; Apptd and Recog. Teachers in Path., Charing Cross Hosp. Med. Sch., 1980–82; Examiner: Univ. of Riyadh, Saudi Arabia, 1978–81; on Forensic Med., RCPath, 1976–90; for Diploma of Med. Jurisprudence, Soc. of Apothecaries of London, 1970–93; for MD (Forensic Medicine) and Diploma in Legal Medicine, Univ. of Sri Lanka, 1985. Lectr, Metropolitan Police Trng Coll., Hendon, 1976–84; W. D. L. Fernando Oration to Medical Legal Soc. of Sri Lanka, 1985. Chm., Quality Assce and Scientific Standards Cttee, Adv. Bd for Forensic Pathol., Home Office, 1990–96. Vice-President: Medico-Legal Soc., 1977–90; Medical Defence Union, 1979–91; President: British Assoc. in Forensic Med., 1977–79; W London Medico-Chirurgical Soc., 1987–88; Member: British Academy in Forensic Sci. and Forensic Sci. Soc., 1960–91 (Mem. Council, 1965–67); British Div. of Internat. Acad. of Path., 1974–93; Acad. Internat. de Médecine Légale et de Méd. Sociale, 1976–90; RCPath Adv. Cttee on Forensic Path., 1973–76 and 1980–82. Liveryman, Apothecaries' Soc., 1972–. Vice-Pres., Old Caterhamians Assoc., 1987–88. *Publications:* Body of Evidence (autobiog.), 2003; sci. papers in numerous med., forensic med. and path. jls. *Recreations:* travel, writing. *Address:* 19 Letchmore Road, Radlett, Herts WD7 8HU. *T:* (01923) 856936.

BOWEN, Prof. (David) Keith, DPhil; FRS 1998; FREng; Group Director of Technology, 2000–05, Chief Scientist, since 2006, Bede plc (President, Bede Scientific Inc., 1996–2002); Professor of Engineering, University of Warwick, 1989–97, now Emeritus; *b* 10 May 1940; *s* of Harold Lane Bowen and Muriel Bowen; *m* 1968, Beryl Lodge; one *s*. *Educ:* Christ's Hosp.; St Edmund Hall, Oxford (MA 1966; DPhil Metallurgy 1967; Hon. Fellow 2006); Open Univ. (Dip. Music 2006). FREng (FEng 1997); FIMMM (FIM 1983); CPhys 1998, FInstP 1998. SRC Res. Fellow, Oxford Univ., 1966–68; Department of Engineering, University of Warwick: Lectr, 1968–78; Sen. Lectr, 1978–85; Reader, 1985–89. Visiting Professor: MIT, 1987; Univ. of Durham, 2003–. Pres., Kammermusik Workshops Inc., USA; Chm., Spires Music Ltd, 2007–. *Publications:* (with C. R. Hall) Microscopy of Materials, 1975; (with B. K. Tanner) High Resolution X-Ray Diffractometry and Topography, 1998; X-Ray Metrology in Semiconductor

Manufacturing, 2006; more than 100 articles in learned jls. *Recreations:* music (orchestral and chamber clarinet player and conductor), woodwork. *Address:* c/o Bede plc, Belmont Business Park, Durham DH1 1TW. *T:* (0191) 332 4700; *e-mail:* keith.bowen@bede.com.

BOWEN, Desmond John, CMG 2002; Policy Director, Ministry of Defence, since 2004; *b* 11 Jan. 1949; *s* of John and Deborah Bowen; *m* 1979, Susan Brandt; one *s* one *d*. *Educ:* Charterhouse; University Coll., Oxford (MA). Parachute Regt, 1970–73; joined MoD, 1973; seconded to FCO, 1978–81, 1987–91; Private Sec. to Permanent Under Sec. of State, 1982–85; Dir Gen. of Mktg, Defence Export Services Orgn, 1995–97; Fellow, Center for Internat. Affairs, Harvard Univ., 1997–98; Asst Under Sec. of State (Service Personnel Policy), 1998–99; Dir, Private Office of Sec. Gen., NATO, 1999–2001; Dir Gen. Operational Policy, MoD, 2001–02; on secondment as Dep. Dir, Overseas and Defence Secretariat, Cabinet Office, 2002–04. *Publication:* contrib. Conflict and Terrorism jl. *Recreation:* mountains. *Address:* c/o Ministry of Defence, Whitehall, SW1A 2HB.

BOWEN, Edward Farquharson, TD 1976; QC (Scot.) 1992; Sheriff-Principal of Lothian and Borders, since 2005; Temporary Judge, Court of Session, since 2000; *b* 1 May 1945; *s* of late Stanley Bowen, CBE; *m* 1975, Patricia Margaret Brown, *y d* of Rev. R. Russell Brown, Perth; two *s* two *d*. *Educ:* Melville Coll., Edinburgh; Edinburgh Univ. (LLB 1966). Enrolled as Solicitor in Scotland, 1968; admitted to Faculty of Advocates, 1970. Standing Jun. Counsel: to Scottish Educn Dept, 1977–79; to Home Office in Scotland, 1979; Advocate-Depute, 1979–83; Sheriff of Tayside Central and Fife, 1983–90; Partner, Thorntons, WS, 1990–91; Sheriff-Principal of Glasgow and Strathkelvin, 1997–2005. Chm. (part-time), Industrial Tribunals, 1995–97; Mem. Criminal Injuries Compensation Bd, 1996–97. Chm., Northern Lighthouse Bd, 2003–05 (Comr of Northern Lights, 1997–). Served RAOC (TA and T&AVR), 1964–80. *Recreations:* golf, curling. *Address:* The Old Manse, Lundie, Angus DD2 5NW. *Clubs:* New (Edinburgh); Royal & Ancient Golf (St Andrews); Hon. Company of Edinburgh Golfers; Panmure Golf; Lundie and Auchterhouse Curling.

BOWEN, Sir Geoffrey (Fraser), Kt 1977; Managing Director, Commercial Banking Company of Sydney Ltd, Australia, 1973–76, retired (General Manager, 1970–73); *m* 1st, Ruth (decd), *d* of H. E. Horsburgh; two *s* one *d*; 2nd, Isabel, *d* of H. T. Underwood. *Address:* Apt 35/36 The Cotswolds, 28 Curagul Road, North Turramurra, NSW 2074, Australia.

BOWEN, Geraint Robert Lewis, FRCO; Organist and Director of Music, Hereford Cathedral, since 2001; *b* 11 Jan. 1963; *s* of Kenneth John Bowen and Angela Mary Bowen (*née* Evenden); *m* 1987, Catherine Lucy Dennis; two *s*. *Educ:* Haverstock Sch.; William Ellis Sch.; Jesus Coll., Cambridge (organ schol.; BA 1986, MA 1989); Trinity Coll., Dublin (MusB 1987). FRCO 1987. Assistant Organist: Hampstead Parish Ch and St Clement Danes Ch, 1985–86; St Patrick's Cathedral, Dublin, 1986–89; Hereford Cathedral, 1989–94; Organist and Master of the Choristers, St Davids Cathedral, and Artistic Dir, St Davids Cathedral Fest., 1995–2001. Conductor, Hereford Choral Soc., 2001–; Associate Conductor, Three Choirs Fest. at Gloucester and Worcester, 2002–; Conductor, Three Choirs Fest. at Hereford, 2003–. *Recreations:* growing vegetables, railways, travel, typography, walking. *Address:* 7 College Cloisters, The Close, Hereford HR1 2NG. *T:* (01432) 374238; *e-mail:* organist@herefordcathedral.org.

BOWEN, Janet Margaret; Lord-Lieutenant of Ross and Cromarty, Skye and Lochalsh, since 2007; *b* 12 July 1944; *d* of Capt. Alexander Matheson, RN and Mary Matheson; *m* 1972, Christopher Richard Croasdaile Bowen; one *s* one *d*. *Educ:* Butterstone House Sch.; North Foreland Lodge. Sec., British Red Cross HQ and volunteer, British Red Cross VSO scheme, 1965–68; Sec., Church Soc., 1969–72; Mem., Children's Panel, 1986–2004. Pres., Red Cross, Highland and Western Isles, 2007– (Chm., Volunteer Council, 2000–07). *Recreations:* cherishing temperamental husband, gardening, cooking, succeeding in life without formal qualifications. *Address:* Kinellan House, Strathpeffer, Ross-shire IV14 9ET. *T:* (01997) 421476; *e-mail:* jbowen@redcross.org.uk.

BOWEN, Jeremy Francis John; Middle East Editor, BBC, since 2005; *b* 6 Feb. 1960; *s* of Gareth Bowen and Jennifer Bowen (*née* Delany); partner, Julia Williams; one *s* one *d*. *Educ:* Cardiff High Sch.; University Coll. London (BA Hons Hist.; Fellow 2005); Johns Hopkins Univ. Sch. of Advanced Internat. Studies, Washington and Bologna, Italy (MA Internat. Affairs). Joined BBC, 1984: news trainee, 1984–85; financial news reporter, 1986–87; Foreign Correspondent, 1987–2000: Radio Corresp., Geneva, 1987; Foreign Affairs Corresp., TV, 1988–95; Middle East Corresp., 1995–2000; Presenter, BBC Breakfast, 2000–02; foreign correspondent and television presenter, 2002–05; Rome Corresp., 2005. Journalism award: NY TV Fest., 1993; Monte Carlo TV Fest., 1994; RTS, 1996; BAFTA Award for BBC team coverage of Kosovo Crisis, 1999; Sony Gold Award for coverage of Saddam Hussein's arrest, 2004; Internat. Emmy, BBC Team Award for coverage of 2006 war in Lebanon and Israel, 2007. *Publications:* Six Days: how the 1967 war shaped the Middle East, 2003; War Stories, 2006. *Recreations:* sport, cooking, not travelling. *Address:* c/o BBC News, Television Centre, W12 7RJ.

BOWEN, John Griffith; playwright and novelist; freelance drama producer for television; *b* 5 Nov. 1924; *s* of Hugh Griffith Bowen and Ethel May Cook; unmarried. *Educ:* Queen Elizabeth's Grammar Sch., Crediton; Pembroke Coll., Oxford; St Antony's Coll., Oxford. Frere Exhibition for Indian Studies, Oxford, 1951–52 and 1952–53. Asst Editor, The Sketch, 1954–57; Advertising Copywriter and Copy Chief, 1957–60; Consultant on TV Drama, Associated TV, 1960–67; productions for Thames TV, LWT, BBC. *Publications:* The Truth Will Not Help Us, 1956; After the Rain, 1958; The Centre of the Green, 1959; Storyboard, 1960; The Birdcage, 1962; A World Elsewhere, 1965; The Essay Prize, 1965; Squeak, 1983; The McGuffin, 1984 (filmed for TV, 1986); The Girls, 1986; Fighting Back, 1989; The Precious Gift, 1992; No Retreat, 1994; *plays:* I Love You, Mrs Patterson, 1964; After the Rain, 1967; Fall and Redemption, 1967; Little Boxes, 1968; The Disorderly Women, 1968; The Corsican Brothers, 1970; The Waiting Room, 1970; Robin Redbreast, 1972; Heil Caesar, 1973; Florence Nightingale, 1975; Which Way Are You Facing?, 1976; Singles, 1977; Bondage, 1978; The Inconstant Couple (adaptation of Marivaux, L'Heureux Stratagème), 1978; Uncle Jeremy, 1981; The Geordie Gentleman (adaptation of Molière's Le Bourgeois Gentilhomme), 1987; Cold Salmon, 1998. *Address:* Old Lodge Farm, Sugarswell Lane, Edgehill, Banbury, Oxon OX15 6HP.

BOWEN, Keith; *see* Bowen, D. K.

BOWEN, Hon. Lionel Frost, AC 1991; MHR (Lab) Kingsford-Smith, NSW, 1969–90; Attorney-General of Australia, 1984–90; Chairman, National Gallery, Canberra, 1990–95; *b* 28 Dec. 1922; *m* 1953, Claire Clement; five *s* three *d*. *Educ:* Sydney Univ. (LLB). Alderman, 1948, Mayor, 1949–50, Randwick Council; MLA, NSW, 1962–69; Postmaster Gen., 1972–74; Special Minister of State, 1974–75; Minister for Manufg Industry, 1975; Dep. Leader, Opposition, 1977–83; Minister for Trade, 1983–84; Dep. Prime Minister, 1983–90. *Recreations:* surfing, reading. *Address:* 24 Mooramie Avenue, Kensington, NSW 2033, Australia.

BOWEN, Sir Mark Edward Mortimer, 5th Bt *cr* 1921, of Colworth, Co. Bedford; *b* 17 Oct. 1958; *s* of Sir Thomas Frederic Charles Bowen, 4th Bt and of Jill, *d* of Lloyd Evans; *S* father, 1989; *m* 1983, Kerry Tessa, *d* of Michael Moriarty; one *s* one *d*. *Heir: s* George Edward Michael Bowen, *b* 27 Dec. 1987. *Address:* Bowood, 31 Ashley Road, Thames Ditton, Surrey KT7 0NH.

BOWEN, Most Rev. Michael George; Archbishop and Metropolitan of Southwark, (RC), 1977–2003, now Archbishop Emeritus; *b* 23 April 1930; *s* of late Major C. L. J. Bowen and Maisie Bowen (who *m* 1945, Sir Paul Makins, 4th Bt). *Educ:* Downside; Trinity Coll., Cambridge; Gregorian Univ., Rome. Army, 1948–49, 2nd Lieut Irish Guards; Wine Trade, 1951–52; English Coll., Rome, 1952–59; ordained 1958; Curate at Earlsfield and at Walworth, South London, 1959–63; taught theology, Beda Coll., Rome, 1963–66; Chancellor of Diocese of Arundel and Brighton, 1966–70; Coadjutor Bishop with right of succession to See of Arundel and Brighton, 1970–71; Bishop of Arundel and Brighton, 1971–77. Pres., Bishops' Conf. of England and Wales, 1999–2000 (Vice-Pres., 1996–98). *Recreations:* golf, tennis. *Address:* c/o Archbishop's House, St George's Road, SE1 6HX. *T:* (020) 7928 2495.

BOWEN, Thomas Edward Ifor L.; *see* Lewis-Bowen.

BOWEN, William G(ordon), PhD; President, The Andrew W. Mellon Foundation, 1988–2006, now Senior Research Associate; President, Princeton University, 1972–88, now Emeritus; *b* 6 Oct. 1933; *s* of Albert A. and Bernice C. Bowen; *m* 1956, Mary Ellen Maxwell; one *s* one *d*. *Educ:* Denison Univ. (AB); Princeton Univ. (PhD). Princeton University: Asst Prof. of Economics, Associate Prof. of Economics; Prof. of Econs, 1958–88; Provost, 1967–72; Sen. Fellow, Woodrow Wilson Sch. of Public and Internat. Affairs, 1988. Director: NCR, 1975–91; Reader's Digest, 1985–97; Merck, 1986–; DeWitt and Lila Wallace-Reader's Digest Funds, 1986–97; American Express, 1988–; Teachers' Insce and Annuity Assoc., 1995–; Coll. Retirement Equities Fund, 1995–; JSTOR (first Chm., 1995). Trustee, Center for Advanced Study in the Behavioral Sciences, 1986–92; Regent, Smithsonian Instn, 1980–92; Mem. Bd of Dirs, Denison Univ., 1992– (Trustee, 1992–2000). Hon. LLD: Denison, Rutgers, Pennsylvania and Yale, 1972; Harvard, 1973; Jewish Theol Seminary, 1974; Seton Hall Univ., 1975; Dartmouth and Princeton, 1987; Brown, 1988; Michigan, 1995; Hon. DHL: Morehouse Coll., 1992; Hartwick Coll., 1992; Hon. DSc Lafayette Coll., 1992; Hon. DEconSc Cape Town, 1996; Hon. DCL Oxford, 2001. *Publications:* Economic Aspects of Education, 1964; (with W. J. Baumol) Performing Arts: the Economic Dilemma, 1966; (with T. A. Finegan) Economics of Labor Force Participation, 1969; Ever the Teacher, 1987; (with Julie Ann Sosa) Prospects for Faculty in the Arts & Sciences, 1989; (with N. L. Rudenstine) In Pursuit of the PhD, 1992; Inside the Boardroom: governance by directors and trustees, 1994; (jtly) The Charitable Nonprofits, 1994; (with Derek Bok) The Shape of the River: long-term consequences of considering race in college and university admissions, 1998; (with James Shulman) The Game of Life: college sports and educational values, 2001; (with Sarah A. Levin) Reclaiming the Game: college sports and educational values, 2003; (jtly) Equity and Excellence in American Higher Education, 2005; contribs to Amer. Econ. Review, Economica, Quarterly Jl of Economics, etc. *Address:* Andrew W. Mellon Foundation, 140 E 62 Street, New York, NY 10021–8124, USA. *T:* (212) 8268114.

BOWEN-SIMPKINS, Peter, FRCOG; Consultant Obstetrician and Gynaecologist: Singleton Hospital, Swansea, 1979–98; Swansea NHS Trust, 1999–2002; Medical Director, London Women's Clinic at Singleton Hospital (formerly Cromwell IVF and Fertility Centre), Swansea, since 1992, and in London, since 2005; *b* 28 Oct. 1941; *s* of late Horace John Bowen-Simpkins and of Christine Dulce Bowen-Simpkins (*née* Clarke); *m* 1967, Kathrin Ganguin; two *d*. *Educ:* Malvern Coll.; Selwyn Coll., Cambridge (BA 1963); MA 1967, MB BChir 1967, Cambridge; Guy's Hosp. Med. Sch. LRCP, MRCS 1966; FRCOG 1985; FFSRH (FFFP 2005; MFFP 1993). Leader, Cambridge expedn to Eritrea, 1963; Resident MO, Queen Charlotte's Maternity Hosp., London, 1971; Resident Surg. Officer, Samaritan Hosp. for Women, London, 1972; Sen. Registrar and Lectr, Middlesex Hosp. and Hosp. for Women, Soho Square, 1972–78; Inspector of Nullity for Wales, 1980–. Lectr, Margaret Pyke Centre for Family Planning, 1973–2003. Royal College of Obstetricians and Gynaecologists: Mem. Council, 1993–2005; Hon. Treas., 1998–2005; Mem. Foundn Bd, Fac. of Family Planning, 1995–98; Trustee and Bd Mem., WellBeing, 1998–. Chm. Mgt Bd, BJOG, 1998–2005. Pres., Victor Bonney Soc., 2002–05. Freeman, City of London, 1980; Liveryman: Soc. of Apothecaries, 1976; Welsh Livery Guild, 1995. Handcock Prize for Surgery, RCS, 1966. *Publications:* Pocket Examiner in Obstetrics and Gynaecology, 1983, 2nd edn 1992; A Practice of Obstetrics and Gynaecology, 2000; papers on obstetrics and gynaecol. in BMJ, BJOG, BJA, Fertility and Sterility, etc. *Recreations:* flyfishing, walking, ski-ing, sailing. *Address:* Cysgod-y-Bryn, Brynview Close, Reynoldston, Swansea SA3 1AG; *e-mail:* pbs@reynoldston.com. *Clubs:* Flyfishers'; Gynaecological Travellers.

BOWER, Michael Douglas; Leader, Sheffield Metropolitan District Council, 1992–98; *b* 25 Aug. 1942; *s* of Stanley Arthur Bower and Rachael Farmer; *m*; two *d*. *Educ:* Colwyn Bay Grammar Sch.; Royal Coll. of Advanced Technol., Salford. Civil engr, 1961–64; journalist, 1965–77; with The Star, Sheffield, 1968–77; Regional Organiser, NUJ, 1977–81; Organiser, Sheffield Co-operative Develt Gp, 1981–94. Mem., Press Council, 1976–77. Mem., Sheffield Metropolitan DC, 1976–98 (Chm., Educn Cttee, 1983). Contested (Lab) Hallam Div. of Sheffield, 1979. *Recreations:* walking, golf. *Address:* 350 Walkley Bank Road, Sheffield S6 5AR. *T:* (0114) 233 5753. *Club:* Carlton Working Men's (Gleadless, Sheffield).

BOWER, Thomas Michael; writer and journalist; *b* 28 Sept. 1946; *s* of George Bower and Sylvia Bower; *m* 1st, 1971, Juliet Ann Oddie (marr. diss. 1981); two *s*; 2nd, 1985, Veronica Judith Colleton Wadley, *qv*; one *s* one *d*. *Educ:* William Ellis Sch.; London Sch. of Econs (LLB). Called to the Bar, Gray's Inn, 1969; with BBC TV, 1970–95: researcher, 24 Hours, 1970–72; producer, Midweek, 1972–76; Dep. Ed. and Producer, Panorama, 1976–86; Producer, Documentaries, 1986–95; contributor, Daily Mail, 1996–. Queen Victoria Bronze Medal, RSPCA, 1975; Award for Excellence in Broadcasting, Ohio State Univ., 1979; Best TV Documentary, Fest. dei Popoli, 1987; Fipa d'Or, Cannes, for best TV documentary, The Confession, 1991; Chairman's Award, BPA, 1991. *Publications:* Blind Eye to Murder, a Pledge Betrayed, 1981; Klaus Barbie, Butcher of Lyons, 1984; The Paperclip Conspiracy, 1987; Maxwell the Outsider, 1988; The Red Web, 1989; Tiny Rowland, a Rebel Tycoon, 1993; The Perfect English Spy, Sir Dick White, 1995; Heroes of World War 2, 1995; Maxwell: the Final Verdict, 1995; Blood Money: the Swiss, the Nazis and the looted billions, 1997; Fayed: the unauthorised biography, 1998; Branson, 2000, reissued, 2008; The Paymaster: Geoffrey Robinson, Maxwell and New Labour, 2001; Broken Dreams: vanity, greed and the souring of British football (William Hill Sports Book of the Year), 2003; Gordon Brown, 2004, reissued as Gordon Brown, Prime Minister, 2007; Conrad & Lady Black: dancing on the edge, 2006. *Recreations:* walking, ski-ing, shooting. *Address:* 10 Thurlow Road, NW3 5PL. *T:* (020) 7435 9776. *Clubs:* Garrick, Beefsteak.

BOWER, Veronica Judith Colleton; *see* Wadley, V. J. C.

BOWERING, Christine, DL; MA; Chairman, Nottingham City Hospital NHS Trust, 1998–2006; Headmistress, Nottingham High School for Girls (GPDST), 1984–96; *b* 30 June 1936; *d* of Kenneth Soper and Florence E. W. Soper; *m* 1960, Rev. John Anthony Bowering; one *s* one *d*. *Educ:* St Bernard's Convent, Westcliff-on-Sea; Newnham Coll., Cambridge (MA). Assistant Teacher: St Bernard's Convent; Ursuline Convent, Brentwood; Sheffield High Sch. (GPDST). Mem., Engineering Council, 1988–91. Dir, Queen's Med. Centre, Nottingham, 1993–98. Chairman: Educn Cttee, GSA, 1989–93; Indep. Schs Curriculum Cttee, 1992–94; Mem., Educn Cttee, Goldsmiths' Co., 1992–. Governor: Nottingham Trent Univ. (formerly Nottingham Poly.), 1989–96 (Mem., 1990–, Chm., 1990–96, Employment Cttee); Minster Sch., Southwell, 2004–. Assoc. Mem., Newnham Coll., Cambridge, 1991–2002. Trustee, Southwell Dio. Council for Family Care, 1998– (Chm., 2007–). FRSA 1994. DL Notts, 2000. Freeman, Goldsmiths' Co., 2005. Hon. DLitt Nottingham, 1996. *Address:* Linthwaite Cottage, Main Street, Kirklington, Newark NG22 8ND. *T:* (01636) 816995, *Fax:* (01636) 813743.

BOWERING, Ven. Michael Ernest; Archdeacon of Lindisfarne, 1987–2000; *b* 25 June 1935; *s* of Hubert James and Mary Elizabeth Bowering; *m* 1962, Aileen (*née* Fox); one *s* two *d*. *Educ:* Barnstaple Grammar Sch.; Kelham Theological Coll.; Univ. of Leeds (MA 2006). Curate: St Oswald, Middlesbrough, 1959–62; Huntington with New Earswick, York, 1962–64; Vicar, Brayton with Barlow, 1964–72; RD of Selby, 1971–72; Vicar, Saltburn by the Sea, 1972–81; Canon Residentiary of York Minster and Secretary for Mission and Evangelism, 1981–87. *Recreation:* crosswords. *Address:* Old Timbers, Westway, Crayke, York YO61 4TE. *T:* (01347) 823682.

BOWERS, John Simon; QC 1998; a Recorder, since 2003; *b* 2 Jan. 1956; *s* of Alfred and Irene Bowers; *m* 1982, Suzanne Franks; one *s* two *d*. *Educ:* Matthew Humberstone Comp. Sch., Cleethorpes; Lincoln Coll., Oxford (MA, BCL). Called to the Bar, Middle Temple, 1979, Bencher, 2004; in practice at the Bar, 1979–. Chairman: Employment Appeal Tribunal Users' Gp, 1995–99; (part-time), Employment Tribunals, 2001–02; Mediator, Centre for Dispute Resolution, 1998–. Chairman: Employment Law Bar Assoc., 2001–03; Bar Disciplinary Tribunal, 2001–; Member: Liaison Cttee, Govt Human Rights Task Force, 1999–2001; Bar Council Race Relations Cttee, 1999–2002; Standards Bd for England, 2000–05. *Publications:* Bowers on Employment Law, 1980, 7th edn 2005; (jtly) Atkin's Court Forms, vol. 38, 1986, 2003; (jtly) Modern Law of Strikes, 1987; Industrial Tribunal Procedure, 1987, 2nd edn, as Employment Tribunal Procedure, 1998; (jtly) The Employment Act 1988, 1988; Termination of Employment, 1988, 3rd edn 1995; (jtly) Transfer of Undertakings: the legal pitfalls, 1989, 6th edn 1996; (jtly) Basic Procedure in Courts and Tribunals, 1990; (jtly) Textbook on Employment Law, 1990, 9th edn 2006; (jtly) Employment Law Update, 1991; Transfer of Undertakings Encyclopaedia, 1998; Whistleblowing: the new law, 2000, 2nd edn 2007; Employment Law and Human Rights, 2000; (contrib.) Bullen & Leake on Pleadings; many articles in legal jls. *Recreations:* walking, football. *Address:* Littleton Chambers, 3 King's Bench Walk, Temple, EC4Y 7HR.

BOWERS, Michael John; Managing Director, Tamoil Shipping Ltd, 1995; *b* 1 Oct. 1933; *s* of Arthur Patrick and Lena Frances Bowers; *m* 1959, Caroline (*née* Clifford); two *d*. *Educ:* Cardinal Vaughan Sch., Kensington. BP Group: various appts in Supply, Distribution Planning and Trading, 1951–73; Vice-Pres. and Dir, BP North America Inc. (NY), 1973–76; Man. Dir and Chief Exec. Officer, BP Gas, 1976–81; Dir, BP Shipping/BP Exploration, 1980–81; Regional Co-ordinator, Western Hemisphere, 1981–83; Chief Exec., International Petroleum Exchange of London Ltd, 1983–85; Man. Dir, TW Oil (UK), 1985–88. *Recreations:* gardening, tennis, bridge, chess.

BOWERS, Peter Hammond; His Honour Judge Bowers; a Circuit Judge, since 1995; *b* 22 June 1945; *s* of Edward Hammond Bowers and Elsie Bowers; *m* 1970, Brenda Janet Burgess; two *s* one *d*. *Educ:* Acklam Hall, Middlesbrough. Admitted solicitor, 1966; in private practice, 1966–70; Prosecuting Solicitor, 1970–72; called to the Bar, Inner Temple, 1972; barrister, N Eastern Circuit, 1972–95. *Recreations:* cricket, aspiring artist, antiques, paintings, armchair sportsman. *Address:* Irving House, Appleton Wiske, Northallerton DL6 2AU.

BOWERS, Roger George, CMG 1997; OBE 1984; PhD; Chief Executive, Trinity College, London, 1998–2006 (Member Council, 1997–98); *b* 23 May 1942; *s* of George Albert Bowers and Hilda Mary Bowers (*née* Wells); *m* 1963, Gweneth Iris Pither (marr. diss.); one *s* one *d*. *Educ:* Royal Grammar Sch., Guildford; Wadham Coll., Oxford (BA); Reading Univ. (MPhil; PhD). Joined British Council, 1964; Tutor to Overseas Students, Univ. of Birmingham, 1965; Asst Regl Dir, Cape Coast, Ghana, 1965–69; seconded to Eng. Lang. Trng Inst., Allahabad, 1971–73; Asst Regl Educ. Advr, Calcutta, 1973–76; Eng. Lang. Consultancies Dept, 1978–80; seconded to Ain Shams Univ., Cairo, 1980–84; Dir, Eng. Lang. Services Dept, 1984–85; Dep. Controller, 1985–89, Controller, then Dir, 1989–93, Eng. Lang. and Lit. Div.; Asst Dir-Gen. (Manchester), and Dir of Professional Services, 1993–96. Director: R. G. Bowers & Associates, 1996–; World of Language Ltd, 1997–. Jt Editor, Cambridge Handbooks for Language Teachers, 1985–92; Member: Editorial Cttee, ELT Documents, 1984–93; Bd of Management, ELT Jl, 1985–96. Mem. Corp., Trinity Coll. of Music, 1999–2006. Trustee, A. S. Hornby Educnl Trust, 1997– (Chm., 2007–). FRSA 1993. Hon. FTCL. *Publications:* In Passing, 1976; Talking About Grammar, 1987; Word Play, 1990. *Recreations:* fishing, cooking, eating. *Address:* 25 Hillbrow, Richmond Hill, Surrey TW10 6BH. *T:* (020) 8948 6342.

BOWERS-BROADBENT, Christopher Joseph St George; organist and composer; *b* 13 Jan. 1945; *s* of Henry W. Bowers-Broadbent and Doris E. Bowers-Broadbent (*née* Mizen); *m* 1970, Deirdre Ann Cape; one *s* one *d*. *Educ:* King's Coll., Cambridge (Chorister); Berkhamsted Sch.; Royal Acad. of Music (Rec.Dip.; FRAM 1983). Organist and Choirmaster, St Pancras Parish Church, 1965–88; début recital, 1966; Organist, W London Synagogue, 1973–; Organist and Choirmaster, Gray's Inn, 1983–. Prof., RAM, 1975–92. Numerous recordings. *Publications include:* numerous sacred and secular compositions; chamber operas: The Pied Piper, 1972; The Seacock Bane, 1979; The Last Man, 1983. *Recreations:* sketching, silence. *Address:* 94 Colney Hatch Lane, N10 1EA. *T:* (020) 8883 1933.

BOWERY, Prof. Norman George, PhD; DSc; FBPharmacolS; Vice President, Biology Verona, GlaxoSmithKline SpA, Italy, since 2004; Professor Emeritus, University of Birmingham, since 2004; *b* 23 June 1944; *s* of George Bowery and Olga (*née* Beevers); *m* 1970, Barbara Joyce (*née* Westcott); one *s* two *d*. *Educ:* Christ's Coll., Finchley; NE Surrey Coll. of Technology; St Bartholomew's Med. Coll., Univ. of London (PhD 1974; DSc 1987). MIBiol 1970. Res. Asst, CIBA Labs, 1963–70; Res. Student, St Bart's Med. Coll., London, 1970–73; Postdoctoral Res. Fellow, Sch. of Pharmacy, London Univ., 1973–75; Lectr in Pharmacology, 1975–82, Sen. Lectr in Pharm., 1982–84, St Thomas's Hosp. Med. Sch.; Section Leader, Neuroscience Res. Centre, Merck, Sharp & Dohme, Harlow, 1984–87; Wellcome Prof. of Pharmacol., Sch. of Pharmacy, London Univ., 1987–95; Prof. of Pharmacol., 1995–2004, Head of Neurosci., 1999–2001, Birmingham Univ.

Pres., British Pharmacol. Soc., 1999–2000. Laurea in pharmacy *hc* Florence, 1992. Biological Council Medal, 1991. *Publications:* Actions and Interactions of GABA and Benzodiazepines, 1984; GABAergic Mechanisms in the Mammalian Periphery, 1986; GABA: basic mechanisms to clinical applications, 1989; $GABA_B$ Receptors in Mammalian Function, 1990; GABA: transport, receptors and metabolism, 1996; The GABA Receptors, 1996. *Recreations:* gardening, socializing, walking, family life. *Address:* GlaxoSmithKline SpA, Medicines Research Centre, Via A. Fleming 4, 37135 Verona, Italy. *T:* (045) 8219829.

BOWES, Michael Anthony; QC 2001; a Recorder, since 2000; *b* 22 Dec. 1956; *s* of late Michael Philip Bowes and of Patricia Bowes; *m* 1987, Amanda Wissler; two *d*. *Educ:* St George's Coll., Weybridge; Manchester Univ. (LLB). Called to the Bar, Middle Temple, 1980, Bencher, 2007; in practice, Western Circuit, 1996–; specialising in criminal law, fraud and financial regulatory work. Dir, Bar Mutual Indemnity Fund Ltd, 1994–. Trustee, Michael Sieff Foundn, 2007–. Gov., Knighton House Sch., Dorset, 2008–. *Recreations:* ski-ing, riding, tennis. *Address:* Outer Temple Chambers, 222 Strand, WC2R 1BA. *T:* (020) 7353 6381.

BOWES, Richard Noel; Deputy Chairman, Willis Faber plc and Chairman, Willis Faber and Dumas, 1985–88, retired; *b* 17 Dec. 1928; *m* 1961, Elizabeth Lyle; one *s* two *d*. *Educ:* Epsom College; Worcester Coll., Oxford (MA). Called to the Bar, Gray's Inn, 1950. RN, 1950–53. Willis Faber and Dumas, 1953–88. *Address:* Fairacre, Enton, Godalming, Surrey GU8 5AQ. *T:* (01483) 416544.

BOWES, Roger Norman; Managing Director, Global Information Management Services Ltd, since 2005; *b* 28 Jan. 1943; *s* of late Russell Ernest Bowes and Sybil Caroline Rose Bowes (*née* Bell); *m* 1st, 1961, Denise Hume Windsor (marr. diss. 1974); one *d*; 2nd, 1977, Ann Rosemary O'Connor (*née* Hamstead) (marr. diss. 1988). *Educ:* Chiswick and Dorking Grammar Schools. Advertisement Executive: Associated Newspapers, 1962–67; IPC/Mirror Gp Newspapers, 1967–70; Marketing Exec./Sales Manager, Mirror Gp, 1970–75; Media Dir, McCann Erickson Advertising, 1976–78; Mirror Gp Newspapers: Adv. Dir, 1978–81; Dep. Chief Exec., 1982–83; Chief Exec., 1984; Man. Dir, Guinness Enterprises, 1985; Chief Executive: Express Gp Newspapers, 1985–86; Aslib, 1989–2004; Chm., Citybridge, 1987–97. Mem., Europ. Council of Information Assocs. FRSA 1994. *Recreations:* political and military history, cookery, architectural restoration, classic cars. *Address:* (office) Holywell Centre, 1 Phipp Street, EC2A 4PS. *T:* (020) 7613 3031, *Fax:* (020) 7613 5080.

BOWES LYON, family name of **Earl of Strathmore**.

BOWES LYON, Sir Simon (Alexander), KCVO 2005; FCA; director of investment companies; Lord-Lieutenant of Hertfordshire, 1986–2007; *b* 17 June 1932; *s* of Hon. Sir David Bowes Lyon, KCVO, and Rachel Bowes Lyon (*née* Spender Clay) (*d* 1996); *m* 1966, Caroline, *d* of Rt Rev. Victor Pike, CB, CBE, DD, and of Dorothea Pike; three *s* one *d*. *Educ:* Eton; Magdalen Coll., Oxford (BA). Hon. LLD Herts, 2007. KStJ 1997. *Recreations:* botany, gardening, shooting, music. *Address:* St Paul's Walden Bury, Hitchin, Herts SG4 8BP. *T:* (01438) 871218, *Fax:* (01438) 871341; *e-mail:* spw@boweslyon.demon.co.uk.

BOWETT, Sir Derek (William), Kt 1998; CBE 1983; QC 1978; LLD; FBA 1983; Whewell Professor of International Law, Cambridge University, 1981–91; Professorial Fellow of Queens' College, Cambridge, 1982–91 (Hon. Fellow, 1991); *b* 20 April 1927; *s* of Arnold William Bowett and Marion Wood; *m* 1953, Betty Northall; two *s* one *d*. *Educ:* William Hulme's Sch., Manchester; Downing Coll., Cambridge. MA, LLB, LLD (Cantab), PhD (Manchester). Called to the Bar, Middle Temple, 1953, Hon. Bencher, 1975. Lectr, Law Faculty, Manchester Univ. 1951–59; Legal Officer, United Nations, New York, 1957–59; Cambridge University: Lectr, Law Faculty, 1960–76, Reader, 1976–81; Fellow of Queens' Coll., 1960–69, President 1969–82. Gen. Counsel, UNRWA, Beirut, 1966–68. Member: Royal Commn on Environmental Pollution, 1973–77; Internat. Law Commn, 1991–96. Commander, Order of Dannebrog (Denmark), 1993; Grand Cross, Civil Order, Jose Cecilio del Valle (Honduras), 1993; White Cross (Slovakia), 2005. *Publications:* Self-defence in International Law, 1958; Law of International Institutions, 1964; United Nations Forces, 1964; Law of the Sea, 1967; Search for Peace, 1972; Legal Régime of Islands in International Law, 1978; The International Court of Justice: process, practice and procedure, 1997. *Recreation:* music. *Address:* 228 Hills Road, Cambridge CB2 2QE. *T:* (01223) 210688.

BOWEY, Prof. Angela Marilyn, PhD; Director, Glassencyclopedia.com and Glasstime.com, since 1997; Professor of Business Administration, Strathclyde Business School, University of Strathclyde, Glasgow, 1976–87; *b* 20 Oct. 1940; *d* of Jack Nicholas Peterson and Kathleen (*née* Griffin); *m* 1st, 1960, Miklos Papp; two *s* one *d*; 2nd, 1965, Gregory Bowey (marr. diss. 1980); one *s* one *d*; 3rd, 2001, Andrew William John Thomson, *qv*. *Educ:* Withington Girls Sch., Manchester; Univ. of Manchester (BA Econ, PhD). Technical Asst, Nuclear Power Gp, 1961–62; Asst Lectr, Elizabeth Gaskell Coll. of Educn, 1967–68; Manchester Business School: Res. Associate, 1968–69; Res. Fellow, 1969–72; Lectr, 1972–76; Dir, Pay Advice Res. Centre, Glasgow, 1977–86, Gibraltar, 1987–97. Vis. Professor: Admin. Staff Coll. of India, 1975; Western Australian Inst. of Technology, 1976; Univ. of WA, 1977; Prahran Coll. of Advanced Educn, Australia, 1978; Massey Univ., NZ, 1978. ACAS Arbitrator, 1977–92; Dir, Pay and Rewards Res. Centre, 1978–85; Comr, Equal Opportunities Commn, 1980–86; Member: Scottish Econ. Council, 1980–83; Police Adv. Bd (Scotland) (formerly Adv. Panel on Police), 1983–88. Gov., Scottish Police Coll., 1985–88. Dir, Paihia Gym Ltd, 1993–. Chm., Glass Mus. Trust, Paihia, NZ, 1994–. Editor, Management Decision, 1979–82. Website Ed., Paperweight Collectors' Assoc. Inc., USA, 2007–. *Publications:* Job and Pay Comparisons (with Tom Lupton), 1973, 2nd edn 1974; A Guide to Manpower Planning, 1974, 2nd edn 1977; (with Tom Lupton) Wages and Salaries, 1974, 2nd edn 1982; Handbook of Salary and Wage Systems, 1975, 2nd edn 1982; The Sociology of Organisations, 1976; (with Richard Thorpe and Phil Hellier) Payment Systems and Productivity, 1986; Managing Salary and Wage Systems, 1987; (jtly) Bagley Glass, 2004, 2nd edn 2005; New Zealand Glass, 2005; articles in Brit. Jl of Indust. Relations, Jl of Management Studies, and Management Decision. *Address:* Paihia, Bay of Islands, New Zealand. *Clubs:* Auckland, Rotary (Bay of Islands); Waitangi Golf (New Zealand).

BOWEY, Olwyn, RA 1975 (ARA 1970); practising artist (painter); *b* 10 Feb. 1936; *o d* of James and Olive Bowey. *Educ:* West Hartlepool Sch. of Art; Royal Coll. of Art. One-man shows: Zwemmer Gall., 1961; New Grafton Gall., 1969; also exhibited at Leicester Gall., Royal Academy; work purchased through Chantrey Bequest for Tate Gall., Royal Academy, Min. of Works, etc.

BOWHAY, Rosalind Louise; *see* Smyth, R. L.

BOWIE, Rev. (Alexander) Glen, CBE 1984; Principal Chaplain (Church of Scotland and Free Churches), Royal Air Force, 1980–84, retired; *b* 10 May 1928; *s* of Alexander

Bowie and Annie (*née* McGhie); *m* 1st, 1952, Mary McKillop (*d* 1991); two *d*; 2nd, 2002, Jean Lawson. *Educ:* Stevenston High Sch.; Irvine Royal Acad.; Glasgow Univ. (BSc 1951; Dip Theol 1954); BA Open Univ., 1977. Nat. Service, RAF, 1947–49. Assistant, Beith High Church, 1952–54; ordained, 1954; entered RAF Chaplains' Br., 1955; served: RAF Padgate, 1955–56; Akrotiri, 1956–59; Stafford, 1959–61; Butzweilerhof, 1961–64; Halton, 1964–67; Akrotiri, 1967–70; RAF Coll., Cranwell, 1970–75; Asst Principal Chaplain, 1975; HQ Germany, 1975–76; HQ Support Comd, 1976–80. Officiating Chaplain, RAF Brampton and RAF Wyton, 1985–; Acting Chaplain to Moderator of Church of Scotland, in London, 1985–99; Moderator, Ch of Scotland Presbytery of England, 1988–89. QHC 1980–84; Hon. Chaplain, Royal Scottish Corp., 1981–2001. Editor, Scottish Forces Bulletin, 1985–95. *Recreations:* oil painting, travel, leading Holy Land tours. *Address:* 16 Weir Road, Hemingford Grey, Huntingdon, Cambs PE28 9EH. *T:* (01480) 381425. *Club:* Royal Air Force.

BOWIE, David; international recording artist and performer; film and stage actor; video and film producer; graphic designer; *b* 8 Jan. 1947; *s* of Hayward Stenton Jones and late Margaret Mary Burns; *m* (marr. diss.); one *s*; *m* 1992, Iman Abdul Majid; one *d*. *Educ:* Stansfield Road Sch., Brixton. Artiste from age of 16; many major recordings, 1970–, and video productions, 1979–; numerous live musical stage performances; guest appearances on television shows. Actor: *films:* The Man who Fell to Earth, 1976; Just a Gigolo, 1978; The Hunger, 1982; Merry Christmas, Mr Lawrence, 1983; Ziggy Stardust and the Spiders from Mars, 1983; Absolute Beginners, 1986; Labyrinth, 1986; Into the Night; The Last Temptation of Christ, 1988; The Linguini Incident, 1990; Basquiat, 1997; The Prestige, 2006; *stage:* The Elephant Man, New York, 1980; *television:* Baal, 1982. Recipient of internat. music and entertainment awards. *Recreations:* painting, ski-ing. *Address:* c/o Isolar, Suite 220, 641 5th Avenue, New York, NY 10022, USA.

BOWIE, Rev. Glen; *see* Bowie, Rev. A. G.

BOWIE, Graham Maitland, CBE 1992; Chief Executive, Lothian Regional Council, 1986–94; *b* 11 Nov. 1931; *s* of John Graham Bowie and Agnes Bowie; *m* 1962, Maureen Jennifer O'Sullivan; one *s* two *d*. *Educ:* Alloa Academy; Univ. of St Andrews (MA); Univ. of Glasgow (LLB). National Service, 1956–58. Asst Sec., Glasgow Chamber of Commerce, 1958–60; Product Planner, Ford Motor Co., 1960–64; Edinburgh Corp. Educn Dept, 1964–69; ILEA, 1969–75; Dir of Policy Planning, Lothian Regional Council, 1975–86. Mem., Nat. Lotteries Charities Bd, 1994–97. *Recreations:* walking, travel, the arts. *Address:* 8 Keith Crescent, Edinburgh EH4 3NH.

BOWIS, John Crocket, OBE 1981; Member (C) London Region, European Parliament, since 1999; *b* 2 Aug. 1945; *s* of late Thomas Palin Bowis and Georgiana Joyce (*née* Crocket); *m* 1968, Caroline May (*née* Taylor); two *s* one *d*. *Educ:* Tonbridge Sch.; Brasenose Coll., Oxford (MA). Tutor, Cumberland Lodge, Windsor Great Park, 1966–67; Cons. Party Agent, Peterborough, Derby, Harborough and Blaby, 1968–72; Conservative Central Office: National Organiser, Fedn of Cons. Students, 1972–75; Nat. Organiser, Cons. Trade Unionists, 1975–79; Dir of Community Affairs, 1979–81; Campaign Dir, 1981–82, Public Affairs Dir, 1983–87, British Insurance Brokers Assoc.; Press and Parly Consultant, Nat. Fedn of Self-employed and Small Firms, 1982–83. Councillor (C) Royal Bor. of Kingston upon Thames, 1982–86 (Chm. of Educn, 1985–86). MP (C) Battersea, 1987–97; contested (C) same seat, 1997. PPS to Minister for Local Govt and Inner Cities, DoE, 1989–90, to Sec. of State for Wales, 1990–93; Parly Under-Sec. of State, DoH, 1993–96, Dept of Transport, 1996–97. Mem., Select Cttee on Members' Interests, 1987–90; Vice-Chm., All Party Gp on Social Sci., 1988–93; Chm., All Party Somali Gp, 1991–97. Secretary: Cons. Inner Cities Cttee, 1987–89; Cons. Educn Cttee, 1988–89; Cons. Arts and Heritage Cttee, 1988–89; Parliamentary Adviser to: ACFHE, 1987–93; Assoc. for Coll. Management, 1990–93; ATL (formerly AMMA), 1992–93. European Parliament: Party spokesman on envmt, health and consumer affairs, 1999–; Rapporteur: on food safety, 2000–01; on health and enlargement, 2000–04; on European Centre for Disease Control, 2005–; on patient mobility, 2005–; on mental health, 2006–; Dep. Leader, Cons. MEPs, 2002–04. Chm., Nat. Council for Civil Protection, 1992–93. Internat. Policy Advr to WHO at Inst. of Psychiatry, 1997–; Board Member: Inst. of Psychiatry, 1997–; Internat. Social Service, 1997–2000; Internat. Inst. for Special Needs Offenders, 1998–; Churches Educn and Develt Partnership for SA, 1998–; SANE and Saneline, 2000–; European Men's Health Forum, 2001–. Trustee and Vice-President: Share Community, 1990–; Nat. Aids Trust, 1997–; Epilepsy Res. Foundn, 1997–; Mosaic Clubhouse, 1997–; President: Torche, 1999–; Battersea Cons. Assoc., 2000–. Director: Battersea Arts Centre, 1991–99; Royal Nat. Theatre, 1992–95; South Bank Centre, 1992–95; Royal Acad. of Dancing, 1992–99. Fellow, Industry and Parlt Trust, 1992. Hon. FRCPsych 2003. *Recreations:* theatre, music, art, sport. *Address:* PO Box 262, New Malden KT3 4WJ. *Fax:* (020) 8395 7463; *e-mail:* johnbowis@aol.com.

BOWKER, Prof. John Westerdale; Hon. Canon of Canterbury Cathedral, since 1985; Adjunct Professor of Religion, North Carolina State University, since 1986; Adjunct Professor of Religious Studies, University of Pennsylvania, since 1986; *b* 30 July 1935; *s* of Gordon Westerdale Bowker and Marguerite (*née* Burdick); *m* 1963, Margaret Roper; one *s*. *Educ:* St John's Sch., Leatherhead; Worcester Coll., Oxford (MA); Ripon Hall, Oxford. National Service, RWAFF, N Nigeria, 1953–55. Henry Stephenson Fellow, Sheffield Univ., 1961; Deacon, St Augustine's, Brocco Bank, Sheffield, 1961; Priest and Dean of Chapel, Corpus Christi Coll., Cambridge, 1962; Asst Lectr, 1965, Lectr, 1970, Univ. of Cambridge; Prof. of Religious Studies, Univ. of Lancaster, 1974–85; Dean, 1984–91 and Fellow, 1984–93, Trinity Coll., Cambridge. Gresham Prof. of Divinity, 1992–97; Fellow, Gresham Coll., London, 1997. Lectures: Wilde, Univ. of Oxford, 1972–75; Staley, Rollins Coll., Florida, 1978–79; Public, Univ. of Cardiff, 1984; Riddell, Newcastle Univ., 1985; Boutwood, Univ. of Cambridge, 1985; Harris Meml, Toronto, 1986; Boardman, Univ. of Pa, 1988; Montefiore, Univ. of Southampton, 1989; Scott Holland, London Univ., 1989; Bicentenary, Univ. of Georgetown, Washington, 1989; Heslington, York, 1997; Member: Durham Commn on Religious Educn, 1967–70; Root Commn on Marriage and Divorce, 1967–71; Archbps' Commn on Doctrine, 1977–86; Patron, Marriage Research Inst.; Hon. Pres., Stauros; Vice-President: Inst. on Religion in an Age of Science, 1980; Culture and Animals Foundn, 1984–92; Pres., Christian Action on AIDS, 1987–91. *Publications:* The Targums and Rabbinic Literature, 1969, 2nd edn 1979; Problems of Suffering in Religions of the World, 1970, 3rd edn 1987; Jesus and the Pharisees, 1973; The Sense of God, 1973, 2nd edn 1995; The Religious Imagination and the Sense of God, 1978; Uncle Bolpenny Tries Things Out, 1973; Worlds of Faith, 1983; (ed) Violence and Aggression, 1983; Licensed Insanities: religions and belief in God in the contemporary world, 1987; The Meanings of Death, 1991 (HarperCollins Religious Book Prize, 1993); A Year to Live, 1991; Hallowed Ground: the religious poetry of place, 1993; (ed jtly) Themes in Religious Studies, 1994; Voices of Islam, 1995; Is God a Virus? Genes, Culture and Religion, 1995; World Religions, 1997; The Oxford Dictionary of World Religions, 1997; The Complete Bible Handbook: an illustrated companion, 1998 (Benjamin Franklin Award, 1999); The Concise Oxford Dictionary of World Religions, 2000; The Cambridge Illustrated History of Religions, 2002; God: a brief history, 2002; The Sacred Neuron, 2005; Beliefs that Changed the World, 2007. *Recreations:* books, painting, poetry. *Address:* 14 Bowers Croft, Cambridge CB1 8RP.

BOWKER, (Steven) Richard, CBE 2005; FCILT; FCMA; Chief Executive, National Express Group plc, since 2006; *b* 23 April 1966; *s* of Roger William Bowker and Dr Sylvia Grace Bowker; *m* 2002, Madeline Victoria Ivemy; two *s*. *Educ:* Queen Elizabeth's Grammar Sch., Blackburn; Univ. of Leicester (BA 2nd Cl. Hons Econs and Econ. and Social Hist. 1988). ACMA 1993, FCMA 2003; FCILT (FCIT, FILT 2001). Manager, London Underground Ltd, 1989–96; Principal, Babcock & Brown Ltd, 1996–99; Dir, Quasar Associates Ltd, 1999–2000; Gp Commercial Dir, Virgin Gp, 2000–01; Co-Chm., Virgin Rail Gp Ltd, 2000–01 (non-exec. Dir, 1999–2001); Dir, Virgin Atlantic Airways, 2000–01; Chm. and Chief Exec., Strategic Rail Authy, 2001–04; Chief Exec., Partnerships for Schs, 2005–06. Non-exec. Dir, British Waterways, 2004–. Mem., Internat. Adv. Council, Assoc. of MBAs, 2003–07. Mem. Bd, Countryside Alliance, 2006–. Vice-Pres., London Internat. Piano Competition, 2002–. Trustee, Settle & Carlisle Railway Trust, 2004–; Dep. Pres., Heritage Railway Assoc., 2005–. CCMI (CIMgt 2003); FRSA 2006. *Recreations:* hill walking, piano, canal boating, wine, Blackburn Rovers FC. *Address:* National Express Group plc, 7 Triton Square, NW1 3MG. *T:* (020) 7506 4321.

BOWKETT, Alan John; venture capitalist and organic farmer; *b* 6 Jan. 1951; *er s* of John and Margaret Bowkett; *m* 1975, Joy Dianne Neale; three *s* two *d*. *Educ:* King Charles I Grammar Sch., Kidderminster; University College London (BSc Econ); London Business Sch. (MSc Econ). Corporate Planning Manager, Lex Service, 1977–83; Corporate Develt Manager, BET, 1983–85; Man. Dir, Boulton & Paul, 1985–87; Chief Executive: United Precision Industries, 1987–91; Berisford Internat., then Berisford plc, 1992–99. Director: Anglian Group, 1992–94; Pallasinvest SA (Luxembourg), 1992–98; Greene King, 1993–2006 (Chm., Audit Cttee, 1997–2006); Chairman: Calder Gp Ltd, 1994–96; Acordis BV, 2000–04; Metzeler APS SA, 2000–05; Redrow plc, 2007–. Councillor (C) London Borough of Ealing, 1978–82 (Chm., Social Services); Dep. Chm., Ealing Acton Cons. Assoc., 1982–84. Council Mem., UEA, 1988–94 (Treasurer, 1990–94; Hon. Fellow, 1997). FRSA 1993. *Recreations:* growing vegetables, shooting, opera, Italy, listening to Archers. *Club:* Carlton.

BOWLBY, Prof. Rachel Helena, FBA 2007; Lord Northcliffe Professor of Modern English Literature, University College London, since 2004; *b* 29 Jan. 1957; *d* of Rt Rev. Ronald Oliver Bowlby, *qv*; two *d*. *Educ:* St Anne's Coll., Oxford (1st Cl. Hon. Mods Latin and Greek Lit. 1977; BA 1st Cl. Hons English 1979); Yale Univ. (PhD Comparative Lit. 1983). University of Sussex: Lectr in English, 1984–90; Sen. Lectr, 1990–92; Reader, 1992–94; Prof., 1994–97; Oxford University: Fellow, St Hilda's Coll., 1997–99; Prof. of English, 1998–99; Prof. of English and Related Lit., Univ. of York, 1999–2004. *Publications:* Just Looking, 1985; Virginia Woolf, 1988; Still Crazy After All These Years: women, writing and psychoanalysis, 1992; Shopping with Freud, 1993; Feminist Destinations and Further Essays on Virginia Woolf, 1997; Carried Away: the invention of modern shopping, 2000; Freudian Mythologies: Greek tragedy and modern identities, 2007. *Address:* Department of English, University College London, Gower Street, WC1E 6BT. *T:* (020) 7679 3138; *e-mail:* r.bowlby@ucl.ac.uk.

BOWLBY, Sir Richard Peregrine Longstaff, 3rd Bt *cr* 1923, of Manchester Square, St Marylebone; *b* 11 Aug. 1941; *s* of Edward John Mostyn Bowlby, CBE, MD (*d* 1990), 2nd *s* of Sir Anthony Alfred Bowlby, 1st Bt, KCB, KCMG, KCVO, and Ursula, *d* of Dr T. G. Longstaff; *S* uncle, 1993; *m* 1963, Xenia, *o d* of R. P. A. Garrett; one *s* one *d*. *Heir: s* Benjamin Bowlby [*b* 2 Nov. 1966; *m* 1992, Mylanna Sophia, *er d* of M. C. Colyer; two *s* one *d*]. *Address:* Boundary House, Wyldes Close, NW11 7JB.

BOWLBY, Rt Rev. Ronald Oliver; Assistant Bishop, Diocese of Lichfield, since 1991; *b* 16 Aug. 1926; *s* of Oliver and Helena Bowlby; *m* 1956, Elizabeth Trevelyan Monro; three *s* two *d*. *Educ:* Eton Coll.; Trinity College, Oxford (MA; Hon. Fellow, 1991); Westcott House, Cambridge. Curate of St Luke's, Pallion, Sunderland, 1952–56; Priest-in-charge and Vicar of St Aidan, Billingham, 1956–66; Vicar of Croydon, 1966–72; Bishop of: Newcastle, 1973–80; Southwark, 1980–91. Chairman: Hospital Chaplaincies Council, 1975–82; Social Policy Cttee, Bd for Social Responsibility, 1986–90; Mem., Anglican Consultative Council, 1977–85. President: Nat. Fedn of Housing Assocs, 1988–94; Churches' Nat. Housing Coalition, 1991–94. Hon. Fellow, Newcastle upon Tyne Polytechnic, 1980. *Publications:* contrib. Church without Walls, ed Lindars, 1969; contrib. Church and Politics Today, ed Moyser, 1985. *Recreations:* walking, gardening, history. *Address:* 4 Uppington Avenue, Shrewsbury SY3 7JL.

See also R. H. Bowlby.

BOWLER, Geoffrey, FCIS; Chief General Manager, Sun Alliance & London Insurance Group, 1977–87; *b* 11 July 1924; *s* of James Henry Bowler and Hilda May Bowler. *Educ:* Sloane Sch., Chelsea. FCIS 1952. Dir, British Aviation Insurance Co., 1976–87 (Chm., 1977–83). Dep. Chm., British Insurance Assoc., 1977, Chm. 1979–80. *Address:* 13 Green Lane, Purley, Surrey CR8 3PP. *T:* (020) 8660 0756.

BOWLER, Ian John, CBE 1971 (OBE 1957); Chairman, International Management & Engineering Group Ltd, 1973 (Managing Director, 1964–68); *b* 1920; *s* of Major John Arthur Bowler; *m* 1963, Hamideh, *d* of Prince Yadollah Azodi, GCMG; two *d*, and one step *s* one step *d*. *Educ:* King's Sch., Worcester; privately; Oxford Univ. Director of Constructors, John Brown, 1961–64; Pres., Iranian Management & Engrg Gp, 1965. Director: IMEG (Offshore) Ltd, 1974–; MMC Gas, Kuala Lumpur. Mem., RNLI, 1983–. Sec., Azerbaijan Foundn, 1992. MInstPet. *Publication:* Predator Birds of Iran, 1973. *Recreations:* ornithology, yachting. *Clubs:* Royal Thames Yacht, Ocean Cruising; S.R.R. (La Rochelle, France).

BOWLER, Prof. Peter John, PhD; FBA 2004; Professor of the History of Science, Queen's University, Belfast, since 1992; *b* 8 Oct. 1944; *s* of Wallace Bowler and Florence Edith Bowler (*née* Moon); *m* 1966, Sheila Mary Holt; one *s* one *d*. *Educ:* King's Coll., Cambridge (BA 1966, MA 1971); Univ. of Sussex (MSc 1967); Univ. of Toronto (PhD 1971). Lectr in Humanities, Science Univ. of Malaysia, Penang, 1972–75; Asst Prof. of Hist., Univ. of Winnipeg, 1975–79; Lectr, 1979–87, Reader, 1987–92, in Hist. and the Philos. of Sci., Queen's Univ., Belfast. MRIA 1993. *Publications:* The Eclipse of Darwinism, 1983, 2nd edn 1992; The Non-Darwinian Revolution, 1988; The Invention of Progress, 1990; Charles Darwin: the man and his influence, 1990; The Fontana History of the Environmental Sciences, 1992; Life's Splendid Drama, 1996; Reconciling Science and Religion, 2001. *Recreations:* collecting antiquarian science books, walking (when I can find the time). *Address:* School of History and Anthropology, Queen's University, Belfast BT7 1NN. *T:* (028) 9097 3882, *Fax:* (028) 9097 3700; *e-mail:* p.bowler@qub.ac.uk.

BOWLER, Tim(othy); writer; *b* 14 Nov. 1953; *yr s* of Norman and Doreen Bowler; *m* 1977, Rachel. *Educ:* Chalkwell Hall Primary Sch.; Westcliff High Sch. for Boys; Univ. of E Anglia (BA Hons Swedish and Scandinavian Studies); Kingston Poly. (PGCE French and German). Forester, 1977; EFL teacher, 1978–79; timber salesman, 1979–82; French and German teacher, 1983–90; Swedish translator, 1990–97; full-time writer, 1997–.

Talks on writing, workshops and radio appearances. 12 book awards, both regl and from USA and Europe. *Publications:* Midget, 1994; Dragon's Rock, 1995; River Boy, 1997 (Carnegie Medal, 1998); Shadows, 1999; Storm Catchers, 2001; Starseeker, 2002; Apocalypse, 2004; Blood on Snow, 2004; Walking with the Dead, 2005; Frozen Fire, 2006; Bloodchild, 2008; Blade series: Playing Dead, Book 1, 2008, Closing In, Book 2, 2008, Breaking Free, Book 3, 2009, Running Scared, Book 4, 2009. *Recreations:* reading poetry, listening to music, playing piano and accordion, walking, thinking, dreaming, meditating, playing squash, going to theatre, ballet and cinema, translating Swedish, being with friends, being alone, holding hands with my wife. *Address:* c/o David Higham Associates, 5–8 Lower John Street, Golden Square, W1R 4HA; *e-mail:* tim@timbowler.co.uk; *web:* www.timbowler.co.uk.

BOWLES, Prof. Dianna Joy, OBE 2003; PhD; Weston Professor of Biochemistry, and Director, Centre for Novel Agricultural Products, University of York, since 2001; *b* 1 May 1948; *d* of Bertie James Bowles and Cicely (*née* Mee). *Educ:* Univ. of Newcastle upon Tyne (BSc Hons 1970); New Hall, Cambridge (PhD 1973). Research Fellow: Univ. of Kaiserslautern, 1973–75; Univ. of Regensburg, 1975; Weizmann Inst., 1976; Univ. of Cambridge, 1976–77; EMBL, 1978; University of Leeds, 1979–93, Prof., 1991–93; Prof. of Biochemistry and Co-Founder, Plant Lab., Univ. of York, 1994–2000. Scientific Advr, Ownership Bd, MAFF Central Science Lab., 1995–2001. Member: ODA Scientific Adv. Gp, Plant Scis Prog., 1993–97; BBSRC Cttees, 1995–2000; EU Framework 5 External Adv. Gp, 1998–2002. Founder, 2001, Chm. Bd of Trustees, 2002–, Heritage GeneBank, subseq. Sheep Trust. Founding Ed., and Ed.-in-Chief, Plant Jl, 1991–2002. *Publications:* articles in jls. *Recreations:* Upper Nidderdale, Wasdale Head, Herdwick sheep. *Address:* CNAP, Department of Biology (Area 8), University of York, PO Box 373, York YO10 5YW.

BOWLES, Godfrey Edward; Managing Director, Pearl Group, 1989–94; *b* 21 Dec. 1935; *s* of Llewellyn Crowley Bowles and Florence Jane Edwards; *m* 1958, Elizabeth Madge Dunning; two *s* two *d.* *Educ:* Commonweal Grammar Sch., Swindon; Exeter Coll., Oxford (MA). Emigrated to Australia, 1959; joined Australian Mutual Provident Society: Dep. Manager, Wellington, NZ, 1976; Manager, WA Br., Perth, 1980; Manager, Victoria Br., Melbourne, 1983; Chief Manager, Corporate Services, Sydney, 1986; Gen. Manager, AMP Corporate, Sydney, 1988; returned to UK after acquisition of Pearl Gp by AMP Soc., 1989. Dir, Royal Liver Assce Ltd. Chairman: Gtr Peterborough Partnership; ASBAH. *Recreations:* running, cycling, reading, music, theatre, cinema.

BOWLES, Peter; actor; *b* 16 Oct. 1936; *s* of Herbert Reginald Bowles and Sarah Jane (*née* Harrison); *m* 1961, Susan Alexandra Bennett; two *s* one *d.* *Educ:* High Pavement Grammar Sch., Nottingham; RADA (schol.; Kendal Prize 1955). London début in Romeo and Juliet, Old Vic, 1956; *theatre* includes: Happy Haven, Platonov, Royal Court, 1960; Bonne Soupe, Wyndham's, 1961; Afternoon Men, Arts, 1962; Absent Friends, Garrick, 1975; Dirty Linen, Arts, 1976; Born in the Gardens, Globe, 1980; Some of My Best Friends Are Husbands, nat. tour, 1985; The Entertainer, Shaftesbury, 1986; Canaries Sometimes Sing, Albery, 1987; Man of the Moment, Globe, 1990; Otherwise Engaged (also dir), nat. tour, 1992; Separate Tables, Albery, 1993; Pygmalion, Chichester, 1994; Present Laughter, nat. tour, 1994, Aldwych, 1996; In Praise of Love, Apollo, 1995; Gangster No 1, Almeida, 1995; The School for Wives, Piccadilly, 1997; Major Barbara, The Misanthrope, Piccadilly, 1998; Sleuth, tour, 1999; Hedda Gabler, tour, 1999; The Beau, The Royal Family, Th. Royal, Haymarket, 2001; Sleuth, Apollo, 2002; Our Song, nat. tour, 2003; Wait Until Dark, Garrick, 2003; The Old Masters, Comedy, 2004; The Unexpected Man, nat. tour, 2005; Joe & I, King's Head, 2005; Hay Fever, Th. Royal, Haymarket, 2006; The Waltz of the Toreadors, Chichester, 2007; Relatively Speaking, nat. tour, 2008; *films* include: Blow Up, 1966; The Charge of the Light Brigade, 1967; Laughter in the Dark, 1968; A Day in the Death of Joe Egg, 1970; The Steal, 1994; The Hollywood Ten, 2000; Gangster No 1 (Exec. Producer); Colour Me Kubrick, 2004; Freebird, 2008; The Bank Job, 2008; *TV films* include: Shadow on the Sun, 1988; Running Late (also co-prod), 1992; Little White Lies, 1998; Love and War in the Apennines, 2001; Ballet Shoes, 2007; *television series* include: Rumpole of the Bailey, 1976–92; To the Manor Born, 1979–82, 2007; Only when I Laugh, 1979–82; The Bounder, 1982–83; The Irish RM, 1983–85; Lytton's Diary, 1984–86 (also co-created series); Executive Stress, 1987–88; Perfect Scoundrels, 1990–92 (also co-created series); Jericho, 2005. Comedy Actor of the Year, Pye Awards, 1984; ITV Personality of the Year, Variety Club of GB, 1984. Hon. DLitt Nottingham Trent, 2002. *Recreations:* British art, physical jerks. *Address:* c/o Conway Van Gelder Grant Ltd, 18–21 Jermyn Street, SW1Y 6HP.

BOWLES, Sharon Margaret; Member (Lib Dem) South East Region, European Parliament, since May 2005; *b* 12 June 1953; *d* of Percy Bowles and Florence Bowles (*née* Sutcliffe); *m* 1981, Andrew Horton; two *s.* *Educ:* Our Lady's Convent, Abingdon; Univ. of Reading (BSc Hons Chem. Physics with Maths 1974); Lady Margaret Hall, Oxford (res. into semiconductors). Chartered Patent Attorney; European Patent Attorney. Trng as patent agent, 1978–81; in practice as Patent Attorney and Trade Mark Attorney, 1981–, founded professional practice, subseq. Bowles Horton partnership, 1981. Contested (Lib Dem): Aylesbury, 1992, 1997, Parly elecns; Buckinghamshire and Oxford East, 1994, South East Reg., 1999, 2004, EP elecns. European Parliament: Member: Cttee on Econ. and Monetary Affairs, 2005–; Cttee of Inq. into collapse of Equitable Life Assce Soc., 2006–; Delegn for relns with countries of SE Asia and ASEAN, 2005–. Liberal Democrats: Sec., Chilterns Reg., 1990–95; Co-Chm., Internat Relns Cttee, 2002–06. Vice President: ELDR, 2004–; Liberal Internat., 2005–07. *Recreation:* music. *Address:* Felden House, Dower Mews, High Street, Berkhamsted, Herts HP4 2BL. *T:* (01442) 875962, *Fax:* (01442) 872860; *e-mail:* info@sharonbowles.org.uk. *Club:* National Liberal.

BOWLES, Timothy John; Master of the Supreme Court (Chancery Division), since 1999; *b* 20 March 1951; *s* of late Arthur Ernest Bowles and of Elizabeth Mary Bowles; *m* 1987, Michelle Martine Riley; two *s.* *Educ:* Downside Sch.; Durham Univ. FCIArb 1994. Called to the Bar, Gray's Inn, 1973 (Mould Schol.); in practice at the Bar, 1973–99; Dep. Chancery Master, 1996–99. Legal Chairman: South and South Eastern Rent Assessment Panel, 1994–2001; London Rent Assessment Panel, 1997–2001; Dep. Chm., Agricl Land Tribunal, 1995–. Gov., King Edward VI Grammar Sch. (The Royal Grammar Sch.), Guildford, 2001–04. *Publication:* (ed) Civil Court Practice, annually 2001–. *Recreations:* sailing, cricket. *Address:* Royal Courts of Justice, Strand, WC2A 2LL. *Clubs:* Bar Yacht; St Mawes Sailing; Merrow Cricket.

BOWLEY, Martin Richard; QC 1981; a Recorder of the Crown Court, 1979–88; *b* 29 Dec. 1936; *s* of late Charles Colin Stuart Bowley and Mary Evelyn Bowley; partner, 1976, Julian Marquez Bedoya (*d* 1990). *Educ:* Magdalen Coll. Sch., Oxford; Queen's Coll., Oxford (Styring Exhibnr, 1955; MA; BCL 1961). National Service, 1955–57: commnd Pilot Officer as a Fighter Controller; served 2nd Tactical Air Force, 1956–57. Called to the Bar, Inner Temple, 1962 (Bencher, 1994; Master of the Revels, 2002–); Midland and Oxford Circuit, 1963–2002; Member: Senate and Bar Council, 1985–86; Gen. Council of Bar, 1987–88, 1989–94 (Treas., 1992–94); Chm., Bar Cttee, 1987. Dir, Barco, 2001–05. Member: Lord Chancellor's Standing Commn on Efficiency, 1986–87; Marre Cttee on Future of Legal Profession, 1987–88; Home Office Steering Gp on Sexual Offences Law Reform, 1999–2000; CPS Wkg Pty on Prosecuting Homophobic Hate Crimes, 2002. Pres., Bar Lesbian and Gay Gp, 1994–. Stonewall Lectr, 1994. Chm., Questors Theatre, 1972–84 and 1988–93 (Sec., 1963–72); Mem. Standing Cttee, Little Theatre Guild of GB, 1974–84 (Vice-Chm., 1979–81, Chm., 1981–84; Hon. Associate, 1997). Mem., Stonewall Gp, 1999–. Mem. Editl Bd, Counsel, 1992–. *Publications:* (contrib.) Advising Gay and Lesbian Clients, 1999; contrib. to nat. and legal periodicals. *Recreations:* playing at theatre, watching cricket, island hopping, supporting Stonewall and Terrence Higgins Trust. *Address:* Flat E, 23/24 Great James Street, WC1N 3ES. *T:* (020) 7831 1674. *Clubs:* Garrick, MCC, Surrey CC; Questors.

BOWLING, Frank, RA 2005; artist; *b* 29 Feb. 1936; *s* of Richard Sheridan Bowling and Agatha Elizabeth Franklin Bowling; partner, Rachel Scott; two *s* (and one *s* decd). *Educ:* Royal Coll. of Art (ARCA); Slade Sch., Univ. of London. Tutor, Camberwell Sch. of Arts and Crafts, 1968–83; Lectr, Reading Univ., 1964–66; Instructor, Columbia Univ., NY, 1968–69; Assistant Professor: Douglass Coll., Rutgers Univ., NJ, 1969–70; Massachusetts Coll. of Art, Boston, 1970–71; Artist-in-residence, Rhode Is. Sch. of Design, 1974–75; Lectr, Sch. of Visual Arts, NY, 1975–76; Tutor, Byam Shaw Sch. of Painting and Sculpture, 1975–86; Artist-in-residence, Skowhegan Sch. of Painting and Sculpture, Maine, 1984. John Simon Guggenheim Meml Fellow, 1967 and 1973. *Solo exhibitions:* Grabowski Gall., London, 1962, 1963; Whitney Mus. of Amer. Art, NY, 1971; Gall. Center for Inter-Amer. Relations, 1973–74; Tibor de Nagy, NY, freq. exhibns 1976–89; Serpentine Gall., 1986; Bowling Through the Decade, RWEA, 1989; Nat. Acad. of Scis, Washington, 1993; Bowling Through the Century, De La Warr Pavilion, Bexhill, 1997; Center for Art and Culture, Brooklyn, 1997; Aljira Center for the Arts, Newark, 2003; Frank Bowling: 4 Decades with Color, Phillips Mus. of Art, Lancaster, Pa, 2004; Arts Club, London, 2007. Contributing Ed., Artsmagazine, 1969–72. Jt Founder, Young Commonwealth Artists Gp, 1958–63; Chm., London Gp, 1962–66. Shakespeare Quatro Centenary Commn, 1963. Hon. Fellow, Arts Inst., Bournemouth, 2006. Hon. Dr Wolverhampton, 2007. Grand Prize for Contemporary Art, First World Fest. of Negro Art, Dakar, Senegal, 1966; Pollock Krasner Award, 1992, 1998. *Recreations:* cricket, athletics. *Address:* 8A John Islip Street, SW1P 4PY. *T:* (020) 7821 7065; PO Box 023703, Brooklyn, NY 11202, USA. *T:* (718) 6252579. *Clubs:* Chelsea Arts, Royal Over-Seas League.

BOWMAN; *see* Kellett-Bowman.

BOWMAN, Prof. Alan Keir, PhD; FBA 1994; Camden Professor of Ancient History, and Fellow of Brasenose College, University of Oxford, since 2002; *b* Manchester, 23 May 1944; *s* of late Cyril Bowman and Freda (*née* Bowman); *m* 1966, Jacqueline Frayman; one *s* one *d.* *Educ:* Manchester Grammar Sch.; Queen's Coll., Oxford (MA; Hon Fellow, 2006); Univ. of Toronto (MA, PhD 1969). Canada Council Postdoctoral Fellow, 1969–70; Asst Prof. of Classics, Rutgers Univ., 1970–72; Lectr in Ancient Hist., Manchester Univ., 1972–77; Oxford University: Official Student, Christ Church, 1977–2002, Emeritus Student, 2002; Sen. Censor, Christ Church, 1988–90; Lectr in Ancient Hist., 1977–2002; Dir, Centre for Study of Ancient Documents, 1995–. Vis. Mem., Inst. for Advanced Study, Princeton, 1976, 1981; British Acad. Res. Reader, 1991–93. Chm., Roman Res. Trust, 1990–; Pres., Soc. for the Promotion of Roman Studies, 2001–05. FSA 1999. *Publications:* The Town Councils of Roman Egypt, 1971; (with J. D. Thomas) The Vindolanda Writing-Tablets, 1983, vol. II 1994, vol. III 2003; Egypt after the Pharaohs, 1986, 3rd edn 1996; Life and Letters on the Roman Frontier: Vindolanda and its people, 1994, 2nd edn 1998 (British Archaeological Book Award, 1998), 3rd edn 2003; (jtly) Literacy and Power in the Ancient World, 1994; (ed jtly) The Cambridge Ancient History, 2nd edn, Vol. X 1996, Vol. XI 2000, Vol. XII 2005; (ed jtly) Agriculture in Egypt from Pharaonic to modern times, 1998; contrib. learned jls. *Recreations:* photography, music, cricket, tennis, walking. *Address:* Brasenose College, Oxford OX1 4AJ. *T:* (01865) 277874.

BOWMAN, Claire Margaret; *see* Makin, C. M.

BOWMAN, Sir (Edwin) Geoffrey, KCB 2004 (CB 1991); First Parliamentary Counsel, 2002–06; *b* Blackpool, Lancs, 27 Jan. 1946; *er s* of late John Edwin Bowman and Lillian Joan Bowman (*née* Nield); *m* 1969, Carol Margaret, *er d* of late Alexander Ogilvie and Ethel Ogilvie; two *s* one *d.* *Educ:* Roundhay Sch., Leeds; Trinity Coll., Cambridge (Senior Scholar; BA 1st cl., LLB 1st cl., MA, LLM). Called to Bar, Lincoln's Inn (Cassel Scholar), 1968, Bencher, 2002; in practice, Chancery Bar, 1969–71; joined Parliamentary Counsel Office, 1971 (seconded to Law Commission, 1977–79, 1996–98); Dep. Parly Counsel, 1981–84; Parly Counsel, 1984–2002. Chm., Harrow Choral Soc., 2001–02. Hon. QC 2006. Hon. LLD London, 2007. *Publications:* The Elements of Conveyancing (with E. L. G. Tyler), 1972; contrib. legal jls. *Recreations:* music (bassoon, recorder), history. *Address:* c/o Parliamentary Counsel Office, 36 Whitehall, SW1A 2AY. *T:* (020) 7210 6629. *Club:* Les Amis du Basson Français (Paris).

BOWMAN, Eric Joseph; consultant, since 1986; *b* 1 June 1929; *s* of late Joseph John Bowman and Lilley Bowman; *m* 1951, Esther Kay; one *d.* *Educ:* Stationers' Company's School; College of Estate Management. FRICS. Private practice, 1945–51; Royal Engineers, 1951–53; private practice, 1953–54; Min. of Works, 1954–63; Min. of Housing and Local Govt, 1963–73; Directorate of Diplomatic and Post Office Services, MPBW, later DoE, 1973–80; Directorate of Quantity Surveying Services, DoE, 1980–83; Dir of Building and Quantity Surveying Services, PSA, DoE, 1983–86. *Recreations:* fly fishing, walking, swimming, gardening, reading. *Address:* Mearsons Farm, Hubbersty Head, Crosthwaite, near Kendal, Cumbria LA8 8JB. *T:* (01539) 568400.

BOWMAN, Sir Geoffrey; *see* Bowman, Sir E. G.

BOWMAN, James Thomas, CBE 1997; counter-tenor; *b* Oxford, 6 Nov. 1941; *s* of Benjamin and Cecilia Bowman (*née* Coote). *Educ:* Ely Cathedral Choir Sch.; King's Sch., Ely; New Coll., Oxford (MA (History) 1967; DipEd 1964; Hon. Fellow, 1998). Lay Vicar, Westminster Abbey, 1969–75; Teacher of Voice, GSM, 1983–92; Gentleman in Ordinary, HM Chapel Royal, St James's Palace, 2000–. Many concert performances with Early Music Consort, 1967–76; operatic performances with: English Opera Gp, 1967; Sadler's Wells Opera, 1970–; Glyndebourne Festival Opera, 1970–; Royal Opera, Covent Gdn, 1972; Sydney Opera, Australia, 1978; Opéra Comique, Paris, 1979; Le Châtelet, Paris, 1982; Geneva, 1983; Scottish Opera, 1985; La Scala, Milan, 1988, 1991; La Fenice, Venice, 1991; Paris Opera, 1991; Badisches Staatstheater, Karlsruhe, 1984; in USA at Santa Fe and Wolf Trap Festivals, Dallas and San Francisco Operas; at Aix-en-Provence Fest., 1979; operatic roles include: Oberon, in A Midsummer Night's Dream; Endymion, in La Calisto; the Priest, in Taverner; Polinesso, in Ariodante; Apollo, in Death in Venice; Astron, in The Ice Break; Ruggiero in Alcina; title rôles: Giulio Cesare; Tamerlano; Xerxes; Scipione; Giustino; Orlando; Ottone. Extensive discography of opera, oratorio and contemporary music. Pres., Holst Singers, 1997–; Vice-Pres., Bach Choir, 2006–. Mem., Royal Soc. of Musicians, 2004. Hon. DMus Newcastle, 1996. Medal, City of Paris,

1992. Officier, Ordre des Arts et des Lettres (France), 1995. *Recreations:* ecclesiastical architecture, collecting records. *Address:* 4 Brownlow Road, Redhill RH1 6AW. *Club:* Athenæum.

BOWMAN, Sir Jeffery (Haverstock), Kt 1991; FCA; Chairman: Mid Essex Hospital Services NHS Trust, 1993–99; Masthead Insurance Underwriting PLC, 1993–99; *b* 3 April 1935; *s* of Alfred Haverstock Bowman and Doris Gertrude Bowman; *m* 1963, Susan Claudia Bostock; one *s* two *d*. *Educ:* Winchester Coll. (schol.); Trinity Hall, Cambridge (major schol.; BA Hons 1st cl. in Law). Served RHG, 1953–55 (commnd, 1954). Price Waterhouse: articled in London, 1958; NY, 1963–64; admitted to partnership, 1966; Mem., Policy Cttee, 1972–91; Dir of Tech. Services, 1973–76; Dir, London Office, 1979–81; Sen. Partner, 1982–91; Chm., Price Waterhouse Europe, 1988–93; Jt Chm., Price Waterhouse World Firm, 1992–93. Dir, Gibbs Mew, 1995–97. Auditor, Duchy of Cornwall, 1971–93. Vice-Pres., Union of Indep. Cos, 1983–93; Member: Council, ICAEW, 1986–90 (Mem., Accounting Standards Cttee, 1982–87); Council, Industrial Soc., 1985–93; Economic and Financial Policy Cttee, CBI, 1987–93; City Capital Markets Cttee, 1989–93; Council, Business in the Community, 1985–91. Chairman: Court of Appeal (Civil Div.) Review, 1996–97; Crown Office Review, 1999–2000. Trustee, 1995–2003, Queen's Trustee, 1998–2003, Royal Botanic Gdns, Kew. Gov., Brentwood Sch., 1985–97. FRSA 1989. Hon. Bencher, Inner Temple, 1998. *Recreations:* golf, opera, gardening, sailing. *Address:* The Old Rectory, Church Road, Boreham, Chelmsford, Essex CM3 3EP. *T:* (01245) 467233. *Club:* Garrick.

BOWMAN, Dr John Christopher, CBE 1986; PhD; FIBiol; independent environmental consultant, 1993–2001; Managing Director (Europe and Africa), Brown & Root Environmental, 1991–93; *b* 13 Aug. 1933; *s* of M. C. Bowman and C. V. Simister; *m* 1961, S. J. Lorimer; three *d*. *Educ:* Manchester Grammar Sch.; Univ. of Reading (BSc); Univ. of Edinburgh (PhD). Geneticist, later Chief Geneticist, Thornbers, Mytholmroyd, Yorks, 1958–66. Post-doctoral Fellow, North Carolina State Univ., Raleigh, NC, USA, 1964–65; University of Reading: Prof. of Animal Production, 1966–81; Head of Dept of Agric., 1967–71; Dir, Univ. Farms, 1967–78; Dir, Centre for Agricl Strategy, 1975–81; Sec., NERC, 1981–89; Chief Exec., NRA, 1989–91. Dir, Certa Foundn, 1998–2001. Chm., Sonning Parish Council, 1994–98. Mem., Cannington Coll. Corp., 2002–04. Trustee, Somerset Community Foundn, 2005–. FRSA 1976 (Chair, Forum for Envmtl and Sustainable Develt Awards, 2005–). Hon. DSc Cranfield, 1990. *Publications:* An Introduction to Animal Breeding, 1974; Animals for Man, 1977; (with P. Susmel) The Future of Beef Production in the European Community, 1979; (jtly) Hammond's Farm Animals, 1983. *Recreations:* golf, tennis, gardening, bridge. *Address:* Court Mill, Lower Street, Merriott, Som TA16 5NL.

BOWMAN, Pamela Margaret Munro; Floating Sheriff, based at Glasgow, since 2003; *b* 1 Aug. 1944; *d* of late James M. Wright and Jean Wright; *m* 1967, Bernard Neil Bowman; two *d*. *Educ:* Beacon Sch., Bridge of Allan; St Andrews Univ. (LLB). Admitted as solicitor and NP, 1967; Partner, Bowman, Solicitors, Dundee and Forfar, 1980–97; Temp. Sheriff, 1995–97; Floating Sheriff, 1997–99; Sheriff of Glasgow and Strathkelvin, 1999–2001; Sheriff of Grampian, Highland and Islands at Aberdeen, 2001–03. Member: Scottish Legal Aid Bd, 1994–97; Bd, Scottish Children's Reporter Admin, 2003–. Non-exec. Dir, Angus NHS Trust, 1994–97. Hon. Sec. and Treas., Sheriffs Assoc., 2004–05. *Recreations:* theatre, dancing. *Address:* Sheriff Court, 1 Carlton Place, Glasgow, G5 9DA. *T:* (0141) 429 8888; *e-mail:* sheriff.pbowman@scotcourts.gov.uk.

BOWMAN, Penelope Jill; *see* Watkins, P. J.

BOWMAN, Philip, FCA; Chief Executive, Smiths Group plc, since 2007; *b* 14 Dec. 1952; *s* of Thomas Patrick Bowman and Norma Elizabeth (*née* Deravin). *Educ:* Westminster Sch.; Pembroke Coll., Cambridge (MA). FCA 1983. Price Waterhouse, London, 1974–78; Gibbs Bright & Co. Pty Ltd, Melbourne, 1978–83; Granite Industries Inc., Atlanta, 1983–85; Bass plc, London, 1985–95: Finance Dir, 1991–94; Chief Exec., Retail Div., 1994–95; Finance Dir, Coles Myer Ltd, Melbourne, 1995; Chm., Liberty plc, 1998–2000; Chief Executive: Allied Domecq plc, 1999–2005; Scottish Power plc, 2006–07. Chm., Coral Eurobet Hldgs, 2004–05; non-executive Director: BSkyB Gp plc, 1994–2003; Berry Bros & Rudd, 2006–; Sen. Ind. Dir, Burberry Gp plc, 2002–; Dir, Scottish & Newcastle plc, 2006–. Mem. Adv. Bd, Alchemy Partners, 2000–. *Recreations:* scuba diving, entomology, opera, computers and electronics. *Address:* Smiths Group plc, 765 Finchley Road, NW11 8DS. *Clubs:* Victoria Racing, Royal Automobile of Victoria, National Golf (Melbourne).

BOWMAN, Richard Alan; Master of the Supreme Court, Chancery Division, 1996–2004; *b* 3 Oct. 1943; *s* of Harry Bowman and Gladys Bowman (*née* Croft); *m* 1970, Joanna Mary Lodder; two *s* one *d*. *Educ:* Clifton; St George's Sch., Newport, RI; Keble Coll., Oxford (MA). FCIArb 1995. Admitted solicitor, 1970; Dep. Chancery Master, 1988–96. Chm., Legal Aid Commn, General Synod of C of E, 1996–. Accredited Mediator, 2005–. *Address:* Smithy House, Tormarton, Badminton, S Glos GL9 1HU.

BOWMAN, Sarah Meredith; District Judge, Principal Registry (Family Division), since 1993; *b* 24 May 1949; *d* of Alexander Dennis Bowman and Jean Bowman; *m* 1984, Jake Downey (separated); three *s*. *Educ:* Notting Hill and Ealing High Sch.; Leeds Univ. (BA). Called to the Bar, Middle Temple, 1976; Barrister, 1976–93. *Recreations:* my sons, trying to secure sufficient time to go walking with my dog, preferably in the Lake District. *Address:* Principal Registry Family Division, First Avenue House, 42–49 High Holborn, WC1V 6NP.

BOWMAN, Dr Sheridan Gail Esther, FSA; Keeper, Department of Conservation, Documentation and Science, British Museum, 2002–05; *b* Westlock, Alta, Canada, 11 March 1950; *o d* of late Otto Michael Bowman and of Eva (*née* McKnight). *Educ:* Whitehaven County Grammar Sch., Cumbria; St Anne's Coll., Oxford (Open Scholar; MA; DPhil Physics, 1976); Chelsea Coll., London (MSc Maths, 1981); (extramural) London Univ. (Dip. in Archaeol., 1985). FSA 1987 (a Vice Pres., 1993). British Museum: Scientific Officer, 1976; Keeper, Dept of Scientific Res., 1989–2002. *Publications:* Radiocarbon Dating, 1990; (ed) Science and the Past, 1991; papers on scientific techniques, particularly dating, applied to archaeology. *Recreations:* heath and fell walking, gardening, theatre.

BOWMAN, Victoria Jane, (Vicky); HM Diplomatic Service; Joint Director, Global and Economic Issues, Foreign and Commonwealth Office, since 2008; *b* 12 June 1966; *d* of Dr Frank Neville Hosband Robinson and Daphne Isabel (*née* Coulthard); *m* 1st, 1991, Mark Andrew Bowman (marr. diss. 2001); 2nd, 2006, Htein Lin; one *d*. *Educ:* Oxford High Sch. for Girls; Pembroke Coll., Cambridge (BA Hons Natural Scis); Univ. of Chicago. Entered FCO, 1988; Third, later Second, Sec., Rangoon, 1990–93; FCO, 1993–96; Spokeswoman, UK Repn to EU, 1996–99; Mem., Cabinet of Eur. Comr for Ext. Relns, 1999–2002; Ambassador to Burma (Union of Myanmar), 2002–06; Hd, Africa Dept. (Southern), FCO, 2006–08. *Publication:* On the Road to Mandalay: translation of writings by Mya Than Tint, 1996. *Recreations:* cycling, diving, travel, learning languages, translating Burmese fiction, bridge. *Address:* c/o Foreign and Commonwealth Office, King Charles Street, SW1A 2AH.

BOWMAN-SHAW, Sir (George) Neville, Kt 1984; DL; Chairman: Samuk Ltd, since 1995; Bowman Lift Trucks Ltd, since 1997; *b* 4 Oct. 1930; *s* of George Bowman-Shaw and Hazel Bowman-Shaw (*née* Smyth); *m* 1962, Georgina Mary Blundell; two *s* one *d* (and one *s* decd). *Educ:* Caldicott Preparatory Sch.; then private tutor. Farming Trainee, 1947; Management Trainee in Engineering Co., 1948. Commissioned in 5th Royal Inniskilling Dragoon Guards, 1950. Sales Manager: Matling Ltd, Wolverhampton, 1953; Materials Handling Equipment (GB) Ltd, London, and Matbro Ltd, London, 1955; Chairman: Boss Trucks Ltd, 1959–95; Lancer Boss Gp Ltd, 1966–94; Lancer Boss Ireland Ltd, 1966–94; Lancer Boss Fördergeräte Vertriebsges. (Austria), 1966–94; Boss France SA, 1967–94; Steinbock GmbH, 1983–94; Boss Trucks España SA, 1987–94; FOREXIA (UK) Ltd, 1994–97. Member: Development Commn, 1970–77; Design Council, 1979–84; BOTB, 1982–85. High Sheriff, Bedfordshire, 1987–88; DL Bedfordshire, 2002. *Recreations:* shooting, vintage tractors. *Address:* Toddington Manor, Toddington, Bedfordshire LU5 6HJ. *Clubs:* Cavalry and Guards, MCC.

BOWMONT AND CESSFORD, Marquis of; Charles Robert George Innes-Ker; *b* 18 Feb. 1981; *s* and *heir* of Duke of Roxburghe, *qv* and of Lady Jane Dawnay, *qv*. *Educ:* Eton Coll.; Newcastle Univ. *Recreations:* motor racing, golf, tennis, fishing. *Address:* Floors Castle, Kelso TD5 7RW.

BOWN, Jane Hope, (Mrs M. G. Moss), CBE 1995 (MBE 1985); Photographer for The Observer, since 1950; *b* 13 March 1925; *d* of Charles Wentworth Bell and Daisy Bown; *m* 1954, Martin Grenville Moss, CBE (*d* 2007); two *s* one *d*. *Educ:* William Gibbs Sch., Faversham. Chart corrector, WRNS, 1944–46; student photographer, Guildford School of Art, 1946–50. Hon. DLitt Bradford, 1986. Barry Award, What the Papers Say, 1995. *Publications:* The Gentle Eye: a book of photographs, 1980; Women of Consequence, 1986; Men of Consequence, 1987; The Singular Cat, 1988; Pillars of the Church, 1991; Jane Bown: Observer, 1996; Faces, 2000; Rock, 2003; Unknown Bown, 2007. *Recreations:* restoring old houses, chickens.

BOWN, Prof. Lalage Jean, OBE 1977; FRSE; FEIS; CCIPD; Director, Department of Adult and Continuing Education, University of Glasgow, 1981–92, now Professor Emeritus; *b* 1 April 1927; *d* of Arthur Mervyn Bown, MC and late Dorothy Ethel (*née* Watson); two foster *d*. *Educ:* Wycombe Abbey Sch.; Cheltenham Ladies' Coll.; Somerville Coll., Oxford (MA); Oxford Post-grad. Internship in Adult Education. FEIS 1990; FRSE 1991; CCIPD (FIPD 1993). Resident Tutor: University Coll. of Gold Coast, 1949–55; Makerere University Coll., Uganda, 1955–59; Asst Dir, then Dep. Dir, Extramural Studies, Univ. of Ibadan, Nigeria, 1960–66; Dir, Extramural Studies and Prof. (*ad personam*), Univ., of Zambia, 1966–70; Prof. of Adult Educn, Ahmadu Bello Univ., Nigeria, 1971–76, Univ. of Lagos, Nigeria, 1977–79; Dean of Educn, Univ. of Lagos, 1979–80; Vis. Fellow, Inst. of Development Studies, 1980–81. Hon. Professor: Internat. Centre for Educn in Develt, Warwick Univ., 1992–97; Inst. of Educn, Univ. of London, 1998–99. Member: Bd, British Council, 1981–89; Scottish Community Educn Council, 1982–88; Exec. Cttee, Scottish Inst. of Adult and Continuing Educn, 1982–88; Bd, Network Scotland, 1983–88; Bd of Trustees, Nat. Museums of Scotland, 1987–97; Council, Insite Trust, 1987–95; Bd of Trustees, Womankind Worldwide, 1988–96; Interim Trustee, Books for Develt, 1987–90; British Mem., Commonwealth Standing Cttee on Student Mobility and Higher Educn Co-operation, 1989–94; Trustee, Education Action (formerly World Univ. Service, UK), 1997–2003; Mem. Bd, Council for Educn in the Commonwealth, 2000–07 (Chm., Wkg Gp on Student Mobility, 1998–2000; Jt Dep. Vice-Chair, 2003–06). Governor, Inst. of Develt Studies, 1982–91; President: Develt Studies Assoc., 1984–86; British Comparative and Internat. Educn Soc., 1985–86; Vice-President: WEA, 1989–95 (Hon. Vice-Pres., 1984–88); Commonwealth Assoc. for Educn and Trng of Adults, 1990–93; Hon. Pres., British Assoc. for Literacy in Develt, 1993–98. Patron, African Families Foundn, 2001–; Trustee, Britain Nigeria Educnl (formerly Alhaji Tafawa Balewa Meml) Trust, 2005–. Hon. Vice-Pres., Townswomen's Guilds, 1984–2005. Hon. Life Member: People's Educnl Assoc., Ghana, 1973; African Adult Educn Assoc., 1976; NIACE, 2007. AcSS 2000. DUniv: Open, 1975; Paisley, 1993; Stirling, 1994; Dr (*hc*) Edinburgh, 1993; Hon. DLitt Glasgow, 2002. William Pearson Tolley Medal, Syracuse Univ., USA, 1975; Meritorious Service Award, Nigerian Nat. Council for Adult Educn, 1979; Symons Medal, ACU, 2001; World Teachers' Day Award, Commonwealth Secretariat, 2003. *Publications:* (ed with Michael Crowder) Proceedings of First International Congress of Africanists, 1964; Two Centuries of African English, 1973; (ed) Adult Education in Nigeria: the next 10 years, 1975; A Rusty Person is Worse than Rusty Iron, 1976; Lifelong Learning: prescription for progress, 1979; (ed with S. H. O. Tomori) A Handbook of Adult Education for West Africa, 1980; (ed with J. T. Okedara) An Introduction to Adult Education: a multi-disciplinary and cross-cultural approach for developing countries, 1980; Preparing the Future: women, literacy and development, 1991; (ed) Towards a Commonwealth of Scholars, 1994; (ed) Education in the Commonwealth: the first 40 years, 2003; numerous articles in academic jls. *Recreations:* travel, reading, entertaining friends. *Address:* 1 Dogpole Court, Dogpole, Shrewsbury SY1 1ES. *T:* (01743) 356155, *Fax:* (01743) 233626. *Clubs:* Royal Over-Seas League, Commonwealth.

BOWNE, Anthony Doran; lighting designer; Director, Laban, since 2003; Joint Principal, Trinity Laban Conservatoire of Music and Dance, since 2006; *b* 23 April 1956; *s* of Tony Alfred Bowne and Kathleen Bowne (*née* Doran); *m* 2005, Emma Redding; one *s*. *Educ:* Princethorpe Coll.; Kenilworth Grammar Sch.; Univ. of Southampton (BSc Econs 1977); Bartlett Sch. of Architecture, University Coll. London (MSc Arch. 1992). Sen. Financial Analyst, Rover Cars, 1978–81; Laban: Lectr in Lighting Design, 1983–86; Sen. Lectr, 1987–94; Exec. Dir, Transitions Dance Co., 1992–2002; Dep. Chief Exec., 1994–2003. Sen. Lectr in Th. Lighting Design, Hong Kong Acad. for Performing Arts, 1996–98; Prof. of Dance, Lasalle Coll., Singapore, 2004–. Lighting Designer, 1993–: Carmina Burana, Taiwan, Silent Tongues, Set the Night on Fire, RFH, 1993; Metalcholica, Forgotten Voices, Silence the Pestle Sound, Taiwan, 1994; Swinger, Car, Fierce/Pink/House, 1995; Spring Dance, Hong Kong, 1996; Una Cosa Rara (opera), Dance!! Dance!! Dance!!, Hong Kong, 1997; Vast Desert, Taiwan, 2000; Rite of Spring, Hong Kong, 2001; Now Blind Yourself, Place, London, 2002; Slow-Still-Divided, Place, London, Rite of Spring, Hong Kong Ballet tour, 2003; architectural: G's Club, Shanghai, 1997; Joyce, Dusk 'til Dawn, Hong Kong, 1998; World Finance Centre, Shanghai, 1999; Chijmes, Singapore, 2001. Chair, Cholmondeleys and Featherstoneshaughs Dance Co., 2000–; Board Member: Bonnie Bird Choreography Fund, 1995–; Dance Forum, DCMS, 2006–. Bd Mem., Deptford Creative Village Consortium, 2007–. Board Member: Granada/Univ. of Calif Davis, 2002–07; Bird Coll., 2006–; Gov., Finnish Inst., London, 2006–. FRSA 2002. Designer for the 90s, Lighting Dimensions mag., USA, 1990; London Dance and Performance Award, Time Out mag., 1992. *Recreations:* wine, food, ski-ing, windsurfing. *Address:* Laban, Creekside, SE8 3DZ. *T:* (020) 8691 8600; *e-mail:* a.bowne@laban.org. *Club:* Home House.

BOWNES, Prof. Mary, OBE 2007; DPhil; CBiol, FIBiol, FRES; FRSE; Professor of Developmental Biology, since 1994, and Vice Principal, since 2003, University of Edinburgh; *b* Drewsteignton, 14 Nov. 1948; *d* of Frederick and Florence Bownes; *m* 1973, Michael John Greaves; one *d*. *Educ:* Univ. of Sussex (BSc 1970; DPhil 1973); CBiol, FIBiol 2001; FRES 2001; FRSE 2004. Postdoctoral Associate, Univ. of Freiberg and Univ. of Calif, Irvine, 1973–76; Lectr in Genetics and Develt Biol., Univ. of Essex, 1976–79; University of Edinburgh: Lectr, 1979–89, Sen. Lectr, 1989–91, Reader, 1991–94, in Molecular Biol.; Associate Dean for Postgrads, Faculty of Sci. and Engrg, 1997–98; Hd, Inst. of Cell and Molecular Biol., 1998–2001; mem. of numerous univ. cttees and gps. Dir, Scottish Initiative for Biotechnol. Educn, 2002–. External Examiner: Univ. of Sussex, 1996–2000; Univ. of Oxford, 2001–03; Univ. of York, 2004–06; Univ. of Glasgow, 2005–; Univ. of Leicester, 2007–. Chairman: Steering Cttee, Sci. and Plants for Schs Biotechnol. Scotland Proj., 2000– (Mem., 1998–); Bd, Edinburgh Consortium for Rural Res., 2003– (Mem., 1999–; Mem. Exec. Cttee, 2000–03); Strategy Bd, BBSRC, 2004–07; Studentships and Fellowships Strategy Panel, BBSRC, 2004–07; Member: Bd, Genetics Soc., 1980–83; Cttee, Brit. Soc. for Develtl Biol., 1982–87 (Treas., 1984–89); Adv. Bd, MRC, 2002–03; Cell and Molecular Biol. Section Cttee, 2004–07, Meetings Cttee, 2004–07, Young People's Cttee, 2004–07, RSE; Skills Cttee, SFC, 2006–. Mem. Bd, Highlands and Is Enterprise, 2007–. Mem., Editl Bd, Jl of Endocrinol., 2000–. *Publications:* (ed jtly) Metamorphosis, 1985; (ed) Ecdysone: from metabolism to regulation of gene expression, 1986; over 100 papers in scientific jls and numerous book chapters. *Recreations:* photography, walking. *Address:* Institute of Cell Biology, University of Edinburgh, Darwin Building, The King's Buildings, Edinburgh EH9 3JR. *T:* (0131) 650 5369; *e-mail:* mary.bownes@ed.ac.uk.

BOWNESS, family name of **Baron Bowness**.

BOWNESS, Baron *cr* 1995 (Life Peer), of Warlingham in the County of Surrey and of Croydon in the London Borough of Croydon; **Peter Spencer Bowness,** Kt 1987; CBE 1981; DL; NP 1977; Consultant, Streeter Marshall, Solicitors, Croydon, Purley and Warlingham, since 2002; *b* 19 May 1943; *s* of Hubert Spencer Bowness and Doreen (Peggy) Bowness; *m* 1969, Marianne Hall (marr. diss.); one *d*; *m* 1984, Mrs Patricia Jane Cook; one step *s*. *Educ:* Whitgift Sch., Croydon. Admitted Solicitor, 1966; Partner, Horsley, Weightman, Richardson and Sadler, subseq. Weightman, Sadler, then Streeter Marshall, 1970–2002. Croydon Council: Mem. (C), 1968–98: Leader, 1976–94; Leader of the Opposition, 1994–96; Mayor of Croydon, 1979–80; Chm., London Boroughs Assoc., 1978–94; Dep. Chm., Assoc. of Metropolitan Authorities, 1978–80. Opposition spokesman on the envmt, transport and the regions, H of L, 1997–98; Mem., H of L Select Cttee on EU, 2003–07 (Chm., Foreign Affairs, Defence and Develt Policy Sub Cttee, 2003–06); Mem., Jt Cttee on Human Rights, 2003–07, 2008–; Co-Chm., All-Party Parly Gp on Lithuania, 2001–; Vice-Chm., All-Party Parly Gp on Romania, 2006–; Sec., All-Party Parly Gp on Moldova, 2007–. Member: Audit Commn, 1983–95; London Residuary Body, 1985–93; Nat. Training Task Force, 1989–92; UK Delegn, CLRAE (Council of Europe), 1990–98; UK Mem., Mem. Bureau, and Mem. Transportation and Telecommunications Commn, EC Cttee of the Regions, 1994–98; Member: UK Delegn to EU Charter of Fundamental Rights Drafting Convention, 1999–2000; Parly Assembly, OSCE, 2007–. Gov., Whitgift Foundn, 1982–94. Hon. Col, 151 (Greater London) Transport Regt RCT (V), 1988–93. DL Greater London, 1981; Freeman, City of London, 1984; Hon. Freeman, London Borough of Croydon, 2002. *Recreations:* travel, gardening, our two dachshunds. *Address:* Three Gables, 10 Westview Road, Warlingham, Surrey CR6 9JD. *T:* (office) (01883) 622433.

BOWNESS, Sir Alan, Kt 1988; CBE 1976; Director of the Tate Gallery, 1980–88; Director, Henry Moore Foundation, 1988–94 (Member, Committee of Management, 1984–88 and 1994–2003); *b* 11 Jan. 1928; *er s* of George Bowness and Kathleen (*née* Benton); *m* 1957, Sarah Hepworth-Nicholson, *d* of Ben Nicholson, OM, and Dame Barbara Hepworth, DBE; one *s* one *d*. *Educ:* University Coll. Sch.; Downing Coll., Cambridge (Hon. Fellow 1980); Courtauld Inst. of Art, Univ. of London (Hon. Fellow 1986). Worked with Friends' Ambulance Unit and Friends' Service Council, 1946–50; Reg. Art Officer, Arts Council of GB, 1955–57; Courtauld Inst., 1957–79, Dep. Dir, 1978–79; Reader, 1967–78, Prof. of Hist. of Art, 1978–79, Univ. of London. Vis. Prof., Humanities Seminar, Johns Hopkins Univ., Baltimore, 1969. Exhibitions arranged and catalogued include: 54:64 Painting and Sculpture of a Decade (with L. Gowing), 1964; Dubuffet, 1966; Sculpture in Battersea Park, 1966; Van Gogh, 1968; Rodin, 1970; William Scott, 1972; French Symbolist Painters (with G. Lacambre), 1972; Ceri Richards, 1975; Courbet (with M. Laclotte), 1977. Mem. Internat. Juries: Premio Di Tella, Buenos Aires, 1965; São Paulo Bienal, 1967; Venice Biennale, 1986; Lehmbruck Prize, Duisburg, 1970; Rembrandt Prize, 1979–88; Heiliger Prize, 1998. Arts Council: Mem., 1973–75 and 1978–80; Mem., Art Panel, 1960–80 (Vice-Chm., 1973–75, Chm., 1978–80); Mem., Arts Film Cttee, 1968–77 (Chm., 1972–75). Member: Fine Arts Cttee, Brit. Council, 1960–69 and 1970–92 (Chm., 1981–92); Exec. Cttee, Contemp. Art Soc., 1961–69 and 1970–86; Kettle's Yard Cttee, Univ. of Cambridge, 1970–99; Cultural Adv. Cttee, UK National Commn for UNESCO, 1973–82. Governor, Chelsea Sch. of Art, 1965–93; Hon. Sec., Assoc. of Art Historians, 1973–76; Dir, Barbara Hepworth Museum, St Ives, Cornwall, 1976–88. Mem. Council, RCA, 1978–99 (Hon. Fellow 1984). Trustee: Yorkshire Sculpture Park, 1979–; Handel House, 1994–2001 (Chm., 1997–2001). Hon. Fellow, Bristol Polytechnic, 1980. Hon. FRIBA 1994. Hon. DLit Liverpool, 1988; Hon. DLitt: Leeds, 1995; Exeter, 1996. Chevalier, l'Ordre des Arts et des Lettres, France, 1973. *Publications:* William Scott Paintings, 1964; Impressionists and Post Impressionists, 1965; (ed) Henry Moore: complete sculpture 1955–64 (vol. 3) 1965, 1964–73 (vol. 4) 1977, 1974–80 (vol. 5) 1983, 1949–54 (vol. 2) 1987, 1980–86 (vol. 6) 1988; Modern Sculpture, 1965; Barbara Hepworth Drawings, 1966; Alan Davie, 1967; Recent British Painting, 1968; Gauguin, 1971; Barbara Hepworth: complete sculpture 1960–70, 1971; Modern European Art, 1972; Ivon Hitchens, 1973; (contrib.) Picasso 1881–1973, ed R. Penrose, 1973; (contrib.) The Genius of British Painting, ed D. Piper, 1975; The Conditions of Success, 1989; Bernard Meadows, 1994; articles in Burlington Magazine, TLS, Observer, and Annual Register. *Recreations:* going to concerts, theatre, opera. *Address:* 91 Castelnau, SW13 9EL. *T:* (020) 8846 8520; 16 Piazza, St Ives, Cornwall TR26 1NQ. *T:* (01736) 795444.

BOWRING, Air Vice-Marshal John Ivan Roy, CB 1977; CBE 1971; CEng, FRAeS; FCMI; management consultant, aircraft maintenance, retired; Head of Technical Training and Maintenance, British Aerospace (formerly British Aircraft Corporation), Riyadh, Saudi Arabia, 1978–88, retired; *b* 28 March 1923; *s* of Hugh Passmore Bowring and Ethel Grace Bowring; *m* 1945, Irene Mary Rance; two *d*. *Educ:* Great Yarmouth Grammar Sch., Norfolk; Aircraft Apprentice, RAF Halton-Cosford, 1938–40; Leicester Tech. Coll. Commissioned, RAF, 1944; NW Europe, 1944–47; RAF, Horsham St Faith's, Engrg duties, 1947–48; RAF South Cerney, Pilot trng, 1949; Engr Officer: RAF Finningly, 1950–51; RAF Kai-Tak, 1951–53; Staff Officer, AHQ Hong Kong, ADC to Governor, Hong Kong, 1953–54; Sen. Engr Officer, RAF Coltishall, 1954–56; exchange duties with US Air Force, Research and Develt, Wright Patterson Air Force Base, Ohio, 1956–60; RAF Staff Coll., Bracknell, 1960; Air Min. Opl Requirements, 1961–64; OC Engrg Wing, RAF St Mawgan, 1964–67; Head of F111 Procurement Team, USA, 1967–68; OC RAF Aldergrove, NI, 1968–70; RCDS, 1971; Dir of Engrg Policy, MoD, 1972–73; AO Engrg, RAF Germany, 1973–74; SASO, RAF Support Comd, 1974–77; AO Maintenance, 1977. *Recreations:* sailing, golf. *Club:* Royal Air Force.

BOWRING, Peter, CBE 1993; Chairman, C. T. Bowring & Co. Ltd, 1978–82; Director, Marsh & McLennan Cos Inc., New York, 1980–85 (Vice-Chairman, 1982–84); *b* 22 April 1923; *e s* of Frederick Clive Bowring and Agnes Walker (*née* Cairns); *m* 1946, Barbara Ekaterina Brewis (marr. diss.; she *d* 2005); one *s* one *d*; *m* 1986, Mrs Carole Dear. *Educ:* Shrewsbury Sch. Served War, 1939–45: commnd Rifle Bde, 1942; served in Egypt, N Africa, Italy, Austria (mentioned in despatches, 1945); demobilised 1946. Joined Bowring Group of Cos, 1947: Dir, C. T. Bowring & Co. Ltd, 1956–84, Dep. Chm. 1973–78; Chairman: C. T. Bowring Trading (Holdings) Ltd, 1967–84; Bowmaker (Plant) Ltd, 1972–83; Bowring Steamship Co. Ltd, 1974–82; Bowmaker Ltd, 1978–82; C. T. Bowring (UK) Ltd, 1980–84. Director: City Arts Trust Ltd, 1984–94 (Chm., 1987–94); Independent Primary and Secondary Educn Trust, 1986–2006. Mem. of Lloyd's, 1968–98. Chm., Help the Aged Ltd, 1977–87, Pres., 1988–2000. Dir, Centre for Policy Studies, 1983–88. Vice Pres., Aldeburgh Foundn, 1989– (Chm., 1982–89). Chairman: Inter-Action Social Enterprise Trust, 1989–91; Bd of Governors, St Dunstan's Educnl Foundn, 1977–91; Dulwich Picture Gall. Consultative Cttee, 1989–96; Mem. Bd of Governors, Shrewsbury Sch., 1969–97. Trustee: Ironbridge Gorge Mus. Develt Trust, 1989–93; Spry Trust (formerly Upper Severn Navigation Trust), 1989–; Third Age Challenge (formerly ReAction Trust), 1991–96; Wakefield (Tower Hill, Trinity Square) Trust, 1986–2007 (Chm., 2002–05). Mem., Guild of Freemen of City of London; Liveryman: Co. of World Traders (Master, 1989–90); Insurers' Co.; Freeman, Co. of Watermen and Lightermen. FRSA; FZS; FInstD. *Publications:* The Last Minute, 2000; A Thicket of Business, 2007. *Recreations:* sailing, motoring, listening to music, photography, cooking, travel. *Address:* Flat 79, New Concordia Wharf, Mill Street, SE1 2BB. *T:* (020) 7237 0818. *Clubs:* Royal Thames Yacht, Little Ship, Royal Green Jackets, City Livery.

BOWRING, Prof. Richard John; Master, Selwyn College, Cambridge, since 2000; Professor of Japanese Studies, University of Cambridge, since 1985; *b* 6 Feb. 1947; *s* of late Richard Arthur Bowring and of Mabel Bowring (*née* Eddy); *m* 1970, Susan (*née* Povey); one *d*. *Educ:* Blundell's Sch.; Downing Coll., Cambridge (PhD 1973; LittD 1997). Lectr in Japanese, Monash Univ., 1973–75; Asst Prof. of Japanese, Columbia Univ., NY, 1978–79; Associate Prof. of Japanese, Princeton Univ., NJ, 1979–84; Cambridge University: Lectr in Japanese, 1984; Chm., Faculty Bd of Oriental Studies, 1987–89, 1998–2000; Fellow, Downing Coll., 1985–2000; Hon. Fellow, 2000. British Acad. Reader, 1995–97. Trustee, Cambridge Foundn, 1989–98. Advr, UFC, subseq. HEFCE, 1992–94. Gov., SOAS, 1994–99. *Publications:* Mori Ogai and the Modernization of Japanese Culture, 1979; trans., Murasaki Shikibu: her diary and poetic memoirs, 1982; Murasaki Shikibu: The Tale of Genji, 1988, 2nd edn 2004; (jtly) An Introduction to Modern Japanese, 1992; (ed) Cambridge Encyclopedia of Japan, 1993; The Diary of Lady Murasaki, 1996; (jtly) Cambridge Intermediate Japanese, 2002; The Religious Traditions of Japan 500–1600, 2005. *Address:* The Master's Lodge, Selwyn College, Cambridge CB3 9DQ.

BOWRON, John Lewis, CBE 1986; solicitor; Secretary-General, The Law Society, 1974–87; *b* 1 Feb. 1924; *e s* of John Henry and Lavinia Bowron; *m* 1950, Patricia, *d* of Arthur Cobby; two *d*. *Educ:* Grangefield Grammar Sch., Stockton-on-Tees; King's Coll., London (LLB, FKC 1976). Principal in Malcolm Wilson & Cobby, Solicitors, Worthing, 1952–74. Member of the Council of the Law Society, 1969–74. Chm. (part-time), Social Security Appeal Tribunals, 1988–96; Agent (part-time) Crown Prosecution Service, 1988–93. *Address:* Hurworth, Sanctuary Lane, Storrington, Pulborough, West Sussex RH20 3JD. *T:* (01903) 746949.

See also M. R. Bowron.

BOWRON, Margaret Ruth, (Mrs A. T. Davy); QC 2001; *b* 8 July 1956; *d* of John Lewis Bowron, *qv* and Patricia (*née* Cobby); *m* 1988, Anthony Tallents Davy; two *d*. *Educ:* Convent of Our Lady of Sion, Worthing; Brighton and Hove High Sch., Brighton; King's Coll., London (LLB 1977). Called to the Bar, Inner Temple, 1978, Bencher, 2008; in practice as barrister, specialising in clinical negligence and related work, 1978–. *Recreations:* walking, theatre, travel. *Address:* (chambers) 1 Crown Office Row, Temple, EC4Y 7HH. *T:* (020) 7797 7500.

BOWRON, Michael, QPM 2007; Commissioner, City of London Police, since 2006 (Assistant Commissioner, 2002–06); *b* 8 Sept. 1957; *s* of Ronald and Christina Bowron; *m* 1994, Karen Elizabeth Purkiss. *Educ:* Ernest Bevin Comprehensive Sch., Tooting; Sussex Univ. (BA Hons (Sociol.) 1989). Sussex Police: Constable 1980; Sergeant 1984; Insp. 1985; Bramshill Schol., Sussex Univ., 1986–89; Chief Insp. 1990; Supt 1991; Asst Chief Constable, Kent Police, 1997–2002. *Recreations:* athletics, cross-country running, horse riding, travel. *Address:* City of London Police HQ, PO Box 36451, EC2M 4WN. *T:* (020) 7601 2001, *Fax:* (020) 7601 2060; *e-mail:* mike.bowron@city-of-london.pnn.police.uk. *Club:* Guildhall.

BOWSER of Argaty and the King's Lundies, David Stewart, JP; a Forestry Commissioner, 1974–82; *b* 11 March 1926; *s* of late David Charles Bowser, CBE and Maysie Murray Bowser (*née* Henderson); *m* 1951, Judith Crabbe; one *s* four *d*. *Educ:* Harrow; Trinity Coll., Cambridge (BA Agric). Captain, Scots Guards, 1944–47. Member: Nat. Bd of Timber Growers Scotland Ltd (formerly Scottish Woodland Owners' Assoc.), 1960–82 (Chm. 1972–74); Regional Adv. Cttee, West Scotland Conservancy, Forestry Commn, 1964–74 (Chm. 1970–74). Chm., Scottish Council, British Deer Soc., 1989–94; Mem., Blackface Sheep Breeders' Assoc. (Vice-Pres., 1981–83; Pres., 1983–84); Pres., Highland Cattle Soc., 1970–72. Trustee, Scottish Forestry Trust, 1983–89. Mem. Perth CC, 1954–61; JP Co. Perth, 1956. *Recreation:* fishing. *Address:* Auchlyne, Killin, Perthshire FK21 8RG.

BOWSHER, Michael Frederick Thomas; QC 2006; *b* 22 Nov. 1963; *s* of His Honour Peter Charles Bowsher, *qv*; *m* 1990, Haylee Fiona, *d* of Terrence and Mary O'Brien, Aberdare; two *s* one *d*. *Educ:* St George's Sch., Windsor Castle; Radley Coll.; Brasenose Coll., Oxford (BA). FCIArb 2000; Chartered Arbitrator, 2002. Called to the Bar: Middle Temple, 1985; NI, 2000; in practice, Chambers of Donald Keating, QC, then Keating Chambers, 1986–88 and 1992–2001; Associate, Cleary, Gottlieb, Steen & Hamilton (Brussels), 1988–92; in practice, Monckton Chambers, 2001–. Vice-Chm., ICC Task Force on Public Procurement, 2007–. *Publications:* (contrib.) Keating on Building Contracts, 5th edn 1991 to 7th edn 2001; (contrib.) Ward & Smith, Competition Litigation in the UK, 2005; articles on public procurement and competition law in Public Procurement Law Rev., Current Competition Law and Internat. Construction Law Rev. *Recreations:* choral music, watching sports, reading. *Address:* Monckton Chambers, 1 & 2 Raymond Buildings, Gray's Inn, WC1R 5NR. *T:* (020) 7405 7211, *Fax:* (020) 7405 2084; *e-mail:* mbowsher@monckton.com. *Clubs:* Brooks's; Leander (Henley-on-Thames).

BOWSHER, His Honour Peter Charles; QC 1978; FCIArb; arbitrator; a Judge of the Technology and Construction Court of the High Court, 1998–2003 (an Official Referee, 1987–98); *b* 9 Feb. 1935; *s* of Charles and Ellen Bowsher; *m* 1960, Deborah, *d* of Frederick Wilkins and Isobel Wilkins (*née* Copp), Vancouver; two *s*. *Educ:* Ardingly; Oriel Coll., Oxford (MA). FCIArb 1990; Chartered Arbitrator, 2000–. Commnd Royal Artillery, 1954; Territorial Army XX Rifle Team, 1957. Called to the Bar, Middle Temple, 1959, Bencher, 1985. Harmsworth Scholar; Blackstone Entrance Scholar. A Legal Assessor to GMC and GDC, 1979–87; a Recorder, 1983–87. Indep. Review Body, Modified Colliery Review Procedure, 1986–87; Adjudicator, Crown Prosecution Service (Transfer of Staff) Regulations, 1985, 1986–87. Member: IT and the Courts Cttee, 1991–2003; Judicial Cttee, British Acad. of Experts, 1992–2003; Arbrix, 2004–. Member: Soc. for Computers and Law, 1990–95; Soc. of Construction Arbitrators, 2005–. *Recreations:* photography, music. *Address:* Keating Chambers, 15 Essex Street, WC2R 3AU. *Clubs:* Brooks's, Royal Automobile.
See also M. F. T. Bowsher.

BOWTELL, Dame Ann (Elizabeth), DCB 1997 (CB 1989); Permanent Secretary, Department of Social Security, 1995–99; *b* 25 April 1938; *d* of John Albert and Olive Rose Kewell; *m* 1961, Michael John Bowtell; two *s* two *d*. *Educ:* Kendrick Girls' Sch., Reading; Girton Coll., Cambridge (MA; Hon. Fellow, 1997); Royal Holloway, Univ. of London (MA 2001). Asst Principal, Nat. Assistance Board, 1960; Principal: Nat. Assistance Board, 1964; Min. of Social Security, 1966; DHSS, 1968; Asst Sec., 1973, Under Sec., 1980, DHSS; Dep. Sec., DHSS, later DSS, 1986; Principal Establishment and Finance Officer, DoH (on secondment), 1990–93; First Civil Service Comr and Dep. Sec., Cabinet Office, 1993–95; Dep. Sec., DSS, 1995. Trustee, Joseph Rowntree Foundn, 2001–. Hon. Dr Middlesex, 1996. *Recreations:* bird watching, medieval history, music, walking. *Address:* 26 Sidney Road, Walton-on-Thames, Surrey KT12 2NA.

BOWYER, family name of **Baron Denham**.

BOWYER, Gordon Arthur, OBE 1970; RIBA; FCSD; Partner, Bowyer Langlands Batchelor (formerly Gordon Bowyer & Partners), Chartered Architects, 1948–92; *b* 21 March 1923; *s* of Arthur Bowyer and Kathleen Mary Bowyer; *m* 1950, Ursula Meyer; one *s* one *d*. *Educ:* Dauntsey's Sch.; Polytechnic of Central London. Architect and designer in private practice, in partnership with Ursula Bowyer, Iain Langlands and Stephen Batchelor, 1948–92. Practice started with design of Sports Section, South Bank Exhibn, Fest. of Britain, 1951; schs and hostel for handicapped children in Peckham, Bermondsey and Dulwich, 1966–75; housing for Southwark, GLC, Family Housing Assoc., London & Quadrant Housing Assoc. and Greenwich Housing Soc., 1969–83; numerous office conversions for IBM (UK), 1969–89; Peckham Methodist Church, 1975; new offices and shops for Rank City Wall at Brighton, 1975 and Folkestone, 1976; Treasury at Gloucester Cathedral, 1976; conservation at Vanbrugh Castle, Greenwich, 1973, Charlton Assembly Rooms, 1980, Hill Hall, Essex, 1982; lecture theatre, library and accommodation, Jt Services Defence Coll., RNC, Greenwich, 1983; Cabinet War Rooms Museum, Whitehall (with Alan Irvine), 1984; refurbishment of Barry Rooms at Nat. Gall., Stuart & Georgian Galls at Nat. Portrait Gall. and East Hall of Science Museum; new Prints & Drawings and Japanese Gall. at BM; gall. for Japanese prints, Fitzwilliam Mus. Advisory architect: Science Mus., 1992–96; Trustees' Buildings Cttee, Nat. Maritime Mus., 1993–96. Hon. Sec., SIAD, 1957–58. Mem. Council, Friends of the Nat. Maritime Mus., 1985–2003; Trustee, Nat. Maritime Museum, 1977–93. *Address:* 111 Maze Hill, SE10 8XQ. *Club:* Arts.

BOWYER, William, RA 1981 (ARA 1974); NEAC, RWS; Head of Fine Art, Maidstone College of Art, 1971–82; *b* 25 May 1926; *m* 1951, Vera Mary Small; two *s* one *d*. *Educ:* Burslem School of Art; Royal College of Art (ARCA). Former Hon. Sec., New English Art Club. Retrospective exhibn, Messum's, London, W1, 2003. *Recreations:* cricket (Chiswick and Old Meadonians Cricket Clubs), snooker. *Address:* 12 Cleveland Avenue, Chiswick, W4 1SN. *T:* (020) 8994 0346. *Club:* Arts.

BOWYER-SMYTH, Sir Thomas Weyland; *see* Smyth.

BOX, Prof. George Edward Pelham, BEM 1946; FRS 1985; Emeritus Professor of Statistics and Engineering, since 1992, and Director of Research, Center for Quality and Productivity, since 1990, University of Wisconsin-Madison; *b* 18 Oct. 1919; *s* of Harry and Helen (Martin) Box; *m* 1st, 1945, Jessie Ward; 2nd, 1959, Joan G. Fisher; one *s* one *d*; 3rd, 1985, Claire Louise Quist. *Educ:* London University (BSc Maths and Statistics 1947, PhD 1952, DSc 1961). Served War of 1939–45 in Army; res. at Chemical Defence Exptl Station, Porton. Statistician and Head Statistician, Statistical Res. Section, ICI, Blackley, 1948–56; Dir, Stats Tech. Res. Group, Princeton Univ., 1956–60; Prof. of Stats, 1960–92, and Vilas Res. Prof., Dept of Stats, 1980–92, Univ. of Wisconsin-Madison. Res. Prof., Univ. of N Carolina, 1952–53; Ford Foundn Vis. Prof., Harvard Business Sch., 1965–66; Vis. Prof., Univ. of Essex, 1970–71. President: Amer. Statistical Assoc., 1978; Inst. of Mathematical Statistics, 1979. Fellow, Amer. Acad. of Arts and Scis, 1974. Hon. DSc: Rochester, NY, 1975; Carnegie Mellon, 1989; Don Carlos III, Madrid, 1995; Waterloo, Canada, 1999; Conservatoire nat. des arts et métiers, Paris, 2000. Numerous medals and awards. *Publications:* Statistical Methods in Research and Production, 1957; Design and Analysis of Industrial Experiments, 1959; Evolutionary Operation: a statistical method for process improvement, 1969; Time Series Analysis Forecasting and Control, 1970; Bayesian Inference in Statistical Analysis, 1973; Statistics for Experimenters, 1977; Empirical Model Building and Response Surfaces, 1986; Statistical Control by Monitoring and Feedback Adjustment, 1997; Box on Quality and Discovery, 2000. *Address:* 911 Western Road, Madison, WI 53705, USA. *T:* (608) 4419905.

BOXALL, Barbara Ann, (Mrs Lewis Boxall); *see* Buss, B. A.

BOXER, Anna; *see* Ford, A.

BOXER, Charles Ian; *b* 11 Feb. 1926; *s* of Rev. William Neville Gordon Boxer and Margaret Boxer; *m* 1968, Hilary Fabienne Boxer. *Educ:* Glasgow High Sch.; Edinburgh Univ. (BL). Church of England ministry, 1950–54; apprentice to solicitors, 1954–58; Mem., Dominican Order (RC), 1958–67; Sen. Community Relations Officer for Wandsworth, 1967–77; Dir, Community Affairs and Liaison Div., Commn for Racial Equality, 1977–81. Communicator of the Year, BAIE Awards, 1976. *Recreation:* music. *Address:* Parish Farmhouse, Hassell Street, Hastingleigh, near Ashford, Kent TN25 5JE. *T:* (01233) 750219.

BOXSHALL, Dr Geoffrey Allan, FRS 1994; Deputy Chief Scientific Officer, Natural History Museum, since 1997; *b* 13 June 1950; *s* of John Edward Boxshall and Sybil Irene Boxshall (*née* Baker); *m* 1972, Roberta Gabriel Smith; one *s* three *d*. *Educ:* Churcher's Coll., Petersfield; Leeds Univ. (BSc, PhD). British Museum (Natural History), subseq. Natural History Museum: Higher SO, 1974–76; SSO, 1976–80; PSO, 1980–91; SPSO, 1991–97. *Publications:* (jtly) Dictionary of Ecology, Evolution and Systematics, 1982, 2nd edn 1998; (jtly) Cambridge Illustrated Dictionary of Natural History, 1987; (ed jtly) Biology of Copepods, 1988; (jtly) Copepod Evolution, 1991; (ed jtly) Pathogens of Wild and Farmed Fish: sea lice, 1993; An Introduction to Copepod Diversity, 2004; numerous papers in scientific jls. *Recreations:* tennis, reading, lexicography, travel. *Address:* Department of Zoology, Natural History Museum, Cromwell Road, SW7 5BD. *T:* (020) 7942 5749.

BOYACK, Sarah; Member (Lab) Edinburgh Central, Scottish Parliament, since 1999; *b* 16 May 1961; *d* of late Jim Boyack. *Educ:* Royal High Sch., Edinburgh; Glasgow Univ. (MA); Heriot-Watt Univ. (DipT&CP). MRTPI. Planning Asst, London Borough of Brent, 1986–88; Sen. Planning Officer, Central Regl Council, 1988–92; Lectr in Planning, Edinburgh Coll. of Art, 1992–99. Scottish Executive: Minister for Transport and the Envmt, 1999–2000, for Transport, 2000–01, for Transport and Planning, 2001; Dep. Minister for Envmt and Rural Develt, 2007. Scottish Parliament: shadow spokesperson on rural affairs, environment and climate change, 2007–; Convener, Envmt and Rural Develt Cttee, 2003–07; Mem., Rural Affairs and Envmt Cttee, 2007. *Address:* Scottish Parliament, Edinburgh EH99 1SP.

BOYCE, family name of **Baron Boyce**.

BOYCE, Baron *cr* 2003 (Life Peer), of Pimlico in the City of Westminster; **Adm. Michael Cecil Boyce,** GCB 1999 (KCB 1995); OBE 1982; DL; Lord Warden and Admiral of the Cinque Ports, and Constable of Dover Castle, since 2004; *b* 2 April 1943; *s* of late Comdr Hugh Boyce, DSC, RN and Madeleine Boyce (*née* Manley); *m* 1st, 1971, Harriette Gail Fletcher (separated 1994; marr. diss. 2005); one *s* one *d*; 2nd, 2006, Fleur Margaret Anne (*née* Smith), *widow* of Vice Adm. Malcolm Rutherford, CBE. *Educ:* Hurstpierpoint Coll.; BRNC, Dartmouth. Joined RN, 1961; qualified Submarines, 1965 and TAS, 1970; served in HM Submarines Anchorite, Valiant, and Conqueror, 1965–72; commanded: HM Submarines: Oberon, 1973–74; Opossum, 1974–75; Superb, 1979–81; HMS Brilliant, 1983–84; Captain (SM), Submarine Sea Training, 1984–86; RCDS, 1988; Sen. Naval Officer, ME, 1989; Dir Naval Staff Duties, 1989–91; Flag Officer: Sea Training, 1991–92; Surface Flotilla, 1992–95; Comdr, Anti-Submarine Warfare Striking Force, 1992–94; Second Sea Lord, and C-in-C Naval Home Comd, 1995–97; C-in-C Fleet, C-in-C Eastern Atlantic Area and Comdr Naval Forces N Western Europe, 1997–98; First Sea Lord and Chief of Naval Staff, and First and Principal Naval ADC to the Queen, 1998–2001; Chief of the Defence Staff, 2001–03; ADC to the Queen, 2001–03. Col Comdt, SBS, 2003–. Non-executive Director: VT Gp plc, 2004–; W. S. Atkins plc, 2004–. President: Officers' Assoc., 2003–; London Br., St John Ambulance, 2003–; RN Submarine Mus., 2005–; Member of Council: White Ensign Assoc., 2003– (Chm., 2007–); RNLI, 2004– (Trustee, 2006–; Chm., 2008–); Trustee, Nat. Maritime Mus., 2005–; Patron: Sail4Cancer, 2003–; Submariners Assoc., 2003–. Gov., Alleyn's Sch., 1995–2005. Freeman, City of London, 1999; Hon. Freeman, Drapers' Co., 2005. Elder Brother, Trinity House, 2006 (Yr Brother, 1999–2006). DL Greater London, 2003. KStJ 2002. Hon. LLD Portsmouth, 2005. Comdr, Legion of Merit (US), 1999 (Bronze Oak Leaf, 2003). *Recreations:* squash, tennis, Real tennis, sailing, windsurfing, opera. *Address:* House of Lords, SW1A 0PW. *Club:* Naval and Military (Dir, 2003–; Vice Chm., 2005–).
See also Sir G. H. Boyce.

BOYCE, Sir Graham (Hugh), KCMG 2001 (CMG 1991); HM Diplomatic Service, retired; Chairman, Middle East Advisory Board, Lehman Brothers, 2006–08; *b* 6 Oct. 1945; *s* of late Comdr Hugh Boyce, DSC, RN and Madeleine Boyce (*née* Manley); *m* 1970, Janet Elizabeth Spencer; one *s* three *d*. *Educ:* Hurstpierpoint Coll.; Jesus Coll., Cambridge (MA). VSO, Antigua, 1967; HM Diplomatic Service, 1968; Ottawa, 1971; MECAS, 1972–74; 1st Sec., Tripoli, Libya, 1974–77; FCO, 1977–81; Kuwait, 1981–85; Asst Hd of ME Dept, FCO, 1985–86; Counsellor and Consul-Gen., Stockholm, 1987–90; Ambassador and Consul-Gen., Doha, 1990–93; Counsellor, FCO, 1993–96; Ambassador to Kuwait, 1996–99; Ambassador to Egypt, 1999–2001. Chm., Middle East Adv. Bd, Invensys, 2005–; Vice Chm., VT Internat. Services, 2002–06; Member: Adv. Bd, Kuwait Investment Office, 2004–; Eur. Adv. Council, Air Products, 2007–; Jt Chm., Windsor Energy Gp, 2005–; various consultancies. Mem. Internat. Adv. Bd, SOAS, 2007–. *Recreations:* tennis, golf, reading. *Club:* Oxford and Cambridge.
See also Baron Boyce.

BOYCE, Joseph Frederick, JP; FRICS; General Manager, Telford Development Corporation, 1980–86; *b* 10 Aug. 1926; *s* of Frederick Arthur and Rosalie Mary Boyce; *m* 1953, Nina Margaret, *o d* of A. F. Tebb, Leeds; two *s*. *Educ:* Roundhay Sch., Leeds; Leeds Coll. of Technology. Articled Pupil and Sen. Assistant, Rex Procter & Miller, Chartered Quantity Surveyors, 1942–53; Sen. Quantity Surveyor, Bedford Corp., 1953–55; Group Quantity Surveyor, Somerset CC, 1955–60; Principal Quantity Surveyor, Shropshire CC, 1960–64; Telford Development Corporation: Chief Quantity Surveyor, 1964–71; Technical Dir, 1971–76; Dep. Gen. Manager, 1976–80. JP Shrewsbury, 1975. *Publications:* technical articles and publications on new towns, in learned journals. *Recreations:* gardening, hill walking, music, fine wine. *Address:* Grasse, Alpes-Maritimes, France.

BOYCE, Michael David; DL; FRWCMD; Chief Executive, Cardiff Bay Development Corporation, 1992–2000; *b* 27 May 1937; *s* of Clifford and Vera Boyce; *m* 1962, Audrey May Gregory; one *s* one *d*. *Educ:* Queen Elizabeth's Sch., Crediton. DMA 1962; Dip. in French, UC Cardiff, 1984. Admitted Solicitor, 1968. Asst Solicitor, 1968–69, Sen. Asst Solicitor, and Asst Clerk of the Peace, 1969–71, Exeter CC; Dep. Town Clerk, 1971–73, Dep. Chief Exec., 1973–74, Newport, Gwent; County Solicitor, S Glam, 1974–87; Chief Exec., S Glam CC, and Clerk to Lieutenancy, 1987–92. Mem., Home Office Adv. Council on Fire Service Pensions, 1976–87; Sec., Lord Chancellor's Adv. Cttee, 1987–92. Director: Cardiff Marketing Ltd, 1990–94; Cardiff Business Technology Centre Ltd, 1979–87; S Glam Youth Opportunities Ltd, 1979–87; New Openings Ltd, 1979–87; S Glam Investments Ltd, 1979–87. Member: Prince's Trust, 1987–92; Bd, S Glam TEC, 1987–95; Cardiff Chamber of Commerce & Trade, 1987–2000; S and Mid Glam Area Manpower Bd, 1976–79; Council, Cardiff Common Purpose, 1995–2000; Bd, Sgrîn Media Agency for Wales, 2002–04. Dir, Earthfall Dance Co. Ltd, 2003–. Advr, ACC, 1976–87; Legal Adviser: Assembly of Welsh Counties, 1976–87; Council of Museums in Wales, 1979–85; Hon. Solicitor, S Glam Probation and After-care Cttee, 1974–85. Member: Sports Council for Wales, 1980–82; BBC Wales Indep. Assessment Panel on Sport, 1997; Legal Advr, BBB of C, 2003–. Trustee: Glam County History Trust Ltd, 1974–85; S Wales Community Foundn, 1996–99; Trustee and Hon. Legal Advisor: STAR Recreation Trust, 1982–2002; Millennium Stadium Charitable Trust, 2002–04; Trustee and Presenter, Hosp. Radio Glamorgan, 2002–; Chm., Old St Mellons Community Council, 2000–. Mem. Council, Univ. of Wales Coll. of Cardiff, 1987–93; Governor: Royal Welsh Coll. of Music and Drama, 1992–98; St Mellons Ch in Wales Primary Sch., 2003–. Chm., Cardiff City AFC, 1993–95. Mem., TAVRA (Wales), 1987–92. FRWCMD (FWCMD 1999). DL S Glam, 1993. *Recreations:* France and French, Association Football, music, railways, travel. *Address:* 1 White Oaks Drive, Old St Mellons, Cardiff CF3 5EX. *T:* (029) 2079 1927.

BOYCE, Peter John, AO 1995; PhD; Vice-Chancellor, Murdoch University, Western Australia, 1985–96; Hon. Research Fellow, University of Tasmania, since 2004 (Visiting

Professor, 1996–2000; Hon. Professor of Political Science, 2000–04); *b* 20 Feb. 1935; *s* of Oswald and Marjorie Boyce; *m* 1962, Lorinne Peet; one *s* two *d*. *Educ:* Wesley Coll., Perth, WA; Univ. of Western Australia (MA); Duke Univ., USA (PhD). Res. Fellow, then Fellow, Dept of Internat. Relns, ANU, 1964–66; Nuffield Fellow, St Antony's Coll., Oxford, 1966–67; Sen. Lectr, then Reader, in Political Science, Tasmania Univ., 1967–75; Prof. of Pol. Science and Hd, Dept of Govt, Queensland Univ., 1976–79; Prof. of Politics and Hd of Dept, Univ. of W Australia, 1980–84. Visiting Fellow: Corpus Christi Coll., Cambridge, 1989; Merton Coll., Oxford, 1996; Christ Church, Oxford, 1997. Interim Principal, Aust. Maritime Coll., 2005–06. Exec. Mem., Aust.-NZ Foundn, 1979–83; Member: Aust. Human Rights Commn, 1981–86; Consultative Cttee on Relns with Japan, 1983–85; Asia Business Council of WA, 1993–96. Lay Canon of St George's Cath., Perth, 1986–96. Editor, Australian Outlook, 1973–77. Hon. LLD Tasmania, 2006. *Publications:* Malaysia and Singapore in International Diplomacy, 1968; Foreign Affairs for New States, 1977; (co-ord. ed.) Dictionary of Australian Politics, 1980; (co-ord. ed.) Politics in Queensland, 1980; (co-ord. ed.) The Torres Strait Treaty, 1981; (ed) Independence and Alliance, 1983; Diplomacy in the Market Place, 1991; Honest and Unsullied Days, 2001. *Recreations:* gardening, walking, church music. *Address:* Windrush, 20 Fisher Avenue, Lower Sandy Bay, Tas 7005, Australia. *T:* (03) 62252009.

BOYCE, Most Rev. Philip; *see* Raphoe, Bishop of, (RC).

BOYCE, Sir Robert (Leslie), 3rd Bt *cr* 1952; FRCSEd (Ophth); Consultant Ophthalmic and Oculoplastic Surgeon, Sunderland Eye Infirmary, since 2003; *b* 2 May 1962; *s* of Sir Richard (Leslie) Boyce, 2nd Bt, and of Jacqueline Anne (who *m* 2nd, 1974, Christopher Boyce-Dennis), *o d* of Roland A. Hill; *S* father, 1968; *m* 1985, Fiona, second *d* of John Savage, Whitmore Park, Coventry; one *s* one *d*. *Educ:* Cheltenham Coll.; Salford Univ. (BSc 1984, 1st cl. hons); Nottingham Univ. (BMedSci 1991, 1st cl. hons; BM BS 1993). FRCSEd (Ophth) 1998. Sen. House Officer, Manchester Royal Eye Hosp., 1995–98; Specialist Registrar in Ophthalmology, Royal Victoria Infirmary, Sunderland Eye Infirmary and N Riding Infirmary, 1998–2003. *Heir: s* Thomas Leslie Boyce, *b* 3 Sept. 1993.

BOYCE, Walter Edwin, OBE 1970; Director of Social Services, Essex County Council, 1970–78; *b* 30 July 1918; *s* of Rev. Joseph Edwin Boyce and Alice Elizabeth Boyce; *m* 1942, Edna Lane (*née* Gargett) (*d* 2001); two *d*. *Educ:* High Sch. for Boys, Trowbridge, Wilts. Admin. Officer, Warwickshire CC, 1938–49. Served war, commnd RA; Gunnery sc, 1943; demob. rank Major, 1946. Dep. County Welfare Officer: Shropshire, 1949–52; Cheshire, 1952–57; Co. Welfare Officer, Essex, 1957–70. Adviser to Assoc. of County Councils, 1965–78; Mem., Sec. of State's Adv. Personal Social Services Council, 1973 until disbanded, 1980 (Chm., People with handicaps Gp); Mem., nat. working parties on: Health Service collaboration, 1972–74; residential accommodation for elderly and mentally handicapped, 1974–78; boarding houses, 1981. Pres., County Welfare Officers Soc., 1967–68. Governor, Queen Elizabeth's Foundn for the Disabled, 1980–. *Recreations:* sailing, golf, in sports, particularly Rugby and athletics, voluntary services, travel. *Address:* Highlanders Barn, Newmans Green, Long Melford, Suffolk CO10 0AD.

BOYCE, William; QC 2001; a Recorder, since 1997; *b* 29 July 1951. *Educ:* St Joseph's Acad. Grammar Sch., Blackheath; Univ. of Kent (BA). Called to the Bar, Gray's Inn, 1976, Bencher, 2007; Jun. Treasury Counsel, 1991–97, Sen. Treasury Counsel, 1997–2001, CCC. *Address:* Queen Elizabeth Building, Temple, EC4Y 9BS. *T:* (020) 7583 5766.

BOYCOTT, Geoffrey; cricket commentator; *b* 21 Oct. 1940; *s* of late Thomas Wilfred Boycott and Jane Boycott; *m* 2003, Rachael Swinglehurst; one *d*. *Educ:* Kinsley Modern Sch.; Hemsworth Grammar Sch. Played cricket for Yorkshire, 1962–86, received County Cap, 1963, Captain of Yorkshire, 1970–78. Played for England, 1964–74, 1977–82; scored 100th first-class hundred, England v Australia, 1977, 150th hundred, 1986; passed former world record no of runs scored in Test Matches, Delhi, Dec. 1981. Mem., General Cttee, Yorks CCC, 1984–93. Commentator: BBC TV; Trans World Internat.; Channel 9; SABC; Talk Radio; ESPN Star; Channel 4, 2004–05; BBC Radio, 2004–; Ten Sports, 2006–; Five (formerly Channel 5), 2006–. Columnist, Daily Telegraph. *Publications:* Geoff Boycott's Book for Young Cricketers, 1976; Put to the Test: England in Australia 1978–79, 1979; Geoff Boycott's Cricket Quiz, 1979; On Batting, 1980; Opening Up, 1980; In the Fast Lane, 1981; Master Class, 1982; Boycott, The Autobiography, 1987; Boycott on Cricket, 1990; Geoffrey Boycott on Cricket, 1999. *Recreation:* golf. *Address:* c/o Yorkshire County Cricket Club, Headingley Cricket Ground, Leeds, Yorks LS6 3BY.

BOYCOTT, Rosie; Editor, The Express, 1998–2001; *b* 13 May 1951; *d* of late Charles Boycott and of Betty Boycott; *m* 1983, David Leitch (marr. diss. 1998; he *d* 2004); one *d*; *m* 1999, Charles Anthony Frederick Howard, *qv*. *Educ:* Cheltenham Ladies' Coll.; Kent Univ. (pure maths). Has worked on: Frendz mag., 1971; Spare Rib (Founder and Editor), 1971–72; Luka (Buddhist Jl of America), 1973–75; Osrati (Kuwait), 1976–79; Honey mag., 1979–81 (Dep. Ed.); Daily Mail, 1984–85; Sunday Telegraph, Harpers & Queen, 1989–92; Editor: Esquire, 1992–96; Independent on Sunday, 1996–98; The Independent, 1998. Regular appearances on The Late Review (BBC2) and The Moral Maze (BBC Radio 4). Dir, Dillington Park Nurseries, 2005–. Bd Mem., Old Vic, 2002–05; Trustee, Hay-on-Wye Literary Fest., 2000–. Trustee, Warchild. Editor of Year (Magazines), 1994, 1995. *Publications:* Batty, Bloomers & Boycott, 1982; A Nice Girl Like Me, 1984; All for Love, 1987; Our Farm, 2007. *Recreations:* riding, ski-ing, tennis, reading, arts. *Club:* Groucho.

BOYD; *see* Lennox-Boyd.

BOYD, family name of **Barons Boyd of Duncansby** and **Kilmarnock**.

BOYD OF DUNCANSBY, Baron *cr* 2006 (Life Peer), of Duncansby in Caithness; **Colin David Boyd;** PC 2000; Lord Advocate, Scottish Executive, 2000–06; *b* 7 June 1953; *s* of Dr David Hugh Aird Boyd and Betty Meldrum Boyd; *m* 1979, Fiona Margaret MacLeod; two *s* one *d*. *Educ:* Wick High Sch.; George Watson's Coll., Edinburgh; Manchester Univ. (BA Econ); Edinburgh Univ. (LLB). Solicitor, 1978–82; called to the Bar, Scotland, 1983; Legal Associate, Royal Town Planning Inst., 1990; Advocate Depute, 1993–95; QC (Scot.) 1995; Solicitor General: for Scotland, 1997–99; Scottish Exec., 1999–2000. FRSA 2000. *Publication:* (contrib.) The Legal Aspects of Devolution, 1997. *Recreations:* walking, reading, watching Rugby. *Address:* House of Lords, SW1A 0PW.

BOYD OF MERTON, 2nd Viscount *cr* 1960, of Merton-in-Penninghame, Co. Wigtown; **Simon Donald Rupert Neville Lennox-Boyd;** *b* 7 Dec. 1939; *e s* of 1st Viscount Boyd of Merton, CH, PC, and Lady Patricia Guinness, *d* of 2nd Earl of Iveagh, KG, CB, CMG, FRS; *S* father, 1983; *m* 1962, Alice Mary (JP, DL, High Sheriff of Cornwall, 1987–88), *d* of late Major M. G. D. Clive and of Lady Mary Clive; two *s* two *d*. *Educ:* Eton; Christ Church, Oxford. Dep. Chm., Arthur Guinness & Sons, 1981–86. Chairman: SCF, 1987–92 (Vice-Chm., 1979–82); Stonham Housing Assoc., 1992–99; Iveagh Trustees Ltd, 1992–2003; Trustee, Guinness Trust, 1974–2004. *Heir: s* Hon. Benjamin Alan Lennox-Boyd [*b* 21 Oct. 1964; *m* 1993, Sheila Carroll; two *s* one *d*]. *Address:* Ince Castle, Saltash, Cornwall PL12 4QZ. *T:* (01752) 842672.

See also Baron Spens.

BOYD, Alan Robb; NP; Director, Public Law, McGrigors LLP (formerly McGrigor Donald), solicitors, since 1997; *b* 30 July 1953; *er s* of Alexander Boyd and Mary Herd Boyd; *m* 1973, Frances Helen Donaldson; two *d*. *Educ:* Irvine Royal Acad.; Univ. of Dundee (LLB 1974); Open Univ. (BA 1985). Admitted solicitor, 1976; Principal Legal Asst, Shetland Is Council, 1979–81; Principal Solicitor, Glenrothes Develt Corp., 1981–84; Legal Advr, Irvine Develt Corp., 1984–97. Mem. Council, Law Soc. of Scotland, 1985–97 (Vice-Pres., 1994–95; Pres., 1995–96); Bd Mem., 1988–94, Pres., 1992–94, European Company Lawyers' Assoc.; Chm., Assoc. for Scottish Public Affairs, 1998–2000. *Recreations:* golf, music, gardening. *Address:* 45 Craigholm Road, Ayr KA7 3LJ. *T:* (01292) 262542. *Club:* Turnberry Golf.

BOYD, Sir Alexander Walter, 3rd Bt *cr* 1916; *b* 16 June 1934; *s* of late Cecil Anderson Boyd, MC, MD, and Marjorie Catharine, *e d* of late Francis Kinloch, JP, Shipka Lodge, North Berwick; *S* uncle, 1948; *m* 1958, Molly Madeline, *d* of late Ernest Arthur Rendell; two *s* three *d*. *Heir: s* Ian Walter Rendell Boyd [*b* 14 March 1964; *m* 1986, LeeAnn Dillon; three *s*].

BOYD, Andrew Jonathan Corrie, CMG 2005; OBE 1992; HM Diplomatic Service, retired; Director, Special Projects, QinetiQ plc, since 2005; *b* 5 May 1950; *s* of John Ronald Boyd and Jane Rhiain Boyd (*née* Morgan); *m* 1979, Ginette Anne Vischer; two *s* one *d*. *Educ:* Tonbridge Sch.; BRNC Dartmouth; St John's Coll., Oxford (BA Hons PPE). Served RN, Submarine Service, 1968–80. Entered FCO, 1980; First Secretary: FCO, 1980; (Econ.), Accra, 1981–84; (Chancery), Mexico City, 1988–91; Political Counsellor, Islamabad, 1996–99; Counsellor, FCO, 1999–2005. *Recreations:* mountain walking, sea swimming, military history. *Address:* c/o Foreign and Commonwealth Office, King Charles Street, SW1A 2AH.

BOYD, Atarah, (Mrs Douglas Boyd); *see* Ben-Tovim, A.

BOYD, (David) John; QC 1982; arbitrator; accredited mediator; Chairman, Axxia Systems Ltd, 1995–2008; *b* 11 Feb. 1935; *s* of David Boyd and Ellen Jane Boyd (*née* Gruer); *m* 1960, Raija Sinikka Lindholm, Finland; one *s* one *d*. *Educ:* Eastbourne Coll.; St George's Sch., Newport, USA (British-Amer. schoolboy schol.); Gonville and Caius Coll., Cambridge (MA). FCIArb 1979. Various secretarial posts, ICI, 1957–62; Legal Asst, Pfizer, 1962–66; called to the Bar, Gray's Inn, 1963, Bencher, 1988; Sec. and Legal Officer, Henry Wiggin & Co., 1966; Asst Sec. and Sen. Legal Officer (UK), Internat. Nickel, 1968; Dir, Impala Platinum, 1972–78; Sec. and Chief Legal Officer, 1972–86, and Dir, 1984–86, Inco Europe; practising barrister, 1986; Director: Legal Services, 1986–93, Public Affairs and Communications, 1993–95, Digital Equipment Co.; Digital Equipment Scotland, 1987–95. Gen. Comr of Income Tax, 1978–83; Immigration Adjudicator, 1995–2005; Immigration Judge, 2005–08; Vice-Pres., Council of Immigration Judges, 1998–2000. Chm., Bar Assoc. for Commerce, Finance and Industry, 1980–81; Mem., Senate of Inns of Court and Bar, 1978–81. Sec. Gen., Assoc. des Juristes d'Entreprise Européens (European Company Lawyers Assoc.), 1983–84. Dir, Centre for European Dispute Resolution, 1991–94. Legal Advisor to Review Bd for Govt Contracts, 1984–91. Chm., CBI Competition Panel, 1988–93; Mem., Electricity Panel, Monopolies and Mergers Commn, 1991–98. Mem., Exec. Cttee, Royal Acad. of Dancing, 1991–98; Chm., The Place Th. and Contemp. Dance Trust, 1995–98; Dir, Oxford Orch. da Camera, 1996–2001. Treas., Upton Bishop PCC, 2003–. *Recreations:* holidaying in France, viticulture. *Address:* Beeches, Upton Bishop, Ross-on-Wye, Herefordshire HR9 7UD. *T:* (01989) 780214, *Fax:* (01989) 780538; *e-mail:* boyd456@btinternet.com.

BOYD, Dennis Galt, CBE 1988; Chief Conciliation Officer, Advisory, Conciliation and Arbitration Service, 1980–92; *b* 3 Feb. 1931; *s* of late Thomas Ayre Boyd and Minnie (*née* Galt); *m* 1953, Pamela Mary McLean; one *s* one *d*. *Educ:* South Shields High School for Boys. National Service, 1949–51; Executive Officer, Civil Service: Min. of Supply/Min. of Defence, 1951–66; Board of Trade, 1966–69; Personnel Officer, Forestry Commission, 1969–75; Director of Corporate Services Health and Safety Executive, Dept of Employment, 1975–79; Director of Conciliation (ACAS), 1979–80. Hon. FIPM 1985. *Recreation:* compulsory gardening. *Address:* Dunelm, Silchester Road, Little London, Tadley RG26 5EW.

BOYD, Prof. Ian Lamont, DSc; FRSE; Professor of Biology, and Director, NERC Sea Mammal Research Unit, University of St Andrews, since 2001; *b* 9 Feb. 1957; *s* of late Dr John Morton Boyd, CBE, FRSE and of Winifred Isobel Boyd; *m* 1982, Sheila M. E. Aitken; one *s* two *d*. *Educ:* George Heriot's Sch., Edinburgh; Univ. of Aberdeen (BSc 1st Cl. Hons 1979; DSc 1996); St John's Coll., Cambridge (PhD 1983). Churchill Fellow, 1980; SSO, Inst. of Terrestrial Ecol., 1982–87, SPSO, British Antarctic Survey, 1987–2001, NERC. Hon. Prof., Univ. of Birmingham, 1997–. Chm., Marine Sci. Scotland, 2005–; Member, Council of Management: Hebridean Trust, 1990–; Seamark Trust, 1993–; Scottish Assoc. for Marine Sci., 2004–; Scottish Sustainable Seas Task Force, 2008; Mem. Adv. Council, Nat. Oceanography Centre, Southampton, 2008–. Ed., 2000–06, Ed.-in-Chief, 2006–07, Jl of Zoology. FRSE 2002. US Antarctic Medal, 1995; Bruce Medal, RSE, 1996; Scientific Medal, Zool Soc. of London, 1998; Marsh Award for Marine & Freshwater Conservation, Zool Soc. of London, 2006. *Publications:* The Hebrides: a natural history, 1990; Marine Mammals: advances in behavioural and population biology, 1993; The Hebrides: a mosaic of islands, 1996; The Hebrides: a natural tapestry, 1996; The Hebrides: a habitable land, 1996; Conserving Nature: Scotland and the wider world, 2005; Top Predators in Marine Ecosystems, 2006; contrib. numerous papers to scientific jls. *Recreations:* walking, sailing, photography, Rugby. *Address:* Sea Mammal Research Unit, Gatty Marine Laboratory, University of St Andrews, St Andrews, Fife KY16 8LB. *T:* (01334) 462630, *Fax:* (01334) 462632; *e-mail:* ilb@st-andrews.ac.uk.

BOYD, Ian Robertson; HM Stipendiary Magistrate, West Yorkshire, 1982–89; a Recorder of the Crown Court, 1983–88; *b* 18 Oct. 1922; *s* of Arthur Robertson Boyd, Edinburgh, and Florence May Boyd (*née* Kinghorn), Leeds; *m* 1952, Joyce Mary Boyd (*née* Crabtree); one *s* one *d*. *Educ:* Roundhay Sch.; Leeds Univ. (LLB (Hons)). Served Army, 1942–47: Captain Green Howards; Royal Lincolnshire Regt in India, Burma, Malaya, Dutch East Indies. Leeds Univ., 1947; called to Bar, Middle Temple, 1952; practised North Eastern Circuit, 1952–72; HM Stipendiary Magistrate, sitting at Hull, 1972–82. Sometime Asst/Dep. Recorder of Doncaster, Newcastle, Hull and York. *Recreation:* gardener manqué.

BOYD, James Edward, CA; Director and Financial Adviser, Denholm group of companies, 1968–96; *b* 14 Sept. 1928; *s* of Robert Edward Boyd and Elizabeth Reid Sinclair; *m* 1956, Judy Ann Christey Scott; two *s* two *d*. *Educ:* Kelvinside Academy; The Leys Sch., Cambridge. CA Scot. (dist.) 1951. Director: Lithgows (Hldgs), 1962–87; Ayrshire Metal Products plc, 1965–93 (Chm., 1991–93); Invergordon Distillers (Holdings) plc, 1966–88; GB Papers plc, 1977–87; Jebsens Drilling plc, 1978–85; Scottish

Widows' Fund & Life Assurance Soc., 1981–93 (Dep. Chm., 1988–93); Shanks & McEwan Gp Ltd, 1983–94; Scottish Exhibn Centre Ltd, 1983–89; British Linen Bank Ltd, 1983–94 (Gov., 1986–94); Bank of Scotland, 1984–94; Yarrow PLC, 1984–86 (Chm., 1985–86); Bank of Wales, 1986–88; Save and Prosper Gp Ltd, 1987–89; James River UK Hldgs Ltd, 1987–90; Chairman: London & Gartmore Investment Trust plc, 1978–91; English & Caledonian Investment plc, 1981–91. Partner, McClelland Ker & Co. CA (subseq. McClelland Moores & Co.), 1953–61; Finance Director: Lithgows Ltd, 1962–69; Scott Lithgow Ltd, 1970–78; Chm., Fairfield Shipbuilding & Engrg Co. Ltd, 1964–65; Man. Dir, Invergordon Distillers (Holdings) Ltd, 1966–67; Director: Nairn & Williamson (Holdings) Ltd, 1968–75; Carlton Industries plc, 1978–84. Dep. Chm., BAA plc (formerly British Airports Authority), 1985–94; Member: CAA (part-time), 1984–85; Clyde Port Authority, 1974–80; Working Party on Scope and Aims of Financial Accounts (the Corporate Report), 1974–75; Exec. Cttee, Accountants Jt Disciplinary Scheme, 1979–81; Mem. Council, Inst. of Chartered Accountants of Scotland, 1977–83 (Vice-Pres., 1980–82, Pres., 1982–83). Mem. Council, Glenalmond Coll., 1983–92. *Recreations:* tennis, golf, gardening, painting. *Address:* Dunard, Station Road, Rhu, Dunbartonshire, Scotland G84 8LW. *T:* (01436) 820441.

BOYD, John; *see* Boyd, D. J.

BOYD, Sir John (Dixon Iklé), KCMG 1992 (CMG 1985); HM Diplomatic Service, retired; Fellow, Churchill College, Cambridge, since 2006 (Master, 1996–2006); Chairman, Trustees, British Museum, 2002–06 (Trustee, 1996–2006, now Trustee Emeritus); *b* 17 Jan. 1936; *s* of Prof. James Dixon Boyd and late Amélie Lowenthal; *m* 1st, 1968, Gunilla Kristina Ingegerd Rönngren; one *s* one *d*; 2nd, 1977, Julia Daphne Raynsford; three *d*. *Educ:* Westminster Sch. (Hon. Fellow, 2003); Clare Coll., Cambridge (BA; Hon. Fellow, 1994); Yale Univ. (MA). Joined HM Foreign Service, 1962; Hong Kong, 1962–64; Peking, 1965–67; Foreign Office, 1967–69; Washington, 1969–73; 1st Sec., Peking, 1973–75; secondment to HM Treasury, 1976; Counsellor: (Economic), Bonn, 1977–81; (Economic and Soc. Affairs), UK Mission to UN, 1981–84; Asst Under-Sec. of State, FCO, 1984; Political Advr, Hong Kong, 1985–87; Dep. Under-Sec. of State, FCO, 1987–89; Chief Clerk, FCO, 1989–92; Ambassador to Japan, 1992–96. Non-exec. Dir, BNFL, 1997–2000. UK Rep., ASEM Vision Gp, 1998–2000; Mem., All Nippon Airways Adv. Gp, 2003–. Co-Chm., Nuffield Langs Inquiry, 1998–2000. Syndic, Fitzwilliam Mus., 1997–2002. Trustee: Sir Winston Churchill Archive Trust, 1996–2006; Wordsworth Trust, 1997–; Margaret Thatcher Archive Trust, 1997–2006; Cambridge Foundn, 1997–2005; GB Sasakawa Foundn, 2001–; RAND Europe (UK), 2001–; Huang Hsing Foundn, 2001–; Joseph Needham Res. Inst., 2005– (Chm., 2008–). Gov., RSC, 1996–2005. Member: Council, Cambridge Univ. Senate, 2001–04; Bd, and Advr, E Asia Inst., Cambridge Univ., 1998–2006; Internat. Adv. Council, Asia House, 2001–; Bd, UK-Japan 21st Century Gp, 2006–; Emeritus Fellow, British Assoc. for Japanese Studies, 2007–. Chairman: Bd of Govs, Bedales Sch., 1996–2001; David Davies Meml Inst., 1997–2001; Trustees, Cambridge Union Soc., 1997–2006. Vice-Chm., Yehudi Menuhin Internat. Violin Trust Ltd, 1996–. Vice Pres., Lakeland Housing Trust, 2007–. Grand Cordon, Order of the Rising Sun (Japan), 2007. *Recreations:* music, fly fishing. *Clubs:* Athenæum, Beefsteak.

See also Sir R. D. H. Boyd.

BOYD, John MacInnes, CBE 1990; QPM 1984; HM Chief Inspector of Constabulary for Scotland, 1993–96; *b* 14 Oct. 1933; *s* of late F. Duncan Boyd and M. Catherine MacInnes; *m* 1957, Sheila MacSporran; two *s*. *Educ:* Oban High School. Paisley Burgh Police, 1956–67; Renfrew and Bute Constabulary, 1967–75; Strathclyde Police, 1975–84 (Asst Chief Constable, 1979–84); Chief Constable, Dumfries and Galloway Constabulary, 1984–89; HM Inspector of Constabulary for Scotland, 1989–93. Pres., Scotland, ACPO, 1988–89. *Recreations:* golf, gardening, reading, photography. *Address:* Beechwood, Lochwinnoch Road, Kilmacolm PA13 4DZ.

BOYD, (John) Michael; Artistic Director, Royal Shakespeare Company, since 2003 (Associate Director, 1996–2003); *b* 6 July 1955; *s* of John Truesdale Boyd and Sheila Boyd; one *s* one *d* by Marcella Evaristi; one *d* by Caroline Hall. *Educ:* Latymer Upper Sch.; Daniel Stewart's Coll.; Univ. of Edinburgh (MA English Lit.). Trainee Dir, Malaya Bronnaya Th., Moscow, 1979; Asst Dir, Belgrade Th., Coventry, 1980–82; Associate Dir, Crucible Th., Sheffield, 1982–84; Founding Artistic Dir, Tron Th., Glasgow, 1985–96. Hon. Prof., Univ. of Michigan, 2001–04. *Productions:* for Tron Theatre: The Guid Sisters, 1989, Tremblay's The Real World, 1991 (also Toronto, NY and Montreal); (with I. Glen) Macbeth, 1993; The Trick is to Keep Breathing (also Royal Court and World Stage Fest., Toronto), 1995; for Royal Shakespeare Co.: The Broken Heart, 1994; The Spanish Tragedy, 1996; Measure for Measure, 1997; Troilus and Cressida (also Tel Aviv and USA), 1999; A Midsummer Night's Dream (also NY), 1999; Romeo and Juliet, 2000; Henry VI, Parts 1, 2 and 3, and Richard III (also USA), 2001; The Tempest, 2002; Hamlet, transf. Albery, 2004; Twelfth Night, transf. Novello, 2005; The Histories, 2006–08, transf. Roundhouse, 2008; West End: Miss Julie, Haymarket, 2000. *Recreations:* cooking, walking, swimming, reading, music. *Address:* c/o Royal Shakespeare Theatre, Waterside, Stratford upon Avon, Warks CV37 6BB. *T:* (01789) 296655.

BOYD, Morgan Alistair, CMG 1990; Adviser, Commonwealth Development Corporation, 1994–2000; *b* 1 May 1934; *s* of Norman Robert Boyd and Kathleen Muriel Boyd; *m* 1959, Judith Mary Martin. *Educ:* Marlborough College; Wadham College, Oxford (BA, MA 1955). FRGS 1957. Commonwealth Development Corporation: Management trainee, 1957; Exec., Malaysia, 1958–66; Manager, East Caribbean Housing, Barbados, 1967–70; Gen. Manager, Tanganyika Develt Finance Co., 1970–74; Advr, Industrial Develt Bank, Kenya, 1975; Regl Controller, Central Africa, 1976–80, East Africa, 1981–82; Dep. Gen. Manager, Investigations, London, 1983–84; Dir of Ops, 1985–89; Dep. Gen. Manager, 1989–91; Dep. Chief Exec., 1991–94. Director: EDESA Management, Switzerland, 1995–97; Tea Plantations Investment Trust PLC, 1998–; AMREF UK, 1999–2007 (Chm., 2001–07); Chm., Gateway to Growth Ltd, 2005–. Chm., Southern Africa Business Assoc., 1995–2007. Member: RSA 1990–; Council, Royal African Soc., 1992– (Vice-Chm., 1996–); Management Council, Africa Centre, 1995–2002. *Publication:* Royal Challenge Accepted, 1962. *Recreations:* music, sailing, travel. *Address:* 7 South Hill Mansions, South Hill Park, NW3 2SL. *T:* (020) 7435 1082. *Clubs:* Naval, English-Speaking Union.

BOYD, Norman Jonathan; Member, Antrim South, Northern Ireland Assembly, 1998–2003 (UKU, 1998–99, NIU, 1999–2003); *b* 16 Oct. 1961; *s* of William and Jean Boyd; *m* 1984, Sylvia Christine (*née* Brindley); one *s* one *d*. *Educ:* Belfast High Sch.; Newtownabbey Technical Coll. (BEC Nat. Cert. in Business Studies with Distinction, 1982). Joined Halifax Bldg Soc., later Halifax plc, 1980: posts included Deptl Manager, Asst Branch Manager, and Manager. NIUP Whip, NI Assembly, 1999–2002. Member: Kilroot True Blues Loyal Orange Lodge, 1988–; Kilroot Royal Arch Purple Chapter, 1989–; Royal Black Instn, Carrickfergus, 1993–. Formerly Mem., Boys' Bde (President's Badge, 1979; Queen's Badge, 1980). *Recreations:* sport - soccer, caravanning, theatre, cinema, programme collecting. *Address:* 18 Woodford Park, Newtownabbey, Co. Antrim BT36 6TJ. *T:* (028) 9084 4297, *Fax:* (028) 9083 6644.

BOYD, Sir Robert (David Hugh), Kt 2004; FRCP, FFPH, FRCPCH, FMedSci; Principal, St George's Hospital Medical School, University of London, 1996–2003; Professor of Paediatrics, 1996–2003, Pro-Vice Chancellor (Medicine), 2000–03, and Deputy Vice-Chancellor, 2002–03, University of London; *b* 14 May 1938; *s* of James Dixon Boyd and Amélie Boyd; *m* 1966, Meriel Cornelia Talbot; one *s* two *d*. *Educ:* Ley's Sch.; Clare Coll., Cambridge (MA; MB, BChir); University Coll. Hosp., London. FRCP 1977; FFPH (FFPHM 1997); FRCPCH 1997. Jun. med. posts, Hosp. for Sick Children, Gt Ormond St, Brompton Hosp., UCH, 1962–65; Sir Stuart Halley Res. Fellow and Sen. Registrar, UC Hosp. and Med. Sch., 1966–71; Goldsmith's MRC Travelling Fellow, Univ. of Colo Med. Center, 1971–72; Sen. Lectr and Hon. Consultant, UCH Med. Sch., 1972–80; Asst Registrar, RCP, 1980–81; University of Manchester Medical School: Prof. of Paediatrics, 1981–96; Dean, 1989–93; Vis. Prof., 1996–; Hon. Consultant: St Mary's Hosp., Manchester and Booth Hall Children's Hosp., Manchester, 1981–96; St George's Healthcare NHS Trust, 1996–2003. Chm., Nat. Primary Care R&D Centre, Manchester, Salford and York Univs, 1994–96. Vis. Prof., Oregon Health Sci. Univ., 1988. Ed., Placenta, 1989–95. Chm., Manchester HA, 1994–96. Member: Standing Med. Adv. Cttee, 1988–92; Standing Cttee on Postgrad. Med. and Dental Educn, 1995–99; Jt Med. Adv. Cttee, HEFCs, 1994–99; Univs UK (formerly CVCP), 1997–2003 (Mem. Health Cttee, 1997–2003); Scientific Adv. Cttee, AMRC, 1996–2003; Council, RVC, 1999–2004; Chm., Council of Heads of UK Med. Schs, 2001–03; Dir, Gtr Manchester Res. Alliance, 2004–. Chair: Lloyds TSB Foundn for England & Wales, 2003–; Council for Assisting Refugee Academics, 2004–. Non-exec. Chm., Nuovoprobe, 2007–. Mem., Taskforce supporting R & D in NHS (Culyer Cttee), 1994. Sec., 1977–80, Chm., 1987–90, Acad. Bd, BPA. Co-opted Gov., Kingston Univ., 1998–2003; Gov., Univ. of Manchester, 2004–. Pres., 1942 Club, 1998–99. Hon. Mem., Amer. Pediatric Soc., 2006. Founder FMedSci 1998. Hon. DSc: Kingston, 2003; Keele, 2005. *Publications:* (jtly) Paediatric Problems in General Practice, 1982, 3rd edn 1996; contribs to Placental and Fetal Physiol. and Paediatrics. *Recreations:* flute, tennis, cooking, reading, holidays. *Address:* The Stone House, Adlington, Macclesfield, Cheshire SK10 4NU. *T:* (01625) 872400.

See also Sir J. D. I. Boyd.

BOYD, Robert Stanley, CB 1982; Solicitor of Inland Revenue, 1979–86; *b* 6 March 1927; *s* of Robert Reginald Boyd (formerly Indian Police) and Agnes Maria Dorothea, *d* of Lt-Col Charles H. Harrison; *m* 1965, Ann, *d* of Daniel Hopkin. *Educ:* Wellington; Trinity Coll., Dublin (BA, LLB). Served RN, 1945–48. Called to Bar, Inner Temple, 1954. Joined Inland Revenue, 1959; Prin. Asst Solicitor, 1971–79. *Address:* Great Beere, North Tawton, Devon EX20 2BS.

BOYD, Stewart Craufurd, CBE 2005; QC 1981; a Recorder, since 1994; *b* 25 Oct. 1943; *s* of late Leslie Balfour Boyd, CBE, and Wendy Marie Boyd; *m* 1970, Catherine Jay; one *s* three *d*. *Educ:* Winchester Coll.; Trinity Coll., Cambridge (MA). Called to the Bar, Middle Temple, 1967, Bencher, 1989. Dep. Chm., FSA, 1999–. *Publications:* (ed) Scrutton, Charterparties, 18th edn 1972, 19th edn 1984; (with Sir Michael Mustill) The Law and Practice of Commercial Arbitration, 1982, 1989; contrib. Civil Justice Rev., Arbitration Internat., Lloyd's Commercial and Maritime Law Qly. *Recreations:* boats, pianos, gardens. *Address:* 1 Gayton Crescent, NW3 1TT. *T:* (020) 7431 1581.

BOYD, Dame Vivienne (Myra), DBE 1986 (CBE 1983); Vice Chairperson, Hutt Diabetic Foundation, since 1992; *b* 11 April 1926; *d* of Hugh France Lowe and Winifred May Lowe (*née* Shearer); *m* 1948, Robert Macdonald Boyd; three *d* (one *s* decd). *Educ:* Eastern Hutt Sch.; Hutt Valley High Sch.; Victoria Coll., Univ. of New Zealand (MSc (Hons)). President: Dunedin Free Kindergarten Assoc., 1965; NZ Baptist Women's League, 1966; Nat. Council of Women of NZ, 1978–82; NZ Baptist Union of Churches and Missionary Soc., 1984–85; Wellington Br., NZ Epilepsy Assoc., 1994–96; Hutt Valley Br., NZ Fedn of Graduate Women, 2002–04. Member: Royal Commn on Nuclear Power Generation, 1976–78; Equal Opportunities Tribunal, 1979–89; Advertising Standards Council, subseq. Advertising Standards Complaints Bd, 1988–97; Envmtl Choice Mgt Adv. Cttee, 1990–98; chaired: Abortion Supervisory Cttee, 1979–80; Women and Recreation Conf., 1981; Review of Preparation and Initial Employment of Nurses, 1986–92; Consumer Council, NZ, 1983–88 (Mem., 1975–88); Consumers' Inst. of NZ Inc., 1988–89 (Mem. Bd, 1989–90); Convener, Internat. Council of Women Standing Cttee on Social Welfare, 1982–88. Mem., NZ Medic Alert Trust Bd, 1995–. Chm., Taita Home and Hosp. for the Elderly, 1989–92. Trustee, Celebrating Women Trust, 1998–2003. Silver Jubilee Medal, 1977. *Recreations:* reading, gardening.

BOYD, William Andrew Murray, CBE 2005; FRSL; author; *b* 7 March 1952; *s* of Dr Alexander Murray Boyd and Evelyn Boyd; *m* 1975, Susan Anne (*née* Wilson). *Educ:* Gordonstoun Sch.; Glasgow Univ. (MA Hons English and Philosophy); Jesus Coll., Oxford (Hon. Fellow, 2007). Lecturer in English, St Hilda's Coll., Oxford, 1980–83; Television Critic, New Statesman, 1981–83. *Screenplays:* Good and Bad at Games (TV), 1983; Dutch Girls (TV), 1985; Scoop (TV), 1987; Stars and Bars, 1988; Aunt Julia and the Scriptwriter, 1990; Mr Johnson, 1990; Chaplin, 1992; A Good Man in Africa, 1994; The Trench, 1999 (also Dir); Sword of Honour (TV), 2001; Armadillo (TV), 2001; Man to Man, 2005; A Waste of Shame (TV), 2005. FRSL 1983. Hon. DLitt: St Andrews, 1997; Stirling, 1997; Glasgow, 2000; Dundee, 2008. Officier de l'Ordre des Arts et des Lettres (France), 2005. *Publications:* A Good Man in Africa, 1981 (Whitbread Prize 1981, Somerset Maugham Award 1982); On the Yankee Station (short stories), 1981; An Ice-Cream War, 1982 (John Llewellyn Rhys Prize, 1982); Stars and Bars, 1984; School Ties (screenplays: Good and Bad at Games; Dutch Girls), 1985; The New Confessions, 1987; Brazzaville Beach, 1990 (James Tait Black Meml Prize, 1990; McVitie's Prize, 1991); The Blue Afternoon, 1993 (Sunday Express Book of the Year Award, 1993; LA Times Book Award for Fiction, 1995); The Destiny of Nathalie X (short stories), 1995; Armadillo, 1998; Nat Tate: an American artist, 1998; Any Human Heart, 2002 (Prix Jean Monnet, 2003); Fascination (short stories), 2004; Bamboo, 2005; Restless (Costa Novel Award), 2006; The Dream Lover (short stories), 2008. *Recreations:* tennis, strolling. *Address:* c/o The Agency, 24 Pottery Lane, Holland Park, W11 4LZ.

BOYD-CARPENTER, Sir (Marsom) Henry, KCVO 2002 (CVO 1994); Senior Partner, Farrer & Co., Solicitors, 2000–02 (Partner, 1968–2002); Private Solicitor to the Queen, 1995–2002; *b* 11 Oct. 1939; *s* of Francis Henry Boyd-Carpenter and Nina Boyd-Carpenter (*née* Townshend); *m* 1971, Lesley Ann Davies; one *s* one *d*. *Educ:* Charterhouse; Balliol Coll., Oxford (BA 1962; MA 1967). Admitted solicitor, 1966; Solicitor to Duchy of Cornwall, 1976–94. Law Society: Mem., 1966–; Hon. Auditor, 1979–81. Member: Council, Prince of Wales's Inst. of Architecture, 1995–99; Bd, British Library, 1999–2007 (Dep. Chm., 2003–07; Mem. Council, Friends, 2005–07). Hon. Steward, Westminster Abbey, 1980–; Hon. Legal Advr, Canterbury Cathedral Trust Fund, 1994–2001. Mem. Governing Body, Charterhouse, 1981–2004 (Chm., 2000–04); Governor: St Mary's Sch., Gerrards Cross, 1967–70; Sutton's Hosp. in Charterhouse, 1994–2005. Member: RHS Governance Wkg Party, 2000–01; Council, Chelsea Physic Garden, 1983–2002; Trustee:

Nat. Gardens Scheme, 1998–2003; Merlin Trust, 1998–2003; Mem., Bd of Trustees, Inst. of Cancer Res., 2001–07. Pres., Wood Green Animal Shelters, 2001–. *Recreations:* reading, gardening, listening to music, hill-walking. *Address:* Llanvapley Court, Llanvapley, near Abergavenny, Monmouthshire NP7 8SG.

BOYD-CARPENTER, Hon. Sir Thomas (Patrick John), KBE 1993 (MBE 1973); Chairman, Moorfields Eye Hospital NHS Foundation Trust, 2001–08; senior consultant, since 1996 and Director, since 1997, People in Business; *b* 16 June 1938; *s* of Baron Boyd-Carpenter, PC; *m* 1972, Mary-Jean (*née* Duffield); one *s* two *d. Educ:* Stowe. Commnd 1957; served UK, Oman, Malaya, Borneo and Germany; Instr, Staff Coll., 1975–77; Defence Fellowship, Aberdeen Univ., 1977–78; CO 1st Bn Scots Guards, 1979–81; Comdr 24 Inf. Brigade, 1983–84; Dir, Defence Policy, 1985–87; COS, HQ BAOR, 1988–89; ACDS (Programmes), 1989–92; DCDS (Progs and Personnel), 1992–96; retd in rank of Lt-Gen. Chairman: Social Security Adv. Cttee, 1995–2004; Kensington & Chelsea and Westminster HA, 1996–2001; Adv. Bd on Family Law, 1997–2002. *Publication:* Conventional Deterrence: into the 1990s, 1989. *Recreations:* reading, gardening. *Address:* c/o Barclays Bank, 6 Market Place, Newbury, Berks RG14 5AY.
See also Baroness Hogg.

BOYD-LEE, Paul Winston Michael; Director, Bible Truth Publishers, since 1974; *b* 3 May 1941; *s* of Harry William Lee and Violet Cynthia (*née* Cabrera); *m* 1962, Jean Warburton; one *s. Educ:* Brighton Coll.; Open Univ. (BA); Exeter Univ. (DipTh). Entertainments manager, 1963–66; credit controller, 1966–72; farmer, 1973–88; publisher, 1988–. Mem., Dir's Bd, Church Army, 1999–. Member: Gen. Synod of C of E, 1991–; Archbp's Council, 2006–. *Publication:* Israel and the New Testament, 1981, 2nd edn 1996. *Recreations:* fruit culture, canal drawing. *Address:* Manor Barn, Horsington, Som BA8 0ET. *T:* (01963) 371137; *e-mail:* paulbl@classicfm.net.

BOYDE, Prof. Patrick, PhD; FBA 1987; Serena Professor of Italian, 1981–2002, and Fellow of St John's College, since 1965, University of Cambridge; *b* 30 Nov. 1934; *s* of late Harry Caine Boyde and Florence Colonna Boyde; *m* 1956, Catherine Taylor; four *s. Educ:* Braintree County High Sch.; Wanstead County High Sch.; St John's Coll., Cambridge. BA 1956, MA 1960, PhD 1963. Nat. service, commnd RA, 1956–58. Research, St John's Coll., Cambridge, 1958–61; Asst Lectr in Italian, Univ. of Leeds, 1961–62; Asst Lectr, later Lectr, Univ. of Cambridge, 1962–81. Corresp. Fellow, Accademia Nazionale dei Lincei, 1986. *Publications:* Dante's Lyric Poetry (with K. Foster), 1967; Dante's Style in his Lyric Poetry, 1971; Dante Philomythes and Philosopher: Man in the Cosmos, 1981; Perception and Passion in Dante's Comedy, 1993; Human Vices and Human Worth in Dante's Comedy, 2000. *Recreations:* dramatising Homer, music.

BOYER, Prof. Paul Delos, PhD; Professor of Biochemistry, University of California at Los Angeles, 1963–89, now Emeritus; *b* 31 July 1918; *s* of Dell Delos Boyer and Grace Guymon; *m* 1939, Lyda Whicker; one *s* two *d. Educ:* Brigham Young Univ.; Univ. of Wisconsin (PhD 1943). Res. Asst, Univ. of Wisconsin, 1939–43; Instructor, Stanford Univ., 1943–45; University of Minnesota: Associate Prof., 1946–53; Prof., 1953–56; Hill Prof. of Biochemistry, 1956–63; Dir, Molecular Biology Inst., 1965–83, Biotechnology Prog., 1985–89, UCLA. Editor, Annual Biochemistry Review, 1964–89. ACS Award, 1955; Tolman Medal, ACS, 1981; Rose Award, Amer. Soc. of Biochemistry and Molecular Biology, 1989; (jtly) Nobel Prize for Chemistry, 1997. *Publications:* (ed jtly) The Enzymes, vol. 2, 1970 to vol. 20, 1992; papers on biochem. and molecular biology. *Address:* University of California, Los Angeles, Molecular Biology Institute, 408 Milgard Avenue, Los Angeles, CA 90024, USA; 1033 Somera Road, Los Angeles, CA 90077–2625, USA.

BOYERS, (Raphael) Howard, DFC 1945; Regional Chairman of Industrial Tribunals, Sheffield, 1984–87, retired 1988; *b* 20 Oct. 1915; *yr s* of late Bernard Boyers and Jennie Boyers; *m* 1st, 1949, Anna Moyra Cowan (*d* 1984); three *d*; 2nd, 1985, Estelle Wolman (*née* Davidson), JP; two step *s* one step *d. Educ:* King Edward VI Grammar School, Retford. Admitted Solicitor, 1939. Served War, RAF, 1940–45; 130 Sqdn, 10 Gp Fighter Comd, 1941; 51 Sqdn, 4 Gp Bomber Comd, 1944–45. Sen. Partner, Boyers Howson & Co., 1944–72. Clerk of the Peace, City of Sheffield, 1964–71; Chairman: VAT Tribunals, 1972–75; Industrial Tribunals, 1975–80; acting Regional Chm., 1980–84. Pres., Rep. Council of Sheffield and Dist Jews, 1963–67 and 1973–74. *Recreations:* theatre, music, watching football. *Address:* 8 Paragon Court, Holders Hill Road, Hendon, NW4 1LH. *T:* (020) 8343 4651. *Club:* Royal Air Force.

BOYES, Kate Emily Tyrrell, (Mrs C. W. Sanders); Chairman, Civil Service Selection Boards, 1978; *b* 22 April 1918; *e d* of S. F. Boyes, Sandiacre, Derbyshire; *m* 1944, Cyril Woods Sanders, CB; one *s* three *d. Educ:* Long Eaton Grammar Sch.; (Scholar) Newnham Coll., Cambridge. Economics Tripos, 1939; MA (Cantab). Administrative Class, BoT, Home Civil Service, 1939; Private Sec. to Parly Sec., 1942–45; Principal, 1945; Sec. to Council on Prices, Productivity and Incomes, 1958–60; Asst Sec., 1961; Speechwriter to President of BoT, 1963–64; Under-Sec., Europe, Industry and Technology Div., DTI, later Dept of Trade, 1972–78. Member: Council, National Trust, 1967–79; Exec., Keep Britain Tidy Gp, 1980–. *Recreations:* climbing, sailing, ski-ing, archæology. *Address:* 41 Smith Street, SW3 4EP. *T:* (020) 7352 8053; Giles Point, Winchelsea, Sussex TN36 4AA. *T:* (01797) 226431; Canower, Cashel, Connemara, Ireland. *Clubs:* Ski Club of Gt Britain; Island Cruising (Salcombe).

BOYLAN, Prof. Patrick John, PhD; FMA; FGS; Professor of Heritage Policy and Management, Department of Cultural Policy and Management, City University, 1996–2004, now Emeritus; *b* 17 Aug. 1939; *s* of Francis Boylan and Mary Doreen (*née* Haxby), Hull, Yorks; *m* 1st, Ann Elizabeth, *o d* of late Alfred William and Elizabeth Worsfold (marr. diss.); four *s*; 2nd, Pamela Mary, *o d* of late Rev. Robert William Jack and Mary Inder; three *s. Educ:* Marist Coll., Hull; Univ. of Hull (BSc 1960; PGCE 1961); Univ. of Leicester (PhD 1985); Museums Diploma (with Distinction), Museums Assoc., 1966. FMA 1972; FGS 1973; FCMI (FBIM 1990; MBIM 1975). Asst Master, Marist Coll., Hull, 1961–63; Keeper of Geology and Natural History, Kingston upon Hull Museums, 1964–68; Dir of Museums and Art Gallery, Exeter City Council, 1968–72; Dir of Museums and Art Gall., Leicester City Council, 1972–74; Dir of Museums and Arts, Leics County Council, 1974–90; Prof. of Arts Policy Mgt and Hd, Dept of Cultural Policy and Mgt, City Univ., 1990–96. International Council of Museums: Chm., Internat. Cttee for Training of Personnel, 1983–89 and 1998–2004; Chm., UK Nat. Cttee, 1987–93; Mem., Adv. Cttee, 1983–93; Chm., Ethics Cttee, 1984–90; Mem., Exec. Council, 1989–92; Vice-Pres., 1992–98; Chm., Legal Affairs Cttee, 2004–08; Hon. Mem., 2004. Councillor, Museums Assoc., 1970–71 and 1986–92 (Centenary Pres., 1988–90); Sec., Soc. of County Museum Dirs, 1974–78; Chm., Library Cttee, Geol Soc., 1984–87. Consultant: UNESCO; Jt UN/UNESCO World Commn on Culture and Develt; Council of Europe; World Bank; British Council, etc. Freeman, City of London, 1991; Liveryman, Framework Knitters' Co., 1991–. FCMI (FBIM 1990; MBIM 1975). High Order of Merit 'Danica' (Croatia) 1997. *Publications:* Ice Age in Yorkshire and Humberside, 1983; The Changing World of Museums and Art Galleries, 1986; Museums 2000: politics, people, professionals and profit, 1991; Review of Convention on Protection of Cultural Property in the Event of Armed Conflict, 1993; Running a Museum: a practical handbook, 2005 (trans. Arabic, French); (with A. V. R. Woolard) Trainer's Manual: for use with Running a Museum: a practical handbook, 2006 (trans. Arabic, French); over 200 papers in learned jls, professional pubns and chapters in books on museums, cultural policy, mgt, prof. training, geology, natural history, history of science and history of music. *Recreations:* the arts (especially opera and contemporary arts and crafts), research on history of science and music, Rotary (Vice-Pres., Rotary Club of Leicester). *Address:* Department of Cultural Policy and Management, City University, Northampton Square, EC1V 0HB; *e-mail:* p.boylan@city.ac.uk; 2A Compass Road, Leicester LE5 2HF. *T:* (0116) 220 5496.

BOYLE, family name of **Earls of Cork, Glasgow,** and **Shannon**.

BOYLE, Viscount; Richard Henry John Boyle; *b* 19 Jan. 1960; *s* and *heir* of 9th Earl of Shannon, *qv*. *Address:* Edington House, Edington, Bridgwater, Somerset TA7 9JS.

BOYLE, Alan Gordon; QC 1991; *b* 31 March 1949; *s* of late Dr Michael Morris Boyle and of Hazel Irene Boyle; *m* 1981, Claudine-Aimée Minne-Vercruysse; two *d. Educ:* Royal Shrewsbury Sch.; St Catherine's Coll., Oxford (MA). Called to the Bar, Lincoln's Inn, 1972, Bencher, 2003; Head of Chambers, 2008. *Recreations:* walking, music. *Address:* Serle Court Chambers, 6 New Square, Lincoln's Inn, WC2A 3QS. *T:* (020) 7242 6105.
See also R. M. Boyle.

BOYLE, James; Trustee, Edinburgh UNESCO City of Literature, since 2007 (Chairman, 2004–07); *b* 29 March 1946; *s* of James Boyle and Margaret Halliday Crilly; *m* 1969, Marie Teresa McNamara; three *s. Educ:* Strathclyde Univ. (BA Hons (1st cl.) 1969); Univ. of East Anglia (MA 1971). Adult educn lectr, 1971–75; BBC: Educn Officer, 1975–83; Head of Educnl Broadcasting, then Sec. and Head of Press, Scotland, 1983–93; Hd, BBC Radio Scotland, 1992–96; Chief Advr, Editorial Policy, 1996; Controller, Radio 4, 1996–2001; Chm., Scottish Arts Council, 2001–04. A CS Comr, 2001–04, 2007–. Non-exec. Dir, Franklin Rae Communications, 2004–. Hon. Lectr, Stirling Univ., 1994. Hon. DArts: Napier, 2002; Edinburgh, 2005; Hon. LLD Aberdeen, 2005. *Publications:* extensive writing for newspapers; six TV plays for school children; radio scripts. *Recreations:* collecting modern first editions, World War I memorabilia. *Address:* 69 Morningside Drive, Edinburgh EH10 5NJ. *T:* (0131) 447 2121; *e-mail:* jamesboyle@btinternet.com.

BOYLE, Michael David; Director of Strategy, National Probation Directorate, Home Office, 2002–04; *b* 23 Jan. 1954; *s* of Robert Brian Boyle and Kathleen Boyle; *m* 1977, Clare Gillard. *Educ:* Regent House Grammar Sch., Newtownards, Co. Down; Univ. of St Andrews (MA 1976). Home Office, 1976–2004: Private Sec. to Parly Under-Sec. of State, 1980–81; Prison Dept, 1981–85; Immigration and Nationality Dept, 1985–89; Criminal Policy Dept, 1989–90; Grade 5, Police Dept, 1990–93; Estabt Dept, 1993–96; Criminal Dept, 1996–2001; Actg Dir, Community Policy, 2001; Dir, Criminal Law and Policy, 2001–02. FRSA 1999. Patron, Revolving Doors Agency, 2004–. *Recreations:* dog-walking, foreign travel, Crystal Palace Football Club. *Address:* 3 Highclere Close, Kenley, Surrey CR8 5JU.

BOYLE, Prof. Nicholas, LittD; FBA 2001; Schröder Professor of German, University of Cambridge, since 2006 (Professor of German Literary and Intellectual History, 2000–06); Fellow, since 1968, and President, since 2006, Magdalene College, Cambridge; *b* 18 June 1946; *e s* of late Hugh Boyle and Margaret Mary Faith (*née* Hopkins, then Mrs R. G. Boothroyd); *m* 1983, Rosemary Angela Devlin; one *s* three *d. Educ:* King's Sch., Worcester; Magdalene Coll., Cambridge (schol.; BA 1967; MA; PhD 1976; LittD 2004). University of Cambridge: Res. Fellow in German, Magdalene Coll., 1968–72; Lectr in German, Magdalene and Girton Colls, 1972–74; Univ. Asst Lectr in German, 1974–79, Lectr, 1979–93, Reader, 1993–2000, Hd of Dept, 1996–2001; Sec., Faculty Bd of Mod. and Medieval Langs, 1982–85; Tutor, Magdalene Coll., 1984–93. Scholar, Alexander von Humboldt Foundn, 1978, 1980–81; British Acad. Res. Reader in Humanities, 1990–92; Res. Fellow, John Rylands Res. Inst., Univ. of Manchester, 1993; Fellow, Wissenschaftskolleg, Berlin, 1994–95; Erasmus Lectr, Univ. of Notre Dame, 2002–03. Hon. DHL Georgetown, 2004. W. Heinemann Prize, RSL, 1992; J. G. Robertson Meml Prize, Univ. of London, 1994; Goethe Medal, 2000; Annibel Jenkins Prize, Amer. Soc. for Eighteenth Century Studies, 2002. *Publications:* (ed with M. Swales) Realism in European Literature: essays in honour of J. P. Stern, 1986; Goethe: Faust, Part One, 1987; Goethe: the poet and the age, Vol. 1, 1991 (trans. German 1995), Vol. 2, 2000 (trans. German, 1999); Who Are We Now? Christian humanism and the global market from Hegel to Heaney, 1998; (ed) Goethe: selected works, 1999; (ed with J. Guthrie) Goethe and the English-Speaking World, 2002; Sacred and Secular Scriptures: a Catholic approach to literature, 2004; German Literature: a very short introduction, 2008; articles in New Blackfriars, German Life and Letters, French Studies, etc. *Recreation:* enjoying other people's gardens. *Address:* Magdalene College, Cambridge CB3 0AG. *T:* (01223) 332137; 20 Alpha Road, Cambridge CB4 3DG. *T:* (01223) 364310.

BOYLE, Paul Vincent, CA; Chief Executive, Financial Reporting Council, since 2004; *b* Glasgow, 27 July 1959; *s* of Gerrard Boyle and Joan Boyle (*née* O'Donnell); *m* 1991, Claire Andrews; two *d* and one step *s. Educ:* Univ. of Glasgow (BAcc 1st Cl. Hons 1980). CA 1983. Coopers & Lybrand, 1980–88; Gp Financial Controller, W H Smith Gp plc, 1988–90; posts with Cadbury Schweppes plc, 1991–98; Chief Operating Officer, FSA, 1998–2004. *Recreations:* golf, tennis. *Address:* Financial Reporting Council, Aldwych House, 71-91 Aldwych, WC2B 4HN. *T:* (020) 7492 2390; *e-mail:* p.boyle@frc.org.uk. *Clubs:* Caledonian; Denham Golf.

BOYLE, Dr Peter, PhD, DSc; FRCPSGlas, FFPH, FRCPE; FRSE; Director, International Agency for Research on Cancer, World Health Organisation, since 2004; *b* 8 June 1951; *s* of Simon and Brigid Boyle; *m* 1976, Helena Mary McNicol; three *d. Educ:* Glasgow Univ. (BSc 1974; PhD 1985, DSc (Med) 2006). FRCPSGlas 2003; FFPH 2004; FRCPE 2006. Res. Asst, Dept of Medicine, Univ. of Glasgow, 1974–77; Sen. Statistician, W Scotland Cancer Surveillance Unit, Glasgow, 1977–84; Instructor and Asst Prof., Depts of Biostats and Epidemiol., Harvard Sch. of Public Health, 1984–86; Sen. Scientist, Internat. Agency for Res. on Cancer, Lyon, 1986–91; Dir, Div. of Epidemiol. and Biostats, Eur. Inst. Oncology, Milan, 1991–2004. Hon. Professor: of Cancer Epidemiol., Birmingham Univ., 1996–; of Cancer Prevention and Control, Oxford Univ., 2003–; Vis. Prof., Glasgow Univ., 2000–. FRSE 2000; FMedSci 2006. Hon. DSc Aberdeen, 2006. Kt's Cross, Order of Merit (Poland), 2000. *Publications: jointly:* Cancer Incidence in Scotland: atlas and epidemiological perspective, 1985; Textbooks for General Practitioners, II: Breast Cancer, 1990; Cancer Mortality Atlas in Central Europe, 1996; Nutrition and Cancer, 1996; Tobacco: public health disaster of the twentieth century, 2004; *edited jointly:* Cancer Mapping, 1989; Cancer Epidemiology: vital statistics through prevention, 1990; Cancer Mortality Atlas of EEC, 1993; Statistical Methods in Cancer Research, 1996; Textbook of Benign Prostatic Hyperplasia, 1996 (Ipertrofia Prostatica Benigna, vol I–II, 1997); Monographs in Oncology, vol. I, Colorectal Cancer, 2000; contribs to scientific jls. *Recreations:* family, music, football. *Address:* International Agency for Research on Cancer, 150 cours Albert Thomas, 69372 Lyon cedex 08, France. *T:* (4) 72738485; *e-mail:* director@iarc.fr. *Club:* Celtic (Glasgow).

BOYLE, Roger Michael, CBE 2004; FRCP, FRCPE, FESC; Consultant Cardiologist, York District Hospital, since 1983 (on secondment); National Director for Heart Disease, since 2000, and for Stroke, since 2006; *b* 27 Jan. 1948; *s* of late Dr Michael Maurice Boyle and of Hazel Irene Boyle; *m* 1975, Susan Scutt (marr. diss.); three *s*; *m* 2002, Margo Bispham Cox; one *d*. *Educ:* Shrewsbury Sch.; London Hosp. Med. Sch., London Univ. (MB BS 1972). House physician and surgeon, then SHO, London Hosp., 1972–75; Registrar, Chelmsford Hosp., 1975–78; Res. Fellow, Wythenshawe Hosp., Manchester, 1978–80; Lectr in Cardiovascular Studies, Univ. of Leeds, 1980–83. Hon. Prof., Dept of Surgery, UCH, 2005–. Hon. Consultant Cardiologist, St Mary's Hosp., London, 2004–. FRSA. Hon. FFPH. *Publications:* contribs to cardiovascular jls on coronary heart disease and trng in cardiology. *Recreations:* sailing, playing the piano, walking. *Address:* 68 Bushwood Road, Kew, Richmond, Surrey TW9 3BQ. *Clubs:* Percuil Sailing, Mantoloking Yacht (USA).

See also A. G. Boyle.

BOYLE, Simon Hugh Patrick; Lord-Lieutenant for Gwent, since 2001; *b* 22 March 1941; *s* of late Lt Col P. J. S. Boyle (killed in action 1944) and Mary Elizabeth Boyle (later Mrs Charles Floyd); *m* 1970, Catriona Gordon; four *d*. *Educ:* Eton Coll. Industrial career with: Stewarts & Lloyds, Australia and UK, 1959–65; Avon Rubber Co. Ltd, 1966–69; British Steel, 1970–2001. Chm., Gwent Criminal Justice Bd, 2003–05. Chm., Monmouth Diocesan Parsonage Bd, 1997–2008; Vice Chm., Monmouth Diocesan Bd of Finance, 2001–. Trustee, St David's Foundn Hospice Care, 1999–. DL 1997, JP 2002, Gwent. CStJ 2002. *Recreations:* gardening, sailing. *Address:* Penpergwm Lodge, Abergavenny, Gwent NP7 9AS. *T:* (01873) 840208; *e-mail:* boyle@penpergwm.co.uk.

BOYLE, Sir Stephen Gurney, 5th Bt *cr* 1904; *b* 15 Jan. 1962; *s* of Sir Richard Gurney Boyle, 4th Bt, and of Elizabeth Ann, *yr d* of Norman Dennes; *S* father, 1983. Chm., Co-operative property services. *Recreations:* music, watching cricket, bridge. *Heir: b* Michael Desmond Boyle, *b* 16 Sept. 1963. *Address:* 19 Fern Hill Lane, Gibb Croft, Harlow, Essex CM18 7JL.

BOYLING, Very Rev. Mark Christopher; Dean of Carlisle, since 2004; *b* 14 Oct. 1952; *s* of Denis and Margaret Boyling; *m* 1991, Helen Mary (*née* Enoch); one *s* one *d*. *Educ:* Keble Coll., Oxford (BA (Modern Hist.) 1974, BA (Theol.) 1976; MA 1978); Cuddesdon Theol Coll. Ordained deacon, 1977, priest, 1978; Asst Curate, Kirkby, 1977–79; Priest i/c, 1979–80, Team Vicar, 1980–85, St Mark, Kirkby; Chaplain to Bp of Liverpool, 1985–89; Vicar, St Peter, Formby, 1989–94; Canon Residentiary, Liverpool Cathedral, 1994–2004. *Recreations:* travel, cooking. *Address:* The Deanery, Carlisle CA3 8TZ. *T:* (01228) 523335, *Fax:* (01228) 547049; *e-mail:* dean@carlislecathedral.org.uk.

BOYNE, 11th Viscount *cr* 1717 (Ire.); **Gustavus Michael Stucley Hamilton-Russell;** Baron Hamilton 1715; Baron Brancepeth (UK) 1866; *b* 27 May 1965; *o s* of 10th Viscount Boyne and of Rosemary Anne, *d* of Sir Dennis Stucley, 5th Bt; *S* father, 1995; *m* 1991, Lucy, *d* of George Potter; three *s* one *d* (incl. twin *s*). *Educ:* Harrow; RAC Cirencester. Dip. Rural Estate Management; MRICS (ARICS 1991). Chartered Surveyor with Carter Jonas. *Recreations:* country sports, tennis, ski-ing. *Heir: s* Hon. Gustavus Archie Edward Hamilton-Russell, *b* 30 June 1999. *Address:* Burwarton House, Bridgnorth, Shropshire WV16 6QH. *T:* (01746) 787221. *Club:* Turf.

BOYNE, Maj.-Gen. John, CB 1987; MBE 1965; CEng, FIMechE; company director, since 1988; *b* 7 Nov. 1932; *s* of John Grant Boyne and Agnes Crawford (*née* Forrester); *m* 1956, Norma Beech (*d* 2002); two *s*. *Educ:* King's Sch., Chester; Royal Military Coll. of Science, Shrivenham (BScEng 1st Cl. Hons). CEng, FIMechE 1975. Served in Egypt, Cyprus, Libya and UK, 1951–62; Staff Coll., Camberley, 1963; DAQMG(Ops) HQ MEC, Aden, 1964–66; OC 11 Infantry Workshop, REME, BAOR, 1966–67; Jt Services Staff Coll., 1968; GSO2 MoD, 1968–70; GSO1 (DS), Staff Coll., 1970–72; Comdr REME, 2nd Div., BAOR, 1972–73; AAG MoD, 1973–75; CSO (Personnel) to CPL, MoD, 1975–76; Dep. Dir Elec. and Mech. Engrg, 1st British Corps, 1976–78; RCDS, 1979; Dep. Dir Personal Services (Army), MoD, 1980–82; Vice Adjutant Gen. and Dir of Manning (Army), MoD, 1982–85; Dir Gen., Electrical and Mechanical Engrg, Logistic Executive (Army), MoD, 1985–88. Col Comdt, REME, 1988–93 (Rep. Col Comdt, 1989–90). Trustee, Army Benevolent Fund, 1986–2005. Vice Pres., Army Football Assoc., 1988–. FCMI (FBIM 1975). *Recreations:* music, philately, football. *Address:* c/o HSBC, 48 High Street, Runcorn, Cheshire WA7 1AN.

BOYS, Rt Hon. Sir Michael H.; *see* Hardie Boys.

BOYS, Penelope Ann, (Mrs D. C. H. Wright), CB 2005; Executive Director, Office of Fair Trading, 2003–05 (Deputy Director General, 2000–03); Member: Water Services Regulation Authority, since 2006; Horserace Betting Levy Board, since 2006; *b* 11 June 1947; *d* of late Hubert John Boys and Mollie Blackman Boys; *m* 1977, David Charles Henshaw Wright. *Educ:* Guildford County Sch. for Girls. Exec. Officer, DES, 1966–69; Asst Principal, Min. of Power, 1969–72; Private Sec., Minister without Portfolio, 1972–73; Principal, Dept of Energy, 1973–78; seconded to BNOC, 1978–80; Head of Internat. Unit, Dept of Energy, 1981–85; seconded to HM Treasury as Head, ST2 Div., 1985–87; Dir of Personnel, Dept of Energy, 1987–89; Dep. Dir Gen., Office of Electricity Regulation, 1989–93; Head of Personnel, DTI, 1993–96; Sec., Monopolies and Mergers, later Competition, Commn, 1996–2000. *Recreations:* entertaining, racing, music.

BOYS-GREENE, Jenny; *see* Greene, J.

BOYS SMITH, Stephen Wynn, CB 2001; Joint-Secretary, Independent Monitoring Commission, Northern Ireland, since 2004; Member, Civil Service Appeal Board, since 2004; *b* 4 May 1946; *s* of late Rev. Dr John Sandwith Boys Smith and Gwendolen Sara Boys Smith (*née* Wynn); *m* 1971, Linda Elaine Price; one *s* one *d*. *Educ:* Sherborne Sch.; St John's Coll., Cambridge (MA); Univ. of British Columbia (MA). Home Office, 1968; Asst Private Sec. to Home Sec., 1971–73; Central Policy Review Staff, Cabinet Office, 1977; Home Office, 1979; Private Sec. to Home Sec., 1980–81; NI Office, 1981; Principal Private Sec. to Sec. of State for NI, 1981–82; Home Office, 1984; Principal Private Sec. to Home Sec., 1985–87; Asst Under Sec. of State, Home Office, 1989–92; Under Sec., HM Treasury, 1992–95; Home Office: Dep. Sec. and Head of Police Dept, 1995–96; Dir, Police Policy, 1996–98; Dir-Gen., Immigration and Nationality Directorate, 1998–2002; Dir-Gen., Organised Crime, Drugs and Internat. Gp, 2002–03. *Recreations:* gardening, reading. *Address:* (office) PO Box 709, Belfast BT2 8YB.

BOYSON, Rt Hon. Sir Rhodes, Kt 1987; PC 1987; *b* 11 May 1925; *s* of Alderman William Boyson, MBE, JP and Mrs Bertha Boyson, Haslingden, Rossendale, Lancs; *m* 1st, 1946, Violet Burletson (marr. diss.); two *d*; 2nd, 1971, Florette MacFarlane. *Educ:* Haslingden Grammar Sch.; UC Cardiff; Manchester Univ. (BA, MA); LSE (PhD); Corpus Christi Coll., Cambridge. Served with Royal Navy. Headmaster: Lea Bank Secondary Modern Sch., Rossendale, 1955–61; Robert Montefiore Secondary Sch., Stepney, 1961–66; Highbury Grammar Sch., 1966–67; Highbury Grove Sch., 1967–74. Chm., Nat. Council for Educnl Standards, 1974–79. Chm., Churchill Press and Constitutional Book Club, 1969–79. Councillor: Haslingden, 1957–61; Waltham Forest, 1968–74 (Chm. Establishment Cttee, 1968–71); Chm., London Boroughs Management Services Unit, 1968–70. Formerly Youth Warden, Lancs Youth Clubs. Contested (C) Eccles, 1970. MP (C) Brent North, Feb. 1974–1997; contested (C) same seat, 1997. Vice-Chm., Cons Parly Educn Cttee, 1975–76; Hon. Sec. Cons. Adv. Cttee on Educn, 1975–78; Opposition spokesman on educn, 1976–79; Parly Under-Sec. of State, DES, 1979–83; Minister of State: for Social Security, DHSS, 1983–84; NI Office, 1984–86; for Local Govt, DoE, 1986–87. Non-executive Dir, Black's Leisure, 1998–2001. *Publications:* The North-East Lancashire Poor Law 1838–1871, 1965; The Ashworth Cotton Enterprise, 1970; (ed) Right Turn, 1970; (ed) Down with the Poor, 1971; (ed) Goodbye to Nationalisation, 1972; (ed) Education: Threatened Standards, 1972; (ed) The Accountability of Schools, 1973; Oversubscribed: the story of Highbury Grove, 1974; Crisis in Education, 1975; (jt ed) Black Papers on Education, 1969–77; (ed) 1985: An Escape from Orwell's 1984, 1975; Centre Forward, 1978; Speaking My Mind (autobiog.), 1995; Boyson on Education, 1996. *Recreations:* reading, writing, talk, hard work, meeting friends, inciting the millenialist Left in education and politics. *Address:* 71 Paines Lane, Pinner, Middx HA5 3BX. *T:* (020) 8866 2071. *Clubs:* Carlton; Churchill (N Wembley), Wembley Conservative.

BRABAZON, family name of **Earl of Meath**.

BRABAZON OF TARA, 3rd Baron *cr* 1942; **Ivon Anthony Moore-Brabazon;** DL; *b* 20 Dec. 1946; *s* of 2nd Baron Brabazon of Tara, CBE, and Henriette Mary (*d* 1985), *d* of late Sir Rowland Clegg; *S* father, 1974; *m* 1979, Harriet Frances, *o d* of Mervyn P. de Courcy Hamilton, Salisbury, Zimbabwe; one *s* one *d*. *Educ:* Harrow. Mem., Stock Exchange, 1972–84. A Lord in Waiting (Govt Whip), 1984–86; Parly Under-Sec. of State, Dept of Transport, 1986–89; Minister of State: FCO, 1989–90; Dept of Transport, 1990–92; Opposition spokesman on Transport, H of L, 1998–2001; elected Mem., H of L, 1999; Principal Dep. Chm. of Cttees, 2001–02, Chm. of Cttees, 2002–, H of L; Chm., EU Select Cttee, H of L, 2001–02. Mem., RAC Public Policy Cttee, 1992–99. Dep. Chm., Foundn for Sport and the Arts, 1992–. President: UK Warehousing Assoc., 1992–; British Internat. Freight Assoc., 1997–99; Inst. of the Motor Industry, 1998–2004. DL Isle of Wight, 1993. *Recreations:* sailing, Cresta Run. *Heir: s* Hon. Benjamin Ralph Moore-Brabazon, *b* 15 March 1983. *Address:* House of Lords, SW1A 0PW. *Clubs:* Royal Yacht Squadron; Bembridge Sailing, St Moritz Tobogganing.

BRABBINS, Martyn Charles; freelance orchestral and opera conductor; Conductor Laureate, Huddersfield Choral Society, since 2006 (Principal Conductor, 1998–2006); *b* 13 Aug. 1959; *s* of Herbert Henry Brabbins and Enid Caroline Brabbins; *m* 1985, Karen Maria Evans; two *s* one *d*. *Educ:* Goldsmiths' Coll., Univ. of London (BMus, MMus; Hon. Fellow, 2004); Leningrad State Conservatoire. Professional début with Scottish Chamber Orch., 1988; Associate Conductor, 1992–94, Associate Prin. Conductor, 1994–2005, BBC Scottish SO; Principal Conductor, Sinfonia 21, 1994–2001; Conducting Consultant, RSAMD, 1996–2002; Artistic Dir, Cheltenham Fest., 2005–07; has conducted most major British orchestras, and orchestras abroad, incl. NDR Hanover, Orch. Philharmonic Gran Canaria, Lahti SO, Tapiola Sinfonietta, St Petersburg Philharmonic, Bergen Philharmonic, Ensemble Intercontemporain, Amsterdam Concertgebouw; also conducted: Don Giovanni, Kirov Opera, 1988; Magic Flute, ENO, 1995; Montpellier Opera, 1999; Netherlands Opera, 2001; Deutsche Oper, 2001; Frankfurt Opera, 2003, 2007; Hamburg State Opera, 2006. Has made 60 recordings. Winner, Leeds Conductors Competition, 1988. *Recreation:* family. *Address:* c/o Intermusica, 16 Duncan Terrace, N1 8BZ. *T:* (020) 7278 5455.

BRABEN, David John; Founder and Chairman, Frontier Developments Ltd, since 1994; *b* 2 Jan. 1964; *s* of Prof. Don Braben and Shirley Braben; *m* 1993, Kathy Dickinson (marr. diss. 1996). *Educ:* Stockton Heath Primary Sch.; Royal Kent Primary Sch.; Buckhurst Hill Co. High Sch.; Jesus Coll., Cambridge (BA 1985; MA Hons Electrical Scis; Dip. Computer Sci.). Freelance software designer and writer, 1982–94: Elite, Zarch, Virus, Frontier. *Recreations:* sailing, movies, board games, computer games, walking my dog. *Address:* c/o Frontier Developments, 306 Science Park, Milton Road, Cambridge CB4 0WG. *T:* (01223) 394300; *e-mail:* dbraben@frontier.co.uk.

BRABHAM, Sir John Arthur, (Sir Jack), Kt 1979; AO 2008; OBE 1966; retired, 1970, as professional racing driver; Director, Engine Developments Ltd, 1964–2002; *b* Sydney, Australia, 2 April 1926; *m* 1st, Betty Evelyn Beresford (marr. diss.); three *s*; 2nd, Margaret Taylor. *Educ:* Hurstville Technical Coll., Sydney. Served in RAAF, 1944–46. Started own engineering business, 1946; Midget Speedway racing, 1947–54; several championships (Australian, NSW, South Australian); numerous wins driving a Cooper-Bristol, Australia, 1953–54; to Europe, 1955; Australian Grand Prix, 1955, 1963 (debut of Repco Brabham) and 1965; World Champion Formula II, 1958, also many firsts including Casablanca, Goodwood, Brands Hatch, NZ Grand Prix (three times), Belgian Grand Prix; Formula II Champion of France, 1964–66. World Champion Driver: (after first full Formula I Season with 2·5-litre car), 1959–60, 1960–61, 1966. First in Monaco and British Grandes Epreuves, 1959; won Grand Prix of: Holland, Belgium, France, Britain, Portugal, Denmark, 1960; Belgium, 1961. Elected Driver of the Year by Guild of Motoring Writers, 1959, 1966 and 1970, Sportsman of the Year by Australian Broadcasting Co., 1959; left Cooper to take up building own Grand Prix cars, 1961; debut, 1962; first ever constructor/driver to score world championship points, 1963; cars finished first: French GP; Mexican GP, 1964; Formula II and Formula III cars world-wide success, 1963; awarded Ferodo Trophy, 1964 and again, 1966; British Saloon Car Championship, 1965; won French Grand Prix and British Grand Prix, 1966; won French Grand Prix, 1967. RAC Gold Medal, 1966; BARC Gold Star, 1959, 1960 and 1966; Formula I Manufacturers' Championship, 1966, 1967. *Publications:* Jack Brabham's Book of Motor Racing, 1960; When the Flag Drops, 1971; The Jack Brabham Story, 2004; contribs to British journals. *Recreations:* photography, water ski-ing, under-water swimming, flying. *Address:* Suite 404, Bag no 1, Robina Town Centre, Qld 4230, Australia. *Clubs:* Royal Automobile, British Racing and Sports Car, British Racing Drivers'; Australian Racing Drivers'.

BRABOURNE, 8th Baron *cr* 1880; **Norton Louis Philip Knatchbull;** Bt 1641; *b* 8 Oct. 1947; *s* of 7th Baron Brabourne, CBE and of Countess Mountbatten of Burma, *qv*; *S* father, 2005; *m* 1979, Penelope Eastwood; one *s* one *d* (and one *d* decd). *Educ:* Dragon School, Oxford; Gordonstoun; University of Kent (BA Politics). *Heir: s* Hon. Nicholas Louis Charles Norton Knatchbull, *b* 15 May 1981. *Address:* Broadlands, Romsey, Hants SO51 9ZD. *T:* (01794) 505030.

BRACADALE, Hon. Lord; Alastair Peter Campbell; a Senator of the College of Justice in Scotland, since 2003; *b* 18 Sept. 1949; *s* of Rev. Donald Campbell and Margaret Campbell (*née* Montgomery); *m* 1973, Flora Beaton; one *s* two *d*. *Educ:* George Watson's Coll.; Aberdeen Univ. (MA); Strathclyde Univ. (LLB). Teacher of English, 1973–75; Solicitor, Procurator Fiscal Service, 1979–84; Advocate, 1985; Advocate Depute,

1990–93; called to the Bar, Inner Temple, 1990; QC (Scot.) 1995; Standing Jun. Counsel in Scotland to HM Customs and Excise, 1995; Home Advocate Depute, 1997–98; Crown Counsel, Scottish Court in the Netherlands, 2000–02. Member: Criminal Justice Forum, 1996–97; Scottish Criminal Rules Council, 1996–98; Criminal Injuries Compensation Bd, 1997. *Recreations:* walking, sailing, golf. *Address:* Cerna, 69 Dirleton Avenue, North Berwick EH39 4QL. *T:* (01620) 894288; Court of Session, Parliament House, Edinburgh EH1 1RQ.

BRACE, Michael Thomas, OBE 2005; Chief Executive: Vision 2020 UK, since 2001; OPSIS, since 2002; Chairman, British Paralympic Association, since 2001; *b* 19 June 1950; *s* of Thomas Brace and Rosina Brace (now Taylor); *m* 1972, Maureen Browne. *Educ:* London Univ. (CQSW DipSW 1976; DipMgt 1996). Tower Hamlets BC, 1976–81; Hackney BC, 1981–83; Area Manager, Islington BC, 1983–89; Service Manager, RBK&C, 1989–2001. Mem. Bd, London 2012, 2003–. Gov., UEL, 2006–. *Publication:* Where There's a Will, 1980. *Recreations:* playing cricket, after dinner speaking, ski-ing, reading, music. *Address:* 80 Elms Farm Road, Hornchurch, Essex RM12 5RD. *T:* (01708) 456832, *Fax:* (01708) 446310; *e-mail:* m.brace@vision2020uk.org.uk.

BRACEGIRDLE, Dr Brian, FSA, FRPS, FIBiol; Research Consultant in microscopy, and Fellow, Science Museum, 1990–2005; *b* 31 May 1933; *o c* of Alfred Bracegirdle; *m* 1st, 1958, Margaret Lucy Merrett (marr. diss. 1974); one *d*; 2nd, 1975, Patricia Helen Miles; no *c*. *Educ:* King's Sch., Macclesfield; Univ. of London (BSc); PhD 1975 (UCL). DipRMS 1975. FRPS 1969; FBIPP (FIIP 1970); FIBiol 1976; FSA 1981. Technician in industry, 1950–57; Biology Master, Erith Grammar Sch., 1958–61; Sen. Lectr in Biol., S Katharine's Coll., London, 1961–64; Head, Depts of Nat. Science and Learning Resources, Coll. of All Saints, London, 1964–77; Science Museum: Keeper, Wellcome Mus. of Hist. of Medicine, 1977; Head of Dept of Med. Scis, and Head of Collections Management Div., 1987–89; Asst Dir, 1987–89. Hon. Lectr in History of Medicine, UCL, 1978–90; Hon. Res. Fellow in Hist. of Sci., Imperial Coll., 1990–93. Hon. Treasurer, ICOM (UK), 1978–89. Chm., Inst. of Medical and Biological Illustration, 1983–84; President: Assoc. Européenne de Musées de l'Histoire des Sciences Medicales, 1983–90; Quekett Microscopical Club, 1985–88; Vice-Pres., Royal Microscopical Soc., 1988–90. Ed., Quekett Jl of Microscopy, 1998–2008. *Publications:* Photography for Books and Reports, 1970; The Archaeology of the Industrial Revolution, 1973; The Evolution of Microtechnique, 1978, 1987; (ed) Beads of Glass: Leeuwenhoek and the early microscope, 1984; Scientific Photomacrography, 1995; Notes on Modern Microscope Manufacturers, 1996; Microscopical Mounts and Mounters, 1998; A Catalogue of the Microscopy Collections at the Science Museum, 2005; (with W. H. Freeman): An Atlas of Embryology, 1963, 1978; An Atlas of Histology, 1966; An Atlas of Invertebrate Structure, 1971; An Advanced Atlas of Histology, 1976; (with P. H. Miles): An Atlas of Plant Structure, vol. I, 1971; An Atlas of Plant Structure, Vol. II, 1973; Thomas Telford, 1973; The Darbys and the Ironbridge Gorge, 1974; An Atlas of Chordate Structure, 1977; (with J. B. McCormick) The Microscopic Photographs of J. B. Dancer, 1993; (with S. Bradbury): Modern Photomicrography, 1995; Introduction to Light Microscopy, 1998; papers on photography for life sciences, on scientific topics, and on history of science/medicine. *Recreations:* walking, music, travel, shouting at the television set. *Address:* 22 Montpellier Spa Road, Cheltenham, Glos GL50 1UL. *T:* (01242) 517478.

BRACEWELL, Julia Helen, OBE 1999; Chair, sportscotland, 2005–08; *b* 26 April 1964; *d* of Herbert and Joan Bracewell; one *s* one *d*. *Educ:* Bristol Univ. (LLB). Called to the Bar, Lincoln's Inn, 1997 (non-practising barrister); admitted solicitor, 1998 (non-practising solicitor). Partner, Brobeck Hale & Dorr, 1997–2000; Morrison & Forester, 2000–02. Mem., Sports Council, GB, 1993–96, Sport England, 1996–2001; Chm., Scottish Steering Gp for 2012 Olympic Games, 2005–08; Board Director: Scottish Inst. of Sport, 2005–08; UK Sport, 2005–08. Fencing competitor: Commonwealth Championships, 1986 (Bronze Medal), 1990 (Bronze Medal); Olympic Games, Barcelona, 1992. Sailed across Atlantic, 1995. *Recreations:* ski-ing, sailing, racket sports, fencing. *Club:* British Olympians.

BRACEWELL-SMITH, Sir Charles, 4th Bt *cr* 1947, of Keighley; *b* 13 Oct. 1955; *s* of Sir George Bracewell Smith, 2nd Bt, MBE, and Helene Marie (*d* 1975), *d* of late John Frederick Hydock, Philadelphia, USA; *S* brother, 1983; *m* 1977, Carol Vivien Hough (*d* 1994); *m* 1996, Nina Kakkar. Former Dir, Park Lane Hotel Ltd. Founder, Homestead Charitable Trust, 1990. *Recreations:* mysticism, theology, philosophy, psychology, poetry, writing, music. *Heir:* none. *Address:* The Hermitage, 7 Clarence Gate Gardens, Glentworth Street, NW1 6AY. *Clubs:* Royal Automobile, Arsenal Football.

BRACK, Rodney Lee, CBE 2006; Chief Executive, Horserace Betting Levy Board, 1993–2005; *b* 16 Aug. 1945; *s* of Sydney William Brack and Mary Alice Brack (*née* Quested); *m* 1973, Marilyn Carol Martin; two *s* one *d*. *Educ:* Whitgift Sch. FCA 1979. Chartered Accountant, 1963–68; Finance Manager, Daily Mirror Gp, 1969–75; Man. Dir, Leisure Div., EMI, 1976–80; Dir, Leisure Div., Lonrho, 1981–84; Financial Controller and Dep. Chief Exec., Horserace Betting Levy Bd, 1985–92. Dir, Horseracing Forensic Lab., 1986–2005. Mem., Lord Donoughue's Future Funding of Racing Review Gp, 2005–06. *Recreations:* music, theatre, cricket, golf. *Address:* 3 Redcliffe Road, Chelsea, SW10 9NR. *T:* (020) 7352 7630; *e-mail:* rodneybrack@hotmail.com. *Clubs:* MCC, Royal Automobile.

BRACK, Terence John, CB 1994; Assistant Under-Secretary of State (General Finance), Ministry of Defence, 1989–94; *b* 17 April 1938; *s* of late Noël D. J. Brack and Tertia Brack; *m* 1983, Christine Mary, *d* of late Douglas and Evelyn Cashin. *Educ:* Bradfield Coll., Berkshire; Caius Coll., Cambridge Univ. (BA Hist. (1st cl. Hons), MA). Pilot Officer, Secretarial Br., RAF, 1956–58. Entered Air Ministry, subseq. MoD, 1961; Private Sec. to Parly Under-Sec. of State for Defence (RAF), 1964–66; Principal, 1966; seconded to HM Treasury, 1968–72; Asst Sec., 1973; Head, Finance and Sec. Div. for Controller of the Navy, 1975–78; Head, Defence Secretariat Div. for Equipment Requirements, 1978–81; RCDS, 1982; Head, Finance and Sec. Div. (Air Launched Guided Weapons and Electronics), 1983–84; Asst Under-Sec. of State (Naval Personnel), 1985–89. Vice-Chm., Management Bd, Royal Hosp. Sch., Holbrook, 1985–89. Pres., London Manx Soc., 2001–02. *Recreations:* walking, travel, family history projects.

BRACKENBURY, (Frederick Edwin) John (Gedge), CBE 2000; Chairman: Brackenbury Leisure Ltd, since 1996; Avanti Communications Group, since 2007; *b* 9 Feb. 1936; *s* of Claude Russell Brackenbury and Florence Edna Brackenbury; *m* 1st, 1958, Pauline Hinchliffe (marr. diss. 1977); one *s* two *d*; 2nd, 1978, Desiree Sally Taylor; one *s*. *Educ:* Mercers Sch., London. Justerini & Brooks Ltd, 1954–62 (Dir, 1958–62); Man. Dir, City Cellars, 1962–65; Chm., Morgan Furze, 1965–67; Dir, IDV Ltd, 1967–72; Founder, Brackenbury consultancy co., 1972–75; Exec. Dir, G. & W. Walker, 1975–83 (Gp Operational Dir, Brent Walker, 1976–83); Man. Dir, All Weather Sports Activities Ltd, 1983–88; Exec. Dir, Brent Walker Gp Plc, 1988–96. Chm., 1991–2002, Dep. Chm., 2002–03, Pubmaster Gp Ltd; Chairman: Active Media Capital Ltd, 2000–07; Avanti Screenmedia Gp plc, 2003–07; non-executive Director: Western Wines Ltd, 1997–2002; Aspen Gp Plc, 1997–99; Hotel and Catering Trng Co., 1998–2002; SFI Gp Plc, 1998–2005; Holsten (UK) Ltd, 2000–04; Isle of Capri Casinos Inc. (USA), 2004–; The Isle Casinos Ltd, 2004– (Chm.); Blue Chip Casinos, 2006–. Chairman: Business in Sport & Leisure, 1985–2005 (Life Pres., 2005–); Hospitality Trng Foundn, 1997–2004; People 1st, 2004–05; Dir, Springboard (formerly Tourism & Hospitality) Educn Trust, 1999–. *Recreations:* golf, tennis, viticulture. *Address:* 8 Moore Street, SW3 2QN. *Clubs:* Carlton, Hurlingham; Walton Heath Golf (Surrey).

BRACKENBURY, Air Vice-Marshal Ian, CB 2000; OBE 1987; CEng, FIMechE; Director, Rolls-Royce Defence Aerospace (Europe), since 2001; *b* 28 Aug. 1945; *s* of late Capt. D. E. Brackenbury and of R. Brackenbury (*née* Grant). Directorate of Aircraft Engrg, 1975; Engrg Staff, Strike Comd, 1981; joined Dept for Supply and Orgn, 1986, Dir of Support Mgt, 1993; Dir of Support Mgt, HQ Logistics Comd, 1994; Dir, Helicopter Support, Chief of Fleet Support, 1995–97; Air Officer Engrg and Supply, Strike Comd, 1997–98; Dir Gen. Defence Logistics (Ops and Policy), MoD, 1998–2000. *Address:* PO Box 3, Filton, Bristol BS34 7QE. *Club:* Royal Air Force.

BRACKENBURY, John; *see* Brackenbury, F. E. J. G.

BRACKENBURY, Ven. Michael Palmer; Archdeacon of Lincoln, 1988–95, now Emeritus; *b* 6 July 1930; *s* of Frank Brackenbury and Constance Mary (*née* Palmer); *m* 1953, Jean Margaret, *d* of Oscar Arnold Harrison and May (*née* Norton). *Educ:* Norwich School; Lincoln Theological Coll. ACII 1956. RAF, 1948–50. Asst Curate, South Ormsby Group, 1966–69; Rector of Sudbrooke with Scothern, 1969–77; RD of Lawres, 1973–78; Diocesan Dir of Ordinands, Lincoln, 1977–87; Personal Assistant to Bishop of Lincoln, 1977–88; Canon and Prebendary of Lincoln, 1979–95; Diocesan Lay Ministry Adviser, Lincoln, 1986–87. Mem., Gen. Synod of C of E, 1989–95. Mem., Ecclesiastical Law Soc., 1988–. Chm. Lincs Award Bd, Prince's Trust, 1996–2001. *Recreations:* music, reading, travel. *Address:* 18 Lea View, Ryhall, Stamford, Lincs PE9 4HZ. *T:* (01780) 752415.

BRACKLEY, Rt Rev. Ian James; *see* Dorking, Bishop Suffragan of.

BRACKS, Hon. Stephen (Phillip); Senior Adviser: to Prime Minister of East Timor, since 2007; to KPMG, since 2007; Premier of Victoria, and Minister for Multicultural Affairs, 1999–2007; *b* 15 Oct. 1954; *m* 1983, Terry Horsfall; two *s* one *d*. *Educ:* St Patrick's Coll., Ballarat; Ballarat Univ. (Dip. Business Studies, Grad. DipEd). Secondary commerce teacher, 1976–81; employment project worker and municipal recreation officer, 1981–85; Exec. Dir, Ballarat Educn Centre, 1985–89; Statewide Manager, Victoria's Employment Progs, 1989–93 (on secondment as Ministerial Advr to Premiers of Victoria, 1990); Principal Advr to Fed. Parly Sec. for Transport and Communications, 1993; Exec. Dir, Victorian Printing Industry Trng Bd, 1993–94. MLA (ALP) Williamstown, Vic, 1994–2007; Shadow Minister for Employment, Industrial Relns and Tourism, 1994–96; Shadow Treas. and Shadow Minister for Finance and Industrial Relns, 1996–99; Dep. Chm., Public Accounts and Estimates Cttee, 1996–99; Shadow Treas. and Shadow Minister for Multicultural Affairs, March–Oct. 1999; Treas., 1999–2000. Leader, State Parly Labor Party, March–Oct. 1999. Non-exec. Dir, Jardine Lloyd Thompson Australia; Vice Chm., Adv. Bd, AIMS Financial Gp. Hon. Professorial Fellow, Univ. of Melbourne. Hon. Dr Ballarat. *Recreations:* camping, distance swimming, tennis, football supporter. *Address:* Old Treasury Building, 20 Spring Street, Melbourne, Vic 3000, Australia; *e-mail:* info@stevebracks.com.au.

BRADBEER, Sir (John) Derek (Richardson), Kt 1988; OBE 1973; TD 1965; DL; Partner, Wilkinson Maughan (formerly Wilkinson Marshall Clayton & Gibson), 1961–97; President of the Law Society, 1987–88; *b* 29 Oct. 1931; *s* of late William Bertram Bradbeer and Winifred (*née* Richardson); *m* 1962, Margaret Elizabeth Chantler (DL Northumberland); one *s* one *d*. *Educ:* Canford Sch.; Sidney Sussex Coll., Cambridge (MA). Nat. Service, 2nd Lieut RA, 1951–52; TA, 1952–77: Lt-Col Comdg 101 (N) Med. Regt RA(V), 1970–73; Col, Dep. Comdr 21 and 23 Artillery Bdes, 1973–76; Hon. Col, 101 (N) Field Regt, RA(V), 1986–91. Admitted Solicitor, 1959. Member: Criminal Injuries Compensation Bd, 1988–2000; Criminal Injuries Compensation Appeals Panel, 1996–2008. Member: Disciplinary Cttee, Inst. of Actuaries, 1989–96; Insurance Brokers Registration Council, 1992–96. Mem. Council, 1973–94, Vice-Pres., 1986–87, Law Soc.; Pres., Newcastle upon Tyne Incorp. Law Soc., 1982–83; Gov., Coll. of Law, 1983–2002 (Chm., 1990–99). Director: Newcastle and Gateshead Water plc, 1978–90; Sunderland and South Shields Water plc, 1990–2002; Chm., North East Water, 1992–2002; Dep. Chm., Northumbrian Water Gp, 1996–2002. UK Vice-Pres., Union Internationale des Avocats, 1988–92. Chm., N of England TA&VRA, 1990–96 (Vice-Chm., 1988–90). DL Tyne and Wear, 1988. DUniv Open, 2000; Hon. DLaws Coll. of Law, 2007. *Recreations:* reading, gardening, sport. *Address:* Forge Cottage, Shilvington, Newcastle upon Tyne NE20 0AP. *T:* (01670) 775214. *Clubs:* Army and Navy, Garrick.

BRADBOURN, Philip Charles, OBE 1994; Member (C) West Midlands Region, European Parliament, since 1999; *b* 9 Aug. 1951; *s* of Horace and Elizabeth Bradbourn. *Educ:* Tipton Grammar Sch.; Worcester Coll. of Higher Educn; Wulfrun Coll. of Further Educn, Wolverhampton (DMA 1972). Local govt officer, 1967–87; Advr to Leader of Opposition, Wolverhampton BC, 1987–99. *Recreation:* gardening. *Address:* (office) 285 Kenilworth Road, Balsall Common, Coventry, Warwickshire CV7 7EL. *T:* (01676) 530621.

BRADBURY, family name of **Baron Bradbury**.

BRADBURY, 3rd Baron *cr* 1925, of Winsford, Co. Chester; **John Bradbury;** *b* 17 March 1940; *s* of 2nd Baron Bradbury and of his 1st wife, Joan, *o d* of W. D. Knight; *S* father, 1994; *m* 1968, Susan, *d* of late W. Liddiard; two *s*. *Educ:* Gresham's Sch.; Univ. of Bristol. *Heir:* *s* Hon. John Timothy Bradbury, *b* 16 Jan. 1973.

BRADBURY, Anita Jean, (Mrs Philip Bradbury); *see* Pollack, A. J.

BRADBURY, His Honour Anthony Vincent; a Circuit Judge, 1992–2006; Resident Judge, Bow County Court, 1998–2006; *b* 29 Sept. 1941; *s* of late Alfred Charles Bradbury, OBE and Noreen Vincent Bradbury; *m* 1966, Rosalie Anne Buttrey; one *d*. *Educ:* Kent College, Canterbury; Univ. of Birmingham (Sir Henry Barber Law Scholar; LLB). Solicitor 1965; Principal, Bradbury & Co., 1970–81; Registrar, then Dist Judge, Ilford County Court, 1981–91; a Recorder of the Crown Court, 1990; authorised to sit as a Judge of the High Court, Queen's Bench, Chancery and Family Divs, 1998–2006. Wandsworth Mem., GLC and ILEA, 1967–70. Contested (C): N Battersea, 1970; S Battersea, Feb. 1974. *Publications:* contribs to cricketing periodicals. *Recreations:* walking, Yorkshire cricket, writing for pleasure, travelling. *Clubs:* Reform, MCC; Yorkshire CC; Cricket Writers'.

BRADBURY, David Anthony Gaunt; Director of Libraries, Archives and Guildhall Art Gallery, City of London Corporation (formerly Corporation of London), since 2005; *b* 1 Nov. 1947; *s* of Peter Bradbury and late Iris Bradbury (*née* Tweedale); *m* 1974, Ellen Williams; three *s* one *d*. *Educ:* Repton Sch.; Univ. of Sussex (BA Russian Studies 1970, MA Contemp. Eur. Studies 1972). MCLIP. Grad. trainee, BM liby, 1972–73; British

Library: Lending Div., 1975–86; Dep. Dir (Services), 1986–89, Dir, 1989–95, Document Supply Centre; Dir-Gen., Collections and Services, 1996–2001; Mem. Bd, 1996–2001; Dir, Libraries and Guildhall Art Gall., Corp. of London, 2002–05. Member: Bd, London Univ. Sch. of Advanced Study, 2000–01; Adv. Cttee, Univ. of London Centre for Metropolitan Hist., 2005–. Mem. Conseil, Projet d'Etablissement de la Bibliothèque nationale de France, 1999–2000. Chm., Saga Trust, 1996–2001. Trustee, London Jl, 2005–. *Publications:* contrib. jl articles on future of libraries, library co-operation, publishing, digital information. *Recreations:* languages, walking, Scrabble, history of Saddleworth. *Address:* Guildhall Library, Aldermanbury, EC2P 2EJ. *T:* (020) 7332 1850, *Fax:* (020) 7600 3384; *e-mail:* david.bradbury@cityoflondon.gov.uk.

BRADBURY, Edgar; Managing Director, Skelmersdale Development Corporation, 1976–85; *b* 5 June 1927; *s* of Edgar Furniss Bradbury and Mary Bradbury; *m* 1954, Janet Mary Bouchier Lisle; two *s* one *d.* *Educ:* Grove Park Sch., Wrexham; The High Sch., Newcastle, Staffs; King's Coll., Durham Univ. LLB (Hons). Solicitor. Asst Solicitor: Scarborough BC, 1952–54; St Helens CBC, 1954–57; Dep. Town Clerk, Loughborough, 1957–59; Town Clerk and Clerk of the Peace, Deal, 1960–63; Legal Dir, Skelmersdale Develt Corp., 1963–76. Vice-Chm., W Lancs Health Authority, 1984–94 (Mem., 1982–94). *Recreations:* tennis, bridge. *Address:* 1 Butterfield Gardens, Aughton, Ormskirk, Lancs L39 4XN. *T:* (01695) 580840.

BRADBURY, Ray Douglas; author; *b* Waukegan, Ill, USA, 22 Aug. 1920; *s* of Leonard S. Bradbury and Esther Moberg; *m* 1947, Marguerite Susan McClure (*d* 2003); four *d.* *Educ:* Los Angeles High Sch. First Science-Fiction stories, 1941–44; stories sold to Harpers', Mademoiselle, The New Yorker, etc., 1945–56. Stories selected for: Best American Short Stories, 1946, 1948, 1952, 1958; O. Henry Prize Stories, 1947, 1948; and for inclusion in numerous anthologies. *Screenplays:* Moby Dick, 1954; Icarus Montgolfier Wright, 1961; The Martian Chronicles, 1964; The Picasso Summer, 1968; The Halloween Tree, 1968; The Dreamers; And The Rock Cried Out. Benjamin Franklin Award for Best Story Published in an Amer. Magazine of General Circulation, 1954; 1000 dollar Grant from Inst. of Arts and Letters, 1954. *Publications: novels:* Dark Carnival, 1947; Fahrenheit 451, 1953 (filmed); (for children) Switch on the Night, 1955; Dandelion Wine, 1957; Something Wicked This Way Comes, 1962 (filmed 1983; adapted for stage, 1986); The Small Assassin, 1973; Mars and the Minds of Man, 1973; The Mummies of Guanajuato, 1978; The Ghosts of Forever, 1981; Death is a Lonely Business, 1986; The Toynbee Convector, 1989; A Graveyard for Lunatics, 1990; Green Shadows, White Whale, 1992; From the Dust Returned, 2001; Let's All Kill Constance, 2003; Farewell Summer, 2006; Now and Forever: somewhere a band is playing and Leviathan '99, 2007; *short stories:* The Martian Chronicles, 1950 (English edn, The Silver Locusts, 1957); The Illustrated Man, 1951 (filmed with The Day It Rained Forever); The Golden Apples of the Sun, 1953; The October Country, 1955; A Medicine for Melancholy (English edn, The Day It Rained Forever), 1959; (for children) R Is For Rocket, 1962; (for children) S Is For Space, 1962; The Machineries of Joy, 1964; The Autumn People, 1965; The Vintage Bradbury, 1965; Tomorrow Midnight, 1966; Twice Twenty-Two, 1966; I Sing the Body Electric!, 1969; Long After Midnight, 1976; Quicker than the Eye, 1998; Driving Blind, 1998; One More for the Road, 2001; (for children) The Cat's Pajamas, 2004; A Sound of Thunder and other stories, 2005; The Homecoming, 2006; *general:* Zen and the Art of Writing, 1973; Bradbury Speaks: too soon from the cave, too far from the stars, 2005; *poems:* When Elephants Last in the Dooryard Bloomed, 1973; Where Robot Mice and Robot Men Run Round in Robot Towns, 1977; This Attic where the Meadow Greens, 1980; The Haunted Computer and the Android Pope, 1981; *plays:* The Meadow, 1947; The Anthem Sprinters (one-act), 1963; The World of Ray Bradbury (one-act), 1964; The Wonderful Ice Cream Suit and Other Plays (one-act), 1965; Any Friend of Nicholas Nickleby's is a Friend of Mine, 1968; Pillar of Fire, 1975. *Recreations:* oil painting, ceramics, collecting native masks. *Address:* 10265 Cheviot Drive, Los Angeles, CA 90064, USA.

BRADBURY, Richard Edward, CBE 2008; Chief Executive, River Island, since 2008; *b* Bedford, 4 Feb. 1956; *s* of Albert Edward and Lily Bradbury; *m* 1981, Susan Price; two *d.* *Educ:* Bedford Modern Sch.; Luton Poly. Mgt trainee, Barnaby Rudge, 1975–76; Merchandiser, Harry Fenton Menswear, 1977–79; Burton Group: Merchandiser, 1979–81; Buyer, 1981–84; Buying and Merchandising Controller, 1984–86; Buying Dir, 1986–89; River Island: Man. Dir, Womenswear, 1989–98; Gp Man. Dir, 1998–2007. *Recreations:* golf, music, wine, eating out, retail. *Address:* River Island, Chelsea House, Westgate, W5 1DR. *T:* (020) 8991 4500.

BRADBURY, Susan Alison, (Mrs J. C. Whitley); Editor-in-Chief, Folio Society, since 2006; *b* 15 June 1947; *d* of John Donovan and Mary Alison Bradbury; *m* 1984, John Christopher Whitley; one step *s.* *Educ:* Nottingham High Sch. for Girls (GPDST); Bretton Hall Coll. of Educn; Leeds Univ. (BEd Hons). Teacher: British Sch., Gran Canaria, Canary Is, 1969–71; Haydon Rd Jun. Sch., 1971–72; Governess, Seville, 1972–73; Folio Society: Membership Sec., Production Asst, Picture Researcher, Asst Editor, then Sen. Editor, 1973–83; Associate Editl Dir, 1983–84; Editl Dir, 1984–2006; Dep. Man. Dir, 1991–2006; Acting Man. Dir, 1992–96. Hon. Sec., Soc. of Bookmen, 2000–04 and 2007–. *Publications:* (trans.) Three Tragedies, by Federico Garcia Lorca, 1977; (ed and transcribed) Sir Thomas Malory's Chronicles of King Arthur, 1982; (with Urgunge Onon) Chinngis Khan, 1993; Midnight Madonna (novel), 1995; anthologies: (with John Letts) A Few Royal Occasions, 1977; Fifty Folio Epigrams, 1996; Christmas Crime Stories, 2004; Christmas Ghost Stories, 2005; A Traveller's Christmas, 2006; selected and introduced: Short Stories by Somerset Maugham, 1985; Dream Street: short stories by Damon Runyan, 1989; Love Poems by Robert Graves, 1990. *Recreations:* travel, drawing, reading, opera, playing flamenco guitar, riding elderly motorbike. *Address:* c/o The Folio Society Ltd, 44 Eagle Street, WC1R 4FS. *T:* (020) 7400 4302, *Fax:* (020) 7400 4246; *e-mail:* sueb@foliosociety.com. *Club:* Reform.

BRADBURY, Rear-Adm. Thomas Henry, CB 1979; *b* 4 Dec. 1922; *s* of Thomas Henry Bradbury and Violet Buckingham; *m* 1st, 1945, Beryl Doreen Evans (marr. diss. 1979; she *d* 1985); one *s* one *d*; 2nd, 1979, Sarah Catherine, *d* of Harley Hillier and Mrs Susan Hillier. *Educ:* Christ's Hosp. CO HMS Jufair, 1960–62; Supply Officer, HMS Hermes, 1965–67; Sec. to Controller of Navy, MoD, 1967–70; CO HMS Terror, 1970–71; RCDS, 1972; Dir, Naval Admin. Planning, MoD, 1974–76; Flag Officer, Admiralty Interview Bd, 1977–79. Gp Personnel Dir, Inchcape Gp of Cos, 1979–86; Gp Personnel Exec., Davy Corp., 1987–91. Non-exec. Dir, Eastbourne HA, 1990–93. *Recreation:* gardening in Sussex and Andalucia. *Address:* Padgham Down, Dallington, Heathfield, E Sussex TN21 9NS. *T:* (01435) 830208.

BRADBY, Prof. David Henry, PhD; Professor of Drama and Theatre Studies, 1988–2007, now Emeritus, and Dean of Arts, 2000–02, University of London, at Royal Holloway (formerly Royal Holloway and Bedford New College); *b* 27 Feb. 1942; *s* of late Edward Lawrence Bradby; *m* 1965, Rachel Anderson, writer; three *s* one *d.* *Educ:* Rugby Sch.; Trinity College, Oxford (MA); PhD Glasgow; CertEd Bristol. Lectr, Glasgow Univ., 1966–70; University of Kent at Canterbury: Lectr, 1971; Sen. Lectr, 1979–85; Reader in French Theatre Studies, 1985–88; Prof. of Theatre Studies, Univ. of Caen, 1983–84. Dir, Orange Tree Theatre, Richmond, 1990–2002. Ed., Contemporary Theatre Review, 2003–. Chevalier des Arts et des Lettres (France), 1997. *Publications:* People's Theatre (with John McCormick), 1978; The Theatre of Roger Planchon, 1984; Modern French Drama 1940–1980, 1984, 2nd edn, as Modern French Drama 1940–1990, 1991; (with David Williams) Directors' Theatre, 1988; Le Théâtre Français Contemporain, 1990; The Theatre of Michael Vinaver, 1993; (with Annie Sparks) Mise en Scène: French theatre now, 1997; Beckett: Waiting for Godot, 2001; Le Théâtre en France de 1968 à 2000, 2007. *Recreation:* forestry. *Address:* Department of Drama and Theatre Studies, Royal Holloway, University of London, Egham, Surrey TW20 0EX.

BRADBY, Thomas; Political Editor, ITV News, since 2005; *b* 13 Jan. 1967; *s* of Daniel James Bradby and Sarah Ley Bradby; *m* 1994, Claudia Hill-Norton; two *s* one *d.* *Educ:* Sherborne Sch.; Edinburgh Univ. (MA Hons Hist.). ITN trainee, 1990–92; ITV News: political producer, 1992–93; Ireland Corresp., 1993–96; Political Corresp., 1996–98; Asia Corresp., 1998–2001; Royal Corresp., 2001–03; UK Ed., 2003–05. *Publications: novels:* Shadow Dancer, 1998; The Sleep of the Dead, 2001; The Master of Rain, 2002; The White Russian, 2003; The God of Chaos, 2005; Blood Money, 2009. *Recreations:* ski-ing, writing, walking, soccer. *Address:* c/o ITV News, Press Gallery, House of Commons, SW1A 0AA. *T:* (020) 7430 4991; *e-mail:* tom.bradby@itn.co.uk. *Club:* Royal Automobile.

BRADDICK, Prof. Oliver John, PhD; Professor of Psychology and Head, Department of Experimental Psychology, Oxford University, since 2001; Fellow, Magdalen College, Oxford, since 2001; *b* 16 Nov. 1944; *s* of Henry John James Braddick and Edith Muriel Braddick; *m* 1979, Prof. Janette Atkinson; two *s* two *d.* *Educ:* Trinity Coll., Cambridge (MA; PhD 1968). Cambridge University: Lectr, 1969–86; Reader in Vision, 1986–93; Fellow, Trinity Coll., 1968–72; University College London: Prof. of Psychol., 1993–2001; Hd of Dept, 1998–2001. Associate, Brown Univ., USA, 1968–69. FMedSci 2001. Trustee, Assoc. for Res. in Vision and Ophthalmol., 1999–2004. *Publications:* numerous articles on vision and its develt in scientific jls and books. *Recreations:* family life, the arts. *Address:* Department of Experimental Psychology, University of Oxford, South Parks Road, Oxford OX1 3UD. *T:* (01865) 271355.

BRADEN, Hugh Reginald, CMG 1980; DL; Mayor of Worthing, 1991–92; *b* 30 Jan. 1923; *s* of late Reginald Henry Braden and Mabel Braden (*née* Selby); *m* 1946, Phyllis Grace Barnes; one *d.* *Educ:* Worthing High School for Boys; Brighton College of Technology. Joined War Office, 1939; served War, Royal Navy, 1942–45; Far East Land Forces, 1946–50; British Army of the Rhine, 1953–56; War Office and Min. of Defence, 1956–66; jssc 1967; British Embassy, Washington, 1968–70; Min. of Defence, 1971–80 (Asst Under Sec. of State, 1978–80). Dir, A. B. Jay, 1981–90. Borough Councillor, Worthing, 1983–95; Chm., Worthing Cons. Assoc., 1992–95. DL W Sussex, 1993. *Address:* Field House, Honeysuckle Lane, High Salvington, Worthing, West Sussex BN13 3BT. *T:* (01903) 260203.

BRADES, Susan Deborah F.; *see* Ferleger Brades.

BRADFIELD, Sir John (Richard Grenfell), Kt 2007; CBE 1986; PhD; Senior Bursar, Trinity College, Cambridge, 1956–92; Founder, and Manager, Cambridge Science Park, 1970–92; *b* 20 May 1925; *s* of Horace and Ada Bradfield; *m* 1951, Jane Wood; one *s.* *Educ:* Trinity Coll., Cambridge (schol. 1942; MA, PhD). Research Fellow in Cell Biology, Trinity Coll., Cambridge, 1947; Commonwealth (Harkness) Fellow, Chicago, 1948; Jun. Bursar, Trinity Coll., Cambridge, 1951. Director: Cambridge Water Co., 1965–95; Cambridge Building Soc., 1968–95; Biotechnology Investments, 1989–2000; Anglian Water, 1989–93 (Bd Mem., 1975–89); 3i Bioscience Investment Trust, 2000–02 (Consultant, 2002–04); Chm., Abbotstone Agricl Property Unit Trust, 1975–2002. Chairman: Addenbrooke's NHS Trust, 1993–96; Commn for the New Towns, 1995–98. Darwin College, Cambridge: proposed foundn, 1963; Hon. Fellow, 1973. Hon. LLD Cambridge, 1992. FRSA 1990. *Publications:* scientific papers on cell biology. *Recreations:* walking, arboretum-visiting. *Address:* Trinity College, Cambridge CB2 1TQ. *T:* (01223) 338400.

BRADFORD, 7th Earl of, *cr* 1815; **Richard Thomas Orlando Bridgeman;** Bt 1660; Baron Bradford, 1794; Viscount Newport, 1815; *b* 3 Oct. 1947; *s* of 6th Earl of Bradford, TD, and Mary Willoughby (*d* 1986), *er d* of Lt-Col T. H. Montgomery, DSO; *S* father, 1981; *m* 1979, Joanne Elizabeth (marr. diss. 2006), *d* of B. Miller; three *s* one *d.* *Educ:* Harrow; Trinity College, Cambridge. Owner of Porters English Restaurant of Covent Garden, Covent Garden Grill and The Countess's Arms, Shropshire. *Publications:* (compiled) My Private Parts and the Stuffed Parrot, 1984; The Eccentric Cookbook, 1985; Stately Secrets, 1994; (with Carol Wilson) Porters English Cookery Bible: Ancient and Modern, 2004; (with Carol Wilson) Porters Seasonal Celebrations, 2007. *Heir: s* Viscount Newport, *qv.* *Address:* Woodlands House, Weston-under-Lizard, Shifnal, Salop TF11 8PX. *T:* (office) (01952) 850566, *Fax:* (01952) 850697; *e-mail:* bradfordr@porters.uk.com.

BRADFORD, Bishop of, since 2002; **Rt Rev. David Charles James,** PhD; *b* 6 March 1945; *s* of Charles George Frederick James and Cecilia Lily James; *m* 1971, Gillian Patricia Harrop; four *d.* *Educ:* Nottingham High Sch.; Exeter Univ. (BSc 1966; PhD 1971); Nottingham Univ. (BA 1973); St John's Theol Coll., Nottingham. Asst Lectr in Chemistry, Southampton Univ., 1969–70. Ordained deacon, 1973, priest, 1974; Curate: Highfield Church, Southampton, 1973–76; Goring by Sea, Worthing, 1976–78; Anglican Chaplain, UEA, 1978–82; Vicar of Ecclesfield, Sheffield, 1982–90; RD, Ecclesfield, 1987–90; Vicar of Highfield, Southampton, 1990–98; Bp Suffragan of Pontefract, 1998–2002. Hon. Canon of Winchester, 1998. Gov., King Alfred's UC, Winchester, 1992–97. *Address:* Bishopscroft, Ashwell Road, Bradford, W Yorks BD9 4AU.

BRADFORD, Dean of; *see* Ison, Very Rev. D. J.

BRADFORD, Archdeacon of; *see* Lee, Ven. D. J.

BRADFORD, Barbara Taylor, OBE 2007; author; *b* Leeds, 10 May; *d* of late Winston and Freda Taylor; *m* 1963, Robert Bradford. Jun. Reporter, 1949–51, Women's Editor, 1951–53, Yorkshire Evening Post; Fashion Editor, Woman's Own, 1953–54; columnist, London Evening News, 1955–57; Exec. Editor, London American, 1959–62; moved to USA, 1964; Editor, National Design Center Magazine, 1965–69; syndicated columnist, 1968–81. Hon. DLitt: Leeds, 1989; Bradford, 1995; Hon. DHL Teikyo Post, Conn, 1996. *Publications:* Complete Encyclopedia of Homemaking Ideas, 1968; A Garland of Children's Verse, 1968; How to be the Perfect Wife, 1969; Easy Steps to Successful Decorating, 1971; How to Solve Your Decorating Problems, 1976; Decorating Ideas for Casual Living, 1977; Making Space Grow, 1979; Luxury Designs for Apartment Living, 1981; *novels:* A Woman of Substance, 1979 (televised, 1985); Voice of the Heart, 1983; Hold the Dream, 1985 (televised, 1986); Act of Will, 1986; To Be the Best, 1988; The Women in His Life, 1990; Remember, 1991; Angel, 1993; Everything to Gain, 1994;

Dangerous to Know, 1995; Love in Another Town, 1995; Her Own Rules, 1996; A Secret Affair, 1996; Power of a Woman, 1997; A Sudden Change of Heart, 1999; Where You Belong, 2000; The Triumph of Katie Byrne, 2001; Emma's Secret, 2003; Unexpected Blessings, 2004; Just Rewards, 2005; The Ravenscar Dynasty, 2006; Heirs of Ravenscar, 2007. *Address:* Bradford Enterprises, 450 Park Avenue, New York, NY 10022–2605, USA. *T:* (212) 308 7390, *Fax:* (212) 935 1636.

BRADFORD, (Sir) Edward Alexander Slade, 5th Bt, *cr* 1902 (but does not use the title); *b* 18 June 1952; *s* of Major Sir Edward Montagu Andrew Bradford, 3rd Bt (*d* 1952) and his 2nd wife, Marjorie Edith (*née* Bere); *S* half-brother, Sir John Ridley Evelyn Bradford, 4th Bt, 1954; *m* 1990, Jacqueline W. Bolton. *Heir: cousin* Robert Berenger Pickering Bradford, *b* 12 Aug. 1952.

BRADFORD, Prof. Eric Watts, MDS (Sheffield); DDSc (St Andrews); Professor of Dental Surgery, 1959–85, now Emeritus, and Pro-Vice-Chancellor, 1983–85, University of Bristol; *b* 4 Nov. 1919; *e s* of E. J. G. and C. M. Bradford; *m* 1946, Norah Mary Longmuir; two *s* three *d. Educ:* King Edward VII Sch., Sheffield; High Storrs Grammar Sch., Sheffield; Univ. of Sheffield (Robert Styring Scholar). LDS, Sheffield, 1943; BDS, Sheffield, 1944; MDS, Sheffield, 1950; DDSc St Andrews, 1954. Lieut, Army Dental Corps, Nov. 1944; Capt., Nov. 1945. Lectr, Univ. of Sheffield, 1947–52; Senior Lectr, Univ. of St Andrews, 1952–59; Dean, Faculty of Medicine, Bristol University, 1975–79. Mem., Gen. Dental Council, 1979–85. *Publications:* many papers on dental anatomy in British and other journals. *Address:* 9 Cedar Court, Glenavon Park, Sneyd Park, Bristol BS9 1RL. *T:* (0117) 968 1849.

BRADFORD, Hon. Max(well Robert); World Bank consultant and economic consultant, since 2002; company director; Minister of Defence, 1997–99, Minister for Tertiary Education, 1999, New Zealand; *b* 19 Jan. 1942; *s* of Robert and Ella Bradford; *m* 1st, 1967, Dr Janet Grieve (marr. diss. 1988); 2nd, 1991, Rosemary Young; two step *d. Educ:* Christchurch Boys' High Sch.; Univ. of Canterbury, NZ (MCom Hons). NZ Treasury, 1966–69, 1973–78; Economist, IMF, Washington, 1969–73; Dir of Advocacy, Employers' Fedn, 1978–85; Chief Exec., Bankers Assoc., 1985–87; Sec.-Gen., Nat. Party, 1987–89; MP (Nat. Party): Tarawera, 1990–96; Rotorua, 1996–99; List, 1999–2002; Minister for Enterprise, Commerce, Labour, Energy and Revenue, 1996–99. *Recreations:* sailing, music, reading, fishing, ski-ing. *Address:* PO Box 8040, Wellington 6145, New Zealand. *T:* (4) 4721345, (mobile) (21) 570854. *Club:* Wellington.

BRADFORD, Sarah Mary Malet Ward, (Viscountess Bangor); historian and biographer, critic, broadcaster and journalist; *b* 3 Sept. 1938; *d* of late Brig. Hilary Anthony Hayes, DSO, OBE, and Mary Beatrice de Carteret (*née* Malet), who *m* 2nd, Keith Murray; *m* 1st, 1959, Anthony John Bradford (marr. diss. 1976); one *s* one *d*; 2nd, 1976, Viscount Bangor, qv. *Educ:* St Mary's Convent, Shaftesbury; Lady Margaret Hall, Oxford (schol.). Manuscript Expert, Christies, 1974–78; Consultant, Manuscript Dept, Sotheby's, 1979–81. *Publications:* The Englishman's Wine, 1969, new edn as The Story of Port, 1978, 2nd edn 1983; Portugal and Madeira, 1969; Portugal, 1973; Cesare Borgia, 1976, 2nd edn 2001; Disraeli, 1982, 2nd edn 1996; Princess Grace, 1984; King George VI, 1989, revised edn 2001; Sacheverell Sitwell, 1993; Elizabeth, A Biography of Her Majesty The Queen, 1996, revised edn 2001; America's Queen, The Life of Jacqueline Kennedy Onassis, 2000; Lucrezia Borgia: life, love and death in Renaissance Italy, 2004; Diana, 2006. *Recreations:* reading biographies, diaries and letters, gardening, travelling, watching Liverpool FC. *Address:* c/o Aitken Alexander Associates, 18–21 Cavaye Place, SW10 9PT. *T:* (020) 7373 8672, *Fax:* (020) 7373 6002.

BRADING, Prof. David Anthony, PhD, LittD; FBA 1995; Professor of Mexican History, University of Cambridge, 1999–2004; Fellow of Clare Hall, Cambridge, 1995–2004; *b* 26 Aug. 1936; *s* of Ernest Arthur Brading and Amy Mary (*née* Driscoll); *m* 1966, Celia Wu; one *s. Educ:* Pembroke Coll., Cambridge (BA 1960; LittD 1991); UCL (PhD 1965). Asst. Prof., Univ. of Calif, Berkeley, 1965–71; Associate Prof., Yale Univ., 1971–73; Cambridge University: Lectr, 1973–92; Reader in Latin American Hist., 1992–99. Hon. Prof., Univ. of Lima, 1993. Order of the Aztec Eagle (Mexico), 2003. *Publications:* Miners and Merchants in Bourbon Mexico, 1971; Haciendas and Ranchos in the Mexican Bajío, 1979; The Origins of Mexican Nationalism, 1985; The First America, 1991; Church and State in Bourbon Mexico, 1994; Mexican Phoenix, 2001. *Recreations:* music, walking. *Address:* 28 Storey's Way, Cambridge CB3 0DT. *T:* (01223) 352098. *Club:* Oxford and Cambridge.

BRADLEY, family name of **Baron Bradley**.

BRADLEY, Baron *cr* 2006 (Life Peer), of Withington in the County of Greater Manchester; **Keith John Charles Bradley;** PC 2001; *b* 17 May 1950; *m* 1987, Rhona Graham; two *s* one *d. Educ:* Manchester Polytechnic (BA Hons); York Univ. (MPhil). Former health service administrator, North West RHA. Mem., Manchester City Council, 1983–88. MP (Lab) Manchester, Withington, 1987–2005; contested (Lab) same seat, 2005. Opposition spokesman on social security, 1991–96, on transport, 1996–97; Parly Under-Sec. of State, DSS, 1997–98; Treasurer of HM Household (Dep. Chief Whip), 1998–2001; Minister of State, Home Office, 2001–02. Joined Labour Party, 1973; Mem., Manchester Withington Co-op Party. Mem., Unite. *Address:* House of Lords, SW1A 0PW.

BRADLEY, Prof. Allan, PhD; FRS 2002; Director, The Sanger Centre (for genome research), Hinxton, Cambridge, since 2000. *Educ:* Trinity Coll., Cambridge (BA Hons 1981; PhD 1986). Baylor College of Medicine, Houston, Texas: Asst Prof., 1987–92, Associate Prof., 1992–95, Cullen Prof. of Genetics, 1995–2000, Dept of Molecular and Human Genetics; Associate Investigator, Howard Hughes Med. Inst., 1993–2000. Mem., EMBO, 2006. *Publications:* articles in jls. *Address:* The Sanger Centre, Wellcome Trust Genome Campus, Hinxton, Saffron Walden, Cambs CB10 1SA.

BRADLEY, Andrew; see Bradley, J. A.

BRADLEY, Anna Louise; Chairman, Consumer Panel, Office of Communications, since 2008; *b* 29 July 1957; *d* of Donald Bradley and Angela Lucy Bradley (*née* Bradley, now Ratcliffe); *m* 1995, Norman Howard Jones; one *s* one *d. Educ:* Camden Sch. for Girls; Warwick Univ. (BA Phil, 1978; MBA 1994). Sen. Sub-Editor, Marshall Cavendish Partworks Ltd, 1978–82; Consumers' Association: Sen. Project Leader, 1982–87; Project Manager, Food and Health, 1987–88; Head, Food and Health, 1988–91; Dep. Research Dir, 1991–93; Exec. Dir and Co. Sec., Inst. for the Study of Drug Dependence Ltd, 1993–98; Dir, Nat. Consumer Council, 1999–2002; Dir of Consumer Affairs, then of Retail Themes and Consumer Sector Leader, Financial Services Authy, 2002–05. Chair, Organic Standards Bd, 2006–; non-exec. Dir, Soil Assoc. Certification Ltd, 2007–. Member: Adv. Council on the Misuse of Drugs, 1996–98; Agriculture, Envmt and Biotechnol. Commn, 2000–05; Sci. Adv. Council, 2004–05. Adv. Consultant, Fishburn Hedges, 2006. Trustee, Addaction, 2006–; non-exec. Dir, Life Trust Foundn, 2008. Mem., Mgt Cttee, Patients' Assoc., 1985–88. *Publications:* Healthy Eating, 1989; (ed)

Understanding Additives, 1988; acad. and research papers in Lancet, Jl Human Nutrition, Dietetics, etc.

BRADLEY, Anne; see Smith, A.

BRADLEY, Anthony Wilfred; barrister and constitutional lawyer; *b* 6 Feb. 1934; *s* of David and Olive Bradley (*née* Bonsey); *m* 1959, Kathleen Bryce; one *s* three *d. Educ:* Dover Grammar Sch.; Emmanuel Coll., Cambridge (BA 1957, LLB 1958, MA 1961). Solicitor of the Supreme Court, 1960 (Clifford's Inn Prize); called to the Bar, Inner Temple, 1989. Asst Lectr, 1960–64, Lectr, 1964–68, Cambridge, and Fellow of Trinity Hall, 1960–68; Prof. of Constitutional Law, 1968–89, Dean, Faculty of Law, 1979–82, Prof. Emeritus, 1990, Univ. of Edinburgh. Vis. Reader in Law, UC, Dar es Salaam, 1966–67; Vis. Prof. of Public Law, Univ. of Florence, 1984. Chairman: Edinburgh Council for Single Homeless, 1984–88; Social Security Appeal Tribunal, 1984–89; Member: Wolfenden Cttee on Voluntary Orgns, 1974–78; Social Scis and Law Cttee, SSRC, 1975–79; Social Studies Sub-Cttee, UGC, 1985–89; Cttee of Inquiry into Local Govt in Scotland, 1980; Cttee to review local govt in Islands of Scotland, 1983–84. Mem. Exec. Cttee, Internat. Assoc. of Constitutional Law, 1999–2007. Legal Advr, H of L Select Cttee on the Constitution, 2002–05; Alternate Mem. (UK), Venice Commn for Democracy Through Law, 2003–. Ed., Public Law, 1986–92. Hon. LLD: Staffordshire, 1993; Edinburgh, 1998. *Publications:* (with M. Adler) Justice, Discretion and Poverty, 1976; (ed) Wade and Bradley, Constitutional and Administrative Law, 9th edn 1978 to 11th edn 1993, subseq. Bradley and Ewing, Constitutional and Administrative Law, 12th edn 1997 to 14th edn 2006; The Scotland Act 1978, 1979; Administrative Law (in Stair Meml Encyc. of the Laws of Scotland), 1987, 2nd edn 2000; (with J. S. Bell) Governmental Liability, 1991; (jtly) European Human Rights Law: text and materials, 1995, 3rd edn 2008; articles in legal jls. *Recreation:* music. *Address:* Cloisters, 1 Pump Court, Temple, EC4Y 7AA. *T:* (020) 7827 4000; Morland, Sheepstead Road, near Marcham, Abingdon, Oxon OX13 6QG. *T:* (01865) 390774.

BRADLEY, Averil Olive, (Mrs J. W. P. Bradley); see Mansfield, A. O.

BRADLEY, Prof. Benjamin Arthur de Burgh, PhD; FRCP, FRCPath; Director, Shannon Applied Biotechnology Centre, Ireland, since 2008; Professor of Transplantation Sciences, and Director, Department of Transplantation Sciences, University of Bristol, 1992–2004; *b* 17 Sept. 1942; *s* of Reuben Stephen Bradley and Elsie Marjorie Bradley (*née* Burke); *m* 1968, Anne White; four *d. Educ:* Silcoates Sch., Wakefield; Bilston Grammar Sch.; Birmingham Univ. Med. Sch. (MB ChB 1965); Birmingham Univ. (MSc 1967; PhD 1970). FRCPath 1986 (MRCPath 1974); FRCP 1999. House surgeon and house physician, United Birmingham Hosps, 1965–66; MRC Res. Fellow, Dept of Surgery and Exptl Pathology, Univ. of Birmingham, 1967–70; Asst Dir of Res., Dept of Surgery, Univ. of Cambridge, 1970–75; Asst Prof., Dept of Immunohaematology, Univ. of Leiden, 1975–79; Dir, UK Transplant Service, 1979–92. Prof. of Transplantation Immunology, Univ. of Bristol, 1988. Dir of Immunol., Ximerex Inc., 2006–07. Member: Scientific Policy Adv. Cttee, Nat. Inst. for Biol Standards, 1991–96; Bd, Jenner Educnl Trust, 1992–2000; Scientific Cttee, Foundn for Nephrology, 1992–2004. President: Eur. Foundn for Immunogenetics, 1988–89; British Soc. for Histocompatibility and Immunogenetics, 1996–98. Hon. Consultant in Transplantation Scis, N Bristol NHS Trust, 1979–. Chm., Editl Bd, European Jl Immunogenetics, 1989–2004. Hon. MA Cantab, 1974. *Publications:* (with S. M. Gore) Renal Transplantation: sense and sensitization, 1986; Editor and contributor to annual reports of: UK Transplant Service, 1979–90; Transplantation Services and Statistics in UK and Eire, 1991; contrib. textbooks and med. jls on clinical organ and tissue transplantation and immunology and genetics of transplantation and blood transfusion. *Recreation:* competitive sailing. *Address:* East Barn, The Pound, Lower Almondsbury, Bristol BS32 4EF. *T:* (01454) 201077; Shannon Applied Biotechnology Centre, Institute of Technology Tralee, Tralee, Co. Kerry, Ireland. *T:* (066) 7144217; *e-mail:* benjaminbzone-whoswho2009@yahoo.co.uk.

BRADLEY, Dr (Charles) Clive; Managing Director, 1990–99, and Consultant, 1999–2000, Sharp Laboratories of Europe Ltd; *b* 11 April 1937; *s* of late Charles William Bradley and Winifred Smith; *m* 1965, Vivien Audrey Godley; one *s* one *d. Educ:* Longton High Sch.; Birmingham Univ. (BSc Hons in Physics, 1958); Emmanuel Coll., Cambridge (PhD 1962). FInstP 1997. Nat. Phys. Lab., 1961–67; MIT, USA, 1967, 1969; Nat. Bureau of Standards, USA, 1968; Nat. Phys. Lab., 1969–75; DoI, 1975–82, SPSO and Head of Energy Unit, 1978–82; Counsellor (Science and Technology), British Embassy, Tokyo, 1982–88; DCSO and Head of Secretariat, ACOST, Cabinet Office, 1988–90. Dir, Birds Hill Oxshott Estate Co., 2000–. Vis. Prof., Univ. of Oxford, 1999–2002. Chm., Industrial Energy Conservation Cttee, Internat. Energy Agency, 1980–82. Dep. Comr Gen. for Britain, Sci. Expo Tokyo, 1985. Mem., Oxford Univ. Adv. Council on Continuing Educn, 1993–2001. Treas. and Mem. Council, Japan Soc., 2001–07. A. F. Bulgin Prize, IERE, 1972. *Publications:* High Pressure Methods in Solid State Research, 1969; contribs to jls on lasers, metals and semiconductors. *Recreations:* tennis, gardening. *Address:* 8 Montrose Gardens, Oxshott, Surrey KT22 0UU. *Club:* Athenæum.

BRADLEY, (Charles) Stuart, CBE 1990; Managing Director, Associated British Ports, 1988–95; Director, Associated British Ports Holdings, 1988–2001; *b* 11 Jan. 1936; *s* of Captain Charles Bradley, OBE and Amelia Jane Bradley; *m* 1959, Kathleen Marina (*née* Loraine); one *s* one *d* (and one *s* decd). *Educ:* Penarth County Sch.; University Coll. Southampton (Warsash). Master Mariner, 1961; FCILT (FCIT 1978). Deck Officer, P&OSN Co., 1952–64; joined British Transport Docks Bd, subseq. Associated British Ports, 1964; Dock and Harbour Master, Silloth, 1968–70; Dock Master, 1970–74, Dock and Marine Superintendent, 1974–76, Plymouth; Docks Manager, Lowestoft, 1976–78; Port Manager, Barry, 1978–80; Dep. Port Manager, 1980–85, Port Manager, 1985–87, Hull; Asst Man. Dir (Resources), 1987–88; Chm., Red Funnel Gp, 1989–2000. Younger Brother, Trinity House, 1994–. *Recreations:* Welsh Rugby football, cycling, walking, theatre. *Clubs:* Oriental, Honourable Company of Master Mariners.

BRADLEY, Clive; see Bradley, Charles C.

BRADLEY, Clive, CBE 1996; Chief Executive, The Publishers Association, 1976–97; Convenor, Confederation of Information Communication Industries, since 1984; *b* 25 July 1934; *s* of late Alfred and Kathleen Bradley. *Educ:* Felsted Sch., Essex; Clare Coll., Cambridge (Scholar; MA). Yale Univ. (Mellon Fellow). Called to the Bar, Middle Temple. Current Affairs Producer, BBC, 1961–63; Broadcasting Officer, Labour Party, 1963–64; Political Editor, The Statist, 1965–67; Gp Labour Adviser, IPC, 1967–69; Dep. Gen. Man., Daily and Sunday Mirror, 1969–71; Controller of Admin, IPC Newspapers, 1971–72; i/c IPC local radio applications, 1972–73; Dir i/c new prodn arrangements, The Observer, 1973–75. Dep. Chm., Central London Valuation Tribunal, 1973–2006; Director: Organising Cttee, World Congress on Books, London, 1982; Don't Tax Reading campaign, 1984–85; Organiser, IPA Congress, London, 1984; DTI Inf. Age Partnership, 1997–2001. Chair, Richmond upon Thames Arts Council, 2003–. Trustee: Age Concern, Richmond, 1998– (Chm., 2001–03); Garrick's Temple to Shakespeare, Hampton, 2006–. Gov., Felsted Sch., 1973–. *Publications:* Which Way?, 1970; (ed) The

Future of the Book, 1982; articles on politics, economics, the press, television, industrial relations. *Recreations:* reading, travel. *Address:* 8 Northumberland Place, Richmond, Surrey TW10 6TS. *T:* (020) 8940 7172; *e-mail:* bradley_clive@btopenworld.com.

BRADLEY, Prof. Daniel Joseph, PhD; FRS 1976; FInstP; Professor of Optical Electronics, Trinity College Dublin, 1980–83, now Emeritus; Emeritus Professor of Optics, London University, 1980; *b* 18 Jan. 1928; *s* of late John Columba Bradley and Margaret Mary Bradley; *m* 1958, Winefride Marie Therese O'Connor; four *s* one *d. Educ:* St Columb's Coll., Derry; St Mary's Trng Coll., Belfast; Birkbeck and Royal Holloway Colls, London (BSc Maths, BSc Physics, PhD). Primary Sch. Teacher, Derry, 1947–53; Secondary Sch. Teacher, London area, 1953–57; Asst Lectr, Royal Holloway Coll., 1957–60; Lectr, Imperial Coll. of Science and Technol., 1960–64; Reader, Royal Holloway Coll., 1964–66; Prof. and Head of Dept of Pure and Applied Physics, QUB, 1966–73; Prof. of Optics, 1973–80, and Head of Physics Dept, 1976–80, Imperial Coll., London. Vis. Scientist, MIT, 1965; Consultant, Harvard Observatory, 1966. Lectures: Scott, Cambridge, 1977; Tolansky Meml, RSA, 1977. Chairman: Laser Facility Cttee, SRC, 1976–79; British Nat. Cttee for Physics, 1979–80; Quantum Electronics Commn, IUPAP, 1982–85; Member: Rutherford Lab. Estab. Cttee, SRC, 1977–79; Science Bd, SRC, 1977–80; Council, Royal Soc., 1979–80. Gov., Sch. of Cosmic Physics, DIAS, 1981–95. MRIA 1969; Fellow, Optical Soc. of America, 1975. Hon. DSc: NUU, 1983; QUB, 1986. Thomas Young Medal, Inst. of Physics, 1975; Royal Medal, Royal Soc., 1983; C. H. Townes Award, Optical Soc. of America, 1989; Cunningham Medal, RIA, 2001. *Publications:* papers on optics, lasers, spectroscopy, chronoscopy and astronomy in Proc. Roy. Soc., Phil. Mag., Phys. Rev., J. Opt. Soc. Amer., Proc. IEEE, Chem. Phys. Letts, Optics Communications. *Recreations:* television, walking, DIY. *Address:* Trinity College, Dublin 2, Ireland.

See also D. D. C. Bradley.

BRADLEY, Prof. David John, DM; FRCP, FRCPath, FFPH, FMedSci; FIBiol; Director, Ross Institute, London School of Hygiene and Tropical Medicine, and Professor of Tropical Hygiene, University of London, 1974–2000, now Ross Professor Emeritus of Tropical Public Health; *b* 12 Jan. 1937; *s* of late Harold Robert and of Mona Bradley; *m* 1961, Lorne Marie, *d* of late Major L. G. Farquhar and Marie Farquhar; two *s* two *d. Educ:* Wyggeston Sch., Leicester; Selwyn Coll., Cambridge (Scholar); University Coll. Hosp. Med. Sch. (Atchison Schol., Magrath Schol., Trotter Medal in Surgery, Liston Gold Medal in Surgery, BA Nat. Scis Tripos, Med. Scis and Zoology, 1st cl. Hons, Frank Smart Prize Zool.; MB, BChir, MA 1960); DM Oxon 1972. FIBiol 1974; FFPH (FFCM 1979); FRCPath 1981; FRCP 1985. Med. Res. Officer, Ross Inst. Bilharzia Res. Unit, Tanzania, 1961–64; Lectr, 1964–66, Sen. Lectr, 1966–69, Makerere Univ. of East Africa, Uganda; Trop. Res. Fellow of Royal Soc., Sir William Dunn Sch. of Pathology, Oxford, 1969–73; Sen. Res. Fellow, Staines Med. Fellow, Exeter Coll., Oxford, 1971–74; Clinical Reader in Path., Oxford Clinical Med. Sch., 1973–74; Chm., Div. of Communicable and Tropical Diseases, LSHTM, 1982–88. Vis. Prof., Univ. of Wales Coll. of Medicine, 1994–. Co-Director, Malaria Ref. Lab., HPA (formerly PHLS), 1974–2003; Hon. Consultant in Public Health Medicine, HPA (formerly PHLS) and to Westminster PCT (formerly to Kensington, Chelsea and Westminster), 1974–; Hon. Consultant in Trop. and Communicable Diseases, Bloomsbury DHA, 1983–2001; Dir, WHO Collaborating Centre Envtl Control of Vectors, 1983–; Mem., Bd of Trustees, Internat. Centre for Diarrhoeal Disease Res., Bangladesh, 1979–85 (Chm., 1982–83); Consultant Advisor to Dir, Royal Tropical Inst., Amsterdam, 1980–90; Advr, Indep. Internat. Commn on Health Res.; Member: WHO Expert Adv. Panel on Parasitic Diseases, 1972–; Tech. Adv. Gp, Diarrhoea Programme, 1979–85; Panel of Experts on Envtl Management, 1981–; External Review Gp on Trop. Diseases Programme, 1987; Task Force on Health Res. for Develt, 1991–93; Chm., Rev. Cttee, Swiss Tropical Inst., 1994–. Editor, Jl of Trop. Med. and Hygiene, 1981–; Founding Ed., Tropical Medicine and Internat. Health. Pres., RSTM&H, 1999–2001. FMedSci 1999; For. Corresp. Mem., Royal Belgian Acad. of Medicine, 1984; Corresp. Mem., German Tropenmediziningesellschaft, 1980; Hon. FIWEM (Hon. FIPHE, 1981). Hon. DSc Leicester, 2004. Chalmers Medal, 1980, Macdonald Medal, 1996, RSTM&H; Harben Gold Medal, RIPH, 2002. *Publications:* (with G. F. and A. U. White) Drawers of Water, 1972; (with E. E. Sabben-Clare and B. Kirkwood) Health in Tropical Africa during the Colonial Period, 1980; (with R. G. Feachem, D. D. Mara and H. Garelick) Sanitation and Disease, 1983; (jtly) Travel Medicine, 1989; (jtly) The Impact of Development Policies on Health, 1990; (jtly) The Malaria Challenge, 1999; papers in learned jls. *Recreations:* natural history, landscape gardens, travel. *Address:* Ross Institute, London School of Hygiene and Tropical Medicine, Keppel Street, WC1E 7HT. *T:* (020) 7927 2216.

BRADLEY, David Rice; Director of Development, King's College School, Wimbledon, 2000–07; *b* 9 Jan. 1938; *s* of George Leonard Bradley and Evelyn Annie Bradley; *m* 1962, Josephine Elizabeth Turnbull Fricker (*née* Harries); two *s. Educ:* Christ Coll., Brecon; St Catharine's Coll., Cambridge (Exhibnr; MA English); Edinburgh Univ. (Dip. in Applied Linguistics). Nat. service commn, S Wales Borderers. British Council: served: Dacca, 1962–65; Allahabad, 1966–69; New Delhi, 1969–70; Dir of Studies, British Inst., Madrid, 1970–73; Department of the Environment: Principal, Res. Admin, 1973–76; Planning, Develt Control, 1976–78; Inner Cities, 1978–79; Rayner Study (develt of Management Inf. System for Ministers), 1979–80; Central Policy Planning Unit, 1980–81; Study of Local Govt Finance (Grade 5), 1981–82; on special leave, Gwilym Gibbon Res. Fellow, Nuffield Coll., Oxford, 1982–83; Finance, Envmtl Servs, 1983–86; London Urban Develt, sponsorship of LDDC, 1986–88; Dir (G3), Merseyside Task Force, DoE, 1988–90; Chief Exec., London Borough of Havering, 1990–95; Man. Consultant, CSC Computer Scis Ltd, 1995–96; Head, Corporate Funding, Univ. of Oxford, 1997–2000. Vis. Fellow, Nuffield Coll., Oxford, 1993–2001. Mem., DoE Adv. Panel on appointments to Sponsored Bodies, 1996–98; non-exec. Dir, E Thames Housing Gp, 1997–98. Mem. Mgt Bd, Bankside Gall., 2002–03. Mem. Council, Sch. of Mgt Studies, Oxford Univ., 1995–98. Hon. Sec., London Planning and Develt Forum, 1990–2003. *Recreations:* painting, gardening. *Address:* 29 York Court, Albany Park Road, Kingston upon Thames, Surrey KT2 5ST. *T:* (020) 8547 1573.

BRADLEY, Prof. Denise Irene, AC 2008 (AO 1995); Vice Chancellor and President, University of South Australia, 1997–2007, now Emeritus Professor; *b* 23 March 1942; *d* of Richard Francis Haren and Lillian Irene (*née* Ward); *m* 1st, 1962, Michael Charles Bradley (marr. diss. 1985); four *s*; 2nd, 1987, Bruce Simpson King. *Educ:* Sydney Univ. (BA); Adelaide Univ. (DipEd 1964); Univ. of NSW (DipLib 1973); Flinders Univ. (MSocAdmin 1986). Women's Advr, Dept of Educn, S Australia, 1977–80; South Australia College of Advanced Education: Dean, Faculty of Educn and Humanities, 1983–86; Dir (Academic), 1986–88; Dep. Principal, 1988–90; Principal, 1990; University of South Australia: Dep. Vice Chancellor, 1991–92; Dep. Vice Chancellor (Academic), 1992–95; Dep. Vice Chancellor and Vice Pres., 1995–96. SA Great, 2005 South Australian of the Year. *Recreation:* reading. *Address:* University of South Australia, GPO Box 2471, Adelaide, SA 5001, Australia.

BRADLEY, Dominic; Member (SDLP) Newry and Armagh, Northern Ireland Assembly, since 2003; *b* 18 Nov. 1954; *s* of William J. Bradley and Sarah McKeown; *m* Mary McManus; one *s. Educ:* St Paul's High Sch., Bessbrook; Abbey Christian Brothers Grammar Sch., Newry; Queen's Univ. Belfast (BA Hons); Univ. of Ulster (MA). Teacher, St Paul's High Sch., Bessbrook, 1978–89 and 1991–2003; Southern Educn and Library Bd, 1989–91. Northern Ireland Assembly: SDLP spokesperson on educn; Dep. Chm., Educn Cttee; Mem., Culture, Arts and Leisure Cttee. *Recreations:* walking, swimming, reading. *Address:* (office) 15 Trevor Hill, Newry BT34 1DN. *T:* (028) 3026 7933, *Fax:* (028) 3026 7828; *e-mail:* dominicobrolchain@btinternet.com. *Club:* St Patrick's Gaelic Athletic (Carrickcruppen, Co. Armagh).

BRADLEY, Prof. Donal Donat Conor, PhD; FRS 2004; CPhys; Lee-Lucas Professor of Experimental Physics, since 2006 and Head of Department of Physics, since 2005, Imperial College London; *b* 3 Jan. 1962; *s* of Daniel Joseph Bradley, *qv*; *m* 1989, Beverley Diane Hirst; one *s* two *d. Educ:* Wimbledon Coll., London; Imperial Coll., Univ. of London (BSc 1st Cl. Hons 1983; ARCS); Cavendish Lab., Univ. of Cambridge (PhD 1987). MInstP 1990, FInstP 2005. Unilever Res. Fellow in Chem. Physics, Corpus Christi Coll., Cambridge, 1987–89; Toshiba Res. Fellow, Toshiba R&D Center, Kawasaki, Japan, 1987–88; Asst Lectr in Physics, Univ. of Cambridge, 1989–93; Churchill College, Cambridge: Lectr and Fellow, 1989–93; Dir of Studies, 1992–93; Tutor, 1992–93; University of Sheffield: Reader in Physics, 1993–95; Warden, Tapton Hall, 1994–99; Prof. of Physics, 1995–2000; Dir, Centre for Molecular Materials, 1995–2000; Royal Soc. Amersham Internat. Sen. Res. Fellow, 1996–97; Leverhulme Trust Res. Fellow, 1997–98; Prof. of Exptl Solid State Physics, 2000–06, and Dep. Dir, Centre for Electronic Materials and Devices, and Hd of Exptl Solid State Gp, 2001–05, Imperial Coll., Univ. of London. Member: SERC/EPSRC Laser Facility Cttee Panel, 1991–95; EPSRC Functional Materials Coll., 1995–; ESF EUROCORES Cttee, 2006; Jury Cttee, Degussa European Sci. to Business Award, 2006. Co-inventor, conjugated polymer electroluminescence; co-founder: Cambridge Display Technol. Ltd; Molecular Vision Ltd (Dir, 2001–); Dir, Imperial Coll. London Consultants Ltd, 2005–06. Ed., Organic Electronics, 2000–05. FRSA 1983. RSA Silver Medal, Outstanding Grad., RCS, 1983; Daiwa Award for Anglo-Japanese Collaboration, 1994; Descartes Prize, EU, 2003; Jan Rajchman Prize, Soc. for Inf. Display, 2005; European Latsis Prize, ESF, 2005; Res. Excellence Award, Imperial Coll., London, 2006; Brian Mercer Award for Innovation, Royal Soc., 2007. *Publications:* numerous papers in learned jls and 16 patents on polymer optoelectronics. *Recreations:* DIY, cinema, music, military history. *Address:* Blackett Laboratory, Imperial College London, Prince Consort Road, SW7 2AZ.

BRADLEY, Prof. Donald Charlton, CChem, FRSC; FRS 1980; Professor of Inorganic Chemistry, 1965–87, and Head of Chemistry Department, 1978–82, Fellow, 1988, Queen Mary College, University of London; Emeritus Professor, University of London, since 1988; *b* 7 Nov. 1924; *m* 1st, 1948, Constance Joy Hazeldean (*d* 1985); one *s*; 2nd, 1990, Ann Levy (*née* MacDonald). *Educ:* Hove County School for Boys; Birkbeck Coll., Univ. of London (BSc 1st Cl. Hons Chemistry, PhD, DSc; Fellow, 2006). Research Asst, British Electrical and Allied Industries Research Assoc., 1941–47; Asst Lectr in Chemistry, 1949–52, Lectr in Chemistry, 1952–59, Birkbeck Coll.; Prof. of Chemistry, Univ. of Western Ontario, Canada, 1959–64. Univ. of London: Chm., Bd of Studies in Chemistry and Chemical Industries, 1977–79; Mem. Senate, 1981–87. MRI 1979 (Mem. Council, 1987–93; Hon. Sec., 1988–93); Royal Society of Chemistry: Pres. Dalton Div., 1983–85; Ludwig Mond Medal and Lectr, 1987. Exec. Editor, Polyhedron, 1982–97. Gov., Haberdashers' Aske's Schs, Elstree, 1973–95. Freeman: Haberdashers' Co., 1995; City of London, 1996. Member: Samuel Pepys Club, 1995–; Aldersgate Ward Club, 1996–. FRSA 1982. Royal Medal, Royal Soc., 1998. *Publications:* (jtly) Metal Alkoxides, 1978; Alkoxo and Aryloxo Derivatives of Metals, 2001; numerous pubns on synthesis and structure of metallo-organic compounds, co-ordination chemistry and inorganic polymers, mainly in Jl of Chemical Soc. *Recreations:* travelling, theatre, listening to music, amateur interest in archaeology. *Address:* 171 Shakespeare Tower, Barbican, EC2Y 8DR.

BRADLEY, Edgar Leonard, OBE 1979; Metropolitan Stipendiary Magistrate, 1967–83; *b* 17 Nov. 1917; 2nd *s* of Ernest Henry and Letitia Bradley, W Felton, Oswestry; *m* 1942, Elsa, *o d* of Colin and Elizabeth Matheson, Edinburgh; two *s* three *d. Educ:* Malvern Coll.; Trinity Hall, Cambridge. BA 1939; MA 1944. Called to Bar, Middle Temple, 1940. Served 1940–46, RA; Capt. and Adjt, 1943–45; Major, GSO2, Mil. Govt of Germany, 1946. Practised at Bar, 1946–51, SE Circuit, Central Criminal Ct, S London and Surrey Sessions. Legal Dept of Home Office, 1951–54. Sec., Departmental Cttee on Magistrates' Courts Bill, 1952; Sec. of Magistrates' Courts Rule Cttee, 1952–54; Clerk to Justices: Wrexham and Bromfield, 1954–57; Poole, 1957–67. Justices' Clerks Society: Mem. Council, 1957–67; Hon. Sec., 1963–67. Mem., Nat. Adv. Council on Trng of Magistrates, 1965–67; Magistrates' Association: Vice Pres., 1984–; Mem. Council, 1968–84; Chm. Legal Cttee, 1973–82. Adv. tour of Magistrates' Courts in Ghana, 1970. *Publications:* (with J. J. Senior) Bail in Magistrates' Courts, 1977; articles in legal jls. *Recreations:* travel, music. *Address:* 55 St Germains, Bearsden, Glasgow G61 2RS. *T:* (0141) 942 5831.

BRADLEY, Prof. (John) Andrew, PhD; FRCSGlas; Professor of Surgery, University of Cambridge, since 1997; Hon. Consultant Surgeon, Addenbrooke's Hospital, Cambridge, since 1997; *b* 24 Oct. 1950; *s* of Colin Bradley and Christine Bradley (*née* Johnstone Miller); *m* 1987, Eleanor Mary Bolton; two *s. Educ:* Salendine Nook Secondary Sch., Huddersfield; Huddersfield Coll. of Tech.; Univ. of Leeds (MB ChB 1975); Univ. of Glasgow (PhD 1982). FRCSGlas 1979. Lectr in Surgery, Glasgow Univ., 1978–84; Cons. Surgeon, Western Infirmary, Glasgow, 1984–94; Prof. of Surgery, Univ. of Glasgow, 1994–97; Hon. Cons. Surgeon, Western Infirmary, Glasgow, 1994–97. Pres., British Transplantation Soc., 1999–2002. Founder FMedSci 1998; FRCS *ad eundem* 1999. *Publications:* articles in sci. jls, mainly in the field of organ transplantation and immunology. *Recreations:* ski-ing, mountaineering. *Address:* University Department of Surgery, Box 202, Level 9, Addenbrooke's Hospital, Cambridge CB2 2QQ.

BRADLEY, Michael John, CMG 1990; QC (Cayman Islands) 1983; Constitutional Adviser, Overseas Territories Department, Foreign and Commonwealth Office, since 2001; Law Revision Commissioner for the Cayman Islands, since 1994; *b* 11 June 1933; *s* of late Joseph Bradley and Catherine Bradley (*née* Cleary); *m* 1965, Patricia Elizabeth Macauley, MBE; one *s. Educ:* St Malachy's Coll., Belfast; Queen's Univ., Belfast (LLB Hons). Solicitor, Law Soc. of NI, 1964; Attorney, Supreme Ct, Turks and Caicos Is, 1980; Barrister-at-law, Eastern Caribbean Supreme Ct, 1982. Solicitor, NI, 1964–67; State Counsel, Malawi, 1967–69; Volume Editor, Halsbury's Laws, 1970; Sen., later Chief, Parly Draftsman, Botswana, 1970–72; UN Legal Advr to Govt of Antigua, 1973–76; Reg. Legal Draftsman to Govts of E Caribbean, British Develt Div. in the Caribbean, FCO, 1976–82; Attorney General: British Virgin Is, 1977–78; Turks and Caicos Is, 1980; Montserrat, 1981; Cayman Is, 1982–87; Gov., Turks and Caicos Is, 1987–93. British Dependent Territories Law Reform and Law Revision Consultant, 1993. Pres., Cayman Is Gaelic FC, 2000–07; Chm., Cayman Is Celtic Supporters Club, 2004–. *Recreations:* reading, philately, travel, good wine. *Address:* 11 The Lays, Goose Street, Beckington,

Somerset BA11 6RS. *T:* and *Fax:* (01373) 831059; c/o Law Revision Commission, PO Box 2394, George Town, Grand Cayman KY1–1105, Cayman Islands, West Indies. *T:* 9454731, *Fax:* 9455925; *e-mail:* michael.bradley@gov.ky. *Clubs:* Civil Service, Royal Over-Seas League.

BRADLEY, Peadar John; Member (SDLP) Down South, Northern Ireland Assembly, since 1998; *b* 28 April 1940; *s* of William T. Bradley and Annie E. Barry; *m* 1962, Leontia Martin; three *s* five *d*. *Educ:* Carrick Primary Sch.; St Colman's Coll., Newry, Co. Down; Warrenpoint Tech. Centre. Mem., Irish Auctioneers and Valuers Inst., 1986 (Fellow, 2000). Salesman, 1958–65; Agricl Rep., 1965–78; Property Negotiator, 1978–81; self-employed Estate Agent, 1981–99. Mem., Newry and Mourne DC, 1981–2005. *Recreations:* Gaelic games, part-time farming, travel. *Address:* 10 Corrogs Road, Newry, Co. Down BT34 2NJ. *T:* (028) 3026 2062; (office) (028) 4177 2228. *Club:* Naomh Mhuire, Cumann Luth Chleas Gael (Boireann).

BRADLEY, Peter Charles Stephen; Director, Speakers' Corner Trust, since 2007; Member, Affordable Rural Housing Commission, 2005–06; *b* 12 April 1953; *s* of Fred and Trudie Bradley; *m* 2000, Annie Hart; one *s* one *d* (twins). *Educ:* Abingdon Sch.; Univ. of Sussex (BA Hons 1975); Occidental Coll., LA. Res. Dir, Centre for Contemporary Studies, 1979–85; Dir, Good Relations Ltd, 1985–93; Man. Dir, Millbank Consultants Ltd, 1993–97. Mem. (Lab), Westminster CC, 1986–96 (Dep. Leader, Labour Gp, 1990–96). MP (Lab) The Wrekin, 1997–2005; contested (Lab) same seat, 2005. PPS to Minister of State for Rural Affairs, 2001–05. Mem., Select Cttee on Public Admin, 1997–99; Chm., Rural Gp of Labour MPs, 1997–2001. Chair, Community Stations Initiative, 2004–. Hon. Patron, AFC Telford Utd, 2004–. *Recreations:* playing/watching cricket, supporting Aston Villa, walking and reading (both slowly). *Address:* 7 Tern Cottages, Crudgington, Telford TF6 6HZ. *Club:* Warwickshire County Cricket.

BRADLEY, Ven. Peter David Douglas; Archdeacon of Warrington, since 2001; Team Rector, Upholland, since 1994; *b* 4 June 1949; *m* 1970, Pat Dutton; three *s*. *Educ:* Brookfield Comp. Sch., Kirkby; Lincoln Theol Coll.; Ian Ramsey Coll., Brasted; Nottingham Univ. (BTh 1979). Ordained deacon, 1979, priest, 1980; Curate, Upholland Team, 1979–83; Vicar, Holy Spirit, Dovecot, Liverpool, 1983–94; Dir, Continuing Ministerial Educn, dio. Liverpool, 1989–2001. Mem., Gen. Synod of C of E, 1990–. Hon. Canon, Liverpool Cathedral, 2000. *Recreations:* walking, reading. *Address:* The Rectory, 1a College Road, Upholland, Skelmersdale WN8 0PY. *T:* (01695) 622936.

BRADLEY, Very Rev. Peter Edward; Dean of Sheffield, since 2003; *b* 26 June 1964; *s* of William Charles Basil Bradley and Elizabeth Alexandra Bradley. *Educ:* Royal Belfast Academical Instn; Trinity Hall, Cambridge (BA Theol. and Religious Studies 1986, MA 1989); Ripon Coll., Cuddesdon. Ordained deacon, 1988, priest, 1989; Chaplain, Gonville and Caius Coll., Cambridge, 1990–95; Team Vicar: St Michael and All Angels, Abingdon, 1995–98; All Saints', High Wycombe, 1998–2003; Team Rector, High Wycombe, 2003. FRSA 2002. *Recreations:* cinema, painting, walking, living beyond my means, being Irish. *Address:* The Cathedral, Church Street, Sheffield S1 1HA. *T:* (0114) 263 6063, *Fax:* (0114) 279 7412; *e-mail:* enquiries@sheffield-cathedral.org.uk.

BRADLEY, Maj.-Gen. Peter Edward Moore, CB 1968; CBE 1964 (OBE 1955); DSO 1946; Trustee, Vindolanda Trust, 1982–85 (Secretary, 1975–82); *b* 12 Dec. 1914; *s* of late Col Edward de Winton Herbert Bradley, CBE, DSO, MC, DL; *m* Margaret, *d* of late Norman Wardhaugh of Haydon Bridge, Northumberland; three *s*. *Educ:* Marlborough; Royal Military Academy, Woolwich. 2nd Lieut, Royal Signals, 1934. Served War of 1939–45; India, Middle East, Italy and North West Europe (DSO 6th Airborne Div.). Lieut-Col 1954; Col 1957; Brig. 1962; Maj.-Gen. 1965; Signal Officer in Chief (Army), Ministry of Defence, 1965–67; Chief of Staff to C-in-C Allied Forces Northern Europe, Oslo, 1968–70, retired. Dunlop Ltd, 1970–75. Col Comdt, Royal Signals, 1967–82, Master of Signals, 1970–82; Col Gurkha Signals, 1967–74. CEng, FIET (FIEE, 1966). *Address:* c/o RHQ Royal Signals, Blandford Camp, Blandford Forum, DT11 8RH.
See also S. E. Bradley.

BRADLEY, Peter Richard, CBE 2005; Chief Executive, London Ambulance Service NHS Trust, since 2000, and National Ambulance Adviser, Department of Health, since 2004; *b* 28 Dec. 1957; *s* of John and Mary Bradley; *m* 1978, Mary Elisabeth Verhoeff (marr. diss.); one *s* two *d*. *Educ:* Temple Moor Grammar Sch., Leeds; Otago Univ., NZ (MBA). With Commercial Bank of Australia, Auckland, 1973–76; St John Ambulance Service, Auckland, 1976–95; qualified paramedic, 1986; Chief Ambulance Officer, 1993–95; joined London Ambulance Service NHS Trust, 1996; Dir of Ops, 1998–2000. FNZIM 1999. OStJ 1994 (SBStJ 1992). *Recreations:* reading, sport, music. *Address:* London Ambulance Service NHS Trust, 220 Waterloo Road, SE1 8SD.

BRADLEY, Richard Alan; Headmaster, Rivers Country Day School, Massachusetts, USA, 1981–91, retired; *b* 6 Oct. 1925; *s* of late Reginald Livingstone Bradley, CBE, MC, and of Phyllis Mary Richardson; *m* 1971, Mary Ann Vicary; one *s* two *d* by previous marriage. *Educ:* Marlborough Coll.; Trinity Coll., Oxford (Scholar). 2nd cl. hons Mod. History. Royal Marines, 1944–46; Oxford, 1946–48; Club Manager, Oxford and Bermondsey Club, 1949. Asst Master: Dulwich Coll., 1949–50; Tonbridge Sch., 1950–66 (Head of History Dept, 1957–66; Housemaster of Ferox Hall, 1961–66); Warden of St Edward's Sch., Oxford, 1966–71; Headmaster, Ridley Coll., Canada, 1971–81. *Recreations:* games, dramatics, mountains. *Address:* 10 Carver Hill Court, South Natick, MA 01760–5531, USA. *Club:* Vincent's (Oxford).

BRADLEY, Prof. Richard John, FSA, FSAScot; FBA 1995; Professor of Archaeology, Reading University, since 1987; *b* 18 Nov. 1946; *s* of John Newsum Bradley and Margaret Bradley (*née* Saul); *m* 1976, Katherine Bowden. *Educ:* Portsmouth Grammar Sch.; Magdalen Coll., Oxford (MA). MIFA. Lectr in Archaeology, 1971–84, Reader, 1984–87, Reading Univ. Mem., Royal Commn on Historical Monuments of England, 1987–99. Hon. FSAScot 2007. Hon. Dr Univ. of Lund, 2002. *Publications:* (with A. Ellison) Rams Hill: a Bronze Age Defended Enclosure and its Landscape, 1975; The Prehistoric Settlement of Britain, 1978; (ed with J. Barrett) Settlement and Society in the British Later Bronze Age, 1980; The Social Foundations of Prehistoric Britain, 1984; (ed with J. Gardiner) Neolithic Studies, 1984; The Passage of Arms: an archæological analysis of prehistoric hoards and votive deposits, 1990, rev. edn 1998; (with J. Barrett and M. Green) Landscape, Monuments and Society, 1991; (ed with J. Barrett and M. Hall) Papers on the Prehistoric Archaeology of Cranborne Chase, 1991; Altering the Earth: the origins of monuments in Britain and Continental Europe, 1993; (with M. Edmonds) Interpreting the Axe Trade: production and exchange in Neolithic Britain, 1993; (jtly) Prehistoric Land Divisions on Salisbury Plain: the work of the Wessex Linear Ditches Project, 1994; Rock Art and the Prehistory of Atlantic Europe, 1997; The Significance of Monuments, 1998; An Archaeology of Natural Places, 2000; The Good Stones: a new investigation of the Clava Cairns, 2000; The Past in Prehistoric Society, 2002; The Moon and the Bonfire: an investigation of three stone circles in north-east Scotland, 2004; Ritual and Domestic Life in Prehistoric Europe, 2005; The Prehistory of Britain and Ireland, 2007; contribs to learned jls. *Recreations:* literature, contemporary classical music, watercolours, antiquarian bookshops. *Address:* Department of Archaeology, The University, Whiteknights, Reading RG6 6AB. *T:* (0118) 378 8130.

BRADLEY, Robin Alistair, CBE 2000; CEng; Chief Executive, Atomic Weapons Establishment, Aldermaston, 1997–2000; *b* 3 Aug. 1938; *s* of Cyril Robert Bradley and Phyllis Mary (*née* Stalham); *m* 1964, Marguerite Loftus; one *s* two *d*. MIMechE 1972; CEng 1972. MoD, 1962–65; Hunting Engrg, Ampthill, 1965–72; Manager, Defence Progs (Australia), Hunting Systems, S Australia, 1972–75; Chief Project Engr, Project Manager, then Divl Manager Engrg, Hunting Engrg, Ampthill, 1975–90; Ops Director, AWE/Hunting Brown Root/AEA, Aldermaston (originally on secondment), 1990–96. *Recreations:* athletics, climbing, gardening. *Address:* c/o Hunting plc, 3 Cockspur Street, SW1 5BQ.

BRADLEY, Roger Thubron, FICFor; FIWSc; Chairman, Loch Lomond and Trossachs National Park Fisheries Forum, since 2005; *b* 5 July 1936; *s* of Ivor Lewis Bradley and Elizabeth Thubron; *m* 1959, Ailsa Mary Walkden; one *s* one *d*. *Educ:* Lancaster Royal Grammar Sch.; St Peter's Coll., Oxford (MA). FICFor 1980; FIWSc 1985. Asst District Officer, Kendal, 1960; Mensuration Officer, Alice Holt, 1961; Working Plans Officer, 1967; District Officer, North Argyll, 1970; Asst Conservator, South Wales, 1974; Conservator, North Wales, 1977; Forestry Commission: Dir, and Sen. Officer for Wales, 1982–83; Dir, Harvesting and Marketing, Edinburgh, 1983–85; Forestry Comr, 1985–95; Hd of Forestry Authy, 1992–95; Dir, Scottish Greenbelt Foundn, 1996–2006. Chairman: UK Forestry Accord, 1996–2002; Forth Dist Salmon Fishery Bd, 1998–2003. Chm., Edinburgh Centre for Tropical Forestry, 1996–99. Chm., Commonwealth Forestry Assoc., 1988–90; Pres., Inst. of Chartered Foresters, 1996–98. *Publications:* Forest Management Tables, 1966, 2nd edn 1971; Forest Planning, 1967; Thinning Control in British Forestry, 1967, 2nd edn 1971; various articles in Forestry, etc. *Recreation:* sailing. *Club:* 1970 (Edinburgh).

BRADLEY, Stanley Walter; business consultant, since 1988; Director, W. Hart & Son (Saffron Walden) Ltd, since 1991; Director General, British Printing Industries Federation, 1983–88; *b* 9 Sept. 1927; *s* of Walter Bradley; *m* 1955, Jean Brewster; three *s* one *d*. *Educ:* Boys' British Sch., Saffron Walden. Joined Spicers Ltd, 1948: held posts in prodn, marketing and gen. management; Personnel Dir, 1973–83; Dir, Capital Spicers Ltd, Eire, 1971–83. Dir, Harman Gp, 1988–91. Chm., BPIF Manufg Stationery Industry Gp, 1977–81; Pres., E Anglian Printing Industries Alliance, 1978–79; Mem., Printing Industries Sector Working Party, 1979–87, Chm., Communications Action Team, 1980–85, NEDC. *Recreations:* painting, golf, fishing. *Address:* 5 Edward Bawden Court, Park Lane, Saffron Walden, Essex CB10 1FP. *T:* (01799) 529209.

BRADLEY, Stephen Edward; HM Diplomatic Service; Consul-General, Hong Kong, 2003–08; *b* 4 April 1958; *s* of Maj.-Gen. Peter Edward Moore Bradley, *qv*; *m* 1982, Elizabeth Gomersall; one *s* one *d*. *Educ:* Marlborough Coll.; Balliol Coll., Oxford; Fudan Univ., Shanghai. South Asian Dept, FCO, 1982; Tokyo, 1983–87; Guinness Peat Aviation, 1987–88; Dep. Political Advr, Hong Kong Govt, 1988–93; Lloyd George Investment Management, 1994–95; Near East and North Africa Dept, FCO, 1995–97; West Indian and Atlantic Dept, FCO, 1997–98; New Millennium Experience Co., 1998–99; Paris, 1999–2002; Minister, Beijing, 2002–03. *Recreations:* books, gardens, travel. *Address:* c/o Foreign and Commonwealth Office, King Charles Street, SW1A 2AH. *Club:* Oxford and Cambridge.

BRADLEY, Stuart; *see* Bradley, C. S.

BRADLEY GOODMAN, Michael; *see* Goodman, M. B.

BRADMAN, Godfrey Michael, FCA; company director; *b* 9 Sept. 1936; *s* of William I. Bradman and Anne Bradman (*née* Goldsweig); *m* 1975, Susan Bennett; two *s* three *d*. FCA 1961. Sen. Partner, Godfrey Bradman and Co. (Chartered Accountants), 1961–69; Chm. and Chief Exec., London Mercantile Corp. (Bankers), 1969; Chm., Rosehaugh plc, 1979–91; Joint Chairman: Broadgate Develts, 1984–91; Victoria Quay Ltd, 1993; Chairman: Eur. Land & Property Corp. plc, 1992; Ashpost Finance, 1993; Pondbridge Europe Ltd, 1994; Dep. Chm., Kyp Hldgs plc, 2003–; Director: Property & Land Investment Corp. plc, 2001–; Midatech Ltd, 2004–; Metropolitan & Suburban, 2006–. Founder and Mem., CLEAR (Campaign for Lead-Free Air) Ltd, 1981–91; Jt Founder, 1983, and Hon. Pres., Campaign for Freedom of Information, 1983; Founder and Chm., Citizen Action and European Citizen Action, 1983–91 (Dir, AIDS Policy Unit, 1987–90); Chm., Friends of the Earth Trust, 1983–91; Council Mem., UN Internat. Year of Shelter for the Homeless, 1987; Pres., Soc. for the Protection of Unborn Children Educnl Res. Trust, 1987; Trustee, Right To Life Charitable Trust; Founder and Jt Chm., Parents Against Tobacco Campaign; Founder, Opren Victims Campaign. Mem. governing body, LSHTM, 1988–91. Hon. Fellow, Downing Coll., Cambridge, 1997 (Wilkins Fellow, 1999); Hon. FKC. Hon. DSc Salford. *Recreation:* reading. *Address:* 1 Berkeley Street, W1J 8DJ. *T:* (020) 7706 0189; *e-mail:* gb@godfreybradman.com.

BRADNEY, John Robert; HM Diplomatic Service, retired; *b* 24 July 1931; *s* of Rev. Samuel Bradney, Canon Emeritus of St Alban's Abbey, and Constance Bradney (*née* Partington); *m* 1st, Jean Marion Halls (marr. diss. 1971); one *s* two *d*; 2nd, 1974, Sandra Cherry Smith, JP, *d* of Richard Arthur Amyus Smith, MC. *Educ:* Christ's Hospital. HM Forces, 1949–51, Herts Regt and RWAFF; Colonial Police, Nigeria, 1953–65; HM Diplomatic Service, 1965–86: First Sec., Lagos, 1974; FCO, 1977–86 (Counsellor, 1985); Advr, Govt of Oman, 1986–89. Chm., Carlisle Cathedral Develt Trust, 2007–08. DSM Oman, 1989. *Recreations:* salmon and trout fishing, gardening, ornithology. *Address:* Barclays Bank PLC, Penrith, Cumbria CA11 7YB. *Club:* Royal Over-Seas League.

BRADSHAW, family name of **Baron Bradshaw**.

BRADSHAW, Baron *cr* 1999 (Life Peer), of Wallingford in the county of Oxfordshire; **William Peter Bradshaw;** Senior Visiting Research Fellow, Centre for Socio-Legal Studies, Wolfson College, Oxford, 1985–2000; Honorary Fellow, Wolfson College, Oxford, since 2004 (Supernumerary Fellow, 1988–2003); *b* 9 Sept. 1936; *s* of Leonard Charles Bradshaw and Ivy Doris Bradshaw; *m* 1st, 1957, Jill Hayward (*d* 2002); one *s* one *d*; 2nd, 2003, Diana Mary Ayris. *Educ:* Univ. of Reading (BA Pol Economy, 1957; MA 1960). FCIT 1987 (MCIT 1966). Joined Western Region of British Railways as Management Trainee, 1959; various appts, London and W of England Divs; Divl Manager, Liverpool, 1973; Chief Operating Man., LMR, 1976, Dep. Gen. Man. 1977; Chief Ops Man., BR HQ, 1978; Dir, Policy Unit, 1980; Gen. Man., Western Region, BR, 1983–85; Prof. of Transport Mgt, Univ. of Salford, 1986–92; Chm., Ulsterbus and Citybus Ltd, 1987–93. Member: Thames Valley Police Authority, 1997–2008 (Vice Chm., 1999–2003); BRB, later Strategic Rail Authy, 1999–2001; Commn for Integrated Transport, 1999–2001; Chm., Bus Appeals Body, 1998–2000. Mem. (Lib Dem) Oxfordshire CC, 1993–2008. Special Advr to Transport Select Cttee, H of C, 1992–97; Lib Dem spokesman on transport, H of L, 2001–. *Recreations:* growing hardy plants, playing member of a brass band. *Address:* House of Lords, SW1A 0PW. *Club:* National Liberal.

BRADSHAW, Prof. Alexander Marian, CBE 2007; PhD; FRS 2008; Scientific Director, Max-Planck-Institut für Plasmaphysik, Garching and Greifswald, since 1999; *b* 12 July 1944. *Educ:* Queen Mary Coll., London (BSc 1965; PhD 1969). Scientific Mem., Fritz-Haber Institute of Max-Planck Soc., Berlin, 1980–98. Adjunct Professor of Physics: Technical Univ. of Berlin, 1997; Technical Univ. of Munich, 2000. Pres., German Physical Soc., 1998–2000. Fellow, German Nat. Acad. of Scis (formerly German Acad. of Scis Leopoldina), 2002. *Publications:* articles in learned jls. *Address:* Max-Planck-Institut für Plasmaphysik, Boltzmannstrasse 2, 85748 Garching, Germany. *T:* (89) 32991342, *Fax:* (89) 32991001; *e-mail:* alex.bradshaw@ipp.mpg.de.

BRADSHAW, Prof. Anthony David, PhD; FRS 1982; Holbrook Gaskell Professor of Botany, University of Liverpool, 1968–88, now Emeritus; *b* 17 Jan. 1926; *m* Betty Margaret Bradshaw; three *d. Educ:* St Paul's Sch., Hammersmith; Jesus Coll., Cambridge (BA 1947; MA 1951); PhD Wales 1959. FIBiol 1971. Lectr, 1952–63, Sen. Lectr, 1963–64, Reader in Agricl Botany, 1964–68, UCNW, Bangor. Member: Nature Conservancy Council, 1969–78; Natural Environment Res. Council, 1969–74; Bd of Management, Sports Turf Res. Inst., 1976– (Vice Pres., 1982–). President: British Ecological Soc., 1981–83; Inst. Ecology and Envmtl Management, 1991–94; Merseyside Envmtl Trust, 1998–. Trustee, Nat. Museums and Galls on Merseyside, 1986–96 (Vice Chm., 1995–96). Mem. Bd, Groundwork Trust St Helens, 1981–2006. Hon. Fellow, Indian Nat. Acad. Sci., 1990. FLS 1982; FIEEM 1994 (MIEEM 1991). Hon. DSc: Lancaster, 1998; Hong Kong Baptist Univ., 2000. *Publications:* (ed jtly) Teaching Genetics, 1963; (with M. J. Chadwick) The Restoration of Land, 1980; (with others) Quarry Reclamation, 1982; (with others) Mine Wastes Reclamation, 1982; (with R. A. Dutton) Land Reclamation in Cities, 1982; (with Alison Burt) Transforming our Waste Land: the way forward, 1986; (ed jtly) Ecology and Design in Landscape, 1986; (ed jtly) The Treatment and Handling of Wastes, 1992; (with B. Hunt and T. J. Walmsley) Trees in the Urban Landscape, 1995; contribs to symposia and learned jls. *Recreations:* sailing, gardening, appreciating land. *Address:* 58 Knowsley Road, Liverpool L19 0PG.

BRADSHAW, Benjamin Peter James; MP (Lab) Exeter, since 1997; Minister of State, Department of Health, and Minister for the South West, since 2007; *b* 30 Aug. 1960; *s* of late Canon Peter Bradshaw and Daphne Bradshaw (*née* Murphy); civil partnership 2006, Neal Thomas Dalgleish. *Educ:* Thorpe St Andrew Sch., Norwich; Univ. of Sussex (BA Hons). Reporter: Express and Echo, Exeter, 1984–85; Eastern Daily Press, Norwich, 1985–86; BBC Radio Devon, Exeter, 1986–89; BBC Radio Corresp., Berlin, 1989–91; reporter, World At One and World This Weekend, BBC Radio 4, 1991–97. Parly Under-Sec. of State, FCO, 2001–02; Parly Sec., Privy Council Office, 2002–03; Parly Under-Sec. of State, 2003–06, Minister of State, 2006–07, DEFRA. Member: European Legislation Select Cttee, 1997–2001; Ecclesiastical Cttee, 1997–2001. Member: Christian Socialist Movement, 1997–; Lab. Campaign for Electoral Reform, 1997–. Mem., Inst. of Internat. and Foreign Affairs. Consumer Journalist of Year, Argos, 1988; Journalist of Year, Anglo-German Foundn, 1990; Sony News Reporter Award, 1993. *Recreations:* cycling, walking in Devon, classical music, cooking, gardening. *Address:* House of Commons, SW1A 0AA. *T:* (020) 7219 6597, (constituency office) (01392) 424464. *Club:* Whipton Labour (Exeter).

BRADSHAW, Ian Cameron; Chief Executive, NHS Logistics Authority, 2000–01; *b* 12 Sept. 1941; *s* of Kenneth Bradshaw and Margaret Bradshaw (*née* Pirie); *m* 1962, Margaret Gilmour Milligan. *Educ:* Coatbridge High Sch.; Burnbank Coll. of Engrg. MCIPS 1990; FILog 1997; FCIT 1999. Engrg Apprentice, NCB, 1956–62; Traffic Div., Strathclyde Police, 1962–69; gen. mgt trainee, subseq. Gen. Manager, 1969–76, Distribution Dir, 1976–79, Man. Dir, 1979–83, Glasgow Hiring Co. (Transport Develt Gp plc); Trent Regional Health Authority: Project Manager, 1984–88; Regl Supplies Officer, 1988–89; Chief Exec., Trent Purchasing Agency, 1989–92; NHS Supplies Authority: Chief Exec., Central Div., 1992–94; Nat. Dir of Logistics, 1994–96; Man. Dir, Wholesaling Div., 1996–2000. FCMI (FIMgt) 1980. *Recreations:* fly fishing, gardening, all forms of woodworking, dining out, listening to classical music. *Address:* The Gables, 178 Derby Road, Cromford, Matlock, Derbys DE4 3RN. *T:* (01629) 822782.

BRADSHAW, Martin Clark; Planning consultant, MB Consultants, 1995–2005; Director, Civic Trust, 1987–95; *b* 25 Aug. 1935; *s* of late Cyril Bradshaw and Nina Isabel Bradshaw; *m* 1st, 1959, Patricia Anne Leggatt (*d* 1981); two *s* one *d*; 2nd, 1986, Gillian Rosemary Payne; three step *s* one step *d. Educ:* King's Sch., Macclesfield; St John's Coll., Cambridge (MA); Univ. of Manchester (DipTP); MRTPI. Staff Surveyor, Lands and Surveys Dept, Uganda Protectorate, 1958–63; Asst Planning Officer, Planning Dept, City of Manchester, 1963–67; Asst Dir, City of Toronto Planning Bd, 1967–70; Asst Chief Planner, Cheshire CC, 1970–72; Asst County Planning Officer, Leics CC, 1972–73; Exec. Dir, Planning and Transport, 1973–81, Dir of Planning, 1981–86, W Yorks MCC; DoE Local Plans Inspectorate, 1986–87. Mem. Council, 1989–2001, Pres., 1993, RTPI. Gen. Comr for Income Tax, Bedford, 1987–96, Oxford, 2000–. Hon. FRIBA 1995. *Recreations:* theatre, art, golf.

BRADSHAW, Prof. Peter, FRS 1981; Thomas V. Jones Professor of Engineering, Department of Mechanical Engineering, Stanford University, 1988–95, now Emeritus; *b* 26 Dec. 1935; *s* of Joseph W. N. Bradshaw and Frances W. G. Bradshaw; *m* 1968, Sheila Dorothy (*née* Brown). *Educ:* Torquay Grammar Sch.; St John's Coll., Cambridge (BA). Scientific Officer, Aerodynamics Div., National Physical Lab., 1957–69; Imperial College, London: Sen. Lectr, Dept of Aeronautics, 1969–71; Reader, 1971–78; Prof. of Experimental Aerodynamics, 1978–88. *Publications:* Experimental Fluid Mechanics, 1964, 2nd edn 1971; An Introduction to Turbulence and its Measurement, 1971, 2nd edn 1975; (with T. Cebeci) Momentum Transfer in Boundary Layers, 1977; (ed) Topics in Applied Physics: Turbulence, 1978; (with T. Cebeci and J. H. Whitelaw) Engineering Calculation Methods for Turbulent Flow, 1981; (with T. Cebeci) Convective Heat Transfer, 1984; author or co-author of over 100 papers in Jl of Fluid Mechanics, AIAA Jl, etc. *Recreations:* ancient history, walking. *Address:* c/o Department of Mechanical Engineering, Stanford University, Stanford, CA 94305–3032, USA.

BRADSHAW, Peter Nicholas; film critic, The Guardian, since 1999; *b* 19 June 1962; *s* of late Albert Desmond Bradshaw and of Mollie Bradshaw (*née* Fine); *m* 2007, Dr Caroline Hill; one *s. Educ:* Haberdashers' Aske's Sch., Elstree; Pembroke Coll., Cambridge (BA 1st Cl. Hons 1984; PhD 1989). Evening Standard: reporter, Londoner's Diary, 1989–92; leader writer and columnist, 1992–99. Radio: The Skivers, 1995; For One Horrible Moment, 1999; Heresy, 2003; television, Baddiel's Syndrome, 2001. *Publications:* Not Alan Clark's Diaries, 1998; Lucky Baby Jesus, 1999; Dr Sweet and his Daughter, 2003. *Recreations:* swimming, dozing. *Address:* The Guardian, Kings Place, 90 York Way, N1 9AG. *Club:* Soho House.

BRADTKE, Hon. Robert Anthony; United States Ambassador to Croatia, since 2006; *b* 11 Oct. 1949; *s* of Albert Bradtke and Lucille Bradtke (*née* Gale); *m* 1983, Marsha Barnes. *Educ:* Univ. of Notre Dame; Bologna Center; Johns Hopkins Univ.; Univ. of Virginia. Joined Foreign Service, US Dept of State, 1973; served in: Georgetown, 1973–75; Zagreb, 1976–78; Office of Eastern European Affairs, Dept of State, 1978–81; Moscow, 1983–86; Bonn, 1986–90; Office of Congressional Affairs, Dept of State, 1990–94 (Dep. Asst Sec. of State, 1992–94); Exec. Asst to Sec. of State, 1994–96; Minister and Dep. Chief of Mission, London, 1996–99; Exec. Sec., Nat. Security Council, 1999–2001; Dep. Asst Sec. of State for European and Eurasian Affairs, 2002–05. Superior Honor Award, Dept of State, 1988, 1996. *Recreations:* hiking, reading, baseball. *Address:* American Embassy, 2 Thomas Jefferson Street, 10010 Zagreb, Croatia.

BRADWELL, Area Bishop of, since 1993; **Rt Rev. Dr Laurence Alexander Green, (Laurie);** *b* 26 Dec. 1945; *s* of Leonard Alexander and Laura Elizabeth Green; *m* 1969, J. Victoria Bussell; two *d. Educ:* King's Coll. London (BD Hons, AKC); New York Theological Seminary, NY State Univ. (STM, DMin); St Augustine's Coll., Canterbury. Curate, St Mark, Kingstanding, Birmingham, 1970–73; Vicar, St Chad, Erdington, Birmingham, 1973–83; Industrial Chaplain, British Steel Corp., 1975–83; Lectr in Urban Studies, Urban Theol. Unit, Sheffield, 1976–82; Principal, Aston Training Scheme, 1983–89; Hon. Curate, Holy Trinity, Birchfield, Handsworth, 1983–89; Team Rector, All Saints, Poplar, 1989–93; Tutor in Urban Theology, Sheffield Univ., 1989–93. *Publications:* Power to the Powerless, 1987; (jtly) A Thing Called Aston (ed Todd), 1987; Let's Do Theology, 1989; God in the Inner City, 1993; (jtly) God in the City, 1995; (contrib.) Urban Christ, 1997; (contrib.) Gospel from the City, 1997; (jtly) A Reader in Urban Theology, 1998; The Impact of the Global: an urban theology, 2001 (trans. Japanese, Spanish, Tamil, Portuguese); Urban Ministry and the Kingdom of God, 2003; contrib. St George's Windsor Review. *Recreations:* folk and jazz music, classical guitar, sailing. *Address:* Bishop's House, Orsett Road, Horndon-on-the-Hill, Essex SS17 8NS. *T:* (01375) 673806, *Fax:* (01375) 674222; *e-mail:* b.bradwell@chelmsford.anglican.org.

BRADY, Angela Maria, RIBA; Partner, Brady Mallalieu Architects Ltd, since 1987; *d* of Peter Gerard Brady, FRCSI and Deirdre (*née* Rowan); *m* 1987, Robin Mallalieu; one *s* one *d. Educ:* Dublin Sch. of Architecture (BArch Sc; DipArch); Royal Danish Acad., Copenhagen; Univ. of Westminster. RIBA 1986. Work with: William Strong and Associates, Toronto, 1981; Arthur Erikson Architects, Toronto, 1982; Brady, Shipman Martin Architects, Dublin, 1983–84; GMW Partnership, 1983–85; Lewis and Hickey Architects, London, 1985–87; Shepherd, Epstein and Hunter, 1987–91. Brady Mallalieu projects include: Barra Park Open Air Th. (RIAI Award); a Victorian house renovation (RIAI Award); new Sch. of Architecture for Metropolitan Univ., London (RIAI Award); St Catherine's Foyer and sports centre, Dublin; housing and healthcare projects for the private and public sector in UK and Ireland. Curator, Diversity Exhibn, Architects for Change, touring UK and world cities, 2003–08. Designer and co-presenter, Building the Dream, TV series, 2004. Member: CABE/English Heritage Urban Panel, 2001–08; Bd, London Develt Agency, 2006–08 (Design Champion). Chair, Women in Architecture, RIBA, 2000–05; Co-Founder, 1986, Chair, 2007–, RIAI London Forum; Mem. Council, RIAI, 2007, 2008. Chm., Finsbury Park Community Forum, 2001–03. Trustee Dir, Building Exploratory, Hackney, 1998–2008. SETnet Ambassador, 2004–08. Judge/Advr, Nat. Panel, Civic Trust, 2000–08. Ext. Examr, Brighton Univ., Liverpool Univ. and Dublin Sch. of Architecture. Mem., Women's Irish Network, 2003–08. Hon. FRIAI 1999; Hon. FRSA 2003. *Publication:* (with R. Mallalieu) Dublin: a guide to recent architecture, 1997. *Address:* Brady Mallalieu Architects, 90 Queen's Drive, N4 2HW; *e-mail:* info@bradymallalieu.com; *web:* www.bradymallalieu.com.

BRADY, Graham Stuart; MP (C) Altrincham and Sale West, since 1997; *b* 20 May 1967; *s* of John Brady and Maureen Brady (*née* Birch); *m* 1992, Victoria Anne Lowther; one *s* one *d. Educ:* Altrincham Grammar Sch.; Univ. of Durham (BA Hons Law 1989). Chm., Durham Univ. Cons. Assoc., 1987; Chm., Northern Area Cons. Collegiate Forum, 1987–89. Shandwick plc, 1989–90; Centre for Policy Studies, 1990–92; Public Affairs Dir, Waterfront Partnership, 1992–97. PPS to Chm. Cons. Party, 1999–2000; an Opposition Whip, 2000; Opposition frontbench spokesman on educn and employment, 2000–01, on educn, 2001–03; PPS to Leader of the Opposition, 2003–04; Shadow Minister for Europe, 2004–07. Member: Educn and Employment Select Cttee, 1997–2001; Treasury Select Cttee, 2007–; Jt Chm., All Party Railfreight Gp, 1998–99; Vice-Chm., All Party Gp on Advertising, 1999–. Sec., Cons. backbench Educn and Employment Cttee, 1997–2000; Mem. Exec., 1922 Cttee, 1998–2000, 2007–. Vice-Chm., E Berks Cons. Assoc., 1992–95. Patron, Family Contact Line; Vice Patron, Friends of Rosie; Trustee, Jubilee Centre. Vice Pres., Gtr Altincham Chamber of Commerce. *Recreations:* family, friends, garden. *Address:* House of Commons, SW1A 0AA.

BRADY, Sir (John) Michael, Kt 2004; FRS 1997; FREng; BP Professor of Information Engineering, Oxford University, since 1985; Fellow of Keble College, Oxford, since 1985; *b* 30 April 1945; *s* of late John and of Priscilla Mansfield; *m* 1967, Naomi Friedlander; two *d. Educ:* Manchester Univ. (BSc (1st Cl. Hons Mathematics) 1966; Renold Prize 1967; MSc 1968); Australian National Univ. (PhD 1970). FREng (FEng 1992); FIET (FIEE 1992); FInstP 1997. Lectr, Computer Science, 1970, Sen. Lectr 1979, Essex Univ.; Sen. Res. Scientist, MIT, 1980; EPSRC Sen. Fellow, 1994–99. Member: ACOST, 1990–93; Bd, UKAEA, 1994–95; Nat. Technology Foresight Steering Gp, 1994–97; Royal Commn for Exhibn of 1851, 2007–; Chm., IT Adv. Bd, 1989–94. Member Board: Guidance and Control Systems, 1991–; Oxford Instruments, 1995–; AEA Technology, 1995–2003; Surgistar, 1997–; Mirada Solutions, 2001– (Oxford Med. Image Analysis, 1997–2001; OXIVA, 1999–2001); IXICO, 2006–; Dexela, 2006–. DU Essex, 1996; Hon. DSc: Manchester, 1998; Southampton, 1999; Hon. DEng Liverpool, 1999; Dr (*hc*) Univ. Paul Sabatier, Toulouse, 2000; Oxford Brookes, 2006. Faraday Medal, IEE, 2000; Millennium Medal, IEEE, 2000. *Publications:* Theory of Computer Science, 1975; Computer Vision, 1981; Robot Motion, 1982; Computational Theory of Discourse, 1982; Robotics Research, 1984; Artificial Intelligence and Robotics, 1984; Robotics Science, 1989; Mammographic Image Analysis, 1999; Images and Artefacts of the Ancient World, 2004; Digital Mammography, 2006; contribs to jls on computer vision, medical image analysis, robotics, artificial intelligence, computer science. *Recreations:* squash, music, wine tasting.

BRADY, Nicholas Frederick; Secretary of the US Treasury, 1988–93; Chairman: Darby Overseas Investments Ltd, since 1994; Darby Emerging Markets Investments, LDC, since 1994; *b* 11 April 1930; *s* of James Brady and Eliot Brady; *m* 1952, Katherine Douglas; three *s* one *d. Educ:* Yale Univ. (BA 1952); Harvard Univ. (MBA 1954). Joined Dillon Read & Co. Inc., 1954; Vice-Pres., 1961; Pres. and Chief Exec. Officer, 1971; Chm. and Chief Exec. Officer, 1982–88. Mem., US Senate, Apr.–Dec. 1982. Posts on federal commns include: Chairman: Commn on Executive, Legislative and Judicial Salaries, 1984; Task Force on Market Mechanisms, 1987–88; Member: Commn on Strategic Forces, 1983; Bipartisan Commn on Central America, 1984; Commn on Defense Mgt, 1986. Chm., Templeton Emerging Markets Investment Trust, 1994–; Director: C-2 Inc., 1993–; H. J. Heinz Co., 1993–; Amerada Hess Corp., 1994–. *Address:* c/o Darby Overseas Investments Ltd, 1133 Connecticut Avenue NW, Suite 400, Washington, DC 20036, USA.

BRADY, Dr Paul A.; Head of International Communications Group, Scottish Executive, 2004–05; *b* 28 July 1949; two *s* one *d*. *Educ:* St Mungo's Acad., Glasgow; Univ. of Glasgow (BSc Hons; PhD 1974). Joined Scottish Office, 1974; Hd, electricity privatisation team, 1988–90; leader, higher educn reforms, 1991–92; Dir of Policy, SHEFC, 1992–93; Hd, Finance Div., Scottish Office, 1993–94; Dir, Finance and Planning, Scottish Enterprise, 1994–98; Dir of Finance, Mgt Exec., NHS in Scotland, 1998–99; Hd, Fisheries and Rural Develt Gp, Envmt and Rural Affairs Dept, Scottish Exec., 1999–2003. *Recreations:* walking, music, family. *Address:* 32 Grange Road, Edinburgh EH9 1UL; *e-mail:* pabrady@gmail.com.

BRADY, Robin James; Chief Executive, Crusaid, since 2003; *b* 26 June 1971; *s* of Peter Robin Brady and Brenda Patricia Brady (*née* Worth). *Educ:* Univ. of Witwatersrand, Johannesburg (BA (Dramatic Art) 1992). Singer and dancer, 1990–94; Asst Dept Manager, Harrods, 1994–96; retail consultant, 1996–99; Capital Services Officer, Arts Council England, 2000–03. Consultant (pt-time), Crusaid, 2001–03. Certified Mem., Inst. of Fundraising, 2006. FRSA 2003. *Recreations:* theatre, opera, film, literature, wine. *Address:* Crusaid, 1–5 Curtain Road, EC2A 3JX. *T:* (020) 7539 3880, *Fax:* (020) 7539 3890; *e-mail:* robinb@crusaid.org.uk.

BRADY, Scott; QC (Scot.) 2000; *b* 31 Oct. 1962; *s* of late John Brady and Miriam Cameron Brady (*née* Brown). *Educ:* Ardrossan Acad., Ayrshire; Edinburgh Univ. (LLB); Glasgow Univ. (DipLP). Admitted Advocate, Scottish Bar, 1987; Advocate Depute, 1993–97; called to the Bar, Middle Temple, 1998. *Address:* c/o Advocates' Library, Parliament House, Edinburgh EH1 1RF. *T:* (0131) 226 5071. *Clubs:* Lansdowne; Scottish Arts (Edinburgh).

BRADY, His Eminence Cardinal Seán; *see* Armagh, Archbishop of, (RC).

BRADY, Terence Joseph; playwright, novelist, artist and actor, since 1962; *b* 13 March 1939; *s* of late Frederick Arthur Noel and Elizabeth Mary Brady; *m* Charlotte Mary Thérèse Bingham, *qv*; one *s* one *d*. *Educ:* Merchant Taylors', Northwood; TCD (BA Moderatorship, History and Polit. Science). Actor: Would Anyone who saw the Accident?, The Dumb Waiter, Room at the Top, 1962; Beyond the Fringe, 1962–64; Present from the Corporation, In the Picture, 1967; Quick One 'Ere, 1968; films include: Baby Love; Foreign Exchange; TV appearances include plays, comedy series and shows, incl. Nanny, 1981, and Pig in the Middle, 1981, 1982, 1983. Writer for *radio:* Lines from my Grandfather's Forehead (BBC Radio Writers' Guild Award, Best Radio Entertainment, 1972); *television:* Broad and Narrow; TWTWTW; with Charlotte Bingham: TV series: Boy Meets Girl; Take Three Girls; Upstairs Downstairs; Away From It All; Play for Today; Plays of Marriage; No—Honestly; Yes—Honestly; Thomas and Sarah; Pig in the Middle; The Complete Lack of Charm of the Bourgeoisie; Nanny; Oh Madeline! (USA TV); Father Matthew's Daughter; Forever Green; adapted for television: Love with a Perfect Stranger; Losing Control, 1987; The Seventh Raven, 1987; This Magic Moment, 1988; Lorna Doone, 1997; The Lost Domain (film), 1999; screenwriter with Charlotte Bingham, Riders, 1993; *stage:* Below Stairs, 2001; Anyone for Tennis?, 2003; A Change of Heart, 2005; with Charlotte Bingham: (contrib.) The Sloane Ranger Revue, 1985; I wish I wish, 1989; The Shell Seekers (adapted 1999); exhibitions include: The Actors' Picture Show, NT, 1984–85; Wykenham Gall., 1992. Member: Soc. of Authors, 1988–; Point to Point Owners Assoc., 1988–. Dir, Wincanton Racecourse, 1995–2001. *Publications:* Rehearsal, 1972; The Fight Against Slavery, 1976; Blueprint, 1998; with Charlotte Bingham: Victoria, 1972; Rose's Story, 1973; Victoria and Company, 1974; Yes—Honestly, 1977; (with Michael Felton) Point-to-Point, 1990; regular contribs to Daily Mail, Living, Country Homes and Interiors, Punch, Sunday Express, Mail on Sunday. *Recreations:* painting, music, National Hunt horse racing and breeding. *Address:* c/o United Authors, Garden Studios, 11/15 Betterton Street, WC2H 9BP. *Club:* PEN.

BRAGG, family name of **Baron Bragg**.

BRAGG, Baron *cr* 1998 (Life Peer), of Wigton in the co. of Cumbria; **Melvyn Bragg;** DL; writer; Presenter and Editor, The South Bank Show, for ITV, since 1977; Controller of Arts, London Weekend Television, since 1990 (Head of Arts, 1982–90); *b* 6 Oct. 1939; *s* of late Stanley Bragg and of Mary Ethel (*née* Parks); *m* 1st, 1961, Marie-Elisabeth Roche (*d* 1971); one *d*; 2nd, 1973, Catherine Mary Haste; one *s* one *d*. *Educ:* Nelson-Thomlinson Grammar Sch., Wigton; Wadham Coll., Oxford (MA; Hon. Fellow, 1995). BBC Radio and TV Producer, 1961–67; writer and broadcaster, 1967–. Novelist, 1964–. Presenter: BBC TV series: 2nd House, 1973–77; Read all About It (also editor), 1976–77; ITV series: Two Thousand Years, 1999; Who's Afraid of the Ten Commandments?, 2000; The Apostles, 2001; (also writer) The Adventure of English, 2003; Not Just on Sunday, 2004; The Big Idea, Channel 4 series, 2001; BBC Radio 4: writer/presenter: Start the Week, 1988–98; On Giants' Shoulders, 1998; In Our Time, 1998–; Routes of English, 1999–; Voices of the Powerless, 2002. Dep. Chm., 1985–90, Chm., 1990–95, Border Television. Mem. Arts Council, and Chm. Literature Panel of Arts Council, 1977–80. President: Northern Arts, 1983–87; Nat. Campaign for the Arts, 1986–; Nat. Acad. of Writing, 2000–. Pres., MIND, 1999–; Appeal Chm., RNIB Talking Books Appeal, 2000–. Chancellor, Leeds University, 1999–. Governor, LSE, 1997–. Domus Fellow, St Catherine's Coll., Oxford, 1990. DL Cumbria, 2003. FRSL; FRTS. Hon. FCLIP (Hon. FLA 1994). Hon. Fellow: Lancashire Polytechnic, 1987; Univ. of Wales, Cardiff, 1996. Hon. DLitt: Liverpool, 1986; Lancaster, 1990; CNAA, 1990; South Bank, 1997; DUniv Open, 1987; Hon. LLD St Andrews, 1993; Hon. DCL Northumbria, 1994. *Plays:* Mardi Gras, 1976 (musical); Orion (TV), 1977; The Hired Man, 1984 (musical); King Lear in New York, 1992; *screenplays:* Isadora; Jesus Christ Superstar; (with Ken Russell) Clouds of Glory. *Publications:* Speak for England, 1976; Land of the Lakes, 1983 (televised); Laurence Olivier, 1984; Rich: the life of Richard Burton, 1988; The Seventh Seal: a study on Ingmar Bergman, 1993; On Giants' Shoulders, 1998; The Adventure of English 500AD–2000, 2003; 12 Books that Changed the World, 2006; *novels:* For Want of a Nail, 1965; The Second Inheritance, 1966; Without a City Wall, 1968; The Hired Man, 1969; A Place in England, 1970; The Nerve, 1971; Josh Lawton, 1972; The Silken Net, 1974; A Christmas Child, 1976; Autumn Manoeuvres, 1978; Kingdom Come, 1980; Love and Glory, 1983; The Maid of Buttermere, 1987; A Time to Dance, 1990 (televised 1992); Crystal Rooms, 1992; Credo, 1996; The Soldier's Return, 1999 (W. H. Smith Lit. Award, 2000); A Son of War, 2001; Crossing the Lines, 2003; Remember Me, 2008; articles for various English jls. *Recreations:* walking, books. *Address:* 12 Hampstead Hill Gardens, NW3 2PL. *Clubs:* Garrick, PEN.

BRAGG, Heather Jean; *see* Williams, H. J.

BRAGG, Stephen Lawrence, MA, SM; FREng; FIMechE; FRAeS; Administrator, Cambridge Office, American Friends of Cambridge University, 1988–93; Fellow, Wolfson College, Cambridge, 1982–91, now Emeritus Fellow; *b* 17 Nov. 1923; *e s* of Sir Lawrence Bragg, CH, OBE, MC, FRS and Lady Bragg, CBE; *m* 1951, Maureen Ann (*née* Roberts); three *s*. *Educ:* Rugby Sch.; Cambridge Univ.; Massachusetts Inst. of Technology. BA 1945, MA 1949 (Cambridge); SM 1949 (MIT). FREng (FEng 1981). Rolls-Royce Ltd, 1944–48; Commonwealth Fund Fellow, 1948–49; Wm Jessop Ltd, Steelmakers, 1949–51; Rolls-Royce Ltd, 1951–71: Chief Scientist, 1960–63; Chief Research Engineer, 1964–68; Dir, Aero Div., 1969–71. Vice-Chancellor, Brunel Univ., 1971–81. Eastern Region Broker, SERC, 1981–83. Dir in Industrial Co-operation, Cambridge Univ., 1984–87. Chm., Cambridge DHA, 1982–86. Member: Univ. Grants Cttee, 1966–71; Aeronautical Research Council, 1970–73; Court of ASC, Henley, 1972–81; SRC Engineering Bd, 1976–79; Airworthiness Requirements Bd, 1979–81; Chm., Adv. Cttee on Falsework, 1973–75. Pres., Railway and Canal Histl Soc., 1998–2000. Corresp. Mem., Venezuelan Acad. Sci., 1975. Hon. DEng Sheffield, 1969; Hon. DTech Brunel, 1982. *Publications:* Rocket Engines, 1962; articles on Jet Engines, Research Management, University/Industry Collaboration, etc. *Recreation:* railway history. *Address:* 22 Brookside, Cambridge CB2 1JQ. *T:* (01223) 362208. *Club:* Athenæum.

See also D. P. Thomson.

BRAGG, Stephen William, (Billy); singer and songwriter; *b* Barking, Essex, 20 Dec. 1957; partner, Juliet de Valero Wills; one *s*. *Educ:* Barking Abbey Comprehensive Sch. Singer with Riff Raff, 1977–81, The Blokes, 1999–. *Recordings include:* Life's a Riot with Spy vs Spy, 1983; Brewing Up with Billy Bragg, 1984; Between the Wars, 1985; Talking with the Taxman about Poetry, 1986; Back to Basics, 1987; Workers Playtime, 1988; Help Save the Youth of America, 1988; The Internationale, 1990; Don't Try This at Home, 1991; William Bloke, 1996; (with Wilco) Mermaid Avenue, vol. 1, 1998, vol. 2, 2000; Reaching to the Converted, 1999; (with The Blokes) England, Half English, 2002; Mr Love & Justice, 2008. *Publication:* The Progressive Patriot: a search for belonging, 2006. *Recreations:* reading, beachcombing, reforming the House of Lords. *Address:* c/o Sincere Management, 35 Bravington Road, W9 3AB. *T:* (020) 8960 4438; *web:* www.billybragg.co.uk.

BRAGGE, Nicolas William; Master of the Supreme Court, Chancery Division, since 1997; *b* 13 Dec. 1948; *o s* of late Norman Bragge and Nicolette Hilda Bragge (*née* Simms); *m* 1973, Pamela Elizabeth Brett; three *s*. *Educ:* S Kent Coll. of Technol., Ashford; Holborn Coll. of Law and Inns of Court Sch. of Law (LLB Hons London). Called to the Bar, Inner Temple, 1972; in practice, Intellectual Property and Chancery Bars, 1974–97; Dep. Chancery Master, 1993–97. Chm. (part-time), Social Security and Disability Appeal Tribunals, 1990–97; Dep. Social Security Comr, 1996–98. Mem. Cttee, Barristers' Benevolent Assoc., 1995–. Master, Cutlers' Co., 2003–04; Mem. Court, Guild of Freemen, City of London, 2005–. Jt Ed., Civil Procedure, 2001–. *Address:* Royal Courts of Justice, Strand, WC2A 2LL. *Club:* City Livery.

BRAGGINS, Peter Charles Deverell; Senior Lecturer, and Professional Tutor for Teach First, Canterbury Christ Church University, since 2006; *b* 10 July 1945; *s* of Charles and Hilda Braggins; *m* 1968, Julia Cox; three *d*. *Educ:* Bedford Sch.; Christ's Coll., Cambridge (Open Award; BA Hons Hist. 1967). Teacher, Royal Grammar Sch., Newcastle upon Tyne, 1968–72; Head of History: Bootham Sch., York, 1972–77; Bedford Sch., 1977–82; Dep. Headmaster, Wilson's Sch., Sutton, 1982–91; Headmaster, Skinners' Sch., Tunbridge Wells, 1991–2005. Cadet Force Medal, 1998; Golden Jubilee Medal, 2002. *Recreations:* walking, swimming, music, historical research, football.

BRAHAM, Allan John Witney, PhD; Keeper and Deputy Director, the National Gallery, 1978–88; *b* 19 Aug. 1937; *s* of Dudley Braham and Florence Mears; *m* 1963, Helen Clare Butterworth (marr. diss. 2004); two *d*. *Educ:* Dulwich Coll.; Courtauld Inst. of Art, Univ. of London (BA 1960, PhD 1967). Asst Keeper, National Gall., 1962, Dep. Keeper, 1973. Arts Council Exhibn (with Peter Smith), François Mansart, 1970–71; National Gall. Exhibitions: (co-ordinator and editor) The Working of the National Gallery, 1974; Velázquez, The Rokeby Venus, 1976; Giovanni Battista Moroni, 1978; Italian Renaissance Portraits, 1979; El Greco to Goya, 1981; Wright of Derby "Mr and Mrs Coltman", 1986. *Publications:* Dürer, 1965; Murillo (The Masters), 1966; The National Gallery in London: Italian Painting of the High Renaissance, 1971; (with Peter Smith) François Mansart, 1973; Funeral Decorations in Early Eighteenth Century Rome, 1975; (with Hellmut Hager) Carlo Fontana: The Drawings at Windsor Castle, 1977; The Architecture of the French Enlightenment, 1980 (Hitchcock Medal, Banister Fletcher Prize; French edn 1982); National Gall. catalogues: The Spanish School (revised edn), 1970, and booklets: Velázquez, 1972; Rubens, 1972; Architecture, 1976; Italian Paintings of the Sixteenth Century, 1985; contrib. prof. jls, etc. *Recreation:* history of architecture. *Address:* 1 Catherine Lodge, 40 Woodside Park Road, N12 8RP.

BRAHAM, Edward Charles; Partner, Freshfields Bruckhaus Deringer LLP (formerly Freshfields), since 1995; *b* 17 July 1961; *s* of David Gerald Henry Braham, QC and (Margaret) Louise Hastings (*née* Treves); *m* 1988, Isabel Dorothy Gurney; two *s* one *d*. *Educ:* Worcester Coll., Oxford (BA 1983; BCL 1984; Vinerian Scholar 1984). Freshfields: articled clerk, 1985; admitted solicitor, 1987. Liveryman, Goldsmiths' Co., 2004. Mem., Lowtonian Soc., 2006–. *Recreations:* riding, photography, ski-ing, wine, bird watching, shooting. *Address:* Fittleworth House, Fittleworth, Pulborough, W Sussex RH20 1JH. *T:* (01798) 865305; *e-mail:* edward.braham@freshfields.com.

BRAIDEN, Prof. Paul Mayo, PhD; FREng, FIMechE, FIET; CPhys; Sir James Woodeson Professor of Manufacturing Engineering, 1983–2006, now Emeritus Professor of Engineering, and Head, Department of Mechanical, Materials and Manufacturing Engineering, 1992–97, University of Newcastle upon Tyne; *b* 7 Feb. 1941; *s* of late Isaac Braiden and of Lilian Braiden (*née* Mayo); *m* 1st, 1967, Elizabeth Marjorie Spensley (marr. diss. 1993); 2nd, 1993, Lesley Howard. *Educ:* Univ. of Sheffield (BEng, MEng, PhD). CEng, FIMechE 1978; FIET (FIEE 1983); FREng (FEng 1994); CPhys, MInstP 1973. Asst Prof., Carnegie Mellon Univ., Pittsburgh, 1968–70; Atomic Energy Research Establishment, Harwell: SSO, 1970–73; PSO, 1973–76; Lectr, then Sen. Lectr, Dept of Engrg, Univ. of Durham, 1976–83. Science and Engineering Research Council: Chm., Engrg Design Cttee, 1990–94; Member: Engrg Bd, 1990–91; Engrg Res. Commn, 1991–94; Cttee on Electro-Mechanical Engrg, 1989–91; Automotive Design Prog., 1989–91; Panel on the Innovative Manufg Initiative, 1993–94. Chm., DTI Working Party on Advanced Mfg Technol., 1987–89. Chm., Northern Reg. and Council Mem., IProdE, 1988–90; Hon. Sec. for Mechanical Subjects, Royal Acad. Engrg, 1997–2000. Mem. Bd, Entrust, 1984–91. Mem., Nat. Cttee for Revision of Methodist Hymn Book, 1979–82. *Publications:* articles on materials behaviour, stress analysis, manufacturing technol. and systems in various jls. *Recreations:* music, especially opera/oratorio (trained singer, tenor voice), cycling, ski-ing. *Address:* School of Mechanical and Systems Engineering, Newcastle University, Stephenson Building, Claremont Road, Newcastle upon Tyne NE1 7RU. *T:* (0191) 222 6210.

BRAILSFORD, Hon. Lord; (Sidney) Neil Brailsford; a Senator of the College of Justice in Scotland, since 2006; *b* 15 Aug. 1954; *s* of Sidney James Brailsford and Jean Thelma Moar Leighton or Brailsford; *m* 1984, Elaine Nicola Robbie; three *s*. *Educ:* Daniel Stewart's Coll., Edinburgh; Stirling Univ. (BA); Edinburgh Univ. (LLB). Admitted Faculty of Advocates, 1981, Treasurer, 2000; QC (Scot.) 1994; called to the Bar, Lincoln's Inn, 1990. *Recreations:* travel, food and wine, American history, fishing. *Address:* Court of

Session, Parliament House, Parliament Square, Edinburgh EH1 1RQ; 29 Warriston Crescent, Edinburgh EH3 5LB. *T:* (0131) 556 8320; Kidder Hill Road, Grafton, VT 05146, USA. *T:* (802) 8432120. *Club:* New (Edinburgh).

BRAILSFORD, David John, MBE 2005; National Performance Director, British Cycling, since 2003; *b* Derby, 29 Feb. 1964; *s* of John and Barbara Brailsford; partner, Lisa Buckle; one *d* and one step *d. Educ:* Liverpool Univ. (BA Hons Sports Sci. and Psychol.); Sheffield Business Sch. (MBA). Dir, Planet X, 1998–2000; Commercial and Mktg Consultant, BDJ Consultancy Ltd, 1999–2003. *Recreations:* cycling, music, family. *Address:* c/o British Cycling, National Cycling Centre, Stuart Street, Manchester M11 4DQ. *T:* (0161) 274 2092, *Fax:* (0161) 274 2095; *e-mail:* worldclass@britishcycling.org.uk.

BRAILSFORD, (Sidney) Neil; *see* Brailsford, Hon. Lord.

BRAIN, family name of **Baron Brain**.

BRAIN, 2nd Baron *cr* 1962, of Eynsham; **Christopher Langdon Brain;** Bt 1954; *b* 30 Aug. 1926; *s* of 1st Baron Brain, MA, DM, FRS, FRCP and Stella, *er d* of late Reginald L. Langdon-Down; *S* father 1966; *m* 1953, Susan Mary (*d* 2007), *d* of George P. and Ethelbertha Morris; three *d. Educ:* Leighton Park Sch., Reading; New College, Oxford. MA 1956. Royal Navy, 1946–48. Liveryman, 1955, Upper Warden, 1974–75, Asst, 1980–2000, Renter Bailiff, 1983–84, Upper Bailiff, 1984–85, Worshipful Co. of Weavers. Chm., Rhone-Alps Regional Council, British Chamber of Commerce, France, 1967. ARPS 1970. *Recreations:* bird watching, fly-fishing. *Heir: b* Hon. Michael Cottrell Brain, MA, DM, FRCP, FRCP Canada, Prof. of Medicine, McMaster Univ. [*b* 6 Aug. 1928; *m* 1960, Dr the Hon. Elizabeth Ann Herbert, *e d* of Baron Tangley, KBE; one *s* two *d*]. *Address:* Alexandra House, 8 Cross Street, Moretonhampstead, Devon TQ13 8NL. *Club:* Oxford and Cambridge Sailing Society.

See also Area Bishop for Ethiopia and the Horn of Africa.

BRAIN, Albert Edward Arnold; Regional Director (East Midlands), Department of the Environment, and Chairman of Regional Economic Planning Board, 1972–77; *b* 31 Dec. 1917; *s* of Walter Henry and Henrietta Mabel Brain; *m* 1947, Patricia Grace Gallop; two *s* one *d. Educ:* Rendcomb Coll., Cirencester; Loughborough College. BSc (Eng) London, external; DLC hons Loughborough; CEng, MICE, MIMunE. Royal Engineers, 1940–46; Bristol City Corp., 1946–48; Min. of Transport: Asst Engr, London, 1948–54; Civil Engr, Wales, 1954–63; Sen. Engr, HQ, 1963–67; Asst Chief Engr, HQ, 1967–69; Divl Road Engr, W Mids, then Regional Controller (Roads and Transportation), 1969–72. Pres., Old Rendcombian Soc., 1986–91. *Recreation:* gardening. *Address:* Withyholt Lodge, Moorend Road, Charlton Kings, Cheltenham GL53 9BW. *T:* (01242) 576264.

BRAIN, Charlotte; *see* Atkins, C.

BRAIN, Dame Margaret Anne, DBE 1994 (OBE 1989); FRCOG; President, Royal College of Midwives, 1987–94 (Member Council, 1970–96); *b* 23 April 1932; *d* of late Charles and Leonora Brain; *m* 1985, Peter Wheeler (*d* 1988), MBE, FRCS, FRCOG. *Educ:* Northampton High Sch.; Westminster Hosp. (SRN 1953); Northampton and Epsom Hosps (SCM 1956); Sheffield Hosp. (MTD 1966). FRCOG *ad eund* 1991. Med. Missionary, USPG St Columba's Hosp., Hazaribagh, Bihar, India, 1959–65; Dep. Matron, Barratt Maternity Home, Northampton, 1966–68; Prin. Midwifery Officer, Reading HMC, 1968–73; Dist Nursing Officer, W Berks DHA, 1974–77; Chief Admin. Nursing Officer, S Glamorgan HA, 1977–88, retd. Member: Nat. Staff Cttee for Nurses and Midwives, 1978–86; Maternity Services Adv. Cttee, 1981–85; Standing Midwifery Cttee, Welsh Nat. Bd, 1982–87; Perinatal Mortality Initiative Steering Gp for Wales, 1983–85; Standing Nursing and Midwifery Adv. Cttee, 1987–93; Women's Nat. Commn, 1990–92; Alternate Treas., 1972–78, Treas., 1978–90, Internat. Confedn of Midwives. Reader, C of E, 2001–. Hon. DSc City, 1995. *Address:* Squirrels, Castle Farm, Lower Broad Oak Road, West Hill, Ottery St Mary, Devon EX11 1UF. *T:* (01404) 812958.

BRAIN, Rt Rev. Peter Robert; *see* Armidale, Bishop of.

BRAIN, Rt Rev. Terence John; *see* Salford, Bishop of, (RC).

BRAITHWAITE, Eustace Ricardo; writer and lecturer; *b* Georgetown, British Guyana (now Guyana). *Educ:* Cambridge Univ. Served War of 1939–45, Fighter Pilot, RAF. Schoolteacher, London, 1950–57; Welfare Officer, LCC, 1958–60; Human Rights Officer, World Veterans Fedn, Paris, 1960–63; Education Consultant, UNESCO, Paris, 1963–66; Permanent Rep. of Guyana to UN, 1966–68; Ambassador of Guyana to Venezuela, 1968–70. Ainsfield-Wolff Prize, 1967; Franklin Peace Prize, 1968. *Publications:* To Sir With Love, 1959; Paid Servant, 1962; A Kind of Homecoming, 1962; Choice of Straws, 1965; Reluctant Neighbours, 1972; Honorary White, 1976. *Recreations:* tennis, birdwatching.

BRAITHWAITE, Sir Rodric (Quentin), GCMG 1994 (KCMG 1988 CMG 1981); HM Diplomatic Service, retired; Senior Advisor and Managing Director, Deutsche Bank (formerly Deutsche Morgan Grenfell), 1994–2002; *b* 17 May 1932; *s* of Henry Warwick Braithwaite and Lorna Constance Davies; *m* 1961, Gillian Mary Robinson; three *s* one *d* (and one *s* decd). *Educ:* Bedales Sch.; Christ's Coll., Cambridge (1st cl. Mod. Langs, Pts I and II; Hon. Fellow, 1989). Mil. Service, 1950–52. Joined Foreign (subseq. Diplomatic) Service, 1955; served Djakarta, Warsaw and FO, 1957–63; Moscow, 1963–66; Rome, 1966–69; FCO, 1969–72; Vis. Fellow, All Souls Coll., Oxford, 1972–73; Head of European Integration Dept (External), FCO, 1973–75; Head of Chancery, Office of Permanent Rep. to EEC, Brussels, 1975–78; Head of Planning Staff, FCO, 1979–80; Asst Under Sec. of State, FCO, 1981; Minister Commercial, Washington, 1982–84; Dep. Under-Sec. of State, FCO, 1984–88; Ambassador to Russia, 1988–92; Prime Minister's foreign policy advr, and Chm., Jt Intelligence Cttee, 1992–93. Member: European Strategy Bd, ICL plc, 1994–99; Adv. Bd, Sirocco Aerospace, 1999–2003; Bd, OMZ (Moscow), 2002–. Vis. Fellow, Wilson Center, Washington, 2005. Mem., Adv. Council on Nat. Records and Archives, 2005–. Chm. Council, Britain-Russia Centre, 1995–99; Mem. Council, VSO, 1994–99. Dir, ENO, 1992–99. Chm., Moscow Sch. of Political Studies, 1998–. Governor: RAM, 1993–2002 (Chm. of Govs, 1998–2002; Hon. FRAM 1996); Wilton Park, 2002–; Ditchley Park, 2003–. Trustee, BBC Marshall Plan for the Mind, 1995–98. Hon. LLD, 1997, Hon. Prof., 1999, Birmingham. *Publications:* (jtly) Engaging Russia, 1995; Russia in Europe, 1999; Across the Moscow River, 2002; Moscow 1941: a city and its people at war, 2006; various articles.

BRAITHWAITE, William Thomas Scatchard; QC 1992; a Recorder, 1993–99; *b* 20 Jan. 1948; *s* of late John Vernon Braithwaite and Nancy Phyllis Braithwaite; *m* 1972, Sheila Edgecombe; one *s* one *d. Educ:* Gordonstoun Sch.; Liverpool Univ. (LLB Hons). Called to the Bar, Gray's Inn, 1970; joined chambers in Liverpool, 1970; Asst Recorder of the Crown Court, 1990. Consultant Editor, Kemp and Kemp, The Quantum of Damages, 1995–2004. *Publications:* Medical Aspects of Personal Injury Litigation (ed jtly), 1997; Brain and Spine Injuries: the fight for justice, 2001. *Recreations:* cars, wine. *Address:* Exchange Chambers, Pearl Assurance House, Derby Square, Liverpool L2 9XX.

BRAKE, Thomas Anthony; MP (Lib Dem) Carshalton and Wallington, since 1997; *b* 6 May 1962; *s* of Michael and Judy Brake; *m* 1998, Candida Goulden; one *s* one *d. Educ:* Imperial Coll., London (BSc Hons Physics); Lycée International, France (Internat. Baccalauréat). Formerly Principal Consultant, Cap Gemini, (IT services). Mem., Select Cttee on Transport, 2002–03. Lib Dem spokesman: on envmt, 1997–2001; on transport, local govt and the regions, 2001–02; on transport and London, 2002–03; on internat. develt, 2003–05; on transport, 2005–06; on local govt, 2006–07; on London, 2007–; on the Olympics, 2007–; on home affairs, 2008–; a Lib Dem Whip, 2000–01. Mem., Accommodation and Works Cttee, H of C, 2001–02. *Publication:* (jtly) Costing the Earth, 1991. *Recreations:* running, travel, eating, film. *Address:* House of Commons, SW1A 0AA.

BRAMALL, family name of **Baron Bramall**.

BRAMALL, Baron *cr* 1987 (Life Peer), of Bushfield in the County of Hampshire; **Field Marshal Edwin Noel Westby Bramall,** KG 1990; GCB 1979 (KCB 1974); OBE 1965; MC 1945; JP; HM Lord-Lieutenant of Greater London, 1986–98; Chief of the Defence Staff, 1982–85; *b* 18 Dec. 1923; *s* of late Major Edmund Haselden Bramall and Mrs Katherine Bridget Bramall (*née* Westby); *m* 1949, Dorothy Avril Wentworth Vernon; one *s* one *d. Educ:* Eton College. Commnd into KRRC, 1943; served in NW Europe, 1944–45; occupation of Japan, 1946–47; Instructor, Sch. of Infantry, 1949–51; psc 1952; Middle East, 1953–58; Instructor, Army Staff Coll., 1958–61; on staff of Lord Mountbatten at MoD, 1963–64; CO, 2 Green Jackets, KRRC, Malaysia during Indonesian confrontation, 1965–66; comd 5th Airportable Bde, 1967–69; idc 1970; GOC 1st Div. BAOR, 1971–73; Lt-Gen., 1973; Comdr, British Forces, Hong Kong, 1973–76; Gen., 1976; C-in-C, UK Land Forces, 1976–78; Vice-Chief of Defence Staff (Personnel and Logistics), 1978–79; Chief of the General Staff, 1979–82; Field Marshal, 1982. ADC (Gen.), 1979–82. Col Comdt, 3rd Bn Royal Green Jackets, 1973–84; Col, 2nd Goorkhas, 1976–86; President: Greater London TAVRA, 1986–98; Gurkha Bde Assoc., 1987–97. Hon. Life Vice Pres., MCC, 1997 (Mem. Cttee, 1985–94; Pres., 1988–89; Trustee, 1994–97). A Trustee, Imperial War Museum, 1983–98 (Chm., 1989–98). JP London 1986. KStJ 1986. *Publication:* (jtly) The Chiefs, 1993. *Recreations:* cricket, painting, travel. *Address:* House of Lords, SW1A 0PW. *Clubs:* Travellers, Army and Navy, Pratt's, MCC, I Zingari, Free Foresters.

BRAMLEY, Prof. Sir Paul (Anthony), Kt 1984; FRCS, FDSRCS; Professor of Dental Surgery, University of Sheffield, 1969–88, now Emeritus; *b* 24 May 1923; *s* of Charles and Constance Bramley; *m* 1952, Hazel Morag Boyd, MA, MB ChB; one *s* three *d. Educ:* Wyggeston Grammar Sch., Leicester; Univ. of Birmingham. MB ChB, BDS. HS, Queen Elizabeth Hosp., Birmingham, 1945; Capt., RADC, 224 Para Fd Amb., 1946–48; MO, Church of Scotland, Kenya, 1952; Registrar, Rooksdown House, 1953–54; Consultant Oral Surgeon, SW Region Hosp. Bd, 1954–69; Dir, Dept of Oral Surgery and Orthodontics, Plymouth Gen. Hosp. and Truro Royal Infirmary, 1954–69; Civilian Consultant, RN, 1959–88, now Emeritus; Dean, Sch. of Clinical Dentistry, Univ. of Sheffield, 1972–75. Consultant Oral Surgeon, Trent Region, 1969–88. Chm., Dental Protection Ltd, 1989–95. Member: General Dental Council, 1973–89; Council, Medical Protection Soc., 1975–95; Council, RCS, 1975–83 (Tomes Lectr, 1980; Dean of Faculty of Dental Surgery, 1980–83; Colyer Gold Medal, 1988); Royal Commission on NHS, 1976–79; Dental Strategy Review Group; Chm., Standing Dental Adv. Cttee; Consultant Adviser, DHSS, 1970–80; Hon. Sec., British Assoc. of Oral Surgeons, 1968–72, Pres., 1975; President: S Yorks Br., British Dental Assoc., 1975; Oral Surgery Club of GB, 1985–86; Inst. of Maxillofacial Technol., 1987–89; Nat. Pres., BDA, 1988–89. Adviser, Prince of Songkla Univ., Thailand, 1982–; External Examiner to RCS, RCSI, RCSG, RACDS, Univs of Birmingham, Baghdad, Hong Kong, London, Singapore, Trinity College Dublin, Cardiff, NUI. Pres., Norman Rowe Educnl Trust, 1993–95; Chm., Cavendish Br., NADFAS, 1996–99. Lay Reader, dio. of Winchester, 1953–68. Hon. FRACDS. Hon. DDS: Birmingham, 1987; Prince of Songkla Univ., 1989; Hon. MD Sheffield, 1994. Fellow, Internat. Assoc. of Oral and Maxillofacial Surgeons. Bronze Medal, Helsinki Univ., 1990. *Publications:* (with J. Norman) The Temporomandibular Joint: disease, disorders, surgery, 1989; scientific articles in British and foreign medical and dental jls. *Address:* Greenhills, Back Lane, Hathersage S32 1AR.

BRAMLEY, Steven Michael Stuart; Deputy Legal Adviser at the Home Office, since 2004; *b* 18 March 1961; *s* of Michael Frank Rayner Bramley and Patricia Anne Bramley (*née* Easter); *m* 1990, Ann Weir; three *s. Educ:* Royal Grammar Sch., High Wycombe; UCL (LLB Hons). Called to the Bar, Gray's Inn, 1983; Legal Advr's Br., Home Office, 1986–93 and 1996–2003 (Asst Legal Advr, 1997–2003); NI Office, 1993–96; Dep. Legal Sec. to the Law Officers, 2003–04. *Address:* Legal Advisers' Branch, Home Office, Seacole, 2 Marsham Street, SW1P 4DF.

BRAMMA, Harry Wakefield, FRCO; Organist and Director of Music, All Saints', Margaret Street, 1989–2004; Director, Royal School of Church Music, 1989–98; *b* 11 Nov. 1936; *s* of late Fred and Christine Bramma. *Educ:* Bradford Grammar Sch.; Pembroke Coll., Oxford (MA). FRCO 1958 (Harding Prize). Organist, All Saints, Bingley, WR Yorks, 1954–55; Dir of Music, King Edward VI Grammar Sch., Retford, Notts, 1961; Asst Organist, Worcester Cathedral, 1963; Dir of Music, The King's Sch., Worcester, 1965; Organist, Southwark Cathedral, 1976. Vis. Music Supervisor, King's Coll., Cambridge, 1998–2000; Vis. Music Tutor, Christ Church, Oxford, 2000–05. Organist, St Saviour's, E Retford and St Michael's, W Retford, 1961; Asst Conductor and Accompanist, Worcester Fest. Choral Soc., 1963; Organist, Worcester Three Choirs' Fest., 1966, 1969, 1972 and 1975; Conductor, Kidderminster Choral Soc., 1972–79. Examnr, Associated Bd of Royal Schs of Music, 1978–89. Mem. Council, RCO, 1979–96, Hon. Treas., 1987–96; Mem., Archbishops' Commn on Church Music, 1989–92; Organ Advr, Dio. of Southwark, 1976–93 and 1999–; Mem., Ct of Advrs, St Paul's Cathedral, 1993–99. Hon. Sec., Cathedral Organists' Assoc., 1989–98; Pres., Southwark and S London Soc. of Organists, 1976–; Vice Pres., Church Music Soc.; Mem. Cttee, Organists' Benevolent League, 1989–. Patron, Herbert Howells Soc., 1987–. Liveryman, Musicians' Co., 1985–. FGCM 1988; FRSCM 1994. Hon. Mem., Assoc. of Anglican Musicians, USA. Hon. DLitt Bradford, 1995. *Recreations:* travel, walking. *Address:* c/o The Parish Office, 7 Margaret Street, W1W 8JG. *Club:* Athenæum.

BRAMPTON, Sally Jane; novelist; *b* 15 July 1955; *d* of Roy and Pamela Brampton; *m* 1st, 1981, Nigel Cole (marr. diss. 1990); 2nd, 1990, Jonathan Leslie Powell, *qv* (marr. diss. 2007); one *d*; 3rd, 2007, Tom Wnek. *Educ:* Ashford Sch., Ashford, Kent; St Clare's Hall, Oxford; St Martin's School of Art, London. Fashion Writer, Vogue, 1978; Fashion Editor, Observer, 1981; Editor, Elle (UK), 1985–89; Associate Editor, Mirabella, 1990–91; Editor, Red, 2000. Contrib. Ed., Easy Living, 2005–; columnist: Saga mag., 2005–; Sunday Times, 2006–. Vis. Prof., Central St Martin's Coll. of Art and Design, 1997–. TV documentary: Undressed: the history of 20th century fashion, C4, 1998. *Publications: novels:* Good Grief, 1992; Lovesick, 1995; Concerning Lily, 1998; Love, Always, 2000; *non-fiction:* Shoot The Damn Dog: a memoir of depression, 2008.

BRAMSON, David; Consultant, Nabarro Nathanson, 2001–06 (Senior Partner, 1995–2001); *b* 8 Feb. 1942; *s* of late Israel Bramson and Deborah Bramson (*née*

Warshinsky); *m* 1966, Lilian de Wilde; one *s* one *d*. *Educ:* Willesden Co. Grammar Sch.; University Coll. London (LLB). Solicitor: Mobil Oil Co. Ltd, 1966–68; Nabarro Nathanson, 1968–2006 (Partner, 1969–2001). Member, Policy Cttee, British Property Fedn, 1995–2001; Trustee, Investment Property Forum Educnl Trust, 1997–2001. Lectr on commercial property, 1996–2000. Non-exec. Dir, Liberty Internat. plc, 2001–06. Gov. and Vice Chm., Coram Family, 2002–07. Chairman: Home-Start Camden, 2003–08; Westminster Advocacy Service for Sen. Residents, 2006–. *Address: e-mail:* d.bramson@blueyonder.co.uk.

BRAMWELL, Richard Mervyn; QC 1989; *b* 29 Sept. 1944; *s* of Clifford and Dorothy Bramwell; *m* 1968, Susan Green; one *d*. *Educ:* Stretford Grammar Sch.; LSE (LLB, LLM). Called to the Bar, Middle Temple, 1967. *Publications:* Taxation of Companies and Company Reconstructions, 1973, 8th edn 2002; Inheritance Tax on Lifetime Gifts, 1987. *Recreations:* hunting, tennis. *Address:* 3 Temple Gardens, Temple, EC4Y 9AU. *T:* (020) 7353 7884.

BRANAGH, Kenneth Charles; actor and director; *b* 10 Dec. 1960; *s* of William and Frances Branagh; *m* 1st, 1989, Emma Thompson, *qv* (marr. diss. 1997); 2nd, 2003, Lindsey Brunnock. *Educ:* Meadway Comprehensive Sch., Reading; Royal Academy of Dramatic Art (Bancroft Gold Medalist). *Theatre:* Another Country, Queen's, 1982 (SWET Award, Most Promising Newcomer; Plays and Players Award); The Madness; Francis; Henry V, Golden Girls, Hamlet, Love's Labours Lost, 1984–85; Tell Me Honestly (also author); Across the Roaring Hill; The Glass Maze; Hamlet, RSC, 1992; Edmond, NT, 2003; Ivanov, Wyndham's, 2008; directed: The Play What I Wrote, Wyndham's, 2001, NY, 2003; Ducktastic, Albery, 2005; founder dir, Renaissance Theatre Company, 1987–93: Romeo and Juliet (also dir); Public Enemy (also author); Much Ado About Nothing; As You Like It; Hamlet; Look Back in Anger (also televised); A Midsummer Night's Dream (also dir); King Lear (also dir); Coriolanus; Richard III; directed: Twelfth Night (also televised); The Life of Napoleon; (with Peter Egan) Uncle Vanya. *Films include:* A Month in the Country, 1987; High Season, 1987; Henry V (also dir), 1989 (Evening Standard Best Film of the Year, 1989; Oscar, Best Costume Design, 1990; BFI Award, Best Film and Technical Achievement, 1990; Young European Film of the Year, 1990; NY Critics Circle Award, Best New Dir; European Actor of the Year, 1990); Dead Again (also dir), 1991; Peter's Friends (also dir), Swan Song (dir), 1992; Swing Kids, Much Ado About Nothing (also dir), 1993; Mary Shelley's Frankenstein (also dir), 1994; (writer and dir) In the Bleak Midwinter, 1995; Othello, 1995; Hamlet (also dir), 1997; The Proposition, 1997; The Gingerbread Man, 1998; The Theory of Flight, 1998; Celebrity, 1999; Wild Wild West, 1999; Love's Labour's Lost (also dir), 2000; How to Kill Your Neighbor's Dog, 2002; Rabbit-Proof Fence, 2002; Harry Potter and the Chamber of Secrets, 2002; Five Children and It, 2004; As You Like It (dir), 2006; The Magic Flute (also dir), 2006; Sleuth (dir), 2007; *television includes:* Billy Trilogy, 1982; Fortunes of War, 1987; Boy in the Bush; To the Lighthouse; Strange Interlude; Ghosts, 1987; The Lady's Not for Burning; Shadow of a Gunman, 1995; Shackleton, Conspiracy (Emmy Award), 2002; Warm Springs, 2005; *radio includes:* Hamlet, and Romeo and Juliet (both also co-dir); King Lear; Anthem for the Doomed Youth; Diaries of Samuel Pepys; Mary Shelley's Frankenstein. *Publications:* Public Enemy (play), 1988; Beginning (autobiog.), 1989; *screenplays:* Henry V; Much Ado About Nothing; Hamlet; In the Bleak Midwinter. *Recreations:* reading, playing guitar. *Address:* Shepperton Studios, Shepperton, Middx TW17 0QD.

BRANCH, Prof. Michael Arthur, CMG 2000; PhD; Director, School of Slavonic and East European Studies, 1980–2001, and Professor of Finnish, 1986–2001, London University, at University College London; Fellow, University College London, since 2001; *b* 24 March 1940; *s* of Arthur Frederick Branch and Mahala Parker; *m* 1963, Ritva-Riitta Hannele, *d* of Erkki Kari, Heinola, Finland; three *d*. *Educ:* Shene Grammar Sch.; Sch. of Slavonic and East European Studies, Univ. of London (BA 1963; PhD 1967). School of Slavonic and East European Studies: Asst Lectr and Lectr in Finno-Ugrian Studies, 1967–72; Lectr, 1972–77, and Reader in Finnish, 1977; Chm., Dept of East European Language and Literature, 1979–80. Corresponding Member: Finno-Ugrian Soc., 1977; Finnish Literature Soc. (Helsinki), 1980. Hon. PhD Oulu (Finland), 1983. Comdr, Lion of Finland, 1980; Comdr, Polish Order of Merit, 1992; Comdr, Estonian Terra Mariana Cross, 2000; Officer, Order of Lithuanian Grand Duke Gediminas, 2002. *Publications:* A. J. Sjögren, 1973; (jtly) Finnish Folk Poetry: Epic, 1977; (jtly) A Student's Glossary of Finnish, 1980; (ed) Kalevala, 1985; (jtly) Edith Södergran, 1992; (jtly) The Great Bear, 1993; (jtly) Uses of Tradition, 1994; (jtly) Finland and Poland in the Russian Empire, 1995; (ed) The Writing of National History and Identity, 1999. *Recreations:* forestry, walking. *Address:* 33 St Donatt's Road, SE14 6NU. *Club:* Athenæum.

BRAND, family name of **Viscount Hampden**.

BRAND, Prof. Andrea Hilary, PhD; FMedSci; Herchel Smith Professor of Molecular Biology, Wellcome Trust/Cancer Research UK Gurdon Institute and Department of Physiology, Development and Neuroscience, University of Cambridge, since 2007; *b* 9 March 1959; *d* of Howard and Marlene Brand (*née* Nykerk); partner, Dr Jim Haseloff; one *d*. *Educ:* UN Internat. Sch., NY; Brasenose Coll., Oxford (BA Hons Biochem. 1981); MRC Lab. of Molecular Biol. and King's Coll., Cambridge (PhD Molecular Biol. 1986). SERC Post Doctoral Fellow, 1986–87, Helen Hay Whitney Fellow, 1987–89, Harvard Univ.; Leukemia Soc. Special Fellow, Harvard Med. Sch., 1990–93; Cancer Research Campaign Gurdon Institute, subseq. Wellcome Trust/Cancer Research UK Gurdon Institute, University of Cambridge: Wellcome Trust Sen. Fellow in Basic Biomed. Res., 1993–2003; Dir of Res. in Develtl Neurobiol., 2003–07; Sen. Gp Leader, 2005–; Res. Fellow, King's Coll., Cambridge, 1999–2003. Invited Prof., Ecole Normale Supérieure, Paris, 2002; Dietrich Bodenstein Lectr, Univ. of Virginia, 2002. Member, Editorial Board: Bioessays, 2003–; Neural Develt, 2006–; Fly, 2006–. Mem., Internat. Scientific Adv. Bd, Promega Corp., 1999–2004. Mem., Academic Careers Cttee, Acad. Med. Scis, 2003–06. Founding Bd Mem., Rosalind Franklin Soc., 2006–. Mem., EMBO, 2000. FMedSci 2003. Hooke Medal, British Soc. for Cell Biol., 2002; (jtly) William Bate Hardy Prize, Cambridge Philosophical Soc., 2004; Rosalind Franklin Award, Royal Soc., 2006. *Publications:* contribs to scientific jls. *Recreations:* contemporary dance, Arts and Crafts furniture, fast cars. *Address:* Wellcome Trust/Cancer Research UK Gurdon Institute and Department of Physiology, Development and Neuroscience, University of Cambridge, Tennis Court Road, Cambridge CB2 1QN.

BRAND, Prof. Charles Peter, FBA 1990; Professor of Italian, 1966–88, and Vice-Principal, 1984–88, University of Edinburgh; *b* 7 Feb. 1923; *er s* of Charles Frank Brand and Dorothy (*née* Tapping); *m* 1948, Gunvor, *yr d* of Col I. Hellgren, Stockholm; one *s* three *d*. *Educ:* Cambridge High Sch.; Trinity Hall, Cambridge. War Service, Intelligence Corps, 1943–46. Open Maj. Scholar, Trinity Hall, 1940; 1st Class Hons Mod. Languages, Cantab, 1948; PhD Cantab, 1951. Asst Lecturer, Edinburgh Univ., 1952; Cambridge University: Asst Lecturer, subsequently Lecturer, 1952–66; Fellow and Tutor, Trinity Hall, 1958–66. Pres., MHRA, 1995. Cavaliere Ufficiale, 1975, Commendatore, 1988, al Merito della Repubblica Italiana. General Editor, Modern Language Review, 1971–77; Editor, Italian Studies, 1976–81. *Publications:* Italy and the English Romantics, 1957; Torquato Tasso, 1965; Ariosto: a preface to the Orlando Furioso, 1974; (ed) Cambridge History of Italian Literature, 1996; contributions to learned journals. *Recreations:* sport, travel, gardening. *Address:* 21 Succoth Park, Edinburgh EH12 6BX.

BRAND, Geoffrey Arthur; Under-Secretary, Department of Employment, 1972–85; *b* 13 June 1930; *s* of late Arthur William Charles Brand and Muriel Ada Brand; *m* 1954, Joy Trotman; two *d*. *Educ:* Andover Grammar Sch.; University Coll., London. Entered Min. of Labour, 1953; Private Sec. to Parly Sec., 1956–57; Colonial Office, 1957–58; Private Sec. to Minister of Labour, 1965–66; Asst. Sec., Industrial Relations and Research and Planning Divisions, 1966–72. Mem., Archbishop of Canterbury's (later Bishops') Adv. Gp on Urban Priority Areas, 1986–98. FRSA 1985. *Address:* Cedarwood, Seer Green, Beaconsfield, Bucks HP9 2UH. *T:* (01494) 676637.

BRAND, Jo; writer and comedian; *m*; two *d*. Formerly psychiatric nurse. Comedy includes stand-up. Television series: Jo Brand Through the Cakehole, 1995; A Big Slice of Jo Brand, 1996; Jo Brand's Commercial Breakdown, 1999–; Head on Comedy with Jo Brand, 2000; Nobody Likes a Smartass, 2003. Radio series: Windbags (with Donna McPhail); Seven Ages of Man, 2000. Theatre, The Pirates of Penzance, Gielgud, 2008. Former columnist, The Independent; columnist, Nursing Times, 2000. British Comedy Award, 1992. *Publications:* Load of Old Balls: ranking of men in history, 1995; Load of Old Ball Crunchers: women in history, 1996; (with Helen Griffin) Mental (play), 1996; Sorting Out Billy (novel), 2004; It's Different for Girls (novel), 2005. *Address:* c/o Richard Stone Partnership, 2 Henrietta Street, WC2E 8PS.

BRAND, Dr Michael; Director, J. Paul Getty Museum, since 2006; *b* 9 Jan. 1958; *s* of Lindsay and Betty Brand; *m* 1988, Tina Gomes; two *d*. *Educ:* Canberra Grammar Sch.; Maret Sch., Washington, DC; Emerson Prep. Sch., Washington; Australian Nat. Univ. (BA Hons Asian Studies); Harvard Univ. (MA; PhD 1987). Curator, Asian Art, Mus. of Art, Rhode Is. Sch. of Design, 1985–87; Res. Fellow, Arthur M. Sackler Gall., Smithsonian Instn, 1987; Co-Dir, Smithsonian Instn Mughal Garden Project, Lahore, Pakistan, 1988–93; Curator, Asian Art, Nat. Gall., Australia, 1988–96; Asst Dir, Qld Art Gall., Brisbane, 1996–2000; Dir, Virginia Mus. of Fine Arts, USA, 2000–05. *Publications:* (ed with G. D. Lowry) Fatehpur-Sikri: a sourcebook, 1985; (with G. D. Lowry) Akbar's India: art from the Mughal City of Victory, 1985; (ed with G. D. Lowry) Studies on Fatehpur-Sikri, 1987; (jtly) Shalamar Garden Lahore: landscape, form and meaning, 1990; (with C. Phoeurn) The Age of Angkor: treasures from the National Museum of Cambodia, 1992; (ed and contrib.) Traditions of Asian Art (traced through the Collection of the National Gallery of Australia), 1995; The Vision of Kings: art and experience in India, 1995; (ed with C. Roberts) Earth, Spirit, Fire: Korean masterpieces of the Choson Dynasty, 2000; contrib. numerous articles to art catalogues, books and jls. *Address:* J. Paul Getty Museum, 1200 Getty Center Drive, Suite 1000, Los Angeles, CA 90049–1687, USA. *T:* (310) 4406354, *Fax:* (310) 4407718.

BRAND, Dr Paul Anthony, FBA 1998; Senior Research Fellow of All Souls College, Oxford, since 1999; *b* 25 Dec. 1946; *s* of Thomas Joseph Brand and Marjorie Jean Brand (*née* Smith); *m* 1970, Vanessa Carolyn Alexandra Rodrigues. *Educ:* Hampton Grammar Sch.; Magdalen Coll., Oxford (BA 1967; DPhil 1974). Asst Keeper, Public Record Office, 1970–76; Lectr in Law, UCD, 1976–83; research, 1983–93; Res. Fellow, Inst. of Historical Res., Univ. of London, 1993–99; Fellow, All Souls Coll., Oxford, 1997–99. Vis. Fellow, All Souls Coll., Oxford, 1995; Vis. Prof., Columbia Univ. Law Sch., 1995, 2003; Dist. Vis. Prof., Arizona Center for Medieval and Renaissance Studies and Merriam Vis. Prof. of Law, Arizona State Univ., 2000. *Publications:* The Origins of the English Legal Profession, 1992; The Making of the Common Law, 1992; The Earliest English Law Reports, vol. I, vol. II, 1996, vol. III, 2005, vol. IV, 2007; Kings, Barons and Justices: the making and enforcement of legislation in thirteenth century England, 2003; The Parliament Rolls of Medieval England, vols I and II, 2005; Plea Rolls of the Exchequer of the Jews, vol. VI, 2005. *Recreations:* theatre, looking at buildings. *Address:* All Souls College, Oxford OX1 4AL. *T:* (01865) 279286; 155 Kennington Road, SE11 6SF. *T:* (020) 7582 4051.

BRAND, Dr Peter; General Practitioner, Brading, Isle of Wight, since 1977; *b* 16 May 1947; *s* of L. H. Brand and J. Brand (*née* Fredricks); *m* 1972, Jane Vivienne Attlee; two *s*. *Educ:* Thornbury Grammar Sch., Glos; Birmingham Univ. Med. Sch. MRCS; LRCP; DObstRCOG; MRCGP. Chm., IoW Div., BMA, 1980–84. Contested (Lib Dem) Isle of Wight, 1992, 2001; MP (Lib Dem) Isle of Wight, 1997–2001. *Recreations:* boating, building. *Address:* Chain Ferry House, 3 Ferry Road, East Cowes, Isle of Wight PO32 6RA. *Clubs:* National Liberal; Island Sailing, E Cowes Sailing.

BRANDES, Lawrence Henry, CB 1982; Under Secretary and Head of Office of Arts and Libraries, 1978–82; *b* 16 Dec. 1924; *m* 1950, Dorothea Stanyon; one *s* one *d*. *Educ:* Beltane Sch.; London Sch. of Economics. Min. of Health, 1950; Principal Private Sec. to Minister, 1959; Nat. Bd for Prices and Incomes, 1966; Dept of Employment and Productivity, 1969; Under-Sec., DHSS, 1970; HM Treasury, 1975. Director: Dance Umbrella, 1984–94; London Internat. Festival of Theatre, 1985–92. Member: Dulwich Picture Gall. Man. Cttee, 1984–94 (acting Chm., 1992; Chm., 1994); Museums and Galls Commn (Chm., Conservation Cttee), 1988–92. Chm., Textile Conservation Centre, 1993–98. Mem. Delegacy, Goldsmiths' Coll., 1983–88. Trustee, SS Great Britain, 1987–98. *Address:* 4 Hogarth Hill, NW11 6AX.

BRANDON, (David) Stephen; QC 1996; *b* 18 Dec. 1950; *s* of late James Osbaldeston Brandon and Dorothy Brandon (*née* Wright); *m* 1982, (Helen) Beatrice Lee; one *d*. *Educ:* Univ. of Nottingham (BA); Univ. of Keele (LLM). Lectr in Law, Univ. of Keele, 1975–85; called to the Bar, Gray's Inn, 1978; in practice at Revenue Bar, 1981–. *Publications:* Taxation of Non-Resident and Migrant Companies, 1989; Foreign Companies and the Problem of UK Residence, 1991; Taxation of Non-UK Resident Companies and Their Shareholders, 2001; various articles. *Recreations:* art (esp. collecting early woodcuts), opera, nurturing woodlands. *Address:* 15 Old Square, Lincoln's Inn, WC2A 3UE; Clopton Manor, Clopton, Northants NN14 3DZ.

BRANDON, Michael John Hamilton, FNAEA; Senior Partner, since 1992, and Deputy Chairman, since 2005, Jackson-Stops & Staff; *b* Derby, 27 June 1947; *s* of Reginald Brandon and Doris Cecily Brandon; *m* 1975, Rosalind Mary Attwood; one *s* one *d*. *Educ:* Shoreham Grammar Sch.; Chichester Coll. of Art and Technol. FNAEA 1985. Joined Jackson-Stops & Staff Consortium, 1967; Area Dir, Chichester, 1987. *Recreations:* sailing, walking, computing, classic cars, motor racing, horse-racing. *Address:* Jackson-Stops & Staff, 37 South Street, Chichester, W Sussex PO19 1EL. *T:* (01243) 786316, *Fax:* (01243) 533736; *e-mail:* michaelbrandon@jackson-stops.co.uk. *Club:* Goodwood Road Racing.

BRANDON, Prof. Peter Samuel, FRICS; Professor of Quantity and Building Surveying, since 1985, Director of Strategic Programmes and Public Orator, since 2001, University of Salford; Director, Salford University Think Lab, since 2005; *b* 4 June 1943; *s* of Samuel Brandon and Doris Eileen Florence Brandon (*née* Downing); *m* 1968, Mary

Ann Elizabeth Canham; one *s* two *d*. *Educ:* Bournemouth Grammar Sch.; Bristol Univ. (MSc Architecture); DSc Salford 1996. Private practice and local govt, 1963–69; Lectr, Portsmouth Poly., 1969–73; Prin. Lectr, Bristol Poly., 1973–81; Head of Dept, Portsmouth Poly., 1981–85; Salford University: Chm., Surveying Dept, 1985–93; Pro-Vice-Chancellor, 1993–2001; Dir, Res. and Grad. Coll., 1993–2001. Royal Institution of Chartered Surveyors: Chm., Res. Cttee, 1987–91; Mem. Gen. Council representing Gtr Manchester, 1989–93; Mem., Exec. Bd, QS Div., 1991–; Science and Engineering Research Council: Chm., Construction Cttee, 1991–94; Chm., Building Design Technology and Management Sub-Cttee, 1990–91; Member: Engrg Res. Commn, 1991–94; DTI Technology Foresight Panel for Construction, 1994; Chm., Built Envmt Panel for HEFCE RAE, 1996 and 2001. Hon. Mem., ASAQS, 1994. Hon. DEng Heriot-Watt, 2006. *Publications:* Cost Planning of Buildings, 1980, 8th edn 2007; (ed) Building Cost Techniques, 1982; Microcomputers in Building Appraisal, 1983; (ed) Quality and Profit in Building Design, 1984; Computer programs for Building Cost Appraisal, 1985; Building, Cost Modelling and Computers, 1987; Expert Systems: the strategic planning of construction projects, 1988; (ed) Investment, Procurement & Performance in Construction, 1991; (ed) Management, Quality and Economics in Building, 1991; (ed) Integration of Construction Information, 1995; (ed) Client Centered Approach to Knowledge Based Systems, 1995; Evaluation of the Built Environment Sustainability, 1997; (ed) Cities and Sustainability, 2000; Evaluating Sustainable Development in the Built Environment, 2005. *Recreations:* mountain biking alongside canals, walking, travel, modern art. *Address:* School of the Built Environment, Maxwell Building, University of Salford, Salford M5 4WT. *T:* (0161) 295 5164, *Fax:* (0161) 745 5553. *Club:* Royal Over-Seas League.

BRANDON, Stephen; *see* Brandon, D. S.

BRANDON-BRAVO, Martin Maurice, OBE 2002; *b* 25 March 1932; *s* of late Isaac, (Alfred), and Phoebe Brandon-Bravo; *m* 1964, Sally Anne Wallwin; two *s*. *Educ:* Latymer Sch. FCMI (FBIM 1980). Joined Richard Stump Ltd, later Richard Stump (1979), 1952; successively Floor Manager, Factory Manager, Production Dir and Asst Man. Dir; Man. Dir, 1979–83; non-exec. Dir, 1983–; Dir, Hall & Earl Ltd, 1970–83. Mem., Nottingham City Council, 1968–70 and 1976–87; Chm., 1970–73, Pres., 1975–83, Nottingham West Cons. Party Orgn; Dep. Chm., City of Nottingham Cons. Fedn. Contested (C): Nottingham East, 1979; Nottingham South, 1992. MP (C) Nottingham South, 1983–92; PPS to Minister of State for Housing and Urban Affairs, 1985–87, to Minister of State, Home Office, 1987–89, to Home Sec., 1989–90, to Lord Privy Seal and Leader of the House of Lords, 1990–92. Mem., Notts CC, 1993–. Contested (C) Nottingham and Leicestershire NW, Eur. Parly elecns, 1994. Mem., Nat. Water Sport Centre Management Cttee, 1972–83; Pres., Amateur Rowing Assoc., 1993–2001 (Hon. Life Vice Pres., 2001–); Pres. and Trustee, Nottingham and Union Rowing Club, 1983–; Vice Pres., Henley River and Rowing Mus., 2006– (Trustee, 1993–2006). *Recreation:* rowing (held Internat. Umpire licence, now retired). *Address:* The Old Farmhouse, 27 Rectory Place, Barton-in-Fabis, Nottingham NG11 0AL. *T:* (0115) 983 0459, *Fax:* (0115) 983 0457. *Club:* Leander.

BRANDRETH, Gyles Daubeney; author, broadcaster; *b* 8 March 1948; *s* of late Charles Brandreth and of Alice Addison; *m* 1973, Michèle Brown; one *s* two *d*. *Educ:* Lycée Français de Londres; Betteshanger Sch., Kent; Bedales Sch., Hants; New Coll., Oxford (Scholar). Pres. Oxford Union, Editor of Isis. Chairman: Archway Productions Ltd, 1971–74; Victorama Ltd, 1974–93; Complete Editions Ltd, 1988–93; Director: Colin Smythe Ltd, 1971–73; Newarke Wools Ltd, 1988–92; J. W. Spear & Sons, 1992–95. Dep. Chm., Unicorn Heritage, 1987–90; children's publisher, André Deutsch Ltd, 1997–2000; consultant ed., Whitaker's Almanack, 1997–2002. Freelance journalist, 1968–: contrib. Observer, Guardian, Express, Daily Mail, Daily Mirror, Daily Telegraph, Evening Standard, Spectator, Punch, Homes & Gardens, She, Woman's Own; Columnist: Honey, 1968–69; Manchester Evening News, 1971–72; Woman, 1972–73, 1986–88; TV Times, 1989–92; Press Assoc. weekly syndicated column in USA, 1981–85; Ed., Puzzle World, 1989–92; Ed.-at-Large, Sunday Telegraph Review, 1999–2004. MP (C) City of Chester, 1992–97; contested (C) same seat, 1997. PPS to Financial Sec. to Treasury, 1993–94, to Sec. of State for Nat. Heritage, 1994–95, to Sec. of State for Health, 1995; an Asst Govt Whip, 1995–96; a Lord Comr, HM Treasury, 1996–97. Sponsor, 1994 Marriage Act. Broadcaster, 1969–: TV series incl.: Child of the Sixties, 1969; Puzzle Party, 1977; Chatterbox, 1977–78; Memories, 1982; Countdown, 1983–90 and 1997–; TV-am, 1983–90; Railway Carriage Game, 1985; Catchword, 1986; Discovering Gardens, 1990–91; CBS News, 1992–2002; Have I Got News For You, 1997–; Home Shopping Network, 2002–05; This Is Your Life, 2003; Public Opinion, 2004; The One Show, 2007–; (with Hinge and Bracket) Dear Ladies (TV scripts); (with Julian Slade) Now We Are Sixty (play); Theatrical producer, 1971–86: Through the Looking-Glass, 1972; Oxford Theatre Fest., 1974, 1976; The Dame of Sark, Wyndham's, 1974; The Little Hut, Duke of York's, 1974; Dear Daddy, Ambassador's, 1976; Cambridge Fest., 1986; also Son et Lumière; appeared as Baron Hardup in Cinderella, Guildford, 1989, Wimbledon, 1990; writer and performer, Zipp! (musical), Edinburgh Fest., 2002 (Most Popular Show award), Duchess, 2003, UK tour, 2004; Malvolio in Twelfth Night The Musical!, Edinburgh Fest., 2005. Founder: National Scrabble Championships, 1971; British Pantomime Assoc., 1971; Teddy Bear Mus., 1988. Dir, Europ. Movement's People for Europe campaign, 1975; Mem., Better English Campaign, 1995–97. Appeals Chm., 1983–89, Chm., 1989–93, Vice-Pres., 1993–, NPFA. Co-curator, NPG exhibition of children's writers, 2002. Three times holder, world record for longest-ever after-dinner speech (4 hrs 19 mins, 1976; 11 hrs, 1978; 12 hrs 30 mins, 1982). *Publications:* over fifty books since Created in Captivity, 1972; most recent: Under the Jumper (autobiog.), 1993; Who is Nick Saint? (novel), 1996; Venice Midnight (novel), 1998; Breaking the Code (diaries), 1999; John Gielgud, 2000; Brief Encounters: meetings with remarkable people, 2001; Philip and Elizabeth: portrait of a marriage, 2004; Charles and Camilla: portrait of a love affair, 2005; Oscar Wilde and the Candlelight Murders (novel), 2007; Oscar Wilde and the Ring of Death, 2008; over seventy books for children. *Address:* c/o International Artistes, Holborn Hall, 193 High Holborn, WC1V 7BD.

BRANDRICK, David Guy, CBE 1981; Secretary, British Coal Corporation (formerly National Coal Board), 1972–89, retired; Director: Coal Staff Superannuation Scheme Trustees Ltd (formerly British Coal Staff Scheme Superannuation Trustees Ltd), 1989–2002; CMT Pension Trustee Services Ltd, 1993–2002; *b* 17 April 1932; *s* of Harry and Minnie Brandrick; *m* 1956, Eunice Fisher (*d* 1999); one *s* one *d*. *Educ:* Newcastle-under-Lyme High Sch.; St John's Coll., Oxford (MA). Joined National Coal Board, 1955; Chairman's Office, 1957; Principal Private Secretary to Chairman, 1961; Departmental Sec., Production Dept, 1963; Dep. Sec. to the Bd, 1967. *Recreation:* walking.

BRANDT, His Honour (Paul) Nicholas; a Circuit Judge, 1987–2003; *b* 21 Nov. 1937; *s* of late Paul Francis and Barbara Brandt. *Educ:* St Andrew's Sch., Eastbourne; Marlborough Coll.; New Coll., Oxford (BA 2nd Cl. Hons Sch. of Jurisprudence). Called to the Bar, Gray's Inn, 1963; a Recorder, 1983–87. *Recreations:* sailing, shooting, Rugby football. *Address:* c/o Colchester County Court, Falkland House, 25 Southway, Colchester, Essex CO3 3EG. *Clubs:* Royal Harwich Yacht (Woolverstone, Suffolk), Bar Yacht.

BRANDT, Peter Augustus; Chairman, Atkins Fulford Ltd, 1977–2006; *b* 2 July 1931; *s* of late Walter Augustus Brandt and late Dorothy Gray Brandt (*née* Crane); *m* 1962, Elisabeth Margaret (*née* ten Bos); two *s* one *d*. *Educ:* Eton Coll.; Trinity Coll., Cambridge (MA). Joined Wm Brandt's Sons & Co. Ltd, Merchant Bankers, 1954; Mem. Bd, 1960; Chief Executive, 1966; resigned, 1972. Director: London Life Assoc., 1962–89; Corp. of Argentine Meat Producers (CAP) Ltd and affiliates, 1970; Edward Bates (Holdings) Ltd, 1972–77; Edward Bates & Sons Ltd, 1972–77 (Chm., 1974–77). Mem., Nat. Rivers Authy (formerly Nat. Rivers Adv. Cttee), 1988–95. *Recreations:* sailing, rowing, steam engines, wild fowl. *Address:* Spout Farm, Boxford, Suffolk CO10 5HA. *Clubs:* Boodle's; Leander (Henley-on-Thames).

BRANIGAN, Kate Victoria; QC 2006; *b* 3 Sept. 1961; *d* of Cyril and Patricia Branigan; *m* 1983, Robert Solomon; one *s* one *d*. *Educ:* Coopers' Company and Coborn Sch., Upminster; Univ. of Southampton (LLB 1983). Called to the Bar, Inner Temple, 1984; in practice as a barrister specialising in family law, 1984–. *Recreations:* church, entertaining, classical music, reading, theatre, France, walking, ski-ing, being with my family. *Address:* 4 Paper Buildings, Temple, EC4Y 7EX. *T:* (020) 7583 0816, *Fax:* (020) 7353 4979; *e-mail:* kb@4pb.com.

BRANKIN, Rhona; Member (Lab) Midlothian, Scottish Parliament, since 1999; *b* 19 Jan. 1950; *d* of Edward and Joyce Lloyd; *m* 1998, Peter Jones; two *d* by former marriage. *Educ:* Aberdeen Univ. (BEd 1975); Moray House Coll. (Dip. Special Educnl Needs 1989). Teacher, 1975–94; Lectr in Special Educnl Needs, Northern Coll., Dundee, 1994–99. Scottish Executive: Deputy Minister: for Culture and Sport, 1999–2001; for Envmt and Rural Develt, 2000–01 and 2005–07; for Health and Community Care, 2004–05; Minister for Communities, 2007; Shadow Cabinet Sec. for Educn and Lifelong Learning, 2007–. Former Chair, Scottish Labour Party. Hon. FRIBA. *Recreations:* sport, the arts, countryside. *Address:* Scottish Parliament, Edinburgh EH99 1SP.

BRANNAN, Micheline Hadassah; student nurse, Napier University; Head, Civil and International Group, Scottish Executive Justice Department, 2005–07; Head, Social Justice Group, Scottish Executive Development Department, 2006–07; *b* 23 Oct. 1954; *d* of Israel and Halina Moss; *m* 1986, Michael Neilson Brannan; two *s*. *Educ:* St Hilda's Coll., Oxford (BA 1976, MA Lit. Hum. 1978). Scottish Office: admin. trainee, 1976–78; HEO(D), 1978–82; Principal, 1982–91; Head: Parole and Lifer Rev. Div., 1991–95; Civil Law Div., 1995–2001; Hd, Criminal Justice Gp, Scottish Exec. Justice Dept, 2001–05. *Recreations:* Jewish cultural activities and interfaith. *Address:* 31/3 Rattray Grove, Edinburgh EH10 5TL; *e-mail:* michelinehbrannan@msn.com.

BRANNEN, Peter; Visiting Professor in Management, Southampton University, since 2000; Director, International Labour Office, London, 1992–2003; *b* 1 Dec. 1941; *s* of Joseph Brannen and Monica Brannen (*née* Cairns); *m* 1966, Julia Mary Morgan; two *s*. *Educ:* Ushaw Coll., Durham; Univ. of Manchester (BA Hons Econs 1964). Account Exec., McCann Erickson Advertising, 1964; Sen. Res. Asst, Univ. of Durham, 1966–69; Senior Research Fellow: Univ. of Bradford, 1969–72; Univ. of Southampton Med. Sch., 1973; Department of Employment: Special Advr, 1974; Chief Res. Officer, 1975–86; Head of Internat. Relns, 1989–91. Visiting Fellow: ANU, 1987; Nuffield Coll., Oxford, 1988; Sen. Vis. Fellow, PSI, 1988. Mem., Mgt, Indust. Relns and other cttees, SSRC, 1975–81; Chm., British Workplace Indust. Relns Surveys, 1980–89; Member: Admin Bd, European Foundn, 1986–92 (Dep. Chm., 1991); Employment Labour and Social Affairs Cttee, OECD, 1990–92; Employment Cttee, Council of Europe, 1990–92. FRSA 2000. Editl Bd, Work, Employment and Society, 1986–90. *Publications:* Entering the World of Work, 1975; The Worker Directors, 1976; Authority and Participation in Industry, 1983; various contribs to anthologies and learned jls on economic sociology. *Recreations:* sailing, gardening, music. *Club:* Royal Southampton Yacht.

BRANSON, Rear Adm. Cecil Robert Peter Charles, CBE 1975; *b* 30 March 1924; *s* of Cecil Branson and Marcelle Branson; *m* 1945, Sonia Moss; one *d*. *Educ:* RNC, Dartmouth. Served, HMS Dragon, W Africa, S Atlantic, Indian Ocean and Far East (present during time of fall of Singapore and Java), 1941–42; Sub-Lieut's Courses, 1943; qual. as submarine specialist, served in HM S/M Sea Rover, Far East, 1944–45; various appts in S/Ms, 1945–49; First Lieut, HMS Defender, 1953–55; jssc; CO, HMS Roebuck, Dartmouth Trng Sqdn, 1958; Staff, Flag Officer Flotillas Mediterranean, 1959–60; Jt Planning Staff, MoD, 1960–62; Exec. Officer, HMS Victorious, Far East, 1962–64; CO, HMS Rooke, Gibraltar, 1964–65; NATO Def. Coll., 1965; Defence Planning Staff, MoD, 1966–68; CO, HMS Phoebe, and Captain (D) Londonderry Sqdn, 1968–70; Naval Attaché, Paris, 1970–73; CO, HMS Hermes, 1973–74 (Hermes headed RN task force evacuating Brit. and foreign subjects from Cyprus beaches after Turkish invasion, 1973); Asst Chief of Naval Staff (Ops), MoD, 1975–77; retired. Man. Dir, UK Trawlers Mutual Insurance Assoc., 1977–85.

BRANSON, Edward James, MA; public relations and publicity services; a Metropolitan Stipendiary Magistrate, 1971–87; barrister-at-law; *b* 10 March 1918; *s* of late Rt Hon. Sir George Branson, PC, sometime Judge of High Court, and late Lady (Mona) Branson; *m* 1949, Evette Huntley, *e d* of late Rupert Huntley Flindt; one *s* two *d*. *Educ:* Bootham Sch., York; Trinity Coll., Cambridge. Served War, 1939–46, Staffordshire Yeomanry: Palestine, Egypt, and Western Desert, 1941–42; GSO 3 (Ops) attd 2 NZ Div. for Alamein, 1942; GS02 (Ops), attd 6 (US) Corps for Salerno and Anzio landings, 1943–44; subseq. GSO2 (Ops) 53 (W) Div. in Germany. Called to the Bar, Inner Temple, 1950; practised London and SE Circuit. *Recreations:* shooting, fishing, archaeology. *Address:* Cakeham Manor, West Wittering, W Sussex PO20 8LG.

See also Sir R. Branson.

BRANSON, Sir Richard (Charles Nicholas), Kt 2000; Founder and Chairman, Virgin Retail Group, Virgin Communications, Virgin Travel Group, Virgin Hotels Group, Virgin Direct Ltd, Virgin Bride Ltd, Virgin Net Ltd, Virgin Express Holdings Plc and Virgin Mobile; Life President, Virgin Music Group (sold to Thorn-EMI, 1992); *b* 18 July 1950; *s* of Edward James Branson, *qv*; *m* 1st, 1969 (marr. diss.); 2nd, 1989, Joan Templeman; one *s* one *d*. *Educ:* Stowe. Editor, Student magazine, 1968–69; set up Student Advisory Centre (now Help), 1970. Founded Virgin Mail-Order Co., 1969, followed by Virgin Retail, Virgin Record Label, Virgin Music Publishing, Virgin Recording Studios; estabd Virgin Record subsids in 25 countries, 1980–86; founded Virgin Atlantic Airways, 1984; Voyager Gp Ltd formed 1986, encompassing interests in travel, clubs and hotels; Virgin Records launched in US, 1987; founded: Virgin Radio, 1993; Virgin Rail Gp Ltd, 1996; Virgin Games, 2004. Pres., UK 2000, 1988– (Chm., 1986–88); Dir, Intourist Moscow Ltd, 1988–90. Launched charity, The Healthcare Foundn, 1987. Captain, Atlantic Challenger II, winner Blue Riband for fastest crossing of Atlantic by a ship, 1986; with Per Lindstrand, first to cross Atlantic in hot air balloon, 1987, and Pacific, 1991 (longest flight in hot air balloon, 6700 miles, and fastest speed, 200 mph, 1991). *Publication:*

Losing My Virginity: the autobiography, 1998. *Address:* c/o Virgin Group Ltd, 120 Campden Hill Road, W8 7AR. *T:* (020) 7229 1282.

BRANT, Colin Trevor, CMG 1981; CVO 1979; HM Diplomatic Service, retired; *b* 2 June 1929; *m* 1954, Jean Faith Walker; one *s* two *d. Educ:* Christ's Hospital, Horsham; Sidney Sussex Coll., Cambridge (MA). Served Army, 4th Queen's Own Hussars, active service, Malaya, 1948–49; Pilot, Cambridge Univ. Air Squadron, 1951–52. Joined Sen. Br., Foreign Office, 1952; MECAS, Lebanon, 1953–54; Bahrain, 1954; Amman, 1954–56; FO, 1956–59; Stockholm, 1959–61; Cairo, 1961–64; Joint Services Staff Coll., Latimer, Bucks, 1964–65 (jssc); FO, 1965–67; Head of Chancery and Consul, Tunis, 1967–68; Asst Head, Oil Dept, FCO, 1969–71; Counsellor (Commercial), Caracas, 1971–73; Counsellor (Energy), Washington, 1973–78; Ambassador to Qatar, 1978–81; FCO Fellow, St Antony's Coll., Oxford, 1981–82; Consul Gen., and Dir Trade Promotion for S Africa, Johannesburg, 1982–87. Internat. business consultant, 1990–96. Donation Governor, Christ's Hosp., 1980–, Almoner 1989–95; Cttee Mem., Oxfordshire Sect., Christ's Hosp. Club, 1999– (Chm., 2002–04). *Recreations:* music, painting, history. *Address:* Orchard House, 22 Mills Close, Broadway, Worcs WR12 7RB. *Club:* Royal Over-Seas League.

BRASH, Dr Donald Thomas; Chairman, Huljich Wealth Management, since 2007; Director: ANZ National Bank, since 2007; Ocean Partners, since 2008; *b* 24 Sept. 1940; *s* of late Rev. Alan Anderson Brash, OBE; *m* 1st, 1964, Erica Beatty; one *s* one *d*; 2nd, 1989, Je Lan Lee; one *s*. *Educ:* Christchurch Boys' High Sch.; Canterbury Univ., NZ (BA Hist. and Econs 1961; MA 1st Cl. Hons Econs 1962); Australian Nat. Univ. (PhD 1966). IBRD, Washington, 1966–71; Gen. Manager, Broadbank Corp. Ltd, 1971–81; Managing Director: NZ Kiwifruit Authy, 1982–86; Trust Bank Gp, 1986–88; Gov., Reserve Bank of NZ, 1988–2002. MP (Nat.) NZ, 2002–07. Leader of Opposition, and Leader, Nat. Party, NZ, 2003–06. Hon. Dr Canterbury, 1999. NZIER-Qantas Econs Award, 1999. *Publications:* New Zealand's Debt Servicing Capacity, 1964; American Investment in Australian Industry, 1966. *Recreation:* growing kiwifruit. *Address:* Huljich Wealth Management (NZ) Ltd, Level 6, 12 Viaduct Harbour Avenue, Auckland, New Zealand.

BRASLAVSKY, Dr Nicholas Justin; QC 1999; a Recorder, since 2001; *b* 9 Feb. 1959; *s* of late Rev. Cyril and of Stella Braslavsky; *m* 1990, Jane Margolis; two *s* one *d. Educ:* Blackpool Grammar Sch.; High Pavement Grammar Sch., Nottingham; Univ. of Birmingham (LLB Hons 1979; PhD 1982). Called to the Bar, Inner Temple, 1983; in practice at the Bar, 1983–. *Address:* Kings Chambers, 36 Young Street, Manchester M3 3FT; 5 Park Square East, Leeds LS1 2NE; 3 Paper Buildings, Temple, EC4Y 7EU.

BRASNETT, John, CMG 1987; HM Diplomatic Service, retired; Deputy High Commissioner, Bombay, 1985–89; *b* 30 Oct. 1929; *s* of late Norman Vincent Brasnett and of Frances May Brasnett (*née* Hewlett); *m* 1956, Jennifer Ann Reid; one *s* one *d. Educ:* Blundells Sch.; Selwyn Coll., Cambridge (BA). Served Royal Artillery, 1948–49. Colonial Administrative Service, Uganda, 1953–65; retired from HM Overseas CS as Dep. Administrator, Karamoja District, 1965; entered HM Diplomatic Service, 1965; 1st Sec., OECD Delegn, 1968; Dep. High Comr, Freetown, 1970; FCO, 1973; Olympic Attaché, Montreal, 1975–76; Dep. High Comr, Accra, 1977–80; Counsellor (Econ. and Commercial), Ottawa, 1980–85. *Recreations:* reading, photography. *Address:* 8 Croft Way, Sevenoaks, Kent TN13 2JX.

BRASON, Paul, PPRP (RP 1994); RWA 2001; artist, portrait painter; President, Royal Society of Portrait Painters, 2000–02; *b* 17 June 1952; *s* of John Ainsley Brason and Audrey (*née* Wheldon). *Educ:* King James I Grammar Sch., Newport, IoW; Camberwell Coll. of Art. Work in many public and private collections incl. NPG, Royal Collection, Windsor Castle, Bodleian Library, Eton Coll., Mus and Galls Commn, Duke of Westminster, Goodwood House, etc. *Recreation:* early period houses and gardens. *Address:* Blakeleys House, Beechen Cliff, Bath BA2 4QT. *T:* 07799 417255. *Clubs:* Arts, Chelsea Arts.

BRASSE, Glenn Clifford; His Honour Judge Brasse; a Circuit Judge, since 2006; *b* 16 June 1949; *s* of late Robert Brasse and Iris Brasse; *m* 1974, Valerie Hauser, PhD; three *s*. *Educ:* Brighton, Hove and Sussex Grammar Sch.; LSE (LLB Hons). Called to the Bar, Middle Temple, 1972; Actg Stipendiary Magistrate, 1989–94; a Dep. Dist Judge, 1995; a Dist Judge, Principal Registry, Family Div., High Ct of Justice, 1995–2006; a Recorder, SE Circuit, 2002–06. *Publications:* (contrib.) Evidence in Family Proceedings, 1999; (contrib.) Family Law in Practice, 2006; contrib. numerous articles to Family Law. *Recreations:* sport (cycling, squash, mountain walking, ski-ing), classical guitar, drawing and painting, reading, cinema, opera. *Address:* Clerkenwell and Shoreditch County Court, The Gee Street Court House, 29–41 Gee Street, EC1V 3RE.

BRASSEY, family name of **Baron Brassey of Apethorpe**.

BRASSEY OF APETHORPE, 3rd Baron *cr* 1938, of Apethorpe; **David Henry Brassey,** Bt 1922; OBE 1994; JP; Vice Lord-Lieutenant of Northamptonshire, 2000–07; *b* 16 Sept. 1932; *er s* of 2nd Baron Brassey of Apethorpe, MC, TD, and late Lady Brassey of Apethorpe; *S* father, 1967; *m* 1st, 1958, Myrna Elizabeth (*d* 1974), *o d* of late Lt-Col John Baskervyle-Glegg; one *s*; 2nd, 1978, Caroline, *y d* of late Lt-Col G. A. Evill; two *d*. Commissioned, Grenadier Guards, 1951; Major, 1966, retired, 1967. JP 1970, DL 1972, Northants. *Heir: s* Hon. Edward Brassey [*b* 9 March 1964; *m* 2003, Joanna, *e d* of Julian Pardoe; one *s* one *d*]. *Address:* The Manor House, Apethorpe, Peterborough PE8 5DL. *T:* (01780) 470231. *Club:* White's.

BRATHWAITE, James Everett, CBE 2001; Chairman, South East England Development Agency, since 2002; *b* 31 March 1953; *s* of James and Louise Brathwaite; *m* 1977, Barbara Worby; one *s* four *d. Educ:* Sheffield Univ. (BSc Hons Physiol. and Zool.); Open Univ. (Dip. Competent Mgt). Graduate trainee acct, then Sales Trainer, Beecham Pharmaceuticals UK Ltd, 1975–79; a Product Manager, then a Mktg Manager, Antibiotic Mktg Strategy gp, Bayer Pharmaceuticals UK Ltd, 1979–82; founder and Chief Exec., VPS, subseq. Epic Multimedia Group plc, 1982–97; founder Dir and Chief Exec., XL Entertainment plc, 1997–; consultant and CEO, Future Gp Ltd, 1997–98; Chairman: Floella Benjamin Productions Ltd, 1997–2002 (Dir, 1997–2002); Renga Media Ltd, 2001–; Community Alerts Ltd, 2002–; Morgan Everett Ltd, 2003–; Splash FM; Brighton and Hove Radio Ltd; non-exec. Chairman: Business Link Sussex Ltd, 1995–2002; X-Tension Ltd, 1996–98 (Dir); Citizen TV Ltd, 1998–2002; BookLines plc, 2000–01; SEAL Ltd, 2000–; consultant and non-exec. Dir, Amplicon LiveLine Ltd, 1997–99; non-executive Director: Sussex TEC Ltd, subseq. Sussex Enterprise Ltd, 1994–2002; Nat. Business Angels Network, 2003–04; Dir, RSTV, 2007–. Advr on multimedia industry to DTI, 1989; Member: Caribbean Adv. Gp, FCO, 1998–2003 (Treas., 1998–2003); Nat. Business Link Accreditation Adv. Bd, 1999–2000; Small Business Council, 2000–04; Trade Partners UK, subseq. UK Trade and Investment, 2001–; Bd, Envmt Agency. Founder Director: Brit. Interactive Media Assoc. (formerly Brit. Interactive Video Assoc.), 1985–90 (Chm., 1989–90); Wired Sussex, 1996–2002; Dir, Internat. CD-i Assoc., 1993–96. Council Member: Univ. of Sussex, 1995–2001 (Mem. of Ct, 2003–); Univ. of Greenwich, 2003–; C&G, 2006–; Business Rep., Bd, Brighton & Hove Sixth Form Coll., 1995–99 (Chm., Finance Cttee, 1995–99). Board Member: Rockinghorse Charity, 1994–96; Arundel Fest., 1998–2002 (Chm., 1999–2002); Farnham Castle Trustees Ltd; Bd of Trustees, Public Catalogue Foundn. Mem., World Traders' Co., 2007–. Hon. Consul for S Africa in SE England, 2007–. Hon. Fellow, UC Chichester, 2003. Mem., BAFTA; MInstD. Hon. FCGI 2006. *Recreations:* the arts, music, ski-ing, watching cricket, football (Manchester United) and Rugby. *Address:* Church Farm House, Rectory Lane, Angmering, W Sussex BN16 4JU. *T:* (01903) 772648, *Fax:* (01903) 859863; *e-mail:* james@brathwaite.net. *Club:* Royal Commonwealth Society.

BRATHWAITE, Rt Hon. Nicholas (Alexander), Kt 1995; OBE 1975; PC 1994; Prime Minister of Grenada, 1990–95; *b* Carriacou, 8 July 1925; *s* of Charles and Sophia Brathwaite; *m*; three *s* one *d. Educ:* Univ. of W Indies (BEd 1967). Formerly: teacher; Sen. Tutor, then Principal, Teachers' Coll.; Chief Educn Officer, Min. of Social Affairs, Grenada; Regl Dir, Commonwealth Youth Prog., Caribbean Centre, 1974–83; Chm., Interim Council, Grenada, 1983–84; Leader, Nat. Democratic Congress, 1989–95; formerly Minister of: Finance; Home Affairs; Nat. Security; Foreign Affairs; Personnel and Mgt; Carriacou and Petit Martinique Affairs. *Address:* Villa A, St George's, Grenada.

BRATTON, Prof. Jacqueline Susan, DPhil; Professor of Theatre and Cultural History, Royal Holloway, University of London, since 1992 (Head of Drama and Theatre, 1994–2001); *b* 23 April 1945; *d* of Jack Stanley Bratton and Doris Nellie Bratton (*née* Reynolds); partner, Gillian Bush-Bailey. *Educ:* St Anne's Coll., Oxford (BA 1966; DPhil 1969). Lectr, 1969–83, Reader in English Literature, 1983–84, Bedford Coll., Univ. of London; Reader in Theatre and Cultural History, RHBNC, 1984–92. Series Editor, Shakespeare in Production, 1994–; Editor, Nineteenth Century Theatre, 1996–2001. *Publications:* The Victorian Popular Ballad, 1975; The Impact of Victorian Children's Fiction, 1981; (ed) Music Hall: Performance and Style, 1986; King Lear: a stage history edition, 1987; Acts of Supremacy, 1991; (ed) Melodrama: stage picture screen, 1994; New Readings in Theatre History, 2003; The Victorian Clown, 2006. *Address:* Department of Drama, Royal Holloway, University of London, Egham TW20 0EX.

BRATZA, Hon. Sir Nicolas (Dušan), Kt 1998; **Hon. Mr Justice Bratza;** a Judge of the High Court, Queen's Bench Division, since 1998; Judge of the European Court of Human Rights, since 1998 (Section President, 1998–2000, and 2001–07; Vice-President of the Court, since 2007); *b* 3 March 1945; *s* of late Milan Bratza, concert violinist, and Hon. Margaret Bratza (*née* Russell). *Educ:* Wimbledon Coll.; Brasenose Coll., Oxford (BA 1st Cl. Hons, MA). Instructor, Univ. of Pennsylvania Law Sch., 1967–68; called to Bar, Lincoln's Inn, 1969 (Hardwicke and Droop Schol.), Bencher, 1993; Jun. Counsel to the Crown, Common Law, 1979–88; QC 1988; a Recorder, 1993–98; UK Mem., European Commn of Human Rights, 1993–98. Mem., Adv. Council, British Inst. of Human Rights, 2004– (Gov., 1985–2004; Vice-Chm., 1989–98); Mem., Adv. Bd, British Inst. of Internat. and Comparative Law, 2006– (Mem., Bd of Mgt, 1999–2006). Member Editorial Board: European Human Rights Law Review, 1996–; European Law Review, 2004–. DU Essex, 2005; Hon. LLD Glasgow, 2007. *Publications:* (jtly) Contempt of Court, and Crown Proceedings, in Halsbury's Laws of England, 4th edn. *Recreations:* music, cricket. *Address:* European Court of Human Rights, Council of Europe, 67075 Strasbourg, France. *T:* 388412018, *Fax:* 388412730. *Clubs:* Garrick, MCC.

BRAUDE, Prof. Peter Riven, PhD; FRCOG; Professor and Head of Department of Women's Health (formerly Division of Women's and Children's Health), King's College London School of Medicine (formerly Guy's, King's and St Thomas' School of Medicine, King's College, London) (formerly Head of Department of Obstetrics and Gynaecology, United Medical and Dental Schools of Guy's and St Thomas' Hospitals), since 1991; Director, Centre for Pre-implantation Genetic Diagnosis, Guy's and St Thomas' Hospital NHS Trust, since 1999; *b* Johannesburg, 29 May 1948; *s* of Dr Barnett Braude and Sylvia (*née* Grumberg); *m* 1973, Beatrice Louise Roselaar; two *s*. *Educ:* Univ. of Witwatersrand (BSc 1968; MB BCh 1972); Jesus Coll., Cambridge (MA 1975; PhD 1981). DPMSA 1983; MRCOG 1982, FRCOG 1993. Lectr in Physiology and Pharmacology, Univ. of Witwatersrand Med. Sch., 1973; Demonstrator, Dept of Anatomy, Univ. of Cambridge, 1974–79; sen. house officer appts, St Mary's Hosp., London and Addenbrooke's Hosp., Cambridge, 1979–81; Sen. Res. Associate, Dept of Obstetrics and Gynaecol., Univ. of Cambridge, 1981–83; Registrar in Obstetrics and Gynaecol., Rosie Maternity Hosp., Cambridge, 1983–85; University of Cambridge: Clinical Lectr in Obstetrics and Gynaecol., 1985–88; MRC Clinical Res. Consultant, Clinical Sch., 1988–89; Consultant and Sen. Lectr, Dept of Obstetrics and Gynaecol., 1989–90; Clinical Dir for Women's Services, 1993–94, Dir, Assisted Conception Unit and Fertility Service, 1993–99, Guy's and St Thomas' Hosp. NHS Trust. Mem., HFEA, 1999–2004 (Inspector, 1991–99); Chm., Sci. Adv. Cttee, RCOG, 2004–07. Exec. Sec., Assoc. Profs of Obstetrics and Gynaecol., 1993–95. Mem., Med. Adv. Bd, Tommy's Campaign, 1993–99. Member, Editorial Board: Molecular Human Reproduction, 1992–98; Stem Cells, 2005–08. FMedSci 2006. *Publications:* Obstetric and Gynaecologic Dermatology, 1995, 2nd edn 2002; ABC of Subfertility, 2004; contribs to scientific jls on develt of the human embryo *in vitro*, assisted conception techniques, treatment of infertility, ethics and politics of new reproductive technologies and preimplantation diagnosis, human embryonic stem cells. *Recreations:* ski-ing, narrow boating, music, wine-tasting, gardening, Apple Macs. *Address:* King's College London Department of Women's Health, St Thomas' Hospital, Lambeth Palace Road, SE1 7EH. *T:* (020) 7188 4138; *e-mail:* peter.braude@kcl.ac.uk.

BRAUTASET, Tarald Osnes; Ambassador of Norway to the Court of St James's, 2000–05; *b* 28 Sept. 1946; *s* of Alv Brautaset and Birgit Osnes Brautaset; *m* 1975, Elisabeth Mohr; two *d. Educ:* Univ. of Oslo (MA Pol Sci.). Joined Norwegian Diplomatic Service, 1975: 2nd Sec., Abidjan, 1975–77; 1st Sec., Paris, 1977–80; Hd of Div., Min. of Foreign Affairs, Oslo, 1980–88; Counsellor, Mission to EU, Brussels, 1988–94; Dep. Dir Gen., 1994–96, Dir Gen., 1996–98, Dep. Sec. Gen., 1998–2000, Min. of Foreign Affairs, Oslo. Comdr, Order of St Olav (Norway), 2000. *Recreation:* gardening. *Address:* c/o Royal Norwegian Embassy, 25 Belgrave Square, SW1X 8QD.

BRAVO, Martin Maurice B.; *see* Brandon-Bravo.

BRAY, Angela Lavinia; Member (C) West Central, London Assembly, Greater London Authority, 2000–08; *b* 13 Oct. 1953; *d* of Benedict and Patricia Bray. *Educ:* Downe House, Newbury; St Andrews Univ. (MA Hons Medieval Hist.). Presenter, British Forces Broadcasting, Gibraltar, 1979–80; presenter, producer and reporter, LBC Radio, 1980–88; Hd, Broadcasting Unit, Cons. Central Office, 1989–91; Press Officer, Rt Hon. John Major's Leadership Campaign, Nov. 1990; Press Sec. to Chm., Conservative Party, 1991–92; Public Affairs Consultant, 1992–2000. Contested (C) E Ham, 1997. Pres., Kensington and Chelsea Cons. Pol Forum, 2000–03; Vice Pres., Hammersmith and Fulham Cons. Assoc., 2000–. *Recreations:* tennis, music, history, walking my dogs.

BRAY, Charles; artist, mainly in glass; *b* 26 Feb. 1922; *s* of Charles and Minnie Bray; *m* 1955, Margaret Ingram; four *s*. *Educ:* Goldsmiths' Coll., London. University of Sunderland: Principal Lectr in 3D Design, 1962–81; Hd, Glass and Ceramics, 1981. *Solo exhibitions*, including: Ancrum Gall., Fountain Fine Arts, Llandeilo, Carlisle City Art Gall.,

1991; Invetro Galerie, Hanover, 1992; Galerie H. D. Nick, Montpellier, 1993; Pilkington Glass Mus., 1994; Castlegate Gall., Cockermouth, 2001; Sultan Gall., Lancaster, 2002; work in *group exhibitions*, including: England Glass, The Hague, Eur. Glass Sculpture, Liege, Sculpteurs de Lumière, Nimes, 1993; Glass Objects, Art Centre Internat., Holland, 1994; British Glass, Nat. Glass Centre, Sunderland, 1998; Thompson Gallery: Aldermaston, 2000, 2001 and 2002; Stow on the Wold, 2000, 2001 and 2002; Marylebone High St, 2000, 2001 and 2002; work in *collections*, including: Turner Collection, Sheffield; Shipley Art Gall., Gateshead; Ulster Mus., Belfast; Kelvingrove Mus., Glasgow; Royal Scottish Mus., Edinburgh; Glass Mus., Ebeltoft, Denmark; Corning Mus. of Glass, NY. Fellow, Univ. of Sunderland, 1990. Fellow, Soc. of Glass Technol., 1970. FRSA 1965. *Publications:* A Dictionary of Glass, 1995, 2nd edn 2001; Ceramics and Glass: a basic technology, 2000; Glass Blowing, 2003, 2nd edn 2006. *Address:* Prospect House, Farlam, Cumbria CA8 1LA. *T:* and *Fax:* (01697) 746203; *e-mail:* cbglass@freeserve.co.uk.

BRAY, Prof. Kenneth Noel Corbett, PhD; FRS 1991; CEng; Hopkinson and Imperial Chemical Industries Professor of Applied Thermodynamics, 1985–97, now Emeritus, and Fellow of Girton College, 1985–97, Cambridge University; *b* 19 Nov. 1929; *s* of Harold H. Bray and Effie E. Bray; *m* 1958, Shirley Maureen Culver; two *s* one *d*. *Educ:* Univ. of Cambridge (BA); Univ. of Southampton (PhD); MSE Princeton; CEng; MRAeS; MAIAA. Engr in Research Dept, Handley Page Aircraft, 1955–56; University of Southampton, 1956–85: Dean, Faculty of Engrg and Applied Science, 1975–78; Head, Dept of Aeronautics and Astronautics, 1982–85. Vis. appt, Avco-Everett Res. Lab., Mass, USA, 1961–62; Vis. Prof., MIT, 1966–67; Vis. Res. Engr, Univ. of California, San Diego, 1975, 1983. *Publications:* on topics in gas dynamics, chemically reacting flows, molecular energy transfer processes and combustion. *Recreations:* walking, wood carving, gardening. *Address:* 23 De Freville Avenue, Cambridge CB4 1HW.

BRAY, Michael Peter; Partner, Clifford Chance (Chief Executive Officer, 2000–03); *b* 27 March 1947; *s* of William Charles Bray and Ivy Isobel (*née* Ellison); *m* 1970, Elizabeth Ann Harrington (marr. diss. 2007); two *d*. *Educ:* Caterham Sch.; Liverpool Univ. (LLB 1969). Joined Coward Chance, subseq. Clifford Chance, 1970, Partner, 1976; Global Head, Clifford Chance Finance Practice, 1995–2000. *Recreations:* golf, ski-ing, opera, theatre. *Address:* Clifford Chance, 10 Upper Bank Street, E14 5JJ. *T:* (020) 7600 1000; *e-mail:* Michael.Bray@cliffordchance.com.

BRAY, Maj.-Gen. Paul Sheldon, CB 1991; Paymaster-in-Chief and Inspector of Army Pay Services, 1989–92, now retired; *b* 31 Jan. 1936; *s* of Gerald Bray and Doris (*née* Holt); *m* 1958, Marion Diana Naden; one *s* two *d*. *Educ:* Purbrook Park County High Sch.; RMA Sandhurst; Southampton Univ. (BA 1995; MA 1998). ndc, psc†, sq, pfc. Commissioned RA 1956; served BAOR, Cyprus, UK; transf. RAPC 1965; served Malaya, N Wales, MoD, HQ UKLF, HQ Scotland, HQ NE District; OC RAPC Training Centre, 1976–77; NDC 1978; DS RMCS Shrivenham, 1979–82; MoD 1982; Chief Paymaster, Army Pay Office (Officers' Accounts), 1982–83; Comdt, Defence ADP Training Centre, 1983–85; Chief Paymaster ADP, RAPC Computer Centre, 1985–89. Trustee, Winchester Cathedral Trust, 2003–. Governor, King's Sch., Winchester, 1992– (Chm., 1998–). *Recreations:* music, theatre, travel, oenology, digging the allotment. *Address:* c/o Corps HQ, RAPC Worthy Down, Winchester, Hants SO21 2RG.

BRAY, Richard Winston Atterton; His Honour Judge Bray; a Circuit Judge, since 1993; *b* 10 April 1945; *s* of late Winston Bray, CBE and Betty Atterton Bray (*née* Miller); *m* 1978, Judith Elizabeth Margaret Ferguson; one *s* three *d*. *Educ:* Rugby Sch.; Corpus Christi Coll., Oxford (BA). Called to the Bar, Middle Temple, 1970; practised on Midland and Oxford Circuit; Asst Recorder, 1983–87; Recorder, 1987–93. *Recreations:* cricket, Real tennis, gardening. *Address:* c/o Midland Regional Director, PO Box 11772, 6th Floor, Temple Court, Bull Street, Birmingham B4 6WF. *Clubs:* MCC, I Zingari, Frogs.

BRAYBROOKE, 10th Baron *cr* 1788; **Robin Henry Charles Neville;** Lord-Lieutenant of Essex, 1992–2002; Hereditary Visitor of Magdalene College, Cambridge; Patron of three livings; farmer and landowner; *b* 29 Jan. 1932; *s* of 9th Baron Braybrooke and Muriel Evelyn (*d* 1962), *d* of William C. Manning; *S* father, 1990; *m* 1st, 1955, Robin Helen Brockhoff (marr. diss. 1974); four *d* (inc. twins) (and one *d* decd); 2nd, 1974, Linda Norman (marr. diss. 1998); three *d*; 3rd, 1998, Mrs Perina Fordham. *Educ:* Eton; Magdalene Coll., Cambridge (MA); RAC Cirencester. Commnd Rifle Bde, 1951; served 3rd Bn King's African Rifles in Kenya and Malaya, 1951–52. Dir of Essex and Suffolk Insurance Co. until amalgamation with Guardian Royal Exchange. Member: Saffron Walden RDC, 1959–69; for Stansted, Essex CC, 1969–72; Council of CLA, 1965–83; Agricl Land Tribunal, Eastern Area, 1975–. Chairman: Price Trust, 1983–95; Rural Develt Commn for Essex, 1984–90. Pres., Essex Show, 1990. DL Essex, 1980. DU Essex, 2000. *Recreations:* railway and airfield operating, photography, motorcycling. *Heir: kinsman* Richard Ralph Neville, *b* 10 June 1977. *Address:* Abbey House, Audley End, Saffron Walden, Essex CB11 4JB. *T:* (01799) 522484, *Fax:* (01799) 542134. *Clubs:* Boodle's, Farmers'.

See also Earl of Derby.

BRAYBROOKE, Rev. Marcus Christopher Rossi; President, World Congress of Faiths, since 1997 (Chairman, 1978–83 and 1992–99; Vice-President, 1986–97); *b* 16 Nov. 1938; *s* of late Lt-Col Arthur Rossi Braybrooke and Marcia Nona Braybrooke; *m* 1964, Mary Elizabeth Walker, JP, BSc, CQSW; one *s* one *d*. *Educ:* Cranleigh School; Magdalene College, Cambridge (BA, MA); Madras Christian College; Wells Theological College; King's College, London (MPhil). Curate, St Michael's, Highgate, 1964–67; Team Vicar, Strood Clergy Team, 1967–73; Rector, Swainswick, Langridge, Woolley, 1973–79; Dir of Training, Dio. of Bath and Wells, 1979–84; Hon. priest-in-charge, Christ Church, Bath, 1984–91; Exec. Director, Council of Christians and Jews, 1984–87; Preb., Wells Cathedral, 1990–93; Chaplain, Chapel of St Mary Magdalene, Bath, 1992–93; non-stipendiary priest, Marsh and Toot Baldon, Dorchester Team Ministry, Oxford, 1993–2005. Chm., Internat. Cttee, 1988–93, Internat. Interfaith Orgns Co-ordinating Cttee, 1990–93, World Congress of Faiths. Trustee: Interfaith Centre, 1993–2000 (Patron, 2001–); Internat. Peace Council, 1995–2000; Council for Parlt of World Religions, 1995–2001; Three Faiths Forum, 2001–; Patron, Utd Religions Initiative, 2001–; Vice-Patron, Deafway, 2002–. Peace Councillor, 2000–. Examng Chaplain to Bishop of Bath and Wells, 1984–88. Editor: World Faiths Insight, 1976–91; Common Ground, 1987–93. DD Lambeth, 2004. Sir Sigmund Sternberg Award for contributions to Christian-Jewish relations, 1992; Kashi Humanitarian Award, Kashi Ashram, Fla, 2001. *Publications:* Together to the Truth, 1971; The Undiscovered Christ of Hinduism, 1973; Interfaith Worship, 1974; Interfaith Organizations: a historical directory, 1980; Time to Meet, 1990; Wide Embracing Love, 1990; Children of One God, 1991; Pilgrimage of Hope, 1992; Stepping Stones to a Global Ethic, 1992; Be Reconciled, 1992; (ed with Tony Bayfield) Dialogue with a Difference, 1992; Love Without Limit, 1995; Faith in a Global Age, 1995; How to Understand Judaism, 1995; A Wider Vision: a history of the World Congress of Faiths, 1996; The Wisdom of Jesus, 1997; (contrib.) The Miracles of Jesus, 1997; (ed with Jean Potter) All in Good Faith, 1997; (contrib.) The Journeys of St Paul, 1997; The Explorers' Guide to Christianity, 1998; (ed with Peggy Morgan) Testing the Global Ethic, 1999; Christian-Jewish Dialogue: the next steps, 2000; Learn to Pray, 2001; (ed) Bridge of Stars, 2001; What Can We Learn from Hinduism, 2002; What Can We Learn from Islam, 2002; (ed) Lifelines, 2002; (ed) One Thousand World Prayers, 2003; 365 Meditations for a Peaceful Heart and a Peaceful World, 2004; (with Kamran Mofid) Sustaining the Common Good, 2005; A Heart for the World: the interfaith alternative, 2006; (ed) 365 Meditations and Inspirations on Love and Peace, 2006; contrib. to various theol books and jls incl. Theology, Modern Believing (formerly The Modern Churchman), The Tablet, Expository Times, Church Times, Church of England Newspaper, Faith and Freedom. *Recreations:* gardening, swimming, travel, photography. *Address:* 17 Courtiers Green, Clifton Hampden, Abingdon OX14 3EN. *T:* (01865) 407566.

BRAYE, Baroness (8th in line) *cr* 1529, of Eaton Braye, Co. Bedford; **Mary Penelope Aubrey-Fletcher;** DL; *b* 28 Sept. 1941; *d* of 7th Baron Braye and Dorothea (*d* 1994), *yr d* of late Daniel C. Donoghue, Philadelphia; *S* father, 1985; *m* 1981, Lt-Col Edward Henry Lancelot Aubrey-Fletcher, Grenadier Guards. *Educ:* Assumption Convent, Hengrave Hall; Univ. of Warwick. Pres., Blaby Cons. Assoc., 1986–; Dep. Pres., Northants Red Cross, 1983–92; Chm. School Cttee, St Andrew's Occupational Therapy School, 1988–93. Governor: St Andrew's Hosp., Northampton, 1978–; Three Shires Hosp., Northampton, 1983–. High Sheriff of Northants, 1983; JP South Northants, 1981–86; DL Northants 1998. *Co-heiresses: cousins* Linda Kathleen Fothergill [*b* 2 May 1930, *née* Browne; *m* 1965, Comdr Christopher Henry Fothergill, RN; two *s*; Theresa Beatrice Browne *b* 9 Aug. 1934]. *Address:* The Garden House, The Avenue, Flore, Northampton NN7 4LZ.

BRAYFIELD, Celia Frances; author; *b* 21 Aug. 1945; *d* of Felix Francis Brayfield and Helen (Ada Ellen) Brayfield; one *d*. *Educ:* St Paul's Girls' Sch.; Univ. of Grenoble. Feature writer, Daily Mail, 1969–71; TV columnist, Evening Standard, 1974–82; TV critic, The Times, 1984–88; columnist, Sunday Telegraph, 1988–90; feature writer, The Times, 1998–; contrib. to other pubns. Sen. Lectr in Creative Writing, 2005–06, Reader, 2007–, Brunel Univ. Mem., Cttee of Mgt, NCOPF, 1989–2006. Mem., Cttee of Mgt, Soc. of Authors, 1995–98; Dir, Nat. Acad. Writing, 1999–2003. *Publications:* Glitter: the truth about fame, 1985; Bestseller, 1996; Deep France, 2004; Arts Reviews, 2008; *fiction:* Pearls, 1986; The Prince, 1990; White Ice, 1993; Harvest, 1993; Getting Home, 1998; Sunset, 1999; Heartswap, 2000; Mister Fabulous and Friends, 2003; Wild Weekend, 2004. *Recreations:* family life, the arts. *Address:* c/o Curtis Brown Ltd, Haymarket House, 28/29 Haymarket, SW1Y 4SP. *T:* (020) 7396 6600. *Clubs:* Groucho, Chelsea Arts.

BRAYNE, Prof. Carol Elspeth Goodeve, MD; FRCP, FFPH; Professor of Public Health Medicine, University of Cambridge, since 2001; Fellow, Darwin College, Cambridge, since 1995; *b* 6 July 1957; *d* of Thomas and Audrey Brayne; *m* 1984, Paul Calloway; two *s* two *d*. *Educ:* Royal Free Hosp. Sch. of Medicine, London Univ. (MB BS, MD); London Sch. of Hygiene and Tropical Medicine (MSc). FFPH (FFPHM 1998); FRCP 2000. Lectr in Epidemiology, Cambridge Univ., 1991–2001. Hon. Consultant in Public Health Medicine: Cambs HA, 1991–2002; Cambs (formerly Hunts) PCT, 2002–. *Address:* Institute of Public Health, Forvie Site, Robinson Way, Cambridge CB2 0SR; Darwin College, Cambridge CB3 9EU.

BRAZAUSKAS, Dr Algirdas Mykolas; Prime Minister, Republic of Lithuania, 2001–06; *b* Rokishkis, Lithuania, 22 Sept. 1932; *s* of Kazimieras Brazauskas and Zofija Brazauskiene; *m* 1958, Julija Styraite-Brazauskiene; two *d*. *Educ:* Polytech. of Kaunas; Dr 1974. Construction work, Hydro-electric Power Stn, River Nemunas and other constructive orgns, 1956–65; Minister, Lithuanian SSR Bldg Materials Industry, 1965–67; Vice-Chm., Lithuanian SSR Planning Cttee, 1967–77; Dep., Supreme Council of Lithuanian SSR, 1969–90; Sec., 1977–88, First Sec., 1988–90, Central Cttee, Communist Party of Lithuania; Republic of Lithuania: Chm., Democratic Labour Party, 1990–93; Dep., Supreme Council and Parliament, 1990–93; Chm. Presidium, Supreme Council, 1990; Dep. Prime Minister, 1990–91; President, 1993–98; Chm., Social Democratic Party, 2001–. Hon. Dr: Vilnius Tech., Lithuania, 1994; Kiev, Ukraine, 1994. Royal Order of Seraphim (Sweden), 1995; Grand-Croix, Ordre de la Rose Blanche (Finland), 1995; Order of White Eagle (Poland), 1995; Order of Gen. San Martin (Argentina), 1996; Collar, Order of the Libertador (Venezuela), 1996; Gran Cordon de la Medallia de la Republica Oriental de Uruguay, 1996. *Publication:* Lithuanian Divorce, 1992. *Recreations:* yachting, hunting. *Address:* Turniškiu 30, 2016 Vilnius, Lithuania. *T:* (2) 778787.

BRAZIER, Helen; Head of RNIB National Library Service, since 2007; *b* 15 Feb. 1957; *d* of John David Brazier and Nancy (*née* Lloyd); partner, Paul Sutcliffe. *Educ:* Newnham Coll., Cambridge (MA); Sheffield Univ. (MA). MCLIP. Various posts, 1981–97, incl. UN Volunteer Librarian, 1990–92; Liby Services Dir, 1997–2001, Chief Exec., 2002–06, Nat. Liby for the Blind. Chm., Northern Br., Aslib, 1999–2002. Mem. Bd, Share the Vision, 2001–; Cttee Mem., Libraries for the Blind Section, IFLA, 2002–. *Publications:* contrib. various articles to jls. *Recreations:* walking, studio pottery, travel, reading. *Address:* RNIB, Far Cromwell Road, Bredbury, Stockport SK6 2SG. *T:* (0161) 355 2004, *Fax:* (0161) 355 2098; *e-mail:* helen.brazier@rnib.org.uk.

BRAZIER, Julian William Hendy, TD; MP (C) Canterbury, since 1987; *b* 24 July 1953; *s* of Lt-Col P. H. Brazier; *m* 1984, Katharine Elizabeth, *d* of Brig. P. M. Blagden; three *s* (incl. twins). *Educ:* Wellington Coll.; Brasenose Coll., Oxford (schol. in maths; MA); London Business Sch. Chm., Oxford Univ. Cons. Assoc., 1974. Charter Consolidated, 1975–84, Sec., Exec. Cttee of Bd, 1981–84; management consultant to industry, H. B. Maynard, internat. management consultants, 1984–87. Contested (C) Berwick-upon-Tweed, 1983. PPS to Minister of State, HM Treasury, 1990–92, to Sec. of State for Employment, 1992–93; an Opposition Whip, 2001–02; Opposition front bench spokesman: for work and pensions, 2002–03; for internat. develt and overseas trade, 2004–05; for transport (aviation and shipping), 2005–. Mem., Defence Select Cttee, 1997–2001; Vice Chm., Cons. Backbench Defence Cttee, 1993–97; Sec., Cons. Backbench Finance Cttee, 1990. Served 13 yrs in TA, principally with airborne forces. *Publications:* pamphlets on defence, economic policy, social security and family issues. *Recreations:* science, philosophy, cross-country running. *Address:* House of Commons, SW1A 0AA. *Club:* Travellers.

BRAZIER, Prof. Margaret Rosetta, OBE 1997; Professor of Law, University of Manchester, since 1990; *b* 2 Nov. 1950; *d* of Leslie Jacobs and Mary Jacobs (*née* Pickering); *m* 1974, Rodney John Brazier, *qv*; one *d*. *Educ:* Univ. of Manchester (LLB 1971). Called to the Bar, Middle Temple, 1973. University of Manchester: Lectr, 1971–83, Sen. Lectr, 1983–89, Reader, 1989–90, in Law; Dir of Legal Studies, Centre for Social Ethics and Policy, 1987; a founder Dir, Inst. of Medicine, Law and Bioethics, 1996. Chairman: Animal Procedures Cttee, 1993–98; Review of Surrogacy, DoH, 1997–98; Mem., Nuffield Council on Bioethics, 1995. Hon. QC 2008. *Publications:* Medicine, Patients and the Law, 1987, 2nd edn 1993; (jtly) Protecting the Vulnerable: autonomy and health care, 1991; (Gen. Ed.) Clerk & Lindsell on Torts, 17th edn 1995; (ed) Street on Torts, 8th edn to 10th edn 1998. *Recreations:* literature, theatre, cooking. *Address:* Faculty of Law, University of Manchester, Manchester M13 9PL. *T:* (0161) 275 3593.

BRAZIER, Dr Patrick Charles; Director, Contracts and Projects, British Council, Manchester, since 2007; *b* 2 Aug. 1960; *s* of Kenneth and Judith Brazier; *m* 1990, Dr Kathryn Louise Samantha Collyear; three *d. Educ:* Univ. of Liverpool (MSc (Microbiol.) 1981); PCL (PhD (Microbial Genetics) 1987). Consultant in Biotechnol., Inst. of Technol., Bandung, Indonesia, 1987–88; Sci. Policy Res. Officer, Royal Soc., London, 1989–90; British Council, 1990–: Project Officer, London, 1990–91; Dep. Dir, Uganda, 1991–94; Director: Swaziland, 1994–96; Durban, 1996–97; Dep. Regl Dir, Southern Africa, Johannesburg, 1997–2001; Director: Syria, 2001–03; Indonesia, 2003–04; Governance and Develt, Manchester, 2004–07. *Address:* British Council, Bridgewater House, 58 Whitworth Street, Manchester M1 6BB. *T:* (0161) 957 7000, *Fax:* (0161) 957 7079; *e-mail:* Patrick.Brazier@britishcouncil.org.

BRAZIER, Rev. Canon Raymond Venner; Vicar, St Matthew and St Nathanael, Kingsdown, Bristol, 1984–2005; Chaplain to the Queen, since 1998; *b* 12 Oct. 1940; *s* of Harold and Doris Brazier; *m* 1964, Elizabeth Dawn Radford; three *d. Educ:* Brockley County Sch., London; Bishop Otter Coll., Chichester; Wells Theol Coll. Assistant teacher: St Martin's County Secondary Boys' Sch., Shenfield, Essex, 1963–66; Kingswood Secondary Boys' Sch., Kingswood, Bristol, 1966–68; ordained deacon 1971, priest 1972; Curate, St Gregory the Great, Horfield, Bristol, 1971–75; Priest-in-charge, 1975–79, Vicar, 1979–84, St Nathanael with St Katharine, Bristol; also Priest-in-charge, St Matthew, Kingsdown, Bristol, 1980–84; Rural Dean of Horfield, 1985–91; Priest-in-charge, Bishopston, Bristol, 1993–97. Canon Emeritus, Bristol Cathedral, 2006 (Hon. Canon, 1994–2006); Hon. Chaplain, Colston's Girls Sch., Bristol, 1976–2005; Supplementary Chaplain, HM Prison Bristol, 2006. *Recreations:* reading, listening to music, watching sport, cooking, walking. *Address:* 51 Chalks Road, St George, Bristol BS5 9EP. *T:* (0117) 952 3209.

BRAZIER, Prof. Rodney John, FRHistS; Professor of Constitutional Law, University of Manchester, since 1992; *b* 13 May 1946; *s* of late Eric Brazier and Mildred Brazier (*née* Davies); *m* 1974, Margaret Rosetta Jacobs (*see* M. R. Brazier); one *d. Educ:* Buckhurst Hill County High Sch.; Univ. of Southampton (LLB 1968; LLD 2008). Called to the Bar, Lincoln's Inn, 1970, Bencher, 2000. University of Manchester: Asst Lectr, 1968–70; Lectr, 1970–78; Sen. Lectr in Law, 1978–89; Reader in Constitutional Law, 1989–92; Dean, Faculty of Law, 1992–94. Chm., Consumer Credit Appeals Tribunal, 1992–2006. Specialist Advr, H of C Public Admin Select Cttee, 2003–04. JP Manchester, 1982–89. FRHistS 1994. *Publications:* Constitutional Practice, 1988, 3rd edn 1999; Constitutional Texts, 1990; Constitutional Reform: reshaping the British political system, 1991, 3rd edn 2008; Ministers of the Crown, 1997; (jtly) Constitutional & Administrative Law, 8th edn 1998; articles in legal jls. *Recreations:* family, reading, television. *Address:* School of Law, University of Manchester, Oxford Road, Manchester M13 9PL. *T:* (0161) 275 3575.

BREADALBANE AND HOLLAND, Earldom of, *cr* 1677; dormant since 1995.

BREADEN, Very Rev. Robert William; Priest-in-charge, St Columba's, Portree, Isle of Skye, since 2007; *b* 7 Nov. 1937; *s* of Moses and Martha Breaden; *m* 1970, Glenice Sutton Martin; one *s* four *d. Educ:* The King's Hospital, Dublin; Edinburgh Theological Coll. Deacon 1961, priest 1962; Asst Curate, St Mary's, Broughty Ferry, 1961–65; Rector: Church of the Holy Rood, Carnoustie, 1965–72; St Mary's, Broughty Ferry, 1972–2007; Canon of St Paul's Cathedral, Dundee, 1977; Dean of Brechin, 1984–2007. OStJ 2001. *Recreations:* gardening, horse riding, Rugby enthusiast. *Address:* St Columba's Rectory, Somerled Square, Portree, Isle of Skye IV51 9EH. *T:* (01478) 613135; *e-mail:* ateallach@aol.com.

BREAKWELL, Prof. Glynis Marie, PhD, DSc; CPsychol, FBPsS; AcSS; Vice Chancellor and Professor, University of Bath, since 2001; *b* 26 July 1952; *d* of Harold and Vera Breakwell; partner, Colin Rowett. *Educ:* Univ. of Leicester (BA); Univ. of Strathclyde (MSc); Univ. of Bristol (PhD 1976); Nuffield Coll., Oxford (MA; DSc 1995). FBPsS 1987 (Hon. FBPsS 2006); CPsychol 1988. Prize Fellow, Nuffield Coll., Oxford, 1978–82; University of Surrey: Lectr in Psychol., 1981–87; Sen. Lectr, 1987–88; Reader, 1988–91; Prof., 1991–2001; Pro-Vice Chancellor, 1994–2001. Res. Advr to MAFF and Food Standards Agency, 1991–2001. Member: Coll. of Postgrad. Trng Assessors, ESRC, 1996–2001; CVCP/HEFCE Steering Gp on costing and pricing, 1997; HEFCE Leadership Governance and Mgt Cttee, 2004; Bd, Higher Educn Career Services Unit, 2007; Dir, UUK, 2005; Chm., HERDA-SW, 2006. Pres., Psychol. Section, BAAS, 1994–95. Mem., SW Sci. and Industry Council, 2006. Dir, New Swindon Co., 2002–07. Dir, Theatre Royal, Bath, 2001–06; Chm., Bath Fests, 2006. FRSA 1997; AcSS 2002. Hon. Prof., Univ. of Shandong, China, 2004. Hon. LLD Bristol, 2003. *Publications:* The Quiet Rebel, 1985; Coping with Threatened Identities, 1986; Facing Physical Violence, 1989; Interviewing, 1990; Coping with Aggressive Behaviour, 1997; The Psychology of Risk, 2007; *edited:* Threatened Identities, 1983; Human Behavior: encyclopedia of personal relationships, vols 17 and 18, 1990; Social Psychology of Political and Economic Cognition, 1991; Social Psychology of Identity and the Self Concept, 1992; (with D. V. Canter) Empirical Approaches to Social Representations, 1993; (jtly) Research Methods in Psychology, 2000; Doing Social Psychology, 2004; (jtly) Research Methods in Psychology, 2006. *Recreations:* racket sports, painting. *Address:* University of Bath, Bath BA2 7AY. *T:* (01225) 386262, *Fax:* (01225) 386626; *e-mail:* g.breakwell@bath.ac.uk. *Club:* Athenæum.

BREALEY, Mark Philip; QC 2002; barrister; *b* 26 Jan. 1960; *s* of Leonard and Shirley Brealey. *Educ:* Reading Univ. (LLB); University Coll. London (LLM). Called to the Bar, Middle Temple, 1984. *Publication:* (with M. Hoskins) Remedies in EC Law, 1994, 2nd edn 1998. *Address:* Brick Court Chambers, 7–8 Essex Street, WC2R 3LD. *T:* (020) 7379 3550. *Clubs:* Royal Ascot Racing; Tottenham Hotspur Football.

BREALEY, Prof. Richard Arthur, FBA 1999; Special Adviser to the Governor, Bank of England, 1998–2001; Professor of Finance, London Business School, 1974–98, Professor Emeritus, since 2001; *b* 9 June 1936; *s* of late Albert Brealey and of Irene Brealey; *m* 1967, Diana Cecily Brown Kelly; two *s. Educ:* Queen Elizabeth's, Barnet; Exeter Coll., Oxford (MA, 1st Cl. Hons PPE). Sun Life Assce Co. of Canada, 1959–66; Keystone Custodian Funds of Boston, 1966–68; London Business School: Prudential Res. Fellow, 1968–74; Sen. Lectr, 1972–74; Barclaytrust Prof. of Investment, 1974–82; Midland Bank Prof. of Corporate Finance, 1982–91; Tokai Bank Prof. of Finance, 1993–98; Dep. Prin., 1984–88; Governor, 1984–88. Director: Swiss Helvetia Fund Inc., 1987–96; Sun Life Assurance Co. of Canada UK Hldgs plc, 1994–97; Tokai Derivative Products, 1995–97. Trustee, HSBC Investor Family of Funds, 2005–. Pres., European Finance Assoc., 1975; Dir, Amer. Finance Assoc., 1979–81. *Publications:* An Introduction to Risk and Return from Common Stocks, 1969, 2nd edn 1983; Security Prices in a Competitive Market, 1971; (with J. Lorie) Modern Developments in Investment Management, 1972, 2nd edn 1978; (with S. C. Myers) Principles of Corporate Finance, 1981, (with S. C Myers and F. Allen) 9th edn 2008; (with S. C. Myers and A. J. Marcus) Fundamentals of Corporate Finance, 1995, 5th edn 2007; articles in professional jls. *Recreations:* ski-ing, rock climbing, horse riding. *Address:* Haydens Cottage, The Pound, Cookham, Berks SL6 9QE. *T:* (01628) 520143.

BREAM, Julian, CBE 1985 (OBE 1964); guitarist and lutenist; *b* 15 July 1933; *e s* of Henry G. Bream; *m* 1st, Margaret Williamson; one adopted *s*; 2nd, 1980, Isobel Sanchez. *Educ:* Royal College of Music (Junior Exhibition Award, 1945 and Scholarship, 1948). Began professional career at Cheltenham, 1947; London début, Wigmore Hall, 1950; subsequently has appeared in leading world festivals in Europe, USA, Australia and Far East. A leader in revival of interest in Elizabethan Lute music, on which he has done much research; has encouraged contemporary English compositions for the guitar. Formed Julian Bream Consort, 1960; inaugurated Semley Festival of Music and Poetry, 1971. DUniv Surrey, 1968. Villa-Lobos Gold Medal, 1976. *Recreations:* playing the guitar; cricket, table tennis, gardening, backgammon. *Address:* c/o Hazard Chase, 25 City Road, Cambridge CB1 1DP.

BREARLEY, Christopher John Scott, CB 1994; DL; Chairman, National Retail Planning Forum, since 2005; *b* 25 May 1943; *s* of Geoffrey Brearley and Winifred (*née* Scott); *m* 1971, Rosemary Stockbridge; two *s. Educ:* King Edward VII Sch., Sheffield; Trinity Coll., Oxford. MA 1964, BPhil 1966. Entered Ministry of Transport, 1966; Private Sec. to Perm. Sec., 1969–70; Principal, DoE, 1970; Sec. to Review of Develt Control Procedures (Dobry), DoE, 1973–74; Private Sec. to the Secretary of the Cabinet, Cabinet Office, 1974–76; Asst Sec., 1977; Under Sec., 1981; Dir of Scottish Services, PSA, 1981–83; Cabinet Office, 1983–85; Department of the Environment, 1985–97: Deputy Secretary: Local Govt, 1990–94; Local Govt and Planning, 1994–95; Local and Regl Develt, 1996–97; Dep. Sec., later Dir Gen., Planning, Roads and Local Transport, DETR, 1997–2000. Mem. (Lib Dem), Three Rivers DC, 2003–07. Sec., Review of Child Protection in the Catholic Ch, 2000–01. Member: Policy Cttee, CPRE, 2001–07 (Chm., Herts Br., 2005–); Chiltern Conservation Bd, 2005–07. Governor, Watford Grammar Sch. for Boys, 1988–2004 (Chm. of Govs, 1998–2004); Trustee, Watford Grammar Schs, 1992–2004. Trustee: Motability Tenth Anniv. Trust, 2001–; Motorway Archive Trust, 2001–; Gov., Oxfordshire and Bucks Mental Health Foundn Trust, 2008–. Freeman, City of London, 1998. DL Herts, 2007. Hon. Fellow, Sch. of Public Policy, Birmingham Univ., 2001–03. *Recreations:* crosswords, sudoku, vernacular architecture. *Address:* Middlemount, 35 South Road, Chorleywood, Herts WD3 5AS. *T:* (01923) 283848. *Clubs:* Oxford and Cambridge; New (Edinburgh).

BREARLEY, (John) Michael, OBE 1978; psychoanalyst; *b* 28 April 1942; *s* of late Horace and Midge Brearley; lives with Mana Sarabhai; two *c. Educ:* City of London Sch.; St John's Coll., Cambridge (MA; Hon. Fellow, 1998). Lectr in Philosophy, Univ. of Newcastle upon Tyne, 1968–71. Middlesex County Cricketer, intermittently, 1961–82, capped 1964, Captain, 1971–82; played first Test Match, 1976; Captain of England XI, 1977–80, 1981. Mem., British Psycho-Analytical Soc., 1991 (Associate Mem., 1985). Hon. LLD Lancaster, 1999; DUniv Oxford Brookes, 2006. *Publications:* (with Dudley Doust) The Return of the Ashes, 1978; (with Dudley Doust) The Ashes Retained, 1979; Phoenix: the series that rose from the ashes, 1982; The Art of Captaincy, 1985, 2nd edn 2001; (with John Arlott) Arlott in Conversation with Mike Brearley, 1986; articles for The Observer. *Club:* MCC (Hon. Life Mem.; Pres., 2007–08).

BREARLEY-SMITH, Anne Margaret; *see* Luther, A. M.

BREARS, Peter Charles David, FMA, FSA; writer and museums consultant, since 1994; *b* 30 Aug. 1944; *s* of Charles Brears and Mary (*née* Fett). *Educ:* Castleford Technical High Sch.; Leeds Coll. of Art (DipAD 1967). FMA 1980; FSA 1980. Hon. Asst, Wakefield City Museum, 1957–66; Keeper of Folk Life, Hampshire CC, 1967–69; Curator: Shibden Hall, Halifax, 1969–72; Clarke Hall, Wakefield, 1972–75; Castle Museum, York, 1975–79; Dir, Leeds City Museums, 1979–94. Founder, 1975, and Mem., 1975–, Group for Regional Studies in Museums, subseq. Social Hist. Curators Gp, 1975; Mem., Social History and Industrial Classification Wkg Party, 1978–; Pres., Soc. for Folk Life Studies, 1995–96. Sophie Coe Prize for food writing, Oxford Symposium for Food History, 1997. *Publications:* The English Country Pottery, 1971; Yorkshire Probate Inventories, 1972; The Collectors' Book of English Country Pottery, 1974; Horse Brasses, 1981; The Gentlewoman's Kitchen, 1984; Traditional Food in Yorkshire, 1987; North Country Folk Art, 1989; Of Curiosities and Rare Things, 1989; Treasures for the People, 1989; Images of Leeds, 1992; Leeds Describ'd, 1993; Leeds Waterfront, 1994; The Country House Kitchen, 1996; Ryedale Recipes, 1998; A Taste of Leeds, 1998; The Old Devon Farmhouse, 1998; All the King's Cooks, 1999; The Compleat Housekeeper, 2000; The Boke of Kervynge, 2003; A New and Easy Method of Cookery, 2005; Cooking and Dining in Medieval England, 2008; articles in Folk Life, Post-Medieval Archaeology, etc; museum guides and catalogues. *Recreations:* hill walking, drawing, cookery. *Address:* 4 Woodbine Terrace, Headingley, Leeds LS6 4AF. *T:* (0113) 275 6537.

BRECHIN, Bishop of, since 2005; **Rt Rev. John Ambrose Cyril Mantle,** PhD; FRHistS; *b* 3 April 1946; *s* of Rupert Mantle and Jean (*née* Bailey); *m* 1969, Gillian Armstrong; one *s* one *d. Educ:* Grove Acad., Broughty Ferry, Dundee; St Andrews Univ. (MTheol 1974); Dundee Coll. of Educn (PGCE 1975); Univ. of Kent (MA 1990); Leeds Univ. (PhD 1998). FRHistS 2001. Ordained deacon, 1969, priest, 1970; Curate: Broughty Ferry, 1969–71; All Saints, St Andrews, 1971–75; SS Philip and James, Edinburgh, 1975–77; Master, Royal High Sch., Edinburgh, 1975–77; Anglican Chaplain, St Andrews Univ., 1977–80; Priest-in-charge: Pittenweem, 1978–80; Elie and Earlsferry, 1978–80; Chaplain, Fitzwilliam Coll., Cambridge, 1980–86 (Fellow, 1984–86); Hon. Curate, Ascension, Cambridge, 1980–86; Staff Tutor and Vice-Principal, Canterbury Sch. of Ministry, 1986–94; Curate, Boxley with Detling, 1986–93; Adult Educn Advr, dio. Chichester, 1994–99; Archbishops' Advr for Bishops' Ministry, 1999–2005. *Publications:* Britain's First Worker-Priests, 2000; contribs to jls. *Recreations:* walking, travel, drawing, painting, film, jazz. *Address:* 5 Glamis Drive, Dundee DD2 1QG.

BRECHIN, Dean of; *see* Stewart, Very Rev. I. G.

BRECKENRIDGE, Sir Alasdair (Muir), Kt 2004; CBE 1995; MD; FRCP, FRCPE; FRSE; FMedSci; Chairman, Medicines and Healthcare Products Regulatory Agency, since 2003; Professor of Clinical Pharmacology, University of Liverpool, 1974–2002; *b* 7 May 1937; *s* of Thomas and Jane Breckenridge; *m* 1967, Jean Margaret Boyle; two *s. Educ:* Bell Baxter Sch., Cupar, Fife; Univ. of St Andrews (MB, ChB Hons 1961); Univ. of London (MSc 1968); Univ. of Dundee (MD Hons 1974). FRCP 1974; FRCPE 1988; FRSE 1991. House Phys. and Surg., Dundee Royal Infirm., 1961–62; Asst, Dept of Medicine, Univ. of St Andrews, 1962–63; successively House Phys., Registrar, Sen. Registrar, Tutor, Lectr and Sen. Lectr, Hammersmith Hosp. and RPMS, 1964–74. Non-exec. Dir, 1990–94, Vice Chm., 1993–94, Mersey RHA (Chm., Jan.–July 1993; Chm., Res. Cttee, 1987–91); Vice Chm., NW RHA, 1994–96 (Dir of R & D, 1994–96); Chm., NW Reg., NHS Exec., 1996–99. NHS Advr in Clin. Pharm. to CMO, 1982–94; Mem., NHS Adv. Cttee on Drugs, 1985–98 (Vice Chm., 1986–98). Committee on Safety of Medicines: Mem., 1982–2003 (Vice Chm., 1996–98; Chm., 1999–2003); Chm., Adverse Reactions Subgroup, 1987–92; Chm., Adverse Reactions to Vaccination and Immunisation Sub Cttee, 1989–92; Chm., Sub Cttee on Safety and Efficacy, 1993–95. Medical Research Council: Mem., 1992–96; Member: Clin. Trials Cttee, 1983–; Physiol Systems and Disorders Bd, 1987–91 (Vice Chm., 1990–91); AIDS Therapeutic Cttee,

1989– (Chm., 1993–). Royal College of Physicians: Mem. Council, 1983–86; Mem., Res. Cttee, 1983–88; Mem., Clin. Pharm. Cttee, 1990–95; Mem. Adv. Res. Cttee, 1993–98; Goulstonian Lectr, 1975; William Withering Lectr, 2006. British Pharmacological Society: Mem., 1972–; Foreign Sec., 1984–91; Chm., Clin. Section, 1988–93; Lilly Medal, 1994; Chm. Editl Bd, British Jl of Clin. Pharmacol., 1983–87. Member: Panel on Tropical and Infectious Disease, Wellcome Trust, 1984–87; Res. Cttee, British Heart Foundn, 1977–82; Steering Cttee for Chemotherapy of Malaria, WHO, 1987–91; Exec. Cttee, Internat. Union of Pharm., 1981–87; Central R&D Cttee, NHS, 1991–94; Jt Med. Adv. Cttee, HEFCE, 1995–2002 (Chm., 1998–2002); Cttee on Proprietary Medicinal Products of EU, 2001–02. Mem., Assoc. of Physicians, 1975–. Founder FMedSci 1998. Hon. DSc: St Andrews, 2005; Keele, 2005; Hon. LLD Dundee, 2005; Hon. MD Liverpool, 2007. Paul Martini Prize in Clin. Pharm., Paul Martini Foundn, 1974; Poulson Medal, Norwegian Pharmacol Soc., 1988. Exec. Editor, Pharmacology and Therapeutics, 1982–98. *Publications:* papers on clinical pharmacology in various jls. *Recreations:* hill-walking, golf, music. *Address:* Cree Cottage, Feather Lane, Heswall, Wirral L60 4RL. *T:* (0151) 342 1096. *Club:* Athenæum.

BRECKNOCK, Earl of; James William John Pratt; *b* 11 Dec. 1965; *s* and *heir* of Marquess Camden, *qv. Educ:* Eton.

BRECON, Dean of; *see* Marshall, Very Rev. G. O.

BREED, Colin Edward; MP (Lib Dem) Cornwall South East, since 1997; *b* 4 May 1947; *s* of Alfred Breed and Edith Violet Breed; *m* 1968, Janet Courtiour; one *s* one *d. Educ:* Torquay GS. ACIB. Junior, to Area Manager, Midland Bank plc, 1964–81; Manager, Venture Capital Fund, later Man. Dir, Dartington & Co. Ltd, 1981–91; Consultant, Corporate Finance, Allied Provincial Stockbrokers, 1991–92; Dir, Gemini Abrasives Ltd, 1992–97. Mem., GMC, 1999–. *Recreations:* golf, watching live sport. *Address:* 10 Dunheved Road, Saltash, Cornwall PL12 4BW.

BREEDON, Timothy James; Group Chief Executive, Legal & General Group plc, since 2006; *b* 14 Feb. 1958; *s* of Peter and Ruth Breedon; *m* 1982, Susan Hopkins; three *s. Educ:* Worcester Coll., Oxford (MA); London Business Sch. (MSc). Standard Chartered Bank, 1981–85; Legal & General Group, 1987–: Gp Dir (Investments), 2002–05; Dep. Chief Exec., 2005. Dir, Financial Reporting Council, 2004–07. *Address:* Legal and General Group plc, One Coleman Street, EC2R 5AA.

BREEN, His Honour Geoffrey Brian; a Circuit Judge, 2000–08; *b* 3 June 1944; *s* of Ivor James Breen and late Doreen Odessa Breen; *m* 1978, Lucy Bolaños (marr. diss. 1999); one *s* one *d. Educ:* Harrow High School. Articled to Stiles Wood & Co., Harrow, 1962–67; admitted Solicitor, 1967; Partner, Stiles, Wood, Head & Co., 1970–75; Sen. Partner, Stiles, Breen & Partners, 1976–86; Partner, Blaser Mills & Newman, Bucks and Herts, 1976–86; a Metropolitan Stipendiary Magistrate, subseq. Dist Judge (Magistrates' Courts), 1986–2000; Asst Recorder, 1989–93; Recorder, 1993–2000. Chairman: Youth Courts, 1989–93; Family Proceedings Courts, 1991–2000; Pres., Mental Health Tribunals, 2006–; Mem., Parole Bd, 2007–. Mem., British Acad. of Forensic Scis, 1989–. *Recreations:* classical guitar, reading, relaxing in Spain. *Address:* c/o Luton Crown Court, 7 George Street, Luton, Beds LU1 2AA.

BREEN, Mary; Headmistress, St Mary's School Ascot, since 1999; *b* Lancs, 4 Jan. 1964; *d* of Gerard Hayes and Mary Hayes; *m* 1988, James Breen; *Educ:* Univ. of Exeter (BSc Hons 1985); Univ. of Manchester (MSc 1987). Teacher of Physics: Wellington Coll., 1988–89; Abbey Sch., Reading, 1989–91; Eton Coll., 1991–92; St Mary's Sch. Ascot, 1992; Eton Coll., 1992–98, Head of Physics, 1996–98. *Recreations:* travel, cooking, reading, racing, walking, wine. *Address:* St Mary's School Ascot, St Mary's Road, Ascot, Berks SL5 9LL. *T:* (01344) 627788; *e-mail:* mbreen@st-marys-ascot.co.uk. *Club:* Athenæum.

BREEN, Prof. Richard James, PhD; FBA 1999; Professor of Sociology, Yale University, since 2007; *b* 25 Aug. 1954; *s* of Edward Francis Breen and Emily Breen (*née* Wolstenholme); *m* 1st, 1981, Eleanor Burgess (marr. diss. 1993); 2nd, 1997, Mary Christine O'Sullivan. *Educ:* St Thomas Aquinas Grammar Sch., Leeds; Fitzwilliam Coll., Cambridge (BA 1976; MA 1979; PhD 1981). Research Officer, then Sen. Research Officer, Economic and Social Research Inst., Dublin, 1980–91; Professor of Sociology: QUB, 1991–2000; European Univ. Inst., Florence, 1997–2001; Official Fellow, Nuffield Coll., Oxford, 2000–06. MRIA 1998. *Publications:* Understanding Contemporary Ireland, 1990; Social Class and Social Mobility in the Republic of Ireland, 1996; Social Mobility in Europe, 2005; numerous contribs to learned jls. *Recreations:* music, chess, reading, hill walking. *Address:* Department of Sociology, Yale University, PO Box 208265, New Haven, CT 06520–8265, USA. *T:* (203) 4323324.

BREEZE, Alastair Jon, CMG 1990; HM Diplomatic Service, retired; Counsellor, Foreign and Commonwealth Office, 1987–94; *b* 1 June 1934; *s* of Samuel Wilfred Breeze and Gladys Elizabeth Breeze; *m* 1960, Helen Burns Shaw; two *s* one *d. Educ:* Mill Hill School; Christ's College, Cambridge (Scholar; MA 1959). Served Royal Marines, 1953–55. Foreign Office, 1958; 3rd Sec., Jakarta, 1960–62; FO, 1962–64; 2nd Sec., seconded to Colonial Office for service in Georgetown, 1964–66; 1st Sec., Tehran, 1967–71; FCO, 1971–72; 1st Sec., Islamabad, 1972–75, Lagos, 1976–79; FCO, 1979–83; Counsellor, UK Mission to UN, NY, 1983–87. *Recreations:* sailing, ornithology. *Address:* La Vieille Boucherie, Puntous, 65230 France.

BREEZE, Dr David John, FSA, FSAScot, FRSE; Chief Inspector of Ancient Monuments, 1989–2005, Head, Special Heritage Projects, since 2005, Historic Scotland; *b* Blackpool, 25 July 1944; *s* of Reginald C. Breeze and Marian (*née* Lawson); *m* 1972, Pamela Diane Silvester; two *s. Educ:* Blackpool Grammar Sch.; University Coll., Durham Univ. (BA; PhD 1970). FSAScot 1970 (Hon. FSAScot 2005); FSA 1975; FRSE 1991; MIFA 1990 (Hon. MIFA 2006). Inspector of Ancient Monuments, Scotland, 1969–88; Principal Inspector, 1988–89. Vis. Prof., Durham Univ., 1994–; Hon. Professor: Edinburgh Univ., 1996–; Newcastle Univ., 2003–. Chairman: Hadrian's Wall Pilgrimage, 1989 and 1999; British Archaeol Awards, 1993–; Member: Hadrian's Wall Adv. Cttee, English Heritage, 1977–97; Internat. Cttee, Congress of Roman Frontier Studies, 1983–; President: South Shields Archaeol and Historical Soc., 1983–85; Soc. of Antiquaries of Scotland, 1987–90; Soc. of Antiquaries of Newcastle upon Tyne, 2008–; Vice-Pres., Cumberland and Westmorland Antiquarian and Archaeol Soc., 2003–April 2009. Trustee, Senhouse Museum Trust, 1985–. F.R.S.A. Corresp. Mem., German Archaeol Inst., 1979. Hon. DLitt Glasgow, 2008. *Publications:* (with Brian Dobson) Hadrian's Wall, 1976, 4th edn 2000; (with D. V. Clarke and G. Mackay) The Romans in Scotland, 1980; The Northern Frontiers of Roman Britain, 1982; Roman Forts in Britain, 1983, 2nd edn 2002; (ed) Studies in Scottish Antiquity, 1984; Hadrian's Wall, a Souvenir Guide, 1987, 2nd edn 2003; A Queen's Progress, 1987; The Second Augustan Legion in North Britain, 1989; (ed) Service in the Roman Army, 1989; (with Anna Ritchie) Invaders of Scotland, 1991; (with Brian Dobson) Roman Officers and Frontiers, 1993; Roman Scotland: frontier country, 1996, 2nd edn 2006; (with G. Munro) The Stone of Destiny, 1997; Historic Scotland, 1998; Historic Scotland: peoples and places, 2002; (ed with R. Welander and T.

Clancy) The Stone of Destiny: artefact and icon, 2003; (with Sonja Jilek and Andreas Thiel) Frontiers of the Roman Empire, 2005; Handbook to the Roman Wall, 14th edn, 2006; The Antonine Wall, 2006; Roman Frontiers in Britain, 2007; Edge of Empire: Rome's Scottish frontier, the Antonine Wall, 2008; (ed with Sonja Jilek) Frontier of the Roman Empire: the European dimension of a world heritage site, 2008; contribs to British and foreign jls. *Recreations:* reading, walking, travel. *Address:* Historic Scotland, Longmore House, Salisbury Place, Edinburgh EH9 1SH. *T:* (0131) 668 8724.

BREEZE, Stevan William; Chief Executive, BSI Group, since 2002; *b* 4 June 1951; *s* of William and Gwendoline Breeze; *m* 1973, Diana Julie Farthing; one *s* one *d.* Man. Dir, Tefal UK Ltd, 1984–87; Divl Dir, Polly Peck Internat., 1987–90; Divl Gp Man. Dir, BTR plc, 1990–98; Divl Man. Dir, Jarvis plc, 1999–2002. *Recreations:* tennis, ski-ing, travel. *Address:* BSI Group, 389 Chiswick High Road, W4 4AL; *e-mail:* stevanbreeze@yahoo.co.uk.

BREHONY, Dr John Albert Noel, CMG 1991; Chairman, Menas Associates, since 2001; *b* 11 Dec. 1936; *s* of Patrick Paul Brehony and Agnes Maher; *m* 1961, Jennifer Ann (*née* Cox); one *s* one *d. Educ:* London Oratory Sch.; Univ. of Durham (BA, PhD). Tutor, Durham Univ., 1960; Economist Intell. Unit, 1961; Res. Fellow, Jerusalem (Jordan), 1962; Lectr, Univ. of Libya, 1965–66; FO, 1966; Kuwait, 1967–69; Aden, 1970–71; Amman, 1973–77; Cairo, 1981–84; Counsellor, FCO, 1984–92; Dir of Middle East Affairs, 1992–99, Advr to Bd on ME Affairs, 1999–, Rolls-Royce PLC. Chm., Middle East Assoc., 1996–97; Pres., British Soc. of ME Studies, 2000–06; Mem. Council, Brit. Egyptian Soc., 2003–. Chairman: British Inst. at Amman for Archaeol. and Hist., 1992–99; Council for British Res. in the Levant, 2004–. Mem. Adv. Bd, London Middle East Inst., SOAS, 1999–; Internat. Advr to Gaza 2010 Project, Harvard Univ., 2005–. *Publication:* (ed with Ayman El-Desouky) British-Egyptian Relations from Suez to the Present Day, 2007. *Recreations:* Middle Eastern history, tennis, golf, opera. *Address:* (office) PO Box 444, Berkhamsted, Herts HP4 3DL. *Club:* Athenæum.

BREHONY, Rosemary; *see* Deem, R.

BREMER de MARTINO, Juan José, Hon. CVO 1975; Ambassador of Mexico to the Court of St James's, since 2004; *b* 22 March 1944; *s* of Juan José Bremer Barrera and Cristina de Martino Noriega; *m* Marcela Sánchez de Bremer Science; two *s. Educ:* Nat. Autonomous Univ. of Mexico (law degree 1966). Private Sec. to Pres. of Mexico, 1972–75; Dep. Sec., Ministry of the Presidency, 1975–76; Hd, Nat. Fine Arts Inst., Mexico, 1976–82; Dep. Sec. for Cultural Affairs, Ministry of Educn, 1982; Ambassador to Sweden, 1982; Mem., Mexican Legislature, 1985–88 (Pres., Foreign Affairs Cttee, Chamber of Deputies); Ambassador to: Soviet Union, 1988–90; FRG, 1990–98; Spain, 1998–2000; USA, 2000–04. Mem., Commn to Study the Future of Mexican-Amer. Relns, 1986–88. Pres., Cervantino Internat. Fest., 1983; guest lectr at US, Mexican and European univs. *Address:* 48 Belgrave Square, Belgravia, SW1X 8QR. *T:* (020) 7235 6515, (020) 7235 9165, *Fax:* (020) 7259 5028; *e-mail:* mexuk@easynet.co.uk.

BREMNER, Rory Keith Ogilvy; satirical impressionist and writer; *b* 6 April 1961; *s* of late Major Donald Stuart Ogilvy Bremner and Anne Ulithorne Bremner (*née* Simpson); *m* 1987, Susan Shackleton (marr. diss. 1994); *m* 1999, Tessa Campbell Fraser; two *d. Educ:* Wellington Coll.; King's Coll. London (BA Hons French and German 1983; FKC 2005; Hon. Fellow 2006). Television: Now... Something Else, 1986–87; Rory Bremner, 1988–92; Rory Bremner...Who Else?, 1993–99; Bremner, Bird and Fortune, 1999–2007 (also stage version, Albery, 2002); Between Iraq and a Hard Place, 2003. Opera translations: Silver Lake (Weill), 1999; Carmen (Bizet), 2001; trans. Brecht, A Respectable Wedding, Young Vic, 2007. British Comedy Award, 1993; BAFTA Award for Best Light Entertainment Performance, 1995, 1996; RTS Awards for Best Television Perf., 1995, 1999, 2000; Channel 4 political humorist of the year, 1998, 2000. *Publication:* (with John Bird and John Fortune) You Are Here, 2004. *Recreations:* cricket, opera, travel. *Address:* c/o Richard Stone Partnership, 2 Henrietta Street, WC2E 8PS. *T:* (020) 7497 0849. *Club:* Lord's Taverners.

BRENCHLEY, Dr Thomas Frank, CMG 1964; HM Diplomatic Service, retired; *b* 9 April 1918; *m* 1946, Edith Helen Helfand (*d* 1980); three *d. Educ:* privately and at Sir William Turner's Sch., Coatham; Merton Coll., Oxford (Modern History postmastership; Classical Hon. Mods, 1938; MA Philos. and Ancient Hist., 1946; Mem., Sen. Common Room, 1987; Hon. Fellow 1991; DPhil 2001); Open Univ. (BA 1986; BSc 1996). CS quals in Arabic, Norwegian and Polish. Served with Royal Corps of Signals, 1939–46; Major on Staff of Military Attaché, Ankara, 1943–45; Director, Telecommunications Liaison Directorate, Syria and Lebanon, 1945–46. Civil Servant, GCHQ, 1947; transferred to Foreign Office, 1949; First Secretary: Singapore, 1950–53; Cairo, 1953–56; FO, 1956–58; MECAS, 1958–60; Counsellor, Khartoum, 1960–63; Chargé d'Affaires, Jedda, 1963; Head of Arabian Department, Foreign Office, 1963–67; Assistant Under-Secretary of State, Foreign Office, 1967–68; Ambassador to: Norway, 1968–72; Poland, 1972–74; Vis. Fellow, Inst. for Study of Conflict, 1974–75; Dep. Sec., Cabinet Office, 1975–76. Dep. Sec. Gen. and Chief Exec., Arab-British Chamber of Commerce, 1976–83; Chairman: Institute for Study of Conflict, 1983–89; Res. Inst. for Study of Conflict and Terrorism, 1989–94; Pres., Internat. Inst. for Study of Conflict, Geneva, 1989–91. Dir, Center for Security Studies, Washington DC, 1988–90. *Publications:* New Dimensions of European Security (ed), 1975; Norway and her Soviet Neighbour: NATO's Arctic Frontier, 1982; Diplomatic Immunities and State-sponsored Terrorism, 1984; Living With Terrorism: the problem of air piracy, 1986; Britain and the Middle East: an economic history 1945–87, 1989; Aegean Conflict and the Law of the Sea, 1990; Britain, the Six-Day War and its Aftermath, 2005. *Recreation:* collecting (and sometimes reading) books. *Address:* 19 Ennismore Gardens, SW7 1AA. *Club:* Travellers (Chm., 1991–94).

BRENDEL, Alfred, Hon. KBE 1989; concert pianist since 1948; *b* 5 Jan. 1931; *s* of Albert Brendel and Ida Brendel (*née* Wieltschnig); *m* 1960, Iris Heymann-Gonzala (marr. diss. 1972); one *d; m* 1975, Irene Semler; one *s* two *d. Educ:* Studied piano with: S. Deželić, 1937–43; L. V. Kaan, 1943–47; also under Edwin Fischer, P. Baumgartner and E. Steuermann; composition with Artur Michl, harmony with Franjo Dugan, Zagreb. Vienna State Diploma, 1947; Premio Bolzano Concorso Busoni, 1949. Concerts: most European countries, North and Latin America, Australia and New Zealand, also N and S Africa and Near and Far East. Many appearances Vienna and Salzburg Festivals, 1960–. Other Festivals: Athens, Granada, Bregenz, Würzburg, Aldeburgh, York, Cheltenham, Edinburgh, Bath, Puerto Rico, Barcelona, Prague, Lucerne, Dubrovnik, etc. Many long playing records (Bach to Schoenberg) incl. first complete recording of Beethoven's piano works (Grand Prix du Disque, 1965). Cycle of Beethoven Sonatas: London, 1962, 1977, 1982–83, 1992–95; Copenhagen, 1964; Vienna, 1965, 1982–83; Puerto Rico, 1968; BBC and Rome, 1970; Munich and Stuttgart, 1977; Amsterdam, Paris and Berlin, 1982–83; New York, 1983; 14 Eur. and 4 N Amer. cities, 1992–96; Cycle of Schubert piano works 1822–28 in 19 cities, incl. London, Paris, Amsterdam, Berlin, Vienna, New York, Los Angeles, 1987–88. *Television (series):* Schubert Piano Music (13 films), Bremen, 1978; Alfred Brendel Masterclass, BBC, 1983; Liszt Années de Pèlerinage, BBC, 1986; Schubert

Last Three Sonatas, BBC, 1988. Hon. RAM; FRNCM 1990; Hon. RCM 1999; Hon. Mem., Amer. Acad. of Arts and Sciences, 1984; Korrespondierendes Mitglied, Bayer. Akad. der Wissenschaften; Hon. Fellow, Exeter Coll., Oxford, 1987; Hon. DMus: London, 1978; Sussex, 1980; Oxford, 1983; Warwick, 1991; Yale, 1992; Cologne, 1995; Exeter, 1998. Busoni Foundn Award, 1990; Hans von Bülow Medal, Kameradschaft der Berliner Philharmoniker eV, 1992; Gold Medal, Royal Philharmonic Soc., 1993; Ehrenmitgliedschaft der Wiener Philharmoniker, 1998; Léonie Sonnings Musikpris, Denmark, 2002; Ernst von Siemens Musikpreis, 2004. Chevalier des Arts et des Lettres, 2004; Orden pour le Mérite für Wissenschaften und Künste, 1991. *Publications:* Musical Thoughts and Afterthoughts (Essays), 1976; Music Sounded Out, 1990; Fingerzeig, 1996; Störendes Lachen während des Jaworts, 1997; One Finger Too Many, 1998; Kleine Teufel, 1999; Ausgerechnet Ich, 2000; Alfred Brendel on Music: collected essays, 2001; The Veil of Order: Alfred Brendel in conversation with Martin Meyer, 2002; Spiegelbild und schwarzer Spuk (poems), 2003; Cursing Bagels (poems), 2004; essays on music in: HiFi Stereophonie, Music and Musicians, Phono, Fono Forum, Osterreichische Musikzeitschrift, Gramophone, Die Zeit, New York Rev. of Books, Frankfurter Allgemeine, Neue Zürcher Zeitung, etc. *Recreations:* literature, art galleries, architecture, unintentional humour, "kitsch". *Address:* Ingpen & Williams, 7 St George's Court, 131 Putney Bridge Road, SW15 2PA. *T:* (020) 8874 3222.

BRENIKOV, Prof. Paul, FRTPI; Professor and Head of Department of Town and Country Planning, University of Newcastle upon Tyne, 1964–86, now Professor Emeritus; *b* 13 July 1921; *o s* of Pavel Brenikov and Joyce Mildred Jackson, Liverpool; *m* 1943, Margaret (*d* 1994), *e d* of Albert McLevy, Burnley, Lancs; two *s* one *d*. *Educ:* St Peter's Sch., York; Liverpool Coll.; Univ. of Liverpool (BA (Hons Geog.), MA, DipCD); Univ. of Sunderland (BA Fine Art 2006). War service with RNAS, 1941–46. Sen. Planning Officer, Lancs CC, 1950–55; Lectr, Dept of Civic Design, Univ. of Liverpool, 1955–64; Planning Corresp., Architect's Jl, 1957–63; Environmental Planning Consultant: in UK, for former Bootle CB, 1957–64; Govt of Ireland, 1963–67; overseas, for UN: Chile, 1960–61; E Africa, 1964; OECD; Turkey, 1968. Royal Town Planning Institute: Mem. Council, 1967–78; Chm., Northern Br., 1973–74. Member: Subject Cttee of UGC, 1975–86; DoE Local Plans Inspector's Panel, 1985–. FRSA 1979 (Chm., NE Region, RSA, and Council Mem., 1997–2000). *Publications:* contrib. Social Aspects of a Town Development Plan, 1951; contrib. Land Use in an Urban Environment, 1961; (jtly) The Dublin Region: preliminary and final reports, 1965 and 1967; other technical pubns in architectural, geographical, planning and sociological jls. *Recreations:* drawing, painting, listening to music, walking, reading. *Address:* 46 Mitchell Avenue, Jesmond, Newcastle upon Tyne NE2 3LA. *T:* (0191) 281 2773.

BRENNAN, family name of **Baron Brennan**.

BRENNAN, Baron *cr* 2000 (Life Peer), of Bibury in the co. of Gloucestershire; **Daniel Joseph Brennan;** QC 1985; a Recorder of the Crown Court, since 1982; a Deputy High Court Judge, since 1994; *b* 19 March 1942; *s* of late Daniel Brennan and Mary Brennan; *m* 1968, Pilar, *d* of late Luis Sanchez Hernandez; four *s*. *Educ:* St Bede's Grammar Sch., Bradford; Victoria University of Manchester (LLB Hons). President, University Union, 1964–65. Called to the Bar: Gray's Inn, 1967 (Bencher, 1993); King's Inns, Dublin, 1990; NI, 2001. Mem., Criminal Injuries Compensation Bd, 1989–97; Indep. Assessor to MoD and MoJ (formerly to Home Sec.) on miscarriages of justice, 2001–. Chm., Gen. Council of the Bar, 1999 (Vice Chm., 1998). President: Catholic Union of GB, 2001–; UK Consortium for Street Children, 2003–; Canning House, 2008– (Vice Pres., 2002–08). Chm., Caux Round Table, 2005–. FRSA 2000. Hon. LLD: Nottingham Trent, 1999; Manchester, 2000; Bradford, 2007. Delegate for GB and Ireland, Sacred Military Constantinian Order of St George, 2006–. Cross of St Raimond de Penafort (Spain), 2000; Order of Bernardo O'Higgins (Chile), 2005. *Publication:* (gen. ed) Bullen and Leake, Precedents of Pleading, 14th edn 2001 to 15th edn 2007. *Address:* Matrix Chambers, Gray's Inn, WC1R 5LN. *T:* (020) 7404 3447, *Fax:* (020) 7404 3448.

BRENNAN, Anthony John Edward, CB 1981; Deputy Secretary, Northern Ireland Office, 1982–87; *b* 24 Jan. 1927; 2nd *s* of late Edward Joseph Brennan and Mabel Brennan (*née* West); *m* 1958, Pauline Margery, *d* of late Percy Clegg Lees and Mildred (*née* Middleton); two *s* one *d*. *Educ:* St Joseph's; London Sch. of Economics (Leverhulme Schol.). BSc Econ 1946. Served Army, RA, RAEC, 1946–49; Asst Principal, Home Office, 1949; Private Sec. to Parly Under-Sec. of State, 1953–54; Principal, 1954; Principal Private Sec. to Home Sec., 1963; Asst Sec., 1963; Asst Under Sec. of State, Criminal Dept, 1971–75, Immigration Dept, 1975–77; Dep. Under-Sec. of State, Home Office, 1977–82. Sec., Royal Commn on Penal System, 1964–66; Mem., UN Cttee on Crime Prevention and Control, 1979–84. *Recreations:* reading, poetry, music; past Chm. of, and active in, athletics, dramatic and bridge clubs. *Club:* Athenæum.

BRENNAN, Archibald Orr, (Archie), OBE 1981; designer, weaver, teacher and lecturer, since 1984; *b* 7 Dec. 1931; *s* of James and Jessie Brennan; *m* 1956, Elizabeth Hewitt Carmichael (marr. diss.); three *d*. *Educ:* Boroughmuir Sch., Edinburgh; Edinburgh College of Art (DA). Training as tapestry weaver/student, 1947–62; Lectr, Edinburgh College of Art, 1962–78; Dir, Edin. Tapestry Co., 1962–77; co-ordinator/designer of all embellishment, new Nat. Parlt Bldg, PNG, 1978–84; Artist in residence, 1977, established production dept, 1978–84, Nat. Arts Sch., PNG. Pres., Soc. of Scottish Artists, 1977–78; Chm., British Craft Centre, 1977–78; travelling lectr, UK, USA, Canada, Australia, PNG, 1962–. Fellow, ANU, 1974–75. *Publications:* articles in various jls.

BRENNAN, Denis; Ceremonial Officer, Cabinet Office, since 2005; *b* 4 Nov. 1951; *s* of Michael and Mary Brennan; *m* 1975, Ursula Mary Brennan, *qv*. *Educ:* Gonville and Caius Coll., Cambridge (BA Philos. 1973). Ministry of Defence, 1973–94: Private Sec. to Parly Sec., RAF, 1977–78; policy posts incl. secondment to Cabinet Office, 1978–84; Private Sec. to Sec. of State, 1984–86; Head: Air Staff Secretariat, 1987–90; Housing Task Force, 1990–94; Cabinet Office: Hd, Infrastructure, Defence and Overseas Secretariat, 1994–2002; on loan to DEFRA, 2003–04. *Address:* Ceremonial Secretariat, Cabinet Office, 35 Great Smith Street, SW1P 3BQ.

BRENNAN, Hon. Sir (Francis) Gerard, AC 1988; KBE 1981; Non-Permanent Judge, Court of Final Appeal of Hong Kong, since 2000; Chancellor, University of Technology, Sydney, 1998–2004; *b* 22 May 1928; *s* of Hon. Mr Justice (Frank Tenison) Brennan and Mrs Gertrude Brennan; *m* 1953, Dr Patricia (*née* O'Hara); three *s* four *d*. *Educ:* Christian Brothers Coll., Rockhampton, Qld; Downlands Coll., Toowoomba, Qld; Univ. of Qld (BA, LLB). Called to the Queensland Bar, 1951; QC (Australia) 1965. Judge, Aust. Indust. Court, and Additional Judge of Supreme Court of ACT, 1976–81; Judge, Fed. Court of Australia, 1977–81; Justice of the High Court, 1981–95; Chief Justice of Australia, 1995–98; Foundn Scientia Prof. of Law, Univ. of NSW, 1998–99; external Judge, Supreme Court, Republic of Fiji, 1999–2000. President: Admin. Appeals Tribunal, 1976–79; Admin. Review Council, 1976–79; Bar Assoc. of Qld, 1974–76; Aust. Bar Assoc., 1975–76; National Union of Aust. Univ. Students, 1949. Member: Exec. Law Council of Australia, 1974–76; Aust. Law Reform Commn, 1975–77. Hon. LLD: TCD, 1988; Queensland, 1996; ANU, 1996; Melbourne, 1998; UTS, 1998; NSW, 2005; Hon. DLitt Central Queensland, 1996; DUniv: Griffith, 1996; UTS, 2005. *Address:* (office) Suite 3003, Piccadilly Tower, 133 Castlereagh Street, Sydney, NSW 2000, Australia. *T:* (2) 92618704, *Fax:* (2) 92618113. *Club:* Australian (Sydney).

BRENNAN, John James Edward, OBE 1990; Chairman, Associated Textiles Co. Ltd, Bradford, since 1970; Vice Lord-Lieutenant, West Yorkshire, since 2004; *b* 14 Nov. 1941; *s* of Joseph Edward Brennan, KSG and Mary Jane Brennan; *m* 1984, Claire Elizabeth Linnell; two *s* one *d*. *Educ:* Ampleforth; Keble Coll., Oxford. Mem. (C), Bradford CC, 1965–68. Chm., Bradford Conservative Fedn, 1978–98. Yorkshire Agricultural Society: Mem. Council, 1997–; Chm., Finance Cttee, 2001–06; Chm., Audit and Investment Cttee, 2006–; Trustee, 2006–. Chm., British Wool Fedn, 1996–98. Pres., Leeds Business Br., RNLI, 2003–; Vice Pres., Hosp. Heartbeat Appeal, Leeds, 2008–. DL 1991, High Sheriff, 1998–99, W Yorks. *Recreations:* cricket (watching), golf (playing), French property (restoring). *Address:* Lieutenancy Office, Bowcliffe Hall, Bramham, W Yorks LS23 6LP. *Clubs:* White's; Alwoodley Golf (Chm., 2006–), Swinley Forest Golf.

BRENNAN, Kevin Denis; MP (Lab) Cardiff West, since 2001; a Parliamentary Secretary and Minister for the Third Sector, Cabinet Office, and Minister for the East Midlands, since 2008; *b* 16 Oct. 1959; *s* of Michael John Brennan and Beryl Marie Brennan (*née* Evans); *m* 1988, Amy Lynn Wack; one *d*. *Educ:* St Alban's RC Comprehensive Sch., Pontypool; Pembroke Coll., Oxford (BA); UC, Cardiff (PGCE); Univ. of Glamorgan (MSc). Volunteer organiser/news ed., Cwmbran Community Press, 1982–84; Hd, Econs and Business Studies, Radyr Comprehensive Sch., 1985–94; Res. Officer for Rhodri Morgan, MP, 1995–2000; Special Advr to First Minister, Nat. Assembly for Wales, 2000. An Asst Govt Whip, 2005–06; a Lord Comr of HM Treasury (Govt Whip), 2006–07; Parly Under-Sec. of State, DCSF, 2007–08. *Recreations:* Rugby (watching now), music (Mem., parly rock gp MP4). *Address:* House of Commons, SW1A 0AA; Transport House, 1 Cathedral Road, Cardiff CF11 9SD. *Club:* Canton Labour (Cardiff).

BRENNAN, Dame Maureen, DBE 2005; Headteacher, Barr Beacon Language College, Walsall, since 2007; *b* 26 March 1954; *d* of Joseph and Elizabeth Eddy; *m* 1989, Denis Brennan; one *s*. *Educ:* St Agnes' RC Grammar Sch. for Girls; Newman Coll., Birmingham (BEd). Teacher, St Chad's RC Comprehensive Sch., Birmingham, 1976–80; Hd of Dept, Ladywood Sch., 1980–85; Staff Develt Tutor, Equal Opportunities Co-ordinator, Birmingham Adv. Service, 1985–90; Dep. Hd, Great Barr Sch., 1990–2000; Principal, Hillcrest Sch. and Community Coll., Dudley, 2000–07. *Address:* Barr Beacon Language College, Old Hall Lane, Aldridge, W Midlands WS9 0RF. *T:* (0121) 366 6600, *Fax:* (0121) 366 6876; *e-mail:* mbrennan@barrbeacon.walsall.sch.uk. *Club:* Lichfield RFU.

BRENNAN, Timothy Roger; QC 2001; a Recorder, since 2000; a Deputy High Court Judge, since 2008; *b* 11 April 1958. *Educ:* Olchfa Sch., Swansea; Balliol Coll., Oxford (BCL, MA). Called to the Bar, Gray's Inn, 1981 (Atkin Schol. 1981; Bencher, 2006); Addnl Jun. Counsel to Inland Revenue (Common Law), 1991–97, Jun. Counsel, 1997–2001; Asst Recorder, 1997–2000; a Judge of the Employment Appeal Tribunal, 2002–04. Mem., Gen. Council of the Bar, 1987, 1988 (Mem., Conduct Cttee, 1989, 1995–98 and 2005; Vice-Chm., Complaints Cttee, 2006–). *Publications:* contribs to various tech. legal pubns. *Address:* Devereux Chambers, Devereux Court, WC2R 3JH. *T:* (020) 7353 7534.

BRENNAN, Ursula Mary; Second Permanent Under-Secretary of State, Ministry of Defence, since 2008; *b* 28 Oct. 1952; *d* of Philip and Mary Burns; *m* 1975, Denis Brennan, *qv*. *Educ:* Univ. of Kent at Canterbury (BA Hons English and Amer. Lit). ILEA, 1973–75; Department of Health and Social Security, later of Social Security, 1975–2001; Head, Disability Benefits Policy, 1990–93; Dir, IT Services Agency, 1993–95; Dir, Change Management, Benefits Agency, 1995–97; Gp Dir, Working Age Services, 1997–2001; Gp Dir, Working Age and Children Strategy, DWP, 2001–04; Dir Gen., Natural Resources and Rural Affairs, DEFRA, 2004–05; Chief Exec., Office for Criminal Justice Reform, 2006–08; Dir Gen., Corporate Performance, MoJ, 2008. *Address:* Ministry of Defence, Whitehall, SW1A 2HB.

BRENNER, Sydney, CH 1987; DPhil; FRCP; FRS 1965; Distinguished Research Professor, Salk Institute, La Jolla, California, since 2001; Member of Scientific Staff, MRC, 1957–92; Fellow of King's College, Cambridge, since 1959; *b* Germiston, South Africa, 13 Jan. 1927; *s* of Morris Brenner and Lena (*née* Blacher); *m* 1952, May Woolf Balkind; one *s* two *d* (and one step *s*). *Educ:* Germiston High School; University of the Witwatersrand, S Africa; Oxford University (Hon. Fellow, Exeter Coll., 1985). MSc 1947, MB, BCh 1951, Univ. of the Witwatersrand; DPhil Oxon, 1954; FRCP 1979; Hon. FRCPath 1990. Director: MRC Lab. of Molecular Biol., Cambridge, 1979–86; MRC Molecular Genetics Unit, Cambridge, 1986–92; Mem., Scripps Res. Inst., La Jolla, 1992–94. Pres. and Dir of Res., Molecular Scis Inst., Berkeley, Calif, 1996–2001. Mem., MRC, 1978–82, 1986–90. Hon. Prof. of Genetic Medicine, Cambridge Univ., 1989–97. Carter-Wallace Lectr, Princeton, 1966, 1971; Gifford Lectr, Glasgow, 1978–79; Dunham Lectr, Harvard, 1984; Croonian Lectr, Royal Soc., 1986. External Scientific Mem., Max-Planck Soc., 1988; Mem., Academia Europaea, 1989; Foreign Hon. Member, American Academy of Arts and Sciences, 1965; Foreign Associate: Nat. Acad. of Sciences, USA, 1977; Royal Soc. of S Africa, 1983; Académie des Sciences, Paris, 1992; Mem., Deutsche Akademie der Naturforscher, Leopoldina, 1975 (Gregor Mendel Medal, 1970); Foreign Member: Amer. Philosophical Soc., 1979; Real Academia de Ciencias, Spain, 1985; Correspondant Scientifique Emerite, Institut National de la Santé et de la Recherche Médicale, Paris, 1991; Hon. Member: Chinese Soc. of Genetics, 1989; Assoc. of Physicians of GB and Ireland, 1991; Alpha Omega Alpha Honor Med. Soc., 1994; German Soc. Cell Biol., 1999. Fellow, Amer. Acad. of Microbiol., 1996. Hon. FRSE 1979. Hon. FIASc 1989; Hon. Fellow, UCL, 2005. Hon. DSc: Dublin, 1967; Witwatersrand, 1972; Chicago, 1976; London, 1982; Leicester, 1983; Oxford, 1985; Rockefeller, 1996; Columbia, 1997; La Trobe, 1999; Harvard, 2002; Yale, 2003; BC, 2004; Hon. LLD: Glasgow, 1981; Cambridge, 2001; Hon. DLitt Nat. Univ. of Singapore, 1995; Dr rer. nat. *hc* Jena, 1998; Hon. Dr Oporto, 2003. Warren Triennial Prize, 1968; William Bate Hardy Prize, Cambridge Philosophical Soc., 1969; (jtly) Lasker Award for Basic Medical Research, 1971; Royal Medal, Royal Soc., 1974; (jtly) Prix Charles Leopold Mayer, French Acad. of Science, 1975; Gairdner Foundn Annual Award, 1978; Krebs Medal, FEBS, 1980; CIBA Medal, Biochem. Soc., 1981; Feldberg Foundn Prize, 1983; Neil Hamilton Fairley Medal, RCP, 1985; Rosenstiel Award, Brandeis Univ., 1986; Prix Louis Jeantet de Médecine, Switzerland, 1987; Genetics Soc. of America Medal, 1987; Harvey Prize, Technion-Israel Inst. of Technol., 1987; Hughlings Jackson Medal, RSocMed, 1987; Waterford Bio-Medical Sci. Award, Res. Inst. of Scripps Clinic, USA, 1988; Kyoto Prize, Inamori Foundn, 1990; Gairdner Foundn Internat. Award, Canada, 1991; Copley Medal, Royal Soc., 1991; King Faisal Internat. Prize for Science, King Faisal Foundn, Saudi Arabia, 1992; Bristol-Myers Squibb Award for Dist. Achievement in Neurosci. Res., NY, 1992; Albert Lasker Award for Special Achievement, 2000; Novartis Drew Award, 2001; (jtly) Nobel Prize for Physiology or Medicine, 2002; Dist. Service Award, Miami Nature Biotechnol., 2002; March of Dimes Prize, 2002; Dan David Prize, 2002; Clinical Sci. Prize, UCL, 2003; Scientist of the Year, ARCS Foundn, Calif, 2004;

Rocovich Gold Medal, 2004; Phillip Tobias Lect. Medal, 2004; (jtly) Nat. Sci. Award, Singapore, 2004. Holds various foreign orders and decorations. *Publications:* papers in scientific journals. *Recreation:* rumination. *Address:* King's College, Cambridge CB2 1ST.

BRENT, Prof. Leslie Baruch, FIBiol; Professor Emeritus, University of London, since 1990; *b* Köslin, Germany, 5 July 1925; *s* of Charlotte and Arthur Baruch; arrived UK in Kindertransport, 1938; *m* 1st, 1954, Joanne Elisabeth Manley (marr. diss. 1991); one *s* two *d*; 2nd, 1991, Carol Pamela Martin. *Educ:* Bunce Court Sch., Kent; Birmingham Central Technical Coll.; Univ. of Birmingham; UCL. BSc Birmingham, PhD London; FIBiol 1964. Laboratory technician, 1941–43; Army service, 1943–47, Captain; Lectr, Dept of Zoology, UCL, 1954–62; Rockefeller Res. Fellow, Calif Inst. of Technology, 1956–57; Res. scientist, Nat. Inst. for Med. Res., 1962–65; Prof. of Zoology, Univ. of Southampton, 1965–69; Prof. of Immunology, St Mary's Hosp. Med. Sch., London, 1969–90. European Editor, Transplantation, 1963–68; Gen. Sec., British Transplantation Soc., 1971–75; Pres., The Transplantation Society, 1976–78; Chairman: Wessex Br., Inst. of Biol., 1966–68; Organising Cttee, 9th Internat. Congress of The Transplantation Soc., 1978–82; Fellowships Cttee, Inst. of Biol., 1982–85; Art Cttee, St Mary's Hosp. Med. Sch., 1988–92. Pres., Guild of Undergrads, Birmingham Univ., 1950–51. Chairman: Haringey Community Relations Council, 1979–80; Haringey SDP, 1981–83. Governor: Creighton Sch., 1974–79; Yerbury Sch., 1999–2006; Mem., Islington Schs Ind. Appeals Panel, 2001–06. Trustee, British Scholarship Trust for Former Yugoslavian Territories, 1997–. Mem., Eur. Acad. for Scis and Arts (Salzburg), 2002. Hon. MRCP 1986; Hon. Mem., Koszalin Regl Chamber of Physicians (Poland), 2005. Hon. Mem., British Transplantation Soc., 1988; hon. mem. of several foreign scientific socs. FZS. Vice-Chancellor's Prize, Birmingham Univ., 1951; Scientific Medal, Zool Soc., 1963; Peter Medawar Medal and Prize, Internat. Transplantation Soc., 1994. Played hockey for UAU and Staffs, 1949–51. Co-editor, Immunology Letters, 1983–90. *Publications:* (ed jtly) Organ Transplantation: current clinical and immunological concepts, 1989; History of Transplantation Immunology, 1997; articles in scientific and med. jls on transplantation immunology. *Recreations:* music, fell-walking, novels, politics. *Address:* 30 Hugo Road, N19 5EU.

BRENT, Michael Leon; QC 1983; a Recorder, 1990–2000; a Deputy High Court Judge, 1994–2000; *b* 8 June 1936; *m* 1965, Rosalind Keller; two *d*. *Educ:* Manchester Grammar Sch.; Manchester Univ. (LLB Hons). Called to the Bar, Gray's Inn, 1961; practised on: Northern Circuit, 1961–67 (Circuit Junior, 1964); Midland and Oxford Circuit, 1967–2000. Mem. Bd, Criminal Injuries Compensation Appeals Panel, 1999–2002. *Address:* 9 Gough Square, EC4A 3DG.

BRENT, Prof. Richard Peirce, PhD, DSc; Federation Fellow, Mathematical Sciences Institute, Australian National University, since 2005; *b* 20 April 1946; *s* of Oscar and Nancy Brent; *m* 1969, Erin O'Connor (*d* 2005); two *s*; *m* 2007, Judy-anne Osborn. *Educ:* Melbourne Grammar Sch.; Monash Univ. (BSc 1968; DSc 1981); Stanford Univ. (PhD 1971). FAA 1982; FIEEE 1991. IBM Res., Yorktown Heights, NY, 1971–72; Australian National University: Res. Fellow, 1972–73; Fellow, 1973–76; Sen. Fellow, 1976–78; Foundation Prof. of Computer Science, 1978–98; Prof. of Computing Sci., Univ. of Oxford, and Fellow of St Hugh's Coll., Oxford, 1998–2005. Visiting Professor: Stanford Univ., 1974–75; Univ. of Calif at Berkeley, 1977–78; Harvard Univ., 1997. Fellow, ACM, 1994. Aust. Math. Soc. Medal, 1984; Hannan Medal, Aust. Acad. of Sci., 2005. *Publications:* Algorithms for Minimization without Derivatives, 1973, repr. 2002; Computational Complexity and the Analysis of Algorithms, 1980. *Recreations:* music, chess, bridge. *Address:* Mathematical Sciences Institute, Australian National University, ACT 0200, Australia.

BRENTFORD, 4th Viscount *cr* 1929, of Newick; **Crispin William Joynson-Hicks;** Bt of Holmbury, 1919; Bt of Newick, 1956; Partner, Taylor Joynson Garrett (formerly Joynson-Hicks), 1961–95; *b* 7 April 1933; *s* of 3rd Viscount Brentford and Phyllis (*d* 1979), *o d* of late Major Herbert Allfrey, Tetbury, Glos; *S* father, 1983; *m* 1964, Gillian Evelyn Schluter (*see* Viscountess Brentford); one *s* three *d*. *Educ:* Eton; New College, Oxford. Admitted solicitor, 1960. Master, Girdlers' Co., 1983–84. *Heir:* *s* Hon. Paul William Joynson-Hicks [*b* 18 April 1971; *m* 2006, Catharine, *d* of Richard James Kay Muir, *qv*; one *d*]. *Address:* Springhill, Broad Oak, Heathfield, East Sussex TN21 8XJ. *T:* (01435) 867161.

BRENTFORD, Viscountess; Gillian Evelyn Joynson-Hicks, OBE 1996; FCA; Third Church Estates Commissioner, 1999–2005; *b* 22 Nov. 1942; *d* of Gerald Edward Schluter, OBE; *m* 1964, Crispin William Joynson-Hicks (*see* Viscount Brentford); one *s* three *d*. *Educ:* West Heath Sch. FCA 1965. Director: Edward Schluter & Co. (London) Ltd, 1971–88; M. A. F. Europe, 1990–97. Mem., General Synod of C of E, 1990–2005; a Church Comr, 1991–98 (Mem., Bd of Govs, 1993–98); Chm., House of Laity, Chichester dio., 1991–99; Mem., Crown Appts Commn, 1995–2002. Pres., CMS, 1998–2007. High Sheriff, E Sussex, 1998–99. *Recreations:* family, gardens, travel. *Address:* Springhill, Broad Oak, Heathfield, East Sussex TN21 8XJ.

BRENTON, Sir Anthony Russell, KCMG 2007 (CMG 2001); HM Diplomatic Service; Ambassador to Russia, 2004–08; *b* 1 Jan. 1950; *s* of Ivan Bernard Brenton and Jean Sylvia (*née* Rostgard); *m* 1981, Susan Mary Penrose; one *s* two *d*. *Educ:* Queens' Coll. Cambridge (BA); Open Univ. (MPhil). Joined HM Diplomatic Service, 1975; Cairo, 1978–81; European Communities Dept, FCO, 1981–85; with UK Perm. Repn to EC, 1985–86; Dep. Chef de Cabinet, EC, 1986–89; Counsellor, 1989; Head: UN Dept, FCO, 1989–90; Envmt, Sci. and Energy Dept, FCO, 1990–92; Fellow, Centre for Internat. Affairs, Harvard Univ., 1992–93; Counsellor, Moscow, 1994–98; Dir, FCO, 1998–2001; Minister, Washington, 2001–04. *Publication:* The Greening of Machiavelli, 1994. *Recreation:* history. *Address:* c/o Foreign and Commonwealth Office, King Charles Street, SW1A 2AH.

BRENTON, Howard; playwright; *b* 13 Dec. 1942; *s* of Donald Henry Brenton and Rose Lilian (*née* Lewis); *m* 1970, Jane Fry; two *s*. *Educ:* Chichester High Sch. for Boys; St Catharine's Coll., Cambridge (BA Hons English). Hon. Dr North London; Hon. DLit Westminster, 2002. *Full-length stage plays:* Revenge, 1969; Hitler Dances, and Measure for Measure (after Shakespeare), 1972; Magnificence, 1973; The Churchill Play, 1974; Government Property, 1975; Weapons of Happiness, 1976 (Evening Standard Award); Epsom Downs, 1977; Sore Throats, 1979; The Romans in Britain, 1980; Thirteenth Night, 1981; The Genius, 1983; Bloody Poetry, 1984; Greenland, 1988; H. I. D. (Hess is Dead), 1989; Berlin Bertie, 1992; Kit's Play, 2000; Paul, 2005; In Extremis, 2006; Never So Good, 2008; *one-act stage plays:* Gum and Goo, Heads, The Education of Skinny Spew, and Christie in Love, 1969; Wesley, 1970; Scott of the Antarctic, and A Sky-blue Life, 1971; How Beautiful with Badges, 1972; Mug, 1973; The Thing (for children), 1982; *collaborations:* (with six others) Lay-By, 1970; (with six others) England's Ireland, 1971; (with David Hare) Brassneck, 1973; (with Trevor Griffiths, David Hare and Ken Campbell), Deeds, 1978; (with Tony Howard) A Short Sharp Shock, 1980; (with Tunde Ikoli) Sleeping Policemen, 1983; (with David Hare) Pravda, 1985 (London Standard Award); Playing Away (opera), 1994 (score by Benedict Mason); Bacchae/Backup, 2001; *with Tariq Ali:* Iranian Nights, 1989; Moscow Gold, 1990; Ugly Rumours, 1998; *with Tariq Ali and Andy de la Tour:* Collateral Damage, 1999; Snogging Ken, 2000; *television plays:* Lushly, 1971; Brassneck (adaptation of stage play), 1974; The Saliva Milkshake, 1975 (also perf. theatre); The Paradise Run, 1976; Desert of Lies, 1984; *television series:* Dead Head, 1986; (with David Wolstencroft and Simon Mirren) Spooks, 2002–03 (BAFTA award for Best TV Drama series); *radio play:* Nasser's Eden, 1998; *translations:* Bertolt Brecht, The Life of Galileo, 1980; Georg Buchner, Danton's Death, 1982; Bertolt Brecht, Conversations in Exile, 1982; Goethe, Faust, 1995. *Publications:* Diving for Pearls (novel), 1989; Hot Irons: diaries, essays, journalism, 1995; many plays published. *Recreation:* painting. *Address:* c/o Casarotto Ramsay Ltd, Waverley House, 7–12 Noel Street, W1F 8GQ. *T:* (020) 7287 4450.

BRENTON, Timothy Deane; QC 1998; *b* 4 Nov. 1957; *s* of late Comdr R. W. Brenton, RN and of P. C. D. Brenton; *m* 1981, Annabel Louisa Robson; one *s* one *d*. *Educ:* King's Sch., Rochester; BRNC, Dartmouth; Bristol Univ. (LLB 1st cl. Hons 1979). RN, 1975–79; Lectr in Law, King's Coll. London, 1980; called to the Bar, Middle Temple, 1981; in practice at the Bar, 1981–. Mem., Editl Bd, International Maritime Law, 1994–2001. Hon. Counsel and Trustee, King George's Fund for Sailors, 2000–. *Recreations:* golf, country pursuits, ski-ing, music. *Address:* 7 King's Bench Walk, Inner Temple, EC4Y 7DS. *T:* (020) 7910 8300.

BRENTWOOD, Bishop of, (RC), since 1980; **Rt Rev. Thomas McMahon;** Parish Priest, Stock, since 1969; *b* 17 June 1936. *Educ:* St Bede's GS, Manchester; St Sulpice, Paris; Wonersh. Ordained priest, 1959; Asst Priest, Colchester, 1959–64; Priest, Westcliff-on-Sea, 1964–69; Chaplain, Univ. of Essex, 1972–80. Hon. Ecumenical Canon, Chelmsford Cathedral, 2005–. Former Member: Nat. Ecumenical Commn; Liturgical Commn; Mem., Churches Together in Essex & E London, 1991– (Chm., 1984–93); Chairman: Brentwood Ecumenical Commn, 1979; Cttee for Pastoral Liturgy, 1983–97; Essex Churches Consultative Council, 1984–; Cttee for Church Music, 1997–2001; Bishop's Patrimony Cttee, 2001–; Mem., London Church Leaders Gp, 1980–; Rep. of Bps' Conf. on Council of St George's House, Windsor, 2005–. Founder Mem., Movt for Christian Democracy, 1999–. Pres., Essex Show, 1992. Vice-President: Pax Christi, 1987–; Friends of Cathedral Music, 2005–. Hon. Fellow, Hertford Coll., Oxford, 2004. DU: Essex, 1991; Anglia, 2001. *Address:* Bishop's House, Stock, Ingatestone, Essex CM4 9BU. *T:* (01277) 840268.

BRERETON, Donald, CB 2001; Director, Motability, since 2004; *b* 18 July 1945; *s* of Clarence Vivian and Alice Gwendolin Brereton; *m* 1969, Mary Frances Turley; one *s* two *d*. *Educ:* Plymouth Coll.; Univ. of Newcastle upon Tyne (BA Hons Pol. and Soc. Admin). VSO, Malaysia, 1963–64. Asst Principal, Min. of Health, 1968; Asst Private Sec. to Sec. of State for Social Services, 1971; Private Sec. to Perm. Sec., DHSS, 1972; Prin., Health Services Planning, 1973; Private Sec. to Sec. of State for Social Services, 1979–82; Asst Sec., DHSS Policy Strategy Unit, 1982–83; Sec. to Housing Benefit Rev. Team, 1984; Asst Sec., Housing Benefit, 1985–89; Under Sec., Head of Prime Minister's Efficiency Unit, 1989–93; Under Sec., Social Security Policy Gp, DSS, 1993–2000; Dir, Disability, DSS, then Gp Dir, Disability and Carers, DWP, 2000–03. Chm., Carers UK, 2005–. *Recreations:* squash, holidays, books, gardening, bridge. *Address:* Motability, Warwick House, Roydon Road, Harlow, Essex CM19 5PX.

BRESLAND, (David) Allan; Member (DemU) West Tyrone, Northern Ireland Assembly, since 2007; *b* 16 Aug. 1945; *s* of Hugh and May Bresland; *m* 1966, Mary Elizabeth Martin; four *d*. *Educ:* Ballylaw Primary Sch. Lorry driver: R. J. Hemphill, 1967–76; Water Service, 1976–2001. UDR (pt-time), 1970–85. Mem. (DemU), Strathbane DC, 1993–. *Recreation:* watching and following cricket. *Address:* 41 Millhaven, Sion Mills, Co. Tyrone BT82 9FG. *T:* (028) 8165 8579, *Fax:* (028) 8165 9177; *e-mail:* a.bresland@btconnect.com.

BRETHERTON, James Russell; Secretary, 1989–2003, and Director of Corporate Services, 1998–2003, United Kingdom Atomic Energy Authority; *b* 28 March 1943; *y s* of Russell Frederick Bretherton, CB and Jocelyn Nina Mathews; *m* 1968, Harriet Grace Drew, *d* of Sir Arthur Charles Walter Drew, KCB; two *s*. *Educ:* King's Sch., Canterbury; Wadham Coll., Oxford (MA History). Voluntary Service as Asst Dist Officer, Nigeria, 1965–66; Asst Principal, Min. of Fuel and Power, 1966–70; Principal, Min. of Technol., 1970–76; Principal Private Sec. to Sec. of State for Energy, 1976–78; Head of Oil Industry Div., Internat. Energy Agency, Paris, 1980–82; Asst Sec., Dept of Energy, 1983–86; United Kingdom Atomic Energy Authority: Principal Finance and Programmes Officer, 1986–89; Commercial and Planning Dir, 1990–94; Dir, Property Mgt and Services, 1994–98. *Recreations:* gardening, walking, bassoon playing (St Giles Orch.). *Address:* Highview, 15 Hid's Copse Road, Oxford OX2 9JJ. *T:* (01865) 863388; Authers Cottage, Cotleigh, Honiton, Devon EX14 9HD. *T:* (01404) 831243.

See also P. C. Drew.

BRETSCHER, Barbara Mary Frances, (Mrs M. S. Bretscher); *see* Pearse, B. M. F.

BRETSCHER, Mark Steven, PhD; FRS 1985; Visitor, Division of Cell Biology, Medical Research Council Laboratory of Molecular Biology, Cambridge, since 2005 (Member of Scientific Staff, 1965–2005; Head of Division, 1984–95); *b* 8 Jan. 1940; *s* of late Egon Bretscher, CBE and Hanni (*née* Greminger); *m* 1978, Barbara Mary Frances Pearse, *qv*; one *s* one *d*. *Educ:* Abingdon Sch., Berks; Gonville and Caius Coll., Cambridge (MA, PhD). Res. Fellow, Gonville and Caius Coll., Cambridge, 1964–70. Vis. Professor: Harvard Univ., 1975; Stanford Univ., 1984. Friedrich Miescher Prize, Swiss Biochemical Soc., 1979. *Publications:* papers in scientific jls on protein biosynthesis, membrane structure and cell locomotion. *Recreation:* gardening. *Address:* Ram Cottage, Commercial End, Swaffham Bulbeck, Cambridge CB5 0ND. *T:* (01223) 811276; *e-mail:* msb@mrc-lmb.cam.ac.uk.

BRETT, family name of **Viscount Esher** and **Baron Brett**.

BRETT, Baron *cr* 1999 (Life Peer), of Lydd in the county of Kent; **William Henry Brett;** a Lord in Waiting (Government Whip), since 2008; *b* 6 March 1942; *s* of William Joseph Brett and Mary Brett (*née* Murphy); *m* 1st, 1961, Jean Valerie (marr. diss. 1986); one *s* one *d*; 2nd, 1994, Janet Winters (marr. diss. 2006); two *d*. *Educ:* Radcliffe Secondary Technical College, Manchester. British Railways, 1958–64; TSSA, 1964–66; NW Organiser, NUBE (now AMICUS, previously UNIFI), 1966–68; E Midlands Divl Officer, ASTMS, 1968–74; Institution of Professionals, Managers and Specialists (formerly IPCS): Asst Sec.; Asst Gen. Sec., 1980; elected Gen. Sec., 1988, Gen. Sec., 1989–99. Mem., Gen. Council, TUC, 1989–99. Exec. Sec., Internat. Fedn of Air Traffic Electronic Assocs, 1984–92; Mem. Public Services Internat. Exec. Cttee, 1989–99. International Labour Organisation: Mem. Governing Body, Geneva, 1991–2002 (Vice Pres., 1993–2002); Pres., Worker Group, 1993–2002; Chm., Governing Body, 2002–03; Dir, 2004–08. FRSA. Hon. Sen. Fellow, Sullivan Univ., Louisville, Kentucky, 2004– (Hon. DBA, 2004). *Publication:* International Labour in the 21st Century, 1994. *Recreations:* travelling, reading. *Address:* 310 Nelson House, Dolphin Square, SW1V 3NY; *e-mail:* billbrett70@hotmail.com.

BRETT, Michael John Lee; freelance financial journalist, part-time lecturer and writer, since 1982; *b* 23 May 1939; *s* of late John Brett and Margaret Brett (*née* Lee). *Educ:* King's Coll. Sch., Wimbledon; Wadham Coll., Oxford (BA Modern Langs). Investors Review, 1962–64; Fire Protection Assoc., 1964–68; Investors Chronicle, 1968–82: Dep. Editor, 1973–77; Editor, 1977–82. Past Director: Throgmorton Publications; Financial Times Business Publishing Div. *Publications:* Finance for Business: private sector finance; (contrib.) Valuation and Investment Appraisal; How to Read the Financial Pages; Property and Money, 1990; How to Figure Out Company Accounts, 2003. *Recreations:* travelling, reading.

See also S. A. L. Brett.

BRETT, Richard John; Finance Manager, Age Concern Torbay, since 2005; Consultant, Aston Group UK, since 2002 (Director, 2000–01; Joint Managing Director, 2001–02); *b* 23 Oct. 1947; *s* of Henry William Brett and Dorothy Ada Brett; *m* 1st, 1972, Alison Elizabeth Lambert (marr. diss. 1991); one *d*; 2nd, 1991, Maria Antoinette Brown. *Educ:* Univ. of Bradford (MSc). FCA; Associate, Inst. of Taxation. Leonard C. Bye, Chartered Accountants, Middlesbrough, 1964; ICI Petro-chemicals, 1971; Finance Director: Chloride Shires, 1976; Chloride Automotive Batteries, 1979; Westpark, 1981; Thorn EMI Datatech, 1985–88; Gp Dir, Finance and Mgt Services, CAA, 1988–96; Man. Dir, Solution Partners Ltd, 1996–2000. *Recreation:* music.

BRETT, Simon Anthony Lee; writer; *b* 28 Oct. 1945; *s* of late Alan John Brett and Margaret Agnes Brett (*née* Lee); *m* 1971, Lucy Victoria McLaren; two *s* one *d*. *Educ:* Dulwich College; Wadham College, Oxford (BA Hons). Department store Father Christmas, 1967; BBC Radio Producer, 1968–77; LWT Producer, 1977–79. Chm., Adv. Cttee, PLR, 2003–. Chm., Soc. of Authors, 1995–97; Pres., Detection Club, 2001–. Radio and television scripts, incl. After Henry, No Commitments, Smelling of Roses. *Publications: Charles Paris crime novels:* Cast, In Order of Disappearance, 1975; So Much Blood, 1976; Star Trap, 1977; An Amateur Corpse, 1978; A Comedian Dies, 1979; The Dead Side of the Mike, 1980; Situation Tragedy, 1981; Murder Unprompted, 1982; Murder in the Title, 1983; Not Dead, Only Resting, 1984; Dead Giveaway, 1985; What Bloody Man Is That?, 1987; A Series of Murders, 1989; Corporate Bodies, 1991; A Reconstructed Corpse, 1993; Sicken And So Die, 1995; Dead Room Farce, 1997; *Mrs Pargeter crime novels:* A Nice Class of Corpse, 1986; Mrs, Presumed Dead, 1988; Mrs Pargeter's Package, 1990; Mrs Pargeter's Pound of Flesh, 1992; Mrs Pargeter's Plot, 1996; Mrs Pargeter's Point of Honour, 1998; *other crime novels:* A Shock to the System, 1984; Dead Romantic, 1985; The Three Detectives and the Missing Superstar, 1986; The Three Detectives and the Knight-in-Armour, 1987; The Christmas Crimes at Puzzel Manor, 1991; Singled Out, 1995; The Body on the Beach, 2000; Death on the Downs, 2001; The Torso in the Town, 2002; Murder in the Museum, 2003; The Hanging in the Hotel, 2004; The Witness at the Wedding, 2005; The Stabbing in the Stables, 2006; Death Under the Dryer, 2007; Blood at the Bookies, 2008; *crime short stories:* A Box of Tricks, 1985; Crime Writers and Other Animals, 1998; *humorous books:* The Child-Owner's Handbook, 1983; Molesworth Rites Again, 1983; Bad Form, 1984; People-Spotting, 1985; The Wastepaper Basket Archive, 1986; How to Stay Topp, 1987; After Henry, 1987; The Booker Book, 1989; How to be a Little Sod, 1992; Look Who's Walking, 1994; Not Another Little Sod!, 1997; The Penultimate Chance Saloon, 2006; On Second Thoughts, 2006; *anthologies:* The Faber Book of Useful Verse, 1981; (with Frank Muir) The Book of Comedy Sketches, 1982; Take a Spare Truss, 1983; The Faber Book of Parodies, 1984; The Faber Book of Diaries, 1987; *stage play:* Silhouette, 1998. *Recreations:* writing, reading, Real tennis, unreal fantasies. *Address:* Frith House, Burpham, Arundel, West Sussex BN18 9RR. *T:* (01903) 882257. *Clubs:* Garrick, Groucho.

See also M. J. L. Brett.

BRETT, Simon Baliol, RE 1991 (ARE 1986); wood engraver, printmaker and illustrator; writer on wood engraving; *b* 27 May 1943; *s* of late Antony Baliol Brett and Bay Helen (*née* Brownell); *m* 1974, Juliet Shirley-Smith (*née* Wood); one *d*, and three step *s* one step *d*. *Educ:* Ampleforth Coll.; St Martin's Sch. of Art (NDD 1964). Teacher, Marlborough Coll. Art Sch., 1971–89; publisher, under own Paulinus Print imprint, 1981–88. Editl Advr, Printmaking Today, 1994–. Society of Wood Engravers: Mem., 1984–; Chm., 1986–92; Treas., 1990–2002. Occasional exhibns; presentation print commnd by Medical Household for Golden Wedding of the Queen and Duke of Edinburgh, 1997. Exhibitions curated: Wood Engraving Then and Now, 1987; Out of the Wood, 1991; Wood Engraving Here and Now, 1995. *Publications:* Engravers, 1987; Engravers Two, 1992; Mr Derrick Harris, 1999; An Engraver's Globe, 2002; Wood Engraving - How to Do it, 1994, rev. edn 2000; *books illustrated include:* The Animals of St Gregory (Francis Williams/V&A/NBL Illustration Award), 1981; To the Cross, 1984; Shakespeare's Sonnets, 1989; The Reader's Digest Illustrated Bible, 1990; Clarissa, 1991; Jane Eyre, 1991; The Confessions of Saint Augustine, 1993; Amelia, 1995; Shakespeare, The Classical Plays, 1997; (also picture ed.) The Folio Golden Treasury, 1997; Middlemarch, 1999; The Poetry of John Keats, 2001; The Meditations of Marcus Aurelius, 2002; Legends of the Ring, 2004; The Gypsies, 2006; Legends of the Grail, 2007; Shelley, 2008. *Address:* 12 Blowhorn Street, Marlborough, Wilts SN8 1BT. *T:* (01672) 512905; *e-mail:* simon@simonbrett-woodengraver.co.uk.

BRETT, Timothy Edward William; Member (Lib Dem), Fife Unitary Council, since 2003; *b* 28 March 1949; *s* of Reuben Brett and Edna Brett (*née* Waterman); *m* 1972, Barbara Jane Turnbull; two *s* one *d* (and one *s* decd). *Educ:* Gravesend GS for Boys; Bristol Univ. (BSc Hons). CIHM, CCIPD, FFPH. VSO Teacher, Min. of Educn, Sierra Leone, 1971–73; Nat. Admin. Trainee, Leeds RBH, later Yorks RHA, 1973–75; Sen. Admin. Asst (Planning & Personnel), Leeds AHA, 1975–76; Business Manager, Nixon Meml Hosp., Methodist Church-Overseas Div., Segbwema, Sierra Leone, 1976–78; Community Services Adminr, Humberside AHA, 1978; Dep. Adminr, Derbyshire Royal Infirmary, 1979–80; Unit Adminr, Plymouth Gen. Hosp., 1981–85; Unit Adminr, 1985–87, Unit Gen. Manager, 1987–93, Dundee Gen. Hosps Unit; Chief Exec., Dundee Teaching Hosps NHS Trust, 1993–98; Gen. Manager, then Chief Exec., Tayside Health Board, 1998–2001; Dir, Health Protection Scotland, 2002–07. Chm., Social Work and Health Cttee, Fife Council, 2007–. *Recreations:* hill-walking, swimming, theatre, church activities. *Address:* Woodend Cottage, Hazelton Walls, Cupar, Fife KY15 4QL. *T:* (01382) 330629.

BRETT-HOLT, Alexis Fayrer; Legal Adviser, Health and Safety Executive, since 2004; *b* 7 March 1950; *d* of late Raymond Arthur Brett-Holt and Jacqueline Fayrer Brett-Holt (*née* Fayrer Hosken); *m* 1980, (John) Gareth Roscoe, *qv*; one *s* one *d*. *Educ:* Wimbledon High Sch.; St Anne's Coll., Oxford (BA). Called to the Bar, Lincoln's Inn, 1973, Additional Bencher, 2007; Department of the Environment: Legal Asst, 1974–78; Sen. Legal Asst, 1978–85; Asst Solicitor, 1985–89; Assistant Solicitor: DoH, 1989–93; DoE, 1993–97; Dir, Legal Services C, 1997–2001, Legal Services B, 2001–04, DTI. *Address:* Legal Adviser's Office, Health and Safety Executive, Rose Court, 2 Southwark Bridge, SE1 9HS. *T:* (020) 7717 6650. *Club:* CWIL.

BRETTEN, George Rex; QC 1980; barrister-at-law; *b* 21 Feb. 1942; *s* of Horace Victor Bretten and Kathleen Edna Betty Bretten; *m* 1965, Maureen Gillian Crowhurst; one *d*. *Educ:* King Edward VII Sch., King's Lynn; Sidney Sussex Coll., Cambridge (MA, LLM). Lectr, Nottingham Univ., 1964–68; Asst Director, Inst. of Law Research and Reform, Alberta, Canada, 1968–70; called to the Bar, Lincoln's Inn, 1965, a Bencher 1989; in practice, 1971–. *Publication:* Special Reasons, 1977. *Recreations:* gardening, walking, tennis. *Address:* Stonehill House, Horam, Heathfield, East Sussex TN21 0JN. *T:* (01825) 872820. *Club:* Athenæum.

BREW, David Allan; Head, Rural Communities Division, Scottish Government (formerly Scottish Executive), since 2006; *b* 19 Feb. 1953; *s* of Kenneth Frederick Cecil Brew and Iris May (*née* Sharpe). *Educ:* Kettering Grammar Sch.; Heriot-Watt Univ. (BA 1st Cl. Hons 1974; Pres., Students' Assoc., 1974–75); Univ. of Strathclyde (MSc 1976); European Univ. Inst., Florence. Scottish Office, 1979–81; Adminr, Directorate-Gen. V, EC, Brussels, 1981–84; Scottish Office: Principal, Glasgow, 1984–88, Edinburgh, 1988–90; Head: Electricity Privatisation Div., 1990–91; Eur. Funds and Co-ordination Div., 1991–95; Sea Fisheries Div., 1995–98; Devolution Team, Constitution Secretariat, Cabinet Office, 1998–2000; Chief Exec., ICAS, 2000–03; Hd, Cultural Policy Div., Scottish Exec., 2004–06. Mem. Court, Heriot-Watt Univ., 1985–91, 2000–06. *Publications:* (contrib.) Changing Patterns of Relations between the National Parliaments and the European Parliament, 1979; (contrib.) European Electoral Systems Handbook, 1979; (contrib.) The European Parliament: towards a uniform procedure for direct elections, 1981. *Recreations:* languages, music, film, gastronomy. *Address:* 1 Dundas Street, Edinburgh EH3 6QG. *T:* (0131) 556 4692.

BREW, Richard Maddock, CBE 1982; DL; Chairman, Budget Boilers Ltd, since 1984; *b* 13 Dec. 1930; *s* of late Leslie Maddock Brew and Phyllis Evelyn Huntsman; *m* 1953, Judith Anne, *d* of late P. E. Thompson Hancock, FRCP; two *s* two *d*. *Educ:* Rugby Sch.; Magdalene Coll., Cambridge (BA). Called to the Bar, Inner Temple, 1955. After practising for short time at the Bar, joined family business, Brew Brothers Ltd, SW7, 1955, and remained until takeover, 1972. Chm., Monks Dormitory Ltd, 1979–93; Regl Dir, Lloyds Bank, 1988–91. Mem., NE Thames RHA, 1982–90 (Vice-Chm., 1982–86); Chm., Tower Hamlets DHA, 1990–93. Farms in Essex. Member: Royal Borough of Kensington Council, 1959–65; Royal Borough of Kensington and Chelsea Council, 1964–70; Greater London Council: Mem., 1968–86; Alderman, 1968–73; Vice-Chm., Strategic Planning Cttee, 1969–71; Chm., Covent Garden Jt Development Cttee, 1970–71 and Environmental Planning Cttee, 1971–73; Mem. for Chingford, 1973–86; Dep. Leader of Council and Leader, Policy and Resources Cttee, 1977–81; Dep. Leader, Cons. Party and Opposition Spokesman on Finance, 1981–82; Leader of the Opposition, 1982–83. Mem., Nat. Theatre Bd, 1982–86. Mem., Pony Club Council, 1975–93. High Sheriff, Greater London, 1988–89. DL Greater London, 1989. *Recreations:* hunting, gardening. *Address:* Holm Close, Kilton, Somerset TA5 1ST. *T:* (01278) 741293. *Clubs:* Carlton, MCC.

BREWER, Sir David (William), Kt 2007; CMG 1999; JP; FCII; Lord-Lieutenant of Greater London, since 2008; Chairman, China-Britain Business Council, since 2007; Vice-President, GB-China Centre, since 2004 (Chairman, 1997–2004); non-executive Vice-Chairman, Marsh Ltd, since 2007; Lord Mayor of London, 2005–06; *b* 28 May 1940; *s* of Dr H. F. Brewer and Elizabeth Brewer (*née* Nickell-Lean); *m* 1985, Tessa Suzanne Mary Jordá; two *d*. *Educ:* St Paul's Sch.; Univ. of Grenoble. FCII 1966. Joined Sedgwick Group, 1959: Rep., Japan, 1976–78; Director: Sedgwick Far East Ltd, 1982–99 (Chm., 1993–97); Develt Cos, 1982–98; Sedgwick Internat. Risk Mgt Inc., 1990–99; Chairman: Sedgwick Insce and Risk Mgt Consultants (China) Ltd, 1993–97; Sedgwick Japan Ltd, 1994–97. Dir, Sumitomo Marine & Fire Insce Co. (Europe) Ltd, 1985–98; non-executive Director: Tullett Prebon SITICO (China) Ltd, 2007–; Sen. Consultant, Internat. Financial Services, London, 2001–; Dir and Sen. Consultant, British Invisibles, 1998–2001. Mem., Action Japan Cttee, DTI, 1996–2000. Mem. Bd and Hon. Treas., China-Britain Business Council, 1991–2007; Chm., International Financial Services, London/China-Britain Business Council Financial Services Cttee, 1993–; Mem. Bd, UK-India Business Council, 2008–; UK Chm., Care for Children (China), 1998–. Internat. Envoy for London, Think London, 2005–. Pres., City of London Br., IoD, 2008– (Chm., 1999–2008); Pres., Insce Inst. of London, 2006–07 (Vice-Pres., 2005–06); Mem. Bd, Securities and Investment Trust, 2006– (Hon. Fellow, 2006). Dir, City of London Sinfonia, 1988–; Mem., Adv. Council, LSO, 1999–. Pres., City of London Br., RNLI, 2007– (Chm., 1997–2007); Vice-Pres., City of London Sector, BRCS, 1986–. Governor: City of London Poly., 1979–90; Sons of the Clergy, 1993– (Treas., 2008–09); SOAS, 2000–; Mem., Internat. Bd of Overseers, Cass Business Sch., City Univ., 2003–. Almoner, Christ's Hosp., 1998–2004. Trustee, Daiwa Anglo-Japanese Foundn, 2008–; Dir, Guildhall Sch. Trust, 1999–. Alderman, City of London, Ward of Bassishaw, 1996– (Mem. Ct of Common Council, 1992–96; Pres., Bassishaw Ward Club, 1996–); Sheriff, City of London, 2002–03; HM Comr of Lieutenancy, City of London, 2005–; Liveryman: Merchant Taylors' Co., 1968– (Mem., Ct of Assts, 1985–; Master, 2001–02); Insurers' Co., 2001– (Mem., Ct of Assts, 2004–); Mem., Ct of Assts, Blacksmiths' Co., 2007– (Hon. Mem., 2001–07); Hon. Liveryman, Security Professionals' Co., 2008 (Hon. Freeman, 2003–08); Mem., Parish Clerks' Co., 2006–; Pres., Soc. of Young Freemen, 2003–08. Pres., London Cornish Assoc., 2005–. Churchwarden, St Lawrence Jewry, 1996–. JP City of London, 1979. Hon. Bencher, Gray's Inn, 2004–. Hon. DPhil London Metropolitan, 2005; Hon. DSc City, 2006; Hon. LLD Exeter, 2008; Hon. DSc (Econs) London, 2008. Magnolia Gold Award, Mayor of Shanghai, 2006. *Recreations:* music (especially opera and choral music), golf, mechanical gardening, chocolate, paronomasia. *Address:* 16 Cowley Street, SW1P 3LZ. *T:* (020) 7222 5481; Orchard Cottage, Hellandbridge, Bodmin, Cornwall PL30 4QR. *T:* (01208) 841268. *Clubs:* Garrick, City of London, MCC; St Enodoc Golf.

BREWER, Prof. Derek Stanley, LittD; Master of Emmanuel College, Cambridge, 1977–90; Professor of English, University of Cambridge, 1983–90, now Emeritus Professor; *b* 13 July 1923; *s* of Stanley Leonard Brewer and Winifred Helen Forbes; *m* 1951, Lucie Elisabeth Hoole; three *s* two *d*. *Educ:* elementary school; The Crypt Grammar Sch.; Magdalen Coll., Oxford (Matthew Arnold Essay Prize, 1948; BA, MA 1948); Birmingham Univ. (PhD 1956); LittD Cantab 1980. Commnd 2nd Lieut, Worcestershire Regt, 1942; Captain and Adjt, 1st Bn Royal Fusiliers, 1944–45. Asst Lectr and Lectr in English, Univ. of Birmingham, 1949–56; Prof. of English, Internat. Christian Univ., Tokyo, 1956–58; Lectr and Sen. Lectr, Univ. of Birmingham, 1958–64; Lectr in English, Univ. of Cambridge, 1965–76, Reader in Medieval English, 1976–83; Fellow of Emmanuel Coll., Cambridge, 1965–77, Life Fellow 1990. Founder, D. S. Brewer Ltd, for the publication of academic books, 1972; now part of Boydell and Brewer Ltd (Dir, 1979–96). Mem., Council of the Senate, Cambridge, 1978–83; Chairman: Fitzwilliam Museum Enterprises Ltd, 1978–90; Univ. Library Synd., 1980–93; English Faculty Bd, Cambridge, 1984–86, 1989. Lectures: Sir Israel Gollancz Meml, British Academy, 1974; first William Matthews, Univ. of London, 1982; first Geoffrey Shepherd Meml, Univ. of Birmingham, 1983; Ballard Mathews, Univ. of Wales, Bangor, 1996. Sandars Reader, Univ. of Cambridge, 1991. First British Council Vis. Prof. of English to Japan, 1987; Vis. Prof., Japan Soc. for Promotion of Science, 1988; Cline Distinguished Vis. Prof., Univ. of

Texas at Austin, 1992; Francqui Internat. Chair in Human Sciences, univs in Belgium, 1998. President: The English Assoc., 1982–83, 1987–90 (Hon. Fellow, 2001); Internat. Chaucer Soc., 1982–84; Chairman Trustees: Chaucer Heritage Trust, 1992–98; British Taiwan Cultural Inst., 1990–98; Trustee (Treas.), SOS Villages (UK), 1990–2002; Hon. Trustee, Osaka Univ. of Arts, 1987–. Hon. Mem., Japan Acad., 1981 (Commemorative Medal, 1997); Corresp. Fellow, Medieval Soc. of America, 1987. Hon. LLD: Keio Univ., Tokyo, 1982; Harvard Univ., 1984; Hon. DLitt: Birmingham, 1985; Williams Coll., USA, 1990; DUniv: York, 1985; Sorbonne, 1988; Univ. of Liège, 1990. Seatonian Prize, Univ. of Cambridge, 1969, 1972, 1983, 1986, 1988, 1993, 1999, (jtly) 1979, 1980, 1992, (*prox. acc.*) 1985, 1990. Editor, The Cambridge Review, 1981–86. *Publications:* Chaucer, 1953, 3rd edn 1973; Proteus, 1958 (Tokyo); (ed) The Parlement of Foulys, 1960; Chaucer in his Time, 1963; (ed and contrib.) Chaucer and Chaucerians, 1966; (ed) Malory's Morte Darthur: Parts Seven and Eight, 1968; (ed and contrib.) Writers and their Backgrounds: Chaucer, 1974; (ed) Chaucer: the Critical Heritage, 1978; Chaucer and his World, 1978; Symbolic Stories, 1980, 2nd edn 1988; (ed jtly) Aspects of Malory, 1981; English Gothic Literature, 1983; Tradition and Innovation in Chaucer, 1983; Chaucer: the Poet as Storyteller, 1984; Chaucer: an introduction, 1984; (ed) Beardsley's Le Morte Darthur, 1985; (with E. Frankl) Arthur's Britain: the land and the legend, 1985; (ed) Studies in Medieval English Romances, 1988; (ed) Medieval Comic Tales, 1996; (ed) A Critical Companion to the Gawain-poet, 1997; (ed) The Middle Ages after the Middle Ages, 1997; A New Introduction to Chaucer, 1998; Seatonian Exercises and Other Verses, 2000; Chaucer's World, 2000; numerous articles in learned jls, reviews, etc. *Recreations:* reading, travelling, publishing other people's books. *Address:* 240 Hills Road, Cambridge CB2 2QE; Emmanuel College, Cambridge CB2 3AP. *T:* (01223) 334200.

BREWER, Dr Nicola Mary, (Mrs G. C. Gillham), CMG 2002; Chief Executive, Equality and Human Rights Commission, since 2007; *b* 14 Nov. 1957; *d* of Trevor James Brewer and late Mary Margaret Eleanor Brewer (*née* Jones); *m* 1991, Geoffrey Charles Gillham, *qv*; one *s* one *d*. *Educ:* Univ. of Leeds (BA 1980; PhD 1988). Entered FCO, 1983: Second Sec., Mexico City, 1984–87; First Secretary: FCO, 1987–91; (Econ.), Paris, 1991–94; Counsellor: FCO, 1995–98; New Delhi, 1998–2001; Dir, Global Issues, FCO, 2001–02; Dir Gen., Regl Progs, DFID, 2002–04 (on secondment); Dir Gen., Europe, FCO, 2004–07. *Recreations:* reading novels, cycling, riding. *Address:* c/o Equality and Human Rights Commission, 3 More London, Riverside Tooley Street, SE1 2RG.

BREWER, Richard John, FSA; Keeper of Archaeology & Numismatics, Amgueddfa Cymru - National Museum Wales, since 1996; *b* 23 Oct. 1954; *s* of Kenneth Arthur Brewer and Constance Brewer (*née* Crooks). *Educ:* Birchgrove Primary Sch., Cardiff; Cathays High Sch., Cardiff; Inst. of Archaeol., Univ. of London (BA Hons Archaeol. 1976). National Museum of Wales: Res. Asst, 1978–85; Asst Keeper, Roman Archaeol., 1985–96. Res. Fellow, Sch. of Hist. and Archaeol., Cardiff Univ., 2005–. Chm., Ancient Monuments Adv. Bd for Wales, 2005– (Mem., 1997–). Mem. Council and Review Ed., Soc. for Promotion of Roman Studies, 2004–. Chm., Adv. Cttee, Young Archaeologists' Club, 2002–. FSA 1986. *Publications:* Corpus of Sculpture of the Roman World: Great Britain, Wales, 1986; Caerwent Roman Town, 1993, 3rd edn 2006; Roman Fortresses and Their Legions, 2000; Caerleon and the Roman Army, 2000; The Second Augustan Legion and the Roman Military Machine, 2002; The Romans in Gwent, 2004. *Recreations:* ultra distance and marathon running, crime fiction, travel, Association Football (Cardiff City). *Address:* Department of Archaeology & Numismatics, Amgueddfa Cymru - National Museum Wales, Cathays Park, Cardiff CF10 3NP. *T:* (029) 2057 3247; *e-mail:* richard.brewer@museumwales.ac.uk. *Club:* Les Croupiers Running (Cardiff).

BREWERTON, Prof. Andrew John; Honorary Professor of Fine Art, Shanghai University, since 2000; Principal, Dartington College of Arts, 2004–08; *b* 8 Feb. 1958; *s* of Peter John Thomas Brewerton and Jean Patricia Brewerton (*née* Cameron); *m* 1983, Jan Beaver; two *d*. *Educ:* Wolverhampton Grammar Sch.; Sidney Sussex Coll., Cambridge (R. E. Hentsch Schol.; BA Hons English, MA). Lettore in English, Univ. dell' Aquila, Italy, 1980–82; Glasshouse, Ops, and Prodn Manager, Stuart Crystal, 1984–89; Head of Design and Develt, Dartington Crystal, 1989–94; University of Wolverhampton: Principal Lectr and Hd of Glass, Sch. of Art and Design, 1994–96; Dean, Art and Design, and Prof. of Glass, 1996–2004. Exec. Mem., Council for Higher Educn in Art and Design, 2001–06; Mem., Strategic Adv. Cttee (Business and Community), HEFCE, 2005–; Bd Mem., Higher Educn Stats Agency, 2006–08; Vice-Chair, Prime Minister's Initiative Higher Educn Adv. Gp, 2006–. Mem. Council and SW Regl Chm., Arts Council England, 2007–. Chair, Jury Panel, British Glass Biennale Exhibn, 2004. Chair, Foundn for Higher Educn in Art & Design, 2005– (Trustee, 1999–); Trustee, New Art Gall., Walsall, 1997–2004. *Publications: poetry:* Sirius, 1995; Cade l'uliva, 2003; Raag Leaves for Paresh Chakraborty, 2008; contrib. numerous jl articles and catalogue essays on contemporary art. *Recreation:* fresh air. *T:* 07977 462370; *e-mail:* a.j.brewerton@btinternet.com.

BREWIS, Marion Teresa; JP; Lord-Lieutenant for Wigtown, since 2006; *d* of Robert and Anna Anderson; *m* 1981, Francis Roger Mactaggart Brewis. *Educ:* Convent of Sacred Heart High Sch., Hammersmith. Civil Servant, resigned 1989 to move to Scotland to assist in running Ardwell Estates; Dir, Ardwell Estates, 1997–. Lay Chm., NHS Appeals Tribunal, 1993. JP Wigtown, 1991. *Recreations:* walking, singing, cooking. *Address:* Ardwell House, Ardwell, by Stranraer, Wigtownshire DG9 9LY. *T:* (01776) 860227, *Fax:* (01776) 860288. *Club:* New (Edinburgh).

BREWSTER, (Elsie) Yvonne, OBE 1993; Artistic Director, Talawa Theatre Co., 1986–2003; *b* 7 Oct. 1938; *d* of Claude Noel Clarke and Kathleen Vanessa Clarke; *m* 1st, 1961, John Roger Francis Jones (marr. diss. 1965); 2nd, 1971, Starr Edmund Francis Home Brewster; one *s*. *Educ:* Rose Bruford Coll. of Speech and Drama (Dip.; Fellow, 2004). LRAM. Stage, TV and radio actress, 1960–; theatre, film, TV and radio director, 1965–; Drama Officer, Arts Council of GB, 1982–84. Mem., London Arts Bd, 1993–99; Trustee, Theatres Trust, 1992–; Patron, Rose Bruford Coll., 1994–. Non-executive Director: Riverside Mental Health NHS Trust, 1994–99; Kensington, Chelsea, Westminster and Brent NHS Trust, 1999–2001. Juror, Commonwealth Writers' Prize, 2005. Fellow: Rose Bruford Coll., 2004; Central Sch. of Speech and Drama, 2005. FRSA 1992. DUniv Open, 2002. *Publications:* Black Plays, Vol. 1, 1987, Vol. 2, 1989, Vol. 3, 1995; The Undertaker's Daughter (autobiog.), 2004. *Recreations:* reading, London. *Address:* 41B Dyne Road, NW6 7XG. *T:* (020) 7328 9306.

BREWSTER, Richard Philip; Executive Director, National Center on Nonprofit Enterprise, Alexandria, since 2003; *b* 25 May 1952; *s* of Peter and Patricia Brewster; *m* 1975, Lindy Udale; three *s* one *d*. *Educ:* Leeds Grammar Sch.; Trinity Coll., Oxford (BA Hons). ICI, 1976–86: Sales Rep., 1976–79; Product Man., 1979–81; Purchasing Man., 1981–83; Marketing Man., 1983–86; Nat. Appeals Manager, Oxfam, 1986–89; Dir of Mkting, Spastics Soc., then Scope, 1989–95; Chief Exec., Scope, 1995–2003. *Recreations:* arts, watching sport. *Address:* 1851 Stratford Park Place (107), Reston, VA 20190, USA.

BREYER, Stephen Gerald; Associate Justice, Supreme Court of the United States, since 1994; *b* 15 Aug. 1938; *s* of Irving Breyer and Anne (*née* Roberts); *m* 1967, Joanna Hare; one *s* two *d*. *Educ:* Stanford Univ. (AM 1959); Magdalen Coll., Oxford (Marshall Schol.; BA 1st Cl. Hons PPE 1961; Hon Fellow 1995); Harvard Law Sch. (LLB 1964). Law Clerk, US Supreme Court, 1964–65; Special Asst to Asst Attorney Gen., US Dept of Justice, 1965–67; Harvard University: Asst Prof. of Law, 1967–70; Prof. of Law, Harvard Law Sch., 1970–80, Lectr, 1981–; Prof., Kennedy Sch. of Govt, 1977–80; Asst Special Prosecutor, Watergate Special Prosecution Force, 1973; US Court of Appeals for First Circuit: Circuit Judge, 1980–94; Chief Judge, 1990–94. US Senate Judiciary Committee: Special Counsel, Admin. Practices Subcttee, 1974–75; Chief Counsel, 1979–80; Mem., US Sentencing Commn, 1985–89. Vis. Lectr, Coll. of Law, Sydney, Aust., 1975; Vis. Prof., Univ. of Rome, 1993. Fellow: Amer. Acad. of Arts and Scis; Amer Bar Foundn. *Publications:* (with P. MacAvoy) The Federal Power Commission and the Regulation of Energy, 1974; (with R. Stewart) Administrative Law and Regulatory Policy, 1979, 3rd edn 1992; Regulation and its Reform, 1982; Breaking the Vicious Circle: toward effective risk regulation, 1993; contrib. chapters in books; numerous articles in law jls and reviews. *Address:* Supreme Court Building, One First Street NE, Washington, DC 20543–0001, USA. *T:* (202) 4793000.

BRIAULT, Clive Bramwell; Managing Director, Retail Markets, Financial Services Authority, 2004–08; *b* 19 Sept. 1957. *Educ:* Merton Coll., Oxford (BA PPE 1978); Nuffield Coll., Oxford (MPhil Econs 1980). Bank of England, 1980–98; FSA, 1998–2008.

BRICE, (Ann) Nuala, PhD; Special Commissioner of Taxes, since 1999 (Deputy Special Commissioner, 1992–99); Chairman: VAT and Duties Tribunals (formerly VAT Tribunals), since 1999 (part-time Chairman, 1992–99); Financial Services and Markets Tribunal, since 2001; Pensions Regulator Tribunal, since 2005; Claims Management Services Tribunal, since 2007; *d* of William Connor and Rosaleen Gertrude Connor; *m* 1963, Geoffrey James Barrington Groves Brice, QC (*d* 1999); one *s*. *Educ:* Loreto Convent, Manchester; University Coll. London. LLB (Hons), LLM 1976, PhD 1982, London. Admitted Solicitor of the Supreme Court, 1963 (Stephen Heelis Gold Medal and John Peacock Conveyancing Prize, 1963). The Law Society: Asst Solicitor, 1963; Asst Sec., 1964; Sen. Asst Sec., 1973; Deptl Sec., 1982; Asst Sec.-Gen., 1987–92. Sec., Revenue Law Cttee, 1972–82. Vis. Associate Prof. of Law, Tulane Univ., 1990–99; Vis. Prof. of Law, Univ. of Natal, 1999. MRI 1965. *Recreations:* reading, music, gardening. *Address:* (office) 15/19 Bedford Avenue, WC1B 3AS. *T:* (020) 7612 9700. *Club:* University Women's.

BRICE, Air Cdre Eric John, CBE 1971 (OBE 1957); CEng; AFRAeS; RAF retd; stockbroker; *b* 12 Feb. 1917; *s* of Courtenay Percy Please Brice and Lilie Alice Louise Brice (*née* Grey); *m* 1942, Janet Parks, Roundhay, Leeds, Yorks; two *s* one *d*. *Educ:* Loughborough Coll. (DLC). Joined RAF, 1939; served War, MEAF, 1943–46 (Sqdn Ldr). Air Ministry, 1946–50; Parachute Trg Sch., 1950–52; Wing Comdr, 1952; RAE, Farnborough, 1952–58; Comd, Parachute Trg Sch., 1958–60; RAF Coll., Cranwell, 1960–61; Gp Capt., 1961; RAF Halton, 1961–64; Comd, RAF Innsworth, Glos, 1964–66; Dir, Physical Educn, RAF, MoD, 1966–68; Air Cdre, 1968; Dep. AOA, RAF HQ, Maintenance Comd, 1968–71; April 1971, retd prematurely. MCMI. *Recreations:* athletics (Combined Services and RAF athletic blues); Rugby football (RAF trialist and Blackheath Rugby Club); captained Loughborough Coll. in three sports. *Address:* Durns, Boldre, Lymington, Hampshire SO41 8NE. *T:* (01590) 672196. *Club:* Royal Lymington Yacht.

BRICE, Nuala; *see* Brice, A. N.

BRICHTO, Rabbi Dr Sidney; Senior Vice-President, Union of Liberal and Progressive Synagogues, since 1992; *b* 21 July 1936; *s* of Solomon and Rivka Brichto; *m* 1st, 1959, Frances Goldstein (decd); one *s* one *d*; 2nd, 1971, Cathryn Goldhill; two *s*. *Educ:* New York Univ. (BA); Hebrew Union Coll., NY (MA, MHL, DD); University College London (Study Fellowship). Associate Minister, Liberal Jewish Synagogue, 1961–64; Founder and Principal, Evening Inst. for Study of Judaism, 1962–65; Exec. Vice-Pres. and Dir, ULPS, 1964–89; Lectr, Oxford Centre for Postgrad. Hebrew Studies, 1991–96; Dir, Joseph Levy Charitable Foundn, 1989–99. Chairman: Conf. of Rabbis, ULPS, 1969–70, 1974–75; Council of Reform and Liberal Rabbis, 1974–76; Chief Rabbi's Consultative Cttee on Jewish-non-Jewish Relations, 1976–78. Vice-Pres., Nat. Assoc. of Bereavement Services, 1992–98. Founder and Chm., Adv. Cttee, Israel Diaspora Trust, 1982–; Mem. Exec. Council, Leo Baeck Coll., 1964–74; Dir, Inst. for Jewish Policy Res., 1996–99; Gov., Oxford Centre for Hebrew and Jewish Studies, 1994–2003. *Publications:* Funny…you don't look Jewish, 1995; (ed jtly) Two Cheers for Secularism, 1998; Ritual Slaughter, 2001; (ed jtly) He Kissed Him and They Wept, 2001; (ed and trans.) The People's Bible: Genesis, 2000; Samuel, 2000; Song of Songs, 2000; St Luke and the Apostles, 2000; The Conquest of Canaan, 2001; The Genius of Paul, 2001; Moses, Man of God and the Laws of Moses, 2003; Apocalypse, 2004; contribs to Service of the Heart (Liberal Jewish Prayer Book) and to national and Jewish jls. *Recreations:* pleasant lunches, reading, writing. *T:* (020) 8933 6216; *e-mail:* sidney@brichto.com. *Club:* Athenæum.

BRICKELL, Christopher David, CBE 1991; VMH 1976; Director General, Royal Horticultural Society, 1985–93; *b* 29 June 1932; *s* of Bertram Tom Brickell and Kathleen Alice Brickell; *m* 1963, Jeanette Scargill Flecknoe; two *d*. *Educ:* Queen's College, Taunton; Reading Univ. (BSc Horticulture). Joined Royal Horticultural Society Garden, Wisley, 1958: Asst Botanist, 1958; Botanist, 1960; Sen. Scientific Officer, 1964; Dep. Dir, 1968; Dir, 1969–85. Pres., Internat. Soc. for Hortl Sci., 1998–2002. George Robert White Medal of Honor, Mass Hort. Soc., 1988; Inst. of Horticulture Award, 1997. *Publications:* Daphne: the genus in cultivation, 1976; Pruning, 1979; The Vanishing Garden, 1986; An English Florilegium, 1987; (ed and contrib.) The Gardener's Encyclopaedia of Plants and Flowers, 1989, 4th edn 2006; (ed and contrib.) The RHS Encyclopaedia of Gardening, 1992, 2nd edn 2002; Garden Plants, 1995; (ed and contrib.) The RHS A-Z of Garden Plants, 1996, 2nd edn 2003; botanical papers in Flora Europaea, European Garden Flora, and Flora of Turkey; horticultural and botanical papers in RHS Jl, The New Plantsman and Alpine Garden Soc. Bulletin. *Recreations:* gardening, sailing, squash, tennis. *Address:* The Camber, Nutbourne, Pulborough, West Sussex RH20 2HE.

BRIDEN, Prof. James Christopher, PhD, DSc; FGS; Professor of Environmental Studies and Director of the Environmental Change Institute, University of Oxford, 1997–2003, now Professor Emeritus; Fellow, Linacre College, Oxford, 1997–2003, now Fellow Emeritus; *b* 30 Dec. 1938; *s* of late Henry Charles Briden and Gladys Elizabeth (*née* Jefkins); *m* 1968, Caroline Mary (*née* Gillmore); one *s* one *d*. *Educ:* Royal Grammar Sch., High Wycombe; St Catherine's Coll., Oxford (MA); ANU (PhD 1965; DSc 1994). FGS 1962; CGeol 1990. Research Fellow: Univ. of Rhodesia, 1965–66; Univ. of Oxford, 1966–67; Univ. of Birmingham, 1967–68; University of Leeds: Lectr, 1968–73; Reader, 1973–75; Prof. of Geophysics, 1975–86; Head, Dept of Earth Sciences, 1976–79 and 1982–85; Dir of Earth Scis, NERC, 1986–94; Vis. Prof. (NERC Res. Prof.), Univ. of Oxford, 1994–96. Canadian Commonwealth Fellow and Vis. Prof., Univ. of Western Ontario, 1979–80; Hon. Prof., Leeds Univ., 1986–94. Mem., NERC, 1981–86; Chairman: Jt Assoc. for Geophysics, 1981–84 (Chm., Founding Cttee, 1978–79); Exec. Cttee, Ocean Drilling Prog., 1994–96; Member: Science and Engrg (formerly Science) Cttee, British Council, 1990–96; Governing Council, Internat. Seismol Centre, 1978–83;

Council: Eur. Geophysical Soc., 1976–84; RAS, 1978–79 (FRAS 1962); Geol Soc., 1992–95. Fellow, Amer. Geophysical Union, 1994. Murchison Medal, Geol Soc., 1984. Editor, Earth and Planetary Science Letters, 1971–97; Ed.-in-chief, Envmtl Sci. and Policy, 2001–. *Publications:* (with A. G. Smith) Mesozoic and Cenozoic Palaeocontinental World Maps, 1977; (with A. G. Smith and A. M. Hurley) Phanerozoic Palaeocontinental World Maps, 1981; over 90 papers on palaeomagnetism, palaeoclimates, tectonics and aspects of geophysics. *Recreations:* music- and theatre-going, gentle walking, bad golf, mild gardening. *Address:* Stoneleigh House, 1 Paternoster Court, Cassington Road, Yarnton, Oxon OX5 1QB.

BRIDEN, Timothy John; Vicar-General, Province of Canterbury, since 2005; *b* 29 Oct. 1951; *s* of Thomas Dan Briden and Joan Briden (*née* Garratt); *m* 1989, Susanne. *Educ:* Ipswich Sch.; Downing Coll., Cambridge (BA 1974, MA 1978; LLB 1975). Called to the Bar, Inner Temple, 1976; Chancellor: Dio. Bath and Wells, 1993–; Dio. Truro, 1998–. Mem., Legal Adv. Cttee, Gen. Synod of C of E, 1986–. Sec., Ecclesiastical Judges Assoc., 1997–. Ed., Macmorran's Handbook for Church Wardens and Parochial Church Councillors, 1989–. *Address:* Lamb Chambers, Elm Court, Temple, EC4Y 7AS. *T:* (020) 7797 8300, *Fax:* (020) 7797 8308.

BRIDGE, Dame Jill; *see* Macleod Clark, Dame J.

BRIDGE, John Neville, PhD; Chairman: Endeavour-SCH plc, since 2001; Agricultural and Horticultural Development Board (formerly Levy Board (UK)), since 2006; *b* 18 Sept. 1942; *s* of Tom and Eunice Bridge; *m* 1966, Rosalind Forrester; one *s* one *d*. *Educ:* Lancaster Royal Grammar Sch.; Durham Univ. (BA Geog. 1964; PhD Econs 1974); Indiana Univ. (MA Econs 1965). Lectr in Econs and Fellow, Centre for Middle Eastern and Islamic Studies, 1966–74; Hd of Industrial Develt, N of England Develt Council, 1975–84; Chief Executive: Yorks and Humberside Develt Agency, 1984–88; Northern Develt Co., 1988–98; Chm., One Northeast, 1998–2003. Consultant, PriceWaterhouseCoopers, 2004–07. Non-executive Director: Tanfield Gp (formerly Comeleon) plc, 2001–; Kenmore (UK) Ltd, 2001–05; Watson Burton LLP, 2004–06. Member: Bd, English Partnerships, 2000–03; Urban Sounding Bd, 2001–03; Bd, UK Trade and Investment, 2001–03; Treas. Adv. Council, Partnerships UK, 2001–03. Chairman: Northern Sights, 1996–; Council, Durham Cathedral, 2001–; NE Seedcorn Fund, 2001–04; Alnwick Garden Trust, 2003–; Yorks and NE Reg., Nat. Trust, 2003–; Land Restoration Trust, 2004–; Calvert Trust Kielder, 2004–; Spirit of Enterprise Trust, 2004–; Consultant, Northumbrian Leisure, 2007–. Visiting Professor: Newcastle Business Sch., 1996–; Durham Univ. Business Sch., 1998–. Member: Adv. Bd, Durham Business Sch., 2003–; Hatfield Coll. Council and Trust, 2006–. Hon. Fellow, Univ. of Sunderland, 1993. Hon. DCL: Durham, 2005; Northumbria, 2005. *Recreations:* walking, gardening, travel. *Address:* The Granary, Fenwick Shield, Matfen, Northumberland NE18 0QS. *T:* (01661) 886522, *Fax:* (01661) 886466; *e-mail:* john@bridgedev.co.uk. *Club:* Reform.

BRIDGE, Keith James, CBE 1997; consultant; *b* 21 Aug. 1929; *s* of late James Henry Bridge and Lilian Elizabeth (*née* Nichols); *m* 1960, Thelma Ruby (*née* Hubble); three *d* (and one *s* decd). *Educ:* Sir George Monoux Grammar Sch., Walthamstow; Corpus Christi Coll., Oxford (MA); Univ. of Hull (BTh 2001). CIPFA 1959; CCMI (CBIM 1978). Local govt service, 1953; Dep. City Treasurer, York, 1965; Borough Treas., Bolton, 1967; City Treas., Manchester, 1971; County Treasurer, Greater Manchester Council, 1973; Chief Exec., Humberside CC, 1978–83. Mem., W Yorks Residuary Body, 1985–91. Financial Adviser to Assoc. of Metrop. Authorities, 1971–78; Mem. Council, 1972–84, Pres., 1982–83, Chartered Inst. of Public Finance and Accountancy; Pres., Soc. of Metropolitan Treasurers, 1977–78. Member: Audit Commn for Local Authorities in Eng. and Wales, 1983–86; Exec. Council, Business in the Community, 1982–84; Bd, Public Finance Foundn, 1984–90; Educn Transfer Council (formerly Educn Assets Bd), 1988–2000 (Chm., 1996–2000); Football Licensing Authy, 1990–96. Dir, Phillips & Drew, 1987–89. Chm., York Diocesan Pastoral Cttee, 1989–94. Governor: Univ. of Lincolnshire and Humberside (formerly Humberside Poly.), 1989–98; E Yorks Coll., 2000–01. Hon. LLD Lincs and Humberside, 1999. Freeman, City of London, 1986. *Publications:* papers in professional jls. *Recreations:* gardening, literature, music. *Address:* 1 Fairlawn, Molescroft, Beverley, E Yorks HU17 7DD. *T:* (01482) 887652.

BRIDGE, Prof. Michael Greenhalgh; Professor of Law, London School of Economics, since 2007; *b* 3 Nov. 1947; *s* of Louis and Sarah Bridge; *m* 1971, Rowena Austin; one *s* one *d*. *Educ:* LSE (LLB 1969; LLM 1970). Called to the Bar, Middle Temple, 1975; Associate Prof., 1977–86, Prof. of Law, 1987–88, McGill Univ., Montreal; Hind Prof. of Commercial Law, Univ. of Nottingham, 1988–2000; Prof. of Commercial Law, UCL, 2000–07. *Publications:* Sales and Sales Financing in Canada, 1981; The Sale of Goods, 1988, 2nd edn 1998; (jtly) The Companies Act 1989, 1989; Personal Property Law, 1993, 3rd edn 2002; The International Sale of Goods, 1999; (with R. Stevens) Cross-Border Security and Insolvency, 2001; (jtly) International Sale of Goods in the Conflict of Laws, 2005; (jtly) Personal Property Security, 2007. *Recreations:* travel, wine, music (opera, orchestral, chamber), art. *Address:* Department of Law, London School of Economics, Houghton Street, WC2A 2AE. *T:* (020) 7955 6255, *Fax:* (020) 7955 7366; *e-mail:* m.g.bridge@lse.ac.uk.

BRIDGE, Stuart Nigel; Fellow, Queens' College, and Lecturer in Law, University of Cambridge, since 1990; a Recorder, since 2004; *b* 12 Aug. 1958; *s* of Albert and Nora Bridge; *m* 1st, 1982, Anabelle Jane Baker (marr. diss. 2001); one *s* one *d*; 2nd, 2003, Dr Beverley Glover; one *s*. *Educ:* Lawnswood Sch., Leeds; Queens' Coll., Cambridge (BA 1980, MA 1984). Called to the Bar, Middle Temple, 1981; Lectr in Law, Univ. of Leeds, 1985–89; a Law Comr, 2001–08; Vis. Prof., Cornell Law Sch., 1994. *Publications:* Residential Leases, 1994; Assured Tenancies, 1999; (ed) Theobald on Wills, 16th edn 2001. *Recreations:* walking, football, music, literature. *Address:* Queens' College, Cambridge CB3 9ET. *T:* (01223) 335511; *e-mail:* snb1000@cam.ac.uk.

BRIDGE, Timothy John Walter; DL; Chairman, Greene King plc, since 2005; *b* 1 Feb. 1949; *s* of Walter John Blencowe Bridge and Susan Mary Bridge (*née* Rushbrooke). *Educ:* Twyford Sch.; Repton Sch.; Univ. of Exeter (BA). Joined Greene King plc, 1970: Dir, 1977–; Man. Dir, 1990–94; Chief Exec., 1994–2005. Non-executive Director: Weatherbys Ventures Ltd, 2006–; William Ransom & Son plc, 2006–. Pres., Gentlemen of Suffolk CC, 1996–. DL Suffolk, 2004. *Recreations:* fishing, shooting, racing, cricket. *Address:* Priory Farm, Shudy Camps, Cambs CB21 4RE.

BRIDGEMAN, family name of **Earl of Bradford** and **Viscount Bridgeman**.

BRIDGEMAN, 3rd Viscount *cr* 1929, of Leigh; **Robin John Orlando Bridgeman,** CA; *b* 5 Dec. 1930; *s* of Hon. Geoffrey John Orlando Bridgeman, MC, FRCS (*d* 1974) (2nd *s* of 1st Viscount) and Mary Meriel Gertrude Bridgeman (*d* 1974), *d* of Rt Hon. Sir George John Talbot; *S* uncle, 1982; *m* 1966, (Victoria) Harriet Lucy, *d* of Ralph Meredyth Turton; three s (and one *s* decd). *Educ:* Eton. CA 1958. 2nd Lieut, Rifle Bde, 1950–51. Partner: Fenn & Crosthwaite, 1973; Henderson Crosthwaite & Co., 1975–86; Director: Nestor-BNA plc, 1988–94; Guinness Mahon & Co. Ltd, 1988–90; Chm., Asset Management Investment Co. plc, 1994–2001. Opposition Whip, H of L, 1999–; elected Mem., H of L, 1999. Dir., Bridgeman Art Library Ltd, 1972–; Chm., Friends of Lambeth Palace Liby, 1992–. Chm., Hosp. of St John and St Elizabeth, 1999–2007; Special Trustee, Hammersmith Hosp., 1986–99; Treasurer, Florence Nightingale Aid in Sickness Trust, 1995–2006. Trustee, Music at Winchester, 1995–2006. Gov., Reed's Sch., 1994–2002 (Chm.). Mem. Court, New England Co., 1986– (Treas., 1996–2007). *Recreations:* music, gardening, shooting. *Heir:* *s* Hon. Luke Robinson Orlando Bridgeman [*b* 1 May 1971; *m* 1996, Victoria Rose, *y d* of late Henry Frost; two *s* one *d*]. *Address:* 19 Chepstow Road, W2 5BP. *T:* (020) 7727 5400; Watley House, Sparsholt, Winchester SO21 2LU. *T:* (01962) 776297. *Clubs:* Beefsteak, MCC; Pitt.

BRIDGEMAN, (John) Michael, CB 1988; Chief Registrar of Friendly Societies and Industrial Assurance Commissioner, 1982–91; First Commissioner (Chairman), Building Societies Commission, 1986–91; *b* 26 April 1931; *s* of late John Wilfred Bridgeman, CBE and Mary Bridgeman (*née* Wallace); *m* 1958, June Bridgeman, *qv*; one *s* four *d*. *Educ:* Marlborough Coll.; Trinity Coll., Cambridge. Asst Principal, BoT, 1954; HM Treasury, 1956–81, Under Sec., 1975–81. *Address:* Bridge House, Culverden Park Road, Tunbridge Wells, Kent TN4 9QX.

BRIDGEMAN, John Stuart, CBE 2001; TD 1995; DL; Chairman: Regulatory Committee, British Horseracing Authority, since 2007; howtocomplain.com Ltd, since 2000; *b* 5 Oct. 1944; *s* of late James Alfred George Bridgeman, Master Mariner, and Edith Celia (*née* Watkins); *m* 1967, Lindy Jane Fillmore; three *d*. *Educ:* Whitchurch Sch., Cardiff; University Coll., Swansea (BSc) (Hon. Fellow, Univ. of Wales, Swansea, 1997); McGill Univ., Montreal. Alcan Inds, 1966–69; Aluminium Co. of Canada, 1969–70; Alcan Australia, 1970; Commercial Dir, Alcan UK, 1977–80; Vice-Pres. (Europe), Alcan Basic Raw Materials, 1978–82; Dir, Saguenay Shipping, 1979–82; Divl Man. Dir, Alcan Aluminium (UK) Ltd, 1981–82; Managing Director: Extrusion Div., Brit. Alcan Aluminium plc, 1983–87; Brit. Alcan Enterprises, 1987–91; Chm., Luxfer Hldgs, 1988–91; Dir, Corporate Planning, Alcan Aluminium Ltd, Montreal, 1992–93; Man. Dir, British Alcan Aluminium plc, 1993–95; Dir-Gen. of Fair Trading, 1995–2000; Chm., GPC Europe, 2000–01; Dir, Regulatory Impact Unit, Cardew & Co., 2001–03. Chm., HRA, 2005–07; Member: British Airways NE Consumer Council, 1978–86; Monopolies and Mergers Commn, 1990–95; Adv. Council, Consumer Policy Inst., 2000–04; Bd, British Waterways, 2006– (Chm., Fair Trading Cttee); Ind. Appeals Comr, Direct Marketing Authy (Chm., 2000–06); Ind. Complaints Adjudicator, Assoc. for Television On-Demand, 2007–. Vis. Prof. of Mgt, Keele Univ., 1992–; Vis. Prof., Univ. of Surrey, 2004–07. Vice-President: Aluminium Fedn, 1995; Trading Standards Inst., 2001–. Chairman: N Oxon Business Gp, 1984–92; Enterprise Cherwell Ltd, 1985–91; Oxfordshire Economic Partnership, 2000–06; Dir, Heart of England TEC, 1989–2002 (Chm., 2000–02). Chm., Audit and Standards Cttee, Warwicks CC, 2000–. Commnd TA and Reserve Forces, 1978; QOY, 1981–84; Maj. REME (V), 1985–94; Staff Coll., 1986; SO2 Employer Support SE Dist, 1994–95. Hon. Col, 5 (QOOH) Sqdn, 39 (Skinners), later 31 (City of London) Signal Regt (V), 1996–. Mem., TAVRA Oxon and E Wessex, 1985–. Member: Defence Science Adv. Council, 1991–94; Nat. Employer Liaison Cttee for Reserve Forces, 1992–2002 (Chm., 1998–2002); SE RFCA, 2001–. Member: UK-Canada Colloquium, 1993– (Treas., 2005); UK-Canada Chamber of Commerce, 1993– (Vice-Pres., 1995–96; Pres., 1997–98); Canada Club, 1994–. Gov., N Oxon Coll., 1985–99 (Chm., 1989; Vice Chm., 1997–99). Trustee: Oxfordshire Community Foundn, 1995–2002; Oxford Orch. da Camera, 1996–2001; Foundn for Canadian Studies, 1996– (Vice-Chm., 2005–06; Chm., 2007–); Oxfordshire Yeomanry Trust, 1997–. Pres., Oxfordshire Gliding Club, 1998–. CCMI; FInstD, FRGS, FRSA. Court Asst, Turners' Co. DL Oxon, 1989; High Sheriff, Oxon, 1995–96. Hon. Dr Sheffield Hallam, 1996. US Aluminium Assoc. Prize, 1988. *Recreations:* Queen's Own Oxfordshire Hussars, horseracing, gardening, genealogy, shooting, ski-ing. *Address:* c/o British Horseracing Authority, 151 Shaftesbury Avenue, WC2H 8AL. *T:* (020) 7189 3800. *Clubs:* Reform; Glamorgan County Cricket.

BRIDGEMAN, Mrs June, CB 1990; Deputy Chair, Equal Opportunities Commission, 1991–94; *b* 26 June 1932; *d* of Gordon and Elsie Forbes; *m* 1958, John Michael Bridgeman, *qv*; one *s* four *d*. *Educ:* variously, England and Scotland; Westfield Coll., London Univ. (BA; Fellow, QMW, 1993–2001). Asst Principal, BoT, 1954; subseq. served in DEA, NBPI, Min. of Housing and Local Govt, DoE; Under Secretary: DoE 1974–76; Central Policy Review Staff, Cabinet Office, 1976–79; Dept of Transport, 1979–90. Mem., BSE Inquiry, 1998–2000. Mem., Central Bd of Finance, C of E, 1979–83; Bishops Selector for ACCM, 1974–89. Member of Council: PSI, 1984–90; NCOPF, 1994–2001; GDST (formerly GPDST), 1995–2002. Vice-Pres., Fawcett Soc., 1994–. Trustee, Rees Jeffreys Road Fund, 1992–. FRSA 1991. *Recreations:* feminism, learning the piano accordion. *Address:* Bridge House, Culverden Park Road, Tunbridge Wells TN4 9QX. *T:* (01892) 525578.

BRIDGEMAN, Michael; *see* Bridgeman, J. M.

BRIDGER, Rev. Dr Francis William; Executive Director, Center for Anglican Communion Studies, and Professor of Anglican Studies, Fuller Theological Seminary, Pasadena, California, since 2006; *b* 27 May 1951; *s* of Harry Edward George Bridger and Harriet Rose Bridger; *m* 1st, 1975, Renee Winifred (*d* 2003); one *s* two *d*; 2nd, 2004, Helen Foster. *Educ:* Pembroke Coll., Oxford (BA 1973; MA 1978); Trinity Coll., Bristol; Bristol Univ. (PhD 1981). Ordained deacon, 1978, priest, 1979; Asst Curate, St Jude, Mildmay Park and St Paul, Canonbury, 1978–82; Lectr and Tutor, St John's Coll., Nottingham, 1982–90; Vicar, St Mark, Woodthorpe, 1990–99; Principal, Trinity Theol Coll., Bristol, 1999–2005. Vis. Prof. of Pastoral Care and Counselling, 1999–2005, of Practical Theol., 2005–06, Fuller Theol Seminary, Calif. Mem., Gen. Synod of C of E, 1998–. Theol Advr to Archbishop of Burundi, 2007–. *Publications:* The Cross and the Bomb, 1983; Videos, Permissiveness and the Law, 1984; Children Finding Faith, 1988, 2nd edn 2000 (trans. French and German, 1995); Counselling in Context, 1995, 2nd edn 1998; Celebrating the Family, 1995; Why Can't I have Faith?, 1998; The Diana Phenomenon, 1998; A Charmed Life: the spirituality of Potterworld, 2001; 23 Days: a story of love, death and God, 2004; contrib. to Tyndale Bull., Anvil, Theology, Jl of Christian Educn, Church Times. *Recreations:* politics, current affairs, media, Star Trek. *Address:* 700 Locust Street, Pasadena, CA 91101, USA; *e-mail:* fbridger@yahoo.ie.

BRIDGER, Rev. Canon Gordon Frederick; Principal, Oak Hill Theological College, 1987–96; *b* 5 Feb. 1932; *s* of late Dr John Dell Bridger and Hilda Bridger; *m* 1962, Elizabeth Doris Bewes; three *d*. *Educ:* Christ's Hospital, Horsham; Selwyn Coll., Cambridge (MA Hons Theology); Ridley Hall, Cambridge. Curate, Islington Parish Church, 1956–59; Curate, Holy Sepulchre Church, Cambridge, 1959–62; Vicar, St Mary, North End, Fulham, 1962–69; Chaplain, St Thomas's Episcopal Church, Edinburgh, 1969–76; Rector, Holy Trinity Church, Heigham, Norwich, 1976–87; RD Norwich (South), 1981–86; Exam. Chaplain to Bishop of Norwich, 1981–86; Hon. Canon, Norwich Cathedral, 1984–87, now Hon. Canon Emeritus. Dir, Open Theol Coll., 1993–97; Mem. Court, Middlesex Univ., 1996–2000. Trustee, Jerusalem Trust,

1998–2006. Fellow, 1996–98, Associate Fellow, 1999–, Coll. of Preachers. Hon. MA Middlesex, 1996. *Publications:* The Man from Outside, 1969, rev. edn 1978; A Day that Changed the World, 1975; A Bible Study Commentary (I Corinthians—Galatians), 1985; reviews in The Churchman, Anvil and other Christian papers and magazines. *Recreations:* music, sport, reading. *Address:* 4 Common Lane, Sheringham, Norfolk NR26 8PL.

BRIDGER, Timothy Peter M.; *see* Moore-Bridger.

BRIDGES, family name of **Baron Bridges**.

BRIDGES, 2nd Baron *cr* 1957; **Thomas Edward Bridges,** GCMG 1988 (KCMG 1983; CMG 1975); HM Diplomatic Service, retired; *b* 27 Nov. 1927; *s* of 1st Baron Bridges, KG, PC, GCB, GCVO, MC, FRS, and late Hon. Katharine Dianthe, *d* of 2nd Baron Farrer; *S* father, 1969; *m* 1953, Rachel Mary (*d* 2005), *y d* of late Sir Henry Bunbury, KCB; two *s* one *d*. *Educ:* Eton; New Coll., Oxford. Entered Foreign Service, 1951; served in Bonn, Berlin, Rio de Janeiro and at FO (Asst Private Sec. to Foreign Secretary, 1963–66); Head of Chancery, Athens, 1966–68; Counsellor, Moscow, 1969–71; Private Sec. (Overseas Affairs) to Prime Minister, 1972–74; RCDS 1975; Minister (Commercial), Washington, 1976–79; Dep. Under Sec. of State, FCO, 1979–82; Ambassador to Italy, 1983–87. Mem., Select Cttee on Eur. Communities, H of L, 1988–92 and 1994–98; elected Mem., H of L, 1999. Dir, Consolidated Gold Fields, 1988–89. Indep. Bd Mem., Securities and Futures Authority (formerly Securities Assoc.), 1989–97. Chairman: UK Nat. Cttee for UNICEF, 1989–97; British-Italian Soc., 1991–97. Mem., E Anglian Regl Cttee, NT, 1988–97. Pres., Dolmetsch Foundn. Trustee, Rayne Foundn, 1995–. *Heir: s* Hon. Mark Thomas Bridges, *qv*. *Address:* 56 Church Street, Orford, Woodbridge, Suffolk IP12 2NT.

See also M. E. Aston.

BRIDGES, Andrew Michael, CBE 2007; HM Chief Inspector of Probation, since 2004; *b* Bath, 2 June 1951; *s* of Michael and Peggy Bridges; partner, Lesley Corina; two *s*. *Educ:* City of Bath Boys' Sch.; Univ. of York (BA Hist. 1972); Univ. of Leicester (DipSW 1975); Bristol Poly. (MA 1984); Univ. of Bath (MPhil 1991). Probation Officer, Wilts, 1975–83; Sen. Probation Officer, Gwent, 1983–89; Asst Chief Probation Officer, 1989–98, Chief Probation Officer, 1998–2001, Berks; HM Inspector of Probation, 2001–03; HM Dep. Chief Inspector of Probation, 2003–04. Res. Fellow (pt-time), Univ. of Oxford, 1996. Chm., Interdeptl Nat. Offender Employment Forum, 1998–2001. *Publication:* Increasing the Employability of Offenders: an inquiry into Probation Service effectiveness, 1998. *Recreations:* early morning running (slowly), travelling to sometimes unusual destinations, occasionally continuing to enjoy the Grateful Dead, persistently using a Reading FC season ticket since 1995. *Address:* HM Inspector of Probation, 2nd Floor, Ashley House, 2 Monck Street, SW1P 2BQ. *T:* (020) 7035 2200, *Fax:* (020) 7035 2237; *e-mail:* Andrew.bridges@hmiprobation.gsi.gov.uk.

BRIDGES, Rt Rev. Dewi Morris; Bishop of Swansea and Brecon, 1988–98; *b* 18 Nov. 1933; *s* of Harold Davies Bridges and Elsie Margaret Bridges; *m* 1959, Rhiannon Williams; one *s* one *d*. *Educ:* St David's University College, Lampeter (BA 1954, 1st cl. Hons History); Corpus Christi Coll., Cambridge (BA 1956 II 1, Pt 2 Theol. Tripos, MA 1960); Westcott House, Cambridge. Assistant Curate: Rhymney, Gwent, 1957–60; Chepstow, 1960–63; Vicar of St James', Tredegar, 1963–65; Lecturer and Senior Lectr, Summerfield Coll. of Education, Kidderminster, 1965–69; Vicar of Kempsey, Worcester, 1969–79; RD of Upton-upon-Severn, 1974–79; Rector of Tenby, Pembs, 1979–88; RD of Narberth, 1980–82; Archdeacon of St Davids, 1982–88. Member: Court, 1989–98, and Council, 1989–95, UCW, Swansea; Council, Univ. of Wales, Lampeter (formerly St David's UC, Lampeter), 1992–98. *Recreations:* walking, gardening, photography. *Address:* Hafan Dawel, 4 St Mary's Hill, Heywood Lane, Tenby, Pembrokeshire SA70 8BG. *T:* (01834) 844087.

BRIDGES, Prof. James Wilfrid; Professor of Toxicology and Environmental Health, University of Surrey, 1979–2003, Professor Emeritus, since 2004; *b* 9 Aug. 1938; *s* of Wilfrid Edward Seymour Bridges and Mary Winifred Cameron. *Educ:* Bromley Grammar Sch.; Queen Elizabeth Coll., London Univ.; St Mary's Hosp. Med. Sch., London Univ. (BSc, DSc, PhD). Lectr, St Mary's Hosp. Med. Sch., 1962–68; University of Surrey: Senior Lectr then Reader, Dept of Biochemistry, 1968–78; Res. Dir, Robens Inst. of Industrial and Envmtl Health and Safety, 1978–95; Dean, Faculty of Science, 1988–92; Hd, European Inst. of Health and Med. Scis, 1995–2000; Dean for Internat. Strategy, 2000–03. Visiting Professor: Univ. of Texas at Dallas, 1973, 1979; Univ. of Rochester, NY, 1974; Mexico City, 1991; Sen. Scientist, Nat. Inst. of Envtl Health Scis, N Carolina, 1976. Chm., British Toxicology Soc., 1980–81; First Pres., Fedn of European Toxicology Socs, 1985–88. Member: Vet. Products Cttee, 1982–96; HSE WATCH Cttee, 1982–2005; EC Scientific Cttee on Animal Nutrition, 1991–97; EU Scientific Steering Cttee (Public Health), 1997–2004; EU Mirror Gp, 2006–; DG SANCO Scientific Cttee Co-ordination Gp, 2004–; various EFSA working gps, 2004–; former Member: Novel and Irradiated Foods Cttee; Med. Aspects of Water Quality Cttee; Adv. Cttee on Toxic Substances; Chairman: Vet. Residues Cttee, 2001–04; EU Harmonisation of Risk Assessment Working Party, 1998–2004; President: EU Scientific Adv. Cttee on Toxicology, Ecotoxicology and the Envmt, 1997–2004; EU Scientific Cttee on Emerging and Newly Identified Health Risks, 2004–. Founder, Eur. Drug Metabolism Workshops. Hon. Mem., Soc. of Occup. Med.; Hon. Fellow, Europ. Soc. of Toxicol. Hon. DSc Baptist Univ. of Hong Kong. *Publications:* (ed jtly) Progress in Drug Metabolism, 10 vols, 1976–88; (with Dr Olga Bridges) Losing Hope: the environment and health in Russia, 1996; over 400 research papers and reviews in scientific jls. *Recreations:* theatre going, various sports. *Address:* Liddington Lodge, Liddington Hall Drive, Guildford GU3 3AE.

BRIDGES, Hon. Mark Thomas; Private Solicitor to the Queen, since 2002; *b* 25 July 1954; *er s* and *heir* of Baron Bridges, *qv*; *m* 1978, Angela Margaret, *er d* of late John Leigh Collinson; one *s* three *d*. *Educ:* Eton Coll.; Corpus Christi Coll., Cambridge (Choral Exhibition). Partner, Farrer & Co., 1985–; Solicitor, Duchy of Lancaster affairs, 1998–. Mem. Council, RSCM, 1989–97; Treas., Bach Choir, 1992–97; Chm., Music in Country Churches, 2006–; Trustee: UCL Hospitals Charity, 1992–; Leeds Castle Foundn, 2007–. Chm. Govs, Hanford Sch., 2004–; Governor: Purcell Sch., 2000–; Sherborne Sch. for Girls, 2001–. Academician, Internat. Acad. of Estate and Trust Law, 2005. Mem., Court of Assistants, Goldsmiths' Co., 2006–. *Publication:* (ed) International Succession Laws, 2001. *Recreations:* music, sailing. *Address:* Farrer & Co., 66 Lincoln's Inn Fields, WC2A 3LH. *T:* (020) 7242 2022, *Fax:* (020) 7242 9899; *e-mail:* mtb@farrer.co.uk. *Clubs:* Brooks's, House of Lords Yacht, Noblemen and Gentlemen's Catch.

BRIDGES, Dame Mary (Patricia), DBE 1981; *b* 6 June 1930; *d* of Austin Edward and Lena Mabel Fawkes; *m* 1951, Bertram Marsdin Bridges; one step *s*. Chm., Honiton Div. Cons. Assoc., 1968–71; Pres., Western Provincial Area, Nat. Union of Cons. and Unionist Assocs, 1987–. Women's Section of Royal British Legion: Pres., Exmouth Br., 1965–; Chm., Devon County Women's Section, 1979–91; County Vice Pres., 1991; County Pres., 1997–; SW Area Rep. to Central Cttee, 1985–89; Nat. Vice-Chm., 1989–92; Nat. Chm., 1992–95; Nat. Life Vice-Pres., 1999; Mem. House Cttee, Dunkirk Meml House, 1994–99. Mem., SW Electricity Consultative Council, 1982–90 (Chm., Devon Cttee, 1986–90). Former Mem., Exe Vale HMC; Pres., Exmouth Council of Voluntary Service (Founder Chm., 1975). Member: Exec., Resthaven, Exmouth, 1970–2001 (Chm., League of Friends, 1971–90); Devon FPC, 1985–91; President: Exmouth and Budleigh Salterton Br., CRUSE, 1980–88; Exmouth Campaign Cttee, Cancer Research, 1981– (Chm., 1975–81); Founder Pres., Exmouth Br., British Heart Foundn, 1984–2004. Mem., Exmouth Cttee, LEPRA, 1962–87 (Hon. Sec., 1964–87); Dir, Home Care Trust, 1988–90; Co-optative Trustee, Exmouth Welfare Trust, 1979–2005; Co-founder, and Trustee, Exmouth and Lympstone Hospiscare, 1986– (Pres., 1994–2004); founder Trustee, Exmouth Adventure Trust for Girls, 1987–90 (Patron, 1990–); Exec. Mem., St Loye's Coll. Foundn for Trng the Disabled for Commerce and Industry, 1988–2001; Governor, Rolle Coll., Exmouth, 1982–88. Hon. Life Member: Retford Cricket Club, 1951; Exmouth Cricket Club, 1997 (Hon. Vice-Pres., 1981; Pres., 1992–2001). *Recreations:* cricket, reading. *Address:* Walton House, Fairfield Close, Exmouth, Devon EX8 2BN. *T:* (01395) 265317.

BRIDGES, Ven. Peter Sydney Godfrey; Archdeacon of Warwick, 1983–90, now Emeritus; Canon-Theologian of Coventry Cathedral, 1977–90, now Emeritus; *b* 30 Jan. 1925; *s* of Sidney Clifford Bridges and Winifred (*née* Livette); *m* 1952, Joan Penlerick (*née* Madge); two *s*. *Educ:* Raynes Park Grammar Sch.; Kingston upon Thames Sch. of Architecture; Lincoln Theol College. ARIBA 1950, Dip. Liturgy and Architecture 1967. Gen. and ecclesiastical practice, 1950–54; Lectr, Nottingham Sch. of Architecture, 1954–56. Deacon, 1958; Priest, 1959. Asst Curate, Hemel Hempstead, 1958–64; Res. Fellow, Inst. for Study of Worship and Religious Architecture, Univ. of Birmingham, 1964–67 (Hon. Fellow, 1967–72 and 1978); Warden, Anglican Chaplaincy and Chaplain to Univ. of Birmingham, 1965–68; Lectr, Birmingham Sch. of Arch., 1967–72; eccles. architect and planning consultant, 1968–75; Chm., New Town Ministers Assoc., 1968–72; Co-Dir, Midlands Socio-Religious Res. Gp, 1968–75; Dir, Chelmsford Diocesan R&D Unit, 1972–77; Archdeacon of Southend, 1972–77; Archdeacon of Coventry, 1977–83. Advr for Christian Spirituality, Dio. of Coventry, 1990–93. Mem., Cathedrals Advisory Commn for England, 1981–86. Chm., Painting and Prayer, 1989–94. *Publications:* Socio-Religious Institutes, Lay Academies, etc, 1967; contrib. Church Building, res. bulletins (Inst. for Study of Worship and Relig. Arch.), Clergy Review, Prism, Christian Ministry in New Towns, Cathedral and Mission, Church Architecture and Social Responsibility. *Recreations:* architecture, singing, painting. *Address:* Saint Clare, 25 Rivermead Close, Romsey, Hants SO51 8HQ. *T:* (01794) 512889.

BRIDGES, Stephen John, LVO 1998; HM Diplomatic Service; Director, Carbon Mining plc and Delta Pacific Mining plc, since 2007; *b* 19 June 1960; *s* of Gordon Alfred Richard Bridges and Audrey Middleton; *m* 1990, Kyung Mi. *Educ:* Devonport High Sch.; London Univ. (International Relations). Joined FCO, 1980; Third Sec., Luanda, 1984–87; Third, later Second, Sec., Seoul, 1987–91; Second, later First, Sec., UN and SE Asia Dept, FCO, 1991–96; First Sec., and Head, Political Section, Kuala Lumpur, 1996–2000; Ambassador to Cambodia, 2000–05; Dep. High Comr, Dhaka, Bangladesh, 2005–07. *Recreations:* golf, food and wine, Coco and Montague - the dogs. *Address:* c/o Foreign and Commonwealth Office, King Charles Street, SW1A 2AH; *e-mail:* bridgeskm@hotmail.com.

BRIDGEWATER, Allan, CBE 1998; LVO 2008; Chairman, Swiss Re GB plc (formerly Swiss Re Group UK), 1998–2008; *b* 26 Aug. 1936; *m* 1960, Janet Bridgewater; three *d*. *Educ:* Wyggeston Grammar Sch., Leicester. ACII, Chartered Insurer, FCIPD, CCMI. Norwich Union Insurance Group: Dir, 1985–97; Group Chief Exec., 1989–97. Director: Riggs Bank Europe, 1991–; Fox Pitt Kelton, 2000–. Pres., Chartered Insurance Inst., 1989–90; Chm., Assoc. of British Insurers, 1993–95. Pres., Endeavour Training, 1997–2005 (Chm., 1987–97); Chm., C of E Pensions Bd, 1998–. Special Prof., Business Sch., Univ. of Nottingham, 1995–. Trustee: Duke of Edinburgh's Commonwealth Study Conf., 1993– (Vice Chm.); Industry in Educn, 1993–97; Soc. for the Protection of Life from Fire, 1991–. Gov., Chartered Insurance Inst. College, 1985–. FRSA 1989. Freeman, City of London, 1991; Liveryman, Insurers' Co., 1991– (Mem., Ct of Assistants).

BRIDGLAND, Milton Deane, AO 1987; FTSE; Chairman, ICI Australia Ltd, 1980–93; *b* 8 July 1922; *s* of late Frederick H. and Muriel E. Bridgland, Adelaide; *m* 1945, Christine L. Cowell; three *d*. *Educ:* St Peter's Coll., Adelaide; Adelaide Univ. (BSc). FRACI, FAIM. Joined ICI Australia Ltd, 1945; Technical Manager, Plastics Gp, 1955–62; Ops Dir, 1962–67, Man. Dir, 1967–71, Dulux Australia Ltd; Exec. Dir 1971, Man. Dir, 1978–84, ICI Australia Ltd. Chairman: Jennings Properties, later Centro Properties Ltd, 1985–92; ANZ Banking Group Ltd, 1989–92 (Dir, 1982–92; Dep. Chm., 1987–89); Director: Jennings Group (formerly Industries) Ltd, 1984–92; Freeport-McMoRan Australia Ltd, 1987–89. President: Aust. Chemical Industry Council, 1977; Aust. Industry Develt Assoc., 1982–83. Vice President: Aust. Business Roundtable, 1983; Business Council of Australia, 1983–84; Dir, Aust. Inst. of Petroleum, 1980–84; Mem., National Energy Adv. Cttee, 1977–80. Member, Board of Management: Univ. of Melbourne Grad. Sch. of Management, 1983–86; Crawford Fund for Internat. Agricl Res., 1989–94. Chm. Adv. Bd, Salvation Army, Southern Territory, 1986–90. Mem., Cook Soc. *Recreations:* the arts, gardening. *Address:* 1/42 Glen Street, Hawthorn, Vic 3122, Australia. *T:* (3) 98193939.

BRIDGWATER, Prof. John, FREng, FIChemE; Shell Professor of Chemical Engineering, Cambridge University, 1993–2004, now Professor Emeritus; Professorial Fellow, 1993–2004 and Senior Tutor, 2004, St Catharine's College, Cambridge; *b* 10 Jan. 1938; *s* of Eric and Mary Bridgwater; *m* 1962, Diane Louise Tucker; one *s* one *d*. *Educ:* Solihull Sch.; St Catharine's Coll., Cambridge (Major Scholar; MA, PhD, ScD); Princeton Univ. (MSE). FREng (FEng 1987). Chemical Engineer, Courtaulds, 1961–64; University of Cambridge: Demonstrator in Chem. Engrg, 1964–69; Univ. Lectr in Chem. Engrg and Fellow, St Catharine's Coll., 1969–71; Esso Res. Fellow in Chem. Engrg, Hertford Coll., Oxford, 1971–73; Univ. Lectr in Engrg Sci., Univ. of Oxford and Lubbock Fellow in Engrg, Balliol Coll., 1973–80; University of Birmingham: Prof., 1980–93; Head, Sch. of Chem. Engrg, 1983–89; Dean, Faculty of Engrg, 1989–92; Gp Leader in Inter-Disciplinary Res. Centre in Materials for High Performance Applications, 1989–93; Hd, Dept of Chemical Engrg, Cambridge Univ., 1993–98. Dir, Tunkhu Abdul Rahman Fund, 2005–06. Vis. Associate Prof., Univ. of British Columbia, 1970–71; Vis. Prof., Univ. of Calif at Berkeley, 1992–93; Erskine Vis. Fellow, Univ. of Canterbury, NZ, 2002; Vis. Fellow, Univ. of NSW, 2004–. Mem., Engrg Bd, SERC, 1986–89; Chm., Process Engrg Cttee, SERC, 1986–89. Pres., IChemE, 1997–98 (Vice-Pres., 1995–97). Chm., Editl Bd, Chem. Engrg Science, 1996–2003 (Exec. Editor, 1983–96). *Publications:* (with J. J. Benbow) Paste Flow and Extrusion, 1993; papers on chem. and process engineering in professional jls. *Address:* St Catharine's College, Cambridge CB2 1RL.

BRIDLE, Rear-Adm. Gordon Walter, CB 1977; MBE 1952; *b* 14 May 1923; *s* of Percy Gordon Bridle and Dorothy Agnes Bridle; *m* 1944, Phyllis Audrey Page; three *s*. *Educ:* King Edward's Grammar Sch., Aston, Birmingham; Northern Grammar Sch., Portsmouth; Royal Dockyard Sch., Portsmouth (Whitworth Scholar); Imperial Coll., London (ACGI). CEng, FIET. jssc. Loan Service, Pakistan, 1950–52; served HM Ships: Implacable, St James, Gambia, Newfoundland, Devonshire; Proj. Manager, Sea Slug and

Sea Dart, Mins of Aviation/Technol.; comd HMS Collingwood, 1969–71; Dir, Surface Weapons Projects, ASWE; Asst Controller of the Navy, 1974–77. *Address:* 25 Heatherwood, Midhurst, Sussex GU29 9LH. *T:* (01730) 812838.

BRIDLE, Ronald Jarman, FREng; private consultant and inventor, Cardiff University Industry Centre, since 1989, and Hon. Professor, Cardiff University, since 1991; *b* 27 Jan. 1930; *s* of Raymond Bridle and Dorothy (*née* Jarman); *m* Beryl Eunice (*née* Doe); two *d. Educ:* West Monmouth Grammar Sch.; Bristol Univ. (BSc). FREng (FEng 1979); FICE, FIHE. Graduate Asst, Monmouthshire CC, 1953–55; Exec. Engr, Gold Coast Govt, 1955–57; Sen. Engr, Cwmbran Develt Corp., 1957–60; Principal Designer, Cardiff City, 1960–62; Project Engr, Sheffield-Leeds Motorway, West Riding CC, 1962–65; Dep. County Surveyor II, Cheshire CC, 1965–67; Dir, Midland RCU, DoE, 1967–71; Dep. Chief Highway Engr, 1971–73, Under-Sec., Highways 1, 1973–75, Chief Highway Engr, 1975–76, DoE; Chief Highway Engr, Dept of Transport, 1976–80; Controller of R&D, Dept of Transport, and Dir, Transport and Road Res. Lab., 1980–84; Dir, Key Resources Internat., 1984–87. Dir (Technology and Develt), Mitchell Cotts PLC, 1984–86; Chm., Permanent Formwork Ltd, 1987–89. FRSA. Former Member: Council, ICE; EDC for Civil Engrg; Past Pres., IHE; Mem. Bd., BSI, 1979–85; Chm., Building and Civil Engineering Council, BSI, 1979–85. *Publications:* papers in jls of ICE, IHE and internat. confs. *Recreations:* golf, painting. *Address:* Parsonage Farm, Kemeys Commander, Usk, Gwent NP5 1SU. *T:* (01873) 880929; *e-mail:* ron@kolvox.net. *Club:* Royal Automobile.

BRIDPORT, 4th Viscount, *cr* 1868; **Alexander Nelson Hood;** Baron Bridport, 1794; 7th Duke of Bronte in Sicily (*cr* 1799); Managing Partner, Bridport & Cie SA, since 1991; *b* 17 March 1948; *s* of 3rd Viscount Bridport and Sheila Jeanne Agatha (*d* 1996), *d* of Johann van Meurs; *S* father, 1969; *m* 1st, 1972, Linda Jacqueline Paravicini (marr. diss.), *d* of Lt-Col and Mrs V. R. Paravicini; one *s;* 2nd, 1979, Mrs Nina Rindt-Martyn (marr. diss. 1999); one *s. Educ:* Eton; Sorbonne. *Heir: s* Hon. Peregrine Alexander Nelson Hood, *b* 30 Aug. 1974. *Address:* 1 Place Longemalle, 1204 Geneva, Switzerland. *T:* (22) 8177000, *Fax:* (22) 8177050. *Club:* Brooks's.

BRIEGEL, Geoffrey Michael Olver; Deputy Master of the Court of Protection, 1977–83; *b* 13 July 1923; *s* of late Roy C. Briegel, TD, and Veria Lindsey Briegel; *m* 1947, Barbara Mary Richardson; three *s* one *d. Educ:* Highgate Sch. Served War, RAF, 1942–46 (514 Sqdn Bomber Command). Called to Bar, Lincoln's Inn, 1950; Public Trustee Office, 1954; Clerk of the Lists, Queen's Bench Div., and Legal Sec. to Lord Chief Justice of England, 1963; Dep. Circuit Administrator, South Eastern Circuit, 1971. Legacy Officer, Inst. of Cancer Res., Royal Cancer Hosp., 1983–97; Legacy Consultant, Imperial Cancer Res. Fund, 1998. *Recreations:* theatre, cinema, music, boating, all sports. *Club:* Royal Air Force.

BRIERLEY, David, CBE 1986; Hon. Associate Artist, Royal Shakespeare Company, since 2004; *b* 26 July 1936; *s* of Ernest William Brierley and Jessie Brierley; *m* 1962, Ann Fosbrooke Potter; two *s. Educ:* Romiley County Primary Sch.; Stockport GS; Clare Coll., Cambridge (Exhibnr; Cert Ed 1959; MA; Pres., 1958–59, Trustee, 1969–, CU Amateur Dramatic Club). Teacher: Perse Sch., Cambridge, 1958–59; King Edward VI Sch., Macclesfield, 1959–61; Royal Shakespeare Company: Asst Stage Manager, and Stage Manager, Royal Shakespeare Theatre, 1961–63; Gen. Stage Manager, 1963–66; Asst to Dir, 1966–68; Gen. Manager, Sec. to Govs and Dir, various associated cos, 1968–96; Adv. Dir, 1996–2004. Member: Council of Mgt, Royal Shakespeare Theatre Trust, 1982–; Trustees and Guardians, Shakespeare's Birthplace, 1984–96. Director: West End Theatre Managers Ltd, 1975–96; Theatre Royal, Plymouth, 1997–; Gov., Clwyd Theatr Cymru, 1997–. Chairman: Grant Aided Theatres Standing Cttee, Soc. of London Theatre, 1975–96; Theatres Nat. Cttee, 1986–96; Mem., Theatres Trust, 1996–2002; Adv. Bd Actors Centre, 1996–. Mem. and chm. of panels and cttees, Arts Council of GB, 1975–94; Arts Council England (formerly Arts Council of England): Member: Drama Adv. Panel, 1994–96; Capital Adv. Panel, 1996–2006; Council, 1997–2002; Audit Cttee, 1998–; Chm., Stabilisation Adv. Panel, 1996–2006; Chairman: Drama and Dance Adv. Cttee, British Council, 1997–2006; South West Arts, 1997–98. Trustee, Hall for Cornwall Trust, 1999– (Chm., 2003–06). Member: Cambridge Univ. Careers Service Syndicate, 1980–88; Council, Warwick Univ., 1984–91; Gov., Stratford-upon-Avon Coll., 1971–96. Hon. DLitt Warwick, 1996. Special Award, 10th Internat. Congress, Internat. Soc. for the Performing Arts, 1996. *Recreation:* reading. *Address:* Headland, 8 Pear Tree Close, Chipping Camden, Glos GL55 6DB. *T:* (01386) 840361.

BRIERLEY, Ven. David James; Archdeacon of Sudbury, since 2006; *b* 12 Dec. 1953; *s* of Jack Brierley and Mary Brierley (*née* Connearn); *m* 1976, Gill Eatough; one *s* two *d. Educ:* Bristol Univ. (BA Hons Theol.); Oak Hill Theol Coll. (DPS). Ordained deacon, 1977, priest, 1978; Curate, Rochdale, 1977–80; Vicar: St Andrew, Eccles, 1980–85; Harwood, 1985–95; Vicar and RD, Walmsley, 1995–2002; Residentiary Canon, Bradford Cathedral, 2002–04; Diocesan Missioner, Bradford, 2004–06. Manchester Diocesan Ecumenical Officer, 1981–88; Chm., Decade of Evangelism Steering Cttee, 1999–2000. *Publications:* two working booklets. *Recreations:* walking (Labrador dogs), biographies (Churchill), ornithology, 'soaps', the amber nectar. *Address:* Sudbury Lodge, Stanningfield Road, Great Whelnetham, Suffolk IP30 0TL. *T:* (01284) 386942; *e-mail:* archdeacon.david@stedmundsbury.anglican.org.

BRIERLEY, Sir Ronald (Alfred), Kt 1988; Chairman, Guinness Peat Group plc (formerly GPG plc), since 1990; *b* Wellington, 2 Aug. 1937; *s* of J. R. Brierley. *Educ:* Wellington Coll. Editor, New Zealand Stocks and Shares, 1957–63; Chairman: Brierley Investments Ltd, 1961–89 (Founder, 1961; Founder Pres. 1989–); Industrial Equity Ltd, 1966–89; Chm., Bank of New Zealand, 1987–88 (Dir, 1985–88; Dep. Chm., 1986). *Address:* Guinness Peat Group plc, First Floor, Times Place, 45 Pall Mall, SW1Y 5GP. *Clubs:* American National, City Tattersall's (NSW).

BRIERS, Richard David, CBE 2003 (OBE 1989); actor since 1955; *b* 14 Jan. 1934; *s* of Joseph Briers and Morna Richardson; *m* 1957, Ann Davies; two *d. Educ:* Rokeby Prep. Sch., Wimbledon; Ridgeway Sch., Wimbledon. RADA, 1954–56 (silver medal). First appearance in London in Gilt and Gingerbread, Duke of York's, 1959. *Plays:* (major parts in): Present Laughter, Queen's, 1964; Arsenic and Old Lace, Vaudeville, 1965; Relatively Speaking, Duke of York's, 1966; The Real Inspector Hound, Criterion, 1968; Cat Among the Pigeons, Prince of Wales, 1969; The Two of Us, Garrick, 1970; Butley, Criterion, 1972; Absurd Person Singular, Criterion, 1973; Absent Friends, Garrick, 1975; Middle Age Spread, Lyric, 1979; The Wild Duck, Lyric, Hammersmith, 1980; Arms and the Man, Lyric, 1981; Run for Your Wife, Shaftesbury, 1983; Why Me?, Strand, 1985; The Relapse, Chichester, 1986; Twelfth Night, Riverside Studios, 1987 (televised 1988); Midsummer Night's Dream, and King Lear, Renaissance Theatre world tour, 1990; Wind in the Willows, Nat. Theatre, 1991; Uncle Vanya, Lyric, Hammersmith, 1991; Coriolanus, Chichester, 1992; Home, Wyndham's, 1994; A Christmas Carol, Lyric, Hammersmith, 1996; The Chairs, Duke of York's and NY, 1997; Spike, Southampton, 2001; Bedroom Farce, Aldwych, 2002; The Tempest, nat. tour, 2002. *Television series:* Brothers-in-Law; Marriage Lines; The Good Life; OneUpManShip; The Other One; Norman Conquests; Ever-Decreasing Circles; All In Good Faith; Monarch of the Glen. *Films:* Henry V, 1989; Much Ado About Nothing, Swan Song, 1993; Mary Shelley's Frankenstein, 1994; In the Bleak Midwinter, 1995; Hamlet, 1997; Love's Labours Lost, 1999; Peter Pan, 2003; As You Like It, 2007. *Publications:* Natter Natter, 1981; Coward and Company, 1987; A Little Light Weeding, 1993; A Taste of the Good Life, 1995. *Recreations:* reading, gardening. *Address:* c/o Hamilton Hodell Ltd, Fifth Floor, 66–68 Margaret Street, W1W 8SR.

BRIGGS, family name of **Baron Briggs**.

BRIGGS, Baron *cr* 1976 (Life Peer), of Lewes, E Sussex; **Asa Briggs,** MA, BSc (Econ); FBA 1980; Provost, Worcester College, Oxford, 1976–91; Chancellor, Open University, 1978–94; *b* 7 May 1921; *o s* of William Walker Briggs and Jane Briggs, Keighley, Yorks; *m* 1955, Susan Anne Banwell, *o d* of late Donald I. Banwell, Keevil, Wiltshire; two *s* two *d. Educ:* Keighley Grammar School; Sidney Sussex College, Cambridge (1st cl. History Tripos, Pts I and II, 1940, 1941; Hon. Fellow, 1968); 1st cl. BSc (Econ.), Lond., 1941. Gerstenberg studentship in Economics, London, 1941. Served in Intelligence Corps, Bletchley Park, 1942–45. Fellow of Worcester College, Oxford, 1945–55; Reader in Recent Social and Economic History, Oxford, 1950–55; Member, Institute for Advanced Study, Princeton, USA, 1953–54; Faculty Fellow of Nuffield College, Oxford, 1953–55; Professor of Modern History, Leeds Univ., 1955–61; University of Sussex: Professor of History, 1961–76; Dean, School of Social Studies, 1961–65; Pro Vice-Chancellor, 1961–67; Vice-Chancellor, 1967–76. Chm. Bd of Governors, Inst. of Develt Studies, 1967–76. Visiting Professor: ANU, 1960; Chicago Univ., 1966, 1972; Sen. Gannett Fellow, Columbia Univ., 1988, 1996; Dist. Sen. Kluge Prof., Liby of Congress, Washington, 2005. Lectures: Gregynog, Univ. of Wales, 1981; Ford, Oxford Univ., 1991; Ellen McArthur, Cambridge Univ., 1992. Dep. Pres., WEA, 1954–58, Pres., 1958–67. Mem., UGC, 1959–67; Chm., Cttee on Nursing, 1970–72 (Cmnd 5115, 1972). Trustee: Glyndebourne Arts Trust, 1966–91; Internat. Broadcasting Inst., 1968–87 (Hon. Trustee, 1991–); (Chm.) Heritage Educn Gp, 1976–86; Civic Trust, 1976–86; Chairman: Standing Conf. for Study of Local History, 1969–76; Council, European Inst. of Education, 1975–90; Commonwealth of Learning, 1988–93 (Hon. Dist. Fellow, 2003); Govs and Trustees, Brighton Pavilion, 1975–; Adv. Bd for Redundant Churches, 1983–89; Eurydice Consultative Gp, 1996–2001; Vice-Chm. of Council, UN Univ., 1974–80; Governor, British Film Institute, 1970–77; President: Social History Soc., 1976–; Victorian Soc., 1983–; The Ephemera Soc., 1984–; Brontë Soc., 1989–96; British Assoc. for Local History, 1984–86; Assoc. of Research Associations, 1986–88; Vice-Pres., Historical Assoc., 1986–. Mem., Ct of Governors, Administrative Staff Coll., 1971–91. Mem., Amer. Acad. of Arts and Sciences, 1970. Hon. FRCP 2005; Hon. Fellow: Worcester Coll., Oxford, 1969; St Catharine's Coll., Cambridge, 1977. Hon. DLitt: East Anglia, 1966; Strathclyde, 1973; Leeds, 1974; Cincinnati, 1977; Liverpool, 1977; Open Univ., 1979; Birmingham, 1989; Missouri, Teesside, 1993; Hon. DSc Florida Presbyterian, 1966; Hon. LLD: York, Canada, 1968; New England, 1972; Sussex, 1976; Bradford, 1978; Rochester, NY, 1980; Ball State, 1985; E Asia, 1987; George Washington, 1988; Southampton, 1995; Tulane, 1996; London, 2001. Marconi Medal for Communications History, 1975; Médaille de Vermeil de la Formation, Fondation de l'Académie d'Architecture, 1979; Snow Medal, Royal Coll. of Anaesthetists, 1991. *Publications:* Patterns of Peace-making (with D. Thomson and E. Meyer), 1945; History of Birmingham (1865–1938), 1952; Victorian People, 1954; Friends of the People, 1956; The Age of Improvement, 1959, rev. edn 2000; (ed) Chartist Studies, 1959; (ed with John Saville) Essays in Labour History, Vol. I, 1960, Vol. II, 1971, Vol. III, 1977; (ed) They Saw it Happen, 1897–1940, 1961; A Study of the Work of Seebohm Rowntree, 1871–1954, 1961; History of Broadcasting in the United Kingdom: vol. I, The Birth of Broadcasting, 1961; vol. II, The Golden Age of Wireless, 1965; vol. III, The War of Words, 1970; vol. IV, Sound and Vision, 1979; vol. V, Competition 1955–1974, 1995; Victorian Cities, 1963, 2nd edn 1996; William Cobbett, 1967; How They Lived, 1700–1815, 1969; (ed) The Nineteenth Century, 1970; (ed with Susan Briggs) Cap and Bell, 1973; (ed) Essays in the History of Publishing, 1974; Iron Bridge to Crystal Palace: impact and images of the Industrial Revolution, 1979; Governing the BBC, 1979; The Power of Steam, 1982; Marx in London, 1982; A Social History of England, 1983, 3rd edn 1999; Toynbee Hall, 1984; Collected Essays, 2 vols, 1985, vol. III 1991; The BBC: the first fifty years, 1985; (with Joanna Spicer) The Franchise Affair, 1986; Victorian Things, 1988, 2nd edn 1996; Haut Brion, 1994; The Channel Islands, Occupation and Liberation 1940–1945, 1995; (ed jtly) Fins de Siècle: how centuries end 1400–2000, 1996; (with Patricia Clavin) Modern Europe 1789–1989, 1997, 2nd edn, 1789–2003, 2003; Chartism, 1998; Go To It!: working for victory on the Home Front 1939–1945, 2000; Michael Young; social entrepreneur, 2001, 2nd edn 2005; (with Peter Burke) A Social History of the Media from Gutenberg to the Internet, 2002, 2nd edn 2005; A History of the Royal College of Physicians of London, vol. 4, 2005. *Recreation:* travelling. *Address:* The Caprons, Keere Street, Lewes, Sussex BN7 1TY. *Clubs:* Beefsteak, Oxford and Cambridge.

BRIGGS, Andrew; *see* Briggs, G. A. D.

BRIGGS, David John, FRCO; freelance composer and concert organist, since 2002; *b* 1 Nov. 1962; *s* of late J. R. Briggs and of J. A. Briggs (*née* Jones); *m* 1st, 1986, Elisabeth Anne Baker; one *d;* 2nd, 2004, Madge Nimocks. *Educ:* Solihull Sch. (Music Schol.); King's Coll., Cambridge (Organ Schol.; MA 1987). FRCO 1980; ARCM 1986. Asst Organist, Hereford Cathedral, 1985–88; Organist: Truro Cathedral, 1989–94; Gloucester Cathedral, 1994–2002. Vis. Tutor in Improvisation, RNCM, 1995–; Vis. Prof. of Improvisation, RAM, 2001–. Festival Conductor, Gloucester Three Choirs Fest., 1995. Recital tours, Australia, NZ and USA, 1997. Has made numerous recordings. FRSA 1993. *Publications: compositions:* Truro Eucharist, 1990; The Music Mountain, 1991; Te Deum Laudamus, 1998; Creation, 2000; *transcriptions:* Cochereau, Improvisations on Alouette, gentille Alouette, 1993; Cantem toto la Gloria, 1997; Suite de Danses improvisées, 1998; Improvisations sur Venez, Divin Messie, 1998; Triptique Symphonique, 1998; (for organ) Mahler, Symphony No 5. *Recreation:* training for private pilot's licence.

BRIGGS, Prof. Derek Ernest Gilmor, PhD; FRS 1999; Frederick William Beinecke Professor of Geology and Geophysics, since 2006 (Professor of Geology and Geophysics, 2003–06) and Curator in Charge of Invertebrate Paleontology, Peabody Museum, since 2003, Yale University; Director, Yale Peabody Museum of Natural History, since 2008; *b* 10 Jan. 1950; *s* of John Gilmor Briggs and Olive Evelyn Briggs (*née* Scanlon); *m* 1972, Jennifer Olive Kershaw; three *s. Educ:* Sandford Park Sch., Dublin; Trinity Coll., Dublin (Foundn Scholar; BA Geology); Sidney Sussex Coll., Cambridge (MA, PhD). Res. Fellow, Cambridge, 1974–77; Goldsmiths' College, London University: Department of Geology: Lectr, 1977; Sen. Lectr, 1980; Principal Lectr and Dep. Dean of Sci. and Maths, 1982–85; Department of Earth Sciences, Bristol University: Lectr, 1985; Reader, 1988; Prof. of Palaeontol., 1994–2002; Head of Dept, 1997–2001; Asst Dir, Biogeochemistry Res. Centre, 1990–97; Dir, Yale Inst. for Biospheric Studies, 2004–06. Res. Associate, Royal Ontario Mus., Toronto, 1983–; Vis. Scientist, Field Mus. of Nat. History, Chicago, 1983; Dist. Vis. Scholar, Univ. of Adelaide, 1994; Vis. Prof., Univ. of Chicago and Field Mus. of Nat. History, Chicago, 2001–02. Lectures: Benedum, Univ. of W Virginia, 1994;

Case Meml, Michigan Univ., 2004; Darwin, Duquesne Univ., 2006; Walther Arndt Meml, Berlin, 2008. Editor, Palaeontology and Special Papers in Palaeontology, 1982–86. President: Palaeontolog. Assoc., 2002–04; Paleontolog. Soc., 2006–08. Hon. MRIA 2003. Lyell Medal, Geol Soc., 2000; Boyle Medal, Royal Dublin Soc./Irish Times, 2001; Premio Capo d'Orlando, Italy, 2000; Humboldt Res. Award, Alexander von Humboldt Foundn, 2008. *Publications:* (ed with K. C. Allen) Evolution and the Fossil Record, 1989; (ed with P. R. Crowther) Palaeobiology: a synthesis, 1990; (ed with P. A. Allison) Taphonomy: releasing the data locked in the fossil record, 1991; (jtly) The Fossils of the Burgess Shale, 1994; The Fossils of the Hunsrück Slate, 1998; (ed with P. R. Crowther) Palaeobiology II, 2001; (jtly) Evolution, 2007; contribs to learned jls. *Recreations:* the outdoors, natural history, golf. *Address:* Department of Geology and Geophysics, Yale University, PO Box 208109, New Haven, CT 06520–8109, USA. *T:* (203) 4328590; Flat 4, 65 Pembroke Road, Clifton, Bristol BS8 3DW.

BRIGGS, Prof. (George) Andrew (Davidson), PhD; FInstP; Professor of Nanomaterials, University of Oxford, and Fellow, St Anne's College, Oxford, since 2002; Director, Quantum Information Processing Interdisciplinary Research Collaboration, and Professorial Research Fellow, Engineering and Physical Sciences Research Council, since 2002; *b* 3 June 1950; *s* of John Davidson Briggs and Catherine Mary Briggs (*née* Lormer); *m* 1981, Diana Margaret Ashley Johnson; two *d. Educ:* King's Coll. Sch., Cambridge; Leys Sch., Cambridge; St Catherine's Coll., Oxford (Clothworkers' Schol.; BA, MA); Queens' Coll., Cambridge (PhD 1977); Ridley Hall, Cambridge. FInstP 2004. Physics and RE, House Tutor, Canford Sch., 1971–73; Res. Asst, Engrg Dept, Univ. of Cambridge, 1979; University of Oxford: Res. Fellow, Dept of Metallurgy, 1980–82; Lectr in Physics, 1981–93, Res. Associate, 1982–84, St Catherine's Coll.; Royal Soc. Res. Fellow in Physical Scis, 1983–84; Lectr in Metallurgy and Sci. of Materials, 1984–96; Fellow, Wolfson Coll., 1984–96, now Emeritus; Reader in Materials, 1996–99; Prof. of Materials, 1999–2002. Founding Dir and Vice-Chm., OxLoc Ltd, 2000–. Vis. Faculty, Center for Quantized Electronic Structures, Univ. of Calif, Santa Barbara, 1990, 1993; Prof. invité, Ecole polytechnique fédérale de Lausanne, 1992–2002; Vis. Scientist, Hewlett-Packard Labs, Palo Alto, 1997–98; Vis. Prof., Univ. of NSW, 2002; Guest Prof., State Key Lab., Wuhan Univ. of Technol., 2005–. Member, Editorial Board: Sci. and Christian Belief, 2001–; Current Opinion in Solid State and Materials Sci., 2002–; Nanotechnology, 2005–06. Sci. Scholarships Cttee, Royal Commn for the Exhibn of 1891, 2006–; Peer Rev. Coll., EPSRC, 2006–. Dir, Oxford Toppan Centre, 1996–2006; Member: Bd of Mgt, Ian Ramsey Centre, 2001–; Internat. Bd of Advrs, John Templeton Foundn, 2007–. Hon. Fellow, Royal Microscopical Soc. (Chm. Materials Section, Council, 1986–91; Hon. Treas., 1989–91). Liveryman, Clothworkers' Co., 2005–. Holliday Prize, Inst. of Metals, 1986; (jtly) Metrology for World Class Manfg Award, 1999. *Publications:* An Introduction to Scanning Acoustic Microscopy, 1985; Acoustic Microscopy, 1992, 2nd edn 2008; (ed) The Science of New Materials, 1992; (ed) Advances in Acoustic Microscopy 1, 1995, 2, 1996; numerous contribs to learned jls. *Recreations:* Christian theology, opera, ski-ing, sailing, flying. *Address:* 5 Northmoor Road, Oxford OX2 6UW. *T:* (01865) 273725, *Fax:* (01865) 273730; *e-mail:* andrew.briggs@materials.ox.ac.uk.

BRIGGS, Very Rev. George Peter N.; *see* Nairn-Briggs.

BRIGGS, Isabel Diana, (Mrs Michael Briggs); *see* Colegate, I. D.

BRIGGS, John; *see* Briggs, P. J.

BRIGGS, Martin Paul; Chief Executive, East Midlands Development Agency, 1999–2004; *b* 17 April 1948; *s* of late Maurice William John Briggs and Beryl Edna Briggs; *m* 1999, Angela Byrne; three *s* one *d* and two step *s* one step *d. Educ:* Forest Sch., Snaresbrook; Univ. of E Anglia (BA Hons Social Studies). Department of Trade and Industry: Res. Officer and other res. posts, 1970–82; Hd, Location/Inward Investment, E Midlands, 1982–87; Dir, Industry, W Midlands, 1987–91; Director: English Unit, Investment in Britain Bureau, 1991–93; Trade and Industry, Govt Office for E Midlands, 1994–98; Business Links, DTI, 1998–99. Special Prof., Nottingham Univ. *Recreations:* recorded music, tastes catholic, travel, philosophy/theology, family pursuits.

BRIGGS, Dr (Michael) Peter; Pro Vice-Chancellor, Roehampton University (formerly Pro-Rector, University of Surrey Roehampton), and Principal, Southlands College, since 2002; *b* 3 Dec. 1944; *s* of late Hewieson Briggs and of Doris (*née* Habberley); *m* 1969, Jennifer Elizabeth Watts; one *s* one *d. Educ:* Abbeydale Boys' Grammar Sch., Sheffield; Univ. of Sussex (BSc, DPhil). Jun. Res. Fellow in Theoretical Chem., Univ. of Sheffield, 1969–71; Res. Assistant, Dept of Architecture, Univ. of Bristol, 1971–73; Deputation Sec., Methodist Church Overseas Div., 1973–77; Area Sec. (Herts and Essex), Christian Aid, BCC, 1977–80; British Association for the Advancement of Science: Educn Manager, 1980–86; Public Affairs Man., 1986–88; Dep. Sec., 1988–90; Exec. Sec., then Chief Exec., 1990–2002. Mem. Council, Internat. Council for Advancement of Scientific Literacy, 1992–. Chairman: Management Cttee, Methodist Church Div. of Social Responsibility, 1983–86; Methodist Youth World Affairs Management Cttee, 1984–92. FRSA 1990. Hon. DSc Leicester, 2002. *Recreation:* walking. *Address:* Southlands College, Roehampton University, 80 Roehampton Lane, SW15 5SL. *T:* (020) 8392 3411. *Club:* Athenæum.

BRIGGS, Hon. Sir Michael Townley Featherstone, Kt 2006; **Hon. Mr Justice Briggs;** a Judge of the High Court of Justice, Chancery Division, since 2006; *b* 23 Dec. 1954; *s* of Capt. James William Featherstone Briggs, RN and late Barbara Nadine Briggs (*née* Pelham Groom); *m* 1981, Beverly Ann Rogers; three *s* one *d. Educ:* Charterhouse; Magdalen Coll., Oxford (BA History). Called to the Bar, Lincoln's Inn, 1978, Bencher, 2001; Jun. Counsel to Crown Chancery, 1990–94; QC 1994; Attorney Gen., Duchy of Lancaster, 2001–06. *Recreations:* sailing, singing (solo and choral), cooking, classic cars, garden railways. *Address:* Royal Courts of Justice, Strand, WC2A 2LL. *Clubs:* Bar Yacht; British Classic Yacht; Royal Yacht Squadron.

BRIGGS, Patrick David, MA; Principal, Kolej Tuanku Ja'afar, Malaysia, 1997–2005; *b* 24 Aug. 1940; *s* of late Denis Patrick Briggs and of Nancy Sylvester (*née* Jackson); *m* 1968, Alicia Dorothy O'Donnell; two *s* one *d. Educ:* Pocklington Sch.; Christ's Coll., Cambridge (MA). Bedford Sch., 1965–87 (Sen. Housemaster, 1983–87); Head Master, William Hulme's GS, 1987–97. Rugby Blue, Cambridge, 1962; England Rugby trialist, 1968 and 1969; Mem. Barbarians, 1968–69; RFU staff coach, 1973–95; England Under-23 Rugby coach, 1975–80; Team Manager, England Students Rugby, 1988–95. *Publication:* The Parents' Guide to Independent Schools, 1979. *Recreations:* cricket, Rugby, golf, fell walking, poetry, theatre, canal-boating. *Address:* 14 Cockburn Street, Cambridge CB1 3NB. *T:* (01223) 476108. *Clubs:* East India, Devonshire, Sports and Public Schools, XL; Hawks (Cambridge); Quidnuncs, Cheshire County Cricket, Lancashire County Cricket; Royal Selangor (Kuala Lumpur).

BRIGGS, Peter; *see* Briggs, M. P.

BRIGGS, (Peter) John; a Recorder of the Crown Court, 1978–97; *b* 15 May 1928; *s* of late Percy Briggs and Annie M. Folker; *m* 1956, Sheila Phyllis Walton; one *s* three *d. Educ:* King's Sch., Peterborough; Balliol Coll., Oxford. MA, BCL. Called to the Bar, Inner Temple, 1953. Legal Member: Mersey Mental Health Review Tribunal, 1969 (Dep. Chm., 1971, Chm., 1981–94); North-West Mental Health Review Tribunal, 1994–98; NW and W Midlands Mental Health Review Tribunal, 1998–2000. Pres., Merseyside Medico-Legal Soc., 1982–84. Chm., Merseyside Opera, 1996–99. *Recreation:* music, particularly amateur operatics. *Address:* 15 Dean's Lawn, Berkhamsted, Herts HP4 3AZ. *T:* (01442) 871488.

BRIGGS, Raymond Redvers, DFA; FCSD; FRSL; freelance illustrator, since 1957; author, since 1961; *b* 18 Jan. 1934; *s* of late Ernest Redvers Briggs and Ethel Bowyer; *m* 1963, Jean Taprell Clark (*d* 1973). *Educ:* Rutlish Sch., Merton; Wimbledon School of Art; Slade School of Fine Art. NDD; DFA London. Part-time Lecturer in Illustration, Faculty of Art, Brighton Polytechnic, 1961–87. FRSL 2005. *Publications:* The Strange House, 1961; Midnight Adventure, 1961; Ring-A-Ring O'Roses, 1962; Sledges to the Rescue, 1963; The White Land, 1963; Fee Fi Fo Fum, 1964; The Mother Goose Treasury, 1966 (Kate Greenaway Medal, 1966); Jim and the Beanstalk, 1970; The Fairy Tale Treasury, 1972; Father Christmas, 1973 (Kate Greenaway Medal, 1973); Father Christmas Goes On Holiday, 1975; Fungus The Bogeyman, 1977 (adapted for BBC TV, 2004); The Snowman, 1978 (animated film, 1982); Gentleman Jim, 1980 (play, Nottingham Playhouse, 1985); When the Wind Blows, 1982 (play, BBC Radio and Whitehall Th., 1983; text publd 1983; cassette 1984; animated film, 1987); Fungus the Bogeyman Plop-Up Book, 1982; The Tin-Pot Foreign General and the Old Iron Woman, 1984; The Snowman Pop-Up, 1986; Unlucky Wally, 1987; Unlucky Wally Twenty Years On, 1989; The Man, 1992; The Bear, 1994; Ethel & Ernest, 1998; UG, Boy Genius of the Stone Age, 2001; Blooming Books, 2003; The Puddleman, 2004. *Recreations:* gardening, reading, walking, second-hand bookshops. *Address:* Weston, Underhill Lane, Westmeston, Hassocks, Sussex BN6 8XG. *Clubs:* Groucho, Royal Over-Seas League.

BRIGHOUSE, Prof. Timothy Robert Peter; Chief Adviser for London Schools, Department for Education and Skills, since 2003–07; *b* 15 Jan. 1940; *s* of Denison Brighouse and Mary Howard Brighouse; *m* 1st, 1962, Mary Elizabeth Demers (marr. diss. 1988); one *s* one *d*; 2nd, 1989, Elizabeth Ann (formerly Kearney). *Educ:* St Catherine's College, Oxford (MA Modern History); DipEd. Head of History Dept, Cavendish Grammar Sch., Buxton, 1962–64; Dep. Head and Warden, Chepstow Comm. Coll., 1964–66; Asst Educn Officer, Monmouthshire Educn Dept, 1966–69; Sen. Asst Educn Officer, Bucks Educn Dept, 1969–74; Under-Sec., Educn, ACC, 1974–76; Dep. Educn Officer, ILEA, 1976–78; Chief Educn Officer, Oxon, 1978–89; Prof. of Educn and Hd of Dept, Keele Univ., 1989–93; Chief Educn Officer, Birmingham CC, 1993–2002. Jt Vice-Chm., Standards Task Force, 1997–99. Visiting Professor: Keele Univ., 1993–2002; London Univ. Inst. of Educn, 2002–; Hon. Prof., Birmingham Univ., 1996. Non-exec. Dir, RM Education plc, 2005–. Hon. DEd (CNAA) Oxford Poly., 1989; Hon. PhD UCE, 1996; Hon. DLitt: Exeter, 1996; Birmingham, 1999; Sheffield Hallam, 2001; Hon. MA Open Univ., 1997; Hon. EdD UWE, 2002; Hon. Dr: Greenwich, 2003; Middlesex 2004; Wolverhampton, 2006; Sunderland, 2007. *Publications:* Revolution in Education and Training (jt editor and author), 1986; Managing the National Curriculum (jt editor and author), 1990; What Makes a Good School, 1991; Successful Schooling, 1991; (jtly) How to Improve Your School, 1999. *Recreations:* gardening, politics, golf. *Address:* Institute of Education, 10 Woburn Square, WC1H 0NS; Willowbank, Old Road, Headington, Oxford OX3 8TA. *T:* (01865) 766995.

BRIGHT, Andrew John; QC 2000; **His Honour Judge Bright;** a Circuit Judge, since 2007; *b* 12 April 1951; *e s* of late J. H. Bright and of Freda Bright (*née* Cotton); *m* 1976, Sally Elizabeth Carter; three *s* one *d. Educ:* Wells Cathedral Sch.; University Coll. London (LLB Hons). Called to the Bar, Middle Temple, 1973; in practice at the Bar in field of criminal law, S Eastern Circuit, 1975–2007; Recorder, 2000–07. Co-opted Mem. Cttee, Criminal Bar Assoc., 1993–95. *Recreations:* river and canal boating, fishing, music. *Address:* Luton Crown Court, 7 George Street, Luton, Beds LU1 2AA.

BRIGHT, Colin Charles; HM Diplomatic Service, retired; Counsellor, Foreign and Commonwealth Office, 2006; *b* 2 Jan. 1948; *s* of William Charles John Bright and Doris (*née* Sutton); *m* 1st, 1978, Helen-Anne Michie; 2nd, 1990, Jane Elizabeth Gurney Pease; one *s* one *d* (and one *d* decd). *Educ:* Christ's Hospital; St Andrews Univ. (MA Hons 1971). FCO, 1975–77; Bonn, 1977–79; FCO, 1979–83; seconded to Cabinet Office, 1983–85; British Trade Develt Office, NY, 1985–88; Dep. Head of Mission, Berne, 1989–93; Consul Gen., Frankfurt, 1993–97; Hd of Commonwealth Co-ordination Dept, FCO, 1998–2002; Counsellor, FCO, 2002–03; Consul Gen., Lyon, 2004–06.

BRIGHT, Sir Graham (Frank James), Kt 1994; Chairman, since 1977, Managing Director, since 1970, Dietary Foods Ltd; Chairman, International Sweeteners Association, since 1997; *b* 2 April 1942; *s* of late Robert Frank Bright and Agnes Mary (*née* Graham); *m* 1972, Valerie, *d* of late E. H. Woolliams; one *s. Educ:* Hassenbrook County Sch.; Thurrock Technical Coll. Marketing Exec., Pauls & White Ltd, 1958–70. Contested (C): Thurrock, 1970 and Feb. 1974; Dartford, Oct. 1974. MP (C) Luton East, 1979–83, Luton South, 1983–97; contested (C) Luton South, 1997; contested (C) Eastern Region, EP elecns, 1999. PPS to Ministers of State, Home Office, 1984–87, DoE, 1988–89, to Paymaster Gen., 1989–90, to Prime Minister, 1990–94. Mem. Select Cttee on House of Commons Services, 1982–84. Jt Sec. to Parly Aviation Gp, 1984–90; Chm., Cons. Backbench Smaller Businesses Cttee, 1983–84, 1987–88 (Vice-Chm., 1980–83; Sec., 1979–80); Vice-Chairman: Cons. Backbench Food and Drink Sub-Cttee, 1983 (Sec., 1983–85); Backbench Aviation Cttee, 1987–88; former Sec., Space Sub-Cttee; Introduced Private Member's Bills: Video Recordings Act, 1984; Entertainment (Increased Penalties) Act, 1990. Member: Thurrock Bor. Council, 1966–79; Essex CC, 1967–70. Chm., Eastern Area CPC, 1977–79; Mem., Nat. CPC, 1980–97; Vice Chm., YC Org., 1970–72; Pres., Eastern Area YCs, 1981–98; Conservative Party: a Vice-Chm., 1994–97; Chm., Eastern Reg., 2006–. Vice-Chm., Small Business Bureau, 1980–89, and 1991–97 (Dir, 1989–91). *Publications:* pamphlets on airports, small businesses, education. *Recreations:* golf, gardening. *Address:* Cumberland Place, Mill Lane, Fordham, Cambs CB7 5NQ. *Club:* Carlton.

BRIGHT, Jonathan Steven Noel; Regional Director, Government Office for the South West, since 2008; *b* Gloucester, 26 Dec. 1951; *s* of Stanley and Suzanne Bright; *m* 1990, Suzanne Lingard; two *s* one *d. Educ:* Hardyes Grammar Sch.; Magdalene Coll., Cambridge (BA Social and Pol Sci. 1974); Leicester Univ. (PGCE). Dir, Safe Neighbourhood Unit, NACRO, 1981–90; Dir of Ops, Crime Concern, 1990–97; Deputy Director: Social Exclusion Unit, Cabinet Office, 1997–2000; Neighbourhood Renewal Unit, ODPM, 2001–06; Dir of Policy, Birmingham CC, 2006–07. Harkness Fellow, Michigan, 1990–91. Fellow, Australian Inst. Criminol., 1996. FRSA. *Publications:* Crime Prevention in the United States: a British perspective, 1993; Turning the Tide: crime, prevention and neighbourhoods, 1997. *Recreations:* wild swimming, cycling, mountain-walking, architecture. *Address:* c/o Government Office for the South West, 2 Rivergate, Temple Quay, Bristol BS1 6EH. *T:* (0117) 900 1701; *e-mail:* jon.bright@gosw.gsi.gov.uk.

BRIGHT, Robert Graham; QC 2007; barrister; *b* 22 Aug. 1964; *s* of John and Elizabeth Bright; *m* Susan; three *d. Educ:* St Paul's Sch.; St John's Coll., Oxford (BA Juris., BCL). Called to the Bar, Gray's Inn, 1987. *Recreation:* murdering Schubert. *Address:* 7 King's Bench Walk, Temple, EC4Y 7DS.

BRIGHT, Roger Martin Francis; Second Commissioner and Chief Executive, Crown Estate, since 2001; *b* 2 May 1951. *Educ:* Christ's Hosp.; Trinity Hall, Cambridge (BA 1973). Joined DoE, 1973; posts held include: Hd, Envmtl Policy Co-ordination Div.; Hd, Housing Policy Studies Div.; Hd, Local Govt Review Div.; Principal Private Sec. to Sec. of State for the Envmt, 1989–90; Dir of Information, 1990; Dep. Chief Exec., Housing Corp., 1991–95; Dir of Ops and Finance, 1995–97, Chief Exec., 1998, PIA; Hd of Investment Business Dept (PIA firms), FSA, 1998–99; Dir of Finance and Admin, 1999–2001, a Comr, 2000–, Crown Estate. *Address:* (office) 16 New Burlington Place, W1S 2HX.

BRIGHTLING, Peter Henry Miller; Assistant Under Secretary of State, Ministry of Defence, 1973–81; *b* 12 Sept. 1921; *o s* of late Henry Miller Brightling and Eva Emily Brightling (*née* Fry); *m* 1951, Pamela Cheeseright; two *s* two *d. Educ:* City of London Sch.; BSc(Econ), London. War of 1939–45: Air Ministry, 1939–40; MAP, 1940–41; served in RAF, 1941–46. Ministry of: Supply, 1946–59; Aviation, 1959–67; Technology, 1967–70; Aviation Supply, 1970–71; MoD (Procurement Executive), 1971. *Address:* 39 Thetford Road, New Malden, Surrey KT3 5DP.

BRIGHTMAN, Dr David Kenneth, CBiol, FIBiol; Partner, Brightman Farms, since 1982; *b* 12 Aug. 1954; *s* of late Brian George Brightman and Dorothy Brightman; partner, Gillian Theresa Bolton; two *s. Educ:* Univ. of Reading; Univ. of Newcastle upon Tyne (BSc Hons (Agric.) 1977); Univ. of Nottingham (PhD 1983). CBiol, FIBiol 2005; ARAgS 2005. Lectr in Crop Prodn, Brooksby Coll., 1980–82. Dir and Co. Sec., Arable Crop Storage Ltd, 1995–; Co. Sec., Arable Crop Services Ltd, 1995–. Mem. Council, BBSRC, 2003–. Ministry of Agriculture, Fisheries and Food, later Department for Environment, Food and Rural Affairs: Chm., MAFF/ADAS Drayton Experimental Husbandry Farm Adv. Cttee, 1990–92; Member: Pesticides Forum, 1995–98; Sustainable Arable LINK Prog. Mgt Cttee, 1997–2003; Sub-gp on Biodiversity, Adv. Cttee on Releases to the Envmt, 1999–2001; Agricl Forum, 2008–. Mem., NFU Pesticides Wkg Gp, 1991–2003 (Chm., 1993–2003). Dir, Rothamsted Res. Assoc., 1990–2005 (Chm., 2001–03); Dir and Trustee, Rothamsted Res. Ltd, 2005–. Dir, Mid-Tak/CMR Ltd Machinery Rings. Formerly Chairman: Warks Farm Mgt Assoc.; Southam Agricl Discussion Club; Chm., Fenny Compton NFU, 1988–90; mem., various cttees, panels and wkg gps. *Publications:* Dietary Nitrogen Requirements of Entire Male Cattle, 1983; conf. papers in Animal Prodn and for BCPC annual conf., and articles in farming press. *Recreations:* playing golf, ski-ing, watching sport, watching people.

BRIGHTON, Wing Comdr Peter, BSc; CEng, FRAeS; independent consultant; *b* 26 March 1933; *s* of late Henry Charles Brighton and Ivy Irene Brighton (*née* Crane); *m* 1959, Anne Maureen Lewis Jones (*d* 2007); one *d* (one *s* decd). *Educ:* Wisbech Grammar Sch.; Reading Univ. (BSc); RAF Technical Coll. and Staff Coll. CEng 1966; FIET (FIEE 1980); FRAeS 1981. Pilot, Engr and Attaché, RAF, 1955–71. Man. Dir, Rockwell-Collins UK, 1974–77; Regional Man. Dir, Plessey Co., 1977–78; Man. Dir, Cossor Electronics Ltd, 1978–85; British Aerospace PLC: Divl Man. Dir, 1985–87; Co. Dir of Operations, 1988; Dir Gen., EEF, 1989–91. Chm., Princess Alexandra Hosp. NHS Trust, 1996–97. Pres., Electronic Engineering Assoc., 1984–85. Mem. Ct, Cranfield Inst. of Technology, 1989–92. CCMI (CBIM 1984). Liveryman, Coachmakers and Coach Harness Makers Co., 1989; Freeman of City of London, 1989. *Publications:* articles on aviation topics in learned jls. *Recreations:* bridge, golf. *Address:* St Andrew's Cottage, Church Lane, Much Hadham, Herts SG10 6DH. *T:* (01279) 842309. *Club:* Royal Air Force.

BRIGHTY, (Anthony) David, CMG 1984; CVO 1985; HM Diplomatic Service, retired; Ambassador to Spain, and concurrently (non resident) to Andorra, 1994–98; *b* 7 Feb. 1939; *s* of C. P. J. Brighty and Winifred (*née* Turner); *m* 1963, Diana Porteous (marr. diss. 1979; she *d* 1993); two *s* two *d*; *m* 1997, Susan Olivier. *Educ:* Northgate Grammar Sch., Ipswich; Clare Coll., Cambridge (BA). Entered FO, 1961; Brussels, 1962–63; Havana, 1964–66; FO, 1967–69, resigned; joined S. G. Warburg & Co., 1969; reinstated in FCO, 1971; Saigon, 1973–74; UK Mission to UN, NY, 1975–78; RCDS, 1979; Head of Personnel Operations Dept, FCO, 1980–83; Counsellor, Lisbon, 1983–86; Dir, Cabinet of Sec.-Gen. of NATO, 1986–87; Resident Chm., CSSB, 1988; Ambassador to Cuba, 1989–91; Ambassador to Czech and Slovak Fed. Republic, later to Czech Republic and (non-resident) to Slovakia, 1991–94. Non-executive Director: EFG Private Bank Ltd, 1999–2005; Henderson EuroMicro Investment Trust, 2000–04. Chairman: Co-ordinating (formerly Consultative) Cttee on Remuneration (NATO, OECD, etc), 1999–2006; Cañada Blanch Foundn (UK), 2006–. Robin Humphreys Fellow, Inst. for Latin Amer. Studies, London Univ., 2003. Chairman: Anglo-Spanish Soc., 2001–07; Friends of British Liby, 2004–07. *Address:* 15 Provost Road, NW3 4ST.

BRIGSTOCKE, Dr Hugh Nicholas Andrew; freelance writer and art historian; *b* 7 May 1943; *s* of late Rev. Canon George Edward Brigstocke and Mollie (*née* Sandford); *m* 1969, Anthea Elizabeth White; one *s* one *d. Educ:* Marlborough Coll., Wilts; Magdalene Coll., Cambridge (MA Modern Hist.); Univ. of Edinburgh (PhD Art Hist. 1976). Curator, Italian, Spanish and French Paintings, National Gall. of Scotland, Edinburgh, 1968–83; Editor-in-Chief, 1983–87, Consulting Ed., 1987–89, Hon. Consulting Ed., 1989–96, Grove Dictionary of Art; Old Master Paintings, Sotheby's, London, 1989–95: Dir, 1990–95; Hd of Dept, 1993–94; Sen. Expert, 1994–95; Ed. (freelance), Oxford Companion to Western Art, 1995–2001. Paul Mellon Fellow, British Sch. at Rome, 2001. Ed., Walpole Soc., 2000–. *Publications:* A Critical Catalogue of the Italian and Spanish Paintings, National Gallery of Scotland, 1978, 2nd edn 1993; William Buchanan and the 19th Century Art Trade: 100 letters to his agents in London and Italy, 1979; (ed) Oxford Companion to Western Art, 2001; *exhibition catalogues:* (jtly) Poussin Bacchanals and Sacraments, 1981; A Loan Exhibition of Poussin Drawings from British Collections, 1990; (jtly) Masterpieces from Yorkshire Houses: Yorkshire families at home and abroad 1700–1850, 1994; (jtly) Italian Paintings from Burghley House, 1995; (jtly) En Torno a Velázquez, 1999; (jtly) A Poet in Paradise: Lord Lindsay and Christian Art, 2000; Procaccini in America, 2002; contrib. articles to various jls incl. Burlington Mag., Apollo, Walpole Soc., Revue de l'Art, Paragone, Revue du Louvre, Jahrbuch der Berliner Mus., Münchner Jahrbuch, etc. *Recreations:* opera, theatre, wine, horse-racing. *Address:* 118 Micklegate, York YO1 6JX. *T:* (01904) 626013; *e-mail:* hugh.brigstocke@zen.co.uk.

See also Adm. Sir J. R. Brigstocke.

BRIGSTOCKE, Adm. Sir John (Richard), KCB 1997; Judicial Appointments and Conduct Ombudsman, since 2006; Chairman, NHS East Midlands (East Midlands Strategic Health Authority), since 2006; *b* 30 July 1945; *s* of late Rev. Canon George Edward Brigstocke and Molly Brigstocke (*née* Sandford); *m* 1979, Heather, *d* of late Dennis and Muriel Day (*née* Glossop); two *s. Educ:* Marlborough Coll.; BRNC, Dartmouth; RNC Greenwich; RCDS. Joined RN, 1962; trng, 1962–66; HMS Caprice, 1966–69; HMY Britannia, 1969; HMS Whitby, 1969–70; i/c HMS Upton, 1970–71; long gunnery course, HMS Excellent, 1971–72; HMS Minerva, 1972–74; RNSC Greenwich, 1974; Staff, BRNC Dartmouth, 1974–76; First Lieut, HMS Ariadne, 1976–78; i/c HMS Bacchante, 1978–79; Directorate of Naval Plans, MoD, 1980–81 and 1982–84; Comdr Sea Trng, Portland, 1981–82; i/c HMS York and Capt. (D) 3rd Destroyer Sqn, 1986–87; Capt., BRNC Dartmouth, 1987–88; i/c HMS Ark Royal, 1989–90; FO, 2nd Flotilla, 1991–92; Comdr, UK Task Gp, 1992–93; ACNS and Mem. Admiralty Bd, 1993–95; Adm. Pres., RNC, Greenwich, 1994–95; Flag Officer, Surface Flotilla, 1995–97; Second Sea Lord, Mem. Admiralty Bd, C-in-C Naval Home Comd, and Flag ADC to the Queen, 1997–2000. Chief Exec., St Andrew's Gp of Hosps, 2000–04; Director: Ind. Healthcare Assoc., 2000–03; Three Shires Hosp. Ltd, 2000–04. Trustee, Nuffield Trust for the Forces of the Crown, 2003–. Chm. Council, Univ. of Buckingham, 2005–08 (Mem., 2004–05). Younger Brother, Trinity House, 1981. Freeman, City of London, 1995. *Recreations:* ski-ing, riding. *Address:* c/o Naval Secretary, Sir Henry Leach Building, Whale Island, Portsmouth PO2 8BY.

See also H. N. A. Brigstocke.

BRIKHO, Samir Yacoub; Chief Executive, AMEC plc, since 2006; *b* 3 May 1958; *s* of Jacob and Viktoria Brikho; two *s. Educ:* Royal High Sch. of Technol., Stockholm (MSc Thermal Technol.); INSEAD (Young Managers Prog.); Stamford Univ. (Sen. Exec. Prog. 2000). Sen. Vice Pres., ABB, 1993–95; Sen. Vice Pres. and Man. Dir, ABB Kraftwerke, 1995–99; CEO, ABB Alstom Kraftwerke, 1999–2001; Sen. Vice Pres., Internat. Business and Chief Internat. Ops Officer, Alstom Power, 2000–03; Chief Exec., ABB Lummus Global, Switzerland, 2003–05; Mem. Exec. Bd, ABB, Hd, Power Systems Div. and Chm., ABB Lummus Global, 2005–06. *Recreations:* sports, music, dance. *Address:* AMEC plc, 76–78 Old Street, EC1V 9RU. *T:* (020) 7539 1681, *Fax:* (020) 7539 1655; *e-mail:* samir.brikho@amec.com. *Clubs:* Cavalry and Guards; Wentworth Golf.

BRILL, Elaine; *see* Bedell, E.

BRIMACOMBE, Prof. John Stuart, FRSE, FRSC; Roscoe Professor of Chemistry, University of Dundee, 1969–2002; *b* Falmouth, Cornwall, 18 Aug. 1935; *s* of Stanley Poole Brimacombe and Lillian May Kathleen Brimacombe (*née* Candy); *m* 1959, Eileen (*née* Gibson); four *d. Educ:* Falmouth Grammar Sch.; Birmingham Univ. (DSc); DSc Dundee Univ. Lectr in Chemistry, Birmingham Univ., 1961–69. Meldola Medallist, 1964, Haworth Lect. and Medal, 2007, RSC. *Publications:* (co-author) Mucopolysaccharides, 1964; numerous papers, reviews, etc., in: Jl Chem. Soc., Carbohydrate Research, etc. *Recreations:* sport, swimming. *Address:* 29 Dalhousie Road, Barnhill, Dundee DD5 2SP. *T:* (01382) 779214.

BRIMELOW, Alison Jane, CBE 2005; President, European Patent Office, since 2007 (President-elect, and Vice-Chair of Administrative Council, 2004–07); *b* 6 June 1949. HM Diplomatic Service, 1973–76; DTI, 1976–2003; Comptroller Gen. and Chief Exec., Patent Office, 1999–2003. Associate Fellow, Saïd Business Sch. (formerly Templeton Coll.), Oxford, 2005–. Hon. LLD Wolverhampton, 2007. *Address:* c/o European Patent Office, 80298 München, Germany. *Club:* Athenæum.

BRIMS, Lt Gen. Robin Vaughan, CB 2007; CBE 1999 (OBE 1991; MBE 1986); DSO 2003; Commander, Field Army, Land Command, 2005–07; *b* 27 June 1951; *s* of late David Vaughan Brims and of Eve Georgina Mary Brims. *Educ:* Winchester Coll. Commissioned LI, 1970; sc 1982–83; CO 3rd Bn LI, 1989–91; Comdr, 24 Airmobile Bde, 1995–96; COS, NI, 1997–98; Dir, Army Resources and Plans, 1999; Comdr, Multinat. Div. (South West), 2000; GOC 1 (UK) Armoured Div., 2000–03; Dep. Chief of Jt Ops, MoD, 2003–05; Dep. Commanding Gen., Multinational Force, Iraq, 2005 (on detachment). Officer, Legion of Merit (USA), 2006. *Recreation:* sport. *Address:* c/o RHQ The Rifles, Peninsula Barracks, Romsey Road, Winchester, Hants SO23 8TS.

BRIMSON-LEWIS, Stephen John; freelance theatre designer, since 1985; *b* 15 Feb. 1963; *s* of David and Doris Lewis; adopted stage name Brimson-Lewis. *Educ:* Central Sch. of Art and Design (BA Hons). Designer of productions: for RNT, incl. Les Parents Terribles (Olivier Award for Best Set Design), 1995, A Little Night Music, 1996; for RSC, 1999–, incl. A Midsummer Night's Dream, 2005, Antony and Cleopatra, 2006; Design for Living (Olivier Award for Best Set Design), Donmar Warehouse, 1995; Dirty Dancing, Aldwych, 2006; also for maj. internat. opera and ballet cos. *Address:* c/o Clare Vidal-Hall, 57 Carthew Road, W6 0DU. *T:* (020) 8741 7647; *e-mail:* cvh@clarevidalhall.com.

BRINCKMAN, Sir Theodore (George Roderick), 6th Bt *cr* 1831; retired antiquarian bookseller; *b* 20 March 1932; *s* of Col. Sir Roderick Napoleon Brinckman, 5th Bt, DSO, MC, and Margaret Wilson Southam; *S* father, 1985; *m* 1st, 1958, Helen Mary Anne Cook (marr. diss. 1983), *d* of Arnold Cook; two *s* one *d*; 2nd, 1983, Hon. Sheira Murray (marr. diss. 2001), formerly wife of Christopher Murray, and *d* of Baron Harvington, AE, PC; 3rd, 2001, Margaret Kindersley, formerly wife of Gay Kindersley, and *d* of Hugh Wakefield. *Educ:* Trinity College School, Port Hope, Ontario; Millfield; Christ Church, Oxford; Trinity Coll., Toronto (BA). *Heir: s* Theodore Jonathan Brinckman, *b* 19 Feb. 1960. *Address:* Monk Bretton, Barnsley, Cirencester, Glos GL7 5EJ. *T:* (01285) 740564.

BRIND, (Arthur) Henry, CMG 1973; HM Diplomatic Service, retired; *b* 4 July 1927; *o s* of late T. H. Brind and late N. W. B. Brind; *m* 1954, Barbara Harrison; one *s* one *d. Educ:* Barry; St John's Coll., Cambridge. HM Forces, 1947–49. Colonial Administrative Service: Gold Coast/Ghana, 1950–60; Regional Sec., Trans-Volta Togoland, 1959. HM Diplomatic Service, 1960–87: Acting High Comr, Uganda, 1972–73; High Comr, Mauritius, 1974–77; Ambassador to Somali Democratic Republic, 1977–80; Vis. Research Fellow, RIIA, 1981–82; High Comr, Malaŵi, 1983–87. Grand Comdr, Order of Lion of Malaŵi, 1985. *Publication:* Lying Abroad (memoirs), 1999. *Recreations:* walking, swimming, books. *Address:* 20 Grove Terrace, NW5 1PH. *T:* (020) 7267 1190. *Club:* Reform.

BRINDED, Malcolm Arthur, CBE 2002; FREng; Member of the Board, Royal Dutch/Shell plc, since 2003; Executive Director, Shell Exploration and Production, since 2004; *b* 18 March 1953; *s* of Cliff and Gwen Brinded; *m* 1975, Carola Telford; three *s. Educ:* Churchill Coll., Cambridge (MA Engrg). Shell Internat., The Hague, 1974–75; Project Engr, Brunei Shell Petroleum, 1975–80; Facilities Engr, Shell UK Exploration and Prodn, 1980–82; on secondment to Dept of Energy as Policy Advr, 1982–84; Nederlands Aardolie MIJ, 1984–86; Shell Gp, 1987–88; Business Unit Dir, Petroleum Devclt, Shell Oman, 1988–92; Shell UK Exploration and Prodn, 1993–2001 (Man. Dir, 1998–2001); Country Chm., Shell UK Ltd, 1999–2002; Dir, Planning, HSE and External Affairs, Shell Internat., 2001–02; Gp Man. Dir, 2002–03, Vice Chm., Cttee of Man. Dirs, 2003, Royal Dutch/Shell Gp of Cos; CEO, Shell Gas & Power, 2003. FICE; FREng 2002. Hon. FIMechE 2003. Alec Buchanan Smith Award for contrib. to Scottish oil and gas industry,

2001. *Recreations:* music, mountain biking, Rugby. *Address:* Shell International, PO Box 162, 2501 AN, The Hague, Netherlands.

BRINDLE, Ian; Deputy Chairman, Financial Reporting Review Panel, since 2001; *b* 17 Aug. 1943; *s* of John Brindle and Mabel Brindle (*née* Walsh); *m* 1967, Frances Elisabeth Moseby; two *s* one *d*. *Educ:* Blundells School; Manchester Univ. (BA Econ). FCA 1969. Price Waterhouse: articled in London, 1965; Toronto, 1971; admitted to partnership, 1976; Mem., Supervisory Cttee, 1988–98; Dir, Audit and Business Advisory Services, 1990–91; Mem., UK Exec., 1990–98; Sen. Partner, 1991–98; company merged with Coopers & Lybrand, 1998; UK Chm., PricewaterhouseCoopers, 1998–2001. Member: Auditing Practices Cttee, CCAB, 1986–90 (Chm., 1990); Accounting Standards Bd, 1993–2001 (Mem. Urgent Issues Task Force, 1991–93); Council, ICAEW, 1994–97; Financial Reporting Council, 1995–. Auditor, Duchy of Cornwall, 1993–. *Recreations:* tennis, golf. *Address:* Milestones, Packhorse Road, Bessels Green, Sevenoaks, Kent TN13 2QP.

BRINDLE, Jane; *see* Cox, Josephine.

BRINDLE, Michael John; QC 1992; a Recorder, since 2000; a Deputy High Court Judge; *b* 23 June 1952; *s* of John Arthur Brindle and Muriel Jones; *m* 1st, 1988, Heather Mary (*née* Pearce) (marr. diss. 2005); one *s* two *d*; 2nd, 2007, Alison Jane (*née* Slann). *Educ:* Westminster Sch.; New Coll., Oxford (Ella Stephens Schol. in Classics; 1st Cl. Hons Mods, 1972; 1st Cl. Jurisprudence, 1974; MA). Called to the Bar, Lincoln's Inn, 1975 (Hardwicke Scholar), Bencher, 2002. Chairman: Commercial Bar Assoc., 2001–02 (Treas., 1999–2001); Bar Educn and Trng Cttee, 2003–05; Bar Council Internat. Cttee, 2008–. Member: Financial Reporting Review Panel, 1998–; Financial Markets Law Cttee, 2004–. Chm. Adv. Council, Public Concern at Work, 2001– (Chm. Trustees, 1997–2001). *Recreations:* classical music, travel, bridge. *Address:* Fountain Court, Temple, EC4Y 9DH.

BRINDLE, Dr Michael John, CBE 1998; FRCP, FRCR, FRCPC, FRCPE, FRCSE; Consultant Radiologist, The Queen Elizabeth Hospital, King's Lynn, 1972–98; President, Royal College of Radiologists, 1995–98; *b* 18 Nov. 1934; *s* of Dr W. S. Brindle and P. M. Brindle; *m* 1960, Muriel Eileen Hayward; two *s* two *d*. *Educ:* Liverpool Univ. (MB ChB 1958; MD 1967; MRad 1971). FRCPC 1972; FRCR 1989; FRCP 1998; FRCPE 1999; FRCSE 1999. Surgeon Lieut, RN, 1959–62. Consultant, Royal Alexandra Hosp., Edmonton, Alberta, 1966–72. Treas., RCR, 1990–95. LRPS 2007. Hon. FRCGP 1998. *Recreations:* bird-watching, golf, photography.

BRINDLEY, Very Rev. David Charles; Dean of Portsmouth, since 2002; *b* 11 June 1953; *m* 1975, Gillian Griffin; one *s* two *d*. *Educ:* Wednesfield Grammar Sch.; King's Coll., London (BD, AKC 1975; MTh 1976; MPhil 1980). VSO, Lebanon, 1971–72. Ordained deacon, 1976, priest, 1977; Curate, Epping, 1976–79; Lectr, Coll. of St Paul and St Mary, Cheltenham, 1979–82; Vicar, Quorn, and Dir of Clergy Trng, dio. Leicester, 1982–86; Principal, W of England Ministerial Trng Course, 1987–94; Team Rector, Warwick, 1994–2002. *Publications:* Stepping Aside, 1993; Story, Song and Law, 1996; Richard Beauchamp: medieval England's greatest knight, 2001; *for children:* (with Gillian Brindley): Moses, 1985; Joseph, 1985. *Recreations:* morris dancing, folk music, modern literature, theatre, walking the dog. *Address:* The Deanery, Pembroke Road, Portsmouth PO1 2NS. *T:* (home) (023) 9282 4400, (office) (023) 9234 7605, *Fax:* (023) 9229 5480; *e-mail:* david.brindley@portsmouthcathedral.org.uk. *Clubs:* Athenæum, Royal Naval.

BRINDLEY, Prof. Giles Skey, MA, MD; FRS 1965; FRCP; Professor of Physiology in the University of London at the Institute of Psychiatry, 1968–91, now Emeritus; *b* 30 April 1926; *s* of late Arthur James Benet Skey and Dr Margaret Beatrice Marion Skey (*née* Dewhurst), later Brindley; *m* 1st, 1959, Lucy Dunk Bennell (marr. diss.); 2nd, 1964, Dr Hilary Richards; one *s* one *d*. *Educ:* Leyton County High School; Downing College, Cambridge (Hon. Fellow, 1969); London Hospital Medical College. Various jun. clin. and res. posts, 1950–54; Russian lang. abstractor, British Abstracts of Medical Sciences, 1953–56; successively Demonstrator, Lectr and Reader in Physiology, Univ. of Cambridge, 1954–68; Fellow: King's Coll., Cambridge, 1959–62; Trinity Coll., Cambridge, 1963–68. Hon. Dir, MRC Neurological Prostheses Unit, 1968–92; Hon. Consultant Physician, Maudsley Hosp., 1971–92. Chm. of Editorial Board, Journal of Physiology, 1964–66 (Member 1959–64). Visiting Prof., Univ. of California, Berkeley, 1968. Hon. FRCS 1988; Hon. FRCSE 2000. Liebrecht-Franceschetti Prize, German Ophthalmological Soc., 1971; Feldberg Prize, Feldberg Foundn, 1974; St Peter's Medal, British Assoc. of Urological Surgeons, 1987. *Publications:* Physiology of the Retina and Visual Pathway, 1960, 2nd edn 1970; papers in scientific, musicological and medical journals. *Recreations:* cross-country and track running (silver medallist, 2000m steeplechase and 800m (men over 65), World Veterans' Track and Field Championships, Finland, 1991), designing, making and playing various musical instruments (inventor of the logical bassoon), composing chamber music and songs. *Address:* 102 Ferndene Road, SE24 0AA. *T:* (020) 7274 2598.

BRINDLEY, John Frederick, CB 1996; Circuit Administrator, South Eastern Circuit, 1995–97; *b* 25 Sept. 1937; *s* of Harold and Eva Brindley; *m* 1960, Judith Ann Sherratt; one *d*. *Educ:* Leek Grammar Sch. Lord Chancellor's Department: Court Business Officer, Midland and Oxford Circuit, 1971; HQ Personnel Officer, 1976; Courts Administrator, Exeter Group, 1981; Head, Civil Business Div. HQ, 1987; Court Service Management Gp, 1988; Court Service Business Gp, 1991. Chm., CSSB, 1998–2004. *Recreations:* hockey, cricket, amateur theatricals, choral and solo singing. *Address:* Sidmouth, Devon. *Club:* Athenæum.

BRINDLEY, Kate Victoria; Director of Museums, Galleries & Archives, Bristol City Council, since 2005; *b* Sheffield, 27 May 1970; *d* of Roger and Carol Manning. *Educ:* Silverdale Sch., Sheffield; Univ. of Leeds (BA Jt Hons Hist. of Art and Religious Studies); Univ. of Manchester (Dip. Mus and Gall. Studies). Curatorial asst, Mead Gall., Warwick Univ., 1992–96; Exhibns Officer, Leamington Spa Art Gall., 1994–98; Art and Exhibns Officer, Rugby Art Gall. and Mus., 1998–2000; freelance curator and consultant, 2000–02; Hd of Arts and Mus., Wolverhampton CC, 2002–05. Advr, Visual Art, Arts Council England, W Midlands, 1996–2002. Lead, SW Hub for Mus, 2005–. Arts Advr, Paul Hamlyn Foundn, 2008–. Trustee, CraftSpace touring, 2002–05. *Recreations:* shopping, drinking lattes and wine, watching movies, seeking the sun. *Address:* Bristol City Museum & Art Gallery, Queen's Road, Bristol BS8 1RL. *T:* (0117) 922 3586, *Fax:* (0117) 922 2047; *e-mail:* kate.brindley@bristol.gov.uk.

BRINDLEY, Dame Lynne (Janie), DBE 2008; Chief Executive, British Library, since 2000; *b* 2 July 1950; *d* of Ivan Blowers and Janie Blowers (*née* Williams); adopted *d* of Ronald Williams and Elaine Williams (*née* Chapman), 1958; *m* 1972, Timothy Stuart Brindley. *Educ:* Truro High Sch.; Univ. of Reading (BA 1971); UCL (MA 1975; Hon. Fellow, 2002). FIInfSc 1990; FCLIP (FLA 1990). Head of Mktg and of Chief Exec.'s Office, British Library, 1979–85; Dir of Library and Information Services, and Pro-Vice Chancellor, Aston Univ., 1985–90; Principal Consultant, KPMG, 1990–92; Librarian and

Dir of Information Services, LSE, 1992–97; Librarian and Pro-Vice Chancellor, Univ. of Leeds, 1997–2000. Visiting Professor: Knowledge Mgt, Univ. of Leeds, 2000–; City Univ., 2002–. Member: Lord Chancellor's Adv. Cttee on Public Records, 1992–98; Jt Inf. Systems Cttee, HEFCs, 1992–98 (Chair, Electronic Libraries Prog., 1993–98); Review of Higher Educn Libraries, HEFCs, 1992–93; Internat. Cttee on Social Sci. Inf., UNESCO, 1992–97; Res. Resources Bd, 1994–2001, Communications and Inf. Cttee, 2004–, ESRC; Liby and Inf. Commn, DCMS, 1999–2000; Stanford Univ. Adv. Council for Libraries and Inf. Resources, 1999–. Trustee, Thackray Med. Mus., Leeds, 1999–2001. FRSA 1993. CCMI 2004. Freeman, City of London, 1989; Liveryman, Goldsmiths' Co., 1993– (Mem., Court of Assts, 2006–). Hon. Fellow, Univ. of Wales, Aberystwyth, 2007. Hon. DLitt: Nottingham Trent, 2001; Oxford, Leicester, London Guildhall, 2002; Reading, Sheffield, 2004; Aston, 2008; Hon. DSc: City, 2005; Leeds, 2006; DUniv Open, 2006. *Publications:* numerous articles on electronic libraries and information mgt. *Recreations:* classical music, theatre, modern art, hill walking. *Address:* British Library, 96 Euston Road, NW1 2DB. *Club:* Reform.

BRINDLEY, Stephen, FCIH; therapeutic counsellor/psychotherapist; Chief Executive, North Hull Housing Action Trust, 1991–99; *b* 18 April 1947; *s* of Bernard Patrick and Marjorie Yvonne Brindley; *m* 1969, Elaine Gillian Hill (*d* 1998); two *d*. *Educ:* Wolverhampton Grammar Tech. Sch.; Univ. of Essex. FCIH 1981. Various local govt housing positions, 1969–81; Dir of Housing, Hull CC, 1981–91. *Recreation:* music. *Address:* The Old Farmhouse, 47 Main Street, Brandesburton, Driffield, E Yorks YO25 8RL.

BRINK, Prof. André Philippus, DLitt; Professor of English, University of Cape Town, since 1991; *b* 29 May 1935; *s* of Daniel Brink and Aletta Wilhelmina Wolmarans; *m*; three *s* one *d*. *Educ:* Potchefstroom Univ. (MA Eng. Lit. 1958, MA Afr. Lit. 1959); Rhodes Univ. (DLitt 1975). Rhodes University: Lectr, 1961; Sen. Lectr, 1975; Associate Prof., 1977; Prof. of Afrikaans and Dutch Literature, 1980–90. Hon. DLitt Witwatersrand, 1985. Prix Médicis étranger, 1981; Martin Luther King Meml Prize, 1981. Chevalier de la Légion d'honneur, 1982; Commandeur, l'Ordre des Arts et des Lettres, 1992. *Publications:* in Afrikaans: Die meul teen die hang, 1958; over 40 titles (novels, plays, travel books, literary criticism, humour); in English: Looking on Darkness, 1974; An Instant in the Wind, 1976; Rumours of Rain, 1978; A Dry White Season, 1979; A Chain of Voices, 1982; Mapmakers (essays), 1983; The Wall of the Plague, 1984; The Ambassador, 1985; (ed with J. M. Coetzee) A Land Apart, 1986; States of Emergency, 1988; An Act of Terror, 1991; The First Life of Adamastor, 1993; On the Contrary, 1993; Imaginings of Sand, 1996; Reinventing a Continent (essays), 1996; Devil's Valley, 1998; The Rights of Desire, 2000; The Other Side of Silence, 2002; Before I Forget, 2004; Praying Mantis, 2005. *Address:* Department of English, University of Cape Town, Rondebosch, 7701, South Africa.

BRINK, Prof. Christoffel Hendrik, PhD, DPhil; Vice-Chancellor, Newcastle University, since 2007; *b* Upington, CP, S Africa, 31 Jan. 1951; *s* of Petrus Johannes Brink and Hester Brink; *m* 1981, Tobea du Preez; one *s* two *d*. *Educ:* Upington Primary and Secondary Sch., SA; Rand Afrikaans Univ., Johannesburg (BSc Maths and Computer Sci. 1972; DPhil 1992); Rhodes Univ. (BSc Hons Maths 1973; MSc Maths 1974; MA Phil. 1975); PhD Algebraic Logic Cambridge 1978. Mil. trng, Army Gymnasium Heidelberg, 1969 (2nd Lt). Lectr in Maths, 1979–80; Sen. Lectr, 1980–86, Univ. of Stellenbosch; Associate Prof. of Maths, Univ. of Cape Town, 1987–92; Sen. Res. Fellow, ANU, 1988–90; University of Cape Town: Hd, Dept of Maths, 1991–94; Prof. of Maths, 1993–99; Hd, Dept of Maths and Applied Maths, 1995–99; Dir, Lab. for Formal Aspects and Complexity in Computer Sci., 1994–99; Coordinator of Strategic Planning, 1997; Pro Vice-Chancellor (Res.) and Prof. of Maths, Univ. of Wollongong, NSW, 1999–2001; Vice-Chancellor and Rector, Stellenbosch Univ., 2002–07. Founder Mem., Acad. of Sci. of SA, 1995; FRSSAf 1995. Hon. Col, Mil. Acad. of SA, 2004. *Publications:* (jtly) Wiskunde vir Wetenskapstudente (Mathematics for Science Students), 1983; (ed jtly) Relational Methods in Computer Science, 1997; (with I. M. Rewitzky) A Paradigm for Program Semantics: power structures and duality, 2001; No Lesser Place: the taaldebat at Stellenbosch, 2006. *Address:* Newcastle University, 6 Kensington Terrace, Newcastle upon Tyne NE1 7RU. *T:* (0191) 222 6064, *Fax:* (0191) 222 6828; *e-mail:* chris.brink@ncl.ac.uk. *Club:* Northern Counties (Newcastle upon Tyne).

BRINK, Prof. David Maurice, DPhil; FRS 1981; Professor of History of Physics, University of Trento, Italy, 1993–98; *b* 20 July 1930; *s* of Maurice Ossian Brink and Victoria May Finlayson; *m* 1958, Verena Wehrli; one *s* two *d*. *Educ:* Friends' Sch., Hobart; Univ. of Tasmania (BSc); Univ. of Oxford (DPhil). Rhodes Scholar, 1951–54; Rutherford Scholar, 1954–58; Lectr, 1954–58, Fellow and Tutor, 1958–93, Balliol Coll., Oxford; Univ. Lectr, 1958–89, H. J. G. Moseley Reader in Physics, 1989–93, Oxford Univ., retd. Instructor, MIT, 1956–57. Rutherford Medal and Prize, Inst. of Physics, 1982; Lise Meitner Prize for Nuclear Physics, Eur. Physical Soc., 2006. *Publications:* Angular Momentum, 1962, 3rd edn 1993; Nuclear Forces, 1965; Semi-classical Methods in Nucleus-Nucleus Scattering, 1985; (with R. Broglia) Nuclear Superfluidity, 2004. *Recreations:* birdwatching, walking. *Address:* 34 Minster Road, Oxford OX4 1LY. *T:* (01865) 246127.

BRINKLEY, Robert Edward, CMG 2006; HM Diplomatic Service; High Commissioner to Pakistan, since 2006; *b* 21 Jan. 1954; *s* of Thomas Edward Brinkley and Sheila Doris Brinkley (*née* Gearing); *m* 1982, (Frances) Mary Webster (*née* Edwards); three *s*. *Educ:* Stonyhurst Coll.; Corpus Christi Coll., Oxford (MA). Entered HM Diplomatic Service, 1977: FCO, 1977–78; Mem., UK Delegn to Comprehensive Test Ban Negotiations, Geneva, 1978; Second Sec., Moscow, 1979–82; First Secretary: FCO, 1982–88; Bonn, 1988–92; FCO, 1992–95; Counsellor and Head, Fundamental Expenditure Rev. Unit, FCO, 1995–96; Political Counsellor, Moscow, 1996–99; Head, FCO/Home Office Jt Entry Clearance Unit, 2000–02; Ambassador to Ukraine, 2002–06. *Recreations:* walking, reading, music (violin). *Address:* c/o Foreign and Commonwealth Office, King Charles Street, SW1A 2AH.

BRINLEY JONES, Robert; *see* Jones.

BRINSDEN, Peter Robert, FRCOG; Consultant, since 1989 and Medical Director, 1989–2005, now Consultant Medical Director, Bourn Hall Clinic, Cambridge; *b* 2 Sept. 1940; *s* of Dudley and Geraldine Brinsden; *m* 1967, Gillian Susan Heather; two *s*. *Educ:* Rugby Sch.; King's Coll. London; St George's Hosp., London (MB BS 1966). MRCS 1966; LRCP 1966; FRCOG 1989. House officer appts, 1967; Medical Officer, Royal Navy, 1966–82: appointments: HMS Glamorgan, 1967–68; RN Hosps, Haslar, Plymouth, Malta and Gibraltar, 1968–78; civilian hosps, Southampton and Portsmouth, 1972–74; Surgeon Comdr, 1976; Consultant Obstetrician and Gynaecologist, RN Hosps, Portsmouth and Plymouth, 1978–82; retd 1982; Consultant: King Fahd Hosp., Riyadh, 1982–84; Bourn Hall and Wellington Hosp., 1985–89. Affiliated Lectr, Univ. of Cambridge Clinical Sch., Addenbrooke's Hosp., 1992–2007. Vis. Prof. in Gynaecology and Fertility, Capital Medical Univ., Beijing, 2001–. Inspector, HFEA, 1997–. Gov., Newton Primary Sch., Cambs, 1998–2001. *Publications:* (ed) A Textbook of In-Vitro

Fertilization and Assisted Reproduction, 1992, 3rd edn 2005; contrib. numerous medical articles and book chapters on infertility and assisted reproduction. *Recreations:* sailing, sub-aqua diving, computing, photography. *Address:* Manor Farm, Yelling, Cambs PE19 6SD. *T:* (01480) 880272; *e-mail:* peter@brinsden.net.

BRINTON, Helen Rosemary; *see* Clark, H. R.

BRINTON, Michael Ashley Cecil; Director, since 1970, Chairman, since 1991, Brintons Ltd; Lord-Lieutenant of Worcestershire, since 2001; *b* 6 Oct. 1941; *s* of Maj. Sir (Esme) Tatton (Cecil) Brinton and Mary Elizabeth Brinton (*née* Fahnestock); *m* 1966, Angela Elizabeth Ludlow; two *s* one *d*. *Educ:* Arden House, Henley in Arden; Eton; lang. studies at univs of Vienna, Perugia and Aix-en-Provence. Joined Brintons Ltd, 1962. Chm., Export Council, 1984–95, Vice Pres., 1996–98, Pres., 1998–2000, British Carpet Manufr's Assoc.; President: Confedn Internat. de Tapis et Tissus d'Ameublement, 1987–91; Qualitas Council, 1992–94. Chm., Hereford and Worcester, CBI, 1998–. High Sheriff, 1990–91, DL 1991–2001, Hereford and Worcs. KStJ 2002. *Recreations:* shooting, fishing, old cars. *Address:* Brintons Ltd, PO Box 16, Kidderminster, Worcs DY10 1AG. *T:* (01562) 635021, *Fax:* (01562) 822225; *e-mail:* mbrinton@brintons.co.uk.

BRINTON, Timothy Denis; self-employed broadcasting consultant, presentation tutor and communications adviser, retired 1999; *b* 24 Dec. 1929; *s* of late Dr Denis Hubert Brinton; *m* 1st, 1954, Jane-Mari Coningham; one *s* three *d*; 2nd, 1965, Jeanne Frances Wedge; two *d*. *Educ:* Summer Fields, Oxford; Eton Coll., Windsor; Geneva Univ.; Central Sch. of Speech and Drama. BBC staff, 1951–59; ITN, 1959–62; freelance, 1962–99. Mem., Kent CC, 1974–81. Chm., Dartford Gravesham HA, 1988–90. MP (C): Gravesend, 1979–83; Gravesham, 1983–87. Member: Court, 1979–95, Council, 1995–98, Univ. of London; Med. Sch. Council, St Mary's Hosp., Paddington, 1983–88; Gov., Wye Coll., London Univ., 1989–97. Mem., RTS. *Address:* 4/21 Grimston Gardens, Folkestone, Kent CT20 2PU. *T:* (01303) 226558.

BRISBANE, Archbishop of, and Metropolitan of the Province of Queensland, since 2002, and Primate of Australia, since 2005; **Most Rev. Dr Phillip John Aspinall;** *b* 17 Dec. 1959; *m* 1982, Christa Schmitt; two *s*. *Educ:* Univ. of Tasmania (BSc 1980); Brisbane Coll. of Advanced Educn (GradDipRE 1985); Ecumenical Inst., Geneva (Cert. 1987); Trinity Coll., Melbourne Coll. of Divinity (BD (Hons) 1988); Monash Univ. (PhD 1989); Deakin Univ. (MBA 1998). Field Officer, C of E Boys' Soc., 1980; Diocesan Youth and Educn Officer, 1981–84; Dep. Warden, Christ Coll., Dio. Tasmania, 1983–84; Dir, Parish Educn, St Stephen's, Mt Waverley, Dio. Melbourne, 1985–88; ordained deacon, 1988, priest, 1989; Asst Curate, St Mark-on-the-Hill, 1988–89; Asst Priest, Brighton, 1989–91; Priest in charge, Bridgewater-Gagebrook, 1991–94; Dir, Anglicare, Tasmania, 1994–98; Acting Archdeacon of Clarence, 1997; Archdeacon for Church and Society, Dio. Tasmania, 1997–98; Asst Bp, Dio. Adelaide, 1998–2002. Member: Standing Cttee, Primates' Meeting of the Anglican Communion, 2007–; (*ex-officio*) ACC, 2007–. *Address:* Bishopsbourne, Box 421, GPO, Brisbane, Qld 4001, Australia.

BRISBANE, Archbishop of, (RC), since 1992; **Most Rev. John Alexius Bathersby,** AO 2008; STD; *b* 26 July 1936; *s* of John Thomas Bathersby and Grace Maud Bathersby (*née* Conquest). *Educ:* Pius XII Seminary, Banyo, Qld, Australia; Gregorian Univ., Rome (STL, STD). Priest, 1961; Asst Priest, Goondiwindi, 1962–68; Spiritual Dir, Banyo Seminary, 1973–86; Bishop of Cairns, 1986–92. *Recreation:* bush walking. *Address:* Wynberg, 790 Brunswick Street, Brisbane, Qld 4005, Australia. *T:* (7) 31315500.

BRISBANE, Assistant Bishop of; *see* Holland, Rt Rev. Dr J. C.

BRISBY, John Constant Shannon McBurney; QC 1996; a Deputy High Court Judge, since 2004; *b* 8 May 1956; *s* of late Michael Douglas James McBurney Brisby and Liliana Daneva–Hadjikaltcheva Drenska; *m* 1985, Claire Alexandra Anne, *d* of Sir Donald Logan, *qv. Educ:* Westminster Sch.; Christ Church, Oxford (Schol.; MA). 2nd Lieut, 5th Royal Inniskilling Dragoon Guards, 1974. Called to the Bar, Lincoln's Inn, 1978 (Mansfield Schol.; Bencher, 2005); in practice as barrister, 1980–. Member, Executive Council: Friends of Bulgaria, 1991–; British-Bulgarian Legal Assoc., 1991–. *Publications:* (contrib.) Butterworth's Company Law Precedents, 4th edn; Konstantin Hadjikaltchoff 1856–1940, 2006. *Recreations:* hunting, shooting, ski-ing, tennis, music, reading, art and architecture. *Address:* 4 Stone Buildings, Lincoln's Inn, WC2A 3XT. *T:* (020) 7242 5524.

BRISCO, Sir Campbell Howard, 9th Bt *cr* 1982, of Crofton Place, Cumberland; livestock farmer and manager; *b* 11 Dec. 1944; *s* of Gilfred Rimington Brisco (*d* 1981) and Constance Freda Brisco (*d* 1980), 2nd *d* of Charles John Polson, Masterton, NZ; *S* cousin, 1995, but his name does not appear on the Official Roll of the Baronetage; *m* 1969, Kaye Janette, *d* of Ewan William McFadzien; two *s* one *d*. *Educ:* Southland Boys' High Sch. *Recreation:* sport. *Heir:* *s* Kent Rimington Brisco, *b* 24 Sept. 1972. *Address:* 134 Park Street, Winton, Southland, New Zealand. *T:* (3) 2369068.

BRISCOE, Sir Brian (Anthony), Kt 2002; Chief Executive, Local Government Association, 1996–2006; *b* 29 July 1945; *s* of Anthony Brown Briscoe and Lily Briscoe; *m* 1969, Sheila Mary Cheyne; three *s*. *Educ:* Newcastle Royal Grammar Sch.; St Catharine's Coll., Cambridge (MA, DipTP). MRTPI, MRICS. Asst Planner, Derbyshire CC, 1967–71; Section Head, Herefordshire CC, 1971–74; Asst Chief Planner, W Yorks CC, 1974–79; Dep. County Planning Officer, Herts CC, 1979–88; County Planning Officer, Kent CC, 1988–90; Chief Exec., Herts CC, 1990–96. Hon. DLaws. FRSA; CCMI. *Publications:* contribs to planning and property jls; chapter in English Structure Planning, 1982. *Recreations:* family, golf, Newcastle United FC. *Address:* 132 Marsham Court, Marsham Street, SW1P 4LB.

BRISCOE, Constance; a part-time Recorder, since 1996; barrister; author, since 2003; *b* London, 18 May 1957; *d* of George and Carmen Briscoe; one *s* one *d*; partner, 1999, Anthony Arlidge, QC. *Educ:* Sacred Heart Sch., Camberwell; Univ. of Newcastle upon Tyne (LLB Hons Law); Council of Legal Educn (Bar Finals). Called to the Bar, Inner Temple, 1983. *Publications:* Ugly, 2006; Beyond Ugly, 2008. *Recreations:* gardening, reading, Billy Holliday, writing. *Address:* 9–12 Bell Yard, WC2 2JR. *T:* (020) 7400 1800, *Fax:* (020) 7404 1405; *e-mail:* constance.briscoe@googlemail.com.

BRISCOE, Sir John Geoffrey James, 6th Bt *cr* 1910, of Bourn Hall, Bourn, Cambridge; *b* (posthumously) 4 Nov. 1994; *o s* of Sir (John) James Briscoe, 5th Bt and of Felicity Mary (now Mrs Christopher Edward Whitley), *e d* of David Melville Watkinson; *S father*, 1994. *Heir:* uncle: Edward Home Briscoe [*b* 27 March 1955; *m* 1st, 1979, Anne Lister (marr. diss. 1989); one *s* one *d*; 2nd, 1994, Sandy Elizabeth King (*née* Lloyd)].

BRISCOE, John Hubert Daly, LVO 1997; FRCGP; Apothecary to HM Household, Windsor, and to HM the Queen Mother's Household at Royal Lodge, 1986–97; Master, Worshipful Society of Apothecaries of London, 2000–01; *b* 19 March 1933; only *s* of late Dr Arnold Daly Briscoe and Doris Winifred Briscoe (*née* Nicholson); *m* 1958, Janet Anne Earlam; one *s* four *d*. *Educ:* St Andrew's Sch., Eastbourne; Winchester Coll.; St John's Coll., Cambridge (MA); St Thomas's Hosp. (MB BChir); DObstRCOG 1959; MRCGP

1968, FRCGP 2006. MO, Overseas CS, Basutoland, 1959–62; Asst in gen. practice, Aldeburgh, 1963–65; Principal in gen. practice, Eton, 1965–97; Medical Officer: Eton Coll., 1965–97; St George's Sch., Windsor Castle, 1976–97. Fellow, MOs of Schs Assoc., 2002 (Pres., 1989–91). FRSocMed 1995. Hon. MO, Guards' Polo Club, 1966–83. Hon. Mem., Windsor and Dist Med. Soc., 1999. Hon. Auditor, Eur. Union of Sch. and Univ. Health and Medicine, 1981–89. Lay Steward, St George's Chapel, Windsor Castle, 1999. Bridgemaster, Baldwin's Bridge Trust, Eton, 1988–89 and 2002–03. Pres., Omar Khayyam Club, 2005. Hon. Licentiate, Apothecaries' Hall, Dublin, 2001. *Publications:* contrib. papers on influenza vaccination and adolescent medicine. *Recreations:* growing vegetables, pictures. *Address:* Wistaria House, 54/56 Kings Road, Windsor, Berks SL4 2AH. *T:* (01753) 855321. *Club:* Athenæum.

BRISE, Sir Timothy Edward R.; *see* Ruggles-Brise.

BRISON, Ven. William Stanley; Team Rector, Pendleton, Manchester, 1994–98; permission to officiate, diocese of Manchester, since 1999; *b* 20 Nov. 1929; *s* of William P. Brison and Marion A. Wilber; *m* 1951, Marguerite, (Peggy), Adelia Nettleton; two *s* two *d*. *Educ:* Alfred Univ., New York (BS Eng); Berkeley Divinity School, New Haven, Conn (STM, MDiv). United States Marine Corps, Captain (Reserve), 1951–53. Engineer, Norton Co., Worcester, Mass, 1953–54. Vicar, then Rector, Christ Church, Bethany, Conn, 1957–69; Archdeacon of New Haven, Conn, 1967–69; Rector, Emmanuel Episcopal Church, Stamford, Conn, 1969–72; Vicar, Christ Church, Davyhulme, Manchester, 1972–81; Rector, All Saints', Newton Heath, Manchester, 1981–85; Area Dean of North Manchester, 1981–85; Archdeacon of Bolton, 1985–92, then Archdeacon Emeritus; CMS Missionary, Nigeria, 1992–94; Lectr, St Francis of Assisi Theol Coll., Zaria, 1992–94. Chairman: Bury Christian Aid, 2002–; Goshen and Blackford Bridge Tenants' and Residents' Assoc., 2003–. *Publication:* (with Peggy Brison) A Tale of Two Visits to Chechnya, 2005. *Recreations:* squash, grandchildren. *Address:* 2 Scott Avenue, Bury, Lancs BL9 9RS. *T:* (0161) 764 3998.

BRISTER, William Arthur Francis, CB 1984; Deputy Director General of Prison Service, 1982–85; *b* 10 Feb. 1925; *s* of Arthur John Brister and Velda Mirandoli; *m* 1949, Mary Speakman; one *s* one *d* (and one *s* decd). *Educ:* Douai Sch.; Brasenose Coll., Oxford (MA 1949). Asst Governor Cl. II, HM Borstal, Lowdham Grange, 1949–52; Asst Principal, Imperial Trng Sch., Wakefield, 1952–55; Asst Governor II, HM Prison, Parkhurst, 1955–57; Dep. Governor, HM Prison: Camp Hill, 1957–60; Manchester, 1960–62; Governor, HM Borstal: Morton Hall, 1962–67; Dover, 1967–69; Governor II, Prison Dept HQ, 1969–71; Governor, HM Remand Centre, Ashford, 1971–73; Governor I, Prison Dept HQ, 1973–75, Asst Controller, 1975–79; Chief Inspector of the Prison Service, 1979–81; HM Dep. Chief Inspector of Prisons, 1981–82. Mem., Parole Board, 1986–89. Nuffield Travelling Fellow, Canada and Mexico, 1966–67. *Recreations:* shooting, music, Venetian history. *Clubs:* Oxford and Cambridge, English-Speaking Union.

BRISTOL, 8th Marquess of, *cr* 1826; **Frederick William Augustus Hervey;** Baron Hervey of Ickworth, 1703; Earl of Bristol, 1714; Earl Jermyn of Horningsheath, 1826; Hereditary High Steward of the Liberty of St Edmund; Patron of 30 Livings; *b* 19 Oct. 1979; *s* of 6th Marquess of Bristol and of his 3rd wife, Yvonne Marie, *d* of Anthony Sutton; *S half-brother*, 1999. *Educ:* Eton Coll.; Edinburgh Univ. (BCom). Dir, Bristol & Stone Real Estate Investment Co., 2004–. Trustee, Gen. Hervey's Charitable Trust, 1999–. Patron: Gwrych Castle Preservation Trust, 2002–; Athenaeum, Bury St Edmunds, 2006–; A Heart for Russia Foundn, 2006–. *Recreations:* emerging markets, reading, shooting, travel. *Address:* 65b Eaton Square, SW1W 9BQ. *Club:* Turf.

BRISTOL, Bishop of, since 2003; **Rt Rev. Michael Arthur Hill;** *b* 17 April 1949; *s* of Arthur and Hilda Hill; *m* 1972, Anthea Jean Hill (*née* Longridge); one *s* four *d*. *Educ:* N Cheshire Coll. of FE (Dip. in Business Studies); Brasted Place Coll.; Ridley Hall, Cambridge (GOE); Fitzwilliam Coll., Cambridge (Postgrad. Cert. in Theology). Junior Exec. in printing industry, 1968–72. Mem., Scargill House Community, 1972–73; ordained deacon, 1977, priest, 1978; Curate: St Mary Magdalene, Addiscombe, Croydon, 1977–80; St Paul, Slough, 1980–83; Priest in charge, 1983–90, Rector, 1990–92, St Leonard, Chesham Bois; RD, Amersham, 1990–92; Archdeacon of Berkshire, 1992–98; Area Bishop of Buckingham, 1998–2003. *Publications:* Reaching the Unchurched, 1992; Lifelines, 1997. *Recreations:* playing guitar, listening to music, cricket, soccer, Rugby League and Union, reading. *Address:* Wethered House, 11 The Avenue, Clifton, Bristol, BS8 3HG.

BRISTOL, Dean of; *see* Grimley, Very Rev. R. W.

BRISTOL, Archdeacon of; *see* McClure, Ven. T. E.

BRISTOW, Alan Edgar, OBE 1966; FRAeS; Managing Director, then Chairman, Bristow Helicopters Ltd, 1954–85; *b* 3 Sept. 1923; *m* 1945; one *s* one *d*. *Educ:* Portsmouth Grammar School. Cadet, British India Steam Navigation Co., 1939–43; Pilot, Fleet Air Arm, 1943–46; Test Pilot, Westland Aircraft Ltd, 1946–49; Helicopair, Paris/Indo-China, 1949–51; Man. Dir, Air Whaling Ltd (Antarctic Whaling Expedns), 1951–54; Dir, British United Airways Ltd, 1960–70, Man. Dir 1967–70; Chairman: Briway Transit Systems Ltd, 1987–94; Alanta Ltd, 1996–. Invented water beds for cows and horses, 1995, patented 1997. Cierva Memorial Lectr, RAeS, 1967. FRAeS 1967. Croix de Guerre (France), 1950. *Publications:* papers to RAeS. *Recreations:* flying, shooting, sailing. *Address:* Meadowfield, Barhatch Road, Cranleigh, Surrey GU6 7DJ. *T:* (01483) 274674.

BRISTOW, Dr Laurence Stanley Charles; HM Diplomatic Service; Deputy Head of Mission, Moscow, since 2007; *b* 23 Nov. 1963; *s* of Stanley and Hilary Bristow; *m* 1988, Fiona MacCallum; two *s*. *Educ:* Colchester Royal Grammar Sch.; Trinity Coll., Cambridge (BA 1986; PhD 1991); Open Univ. (MBA 2001). Entered FCO, 1990; Second Sec., Bucharest, 1992–95; First Secretary: FCO, 1995–99; Ankara, 1999–2002; NATO Defence Coll., Rome, 2002–03; FCO, 2003; Ambassador to Azerbaijan, 2004–07. *Address:* c/o Foreign and Commonwealth Office, King Charles Street, SW1A 2AH.

BRITNELL, Mark Douglas; Director General, Commissioning and System Management, Department of Health, since 2007; *b* 5 Jan. 1966; *s* of late Robert Britnell and of Veronica Britnell, now Leigh; *m* 2005, Stephanie Joy; one *d*. *Educ:* Univ. of Warwick (BA Hons 1988). NHS Mgt Trng Scheme, 1989–92; Gen. Manager, St Mary's Hosp., London, 1992–95; Exec. Dir, Central Middlesex Hosp., London, 1995–98; Chief Executive: Univ. Hosp. Birmingham NHS, then NHS Foundn, Trust, 1998–2006; NHS S Central Strategic HA, 2006–07. Non-exec. Dir, Dr Foster Ltd, 2004–07. Sen. Associate, King's Fund, 2004–. Hon. Sen. Fellow, Univ. of Birmingham, 2006–. *Recreations:* sport, current affairs, family. *Address:* Department of Health, Richmond House, 79 Whitehall, SW1A 2NS. *Club:* Reform.

BRITNELL, Prof. Richard Hugh, PhD; FBA 2005; FRHistS; Professor of History, University of Durham, 1997–2003, now Professor Emeritus; *b* 21 April 1944; *s* of Ronald

Frank Britnell and Edith Britnell (*née* Manson); *m* 1973, Jennifer Joan Beard; two *s*. *Educ:* Sir William Borlase Sch.; Bedford Modern Sch.; Clare Coll., Cambridge (BA 1964; PhD 1970). FRHistS 1988. University of Durham: Lectr in Econ. Hist., 1966–85; Lectr in Hist., 1985–86; Sen. Lectr, 1986–94; Reader in Hist., 1994–97. Jt Ed., Surtees Soc., 1999–. *Publications:* Growth and Decline in Colchester 1300–1525, 1986; The Commercialisation of English Society 1000–1500, 1993, 2nd edn 1996; The Closing of the Middle Ages? England 1471–1529, 1997; Britain and Ireland 1050–1530: economy and society, 2004. *Recreations:* amateur dramatics, keyboard playing (clavichord, piano, organ), cooking, gardening, swimming. *Address:* 25 Orchard House, New Elvet, Durham DH1 3DB. *T:* (0191) 383 0409; *e-mail:* R.H.Britnell@durham.ac.uk; 2 Parkside, Durham DH1 4RE. *T:* (0191) 384 2017.

BRITTAIN, Barbara Jane; *see* Moorhouse, B. J.

BRITTAIN, Clive Edward; racehorse trainer, since 1972; *b* 15 Dec. 1933; *s* of Edward John Brittain and Priscilla Rosalind (*née* Winzer); *m* 1957, Maureen Helen Robinson. *Educ:* Calne Secondary Mod. Sch. Winning horses trained include: Julio Mariner, St Leger, 1978; Pebbles, 1000 Guineas, 1984; Eclipse, Dubai Champion and Breeders Cup Turf, 1985; Jupiter Island, Japan Cup, Tokyo, 1986; Mystiko, 2000 Guineas, 1991; Terimon, Juddmonte Internat., 1991; User Friendly, Oaks, Irish Oaks, Yorkshire Oaks, St Leger, 1992; Sayyedati, 1000 Guineas, and Jacque le Marois, 1993, Sussex Stakes, 1995; Luso, Hong Kong Vase, 1996 and 1997; Crimplene, Irish 1000 Guineas, 2000; Var, Prix de l'Abbaye, Longchamp, 2004; Warrsan, Coronation Cup, 2003 and 2004, and Grosser Prix von Baden, 2004 and 2005. *Recreation:* shooting. *Address:* Carlburg, 49 Bury Road, Newmarket, Suffolk CB8 7BY. *T:* (01638) 664347. *Club:* Jockey Club Rooms (Newmarket).

BRITTAN OF SPENNITHORNE, Baron *cr* 2000 (Life Peer), of Spennithorne in the County of North Yorkshire; **Leon Brittan**, Kt 1989; PC 1981; QC 1978; DL; Vice-Chairman, UBS Investment Bank (formerly UBS Warburg), since 2000; Member, 1989–99, a Vice-President, 1989–93 and 1995–99, European Commission (formerly Commission of the European Communities); *b* 25 Sept. 1939; *s* of late Dr Joseph Brittan and Mrs Rebecca Brittan; *m* 1980, Diana Peterson (*see* Lady Brittan of Spennithorne); two step *d*. *Educ:* Haberdashers' Aske's Sch.; Trinity Coll., Cambridge (MA); Yale Univ. (Henry Fellow). Chm., Cambridge Univ. Conservative Assoc., 1960; Pres., Cambridge Union, 1960; debating tour of USA for Cambridge Union, 1961. Called to Bar, Inner Temple, 1962; Bencher, 1983. Chm., Bow Group, 1964–65; contested (C) North Kensington, 1966 and 1970. MP (C): Cleveland and Whitby, Feb. 1974–1983; Richmond, Yorks, 1983–88. Editor, Crossbow, 1966–68; formerly Mem. Political Cttee, Carlton Club; Vice-Chm. of Governors, Isaac Newton Sch., 1968–71; Mem. European North American Cttee, 1970–78; Vice-Chm., Nat. Assoc. of School Governors and Managers, 1970–78; Vice-Chm., Parly Cons. Party Employment Cttee, 1974–76; opposition front bench spokesman on Devolution, 1976–79, on employment, 1978–79; Minister of State, Home Office, 1979–81; Chief Sec. to the Treasury, 1981–83; Sec. of State for Home Dept, 1983–85; Sec. of State for Trade and Industry, 1985–86. Chm., Cons. Gp for Europe, 2000–03. Consultant, Herbert Smith, 2000–06; non-exec. Dir, Unilever, 2004– (Adv. Dir, 2000–04). Distinguished Vis. Scholar, Yale Univ., 2000–02. Chancellor, Univ. of Teesside, 1993–2005. Chm., Soc. of Cons. Lawyers, 1986–88. DL N Yorks, 2001. Hon. DCL: Newcastle, 1990; Durham, 1992; Hon. LLD: Hull, 1990; Bath, 1995; Dr *hc* Edinburgh, 1991; Hon. DLitt Bradford, 1992; Hon. DEc Korea, 1997. *Publications:* Defence and Arms Control in a Changing Era, 1988; Hersch Lauterpacht Memorial Lectures, 1990; European Competition Policy, 1992; The Europe We Need, 1994; Globalisation *vs* Sovereignty (Rede Lect., 1997); A Diet of Brussels, 2000; (contrib.) The Conservative Opportunity; pamphlets: Millstones for the Sixties (jtly), Rough Justice, Infancy and the Law, How to Save Your Schools, To spur, not to mould, A New Deal for Health Care, Discussions on Policy, Monetary Union. *Recreations:* opera, art, cricket, walking. *Address:* c/o House of Lords, SW1A 0PW. *Clubs:* Carlton, White's, Pratts, MCC.

See also Sir Samuel Brittan.

BRITTAN OF SPENNITHORNE, Lady; Diana Brittan, DBE 2004 (CBE 1995); JP; Chairman, Community Fund (formerly National Lottery Charities Board), 1999–2004; *b* 14 Oct. 1940; *d* of Leslie Howell Clemetson and Elizabeth Agnes Clemetson (*née* Leonard); *m* 1st, 1965, Dr Richard Peterson (marr. diss. 1979); two *d*; 2nd, 1980, Leon Brittan (*see* Baron Brittan of Spennithorne). *Educ:* Westonbirt Sch., Tetbury. Man. Editor, Eibis Internat., London, 1977–88. Deputy Chairman: HFEA, 1990–97; EOC, 1994–96 (Comr, 1989–94); Mem., Lord Chancellor's Adv. Cttee on Legal Educn and Conduct, 1997–99. Chairman: Rathbone Training, 1991–2002; Nat. Family Mediation, 2001–07; Trustee: Action on Addiction, 1993–98; Runnymede Trust, 1995– (Chm., 1998–99); Open Univ. Foundn, 1996–2000; Multiple Birth Foundn, 1998–; The Connection at St Martin's, 2005–; Chm., Carnegie Commn for Rural Community Develt, 2006–07 (Vice-Chm., 2004–06); President: Townswomen's Guild, 1996–; Nat. Assoc. of Connexions Partnerships, 2005–08. Mem., Bd of Mgt, British Sch. of Brussels, 1989–99. JP City of London, 1984. Distinguished Associate, Darwin Coll., Cambridge, 1998. *Recreations:* botany, travel, cinema, cards, walking.

BRITTAN, Sir Samuel, Kt 1993; columnist, Financial Times, since 1966 (Assistant Editor, 1978–95); *b* 29 Dec. 1933; *s* of late Joseph Brittan, MD, and Rebecca Brittan (*née* Lipetz). *Educ:* Kilburn Grammar Sch.; Jesus Coll., Cambridge (Hon. Fellow, 1988). 1st Class in Economics, 1955; MA Cantab. Various posts in Financial Times, 1955–61; Economics Editor, Observer, 1961–64; Adviser, DEA, 1965. Fellow, Nuffield Coll., Oxford, 1973–74, Vis. Fellow, 1974–82; Vis. Prof. of Economics, Chicago Law Sch., 1978; Hon. Prof. of Politics, Warwick Univ., 1987–92. Mem., Peacock Cttee on Financing the BBC, 1985–86. Pres., David Hume Soc., 1996–99. Hon. DLitt Heriot-Watt, 1985; DU Essex, 1994. Financial Journalist of the Year Award 1971; George Orwell Prize (for political journalism), 1980; Ludwig Erhard Prize (for economic writing), 1988. Chevalier de la Légion d'Honneur, 1993. *Publications:* The Treasury under the Tories, 1964, rev. edn, Steering the Economy, 1969, 1971; Left or Right: The Bogus Dilemma, 1968; The Price of Economic Freedom, 1970; Capitalism and the Permissive Society, 1973, rev. edn as A Restatement of Economic Liberalism, 1988; Is There an Economic Consensus?, 1973; (with P. Lilley) The Delusion of Incomes Policy, 1977; The Economic Consequences of Democracy, 1977; How to End the Monetarist Controversy, 1981; The Role and Limits of Government, 1983; Capitalism with a Human Face, 1995; Essays: Moral, Political and Economic, 1998; Against the Flow, 2005; articles in various jls. *Address:* c/o Financial Times, Number One Southwark Bridge, SE1 9HL.

See also Baron Brittan of Spennithorne.

BRITTEN, Alan Edward Marsh, CBE 2003; Chairman, English Tourism Council, 1999–2003; Board Member, British Tourist Authority, 1997–2003; *b* 26 Feb. 1938; *s* of Robert Harry Marsh Britten and Helen Marjorie (*née* Goldson); *m* 1967, Judith Clare Akerman; two *d*. *Educ:* Radley; Emmanuel Coll., Cambridge (MA English); Williams Coll., Mass (American Studies). Mobil Oil Co.: joined 1961; marketing and planning, UK, USA, Italy; Chief Exec., Mobil Cos in E Africa, 1975–77, Denmark, 1980–81, Portugal, 1982–84, Benelux, 1984–86; Managing Dir, Mobil Oil Co., 1987–89; Manager, Internat. Planning, Mobil Oil Corp., 1989–90; Vice-President: Mobil Europe, 1991–97; Country Management, 1993–97; non-exec. Dir, Mobil Oil Co. Ltd, 1997–2001. Dir, Europia, 1994–97. Member: Council for Aldeburgh Foundn, 1989–99; Develt Cttee, Britten-Pears Foundn, 2006–; Pres., Friends of Aldeburgh Prodns, 2000–. Member: Council, Royal Warrant Holders' Assoc. (Pres., 1997–98); Adv. Board, Ten Days at Princeton; Council, UEA, 1996–2005 (Vice-Chm., 2003–05); Chm., Tourism Quality Review, 2003–. Trustee: Queen Elizabeth Scholarship Trust, 1997–2003 (Chm., 1999–2003); Leeds Castle Foundn, 2005–; Integrated Neurological Services, 2006–; Transglobe Expedition Trust, 2006–. Governor: Trinity Laban (formerly Trinity Coll. of Music), 2001– (Chm., Audit Cttee, 2005–); Trinity Coll., London, 2004–. *Recreations:* music, travel, gardening, letter writing. *Clubs:* Garrick, Noblemen & Gentlemen's Catch; Aldeburgh Golf.

BRITTENDEN, (Charles) Arthur; Senior Consultant, Bell Pottinger (formerly Lowe Bell) Communications Ltd, 1988–2003; Director of Corporate Relations, News International, 1981–87; General Manager (Editorial), Times Newspapers, 1982–87; Director, Times Newspapers Ltd, 1982–87; *b* 23 Oct. 1924; *o s* of late Tom Edwin Brittenden and Caroline (*née* Scrivener); *m* 1st, 1953, Sylvia Penelope Cadman (marr. diss. 1960); 2nd, 1966, Ann Patricia Kenny (marr. diss. 1972); 3rd, 1975, Valerie Arnison (*d* 2002). *Educ:* Leeds Grammar School. Served in Reconnaissance Corps, 1943–46. Yorkshire Post, 1940–43, 1946–49; News Chronicle, 1949–55; joined Sunday Express, 1955: Foreign Editor, 1959–62; Northern Editor, Daily Express, 1962–63; Dep. Editor, Sunday Express, 1963–64; Exec. Editor, 1964–66, Editor, 1966–71, Daily Mail; Dep. Editor, The Sun, 1972–81. Dir, Harmsworth Publications Ltd, 1967–71; Man. Dir, Wigmore Cassettes, 1971–72. Dir, Dowson-Shurman Associates Ltd, 1990–. Mem., 1982–86, Jt Vice-Chm., 1983–86, Press Council. *Address:* 22 Park Street, Woodstock, Oxon OX20 1SP.

BRITTLE, (Benjamin) Cliff; Chairman, Management Board, Rugby Football Union, 1996–98; *b* 11 Jan. 1942; *s* of Benjamin James Brittle and Amy Brittle; *m* (marr. diss.). *Educ:* Longton High Sch., Stoke-on-Trent. With NCR, 1960–62; started business, 1962, retd 1987. FCMI. *Recreations:* golf, Rugby. *Address:* The Hollies, Main Road, Baldrine, Isle of Man IM4 6DQ. *T:* (01624) 861011.

BRITTON, Alison Claire, OBE 1990; ceramic artist, since 1973; tutor, Royal College of Art, since 1984; *b* 4 May 1948; *d* of Prof. James Nimmo Britton and Jessie Muriel Britton (*née* Robertson); two *d*. *Educ:* N London Collegiate Sch.; Leeds Coll. of Art; Central Sch. of Art and Design (DipAD); Royal Coll. of Art (MA). Solo exhibitions: Crafts Council, 1979; Miharudo Gall., Tokyo, 1985; Contemp. Applied Arts, 1987, 1990; Craft Centre Gall., Sydney, 1988; Marianne Heller Galerie, Sandhausen, Germany, 1995; Australian tour, 1996; Barrett Marsden Gall., London, 1998, 2000, 2003, 2005, 2007; Glynn Vivian Art Gall., Swansea, 2003; retrospective exhibn (tour), 1990–91. Work in internat. public and private collections. Co-curator, The Raw and the Cooked, MOMA, Oxford and tour, 1993. *Recreations:* film, walking. *Address:* c/o Barrett Marsden Gallery, 17–18 Great Sutton Street, EC1V 0DN. *T:* (020) 7336 6396.

See also C. M. Britton.

BRITTON, Andrew James Christie; Chairman, Finance Committee, Archbishops' Council, since 2007; *b* 1 Dec. 1940; *s* of late Prof. Karl William Britton and Sheila Margaret Christie; *m* 1963, Pamela Anne, *d* of His Honour Edward Sutcliffe, QC; three *d*. *Educ:* Royal Grammar Sch., Newcastle upon Tyne; Oriel Coll., Oxford (BA); LSE (MSc). Joined HM Treasury as Cadet Economist, 1966; Econ. Asst, 1968; Econ. Adviser, 1970; Sen. Econ. Adviser: DHSS, 1973; HM Treasury, 1975; London Business Sch., 1978–79; Under Sec., HM Treasury, 1980–82; Dir, NIESR, 1982–95. Mem., Treasury Panel of Indep. Forecasters, 1993–95. Vis. Prof., Univ. of Bath, 1998–2001. Licensed Reader, Dio. of Southwark, 1986–; Lay Canon, Southwark Cathedral, 2004–. Mem., Bd of Finance, Dio. of Southwark, 1998–2007 (Vice Chm., 1999–2000; Chm., 2000–07). Exec. Sec., Churches' Enquiry into Unemployment and the Future of Work, 1995–97. *Publications:* (ed) Employment, Output and Inflation, 1983; The Trade Cycle in Britain, 1986; (ed) Policymaking with Macroeconomic Models, 1989; Macroeconomic Policy in Britain 1974–87, 1991; Monetary Regimes of the Twentieth Century, 2001; (jtly) Economic Theory and Christian Belief, 2003. *Address:* 2 Shabden Park, High Road, Chipstead, Surrey CR5 3SF.

BRITTON, Prof. Celia Margaret, PhD; FBA 2000; Professor of French, University College London, since 2003; *b* 20 March 1946; *d* of Prof. James Nimmo Britton and Jessie Muriel Britton. *Educ:* New Hall, Cambridge (MA Mod. and Medieval Langs 1969; Postgrad. Dip. Linguistics 1970); Univ. of Essex (PhD Literary Stylistics 1973. Temp. Lectr in French, KCL, 1972–74; Lectr in French Studies, Univ. of Reading, 1974–91; Carnegie Prof. of French, Univ. of Aberdeen, 1991–2002. Chair, RAE French Panel, 2001. Pres., Soc. for French Studies, 1996–98. Chevalier, Ordre des Palmes Académiques (France), 2003. *Publications:* Claude Simon: writing the visible, 1987; The Nouveau Roman: fiction, theory and politics, 1992; Edouard Glissant and Postcolonial Theory, 1999; Race and the Unconscious, 2002; The Sense of Community in French Caribbean Fiction, 2008; numerous articles on French and Francophone literature and film. *Recreations:* travel, cinema, cookery. *Address:* University College London, Gower Street, WC1E 6BT.

See also A. C. Britton.

BRITTON, John William; independent consultant, since 1993; *b* 13 Dec. 1936; *s* of John Ferguson and Dinah Britton; *m* 1961, Maisie Rubython; one *s* one *d*. *Educ:* Bedlington Grammar Sch.; Bristol Univ. (BScEng 1st Cl. Hons). Royal Aircraft Establishment, Bedford, 1959–83: Hd, Flight Res. Div., 1978–80; Chief Supt and Hd, Flight Systems Bedford Dept, 1981–83; RCDS 1984; Dir, Avionic Equipment and Systems, MoD PE, 1985–86; Science and Technology Assessment Office, Cabinet Office, 1987; Dir Gen. Aircraft 3, MoD PE, 1987–90; Asst Chief Scientific Advr (Projects), MoD, 1990–92, retd. *Recreations:* wine, painting, motor racing (watching), gardening (especially dahlias and fuchsias). *Address:* 6 The Drive, Sharnbrook, Bedford MK44 1HU.

BRITTON, Mark Gordon, MD; FRCP; Consultant Physician in respiratory medicine, Ashford and St Peter's Hospitals NHS Trust (formerly St Peter's Hospital, Chertsey), since 1983; *b* 23 Nov. 1946; *s* of late Capt. Gordon Berry Cowley Britton, CBE and Vera Britton (*née* Hyman); *m* 1972, Gillian Vaughan Davies; three *s*. *Educ:* Ipswich Sch.; Med. Coll. of St Bartholomew's Hosp., London; London Univ. (MB BS 1970, MSc 1981, MD 1982). DIH 1981; FRCP 1990. Surg. Lt Comdr, RNR, 1970–90. Hon. Consultant, King Edward VII's Hosp., London, 1980–; Hon. Consultant and Sen. Lectr, St George's Hosp., London, 1983–; Med. Dir, St Peter's Hosp. NHS Trust, 1994–97; Hon. Sen. Lectr, Imperial Coll., London, 2001–. Vis. Prof., Faculty of Health and Med. Scis (formerly Faculty of Medicine), Univ. of Surrey, 2006–. Member: Med. Reference Panel (Coal Bd), DTI, 2000–; Industrial Injuries Adv. Council, 2003–. Chm., Bd of Trustees, 1999–2005, Mem. Council, 2005–, Vice Pres., 2006–, British Lung Foundn. Trustee, Nat. Confidential Enquiry into Patient Outcome and Death, 2005–. Freeman, City of London,

1983; Mem., Soc. of Apothecaries, 1979–. *Publications:* contrib. various chapters and papers in learned jls on mgt and treatment of asthma, chronic obstructive airways disease and asbestos related diseases. *Recreations:* Rugby football, golf, sailing, gardening, British stamps, Pembrokeshire cottage. *Address:* Woodham House, 92 Ashley Road, Walton-on-Thames, Surrey KT12 1HP. *T:* (01932) 225472, *Fax:* (01932) 244127; *e-mail:* markbritton@btinternet.com. *Club:* Burhill Golf.

BRITTON, Paul John James, CB 2001; Head, Economic and Domestic Affairs Secretariat, since 2001, and Director General, Domestic Policy and Strategy Group, since 2006, Cabinet Office; Appointments Secretary to the Prime Minister for senior ecclesiastical appointments, since 2008; *b* 17 April 1949; *s* of Leonard Britton and Maureen Britton (*née* Vowles); *m* 1972, Pauline Bruce; one *s* one *d. Educ:* Clifton Coll.; Magdalene Coll., Cambridge (BA 1971; MA 1974). Department of the Environment: Admin trainee, 1971–75; Private Sec. to Second Perm. Sec., 1975–77; Principal, 1977; Dept of Transport, 1979–81; DoE, 1981–97: Private Sec. to Minister for Housing and Construction, 1983–84; Asst Sec., 1984; Grade 4, 1991; Dir of Local Govt Finance Policy, 1991–96; Under Sec., 1992; Dir, Envmt Protection Strategy, 1996–97; Dep. Dir, Constitution Secretariat, 1997–98, Dep. Head, Econ. and Domestic Affairs Secretariat, 1998–2001, Cabinet Office; Dir, Town and Country Planning, DTLR, 2001. *Recreations:* architectural history, photography, topography. *Address:* Cabinet Office, 70 Whitehall, SW1A 2AS. *T:* (020) 7270 0140.

BRITZ, Lewis; Executive Councillor, Electrical, Electronic, Telecommunication & Plumbing Union, 1984–95; Member, Industrial Tribunals, 1990–2003; *b* 7 Jan. 1933; *s* of Alfred and Hetty Britz; *m* 1960, Hadassah Rosenberg; four *d. Educ:* Hackney Downs Grammar Sch.; Acton Technical Coll. (OND Elec. Engrg); Nottingham Univ. (BSc (Hons) Engrg); Birkbeck Coll., London Univ. (BA Hons Eng 2002). Head of Research, 1967–71, Nat. Officer, 1971–83, EETPU. Director: LEB, 1977–87; British Internat. Helicopters, 1987–92; Esca Services, 1990–; Chm., JIB Pension Scheme Trustee Co. Ltd, 1997–. Mem., Monopolies and Mergers Commn, 1986–92. Sat in Restrictive Practices Court, 1989. *Recreation:* philately. *Address:* 30 Braemar Gardens, West Wickham, Kent BR4 0JW. *T:* (020) 8777 5986.

BRIXWORTH, Bishop Suffragan of, since 2002; **Rt Rev. Francis, (Frank), White;** *b* 26 May 1949; *s* of John Edward White and Mary Ellen White; *m* 1982, Alison Mary, *d* of Dr K. R. Dumbell, *qv. Educ:* St Cuthbert's GS, Newcastle upon Tyne; Consett Tech. Coll.; UWIST, Cardiff (BScEcon); UC Cardiff (DipSocSci); St John's Coll., Nottingham (Dip. Pastoral Studies); Nottingham Univ. (DipTh). Dir, Youth Action York, 1971–73; Detached Youth Worker, Manchester, 1973–77; Asst Curate, St Nicholas, Durham, 1980–84; Sen. Curate, St Mary and St Cuthbert, Chester-le-Street, 1984–87; Chaplain, Durham HA Hosps, 1987–89; Vicar, St John the Evangelist, Birtley, 1989–97; RD of Chester-le-Street, 1993–97; Archdeacon of Sunderland, 1997–2002. Proctor in Convocation, Gen. Synod of C of E, 1987–2000. Hon. Canon: Durham Cathedral, 1997–2002; Peterborough Cathedral, 2002–. *Recreations:* birdwatching, walking, motor cars, theatre, soccer. *Address:* 4 The Avenue, Dallington, Northampton NN5 7AN. *T:* (01604) 759423, *Fax:* (01604) 750925.

BROAD, Rev. Canon Hugh Duncan; Priest-in-charge, Costa Almeria and Costa Calida, Spain, since 2003; Area Dean, Gibraltar, since 2008; Member, Crown Appointments Commission, 1997–2003; *b* 28 Oct. 1937; *s* of Horace Edward Broad and Lucy Broad; *m* 1988, Jacqueline Lissaman; two *d. Educ:* Shropshire Inst. of Agriculture; Bernard Gilpin Soc., Durham Univ.; Lichfield Theol Coll.; Hereford Coll. of Education. Curate, Holy Trinity, Hereford, 1967–72; Asst Master, Bishop of Hereford's Bluecoat Sch., 1972–74; Curate, St Peter and St Paul, Fareham, 1974–76; Vicar, All Saints with St Barnabas, Hereford, 1976–90; Rector, Matson, 1990–97; Vicar, St George, Gloucester and St Margaret, Whaddon, 1997–2003. Chaplain: Victoria Eye Hosp., Hereford, 1976–90; Selwyn Sch., Gloucester, 1990–97. Mem., Gen. Synod, C of E, 1995–2003. Hon. Canon, Gloucester Cathedral, 2002–03, now Emeritus. *Recreations:* theatre, music, cricket. *Address:* Apartado 617, Mojácar Playa, 04638 Almeria, Spain. *T:* (950) 478432; *e-mail:* hughbroad996@hotmail.com.

BROADBENT, Adam Humphrey Charles; Chairman, Emap plc, 2001–06; *b* 21 June 1936; *s* of Harold and Celia Broadbent; *m* 1963, Sara Peregrine (*née* Meredith); four *s. Educ:* Stonyhurst Coll.; Magdalen Coll., Oxford (MA); London Sch. of Economics (MSc Econ). 2nd Lieut, 1st RTR, 1957–59. Bank of London and South America, 1960–63; COI, 1963–66; NIESR, 1966–68; Schroders plc, 1968–96: Dir, J. Henry Schroder Wagg & Co. Ltd, 1984–96; Dir, 1990–96; Group Managing Director: Corporate Finance, 1990–96; Investment Banking, 1994–96; Chm., Arcadia Gp plc, 1998–2002. Director: Carclo, 1997–2003; REL Consultancy Gp, 1997–2005; Capital One Bank (Europe), 2000–. Chm., Dover Harbour Bd, 1996–2000. Gov., NIESR, 2002–. Dir, Acad. of Ancient Music, 2003–. *Club:* Brooks's.

BROADBENT, Sir Andrew George, 5th Bt *cr* 1893, of Brook Street, co. London and Longwood, co. Yorkshire; *b* 26 Jan. 1963; *s* of Sqn Ldr Sir George Broadbent, AFC, RAF, 4th Bt and Valerie Anne, *o d* of Cecil Frank Ward; *S* father, 1992, but his name does not appear on the Official Roll of the Baronetage. *Educ:* Oakley Hall Prep. Sch., Cirencester; Monkton Combe Sch.; RMA, Sandhurst. Capt., PWO Regt Yorks, 1984; retd 1994. *Recreations:* music, reading, walking, following sport. *Heir: uncle* Robert John Dendy Broadbent, *b* 4 Nov. 1938.

BROADBENT, Christopher Joseph St George B.; *see* Bowers-Broadbent.

BROADBENT, James, (Jim); actor, since 1972; *b* Lincoln, 24 May 1949; *s* of late Roy Broadbent and Dee (*née* Findlay); *m* 1987, Anastasia Lewis; two step *s. Educ:* Leighton Park Sch., Reading; Hammersmith Coll. of Art; LAMDA. Joined Nat. Theatre of Brent, 1983, appeared in: The Messiah, 1983; (jt writer) The Complete Guide to Sex, 1984; (jt writer) The Greatest Story Ever Told, 1987; Founder Member, Science Fiction Theatre of Liverpool: Illuminatus!, 1976; The Warp, 1978; *other theatre* includes: Hampstead Theatre: Ecstasy, 1979; Goose Pimples, 1980; Royal Shakespeare Co.: Our Friends in the North, Clay, 1981; National Theatre: The Government Inspector, 1984; A Place with the Pigs, 1988; The Pillowman, 2003; Theatre of Blood, 2005; Royal Court: Kafka's Dick, 1986; The Recruiting Officer, Our Country's Good, 1988; Old Vic: A Flea in Her Ear, 1989; Donmar: Habeas Corpus, 1996; *films* include: The Time Bandits, 1981; Brazil, 1985; The Good Father, 1986; Life is Sweet, Enchanted April, 1991; A Sense of History (also writer), The Crying Game, 1992; Widow's Peak, 1993; Princess Caraboo, Bullets over Broadway, Wide Eyed and Legless, 1994; Richard III, 1995; The Borrowers, 1997; The Avengers, Little Voice, 1998; Topsy-Turvy, 1999 (Best Actor, Venice Film Fest., Evening Standard British Film Awards, London Film Critics' Circle, 2001); Bridget Jones's Diary, Moulin Rouge, 2001 (Best Supporting Actor, Nat. Bd of Review, LA Film Critics Assoc., 2001, BAFTA, 2002); Iris, 2002 (Best Supporting Actor, Nat. Bd of Review, LA Film Critics Assoc., 2001, Golden Globe, Acad. Award, 2002); Gangs of New York, Nicholas Nickleby, Bright Young Things, 2003; Around the World in 80 Days, Bridget Jones: The Edge of Reason, Vera Drake, 2004; Vanity Fair, The Chronicles of Narnia: The Lion the Witch and the Wardrobe, 2005; Art School Confidential, 2006; And When Did You Last See Your Father?, Hot Fuzz, Inkheart, 2007; *television series* include: Victoria Wood as Seen on TV; Blackadder; Only Fools and Horses; Gone to the Dogs; Gone to Seed; The Peter Principle; The Gathering Storm, 2002; The Street, 2006, 2007 (Emmy Award, 2007); Longford, 2006 (Best Actor, BAFTA, 2007; Golden Globe Award, 2008). *Recreations:* walking, cooking, golf, wood carving, cinema, reading. *Address:* c/o Independent Talent Group Ltd, Oxford House, 76 Oxford Street, W1D 1BS. *T:* (020) 7636 6565. *Club:* Two Brydges.

BROADBENT, (John) Michael; wine writer; Senior Consultant, Christie's Wine Department; *b* 2 May 1927; *s* of late John Fred Broadbent and Hilary Louise Broadbent; *m* 1954, Daphne Joste; one *s* one *d. Educ:* Rishworth Sch., Yorks; Bartlett Sch. of Architecture, UCL (Cert. in Architecture 1952). Commissioned RA, 1945–48 (Nat. Service). Trainee, Laytons Wine Merchants, 1952–53; Saccone & Speed, 1953–55; John Harvey & Sons, Bristol, 1955–66 (Dir, 1963); Head, Wine Dept, Christie's, 1966–92. Director: Christie Manson & Woods, 1967–99; Christie's Fine Art Ltd, 1998–2001; Christie's Internat. (UK) Ltd, 2001–07. Wine Trade Art Society: Founder Mem., 1955; Chm., 1972–2006; Institute of Masters of Wine: Mem. Council, 1966–78; Chm., 1971–72. Distillers' Company: Liveryman, 1964–80; Master, 1990–91; Vintners' Company: Hon. Freeman, 2001; Liveryman, 2005–. International Wine and Food Society: Life Mem.; Mem. Council, 1969–92; Internat. Pres., 1985–92; Gold Medal, 1989; Chm., Wine and Spirit Benevolent Soc., 1991–92. Hon. Pres., Wine and Spirit Educn. Trust, 2007–. Numerous awards from wine socs and other instns. Chevalier, l'Ordre National du Mérite, 1979; La Médaille de la Ville de Paris, Echelon Vermeil, 1989; Wine Spectator Annual Lifetime Achievement Award, 1991; Man of the Year, Decanter magazine, 1993; Glenfiddich Wine Writer of the Year, 2001. *Publications:* Wine Tasting, 1st edn 1968 (numerous foreign edns); The Great Vintage Wine Book, 1980 (foreign edns); Pocket Guide to Wine Tasting, 1988; The Great Vintage Wine Book II, 1991; Pocket Guide to Wine Vintages, 1992; The Bordeaux Atlas, 1997; Vintage Wine, 2003 (also German edn; four top internat. awards); Wine Tasting, 2003; Wine Vintages, 2003; Vintage Wine Companion, 2006; Michael Broadbent's Pocket Vintage Wine Companion, 2007; contribs to Decanter and other jls. *Recreations:* piano, painting. *Address:* 87/88 Rosebank, Holyport Road, SW6 6LJ. *T:* (020) 7381 0858. *Clubs:* Brooks's, Saintsbury.

See also E. L. Arbuthnot.

BROADBENT, Miles Anthony Le Messurier; Chairman, The Miles Partnership, since 1996; *b* 1936; *m* 1980, Robin Anne Beveridge; two *s* two *d. Educ:* Shrewsbury Sch.; Magdalene Coll., Cambridge Univ. (MA); Harvard Bus. Sch. (MBA). *Recreations:* tennis, golf. *Address:* Brackendene, Golf Club Road, St George's Hill, Weybridge, Surrey KT13 0NJ. *T:* (01932) 844159. *Clubs:* Boodle's; St George's Hill Tennis; St George's Hill Golf, Royal Cape Golf (Cape Town).

BROADBENT, Rt Rev. Peter Alan; *see* Willesden, Area Bishop of.

BROADBENT, Sir Richard (John), KCB 2003; Chairman, Arriva plc, since 2004; Senior Independent Director, Barclays plc, since 2003; *b* 22 April 1953; *s* of John Barclay Broadbent and Faith Joan Laurie Broadbent (*née* Fisher); *m* 2007, Jill (née McLoughlin). *Educ:* Queen Mary Coll., Univ. of London (BSc); Univ. of Manchester (MA). HM Treasury, 1975–86; Harkness Fellow, 1983–84; Schroders plc, 1986–99: Head, European Corporate Finance, 1995–99; Gp Man. Dir, Corporate Finance, and Mem., Gp Exec. Cttee, 1998–99; Chm., HM Customs and Excise, 2000–03. MSI. *Address:* Arriva plc, Admiral Way, Doxford International Business Park, Sunderland SR3 3XP.

BROADBENT, Simon Hope; Visiting Fellow, National Institute of Economic and Social Research, since 1994; *b* 4 June 1942; *s* of Edmund Urquhart Broadbent, CBE and late Doris Hope; *m* 1966, Margaret Ann Taylor; two *s* one *d. Educ:* University College School; Hatfield College, Durham (BA); Magdalen College, Oxford (BPhil). Malawi Civil Service, 1964; FCO, 1971; UK Treasury and Supply delegn, Washington, 1974; seconded to Bank of England, 1977; Joint Head, Economists Dept, FCO, 1978; Centre for Econ. Policy Res., and Graduate Inst. of Internat. Studies, Geneva, 1984. Hd of Econ. Advrs, later Chief Econ. Advr, FCO, 1984–93. Trustee, Anglo-German Foundn, 1994–. *Recreation:* boating. *Address:* Manor House, Dorchester-on-Thames, Oxon OX10 7HZ. *T:* (01865) 340101.

BROADBRIDGE, family name of **Baron Broadbridge**.

BROADBRIDGE, 4th Baron *cr* 1945, of Brighton, co. Sussex; **Martin Hugh Broadbridge;** Bt 1937; *b* 29 Nov. 1929; *s* of Hon. Hugh Broadbridge and Marjorie Broadbridge; *S* cousin, 2000; *m* 1st, 1954, Norma Sheffield (marr. diss. 1967); one *s* one *d*; 2nd, 1968, Elizabeth Trotman (*d* 2007). *Educ:* St George's Coll., Weybridge; Univ. of Birmingham (BSc 1954). Dist Officer, Northern Nigeria, HMOCS, 1954–63; Dir and Manager, specialist road surface treatments co., 1963–92; consultant, 1992–95. *Recreations:* game fishing, natural history. *Heir: s* Hon. Richard John Martin Broadbridge [*b* 20 Jan. 1959; *m* 1980, Jacqueline Roberts; one *s* one *d*]. *Address:* 23A Westfield Road, Barton-on-Humber, North Lincolnshire DN18 5AA. *T:* (01652) 632895.

BROADFOOT, Prof. Patricia Mary, CBE 2006; DSc, PhD; Vice-Chancellor, University of Gloucestershire, since 2006; *b* 13 July 1949; *d* of late Norman John Cole, VRD, sometime MP and Margaret Grace Cole (*née* Potter); *m* 1971, John Ledingham Broadfoot (marr. diss. 1977); *m* 1980, David Charles Rockey, *yr s* of Prof. Kenneth Rockey; two *s* one *d. Educ:* Queen Elizabeth's Girls' Grammar Sch., Barnet; Leeds Univ. (BA 1970); Edinburgh Univ. (MEd 1977); Open Univ. (PhD 1984); PGCE London 1971; DSc Univ. of Bristol 2000. Teacher, Wolmer's Boys' Sch., Jamaica, 1971–73; Researcher, Scottish Council for Res. in Educn, 1973–77; Lectr and Sen. Lectr, Westhill Coll., Birmingham, 1977–81; University of Bristol: Lectr, 1981–90; Reader, 1990–91; Prof. of Educn, 1991–2006; Hd, Sch. of Educn, 1993–97; Dean of Social Scis, 1999–2002; Pro-Vice-Chancellor, 2002–05, Sen. Pro-Vice-Chancellor, 2005–06. Visiting Scholar: Macquarie Univ., Aust., 1987; Univ. of Western Sydney, 1992. Member: Conseil Scientifique de l'Institut Nat. de Recherche Pedagogique, 1998–99; Council, ESRC, 2001–06 (Mem., Res. Grants Bd, 1998–99; Chair, Internat. Cttee, 2002–03; Chair, Research Resources Bd, 2003–06); Top Mgt Prog. Adv. Gp, 2004–, Res. Adv. Panel, 2004–, Leadership Foundn; UUK/SCOP Burgess Steering Gp, 2005–; Quality Assessment Learning and Teaching Cttee, HEFCE, 2005–; Chairman: Teaching and Learning Special Interest Gp, HERDA-SW, 2004–06; Pro-Vice-Chancellors Gp, Worldwide University Network, 2004–06; Co-Chm., Russell Gp Pro-Vice-Chancellors Gp, 2004–06; Director: HEA; UCEA. Chm., Gov. Bd, UK Household Longitudinal Study, 2007–. Mem., Res. Adv. Bd, ETS. President: British Educnl Res. Assoc., 1987–88; British Assoc. for Internat. and Comparative Educn, 1997–98. Trustee, St Monica Trust, 2005–. Mem. Coll. of Fellows, Internat. Bureau of Educn, Geneva, 1999–2004; Founding Mem., Assessment Reform Gp, 1989–2003; Founding AcSS, 1999 (Mem., Commn on Social Scis, 2001–03). Mem. Bd, Gloucestershire Coll. Hon. Canon, Gloucester Cath., 2007–. Editor: Comparative Education, 1993–2004; Assessment in Education,

1994–2002. *Publications:* Assessment, Schools and Society, 1979; (with J. D. Nisbet) The Impact of Research on Education, 1981; (with H. D. Black) Keeping Track of Teaching, 1982; (ed) Selection, Certification and Control, 1984; (ed) Profiles and Records of Achievement, 1986; Introducing Profiling, 1987; (with M. Osborn) Perceptions of Teaching, 1993; (jtly) The Changing English Primary School, 1994; Education, Assessment and Society, 1996; (ed jtly) Learning from Comparing, 1999; (jtly) Promoting Quality in Learning, 2000; (jtly) What Teachers Do, 2000; (jtly) Assessment: what's in it for schools?, 2002; (jtly) A World of Difference, 2003; An Introduction to Assessment, 2007. *Recreations:* gardening, horse-riding. *Address:* University of Gloucester, Fulwood House, The Park, Cheltenham GL50 2RH. *T:* (01242) 714169. *Club:* Athenæum.

BROADHURST, Rt Rev. John Charles; *see* Fulham, Bishop Suffragan of.

BROADHURST, Norman Neill, FCA, FCT; Chairman: Chloride Group plc, since 2001; Freightliner Ltd, since 2001; Cattles plc, since 2006 (Deputy Chairman, 2006; non-executive Director, since 2000); *b* 19 Sept. 1941; *s* of Samuel Herbert and Ruth Broadhurst; *m* 1964, Kathleen Muriel Joyce; two *d*. *Educ:* Cheadle Hume Sch. FCA 1975; FCT 1995. Divl Manager, Finance and Admin, China Light Power Co. Ltd, Hong Kong, 1981–86; Finance Dir, United Engineering Steels Ltd, Sheffield, 1986–90; Finance Dir, VSEL plc, Barrow, 1990–94; Finance Dir, Railtrack plc, 1994–2000. Non-executive Director: Old Mutual, 1999–; United Utilities, 1999–; Taylor Woodrow, 2000–03; Tomkins, 2000–06. *Recreation:* golf. *Address:* Hobroyd, Pennybridge, Ulverston, Cumbria LA12 7TD. *T:* (01229) 861226; *e-mail:* norman@hobroyd.ndo.co.uk. *Club:* Ulverston Golf.

BROADIE, Prof. Sarah Jean, PhD; FBA 2003; FRSE; Professor of Philosophy, University of St Andrews, since 2001; *b* 3 Nov. 1941; *d* of Prof. John Conrad Waterlow, *qv*; *m* 1984, Frederick Broadie. *Educ:* Somerville Coll., Oxford (BA, BPhil); Univ. of Edinburgh (PhD 1978). Lectr in Philosophy, Univ. of Edinburgh, 1967–84; Professor of Philosophy: Univ. of Texas, Austin, 1984–86; Yale Univ., 1987–91; Rutgers Univ., 1991–93; Princeton Univ., 1993–2001. Vice-Pres., British Acad., 2006–08. MAE 2006. FRSE 2002; Fellow, Amer. Acad. of Arts and Scis, 1991. *Publications:* Nature, Change and Agency, 1982; Passage and Possibility, 1982; Ethics with Aristotle, 1991; (with C. Rowe) Aristotle: the Nicomachean ethics, 2002; numerous articles on Ancient Greek philosophy. *Recreation:* playing under the auspices of all nine muses. *Address:* Philosophy Departments, University of St Andrews, The Scores, St Andrews KY16 9AL. *T:* (01334) 462486, *Fax:* (01334) 462485; *e-mail:* sjb15@st-andrews.ac.uk.

BROADLEY, Ian R.; *see* Rank-Broadley.

BROADLEY, John Kenneth Elliott, CMG 1988; HM Diplomatic Service, retired; Ambassador to the Holy See, 1988–91; *b* 10 June 1936; *s* of late Kenneth Broadley and late Rosamund Venn (*née* Elliott); *m* 1961, Jane Alice Rachel (*née* Gee); one *s* two *d*. *Educ:* Winchester Coll.; Balliol Coll., Oxford (Exhibnr, MA). Served Army, 1st RHA, 1954–56. Entered HM Diplomatic Service, 1960; Washington, 1963–65; La Paz, 1965–68; FCO, 1968–73; UK Mission to UN, Geneva, 1973–76; Counsellor, Amman, 1976–79; FCO, 1979–84; Dep. Governor, Gibraltar, 1984–88. Non-Service Mem., Home Office Extended Interview Panel, 1994–. Trustee: Kainos Community, 1999–; SAT-7 (UK) Trust, 1999– (Chm., 2003–); Concordis Internat., 2003–. Reader, St Saviour and St Nicholas, Brockenhurst, 1998–. Chm. of Govs, Ballard Sch., 1998–2002. *Recreations:* golf, tennis, sailing. *Address:* The Thatched Cottage, Tile Barn Lane, Brockenhurst, Hants SO42 7UE.

BROCK, George Laurence; Saturday Editor, The Times, since 2004; *b* 7 Nov. 1951; *s* of Michael George Brock, *qv*; *m* 1978, Katharine Sandeman (*see* K. Brock); two *s*. *Educ:* Winchester Coll.; Corpus Christi Coll., Oxford (MA). Reporter: Yorks Evening Press, 1973–76; The Observer, 1976–81; The Times: feature writer and ed., 1981–84; Opinion Page Ed., 1984–87; Foreign Ed., 1987–90; Bureau Chief, Brussels, 1991–95; Eur. Ed., 1995–97; Managing Ed., 1997–2004. Mem., Defence, Press and Broadcasting Adv. Cttee, 1998–2004. World Editors Forum: Bd Mem., 2001–; Pres., 2004–08. Mem., British Exec., Internat. Press Inst., 2000–. Gov., Ditchley Foundn, 2003– (Mem., Prog. Cttee, 1995–2003). Judge, Olivier Th. Awards, 2004. FRSA 2004. *Publications:* (jtly) Siege: six days at the Iranian Embassy, 1980; (with N. Wapshott) Thatcher, 1983. *Recreations:* theatre, cities, walking, music. *Address:* c/o The Times, 1 Pennington Street, E98 1TT. *T:* (020) 7782 5000.

BROCK, Katharine, (Kay), LVO 2002; Private Secretary and Chief of Staff (formerly Private Secretary) to the Lord Mayor of London, since 2004; *b* 23 May 1953; *d* of George Roland Stewart Sandeman and Helen Stewart Sandeman (*née* McLaren); *m* 1978, George Laurence Brock, *qv*; two *s*. *Educ:* Sherborne Sch. for Girls; Somerville Coll., Oxford (BA Hons 1975); London Business Sch. (MBA 1988). MAFF, 1975–85 (Private Sec. to Perm. Sec., 1980–81); consultant in internat. trade, 1985–88; Spicers Consulting Gp, 1988–89; Dir, PDN Ltd, 1990–91; Ext. Relns Directorate, EC, 1992–95; Advr to UK Knowhow Fund and EBRD, 1995–99; Asst Private Sec. to the Queen, 1999–2002. Mem., Ind. Monitoring Bd, Wandsworth Prison, 2003–04. Pres., Somerville Coll. alumni, 2004–08. Chm., Dance United, 2008–. Liveryman, Founders' Co., 2005–. *Recreations:* music, Italy, cycling. *Address:* 99 East Sheen Avenue, SW14 8AX. *Clubs:* Farmers, Walbrook.

BROCK, Michael George, CBE 1981; Warden of St George's House, Windsor Castle, 1988–93; *b* 9 March 1920; *s* of late Sir Laurence George Brock and Ellen Margery Brock (*née* Williams); *m* 1949, Eleanor Hope Morrison; three *s*. *Educ:* Wellington Coll. (Schol.); Corpus Christi Coll., Oxford (Open Schol.; First Cl. Hons Mod. Hist. 1948; MA 1948); DLitt Oxon 2002. FRHistS 1965; FRSL 1983. War service (Middlesex Regt), 1940–45. Corpus Christi Coll., Oxford: Jun. Res. Fellow, 1948–50; Fellow and Tutor in Modern History and Politics, 1950–66, Fellow Emeritus, 1977; Hon. Fellow, 1982; Oxford University: Jun. Proctor, 1956–57; Univ. Lectr, 1951–70; Mem., Hebdomadal Council, 1965–76, 1978–86; Vice Pres. and Bursar, Wolfson Coll., Oxford, 1967–76; Prof. of Educn and Dir, Sch. of Educn, Exeter Univ., 1977–78; Warden of Nuffield Coll., Oxford, 1978–88; Pro-Vice-Chancellor, Oxford Univ., 1980–88. Church Comr, 1990–93. Hon. Fellow: Wolfson Coll., Oxford, 1977; Nuffield Coll., Oxford, 1988; Hon. FSRHE 1986–06. Hon. DLitt Exeter, 1982. *Publications:* The Great Reform Act, 1973; (ed with Eleanor Brock) H. H. Asquith: Letters to Venetia Stanley, 1982; (ed with M. Curthoys) The History of the University of Oxford, vols vi and vii: Nineteenth-Century Oxford, Part 1, 1997, Part 2, 2000; many articles on historical topics and on higher education. *Address:* Flat 1, Ritchie Court, 380 Banbury Road, Oxford OX2 7PW. *Club:* Oxford Union.

See also G. L. Brock.

BROCK, Dr Sebastian Paul, FBA 1977; Reader in Syriac Studies, University of Oxford, 1990–2003; Fellow of Wolfson College, Oxford, 1974–2003, now Emeritus; *b* 24 Feb. 1938; *m* 1966, Helen M. C. (*née* Hughes). *Educ:* Eton College; Trinity Coll., Cambridge (BA 1962, MA 1965); MA and DPhil Oxon 1966. Asst Lectr, 1964–66, Lectr, 1966–67, Dept of Theology, Univ. of Birmingham; Fellow, Selwyn Coll., Cambridge, 1967–72; Lectr, Hebrew and Aramaic, Univ. of Cambridge, 1967–74; Lectr in Aramaic and Syriac, Univ. of Oxford, 1974–90. Corresp. Mem., Syriac Section, Iraqi Acad., 1979. Editor, JSS, 1987–90. Hon. Dr: Pontificio Istituto Orientale, Rome, 1992; St Ephrem Ecumenical Res. Inst., Mahatma Gandhi Univ. of Kottayam, India, 2004; Univ. Saint Esprit, Kaslik, Lebanon, 2004; Hon. DLitt Birmingham, 1998. *Publications:* Pseudepigrapha Veteris Testamenti Graece II; Testamentum Iobi, 1967; The Syriac Version of the Pseudo-Nonnos Mythological Scholia, 1971; (with C. T. Fritsch and S. Jellicoe) A Classified Bibliography of the Septuagint, 1973; The Harp of the Spirit: Poems of St Ephrem, 1975, 2nd edn 1983; The Holy Spirit in Syrian Baptismal Tradition, 1979; Sughyotho Mgabyotho, 1982; Syriac Perspectives on Late Antiquity, 1984; Turgome d'Mor Ya'qub da-Srug, 1984; The Luminous Eye: the spiritual world vision of St Ephrem, 1985, 2nd edn 1992; (with S. A. Harvey) Holy Women of the Syrian Orient, 1987; Vetus Testamentum Syriace III. 1: Liber Isaiae, 1987; The Syriac Fathers on Prayer and the Spiritual Life, 1987; Malpanuto d-abohoto suryoye d-'al ṣluto, 1988; St Ephrem: Hymns on Paradise, 1990; Studies in Syriac Christianity, 1992; Luqoṭo d-Mimre, 1993; Bride of Light: hymns on Mary from the Syriac churches, 1994; Isaac of Nineveh: the second part, ch. IV–XLI, 1995; Catalogue of Syriac Fragments (New finds) in the Library of the Monastery of St Catherine, Mount Sinai, 1995; The Recensions of the Septuaginta Version of I Samuel, 1996; A Brief Outline of Syriac Literature, 1997; From Ephrem to Romanos: interactions between Syriac and Greek in late antiquity, 1999; (with D. G. K. Taylor and W. Witakowski) The Hidden Pearl: the Syrian Orthodox Church and its Ancient Aramaic Heritage (3 vols), 2001; (with G Kiraz) Ephrem the Syrian: select poems, 2006; Fire from Heaven: studies in Syriac theology and liturgy, 2006; The Bible in the Syriac Tradition, 2006; An Introduction to Syriac Studies, 2006; contrib. Jl of Semitic Studies, JTS, Le Muséon, Oriens Christianus, Orientalia Christiana Periodica, Parole de l'Orient, Revue des études arméniennes. *Address:* Wolfson College, Oxford OX2 6UD; Oriental Institute, Pusey Lane, Oxford OX1 2LE.

BROCK, Timothy Hugh C.; *see* Clutton-Brock.

BROCK, Prof. William Ranulf, FBA 1990; Fellow of Selwyn College, Cambridge, since 1947; Professor of Modern History, University of Glasgow, 1967–81, now Emeritus; *b* 16 May 1916; *s* of Stewart Ernst Brock and Katherine Helen (*née* Temple Roberts); *m* 1950, Constance Helen (*née* Brown) (*d* 2000); one *s* one *d*. *Educ:* Christ's Hosp.; Trinity Coll., Cambridge (MA, PhD). Prize Fellow 1940 (in absentia). Military service (Army), 1939–45; Asst Master, Eton Coll., 1946–47. Commonwealth Fund Fellow, Berkeley, Calif, Yale and Johns Hopkins, 1952–53, 1958; Vis. Professor: Michigan Univ., 1968; Washington Univ., 1970; Maryland Univ., 1980; Charles Warren Fellow, Harvard Univ., 1976; Leverhulme Emeritus Fellow, 1981. Hon. LittD Keele, 1998. *Publications:* Lord Liverpool and Liberal Toryism, 1941; The Character of American History, 1960; An American Crisis, 1963; The Evolution of American Democracy, 1970; Conflict and Transformation 1844–1877, 1973; The Sources of History: the United States 1790–1890, 1975; Parties and Political Conscience, 1979; Scotus Americanus, 1982; Investigation and Responsibility, 1985; Welfare, Democracy and the New Deal, 1988; (with P. H. M. Cooper) Selwyn College: a history, 1994; contrib. New Cambridge Mod. History, Vols VII and XI; articles and reviews in Proc. of British Acad., Jl Amer. Studies, Jl Amer. Hist., Amer. Nineteenth Cent. Hist., etc. *Recreation:* antiques. *Address:* 49 Barton Road, Cambridge CB3 9LG. *T:* (01223) 529655; *e-mail:* wrb20@cam.ac.uk.

BROCKES, Prof. Jeremy Patrick, PhD; FRS 1994; MRC Research Professor, Department of Biochemistry and Molecular Biology, University College London, since 1997; Member, Ludwig Institute for Cancer Research, 1991–97; *b* 29 Feb. 1948; *s* of Bernard A. Brockes and Edna (*née* Heaney). *Educ:* Winchester Coll.; St John's Coll., Cambridge (BA 1969); Edinburgh Univ. (PhD 1972). Muscular Dystrophy Assoc. of America Postdoctoral Fellow, Dept of Neurobiology, Harvard Med. Sch., 1972–75; Research Fellow, MRC Neuroimmunology Project, UCL, 1975–78; Asst, then Associate, Prof., Div. of Biology, CIT, 1978–83; Staff Mem., MRC Biophysics Unit, KCL, 1983–88; scientific staff, Ludwig Inst. for Cancer Res., UCL/Middlesex Hosp. Br., 1988–97; Prof. of Cell Biology, UCL, 1991–97. Mem. Scientific Adv. Bd, Cambridge Neuroscience Inc., 1987–2000. Brooks Lectr, Harvard Med. Sch., 1997. MAE 1989. Scientific Medal: Zool Soc. of London, 1986; Biol Council, 1990. *Publications:* Neuroimmunology, 1982; papers in scientific jls. *Recreation:* soprano saxophone. *Address:* Department of Biochemistry, University College London, Gower Street, WC1E 6BT. *T:* (020) 7679 4483.

BROCKET, 3rd Baron, *cr* 1933; **Charles Ronald George Nall-Cain;** Bt 1921; *b* 12 Feb. 1952; *s* of Hon. Ronald Charles Manus Nall-Cain (*d* 1961), and of Elizabeth Mary (who *m* 2nd, 1964, Colin John Richard Trotter), *d* of R. J. Stallard; *S* grandfather, 1967; *m* 1st, 1982, Isabell Maria Lorenzo (marr. diss. 1994), *o d* of Gustavo Lorenzo, New York; two *s* one *d*; 2nd, 2006, Harriet Warren. *Educ:* Eton. 14/20 Hussars, 1970–75 (Lieut). Pres., Herts Chamber of Commerce and Industry, 1992; Chm., Business Link Hertfordshire, 1994. Chm., Trust for Information and Prevention (drug prevention initiatives), 1993. Chm., British Motor Centenary Trust; Dir, De Havilland Museum Trust; Patron, Guild of Guide Lectrs, 1992. *Publication:* Call Me Charlie (autobiog.), 2004. *Heir:* *s* Hon. Alexander Christopher Charles Nall-Cain, *b* 30 Sept. 1984.

BROCKLEBANK, Sir Aubrey (Thomas), 6th Bt *cr* 1885; ACA; director of various companies; *b* 29 Jan. 1952; *s* of Sir John Montague Brocklebank, 5th Bt, TD, and Pamela Sue, *d* of late William Harold Pierce, OBE; *S* father, 1974; *m* 1st, 1979, Dr Anna-Marie Dunnet (marr. diss. 1989); two *s*; 2nd, 1997, Hazel Catherine, *yr d* of Brian Roden; one *s*. *Educ:* Eton; University Coll., Durham (BSc Psychology). With Guinness Mahon & Co., 1981–86; Director: Venture Founders, 1986–90; Dartington & Co., 1990–92; Manager, Avon Enterprise Fund, 1990–97. *Recreations:* deep sea tadpole wrestling, shooting, motor racing. *Heir:* *s* Aubrey William Thomas Brocklebank, *b* 15 Dec. 1980. *Address:* Hunters Lodge, St Andrews Lane, Titchmarsh, Northants NN14 3DN. *Club:* Brooks's.

BROCKLEBANK, Edward; Member (C) Mid Scotland and Fife, Scottish Parliament, since 2003; *b* 24 Sept. 1942; *s* of Fred Brocklebank and Nancy Mitchell Ainslie Brocklebank; *m* 1965, Lesley Beverley Davidson (marr. diss. 1978); two *s*. *Educ:* Madras Coll.; St Andrews. Trainee journalist, D. C. Thomson, Dundee, newspaper publishers, 1960–63; freelance journalist, Fleet St, 1963–65; press officer, Scottish TV, Glasgow, 1965–70; Grampian TV, Aberdeen: reporter, 1970–76; Head: News and Current Affairs, 1977–85; Documentaries and Features, 1985–95; Man. Dir, Greyfriars Prodns, St Andrews, 1995–2001. *Recreations:* ornithology, oil painting, walking, Rugby football. *Address:* Westlands, Kennedy Gardens, St Andrews, Fife KY16 9DJ. *T:* and *Fax:* (01334) 475596; *e-mail:* ted.brocklebank.msp@ scottish.parliament.uk. *Clubs:* New (Edinburgh); Royal & Ancient Golf (St Andrews).

BROCKLEBANK-FOWLER, Christopher; certified management consultant; *b* 13 Jan. 1934; 2nd *s* of Sidney Straton Brocklebank Fowler, MA, LLB Cantab; *m* 1st, 1957, Joan Nowland (marr. diss. 1975; she *d* 2006); two *s*; 2nd, 1975, Mrs Mary Berry (marr. diss. 1986); 3rd, 1996, Mrs Dorothea Rycroft (marr. diss. 2000). *Educ:* Perse Sch., Cambridge; DipAgr Agricl Corresp. Coll., Oxford, 1952. Farm pupil on farms in Suffolk,

Cambridgeshire and Norfolk, 1950–55. National service (submarines), Sub-Lt, RNVR, 1952–54. Farm Manager, Kenya, 1955–57; Lever Bros Ltd (Unilever Cos Management Trainee), 1957–59; advertising and marketing consultant, 1959–79; Chm., Overseas Trade and Develt Agency Ltd, 1979–83; Man. Dir, Cambridge Corporate Consultants Ltd, 1985–87. Mem. Bow Group, 1961–81 (Chm., 1968–69; Dir, Bow Publications, 1968–71). Mem. London Conciliation Cttee, 1966–67; Vice-Chm. Information Panel, Nat. Cttee for Commonwealth Immigrants, 1966–67; Mem. Exec. Cttee, Africa Bureau, 1970–74; Chm., SOS Children's Villages, 1978–84. MP King's Lynn, 1970–74, Norfolk North West, 1974–83 (C, 1970–81, SDP, 1981–83); Chm., Conservative Parly Sub-Cttee on Horticulture, 1972–74; Vice-Chairman: Cons. Parly Cttee on Agriculture, 1974–75; Cons. Parly Foreign and Commonwealth Affairs Cttee, 1979 (Jt Sec., 1974–75, 1976–77); Cons. Parly Trade Cttee, 1979–80; SDP Agriculture Policy Cttee, 1982–83; Chairman: UN Parly Gp, 1979–83 (Jt Sec., 1971–78); Cons. Parly Overseas Develt Sub-Cttee, 1979–81; SDP Third World Policy Cttee, 1981–87; Member: Select Cttee for Overseas Develt, 1973–79; Select Cttee on Foreign Affairs, 1979–81; SDP Nat. Steering Cttee, 1981–82; SDP Nat. Cttee, 1982; SDP Parly spokesman on Agriculture, 1981–82, on Overseas Develt, 1981–83, on Foreign Affairs, 1982–83. Contested: (C) West Ham (North), 1964; (SDP) 1983, (SDP/Alliance) 1987, Norfolk North West; (Lib. Dem.) Norfolk South, 1992. Mem., Labour Party, 1996–. Vice Chm., Centre for World Develt Educn, 1980–83; Governor, Inst. of Develt Studies, 1978–81. Vice Pres., Inst. of Mgt Consultancy, 1999. Fellow, De Montfort Univ., 1992. MCIM; MCAM; FCMI; FCMC; Hon. Fellow IDS. *Publications:* pamphlets and articles on race relations, African affairs, overseas development. *Recreations:* painting, fishing, shooting, swimming.

BROCKLEHURST, Prof. John Charles, CBE 1988; FRCP, FRCPE, FRCPGlas; Professor of Geriatric Medicine, University of Manchester, 1970–89, now Emeritus; Associate Director, Research Unit, Royal College of Physicians, 1989–98; *b* 31 May 1924; *s* of late Harold John Brocklehurst and Dorothy Brocklehurst; *m* 1956, Susan Engle; two *s* one *d*. *Educ:* Glasgow High Sch.; Ayr Academy; Univ. of Glasgow (MB ChB 1947; MD Hons 1950). Christine Hansen Research Fellow, Glasgow Univ., 1948–49; RAMC (to rank of Major), 1949–51; Medical Registrar, Stobhill Hosp., and Asst Lectr, Dept of Materia Medica and Therapeutics, Glasgow Univ., 1952–53 and 1958–59; MO, Grenfell Mission, Northern Newfoundland and Labrador, 1955–57; Cons. Geriatrician, Bromley Hosp. Gp and Cray Valley and Sevenoaks Hosp. Gp, 1960–69; Cons. in Geriatric and Gen. Med., Guy's Hosp., London, 1969–70. Dir, Univ. of Manchester Unit for Biological Aging Research (formerly Geigy Unit for Res. in Aging), 1974–89. Chm., Age Concern England, 1973–77, Hon. Vice-Pres., 1980–; Governor, Research into Ageing (formerly British Foundn for Age Research), 1980–97; President: Soc. of Chiropodists, 1977–83; British Geriatrics Soc., 1984–86; Trustee, Continence Foundn, 1992–97. Vis. Professor of Geriatric Med. and Chm., Div. of Geriatric Med., Univ. of Saskatchewan, Canada, 1978–79. Hon. Fellow, Manchester Med. Soc. Hon. MSc Manchester 1974. Bellahouston Gold Medal, Univ. of Glasgow, 1950; Willard Thomson Gold Medal, Amer. Geriatrics Soc., 1978; Sandoz Prize, Internat. Assoc. of Gerontology, 1989; Founder's Medal, British Geriatrics Soc., 1990. *Publications:* Incontinence in Old People, 1951; The Geriatric Day Hospital, 1971; ed and part author, Textbook of Geriatric Medicine and Gerontology, 1973, 6th edn 2003; Geriatric Care in Advanced Societies, 1975; (jtly) Geriatric Medicine for Students, 1976, 3rd edn, 1986; (jtly) Progress in Geriatric Day Care, 1980; (jtly) Colour Atlas of Geriatric Medicine, 1983, 2nd edn 1991; (ed and part author) Urology: the elderly, 1985; Geriatric Pharmacology and Therapeutics, 1985; (jtly) British Geriatric Medicine in the 1980s, 1987; 125 Years an Art Club: the ups and downs of the Manchester Graphic Club 1876–2001, 2001. *Recreations:* painting, the mandoline. *Address:* 59 Stanneylands Road, Wilmslow, Cheshire SK9 4EX. *Club:* East India and Devonshire.

BROCKLESBY, Prof. David William, CMG 1991; FRCVS; Professor of Tropical Animal Health and Director of Centre for Tropical Veterinary Medicine, Royal (Dick) School of Veterinary Studies, University of Edinburgh, 1978–90, now Emeritus; *b* 12 Feb. 1929; *s* of late David Layton Brocklesby, AFC, and Katherine Jessie (*née* Mudd); *m* 1957, Jennifer Mary Hubble, MB, BS; one *s* three *d*. *Educ:* Terrington Hall Sch.; Sedbergh Sch.; Royal Vet. Coll., Univ. of London; London Sch. of Hygiene and Tropical Med. MRCVS 1954; FRCVS (by election) 1984; MRCPath 1964, FRCPath 1982; DrMedVet Zürich 1965. Nat. Service, 4th Queen's Own Hussars (RAC), 1947–49. Vet. Res. Officer (Protozoologist), E Afr. Vet. Res. Org., Muguga, Kenya, 1955–66; Hd of Animal Health Res. Dept, Fisons Pest Control, 1966–67; joined ARC Inst. for Res. on Animal Diseases, Compton, as Parasitologist, 1967; Hd of Parasitology Dept, IRAD, 1969–78. Member: Senatus Academicus, Univ. of Edinburgh, 1978–90; Governing Body, Animal Virus Res. Inst., Pirbright, 1979–86; Bd, Edinburgh Centre of Rural Economy, 1981–88; Council, RCVS, 1985–89. Mem. Editorial Board: Research in Veterinary Science, 1970–88; Tropical Animal Health and Production, 1978–90; British Vet. Jl, 1982–90. *Publications:* papers in sci. jls and chapters in review books, mainly on tropical and veterinary protozoa. *Recreations:* formerly squash and golf, now TV and The Times. *Address:* Lynwood, Honeyfield Road, Jedburgh, Borders TD8 6JN. *T:* (01835) 863472.

BROCKLISS, Prof. Laurence William Beaumont, PhD; Professor of Early Modern French History, University of Oxford, since 2002; Tutor and Fellow in Modern History, Magdalen College, Oxford, since 1984; *b* 20 March 1950; *s* of Henry Richard Brockliss and Rosemary Brockliss (*née* Beaumont); *m* 1974, Alison Jane Gordon; one *s* two *d*. *Educ:* Dulwich Coll.; Gonville and Caius Coll., Cambridge (BA 1971; PhD 1976). Lectr in Hist., Univ. of Hull, 1974–84; CUF Lectr in Mod. Hist., 1984–97, Reader, 1997–2002, Univ. of Oxford. Sarton Prof. in Hist. of Scis, Univ. of Ghent, 1996–97 (Sarton Medal, 1996); Jean Leclerc Prof. of Sociol., Univ. of Louvain-la-Neuve, 2000–01. Ed., Hist. of Univs, 1988–93. *Publications:* French Higher Education in the Seventeenth and Eighteenth Centuries, 1987; (ed with J. Bergin) Richelieu and His Age, 1992; (with C. Jones) The Medical World of Early Modern France, 1997; (ed with D. Eastwood) A Union of Multiple Identities: the British Isles *c* 1750–*c* 1850, 1997; (ed with Sir John Elliott) The World of the Favourite, 1999; Calvet's Web: enlightenment and the republic of letters in eighteenth-century France, 2002; (ed jtly) Nelson's Surgeon: William Beatty, naval medicine, and the Battle of Trafalgar, 2005. *Recreations:* walking, gardening, camping. *Address:* 85 Whitecross, Wootton, Abingdon, Oxon OX13 6BS. *T:* (01235) 529214; *e-mail:* laurence.brockliss@magdalen.ox.ac.uk.

BROCKMAN, Rev. John St Leger, CB 1988; Permanent Deacon, St Joseph's RC Church, Epsom, since 1988; Assistant Director for Permanent Diaconate, Diocese of Arundel and Brighton, 1996–2002; *b* 24 March 1928; *s* of late Prof. Ralph St Leger Brockman and Estelle Wilson; *m* 1954, Sheila Elizabeth Jordan; one *s* two *d* (and one *d* decd). *Educ:* Ampleforth; Gonville and Caius Coll., Cambridge. MA, LLB. Called to the Bar, Gray's Inn, 1952. Legal Asst, Min. of National Insurance, 1953; Sen. Legal Asst, Min. of Pensions and National Insurance, 1964; Asst Solicitor, DHSS, 1973; Under Sec. and Principal Asst Solicitor, DHSS, 1978; Solicitor to DHSS, to Registrar General and to OPCS, 1985–89. *Publications:* compiled and edited: The Law relating to Family Allowances and National Insurance, 1961; The Law relating to National Insurance (Industrial Injuries), 1961. *Address:* 304 The Greenway, Epsom, Surrey KT18 7JF. *T:* (01372) 812915.

BRÖDER, Ernst-Günther, DEcon; German economist and financial executive; international consultant; *b* Cologne, 6 Jan. 1927. *Educ:* Univs of Cologne, Mayence, Freiburg and Paris. Corporate staff, Bayer AG Leverkusen, 1956–61; Projects Dept, World Bank, 1961–64; Kreditanstalt für Wiederaufbau, 1964–84: Manager, 1969–75; Mem., Bd of Management, 1975–84; Bd of Management Spokesman, 1980–84; European Investment Bank: a Dir, 1980–84; Pres., and Chm. of Bd of Dirs, 1984–93; Hon. Pres., 1993–; Chm., 1994–96, 1998–99, Mem., 1997–98, 1999, Inspection Panel, World Bank. Member: Special Adv. Gp, Asian Develt Bank, 1981–82; Panel of Conciliators, Internat. Centre for Settlement of Investment Disputes, 1976–. *Address:* Büelstrasse 12, 6052 Hergiswil NW, Switzerland.

BRODIE, Hon. Lord; Philip Hope Brodie; a Senator of the College of Justice in Scotland, since 2002; *b* 14 July 1950; *s* of Very Rev. Peter Philip Brodie and Constance Lindsay Hope; *m* 1983, Carol Dora McLeish; two *s* one *d*. *Educ:* Dollar Academy; Edinburgh Univ. (LLB Hons); Univ. of Virginia (LLM). Admitted Faculty of Advocates, 1976; QC (Scot.) 1987; called to the Bar, Lincoln's Inn, 1991; Standing Junior Counsel, MoD (Scotland) PE, and HSE, 1983–87; Advocate-Depute, 1997–99. Mem., Mental Welfare Commn for Scotland, 1985–96. Part-time Chairman: Industrial Tribunals, 1987–91; Medical Appeal Tribunals, 1991–96; Employment Tribunals, 2002; Judicial Studies Cttee, 2006–. *Recreations:* fencing, walking, reading. *Address:* 2 Cobden Crescent, Edinburgh EH9 2BG; Court of Session, Parliament House, Parliament Square, Edinburgh EH1 1RQ.

BRODIE, Sir Benjamin David Ross, 5th Bt *cr* 1834; *b* 29 May 1925; *s* of Sir Benjamin Collins Brodie, 4th Bt, MC, and Mary Charlotte (*d* 1940), *e d* of R. E. Palmer, Ballyheigue, Co. Kerry; *S* father, 1971, but his name does not appear on the Official Roll of the Baronetage; *m*; one *s* one *d*. *Educ:* Eton. Formerly Royal Corps of Signals. *Heir: s* Alan Ross Brodie [*b* 7 July 1960; *m* 1993, Jutta Maria Herrmann].

BRODIE of Lethen, Ewen John; Lord Lieutenant of Nairnshire, since 1999; Director, John Gordon & Son, since 1992; *b* 16 Dec. 1942; *s* of Major David J. Brodie of Lethen, OBE and Diana, *d* of Maj. Gen. Sir John Davidson, KCMG, CB, DSO; *m* 1967, Mariota, *yr d* of Lt-Col Ronald Steuart-Menzies of Culdares; three *d*. *Educ:* Harrow. Lieut, Grenadier Guards, 1961–64; IBM (UK) Ltd, 1965–74; estate mgt, 1975–. Vice Chm., Timber Growers Scotland, 1979–82; Chm., Findhorn Dist Salmon Fishing Bd, 2001–07. Mem., N Scotland Regl Adv. Cttee, Forestry Commn, 1977–89. DL Nairn, 1980. *Recreation:* countryside sports. *Address:* Dunearn Farm, Glenferness, Nairn IV12 5UR. *T:* (01309) 651249. *Club:* New (Edinburgh).

BRODIE, Huw David; Director for Rural Affairs and for Heritage, Welsh Assembly Government, since 2007; *b* 20 July 1958; *s* of John Handel James Brodie and June (*née* Mustow); *m* 1985, Benita Humphries (*d* 2003); one *s*; *m* 2006, Anna Wizley. *Educ:* Trinity Coll., Cambridge (MA Hist.). Joined Dept of Employment, 1980; MSC and Trng Agency, 1983–90; Head of Policy Analysis Br., Trng Agency, 1987; TEC Policy Team, 1988; Asst Dir, Trng Agency, Wales, 1990–92; joined Welsh Office, 1992: Trng, Educn and Enterprise Dept, 1992–94; Head of Industrial and Trng Policy Div., Industry and Trng Dept, 1994–97; Agriculture Dept, 1997–99; Dir, Agric. Dept, Nat. Assembly for Wales, 1999–2003; Dir, Strategy and Communications, subseq. Strategy, Equality and Communications, Welsh Assembly Govt, 2003–07. *Recreations:* history, archaeology, hill walking. *Address:* Welsh Assembly Government, Cathays Park, Cardiff CF10 3NQ.

BRODIE, Philip Hope; *see* Brodie, Hon. Lord.

BRODIE, Robert, CB 1990; Solicitor to the Secretary of State for Scotland, 1987–98; *b* 9 April 1938; *s* of Robert Brodie, MBE and Helen Ford Bayne Grieve; *m* 1970, Jean Margaret McDonald; two *s* two *d*. *Educ:* Morgan Acad., Dundee; St Andrews Univ. (MA 1959, LLB 1962). Admitted Solicitor, 1962. Office of Solicitor to the Sec. of State for Scotland: Legal Asst, 1965; Sen. Legal Asst, 1970; Asst Solicitor, 1975; Dep. Dir, Scottish Courts Admin, 1975–82; Dep. Solicitor to Sec. of State for Scotland, 1984–87. Temporary Sheriff, 1999; part-time Sheriff, 2000–08; part-time Chm., Employment Tribunals (Scotland), 2000–03. Chm., Scottish Assoc. of CABx, 1999–2004. *Recreations:* music, hill-walking. *Address:* 8 York Road, Edinburgh EH5 3EH. *T:* (0131) 552 2028.

BRODIE, Stanley Eric; QC 1975; a Recorder of the Crown Court, 1975–89; *b* 2 July 1930; *s* of late Abraham Brodie, MB, BS and Cissie Rachel Brodie; *m* 1956, Gillian Rosemary Joseph; two *d*; *m* 1973, Elizabeth Gloster (*see* Hon. Dame E. Gloster) (marr. diss. 2005); one *s* one *d*. *Educ:* Bradford Grammar Sch.; Balliol Coll., Oxford (MA). Pres., Oxford Univ. Law Soc., 1952. Called to Bar, Inner Temple, 1954 (Bencher, 1984, Reader, 1999, Treas., 2000); Mem. NE Circuit, 1954; Lectr in Law, Univ. of Southampton, 1954–55. Mem., Bar Council, 1987–89. Mem., River Doon Fishery Bd, 1990–. *Publication:* (jtly) Inner Temple Millennium Lectures, 2002. *Recreations:* opera, boating, winter sports, fishing. *Address:* Skeldon House, Dalrymple, Ayrshire KA6 6ED. *T:* (01292) 560223; 9 King's Bench Walk, Temple, EC4Y 7DX. *T:* (020) 7797 8270. *Clubs:* Athenæum, Flyfishers', Beefsteak.

BRODIE-HALL, Sir Laurence (Charles), Kt 1982; AO 1993; CMG 1976; Director, 1962–82, Consultant, 1975–82, Western Mining Corporation; Chairman, West Australian Foundation for the Museum of Science and Technology; *b* 10 June 1910; *m* 1st, 1940, Dorothy Jolly (decd); three *s* two *d*; 2nd, 1978, Jean Verschuer (AM 2001). *Educ:* Sch. of Mines, Kalgoorlie (Dip. Metallurgy 1947, DipME 1948). Served War, RAE. Geologist, Central Norseman Gold Corp., 1948–49; Tech. Asst to Man. Dir, Western Mining Corp., 1950–51; Gen. Supt, Gt Western Consolidated, 1951–58; Gen. Supt, 1958–68, Exec. Dir, WA, 1967–75, Western Mining Corp.; Chairman: Gold Mines of Kalgoorlie (Aust.) Ltd, 1974–82; Central Norseman Gold Corp. NL, 1974–82; Westintech Innovation Corp. Ltd, 1984–88; Director: Ansett WA (formerly Airlines WA), 1983–93; Coolgardie Gold NL, 1985–93; former Chm. or Dir of many subsidiaries, and Dir, Alcoa of Australia Ltd, 1971–83. Pres., WA Chamber of Mines, 1970–75 (Life Mem.); Past Pres., Australasian Inst. of Mining and Metallurgy (Institute Medal, 1977, Hon. Life Mem., 1987); Chairman: WA State Cttee, CSIRO, 1971–81; Bd of Management, WA Sch. of Mines, to 1991. Hon. DTech, WA Inst. Technology, 1978. *Address:* (office) 2 Cliff Street, West Perth, WA 6005, Australia. *Club:* Weld (Perth).

BRODRICK, family name of **Viscount Midleton**.

BRODRICK, Michael John Lee; His Honour Judge Brodrick; a Senior Circuit Judge, since 2002 (a Circuit Judge, since 1987); Resident Judge, Winchester Combined Court, since 1999; *b* 12 Oct. 1941; *s* of His Honour Norman John Lee Brodrick, QC and late Ruth, *d* of Sir Stanley Unwin, KCMG; *m* 1969, Valerie Lois Stroud; one *s* one *d*. *Educ:* Charterhouse; Merton Coll., Oxford (2nd Jurisp.). Called to the Bar, Lincoln's Inn, 1965, Bencher, 2000; Western Circuit; a Recorder, 1981–87; Liaison Judge to SE Hants Magistrates, 1989–93, to IoW Magistrates, 1989–94, to NE and NW Hants Magistrates, 1999–2007; Hon. Recorder of Winchester, 2005–. Judicial Mem., Transport Tribunal, 1986–. Member: Senate of Inns of Court and Bar, 1979, served 1979–82; Wine Cttee,

Western Circuit, 1982–86; Cttee, Council of Circuit Judges, 1990–2003 (Pres., 2003). Mem., Lord Chancellor's Adv. Cttee for the Appointment of Magistrates, for Portsmouth, 1990–93, for SE Hants, 1993–2000. Chm., Area Judicial Forum for Hants, 2004–. Counsellor to Dean and Chapter, Winchester Cathedral, 1993–. *Recreation:* gardening.

BRODY, William Ralph, PhD, MD; FIEEE; President, Johns Hopkins University, 1996–2008; *b* 4 Jan. 1944; *m* Wendyce H.; one *s* one *d*. *Educ:* Massachusetts Inst. of Technol. (BS Electrical Engrg 1965; MS 1966); Stanford Univ. Sch. of Medicine (MD 1970); Stanford Univ. (PhD Electrical Engrg 1972). Dip. Amer. Bd Radiol., 1977. Stanford University School of Medicine: Fellow, Dept of Cardiovascular Surgery, 1970–71; Intern, Dept of Surgery, 1971–72; Resident, Dept of Cardiovascular Surgery, 1972–73; Clin. Associate, Nat. Heart, Lung and Blood Inst., Bethesda, Md, 1973–75; Resident, Dept of Radiol., Univ. of Calif, San Francisco, 1975–77; Stanford University School of Medicine: Dir, Res. Labs, Div. of Diagnostic Radiol., 1977–84; Associate Prof. of Radiol., 1977–82; Dir, Advance Imaging Techniques Lab., 1978–84; Prof. of Radiol., 1982–86 (on leave of absence, 1984–86); Radiologist-in-Chief, Johns Hopkins Hosp., 1987–94; Johns Hopkins University School of Medicine: Martin Donner Prof. and Dir, Dept of Radiol., 1987–94; secondary appt in biomed. engrg and jt appt in electrical and computer engrg, 1987–94; Prof. of Radiol., Univ. of Minn, 1994–96. Founder, Resonex Inc., 1983: Consultant, 1983–84; Pres., 1984–86; Pres. and CEO, 1986–87; Chm., 1987–89. Mem., Inst. of Medicine, NAS. Founding Fellow, Amer. Inst. Med. and Biol Engrg; Fellow: Amer. Coll. Cardiol.; Amer. Coll. Radiol.; Council on Cardiovascular Radiol., Amer. Heart Assoc.; Internat. Soc. Magnetic Resonance in Medicine. *Publications:* (ed) Digital Radiography: proceedings of the Stanford Conference on digital radiography, 1981; Digital Radiography, 1984; (ed with G. S. Johnston) Computer Applications to Assist Radiology, 1992; contrib. numerous book chapters and to conf. proceedings and tech. reports; contrib. numerous articles to jls, incl. Radiol., Jl Thoracic Cardiovascular Surgery, Med. Phys., IEEE Trans Biomed. Engrg, Investigative Radiol., Amer. Jl Radiol. *Address:* c/o Johns Hopkins University, 242 Garland Hall, 3400 North Charles Street, Baltimore, MD 21218, USA.

BROERS, family name of **Baron Broers**.

BROERS, Baron *cr* 2004 (Life Peer), of Cambridge in the County of Cambridgeshire; **Alec Nigel Broers,** Kt 1998; DL; PhD, ScD; FRS 1986; FREng; FIET; FInstP; President, Royal Academy of Engineering, 2001–06; Professor of Electrical Engineering, Cambridge University, 1984–96, now Emeritus; Vice-Chancellor, Cambridge University, 1996–2003, now Emeritus; Fellow, Churchill College, Cambridge, since 1990 (Master, 1990–96); *b* 17 Sept. 1938; *s* of late Alec William Broers and of Constance Amy (*née* Cox); *m* 1964, Mary Therese Phelan; two *s*. *Educ:* Geelong Grammar School; Melbourne Univ. (BSc Physics 1958, Electronics 1959); Gonville and Caius College, Cambridge (BA Mech Scis 1962; PhD Mech Scis 1966; ScD 1991; Hon. Fellow, 1996). FIET (FIEE 1984); FREng (FEng 1985); FInstP 1991. IBM Thomas Watson Research Center: Research Staff Mem., 1965–67; Manager, Electron Beam Technology, 1967–72; Manager, Photon and Electron Optics, 1972–80; IBM Fellow, 1977; IBM East Fishkill Laboratory: Manager, Lithography Systems and Technology Tools, 1981–82; Manager, Semiconductor Lithography and Process Develt, 1982–83; Manager, Advanced Develt, 1983–84; Mem., Corporate Tech. Cttee, IBM Corporate HQ, 1984; Cambridge University: Hd of Electrical Div., 1984–92, and of Dept of Engrg, 1992–96; Fellow, Trinity Coll., 1985–90 (Hon. Fellow, 1999). BBC Reith Lectures, 2005. Non-exec. Dir, Vodafone (then Vodafone AirTouch, subseq. reverted to Vodafone) plc, 1998–2007. Mem., EPSRC, 1994–2000. Chm., H of L Sci. and Technol. Select Cttee, 2004–07. Trustee, BM, 2004–. Mem. Council, Univ. of Melbourne. Mem. Council, Royal Acad. of Engineering, 1993–96. Foreign Associate, Nat. Acad. of Engrg, USA, 1994; Mem., Amer. Philosophical Soc., 2001; Foreign Mem., Chinese Acad. Engrg, 2006. DL Cambs, 2000. Hon. Fellow: Univ. of Wales, Cardiff, 2001; St Edmund's Coll., Cambridge, 2003; FIC 2004. Hon. FIEE 1996; Hon. FTSE 2002; Hon. FIMechE 2004. Hon. DEng: Glasgow, 1996; Trinity Coll., Dublin, 2005; Sheffield, 2007; Durham, 2007; Tufts, 2007; Hon. DSc: Warwick, 1997; UMIST, 2002; Hon. LLD Melbourne, 2000; Hon. DTech Greenwich, 2000; DUniv Anglia Polytech. Univ., 2000; Hon. PhD Peking, 2002. Prize for Industrial Applications of Physics, Amer. Inst. of Physics, 1982; Cledo Brunetti Award, IEEE, 1985; Prince Philip Medal, Royal Acad. Engrg, 2001. *Publications:* patents and papers on electron microscopy, electron beam lithography, integrated circuit fabrication. *Recreations:* music, sailing, tennis. *Address:* House of Lords, SW1A 0PW.

BROGAN, Prof. (Denis) Hugh (Vercingetorix); R. A. Butler Professor of History, University of Essex, 1992–98, now Research Professor; *b* 20 March 1936; *s* of Prof. Sir Denis Brogan, FBA and late Olwen Brogan (*née* Kendall). *Educ:* St Faith's Sch., Cambridge; Repton Sch.; St John's Coll., Cambridge (BA Hist. 1959; MA 1964). Staff mem., The Economist, 1960–63; Harkness Fellow, 1962–64; Fellow, St John's Coll., Cambridge, 1963–74; Lectr, then Reader, Dept of Hist., Univ. of Essex, 1974–92. DUniv Essex, 2007. *Publications:* Tocqueville, 1973; The Times Reports The American Civil War, 1975; The Life of Arthur Ransome, 1984; The Longman History of the United States of America, 1985, repr. as The Penguin History of the United States of America, 1990; Mowgli's Sons: Kipling and Baden-Powell's Scouts, 1987; (with Anne P. Kerr) Correspondance et Conversations d'Alexis de Tocqueville et Nassau William Senior, 1991; Kennedy, 1996; (ed) Signalling from Mars: the letters of Arthur Ransome, 1997; Alexis de Tocqueville: a biography, 2006. *Recreation:* collecting English epitaphs. *Address:* Department of History, University of Essex, Colchester, Essex CO4 3SQ. *T:* (01206) 872232. *Club:* Reform.

BROGAN, Melanie Henrietta; *see* Dawes, M. H.

BROKE; *see* Willoughby de Broke.

BROKE, Col George Robin Straton, LVO 1977; Director, Association of Leading Visitor Attractions, since 1996; Equerry-in-Waiting to the Queen, 1974–77; *b* 31 March 1946; *s* of Maj.-Gen. Robert Straton Broke, CB, OBE, MC; *m* 1978, Patricia Thornhill Shann, *d* of Thomas Thornhill Shann; one *s*. *Educ:* Eton. Commissioned into Royal Artillery, 1965; CO 3 RHA, 1987–89. Mem., HM Bodyguard, Hon. Corps of Gentlemen-at-Arms, 1997–. Mem. Bd of Management, King Edward VII's Hosp., London, 1994–96; Mem., Grants Cttee, Army Benevolent Fund, 1994–. Trustee, Hedley Foundn, 1998–. *Recreation:* country pursuits. *Address:* St Mary's Lodge, Bircham, King's Lynn, Norfolk PE31 6QR. *T:* (01485) 578402. *Clubs:* Cavalry and Guards, Queen's.

BROKENSHIRE, James Peter; MP (C) Hornchurch, since 2005; *b* 8 Jan. 1968; *m* Cathrine; one *s* two *d*. *Educ:* Davenant Foundn Grammar Sch.; Cambridge Centre for Sixth Form Studies; Univ. of Exeter (LLB). Solicitor with Jones Day Gouldens, 1991–2005. Opposition front bench spokesman on home affairs, 2006–. *Address:* House of Commons, SW1A 0AA; (office) 23 Butts Green Road, Hornchurch, Essex RM11 2JS.

BROMHEAD, (Sir) John Desmond Gonville, (6th Bt *cr* 1806); *S* father, 1981, but does not use title. *Heir: cousin* John Edmund de Gonville Bromhead [*b* 10 Oct. 1939; *m* 1965, Janet Frances, *e d* of Harry Vernon Brotherton, Moreton-in-Marsh, Glos; one *s* one *d*].

BROMILOW, Richard Bruce Davies; His Honour Judge Bromilow; a Circuit Judge, since 2005; *b* 6 May 1954; *s* of Comdr Frank Bromilow and Joyce Bromilow (*née* Davies); *m* 1985, Alison Nina Whitaker Bell; one *s* one *d*. *Educ:* Aldwickbury Sch., Harpenden; Bedford Sch.; Southampton Univ. (LLB); Inns of Court Sch. of Law. Called to the Bar, Gray's Inn, 1977; in practice as barrister, St John's Chambers, Bristol, 1985–2005; Asst Recorder, 1998–2000; Recorder, 2000–05. *Recreations:* bridge, cricket, cycling, golf, opera. *Address:* The Law Courts, Small Street, Bristol BS1 1DW. *Clubs:* Bristol and Clifton Golf; Gloucestershire County Cricket.

BROMLEY AND BEXLEY, Archdeacon of; *see* Wright, Ven. P.

BROMLEY, Lance Lee, MA; MChir; FRCS; Director of Medical and Health Services, Gibraltar, 1982–85; Honorary Consultant Cardiothoracic Surgeon, St Mary's Hospital, W2; *b* 16 Feb. 1920; *s* of late Lancelot Bromley, MChir, FRCS, of London and Seaford, Sussex, and Dora Ridgway Bromley, Dewsbury, Yorks; *m* 1952, Rosemary Anne Holbrook; three *d*. *Educ:* St Paul's School; Caius Coll., Cambridge. Late Capt. RAMC. Late Travelling Fell. Amer. Assoc. for Thoracic Surgery. Consultant Thoracic Surgeon, St Mary's Hosp., 1953–80; Consultant Gen. Surgeon, Teddington Hosp., 1953–80. *Publications:* various contributions to medical journals. *Recreations:* sailing, golf. *Address:* 26 Molyneux Street, W1H 5HW. *T:* (020) 7262 7175. *Club:* Royal Ocean Racing.

See also Sir C. F. Knowles, Bt.

BROMLEY, Sir Michael (Roger), KBE 1998; Chairman and Chief Executive Officer, Collins & Leahy Pty Ltd, 1998–2000; Director, Steamships Trading Co. Ltd, 1986–96 and since 2000; *b* 19 July 1948; *s* of Harry and Joan Margaret Bromley; *m* 1st, 1972, Thierrine Brands (marr. diss. 1976); one *d*; 2nd, 1982, Peta Lynette Baynes (marr. diss. 1998); one *s* three *d*. *Educ:* Kikori Bush Sch., PNG, by corresp.; Mount Hagen Park Sch., PNG; Southport Sch., Qld, Australia. Collins & Leahy: Merchandise Operator, then Night Security, then truck driver, 1966–73; Man. Dir, 1982–98; Gen. Manager, Bromley & Manton, 1973–82. Former Chm., Air Niugini. *Recreations:* polocrosse, flying (pilot), scuba diving, sailing. *Club:* Goroka Polocrosse.

BROMLEY, Prof. Peter Mann; Professor of English Law, University of Manchester, 1985–86 (Professor of Law, 1965–85), now Professor Emeritus; *b* 20 Nov. 1922; *s* of Frank Bromley and Marion Maud (*née* Moy); *m* 1963, Beatrice Mary, *d* of Eric Charles Cassels Hunter and Amy Madeleine (*née* Renold). *Educ:* Ealing Grammar Sch.; The Queen's College, Oxford (MA 1948). Called to the Bar, Middle Temple, 1951. Served War, Royal Artillery, 1942–45. University of Manchester: Asst Lectr 1947–50, Lectr 1950–61, Sen. Lectr 1961–65; Dean, Faculty of Law, 1966–68, 1972–74 and 1981–83; Pro-Vice-Chancellor, 1977–81; Principal, Dalton Hall, 1958–65. Vis. Prof. of Law, Univ. of Buckingham, 1987–88. Chm., Cttee on Professional Legal Educn in NI, 1983–85; Member: Adv. Cttee on Legal Educn, 1972–75; University Grants Cttee, 1978–85 (Chm., Social Studies Sub-cttee, 1979–85); Commonwealth Scholarship Commn, 1986–92. Editor, Butterworths Family Law Service, 1983–96. *Publications:* Family Law, 1957, 8th edn with N. V. Lowe, 1992; (contrib.) Parental Custody and Matrimonial Maintenance, 1966; (contrib.) Das Erbrecht von Familienangehörigen, 1971; (contrib.) The Child and the Courts, 1978; (contrib.) Adoption, 1984; (contrib.) Children and the Law, 1990; (contrib.) Droit Sans Frontières, 1991; articles in various legal jls. *Recreations:* walking, theatre, listening to music. *Address:* 7A Hawthorn Avenue, Wilmslow, Cheshire SK9 5BR. *T:* (01625) 526516. *Club:* Oxford and Cambridge.

BROMLEY, Sir Rupert Charles, 10th Bt *cr* 1757; *b* 2 April 1936; *s* of Major Sir Rupert Howe Bromley, MC, 9th Bt, and Dorothy Vera (*d* 1982), *d* of late Sir Walford Selby, KCMG, CB, CVO; *S* father, 1966; *m* 1962, Priscilla Hazel, *d* of late Maj. Howard Bourne, HAC; three *s*. *Educ:* Michaelhouse, Natal; Rhodes Univ.; Christ Church, Oxford. Called to the Bar, Inner Temple, 1959. *Recreations:* equestrian. *Heir: s* Charles Howard Bromley [*b* 31 July 1963; *m* 1998, Marie, *d* of W. J. Taylor; one *s* one *d*]. *Address:* The Old Manse, Glencairn, Simon's Town, 7975, South Africa.

BROMLEY-DAVENPORT, John; QC 2002; a Recorder of the Crown Court, since 1989; *b* 13 March 1947; *s* of Togo and Elizabeth Bromley-Davenport; *m* 1971, Judy Francis; one *s* two *d*. *Educ:* Eton Coll.; LAMDA; College of Law. Called to the Bar, Gray's Inn, 1972. *Publication:* Sober in the Morning (anthology of drink and drinking), 2004. *Recreations:* acting, cricket, shooting, fishing, golf, wine and gormandise. *Address:* Dean's Court Chambers, 24 St John Street, Manchester M3 4DF. *T:* (0161) 214 6000, *Fax:* (0161) 214 6001; *e-mail:* bromley@deanscourt.co.uk. 3 Paper Buildings, Temple, EC4Y 7EU. *T:* (020) 7583 8055, *Fax:* (020) 7353 6271; *e-mail:* john.bromley-davenport@3paper.co.uk. *Clubs:* Tarporley Hunt; Manchester Tennis and Racquet; Delamere Forest Golf, Royal Liverpool Golf.

BROMLEY-DAVENPORT, William Arthur; landowner; chartered accountant; Lord-Lieutenant of Cheshire, since 1990; *b* 7 March 1935; *o s* of Lt-Col Sir Walter Bromley-Davenport, TD, DL and Lenette, *d* of Joseph Y. Jeanes, Philadelphia; *m* 1962, Elizabeth Watts, Oldwick, NJ; one *s* one *d*. *Educ:* Eton; Cornell Univ., NY. Mem. ICA, 1966. National Service, 2nd Batt. Grenadier Guards, 1953–54; Hon. Col 3rd (Vol.) Batt. 22nd (Cheshire) Regt, 1985. Owns land in UK and Norway. Mem. Cttee (past Chm.) Cheshire Br., CLA, 1962–. Pres., Cheshire Scout Council, 1990– (Chm., 1981–90). Chm. of Govs, King's Sch., Macclesfield, 1986–. JP 1975, DL 1982, High Sheriff 1983–84, Cheshire. *Address:* Capesthorne Hall, Macclesfield SK11 9JY; Fiva, Aandalsnes, Norway.

BROMLEY-MARTIN, Michael Granville; QC 2002; a Recorder, since 2003; *b* 27 April 1955; *s* of late Captain David Eliot Bromley-Martin, RN, and of Angela Felicity Bromley-Martin (*née* Hampden-Ross); *m* 1983, Anna Frances Birley; one *s* two *d*. *Educ:* Eton; Southampton Univ. (BSc Civil Eng). Called to the Bar, Gray's Inn, 1979. Inspector, DTI, 1989, 1990. *Recreations:* sailing, shooting, fishing, arts. *Address:* 3 Raymond Buildings, Gray's Inn, WC1R 5BH. *T:* (020) 7400 6400, *Fax:* (020) 7400 6464; *e-mail:* chambers@3raymondbuildings.com. *Clubs:* Garrick, Royal Ocean Racing; Itchenor Sailing.

BROMPTON, Michael John; QC 2003; a Recorder, since 2006; *b* 6 Sept. 1950; *s* of Harry and Lena Brompton; *m* 1st, 1983, Sally Elizabeth Mary O'Brien (marr. diss. 1997); two *d*; 2nd, 2003, Clare Elizabeth Gilbert. *Educ:* Stowe Sch., Buckingham; Univ. of Sussex (BA Hons Hist.); Coll. of Law, London. Called to the Bar, Middle Temple, 1973; in practice, specialising in law of crime, fraud, money-laundering and confiscation of assets. Standing Counsel to HM Customs and Excise (Crime), S Eastern Circuit, 1994–2003. *Address:* 5 Paper Buildings, Temple, EC4Y 7HB. *T:* (020) 7583 6117, *Fax:* (020) 7353 0075.

BROMWICH, Prof. Michael; CIMA Professor of Accounting and Financial Management, London School of Economics and Political Science, 1985–2006, now

Emeritus; *b* 29 Jan. 1941; *s* of William James Bromwich and Margery (*née* Townley); *m* 1972, Christine Margaret Elizabeth Whitehead (OBE 1991). *Educ:* Wentworth High Sch., Southend; London School of Economics (BScEcon 1965); FCMA. Ford Motor Co., 1958–62 and 1965–66; Lectr, LSE, 1966–70; Professor: UWIST, 1971–77; Univ. of Reading, 1977–85. Mem. Council, ICMA, 1980–85; Vice Pres., ICMA, later CIMA, 1985–87, Pres., CIMA, 1987–88. Accounting Advr, OFT, 2001–. Mem., Accounting Standards Cttee, 1981–84; Additional Mem., Monopolies and Mergers Commn, 1992–2000; Research Grants Bd, ESRC, 1992–96. Hon. Treas., Disability Alliance, 2007–. Hon. DEcon Lund Univ., Sweden, 1993. *Publications:* Economics of Capital Budgeting, 1976; Economics of Accounting Standard Setting, 1985; (jtly) Management Accounting: evolution not revolution, 1989; (jtly) Housing Association Accounting, 1990; Financial Reporting, Information and Capital Markets, 1992; Management Accounting: pathways to progress, 1994; Accounting for Overheads: critique and reforms, 1997; (jtly) Following the Money: the Enron failure and the state of corporate disclosure, 2003; (jtly) Worldwide Financial Reporting: the development and future of accounting standards, 2006; co-ed others, incl. Essays in British Accounting Research; many articles. *Recreations:* working and eating in restaurants. *Address:* 14 Thornhill Road, N1 1HW. *T:* (020) 7607 9323.

BRON, Prof. Anthony John, FRCS, FCOphth, FMedSci; Head, Nuffield Laboratory of Ophthalmology, 1973–2003, and Clinical Professor of Ophthalmology, 1989–2003, University of Oxford, now Professor Emeritus; Fellow of Linacre College, Oxford, 1975–2003; *b* 3 Feb. 1936; *s* of late Sydney and Fagah Bron; *m* 1st, 1961, Sandra Ruth Shoot (*d* 1976); one *s* one *d* (and one *s* decd); 2nd, 1981, Diana S. Shortt; one step *s* three step *d*. *Educ:* London Univ. (BSc 1957; MB BS 1961); Guy's Hosp. (DO 1964). LRCP 1960; MRCS 1960, FRCS 1968; FCOphth 1989. Guy's Hosp., 1961–63; Clin. Fellow in Ophthalmol., Wilmer Inst., Johns Hopkins Univ., 1964–65; Res. Assistant, Inst. of Ophthalmol., 1965; Moorfields Eye Hospital: Chief Clin. Assistant, 1965; Resident Surg. Officer, 1965–68; Lectr, 1968–70; Sen. Lectr and Hon. Consultant, 1970–73; Margaret Ogilvie's Reader in Ophthalmol., Oxford Univ., 1973–2003; Hon. Consultant, Oxford Eye Hosp., 1989–. Pres., Ophthalmic Section, RSM, 1986; Vice Pres., Jt Eur. Res. Meetings in Ophthal. and Vision, 1994–95; Chm., Assoc. for Eye Res., 1993–95; Chm. Cornea Sect., 1998–2002, Pres., 2002–03, Eur. Assoc. for Vision and Eye Res. Mem., Soc. of Scholars, Johns Hopkins Univ., 1991; Chm. and Co-organiser, Internat. Dry Eye Workshop, 2007. Founder FMedSci 1998. Hon. MA Oxon, 1973. *Publications:* (contrib.) The Inborn Errors of Metabolism, 1974; The Unquiet Eye, 1983, 2nd edn 1987; (jtly) Lens Disorders, 1996; (ed and contrib.) Wolff's Anatomy of the Eye and Orbit, 1997; (jtly) Lecture Notes in Ophthalmology, 2007; papers on the cornea, tears and crystalline lens. *Recreations:* drawing, photography, musing on Life. *Address:* Nuffield Laboratory of Ophthalmology, Walton Street, Oxford OX2 6AW. *T:* (01865) 248996. *Club:* Athenæum.

See also E. Bron.

BRON, Eleanor; actress and writer; *d* of late Sydney and Fagah Bron. *Educ:* North London Collegiate Sch., Canons, Edgware; Newnham Coll., Cambridge (BA Hons Mod. Langs). De La Rue Co., 1961. Director: Actors Centre, 1982–93; Soho Theatre Co., 1993–2000. Appearances include: revue, Establishment Nightclub, Soho, 1962, and New York, 1963; Not so much a Programme, More a Way of Life, BBC TV, 1964; several TV series written with John Fortune, and TV series: Making Faces, written by Michael Frayn, 1976; Pinkerton's Progress, 1983; Absolutely Fabulous, 1992; Fat Friends, 2002; *TV plays and films include:* Nina, 1978; My Dear Palestrina, 1980; A Month in the Country, 1985; Quartermaine's Terms, 1987; Changing Step, 1989; The Hour of the Lynx, 1990; The Blue Boy, 1994; Vanity Fair, 1998; Gypsy Girl, Randall & Hopkirk (Deceased), 2001; Ted and Alice, 2002. *Stage roles include:* Jennifer Dubedat, The Doctor's Dilemma, 1966; Jean Brodie, The Prime of Miss Jean Brodie, 1967, 1984; title role, Hedda Gabler, 1969; Portia, The Merchant of Venice, 1975; Amanda, Private Lives, 1976; Elena, Uncle Vanya, 1977; Charlotte, The Cherry Orchard, 1978; Margaret, A Family, 1978; On Her Own, 1980; Goody Biddy Bean; The Amusing Spectacle of Cinderella and her Naughty, Naughty Sisters, 1980; Betrayal, 1981; Heartbreak House, 1981; Duet for One, 1982; The Duchess of Malfi, 1985; The Real Inspector Hound, and The Critic (double bill), 1985; Jocasta and Ismene, Oedipus and Oedipus at Colonus, 1987; Infidelities, 1987; The Madwoman of Chaillot, 1988; The Chalk Garden, 1989; The Miser, and The White Devils, 1991; opera, Die Glückliche Hand, Nederlandse Oper, Amsterdam, 1991; Desdemona—if you had only spoken! (one-woman show), 1992; Gertrude, Hamlet, 1993; Agnes, A Delicate Balance, 1996; A Perfect Ganesh, 1996; Doña Rosita: the Spinster, 1997; Be My Baby, 1998; Making Noise Quietly, 1999; Tuppence to Cross the Mersey, 2005; The Clean House, 2006, tour, 2008; In Extremis, 2007. *Films include:* Help!; Alfie; Two for the Road; Bedazzled; Women in Love; The National Health; The Day that Christ Died, 1980; Turtle Diary, 1985; Little Dorrit, 1987; The Attic, 1988; Deadly Advice, 1994; Black Beauty, A Little Princess, 1995; The House of Mirth, 2000; The Heart of Me, 2001; Love's Brother, 2003; Wimbledon, 2004. Author: song-cycle with John Dankworth, 1973; verses for Saint-Saens' Carnival of the Animals, 1975 (recorded). *Publications:* Is Your Marriage Really Necessary (with John Fortune), 1972; (contrib.) My Cambridge, 1976; (contrib.) More Words, 1977; Life and Other Punctures, 1978; The Pillow Book of Eleanor Bron, 1985; (trans.) Desdemona—if you had only spoken!, by Christine Brückner, 1992; Double Take, 1996. *Address:* c/o Rebecca Blond Associates, 69A King's Road, SW3 4NX.

See also A. J. Bron.

BRONFMAN, Edgar Miles; Chief Executive, Warner Music Group; *b* 20 June 1929; *s* of late Samuel Bronfman and of Saidye Rosner. *Educ:* Trinity College Sch., Port Hope, Ont., Canada; Williams Coll., Williamstown, Mass, US; McGill Univ., Montreal (BA 1951). Chm., Joseph E. Seagram & Sons, Inc. (Pres., 1957); Pres., 1971, CEO, 1975–94, Chm., 1975–2000, The Seagram Company Ltd; Exec. Vice Chm., 2000–01, Vice Chm., 2001–03, Vivendi Universal; Dir, E. I. duPont de Nemours & Co. Pres., World Jewish Congress, 1980–. Hon. LHD Pace Univ., NY, 1982; Hon. Dr Laws Williams Coll., Williamstown, 1986. *Address:* 375 Park Avenue, 17th Floor, New York, NY 10152, USA. *T:* (212) 572719.

BRONNERT, Deborah Jane; Joint Director, Global and Economic Issues, Foreign and Commonwealth Office, since 2008; *b* Stockport, 31 Jan. 1967; *d* of Rev. Preb. Dr David Bronnert and Beryl Bronnert; *m* 2006, Alfonso Torrents; one *s*. *Educ:* Featherstone High Sch., Southall; Univ. of Bristol (BSc Hons Maths); University Coll. London (MA Pol Econ. of Russia and E Europe). DoE, 1989–91; Second Sec., Envmt, UK Repn to EC, Brussels, 1991–93; DoE, then FCO, 1993–95; Mem. of Cabinet, EC, Brussels, 1995–99; Dep. Hd, S Eur. Dept, FCO, 1999–2001; Econ. and Trade Counsellor, Moscow, 2002–05; Hd, Future of Europe Gp, then Hd, Europe Delivery Gp, FCO, 2006–08. *Recreations:* travel, running, hill walking, politics. *Address:* Foreign and Commonwealth Office, King Charles Street, SW1A 2AH.

BROOK, Anthony Donald, FCA; Chairman, Ocean Radio Group Ltd, 1994–2000; *b* 24 Sept. 1936; *s* of Donald Charles Brook and Doris Ellen (*née* Emmett); *m* 1st, 1965, Ann Mary Reeves (*d* 2000); two *d*; 2nd, 2005, Jean Curtis. *Educ:* Eastbourne Coll. FCA 1970 (ACA 1960). Joined Associated Television Ltd, 1966; Financial Controller, ATV Network Ltd, 1969; Dir of External Finance, IBA, 1974; Finance Dir/Gen. Man., ITC Entertainment Ltd, 1978; Dep. Man. Dir, Television South plc, 1981; Man. Dir (Television), TVS Entertainment, 1984–89, Man. Dir Broadcasting, 1989–91; Man. Dir, TVS Television Ltd, 1986–89; Dep. Chm. and Man. Dir, TVS Entertainment plc, 1991–93; Chairman: SelecTV, 1993–95; Advanced Media Gp plc, 1994–95; Southern Screen Commn, 1996–99. *Recreations:* sailing, travel, golf. *Address:* 20 Meadow Lane, Hamble, Southampton SO31 4RD. *Clubs:* Royal Southern Yacht (Hamble, Hants); Tamesis (Teddington, Middx).

BROOK, Prof. Charles Groves Darville, MD; FRCP, FRCPH; JP; Professor of Paediatric Endocrinology, University College London, 1989–2000, now Emeritus; Consultant Paediatrician, Middlesex Hospital, 1974–2000, and Gt Ormond Street Hospital, 1994–2000, now Hon. Consulting Paediatric Endocrinologist; Director, London Centre for Paediatric Endocrinology, 1994–2000; *b* 15 Jan. 1940; *s* of Air Vice-Marshal William Arthur Darville Brook, CB, CBE, and Marjorie Jean Brook (*née* Grant, later Hamilton); *m* 1963, Hon. Catherine Mary Hawke, *d* of 9th Baron Hawke; two *d*. *Educ:* Rugby Sch.; Magdalene Coll., Cambridge (MA); St Thomas's Hosp. Med. Sch. (MD 1964). FRCP 1979; FRCPCH 1997. Resident posts at St Thomas' and Gt Ormond St Hosps, 1964–74; Res. Fellow, Kinderspital, Zurich, 1972; University College London: Sen. Lectr in Paediatric Endocrinology, 1983–89; Academic Dir of Endocrinology, 1997–2000. Fellow, UCL Hosps, 2000. Vice Pres., 2004–06, Trustee, 2006–, St Margaret's Somerset Hospice. Member: Pitcombe Parish Council, 2001–07 (Chm., 2003–07); Pitcombe PCC, 2002– (Sec., 2003–; Church Warden 2007–). JP Avon and Som, 2002. Andrea Prader Prize, European Soc. for Paediatric Endocrinology, 2000. *Publications:* Practical Paediatric Endocrinology, 1978; Clinical Paediatric Endocrinology, 1981, 6th edn as Brook's Clinical Pediatric Endocrinology, 2009; Essential Endocrinology, 1982, 4th edn 2001; Growth Assessment in Childhood and Adolescence, 1982; All About Adolescence, 1985; Current Concepts in Paediatric Endocrinology, 1987; The Practice of Medicine in Adolescence, 1993; A Guide to the Practice of Paediatric Endocrinology, 1993; Essential Endocrinology, 1996; Handbook of Pediatric Endocrinology, 2007; numerous papers on endocrinology in med. jls. *Recreations:* gardening, DIY. *Address:* Hadspen Farm, Castle Cary, Som BA7 7LX. *T:* (01963) 351492; *e-mail:* c.brook@ucl.ac.uk.

See also Air Vice-Marshal D. C. G. Brook.

BROOK, Air Vice-Marshal David Conway Grant, CB 1990; CBE 1983; *b* 23 Dec. 1935; *s* of late Air Vice-Marshal William Arthur Darville Brook, CB, CBE and Jean Brook (later Jean Hamilton); *m* 1961, Jessica (*née* Lubbock); one *s* one *d*. *Educ:* Marlborough Coll.; RAF Coll. Pilot, Nos 263, 1 (Fighter) and 14 Sqdns, 1957–62 (Hunter aircraft; fighter combat leader); ADC to AOC-in-C Near East Air Force, 1962–64; CO No 1 (Fighter) Sqdn, 1964–66 (Hunter Mk 9); RN Staff Course, 1967 (psc); RAF Adviser to Dir Land/Air Warfare (MoD Army), 1968–69; Wing Comdr Offensive Support, Jt Warfare Estab., 1970–72; CO No 20 (Army Cooperation) Sqdn, 1974–76 (Harrier); Station Comdr, RAF Wittering, 1976–78 (Harrier); RCDS, 1979 (rcds); Principal Staff Officer to Chief of Defence Staff, 1980–82; SASO, HQ RAF Germany, 1982–85; Air Officer Scotland and NI, 1986–89. Civil Emergencies Advr, Home Office, 1989–93. Mem., Lord Chancellor's Panel of Ind. (Highway) Inspectors, 1994–2003. Chm., Broad Campden Village Hall Cttee, 1993–2006. *Publications:* contrib. to Brasseys Annual. *Recreations:* golf, music, walking. *Address:* Cherry Orchard Cottage, Broad Campden, Chipping Campden, Glos GL55 6UU. *Club:* Royal Air Force.

See also Prof. C. G. D. Brook.

BROOK, (Gerald) Robert, CBE 1981; Chief Executive, 1977–86, and Chairman, 1985–86, National Bus Company (Deputy Chairman, 1978–85); *b* 19 Dec. 1928; *s* of Charles Pollard Brook and Doris Brook (*née* Senior); *m* 1957, Joan Marjorie Oldfield; two *s* one *d*. *Educ:* King James Grammar Sch., Knaresborough. FCIS, FCIT. Served Duke of Wellington's Regt, 1947–49. Appointments in bus companies, from 1950; Company Secretary: Cumberland Motor Services Ltd, 1960; Thames Valley Traction Co. Ltd, 1963; General Manager: North Western Road Car Co. Ltd, 1968; Midland Red Omnibus Co. Ltd, 1972; Regional Director, National Bus Company, 1974; Chm., Fleetsoftware Ltd, 1998–. Pres., CIT, 1987–88. *Publications:* papers for professional instns and learned socs. *Recreation:* reading military history. *Address:* Pleinmont, 24 Hookstone Drive, Harrogate, N Yorks HG2 8PP. *Club:* Army and Navy.

BROOK, Air Vice-Marshal John Michael, CB 1993; FRCGP; Director General, Royal Air Force Medical Services, 1991–94, retired; *b* 26 May 1934; *s* of late Norman Brook and Nellie Brook (*née* Burns); *m* 1959, Edna Kilburn; one *s* three *d*. *Educ:* Mirfield Grammar Sch.; Leeds Univ. (MB ChB 1957). MRCGP 1972, FRCGP 1992; Dip AvMed RCP 1974; MFOM 1981. Commissioned 1959; served Laarbruch, Stafford, Muharraq, Watton, Linton-on-Ouse, MoD; SMO, RAF Finningley, 1974–76; MoD, 1976; SMO RAF Brize Norton, 1978–81; OC RAF Av. Med. Trng Centre, 1981–83; RAF Exchange Officer, USAF HQ Systems Command, 1983–86; OC Defence Services Med. Rehabilitation Unit, 1986–87; OC Central Med. Estabt, 1987–89; Dep. Principal MO, HQ Strike Comd, 1989–91; Dep. Surgeon Gen., Health Services, 1991–93. QHS 1991–94. OStJ 1980. *Recreations:* all music, travel, walking. *Address:* 2 Vicarage Fields, Hemingford Grey, Cambs PE28 9BY. *Club:* Royal Air Force.

BROOK, Peter Stephen Paul, CH 1998; CBE 1965; producer; Co-Director, The Royal Shakespeare Theatre; *b* 21 March 1925; 2nd *s* of Simon and Ida Brook; *m* 1951, Natasha Parry, stage and film star; one *s* one *d*. *Educ:* Westminster; Greshams; Magdalen College, Oxford (Hon. Fellow, 1991). Productions include: The Tragedy of Dr Faustus, 1942; The Infernal Machine, 1945; Birmingham Repertory Theatre: Man and Superman, King John, The Lady from the Sea, 1945–46; Stratford: Romeo and Juliet, Love's Labour's Lost, 1947; London: Vicious Circle, Men Without Shadows, Respectable Prostitute, The Brothers Karamazov, 1946; Director of Productions, Royal Opera House, Covent Garden, 1947–50: Boris Godunov, La Bohème, 1948; Marriage of Figaro, The Olympians, Salome, 1949. Dark of the Moon, 1949; Ring Round the Moon, 1950; Measure for Measure, Stratford, 1950, Paris, 1978; The Little Hut, 1950; The Winter's Tale, 1951; Venice Preserved, 1953; The Little Hut, New York, Faust, Metropolitan Opera House, 1953; The Dark is Light Enough; Both Ends Meet, 1954; House of Flowers, New York, 1954; The Lark, 1955; Titus Andronicus, Stratford, 1955; Hamlet, London, Moscow, 1955, Paris 2000, London, 2001; The Power and the Glory, 1956; Family Reunion, 1956; The Tempest, Stratford, 1957; Cat on a Hot Tin Roof, Paris, 1957; View from the Bridge, Paris, 1958; Irma la Douce, London, 1958; The Fighting Cock, New York, 1959; Le Balcon, Paris, 1960; The Visit, Royalty, 1960; King Lear, Stratford, Aldwych and Moscow, 1962; The Physicists, Aldwych, 1963; Sergeant Musgrave's Dance, Paris, 1963; The Persecution and Assassination of Marat..., Aldwych, 1964 (New York, 1966); The Investigation, Aldwych, 1965; US, Aldwych, 1966; Oedipus, National Theatre, 1968; A Midsummer Night's Dream, Stratford, 1970, NY, 1971; Timon of Athens, Paris, 1974 (Grand Prix Dominique, 1975; Brigadier Prize, 1975);

The Ik, Paris, 1975, London, 1976; Ubu Roi, Paris, 1977; Antony and Cleopatra, Stratford, 1978, Aldwych, 1979; Ubu, Young Vic, 1978; Conference of the Birds, France, Australia, NY, 1980; The Cherry Orchard, Paris, 1981, NY, 1988; La tragédie Carmen, Paris, 1981, NY, 1983 (Emmy Award, and Prix Italia, 1984); The Mahabharata, Avignon and Paris, 1985, Glasgow, 1988, televised, 1989 (Internat. Emmy Award 1990); Woza Albert, Paris, 1988; Carmen, Glasgow, 1989; The Tempest, Glasgow and Paris, 1990; Impressions de Pelléas, Paris, 1992; L'Homme Qui, Paris, 1993, The Man Who, Nat. Theatre, 1994, New York, 1995; Qui Est Là, Paris, 1995; Oh les Beaux Jours, Lausanne, Paris, Moscow, Tbilisi, 1995, London, 1997; Don Giovanni, Aix, 1998; Je Suis un Phenomène, Paris, 1998; Le Costume, Paris, 1999, Young Vic, 2001; The Tragedy of Hamlet, Paris, 2000, Young Vic, 2001; La Tragédie d'Hamlet, Paris, 2002; Far Away, Paris, 2002; La Mort de Krishna, Paris and tour, 2002; Ta Main dans la Mienne, Paris and tour, 2003; Tierno Bokar, Paris and NY, 2004; Le Grand Inquisiteur, Paris, 2005, world tour and (as The Grand Inquisitor) Barbican Pit, 2006; Fragments, Paris, 2006, Young Vic, 2007; work with Internat. Centre of Theatre Research, Paris, Iran, W Africa, and USA, 1971, Sahara, Niger and Nigeria, 1972–73. *Directed films:* The Beggar's Opera, 1952; Moderato Cantabile, 1960; Lord of the Flies, 1962; The Marat/Sade, 1967; Tell Me Lies, 1968; King Lear, 1969; Meetings with Remarkable Men, 1979; The Tragedy of Carmen, 1983; (TV film) The Tragedy of Hamlet, 2001. Hon. DLitt: Birmingham; Strathclyde, 1990; Oxford, 1994. SWET award, for outstanding contribn by UK theatre artist to US theatre season, 1983. Freiherr von Stein Foundn Shakespeare Award, 1973. Commandeur de l'Ordre des Arts et des Lettres; Officer of the Legion of Honour (France), 1995. *Publications:* The Empty Space, 1968; The Shifting Point (autobiog.), 1988; Le Diable c'est l'Ennui, 1991; There Are No Secrets, 1993; Threads of Time: a memoir, 1998; Evoking Shakespeare, 1999. *Recreations:* painting, piano playing and travelling by air. *Address:* c/o Théâtre des Bouffes du Nord, 37 bis Boulevard de la Chapelle, 75010 Paris, France.

BROOK, Richard; Chief Executive, Sense, since 2008; *b* 22 Nov. 1956; *s* of Ralph Brook and Doris May Brook; *m* 1979, Sheena Ward; two *d*. *Educ:* Keele Univ. (BSc Hons Biol. 1978); University Coll., Cardiff (CQSW and Dip. Social Work 1981); Essex Univ. (MA Social Service Planning 1992). Asst Dir, Thames Reach Housing Assoc., 1991–94; Dir of Care, Heritage Care, 1994–96; Dir of Care and Community Services, Shaftesbury Soc., 1996–99; Chief Executive: Christian Alliance Housing Assoc., 1999–2001; Mind (Nat. Assoc. for Mental Health), 2001–06; Chief Exec., Public Guardianship Office and Public Guardian designate, 2006–07; Chief Exec. and Public Guardian, Office of the Public Guardian, 2007–08. *Recreations:* gardening, computing. *Address:* Sense, 101 Pentonville Road, N1 9LG.

BROOK, Sir Richard (John), Kt 2002; OBE 1988; ScD; FREng; Director, Leverhulme Trust, since 2001; Professor of Materials Science, Oxford University, 1995–2003, now Professor Emeritus; Professorial Fellow, St Cross College, Oxford, 1991–2003, now Hon. Fellow; *b* 12 March 1938; *s* of Frank Brook and Emily Sarah (*née* Lytle); *m* 1961, Elizabeth Christine Aldred; one *s* one *d*. *Educ:* Univ. of Leeds (BSc Ceramics); MIT (ScD Ceramics). FREng (FEng 1998). Res. Asst, MIT, 1962–66; Asst Prof. of Materials Science, Univ. of S California, 1966–70; Gp Leader, AERE, 1970–74; Prof. and Head of Dept of Ceramics, Univ. of Leeds, 1974–88; Scientific Mem., Max Planck Soc. and Dir, Max Planck Inst. Metallforschung, Stuttgart, 1988–91; Cookson Prof. of Materials Sci., 1991–95, and Head, Dept of Materials, 1992–94, Oxford Univ.; Chief Exec., EPSRC, 1994–2001. Chairman, Materials Cttee, 1985–88, Materials Commn, 1992–94, SERC; Ext. Mem., Res. Cttee, British Gas, 1989–98; Mem., ESTA, 1994–98; Chm., EU Res. Orgns Hds of Res. Councils, 1997–99. Non-executive Director and Board Member: Carbon Trust, 2002–; ERA Foundn, 2002–. Mem., Curatorium, Körber Award, 1995–2003. Editor, Jl of European Ceramic Soc., 1989–. Pres., British Ceramic Soc., 1984–86; Vice-Pres., Inst. of Materials, 1993–95; Fellow, Inst. of Ceramics, 1978 (Pres., 1984–86); Dist. Life Fellow, American Ceramic Soc., 1995; Mem. d'Honneur, Soc. Française Métallurgie Matériaux, 1995–. Mem. Senate, Max Planck Soc., 1999–. Hon. Prof., Univ. of Stuttgart, 1990–. Mellor Meml Lectr, Swansea, 1989; Stuijts Meml Lectr, Maastricht, 1989. Mem., Deutsche Akad. der Naturforscher Leopoldina, 2002. Dr *hc*: Aveiro, 1995; Limoges, 2003; Hon. DSc: Bradford, 1996; Loughborough, 2000; Brunel, Nottingham Trent, 2001; Strathclyde, 2002. *Publications:* papers in publications of Inst. of Materials, Amer. Ceramic Soc., European Ceramic Soc. *Recreation:* Europe. *Address:* Leverhulme Trust, 1 Pemberton Row, EC4A 3BG.

BROOK, Robert; *see* Brook, G. R.

BROOK, (Rowland) Stuart; Director of Consulting, Tribal Consulting, 2006–07; *b* 17 Nov. 1949; *s* of Geoffrey Brook and Eileen Brook; *m* 1971, Susan Heward; three *s* one *d*. *Educ:* Warwick Univ.; Hull Univ.; Bradford Univ. (MA). Probation Officer, Humberside Probation Service, 1973–77; Humberside County Council: Sen. Social Worker, 1977–81; Area Manager, 1981–84; Principal Officer, Dyfed CC, 1984–87; Asst Dir (Ops), Rotherham MBC, 1987–89; Asst Dir, Bradford MBC, 1989–92; Dep. Dir, 1992–94, Dir, 1995–2005, Notts CC Social Services Dept. Non-exec. Dir, Notts County NHS PCT, 2007–. Chm., Nat. Homecare Council, 2003–05. *Recreations:* family, sport, music. *Address:* Plumtree House, Station Road, Plumtree, Notts NG12 5NA.

BROOK, Prof. Timothy James, PhD; Shaw Professor of Chinese, University of Oxford, since 2007; Principal, St John's College, University of British Columbia, 2004–June 2009; *b* 6 Jan. 1951; *s* of John and Barbara Brook; *m* 1989, Fay Sims; two *s* two *d*. *Educ:* Univ. of Toronto (BA 1973); Harvard Univ. (AM 1977; PhD 1984). Mactaggart Fellow, Dept of Hist., Univ. of Alberta, 1984–86; Professor: Dept of Hist., Univ. of Toronto, 1986–97, 1999–2004; Dept of Hist., Stanford Univ., 1997–99. Guggenheim Meml Fellowship, 2006. François-Xavier Garneau Medal, Canadian Histl Assoc., 2005. *Publications:* Geographical Sources of Ming-Qing History, 1988, 2nd edn 2002; The Asiatic Mode of Production, 1989; Quelling the People: the military suppression of the Beijing democracy movement, 1992; Praying for Power: Buddhism and the formation of gentry society in Late-Ming China, 1993; (with Hy Van Luong) Culture and Economy: the shaping of capitalism in Eastern Asia, 1997; (with B. Michael Frolic) Civil Society in China, 1997; The Confusions of Pleasure: commerce and culture in Ming China, 1998; Documents on the Rape of Nanking, 1999; (with Gregory Blue) China and Historical Capitalism: genealogies of Sinological knowledge, 1999; (with Andre Schmid) Nation Work: Asian elites and national identities, 2000; (with Bob Tadashi Wakabayashi) Opium Regimes: China, Britain, and Japan, 2000; The Chinese State in Ming Society, 2005; Collaboration: Japanese agents and Chinese elites in wartime China, 2005; (with Jérôme Bourgon and Gregory Blue) Death by a Thousand Cuts, 2008; Vermeer's Hat: the seventeenth century and the dawn of the global world, 2008. *Recreations:* music, travel, poetry. *Address:* Institute for Chinese Studies, University of Oxford, Walton Road, Oxford OX1 2HG. *T:* (01865) 280387, *Fax:* (01865) 280435.

BROOK-PARTRIDGE, Bernard; Deputy Chairman, Central London Masonic Centre Ltd, since 2000; *b* Croydon, 1927; *o s* of late Leslie Brook-Partridge and late Gladys Vere Burchell (*née* Brooks), Sanderstead; *m* 1st, 1951, Enid Elizabeth Hatfield (marr. diss. 1965); one *d* (and one *d* decd); 2nd, 1967, Carol Devonald, *o d* of late Arnold Devonald Francis Lewis and late Patricia (*née* Thomas), Gower, S Wales; two *s*. *Educ:* Selsdon County Grammar Sch.; Cambridgeshire Tech. Coll.; Cambridge Univ.; London Univ.; Gray's Inn. Military Service, 1945–48. Studies, 1948–50. Cashier/Accountant, Dominion Rubber Co. Ltd, 1950–51; Asst Export Manager, British & General Tube Co. Ltd, 1951–52; Asst Sec., Assoc. of Internat. Accountants, 1952–59; Sec.-Gen., Institute of Linguists, 1959–62; various teaching posts, Federal Republic of Germany, 1962–66; Special Asst to Man. Dir, M. G. Scott Ltd, 1966–68; business consultancy work on own account, incl. various dirships with several client cos, 1968–72; Partner, Carsons, Brook-Partridge & Co. (Planning Consultants), 1972–2004. Chairman: Brompton Troika Ltd, 1985–; Daldorch Estates Ltd, 1995–98; Dep. Chm., World Trade Centre Ltd, 1997–2002; Director: Edmund Nuttall Ltd, 1986–92; Kyle Stewart, 1989–92; Paramount Hill Ltd, 2003–; Location of Industry Bureau Ltd, 2004–06. Local Govt and Pol Advisor to Transmanche-Link UK, 1988 and 1989. Contested (C) St Pancras North, LCC, 1958; Mem. (C) St Pancras Metropolitan Borough Council, 1959–62. Prospective Parly Cand. (C), Shoreditch and Finsbury, 1960–62; contested (C) Nottingham Central, 1970. Greater London Council: Mem. for Havering, 1967–73, for Havering (Romford), 1973–85; Chm., 1980–81; Chairman: Planning and Transportation (NE) Area Bd, 1967–71; Town Develt Cttee, 1971–73; Arts Cttee, 1977–78; Public Services and Safety Cttee, 1978–79; Opposition spokesman: for Arts and Recreation, 1973–77; for Police Matters, 1983–85; Member: Exec. Cttee, Greater London Arts Assoc., 1973–78; Council and Exec., Greater London and SE Council for Sport and Recreation, 1977–78; GLC Leaders' Cttee with special responsibility for Law and Order and Police Liaison matters, 1977–79; Dep. Leader, Recreation and Community Services Policy Cttee, 1977–79. Vice-Pres., SPCK, 1993– (Gov. and Trustee, 1976–93); Member: BBC Radio London Adv. Council, 1974–79; Gen. Council, Poetry Soc., 1977–86 (Treas., 1982–84); Board Member: Peterborough Develt Corp., 1972–88 (Chm., Queensgate Management Services); London Festival Ballet (and Trustee), 1977–79; Young Vic Theatre Ltd, 1977–88 (Chm., 1983–87); London Orchestral Concert Bd Ltd, 1977–78; ENO, 1977–78; London Contemp. Dance Trust, 1979–84; Governor and Trustee, Sadler's Wells Foundn, 1977–79; Chairman: London Music Hall Trust, 1983–96; London Symphony Chorus Develt Cttee, 1981–88; Samuel Lewis Housing Trust, 1985–92 (Trustee, 1976–94); Council, Royal Philharmonic Soc., 1991–99 (Chm., 1991–95); Exec. Cttee, Henley Soc., 1994–2004; Old Sessions House Charitable Trust, 2004–; Pres., British Sch. of Osteopathy Appeal Fund, 1980–84. President: City of London Rifle League, 1980–2004; Gtr London Horse Show, 1982–85; Gtr London (County Hall), subseq. GLA City Hall, Br., Royal British Legion, 1988–2006. An active Freemason, 1973–. FCIS (Mem. Council, 1981–97, Treas., 1984, Vice-Pres. 1985, Pres., 1986); MCMI. Hon. FIIT. Hon. PhD Columbia Pacific, 1982. Order of Gorkha Dakshina Bahu (2nd cl.), Nepal, 1981. *Publications:* Europe—Power and Responsibility: Direct Elections to the European Parliament (with David Baker), 1972; numerous contribs to learned jls and periodicals on linguistics and translation, the use of language, political science and contemporary politics. *Recreations:* conversation, opera, classical music and being difficult. *Address:* 28 Elizabeth Road, Henley-on-Thames, Oxfordshire RG9 1RG. *T:* (01491) 412080; *e-mail:* bernard@brook-partridge.freeserve.co.uk. *Clubs:* Athenæum; Leander (Henley).

BROOK SMITH, Philip Andrew; QC 2002; a Recorder, since 2006; *b* 6 March 1957; *s* of Alan and Beryl Smith; adopted surname Brook Smith, 1981; *m* 1981, Charlotte Brook; two *s* one *d*. *Educ:* London Sch. of Econs (BSc 1st Cl. Hons Maths; MSc Maths Dist.). Called to the Bar, Middle Temple, 1982; in practice at the Bar, specialising in commercial law, 1983–. *Address:* (chambers) Fountain Court, Temple, EC4Y 9DH. *T:* (020) 7583 3335, *Fax:* (020) 7353 0329; *e-mail:* pbs@fountaincourt.co.uk.

BROOKE, family name of **Viscounts Alanbrooke and Brookeborough and Baron Brooke of Sutton Mandeville**.

BROOKE, Lord; Charles Fulke Chester Greville; *b* 27 July 1982; *s* and *heir* of Earl of Warwick, *qv*. *Educ:* Eton.

BROOKE OF ALVERTHORPE, Baron *cr* 1997 (Life Peer), of Alverthorpe in the co. of West Yorkshire; **Clive Brooke;** Joint General Secretary, Public Services Tax and Commerce Union, 1996–98; *b* 21 June 1942; *s* of Mary Brooke (*née* Colbeck) and John Brooke; *m* 1967, Lorna Hopkin Roberts. *Educ:* Thornes House School, Wakefield. Asst Sec., 1964–82, Dep. Gen. Sec., 1982–88, Gen. Sec., 1988–95, Inland Revenue Staff Fedn. Trade Union Congress: Member: Gen. Council, 1989–96; Exec. Cttee, 1993–96. Govt Partnership Dir, NATS Ltd, 2001–06; Adviser: Accenture, 1997–; Liverpool Victoria Friendly Soc., 2002–. Member: Council of Civil Service Unions, 1982–97 (Chm., Major Policy Cttee, 1996–97); H of C Speaker's Commn on Citizenship, 1988; Exec. Cttee, Involvement and Participation Assoc., 1991–97; Council, Inst. for Manpower Studies, 1994–2001; Pensions Compensation Bd, 1996–2006. Member: H of L EU Select Cttee, 1999–2002, and Chm., Sub-Cttee B (Energy, Industry and Transport), 1998–2002; Jt Cttee on H of L Reform, 2002–03; H of L EU Select Cttee D (Agriculture, Environment and Fisheries), 2007–; H of L Select Cttee on Crossrail Bill, 2008. Mem., Labour Party. Mem., Churches Enquiry on Employment and Future of Work, 1995–96. Trustee: Duke of Edinburgh Study Conf., 1993– (Mem., Canada Conf., 1980); Community Services Volunteers, 1989–; IPPR, 1997–; Action on Addiction, 2002–. Jt Patron, Neighbourhood Initiatives Foundn, 1999–2007; Patron: European Assoc. for the Treatment of Addiction (UK), 2001–; Fedn of Drug and Alcohol Professionals, 2002–; Kenward Trust, 2006–. *Recreations:* painting, reading, watching soccer and Rugby League, walking my cairn terriers. *Address:* House of Lords, SW1A 0PW. *T:* (020) 7219 0478.

BROOKE OF SUTTON MANDEVILLE, Baron *cr* 2001 (Life Peer), of Sutton Mandeville in the County of Wiltshire; **Peter Leonard Brooke,** CH 1992; PC 1988; *b* 3 March 1934; *s* of Lord Brooke of Cumnor, PC, CH and Lady Brooke of Ystradfellte, DBE; *m* 1st, 1964, Joan Margaret Smith (*d* 1985); three *s* (and one *s* decd); 2nd, 1991, Lindsay Allinson. *Educ:* Marlborough; Balliol College, Oxford (MA); Harvard Business School (MBA). Vice-Pres., Nat. Union of Students, 1955–56; Chm., Nat. Conf., Student Christian Movement, 1956; Pres., Oxford Union, 1957; Commonwealth Fund Fellow, 1957–59. Research Assistant, IMEDE, Lausanne, 1960–61; Spencer Stuart & Associates, Management Consultants, 1961–79 (Director of parent company, 1965–79, Chairman 1974–79); worked in NY and Brussels, 1969–73. Dir, Hambros plc, 1997–98. Mem., Camden Borough Council, 1968–69. Chm., St Pancras N Cons. Assoc., 1976–77. Contested (C) Bedwellty, Oct. 1974; MP (C) City of London and Westminster South, Feb. 1977–1997, Cities of London and Westminster, 1997–2001. An Asst Govt Whip, 1979–81; a Lord Comr of HM Treasury, 1981–83; Parly Under Sec. of State, DES, 1983–85; Minister of State, HM Treasury, 1985–87; Paymaster Gen., HM Treasury, 1987–89; Chm., Conservative Party, 1987–89; Secretary of State: for NI, 1989–92; for Nat. Heritage, 1992–94. Chm., H of C Select Cttee on NI, 1997–2001. Mem., British Irish Parly Body, 1997–2007. Chm., Assoc. of Cons. Peers, 2004–06. Chm., Building Socs Ombudsman Council, 1996–2001. President: British Antique Dealers Assoc., 1995–2005; British Art Market Fedn, 1996–; IAPS, 1980–83; Mem. Council, Marlborough Coll., 1977–83, 1992–95; Lay Mem., Univ. of London Council, 1994–2006 (Dep. Chm., 2001–02; Chm. and Pro-Chancellor, 2002–06). Chm., Churches Conservation Trust,

1995–98. Trustee: Wordsworth Trust, 1974–2001; Cusichaca Project, 1978–98; Conf. on Trng in Archtl Conservation, 1994–97. Pres., St Andrew's Youth Club, 1998–2006. FSA 1998. Sen. Fellow, RCA, 1987; Presentation Fellow, KCL, 1989; Hon. Fellow: QMW, 1996; Univ. of Wales, Lampeter, 2008. Hon. DLitt: Westminster, 1999; London Guildhall, 2001; Hon. LLD London, 2006. *Recreations:* churches, conservation, cricket, visual arts. *Address:* c/o House of Lords, SW1A 0PW. *Clubs:* Beefsteak, Brooks's, Grillions, MCC, I Zingari.

See also Rt Hon. Sir H. Brooke.

BROOKE, Sir Alistair Weston, 4th Bt *cr* 1919, of Almondbury; *b* 12 Sept. 1947; *s* of Major Sir John Weston Brooke, 3rd Bt, TD, and Rosemary (*d* 1979), *d* of late Percy Nevill, Birling House, West Malling, Kent; *S* father, 1983, but his name does not appear on the Official Roll of the Baronetage; *m* 1982, Susan Mary, *d* of Barry Charles Roger Griffiths, MRCVS, Church House, Norton, Powys; one *d. Educ:* Repton; Royal Agricultural Coll., Cirencester. *Recreations:* shooting, farming, racehorse training. *Heir: b* Charles Weston Brooke [*b* 27 Jan. 1951; *m* 1984, Tanya Elizabeth, *d* of Antony Thelwell Maurice; one *s* two *d*].

BROOKE, Annette Lesley; MP (Lib Dem) Dorset Mid and Poole North, since 2001; *b* 7 June 1947; *m* Mike Brooke; two *d. Educ:* Romford Tech. Sch.; LSE (BSc Econ); Hughes Hall, Cambridge (Cert Ed). Teacher of econs and social scis in schs and colls in Reading, Aylesbury and Poole; Hd of Econs, Talbot Heath Sch., Bournemouth, 1984–94; Tutor, Open Univ., 1971–91. Partner, Broadstone Minerals. Poole Borough Council: Mem. (Lib Dem), 1986–2003; Chairman: Planning Cttee, 1991–96; Educn Cttee, 1996–2000; Dep. Gp Leader, 1995–97, 1998–2000; Mayor, 1997–98. Lib Dem spokesman on children, 2004–. *Address:* (office) 14 York Road, Broadstone, Dorset BH18 8ET; c/o House of Commons, SW1A 0AA.

BROOKE, Prof. Christopher Nugent Lawrence, CBE 1995; MA; LittD; FSA; FRHistS; FBA 1970; Dixie Professor of Ecclesiastical History, University of Cambridge, 1977–94, now Dixie Professor Emeritus; Fellow, Gonville and Caius College, Cambridge, 1949–56 and since 1977 (Life Fellow, 1994); *b* 23 June 1927; *y s* of late Professor Zachary Nugent Brooke and Rosa Grace Brooke; *m* 1951, Rosalind Beckford, *d* of Dr and Mrs L. H. S. Clark; two *s* (and one *s* decd). *Educ:* Winchester College (Scholar); Gonville and Caius College, Cambridge (Major Scholar). BA 1948; MA 1952; LittD 1973. Army service in RAEC, Temp. Captain 1949. Cambridge University: College Lecturer in History, 1953–56; Praelector Rhetoricus, 1955–56; Asst Lectr in History, 1953–54; Lectr, 1954–56; Prof. of Mediæval History, University of Liverpool, 1956–67; Prof. of History, Westfield Coll., Univ. of London, 1967–77. Member: Royal Commn on Historical Monuments (England), 1977–83; Reviewing Cttee on Export of Works of Art, 1979–82. Vice-Pres., Soc. of Antiquaries, 1975–79, Pres., 1981–84. Corresp. Fellow, Medieval Acad. of America, 1981; Corresponding Member: Monumenta Germaniae Historica, 1988; Bavarian Acad. of Scis, 1997. DUniv York, 1984. Lord Mayor's Midsummer Prize, City of London, 1981. *Publications:* The Dullness of the Past, 1957; From Alfred to Henry III, 1961; The Saxon and Norman Kings, 1963, 3rd edn 2001; Europe in the Central Middle Ages, 1964, 3rd edn 2000; Time the Archsatirist, 1968; The Twelfth Century Renaissance, 1970; Structure of Medieval Society, 1971; Medieval Church and Society (sel. papers), 1971; (with W. Swaan) The Monastic World, 1974, new edn as The Age of the Cloister, 2004, as The Rise and Fall of the Medieval Monastery, 2006; (with G. Keir) London, 800–1216, 1975; Marriage in Christian History, 1977; (with R. B. Brooke) Popular Religion in the Middle Ages, 1000–1300, 1984; A History of Gonville and Caius College, 1985; The Church and the Welsh Border, 1986; (with J. R. L. Highfield and W. Swaan) Oxford and Cambridge, 1988; The Medieval Idea of Marriage, 1989; (jtly) David Knowles Remembered, 1991; A History of the University of Cambridge, vol. IV, 1870–1990, 1993, (jtly) vol. II, 1546–1750, 2004; Jane Austen: illusion and reality, 1999; (with R. B. Brooke) Churches and Churchmen in Medieval Europe (selected papers), 1999; (jtly) A History of Emmanuel College, Cambridge, 1999; part Editor: The Book of William Morton, 1954; The Letters of John of Salisbury, vol. I, 1955, vol. II, 1979; Carte Nativorum, 1960; (with A. Morey) Gilbert Foliot and his letters, 1965 and (ed jtly) The Letters and Charters of Gilbert Foliot, 1967; (with D. Knowles and V. London) Heads of Religious Houses, England and Wales 940–1216, 1972, 2nd edn 2001; (with D. Whitelock and M. Brett) Councils and Synods, vol. I, 1981; (with Sir Roger Mynors) Walter Map, De Nugis Curialium (revision of M. R. James edn), 1983; (with M. Brett and M. Winterbottom) Hugh the Chanter, History of the Church of York (revision of C. Johnson edn), 1990; (with D. Knowles) The Monastic Constitutions of Lanfranc, 2002; (jtly) English Episcopal Acta 33, Worcester 1062–1185; contributed to: A History of St Paul's Cathedral, 1957; A History of York Minster, 1977; general editor: Oxford (formerly Nelson's) Medieval Texts, 1959–87; A History of the University of Cambridge, 4 vols 1988–2004; Nelson's History of England, etc.; articles and reviews in English Historical Review, Cambridge Historical Journal, Studies in Church History, Bulletin of Inst. of Historical Research, Downside Review, Traditio, Bulletin of John Rylands Library, Jl of Soc. of Archivists, etc. *Address:* Gonville and Caius College, Cambridge CB2 1TA.

BROOKE, (Christopher) Roger (Ettrick), OBE 2005; Chairman, Innisfree Group Ltd, 1995–2006; *b* 2 Feb. 1931; *s* of late Ralph Brooke and Marjorie (*née* Lee); *m* 1958, Nancy Belle Lowenthal; three *s* one *d. Educ:* Tonbridge; Trinity Coll., Oxford (MA). Served HM Diplomatic Service: Bonn, 1955–57; Southern Dept, FO, 1958–60; Washington, 1960–63; Tel Aviv, 1963–66. Dep. Man. Dir, IRC, 1966–69; Man. Dir, Scienta SA, 1969–71; Dir, Pearson Gp, 1971–79; Gp Man. Dir, EMI, 1979–80; Chief Exec., 1980–90, and Chm., 1991–99, Candover Investments plc. Chm., Audit Commn, 1995–98. Director: Slough Estates plc, 1980–2001; Lambert Fenchurch Gp (formerly Lowndes Lambert Gp Holdings) PLC, 1991–99; Tarmac plc, 1994–99; Wembley PLC, 1995–99; Ethos Private Equity (South Africa), 1998–2007; Beeson Gregory Gp, 2000–02; IP Gp (formerly IP2IPO) plc, 2001–; RL Automotive, 2007–, and various other cos; Dep. Chm., Carillion plc, 1999–2001; Chairman: Accord plc, 1999–2005; Foresight 4VCT, 2004–. Mem., Southampton Univ. Develt Trust, 2006–. *Publication:* Santa's Christmas Journey, 1985. *Recreations:* golf, tennis, theatre, reading, travel. *Address:* Water Meadow, Swarraton, near Alresford, Hants SO24 9TQ. *T:* (01962) 732259. *Club:* East India.

BROOKE, Sir Francis (George Windham), 4th Bt *cr* 1903; Director, Troy Asset Management Ltd, since 2004; *b* 15 Oct. 1963; *s* of Sir George Cecil Francis Brooke, 3rd Bt, MBE, and of Lady Melissa Brooke, *er d* of 6th Earl of Dunraven and Mount-Earl, CB, CBE, MC; *S* father, 1982; *m* 1989, Hon. Katharine Elizabeth, *o d* of Baron Hussey of North Bradley and of Lady Susan Hussey, *qv*; one *s* two *d. Educ:* Eton; Edinburgh University (MA Hons). AIIMR 1993. Director: Foreign & Colonial Mgt Ltd, 1994–97; UK Equities, Merrill Lynch Investment Managers, 1997–2004. *Heir: s* George Francis Geoffrey Brooke, *b* 10 Sept. 1991. *Address:* 65 Sterndale Road, W14 0HU; Glenbevan, Croom, Co. Limerick, Ireland. *Clubs:* Turf, White's; Royal St George's (Sandwich).

BROOKE, Prof. George John, PhD; Rylands Professor of Biblical Criticism and Exegesis, University of Manchester, since 1998; *b* 27 April 1952; *s* of Comdr Henry John Allen Brooke, MBE, DSC, and Lesley Mary Brooke (*née* Noble); *m* 1976, (Rosemary)

Jane Peacocke; two *s* one *d. Educ:* Wellington Coll.; St Peter's Coll., Oxford (BA 1973); St John's Coll., Cambridge (PGCE 1974); Claremont Graduate Sch., Claremont, Calif (PhD 1978). Fulbright Scholar, 1974–77; Jun. Fellow, Oxford Univ. Centre for Postgrad. Hebrew Studies, 1977–78; Lectr in New Testament Studies, 1978–84, Vice-Principal, 1982–84, Salisbury and Wells Theol Coll.; University of Manchester: Lectr in Intertestamental Lit., 1984–94, Sen. Lectr, 1994–97; Prof. of Biblical Studies, 1997–98. Res. Scholar, Ecumenical Inst., Tantur, 1983; Sen. Res. Fellow, Annenberg Inst., Philadelphia, 1992; Guest Prof., Univ. of Aarhus, 2007. Pres., British Assoc. of Jewish Studies, 1999. Founding Editor, Dead Sea Discoveries, 1994–; Editor, SOTS Book List, 2000–06. *Publications:* Exegesis at Qumran: 4QFlorilegium in its Jewish context, 1985; The Allegro Qumran Collection, 1996; (jtly) The Complete World of the Dead Sea Scrolls, 2002; Qumran and the Jewish Jesus, 2005; The Dead Sea Scrolls and the New Testament: essays in mutual illumination, 2005. *Recreations:* cooking, hill walking. *Address:* Department of Religions and Theology, Samuel Alexander Building, University of Manchester, Oxford Road, Manchester M13 9PL. *T:* (0161) 275 3609, *Fax:* (0161) 306 1241; *e-mail:* george.brooke@manchester.ac.uk.

BROOKE, Rt Hon. Sir Henry, Kt 1988; PC 1996; a Lord Justice of Appeal, 1996–2006; Vice-President, Court of Appeal (Civil Division), 2003–06; *b* 19 July 1936; *s* of Lord Brooke of Cumnor, PC, CH and Lady Brooke of Ystradfellte, DBE; *m* 1966, Bridget Mary Kalaugher; three *s* one *d. Educ:* Marlborough College; Balliol Coll., Oxford. MA (1st Cl. Classical Hon. Mods, 1st Cl. Lit. Hum.). Called to the Bar, Inner Temple, 1963, Bencher, 1987; Junior Counsel to the Crown, Common Law, 1978–81; QC 1981; a Recorder, 1983–88; a Judge of the High Court, QBD, 1988–96; Judge i/c modernisation, 2001–04. Chm., Law Commn, 1993–95; Counsel to the Inquiry, Sizewell 'B' Nuclear Reactor Inquiry, 1983–85; DTI Inspector, House of Fraser Hldgs plc, 1987–88. Mem., Bar Council, 1987–88 (Chairman: Professional Standards Cttee, 1987–88; Race Relations Cttee, 1989–91); Chairman: Computer Cttee, Senate of the Inns of Court and the Bar, 1985–86; London Common Law and Commercial Bar Assoc., 1988 (Vice-Chm., 1986–87); Ethnic Minority Adv. Cttee, Judicial Studies Bd, 1991–94; Council, Centre for Crime and Justice Studies (formerly Inst. for Study and Treatment of Delinquency), 1997–2001; Civil Mediation Council, 2007–; Exec. Vice-Pres., Commonwealth Magistrates' and Judges' Assoc., 2006–. Member: Information Technology and the Courts Cttee, 1986–87, 1990–96; Judicial Studies Bd, 1992–94; Courts and Tribunals Modernisation Prog. Bd, 2001–04. Pres., Soc. for Computers and Law, 1992–2001. Chm. Trustees, British and Irish Legal Inf. Inst., 2001–. Fellow, Wordsworth Trust, 2002– (Trustee, 1995–2001). *Publications:* Institute Cargo Clauses (Air), 1986; (contrib.) Halsbury's Laws of England, 4th edn, and to legal jls. *Address:* Royal Courts of Justice, Strand, WC2A 2LL. *Club:* Brooks's.
See also Baron Brooke of Sutton Mandeville.

BROOKE, Ian Richard, CB 2002; various posts with Ministry of Defence, 1971–2003; *b* 14 Aug. 1946; *s* of Richard Leslie Frederick Brooke and Betty Margaret (*née* Holliday); *m* 1970, Rachel Grace Wade; two *s. Educ:* St Clement Danes Grammar Sch.; Southampton Univ. (BSc(Eng)). FCO, 1967–71. Mem., St Albans Diocesan Synod, 2000–03; Churchwarden, 2003–07. *Recreations:* genealogy, walking, visiting cathedrals.

BROOKE, Prof. John Hedley, PhD; Andreas Idreos Professor of Science and Religion, and Director, Ian Ramsey Centre, Oxford University, 1999–2006; Fellow of Harris Manchester College, Oxford, 1999–2006, now Fellow Emeritus; *b* 20 May 1944; *s* of Hedley Joseph Brooke and Margaret Brooke (*née* Brown); *m* 1972, Janice Marian Heffer. *Educ:* Fitzwilliam Coll., Cambridge (MA; PhD 1969). Res. Fellow, Fitzwilliam Coll., Cambridge, 1967–68; Tutorial Fellow, Univ. of Sussex, 1968–69; Lancaster University: Lectr, 1969–80; Sen. Lectr, 1980–91; Reader in History of Science, 1991–92; Prof. of History of Science, 1992–99. Co-ordinator, ESF Network on Sci. and Human Values, 2000–04; Co-Dir, Templeton Project on Sci. and Religion in Schs, 2002–06. (Jtly) Gifford Lectr, Glasgow Univ., 1995–96; Alister Hardy Meml Lectr, Oxford Univ., 2000; Dist. Lectr, Amer. Hist. of Sci. Soc., 2001; Select Preacher, Oxford Univ., 2001. Foundn Fellow, Inst. for Advanced Studies, Durham Univ., 2007. President: Historical Section, BAAS, 1996–97; British Soc. for History of Science, 1996–98; Science and Religion Forum, 2006–; Foundn Mem. and Mem. Exec. Cttee, Internat. Soc. for Sci. and Religion, 2002–; Corresp. Mem., Internat. Acad. of History of Science, 1993. Ed., British Jl for the History of Science, 1989–93. *Publications:* Science and Religion: some historical perspectives, 1991; Thinking about Matter: studies in the history of chemical philosophy, 1995; (jtly) Reconstructing Nature: the engagement of science and religion, 1998; (ed jtly) Science in Theistic Contexts, 2001; (ed jtly) Heterodoxy in Early Modern Science and Religion, 2005; (ed jtly) Religious Values and the Rise of Science in Europe, 2005; many articles on history of chemistry and history of natural theology. *Recreations:* music (opera), foreign travel, chess, walking, rhododendrons. *Address:* Harris Manchester College, Oxford OX1 3TD. *T:* (01865) 271006.

BROOKE, John Stephen P.; see Pitt-Brooke.

BROOKE, Michael Eccles Macklin; QC 1994; **His Honour Judge Brooke;** a Circuit Judge, since 2004; *b* 8 May 1942; *s* of late Reginald Eccles Joseph Brooke and Beryl Cicely Brooke (*née* Riggs); *m* 1st, 1972, Annie Sophie (marr. diss. 1985), *d* of André Vautier; three *s;* 2nd, 1996, Mireille, *d* of late Colin Colahan; two step *d. Educ:* Froebel Sch., Datchet; Lycée Français de Londres; Edinburgh Univ. (LLB). Called to the Bar, Gray's Inn, 1968 (Bencher, 2002); in practice, 1968–2004; a Recorder, 2000–04; Avocat, Cour d'appel, Paris, 1987–2004. *Recreations:* boating, travelling, comparing England and France. *Clubs:* Bar Yacht, Travellers.

BROOKE, Sir Richard (David Christopher), 11th Bt *cr* 1662, of Norton Priory, Cheshire; *b* 23 Oct. 1938; *s* of Sir Richard (Neville) Brooke, 10th Bt and Lady Mabel Kathleen Brooke (*d* 1985), *d* of 8th Earl of Roden; *S* father, 1997; *m* 1st, 1963, Carola Marion (marr. diss. 1978), *e d* of Sir Robert Erskine-Hill, 2nd Bt; two *s;* 2nd, 1979, Lucinda, *d* of John Frederick Voelcker. *Educ:* Eton College. MSI. Lt, Scots Guards, 1957–58. Partner, Rowe & Pitman, 1968–86; Dir, S. G. Warburg Gp and Dep. Chm., S. G. Warburg Securities, 1986–90; Pres. and Chm., S. G. Warburg (USA) Inc., 1988–90; Chm., J. O. Hambro & Partners, 1990–97. Director: Potter Partners, 1987–90; Govett Atlantic Investment Trust plc, 1990–92; Contracyclical Investment Trust, 1990–96; J. O. Hambro & Co., 1990–97; Exeter Preferred Capital Investment Trust plc, 1991–2000; Gartmore American Securities plc, 1991–95; Govett American Smaller Companies Investment Trust plc, 1992–98; HCG Lloyd's Investment Trust plc, 1994–96; Templeton Emerging Markets Investment Trust plc, 1994–2003; Templeton Latin America Investment Trust plc, 1994–2001; Templeton Central and Eastern European Investment Trust plc, 1995–98; Avocet Mining plc, 1995–; Fidelity Special Values plc, 1995–; Exeter Selective Assets Investment Trust, 1996–2001; Chairman: Armstrong International Ltd, 1990–2001; N Atlantic Smaller Cos Investment Trust plc, 1993–98; Govett Global Smaller Cos Investment Trust plc, 1994–97; Tai Chi Fund Ltd, 2006–; Johim IDF LLC, 2006–. Member: Internat. Capital Mkts Adv. Bd, NY Stock Exchange, 1987–89; Cttee, Soc. of Merchants Trading into Europe, 1988–2005; National Association of Securities

Dealers Inc.: Chm., Internat. Markets Adv. Bd, 1991–95; Vice Chm. Bd of Governors, 1994–95. *Recreations:* travel, antiques and fine art, wines, boating. *Heir: er s* Richard Christopher Brooke [*b* 10 July 1966; *m* 1st, 1995, Sophie Scott (marr. diss. 1997); one *d*; 2nd, 2002, Sarah Montague; three *d*]. *Address:* Château Rouzaud, St Victor-Rouzaud, 09100 Pamiers, France. *Clubs:* Boodle's, Pratt's; Tarporley Hunt (Cheshire).

BROOKE, Sir Rodney (George), Kt 2007; CBE 1996; DL; Chairman, General Social Care Council, since 2002; *b* 22 Oct. 1939; *s* of George Sidney Brooke and Amy Brooke; *m* 1967, Dr Clare Margaret Cox; one *s* one *d*. *Educ:* Queen Elizabeth's Grammar Sch., Wakefield. Admitted solicitor (hons), 1962. Rochdale County Bor. Council, 1962–63; Leicester CC, 1963–65; Stockport County Bor. Council, 1965–73; West Yorkshire Metropolitan County Council: Dir of Admin, 1973–81; Chief Exec. and Clerk, 1981–84; Clerk to W Yorks Lieutenancy, 1981–84; Chief Exec., Westminster City Council, 1984–89; Clerk to Gtr London Lieutenancy, 1987–89; Sec., AMA, 1990–97. Chm., Bradford HA, 1989–90; Director: Riverside Health Trust, 2000–02; Westminster PCT, 2002–06. Secretary: Yorks and Humberside Tourist Board, 1974–84; Yorks and Humberside Develt Assoc., 1974–84; Hon. Sec., London Boroughs Assoc., 1984–90; Dir, Foundn for IT in Local Govt, 1988–92; Chairman: Electricity Consumers' Cttee (Yorks), 1997–2000; National Electricity Consumers Council, 1999–2000. Associate: Local Govt Mgt Bd, 1997–2000; Politics Internat., 1998–2000. Member: Action London, 1988–90; Exec., SOLACE, 1981–84, 1987–89; CS Final Selection Bd, 1991–2000; Ethics Standards Bd for Accountants, 2001–03; Nat. Inf. Governance Bd for Health Records, 2007–. Chm., Durham Univ. Centre for Public Management Res., 1994–97; Vis. Res. Fellow, RIPA, 1989–92; Vis. Fellow, Nuffield Inst. for Health Studies, Leeds Univ., 1989–96; Sen. Vis. Res. Fellow, Sch. of Public Policy, Birmingham Univ., 1997–. Dir, Dolphin Square Trust, 1987– (Chm., 2002–); Chm., London NE, Royal Jubilee and Prince's Trusts, 1984–91. Trustee: Community Develt Foundn, 1996–2000; Dolphin Square Charitable Foundn, 2005–; Internet Watch Foundn, 2007–. Associate, Ernst & Young, 1989–90. Editl Advr, Longman Gp, 1989–90. Mem. Council, Tavistock Inst., 2006–. Gov., Pimlico Sch., 2000–07 (Chm., 2003–05). Hon. Fellow, Inst. of Govt Studies, Birmingham Univ. FRSA. Freeman, City of London, 1993. DL Greater London, 1989. National Order of Merit (France), 1984; Nat. Order of Aztec Eagle (Mexico), 1985; Medal of Merit (Qatar), 1985; Order of Merit (Germany), 1986; Legion of Merit (Senegal), 1988. *Publications:* Managing the Enabling Authority, 1989; The Environmental Role of Local Government, 1990; (jtly) City Futures in Britain and Canada, 1990; (jtly) The Public Service Manager's Handbook, 1992; (jtly) Strengthening Local Government in the 1990s, 1997; (jtly) Ethics in Public Service for the New Millennium, 2000; The Consumers-Eye View of Utilities, 2000; The Councillor: victim or vulgarian, 2005; articles on local govt and social care. *Recreations:* ski-ing, opera, Byzantium. *Address:* Stubham Lodge, Clifford Road, Middleton, Ilkley, West Yorks LS29 0AX. *T:* (01943) 601869; 706 Grenville House, Dolphin Square, SW1V 3LR. *T:* (020) 7798 8086. *Clubs:* Athenæum, Ski Club of Great Britain.

BROOKE, Roger; *see* Brooke, C. R. E.

BROOKE, Sarah Anne Louise; *see* Montague, S. A. L.

BROOKE-ROSE, Prof. Christine; novelist and critic; Professor of English Language and Literature, University of Paris, 1975–88 (Lecturer, 1968–75); *b* 16 Jan. 1923. *Educ:* Somerville Coll., Oxford (MA 1953; Hon. Fellow, 1997); PhD London 1954. WAAF Intelligence Officer, Bletchley Park Decoding Centre, 1942–45. Research and criticism, 1955–. Reviewer for: The Times Literary Supplement, The Times, The Observer, The Sunday Times, The Listener, The Spectator, and The London Magazine, 1956–68; at Univ. of Paris VIII, Vincennes, 1968–88. Has broadcast in book programmes on BBC, and on 'The Critics', and ABC Television. Hon. LittD East Anglia, 1988. Travelling Prize of Society of Authors, 1964; James Tait Black Memorial Prize, 1966; Arts Council Translation Prize, 1969. *Publications: novels:* The Languages of Love, 1957; The Sycamore Tree, 1958; The Dear Deceit, 1960; The Middlemen, 1961; Out, 1964; Such, 1965; Between, 1968; Thru, 1975; Amalgamemnon, 1984; Xorandor, 1986; Verbivore, 1990; Textermination, 1991; Remake, 1996; Next, 1998; Subscript, 1999; Life, End of, 2006; *criticism:* A Grammar of Metaphor, 1958; A ZBC of Ezra Pound, 1971; A Rhetoric of the Unreal, 1981; Stories, Theories and Things, 1991; Invisible Author, last essays, 2002; *short stories:* Go when you see the Green Man Walking, 1969; short stories and essays in various magazines, etc. *Recreations:* people, books. *Address:* c/o Cambridge University Press, PO Box 110, Cambridge CB2 3RL.

BROOKE TURNER, Alan, CMG 1980; HM Diplomatic Service, retired; Director, British Association for Central and Eastern Europe (formerly Great Britain/East Europe Centre), 1987–95; *b* 4 Jan. 1926; *s* of late Arthur Brooke Turner, MC; *m* 1954, Hazel Alexandra Rowan Henderson; two *s* two *d*. *Educ:* Marlborough; Balliol Coll., Oxford (Sen. Schol.). 1st cl Hon. Mods 1949; 1st cl. Lit. Hum. 1951. Served in RAF, 1944–48. Entered HM Foreign (subseq. Diplomatic) Service, 1951; FO, 1951; Warsaw, 1953; 3rd, later 2nd Sec. (Commercial), Jedda, 1954; Lisbon, 1957; 1st Sec., FO, 1959 (UK Delegn to Nuclear Tests Conf., Geneva, 1962); Cultural Attaché, Moscow, 1962; FO, 1965; Fellow, Center for Internat. Affairs, Harvard Univ., 1968; Counsellor, Rio de Janeiro, 1969–71; Head of Southern European Dept, FCO, 1972–73; Counsellor and Head of Chancery, British Embassy, Rome, 1973–76; Civil Dep. Comdt and Dir of Studies, NATO Defense Coll., Rome, 1976–78; Internat. Inst. for Strategic Studies, 1978–79; Minister, Moscow, 1979–82; Ambassador to Finland, 1983–85. Member: Council, Anglican Centre, Rome, 1976–77; Anglican Synod Wkg Gp on Peacemaking, 1986–88; Southwark Diocesan Synod, 2000–06. Mem. Council, SSEES, 1987–95 (Chm., 1989–92). *Recreations:* music, reading. *Address:* Poultons, Moor Lane, Dormansland, Lingfield, Surrey RH7 6NX; *e-mail:* alan.brooketurner@btopenworld.com. *Club:* Travellers.

BROOKEBOROUGH, 3rd Viscount *cr* 1952, of Colebrooke; **Alan Henry Brooke,** Bt 1822; DL; farmer; a Personal Lord in Waiting to the Queen, since 1997; *b* 30 June 1952; *s* of 2nd Viscount Brookeborough, PC and Rosemary Hilda (*née* Chichester); *S* father, 1987; *m* 1980, Janet Elizabeth, *d* of J. P. Cooke, Doagh, Ballyclare. *Educ:* Harrow; Millfield. Commissioned 17th/21st Lancers, 1971; transferred 4th (County Fermanagh) Bn, UDR, 1977; Company Commander, 1981–83; Royal Irish Regt (Co. Comdr, 1988–93); Lt-Col, 1993, transf. to RARO. Now farms and runs an estate with a shooting/fishing tourist enterprise. Member: EEC Agricl Sub-Cttee, House of Lords, 1988–92, 1993–97; EC Select Cttee and Sub-Cttee B (energy, industry and transport), H of L, 1998–; elected Mem., H of L, 1999. Non-exec. Director: Green Park Unit Hosp. Trust, 1993–2001; Basel International (Jersey), 2000– (Chm., 1996–2000). Mem., NI Policing Bd, 2001–. Hon. Col, 4th/5th Bn, Royal Irish Rangers, 1997–. DL 1987, High Sheriff 1995, Co. Fermanagh. *Recreations:* shooting, fishing. *Heir: b* Hon. Christopher Arthur Brooke [*b* 16 May 1954; *m* 1990, Amanda Hodges; four *s*]. *Address:* Colebrooke Park, Brookeborough, Co. Fermanagh, N Ireland BT94 4DW. *T:* (01365) 531402. *Club:* Cavalry and Guards.

BROOKER, Alan Bernard; JP, DL; FCA; Chairman: Kode International, 1988–98; E. T. Heron & Co., 1991–96; *b* 24 Aug. 1931; *s* of late Bernard John Brooker and of Gwendoline Ada (*née* Launchbury); *m* 1957, Diana (*née* Coles); one *s* two *d*. *Educ:* Chigwell School, Essex. FCA 1954. Served 2nd RHA (2nd Lieut), 1954–56. Articled, Cole, Dickin & Hills, Chartered Accountants, 1949–54, qualified 1954; Manager, Cole, Dickin & Hills, 1956–58; Accountant, Independent Dairies, 1958–59; Asst Accountant, Exchange Telegraph Co., 1959–64; Dir, 1964–87, Chm. and Chief Exec., 1980–87, Extel Group. Chm., Serif Cowells, then Serif, 1990–93; Vice-Chairman: Provident Financial, 1983–94; James Martin Associates, 1987–89; non-executive Director: Pauls plc, 1984–85; Aukett Associates, 1988–2002; Plysu, 1988–99; PNA Holdings, 1988–89; Addison Worldwide, 1990–94; Eastern Counties Newspapers (formerly East Anglian Daily Times), 1990–96; ACAL plc, 1996–2002. Member: Council, CBI London Region, 1980–83; Companies Cttee, CBI, 1979–83; Council, CPU, 1975–88. Appeal Chm., Newspaper Press Fund, 1985–86. Governor: Chigwell School, 1968–2006 (Chm., 1978–99); Felixstowe Coll., 1986–94. Essex Pres., RBL, 2002–05. Freeman, City of London; Liveryman, Stationers and Newspapermakers' Co. (Court Asst, 1985–2007; Master, 1995–96). Churchwarden, St Bride's, Fleet Street, 1986–2002. JP Essex 1972 (Chm. of Bench, Epping and Ongar, 1995–99); DL Essex 1982. FRSA 1980. *Recreations:* cricket, golf. *Address:* Silkwater, East Hill, Evershot, Dorset DT2 0LB. *Clubs:* East India, MCC; Royal Worlington and Newmarket Golf.

BROOKER, Mervyn Edward William; Headmaster, Bolton School Boys' Division, since 2003; *b* 24 March 1954; *s* of Derek and Hazel Brooker; *m* 1976, Brigid Mary O'Rorke; two *d*. *Educ:* Lancaster Royal Grammar Sch.; Burnley Grammar Sch.; Jesus Coll., Cambridge (BA Hons Geography 1975; PGCE 1976; cricket blue, 1976). Teacher (Geography and Games): County High Sch., Saffron Walden, 1976–80; Royal Grammar Sch., Worcester, 1980–88; Highfields Sch., Wolverhampton, 1988–91; King Edward VI Camp Hill Sch. for Boys: Teacher, 1992–2002; Dep. Headmaster, 1992–95; Headmaster, 1995–2002; Played cricket for: Combined Univs CC, 1976; Cambs CCC, 1976–80 (county cap, 1978); Staffs CCC, 1982–86; Birmingham Cricket League XI, 1984; Midlands Clubs Cricket Conf., 1986–90; Hereford and Worcester Cricket Assoc., 1981–86; Staffs Club Cricket League XI, 1994. *Recreations:* cricket, sport in general, hill walking, foreign travel. *Address:* Bolton School Boys' Division, Chorley New Road, Bolton BL1 4PA. *Clubs:* Edgworth Cricket (Bolton); Tything Tramps (Worcester).

BROOKES, Beata Ann, CBE 1996; *b* 21 Jan. 1931. *Educ:* Lowther College, Abergele; Univ. of Wales, Bangor; studied politics in USA (US State Dept Scholarship). Former social worker, Denbighshire CC; company secretary and farmer. Contested (C) Widnes, 1955, Warrington, 1963, Manchester Exchange, 1964. Contested (C) N Wales, European Parly Elecn, 1989. MEP (C) N Wales, 1979–89; Mem., Educn and Agricl Cttees. Member: Clwyd AHA, 1973–80 (Mem., Welsh Hosp. Bd, 1963–74); Clwyd Family Practitioner Cttee; Clwyd CC Social Services Cttee, 1973–81; Flintshire Soc. for Mentally Handicapped; N Wales Council for Mentally Handicapped; Council for Professions Supplementary to Medicine; Exec. Cttee, N Wales Cons. Group. Pres., N Wales Assoc. for the Disabled. *Address:* The Cottage, Wayside Acres, Bodelwyddan, near Rhyl, North Wales.

BROOKES, James Robert; non-executive Chairman, HomeWorkBase Ltd, since 2005; Consultant, SOCITM, since 1998; *b* 2 Sept. 1941; *s* of James Brookes and Hettie Brookes (*née* Colley); *m* 1964, Patricia Gaskell; three *d*. *Educ:* Manchester Grammar Sch.; Corpus Christi Coll., Oxford (MA Maths). FBCS; CEng 1990; Eur Ing, 1991. Various posts as systems and applications programmer in develt, tech. support and sales; Northern Branch Manager, Univs and Nat. Research Region, Ferranti/Internat. Computers, 1962–67; Computer Services Manager, Queen's Univ. Belfast, 1967–69; Operations Manager, Univ. of Manchester Regional Computer Centre, 1969–75; Director: SW Univs Regional Computer Centre, 1975–87; Bath Univ. Computer Service, 1983–87; Inf. Services Orgn, Portsmouth Univ., 1992–95; Head of Information Systems, Avon and Somerset Constabulary, 1995–98. Co-founder and non-exec. Chm., Praxis Systems, 1983; Chief Exec., 1986–91, Consultant, 1991–92, BCS; non-executive Director: The Knowledge Gp, 1998–2002; Smart South West, 1999–2004; RMS Ltd, 2006–. Vis. Prof., Business Sch., Strathclyde Univ., 1991–98. Mem. Council, PITCOM, 1989– (Prog. Exec., 1997–2000); Hon. Sec., Council of European Professional Information Socs, 1991–93. Trustee, Young Electronic Designer Awards, 1994–2005. FRSA 1988. Freeman, City of London, 1989; Liveryman, Information Technologists' Co. (Mem., 1988). *Recreations:* sailing, fellwalking, cycling, bridge, reading, theatre. *Address:* 29 High Street, Marshfield, Chippenham, Wilts SN14 8LR. *T:* (home) (01225) 891294; *e-mail:* jr.brookes@btinternet.com. *Club:* Oxford and Cambridge.

BROOKES, John Andrew, MBE 2004; landscape designer; *b* 11 Oct. 1933; *s* of Edward Percy Brookes and Margaret Alexandra Brookes. *Educ:* Durham; University Coll. London (Dip. Landscape). Asst to Brenda Colvin, 1957, to Dame Sylvia Crowe, 1958–61; private practice, 1964–; Director: Inchbald Sch. of Garden Design, 1970–78; Inchbald Sch. of Interior Design, Tehran, 1978–80; founded Clock House Sch. of Garden Design, Sussex, 1980; gardening corresp., Evening Standard, 1988–89; Principal Lectr, Kew Sch. of Garden Design, 1990–93. Chm., Soc. of Garden Designers, 1997–2000. Design workshops and lectures, UK and overseas; design and construction of gardens, and consultancies, UK, Europe, Japan, USA. DU Essex, 2006. *Publications:* Room Outside, 1969; Gardens for Small Spaces, 1970; Garden Design and Layout, 1970; Living in the Garden, 1971; Financial Times Book of Garden Design, 1975; Improve Your Lot, 1977; The Small Garden, 1977; The Garden Book, 1984; A Place in the Country, 1984; The Indoor Garden Book, 1986; Gardens of Paradise, 1987; The Country Garden, 1987; The New Small Garden Book, 1989; Garden Design, 1991, 2nd edn 2001; Planting the Country Way, 1994; Garden Design Workbook, 1994; Home and Garden Style, 1996; The New Garden, 1998; Garden Masterclass, 2002. *Recreations:* reading, pottering, entertaining. *Address:* Clock House, Denmans, Fontwell, near Arundel, West Sussex BN18 0SU. *T:* (01243) 542808, *Fax:* (01243) 544064; *e-mail:* jbrookes@denmans-garden.co.uk.

BROOKES, Michael John Patrick; General Secretary, National Association of Head Teachers, since 2005; *b* 12 May 1948; *s* of Percival John Brookes and Joan Brookes; *m* 2000, Karen Jane Mann; one *s*. *Educ:* King Alfred's Coll., Winchester (Cert Ed); Open Univ. (BA); Nottingham Univ. (MEd). Teacher: Kanes Hill First Sch., Southampton, 1969–70; Liss Jun. Sch., Hants, 1971–74; Dep. Hd, Gosberton Primary Sch., Lincs, 1975–78; Head: Gosberton Clough & Risegate Sch., Lincs, 1978–85; Sherwood Jun. Sch., Notts, 1985–2005. *Recreations:* walking, motorcycling, music. *Address:* 10 Charnwood Close, Ravenshead, Notts NG15 9BZ; *e-mail:* mickb@naht.org.uk.

BROOKES, Nicholas Kelvin, FCA; Chairman, De La Rue plc, since 2004 (non-executive Director, since 1997); *b* 19 May 1947; *s* of Stanley Brookes and Jean (*née* Wigley); *m* 1968, Maria Rosa Crespo; two *s* one *d*. *Educ:* Harrow Sch. FCA 1971. Articles for ACA, Hart Bros Reddall & Co., London, 1965–69; joined Texas Instruments, 1975; Man. Dir, Canada, 1980–85; Man. Dir, Europe, 1985–92; Vice-Pres., Texas Instruments

Inc. and Pres., Materials and Controls Gp, 1992–95; Chief Exec., Bowthorpe, then Spirent, plc, 1995–2004. Non-executive Director: Corp. Financiera ALBA SA, Spain, 1999–; Axel-Johnson Inc., Sweden, 2005–. Non-exec. Dir, Inst. of Directors, 2007–. FInstD. *Recreations:* tennis, badminton, opera. *Address:* De La Rue plc, De La Rue House, Jays Close, Basingstoke, Hants RG22 4BS. *Club:* Reform.

BROOKES, Peter C.; *see* Cannon-Brookes.

BROOKES, Peter Derek, RDI 2002; Political Cartoonist, The Times, since 1993; *b* 28 Sept. 1943; *s* of George Henry Brookes and Joan Elizabeth Brookes; *m* 1971, Angela Harrison; two *s*. *Educ:* Heversham Grammar Sch., Westmorland; RAF Coll., Cranwell (BA London Ext.); Central School of Art and Design (BA). Freelance illustrator, 1969–; Cover Artist, The Spectator, 1986–98, 2005–; stamp designs for Royal Mail, 1995, 1999 and 2003; contributor to: The Times, Sunday Times, Radio Times, New Statesman, The Listener, Spectator, TLS and Glyndebourne Fest. Opera Books. Illustration Tutor: Central Sch. of Art and Design, 1977–79; RCA, 1979–89. Mem., AGI, 1988–. FRSA 2000. Political Cartoonist of the Year, Cartoon Art Trust Awards, 1996, 1998 and 2006; Cartoonist of Year, British Press Awards, 2002 and 2007; Cartoonist of the Year, What the Papers Say Awards, 2005; Cartoonist of the Year, Political Cartoon Soc., 2006. *Publications:* Nature Notes, 1997; Nature Notes: the new collection, 1999; Nature Notes III, 2001; Peter Brookes of The Times, 2002; Nature Notes IV, 2004. *Recreations:* music, QPR, arguing. *Address:* 30 Vanbrugh Hill, Blackheath, SE3 7UF. *T:* (020) 8858 9022.

BROOKING, Barry Alfred, MBE 1972; JP; Chief Executive, British Psychological Society, 2000–04; *b* 2 Feb. 1944; *s* of Alfred Brooking and Winifred Joan Brooking; *m* 1978, Julia Irene McBride (marr. diss. 1993). *Educ:* Milford Haven GS; Sir Joseph Williamson's Math. Sch., Rochester; Birkbeck Coll., London Univ. (BA 1976, MA 1980). MInstM, MIPD, ACP. Royal Navy, 1965–81: BRNC Dartmouth, 1965; HMS Pembroke, 1966–67; HMS Diamond, 1968–69; CTC RM, Lympstone, 1969; 41 Cdo RM, 1969–70; 40 Cdo RM, 1970–72; HMS Raleigh, 1972–75; RN Sch. of Educnl and Trng Technol., 1976–78; ARE, 1978–81. Business Adminr, Med. Protection Soc., 1981–91; Regl Dir, St John Ambulance, 1992–95; Chief Exec., Parkinson's Disease Soc., 1995–99. Member: Surrey Magistrates' Soc., 1985–2000; Surrey Magistrates' Courts Cttee, 1993–95; Surrey Probation Cttee, 1993–95; Surrey Magistrates' Club, 1995–; Dep. Chm., North and East PSD, Surrey, 1995–97. Pres., Brooking Soc., 2004– (Mem., 1980–; Chm., 1993–2004). MRTS. JP Surrey, 1985–2000, Leics, 2001–04, Plymouth and Dist, 2004. Business Develt Award, Surrey TEC, 1994. *Publications:* Naval Mathematics Self-Tuition Text, 1966; Naval English Self-Tuition Text, 1966; Naval Mathematics Programmed-Learning Text, 1967; Royal Navy CCTV Production Techniques Handbook, 1977; (contrib.) Educational Technology in a Changing World: aspects of educational technology Vol. XII, 1978; ARE reports, booklets, articles in jls. *Recreations:* travel, theatre, cinema, music, history, sport. *Address:* 9 Hawkmoor Parke, Bovey Tracey, Devon TQ13 9NL.

BROOKING, Maj.-Gen. Patrick Guy, CB 1988; CMG 1997; MBE 1975; DL; *b* 4 April 1937; *s* of late Captain C. A. H. Brooking, CBE, RN, and G. M. J. White (*née* Coleridge); *m* 1964, Pamela Mary Walford; one *s* one *d*. *Educ:* Charterhouse Sch.; Alliance Française, Paris, 1955. Commnd 5th Royal Inniskilling Dragoon Guards, 1956; early career served in England, W Germany, NI, Cyprus (UN); Staff Coll., Camberley, 1969; Mil. Asst to Comdr 1st British Corps, 1970–71; Bde Major 39 Bde, Belfast, 1974–75; comd his regt, 1975–77; Instr Army Staff Coll., 1978; COS, 4 Armd Div., 1979–80; RCDS 1981; Comdr 33 Armd Bde, Paderborn Garrison, 1982–83; Dep. COS, HQ UKLF, 1984–85; Commandant and GOC Berlin (British Sector), 1985–89; Dir Gen., Army Manning and Recruiting, 1990; retd 1991. Chief Exec. Officer, Worldwide Subsidiaries, KRONE AG, Berlin, 1991–97. Colonel: 5th Royal Inniskilling Dragoon Guards, 1991–92; Royal Dragoon Guards (on foundn), 1992–94. Chm., British-German Assoc., 2000–04; Life Pres., Internat. Club, Berlin, 2001 (Chm., 1994–2001). Mem., Salisbury Cathedral Chapter, 2001–07. Freeman, City of London, 1964; Liveryman, Broderers' Co., 1964– (Master, 2003–04). DL Wilts, 1997. Verdienstorden des Landes, Berlin, 1996; Bundesverdienstkreuz 1st cl. (Germany), 2004. *Recreations:* golf, choral singing, painting. *Address:* c/o National Westminster Bank, PO Box 411, 34 Henrietta Street, WC2E 8NN. *Club:* Cavalry and Guards.

BROOKING, Sir Trevor (David), Kt 2004; CBE 1999 (MBE 1981); football broadcaster, since 1984; Director of Football Development, Football Association, since 2004; *b* 2 Oct. 1948; *s* of Henry and Margaret Brooking; *m* 1970, Hilkka Helina Helakorpi; one *s* one *d*. *Educ:* Ilford County High Sch. Professional footballer with West Ham United, 1965–84: played 642 games; scored 111 goals; FA Cup winner, 1975, *v* Fulham, 1980, *v* Arsenal (scoring only goal); won Football League Div. 2, 1980–81; 47 appearances for England, 1974–82. Chm., Eastern Council for Sport and Recreation, 1986–95; Sports Council, then English Sports Council, subseq. Sport England: Mem., 1989–2002; Vice-Chm., 1994–96; Chm., 1998–2002. *Publications:* Trevor Brooking (autobiog.), 1981; Trevor Brooking's 100 Great British Footballers, 1988. *Recreations:* golf, tennis.

BROOKMAN, family name of **Baron Brookman**.

BROOKMAN, Baron *cr* 1998 (Life Peer), of Ebbw Vale in the co. of Gwent; **David Keith Brookman;** General Secretary, Iron and Steel Trades Confederation, 1993–99; *b* 3 Jan. 1937; *s* of George Henry Brookman, MM and Blodwin Brookman (*née* Nash); *m* 1958, Patricia Worthington; three *d*. *Educ:* Nantyglo Grammar Sch., Gwent. Nat. Service, RAF, 1955–57. Steel worker, Richard Thomas & Baldwin, Ebbw Vale, 1953–55 and 1957–73; Iron & Steel Trades Confederation: Organiser, 1973–85; Asst Gen. Sec., 1985–93. Trades Union Congress: Member: Educn Adv. Cttee for Wales, 1976–82; Steel Cttee, 1985–90; Gen. Council, 1992–99. Member: Brit. Steel Jt Accident Prevention Adv. Cttee, 1985–93; Brit. Steel Adv. Cttee on Educn and Trng, 1986–93; Nat. Steel Co-ordinating Cttee, 1991–99 (Chm., 1993–99); Consultative Cttee, ECSC, 1993–2002; Operatives' Secretary: Jt Ind. Council for Slag Ind., 1985–93; Brit. Steel Long Products portfolio of cos Jt Standing Cttee, 1993–98; Brit. Steel Strip Trade Bd, 1993–98; Mem. Bd, UK Steel Enterprise (formerly Brit. Steel (Ind.) Ltd), 1993–; Jt Sec., European Works Council, British Steel, 1996–98. Member Executive Council: European Metalworkers' Fedn, 1985–95 (Mem., Steel Cttee, 1994–99); CSEU, 1989–93; International Metalworkers' Federation: Hon. Sec., Brit. Section, 1993–99; Pres., Iron and Steel and Non-Ferrous Metals Dept, 1993–99. Labour Party: Member: Exec. Cttee, Wales, 1982–85; Nat. Constitutional Cttee, 1987–91; NEC, 1991–92. Trustee, Julian Melchett Trust, 1985–95. Gov., Gwent Coll. of HE, 1980–84. *Recreations:* cricket, Rugby, reading, keep fit, golf.

BROOKNER, Dr Anita, CBE 1990; Reader, Courtauld Institute of Art, 1977–88; *b* 16 July 1928; *o c* of Newson and Maude Brookner. *Educ:* James Allen's Girls' Sch.; King's Coll., Univ. of London (FKC 1990); Courtauld Inst.; Paris. Vis. Lectr, Univ. of Reading, 1959–64; Slade Professor, Univ. of Cambridge, 1967–68; Lectr, Courtauld Inst. of Art, 1964. Fellow, New Hall, Cambridge. *Publications:* Watteau, 1968; The Genius of the Future, 1971; Greuze: the rise and fall of an Eighteenth Century Phenomenon, 1972; Jacques-Louis David, 1980; (ed) The Stories of Edith Wharton, Vol. 1, 1988, Vol. 2, 1989; Soundings, 1997; Romanticism and its Discontents, 2000; *novels:* A Start in Life, 1981; Providence, 1982; Look at Me, 1983; Hotel du Lac, 1984 (Booker McConnell Prize; filmed for TV, 1986); Family and Friends, 1985; A Misalliance, 1986; A Friend from England, 1987; Latecomers, 1988; Lewis Percy, 1989; Brief Lives, 1990; A Closed Eye, 1991; Fraud, 1992; A Family Romance, 1993; A Private View, 1994; Incidents in the Rue Laugier, 1995; Altered States, 1996; Visitors, 1997; Falling Slowly, 1998; Undue Influence, 1999; The Bay of Angels, 2001; The Next Big Thing, 2002; The Rules of Engagement, 2003; Leaving Home, 2005; articles in Burlington Magazine, etc. *Address:* 68 Elm Park Gardens, SW10 9PB. *T:* (020) 7352 6894.

BROOKS, family name of **Barons Brooks of Tremorfa and Crawshaw**.

BROOKS OF TREMORFA, Baron *cr* 1979 (Life Peer), of Tremorfa in the County of South Glamorgan; **John Edward Brooks;** DL; *b* 12 April 1927; *s* of Edward George Brooks and Rachel Brooks (*née* White); *m* 1948 (marr. diss. 1956); one *s* one *d*; *m* 1958, Margaret Pringle; two *s*. *Educ:* elementary schools; Coleg Harlech. Secretary, Cardiff South East Labour Party, 1966–84; Member, South Glamorgan CC, 1973–93 (Leader, 1973–77, 1986–92; Chm., 1981–82). Contested (Lab) Barry, Feb. and Oct. 1974; Parliamentary Agent to Rt Hon. James Callaghan, MP, Gen. Elections, 1970, 1979. Chm., Labour Party, Wales, 1978–79. Opposition defence spokesman, 1980–81. British Boxing Board of Control: Steward, 1986–; Vice Chm., 1999–2000; Chm., 2000–04; Pres., 2004–. Chairman: Welsh Sports Hall of Fame, 1988–; Sportsmatch Wales, 1992–. DL S Glam, 1994. *Recreations:* reading, most sports. *Address:* 40 Kennerleigh Road, Rumney, Cardiff, S Glam CF3 9BJ.

BROOKS, Alan; Director, Horace Clarkson plc, 1993–2001; *b* 30 Dec. 1935; *s* of Charles and Annie Brooks; *m* 1959, Marie Curtis; one *s* two *d*. *Educ:* Leeds Univ. (BSc 1st Cl. Mining Engineering; 1st Cl. Cert. of Competency, Mines and Quarries). Asst Mine Manager, Winsford Salt Mine, ICI, 1961–66; British Gypsum: Dep. Mines Agent, 1966–71; Dir, Midland Region, 1971–74; Production Dir, 1974–77; Dep. Man. Dir, 1977–85; Man. Dir, 1985–88; Chm., 1988; Gp Man. Dir, Gypsum Products, BPB Industries, subseq. BPB Gypsum Industries, 1988–93; Chm., Anglo United plc, 1993–98. Chairman: Westroc Industries, Canada, 1988; Inveryeso, Spain, 1991; Dir, Falkland Is Hldgs, 1998–2000. *Recreation:* fell walking.

BROOKS, Prof. David James, MD, DSc; FRCP, FMedSci; Hartnett Professor of Neurology, Faculty of Medicine, Imperial College, London University at Hammersmith Hospital, since 1993; Hon. Consultant, Hammersmith Hospital, since 1993; *b* 4 Dec. 1949; *s* of late Prof. James Leslie Brooks and Doris Margaret Adeline Brooks (*née* Welply); *m* 1987, Prof. Gillian Patricia Rowlands; two *s*. *Educ:* Newcastle Royal Grammar Sch.; Christ Church and Wolfson Coll., Oxford (BA 1st Cl. Hons Chem. 1972); University Coll. London (MB BS 1979, MD 1986; DSc Medicine 1998). MRCP 1982, FRCP 1993. Hon. Sen. Lectr, Inst. of Psychiatry, London, 1993; Hammersmith Hospital: Hd, Neurol. Gp, MRC Clinical Scis Centre, 1993–; Clinical Dir, Hammersmith Imanet (formerly Imaging Res. Solutions Ltd), 2001–. Hd of Neurol., Medical Diagnostics, GE Healthcare, 2007–. Chm., Scientific Issues Cttee, Movt Disorder Soc., 1998–2002; Member: Wellcome Trust Neurosci. Panel, 2000–03; Med. Adv. Panel, UK Huntington's Disease Assoc., 1996–; Med. Adv. Bd, 1997–2000, Neuroscis Bd, 2004–, MRC. UK Parkinson's Disease Association: Mem., Res. Adv. Panel, 1995– (Chm., 1996–97); Trustee, Council of Mgt, 1996–99 (Chm., 1997–98). Member: Internat. Adv. Panel, Michael J. Fox Foundn for Parkinson's Disease Res., 2002–06; Adv. Bd, Eur. Soc. for Clinical Neuropharmacol., 2000–; Internat. Adv. Bd for German Parkinson Network, 2001–05; Internat. Adv. Bd for German Dementia Network, 2006–. Patron: Alzheimer's Soc., 2006–; Alzheimer Disease Soc., 2007–. FMedSci 2001. *Publications:* contrib. numerous peer-reviewed pubns to learned jls. *Recreations:* golf, music, supporting Arsenal FC. *Address:* Cyclotron Building, Hammersmith Hospital, Du Cane Road, W12 0NN. *T:* (020) 8383 3172, *Fax:* (020) 8383 1783; *e-mail:* david.brooks@csc.mrc.ac.uk. *Clubs:* Athenæum; West Middlesex Golf.

BROOKS, Diana D., (Dede); President and Chief Executive Officer: Sotheby's Holdings Inc., 1994–2000 (also Director); Sotheby's North and South America, 1990–2000; *m* Michael C. Brooks; one *s* one *d*. *Educ:* Miss Porter's Sch., Farmington; Yale Univ. (BA Amer. Studies, 1973). Lending officer, Nat. Banking Gp, Citibank, 1973–79; joined Sotheby's New York, 1979; Sotheby's North America: Sen. Vice Pres. and Chief Financial and Admin. Officer, 1982; Exec. Vice Pres., 1984; Chief Operating Officer, 1985; Pres., 1987; Chief Exec. Officer, 1990. Trustee: Yale Univ.; Deerfield Acad., Mass; Henry Francis du Pont Winterthur Mus.; Meml Sloan-Kettering Cancer Center; Discover & Co.; Central Park Conservatory.

BROOKS, Douglas; Chairman, Ledbury Poetry Festival Ltd, since 2001; *b* 3 Sept. 1928; *s* of Oliver Brooks and Olive Brooks; *m* 1952, June Anne (*née* Branch); one *s* one *d*. *Educ:* Newbridge Grammar Sch.; University Coll., Cardiff (Dip. SocSc.). CCIPD. Girling Ltd: factory operative, 1951–53; Employment Officer, 1953–56; Hoover Ltd: Personnel Off., 1956–60; Sen. Personnel Off., 1960–63; Dep. Personnel Man., 1963–66; Indust. Relations Advr, 1966–69; Gp Personnel Man., 1969–73; Personnel Dir, 1973–78; Group Personnel Manager, Tarmac Ltd, 1979–80; Director: Walker Brooks and Partners Ltd, 1980–91; Flexello Castors & Wheels plc, 1987–91; Consultant, Douglas Brooks Associates, 1992–98. Member: Council, SSRC, later ESRC, 1976–82; BBC Consultative Gp on social effects of television, 1978–80; Hon. Soc. Cymmrodorion, 1981– (Mem. Council, 1992–). Vis. Fellow, PSI, 1982–84. Vice-Pres., IPM, 1972–74. Chm., Wooburn Fest. Soc. Ltd, 1978–86. *Publications:* (with M. Fogarty) Trade Unions and British Industrial Development, 1986; various articles in professional jls. *Recreations:* talking, music, reading, gardening, cooking. *Address:* 5 Queensholme, Pittville Circus Road, Cheltenham, Glos GL52 2QE. *Club:* Reform.

BROOKS, Edwin, PhD; FAIM, FCIM; Deputy Principal, Charles Sturt University, 1988–89; *b* Barry, Glamorgan, 1 Dec. 1929; *s* of Edwin Brooks and Agnes Elizabeth (*née* Campbell); *m* 1956, Winifred Hazel Soundie; four *s* two *d*. *Educ:* Barry Grammar Sch.; St John's Coll., Cambridge; PhD Cantab 1958. National Service, Singapore, 1948–49. MP (Lab) Bebington, 1966–70. Univ. of Liverpool: Lectr, Dept of Geography, 1954–66 and 1970–72; Sen. Lectr, 1972–77; Dean, College Studies, 1975–77; Riverina College of Advanced Education, later Riverina-Murray Institute of Higher Education, then Charles Sturt University: Dean of Business and Liberal Studies, 1977–82; Dean of Commerce, 1982–88; Dir, Albury-Wodonga Campus, 1982; Dean Emeritus, 1990. Wagga Wagga Base Hospital: Dir, 1989–96; Dep. Chm., 1989–93; Chm., 1995–96; Riverina Dist Health Service: Dir and Dep. Chm., 1994–96; Treas., 1995–96. Councillor, Birkenhead, 1958–67. Mem., Courses Cttee, Higher Educn Bd of NSW, 1978–82; Dir, Australian Business Educn Council, 1986–89. Pres., Wagga Wagga Chamber of Commerce, 1988–90. FAIM 1983; FCIM 1989; ACIS 1995. *Publications:* This Crowded Kingdom, 1973; (ed) Tribes of the Amazon Basin in Brazil, 1973. *Recreations:* gardening, listening to music, computing. *Address:* Inchnadamph, 4 Gregadoo Road, Wagga Wagga, NSW 2650, Australia. *T:* (2) 69226798.

BROOKS, Most Rev. Francis Gerard, DD, DCL; Bishop of Dromore (RC), 1976–99, now Bishop Emeritus; *b* 14 Jan. 1924. Ordained, 1949; priest of Dromore, 1949–75. Formerly President, St Colman's Coll., Violet Hill, Newry. *Address:* Drumiller House, Jerrettspass, Newry, Co. Down BT34 1TF. *T:* (028) 3082 1508, (028) 3082 1367.

BROOKS, James Wallace; Executive Director, Sector Treasury Ltd, since 2004; *b* 15 Sept. 1952; *s* of Leslie Duncan Brooks and Elizabeth June Brooks; *m* 1999, Kim Campbell; one *d. Educ:* Bolton Sch.; Univ. of Nottingham (BA); Liverpool Poly. CIPFA 1977. Dep. Dir. of Finance, Bolton MBC, 1985–89; City Treasurer, Manchester CC, 1989–93; Chief Executive: Poole BC, 1993–2002; Kingston upon Hull CC, 2002–03. *Recreations:* family, music. *Address:* Sector Treasury Services Ltd, 17 Rochester Row, SW1P 1QT.

BROOKS, John Ashton, CBE 1989; FCIB; Director: Midland Bank plc, 1981–91; Hongkong and Shanghai Banking Corp., 1989–91; Thomas Cook Group Ltd, 1983–94 (Chairman, 1988–92); *b* 24 Oct. 1928; *s* of Victor Brooks and Annie (*née* Ashton); *m* 1959, Sheila (*née* Hulse); one *s* one *d. Educ:* Merchant Taylors' Sch., Northwood. Joined Midland Bank, 1949; Manager: 22 Victoria Street Br., 1970; Threadneedle Street Br., 1972; Gen. Man., Computer Operations, 1975; Dep. Gp Chief Exec., Midland Group, 1981–89. President: Chartered Inst. of Bankers, 1987–89; Assoc. of Banking Teachers, 1990–98. Trustee, Charities Aid Foundn, 1990–99; Dir and Chm., CafCash Ltd (formerly Charities Aid Foundn Money Management Ltd), 1993–99. *Recreations:* reading, walking. *Club:* Institute of Directors.

BROOKS, Prof. John Stuart, PhD, DSc; FInstP; Vice-Chancellor, Manchester Metropolitan University, since 2005; *b* 8 March 1949; *s* of Ernest and Maude Brooks; *m* 1971, Jill Everil (*née* Pusey); two *s. Educ:* Cheshunt Grammar Sch.; Sheffield Univ. (BSc; PhD 1973; DSc 1998). CPhys, FInstP 1985; CEng 1992. Lectr, Sheffield City Poly., 1973–84; Head of Applied Physics Dept, 1984–90; Dir, Materials Res. Inst., 1990–92; Asst Principal, Sheffield Hallam Univ., 1992–98; Vice-Chancellor, Univ. of Wolverhampton, 1998–2005. *Publications:* 75 papers on materials and spectroscopy in learned jls. *Recreations:* travel, walking, music, bridge. *Address:* Manchester Metropolitan University, All Saints Building, All Saints, Manchester M15 6BH. *T:* (0161) 247 1559.

BROOKS, Louise Méarie; *see* Taylor, L. M.

BROOKS, Mel; producer, writer, director, actor; *b* Brooklyn, 28 June 1926; *m* Florence Baum; two *s* one *d*; *m* 1964, Anne Bancroft (*d* 2005); one *s*. TV script writer for series: Your Show of Shows, 1950–54; Caesar's Hour, 1954–57; (co-created) Get Smart, 1965. Films: (cartoon) The Critic (Academy Award), 1964; writer and director: The Producers (Academy Award), 1968 (adapted for stage, NY, 2001 (3 Tony Awards), Th. Royal, London, 2004 (Critics' Circle Award, Olivier Award, 2005)); Young Frankenstein, 1974; writer, director and actor: The Twelve Chairs, 1970; Blazing Saddles, 1974; Silent Movie, 1976; writer, director, actor and producer: High Anxiety, 1977; History of the World Part 1, 1981; Spaceballs, 1987; Life Stinks, 1991; Robin Hood: Men in Tights, 1993; Dracula: Dead and Loving It, 1995; actor, producer: To Be Or Not To Be, 1983. Film productions include: The Elephant Man, 1980; The Fly; Frances; My Favorite Year; 84 Charing Cross Road. Several album recordings. *Address:* c/o The Culver Studios, 9336 W Washington Boulevard, Culver City, CA 90232–2600, USA.

BROOKS, Michael James; freelance business consultant, interim manager and writer, since 1999; *b* Edgware, Middx, 16 July 1946; *s* of James and Doreen Brooks; *m* 1973, Susan Elizabeth Dickens; two *d. Educ:* Harrow Weald Grammar Sch.; Bushey Grammar Sch.; Portsmouth Coll. of Technol. (Dip. Business Studies 1967); London Sch. of Econs and Pol Sci. (MSc Accounting and Finance 1987). Internal Auditor, BP, 1967–70; Mgt Accountant, ICL, 1970–72; Chief Accountant, Santa Fe Drilling Co., Saudi Arabia and Australia, 1972–77; Consultant, Coopers & Lybrand, 1977–79; Royal Dutch Shell Group: Financial Reporting Manager, Shell UK, 1980–81; Budget Controller, Shell UK Expro, 1981–84; Accounting Res., Shell Internat., and Sec., Oil Industry Accounting Cttee, 1984–87; Hd of Financial Forecasts and Appraisals, Shell Internat., 1987–89; Hd of Finance, Shell Gas, 1989–92; Treas., Nigeria LNG, 1992–96; Sen. Finance Rep., M&A Team, Shell Chemicals, 1996–99. Mem., MRC, 2005–. Gov., Univ. of Portsmouth, 2005–. FCMA; FCCA. *Publications:* contrib. numerous articles to professional accounting jls. *Recreations:* watching cricket, listening to opera and Blondie, wine, food, real ale, walking. *Address:* c/o St Omer Consulting Ltd, 10 St Omer Road, Guildford, Surrey GU1 2DB. *T:* (01483) 560800; *e-mail:* mikebrooks@gatehouse10.demon.co.uk. *Clubs:* Middlesex County Cricket, Surrey County Cricket.

BROOKS, Prof. Nicholas Peter, DPhil; FSA, FRHistS; FBA 1989; Professor of Medieval History, University of Birmingham, 1985–2004, now Emeritus; *b* 14 Jan. 1941; *s* of late W. D. W. Brooks, CBE; *m* 1967, Chloë Carolyn Willis; one *s* one *d. Educ:* Winchester Coll.; Magdalen Coll., Oxford (Demy; MA DPhil). FRHistS 1970; FSAScot 1970–85; FSA 1974. Lectr in Medieval Hist., 1964–78, Sen. Lectr, 1978–85, St Andrews Univ.; Birmingham University: Chm., Sch. of History, 1987–89; Chm., Jun. Year Abroad prog., 1988–95; Dean, Faculty of Arts, 1992–95; Hd, Dept of Medieval History, 1985–2001. Chm., British Acad./RHistS Anglo-Saxon Charters Project, 1994–. General Editor: Studies in the Early Hist. of Britain, 1978–2000; Studies in Early Medieval Britain, 1999–. *Publications:* (ed) Latin and the Vernacular Languages in Early Medieval Britain, 1981; The Early History of the Church of Canterbury, 1984; (ed) St Oswald of Worcester, 1996; Anglo-Saxon Myths: State and Church 400–1066, 2000; Communities and Warfare 700–1400, 2000; (ed) St Wulfstan and his World, 2005; numerous articles in festschriften, Medieval Archaeology, Anglo-Saxon England, Trans of RHistS, etc. *Recreations:* gardening, bridge, walking. *Address:* Department of Medieval History, University of Birmingham, Edgbaston, Birmingham B15 2TT. *T:* (0121) 414 5736.

BROOKS, Peter Malcolm; Chairman, Enodis plc, since 2000 (non-executive Director, since 1998); *b* 12 Feb. 1947; *s* of Roger Morrison Brooks and Phyllis Fuller Brooks (*née* Hopkinson); *m* 1987, Patricia Margaret Garrett; one *s*; and one *s* by a previous marriage. *Educ:* Marlborough Coll.; Southampton Univ. (LLB). Solicitor, Macfarlanes, 1970–84 (Partner, 1977–84); Clifford Chance: Partner, 1984–96; Hd of Corporate Practice, 1992–96; General Counsel, Deutsche Morgan Grenfell, 1997–99. Dir, Genting Internat. (UK) Ltd, 2004–; non-executive Director: NCL Holdings ASA, 2000–02; Code Securities Ltd, 2004–05. *Recreations:* opera, theatre, travel, cricket, rackets. *Address:* c/o Enodis plc, thePlace, 175 High Holborn, WC1V 7AA. *Club:* Brooks's.

BROOKS, Richard John; Arts Editor, Sunday Times, since 1999; *b* 5 Feb. 1946; *s* of late Peter John Brooks and Joan Brooks; *m* 1978, Jane Mannion; two *d. Educ:* University College Sch.; Bristol Univ. (BA). Reporter, Bristol Evening Post, 1968–71; Journalist: BBC Radio, 1972–79; Economist, 1979–80; Sunday Times, 1980–85; Media and Culture Editor, Observer, 1986–99. *Recreations:* playing golf and tennis, supporting Arsenal, watching films. *Address:* Sunday Times, 1 Pennington Street, E98 1ST. *T:* (020) 7782 5735.

BROOKS, Robert; Chairman, Bonhams, since 2000; *b* 1 Oct. 1956; *s* of William Frederick Brooks and Joan Patricia (*née* Marshall); *m* 1981, Evelyn Rachel Durnford; two *s* one *d. Educ:* St Benedict's Sch., Ealing. Joined Christie's South Kensington Ltd, 1975, Dir, 1984–87; Dir, Christie Manson and Woods Ltd, 1987–89; established Brooks (Auctioneers) Ltd, 1989; acquired W. & F. C. Bonham and Sons Ltd, 2000. FIA Gp N European Touring Car Champion, 1999. *Recreations:* motor racing, golf, cricket. *Address:* Bonhams, 101 New Bond Street, W1S 1SR. *T:* (020) 7468 8220. *Club:* British Racing Drivers'.

BROOKS, Simon Jeremy, CB 2006; Vice President, European Investment Bank, since 2006; *b* 1 Aug. 1954; *s* of Stanley William Brooks and Jane Brooks; *m* 1990, Caroline Turk; one *s* one *d. Educ:* Queen's Coll., Oxford (BA PPE 1975); Nuffield Coll., Oxford (BPhil Econs 1977). NIESR, 1978–85; HM Treasury, 1985–2006: Econ. Advr, 1985–92; Head: Econ. Analysis 2 Div., 1992–94; Regl and Country Analysis/World Econ. Issues Teams, 1994–98; EU Finance Team, 1998–2000; Dir of Macroeconomics, 2000–06. *Address:* European Investment Bank, 100 boulevard Konrad Adenauer, 2950 Luxembourg. *T:* 437994424.

BROOKS, Stuart Armitage, CMG 2001; OBE 1991; HM Diplomatic Service; Counsellor, Foreign and Commonwealth Office, 1997–2001; *b* 15 May 1948; *s* of Frank and Audrey Brooks; *m* 1975, Mary-Margaret Elliott; two *d. Educ:* Churchill Coll., Cambridge (MA). Entered FCO, 1970: Vice-Consul, Rio de Janeiro, 1972–74; Second Sec., on secondment to Home CS, 1974–75; Second, later First, Sec., Lisbon, 1975–78; First Secretary: FCO, 1978; Moscow, 1979–82; FCO, 1982–87; Stockholm, 1987–91; FCO, 1991–93; Counsellor, Vienna, 1993–97. *Recreations:* music, horticulture. *Address:* c/o Foreign and Commonwealth Office, King Charles Street, SW1A 2AH.

BROOKS, Sir Timothy (Gerald Martin), KCVO 2003; JP; farmer; Lord-Lieutenant of Leicestershire, 1989–2003; *b* 20 March 1929; *s* of late Hon. Herbert William Brooks, *s* of 2nd Baron Crawshaw, and of Hilda Muriel (*née* Steel); *m* 1951, Hon. Ann Fremantle, *d* of 4th Baron Cottesloe, GBE, TD and late Lady Elizabeth Harris; three *s* two *d. Educ:* Eton; RAC, Cirencester (NDA). Set up farm and garden centre, Wistow, 1953; Dir, Thomas Tapling & Co. Ltd, 1963–2007. Mem., Harborough DC, 1975–89 (Chm., 1983–84). Chm. Governors, Wyggeston's Hosp., Leicester, 1988–96. Churchwarden, St Wistan's, Wistow. JP 1960, High Sheriff, 1979–80, Leics. Hon. DLitt Loughborough, 1997; Hon. LLD: De Montfort, 1997; Leicester, 2002. KStJ 1992. *Recreations:* arts, travel. *Address:* Garden Cottage, Wistow, Leicester LE8 0QF.

BROOKSBANK, Sir (Edward) Nicholas, 3rd Bt *cr* 1919; with Christie's, 1974–97; *b* 4 Oct. 1944; *s* of Sir Edward William Brooksbank, 2nd Bt, TD, and of Ann, 2nd *d* of Col T. Clitherow; *S* father, 1983; *m* 1970, Emma, *d* of Rt Hon. Baron Holderness, PC; one *s* one *d. Educ:* Eton. Royal Dragoons, 1963–69; Blues and Royals, 1969–73; Adjutant, 1971–73. *Heir: s* (Florian) Tom (Charles) Brooksbank, *b* 9 Aug. 1982. *Address:* Menethorpe Hall, Malton, North Yorks YO17 9QX.

BROOKSBANK, Sir Nicholas; *see* Brooksbank, Sir E. N.

BROOM, Prof. Donald Maurice; Colleen Macleod Professor of Animal Welfare, University of Cambridge, since 1986; Fellow, St Catharine's College, Cambridge, since 1987 (President, 2001–04); *b* 14 July 1942; *s* of late Donald Edward Broom and Mavis Edith Rose Broom; *m* 1971, Sally Elizabeth Mary Riordan; three *s. Educ:* Whitgift Sch.; St Catharine's Coll., Cambridge (MA, PhD, ScD). Lectr, 1967, Sen. Lectr, 1979, Reader, 1982, Dept of Pure and Applied Zoology, Univ. of Reading. Vis. Asst Prof., Univ. of California, Berkeley, 1969; Vis. Lectr, Univ. of W Indies, Trinidad, 1972; Vis. Scientist, CSIRO Div. of Animal Prodn, Perth, WA, 1983. Member: EEC Farm Animal Welfare Expert Gp, 1981–89; EU Scientific Cttee on Animal Health and Animal Welfare, 1997–2003; Chm., EU Scientific Veterinary Cttee on Animal Welfare, 1990–97; Vice-Chm., Eur. Food Safety Authy Scientific Panel on Animal Health and Welfare, 2003–; Scientific Advr, Council of Europe Standing Cttee of Eur. Convention for Protection of Animals kept for Farming Purposes, 1987–2000; EU Rep., Quadripartite Wkg Gp on Humane Trapping Standards, 1995–96. Hon. Res. Associate, BBSRC Inst. of Grassland and Envmtl Res. (formerly AFRC Inst. for Grassland and Animal Production), 1985–. Member: Council, Assoc. for Study of Animal Behaviour, 1971–83 (Hon. Treas., 1971–80); Internat. Ethological Cttee, 1976–79; Council, Soc. for Vet. Ethology, 1981–89 (Vice-Pres., 1986–87, 1989–91; Pres., 1987–89); Animal Welfare Cttee, Zool Soc., 1986–95; NERC Special Cttee on Seals, 1986–96; Farm Animal Welfare Council, MAFF, 1991–99; BSI Panel on ISO Animal (Mammal) Traps, 1993–98; Animal Procedures Cttee, Home Office, 1998–2006; Chm., Gp on Land Transport, Orgn Internat. des Epizooties, 2003–. Trustee, Farm Animal Care Trust, 1986– (Chm., 1999–). Hon. Coll. Fellow, Myerscough Coll., Univ. of Central Lancs, 1999; Hon. Prof., Univ. Salvador, Buenos Aires, 2004. Hon. Socio Corrispondenti, Accad. Peloritana dei Pericolanti Messina, 2005. Vice-Pres., Old Whitgiftian Assoc., 2000–; Vice-Pres., 2004–05, Pres., 2005–06, St Catharine's Soc. FZS 1986. Hon. DSc De Montfort, 2000; Hon. Dr, Norwegian Univ. of Life Scis, 2005. George Fleming Prize, British Vet. Jl, 1990; British Soc. of Animal Sci./RSPCA Award for Innovative Develts in Animal Welfare, 2000; Eurogroup Medal, 2001; Michael Kay Award, RSPCA, 2007. *Publications:* Birds and their Behaviour, 1977; Biology of Behaviour, 1981; (ed jtly) The Encyclopaedia of Domestic Animals, 1986; (ed) Farmed Animals, 1986; (with A. F. Fraser) Farm Animal Behaviour and Welfare, 1990; (with K. G. Johnson) Stress and Animal Welfare, 1993; (ed) Coping with Challenge: welfare in animals including humans, 2001; The Evolution of Morality and Religion, 2003; (with A. F. Fraser) Domestic Animal Behaviour and Welfare, 2007; over 300 papers in behaviour, psychol, zool, ornithol, agricl and vet. jls. *Recreations:* squash, water-polo, modern pentathlon, ornithology. *Address:* Department of Veterinary Medicine, University of Cambridge, Madingley Road, Cambridge CB3 0ES. *T:* (01223) 337697; *e-mail:* dmb16@cam.ac.uk. *Club:* Hawks (Cambridge).

BROOM, Peter David; HM Diplomatic Service; Deputy Consul General, San Francisco, since 2003; *b* 7 Aug. 1953; *s* of Albert Leslie Broom and Annie Myfannwy Broom; *m* 1976, Vivienne Louise Pyatt; five *d. Educ:* Hillside Sch., Finchley. Entered FCO, 1970; Attaché: Oslo, 1974–77; Jedda, 1977–79; Islamabad, 1979–81; FCO, 1981–84; Mbabane, 1984–87; New Delhi, 1987–89; Second Sec., FCO, 1989–91; Consul (Commercial), Brisbane, 1991–97; Consul and Dep. High Comr, Yaoundé, 1997–2000; Consul Gen., Cape Town, 2000–02. *Recreations:* sport, history. *Address:* c/o Foreign and Commonwealth Office, King Charles Street, SW1A 2AH; 7 Sunny Hill, Waldringfield, Suffolk IP12 4QS.

BROOME, David McPherson, CBE 1995 (OBE 1970); farmer; British professional show jumper; *b* Cardiff, 1 March 1940; *s* of Fred and Amelia Broome, Chepstow, Gwent; *m* 1976, Elizabeth, *d* of K. W. Fletcher, Thirsk, N Yorkshire; three *s. Educ:* Monmouth Grammar Sch. for Boys. European Show Jumping Champion (3 times); World Show Jumping Champion, La Baule, 1970; Olympic Medallist (Bronze) twice, 1960, 1968; King George V Gold Cup 6 times (a record, in 1990). Mounts include: Sunsalve, Aachen, 1961; Mr Softee, Rotterdam, 1967, and Hickstead, 1969; Beethoven, La Baule, France, 1970, as

(1st British) World Champion; Sportsman and Philco, Cardiff, 1974; Professional Champion of the World. *Publications:* Jump-Off, 1971; (with S. Hadley) Horsemanship, 1983. *Recreation:* shooting. *Address:* Mount Ballan Manor, Port Skewett, Caldicot, Monmouthshire, Wales NP26 5XP.

BROOME, Prof. John, PhD; FBA 2000; FRSE; White's Professor of Moral Philosophy, University of Oxford, since 2000; Fellow, Corpus Christi College, Oxford, since 2000; *b* 17 May 1947; *s* of Richard and Tamsin Broome; *m* 1970, Ann Rowland; one *s* one *d*. *Educ:* Trinity Hall, Cambridge (BA); Bedford Coll., Univ. of London (MA); Massachusetts Inst. Technol. (PhD 1972). Lectr in Econs, Birkbeck Coll., London Univ., 1972–78; Reader in Econs, 1979–92, Prof. of Econs and Philosophy, 1992–95, Univ. of Bristol; Prof. of Philosophy, Univ. of St Andrews, 1996–2000. Visiting posts: Univ. of Va, 1975; All Souls Coll., Oxford, 1982–83; ANU, 1986, 1993, 2001, 2007; Princeton Univ., 1987–89; Univ. of Washington, 1988; Univ. of BC, 1993–94; Uppsala Univ., 1997–98, 2004; Univ. of Canterbury, NZ, 2005. Ed., Economics and Philosophy, 1994–99. Mem., Royal Swedish Acad. of Scis. FRSE 1999. *Publications:* The Microeconomics of Capitalism, 1983; Weighing Goods, 1991; Counting the Cost of Global Warming, 1992; Ethics Out of Economics, 1999; Weighing Lives, 2004. *Recreation:* sailing. *Address:* Corpus Christi College, Oxford OX1 4JF.

BROOME, John Lawson, CBE 1987; Founder and Chairman, Alton Towers Theme Park, since 1980 (Chief Executive, 1980–90); *b* 2 Aug. 1943; *s* of late Albert Henry and Mary Elizabeth Broome; *m* 1972, Jane Myott Bagshaw; one *s* two *d*. *Educ:* Rossall School. School master, 1960–65; Dir, JLB Investment Property Group, 1961–, and numerous other companies; Chm. and Chief Exec., Adventure World Theme Park, 1997–99; Chairman: London Launch Ltd, 2000–; Launch Hldgs, 2005–. Member: ETB and BTA, 1982–92; Internat. Assoc. of Amusement Parks and Attractions, USA, 1986–89 (Chm., Internat. Cttee; Chm., Internat. Council, 1986–89). Vice-Pres., Ironbridge Gorge Museum Trust. Governor, Staffordshire Univ. (formerly N Staffs Poly.), 1984–95. Vis. Prof., Sunderland Univ., 1996–. *Recreations:* ski-ing, travelling, antiques, old paintings, objets d'art, fine gardens, restoration of historic properties.

BROOMFIELD, Alexander Bryan; Chairman, Aberdeen Royal Hospitals NHS Trust, 1992–96; *b* 13 Jan. 1937; *s* of late William P. Broomfield, OBE and Eliza M. Broomfield; *m* 1960, Morag Carruthers. *Educ:* Aberdeen Grammar Sch. 26 years with Town & County Motor Garage Ltd; Man. Dir, retired 1992. Member: Grampian Health Bd, 1990–92; Bd, Scottish SHA, 1980–88; Council, Aberdeen Chamber of Commerce, to 1995 (Pres., 1978–79); Vice-Chm., Aberdeen Airport Consultative Cttee, 1990–. *Recreations:* walking, fishing, golf. *Address:* 5 Carnegie Gardens, Aberdeen AB15 4AW. *Clubs:* Royal Northern and University (Aberdeen); Royal Aberdeen Golf.

BROOMFIELD, Sir Nigel (Hugh Robert Allen), KCMG 1993 (CMG 1986); HM Diplomatic Service, retired; Chairman, Leonard Cheshire Disability (formerly Leonard Cheshire), since 2005; *b* 19 March 1937; *s* of Col Arthur Allen Broomfield and Ruth Sheilagh Broomfield; *m* 1963, Valerie Fenton; two *s*. *Educ:* Haileybury Coll.; Trinity Coll., Cambridge (BA (Hons) English Lit.). Commnd 17/21 Lancers, 1959, retired as Major, 1968. Joined FCO as First Sec., 1969; First Secretary: British Embassy, Bonn, 1970–72; British Embassy, Moscow, 1972–74; European Communities Dept, London, 1975–77; RCDS, 1978; Political Advr and Head of Chancery, British Mil. Govt, Berlin, 1979–81; Head of Eastern European and Soviet Dept, 1981–83, and Head of Soviet Dept, 1983–85, FCO; Dep. High Comr and Minister, New Delhi, 1985–88; Ambassador to GDR, 1988–90; Dep. Under Sec. of State (Defence), FCO, 1990–92; Ambassador to Germany, 1993–97. Dir, Ditchley Foundn, 1999–2004. Non-exec. Dir, C & W (Jersey) Ltd, 2005–; Chm., Yatra (Jersey) Ltd, 2006–. Advr, Smiths Detection. Captain, Cambridge Squash Rackets and Real Tennis, 1957–58; British Amateur Squash Champion, 1958–59 (played for England, 1957–60). *Recreations:* tennis, golf, reading, music. *Address:* Huntington House, Rue du Clos Fallu, Trinity, Jersey JE3 5BG. *Clubs:* Royal Automobile, MCC, All England Lawn Tennis; Hawks (Cambridge).

BROOMHEAD, Steven John; Chief Executive, North West Development Agency, since 2003; *b* 15 Jan. 1956; *s* of Brian and Hazel Broomhead; *m* 1990, Linda Whelan; one *d*. *Educ:* W Glam Inst. of HE (BEd (Hons) Wales); Univ. of Leicester (MA); UC Swansea (CertEd). Lectr in Social Sciences, W Bridgford Coll., Nottingham, 1979; Sen. Lectr, Arnold and Carlton Coll., Nottingham, 1981; Vice-Principal, Skelmersdale Coll., Lancashire, 1986; Principal: Peterlee Coll., 1990–94; Warrington Collegiate Inst., 1994–97; Chief Exec., Warrington BC (Unitary), 1997–2003. Chm., NW Chamber of Commerce, 2002–; Board Member: Basic Skills Agency, 1996–; Learning and Skills Devlt Agency, 2001–; Mem., Nat. Skills Alliance, 2003–; Policy Advr to DfES, 2000–03. Chm., Connexions, Chester and Warrington, 2001–; Mem. NW Regl Exec., Prince's Trust, 2001–. Governor: Univ. of Central Lancs, 2005–; Skelmersdale Coll. (Chm., 2006–). CCMI; FCGI; FRSA. Patron, Campaign for Learning, 2001. *Recreations:* railway history, walking, Notts County FC, Warrington RL FC (Dep. Chm.). *Address:* Principal's Lodge, 32 Blackhurst Avenue, Hutton, Preston PR4 4BG; *e-mail:* Steven.Broomhead@NWDA.co.uk.

BROPHY, Michael John Mary; Director, Help For All Trust, since 2002; *b* 24 June 1937; *s* of Gerald and Mary Brophy; *m* 1962, Sarah Rowe; three *s* one *d*. *Educ:* Ampleforth Coll.; Royal Naval Coll., Dartmouth. Entered Royal Navy, 1955; retired as Lt-Comdr, 1966. Associate Dir, J. Walter Thompson, 1967–74; Appeals Dir, Spastics Soc., 1974–82; Chief Exec., CAF, 1982–2002. Dir, European Foundn Centre, 1989–98 (Chm., 1994–95); Chm., Euro Citizens Action Service, 1996–2002. Trustee: Capital Community Foundn, 2006–; Charity Employees Benevolent Fund, 2007–; Chm., United Trusts, 2006–08. *Publication:* Citizen Power, 2005. *Address:* 8 Oldlands Hall, Herons' Ghyll, Uckfield, E Sussex TN22 3DA; *e-mail:* thebrophys@waitrose.com.

BROSNAN, Pierce, Hon. OBE 2003; actor; *b* Navan, Co. Meath, 16 May 1953; *s* of Tom Brosnan and May Smith; *m* 1977, Cassandra Harris (*d* 1991); one *s*, and one step *s* one step *d*; *m* 2001, Keely Shaye Smith; two *s*. *Educ:* Drama Centre, London. Asst stage manager, Theatre Royal, York; *stage* appearances include: Red Devil Battery Sign; Filumena; Wait Until Dark; *television* includes: The Manions of America series, 1981; Remington Steele series (title rôle), 1982–87; Nancy Astor, 1984; Noble House 1988; Around the World in 80 Days, 1989; Robinson Crusoe, 1996; *films* include: Nomads, 1986; The Fourth Protocol, 1987; The Deceivers, 1988; Mr Johnson, 1991; Lawnmower Man, 1992; Mrs Doubtfire, 1993; Love Affair, 1994; The Mirror has Two Faces, Mars Attacks!, 1996; Dante's Peak, 1997; The Nephew, 1998 (also prod); The Thomas Crown Affair, 1999 (also prod); Grey Owl, 2000; The Taylor of Panama, 2001; Evelyn, 2003; Laws of Attraction, After the Sunset, 2004; The Matador, 2006; Seraphim Falls, 2007; Mamma Mia!, Married Life, 2008; rôle of James Bond in: GoldenEye, 1995; Tomorrow Never Dies, 1997; The World is Not Enough, 1999; Die Another Day, 2002. *Address:* c/o Guttman Associates, 118 South Beverly Drive, Suite 201, Beverly Hills, CA 90212, USA.

BROTHERS, Air Cdre Peter Malam, CBE 1964; DSO 1944; DFC 1940, and Bar, 1943; Managing Director, Peter Brothers Consultants Ltd, 1973–86; *b* 30 Sept. 1917; *s* of late John Malam Brothers; *m* 1939, Annette (*d* 2005), *d* of late James Wilson; three *d*. *Educ:* N Manchester Sch. (Br. of Manchester Grammar). Joined RAF, 1936; Flt-Lieut 1939; RAF Biggin Hill, Battle of Britain, 1940; Sqdn-Ldr 1941; Wing Comdr 1942; Tangmere Fighter Wing Ldr, 1942–43; Staff HQ No. 10 Gp, 1943; Exeter Wing Ldr, 1944; US Comd and Gen. Staff Sch., 1944–45; Central Fighter Estab., 1945–46; Colonial Service, Kenya, 1947–49; RAF Bomber Sqdn, 1949–52; HQ No. 3 Gp, 1952–54; RAF Staff Coll., 1954; HQ Fighter Comd, 1955–57; Bomber Stn, 1957–59; Gp Capt., and Staff Officer, SHAPE, 1959–62; Dir of Ops (Overseas), 1962–65; Air Cdre, and AOC Mil. Air Traffic Ops, 1965–68; Dir of Public Relations (RAF), MoD (Air), 1968–73; retired 1973. Freeman, Guild Air Pilots and Air Navigators, 1966 (Liveryman, 1968; Warden, 1971; Master, 1974–75); Freeman, City of London, 1967. Editorial Adviser, Defence and Foreign Affairs publications, 1973–76. Chm., Battle of Britain Fighter Assoc., 2003– (Dep. Chm., 1993–2003); Patron, Spitfire Assoc., Australia, 1971–; Vice-President: Spitfire Soc., 1984–; Devon Emergency Volunteers, 1980–93 (Chm., 1981–93); Life Vice-Pres., Battle of Britain Meml Trust, 2003–; President: Hungerford Br., Aircrew Assoc., 2001–; Battle of Britain Histl Soc., 2003–. *Recreations:* golf, sailing, fishing, swimming, flying. *Address:* 11 Downs Close, Eastbury, W Berks RG17 7JW. *Clubs:* Royal Air Force; Deanwood Park Golf.

BROTHERSTON, Leslie William, (Lez); freelance production designer, since 1984; *b* 6 Oct. 1961; *s* of L. Brotherston and Irene Richardson. *Educ:* Prescot Grammar Sch., Prescot, Liverpool; Central Sch. of Art and Design (BA Hons Th. Design 1984). First design for Letter to Brezhnev (film); work with Northern Ballet Theatre includes: The Brontes, Strange Meeting, Romeo and Juliet; Giselle, 1997; Dracula, 1997; The Hunchback of Notre Dame, 1998; Carmen (Barclays Th. Award for Outstanding Achievement in Dance, TMA Award), 1999; A Christmas Carol, 2001; designs for *dance* include: for Adventures in Motion Pictures: Highland Fling, 1994; Swan Lake, Piccadilly, 1995, transf. NY (Tony Award for Best Costume Design, Drama Desk Awards for Best Costume Design and Best Set Design, Outer Critics Award for Outstanding Costume Design, 1999); Cinderella, Piccadilly, 1997 (Olivier Award for Outstanding Achievement in Dance, 1998); Greymatter, Rambert; for Scottish Ballet: Just Scratchin' the Surface, Nightlife, 1999; 6 Faces, K-Ballet, Japan; Bounce, Eur. tour, 2000; Play Without Words, NT, 2002; for Adam Cooper Co.: Les Liaisons Dangereuses (also Co-Dir and writer), Japan, then Sadler's Wells, 2005; for New Adventures: Edward Scissorhands, Sadler's Wells, 2005; *theatre* includes: Jane Eyre, tour; Greenwich: Prisoner of Zenda, 1992; The Sisters Rosensweig, 1994, transf. Old Vic; Handling Bach, 1995; The Last Romantics, Northanger Abbey, 1996; David Copperfield, 1997; Neville's Island, Apollo, 1994; Rosencrantz and Guildenstern are Dead, RNT, 1995; Alarms and Excursions, Gielgud, 1998; Spend, Spend, Spend, Piccadilly, 1999; A Midsummer Night's Dream, Albery, 2000; French and Saunders Live, UK tour, 2000; Little Foxes, Donmar Warehouse, 2001; Victoria Wood - At It Again, Royal Albert Hall, 2001; Bedroom Farce, Aldwych, 2002; Royal Exchange, Manchester: A Woman of No Importance, 2000; Sex, Chips and Rock 'n' Roll, Design for Living, 2002; Volpone, 2004; The Vortex, 2007; *opera* includes prodns for Opera Zuid, Hong Kong Arts Fest., Opera North, Glyndebourne Touring Opera, Teatro Bellini, Royal Danish Opera, Opera NI; *musicals* include: Side by Side by Sondheim, Greenwich, 1997; Cabaret, Sheffield Crucible; Maria Friedman by Special Arrangement, Donmar Warehouse; My One and Only, Piccadilly, 2002; Brighton Rock, Almeida, 2004; Acorn Antiques, Haymarket, 2005; The Far Pavilions, Shaftesbury, 2005. *Address:* c/o Cassie Mayer Management, 11 Wells Mews, W1T 3HD. *T:* (020) 7462 0040; 26 Bow Brook, Mace Street, Bethnal Green, E2 0PW. *T:* (020) 8981 8764. *Club:* Soho House.

BROTHERTON, Ven. (John) Michael; Archdeacon of Chichester and Canon Residentiary of Chichester Cathedral, 1991–2002; *b* 7 Dec. 1935; *s* of late Clifford and Minnie Brotherton; *m* 1963, Daphne Margaret Yvonne, *d* of Sir Geoffrey Meade, KBE, CMG, CVO; three *s* one *d*. *Educ:* St John's Coll., Cambridge (MA); Cuddesdon Coll., Oxford; Univ. of London Inst. of Educn (PGCE). Ordained: deacon, 1961; priest, 1962; Asst Curate, St Nicolas, Chiswick, 1961–64; Chaplain, Trinity Coll., Port of Spain, Trinidad, 1965–69; Rector of St Michael's, Diego Martin, Trinidad, 1969–75; Vicar, St Mary and St John, Oxford, and Chaplain, St Hilda's Coll., Oxford, 1976–81; Rural Dean of Cowley, 1978–81; Vicar, St Mary, Portsea, 1981–91. Mem., Legal Adv. Commn, C of E, 1996–2001. Hon. Canon, St Michael's Cathedral, Kobe, Japan, 1986. Proctor in Convocation, 1995–2002. *Recreations:* travel, walking. *Address:* Flat 2, 23 Gledhow Gardens, SW5 0AZ. *T:* (020) 7373 5147; *e-mail:* jmbrotherton@amserve.com.

BROTHERTON, Michael Lewis; formed Michael Brotherton Associates, Parliamentary Consultants, 1986; *b* 26 May 1931; *s* of late John Basil Brotherton and Maud Brotherton; *m* 1968, Julia, *d* of Austin Gerald Comyn King and Katherine Elizabeth King, Bath; three *s* one *d*. *Educ:* Prior Park; RNC Dartmouth. Served RN, 1949–64: qual. Observer 1955; Cyprus, 1957 (despatches); Lt-Comdr 1964, retd. Times Newspapers, 1967–74. Chm., Beckenham Conservative Political Cttee, 1967–68; contested (C) Deptford, 1970; MP (C) Louth, Oct. 1974–1983. Pres., Hyde Park Tories, 1975. Mem., Select Cttee on violence in the family, 1975–76. Chm., Friends, 1995–99, Chm., Library Cttee, 1997–99, Boston Parish Church. *Recreations:* cricket, cooking, gardening, talking. *Address:* Ava Cottage, 46 The Butts, Chippenham, Wilts SN15 3JS. *T:* (01249) 651783. *Clubs:* Conservative Working Men's, Louth; Castaways; Cleethorpes Conservative; Immingham Conservative.

BROTHWOOD, Rev. John, MRCP, FRCPsych, FFOM; Hon. Curate, St Barnabas, Dulwich, 1991–99; *b* 23 Feb. 1931; *s* of late Wilfred Cyril Vernon Brothwood and Emma Bailey; *m* 1957, Dr Margaret Stirling Meyer (*d* 2008); one *d* (one *s* decd). *Educ:* Marlborough Coll.; Peterhouse, Cambridge (Schol.); Middlesex Hosp. MB BChir (Cantab) 1955; MRCP 1960, DPM (London) 1964, FFCM 1972, FRCPsych 1976, FFOM 1988. Various posts in clinical medicine, 1955–64; joined DHSS (then Min. of Health) as MO, 1964; SPMO and Under Secretary, DHSS, 1975–78; CMO, Esso Petroleum (UK) and Esso, subseq. Exxon, Chemicals, 1979–90. Lay Reader, Parish of St Barnabas, Dulwich, 1982–91; Southwark Ordination Course, 1988–91; deacon, 1991; priest, 1992. Mem. Council, Missions to Seamen, 1994–2001. *Publications:* various. *Recreations:* diverse. *Address:* 98 Woodwarde Road, SE22 8UT. *T:* (020) 8693 8273.

BROUCHER, David Stuart; HM Diplomatic Service, retired; Advisor on European Union enlargement to Birmingham University, since 2006; *b* 5 Oct. 1944; *s* of late Clifford Broucher and of Betty Broucher (*née* Jordan); *m* 1971, Marion Monika Blackwell; one *s*. *Educ:* Manchester Grammar School; Trinity Hall, Cambridge (MA Modern Languages). Foreign Office, 1966; British Military Govt, Berlin, 1968; Cabinet Office, 1972; Prague, 1975; FCO, 1978; UK Perm. Rep. to EC, 1983; Counsellor, Jakarta, 1985–89; Economic Counsellor, Bonn, 1989–93; Counsellor, FCO, 1994; Asst Under Sec. of State, FCO, 1995–97; Ambassador to Czech Republic, 1997–2001; UK Perm. Rep. to Conf. on Disarmament, Geneva (with personal rank of Ambassador), 2001–04. Advr to Pres. of Romania on EU accession, 2005. Vis. Fellow, Southampton Univ., 2006–. *Recreations:* music, golf, sailing. *Address:* *e-mail:* dbroucher@btinternet.com.

BROUGH, Dr Colin, FRCPE; FFCM; Chief Administrative Medical Officer, Lothian Health Board, 1980–88; *b* 4 Jan. 1932; *s* of Peter Brough and Elizabeth C. C. Chalmers; *m* 1957, Maureen Jennings; four *s* one *d*. *Educ:* Bell Baxter Sch., Cupar; Univ. of Edinburgh (MB ChB 1956). DPH 1965; DIH 1965; FFCM 1978; MRCPE 1981; FRCPE 1982. House Officer, Leicester General Hosp. and Royal Infirmary of Edinburgh, 1956–57; Surg.-Lieut, Royal Navy, 1957–60; General Practitioner, Leith and Fife, 1960–64; Dep. Medical Supt, Royal Inf. of Edinburgh, 1965–67; ASMO, PASMO, Dep. SAMO, South-Eastern Regional Hosp. Board, Scotland, 1967–74; Community Medicine Specialist, Lothian Health Board, 1974–80. *Recreations:* golf, shooting, fishing, first aid. *Address:* The Saughs, Gullane, East Lothian EH31 2AL. *T:* (01620) 842179.

BROUGH, Jonathan; Head, Preparatory Department, City of London School for Girls, since 2004; *b* Bedford, 2 Feb. 1971; *s* of George Ernest Brough and Amy Elizabeth Brough; civil partnership 2006, Harry Small. *Educ:* Walmsley House Sch.; Bedford Sch.; Colyton Grammar Sch.; Homerton Coll., Cambridge (BEd Hons 1994); Nat. Coll. for Sch. Leadership (NPQH 2002). Head of English: York House Sch., Rickmansworth, 1994–96; Cumnor Hse Sch., Croydon, 1996–99; Dep. Hd (Dir of Studies), Bute Hse Prep. Sch. for Girls, Hammersmith, 1999–2004. Team Inspector, ISI, 2006–. Gov., Fairley Hse Sch., Pimlico, 2006–. *Recreations:* believing a book in the hand is worth two on the shelf, getting lost in hidden corners of London, New York and San Francisco, enjoying fine wine, good food and good company. *Address:* Preparatory Department, City of London School for Girls, St Giles' Terrace, Barbican, EC2Y 8BB. *T:* (020) 7847 5540, *Fax:* (020) 7638 3212; *e-mail:* broughj@clsg.org.uk.

BROUGHAM, family name of **Baron Brougham and Vaux**.

BROUGHAM AND VAUX, 5th Baron *cr* 1860; **Michael John Brougham,** CBE 1995; *b* 2 Aug. 1938; *s* of 4th Baron and Jean (*d* 1992), *d* of late Brig.-Gen. G. B. S. Follett, DSO, MVO; *S* father, 1967; *m* 1st, 1963, Olivia Susan (marr. diss. 1968; she *d* 1986), *d* of Rear-Admiral Gordon Thomas Seccombe Gray, CB, DSC; one *d*; 2nd, 1969, Catherine Gulliver (marr. diss. 1981), *d* of late W. Gulliver; one *s*. *Educ:* Lycée Jaccard, Lausanne; Millfield School. Dep. Chm. of Cttees, H of L, 1992–; a Dep. Speaker, H of L, 1995–; elected Mem., H of L, 1999; Member: Select Cttee on H of L Officers, 1997–99, on Hybrid Instruments, 1999–2001; Statutory Instruments Jt Cttee, 2001–07; Information Cttee, 2006–; Vice-Chm., Assoc. of Cons. Peers, 1998–2002, 2003–07. President: RoSPA, 1986–89; Nat. Health and Safety Gps Council, 1994–. Chm., Tax Payers Soc., 1989–91. Chm., European Secure Vehicle Alliance, 1992–. *Heir: s* Hon. Charles William Brougham, *b* 9 Nov. 1971. *Address:* 11 Westminster Gardens, Marsham Street, SW1P 4JA.

BROUGHAM, Christopher John; QC 1988; *b* 11 Jan. 1947; *s* of late Lt-Comdr Patrick Brougham and of Elizabeth Anne (*née* Vestey); *m* 1974, Mary Olwen (*née* Corker); one *s* three *d*. *Educ:* Radley Coll.; Worcester Coll., Oxford (BA Hons). Called to the Bar, Inner Temple, 1969, Bencher, 2007; Dep. High Court Bankruptcy Registrar, 1984. Dep. Churchwarden, Christ Church, Kensington, 1980–95. *Publications:* (contrib.) Encyclopedia of Financial Provision in Family Matters, 1998–; (jtly) Muir Hunter on Personal Insolvency, 2000–. *Recreations:* music, crossword puzzles. *Address:* 3–4 South Square, Gray's Inn, WC1R 5HP. *T:* (020) 7696 9900.

BROUGHER, Kerry; Director of Art and Programs and Chief Curator, Hirshhorn Museum and Sculpture Garden, since 2001; *b* 25 Sept. 1952; *s* of Russell Brougher and Margaret Brougher (*née* Smith); *m* 1987, Nora Halpern; two *d*. *Educ:* Univ. of Calif at Irvine (BA 1974); UCLA (MA 1978). Museum of Contemporary Art, Los Angeles: Asst Curator, 1982–87; Associate Curator, 1987–93; Curator, 1993–97; Dir, MOMA, Oxford, 1997–2000. Co-Artistic Dir, Gwangju Biennale, Korea, 2004. Visitor, Ashmolean Mus., Univ. of Oxford, 1998–; Vis. Fellow, Nuffield Coll., Oxford, 1999–. Mem. Bd of Advrs, Filmforum, Los Angeles, 1994–. FRSA 2000. *Publications:* The Image of Abstraction, 1988; The Beatrice and Philip Gersh Collection, 1989; Wolfgang Laib, 1992; Robert Irwin, 1993; Hiroshi Sugimoto, 1993; Hall of Mirrors: art and film since 1945, 1996; Jeff Wall, 1997; Gustav Metzger, 1998; Notorious: Alfred Hitchcock and contemporary art, 1999; Ed Ruscha, 2000; Enclosed and Enchanted, 2000; Open City: street photographs since 1950, 2001; Visual Music, 2005; Hiroshi Sugimoto, 2005. *Address:* Hirshhorn Museum and Sculpture Garden, PO Box 37012, MRC 350, Washington, DC 20013–7012, USA.

BROUGHTON, family name of **Baron Fairhaven**.

BROUGHTON, Sir David (Delves), 13th Bt *cr* 1660, of Broughton, Staffordshire; *b* 7 May 1942; *s* of Lt-Comdr P. J. D. Broughton, RN, *g g g s* of Rev. Sir Henry Delves Broughton, 8th Bt, and of his 1st wife, Nancy Rosemary, *yr d* of J. E. Paterson; *S* kinsman, 1993, but his name does not appear on the Official Roll of the Baronetage; *m* 1969, Diane, *d* of R. L. Nicol. *Heir: half b* Geoffrey Delves Broughton [*b* 1962; *m* 1986, Karen Louise Wright; two *s* two *d*]. *Address:* 31 Mayfield Court, Sandy, Beds SG19 1NF.

BROUGHTON, Martin Faulkner, FCA; Chairman, British Airways, since 2004 (Director, since 2000); President, Confederation of British Industry, since 2007; *b* 15 April 1947; *m* 1974, Jocelyn Mary Rodgers; one *s* one *d*. *Educ:* Westminster City Grammar Sch. FCA 1969. Career in BAT Group: British-American Tobacco Co.: travelling auditor, 1971–74; Head Office, 1974–80; Souza Cruz, Brazil, 1980–85; Eagle Star, 1985–88 and (Chm.) 1992–93; Chm., Wiggins Teape Gp, 1989–90; Finance Dir, 1988–92; Man. Dir, Financial Services, 1992–98; Gp Chief Exec. and Dep. Chm., BAT Industries, 1993–98; Chm., 1998–2004. Non-exec. Dir, Whitbread, 1993–2000. Ind. Dir, 1999–2007, Chm., 2004–07, British Horseracing Bd. Member: Takeover Panel, 1996–99; Financial Reporting Council, 1998–2004. Co-Chm., TransAtlantic Business Dialogue, 2006–08. *Recreations:* theatre, golf, horseracing. *Address:* British Airways plc, Waterside HBB3, PO Box 365, Harmondsworth UB7 0GB. *Club:* Tandridge Golf.

BROUGHTON, Dr Peter, FREng; Consultant, Peter Fraenkel and Partners (formerly Peter Fraenkel Maritime), since 2003; *b* 1944; *s* of late Thomas Frederick Broughton and Mary Theodosia Broughton; *m* 1968, Janet Mary, *d* of late Ronald George Silveston and Molly Silveston; two *s*. *Educ:* Rowlinson Technical Sch., Sheffield; Manchester Univ. (BSc 1966; PhD 1970). FICE; FIStructE; FIMarEST; FRINA; FREng (FEng 1996). Engrg Surveyor, Lloyd's Register of Shipping, 1971–74; Partner, Campbell Reith and Partners, 1974–75; Sen. Structural Engr, Burmah Oil Development, 1975–76; Supervising Structural Engr, BNOC, 1977–79; Phillips Petroleum Co., 1979–2003: Sen Structl Engr, 1979–82, Civil Engrg Supervisor, 1982–86, UK; Project Engr and Co. Rep., Ekofisk Protective Barrier Project, Norway, 1986–90; Engrg and Procurement Manager, Judy/Joanne Develt Project, UK, 1990–94; Project Manager: for Substructures, Ekofisk II Develt Project, Norway, 1994–98; Maureen Platform Re-Float and Decommng Project, UK, 1998–2003. Vis. Prof., Dept of Civil Engrg, ICSTM, 1991–2005; Royal Acad. of Engrg Vis. Prof., Oxford Univ., 2004–07. Stanley Grey Award, IMarE, 1992; George Stephenson Medal, 1993, Bill Curtin Medal, 1997, Overseas Premium, 1998, David Hislop Award, 1999, Contribution to Institution Activity Award, 2002, ICE. *Publications:* The Analysis of Cable and Catenary Structures, 1994; numerous technical papers on offshore structures. *Recreations:* walking, fishing, swimming. *Address:* Peter Fraenkel and Partners, Consulting Engineers, South House, South Street, Dorking RH4 2JZ.

BROUN, Sir Wayne (Hercules), 14th Bt *cr* 1686 (NS) of Colstoun, Haddingtonshire; Chief Executive Officer, Australian Asian Pacific Services Pty Ltd, since 2002; *b* 23 Jan. 1952; *s* of Hulance Haddington Broun and Joy Maude Broun (*née* Stack); *S* uncle, 2007; *m* 1st, 1976 (marr. diss. 1998); one *s* one *d*; 2nd, 2001, Caroline Mary Lavender; one *d*. *Educ:* Sydney Grammar Sch. Queen's Commn (Army), OTU; Lieut, Royal Australian Regt, 1973. Dist Mgr, G. M. Holden, 1976; Man. Dir, Lorimar Telepictures, 1985; Man. Dir and Vice Pres., Warner Bros Internat. Television, Australia/NZ Asia Pacific, 1990; Chm., Warner Bros Australia, 1991. Nat. Service Medal, 2004; Australian Defence Medal, 2006. *Recreations:* sport, reading, travel. *Heir: s* Richard Haddington Broun, *b* 3 May 1984. *Address:* 112 Narrabeen Park Parade, Warriewood Beach, NSW 2102, Australia. *T:* (2) 99974175; *e-mail:* aapswayne@bigpond.com. *Clubs:* Royal Automobile of Australia (Sydney); Royal Motor Yacht (Broken Bay); Bayview Golf; Millbrook Golf (NZ).

BROWALDH, Tore; Grand Cross, Order of Star of the North, 1974; Kt Comdr's Cross, Order of Vasa, 1963; Hon. Chairman, Svenska Handelsbanken, since 1988; Deputy Chairman, Nobel Foundation, 1966–88; *b* 23 Aug. 1917; *s* of Knut Ernfrid Browaldh and Ingrid Gezelius; *m* 1942, Gunnel Eva Ericson; three *s* one *d*. *Educ:* Stockholm Univ. (MA Politics, Economics and Law, 1941). Financial Attaché, Washington, 1943; Asst Sec., Royal Cttee of Post-War Econ. Planning, and Admin. Sec., Industrial Inst. for Econ. and Social Res., 1944–45; Sec. to Bd of Management, Svenska Handelsbanken, 1946–49; Dir of Econ., Social, Cultural and Refugee Dept, Secretariat Gen., Council of Europe, Strasbourg, 1949–51; Exec. Vice Pres., Confedn of Swedish Employers, 1951–54; Chief Gen. Man., Svenska Handelsbanken, 1955–66, Chm., 1966–78, Vice-Chm., 1978–88. Chairman: Svenska Cellulosa AB, 1965–88; Sandrew theater and movie AB, 1963–; Swedish IBM, 1978–; Swedish Unilever AB, 1977–; Industrivärden, 1976–88; Deputy Chairman: Beijerinvest AB, 1975–82; AB Volvo, 1977–88; Director: Volvo Internat. Adv. Bd, 1980–88; IBM World Trade Corp., Europe/ME/Africa, New York, 1979–88; Unilever Adv. Bd, Rotterdam and London, 1976–88. Member: Swedish Govt's Econ. Planning Commn, 1962–73 and Res. Adv. Bd, 1966–70; Consultative Cttee, Internat. Fedn of Insts for Advanced Study, 1972–; UN Gp of Eminent Persons on Multinational Corporations, 1973–74. Member: Royal Swedish Acad. of Sciences; Hudson Inst., USA; Soc. of Scientists and Members of Parlt, Sweden; Royal Swedish Acad. of Engrg Sciences; Royal Acad. of Arts and Sciences, Uppsala; World Acad. of Art and Scis. Dr of Technol. *hc* Royal Inst. of Technol., 1967; Dr of Econs *hc* Gothenburg, 1980. St Erik's Medal, Sweden, 1961; Gold Medal for public service, Sweden, 1981. *Publications:* Management and Society, 1961; (autobiography): vol. I, The Pilgrimage of a Journeyman, 1976; vol. II, The Long Road, 1980; vol. III, Against the Wind, 1984. *Recreations:* jazz, piano, golf, chess. *Address:* (office) Svenska Handelsbanken, Kungsträdgårdsgatan 2, 10670 Stockholm, Sweden. *T:* (8) 229220; (home) Sturegatan 14, 11436 Stockholm, Sweden. *T:* (8) 6619643. *Club:* Sällskapet (Stockholm).

BROWN; *see* Malloch-Brown, family name of Baron Malloch-Brown.

BROWN, family name of **Baron Brown of Eaton-under-Heywood**.

BROWN OF EATON-UNDER-HEYWOOD, Baron *cr* 2004 (Life Peer), of Eaton-under-Heywood in the county of Shropshire; **Simon Denis Brown,** Kt 1984; PC 1992; a Lord of Appeal in Ordinary, since 2004; *b* 9 April 1937; *s* of late Denis Baer Brown and Edna Elizabeth (*née* Abrahams); *m* 1963, Jennifer Buddicom; two *s* one *d*. *Educ:* Stowe Sch.; Worcester Coll., Oxford (Hon. Fellow, 1993). Commnd 2nd Lt RA, 1955–57. Called to the Bar, Middle Temple, 1961 (Harmsworth Schol.); Master of the Bench, Hon. Soc. of Middle Temple, 1980; a Recorder, 1979–84; First Jun. Treasury Counsel, Common Law, 1979–84; a Judge of the High Court of Justice, QBD, 1984–92; a Lord Justice of Appeal, 1992–2004; Vice-Pres., Court of Appeal (Civil Div.), 2001–03. President: Security Service Tribunal, 1989–2000; Intelligence Services Tribunal, 1995–2000; Intelligence Services Comr, 2000–06. Chm., Sub-Cttee E (Law and Instns), H of L Select Cttee on EU, 2005–07. *Recreations:* golf, theatre, reading. *Address:* House of Lords, SW1A 0PW. *Clubs:* Garrick; Denham Golf.

BROWN, Hon. Alan John; Chairman: Apprenticeships Plus, Victoria, since 2000; Work & Training Ltd, since 2004; *b* Wonthaggi, Vic, 25 Jan. 1946; *m* 1972, Paula McBurnie; three *s* one *d*. Councillor, Wonthaggi BC, 1970–78, Mayor, 1974–77; MLA (L): Westernport, Vic, 1979–85; Gippsland W, Vic, 1985–96; Victorian Shadow Minister for: Youth, Sport and Recreation, 1982; Aboriginal Affairs and Housing, 1982–85; Correctional Services, 1984–85; Resources, 1985; Tspt, 1985–89; Dep. Leader of Opposition, 1987–89; Leader of Opposition, 1989–91; Shadow Minister for Transport, 1991–92; Minister for Transport, 1992–96; Agent-Gen. for Victoria in UK, 1997–2000. Bd Mem., Traffic Technologies Ltd, 2004–. Chairman: Bass Coast Community Foundn, 2002–; Inner North Community Foundn, 2008–. *Recreations:* motor cycle riding, vintage cars, farming. *Address:* Bridgewater Park, Wattle Bank, Vic 3995, Australia.

BROWN, Alan Thomas, CBE 1978; DL; Chief Executive, Oxfordshire County Council, 1973–88; *b* 18 April 1928; *s* of Thomas Henry Brown and Lucy Lilian (*née* Betts); *m* 1962, Marie Christine East; two *d*. *Educ:* Wyggeston Grammar Sch., Leicester; Sidney Sussex Coll., Cambridge (Wrangler, Maths Tripos 1950, MA 1953). Fellow CIPFA, 1961. Asst, Bor. Treasurer's Dept, Wolverhampton, 1950–56; Asst Sec., IMTA, 1956–58; Dep. Co. Treas., Berks CC, 1958–61; Co. Treas., Cumberland CC, 1961–66; Town Clerk and Chief Exec., Oxford City Council, 1966–73. Member: SE Econ. Planning Council, 1975–79; Audit Commn, 1989–95. DL Oxon 1978. *Recreations:* chess, horticulture, music, reading. *Address:* 4 Malkin Drive, Beaconsfield, Bucks HP9 1JN. *T:* (01494) 677933.

BROWN, Alan Winthrop, CB 1992; Head of Health Policy Division, Health and Safety Executive, 1992–94; *b* 14 March 1934; *s* of James Brown and Evelyn V. Brown (*née* Winthrop); *m* 1959, Rut Berit (*née* Ohlson); two *s* one *d*. *Educ:* Bedford Sch.; Pembroke Coll., Cambridge (BA Hons); Cornell Univ., NY (MSc). Joined Min. of Labour, 1959; Private Sec. to Minister, 1961–62; Principal, 1963; Asst Sec., 1969. Dir of Planning, Employment Service Agency, 1973–74; Under-Sec. and Head of Incomes Div., DoE, 1975; Chief Exec., Employment Service Div., 1976–79, Trng Services Div., 1979–82, MSC; Hd Electricity Div., Dept of Energy, 1983–85; Dir, Personnel and Management Services, Dept of Employment, 1985–89; Dir, Resources and Planning, HSE, 1989–92. Chm., Godalming Trust, 1999–2005. Lay Mem., Waverley Primary Care Gp, 2000–02. *Publications:* papers on occupational psychology and industrial training. *Recreations:* history of art, literature, gardening, croquet. *Address:* Groton, Ballfield Road, Godalming, Surrey GU7 2HE.

BROWN, Alexander Douglas G.; *see* Gordon-Brown.

BROWN, Prof. Alice, PhD; Scottish Public Services Ombudsman, 2002–March 2009; Professor of Politics, University of Edinburgh, since 1997 (on leave of absence); *b* 30 Sept.

1946; *d* of Robert Wilson and Alice (*née* Morgan); *m* 1965, Alan James Brown; two *d*. *Educ:* Boroughmuir High Sch., Edinburgh; Stevenson Coll., Edinburgh; Univ. of Edinburgh (MA 1983; PhD 1990). Lectr in Econs, Univ. of Stirling, 1984–85; University of Edinburgh: Lectr, 1985–92; Sen. Lectr in Politics, 1992–97; Hd, Dept of Politics, 1995; Hd, Planning Unit, 1996; Co-Dir, Governance of Scotland Forum, subseq. Inst. of Governance, 1998–2002 ; Vice-Principal, 1999–2002; Chm., Mergers Cttee, 2001–02. Chm., Community Planning Task Force (Scotland), 2001–02; Member: SHEFC, 1998–2002; Cttee on Standards in Public Life, 1999–2003; Res. Grants Bd, ESRC; Adv. Gp, EOC, Scotland, 1995–; Adv. Bd, CRE, Scotland, 2003–. Founder Member: Engender (women's res. and campaigning gp), 1991–; Scottish Women's Co-ordination Gp, 1992–. Bd Mem., Centre for Scottish Public Policy (formerly John Wheatley Centre), 1992; Mem., Lay Adv. Gp, RCPE, 2003–. Asst Ed., Scottish Affairs jl, 1992–. FRSE 2002; AcSS 2002; Mem., CIPFA, 2004. *Publications:* (co-ed) The Scottish Government Yearbook, 1989–91; The New Scottish Politics, 2002; jointly: A Major Crisis?, 1996; Politics and Society in Scotland, 1996; Gender Equality in Scotland, 1997; The Scottish Electorate, 1999; New Scotland, New Politics?, 2001. *Address:* (until March 2009) (office) 4 Melville Street, Edinburgh EH3 7NS.

BROWN, Andrew Charles, FRICS; Secretary to the Church Commissioners, since 2003; *b* 30 Oct. 1957; *s* of Gordon Charles Brown and Joan Finch Trail Brown (*née* Tomlin); *m* 1983, Marion Denise Chamberlain; one *s* one *d*. *Educ:* Ashmole Sch.; South Bank Poly. (BSc Hons). FRICS 1994. Property Negotiator, Healey and Baker, 1981–84; Investment Surveyor, 1984–87, Associate Partner, 1987–91, Partner, 1991–94, St Quintin; Chief Surveyor, Church Commissioners, 1994–2003. Mem. Council, Westminster Property Owners' Assoc., 1997–2003; Mem., LionHeart Administration, Investment and Finance Cttee, 2006–; Dir, William Leech Foundn, William Leech (Investments) Ltd, 2007–; Chm. Trustees, 2:67 Project, 2007–. Hon. Secretary: Christians in Property, 1991–2003; 1894 Club, 2006–. *Recreations:* family, local church, golf, sport, Chelsea FC, Pathfinder camps/ventures. *Address:* Church Commissioners, Church House, Great Smith Street, SW1P 3AZ. *T:* (020) 7898 1000; *e-mail:* andrew.brown@c-of-e.org.uk.

BROWN, Dr Andrew Edward; international environmental consultant; Chief Executive, English Nature, 2003–06; *b* 9 May 1954; *s* of James Andrew Brown and Gwyneth Brown (*née* Watkins); *m* 1980, Christina Joyce Binks; two *d*. *Educ:* University Coll., Cardiff (BSc Zool. and Envmtl Studies); Leicester Poly. (PhD Freshwater Ecol.). Res. Officer and Tutor, Sussex Univ., 1980–81; Lectr, Bayero Univ., Kano, Nigeria, 1981–83; Nature Conservancy Council: Asst Regl Officer, Cheshire, 1983–86; Develt Officer, Scotland, 1986–89; Sen. Officer, York, 1989–90; English Nature: Strategic Planner, 1990–94; Corporate Manager, 1994–96; Chief Officer, Jt Nature Conservation Cttee, 1996–98; a Dir, English Nature, 1998–2002. Mem., Broads Authority, 1999–2005; non-exec. Bd Mem., Envmt Agency, 2006–. Chairman: UK Cttee, IUCN, 2005–07; Policy Cttee, CPRE, 2006–; Mem. Council, RSPB, 2006–; Trustee, Wildfowl and Wetlands Trust, 2008–. Fellow and Mem. Council, Linnean Soc., 2007. FIBiol 2006. *Publications:* contrib. to books on freshwater ecology; papers in scientific jls. *Recreations:* reading, DIY, walking, travel, ski-ing. *Address:* 1A The Lane, West Deeping, Peterborough PE6 9HS. *T:* (01778) 343229.

BROWN, Andrew Edwin, FRCS; FDSRCS, FDSRCPSGlas; Consultant Maxillofacial Surgeon, Queen Victoria Hospital, East Grinstead, since 1981; *b* 22 Aug. 1945; *s* of Edwin and Kathleen Brown; *m* 1969, Joan Elizabeth Phillips; one *s* two *d*. *Educ:* Sir Joseph Williamson's Mathematical Sch., Rochester; Guy's Hosp., Univ. of London (BDS Hons 1969; MB BS 1973). LDSRCS 1968, FDSRCS 1975; LRCP, MRCS 1973, FRCS 1986; FDSRCPSGlas 1975. Registrar, Dept of Oral and Maxillofacial Surgery, Eastman Dental Hosp. and Inst. of Dental Surgery, Univ. of London, 1974–76; Sen. Registrar, Dept of Oral and Maxillofacial Surgery, Queen Victoria Hosp., E Grinstead, 1976–81. Hon. Civil Consultant in Oral and Maxillofacial Surgery, RAF, 2000–. Chm., Specialist Adv. Cttee in Oral and Maxillofacial Surgery, 2003–05. President: Inst. of Maxillofacial Prosthetists and Technologists, 2002–03; BOAMS, 2006–07. *Publications:* (with P. Banks) Fractures of the Facial Skeleton, 2001; chapters in: Operative Maxillofacial Surgery, 1998; Maxillofacial Surgery, 1999, 2nd edn 2007; papers on facial trauma, reconstruction, etc in learned jls. *Recreations:* art and graphic design, travel, ski-ing, swimming, reading history and biography, lay preaching. *Address:* c/o Department of Maxillofacial Surgery, Queen Victoria Hospital, E Grinstead, W Sussex RH19 3DZ. *T:* (01342) 414305; *e-mail:* andrew.brown@qvh.nhs.uk.

BROWN, Andrew Gibson, CBE 2003; QPM 1997; HM Chief Inspector of Constabulary for Scotland, 2004–07; *b* 11 April 1945; *s* of Alexander Brown and Euphemia Brown; *m* 1988, Fiona McMillan; one *s* one *d*. *Educ:* Kelso High Sch. Police Cadet, 1961; Police Constable, 1964; Detective Chief Supt, 1992; Asst Chief Constable (Crime), Lothian and Borders Police, 1993–98; Chief Constable, Grampian Police, 1998–2004. *Recreations:* spectating Rugby, Prince's Trust, Common Purpose. *Club:* Melrose Rugby Football.

BROWN, Andrew William; Director General, Advertising Association, 1993–2006; *b* 3 March 1946; *s* of Harry Brown and Geraldine (*née* O'Leary); *m* 1977, Shelby Ann Hill. *Educ:* St Edmund's Coll., Ware, Herts. J. Walter Thompson Co. Ltd. 1965–93, Board Dir, 1982–93. Chm., CAM Foundn, 1994–96. Director: Advertising Standards Bd of Finance, 1993–; Broadcast Advertising Standards Bd of Finance Ltd, 2004–; Chairman: Cttee of Advertising Practice, 1999–; Broadcast Cttee of Advertising Practice, 2004– (Mem., Advertising Adv. Cttee, 2004–); Mem., ITC Advertising Adv. Cttee, 1999–2003. *Recreations:* cricket, theatre, London, Bodmin Moor. *Address:* 81 Westbourne Terrace, W2 6QS. *Clubs:* Reform, MCC; XL.

BROWN, Prof. Archibald Haworth, CMG 2005; FBA 1991; Professor of Politics, University of Oxford, 1989–2005, now Professor Emeritus; Fellow, St Antony's College, Oxford, 1971–2005, now Fellow Emeritus (Sub-Warden, 1995–97); Director, Russian and East European Centre, St Antony's College, 1991–94 and 1999–2001; *b* 10 May 1938; *s* of late Rev. Alexander Douglas Brown and Mary Brown (*née* Yates); *m* 1963, Patricia Susan Cornwell; one *s* one *d*. *Educ:* Annan Acad.; Dumfries Acad.; City of Westminster Coll.; LSE (BSc Econ, 1st Cl. Hons 1962). MA Oxon 1972. Reporter, Annandale Herald and Annandale Observer, 1954–56. National Service, 1956–58. Lectr in Politics, Glasgow Univ., 1964–71; British Council exchange scholar, Moscow Univ., 1967–68; Lectr in Soviet Instns, Univ. of Oxford, 1971–89. Visiting Professor: of Political Science, Yale Univ. and Univ. of Connecticut, 1980; Columbia Univ., NY, 1985; Univ. of Texas, Austin, 1990–91; INSEAD, 1991; Distinguished Vis. Fellow, Kellogg Inst. for Internat. Studies, Univ. of Notre Dame, 1998; Henry L. Stimson Lectures, Yale Univ., 1980. Mem. Council, SSEES, Univ. of London, 1992–98. Founder AcSS 1999. For. Hon. Mem., Amer. Acad. of Arts and Scis, 2003. *Publications:* Soviet Politics and Political Science, 1974; (ed jtly and contrib.) The Soviet Union since the Fall of Khrushchev, 1975, 2nd edn 1978; (ed jtly and contrib.) Political Culture and Political Change in Communist States, 1977, 2nd edn 1979; (ed jtly and contrib.) Authority, Power and Policy in the USSR: essays dedicated to Leonard Schapiro, 1980; (ed jtly and contrib.) The Cambridge Encyclopedia of Russia and the Soviet Union, 1982; (ed jtly and contrib.) Soviet Policy for the 1980s, 1982; (ed and contrib.) Political Culture and Communist Studies, 1984; (ed and contrib.) Political Leadership in the Soviet Union, 1989; (ed and contrib.) The Soviet Union: a biographical dictionary, 1990; (ed and contrib.) New Thinking in Soviet Politics, 1992; (ed jtly and contrib.) The Cambridge Encyclopedia of Russia and the Former Soviet Union, 1994; The Gorbachev Factor, 1996 (W. J. M. Mackenzie Prize, Pol Studies Assoc., 1998; Alec Nove Prize, British Assoc. for Slavonic and E Eur. Studies, 1998); (ed jtly and contrib.) The British Study of Politics in the Twentieth Century, 1999; (ed and contrib.) Contemporary Russian Politics: a reader, 2001; (ed jtly and contrib.) Gorbachev, Yeltsin and Putin: political leadership in Russia's transition, 2001; (ed and contrib.) The Demise of Marxism-Leninism in Russia, 2004; Seven Years that Changed the World: Perestroika in perspective, 2007; The Rise and Fall of Communism, 2009; papers in academic jls and symposia; *festschrift:* Leading Russia - Putin in Perspective: essays in honour of Archie Brown, ed Alex Pravda, 2005. *Recreations:* novels and political memoirs, opera, watching football and cricket. *Address:* St Antony's College, Oxford OX2 6JF.

BROWN, Rt Rev. Arthur Durrant; a Suffragan Bishop of Toronto, 1981–93 (Bishop of York-Scarborough); *b* 7 March 1926; *s* of Edward S. Brown and Laura A. Durrant; *m* 1949, Norma Inez Rafuse (*d* 2005); three *d*. *Educ:* Univ. of Western Ontario (BA 1949); Huron College (LTh 1949). Ordained deacon, 1949; priest, 1950, Huron. Rector: of Paisley with Cargill and Pinkerton, 1948–50; of Glenworth and St Stephen, London, Ont., 1950–53; of St John, Sandwich, Windsor, Ont., 1953–63; of St Michael and All Angels, Toronto, 1963–80; Canon of Toronto, 1972–74; Archdeacon of York, Toronto, 1974–80. Member: Nat. Exec. Council, Anglican Church of Canada, 1969–81; Judicial Council of Ontario, 1978–85; Multi-Cultural Council of Ontario, 1985–87; Press Council of Ontario, 1986. Hon. Chm. Adv. Bd, Cdn Foundn on Compulsive Gambling (Ontario), 1983–; Chairman: Canadian Friends to West Indian Christians, 1982–; Royal Visit Children's Fund, 1984–. Columnist, Toronto Sunday Sun, 1974–86. Mem., Corp. of Huron Coll., 1961–86; Chancellor, Renison Coll., 1994–2001, Chancellor Emeritus, 2001. City of Toronto Civic Award, 1981. Hon. DD: Huron Coll., 1976; Wycliffe Coll., 1981; Trinity Coll., 1999. Distinguished Service Award, 5th Caribbean Anglican Consultation, 1999. *Address:* 45 Livingston Road # 810, Scarborough, ON M1E 1K8, Canada.

BROWN, Sir (Austen) Patrick, KCB 1995; Chairman: Go-Ahead Group, since 2002 (Director, since 1999); Amey plc, since 2004; *b* 14 April 1940; *m* 1966, Mary (*née* Bulger); one *d*. *Educ:* Royal Grammar School, Newcastle upon Tyne; School of Slavonic and East European Studies, Univ. of London. Carreras Ltd, 1961–69 (Cyprus, 1965–66, Belgium, 1967–68); Management Consultant, Urwick Orr & Partners, UK, France, Portugal, Sweden, 1969–72; DoE, 1972; Asst. Sec., Property Services Agency, 1976–80, Dept of Transport, 1980–83; Under Sec., Dept of Transport, 1983–88; Dep. Sec., DoE, 1988–90; Second Perm. Sec., and Chief Exec., PSA, DoE, 1990–91; Perm. Sec., Dept of Transport, 1991–97. Dep. Chm., Kvaerner Corporate Develt, 1998–99; Director: Hunting PLC, 1998–2001; Arlington Securities plc, 1999–2004; Northumbrian Water Gp plc, 2003–. Chm., Ind. Transport Commn, 1999–. Vis. Prof., Newcastle Univ., 1998–. Leader, Way Ahead Study into Ex-Service Charities, 2001–02. Trustee, Charities Aid Foundn, 1998–2006; Chm. Trustees, Mobility Choice, 1998–. *Club:* Royal Automobile.

BROWN, Barry; *see* Brown, James B. C.

BROWN, Benjamin Robert; Special Correspondent, BBC Television News, since 1998; *b* 26 May 1960; *s* of late Antony Victor Brown and of Sheila Mary Brown; *m* 1991, Geraldine Anne Ryan; one *s* two *d*. *Educ:* Sutton Valence Sch., Kent; Keble Coll., Oxford (BA Hons PPE); Centre for Journalism Studies, UC, Cardiff. Reporter: Radio Clyde, 1982; Radio City, 1982–85; Independent Radio News, 1985–88; BBC Television News: Corresp., 1988–91; Moscow Corresp., 1991–94; Foreign Affairs Corresp., 1994–98. *Publication:* (with D. Shukman) All Necessary Means: inside the Gulf War, 1991. *Recreations:* reading, cinema, following Liverpool Football Club. *Address:* c/o BBC Television News, World Affairs Unit, Room 2505, Television Centre, Wood Lane, W12 7RJ.

BROWN, Adm. Sir Brian (Thomas), KCB 1989; CBE 1983; Chairman, P-E International plc, 1995–98; Director: Cray Electronics plc, 1991–96; Lorien plc, 1996–2007; *b* 31 Aug. 1934; *s* of late Walter Brown and Gladys (*née* Baddeley); *m* 1959, Veronica, *d* of late Wing Comdr and Mrs J. D. Bird; two *s*. *Educ:* Peter Symonds' School. Joined RN 1952; pilot in 898 and 848 Sqdns, 1959–62; Dep. Supply Officer, HMY Britannia, 1966–68; Supply Officer, HMS Tiger, 1973–75; Secretary: to VCNS, 1975–78; to First Sea Lord, 1979–82; rcds 1983; CO HMS Raleigh, 1984–85; DGNPS, 1986; Dir Gen., Naval Manpower and Trng, 1986–88, and Chief Naval Supply and Secretariat Officer, 1987–88; Chief of Naval Personnel, Second Sea Lord and Admiral Pres., RNC, Greenwich, 1988–91, retired. Chairman: King George's Fund for Sailors, 1993–2003; Exec. Cttee, Nuffield Trust for Forces of the Crown, 1996–2003; Michael May Young Cricketers Foundn, 1993–2008; President: Victory Services Assoc., 1993–2002; Friends of RN Mus. and HMS Victory, 1993–2003; Portsmouth Services Fly Fishing Assoc., 2005–; CPRE Hants, 2008–. Churchwarden, Froxfield with Privett, 1999–2008. CCMI (CBIM 1989); FIPD (FIPM 1990). Hon. DEd CNAA, 1990. Freeman, City of London, 1989; Liveryman, Gardeners' Co., 1991. Jt Master, Clinkard Meon Valley Beagles, 2003–. *Recreations:* cricket, gardening, fishing. *Address:* The Old Dairy, Stoner Hill Road, Froxfield, Petersfield, Hants GU32 1DX. *Club:* Army and Navy.

BROWN, Bruce; *see* Brown, John B.

BROWN, Prof. Bruce; Professor of Graphic Design, since 1989, and Pro-Vice Chancellor (Research) since 2006, University of Brighton; *b* 14 June 1949; *s* of George and Grace Brown; *m* 1976, Morag Ross; two *d*. *Educ:* Liverpool Coll. of Art (Foundn Cert. 1968); Canterbury Coll. of Art (DipAD 1971); Royal Coll. of Art (MA 1978). Lectr, RCA, 1978–81; Head, Department of Graphic Design: Norwich Sch. of Art, 1981–84; Brighton Poly., 1984–89; Dean, Faculty of Arts and Architecture, Univ. of Brighton, 1989–2006. Dir, Subject Centre for Art, Design & Media, Higher Educn Acad., York, 1999–. Indep. design consultant and Art Dir, Crafts mag., Crafts Council, 1978–84. Chm., Main Panel O, 2008 RAE, 2005–; Mem., Hong Kong Council for Acad. Accreditation, 1991–. FRSA 1973. Hon. FRCA 2004; Hon. Fellow, Kent Inst. of Art & Design, 2005. *Publications:* Brown's Index to Photocomposition Typography, 1983; Graphic Memory, 2000. *Recreations:* music, travel, food, wine. *Address:* Faculty of Arts and Architecture, University of Brighton, Grand Parade, Brighton, East Sussex BN2 2JY; *e-mail:* b.brown@brighton.ac.uk. *Clubs:* Chelsea Arts, Double Crown, Wynkyn de Worde Society.

BROWN, Bruce Macdonald, QSO 1998; National Vice-President, New Zealand Institute of International Affairs, since 2004 (Director, 1993–97; Chairman, Research Committee, 1993–2004); *b* 24 Jan. 1930; *s* of John Albert Brown and Caroline Dorothea Brown (*née* Jorgensen); *m* 1st, 1953, Edith Irene (*née* Raynor) (*d* 1989); two *s* one *d*; 2nd, 1990, Françoise Rousseau (*d* 1995); 3rd, 2006, Josephine Stening. *Educ:* Victoria

University of Wellington (MA Hons). Private Secretary to Prime Minister, 1957–59; Second Sec., Kuala Lumpur, 1960–62; First Sec. (later Counsellor and Dep. Perm. Rep.), New Zealand Mission to UN, New York, 1963–67; Head of Administration, Min. of Foreign Affairs, Wellington, 1967–68; Director, NZ Inst. of International Affairs, 1969–71; NZ Dep. High Commissioner, Canberra, 1972–75; Ambassador to Iran, 1975–78, and Pakistan, 1976–78; Asst Sec., Min. of Foreign Affairs, 1978–81; Dep. High Comr in London, 1981–85; Ambassador to Thailand, Vietnam and Laos, 1985–88, to Burma, 1986–88; High Comr to Canada, also accredited to Barbados, Guyana, Jamaica and Trinidad and Tobago, 1988–92. Sen. Fellow, Centre for Strategic Studies, Victoria University of Wellington, 2003–. *Publications:* The Rise of New Zealand Labour, 1962; (ed) Asia and the Pacific in the 1970s, 1971; (ed) New Zealand in World Affairs, Vol. III, 1972–1990, 1999. *Recreations:* reading, golf. *Address:* New Zealand Institute of International Affairs, PO Box 600, Wellington, New Zealand.

BROWN, Cedric Harold, FREng, FIGEM, FICE; consultant; Chairman: CB Consultants, since 1996; Atlantic Caspian Resources plc, since 1999; Intellipower, since 2003; *b* 7 March 1935; *s* of late William Herbert Brown and Constance Dorothy Brown (*née* Frances); *m* 1956, Joan Hendry; one *s* three *d*. *Educ:* Sheffield, Rotherham and Derby Colleges of Technology. Pupil Gas Distribution Engineer, E Midlands Gas Bd, 1953–58, Tech. Asst, 1958–59; Engineering Asst, Tunbridge Wells Borough Council, 1959–60; engineering posts, E Midlands Gas Bd, 1960–75 (Chief Engineer, 1973–75); Dir of Engineering, E Midlands Gas, 1975–78; British Gas Corp., subseq. British Gas plc: Asst Dir (Ops) and Dir (Construction), 1978–79; Dir, Morecambe Bay Project, 1980–87; Regl Chm., British Gas W Midlands, 1987–89; Dir, Man. Dir, Exploration and Production, 1989; Man. Dir, Regl Services, 1989–91; Sen. Man. Dir, 1991–92; Chief Exec., 1992–96. Chairman: Business Champions-E Midlands Develt Agency, 2001–04; Lachesis Investment Adv. Cttee, 2002–. Pres., IGasE, 1996–97. FREng (FEng 1990). Liveryman, Engineers' Co., 1988–. *Publications:* tech. papers to professional bodies. *Recreations:* sport, countryside, places of historic interest. *Address:* Atlantic Caspian Resources plc, 1 Grosvenor Crescent, SW1X 7EF.

BROWN, (Cedric Wilfred) George E.; *see* Edmonds-Brown.

BROWN, Charles Dargie, FREng; consulting engineer, retired; Joint Chairman, Mott, Hay & Anderson, Consulting Engineers, 1981–89; *b* 13 April 1927; *s* of William Henry Brown and Jean Dargie; *m* 1952, Sylvia Margaret Vallis; one *s* one *d*. *Educ:* Harris Acad., Dundee; St Andrews Univ. (BScEng, 1st Cl. Hons.). FICE; FREng (FEng 1981). Joined staff of Mott, Hay & Anderson, 1947; engaged on highways, tunnels and bridge works, incl. Tamar Bridge, Forth Road Bridge, George Street Bridge, Newport, Kingsferry and Queensferry Bridges, 1947–65; Partner and Director, 1965. Principally concerned with planning, design and supervision of major works, 1965–89, incl. Mersey Queensway tunnels and new London Bridge, and projects in Hong Kong (Tsing Ma Bridge), Malaysia (Pahang River Bridges), highway and bridge works in Indonesia and USA; participated in devel of underground rly systems in Melbourne and Singapore. Member, Smeatonian Soc. of Civil Engrs, 1984–. Hon. LLD Dundee, 1982. *Publications:* papers to Instn of Civil Engrs, on Kingsferry Bridge, George St Bridge, London Bridge and Mersey tunnels; also various papers to engrg confs. *Recreations:* golf, gardening, bird watching, reading. *Address:* Mallards Mere, Russell Way, Petersfield, Hants GU31 4LD. *T:* (01730) 267820. *Club:* Royal Automobile.

BROWN, Christina Hambley, (Lady Evans); *see* Brown, Tina.

BROWN, Christopher; Director and Chief Executive, National Society for Prevention of Cruelty to Children, 1989–95; *b* 21 June 1938; *s* of Reginald Frank Greenwood Brown and Margaret Eleanor Brown; *m* 1968, Helen Margaret, *d* of George A. Woolsey and Hilda M. Woolsey; three *s* one *d*. *Educ:* Hertford Grammar Sch.; King's Coll., London (AKC); Heythrop Coll., London (MA 2005). Home Office Cert. in Probation. Ordained deacon, 1963, priest, 1964; Assistant Curate, Diocese of Southwark: St Hilda's, Crofton Park, 1963; St Michael's, Wallington, 1964–67. Probation Officer, Nottingham, 1968–72; Sen. Probation Officer, W Midlands, 1972–74; Asst Dir, Social Services, Solihull, 1974–76; Asst Chief Probation Officer, Hereford and Worcester, 1976–79; Chief Probation Officer: Oxfordshire, 1979–86; Essex, 1986–89. Member: Parole Bd, 1985–87; Trng Cttee, Inst. for Study and Treatment of Delinquency, 1986–89; Professional Adv. Cttee, NSPCC, 1986–89; Chm., Social Issues Cttee, Assoc. of Chief Officers of Probation, 1985–87. Mem., Green Coll., Oxford, 1981–86. Licensed to officiate, Dio. Chelmsford, 1986–. FRSA 2008. *Publications:* contribs to various jls on social work practice and community issues, 1971–, on Christian/Muslim relations, and to Christian/Islamic studies and dialogues, 2005–. *Recreations:* walking, reading, music, conversation, gardening. *Address:* 7 Baronia Croft, Colchester, Essex CO4 9EE; *e-mail:* chribrow@yahoo.co.uk.

BROWN, Maj. Gen. Christopher Charles, CBE 1999; General Officer Commanding Northern Ireland, since 2007; *b* 26 Oct. 1955; *s* of Philip Alexander George Brown and Gladys Maud Brown; *m* 1983, Leigh Margaret Kennedy; two *s*. *Educ:* University Coll. Cardiff (LLB); Peterhouse, Cambridge (MPhil). Battery Comdr, Chestnut Troop, RHA, 1990–91; UN Mil. Observer, Western Sahara, 1991–92; Directing Staff, Staff Coll., 1992–94; CO, 7th Parachute Regt, RHA, 1994–96; ACOS Plans, HQ ARRC, 1996–99; Comdr RA, 1st Armd Div., 1999–2002; Dep. Sen. British Mil. Advr, US Central Comd, 2002; ADC to the Queen, 2002–03; Director: RA, 2002–03; Mil. Ops, MoD, 2003; COS, Allied Comd Europe RRC, 2004–06; COS, NATO Internat. Security and Assistance Force, Afghanistan, 2006–07. QCVS 2007. *Recreations:* cross-country ski-ing (Bd Mem., British Biathlon Union), orienteering, mountaineering, fishing, sailing. *Address:* GOC NI, BFPO 825.

BROWN, Christopher David, MA; Headmaster, Norwich School, 1984–2002; *b* 8 July 1944; *s* of E. K. Brown; *m* 1972, Caroline Dunkerley; two *d*. *Educ:* Plymouth College; Fitzwilliam College, Cambridge (MA). Assistant Master: The Leys School, Cambridge, 1967–71; Pangbourne College, 1971–73; Radley College, 1973–84 (Head of English, 1975–84). Chairman: Choir Schs Assoc., 1997–99; HMC, 2001; Dep. Chm., ISC, 2003–06.

BROWN, Christopher Ledwith, OBE 2004; FRGS; Director, Turkey, British Council, since 2003; *b* 15 March 1953; *s* of Peter and Joanna Brown; *m* 1977, Elizabeth Varrall; one *s* two *d*. *Educ:* Leicester Univ. (BSc Geol.). Served RN, 1974–79; with British Council, 1979–: posts in Nigeria, Nepal, Spain and UK, 1979–95; Dir, Peru, 1995–99; Regl Dir, Western and Southern Europe, 1999–2003. FRGS 1978. *Recreations:* bricklaying, herding penguins. *Address:* c/o Foreign and Commonwealth Office, King Charles Street, SW1A 2AH; *e-mail:* chris.brown@britishcouncil.org.tr.

BROWN, Dr Christopher Paul Hadley; Director, Ashmolean Museum, and Fellow, Worcester College, Oxford, since 1998; *b* 15 April 1948; *s* of late Arthur Edgar Brown and of Florence Marjorie Brown; *m* 1975, Sally Madeleine Stockton; one *s* one *d*. *Educ:* Merchant Taylors' Sch.; St Catherine's Coll., Oxford (BA Hons Modern History, Dip. History of Art); Courtauld Inst. of Art, Univ. of London (PhD). National Gallery: Asst Keeper, 1971, with responsibility for Dutch and Flemish 17th cent. paintings; Dep. Keeper, 1979; Keeper, then Chief Curator, 1989–98. Trustee, Dulwich Picture Gall., 1993–2001. Visiting Professor: Univ. of St Andrews, 1996–2008; Centre for Golden Age Studies, Univ. of Amsterdam, 2002. Lectures: Ferens Fine Art, Univ. of Hull, 1980; Cargill, Univ. of Glasgow, 1987; Jasper Walls, Pierpont Morgan Library, NY, 1991; Visual Arts, QUB, 1999. Fellow, Netherlands Inst. for Advanced Study, Wassenaar, 1993–94. Member: Consultative Cttee, Burlington Mag., 1994–; Cttee of Mgt, Royal Mus. of Fine Arts, Antwerp, 1997–. *Publications:* Carel Fabritius, 1981; Van Dyck, 1982; Scenes of Everyday Life: seventeenth-century Dutch genre painting, 1984; Dutch Landscape (catalogue), 1986; The Drawings of Anthony van Dyck, 1991; (jtly) Rembrandt: the master and his workshop (catalogue), 1991; Making and Meaning: Rubens's landscapes, 1996; (jtly) Van Dyck 1599–1641, 1999; National Gallery catalogues, incl. The Dutch School 1600–1900, 1990; contribs to art magazines, UK and overseas. *Address:* Ashmolean Museum, Oxford OX1 2PH. *T:* (01865) 278005, *Fax:* (01865) 278018; *e-mail:* christopher.brown@ashmus.ox.ac.uk.

BROWN, Colin James; British Film Commissioner, since 2007; *b* 27 Nov. 1950; *s* of Gordon and Jeanne Brown; *m* 1st, 1972, Marie-Laure Delvaux (marr. diss. 1984); one *d*; 2nd, 1985, Bendicte Marie Granier; two *s*. *Educ:* George Watson's Boys' Coll., Edinburgh; RMA, Sandhurst; Reading Univ. (BA Hons Hist.). Served RWF, 1971–80 (Captain). Alexander Proudfoot, Paris, 1980–81; Rank Xerox, 1981–82; Bell and Howell, 1982–84; Rank Cintel Ltd, 1984–86; Exec. Vice Pres., Rank Cintel Inc., 1986–89; Man. Dir, Molinare, 1989–92; Divl Man. Dir, Eur. Television Networks, 1992–94; Man. Dir, Cinesite Europe Ltd, 1994–2000; CEO, Cinesite Worldwide, 2000–07. Member: Bd, UK Film Council, 2003–07; Bd, Nat. Film and TV Sch., 2005–. *Recreations:* travelling, sailing, gastronomy. *Address:* 27 Ennismore Avenue, W4 1SE. *T:* (020) 7861 7905; *e-mail:* brown@ukfilmcouncil.org.uk. *Clubs:* Soho House, Union.

BROWN, Craig; *see* Brown, J. C.

BROWN, Craig Edward Moncrieff; freelance writer, since 1977; *b* 23 May 1957; *s* of Peter Brown and Jennifer (*née* Bethell); *m* 1987, Frances Welch; one *s* one *d*. *Educ:* Farleigh House; Eton Coll.; Bristol Univ. Drama Dept. Columnist on: Sunday Telegraph, Daily Telegraph, Private Eye, Independent on Sunday, Guardian (as Wallace Arnold, and Bel Littlejohn); specializing in parody and satire. What the Papers Say Gen. Pleasure Award, 1996. *Publications:* The Marsh-Marlow Letters, 1984; A Year Inside, 1989; The Agreeable World of Wallace Arnold, 1990; Rear Columns, 1992; Welcome to My Worlds!, 1993; Craig Brown's Greatest Hits, 1993; The Hounding of John Thomas, 1994; The Private Eye Book of Craig Brown Parodies, 1995; (ed jtly) Colin Welch, The Odd Thing About the Colonel and Other Pieces, 1997; Hug Me While I Weep (For I Weep For the World): the lonely struggles of Bel Littlejohn, 1998; This is Craig Brown, 2003; Craig Brown's Imaginary Friends, 2005; 1966 and All That, 2005; The Tony Years, 2006. *Recreations:* swimming in the sea, drinking, shopping. *Address:* c/o Private Eye, 6 Carlisle Street, W1D 3BN.

BROWN, Sir (Cyril) Maxwell Palmer, (Sir Max), KCB 1969 (CB 1965); CMG 1957; Permanent Secretary, Department of Trade, March–June 1974; *b* 30 June 1914; *s* of late Cyril Palmer Brown; *m* 1940, Margaret May Gillhespy (*d* 2006); three *s* one *d*. *Educ:* Wanganui College; Victoria University College, NZ; Clare College, Cambridge. Princ. Private Secretary to Pres. Board of Trade, 1946–49; Monopolies Commn, 1951–55; Counsellor (Commercial) Washington, 1955–57; returned to Board of Trade; Second Permanent Sec., 1968–70; Sec. (Trade), DTI, 1970–74; Mem., 1975–81, Dep. Chm., 1976–81, Monopolies and Mergers Commn. Director: John Brown & Co., 1975–82; ERA Technology Ltd, 1974–86; RHP Gp plc (formerly Ransome Hoffmann Pollard Ltd), 1975–88. *Address:* 20 Cottenham Park Road, Wimbledon, SW20 0RZ. *T:* (020) 8946 7237.

BROWN, Dr Daniel McGillivray, BSc, PhD, ScD; FRS 1982; FRSC; Emeritus Reader in Organic Chemistry, Cambridge University, since 1983; Fellow of King's College, Cambridge, since 1953; Attached Scientist, MRC Laboratory of Molecular Biology, 1983–2002; *b* 3 Feb. 1923; *s* of David Cunninghame Brown and Catherine Stewart (*née* McGillivray); *m* 1953, Margaret Joyce Herbert; three *d* (one *s* decd). *Educ:* Glasgow Acad.; Glasgow Univ. (BSc); London Univ. (PhD); Cambridge Univ. (PhD, ScD). FRSC 2001. Res. Chemist, Chester Beatty Res. Inst., 1945–53; Asst Dir of Res., 1953–58, Lectr, 1959–67, Reader in Org. Chem., 1967–83, Cambridge Univ.; Vice-Provost, King's Coll., Cambridge, 1974–81. Vis. Professor: Univ. of Calif, LA, 1959–60; Brandeis Univ., 1966–67. *Publications:* scientific papers, mainly in chemical and molecular biology jls. *Recreations:* modern art, gardening. *Address:* 60 Hartington Grove, Cambridge CB1 7UE. *T:* (01223) 245304.

BROWN, Prof. David Anthony, PhD; FRS 1990; FIBiol; Research Professor, Department of Pharmacology, University College London, since 2005; *b* 10 Feb. 1936; *s* of Alfred William and Florence Brown; *m* Susan Hames; two *s* one *d*. *Educ:* Univ. of London (BSc, BSc, PhD). University of London: Asst Lectr 1961–65, Lectr 1965–73, Dept of Pharmacology, St Bart's Hosp. Med. Coll.; Dept of Pharmacology, School of Pharmacy: Sen. Lectr, 1973–74; Reader, 1974–77; Professor, 1977–79; Wellcome Professor, 1979–87; Prof. of Pharmacol., Middx Hosp. Med. Sch., then University Coll. and Middx Sch. of Medicine, UCL, 1987–2005 (Hd, Dept of Pharmacol., 1987–2002). Visiting Professor: Univ. of Chicago, 1970; Univ. of Iowa, 1971, 1973; Univ. of Texas, 1979, 1980, 1981; Vis. Scientist, Armed Forces Radiobiology Res. Inst., Bethesda, Md, 1976; Fogarty Schol.-in-Residence, NIH, Bethesda, 1985–86. Member: Physiological Soc., 1970; British Pharmacological Soc., 1965– (Hon. Fellow 2005); Biochemical Soc., 1969–; Academia Europaea, 1990. *Publications:* contribs to Jl of Physiology, British Jl of Pharmacology. *Recreation:* filling in forms. *Address:* Department of Pharmacology, University College London, Gower Street, WC1E 6BT.

BROWN, Prof. David Clifford; writer on music; Professor of Musicology, Southampton University, 1983–89, now Professor Emeritus; *b* 8 July 1929; *s* of Bertram and Constance Brown; *m* 1953, Elizabeth (*née* Valentine); two *d*. *Educ:* Sheffield Univ. (BA, MA, BMus); PhD Southampton Univ. LTCL. RAF 1952–54. Schoolmaster, 1954–59; Music Librarian, London Univ., 1959–62; Southampton University: Lectr in Music, 1962; Sen. Lectr, 1970; Reader, 1975. Many broadcast talks and scripts incl. series: Tchaikovsky and his World, 1980; Tchaikovsky: a fateful gift, 1984; A Sympathetic Person, 1989–90. Mem. Editl Cttee, Musica Britannica, 1980–2005. *Publications:* (ed jtly) Thomas Weelkes: collected anthems, 1966; Thomas Weelkes, 1969; Mikhail Glinka, 1974; John Wilbye, 1974; Tchaikovsky, vol. 1, 1978, vol. 2, 1982 (Derek Allen Prize, British Acad.), vol. 3, 1986, vol. 4, 1991 (Yorkshire Post Music Book Award, 1991); Tchaikovsky Remembered, 1993; Musorgsky, 2003; Tchaikovsky: the man and his music, 2006; contribs to jls and periodicals. *Recreation:* walking. *Address:* Braishfield Lodge West, Braishfield, Romsey, Hants SO51 0PS. *T:* (01794) 368163.

BROWN, David Colin, CMG 1995; HM Diplomatic Service, retired; Consultant, Home Estates Department, Foreign and Commonwealth Office, 1997 (Head, 1989–97); Project Director, Refurbishment of Foreign Office, Whitehall, 1989–97; *b* 10 Aug. 1939; *yr s* of Alan James Brown and Catherine Mary Brown; *m* 1960, Ann Jackson; two *s* one *d*. *Educ:* Lymm Grammar Sch. Joined CRO, 1960; Tech. Aid Administrator, Lagos, 1960–63; Admin Officer, Kingston, Jamaica, 1964–66; Diplomatic Service Admin Office, 1966–68; Second Sec., FCO, 1968; Vice-Consul (Commercial), Johannesburg, 1969–73; seconded to Commn on Rhodesian Opinion, Bulawayo, 1971; News Dept, FCO, 1974–77; Dep. High Comr, Port Louis, 1977–81; Overseas Inspectorate, 1981–83; Asst Hd, W Indian and Atlantic Dept, FCO, 1983–86; Dep. Consul Gen., Milan, 1986–89; Counsellor, 1989. *Recreations:* walking, gardening, building conservation.

BROWN, Dr David John, CPhys, FInstP, CSci; Chief Executive, Institution of Chemical Engineers, since 2006; *b* 10 March 1956; *s* of Colin and Patricia Brown; *m* 1985, Vivienne Burges; two *s* one *d*. *Educ:* Aylesbury Grammar Sch.; Queens' Coll., Cambridge (BA Natural Scis 1978; PhD 1982). CPhys 2001; FInstP 2001; CSci 2004. Various posts, ICI PLC, 1983–93; Dir, Warwick Res. Inst., Univ. of Warwick, 1992–97; Arthur D. Little Ltd, 1997–2006 (Dir and Hd, Technol. and Innovation, 2002–06). Dir, Chemistry Innovation Ltd, 2007–. Member: Bd, Advantage W Midlands, 2006–; Bd, Central Technol. Belt, 2006–; W Midlands Innovation and Technol. Council, 2006–; Bd, W Midlands in Europe, 2006–; Bd, Birmingham Sci. City Partnership, 2007–. Non-exec. Dir, Coventry Refugee Centre, 2007–. *Publications:* various, on scientific and mgt subjects. *Recreations:* cooking, Church activities. *Address:* Institution of Chemical Engineers, One Portland Place, W1B 1PN; *e-mail:* dbrown@icheme.org; Institution of Chemical Engineers, Davis Building, Railway Terrace, Rugby CV21 3HQ. *T:* (01788) 534411, *Fax:* (01788) 550904.

BROWN, Sir David (Martin), Kt 2001; FREng, FIET; Chairman, Motorola Ltd, 1997–2008; *b* 14 May 1950; *s* of Alan Brown and Laura Marjorie Brown (*née* Richardson); *m* 1975, Denise Frances Bowers; two *s*. *Educ:* Portsmouth Poly. (BSc Electrical Engrg); CEng 1980; FIET (FIEE 1985); FREng 1999. With Standard Telephones and Cables, 1979–91; joined Motorola, 1991: Director: UK Ops, Cellular Infrastructure, 1991–93; GSM Product Mgt, 1993–95; Sen. Dir, Radio Access, 1995–97. Non-executive Director: P&OSN Co., 2002–06; Ceres Power Hldgs plc, 2008–; Domino Printing Scis plc, 2008–; Dep. Chm., DRS Data & Res. Services plc, 2008–. President: ASE, 1998; Fedn of Electronics Industry, 1999–2000; IEE, 2003–04 (Mem. Council, 1986–90, 1997–2001; Dep. Pres., 2001–03); CQI, 2007– (Hon. FCQI 2007). CCMI (MBIM 1976). DUniv Surrey, 2004; Hon. DEng Bath, 2004; Hon. DSc Portsmouth, 2005; Hon. DTech Kingston, 2006. *Recreations:* literature, art, theatre. *Address:* Bridleway Cottage, Stanmore, Newbury, Berks RG20 8SR.

BROWN, David Rodney H.; *see* Heath-Brown.

BROWN, Rev. Prof. David William, PhD; FBA 2002; Wardlaw Professor of Theology, Aesthetics and Culture, University of St Andrews, since 2007; *b* 1 July 1948; *s* of David William Brown and Catherine Smith. *Educ:* Keil Sch., Dumbarton; Edinburgh Univ. (MA 1st cl. Classics 1970); Oriel Coll., Oxford (BA 1st cl. Phil. and Theol. 1972); Clare Coll., Cambridge (PhD 1976); Westcott House, Cambridge. Fellow, Chaplain and Tutor in Theol. and Phil., Oriel Coll., Oxford and Univ. Lectr in Theol., 1976–90; Van Mildert Prof. of Divinity, Univ. of Durham and Canon of Durham Cathedral, 1990–2007. Vice-Chm., Doctrine Commn of C of E, 1990–95. *Publications:* Choices: ethics and the Christian, 1983; The Divine Trinity, 1985; Continental Philosophy and Modern Theology, 1987; Invitation to Theology, 1989; (ed) Newman: a man for our time, 1990; The Word To Set You Free, 1995; (ed jtly) The Sense of the Sacramental, 1995; (with D. Fuller) Signs of Grace, 1995; (ed jtly) Christ: the Sacramental Word, 1996; Tradition and Imagination: revelation and change, 1999; Discipleship and Imagination: Christian tradition and truth, 2000; God and Enchantment of Place, 2004; Through the Eyes of the Saints, 2005; God and Grace of Body, 2007; God and Mystery in Words, 2008. *Recreations:* dog and cat, art, listening to music. *Address:* Mansfield, 1A Grey Street, Tayport, Fife DD6 9JF. *T:* (01382) 550063; School of Divinity, St Mary's College, St Andrews, Fife KY16 9JU. *T:* (01334) 462850.

BROWN, Hon. Dean Craig, AO 2008; company director, since 2006; Chairman, Hillgrove Resources Ltd, since 2006; *b* Adelaide, 5 Aug. 1943; *m* 1979, Rosslyn Judith Wadey; one *s* one *d*. *Educ:* Unley High Sch.; Univ. of New England, NSW (BRurSc, MRurSc); Australian Admin. Staff Coll.; S Australian Inst. of Technol. (Fellowship Dip. in Business Admin). Parliament of South Australia: MP (L) Davenport, 1973–85; Shadow Minister for Industrial Affairs, 1975–79; Minister for Industrial Affairs and for Public Works, 1979–82; Shadow Minister, 1982–85, for: Public Works; Transport; Technology; agricl consultant, 1986–92; MP (L) Alexandra, 1992–93, Finniss, 1993–2006; Leader of Opposition, 1992–93; Shadow Minister for Multicultural and Ethnic Affairs, 1992–93; Premier of SA, and Minister for Multicultural and Ethnic Affairs, 1993–96; Minister: for IT, 1995–96; for Industrial Affairs, Aboriginal Affairs, and Inf. and Contract Services, 1996–97; for Human Services, 1997–2002; Dep. Premier of SA, 2001–02; Dep. Leader of the Opposition, 2002–05. A Dir of state and federal govt bds, company bds and community bds. *Publications:* contribs to political, technical and scientific jls. *Recreations:* jogging, fishing, gardening. *Address:* 11 Leonard Terrace, Torrens Park, SA 5062, Australia.

BROWN, Sir Derrick H.; *see* Holden-Brown.

BROWN, Douglas Allan; all-Scotland floating Sheriff, since 2004; *b* 18 June 1951; *s* of Thomas T. Brown and Thelma R. Cheney or Brown; *m* 1978, Elaine Ann Currie; one *s* one *d*. *Educ:* Glasgow Univ. (LLB Hons). Procurator Fiscal Depute, Dumbarton and Glasgow, 1977–87; Sen. Procurator Fiscal Depute, Edinburgh, 1987–91; Asst Solicitor, Crown Office, 1991–94; Procurator Fiscal, Ayr, 1994–96; Sen. Asst Procurator Fiscal, Glasgow, 1996–99; Regl Procurator Fiscal, S Strathclyde, Dumfries and Galloway, 1999–2002; Area Procurator Fiscal, Lothian and Borders, 2002–04. *Recreations:* music, tennis, swimming, gardening. *Address:* Hamilton Sheriff Court, Beckford Street, Hamilton ML3 0BT. *T:* (01698) 282957, *Fax:* (01698) 284403; *e-mail:* sheriffdbrown@scotcourts.gov.uk.

BROWN, Hon. Sir Douglas (Dunlop), Kt 1989; a Judge of the High Court of Justice, Queen's Bench Division, 1996–2005 (Family Division, 1989–96); Judge of Employment Appeal Tribunal, 2001–05; *b* 22 Dec. 1931; *s* of late Robert Dunlop Brown, MICE, and Anne Cameron Brown; *m* 1960, June Margaret Elizabeth McNamara; one *s*. *Educ:* Ryleys Sch., Alderley Edge; Manchester Grammar Sch.; Manchester Univ. (LLB). Served in RN, 1953–55; Lieut, RNR. Called to Bar, Gray's Inn, 1953; Bencher, 1989; practised Northern Circuit from 1955; Mem. General Council of Bar, 1967–71; Asst Recorder, Salford City QS, 1971; a Recorder of the Crown Court, 1972–80; QC 1976; a Circuit Judge, 1980–88; Family Div. Liaison Judge, Northern Circuit, 1990–95; Presiding Judge, Northern Circuit, 1998–2001. Mem., Parole Bd for England and Wales, 1985–87.

Recreations: cricket, golf, music. *Address:* c/o Royal Courts of Justice, Strand, WC2A 2LL. *Clubs:* St James's (Manchester); Wilmslow Golf; Royal Porthcawl Golf.

BROWN, Edmund Gerald, Jr, (Jerry Brown); lawyer, writer and politician; Mayor of Oakland, California, 1999–2006; *b* 7 April 1938; *s* of late Edmund Gerald Brown and of Bernice (*née* Layne). *Educ:* Univ. of California at Berkeley (BA 1961); Yale Law School (JD 1964). Admitted to California Bar, 1965; Research Attorney, Calif. Supreme Court, 1964–65; with Tuttle & Taylor, LA, 1966–69; Sec. of State, Calif., 1970–74; Gov. of California, 1975–83; Attorney with Fulbright Jaworski, 1986–91. Democratic Candidate for US Senator from California, 1982; Chm., California Democratic Party, 1989–91; Candidate for Democratic Presidential Nomination, 1992. Founder and Chm., We the People Legal Foundn, 1992. Trustee, Los Angeles Community Colls, 1969–70. *Address:* (office) 1 Frank H. Ogawa Plaza, 3rd Floor, Oakland, CA 94612–1997, USA.

BROWN, Edmund Walter F.; *see* Fitton-Brown.

BROWN, Edward Francis Trevenen; QC 2008; Senior Treasury Counsel, Central Criminal Court, since 2006; a Recorder, since 2000; *b* 17 Jan. 1958; *s* of Francis Brown and late Ruth Brown; *m* 1989, Victoria Bell; one *s* two *d*. *Educ:* Eton Coll.; University Coll. at Buckingham (LLB). Caelt Gall., London, 1978–80; Pres., Weighouse Gall., LA, 1979–80. Called to the Bar, Gray's Inn, 1983; Jun. Treasury Counsel, 2001–06. Mem., UN Detention Commn, Kosovo, 2001. *Recreations:* paintings, architecture. *Address:* Hollis Whiteman Chambers, Queen Elizabeth Building, Temple, EC4Y 9BS. *T:* (020) 7583 5766, *Fax:* (020) 7353 0339; *e-mail:* edward.brown@qebholliswhiteman.co.uk.

BROWN, Prof. Edwin Thomas, AC 2001; PhD, DSc Eng; FREng; FTSE; FIEAust; FIMMM; Senior Consultant, Golder Associates Pty Ltd, since 2001; Director, Port of Brisbane Corporation, since 2005; Senior Deputy Vice-Chancellor, University of Queensland, Australia, 1996–2001 (Deputy Vice-Chancellor, 1990–96; Dean of Engineering, 1987–90); *b* 4 Dec. 1938; *s* of George O. and Bessie M. Brown. *Educ:* Castlemaine High Sch.; Univ. of Melbourne (BE 1960, MEngSc 1964); Univ. of Queensland (PhD 1969); Univ. of London (DSc Eng 1985). MICE 1976; MASCE 1965; FIMMM (FIMM 1980); FIEAust 1987 (MIEAust 1965); FTSE (FTS 1990). Engr, State Electricity Commn of Victoria, 1960–64; James Cook Univ. of North Queensland (formerly UC of Townsville): Lectr, 1965–69; Sen. Lectr, 1969–72; Associate Prof. of Civil Engrg, 1972–75; Imperial College, Univ. of London: Reader in Rock Mechanics, 1975–79; Prof. of Rock Mechanics, 1979–87; Dean, RSM, 1983–86; Hd, Dept of Mineral Resources Engrg, 1985–87. Res. Associate, Dept of Civil and Mineral Engrg, Univ. of Minnesota, 1970; Sen. Visitor, Dept of Engrg, Univ. of Cambridge, 1974; Vis. Prof., Dept of Mining and Fuels Engrg, Univ. of Utah, 1979. Dir, Queensland Rail, 2001–05. Editor-in-Chief, Internat. Jl of Rock Mechanics and Mining Sciences, 1975–82. Chm., British Geotechnical Soc., 1982–83; Pres., Internat. Soc. for Rock Mechanics, 1983–87; Mem. Council, AATSE, 1997–98 and 2002–03. Foreign Mem., Royal Acad. (formerly Fellowship) of Engrg, 1989. Instn of Mining and Metallurgy: Consolidated Gold Fields Gold Medal, 1984; Sir Julius Wernher Meml Lecture, 1985; John Jaeger Meml Award, Aust. Geomechanics Soc., 2004; Müller Award, Internat. Soc. for Rock Mechanics, 2007. *Publications:* (with E. Hoek) Underground Excavations in Rock, 1980; (ed) Rock Characterization, Testing and Monitoring, 1981; (with B. H. G. Brady) Rock Mechanics for Underground Mining, 1985, 3rd edn 2004; (ed) Analytical and Computational Methods in Engineering Rock Mechanics, 1987; Block Caving Geomechanics, 2003, 2nd edn 2007; papers on rock mechanics in civil engrg and mining jls. *Recreations:* cricket, jazz. *Address:* 5121 Bridgewater Crest, 55 Baildon Street, Kangaroo Point, Qld 4169, Australia. *T:* (7) 38919833. *Club:* Queensland (Brisbane).

BROWN, Elizabeth, (Mrs Ray Brown); *see* Vaughan, E.

BROWN, Prof. Eric Herbert, PhD; Professor of Geography, University College London, 1966–88, Honorary Research Fellow, since 1988; *b* 8 Dec. 1922; *s* of Samuel Brown and Ada Brown, Melton Mowbray, Leics; *m* 1945, Eileen (*née* Reynolds) (*d* 1984), Llanhowell, Dyfed; two *d*. *Educ:* King Edward VII Grammar Sch., Melton Mowbray; King's Coll., London (BSc 1st Cl. Hons); MSc Wales, PhD London. Served War: RAF Pilot, Coastal Comd, 1941–45. Asst Lectr, then Lectr in Geography, University Coll. of Wales, Aberystwyth, 1947–49; University College London: Lectr, then Reader in Geog., 1950–66; Dean of Students, 1972–75; Alumnus Dir, 1989–91; Mem. Senate, Univ. of London, 1981–86. Vis. Lectr, Indiana Univ., USA, 1953–54; Vis. Prof., Monash Univ., Melbourne, 1971. Mem., NERC, 1981–84. Geographical Adviser, Govt of Argentina, 1965–66, 1992–94; Hon. Mem., Geograph. Soc. of Argentina, 1968. Chairman: British Geomorphol Res. Group, 1971–72; British Nat. Cttee for Geog., 1985–90. Royal Geographical Society: Back Grant, 1961; Hon. Sec., 1977–87; Vice-Pres., 1988–89, Hon. Vice-Pres., 1989; Hon. Fellow, 1989; Pres., Inst. of British Geographers, 1978. Foreign Mem., Polish Acad. of Scis and Letters, 1992. DUniv York, 2002. *Publications:* The Relief and Drainage of Wales, 1961; (with W. R. Mead) The USA and Canada, 1962; (ed) Geography Yesterday and Tomorrow, 1980; contrib. Geog. Jl, Phil. Trans Royal Soc., Proc. Geologists' Assoc., Trans Inst. of British Geographers, and Geography. *Recreations:* watching Rugby football, wine. *Address:* Monterey, 13 Castle Hill, Berkhamsted, Herts HP4 1HE. *T:* (01442) 864077. *Clubs:* Athenæum, Geographical.

BROWN, Captain Eric Melrose, CBE 1970 (OBE 1945; MBE 1944); DSC 1942; AFC 1947; QCVSA 1949; RN; Vice-President, European Helicopter Association, since 1992 (Chief Executive, 1980–92); *b* 21 Jan. 1919; *s* of Robert John Brown and Euphemia (*née* Melrose); *m* 1942, Evelyn Jean Margaret Macrory (*d* 1998); one *s*. *Educ:* Royal High Sch., Edinburgh; Edinburgh University. MA 1947. Joined Fleet Air Arm as Pilot, 1939; Chief Naval Test Pilot, 1944–49 (RN Boyd Trophy, 1948); Resident British Test Pilot at USN Air Test Center, Patuxent River, 1951–52; CO No 804 Sqdn, 1953–54; Comdr (Air), RN Air Stn, Brawdy, 1954–56; Head of British Naval Air Mission to Germany, 1958–60; Dep. Dir (Air), Gunnery Div., Admty, 1961; Dep. Dir, Naval Air Warfare and Adviser on Aircraft Accidents, Admty, 1962–64; Naval Attaché, Bonn, 1965–67; CO, RN Air Stn, Lossiemouth, 1967–70. Chief Exec., British Helicopter Adv. Bd, 1970–87, Vice-Pres., 1988–. Chm., British Aviation Bicentenary Exec. Cttee, 1984. Hon. FRAeS 2004 (FRAeS 1964; Pres., 1982–83; Chm., RAeS Rotorcraft Sect., 1973–76). Hon. FEng (Pakistan) 1984; Hon. Fellow, Soc. of Experimental Test Pilots, 1984. Hon. PhD 2007. Liveryman, GAPAN, 1978. British Silver Medal for Practical Achievement in Aeronautics, 1949; Anglo-French Breguet Trophy, 1983; Bronze Medal, Fédération Aéronautique Internationale, 1986; US Carrier Aviation Test Pilot Hall of Honor, 1995; Gold Medal, British Assoc. of Aviation Consultants, 1997; Award of Honour, GAPAN, 2006. *Publications:* Wings on My Sleeve, 1961, 4th edn 2006; (jtly) Aircraft Carriers, 1969; Wings of the Luftwaffe, 1977; Wings of the Navy, 1980; The Helicopter in Civil Operations, 1981; Wings of the Weird and the Wonderful, vol. 1, 1982, vol. 2, 1985; Duels in the Sky, 1989; Testing for Combat, 1994. *Recreations:* travel, philately, bridge. *Address:* Carousel, Herons Close, Copthorne, W Sussex RH10 3HF. *T:* (01342) 712610. *Clubs:* Naval and Military, Royal Air Force, City Livery; Explorers' (NY).

BROWN, Hon. Dr Ewart Frederick; JP; MP (PLP), Bermuda, since 1993; Premier and Minister of Tourism and Transport, Bermuda, since 2006; Leader, Progressive Labour Party, since 2006; *b* 17 May 1946; *s* of Ewart D. A. Brown and Helene A. Brown; *m* 2003, Wanda Henton; four *s* from previous marr. *Educ:* Howard Univ. (BSc, MD); Univ. of Calif, Los Angeles (MPH). Med. Dir, Vermont-Century Med. Clinic, Calif, 1974–93; Med. Dir, 1993–2006, Pres. and Chm. Bd, 1993–, Bermuda Healthcare Services. Minister of Transport, 1998–2004, of Tourism and Transport, 2004–06; Dep. Premier, 2003–06. *Recreation:* golf. *Address:* Cabinet Office, 105 Front Street, Hamilton HM12, Bermuda. *T:* 2925501, *Fax:* 2920304; *e-mail:* ebrown@gov.bm.

BROWN, Frank Henry, OBE 1975; HM Diplomatic Service, retired; *b* 6 Sept. 1923; *s* of late Thomas Henry Brown and Ada Katherine Brown (*née* Clifton); *m* 1943, Sheila Desiree (*d* 1997), *d* of late Rev. Canon John Rees and Elsie Rees; one *s* three *d*. *Educ:* LCC Bonneville Road, Clapham; Bec Sch., Tooting Bec. C. & E. Morton Ltd, 1940; Colonial Office, 1940–42; RN, 1942–46; Colonial Office, subseq. Commonwealth Office, then Foreign and Commonwealth Office, 1946–83: St Helena, 1948–50; Gold Coast/Ghana, 1954–57; Financial Sec., New Hebrides, 1971–75; Dep. High Comr, Guyana, 1978–80; Asst Head, Nationality and Treaty Dept, FCO, 1980–83. *Recreations:* Christian service, family solidarity, happy great-grandfather, appreciating creation. *Address:* Abbeyfield House, 8 Purley Knoll, Purley, Surrey CR8 3AE. *T:* (020) 8660 0939. *Club:* Civil Service.

BROWN, Prof. Gavin, AO 2006; PhD; FAA; Vice-Chancellor and Principal, University of Sydney, since 1996; *b* Fife, Scotland, 27 Feb. 1942; *s* of F. B. D. and A. D. D. Brown; *m* 1st, 1966, Barbara Routh (*d* 2001); one *s* one *d*; 2nd, 2004, Diané Ranck. *Educ:* Univ. of St Andrews (MA); Univ. of Newcastle upon Tyne (PhD 1966). FAA 1981. Asst Lectr, then Lectr, and Sen. Lectr in Maths, Liverpool Univ., 1966–75; University of New South Wales: Prof. of Pure Maths, 1976–92, now Emeritus; Hd, Dept of Pure Maths, 1976–81, 1986–89; Hd, Sch. of Maths, 1981–85; Dean: Faculty of Sci., 1989–92; Bd of Studies in Sci. & Maths, 1990–92; Dep. Vice-Chancellor, 1992–93, Vice-Chancellor, 1994–96, Univ. of Adelaide. Visiting Professor: Univ. of Paris, 1975; Univ. of York, 1979; Univ. of Cambridge, 1986. Corresp. FRSE 2007. Hon. LLD: St Andrews, 1998; Dundee, 2004. *Publications:* numerous contribs to various maths jls. *Recreation:* racing. *Address:* University of Sydney, NSW 2006, Australia. *T:* (2) 93513058.

BROWN, Gavin Lindberg; Member (C) Lothians, Scottish Parliament, since 2007; *b* 4 June 1975; *s* of William and Jacqueline Brown; *m* 2006, Hilary Fergus; one *d*. *Educ:* Boundary Jun. Sch., Hong Kong; Fettes Coll.; Univ. of Strathclyde (LLB Hons 1997; DipLP 1998). Trainee solicitor, 1998–2000, solicitor, 2000–02, McGrigor Donald; Man. Dir, Speak With Impact Ltd, 2002–. Shadow spokesman for enterprise, energy and tourism, Scottish Parlt, 2007–. *Recreations:* tae kwon-do (black belt), motivational speaking. *Address:* Scottish Parliament, Edinburgh EH99 1SP. *T:* (0131) 348 5000; *e-mail:* gavin.brown.msp@scottish.parliament.uk.

BROWN, Rev. Canon Geoffrey Harold; Vicar of St Martin-in-the-Fields, 1985–95; *b* 1 April 1930; *s* of Harry and Ada Brown; *m* 1963, Elizabeth Jane Williams; two *d*. *Educ:* Monmouth Sch.; Trinity Hall, Cambridge (MA). Asst Curate, St Andrew's, Plaistow, 1954–60; Asst Curate, St Peter's, Birmingham and Sub-Warden of Pre-Ordination Training Scheme, 1960–63; Rector: St George's, Newtown, Birmingham, 1963–73; Grimsby, 1973–85. Hon. Canon Lincoln Cathedral, 1978; Canon Emeritus, 1985. FRSA 1991. *Recreations:* the countryside, photography, theatre. *Address:* 8 Worcester Close, Hagley, near Stourbridge, W Midlands DY9 0NP.

BROWN, Geoffrey Howard; journalist, The Times; *b* 1 March 1949; *s* of John Howard Brown and Nancy (*née* Fardoe); *m* 1985, Catherine Ann Surowiec. *Educ:* King Henry VIII Grammar Sch., Coventry; Pembroke Coll., Cambridge (BA); Royal Coll. of Art (Sch. of Film and TV, MA). Dep. Film Critic, Financial Times, 1977–81; Film Critic, Radio Times, 1981–89; Dep. Film Critic, 1981–90, Film Critic, 1990–98, The Times. *Publications:* Walter Forde, 1977; Launder and Gilliat, 1977; Der Produzent: Michael Balcon und der Englische Film, 1981; (contrib.) Michael Balcon: the pursuit of British cinema, 1984; The Common Touch: the films of John Baxter, 1989; (contrib.) The British Cinema Book, 1997; (contrib.) The Unknown 1930s, 1998; (contrib.) British Cinema of the 90s, 2000; (contrib.) The Cinema of Britain and Ireland, 2005; Directors in British and Irish Cinema: a reference guide, 2006. *Recreations:* art exhibits, children's books. *Address:* The Times, 1 Pennington Street, E98 1TT. *T:* (020) 7782 5167.

BROWN, Geoffrey Robert C.; *see* Clifton-Brown.

BROWN, Sir George (Francis) Richmond, 5th Bt *cr* 1863, of Richmond Hill; *b* 3 Feb. 1938; *o s* of Sir Charles Frederick Richmond Brown, 4th Bt and of Audrey Baring; *S* father, 1995; *m* 1978, Philippa Willcox; three *s*. *Educ:* Eton. Served Welsh Guards, 1956–70; Extra Equerry to HRH The Duke of Edinburgh, 1961–63; ADC to Governor of Queensland, 1964–66; Adjt, 1st Bn Welsh Guards, 1967–69. *Heir: s* Sam George Richmond Brown, *b* 27 Dec. 1979. *Address:* Mas de Sudre, 81600 Gaillac, France. *T:* 563410132. *Clubs:* Pratt's, Cavalry and Guards.

BROWN, Prof. George William, OBE 1995; FBA 1986; Member, External Scientific Staff, Medical Research Council, since 1980; Hon. Professor of Sociology, Royal Holloway and Bedford New College, London University, since 1980; *b* 15 Nov. 1930; *s* of late William G. Brown and Lily Jane (*née* Hillier); *m* 1st, 1954, Gillian M. Hole (marr. diss. 1970); one *s* one *d*; 2nd, 1978, Seija T. Sandberg (marr. diss. 1987); one *d*; 3rd, 1990, Elizabeth A. Davies; one *s*. *Educ:* Kilburn Grammar Sch.; University Coll. London (BA Anthropol. 1954); LSE (PhD 1961). Scientific Staff, DSIR, 1955–56; MRC Social Psychiatry Res. Unit, Inst. of Psychiatry, 1956–67; joined Social Res. Unit, Bedford Coll., London Univ., 1967; Prof. of Sociology, London Univ. and Jt Dir, Social Res. Unit, Bedford Coll., 1973–80. Mem., Inst. Medicine, 2005. Mem., Academia Europaea, 1990. Founder FMedSci 1998. Hon. FRCPsych, 1987. *Publications:* (jtly) Schizophrenia and Social Care, 1966; (with J. K. Wing) Institutionalism and Schizophrenia, 1970; (with T. O. Harris) Social Origins of Depression, 1978; Life Events and Illness, 1989; numerous contribs to jls. *Address:* 1 Redberry Grove, SE26 4DA. *T:* (020) 8699 0120.

BROWN, Prof. Gillian, CBE 1992; Professor of English as an International Language, University of Cambridge, 1988–2004; Fellow of Clare College, Cambridge, 1988–2007, now Emeritus; *b* 23 Jan. 1937; *d* of Geoffrey Rencher Read and Elsie Olive Chapman; *m* 1959, Edward Keith Brown; three *d*. *Educ:* Perse Sch. for Girls; Girton Coll., Cambridge (MA); Univ. of Edinburgh (PhD 1971); LittD Cantab 1997. Lectr, University Coll. of Cape Coast, Ghana, 1962–64; Lectr, 1965–81, Reader, 1981–83, Univ. of Edinburgh; Prof., Univ. of Essex, 1983–88 (Dean of Social Scis, 1985–88); Dir, Res. Centre for English and Applied Linguistics, Univ. of Cambridge, 1988–2004. Mem., ESRC Educn and Human Develt Cttee, 1983–87; Chm., Research Grants Board, ESRC, 1987–90; Member: Kingman Cttee, 1987–88; UGC, subseq. UFC, 1988–91; Council, Philological Soc., 1988–93; British Council English Teaching Adv. Cttee, 1989–94; Cttee of Mgt, British Inst. in Paris, 1990–2004. Curator, Sch. of Advanced Studies, Univ. of London, 1994–2005. Gov., Bell Educnl Trust, 1987–92. Dr *hc* Univ. of Lyon, 1987. Member, Editorial Boards: Jl of Semantics; Jl of Applied Linguistics; Second Language Acquisition Res. *Publications:* Phonological Rules and Dialect Variation, 1972; Listening to Spoken English, 1977; (with George Yule) Discourse Analysis, 1983; Speakers, Listeners and Communication, 1995; articles in learned jls. *Address:* Clare College, Cambridge CB2 1TL.

BROWN, Gillian Margaret S.; *see* Stuart-Brown.

BROWN, Prof. Godfrey Norman; Professor of Education, University of Keele, 1967–80, now Emeritus; Director, Betley Court Gallery, 1980–94; *b* 13 July 1926; *s* of Percy Charles and Margaret Elizabeth Brown; *m* 1960, Dr Freda Bowyer; three *s*. *Educ:* Whitgift Sch.; School of Oriental and African Studies, London; Merton Coll., Oxford (MA, DPhil). Army service, RAC and Intelligence Corps, 1944–48. Social Affairs Officer, UN Headquarters, NY, 1953–54; Sen. History Master, Barking Abbey Sch., Essex, 1954–57; Lectr in Educn, University Coll. of Ghana, 1958–61; Sen. Lectr, 1961, Prof., 1963, Univ. of Ibadan, Nigeria; Dir, Univ. of Keele Inst. of Educn, 1967–80. Visiting Prof., Univ. of Rhodesia and Nyasaland, 1963; Chm., Assoc. for Recurrent Educn, 1976–77; Mem., Exec. Cttee and Bd of Dirs, World Council for Curriculum and Instruction, 1974–77. OECD Consultant on teacher education, Portugal, 1980. Vice-Pres., Community Council of Staffs, 1984–. Collector of the Year Award, Art and Antiques, 1981; Newcastle-under-Lyme Civic Award for Conservation, 1990. *Publications:* An Active History of Ghana, 2 vols, 1961 and 1964; Living History, 1967; Apartheid, a Teacher's Guide, 1981; Betley Through the Centuries, 1985; This Old House: a domestic biography, 1987; Betley's Cultural Heritage, 2002; edited: (with J. C. Anene) Africa in the Nineteenth and Twentieth Centuries, 1966; Towards a Learning Community, 1971; (with M. Hiskett) Conflict and Harmony in Education in Tropical Africa, 1975; Eccentric Harmony, 2003; contrib. educnl and cultural jls. *Recreations:* family life, art history, conservation, writing. *Address:* Betley Court, Betley, near Crewe, Cheshire CW3 9BH. *T:* (01270) 820652.

BROWN, Rt Hon. Gordon; *see* Brown, Rt Hon. James G.

BROWN, Harold, PhD; Partner, Warburg Pincus & Co., 1990–2008; Counselor, Center for Strategic and International Studies, since 1992; *b* 19 Sept. 1927; *s* of A. H. Brown and Gertrude Cohen Brown; *m* 1953, Colene McDowell; two *d*. *Educ:* Columbia Univ. (BA 1945, MA 1946, PhD in Physics 1949). Res. Scientist, Columbia Univ., 1945–50, Lectr in Physics, 1947–48; Lectr in Physics, Stevens Inst. of Technol., 1949–50; Res. Scientist, Radiation Lab., Univ. of Calif, Berkeley, 1951–52; Gp Leader, Radiation Lab., Livermore, 1952–61; Dir, Def. Res. and Engrg, Dept of Def., 1961–65; Sec. of Air Force, 1965–69; Pres., Calif Inst. of Technol., Pasadena, 1969–77; Sec. of Defense, USA, 1977–81; Vis. Prof., 1981–84, Chm., 1984–92, Johns Hopkins Foreign Policy Inst., Sch. of Advanced Internat. Studies. Sen. Sci. Adviser, Conf. on Discontinuance of Nuclear Tests, 1958–59; Delegate, Strategic Arms Limitations Talks, Helsinki, Vienna and Geneva, 1969–77. Member: Polaris Steering Cttee, 1956–58; Air Force Sci. Adv. Bd, 1956–61; (also Consultant) President's Sci. Adv. Cttee, 1958–61. Chm., Commn on Roles and Capabilities, US Intelligence Cttee, 1995–96. Hon. DEng Stevens Inst. of Technol., 1964; Hon. LLD: Long Island Univ., 1966; Gettysburg Coll., 1967; Occidental Coll., 1969; Univ. of Calif, 1969; Hon. ScD: Univ. of Rochester, 1975; Brown Univ., 1977; Univ. of the Pacific, 1978; Univ. of S Carolina, 1979; Franklin and Marshall Coll., 1982; Chung Ang Univ. (Seoul, Korea), 1983. Member: Amer. Phys. Soc., 1946; Nat. Acad. of Engrg, 1967; Amer. Acad. of Arts and Scis, 1969; Nat. Acad. of Scis, 1977. One of Ten Outstanding Young Men of Year, US Jun. Chamber of Commerce, 1961; Columbia Univ. Medal of Excellence, 1963; Air Force Exceptl Civil. Service Award, 1969; Dept of Def. Award for Exceptionally Meritorious Service, 1969; Joseph C. Wilson Award, 1976; Presidential Medal of Freedom, 1981; Enrico Fermi Award, US Dept of Energy, 1993. *Publications:* Thinking About National Security: defense and foreign policy in a dangerous world, 1983; (ed) The Strategic Defense Initiative: shield or snare?, 1987. *Address:* Center for Strategic and International Studies, Suite 400, 1800 K Street, NW, Washington, DC 20006–2202, USA. *Club:* City Tavern (Washington, DC).

BROWN, (Harold) Vivian (Bigley), CB 2004; Micro-credit Adviser, Lea Toto Program, Nairobi, since 2007; *b* 20 Aug. 1945; *s* of late Alec Sidney Brown and Joyce Brown (*née* Bigley); *m* 1970, Jean Josephine Bowyer, *yr d* of Sir Eric Bowyer, KCB, KBE and Lady Bowyer; two *s*. *Educ:* Leeds Grammar Sch.; St John's Coll., Oxford (BA); St Cross Coll., Oxford (BPhil Islamic Philosophy). Min. of Technology, 1970; DTI, 1972–74 (Private Sec. to Permanent Sec., 1972–73); FCO, 1975–79 (First Sec. Commercial Jeddah); DTI, 1979–86; Hd of Sci. and Technol. Assessment Office, Cabinet Office, 1986–89; Hd of Competition Policy Div., 1989–91; Hd of Investigations Div., 1991–92, of Deregulation Unit, 1992–94, of Small Firms and Business Link, 1994–96, DTI; Dep. Dir Gen. and Dir, Business Link, DTI, 1996–97; Chief Exec., ECGD, 1997–2004; Advr to Minister of Finance, Bahrain, 2004–06. *Publication:* (with S. M. Stern and A. Hourani) Islamic Philosophy and the Classical Tradition, 1972. *Recreations:* playing piano, cycling, cooking. *Address:* PO Box 24970, 00502 Nairobi, Kenya.

BROWN, Prof. Harvey Robert, PhD; FBA 2007; Professor of Philosophy of Physics, University of Oxford, since 2006; Fellow of Wolfson College, Oxford, since 1984; *b* 4 April 1950; *s* of Harvey C. Brown and M. Katrine Brown; *m* 1980, Maria Rita Kessler; one *s* one *d*. *Educ:* Univ. of Canterbury, NZ (BSc Hons 1971); Univ. of London (PhD 1978). Asst Prof., Dept of Philos. and Mem., Centro de Lógica, Epistemologia e História da Ciência, São Paulo State Univ. at Campinas, 1978–84; Lectr in Philos. of Physics, 1984–96, Reader in Philos., 1996–2006, Univ. of Oxford. Long-term Visitor, Perimeter Inst. for Theoretical Physics, Waterloo, Ont, 2007–08. Pres., British Soc. for the Philos. of Sci., 2007–July 2009. *Publications:* Albert Einstein. Um simples homem de visão, 1984; Physical Relativity: space-time structure from a dynamical perspective, 2005 (Lakatos Award in the Philosophy of Science (jtly), 2006); numerous contribns to learned jls. *Recreations:* drawing, swimming, motorcycles, cooking, things Brazilian. *Address:* Philosophy Centre, University of Oxford, 10 Merton Street, Oxford OX1 4JJ. *T:* (01865) 276930, *Fax:* (01865) 276932; *e-mail:* harvey.brown@philosophy.ox.ac.uk.

BROWN, Hazel Christine P.; *see* Parker-Brown.

BROWN, Henry Thomas C.; *see* Cadbury-Brown.

BROWN, Col Hugh Goundry, TD 1968; FRCS; Vice Lord-Lieutenant, Tyne & Wear, 1993–2002; *b* 25 Feb. 1927; *s* of Charles Frank Brown and Edith Temple Brown (*née* Smithson); *m* 1961, Ann Mary Crump; one *s* two *d*. *Educ:* Durham Univ. (MB BS 1949). FRCS 1958. Nat. Service, RMO, 1 (Nyasaland) Bn, KAR, 1950–52. TA 1 (N) Gen. Hosp., 1952–73; OC, 201 (N) Gen. Hosp., 1970–73, Hon. Col, 1982–87. Consultant Plastic Surgeon, Royal Victoria Inf., Newcastle upon Tyne and Sen. Lectr in plastic surgery, Univ. of Newcastle upon Tyne, 1968–92. President: Brit. Soc. for Surgery of the Hand, 1985; Brit. Assoc. Plastic Surgeons, 1988; Brit. Assoc. Clinical Anatomists, 1989. QHS 1972. Tyne & Wear: DL 1986; High Sheriff, 1992. *Publications:* contrib. Brit. Jl

Plastic Surgery, Hand, Brit. Jl Anaesthesia. *Recreations:* family, fell-walking. *Address:* 12 Lindisfarne Road, Jesmond, Newcastle upon Tyne NE22 2HE. *T:* (0191) 281 4141. *Club:* Northern Counties (Newcastle).

BROWN, Ian James Morris, PhD; playwright; poet; freelance arts and education consultant; *b* 28 Feb. 1945; *s* of Bruce Beveridge Brown and Eileen Frances Scott Carnegie; *m* 1st, 1968, Judith Ellen Sidaway (marr. diss. 1997); one *s* one *d*; 2nd, 1997, Nicola Dawn Axford. *Educ:* Dollar Academy; Edinburgh Univ. MA Hons, MLitt, DipEd; Crewe and Alsager Coll. (PhD). Playwright, 1969–; Schoolmaster, 1967–69, 1970–71; Lectr in Drama, Dunfermline Coll., 1971–76; British Council: Asst Rep., Scotland, 1976–77; Asst Regional Dir, Istanbul, 1977–78; Crewe and Alsager College: Head of Drama, 1978–79; Head of Performance Arts, 1979–82; Programme Leader, BA Hons Drama Studies, 1982–86; Programme Dir, Alsager Arts Centre, 1980–86; Drama Dir, Arts Council of GB, 1986–94; Queen Margaret College, subseq. Queen Margaret University College, Edinburgh: Reader, 1994–95; Prof. of Drama, 1995–2002; Head, Dept of Drama, 1995–99; Dir, Scottish Centre for Cultural Mgt and Policy, 1996–2002; Dean of Arts, 1999–2002. Vis. Prof. (Hon. Sen. Res. Fellow), Dept of Scottish Lit., Univ. of Glasgow, 2007–; Vis. Prof., Centre for the Study of Media and Culture in Small Nations, 2007–. Chm., Scottish Soc. of Playwrights, 1973–75, 1984–87, 1997–99 (Mem. Council, 1999–2007); convenor, NW Playwrights' Workshop, 1982–85; Member: NW Arts Assoc. Drama panel, 1980–83, General Arts panel, 1983–86; Arts Council of GB Drama panel, 1985–86; British Theatre Institute: Vice-Chm., 1983–85; Chm., 1985–87. Chairman: Dionysia World Fest. of Contemp. Theatre, Chianti, Italy, 1991–94; Highlands and Islands Theatre Network, 2005–; Dràma Na h-Alba, Scotland's Internat. Theatre Fest. and Forum, 2006–. Productions: Antigone, 1969; Mother Earth, 1970; The Bacchae, 1972; Positively the Last Final Farewell Performance (ballet), 1972; Rune (choral work), 1973; Carnegie, 1973; The Knife, 1973; The Fork, 1976; New Reekie, 1977; Mary, 1977; Runners, 1978; Mary Queen and the Loch Tower, 1979; Joker in the Pack, 1983; Beatrice, 1989; (jtly) First Strike, 1990; The Scotch Play, 1991; Bacchai, 1991; Wasting Reality, 1992; Margaret, 2000; A Great Reckonin, 2000. FRSA 1991. Series Ed., The Edinburgh Companions to Scottish Literature, 2007–. *Publications:* (ed) An Anthology of Contemporary Scottish Drama (in Croatian), 1999; (ed) Cultural Tourism: the convergence of culture and tourism at the start of the 21st century (in Russian), 2001; Poems for Joan, 2001; (ed) Journey's Beginning: the Gateway Theatre building and company 1884–1965, 2004; (ed) The Edinburgh History of Scottish Literature, 2007; (ed) Changing Identities – Ancient Roots: the history of West Dunbartonshire from earliest times, 2006; articles on drama, theatre and arts policy. *Recreations:* theatre, sport, travel, cooking. *Address:* New Balghoulan, 5 Fenton Terrace, Pitlochry, Perthshire PH16 5DP.

BROWN, Col James, CVO 1985; RNZAC (retd); *b* 15 Aug. 1925; *y s* of late John Brown and Eveline Bertha (*née* Cooper), Russells Flat, North Canterbury, NZ; *m* 1952, Patricia Sutton; two *d*. *Educ:* Christchurch Boys' High Sch., NZ; Royal Military Coll., Duntroon, Australia (grad 1947). NZ Regular Army, 1947–71: active service, Korea, 1951–52; Comptroller of Household to Gov.-Gen. of NZ, 1961–62; Reg. Comr of Civil Defence, Dept of Internal Affairs, NZ, 1971–77; Official Sec. to Governor-Gen. of NZ, 1977–85; Gen. Sec., Duke of Edinburgh's Award Scheme in NZ, 1986–94. Col Comdt, RNZAC, 1982–86; Pres., NZ Army Assoc., 1986–94. *Recreations:* fishing, shooting. *Address:* 2 Te Maku Grove, Waikanae, New Zealand. *Club:* Wellington (Wellington).

BROWN, Hon. James Anthony, (Hon. Tony); Chief Minister, Isle of Man, since 2006; MHK Castletown, since 1981 (Speaker, House of Keys, 2001–06); *b* 5 Jan. 1950; *s* of Margaret Brown; *m* 1979, Rachel (*née* Smith); one *s* one *d*. *Educ:* Victoria Road Primary Sch., Castletown; Castle Rushen High Sch., Castletown. Apprentice electrician, 1965–70, electrician, 1970–80, IOM Electricity Bd; self-employed electrician, 1980–81; Proprietor, Tony Brown Electrics, 1981–. Mem., Castletown Town Commn, 1976–81 (Chm., 1980–81). Manx Government: Minister: for Health and Social Security, 1986–89; for Local Govt and Envmt, 1989–94; for Tourism and Leisure, 1994–96; for Transport, 1996–2001; Dep. Pres., Tynwald, 2002–06. Pres., Castletown Chamber of Trade and Commerce, 1987–. Pres., 1984, Pres. and Chm., 1990–, Castletown and District Over 60s Club; Vice-Pres., Castletown Rifle Club, 1994–. *Recreations:* photography, history, historic architecture, motorcycle racing (marshal and spectator), heritage. *Address:* 20 Kissack Road, Castletown, Isle of Man IM9 1NW. *T:* (01624) 824393, (business) (01624) 822148, *Fax:* (01624) 823828; (office) Legislative Buildings, Douglas, Isle of Man IM1 3PW. *T:* (01624) 685500, *Fax:* (01624) 685504; *e-mail:* chief.minister@cso.gov.im.

BROWN, Dr (James) Barry (Conway), OBE 1978; Subject Assessor, Higher Education Funding Council for England, 1995–97; *b* 3 July 1937; *s* of Frederick Clarence and Alys Brown; *m* 1963, Anne Rosemary Clough (*d* 2007); two *s* one *d*. *Educ:* Cambridge Univ. (BA Nat. Sci 1959; MA 1963); Birmingham Univ. (MSc 1960; PhD 1963). Research Officer, CEGB, Berkeley Nuclear Labs, 1963–67; British Council: Sen. Sci. Officer, Sci. Dept, 1967–69; Sci. Officer, Madrid, 1969–72, Paris, 1972–78; Head, Sci. and Technology Group, 1978–81; Rep. and Cultural Counsellor, Mexico, 1981–85; Dep. Controller (Higher Educn Div.), 1985–89; Dir, EC Liaison Unit (Higher Education), Brussels, 1989–91; Dir, Poland, 1992–94. Treas., St Mary's Church, Purley-on-Thames, 1994–2000. Mem., Pangbourne Choral Soc., 2001–. *Recreations:* music, travel in (and study of) countries of posting, singing, reading. *Address:* 42 Hazel Road, Purley-on-Thames, Reading RG8 8BB. *T:* (0118) 941 7581.

BROWN, (James) Craig, CBE 1999; International Team Manager, Scottish Football Association, 1993–2001; *b* 1 July 1940; *s* of Hugh and Margaret Brown; *m* 1964 (separated 1981); two *s* one *d*. *Educ:* Scottish Sch. of Physical Educn (DipPE (Distinction)); BA Open Univ. 1976. Lectr in Primary Educn, Craigie Coll. of Educn, 1969–86. Professional footballer: Rangers FC, 1958–60; Dundee FC, 1960–65; Falkirk FC, 1965–67; Asst Manager, Motherwell FC, 1974–77; Manager, Clyde FC, 1977–86; Scottish Football Association: Asst Nat. Coach, 1986–93; Nat. Coach and Dir, Football Develt, 1993–2002; Manager, Preston North End FC, 2002–04. DUniv Paisley, 1998; Hon. DArts Abertay Dundee, 2000. *Publications:* (jtly) Activity Methods in the Middle Years, 1975; Craig Brown (autobiog.), 1998, repr. as The Game of My Life, 2001. *Recreations:* golf, reading, travel. *Address:* 28 Victoria Mansions, Navigation Way, Ashton-on-Ribble, Preston PR2 2YY.

BROWN, Rt Hon. (James) Gordon; PC 1996; MP (Lab) Kirkcaldy and Cowdenbeath, since 2005 (Dunfermline East, 1983–2005); Prime Minister and First Lord of the Treasury, since 2007; Leader of the Labour Party, since 2007; *b* 20 Feb. 1951; *s* of late Rev. Dr John Brown and J. Elizabeth Brown; *m* 2000, Sarah Jane Macaulay; two *s* (one *d* decd). *Educ:* Kirkcaldy High Sch.; Edinburgh Univ. MA 1972; PhD 1982. Rector, Edinburgh Univ., 1972–75; Temp. Lectr, Edinburgh Univ., 1976; Lectr, Glasgow Coll. of Technology, 1976–80; Journalist and Current Affairs Editor, Scottish TV, 1980–83. Mem., TGWU. Chm., Labour Party Scottish Council, 1983–84; Opposition Chief Sec. to the Treasury, 1987–89; Opposition Trade and Industry Sec., 1989–92; Opposition Treasury Sec., 1992–97; Chancellor of the Exchequer, 1997–2007. Contested (Lab) S Edinburgh, 1979. *Publications:* (ed) The Red Paper on Scotland, 1975; (with H. M. Drucker) The Politics of Nationalism and Devolution, 1980; (ed) Scotland: the real divide, 1983; Maxton, 1986; Where There is Greed, 1989; (with J. Naughtie) John Smith: Life and Soul of the Party, 1994; (with T. Wright) Values, Visions and Voices, 1995; Speeches 1997–2006, 2006; Moving Britain Forward: selected speeches 1997–2006, 2006; Courage: eight portraits, 2007; Britain's Ordinary Heroes, 2007. *Recreations:* reading and writing, football and tennis. *Address:* 10 Downing Street, SW1A 2AA.

BROWN, Jerry; *see* Brown, E. G.

BROWN, Joe, MBE 1975; freelance guide and climber, and film maker for television and cinema; *b* 26 Sept. 1930; *s* of J. Brown, Longsight, Manchester; *m* 1957, Valerie Gray; two *d*. *Educ:* Stanley Grove, Manchester. Started climbing while working as plumber in Manchester; pioneered new climbs in Wales in early 1950's; gained internat. reputation after climbing West Face of Petit Dru, 1954; climbed Kanchenjunga, 1955; Mustagh Tower, 1956; Mt Communism, USSR, 1962; Trango Tower, 1976; Cotaphxi, 1979; Mt Kenya, 1984; Mt McInley, 1986; other expdns: El Torro, 1970; Bramah 2, 1978; Thalaysagar, 1982; Everest NE Ridge, 1986 and 1988. Climbing Instructor, Whitehall, Derbs, 1961–65; opened climbing equipment shops, Llanberis, 1965, Capel Curig, 1970; Leader of United Newspapers Andean Expedn, 1970; Roraima Expedn, 1973. Hon. Fellow, Manchester Polytechnic, 1970. *Publication:* (autobiog.) The Hard Years, 1967. *Recreations:* mountaineering, ski-ing, fishing. *Address:* Allandale, Llanberis, Gwynedd LL55 4TF. *T:* (01286) 870727. *Clubs:* Alpine (Hon. Mem.), Climbers' (Hon. Mem.).

BROWN, John, CBE 1982; FREng; Part-time Dean of Technology, Brunel University, 1988–91; *b* 17 July 1923; *s* of George Brown and Margaret Ditchburn Brown; *m* 1st, 1947, Maureen Dorothy Moore (*d* 1991); one *d*; 2nd, 1992, Dr Helen Crawford Gladstone. *Educ:* Edinburgh University. Radar Research and Development Estabt, 1944–51; Lectr, Imperial Coll., 1951–54; University Coll., London: Lectr, 1954–56; Reader, 1956–64; Prof., 1964–67; seconded to Indian Inst. of Technology as Prof. of Electrical Engrg, 1962–65; Prof. of Elect. Engineering, Imperial Coll. of Science and Technology, 1967–81 (Head of Dept, 1967–79); Tech. Dir, Marconi Electrical Devices Ltd, 1981–83; Dir, Univ. and Schs Liaison, GEC, 1983–88. Mem., SRC, 1977–81 (Chm., Engrg Bd, 1977–81); Chm., Joint ESRC–SERC Cttee, 1988–91; Member: Engrg Group, Nat. Advisory Bd, 1983–84; Engrg Cttee, CNAA, 1985–87; Accreditation Cttee, CNAA, 1987–89. Pres., IEE, 1979–80 (Vice-Pres., 1975–78; Dep. Pres., 1978–79); Pres., IEEIE, 1981–85 (Treasurer, 1989–99). Treas., Church Monuments Soc., 2000–07. Governor: S Bank Polytechnic, 1985–90; Willesden Coll. of Technology, 1985–86. FREng (FEng 1984). Hon. FIET (Hon. FIEIE 1986). Hon. DLitt Nanyang Technol Univ., Singapore, 1996. *Publications:* Microwave Lenses, 1953; (with H. M. Barlow) Radio Surface Waves, 1962; Telecommunications, 1964; (with R. H. Clarke) Diffraction Theory and Antennas, 1980; papers in Proc. IEE, etc. *Recreation:* gardening. *Address:* 28 Dale Side, Gerrards Cross, Bucks SL9 7JE.

BROWN, John, CMG 1989; HM Diplomatic Service, retired; *b* 13 July 1931; *s* of John Coultas Scofield Brown and Sarah Ellen Brown (*née* Brown); *m* 1955, Christine Ann Batchelor; one *d*. Export Credits Guarantee Dept, 1949; Nat. service, Grenadier Guards, 1949–51; Board of Trade, 1967; seconded to HM Diplomatic Service, 1969; Diplomatic Service, 1975; First Secretary and Head of Chancery, Accra, 1977; FCO, 1979, Counsellor, 1981; Counsellor (Commercial) and Dir of Trade Promotion, British Trade Develt Office, NY, 1984; Consul-Gen., Toronto, and Dir, Trade Promotion and Investment, 1989–91. *Recreations:* walking, public speaking. *Club:* Royal Over-Seas League.

BROWN, (John) Bruce, FRICS; Chairman, Lambert Smith Hampton, since 1988; *b* 15 June 1944; *s* of late Bruce Brown and Margaret Mary (*née* Roberts); *m* 1967, Daphne Jane Walker; one *s* two *d*. *Educ:* Acton Park, Wrexham; Grove Park, Wrexham; Coll. of Estate Management, London Univ. (BSc). FRICS 1977. Surveyor, Samuel Walker & Son, 1967–68; Estates Surveyor, Bracknell Develt Corp., 1968–69; Sen. Develt Surveyor, Town & City Properties, 1969–71; Sen. Partner, Anthony Brown Stewart, 1971–88. *Recreations:* motor-racing, vintage and veteran cars. *Address:* United Kingdom House, 180 Oxford Street, W1D 1NN. *T:* (020) 7198 2000; Radmore Farm, Wappenham, Towcester, Northants NN12 8SX.

BROWN, Prof. John Campbell, PhD; DSc; Regius Professor of Astronomy, University of Glasgow, since 1996; Astronomer Royal for Scotland, since 1995; *b* 4 Feb. 1947; *s* of John Brown and Jane Livingston Stewart Brown (*née* Campbell); *m* 1972, Dr Margaret Isobel Logan; one *s* one *d*. *Educ:* Hartfield Primary; Dumbarton Acad.; Glasgow Univ. (BSc 1st Cl. Hons Physics and Astronomy 1968; PhD 1973; DSc 1984). University of Glasgow: Research Asst, 1968–70; Lectr, 1970–78; Sen. Lectr, 1978–80; Reader, 1980–84; Prof. of Astrophysics, 1984–96. Fellow: Univ. of Tubingen, 1971–72; Univ. of Utrecht, 1973–74; Vis. Fellow, Nat. Center for Atmospheric Res., Colorado, 1977; NASA Associate Prof., Univ. of Md, 1980; Nuffield/NSF Fellow, UCSD and Univ. of Amsterdam, 1984; Brittingham Prof., Univ. of Wisconsin-Madison, 1987; Visiting Fellow, 1999: Univ. of Amsterdam; ETH Zürich; Observatoire de Paris; NASA Goddard SFC; Univ. of Wisconsin-Madison, 2003; Univ. of Alabama-Huntsville; Univ. of Calif, Berkeley, 2006. Hon. Professor: Univ. of Edinburgh, 1996–; Univ. of Aberdeen, 1998–. Marlar Lectr, Rice Univ., Texas, 2006. Time & Space Project Astronomer, Royal Observatory, Greenwich, 2004–06. Pres., Physics Section, BAAS, 2001. FRAS 1973 (Vice Pres., 1986–87); FRSE 1984 (Mem. Council, 1997–2000); FInstP 1996; Associate Mem., Brazilian Acad. of Scis, 1988. Kelvin Prize and Medal, Univ. of Glasgow, 1984; Kelvin Medal, Royal Philosophical Soc., Glasgow, 1996; Robinson Lectr and Medal, Armagh Observatory, 1998; Promotion of Physics Award, Inst. of Physics, 2003. *Publications:* (with I. J. D. Craig) Inverse Problems in Astronomy, 1986; (ed with J. T. Schmeltz) The Sun: a laboratory for astrophysics, 1992; numerous papers in Astrophysical Jl, Astronomy and Astrophysics, Solar Physic, Nature, etc. *Recreations:* oil-painting, lapidary and silvercraft, woodwork, photography, conjuring, reading, cycling, hiking. *Address:* Department of Physics and Astronomy, University of Glasgow, Glasgow G12 8QQ. *T:* (0141) 330 5182; 21 Bradfield Avenue, Glasgow G12 0QH. *T:* (0141) 339 1688.

BROWN, John Domenic Weare; Chairman: John Brown Enterprises; John Brown Publishing Ltd, 1987–2004 (Managing Director, 1987–99); John Brown Citrus Publishing, 2002–04; Bob Books Ltd, since 2006; *b* 29 May 1953; *s* of Sir John Gilbert Newton Brown, CBE and of Virginia (*née* Braddell); *m* 1987, Claudia Zeff; one *s* one *d*. *Educ:* Westminster Sch.; London Coll. of Printing. Managing Director: Eel Pie Publishing, 1982; Virgin Books, 1983–87; Founder, John Brown Publishing Ltd (magazine publisher), 1987. Director: John Wisden and Co., 2003–; Wisden Gp, 2003–; Aurenis, 2007; The Sound Agency Ltd, 2008; non-executive Director: Wanderlust Ltd, 2003–; Oldie Pubns, 2003; non-exec. Chm., Wild Frontiers, 2008. Chm., Portobello Centre. Non-exec. Dir, Notting Hill Prep. Sch., 2003–. Marcus Morris Award, PPA, 1997. *Recreations:* sport (mainly watching), music (mainly listening). *Address:* c/o John Brown Enterprises, 241a Portobello Road, W11 1LT. *T:* (020) 7243 7402. *Clubs:* Soho House, Garrick.

BROWN, Rt Rev. John Edward; Bishop in Cyprus and the Gulf, 1987–95; Episcopal Canon, St George's Cathedral, Jerusalem, 1987–95; an Assistant Bishop, Diocese of Lincoln, since 1995; *b* 13 July 1930; *s* of Edward and Muriel Brown; *m* 1956, Rosemary (*née* Wood); one *s*. *Educ:* Wintringham Grammar Sch., Grimsby; Kelham Theological Coll., Notts. BD London. Deacon 1955, priest 1956; Master, St George's School, Jerusalem; Curate, St George's Cathedral, Jerusalem; Chaplain of Amman, Jordan, 1954–57; Curate-in-Charge, All Saints, Reading, 1957–60; Missionary and Chaplain, All Saints Cathedral, Khartoum, Sudan, 1960–64; Vicar: Stewkley, Buckingham, 1964–69; St Luke's, Maidenhead, 1969–73; Bracknell, Berkshire, 1973–77; Rural Dean of Sonning, 1974–77; Archdeacon of Berkshire, 1978–86; Rural Dean, Grimsby and Cleethorpes, 2003–04. *Recreations:* walking; Middle East and African studies. *Address:* 130 Oxford Street, Cleethorpes DN35 0BP. *T:* (01472) 698840; *e-mail:* bishopjohn6@hotmail.com.

BROWN, (John) Michael, CBE 1986; HM Diplomatic Service, retired; *b* 16 Nov. 1929; *m* 1955, Elizabeth Fitton; one *s* one *d*. *Educ:* Sch. of Oriental and African Studies, London. MECAS, 1953. Served at: Cairo, 1954–55; Doha, 1956–57; FO, 1957–60; Havana, 1960–62; FO, 1962–64; Jedda, 1965–66; Maseru, 1966–67; Bogotá, 1967–69; FCO, 1969–71; Ankara, 1971–73; Counsellor, Tripoli, 1973–75; FCO, 1976–79; Ambassador to Costa Rica and Nicaragua, 1979–82; Consul-Gen., Geneva, 1983–85. *Address:* 26 Silchester Place, Winchester, Hants SO23 7FT.

BROWN, Dr John Michael, FRS 1996; Lecturer and Tutor in Chemistry, Chemical Research Laboratory, Oxford University, 1974–2008; Fellow of Wadham College, Oxford1974–2007, now Emeritus; *b* 24 Dec. 1939; *s* of John Caulfield Brown and Winefride Brown; *m* 1963, Una Horner; one *s* one *d*. *Educ:* Manchester Univ. (BSc 1960; PhD 1963). Various postdoctoral appts, 1963–66; Lectr in Chemistry, Warwick Univ., 1966–74. Tilden Lectr, RSC, 1991. Organometallic Prize, RSC, 1993; (jtly) Descartes Prize, EU, 2001; Horst Pracejus Prize, 2005. *Publications:* (jtly) Mechanism in Organic Chemistry, 1971; articles and reviews in UK, US and European jls. *Recreations:* countryside (UK and France), good writing, grandchildren, Man Utd. *Address:* Chemical Research Laboratory, Mansfield Road, Oxford OX1 3TA. *T:* (01865) 275642, *Fax:* (01865) 285002; *e-mail:* john.brown@chem.ox.ac.uk.

BROWN, John Michael; Chairman, William Hill Organisation, 1989–2004; *b* 17 Sept. 1942; *s* of John Lawrence Brown and Iris May Brown; *m* 1st, 1964, Jennifer Kathleen Dixon (*d* 1993); one *d*; 2nd, 2002, Christine Shine. *Educ:* Stratford Grammar Sch., London. Joined William Hill Orgn, 1959. Dir, Brent Walker, 1991–98. Non-exec. Dir, Satellite Inf. Services, 1989–. Dep. Chm., Bookmakers' Cttee, 2000. *Recreation:* horse racing. *Address:* Milford Court, Milford Road, South Milford, Leeds LS25 5AD. *T:* (01997) 689703; *e-mail:* johnbrown@dial.pipex.com.

BROWN, Prof. John Milton, PhD; FRS 2003; Professor of Chemistry, Oxford University, 1996–2008; Fellow, Exeter College, Oxford, since 1983; *b* 12 Sept. 1941; *s* of Arthur Godfrey Kilner Brown and Mary Denholm Brown; *m* 1964, Monika Bergstrom; two *s* one *d*. *Educ:* Cheltenham Coll.; Peterhouse, Cambridge (BA 1963; PhD 1966); MA Oxon. Lectr, 1970–82, Reader, 1982–83, Southampton Univ.; Lectr, Oxford Univ., 1983–96. *Publications:* Molecular Spectroscopy, 1998; Rotational Spectroscopy of Diatomic Molecules, 2003. *Recreations:* walking in mountains, bicycling, running. *Address:* Physical and Theoretical Chemistry Laboratory, South Parks Road, Oxford OX1 3QZ. *T:* (office) (01865) 275403, *Fax:* (01865) 275410; *e-mail:* jmb@physchem.ox.ac.uk. *Club:* Achilles.

BROWN, John Russell; Honorary Visiting Professor, University College London, since 2008; *b* 15 Sept. 1923; *yr s* of Russell Alan and Olive Helen Brown, Coombe Wood, Somerset; *m* 1961, Hilary Sue Baker; one *s* two *d*. *Educ:* Monkton Combe Sch.; Keble Coll., Oxford. Sub-Lieut (AE) RNVR, 1944–46. Fellow, Shakespeare Inst., Stratford-upon-Avon, 1951–55; Lectr and Sen. Lectr, Dept of English, Birmingham Univ., 1955–63; Prof. and Hd of Dept of Drama and Theatre Arts, Univ. of Birmingham, 1964–71; Prof. of English, Sussex Univ., 1971–82; Prof. of Theatre Arts, State Univ. of NY at Stony Brook, 1982–85; Prof. of Theatre, Univ. of Michigan, Ann Arbor, 1985–97; Artistic Dir, Project Theatre, Michigan Univ., 1985–89. Reynolds Lectr, Colorado Univ., 1957; Vis. Prof. Graduate Sch., New York Univ., 1959; Mellon Prof. of Drama, Carnegie Inst., Pittsburgh, 1964; Vis. Prof., Zürich Univ., 1969–70; Univ. Lectr in Drama, Univ. of Toronto, 1970; Vis. Prof., Columbia Univ., NY, 1998 and 2002; Research Consultant, 1994–2000, Vis. Prof. of Theatre 2000–08, Middlesex Univ. Robb Lectr, Univ. of Auckland, 1976; Lansdowne Visitor, Univ. of Victoria, BC, 1990. Associate, NT, 1973–88. Member: Adv. Council of Victoria and Albert Museum, 1980–83; Adv. Council of Theatre Museum, 1974–83 (Chm., 1979–83); Arts Council of GB, 1980–83, and Chm. Drama Panel, 1980–83 (formerly Dep. Chm.). *Theatre productions include:* Twelfth Night, Playhouse, Pittsburgh, 1964; Macbeth, Everyman, Liverpool, 1965; The White Devil, Everyman, 1969; Crossing Niagara, Nat. Theatre at the ICA, 1975; They Are Dying Out, Young Vic, 1976; Old Times, British Council tour of Poland, 1976; Judgement, Nat. Theatre, 1977; Hamlet (tour), 1978; Macbeth, Nat. Theatre (co-director), 1978; The Vienna Notes and The Nest, Crucible, Sheffield, 1979; Company, Nat. Theatre, 1980; Faith Healer, Nat. Theatre and Santa Fe, 1982, and, with Candida, British Council tour of India, 1983; The Double Bass, Nat. Theatre, 1984; The Daughter-in-Law, Antique Pink, Oedipus, Waiting for Godot, Don Juan, Every Good Boy, Project Theater, Ann Arbor, Mich, USA, 1985–89; Richard II, Nat. Theatre, Educn Project Tour, 1987; Much Ado About Nothing, Playhouse, Cincinnati, 1989; Burn This, 1989, On the Verge, 1991, Dunedin, NZ; Arden of Faversham, Empty Space, Seattle, 1991; Life Sentences, Group Theater of Mich, 1994. General Editor: Stratford-upon-Avon Studies, 1960–67; Stratford-upon-Avon Library, 1964–69; Theatre Production Studies, 1981–2002; Theatre Concepts, 1992–95; Theatres of the World, 2001–; Shakespeare Handbooks, 2002–. *Publications:* (ed) The Merchant of Venice, 1955; Shakespeare and his Comedies, 1957; (ed) The White Devil, 1960; Shakespeare: The Tragedy of Macbeth, 1963; (ed) The Duchess of Malfi, 1965; (ed) Henry V, 1965; Shakespeare's Plays in Performance, 1966; Effective Theatre, 1969; Shakespeare's The Tempest, 1969; Shakespeare's Dramatic Style, 1970; Theatre Language, 1972; Free Shakespeare, 1974; Discovering Shakespeare, 1981; Shakespeare and his Theatre, 1982; A Short Guide to Modern British Drama, 1983; Shakescenes, 1993; (ed) Oxford Illustrated History of Theatre, 1995; William Shakespeare: writing for performance, 1996; What is Theatre?, 1997; New Sites for Shakespeare: theatre, the audience and Asia, 1999; Shakespeare: the Tragedies, 2001; Shakespeare and the Theatrical Event, 2002; Shakespeare Dancing: a theatrical study of the plays, 2004; (ed) Directors' Shakespeare, 2008; articles in Shakespeare Survey, Critical Quarterly, Tulane Drama Review, Studies in Bibliography, New Theatre Qly, Theatre Res. Internat., etc. *Recreations:* gardening, travel.

BROWN, Joseph Lawler, CBE 1978; TD 1953; FMIC; DL; Chairman and Managing Director, The Birmingham Post & Mail Ltd, 1973–77; *b* 22 March 1921; *s* of late Neil Brown; *m* 1950, Mabel Smith, SRN, SCM; one *s* one *d*. *Educ:* Peebles; Heriot-Watt Coll., Edinburgh. BA Hons Open Univ. FCIM (FInstM 1976); CCMI (FBIM 1978). Served War, The Royal Scots, 1939–47 (Major). The Scotsman Publications Ltd, 1947–60; Coventry Newspapers Ltd: Gen. Man., 1960; Jt Man. Dir, 1961; Man. Dir, 1964–69; The Birmingham Post & Mail Ltd: Dep. Man. Dir, 1970; Man. Dir, 1971. Director: Cambridge Newspapers Ltd, 1965–69; Press Assoc., 1968–75 (Chm. 1972); Reuters Ltd, 1972–75; BPM (Holdings) Ltd, 1973–81. Pres., Birmingham Chamber of Industry and Commerce, 1979–80. Exec. Chm., Birmingham Venture, 1981–85. Mem., Bromsgrove and Redditch DHA, 1982–84; Mem., Hereford and Worcester Family Practitioner Cttee, 1982–83. Mem. Council, Regular Forces Employment Assoc., 1983–87; Warden, Neidpath Castle, Peebles, 1983–84. Mem., Peebles Guildry Corp., 1991–97. Life Mem., Court, Birmingham Univ., 1980; Bailiff, Schs of King Edward the Sixth in Birmingham, 1987–88. Hon. Callant of Peebles, 2007. FRSA 1975. DL County of W Midlands, 1976. Kt, Mark Twain Soc., 1979. Commendatore, Order Al Merito Della Repubblica Italiana, 1973. *Publication:* (with J. C. Lawson) History of Peebles 1850–1990, 1990. *Address:* 1 Norbury Close, Church Hill North, Redditch, Worcs B98 8RP. *T:* (01527) 597887.

BROWN, Prof. Judith Margaret, (Mrs P. J. Diggle), FRHistS; Beit Professor of Commonwealth History and Fellow of Balliol College, University of Oxford, since 1990; *b* India, 9 July 1944; *d* of late Rev. Wilfred George Brown and Joan M. Brown; *m* 1984, Peter James Diggle; one *s*. *Educ:* Sherborne Sch. for Girls; Girton Coll., Cambridge (BA 1965; PhD 1968; MA 1969); MA, DPhil Oxon 1990. Research Fellow, Official Fellow and Dir of Studies in History, Girton Coll., Cambridge, 1968–71; Lectr, Sen. Lectr, Reader Elect in History, Univ. of Manchester, 1971–90. Trustee, Charles Wallace (India) Trust, 1996–2008; Chm. Trustees, Friends of Delhi Brotherhood Soc., 1997–99. Governor: Bath Spa UC, 1997–; SOAS, London Univ., 1999–2006; Sherborne Sch. for Girls, 2003–. Hon. DSocSc Natal, 2001. *Publications:* Gandhi's Rise to Power: Indian politics 1915–1922, 1972; Gandhi and Civil Disobedience: the Mahatma in Indian politics 1928–1934, 1977; Men and Gods in a Changing World, 1980; Modern India: the origins of an Asian democracy, 1984, 2nd edn 1994; Gandhi: prisoner of hope, 1989, 2nd edn 1998 (trans. Italian, 1995); (ed with R. Foot) Migration: the Asian experience, 1994; (ed with M. Prozesky) Gandhi and South Africa: principles and politics, 1996; (ed with R. Foot) Hong Kong's Transitions 1842–1997, 1997; Nehru, 1999; (ed with W. R. Louis) The Oxford History of the British Empire, vol. IV: the twentieth century, 1999; (ed with R. E. Frykenberg) Christians, Cultural Interactions and India's Religious Traditions, 2002; Nehru: a political life, 2003; Global South Asians: introducing the modern diaspora, 2006; (ed) The Essential Writings of Mahatma Gandhi, 2008. *Recreations:* classical music, gardening, walking. *Address:* Balliol College, Oxford OX1 3BJ. *T:* (01865) 277736.

See also P. W. H. Brown.

BROWN, Julia Elizabeth; *see* King, J. E.

BROWN, Julian Francis, RDI 1998; owner, StudioBrown, since 1990; *b* 8 Sept. 1955; *s* of Oliver and Barbara Brown; *m* 1986, Louise Mary Aron; two *s* one *d*. *Educ:* Leicester Poly. (BA Hons Industrial Design 1978); RCA (MDes 1983). Designer: David Carter Associates, 1979–80; Porsche Design, Austria, 1983–86; Partner, Lovegrove & Brown, 1986–90. Guest Professor: Hochschule der Kunste, Berlin, 1991–92; Essen-Duisburg Univ., 2003–04. External Examiner in Industrial Design: RCA, 1997–99; Glasgow Sch. of Art, 1998–2003. *Address:* StudioBrown, 4 The Wharf, Lacock, N Wilts SN15 2PQ. *T:* (01249) 730670.

BROWN, June Marion; *see* Venters, J. M.

BROWN, June P.; *see* Paterson-Brown.

BROWN, Keith James; Member (SNP) Ochil, Scottish Parliament, since 2007; *b* 20 Dec. 1961; *s* of Atholl Brown and Carole Brown; *m* 1990, Tammy Joyce (separated 2006); two *s* one *d*. *Educ:* Univ. of Dundee (MA Hons 1988); Univ. of Prince Edward Is. (MA Hons). Royal Marines, 1980–83. Clerk, Edinburgh DC, 1988–90; Admin. Officer, 1990–96, Civic Officer, 1996–2007, Stirling DC, then Stirling Council. Mem. (SNP), Clackmannanshire Council, 1996–2007. Mem., European Cttee of the Regions, 1999–2006, 2008–. *Recreations:* smoking Cuban cigars, Hibernian FC. *Address:* c/o Scottish Parliament, Edinburgh EH99 1SP. *T:* (0131) 348 6335; *e-mail:* keith.brown.msp@scottish.parliament.uk.

BROWN, (Laurence Frederick) Mark; His Honour Judge Mark Brown; a Circuit Judge, since 2000; *b* 16 March 1953; *s* of Rt Rev. Ronald Brown, *qv* and late Joyce Brown; *m* 1978, Jane Margaret Boardman; one *s*. *Educ:* Bolton Sch.; St John's Coll., Univ. of Durham (BA Jt Hons Law/Econs; Adam Smith Prize in Econs). Called to the Bar, Inner Temple, 1975; practised, Northern Circuit, 1976–2000; Asst Recorder, 1993–97, a Recorder, 1997–2000; Asst Boundary Comr, England and Wales, 2000. Ethnic Minority Liaison Judge, Liverpool, 2002–05; Liaison Judge, Knowsley Magistrates' Ct, 2002–; Investigating Judge, 2007–. Pt-time tutor in Law, Univ. of Liverpool, 1977–82; Head of advocacy training, Northern Circuit, 1998–2001. Counsel to Chief Constable at Police Disciplinary Hearings, 1989–2000; Member: Panel, Disciplinary Tribunals of Council of Inns of Court, 1994–2000; Merseyside Area Criminal Justice Strategy Cttee, 1997–2000; Parole Bd, 2003–; Judicial Panel for Judicial Appts, 2004–. *Recreations:* golf, ballroom dancing, gardening. *Address:* Liverpool Crown Court, Queen Elizabeth II Law Courts, Derby Square, Liverpool L2 1XA. *T:* (0151) 473 7373. *Club:* Royal Liverpool Golf.

BROWN, Prof. Lawrence Michael, ScD; FRS 1982; Professor of Physics, University of Cambridge, 1990–2001, now Emeritus; Founding Fellow, Robinson College, Cambridge, since 1977; *b* 18 March 1936; *s* of Bertson Waterworth Brown and Edith Waghorne; *m* 1965, Susan Drucker; one *s* two *d*. *Educ:* Univ. of Toronto (BASc); Univ. of Birmingham (PhD); ScD Cantab 1992. Athlone Fellow, Univ. of Birmingham, 1957; W. M. Tapp Research Fellow, Gonville and Caius Coll., Cambridge, 1963; University Demonstrator, Cavendish Laboratory, 1965; Lectr, 1970–83, Reader, 1983–90, Cambridge Univ.; Lectr, Robinson Coll., Cambridge, 1977–90. *Publications:* many papers on structure and properties of materials and electron microscopy in Acta Metallurgica and Philosophical Magazine. *Address:* 74 Alpha Road, Cambridge CB4 3DG. *T:* (01223) 337336.

BROWN, Prof. L(ionel) Neville, OBE 1988; Professor of Comparative Law, University of Birmingham, 1966–90, Emeritus Professor, since 1990; Leverhulme Fellow, 1990–92; *b* 29 July 1923; *s* of Reginald P. N. Brown and Fanny Brown (*née* Carver); *m* 1957, Mary Patricia Vowles; three *s* one *d*. *Educ:* Wolverhampton Grammar Sch.; Pembroke Coll., Cambridge (Scholar; 1st Cl. Class. Tripos Pt I and Law Tripos Pt II; MA, LLM); Lyons Univ. (Dr en Droit). RAF, 1942–45; Cambridge, 1945–48; articled to Wolverhampton solicitor, 1948–50; Rotary Foundn Fellow, Lyons Univ., 1951–52; Lectr in Law, Sheffield Univ., 1953–55; Lectr in Comparative Law, Birmingham Univ., 1956, Sen. Lectr, 1957; Sen. Res. Fellow, Univ. of Michigan, 1960. Mem., Council on Tribunals, 1982–88; Chm., Birmingham Social Security Appeal Tribunal, 1988–96. Visiting Professor: Univ. of Tulane, New Orleans, 1968; Univ. of Nairobi, 1974; Laval, 1975, 1979, 1983, 1990; Limoges, 1986; Mauritius, 1988, 1989; Aix-en-Provence, 1991. Commonwealth Foundn Lectr (Caribbean), 1975–76. Pres., SPTL, 1984–85. Reader, C of E, Lichfield Dio., 1971–. Dr *hc* Limoges, 1989; Hon. LLD Laval, 1992. Commandeur, Ordre des Palmes

Académiques (France), 2006 (Officier, 1987). *Publications:* (with F. H. Lawson and A. E. Anton) Amos and Walton's Introduction to French Law, 2nd edn 1963 and 3rd edn 1967; (with J. F. Garner) French Administrative Law, 1967, 5th edn (with J. S. Bell) 1998; (with F. G. Jacobs) Court of Justice of the European Communities, 1977, 5th edn (with T. Kennedy), 2000. *Recreations:* landscape gardening, country walking, music. *Address:* Willow Rise, 14 Waterdale, Compton Road West, Wolverhampton, West Midlands WV3 9DY. *T:* (01902) 426666. *Club:* Oxford and Cambridge.

BROWN, Dr Lydia Akrigg, (Mrs J. H. Seamer), FRCVS; CBiol, FIBiol; Managing Director, UK and Ireland, PHARMAQ Ltd (formerly Alpharma Animal Health Ltd), since 2000; *b* 28 June 1954; *d* of late Tom Brown and of Barbara Brown (*née* Blackmore); *m* 1988, John Heckford Seamer (*d* 2007). *Educ:* Childwall Valley High Sch. for Girls, Liverpool; Univ. of Liverpool (BVSc 1978); Univ. of Stirling (PhD 1983); BA Open 1992; Univ. of Warwick (MBA 2002). MRCVS 1978, FRCVS 1987; CBiol, FIBiol 2002. Wellcome Trust res. schol., 1978–81; Technical Manager: Ewos Aquaculture, 1982–83; Willows Francis, 1984–85; Asst Prof., Coll. of Veterinary Medicine, Mississippi State Univ., 1985–87; Man. Dir, Biological Labs (UK) Ltd, 1987–89; Eur. Tech. Manager, then UK Country Manager, Abbott Labs, 1989–2000. Hon. Lectr, Univs of Liverpool and London. Mem., Medicines Commn, 2000–05. RCVS specialist in fish health and prodn, 1989–94, 2007–. Royal College of Veterinary Surgeons: Mem. Council, 1991–2007; Chm., various cttees; Pres., 1998–99; Mem., Parly and Scientific Cttee, 1998–2003, 2007–; Chm., RCVS Trust, 1998–2004; Pres., Veterinary Benevolent Fund, 2006–; RCVS rep., Fedn of Veterinarians in Europe, 1998–2000. Non-exec. Dir, Salisbury NHS Foundn Trust, 2008–. Mem. Council, Univ. Fedn of Animal Welfare, 2005–. Founder Trustee, Veterinary Surgeons Health Support Prog., 1999–; Trustee, Humane Slaughter Assoc., 2005–. Mem., Steering Cttee, Vet Helpline, 1993–98, 2008–. Pres., Southern Counties Veterinary Assoc., 1994–95. MInstD 2001. Gov., Salisbury Cathedral Sch., 2005–. Lay Canon, Salisbury Cathedral, 2007–. *Publications:* (ed) Rearing Healthy Fish under Primitive Conditions, 1987; The Aquaculture Market, 1989; (ed) Aquaculture for Veterinarians, 1993; contrib. papers and chapters on surgical techniques, anaesthesia, pharmacology and husbandry related to aquaculture. *Recreations:* travel, scuba diving, photography. *Address:* Mill Leat, W Gomeldon, Salisbury, Wilts SP4 6JY. *T:* (01980) 611438, *Fax:* (01980) 611611; *e-mail:* lydia.brown@btinternet.com. *Club:* Farmers, Royal Society of Medicine.

BROWN, Lyn Carol; MP (Lab) West Ham, since 2005; *b* 13 April 1960. *Educ:* Univ. of London (BA). Residential Social Worker, Ealing. Mem. (Lab) Newham BC, 1988. Founder and Chm., London Libraries Develt Agency, 2000–. Contested (Lab) Wanstead and Woodford, 1992. *Address:* House of Commons, SW1A 0AA.

BROWN, Rev. Dr Malcolm Arthur; Director of Mission and Public Affairs, Church of England, since 2007; *b* Sept. 1954; *s* of Arthur Leslie and Gwendolen Mary Brown; *m* 1983, Angela Josephine; one *s*, and one step *s*. *Educ:* Eltham Coll.; Oriel Coll., Oxford (BA 1976; MA 1982); Westcott House; Univ. of Manchester (PhD 2000). Ordained deacon, 1979, priest, 1980; Asst Curate, Riverhead with Dunton Green, 1979–83; Team Vicar and Industrial Missioner, Southampton City Centre, 1983–90; Exec. Sec., William Temple Foundn, 1990–2000; Principal, E Anglian Ministerial Trng Course, then Eastern Reg. Ministry Course, 2000–07. Honorary Lecturer: Univ. of Manchester, 1993–2000; Univ. of Wales, Bangor, 2000–06; Anglia Ruskin Univ., 2005–; Sen. Associate, Cambridge Theol Fedn, 2007–. FHEA 2007. *Publications:* After the Market, 2004; (with P. Ballard) The Church and Economic Life, 2006; contrib. numerous essays and articles in academic jls. *Recreations:* driving steam trains, metal bashing, rowing. *Address:* Church House, Great Smith Street, SW1P 3NZ. *T:* (020) 7898 1468; *e-mail:* malcolm.brown@c-of-e.org.uk.

BROWN, Prof. Malcolm Watson, PhD; FRS 2004; Professor of Anatomy and Cognitive Neuroscience, since 1998, Research Director, Faculty of Medicine and Veterinary Sciences, since 2003, University of Bristol; *b* 24 Feb. 1946; *s* of Denis and Vivian Irene Brown; *m* 1974, Geraldine Ruth Hassall; one *s* one *d*. *Educ:* Crewkerne Sch., Som.; St John's Coll., Cambridge (BA 1st Cl. Natural Scis Tripos, Theoretical Physics 1968; MA 1972; PhD 1974). Asst in Res., Dept of Anatomy, Univ. of Cambridge, 1972–74; Res. Fellow, Downing Coll., Cambridge, 1973–74; Department of Anatomy, University of Bristol: Lectr, 1975–91; Sen. Lectr, 1991–94; Reader in Anatomy and Cognitive Neurosci., 1994–98; Dep. Hd, 1996–98; Hd, 1998–2006. Special Res. Fellow, AFRC, 1991–92. Exec. Mem., Mgt Cttee, MRC Centre for Synaptic Plasticity, 1999–. Member: Brain Res., subseq. British Neurosci., Assoc., 1970–; Eur. Brain and Behaviour Soc., 1984–; Anatomical Soc. of GB and Ireland, 2000–. *Publications:* (contrib.) A Textbook of Head and Neck Anatomy, 1988; contrib. scientific papers and reviews to learned jls. *Recreations:* foreign travel, local church responsibilities. *Address:* University of Bristol, Department of Anatomy, School of Medical Sciences, Bristol BS8 1TD. *T:* (0117) 928 7408, *Fax:* (0117) 929 1687; *e-mail:* M.W.Brown@bris.ac.uk.

BROWN, Prof. Margaret Louise, PhD; AcSS; Professor of Mathematics Education, King's College, London, since 1990; *b* 30 Sept. 1943; *d* of (Frederick) Harold Seed and Louisa Seed (*née* Shearer); *m* 1970, Hugh Palmer Brown; three *s*. *Educ:* Merchant Taylors' Sch. for Girls, Liverpool; Newnham Coll., Cambridge (BA Math. 1965; MA 1968); Inst. of Education, London Univ. (PGCE 1966); Chelsea Coll., Univ. of London (PhD 1981). Math. Teacher, Cavendish Sch., Hemel Hempstead, 1966–69; Lectr in Math. Educn, 1969–83, Sen. Lectr, 1983–86, Chelsea Coll., Univ. of London; Reader in Math. Educn, 1986–90, Head of Sch. of Educn, 1992–96, KCL; FKC 1996. Member: Nat. Curriculum Math. Wkg Gp, 1987–88; Numeracy Task Force, 1997–98; Adv. Cttee on Maths Educn, 2005–; Chair: Jt Math. Council of UK, 1991–95; Trustees, School Math. Project, 1996–2006; Educn Sub-Panel, RAE 2008, 2004–; President: Math. Assoc., 1990–91; British Educnl Res. Assoc., 1997–98. AcSS 2000. Hon. EdD Kingston, 2002. *Publications:* (jtly) Statistics and Probability, 1972, 2nd edn 1977; (jtly) Low Attainers in Mathematics 5–16, 1982; (jtly) Children Learning Mathematics, 1984; Graded Assessment in Mathematics, 1992; (jtly) Intuition or Evidence?, 1995; (jtly) Effective Teachers of Numeracy, 1997; papers in jls and contribs to books on math. educn. *Recreations:* walking, music. *Address:* Department of Education and Professional Studies, King's College London, Franklin Wilkins Building, Waterloo Road, SE1 9NN. *T:* (020) 7848 3088; (home) 34 Girdwood Road, SW18 5QS. *T:* (020) 8789 4344.

BROWN, (Marion) Patricia; Under-Secretary (Economics), Treasury, 1972–85; *b* 2 Feb. 1927; *d* of late Henry Oswald Brown and Elsie Elizabeth (*née* Thompson). *Educ:* Norwich High Sch. for Girls; Newnham Coll., Cambridge. Central Economic Planning Staff, Cabinet Office, 1947; Treasury, 1948–54; United States Embassy, London, 1956–59; Treasury, 1959–85. Mem. Council, Royal Holloway and Bedford New Coll., London Univ., 1985–98 (Hon. Fellow, 1999). *Recreations:* bird watching, walking.

BROWN, Mark; *see* Brown, L. F. M.

BROWN, Martin; Director, Eurocustoms, since 2002 (on secondment from HM Revenue and Customs (formerly HM Customs and Excise)); *b* 26 Jan. 1949; *s* of late Clarence and Anne Brown; *m* 1971, Frances Leithead; two *s*. *Educ:* Bolton Sch.; New Coll., Oxford (MA). Joined Customs and Excise as Admin. Trainee, 1971; Private Sec. to Minister of State and to Financial Sec., HM Treasury, 1974–76; Principal, HM Customs and Excise, 1976; Customs adviser to Barbados Govt, 1984–86; HM Customs and Excise: Asst Sec., 1987; Comr, 1993–2002; Director: Customs, 1993; Central Ops, 1994–96; VAT Policy, 1996–2000; Customs and Tax Practice, 2001–02. *Recreations:* theatre, singing, walking, gardening, pottering. *Address:* Eurocustoms, Bureau E1, DGDDI, 5–11 rue des Deux Communes, 93100 Montreuil sous Bois, France; *e-mail:* martin.brown@eurocustoms.org.

BROWN, Martin; a District Judge (Magistrates' Courts), since 2005; *b* 31 Aug. 1958; *s* of Raymond Brown and Beryl Brown (*née* Yorath); *m* 1983, Anne Elizabeth Pooley; one *d*. *Educ:* Univ. of Wales, Aberystwyth (LLB 1979). Admitted solicitor, 1982; High Court (Criminal) Advocate, 1994–2005; Actg Stipendiary Magistrate, subseq. Dep. Dist Judge, 1999–2004. Mem., Test Bd, Centre for Professional Legal Studies, 1998–2005 (Duty Solicitor accreditation scheme). *Recreations:* hill-walking, squash, bird-watching, enthusiastic Terry Wogan fan. *Club:* Wolverhampton Lawn Tennis and Squash.

BROWN, Sir Max; *see* Brown, Sir C. M. P.

BROWN, Sir Mervyn, KCMG 1981 (CMG 1975); OBE 1963; HM Diplomatic Service, retired; *b* 24 Sept. 1923; *m* 1949, Elizabeth Gittings. *Educ:* Ryhope Gram. Sch., Sunderland; St John's Coll., Oxford. Served in RA, 1942–45. Entered HM Foreign Service, 1949; Third Secretary, Buenos Aires, 1950; Second Secretary, UK Mission to UN, New York, 1953; First Secretary, Foreign Office, 1956; Singapore, 1959; Vientiane, 1960; again in Foreign Office, 1963–67; Ambassador to Madagascar, 1967–70; Inspector, FCO, 1970–72; Head of Communications Operations Dept, FCO, 1973–74; Asst Under-Sec. of State (Dir of Communications), 1974; High Comr in Tanzania, 1975–78, and concurrently Ambassador to Madagascar; Minister and Dep. Perm. Representative to UN, 1978; High Comr in Nigeria, 1979–83, and concurrently Ambassador to Benin. Chairman: Visiting Arts Unit of GB, 1983–89; Council, King's Coll., Madrid, 1995–2003; Vice-Pres., Commonwealth Youth Exchange Council, 1984–87. Pres., Britain-Nigeria Assoc., 2000–03; Chm., Anglo-Malagasy Soc., 1986–. Associate Mem., Acad. Malgache. Officier, Ordre National (Madagascar). *Publications:* Madagascar Rediscovered, 1978; A History of Madagascar, 1995; War in Shangri-La, 2001. *Recreations:* music, tennis, history, cooking. *Address:* 195 Queen's Gate, SW7 5EU. *Clubs:* Royal Commonwealth Society, Hurlingham, All England Lawn Tennis.

BROWN, Michael; *see* Brown, J. M.

BROWN, Prof. Michael Alan, CBE 2008; PhD; CPhys, CEng; DL; Vice-Chancellor and Chief Executive, Liverpool John Moores University, since 2000; *b* 19 May 1946; *s* of Reginald Leslie Brown and Barbara Evelyn Brown; *m* 1966, Andrea Kathleen Evans; one *s* one *d*. *Educ:* Bridgend Boys' Tech./Grammar Sch.; Nottingham Univ. (BSc Physics; PhD 1971). Eur Ing 1991; MInstP 1980, FInstP 2003; CPhys 1980; MIEE 1984, FIET (FIEE 2002); CEng 1984. Demonstrator, Nottingham Univ., 1967–71; Royal Soc. Post-doctoral Eur. Fellow, Grenoble, 1971–72; Lectr, then Sen. Lectr, in Physics, Loughborough Univ., 1972–86; Gen. Manager, Loughborough Consultants Ltd, 1986–87; Pro Vice-Chancellor, Leicester Poly., then De Montfort Univ., 1987–2000. Dir, UCAS, 2001–05. Mem., Cttee for S African Trade, DTI, 1995–2001. Eur. Trng Consultant to Intel Corp., 1981–87. Mem. and Dir, De Montfort Expertise Ltd, 1989–2000 (Man. Dir, 1989–96); Mem., Dir and Co. Sec., E Midlands Regl Technol. Network Ltd, 1989–96; Mem. and Dir, E Midlands Regl Mgt Centre Ltd, 1991–92; Man. Dir, Flexible Learning Systems Ltd, 1992–2000; Dir, Higher Educn Subscription Fund Ltd, 1994–2000; Dir, Leicester Promotions Ltd, 1996–2000; Exec. Chm., De Montfort Univ., S Africa, 1998–2000; Member: Internat. Sub-Cttee, 2002–07, Finance Sub-Cttee, 2003–07, UUK; Steering Gp for Jt Masters Progs, European Univs Assoc., 2002–. Ind. Chm., Forum for a Better Leics, 1995–2000; Vice-Pres., Personal Service Soc., Liverpool, 2000–; Member: Bd, Liverpool First, 2001–; Liverpool Capital of Culture Ltd, 2003–07; Mem., Monitoring Cttee, Merseyside Objective One Prog., 2002– (Chairman: Strategy Sub-Cttee, 2002–05; Strategy and Monitoring Sub-Cttee, 2005–); Director: Merseyside Partnership Ltd, 2002–; Liverpool Vision, 2003–; Liverpool Ventures Ltd, 2004–05; Chairman: Merseyside and Liverpool Theatres Trust Ltd, 2002–; Liverpool Science Park, 2003–. Mem. and Trustee, Africa Now, 1997–2002. FCMI (FIMgt 1991); FCIM 2000. FRSA 1996. Freeman, City of London, 2007; Liveryman, Engineers' Co., 2007–. DL Merseyside, 2005. Mem. Editl Bd, Laboratory Microcomputer, 1988–93. *Publications:* (contrib.) Collaboration between Business and Higher Education, 1990; (contrib.) The Funding of Higher Education, 1993; (contrib.) Preparing Students for Career Employment, 1998; numerous contribs to learned jls and internat. conf. proc. on physics, mktg and higher educn mgt. *Recreations:* cinema, theatre, travel, spending time with my wife. *Address:* Dawstone Croft, Dawstone Road, Heswall, Wirral, Merseyside CH60 0BU; *e-mail:* vc@livjm.ac.uk. *Clubs:* Institute of Directors; Athenaeum (Liverpool).

BROWN, Air Vice-Marshal Michael John Douglas; consulting engineer; *b* 9 May 1936; *s* of late N. H. B. Brown, AMIERE; *m* 1st, 1961, Audrey (*d* 1994); one *s*; 2nd, 1997, Ruth, *d* of late H. G. Willey, Weobley, Herefordshire. *Educ:* Drayton Manor, W7; RAF Technical Coll., Henlow; Trinity Hall, Cambridge (MA). CEng 1968; CMath, FIMA 1991; FRIN 1998; FRAeS 2000; CSci 2005. Commnd RAF Technical Br., 1954; Cambridge Univ. Air Sqdn, 1954–57; RAF pilot trng, 1958–59; served in Bomber Comd, 1959–61; signals duties in Kenya (also assisted with formation of Kenya Air Force), 1961–64; advanced weapons course, 1965–66; Defence Operational Analysis Estabt, 1966–69; RAF Staff Coll., 1970; MoD Operational Requirements Staff, 1971–73; RAF Boulmer, 1973–75; USAF Air War Coll., 1975–76; HQ RAF Strike Comd, 1976–78; Comdr, RAF N Luffenham, 1978–80; rcds 1981; Dir, Air Guided Weapons, MoD (PE), 1983–86; Dir Gen., Strategic Electronic Systems, MoD (PE), 1986–91. Non-exec. Dir, CSE International Ltd, 1993–2002. Mem. Council, Royal Inst. Navigation, 2006–. Vice-Chm., Herefordshire RBL, 1997–2000; Vice-President: SSAFA, Powys, 1993–2001; RAFA, Hereford, 1997–2001; Regl Rep. for S Wales, SSAFA Nat. Council, 1997–2001; Pres., RAFA, Peterborough, 2002–. Chairman: Cambridge Soc., Peterborough, 2002–; Peterborough Astronomical Soc., 2004–; Peterborough Art Soc., 2006–. Freeman, City of London, 2000; Freeman, 2000, Liveryman, 2001, Engineers' Co. *Club:* Royal Air Force.

BROWN, Michael Russell; journalist; *b* 3 July 1951; *s* of Frederick Alfred Brown and Greta Mary Brown, OBE (*née* Russell). *Educ:* Andrew Cairns Secondary Modern Sch., Sussex; Univ. of York (BA (Hons) Economics and Politics). Graduate Management Trainee, Barclays Bank Ltd, 1972–74; Lecturer and Tutor, Swinton Conservative Coll., 1974–75; part-time Asst to Michael Marshall, MP, 1975–76; Law Student, 1976–77, Member of Middle Temple; Personal Asst to Nicholas Winterton, MP, 1976–79. MP (C) Brigg and Scunthorpe, 1979–83, Brigg and Cleethorpes, 1983–97; contested (C) Cleethorpes, 1997. PPS to Hon. Douglas Hogg, Minister of State, DTI, 1989–90, FCO, 1990–92; PPS to Sir Patrick Mayhew, Sec. of State for NI, 1992–93; an Asst Govt Whip, 1993–94. Mem., Energy Select Cttee, 1986–89; Sec., 1981–87, Vice-Chm., 1987–89,

Conservative Parly N Ireland Cttee. Political columnist, The Independent, 1998–. *Recreations:* cricket, walking. *Address:* 78 Lupus Street, SW1V 3EL. *T:* (020) 7630 9045. *Club:* Reform.

BROWN, Prof. Michael Stuart, MD; Regental Professor, University of Texas; Paul J. Thomas Chair in Medicine, Jonsson Center for Molecular Genetics, since 1977, and W. A. Moncrief Distinguished Chair in Cholesterol and Arteriosclerosis Research, since 1989, University of Texas Southwestern Medical School at Dallas; *b* 13 April 1941; *s* of Harvey and Evelyn Brown; *m* 1964, Alice Lapin; two *d. Educ:* Univ. of Pennsylvania (AB 1962, MD 1966). Resident in Internal Medicine, Mass. Gen. Hosp., Boston, 1966–68; Research Scientist, NIH, Bethesda, 1968–71; Asst Prof., Univ. of Texas Southwestern Med. Sch. at Dallas, 1971–74; Associate Prof., 1974–76. Member Board of Directors: Regeneron Inc., 1991–; Pfizer Inc., 1996–. For. Mem., Royal Soc., 1991. Lounsbery Award, 1979; Albert D. Lasker Award, 1985; (jtly) Nobel Prize in Medicine or Physiology for the discovery of receptors for Low Density Lipoproteins, a fundamental advance in the understanding of cholesterol metabolism, 1985; US Nat. Medal of Science, 1987. *Publications:* numerous papers to learned jls. *Address:* Department of Molecular Genetics, University of Texas Southwestern Medical School, 5323 Harry Hines Boulevard, Dallas, TX 75390–9046, USA.

BROWN, Moira; *see* Brown, S. M.

BROWN, Prof. Morris Jonathan, FRCP; Professor of Clinical Pharmacology, Cambridge University, and Hon. Consultant Physician, Addenbrooke's Hospital, since 1985; Fellow of Gonville and Caius College, and Director of Clinical Studies, Cambridge, since 1989; *b* 18 Jan. 1951; *s* of Arnold and Irene Brown; *m* 1977, Diana Phylactou; three *d. Educ:* Harrow; Trinity College, Cambridge (MA, MD); MSc London. FRCP 1987. Lectr, Royal Postgraduate Medical School, 1979–82; Senior Fellow, MRC, 1982–85. Oliver-Sharpey Lectr, RCP, 1992. Chm., Med. Res. Soc., 1991–97; Pres., British Hypertension Soc., 2005–07. FMedSci 1999. Hospital Doctor of the Year, Elsevier Press, 2003; Lilly Gold Medal, British Pharmacol Soc., 2002; Walter Somerville Medal, British Cardiac Soc., 2006. *Publications:* Advanced Medicine 21, 1985; (jtly) Clinical Pharmacology, 8th edn 1996, 9th edn 2003; articles on adrenaline and cardiovascular disease, genetics and therapy of hypertension, prevention of myocardial infarction by vitamin E. *Recreations:* violin and oboe playing, tennis. *Address:* 104 Grange Road, Cambridge CB3 9AA.

BROWN, Rt Hon. Nicholas (Hugh); PC 1997; MP (Lab) Newcastle upon Tyne East and Wallsend, since 1997 (Newcastle upon Tyne East, 1983–97); Parliamentary Secretary to HM Treasury (Government Chief Whip), since 2008; Minister for the North East of England, since 2007; *b* 13 June 1950; *s* of late R. C. Brown and of G. K. Brown (*née* Tester). *Educ:* Swatenden Secondary Modern Sch.; Tunbridge Wells Tech. High Sch.; Manchester Univ. (BA 1971). Trade Union Officer, GMWU Northern Region, 1978–83. Mem., Newcastle upon Tyne City Council, 1980–84. Opposition front-bench spokesman: on legal affairs, 1984–87; on Treasury affairs, 1987–94; on health, 1994–95; Dep. Chief Opposition Whip, 1995–97; Parly Sec. to HM Treasury (Govt Chief Whip), 1997–98; Minister, Agriculture, Fisheries and Food, 1998–2001; Minister of State (Minister for Work), DWP, 2001–03; Treasurer of HM Household (Dep. Chief Whip), 2007–08. *Address:* House of Commons, SW1A 0AA. *Clubs:* Shieldfield Working Men's, West Walker Social, Newcastle Labour (Newcastle); Lindisfarne (Wallsend).

BROWN, Nicolas Jerome Danton; Director, Drama Production, BBC, since 2006; *b* 11 Sept. 1965; *s* of Simon and Rosemary Brown; *m* 1998, Sarah Barker; two *s. Educ:* Portswood Primary Sch., Southampton; St John's Sch., Leatherhead; Choate Rosemary Hall, Conn.; Clare Coll., Cambridge (BA Hist. 1987). Trainee, Central TV, 1987–89; Develt Exec., 1989–91, Production Exec., 1991–94, Central Films; freelance producer, 1995–2006. Producer: *television:* Insiders, 1997; London Bridge, 1998; Hope and Glory, 1999; Deceit, 1999; Nicholas Nickleby, 2000; White Teeth, 2001–02; Friends and Crocodiles, 2003; Gideon's Daughter, 2004; Bradford Riots, 2005; *film:* Ladies in Lavender, 2004. *Recreation:* sailing. *Address:* c/o Sam Putt Associates, Shepperton Studios, Shepperton, Middx TW17 0QD.

BROWN, Prof. Nigel Leslie, PhD; Vice-Principal, and Head, College of Science and Engineering, University of Edinburgh, since 2008; *b* 19 Dec. 1948; *s* of Leslie Charles Brown and Beryl (*née* Brown); *m* 1971, Gayle Lynnette Blackah; three *d. Educ:* Beverley Grammar Sch.; Univ. of Leeds (BSc 1971; PhD 1974). CBiol, FIBiol 1989; CChem, FRSC 1990. ICI Fellow, MRC Lab. of Molecular Biology, Cambridge, 1974–76; Lectr in Biochemistry, 1976–81, Royal Soc. EPA Cephalosporin Fund Sen. Res. Fellow, 1981–88, Univ. of Bristol; University of Birmingham: Prof. of Molecular Genetics and Microbiol., 1988–2008; Hd, 1994–99, Dep. Hd, 1999–2000, Sch. of Biol Scis; Hd, Sch. of Chemistry, 2003–04; Dir of Sci. and Technol., BBSRC, 2004–08. Vis. Fellow in Genetics, Univ. of Melbourne, 1987–88; Leverhulme Trust Res. Fellow, 2000–01. Biotechnology and Biological Sciences Research Council: Chairman: Genes and Develtl Biology Cttee, 1997–2000; Studentships and Fellowships Cttee, 2000–04. Mem., Res. Careers Initiative, 1997–98. Hon. Pres., W Midlands Reg., ASE, 1997–98. Mem. Editl Bd, Molecular Microbiology, 1986–97; Chief Ed., Fedn of Eur. Microbiology Socs Microbiology Reviews, 2000–04. FRSA 2001. *Publications:* contribs to scientific jls and books. *Recreations:* travel, house renovation. *Address:* College of Science and Engineering, University of Edinburgh, The King's Buildings, West Mains Road, Edinburgh EH9 3JY. *T:* (0131) 650 5754.

BROWN, Patricia; *see* Brown, M. P.

BROWN, Sir Patrick; *see* Brown, Sir A. P.

BROWN, Paul Campbell, CBE 2003; Chairman, RadioCentre, since 2006; *b* 6 Nov. 1945; *s* of James Henry Brown and Edna May Brown (*née* Howell); *m* 1970, Sarah Hunter Bailey; two *s. Educ:* Portsmouth Grammar Sch.; RMA Sandhurst; Balliol Coll., Oxford (BA Hons). Served Army, as Officer, 1966–74. British Forces Broadcasting Service, 1974–78; Ops Manager, BRMB Radio, 1979–81; Prog. and News Dir, Radio Victory, 1981–84; Hd, Radio Programming, IBA, 1984–90; Dep. Chief Exec., Radio Authy, 1990–95; Chief Exec., Commercial Radio Cos Assoc., 1995–2006. Director: Rajar, 1996–2006; Skillset, 2004–08. Chm., UK Digital Radio Forum, 2000–01; Pres., Assoc. of European Radios, 1998–2000; Vice Pres., World DAB Forum, 2000–05. FRA 1996 (Chm. Council, 2001–04); FRSA 2000. *Recreations:* sailing, tennis, walking, reading. *Address:* RadioCentre, 77 Shaftesbury Avenue, W1D 5DU. *Clubs:* Army and Navy; Thorney Island Sailing (Vice Commodore, 2005–07, Commodore, 2007–08).

BROWN, Paul G.; Executive Director, UK Retail Banking, Lloyds Bank plc, 1991–97, retired; *b* 10 Sept. 1942; *s* of Col E. G. Brown and Alice Brown (*née* Van Weyenberghe); *m* 1969, Jessica Faunce; one *s* two *d. Educ:* Belgium, Germany and UK. Management appts with Lloyds Bank plc in Germany, Switzerland, USA and UK, 1960–97. *Recreations:* sailing, ski-ing.

BROWN, Sir Peter (Randolph), Kt 1997; Conservative Constituency Agent for Huntingdon, since 1985; *b* 30 Aug. 1945; *s* of Stanley Percival Brown and late Dorothy Ida Brown (*née* Bagge); *m* 1983, Antonia Brenda Taylor; one *s* one *d. Educ:* Bushey Sch., New Malden, Surrey. With Inland Revenue, 1961–67; Conservative Constituency Agent: London Bor. of Newham, 1967–70; Lambeth, Norwood, 1970–74; Kingston upon Thames, 1974–85; Cons. Eur. Constituency Agent, Cambridge and N Beds, 1987–90. Dir, PRB Consultancy Services Ltd, 2002–. Qualified Mem., Nat. Soc. of Cons. and Unionist Agents, 1968; Mem., Inst. of Supervisory Mgt, 1994. Freeman, City of London, 1992. *Recreations:* reading, following international tennis, gardening. *Address:* Huntingdon Constituency Conservative Association, Archers Court, 8 Stukeley Road, Huntingdon PE29 6XG. *Club:* St Neots Conservative.

BROWN, Prof. Peter Robert Lamont, FBA 1971; FRHistS; Rollins Professor of History, since 1986, and Director, Program in Hellenic Studies, Princeton University (Visiting Professor, 1983–86); *b* 26 July 1935; *s* of James Lamont and Sheila Brown, Dublin; *m* 1st, 1959, Friedl Esther (*née* Löw-Beer); two *d*; 2nd, 1980, Patricia Ann Fortini; 3rd, 1989, Elizabeth Gilliam. *Educ:* Aravon Sch., Bray, Co. Wicklow, Ireland; Shrewsbury Sch.; New Coll., Oxford (MA). Harmsworth Senior Scholar, Merton Coll., Oxford and Prize Fellow, All Souls Coll., Oxford, 1956; Junior Research Fellow, 1963, Sen. Res. Fellow, 1970–73, All Souls Coll.; Fellow, All Souls Coll., 1956–75; Lectr in Medieval History, Merton Coll. Oxford, 1970–75; Special Lectr in late Roman and early Byzantine History, 1970–73, Reader, 1973–75, Univ. of Oxford; Prof. of History, Royal Holloway Coll., London Univ., 1975–78; Prof. of History and Classics, Univ. of Calif. at Berkeley, 1978–86. Fellow, Amer. Acad. of Arts and Scis, 1978. Hon. DTheol Fribourg, 1975; Hon. DHL Chicago, 1978; Hon. DLitt: TCD, 1990; Wesleyan Univ., Conn, 1993; Columbia Univ., NY, 2001; Pisa, 2001. *Publications:* Augustine of Hippo: a biography, 1967; The World of Late Antiquity, 1971; Religion and Society in the Age of St Augustine, 1971; The Making of Late Antiquity, 1978; The Cult of the Saints: its rise and function in Latin Christianity, 1980; Society and the Holy in Late Antiquity, 1982; The Body and Society: men, women and sexual renunciation in Early Christianity, 1989; Power and Persuasion in Late Antiquity: towards a Christian Empire, 1992; Authority and the Sacred: aspects of the christianization of the Roman world, 1995; The Rise of Western Christendom: triumph and diversity, AD 200–1000, 1996; Poverty and Leadership in the Later Roman Empire, 2002. *Address:* Department of History, 135 Dickinson Hall, Princeton University, Princeton, NJ 08544–1017, USA.

BROWN, Peter Wilfred Henry, CBE 1996; Secretary of the British Academy, 1983–2006; *b* 4 June 1941; *s* of late Rev. Wilfred George Brown and Joan Margaret (*née* Adams); *m* 1968, Kathleen Clarke (marr. diss.); one *d. Educ:* Marlborough Coll.; Jesus Coll., Cambridge (Rustat Schol.). Assistant Master in Classics, Birkenhead Sch., 1963–66; Lectr in Classics, Fourah Bay Coll., Univ. of Sierra Leone, 1966–68; Asst Sec., School of Oriental and African Studies, Univ. of London, 1968–75; Dep. Sec., British Academy, 1975–83 (Actg Sec., 1976–77). Member: British Library Adv. Council, 1983–88; CNAA Cttee for Arts and Humanities, 1985–87; Cttee for Research, 1987–89; Council, Council for Assisting Refugee Academics (formerly Soc. for Protection of Sci. and Learning), 1997–. Member: Governing Body, British Assoc. for Central and Eastern Europe (formerly GB/E Europe Centre), 1983–96; Conseil Internat. de la Maison Suger, Paris, 1988–2002; Council: Britain-Russia Centre (formerly GB/USSR Assoc.), 1983–94; British Inst. in Eastern Africa, 1983–; SSEES, Univ. of London, 1984–99; Committee of Management: Inst. of Archaeol., Univ. of London, 1984–86; Inst. of Classical Studies, Univ. of London, 1984–99; Warburg Inst., Univ. of London, 1987–93; Bd, Inst. of Histl Res., London Univ., 1994–99. Fellow, National Humanities Center, N Carolina, 1978; Hon. Fellow, British Sch. at Rome, 2007. Hon. DLitt: Birmingham, 1995; Sheffield, 2007. Kt Grand Cross, Order of Merit (Poland), 1995. *Recreations:* travel on business, reading, listening to classical music, photography. *Address:* 34 Victoria Road, NW6 6PX. *Club:* Athenæum.

See also J. M. Brown.

BROWN, Philip Anthony Russell, CB 1977; Director of Policy, Investment Management Regulatory Organisation, 1985–93; *b* 18 May 1924; *e s* of late Sir William Brown, KCB, KCMG, CBE, and of Elizabeth Mabel (*née* Scott); *m* 1954, Eileen (*d* 1976), *d* of late J. Brennan; *m* 1976, Sarah Elizabeth Dean (*see* S. E. Brown). *Educ:* Malvern; King's Coll., Cambridge. Entered Home Civil Service, Board of Trade, 1947; Private Sec. to Perm. Sec., 1949; Principal, 1952; Private Sec. to Minister of State, 1953; Observer, Civil Service Selection Board, 1957; returned to BoT, 1959; Asst Sec., 1963; Head of Overseas Information Co-ordination Office, 1963; BoT, 1964; Under-Sec., 1969; Head of Establishments Div. 1, BoT, later DTI, 1969; Head of Cos Div., DTI, 1971; Dep. Sec., Dept of Trade, 1974–83. Head of External Relations, Lloyd's of London, 1983–85; Dir, NPI, 1985–90. Mem., Disciplinary Cttee, ICA, 1985–96. Mem., London Adv. Bd, Salvation Army, 1982–92. *Publications:* (contrib.) Multinational Approaches: corporate insiders, 1976; Poems from Square Mile, 1992; articles in various jls. *Recreations:* reading, gardening, music. *Address:* Christmas Croft, Hopgarden Lane, Sevenoaks, Kent TN13 1PX. *Club:* Oxford and Cambridge.

BROWN, Ralph, RA 1972 (ARA 1968); sculptor; *b* 24 April 1928; *m* 1st, 1952, M. E. Taylor (marr. diss. 1963); one *s* one *d*; 2nd, 1964, Caroline Ann Clifton-Trigg; one *s. Educ:* Leeds Grammar School. RAF, 1946–48. Studied Royal College of Art, 1948–56; in Paris with Zadkine, 1954; travel scholarships to Greece 1955, Italy 1957. Tutor, RCA, 1958–64. Sculpture Prof., Salzburg Festival, Summer 1972. Work exhibited: John Moores, Liverpool (prizewinner 1957), Tate Gallery, Religious Theme 1958, Arnhem Internat. Open Air Sculpture, 1958; Middelheim Open Air Sculpture, 1959; Battersea Park Open Air Sculpture, 1960, 1963, 1966, 1977; Tokyo Biennale, 1963; British Sculptors '72, RA, 1972; Holland Park Open Air, 1975; Sculpture of the Century, Salisbury Cathedral and Canary Wharf, London, 1999. One man shows: Leicester Galls, 1961, 1963; Archer Gall., 1972; Salzburg 1972; Munich 1973; Montpellier 1974; Marseilles 1975; Oxford 1975; Taranman Gall., 1979; Browse & Darby Gall., 1979; Beaux Arts, Bath, 1983, 1987; Charles Foley Gall., Columbus, US, 1984; Lloyd Shine Gall., Chicago, 1984; Falle Gall., Jersey, 1995; Bruton Gall., Leeds, 1999; Number 9 the Gall., Birmingham, 2005; Retrospective: Leeds City Art Gall. and Warwick Arts Centre, 1988; Pangolin London, 2009. Work in Collections: Tate Britain, Arts Council, Contemp. Art Society, Kröller-Müller, Gallery of NSW, Stuyvesant Foundation, City of Salzburg, Nat. Gallery of Wales, Allbright-Knox Gall., and at Leeds, Bristol, Norwich, Aberdeen, etc; public sculpture in Harlow New Town Market Square and Jersey Zoo. *Address:* Southanger Farm, Chalford, Glos GL6 8HP. *T:* (01285) 760243; *e-mail:* ralph@ralphbrown.co.uk.

BROWN, Rt Rev. Mgr Ralph, JCD; Vicar General, Archdiocese of Westminster, 1977–99; *b* 30 June 1931; *s* of John William and Elizabeth Josephine Brown. *Educ:* Highgate Sch.; St Edmund's Coll., Old Hall Green, Herts; Pontifical Gregorian Univ., Rome. Licence in Canon Law, 1961, Doctorate, 1963. Commnd Middlesex Regt, 1949; Korea, 1950. Ordained priest, Westminster Cathedral, 1959; Vice-Chancellor, Vice Officialis, dio. of Westminster, 1964–69; Officialis, 1969–76, Officialis, subseq. Judicial

Vicar, 1988–2006, Westminster; Judicial Vicar: Oslo, 2006–; Oslo Coll. of Consultors, 2007–; Canonical Adviser: to British Mil. Ordinariate, 1987–; to Polish Catholic Mission in England and Wales, 2006–. Pres., Canon Law Soc. of GB and Ireland, 1980–86, Sec., 1986–89. Apptd Papal Chamberlain, 1972; National Co-ordinator for Papal Visit to England and Wales, 1982; Prelate of Honour to HH the Pope, 1987; Protonotary Apostolic, 1999. Elected to Old Brotherhood of English Secular Clergy, 1987 (Sec., 1989). Hon. Member: Canon Law Soc. of Aust. and NZ, 1975; Canadian Canon Law Soc., 1979; Canon Law Soc. of America, 1979; Canon Law Soc. of GB and Ireland, 2006. KHS 1985; KCHS 1991 (Prior, Westminster sect., 1996). Silver Palm of Jerusalem, 1999; Cross, Pro Piis Meritis, Order of Malta, 2000. *Publications:* Marriage Annulment, 1969, rev. edn 1990; (ed) Matrimonial Decisions of Great Britain and Ireland, 1969–; co-translator, The Code of Canon Law in English Translation, 1983; (ed jtly) The Canon Law: Letter and Spirit: a practical guide to the Code of Canon Law, 1995; articles in Heythrop Jl, Studia Canonica, Theological Digest, The Jurist. *Address:* Flat 3, 8 Morpeth Terrace, SW1P 1EQ. *T:* (020) 7798 9020. *Club:* Anglo-Belgian.

BROWN, Rev. Raymond; *see* Brown, Rev. Robert R.

BROWN, Rev. Raymond, PhD; Senior Minister, Victoria Baptist Church, Eastbourne, 1987–93, retired; *b* 3 March 1928; *s* of Frank Stevenson Brown and Florence Mansfield; *m* 1966, Christine Mary Smallman; one *s* one *d*. *Educ:* Spurgeon's Coll., London (BD, MTh); Fitzwilliam Coll., Cambridge (MA, BD, PhD). Minister: Zion Baptist Church, Cambridge, 1956–62; Upton Vale Baptist Church, Torquay, 1964–71; Tutor in Church History, Spurgeon's Coll., London, 1971–73, Principal 1973–86. Pres., Evangelical Alliance, 1975–76; Trustee, Dr Daniel Williams's Charity, 1980–; Nat. Chaplain, Girls' Brigade, 1986–90. *Publications:* Their Problems and Ours, 1969; Let's Read the Old Testament, 1971; Skilful Hands, 1972; Christ Above All: the message of Hebrews, 1982; Bible Study Commentary: 1 Timothy-James, 1983; The English Baptists of the Eighteenth Century, 1986; The Bible Book by Book, 1987; Be My Disciple, 1992; The Message of Deuteronomy: not by bread alone, 1993; Collins Gem Bible Guide, 1993; Four Spiritual Giants, 1997 (US edn as Giants of the Faith, 1997); The Message of Nehemiah: God's servant in a time of change, 1998; The Message of Numbers: journey to the promised land, 2002; contribs to: What the Bible Says, 1974; Dictionary of Christian Spirituality, 1983; My Call to Preach, 1986; Encyclopedia of World Faiths, 1987; New Dictionary of Theology, 1988; The Empty Cross, 1989; Dictionary of Evangelical Biography, 1995; Oxford Dictionary of World Religions, 1997; Oxford Dictionary of the Christian Church, 1998; Called to One Hope, 2000; A Protestant Catholic Church of Christ: essays on the history and life of New Road Baptist Church, Oxford, 2003. *Recreations:* music, walking. *Address:* 200B Perne Road, Cambridge CB1 3NX. *T:* (01223) 700110.

BROWN, Richard George; His Honour Judge Richard Brown; DL; a Circuit Judge, since 1992, a Senior Circuit Judge, since 2007; *b* Durham, 10 April 1945; *m* 1969, Ann Patricia Bridget Wade; one *s* one *d* (and one *s* decd). *Educ:* Bournville Grammar Sch.; Technical Sch., Birmingham; London Sch. of Economics (LLB Hons); Inns of Court Sch. of Law. Insurance clerk, 1961–62; shop assistant, 1962–63; bus conductor, 1963–64; Trainee Radio Officer, Merchant Navy, 1964–65; taxi driver, 1965–66; assistant, school for maladjusted children, 1966–67; bus driver, 1967–68. Called to the Bar, Middle Temple, 1972 (Blackstone Entrance Exhibnr). Asst Recorder, 1986–90; a Recorder of the Crown Court, 1990–92. Resident and Liaison Judge, Crown Courts in E Sussex, 1996–. Vice Pres., E Sussex Magistrates' Assoc., 1997–. Hon. Recorder, Brighton and Hove, 2008–. Chm., Bd of Govs, Farney Close Sch., 1984–86. DL E Sussex, 2004. *Recreations:* watching sport, travel, being with the family. *Address:* Lewes Crown Court, High Street, Lewes, East Sussex BN7 1YB. *T:* (01273) 480400.

BROWN, Robert; His Honour Judge Robert Brown; a Circuit Judge, since 1988; *b* 21 June 1943; *s* of Robert and Mary Brown. *Educ:* Arnold Sch., Blackpool; Downing Coll., Cambridge (Exhibnr; BA, LLB). Called to Bar, Inner Temple, 1968 (Major Schol.); a Recorder, 1983–88. *Recreation:* golf. *Address:* c/o Preston Crown Court, Openshaw Place, Ringway, Preston, Lancs PR1 2LL. *Club:* Royal Lytham St Annes Golf.

BROWN, Robert; Member (Lib Dem) Glasgow, Scottish Parliament, since 1999; *b* 25 Dec. 1947; *s* of Albert Edward Brown and Joan Brown; *m* 1977, Gwen Morris; one *s* one *d*. *Educ:* Gordon Schools, Huntly; Univ. of Aberdeen (LLB 1st Cl. Hons). Legal Apprentice and Asst, Edmonds and Ledingham, Solicitors, Aberdeen, 1969–72; Procurator Fiscal, Dumbarton, 1972–74; Asst, 1974–75, Partner, 1975–99, Consultant, 1999–2004, Ross Harper and Murphy, Solicitors, Glasgow. Dep. Minister for Educn and Young People, Scottish Exec., 2005–07. Scottish Parliament: Lib Dem spokesman on communities and housing, 1999–2003, on education, 2003–05; Convenor, Educn and Young People Cttee, 2003–05; Business Manager, Lib Dem Gp, 2007–. Convenor, Scottish Lib Dem Policy Cttee, 2002–07. *Recreations:* history, science fiction. *Address:* 1 Douglas Avenue, Burnside, Rutherglen, Glasgow G73 4RA; (constituency) Olympic House, 2nd Floor, 142 Queen Street, Glasgow G1 1BU. *T:* (0141) 243 2421; *e-mail:* robert.brown.msp@scottish.parliament.uk.

BROWN, Sir Robert C.; *see* Crichton-Brown.

BROWN, Robert Glencairn; Director (formerly Deputy Chief Officer), Housing Corporation, 1986–91; *b* 19 July 1930; *s* of William and Marion Brown (*née* Cockburn); *m* 1957, Florence May Stalker; two *s*. *Educ:* Hillhead High Sch., Glasgow. Commnd, RCS, 1949–51. Forestry Commn, 1947–68; seconded to CS Pay Res. Unit, 1963–64 and to Min. of Land and Natural Resources, 1964–68; Min. of Housing and Local Govt, later DoE, 1968–71; seconded to Nat. Whitley Council, Staff Side, 1969; Asst Dir, Countryside Commn, 1971–77; Department of the Environment: Asst Sec., 1977–83; Under Sec., 1983–86. Chm., W Middx Centre, Nat. Trust, 1989–93. *Recreations:* golfing, gardening, walking, reading. *Address:* 35 The Forresters, Winslow Close, Pinner, Middx HA5 2QX. *T:* (020) 8866 1057. *Club:* Pinner Hill Golf.

BROWN, Rev. (Robert) Raymond; Methodist Minister, responsible for lay training and development, Melton Mowbray, 1994–99; *b* 24 March 1936; *s* of Robert Brown and Elsie (*née* Dudson); *m* 1959, Barbara (*née* Johnson); three *s* one *d*. *Educ:* Stockport Sch.; Univ. of Leeds (BA Hons Philosophy); Univ. of Manchester (BD Hons Theology). Ordained Methodist minister, 1959; Minister: Luton Industrial Coll. and Mission, 1959–64; Heald Green and Handforth, 1964–67; commnd RAF Chaplain, 1967; Vice Principal, RAF Chaplains' Sch., 1978–83; Comd Chaplain, RAF Germany, 1983–87; Asst Prin. Chaplain, 1987–90, Prin. Chaplain, 1990–94, Ch of Scotland and Free Churches, RAF. QHC 1990–94. *Recreations:* music and drama (amateur singer and actor), writing for pleasure. *Address:* 1 Hazlebadge Close, Poynton, Stockport, Cheshire SK12 1HD. *T:* (01625) 879699; *e-mail:* ray.brown980@ntlworld.com. *Club:* Royal Air Force.

BROWN, Prof. Roger John, PhD; Professor of Higher Education Policy, and Co-Director, Centre for Research and Development in Higher Education, Liverpool Hope University, since 2007; *b* 26 June 1947; *s* of John Richard Brown and Beatrice Anne (*née* Clamp); *m* 1st, 1971, Mary Elizabeth George (*see* M. E. Francis) (marr. diss. 1991); 2nd, 1992, Josephine Ann Titcomb. *Educ:* St Olave's Grammar Sch., Bermondsey; Queens' Coll., Cambridge (Haynes Exhibnr in History; MA); Inst. of Educn, Univ. of London (PhD). Admin. Officer, ILEA, 1969–75; Sec., William Tyndale Schs' Inquiry, 1975–76; Principal, Dept Industry, Dept Trade, Cabinet Office, OFT, DTI, 1976–84; Assistant Secretary: DoE, 1984–86; DTI, 1986–90; Sec., PCFC, 1990–91; Chief Exec., Cttee of Dirs of Polytechnics, 1991–93; Chief Exec., HEQC, 1993–97; Principal, Southampton Inst., 1998–2005; Prof. of Higher Educn Policy, Southampton Inst., subseq. Southampton Solent Univ., 2004–07; Vice-Chancellor, Southampton Solent Univ., 2005–07. Visiting Professor: Univ. of London Inst. of Educn, 1996–98; Middx Univ., 1997–99; Goldsmiths' Coll., 1997–99; Univ. of Surrey Roehampton (formerly Roehampton Inst.), 1997–; Univ. of East London, 2000–; City Univ., 2001–; Univ. of Southampton, 2006–; Napier Univ., Edinburgh, 2007–; Vis. Fellow, Oxford Centre for Higher Educn Policy Studies, 2007–; Hon. Vis. Fellow, Inst. for Policy Studies in Educn, London Metropolitan Univ., 2007–. Vice-Chm., Standing Conf. of Principals, 1999–2003; Vice-Pres., SRHE, 2007–. DUniv: Southampton Solent, 2007; Southampton, 2007. *Publications:* Educational Policy Making: an analysis, 1983; The Post-Dearing Quality Agenda, 1998; Quality Assurance in Higher Education: the UK experience since 1992, 2004; contribs to educnl jls. *Recreations:* opera, cinema, jazz, collecting books about music. *Address:* 9 Bleinheim Avenue, Southampton SO17 1DW.

BROWN, Roland George MacCormack; Legal Adviser, Technical Assistance Group, Commonwealth Secretariat, 1975–87; *b* 27 Dec. 1924; 2nd *s* of late Oliver and of Mona Brown; *m* 1964, Irene Constance (*d* 2000), *d* of Rev. Claude Coltman; two *s* one *d*. *Educ:* Ampleforth College; Trinity College, Cambridge. Called to the Bar, Gray's Inn, Nov. 1949. Practised at the Bar, Nov. 1949–May 1961; Attorney-Gen., Tanganyika, later Tanzania, 1961–65; Legal Consultant to Govt of Tanzania, 1965–72; Fellow, Inst. of Develt Studies, Sussex Univ., 1973–75; on secondment as Special Adviser to Sec. of State for Trade, 1974. *Publication:* (with Richard O'Sullivan, QC) The Law of Defamation. *Recreation:* swimming.

BROWN, Rt Rev. Ronald; Bishop Suffragan of Birkenhead, 1974–92; Hon. Assistant Bishop of Liverpool, 1992–2003; *b* 7 Aug. 1926; *s* of Fred and Ellen Brown; *m* 1951, Joyce Hymers (*d* 1987); one *s* one *d*. *Educ:* Kirkham Grammar Sch.; Durham Univ. (BA, DipTh). Vicar of Whittle-le-Woods, 1956; Vicar of St Thomas, Halliwell, Bolton, 1961; Rector and Rural Dean of Ashton-under-Lyne, 1970. *Publications:* Bishop's Brew, 1989; Good Lord, 1992; Bishop's Broth, 2000. *Recreations:* antiques and golf. *Address:* 16 Andrew Crescent, Queen's Park, Chester CH4 7BQ. *T:* (01244) 629955.

See also L. F. M. Brown.

BROWN, Rosemary Jean, (Rosie); *see* Atkins, R. J.

BROWN, Roswyn Ann H.; *see* Hakesley-Brown.

BROWN, Rowland Percival, OBE 1993; MA; JP; legal consultant, Secondary Heads Association, 1993–2002; Headmaster, Royal Grammar School, High Wycombe, 1975–93; *b* 8 Jan. 1933; *s* of late Percy and Gladys Mabel Brown; *m* 1959, Jessie Doig Connell; three *d*. *Educ:* Queen Mary's Sch., Basingstoke; Worcester Coll., Oxford (MA French and Russian, 1956). Called to the Bar, Inner Temple, 1966; ESU Walter Page Scholar, 1976. Intelligence Corps, 1951–53, Second Lieut. Hampton Sch., 1957–62; Head of Modern Langs, Tudor Grange Grammar Sch., Solihull, 1962–67; Head Master, King Edward VI Sch., Nuneaton, 1967–75. Legal Sec., Headmasters' Assoc. and SHA, 1975–85; Pres., SHA, 1985–86. Oxford Univ. Delegacy of Local Exams, 1986–96; Mem., RAF OASC Selection Bd, 1970–96. Educnl Advr, World Challenge Expedns, 1993–2001. Liveryman, Feltmakers' Co., 1991–. JP Bucks, 1978. *Publications:* Heads Legal Guide, 1984; The School Management Handbook, 1993; The Education Acts, 1998. *Recreations:* golf, walking, theatre, following sport. *Address:* Wildwood, Manor Road, Penn, Bucks HP10 8JA. *Club:* Phyllis Court (Henley).

BROWN, Roy Drysdale, CEng, FIMechE, FIET; Chairman, GKN plc, since 2004 (Director, since 1996); *b* 4 Dec. 1946; *s* of late William Andrew Brown and Isabelle Drysdale (*née* Davidson); *m* 1978, Carol Wallace; two *s*. *Educ:* Tonbridge Sch.; UCL (GEC Schol.; BSc Mech. Eng); Harvard Business Sch. (MBA). CEng, FIMechE 1983; FIET (FIEE 1990). Commercial Gen. Manager, Vosper Thorneycroft Ltd, 1972–74; Unilever plc, 1974–2001: various financial, mktg and tech. posts, 1974–82; Chairman: Pamol Plantations Sdn Bhd, Malaysia, 1982–86; PBI Cambridge Ltd, 1987–88; Tech. Dir, Birds Eye Walls Ltd, 1988–90; Chm., Lever Bros Ltd, 1991–92; Regional Director: Africa, ME, Central and Eastern Europe, 1992–96; Foods and Beverages Europe, 1996–2001; Dir, Unilever plc and NV, 1992–2001; retd, 2001. Non-executive Director: Brambles Industries Ltd & plc, 2001–06; BUPA, 2001–07; HMV Gp plc, 2002–; Lloyds Franchise Bd, 2003–; Alliance & Leicester plc, 2007– (Vice-Chm., 2007–). *Recreations:* military history, wild life photography, classical music, opera, woodworking. *Address:* GKN plc, 2nd Floor, 50 Pall Mall, SW1Y 5JH. *T:* (020) 7463 2322, *Fax:* (020) 7463 2404. *Clubs:* Carlton, Royal Automobile; Leander (Henley); Harvard (NY).

BROWN, Russell; *see* Brown, J. R.

BROWN, Russell Leslie; MP (Lab) Dumfries and Galloway, since 2005 (Dumfries, 1997–2005); *b* 17 Sept. 1951; *s* of Howard Russell Brown and Muriel Brown (*née* Anderson); *m* 1973, Christine Margaret Calvert; two *d*. *Educ:* Annan Acad. Various posts with ICI, 1974–97, Plant Operative, 1992–97. Member: Dumfries and Galloway Regl Council, 1986–96 (Chm., Public Protection Cttee, 1990–94); Annandale and Eskdale DC, 1988–96; Dumfries and Galloway UA, 1995–97. PPS to Sec. of State for Scotland, 2005–. *Recreations:* walking, football. *Address:* 46 Northfield Park, Annan DG12 5EZ. *T:* (01461) 205365.

BROWN, Prof. Sara Ann, (Sally), OBE 2002; PhD; FRSE, AcSS; Professor of Education, 1990–2001, now Emeritus, and Deputy Principal, 1996–2001, University of Stirling; *b* 15 Dec. 1935; *d* of Fred Compigné-Cook and Gwendoline Cook (*née* Barrett); *m* 1959, Charles Victor Brown (*d* 1991); two *s*. *Educ:* Bromley High Sch.; University College London (BSc Hons 1957); Smith Coll., Mass (MA 1958); Jordanhill Coll., Glasgow (Teaching Cert. 1966); Univ. of Stirling (PhD 1975). Lectr in Physics, Univ. of Ife and Nigerian Coll. of Tech., 1960–64; Principal Teacher of Science, Helensburgh, 1964–70; Sen. Res. Fellow, Univ. of Stirling, 1970–80; Consultant and Adviser, Scottish Educn Dept, 1980–84; Dir, Scottish Council for Res. in Educn, 1986–90 (Fellow, 1992). Chair: Univs' Assoc. for Continuing Educn (Scotland), 2000–02; Educn Panel, 2001 RAE; Teacher Support Scotland Forum, 2002–; Scottish Arts Council Educn Forum, 2003–04; Vice-Chair, ESRC Teaching and Learning Res. prog., 1998–. Chair Adv. Bd, Leirsinn Gaelic res. centre, 2000–; Mem. Academic Council, UHI Millennium Inst., 2001–05. Gov., Queen Margaret UC, Edinburgh, 1999– (Vice Chm., 2005–). FRSA 1989; FRSE 1996; FEIS 1997; AcSS 2000. Hon. Fellow UHI Millennium Inst., 2005. DUniv: Stirling, 2002; Open, 2004; Hon. DEd Edinburgh, 2003. *Publications:* What Do They Know?, 1980; Making Sense of Teaching, 1993; Special Needs Policy in the 1990s, 1994; numerous academic works. *Recreations:* theatre, music, golf. *Address:* 30A Chalton

Road, Bridge of Allan, Stirling FK9 4EF. *T:* (01786) 833671; *e-mail:* s.a.brown@stir.ac.uk; Institute of Education, University of Stirling, Stirling FK9 4LA. *T:* (01786) 467600.

BROWN, Sarah Elizabeth, OBE 2004; Member, Competition (formerly Monopolies and Mergers) Commission, 1998–2007; *b* 30 Dec. 1943; *d* of Sir Maurice Dean, KCB, KCMG and Anne (*née* Gibson); *m* 1976, Philip Anthony Russell Brown, *qv*. *Educ:* St Paul's Girls' Sch.; Newnham Coll., Cambridge (BA Nat. Sci.). Joined BoT as Asst Principal, 1965; Private Sec. to Second Perm. Sec., 1968; Principal, 1970; DTI, 1971–96: Asst. Sec., 1978; Sec. to Crown Agents Tribunal, 1978–82; Personnel Management Div., 1982–84; Head of Financial Services Bill team, 1984–86; Under Sec., 1986; Head of Companies Div., 1986–91; Head of Enterprise Initiative Div., 1991–93, and Small Firms Div., 1992–93; Head of Small Firms and Business Link Div., 1993–94; Head of Companies Div., 1994–96; Dir, Company Law, 1996. Comr, Friendly Socs Commn, 1997–2001. Dir, Remploy Ltd, 1997–2000; Mem. Bd, Look Ahead Housing Assoc., 1996–2008; Associate Mem., Kensington & Chelsea and Westminster HA, 1996–99; non-executive Director: Kent and Sussex Weald NHS Trust, 1999–2000; Financial Services Compensation Scheme, 2000–07; SW Kent Primary Care Trust, 2001–06; Accountancy and Actuarial Discipline (formerly Accountants Investigation and Discipline) Bd Ltd, 2001–; Revenue and Customs Prosecutions Office, 2005–. Mem., Civil Service Appeals Bd, 1998–2004; Lay Mem., Bar Standards Bd, 2006–; Mem., Investigations Cttee, RPSGB, 2007–. Trustee, Horder Centre, 2007–. *Recreations:* travel, theatre, gardening. *Address:* 32 Cumberland Street, SW1V 4LX.

BROWN, Sarah Elizabeth; writer and broadcaster; Flexible Learning Co-ordinator, Christ's School, Richmond, since 2004; *b* 13 Sept. 1952; *d* of Lewis William Brown, OBE and Gweneth Elizabeth Brown (*née* Richards); *m* 1989, Paul Malcolm Street; two *s*. *Educ:* Brighton and Hove High Sch.; I. M. Marsh Coll., Liverpool (Cert Ed Dance and Drama 1973); London Sch. of Contemporary Dance. TV and theatre work, 1976–78; restaurateur and wholefood shop proprietor, 1978–88; Presenter, Vegetarian Kitchen (series), BBC TV, 1983; vegetarian cookery writer and broadcaster, 1984–. Mem. steering gp, Focus on Food, RSA/Waitrose, 1998–2003. Mem., Guild of Food Writers, 1986–2006. Manager, England Over 35s Orienteering Team, 1998–. Egon Ronay Cellnet Award, 1987; Glenfiddich Special Award for Writing, 1988. *Publications:* Vegetarian Kitchen, 1984; Sarah Brown's Vegetarian Cookbook, 1984; Sarah Brown's Healthy Living Cookbook, 1986; Sarah Brown's Vegetarian Microwave Cookbook, 1987; Sarah Brown's New Vegetarian Kitchen, 1987; Sarah Brown's Quick and Easy Vegetarian Cookery, 1989; Secret England, 1989; Outdoor London, 1991; Sarah Brown's Healthy Pregnancy, 1992; Sarah Brown's Fresh Vegetarian Cookery, 1995; No Fuss Vegetarian Cooking, 1998; The Complete Vegetarian Cookbook, 2002; Sarah Brown's World Vegetarian Cookbook, 2004. *Recreations:* orienteering, listening to TMS, playing German board games.

BROWN, Simon Staley; QC 1995; **His Honour Judge Simon Brown;** a Deputy High Court Judge, Senior Circuit Judge and a Specialist Mercantile Judge, Midland Circuit, since 2006; *b* 23 Aug. 1952; *s* of Peter Brown and late Celia Rosamond Brown; *m* 1981, Kathleen Margaret Wain, PhD (Kathy Brown, garden owner, writer and designer); one *s* one *d*. *Educ:* Harrow Sch.; Queens' Coll., Cambridge (MA). Called to the Bar, Inner Temple, 1976 (Bencher and Master of the Garden). A Recorder, 2000. Asst Boundary Comr, 2000–05. Mem., Bar Assocs of Professional Negligence, Technology and Construction, London Common Law, and Commercial Law. Chm. of Govs, Bedford Sch.; Trustee, The Bedford Charity (The Harpur Trust). *Recreation:* gardening. *Address:* Birmingham Civil Justice Centre, 33 Bull Street, Birmingham B4 6DS. *T:* (Clerk) (0121) 681 3035; *e-mail:* HHJudge.Brownqc@judiciary.gsi.gov.uk.

BROWN, Rt Hon. Sir Stephen, GBE 1999; Kt 1975; PC 1983; a Lord Justice of Appeal, 1983–88; President of the Family Division, 1988–99; *b* 3 Oct. 1924; *s* of Wilfrid Brown and Nora Elizabeth Brown, Longdon Green, Staffordshire; *m* 1951, Patricia Ann, *d* of Richard Good, Tenbury Wells, Worcs; two *s* (twins) three *d*. *Educ:* Malvern College; Queens' College, Cambridge (Hon. Fellow, 1984). Served RNVR (Lieut), 1943–46. Barrister, Inner Temple, 1949; Bencher, 1974; Treas., 1994. Dep. Chairman, Staffs QS, 1963–71; Recorder of West Bromwich, 1965–71; QC 1966; a Recorder, and Honorary Recorder of West Bromwich, 1972–75; a Judge of the High Court, Family Div., 1975–77, QBD, 1977–83; Presiding Judge, Midland and Oxford Circuit, 1977–81. Member: Parole Board, England and Wales, 1967–71; Butler Cttee on mentally abnormal offenders, 1972–75; Adv. Council on Penal System, 1977; Chm., Adv. Cttee on Conscientious Objectors, 1971–75. Chm. Council, Malvern Coll., 1976–94; President: Edgbaston High Sch., 1989–; Malvernian Soc., 1998–. Hon. FRCPsych 2000. Hon. LLD: Birmingham, 1985; Leicester, 1997; UWE, 2000. *Recreation:* sailing. *Address:* 78 Hamilton Avenue, Harborne, Birmingham B17 8AR. *Club:* Garrick.

BROWN, Sir Stephen (David Reid), KCVO 1999; HM Diplomatic Service, retired; advisor to Vermilion Partners, Oxford Intelligence, and The D Group, since 2006; *b* 26 Dec. 1945; *s* of Albert Senior Brown and Edna Brown; *m* 1966, Pamela Denise Gaunt; one *s* one *d*. *Educ:* Leeds Grammar Sch.; RMA Sandhurst; Univ. of Sussex (BA Hons). Served HM Forces, RA, 1966–76; FCO, 1976–77; 1st Sec., Nicosia, 1977–80; 1st Sec. (Commercial), Paris, 1980–85; FCO, 1985–89; DTI, 1989; Consul-Gen., Melbourne, 1989–94; Commercial Counsellor and Dir of Trade Promotion, Peking, 1994–97; Ambassador, Republic of Korea, 1997–2000; High Comr, Singapore, 2001–02; Chief Exec. (Permanent Sec.), British Trade Internat., then UK Trade & Investment, 2002–05. Hon. Chm., Anglo-Korean Soc., 2007–. *Recreations:* reading, ski-ing, motor sport.

BROWN, Stuart Christopher; QC 1991; a Recorder, since 1992; a Deputy High Court Judge, since 1994; *b* 4 Sept. 1950; *s* of late Geoffrey Howard Brown and of Olive Baum; *m* 1973, Imogen Lucas; two *d*. *Educ:* Acklam High Sch., Middlesbrough; Worcester Coll., Oxford (BA, BCL). Called to the Bar, Inner Temple, 1974, Bencher, 1998. Practises on NE Circuit. Pres., Mental Health Rev. Tribunal, 2000–. *Recreations:* family, theatre, walking. *Address:* Cherry Hill, Staircase Lane, Leeds LS16 9JD; Park Lane Chambers, 19 Westgate, Leeds LS1 2RD.

BROWN, Susan Mary; *see* Spindler, S. M.

BROWN, Prof. (Susanne) Moira, OBE 2007; PhD; FRCPath; FRSE; Director, Crusade Laboratories Ltd, Glasgow, since 2000; *b* 21 March 1946; *d* of Edmund and Elizabeth Mitchell; *m* 1970, Alasdair MacDougall Brown. *Educ:* Queen's Univ., Belfast (BSc 1968); Univ. of Glasgow (PhD 1971). FRCPath 1997. Sen. Scientist, MRC Virology Unit, Glasgow, 1972–95; Prof. of Neurovirology, Univ. of Glasgow, 1995–2004, Prof. Emeritus, 2004. Chm., Med. Res. Scotland (formerly Scottish Hosp. Endowments Res. Trust), 2001–. FRSE 1999 (Convener, Cell and Molecular Biol Fellowships Cttee, 2001–06). *Publication:* Methods in Molecular Medicine: herpes simplex virus, 1998. *Recreations:* walking, travel, reading, Christian faith, Scottish painters, beagles. *Address:* Kilure, The Steading, Croy Cunningham, Killearn G63 9QY. *T:* (01360) 551715, *Fax:* (01360) 551716; *e-mail:* smbrown@crusadelabs.co.uk. *Clubs:* Athenæum; Western (Glasgow).

BROWN, Rt Rev. Thomas John; *see* Wellington (NZ), Bishop of.

BROWN, Timothy Charles; Fellow, and Director of Music, Clare College, Cambridge, since 1979; *b* 9 Dec. 1946; *s* of Roland Frederick John Brown and Ruth Margery Brown (*née* Dawe). *Educ:* Westminster Abbey Choir Sch.; Dean Close Sch., Cheltenham; King's Coll., Cambridge (alto choral schol.; MA); Westminster Coll., Oxford (DipEd). Music Master, Hinchingbrooke Sch., Huntingdon, 1969–72; Dir of Music, Oundle Sch., 1972–79. Mem., Scholars' Vocal Ensemble, 1969–72. Director: Choir of Clare Coll., Cambridge, 1979–; Cambridge Univ. Chamber Choir, 1986–2000; English Voices, 1995–. *Publication:* (ed) William Walton: shorter choral works, 1999. *Recreations:* foreign travel, gardens and gardening, walking. *Address:* Clare College, Cambridge CB2 1TL. *T:* (01223) 333264.

BROWN, Timothy William Trelawny T.; *see* Tatton-Brown.

BROWN, Tina, (Christina Hambley Brown), (Lady Evans), CBE 2000; writer and journalist; Partner and Chairman, Talk Media, 1998–2002; *b* 21 Nov. 1953; *d* of late Bettina Iris Mary Kohr Brown and George Hambley Brown; *m* 1981, Sir Harold Matthew Evans, *qv*; one *s* one *d*. *Educ:* Univ. of Oxford (MA). Columnist for Punch, 1978; Editor, Tatler, 1979–83; Editor in Chief, Vanity Fair Magazine, 1984–92; Editor, The New Yorker, 1992–98; Chm. and Editor in Chief, Talk magazine, 1998–2002. Columnist: The Times, 2002; Washington Post, 2003–. Catherine Pakenham Prize, Most Promising Female Journalist (Sunday Times), 1973; Young Journalist of the Year, 1978. *Plays:* Under the Bamboo Tree (Sunday Times Drama Award), 1973; Happy Yellow, 1977. *Publications:* Loose Talk, 1979; Life as a Party, 1983; The Diana Chronicles, 2007.

BROWN, Hon. Tony; *see* Brown, Hon. J. A.

BROWN, Prof. Valerie Kathleen, PhD; Director, Centre for Agri-Environmental Research, and Research Professor in Agro-Ecology, University of Reading, 2000–04; *b* 11 May 1944; *d* of Reginald Brown and Kathleen (*née* Southerton); *m* 1970, Dr Clive Wall. *Educ:* Imperial Coll., London Univ. (BSc Zoology 1966; ARCS 1966; PhD Entomology 1969; DIC 1969). Lectr, Royal Holloway Coll., London Univ., 1969–74; Imperial College of Science, Technology and Medicine: Lectr, 1975–84; Sen. Lectr, 1984–89; Reader, 1989–94; CAB International: Dir, Internat. Inst. of Entomology, 1994–98; Dir, CABI Bioscience: Environment, 1998–2000. Member: Council, NERC, 2002–04; Sci. Adv. Gp, 2002–03, Res. and Priorities Bd, 2003–04, DEFRA; Nat. Scis Adv. Gp, English Nature, 2002–06; Special Advr, Grasslands, DEFRA, 2000–. Member: Bd, Internat. Assoc. for Ecology, 1997–2006; Nat. Cttee, Internat. Geosphere-Biosphere Prog., 2001–04; Council, RSPB, 2005–; Chair, Nat. Moth Recording Scheme Steering Gp, 2006–. *Publications:* Grasshoppers, 1983, 2nd edn 1992; (ed) Insect Life History Strategies, 1983; Multitrophic Interactions, 1997; (ed) Herbivores between Plants and Predators, 1999. *Recreations:* bird watching, cultivation of alpine plants, wine tasting. *Address:* Woodpeckers, Stawley, Wellington, Som TA21 0HN. *T:* and *Fax:* (01823) 672063; *e-mail:* valeriebrown@letour.fsnet.co.uk.

BROWN, Vivian; *see* Brown, H. V. B.

BROWN, Prof. William Arthur, CBE 2002; Montague Burton Professor of Industrial Relations, University of Cambridge, since 1985; Master, Darwin College, Cambridge, since 2000; *b* 22 April 1945; *s* of late Prof. Arthur Joseph Brown, CBE, FBA and Joan H. M. (*née* Taylor); *m* 1993, Kim Hewitt; two step *d*. *Educ:* Leeds Grammar Sch.; Wadham Coll., Oxford (BA Hons). Economic Asst, NBPI, 1966–68; Res. Associate, Univ. of Warwick, 1968–70; SSRC's Industrial Relations Research Unit, University of Warwick: Res. Fellow, 1970–79; Dep. Dir, 1979–81; Dir, 1981–85; University of Cambridge: Fellow, Wolfson Coll., 1985–2000; Chairman: Faculty of Econs and Politics, 1992–96; Sch. of Humanities and Soc. Scis, 1993–96; Bd of Graduate Studies, 2000–; Faculty of Social and Political Sci., 2003–08; Colleges' Cttee, 2005–07 (Sec., 2003–05). Ind. Chm., Nat. Fire Brigades Disputes Cttee, 1998–. Member: Low Pay Commn, 1997–2007; Council, ACAS, 1998–2004. *Publications:* Piecework Bargaining, 1973; The Changing Contours of British Industrial Relations, 1981; The Individualisation of Employment Contracts in Britain, 1999; articles in industrial relations jls, etc. *Recreations:* walking, gardening. *Address:* Darwin College, Cambridge CB3 9EU.

BROWN, Sir William Brian P.; *see* Pigott-Brown.

BROWN, William Charles Langdon, CBE 1992 (OBE 1982); Deputy Group Chief Executive and Deputy Chairman, Standard Chartered PLC, 1988–91 (Director, 1987–94); Deputy Chairman, Standard Chartered Bank, 1989–91; *b* 9 Sept. 1931; *s* of Charles Leonard Brown and Kathleen May Tizzard; *m* 1959, Nachiko Sagawa; one *s* two *d*. *Educ:* John Ruskin Sch., Croydon; Ashbourne Grammar Sch., Derbyshire. Joined Westminster Bank, 1947; transf. to Standard Chartered Bank (formerly Chartered Bank of India, Australia and China, the predecessor of Chartered Bank), 1954; Standard Chartered Bank: Tokyo, 1954–59; Bangkok, 1959–62; Hong Kong, 1962–69; Man., Singapore, 1969–72; Country Man., Bangkok, 1972–75; Area Gen. Man., Hong Kong, 1975–87. Various additional positions in Hong Kong, 1975–87, include: MLC Hong Kong; Chm., Hong Kong Export Credit Insce Corp. Adv. Bd; Mem. Council, Hong Kong Trade Develt Council; Chm., Hong Kong Assoc. of Banks; Director: Mass Railway Corp.; Wing Lung Bank Ltd. Director: Hong Kong Investment Trust, 1991–96; Kexim Bank (UK) Ltd, 1992–2002; Arbuthnot Latham & Co. Ltd, 1993–99; Chm., Atlantis Japan Growth Fund Ltd, 1996–2002. Treas., Royal Commonwealth Soc. and Commonwealth Trust, 1991–96. FCIB 1984; FInstD 1988. Hon. DSSc Chinese Univ. of Hong Kong, 1987. *Recreations:* mountain walking, snow ski-ing, yoga, philately, photography, calligraphy, classical music. *Address:* Appleshaw, 11 Central Avenue, Findon Valley, Worthing, Sussex BN14 0DS. *T:* (01903) 873175; Penthouse B, 15 Portman Square, W1H 6LJ. *T:* (020) 7487 5741, *Fax:* (020) 7486 3005. *Clubs:* Oriental, Royal Automobile; Hong Kong, Shek-O, Ladies Recreation (Hong Kong); Tanglin (Singapore).

BROWN, Yasmin A.; *see* Alibhai-Brown.

BROWNBILL, David John; QC 2008; *b* 26 Sept. 1951; *s* of late Joseph Brownbill and Veronica Brownbill; *m* 1974, Carol Ann Allen; two *d*. *Educ:* Univ. of Nottingham (LLB). Admitted solicitor, 1980; called to the Bar: Gray's Inn, 1989; Lincoln's Inn, 2007; E Caribbean Supreme Court, 2005. Editor: Jl of Internat. Trust and Corporate Planning; International Trust Laws. *Address:* (chambers) 24 Old Buildings, Lincoln's Inn, WC2A 3UP. *T:* (020) 7691 2424, *Fax:* (020) 7405 1360.

BROWNBILL, Timothy Patrick; HM Diplomatic Service; Head of Mission, Ho Chi Minh City, Vietnam, since 2008; *b* 6 Feb. 1960; *s* of George and Helen Brownbill. *Educ:* Sandbach Sch. MIL. Entered HM Diplomatic Service, 1979; Commercial Attaché, Lagos, 1982–86; Vice Consul, Madrid, 1986–90; Dep. Hd of Mission, Vilnius, 1992–94; Commercial Sec., Havana, 1996–98; Internat. Trade Dir, Trade Partners UK, 2000–02; Ambassador to Nicaragua, 2002–04; Dir for Trade Promotion, subseq. Dep. Hd of

Mission, Düsseldorf, 2004–08. *Recreations:* music, literature, sports, film. *Address:* c/o Foreign and Commonwealth Office, King Charles Street, SW1A 2AH.

BROWNE, family name of **Barons Kilmaine, Oranmore and Browne,** and **Marquess of Sligo**.

BROWNE OF BELMONT, Baron *cr* 2006 (Life Peer), of Belmont in the County of Antrim; **Wallace Hamilton Browne;** Member (DemU) Belfast East, Northern Ireland Assembly, since 2007; *b* 29 Oct. 1947; *s* of Gerald and Phyllis Hamilton Browne. *Educ:* Campbell Coll., Belfast; QUB (BSc (Hons) Zoology 1970). Biology teacher, Raney Endowed Sch., Magherafelt, 1970–2000. Mem. (DemU), Belfast City Council, 1985–; Lord Mayor of Belfast, 2005–06. Trustee, Somme Assoc., NI. High Sheriff, Belfast, 2002. *Address:* House of Lords, SW1A 0PW.

BROWNE OF MADINGLEY, Baron *cr* 2001 (Life Peer), of Cambridge in the County of Cambridgeshire; **Edmund John Phillip Browne,** Kt 1998; FRS 2006; FREng, FIMMM, FInstPet; FInstP; President, Royal Academy of Engineering, since 2006; Managing Director and Managing Partner (Europe), Riverstone Holdings LLC, since 2007; *b* 20 Feb. 1948; *s* of late Edmund John Browne and Paula (*née* Wesz). *Educ:* King's Sch., Ely; St John's Coll., Cambridge (MA Hons; Hon. Fellow, 1997); Stanford Grad. Sch. of Business (MS Business). FIMMM (FIMM 1987); FREng (FEng 1993); FInstPet 1992; FInstP 1992. Joined British Petroleum Co., 1966; Gp Treasurer and Chief Exec., BP Finance Internat., 1984–86; Executive Vice-President and Chief Financial Officer: Standard Oil Co., 1986–87; BP America, 1987–89; Chief Exec. Officer, Standard Oil Prodn Co., 1987–89; Man. Dir and CEO, BP Exploration Co., 1989–95; Man. Dir, 1991–2007, and Gp Chief Exec., 1995–2007, British Petroleum Co. plc, subseq. BP Amoco, later BP plc. Chm. Adv. Bd, Apax Partners, 2007; non-executive Director: SmithKline Beecham, 1995–99; Intel Corp., 1997–2006; Goldman Sachs, 1999–2007; Foster + Partners, 2007–; Mem. Supervisory Bd, DaimlerChrysler AG, 1998–2001. Trustee: BM, 1995–2005; Cicely Saunders Foundn, 2001–; Tate Gall., 2007–. Pres., BAAS, 2006–07. Chm., Adv. Bd, Stanford Grad. Sch. of Business, 1995–97, now Chm. Emeritus; Mem. Governing Body, London Business Sch., 1996–2000; Chm., Adv. Bd, Judge Business Sch., Cambridge (Judge Inst. of Mgt Studies), 2002–. A Vice Pres., Prince of Wales Business Leaders Forum. Hon. Trustee, Chicago SO; Hon. Counsellor, Conference Bd Inc. CCMI (CIMgt 1993). Hon. FIChemE; Hon. FIMechE 2001; Hon. FRSC 2002; Hon. FGS 1999; Foreign Fellow, Amer. Acad. Arts and Scis, 2003. Holds numerous hon. degrees. Prince Philip Medal, Royal Acad. of Engrg, 1999; Ernest C. Arbuckle Award, Stanford Univ., 2001; Gold Medal, Inst. of Mgt, 2001. *Recreations:* opera, photography, books, pre-Columbian art, 18th century Venetian books and works on paper. *Address:* Riverstone Europe, 3 Burlington Gardens, W1S 3EP. *Clubs:* Athenæum, Savile.

BROWNE, Sir Anthony Arthur Duncan M.; *see* Montague Browne.

BROWNE, Anthony Edward Tudor; author and illustrator of children's books, since 1976; *b* 11 Sept. 1946; *s* of Jack and Doris Browne; *m* 1980, Jane Franklin; one *s* one *d*. *Educ:* Whitcliffe Mount GS, Cleckheaton; Leeds Coll. of Art (BA 1967). Medical Artist, Manchester Royal Infirmary, 1969–71; designer of greetings cards, Gordon Fraser Gall., 1972–86. Hon. DEd Kingston, 2005. Silver Medal, US Soc. of Illustrators, 1994; Hans Christian Andersen Award, 2000. *Publications: author and illustrator:* Through the Magic Mirror, 1976; Walk in the Park, 1977; Bear Hunt, 1979; Bear Goes to Town, 1982; Gorilla, 1983 (Kurt Maschler Award, 1983; Kate Greenaway Medal, 1984; Boston Globe Horn Book Award, 1986; Netherlands Silver Pencil Award, 1989); Willy the Wimp, 1984; Piggybook, 1985; Willy the Champ, 1985; I Like Books, 1988; The Tunnel, 1989 (Netherlands Silver Pencil Award, 1990); Changes, 1990; Willy and Hugh, 1991; Zoo, 1992 (Kate Greenaway Medal, 1992); Big Baby, 1993; Willy the Wizard, 1995; Look What I've Got!, 1996; Things I Like, 1997; Willy the Dreamer, 1997; Voices in the Park, 1998 (Kurt Maschler Award, 1998); Willy's Pictures, 1999; My Dad, 2000; The Shape Game, 2003; Into the Forest, 2004; My Mum, 2005; Silly Billy, 2006; My Brother, 2007; Little Beauty, 2008; *illustrator:* Hansel and Gretel (adapted from trans. by Eleanor Quarrie), 1981; Annalena McAfee, The Visitors Who Came to Stay, 1984; Sally Grindley, Knock, Knock!, Who's There?, 1985; Annalena McAfee, Kirsty Knows Best, 1987; Lewis Carroll, Alice's Adventures in Wonderland, 1988 (Kurt Maschler Award, 1988); Gwen Strauss, Trail of Stones (poems), 1990; Gwen Strauss, The Night Shimmy, 1991; Janni Howker, The Topiary Garden, 1993; King Kong (from story by Edgar Wallace and Merian C. Cooper), 1994; Ian McEwan, The Daydreamer, 1994; Animal Fair (traditional), 2002. *Recreations:* playing cricket, swimming, being with my children. *Address:* c/o Walker Books Ltd, 87 Vauxhall Walk, SE11 5HJ. *T:* (020) 7793 0909. *Club:* St Nicholas at Wade Cricket.

BROWNE, Anthony Percy Scott; Chairman, British Art Market Federation, since 1996; *b* 8 Jan. 1949; *s* of late Percy Browne and Pamela Browne (*née* Exham); *m* 1976, Annabel Louise Hankinson; three *d*. *Educ:* Eton Coll.; Christ Church, Oxford (MA Modern Hist.). Dir, Christie's, 1978–96; Sen. Consultant, Christie's Internat., 1996–. Member: Cultural Industries Export Adv. Gp, 1998–2001; Ministerial Adv. Panel on Illicit Trade, 1999–2003. Mem. Bd, Eur. Fine Art Foundn, 1999–. Hon. Associate, Soc. of Fine Art Auctioneers, 2005. Vice Chm., Art Fortnight London, 2004–05. Trustee, Raise from the Ruins, 1978–80. *Recreations:* fishing, gardening. *Address:* British Art Market Federation, 10 Bury Street, SW1Y 6AA. *T:* (020) 7389 2148. *Clubs:* Turf, Pratt's.

BROWNE, Benjamin James; QC 1996; a Recorder, since 2000; *b* 25 April 1954; *s* of late Percy Basil Browne and of Jenefer Mary Browne; *m* 1987, Juliet Mary Heywood; one *s* one *d*. *Educ:* Eton Coll.; Christ Church, Oxford (MA). Called to the Bar, Inner Temple, 1976; Hd of Chambers, 2 Temple Gdns, 2005–. An Asst Recorder, 1998–2000. *Recreations:* country pursuits, gardening. *Address:* 2 Temple Gardens, Temple, EC4Y 9AY. *T:* (020) 7583 6041. *Club:* Boodle's.

BROWNE, Bernard Peter Francis K.; *see* Kenworthy-Browne.

BROWNE, Carolyn; HM Diplomatic Service; Ambassador to Azerbaijan, since 2007; *b* 19 Oct. 1958; *d* of late Brig. C. C. Ll. Browne and of Margaret Browne (*née* Howard). *Educ:* Godolphin Sch.; S Wilts Grammar Sch., Salisbury; Bristol Univ. (BSc Hons Microbiol.); Linacre Coll., Oxford (DPhil Bacterial Genetics 1985). Joined HM Diplomatic Service, 1985; Second, later First, Sec., Moscow, 1988–91; FCO, 1991–93; UKMIS to UN, NY, 1993–97; FCO, 1997–99; Hd, Human Rights Policy Dept, FCO, 1999–2002; Counsellor (External Relns), UK Perm. Repn to EU, Brussels, 2002–05; FCO, 2005–07. *Address:* c/o Foreign and Commonwealth Office, King Charles Street, SW1A 2AH.

BROWNE, Air Cdre Charles Duncan Alfred, CB 1971; DFC 1944; RAF, retired; *b* 8 July 1922; *m* 1946, Una Felicité Leader (*d* 2001); (one *s* decd). War of 1939–45: served Western Desert, Italy, Corsica and S France in Hurricane and Spitfire Sqdns; post war service in Home, Flying Training, Bomber and Strike Commands; MoD; CO, RAF Brüggen, Germany, 1966–68; Comdt, Aeroplane and Armament Exp. Estab., 1968–71; Air Officer i/c Central Tactics and Trials Orgn, 1971–72. *Club:* Royal Air Force.

BROWNE, Colin; *see* Browne, J. C. C.

BROWNE, Most Rev. Denis George; *see* Hamilton (NZ), Bishop of, (RC).

BROWNE, Rt Hon. Desmond (Henry); PC 2005; MP (Lab) Kilmarnock and Loudoun, since 1997; *b* 22 March 1952; *s* of Peter and Maureen Browne. *Educ:* St Michael's Acad., Kilwinning; Univ. of Glasgow. Apprentice Solicitor, Jas Campbell & Co., 1974–76; Solicitor, 1976; Asst Solicitor, 1976–80, Partner, 1980–85, Ross Harper & Murphy; Partner, McCluskey Browne, 1985–92; admitted, Faculty of Advocates, 1993. Contested (Lab) Argyll and Bute, 1992. Parly Under-Sec. of State, NI Office, 2001–03; Minister of State: (Minister for Work), DWP, 2003–04; Home Office, 2004–05; Chief Sec. to HM Treasury, 2005–06; Secretary of State: for Defence, 2006–08; for Scotland, 2007–08. *Recreations:* football, reading. *Address:* House of Commons, SW1A 0AA.

BROWNE, Desmond John Michael; QC 1990; Recorder, since 1994; *b* 5 April 1947; *s* of Sir Denis John Browne, KCVO, FRCS and of Lady Moyra Browne, *qv*; *m* 1973, Jennifer Mary Wilmore; two *d*. *Educ:* Eton College; New College, Oxford (Scholar). Called to the Bar, Gray's Inn, 1969, Bencher, 1999. Vice-Chm., Bar Council, 2008–. *Recreations:* Australiana, Venice, Sussex Downs. *Address:* 5 Raymond Buildings, Gray's Inn, WC1R 5BP. *T:* (020) 7242 2902. *Clubs:* Brooks's, Beefsteak.

BROWNE, Prof. (Elizabeth) Janet, (Janet Bell), PhD; FLS; Aramont Professor of the History of Science, Harvard University, since 2006; *b* 30 March 1950; *d* of Douglas Maurice Bell and Elizabeth Mary Bell (*née* Edelsten); *m* 1972, Nicholas Browne; two *d*. *Educ:* Trinity Coll., Dublin (BA Hons 1972); Imperial Coll., London (MSc 1973; PhD 1978). Antiquarian bookseller, 1973–75; Wellcome Inst. for Hist. of Medicine, 1979–83 and 1993–2006, Lectr, then Reader, 1993–2002; Prof. in Hist. of Biology, Wellcome Trust Centre for Hist. of Medicine at UCL, 2002–06. Associate Ed., Correspondence of Charles Darwin, 1983–91. Vis. Sen. Res. Fellow, King's Coll., Cambridge, 1996–97. Member: Blue Plaque Panel, English Heritage, 1999–2006; Liby Cttee, Royal Soc., 2001–05. Pres., British Soc. for Hist. of Sci., 2002–04; Mem., Acad. Internat. d'histoire des Scis, 2005. FLS 2003. Ed., British Jl for Hist. of Sci., 1993–99. Founders' Medal, Soc. for Hist. of Natural Hist., 2003. *Publications:* The Secular Ark: studies in the history of biogeography, 1983; (jtly) Dictionary of the History of Science, 1981; Charles Darwin: voyaging, 1995; Charles Darwin: the power of place, 2002 (winner, Biog. Section, Nat. Book Critics Circle, 2002; W. H. Heinemann Award, RSL, 2003; James Tait Black Prize (Biog.), 2004; Pfizer Prize, Hist. of Sci. Soc., 2004). *Recreation:* gardening. *Address:* Science Center 371, Department of the History of Science, Harvard University, 1 Oxford Street, Cambridge, MA 02138, USA.

BROWNE, Gillian Brenda B.; *see* Babington-Browne.

BROWNE, Graham David; Principal, Estover Community College, Plymouth, since 1995; *b* 6 July 1953; *s* of Edwin and Pamela Browne; *m* 1977, Janet Manning; two *d*. *Educ:* Coll. of St Mark and St John (BEd Geog., Educn, Geol.). Teacher, Prendergast Sch., Catford, 1975–80; with Murdo Maclean & Sons Ltd, Stornoway, 1980–84; Hd of Year, Barnwell Sch., Stevenage, 1984–88; Sen. Teacher, John Bunyan Upper Sch., Bedford, 1988–91; Dep. Hd, Beaumont Sch., St Albans, 1991–95. Regl Leader, Nat. Coll. Sch. Leadership, 2006–07; Associate Headteacher, Specialist Schs and Academies Trust; Chairman: Plymouth Assoc. of Headteachers, 2006–07; WISE Adv. Gp, Plymouth CC, 2007. Advr, Letts Publishers, 1986–87. Trustee, Abbey Chapel, Tavistock, 2003–. Teacher of Year Award, SW Reg., Leadership, 2002. *Recreations:* building, orchards, soccer (West Ham United supporter), travel, writing, film, music. *Address:* Estover Community College, Miller Way, Estover, Plymouth PL6 8UN.

BROWNE, Rev. Dr Herman Beseah; Head of Theology Department, Cuttington University Graduate School, Liberia, since 2005; *b* 11 March 1965; *s* of George D. Browne and Clavender Railey Browne; *m* 1992, Versia Karpeh; (one *s* decd). *Educ:* Cuttington UC, Liberia (BA Theol.); King's Coll., London (BD; AKC); Heythrop Coll., London (DPhil 1994). Ordained priest, 1987; Co-ordinator of Studies, Simon of Cyrene Theol Inst., London, 1994–96; Archbp's Asst Sec. for Anglican Communion and Ecumenical Affairs, 1996–2001; Archbishop of Canterbury's Sec. for Anglican Communion Affairs, 2001–05. Canon of Canterbury Cathedral, 2001–05, now Emeritus. Chm., Liberian Community Orgn, UK, 1995–96. *Publications:* Theological Anthropology: a dialectic study of the African and Liberian traditions, 1996, 2nd edn 1998; (ed with G. Griffith-Dickson) Passion for Critique: essays in honour of F. J. Laishley, 1997. *Recreations:* photography, table tennis, movies, music... and often upsetting those I love most. *Address:* Cuttington University, PO Box 277, Monrovia, Liberia. *T:* 77040595; *e-mail:* herman_gblayon@yahoo.com.

BROWNE, (James) Nicholas; QC 1995; **His Honour Judge Nicholas Browne;** a Circuit Judge, since 2006; *b* 25 April 1947; *o s* of late James Christopher Browne, MC and Winifred Browne (*née* Pirie); *m* 1981, Angelica Elizabeth Mitchell, a Circuit Judge (*d* 2006); two *d*. *Educ:* Cheltenham Coll.; Liverpool Univ. (LLB 1969). Called to the Bar, Inner Temple, 1971 (Duke of Edinburgh Entrance Schol.); Bencher 2002; Midland (formerly Midland and Oxford) Circuit, 1971–2006; Asst Recorder, 1990–93; a Recorder, 1993–2006. Mem., Bar Council, 1992–94 (Mem., Professional Conduct Cttee, 1993–94). Chairman, Code of Practice Appeal Board: Prescription Medicines Code of Practice Authy, 2000–05; Assoc. of British Pharmaceutical Industry, 2000–05. *Recreations:* cricket, squash, theatre, spending time with family and friends. *Address:* Wood Green Crown Court, Lordship Lane, N22 5LF. *T:* (020) 8826 4100. *Club:* Cumberland Lawn Tennis.

BROWNE, Janet; *see* Browne, E. J.

BROWNE, Jeremy Richard; MP (Lib Dem) Taunton, since 2005; *b* 17 May 1970; *s* of Sir Nicholas Walker Browne, *qv* and Diana (*née* Aldwinckle); *m* 2004, Charlotte (*née* Callen). *Educ:* Univ. of Nottingham (BA 1992). Dewe Rogerson Ltd, 1994–96; Dir of Press and Broadcasting, Lib Dem Party, 1997–2000; Edelman Communications Worldwide, 2000–02; Associate Dir, Reputation Inc., 2003–04. Lib Dem spokesman on foreign affairs, 2005–06; Lib Dem dep. spokesman on home affairs, 2006–07; Lib Dem Shadow Chief Sec. to Treasury, 2007–. Mem., Home Affairs Select Cttee, 2005–08. Contested (Lib Dem) Enfield Southgate, 1997. *Address:* (office) Masons House, Magdalene Street, Taunton TA1 1SG; House of Commons, SW1A 0AA.

BROWNE, John Anthony; a District Judge (Magistrates' Courts) (formerly Stipendiary Magistrate), S Yorkshire, since 1992; *b* 25 Aug. 1948; *s* of George Henry Browne and Margaret Browne (now Wheeler); *m* 1971, Dr Jill Lesley Atfield; one *s* three *d*. *Educ:* St Peter's de la Salle, Bournemouth; Sheffield Univ. (LLB Hons). Admitted solicitor, 1975; in private practice with Elliot Mather Smith, Chesterfield and Mansfield, 1975–92. *Recreations:* tennis, hill-walking, ski-ing, running (slowly), reading, supporting Sheffield

Wednesday. *Address:* The Magistrates' Court, Castle Street, Sheffield S3 8LU. *T:* (0114) 276 0760.

BROWNE, (John) Colin (Clarke); Partner, The Maitland Consultancy, since 2000; *b* 25 Oct. 1945; *s* of late Ernest Browne, JP and Isobel Sarah Browne (*née* McVitie); *m* 1984, Karen Lascelles Barr; one *s*. *Educ:* Wallace High Sch., Lisburn, Co. Antrim; Trinity Coll., Dublin (BA). Post Office, then British Telecommunications, 1969–94: Dir, Chairman's Office, 1980–85; Chief Exec., Broadband Services, 1985–86; Dir, Corporate Relations, 1986–94; Dir of Corporate Affairs, BBC, 1994–2000. Member: HDA (formerly HEA), 1996–2003; Spongiform Encephalopathy Cttee, 2003–04. Mem., Govt Communications Review Gp, 2003. Trustee: BBC Children in Need, 1994–2000; One World Broadcasting Trust, 1997–2003; Mem. Bd Trustees, Inst. of Internat. Communications, 1998–2000. FCIPR. *Recreations:* sport, music, reading. *Address:* The Maitland Consultancy, Orion House, 5 Upper St Martin's Lane, WC2H 9EA. *T:* (020) 7379 5151.

BROWNE, John Ernest Douglas Delavalette; Senior Investment Strategist, Euro-Pacific Capital (New York), since 2008; Op-ed Columnist, Pittsburgh Tribune Review, since 2008; Visiting Fellow, Heritage Foundation, Washington DC, since 2008; *b* Hampshire, 17 Oct. 1938; *s* of late Col Ernest Coigny Delavalette Browne, OBE, and Victoria Mary Eugene (*née* Douglas); *m* 1st, 1965, Elizabeth Jeannette Marguerite Garthwaite (marr. diss.); 2nd, 1986, Elaine Margaret Schmid Boylen (marr. diss. 2003). *Educ:* Malvern; RMA Sandhurst; Cranfield Inst. of Technology (MSc); Harvard Business Sch. (MBA). Served Grenadier Guards, British Guiana (Battalion Pilot), Cyprus, BAOR, 1959–67; Captain 1963; TA, Grenadier Guards (Volunteers), 1981–91, Major 1985. Associate, Morgan Stanley & Co., New York, 1969–72; Pember & Boyle, 1972–74; Dir, ME Ops, Eur. Banking Co., 1974–78; Man. Dir, Falcon Finance Mgt Ltd, 1978–95; Vice Pres., Investments, Salomon Smith Barney, subseq. Smith Barney Inc., 1995–2004. Editor, Financial Intelligence Report, Newswax Media Inc., 2006–08. Director: Worms Investments, 1981–83; Scansat (Broadcasting) Ltd, 1988–93; Internat. Bd, World Times (Boston), 1988–2001; Tijari Finance Ltd, 1989–92; Adviser: Barclays Bank Ltd, 1978–84; Trustees Household Div., 1979–83. Director: Churchill Private Clinic, 1980–91; Drug Free America, 1998–; Greater Palm Beach Symphony, 1998–2003; World Affairs Council, Palm Beaches, 2003–. Councillor (C), Westminster Council, 1974–78. MP (C) Winchester, 1979–92; introduced: Trades Description Act (Amendment) Bill, 1988; Protection of Animals (Amendment) Act, 1988; Protection of Privacy Bill, 1989; Armed Forces (Liability for Injury) Bill, 1991. Member: H of C Treasury Select Cttee, 1982–87; Social Services Select Cttee, 1991–92; Secretary: Conservative Finance Cttee, 1982–84; Conservative Defence Cttee, 1982–83; Chairman: Conservative Smaller Business Cttee, 1987–90 (Sec., 1984–87); Lords and Commons Anglo-Swiss Soc., 1979–92 (Treas., 1984–87; Sec., 1987–92); UK deleg. to N Atlantic Assembly, 1986–92 (rapporteur on human rights, 1989–92). Contested: (Ind. C) Winchester, 1992; (Ind. Against a Federal Europe) Hampshire South and Wight, EP election, 1994; (UK Ind.): Falmouth and Camborne, 2001; NE, EP election, 2004; N Devon, 2005. Mem., NFU. Mem., Winchester Preservation Trust, 1980–90; Patron, Winchester Cadets Assoc., 1980–90; Trustee, Winnall Community Assoc., 1981–94; President: Winchester Gp for Disabled People, 1982–92; Hursley Cricket Club, 1985–90. Mem. Court, Univ. of Southampton, 1979–90; Governor, Malvern Coll., 1982–. Liveryman, Goldsmiths' Co., 1982–. OStJ 1979 (Mem., Chapter Gen., 1985–90). Interests include: economics, gold and internat. monetary affairs, defence, broadcasting. *Publications:* Tarantula: an Anglo American Special Forces hunt for bin Laden, 2003; Grenadier Grins, 2006; A Frozen Account of the Romanovs, 2008; various articles on finance, gold (A New European Currency—The Karl, ₭), defence, Middle East, Soviet leadership. *Recreations:* golf, riding, sailing, shooting, ski-ing. *Address:* e-mail: johnbrowne@post.harvard.edu. *Clubs:* Boodle's, Turf, Special Forces; Fishers Island (New York).

BROWNE, Air Vice-Marshal John Philip Ravenscroft, CBE 1985; *b* 27 April 1937; *s* of late Charles Harold Browne and Lorna Browne (*née* Bailey); *m* 1962, Gillian Dorothy Smith; two *s*. *Educ:* Brockenhurst County High Sch.; Southampton Univ. (BSc(Eng)). CEng, FICE, FRAeS. Commissioned Airfield Construction Branch, RAF, 1958; appts in NEAF and UK, 1959–66; transf. to Engineer Branch, 1966; RAF Coll., Cranwell, 1966–67; aircraft engineering appts, RAF Valley and MoD, 1967–71; RAF Staff Coll., 1972; OC Engrg Wing, RAF Valley, 1973–75; staff appts, MoD and HQ RAF Germany, 1975–82; MoD (PE), 1982–89: Asst Dir, Harrier Projects, 1982–85, Dir, Electronics Radar Airborne, 1985–86, Dir, Airborne Early Warning, 1986–89; Dir Gen. Support Services (RAF), MoD, 1989–92; RAF retd, 1992; Dir Engrg, 1992–95, Dir Systems, 1995–96, NATS, CAA. Trustee, Bletchley Park Trust, 2000–. FCMI. *Publication:* (with M. T. Thurbon) Electronic Warfare, 1998. *Recreations:* reading, writing, aviation, military history, photography, music. *Address:* c/o Lloyds TSB, New Milton, Hants BH25 6HU. *Club:* Royal Air Force.

BROWNE, Lady Moyra (Blanche Madeleine), DBE 1977 (OBE 1962); Governor, 1987–99, Vice President, since 1999, Research into Ageing (formerly British Foundation for Age Research) (National Chairman, Support Groups, 1987–93); *b* 2 March 1918; *d* of 9th Earl of Bessborough, PC, GCMG; *m* 1945, Sir Denis John Browne, KCVO, FRCS (*d* 1967); one *s* one *d*. *Educ:* privately. Enrolled Nurse (General) (State Enrolled Nurse, 1946). Dep. Supt-in-Chief, 1964, Supt-in-Chief, 1970–83, St John Amb. Bde. Vice-Chm. Central Council, Victoria League, 1961–65; Vice-Pres., Royal Coll. of Nursing, 1970–85. Hon. Mem., British Assoc. of Paediatric Surgeons, 1990. GCStJ 1984 (Mem., Chapter Gen., subseq. Chapter, Priory of England and Islands, 1983–). *Recreations:* music, fishing, travel. *Address:* 16 Wilton Street, SW1X 7AX. *T:* (020) 7235 1419.

See also D. J. M. Browne.

BROWNE, Nicholas; *see* Browne, James N.

BROWNE, Sir Nicholas (Walker), KBE 2002; CMG 1999; HM Diplomatic Service; Ambassador to Denmark, 2003–06; *b* 17 Dec. 1947; *s* of Gordon Browne and Molly (*née* Gray); *m* 1969, Diana Aldwinckle; two *s* two *d*. *Educ:* Cheltenham Coll.; University Coll., Oxford (Open Scholar) (BA). Third Sec., FCO, 1969–71; Tehran, 1971–74; Second, later First Sec., FCO, 1974–76; on loan to Cabinet Office, 1976–80; First Sec. and Head of Chancery, Salisbury, 1980–81; First Sec., FCO, 1981–84; First Sec. (Envmt), Office of UK Rep., Brussels, 1984–89; Chargé d'Affaires, Tehran, 1989; Counsellor, FCO, 1989–90; Counsellor (Press and Public Affairs), Washington, and Hd of British Information Services, NY, 1990–94; Hd of Middle East Dept, FCO, 1994–97; Chargé d'Affaires, Tehran, 1997–99; Ambassador to Iran, 1999–2002; Sen. Dir (Civil), RCDS, 2002–03. *Recreations:* travel, theatre, log fires. *Address:* c/o Foreign and Commonwealth Office, King Charles Street, SW1A 2AH.

See also J. R. Browne.

BROWNE, Peter K.; *see* Kenworthy-Browne.

BROWNE, Robert William M.; *see* Moxon Browne.

BROWNE, Sheila Jeanne, CB 1977; Principal, Newnham College, Cambridge, 1983–92; *b* 25 Dec. 1924; *d* of Edward Elliott Browne. *Educ:* Lady Margaret Hall, Oxford (MA; Hon. Fellow 1978); Ecole des Chartes, Paris. Asst Lectr, Royal Holloway Coll., Univ. of London, 1947–51; Tutor and Fellow of St Hilda's Coll., Oxford and Univ. Lectr in French, Oxford, 1951–61, Hon. Fellow, St Hilda's Coll., 1978; HM Inspector of Schools, 1961–70; Staff Inspector, Secondary Educn, 1970–72; Chief Inspector, Secondary Educn, 1972; Dep. Sen. Chief Inspector, DES, 1972–74, Senior Chief Inspector, 1974–83. Member: CNAA, 1985–93; Franco-British Council, 1987–95; Marshall Aid Commemoration Comr, 1987–92. Trustee, Gladstone Meml Trust, 1991–. Chairman: Council, Selly Oak Colls, 1992–93; Govs, Morley Coll., 2000–04. Hon. Fellow: Thames Valley Univ. (formerly Ealing Tech. Coll., then Poly. of W London), 1984; RHBNC, 1987; Lancashire Polytechnic, 1989; Univ. (formerly Poly.) of N London, 1989. Hon. DLitt Warwick, 1981; Hon. LLD: Exeter, 1984; Birmingham, 1987. *Recreations:* medieval France, enjoying Oxford. *Address:* 101 Walton Street, Oxford OX2 6EB. *T:* (01865) 511128.

BROWNE-CAVE, Sir Robert C.; *see* Cave-Browne-Cave.

BROWNE-WILKINSON, family name of **Baron Browne-Wilkinson**.

BROWNE-WILKINSON, Baron *cr* 1991 (Life Peer), of Camden, in the London Borough of Camden; **Nicolas Christopher Henry Browne-Wilkinson,** Kt 1977; PC 1983; a Lord of Appeal in Ordinary, 1991–2000; Senior Law Lord, 1999–2000; *b* 30 March 1930; *s* of late Canon A. R. Browne-Wilkinson and Molly Browne-Wilkinson; *m* 1st, 1955, Ursula de Lacy Bacon (*d* 1987); three *s* two *d*; 2nd, 1990, Mrs Hilary Tuckwell. *Educ:* Lancing; Magdalen Coll., Oxford (BA; Hon. Fellow, 1993). Called to Bar, Lincoln's Inn, 1953 (Bencher, 1977); QC 1972. Junior Counsel: to Registrar of Restrictive Trading Agreements, 1964–66; to Attorney-General in Charity Matters, 1966–72; in bankruptcy, to Dept of Trade and Industry, 1966–72; a Judge of the Courts of Appeal of Jersey and Guernsey, 1976–77; a Judge of the High Court, Chancery Div., 1977–83; a Lord Justice of Appeal, 1983–85; Vice-Chancellor of the Supreme Court, 1985–91. Pres., Employment Appeal Tribunal, 1981–83. Pres., Senate of the Inns of Court and the Bar, 1984–86. Hon. Fellow, St Edmund Hall, Oxford, 1987. *Recreation:* gardening. *Address:* House of Lords, SW1A 0PW.

See also S. Browne-Wilkinson.

BROWNE-WILKINSON, Simon; QC 1998; a Recorder, since 2004; barrister; *b* 18 Aug. 1957; *s* of Baron Browne-Wilkinson, *qv*; *m* 1988, Megan Tresidder (*d* 2001); one *s* one *d*. *Educ:* City of London Sch.; Magdalen Coll., Oxford (BA Jurisprudence 1979). Called to the Bar, Lincoln's Inn, 1981, Bencher, 2008; in practice at the Bar, 1981–. *Recreation:* sailing. *Address:* Fountain Court, Temple, EC4Y 9DH. *T:* (020) 7583 3335.

BROWNING, Angela Frances; MP (C) Tiverton and Honiton, since 1997 (Tiverton, 1992–97); Deputy Chairman of Conservative Party, since 2006; *b* 4 Dec. 1946; *d* of late Thomas Pearson and Linda Pearson (later Chamberlain); *m* 1968, David Browning; two *s*. *Educ:* Westwood Girls' Grammar Sch.; Reading Coll. of Technol.; Bournemouth Coll. of Technol. FInstSMM. Management Consultant. Parly Sec., MAFF, 1994–97; Opposition spokesman: on educn and disability, 1997–98; on trade and industry, 1999–2000; Shadow Leader, H of C, 2000–01. Vice Pres., InstSMM, 1997–. Mem. and Vice Pres., Nat. Autistic Soc.; Nat. Vice Pres., Alzheimer's Disease Soc., 1997–. *Recreations:* theatre, opera. *Address:* House of Commons, SW1A 0AA. *T:* (020) 7219 5067.

BROWNING, (David) Peter (James), CBE 1984; MA; Chief Education Officer: Southampton, 1969–73; Bedfordshire, 1973–89; *b* 29 May 1927; *s* of late Frank Browning and Lucie A. (*née* Hiscock); *m* 1953, Eleanor Berry, *d* of late J. H. Forshaw, CB, FRIBA; three *s*. *Educ:* Christ's Coll., Cambridge (Engl. and Mod. Langs Tripos); Sorbonne; Univs of Strasbourg and Perugia. Personal Asst to Vice-Chancellor, Liverpool Univ., 1952–56; Teacher, Willenhall Comprehensive Sch., 1956–59; Sen. Admin. Asst, Somerset LEA, 1959–62; Asst Dir of Educn, Cumberland LEA, 1962–66; Dep. Chief Educn Officer, Southampton LEA, 1966–69. Member: Schools Council Governing Council and 5–13 Steering Cttee, 1969–75; Council, Univ. of Southampton, 1970–73; C of E Bd of Educn Schools Cttee, 1970–75; Council, Nat. Youth Orch., 1972–77; Merchant Navy Trng Bd, 1973–77; British Educnl Administration Soc. (Chm., 1974–78; Founder Mem., Council of Management); UGC, 1974–79; Taylor Cttee of Enquiry into Management and Govt of Schs, 1975–77; Governing Body, Centre for Inf. on Language Teaching and Research, 1975–80; European Forum for Educational Admin (Founder Chm., 1977–84); Library Adv. Council (England), 1978–81; Bd of Governors, Camb. Inst. of Educn (Vice-Chm., 1980–89); Univ. of Cambridge Faculty Bd of Educn, 1983–92; Council of Management, British Sch. Tech., 1984–87, Trust Dir, 1987–92; Lancaster Univ. Council, 1988–97 (Treas., 1993–97); Dir, Nat. Educnl Resources Inf. Service, 1988–91; Member: Carlisle Diocesan Bd of Educn, 1989–97 (Chm., 1992–97); Council, Open Coll. of NW, 1991–94; Cumbria Arts in Educn Trust, 1992–95 (Chm., 1992–95); Chairman: Carlisle DAC for Care of Churches, 1993–2000; Armitt (Liby and Mus.) Trust, 1994–2000 (Mem., 1992–2002); Armitt Liby and Mus. Centre Co., 1996–2000 (Mem., 1996–2001); Armitt Centre Enterprises Co., 1997–2001. Dir, Wordsworth Meml Lects and Rydal Bach Celebrity Concerts, 1993–95. Governor: Gordonstoun Sch., 1985–92; Lakes Sch., Windermere, 1988–92; Charlotte Mason Coll. of Higher Educn, Ambleside, 1988–92; London Coll. of Dance, 1990–93. Consultant, Ministry of Education: Sudan, 1976; Cyprus, 1977; Italy, 1981. Sir James Matthews Meml Lecture, Univ. of Southampton, 1983. FRSA 1981–93. Cavalier, Order of Merit (Republic of Italy), 1985; Médaille d'honneur de l'Oise, 1988; Commandeur, Ordre des Palmes Académiques (Republic of France), 1989 (Officier, 1985). *Publications:* Editor: Julius Caesar for German Students, 1957; Macbeth for German Students, 1959; contrib. London Educn Rev., Educnl Administration jl, and other educnl jls. *Recreations:* music, theatre, travel, conversation, walking. *Address:* Park Fell, Skelwith Bridge, near Ambleside LA22 9NP. *T:* (015394) 33978; 43/45 Chilkwell Street, Glastonbury BA6 8DE. *T:* (01458) 832514.

BROWNING, Most Rev. Edmond Lee; Presiding Bishop of the Episcopal Church in the United States, 1986–97; *b* 11 March 1929; *s* of Edmond Lucian Browning and Cora Mae Lee; *m* 1953, Patricia A. Sparks; four *s* one *d*. *Educ:* Univ. of the South (BA 1952); School of Theology, Sewanee, Tenn (BD 1954). Curate, Good Shepherd, Corpus Christi, Texas, 1954–56; Rector, Redeemer, Eagle Pass, Texas, 1956–59; Rector, All Souls, Okinawa, 1959–63; Japanese Lang. School, Kobe, Japan, 1963–65; Rector, St Matthews, Okinawa, 1965–67; Archdeacon of Episcopal Church, Okinawa, 1965–67; first Bishop of Okinawa, 1967–71; Bishop of American Convocation, 1971–73; Executive for National and World Mission, on Presiding Bishop's Staff, United States Episcopal Church, 1974–76; Bishop of Hawaii, 1976–85. Chm., Standing Commn on World Mission, 1979–82. Member: Exec. Council, Episcopal Church, 1982–85; Anglican Consultative Council, 1982–91. Hon. DD: Univ. of the South, Sewanee, Tenn, 1970; Gen. Theol Seminary, 1986; Church Divinity Sch. of the Pacific, 1987; Seabury Western Seminary, 1987; Hon. DHL: Chaminade Univ., Honolulu, 1985; St Paul's Coll., Lawrenceville, Va, 1987. *Publication:* Essay on World Mission, 1977. *Address:* 5164 Imai Road, Hood River, OR 97031, USA. *T:* (212) 9225322.

BROWNING, Rt Rev. George Victor; Priest-in-charge, Wriggle Valley, Salisbury, since 2008; Bishop of Canberra and Goulburn, 1993–2008; *b* 28 Sept. 1942; *s* of John and Barbara Browning; *m* 1965, Margaret Rowland; three *s*. *Educ:* Ardingly Coll.; Lewes County Grammar Sch., Sussex; St John's Coll., Morpeth, NSW (ThL 1st cl. Hons 1965); Charles Sturt Univ. (DLitt 2007). Curate: Inverell, 1966–68; Armidale, 1968–69; Vicar, Warialda, 1969–73; Vice Warden and Lectr in Old Testament Studies and Pastoral Theol., St John's Coll., Morpeth, 1973–75 (Acting Warden, 1974); Rector of Singleton, Rural Dean and Archdeacon of the Upper Hunter, 1976–84; Rector of Woy Woy and Archdeacon of the Central Coast, 1984–85; Bishop of the Northern Reg., Brisbane, 1985–92; Principal, St Francis' Theol Coll., 1988–92; Bishop of the Coastal Reg., and Asst Bishop, dio. of Brisbane, 1992–93. *Recreations:* reading, running (anything that presents a challenge).

BROWNING, Helen Mary, OBE 1998; farmer and business woman; Chairman, Eastbrook Farms Organic Meat, since 1997; *b* 22 Nov. 1961; *d* of Robert Roland Browning and Sheila Mary Browning (*née* Harris); *m* 1989, Henry George Stoye (separated); one *d*. *Educ:* Harper Adams Agricl Coll. (BSc Agricl Technol.). Chairman: British Organic Farmers, 1991–97; Soil Assoc., 1997–2001 (Dir, Food and Farming, 2004–). Member: MLC, 1998–; Agric. and Envmt Biotechnol. Commn, 1998–2005; Policy Commn on Future of Food and Farming, 2001–02; Chairman: Food Ethics Council, 2000–; Animal Health and Welfare England Implementation Gp, 2005–. Member: Steering Cttee, Food Chain Centre, 2002–05; Bd, Organic Milk Suppliers Co-op., 2002–. MInstD 2000. *Recreations:* sport, especially squash, walking, food, reading, travel. *Address:* Eastbrook Farm, Bishopstone, Swindon, Wilts SN6 8PW. *T:* (01793) 792042, *Fax:* (01793) 791239; *e-mail:* helen@helenbrowningorganics.co.uk. *Club:* Farmers.

BROWNING, Ian Andrew; DL; Chief Executive, Wiltshire County Council, 1984–96; Clerk to the Wiltshire Police Authority, 1976–2002; *b* 28 Aug. 1941; *m* 1967, Ann Carter; two *s*. *Educ:* Liverpool Univ. (BA Hons Pol Theory and Instns). Solicitor. Swindon BC, 1964–70; WR, Yorks, 1970–73; S Yorks CC, 1973–76; Wilts CC, 1976–96. DL Wilts, 1996. *Recreations:* golf, travel, ornithology. *Address:* 10 The Picquet, Bratton, Westbury, Wiltshire BA13 4RU.

BROWNING, Prof. Keith Anthony, PhD; FRS 1978; CMet, FRMetS; Director, Joint Centre for Mesoscale Meteorology, 1992–2003, and Professor in Department of Meteorology, 1995–2003, now Professor Emeritus, University of Reading; *b* 31 July 1938; *s* of late Sqdn Ldr James Anthony Browning and Amy Hilda (*née* Greenwood); *m* 1962, Ann Muriel (*née* Baish), BSc, MSc; one *s* two *d*. *Educ:* Commonweal Grammar Sch., Swindon, Wilts; Imperial Coll. of Science and Technology, Univ. of London. BSc, ARCS, PhD, DIC. FRMetS 1962 (Hon. FRMetS 2006); CMet 1994. Research atmospheric physicist, Air Force Cambridge Research Laboratories, Mass, USA, 1962–66; in charge of Meteorological Office Radar Research Lab., RSRE, Malvern, 1966–85; Dep. Dir (Phys. Res.), 1985–89, Dir of Res., 1989–91, Met. Office, Bracknell; Principal Research Fellow, 1966–69; Principal Scientific Officer, 1969–72; Sen. Principal Scientific Officer, 1972–79; Dep. Chief Scientific Officer, 1979–89; Chief Scientific Officer, 1989–91. Director: NERC Univs Weather Res. Network, 2000–03; NERC Univs Facility for Atmospheric Measurements, 2001–03. Ch. Scientist, Nat. Hail Res. Experiment, USA, 1974–75. Visiting Professor: Dept of Meteorology, Reading Univ., 1988–94; Leeds Univ., 2006–July 2009. World Climate Research Programme: Member: British Nat. Cttee, 1988–89; Scientific Steering Gp, Global Energy and Water Cycle Expmt, 1988–96 (Chm., Cloud System Sci. Study, 1992–96); WMO/ICSU Jt Scientific Cttee, 1990–94; World Weather Research Programme: Mem., WMO Interim Sci. Steering Cttee, 1996–98; Mem., Sci. Steering Cttee, 1998–2005. Royal Meteorological Society: Mem. Council, 1971–74, 1979–81, 1987–91 and 1994–99 (Vice-Pres., 1979–81, 1987–88 and 1990–91; Pres., 1988–90); Mem., Accreditation Bd, 1993–99; Chm., 1994–99; Member: Editing Cttee, Qly Jl RMetS, 1975–78; Inter-Union Commn on Radio Meteorology, 1975–78; Internat. Commn on Cloud Physics, 1976–84; British Nat. Cttee for Physics, 1979–84; British Nat. Cttee for Geodesy and Geophysics, 1983–89 (Chm., Met. and Atmos. Phys. Sub-Cttee, 1985–89, Vice-Chm., 1979–84); NERC, 1984–87; British Nat. Cttee for Space Res., 1986–89 (Remote Sensing Sub-Cttee, 1986–89); Royal Soc. Interdisciplinary Sci. Cttee for Space Res., 1990–91. MAE, 1989; For. Associate, US Nat. Acad. of Engrg, 1992. UK Nat. Correspondent, Internat. Assoc. of Meteorology and Atmospheric Physics, 1991–94. L. F. Richardson Prize, 1968, Buchan Prize, 1972, William Gaskell Meml Medal, 1982, Symons Gold Medal, 2001, RMetS; L. G. Groves Meml Prize for Meteorology, Met. Office, 1969; Meisinger Award, 1974, Jule Charney Award, 1985, Rossby Medal, 2003, Amer. Met. Soc. (Fellow of the Society, 1975); Charles Chree Medal and Prize, Inst. of Physics, 1981. *Publications:* (ed) Nowcasting, 1982; (ed jtly) Global Energy and Water Cycles, 1999; meteorological papers in learned jls, mainly in Britain and USA. *Recreations:* photography, home and garden.

BROWNING, Prof. Martin James, PhD; FBA 2008; Professor of Economics, University of Oxford, since 2006; Fellow, Nuffield College, Oxford, since 2006; *b* Loughborough, 27 Aug. 1946; *s* of George and Daisy Browning; *m* 1969, Lisbeth Hammer; two *s* one *d*. *Educ:* London School of Econs (MSc 1979); Tilburg Univ. (PhD 1993). Lectr, Bristol Univ., 1979–84; Prof. of Econs, McMaster Univ., 1984–97; Prof. of Econs, 1997–2006, Dir, Centre for Applied Microeconometrics, 2001–08, Univ. of Copenhagen. Fellow, Econometric Soc. *Publications:* over 50 articles. *Address:* 35 The Stream Edge, Oxford OX1 1HT; *e-mail:* martin.browning@economics.ox.ac.uk.

BROWNING, Peter; *see* Browning, D. P. J.

BROWNING, Philip Harold Roger; a District Judge (Magistrates' Courts), Norfolk, since 2004; *b* 25 Aug. 1946; *s* of Harold and late Barbara Browning; *m* 1972, Linda; two *s*. *Educ:* Hele's Sch., Exeter; Surbiton County Grammar Sch.; Windsor Grammar Sch.; Coll. of Law. Articled T. W. Stuchbery & Son, Windsor and Maidenhead, 1964–69; admitted solicitor, 1969; Asst Solicitor, Baily, Williams & Lucas, Saffron Walden, 1969–71; Prosecuting Solicitor, Devon, 1972–81; Clerk to Justices: Axminster, Exmouth, Honiton and Wonford, 1981–85; Norwich, 1985–94; a Stipendiary Magistrate, subseq. Dist Judge (Magistrates' Courts), Shropshire, 1994–2000; a District Judge (Magistrates' Courts): West Mercia, 2000–03; Wolverhampton, 2003–04. Course Dir, continuation trng for Dist Judges (Magistrates' Courts), Judicial Studies Bd, 1997–2004. *Recreations:* books, music. *Address:* Norwich Magistrates' Court, Bishopgate, Norwich NR3 1UP. *T:* (01603) 679500.

BROWNING, Rex Alan, CB 1984; Deputy Secretary, Overseas Development Administration, 1981–86, retired; *b* 22 July 1930; *s* of Gilbert H. W. Browning and Gladys (*née* Smith); *m* 1961, Paula McKain; three *d*. *Educ:* Bristol Grammar Sch.; Merton Coll., Oxford (Postmaster) (MA). HM Inspector of Taxes, 1952; Asst Principal, Colonial Office, 1957; Private Sec. to Parly Under-Sec. for the Colonies, 1960; Principal, Dept of Techn. Co-operation, 1961; transf. ODM, 1964; seconded to Diplomatic Service as First Sec. (Aid), British High Commn, Singapore, 1969; Asst Sec., 1971; Counsellor, Overseas Develt, Washington, and Alternate UK Exec. Dir, IBRD, 1973–76; Under-Secretary: ODM, 1976–78; Dept of Trade, 1978–80; ODA, 1980–81. *Address:* 19 Lingdale Road, Prenton, Merseyside CH43 8TE.

BROWNING, Rev. Canon Wilfrid Robert Francis; Canon Residentiary of Christ Church Cathedral, Oxford, 1965–87, Hon. Canon since 1987; *b* 29 May 1918; *s* of Charles Robert and Mabel Elizabeth Browning; *m* 1948, Elizabeth Beeston; two *s* two *d*. *Educ:* Westminster School; Christ Church, Oxford (Squire Scholar); Cuddesdon Coll., Oxford. MA, BD Oxon. Deacon 1941, priest 1942, dio. of Peterborough; on staff of St Deiniol's Library, Hawarden, 1946–48; Vicar of St Richard's, Hove, 1948–51; Rector of Great Haseley, 1951–59; Lectr, Cuddesdon Coll., Oxford, 1951–59 and 1965–70; Canon Residentiary of Blackburn Cath. and Warden of Whalley Abbey, Lancs, 1959–65; Director of Ordinands and Post-Ordination Trng (Oxford dio.), 1965–85; Dir of Trng for Non-Stipendiary Ordinands and Clergy, 1972–88; Tutor, Westminster Coll., Oxford, 1993–99. Examining Chaplain: Blackburn, 1960–70; Manchester, 1970–78; Oxford, 1965–89. Member of General Synod, 1973–85; Select Preacher, Oxford Univ., 1972, 1981. *Publications:* Commentary on St Luke's Gospel, 1960, 6th edn 1981; Meet the New Testament, 1964; ed, The Anglican Synthesis, 1965; Handbook of the Ministry, 1985; A Dictionary of the Bible, 1996, 2nd edn 2004. *Address:* 33 Dunstone Road, Plymstock, Plymouth PL9 8RJ. *T:* (01752) 403039; 42 Alexandra Road, Oxford OX2 0DB. *T:* (01865) 723464.

BROWNJOHN, Alan Charles; poet, novelist and critic; *b* 28 July 1931; *s* of Charles Henry Brownjohn and Dorothy Brownjohn (*née* Mulligan); *m* 1st, 1960, (Kathleen) Shirley Toulson; one *s*, and one step *s* one step *d*; 2nd, 1972, Sandra Lesley Willingham (marr. diss. 2005). *Educ:* Brockley County Sch.; Merton Coll., Oxford (BA Hons Mod. Hist. 1953; MA 1961). Asst Master, Beckenham and Penge Boys' Grammar Sch., 1958–65; Lectr, then Sen. Lectr, Battersea Coll. of Educn, subseq. S Bank Poly., 1965–79. Visiting Lecturer: in Poetry, Polytechnic of North London, 1981–83; in Creative Writing, Univ. of N London, then London Metropolitan Univ., 2000–03. Poetry Critic: New Statesman, 1968–74; Encounter, 1978–82; Sunday Times, 1990–. Special Award, Writers' Guild Bks Cttee, 2007. *Publications: poetry:* The Railings, 1961; The Lions' Mouths, 1967; Sandgrains on a Tray, 1969; Warrior's Career, 1972; A Song of Good Life, 1975; A Night in the Gazebo, 1980; Collected Poems, 1983, 3rd edn 2006; The Old Flea-Pit, 1987; The Observation Car, 1990; In the Cruel Arcade, 1994; The Cat Without E-Mail, 2001; The Men Around Her Bed, 2004; *novels:* The Way You Tell Them, 1990 (Authors' Club prize, 1991); The Long Shadows, 1997; A Funny Old Year, 2001; *translations:* Goethe, Torquato Tasso (with Sandra Brownjohn), 1986; Corneille, Horace, 1995. *Recreations:* walking, listening to music, left-wing censoriousness. *Address:* 2 Belsize Park, NW3 4ET. *T:* (020) 7794 2479.

BROWNLEE, Derek Scott; Member (C) South of Scotland, Scottish Parliament, since June 2005; *b* 10 Aug. 1974; *s* of David Melville Brownlee and Jean Chisholm Brownlee. *Educ:* Selkirk High Sch.; Univ. of Aberdeen (LLB 1st Cl. Hons). CA 1999. Ernst & Young: Accountant, 1996–99; Consultant, 1999–2001; Sen. Consultant, 2001–02; Hd, Taxation and Pensions Policy, Inst. Dirs, 2002–04; Manager, Deloitte, 2004–05. Scottish Parliament: Member: Finance Cttee, 2005–; Scottish Commn for Public Audit, 2007–. Contested (C) Tweeddale, Ettrick and Lauderdale, Scottish Parlt, 2003, 2007. *Recreation:* beer and whisky. *Address:* Scottish Parliament, Edinburgh EH99 1SP. *T:* (0131) 348 5635, *Fax:* (0131) 348 5932; *e-mail:* Derek.Brownlee.msp@scottish.parliament.uk. *Club:* Selkirk Conservative.

BROWNLEE, Prof. George; Professor of Pharmacology, King's College, University of London, 1958–78, retired; now Emeritus Professor; *b* 8 Sept. 1911; *s* of late George R. Brownlee and of Mary C. C. Gow, Edinburgh; *m* 1940, Margaret P. M. Cochrane (*d* 1970), 2nd *d* of Thomas W. P. Cochrane and Margaret P. M. S. Milne, Bo'ness, Scotland; three *s*; 2nd, 1977, Betty Jean Gaydon (marr. diss. 1981), *o d* of Stanley H. Clutterham and Margaret M. Fox, Sidney, Australia. *Educ:* Tynecastle Sch.; Heriot Watt Coll., Edinburgh, BSc 1936, DSc 1950, Glasgow; PhD 1939, London. Rammell Schol., Biological Standardization Labs of Pharmaceutical Soc., London; subseq. Head of Chemotherapeutic Div., Wellcome Res. Labs, Beckenham; Reader in Pharmacology, King's Coll., Univ. of London, 1949. Editor, Jl of Pharmacy and Pharmacology, 1955–72. FKC, 1971. *Publications:* (with Prof. J. P. Quilliam) Experimental Pharmacology, 1952; papers on: chemotherapy of tuberculosis and leprosy; structure and pharmacology of the polymyxins; endocrinology; toxicity of drugs; neurohumoral transmitters in smooth muscle, etc., in: Brit. Jl Pharmacology; Jl Physiology; Biochem. Jl; Nature; Lancet; Annals NY Acad. of Science; Pharmacological Reviews, etc. *Recreations:* collecting books, making things. *Address:* 602 Gilbert House, Barbican, EC2Y 8BD. *T:* (020) 7638 9543. *Club:* Athenæum.
See also G. G. Brownlee.

BROWNLEE, Prof. George Gow, PhD; FMedSci; FRS 1987; E. P. Abraham Professor of Chemical Pathology, Sir William Dunn School of Pathology, University of Oxford, 1980–2008; Fellow of Lincoln College, Oxford, since 1980; *b* 13 Jan. 1942; *s* of Prof. George Brownlee, *qv*; *m* 1966, Margaret Susan Kemp; one *d* (one *s* decd). *Educ:* Dulwich College; Emmanuel Coll., Cambridge (MA, PhD). Scientific staff of MRC at Laboratory of Molecular Biology, Cambridge, 1966–80. Fellow, Emmanuel Coll., Cambridge, 1967–71. Founder FMedSci 1998. Colworth Medal, 1977, Wellcome Trust Award, 1985, Biochemical Soc.; Owren Medal (Norway), 1987; Haemophilia Medal (France), 1988. *Publications:* Determination of Sequences in RNA (Vol. 3, Part I of Laboratory Techniques in Biochemistry and Molecular Biology), 1972; scientific papers in Jl of Molecular Biology, Nature, Cell, Nucleic Acids Research, etc. *Recreations:* gardening, cricket.

BROWNLIE, Albert Dempster; Vice-Chancellor, University of Canterbury, Christchurch, New Zealand, 1977–98; *b* 3 Sept. 1932; *s* of Albert Newman and Netia Brownlie; *m* 1955, Noelene Eunice (*née* Meyer); two *d*. *Educ:* Univ. of Auckland, NZ (MCom). Economist, NZ Treasury, 1954–55. Lecturer, Sen. Lectr, Associate Prof. in Economics, Univ. of Auckland, 1956–64; Prof. and Head of Dept of Economics, Univ. of Canterbury, Christchurch, 1965–77. Chairman: Monetary and Economic Council, 1972–78; Australia–NZ Foundn, 1979–83; UGC Cttee to Review NZ Univ. Educn, 1980–82; NZ Vice-Chancellors' Cttee, 1983–84, 1993; Member: Commonwealth Experts Group on New Internat. Economic Order, 1975–77; Commonwealth Experts Gp on Econ. Growth, 1980; Wage Hearing Tribunal, 1976. Silver Jubilee Medal, 1977. *Publications:* articles in learned jls. *Address:* 66 Clyde Road, Christchurch 4, New Zealand. *T:* (3) 3487629.

BROWNLIE, Ian, CBE 1993; QC; DCL; FBA; International Law practitioner; Chichele Professor of Public International Law, now Emeritus, and Fellow of All Souls College, University of Oxford, 1980–99 (Distinguished Fellow, 2004); *b* 19 Sept. 1932; *s* of John Nason Brownlie and Amy Isabella (*née* Atherton); *m* 1st, 1957, Jocelyn Gale; one *s* two *d*; 2nd, 1978, C. J. Apperley, LLM. *Educ:* Alsop High Sch., Liverpool; Hertford Coll., Oxford (Gibbs Scholar, 1952; BA 1953); King's Coll., Cambridge (Humanitarian Trust Student, 1955). DPhil Oxford, 1961; DCL Oxford, 1976. Called to the Bar, Gray's Inn, 1958, Bencher, 1987; QC 1979. Lectr, Nottingham Univ., 1957–63; Fellow and Tutor in Law, Wadham Coll., Oxford, 1963–76 and Lectr, Oxford Univ., 1964–76; Prof. of

Internat. Law, LSE, Univ. of London, 1976–80. Reader in Public Internat. Law, Inns of Ct Sch. of Law, 1973–76; Dir of Studies, Internat. Law Assoc., 1982–91. Member: Panel of Conciliators and Panel of Arbitrators, ICSID (World Bank), 1988–98; Internat. Law Commn, UN, 1996– (Chm., 2007–08); Judge, 1995–, Pres., 1996–, Eur. Nuclear Energy Tribunal. Delegate, OUP, 1984–94. Lectr, Hague Acad. of Internat. Law, 1979, 1995. Editor, British Year Book of International Law, 1974–99. Mem., Inst. of Internat. Law, 1985– (Associate Mem., 1977; Third Vice-Pres., 2001–). Hon. Mem., Amer. Soc. of Internat. Law, 2004. FBA 1979. Japan Foundn Award, 1978. Comdr, Royal Norwegian OM, 1993. *Publications:* International Law and the Use of Force by States, 1963; Principles of Public International Law, 1966, 6th edn 2003 (Russian edn, ed G. I. Tunkin, 1977; Japanese edn, 1989; Portuguese edn, 1998; Chinese edn, 2003; Certif. of Merit, Amer. Soc. of Internat. Law, 1976); Basic Documents in International Law, 1967, 5th edn 2002; The Law Relating to Public Order, 1968; Basic Documents on Human Rights, 1971, 5th edn 2006; Basic Documents on African Affairs, 1971; African Boundaries, a legal and diplomatic encyclopaedia, 1979; State Responsibility, part 1, 1983; (ed jtly) Liber Amicorum for Lord Wilberforce, 1987. *Recreation:* travel. *Address:* Blackstone Chambers, Blackstone House, Temple, EC4Y 9BW. *T:* (020) 7583 1770.

BROWNLOW, 7th Baron *cr* 1776; **Edward John Peregrine Cust;** Bt 1677; Chairman and Managing Director of Harris & Dixon (Underwriting Agencies) Ltd, 1976–82; *b* 25 March 1936; *o s* of 6th Baron Brownlow and Katherine Hariot (*d* 1952), 2nd *d* of Sir David Alexander Kinloch, 11th Bt, CB, MVO; *S* father, 1978; *m* 1964, Shirlie Edith, 2nd *d* of late John Yeomans, The Manor Farm, Hill Croome, Upton-on-Severn, Worcs; one *s*. *Educ:* Eton. Member of Lloyd's, 1961–88, and 1993–96; Director: Hand-in-Hand Fire and Life Insurance Soc. (branch office of Commercial Union Assurance Co. Ltd), 1962–82; Ermitage International Ltd, 1988–99; Vice Chm., Ermitage Global Wealth Mgt Jersey Ltd, 2007–. High Sheriff of Lincolnshire, 1978–79. CStJ 1999 (Chm. Council, Jersey, 1996–2005). *Heir: s* Hon. Peregrine Edward Quintin Cust, *b* 9 July 1974. *Address:* La Maison des Prés, St Peter, Jersey JE3 7EL. *Clubs:* White's; United, Victoria (Jersey).

BROWNLOW, Air Vice-Marshal Bertrand, (John), CB 1982; OBE 1967; AFC 1962; FRAeS; aviation consultant, since 1997; *b* 13 Jan. 1929; *s* of Robert John Brownlow and Helen Louise Brownlow; *m* 1958, Kathleen Shannon; one *s* one *d* (and one *s* decd). *Educ:* Beaufort Lodge Sch. Joined RAF, 1947; 12 and 101 Sqdns, ADC to AOC 1 Gp, 103 Sqdn, 213 Sqdn, Empire Test Pilots' Sch., OC Structures and Mech. Eng Flt RAE Farnborough, RAF Staff Coll., Air Min. Op. Requirements, 1949–64; Wing Comdr Ops, RAF Lyneham, 1964–66; Jt Services Staff Coll., 1966–67; DS RAF Staff Coll., 1967–68; Def. and Air Attaché, Stockholm, 1969–71; CO Experimental Flying, RAE Farnborough, 1971–73; Asst Comdt, Office and Flying Trng, RAF Coll., Cranwell, 1973–74; Dir of Flying (R&D), MoD, 1974–77; Comdt, A&AEE, 1977–80; Comdt, RAF Coll., Cranwell, 1980–82; Dir Gen., Trng, RAF, 1982–83, retired 1984. Exec. Dir, Marshall of Cambridge (Engineering), subseq. Dir, Marshall Aerospace, 1987–94. Mem., CAA, 1994–96. Gov., Papworth Hosp. NHS Foundn Trust, 2004–. FRAeS 1981. Silver Medal, Royal Aero Club, 1983, for servs to RAF gliding; Sword of Honour, GAPAN, 2000. *Recreations:* squash, tennis, golf, gliding (Gold C with two diamonds). *Address:* Woodside, Abbotsley Road, Croxton, St Neots PE19 6SZ. *T:* (01480) 880663; *e-mail:* john.brownlow1@btinternet.com. *Club:* Royal Air Force.

BROWNLOW, James Hilton, CBE 1984; QPM 1978; Adviser on Ground Control, Football Association, 1990–94; HM Inspector of Constabulary for North Eastern England, 1983–89; *b* 19 Oct. 1925; *s* of late Ernest Cuthbert Brownlow and Beatrice Annie Elizabeth Brownlow; *m* 1947, Joyce Key; two *d*. *Educ:* Worksop Central School. Solicitor's Clerk, 1941–43; served war, RAF, Flt/Sgt (Air Gunner), 1943–47. Police Constable, Leicester City Police, 1947; Police Constable to Det. Chief Supt, Kent County Constabulary, 1947–69; Asst Chief Constable, Hertfordshire Constabulary, 1969–75; Asst to HM Chief Inspector of Constabulary, Home Office, 1975–76; Dep. Chief Constable, Greater Manchester Police, 1976–79; Chief Constable, S Yorks Police, 1979–82. Mem., Parole Bd, 1991–94. Queen's Commendation for Brave Conduct, 1972. Officer Brother OStJ 1981. *Recreations:* golf, gardening.

BROWNLOW, Air Vice-Marshal John; *see* Brownlow, Air Vice-Marshal B.

BROWNLOW, Kevin; author; film director; *b* 2 June 1938; *s* of Thomas and Niña Brownlow; *m* 1969, Virginia Keane; one *d*. *Educ:* University College School. Entered documentaries, 1955; became film editor, 1958, and edited many documentaries; with Andrew Mollo dir. feature films: It Happened Here, 1964; Winstanley, 1975; dir. Charm of Dynamite, 1967, about Abel Gance, and restored his classic film Napoleon (first shown London, Nov. 1980, NY, Jan. 1981). Directed TV documentaries: Universal Horror, 1998; Lon Chaney: a thousand faces, 2000; Cecil B. DeMille: American Epic, 2003; with David Gill: Hollywood, 1980; Thames Silents, 1981–90 (incl. The Big Parade); Channel Four Silents, 1991–99 (incl. Sunrise); Unknown Chaplin, 1983; British Cinema—Personal View, 1986; Buster Keaton: a Hard Act to Follow, 1987; Harold Lloyd—The Third Genius, 1990; D. W. Griffith, Father of Film, 1993; Cinema Europe—The Other Hollywood, 1995; with Michael Kloft: The Tramp and the Dictator, 2002; with Christopher Bird: Buster Keaton—So Funny It Hurt, 2004; Garbo, 2005; I'm King Kong!—The Exploits of Merian C. Cooper, 2005. *Publications:* The Parade's Gone By…, 1968; How it Happened Here, 1968; The War, the West and the Wilderness, 1978; Hollywood: the Pioneers, 1979; Napoleon: Abel Gance's classic film, 1983; Behind The Mask of Innocence, 1991; David Lean: a biography, 1996; Mary Pickford Rediscovered, 1999; The Search for Charlie Chaplin, 2005; many articles on film history. *Recreation:* motion pictures. *Address:* Photoplay Productions, 21 Princess Road, NW1 8JR.

BROWNLOW, Peter; Managing Director and Financial Director, Border Television plc, 1996–2000; *b* 4 June 1945; *s* of Frederick and Margaret Brownlow; *m* 1972, Judith Margaret Alton; two *s*. *Educ:* Rothwell Grammar Sch.; Leeds Poly. ACMA 1970. Company Accountant: John Menzies plc, 1967–70; United Newspapers, 1970–82; Co. Sec., Border Television plc, 1982–84; Financial Dir, 1984–96, non-exec. Dep. Chm., 1995–2006, Cumberland Building Soc. Director: Century Radio Ltd, 1993–2000; Century Radio 106 Ltd, 1996–2000; Century Radio 105 Ltd, 1997–2000; Sun FM Ltd, 1997–2000; Border Radio Hldgs, 1997–2000. *Recreations:* sailing, fell walking, gardening. *Address:* Quarry Bank, Capon Hill, Brampton, Cumbria CA8 1QN.

BROWNRIGG, Sir Nicholas (Gawen), 5th Bt *cr* 1816; *b* 22 Dec. 1932; *s* of late Gawen Egremont Brownrigg and Baroness Lucia von Borosini, *o d* of Baron Victor von Borosini, California; *S* grandfather, 1939; *m* 1959, Linda Louise Lovelace (marr. diss. 1965), Beverly Hills, California; one *s* one *d*; *m* 1971, Valerie Ann, *d* of Julian A. Arden, Livonia, Michigan, USA. *Educ:* Midland Sch.; Stanford Univ. *Heir: s* Michael Gawen Brownrigg [*b* 11 Oct. 1961; *m* 1990, Margaret Dillon, *d* of Dr Clay Burchell; three *s* one *d*]. *Address:* PO Box 1847, Fort Bragg, CA 95437, USA.

BROWNSWORD, Andrew; Chairman and Chief Executive, Andrew Brownsword Group, since 1993; Chairman: Bath Priory Group Ltd, since 1992; Bath Rugby plc, since 1996; Paxton & Whitfield Ltd, since 2002; Snow & Rock Ltd; Andrew Brownsword Hotels Ltd; *s* of Douglas and Eileen Brownsword; *m* 1983, Christina Brenchley; two *d*. *Educ:* Harvey Grammar Sch., Folkestone. Formed A. Brownsword and Co., wholesale distributors of greetings cards and stationery, 1971; formed the Andrew Brownsword Collection Ltd, 1975; acquired Gordon Fraser Gallery, 1989; greetings cards business acquired by Hallmark Cards, 1994. *Recreations:* sailing, ski-ing, hill-walking. *Address:* 4 Queen Square, Bath BA1 2HA.

BROWSE, Sir Norman (Leslie), Kt 1994; MD; FRCS, FRCP; President of the States of Alderney, since 2002; Professor of Surgery and Senior Consultant Surgeon, St Thomas's Hospital Medical School, 1981–96, now Professor Emeritus; Consulting Surgeon, St Thomas' Hospital, since 1996; President, Royal College of Surgeons, 1992–95; *b* 1 Dec. 1931; *s* of Reginald and Margaret Browse; *m* 1957, Dr Jeanne Menage; one *s* one *d*. *Educ:* St Bartholomew's Hosp. Med. Coll. (MB BS 1955); Bristol Univ. (MD 1961). FRCS 1959; FRCP 1993. Capt. RAMC, Cyprus, 1957–59 (GSM 1958). Lectr in Surgery, Westminster Hosp., 1962–64; Harkness Fellow, Res. Associate, Mayo Clinic, Rochester, Minn, 1964–65; St Thomas's Hospital Medical School: Reader in Surgery, 1965–72; Prof. of Vascular Surgery, 1972–81. Hon. Consultant (Vascular Surgery) to: Army, 1980–96; RAF, 1982–96. President: European Soc. for Cardiovascular Surgery, 1982–84; Assoc. of Profs of Surgery, 1985–87; Surgical Res. Soc., 1990–92; Venous Forum, RSM, 1989–91; Vascular Surgical Soc. of GB and Ireland, 1991–92; Mem. Council, RCS, 1986–95 (Mem., Ct of Patrons, 1996–); Co-Chm., Senate of Surgery, 1993–95; Chm., Jt Consultants Cttee, 1994–98. Chairman: British Atherosclerosis Soc., 1988–91; Lord Brock Meml Trust, 1994–2001; Vice-Chm., British Vascular Foundn, 1997–2002. Trustee, Restoration of Appearance and Function Trust, 1996–2001; Patron: INPUT Trust, 1999–2004; HOPE, Wessex Med. Trust, 2002–. Gov., Amer. Coll. of Surgeons, 1997–2002. Mem. Council, Marlborough Coll., 1990–2001. Sims Travelling Prof., 1990; Lectures: Arris & Gale, 1966, Vicary, 2000, RCS; Marjory Budd, Bristol, 1982; Pierce Golding, London, Leriche, Madrid, 1986; Abraham Colles (also Medal), 1990, Kinmonth (also Medal), 1991, Dublin; Bernstein, La Jolla, 1996; James Mousley, Winchester, 1997; John Clewes, Ann Arbor, Charles Robb, Washington, 1998; Ratschow (also Medal), Mainz, 2007. FKC 2000. Hon. FRCP&SGlas 1993; Hon. FSACM 1993; Hon. FRACS 1994; Hon. FDS RCS 1994; Hon. FCEM (Hon. FFAEM 1994); Hon. FRSCI 1995; Hon. FACS 1995; Hon. FRCSE 1996. Hon. Member: Amer. Surgical Vascular Soc., 1987; Australian Vascular Soc., 1987; Amer. Vascular Biol. Soc., 1988; Amer. Venous Forum, 1991; Soc. for Clin. Vascular Surg., USA, 1993. Distinguished Alumnus, Mayo Clinic, 1993; Hon. Academician, Acad. of Athens, 1995. Hon. Freeman, Barbers' Co., 1997. *Publications:* Physiology and Pathology of Bed Rest, 1964; Symptoms and Signs of Surgical Disease, 1978, 4th edn 2005; Reducing Operations for Lymphoedema, 1986; Diseases of the Veins, 1988, 2nd edn 1999; Diseases of the Lymphatics, 2003; papers on all aspects of vascular disease. *Recreations:* marine art, mediaeval history, sailing. *Address:* Corbet House, Butes Lane, Alderney, Channel Islands GY9 3UW. *T:* (01481) 823716.

BRUBECK, David Warren; jazz musician, composer; *b* Concord, Calif, 6 Dec. 1920; *s* of Howard Brubeck and Elizabeth Ivey; *m* 1942, Iola Whitlock; five *s* one *d*. *Educ:* Univ. of the Pacific (BA); graduate study with Darius Milhaud, Mills Coll. Leader, Dave Brubeck Octet, and Trio, 1946–; formed Dave Brubeck Quartet, 1951; played colls, fests, clubs and symphony orchs; 3 month tour of Europe and Middle East (for US State Dept) and tours in Aust., Japan, USSR and S America. Numerous recordings. Has composed: *ballet:* Points on Jazz, 1962; Glances, 1976; *orchestral:* Elementals, 1963; They All Sang Yankee Doodle, 1976; *flute and guitar:* Tritonis, 1979; *piano:* Reminiscences of the Cattle Country, 1946; Four by Four, 1946; *oratorios:* The Light in the Wilderness, 1968; Beloved Son, 1978; The Voice of the Holy Spirit, 1985; *cantatas:* Gates of Justice, 1969; Truth is Fallen, 1971; La Fiesta de la Posada, 1975; In Praise of Mary, 1989; *chorus and orchestra:* Pange Lingua Variations, 1983; Upon This Rock Chorale and Fugue, 1987; Lenten Triptych, 1988; Joy in the Morning, 1991; *mass:* To Hope!, a celebration, 1980; *SATB Chorus:* I See Satie, 1987; Four New England Pieces, 1988; Earth is our mother (with chamber orch.), 1992; *jazz opera:* Cannery Row Suite, 2006; over 250 *jazz* compositions incl. Blue Rondo à la Turk; In Your Own Sweet Way; The Duke. Duke Ellington Fellow, Yale Univ., 1973. Hon. PhD: Univ. of Pacific; Fairfield Univ.; Bridgeport Univ., 1982; Mills Coll., 1982; Niagara Univ., 1989; Kalamazoo Coll., 1991. Hollywood Walk of Fame. Winner, jazz polls conducted by Downbeat, Melody Maker, Cashbox, Billboard and Playboy magazines, 1952–55; Broadcast Music Inc. Jazz Pioneer Award, 1985; Compostela Humanitarian award, 1986; Connecticut Arts award, 1987; American Eagle award, Nat. Music Council, 1988; Pantheon of the Arts, Univ. of the Pacific, 1989; Gerard Manley Hopkins Award, Fairfield Univ., 1990; Distinguished Achievement Award, Simon's Rock Coll., 1991; Connecticut Bar Assoc. Award, 1992; Nat. Medal of the Arts, USA, 1994; Lifetime Achievement Award, Nat. Acad. of Recording Arts and Scis, 1996. Officier de l'Ordre des Arts et des Lettres (France), 1990. *Address:* Derry Music, 601 Montgomery Street, Suite 800, San Francisco, CA 94111, USA; c/o Sutton Artists Corporation, 20 West Park Avenue, Suite 305, Long Beach, NY 11561, USA; Box 216, Wilton, CT 06897, USA.

BRUCE; *see* Hovell-Thurlow-Cumming-Bruce.

BRUCE, family name of **Baron Aberdare,** of **Lord Balfour of Burleigh,** and of **Earl of Elgin.**

BRUCE, Lord; Charles Edward Bruce; DL; Director: Scottish Lime Centre Trust; Environmental Trust for Scotland; Ashra Group Ltd (Environmental Consultants); *b* 19 Oct. 1961; *s* and *heir* of 11th Earl of Elgin, *qv*; *m* 1st, 1990, Amanda (marr. diss. 2000), *yr d* of James Movius; two *s* one *d*; 2nd, 2001, Dr Alice Enders; one *s*. *Educ:* Eton College; Univ. of St Andrews (MA Hons). A Page of Honour to HM the Queen Mother, 1975–77. Former Dir, Assoc. for Protection of Rural Scotland. Trustee, Historic Scotland Foundn; Chm. Patrons, Nat. Galls of Scotland. Dir, Canadian Friends of Scotland Foundn; Hon. Vice Pres., St Andrew Soc. Mem., Queen's Bodyguard for Scotland, Royal Co. of Archers. DL Fife, 1997. Hon. Major, 31 Combat Engr Regt (The Elgins), Canadian Forces; Officer, 78th Fraser Highlanders, Ile St Hélène Garrison, Montreal. *Heir: s* Hon. James Andrew Charles Robert Bruce, Master of Bruce, *b* 16 Nov. 1991. *Address:* The Abbey House, Culross, Fife KY12 8JB. *T:* (01383) 880333, *Fax:* (01383) 881218. *Club:* Dunfermline United Burns (Pres.).

BRUCE, Prof. Alistair Cameron, PhD; Professor of Decision and Risk Analysis, University of Nottingham, since 1999; Director, Nottingham University Business School, 2003–07; *b* 21 May 1955; *s* of Ian Paterson Bruce and Margaret Muriel Bruce; *m* 1989, Gillian Amy Tinker; one *s* two *d*. *Educ:* Univ. of St Andrews (MA Hons Econs 1977); Heriot-Watt Univ. (PhD Econs 1982). Lectr, Heriot-Watt Univ., 1980–81; University of Nottingham: Lectr, 1981–94; Sen. Lectr, 1994–99. *Publications:* Decision, Risk and Reward (with J. E. V. Johnson), 2007; articles in learned jls in areas of econs, mgt, organisational behaviour, decision making and psychology. *Recreations:* horseracing, football, visiting pubs, gardening, cooking, wine, railway history. *Address:* Nottingham University Business School, Jubilee Campus, Nottingham NG8 1BB. *T:* (0115) 951 5505; *e-mail:* alistair.bruce@nottingham.ac.uk.

BRUCE, Christopher, CBE 1998; dancer, choreographer, opera producer; Artistic Director, Rambert Dance Company, 1994–2002; Resident Choreographer, Houston Ballet, since 1989; *b* Leicester, 3 Oct. 1945; *m* Marian Bruce; two *s* one *d*. *Educ:* Ballet Rambert Sch. Joined Ballet Rambert Company, 1963; leading dancer with co. when re-formed as modern dance co., 1966; Associate Dir, 1975–79; Associate Choreographer, 1979–87; Associate Choreographer, London Fest. Ballet, later English Nat. Ballet, 1986–91. Leading roles include: Pierrot Lunaire, The Tempest (Tetley); L'Apres-Midi d'un Faune (Nijinsky); Cruel Garden (also choreographed with Lindsay Kemp); choreographed: for Ballet Rambert: George Frideric (1st work), 1969; For These Who Die as Cattle, 1971; There Was a Time, 1972; Weekend, 1974; Ancient Voices of Children, 1975; Black Angels, 1976; Cruel Garden, 1977; Night with Waning Moon, 1979; Dancing Day, 1981; Ghost Dances, 1981; Berlin Requiem, 1982; Concertino, 1983; Intimate Pages, 1984; Sergeant Early's Dream, 1984; Ceremonies, 1986; Crossing, 1994; Meeting Point, 1995; Quicksilver, 1996; Stream, 1997; Four Scenes, 1998; God's Plenty, 1999; Grinning in Your Face, 2001; A Steel Garden, 2005; for London Festival Ballet, later English National Ballet: Land, 1985; The World Again, 1986; The Dream is Over, 1987; Swansong, 1987; Symphony in Three Movements, 1989; for Tanz Forum, Cologne: Wings, 1970; Cantata, 1981; for Nederlands Dans Theater: Village Songs, 1981; Curses and Blessings, 1983; Moonshine, 1993; for Houston Ballet: Gautama Buddha, 1989; Journey, 1990; Nature Dances, 1992; Hush, 2005; for Geneva: Rooster, 1991 (restaged for London Contemporary Dance Theatre, 1992); Kingdom, 1993; for London Contemporary Dance Theatre, Waiting, 1993; for Royal Ballet, Three Songs, Two Voices, 2005; works for Batsheva Dance Co., Munich Opera Ballet, Gulbenkian Ballet Co., Australian Dance Theatre, Royal Danish Ballet, Royal Swedish Ballet. Kent Opera: choreographed and produced: Monteverdi's Il Ballo delle Ingrate, 1980; Combattimento di Tancredi e Clorinda, 1981; chor. John Blow's Venus and Adonis, 1980; co-prod Handel's Agrippina, 1982. Choreographed Mutiny (musical), Piccadilly, 1985. TV productions: Ancient Voices of Children, BBC, 1977; Cruel Garden, BBC, 1981–82; Ghost Dances, Channel 4, 1982, Danmark Radio, 1990; Requiem, Danish-German co-prodn, 1982; Silence is the end of our Song, Danish TV, 1984. Hon. Life Mem., Amnesty Internat., 2002. Hon. DArt De Montfort, 2000; Hon. DLitt Exeter, 2001. Evening Standard's inaugural Dance Award, 1974; Internat. Theatre Inst. Award, 1993; Evening Standard Ballet Award for outstanding artistic achievement, 1996; de Valois Award, Critics' Circle Nat. Dance Awards, 2003. *Address:* c/o Rambert Dance Co., 94 Chiswick High Road, W4 1SH; Houston Ballet, 1916 West Gray, PO 13150, Houston, TX 77219–3150, USA.

BRUCE, David, CA; Partner, Deloitte Haskins & Sells, 1974–87; *b* 21 Jan. 1927; *s* of David Bruce and Margaret (*née* Gregson); *m* 1955, Joy Robertson McAslan (*d* 1999); four *d*. *Educ:* High School of Glasgow. Commissioned, Royal Corps of Signals, 1947–49. Qualified as Chartered Accountant, 1955; Partner, Kerr McLeod & Co., Chartered Accountants, 1961 (merged with Deloitte Haskins & Sells, 1974); retired 1987. Vice-Pres., Inst. of Chartered Accountants of Scotland, 1978–79 and 1979–80, Pres. 1980–81. Mem., Council on Tribunals, 1984–90 (Mem., Scottish Cttee, 1984–90). *Address:* 8 Beechwood Court, Bearsden, Glasgow G61 2RY.

BRUCE, Fiona; Presenter: BBC Television News, since 1999; Antiques Roadshow, since 2008; *b* 25 April 1964; *d* of John and Rosemary Bruce; *m* 1995, Nigel; one *s* one *d*. *Educ:* Hertford Coll., Oxford (MA French/Italian). Joined BBC, 1989: researcher, Panorama, 1989–91; reporter: Breakfast News, 1991–92; First Sight, 1992–93; Public Eye, 1993–95; Newsnight, 1995–98; Presenter: Antiques Show, 1998–2000; Six O'Clock News, 1999; Ten O'Clock News, 1999–; Crimewatch UK, 2000–08; Real Story, 2003–07; Call My Bluff, 2003–. *Recreation:* playing with my children. *Address:* c/o BBC News, TV Centre, Wood Lane, W12 7RJ.

BRUCE, Sir (Francis) Michael Ian; *see* Bruce, Sir Michael Ian.

BRUCE, George John Done, RP 1959; painter of portraits, landscapes, still life, flowers; *b* 28 March 1930; *s* of 11th Lord Balfour of Burleigh, Brucefield, Clackmannan, Scotland and Violet Dorothy, *d* of Richard Henry Done, Tarporley, Cheshire; *b* of 12th Lord Balfour of Burleigh, *qv*. *Educ:* Byam Shaw Sch. of Drawing and Painting; by his portrait sitters. Pres., Royal Soc. of Portrait Painters, 1991–94 (Hon. Sec., 1970–84; Vice-Pres., 1984–89). *Recreations:* ski-ing, windsurfing, talking books. *Address:* 6 Pembroke Walk, W8 6PQ. *T:* (020) 7937 1493. *Club:* Athenæum.

BRUCE, Rt Rev. George Lindsey Russell; *see* Ontario, Bishop of.

BRUCE, Sir Hervey (James Hugh); *see* Bruce-Clifton, Sir H. J. H.

BRUCE, Ian Cameron; Chairman, Ian Bruce Associates Ltd, management consultancy and property co., since 1975; *b* 14 March 1947; *s* of Henry Bruce and Ellen Flora Bruce (*née* Bingham); *m* 1969, Hazel Bruce (*née* Roberts); one *s* three *d*. *Educ:* Chelmsford Tech. High Sch.; Bradford Univ.; Mid-Essex Tech. Coll. Mem., Inst. of Management Services. Student apprentice, Marconi, 1965–67; Work Study Engineer: Marconi, 1967–69; Pye Unicam, 1969–70; Haverhill Meat Products, 1970–71; Factory Manager and Work Study Manager, BEPI (Pye), 1971–74; Factory Manager, Sinclair Electronics, 1974–75; Chm. and Founder, gp of employment agencies and management consultants, 1975–. MP (C) Dorset South, 1987–2001; contested (C) same seat, 2001. PPS to Social Security Ministers, 1992–94. Member, Select Committee: on Employment, 1990–92; on Science and Technol., 1995–97; on Information, 1997–2001; Vice-Chm., PITCOM, 1997–2001; Jt Chm., All Party Street Children Gp, 1992–2001; Vice Chairman: Cons. Employment Cttee, 1992; Cons. Social Security Cttee, 1995–97 (Sec., 1991–92); Cons. Educn and Employment Cttee, 1995–2001; Cons. Trade and Industry Cttee, 1999–2001; Pres., Cons. Technol. Forum, 1999–2001. Jt Chm., British Cayman Island Gp, 1995–2001; Vice Chm., British-Nepal Gp, 1993–2001; Secretary: British-Finnish Gp, 1995–2001; British-Romanian Gp, 1995–2001; Chm., European Informatics Market, 1993–2002. Parly Consultant to Telecommunication Managers Assoc., 1989–2001, to Trevor Gilbert Associates, 1993–2002, to Fedn of Recruitment and Employment Services, 1996–97. ICT Consultant, Engrg Manufg Trng Authy, 2001–05; Employment Expert Witness, TGA, 2001–04. Foster parent, 1974–77 and 2006–. Knight, First Class, Order of Lion of Finland, 2001. *Publications:* numerous articles in press and magazines, both technical and political. *Recreations:* scouting, badminton, writing, wind surfing, sailing, camping, squash, ski-ing. *Address:* 14 Preston Road, Weymouth, Dorset DT3 6PZ. *T:* (01305) 833320; *e-mail:* iancbruce@tiscali.co.uk.

BRUCE, Ian Waugh, CBE 2004; Vice-President, Royal National Institute of Blind People, since 2003 (Director-General, 1983–2003); Founder Director, and Visiting Professor, Centre for Charity Effectiveness, Sir John Cass Business School, City of London (formerly VOLPROF, the Centre for Voluntary Sector and Not-for-Profit Management, City University Business School), since 1991; *b* 21 April 1945; *s* of Thomas Waugh Bruce and Una (*née* Eagle); *m* 1971, Anthea Christine, (Tina), *d* of Dr P. R. Rowland, FRSC; one *s* one *d*. *Educ:* King Edward VI Sch., Southampton; Central High Sch., Arizona; Univ. of Birmingham (BSocSc Hons 1968). Apprentice Chem. Engr, Courtaulds, 1964–65; Marketing Trainee, then Manager, Unilever, 1968–70; Appeals and PR Officer, then Asst Dir, Age Concern England, 1970–74; Dir, The Volunteer Centre UK, 1975–81; Controller of Secretariat, then Asst Chief Exec., Bor. of Hammersmith and Fulham, 1981–83. Chm., Coventry Internat. Centre, 1964; spokesman, Artists Now, 1973–77. Consultant, UN Div. of Social Affairs, 1970–72; Mem., Prime Minister's Gp on Voluntary Action, 1978–79; Founding Sec., Volunteurope, Brussels, 1979–81; Adviser, BBC Community Progs Unit, 1979–81. Member: Art Panel, Art Film Cttee and New Activities Cttee, Arts Council of GB, 1967–71; National Good Neighbour Campaign, 1977–79; Exec. Cttee, 1978–81, 1990–94, Adv. Council, 1998–, NCVO; Council, Retired Executives Action Clearing House, 1978–83; Adv. Council, Centre for Policy on Ageing, 1979–83; Educn Adv. Council, IBA, 1981–83; Disability Alliance Steering Cttee, 1985–93; Exec. Cttee, Age Concern England, 1986–92, 2002–04; Nat. Adv. Council on Employment of People with Disabilities, 1987–98; DHSS Cttee on Inter-Agency Collaboration on Visual Handicap, 1987–88; Bd, Central London TEC, 1990–97 (Dep. Chm., 1996–97); Bd, Focus TEC, 1997–99; Founding Co-Chair, Disability Benefits Consortium, 1988–2001; Chair: Nat. Adv. Cttee, Johns Hopkins Univ. Comparative Non Profit Study, 1996–99; Res. Cttee, Nat. Giving Campaign, 2001–04; Sec., World Nonprofit Academic Centres' Council, 2008–. CCMI (CIMgt 1991); FRSA 1991. Hon. DSocSc Birmingham, 1995. Sir Raymond Priestley Expeditionary Award, Univ. of Birmingham, 1968; UK Charity Lifetime Achievement Award, 2001 and 2003. *Publications:* Public Relations and the Social Services, 1972; (jtly) Patronage of the Creative Artist, 1974; Blind and Partially Sighted Adults in Britain, 1991; Meeting Need: successful charity marketing, 1994, 3rd edn 2005; papers on vision impairment, voluntary and community work, older people, contemporary art, management and marketing. *Recreations:* the arts, the countryside. *Address:* Ormond House Cottage, Ormond Road, Richmond, Surrey TW10 6TH. *Club:* ICA.

BRUCE, Hon. James Michael Edward, CBE 1992; Founder and Chairman, Scottish Woodlands Ltd, 1967–93; *b* 26 Aug. 1927; *s* of 10th Earl of Elgin, KT, CMG, TD and Hon. Katherine Elizabeth Cochrane, Countess of Elgin, DBE (*d* 1989); *m* 1st, 1950, Hon. (Margaret) Jean Dagbjørt Coats (marr. diss.), *d* of 2nd Baron Glentanar; two *s* one *d* (and one *s* decd); 2nd, 1975, Morven-Anne Macdonald (*d* 1994); two *s* two *d*; 3rd, 2000, Mrs Mary Elizabeth Hamilton. *Educ:* Eton; RAC, Cirencester (Goldstand Medal). FInstD. Served Scots Guards, 2nd Lieut. Mem., Home Grown Timber Adv. Cttee, 1969–93; Dir, Forest Industry Cttee, 1989–93. Vice-Pres., Scottish Opera, 1985–94. FRSA (Council Mem., 1988–95); Hon. Fellow: Game Conservancy, 1993; Scottish Council for Development and Industry, 1993. JP Perth, 1962–2002. *Recreations:* gardens, boats, fishing, shooting. *Address:* Dron House, Balmanno, Perth PH2 9HG. *T:* (01738) 812786. *Clubs:* Pratt's; New (Edinburgh).

BRUCE, Karen; choreographer and director; *b* 25 March 1963; *d* of George and Elizabeth Bruce. *Educ:* Betty Laine Theatre Arts. *Theatre:* assistant director: Annie, Crucible, Sheffield; Hello Dolly!, My One and Only, Palladium; Dir and Associate Choreographer, Fame, Cambridge Th. and tour, 1996–2007, Aldwych, 2006; Associate Dir and Choreographer, Saturday Night Fever, Palladium, UK and world tour, 1998–99, NY, 1999–2000; Choreographer: Chorus Line, 2003, Sweet Charity, 2004, Crucible, Sheffield; Pacific Overtures, Donmar Warehouse, 2004 (Olivier Award for Best Choreography); Annie Get Your Gun, tour, 2005; Brighton Rock, Almeida, 2005; Far Pavilions, Shaftesbury, 2005; Dir and Choreographer, Footloose, Novello and tour, 2006; has also choreographed for TV; choreographer, opening ceremony for Commonwealth Games, Manchester, 2002. *Address:* 2 Lavell Street, N16 9LS. *T:* (020) 7249 9180; *e-mail:* BKarenbruce99@aol.com.

BRUCE, Rt Hon. Malcolm (Gray); PC 2006; MP Gordon, since 1983 (L 1983–88, Lib Dem since 1988); *b* 17 Nov. 1944; *s* of David Stewart Bruce and Kathleen Elmslie (*née* Delf); *m* 1st, 1969, Veronica Jane Wilson (marr. diss. 1992); one *s* one *d*; 2nd, 1998, Rosemary Vetterlein; one *s* two *d*. *Educ:* Wrekin Coll., Shropshire; St Andrews Univ. (MA 1966); Strathclyde Univ. (MSc 1970). Liverpool Daily Post, 1966–67; Buyer, Boots Pure Drug Co., 1967–68; A. Goldberg & Son, 1968–69; Res. Information Officer, NE Scotland Develt Authority, 1971–75; Marketing Dir, Noroil Publishing House (UK), 1975–81; Jt Editor/Publisher/ Dir, Aberdeen Petroleum Publishing, 1981–84. Called to the Bar, Gray's Inn, 1995. Dep. Chm., Scottish Liberal Party, 1975–84 (Energy Spokesman, 1975–83); Liberal Parly Spokesman on Scottish Affairs, 1983–85, on Energy, 1985–87, on Trade and Industry, 1987–88; Alliance Parly Spokesman on Employment, 1987; Lib Dem Spokesman on Natural Resources (energy and conservation), 1988–90, on Trade and Industry, 1992–94, 2003–05, on Treasury affairs, 1994–99; Chm., Parly Lib Dems, 1999–2001; Lib Dem Spokesman on envmt, food and rural affairs, 2001–02. Member: Select Cttee on Trade and Industry, 1992–94, Treasury, 1994–98; Standards and Privileges Cttee, 1999–2001; Chair, Select Cttee on Internat. Develt, 2005–. Leader, Scottish Liberal Democrats, 1988–92. Mem. Bd, Britain in Europe, 2004–05. Rector of Dundee Univ., 1986–89. Vice-Pres., Nat. Deaf Children's Soc., 1990– (Pres., Grampian Br., 1985–); Trustee, RNID, 2004–. *Publications:* A New Life for the Country: a rural development programme for West Aberdeenshire, 1978; Putting Energy to Work, 1981; (with others) A New Deal for Rural Scotland, 1983; (with Paddy Ashdown) Growth from the Grassroots, 1985; (with Ray Michie) Toward a Federal UK, 1997. *Recreations:* theatre, music, travel, fresh Scottish air. *Address:* Grove Cottage, Grove Lane, Torphins AB31 4HJ. *T:* (01339) 889120.

BRUCE, Sir Michael Ian, 12th Bt *cr* 1628; partner, Gossard-Bruce Co., since 1953; President, Newport Sailing Club Inc. and Academy of Sail, Newport Beach, 1978–2000; *b* 3 April 1926; *s* of Sir Michael William Selby Bruce, 11th Bt and Doreen Dalziel, *d* of late W. F. Greenwell; *S* father 1957; holds dual UK and US citizenship; has discontinued first forename, Francis; *m* 1st, 1947, Barbara Stevens (marr. diss., 1957), *d* of Frank J. Lynch; two *s*; 2nd, 1961, Frances Keegan (marr. diss., 1963); 3rd, 1966, Marilyn Ann (marr. diss., 1975), *d* of Carter Mulally; 4th, Patricia Gail (marr. diss. 1991), *d* of Frederich Root; 5th, 1994, Alessandra Conforto, MD. *Educ:* Forman School, Litchfield, Conn; Pomfret, Conn. Served United States Marine Corps, 1943–46 (Letter of Commendation); S Pacific area two years, Bismarck Archipelago, Bougainville, Philippines. Master Mariner's Ticket, 1968; Pres., American Maritime Co., 1981–2000. Mem., US Naval Inst. *Recreations:* sailing, spear-fishing. *Heir:* *s* Michael Ian Richard Bruce, now Ross [*b* 10 Dec. 1950; *m* 2005, Sandra Salemi; one adopted *s*]. *Clubs:* Rockaway Hunt; Lawrence Beach; Balboa Bay (Newport Beach).

BRUCE, Michael Stewart Rae; *see* Marnoch, Rt Hon. Lord.

BRUCE, Prof. Peter George, PhD; FRS 2007; FRSE; FRSC; Wardlaw Professor of Chemistry, University of St Andrews, since 2007; *b* 2 Oct. 1956; *s* of George H. Bruce and Gladys I. Bruce; *m* 1982, Margaret Duncan; one *s* one *d*. *Educ:* Aberdeen Grammar Sch.; Univ. of Aberdeen (BSc 1978; PhD 1982). FRSC 1994; FRSE 1995. Postdoctoral Res. Fellow, Univ. of Oxford, 1982–85; Lectr, Heriot-Watt Univ., 1985–91; University of St Andrews: Reader, 1991–95; Founder and Dir, Centre for Advanced Materials, 1994–97; Prof. of Chemistry, 1995–2007; Hd, Sch. of Chemistry, 1997–2002. RSE Res.

Fellow, 1989–90; Royal Soc. Pickering Res. Fellow, 1990–95; Leverhulme Res. Fellow, 1995–98. Award for Achievements in Materials Chem., 1999, Beilby Medal, 2003, Interdisciplinary Award, 2003, John Jeyes Lect. and Medal, 2004, Solid State Chem. Award, 2005, RSC; Wolfson Merit Award, Royal Soc., 2001; Gunning Victoria Jubilee Prize Lect., RSE, 2004. *Publications:* Solid State Electrochemistry, 1994; articles in Nature, Science, Jl of ACS, Angewandte Chemie. *Recreations:* thinking, dining, music, running. *Address:* School of Chemistry, University of St Andrews, North Haugh, St Andrews, Fife KY16 9ST.

BRUCE, Prof. Steve, PhD; FBA 2003; FRSE; Professor of Sociology, since 1991, and Head, School of Social Science, since 2002, University of Aberdeen; *b* 1 April 1954; *s* of George Bruce and Maria (*née* Ivanova-Savova); *m* 1988, Elizabeth Struthers Duff; one *s* two *d*. *Educ:* Queen Victoria Sch., Dunblane; Univ. of Stirling (BA 1976; PhD 1980). Queen's University, Belfast: Lectr in Sociol., 1978–87; Reader in Sociol., 1987–89; Prof. of Sociol. and Hd, Dept of Sociol., 1989–91. FRSE 2005. *Publications:* No Pope of Rome: militant Protestantism in modern Scotland, 1985; God Save Ulster!: the religion and politics of Paisleyism, 1986; The Rise and Fall of the New Christian Right: Protestant politics in America, 1988; A House Divided: Protestantism, schism and secularization, 1990; Pray TV: televangelism in America, 1990; The Red Hand: loyalist paramilitaries in Northern Ireland, 1992; The Edge of the Union: the Ulster Loyalist political vision, 1994; Religion in Modern Britain, 1995; Religion in the Modern World: from cathedrals to cults, 1996; Conservative, Protestant Politics, 1998; Sociology: a very short introduction, 1999; Choice and Religion: a critique of rational choice theory, 1999; Fundamentalism, 2001; God is Dead: secularization in the West, 2002; Politics and Religion, 2003; (with Steven Yearley) A Dictionary of Sociology, 2004; (jtly) Sectarianism in Scotland, 2004. *Recreation:* playing in the Conglass Ceilidh Band. *Address:* School of Social Science, University of Aberdeen, Aberdeen AB24 3QY. *T:* (01224) 272729, *Fax:* (01224) 273442; *e-mail:* soc108@abdn.ac.uk.

BRUCE, Prof. Victoria Geraldine, OBE 1997; PhD; CPsychol, FBPsS; FRSE; FBA 1999; Head, School of Psychology, Newcastle University, since 2008; *b* 4 Jan. 1953; *d* of Charles Frederick Bruce and Geraldine Cordelia Diane (*née* Giffard); *Educ:* Newcastle upon Tyne Church High Sch.; Newnham Coll., Cambridge (BA Nat. Scis 1974; MA, PhD Psychol. 1978). CPsychol, FBPsS 1989. University of Nottingham: Lectr, 1978–88; Reader, 1988–90; Prof. of Psychology, 1990–92; Prof. of Psychology, 1992–2002, Dep. Principal (Res.), 1995–2001, Stirling Univ.; Vice Principal and Hd, Coll. of Humanities and Social Sci., Univ. of Edinburgh, 2002–08. Member: Neuroscis Bd, MRC, 1989–92; ESRC, 1992–96 (Chm., Res. Progs Bd, 1992–); SHEFC, 1995–2001 (Chm., Res. Policy Adv. Cttee, 1988–2001); Chairman: Psychology Panel, RAE, 1996, 2001, HEFCE; Main Panel K, 2008 RAE, HEFCE. President: Eur. Soc. for Cognitive Psychology, 1996–98; BPsS, 2001–02. Editor, British Jl of Psychology, 1995–2000. FRSE 1996. Hon. Fellow, Cardiff Univ., 2005. Hon. DSc: London, 2002; St Andrews, 2006. *Publications:* (with P. R. Green) Visual Perception: physiology, psychology and ecology, 1985, 4th edn (with P. R. Green and M. Georgeson) 2003; Recognising Faces, 1988; (with G. W. Humphreys) Visual Cognition: computational, experimental and neuropsychological perspectives, 1989; (ed) Face Recognition (special edn of European Jl of Cognitive Psychology), 1991; (ed jtly) Processing the Facial Image, 1992; (ed with A. M. Burton) Processing Images of Faces, 1992; (ed with G. W. Humphreys) Object and Face Recognition (special issue of Visual Cognition), 1994; (with I. Roth) Perception and Representation: current issues, 2nd edn 1995; (ed) Unsolved Mysteries of the Mind: tutorial essays in cognition, 1996; (with A. Young) In the Eye of the Beholder: the science of face perception, 1998; numerous articles in learned jls and edited books. *Recreations:* dogs, walking, games. *Address:* School of Psychology, Newcastle University, Ridley Building, Newcastle upon Tyne NE1 7RU. *T:* (0191) 222 6579.

BRUCE-CLIFTON, Sir Hervey (James Hugh), 7th Bt *cr* 1804; hotelier, Oaklands Country Manor; *b* 3 Sept. 1952; *s* of Sir Hervey John William Bruce, 6th Bt, and Crista, (*d* 1984), *y d* of late Lt-Col Chandos De Paravicini, OBE; changed name to Bruce-Clifton on inheriting Clifton estate, 1996; *S* father, 1971; *m* 1st, 1979, Charlotte (marr. diss. 1991), *e d* of Jack Gore; one *s* one *d*; 2nd, 1992, Joanna, *y d* of Frank Pope; two *s*. *Educ:* Eton; Officer Cadet School, Mons. Major, the Grenadier Guards, 1984–96. *Recreations:* bungee jumping, body surfing, riding, tapestry. *Heir: s* Hervey Hamish Peter Bruce, *b* 20 Nov. 1986. *Address:* PO Box 19, Van Reenen 3372, KwaZulu-Natal, South Africa. *Club:* Cavalry and Guards.

BRUCE-GARDNER, Sir Robert (Henry), 3rd Bt *cr* 1945, of Frilford, Berks; Director, Department of Conservation and Technology, Courtauld Institute, 1990–2000; *b* 10 June 1943; *s* of Sir Douglas Bruce-Gardner, 2nd Bt and of his 1st wife, Monica Flumerfelt (*née* Jefferson; decd); *S* father, 1997; *m* 1979, Veronica Ann Hand Oxborrow; two *s*. *Educ:* Uppingham; Reading Univ. (BA Fine Art); Courtauld Inst., Univ. of London (Dip.). Asst Lectr, Dept of History of Art, Univ. of Manchester, 1968; Courtauld Institute: Asst to Hd, 1970–76, Lectr, 1976–90, Dept of Technol.; Fellow, 2000. *Publications:* catalogue contrib., Metropolitan Mus., NY; contrib. The Conservator. *Recreation:* Himalayan travel. *Heir: s* Edmund Thomas Peter Bruce-Gardner, *b* 28 Jan. 1982. *Address:* 121 Brackenbury Road, W6 0BQ. *T:* (020) 8932 4627. *Club:* Travellers.

BRUCE LOCKHART, Logie, MA; Headmaster of Gresham's School, Holt, 1955–82; *b* 12 Oct. 1921; *s* of late John Harold Bruce Lockhart; *m* 1944, Josephine Agnew; two *s* two *d* (and one *d* decd). *Educ:* Sedbergh School; St John's College, Cambridge (Schol. and Choral Studentship). RMC Sandhurst, 1941; served War of 1939–45; 9th Sherwood Foresters, 1942; 2nd Household Cavalry (Life Guards), 1944–45. Larmor Award, 1947; Asst Master, Tonbridge School, 1947–55. Sponsor, Nat. Council for Educnl Standards. *Publications:* The Pleasures of Fishing, 1981; Stuff and Nonsense, 1996. *Recreations:* fishing, writing, music, natural history, games; Blue for Rugby football, 1945, 1946, Scottish International, 1948, 1950, 1953; squash for Cambridge, 1946. *Address:* Mead Barn, New Road, Blakeney, Norfolk NR25 7PA. *T:* (01263) 740588.

BRUDENELL-BRUCE, family name of **Marquess of Ailesbury**.

BRÜGGEN, Frans; conductor; formerly recorder player; Founder and conductor, Orchestra of the Eighteenth Century, since 1981; *b* Amsterdam, 30 Oct. 1934. *Educ:* Conservatory and Univ. of Amsterdam. Prof., Royal Hague Conservatoire, 1955; formerly: Erasmus Prof., Harvard Univ.; Regents Prof., Univ. of Calif, Berkeley. Artistic Dir, Stavanger Symphony Orch., 1990–94; Principal Guest Conductor, Orchestre de Paris, 1998–2000; former Chief Conductor, Radio Kamer Filharmonie, now Conductor Emeritus; guest conductor: Concertgebouw Orch., Amsterdam; Vienna Philharmonic Orch.; Rotterdam Philharmonic Orch.; Orch. of the Age of Enlightenment; Birmingham Philharmonic Orch.; Stockholm Philharmonic Orch. Hon. RCM. UNESCO Music Prize, 1997. *Address:* c/o Askonas Holt Ltd, Lincoln House, 300 High Holborn, WC1V 7JH.

BRUINVELS, Canon Peter Nigel Edward; Principal, Peter Bruinvels Associates, media management and public affairs consultants, founded 1986; Managing Director, Bruinvels News & Media, since 1992; news broadcaster, political commentator and freelance journalist; *b* 30 March 1950; *er s* of Stanley and late Ninette Maud Bruinvels; *m* 1980, Alison Margaret, *o d* of Major David Gilmore Bacon, RA retd; two *d*. *Educ:* St John's Sch., Leatherhead; London Univ. (LLB Hons); Council of Legal Educn. Co. Sec., BPC Publishing, 1978–81; Sec./Lawyer, Amari PLC, 1981–82; Management Consultant and company director, 1982–. Chm., Dorking CPC, 1979–83; Mem., Cons. Nat. Union Exec., 1976–81. MP (C) Leicester E, 1983–87; contested (C): Leicester E, 1987; The Wrekin, 1997. Jt Chm., British Parly Lighting Gp; Vice-Chairman: Cons. Backbench Cttee on Urban Affairs and New Towns, 1984–87; Cons. Backbench Cttee on Education, 1985–87; Sec., Anglo-Netherlands Parly Gp, 1983–87; Chm., British-Malta Parly Gp, 1984–87; Member: Cons. Backbench Cttee on Home Affairs, 1983–87; Cons. Backbench Cttee on NI, 1983–87; Life Mem., British-Amer. Parly Gp, 1983. Promoter, Crossbows Act, 1987. Campaign Co-ordinator, Eastbourne, gen. election, 1992. Pres., Dorking Conservatives, 1995– (Chm., 1992–95). Director: Aalco Nottingham Ltd, 1983–88; Radio Mercury and Allied Radio, 1994–97. Special Advr, DTI Deregulation Task Force on Pharmaceuticals and Chemicals, 1993. Ind. Lay Chm., NHS Complaints Procedure, 1999–2006; Member: Social Security Appeals Tribunal, 1994–99; Child Support Appeals Tribunal, 1995–99. Non-exec. Dir, E Elmbridge and Mid Surrey PCT, 2002–07. Mem., Surrey LEA, 1997–2007 (Admissions Adjudicator). Inspector, Denominational Ch Schs, OFSTED, 1994–; Mem., Dearing Implementation Gp for Ch Schs, 2001–. Church Comr, 1992– (Member: Pastoral and Houses Cttee, 1993–; Bd of Govs, 1998–; Mgt Adv. Cttee, 1999–); Dir, Church Army, 1999–2004 (Chm., Remuneration Cttee, 1999–2004); Member: Guildford Dio. Synod, 1974– (Vice-Pres., 2003–; Chm., House of Laity, 2003–); Gen. Synod, 1985– (Mem. Legislative Cttee, 1991–96 and 2000–); Guildford Diocesan Bd of Educn, 1994– (Chm., 2005–08); Gen. Synod Bd of Educn, 1996–2006; Clergy Discipline (Doctrine) Gp, 1999–; Guildford Crown Nominations Commn, 2003–; Lay Canon, 2002–, Mem. Coll. of Canons, 2002–, Mem. Council, 2006–, Guildford Cathedral. Mem., Cathedrals Fabric Commn for England, 2006–. Mem., SE England War Pensions Cttee, 2003–; Chm., Surrey Jt Services' Charities Cttee, 2004–; Hon. Sec., Surrey County Appeals Cttee, 2002–. Mem., Jersey Wildlife Preservation Trust. Chm., Surrey Schs Orgn Cttee, 2000–07. Governor: York St John Univ. (formerly Ripon and York St John, then UC of York St John), 1998–2007; Whitelands Coll., Roehampton Univ., 2007–; Mem. Ct, Univ. of Sussex, 2000–08. Co. Field Officer, Surrey, RBL, 2002–. MCIPR (MIPR 1981); FRSA 1986; FCIM 1998 (Hon. MCIM 1987; Pres., Norwest Midlands, 1997–98); MCIJ (MJI 1988); Fellow, Industry and Parliament Trust. Granted Freedom, City of London, 1980. *Publications:* Zoning in on Enterprise, 1982; Light up the Roads, 1984; Sharing in Britain's Success—a Study in Widening Share Ownership, Through Privatisation, 1987; Investing in Enterprise—a Comprehensive Guide to Inner City Regeneration and Urban Renewal, 1989. *Recreations:* political campaigning, the media, Church of England. *Address:* 14 High Meadow Close, Dorking, Surrey RH4 2LG. *T:* (01306) 887082, (office) 887680, (01372) 386500, *Fax:* 0870 133 1756, (office) (01372) 375843. *Clubs:* Carlton, Inner Temple, Corporation of Church House.

BRUMBY, Hon. John Mansfield; MLA (ALP) Broadmeadows, Victoria, Australia, since 1993; Premier of Victoria, and Minister for Veterans' Affairs and for Multicultural Affairs, since 2007; *b* Melbourne, 21 April 1953; *s* of Malcolm Mansfield and Alison Jessie Brumby; *m* 1985, Rosemary McKenzie; one *s* two *d*. *Educ:* Melbourne Grammar Sch.; Univ. of Melbourne (BCom 1974); State Coll. of Victoria (DipEd 1975). Secondary sch. teacher, 1976–80; Union Organiser, Victorian Teachers' Union, 1981–83. Consultant to finance and banking industry, 1990; COS to Federal Minister for Tourism and Resources, 1991–92. MHR (ALP) Bendigo, 1983–90; Chm., Parly Standing Cttee on Employment, Educn and Trng, 1986–90. Shadow Minister for Arts and Ethnic Affairs, 1993–94; Shadow Treas., 1994–96; Shadow Minister: for Agric. and Rural Affairs, 1996–99; for Racing, 1996–99; for Multicultural and Ethnic Affairs, 1997–99; for Primary Industries, 1999; for State and Regl Develt, 1999; of Finance, 1999; Leader of the Opposition, Victoria, 1993–99; Minister: for Finance, and Asst Treas., 1999–2000; for State and Regl Develt, 1999–2006; for Regl and Rural Develt, 2006–07; for Innovation, 2002–07; Treas. of Victoria, 2000–07. Centenary Medal, 2001. *Publications:* Bendigo Almanac and Tourist Guide, 1981; Restoring Democracy, 1999. *Recreations:* tennis, Australian football, Australian film. *Address:* Office of the Premier, Level 1, 1 Treasury Place, East Melbourne, Vic 3002, Australia. *T:* (3) 96515000, *Fax:* (3) 96515054; *e-mail:* premier@dpc.vic.gov.au.

BRUMMELL, David, CB 2005; Legal Secretary to the Law Officers, 2000–04; *b* 18 Dec. 1947; *s* of late Ernest Brummell and Florence Elizabeth Brummell (*née* Martin). *Educ:* Nottingham High Sch.; Queens' Coll., Cambridge (MA Law 1973); Inst. of Linguistics (Dips in French, German and Spanish). Articled clerk, 1971–73, Asst Solicitor, 1973–75, Simmons & Simmons, Solicitors, London; Legal Adviser: Devon CC, 1975–77; W Sussex CC, 1977–79; Legal Asst, then Sen. Legal Asst, OFT, 1979–84; Treasury Solicitor's Department: Sen. Legal Asst, 1984–86, Grade 6, 1986, Central Adv. Div.; Grade 5, 1986–89; Litigation Div., 1989–2000, Head, 1995–2000. *Recreations:* tennis, walking, music, languages, poetry. *Address:* 14A The Gateways, Park Lane, Richmond, Surrey TW9 2RB. *T:* (020) 8948 1247. *Clubs:* Athenæum; Thames Hare and Hounds.

BRUMMELL, Paul; HM Diplomatic Service; Ambassador to Kazakhstan, since 2005 and concurrently (non-resident) to the Kyrgyz Republic; *b* 28 Aug. 1965; *s* of late Robert George Brummell and June Brummell (*née* Rawlins). *Educ:* St Albans Sch.; St Catharine's Coll., Cambridge (BA Hons Geog.). Joined HM Diplomatic Service, 1987; Third, later Second, Sec., Islamabad, 1989–92; FCO, 1993–94; First Sec., Rome, 1995–2000; Dep. Hd, Eastern Dept, FCO, 2000–01; Ambassador to Turkmenistan, 2002–05. *Publication:* Turkmenistan—The Bradt Travel Guide, 2005. *Recreations:* travel writing, glam rock. *Address:* c/o Foreign and Commonwealth Office, King Charles Street, SW1A 2AH.

BRUMMER, Alexander; City Editor, Daily Mail, since 2000; *b* 25 May 1949; *s* of Michael Brummer and Hilda (*née* Lyons); *m* 1975, Patricia Lyndsey Magrill; two *s* one *d*. *Educ:* Univ. of Southampton (BSc Econ. Politics); Univ. of Bradford Mgt Centre (MSc Business Admin). The Guardian: Financial Corresp., 1973–79; Washington Ed., 1979–89; Foreign Ed., 1989–90; Financial Ed., 1990–99; Associate Ed., 1998–99; Consultant Ed., Mail on Sunday, 1999. Awards include: Financial Journalist of Year, British Press Awards, 1999; Best City Journalist, Media Awards, 2000; Wincott Award for Sen. Financial Journalist of Year, 2001; Newspaper Journalist of Year, 2002, Columnist of the Year, 2007, Workworld Media Awards; Business Journalist of Year, World Leadership Forum, 2006. *Publications:* Hanson: a biography, 1994; Weinstock: the life and times, 1999; The Crunch, 2007. *Recreations:* reading, antiques, football. *Address:* Daily Mail, City Office, Northcliffe House, 2 Derry Street, W8 5TT. *T:* (020) 7938 6990; *e-mail:* alex.brummer@dailymail.co.uk.

BRUNA, Dick; graphic designer; writer and illustrator of children's books; *b* 23 Aug. 1927; *s* of A. W. Bruna and J. C. C. Erdbrink; *m* 1953, Irene de Jongh; two *s* one *d*. *Educ:* Primary Sch. and Gymnasium, Utrecht, Holland; autodidact. Designer of book jackets, 1945–, and of posters, 1947– (many prizes); writer and illustrator of children's books, 1953– (1st book, The Apple); also designer of postage stamps, murals, greeting cards and picture postcards. Exhibn based on Miffy (best-known character in children's books): Gemeentemuseum, Arnhem, 1977; Frans Halsmus. Haarlem, 1989; Centre Pompidou, Paris, 1991. Member: Netherlands Graphic Designers; Authors League of America Inc.; PEN Internat.; Alliance Graphique Internat. *Publications*: 100 titles published and 100 million copies printed by 2000; children's books translated into 41 languages. *Address*: (studio) 3 Jeruzalemstraat, 3512 KW, Utrecht. *T*: (30) 2316042. *Club*: Art Directors (Netherlands).

BRUNDIN, Clark Lannerdahl, PhD; Director, School of Management Studies, University of Oxford, 1992–96; President, Templeton College, Oxford, 1992–96; *b* 21 March 1931; *s* of late Ernest Walfrid Brundin and Elinor Brundin (*née* Clark); *m* 1959, Judith Anne (*née* Maloney); two *s* two *d*. *Educ*: Whittier High Sch., California; California Inst. of Technology; Univ. of California, Berkeley (BSc, PhD); MA Oxford. Electronics Petty Officer, US Navy, 1951–55. Associate in Mech. Engrg, UC Berkeley, 1956–57; Demonstr. Dept of Engrg Science, Univ. of Oxford, 1957–58; Res. Engr, Inst. of Engrg Res., UC Berkeley, 1959–63; Univ. Lectr, Dept of Engrg Sci., Univ. of Oxford, 1963–85, Vice-Chm., Gen. Bd of the Faculties, 1984–85; Jesus College, Oxford: Fellow and Tutor in Engrg, 1964–85; Sen. Tutor, 1974–77; Estates Bursar, 1978–84; Hon. Fellow, 1985; Vice Chancellor, Univ. of Warwick, 1985–92. Vis. Prof., Univ. of Calif Santa Barbara, 1978; Vis. Schol., Center for Studies in Higher Educn, UC Berkeley, 1997–. Member: Engrg Bd, CNAA, 1976–82; CICHE, 1987–96. Director: Cokethorpe Sch. Educnl Trust, 1983–96; Heritage Projects (Oxford) Ltd, 1985–97; Blackwell Science Ltd, 1990–98; Finsbury Growth Trust plc, 1995–2000; CAF America, 1997–2000 (Pres., 1998–2000); Chm., Anchor Housing Assoc., 1985–91 (Bd Mem., 1985–94). Mem. (Lib Dem) Oxford City Council, 2004–. Governor: Oxford Poly., 1979–84; Magdalen College Sch., 1987–99; Coventry Sch. Foundn, 1991–99. Hon. LLD Warwick, 2005. *Publications*: articles on rarefied gas dynamics. *Recreations*: sailing, mending old machinery, music of all sorts. *Address*: 28 Observatory Street, Oxford OX2 6EW.

BRUNDLE, Martin John; racing driver; presenter and commentator, Formula One, ITV, 1997–2008; *b* 1 June 1959; *s* of late Alfred Edward John Brundle and of Alma Brundle (*née* Coe); *m* 1981, Elizabeth Mary Anthony; one *s* one *d*. *Educ*: King Edward VII Grammar Sch., King's Lynn; Norfolk Coll. of Arts and Technol. Formula One racing driver, 1984–96 (158 Grands Prix): World Sportscar Champion, 1988; winner: Daytona 24 hours, 1988; Le Mans 24 hours, 1990. Chm., British Racing Drivers' Club, 2000–03. Grovewood Award, 1982; Segrave Trophy, 1988; RTS Sports Award, 1998, 1999, 2005 and 2007. *Recreations*: helicopter flying, motor biking. *Club*: British Racing Drivers' (Silverstone).

BRUNDTLAND, Gro Harlem, MD; Norwegian physician and politician; United Nations Special Envoy for Climate Change, since 2007; Director General, World Health Organisation, 1998–2003; *b* 20 April 1939; *d* of Gudmund and Inga Harlem; *m* 1960, Arne Olav Brundtland; two *s* one *d* (and one *s* decd). *Educ*: Oslo and Harvard Univs. MPH. MO, Directorate of Health, 1966–68; Asst Med. Dir, Oslo Bd of Health, 1968–74; Minister of Environment, 1974–79; MP (Lab) Oslo, 1977–96; Dep. Leader, Labour Party, 1975–81; Dep. Leader, Labour Parly Gp, 1979–81, Leader, 1981–90; Prime Minister of Norway, Feb.–Oct. 1981, 1986–89 and 1990–96. Mem., Indep. Commn on Disarmament and Security Issues; Vice-Pres., Socialist Internat.; Chm., UN World Commn on Envmt and Develt, 2003–05. Hon. DCL Oxon, 2001. Third World Prize; Indira Gandhi Prize; Blue Planet Prize. *Publications*: articles on preventive medicine, school health and growth studies, internat. issues. *Recreation*: cross-country ski-ing. *Address*: 241 Route de Bellet, 06200 Nice, France.

BRUNEI, HM Sultan of; *see* Negara Brunei Darussalam.

BRUNER, Jerome Seymour, MA, PhD; University Professor, New York University, since 1998 (Research Professor of Psychology, 1987–98; Adjunct Professor of Law, 1991–98); Fellow, New York Institute for the Humanities; *b* New York, 1 Oct. 1915; *s* of Herman and Rose Bruner; *m* 1st, 1940, Katherine Frost (marr. diss. 1956); one *s* one *d*; 2nd, 1960, Blanche Marshall McLane (marr. diss. 1984); 3rd, 1987, Carol Fleisher Feldman. *Educ*: Duke Univ. (AB 1937); Harvard Univ. (AM 1939, PhD 1941). US Intelligence, 1941; Assoc. Dir, Office Public Opinion Research, Princeton, 1942–44; govt public opinion surveys on war problems, 1942–43; political intelligence, France, 1943; Harvard University: research, 1945–72; Prof. of Psychology, 1952–72; Dir, Centre for Cognitive Studies, 1961–72; Watts Prof. of Psychology, Univ. of Oxford, 1972–80; G. H. Mead Univ. Prof., New Sch. for Social Res., NY, 1980–88. Lectr, Salzburg Seminar, 1952; Bacon Prof., Univ. of Aix-en-Provence, 1965. Editor, Public Opinion Quarterly, 1943–44; Syndic, Harvard Univ. Press, 1962–74. Member: Inst. Advanced Study, 1951; White House Panel on Educnl Research and Develt. Guggenheim Fellow, Cambridge Univ., 1955; Fellow: Amer. Psychol Assoc. (Pres., 1964–65; Distinguished Scientific Contrib. award, 1962); Amer. Acad. Arts and Sciences; Swiss Psychol Soc. (hon.); Soc. Psychol Study Social Issues (past Pres.); Amer. Assoc. Univ. Profs; Puerto Rican Acad. Arts and Sciences (hon.); Corresp. FBA 2003. Hon. DHL Lesley Coll., 1964; Hon. DSc: Northwestern Univ., 1965; Sheffield, 1970; Bristol, 1975; Hon. MA, Oxford, 1972; Hon. DSocSci, Yale, 1975; Hon. LLD: Temple Univ., 1965; Univ. of Cincinnati, 1966; Univ. of New Brunswick, 1969; Hon. DLitt: North Michigan Univ., 1969; Duke Univ., 1969; Dr *hc* Sorbonne, 1974; Leuven, 1976; Ghent, 1977; Madrid, 1987; Free Univ., Berlin, 1988; Columbia, 1988; Stirling, 1990; Rome, 1992; Harvard, Bologna, Geneva, 1996; Salerno, Crete, 2002. Internat. Balzan Prize, Fondazione Balzan, 1987. *Publications*: Mandate from the People, 1944; (with Krech) Perception and Personality: A Symposium, 1950; (with Goodnow and Austin) A Study of Thinking, 1956; (with Smith and White) Opinions and Personality, 1956; (with Bresson, Morf and Piaget) Logique et Perception, 1958; The Process of Education, 1960; On Knowing: Essays for the Left Hand, 1962; (jtly) Studies in Cognitive Growth, 1966; Toward a Theory of Instruction, 1966; Processes of Cognitive Growth: Infancy, Vol III, 1968; The Relevance of Education, 1971; (ed Anglin) Beyond the Information Given: selected papers of Jerome S. Bruner, 1973; (with Connolly) The Growth of Competence, 1974; (with Jolly and Sylva) Play: its role in evolution and development, 1976; Under Five in Britain, 1980; Communication as Language, 1982; In Search of Mind: essays in autobiography, 1983; Child's Talk, 1983; Actual Minds, Possible Worlds, 1986; Acts of Meaning, 1990; The Culture of Education, 1996; (with A. G. Amsterdam) Minding the Law, 2000; Making Stories, 2002; contribs technical and professional jls. *Recreation*: sailing. *Address*: 200 Mercer Street, New York, NY 10012, USA. *Clubs*: Royal Cruising; Century (New York); Cruising Club of America.

BRUNNER, Adrian John Nelson; QC 1994; a Recorder, since 1990; *b* 18 June 1946; *s* of late Comdr Hugh Brunner, DSC, RN and of Elizabeth Brunner; *m* 1970, Christine Anne Hughes; one *s* four *d*. *Educ*: Ampleforth Coll.; BRNC; Coll. of Law. Served RN, 1963–66. Called to the Bar, Inner Temple, 1968 (Major Schol., 1967), Bencher, 2006. *Recreations*: yachting, shooting. *Address*: Furneaux Pelham Hall, Buntingford, Herts SG9 0LB; Holborn Head Farm, Scrabster, Caithness KW14 7UW. *Clubs*: Royal Yacht Squadron, Bar Yacht.

BRUNNER, Sir Hugo Laurence Joseph, KCVO 2008; JP; Lord-Lieutenant of Oxfordshire, 1996–2008; *b* 17 Aug. 1935; *s* of Sir Felix Brunner, 3rd Bt and late Dorothea Elizabeth (*née* Irving); *m* 1967, Mary Rose Pollen; five *s* one *d*. *Educ*: Eton; Trinity Coll., Oxford (MA Hons; Hon. Fellow, 1994). With OUP, 1958–65 (First Rep., Hong Kong, 1960–62); Sales Dir, Chatto & Windus, publishers, 1966–76; Dep. Gen. Publisher, OUP, 1977–79; Man. Dir, then Chm., Chatto & Windus, 1979–85. Director: Caithness Glass Ltd, 1966–96 (Chm., 1984–91); Brunner Investment Trust PLC, 1987–99; SCM Press Ltd, 1991–97. Contested (L) Torquay, 1964 and 1966. Chm., Oxford DAC for Care of Churches, 1985–98. Governor: St Edward's Sch., Oxford, 1991–2005; Ripon Coll. Cuddesdon, 1992–2005. Dep. Steward, Univ. of Oxford, 2001–. High Sheriff, 1988–89, DL 1993, JP 1996, Oxon. Mem., Order of St Frideswide, 2006. Hon. LLD Oxford Brookes, 1999. *Recreations*: hill-walking, church visiting, study of animal-powered engines. *Address*: 26 Norham Road, Oxford OX2 6SF. *T*: (01865) 316431. *Clubs*: Reform, Chelsea Arts.

BRUNNER, Sir John Henry Kilian, 4th Bt *cr* 1895; *b* 1 June 1927; *s* of Sir Felix John Morgan Brunner, 3rd Bt, and Dorothea Elizabeth, OBE, *d* of Henry Brodribb Irving; *S* father, 1982, but his name does not appear on the Official Roll of the Baronetage; *m* 1955, Jasmine Cecily, *d* of late John Wardrop Moore; two *s* one *d*. *Educ*: Eton; Trinity Coll., Oxford (BA 1950). Served as Lieut RA. On staff, PEP, 1950–53; Talks producer, 1953; Economic Adviser, Treasury, 1958–61; Asst Manager, Observer, 1961. *Heir*: *s* Nicholas Felix Minturn Brunner, *b* 16 Jan. 1960. *Address*: 138 Victoria Avenue, Dalkeith, WA 6009, Australia.

BRUNNING, His Honour David Wilfrid; a Circuit Judge, 1988–2008; Designated Family Judge, Leicester County Court, 2004–08; *b* 10 April 1943; *s* of Wilfred and Marion Brunning; *m* 1967, Deirdre Ann Shotton; three *s*. *Educ*: Burton upon Trent Grammar Sch.; Worcester Coll., Oxford (BA (Modern History) 1965; DPA 1966). Called to the Bar, Middle Temple, 1969; Midland and Oxford Circuit, 1970–88; Assigned Judge, Designated Family Judge and Designated Civil Judge, Nottingham; Judge of the Technology and Construction Court at Nottingham, 1995–2004; Dep. Judge, QBD and Family Div., 1995–2008. Mem. Council, Leicester Univ., 2003–. *Recreations*: campanology, walking, wine, military history.

BRUNO, Franklin Roy, (Frank), MBE 1990; professional boxer, 1982–96; *b* 16 Nov. 1961; *s* of late Robert Bruno and of Lynette Bruno (*née* Campbell); *m* 1990, Laura Frances Mooney (marr. diss. 2001); one *s* two *d*; one *d* by Yvonne Clydesdale. *Educ*: Oak Hall Sch., Sussex. Amateur boxer, Sir Philip Game Amateur Boxing Club, 1977–80: 21 contests, 20 victories; London ABA and Nat. ABA Heavyweight Champion, 1980; professional career, 1982–96: 45 contests, 40 victories; European Champion, 1985–86; WBC World Heavyweight Champion, 1995. Pantomime appearances: Aladdin, Dominion, 1989, Nottingham, 1990, Wycombe, 2003; Robin Hood, Bristol, 1991; Jack and the Beanstalk, Bradford, 1996; Goldilocks, Birmingham, 1997, Southampton, 1999, Wolverhampton, 2001. Sports Personality of Year, Stars Orgn for Spastics, 1989, 1990. *Publications*: Know What I Mean?, 1987; Eye of the Tiger, 1992; From Zero to Hero, 1996; Frank: fighting back, 2005. *Recreations*: swimming, training, driving, eating, shopping for good clothes.

BRUNSDEN, Prof. Denys, OBE 2004; PhD; Professor of Geography, Department of Geography, King's College, University of London, 1983–96, now Emeritus; *b* 14 March 1936; *s* of Francis Stephen Brunsden and Mabel Florence (*née* Martin); *m* 1961, Elizabeth Mary Philippa (*née* Wright); one *s* one *d*. *Educ*: Torquay Grammar Sch. for Boys; King's Coll., Univ. of London (BSc Hons Geography; PhD 1963). King's College, London: Tutorial Student, 1959–60; Asst Lectr, 1960–63; Lectr, 1963–75; Reader, 1975–83; Fellow, 1998. Vis. Lectr, 1964–65, Erskine Fellow, 1988, Univ. of Canterbury, NZ; Vis. Associate Prof., Louisiana State Univ., 1971; Visiting Professor: Univ. of Durham, 1996–2002; Bournemouth Univ., 1999–2005. Founder Consultant, Geomorphological Services Ltd, 1972. Chairman: British Geomorphol Res. Gp, 1985–86; Wkg Pty for Collaboration in Internat. Geomorphology, 1985–; President: Geographical Assoc., 1986–87 (Hon. Mem., 1996); Internat. Assoc. of Geomorphologists, 1989–93 (Sen. Past Pres., 1993–97; Hon. Fellow 1997); Vice-Pres., RGS, 1984–87; Hon. Mem., Polish Assoc. of Geomorphologists, 1993. Member: St George's House Consultation, 1989; Nat. Curriculum Wkg Party for Physical Educn, 1990–92. Mem. Steering Cttee, successful bid for World Heritage Site status for Dorset and E Devon Coast, 1993–; Chm., Dorset Coast Forum, 1995– (Trustee, 2005–). Hon. DSc: Plymouth, 2000; Bournemouth, 2002. Gill Meml Award, RGS (for contribs to study of mass movement and fieldwork), 1977; Republic of China Award Lectr, 1988–89; Assoc. of American Geographers Honours, 1991; Linton Award, British Geomorphological Res. Gp, 1993; William Smith Medal, Geol Soc. of London, 2000; Glossop Lect. and Medal, Geol Soc., 2001. *Publications*: Dartmoor, 1968; Slopes, Forms and Process, 1970; (with J. C. Doornkamp) The Unquiet Landscape, 1971 (USA 1976, Australia 1976, Germany 1977); (with J. B. Thornes) Geomorphology and Time, 1977; (with C. Embleton and D. K. C. Jones) Geomorphology: present problems, future prospects, 1978; (with J. C. Doornkamp and D. K. C. Jones) The Geology, Geomorphology and Pedology of Bahrain, 1980; (with R. U. Cooke, J. C. Doornkamp and D. K. C. Jones) The Urban Geomorphology of Drylands, 1982; (with D. B. Prior) Slope Instability, 1984; (with R. Gardner, A. S. Goudie and D. K. C. Jones) Landshapes, 1989; Natural Disasters, 1990; (with A. S. Goudie) The Environment of the British Isles: an Atlas, 1995; (with R. Dikau) Landslide Recognition, 1996. *Recreations*: making walking sticks and shepherd's-crooks, painting, reading thrillers, watching TV, enjoying dinner parties and fine wine, talking, travelling to exotic places, eating, drinking and relaxing in the Drôme. *Address*: Department of Geography, King's College London, Strand, WC2R 2LS. *Club*: Geographical.

BRUNSDON, Norman Keith, AM 2000; Chairman and Senior Partner, Price Waterhouse, Australia, 1982–86; *b* 11 Jan. 1930; *s* of late G. A. Brunsdon; *m* 1953, Ruth, *d* of late W. Legg; one *s* one *d*. *Educ*: Wagga Wagga High Sch., NSW. FCA. Price Waterhouse, Australia: joined, 1951; Partner, 1963; Mem. Policy Cttee (Bd), 1970–86; Partner-in-Charge, Sydney, 1975–81; Mem., World Firm Policy Cttee (Bd) and Council of Firms, 1979–86; Agent Gen. for NSW in London, 1989–91. Dir, Arthur Yates & Co. Ltd, 1993–2001. Chm., Aust. Govt's Taxation Adv. Cttee, 1979–83; Trustee, Econ. Develt of Aust. Cttee, 1977–86. Vice-Pres., Thai-Aust. Chamber of Commerce & Industry, 1982–85; Member: Pacific Basin Econ. Council, 1982–86; Aust. Japan Business Co-op. Cttee, 1982–86. Member: Standing Cttee, C of E Dio. Sydney, 1969–74; C of E Children's Homes Cttee, 1974–84 (Treasurer, 1969–75; Acting Chm., 1972–73); Chairman: Anglican Retirement Villages, dio. Sydney, 1991–98; Anglican Foundn for Aged Care, 1993–2001. Governor, King's Sch., Parramatta, 1977–86; Trustee, Bark Endeavour Foundn Pty Ltd, 1992–2001. Hon. Mem., Cook Soc. Freeman, City of London, 1989. *Recreations*: music, opera, theatre, reading, sailing, golf. *Address*: PO Box 675, Northbridge, NSW 2063, Australia. *T*: (2) 99580641. *Clubs*: Australian (Sydney); Royal Sydney Yacht Squadron.

BRUNSKILL, Ronald William, OBE 1990; MA, PhD; FSA; lecturer and author; Professor, Centre for Conservation Studies, School of Architecture (formerly School of the Built Environment), De Montfort University, 1995–2001; *b* 3 Jan. 1929; *s* of William Brunskill and Elizabeth Hannah Brunskill; *m* 1960, Miriam Allsopp; two *d*. *Educ:* Bury High Sch.; Univ. of Manchester (BA Hons Arch. 1951, MA 1952, PhD 1963). Registered Architect and ARIBA, 1951; FSA 1975. National Service, 2nd Lieut RE, 1953–55. Studio Asst in Arch., Univ. of Manchester, 1951–53; Architectural Asst, LCC, 1955; Asst in Arch., Univ. of Manchester, 1955–56; Commonwealth Fund Fellow (arch. and town planning), MIT, 1956–57; Architect to Williams Deacon's Bank, 1957–60; Manchester University: Lectr, 1960–73; Sen. Lectr, 1973–84; Reader in Architecture, 1984–89; Hon. Fellow, Sch. of Architecture, 1989–95; Architect in private practice, 1960–66; Partner, Carter, Brunskill & Associates, chartered architects, 1966–69, Consultant, 1969–73. Vis. Prof., Univ. of Florida, Gainesville, 1969–70; Hon. Vis. Prof., De Montfort Univ., 1994–95. President: Vernacular Arch. Gp, 1974–77; Cumberland and Westmorland Antiquarian and Archaeol Soc., 1990–93 (Vice-Pres., 1975–90); Friends of Friendless Churches, 1999– (Chm., 1990–98); Ancient Monuments Soc., 2004– (Hon. Architect, 1983–88; Vice-Chm., 1988–90; Chm., 1990–2000; Vice-Pres., 2000–04); Vice-Pres., Weald and Downland Museum Trust, 1980–; Chm., Urban Parks Adv. Panel, Heritage Lottery Fund, 1995–99; Member: Historic Bldgs Council for England, 1978–84; Royal Commn on Ancient and Historical Monuments of Wales, 1983–97 (Vice Chm., 1993–97); Historic Buildings and Monuments Commn (English Heritage), 1989–95 (Member: Historic Buildings Adv. Cttee, 1984–95 (Chm., 1989–95); Ancient Monuments Adv. Cttee, 1984–90; Chm., Cathedrals and Churches Adv. Cttee, 1989–95); Cathedrals Adv. Commn for England, 1981–91; Cathedrals Fabric Commn for England, 1991–96; Manchester DAC for Care of Churches, 1973–79 and 1987–93; Manchester Cathedral Fabric Cttee, 1987–96; Blackburn Cathedral Fabric Cttee, 1989–96 (Chm.); Chester Cathedral Fabric Cttee, 1989–94 and 2004–; Council, Soc. for Folk Life Studies, 1969–72 and 1980–83. Trustee, British Historic Buildings Trust, 1985–92. Hon. DArt De Montfort, 2001. Neale Bursar, RIBA, 1962; President's Award, Manchester Soc. of Architects, 1977. *Publications:* Illustrated Handbook of Vernacular Architecture, 1971, 3rd edn (enlarged) 1987; Vernacular Architecture of the Lake Counties, 1974; (with Alec Clifton-Taylor) English Brickwork, 1977; Traditional Buildings of Britain, 1981, 3rd edn (enlarged) 2004; Houses (in series, Collins Archaeology), 1982; Traditional Farm Buildings of Britain, 1982, 2nd edn (enlarged) 1987; Timber Building in Britain, 1985, 2nd edn (enlarged) 1994; Brick Building in Britain, 1990; Houses and Cottages of Britain, 1997; Traditional Farm Buildings and their Conservation, 1999; Vernacular Architecture: an illustrated handbook, 2000; Traditional Buildings of Cumbria, 2002; Brick and Clay Buildings of Britain, 2008; articles and reviews in archaeol and architectural jls. *Recreation:* enjoying the countryside. *Address:* Three Trees, 8 Overhill Road, Wilmslow SK9 2BE. *T:* (01625) 522099. *Club:* Athenæum.

BRUNSON, Michael John, OBE 2000; broadcaster and journalist; Political Editor, ITN, 1986–2000; *b* 12 Aug. 1940; *s* of Geoffrey Brunson and Ethel (*née* Mills); *m* 1965, Susan Margaret Brown; two *s*. *Educ:* Bedford Sch.; Queen's Coll., Oxford (BA Theol. 1963; MA). VSO, Sierra Leone, 1963–64; BBC General Trainee, 1964–65; Reporter, BBC SE Radio News, 1965–66; Asst Producer, BBC TV Current Affairs, 1966–68; Independent Television News: Reporter, 1968–72; Washington Corresp., 1972–77; Reporter, 1977–80; Diplomatic Editor, 1980–86; Campaign Reporter with Mrs Thatcher, 1979 and 1983 Gen. Elections. Chairman: Parly Lobby Journalists, 1994; Parly Press Gall., 1999. Member: Govt Adv. Gp on Citizenship Educn, 1997–98; Preparation for Adult Life Gp, QCA, 1998; Adult Learning Cttee, Learning and Skills Council, 2001–03. Trustee, Citizenship Foundn, 2000–06. Columnist: The House Mag. (H of C), 1989–90, 1997–99; Saga Magazine, 2000–05. Hon. LittD UEA, 2003. RTS News Event Award, 1994; RTS Judges' Award for lifetime achievement, 2000. *Publication:* A Ringside Seat (autobiog.), 2000. *Recreations:* caring for my garden, my classic sports car, Norwich City FC. *Address:* c/o Knight Ayton Management, 114 St Martin's Lane, WC2N 4AZ. *T:* (020) 7836 5333. *Clubs:* Oxford and Cambridge; Norfolk (Norwich).

BRUNT, Rev. Prof. Peter William, CVO 2001; OBE 1994; MD, FRCP, FRCPE; Physician to the Queen in Scotland, 1983–2001; Consultant Physician and Gastroenterologist, Grampian Health Board, Aberdeen, 1970–2001; Clinical Professor of Medicine, University of Aberdeen, 1996–2001; Non-Stipendiary Minister, diocese of Aberdeen, Scottish Episcopal Church, since 1996; *b* 18 Jan. 1936; *s* of late Harry Brunt and Florence J. J. Airey; *m* 1961, Dr Anne Lewis, *d* of Rev. R. H. Lewis; three *d*. *Educ:* Manchester Grammar Sch.; Cheadle Hulme Sch.; King George V Sch.; Univ. of Liverpool (MB, ChB 1959; MD 1967). Gen. Med. training, Liverpool Royal Infirmary and Liverpool Hosps, 1959–64; Research Fellow, Johns Hopkins Univ. Sch. of Medicine, Baltimore, USA, 1965–67; Lectr in Medicine, Edinburgh Univ., 1967–68; Senior Registrar, Gastrointestinal Unit, Western Gen. Hosp., Edinburgh, 1968–69; Clin. Sen. Lectr in Medicine, Aberdeen Univ., 1970–96. Hon. Lectr in Medicine, Royal Free Hosp. Sch. of Medicine, Univ. of London, 1969–70. Medical Dir, Scottish Adv. Cttee on Distinction Awards, 2000–05; Chairman: Med. Council on Alcohol, 2004–; Alcohol Focus Scotland, 2005–. Mem., Assoc. of Physicians of GB and Ireland (Pres., 1995–96); Jt Vice-Pres., RCPE, 2005–. Ordained deacon, 1996, priest, 1997, Scottish Episcopal Church. *Publications:* (with M. Losowsky and A. E. Read) Diseases of the Liver and Biliary System, 1984; (with P. F. Jones and N. A. G. Mowat) Gastroenterology, 1984. *Recreations:* mountaineering, music, operatics. *Address:* Flat 4, 1 Hillpark Rise, Blackhall, Edinburgh EH4 7BB. *T:* (0131) 312 6687.

BRUNTISFIELD, 3rd Baron *cr* 1942, of Boroughmuir; **Michael John Victor Warrender;** Bt 1715; *b* 9 Jan. 1949; *s* of 2nd Baron Bruntisfield and Anne Moireen, 2nd *d* of Sir Walter Campbell, KCIE; *S* father, 2007; *m* 1978, Baroness Walburga von Twickel; one *s*. *Educ:* Downside; RMA Sandhurst; Durham Univ. (BA 1972). Major, Irish Guards, 1967–86. *Heir:* *s* Hon. John Michael Patrick Caspar Warrender, *b* 1 June 1996.

BRUNTON, Sir Gordon (Charles), Kt 1985; Chairman: Communications and General Consultants, since 1985; Green Field Leisure Group Ltd, since 1992; Stock Productions Ltd, since 1999; Galahad Gold plc, 2003–07; *b* 27 Dec. 1921; *s* of late Charles Arthur Brunton and late Hylda Pritchard; *m* 1st, 1946, Nadine Lucile Paula Sohr (marr. diss. 1965); one *s* two *d* (and one *s* decd); 2nd, 1966, Gillian Agnes Kirk; one *s* one *d*. *Educ:* Cranleigh Sch.; London Sch. of Economics. Commnd into RA, 1942; served Indian Army, Far East; Mil. Govt, Germany, 1946. Joined Tothill Press, 1947; Exec. Dir, Tothill, 1956; Man. Dir, Tower Press Gp of Cos, 1958; Exec. Dir, Odhams Press, 1961; joined Thomson Organisation, 1961; Man. Dir, Thomson Publications, 1961; Dir, Thomson Organisation, 1963; Chm., Thomson Travel, 1965–68; Man. Dir and Chief Exec., Internat. Thomson Orgn plc (formerly Thomson British Hldgs) and The Thomson Orgn Ltd, 1968–84; Pres., Internat. Thomson Orgn Ltd, 1978–84. Director: Times Newspapers Ltd, 1967–81; Sotheby Parke Bernet Group, 1978–83 (Chm., 1982–83, Chm. Emeritus, Sotheby's Holding Inc., 1983); Cable and Wireless plc, 1981–91; Yattendon Investment Trust, 1985–2001; Chairman: Bemrose Corp., 1978–91; Martin Currie Pacific Trust, 1985–92; Community Industry, 1985–92; Euram Consulting, 1985–92; Cavendish Shops, 1985–93; The Racing Post plc, 1985–97; Mercury Communications, 1986–90; Cavendish Retail, 1987–94; Ingersoll Publications, 1988–91; Wharfedale, then Verity Gp, 1991–97; PhoneLink, then Telme.com, 1993–2001. President: Periodical Publishers Assoc., 1972–74, 1981–83; Nat. Advertising Benevolent Soc., 1973–75 (Trustee, 1980–); History of Advertising Trust, 1981–84; CPU, 1991–94; Chm., EDC for Civil Engrg, 1978–84; Member: Printing and Publishing Ind. Trng Bd, 1974–78; Supervisory Bd, CBI Special Programmes Unit, 1980–84; Business in the Community Council, 1981–84; Chm., Independent Adoption Service, 1986–. Mem., South Bank Bd, Arts Council, 1985–92. Governor: LSE, 1971–95 (Fellow, 1978); Ashridge Management Coll., 1983–86; Ct of Governors, Henley—The Management Coll., 1983–85; Mem. Council, Templeton College (formerly Oxford Centre for Management Studies), 1976–95; Mem., Finance Cttee, OUP, 1985–91. *Recreations:* books, breeding horses. *Address:* (office) North Munstead, North Munstead Lane, Godalming, Surrey GU8 4AX. *T:* (01483) 424181, *Fax:* (01483) 426043. *Club:* Garrick.

BRUNTON, Sir James (Lauder), 4th Bt *cr* 1908, of Stratford Place, St Marylebone; MD; FRCPC; Professor of Medicine, and Head of Division of Infectious Diseases, Department of Medicine, University of Toronto; *b* 24 Sept. 1947; *s* of Sir (Edward Francis) Lauder Brunton, 3rd Bt, physician, and of Marjorie, *o d* of David Sclater Lewis, MSc, MD, CM, FRCPC; *S* father, 2007; *m* 1st, 1967, Susan Elizabeth (marr. diss. 1983), *o d* of Charles Hons; one *s* one *d*; 2nd, 1984, Beverly Anne Freedman; one *s*. *Educ:* Bishops Coll. Sch., Montreal; McGill Univ. (BSc 1968); MD. *Heir:* *s* Douglas Lauder Brunton, *b* 1968.

BRUTON, John (Gerard); European Union Ambassador to Washington, since 2004; *b* 18 May 1947; *s* of Matthew Joseph Bruton and Doris Bruton (*née* Delany); *m* 1981, Finola Gill; one *s* three *d*. *Educ:* St Dominic's Coll., Dublin; Clongowes Wood Coll., Co. Kildare; University Coll., Dublin (BA, BL). King's Inns, Dublin; called to the Bar, 1972. National Secretary, Fine Gael Youth Group, 1966–69. TD (Fine Gael), Meath, 1969–2004. Mem., Dáil Committee of Procedure and Privileges, 1969–73, 1982; Fine Gael Spokesman on Agriculture, 1972–73; Parliamentary Secretary: to Minister for Education, 1973–77; to Minister for Industry and Commerce, 1975–77; Fine Gael Spokesman: on Agriculture, 1977–81; on Finance, Jan.–June 1981; Minister: for Finance, 1981–82, for Industry and Energy, 1982–83, for Industry, Trade, Commerce and Tourism, 1983–86, for Finance, 1986–87; Fine Gael Spokesman on Industry and Commerce, 1987–89, on education, 1989; Leader of the House, 1982–86; Taoiseach (Prime Minister of Ireland), 1994–97; Leader of the Opposition, 1997–2001. Dep. Leader, 1987–90, Leader, 1990–2001, Fine Gael. Pres., EEC Industry, Research and Internal Market Councils, July–Dec. 1984. Member: Parly Assembly, Council of Europe, 1989–90; British-Irish Parly Body, 1993–94; Parly Assembly, WEU, 1997–98; Præsidium, Convention on the Future of Europe, 2002–. Vice President: Christian Democrat Internat., 1998–2001; EPP, 1999–2005. Hon. DLaw: Memorial Univ., Newfoundland; NUI. Schumann Medal, 1998. *Recreations:* reading history, tennis. *Address:* Delegation of the European Commission, 2300 M Street NW, Suite 300, Washington, DC 20037, USA. *T:* (202) 8629510.

BRYAN, Sir Arthur, Kt 1976; Lord-Lieutenant of Staffordshire, 1968–93; President, Waterford Wedgwood Holdings plc and a Director, Waterford Glass Group plc, 1986–88 (Managing Director, 1963–85, Chairman, 1968–86, Wedgwood); *b* 4 March 1923; *s* of William Woodall Bryan and Isobel Alan (*née* Tweedie); *m* 1947, Betty Ratford; one *s* one *d*. *Educ:* Longton High Sch., Stoke-on-Trent. Served with RAFVR, 1941–45. Joined Josiah Wedgwood & Sons Ltd, 1947; London Man., 1953–57; General Sales Man., 1959–60; Director and President, Josiah Wedgwood & Sons Inc. of America, 1960–62; Director: Josiah Wedgwood & Sons Ltd, Barlaston, 1962; Josiah Wedgwood & Sons (Canada) Ltd; Josiah Wedgwood & Sons (Australia) Pty Ltd; Phoenix Assurance Co., 1976–85; Friends' Provident Life Office, 1985–92; Rank Organisation, 1985–94; United Kingdom Fund Inc., 1987–2001. Member: BOTB, 1978–82 (Chm., N American Adv. Gp, 1973–82); British-American Associates, 1988–94; Marshall Aid Commem. Cttee, 1988–94. Pres., British Ceramic Manufacturers' Fedn, 1970–71; Mem., Design Council, 1977–82. Mem. Ct, Univ. of Keele. Fellow, Inst. of Marketing (grad. 1950); CCMI (FBIM 1968); Comp. Inst. Ceramics. KStJ 1972. Hon. MUniv Keele, 1978; Hon. DLitt Staffordshire, 1993. *Recreations:* walking, reading. *Address:* Parkfields Cottage, Tittensor, Stoke-on-Trent, Staffs ST12 9HQ. *T:* (01782) 372686.

BRYAN, Dora May, (Mrs William Lawton), OBE 1996; actress; *b* 7 Feb. 1924; *d* of Albert Broadbent and Georgina (*née* Hill); *m* 1954, William Lawton; one *s* (and one *s* one *d* adopted). *Educ:* Hathershaw Council Sch., Lancs. Pantomimes: London Hippodrome, 1936; Manchester Palace, 1937; Alhambra, Glasgow, 1938; Oldham Repertory, 1939–44; followed by Peterborough, Colchester, Westcliff-on-Sea. ENSA, Italy, during War of 1939–45. Came to London, 1945, and appeared in West End Theatres: Peace in our Time; Travellers' Joy; Accolade; Lyric Revue; Globe Revue; Simon and Laura; The Water Gypsies; Gentlemen Prefer Blondes; Six of One; Too True to be Good; Hello, Dolly!; They Don't Grow on Trees; Rookery Nook, Her Majesty's, 1979; The Merry Wives of Windsor, Regent's Park, 1984; She Stoops to Conquer, Nat. Theatre, 1985; The Apple Cart, Haymarket, 1986; Charlie Girl, Victoria Palace, 1986, Birmingham, 1988; Pygmalion, Plymouth, New York, 1987; 70, Girls, 70, Vaudeville, 1991; The Birthday Party, NT, 1994; Hello Dora (one-woman show), tour, 1996; Miss Prism, in The Importance of Being Earnest, tour, 1999; Talking Heads, tour, 2000; The Full Monty, Prince of Wales, 2002; Chichester Festival seasons, 1971–74 and 1995–97; London Palladium season, 1971; London Palladium Pantomime season, 1973–74. *Films include:* The Fallen Idol, 1949; A Taste of Honey, 1961 (British Acad. Award); Two a Penny, 1968; Great St Trinian's Train Robbery, 1970; Apartment Zero, 1989; Angel for May, 2002. *TV series:* appearances on A to Z; Sunday Night at the London Palladium; According to Dora, 1968; Both Ends Meet, 1972; Mother's Ruin, 1994; Last of the Summer Wine, 2001. Cabaret in Canada, Hong Kong and Britain. Has made recordings. *Publication:* According to Dora (autobiog.), 1987, 2nd edn 1996. *Recreations:* reading, patchwork quilts, cooking, dog walking, tapestry. *Address:* 118 Marine Parade, Brighton BN2 1DD. *T:* (01273) 603235.

BRYAN, Gerald Jackson, CMG 1964; CVO 1966; OBE 1960; MC 1941; Member, Lord Chancellor's Panel of Independent Inquiry Inspectors, 1982–91; *b* 2 April 1921; *yr s* of late George Bryan, OBE, LLD, and Ruby Evelyn (*née* Jackson), Belfast; *m* 1947, Georgiana Wendy Cockburn, OStJ, Hon. Belonger, BVI, *d* of late William Barraud and Winnifred Hull; one *s* two *d*. *Educ:* Wrekin Coll.; RMA, Woolwich; New Coll., Oxford. Regular Commn, RE, 1940; served Middle East with No 11 (Scottish) Commando, 1941; retd 1944, Capt. (temp. Maj.). Apptd Colonial Service, 1944; Asst District Comr, Swaziland, 1944; Asst Colonial Sec., Barbados, 1950; Estabt Sec., Mauritius, 1954; Administrator, Brit. Virgin Is, 1959; Administrator of St Lucia, 1962–67, retired; Govt Sec. and Head of Isle of Man Civil Service, 1967–69; General Manager: Londonderry Develt Commn, NI, 1969–73; Bracknell Develt Corp., 1973–82. Director: Lovaux Engrg Co. Ltd, 1982–88; MDSL Estates Ltd, 1988–2001. Sec. Gen., Assoc. of Contact Lens Manufacturers, 1983–88. Mem. (C), Berks CC, 1983–85. Treasurer, 1979–99, Vice-Chm., 1999–2002, Gordon Foundn; Gov., Gordon's Sch. (formerly Gordon Boys' Home), Woking, 1979–2002. Chm., St John Council for Berks, 1981–88. KStJ 1985,

Mem., Chapter Gen., 1987–96. Hon. Belonger, BVI, 2000. *Recreation:* swimming. *Address:* Whitehouse, Murrell Hill Lane, Binfield, Bracknell, Berks RG42 4BY. *T:* (01344) 425447. *Clubs:* Royal Commonwealth Society; Leander.

BRYAN, Katharine Ann; Chief Executive, Northern Ireland Water (formerly Water Service, Northern Ireland), since 2004; *b* 25 Nov. 1952; *d* of John and Dorothy Ludlow; *m* 1974, Michael Bryan; two *d. Educ:* Univ. of Durham (BSc Jt Hons Botany and Geog.); Univ. of Aston in Birmingham (MSc Biol. of Water Mgt). National Rivers Authority: Manager, Regl Fisheries, Conservation and Recreation, Severn-Trent Reg., 1988–92; Regl Gen. Manager (SW), 1992–95; Regl Dir (SW), Envmt Agency, 1995–2000; Chief Exec., N of Scotland Water Authy, 2000–02; Chm., Jt Nature Conservation Cttee, 2002–03. Mem., CIWEM, 1995. *Address:* Northern Ireland Water, Northland House, 3 Frederick Street, Belfast BT1 2NR. *T:* (028) 9035 4749; *e-mail:* katharine.bryan@niwater.com.

BRYAN, Kenneth John; Chairman, Southampton University Hospitals NHS Trust, 1996–2001; *b* 22 July 1939; *s* of late Patrick Joseph Bryan and Elsie May Bryan; *m* 1962 (marr. diss. 1999); one *d*; *m* Gillian. *Educ:* De La Salle Coll.; Farnborough GS. Insurance Broker, Lloyds, 1957–59; Major, British Army, 1959–78; Sen. Mgt Cons., KPMG, 1978–79; Hongkong and Shanghai Banking Corporation: Financial Controller, Hong Kong office, 1979–86; Sen. Manager, Banking Services, 1986–88; Hd of Gp Finances, 1988–93; Chief Financial Officer, Midland Bank, 1993–96; Dir Gen., Southampton and Fareham Chamber of Commerce and Industry, 2001–04. Chm. Trustees, Hampshire Autistic Soc., 2001–02 (Trustee, 1996–2002). Gov., Barton Peverill Coll., 1998–2002. Mem., Pangbourne Parish Council, 2007–. *Recreations:* golf, fly fishing. *Club:* Army and Navy.

BRYAN, Margaret, CMG 1988; HM Diplomatic Service, retired; Ambassador to Panama, 1986–89; *b* 26 Sept. 1929; *d* of James Grant and Dorothy Rebecca Galloway; *m* 1952, Peter Bernard Bryan (marr. diss. 1981). *Educ:* Cathedral Sch., Shanghai; Croydon High Sch.; Girton Coll., Cambridge (MA Modern Languages). Second, later First, Secretary, FCO, 1962–80; Head of Chancery and Consul, Kinshasa, 1980–83; Counsellor, Havana, 1983–86. *Recreations:* theatre, travel, opera. *Club:* Royal Over-Seas League.

BRYAN, Robert Patrick, OBE 1980; security consultant; Police Adviser to Foreign and Commonwealth Office, and Inspector General of Dependent Territories Police, 1980–85, retired; *b* 29 June 1926; *s* of Maurice Bryan and Elizabeth (*née* Waite); *m* 1948, Hazel Audrey (*née* Braine) (*d* 1990); three *s. Educ:* Plaistow Secondary Sch.; Wanstead County High Sch. Indian Army (Mahratta LI), 1944–47. Bank of Nova Scotia, 1948–49; Metropolitan Police: Constable, 1950; Dep. Asst Commissioner, 1977, retired 1980. National Police College: Intermediate Comd Course, 1965; Sen. Comd Course, 1969; occasional lecturer. RCDS 1974. Non-exec. Dir, Control Risks Internat. Ltd, 1986–87; Corporate Security Advr, Unilever, 1986–99; Chm., Los Zapateros (cobblers), 1998–99. Chm., Food Distribn Security Assoc., 1988–99. Gov., Corps of Commissionaires, 1993–97. Governor, Hampton Sch., 1978–97. *Publications:* contribs to police and related pubns, particularly on community relations and juvenile delinquency. *Address:* 28 Bolton Gardens, Teddington, Middx TW11 9AY.

BRYAN, Simon James; QC 2006; *b* 23 Nov. 1965; *s* of James and Dorothy Bryan; *m* 1989, Katharine Hilton; one *s* one *d. Educ:* Arnold Sch.; Magdalene Coll., Cambridge (Schol.; Maxwell Prize, George Long Prize; BA Double 1st Law Tripos 1987). Council of Legal Educn Studentship, 1986; called to the Bar, Lincoln's Inn, 1988 (Denning Schol.); Supervisor in Law, Magdalene Coll., Cambridge, 1988–89; in practice as a barrister specialising in commercial law, 1989–. CEDR Accredited Mediator, 2006; MCIArb 2007. Freeman, City of London, 2002; Liveryman, Co. of Gardeners, 2002–. *Publication:* (Asst Ed. and contrib.) Encyclopedia of International Commercial Litigation, 2008. *Recreations:* winter sports, travel, gardening, dogs. *Address:* Essex Court Chambers, 24 Lincoln's Inn Fields, WC2A 3EG. *T:* (020) 7813 8000, *Fax:* (020) 7813 8080; *e-mail:* sjbryan@essexcourt.net. *Club:* Travellers.

BRYANT, (Alan) Christopher, OBE 1995; Life President, Bryant Group plc (formerly Bryant Holdings Ltd), since 1992 (Managing Director, 1960–88; Chairman, 1962–92); *b* 28 July 1923; *s* of Ebenezer John Bryant and Ivy Maud Bryant (*née* Seymour); *m* 1951, Jean Mary Nock (*d* 2002); four *d. Educ:* West House School, Birmingham; Malvern Coll.; Birmingham Univ. (BSc (Hons)). FCIOB 1958. Engineer Officer, Fleet Air Arm, 1944–47 (Sub-Lieut, RNVR); Project Manager, 1946–48, Director, 1948–86, C. Bryant & Son Ltd. Non-exec. Dir, BSG International plc, 1985–94. Chm., 1969–95, Pres., 1987–, Birmingham YMCA; Hon. Treas., Nat. Council of YMCAs, 1991–95. Hon. DEng Birmingham, 1992. *Recreations:* sailing, walking. *Clubs:* Naval; South Caernarvonshire Yacht.

BRYANT, Christopher; *see* Bryant, A. C.

BRYANT, Christopher John; MP (Lab) Rhondda, since 2001; *b* 11 Jan. 1962; *s* of Rees Bryant and Anne Gracie Bryant (*née* Goodwin). *Educ:* Cheltenham Coll.; Mansfield Coll., Oxford (MA); Ripon Coll., Cuddesdon (MA, DipTh). Ordained deacon, 1986, priest, 1987; Asst Curate, All Saints, High Wycombe, 1986–89; Youth Chaplain, Dio. Peterborough, 1989–91; Organiser, Holborn & St Pancras Lab. Party, 1991–93; Local Govt Devlt Officer, Lab. Party, 1993–94. London Manager, Common Purpose, 1994–96; freelance writer, 1996–98; Hd, Eur. Affairs, BBC, 1998–2000. *Publications:* (ed) Reclaiming the Ground, 1993; (ed) John Smith: an appreciation, 1995; Possible Dreams, 1996; Stafford Cripps: the first modern Chancellor, 1997; Glenda Jackson: the biography, 1998. *Recreations:* theatre, modern art, Spain. *Address:* House of Commons, SW1A 0AA. *T:* (020) 7219 8315; *e-mail:* bryantc@parliament.uk. *Club:* Ferndale Rugby Football (Vice-Pres.) (Rhondda).

BRYANT, David John, CBE 1980 (MBE 1969); international bowler, 1958–92; *b* 27 Oct. 1931; *s* of Reginald Samuel Harold Bryant and Evelyn Claire (*née* Weaver); *m* 1960, Ruth Georgina (*née* Roberts); two *d. Educ:* Weston Grammar Sch.; St Paul's Coll., Cheltenham; Redland Coll., Bristol (teacher training colls). National Service, RAF, 1950–52; teacher trng, 1953–55; schoolmaster, 1955–71; company director, sports business, 1971–78; Dir, Drakelite Ltd (Internat. Bowls Consultant), 1978–97. Hon. Pres., English Bowling Assoc. Charity Trust, 2002–. Patron, Francis Drake Fellowship, 1994–. World Singles Champion, 1966, 1980 and 1988; World Indoor Singles Champion, 1979, 1980 and 1981; World Indoor Pairs Champion, 1986, 1987, 1989, 1990, 1991 and 1992; Kodak Masters International Singles Champion, 1978, 1979 and 1982; Gateway International Masters Singles Champion, 1984, 1985, 1986, 1987; Woolwich International Singles Champion, 1988, 1989; World Triples Champion, 1980; Commonwealth Games Gold Medallist: Singles: 1962, 1970, 1974 and 1978; Fours: 1962. Numerous national and British Isles titles, both indoor and outdoor. England Indoor Team Captain, 1993, 1994. *Publications:* Bryant on Bowls, 1966; Bowl with Bryant, 1984; Bryant on Bowls, 1985; The Game of Bowls, 1990; Bowl to Win, 1994. *Recreations:* angling, gardening. *Address:* 47 Esmond Grove, Clevedon, Somerset BS21 7HP. *Clubs:* Clevedon Bowling, Clevedon Conservative.

BRYANT, His Honour David Michael Arton; a Circuit Judge, 1989–2007; *b* 27 Jan. 1942; *s* of Lt-Col and Mrs A. D. Bryant; *m* 1969, Diana Caroline, *d* of Brig. and Mrs W. C. W. Sloan; two *s* one *d. Educ:* Wellington Coll.; Oriel Coll., Oxford (Open Scholar; MA). Called to the Bar, Inner Temple, 1964; practised North Eastern Circuit, 1965–89. Recorder, 1985–89. *Recreations:* gardening, shooting, tennis, Byzantine history. *Address:* Sleningford Park, Ripon, N Yorks HG4 3JA. *Club:* Carlton.

BRYANT, Air Vice-Marshal Derek Thomas, CB 1987; OBE 1974; Air Officer Commanding, Headquarters Command and Staff Training and Commandant, Royal Air Force Staff College, 1987–89, retired; *b* 1 Nov. 1933; *s* of Thomas Bryant and Mary (*née* Thurley); *m* 1956, Patricia Dodge; one *s* one *d. Educ:* Latymer Upper Grammar Sch., Hammersmith. Fighter pilot, 1953; Qualified Flying Instructor, 1957; Sqdn Comdr, 1968–74; OC RAF Coningsby, 1976–78; SASO HQ 38 Gp, 1982–84; Dep. Comdr, RAF Germany, 1984–87; various courses and staff appts. *Recreations:* gardening, golf. *Address:* The Old Stables, Lower Swell, Fivehead, Taunton, Somerset TA3 6PH. *Club:* Royal Air Force.

BRYANT, Prof. Greyham Frank, PhD; FREng, FIET; FIMA; Professor of Control, Imperial College, London University, 1982–98, now Professor Emeritus and Senior Research Fellow; *b* 3 June 1931; *s* of Ernest Noel Bryant and Florence Ivy (*née* Russell); *m* 1955, Iris Sybil Jardine; two *s. Educ:* Reading Univ.; Imperial Coll. (PhD). FIMA 1973; FIET (FIEE 1987); FREng (FEng 1988). Sen. Scientific Officer, Iron and Steel Res., London, 1959–64; Imperial College: Res. Fellow, 1964–67; Reader in Industrial Control, 1975–82. Chm., Broner Consultants, 1979–88; Director: Greycon Consultants, 1985–2000; Circulation Research, 1989–. *Publications:* Automation of Tandem Mills (jtly), 1973; (with L. F. Yeung) Multivariable Control and System Design Techniques, 1996; papers on design of management control schemes, multivariable control and modelling, in learned jls. *Recreations:* music, oil painting. *Address:* 18 Wimborne Avenue, Norwood Green, Middlesex UB2 4HB. *T:* (020) 8574 5648. *Club:* Athenæum.

BRYANT, John Martin, FREng, FIMMM; Joint Chief Executive, Corus Group plc, 1999–2000; *b* 28 Sept. 1943; *s* of William George Bryant and Doris Bryant; *m* 1965, Andrea Irene Emmons; two *s* one *d. Educ:* West Monmouth Sch.; St Catharine's Coll., Cambridge (BA Nat. Sci. 1965; MA). CEng 1993; FIMMM (FIM 1993). Trainee, Steel Co. of Wales, 1965; British Steel, 1967–99: Production/Technical Mgt, Port Talbot works, 1967–78; Works Manager, Hot Rolled Products, Port Talbot, 1978–87; Project Manager, Hot Strip Mill Develt, 1982–87; Works Manager, Cold Rolled Products, Shotton, 1987–88; Dir, Coated Products, 1988–90; Dir, Tinplate, 1990–92; Man. Dir, Strip Products, 1992–96; Exec. Dir, 1996–99; Chief Exec., 1999. Director: ASW plc, 1993–95; Bank of Wales plc, 1996–2001; Welsh Water plc, 2001–; Glas Cymru Ltd, 2001–; Costain Gp plc, 2002–. Trustee, Ogmore Centre, 2003–. FREng 2000. Hon. DSc Wales, 2000. *Recreations:* Rugby, cricket, theatre, opera, family. *Address:* Broadway Farm, 24 Rogers Lane, Laleston, Bridgend CF32 0LA.

BRYANT, John William; Editor-in-Chief, The Daily Telegraph and The Sunday Telegraph, 2005–06; *b* 25 April 1944; *s* of late James Douglas John Bryant and Mollie Bryant; *m* 1968, Carol Leffman; two *s. Educ:* Sexey's Sch., Bruton; Queen's Coll., Oxford (BA Hons 1966). Edinburgh Evening News, 1967–70; Daily Mail, 1971–86, Exec. Editor, 1980–86; The Times: Man. Editor, 1986–88; Dep. Editor, 1988–90; Editor: Sunday Correspondent, 1990; The European, 1991; Dep. Editor, The Times, 1991–2000; Consultant Editor, Daily Mail, 2000–05. Chm., Press Assoc. Trust, 2008. Trustee, London Marathon, 2007–. *Publications:* Jogging, 1979; 3:59.4: The Quest to Break the Four Minute Mile, 2004; The London Marathon, 2005; The Marathon Makers, 2008. *Recreations:* athletics, cross-country and road running, singing (scrumpy'n western). *Address:* 18 Wonford Close, Coombe Lane, Kingston-upon-Thames, Surrey KT2 7XA. *Clubs:* Travellers'; Vincent's (Oxford); Thames Hare and Hounds.

BRYANT, Judith Marie, (Mrs H. M. Hodkinson), RGN; retired; Fellow, King's Fund College, 1990–94 (part-time Fellow, 1986–90); *b* 31 Dec. 1942; *d* of Frederic John Bryant and Joan Marion (*née* Summerfield); *m* 1986, Prof. Henry Malcolm Hodkinson, *qv. Educ:* City of London Sch. for Girls; The London Hosp. (RGN 1964); Brunel Univ. (MPhil 1983). Ward Sister, UCH, 1965–69; Nursing Officer, subseq. Sen. Nursing Officer, Northwick Park Hosp., Harrow, 1969–75; Divl Nursing Officer, Harrow, 1975–78; Dist Nursing Officer, Enfield, 1978–82, Victoria, 1982–85; Chief Nursing Officer and Dir of Quality Assurance, Riverside HA, 1985–86; Regl Nursing Officer, NE Thames RHA, 1986–90. Florence Nightingale Meml Scholar, USA and Canada, 1970. Adviser, DHSS Res. Liaison Cttee for the Elderly, 1977–83; Member: SW Herts DHA, 1981–86; NHS Training Authority, Nurses and Midwives Staff Training Cttee, 1986–89; 1930 Fund for Dist Nurses, 1985–2004; Cttee, Nurseline, 1996–2000. Mem., Criminal Injuries Compensation Appeals Panel, 1999–. *Publication:* (with H. M. Hodkinson) Sherratt? A Natural Family of Staffordshire Figures, 1991. *Recreations:* opera, gardening. *Address:* 8 Chiswick Square, Burlington Lane, W4 2QG. *T:* (020) 8747 0239.

BRYANT, Julius John Victor, FSA; Keeper of Word & Image, Victoria & Albert Museum, since 2005; *b* 17 Dec. 1957; *s* of late Robert Bryant and of Dena Bryant (*née* Bond); *m* 1984, Barbara Ann Coffey; one *s. Educ:* St Alban's Sch.; University College London; Courtauld Inst. of Art. Paintings Cataloguer, Sotheby's, 1980–81; Mus. Asst, V&A Mus., 1982–83; Asst Curator, 1983–88, Curator, 1989–90, Iveagh Bequest, Kenwood; English Heritage: Hd of Museums Div. and Dir of London Historic Properties, 1990–95; Dir of Museums and Collections, 1995–2002; Chief Curator, 2003–05. Visiting Fellow: Yale Center for British Art, 1985; Huntington Liby and Art Gall., Calif, 1992; British Council Res. Scholar, Leningrad, 1989. Guest Curator, Sir John Soane's Mus., 2002–05. Member: London Museums Consultative Cttee, 1989–99; Exec. Council, Area Museums Service for SE England, 1992–95; Art Museum Directors' Conf. (formerly Conf. of Nat. and Regl Mus. Dirs), 1998–2005; Hampstead Heath Mgt Cttee, 1990–95; Council, Furniture History Soc., 1998–2000; Mgt Cttee, AHRC (formerly AHRB) Centre for Study of the Domestic Interior, 2002–05; Anglo Sikh Heritage Trail Adv. Gp, 2003–; Adv. Council, Paul Mellon Centre for Studies in British Art, Yale Univ., 2004–; Internat. Adv. Cttee of Keepers of Public Collections of Graphic Art, 2006–; Dep. Chm., Cttee for Historic House Museums, ICOM, 2002– (Mem., 1999–). Pres., Hampstead Heath DFAS, 1989–. FSA 1999. Editor, Collections Review, 1997–2003. *Publications:* Marble Hill: the design and use of a Palladian estate, 1986; Finest Prospects, 1986; The Victoria and Albert Museum Guide, 1986; Marble Hill House, 1988; Mrs Howard: a woman of reason, 1988; (jtly) The Landscape of Kenwood, 1990; The Iveagh Bequest, Kenwood, 1990; Robert Adam, 1992; London's Country House Collections, 1993; (jtly) The Trojan War: sculptures by Anthony Caro, 1994, 3rd edn 1998; Turner: painting the nation, 1996; Marble Hill, 2002; The Wernher Collection, 2002; (ed) Decorative Arts from the Wernher Collection, 2002; Catalogue of Paintings in the Iveagh Bequest, Kenwood, 2003; Anthony Caro: a life in sculpture, 2004; Thomas Banks (1735–1805): Britain's first modern sculptor, 2005; Apsley House: the Wellington Collection, 2005; The

English Grand Tour, 2005; The Complete Works of Barry Martin, 2007; contribs to Oxford DNB, Grove Dictionary of Art; exhibn catalogues; articles in jls. *Recreations:* running around Hampstead Heath, family life. *Address:* Victoria & Albert Museum, Knightsbridge, SW7 2RL.

BRYANT, Rt Rev. Mark Watts; *see* Jarrow, Bishop Suffragan of.

BRYANT, Martin Warwick; Chief Executive, Shareholder Executive, 2006–07; *b* 30 June 1952; *s* of Douglas and Marjorie Bryant; *m* 1979, Hilary Mary Southall; one *s* two *d*. *Educ:* Christ Church, Oxford (MA Hist. and Econs 1975); Univ. of Leeds (MA Econs 1978); Cranfield Sch. of Mgt (MBA 1983). Planning Manager, BOC Gp, 1983–87; Dir of Corporate Develt, Charles Barker plc, 1987–89; Dir of Corporate Develt, Boots Co. plc, 1989–95; Man. Dir, Boots Opticians Ltd, 1995–97; Ops Dir, Boots The Chemists, 1997–2000; Man. Dir, Boots Retail Internat., 2000; Dir of Business Develt, Boots Co. plc, 2000–02; Chief Operating Officer, BP Retail (UK), 2002–04; Dir of Strategy, Home Office, 2004–06. *Recreations:* golf, ski-ing, vintage motor cars. *Address:* Upton Grange, Upton, Newark, Notts NG23 5SY. *T:* (01636) 812901; *e-mail:* martinwbryant@aol.com.

BRYANT, Prof. Peter Elwood, FRS 1991; Watts Professor of Psychology, Oxford University, 1980–2004; Fellow of Wolfson College, Oxford, 1980–2004, now Emeritus; *b* 24 June 1937; *s* of Michael Bryant; *m* (marr. diss.); one *s* two *d*; *m* 1995, Prof. Terezinha Nunes, *qv*. *Educ:* Blundell's Sch.; Clare College, Cambridge (BA 1963; MA 1967); London Univ. (PhD). University Lecturer in Human Experimental Psychology, Oxford, 1967–80; Fellow, St John's Coll., Oxford, 1967–80. Vis. Prof., Oxford Brookes Univ. Editor: British Jl of Developmental Psychol., 1982–88; Cognitive Development, 2000–. President's award, BPsS, 1984; Dist. Scientific Contribn Award, Soc. for Scientific Study of Reading, 1999. *Publications:* Perception and Understanding in Young Children, 1974; (with L. Bradley) Children's Reading Problems, 1985; (with U. Goswami) Phonological Skills and Learning to Read, 1990; with T. Nunes: Children Doing Mathematics, 1996; Learning & Teaching Mathematics: an international perspective, 1997; Improving Literacy Through Teaching Morphemes, 2006; Children's Reading and Spelling: beyond the first steps, 2008. *Address:* Wolfson College, Oxford OX2 6UD.

BRYANT, Peter George Francis; Under Secretary, Department of Trade and Industry, 1989–92; *b* 10 May 1932; *s* of late George Bryant, CBE and Margaret Bryant; *m* 1961, Jean (*née* Morriss); one *s* one *d*. *Educ:* Sutton Valence Sch.; Birkbeck Coll., London Univ. (BA). Min. of Supply, 1953–55; BoT, 1955–69; 1st Sec. (Commercial), Vienna (on secondment), 1970–72; Dir of British Trade Drive in S Germany, 1973; Department of Trade (later Department of Trade and Industry), 1974–85; seconded to HM Diplomatic Service as Consul-Gen., Düsseldorf, 1985–88, and Dir-Gen. of Trade and Investment Promotion, FRG, 1988.

BRYANT, Air Vice-Marshal Simon, CBE 2005; Chief of Staff Personnel and Air Secretary, since 2006; *b* 20 June 1956; *s* of Robert Francis and Audrey Ethel Ashby Bryant; *m* 1984, Helen Burns; one *s* one *d*. *Educ:* Stamford Sch.; Nottingham Univ. (BA Hons Geog. 1977); King's Coll. London (MA Defence Studies). Joined RAF, 1974; served with Fighter Sqdns Nos 19, 56 and 23, 1979–89, and VF-101 USN, 1984–87; RAF Personnel Mgt Centre, 1989–91; RAF Staff Coll., 1992; MoD, 1992–95; No 43 (Fighter) Sqdn, 1996–2001, OC, 1999–2001; Personal Staff Officer to Dep. Comdr, SHAPE, 2001–03; AO Scotland and CO, RAF Leuchars, 2003–05; Dir, Jt Capability, 2005–06. *Recreations:* tennis, squash, golf. *Address:* Hurricane Block, 1N77, RAF High Wycombe, Bucks HP14 4UE.

BRYANT, Thomas, CMG 1995; HM Diplomatic Service, retired; Consul General, Zürich, 1991–95; *b* 1 Nov. 1938; *s* of George Edward Bryant and Ethel May Bryant (*née* Rogers); *m* 1st, 1961, Vivien Mary Theresa Hill (marr. diss. 2002); twin *s* one *d*; 2nd, 2002, Jean Hilary Todd (*née* Colbert). *Educ:* William Ellis Sch., London; Polytechnic of Central London (DMS). Nat. service, Army, 1957–59. Entered FO, 1957; Hong Kong, 1963; Peking, 1963–65; Vice Consul, Frankfurt, 1966–68; Second Sec., Tel Aviv, 1968–72; First Sec., FCO, 1973–76; Vienna, 1976–80; FCO, 1980–82, Counsellor, 1982; Hd of Finance Dept, 1982–84; Consul-Gen., Munich, 1984–88; Dep. High Comr, Nairobi, 1988–91. *Recreations:* cricket, soccer, tennis, classical music, laughter. *Address:* 36 Fulmar Drive, East Grinstead, W Sussex RH19 3NN.

BRYARS, Donald Leonard; Commissioner of Customs and Excise, 1978–84 and Director, Personnel, 1979–84, retired; *b* 31 March 1929; *s* of late Leonard and Marie Bryars; *m* 1953, Joan (*née* Yealand); one *d*. *Educ:* Goole Grammar Sch.; Leeds Univ. Joined Customs and Excise as Executive Officer, 1953, Principal, 1964, Asst Sec., 1971; on loan to Cabinet Office, 1976–78; Director, General Customs, 1978–79. Dir (non-exec.), The Customs Annuity Benevolent Fund Inc., 1986–2004. Trustee, Milton's Cottage Trust, 1993–2002. *Address:* 15 Cedars Walk, Chorleywood, Rickmansworth, Herts WD3 5GD. *T:* (01923) 446752. *Club:* Civil Service (Chm., 1981–85).

BRYARS, Gavin; *see* Bryars, R. G.

BRYARS, (Richard) Gavin; composer; *b* 16 Jan. 1943; *s* of Walter Joseph Bryars and Miriam Eleanor Bryars (*née* Hopley); *m* 1st, 1971, Angela Margaret Bigley (marr. diss. 1993); two *d*; 2nd, 1999, Anna Tchernakova; one *s*, and one step *d*. *Educ:* Goole Grammar Sch.; Sheffield Univ. (BA Hons Philosophy). Freelance bassist, 1963–66; Mem. trio, Joseph Holbrooke (improvising), 1964–66, 1998–; Lecturer: Northampton Tech. Coll. and Sch. of Art, 1966–67; Portsmouth Coll. of Art, 1969–70; Sen. Lectr, Leicester Poly., 1970–85; Prof. of Music, Leicester Poly., later De Montfort Univ., 1985–96 (part-time, 1994–96). Visiting Professor: Univ. of Victoria, BC, 1999–2001; Univ. of Hertfordshire, 1999–2004; Associate Res. Fellow, Dartington Coll. of Arts, 2005–. Founder and Dir, Gavin Bryars Ensemble, 1979–. Mem., Collège de Pataphysique, France, 1974– (Pres., sous-commn des Cliques Claques, 1984–; Regent, 2002–). *Compositions* include: The Sinking of the Titanic, 1969; Jesus' Blood Never Failed Me Yet, 1971; Out of Zaleski's Gazebo, 1977; My First Homage, 1978; The Cross Channel Ferry, 1979; The Vespertine Park, The English Mail-Coach, 1980; Les Fiançailles, Allegrasco, 1983; On Photography, Effarene, 1984; String quartet No 1, 1985; Pico's Flight, Sub Rosa, 1986; By the Vaar, The Old Tower of Löbenicht, 1987; Invention of Tradition, Glorious Hill, Doctor Ox's Experiment (Epilogue), 1988; Incipit Vita Nova, 1989; Cadman Requiem, 1989, revd 1996; Alaric I or II, 1989; After the Requiem, String Quartet No 2, 1990; The Black River, The Green Ray, 1991; The White Lodge, 1991; (with Juan Munoz) A Man in a Room Gambling, Die Letzen Tage, 1992; The War in Heaven, The North Shore, 1993; Three Elegies for Nine Clarinets, One Last Bar Then Joe Can Sing, The East Coast, 1994; The South Downs, In Nomine (after Purcell), After Handel's Vesper, Cello Concerto, 1995; The Adnan Songbook, 1996; The Island Chapel, And so ended Kant's travelling in this world, 1997; String Quartet no 3, 1998; First Book of Madrigals, 1998–99; The Porazzi Fragment, 1999; Violin Concerto, 2000; Second Book of Madrigals, 2002; Double Bass Concerto, 2002; Laude Cortonese, vols I and II, 2002–04; Third Book of Madrigals, 2003–04; New York (concerto for percussion quintet and orch.), 2004; Lachrymae (viol consort), 2004; From Egil's Saga, 2004; Eight Irish Madrigals, 2004; Creamer Etudes, 2005; Nine Irish Madrigals, 2006; Silva Caledonia, 2006; The Paper Nautilus, 2006; Nothing Like the Sun, 2007; The Church Closest to the Sea, 2007; Sonnets from Scotland, 2008; Ian in the Broch, 2008; Lón Anama, 2008; In Praise of Trond, 2008; *opera:* Medea, for Opéra de Lyon, 1982, revd 1984, 1995; Doctor Ox's Experiment, for ENO, 1998; G, for Staatstheater Mainz, 2002; *ballet:* Four Elements, 1990; Wonderlawn, 1994; 2, 1995; BIPED, 2000; Writings on Water, 2002; Amjad, 2007; *theatre:* To Define Happiness, Tallinn, 2007; *film music:* Last Summer, 2000; Sea and Stars, 2002. Has made recordings. Hon. DArts Plymouth, 2006. *Recreations:* supporting, from a distance, Yorkshire CCC and Queen's Park Rangers FC; dalmatians. *Address:* c/o Schott Music, 48 Great Marlborough Street, W1F 2BB. *T:* (020) 7534 0750; *web:* www.gavinbryars.com.

BRYCE, Gabe Robb, OBE 1959; Sales Manager (Operations) British Aircraft Corporation, 1965–75; occupied in breeding dogs and boarding cats, until retirement from animal world, 1987; *b* 27 April 1921; *m* 1943, Agnes Lindsay; one *s* one *d*. *Educ:* Glasgow High School. Served in RAF, 1939–46. Vickers-Armstrongs (Aircraft) Ltd, 1946–60 (Chief Test Pilot, 1951–60). Participated as First or Second Pilot, in Maiden Flights of following British Aircraft: Varsity; Nene Viking; Viscount 630, 700 and 800; Tay Viscount; Valiant; Pathfinder; Vanguard; VC-10; BAC 1–11; Chief Test Pilot, British Aircraft Corporation, 1960–64. Fellow Soc. of Experimental Test Pilots (USA), 1967. Sir Barnes Wallis Meml Medal, GAPAN, 1980. *Recreations:* squash, tennis. *Address:* 8 Rowan Green, Rosslyn Park, Weybridge, Surrey KT13 9NF. *T:* (01932) 858996.

BRYCE, Gordon, RSA 1993 (ARSA 1976); RSW 1976; painter; Head of Fine Art, Gray's School of Art, Aberdeen, 1986–95; *b* 30 June 1943; *s* of George and Annie Bryce; *m* 1st, 1966, Margaret Lothian (marr. diss. 1976); two *s*; 2nd, 1984, Hilary Duthie; one *s* two *d*. *Educ:* Edinburgh Acad.; George Watson's Coll., Edinburgh; Edinburgh Coll. of Art. Dip. in Art. Exhibited widely in UK, Europe and USA, 1965–, esp. Scottish Gall., Edinburgh and Thackeray Gall., London; 30 one-man exhibns of painting, UK and overseas; paintings in public and private collections, UK, Europe, USA, Canada. *Recreation:* fly fishing. *Address:* Sylva Cottage, 2 Culter House Road, Milltimber, Aberdeen AB1 0EN. *T:* (01224) 733274.

BRYCE, Ian James G.; *see* Graham-Bryce.

BRYCE, Rt Rev. Jabez Leslie; *see* Polynesia, Bishop in.

BRYCE, Quentin Alice Louise, AC 2003 (AO 1988); Governor-General of Australia, since 2008; *b* 23 Dec. 1942; *d* of Norman Walter Strachan and Edwina Naida Strachan (*née* Wetzel); *m* 1964, Michael John Strachan Bryce, AE; three *s* two *d*. *Educ:* Moreton Bay Coll., Queensland; Univ. of Queensland (BA 1962; LLB 1965). Admitted to Qld Bar, 1965; Lectr and Tutor, Law Sch., Univ. of Qld, 1968–82; Dir, Women's Inf. Service Qld, Dept of PM and Cabinet, 1984–87; Qld Dir, Human Rights and Equal Opportunity Commn, 1987; Fed. Sex Discrimination Comr, 1988–93; Chm. and CEO, Nat. Childcare Accreditation Council, 1993–96; Principal and CEO, The Women's Coll., Univ. of Sydney, 1997–2003; Governor of Qld, 2003–08. US State Dept Visitor, 1978; Mem., Aust. Delegn to UN Human Rights Commn, Geneva, 1989–92. Nat. Pres., Assoc. for Welfare of Children in Hosp., 1978–81; Vice Pres., Qld Council for Civil Liberties, 1979–80; Pres., Women's Cricket Australia, 1999–2003; Director: Aust. Children's TV Foundn Bd, 1982–92; YWCA, Sydney, 1997–2000; Bradman Foundn, 2002–03; Convener, Nat. Women's Adv. Council, 1982–83 (Mem., 1978–81); Chairman: Jessie Street Nat. Women's Liby, 1996–98; Nat. Breast Cancer Centre Adv. Network, 1996–2003; Member: Internat. Yr for Disabled Persons Legal Cttee, Qld, 1981; Family Planning Council, Qld, 1981–92; Nat. Cttee on Discrimination in Employment and Occupation, 1982–86; Bd, Schizophrenia Foundn Aust., 1987–90; Bd, Abused Child Trust, Qld, 1988–89; Bd, Mindcare Mental Health Foundn, 1990–95; Nat. Alternative Dispute Resolution Adv. Council, 1995–97; Bd, Plan Internat., 1996–2003; Sydney IVF Ethics Cttee, 2000–03. Presiding Mem., Bd of Mgt, Dip. of Policing Practice, NSW, 1998–2001. Mem. Council, Central Qld Univ., 1999–2001. Patron, Nat. Alliance of Girls' Schs, 2001–. Hon. LLD: Macquarie, 1998; Qld, 2006; Hon. DLitt Charles Sturt, 2002; DUniv: Griffith, 2003; Qld Univ. of Technol., 2004. *Address:* Government House, Canberra, ACT 2600, Australia.

BRYCE-SMITH, Prof. Derek, PhD, DSc; CChem, FRSC; Professor of Organic Chemistry, University of Reading, 1965–89, part-time, 1989–91, now Emeritus; *b* 29 April 1926; *s* of Charles Philip and Amelia Smith; *m* 1st, 1956, Marjorie Mary Anne Stewart (*d* 1966); two *s* two *d*; 2nd, 1969, Pamela Joyce Morgan; two step *d*. *Educ:* Bancrofts Sch., Woodford Wells; SW Essex Tech. Coll.; West Ham Municipal Coll.; Bedford Coll., London. Research Chemist: Powell Duffryn Res. Ltd, 1945–46; Dufay-Chromex Ltd, 1946–48; Inst. of Petroleum Student, Bedford Coll., 1948–51; ICI Post-doctoral Fellow, KCL, 1951–55; Asst Lectr in Chem., KCL, 1955–56; Lectr in Chem., 1956–63, Reader, 1963–65, Reading Univ. Founding Chm., European Photochem. Assoc., 1970–72; Founding Vice-Chm., UK Br., Internat. Solar Energy Soc., 1973–74; Chm., RSC Photochemistry Gp, 1981–92. John Jeyes Endowed Lectureship and Silver Medal, RSC, 1984–85. *Publications:* (with R. Stephens) Lead or Health, 1980, 2nd edn 1981; (with E. Hodgkinson) The Zinc Solution, 1986; (RSC Senior Reporter and contrib.) Photochemistry: a review of chemical literature, vols 1–25, 1970–94; contribs to learned jls in the fields of photochem., organometallic chem., environmental chem. and philosophy of sci. *Recreations:* gardening, making music. *Address:* Highland Wood House, Mill Lane, Kidmore End, Reading, Berks RG4 9HB. *T:* (0118) 972 3132.

BRYDEN, David John, PhD; FSA; Property Manager, Felbrigg Hall and Sheringham Park, National Trust, 1997–2001; *b* 23 Nov. 1943; *s* of George Bryden and Marion (*née* Bellingham); *m* 1964, Helen Margaret Willison; two *s*. *Educ:* Univ. of Leicester (BSc(Engrg)); Linacre Coll., Oxford (Dip. in Hist. and Philos. of Sci.); Gonville and Caius Coll., Cambridge (MA 1973); St Edmund's Coll., Cambridge (PhD 1993). FSA 1993. Asst Keeper II, Royal Scottish Mus., 1966–70; Curator, Whipple Mus. of Hist. of Sci., Univ. of Cambridge, 1970–78; Fellow and Steward, St Edmund's House, 1977–78; Asst Keeper I, Science Mus. Library, 1979–87; Academic Administrator, Gresham Coll., 1987–88; Keeper, Dept of Sci., Technol. and Working Life, Nat. Museums of Scotland, 1988–96. *Publications:* Scottish Scientific Instrument Makers 1600–1900, 1972; Napier's Bones: a history and instruction manual, 1992; (jtly) A Classified Bibliography on the history of scientific instruments, 1997; articles on early scientific instruments, history of science and technology, printing history and bibliography, numismatics. *Address:* 11 Pensham Hill, Pershore, Worcs WR10 3HA.

BRYDEN, Prof. Harry Leonard, PhD; FRS 2005; Professor of Physical Oceanography, University of Southampton, since 2000; *b* 9 July 1946; *s* of Harry L. and Ruth F. Bryden; *m* 1988, Mary E. Woodgate-Jones; four *s*. *Educ:* Dartmouth Coll. (AB Maths 1968); Massachusetts Inst. of Technol. and Woods Hole Oceanographic Instn (PhD Oceanography 1975). Postdoctoral Res. Associate, Oregon State Univ., 1975–77; Woods Hole Oceanographic Institution: Asst Scientist, 1977–80; Associate Scientist, 1980–88; Sen. Scientist, 1988–92; Physical Oceanographer: Inst. of Oceanographic Scis, Surrey,

1993–95; Southampton Oceanography Centre, 1995–2000. Vis. Fellow, Wolfson Coll., Oxford Univ., 1988–89. Henry Stommel Res. Medal, American Meteorol Soc., 2003. *Publications:* numerous refereed scientific pubns on role of the ocean in climate, ocean heat and freshwater transports, exchange between Atlantic and Mediterranean through the Strait of Gibraltar. *Recreation:* walking in the country. *Address:* School of Ocean and Earth Science, University of Southampton, Empress Dock, Southampton SO14 3ZH. *T:* (023) 8059 6437, *Fax:* (023) 8059 6204.

BRYDEN, William Campbell Rough, (Bill Bryden), CBE 1993; director and writer; Head of Drama Television, BBC Scotland, 1984–93; *b* 12 April 1942; *s* of late George Bryden and of Catherine Bryden; *m* 1971, Hon. Deborah Morris, *d* of Baron Killanin, MBE, TD; one *s* one *d*. *Educ:* Hillend Public Sch.; Greenock High Sch. Documentary writer, Scottish Television, 1963–64; Assistant Director: Belgrade Theatre, Coventry, 1965–67; Royal Court Th., London, 1967–69; Associate Director: Royal Lyceum Th., Edinburgh, 1971–74; National Th., subseq. RNT, 1975–85; Dir, Cottesloe Theatre (Nat. Theatre), 1978–80. Director: *opera:* Parsifal, 1988, The Cunning Little Vixen, 1990, 2003, Royal Opera House, Covent Garden; The Silver Tassie, Coliseum, 2000; *stage:* Bernstein's Mass, GSMD, 1987; A Life in the Theatre, Haymarket, 1989; The Ship, Harland and Wolff Shipyard, Glasgow, 1990; Cops, Greenwich, 1991; A Month in the Country, Albery, 1994; The Big Picnic, Harland and Wolff Shipyard, Glasgow (also writer), 1994 (televised 1996); Son of Man, RSC, 1995; Uncle Vanya, Chichester, 1996; Three Sisters, Birmingham, 1998; The Good Hope, NT, 2001. *Television:* Exec. Producer: Tutti Frutti, by John Byrne, 1987 (Best Series, BAFTA awards); The Play on 1 (series), 1989; Dir, The Shawl, by David Mamet, 1989. *Radio:* includes, 2000–: HMS Ulysses, Daisy Miller, The Plutocrat, Charge of the Light Brigade. Member Board, Scottish Television, 1979–85. Dir of the Year, Laurence Olivier Awards, 1985, Best Dir, Brit. Th. Assoc. and Drama Magazine Awards, 1986, and Evening Standard Best Dir Award, 1985 (for The Mysteries, NT, 1985). Hon. FGSM; Hon. Fellow: Rose Bruford Coll.; Queen Margaret Coll., Edinburgh. DUniv Stirling 1991. *Publications: plays:* Willie Rough, 1972; Benny Lynch, 1974; Old Movies, 1977; *screenplay:* The Long Riders, 1980; *films:* (writer and director) Ill Fares The Land, 1982; The Holy City (for TV), 1985; Aria, 1987. *Recreation:* music.

BRYDIE, Isobel Gunning, MBE 1997; Lord-Lieutenant for West Lothian, since 2002; *b* 20 Sept. 1942; *d* of Thomas and Sarah Hardie; *m* 1965, John Lawrie Brydie; one *s* one *d* (and one *s* decd). *Educ:* Broxburn High Sch. Mem. Bd, Livingston Develt Corp., 1982–96; Mem. Bd, 1996, Chm., 1997–99, W Lothian NHS Trust. *Recreations:* walking, curling, equestrian. *Address:* Limekilns, 29 Main Street, East Calder, West Lothian EH53 0ES. *T:* (01506) 880800. *Club:* Mid Calder Curling.

BRYDON, Donald Hood, CBE 2004 (OBE 1993); Chairman: London Metal Exchange, since 2003; Smiths Group plc, since 2004; Taylor Nelson Sofres plc, since 2006; AXA Framlington, since 2006; *b* 25 May 1945; *s* of James Hood Brydon and Mary Duncanson (*née* Young); *m* 1st, 1971, Joan Victoria (marr. diss. 1995); one *s* one *d*; 2nd, 1996, Corrine Susan Jane Green. *Educ:* George Watson's Coll., Edinburgh; Univ. of Edinburgh (BSc). Econs Dept, Univ. of Edinburgh, 1967–70; British Airways Pension Fund, 1970–77; Barclays Investment Manager's Office, 1977–81; Dep. Man. Dir, Barclays Investment Mgt Ltd, 1981–86; BZW Investment Management Ltd: Dir, 1986–88; Man. Dir, 1988–91; BZW Asset Management Ltd: Chm. and Chief Exec., 1991–94; non-exec. Chm., 1994–95; Barclays de Zoete Wedd: Dep. Chief Exec., 1994–96; Acting Chief Exec., 1996; AXA Investment Managers SA: Chief Exec., 1997–2002; Chm., 1997–2006. Director: London Stock Exchange, 1991–98; Edinburgh Inca Investment Trust, 1996–2001; Allied Domecq, 1997–2005; Amersham (formerly Nycomed Amersham), 1997–2004 (Chm., 2003–04); Edinburgh UK Tracker Trust, 1997–2006; AXA UK (formerly Sun Life and Provincial Hldgs), 1997–2007. Chairman: Financial Services Practitioner Panel, 2001–04; Code Cttee, Panel on Takeovers and Mergers, 2002–06. Pres., Eur. Asset Mgt Assoc., 1999–2001. Dep. Pres., Inst. for Financial Services, 2005–06; Chm., *ifs* Sch. of Finance, 2006–. Chairman: Eur. Children's Trust, 1999–2001; EveryChild, 2003–08; David Rattray Meml Trust (UK), 2007–. *Publications:* (jtly) Economics of Technical Information Services, 1972; (jtly) Pension Fund Investment, 1988. *Recreation:* golf. *Address:* (office) 7 Newgate Street, EC1A 7NX. *Clubs:* Caledonian; Golf House (Elie), Highgate Golf.

BRYDON, Robert; actor and writer; *b* Swansea, 3 May 1965; *s* of Howard Jones and Joy Brydon Jones; *m* 1st; one *s* two *d*; 2nd, 2006, Claire Holland; one *s*. *Educ:* St John's Sch., Porthcawl; Dumbarton House Sch., Swansea; Porthcawl Comp. Sch.; Royal Welsh Coll. of Music and Drama (Hon. Fellow, 2004). Radio and TV presenter, BBC Wales, 1986–92. *Television:* actor and writer: Marion and Geoff, 2000–03; Human Remains, 2000; Director's Commentary, 2004; The Keith Barret Show, 2004–05; Rob Brydon's Annually Retentive, 2006–07; Rob Brydon's Identity Crisis, 2008; actor: The Way We Live Now, 2001; Cruise of the Gods, 2002; Little Britain, 2005; Kenneth Tynan, In Praise of Hardcore, 2005; Supernova, 2005–06; Gavin and Stacey, 2007–; Heroes & Villains: Napoleon, 2007; *films:* First Knight, 1995; Lock, Stock and Two Smoking Barrels, 1998; 24 Hour Party People, 2002; MirrorMask, 2005; A Cock and Bull Story, 2005. *Publication:* (as Keith Barret) Making Divorce Work, 2004. *Recreations:* playing the guitar badly, Apple gadgets, country walks, drinking milk and eating biscuits, thinking about Sydney. *Address:* c/o United Agents, 12–26 Lexington Street, W1F 0LE; *e-mail:* mvincent@unitedagents.co.uk.

BRYER, Prof. Anthony Applemore Mornington, FSA 1972; Professor of Byzantine Studies, University of Birmingham, 1980–99, now Emeritus; Senior Research Fellow, King's College London, since 1996; *b* 31 Oct. 1937; *e s* of late Group Captain Gerald Mornington Bryer, OBE and of Joan Evelyn (*née* Grigsby); *m* 1st, 1961, Elizabeth Lipscomb (*d* 1995); three *d*; 2nd, 1998, Jennifer Ann Banks, widow. *Educ:* Canford Sch.; Sorbonne Univ.; Balliol Coll., Oxford (Scholar; BA, MA; DPhil 1967); Athens Univ. Nat. Service, RAF (Adjutant), 1956–58. University of Birmingham: Research Fellow, 1964–65, Lectr, 1965–73, Sen. Lectr, 1973–76, in Medieval History; Reader in Byzantine Studies, 1976–79; Dir of Byzantine Studies, 1969–76; Dir, Centre for Byzantine, Ottoman and Modern Greek Studies, 1976–94; Public Orator, 1991–98. Fellow, Inst. for Advanced Res. in Humanities, Univ. of Birmingham, 1999–. Visiting Fellow: Dumbarton Oaks, Harvard, 1971–; Merton Coll., Oxford, 1985. Founder and Dir, annual British Byzantine Symposia, 1966–; Chm., British Nat. Cttee, Internat. Byzantine Assoc., 1989–95 (Sec., 1976–89); former Vice-Pres., Nat. Trust for Greece; Pres., British Inst. of Archaeology, Ankara, 2002–07; Consultant to Cyprus Govt on res. in humanities, 1988–89; field trips to Trebizond and Pontos, 1959–; Hellenic Cruise lectr, 1967–; British Council specialist lectr, Greece, Turkey, Latvia, Albania and Australia; Loeb Lectr, Harvard, 1979; Vis. Byzantinist, Medieval Acad. of America, 1987; Wiles Lectr, QUB, 1990; Runciman Lectr, KCL, 1997. Convenor, Internat. Congress of Byzantine Studies, 2006. Chm., Runciman Award, 1999. Co-founder, Byzantine and Modern Greek Studies, 1975–. *Publications:* Byzantium and the Ancient East, 1970; Iconoclasm, 1977; The Empire of Trebizond and the Pontos, 1980; (with David Winfield) The Byzantine Monuments and Topography of the Pontos, 2 vols, 1985; (with Heath Lowry) Continuity and Change in late Byzantine and Early Ottoman Society, 1986; Peoples and Settlement in Anatolia and the Caucasus 800–1900, 1988; The Sweet Land of Cyprus, 1993; Mount Athos, 1996; The Post-Byzantine Monuments of the Pontos, 2002; articles in learned jls. *Recreation:* cricket in Albania. *Address:* 33 Crosbie Road, Harborne, Birmingham B17 9BG. *T:* (0121) 427 1207. *Clubs:* Buckland (Birmingham); Lochaline Social (Morvern); Black Sea (Trabzon).

BRYER, Dr David Ronald William, CMG 1996; Chairman, Home-Start International, since 2008; *b* 15 March 1944; *s* of Ronald Bryer and Betty Bryer (*née* Rawlinson); *m* 1980, Margaret Isabel, *e d* of Sir Eric Bowyer, KCB, KBE and Elizabeth (*née* Nicholls); one *s* one *d*. *Educ:* King's Sch., Worcester; Worcester Coll., Oxford (MA, DPhil); Manchester Univ. (Dip. Teaching English Overseas). Teaching and research, Lebanon and Britain, 1964–65, 1967–74 and 1979–81; Asst Keeper, Ashmolean Museum, 1972–74; Oxfam, 1975–2001: Field Dir, Middle East, 1975–79; Co-ordinator, Africa, 1981–84; Overseas Dir, 1984–91; Dir, 1992–2001; Sen. Advr, Henry Dunant Centre for Humanitarian Dialogue 2001–03; Chm., Oxfam Internat., 2003–07. Vis. Fellow, British Acad., 1972. Chm., Steering Cttee for Humanitarian Response, Geneva, 1995–97. Chairman: Eurostep, 1993–94; British Overseas Aid Gp, 1998–2000. Mem., UN High Level Panel on financing for develt, 2001. Member: Council, VSO, 1992–; Wilton Park Academic Council, 1999–; Court, Oxford Brookes Univ., 1999–2003. Board Member: Save the Children UK, 2002–; Oxfam America, 2003–07. *Publications:* The Origins of the Druze Religion, in Der Islam, 1975; articles on humanitarian and development issues. *Recreations:* family and friends, travel, esp. Eastern Mediterranean, walking. *Address:* Bracken Lodge, Eaton Road, Malvern Wells, Worcs, WR14 4PE.

BRYN, Kare; Secretary-General, European Free Trade Association, since 2006; *b* 12 March 1944; *m*; four *c*. *Educ:* Norwegian Sch. of Econs and Business Admin. Joined Norwegian Foreign Service, 1969; served in London, Belgrade, Oslo, Geneva, 1971–84; Hd of Div., 1984, Asst Dir Gen., 1985–89, Multilateral Econ. Co-operation; Dir Gen., Dept for Natural Resources and Envmtl Affairs, 1989–99; Ambassador: to WTO and EFTA, Geneva, 1999–2003; to Netherlands, 2003–06. Comdr, Order of St Olav (Norway), 1998. *Address:* European Free Trade Association, 9–11 rue de Varembé, 1211 Geneva 20, Switzerland. *T:* (22) 3322601; *e-mail:* kbn@efta.int.

BRYSON, Col (James) Graeme, OBE (mil.) 1954; TD 1949; JP; Vice Lord-Lieutenant of Merseyside, 1979–89; *b* 4 Feb. 1913; 3rd *s* of John Conway Bryson and Oletta Bryson; *m* Jean (*d* 1981), *d* of Walter Glendinning; two *s* four *d* (and one *s* decd). *Educ:* St Edward's Coll.; Liverpool Univ. (LLM); Open Univ. (BSc 1994). Admitted solicitor, 1935. Commnd 89th Field Bde RA (TA), 1936; served War, RA, 1939–45 (Lt-Col 1944); comd 470 (3W/Lancs) HAA Regt, 1947–52, and 626 HAA Regt, 1952–55; Bt-Col 1955; Hon. Col 33 Signal Regt (V), 1975–81. Sen. Jt Dist Registrar and Liverpool Admiralty Registrar, High Court of Justice, Liverpool, and Registrar of Liverpool County Court, 1947–78; Dep. Circuit Judge, Northern Circuit, 1978–82. A Gen. Comr of Income Tax, 1968–88 (Chm., Merseyside Adv. Cttee, 1979–88). President: Assoc. of County Court Registrars, 1969; Liverpool Law Soc., 1969; W Lancs Co., 1959–79 (Hon. Life Pres., 1993), City of Liverpool, 1965–, NW Area, 1979–90, Royal British Legion; Merseyside Council of Ex-Service and Regtl Assocs, 1975–89 (Hon. Life Pres., 1989). Chm., Med. Appeal Tribunal, 1978–85; Member: Lord Chancellor's Cttee for enforcement of debts (Payne), 1965–69; IOM Commn to reform enforcement laws, 1972–74; Vice-Patron, Nat. Assoc. for Employment of Regular Sailors, Soldiers and Airmen, 1989– (Mem. Council, 1952–89); Life Vice President: RA Officers Assoc., 1996; RA Assoc., Liverpool, 1996. Kt, Hon. Soc. of Knights of the Round Table, 1987–. FRSA 1989. JP Liverpool, 1956; DL Lancs, 1965, later Merseyside. QCB 1961. KHS 1974; KCHS 1990; KCSG 1996. *Publications:* (jtly) Execution, in Halsbury's Laws of England, 3rd edn 1976; Shakespeare in Lancashire, 1997; A Cathedral in My Time, 2000; (jtly) Liverpool Lawyers of the 20th Century, 2001; There's Poetry in my Veins, 2003; (contrib.) Oxford DNB. *Recreations:* local history, boating. *Address:* 36 Hillary Court, Freshfield Road, Formby, Merseyside L37 3PS. *T:* (01704) 834711. *Clubs:* Athenæum (Liverpool; Pres., 1969); Lancashire County Cricket.

BUBB, Stephen John Limrick; JP; Chief Executive, Association of Chief Executives of Voluntary Organisations, since 2000; Secretary General, Euclid, European Third Sector Leaders Network, since 2006; *b* 5 Nov. 1952; *s* of John William Edward Bubb and Diana Rosemary Bubb (*née* Willatts). *Educ:* Gillingham Grammar Sch.; Christ Church, Oxford (MA PPE 1975). FCIPD 2004. Economist, NEDO, 1975–76; Res. Officer, TGWU, 1976–80; Negotiations Officer, NUT, 1980–87; Hd, Pay Negotiations for Local Govt, AMA, 1987–95; Founding Dir, Nat. Lottery Charities Bd, 1995–2000. Chairman: Adventure Capital Fund, 2006–; Future Builders England, 2008–. Pt-time tutor, Open Univ., 1982–87. Founder Dir, Metropolitan Authorities Recruitment Agency, 1990–95. Mem. (Lab), Lambeth Council, 1982–86 (Chief Whip). Mem., W Lambeth HA, 1982–89; non-exec. Mem., Lambeth, Lewisham and Southwark HA, 1998–2002. Indep. Assessor for Govt Appts, 1999–; Member: Tyson Task Force on Non-exec. Dir Appts, 2002; Honours Cttee, Cabinet Office, 2005–; Civil Soc. Cttee, Commonwealth Foundn, 2008–. Chm., Strategy Cttee, Govs of Guy's and St Thomas' Trust, 2004–07. Founding Mem., Pakistan Develt Network, 2006–07. Youth Court Magistrate for Inner London, 1980–2000. Founder Chair, Lambeth Landmark, 1982–88. Chm., City of Oxford Orch., 1993–95. FRSA 1998. *Publications:* People are Key?, 2003; And Why Not?: tapping the talent of not-for-profit chief executives, 2004; Only Connect: a leader's guide to networking, 2005; Choice and Voice: Third Sector role in service delivery, 2006; Public Matters, 2007. *Recreations:* genealogy, travel, fine art and fine wine, the Anglican church, making a difference. *Address:* Armada Cottage, Thames Street, Charlbury, Oxon OX7 3QQ; *e-mail:* stephen.bubb@acevo.org.uk. *Clubs:* Oxford and Cambridge, New Cavendish.

BUCCLEUCH, 10th Duke of, *cr* 1663, **AND QUEENSBERRY,** 12th Duke of, *cr* 1684; **Richard Walter John Montagu Douglas Scott,** KBE 2000; DL; FRSE, FRSGS; Baron Scott of Buccleuch, 1606; Earl of Buccleuch, Baron Scott of Whitchester and Eskdaill, 1619; Earl of Doncaster and Baron Tynedale (Eng.), 1662; Earl of Dalkeith, 1663; Marquis of Dumfriesshire, Earl of Drumlanrig and Sanquhar, Viscount of Nith, Torthorwold and Ross, Baron Douglas, 1684; *b* 14 Feb. 1954; *e s* of 9th Duke of Buccleuch, KT, VRD and of Jane (*née* McNeill); *S* father, 2007; *m* 1981, Lady Elizabeth Kerr (*see* Duchess of Buccleuch); two *s* two *d*. *Educ:* Eton; Christ Church, Oxford. Dir, Border Television, 1989–90, 2000. Member: Nature Conservancy Council, 1989–91; Scottish Natural Heritage, 1992–95 (Chm., SW Reg., 1992–95); ITC, 1991–98 (Dep. Chm., 1996–98); Millennium Commn, 1994–2003. Trustee: Nat. Heritage Meml Fund, 2000–05; President: RSGS, 1999–2005; NT for Scotland, 2002–; Royal Scottish Agricultural Benevolent Inst.; Royal Blind and Scottish Nat. Inst. for War Blinded. Mem. Council, Winston Churchill Meml Trust, 1993–2005. Dist Councillor, Nithsdale, 1984–90. DL Nithsdale and Annandale and Eskdale, 1987. FRSGS 2006; FRSE 2007. Hon. Fellow, UHI, 2002. *Heir:* *s* Earl of Dalkeith, *qv*. *Address:* Dabton, Thornhill, Dumfriesshire DG3 5AR. *T:* (01848) 330467; 24 Lansdowne Road, W11 3LL. *T:* (020) 7727 6573.

BUCCLEUCH, Duchess of; Elizabeth Marian Frances Montagu Douglas Scott; Trustee, British Museum, since 1999; *b* 8 June 1954; *y d* of 12th Marquess of Lothian, KCVO and of Antonella (*née* Newland), OBE; *m* 1981, Earl of Dalkeith (*see* Duke of Buccleuch and Queensberry); two *s* two *d*. *Educ:* London Sch. of Economics (BSc 1975). Radio journalist, BBC R4, 1977–81. Chairman: Scottish Ballet, 1990–95; Heritage Educn Trust, 1999–. Mem. Council, National Trust, 2000–. Trustee, Nat. Museums of Scotland, 1991–99. Chm. Council of Mgt, Arts Educnl Schs, London, 1999–. *Recreations:* reading, theatre, music, gardening. *Address:* 24 Lansdowne Road, W11 3LL. *T:* (020) 7727 6573, *Fax:* (020) 7229 7279.

See also Earl of Dalkeith.

BUCHAN, family name of **Baron Tweedsmuir**.

BUCHAN, 17th Earl of, *cr* 1469; **Malcolm Harry Erskine;** Lord Auchterhouse, 1469; Lord Cardross, 1610; Baron Erskine, 1806; *b* 4 July 1930; *s* of 16th Earl of Buchan and Christina, Dowager Countess of Buchan (*d* 1994), *d* of late Hugh Woolner and adopted *d* of late Lloyd Baxendale; *S* father, 1984; *m* 1957, Hilary Diana Cecil, *d* of late Sir Ivan McLannahan Power, 2nd Bt; two *s* two *d*. *Educ:* Eton. JP Westminster, 1972–2000. *Heir: s* Lord Cardross, *qv*. *Address:* Newnham House, Newnham, Hook, Hants RG27 9AS. *Club:* Carlton.

BUCHAN, Prof. Alastair Mitchell; Professor of Clinical Geratology and Hon. Consultant Neurologist, University of Oxford, and Fellow of Green Templeton College (formerly Green College), Oxford, since 2004; *b* 16 Oct. 1955; *s* of Prof. Alan Robson Buchan and Dorothy Mitchell; *m* 1999, Angelika S. Kaiser; two *d*. *Educ:* Repton Sch.; Sidney Sussex Coll., Cambridge (BA 1977, MA 1981); University Coll., Oxford (BM BCh 1980). Radcliffe Travelling Fellow, UC, Oxford, 1983–85; MRC Centennial Fellow, Cornell Univ., NY, 1985–88; Asst Prof. of Neurology, Univ. of Western Ontario, 1988–91; Associate Prof. of Medicine and Anatomy, Univ. of Ottawa, 1991–95; Prof. of Neurology and Heart and Stroke Foundn Prof. of Stroke Res., Univ. of Calgary, 1995–2004. Director: Canadian Stroke Network, 1999–2004; UK Stroke Network, 2005–. R&D Chair, Canadian Stroke Consortium, 1993–. FMedSci 2007. *Publications:* Maturation Phenomenon of Cerebral Ischaemic Injury, 2003; contrib. Lancet, New England Jl of Medicine, Nature, Jl of Cerebral Blood Flow and Metabolism, Stroke, Jl of Neurosci. *Recreations:* archaeology, antiquities, art history. *Address:* Nuffield Department of Clinical Medicine, University of Oxford, John Radcliffe Hospital, Level 7, Headington, Oxford OX3 9DU. *T:* (01865) 222301, *Fax:* (01865) 221354; *e-mail:* alastair.buchan@ndm.ox.ac.uk. *Club:* Osler House (Oxford).

BUCHAN of Auchmacoy, Captain David William Sinclair; Chief of the Name of Buchan; *b* 18 Sept. 1929; *o s* of late Captain S. L. Trevor, late of Lathbury Park, Bucks, and late Lady Olivia Trevor, *e d* of 18th Earl of Caithness; changed name from Trevor through Court of Lord Lyon King of Arms, 1949, succeeding 18th Earl of Caithness as Chief of Buchan Clan; *m* 1961, Susan Blanche Fionodbhar Scott-Ellis, *d* of 9th Baron Howard de Walden and 5th Baron Seaford, TD; four *s* one *d*. *Educ:* Eton; RMA Sandhurst. Commissioned 1949 into Gordon Highlanders; served Berlin, BAOR and Malaya; ADC to GOC, Singapore, 1951–53; retired 1955. Member of London Stock Exchange. Sen. Partner, Messrs Gow and Parsons, 1963–72. Comr, Inland Revenue, 1974–76. Member: Queen's Body Guard for Scotland; The Pilgrims; Friends of Malta GC; Cook Soc., 1982–; Council, Royal Sch. of Needlework, 1987–96; Cons. Industrial Fund Cttee, 1988–97. Gov., London Clinic, 1988–95. Mem., Worshipful Company of Broderers (Master, 1992). Vice-President: Aberdeenshire CCC, 1962–; Bucks CCC, 1984–. JP Aberdeenshire, 1959–96; JP London, 1972–95. KStJ 1987 (OStJ 1981). *Recreations:* bridge, reading. *Address:* 30 Chipstead Street, SW6 3SS; North Court, Clanfield, Oxon OX18 2RG. *Clubs:* Turf, MCC, Pitt.

BUCHAN, Dennis Thorne, RSA 1991 (ARSA 1975); painter; *b* 25 April 1937; *s* of David S. Buchan and Mary Buchan (*née* Clark); *m* 1965, Elizabeth Watson (marr. diss. 1977); one *s* one *d*. *Educ:* Arbroath High Sch.; Dundee Coll. of Art; Patrick Allan Fraser Coll., Arbroath; Dundee Coll. of Art (DA 1958). Nat. Service, RAEC, 1960–62. Lectr in Drawing and Painting, Duncan of Jordanstone Coll. of Art, 1965–94. Mem., SSA, 1961–74. *Solo exhibitions:* Douglas and Foulis Gall., 1965; Saltire Soc., Edinburgh Fest., 1974; Compass Gall., 1975, A Span of Shores, 1994; *group exhibitions* include: Six Coastal Artists, Demarco Gall., Edinburgh, 1965; Seven Painters in Dundee, Scottish Nat. Gall. of Modern Art, and tour, 1972; Compass Contribution, Tramway, Glasgow, 1990; Scottish Contemporary Painting, Flowers East, London, 1993; Five Scottish Artists, Centre d'Art en l'Ile, Geneva, 1994; work in private and public collections throughout UK and USA. Keith Prize, 1962, Latimer, 1973, William McCauley Award, 1988, Gillies Bequest, 1991, Royal Scottish Acad. *Recreations:* non specific. *Address:* 8 Inchcape Road, Arbroath, Angus DD11 2DF. *T:* (01241) 873080.

BUCHAN, Janey, (Jane O'Neil Buchan); Member (Lab) Glasgow, European Parliament, 1979–94; *b* 30 April 1926; *d* of Joseph and Christina Kent; *m* 1945, Norman Findlay Buchan, MP (*d* 1990); one *s*. *Educ:* secondary sch.; commercial coll. Mem., Strathclyde Regl Council, 1974–79 (Vice-Chm., Educn Cttee). Former Chm., local consumer gp, Scottish Gas Consumers' Council. Trustee, Smith Art Gall. and Mus., Stirling, 1996–. Founder, Centre for Political Song, Glasgow Caledonian Univ. *Recreations:* books, music, theatre, watching television more carefully than ever especially after the Hutton enquiry.

BUCHAN, Hon. Ursula Margaret Bridget, (Hon. Mrs Wide); JP; gardening journalist and author; *b* 25 June 1953; twin *d* of 3rd Baron Tweedsmuir and Barbara (*née* Ensor); *m* 1979, Charles Thomas Wide, *qv*; one *s* one *d*. *Educ:* Littlemore Grammar Sch.; Oxford High Sch. for Girls; New Hall, Cambridge (MA); Royal Botanic Gardens, Kew (Dip. Hort.). Freelance journalist, 1980–; gardening columnist: Spectator, 1984–; Observer, 1987–93; Sunday Telegraph, 1993–97; Independent, 1998–2003; Daily Telegraph, 2004–. JP 2004. *Publications:* An Anthology of Garden Writing, 1986; The Pleasures of Gardening, 1987; (with Nigel Colborn) The Classic Horticulturist, 1987; Foliage Plants, 1988, 2nd edn 1993; The Village Show, 1990; Wall Plants and Climbers, 1992; (with David Stevens) The Garden Book, 1994; Gardening for Pleasure, 1996; Plants for All Seasons, 1999, 2nd edn 2004; Good in a Bed: garden writings from The Spectator, 2001; Better Against a Wall, 2003; The English Garden, 2006; Garden People, 2007. *Recreations:* gardening, fell walking, watching Rugby Union and cricket. *Address:* c/o Felicity Bryan Literary Agency, 2a North Parade Avenue, Oxford OX2 6LX.

BUCHAN-HEPBURN, Sir (John) Alastair (Trant Kidd), 7th Bt *cr* 1815, of Smeaton Hepburn, Haddingtonshire; *b* 27 June 1931; *s* of John Trant Buchan-Hepburn (*d* 1953), *g g s* of 2nd Bt, and Edith Margaret Mitchell (*née* Robb) (*d* 1980); *S* cousin, 1992; *m* 1957, Georgina Elizabeth, *d* of late Oswald Morris Turner, MC; one *s* three *d*. *Educ:* Charterhouse; St Andrews Univ.; RMA, Sandhurst. 1st King's Dragoon Guards, 1952–57; Captain, 1954; ADC to GOC-in-C, Malaya, 1954–57. Arthur Guinness & Son Co. Ltd, 1958–86; Director: Broughton Brewery Ltd, 1987–95; Broughton Ales Ltd, 1995–2001; Chairman: Valentine Marketing Ltd, 2002–03; Valentine Holdings Ltd, 2002–03. Member: Cttee, St Andrews Br., RBL; St Andrews Cttee, Macmillan Cancer Relief Fund Raising, 2002–05; Nat. Trust for Scotland, 2007–; Historic Scotland, 2007–. Life Mem., St Andrews Preservation Trust, 1984–; Mem., Baronets' Trust, 1992–. Trustee, Dundee Industrial Heritage Trust, 1999–2006. Vice-Pres., Maritime Volunteer Service, 2001–07. Member: Regtl Assoc., 1st Queen's Dragoon Guards, 1958–; Vestry, All Saints Scottish Episcopal Ch, St Andrews, 2002–06. Mem., Royal Stuart Soc., 2005. Mem., St Andrews Loches Alliance—La Nouvelle Alliance, 2005–. Mem., Kate Kennedy Club, 1950–, After Many Days Club, 2002–, Sports Club, 2006–, St Andrews Univ. Member: St Andrews Shoot, 1990–2005; Logiealmond Shoot, 2004–07. Chief Marshal: Dunhill Championship, St Andrews, 1999–2005; Open Championship, St Andrews, 2000 and 2006. *Recreations:* golf, fishing, shooting, tennis, badminton, travel in France and other European countries, antiquities, Buchan and Hepburn genealogical history; leading European effort to have remains of James Hepburn, 4th Earl of Bothwell and 3rd husband of Mary, Queen of Scots returned to Scotland. *Heir: s* (John) Christopher (Alastair) Buchan-Hepburn [*b* 9 March 1963; *m* 1990, Andrea Unwin]. *Address:* Chagford, 60 Argyle Street, St Andrews, Fife KY16 9BU. *T:* and *Fax:* (01334) 472161, *T:* 07939 139545; *e-mail:* alastairbh@googlemail.com. *Clubs:* New, Royal Scots (Edinburgh); Royal and Ancient Golf (St Andrews).

BUCHANAN, Alistair George, FCA; Chief Executive, Office of Gas and Electricity Markets, since 2003; *b* 22 Dec. 1961; *s* of Colin and Isobel Buchanan; *m* 1988, Linda Pollock; one *s* two *d*. *Educ:* Malvern Coll.; Durham Univ. (BA Hons). FCA 1986. Chartered Accountant, KPMG, 1983–87; Head: UK Utilities Res., Smith New Court, 1987–94; UK, European and Global Res. Div., BZW, 1994–97; USA Utilities Res., Salomon Smith Barney, NY, 1997–2000; European Res., London, Donaldson, Lufkin & Jenrette (DLJ), 2000–01; ABN AMRO, 2001–03. *Recreations:* season ticket holder London Wasps, school governor, classical music, all sports. *Address:* Office of Gas and Electricity Markets, 9 Millbank, SW1P 3GE. *T:* (020) 7901 7357, *Fax:* (020) 7901 7062; *e-mail:* alistair.buchanan@ofgem.gov.uk.

BUCHANAN, Sir Andrew George, 5th Bt *cr* 1878; farmer; Lord-Lieutenant and Keeper of the Rolls for Nottinghamshire, since 1991; *b* 21 July 1937; *s* of Major Sir Charles Buchanan, 4th Bt, and Barbara Helen (*d* 1986), *o d* of late Lt-Col Rt Hon. Sir George Stanley, PC, GCSI, GCIE; *S* father, 1984; *m* 1966, Belinda Jane Virginia (*née* Maclean), JP, DL, *widow* of Gresham Neilus Vaughan; one *s* one *d*, and one step *s* one step *d*. *Educ:* Eton; Trinity Coll., Cambridge; Wye Coll., Univ. of London. Nat. Service, 2nd Lieut, Coldstream Guards, 1956–58. Chartered Surveyor with Smith-Woolley & Co., 1965–70. Chm., Bd of Visitors, HM Prison Ranby, 1983 (Vice-Chm. 1982). Commanded A Squadron (SRY), 3rd Bn Worcs and Sherwood Foresters (TA), 1971–74; Hon. Col, B Sqn (SRY), Queen's Own Yeo., 1989–94; Hon. Col, Notts ACF, 2001–07. High Sheriff, Notts, 1976–77; DL Notts, 1985. KStJ 1991. *Recreations:* ski-ing, walking, forestry. *Heir: s* George Charles Mellish Buchanan [*b* 27 Jan. 1975; *m* 2002, Katharine, *d* of late Tom Price]. *Address:* Hodsock Priory Farm, Blyth, Worksop, Notts S81 0TY. *T:* (01909) 591227, *Fax:* (01909) 591947; *e-mail:* andrew.buchanan@hodsock.com. *Club:* Boodle's.

BUCHANAN, Rt Rev. Colin Ogilvie; Area Bishop of Woolwich, 1996–2004; Hon. Assistant Bishop of Bradford, 2004–06; *b* 9 Aug. 1934; *s* of late Prof. Robert Ogilvie Buchanan and of Kathleen Mary (*née* Parnell); *m* 1963; two *d*. *Educ:* Whitgift Sch., S Croydon; Lincoln Coll., Oxford (BA, 2nd Cl. Lit. Hum., MA). Theological training at Tyndale Hall, Bristol, 1959–61; deacon, 1961; priest, 1962; Curate, Cheadle, Cheshire, 1961–64; joined staff of London Coll. of Divinity (now St John's Coll., Nottingham), 1964; posts held: Librarian, 1964–69; Registrar, 1969–74; Director of Studies, 1974–75; Vice-Principal, 1975–78; Principal, 1979–85; Hon. Canon of Southwell Minster, 1982–85; Bishop Suffragan of Aston, 1985–89; Hon. Asst Bishop, dio. of Rochester, 1989–96; Vicar, St Mark's, Gillingham, Kent, 1991–96. Member: Church of England Liturgical Commn, 1964–86; Doctrinal Commn, 1986–91; House of Clergy, 1970–85, House of Bishops, 1990–2004, General Synod of C of E; Assembly of British Council of Churches, 1971–80; Steering Cttee, CCBI, 1990–92; Council for Christian Unity, 1991–2001; Steering Gp, Internat. Anglican Liturgical Consultations, 1995–2001. Mem., Lambeth Conf., 1988, 1998 (Mem., Chaplaincy Team, 1998). Chm., Millennium Dome Chaplaincy Gp, 1999–2000. Pres., Movt for Reform of Infant Baptism, 1988–. Vice-Pres., 1987–2005, Pres., 2005–, Electoral Reform Soc. Grove Books: Proprietor, 1970–85; Hon. Manager, 1985–93; Editorial Consultant, 1993–. DD Lambeth, 1993. *Publications:* (ed) Modern Anglican Liturgies 1958–1968, 1968; (ed) Further Anglican Liturgies 1968–1975, 1975; (jtly) Growing into Union, 1970; (ed jtly) Anglican Worship Today, 1980; (ed) Latest Anglican Liturgies 1976–1984, 1985; (jtly) Reforming Infant Baptism, 1990; Open to Others, 1992; Infant Baptism and the Gospel, 1993; Cut the Connection, 1994; Is the Church of England Biblical?, 1998; (ed) Michael Vasey—Liturgist and Friend, 1999; Historical Dictionary of Anglicanism, 2006; Taking the Long View, 2006; editor: Grove Booklets on Ministry and Worship, 1972–2002; Grove Liturgical Studies, 1975–86; Alcuin/GROW Joint Liturgical Studies, 1987– (regular author in these series); News of Liturgy, 1975–2003; contrib. learned jls. *Recreations:* interested in electoral reform, sport, etc.

BUCHANAN, Prof. David Alan, PhD; Professor of Organizational Behaviour, School of Management, Cranfield University, since 2005; *b* 26 July 1949; *s* of David Stewart and Harriet Buchanan; *m* 1974, Lesley Fiddes Fulton; one *s* one *d*. *Educ:* Heriot-Watt Univ. (BA Hons); Univ. of Edinburgh (PhD). Personnel Asst, Lothian Regl Council, Edinburgh, 1976–77; Lecturer in Organizational Behaviour: Napier Poly., Edinburgh, 1977–79; Univ. of Glasgow, 1979–86, Sen. Lectr, 1986–89; Prof. of Human Resource Management, Loughborough Univ. of Technology, 1989–95; Dir, Loughborough Univ. Business Sch., 1992–95; Prof. of Organizational Behaviour, Leicester Business Sch., De Montfort Univ., 1995–2005. FCIPD; FRSA; FBAM. *Publications:* The Development of Job Design Theories and Techniques, 1979; (with A. A. Huczynski) Organizational Behaviour: an introductory text, 1985, 5th edn 2004, Student Workbook, 1994, Instructor's Manual, 1994, 6th edn 2007; (ed jtly) The New Management Challenge: information systems for improved performance, 1988; (with J. McCalman) High Performance Work Systems: the digital experience, 1989; (with R. Badham) Power, Politics, and Organizational Change, 1999, 2nd edn 2008; (ed jtly) The Sustainability and Spread of Organizational Change, 2007; with D. Boddy: Organizations in the Computer Age: technological imperatives and strategic choice, 1983; Managing New Technology, 1986; The Technical Change Audit: action for results, 1987; Take the Lead: interpersonal skills for project managers, 1992; The Expertise of the Change Agent: public performance and backstage activity, 1992; numerous contribs to learned jls. *Recreations:* music, reading, photography, diving, fitness. *Address:* 18 Ascott Gardens, West Bridgford, Nottingham NG2 7TH.

BUCHANAN, Rt Rev. Duncan; *see* Buchanan, Rt Rev. G. D.

BUCHANAN, Rt Rev. (George) Duncan; Bishop of Johannesburg, 1986–2000; Priest-in-charge, St John's Parish, Houghton, since 2001; *b* 23 April 1935; *s* of Wyndam Kelsey Fraser Buchanan and Phyllis Rhoda Dale Buchanan (*née* Nichols); *m* 1959, Diana Margaret

Dacombe; two *d. Educ:* St John's Coll., Johannesburg; Rhodes Univ., Grahamstown (BA 1957); Ripon Hall, Oxford (GOE 1958); Gen. Theological Seminary (MDiv 1959). Curate, St Paul's Church, Durban, 1960; Rector, Parish of Kingsway, Natal, 1961–65; Diocesan Theol Tutor, Dio. Natal, 1963–65; Sub Warden, St Paul's Theol Coll., Grahamstown, 1966–76, Warden, 1976–86; Dean, St Mary's Cathedral, Johannesburg, May–Sept. 1986; Archdeacon of Albany, Diocese of Grahamstown, 1975–86. Chairman: Church Unity Commn, 1989–2000; Theol Educn by Extension Coll., 1993–2000; SA Anglican Theol Commn, 1995–2000; Co-ordinator, St Thomas Inst. for Leadership in Ministry, Dio. of Johannesburg, 2001–07. Hon. DD General Theological Seminary, 1987. *Publications:* The Counselling of Jesus, 1985; (ed) Meeting the Future: Christian leadership in South Africa, 1995. *Recreations:* carpentry, reading. *Address:* 35 East Street, East Town, Johannesburg 2195, South Africa. *T:* and *Fax:* (11) 7829201.

BUCHANAN, Sir Gordon Kelly McNicol L.; *see* Leith-Buchanan.

BUCHANAN, Isobel Wilson, (Mrs Jonathan King); soprano; *b* 15 March 1954; *d* of Stewart and Mary Buchanan; *m* 1980, Jonathan Stephen Geoffrey King (otherwise Jonathan Hyde, actor); two *d. Educ:* Cumbernauld High Sch.; Royal Scottish Academy of Music and Drama (DRSAMD 1974). Australian Opera principal singer, 1975–78; freelance singer, 1978–; British debut, Glyndebourne, 1978; Vienna Staatsoper debut, 1978; American debut: Santa Fé, 1979; Chicago, 1979; New York, 1979; German debut, Cologne, 1979; French debut, Aix-en-Provence, 1981; ENO debut, 1985; Paris Opera debut, 1986. Performances also with Scottish Opera, Covent Garden, Munich Radio, Belgium, Norway, etc. Various operatic recordings. *Recreations:* reading, gardening, cooking, yoga.

BUCHANAN, Prof. James McGill; Holbert L. Harris University Professor, 1983–99, now Emeritus Professor, and Advisory General Director, Center for the Study of Public Choice, since 1988 (General Director, 1969–88), George Mason University; *b* 2 Oct. 1919; *s* of James Buchanan and Lila Scott; *m* 1945, Anne Bakke. *Educ:* Middle Tennessee State Coll. (BS 1940); Univ. of Tennessee (MA 1941); Univ. of Chicago (PhD 1948). Lieut, USNR, 1941–46. Professor of Economics: Univ. of Tennessee, 1950–51; Florida State Univ., 1951–56; Univ. of Virginia, 1956–62, 1962–68 (Paul G. McIntyre Prof.); UCLA, 1968–69; Virginia Polytechnic Inst., 1969–83 (Univ. Dist. Prof.). Fulbright Res. Scholar, Italy, 1955–56; Ford Faculty Res. Fellow, 1959–60; Fulbright Vis. Prof., Univ. of Cambridge, 1961–62. Fellow, Amer. Acad. of Arts and Scis; Dist. Fellow, Amer. Econ. Assoc. (Seidman Award, 1984). Hon. Dr, US and overseas Univs. Nobel Prize for Economics, 1986. *Publications:* Prices, Incomes and Public Policy (jtly), 1954; Public Principles of Public Debt, 1958; The Public Finances, 1960; Fiscal Theory and Political Economy, 1960; (with G. Tullock) The Calculus of Consent, 1962; Public Finance in Democratic Process, 1966; The Demand and Supply of Public Goods, 1968; Cost and Choice, 1969; (with N. Devletoglou) Academia in Anarchy, 1970; (ed jtly) Theory of Public Choice, 1972; (with G. F. Thirlby) LSE Essays on Cost, 1973; The Limits of Liberty, 1975; (with R. Wagner) Democracy in Deficit, 1977; Freedom in Constitutional Contract, 1978; What Should Economists Do?, 1979; (with G. Brennan) The Power to Tax, 1980; (ed jtly) Towards a Theory of the Rent-Seeking Society, 1980; (ed jtly) The Theory of Public Choice II, 1984; (with G. Brennan) The Reason of Rules, 1985; Liberty Market and State, 1985; (jtly) El Analisis Economico de lo Politico, 1985; (ed jtly) Deficits, 1987; Economics: between predictive science and moral philosophy, 1987; Economía y Política, 1987; Maktens Gränser, 1988; (ed) Explorations into Constitutional Economics, 1989; Essays on the Political Economy, 1989; Stato, mercato e libertà, 1989; The Economics and the Ethics of Constitutional Order, 1991; Constitutional Economics, 1991; Better than Plowing and Other Personal Essays, 1992; Ethics and Economic Progress, 1994; (ed jtly) Return to Increasing Returns, 1994; Post-Socialist Political Economy, 1997; (with R. Congleton) Politics by Principle, not Interest, 1998. *Address:* Center for the Study of Public Choice, Buchanan House, George Mason University, Fairfax, VA 22030–4444, USA; PO Drawer G, Blacksburg, VA 24063–1021, USA.

BUCHANAN, Dr John Gordon St Clair; Chairman, Smith & Nephew plc, since 2006 (Deputy Chairman, 2005–06); Deputy Chairman, Vodafone plc, since 2006 (non-executive Director, since 2003); *b* Auckland, NZ, 9 June 1943; *s* of Russell Penman Buchanan and Marguerite, (Ginette), St Clair Stuart (*née* Cabouret); *m* 1967, Rosemary June Johnston; one *s* one *d. Educ:* Auckland Grammar Sch.; Univ. of Auckland (MSc Hons I, PhD Organic Chemistry); Harvard Business Sch. (PMD 1977). Post-Doctoral Res. Fellow, Wolfson Coll., Oxford, 1968–69; British Petroleum, 1970–2003: various operational, commercial, and marketing posts for BP Oil, 1970–76; seconded to Central Policy Rev. Staff, Cabinet Office, 1976–77; BP Switzerland, 1978–80; Manager, Mkting and Ops, BP NZ, 1980–82; Asst Gen. Manager, Supply Dept, 1982–85; Gen. Manager, Gp Corporate Planning, 1985–88; Chief Operating Officer and Dep. Chief Exec., BP Chemicals, 1988–95; Gp Treas. and Chief Exec., BP Finance, 1995–96; Exec. Dir and Chief Financial Officer, BP (formerly BP Amoco) plc, 1996–2002. Non-executive Director: Boots Co., 1997–2003; Astra Zeneca plc, 2002–; Sen. Ind. Dir, BHP Billiton plc, 2003–. Mem., Accounting Standards Bd, 1997–2001. Vice-Pres., SCI, 1991–93. Mem., Main Cttee, Hundred Gp of Finance Dirs, 1998–2002. Chm., Univ. of Auckland UK Trust, 2001–; Trustee, UK Friends of Auckland Grammar Sch., 2005–. *Recreations:* golf, ski-ing, Polynesian culture. *Address:* Smith & Nephew plc, 15 Adam Street, WC2N 6LA. *Clubs:* Tandridge Golf (Surrey); Remuera Golf (Auckland, NZ).

BUCHANAN, John M.; *see* Macdonald-Buchanan.

BUCHANAN, Vice-Adm. Sir Peter (William), KBE 1980; *b* 14 May 1925; *s* of Lt-Col Francis Henry Theodore Buchanan and Gwendolen May Isobel (*née* Hunt); *m* 1953, Audrey Rowena Mary (*née* Edmondson); three *s* one *d. Educ:* Malvern Coll. Joined RN, 1943; served in HM Ships King George V, Birmingham, destroyers and frigates; comd HMS Scarborough 1961–63; Ops Officer, Far East Fleet, 1963–65 (despatches); HMS Victorious, 1965–67; British Antarctic Survey, 1967–68; comd HMS Endurance, 1968–70; MoD, 1970–72; comd HMS Devonshire, 1972–74; MoD, 1974–76; ADC to the Queen, 1975–76; Rear-Adm. 1976; Naval Sec., 1976–78; Vice-Adm., 1979; Chief of Staff, Allied Naval Forces Southern Europe, 1979–82. Mem., Lord Chancellor's Panel of Independent Inspectors, 1983–95. Younger Brother of Trinity House, 1963. Liveryman, Shipwrights' Co., 1984; Master, Guild of Freemen of City of London, 1996. MRIN; FNI. *Recreation:* sailing. *Clubs:* Caledonian; Royal Yacht Squadron.

BUCHANAN, Prof. Robert Angus, OBE 1993; PhD; FSA; FRHistS; Founder and Director, Centre for the History of Technology, Science and Society, 1964–95, Professor of the History of Technology, 1990–95, University of Bath, now Emeritus Professor; Director, National Cataloguing Unit for the Archives of Contemporary Scientists, 1987–95; *b* 5 June 1930; *s* of Roy Graham Buchanan and Bertha (*née* Davis); *m* 1955, Brenda June Wade; two *s. Educ:* High Storrs Grammar Sch. for Boys, Sheffield; St Catharine's Coll., Cambridge (MA, PhD). FRHistS 1978; FSA 1990. Educn Officer to Royal Foundn of St Katharine, Stepney, 1956–60 (Co-opted Mem., LCC Educn Cttee, 1958–60); Asst Lectr, Dept of Gen. Studies, Bristol Coll. of Science and Technol. (now Univ. of Bath), 1960; Lectr, 1961, Sen. Lectr, 1966, Head of Humanities Gp, Sch. of Humanities and Social Scis, 1970–95, Reader in Hist. of Technol., 1981–90, Univ. of Bath. Vis. Lectr, Univ. of Delaware, USA, 1969; Vis. Fellow, ANU, Canberra, 1981; Vis. Lectr, Huazhong (Central China) Univ. of Science and Tech., Wuhan, People's Repub. of China, 1983; Jubilee Chair in History of Technol., Chalmers Univ., Göteborg, Sweden, Autumn term, 1984. Royal Comr, Royal Commn on Historical Monuments (England), 1979–93; Sec., Res. Cttee on Indust. Archaeology, Council for British Archaeology, 1972–79; President: (Founding), Bristol Indust. Archaeology Soc., 1967–70; Assoc. for Indust. Archaeology, 1974–77; Newcomen Soc. for History of Engrg and Technol., 1981–83; Internat. Cttee for History of Technol., 1993–97 (Sec.-Gen., 1981–93); Vice Pres., Soc. of Antiquaries, 1995–99; Chm., Water Space Amenity Commn's Working Party on Indust. Archaeology, 1982–83; Member: Properties Cttee, National Trust, 1974–2002; Technol Preservation Awards Cttee, Science Museum, 1973–81. FRSA 1993–99. Hon. Fellow, Science Mus., 1992. Hon. DSc (Engrg) Chalmers Univ., Göteborg, Sweden, 1986. Leonardo da Vinci Medal, Soc. for Hist. of Technol., 1989. *Publications:* Technology and Social Progress, 1965; (with Neil Cossons) Industrial Archaeology of the Bristol Region, 1969; Industrial Archaeology in Britain, 1972, 2nd edn 1982; (with George Watkins) Industrial Archaeology of the Stationary Steam Engine, 1976; History and Industrial Civilization, 1979; (with C. A. Buchanan) Industrial Archaeology of Central Southern England, 1980; (with Michael Williams) Brunel's Bristol, 1982; The Engineers: a history of the engineering profession in Britain, 1989; The Power of the Machine, 1992; Brunel: the life and times of I. K. Brunel, 2002. *Recreations:* Cambridge Judo half-blue, 1955; rambling, travelling, exploring. *Address:* 13 Hensley Road, Bath BA2 2DR. *T:* (01225) 311508.

BUCHANAN, Sir Robert Wilson, (Sir Robin), Kt 1991; DL; CA; Chairman, NHS Supplies Authority, 1991–95; *b* 28 Sept. 1930; *s* of Robert Downie and Mary Hobson Buchanan; *m* Naomi Pauline (*née* Lewis); three *d. Educ:* Dumbarton Acad.; Glasgow Acad. Mem., Inst. of Chartered Accts of Scotland, 1953. CA, Bath, 1965–. Chairman: Bath DHA, 1982–88; Wessex RHA, 1988–93; Vice-Chm., NHS Training Authy, 1983–88; Mem., Bath City Council, 1978–86. Mem. Council, Bath Internat. Fest., 1970–88 (Chm., 1982–86, 1988); Trustee, Robin Buchanan Charitable Trust, 1985–. Mem. Council, 1985–2001, Treasurer, 1995–2001, Bath Univ.; Mem. Council, Southampton Univ., 1990–93; Gov., Millfield Sch., 1992–2000 (Treas., 1963–92; Chm., 1997–2000). DL Avon, 1992, Somerset, 1996. *Recreations:* golf, beach walking. *Address:* Belmont Cottage, Belmont Road, Combe Down, Bath BA2 5JR. *T:* (01225) 833768; Cassia Heights, Royal Westmoreland, Barbados.

BUCHANAN, Robin William Turnbull, FCA; Dean, London Business School, since 2007; *b* 2 April 1952; *s* of Iain Buchanan and Gillian Pamela Buchanan (*née* Hughes-Hallett); *m* 1986, Diana Tei Tanaka; one *s* one *d. Educ:* Harvard Business Sch. (MBA, Baker Scholar). Mann Judd Landau, subseq. Deloitte & Touche, 1970–77; American Express Internat. Banking Corp., 1979–82; Bain & Company Inc., 1982–: Bain Capital, 1982–84; Man. Partner, London, 1990–96; Sen. Partner, London, 1996–2007; Sen. Advr, 2007–. Non-executive Director: Liberty Internat. plc, 1997–; Shire plc (formerly Shire Pharmaceuticals Gp plc), 2003–. Member: Trilateral Commn; Professional Standards Adv. Bd, IoD; Adv. Council, Prince's Trust. Mem. Editl Bd, European Business Jl. Fellow, Salzburg Seminar. Mem., Northern Meeting. FRSA. Liveryman, Co. of Ironmongers. *Recreations:* farming, forestry, shooting, collecting old children's books. *Address:* London Business School, Regent's Park, NW1 4SA. *T:* (020) 7700 7014. *Clubs:* Boodle's, Beefsteak, Pilgrims.

BUCHANAN-DUNLOP, Richard; QC 1966; *b* 19 April 1919; *s* of late Canon W. R. Buchanan-Dunlop and Mrs R. E. Buchanan-Dunlop (*née* Mead); *m* 1948, Helen Murray Dunlop (*d* 2006); three *d. Educ:* Marlborough College; Magdalene College, Cambridge. Served in Royal Corps of Signals, 1939–46 (Hon. Major). BA (Hons) Law, Cambridge, 1949; Harmsworth Scholar, 1950. Called to the Bar, 1951. *Publications:* Skiathos and other Poems, 1984; Old Olive Men, 1986; Hie Paeeon: songs from the Greek Isles, 1989; The Painted Veil, 2003. *Recreations:* painting, writing. *Address:* Skiathos, Greece.

BUCHANAN-DUNLOP, Col Robert Daubeny, (Robin), CBE 1987 (OBE 1982); Clerk, Goldsmiths' Company, 1988–2004; *b* 11 Aug. 1939; *o s* of late Col Robert Arthur Buchanan-Dunlop of Drumhead, OBE, The Cameronians (Scottish Rifles) and Patricia Buchanan-Dunlop (*née* Upton); *m* 1972, Nicola Jane Goodhart; two *s. Educ:* Loretto Sch. National Service, The Cameronians (Scottish Rifles), 1959–61; Regular Commission, 1961; transf. to Scots Guards; served Kenya, Aden, Sharjah, Germany, NI (despatches); Staff Coll., 1971; HQ 1 Div., 1973–75; Armed Forces Staff Coll., USA, 1978; Directing Staff, Canadian Land Forces Staff Coll., 1978–79; CO 8th (Co. Tyrone) Bn, UDR, 1979–81; COS 52 Lowland Bde, 1982–84; COS NI, 1984–86; Dep. Dir, UK C-in-C Cttees, 1987; retired. Mem., Queen's Body Guard for Scotland (Royal Company of Archers), 1987–. Chm., Lead Body, Jewellery and Allied Industries, 1994–98. Mem., British Hallmarking Council, 1988–2004. Member: Council, Goldsmiths' Coll., 1989–2004; Governing Body: Imperial Coll., 1989–2001; London Guildhall Univ., 1997–2002. Hon. MA London Guildhall, 1994. *Recreations:* walking, gardening, visual arts. *Address:* Ham Green Cottage, Ham, Marlborough, Wilts SN8 3QR. *T:* (01488) 668846. *Club:* Army and Navy.

BUCHANAN-JARDINE, Sir Andrew Rupert John; *see* Jardine.

BUCK, John Stephen; Ambassador to Portugal, 2004–07; *b* 10 Oct. 1953; *s* of Frederick George Buck and Amelia Ellen Buck (*née* Stevens); *m* 1980, Jean Claire Webb; one *s* one *d. Educ:* East Ham GS; York Univ. (BA History 1975); Wolfson Coll., Oxford (MSc Applied Social Studies, 1979; CQSW 1979). Middlesex Probation Service, 1975–77; social worker, Oxfordshire Social Services, 1979–80; joined HM Diplomatic Service, 1980; Second Sec., Sofia, 1982–84; First Sec., FCO, 1984–88; Head of Chancery, Lisbon, 1988–92; FCO, 1992–94; Counsellor, on loan to Cabinet Office, Prin. Private Sec. to Chancellor of the Duchy of Lancaster, 1994–96; Counsellor and Dep. High Comr, Republic of Cyprus, 1996–2000; Head, Public Diplomacy, FCO, 2000–03; Head, Commns and Information Centre, 10 Downing Street/FCO, 2003; Dir, Iraq, FCO, 2003–04. *Recreations:* music, reading, swimming.

BUCK, Karen Patricia; MP (Lab) Regent's Park and Kensington North, since 1997; *b* 30 Aug. 1958; partner, Barrie Taylor; one *s. Educ:* Chelmsford High Sch.; LSE (BSc, MSc, MA). R&D worker, Outset, 1979–83; London Borough of Hackney: Specialist Officer, Developing Services and Employment for Disabled People, 1983–86; Public Health Officer, 1986–87; Lab. Party Policy Directorate (Health), 1987–92; Co-ordinator, Lab. Party Campaign Strategy, 1992–96. Parly Under-Sec. of State, DfT, 2005–06. Member: Social Security Select Cttee, 1997–2001; Work and Pensions Select Cttee, 2001–05; Home Affairs Select Cttee, 2006–. Chm., London Gp of Labour MPs, 1998–2005. *Address:* House of Commons, SW1A 0AA.

BUCK, Prof. Kenneth William, PhD, DSc; Professor of Plant and Fungal Virology, and Head, Microbiology and Plant Pathology Section, then Plant and Microbial Sciences Section, 1986–2005, and Director of Research, Department of Biological Sciences,

2001–05, Imperial College of Science, Technology and Medicine, University of London; *b* 16 Feb. 1938; *s* of William Buck and Nellie Sebra (*née* Turner); *m* 1961, Gwendoline Maureen Patterson; three *d*. *Educ:* Univ. of Birmingham (BSc 1st Cl. Hons 1959; PhD 1962; DSc 1983). Res. Fellow, Univ. of Birmingham, 1962–65; Imperial College, University of London: Lectr, Dept of Biochem., 1965–81; Reader, Dept of Biol., 1981–86; Chairman: Sub-Bd of Examrs in Microbiol., 1981–98; Bd of Examrs in Biol., 2000–05; Panel of Vis. Examrs in Microbiol., London Univ., 1988–96. Sec., Cttee on Non-Specific Immunity, MRC, 1968–71; Member: Plants and Envmt Res. Grants Bd, AFRC, 1992–94; Plant and Microbial Scis Cttee, BBSRC, 1994–97. International Committee on Taxonomy of Viruses: Mem., Exec. Cttee, 1981–93; Mem., 1975–2005, Chm., 1981–87, Fungal Virus Sub-cttee; Sec., 1984–90; Vice-Pres., 1990–93; Mem., Plant Virus Sub-cttee, 1999–2005; Chm., Narnaviridae Study Gp, 2000–05. Chm. of workshops on fungal virol. and plant virus replication, Internat. Congress of Virology, triennially, 1981–93, 1999, 2002, 2005; Mem., Internat. Adv. Cttee, XII Internat. Congress of Virology, Paris, 2002, XIII, San Francisco, 2005. Mem., Soc. for Gen. Microbiol., 1975–2005. Editor, Jl of Gen. Virology, 1991–96 (Mem., Editl Bd, 1985–90, 1997–2001); Mem., Editl Bd, Virology, 1998–2005. *Publications:* (ed) Fungal Virology, 1986; over 200 papers in scientific jls and books. *Recreations:* genealogy, mountain walking.

BUCK, Linda B., PhD; Member, Division of Basic Sciences, Fred Hutchinson Cancer Research Center, since 2002; Affiliate Professor of Physiology and Biophysics, University of Washington, since 2003; *b* 29 Jan. 1947. *Educ:* Univ. of Washington (BS 1975); Univ. of Texas (PhD 1980). Associate, Howard Hughes Med. Inst., Columbia Univ., 1984–91; Asst Prof., 1991–96, Associate Prof., 1996–2001, Prof., 2001–02, Dept of Neurobiol., Harvard Med. Sch.; Asst Investigator, 1994–97, Associate Investigator, 1997–2000, Investigator, 2001–, Howard Hughes Med. Inst. (Jtly) Nobel Prize in Physiology or Medicine, 2004. *Publications:* articles in learned jls. *Address:* Division of Basic Sciences, Fred Hutchinson Cancer Research Center, 1100 Fairview Avenue North, PO Box 19024, Seattle, WA 98109–1024, USA.

BUCK, Prof. Margaret Ann, OBE 2008; Director, Connecting Creativity, since 2006; *b* 23 Nov. 1948; *d* of late William Ewart Buck and Winifred Annie Buck; *m* 1985, David Martin Burrows; one *s* one *d* (twins). *Educ:* Pate's Grammar Sch. for Girls, Cheltenham; Gloucestershire Coll. of Art and Design (DipAD Fine Art); Royal Coll. of Art (MA Furniture Design). Head of Dept, then Dep. Head of Sch., Central Sch. of Art and Design, 1982–86; Dep. Head of Sch., Camberwell Sch. of Arts and Crafts, 1987–89; London Institute, then University of the Arts, London: Head, Camberwell Coll. of Arts, 1989–91; Asst Rector, 1989–2006; Head of Coll., Central St Martins Coll. of Art & Design, 1991–2006; Mem., Conferments Panel, 1995–2006; exhibitions: Proj. Dir and Curator, Theatre Design and Interpretation, 1986; Proj. Dir, A Century in the Making, 1999; conceived and designed, The Innovation Centre: Arts, Communication, Fashion, Design, Central St Martins Coll. of Art & Design, 2003. Lectr, Wimbledon Sch. of Art, 1978–82; lectr at internat. confs incl. Saga Internat. Design Conf., Japan, 1993 and Handwerkskammer fur München, 1994; various appts as vis. lectr and ext. examnr. Advr on strategic develt of arts and design to Ruler of Sharjah and to Coll. of Fine Arts and Design, Univ. of Sharjah, UAE, 2006–. Exhibitor, Design of the Times exhibn, RCA, 1996. Director: Develts at London Inst., later London Artscom, Ltd, 1989–2006; Cochrane Th. Co., 1990–2006; Design Lab Ltd, 1999–2006. Chair: London and SE, Nat. Standing Conf. for Foundn Educn in Art and Design, 1981–87; Nat. Council for Foundn Educn in Art and Design, 1987–92. Trustee: Arts Foundn, 1998–; V&A Mus., 2000–06 (Mem. Collections Cttee, 2000–, Remuneration Cttee, 2004–, Theatre Mus.). Mem. Council, ESU, 2003– (Chm., Pres.'s Award for Innovation Design and Excellence in the Use of New Freestanding Technologies in the Teaching and Learning of English, 2003–). Ext. Mem., Profs' and Readers' Conferments Panel, Liverpool John Moores Univ., 2004. Member: Internat. Adv. Cttee, Fashion Fringe, 2004–; Internat. Adv. Gp, Shanghai Inst. of Visual Arts, Univ. of Fudan, China, 2005–. Governor, GSMD, 2000–. Hon. Associate, Altagamma Internat. Hon. Council, Italy, 2005. Sanderson Art in Industry Award, 1976, Radford Design Award, 1977, Furniture Makers' Co. *Address: e-mail:* mbuck@connectingcreativity.co.uk. *Fax:* (020) 8299 2031. *Clubs:* Chelsea Arts, Union.

BUCKELS, Prof. John Anthony Charles, CBE 2002; MD; FRCS; Professor of Hepatobiliary and Transplant Surgery, University of Birmingham, since 2005; Consultant Hepatobiliary and Liver Transplant Surgeon, Queen Elizabeth Hospital, Birmingham, since 1986; *b* 4 Jan. 1949; *s* of Noel and Loretta Buckels; *m* 1975, Carol Ann Francis; one *s* four *d*. *Educ:* Birmingham Univ. (MB ChB 1972; MD 1986). FRCS 1977. Raine Vis. Prof., Univ. of Western Australia, 1998; Margery Budd Prof., Univ. of Bristol, 2000. *Publications:* numerous contribs on general surgery and transplantation topics to scientific jls. *Recreations:* French home, fishing, sailing. *Address:* 87 Reddings Road, Moseley, Birmingham B13 8LP. *T:* (0121) 449 3310.

BUCKHURST, Lord; William Herbrand Thomas Sackville; with Cheviot Asset Management, since 2006; *b* 13 June 1979; *s* and *heir* of Earl De La Warr, *qv*. *Educ:* Eton; Newcastle Univ. *Recreations:* racing, shooting, Chelsea FC. *Address:* Buckhurst Park, Withyham, E Sussex TN7 4BL.

BUCKINGHAM, Area Bishop of, since 2003; **Rt Rev. Alan Thomas Lawrence Wilson,** DPhil; *b* 27 March 1955; *s* of Alan Thomas Wilson and Anna Maria Magdalena Wilson; *m* 1984, Lucy Catherine Janet (*née* Richards); two *s* three *d*. *Educ:* Sevenoaks Sch.; St John's Coll., Cambridge (BA 1977, MA 1981); Balliol Coll., Oxford (DPhil 1989); Wycliffe Hall, Oxford. Ordained deacon, 1979, priest, 1980; Hon. Curate, 1979–81, Curate, 1981–82, Eynsham; Priest i/c, St John's, Caversham, and Asst Curate, Caversham and Mapledurham, 1982–89; Vicar, St John's, Caversham, 1989–92; Rector, Sandhurst, 1992–2003. Anglican Substitute Chaplain, HMP Reading, 1990–92; Area Dean, Sonning, 1998–2003; Hon. Canon, Christ Church, Oxford, 2002–03. Visitor, Piper's Corner Sch., 2004–; Mem. Council, Wycombe Abbey Sch., 2008–; Gov., Cressex Community Sch., 2008–. *Recreations:* modern history, art and design, photography, singing, running, France. *Address:* Sheridan, Grimms Hill, Great Missenden, Bucks HP16 9BG. *T:* (01494) 862173, *Fax:* (01494) 890508; *e-mail:* bishopbucks@oxford.anglican.org.

BUCKINGHAM, Archdeacon of; *see* Gorham, Ven. K. M.

BUCKINGHAM, Amyand David, CBE 1997; FRS 1975; Professor of Chemistry, University of Cambridge, 1969–97; Fellow of Pembroke College, Cambridge, 1970–97 (Hon. Fellow, 2005); *b* 28 Jan. 1930; 2nd *s* of late Reginald Joslin Buckingham and late Florence Grace Buckingham (formerly Elliot); *m* 1965, Jillian Bowles; one *s* two *d*. *Educ:* Barker Coll., Hornsby, NSW; Univ. of Sydney; Corpus Christi Coll., Cambridge (Shell Postgraduate Schol.). Univ. Medal 1952, MSc 1953, Sydney; PhD 1956, ScD 1985, Cantab. 1851 Exhibn Sen. Studentship, Oxford Univ., 1955–57; Lectr and subseq. Student and Tutor, Christ Church, Oxford, 1955–65; Univ. Lectr in Inorganic Chem. Lab., Oxford, 1958–65; Prof. of Theoretical Chem., Univ. of Bristol, 1965–69. Vis. Lectr, Harvard, 1961; Visiting Professor: Princeton, 1965; Univ. of California (Los Angeles), 1975; Univ. of Illinois, 1976; Univ. of Wisconsin, 1978; ANU, 1996; Vis. Fellow, ANU, 1979 and 1982; Vis. Erskine Fellow, Univ. of Canterbury, NZ, 1990. FRACI 1961 (Masson Meml Schol. 1952; Rennie Meml Medal, 1958); FRSC (formerly FCS) (Harrison Meml Prize, 1959; Tilden Lectr, 1964; Theoretical Chemistry and Spectroscopy Prize, 1970; Faraday Medal and Lectr, 1997; Mem., Faraday Div. (Pres., 1987–89; Mem. Council, 1965–67, 1975–83, 1987–99)); FInstP (Harrie Massey Medal and Prize, 1995); Fellow: Optical Soc. of America (C. H. Townes Medal, 2001); Amer. Phys. Soc.; Mem., Amer. Chem. Soc.; For. Associate, Nat. Acad. Scis, USA, 1992; Foreign Member: Amer. Acad. of Arts and Scis, 1992; Royal Swedish Acad. Scis, 1996. Editor: Molecular Physics, 1968–72; Chemical Physics Letters, 1978–99. Member: Chemistry Cttee, SRC, 1967–70; Adv. Council, Royal Mil. Coll. of Science, Shrivenham, 1973–87; Council, Royal Soc., 1999–2001. Senior Treasurer: Oxford Univ. Cricket Club, 1959–64; Cambridge Univ. Cricket Club, 1977–90 (Pres., 1990–). Trustee, Henry Fund, 1977–2006. Hon. Dr: Univ. de Nancy I, 1979; Sydney, 1993; Antwerp, 2004. Hughes Medal, Royal Soc., 1996; Ahmed Zewail Prize in Molecular Scis, Elsevier/Chem. Physics Letters, 2007. *Publications:* The Laws and Applications of Thermodynamics, 1964; Organic Liquids, 1978; Principles of Molecular Recognition, 1993; papers in scientific jls. *Recreations:* walking, woodwork, cricket, travel. *Address:* Crossways, 23 The Avenue, Newmarket CB8 9AA.

BUCKINGHAM, David Anthony; Agent General for Victoria, Australia, in London, since 2004; *b* 30 March 1946; *s* of Donald Buckingham and Joyce (*née* Craven); *m* 2001, Kiren Mason; one *s* three *d*. *Educ:* Australian National Univ. (BEc 1st Cl. Hons). Aust. Foreign Service, 1972–83; Advr to Prime Minister, Bob Hawke, 1983–86; Dir, Internat. Educn, 1986–89; First Asst Sec., Aviation Div., Aust. Dept of Transport, 1989–92; Dep. Sec., Aust. Dept of Envmt, 1992–94; Exec. Dir, Minerals Council of Australia, 1994–96; Chief Exec., Business Council of Australia, 1996–2001; CEO, Turnbull Porter Novelli, 2001; Man. Dir, Stratpol Consultants, 2002–04. *Recreations:* fishing, walking. *Address:* Victoria House, Melbourne Place, Strand, WC2B 4LG. *T:* (020) 7836 2656, *Fax:* (020) 7240 6025; *e-mail:* david.buckingham@invest.vic.gov.au. *Club:* Commonwealth (Canberra).

BUCKINGHAM, Ven. Hugh Fletcher; Archdeacon of the East Riding, 1988–98, now Archdeacon Emeritus; *b* 13 Sept. 1932; *s* of Rev. Christopher Leigh Buckingham and Gladys Margaret Buckingham; *m* 1967, Alison Mary Cock; one *s* one *d*. *Educ:* Lancing College; Hertford Coll., Oxford (MA Hons). Curate: St Thomas', Halliwell, Bolton, 1957–60; St Silas', Sheffield, 1960–65; Vicar of Hindolveston and Guestwick, dio. Norwich, 1965–70; Rector of Fakenham, 1970–88. Hon. Canon of Norwich Cathedral, 1985–88. *Publications:* How To Be A Christian In Trying Circumstances, 1985; Feeling Good, 1989; Happy Ever After, 2000. *Recreations:* pottery, gardening. *Address:* Orchard Cottage, Rectory Corner, Brandsby, York YO61 4RJ.

BUCKINGHAM, Prof. Julia Clare, (Mrs S. J. Smith), PhD, DSc; Professor of Pharmacology, since 1997 and Pro-Rector (Education), since 2007, Imperial College London; *b* 18 Oct. 1950; *d* of Jack William Harry Buckingham and Barbara Joan Buckingham; *m* 1974, Simon James Smith. *Educ:* St Mary's Sch., Calne; Univ. of Sheffield (BSc Zool. 1971); Royal Free Hosp. Sch. of Medicine, Univ. of London (PhD Pharmacol. 1974; DSc Neuroendocrine Pharmacol. 1987). Res. Fellow, 1974–80, Sen. Lectr in Pharmacol., 1980–87, Royal Free Hosp. Sch. of Medicine, London; Prof. of Pharmacol., Charing Cross and Westminster Med. Sch., 1987–97 (Pre-clinical Dean, 1992–97); Head, Dept of Neuroendocrinology, 1997–2003, Dean for Non-clinical Medicine, 2000–03, Hd, Div. of Neurosci. and Mental Health, 2003–07, Imperial Coll. London. Mem., Council, Sch. of Pharmacy, London Univ., 2000–05. Pres., British Pharmacol Soc., 2004–05 (Fellow, 2004); Gen. Sec., Soc. for Endocrinol., 2005–March 2009 (Treas., 1996–2001; Chm., March 2009–); Mem. Council, Bioscis Fedn, 2008–. Dir, Bioscientifica, 1996– (Chm., 2001–05). Ed., Jl of Neuroendocrinology, 2004–. Governor: King's Coll. Sch., Wimbledon, 1991–94; St Mary's Sch., Calne, 2003–. FRSA. *Publications:* Stress, Stress Hormones and the Immune System, 1997; contribs to endocrinol. and pharmacol. jls. *Recreations:* music, ski-ing, sailing. *Address:* Faculty Building, Imperial College London, South Kensington Campus, SW7 2AZ. *T:* (020) 7594 8809, *Fax:* (020) 7594 8802; *e-mail:* j.buckingham@imperial.ac.uk. *Clubs:* Sloane, Riverside; Royal Cornwall Yacht.

BUCKINGHAMSHIRE, 10th Earl of, *cr* 1746; **George Miles Hobart-Hampden;** Bt 1611; Baron Hobart 1728; Partner, Watson Wyatt LLP (formerly Watson Wyatt Partners), consulting actuaries, 1995–2004; *b* 15 Dec. 1944; *s* of Cyril Langel Hobart-Hampden (*d* 1972) (*g g s* of 6th Earl), and Margaret Moncrieff Hilborne Hobart-Hampden (*née* Jolliffe) (*d* 1985); *S* cousin, 1983; *m* 2nd, 1975, Alison Wightman, JP, DL (*née* Forrest); two step *s*. *Educ:* Clifton College; Exeter Univ. (BA Hons History); Birkbeck Coll. and Inst. of Commonwealth Studies, Univ. of London (MA Area Studies). With Noble Lowndes and Partners Ltd, 1970–81; Dir, Scottish Pension Trustees Ltd, 1979–81, resigned; Director: Antony Gibbs Pension Services Ltd, 1981–86; Wardley Investment Services (UK) Ltd, 1986–91; Wardley Investment Services International Ltd (Man. Dir, 1988–91); Wardley Investment Services Ltd, 1988–91; Wardley Unit Trust Managers Ltd (Chm.), 1988–91; Wardley Fund Managers (Jersey) Ltd (Chm.), 1988–91; Wardley Investment Services (Luxembourg) SA, 1988–91; Wardley Asia Investment Services (Luxembourg) SA, 1989–91; Wardley Global Selection, 1989–91; Gota Global Selection, 1988–95; Korea Asia Fund, 1990–91; Wyatt Co. (UK) Ltd, 1991–95; Russian Pension Trust Co. Ltd, 1994–2001; Avnet Corporate Trustee Ltd, 2006–; Associate, 2004, Dir, 2005–, BESTrustees plc. House of Lords, 1984–99: Member: Sub-Cttee C, 1985–90, Sub-Cttee A, 1990–93, H of L Select Cttee on European Affairs; H of L Sub-Cttee on Staffing of Community Instns, 1987–88. Pres., Buckingham Cons. Constituency Assoc., 1989–. President: John Hampden Soc., 1993–; Friends of the Vale of Aylesbury, 1994–; Downend Police Community Boxing Club, 2003–. Dir, Britain-Australia Soc., 2004– (Dep. Chm., 2006–); Chm., Cook Soc., 2007. Mem. Council, Buckinghamshire Chilterns UC, 2001–. Gov., Clifton Coll., Bristol, 1991–; Pres., Old Cliftonian Soc., 2000–03. Patron, Chiltern MS Centre, 2005–. FInstD 1983. Affiliate, Inst. of Actuaries, 2001. Patron: Hobart Town (1804) First Settlers Assoc., 1984–; Sleep Apnoea Trust, 1997. Liveryman, Glovers' Co., 2007; Freeman: City of Geneva, USA, 1987; Glasgow, 1991. *Recreations:* music, squash, fishing, Real tennis, Rugby football. *Heir: kinsman* Sir John Vere Hobart, Bt, *qv*. *Address:* The Old Rectory, Church Lane, Edgcott, near Aylesbury, Bucks HP18 0TU. *T:* (01296) 770357, *Fax:* (01296) 770023. *Clubs:* Royal Over-Seas League; Leamington Tennis, Hatfield Tennis (Dir, 2001–06).

BUCKLAND, Sir Ross, Kt 1997; Chief Executive and Director, Unigate plc, 1990–2001; *b* 19 Dec. 1942; *s* of William Arthur Haverfield Buckland and Elizabeth Buckland; *m* 1966, Patricia Ann Bubb; two *s*. *Educ:* Sydney Boys' High Sch. Various positions in cos engaged in banking, engrg and food ind., 1958–66; Dir, Finance and Admin, Elizabeth Arden Pty Ltd, 1966–73; Kellogg (Australia) Pty Ltd, 1973–77, Man. Dir, 1978; Pres. and Chief Exec., Kellogg Salada Canada Inc., 1979–80; Chm., Kellogg Co. of GB Ltd and Dir, European Ops and Vice-Pres., Kellogg Co., USA, 1981–90. Director: RJB Mining, 1997–99; Allied Domecq, 1998–2004; Nat. Australia Bank Europe, 1999–2002; Mayne Gp Ltd, 2001–04; Goodman Fielder Ltd, 2001–03; Clayton Utz, 2002–. FCPA; FCIS; FIGD. *Recreation:* walking. *Address:* 2804 The Tower Apartments, 68 Market Street,

Sydney, NSW 2000, Australia. *Clubs:* Union, Sydney Cricket, Stadium Australia, Royal Sydney Golf (Sydney).

BUCKLAND, Dame Yvonne Helen Elaine, (Dame Yve), DBE 2003; Chair: Consumer Council for Water, since 2005; NHS Institute for Innovation and Improvement, since 2005; *b* 29 Nov. 1956; *d* of George Robert Jones and Margaret Ann Jones (*née* O'Hanlon); *m* 1999, Stephen Freer; two *d. Educ:* Our Lady of Mercy Grammar Sch., Wolverhampton; Leeds Univ. (BA Hons 1977); Univ. of Liverpool (DipArch 1978); Univ. of Central Lancashire (DMS 1984). FFPH (FFPHM 2001). Archivist, 1979–83, Dep. County Archivist, 1983–85, Cheshire CC; Team Leader, Mgt Effectiveness Unit, 1985–88, Asst Dir, Social Services, 1988–92, Birmingham CC; Dep. Chief Exec., Nottingham CC, 1992–99; Chm., Health Educn Authy for England, 1999–2000; Chair, HDA, 2000–05. Non-exec. Dir, S Warwicks Primary Care Trust, 2003–05. Dir, Health Partnership, Warwick Business Sch., 2003–05. Fellow, Warwick Inst. of Govt and Public Mgt, 2001. FRSA 2002. *Recreations:* gardening, bell ringing. *Address:* Consumer Council for Water, Victoria Square House, Victoria Square, Birmingham B2 4AJ; NHS Institute for Innovation and Improvement, Coventry House, University of Warwick, Coventry CV4 7AL.

BUCKLE, Alan Arthur; a Senior Partner and Chief Executive, KPMG Advisory; *b* 19 May 1959; partner, Adèle Anderson; three *s. Educ:* Durham Univ. (BA). ACA 1986. Mem., Bd of Trustees, British Council, 2005–. *Recreations:* family, small mountains, running, football, reading and the usual things. *Address:* KPMG, 8 Salisbury Square, EC4Y 8BB.

BUCKLE, Simon James, CMG 2007; DPhil; FInstP; HM Diplomatic Service; Director, Climate Policy, Grantham Institute for Climate Change, Imperial College London, since 2007; *b* 29 Feb. 1960; *s* of Roy Thomas Buckle and Muriel May Buckle; *m* 1990, Dr Rajeshree Bhatt; one *d. Educ:* Univ. of Bristol (BSc 1st Cl. Jt Hons Physics and Philosophy 1982); Univ. of Sussex (DPhil Theoretical Physics 1985). FInstP 2001. Res. Asst, Dept of Physics, Imperial Coll., London, 1985–86; joined HM Diplomatic Service, 1986; Far East Dept, FCO, 1986–88; MoD, 1988–91; Head of Iran Section, Middle East Dept, FCO, 1992–94; First Sec., Dublin, 1994–97; Political Counsellor and Consul Gen., Seoul, 1997–98; Bank of England, 1998–2002, Sen. Manager (Res.), Market Infrastructure Div., 2001–02; Hd, Res. Analysts, FCO, 2003–04; Political Counsellor, Baghdad, 2004–05; Dep. Hd of Mission, Kabul, 2005–06; Counsellor, Global Issues, Paris, 2006–07. *Recreations:* hill walking, music. *Address:* Grantham Institute for Climate Change, Imperial College London, South Kensington Campus, SW7 2AZ.

BUCKLE, Rt Rev. Terrence Owen; *see* Yukon, Bishop of.

BUCKLER, Very Rev. Philip John Warr; Dean of Lincoln, since 2007; *b* 26 April 1949; *s* of Ernest and Cynthia Buckler; *m* 1977, Linda Marjorie; one *d. Educ:* Highgate Sch.; St Peter's Coll., Oxford (BA, MA); Cuddesdon Theol Coll. Ordained deacon, 1972, priest, 1973; Asst Curate, St Peter's, Bushey Heath, 1972–75; Chaplain, Trinity Coll., Cambridge, 1975–81; Sacrist and Minor Canon, St Paul's Cathedral, 1981–86; Vicar of Hampstead, 1987–99; Area Dean of N Camden, 1993–98; Canon Residentiary, 1999–2007, Treas., 2000–07, St Paul's Cathedral. Chaplain, Actors' Church Union, 1983–92; Hon. Chaplain: Scriveners' Co., 1984–2007; Merchant Taylors' Co., 1986–87; Spectacle Makers' Co., 2000–01; Mem. Court, Corp. of Sons of Clergy, 1996–2004. *Recreations:* cricket, walking, gardening. *Address:* The Deanery, 12 Eastgate, Lincoln LN2 1QG. *T:* (01522) 561611; *e-mail:* dean@lincolncathedral.com. *Clubs:* Athenæum, MCC.

BUCKLES, Nicholas Peter; Chief Executive, Group 4 Securicor, since 2005; *b* 1 Feb. 1961; *s* of Ronald Peter Buckles and Sylvia Mary Buckles; *m* 1988, Loraine Salter; one *s* two *d. Educ:* Coventry Univ. (BA Hons Business Studies). Dowty Engrg Gp, 1979–83; Business Analyst, Avon Cosmetics, 1983–85; joined Securicor, 1985: Project Accountant, 1985–88; Commercial Manager, 1988–91; Dir, Securicor Cash Services, 1991–93; Dep. Man. Dir, Securicor Guarding, 1993–96; Man. Dir, Securicor Cash Services, 1996–98; Chief Executive: Securicor Europe, 1998–99; Security Div., 1999–2002; Securicor, 2002–04. *Recreations:* soccer, tennis, walking. *Address:* Group 4 Securicor, The Manor, Manor Royal, Gatwick, W Sussex RH10 9UN.

BUCKLEY, family name of **Baron Wrenbury**.

BUCKLEY, Edgar Vincent, CB 1999; PhD; Senior Vice-President, European Marketing and Sales, Thales, since 2003; *b* 17 Nov. 1946; *s* of Michael Joseph Buckley and Mary Buckley; *m* 1972, Frances Jacqueline Cheetham; two *s* three *d. Educ:* St Ignatius Coll., London; North-Western Poly., London (BA Hons 1967); Birkbeck Coll., London (PhD 1974). Teacher, Redbridge, 1970–73; joined MoD, 1973; Administration Trainee, 1974–76; Private Sec. to Vice Chief of Air Staff, 1976–78; Principal, 1978–79; Assistant Director: Strategic Systems Finance, 1980–84; Nuclear Policy, 1984–85; Head of Resources and Programmes (Navy), 1985–89; rcds, 1990; Efficiency Study, Cabinet Office, 1991 (on secondment); Head of Defence Arms Control Unit, 1991–92; Defence Counsellor, UK Delegn to NATO, 1992–96 (on secondment); Asst Under-Sec. of State (Home and Overseas), 1996–99; Asst Sec. Gen. for Defence Planning and Operations, NATO, 1999–2003. *Recreations:* running, swimming, reading, home maintenance. *Address:* Thales, 45 rue de Villiers, 92526 Neuilly-sur-Seine Cedex, France.

BUCKLEY, Eric Joseph, MA; FIP3; Printer to the University of Oxford, 1978–83; Emeritus Fellow of Linacre College, Oxford, 1983 (Fellow, 1979–83); *b* 26 June 1920; *s* of Joseph William Buckley and Lillian Elizabeth Major (*née* Drake); *m* 1st, 1945, Joan Alice Kirby (*d* 1973); one *s* one *d*; 2nd, 1978, Harriett (*d* 1995), *d* of Judge and Mrs Robert Williams Hawkins, Caruthersville, Mo, USA. *Educ:* St Bartholomew's, Dover. MA Oxon 1979 (by special resolution; Linacre College). Served War, RAOC and REME, ME and UK, 1939–45. Apprentice, Amalgamated Press, London, 1935; Dir, Pergamon Press Ltd, 1956–74; joined Oxford Univ. Press as Dir, UK Publishing Services, 1974. Liveryman, Stationers and Newspaper Makers Co., 1981; Freeman, City of London, 1980. FIP3 (FIOP 1981). *Recreations:* reading, theatre, cats. *Address:* 43 Sandfield Road, Oxford OX3 7RN. *T:* (01865) 760588.

BUCKLEY, James; Chief Executive, Baltic Exchange, 1992–2004; *b* 5 April 1944; *s* of late Harold Buckley and of Mabel Buckley; *m* 1972, Valerie Elizabeth Powles; one *d. Educ:* Sheffield City Grammar Sch.; Imperial College of Science and Technology (BSc, ARCS). RAF Operational Res., 1965. Principal Scientific Officer, 1971; Asst Sec., CSD; Private Secretary: to Lord Privy Seal, Lord Peart, 1979; to Lord President of Council, Lord Soames, 1979; to Chancellor of Duchy of Lancaster, Baroness Young, 1981; Sec., Civil Service Coll., 1982; Chief Exec., BVA, 1985–87; Dep. Dir Gen., GCBS, 1987–91. *Recreations:* photography, tennis. *Address:* 1 Aldenholme, Weybridge, Surrey KT13 0JF.

BUCKLEY, Martin Christopher Burton; Chief Registrar in Bankruptcy, Companies Court, High Court of Justice, 1997–2001, and Clerk of Restrictive Practices Court, 1988–2001; *b* 5 Oct. 1936; *s* of late Hon. Dr Colin Burton Buckley and Evelyn Joyce Buckley (*née* Webster); *m* 1964, Victoria Gay, *d* of Dr Stanhope Furber; two *s* three *d. Educ:* Rugby School; Trinity College, Oxford (MA). Called to the Bar, Lincoln's Inn, 1961, Bencher, 1996; practised at Chancery Bar, 1962–88; Registrar in Bankruptcy, 1988–97. *Publication:* (ed jtly) Buckley on the Companies Acts, 14th edn 1981 (1st edn 1873–9th edn 1909 by grandfather, Henry Burton Buckley, later 1st Baron Wrenbury). *Recreations:* amateur theatre, choral singing. *Address:* Crouchers, Rudgwick, Horsham, W Sussex RH12 3DD.

BUCKLEY, Martin Howard; Chairman, Leeds Teaching Hospitals NHS Trust, since 2003; *b* 10 Aug. 1945; *s* of Charles and Elma Buckley; *m* 1972, Kay Lesley Rowson; one *s* one *d.* FCA 1969. Man. Dir, packaging subsid., Rexam plc, 1976–79; CEO, NY and Philadelphia Box Plants, LINPAC Containers Internat. Ltd, 1979–85; Waddington plc: Divl Chief Exec., 1985–90; Man. Dir, 1990–92; Chief Exec., 1992–2000. Non-exec. Dir, Magnadata Internat. Ltd, 2002–04. *Recreations:* walking, clay-pigeon shooting. *Address:* Leeds Teaching Hospitals NHS Trust Headquarters, St James's University Hospital, Beckett Street, Leeds, W Yorks LS9 7TF. *T:* (0113) 206 4678, *Fax:* (0113) 206 4954; *e-mail:* martin.buckley@leedsth.nhs.uk.

BUCKLEY, Sir Michael (Sydney), Kt 2002; Parliamentary Commissioner for Administration, and Health Service Commissioner for England, Scotland and Wales, 1997–2002; Scottish Parliamentary Commissioner for Administration and Welsh Administration Ombudsman, 1999–2002; *b* 20 June 1939; *s* of Sydney Dowsett Buckley and Grace Bew Buckley; *m* 1st, 1972, Shirley Stordy (*d* 1991); one *s* one *d*; 2nd, 1992, Judith Cartmell (*née* Cobb); two step *s* one step *d. Educ:* Eltham College; Christ Church, Oxford (MA; Cert. of Stats). Asst Principal, Treasury, 1962; Asst Private Sec. to Chancellor of Exchequer, 1965–66; Principal: Treasury, 1966–68 and 1971–74; CSD, 1968–71; Assistant Secretary: Treasury, 1974–77 and 1980–82; DoI, 1977–80; Under Secretary: Cabinet Office, 1982–85; Dept of Energy, 1985–91; Chm., Dartford and Gravesham NHS Trust, 1995–96. Member: CS Appeal Bd, 1991–96; GMC, 2003–. *Recreations:* photography, listening to music, reading. *Address:* 1 Manor Court, Bearsted, Maidstone, Kent ME14 4BZ.

BUCKLEY, Peter Neville; Chairman, Caledonia Investments plc, since 1994 (Deputy Chairman, 1987–94; Chief Executive, 1987–2002); President, Royal Horticultural Society, since 2006; *b* 23 Sept. 1942; *s* of Maj. Edward Richard Buckley and Ina Heather (*née* Cayzer); *m* 1967, Mary Barabel Stewart; two *d. Educ:* Eton; Manchester Business Sch. (DipBA). Served articles with McClelland Moores & Co. (later Ernst & Young); qualified as Chartered Accountant, 1966; joined Brit. & Commonwealth Shipping Co., later Brit. & Commonwealth Hldgs PLC, 1968; Exec. Dir, 1974–88. Chairman: English & Scottish Investors, 1988–2002; Sterling Inds, 1988–2005; Bristow Helicopter Gp, 1991–2004; Bristow Aviation Hldgs, 1996–; Cayzer Trust Co., 1996–; non-executive Director: RHS Enterprises, 1993–2006; Kerzner Internat. Ltd (formerly Sun Internat. Hotels), 1994–2006; Close Brothers Gp, 1995–2007; Offshore Logistics, subseq. Bristow Gp, Inc., 1996–. *Recreations:* gardening, golf, shooting. *Address:* Caledonia Investments plc, Cayzer House, 30 Buckingham Gate, SW1E 6NN. *T:* (020) 7802 8080.

BUCKLEY, Lt-Comdr Sir (Peter) Richard, KCVO 1982 (CVO 1973; MVO 1968); *b* 31 Jan. 1928; 2nd *s* of late Alfred Buckley and Mrs E. G. Buckley, Crowthorne, Berks; *m* 1958, Theresa Mary Neve; two *s* one *d. Educ:* Wellington Coll. Cadet, RN, 1945. Served in HM Ships: Mauritius, Ulster, Contest, Defender, and BRNC, Dartmouth. Specialised in TA/S. Invalided from RN (Lt-Comdr), 1961. Private Sec. to the Duke and Duchess of Kent, 1961–89; Extra Equerry to the Duke of Kent, 1989–. Director: Vickers Internat., 1981–89; Malcolm McIntyre Consultancy, 1989–92. Governor: Wellington Coll., 1989–98; Eagle House Sch., 1989–98 (Chm. of Govs, 1992–98). FRGS. *Recreations:* fishing, sailing, bee keeping. *Address:* Coppins Cottages, Iver, Bucks SL0 0AT. *T:* (01753) 653004. *Clubs:* Army and Navy; All England Lawn Tennis and Croquet.

BUCKLEY, Hon. Sir Roger (John), Kt 1989; a Judge of the High Court of Justice, Queen's Bench Division, 1989–2004; *b* 26 April 1939; *s* of Harold and Marjorie Buckley; *m* 1965, Margaret Gillian, *d* of Robert and Joan Cowan; one *s* one *d. Educ:* Mill Hill Sch.; Manchester Univ. (LLB (Hons)). Called to the Bar, Middle Temple, 1962 (Harmsworth Schol.); Bencher, Middle Temple, 1987; QC 1979; a Recorder, 1986–89; a Judge of the Employment Appeal Tribunal, 1994–2004; Pres., Restrictive Practices Court, 1994–2001. Mem., Judicial Panel, City Disputes Panel, 2005–. Chm., Jockey Club Appeal Bd, 2005–. Trustee, Painshill Park Trust Ltd, 2005–. *Recreations:* golf, theatre. *Address:* Brick Court Chambers, 2–8 Essex Street, WC2R 3LD. *Club:* Old Mill Hillians.

BUCKMASTER, family name of **Viscount Buckmaster**.

BUCKMASTER, 4th Viscount *cr* 1933, of Cheddington, Buckinghamshire; **Adrian Charles Buckmaster;** Baron 1915; Chief Executive Officer and Director, Avecia Holdings plc, since 2006; *b* 2 Feb. 1949; *s* of Hon. Colin John Buckmaster and of May Buckmaster (*née* Gibbon); *S* uncle, 2007; *m* 1975, Dr Elizabeth Mary Mark; one *s* two *d. Educ:* Charterhouse; Clare Coll., Cambridge (BA 1970; MA 1974). *Heir: s* Hon. Andrew Nicholas Buckmaster, *b* 1980.

BUCKNALL, Maj. Gen. James Jeffrey Corfield, CBE 2004 (MBE 1994); Chief of Staff, Allied Rapid Reaction Corps, Afghanistan, then Germany, since 2006; *b* 29 Nov. 1958; *s* of Captain Robin Bucknall and Diana Bucknall; *m* 1986, Tessa Jane Freemantle (*née* Barrett); two *s. Educ:* Winchester Coll. Joined Army, 1977; commnd Coldstream Guards, 1978; served with 2nd Bn in GB, Germany, NI and Cyprus; Staff Coll., 1990; on staff, HQ NI, 1992–96 (despatches, 1992); CO, 1st Bn, Germany and England, 1996–98; COS, 1st (UK) Armd Div., Bosnia and Germany, 1998–2001; HCSC 2001; Comdr, 39 Inf. Bde, Belfast, 2001–03; Dir, Counter Terrorism and UK Ops, MoD, 2004–06; served with HQ Multi-National Force Iraq, Baghdad, 2006. *Recreations:* shooting, fishing, cricket, military history, long suffering supporter of Newcastle United. *Clubs:* Pratt's, MCC.

BUCKNILL, Thomas Michael, RD 1983; FRCS; Consultant Orthopaedic Surgeon, St Bartholomew's Hospital, since 1977 and Royal London Hospital, since 1995; *b* 11 Jan. 1942; *m* 1968, Rachael Offer (marr. diss. 1998); one *s* three *d*; *m* 1999, Annie Marshall. *Educ:* Douai Sch.; St Bartholomew's Hosp. Med. Coll., London (MB BS 1964). FRCS 1970. House Surgeon, 1965–66, Anatomy Demonstrator, 1966–67, St Bartholomew's Hosp.; Surgical Registrar, St Stephen's Hosp., Chelsea, 1968–70; Registrar, Royal Nat. Orthopaedic Hosp., Stanmore, 1970–76; Clin. Fellow, Harvard Med. Sch., 1976; Cons. Orthopaedic Surgeon, King Edward VII Hosp., London, 1981–. MO, RNR London Div., 1967–93; Surgeon Comdr, RNR, 1987–93, retd; PMO, Royal Marines Reserve, London, 1988–91. FRSocMed 1995. *Publication:* (contrib.) Textbook of General Surgery, 1980. *Recreations:* sailing, golf. *Address:* 134 Harley Street, W1G 7JY. *T:* (020) 7486 2622. *Clubs:* Naval; Moor Park Golf, Royal Southampton Yacht.

BUCKWELL, Prof. Allan Edgar; Chief Economist, Country Land and Business Association, since 2000; *b* 10 April 1947; *s* of George Alfred Donald Buckwell and Jessie Ethel Buckwell (*née* Neave); *m* 1967, Susan Margaret Hopwood (marr. diss. 1990); two *s*;

m 1997, Elizabeth Gay Mitchell. *Educ:* Wye Coll., Univ. of London (BSc Agric.); Manchester Univ. (MA Econ.). Research Associate, Agricl Adjustment Unit, Newcastle Univ., 1970–73; Lectr in Agricl Economics, Newcastle Univ., 1973–84; Prof. of Agricl Econs, Wye Coll., Univ. of London, 1984–99. Kellogg Res. Fellow, Univ. of Wisconsin, Madison, 1974–75; Vis. Prof., Cornell Univ., 1983. Auxilliare, DG VI, EC, 1995–96. *Publications:* (jtly) The Cost of the Common Agricultural Policy, 1982; Chinese Grain Economy and Policy, 1989; Privatisation of Agriculture in New Market Economies: lessons from Bulgaria, 1994; articles in Jl Agricl Economics. *Recreations:* walking, gardening, cycling. *Address:* 51 Joy Lane, Whitstable, Kent CT5 4DE. *T:* (01227) 265684; *e-mail:* allan.buckwell@cla.org.uk.

BUCZACKI, Dr Stefan Tadeusz; biologist, broadcaster and author; *b* 16 Oct. 1945; *o s* of Tadeusz Buczacki and Madeleine Mary Cato Buczacki (*née* Fry); *m* 1970, Beverley Ann Charman; two *s*. *Educ:* Ecclesbourne Sch., Duffield; Univ. of Southampton (BSc 1st cl. Hons Botany, 1968); Linacre Coll., Oxford (DPhil 1971). FIHort 1986; CBiol, FIBiol; ARPS; FLS. Research Biologist, Nat. Vegetable Res. Station, 1971–84; freelance broadcaster, writer, garden designer and consultant, 1984–; Partner, Stefan Buczacki Associates, landscape and garden design, 2001–. *Radio:* Gardeners' Question Time, 1982–94; Classic Gardening Forum, 1994–97; The Gardening Quiz (originator and writer), 1988–93; *television:* Gardeners' Direct Line, 1983–85; That's Gardening, 1989–90, 1992; Bazaar, 1989–93; Gardeners' World, 1990–91; Chelsea Flower Show, 1990–91; Good Morning, 1992–96; Stefan Buczacki's Gardening Britain, 1996; At Home, 1997–98; Stefan's Garden Roadshow, 1998–2000; Open House, 1998–2002; Learn to Garden with Stefan Buczacki, 1999; Stefan's Ultimate Gardens, 2001. President: W Midlands ASE, 1996–97; British Mycological Soc., 1999–2000 (Vice-Pres., 1994, Press Officer, 2002–); Mem. Council, Gardeners' Royal Benevolent Soc., 1990–98. Trustee: Brogdale Horticultural Trust, 1990–95; Hestercombe Gardens Trust, 1996–2006 (Chm., Estates Cttee, 2003–06). Patron: Parrs Wood Rural Trust, 1990–; Dawlish Gardens Trust, 1990–; Warwick Castle Gdns Trust, 1992–; Friends of Hestercombe Gardens, 1994–2006; Nat. Amateur Gardening Show, 1996–98; Southport Flower Show, 1997–. Hon. Prof., Plant Pathology, Liverpool John Moores Univ., 1994–. Honorary Fellow: CABI Bioscience, 2003; Warwicks Coll., 2007. Benefactors' Medal, British Mycological Soc., 1996. DUniv Derby, 2002. *Publications:* (jtly) Collins Guide to the Pests, Diseases and Disorders of Garden Plants, 1981 (shorter Guide, 1983), 3rd edn 2005; Gem Guide to Mushrooms and Toadstools, 1982; (ed) Zoosporic Plant Pathogens, 1983; Beat Garden Pests and Diseases, 1985; Gardeners' Questions Answered, 1985; (jtly) Three Men in a Garden, 1986; Ground Rules for Gardeners, 1986; Beginners Guide to Gardening, 1988; Creating a Victorian Flower Garden, 1988; Garden Warfare, 1988; New Generation Guide to the Fungi of Britain and Europe, 1989; A Garden for all Seasons, 1990; Understanding Your Garden, 1990; The Essential Gardener, 1991; Dr Stefan Buczacki's Gardening Hints, 1992; Mushrooms and Toadstools of Britain and Europe, 1992; The Plant Care Manual, 1992; (ed) The Gardener's Handbook, 1993; The Budget Gardening Year, 1993; Best Climbers, 1994; Best Foliage Shrubs, 1994; Best Shade Plants, 1994; Best Soft Fruit, 1994; (jtly) Classic FM Garden Planner, 1995; Best Water Plants, 1995; Best Herbs, 1995; Best Geraniums, 1998; Best Roses, 1996; Best Container Plants, 1996; Stefan Buczacki's Gardening Britain, 1996; Best Garden Doctor, 1997; Best Summer Flowering Shrubs, 1997; Best Winter Plants, 1997; Best Clematis, 1998; Best Pruning, 1998; Stefan Buczacki's Gardening Dictionary, 1998; Stefan Buczacki's Plant Dictionary, 1998; Best Fuchsias, 1999; Best Evergreens, 1999; First Time Gardener, 2000; Best Water Gardens, 2000; Best Kitchen Herbs, 2000; Essential Garden Answers, 2000; Best Ground Cover, 2000; Best Rock Garden Plants, 2000; Plant Problems: prevention and treatment, 2000; Hamlyn Encyclopaedia of Gardening, 2002; Fauna Britannica, 2002; The Commonsense Gardener, 2004; (jtly) Young Gardener, 2006; Garden Natural History, 2007; Collins Wildlife Gardener, 2007; Churchill and Chartwell: the untold story of Churchill's homes and gardens, 2007; articles in magazines and newspapers; numerous scientific papers in professional jls. *Recreations:* own garden, photography, riding, fishing, natural history, book collecting, theatre, kippers, Derbyshire porcelain, fine music, travelling and then returning to appreciate the British countryside. *Address:* c/o Knight Ayton Management, 114 St Martin's Lane, WC2N 4AZ. *T:* (020) 7836 5333. *Club:* Garrick.

BUD, Dr Robert Franklin; Principal Curator, Medicine, Science Museum, since 2007; *b* 21 April 1952; *s* of Martin Bud and Hanna Bud (*née* Loebl); *m* 1979, Lisa Frierman; one *s*. *Educ:* University Coll. Sch.; Univ. of Manchester (BSc 1st Cl. Liberal Studies in Sci. 1973); Univ. of Pennsylvania (PhD 1980). Science Museum: Asst Keeper, Industrial Chem., 1978–85; Dep. Keeper, Dept of Physical Scis, 1985–89; Hd, Collections Services, 1989–91; Hd, Life and Envmtl Scis, 1991–94; Manager, Life and Commns Technols, and Res. (Collections), subseq. Information and Res., then Electronic Access, 1994–2007. Associate Sen. Res. Fellow, Centre for Evaluation of Public Policy and Practice, Brunel Univ., 1990–95; Adjunct Prof., Univ. of Va, 1993; Associated Scholar, Dept of History and Philosophy of Sci., Univ. of Cambridge, 2002–; Honorary Senior Research Fellow: Dept Sci. and Technol. Studies, UCL, 2003–; Dept History, Classics and Archaeology, Birkbeck Coll., London, 2003–; Hon. Professorial Fellow, Dept History, QMUL, 2008–. Associate Editor, Outlook on Sci. Policy, 1989–91; Member Editorial Board: Brit. Jl for Hist. of Sci., 1982–; History and Technol., 1993–; Mem., Editl Adv. Bd, Oxford Companion to the History of Science, 1998–. Member of Council: Brit. Soc. for Hist. of Sci., 1985–88; Soc. for Hist. of Technol., 1996–98; Mem. Steering Cttee, Hist. of Twentieth Century Medicine Gp, Wellcome Trust, 1998–. Trustee, RN Submarine Mus., 1994–99. FWAAS 1989; FRHistS 1999. (Jtly) Bunge Prize, Hans Jenemann Stiftung, 1998. *Publications:* (with G. K. Roberts) Science versus Practice: chemistry in Victorian Britain, 1984; (jtly) Chemistry in America 1876–1976: historical indicators, 1984; The Uses of Life: a history of biotechnology, 1993 (trans. German 1995); edited jointly: Invisible Connections: instruments, institutions and science, 1992; Guide to the History of Technology in Europe, 1992, 3rd edn 1996; Instruments of Science: an historical encyclopedia, 1998; Manifesting Medicine: bodies and machines, 1999; Cold War, Hot Science: applied research in British defence laboratories 1945–1990, 1999; (jtly) Inventing the Modern World: technology since 1750, 2000; Penicillin: triumph and tragedy, 2007; articles in learned jls. *Recreations:* family life, walking, second-hand bookshops. *Address:* Science Museum, Exhibition Road, SW7 2DD. *T:* (020) 7942 4200; *e-mail:* robert.bud@nmsi.ac.uk.

BUDD, Sir Alan (Peter), Kt 1997; Provost, The Queen's College, Oxford, 1999–2008; *b* 16 Nov. 1937; *s* of late Ernest and Elsie Budd; *m* 1964, Susan (*née* Millott); three *s*. *Educ:* Oundle Sch. (Grocers' Co. Schol.); London School of Economics (Leverhulme Schol.; BScEcon); Churchill Coll., Cambridge (PhD). Lectr, Southampton Univ., 1966–69; Ford Foundn Vis. Prof., Carnegie-Mellon Univ., Pittsburgh, 1969–70; Sen. Economic Advr, HM Treasury, 1970–74; Williams & Glyn's Sen. Res. Fellow, London Business Sch., 1974–78; High Level Cons., OECD, 1976–77; Special Advr, Treasury and CS Cttee, 1979–81; Dir, Centre for Economic Forecasting, 1980–88, Prof. of Econs, 1981–91, Fellow, 1997, London Business Sch.; Gp Economic Advr, Barclays Bank, 1988–91; Chief Economic Advr to HM Treasury, and Head of Govt Economic Service, 1991–97; Mem., Monetary Policy Cttee, Bank of England, 1997–99. Reserve Bank of Aust. Vis. Prof., Univ. of New South Wales, 1983. Member: Securities and Investments Board, 1987–88; ABRC, 1991; Chairman: Gambling Rev. Body, 2000–01; Tax Law Review Cttee, 2006–. Member: Council, Inst. for Fiscal Studies, 1988–91; Council, REconS, 1988–93. Chairman: British Performing Arts Medicine Trust, 1998–2005; Schola Cantorum of Oxford, 2002–08. Governor: LSE, 1994–2002; NIESR, 1998–. Econs columnist, The Independent, 1991. *Publications:* The Politics of Economic Planning, 1978; articles in professional jls. *Recreations:* music, gardening. *Club:* Reform.

BUDD, Sir Colin (Richard), KCMG 2002 (CMG 1991); HM Diplomatic Service, retired; Ambassador to the Netherlands, 2001–05; *b* 31 Aug. 1945; *s* of Bernard Wilfred Budd, QC and Margaret Alison Budd, MBE (*née* Burgin); *m* 1971, Agnes Smit; one *s* one *d*. *Educ:* Kingswood Sch., Bath; Pembroke Coll., Cambridge. Entered HM Diplomatic Service, 1967; CO, 1967–68; Asst Private Sec. to Minister without Portfolio, 1968–69; Warsaw, 1969–72; Islamabad, 1972–75; FCO, 1976–80; The Hague, 1980–84; Asst Private Sec. to Sec. of State for Foreign and Commonwealth Affairs, 1984–87; European Secretariat, Cabinet Office, 1987–88; Counsellor (Political), Bonn, 1989–92; Chef de Cabinet to Sir Leon Brittan, Vice Pres. of EC, 1993–96; Dep. Sec., Cabinet Office (on secondment), 1996–97; Dep. Under-Sec. of State, FCO, 1997–2001. Mem., Commn for Racial Equality, 2006–07. *Recreations:* running, mountains, music (Mozart, chansons, Don McLean). *Address:* *e-mail:* acbudd@hotmail.com.

BUDD, Rt Rev. Mgr Hugh Christopher; *see* Plymouth, Bishop of, (RC).

BUDD, Prof. Malcolm John, PhD; FBA 1995; Grote Professor of Philosophy of Mind and Logic, University College London, 1998–2001, now Emeritus; *b* 23 Dec. 1941; *s* of Edward Charles Budd and Hilare (*née* Campbell). *Educ:* Latymer Upper Sch.; Jesus Coll., Cambridge (BA 1964; MA 1967; PhD 1968). William Stone Research Fellow, Peterhouse, Cambridge, 1966–70; University College London: Lectr in Philosophy, 1970–87; Reader, 1987–90; Prof. of Philosophy, 1990–98. Pres., British Soc. of Aesthetics, 2004–. Editor, Aristotelian Soc., 1989–94. *Publications:* Music and the Emotions, 1985; Wittgenstein's Philosophy of Psychology, 1989; Values of Art, 1995; The Aesthetic Appreciation of Nature, 2002. *Address:* 12 Hardwick Street, Cambridge CB3 9JA.

BUDGE, Keith Joseph; Head, Bedales School, since 2001; *b* 24 May 1957; *s* of William and Megan Budge; *m* 1983, Caroline Ann Gent; two *s* one *d*. *Educ:* Rossall Sch.; University Coll., Oxford (MA Hons English; PGCE). Asst Master, Eastbourne Coll., 1980–84; Marlborough College: Asst Master, 1984–88 and 1989–91; Housemaster, Cotton Hse, 1991–95; Instructor in English, Stevenson Sch., Pebble Beach, CA, 1988–89; Headmaster, Loretto Sch., 1995–2000. *Recreations:* hill-walking, trout-fishing, gadgets, theatre. *Address:* Bedales School, Petersfield, Hants GU32 2DG.

BUDGEN, Keith Graham; Regional Director, South East, HM Courts Service, since 2006; *b* 14 Oct. 1950; *s* of Victor Charles Budgen and Norma Budgen (*née* Day); *m* 1980, Penelope Ann Lane; one *s* two *d*. *Educ:* Claygate Primary Sch.; Wayneflete Sch., Esher. Lord Chancellor's Department, subseq. Department for Constitutional Affairs, 1967–: Group Manager: Newcastle upon Tyne Gp of Courts, 1990–98; London Gp of Crown Courts, 1998–2002; Dir, Criminal Justice Improvement, 2002–06. *Recreations:* renovating houses, gardening, walking, socialising. *Address:* (office) 3rd Floor, Rose Court, 2 Southwark Bridge, SE1 9HS. *T:* (020) 7921 2020; *e-mail:* keith.budgen@hmcourts-service.gsi.gov.uk.

BUDGETT, Richard Gordon McBride, OBE 2003; Chief Medical Officer, London Organising Committee of the Olympic Games, since 2007; *b* 20 March 1959; *s* of Robert and Fiona Budgett; *m* 1987, Sue Moore; one *s* two *d*. *Educ:* Radley Coll.; Selwyn Coll., Cambridge (BA 1980, MA 1984); Middlesex Hosp., London (MB BS 1983); London Hosp. (Dip. Sports Medicine 1989); DCH RCP 1986; DRCOG 1987. MRCGP 1988; FISM 2001. Won Gold Medal for rowing (coxed fours), Los Angeles Olympic Games, 1984. Principal in General Practice, Acton, 1989–2004; CMO, Olympic Medical Centre, 1989–; Dir of Med. Services, British Olympic Assoc., 1994–2008; Sports Physician, English Inst. of Sport, 2003–. MO, Governing Body, British Bobsleigh Assoc., 1989–2007; Dr, Bobsleigh Team, Olympic Winter Games, 1992, 1994; CMO, British Team at Olympic Games, 1996, 1998, 2000, 2002, 2004, 2006. Bd Mem., then Chm., Nat. Sports Medicine Inst., 1994–2000; Examiner, Intercollegiate Academic Bd of Sports and Exercise Medicine, 2000. FFSEM 2003. *Publications:* articles on sports and exercise medicine in med. jls, mainly on 'Unexplained Underperformance Syndrome'. *Recreations:* sailing, ski-ing and ski-touring, cycling, rowing, good food, traditional board games. *Address:* Olympic Medical Institute, Northwick Park Hospital, Watford Road, Harrow, Middx HA1 3UJ.

BUENO, Antonio de Padua Jose Maria; QC 1989; a Recorder, since 1989; *b* 28 June 1942; *s* of late Antonio and Teresita Bueno; *m* 1966, Christine Mary Lees; three *d*. *Educ:* Downside School; Salamanca Univ. Called to the Bar: Middle Temple, 1964, Bencher, 1998; NSW, Ireland and Gibraltar. An Asst Recorder, 1984–89. *Publications:* (ed jtly) Banking section, Atkin's Encyclopaedia of Court Forms, 2nd edn 1976; (Asst Editor, 24th edn 1979 and 25th edn 1983, Jt Editor, 26th edn 1988) Byles on Bills of Exchange; (Asst Editor) Paget's Law of Banking, 9th edn 1982. *Recreations:* fishing, shooting. *Address:* Hammoon House, Hammoon, Sturminster Newton, Dorset DT10 2DB. *T:* (01258) 861704; Equity House, Blackbrook Park Avenue, Taunton, Somerset TA1 2PX. *T:* 0845 0833000; *e-mail:* christinebueno@aol.com. *Clubs:* Athenaeum, MCC; Kildare Street (Dublin).

BUERK, Michael Duncan; foreign correspondent and newscaster, television; *b* 18 Feb. 1946; *s* of Betty Mary Buerk and Gordon Charles Buerk; *m* 1968, Christine Lilley; two *s*. *Educ:* Solihull School. Thomson Newspapers, Cardiff, 1967–69; reporter, Daily Mail, 1969–70; producer, BBC radio, 1970–71; reporter: HTV (West), 1971–72; BBC TV (South), 1972–73; BBC TV London, 1973–76; correspondent, BBC TV: industrial, 1976–77; energy, 1977–79; Scotland, 1979–81; special corresp. and newscaster, 1981–83; Southern Africa, 1983–87; presenter, BBC TV News, 1988–2002; Chm., The Moral Maze, R4, 1997–; presenter, The Choice, Radio 4, 1999–. Hon. MA Bath, 1991; Hon. LLD Bristol, 1994; Hon. DSc Aston, 2000. RTS TV Journalist of the Year and RTS News Award, 1984; UN Hunger Award, 1984; numerous other awards, UK and overseas, 1984, 1985; BAFTA News Award, 1985; James Cameron Meml Award, 1988; Science Writer of the Year Award, 1989; Mungo Park Award, RSGS, 1994. *Publication:* The Road Taken (autobiog.), 2004. *Recreations:* travel, oenophily, sailing. *Address:* c/o BBC Television, W12 7RJ. *T:* (020) 7743 8000. *Clubs:* Reform, Garrick.

BUFORD, William Holmes; staff writer, The New Yorker, since 2006 (Literary and Fiction Editor, 1995–2002); *b* 6 Oct. 1954; *s* of late William H. Buford and of Helen Shiel; *m* 1991, Alicja Kobiernicka (marr. diss. 2000); *m* 2002, Jessica Green; twin *s*. *Educ:* Univ. of California, Berkeley (BA); King's College, Cambridge (MA). Editor, Granta, 1979–95; former Chm., Granta Publications Ltd. *Publications:* (as Bill Buford): Among the Thugs, 1991; (ed) The Best of Granta Travel, 1991; (ed) The Best of Granta Reportage, 1993;

(ed) The Granta Book of the Family, 1995; Heat, 2006. *Address:* New Yorker Magazine, 4 Times Square, New York, NY 10036, USA.

BUHARI, Alhaji Haroun Madani; media relations consultant; High Commissioner for Sierra Leone in London, and Ambassador for Sierra Leone to Sweden, Denmark, Norway, Spain, Portugal, Greece, India and Tunisia, 1995–96; *b* 23 Aug. 1945; *s* of Alhaji Mohammed Buhari and Haja Fatmatta M'balu (*née* Tejan-Sie); *m* 1st, 1975, Haja Sakinatu Onikeh Adams; three *s*; 2nd, 1990, Máriam Zainab Koroma; one *s* one *d*. *Educ:* St Helena Secondary Sch., Freetown; Islamic Missions Inst. at Al-Azhar Univ., Cairo; El Nasr Boys' Coll., Cairo; Univ. of Alexandria, Egypt (BA Hons 1970); Inst. of Social Studies, Univ. of Alexandria; SW London Coll.; Internat. Inst. for Journalism, W Berlin; Diplomatic Acad., Univ. of Westminster (MA 1997). Ministry of Information and Broadcasting, Sierra Leone: Inf. Officer, 1971–78; Sen. Inf. Officer, 1978–82 (Press. Sec., Office of Pres., 1981–82); Asst Controller/Principal Inf. Officer, 1982–90; Editor-in-Chief, Sierra Leone News Agency, 1986–87; Controller, Govt Inf. Services, 1990–91; Asst Dir of Inf., 1991–92 (Press Sec., Office of Pres., 1987–92); High Comr to Gambia and Ambassador to Senegal, Mauritania and Morocco, 1992–95. Founder Mem., Sierra Leone Assoc. of Journalists, 1971 (Chm., Interim Exec., 1992–93). Sec.-Gen., Sierra Leone Islamic Foundn, 1982–85; Exec. Sec. Federation of Sierra Leone Muslim Orgns, 1987. Governor: Commonwealth Foundn, 1995–96; Commonwealth Inst., 1995–96. Vice-Pres., Royal Over-Seas League, 1996–. *Publications:* articles on literary, political, social and religious issues for Sierra Leone and internat. press. *Recreations:* football, reading, travelling. *Address: e-mail:* HarounBuhari@hotmail.com.

BUIST, John Latto Farquharson, (Ian), CB 1990; Under Secretary, Foreign and Commonwealth Office (Overseas Development Administration), retired; *b* 30 May 1930; *s* of late Lt-Col Thomas Powrie Buist, RAMC, and Christian Mary (*née* Robertson); partner, 1981, J. E. Regensburg, (Dennis Regensburg) (*d* 1988). *Educ:* Dalhousie Castle Sch.; Winchester Coll.; New Coll., Oxford (MA). Asst Principal, CO, 1952–54; seconded Kenya Govt, 1954–56; Principal, CO, 1956–61; Dept of Tech. Cooperation, 1961–62; Brit. High Commn, Dar-es-Salaam, 1962–64; Consultant, E African Common Services Org./Community, 1964–69; Sec., Commn on E African Cooperation and related bodies, 1966–69; Asst Sec., Min. of Overseas Develt, 1966–76; Under Sec., FCO (ODA), 1976–90. Director: PLAN International (UK), 1990–; Foster Parents PLAN Inc., 1991–2002. Co-founder, Classical Assoc. of Kenya; Member: Thames Philharmonic (formerly John Bate) Choir; United Reformed Church; Lesbian and Gay Christian Movement. *Recreation:* choral singing. *Address:* 9 West Hill Road, SW18 1LH.

BUITER, Prof. Willem Hendrik, CBE 2000; PhD; FBA 1998; Professor of European Political Economy, London School of Economics and Political Science, University of London, since 2005; *b* 26 Sept. 1949; *s* of Harm Geert Buiter and Hendrien Buiter, *née* van Schooten; *m* 1st, 1973, Jean Archer (marr. diss. 1998); one *s* one *d*; 2nd, 1998, Prof. Anne Sibert. *Educ:* Cambridge Univ. (BA 1971); Yale Univ. (PhD 1975). Asst Prof., Princeton Univ., 1975–76; Lectr, LSE, 1976–77; Asst Prof., Princeton Univ., 1977–79; Prof. of Economics, Univ. of Bristol, 1980–82; Cassel Prof. of Economics, LSE, Univ. of London, 1982–85; Prof. of Econs, 1985–90, Juan T. Trippe Prof. of Internat. Econs, 1990–94, Yale Univ.; Prof. of Internat. Macroecons, and Fellow of Trinity Coll., Cambridge Univ., 1994–2000; Chief Economist, EBRD, 2000–05. Consultant: IMF, 1979–80; World Bank, 1986–; Inter-American Develt Bank, 1992–; EBRD, 1994–2000; Specialist Advr, House of Commons Select Cttee on the Treasury and CS, 1980–84; Advr, Netherlands Min. of Educn and Science, 1985–86; External Mem., Monetary Policy Cttee, Bank of England, 1997–2000; Chm., Netherlands Council of Econ. Advrs, 2005–07. Mem. Council, Royal Economic Soc., 1997–. Associate Editor, Econ. Jl, 1980–84. *Publications:* Temporary and Long Run Equilibrium, 1979; Budgetary Policy, International and Intertemporal Trade in the Global Economy, 1989; Macroeconomic Theory and Stabilization Policy, 1989; Principles of Budgetary and Financial Policy, 1990; International Macroeconomics, 1990; (jtly) Financial Markets and European Monetary Co-operation: the lessons of the 1992–93 ERM crisis, 1998; articles in learned jls. *Recreations:* tennis, poetry, music. *Address:* 24 Micheldever Road, SE12 8LX.

BUKHT, Mirza Michael John, (Michael Barry), OBE 1996; food journalist; Programme Controller, Classic FM Radio, 1992–97; *b* 10 Sept. 1941; *s* of Mirza Jawan Bukht and Lilian Ray Bukht (*née* Oaten); *m* 1964, Jennie Mary Jones; one *s* three *d*. *Educ:* Haberdashers' Aske's Sch.; King's Coll. London (BA Hons). BBC general trainee, 1963; Producer, Tonight prog., 1965; Prog. Controller, JBC, Jamaica, 1967; Dep. Editor, 24 Hours, BBC TV, 1969; Editor, Special Projects, BBC TV, 1970; Prog. Controller, Capital Radio, 1972; Principal, Nat. Broadcasting Sch., 1979; Man. Dir, Invicta Radio, 1985; Gp Prog. Dir, GWR Gp, 1988. Chm., Kentish Fare Bd, 1994–2006. Mem. Cttee, Early Dance Circle, 1991–. Chairman: Canterbury Multi-Cultural Assoc., 2001–04; Ethnic and Minorities Council, 2005–. Gov., St Edmund's Sch., Canterbury, 1997–2006. FRSA 1995; Fellow, Radio Acad., 1996. Hon. DCL Kent, 2002. *Publications:* (as Michael Barry) 5 Food and Drink books, 1984–89; Food Processor Cookery, 1985; Complete Crafty Cook Book, 1988; Exotic Food, 1989, 2nd edn 1996; Michael Barry's Cook Book, 1991; Big Food and Drink Book, 1993; Great House Cookery, 1993; Classic Recipes, 1993; The Radio Times Cookery Guide, 1994; Entertaining with Food and Drink, 1995; Crafty French Cooking, 1995; Italian Food, 1997; The Classic FM Recipes, 2000. *Recreations:* music, dance, sailing, military history, food. *Address:* 6 Chantry Hall, Dane John, Canterbury, Kent CT1 2QS.

BULFIELD, Prof. Grahame, CBE 2001; PhD; FRSE; FIBiol; Vice-Principal, Head of College of Science and Engineering, and Professor of Animal Genetics, University of Edinburgh, since 2002; *b* 12 June 1941; *s* of Frederick Bulfield and Madge (*née* Jones). *Educ:* King's Sch., Macclesfield; Univ. of Leeds (BSc 1964); Univ. of Edinburgh (Dip. Animal Genetics 1965; PhD 1968). FRSE 1992; FIBiol 1995. Fulbright Fellow and NIH Postdoctoral Fellow, Dept of Genetics, Univ. of Calif., Berkeley, 1968–70; SRC Resettlement Fellow, 1970–71, Res. Associate, 1971–76, Inst. of Animal Genetics, Univ. of Edinburgh; Lectr and Convenor of Med. Genetics, Dept of Genetics, Med. Sch. and Sch. of Biol Scis, Univ. of Leicester, 1976–81; Hd, Genetics Gp, AFRC Poultry Res. Centre, Roslin, 1981–86; Hd, Gene Expression Gp, 1986–88, and Hd of Station and Associate Dir, 1988–93, Edinburgh Res. Station of Inst. of Animal Physiology and Genetic Res., Roslin; Dir and Chief Exec., Roslin Inst., BBSRC, 1993–2002. Hon. Fellow, 1981–90, Hon. Prof., 1990–2002, Div. of Biol Scis, Univ. of Edinburgh. Member: Animal Procedures Cttee, Home Office, 1998–2006; Res. Policy Cttee, SHEFC, 2002–05; Res. and Knowledge Transfer Cttee, SFC, 2005–06. Pres., Agric. and Food Section, BAAS, 1999–2000. Mem., Enterprise Fellowship Cttee, Scottish Enterprise/RSE, 2001–. Hon. FRASE 1999. Hon. DSc: Edinburgh, 2000; Abertay, 2003. *Publications:* res. papers, reviews and book chapters on biochemical and molecular genetics. *Recreations:* fell-walking, cricket. *Address:* College of Science and Engineering, University of Edinburgh, The King's Buildings, West Mains Road, Edinburgh EH9 3JY. *T:* (0131) 650 5705.

BULFIELD, Peter William, CA; Deputy Chairman, Yamaichi Bank (UK) PLC, 1991–94 (Managing Director and Chief Executive, 1988–91); *b* 14 June 1930; *s* of Wilfred Bulfield and Doris (*née* Bedford); *m* 1958, Pamela June Beckett; two *d*. *Educ:* Beaumont Coll., Old Windsor. Peat Marwick Mitchell & Co., 1947–59; J. Henry Schroder Wagg & Co., 1959–86, Dir, 1967–86; Director: Schroder Finance, 1966–73; Schroder Darling Hldgs, Sydney, 1973–80; Vice-Chm., Mitsubishi Trust & Banking Corporation (Europe) SA, 1973–84; Jt Dep. Chm., Schroder Internat., 1977–86; Dep. Chm., Crown Agents for Overseas Govts and Admin, 1982–85 (Mem., 1978–85); Director: Yamaichi Internat. PLC, 1986–87; London Italian Bank, 1989–91. Member: Overseas Projects Board, 1983–86; Overseas Promotions Cttee, BIEC, 1984–86; Export Guarantees Adv. Council, 1985–88. Mem., Finance Cttee, CAFOD, 1994–2002; Hon. Treas., W Sussex Assoc. for the Blind, 1998–99. KSG 2001. *Recreations:* sailing, music, painting. *Address:* Snow Goose Cottage, Sandy Lane, East Ashling, W Sussex PO18 9AT. *T:* and *Fax:* (01243) 575298. *Clubs:* Sloane, Royal Thames Yacht.

BULFORD, Anne Judith; *see* Weyman, A. J.

BULKELEY, Sir Richard Thomas W.; *see* Williams-Bulkeley.

BULL, Christopher John; Business Manager, Government Equalities Office, since 2007; *b* 26 July 1954; *s* of George William and Kathleen Bull; *m* 1983, Alison Jane Hughes; two *d*. *Educ:* UCW, Aberystwyth (BA). CPFA 1983. With Nat. Audit Office, 1977–97; Inspector, Benefit Fraud Inspectorate, DSS, 1997–99; Dir, Benefit Fraud Inspectorate, DSS, subseq. DWP, 1999–2007. Ind. Mem., Audit Cttee, CRE, 2006–. FRSA 2000. *Recreations:* books, wood. *Address:* Government Equalities Office, Ashdown House, 123 Victoria Street, SW1E 6DE. *T:* (020) 7944 0612.

BULL, David Neill; Executive Director, UNICEF UK, since 1999; *b* 21 June 1951; *s* of Denis Albert and Doreen Lilian Bull; *m* 1978, Claire Grenger; one *d*. *Educ:* Sussex Univ. (BA Econ); Bath Univ. (MSc Develt Studies). Public Affairs Unit Officer, Oxfam, 1979–84; Dir, Environment Liaison Centre, Nairobi, 1984–87; Gen. Sec., World University Service (UK), 1987–90; Dir, Amnesty Internat. (UK Sect.), 1990–99. Trustee: Refugee Council, 1987–90; Pesticides Trust, 1987–99; Mem., Exec. Cttee, ACENVO, 1994–98. *Publications:* A Growing Problem: pesticides and the Third World Poor, 1982; The Poverty of Diplomacy: Kampuchea and the outside world, 1983. *Recreations:* walking, reading, esp. science fiction, family history, photography. *Address:* UNICEF UK, Africa House, 64–78 Kingsway, WC2B 6NB. *T:* (020) 7405 5592.

BULL, Deborah Clare, CBE 1999; Creative Director, Royal Opera House (formerly first Artistic Director, then Creative Director, ROH2), since 2002; a Governor, BBC, 2003–06; *b* 22 March 1963; *d* of Rev. Michael John Bull and Doreen Audrey Franklin (*née* Plumb). *Educ:* Royal Ballet Sch. Joined Royal Ballet, 1981; Principal Dancer, 1992–2001; Nutrition Teacher, Royal Ballet Sch., 1996–99; Dir, Artists' Develt Initiative, Royal Opera House, 1999–2001. Has danced a wide range of work, incl. leading rôles in: Swan Lake; Sleeping Beauty; Don Quixote; particularly noted for modern rôles, incl. Steptext, and Symbiont(s) (Time Out Outstanding Achievement Award); appeared in Diamonds of World Ballet Gala, Kremlin Palace, Moscow, 1996. Mem., Arts Council, 1998–2004 (Mem., Dance Panel, 1996–98; Annual Lecture, 1996); Gov., S Bank Centre, 1997–2003. Columnist, The Telegraph, 1999–2002; contributing editor, Harpers & Queen, 2000–01. Wrote and presented: *television:* Dance Ballerina Dance, 1998; Travels with my Tutu, 2000; The Dancer's Body, 2002; Saved for the Nation, 2006; *radio:* Leaving Barons Court, 1999; Breaking the Law, 2001; Law in Order, 2002. DUniv: Derby, 1998; Sheffield, 2001; Open, 2005. Prix de Lausanne, 1980. *Publications:* The Vitality Plan, 1998; Dancing Away, 1998; (jtly) Faber Guide to Classical Ballets, 2004; articles in jls and newspapers. *Recreations:* mountain pursuits, food and wine, reading, writing, dancing, cycling. *Address:* Royal Opera House, Covent Garden, WC2E 9DD. *T:* (020) 7240 1200.

BULL, Sir George (Jeffrey), Kt 1998; Chairman, J Sainsbury PLC, 1998–2004; *b* 16 July 1936; *s* of late William Perkins Bull and of Hon. Noreen Bull (*née* Hennessy); *m* 1960, Jane Fleur Thérèse Freeland; four *s* one *d*. *Educ:* Ampleforth Coll.; IDV Ltd: Dir, 1972; Dep. Man. Dir, 1982–84; Chief Exec., 1984–92; Chm., 1988–92; Chm. and Chief Exec., Grand Metropolitan Food Sector, 1992–93; Gp Chief Exec., 1993–96, Chm., 1996–98, Grand Metropolitan PLC; Jt Chm., Diageo, 1997–98. Non-Executive Director: United Newspapers, 1993–98; BNP Paribas Ltd, 2000–04; Maersk Co. Ltd, 2001–. Formerly Dir, BOTB; Dir, Marketing Council, 1996–2000. Mem., Adv. Bd, Marakon, 2002–06. Pres., Advertising Assoc., 1996–2000. FRSA 1992. Chevalier, Légion d'Honneur (France), 1994. *Recreations:* golf, shooting, photography. *Address:* The Old Vicarage, Arkesden, Saffron Walden, Essex CB11 4HB. *T:* (01799) 550445. *Clubs:* Cavalry and Guards; Royal Worlington and Newmarket Golf (Suffolk).

BULL, Gregory; QC 2003; a Recorder, since 2000; *b* 14 Aug. 1953; *s* of Mansel and Joyce Bull; *m* 1983, Helen Ruth Bookes Parsons; one *s* one *d*. *Educ:* Mardy House Church in Wales Secondary Sch.; Aberdare Boys' Grammar Sch.; Univ. of Birmingham (LLB Hons). Called to the Bar, Inner Temple, 1976; in practice, specialising in crime, fraud and common law; Asst Recorder, 1995–2000. *Recreations:* Rugby Union, Freemasonry, walking, politics, music, theatre. *Address:* 2 Paper Buildings, Temple, EC4Y 7ET. *T:* (020) 7556 5500, *Fax:* (020) 7583 3423. *Clubs:* Cardiff and County, United Services Mess (Cardiff).

BULL, John; *see* Bull, R. J.

BULL, His Honour John Michael; DL; QC 1983; a Circuit Judge, 1991–2006; a Deputy Circuit Judge, 2006–08; *b* 31 Jan. 1934; *s* of John Godfrey Bull and Eleanor Bull (*née* Nicholson); *m* 1959, Sonia Maureen, *d* of Frank Edward Woodcock; one *s* three *d*. *Educ:* Norwich Sch. (State Schol.); Corpus Christi Coll., Cambridge (Parker Exhibnr in Modern History; BA 1958; LLM 1959; MA 1963). Called to the Bar, Gray's Inn, 1960; Dep. Circuit Judge, 1972; Standing Counsel to the Board of Inland Revenue, Western Circuit, 1972–83; a Recorder, 1980–91; Resident Judge, Crown Court at Guildford, 1992–2000. Judge, Employment Appeal Tribunal, 1993–2000. Hon. Recorder of Guildford, 1998. Hon. Vis. Prof., Surrey Univ., 1999–2005. DL Surrey, 1996.

BULL, (Oliver) Richard (Silvester); Headmaster, Rugby School, 1985–90; *b* 30 June 1930; *s* of Walter Haverson Bull and Margaret Bridget Bull; *m* 1956, Anne Hay Fife; two *s* four *d*. *Educ:* Rugby Sch.; Brasenose Coll. Oxford (MA). Mil. Service (1st Beds and Herts), 1949–51. Asst Master, Eton Coll., 1955–77 (Housemaster, 1968–77); Headmaster, Oakham Sch., Rutland, 1977–84. *Recreations:* music, walking, reading, ball games. *Address:* Broken Bank Cottage, Gladestry, Kington, Herefords HR5 3NY.

BULL, Prof. (Roger) John, CBE 2002; Chairman: Plymouth Hospitals NHS Trust, since 2002 (non-executive Director, 1993–2002); Devon and Cornwall Learning and Skills Council, since 2002; *b* 31 March 1940; *s* of William Leonard Bull and Margery Bull (*née* Slade); *m* 1964, Margaret Evelyn Clifton; one *s* one *d*. *Educ:* Churchers' Coll.; LSE (BSc Econ). FCCA. Research Fellow, DES/ICA, 1967–68; Principal Lectr in Accounting, Nottingham Poly., 1968–72; Head, Sch. of Accounting and Applied Econs, Leeds Poly., 1972–85; Dep. Dir (Academic), Plymouth Poly., 1986–89; Dir and Chief Exec., Poly. SW, Plymouth, 1989–92; Vice-Chancellor and Chief Exec., Univ. of Plymouth,

1992–2002. Chm., Open Learning Foundn, 1994–97; Dir, HEQC, 1994–97; Hon. Treas., UUK (formerly CVCP), 1994–2002. Non-executive Director/Trustee: UK e-Universities Worldwide Ltd, 2001–04; Universities Superannuation Scheme Ltd, 2004– (Dep. Chm., 2006–). Dir, Plymouth Chamber of Commerce, 1994–97. Member: Council, CNAA, 1981–87; Council for Industry and Higher Educn, 1993–2002. Chm., Dartington Coll. of Arts, 2003– (Gov., 1996–2003). *Publications:* Accounting in Business, 1969, 6th edn 1990; articles on accounting and educnl mgt. *Recreations:* music, walking.

BULL, Sir Simeon (George), 4th Bt *cr* 1922, of Hammersmith; former Senior Partner in legal firm of Bull & Bull, now retired; *b* 1 Aug. 1934; *s* of Sir George Bull, 3rd Bt and of Gabrielle, *d* of late Bramwell Jackson, MC; *S* father, 1986; *m* 1961, Annick Elizabeth Renée Geneviève (*d* 2000), *d* of late Louis Bresson and Mme Bresson, Chandai, France; one *s* two *d*. *Educ:* Eton; Innsbruck; Paris. Admitted solicitor, 1959. *Heir: s* Stephen Louis Bull [*b* 5 April 1966; *m* 1994, Maria Brampton; two *s* (twins) three *d*]. *Club:* Royal Thames Yacht.

BULL, Tony Raymond, FRCS; Consultant Surgeon: Charing Cross Hospital; Royal National Throat Nose and Ear Hospital; King Edward VII's Hospital for Officers; *b* 21 Dec. 1934; *m* 1958, Jill Rosemary Beresford Cook; one *s* two *d*. *Educ:* Monkton Combe School; London Hosp. (MB BS 1958). FRCS 1962. President: Eur. Acad. of Facial Plastic Surgery, 1989–96; Section of Otology, RSocMed, 1993–94; Internat. Fedn of Facial Plastic Surgeons, 1997. Yearsley Lectr, 1982, Semon Lectr, 2000, RSocMed. Sir William Wilde Medal, Irish Otolaryngol Soc., 1993. Editor, Facial Plastic Surgery (Quarterly Monographs), 1983–. *Publications:* Atlas of Ear, Nose and Throat Diagnosis, 1974, 3rd edn 1995; Recent Advances in Otolaryngology, 1978; Plastic Reconstruction in the Head and Neck, 1986; Diagnostic Picture Test, Ear, Nose and Throat, 1990. *Recreations:* tennis, golf. *Address:* 107 Harley Street, W1N 1DG. *T:* (020) 7935 3171; 25 Pembroke Gardens Close, W8 6HR. *T:* (020) 7602 4362. *Clubs:* Savile, MCC, Hurlingham, Queen's.

BULLER; *see* Manningham-Buller.

BULLER; *see* Manningham-Buller, family name of Viscount Dilhorne.

BULLER; *see* Yarde-Buller, family name of Baron Churston.

BULLER, Prof. Arthur John, ERD 1969; FRCP; Emeritus Professor of Physiology, University of Bristol, since 1982; *b* 16 Oct. 1923; *s* of Thomas Alfred Buller, MBE, and Edith May Buller (*née* Wager); *m* 1946, Helena Joan (*née* Pearson) (*d* 2007); one *s* one *d* (and one *d* decd). *Educ:* Duke of York's Royal Military Sch., Dover; St Thomas's Hosp. Med. Sch. (MB, BS; BSc); PhD Bristol 1992; BA Open Univ., 1996. FRCP 1976; FIBiol 1978; FRSA 1979. Kitchener Scholar, 1941–45; Lectr in Physiology, St Thomas' Hosp., 1946–49. Major, RAMC (Specialist in Physiology; Jt Sec., Military Personnel Research Cttee), 1949–53. Lectr in Medicine, St Thomas' Hosp., 1953–57. Royal Society Commonwealth Fellow, Canberra, Aust., 1958–59. Reader in Physiology, King's Coll., London, 1961–65; Gresham Prof. of Physic 1963–65; Prof. of Physiology, Univ. of Bristol, 1965–82, Dean, Fac. of Medicine, 1976–78, on secondment as Chief Scientist, DHSS, 1978–81. Res. Develt Dir, subseq. Dir of Res. and Support Services, Muscular Dystrophy Gp of GB, 1982–90. Hon. Consultant in Clinical Physiology, Bristol Dist Hosp. (T), 1970–82. Vis. Scholar, UCLA, 1966; Visiting Prof., Monash Univ., Aust., 1972. Lectures: Long Fox Meml, Bristol, 1978; Milroy, RCP, 1983; Haig Gudenian Meml, Muscular Dystrophy Gp, 1993. Member: Bd of Governors, Bristol Royal Infirmary, 1968–74; Avon Health Authority (T), 1974–78; MRC, 1975–81; BBC, IBA Central Appeals Adv. Cttee, 1983–88; Neurosciences and Mental Health Bd, MRC, 1973–77 (Chm., 1975–77); Chm., DHSS Working Party on Clinical Accountability, Service Planning and Evaluation, 1981–86; Trustee, Health Promotion Res. Trust, 1983–90. External Scientific Advisor, Rayne Inst., St Thomas' Hosp., 1979–85. *Publications:* contribs to books and various jls on normal and disordered physiology. *Recreations:* clarets and conversation. *Address:* Flat 13, Turnpike Court, Hett Close, Ardingly, West Sussex RH17 6GQ. *T:* (01444) 891873.

BULLERS, Ronald Alfred, CBE 1988; QFSM 1974; FIFireE; consultant fire prevention engineer; Chief Executive Officer, London Fire and Civil Defence Authority, 1986–87; *b* 17 March 1931; *m* 1954, Mary M. Bullers. *Educ:* Queen Mary's Grammar Sch., Walsall. Deputy Asst Chief Officer, Lancashire Fire Brigade, 1971; Dep. Chief Officer, Greater Manchester Fire Brigade, 1974, Chief Officer, 1977; Chief Officer, London Fire Bde, 1981–86. Adviser: Nat. Jt Council for Local Authority Fire Brigades, 1977; Assoc. of Metropolitan Authorities, 1977. FCMI. OStJ. *Recreations:* gardening, travel. *Address:* 31 Pavillion Close, Aldridge, Walsall WS9 8LS.

BULLIMORE, John Wallace MacGregor; His Honour Judge Bullimore; a Circuit Judge, since 1991; *b* 4 Dec. 1945; *s* of late James Wallace Bullimore and Phyllis Violet Emily Bullimore (*née* Brandt); *m* 1975, Rev. Christine Elizabeth Kinch; two *s* (one *d* decd). *Educ:* Queen Elizabeth Grammar School, Wakefield; Univ. of Bristol (LLB). Called to the Bar, Inner Temple, 1968; Chancellor, Diocese of Derby, 1980, of Blackburn, 1990. Mem., Gen. Synod of the Church of England, 1970–. *Address:* c/o North Eastern Circuit Administrator, West Riding House, Albion Street, Leeds LS1 5AA.

BULLMORE, Prof. Edward Thomas, PhD; Professor of Psychiatry, University of Cambridge, since 1999; Hon. Consultant Psychiatrist, Addenbrooke's Hospital, Cambridge, since 1999; Fellow, Wolfson College, Cambridge, since 2002; *b* 27 Sept. 1960; *s* of (John) Jeremy David Bullmore, *qv* and Pamela Audrey Bullmore (*née* Green); *m* 1992, Mary Pitt, *d* of late Arthur Pitt and of Elizabeth Pitt; three *s*. *Educ:* Westminster Sch.; Christ Church, Oxford (BA); St Bartholomew's Hosp. Med. Coll. (MB BS); PhD London 1997; MA Cantab 2000. MRCP 1989; MRCPsych 1992. Lectr in Medicine, Univ. of Hong Kong, 1987–88; SHO in Psychiatry, St George's Hosp., London, 1989–90; Registrar in Psychiatry, Bethlem Royal and Maudsley Hosps, 1990–93; Wellcome Trust Res. Trng Fellow, 1993–96; Advanced Res. Trng Fellow, 1996–99; Hon. Consultant Psychiatrist, Maudsley Hosp., London, 1996–99; Dep. Dir, MRC/Wellcome Trust Behavioural and Clin. Neuroscis Inst., Cambridge; Vice-Pres., Exptl Medicine and Head, Clin. Unit, Cambridge, GlaxoSmithKline, 2005–. Vis. Prof., Inst. of Psychiatry, KCL, 2000–. Mem., MRC Neuroscis and Mental Health Bd, 2002–06. *Publications:* papers on anatomical and functional brain imaging methods and applications to psychiatry and neuroscience. *Recreations:* running, birding. *Address:* Department of Psychiatry, University of Cambridge, Addenbrooke's Hospital, Cambridge CB2 2QQ. *T:* (01223) 336582.

BULLMORE, (John) Jeremy David, CBE 1985; Chairman, J. Walter Thompson Co. Ltd, 1976–87; Director: The Guardian Media Group (formerly The Guardian and Manchester Evening News plc), 1988–2001; WPP Group plc, 1988–2004; *b* 21 Nov. 1929; *s* of Francis Edward Bullmore and Adeline Gabrielle Bullmore (*née* Roscow); *m* 1958, Pamela Audrey Green; two *s* one *d*. *Educ:* Harrow; Christ Church, Oxford. Military service, 1949–50. Joined J. Walter Thompson Co. Ltd, 1954: Dir, 1964; Dep. Chm., 1975; Dir, J. Walter Thompson Co. (USA), 1980–87. Mem., Nat. Cttee for Electoral Reform, 1978–. Chm., Advertising Assoc., 1981–87; President: Nat. Advertising Benevolent Soc., 1999–2001; Market Res. Soc., 2004–. *Publications:* Behind the Scenes in Advertising, 1991, 3rd edn 2003; Another Bad Day at the Office?, 2001; Ask Jeremy, 2004; Apples, Insights and Mad Inventors, 2006. *Address:* 17/20 Embankment Gardens, SW3 4LW. *T:* (020) 7351 2197. *Club:* Arts.

See also E. T. Bullmore.

BULLOCK, Edward Anthony Watson; HM Diplomatic Service, retired; *b* 27 Aug. 1926; *yr s* of late Sir Christopher Bullock, KCB, CBE, and late Lady Bullock (*née* Barbara May Lupton); *m* 1953, Jenifer Myrtle, *er d* of late Sir Richmond Palmer, KCMG, and late Lady Palmer (*née* Margaret Isabel Abel Smith); two *s* one *d*. *Educ:* Rugby Sch. (Scholar; Running VIII); Trinity Coll., Cambridge (Exhibitioner; MA). Chm., Cambridge Univ. Cons. Assoc. Served The Life Guards, 1944–47. Joined Foreign Service, 1950; served: FO, 1950–52; Bucharest, 1952–54; Brussels, 1955–58; FO, 1958–61; La Paz, 1961–65; ODM, 1965–67; FCO, 1967–69; Havana, 1969–72; HM Treasury, 1972–74; Head of Pacific Dependent Territories Dept, FCO, 1974–77; Consul-Gen., Marseilles, 1978–83; Counsellor, FCO, 1983–85. Chm., Buckhorn Weston and Kington Magna Parish Council, 1993–95. *Recreations:* walking, gardening, tree-planting, reading, charity work. *Address:* Weston House, Buckhorn Weston, Gillingham, Dorset SP8 5HG. *Clubs:* Oxford and Cambridge; Union (Cambridge).

BULLOCK, John; Director, Retirement Security Ltd, 2002–05; Joint Senior Partner and Deputy Chairman, Coopers & Lybrand Deloitte, later Coopers & Lybrand, 1989–92; *b* 12 July 1933; *s* of Robert and Doris Bullock; *m* 1960, Ruth Jennifer (*née* Bullock); two *s* (and one *s* decd). *Educ:* Latymer Upper School. FCA; FCMA; FIMC. Smallfield Fitzhugh Tillet & Co., 1949–56 and 1958–61; RAF Commission, 1956–58; Robson Morrow, 1961, Partner, 1965–70; Robson Morrow merged with Deloitte Haskins & Sells; Partner in charge, Deloitte Haskins & Sells Management Consultants, 1971–79; Deloitte Haskins & Sells: Managing Partner, 1979–85; Dep. Senior Partner, 1984–85; Sen. Partner, 1985–90; Vice Chm., Deloitte Haskins & Sells Internat., 1985–89; Chairman: Deloitte Europe, 1985–89; Coopers & Lybrand Europe, 1989–92. Director: Brightreasons, 1993–96; Nuclear Electric, 1993–98; Kingfisher, 1993–2002; British Energy, 1995–99; More Gp, 1997–98. Mem., UKAEA, 1981–93. Mem., Co. of Chartered Accountants' of England and Wales, 1989–. Chm. Govs, Latymer Upper Sch., 2001–05. *Recreations:* ski-ing, walking, opera, ballet. *Address:* Grove House, 15 Clarendon Road, Sevenoaks, Kent TN13 1EU.

BULLOCK, Hon. Matthew Peter Dominic; Chief Executive, Norwich and Peterborough Building Society, since 1999; *b* 9 Sept. 1949; *s* of Baron Bullock, FBA and Hilda Yates Bullock; *m* 1970, Anna-Lena Margareta Hansson; one *s* two *d*. *Educ:* Magdalen College Sch., Oxford; Peterhouse, Cambridge (BA Hist. 1970); Harvard Business Sch. (AMP 1991). CBI, 1970–74; Barclays Bank plc, 1974–98: Corporate Finance Dir, 1983–86; Regl Dir, Yorkshire, 1986–91; Dir, Risk Mgt, 1991–93; Man. Dir, BZW/Barclays Capital, 1993–98. Member: Cabinet Adv. Cttee on Application of R&D, 1983–88; Econ. Policy Cttee, EEF, 1991–97; Industrial Adv. Bd, DTI, 1993–99; Financial Services Practitioner Panel, 2001–07. Chm., Building Socs Assoc., 2006–07. University of Cambridge: Chm. Adv. Bd, Centre for Business Res., 1994–; Mem., Audit Cttee, 2002–; Mem. Adv. Bd, 1985–2002, Chm., Chinese Big Business Prog., 1999–2001, Judge Inst. of Mgt Studies. Governor: Imperial Coll., London, 1981–86; Leeds Univ., 1986–91. *Publication:* Academic Enterprise, Industrial Innovation and the Development of High Technology Financing in the USA, 1981. *Recreations:* walking, gardening, music, opera. *Address:* Easby House, High Street, Great Chesterford, Essex CB10 1PL; *e-mail:* mpdbullock@btconnect.com. *Club:* Oxford and Cambridge.

BULLOCK, Michael; Director, and Chairman, 1979–98, Morgan Grenfell Investment Services; Director, 1979–98, Chief Investment Officer, 1988–98, Morgan Grenfell Asset Management; *b* 1 Nov. 1951; *m* Felicity Hammond; two *s*. *Educ:* Caterham Sch.; Imperial Coll., London (BSc Hons). ARCS 1973. Joined Morgan Grenfell, as Mem., UK Research Dept, 1973; Mem., Internat. Equity Team (specialised in Japan and Far Eastern mkts), 1975–79; Dir, Morgan Grenfell Capital Mgt Inc., 1985–98. *Recreations:* art, scuba-diving. *Club:* Royal Automobile.

BULLOCK, Sir Stephen Michael, Kt 2007; Executive Mayor, London Borough of Lewisham, since 2002; *b* 26 June 1953; *s* of late Fred George Bullock and of Florence (*née* Gott); *m* 1992, Kristyne Margaret Hibbert. *Educ:* Sir William Turner's Sch., Redcar; Leeds Univ. (BA Hons); Goldsmiths' Coll. (PGCE). Greater London Council: Admin. Officer, 1977–79; Dep. Hd, Labour Gp Office, 1979–83; Asst Dir, Public Relns, 1983–86; Chief Officer, Greenwich CHC, 1986–90. Dir, 1993–97, Chm., 1997–2002, Univ. Hosp. Lewisham NHS Trust. London Borough of Lewisham: Councillor (Lab), 1982–98, 2001–02; Leader of Council, 1988–93. Chm., ALA, 1992–93; Dep. Chm., AMA, 1992–94; Hd, Labour Gp Office, LGA, 1997–2002. Board Member: London Pension Fund Authy, 1989–98; London First, 1993–96; Independent Housing Ombudsman Ltd, 1997–2001; Chairman: Deptford City Challenge Ltd, 1992–93; London Connects, 2004–; Vice-Chm., Local Govt Management Bd, 1994–95 (Chm., 1992–93); Dir, Civic Skills Consultancy, 1994–95; Prin. Consultant, Capita Gp, 1995–97. Mem., Commn for Local Democracy, 1994–96. Trustee, Horniman Mus. and Gdns, 1999–. *Publications:* (contrib.) A Transatlantic Policy Exchange, 1993; (with R. Hambleton) Revitalising Local Democracy: the leadership options, 1996; contrib. Municipal Jl. *Recreations:* inland waterways, watching Middlesbrough FC lose, seeking the "Moon under Water". *Address:* Garden Flat, 9 Tyson Road, Forest Hill, SE23 3AA. *T:* (020) 8291 5030; *e-mail:* steve.bullock@lewisham.gov.uk.

BULLOCK, Susan Margaret, FRAM; soprano; *b* 9 Dec. 1958; *d* of late John Robert Bullock and Mair Bullock (*née* Jones); *m* 1983, Lawrence Archer Wallington. *Educ:* Cheadle Hulme Sch.; Royal Northern Coll. of Music Jun. Sch.; Royal Holloway Coll., Univ. of London (BMus Hons; Hon. Fellow, 2004); Royal Acad. of Music (LRAM; FRAM 1997); Nat. Opera Studio. Mem., Glyndebourne Fest. Opera Chorus, 1983–84; Principal Soprano, ENO, 1985–89; freelance internat. soprano, 1989–; *rôles* include: Madama Butterfly (title rôle) with ENO, Houston Grand Opera, Oper der Stadt, Bonn, New Israeli Opera, Portland Opera, USA, NYC Opera and Teatro Colon, Buenos Aires; Jenůfa (title rôle) with ENO, New Israeli Opera, Glyndebourne and Spoleto Fest., USA; Magda Sorel in The Consul with Teatro Colon, Buenos Aires and Spoleto Fest., Italy; Isolde, in Tristan and Isolde, with Opera North, Bochum Symphony, ENO, Rouen and Oper Frankfurt; Brünnhilde, in Der Ring des Nibelungen, Tokyo, and Perth Fest., Aust.; Elektra (title rôle), with Oper Frankfurt and La Monnaie, Brussels; Marie, in Wozzeck, Royal Opera; appears with all major British orchestras and also in Europe, N and S America, and Australia. Frequent broadcasts; has made recordings. *Recreations:* playing the piano, cooking, theatre. *Address:* c/o HarrisonParrott Ltd, 12 Penzance Place, W11 4PA.

BULLOUGH, Dr Ronald, FRS 1985; consultant in UK and USA; Chief Scientist, UK Atomic Energy Authority, 1988–93, and Director for Corporate Research, Harwell, 1990–93; *b* 6 April 1931; *s* of Ronald Bullough and Edna Bullough (*née* Morrow); *m* 1954, Ruth Corbett; four *s*. *Educ:* Univ. of Sheffield. BSc, PhD, DSc. FIMMM (FIM 1964); FInstP 1962. Res. Scientist, AEI Fundamental Res. Lab., Aldermaston Court,

Aldermaston, 1956–63; Theoretical Physicist and Group Leader, Harwell Res. Lab., Didcot, Berks, 1963–84; Hd, Materials Develt Div., Harwell, 1984–88; Dir for Underlying Res., Harwell, 1988–90. Visiting Professor: Univ. of Illinois, USA, 1964, 1973, 1979; Univ. of Wisconsin, USA, 1978; Rensselaer Polytechnical Inst., USA, 1968; UCL, 1994–; Univ. of Liverpool, 1994–; Visiting Scientist: Nat. Bureau of Standards, USA, 1965; Oak Ridge Nat. Lab., USA, 1969, 1979; Comisión Nacional de Energía Atómica, Buenos Aires, Argentina, 1977. Hon. Citizen of Tennessee, 1967. *Publications:* articles in learned jls such as Proc. Roy. Soc., Phil. Mag., Jl of Nucl. Materials etc., on defect properties in crystalline solids, particularly in relation to the irradiation and mechanical response of materials. *Recreations:* golf, walking, reading, music. *Address:* 4 Long Meadow, Manor Road, Goring-on-Thames, Reading, Berkshire RG8 9EG. *T:* (01491) 873266.

BULLOUGH, Prof. William Sydney, PhD, DSc Leeds; Professor of Zoology, Birkbeck College, University of London, 1952–81, now Emeritus; *b* 6 April 1914; *o s* of Rev. Frederick Sydney Bullough and Letitia Anne Cooper, both of Leeds; *m* 1942, Dr Helena F. Gibbs (*d* 1975), Wellington, NZ; one *s* one *d. Educ:* William Hulme Grammar Sch., Manchester; Grammar Sch., Leeds; Univ. of Leeds. Lecturer in Zoology, Univ. of Leeds, 1937–44, McGill Univ., Montreal, 1944–46; Sorby Fellow of Royal Society of London, 1946–51; Research Fellow of British Empire Cancer Campaign, 1951–52; Hon. Fellow: Soc. for Investigative Dermatology (US); AAAS, 1981. Vice-Pres., Zoological Soc., 1983–84. *Publications:* Practical Invertebrate Anatomy, 1950; Vertebrate Sexual Cycles, 1951; (for children) Introducing Animals, 1953; Introducing Animals-with-Backbones, 1954; Introducing Man, 1958; The Evolution of Differentiation, 1967; The Dynamic Body Tissues, 1983; scientific papers on vertebrate reproductive cycles, hormones, and chalones published in a variety of journals. *Recreation:* gardening. *Address:* 75 Hillfield Court, Belsize Avenue, NW3 4BG. *T:* (020) 7435 4558.

BULMER, Derek John; Editor, Great Britain and Ireland Michelin Guide, since 1996; *b* Hampstead, 24 March 1950; *s* of George Henry Bulmer and Barbara Joan Bulmer (*née* Gray); *m* 1979, Lynn Barton; one *s* one *d. Educ:* Christ Church, N Finchley; Westminster Hotel Sch. (HND). Trust Houses Forte, 1977–92; Asst Manager, White Horse Inn, Hertingfordbury, 1992–94; Dep. Manager, Randolph Hotel, Oxford, 1994–96; Personnel Manager, Brown's Hotel, Mayfair, 1996–97; Michelin Guide: Hotel and Restaurant Insp., 1977–90; Dep. Ed., GB and Ireland, 1990–96; Editor: Main Cities of Europe, 1998–; Eating Out in Pubs, 2005–. FRSA 2008. *Recreations:* wine, musical theatre, photography. *Address:* The Michelin Guide, Hannay House, 39 Clarendon Road, Watford, Herts WD17 1JA. *T:* (01923) 205255, *Fax:* (01923) 205241; *e-mail:* derek.bulmer@ uk.michelin.com.

BULMER, Esmond; see Bulmer, J. E.

BULMER, (James) Esmond; Director, H. P. Bulmer Holdings plc, since 1962 (Deputy Chairman, 1980; Chairman, 1982–2000); *b* 19 May 1935; *e s* of late Edward Bulmer and Margaret Rye; *m* 1st, 1959, Morella Kearton; three *s* one *d*; 2nd, 1990, Susan Elizabeth Bower (*née* Murray). *Educ:* Rugby; King's Coll., Cambridge (BA); and abroad. Commissioned Scots Guards, 1954. Dir (non-exec.), Wales and W Midlands Regional Bd, National Westminster Bank PLC, 1982–92. Chm., Hereford DHA, 1987–94. MP (C): Kidderminster, Feb. 1974–1983; Wyre Forest, 1983–87. PPS to Minister of State, Home Office, 1979–81. Mem. Council, CBI, 1998–2002. Mem. Exec. Cttee, Nat. Trust, 1977–87. *Recreations:* gardening, fishing. *Clubs:* Boodle's, Beefsteak.

BULMER, Dr Michael George, FRS 1997; Professor, Department of Biological Sciences, Rutgers University, 1991–95; *b* 10 May 1931; *s* of Dr Ernest and Dr Eileen Mary Bulmer; *m* 1966, Sylvia Ann House. *Educ:* Rugby Sch.; Merton Coll., Oxford (MA, DPhil 1957; DSc 1985). Lectr in Med. Stats, Univ. of Manchester, 1957–59; Lectr in Biomaths, 1959–91, Fellow of Wolfson Coll., 1965–91, now Emeritus, Univ. of Oxford. *Publications:* Principles of Statistics, 1965; The Biology of Twinning in Man, 1970; The Mathematical Theory of Quantitative Genetics, 1980; Theoretical Evolutionary Ecology, 1994; Francis Galton: pioneer of heredity and biometry, 2003; articles in scientific jls on biometry and evolutionary biology. *Recreation:* walking.

BULMER, Prof. Simon John, PhD; Professor of European Politics, University of Sheffield, since 2007; *b* 29 June 1954; *s* of late Dawson Vivian Bulmer and of Kathleen Amy Bulmer; *m* 1986, Helen Margaret Donaldson. *Educ:* Univ. of Loughborough (BA Hons Eur. Studies 1975); Univ. of Hull (MA Eur. Politics 1976); London Sch. of Economics (PhD 1982). Lecturer: in Govt, Heriot-Watt Univ., 1979–83; in Eur. Studies, UMIST, 1983–89; Sen. Lectr, then Reader, in Govt, 1989–94, Prof. of Govt, 1995–2007, Univ. of Manchester. Vis. Prof., Coll. of Europe, Bruges, 1994–99. Mem., Trng and Develt Bd, ESRC, 2005–. AcSS 2001. *Publications:* The Domestic Structure of European Community Policy-Making in West Germany, 1986; (jtly) The European Council, 1987; (jtly) The Federal Republic of Germany and the European Community, 1987; (ed) The Changing Agenda of West German Public Policy, 1989; (ed jtly) The United Kingdom and EC Membership Evaluated, 1992; (ed jtly) Economic and Political Integration in Europe, 1994; (jtly) The Governance of the Single European Market, 1998; (jtly) Germany's European Diplomacy, 2000; (jtly) British Devolution and European Policy-Making, 2002; The Member States of the European Union, 2005; (jtly) Policy Transfer in European Union Governance, 2007; contrib. numerous jl articles. *Recreations:* travel, jazz, current affairs, walking. *Address:* Department of Politics, University of Sheffield, Elmfield, Northumberland Avenue, Sheffield S10 2TU. *T:* (0114) 222 1706, *Fax:* (0114) 222 1717; *e-mail:* S.Bulmer@sheffield.ac.uk.

BULMER-THOMAS, Prof. Victor Gerald, CMG 2007; OBE 1998; DPhil; Director, Royal Institute of International Affairs (Chatham House), 2001–06; Emeritus Professor, London University, since 1998; *b* 23 March 1948; *s* of late Ivor Bulmer-Thomas, CBE and of Margaret Joan Bulmer-Thomas; *m* 1970, Barbara Ann Swasey; two *s* one *d. Educ:* Westminster Sch.; New Coll., Oxford (MA); St Antony's Coll., Oxford (DPhil). Research Fellow, Fraser of Allander Inst., Strathclyde Univ., 1975–78; Queen Mary, subseq. Queen Mary and Westfield, College, London University: Lectr in Econs, 1978–87; Reader in Econs of Latin America, 1987–90; Prof. of Econs, 1990–98; Institute of Latin American Studies, London University: Dir, 1992–98; Sen. Res. Fellow, 1998–2001; Hon. Res. Fellow, 2001–04; Hon. Res. Fellow, Inst. for the Study of the Americas, 2004–. Associate Fellow, Chatham House, 2007–. Vis. Prof., Florida Internat. Univ., Miami, 2007–. Director: Schroders Emerging Countries Fund, 1996–2003; Deutsche Latin American Companies Trust, 2004; New India Investment Trust, 2004–. Dir, UK-Japan 21st Century Gp, 2001–03. Editor, Jl of Latin American Studies, 1986–97. Comdr, Order of San Carlos (Colombia), 1998; Comdr, Order of Southern Cross (Brazil), 1998. *Publications:* Input-Output Analysis for Developing Countries, 1982; The Political Economy of Central America since 1920, 1987; Studies in the Economics of Central America, 1988; (ed) Britain and Latin America, 1989; (jtly) Central American Integration, 1992; (ed jtly) Mexico and the North American Free Trade Agreement: Who Will Benefit?, 1994; The Economic History of Latin America since Independence, 1994, 2nd edn 2003; (jtly) Growth and Development in Brazil: Cardoso's *real* challenge, 1995; (ed)

The New Economic Model in Latin America and its Impact on Income Distribution and Poverty, 1996; (jtly) Rebuilding the State: Mexico after Salinas, 1996; (ed) Thirty Years of Latin American Studies in the United Kingdom, 1997; (jtly) US-Latin American Relations: the new agenda, 1999; (ed) Regional Integration in Latin America and the Caribbean: the political economy of open regionalism, 2001; (ed jtly) The Cambridge Economic History of Latin America, 2 vols, 2006. *Recreations:* tennis, hill-walking, canoeing, music (viola), underwater photography. *Club:* Athenæum.

BUMBRY, Grace; opera singer and concert singer; *b* St Louis, Mo, 4 Jan. 1937. *Educ:* Boston Univ.; Northwestern Univ.; Music Academy of the West (under Lotte Lehmann). Début: Paris Opera, 1960; Bayreuth Fest., 1961; Chicago Lyric Opera, 1962; Royal Opera, Covent Gdn, London, 1963; San Francisco Opera, 1963; Vienna State Opera, 1964; Salzburg Festival, 1964; Metropolitan Opera, 1965; La Scala, 1964; has also appeared in all major opera houses in Europe, S America and USA. Film, Carmen, 1968. Richard Wagner Medal, 1963. Hon. Dr of Humanities, St Louis Univ., 1968; Hon. doctorates: Rust Coll., Holly Spring, Miss; Rockhurst Coll., Kansas City; Univ. of Missouri at St Louis. Has made numerous recordings. *Recreations:* psychology, entertaining. *Address:* c/o David Molnar, Albstrasse 34, 89150 Laichingen, Germany.

BUNBURY; see McClintock-Bunbury, family name of Baron Rathdonnell.

BUNBURY, Bishop of, since 2000; **Rt Rev. William David Hair McCall;** *b* 29 Feb. 1940; *s* of late Rt Rev. Theodore Bruce McCall, ThD, Bishop of Wangaratta, and Helen Christie McCall; *m* 1969, Marion Carmel le Breton; two *s* three *d. Educ:* Launceston and Sydney Grammar Schools; Saint Michael's House, Crafers. Deacon 1963, priest 1964, dio. Riverina; Assistant Curate: St Alban's, Griffith, 1963–64; St Peter's, Broken Hill, 1965–67; Priest-in-charge, Barellan-Weethalle, 1967–73; Rector: St John's, Corowa, 1973–78; St George's, Goodwood, 1978–87; Pastoral Chaplain, St Barnabas' Theol Coll., 1980–87; Bishop of Willochra, 1987–2000. *Recreations:* reading, walking. *Address:* Bishopscourt, PO Box 15, Bunbury, WA 6231, Australia. *T:* (office) (8) 9721 2100, *Fax:* (8) 9791 2300.

BUNBURY, Sir Michael; see Bunbury, Sir R. D. M. R.

BUNBURY, Sir Michael (William), 13th Bt *cr* 1681, of Stanney Hall, Cheshire; KCVO 2005; DL; company director, landowner and farmer; Consultant, Smith & Williamson, since 1997 (Partner, 1974–97; Chairman, 1986–93); *b* 29 Dec. 1946; *s* of Sir John William Napier Bunbury, 12th Bt, and of Pamela, *er d* of late Thomas Alexander Sutton; *S* father, 1985; *m* 1976, Caroline Anne, *d* of Col A. D. S. Mangnall, OBE; two *s* one *d. Educ:* Eton; Trinity College, Cambridge (MA). Buckmaster & Moore, 1968–74. Chairman: Fleming High Income Investment Trust plc, 1996–97 (Dir, 1995–97); HarbourVest Global Private Equity Ltd, 2007–; Director: JP Morgan Fleming Claverhouse Investment Trust plc, 1996– (Chm., 2005–); Foreign & Colonial Investment Trust plc, 1998–; Invesco Perpetual Select Trust plc, 2008–. Mem. Council, Duchy of Lancaster, 1993–2005 (Dep. Chm., 1995–2000, Chm., 2000–05). Mem. Exec. Cttee, CLA, 1992–97 and 1999–2004 (Chm., Taxation Cttee, 1999–2003; Chm. Cttee, Suffolk Br., 1995–97); Pres., Suffolk Agricl Assoc., 2000–02. Trustee, Calthorpe Edgbaston Estate, 1991–. DL 2004, High Sheriff, 2006–07, Suffolk. *Heir:* *s* Henry Michael Napier Bunbury, *b* 4 March 1980. *Address:* Naunton Hall, Rendlesham, Woodbridge, Suffolk IP12 2RD. *T:* (01394) 460235. *Clubs:* Boodle's; Aldeburgh Yacht.

BUNBURY, Lt-Comdr Sir (Richard David) Michael (Richardson-), 5th Bt, *cr* 1787; RN; *b* 27 Oct. 1927; *er s* of Richard Richardson-Bunbury (*d* 1951) and Florence Margaret Gordon (*d* 1993), *d* of late Col Roger Gordon Thomson, CMG, DSO, late RA; *S* kinsman 1953; *m* 1961, Jane Louise, *d* of late Col Alfred William Pulverman, IA; one *s* (and one *s* decd). *Educ:* Royal Naval College, Dartmouth. Midshipman (S), 1945; Sub-Lieut (S), 1947; Lieut (S), 1948; Lieut-Comdr, 1956; retd 1967. Dir, Sandy Laird Ltd, 1988–96. Pres., HMS Sussex Assoc., 1991–2002. *Publication:* A Short History of Crowcombe, 1999. *Heir:* *s* Thomas William Richardson-Bunbury, *b* 4 Aug. 1965. *Address:* Upper House, Crowcombe, Taunton, Somerset TA4 4AG. *T:* (01984) 618223.

BUNCE, Michael John, OBE 2001; Director, since 1997, and Chairman, since 1999, International Broadcasting Convention (Member, Management Committee, 1992–94); *b* 24 April 1935; *er s* of late Roland John Bunce, ARIBA, and Dorrie Bunce (*née* Woods); *m* 1961, Tina Sims; two *s* two *d. Educ:* St Paul's Sch.; Kingston Coll. Nat. Service, RAF. Joined BBC as engineer; subseq. Studio Manager; Producer, People and Politics (World Service); Dir, Gallery; Producer: A Man Apart—The Murderer, 1965; Minorities in Britain; The Younger Generation; Italy and the Italians; Editor: The Money Programme, 1968–70; Nationwide, 1970–75; Chief Asst, TV Current Affairs and Editor, Tonight, 1975–78; Head: Information Services TV, 1978–82; Information Div., 1982–83; Controller, Information Services, 1983–91; Exec. Dir, RTS, 1991–2000. Member: Francis Cttee, 1977; EBU Working Party on Direct Elections, 1978; Adv. Bd, Univ. of Salford Media Centre, 1992–99; Comité d'Honneur, Internat. Television Symposium and Technical Exhibn, Montreux, 1995–98; Chm., Nat. Industries PR Officers Group, 1991–92. Trustee, Elizabeth R Fund, 2002–. Marshall Fund Vis. Fellow, USA, 1975. FRTS 1989. Shell Internat. Television Award, 1969. *Recreations:* gardening, visiting fine buildings, fishing. *Address:* International Broadcasting Convention, Fifth Floor, International Press Centre, 76 Shoe Lane, EC4A 3JB. *Club:* Century.

BUNCE, Rev. Dr Michael John, FSAScot; Chaplain, Santa Margarita, Menorca, since 2000; *b* 5 Dec. 1949; *s* of Harold Christopher and Kathleen June Bunce; *m* 1973, Frances Sutherland; one *s* one *d. Educ:* St Andrews Univ. (MTh); Westcott House and Trinity Hall, Cambridge; Greenwich Univ. (PhD). Glazing clerk, Middleton Glass Merchant, 1965–69; Personnel Labour Controller, Bird's Eye Unilever, 1969–75. Ordained deacon, 1980, priest, 1981; Curate, 1980–83, Hosp. Chaplain and Team Vicar, 1983–85, Grantham Parish Church; Rector, St Andrew's, Brechin with St Drostan's, Tarfside and St Peter's, Auchmithie (Angus), 1985–92; Provost, St Paul's Cathedral, Dundee, 1992–97. FRSA. *Recreations:* tennis, ski-ing, art, antiques. *Address:* Apartado de Correos 102, 07720 Es Castell, Menorca, Spain. *Club:* Edinburgh Angus.

BUNCH, Dr Christopher, FRCP, FRCPE; Consultant Physician, Oxford Radcliffe Hospitals NHS Trust, since 1994 (Medical Director, 1994–2001); Director, British Association of Medical Managers, 1995–2005 (Chairman, 2001–04); *b* 25 Feb. 1947; *s* of Douglas Campbell Bunch and Barbara Bunch (*née* Hall); *m* 1977, Kathleen Josie Andrew; two *d. Educ:* King's School, Worcester; Birmingham Univ. (MB ChB 1969). FRCP 1984; FRCPE 1988. University of Oxford: Clinical Lectr in Medicine, 1975–81; Clinical Reader in Medicine, 1981–94; Professorial Fellow, Wolfson Coll., Oxford, 1981–94, Fellow Emeritus 1994–. Goulstonian Lectr, RCP, 1985. Mem. Council, RCP, 1999–. *Publications:* (ed) Horizons in Medicine I, 1989; contrib. various scientific and medical articles in haematology, especially control of erythropoiesis. *Recreations:* cooking (and eating) SE Asian, French, Spanish and Italian food, music. *Address:* Bayswater Farm House, Headington, Oxford OX3 8BY. *T:* (office) (01865) 221343.

BUNCLE, Thomas Archibald; Managing Director, Yellow Railroad, since 2001; *b* 25 June 1953; *s* of Thomas Edgar Buncle and Helen Elizabeth Buncle; *m* 1979, Janet Michelle Louise Farmer; two *s*. *Educ:* Trinity Coll., Glenalmond; Exeter Univ. (BA Sociology and Law 1975); Sheffield Univ. (MA Criminology 1978). Various posts, incl. Law Tutor, Sheffield Univ., and tour guide, Amer. Leadership Study Gps and Voyages Sans Frontières, 1975–77; British Tourist Authority: graduate trainee, 1978–79; Asst Internat. Advertising Manager, 1979–80; Asst Manager, Western USA, 1981–84; Manager, Norway, 1984–86; Regl Dir, SE Asia, 1986–91; Scottish Tourist Board: Internat. Mktg Dir, 1991–96; Chief Exec., 1996–2000. Dir, Edinburgh Festival Council, 1997–2000; Board Member: Scotland the Brand, 1996–2000; Cairngorm Partnership, 1997–2000; Member: Exec. Council, Scottish Council for Develt and Industry, 1998–2000; Risk Monitoring and Audit Cttee, Scottish Prisons Service, 2004–. *Recreations:* windsurfing, sailing, scuba diving, Rugby, hill walking, cycling.

BUNDRED, Stephen; Chief Executive, Audit Commission, since 2003; *b* 12 Dec. 1952; *s* of George Bundred, CBE, JP, DL and Theresa Bundred (*née* Hynes); *m* 1976, Kathleen McVeigh; one *s*. *Educ:* St Catherine's Coll., Oxford (BA PPE); Birkbeck Coll., London (MSc Econs); Liverpool Poly. (CPFA). Res. Asst to Eric Varley, MP, 1973–74; Special Advr to Sec. of State for Energy, 1974–75; Hd, Res. Dept, NUM, 1975–83; Principal Technical Accountant, Hackney LBC, 1983–87; Chief Accountant, Lewisham LBC, 1987–88; Financial Sec., Birkbeck Coll., Univ. of London, 1988–90; Dep. Dir of Finance, Hackney LBC, 1990–92; Dir of Finance and Dep. Chief Exec., 1992–95, Chief Finance Officer, 1995–99, Chief Exec., 1995–2003, Camden LBC; Clerk, N London Waste Authy, 1995–2003; Exec. Dir, Improvement and Develt Agency, 2003. Chm., Higher Educn Regulation Rev. Gp, 2006–; Member: TEC Assessors Cttee, 1998–99; Rethinking Construction Local Govt Task Force, DETR, 1999–2003; Bd, HEFCE, 1999–2005 (Chm., Audit Cttee, 2002–05); London Central Learning and Skills Council, 2001–03. Member (Lab): Islington LBC, 1975–78; GLC, 1981–86; ILEA, 1981–90. Mem. Council, 1999–, Dep. Pro Chancellor, 2006–, City Univ. Freeman, City of London, 2001. FRSA. Hon. DSc City, 2006. *Publications:* (contrib.) Policing the Riots, 1982; (contrib.) Reinventing Government Again, 2004; contribs to jls. *Address:* Audit Commission, 1st Floor, Millbank Tower, Millbank, SW1P 4HQ. *T:* 0844 798 2103; 3 Colebrooke Row, Islington, N1 8DB.

BUNDY, Prof. Alan Richard, PhD; Professor of Automated Reasoning, University of Edinburgh, since 1990 (Head of Division of Informatics, 1998–2001); *b* 18 May 1947; *s* of Stanley Alfred Bundy and Joan Margaret Bundy; *m* 1967, D. Josephine A. Maule; one *d*. *Educ:* Univ. of Leicester (BSc 1st Cl. Maths 1968; PhD Mathematic Logic 1971). Teaching Asst, Dept of Maths, Univ. of Leicester, 1970–71; University of Edinburgh: Res. Fellow, Metamathematics Unit, 1971–74; Department of Artificial Intelligence: Lectr, 1974–84; Reader, 1984–87; Professorial Fellow, 1987–90. FAAAI 1990; FRSE 1996; FBCS 2002; FIET (FIEE 2005); Fellow: Soc. for Study of Artificial Intelligence and Simulation of Behaviour, 1997; Eur. Co-ordinating Cttee for Artificial Intelligence, 1999. Donald E. Walter Dist. Service Award, 2003, Res. Excellence Award, 2007, Internat. Jt Conf. on Artificial Intelligence. *Publications:* Artificial Intelligence: an introductory course, 1978; The Computer Modelling of Mathematical Reasoning, 1983, 2nd edn 1986; The Benefits and Risks of Knowledge Based Systems, 1989; Eco-logic: logic based approaches to ecological modelling, 1991; Catalogue of Artificial Intelligence Techniques, 1984, 4th edn 1996. *Recreation:* valley walking. *Address:* School of Informatics, University of Edinburgh, Appleton Tower, Crichton Street, Edinburgh EH8 9LE.

BUNDY, Prof. Colin James, DPhil; Principal, Green Templeton College, Oxford, since 2008; *b* 4 Oct. 1944; *s* of Guy Stanhope Bundy and Winifred Constance Bundy (*née* Tooke); *m* 1st, 1969, Carol Ann Neilson (marr. diss. 1993); one *s* one *d*; 2nd, 2001, Evelyn Jeannette Bertelsen. *Educ:* Graeme Coll., Grahamstown; Univ. of Natal (BA); Univ. of Witwatersrand (BA Hons); Merton Coll., Oxford (Rhodes Schol., 1968); MPhil 1970, DPhil 1976, Oxon. Beit Sen. Res. Scholar, St Antony's Coll., Oxford, 1971–73. Lectr and Sen. Lectr in Hist., Manchester Poly., 1973–78; Res. Fellow, Queen Elizabeth House, Oxford, 1979–80; Tutor in Hist., Dept for External Studies, Oxford Univ., 1980–84; Prof. of Hist., Univ. of Cape Town, 1985–86; Prof. of Hist., concurrently Univs of Cape Town and Western Cape, 1987–90; University of Western Cape: Prof. of Hist., 1991–95; Dir, Inst. of Histl Res., 1992–94; Actg Vice-Rector, 1994–95; Vice-Rector (Academic), 1995–97; Vice-Chancellor and Principal, Univ. of Witwatersrand, Johannesburg, 1998–2001; Dir and Principal, SOAS, 2001–06, and Dep. Vice-Chancellor, 2003–06, Univ. of London; Warden, Green Coll., Oxford, 2006–08. Chm., South African Nat. Commn for UNESCO. Mem. Council, Robben Island Mus., 1997–2001. Hon. Fellow, Kellogg Coll., Oxford, 1998. Hon. DLitt: Manchester Metropolitan, 1999; Univ. of Western Cape, 2005. *Publications:* The Rise and Fall of a South African Peasantry, 1979, 2nd edn 1988; (jtly) Hidden Struggles in Rural South Africa, 1988; (contrib.) Encyclopedia Britannica, other books, and periodicals. *Recreations:* hiking, cricket, chess, music. *Address:* Green Templeton College, Oxford OX2 6HG. *T:* (01865) 274775.

BUNGEY, Michael; Chairman and Chief Executive Officer, Bates Worldwide (formerly BSB Worldwide), 1994–2003; Chief Executive Officer, Cordiant Communications Group, 1997–2003; *b* 18 Jan. 1940; *s* of William Frederick George and Irene Edith Bungey; *m* 1976, Darleen Penelope Cecilia Brooks; one *s* two *d*. *Educ:* St Clement Danes Grammar Sch.; LSE (BSc Econ). Marketing with Nestlé, 1961–65; Associate Dir, Crawfords Advertising, 1965–68; Account Dir, S. H. Benson Advertising, 1969–71; Chm., Michael Bungey & Partners, 1972–84; Dep. Chm., Dorland Advertising, 1984; Chm., Bates Dorland Advertising Ltd, 1987–96; Chairman and Chief Executive Officer: DFS Dorland, 1987; Bates Dorland, 1988; Bates Europe, 1989; Pres. and Chief Operating Officer, BSB Worldwide, 1993–94; Chairman: Bates Americas' Reg., 1993; Bates USA, 1993; Kingstreet Media Gp, 2004–05. Dir, Cordiant plc (formerly Saatchi & Saatchi), 1995. *Club:* Hurlingham.

BUNKER, Very Rev. Michael; Dean of Peterborough, 1992–2006, now Dean Emeritus; *b* 22 July 1937; *s* of Murray Bunker and Nora Bunker; *m* 1957, Mary Helena Bunker; four *s*. *Educ:* Acton Technical Coll. and Brunel Coll., Acton (ONC and HNC in Engineering); Oak Hill Theol Coll. Work Study Engr, Napiers of Acton, London, 1956–60. Ordained deacon, 1963, priest, 1964; Assistant Curate: St James' Church, Alperton, Middlesex, 1963–66; Parish Church of St Helen, Merseyside, 1966–70; Incumbent: St Matthew's Church, Muswell Hill, London, 1970–78; St James with St Matthew, Muswell Hill, 1978–92. Prebendary of St Paul's Cathedral, 1990. Chm., Habitat for Humanity GB, 2000–02. Trustee, Nat. Kidney Res. Fund, 1999–2002. *Publications:* The Church on the Hill, 1988; Peterborough Cathedral 2001–2006: from devastation to restoration, 2007. *Recreations:* flyfishing, walking. *Address:* 69 Puffin Way, Broadhaven, Pembrokeshire SA62 3HP. *T:* (01437) 781667.

BUNN, Douglas Henry David; Chairman: All England Jumping Course, Hickstead; White Horse Caravan Co. Ltd; *b* 1 March 1928; *s* of late George Henry Charles Bunn and Alice Ann Bunn; *m* 1st, 1952, Rosemary Pares Wilson; three *d*; 2nd, 1960, Susan Dennis-Smith; two *s* one *d*; 3rd, 1979, Lorna Kirk (*d* 1995); one *s* two *d*. *Educ:* Chichester High Sch.; Trinity Coll., Cambridge (MA). Called to Bar, Lincoln's Inn; practised at Bar, 1953–59; founded Hickstead, 1960; British Show Jumping Team, 1957–68; Pres., BSJA, 2001–05 (Chm., 1969, 1993–96; Vice-Chm., 1969–93; Vice-Pres., 1996–2001). Mem. British Equestrian Fedn; founded White Horse Caravan Co. Ltd, 1958; Chm., Southern Aero Club, 1968–72. Jt Master, 1976–2000, Vice-Chm., 2000–, Mid Surrey Drag Hounds. *Recreations:* horses, flying, books, wine. *Address:* Hickstead Place, Sussex RH17 5NU. *T:* (01273) 834666, *T:* (office) (01273) 834315, *Fax:* (01273) 834452. *Clubs:* Saints and Sinners (Chm., 1989–90), Annabel's, Sussex.

BUNTING, Martin Brian, FCA; company director; *b* 28 Feb. 1934; *s* of late Brian and Renee Bunting; *m* 1959, Veronica Mary Cope; two *s* one *d*. *Educ:* Rugby School. Director, Courage Ltd, 1972, Man. Dir, later Dep. Chm., 1974–84; Dir, Imperial Group plc, 1975–84; Chief Executive, Clifford Foods PLC, 1990–93. Non-executive Director: George Gale & Co. Ltd, 1984–2004; Longman Cartermill Ltd, 1985–90; Norcros plc, 1986–93; Shepherd Neame Ltd, 1986–2004; NAAFI, 1993–98; Hobson plc, 1994–96; Chairman: Inn Business Gp plc, 1996–97; Select Catalogues Ltd, 1996–98; Bluebird Toys plc, 1996–98 (Dir, 1991–98). Member, Monopolies and Mergers Commission, 1982–88. Chm. Trustees and Gov., Lord Wandsworth Coll., 2000–04. *Address:* The Long House, 41 High Street, Odiham, Basingstoke, Hants RG29 1LF. *T:* (01256) 703585, *Fax:* (01256) 703562.

See also Earl of Southesk.

BUNYAN, Dr Peter John; Chief Scientific Adviser to Ministry of Agriculture, Fisheries and Food, 1990–95; *b* London, 13 Jan. 1936; *o s* of Charles and Jenny Bunyan; *m* 1961, June Rose Child; two *s*. *Educ:* Raynes Park County Grammar Sch.; University Coll., Durham Univ. (BSc, DSc); King's Coll., Univ. of London (PhD). FRSC; CChem; FIBiol; FIFST. Research at KCL, 1960–62, at UCL, 1962–63; Ministry of Agriculture, Fisheries and Food: Sen. Scientific Officer, Infestation Control Lab., 1963–69; PSO, Pest Infestation Control Lab., 1969–73, Head of Pest Control Chemistry Dept, 1973–80; Head of Food Science Div., 1980–84; Head of Agricl Sci. Service, ADAS, 1984–87; Dir of R & D Service, ADAS, 1987–90; Dir. Gen., ADAS and Regl Orgn, 1990–91. Member: AFRC, 1990–94; BBSRC, 1994–95; NERC, 1991–95; Chm., British Crop Protection Council, 1998–2002. Special Advr to Vice-Chancellor, Surrey Univ., 1996–. Hon. Sec., Inst. of Biol., 1996–2001. Vis. Prof., Sch. of Agriculture, De Montfort Univ., 1996–2001. *Publications:* numerous scientific papers in wide variety of scientific jls. *Recreations:* gardening, walking. *Address:* Flushings Meadow, Church Road, Great Bookham, Surrey KT23 3JT. *T:* (01372) 456798. *Club:* Farmers'.

BUNYARD, Sir Robert (Sidney), Kt 1991; CBE 1986; QPM 1980; DL; Commandant, Police Staff College, Bramshill and HM Inspector of Constabulary, 1988–93; *b* 20 May 1930; *s* of Albert Percy Bunyard and Nellie Maria Bunyard; *m* 1948, Ruth Martin; two *d*. *Educ:* Queen Elizabeth Grammar Sch., Faversham; Regent Street Polytechnic Management Sch. (Dip. in Man. Studies). BA (Hons) Open Univ. MIPD; CCMI. Metropolitan Police, 1952; Asst Chief Constable, Leics, 1972; rcds, 1977; Dep. Chief Constable, 1977, Chief Constable, 1978–87, Essex Police. Man. Editor, Police Jl, 1981–88. Member: Royal Commn on Criminal Justice, 1991–93; Parole Bd, 1994–98. Chm., Essex Reg., Royal Assoc. in Aid of Deaf People, 1994–95; Dir, Addaction, 1998–2001. Pres., Essex Youth Orch. Assoc., 2001–; Patron, InterAct, 2006– (Trustee, 2003–06). DL Essex, 1997. *Publications:* Police: organization and command, 1978; Police Management Handbook, 1979; (contrib.) Police Leadership in the Twenty-first Century, 2003; contrib. police and music jls. *Recreations:* music, opera, painting. *Address:* Bellmans, Mounthill Avenue, Springfield, Essex CM2 6DB.

BURBIDGE, (Eleanor) Margaret, (Mrs Geoffrey Burbidge), FRS 1964; Professor of Astronomy, 1964–90, University Professor, 1984–90, now Emeritus, and Research Professor, Department of Physics, since 1990, University of California at San Diego; *d* of late Stanley John Peachey, Lectr in Chemistry and Research Chemist, and of Marjorie Peachey; *m* 1948, Geoffrey Burbidge, *qv*; one *d*. *Educ:* Francis Holland Sch., London; University Coll., London (BSc); Univ. of London Observatory (PhD). Asst Director, 1948–50, Actg Director, 1950–51, Univ. of London Observatory; fellowship from Internat. Astron. Union, held at Yerkes Observatory, Univ. of Chicago, 1951–53; Research Fellow, California Inst. of Technology, 1955–57; Shirley Farr Fellow, later Associate Prof., Yerkes Observatory, Univ. of Chicago, 1957–62; Research Astronomer, 1962–64, Dir, Center for Astrophysics and Space Scis, 1979–88, Univ. of California at San Diego; Dir, Royal Greenwich Observatory, 1972–73. Abby Rockefeller Mauzé Vis. Prof., MIT, 1968. Chief scientist, Faint Object Spectrograph team, Hubble Space Telescope, 1990–96. Member: American Acad. of Arts and Scis, 1969; US Nat. Acad. of Scis, 1978; Nat. Acad. of Scis Cttee on Science and Public Policy, 1979–81; Pres., Amer. Astronomical Soc., 1976–78; Chairwoman Bd of Dirs, Amer. Assoc. for Advancement of Science, 1983 (Pres., 1982); Mem., Amer. Philosophical Soc., 1980. Fellow University Coll., London, 1967; Hon. Fellow: Girton Coll., Cambridge, 1970; Lucy Cavendish Collegiate Soc., Cambridge, 1971. Hon. DSc: Smith Coll., Massachusetts, USA, 1963; Sussex, 1970; Bristol, 1972; Leicester, 1972; City, 1974; Michigan, 1978; Massachusetts, 1978; Williams Coll., 1979; State Univ. of NY at Stony Brook, 1984; Rensselaer Poly. Inst., 1986; Notre Dame Univ., 1986; Chicago, 1991. Catherine Wolfe Bruce Medal, Astr. Soc. of the Pacific, 1982; Nat. Medal of Science (awarded by President of USA), 1984; Sesquicentennial Medal, Mt Holyoke Coll., 1987; Einstein Medal, World Cultural Council, 1988; Gold Medal, RAS, 2005. *Publications:* Quasi-Stellar Objects (with Geoffrey Burbidge), 1967 (also USA, 1967); contribs to learned jls (mostly USA), Handbuch der Physik, etc. *Address:* Center for Astrophysics and Space Sciences, 0424, University of California, San Diego, La Jolla, CA 92093, USA. *T:* (858) 5344477.

BURBIDGE, Prof. Geoffrey, FRS 1968; Professor of Physics, University of California, San Diego, since 1988; *b* 24 Sept. 1925; *s* of Leslie and Eveline Burbidge, Chipping Norton, Oxon; *m* 1948, Margaret Peachey (*see* E. M. Burbidge); one *d*. *Educ:* Chipping Norton Grammar Sch.; Bristol University; Univ. Coll., London. BSc (Special Hons Physics) Bristol, 1946; PhD London, 1951. Asst Lectr, UCL, 1950–51; Agassiz Fellow, Harvard Univ., 1951–52; Research Fellow, Univ. of Chicago, 1952–53; Research Fellow, Cavendish Lab., Cambridge, 1953–55; Carnegie Fellow, Mount Wilson and Palomar Observatories, Caltech, 1955–57; Asst Prof., Dept of Astronomy, Univ. of Chicago, 1957–58; Associate Prof., 1958–62; University of California, San Diego: Associate Prof., 1963–64; Prof., 1964–78; Emeritus Prof., 1984–88; Dir, Kitt Peak Nat. Observatory, Arizona, 1978–84. Phillips Vis. Prof., Harvard Univ., 1968. Elected Fellow: UCL, 1970; Amer. Acad. of Arts and Scis, 1970. Pres., Astronomical Soc. of the Pacific, 1974–76 (Catherine Wolfe Bruce Medal, 1999); Trustee, Assoc. Universities Inc., 1973–82. Gold Medal, RAS, 2005. Editor, Annual Review Astronomy and Astrophysics, 1973–2004; Scientific Ed., Astrophysical Jl, 1996–2002. *Publications:* (with Margaret Burbidge) Quasi-Stellar Objects, 1967; (with Sir Fred Hoyle and J. V. Narlikar) A Different Approach to Cosmology, 2000; scientific papers in Astrophysical Jl, Nature, Rev. Mod. Phys, Handbuch der Physik, etc. *Address:* Department of Physics and Center for Astrophysics and Space Sciences, 0424 University of California, San Diego, La Jolla, CA 92093, USA. *T:* (858) 5346626.

BURBIDGE, James Michael; QC 2003; a Recorder, since 2000; *b* 16 June 1957; *s* of George John Burbidge and late Margaret Elizabeth Burbidge; *m* 1998, Denise McCabe; one *d*. *Educ:* Brockley Co. Grammar Sch.; Leicester Univ. (LLB Hons). Called to the Bar, Lincoln's Inn, 1979; specialist in criminal law; Asst Recorder, 1998–2000. *Recreations:* skiing, golf, travel, theatre. *Address:* St Philips Chambers, 55 Temple Row, Birmingham B2 5LS. *T:* (0121) 246 7000, *Fax:* (0121) 246 7001; *e-mail:* jburbidge@st-philips.co.uk. *Club:* Stratford on Avon Golf.

BURBIDGE, Margaret, (Mrs Geoffrey Burbidge); *see* Burbidge, E. M.

BURBIDGE, Sir Peter Dudley, 6th Bt *cr* 1916, of Littleton Park, co. Middlesex; *b* 20 June 1942; *s* of Sir Herbert Dudley Burbidge, 5th Bt and Ruby Bly Burbidge (*née* Taylor); *S* father, 2001; *m* 1967, Peggy Marilyn Anderson; one *s* one *d*. *Educ:* Sir Winston Churchill Sch., Vancouver. *Heir: s* John Peter Burbidge [*b* 1 April 1975; *m* 2000, Jackie Davies].

BURBRIDGE, Very Rev. (John) Paul, MA Oxon and Cantab; FSA; Dean of Norwich, 1983–95, now Emeritus; *b* 21 May 1932; *e s* of late John Henry Gray Burbridge and Dorothy Vera Burbridge; *m* 1956, Olive Denise Grenfell; four *d*. *Educ:* King's Sch., Canterbury; King's Coll., Cambridge; New Coll., Oxford; Wells Theolog. Coll. Nat. Service Commn in RA, 1957. Jun. Curate, 1959, Sen. Curate, 1961, Eastbourne Parish Church; Vicar Choral of York Minster, 1962–66; Chamberlain, 1962–76; Canon Residentiary, 1966–76; Succentor Canonicorum, 1966; Precentor, 1969–76; Archdeacon of Richmond and Canon Residentiary of Ripon Cathedral, 1976–83; Canon Emeritus, 1998. *Recreation:* model engineering. *Address:* The Clachan Bothy, Newtonairds, Dumfries, Scotland DG2 0JL. *T:* (01387) 820403.
See also S. N. Burbridge.

BURBRIDGE, Stephen Nigel, CB 1992; MA; Secretary, Monopolies and Mergers Commission, 1986–93; *b* 18 July 1934; *s* of late John Henry Gray Burbridge and late Dorothy Vera (*née* Pratt). *Educ:* King's Sch., Canterbury; Christ Church, Oxford. National Service, 2 Lieut, RA, 1953–55. Asst Principal, Bd of Trade, 1958–62; Trade Commissioner, Karachi, 1963–65; 1st Secretary (Economic), Rawalpindi, 1965–67; Principal, BoT, 1967–71; CS Selection Bd, 1971; Department of Trade and Industry: Asst Sec., 1971–80; Under Sec., 1980–86. *Publication:* The Days of Our Age, 2007. *Recreation:* books. *Address:* Chesil Cottage, Brede Hill, Brede, near Rye, E Sussex TN31 6HH. *Clubs:* Reform; Rye Golf.
See also J. P. Burbridge.

BURCH, Rear Adm. Jonathan Alexander, CBE 1991; CEng; Chief Executive (formerly Executive Secretary), Royal Academy of Engineering, 2000–03; *b* 18 June 1949; *s* of late Lt Comdr Walter H. Burch and of Mary Angela Burch; *m* 1976, Ursula Georgette Victoria Maria Villiers Bear (*née* Villiers) (*d* 2008); one step *s*. *Educ:* Chorister Sch., Durham; Durham Sch.; BRNC, Dartmouth; RNEC Manadon (BSc). CEng 1972. HM Submarines, 1972–84; Australian Staff Coll., 1984; Assistant Director: Dockyard Privatisation, 1985–88; Commitments (Middle East), 1989–92; Superintendent Ships, Devonport, 1992–94; rcds 1995; Naval Base Comdr, Devonport (Cdre), 1996–98; DG Aircraft (Navy), 1998–2000 and Chief Naval Engr Officer, 1999. FCMI (FIMgt 1989); FIMarEST (FIMarE 2000). President: Devonport Field Gun, 1996–98; RN Volleyball, 1998–2000. *Recreations:* travel, walking, history, music.

BURCH, Maj.-Gen. Keith, CB 1985; CBE 1977 (MBE 1965); Director Personnel, Defence Staff, Ministry of Defence, 1985, retired; Chapter Clerk, York Minster, 1985–95; *b* 31 May 1931; *s* of Christopher Burch and Gwendoline Ada (*née* James); *m* 1957, Sara Vivette Hales; one *s* two *d*. *Educ:* Bedford Modern Sch.; Royal Military Acad., Sandhurst. Commnd Essex Regt, 1951; DS Staff Coll., Camberley, 1968–69; Comd 3rd Bn Royal Anglian Regt, 1969–71; Asst Sec., Chiefs of Staff Cttee, MoD, 1972–75; Col GS HQ 2nd Armoured Div., 1975–78; Dir, Admin. Planning (Army), MoD, 1978–80; Indian National Defence Coll., New Delhi, 1981; Dep. Dir, Army Staff Duties, MoD, 1981–83; ACDS (Personnel and Logistics), 1984. Pres., N Yorks, RBL, 1999–2005. *Recreation:* country pursuits. *Address:* 11 Crowden Place, Harrowfield, Hamilton, New Zealand.

BURCHAM, Prof. William Ernest, CBE 1980; FRS 1957; Emeritus Professor of Physics, Birmingham University, since 1981; *b* 1 Aug. 1913; *er s* of Ernest Barnard and Edith Ellen Burcham; *m* 1st, 1942, Isabella Mary (*d* 1981), *d* of George Richard Todd and of Alice Louisa Todd; one *d* (and one *d* decd); 2nd, 1985, Patricia Newton, *er d* of Frank Harold Newton Marson and Miriam Eliza Marson. *Educ:* City of Norwich Sch.; Trinity Hall, Cambridge. Stokes Student, Pembroke Coll., Cambridge, 1937; Scientific Officer, Ministry of Aircraft Production, 1940, and Directorate of Atomic Energy, 1944; Fellow of Selwyn Coll., Cambridge, 1944; Univ. Demonstrator in Physics, Cambridge, 1945; Univ. Lecturer in Physics, Cambridge, 1946; Oliver Lodge Prof. of Physics, Univ. of Birmingham, 1951–80. Member: SRC, 1974–78; Council, Royal Soc., 1977–79. Hon. Life Fellow, Coventry Polytechnic, 1984. *Publications:* Nuclear Physics: an Introduction, 1963; Elements of Nuclear Physics, 1979; (with M. Jobes) Nuclear and Particle Physics, 1995; papers in Nuclear Physics A, Phys. Letters B, Phys. Rev. Letters. *Address:* 95 Witherford Way, Birmingham B29 4AN. *T:* (0121) 472 1226.

BURCHELL, Andrew; Chief Operating Officer and Director General, Service Transformation Group, Department for Environment, Food and Rural Affairs, since 2005; *b* 26 March 1955; *s* of Joseph Fredrick Bertram Burchell and Myrtle Miriam Burchell; *m* 1974, Susan Margaret Hewing; one *s* one *d*. *Educ:* London School of Economics and Political Science (BSc (Econ) 1976; MSc 1980). Economist, DHSS, 1976–84; Economic Advr, National Audit Office, 1984–85; Economic Advr, 1985–89, Sen. Economic Advr, 1989–90, Dept of Health; Department of Transport, later Department of the Environment, Transport and the Regions: Sen. Economic Advr, Railways, 1990–96; Director: Strategy and Analysis, 1996; Transport Strategy, 1997; Envmt Protection Strategy, 1998–2001; Department for Environment, Food and Rural Affairs: Dir, Envmt Protection Strategy, 2001; Finance Dir, 2001–05. *Publications:* articles on health economics. *Recreations:* golf, playing the guitar, spectating football, reading. *Address:* (office) Nobel House, 17 Smith Square, SW1P 3JR.

BURCHILL, Julie; columnist, The Times, 2004–06; *b* 3 July 1959; *d* of Thomas William Burchill and Bette Doreen Burchill (*née* Thomas). *Educ:* Brislington Comprehensive Sch., Bristol. Columnist: New Musical Express, 1976–80; The Face, 1980–84; Sunday Times, 1984–86; Mail on Sunday, 1986–98; The Guardian, 1998–2003. *Publications:* The Boy Looked at Johnny, 1979; Love It or Shove It, 1985; Girls on Film, 1986; Damaged Gods, 1986; Ambition, 1989; Sex and Sensibility, 1992; No Exit, 1993; I Knew I Was Right (autobiog.), 1998; Diana, 1998; Married Alive, 1999; The Guardian Columns 1998–2000, 2001; Burchill on Beckham, 2001; Sugar Rush, 2004; Sweet, 2007; (with Daniel Raven) Made in Brighton, 2007; (with C. Newkey-Burden) Not In My Name, 2008. *Recreations:* sex and shopping. *Address:* Capel & Land Ltd, 29 Wardour Street, W1D 6PS. *Club:* Sussex Arts (Brighton).

BURD, Michael; Joint Head of Employment and Incentives, Lewis Silkin LLP, since 1994; *b* New York City, 7 Feb. 1958; *s* of Donald and Shane Gale Burd; *m* 1984, Jacqueline Margaret Thomas; three *d*. *Educ:* Columbia Univ. (BA 1980); Clare Coll., Cambridge (MPhil 1982). Admitted as solicitor, 1986; Lewis Silkin LLP: articled clerk, 1984–86; Associate, 1986–88; Partner, 1988–. Pres., City of London Law Soc., 1995–96. Mem. Cttee, London Solicitors' Litigation Assoc., 1997–. *Recreations:* hiking, fine food, wines. *Address:* Lewis Silkin LLP, 5 Chancery Lane, Clifford's Inn, EC4A 1BL. *T:* (020) 7074 8176, *Fax:* (020) 7864 1722; *e-mail:* michael.burd@lewissilkin.com.

BURDEKIN, Prof. Frederick Michael, OBE 2008; FRS 1993; FREng; Professor of Civil and Structural Engineering, University of Manchester Institute of Science and Technology, 1977–2002, now Professor Emeritus, University of Manchester; *b* 5 Feb. 1938; *s* of Leslie and Gwendoline Burdekin; *m* 1965, Jennifer Meadley; two *s*. *Educ:* King's School, Chester; Trinity Hall, Cambridge (MA, PhD). MSc Manchester. FICE, FIMechE, FIStructE, FInstNDT. Welding Inst., 1961–68; Associate, Sandberg, Consulting Engineers, 1968–77. Vice-Principal External Affairs, UMIST, 1983–85. Chm., Manchester Science Park Ltd, 1988–95. Mem., Engrg Council, 1990–93. President: Manchester Assoc. of Engrs, 2003–05; Welding Inst., 2004–06 (Hon. FWeldI). Brooker Medal, Welding Inst., 1996; James Alfred Ewing Medal, ICE, 1997; Gold Medal, IStructE, 1998. *Publications:* numerous papers on fracture, fatigue and welded structures. *Recreations:* music, sport, countryside. *Address:* 27 Springbank, Bollington, Macclesfield, Cheshire SK10 5LQ.

BURDEN, family name of **Baron Burden**.

BURDEN, 4th Baron *cr* 1950, of Hazlebarrow, Derby; **Fraser William Elsworth Burden;** *b* 6 Nov. 1964; *s* of 2nd Baron Burden and of Audrey Elsworth, *d* of Maj. W. E. Sykes; *S* brother, 2000; *m* 1991, June Ellen (marr. diss. 2006), *d* of James Canham. *Heir: b* Hon. Ian Stuart Burden, *b* 24 Oct. 1967.

BURDEN, Sir Anthony (Thomas), Kt 2002; QPM 1995; Chief Constable, South Wales Police, 1996–2003; *b* 28 Jan. 1950; *s* of late Thomas Edward Burden and Nora Burden (*née* Dowding); *m* 1971, Beryl Myra Hill; one *s* two *d*. *Educ:* St Thomas Sch., Salisbury; BSc Hons. Joined Wilts Constabulary, 1969 (Detective Chief Superintendent, 1988–89); Asst Chief Constable, then Dep. Chief Constable, W Mercia Constabulary, 1989–93; Chief Constable, Gwent Constabulary, 1994–96. Member: Morris Inquiry, 2004; Rosemary Nelson Public Inquiry, 2005–. Advr, Police Assistance Mission of EU in Albania, 2005–07. Deputy Chairman: Reliance Secure Task Mgt, 2005–; Reliance Security Services Ltd, 2005–. Pres., ACPO, 2000–01. Life Vice-Pres., Police Sport UK, 2004. Trustee, British Police Symphony Orch., 1994–. CCMI 2002. DUniv Glamorgan, 2004. SBStJ 1998. *Recreations:* cycling, walking, gardening.

BURDEN, Maj.-Gen. David Leslie, CB 1996; CBE 1988; Chapter Clerk and Receiver General, Westminster Abbey, 1999–2008; *b* 14 July 1943; *s* of late Jack Leslie Burden and Elizabeth Mary Burden (*née* Attkins); *m* 1974, Susan Stuart Watson; two *d*. *Educ:* Portsmouth Grammar School. FCILT. Commissioned RASC 1964, RAOC 1965. Served England, Berlin, W Germany, NI, Cyprus and Hong Kong; NDC, 1981; Chief, Personnel and Logistics, UN Force in Cyprus, 1981–83; CO, 1 Ordnance Bn, 1983–85; ACOS, British Forces, Hong Kong, 1985–87; RCDS, 1988; ACOS, BAOR, 1989–91; Dir-Gen., Resettlement, MoD, 1991–92; Dir-Gen., Logistic Support (Army), 1992–95; Dir Gen., Army Manning and Recruiting, 1995; Dir Gen., Army Personnel Centre, 1996–97; Mil. Sec., and Chief Exec. of Army Personnel Centre, 1997–99. Freeman, City of London; Liveryman, Carmen's Co. *Recreations:* golf, cricket, walking, narrowboating, travelling. *Address:* c/o Barclays Bank, 54 Highgate High Street, N6 5JD. *Clubs:* Army and Navy, MCC; Highgate Taverners, Fadeaways.

BURDEN, Derrick Frank; HM Diplomatic Service, retired; Counsellor and Head of Claims Department, Foreign and Commonwealth Office, 1973–78; *b* 4 June 1918; *s* of late Alfred Burden and Louisa Burden (*née* Dean); *m* 1942, Marjorie Adeline Beckley; two *d*. *Educ:* Bec Sch., London. Crown Agents, 1936. Served War, King's Royal Rifle Corps, 1939–41. Joined Foreign Office, 1945; Comr-Gen.'s Office, Singapore, 1950–53; 2nd Sec., Moscow, 1954–56; 2nd Sec., Tokyo, 1957–59; HM Consul, Lourenço Marques, 1959–61; FO, 1962–67 (Asst Head of Protocol Dept, 1965); HM Consul, Khorramshahr (Iran), 1967–69; 1st Sec., Nairobi, 1969–71; HM Consul, Luanda (Angola), 1972–73. *Recreations:* golf, gardening. *Address:* 12 Strathmore Drive, Charvil, Reading, Berks RG10 9QT. *T:* (0118) 934 0564. *Clubs:* Nairobi (Nairobi); Phyllis Court (Henley-on-Thames).

BURDEN, Richard Haines; MP (Lab) Birmingham Northfield, since 1992; *b* 1 Sept. 1954; *s* of late Kenneth Rodney Burden and Pauline Langan Burden (*née* Ronnan); *m* Jane Slowey. *Educ:* Wallasey Technical Grammar Sch.; Bramhall Comprehensive Sch.; St John's Coll. of Further Educn, Manchester; York Univ. (BA Politics); Warwick Univ. (MA Indust. Relations). Pres., York Univ. Students' Union, 1976–77. Br. Organiser, 1979–81, Dist Officer, 1979–92, NALGO; whilst working for NALGO led Midlands campaign against water privatisation. Founder and Sec., Joint Action for Water Services, 1985–90. Contested (Lab) Meriden, 1987. PPS to Minister of State: MAFF, 1997–99; DSS, 1999–2001. Member: Trade and Industry Select Cttee, 2001–05; Internat. Devlt Select Cttee, 2005–; Parly Advr to Sports Minister on Motor Sports, 2002–. Secretary: All Party Parly Water Gp, 1994–97; PLP Trade and Industry Cttee, 1996–97 (Vice-Chm., 1995–96); Chm., Birmingham Gp of Labour MPs, 2001– (Sec., 1997–2001); Chairman: All Party Parly Gp on Electoral Reform, 1997–; All Party Parly Motor Gp, 1998–; Britain-Palestine All Party Parly Gp, 2001–. Chm., Labour Campaign for Electoral Reform, 1996–98 (Vice-Chm., 1998–99). Mem., Austin Br., RBL. *Publications:* Tap Dancing: water, the environment and privatisation, 1988; contribs to Tribune, Chartist and other jls. *Recreations:* motor racing, cinema, reading, food. *Address:* House of Commons, SW1A 0AA. *T:* (020) 7219 3000; (0121) 475 9295; *web:* www.richardburden.com. *Clubs:* Austin Sports and Social, Kingshurst Labour, 750 Motor.

BURDEN, Roger Francis, FCIB; Chairman, Cheltenham & Gloucester plc, 2003–04; *b* 3 June 1946; *s* of Henry A. Burden and Rose K. Burden, SRN; *m* 1970, Julie Hopkins; two *s*. *Educ:* Cheltenham Tech. High Sch. MBCS 1975; FCIB 1983. Cheltenham & Gloucester Building Society, later Cheltenham & Gloucester plc: various appts, 1969–97; Man. Dir, 1997–2003. Chm., Council of Mortgage Lenders, 2001–. Mem. Council, FA, 1995–; Chm., Glos FA, 2002–. Hon. PhD Glos, 2003. *Address:* Football Association, 25 Soho Square, W1D 4FA.

BURDETT, Prof. Richard Michael; Centennial Professor in Architecture and Urbanism, London School of Economics and Political Science, since 2005; *b* 27 Jan. 1956; *s* of Winston Burdett and Giorgina Nathan Burdett; *m* 1986, Mika; one *s* one *d*. *Educ:* Bristol Univ. (BSc Hons Architecture); Bartlett Sch. of Architecture, University Coll. London (DipArch, MSc). Director: 9H Gall., London, 1985–90; Architecture Foundn, London, 1991–95; Cities Prog., LSE, 1995–2005. Architectural Advr to Mayor of London, 2004–06; Chief Advr on Architecture and Urbanism for London 2012 Olympic Games, Olympic Delivery Authy. Dir, Internat. Architecture Exhibn, Venice Biennale,

2006. Mem. Council, RCA. Trustee, Somerset House. *Publications:* (ed) Richard Rogers Partnership, 1994; (ed) Cities, Architecture and Society, 2006; (ed) The Endless City, 2008; regular contribs to Domus, Casabella, Rassegna. *Recreations:* cities, food, culture, skiing. *Address:* 53 Camden Square, NW1 9XE. *T:* (020) 7267 1942; *e-mail:* r.burdett@lse.ac.uk.

BURDETT, Sir Savile (Aylmer), 11th Bt *cr* 1665; Managing Director, Rapaway Energy Ltd, 1977–99; retired; *b* 24 Sept. 1931; *s* of Sir Aylmer Burdett, 10th Bt; *S* father, 1943; *m* 1962, June E. C. Rutherford; one *s* one *d*. *Educ:* Wellington Coll.; Imperial Coll., London. *Heir:* *s* Crispin Peter Burdett, *b* 8 Feb. 1967. *Address:* 2 Knapp Cottages, Gore Lane, Kilmington, Axminster, Devon EX13 7NU. *T:* (01297) 34200; *e-mail:* Savileburdett@tiscali.co.uk.

BURDETT-COUTTS, William Walter; Artistic Director: Assembly Theatre, Edinburgh, since 1981; Riverside Studios, London, since 1993; Brighton Comedy Festival, since 2002; *b* 17 Feb. 1955; *m* 1999, Fiona Jane Keaney; one *s* two *d*. *Educ:* Radley Coll.; Rhodes Univ., SA (BA Hons Drama 1978); Univ. of Essex (MA Drama 1980). Artistic Dir, Mayfest, Glasgow, 1981–90; Hd of Arts, Granada Television, 1989–93; Chief Executive: Assembly Film and Television, 1993–2006; Assembly Media Gp, 2000–; Chm., Kiss 102 and Kiss 105, 1993–97; Chm., Riverside TV Studios, 2002–. *Address:* Riverside Studios, Crisp Road, W6 9RL. *T:* (020) 8237 1000, *Fax:* (020) 8237 1001; *e-mail:* wbc@riversidestudios.co.uk. *Club:* Soho House.

BURDUS, (Julia) Ann, (Mrs D. L. Parker), CBE 2003; non-executive Director, Next, 1993–2004; *b* 4 Sept. 1933; *d* of Gladstone Beaty and Julia W. C. Booth; *m* 1st, 1956, William Burdus (marr. diss. 1961); 2nd, 1981, Ian B. Robertson (*d* 1996); 3rd, 2005, David L. Parker. *Educ:* Durham Univ. (BA Psychology). Clinical psychologist, 1956–60; Res. Exec., Ogilvy, Benson & Mather, 1961–67; Res. Dir, McCann Erickson, 1971–75, Vice Chm., 1975–77; Senior Vice-Pres., McCann Internat., 1977–79; Chm., McCann & Co., 1979–81; Director: Strategic Planning and Development, Interpublic, 1981–83; Audits of Great Britain Ltd, 1983–86; AGB Research, 1986–89; Dir of Communications and Marketing, Olympia & York, Canary Wharf, 1989–92. Non-executive Director: Dawson Internat., 1992–98; Argyll Gp, later Safeway, 1993–99; Prudential plc, 1996–2003. Chairman: Advertising Assoc., 1980–81; EDC for Distributive Trades, 1983–87. Jt Dep. Chm. and Mem., Health Educn Authority, 1987–90; Member: Sen. (formerly Top) Salaries Rev. Bd, 1991–94; Adv. Council on Business and the Envmt, 1993–96; part-time Mem., CAA, 1993–97. Member: Cttee, Automobile Assoc., 1995–99; Council, Inst. of Dirs, 1995–2002. *Recreations:* dog walking, gardening.

BURFORD, Earl of, (known as **Charles Beauclerk**); **Charles Francis Topham de Vere Beauclerk;** *b* 22 Feb. 1965; *s* and *heir* of Duke of St Albans, *qv*; *m* 1994, Louise Anne (marr. diss. 2001), *e d* of Col Malcolm Vernon Robey; one *s*. *Educ:* Sherborne; Hertford Coll., Oxford. Trustee, Shakespearean Authorship Trust; Pres., De Vere Soc.; Vice-Pres., Royal Stuart Soc., 1989–. Trustee, Stringer Lawrence Meml Trust, 1993–. Freeman, City of London, 1986; Liveryman, Drapers' Co., 1990. *Publication:* Nell Gwyn: a biography, 2005. *Heir:* *s* Lord Vere of Hanworth, (known as James Beauclerk), *qv*. *Address:* *e-mail:* Charlesbeauclerk@aol.com.

BURFORD, Jeremy Michael Joseph; QC 1987; **His Honour Judge Burford;** a Circuit Judge, since 1993; *b* 3 June 1942; *s* of Alexander Joseph Burford and Arlene Burford. *Educ:* Rondebosch Boys' High Sch.; Diocesan Coll., Cape Town; BA Cape Town; MA, LLB Cantab; LLM Harvard. Called to the Bar, Inner Temple, 1968; a Recorder, 1991–93.

BURG, Gisela Elisabeth, Hon. CBE 1987 (for services to exports); Managing Director, GEB Enterprises Ltd, since 1995; *b* 12 Oct. 1939; *d* of Friedrich and Gerda Schlüsselburg. *Educ:* Gymnasium Philippinum, Weilburg, Germany; Ladies Coll., Wetzlar, Germany; Polytechnic of Central London. Founded Expotus Ltd, 1968, Man. Dir, 1968–96. Vice-Pres., Fedn of British Audio, 1979–85 (Chm., 1976); Member: NEDO, 1979–84 (Mem. Electronic Sector Working Party); BOTB, 1982–89. Non-exec. Dir, Royal Mint, 1993–2001. CIEx 1992. The Times/Veuve Clicquot Business Woman of the Year, 1981. *Recreations:* golf, horseracing. *Address:* 82 Kensington Heights, Campden Hill Road, W8 7BD. *T:* (020) 7727 8884. *Clubs:* Hampstead Golf; Woburn Golf and Country (Beds); Erinvale Golf (Somerset West, S Africa); Jockey (S Africa).

BURGE, Richard David Arthur; Director (formerly Partner), Kimberley Burge Ltd, since 2003; *b* 5 April 1958; *s* of Col Arthur Burge and Elsie (*née* Kimberley); *m* 1980, Karen Jayne Bush; one *s* one *d*. *Educ:* Adams Grammar Sch., Newport; Univ. of Durham (BSc Hons Zoology 1980). Biology Master and Asst Housemaster, King Edward's Sch., Witley, 1980–83; Commonwealth Res. Schol., Dept of Zoology, Univ. of Peradeniya, Sri Lanka, 1983–86; British Council: Asst Dir, Nigeria, 1986–90; Projects Dir, Develt and Trng, 1990–93; Hd, Africa and ME Develt, 1993–95; Dir Gen., Zoological Soc. of London, 1995–99; Chief Exec., Countryside Alliance, 1999–2003. Dir, Urban and Rural Catalyst Ltd, 2003–06; Dir of Strategy, African Parks Foundn, 2003–06. Dep. Chm., Rural Regeneration Unit, 2003–05; Member, Board: Countryside Agency, 2005–06; Commn for Rural Communities, 2006–. Member: Exec. Cttee, Assoc. of Chief Execs, 1997–2001; Council, Shropshire and W Midlands Agricl Soc., 1997–2003. Non-exec. Dir, Property Merchant Gp, 2008–. Chm. Trustees, Get Hooked on Fishing, 2002–06; Trustee: Television Trust for the Envmt, 1996–99; Iwokrama Rainforest Project, Guyana, 2002–06; Game Conservancy Trust, 2004–. Internat. Expert, Internat. Congress on Game and Conservation, 2004–. Gov., Bridewell Royal Hosp., 2008–. FRSA 2003. Liveryman, Gunmakers' Co., 2001. *Recreations:* theatre, gardening, fishing, shooting, France. *Address:* Kimberley Burge Ltd, 107–109 Great Portland Street, W1W 6QG. *Club:* Flyfishers'.

BURGE, Prof. Ronald Edgar, CPhys; FInstP; Wheatstone Professor of Physics, King's College, London, 1989–2000; Director, Leverhulme Trust Grant to Cavendish Laboratory, University of Cambridge, 1994–98; *b* 3 Oct. 1932; *s* of John Henry Burge and Edith Beatrice Burge (*née* Thompson); *m* 1953, Janet Mary (*née* Pitts); two *s*. *Educ:* Canton High Sch., Cardiff; King's Coll. London (BSc, PhD; FKC 1989); DSc London 1975. FInstP 1963. King's College London: Asst Lectr in Physics, 1954–58; Lectr in Physics, 1958–62; Reader in Biophysics, 1962–63; Prof. and Head of Dept of Physics, Queen Elizabeth Coll., Univ. of London, 1963–84; Prof. of Physics, 1984–89, Head of Dept of Physics, 1984–92, Vice Principal, 1988–92, KCL. Vis. Fellow, 1992, Life Mem., 1993, Clare Hall, Cambridge. Nanyang Prof. of Elect. Engrg, Nanyang Technolog. Univ., Singapore, 2000–01. Member: Swinnerton-Dyer Cttee concerning Academic Governance of Univ. of London, 1979–82; Computer Bd for Univs and Res. Councils (responsible for computer develt in univs in Scotland and, latterly, SW England), 1978–82. MRI 1988. Rodman Medal, RPS, 1993. *Publications:* papers in sci. jls on theory of scattering (electrons, x-rays and radar) and develts in electron microscopy and x-ray microscopy. *Recreations:* gardening, music.

BURGEN, Sir Arnold (Stanley Vincent), Kt 1976; FRCP 1969; FRS 1964; Master of Darwin College, Cambridge, 1982–89 (Hon. Fellow, 1989); Deputy Vice-Chancellor, Cambridge University, 1985–89; *b* 20 March 1922; *s* of late Peter Burgen and Elizabeth Wolfers; *m* 1st, 1946, Judith Browne (*d* 1993); two *s* one *d*; 2nd, 1993, Dr Olga Kennard, *qv*. *Educ:* Christ's Coll., Finchley; student, Middlesex Hospital Med. Sch., 1939–45; MB BS 1945, MD 1950. Ho. Phys., Middlesex Hospital, 1945; Demonstrator, 1945–48, Asst Lectr, 1948–49, in Pharmacology, Middlesex Hospital Med. Sch. Prof. of Physiology, McGill Univ., Montreal, 1949–62; Dep. Dir, Univ. Clinic, Montreal Gen. Hospital, 1957–62; Sheild Prof. of Pharmacology, Univ. of Cambridge, 1962–71; Fellow of Downing Coll., Cambridge, 1962–71, Hon. Fellow 1972; Dir, Nat. Inst. for Med. Res., 1971–82. Medical Research Council: Member, 1969–71, 1973–77; Hon. Dir, Molecular Pharmacology Unit, 1967–72; Chm., Tropical Medicine Res. Bd, 1977–81; Assessor, 1985–86. Pres., Internat. Union of Pharmacology, 1972–75; Member: Council, Royal Soc., 1972–73, 1980–86 (Vice Pres., 1980–86; Foreign Sec., 1981–86); Nat. Biol. Standards Bd, 1975–78; Med. Cttee, British Council, 1973–77; Gen. Cttee, ICSU, 1982–88; Exec. Cttee, Eur. Science Foundn, 1985–90; Bureau, European Science and Technol. Assembly, 1994–; Chm., Adv. Cttee on Irradiated and Novel Foods, 1982–87. Dir, Amersham Internat., 1985–92. Trustee, CIBA Foundn, 1985–. Editor, European Review, 1993–2007. Pres., Academia Europaea, 1988–94. Founder FMedSci 1998. Academico Correspondiente, Royal Acad. of Spain, 1983; Mem., Deutsche Akad. der Naturforscher Leopoldina, 1984; For. Associate, US Nat. Acad. of Scis, 1985; For. Mem., Ukraine Acad. of Scis. Hon. Fellow, Wolfson Coll., Oxford, 1990. Hon. FRCP (C); Hon. Mem., Amer. Assoc. of Physicians; Academician of Finland, 1990. Hon. DSc: Leeds, 1973; McGill, 1973; Liverpool, 1989; Hon. MD: Utrecht, 1983; Zürich, 1983; DUniv. Surrey, 1983. Gold Medal, British Pharmacol Soc., 1999. *Publications:* Physiology of Salivary Glands, 1961; papers in Journals of Physiology and Pharmacology. *Address:* Keelson, 8a Hills Avenue, Cambridge CB1 7XA; *e-mail:* asvb@cam.ac.uk.

BURGES WATSON, Richard Eagleson Gordon; *see* Watson, R. E. G.

BURGESS, Anthony Reginald Frank, (Tony), CVO 1983; consultant on Third World development; HM Diplomatic Service, retired; *b* 27 Jan. 1932; *s* of Beatrice Burgess; *m* 1960, Carlyn Shawyer; one *s*. *Educ:* Ealing Grammar Sch.; University College London (BScEcon). National Service, 1953–55; TA, 16 Airborne Div., 1955–57. Journalism, 1955–62; European Community Civil Service, 1962–65; HM Diplomatic Service, 1966–89: 1st Sec., European Economic Organisations Dept, FCO, 1966–67; 1st Sec. (Political), Dhaka, 1967–69; 1st Sec., SE Asia Dept, FCO, 1970–72; 1st Sec. (Economic), Ottawa, 1972–76; Head of Chancery and HM Consul, Bogota, 1976–79; 1st Sec., Rhodesia Dept, FCO, 1979–80; Asst Head of Information Dept, FCO, 1980–82; Dep. High Comr, Dhaka, 1982–86; Counsellor and Hd of Chancery, Havana, 1989–89. *Publication:* (jtly) The Common Market and the Treaty of Rome Explained, 1967. *Recreations:* travel, photography, shooting. *Address:* 16 Langford Green, Champion Hill, SE5 8BX. *Club:* Brooks's.

BURGESS, Averil, OBE 1994; Chairman, Independent Schools Inspectorate, Independent Schools Council (formerly Accreditation Review and Consultancy Service, Independent Schools Joint Council), 1993–2000; *b* 8 July 1938; *d* of David and Dorothy Evans (*née* Owen); *m* 1959, Clifford Burgess (marr. diss. 1973). *Educ:* Ashby-de-la-Zouch Girls' Grammar Sch.; Queen Mary Coll., Univ. of London. BA Hons History. Assistant Mistress: Langleybury Secondary Modern Sch., 1959–60; Ensham Sch., 1960–62; Hatfield Sch., 1963–65; Fulham County Sch., 1965–69; Wimbledon High Sch., GPDST, 1969–74 (Head of History and Second Mistress); Headmistress, South Hampstead High School, GPDST, 1975–93. Chm., Camden and Islington FHSA, 1993–96. Chm., Policy Gp, ISJC, 1990–97; Member: Council for Accreditation of Teacher Educn, 1990–93; Nat. Commn on Educn, 1991–93. Adv. Panel on Public Appointments, DCMS, 1997–; Lay Mem., Professional Conduct Cttee, Bar Council, 1996–2005. Pres., GSA, 1988–89. Governor: Central Sch. of Speech and Drama, 1981–95; Mus. of London, 1994–2000. *Recreations:* many, including Wales, Welsh, watercolours, birdwatching and good meals. *Address:* 123 North Hill, Highgate, N6 4DP.

BURGESS, Rev. Preb. David John, FSA; Guild Vicar of St Lawrence Jewry Next Guildhall, The Church of the City of London Corporation (formerly Corporation of London), 1987–2008; a Chaplain to The Queen, since 1987; Prebendary of St Paul's Cathedral, since 2002; *b* 4 Aug. 1939; *e s* of Albert Burgess and Mary Burgess (*née* Kelsey); *m* 1976, Dr Kathleen Louise, *d* of Philip Lindsay Costeloe; one *s* one *d*. *Educ:* King's School, Peterborough; Trinity Hall, Cambridge; Cuddesdon Theological Coll. FSA 1992. Orthodox Studentship, Halki, Istanbul, 1963–64. Curate, All Saints, Maidstone, 1965; Assistant Chaplain, University Coll., Oxford, 1966; Fellow, 1969; Chaplain, 1970; Domestic Bursar, 1971; Canon of St George's Chapel, Windsor, 1978–87. Hon. Fellow, Inst. of Clerks of Works, 1978; Churchill Hon. Fellow, Westminster Coll., Fulton, Miss, 1989. *Publications:* articles and reviews. *Recreations:* opera, art, cooking. *Address:* 62 Orbel Street, SW11 3NZ. *T:* (020) 7585 1572. *Club:* Athenæum.

BURGESS, Dilys Averil; *see* Burgess, A.

BURGESS, Gen. Sir Edward (Arthur), KCB 1982; OBE 1972; Deputy Supreme Allied Commander, Europe, 1984–87; Aide-de-Camp General to the Queen, 1985–87; *b* 30 Sept. 1927; *s* of Edward Burgess and Alice Burgess; *m* 1954, Jean Angelique Leslie Henderson; one *s* one *d*. *Educ:* All Saints Sch., Bloxham; Lincoln Coll., Oxford; RMA, Sandhurst. Commnd RA 1948; served Germany and ME, 1949–59; psc 1960; GSO 2 WO, 1961–63; served Germany and Far East, 1963–65; jssc 1966; Mil. Asst to C-in-C BAOR, 1966–67; GSO I (DS) Staff Coll., 1968–70; CO 25 Light Regt, RA, 1970–72; CRA 4th Div., 1972–74; Dir of Army Recruiting, 1975–77; Dir, Combat Development (Army), 1977–79; GOC Artillery Div., 1979–82; Comdr, UK Field Army, and Inspector Gen. TA, 1982–84. Gentleman Usher to the Sword of State, 1988–97. Col Comdt, RA, 1982–92. Hon. Colonel: 6/7 (V) Bn Queen's Regt, 1991–92; 6/7 (V) Bn Princess of Wales's Royal Regt, 1992–97. Dep. Grand Pres., Royal (formerly British) Commonwealth Ex-Services League, 1996–2003; President: Royal British Legion, 1987–93; Army Football Assoc., 1982–88; Hon. Vice Pres., FA, 1982–88. Hon. Life Mem., RSL of Australia, 1991; Hon. Dominion Officer, Royal Canadian Legion, 2003. Freeman, City of London, 1988; Hon. Liveryman, Haberdashers' Co., 1990. *Publications:* articles in military jls. *Recreations:* fishing, music, reading, gardening. *Address:* c/o Lloyds TSB, Haslemere, Surrey GU27 2JG. *Club:* Army and Navy.

See also J. E. R. Burgess.

BURGESS, Geoffrey Harold Orchard; Chief Scientist (Agriculture and Horticulture), Ministry of Agriculture, Fisheries and Food, 1982–86; *b* 28 March 1926; *s* of late Harold Frank and Eva M. F. Burgess, Reading; *m* 1952, Barbara Vernon, *y d* of late Rev. Gilbert Vernon Yonge; two *s*. *Educ:* Reading Sch.; Univ. of Reading; UC Hull. BSc Reading, 1951 (Colin Morley Prizewinner 1950); PhD London, 1955. Special research appt, Univ. of Hull, 1951; Sen. Scientific Officer, DSIR, Humber Lab., Hull, 1954; PSO, Torry Res. Stn, Aberdeen, 1960; Officer i/c, Humber Lab., Hull, 1962; Director, Torry Res. Station, 1969–79; Head of Biology Div., Agricl Science Service, and Officer i/c Slough Lab., MAFF, 1979–82. Hon. Res. Lectr in Fish Technology, Univ. of Aberdeen, 1969–79; Buckland Lectr, 1964; Hon. Lectr in Fish Technology, Univ. of Leeds, 1966–69; Mem.

Adv. Cttee on Food Science, Univ. of Leeds, 1970–86; Mem., Panel of Fish Technology Experts, FAO, 1962–79. *Publications:* Developments in the Handling and Processing of Fish, 1965; (with Lovern, Waterman and Cutting) Fish Handling and Processing, 1965; The Curious World of Frank Buckland, 1967; scientific and technical papers, reviews, reports etc concerning handling, processing, transport and preservation for food, of fish, from catching to consumption. *Recreations:* music, book collecting, walking.

BURGESS, Geoffrey Kelsen; Chief Executive and Clerk, Cornwall County Council, 1982–93 (Deputy Clerk, 1969–82); *b* 4 June 1935; *s* of Monty and Edith Burgess; *m* 1959, Brenda (*née* Martin); three *s*. *Educ:* Central Foundn Boys' Grammar Sch.; London Sch. of Econs and Pol Science (LLB). Admitted solicitor, 1959. Articled with Simon, Haynes, Barlas & Cassels, London, 1956–59; Assistant Solicitor: East Ham CBC, 1960–62; Worcs CC, 1962–63; Northumberland CC, 1963–65; Asst Clerk, Berks CC, 1965–69; Clerk: Cornwall Magistrates' Courts Cttee, 1982–93; Cornwall Sea Fisheries Cttee, 1982–93; Devon and Cornwall Police Authy, 1988–93; Secretary: Adv. Cttee on appt of Magistrates in Cornwall, 1982–93; Cornwall Probation Cttee, 1982–93. Chairman: Jeffrey Kelson Foundn, 1994–2000; Promoting Effective Parenting, 1999–2005; Cornwall Bd for Young Enterprise, 1999–2006. *Recreations:* music, walking.

BURGESS, Rear-Adm. John, CB 1987; LVO 1975; CEng; Director, Rolls-Royce and Associates, since 1987; *b* 13 July 1929; *s* of Albert Burgess and Winifred (*née* Evans); *m* 1952, Avis (*née* Morgan); two *d*. *Educ:* RN Engineering College; Advanced Engineering RN College, Greenwich; nuclear courses, RN College. HM Ships Aisne, Maidstone, Theseus, Implacable, Cumberland, Caprice; Lectr in Thermodynamics, RNEC, 1962–65; HMS Victorious; nuclear reactor design and manufacture at Rolls Royce, 1968–70; Naval Staff, Washington, DC, 1970–72; Royal Yacht Britannia, 1972–75; Head, Forward Design Group, Ship Dept, 1975–77; Naval Asst to Controller of the Navy, 1977–79; in Command, HMS Defiance, 1979–81; in Command, HMS Sultan, 1981–83; Man. Dir, HM Dockyard, Rosyth, 1984–87. Occasional involvement with urban develt and waterfront management cttees. *Publications:* papers to professional bodies. *Recreations:* golf, sailing. *Club:* Cawsand Bay Sailing (Pres., 1999–).

BURGESS, Ven. John Edward; Archdeacon of Bath, 1975–95, now Emeritus; *b* 9 Dec. 1930; *s* of Herbert and Dorothy May Burgess; *m* 1958, Jonquil Marion Bailey; one *s* one *d*. *Educ:* Surbiton County Gram. Sch.; London Univ. (St John's Hall). BD (2nd Cl.), ALCD (1st Cl.). Shell Chemicals Ltd, 1947–53. Asst Curate, St Mary Magdalen, Bermondsey, 1957–60; Asst Curate, St Mary, Southampton, 1960–62; Vicar of Dunston with Coppenhall, Staffs, 1962–67; Chaplain, Staffordshire Coll. of Technology, 1963–67; Vicar of Keynsham with Queen Charlton and Burnett, Somerset, 1967–75; Rural Dean of Keynsham, 1971–74. Mem. Council, Univ. of Bath, 1990–2005 (Chm., Buildings Cttee, 1992–2002; Life Mem., Court, 2005); Vice-Chm. Trustees, Partis Coll., Bath, 2005– (Chm., 1996–2005). Chancellor's Medal, Univ. of Bath, 2003. *Recreation:* history of railways. *Address:* 12 Berryfield Road, Bradford-on-Avon, Wilts BA15 1SX. *T:* (01225) 868905.

BURGESS, John Edward Ramsay; His Honour Judge Burgess; a Circuit Judge, since 2002; *b* 11 March 1956; *s* of Gen. Sir Edward Arthur Burgess, *qv* and Jean Angelique Leslie Burgess (*née* Henderson); *m* 2001, Cherry Anna Searle; one *s* two *d*. *Educ:* St Edward's Sch., Oxford; Exeter Univ. (LLB). Called to the Bar, Middle Temple, 1978; in practice as barrister, 1978–2002; Asst Recorder, 1995–2000; Recorder, 2000–02; Judge Advocate (pt-time), 2001–. *Recreations:* rowing, walking, going to the seaside. *Address:* Midland Circuit Secretariat, The Priory Courts, 33 Bull Street, Birmingham B4 6DW. *Club:* Nottingham Boat.

BURGESS, Sir (Joseph) Stuart, Kt 1994; CBE 1984; PhD; FRSC; Vice-Chairman, Asthma UK (formerly National Asthma Campaign), 2000–07; Chairman, Finsbury Worldwide Pharmaceutical Trust plc, 1995–2004; *b* 20 March 1929; *s* of late Joseph and Emma Burgess (*née* Wollerton); *m* 1955, Valerie Ann Street; one *s* one *d*. *Educ:* Barnsley Holgate Grammar School; University College London (1st Class Hons BSc Chem, PhD; Fellow, 1994). Amersham International plc (formerly The Radiochemical Centre), 1953–89: Chief Exec., 1979–89; Pres., Amersham Corp. USA, 1975–77; Advr, Immuno Internat. AG, 1990–96; Dir, 1992–2003, Chm., 1998–2003, Haemonetics Corp.; Dir, Anagen plc, 1993–96. Chairman: Oxford RHA, 1990–94; Anglia and Oxford RHA, subseq. Anglia and Oxford Reg., NHS Exec., DoH, 1994–97; Mem., NHS Policy Board, 1994–97. Dir, American Chamber of Commerce (UK), 1988–90. Member: Innovation Adv. Bd, DTI, 1988–93; ACOST Med. Res. and Health Cttee, 1991–92; Chm., CBI Res. and Manufacturing Cttee, 1990–93; Mem., CBI Nat. Manufacturing Council, 1991–92. CCMI (CBIM 1986; Mem., 1996, Chm., 1998–2001, Bd of Companions). *Recreations:* golf, music, travel. *Address:* Barrington, Hearn Close, Penn, Bucks HP10 8JT. *T:* (01494) 816387.

BURGESS, Keith, OBE 2004; PhD; Chairman, Europe, Middle East and Africa (EAMA), BearingPoint, since 2006; Vice-Chairman, Public Services Productivity Panel, HM Treasury, since 2000; *b* 1 Sept. 1946; *s* of Bert Burgess and Mary Burgess; *m* 1970, Patricia Mitchell; two *d*. *Educ:* Lewis Sch. for Boys, Pengam; Univ. of Bristol (BSc 1967; PhD 1971). Joined Arthur Andersen & Co., 1971: Partner, 1980–2000; Managing Partner, Andersen Consulting, UK and Ireland, 1989–94; Global Managing Partner: Practice Competency, 1994–97; Business Process Mgt & Enterprises, 1997–99; Sen. Partner, Andersen Consulting UK, 2000; Exec. Chm., QA plc, 2000–06. Non-exec. Dir, MORI, 2003–05. Pres., Mgt Consultancies Assoc., 1994–95. Chm., Corporate Action for the Homeless, 1993–96. Patron, Univ. of Bristol Campaign for Resource, 1991–2001. Master, Guild of Mgt Consultants, 1998–99 (Mem., 1994–). Hon. LLD Bristol, 2000. *Publication:* (jtly) Foundations of Business Systems, 1989, 2nd edn 1992. *Recreations:* shooting, Rugby, cricket. *Address:* Hengrove, The Chivery, Tring, Herts HP23 6LE.

BURGESS, Melvin; author (children and young adults); *b* 25 April 1954; *s* of Chris Burgess and Helen Burgess; *m* 1998, Judith Ligyett; one *s* one *d*, and one step *s*. *Publications:* The Cry of the Wolf, 1990; Burning Issy, 1992; An Angel for May, 1992; The Baby and Fly Pie, 1993; Loving April, 1995; The Earth Giant, 1995; Tiger, Tiger, 1996; Junk, 1996 (Carnegie Medal, 1996; Guardian Fiction Prize, 1997); Kite, 1997; The Copper Treasure, 1998; Bloodtide, 1999 (jt winner, Lancashire County Library Children's Book of the Year, 2001); Old Bag, 1999; The Ghost Behind the Wall, 2000; The Birdman, 2000; Billy Elliot, 2001; Lady, 2001; Doing It, 2003; Robbers on the Road, 2003; Bloodsong, 2005; Sara's Face, 2006. *Recreations:* walking, cooking. *Address:* c/o Andersen Press Ltd, 20 Vauxhall Bridge Road, SW1V 2SA; *e-mail:* melvin.burgess@ntlworld.com.

BURGESS, Prof. Robert George, PhD; Vice-Chancellor, University of Leicester, since 1999; *b* 23 April 1947; *s* of George Burgess and Olive (*née* Andrews); *m* 1974, Hilary Margaret Mary Joyce. *Educ:* Univ. of Durham (Teachers' Cert. 1968; BA 1971); Univ. of Warwick (PhD 1981). University of Warwick: Lectr in Sociol., 1974–84; Sen. Lectr in Sociol., 1984–88; Chair of Dept of Sociol., 1985–88; Dir, Centre for Educnl Develt, Appraisal and Res., 1987–99; Prof. of Sociology, 1988–99; Chair, Faculty of Social Studies, 1988–91; Founding Chair, Graduate Sch., 1991–95; Sen. Pro-Vice-Chancellor, 1995–99. Founding Chair, UK Council for Graduate Educn, 1994–99. Economic and Social Research Council: Member: Res. Resources Bd, 1991–96; Council, 1996–2000; Jt Equality Steering Gp, 2001–03; Chair, Trng Bd, 1997–2000 (Mem., 1989–93). Chm., E Midlands Univs Assoc., 2001–04; Higher Education Funding Council for England: Chm., Quality Assessment Cttee, 2001–03; Member: Res. Libraries Strategy Gp, 2001–02; Quality Assurance Learning and Teaching, 2003–07; Chairman: ESRC/Funding Councils Teaching and Learning Res. Prog., 2003–; Bd, UCAS, 2005– (Mem. Bd, 2001–05); Res. Information Network, 2005–. Mem., British Liby Bd, 2003–. President: British Sociological Assoc., 1989–91; Assoc. for Teaching of Social Scis, 1991–99. Chm., Higher Educn Acad., 2007– (Bd Mem., 2003–07). AcSS 2000. Hon. DLitt Staffordshire, 1998; DUniv Northampton, 2007. *Publications:* Experiencing Comprehensive Education, 1983; In the Field, 1984; Education, Schools and Schooling, 1985; Sociology, Education and Schools, 1986; (jtly) Implementing In-Service Education, 1993; Research Methods, 1993; ed. of twenty books; numerous contribs to social sci. jls. *Recreations:* walking, listening to music, some gardening. *Address:* University of Leicester, University Road, Leicester LE1 7RH. *T:* (0116) 252 2322.

BURGESS, Sally Anne; classical singer; *b* 9 Oct. 1953; *d* of Edna Rushton (formerly Burgess; *née* Sharman) and Douglas Burgess; *m* 1988, Neal Scott Thornton; one *s*. *Educ:* Royal College of Music. ARCM. Joined ENO 1977; for *ENO* rôles incl., as a soprano: Zerlina, Cherubino, Pamina, Mimi, Micaela; as a mezzo: Composer (Ariadne), Sextus (Julius Caesar), Charlotte (Werther), Carmen, Fennimore (Fennimore and Gerda), 1990; Judith (Duke Bluebeard's Castle), 1991; Octavian (Rosenkavalier), 1994; Mrs Begbick (Mahagonny), 1995; Herodias (Salome), 1996; Dulcinée (Don Quixote), 1996; Amelia (Twice Through the Heart), 1997; Baba the Turk (Rake's Progress), Polinesso (Ariodante), 2002; Mistress Quickly (Sir John in Love), 2006; *Opera North:* Amneris (Aida), Dido (Trojans), Julie (Showboat), 1989–90; Orfeo (Glück), 1990; Laura (La Gioconda), 1993; Azucena (Trovatore), 1994; Eboli (Don Carlos), 1998; Margaretha (Genoveva), 2000; Judith (Duke Bluebeard's Castle), 2005; Kabanicha (Katya Kabanova), 2007; *Royal Opera, Covent Garden:* Siebel (Faust), Maddalena (Rigoletto), 1989; *Scottish Opera:* Fricka (Die Walküre), Amneris (Aida), 1991; Mistress Quickly (Sir John in Love), 2008; *New York Metropolitan:* Carmen, 1995; Queen Isabella (The Voyage), 1996; title rôle (Merry Widow), 2003; *Glyndebourne:* Smeraldina (Love for Three Oranges); Witch (Hansel), tour, 2008; *Welsh National Opera:* Ottavia (Coronation of Poppea), 1998 (also televised); Mother Marie (The Carmelites), Kabanicha (Katya Kabanova), Munich, 1999; Fricka (Das Rheingold), 1999, (Die Walküre), 2000, Geneva; Polinesso (Ariodante), Houston, 2002; Fortunata (Satyricon), Nancy, Ghent, Antwerp, 2004; Marta/Pantalis (Mefistofele), Netherlands Opera, 2004; Amneris, Strasbourg, Wiesbaden, Lausanne and Nancy; Carmen, Munich, Oregon, Zürich, Berlin, Paris and NZ; Delilah, Nantes; Bernstein on Broadway (tour), 2007; Sally Burgess' Women (one-woman show), Lyric Th., Hammersmith, 1997; numerous concert appearances; concert tour, NZ, 2005; numerous recordings, incl. Liverpool Oratorio, and jazz. *Recreations:* family, cooking, walking, reading, singing jazz, theatre. *Address:* AOR Management, 6910 Roosevelt Way NE PMB 221, Seattle, WA 98115, USA; *e-mail:* aormanagementuk@earthlink.net.

BURGESS, Sir Stuart; *see* Burgess, Sir J. S.

BURGESS, Rev. Stuart John; Chairman, Commission for Rural Communities, since 2006, and Government's Rural Advocate, since 2004 (Chairman, Countryside Agency, 2004–06); President, Methodist Conference, 1999–2000; *b* 18 March 1940; *s* of Frederick John Burgess and Winifred May (*née* Gowan); *m* 1965, Elisabeth Maud Fowler; two *d*. *Educ:* Moseley Grammar Sch., Birmingham; Univ. of London (BD ext.); Univ. of Nottingham (MEd; MTh). Minister: Headingley Methodist Church, 1965–68; Nottingham W Circuit, and Chaplain, Univ. of Nottingham, 1968–81; Birmingham SW Circuit, and Chaplain, Univ. of Birmingham, 1981–89; Chm., York and Hull Methodist Dist, 1989–2004. Mem., Ethical Cttee, DWP, 2004–. Chm., Patient Liaison Gp, BMA, 2004–07. Hon. Fellow, UC of York St John, 2003. Hon. MA 1989, DUniv 2006, Birmingham; Hon. DD Hull, 2001; DD Lambeth, 2003. *Publications:* Seeds of Joy, 1985; Spiritual Journey of John Wesley, 1988; Stations of the Cross, 1991; Making Connections, 1998; Coming of Age: challenges and opportunities for the 21st century, 1999. *Recreations:* music, tennis. *Address:* 38 Bibury Road, Hall Green, Birmingham B28 0HQ. *T:* 07900 608249.

BURGESS, Tony; *see* Burgess, A. R. F.

BURGH, 8th Baron *cr* 1529 (called out of abeyance, 1916); **Alexander Gregory Disney Leith;** *b* 16 March 1958; *er s* of 7th Baron Burgh and Anita Lorna Burgh (*née* Eldridge); *S* father, 2001; *m* 1st, 1984, Catherine Mary (marr. diss. 1999), *d* of David Parkes; two *s* one *d*; 2nd, 1999, Emma Jane, *d* of Martin Burdick; one *s* one *d*. Patron, Lord Thomas Burgh Retinue. *Heir: s* Hon. Alexander James Strachan Leith, *b* 11 Oct. 1986.

BURGH, Sir John (Charles), KCMG 1982; CB 1975; President, Trinity College, University of Oxford, 1987–96 (Hon. Fellow, 1997); Chairman, Associated Board of the Royal Schools of Music, 1987–94; Director-General, British Council, 1980–87; *b* 9 Dec. 1925; *m* 1957, Ann Sturge; two *d*. *Educ:* Friends' Sch., Sibford; London Sch. of Economics (BSc Econ.; Leverhulme post-intermediate Schol.; Pres. of Union, 1949; Hon. Fellow, 1983). Asst Principal, BoT, 1950; Private Sec. to successive Ministers of State, BoT, 1954–57; Colonial Office, 1959–62; Mem., UK Delegation to UN Conf. on Trade and Develt, 1964; Asst Sec., DEA, 1964; Principal Private Sec. to successive First Secretaries of State and Secretaries of State for Econ. Affairs, 1965–68; Under-Sec., Dept of Employment, 1968–71; Dep.-Chm., Community Relations Commn, 1971–72; Deputy Secretary: Cabinet Office (Central Policy Rev. Staff), 1972–74; Dept of Prices and Consumer Protection, 1974–79; Dept of Trade, 1979–80. Member: Executive, PEP, 1972–78; Council, Policy Studies Inst., 1978–85; Council, RSA, 1982–85; Council, VSO, 1980–87; Acad. Council, Wilton Park, 1984–87; Exec. Cttee, Anglo-Austrian Soc., 1987–2000; Council, RIIA, 1993–95. Chairman: Nat. Opera Co-ordinating Cttee, 1991–2007 (Sec., 1972–91); Oxford Educnl Trust for Develt of the Arts, 1990–96; Dir, English Shakespeare Co., 1988–94. Chm. Ct of Governors, LSE, 1985–87 (Gov., 1980–2004); Vice-Chm., Yehudi Menuhin Sch., 1994–. Chm., New Berlioz Edition, 1993–. FRCM 1994. Hon. RNCM 1986. Hon. LLD Bath, 1987. *Recreations:* friends, music, the arts generally. *Address:* 2 Oak Hill Lodge, Oak Hill Park, NW3 7LN. *Club:* Royal Over-Seas League.

BURGHLEY, Lord; Anthony John Cecil; *b* 9 Aug. 1970; *s* and *heir* of Marquess of Exeter, *qv*; *m* 1996, Holly Stewart; one *d*. *Educ:* Eton; Oxford Univ.

BURGON, Colin; MP (Lab) Elmet, since 1997; *b* 22 April 1948; *s* of Thomas and Winifred Burgon; *m* (marr. diss.); one *d*; partner, Kathryn. *Educ:* St Michael's Coll., Leeds; Carnegie Coll., Leeds; Huddersfield Poly. Former teacher of History, Foxwood High Sch., Leeds; Policy Advr, Wakefield CC, 1987–95. Contested (Lab) Elmet, 1987, 1992. *Address:* House of Commons, SW1A 0AA.

BURGON, Geoffrey; composer; *b* 15 July 1941; *s* of Alan Wybert Burgon and Ada Vera Isom; *m* 1st, 1963, Janice Elizabeth Garwood (marr. diss.); one *s* one *d*; 2nd, 1992, Jacqueline Krofchak; one *s*. *Educ:* Pewley Sch., Guildford; Guildhall School of Music and Drama; studied composition with Peter Wishart, trumpet with Bernard Brown. Freelance trumpeter, 1964–71: Royal Opera House (stage band), Philomusica, London Mozart Players, Northern Sinfonia, Jacques and Capriol Orchestras, also session work, theatres and jazz bands. Full time composer and conductor, 1971–; work in almost every musical genre, particularly orchestral, choral, and music for dance, film & TV; commissions from many Festivals, incl. Bath, Edinburgh, Cheltenham, Southern Cathedrals, Three Choirs, and Camden; also many works for Dance, incl. Ballet Rambert and London Contemporary Dance Theatre; work performed internationally. *Major works:* Gending; Alleluia Nativitas; The World Again; Acquainted with Night; Think on Dreadful Domesday; Canciones del Alma; Requiem; Revelations; Title Divine; Short Mass; The Golden Eternity; The Fire of Heaven, Dos Coros; A Hymn to the Creatures; The Golden Fish; The Calm; Running Figures; Goldbergs Dream; Songs, Lamentations and Praises; Mass; The Trials of Prometheus; Hymn to Venus; Five Sonnets of John Donne; Four Guitars; Six Studies for Solo Cello; Worldes Blisse; Trumpet Concerto: the Turning World; First Was the World; City Adventures; Merciless Beauty; The Wanderer; Piano Concerto; A Different Dawn; Magic Words, Heavenly Things; Three Mysteries; Cello Concerto; *opera:* Hard Times; *film scores:* Life of Brian; Dogs of War; Turtle Diary; Robin Hood; Labyrinth; *television scores:* Tinker, Tailor, Soldier, Spy; Brideshead Revisited; Bleak House; Happy Valley; Chronicles of Narnia; Children of the North; Martin Chuzzlewit; Silent Witness; Cider with Rosie; Longitude (BAFTA award); The Forsyte Saga (BAFTA award); Island at War; Love Lies Bleeding. Prince Pierre of Monaco Award, 1969; Ivor Novello Award, 1979, 1981; Gold Disc for Brideshead record, 1986. *Recreations:* playing jazz, cricket, Bristol motor cars, sleeping. *Address:* c/o Chester Music, 14–15 Berners Street, W1T 3LJ. *T:* (020) 7434 0066.

BURGOYNE, Rear-Adm. (Robert) Michael, CB 1982; *b* 20 March 1927; *s* of Robert and Elizabeth Burgoyne; *m* 1951, Margaret (Hilda) McCook; one *s* one *d*. *Educ:* Bradfield College; Magdalene College, Cambridge. Joined RN 1945; CO HMS Cleopatra, 1967–68; Captain 2nd Frigate Sqdn and CO HMS Undaunted, 1972–73; Dir, Maritime Tactical Sch., 1974–75; CO HMS Antrim, 1975–77; Comdr, British Navy Staff, Washington and UK Rep. to SACLANT, 1977–80; Senior Naval Member, Directing Staff, RCDS, 1980–82. Dir, RIN, 1983–92 (Hon. FRIN 2001). Vice-Pres., Sea Safety Gp (UK), 1992–96. Chm., W Dorset Dist Scout Council, 1995–97. Hon. Treas., Friends of SSAFA, W Dorset, 2002–06.

BURK, Prof. Kathleen Mildred, DPhil; Professor of Modern and Contemporary History, University College London, since 1995; *d* of Wayne Eliot Burk and Martha Ann Burk (*née* Ankney); *m* 1980, Dr Michael Jewess; one *d*. *Educ:* Sanger Union High Sch., California; Univ. of California, Berkeley (BA 1969); St Hugh's Coll., Oxford (MA, DPhil 1977); Dip. in Wine and Spirits, WSET, 2002. Tutorial Asst in Mod. Hist., Univ. of Dundee, 1976–77; Rhodes Res. Fellow for N America and Caribbean, St Hugh's Coll., Oxford, 1977–80; Lectr in Hist. and Politics, Imperial Coll., London, 1980–90; University College London: Lectr in Hist., 1990–93; Reader in Mod. and Contemp. Hist., 1993–95. Visiting Professor: Kyung Hee Univ., Seoul, Korea, 1986; Univ. of Trondheim, 1994; Univ. of Tübingen, 1999; Univ. of Oslo, 2004; Vis. Fellow, All Souls Coll., Oxford, 1998. Gresham Prof. of Rhetoric, 2003–06. Alec Cairncross Lecture, 1994; Commonwealth Fund Lecture in American Hist., 2005; Crabtree Oration, 2006. Wine correspondent, Prospect magazine, 2002–05. Chm., Historians' Press, 1983–99; Founding Co-Editor, Contemporary European History, 1989–2001. FRHistS 1989 (Mem. Council, 1994–97; Hon. Treas., 1997–2001). Foreign Mem., Royal Norwegian Soc. for Scis and Letters, 2002. Judge, Internat. Wine and Spirits Comp., 2005–. *Publications:* (ed and contrib.) War and the State: the transformation of British Government 1914–1919, 1982; Long Wittenham 1800–1920, 1984; Britain, America and the Sinews of War 1914–1918, 1985; The First Privatisation: the politicians, the city and the denationalisation of steel, 1988; Morgan Grenfell 1838–1988: the biography of a merchant bank, 1989; (with Alec Cairncross) Goodbye, Great Britain: the 1976 IMF crisis, 1992; (with Manfred Pohl) The Deutsche Bank in London 1873–1998, 1998; (ed with Melvyn Stokes) The United States and the Western Alliance since 1945, 1999; Troublemaker: the life and history of A. J. P. Taylor, 2000; (ed) The British Isles since 1945, 2003; Old World, New World: the story of Britain and America, 2007; (with Michael Bywater) Is This Bottle Corked? The Secret Life of Wine, 2008; articles in Histl Jl, Econ. Hist. Rev., Internat. Hist. Rev., World of Fine Wine, etc. *Recreations:* collecting antiquarian history books, playing early music, wine. *Address:* The Long Barn, Townsend, Harwell, Oxon OX11 0DX. *T:* (01235) 835637. *Club:* Academy.

BURKE, Most Rev. Austin-Emile; Archbishop of Halifax (NS), (RC), 1991–98, now Emeritus; *b* 11 June 1922. Ordained priest, 1950; Suffragan Bishop of Yarmouth, 1968–91. *Address:* 215 Village Road, Herring Cove, NS B3V 1H2, Canada.

BURKE, Hon. Brian Thomas; Australian Ambassador to Republic of Ireland and to the Holy See, 1988–91; *b* 25 Feb. 1947; *s* of late Thomas Burke (Federal ALP Member for Perth, 1942–55), and Madelaine Burke; *m* 1965, Susanne May Nevill; four *s* two *d*. *Educ:* Brigidine Convent; Marist Brothers' Coll.; Univ. of Western Australia. FAMI. Former journalist. MLA (Lab) Balga, WA, 1973–88; Opposition Shadow Minister, 1976–81; Leader of the Opposition, 1981–83; Premier and Treasurer of WA, 1983–88. AC 1988. *Recreations:* reading, stamp-collecting, writing poetry, swimming, fishing. *Address:* PO Box 668, Scarborough, WA 6019, Australia.

BURKE, David Thomas, (Tom), CBE 1997; Environmental Policy Adviser, Rio Tinto plc, since 1997; *b* 5 Jan. 1947; *s* of J. V. Burke, DSM, and Mary (*née* Bradley). *Educ:* St Boniface's, Plymouth; Liverpool Univ. (BA (Hons) Philosophy). Great George's Community Arts Project, 1969–70; Lecturer: West Cheshire Coll., 1970–71; Old Swan Technical Coll., 1971–73; Friends of the Earth: Local Groups Co-ordinator, 1973–75; Executive Director, 1975–79; Dir of Special Projects, 1979–80; Vice-Chm., 1980–81; Dir, The Green Alliance, 1982–91; Special Advr to Sec. of State for the Envmt, 1991–97; Envmtl Policy Advr, BP Amoco, 1997–2001; Advr, Central Policy Gp, Cabinet Office, 2002; Sen. Advr to Special Representative on Climate Change, 2006–. Founding Dir, E3G, 2003–. Press Officer, European Environment Bureau, 1979–87; Sec., Ecological Studies Inst., 1987–92. Member: Bd of Dirs, Earth Resources Research, 1975–87; Waste Management Adv. Council, 1976–81; Packaging Council, 1978–82; Exec. Cttee, NCVO, 1984–89; UK Nat. Cttee, European Year of the Environment, 1986–88; Exec. Cttee, European Environment Bureau, 1987–91; Council, English Nature, 1999–2006; London Sustainable Develt Commn, 2002–06. Chm., Rev. of Envmtl Governance in NI, 2006–07. Contested (SDP): Brighton Kemptown, 1983; Surbiton, 1987. Vis. Fellow, Cranfield, 1991–94; Vis. Prof., Imperial Coll., 1997–. Hon. Vis. Fellow, Manchester Business Sch., 1984; Hon. Prof., Faculty of Laws, UCL, 2003–. FRSA 1988 (Mem. Council, 1990–92). Royal Humane Society Testimonials: on Vellum, 1966; on Parchment, 1968; Global 500 Laureate, UNEP, 1993. *Publications:* Europe: environment, 1981; (jtly) Pressure Groups in the Global System, 1982; (jtly) Ecology 2000, 1984; (jtly) The Green Capitalists, 1987; (jtly) Green Pages, 1988. *Recreations:* photography, birdwatching. *Address:* Studio 2, Clink Wharf Studios, Clink Street, SE1 9DG. *T:* (020) 7357 9146. *Club:* Reform.

BURKE, Prof. Derek Clissold, CBE 1994; DL; Vice-Chancellor, University of East Anglia, 1987–95; *b* 13 Feb. 1930; *s* of late Harold Burke and Ivy Ruby (*née* Clissold); *m* 1955, Mary Elizabeth Dukeshire, New York; one *s* two *d* (and one *d* decd). *Educ:* Univ. of Birmingham (BSc, PhD, Chemistry). Res. Fellow, Yale Univ., 1953–55; Scientist, Nat. Inst. for Med. Res., London, 1955–60; Lectr and Sen. Lectr, Dept of Biochemistry, Univ. of Aberdeen, 1960–69; Prof. of Biol Scis, 1969–82, Pro-Vice-Chancellor, 1971–73, Univ. of Warwick; Vice-Pres. and Scientific Dir, Allelix Inc., Toronto, 1982–86. Specialist Advr, H of C Select Cttee on Sci. and Technol., 1995–2001. Member: MRC Cell Bd, 1976–79; Scientific Cttee, Cancer Res. Campaign, 1979–82 and of CRC Council, 1987–97; Europ. Molecular Biol Orgn, 1980–; Adv. Cttee on Genetic Modification, HSE, 1987–95; Steering Gp, Technol. Foresight Initiative, OST, 1993–95; Sci. and Engrg Base Bd, 1994–97, Technol. Interaction Bd, 1994–97, BBSRC; EU Eur. Life Scis Gp, 2000–04; EU-US Biotechnol. Consultative Forum, 2000–01. Chm., Adv. Cttee on Novel Foods and Processes, Dept of Health and MAFF, 1989–97. Chm. Council, Paterson Inst. for Cancer Res., 1992–97; Dir, Babraham Inst., Cambridge, 1995–99; Mem. Governing Body, BBSRC Inst. of Food Res., 1995–2002 (Mem. Adv. Bd, AFRC Inst. of Food Res., 1989–95); Member: Societal Issues Panel, EPSRC, 2005–08; Bioscience for Society Strategy Panel, BBSRC, 2008–. Chm., Genome Research Ltd, 1997–98. Mem., Archbishops' Med. Ethics Adv. Gp, 1995–2006. Pres., Soc. for Gen. Microbiology, 1987–90. Hon. Mem., Soc. for Gen. Microbiol., 2001. Editor and Editor in Chief, Journal of General Virology, 1976–87. Trustee: Norfolk and Norwich Fest., 1988–98; Wingfield Arts, 1995–98. Hon. Fellow, St Edmund's Coll., Cambridge, 1997–. Hon. FIBiol 2001. Hon. LLD Aberdeen 1982; Hon. ScD UEA, 1995. DL Norfolk, 1992. *Publications:* Creation and Evolution (ed and contrib.), 1985; (with R. Gill) Strategic Church Leadership, 1996; (ed and contrib.) Cybernauts Awake!, 1999; numerous sci. papers on interferon and animal viruses. *Recreations:* music, walking. *Address:* 12 Cringleford Chase, Norwich, Norfolk NR4 7RS. *Club:* Norfolk.

BURKE, Ian; *see* Burke, M. I.

BURKE, Sir James (Stanley Gilbert), 9th Bt *cr* 1797 (Ire.), of Marble Hill, Galway; *b* 1 July 1956; *s* of Sir Thomas Stanley Burke, 8th Bt and Susanne Margaretha (*d* 1983), *er d* of Otto Salvisberg, Thun, Switzerland; *S* father, 1989; *m* 1980, Laura, *d* of Domingo Branzuela; one *s* one *d*. *Heir:* *s* Martin James Burke, *b* 22 July 1980. *Address:* Bleierstrasse 14, 8942 Oberrieden, Switzerland.

BURKE, Jeffrey Peter; QC 1984; **His Honour Judge Burke;** a Circuit Judge, since 2002; *b* 15 Dec. 1941; *s* of Samuel and Gertrude Burke; *m*; two *s* one *d*; *m* 1994, Joanna Mary Heal; one *s* one *d*. *Educ:* Shrewsbury Sch.; Brasenose Coll., Oxford (BA 1963). Called to the Bar, Inner Temple, 1964, Bencher, 1997. A Recorder, 1983–2002. Legal Mem., Mental Health Review Tribunal, 1994–; Judge, Employment Appeal Tribunal, 2000–. Non-exec. Dir, Royal Marsden Hosp. NHS Foundn Trust, 2002. *Recreations:* sport, wine, charity triathlons, fighting stinging nettles. *Address:* Luton Crown Court, George Street, Luton, Beds LU1 2AA. *Clubs:* De Todeni (Flamstead); Economicals AFC; Flamstead Cricket.

BURKE, Joanna Margaret; Regional Director, China, British Council, since 2007; *b* 2 May 1960; *d* of James Brian Burke and Margaret Ann Burke; *m* 1987, Eliseo Mayoral-Martinez; one *s* one *d*. *Educ:* Beijing Langs Inst.; Tübingen Univ.; Leeds Univ. (BA Chinese and German 1982). British Council: Asst Dir, China, 1990–95; Dep. Dir, Argentina, 1995–99; Dir, Shanghai, 1999–2003; Regl Dir, Americas and Australasia, 2003–04; Dir, Japan, 2005–07. *Recreations:* Beijing history, collecting books and materials on Beijing, travel, music, gardens. *Address:* c/o Foreign and Commonwealth Office, King Charles Street, SW1A 2AH. *T:* (10) 65906903, *Fax:* (10) 65900977; *e-mail:* joanna.burke@britishcouncil.org.cn.

BURKE, His Honour John Kenneth; QC 1985; a Circuit Judge, 1995–2005; *b* 4 Aug. 1939; *s* of Kenneth Burke and Madeline Burke; *m* 1962, Margaret Anne (*née* Scattergood); three *d*. *Educ:* Stockport Grammar Sch. Served Cheshire Regt, 1958–60; TA Parachute Regt, 1962–67. Called to the Bar, Middle Temple, 1965, Bencher, 1992. A Recorder, 1980–95. *Recreations:* painting and drawing, walking.

BURKE, Kathy; actress and director; *b* 13 June 1964. *Educ:* Anne Scher Drama Sch. *Films:* Scrubbers, Forever Young, 1983; Sacred Hearts, 1985; Sid and Nancy, 1986; Straight to Hell, Walker, Eat the Rich, 1987; Work Experience, 1989; Amongst Barbarians, 1990; Sin Bin, 1994; Hello, Hello, Hello, 1995; Nil by Mouth, 1997; Dancing at Lughnasa, Elizabeth, 1998; This Year's Love, 1999; Kevin and Perry Go Large, Love, Honour and Obey, 2000; The Martins, 2001; Once Upon a Time in the Midlands, Anita and Me, 2002. *Television:* Past Caring, 1985; Two of Us, 1987; Harry Enfield's Television Programme (series), 1990; Mr Wroe's Virgins, 1993; Harry Enfield and Chums (series), 1994; Common as Muck (series), 1994–97; Life's a Bitch, 1995; After Miss Julie, 1995; The History of Tom Jones, a Foundling, 1997; Ted & Ralph, 1998; Gimme, Gimme, Gimme (series; also script editor), 1999–2001; Shooting Gallery, 1999; Harry Enfield Presents Kevin's Guide to Being a Teenager, 1999; Harry Enfield Presents Wayne and Waynetta's Guide to Wedded Bliss, 2001. Writer: play, Mr Thomas; film, The End, 1998; writer and dir, TV series, Renegade TV Gets Dazed, 1998. Director: Out in the Open, 2001, Born Bad, 2003, Love Me Tonight, 2004, Hampstead Th.; Kosher Harry, Royal Court, 2002; Betty, Vaudeville, 2002; The Quare Fellow (tour), 2004; Blue/Orange, Crucible, Sheffield, 2005; The God of Hell, Donmar Warehouse, 2005; Smaller, Lyric, 2006. *Address:* c/o Hatton McEwan, PO Box 37385, N1 7XF.

BURKE, Hon. Sir Kerry; *see* Burke, Hon. Sir T. K.

BURKE, (Michael) Ian; Chief Executive, Rank Group Plc, since 2006; *b* 21 June 1956; *s* of Ronald and Rosemary Burke; *m* 1979, Jane McGuinness; one *s* one *d*. *Educ:* Imperial Coll., London (BSc Maths); London Business Sch. (MSc Business Admin). ACMA 1981. With Lever Bros, 1978–81; finance and planning, Esso UK, 1981–86; Gp Planning Manager, Gateway Corp., 1986–90; Bass plc: Commercial Dir, Bass Leisure, 1990–92; Man. Dir, Gala Clubs, 1992–95; Exec. Vice Pres. and Man. Dir, Holiday Inn Worldwide, Europe, ME and Africa, 1995–98; Chief Executive: Thistle Hotels plc, 1998–2003; Health Club Hldgs, 2003–06. Dir, London Tourist Bd, 1998–2003; Bd Mem., BTA, 2000–03. *Recreations:* fell-walking, cycling. *Address:* Rank Group Plc, Statesman House, Stafferton Way, Maidenhead SL6 1AY.

BURKE, Peter; *see* Burke, U. P.

BURKE, Prof. Philip George, CBE 1993; FRS 1978; MRIA 1974; Professor of Mathematical Physics, Queen's University of Belfast, 1967–98, now Emeritus; *b* 18 Oct. 1932; *s* of Henry Burke and Frances Mary Burke (*née* Sprague); *m* 1959, Valerie Mona Martin; four *d*. *Educ:* Wanstead County High Sch.; Univ. Coll. of SW of England, Exeter

(BSc London (ext.) 1953, 1st cl. Hons Physics); University Coll. London (PhD 1956, Fellow 1986). Granville Studentship, London Univ., 1953; Res. Fellow, UCL, 1956–57; Asst Lectr, Univ. of London Computer Unit, 1957–59; Res. Associate, Alvarez Bubble Chamber Gp and Theory Gp, Lawrence Berkeley Lab., Calif, 1959–62; Res. Fellow, then Principal Scientific Officer, later SPSO, Theoretical Physics Div., AERE, Harwell, 1962–67; Queen's University of Belfast: Head, Dept of Applied Maths and Theoretical Physics, 1974–77; Chm., Sch. of Physics and Math. Scis, 1985–86; Dir, Sch. of Maths and Physics, 1988–90. Science, subseq. Science and Engineering, Research Council: Mem., Physics Cttee, 1967–71; Chm., Synchrotron Radiation Panel, 1969–71; Mem., Atlas Comp. Cttee, 1973–76; Hd, Div. of Theory and Computational Sci., Daresbury Lab., 1977–82; Chm., Science Bd Computer Cttee, 1976–77 and 1984–86; Chm., Scientific Computing Adv. Panel, 1989–94; Mem., 1989–94; Chairman: Internat. Conf. on Physics of Electronic and Atomic Collisions, 1973–75; Computational Physics Gp, Europ. Physical Soc., 1976–78; Atomic, Molecular and Optical Physics Div., Inst. of Physics, 1987–90; Allocations and Resources Panel, Jt Res. Councils Supercomputer Cttee, 1988–90; Supercomputing Management Cttee, 1991–94; Inter-Council High Performance Computing Mgt Cttee, 1996–98; Member: ABRC Supercomputing Sub-cttee, 1991–94; Nuclear Res. Adv. Council, MoD, 1997–2007. Mem., Council, Royal Soc., 1990–92. Co-ordinator, EU Human Capital and Mobility Network of nine EU labs and three E European labs, 1993–96. Dir, 1969–2000, Hon. Dir, 2001–, Computer Physics Communications Internat. Program Library. Series Editor: Plenum Series on Physics of Atoms and Molecules (with H. Kleinpoppen), 1974–2004; Springer Series on Atomic, Optical and Plasma Physics, 2005–. Hon. Editor, Computer Physics Communications, 1986– (founding and principal editor, 1969–79). Hon. DSc: Exeter, 1981; QUB, 1999. Guthrie Medal and Prize, 1994, Sir David Bates Prize, 2000, Inst. of Physics. *Publications:* seven books; many research papers in learned journals. *Recreations:* walking, books, music. *Address:* c/o Department of Applied Mathematics and Theoretical Physics, Queen's University of Belfast, Belfast BT7 1NN. *T:* (028) 9097 6034, *Fax:* (028) 9097 9182; (home) Brook House, Norley Lane, Crowton, Northwich, Cheshire CW8 2RR. *T:* (01928) 788301.

BURKE, Richard; President, Canon Foundation in Europe, 1988–98; *b* 29 March 1932; *s* of David Burke and Elisabeth Burke; *m* 1961, Mary Freeley; two *s* three *d*. *Educ:* University Coll., Dublin (MA). Called to the Bar, King's Inns. Mem., Dublin Co. Council, 1967–73 (Chm., 1972–73); Mem. Dail Eireann, for South County Dublin, 1969–77, for Dublin West, 1981–82; Fine Gael Chief Whip and spokesman on Posts and Telegraphs, 1969–73; Minister for Education, 1973–76. Commission of the European Communities: Member with special responsibility for Transport, Taxation, Consumer Protection, Relations with European Parlt, Research, Educ. and Sci., 1977–81, for Greenland, Greek Memorandum, Personnel and Admin, Jt Interpretation and Conf. Service, Statistical Office and Office of Publications, 1982–85; Vice Pres., 1984–85. Associate Fellow, Center for Internat. Affairs, Harvard Univ., 1980–81. Member: Conseil d'Administration, FIDEPS, UNESCO, 1990–98; Develt Council, HEC, Paris, 1990–. Mem., Academia Scientiarum et Artium Europaea, Salzburg, 1996. Chieftain, Burke Clan, 1990, Hon. Life Pres., 1992. President: Harvard Club of Ireland, 2005–; Arts for Peace Foundn, 2006–. FRSA. Pro Merito Europa Medal, 1980. Grand Croix, Leopold II (Belgium), 1981; Grand Croix, Phoenix (Greece), 1983. *Recreations:* music, golf, travel. *Address:* 13 Iris Grove, Mount Merrion, Co. Dublin, Ireland. *T:* (1) 2109830.

BURKE, Simon Paul, FCA; Chairman, Majestic Wine plc, since 2005; *b* 25 Aug. 1958; *s* of Vincent Paul Burke and Beryl Mary Burke (*née* Cregan). *Educ:* St Mary's Coll., Dublin. FCA 1980. Man. Dir, Virgin Retail, 1988–94; Chief Executive: Virgin Our Price, 1994–96; Virgin Entertainment Gp, 1996–99; Chairman: Hamleys plc, 1999–2003; Superquinn Ltd, 2005–. Dir, W H Smith plc, 1995–96. Trustee, Nat. Gall., 2003–; Chm., Nat. Gall. Co. Ltd, 2004–. *Recreations:* 17th century Dutch art, mediaeval history, flying (private pilot), astronomy, travel. *Address:* e-mail: simon.burke@virgin.net.

BURKE, Hon. Sir (Thomas) Kerry, Kt 1990; Member, since 1998, and Chairman, since 2004, Canterbury Regional Council, Christchurch; *b* 24 March 1942; *m* 1st, 1968, Jennifer Shiel (marr. diss. 1984); two *s*; 2nd, 1984, Helen Paske (*d* 1989); one *s*; 3rd, 1997, Fahimeh Rastar; one step *s* two step *d*. *Educ:* Linwood High Sch.; Univ. of Canterbury (BA); Christchurch Teachers' Coll. (Dip. Teaching). General labourer, Auckland, 1965–66; factory deleg., Auckland Labourers' Union; teacher: Rangiora High Sch., 1967–72; Greymouth High Sch., 1975–78; lang. consultant, Vienna, 1991–98. Chm., Rangiora Post-Primary Teachers' Assoc., 1969–71. MP (Lab) Rangiora, NZ, 1972–75, West Coast, 1978–90; Minister of Regional Develt, and of Employment and Immigration, 1984–87; Speaker, NZ House of Reps, 1987–90. *Recreations:* ski-ing, swimming. *Address:* 44 Naseby Street, Christchurch 8014, New Zealand.

BURKE, Tom; *see* Burke, D. T.

BURKE, Trevor Michael; QC 2001; *b* 16 Oct. 1958; *s* of Michael George Burke and Philomena Burke. *Educ:* Handsworth Grammar Sch.; South Bank Univ., (BA Hons Law). Called to the Bar, Middle Temple, 1981. *Recreation:* golf. *Address:* Charter Chambers, 33 John Street, WC1N 2AT. *T:* (020) 7618 4400. *Club:* Brocket Hall Golf.

BURKE, Prof. (Ulick) Peter, FBA 1994; Professor of Cultural History, 1996–2004, now Emeritus, and Fellow of Emmanuel College, since 1979, University of Cambridge; *b* 16 Aug. 1937; *s* of John Burke and Jennie Burke (*née* Colin); *m* 1st, 1972, Susan Patricia Dell (marr. diss. 1983); 2nd, 1989, Maria Lúcia Garcia Pallares. *Educ:* St John's Coll., Oxford; St Antony's Coll., Oxford (MA). Asst Lectr, then Lectr in History, subseq. Reader in Intellectual History, Sussex Univ., 1962–78; Reader in Cultural History, Univ. of Cambridge, 1988–96. *Publications:* The Renaissance Sense of the Past, 1969; Culture and Society in Renaissance Italy, 1972, 3rd edn 1986; Venice and Amsterdam: a study of Seventeenth Century elites, 1974, 2nd edn 1994; Popular Culture in Early Modern Europe, 1978, 2nd edn 1994; Sociology and History, 1980; Montaigne, 1981; Vico, 1985; Historical Anthropology in Early Modern Italy: essays on perception and communication, 1987; The Renaissance, 1987; The French Historical Revolution: the Annales School 1929–89, 1990; The Fabrication of Louis XIV, 1992, 2nd edn 1994; History and Social Theory, 1992; Antwerp, a Metropolis in Europe, 1993; The Art of Conversation, 1993; The Fortunes of the Courtier, 1995; Varieties of Cultural History, 1997; The European Renaissance, 1998; A Social History of Knowledge, 2000; Eyewitnessing, 2001; (jtly) A Social History of the Media, 2002; What is Cultural History?, 2004; Languages and Communities in Early Modern Europe, 2004. *Recreation:* travel. *Address:* Emmanuel College, Cambridge CB2 3AP. *T:* (01223) 334272. *Club:* Paineras de Morumbi (São Paulo).

BURKE-GAFFNEY, John Campion; Director-General, The British Red Cross Society, 1985–90; *b* 27 Feb. 1932; *s* of late Dr Henry Joseph O'Donnell Burke-Gaffney, OBE and Constance May (*née* Bishop); *m* 1956, Margaret Mary Jennifer (*née* Stacpoole); two *s* two *d*. *Educ:* Douai School. Called to the Bar, Gray's Inn, 1956. Served: RAC, 1950–52; E Riding of Yorks Imperial Yeomanry (Wenlock's Horse), 1952–56. Shell-Mex and BP Ltd, 1956–75; Shell UK Ltd, 1976–77; Man. Dir, Shell and BP Zambia Ltd, 1977–81; Gp Public Affairs, Shell Internat. Petroleum Co. Ltd, 1981–85. *Address:* c/o Coutts & Co., 440 Strand, WC2R 0QS.

BURKETT, Mary Elizabeth, OBE 1978; FRGS; FMA; Director of Abbot Hall Art Gallery, and Museum of Lakeland Life and Industry, 1967–86, and Borough Museum, Kendal, 1977–86; retired; *d* of Ridley Burkett and Mary Alice Gaussen. *Educ:* Univ. of Durham (BA, Teachers' Cert.). FRGS 1978; FMA 1980. Taught art, craft, maths, etc, at Wroxall Abbey, 1948–54; Art and Craft Lectr, Charlotte Mason Coll., Ambleside, 1954–62; seven months in Turkey and Iran, 1962; Asst Dir, Abbot Hall, 1963–66. Formerly part-time Teacher of Art, Bela River Prison. Member: numerous cttees including National Trust (NW Region), 1978–85; Carlisle Diocesan Adv. Cttee, 1980–96; Carlisle Cathedral Fabric Cttee, 1991–2001. Dir, Border Television, 1982–93. Round the World trip, lecturing in Hong Kong, Perth (WA), NY as well as seeing the Great Wall of China, 1986. FRSA 1983; Fellow, Huguenot Soc., 1986. Hon. Fellow, Cumbria Inst. of Arts, 2005. Hon. MA Lancaster, 1997. Leverhulme Award (to continue research on Lake District portraits), 1986–88. *Publications:* The Art of the Felt Maker, 1979; Kurt Schwitters (in the Lake District), 1979; (with David Sloss) William Green of Ambleside, 1984; (with David Sloss) Read's Point of View, 1995; (with Val Rickerby) Percy Kelly: a Cumbrian artist, 1997; Sutton and his Circle: the Cockermouth School of painting 1750–1880, 2001; Christopher Steele 1733–67 of Acre Walls, Egremont, George Romney's Teacher, 2003; (with G. Malet de Carteret) The Beckoning East: a journey through Persia and Turkey in 1962, 2006; (with V. M. Rickenby) A Softer Landscape: the life and work of Jenny Cowen, 2007; contrib. art and archaeol jls, and gall. and museum catalogues. *Recreations:* travel, bird watching, photography, writing, doing research into more Cumbrian artists, lecturing, picking up stones. *Address:* Isel Hall, Cockermouth, Cumbria CA13 0QG.

BURKILL, Guy Alexander; QC 2002; *b* 5 March 1957; *s* of Arthur and Helen Burkill; *m* 1984, Lorely Claire Owen; two *s*. *Educ:* Winchester Coll.; Corpus Christi Coll., Cambridge (MA Engrg (Electrical option) 1st Cl. Hons). Called to the Bar, Middle Temple, 1981; in practice at Patent and Intellectual Property Bar, 1981–. *Publication:* (ed jtly) Terrell on the Law of Patents, 15th edn 2000, 16th edn 2005. *Recreations:* violin (performs with London Phoenix Orchestra), programming, trying to mend things. *Address:* 3 New Square, Lincoln's Inn, WC2A 3RS. *T:* (020) 7405 1111, *Fax:* (020) 7405 7800; *e-mail:* clerks@3newsquare.co.uk.

BURLAND, James Alan, RIBA; architect; Principal Partner, Burland TM, architects, since 2000; *b* 25 Sept. 1954; *s* of James Glyn Burland and late Elizabeth Beresford Thompson. *Educ:* King Henry VIII Sch., Coventry; Bath Univ. (BSc 1978; BArch 1980). RIBA 1983. Joined Arup Associates, 1978, Dir and Principal, 1994–2000; projects include: Stockley Park, Heathrow, 1983–2000; Eton Coll. Labs, 1984; Bedford High Sch. Sen. Sch., 1984–85; (with Philip Cox Architects, Sydney) Sydney Olympics 2000 Stadium Studies, 1985–90; City of Manchester Stadium, 1992–2000 (Consultant, 2000–); Plantation Place, Fenchurch Street, London, 1993–2000; Johannesburg Athletics Stadium, 1993–94; new coll., Durham Univ., 1994–2000; Crystal Palace Sports Complex, 1998; BP Solar Showcase G8 Summit, Arup campus building, Birmingham, 1998; private commn, design for Body Shop, including Bath and Brighton, 1982; Burland TM projects include: Ealing Studios, 2000–; Bermondsey Market, 2000–; Spitalfields Refuge and Convent restoration, 2000–; Falcon Wharf apartments, 2000–03; Harlequins RFC, 2002–; Pinewood and Shepperton Studios, 2003–; Billiardrome, 2003–; Portable Olympic Stadium studies, 2003–; Bristol Arena Quarter, 2005–. Bovis/Architects' Jl RA Summer Exhibn Grand Award, 1998. *Recreations:* music, cycle racing, art, architecture. *Address:* (office) 43–45 Charlotte Street, W1P 1HA. *T:* (020) 7255 2070; *e-mail:* jb@burlandtm.com. *Club:* Chelsea Arts.

BURLAND, Prof. John Boscawen, CBE 2005; FRS 1997; FREng; Professor of Soil Mechanics in the University of London, at Imperial College (formerly Imperial College of Science and Technology), 1980–2001, now Emeritus; *b* 4 March 1936; *s* of John Whitmore Burland and Margaret Irene Burland (*née* Boscawen); *m* 1963, Gillian Margaret, *d* of J. K. Miller; two *s* one *d*. *Educ:* Parktown Boys' High Sch., Johannesburg; Univ. of the Witwatersrand (BSc Eng, MSc Eng, DSc Eng); Univ. of Cambridge (PhD). MSAICE; FICE; FIStructE; FREng (FEng 1981). Res. Asst, Univ. of the Witwatersrand, 1960; Engineer, Ove Arup and Partners, London, 1961–63; Res. Student, Cambridge Univ., 63–66; Building Research Station: SSO and PSO, 1966–72; Head of Geotechnics Div., 1972–79; Asst Dir and Head of Materials and Structures Dept, 1979–80. Visiting Prof., Dept of Civil Engineering, Univ. of Strathclyde, 1973–82. Member: Adv. Panel to Sec. of State for Environment on Black Country Limestone, 1983–95; Italian Prime Minister's Commn for stabilising the Leaning Tower of Pisa, 1990–2001. Mem. Council, CIRIA, 1987–95 (Vice Pres., 1995–98); Official Visitor, BRE, 1990–97. Chm., Wheathampstead Churches Together, 1990–97. FIC 2004. Hon. Fellow: Emmanuel Coll., Cambridge, 2004; Cardiff Univ., 2005. Royal Academy of Engineering: Mem. Council, 1994–97; Public Promotion of Engrg Medal, 2006; Institution of Structural Engineers: Mem. of Council, 1979–82; Murray Buxton Silver Medal, 1977; Oscar Faber Bronze Medal, 1979; Gold Medal, 1998; named in Special Award to DoE for Underground Car Park at Palace of Westminster, 1975; Oscar Faber Diploma, 1982; Murray Buxton Diploma, 2002; Sir Arnold Walters Medal, 2006; Murray Buxton Medal, 2007; Institution of Civil Engineers: Vice Pres., 2003–05; Telford Premium, 1972, 1985, 1987; Coopers Hill War Meml Medal, 1985; Baker Medal, 1986; Kelvin Medal, for outstanding contribn to engrg, 1989; Gold Medal, 2001; Brit. Geotechnical Soc. Prize, 1968, 1971, 1974 and 1986; Kevin Nash Gold Medal, Internat. Soc. of Soil Mechanics and Foundn Engrs, 1994; H. Bolton Seed Medal, ASCE, 1996; Gold Medal, World Fedn of Engrg Orgns, 1997; Lord Lloyd of Kilgerran Prize, Foundn for Sci. and Technol., 2002; Dickinson Meml Medal, Newcomen Soc., 2007. Hon. Mem., Japanese Geotechnical Soc., 2005. Hon. DEng: Heriot-Watt, 1994; Glasgow, 2001; Hon. DSc: Nottingham, 1998; Warwick, 2003; Hon. DSc (Eng) Witwatersrand, 2007. Commendatore: Nostro Real Ordine di Francesco 1 (Italy), 2001; Ordine della Stella di Solidarietà Italiana, 2003. *Publications:* numerous papers on soil mechanics and civil engineering. *Recreations:* sailing, golf, painting.

BURLEIGH, Prof. Michael Christopher Bennet, PhD; FRHistS; Distinguished Visiting Fellow, Hoover Institution, Stanford University, since 2006; *b* 3 April 1955; *s* of late Wing Comdr B. G. S. Bennet Burleigh and C. Burleigh; *m* 1990, Linden Mary Brownbridge. *Educ:* University Coll. London (BA 1st Cl. Hons 1977); Bedford Coll., London (PhD 1982). FRHistS 1988. Weston Jun. Res. Fellow, New Coll., Oxford, 1984–87; British Acad. Post-doctoral Fellow, QMC, 1987–88; London School of Economics and Political Science: Lectr, 1988–93; Reader in Internat. Hist., 1993–95; Dist. Res. Prof. in Modern European Hist., Cardiff Univ., 1995–2001. Raoul Wallenberg Vis. Prof. of Human Rights, Rutgers Univ., 1999–2000; William R. Kenan Jr Prof. of Hist., Washington & Lee Univ., 2001–02; Kratter Vis. Prof. of Hist., Stanford Univ., 2003. Cardinal Basil Hume Meml Lectr, Heythrop Coll., 2002; Fisher Lect., Cambridge Univ., 2007. Mem., Academic Adv. Council, Inst. für Zeitgeschichte, Munich, 2004–. Ed., Totalitarian Movements and Political Religions, 2000–05. Writer and presenter, Dark Enlightenment, TV prog., 2006. Chm., Judging Panel, Hessell-Tiltman Prize for

History, PEN Foundn, 2003. Award for Archival Achievement, BFI, 1991; Bronze Medal, NY Film and TV Fest., 1994. *Publications:* Prussian Society and the German Order, 1984; Germany Turns Eastwards, 1988; The Racial State: Germany 1933–45, 1991 (trans. Italian, Japanese); Death and Deliverance: euthanasia in Germany, 1994 (trans. German); (ed) Confronting the Nazi Past, 1996 (trans. Hungarian); Ethics and Extermination: reflections on Nazi genocide, 1997; The Third Reich: a new history, 2000 (Samuel Johnson Prize, 2001) (trans. Estonian, German, Italian, Finnish, French, Spanish, Czech, Hebrew, Polish); Earthly Powers: religion and politics in Europe from the French Revolution to the Great War, 2005 (trans. German, Italian, Spanish, Dutch, French); Sacred Causes: religion and politics from the European dictators to Al-Qaeda, 2006 (trans. Dutch, German, Italian, Spanish, French); Blood and Rage: a cultural history of terrorism, 2008 (trans. Dutch, Danish, German, Italian, Spanish, French). *Recreation:* gardening. *Address:* c/o Wylie Agency Ltd, 17 Bedford Square, WC1B 3JA. *Club:* Athenæum.

BURLEY, Helen; *see* Boaden, H.

BURLEY, Prof. Jeffery, CBE 1991; PhD; Professor of Forestry, 1996–2002, Director, Oxford Forestry Institute, 1985–2002, Oxford University; Professorial Fellow, Green Templeton College (formerly Green College), Oxford, since 1981 (Vice-Warden, 1997–2002; Development Fellow, 2003–07); *b* 16 Oct. 1936; *s* of Jack Burley and Eliza Burley (*née* Creese); *m* 1961, Jean Shirley (*née* Palmer); two *s*. *Educ:* Portsmouth Grammar Sch.; New College, Oxford (BA 1961); Yale (MF 1962; PhD 1965). Lieut, Royal Signals, 1954–57. O i/c and Unesco Expert, Forest Genetics Res. Lab., ARC of Central Africa, 1965–69; Sen. Res. Officer, Commonwealth Forestry Inst., Oxford, 1969–76; Univ. Lectr, 1976–83, Head of Dept of Forestry, 1983–85, Oxford. Pres., Internat. Union of Forestry Res. Orgns, 1996–2000; Chairman: Tropical Forest Resource Gp, 1994–2006; Marcus Wallenberg Prize Selection Cttee, Stockholm, 1998–2006; Commonwealth Forestry Assoc., 2002–05. Chm. Bd, C-Questor plc, 2005–. Mem. Bd, Marcus Wallenberg Foundn, 2006–. Patron, Speedwell and WellBeing Trust, 2000–. Internat. Fellow, Royal Swedish Acad. of Agriculture and Forestry, 1998; Hon. FICFor, 2003; Hon. Fellow, Soc. of Amer. Foresters, 2003. Hon. DSc CATIE, Costa Rica. Ed. in Chief, Encyclopedia of Forest Scis, 2004. *Publications:* (ed jtly) Multipurpose tree germplasm, 1984; (ed jtly) Increasing productivity of multipurpose species, 1985; many book chapters resulting from conference papers; many contribs to periodicals and learned jls on forestry, agroforestry and forest tree breeding. *Recreations:* beekeeping, cricket, gardening. *Address:* Green Templeton College, Woodstock Road, Oxford OX2 6HG. *T:* (01865) 274775.

BURLEY, Lindsay Elizabeth, FRCPE, FRCGP; Chairman, National Waiting Times Centre Board for Scotland, since 2003; *b* Blackpool, 2 Oct. 1950; *d* of William and Elizabeth Lamont; *m* 1972, Robin Burley. *Educ:* Edinburgh Univ. (MB ChB 1973). FRCPE 1985; FRCGP 1995. Sen. Lectr, Univ. of Edinburgh, 1982–87, Hon. Sen. Lectr, 1991–. Consultant Physician, 1982–91, Dir of Planning and Develt, 1991–95, Lothian Health Bd; Chief Exec., Borders Health Bd, 1995–2003. Non-exec. Dir, NHS Educn for Scotland, 2002–. Mem., SFC, 2006–. Partner, Eskhill & Co., 2003–. *Recreations:* gardening, ski-ing, piano playing. *Address:* Eskhill & Co., Eskhill House, 15 Inveresk Village, Musselburgh EH21 7TD. *T:* (0131) 271 4000, 07831 605858; *e-mail:* lindsay@eskhill.com.

BURLIN, Prof. Terence Eric; Rector, University of Westminster (formerly Polytechnic of Central London), 1984–95, Professor Emeritus, 1996; *b* 24 Sept. 1931; *s* of Eric Jonas Burlin and Winifred Kate (*née* Thomas); *m* 1957, Plessey Pamela Carpenter; one *s* one *d*. *Educ:* Acton County School; University of Southampton (BSc); Univ. of London (DSc, PhD, BSc). CPhys, FInstP 1969; FIBiotech 1992. Physicist, Mount Vernon Hosp. and Radium Inst., 1953–57; Sen. Physicist, Hammersmith Hosp., 1957–62; Principal Physicist, St John's Hosp. for Diseases of the Skin, 1960–90; Polytechnic of Central London: Sen. Lectr, 1962; Reader, 1969; Pro-Director, 1971; Sen. Pro-Rector, 1982; Acting Rector, 1982. British Cttee on Radiation Units and Measurements: Mem., 1966–74 and 1979–95; Vice-Chm., 1983–84; Chm., 1984–95; Member: Council, Inst. for Study of Drug Dependence, 1974–86; various Boards, CNAA; Cttee on Practical Determination of Dose Equivalent, Internat. Commn on Radiation Units and Measurements (Chm.), 1979–87; Adv. Council on Adult and Continuing Educn, DES, 1980–83; Cttee on Effects of Ionising Radiation, Physics and Dosimetry Sub-Cttee, MRC, 1983–86; Science Bd, SERC, 1986–89. Mem. Council, BTEC, 1984–86. Member: Council, Westminster Chamber of Commerce, 1994–95; Employment Affairs Cttee, 1994–95, Commercial Educn Trust, 1996–2002, London Chamber of Commerce and Industry. Mem. Bd, Bournemouth Univ., 1996–2002. Hon. FCP 1990. Hon. DSc Westminster, 1996. *Publications:* chapters in Radiation Dosimetry, 1968, 2nd edn 1972; papers on radiation dosimetry, radiological protection, biomechanical properties of skin, radiobiology. *Recreations:* music, swimming. *Club:* Athenæum.

BURLINGTON, Earl of; William Cavendish; photographer; *b* 6 June 1969; *s* and *heir* of Duke of Devonshire, *qv*. *Address:* c/o Chatsworth, Bakewell, Derbyshire DE45 1PP.

BURMAN, Roger Stephen, CBE 1991; DL; Chairman, since 1976, and Managing Director, since 1973, Teledictor; *b* 3 April 1940; *s* of Sir Stephen France Burman, CBE and Lady (Joan Margaret) Burman; *m* 1964, Felicity Jane Crook; four *s*. *Educ:* Oundle Sch.; Univ. of Birmingham (BSc Hon.). Burman & Sons, 1961–72 (Dir, 1965–72); Teledictor, 1972–. Chairman: Nat. Exhibn Centre, 1989–2005 (Dir, 1984–2005); Performances Birmingham Ltd (formerly Symphony Hall (Birmingham) Ltd), 1991–; Director: Black Country Develt Corp., 1992–98; Chrysalis Radio (Midlands), 2001–04; Baugh & Weedon Ltd, 2004–. Gen. Tax Comr, 1973–. Member: British Hallmarking Council, 1980–2006 (Chm., 1989–97); BOTB, 1990–94 and 1996–99; Council, ICC, 1990–2006; Pres., Birmingham Chamber of Commerce, 1984–85; Chm., Assoc. of British Chambers of Commerce, 1988–90. Guardian, 1965–, Chm., 2000–06, Birmingham Assay Office. University of Birmingham: Life Governor, 1983–; Pro-Chancellor, 1994–2001. Liveryman, Goldsmiths' Co., 1993–. DL 1991, High Sheriff 1999, W Midlands. Hon. LLD Birmingham, 1994. *Recreation:* golf. *Address:* Astwood Hill House, Astwood Lane, Astwood Bank, Redditch, Worcs B96 6PT. *T:* (01522) 893951.

BURN, Adrian; *see* Burn, B. A. F.

BURN, Angus Maitland P.; *see* Pelham Burn.

BURN, (Bryan) Adrian (Falconer); *b* 23 May 1945; *s* of Peter and Ruth Burn; *m* 1968, Jeanette Carol; one *s* three *d*. *Educ:* Abingdon Sch. FCA. Whinney Murray, 1963–72; joined Binder Hamlyn, 1972; seconded to DTI, 1975–77; Partner, 1977, Managing Partner, 1988–94, Binder Hamlyn; Partner, Arthur Andersen, 1994–99. Non-executive Chairman: Atlas Gp Hldgs, 1999–2002; Search Holdings Ltd, 2000–06; non-executive Director: Sinclair-Stevenson Ltd, 1990–92; Brent Internat. plc, 1994–99; GE Capital Bank Ltd, 1999–; Pinewood-Shepperton Plc, 2000–; Wolff Olins Ltd, 1999–2001; Strutt and Parker, 1999–2006; Richards Butler, 1999–2006; Smart and Cook Hldgs Ltd, 2004–07; Acentec plc, 2006–. Mem., Financial Adjudication Panel, Second Severn Crossing, 1991–98. Trustee and Hon. Treas., NSPCC, 1999–2008. *Address:* 13 Woodthorpe Road, Putney, SW15 6UQ. *T:* (020) 8788 6383; *e-mail:* email@adrianburn.com. *Club:* Roehampton.

BURN, Prof. John, MD; FRCP, FRCPE, FRCOG, FRCPCH, FMedSci; Professor of Clinical Genetics, since 1991, and Head, Institute of Human Genetics, since 2005, University of Newcastle upon Tyne; *b* 6 Feb. 1952; *s* of Harry and Margaret Burn; *m* 1972, Linda M. Wilson; one *s* one *d*. *Educ:* Barnard Castle Grammar Sch.; Newcastle upon Tyne Univ. (BMedSci 1973; MB BS 1976; MD 1990). FRCP 1989; FRCPCH 1996; FRCOG 1998; FRCPE 2001. Professional trng in medicine and paediatrics, Royal Victoria Infirmary, Newcastle Gen. Hosp., Freeman Hosp., Newcastle, 1976–80; Sen. Registrar, Hosp. for Sick Children, Gt Ormond St, and Clinical Scientific Officer, MRC Genetics Unit, Inst. of Child Health, 1980–84; Consultant Clinical Geneticist, Royal Victoria Infirmary, Newcastle upon Tyne, 1984–91. Mem., Human Genetics Commn, 1989–2005. FMedSci 2000. *Publications:* numerous peer-reviewed contribs in field of clinical genetics with particular interest in birth defects and hereditary cancers. *Recreations:* playing the drums, running, reading, golf. *Address:* 18 Sanderson Road, Jesmond, Newcastle upon Tyne NE2 2DS. *T:* (0191) 241 8611; *e-mail:* john.burn@ncl.ac.uk.

BURN, Lindsay Stuart; His Honour Judge Burn; a Circuit Judge, since 2003; *b* 29 Aug. 1948; *m* 1975, Hon. Anne-Catherine, *d* of Baron Wilberforce, CMG, OBE, PC; one *s* two *d*. *Educ:* Newcastle upon Tyne Univ. (LLB Hons). Called to the Bar, Middle Temple, 1972; barrister, 1972–2003; Asst Recorder, 1995–99, Recorder, 1999–2003; Standing Counsel to DTI, SE Circuit, 1995–2003. *Recreations:* photography, historical novels. *Address:* c/o Court Service, Rose Court, 2 Southwark Bridge, SE1 9HS.

BURN, Michael Clive, MC 1945; writer; *b* 11 Dec. 1912; *s* of late Sir Clive Burn and Phyllis Stoneham; *m* 1947, Mary Booker (*née* Walter) (*d* 1974); no *c*. *Educ:* Winchester; New Coll., Oxford (open scholar); Hons Degree in Soc. Scis, Oxford, 1945, with distinction in all subjects (awarded whilst POW at Colditz). Journalist, The Times, 1936–39; Lieut 1st Bn Queens Westminsters, KRRC, 1939–40; Officer in Independent Companies, Norwegian Campaign, 1940, subseq. Captain No. 2 Commando; taken prisoner in raid on St Nazaire, 1942; prisoner in Germany, 1942–45. Foreign Correspondent for The Times in Vienna, Jugoslavia and Hungary, 1946–49. Mem., Welsh Acad., 2006. Keats Poetry First Prize, 1973. Légion d'Honneur, 5th class (France), 2006. *Plays:* The Modern Everyman (prod. Birmingham Rep., 1947); Beyond the Storm (Midlands Arts Co., and Vienna, 1947); The Night of the Ball (prod. New Theatre, 1956). *Publications: novels:* Yes, Farewell, 1946, repr. 1975; Childhood at Oriol, 1951; The Midnight Diary, 1952; The Trouble with Jake, 1967; *sociological:* Mr Lyward's Answer, 1956; The Debatable Land, 1970; *poems:* Poems to Mary, 1953; The Flying Castle, 1954; Out On A Limb, 1973; Open Day and Night, 1978; *play:* The Modern Everyman, 1948; *non-fiction:* Mary and Richard, 1988; Turned Towards the Sun (autobiog.), 2003; Poems as Accompaniment to a Life, 2006. *Address:* Beudy Gwyn, Minffordd, Gwynedd, N Wales LL48 6EN.

BURN, Rear Adm. Richard Hardy, CB 1992; AFC 1969; Director General Aircraft (Navy), Ministry of Defence, 1990–92; *b* 26 May 1938; *s* of Margaret (*née* Hardy) and Douglas Burn; *m* 1967, Judith Sanderson (*née* Tigg); one *s* one *d*, and one step *s* one step *d*. *Educ:* Berkhamsted; BRNC Dartmouth; RNEC Manadon. MIMechE. HMS Broadsword 1958, fighter pilot, 890 Naval Air Sqdn, HMS Ark Royal, 1961–62; test flying work (incl. 3 years exchange, US Navy), NDC Latimer, to 1975; develt of Sea Harrier, MoD (PE), 1975–78; Ops Officer, A&AEE, 1978–79; Air Eng. Officer, RNAS Yeovilton, 1980; Asst Dir Eng. (N), MoD, 1981–84; RCDS 1985; Dir, Aircraft Maint. and Repair, MoD (N), 1986–87; Dir, Helicopter Projects, MoD (PE), and ADC, 1988–90. Chm., Thomas Heatherley Educnl Trust, 2003–. Mem., Soc. of Experimental Test Pilots. FRAeS 1984. Commendation, US Navy, 1974; Médaille d'Honneur, Soc. d'Encouragement au Progrès, 1989. *Recreations:* ski-ing, golf, painting.

BURNE, Dr Yvonne Ann, OBE 2008; Head, City of London School for Girls, 1995–2007; *b* 29 Aug. 1947; *d* of Archibald Ford and Florence Louise Ford (*née* Knott); *m* 1968, Anthony Richard Burne; one *s* one *d*. *Educ:* Redland High Sch. for Girls, Bristol; Westfield Coll., Univ. of London (BA Hons; PhD). School teacher: Harrow Co. Grammar Sch. for Girls, 1971–74; Lowlands Sixth Form Coll., 1974–77; Hd, Mod. Langs and Careers Guidance, Northwood Coll., 1984–87; Headmistress, St Helen's Sch. for Girls, Northwood, 1987–95. Editor: Educnl Challenges Inc. (VA, USA), 1978–82; Mary Glasgow Pubns, 1983–84; Heinemann Educnl Books, 1984. Mem., Hillingdon FHSA, 1990–96. FRSA 1991. *Publications:* Tomorrow's News, 1979; The Circus Comes to Town, 1979; articles and children's stories. *Recreations:* theatre, entertaining friends, walking.

BURNELL, Dame (Susan) Jocelyn B.; *see* Bell Burnell.

BURNELL-NUGENT, Adm. Sir James (Michael), KCB 2004; CBE 1999; Commander-in-Chief Fleet, and NATO Maritime Component Commander Northwood, 2005–07; Vice-Admiral of the United Kingdom, 2005–07; *b* 20 Nov. 1949; *s* of late Comdr Anthony Frank Burnell-Nugent, DSC, RN and Gian Burnell-Nugent; *m* 1973, Henrietta Mary, (DL, MA, MB BChir), *d* of Rt Rev. R. W. Woods, KCMG, KCVO; three *s* one *d*. *Educ:* Stowe; Corpus Christi Coll., Cambridge (MA Hons; Hon. Fellow, 2006). Joined RN, 1971; BRNC Dartmouth (Queen's Gold Medal); Submarines, 1973–86; Max Horton Prize, 1974; CO HMS Olympus, 1979–80; CO HMS Conqueror, 1984–86; Comdr, 1985; Captain, 1990; Captain, F2 and CO HMS Brilliant, (Bosnia), 1992–93; Cdre, 1994; on secondment to HM Treasury, 1996; Dep. FO Surface Flotilla, 1997; CO HMS Invincible, (Gulf, Kosovo), 1997–99; Rear Adm., 1999; ACNS, MoD, 1999–2001; Mem., Admiralty Bd, 1999–2001 and 2005–07; Dep. Coalition Maritime Comdr, (Op. Enduring Freedom), 2001–02; Comdr UK Maritime Forces, and Comdr Anti Submarine Warfare Striking Force, 2001–02; Second Sea Lord and C-in-C Naval Home Comd, Mem. of Admiralty Bd, and Flag ADC to the Queen, 2003–05. Dir, Orchard Leadership Ltd, 2008–; Trustee and Dir, Plymouth Marine Lab., 2008–. Internat. Advr, Shell Shipping, 2008–; Strategic Advr, Evercore Partners, 2008–; Associate, Hitachi Consulting, 2008–. Gov., Stowe, 2008–. Comp. Inst. of Leadership and Mgt, 2006. Freeman, City of London, 1999. Younger Brother, Trinity House, 2004. *Publications:* pamphlets incl. Leadership in the Office, Keeping an Eye on the Cost of Government; numerous articles in Naval Review and RUSI Jl. *Recreation:* living in the country. *Address:* c/o Naval Secretary, Leach Building, Whale Island, Portsmouth, Hants PO2 8BY. *Club:* Cychod Trefdraeth.

BURNER, (Edward) Alan; HM Diplomatic Service, retired; Ambassador to Senegal and, concurrently, to Guinea Bissau, Cape Verde and Mali, 2000–04; *b* 26 Sept. 1944; *s* of late Douglas Keith Burner and of Mary Burner; *m* 1969, Jane Georgine Du Port; one *s* two *d*. *Educ:* Uppingham Sch., Rutland; Emmanuel Coll., Cambridge (MA Hons Mod. Langs). Volunteer, Nigeria, VSO, 1966–67; joined HM Diplomatic Service, 1967: Sofia, 1970–72; Bonn, 1972–74; Bridgetown, 1974–78; N America Dept, FCO, 1979; Asst Private Sec. to Minister for Overseas Develt, 1979–82; Dep. Head of Recruitment, FCO, 1982–84; Dep. Hd of Mission, Sofia, 1984–87; on loan to ODA, 1987–90; Hd, Med.

Welfare Unit, FCO, 1990–92; Commercial Counsellor, then Dep. Hd of Mission, Lagos, 1992–95; Consul-Gen., Munich, 1995–99. *Recreations:* tennis, walking. *Address:* 12 Hillside Road, Sevenoaks, Kent TN13 3XJ. *T:* (01732) 453885.

BURNET, George Wardlaw, LVO 1981; JP; Lord-Lieutenant of Midlothian, 1992–2002; *b* 26 Dec. 1927; *s* of late Sheriff John Rudolph Wardlaw Burnet, KC and Lucy Margaret Ord Burnet (*née* Wallace); *m* 1951, Jane Elena Moncrieff, *d* of late Malcolm Moncrieff Stuart, CIE, OBE; two *s* one *d*. *Educ:* Edinburgh Acad.; Lincoln Coll., Oxford (BA); Edinburgh Univ. (LLB). Served Black Watch (RHR) TA, retired as Captain, 1957. WS 1954; Partner, Murray Beith and Murray, 1956–90. County Councillor, Midlothian, 1967–76; Elder, 1961–, Convener, Gen. Finance Cttee, 1980–83, Church of Scotland. Chairman: Life Assoc. of Scotland, 1985–93; Caledonian Res. Foundn, 1989–99. Captain, Royal Company of Archers, Queen's Body Guard for Scotland, 2004–. Hon. FRIAS 1980. DL 1975, JP 1991, Midlothian. KStJ. *Recreations:* country pursuits, architecture, gardening. *Address:* Rose Court, Inveresk, Midlothian EH21 7TD. *T:* (0131) 665 2689. *Club:* New (Edinburgh).

BURNET, Sir James William Alexander, (Sir Alastair Burnet), Kt 1984; journalist; *b* 12 July 1928; *s* of late Alexander and Schonaid Burnet, Edinburgh; *m* 1958, Maureen Campbell Sinclair. *Educ:* The Leys Sch., Cambridge; Worcester Coll., Oxford. Sub-editor and leader writer, Glasgow Herald, 1951–58; Commonwealth Fund Fellow, 1956–57; Leader writer, The Economist, 1958–62; Political editor, Independent Television News, 1963–64; Editor, The Economist, 1965–74; Editor, Daily Express, 1974–76; broadcaster with ITN, 1976–91; Assoc. Editor, News at Ten, 1982–91. Ind. Dir, Times Newspapers Hldgs Ltd, 1982–2002; Dir, United Racecourses Hldgs Ltd, 1985–94. Member: Cttee of Award, Commonwealth Fund, 1969–76; Cttee on Reading and Other Uses of English Language, 1972–75; Monopolies Commn specialist panel on newspaper mergers, 1973–91; Council, Banking Ombudsman, 1985–96; Hon. Vice-Pres., Inst. of Journalists, 1990. Richard Dimbleby Award, BAFTA, 1966, 1970, 1979; Judges' Award, 1981, Hall of Fame, 1999, RTS. *Address:* 43 Hornton Court, Campden Hill Road, W8 7NT. *T:* (020) 7937 7563.

BURNET, John Elliot; Chief Executive, Cumbria County Council, 1991–97; *b* 13 Jan. 1947; *m* 1991, Deirdre Eleanor Elizabeth Burton. *Educ:* Barnard Castle Sch.; Nottingham Univ. (BA Law); College of Law, London. Articled, S Shields CBC (Clerk/Asst Solicitor), 1969–73; Sen. Asst Solicitor, S Tyneside MBC, 1973–74; Asst County Clerk, Tyne and Wear CC, 1974–82; Cumbria County Council: Sen. Asst Clerk and Dep. Co. Solicitor, 1982–86; Dir, Econ. Develt and Corporate Policy, 1986–90; Asst Chief Exec., 1990–91. *Recreations:* watching sport, archaeology, historic buildings.

BURNETT, family name of **Baron Burnett**.

BURNETT, Baron *cr* 2006 (Life Peer), of Whitchurch in the County of Devon; **John Patrick Aubone Burnett;** Consultant, Stephens & Scown, since 2005; *b* 19 Sept. 1945; *s* of late Lt-Col Aubone Burnett, OBE and Joan (*née* Bolt); *m* 1971, Elizabeth Sherwood, *d* of Sir Arthur de la Mare, KCMG, KCVO; two *s* two *d*. *Educ:* Ampleforth Coll., Yorks; Britannia RNC, Dartmouth; Coll. of Law, London. Served RM, 1964–70: Troop Comdr, 42 Commando RM, Borneo, 1965–66; Troop Comdr and Co. 2nd in command, 40 Commando RM, FE and ME, 1967–69. Farmer, 1976–98. Admitted Solicitor, 1975; Partner, then Sen. Partner, Burd Pearse, Okehampton, 1976–97. Mem., Law Soc. Revenue Law Cttee, 1984–96. Contested (Lib Dem) Devon West and Torridge, 1987. MP (Lib Dem) Devon West and Torridge, 1997–2005. Lib Dem spokesman on legal affairs, 1997–2002; Lib Dem Shadow Attorney Gen., 2002–05. Mem. Council, Devon Cattle Breeders' Soc., 1985–97 (winner Nat. Herd competition, 1989). *Address:* Stephens & Scown, Curzon House, Southernhay West, Exeter EX1 1RS.

BURNETT, of Leys, Baronetcy of (unclaimed); *see under* Ramsay, Sir Alexander William Burnett, 7th Bt.

BURNETT, Prof. Alan Kenneth, MBE 2008; MD; FRCPGlas, FRCPE, FRCP, FRCPath, FMedSci; Professor of Haematology, Cardiff University (formerly University of Wales College of Medicine), since 1992; *b* 27 May 1946; *s* of George Binnie Burnett and Janet Maloch Burnett (*née* Henderson); *m* 1971, Alison Forrester Liddell; two *s*. *Educ:* Glasgow Acad.; Univ. of Glasgow (ChB; MD Hons 1988). FRCPGlas 1984; FRCPath 1986; FRCPE 1988; FRCP 1993. Res. Fellow, Univ. of Chicago, 1975–76; Consultant Haematologist, Glasgow Royal Infirmary, 1979–92. Visiting Professor: Univ. of Miami, 1994; Northwestern Univ., Chicago, 1999; Univ. of Kuwait, 2000. Chairman: MRC Adult Leukaemia Wkg Party, 1990–; Nat. Cancer Res. Network Gp for Haematolog. Oncology, 2002–; Mem., Med. Advisory Panel, Leukaemia Res. Fund, 1989–93. Pres., British Soc. of Haematol., 1998–99. FMedSci 2000. *Publications:* contrib. papers to medical literature on the subject of leukaemia and bone marrow transplantation. *Recreations:* golf, DIY, irritating NHS overheads. *Address:* 1 Minorca Cottages, Michaelston-Y-Fedw, Cardiff CF3 6XX.

BURNETT, Dr Andrew Michael, FBA 2003; FSA; Deputy Director, British Museum, since 2003; *b* 23 May 1952; *s* of Sir John (Harrison) Burnett and of E. Margaret Burnett, *er d* of Rev. Dr E. W. Bishop; *m* 1978, Susan Jennifer Allix; two *d*. *Educ:* Fettes Coll., Edinburgh; Balliol Coll., Oxford (BA, MA); Inst. of Archaeology, Univ. of London (PhD). Department of Coins and Medals, British Museum: Res. Assistant, 1974–79; Asst Keeper, 1979–90; Dep. Keeper, 1990–92; Keeper, 1992–2003. Secretary: RNS, 1983–90 (Vice-Pres., 1999–2004); Internat. Numismatic Commn, 1992–97 (Pres., 1997–2003). Corresponding Member: Amer. Numismatic Soc., 1982; German Archaeol. Inst., 2001. FSA 1982. Norwegian Numismatic Soc. Medal, 1991; Silver Medal, RNS, 1993; Prix Allier de Hauteroche, Acad. des Inscriptions et Belles-Lettres, 1999; Meshorer Prize, Israel Mus., 2002; Jeton de Vermeil, Soc. Française de Numismatique, 2004; Huntington Medal, Amer. Numismatic Soc., 2008. *Publications:* Coinage in the Roman World, 1987; Interpreting the Past: Coins, 1991; Roman Provincial Coinage, Vol. 1, 1992, Vol. 2, 1999; Behind the Scenes at the British Museum, 2001; contrib. Numismatic Chronicle, Schweizerische Numismatisches Rundschau, Quaderni Ticinesi, Jl Roman Studies, Britannia, etc. *Address:* British Museum, WC1B 3DG. *T:* (020) 7323 8241.

BURNETT, Air Chief Marshal Sir Brian (Kenyon), GCB 1970 (KCB 1965; CB 1961); DFC 1942; AFC 1939; RAF, retired; Chairman, All England Lawn Tennis Club, Wimbledon, 1974–83; *b* 10 March 1913; *s* of late Kenneth Burnett and Anita Catherine Burnett (*née* Evans); *m* 1944, Valerie Mary (*née* St Ludger) (*d* 2003); two *s*. *Educ:* Charterhouse; Wadham Coll., Oxford (BA 1934; Hon. Fellow, 1974). Joined RAFO 1932; RAF 1934; Long Distance Record Flight of 7,158 miles from Egypt to Australia, Nov. 1938. Served War of 1939–45, in Bomber Command, incl. CO 51 Sqdn, 1942, and FTC; Co. 33 Air Navigation Sch., RAF Mounthope, Canada, 1942–43; SASO 25 Gp, 1944; Directing Staff, RAF Staff Coll., 1945–47; UN Military Staff Cttee, New York, 1947–48; Joint Planning Staff, 1949–50; SASO HQ No. 3 (Bomber) Group, 1951–53; CORAF Gaydon, 1954–55; ADC to the Queen, 1953–57; Director of Bomber and Reconnaissance Ops, Air Ministry, 1956–57; Imperial Defence Coll., 1958; Air Officer Administration, HQ Bomber Command, 1959–61; AOC No 3 Gp, Bomber Command, 1961–64; Vice-Chief of the Air Staff, 1964–67; Air Secretary, MoD, 1967–70; C-in-C, Far East Command, Singapore, 1970–71; retired 1972. Air ADC to the Queen, 1969–72. Pres., Squash Rackets Assoc., 1972–75. *Recreations:* tennis, squash rackets, golf, ski-ing. *Address:* Heather Hill, Littleworth Cross, Sands, Farnham, Surrey GU10 1JN. *Clubs:* Royal Air Force; Vincent's (Oxford); All England Lawn Tennis (Vice-Pres., 1983–); Jesters Squash; International Lawn Tennis Clubs of Great Britain, USA, France, Australia, The Netherlands, Spain and Japan.

BURNETT, Sir Charles (David), 4th Bt *cr* 1913, of Selborne House, in the Borough of Croydon; *b* 18 May 1951; *er s* of Sir David Humphery Burnett, 3rd Bt, MBE, TD and Geraldine Elizabeth Mortimer, *d* of Sir Godfrey Fisher, KCMG; *S* father, 2002; *m* 1st, 1989, Victoria Joan Simpson (marr. diss. 1997); one *d*; 2nd, 1998, Kay Rosemary Naylor; one *d*. *Educ:* Harrow; Lincoln Coll., Oxford. *Heir: b* John Godfrey Burnett, *b* 29 March 1954.

BURNETT, Charles John, FSAScot; Ross Herald, since 1988 (Dingwall Pursuivant, 1983); *b* 6 Nov. 1940; *s* of Charles Alexander Urquhart Burnett and Agnes Watt; *m* 1967, Aileen Elizabeth McIntyre; two *s* one *d*. *Educ:* Fraserburgh Academy; Gray's Sch. of Art, Aberdeen (DA); Aberdeen Coll. of Education (Teaching Cert.); MLitt Edinburgh 1992. AMA; FHS Scot. House of Fraser, 1963–64; COI, 1964–68; Asst Dir, Letchworth Mus., 1968–71; Head of Design, Nat. Mus. of Antiquities of Scotland, 1971–85; Curator of Fine Art, Scottish United Services Mus., Edinburgh Castle, 1985–96; Chamberlain, Duff House Country Gall., Banff, 1997–2004. Heraldic Adviser: Girl Guide Assoc. in Scotland, 1978–; NADFAS Church Recorders, Scotland, 2000–; Chm., Banff Preservation and Heritage Soc., 2002–. Vice-Patron, Geneal. Soc. of Queensland, 1986–; Vice-Pres., Soc. of Antiquaries of Scotland, 1992–95; Trustee, St Andrews Fund for Scots Heraldry, 2001–; Pres., Heraldry Soc. of Scotland, 2003–. Pres., Internat. Congress of Geneal and Heraldic Scis, St Andrews, 2006. Trustee, Bield Retirement Housing Trust, 1992–96. Convenor, Companions of the Order of Malta, 1991–94. KStJ 1991; Librarian, Priory of Order of St John in Scotland, 1987–99. Hon. Citizen, Oklahoma, 1989. Kt, Order of SS Maurice and Lazarus, 1999; Kt, Order of Francis I, 2002. *Publications:* Scotland's Heraldic Heritage, 1997; The Order of St John in Scotland, 1997; Thistle Stall Plates, 2001; numerous articles on Scottish heraldry. *Recreations:* reading, visiting places of historical interest. *Address:* Seaview House, Portsoy, Banffshire AB45 2RS. *T:* (01261) 843378.

BURNETT, Prof. Charles Stuart Freeman, PhD; FBA 1998; Professor of the History of Islamic Influences in Europe, Warburg Institute, University of London, since 1999 (Lecturer, 1985–99); *b* 26 Sept. 1951; *m* 1st, 1985, Mitsuri Kamachi (marr. diss. 1991); 2nd, 1995, Tamae Nakamura; two *s*. *Educ:* Manchester Grammar Sch.; St John's Coll., Cambridge (BA 1972; PhD 1976). LGSM 1980. Jun. Res. Fellow, St John's Coll., Cambridge, 1975–79; Sen. Res. Fellow, Warburg Inst., Univ. of London, 1979–82; Leverhulme Res. Fellow, Dept of History, Univ. of Sheffield, 1982–84, 1985; Mem., Inst. for Advanced Study, Princeton, 1984–85. Dist. Vis. Prof., Univ. of Calif, Berkeley, 2003. Corresp. Mem., Internat. Acad. of History of Science. *Publications:* (with Masahiro Takenaka) Jesuit Plays on Japan and English Recusancy, 1995; Magic and Divination in the Middle Ages: texts and techniques in the Islamic and Christian worlds, 1996; The Introduction of Arabic Learning into England, 1997; several edns of Latin and Arabic texts; over 100 articles in learned jls. *Recreations:* playing music (viola, piano, viola da gamba, shakuhachi), hill walking, religious activities (Iona community, Japanese Buddhist and Shinto traditions). *Address:* Warburg Institute, Woburn Square, WC1H 0AB. *T:* (020) 7862 8920.

BURNETT, Hon. Sir Ian Duncan, Kt 2008; **Hon. Mr Justice Burnett;** a Judge of the High Court of Justice, Queen's Bench Division, since 2008; *b* 28 Feb. 1958; *yr s* of late David John Burnett and of Maureen Burnett (*née* O'Brien); *m* 1991, Caroline Ruth Monks; one *s* one *d*. *Educ:* St John's Coll., Southsea; Pembroke Coll., Oxford (MA; Hon. Fellow). Called to the Bar, Middle Temple, 1980, Bencher, 2001; Jun. Crown Counsel, Common Law, 1992–98; QC 1998; Asst Recorder, 1998–2000; Recorder, 2000–08; Hd of Chambers, 2003–08. *Recreations:* history, music, silver, wine. *Address:* Royal Courts of Justice, Strand, WC2A 2LL.

BURNETT, Prof. Keith, CBE 2004; DPhil; FRS 2001; FInstP; Vice-Chancellor, University of Sheffield, since 2007; *b* 30 Sept. 1953; *s* of Royston Ifor Burnett and Jean Marion Burnett; *m* 1975, Elizabeth Anne Mustoe; one *s* one *d*. *Educ:* Brynteg Comprehensive Sch.; Jesus Coll., Oxford (BA 1975; DPhil 1979; Hon. Fellow, 2007). FInstP 1996. Asst Prof., Univ. of Colorado, 1980–84; Fellow, Jt Inst. for Lab. Astrophysics, Colorado Univ. and Nat. Inst. of Standards and Technol., 1981–84; Lectr in Physics, Imperial Coll., London, 1984–88; Oxford University: Lectr in Physics, 1988–96; Prof., 1996–2007; Hd of Atomic and Laser Physics, 1999–2002; Chm. of Physics, 2002–05; Hd of Math., Physical and Life Scis Div., 2005–07; Fellow, St John's Coll., Oxford, 1988–2007, now Hon. Fellow. Member: EPSRC, 1999–2004; CCLRC, 2005–07; STFC, 2007–08. Fellow: APS, 1996; Optical Soc. of America, 1996. Wolfson Merit Award, Royal Soc., 2003. *Publications:* articles in learned jls, incl. Physical Review, Jl Physics B. *Recreations:* reading, music, Chinese. *Address:* University of Sheffield, Firth Court, Western Bank, Sheffield S10 2TN.

BURNETT, Sir Walter (John), Kt 1988; President, Royal National Agricultural and Industrial Association of Queensland, 1983–97; *b* 15 Jan. 1921; *s* of William Henry and Minna Anna Burnett; *m* 1945, Mabel Nestor Dalton; two *d*. *Educ:* Maleny Primary School; Church of England Grammar School; Pharmacy College, Queensland. Conducted own pharmacy business in Maleny for 32 years. Dir, Sunshine Coast Hosps Bd, 1958–. Past Chm., Maleny Br., Qld Ambulance Transport Bde; Vice Patron, Schizophrenia Fellowship of S Qld, 1987. Mem., Electoral Re-distribution Commn, Brisbane City Council, 1984–85. Grand Master, United Grand Lodge of Qld, 1983–86. Past Pres., Maroochy Dist Bowls Assoc. *Recreation:* lawn bowls. *Address:* 62 Zillman Road, Clayfield, Qld 4011, Australia. *T:* (7) 32686529.

BURNETT-STUART, Joseph; Chairman, Robert Fleming Holdings Ltd, 1981–90 (Director, 1963–90); *b* 11 April 1930; *s* of late George Eustace Burnett-Stuart, CBE and Etheldreda Cecily (*née* Edge); *m* 1954, Mary Hermione, *d* of late John A. M. Stewart of Ardvorlich, TD; three *s* one *d*. *Educ:* Eton Coll.; Trinity Coll., Cambridge (BA). Bankers Trust Co., 1953–62. A Church Commissioner, 1984–94. *Recreations:* gardening, shooting, fishing. *Club:* New (Edinburgh).

BURNEY, Sir Nigel (Dennistoun), 4th Bt *cr* 1921, of Preston House, Preston Candover, Southampton; *b* 6 Sept. 1959; *er s* of Sir Cecil Burney, 3rd Bt and Hazel Marguerite de Hamel (*née* Coleman); *S* father, 2002; *m* 1992, Lucy Brooks; two *s* two *d*. *Educ:* Eton; Trinity Coll., Cambridge. *Recreations:* tennis, music, ski-ing. *Heir: s* Max Dennistoun Burney, *b* 15 Sept. 1994. *Address:* e-mail: nigel@nigelburney.com. *Clubs:* White's, Annabel's.

BURNHAM, 7th Baron *cr* 1903, of Hall Barn, Beaconsfield, Bucks; **Harry Frederick Alan Lawson;** Bt 1892; Director, Investment Management, Brewin Dolphin Securities Ltd, since 2000; *b* 22 Feb. 1968; *s* of 6th Baron Burnham and of Lady Burnham (*née* Hilary Margaret Hunter); *S* father, 2005. *Educ:* Summerfield Sch., Oxford; Eton Coll. Associated Newspapers, 1988–95; Williams de Broe plc, 1996–2000. Trustee, Prostate Cancer Res. Centre. Liveryman, Gunmakers' Co. *Recreations:* shooting, horse and dog racing, tobogganing, oenology, golf. *Heir:* none. *Address:* Woodlands Farm, Beaconsfield, Bucks HP9 2SF. *Clubs:* Turf, Pratt's, City Livery; St Moritz Tobogganing; Burnham Beeches Golf.

BURNHAM, Rt Rev. Andrew; *see* Ebbsfleet, Bishop Suffragan of.

BURNHAM, Rt Hon. Andrew Murray; PC 2007; MP (Lab) Leigh, since 2001; Secretary of State for Culture, Media and Sport, since 2008; *b* Liverpool, 7 Jan. 1970; *s* of Kenneth Roy Burnham and Eileen Mary (*née* Murray); *m* 2000, Marie-France van Heel; one *s* two *d. Educ:* St Aelred's RC High Sch., Merseyside; Fitzwilliam Coll., Cambridge (MA Hons Eng.). Researcher to Tessa Jowell, MP, and Labour Health Team, 1994–97; Parly Officer, NHS Confedn, 1997; Advr to Football Task Force, 1997–98; Special Advr to Rt Hon. Chris Smith, MP, DCMS, 1998–2001. PPS to Sec. of State for Home Dept, 2003–05; Parly Under-Sec. of State, Home Office, 2005–06; Minister of State, DoH, 2006–07; Chief Sec. to HM Treasury, 2007–08. Mem., Health Select Cttee, 2001–03. Chm., Supporters Direct, 2002–05. *Recreations:* football (Everton FC), Rugby league (Leigh RLC), cricket. *Address:* House of Commons, SW1A 0AA. *T:* (020) 7219 8250; (constituency office) 10 Market Street, Leigh WN7 1DS. *T:* (01942) 682353. *Clubs:* Lowton, Hindley, Wigan Road and Leigh Labour; Leigh Catholic.

BURNHAM, Rev. Anthony Gerald; Moderator, Free Churches Group (formerly Free Churches' Council), and a President, Churches Together in England, 1999–2003; *b* 2 March 1936; *s* of Selwyn and Sarah Burnham; *m* 1961, Valerie Florence Cleaver; one *s* two *d. Educ:* Silcoates Sch.; Manchester Univ. (BA Admin); Northern Coll., Manchester. Minister: Brownhill Congregational Church, Blackburn, 1961–66; Poulton-le-Fylde and Hambleton Congregational Churches, 1966–69; Lectr, Northern Coll., Manchester, 1969–77; Minister, SW Manchester United Reformed Churches, 1973–81; Moderator, NW Synod, URC, 1981–92; Gen. Sec., URC, 1992–2001. Chm. of Corps, Council for World Mission, 1995–99. Religious broadcasting for radio and TV. *Publications:* In The Quietness, 1981; Say One For Me, 1990. *Recreations:* theatre, jazz. *Address:* 30 Sandhurst Road, Didsbury, Manchester M20 5LR.

BURNHAM, Eleanor; Member (Lib Dem) Wales North, National Assembly for Wales, since March 2001; *b* 17 April 1951; *m* Derek Burnham; one *s* one *d. Educ:* Redbrook Coll., Shrewsbury; Yale Coll., Wrexham; Manchester Metropolitan Univ. (BSc). Worked in social services, healthcare and arts mgt; teacher; lectr in complementary therapy and complementary health practitioner. Formerly Mem., Mental Health Tribunal. Lib Dem spokesman for post 16 educn, 2001, for envmt, planning and transport, 2001–03, for culture, sport and Welsh lang., 2003–, Nat. Assembly for Wales. Contested: (Lib Dem) Alyn and Deeside, 1997; (Lib Dem) Delyn, 1999, Clwyd W, 2003, Nat. Assembly for Wales. JP Wrexham, 1992–2001. *Address:* (constituency office) Rear Office, Kenmar, Chester Road, Rossett LL12 0MW; National Assembly for Wales, Cardiff CF99 1NA.

BURNHAM, Peter Michael; Partner, 1970–93, Consultant, 1993–95, Coopers & Lybrand; *b* 13 May 1935; *s* of late Frank Burnham and Winifred Eileen Burnham (*née* Fyson); *m* 1963, Jill, *d* of Comdr Langton Gowlland, RN; two *d. Educ:* Eltham Coll.; Bristol Univ. (BA 1956). FCA, FCMA, JDipMA. With Sturges Fraser Cave & Co., 1956–59; served as Pilot Officer, RAF, 1959–61 (Sword of Honour); with Coopers & Lybrand, 1961–95: Dep. Man. Dir, Consulting Practice, 1981–88. Bd Mem., Historic Bldgs and Monuments Commn (English Heritage), 1984–88; Dir, UK Council for Computing Develt, 1984–88; Dir and Dep. Chm., E London TEC, 1989–93; Dir, Satellite Observing Systems Ltd, 1993–95, 1998–2005; Mem., Adv. Cttee, HM Inspectorate of Pollution, 1994–95; Mem. Adv. Cttee, 1994–95, Bd Mem., 1995–97, Environment Agency. Member: Archbps' Commn on Cathedrals, 1992–94; Synod Follow-up Gp, 1995–96. *Publications:* various articles in professional jls. *Recreations:* sailing, travelling, listening to music. *Address:* The Old Coach House, Sheep Lane, Midhurst, W Sussex GU29 9NT. *T:* (01730) 812841; La Cumbre, Camino del Morro, 18697 La Herradura, Spain. *T:* and *Fax:* (958) 827426; *e-mail:* pmburnham@waitrose.com. *Clubs:* Royal Air Force, Royal Thames Yacht.

BURNINGHAM, John Mackintosh; free-lance author-designer; *b* 27 April 1936; *s* of Charles Burningham and Jessie Mackintosh; *m* 1964, Helen Gillian Oxenbury, *qv*; one *s* two *d. Educ:* Summerhill School, Leiston, Suffolk; Central School of Art, Holborn, 1956–59 (Diploma). Now free-lance: illustration, poster design, exhibition, animated film puppets, and writing for children. Wall friezes: Birdland, Lionland, Storyland, 1966; Jungleland, Wonderland, 1968; Around the World, 1972. *Publications:* Borka, 1963 (Kate Greenaway Medal, 1963); John Burningham's ABC, 1964; Trubloff, 1964; Humbert, 1965; Cannonball Simp, 1966 (filmed, 1967); Harquin, 1967; The Extraordinary Tug-of-War, 1968; Seasons, 1969; Mr Gumpy's Outing, 1970 (Kate Greenaway Award, 1971); Around the World in Eighty Days, 1972; Mr Gumpy's Motor Car, 1973; "Little Books" series: The Baby, The Rabbit, The School, The Snow, 1974; The Blanket, The Cupboard, The Dog, The Friend, 1975; The Adventures of Humbert, Simp and Harquin, 1976; Come Away from the Water, Shirley, 1977; Time to Get Out of the Bath, Shirley, 1978; Would You Rather, 1978; The Shopping Basket, 1980; Avocado Baby, 1982; John Burningham's Number Play Series, 1983; First Words/Granpa, 1984 (filmed, 1989); Play and Learn Books: abc, 123, Opposites, Colours, 1985; Where's Julius, 1986; John Patrick Norman McHennessy—the Boy who is Always Late, 1987; Rhymetime: A Good Job, The Car Ride, 1988, Animal Chatter, A Grand Band, 1989; Oi! Get off our Train, 1989; Aldo, 1991; England, 1992; Harvey Slumfenburger's Christmas Present, 1993 (jt winner, W. H. Smith Award, 1994); Courtney, 1994; Cloudland, 1996; France, 1998; Whadayamean, 1999; Husherbye, 2000; The Magic Bed, 2003; *illustrated:* Chitty Chitty Bang Bang, 1964; The Wind in the Willows, 1983; (also compiled): The Time of Your Life, 2002; When We Were Young, 2004. *Address:* c/o Jonathan Cape Ltd, 20 Vauxhall Bridge Road, SW1V 2FA.

BURNLEY, Bishop Suffragan of, since 2000; **Rt Rev. John William Goddard;** *b* 8 Sept. 1947; *s* of Rev. Canon William and Anna Elizabeth Goddard; *m* 1970, Vivienne Selby; two *s. Educ:* Durham Univ. (BA Hons Theol 1969; DipTh 1970). Ordained deacon, 1970, priest, 1971; Curate: St John, Southbank, 1970–74; Cayton with Eastfield, 1974–75; Vicar: Ascension, Middlesbrough, 1975–82; All Saints, Middlesbrough, 1982–88; RD, Middlesbrough, 1981–87; Canon and Prebend, York Minster, 1987–88, now Canon Emeritus; Vice-Principal, Edin. Theol Coll., 1988–92; Team Rector, Ribbleton, 1992–2000. *Recreations:* restoring old houses and working with wood, narrow boating. *Address:* Dean House, 449 Padiham Road, Burnley BB12 6TD. *T:* (01282) 470360; *e-mail:* bishop.burnley@ukonline.co.uk.

BURNLEY, Elizabeth; Chief Guide, Girlguiding UK, since 2006; *b* 14 March 1959; *d* of Joan and Jack Noden; *m* 2000, Roger Burnley. *Educ:* Univ. of Nottingham (BSc Hons Psychol.; MSc Occupational Psychol.). Human Resources Manager: British Rail Engrg Ltd, 1982–87; RFS Engrg Ltd, 1987–93; occupational psychologist: Barnes Kavelle Ltd, 1994–98; Boots Co. plc, 1998–2001; HR Manager, Huntsman, 2001–07. Programme Dir, Common Purpose, 2007–. *Recreations:* girlguiding, hill-walking, interesting textile crafts. *Address:* c/o Girlguiding UK, 17–19 Buckingham Palace Road, SW1W 0PT.

BURNS, family name of **Baron Burns**.

BURNS, Baron *cr* 1998 (Life Peer), of Pitshanger in the London Borough of Ealing; **Terence Burns,** GCB 1995; Kt 1983; Chairman: Abbey (formerly Abbey National) plc, since 2002; Marks & Spencer, 2006–08 (Deputy Chairman and Chairman-designate, 2005–06); *b* 13 March 1944; *s* of Patrick Owen and Doris Burns; *m* 1969, Anne Elizabeth Powell; one *s* two *d. Educ:* Houghton-Le-Spring Grammar Sch.; Univ. of Manchester (BAEcon Hons). London Business School: research posts, 1965–70; Lecturer in Economics, 1970–74; Sen. Lectr in Economics, 1974–79; Prof. of Economics, 1979; Director, LBS Centre for Economic Forecasting, 1976–79, Fellow, 1989; Chief Econ. Advr to the Treasury and Hd of Govt Econ. Service, 1980–91; Perm. Sec., HM Treasury, 1991–98. Member, HM Treasury Academic Panel, 1976–79. Chm., Financial Services and Mkts Jt Cttee, 1999. Chm., Cttee of Inquiry into Hunting with Dogs, 2000. Chm., Nat. Lottery Commn, 2000–01. Non-executive Director: Legal & General Group plc, 1999–2001; Pearson plc, 1999–; British Land Co. plc, 2000–05; Glas Cymru Cyfyngedig, 2000–; Dwr Cymru Cyfyngedig, 2001–; Banco Santander Central Hispano SA, 2004–. Pres., NIESR, 2003–. Pres., Soc. of Business Economists, 1999– (Vice-Pres., 1985–99); Vice-Pres., REconS, 1992–. CCMI (CIMgt 1992). Bd Mem., Manchester Business Sch., 1992–98. Dir, Queens Park Rangers FC, 1996–2000. Governor, Royal Acad. of Music, 1998– (Chm. Governing Body). Trustee, Monteverdi Choir and Orch., 1998– (Chm. Trustees). Hon. degrees: Manchester Univ.; Sunderland Univ.; Durham Univ.; Sheffield Univ. *Publications:* various articles in economic jls. *Recreations:* music, golf. *Address:* Abbey plc, Abbey House, 2 Triton Square, Regent's Place, NW1 3AN. *Clubs:* Reform; Ealing Golf.

BURNS, Alison Sarah; Chief Executive Officer, JWT, since 2006; *b* 26 April 1963; *d* of Roy Butler and Judith Cornwell; *m* 1996, Anthony John Burns; one *d. Educ:* Univ. of York (BA Hons 1984). Account Management: Fletcher Shelton Delaney, 1984–86; Boase Massimi Pollitt, 1986–89; Bartle Bogle Hegarty, 1989–92; Young and Rubicam, 1992–93; Global Vice Pres., Mktg, PepsiCo, 1993–96; CEO, Kendall Tarrant, 1996–98; Pres., Fallon McElligott, 1998–2003. *Recreations:* sport, interior design, travel, good food and wine. *Address:* JWT, 1 Knightsbridge Green, SW1X 7NW. *T:* (020) 7656 7520, *Fax:* (020) 7656 7410; *e-mail:* alison.burns@jwt.com.

BURNS, Prof. Alistair Stanyer, MD; FRCP, FRCPsych; Professor of Old Age Psychiatry, and Hon. Consultant Psychiatrist, University of Manchester, since 1992; *b* 4 July 1958; *s* of Richard and Janet Burns; *m* 1986, Alison Wise; two *d. Educ:* Hutchesons' Boys' Grammar Sch., Glasgow; Univ. of Glasgow (MB ChB 1980; MD Hons 1991; DHMSA 1984; MPhil London 1990). FRCPGlas 1993; FRCPsych 1996. Registrar in Psychiatry, Maudsley Hosp., 1983–86; Institute of Psychiatry, London: res. worker/Sen. Registrar, 1986–91; Sen. Lectr, 1991–92. *Publications:* Alzheimer's Disease, 1992; Ageing and Dementia, 1993; Dementia, 1994, 2nd edn 2001; Rating Scales in Old Age Psychiatry, 2000; numerous contribs to med. and scientific jls. *Recreations:* estate management, walking, cars, writing. *Address:* Department of Psychiatry, Education and Research Centre, Wythenshawe Hospital, Manchester M23 9LT. *T:* (0161) 291 5886, *Fax:* (0161) 291 5882; *e-mail:* Alistair.Burns@manchester.ac.uk.

BURNS, Sir Andrew; *see* Burns, Sir R. A.

BURNS, David Allan, CMG 1993; CBE 2003; HM Diplomatic Service, retired; Founder Chairman, Foreign and Commonwealth Office Association, 1999–2003; *b* 20 Sept. 1937; *s* of Allan Robert Desmond Burns, GM, and Gladys Frances Dine; *m* 1971, Inger Ellen Kristiansson; one *s* one *d. Educ:* Sir Anthony Browne's Sch., Brentwood, Essex. Served HM Forces, 1956–58. Language student and Third Secretary, British Embassy, Belgrade, 1962–65; Second Secretary, Bangkok, 1966–68; First Secretary, Washington, 1969–72; Head of Chancery, Belgrade, 1973–76; Asst Head of Arms Control Dept, FCO, 1976–79; Counsellor, Bangkok, 1979–83; Consul General, Boston, 1983–87; Hd of N America Dept, FCO, 1988–91; Ambassador to Cambodia, 1991–94; Ambassador to Finland, 1995–97. Retirement Liaison Officer, FCO, 1998–99. *Recreations:* France, cinema.

BURNS, Elizabeth Kerr, CMG 2005; OBE 1995; President and Chief Executive, International Association for Volunteer Effort, since 2001; *b* 6 Jan. 1939; *d* of Thomas Thomson and Morag Thomson (*née* Cunningham); *m* 1964, William Burns (*d* 2000); two *s* one *d. Educ:* Edinburgh Univ. (MA Hons; DipEd); Moray House Coll. (Cert. Chapter V). Teacher of modern langs, 1962–67; Develt Officer, SCVO, 1981–83; Dir, Volunteer Develt Scotland, 1983–2001. Active in Scottish Playgps' Assoc., 1970–81 (Nat. Chair, 1978–80; Pres., 1986–90). Mem., Govt Strategy Gps, 1994–95, 1999–2000 and 2000–01. Chair, Historic Envmt Adv. Council for Scotland, 2003–May 2009. Board Member: Scottish Community Educn Council, 1998–2000; Learning & Teaching Scotland, 2000–02. Pres., Eur. Volunteer Centre, 1998–2000. *Publications:* contrib. papers to specialist and res. jls in field of volunteering. *Recreations:* reading, reading, reading. *Address:* International Association for Volunteer Effort, Office 1/8, The e-Centre, Cooperage Way Business Village, Alloa FK10 3LP. *T:* (01259) 272161, *Fax:* (01259) 272162; *e-mail:* iavepres@ukonline.co.uk, liz.burns@ukonline.co.uk.

BURNS, Gerard, MBE 1988; Pro-Chancellor, since 2001, and Chairman of Council, since 2002, University of Ulster; *b* 15 Nov. 1934; *s* of Bernard and Sarah Ellen Burns; *m* 1962, Moyra Connolly; three *s* two *d. Educ:* St Mary's Christian Brothers Grammar Sch.; Queen's Univ., Belfast. Divl Inspector, Trading Standards, NI, 1954–68; Lectr in Business Studies, Armagh Coll. of Further and Higher Educn, 1968–76; Chief Exec., Fermanagh DC, 1976–96; Assembly Ombudsman for NI and Comr for Complaints, 1995–2000. Chm., Review Body on Post Primary Educn, NI, 2000–02. Dir, Irish Times Ltd, 1997–2007; Gov., Irish Times Trust Ltd, 1997–2007. Member: EOC, NI, 1979–85; Historic Bldgs Council, 1988–91; Regl Council, Nat. Trust, 1989–1994; Solicitors' Disciplinary Tribunal, NI, 1989–; Local Govt Staff Commn, 1990–95; Standing Adv. Commn on Human Rights, 1996–2000. Mem., NI Tourist Bd, 1992–96. Dir, Fermanagh Training Ltd, 1990–. Chm., Soc. of Local Authority Chief Execs (NI), 1990–92. Chairman: Fermanagh Univ. Foundn, 1998–2005; Fermanagh-Univ. Partnership Bd, 2001–05. Mem., Diocesan Cttee for Catholic Maintained Schools, 1987–95. Trustee, Spirit of Enniskillen Trust, 1988– (Vice-Pres., 2007–); Chm., Enniskillen Civic Trust, 1988–. Patron: Marie Curie Nursing Gp, Co. Fermanagh, 1998–2007; Fermanagh Co. Museum, 1999–. DUniv QUB, 1996. *Recreations:* walking, swimming, the arts. *Address:* 65 Old Rossorry Road, Enniskillen, Northern Ireland BT74 7LF.

BURNS, Dr Henry James Gerard, FRCS, FRCP, FFPH; Chief Medical Officer, Scottish Government (formerly Scottish Executive) Health Department, since 2005; *b* 25 Jan. 1951; *s* of Henry Burns and Mary (*née* Boyle); *m* 1983, Agnes Capaldi; two *s* four *d*. *Educ:* St Aloysius Coll., Glasgow; Glasgow Univ. (MB, ChB). FRCS 1979; MPH 1990; MFPHM 1993, FFPH (FFPHM 2005); FRCP 2000. Glasgow University: Lectr in Surgery, 1975–83; Sen. Lectr, 1983–89; Dir of Public Health, Gtr Glasgow Health, then NHS, Bd, 1994–2005. Mem., MRC, 2007–. *Recreations:* cycling, running. *Address:* Scottish Government Health Department, St Andrew's House, Edinburgh EH1 3DG. *T:* (0131) 244 2317.

BURNS, Ian Morgan, CB 1990; Director-General, Policy (formerly Director of Policy), Lord Chancellor's Department, 1995–99; *b* 3 June 1939; *s* of late Donald George Burns and Margaret Brenda Burns; *m* 1965, Susan Rebecca (*née* Wheeler); two *d*. *Educ:* Bootham, York. LLB, LLM London. HM Forces, 1957–59. Examiner, Estate Duty Office, 1960; Asst Principal, 1965, Principal, 1969, Home Office; Principal, 1972, Asst Sec., 1974, NI Office; Asst Sec., Home Office, 1977; Under Sec., NI Office, 1979–84; Under Sec. (Finance), 1985, and Gen. Manager, Disablement Services, 1986, DHSS; Deputy Under Secretary of State: NI Office, 1987–90; Police Dept, Home Office, 1990–95. FRSA 1993. *Recreations:* travelling, listening to music, adventurous gardening, collecting siurells. *Address:* c/o Department for Constitutional Affairs, Selborne House, 54–60 Victoria Street, SW1E 6QW. *Club:* Athenæum.

BURNS, James; JP; DL; Member, Strathclyde Regional Council, 1974–95 (Convener, 1982–86); *b* 8 Feb. 1931; *s* of late James Burns and of Mary Burns (*née* Magee); *m* 1959, Jean Ward; two *s*. *Educ:* St Patrick's Sch., Shotts; Coatbridge Tech. Coll. Engineer with NCB, 1966–71. Member: Lanark CC, 1967–75; Lanarks Health Bd, 1973–77; Strathclyde Regional Council: Chm., Gen. Purposes Cttee, 1975–82; Vice-Convener, 1978–82. Chm. Vis. Cttee, HM Prison, Shotts, 1980–; Member: Commonwealth Games Council for Scotland, 1982–86; Main Organising Cttee, Commonwealth Games 1986, 1982–86. Vice President: Glasgow Western St Andrew's Youth Club, 1982–86; St Andrew's Ambulance Assoc., 1984–86. Hon. President: Strathclyde CRC, 1982–86; Princess Louise Scottish Hosp. (Erskine Hosp.), 1982–86; Strathclyde Charities Band Assoc., 1982–86; Scottish Retirement Council, 1984–86; Hon. Vice Pres., SNO Chorus, 1982–86; Patron: Strathclyde Youth Club Assoc., 1982–86; YMCA Sports Centre, 1982–86; Scottish Pakistani Assoc., 1984–86. Trustee, The Pearce Institute, 1983–86. JP Motherwell, 1972. DL Monklands, Motherwell, Hamilton, E Kilbride and Clydesdale, 1989. *Recreations:* fishing, golf. *Address:* 57 Springhill Road, Shotts ML7 5JA. *T:* (01501) 820187.

BURNS, Prof. James Henderson, FBA 1992; Professor of the History of Political Thought, University College London, 1966–86, now Emeritus; *b* 10 Nov. 1921; *yr s* of late William Burns and Helen Craig Tait Henderson; *m* 1947, Yvonne Mary Zéla Birnie, *er d* of late Arthur Birnie, MA, and Yvonne Marie Aline Louis; two *s* (and one *d* decd). *Educ:* George Watson's Boys' Coll., Edinburgh; Univ. of Edinburgh (MA); Balliol Coll., Oxford (MA); PhD Aberdeen. Sub-Editor, Home News Dept, BBC, 1944–45; Lectr in Polit. Theory, Univ. of Aberdeen, 1947–60; Head of Dept of Politics, 1952–60; University College London: Reader in the History of Political Thought, 1961–66; Head of History Dept, 1970–75; Hon. Fellow, 1999. John Hinkley Vis. Prof., Dept of History, Johns Hopkins Univ., Baltimore, 1987; Lectures: Creighton, London Univ., 1986; Carlyle, Oxford Univ., 1988; Gifford, Aberdeen Univ., 1994. Gen. Editor, The Collected Works of Jeremy Bentham, 1961–79; Vice-Chm., Bentham Cttee, 1983–92 (Sec., 1966–78); Pres., Internat. Bentham Soc., 1986–92. FRHistS 1962; Hon. Vice-Pres., RHistS, 1986– (Hon. Sec., 1965–70; Vice-Pres., 1978–82). *Publications:* Scottish University (with D. Sutherland Graeme), 1944; Scottish Churchmen and the Council of Basle, 1962; Lordship, Kingship and Empire: the idea of monarchy 1400–1525, 1992; The True Law of Kingship: concepts of monarchy in early-modern Scotland, 1996; *contributor to:* (with S. Rose) The British General Election of 1951, by D. E. Butler, 1952; Essays on the Scottish Reformation, ed D. McRoberts, 1962; Mill: a collection of critical essays, ed J. B. Schneewind, 1968; Bentham on Legal Theory, ed M. H. James, 1973; Jeremy Bentham: ten critical essays, ed B. Parekh, 1974; Absolutism in Seventeenth Century Europe, ed J. Miller, 1990; The Church and Sovereignty c 590–1918, ed D. Wood, 1991; Political Discourse in Early Modern Britain, ed N. Phillipson and Q. Skinner, 1993; Politics, Ideology and the Law in Early Modern Europe, ed A. E. Bakos, 1994; Imperium/Empire/Reich, ed F. Bosbach and H. Hiery, 1999; The Medieval World, ed P. Lineham and J. Nelson, 2001; *edited* (with H. L. A. Hart): Jeremy Bentham, An Introduction in the Principles of Morals and Legislation, 1970; Jeremy Bentham, A Comment on the Commentaries and A Fragment on Government, 1977; (with F. Rosen) Jeremy Bentham, Constitutional Code, vol. I, 1983; The Cambridge History of Medieval Political Thought c350–c1450, 1988; The Cambridge History of Political Thought 1450–1700, 1991; (with T. M. Izbicki) Conciliarism and Papalism, 1997; articles and reviews in: English Historical Review, Scottish Historical Review, Innes Review, Political Studies, History, Trans of RHistSoc, Historical Jl, Jl of Eccles. History, Records of the Scottish Ch History Soc., British Jl for the History of Science, etc. *Address:* 6 Chiltern House, Hillcrest Road, Ealing, W5 1HL. *T:* (020) 8998 9515.

BURNS, Julian Delisle; Chief Operating Officer, All3Media, since 2003; *b* 18 Sept. 1949; *s* of Benedict Delisle Burns, FRS and of Angela Hughesdon (*née* Ricardo); *m* 1976, Cheryl Ann Matthews; one *s* one *d*. *Educ:* Betteshanger Prep. Sch., Kent; Haberdashers' Aske's Sch., Elstree. Manager, Mendel's Garage, Hampstead, 1968–71; musician, various musical groups, 1972–75; Granada Television Ltd, 1976–2004: Prodn Manager, Regl Progs, 1976–80; Manager, Prog. Services, 1980–86; Hd, Business Affairs, 1986–90; Dir, Business and Legal Affairs, 1990–94; Jt Man. Dir, 1994–96; Jt Man. Dir, Granada Production, 1996–2000; Man. Dir, Ops, Granada plc, 2000–02. Dir, Royal Exchange Theatre, Manchester, 1995–2003. Member: Adv. Cttee on Film Finance, DNH, 1996–2001; Adv. Cttee on TV Production, DCMS, 1999–2001; Bd, 2002 Commonwealth Games, 1998–2002; Bd, Liverpool FC, 1999–2007. *Recreations:* walking, reading, music, television, art, the Lake District. *Address:* All3Media, 168–173 High Holborn, WC1V 7AA.

BURNS, Kevin Francis Xavier, CMG 1984; HM Diplomatic Service, retired; *b* 18 Dec. 1930; *s* of late Frank Burns and Winifred Burns (*née* O'Neill); *m* 1st, 1963, Nan Pinto (*d* 1984); one *s* two *d*; 2nd, 1992, Elizabeth Hassell. *Educ:* Finchley Grammar Sch.; Trinity Coll., Cambridge (BA 1953). CRO, 1956–58; Asst Private Sec. to Sec. of State, 1958; 2nd Sec., 1959, 1st Sec., 1960–63, Colombo; CRO/FO, 1963–67; 1st Sec., Head of Chancery and Consul, Montevideo, 1967–70; FCO, 1970–73; Counsellor, UK Mission, Geneva, 1973–79; RCDS, 1979; Head of SE Asian Dept, FCO, 1980–83; High Comr, Ghana, and Ambassador, Togo, 1983–86; High Comr, Barbados and Eastern Caribbean States, 1986–90; Personnel Assessor, FCO, 1991–99. *Address:* 11 Wentworth Hall, The Ridgeway, NW7 1RJ.

BURNS, Michael; Chairman, South Yorkshire County Association, since 1986; *b* 21 Dec. 1917; *s* of Hugh Burns and Jane Ellin Burns; *m* 1939, Vera Williams (*d* 1984); two *d*. *Educ:* Thorne Grammar Sch. Served War, 1940–46: 1939–45 Star, France and Germany Star, War Medal, Defence Medal. Miner, Hatfield Main Colliery, 1934–40 and 1946–66; Thorpe Marsh Power Stn, 1966–70; Sch. Caretaker, Hatfield Travis Sch., 1970–81 (due to wife's illness); retd 1981. Mem., Nat. Cttee, NUPE, 1979–81; Chm., Health and Safety Local Govt Nat. Cttee, NUPE, 1979–81. Member: S Yorks CC, 1973–86 (Chm., 1982–83); Hatfield Town Council, 1995–2007 (Dep. Mayor, 1995–96, 2005–06; Dep. Ldr, 1995; Mayor, 1996–97, 2006–07; Ldr, 2000–07). Mem., Doncaster MBC Robin Hood Doncaster/Sheffield Airport Consultative Cttee, 2005–06. Chairman: Hatfield and Dunscroft Lab Party, 1965–86 (Vice Chm., 1997–); Goole CLP, 1977–83; Doncaster CVS, 1984–92 (Mem., 1977); Thorne No 2 Sub-Div., Police Community Liaison Forum, 1987–; Founder Chm., Doncaster Victim Support Scheme, 1984–95 (Life Pres., 1995); Exec. Mem., Doncaster Intermediate Treatment Orgn, 1990–99; Member: S Yorks Valuation Panel, 1974–89; S Yorks Charity Information Service, 1983–90; Nat. Exec., CVSNA, 1985–87; Doncaster FPC, 1985–86; Doncaster Jt Consultative Cttee, 1985–89; Yorks Local Council Assoc., 1995. Trustee: S Yorks Foundn Charity, 1986–90; Hatfield Church Bldg Trust, 1997–2004; Chm., Friends of S Yorks Training Trust, 1986–2003 (Vice-Pres., 2003–). Pres., Hatfield Br., Arthritic Care, 1980–86. Governor, Hatfield High Sch., 1974–88; Chairman: Hatfield Ash Hill Sch. Bd of Governors, 1974–88 and 1989–92 (Vice-Chm., 1988–89); Govs, Hatfield Sheepdip Lane Sch., 1974–2003; Hatfield Chase Sch. (ESNS), 1983–2003. Hatfield Spiral Youth Club Cttee, 1974–99; Hatfield/Thorne Moors Forum, 1996–2000. Church Warden, Christ Church, Dunscroft, 1964–79. *Recreations:* DIY, oil painting, politics. *Address:* 1 Grange Avenue, Hatfield, Doncaster, South Yorks DN7 6RH. *T:* (01302) 844146.

BURNS, Richard Ronald James; company director; Partner, Baillie Gifford & Co., 1977–2006; *b* Gourock, 5 May 1946; *s* of Ronald and Mary Burns; *m* 1st, 1974, Catriona Douglas Walker (marr. diss. 1994); two *s* one *d*; 2nd, 1994, Catherine Ogilvie Bryson; one *d*. *Educ:* Dundee High Sch.; Craigflower Prep. Sch.; Trinity Coll., Glenalmond; Merton Coll., Oxford (BA Mod. Hist. 1967); Univ. of Edinburgh (LLB 1969). WS 1972. Apprentice and Asst Solicitor, W. & J. Burness, 1969–73; Baillie Gifford & Co., 1973–2006. Director: Mid Wynd International Investment Trust plc, 1981–; EP Global Opportunities Trust plc, 2003–; Bankers Investment Trust plc, 2006–; JPMorgan Indian Investment Trust plc, 2006–; Standard Life Equity Income Trust plc, 2006–. Trustee: Donaldson Trust, 1999–; Nat. Galls of Scotland, 2007–. Mem. Court, Univ. of Dundee, 2006–. *Recreations:* reading, foreign travel, golf. *Address:* 31 Saxe Coburg Place, Edinburgh EH3 5BP. *T:* (0131) 332 5819. *Clubs:* New (Edinburgh); Royal and Ancient Golf (St Andrews).

BURNS, Sir (Robert) Andrew, KCMG 1997 (CMG 1992); HM Diplomatic Service, retired; International Governor, BBC, 2005–06; Director: J. P. Morgan Chinese Investment Trust, since 2003; Aberdeen All Asia Investment Trust, since 2008; *b* 21 July 1943; *e s* of late Robert Burns, CB, CMG and Mary Burns (*née* Goodland); *m* 1973, Sarah Cadogan, JP; two *s* and one step *d*. *Educ:* Highgate Sch.; Trinity Coll., Cambridge. BA (Classics), MA. Entered Diplomatic Service, 1965; UK Mission to UN, NY, 1965; FO 1966; Sch. of Oriental and African Studies, 1966–67; Univ. of Delhi, 1967; served New Delhi, FCO, and UK Delegation to CSCE, 1967–76; First Secretary and Head of Chancery, Bucharest, 1976–78; Private Sec. to Perm. Under Sec. and Head of Diplomatic Service, FCO, 1979–82; Fellow, Center for Internat. Affairs, Harvard Univ., 1982–83; Counsellor (Information), Washington, and Head of British Information Services, NY, 1983–86; Head of S Asian Dept, FCO, 1986–88; Head of News Dept, FCO, 1988–90; Asst Under-Sec. of State (Asia), FCO, 1990–92; Ambassador to Israel, 1992–95; Dep. Under Sec. of State, FCO, 1995–97; Consul-Gen., Hong Kong and Macau, 1997–2000; High Comr to Canada, 2000–03. Chm., Exec. Cttee, Anglo-Israel Assoc., 2004–05; Chm., Adv. Council, British Expertise (formerly British Consultants and Construction Bureau), 2006–; Member: British N Amer. Cttee, 2004–; British N Amer. Res. Assoc., 2004–. Chm. Council, Royal Holloway, Univ. of London, 2004– (Mem., 2003–); Vice-Chm., Cttee of University Chairmen, 2007–; Trustee, UK Foundn, Univ. of BC, 2004–. Pres., Canada UK Colloquia, 2004–. Chm., Hestercombe Gardens Trust, 2004–; Trustee, Internat. Polar Foundn UK, 2006–. FRSA 1997; Fellow, Portland Trust, 2004. *Publication:* Diplomacy, War and Parliamentary Democracy, 1985. *Recreations:* music, theatre, Exmoor. *Address:* Walland Farm, Wheddon Cross, Minehead, Somerset TA24 7EE. *Clubs:* Garrick, Royal Automobile; Hong Kong.

BURNS, Sandra Pauline, CB 1989; Parliamentary Counsel, 1980–91, retired; *b* 19 June 1938; *d* of John Burns and Edith Maud Burns. *Educ:* Manchester Central High Sch.; Somerville Coll., Oxford (BCL, MA). Called to the Bar, Middle Temple, 1964. *Recreation:* painting. *Address:* 30 Diamond Court, 153 Banbury Road, Oxford OX2 7AA.

BURNS, Simon Hugh McGuigan; MP (C) Chelmsford West, since 1997 (Chelmsford, 1987–97); *b* 6 Sept. 1952; *s* of late Brian Stanley Burns, MC, and of Shelagh Mary Nash; *m* 1982, Emma Mary Clifford (marr. diss. 2000); one *s* one *d*. *Educ:* Christ the King Sch., Accra, Ghana; Stamford Sch.; Worcester Coll., Oxford (BA Hons Modern History). Political Adviser to Rt Hon. Sally Oppenheim, 1975–81; Dir, What to Buy Ltd, 1981–83; Policy Exec., Inst. of Dirs, 1983–87. PPS to Minister of State: Dept of Employment, 1989–90; Dept of Educn, 1990–92; DTI, 1992–93; PPS to Minister of Agric., Fisheries and Food, 1993–94; an Asst Govt Whip, 1994–95; a Lord Comr of HM Treasury (Govt Whip), 1995–96; Parly Under-Sec. of State, DoH, 1996–97; Opposition spokesman on: social security, 1997–98; envmt, housing and planning, 1998–99; health, 2001–05; an Opposition Whip, 2005–. Mem., Health Select Cttee, 1999–2005. Treas., 1922 Cttee, 1999–2001 (Mem. Exec., 1999). *Recreations:* American politics, reading, swimming, travelling. *Address:* House of Commons, SW1A 0AA. *T:* (020) 7219 3000. *Clubs:* Essex, Chelmsford Conservative (Patron).

BURNS, Thomas; Member (SDLP) South Antrim, Northern Ireland Assembly, since 2003; *b* Antrim, 19 Aug. 1960; *m* Therese; three *s*. *Educ:* trained as electrical engr. Mem. (SDLP), Antrim BC, 1997– (Vice-Chm., Planning Cttee, 2000–03). Bd Dirs, Antrim Bor. Strategy Partnerships, 2001; Mem., Antrim Dist Policing Partnership, 2004. Founder Mem., Crumlin Credit Union; Dir, Antrim Dist CAB. Governor: Rathenraw Integrated Primary Sch.; St Joseph's Primary Sch.; Crumlin High Sch. Specialist interest in dyslexia and autism support gps. *Recreations:* supporter of recycling and environmental issues, sport (supporter of St James', Aldergrove), committed to GAA youth initiatives and campaigner for development of recreational facilities in South Antrim. *Address:* (constituency office) 17 Main Street, Crumlin, Co. Antrim BT29 4UP. *T:* (028) 9445 3807, *Fax:* (028) 9447 0661; *e-mail:* thomasburnsmla@btconnect.com.

BURNS, Prof. Thomas Patrick, CBE 2006; MD, DSc; FRCPsych; Professor of Social Psychiatry, University of Oxford, and Fellow, Kellogg College, Oxford, since 2003; *b* 20 Sept. 1946; *s* of Reginald Burns and Jane Burns (*née* Cassidy); *m* 1976, Eva Burns-Lundgren; two *d*. *Educ:* Churchfields Comprehensive Sch., West Bromwich; Selwyn Coll., Cambridge (MA 1968, MB BChir 1971); Guy's Hosp., London; MD Cambridge 1984; DSc London 2002. FRCPsych 1984. Consultant Psychiatrist: University Hosp., Uppsala, 1980–83; St George's Hosp., London, 1983–93; Prof. of Community Psychiatry, St George's Hosp. Med. Sch., 1984–2003. Chm. Social Psych. Section, RCPsych,

1988–92. *Publications:* Assertive Outreach in Mental Health, 2002; Community Psychiatric Mental Health Teams: a guide to current practices, 2004; Psychiatry: a very short introduction, 2006; scientific articles on mental health care, anorexia nervosa in men, etc. *Recreations:* theatre, walking, armchair socialism. *Address:* Department of Psychiatry, University of Oxford, Warneford Hospital, Oxford OX3 7JX. *T:* (01865) 226474; *e-mail:* tom.burns@psych.ox.ac.uk. *Club:* Athenæum.

BURNS, Rt Rev. Tom Matthew, SM; Roman Catholic Bishop of the Forces, since 2002; *b* 3 June 1944; *s* of late William James Burns and Louisa Mary Burns (*née* McGarry). *Educ:* Heythrop Coll., London Univ. (BD Hons 1973); BA Open Univ. 1984. Joined SM, 1965; ordained, 1971; Curate, St Anne's, Whitechapel, 1973–74; Head of Econs, St Mary's GS, Sidcup, 1974–78; Head of Econs and Social Scis, St Mary's Sixth-Form Coll., Blackburn, 1979–86; Chaplain, RN, 1986–92; Bursar General, Marist Fathers, Rome, 1992–94; Chaplain, RN, 1994–98; VG 1998–2002; Princ. RC Chaplain, RN, and Dir, Manning (formerly Trng and Progs), Naval Chaplaincy Service, MoD, 1998–2002. Bishop Promoter and Trustee of the Apostleship of the Sea, 2003–; Bd Mem. and Trustee, St Luke's Centre, Manchester, 2005–. *Publication:* pamphlet, Index to the Laws of Rugby Football, 1997. *Recreations:* Rugby (advisor to referees), action novels, film-going. *Address:* c/o Wellington House, St Omer Barracks, Aldershot, Hants GU11 2BG.

BURNS, William Joseph, DPhil; United States Ambassador to Russia, since 2005; *b* 11 April 1956; *s* of William F. and Margaret C. Burns; *m* 1984, Lisa A. Carty; two *d*. *Educ:* LaSalle Univ. (BA Hist. 1978); St John's Coll., Oxford (MPhil 1980; DPhil 1981 Internat. Relns). Special Asst to the President and Sen. Dir for Near East and S Asian Affairs, Nat. Security Council Staff, 1986–89; Actg Dir and Principal Dep. Dir for State Dept's Policy Planning Staff, 1989–93; Minister Counselor for Pol Affairs, Moscow, 1994–95; Exec. Sec. of the State Dept and Special Asst to the Sec. of State, 1996–98; Ambassador to Jordan, 1998–2001; Asst Sec. of State for Near Eastern Affairs, 2001–05. Three hon. degrees. Two Presidential Dist. Service Awards. *Publication:* Economic Aid and American Policy Toward Egypt 1955–1981, 1985. *Recreations:* sports. *Address:* Embassy of the United States of America, Bolshoy Devyatinsky Pereulok 8, 121099 Moscow, Russia.

BURNSIDE, David Wilson Boyd; Member (UU) South Antrim, Northern Ireland Assembly, since 2003; *b* 24 Aug. 1951; *s* of Jack and Betty Burnside; *m* 1999, Fiona Rennie; one *d*; and one *d* by a previous marriage. *Educ:* Coleraine Academical Instn; Queen's Univ. Belfast (BA). Teacher, 1973–74; Press Officer, Vanguard Unionist Party, 1974–76; PR Dir, Inst. of Dirs, 1979–84; Public Affairs Dir, British Airways, 1984–93. Chairman: DBA Ltd, 1993–; New Century Hldgs Ltd, 1995–; New Century Media Ltd, 2007–. MP (UU) South Antrim, 2001–05; contested (UU) same seat, 2005. Mem., RBL, Antrim. *Recreations:* fishing, shooting, motorcycling. *Address:* The Hill, Secon, Ballymoney, Co Antrim BT53 6QB. *Clubs:* Carlton; Portballintrae Boat; Coleraine and District Motor.

BURNSIDE, John, FRSL; writer; *b* 19 March 1955; *m* 1966, Sarah Dunsby; two *s*. Reader in Creative Writing, Univ. of St Andrews, 1999. FRSL 1998. *Publications: poetry:* The Hoop, 1988; Common Knowledge, 1991; Feast Days, 1992; The Myth of the Twin, 1994; Swimming in the Flood, 1995; (jtly) Penguin Modern Poets 9, 1996; A Normal Skin, 1997; The Asylum Dance, 2000; The Light Trap, 2002; (ed with M. Riordan) Wild Reckoning (anthology), 2004; The Good Neighbour, 2005; Selected Poems, 2006; Gift Songs, 2007; *fiction:* The Dumb House, 1997; The Mercy Boys, 1999; Burning Elvis, 2000; The Locust Room, 2001; Living Nowhere, 2003; A Lie About My Father: a memoir, 2006; The Devil's Footprints, 2007; Glister, 2008. *Address:* c/o Jonathan Cape, Random House, 20 Vauxhall Bridge Road, SW1V 2SA.

BURNSTOCK, Prof. Geoffrey, FRS 1986; FAA 1971; Professor of Anatomy, University of London, 1975–2004, now Professor Emeritus; Professor and President, Autonomic Neuroscience Centre, Royal Free and University College Medical School, since 2004; Convener, Centre for Neuroscience, University College London, since 1979; *b* 10 May 1929; *s* of James Burnstock and Nancy Green; *m* 1957, Nomi Hirschfeld; three *d*. *Educ:* King's Coll., London; Melbourne Univ. BSc 1953, PhD 1957 London; DSc Melbourne 1971. National Inst. for Medical Res., Mill Hill, 1956–57; Dept of Pharmacology, Oxford Univ., 1957–59; Rockefeller Travelling Fellowship, Univ. of Ill, 1959; University of Melbourne: Sen. Lectr, 1959–62, Reader, 1962–64, Dept. of Zoology; Prof. of Zoology and Chm. of Dept, 1964–75; Associate Dean (Biological Sciences), 1969–72; Prof. Emeritus, 1993; Head, Dept of Anatomy and Embryology, then Anatomy and Developmental Biology, UCL, 1975–97, Fellow, UCL, 1996; Prof. and Dir, Autonomic Neurosci. Inst., Royal Free Med. Sch., 1997–2004. Vis. Prof., Dept of Pharmacology, Univ. of Calif, LA, 1970. Numerous named lectures, 1976–, including: J. Z. Young, Oxford, 1999; G. W. Harris Prize, Physiol Soc., 1998; Prof. M. Rocha e Silva Award, Caxambu, Brazil, 1999; Horace Davenport Dist., Amer. Physiol. Soc., 2001; Stevenson Meml, London, Ont, 2003. Chm., Scientific Adv. Bd, Eisai London Ltd, 1990–. Editor-in-Chief: Autonomic Neuroscience: Basic & Clinical, 1985–; Purinergic Signalling, 2004–; mem. editl bd of over 20 jls. Vice-Pres., Anatomical Soc. of GB and Ireland, 1990. Member: Academia Europaea, 1992; Russian Soc. of Neuropathology, 1993. Hon. Member: Physiol Soc., 2003; Pharmacol Soc., 2004. Founder FMedSci 1998. Hon. MRCP 1987, Hon. FRCP 2000; Hon. FRCS 1999. Hon. MSc Melbourne 1962; Dr *hc* Antwerp, 2002. Silver Medal, Royal Soc. of Victoria, 1970; Special Award, NIH Conf., Bethesda, USA, 1989; Royal Gold Medal, Royal Soc., 2000; Janssen Award in Gastroenterol., 2000. *Publications:* (with M. Costa) Adrenergic Neurons: their Organisation, Function and Development in the Peripheral Nervous System, 1975; (with Y. Uehara and G. R. Campbell) An Atlas of the Fine Structure of Muscle and its Innervation, 1976; (ed) Purinergic Receptors, 1981; (ed with G. Vrbová and R. O'Brien) Somatic and Autonomic Nerve-Muscle Interactions, 1983; (ed with S. G. Griffith) Nonadrenergic Innervation of Blood Vessels, 1988; (ed with S. Bloom) Peptides: a target for new drug development, 1991; series editor, The Autonomic Nervous System, vols 1–15, 1992–2003; (ed jtly) Nitric Oxide in Health and Disease, 1997; (ed jtly) Cardiovascular Biology of Purines, 1998; papers on smooth muscle and autonomic nervous system, incl. purinergic signalling in health and disease in sci. jls. *Recreations:* tennis, wood sculpture. *Address:* Autonomic Neuroscience Centre, Royal Free and University College Medical School, University College London, Royal Free Campus, Rowland Hill Street, NW3 2PF.

BURNTON, Rt Hon. Sir Stanley Jeffrey, Kt 2000; PC 2008; **Rt Hon. Lord Justice Burnton;** a Lord Justice of Appeal, since 2008; *b* 25 Oct. 1942; *s* of Harry and Fay Burnton; *m* 1971, Gwenyth Frances Castle; one *s* two *d*. *Educ:* Hackney Downs Grammar Sch.; St Edmund Hall, Oxford. MA. Called to the Bar, Middle Temple, 1965, Bencher, 1991; QC 1982; a Recorder, 1994–2000; a Judge of the High Court of Justice, QBD, 2000–08. *Recreations:* music, theatre, wine, travel. *Address:* Royal Courts of Justice, Strand, WC2A 2LL.

BURNYEAT, Myles Fredric, CBE 2007; FBA 1984; Hon. Fellow, Robinson College, Cambridge, since 2006; *b* 1 Jan. 1939; *s* of Peter James Anthony Burnyeat and Cynthia Cherry Warburg; *m* 1st, 1971, Jane Elizabeth Buckley (marr. diss. 1982); one *s* one *d*; 2nd, 1984, Ruth Sophia Padel (marr. diss. 2000); one *d*; 3rd, 2002, Heda Šegvić (*d* 2003); partner, Margaret Hilda Bent, *qv*. *Educ:* Bryanston Sch.; King's Coll., Cambridge (BA). Assistant Lecturer in Philosophy 1964, Lecturer in Philosophy 1965, University Coll. London; Cambridge University: Lectr in Classics, 1978–84; Laurence Prof. of Ancient Philosophy, 1984–96; Fellow, 1978–96, and Lectr in Philosophy, 1978–84, Robinson Coll. Sen. Res. Fellow in Philosophy, All Souls Coll., Oxford, 1996–2006, now Emeritus Fellow. For. Hon. Mem., Amer. Acad. of Arts and Scis, 1992. *Publications:* The Theaetetus of Plato, 1990; A Map of Metaphysics Zeta, 2001; co-editor: Philosophy As It Is, 1979; Doubt and Dogmatism, 1980; Science and Speculation, 1982; The Original Sceptics, 1997; (ed) The Skeptical Tradition, 1983; contribs to classical and philosophical jls. *Recreation:* travel. *Address:* Robinson College, Cambridge CB3 9AN.

BURR, Michael Rodney; His Honour Judge Burr; a Circuit Judge, since 1992; *b* 31 Aug. 1941; *s* of Frank Edward Burr and Aileen Maud Burr; *m* 1963, Rhoda Rule; four *s* one *d*. *Educ:* Brecon County Grammar Sch.; King Edward VI Sch., Chelmsford; Coll. of Law. Solicitor, 1964. Asst Solicitor, Hilliard & Ward, Chelmsford, 1964–69; Sen. Partner, Peter Williams & Co., Swansea, 1972–92; Recorder, 1988. Sec., Incorp. Law Soc. of Swansea and Dist, 1980–83; Law Society: non-Council Member: Professional Purposes Cttee, 1985–86; Adjudication Cttee, 1986–89. *Recreations:* flying, travel.

BURR, Timothy John, CB 2008; Comptroller and Auditor General, National Audit Office, since 2008 (Deputy Comptroller and Auditor General, 2000–08); *b* 31 March 1950; *s* of Eric Cyril Burr and Myrtle Burr (*née* Waters); *m* 1975, Gillian Heather Croot; two *s*. *Educ:* Dulwich Coll. Entered HM Treasury, 1968; Cabinet Office, 1984; Asst Sec., HM Treasury, 1985; Under-Sec., Cabinet Office, 1990; Treasury Officer of Accounts, 1993–94; Asst Auditor Gen., Nat. Audit Office, 1994–2000. *Address:* c/o National Audit Office, Buckingham Palace Road, SW1W 9SP.

BURRELL, Sir Charles Raymond, 10th Bt *cr* 1774, of Valentine House, Essex; *b* 27 Aug. 1962; *s* of Sir (John) Raymond Burrell, 9th Bt, and of Rowena Frances, *d* of late M. H. Pearce; *S* father, 2008, but his name does not appear on the Official Roll of the Baronetage; *m* 1993, Isabella Elizabeth Nancy, adopted *d* of M. L. Tree; one *s* one *d*. *Educ:* Millfield; Royal Agricultural Coll., Cirencester. *Heir: s* Edward Lambert Burrell, *b* 10 Oct. 1996. *Address:* Knepp Castle, West Grinstead, Horsham, W Sussex RH13 8LJ.

BURRELL, Diana Elizabeth Jane; composer; Artistic Director, Spitalfields Festival, since 2006; AHRC Creative Arts Fellow, Royal Academy of Music, since 2006; *b* 25 Oct. 1948; *d* of Bernard Burrell and Audrey (*née* Coleman); *m* 1971, Richard Fallas; one *s* one *d*. *Educ:* Norwich High Sch.; Girton Coll., Cambridge Univ. (BA Hons Music). Music teacher, Sutton High Sch., 1971–75; freelance viola player and teacher, 1978–90; pianist, Holy Trinity Ch, Mile End, 1985–2006; part-time Lectr in Composition and 20th Century Studies, Goldsmiths' Coll., London, 1989–93; Composer-in-residence, Pimlico Sch., London, 1990–91; Living Composer, Eastern Orchestral Bd, 1993–95; Composer-in-Association, City of London Sinfonia, 1994–96; Composition Prof., GSMD, 1999–2006. Recordings of own works (Classic CD Award, 1998, for Viola Concerto and other works). Hon. FTCL 1997. *Compositions* include: The Albatross (opera), 1987; commissions: Landscape, 1988; Resurrection, 1992; Dunkelhvide Månestråler, 1996; Clarinet Concerto (for Northern Sinfonia), 1996; Symphonies of Flocks, Herds and Shoals (for BBC SO), 1997; Flute Concerto (for London Schools SO), 1998. *Recreations:* birdwatching, walking, gardening, 20th Century architecture. *Address:* c/o United Music Publishers, 42 Rivington Street, EC2A 3BN. *T:* (020) 7729 4700.

BURRELL, (Francis) Gary; QC 1996; a Recorder, since 1996; a Deputy High Court Judge, since 2001; *b* 7 Aug. 1953; *s* of Francis Ivan George Burrell and Louisa Shane Burrell; *m* 1979, Heather Young; three *s*. *Educ:* Belfast Boys' Model Sch.; Univ. of Exeter (LLB). Called to the Bar, Inner Temple, 1977, Bencher, 2002; Asst Recorder, 1992–96. Mem., Bar Council, 1995–. Pres., S Yorks Medico-Legal Soc., 1991–92; NE Circuit Rep., Personal Injury Bar Assoc., 1995–2003. *Publications:* various articles on personal injury litigation in Quantum. *Recreations:* sailing, fly fishing. *Address:* 22–26 Paradise Square, Sheffield S1 2DA. *T:* (0114) 273 8951; Thomas More Chambers, Lincoln's Inn Fields, WC2A 3BP.

BURRELL, Mark William; DL; Director, Pearson plc, 1977–97; *b* 9 April 1937; *s* of Sir Walter Burrell, 8th Bt, CBE, TD and Hon. Anne Judith, OBE, *o d* of 3rd Baron Denman, PC, GCMG, KCVO; *m* 1966, Margot Rosemary Pearce; two *s* one *d*. *Educ:* Eton; Pembroke Coll., Cambridge (BA 1st Cl. Hons Engrg). With Sir Alexander Gibb & Partners, 1959, then Vickers, 1960–61; joined Pearson plc, 1963; Whitehall Petroleum: Dir, 1964–88; Chm., 1987–88; joined Lazard Brothers, 1970; Dir, 1974; Man. Dir, 1984–86; non-exec. Dir, 1986–97; Director: BSB Holdings, 1987–99; BSkyB Group plc, 1991–94; Dir, then Chm., Royal Doulton plc, 1993–98; Chm., Millbank Financial Services Ltd, 1986–; non-executive Director: RM plc, 1997–2001; Conafex SA, 1999–2008 (Chm.); Dir, then Chm., Merlin Communications Internat., 1997–2001. Mem. Ct, Sussex Univ. Gov., Northbrook Coll., Sussex, 2004–. High Sheriff, 2002–03, DL, 2004, W Sussex. *Recreations:* hunting, polo, tennis, golf, ski-ing. *Address:* Bakers House, Bakers Lane, Shipley, W Sussex RH13 8GJ. *Clubs:* White's, Boodle's.

BURRELL, Michael Peter; Hon. Mr Justice Burrell; Judge of the Court of First Instance of the High Court (formerly Judge, Supreme Court), Hong Kong, since 1995; *b* 18 July 1948; *s* of Peter Burrell and Gwynneth Burrell; *m* 1975, Anne Hughes; two *d*, and one step *s*. *Educ:* Birkenhead Sch.; Magdalene Coll., Cambridge (MA). Called to the Bar, Inner Temple, 1971; in practice on Northern Circuit, 1972–86 (Junior, 1973); Hong Kong: Perm. Magistrate, 1986–90; Dist Judge, 1991–95. Mem., Hong Kong Judicial Studies Bd, 1992–95; Chm., Hong Kong Insider Dealing Tribunal, 1996–98. Hon. Fellow, HK Inst. of Surveyors, 2004. *Recreations:* sport, reading, walking. *Address:* c/o High Court, Queensway, Hong Kong. *Clubs:* Artists' (Liverpool); Royal Liverpool Golf (Hoylake); Oxton Cricket (Wirral); Hong Kong, Hong Kong Cricket (Hong Kong).

BURRETT, (Frederick) Gordon, CB 1974; Deputy Secretary, Civil Service Department, 1972–81; *b* 31 Oct. 1921; *s* of Frederick Burrett and Marion Knowles; *m* 1943, Joan Giddins; one *s* two *d*. *Educ:* Emanuel Sch.; St Catharine's Coll., Cambridge. Served in Royal Engrs, N Africa, Italy, Yugoslavia, Greece, 1942–45 (despatches). HM Foreign, subseq. Diplomatic, Service, 1946; 3rd Sec., Budapest, 1946–49; FO, 1949–51; Vice-Consul, New York, 1951–54; FO, 1954–57; 1st Sec., Rome, 1957–60; transf. to HM Treasury, 1960; Private Sec. to Chief Sec., Treasury, 1963–64; Asst Secretary: HM Treasury, 1964; Cabinet Office, 1967–68; Secretary: Kindersley Review Body on Doctors' and Dentists' Remuneration; Plowden Cttee on Pay of Higher Civil Service, 1967–68; Civil Service Dept, 1968, Under-Sec. 1969. Mem., Civil Service Pay Res. Unit Bd, 1978–81; conducted govt scrutiny of V&A and Sci. Museums, 1982; Adviser to Govt of Oman on CS reorganisation, 1984; led govt review of policies and operations of Commonwealth Inst., 1986; leader of review team to examine responsibilities and grading of dirs of nat. museums and galls, 1987; conducted review of sen. posts of Arts Council and BFI, 1987–88; Chm., Cttee of Inquiry into CS Pay, Hong Kong, 1988–89. Chairman: Redundant Churches Fund, later Churches Conservation Trust, 1982–95; Wagner Soc.,

1984–88. FSA 1985. Cross of St Augustine, 1995. *Publication:* article on the watercolours of John Massey Wright (1777–1866) in vol. 54 of the Old Water-Colour Society's Club Annual. *Recreations:* music, walking, reading. *Address:* 25 Dalmore Avenue, Claygate, Surrey KT10 0HQ. *T:* (01372) 462783. *Club:* Athenæum.

BURRIDGE, Rev. Dr Richard Alan; Dean, King's College London, since 1994; *b* 11 June 1955; *s* of Alan Burridge and Iris Joyce (*née* Coates); *m* 1979, Susan Morgan; two *d*. *Educ:* University Coll., Oxford (Exhibnr; BA Lit.Hum. 1st Cl. Hons, MA 1981); Univ. of Nottingham (PGCE 1978; Postgrad. DTh 1983; PhD 1989); St John's Coll., Nottingham. Classics Master and House Tutor, Sevenoaks Sch., 1978–82; ordained deacon 1985, priest 1986; Curate, St Peter and St Paul, Bromley, Kent, 1985–87; Lazenby Chaplain, Univ. of Exeter and part-time Lectr, Depts of Theol. and of Classics and Ancient Hist., 1987–94; Dir of NT Studies, Dept of Theol. and Religious Studies, KCL, 1994– (FKC 2002). Mem., Gen. Synod of C of E, 1994–. Member: Council of Mgt, St John's Coll., Nottingham, 1986–99; Council of Ref., Monarch Pubns, Tunbridge Wells, 1992–2000. Mem., Academic Bd (formerly Bd of Studies), N Thames Ministerial Trng Course, 1994–; Ext. Examr, SW Ministerial Trng Course, 1995–99; Commissary, Bp of the High Veld, CPSA, 1997–. Member: SNTS, 1995–; Soc. for Study of Theol., 1995–; Soc. of Biblical Lit., 1996–. Expert Advr (Faith Zone, Greenwich Dome), Nat. Millennium Experience Co., 1998–2000. Chaplain to Hendon Golf Club, 2004–. Trustee: Christian Evidence Soc., 1994– (Chm., 2001–); Foundn of St Catherine, Cumberland Lodge, 1998–. *Publications:* Sex Therapy: some ethical considerations, 1985; What are the Gospels?: a comparison with Graeco-Roman biography, 1992, 2nd edn 2004; Four Gospels, One Jesus?: a symbolic reading, 1994 (also Korean edn, 2000), 2nd edn 2005 (also US and Australian edns); John (People's Bible Commentary), 1998, Lambeth Conference edn 2008 (also US edn, 2007); Faith Odyssey: a journey through Lent, 2000; (ed jtly) The Lectionary Commentary, 2002; Faith Odyssey: a journey through life, 2003 (also Norwegian edn, 2003); (jtly) Jesus Now and Then, 2004; Imitating Jesus: an inclusive approach to New Testament ethics, 2007; *contributor to:* A Dictionary of Biblical Interpretation, 1990; The New Dictionary of Christian Ethics and Pastoral Theology, 1995; A Handbook of Classical Rhetoric in the Hellenistic Period 330 BC–AD 400, 1997; The Gospels for all Christians: rethinking the gospel audiences, 1998; Where Shall We Find God?, 1998; The Lion Handbook to the Bible, 1999; Christology, Community and Controversy, 2000; Dictionary of New Testament Background, 2000; The Story of Christian Spirituality, 2001; Exploring and Proclaiming the Apostles' Creed, 2004; The Dictionary for Theological Interpretation of Scripture, 2005; The Written Gospel, 2005; The Person of Christ, 2005; The Oxford Handbook of Biblical Studies, 2006; The Fourfold Gospel Commentary, 2006; Tutu As I Know Him: on a personal note, 2006; The Dictionary of Biblical Criticism and Interpretation, 2007; articles in Theology, Church Times, St John the Evangelist Mag., C of E Newspaper, THES, Wholeness, Dialogue, The Times, Sewanee Theological Review. *Recreations:* being with my wife and family, sailing, ski-ing, golf, cycling, playing guitar and bass. *Address:* Dean's Office, King's College London, Strand, WC2R 2LS. *T:* (020) 7848 2333/2063, *Fax:* (020) 7848 2344; *e-mail:* dean@kcl.ac.uk.

BURRILL, Timothy; Managing Director, Burrill Productions, since 1966; Chairman, Film Asset Developments Plc, 1987–94; *b* 8 June 1931; *yr s* of L. Peckover Burrill, OBE and Marjorie S. Burrill; *m* 1st, 1959, Philippa (marr. diss. 1966), *o d* of Maurice and Margot Hare; one *d*; 2nd, 1968, Santa (marr. diss. 1993), *e d* of John and Betty Raymond; one *s* two *d*. *Educ:* Eton Coll.; Sorbonne Univ. Served Grenadier Guards, 1949–52: commnd 1950; served 2nd Bn, 1950–52. Jun. management, Cayzer Irvine & Co., 1952–56; entered film industry, 1956; joined Brookfield Prodns, 1965; Dir, World Film Services, 1967–69; first Prodn Administrator, National Film and TV Sch., 1972; Man. Dir, Allied Stars (resp. for Chariots of Fire), 1979–80; Director: Artistry Ltd, 1982–87 (resp. for Superman and Supergirl films); Pathé (formerly Chargeurs) Productions Ltd, 1994–99; Pathé Pictures, 1994–99; Consultant: National Film Develt Fund, 1980–81; Really Useful Group, 1989–90; Script Factory, 1998–. UK Rep., Eurimages, 1994–96. Chairman: BAFTA, 1981–83 (Vice-Chm., 1979–81); First Film Foundn, 1989–98; Producer Mem., Cinematograph Films Council, 1980–85; Member: Gen. Council, ACTT, 1975–76; Exec. Council, British Film and Television Producers Assoc., 1981–89; Exec. Council, The Producers Assoc., 1989–91; Exec. Council, Producers' Alliance for Cinema and Television, 1991–2001 (Vice-Chm., 1993–94); Sir Peter Middleton's Adv. Cttee of Film Finance, 1996–97; Dir, British Film Commn, 1998–2000. Chm., Impact Campaign, 1994–95. Governor: National Film and Television Sch., 1981–92; National Theatre, 1982–88. Films include Tess, The Fourth Protocol, The Pirates of Penzance, The Pianist, Oliver Twist, La Vie en Rose, etc. *Recreation:* theatre. *Address:* 19 Cranbury Road, SW6 2NS. *T:* (020) 7736 8673, *Fax:* (020) 7731 3921; *e-mail:* timothy@timothyburrill.co.uk.

BURRINGTON, Ernest; Deputy Publisher, 1993–95, Vice President, 1995, Globe Communications, USA; Director, 1985–92, Chairman, 1991–92, Mirror Group Newspapers; *b* 13 Dec. 1926; *s* of late Harold Burrington and of Laura Burrington; *m* 1950, Nancy Crossley; one *s* one *d*. Reporter, Oldham Chronicle, 1941–43; Army service, 1944–47; reporter and sub-editor, Oldham Chronicle, 1947–49; sub-editor, Bristol Evening World, 1950; Daily Herald: sub-editor, Manchester, 1950, night editor, 1955; London night editor, 1957; IPC Sun: night editor, 1964; Asst Editor, 1965; Asst Editor and night editor, News International Sun, 1969; dep. night editor, Daily Mirror, 1970; Dep. Editor, 1971, Associate Editor, 1972, Sunday People; Editor, The People, 1985–88 and 1989–90; Dep. Chm. and Asst Publisher, 1988–91, Man. Dir, 1989–91, Mirror Gp Newspapers; Chm., Syndication Internat., 1989–92; Dep. Chm., Mirror Publishing Co., 1989–91; Director: Mirror Group Magazine and Newsday Ltd, 1989–92; Legionstyle Ltd, 1991–92; Mirror Colour Print Ltd, 1991–92; (non-exec.) Sunday Correspondent, 1990; The European, 1990–91; IQ Newsgraphics, 1990–92; Sygma Picture Agency, Paris, 1990–91; Marketing Consultant, 1996–97, Pres., 1996–98, Atlantic Media; Head of Marketing, Harveys plc, 1998–2000. Member: Council, NPA, 1988–92; IPI (Mem., British Exec., 1988–92); Foreign Press Assoc.; Trustee, Internat. Centre for Child Studies, 1986–90. Life Mem., NUJ, 1996. *Recreations:* travel, bridge, Manchester United FC (Hon. Red Devil, 1985). *Address:* 17499 Tiffany Trace Drive, Boca Raton, FL 33487, USA. *T:* (561) 9959897; South Hall, Dene Park, Shipbourne, near Tonbridge TN11 9NS. *T:* (01732) 368517; *e-mail:* burringtone@aol.com.

BURROW, Prof. John Anthony, FBA 1986; Winterstoke Professor of English, University of Bristol, 1976–98, now Emeritus; *b* 3 Aug. 1932; *s* of William and Ada Burrow; *m* 1956, Diana Wynne Jones; three *s*. *Educ:* Buckhurst Hill County High Sch., Essex; Christ Church, Oxford (BA, MA). Asst Lectr, King's Coll., London, 1955–57; Lectr in English, Christ Church, 1957–61, and Brasenose Coll., 1957–59, Oxford; Fellow in English, Jesus Coll., Oxford, 1961–75; Dean of Faculty of Arts, Univ. of Bristol, 1990–93. Vis. Prof., Yale Univ., 1968–69. Hon. Dir, EETS, 1983–2006. *Publications:* A Reading of Sir Gawain and the Green Knight, 1965; Geoffrey Chaucer (critical anthology), 1969; Ricardian Poetry, 1971; (ed) English Verse 1300–1500, 1977; Medieval Writers and their Work, 1982, rev. edn 2008; Essays on Medieval Literature, 1984; The Ages of Man, 1986; (with Thorlac Turville-Petre) A Book of Middle English, 1992; Langland's Fictions, 1993; Thomas Hoccleve, 1994; (ed) Hoccleve's Complaint and Dialogue, 1999; The Gawain-Poet, 2001; Gestures and Looks in Medieval Narrative, 2002; The Poetry of Praise, 2008; articles and reviews in learned jls. *Recreation:* music. *Address:* 9 The Polygon, Clifton, Bristol BS8 4PW. *T:* (0117) 9277845.

BURROW, John Halcrow, CBE 1993 (OBE 1987); QPM 1998; DL; Chief Constable of Essex Police, 1988–98; *b* 1935; *s* of John and Florence Burrow; *m* 1958, Ruth (*née* Taylor); two *s* one *d*. *Educ:* Ulverston Grammar School; University College London (LLB Hons). Lieut, 3rd Kenya Bn, King's African Rifles, 1953–55. Metropolitan Police, 1958–77; Asst/Dep. Chief Constable, Merseyside Police, 1977–88; RCDS, 1979. Pres., ACPO, 1992–93; Chairman: Technical and Res. Cttee, ACPO, 1990–92; ACPO No 5 (SE) Region Cttee, 1991–98; Shotley Training Centre Cttee, 1990–92. Chairman: St John Ambulance, Essex, 2004– (Co. Comdr, 1999–2004); Essex Br., SSAFA, 2001–. DL Essex, 1998. *Recreation:* walking. *Address:* Acorns, Church End, Shalford, Braintree, Essex CM7 5HA. *T:* (01371) 850577.

BURROW, Prof. John Wyon, FBA 1986; FRHistS 1971; Professor of European Thought, and Fellow of Balliol College, University of Oxford, 1995–2000, Emeritus Fellow, since 2001; *b* 4 June 1935; *s* of Charles and Alice Burrow; *m* 1958, Diane Dunnington; one *s* one *d*. *Educ:* Exeter School; Christ's College, Cambridge (MA, PhD). Research Fellow, Christ's College, Cambridge, 1959–62; Fellow, Downing Coll., Cambridge, 1962–65; Lectr, Sch. of European Studies, Univ. of East Anglia, 1965–69; Reader in History, 1969–82, Prof. of Intellectual History, 1982–95, Univ. of Sussex. Vis. Prof., Univ. of California, Berkeley, 1981 and 1989; Visiting Fellow: History of Ideas Unit, ANU, 1983; All Souls Coll., Oxford, 1994–95; Res. Prof. of Intellectual Hist., Univ. of Sussex, 2000–03. Carlyle Lectr, Oxford, 1985; Christian Gauss Seminars, Princeton Univ., 1988. Editor in Chief, History of European Ideas, 1996–2005. Hon. Dr Scienze Politiche, Bologna, 1988. *Publications:* Evolution and Society, 1966; A Liberal Descent, 1981 (Wolfson Prize); (with S. Collini and D. Winch) That Noble Science of Politics, 1983; Gibbon, 1985; Whigs and Liberals, 1988; The Crisis of Reason, 2000; A History of Histories, 2007. *Recreation:* cooking. *Address:* Balliol College, Oxford OX1 3BJ; 22 Bridge Street, Witney, Oxon OX28 1HY. *T:* (01993) 700306.

BURROWES, David John Barrington; MP (C) Enfield Southgate, since 2005; *b* 12 June 1969; *m* 1996, Janet; four *s* two *d* (of whom one *s* one *d* are twins). *Educ:* Highgate Sch.; Univ. of Exeter (LLB 1991). Asst Solicitor, 1995–2005, Consultant, 2005–, Shepherd Harris and Co., Enfield. Mem. (C), Enfield BC, 1994–2006 (Cabinet Mem. for voluntary and community develt, 2003–04). Contested (C) Edmonton, 2001. *Publications:* (jtly) Moral Basis of Conservatism, 1995; Such a Thing as Society: Maggie's children and volunteering, 2006. *Recreations:* sports, particularly football and cricket. *Address:* (office) 1c Chaseville Parade, Chaseville Park Road, Winchmore Hill, N21 1PG. *T:* (020) 8360 0234; *e-mail:* david@davidburrowes.com; House of Commons, SW1A 0AA. *T:* (020) 7219 8144.

BURROWES, Norma Elizabeth; opera and concert singer; *d* of Henry and Caroline Burrowes; *m* 1st, 1969, Steuart Bedford, *qv* (marr. diss.); 2nd, 1987, Emile Belcourt; one *s* one *d*. *Educ:* Sullivan Upper Sch., Holywood, Co. Down; Queen's Univ., Belfast (BA); Royal Academy of Music (FRAM 1992). Operas include: Zerlina in Don Giovanni, Glyndebourne Touring Opera (début); Blöndchen in Die Entführung aus dem Serail, Salzburg Festival, and again Blöndchen, Paris Opera, 1976 (début); Fiakermili, Royal Opera House (début), also Oscar, Despina, Nanetta, Woodbird; Entführung aus dem Serail, Ballo in Maschera, Der Rosenkavalier, Metropolitan, NY; Daughter of the Regiment, Midsummer Night's Dream, Elisir d'Amore, Canada; Cosi Fan Tutte, Romeo and Juliet, France; Marriage of Figaro, Germany; Gianni Schicchi, Switzerland; Marriage of Figaro, La Scala. Television operas include: Nanetta in Falstaff; Susanna in Marriage of Figaro and Lauretta in Gianni Schicchi. Sings regularly with major opera companies, gives concerts and recitals, GB and abroad; many recordings. Hon. DMus Queen's Univ. Belfast, 1979. *Recreations:* swimming, gardening, needlework.

BURROWS, Prof. Andrew Stephen, FBA 2007; Norton Rose Professor of Commercial and Financial Law, and Fellow of St Hugh's College, University of Oxford, since 1999; a Recorder, since 2000; *b* 17 April 1957; *s* of William George Burrows and Dora Burrows; *m* 1982, Rachel Jane Gent; three *s* one *d*. *Educ:* Prescot Grammar Sch.; Brasenose Coll., Oxford (Schol.; Martin Wronker Prize 1978; MA; BCL); Harvard Law Sch. (LLM). Called to the Bar, Middle Temple, 1985 (Hon. Bencher, 2000); Mem., Fountain Court Chambers, Temple. Lectr in Law, Merton Coll., Oxford, 1979–80; Harkness Fellow, Harvard Law Sch., 1980–81; Lectr in Law, Univ. of Manchester, 1981–86; Fellow and CUF Lectr in Law, 1986–94, Hon. Res. Fellow, 1994–, LMH, Oxford; Prof. of English Law, UCL, 1994–99; Law Comr for England and Wales, 1994–99. Hon. QC 2003. Jt winner, Prize for Outstanding Legal Scholarship, SPTL, 1993. *Publications:* Remedies for Torts and Breach of Contract, 1987, 3rd edn 2004; (ed jtly) Clerk and Lindsell on Torts, 16th edn 1989 to 19th edn 2006; Essays on the Law of Restitution (ed Burrows), 1991; The Law of Restitution, 1993, 2nd edn 2002; (ed jtly) Chitty on Contracts, 28th edn 1999, 29th edn 2004; (ed jtly) Scrutton on Charterparties, 20th edn 1996, 21st edn 2008; (jtly) Cases and Materials on the Law of Restitution, 1997, 2nd edn 2007; Understanding the Law of Obligations, 1998; (jtly) English Private Law, 2000, (Gen. Ed.) 2nd edn 2007; (ed jtly) Commercial Remedies, 2003; (ed jtly) Mapping the Law, 2006; (ed jtly) Contract Terms, 2007; A Casebook on Contract, 2007; numerous articles in legal jls. *Recreations:* sport (esp. football), mountain walking. *Address:* St Hugh's College, Oxford OX2 6LE.

BURROWS, Christopher Parker; HM Diplomatic Service; Counsellor, Foreign and Commonwealth Office, since 2006; *b* 12 Sept. 1958; *s* of John Brian and Margaret Katherine Burrows; *m* 1988, Betty Burrows (*née* Cordi); one *s* two *d*. *Educ:* Cleethorpes Grammar Sch.; Liverpool Univ. Entered FCO, 1980; Third Sec., East Berlin, 1982–85; Third, later Second, Sec., Bonn, 1987–89; First Sec. (External), Athens, 1993–96; First Sec., later Counsellor, Brussels, 1998–2002; Counsellor: FCO, 2002–05; New Delhi, 2005–06. *Recreations:* jazz piano, gardening, football. *Address:* Foreign and Commonwealth Office, King Charles Street, SW1A 2AH.

BURROWS, Clive, CEng; FREng, FIET, FIMechE; Group Engineering Director, FirstGroup plc, since 2008; *b* 1 Aug. 1958; *s* of Gordon and Barbara Burrows; *m* 1999, Norma Silvia de Anda Marquez. *Educ:* Univ. of Bath (BSc Hons Electrical and Electronic Engrg). CEng 1992, FREng 2004; MIEE 1992, FIET (FIEE 2002); FIMechE 2002. Intercity Route Fleet Manager, BR, 1989–91; Depot Manager, N Pole Internat., and Project Engr, Eurostar UK, 1991–93; Man. Dir, Transportation Consultants Internat., 1993–98; Gp Rail Engrg Dir, First Gp plc, 1998–2005; Dir, Technical and Professional, DfT, 2005–08. MInstD 1999. *Publications:* contrib. learned jls. *Recreations:* keen student of all matters relating to travel, transport and technology, collector and restorer of preserved rail vehicles and artifacts. *Address:* FirstGroup, Milford House, 1 Milford Street, Swindon SN1 1HL; *e-mail:* Clive.Burrows@firstgroup.com.

BURROWS, General Eva, AC 1994 (AO 1986); General of the Salvation Army, 1986–93, retired; *b* 15 Sept. 1929; *d* of Robert John Burrows and Ella Maria Burrows (*née* Watson). *Educ:* Brisbane State High School; Queensland Univ. (BA); London Univ.

(PGCE); Sydney Univ. (MEd). Salvation Army: Missionary Educator, Howard Inst., Zimbabwe, 1952–67; Principal, Usher Inst., Zimbabwe, 1967–69; Vice-Principal 1970–73, Principal 1974–75, Internat. Coll. for Officers, London; Leader, Women's Social Services in GB and Ireland, 1975–77; Territorial Commander: Sri Lanka, 1977–79; Scotland, 1979–82; Australia, 1982–86. Hon. Dr of Liberal Arts, Ewha Woman's Univ., Seoul, S. Korea, 1988; Hon. LLD: Asbury Coll., USA, 1988; Univ. of NSW, 1996; Hon. DD Olivet Univ., USA, 1993; Hon. DPhil Queensland, 1993; DUniv Griffith, 1994; Hon. STD Melbourne Coll. of Divinity, 2000. *Recreations:* classical music, reading, travel. *Address:* Unit 102, 193 Domain Road, South Yarra, Melbourne, Vic 3141, Australia. *T:* (3) 98209701.

BURROWS, Fred, CMG 1981; PhD; international law consultant, since 1990; *b* 10 Aug. 1925; *s* of late Charles Burrows; *m* 1955, (Jennifer) Winsome Munt; two *s*. *Educ:* Altrincham Grammar Sch.; Trinity Hall, Cambridge (MA). PhD Cantab, 1988. Served in RAF, 1944–47. Called to Bar, Gray's Inn, 1950; Asst Legal Adviser, Foreign Office, 1956–65; Legal Adviser, British Embassy, Bonn, 1965–67; returned to FO, 1967; Legal Counsellor, FCO, 1968–77; Counsellor (Legal Adviser), Office of UK Perm. Rep. to European Communities, 1977–80; Legal Counsellor, FCO, 1980–85; Law Officer (Special Duties), then (International Law), Hong Kong, 1985–90. JP Hong Kong, 1986–90. *Publication:* Free Movement in European Community Law, 1985. *Recreations:* sailing, trombone. *Address:* c/o Foreign and Commonwealth Office, SW1A 2AL.

BURROWS, (George) Richard (William); Governor, Bank of Ireland, since 2005; *b* 16 Jan. 1946; *m* 1970, Sherril Dix; one *s* three *d*. *Educ:* Wesley College, Dublin; Rathmines College of Commerce. FICA. Articled Stokes Bros & Pim, 1963–70; Asst to Man. Dir, Edward Dillon & Co., 1970; Man. Dir, Old Bushmills Distillery Co., 1972; Gen. Manager, Irish Distillers, 1976; Man. Dir, 1978, Chief Exec., 1991–2000, Chm., 1991–2007, Irish Distillers Group; Dir Gen., 2000–05, Bd Dir, 2004–, Pernod Ricard. Non-exec. Dir, Rentokil Initial plc, 2008–. *Recreation:* sailing. *Address:* Bank of Ireland, Lower Baggot Street, Dublin 2, Ireland.

BURROWS, Prof. Malcolm, FRS 1985; Professor of Zoology, University of Cambridge, since 1996, and Fellow of Wolfson College, Cambridge, since 1991; *b* 28 May 1943; *s* of William Roy Burrows and Jean Jones Burrows; *m* 1966, Christine Joan Ellis; one *s* one *d*. *Educ:* Cambridge Univ. (MA; ScD 1983); St Andrews Univ. (PhD 1967). Reader in Neurobiology, 1983–86, Prof. of Neurosci., 1986–96, Univ. of Cambridge. Vis. Prof., Konstanz Univ., 1987; Cornelius Wiersma Vis. Prof., CIT, 1991; Distinguished Vis. Prof., Univ. of California, Davis, 1992. Pres., Internat. Soc. for Neuroethology, 1998–2001. MAE 1992. Mem., Bayerische Akad. der Wissenschaften, 1996. Scientific Medal, Zoological Soc., 1980; Alexander von Humboldt award, 1993. *Publication:* The Neurobiology of an Insect Brain, 1996.

BURROWS, Margaret Ann; *see* Buck, M. A.

BURROWS, Rt Rev. Michael Andrew James; *see* Cashel and Ossory, Bishop of.

BURROWS, Michael Peter; QC 2008; a Recorder, since 2000; *b* Birmingham, 26 June 1957; *s* of Peter and Margaret Burrows; *m* 1990, Gail Burbridge; three *d*. *Educ:* Tudor Grange Grammar Sch., Solihull; Solihull Sixth Form Coll.; Queens' Coll., Cambridge (BA 1978). Called to the Bar, Inner Temple, 1979; in practice at the Bar, specialising in criminal law, 1979–; Asst Recorder, 1997–2000. *Recreations:* walking in the Lake District, holidays in Scotland, theatre and music, especially of Haydn, Beethoven and Mendelssohn. *Address:* 5 Fountain Court, Steelhouse Lane, Birmingham B4 6DR.

BURROWS, Ven. Peter; Archdeacon of Leeds, since 2005; *b* 27 May 1955; *s* of Alfred and Eileen Burrows; *m* 1975, Jane Susan Allsop; one *s* one *d*. *Educ:* Salisbury and Wells Theol Coll.; BTh Southampton (ext.) 1980. Nursing Asst, Derbyshire Royal Infirmary, 1973–76; Clerical Officer, DHSS, 1976–80. Ordained deacon, 1983, priest, 1984; Curate, Baildon, 1983–87; Rector: Broughton Astley, 1987–93; Broughton Astley and Croft with Stoney Stanton, 1993–2000; RD, Guthlaxton First Deanery, 1994–2000; Diocese of Leicester: Dir of Ordinands and Parish Develt Officer, 2000–03; Dep. Dir of Ministry, 2002–03, Dir of Ministry, 2003–05. *Recreations:* cooking Indian food, entertaining and hospitality, theatre, cinema, amateur dramatics, reading, motor sport, travel. *Address:* The Archdeacon's Lodge, 3 West Park Grove, Leeds LS8 2HQ. *T:* (0113) 269 0594.

BURROWS, Richard; *see* Burrows, G. R. W.

BURROWS, Rt Rev. Simon Hedley; Hon. Assistant Bishop, diocese of Winchester, since 1994; Bishop Suffragan of Buckingham, 1974–85, Area Bishop, 1985–94; *b* 8 Nov. 1928; *s* of late Very Rev. H. R. Burrows, and Joan Lumsden, *d* of Rt Rev. E. N. Lovett, CBE; *m* 1960, Janet Woodd; two *s* three *d*. *Educ:* Eton; King's Coll., Cambridge (MA); Westcott House, Cambridge. Curate of St John's Wood, 1954–57; Chaplain of Jesus Coll., Cambridge, 1957–60; Vicar of Wyken, Coventry, 1960–67; Vicar of Holy Trinity, Fareham, 1967–74, and Rector of Team Ministry, 1971–74. Hon. DLitt Buckingham, 1992. Sub-Prelate, Order of St John, 1992–96. *Address:* 8 Quarry Road, Winchester, Hants SO23 0JF. *T:* (01962) 853332.

BURSELL, His Honour Rev. Rupert David Hingston; QC 1986; a Senior Circuit Judge, 2003–08 (a Circuit Judge, 1988–2008); *b* 10 Nov. 1942; *s* of Henry and Cicely Mary Bursell; *m* 1967, Joanna Ruth Gibb; two *s* one *d*. *Educ:* St John's School, Leatherhead; Univ. of Exeter (LLB); St Edmund Hall, Oxford (MA, DPhil). Called to the Bar, Lincoln's Inn, 1968; Sir Thomas More Bursary and Hubert Greenland Studentship, Lincoln's Inn, 1969; a Recorder, 1985–88; an Official Referee, 1992–98; a nominated Judge of the Technology and Construction Court, 1998–2008; Designated Civil Judge, 1999–2008. Chancellor, Vicar-General and Official Principal, Diocese of Durham, 1989–; Chancellor, Dio. of Bath and Wells, 1992; Chancellor, VG and Official Principal, Dio. of St Albans, 1992–2002; Dep. Chancellor, Dio. of York, 1994–2007; Chancellor, VG and Official Principal, Dio. of Oxford, 2002–. Member: Legal Adv. Commn, Gen. Synod, 1990– (Chm., 2007–); Provincial Panels for Canterbury and York, Clergy Discipline Measure, 2006–. Deacon, 1968; Priest, 1969; Hon. Curate: St Marylebone, 1968–69; St Mary the Virgin, Almondsbury, 1969–71; St Francis, Bedminster, 1971–83; Christ Church, and St Stephen, Bristol, 1983–88; St Andrew, Cheddar, 1993–. Hon. Canon, St Albans Cathedral, 1996–2002. Hon. Chaplain, 3rd (Vol.) Military Intelligence Bn, 1996–2001. *Publications:* (contrib.) Atkin's Court Forms, 1972, 2nd edn 1985; (contrib.) Halsbury's Laws of England, 1975; (jtly) Crown Court Practice, 1978; (contrib.) Principles of Dermatitis Litigation, 1985; Liturgy, Order and the Law, 1996; articles in legal jls. *Recreations:* Church music, military history, archaeology of Greece, Turkey and Holy Land, silversmithing. *Address:* The Crown Court, Small Street, Bristol BS1 1DA. *Clubs:* MCC, Army and Navy.

BURSLEM, Dame Alexandra Vivien, (Dame Sandra), DBE 2004 (OBE 1993); DL; Vice-Chancellor, Manchester Metropolitan University, 1997–2005; *b* Shanghai, China, 6 May 1940; *d* of Stanley Morris Thornley, CA and Myrra Thornley (*née* Kimberley); *m* 1st, 1960 (marr. diss. 1971); two *s*; 2nd, 1977, Richard Waywell Burslem, MD, FRCOG (*d* 2001); one *d*. *Educ:* Arnold High Sch. for Girls, Blackpool; Manchester Univ. (BA 1st Cl. Hons Politics and Modern Hist. 1971); Manchester Business Sch. (DipBA 1986). Manchester Polytechnic, later Manchester Metropolitan University: Lectr, 1973, Sen. Lectr, 1975–80 and Principal Lectr, 1980–82, Dept of Social Sci., 1973–82; Hd, Dept of Applied Community Studies, 1982–86; Dean, Faculty of Community Studies and Educn, 1986–88; Academic Dir, 1988–92; Dep. Vice-Chancellor, 1992–97. Vice-Chm., Manchester FPC, 1974–89. Chm., BBC Regl Adv. Council, 1983–92. A Civil Service Comr, 2005–. Member: Council, FEFC, 2000–01; Nat. Learning and Skills Council, 2000–06 (Dep. Chm., 2004–06); Gen. Teaching Council, 2000–02; Council, ACU, 2001–05. Chairman: British Council Education-UK Partnership, 2005–; Educn Honours Cttee, 2005–. Mem. Bd, Anchor Trust, 1995–97; Chm., Manchester and Cheshire Anchor Trust, 1995–97. Gov., Eccles Coll., 1996–98; Feoffee, Chetham's Sch. of Music, 2001– (Chm., Sch. Cttee, 2005–). Mem., Manchester Literary and Philosophical Soc., 1988–. FRSA 1989. JP Inner Manchester, 1981; DL 2004, High Sheriff 2006–07, Greater Manchester. Hon. RNCM 2004. Hon. Fellow, St Martin's UC, 2007. Hon. LLD Manchester, 2001; Hon. DLitt: UMIST, 2004; Salford, 2005; Manchester Metropolitan, 2006. *Recreations:* opera, theatre, reading, travel. *Address:* Lone Oak, Mereside Road, Mere, Knutsford, Cheshire WA16 6QR. *T:* (01565) 830100.

BURSTALL, Dr Clare, FBPsS; Director, National Foundation for Educational Research in England and Wales, 1983–93 (Deputy Director, 1972–83); *b* 3 Sept. 1931; *d* of Alfred and Lily Wells; *m* 1955, Michael Lyle Burstall (marr. diss. 1977); one *s* one *d*. *Educ:* King's Coll. and Birkbeck Coll., Univ. of London (BA Hons French, BA Hons Psychology, PhD Psychology); La Sorbonne, Paris. FBPsS 1975. Project Leader of team evaluating teaching of French in British primary schs, NFER, 1964–72. Charter Fellow, Coll. of Preceptors, 1988; FRSA 1990; Mem., Soc. of Authors, 2000; Hon. Mem., CGLI, 1987. Hon. DSc Hull, 1988; Hon. DEd De Montford, 1993. *Publications:* French from Eight: a national experiment, 1968; French in the Primary School: attitudes and achievement, 1970; Primary French in the Balance, 1974; French from Age Eight or Eleven?, 1975; translated with Vladimir Kisselnikov: Zhitinsky, The Staircase, and Cheops and Nefertiti, 2000; Red Star Under the Baltic, by Viktor Korzh, 2004; Leningrad Under Siege: firsthand accounts of the ordeal, by A. Adamovich and D. Granin, 2006; jl articles on various aspects of educnl research (eg, second language learning, large-scale assessment of achievement, class size, and management of educnl res.). *Recreations:* sailing, art collection, music, needlework. *Address:* Taskalinrinne 4, 49400 Hamina, Finland. *T:* and *Fax:* (5) 388668; *e-mail:* clare.burstall@pp.inet.fi.

BURSTEIN, Joan, CBE 2006; Owner, Browns fashion stores, since 1970; *b* 21 Feb. 1926; *d* of Ashley Jotner and Mary Jotner; *m* 1946, Sidney Burstein; one *s* one *d*. *Educ:* Henrietta Barnet Sch. Owner: Neatawear fashion stores, 1955–67; Feathers boutique, High St Kensington, 1968–70. Hon. Dr Univ. of the Arts, 2007. V&A Award for Outstanding Achievement in Fashion, 2000. *Recreations:* theatre, gardening, travel. *Address:* Browns, 23–27 South Molton Street, W1K 5RD. *T:* (020) 7514 0000, *Fax:* (020) 7408 1281.

BURSTON, Sir Samuel (Gerald Wood), Kt 1977; OBE 1966; Grazier at Noss Estate, Casterton, Victoria, 1945–85; President, Australian Woolgrowers and Graziers Council, 1976–79; *b* 24 April 1915; *s* of Maj.-Gen. Sir Samuel Burston, KBE, CB, DSO, VD, late RAAMC, and late Lady Burston; *m* 1st, 1940, Verna Helen Peebles (*d* 1980); one *s* one *d*; 2nd, 1995, Phyllis Elaine Irwin (*d* 2000). *Educ:* St Peter's Coll., Adelaide (Sch. Captain, 1933). Major, AIF, 1939–45 (despatches). Chm., Country Fire Authority, Vic, 1964–65; Pres., Graziers Assoc. of Vic, 1973–76; Councillor, Nat. Farmers Fedn, 1979–82; Vice-Pres., Confedn of Aust. Industry, 1978–82; Member: Nat. Employers Policy Cttee, 1970–78; Australian Wool Industry Policy Cttee, 1976–78; Aust. Sci. and Technol. Council, 1976–85 (acting Chm., 1982); Aust. Stats Adv. Council, 1976–80; Aust. Govt Econ. Consultative Gp, 1976–82; Nat. Labour Consultative Council, 1976–82; Reserve Bank Bd, 1977–87. Aust. Trade Develt Council, 1979–85; Trade Practices Cons. Council, 1979–82; Aust. Manufacturing Council, 1979–84; Chm., Perpetual Executors & Trustee Co. of Australia, 1981–87. Mem., Victorian Selection Cttee, Winston Churchill Meml Trust, 1967–81; Chm., Aust. Pastoral Res. Trust, 1988–92. *Recreations:* golf, swimming. *Address:* 31/52 Brougham Place, North Adelaide, SA 5006, Australia. *T:* (8) 82672152. *Clubs:* Adelaide, Naval, Military and Air Force of South Australia (Adelaide); Royal Adelaide Golf.

BURSTOW, Paul Kenneth; MP (Lib Dem) Sutton and Cheam, since 1997; *b* 13 May 1962; *s* of Brian Seymour Burstow and Sheila Burstow; *m* 1995, Mary Everdell Kemm. *Educ:* Poly. of South Bank (BA Hons Business Studies). Buying asst, Allied Shoe Repairs, 1985–86; print sales, Kallkwik Printers, 1986–87; research asst (part time), London Borough of Hounslow, 1987–89; Association of Social Democrat, then Liberal Democrat Councillors: Organising Sec. (part time), 1987–89; Councillors Officer, 1989–92; Campaigns Officer, 1992–96; Actg Political Sec., 1996–97. Council, London Borough of Sutton: Mem., 1986–2002; Chm., Envmtl Service Cttee, 1988–91 and 1993–96; Dep. Leader, 1994–97. Contested (Lib Dem) Sutton and Cheam, 1992. Lib Dem Local Govt Team Leader, 1997–99; Lib Dem spokesman on: older people, 1999–2003; health, 2003–05; Lib Dem Chief Whip, 2006–. Mem., Select Cttee on Health, 2003–04, 2005–06. *Recreations:* walking, cooking, gym work. *Address:* House of Commons, SW1A 0AA. *T:* (020) 7219 1196. *Club:* National Liberal.

BURT, Prof. Alastair David, MD; FRCPath; FIBiol; Professor of Pathology, since 1998, and Dean of Clinical Medicine, since 2005, Newcastle University; *b* Dunfermline, 9 March 1957; *s* of George Hoggan Burt and Iris Helen Forrest Burt; *m* 1980, Alison Carol Tweedlie; one *s* one *d*. *Educ:* Hawkhill Prim. Sch., Dundee; Hummersknott Grammar Sch., Darlington; Eastwood High Sch., Newton Mearns; Univ. of Glasgow (BSc 1st Cl. Hons 1979; MB ChB with Commendation 1981; MD Hons and Bellahouston Medal 1991). MRCPath 1988, FRCPath 1997; FIBiol 1996. Jun. House Officer in Medicine and Surgery, 1981–82, Registrar, then Sen. Registrar in Pathol., 1982–89, Western Infirmary, Glasgow and Glasgow Royal Infirmary; Peel Trust Travelling Res. Officer, Free Univ. of Brussels, 1985–86; Newcastle University: Sen. Lectr in Pathol., 1989–95; Personal Prof. in Hepatopathol., 1995–98; Hd, Sch. of Clin. and Lab. Scis, 2002–05. Hon. Clin. Histopathologist, 1989–, Head of Service, Cellular Pathol., 2000–05, Newcastle upon Tyne Hosps NHS Foundn Trust. Hon. Treas. and Trustee, Pathological Soc., 2002–. Ed.-in-Chief, Liver, 1998–2002; Member, Editorial Board: Clinical Science, 2002–; Medical Electron Microscopy, 2002–; Jl of Pathology, 2004–; Hepatology, 2006–; World Jl of Gastroenterology, 2007–. *Publications:* (ed jtly) Pathology of the Liver, 3rd edn, 1994, 4th edn, 2002; (Ed.-in-Chief) MacSween's Pathology of the Liver, 5th edn, 2006; (ed jtly) Muir's Textbook of Pathology, 14th edn, 2007; articles in scientific jls on mechanisms and patterns of liver injury, incl. fatty liver disease, fibrosis and autoimmune disease. *Recreations:* chamber music, walking, Asian cookery, foreign travel. *Address:* Dean of Clinical Medicine's Office, Room 13, Peacock Hall, Royal Victoria Infirmary, Newcastle upon Tyne NE1 4LP. *T:* (0191) 282 0700, *Fax:* (0191) 282 0702; *e-mail:* a.d.burt@ncl.ac.uk. *Club:* Athenæum.

BURT, Alistair James Hendrie; MP (C) Bedfordshire North East, since 2001; *b* 25 May 1955; *s* of James Hendrie Burt, med. practitioner and Mina Christie Robertson; *m* 1983, Eve Alexandra Twite; one *s* one *d*. *Educ:* Bury Grammar Sch.; St John's Coll., Oxford (BA Hons Jurisprudence 1977). Pres., OU Law Soc., Michaelmas term, 1976. Articled Slater Heelis & Co., Manchester, 1978–80; solicitor, Watts, Vallance & Vallance, 1980–92; Consultant, Teeman, Levine and Co. (Solicitors), Leeds, 1992. Councillor, Archway Ward, London Bor. of Haringey, 1982–84. MP (C) Bury North, 1983–97; contested (C) same seat, 1997. Parliamentary Private Secretary: to Sec. of State for the Environment, 1985–86; to Sec. of State for Educn and Science, 1986–89; to Chancellor of Duchy of Lancaster and Chm. of Cons. Party, 1989–90; Parly Under-Sec. of State, DSS, 1992–95; Minister of State (Minister for Disabled People), DSS, 1995–97; Opposition frontbench spokesman on Higher and Further Educn, 2001–02; PPS to Leader of the Opposition, 2002–05; Shadow Minister for Communities and Regeneration, 2005–08; Dep. Chm., Cons. Party, 2007–; Asst Opposition Chief Whip, 2008–. Vice-Chm., 1985–88, Vice Pres., 2003–, Tory Reform Gp. Secretary: NW Cons. MPs Group, 1984–88; Parly Christian Fellowship, 1984–97 (Chm., 2003–06). Consultant, Whitehead Mann plc, 1997–2001. Chm., Enterprise Forum, 1998–2002. *Recreations:* reading left-wing publications, sport (scored a goal at Wembley, playing for northern MPs football team, Nov. 1991), modern art, astronomy. *Address:* c/o House of Commons, SW1A 0AA.

BURT, Charles Anthony J.; *see* Johnstone-Burt.

BURT, Gerald Raymond, OBE 1984; BEM (mil.) 1947; FCILT; Chief Secretary, British Railways Board, 1976–84; *b* 15 Feb. 1926; *s* of Reginald George Burt and Lilian May Burt; *m* 1948, Edna Ivy Elizabeth Sizeland; two *s*. *Educ:* Latymer Upper Sch. FCILT (FCIT 1971). Joined GWR as Booking Clerk, 1942: RE (Movement Control), 1944–47; BR Management Trainee, 1951–54; Gen. Staff, British Transport Commn, 1956–59; Divl Planning Officer, Bristol, 1959–62; Planning Officer, LMR, 1962–64; Divl Man., St Pancras, 1965; Traffic Man., Freightliners, 1967–70; Principal Corporate Planning Officer, British Railways Bd, 1970–76. Member: Council, Chartered Inst. of Transport, 1967–70, 1981–84; British Transport Police Cttee, 1984–88. Governor, British Transport Staff Coll., 1976–82; Trustee, 1984–99, Vice Pres., 2000–, Rly Benevolent Instn. FRSA 1983. Scouting Medal of Merit, 1978. *Recreations:* gardening, the countryside. *Address:* 16 Ravens Court, Castle Village, Berkhamsted, Herts HP4 2GX. *T:* (01442) 871725.

BURT, Lorely Jane; MP (Lib Dem) Solihull, since 2005; *b* 10 Sept. 1954; *d* of Raymond Claude Baker and Hazel June Baker (*née* Abbiss); *m* 1992, Richard George Burt; one *d*, and one step *s*. *Educ:* University Coll., Swansea (BSc Hons Econ.); Open Univ. (MBA). Asst Gov., HM Prison Service; personnel and trng mgt and consultancy; Man. Dir, trng co.; Director: mktg co.; financial services co.; business consultant. Mem. (Lib Dem) Dudley MBC, 1998–2003. *Recreations:* theatre, cinema, socialising with friends. *Address:* House of Commons, SW1A 0AA. *T:* (020) 7219 8269; *e-mail:* burtl@parliament.uk.

BURT, Maurice Edward; Deputy Director, Building Research Establishment, 1975–81, retired; *b* 17 Nov. 1921; *s* of Reginald Edward Burt and Bertha Winifred Burt; *m* 1947, Monica Evelyn Amy; one *s* three *d*. *Educ:* Victoria Coll., Jersey; Taunton's Sch., Southampton; BA Hons London, 1948. CEng, MICE; FRAeS. Aircraft industry, 1938–48; RAE, 1948–66 (Supt, Airworthiness, 1961–66); Head of Structures Dept, Transport and Road Res. Lab., 1966–73; Head of Res. Management, Dept of Environment, 1973–75. *Publications:* technical reports and articles. *Recreations:* golf, walking, gardening.

BURT, Sir Peter (Alexander), Kt 2003; Chairman, Promethean plc, since 2005; Chairman, ITV plc, 2004–07; *b* 6 March 1944; *s* of Robert W. Burt and May H. Rodger; *m* 1971, Alison Mackintosh Turner; three *s*. *Educ:* Merchiston Castle Sch., Edinburgh; Univ. of St Andrews (MA); Univ. of Pennsylvania (MBA). FCIBS (FIB (Scot.) 1987). Hewlett Packard Co., Palo Alto, 1968–70; CSL, Edinburgh, 1970–74; Edward Bates & Sons Ltd, Edinburgh, 1974; joined Bank of Scotland, 1975: Internat. Div., 1975–88; Asst Gen. Manager, 1979–84; Divisional Gen. Manager, 1984–85; Jt Gen. Manager, 1985–88; Treas. and Chief Gen. Manager, 1988–96; Dir, 1995–2001; Chief Exec., 1996–2001; Gov., 2001–03; Dep. Chm., HBOS plc, 2001–03. Chm., Gleacher Shacklock Ltd, 2003–08; Director: Shell Transport and Trading Co., 2002–05; Royal Dutch Shell, 2004–06; TEMIT plc, 2005–. Mem., High Constables and Guard of Honour of Holyroodhouse, Edinburgh. FRSE 2002. Hon. LLD St Andrews, 2001. *Recreations:* golf, ski-ing, gardening, reading. *Clubs:* New (Edinburgh); Hon. Co. of Edinburgh Golfers (Muirfield); Royal & Ancient (St Andrews); Gullane Golf (Gullane); Pine Valley Golf; Sunningdale Golf.

BURTON, 3rd Baron *cr* 1897; **Michael Evan Victor Baillie;** *b* 27 June 1924; *er s* of Brig. Hon. George Evan Michael Baillie, MC, TD (*d* 1941) and *g s* of Baroness Burton (2nd in line); *S* grandmother, 1962; *m* 1st, 1948, Elizabeth Ursula Forster (marr. diss. 1977; she *d* 1993), *er d* of late Capt. A. F. Wise; two *s* four *d*; 2nd, 1978, Coralie Denise, 2nd *d* of late Claud R. Cliffe. *Educ:* Eton. Lieut, Scots Guards, 1944. Mem., CC, 1948–75, JP 1961–75, DL 1963–65, Inverness-shire; Mem., Inverness Dist Council, 1984–92. Grand Master Mason, 1993–99. *Heir: s* Hon. Evan Michael Ronald Baillie [*b* 19 March 1949; *m* 1970, Lucinda (marr. diss. 1984), *e d* of Robert Law, Newmarket; two *s* one *d*; *m* 1998, June Gordon]. *Address:* Dochgarroch Lodge, Inverness IV3 8JG. *T:* (01463) 861252. *Clubs:* Cavalry and Guards; New (Edinburgh).

BURTON, Air Vice-Marshal Andrew John, OBE 1991 (MBE 1986); FCIS, Chartered FCIPD; Bursar and Clerk to the Governors, Sevenoaks School, since 2003; *b* 11 Nov. 1950; *s* of Walter Joseph Burton and Phyllis Jane Burton (*née* Flear); *m* 1977, Sheila Hanson; two *s*. *Educ:* Llanelli Boys' Grammar Sch.; Univ. of Wales Inst. of Sci. and Technol. (BScEcon 1972). FCIS 1993 (ACIS 1982); Chartered FCIPD 2003 (FCIPD 2000). Commnd RAF, 1972; Sqn Leader, 1980; Wing Comdr, 1986; Defence Staff, British Embassy, Washington, 1988–90; Gp Capt., 1991; Station Comdr, RAF Uxbridge, 1994–95; Air Cdre, 1996; Dir of Personnel (RAF), 1995–98; Air Vice-Marshal, 1998; AOA and AOC Directly Administered Units, HQ Strike Comd, 1998–2001, PTC, 2001–03. *Recreations:* golf, sport, theatre. *Address:* Sevenoaks School, Sevenoaks, Kent TN13 1HU. *T:* (01732) 455133. *Club:* Royal Air Force.

BURTON, (Anthony) David, CBE 1992; Chairman, Marshalls Finance Ltd, 1989–98; Director, LIFFE, 1981–94 (Chairman, 1988–92); *b* 2 April 1937; *s* of Leslie Mitchell Burton and Marion Burton (*née* Marsh); *m* 1964, Valerie (*née* Swire); one *s* two *d*. *Educ:* Arnold Sch., Blackpool. FCIB; FCT. Bank of America National Trust and Savings Assoc., 1966–72; S. G. Warburg & Co. Ltd, 1972–92 (Dir, 1977–92). Chairman: Ludgate 181 (Jersey) Ltd (formerly Ludgate 181 plc), 1999–; Ashley House plc, 2004–07; Ashley House Medical Properties plc (formerly Ashley House Properties Ltd), 2004–07; Ludgate Investments Ltd, 2004–; Beechwood House Finance Ltd, 2004–; Dir, Car Crash Line Gp plc, 2003–05. *Recreations:* antique glass, German pottery, music, opera, sport (participating and spectator).

BURTON, Anthony George Graham; author and broadcaster, since 1968; *b* 24 Dec. 1934; *s* of Donald Graham Burton and Irene Burton; *m* 1959, Pip Sharman; two *s* one *d*. *Educ:* King James's Grammar Sch., Knaresborough; Leeds Univ. National Service, RAF, 1955–57. Research chemist, 1958–60; publishing, 1960–68. *Publications:* A Programmed Guide to Office Warfare, 1969; The Jones Report, 1970; The Canal Builders, 1972, 4th edn 2005; Canals in Colour, 1974; Remains of a Revolution, 1975, 2nd edn 2001; Josiah Wedgwood, 1976; (jtly) Canal, 1976; The Miners, 1976; Back Door Britain, 1977; Industrial Archaeological Sites of Britain, 1977; (jtly) The Green Bag Travellers, 1978; The Past At Work, 1980; The Rainhill Story, 1980; The Past Afloat, 1982; The Changing River, 1982; The Shell Book of Curious Britain, 1982; The National Trust Guide to Our Industrial Past, 1983; The Waterways of Britain, 1983; The Rise and Fall of King Cotton, 1984; (ed jtly) Canals: a new look, 1984; Walking the Line, 1985; Wilderness Britain, 1985; (jtly) Britain's Light Railways, 1985; The Shell Book of Undiscovered Britain and Ireland, 1986; (jtly) Landscape Detective, 1986; Britain Revisited, 1986; Opening Time, 1987; Steaming Through Britain, 1987; Walking Through History, 1988; Walk the South Downs, 1988; The Great Days of the Canals, 1989; Cityscapes, 1990; Astonishing Britain, 1990; Slow Roads, 1991; The Railway Builders, 1992; Canal Mania, 1993; (jtly) The Grand Union Canal Walk, 1993; The Railway Empire, 1994; The Rise and Fall of British Shipbuilding, 1994; The Cotswold Way, 1995, new edn 2007; The Dales Way, 1995; The West Highland Way, 1996; The Southern Upland Way, 1997; William Cobbett: Englishman, 1997; The Caledonian Canal, 1998; The Wye Valley Walk, 1998; Best Foot Forward, 1998; The Cumbria Way, 1999; The Wessex Ridgeway, 1999; Thomas Telford, 1999; Weekend Walks Dartmoor and Exmoor, 2000; Weekend Walks the Yorkshire Dales, 2000; Traction Engines, 2000; Richard Trevithick, 2000; Weekend Walks The Peak District, 2001; The Orient Express, 2001; The Anatomy of Canals: the early years, 2001; The Daily Telegraph Guide to Britain's Working Past, 2002; Hadrian's Wall Path, 2003; The Daily Telegraph Guide to Britain's Maritime Past, 2003; The Anatomy of Canals: decline and renewal, 2003; On the Rails, 2004; The Ridgeway, 2005; *novels:* The Reluctant Musketeer, 1973; The Master Idol, 1975; The Navigators, 1976; A Place to Stand, 1977. *Recreations:* walking and travelling in search of steam engines and good beer; cinema. *Address:* c/o Sara Menguc, Literary Agent, 58 Thorkhill Road, Thames Ditton, Surrey KT7 0UG. *T:* (020) 8398 7992.

BURTON, Rt Rev. Anthony John; *see* Saskatchewan, Bishop of.

BURTON, Anthony Philip; Senior Research Fellow in Museology and Museum History, Research Department, Victoria and Albert Museum, 1997–2002; Chairman of Trustees, Charles Dickens Museum, London, 2003–05; *b* 25 Oct. 1942; *s* of late Frank Burton and Lottie Burton (*née* Lax); *m* 1985, Carol Deborah Baker. *Educ:* King's Sch., Macclesfield; Wadham Coll., Oxford (BLitt, MA). Res. Asst, Dept of English, Birkbeck Coll., Univ. of London, 1965–68; Victoria and Albert Museum: Asst Keeper, Nat. Art Liby, 1968–79; Asst Keeper, Directorate, 1979–81; Hd, Bethnal Green Mus. of Childhood, 1981–97. *Publications:* (with S. Haskins) European Art in the Victoria and Albert Museum, 1983; Children's Pleasures: books, toys and games from the Bethnal Green Museum of Childhood, 1996; Vision & Accident: the story of the Victoria and Albert Museum, 1999; (with E. Bonython) The Great Exhibitor: the life and work of Henry Cole, 2003; articles on liby and mus. subjects. *Recreations:* cultural pursuits, reading crime fiction. *Address:* 59 Arlington Avenue, N1 7BA. *T:* (020) 7226 0394.

BURTON, Sir Carlisle (Archibald), Kt 1979; OBE 1968; Barbados High Commissioner to the Bahamas, 1978–93; *b* 29 July 1921; *m* 1946, Hyacinth Marjorie Adelle Barker. *Educ:* Harrison Coll., Barbados, WI; Univ. of London (BA); School of Librarianship, Leeds; Univ. of Pittsburgh (MS Hyg.). MCLIP. Assistant Master, Harrison Coll., Barbados, 1943–50; Sen. Asst Master, Bishop's High Sch., Tobago, 1950–51; Public Librarian, Barbados, 1953–58; Permanent Secretary: Min. of Educn, 1958–63; Min. of Health, 1963–71; Perm. Sec., Prime Minister's Office, and Head of Civil Service, 1972–81; Chm., Public Services Commn, Barbados, 1981–87, Turks and Caicos Islands, 1988–90. Member: Commonwealth Observer Gp at elections in Southern Rhodesia (Zimbabwe), 1980 and in Malaysia, 1990; Caribbean Community Review Team, 1989–91. Director: Barbados National Bank, 1978–86 (Dep. Chm., 1982–86); Insurance Corp. of Barbados, 1978–86 (Chm., 1981–86). Chm., Cave Hill Campus Council, Univ. of the WI, Barbados, 1984–94; Mem. Council, Barbados Mus. and Historical Soc., 1994–2005. Life Mem., Barbados Nat. Trust. Chm., Barbados Assoc. of Retired Persons, 1995–98. Hon. LLD Univ. of WI, 1995. FRSA 1953. *Recreations:* (active) table tennis, swimming, bridge, reading; (spectator) cricket (Life Member, Barbados Cricket Assoc.), athletics (Life Member, Barbados Amateur Athletic Assoc.), soccer. *Address:* Caradelle, Mountjoy Avenue, Pine Gardens, St Michael, Barbados, West Indies. *T:* 4293724.

BURTON, Caroline Oldcorn; *see* Reid, C. O.

BURTON, David; *see* Burton, A. D.

BURTON, David Harold; transport management consultant, 1999–2005; *b* 28 Jan. 1947; *s* of George and Helen Burton; *m* (marr. diss.); one *s*; *m* Julia; one step *s* two step *d*. *Educ:* Bridlington Sch.; Leeds Univ. (BA (Hons) Geography). British Rail: Network Man., S Central Network SE, 1986; Dep. Gen. Man., Southern Region, 1988; Gen. Man., Anglia Region, 1989–91; Gp Dir North, Network SouthEast, 1991–92; Director: Express Parcels, BR Parcels, 1992–93; Restructuring, Network SouthEast, 1993–94; Dir, Product Quality, and Dep. Man. Dir (S & E), BRB, 1994–96; Man. Dir, W Anglia Gt Northern Rly, 1996–99. Mem. Bd, Passenger Focus, 2005–. Non-exec. Dir, Norfolk, Suffolk and Cambs Strategic HA, 2002–06; Gov., Papworth Hosp. Foundn Trust, 2004–06. *Recreations:* spectator sport, lousy golf.

BURTON, Lt-Gen. Sir Edmund Fortescue Gerard, KBE 1999 (OBE); Executive Chairman, Police Information Technology Organisation, 2001–03; *b* 20 Oct. 1943. *Educ:* Trinity Hall, Cambridge (BA 1968; MA 1972). Commissioned RA, 1963; Brig., 1987; Mil. Attaché, Washington, 1990; Maj.-Gen., 1991; Comdt, RMCS, 1991–94; ACDS, Operational Requirements (Land), 1994–97; DCDS (Systems), 1997–99; retd 2000. Vis. Prof., Cranfield Univ., 2000–. Hon. Col, OTC (Cambridge), 1996–2003; Col Comdt, RA, 1998–2004; Hon. Regtl Col, 26 Regt RA, 1999–2006.

BURTON, Dr Frank Patrick; QC 1998; a Recorder, since 2000; *b* 19 June 1950; *s* of Ronald and Ita Burton; *m* 1983, Caroline Oldcorn Reid, *qv*; two *s* one *d*. *Educ:* Salesian Coll., Farnborough; Univ. of Kent at Canterbury (BA 1st Cl. Hons 1971); London School of Economics and Political Science (PhD 1974). Lecturer in Social Science: Brunel Univ., 1976–79; City Univ., 1979–82; called to the Bar, Gray's Inn, 1982, Bencher, 2004; in practice at the Bar, 1982–. Chairman: Law Reform Cttee, Bar Council, 2003–05; Personal Injury Bar Assoc., 2004–06 (Vice Chm., 2002–04). *Publications:* Medical Negligence Case Law, 1990, 2nd edn 1995; Personal Injury Limitation Law, 1994. *Recreations:* sport, reading, Suffolk. *Address:* 12 King's Bench Walk, Temple, EC4Y 7EL.

BURTON, Sir George (Vernon Kennedy), Kt 1977; CBE 1972 (MBE (mil.) 1945); DL; Chairman, Fisons plc, 1973–84 (Chief Executive, 1966–76, Senior Vice-Chairman,

1966–71, Deputy Chairman, 1971–72); *b* 21 April 1916; *s* of late George Ethelbert Earnshaw Burton and Francesca (*née* Holden-White); *g s* of Sir Bunnell Burton, Ipswich; *m* 1st, 1945, Sarah Katherine Tcherniavsky (marr. diss.); two *s*; 2nd, 1975, Priscilla Margaret Gore (MBE 1996), *d* of late Cecil H. King. *Educ:* Charterhouse; Germany. Served RA, 1939–45, N Africa, Sicily, Italy, Austria. Director: Barclays Bank Internat. plc, 1976–82; Thomas Tilling, 1976–83; Rolls-Royce Ltd, 1976–84. Member: Export Council for Europe, 1965–71 (Dep. Chm., 1967–71); Council, CBI, 1970–84 (Chm., CBI Overseas Cttee, 1975–81); BOTB, 1972–73 (BOTB European Trade Cttee, 1972–81; British Overseas Trade Adv. Council, 1975–79); Investment Insce Adv. Cttee, ECGD, 1971–76; Council on Internat. Develt of ODM, 1977–79; Council, BIM, 1968–70 (FBIM); NEDC, 1975–79; Whitford Cttee to Consider Law on Copyright and Designs, 1974–77; Ipswich County Borough Council, 1947–51; Ipswich Gp HMC; Assoc. for Business Sponsorship of the Arts, 1978–84; Governing Body, British National Cttee of Internat. Chamber of Commerce, 1979–86; Governor, Sutton's Hosp. in Charterhouse, 1979–92; Chm., Ipswich Conservative Assoc., 1982–84. FRSA 1978. DL Suffolk, 1980. Commander: Order of Ouissam Alaouite, Morocco, 1968; Order of Léopold II, Belgium, 1974. *Recreation:* music. *Address:* Aldham Mill, Hadleigh, Suffolk IP7 6LE.

BURTON, Sir Graham (Stuart), KCMG 1999 (CMG 1987); HM Diplomatic Service, retired; High Commissioner, Nigeria, also concurrently Ambassador (non-resident) to the Republic of Benin, 1997–2001; *b* 8 April 1941; *s* of late Cyril Stanley Richard Burton and of Jessie Blythe Burton; *m* 1965, Julia Margaret Lappin; one *s* one *d*. *Educ:* Sir William Borlase's Sch., Marlow. Foreign Office, 1961; Abu Dhabi, 1964; Middle East Centre for Arabic Studies, 1967; Kuwait, 1969; FCO, 1972; Tunis, 1975; UK Mission to United Nations, 1978; Counsellor, Tripoli, 1981; Head, Security Co-ordination Dept, FCO, 1984; Consul General, San Francisco, 1987; Ambassador: UAE, 1990; Indonesia, 1994. Director: Magadi Soda Co., Kenya, 2001–; Gulf of Guinea Energy, 2006–; Advr, Control Risks Gp, 2001–. Trustee, Royal Commonwealth Soc. for the Blind, 2005–. *Recreations:* golf, watching cricket, baseball and most other sports; opera. *Club:* MCC.

BURTON, Humphrey McGuire, CBE 2000; writer and broadcaster; *b* 25 March 1931; *s* of Harry (Philip) and Kathleen Burton; *m* 1st, 1957, Gretel (*née* Davis); one *s* one *d*; 2nd, 1970, Christina (*née* Hellstedt); one *s* one *d*. *Educ:* Long Dene Sch., Chiddingstone; Judd Sch., Tonbridge; Fitzwilliam House, Cambridge (BA; Hon. Fellow, Fitzwilliam Coll., 1997). BBC Radio, 1955–58; BBC TV, 1958–67: Editor, Monitor, 1962; Exec. Producer, Music Programmes, 1963; Head of Music and Arts Programmes, 1965–67, productions inc. Workshop, Master Class, In Rehearsal, Britten at 50, Conversations with Glenn Gould; London Weekend TV: Head of Drama, Arts and Music, 1967–69; Editor/Introducer, Aquarius, 1970–75, programmes incl. Mahler Festival, Verdi Requiem, Trouble in Tahiti, The Great Gondola Race, Anatomy of a Record, etc.; Head of Music and Arts, BBC TV, 1975–81; Presenter: Omnibus, 1976–78, 1984–85 (Producer, West Side Story documentary, 1985; RAI Prize, Prix Italia, BAFTA Robert Flaherty Best Documentary Award, 1985); In Performance, 1978–82; Young Musician of the Year, biennially 1978–94; Producer/Director: TV Proms with Giulini and Solti, 1981, and with others, 1982–95; Walton 80th Birthday Concert (Previn); Verdi Requiem (Abbado), and Call me Kiri (Te Kanawa), 1982; Candide, Scottish Opera, Glasgow, 1988 and Barbican (conducted by Leonard Bernstein), 1989; Covent Garden opera relays, incl. Die Fledermaus (Joan Sutherland farewell), 1990; Artistic Dir, 1988–90, Artistic Advr, 1990–93, Barbican Centre. Other productions include: 5 Glyndebourne operas, adapted and produced, Southern TV, 1972–74; The Beach at Falesa, World Première, Harlech TV, 1974; Channel 4 operas include: Eugene Onegin, 1994; Ermione, 1995; Lulu, 1996; The Damnation of Faust, Manon Lescaut, 1997; Rodelinda, Hansel and Gretel, 1998; Pelléas et Mélisande, Flight, 1999; BBC2 opera, Falstaff, 1999; BBC4 drama, Vincent in Brixton, 2002; UN Day Concert with Pablo Casals, 1971, and subseq. UN days, 1972–92; Berlioz' Requiem, at Les Invalides, 1975, The Return of Ulysses, at Aix-en-Provence, 2002, French TV; many free-lance prodns in Austria, Czechoslovakia, Germany, Hungary, Italy, Israel, Poland, Russia and USA, including: Mahler, Brahms, Schumann and Beethoven Cycles with Bernstein and Vienna Philharmonic; concerts with von Karajan and Berlin and Vienna Philharmonic, Giulini and LA Philharmonic, Mehta and NY Philharmonic, Maazel and Bayerisches Rundfunk Orch., Solti and Chicago SO; world première, Epitaph, by Charles Mingus, NY, 1989; Director: Boris Godunov, Kirov, 1990; War and Peace, Kirov, 1991; Mozart Requiem, Vienna Bicentennial 1991; Producer: Leonard Bernstein's 70th Birthday Gala Season, Tanglewood, 1988; Bernstein Meml Concert, Carnegie Hall, 1990; Guest Dir, 1983 Hollywood Bowl Summer Music Fest.; conducting début, Verdi Requiem, Philharmonia Orch., RAH, 2001 (raised £75,000 for Prostate Research); *radio:* writer/presenter of series, incl. Life of Leonard Bernstein, Menuhin-Master Musician, William Walton: the romantic loner, Classic FM, Artist in Focus, etc., BBC. Columnist: Classic FM Magazine, 1995–98; BBC Music Magazine, 1998–99. Chairman: EBU Music Experts Gp, 1976–82; EBU TV Music Working Party, 1982–86; Mem., New Music Sub-Cttee, Arts Council, 1981–83; Advr, Manchester Olympic Fest., 1990; Administrator, Royal Philharmonic Soc.'s Music Awards, 1989–91. Hon. Professorial Fellow, University Coll., Cardiff, 1983–87. Hon. FCSD 1990. Desmond Davis Award, SFTA, 1966; Royal TV Soc. Silver Medal, 1971; Emmy, 1971 for 'Beethoven's Birthday' (CBS TV); Peabody Award, 1972; SFTA Best Specialised Series, 1974; Christopher Award, 1979; Emmy, 1988, for 'Celebrating Gershwin' (PBS/BBC TV). Chevalier de l'Ordre des Arts et des Lettres, 1975. *Publications:* Leonard Bernstein, 1994 (trans. German, Chinese and Japanese; ASCAP book award, 1995); Menuhin: a life, 2000 (trans. German); (jtly) William Walton: the romantic loner, 2002. *Recreations:* music-making, tennis, travel. *Address:* 13 Linden Road, Aldeburgh, Suffolk IP15 5JQ.

BURTON, Iris Grace; Editor-in-Chief: Woman's Realm, 1991–99; Woman's Weekly, 1992–99; Eva, 1994–97; Chat, 1997–99; *d* of Arthur Burton and late Alice Burton; *m*; one *s* one *d*. *Educ:* Roan Girls' Grammar Sch., Greenwich; City of London Coll. Local newspaper, SE London Mercury, until 1966; Writer, then Features Editor, Woman's Own, 1966–78; Asst Editor, TV Times, 1978–80; Editor, Woman's Own, 1980–86; Editor-in-Chief: Prima magazine, 1986–87; Best magazine, 1987–88; Editorial Dir, G+J of the UK publications, 1988–91; Launch Ed., Now mag., 1996. Mem., Press Complaints Commn, 1993–99. *Address:* 13 Wheathill Road, SE20 7XQ.

BURTON, Prof. John Lloyd, MD; FRCP; Professor of Dermatology, University of Bristol, 1992–98; *b* 29 Aug. 1938; *s* of Lloyd Burton and Dorothy Mary Burton (*née* Pacey); *m* 1964, Patricia Anne Crankshaw, DRCOG, FRCPath; one *s* two *d*. *Educ:* Heanor Grammar Sch., Derbys; Manchester Univ. (BSc; MD 1971). FRCP 1978. Trng posts in hosps in Manchester, London, Edinburgh and Newcastle upon Tyne, 1964–73; Consultant Dermatologist, Bristol Royal Infirmary, 1973–98. Numerous guest lectures, including: Dowling Oration, 1980, Deville, 1995, RSM; Parkes-Weber, RCP, 1988; Long-Fox, Bristol Univ., 1994. Advr in Dermatol. to CMO, DoH, 1988–94. Examr, RCP, 1987–92. Chm., Dermatol. Cttee, RCP, 1993–95; President: Dermatol. Sect., RSocMed, 1994–95; Brit. Assoc. Dermatologists, 1995–96. Editor, Brit. Jl Dermatol., 1981–85. *Publications:* Aids to Postgraduate Medicine, 1970, 6th edn 1994; Aids to Undergraduate Medicine, 1973, 6th edn 1997; Essentials of Dermatology, 1979, 3rd edn 1990; (ed jtly) Textbook of Dermatology (4 Vols), 4th edn 1986 to 6th edn 1998; 600 Miseries: the 17th century womb, 2005; numerous chapters and scientific papers. *Recreations:* painting, book-binding. *Address:* Eastfield House, East Street, North Perrott, Somerset TA18 7SW. *T:* (01460) 75156.

BURTON, John Michael, RIBA; Principal Partner, Purcell Miller Tritton, Architects, since 1978; Surveyor to the Fabric, Canterbury Cathedral, since 1990; Surveyor of the Fabric of Westminster Abbey, since 1999; *b* 21 May 1945; *s* of Gerald Victor Burton and Kathleen Blodwen (*née* Harper); *m* 1971, Sally Bason; one *s* one *d*. *Educ:* Duston Secondary Mod. Sch., Northampton; Northampton Coll. of Further Educn; Oxford Sch. of Architecture (DipArch). RIBA 1972. Asst to Surveyor to Ely Cathedral, 1971–73; Parish Architect to numerous churches in E Anglia incl. Long Melford and Thaxted, 1973–; Commissioned Architect to English Heritage, 1983–2002; Architect to NT, Melford Hall, Lavenham Guildhall and Flatford Mill, 1973–96; work on restoration of Colchester Castle, 1984–90; Architect, American Ambassador's Residence, London, 1998–; Conservation Advr to Crown Urban Estate, 2003–. Chm., Cathedral Architects' Assoc., 1997–99. Member: Cathedrals Fabric Commn for England, 1996–2006; Redundant Churches Cttee, Church Comrs, 1999–2002; Places of Worship Panel, 2000–03, Historic Built Envmt Adv. Cttee, 2000–03, English Heritage; Chm., Redundant Churches Uses Cttee, Chelmsford, 1990–. Mem., DAC for Chelmsford, 1977–, St Edmundsbury and Ipswich, 1986–98. Mem. Council, Nat. Trust, 2007–. Dir, Mercury Theatre, Colchester, 1999–2003. Mem., Colchester Trinity Rotary Club. Judge, 1995 and 1997, Chm., 1999, 2003 and 2008, Stone Awards, Stone Fedn of GB. Freeman, City of London, 1996; Court Asst, Masons' Co., 1996–; Liveryman, Carpenters' Co., 2007–. *Recreations:* cycling, ski-ing, woodwork. *Address:* St Mary's Hall, Rawstorn Road, Colchester, Essex CO3 3JH. *T:* (01206) 244844; *e-mail:* johnburton@pmt.co.uk.

BURTON, Prof. Kenneth, FRS 1974; Professor of Biochemistry, 1966–88, now Emeritus, and Dean of Faculty of Science, 1983–86, University of Newcastle upon Tyne; *b* 26 June 1926; *s* of Arthur and Gladys Burton; *m* 1955, Hilda Marsden; one *s* one *d*. *Educ:* High Pavement Sch., Nottingham; Wath-upon-Dearne Grammar Sch.; King's Coll., Cambridge (MA, PhD). Asst Lectr in Biochem., Univ. of Sheffield, 1949, Lectr 1952; Res. Associate, Univ. of Chicago, 1952–54; MRC Unit for Research in Cell Metabolism, Oxford, 1954–66. Vis. Lectr in Medicine, Harvard, 1964; William Evans Vis. Prof., Univ. of Otago, 1977–78. *Publications:* scientific articles, especially on nucleic acids. *Recreations:* music, hill-walking. *Address:* Byways, The Broadway, Alfriston, Polegate, East Sussex BN26 5XH.

BURTON, Hon. Mark; *see* Burton, R. M.

BURTON, Rt Rev. Dr Mark Gregory; Assistant Bishop, Diocese of Perth, Western Australia, since 2006; *b* Sydney, 18 May 1956; *s* of late Kenneth Burton and of Patricia Burton; *m* 1975, Annette Gill; three *d*. *Educ:* Ridley Coll., Melbourne (BTh 1988); Australian Coll. of Theology (ThD 2001). Tutor, Ridley Coll., Melbourne, 1989–97; ordained deacon, 1990, priest, 1990; Asst Curate, Werribee, 1990–91; Priest-in-charge, St James', Glen Iris, 1991–97; Examining Chaplain, Dio. of Melbourne, 1996–2000; Chaplain to Archbishop of Melbourne, and Dir of Ordinands, 1997–2000; Archbishop's Chaplain and Aide, 2000; Chaplain: RAN, 2001; HMAS Cerberus West Port, 2002; HMAS Melbourne, 2003; HMAS Kanimbla/HMAS Adelaide, 2004–05; HMAS Creswell, 2006. Australian Service Medal, 1983; Australian Active Service Medal, 2003; Iraq Campaign Medal, 2003; Humanitarian Overseas Service Medal, 2004; Australian Defence Medal, 2005. *Recreations:* sailing, scuba diving, motorcycling, archery. *Address:* GPO Box W2067, Perth, WA 6846, Australia. *T:* (8) 93257455, *Fax:* (8) 93256741; *e-mail:* mburton@perth.anglican.org.

BURTON, Hon. Sir Michael (John), Kt 1998; **Hon. Mr Justice Burton;** a Judge of the High Court of Justice, Queen's Bench Division, since 1998; Judge of the Employment Appeal Tribunal, since 1999 (President, 2002–05); *b* 12 Nov. 1946; *s* of late Henry Burton, QC, and Hilda Burton; *m* 1972, Corinne Ruth (*d* 1992), *d* of late Dr Jack Cowan, MC, and Dorothy Cowan; four *d*. *Educ:* Eton Coll. (KS, Captain of the School; Fellow, 2004); Balliol Coll., Oxford (MA). President, Balliol JCR, 1967; First President, Oxford Univ. SRC, 1968. Called to Bar, Gray's Inn, 1970, Bencher, 1993; Law Lectr, Balliol Coll., Oxford, 1972–74; QC 1984; Head of Chambers, 1991–98; a Recorder, 1989–98. Chm., Central Arbitration Cttee, 2000–; Pres., Interception of Communications Tribunal, 2000; Vice-Pres., Investigatory Powers Tribunal, 2000–. Contested: (Lab) RBK&C (local elections), 1971; (Lab) Stratford upon Avon, Feb. 1974; (SDP) Putney, GLC, 1981. Hon. Fellow, Goldsmiths Coll., London, 1998. *Publications:* (contrib.) Bullen & Leake & Jacob's Precedents of Pleadings, 13th edn 1990; (ed) Civil Appeals, 2002. *Recreations:* amateur theatricals, lyric writing, singing, bridge. *Address:* Royal Courts of Justice, Strand, WC2A 2LL.

BURTON, Sir Michael (St Edmund), KCVO 1992 (CVO 1979); CMG 1987; HM Diplomatic Service, retired; independent consultant and lecturer; *b* 18 Oct. 1937; *s* of late Brig. G. W. S. Burton, DSO (and two Bars), and Barbara Burton (*née* Kemmis Betty); *m* 1967, Henrietta Jindra Hones; one *s* one *d* (and one *d* decd). *Educ:* Bedford Sch.; Magdalen Coll., Oxford. MA. 2nd Lt, Rifle Brigade, 1955–57. Foreign Office, 1960; Asst Political Agent, Dubai, Trucial States, 1962–64; Private Sec. to Minister of State, FO, 1964–67; Second (later First) Sec. (Information), Khartoum, 1967–69; First Sec. (Inf.), Paris, 1969–72; Asst, Science and Technology Dept, FCO, 1972–75; First Sec. and Head of Chancery, Amman, 1975–77; Counsellor, Kuwait, 1977–79; Head of Maritime, Aviation and Environment Dept, FCO, 1979–81; Head of S Asian Dept, FCO, 1981–84; on secondment to BP as Head of Policy Rev. Unit, 1984–85; Berlin: Minister, 1985–92; Dep. Comdt, BMG, 1985–90; Head of Embassy Office, 1990–92; Asst Under-Sec. of State (ME), FCO, 1993; Ambassador to Czech Republic, 1994–97. Chairman: Eur.-Atlantic Gp, 2001–02 (Pres., 2002–05); British Czech and Slovak Assoc., 2001–; Mem. Council, RSAA, 2001–06, 2007–. Hon. Pres., Hinduja Foundn, 2003–. Order of Merit, Berlin, 1992. *Recreations:* tennis, travel, wine, allotment. *Address:* 6 Napier Court, Ranelagh Gardens, SW6 3UT. *Clubs:* Oxford and Cambridge, Hurlingham (Chm., 2004–07), Pilgrims.

BURTON, Neil Henry, FSA; Director, Architectural History Practice, since 2001; *b* 23 June 1947; *s* of Angus Robert Burton and Joan Burton (*née* Grant); *m* 1989, Susie Barson; one *s* one *d*. *Educ:* Christ's Hosp. Sch., Horsham; Pembroke Coll., Oxford (BA Hons Modern Hist.); Edinburgh Univ. (Dip. Hist. of Art). Historian, Historic Bldgs Div., GLC, 1973–88; Inspector of Historic Bldgs, English Heritage, 1988–94; Sec., Georgian Gp, 1994–2001. Dir, Architects Accredited in Building Conservation, 2000–06; Jt Dir, Attingham Study Week, 2003–07. Trustee, Historic Chapels Trust, 1995–. IHBC 1998; FSA 1998. *Publications:* Historic Houses Handbook, 1981, 3rd edn 1984; Life in the Georgian City, 1990; contrib. articles to Architectural Rev., Country Life, etc. *Recreation:* walking. *Address:* 29 Mount Pleasant Villas, N4 4HH. *T:* and *Fax:* (020) 7263 1715; *e-mail:* neil.burton@architecturalhistory.co.uk.

BURTON, Hon. (Richard) Mark; MP (Lab) Taupo, since 1996 (Tongariro, 1993–96); Deputy Leader of the House, since 1999, and Minister of Justice and of Local Government, since 2005, New Zealand; Minister in Charge of Treaty of Waitangi Negotiations and Responsible for the Law Commission, since 2005; *b* 16 Jan. 1956; *m* 1977, Carol Botherway; two *s* one *d*. *Educ:* Waikato Univ. (Cert. Contg Educn); Massey Univ. (Cert. Social Service Supervision); NZ Council of Recreation and Sport (Dip.). Residential Social Worker, Dept of Social Welfare, 1976–78; Community Recreation Advr, Palmerston North City Corp., 1978–82; Community Educn Organiser, Central Plateau Rural Educn Activities Prog., 1982–93. Lab. Party spokesman for adult and community educn, 1994–99; Sen. Labour Party Whip, 1996–99; Minister: of Internal Affairs and of Veterans' Affairs, 1999–2002; of State Owned Enterprises, 1999–2004; of Defence and of Tourism, 1999–2005. Various posts with NZ Assoc. for Community and Contg Educn, 1983–93; Member: Bd of Studies, Contg Educn, Waikato Univ., 1985–86; Bd, NZ Career Develt and Transition Educn Service, 1990–92. NZ Medal, 1990. *Address:* Parliament Buildings, Wellington, New Zealand.

BURTON, Richard St John Vladimir, CBE 1996; RIBA; Partner, 1961–1985, Director, 1985–2003, Ahrends Burton & Koralek; *b* 3 Nov. 1933; *s* of Percy Basil Harmsworth Burton and Vera (*née* Poliakoff Russell); *m* 1956, Mireille, *d* of Joseph Dernbach-Mayen; three *s* one *d*. *Educ:* Bryanston; AA Sch. of Architecture (AA Dip Hons). RIBA 1957. Founding Partner, Ahrends Burton & Koralek, 1961. Principal works: TCD Library and Arts Bldg, 1967 and 1979; Chalvedon and Northlands Housing, Basildon, 1968 and 1980; Templeton Coll., Oxford, 1969–2007; Nebenzahl House, 1972; extension, Keble Coll., Oxford, 1976; W. H. Smith Head Office Marketing, Swindon, 1985; Burton House, 1987, 1993; Hooke Park Coll., 1990; John Lewis, Kingston-on-Thames, 1991; St Mary's Isle of Wight Low Energy Hosp., 1991; Docklands Light Railway extension, 1993; British Embassy, Moscow, 2000. Chairman: Arts Council Percent for Art Steering Gp, 1989; RIBA Steering Gp on Educn, 1991; Arts Council Adv. Gp on Architecture, 1994–98; Building a 20/20 Vision Future Healthcare Environment, Jt Report of Nuffield Foundn, RIBA and Med. Architectural Res. Unit, 2000–01. Design Advr, NHS Estates, 2003–06. FRSA. *Publications:* Ahrends Burton and Koralek, 1991; (jtly) The Architecture of ABK, 2002. *Recreations:* drawing, writing. *Address:* 1B Lady Margaret Road, NW5 2NE. *T:* (020) 7267 1198; *e-mail:* rsvb@blueyonder.co.uk.

BURTON, Roger; Director of Finance (formerly City Treasurer, then Director of Resources), Birmingham City Council, 1990–97; *b* 12 Oct. 1946; *s* of Norman Burton and Marjorie Rose (*née* Burgin); *m* 1st, 1968, Dorothy May Hey (marr. diss.); one *s* one *d*; 2nd, 1984, Susan Jane Griffiths (marr. diss. 1988); 3rd, 1991, Janet Elizabeth Mauchlen (*née* Davies); two step *s* one step *d*. *Educ:* Doncaster Grammar Sch.; Lanchester Polytechnic (BSc Econs 1968). CIPFA 1972; IRRV 1990. Coventry CC, 1968–79; Birmingham CC, 1979–97. A Public Works Loan Comr, 1996. *Recreations:* sport, walking, photography, Real Ale. *T:* (024) 7640 7480.

BURTON, Sydney Harold; JP; FCIB; Director, Gateway Building Society, 1981–88 (Managing Director, 1975–81); *b* 6 April 1916; *s* of Sydney Collard Burton and Maud Burton; *m* 1st, 1941, Jean Cowling (*d* 1985); one *d*; 2nd, 1986, Irene Robertson (*d* 2008). *Educ:* Belle Vue High Sch., Bradford. Various appts with Bradford Equitable Building Soc. (excl. war years), 1932–63; joined Temperance Permanent Building Soc., 1963; Jt Gen. Manager, 1965; Gen. Man. and Sec., 1972; following merger of Temperance Permanent and Bedfordshire Bldg Socs became Chief Gen. Man. and Sec. of Gateway Bldg Soc., 1974. Pres., Building Societies Inst., 1976–77; Mem. Council, Building Societies Assoc., 1971–81. JP Worthing, 1974. *Recreations:* music and theatre, social and religious work. *Address:* Cherry Trees, 52 Beehive Lane, Ferring, Sussex BN12 5NR. *T:* (01903) 244704.

BURTON, Tim; film director and producer; *b* Burbank, Calif, 25 Aug. 1958; *s* of late Bill Burton and of Jean Burton; *m* 1989, Lena Gieseke; partner, Helena Bonham Carter, *qv*; one *s* one *d*. *Educ:* Calif Inst. of the Arts. Formerly apprentice animator, Walt Disney Studios (projects incl. The Fox and the Hound, 1981; The Black Cauldron, 1985). Animator and dir, Vincent (short film), 1982; *films include: director:* Hansel and Gretel (TV), 1982; Aladdin (TV), 1984; Frankenweenie (short), 1984; Pee-wee's Big Adventure, 1985; Beetlejuice, 1988; Batman, 1989; Sleepy Hollow, 2000; Planet of the Apes, 2001; Big Fish, 2004; Charlie and the Chocolate Factory, 2005; Sweeney Todd: The Demon Barber of Fleet Street, 2008; *director and producer:* Edward Scissorhands, 1991; Batman Returns, 1992; Ed Wood, 1994; Mars Attacks!, 1997; Corpse Bride, 2005; *producer:* The Nightmare Before Christmas, 1993; Cabin Boy, 1994; Batman Forever, 1996; James and the Giant Peach, 1996. *Publications:* My Art and Films, 1993; The Melancholy Death of Oyster Boy and Other Stories, 1997. *Address:* Chapman, Bird & Grey, Suite 200, 1990 South Bundy Drive, Los Angeles, CA 90025, USA.

BURTON, Victoria Geraldine, (Mrs A. M. Burton); see Bruce, V. G.

BURTON-CHADWICK, Sir Joshua (Kenneth), 3rd Bt *cr* 1935, of Bidston; Trainer, The International Academy of Human Relations; *b* 1 Feb. 1954; *s* of Sir Robert Burton-Chadwick, (Sir Peter), 2nd Bt, and of Beryl Joan, *d* of Stanley Frederick J. Brailsford; *S* father, 1983. **Heir:** none.

BURTON-PAGE, Piers John; writer, lecturer, critic and broadcaster; *b* 25 July 1947; *s* of John Garrard Burton-Page and Audrey Ruth Burton-Page (*née* Marley); *m* 1976, Patricia Margaret Cornish; two *s*. *Educ:* Harrow Sch.; Wadham Coll., Oxford (MA); Univ. of Sussex (MA in Russian Studies). Joined BBC, 1971: studio manager, 1971–75; announcer and newsreader, Radio 4, 1975–77; Producer, Gramophone Dept, 1977–83; External Services Music Organiser, 1983–85; Radio 3: Presentation Editor, 1985–90; presenter/producer, 1990–97; Exec. Producer, 1998–2002. Acting Editor, Opera, 1997. (Jtly) Ohio State Award, for series The Elements of Music, 1984. *Publications:* Philharmonic Concerto: the life and music of Sir Malcolm Arnold, 1994; The Allegri at 50: a quartet in 5 movements, 2004. *Recreations:* cricket, theatre, travel, languages, the open air. *Club:* Bushmen.

BURTON-RACE, John William; Co-owner: The New Angel, Dartmouth, since 2004 (1 Michelin star, 2005); New Angel Rooms, since 2005; *b* 1 May 1957; *s* of Keith Burton and Shirley Burton, later Race; *m* (marr. diss. 2008); one *s* one *d*; one *s*. *Educ:* St Mary's Coll., Bitterne; American Sch., Bangkok. Apprentice, Wessex Hotel, Winchester, 1973–75; Commis, Quaglino's Hotel Meurice, London, 1975–76; First Commis, Chewton Glen Hotel, 1976–78; Chef, Olivers, Midhurst, 1978–79; Chef tournant, La Sorbonne, Oxford, 1979–82; Pvte Chef, MacKenzie-Hill Property Develt Internat., 1982–83; Sous Chef, Les Quat' Saisons, Oxford, 1983–84; Head Chef and Manager, Le Petit Blanc, Oxford, 1984–86; Chef-Proprietor, L'Ortolan, Berks, 1986–2000 (1 Michelin star, 1987–90, 2 Michelin stars, 1991–96, 1999); Chef, John Burton-Race at Landmark Hotel, London, 2000–02 (2 Michelin stars, 2001); in France, 2002–03; opened New Angel Cookery Sch., 2005. Television series include: Master Chefs of Europe, 1988; Great British Chefs, 1989; Great European Chefs, 1990; French Leave, 2003; Return of the Chef, 2005; Britain's Best Dish, 2007–08. Many gastronomic awards. *Publications:* Recipes from an English Master Chef, 1994; French Leave, 2003; Coming Home, 2005; First

Crack Your Egg, 2007; Flavour First, 2008; (jtly) Cooking for Beginners, 2008. *Recreations:* Porsche cars, fishing, shooting. *Address:* The New Angel Restaurant, 2 South Embankment, Dartmouth, Devon TQ6 9BH. *T:* (01803) 839425, *Fax:* (01803) 839505; *e-mail:* info@thenewangel.co.uk.

BURY, Viscount; Augustus Sergei Darius Keppel; *b* 8 Feb. 2003; *s* and *heir* of Earl of Albemarle, *qv*.

BURY, (Anne) Carolyn; see Hayman, A. C.

BURY, Lindsay Claude Neils; Chairman, Electric & General Investment Trust (formerly Henderson Electric & Investment Trust), since 2001 (Director, since 1995); *b* 13 Feb. 1939; *s* of Frank James Lindsay Bury and Diana Mary Lewis; *m* 1968, Sarah Ann Ingall; one *s* one *d*. *Educ:* Eton; Trinity College, Cambridge (BA History). J. Henry Schroder Wagg, 1960–66; Singer & Friedlander, 1966–73; Dunbar & Co., 1973–83. Director: ACT (formerly Apricot Computers), 1968–95 (Chm., 1972–89); Portals Holdings, 1973–95; Christie Group, 1989–94; Roxboro Gp, 1993–2001; Sage Gp, 1995–2006; Chairman: Unicorn Internat., 1995–97; Service Power Technologies plc, 1997– (Dir, 1997–); S Staffs Gp (formerly S Staffs Waterworks Co.), 1992–2004 (Dir, 1981–). Trustee, City of Birmingham Touring Opera, 1989–92. Chm. of Govs, Moor Park Sch., 1982–90; Trustee: Millichope Foundn, 1984–; Brazilian Atlantic Rainforest Trust, 2004–; Pres., Fauna and Flora Internat., 2003– (Chm., 1994–2003). High Sheriff, Shropshire, 1998. *Recreations:* music, country pursuits. *Address:* Millichope Park, Munslow, Craven Arms, Shropshire SY7 9HA. *T:* (01584) 841234; Ruantallain Lodge, Island of Jura, Scotland. *Clubs:* Turf, Pratt's, MCC.

BURY, Michael Oswell, OBE 1968; Consultant, Education and Training, Confederation of British Industry, 1986–87; *b* 20 Dec. 1922; *o s* of Lt-Col Thomas Oswell Bury, TD, and Constance Evelyn Bury; *m* 1954, Jean Threlkeld Wood, *d* of late William Threlkeld Wood; two *s* one *d*. *Educ:* Charterhouse; London Sch. of Economics. Served War of 1939–45: The Rifle Brigade (ranks of Rifleman to Captain), 1941–47. Steel Company of Wales, 1947–49; British Iron and Steel Fedn, 1949–64 (Dep. Dir, Labour and Trng, 1962–64); Dir, Iron and Steel Industry Trng Bd, 1964–70; Confederation of British Industry: Director, Educn, Trng and Technol., 1970–81; Dir, Corporate Affairs, 1981–84; Dir, Educn, Trng and Technol., 1985–86. Mem., Manpower Services Commn, 1974–81, 1985–87. *Recreations:* gardening, fishing, travel.

BURY, Very Rev. Nicholas Ayles Stillingfleet; Dean of Gloucester, since 1997; *b* 8 Jan. 1943; *s* of Major John J. S. Bury, MC, RA and Joan A. M. Bury; *m* 1973, Jennifer Anne Newbold; two *s* one *d*. *Educ:* King's Sch., Canterbury; Queens' Coll., Cambridge (MA 1969); MA Oxon 1971; DipEd Oxon; Cuddesdon Theol Coll. Ordained deacon, 1968, priest, 1969; Asst Curate, Our Lady & St Nicholas, Liverpool, 1968–71; Chaplain, Christ Church, Oxford, 1971–75; Vicar: St Mary's, Shephall, Stevenage, Herts, 1975–84; St Peter in Thanet, Broadstairs, 1984–97. Hon. Fellow, Univ. of Gloucester, 2003. *Recreations:* golf, water-colour painting. *Address:* The Deanery, Miller's Green, Gloucester GL1 2BP. *T:* (01452) 524167.

BUSBY, George Benedict Joseph Pascal, OBE 1996; HM Diplomatic Service; Counsellor, Foreign and Commonwealth Office, since 2004; *b* 18 April 1960; *s* of Christopher Raymond Busby and Anne Margaret Busby; *m* 1988, Helen Frances Hurll; one *s* three *d*. *Educ:* Sch. of Slavonic Studies, London Univ. (BA Hons); St Anthony's Coll., Oxford (Diploma). Joined Diplomatic Service, 1987; Second Sec., FCO, 1987; Second, then First Sec., Bonn, 1989–91; First Secretary: FCO, 1991–92; Belgrade, 1992–96; First Sec., then Counsellor, FCO, 1996–2000; Counsellor, Vienna, 2000–04. *Address:* c/o Foreign and Commonwealth Office, King Charles Street, SW1A 2AH.

BUSBY, Prof. Stephen John Williams, DPhil; FRS 2005; Professor of Biochemistry, University of Birmingham, since 1995; *b* 5 March 1951; *s* of Peter Busby and Joan Busby (*née* Williams); *m* 1980, (Elizabeth) Jane Cooper; two *s* one *d*. *Educ:* Moseley Hall Co. Grammar Sch., Cheadle; Sidney Sussex Coll., Cambridge (BA 1972); Merton and St John's Colls, Oxford (DPhil 1975). Postdoctoral scientist, 1975–78, on Scientific Staff, 1979–83, Inst Pasteur, Paris; University of Birmingham: Lectr, 1983–88; Sen. Lectr, 1988–90; Reader, 1990–95; Dean of Sci., then Dean of Life and Health Sci., 2000–04. Vis. Scientist, NIH, Bethesda, USA, 1979–80. *Publications:* contrib. numerous res. papers to learned jls. *Recreations:* family, travel, food, walking, doing nothing! *Address:* School of Biosciences, University of Birmingham, Edgbaston, Birmingham B15 2TT. *T:* (0121) 414 5439; *e-mail:* s.j.w.busby@bham.ac.uk.

BUSCH, Constantinus Albertus Maria; Member, Supervisory Board, Parcom Ventures BV, 1995; *b* 17 Aug. 1937; *m* 1963, Ingrid (*née* Haaksma); two *s* two *d*. *Educ:* in The Netherlands; Amsterdam Univ. (Economics degree). 1st Lieut, Dutch Army, 1962–64; Corporate Finance Dept, NV Philips Eindhoven, 1964–66; Manager, Philips Internat. Finance, Luxembourg, 1966–70; Naarden International NV: Treasurer, 1970–72; Dir of Finance and Mem. Bd of Management, 1973–80; Financial Dir, Philips Electronics UK, 1981–85; Corporate Finance Dir, NV Philips Eindhoven, 1985–87; UK Vice-Chm. and Financial Dir, Philips Electronics, 1988; Chm. and Man. Dir, Philips Electronics and Associated Industries, 1989–90; Corporate Finance Dir, Philips Internat. BV, 1991–92; Mem. Bd of Dirs, Verenigde Nederlandse Uitgeversbedryven BV, 1993–97. *Recreations:* music, particularly clarinet and saxophone; tennis, golf, ski-ing. *Address:* Dirck van Hornelaan 23, Waalre 5581 CZ, Netherlands.

BUSCH, Rolf Trygve; Comdr, Order of St Olav; Hon. GCVO 1988; Norwegian Ambassador to the Court of St James's, 1982–88; *b* 15 Nov. 1920; *s* of Aksel Busch and Alette (*née* Tunby); *m* 1950, Solveig Helle; one *s*. *Educ:* Oslo Univ. (degree in Law); National Defence Coll. Dep. Judge, 1946–47; entered Norwegian Foreign Service, 1947; Min. of For. Affairs, 1947–50; Sec., Cairo, 1950–52; Vice-Consul, New York, 1952–54; Min. of For. Affairs, 1954–56; National Def. Coll., 1956–57; First Sec., Norwegian Delegn to NATO, Paris, 1957–60; Min. of For. Affairs, 1960–65; Counsellor and Dep. Perm. Rep., Norwegian Delegn to NATO, Paris and Brussels, 1965–70; Dir-Gen., Min. of For. Affairs, 1970–71; Perm. Rep. to N Atlantic Council, 1971–77; Ambassador to Fed. Republic of Germany, 1977–82. Officer, Order of the Nile, Egypt; Comdr with Star, Order of the Falcon, Iceland; Grand Cross, Order of Merit, Fed. Republic of Germany. *Address:* 2 Hafrsfjords Gt, 0273 Oslo 2, Norway. *T:* 22431791.

BUSCOMBE, family name of **Baroness Buscombe**.

BUSCOMBE, Baroness *cr* 1998 (Life Peer), of Goring in the co. of Oxfordshire; **Peta Jane Buscombe;** Chief Executive and Director General, Advertising Association, since 2007; Director, Advertising Standards Board of Finance, since 2007; *b* 12 March 1954; *m* 1980, Philip John Buscombe; twin *s* one *d*. *Educ:* Hinchley Wood Sch.; Rosebery Grammar Sch., Epsom; Inns of Ct Sch. of Law. Called to the Bar, Inner Temple, 1977. Legal Advr, Dairy Trade Fedn, 1979–80; lawyer, Barclays Bank International, NY, then Hd Office Lawyer and Inspector, Barclays Bank plc, UK, 1980–84; Asst Sec., Inst. of Practitioners in Advertising, 1984–87. Mem. (C) S Oxfordshire DC, 1995–99. Opposition front bench spokesman, H of L, on trade and industry, social security and legal affairs, 1999–2001, on Cabinet Office affairs, 2000, on home and legal affairs, 2001–, on culture, media and sport, 2002–05; Shadow Minister for Educn and Skills, 2005–06. Vice Chm., All Party Gp for Mgt Consultants, 2001–; Member: British-American All Party Gp, 1998–; All Party Gp for Corporate Social Responsibility, 2001–, for Intellectual Property, 2004–, for Corporate Governance, 2004–; Vice Pres., All Party Parly Gp for Sexual Equality, 2004–. Vice Chm. resp. for Develt, Cons. Party, 1997–99; Founder, Cons. Network and Cons. Cultural Unit; Vice Chm., S Oxfordshire Cons. Assoc., 1995–98; Pres., Slough Cons. Assoc., 1997–. Contested (C) Slough, 1997. Mem. Adv. Bd, Gow and Partners, 2003–05. Non-exec. Dir, Three Valleys plc, 2006–. Chm., Goring and Streatley Amenity Assoc., 1995–98; Mem., Assoc. of Rural Businesses in Oxfordshire, 1994–2002. Vice Pres., Debating Soc., 2005–. Vice Chair, Globe UK, 2007–; Member: RSA Risk Commn, 2006–; Council for Child Internet Safety, 2008–. Patron: Foundn for Internat. Commercial Arbitration and Alternative Dispute Resolution, 1999–; Inns of Ct Sch. of Law Cons. Assoc.; PALS, 2000–; Westminster Media Forum, 2002–; Robert Bowman Gall. Trust, 2004–; Westminster eForum, 2005–; Westminster Educn Forum, 2005–; Founder Patron, Inst. of Paralegals, 2005–; Vice Patron, Abbeyfield House Appeal, 1998–2002; Ambassador, Guide Assoc., 2002–. Vice Pres., Henley Soc.; Mem., Chiltern Soc. FRSA 2004. *Recreations:* theatre, opera, shooting, riding, swimming. *Address:* House of Lords, SW1A 0PW.

BUSE, Diana Anjoli; *see* Garnham, D. A.

BUSH, His Honour Bryan; a Circuit Judge, 1983–2005; *b* 28 Nov. 1936; *s* of Maurice and Hetty Bush; *m* 1963, Jacqueline (*née* Rayman); two *s* one *d*. *Educ:* Leeds Grammar Sch.; Keble Coll., Oxford (MA). Called to the Bar, Gray's Inn, 1961; practising on NE Circuit, 1961–83; a Recorder of the Crown Court, 1978–83. *Recreations:* theatre, golf. *Address:* c/o Leeds Crown Court, Leeds LS1 3BE.

BUSH, Charles Martin Peter, MA; Headmaster, Oundle School, since 2005; *b* 28 June 1952; *s* of late Dr John Peter Bush and of Edith Mary (*née* Farnsworth); *m* 1977, Rosalind Mary Nevin; three *s*. *Educ:* Melbourne C of E Grammar Sch.; Univ. of Melbourne; Trinity Coll., Oxford (MA). Aylesbury Grammar Sch., 1975–78, Hd of Pure Maths, 1977–78; Hd of Maths, Abingdon Sch., 1978–82; Marlborough College, 1982–93: Hd of Maths, 1982–89; Housemaster, B1 House, 1988–93; Headmaster, Eastbourne Coll., 1993–2005. *Publication:* (co-author in SMP Team) Revised Advanced Mathematics (Book 1), 1988. *Recreations:* golf, cricket, mathematics, fell walking. *Address:* Oundle School, New Street, Oundle, Peterborough PE8 4GH. *T:* (01832) 277142. *Clubs:* East India, MCC; Melbourne Cricket.

BUSH, Geoffrey Hubert, CB 1998; DL; Deputy Chairman, Board of Inland Revenue, 1998–99, retired; *b* 5 April 1942; *s* of late Sidney Arthur Bush and Dorothy Elizabeth Bush; *m* 1965, Sylvia Mary Squibb; one *s* one *d*. *Educ:* Cotham Grammar Sch., Bristol. Tax Officer, 1959; Inspector of Taxes, 1968; Dist Inspector of Taxes, 1973; Principal Inspector of Taxes, 1981; Board of Inland Revenue: Under Sec., 1988–94; Dir Gen., 1994–98. Advr, Office of Govt Commerce, 2000–08. Trustee: Devon Co. Agricl Assoc., 2001–; Exeter Univ. Foundn, 2006–. DL Devon, 2008. CStJ 2007 (Chm. Council, Devon, 2001–08). *Recreations:* travel, golf. *Address:* (home) Exmouth, Devon. *Clubs:* Exeter Golf and Country (Devon) (Vice Chm., 2007–); Knowle Lawn Tennis (Bristol).

BUSH, George Herbert Walker, Hon. GCB 1993; President of the United States of America, 1989–93; UN Special Envoy for South Asia Earthquake, since 2005; *b* Milton, Mass, 12 June 1924; *s* of late Prescott Sheldon Bush and Dorothy (*née* Walker); *m* 1945, Barbara, *d* of Marvin Pierce, NY; four *s* one *d*. *Educ:* Phillips Acad., Andover, Mass; Yale Univ. (BA Econs 1948). Served War, USNR, Lieut, pilot (DFC, three Air Medals). Co-founder and Dir, Zapata Petroleum Corp., 1953–59; Founder, Zapata Offshore Co., Houston, 1954, Pres., 1956–64, Chm. Bd, 1964–66. Chm., Republican Party, Harris Co., Texas, 1963–64; Delegate, Republican Nat. Convention, 1964, 1968; Republican cand. US Senator from Texas, 1964, 1970; Mem., 90th and 91st Congresses, 7th District of Texas, 1967–71; US Perm. Rep. to UN, 1971–73; Chm., Republican Party Nat. Cttee, 1973–74; Chief, US Liaison Office, Peking, 1974–75; Dir, US Central Intelligence Agency, 1976–77; Vice-President of the USA, 1981–89. Cand. for Republican Presidential nomination, 1980. Hon. degrees from many colleges and univs. *Publications:* (with Victor Gold) Looking Forward: an autobiography, 1988; (with Gen. Brent Scowcroft) A World Transformed, 1998; All the Best: my life in letters and other writings, 2000. *Recreations:* tennis, jogging, golf, boating, fishing. *Address:* Suite 900, 10000 Memorial Drive, Houston, TX 77024, USA.

See also G. W. Bush.

BUSH, George Walker; President of the United States of America, 2001–09; *b* 6 July 1946; *e s* of George Herbert Walker Bush, *qv*; *m* 1977, Laura Welch; twin *d*. *Educ:* Phillips Acad., Andover; Yale Univ. (BA History 1968); Harvard Business Sch. (MBA 1975). F-102 Pilot, Texas Air Nat. Guard. Founded Bush Exploration, 1975; merged with Spectrum 7 Energy Corp., 1984 (Pres.), subseq. Harken Energy Corp., 1986 (Consultant); advr and speechwriter to father during Presidential campaign, 1986–88; Governor of Texas, 1995–2000. Republican. Part-owner, Texas Rangers baseball team, 1989–98. *Publication:* A Charge to Keep, 1999. *Address:* The White House, Washington, DC 20500, USA.

BUSH, Dr Harry John, CB 2000; Group Director, Economic Regulation, Civil Aviation Authority, since 2003; *b* 26 Aug. 1953; *s* of Harold Leslie Bush and Bridget Bush (*née* Gorman). *Educ:* Quintin Grammar Sch.; Quintin Kynaston Sch.; Merton Coll., Oxford (BA Mod. Hist. and Econs 1974); DPhil Oxon 1980. Nuffield College, Oxford: Student, 1974–77; Prize Res. Fellow, 1977–79; Jun. Dean, 1978–79; HM Treasury, 1979–2003: Private Sec. to Minister of State, 1981–82; Principal, 1982; Dep. Press Sec., 1987–89; Asst Sec., 1989; Head of Privatisation, 1993–97; Dep. Dir, then Dir, and Hd of Enterprise and Growth Unit, 1997–2003. Chm., OECD Privatisation Network, 1996–98; Dir, EIB, 2002–03; Mem., Performance Review Commn, Eurocontrol, 2005–. FRAeS 2007. *Recreations:* political biography, travel, food, wine, moderate exercise. *Address:* Civil Aviation Authority, CAA House, 45–59 Kingsway, WC2B 6TE.

BUSH, Janet Elizabeth; Senior Editor, McKinsey Global Institute, since 2006; *b* Lytham-St-Annes, 2 June 1960; *d* of Arthur and Mary Bush; partner, Nick de Cent; one *d*. *Educ:* Berkhamsted Sch. for Girls; Somerville Coll., Oxford (BA Eng. Lang. and Lit., MA); Centre for Journalism Studies, Cardiff (Reuters schol., postgrad. degree in journalism). Frankfurt Correspondent, 1983–84, Econs writer, 1984–86, Reuters; Dep. Econs Correspondent, 1986–87, NY Correspondent, 1987–90, Financial Times; Presenter, economic documentaries, Money Prog., BBC, 1990–92; Econs Correspondent, 1992–96, Economics Editor, 1997–99, The Times; Director: New Europe, 1999–2003; The No Campaign, 2000–03; Advocacy International Ltd, 2004–05. Harold Wincott Young Financial Journalist of the Year, 1987. *Publications:* (ed) The Real World Economic Outlook, 2003; Consumer Empowerment and Competitiveness, 2004. *Recreations:* good conversation, gardening, politics, family life. *Address:* Blackacre, Colyton, Devon EX24 6SF. *T:* (01404) 871672; *e-mail:* janet@janet-bush.com.

BUSH, John Barnard, OBE 2004; JP; farmer; Lord-Lieutenant of Wiltshire, since 2004; *b* 5 Feb. 1937; *s* of Barnard Bush and Elizabeth (*née* Weeks); *m* 1961, Pamela Bagwell; one *s* one *d*. *Educ:* Monkton Combe Sch.; Balliol Coll., Oxford (MA). Chairman: WMF Ltd, 1995–99; Countrywide Farmers plc, 1999–2004. Chm., Bristol Avon Flood Defences Cttee, 1981–2000. Chm., Wilts Magistrates' Courts Cttee, 2001–05. JP NW Wilts, 1980; High Sheriff, 1997–98, DL 1998, Wilts. Gov., Lackham Coll., 1986–98. *Address:* Fullingbridge Farm, Heywood, Westbury, Wilts BA13 4NB. *T:* and *Fax:* (01373) 824609; *e-mail:* johnbush@btconnect.com. *Club:* Farmers.

BUSH, Adm. Sir John (Fitzroy Duyland), GCB 1970 (KCB 1965 CB 1963); DSC 1941, and Bars, 1941, 1944; Vice-Admiral of the United Kingdom and Lieutenant of the Admiralty, 1979–84; *b* 1 Nov. 1914; *s* of late Fitzroy Bush, Beach, Glos; *m* 1938, Ruth Kennedy Horsey; three *s* two *d*. *Educ:* Clifton Coll. Entered Navy, 1933; served in Destroyers throughout War. Commanded HM Ships: Belvoir, 1942–44; Zephyr, 1944; Chevron, 1945–46. Comdr Dec. 1946; Plans Div., Admiralty, 1946–48; graduated Armed Forces Staff Coll., USA, 1949; Comd, HMS Cadiz, 1950–51; Capt. June 1952; Dep. Sec. Chiefs of Staff Cttee, 1953–55; Capt. (F) Sixth Frigate Sqdn, 1955–56; Cdre, RN Barracks, Chatham, 1957–59; Dir. of Plans, Admiralty, 1959–60; Rear-Adm. 1961; Flag Officer Flotillas (Mediterranean), 1961–62; Vice-Adm. 1963; Comdr, British Naval Staff and Naval Attaché, Washington, 1963–65; Vice-Chief of the Naval Staff, Ministry of Defence, 1965–67; C-in-C Western Fleet, C-in-C Eastern Atlantic, and C-in-C Channel (NATO), 1967–70; Admiral 1968; retd, 1970. Rear-Admiral of the UK, 1976–79. Dir, Gordon A. Friesen International Inc., Washington, DC, 1970–73. Adm., Texas (USA) Navy. Governor, Clifton Coll., 1973– (Chm. Council, 1978–81; Pres., 1982–87). Pres., Old Cliftonians Soc., 1967–69; Vice-Pres., Eighth Army Veterans Assoc., 1984–. Mem., E Hants District Council, 1974–76. *Recreation:* gardening.

BUSH, Maj.-Gen. Peter John, OBE 1968; Controller, Army Benevolent Fund, 1980–87; *b* 31 May 1924; *s* of Clement Charles Victor Bush and Kathleen Mabel Peirce; *m* 1948, Jean Mary Hamilton; two *s* one *d*. *Educ:* Maidenhead County Sch. Commnd Somerset LI, 1944; comd LI Volunteers, 1966; GSO 1 HQ 14 Div./Malaya Dist, 1968; Comdr 3 Inf. Bde, 1971 (mentioned in despatches, 1973); Asst Comdt RMA Sandhurst, 1974; Chief of Staff and Head of UK Delegn to Live Oak, SHAPE, 1977–79, retd. Col, The Light Infantry, 1977–82. *Recreations:* natural history, walking, reading. *Address:* Thorndean, Boyndon Road, Maidenhead, Berks SL6 4EU.

BUSH, Ven. Roger Charles; Archdeacon of Cornwall, since 2006; *b* 22 Nov. 1956; *s* of Harvey John Bush and Edith May Rose Bush (*née* Spurgeon); *m* 1984, Lois Mary (*née* Nichols); one *s* one *d*. *Educ:* King's Coll., London (BA Hons 1978); Univ. of Leeds (BA 1985). Ordained deacon, 1986, priest, 1987; Curate, Newbold with Dunstan, Chesterfield, 1986–90; Team Vicar, Parish of the Resurrection, Leicester, 1990–94; Rector, Redruth with Lanner and Treleigh, Cornwall, 1994–2004; RD, Carnmarth North, 1996–2003; Hon. Canon, 2003–04, Residentiary Canon, 2004–06, Truro Cathedral. *Recreations:* reading history, theology and fiction, music – anything classical (sings tenor in Three Spires Choir), walking, collecting maps. *Address:* Westwood House, Tremorvah Crescent, Truro TR1 1NL. *T:* and *Fax:* (01872) 225630; *e-mail:* rogerbush56@hotmail.com.

BUSH, Prof. Ronald Lee, PhD; Drue Heinz Professor of American Literature and Fellow of St John's College, University of Oxford, since 1997; *b* 16 June 1946; *s* of Raymond J. Bush and Esther Schneyer Bush; *m* 1969, Marilyn Wolin; one *s*. *Educ:* Univ. of Pennsylvania (BA 1968); Pembroke Coll., Cambridge (BA 1970); Princeton Univ. (PhD 1974). Asst Prof., later Associate Prof. of English, Harvard Univ., 1974–82; Associate Prof., later Prof. of Literature, CIT, 1982–97. NEH Fellow, 1977–78, 1992–93; Vis. Fellow, Exeter Coll., Oxford, 1994–95; Fellow, Amer. Civilization Prog., Harvard, 2004. *Publications:* The Genesis of Ezra Pound's Cantos, 1976; T. S. Eliot: a study of character and style, 1984; (ed) T. S. Eliot: the modernist in history, 1991; (ed) Prehistories of the Future, 1995; (ed) Claiming the Stones, 2002. *Recreation:* tennis. *Address:* St John's College, Oxford OX1 3JP. *T:* (01865) 277300.

BUSH, William; Director of Public Policy and Communications, The Premier League (formerly Football Association Premier League), since 2005; *b* 2 Oct. 1951; *s* of Douglas Stewart Murray Bush and Dorothy Yvonne Anna Bush; *m* 1973, Susan Holmes (marr. diss.); one *s*. *Educ:* Bedford Coll. (BA); London Sch. of Econs (MSc Econ). Head: Leader's Office, GLC, 1981–86; of Ext. Relns, ILEA, 1986–89; of Political Res., 1990–97, of Res., 1997–99, BBC News; of Res. and Inf., No 10 Downing St, 1999–2001; Special Advr, DCMS, 2001–05. *Address:* The Premier League, 30 Gloucester Place, W1U 8PL. *T:* (020) 7864 9149; 11 Baptist Gardens, NW5 4ET. *e-mail:* williambush1@hotmail.com. *Club:* London Erratics Cricket.

BUSHE, Frederick Joseph William, OBE 1994; RSA 1986 (ARSA 1977); Founder, 1979, and Director, 1979–96, Scottish Sculpture Workshop; *b* 1 March 1931; *s* of Frederick M. C. Bushe and Kathleen Welch; *m* 1st, 1956, Rosemary R. Beattie; three *s* one *d*; 2nd, 1984, Fiona M. S. Marr; one *d*. *Educ:* Our Lady's High Sch., Motherwell; Glasgow Sch. of Art (DA). Temp. Captain RAEC, 1954–58. Art teacher, Midlothian, 1958–60, Berwickshire, 1960–62; Lectr in Art Educn, Notre Dame, Liverpool, 1962–69, Aberdeen Coll. of Educn, 1969–79. Curator, Scandex, 15th anniv. touring exhibn of Scottish sculpture, 1994–95. Governor, Edinburgh Coll. of Art, 1983–88. Invited Artist: Formaviva Internat. Symposium of Sculptors, Yugoslavia, 1988; Terra Internat. Symposium, Kikinda, Yugoslavia, 1990. Work in numerous public collections; one man exhibitions: Edinburgh, 1962, 1971, 1982; Liverpool, 1966; Glasgow, 1974; Manchester, 1975; Stirling, 1978; group exhibns. *Recreations:* listening to music, cooking. *Address:* Rose Cottage, Lumsden, Huntly, Aberdeenshire AB54 4JJ. *T:* (01464) 861394; Muirhead Private Nursing Home, Muir of Fowlis, by Alford, Aberdeenshire AB33 8NU.

BUSHELL, (Rosalind) Morag; *see* Ellis, R. M.

BUSHILL-MATTHEWS, Philip Rodway; Member (C) West Midlands, European Parliament, since 1999; *b* 15 Jan. 1943; *s* of William Bushill-Matthews, MBE and Phyllis Bushill-Matthews, OBE; *m* 1967, Angela Loveday Bingham; one *s* two *d*. *Educ:* Malvern Coll.; University Coll., Oxford (MA); Harvard Business Sch. (AMP 1987). Joined Birds Eye Foods Ltd, 1965; seconded to Thomas Lipton Inc., USA, 1976; Nat. Accounts Dir, Birds Eye Sales Ltd, 1977–80; Man. Dir, Iglo industrias de gelados, Lisbon, 1980–81; Sales Dir, then Sales and Distribution Dir, Birds Eye Wall's Ltd, 1981–88; Managing Director: Craigmillar Ltd, 1988–91 (also Dir, Van den Bergh & Jurgens Ltd); Red Mill Snack Foods Ltd, 1991–99; Red Mill Co., BV, Netherlands, 1993–99. Dep. Leader, Cons. MEPs, 2007–. FInstD 1994. *Publications:* The Gravy Train, 2003; Who Rules Britannia?, 2005. *Recreations:* bridge, the theatre, enjoying the countryside. *Address:* The Manor House, Harbury, Leamington Spa, Warwicks CV33 9HX. *T:* (01926) 612476; *e-mail:* bushillm@aol.com.

BUSHNELL, Alexander Lynn, CBE 1962; County Clerk and Treasurer, Perth County Council, 1946–75, retired; *b* 13 Aug. 1911; *s* of William and Margaret Bushnell; *m* 1939, Janet Braithwaite Porteous; two *d. Educ:* Dalziel High Sch., Motherwell; Glasgow University. *Recreation:* golf. *Address:* 18 Fairies Road, Perth PH1 1NB. *T:* (01738) 622675.

BUSK, Glennis; *see* Haworth, S. G.

BUSK, Maj.-Gen. Leslie Francis Harry, CB 1990; Director General, British Heart Foundation, 1990–2003; *b* 12 Sept. 1937; *s* of late Lt-Col Charles William Francis Busk and Alice (*née* van Bergen); *m* 1st, 1960, Jennifer Helen Ring (*d* 1992); three *s*; 2nd, 1993, Sheila Glennis McElwain (*see* S. G. Haworth). *Educ:* Wellington Coll.; RMA, Sandhurst; RMCS, Shrivenham (BSc (Eng) London Univ.). Commnd RE, 1957; served in UK, NI, BAOR, India and Singapore; Defence Services Staff Coll., India, 1969; OC 25 Field Sqn, 1971–73; Instr, Staff Coll., Camberley, 1975–77; CO 35 Engr Regt, 1977–79; C of S 2nd Armoured Div., 1979–81; Bde Comd 11 Engr Bde, 1981–83; RCDS, 1984; DMO, MoD, 1985–86; Army Pilots Course, 1986–87; Dir, AAC, 1987–89, retd. Hon. Col, RE Volunteers (Sponsored Units), 1986–91; Col Comdt, RE, 1990–95. Chairman: AMRC, 1991–95, 1999–2002; Eur. Heart Network, 1998–2002. DUniv Glasgow, 2003. *Recreations:* golf, tennis. *Address:* Bushwood, Witheridge Hill Bottom, Highmoor, Henley on Thames, Oxon RG9 5PE. *Club:* Boodle's.

BUSQUIN, Philippe, Member (Soc.), European Parliament, since 2004; *b* 6 Jan. 1941; *m. Educ:* Univ. Libre de Bruxelles (Licence in Phys. Scis 1962; Cand. in Philosophy 1971; post-grad. in Envmt 1976). Asst in Physics, Faculty of Medicine, Univ. Libre de Bruxelles, 1962–77; Prof., Teachers' Coll., Nivelles, 1962–77; Pres., Bd of Dirs, IRE, 1978–80. Deputy: Province of Hainaut, 1977–78; Chamber of Reps, Belgium, 1978–95; Senator, Belgium, 1995–99; Minister of Educn, 1980; Minister for the Interior, 1981; Walloon Minister for Budget and for Energy, 1982–85; Walloon Minister for Economy, 1988; Minister of Social Affairs, 1988–92; Hon. Minister, 1992. Mem., EC, 1999–2004. Mayor of Seneffe, 1995–99. Mem., Community Exec., 1980–81. Pres., Socialist Party, Belgium, 1992–99; Vice-President: Internat. Socialists, 1992–99; European Socialist Party, 1995–97. Chm., Nat. Geographic Inst., 2004–. *Address:* European Parliament, Rue Wiertz 60, 1047 Brussels, Belgium.

BUSS, Barbara Ann, (Mrs Lewis Boxall); freelance journalist, 1976–1992; Editor-in-Chief, Woman magazine, 1974–75; Consultant, IPC Magazines Ltd, 1975–76; *b* 14 Aug. 1932; *d* of late Cecil Edward Buss and Victoria Lilian (*née* Vickers); *m* 1966, Lewis Albert Boxall (*d* 1983); no *c. Educ:* Lady Margaret Sch., London. Sec., Conservative Central Office, 1949–52; Sec./journalist, Good Taste magazine, 1952–56; Journalist: Woman and Beauty, 1956–57; Woman, 1957–59; Asst Editor, Woman's Illustrated, 1959–60; Editor, Woman's Illustrated, 1960–61; Journalist, Daily Herald, 1961; Associate Editor, Woman's Realm, 1961–62; Editor: Woman's Realm, 1962–64; Woman, 1964–74. *Recreations:* reading, theatre, cinema. *Address:* 1 Arlington Avenue, N1 7BE. *T:* (020) 7226 3265.

BUSSELL, Darcey Andrea, CBE 2006 (OBE 1995); Principal Ballerina, 1989–2006, Principal Guest Artist, 2006–07, Royal Ballet; *b* 27 April 1969; *d* of Philip Michael Bussell and Andrea Pemberton (*née* Williams); *m* 1997, Angus Forbes; two *d. Educ:* Arts Educnl Sch.; Royal Ballet Sch. Joined Sadler's Wells Royal Ballet (later Birmingham Royal Ballet), 1987; joined Royal Ballet, 1988: soloist, 1988; first soloist, 1989. *Leading rôles in:* Giselle; Swan Lake; Sleeping Beauty; La Bayadère (also with Kirov and Australian Ballet, 1998); Laurentia pas de six; Song of the Earth; Requiem; Galanteries; Spirit of Fugue; Pursuit; first Royal Ballet perf. of Balanchine's Rubies; Cinderella; Enigma Variations; Nutcracker; MacMillan's Elite Syncopations; Raymonda; Monotones; Symphony in C; first Royal Ballet perf. of Balanchine's Stravinsky Violin Concerto; Agon; Bloodlines; Les Biches; Tchaikovsky pas de deux; Beyond Bach; first perf. of William Forsythe's In the middle, somewhat elevated; Romeo and Juliet; Gong; Sylvia; The Four Temperaments; Kiss; Theme and Variations; *rôles created:* Princess Rose in Prince of the Pagodas, Royal Opera House, 1989; pas de deux (Farewell to Dreams) for HM Queen Mother's 90th Birthday Tribute, Palladium and Royal Opera House, 1990; Masha in Winter Dreams, 1991; Mr Worldly Wise, 1995; Dances With Death, 1996; Pavane pour une infante défunte, 1996; Amores, 1997; Towards Poetry, 1999; Lento, 1999; There Where She Loves, 2000; Dance Variations, 2000; Tryst, 2002; Tryst à Grande Vitesse, 2005. Touring song and dance show, Viva La Diva, 2007–08. Prix de Lausanne, 1986; Variety Club of GB Award for most promising newcomer, 1990; Dancer of Year Award, Dance and Dancers Mag., 1990; Evening Standard Award for dance, 1990. *Publications:* The Young Dancer, 1994; (with Judith Mackrell) Life in Dance (autobiog.), 1998; Pilates For Life, 2005; Dance Body Workout, 2007. *Recreations:* art and painting, reading, swimming. *Address:* c/o The Royal Opera House, Covent Garden, WC2E 9DD.

BUSTANI, José Mauricio; Ambassador of Brazil to France, since 2008; *b* 5 June 1945; *s* of Mauricio José Bustani and Guajá de Figueiredo Bustani; *m* 1971, Janine-Monique Lazaro; two *s* one *d. Educ:* Pontifícia Universidade Católica, Rio de Janeiro (LLB 1967); Brazilian Diplomatic Acad., Rio Branco Inst. Joined Brazilian Foreign Service, 1965; postings include: Moscow, 1970–73; Vienna, 1973–77; UN, NY, 1977–84; Montevideo, 1984–87; Montreal, 1987–92; Dir-Gen., Dept for Internat. Orgns, 1993–97; has held rank of Ambassador, 1995–; Dir-Gen., Orgn for Prohibition of Chem. Weapons, 1997–2002; Ambassador to the Court of St James's, 2003–08. Delegate to international negotiations including: 3rd UN Conf. on Law of the Sea, 1974–82; UN Gen. Assembly, 1977–83, 1993–96; 1st and 2nd Special Sessions of UN Gen. Assembly (Disarmament Affairs), 1978 and 1982; Montreal Protocol on Substances that Deplete the Ozone Layer (Leader), 1989–92; Multilateral Fund for Implementation of Montreal Protocol, 1990–91; 13th and 15th Sessions of Prep. Commn for Orgn for Prohibition of Chem. Weapons (Leader), 1996–97. *Recreation:* classical music. *Address:* Embassy of Brazil, 34 Cours Albert 1er, 75008 Paris, France. *T:* (1) 45616304, *Fax:* (1) 42890345; *e-mail:* ambassadeur@bresil.org.

BUTCHER, Anthony John; QC 1977; a Recorder, 1985–97; *b* 6 April 1934; *s* of late F. W. Butcher and O. M. Butcher (*née* Ansell); *m* 1959, Maureen Workman (*d* 1982); one *s* two *d. Educ:* Cranleigh Sch.; Sidney Sussex Coll., Cambridge (MA, LLB). Called to the Bar, Gray's Inn, 1957, Bencher, 1986; in practice at English Bar, 1957–97. Mem., Bar Council, 1989–91, and 1993–97; Chm., Official Referees Bar Assoc., 1986–92. *Recreations:* enjoying the arts and acquiring useless information. *Address:* Anthony Cottage, Polecat Valley, Hindhead, Surrey GU26 6BE. *T:* (01428) 609053; 1 Atkin Building, Gray's Inn, WC1R 5BQ. *T:* (020) 7404 0102. *Clubs:* Garrick, Beefsteak.

See also C. J. Butcher.

BUTCHER, Christopher John; QC 2001; *b* 14 Aug. 1962; *o s* of Anthony John Butcher, *qv*; *m* 1992, Fiona, *y d* of Prof. Maxwell Gaskin, *qv*; one *s* one *d. Educ:* Charterhouse (Sen. Schol.); Magdalen Coll., Oxford (Demy; Gibbs Prize in Mod. Hist. 1982; BA 1st Cl. Hons Mod. Hist; MA); City Univ. (Dip. Law); King's Coll., London (Dip. EC Law). Fellow, All Souls Coll., Oxford, 1983–98, 2005–07 (Jun. Dean, 1988–90 and 1992–98); Eldon Law Schol., Univ. of Oxford, 1987; called to the Bar, Gray's Inn, 1986 (Bacon Schol., Atkin Schol.; Bencher, 2005). Gov., Berkhamsted Collegiate Sch., 1995–. FRSA 2002. *Publications:* contrib. to various legal pubns. *Recreations:* history, literature, travel, the arts. *Address:* 7 King's Bench Walk, Temple, EC4Y 7DS. *T:* (020) 7583 0404.

BUTCHER, Peter Roderick; HM Diplomatic Service; Ambassador to Turkmenistan, since 2005; *b* 6 Aug. 1947. *Educ:* Univ. of Bath. Entered FCO, 1974; Second Sec., Peru, 1979–83; Madrid, 1983; Second Sec., Bombay, 1983–87; First Sec., FCO, 1987–90; Dep. High Comr, Lesotho, 1990–93; St Vincent and the Grenadines, 1994; First Sec., FCO, 1994–96; Dep. Gov., Port Stanley, 1996; on secondment to DFID, 1997–99; Dep. Hd of Mission, Mozambique, 2000–03. *Address:* c/o Foreign and Commonwealth Office, King Charles Street, SW1A 2AH.

BUTCHER, Philip; Chief Executive, Muscular Dystrophy Campaign, since 2005; *b* 6 June 1965; *s* of Stanley Butcher and Lisette Butcher; *m* 1993, Sally Dean; two *d. Educ:* Rugby Sch.; Univ. of Edinburgh (BSc Hons Electronics and Electrical Engrg); London Business Sch. (MBA). Army Officer, The Light Infantry, 1986–95; Grey Matter: Chief Exec., 1999–2004; Chm., 2004–. Trustee: Neurological Alliance; AMRC. *Recreations:* middle-distance running, fantasising about expensive sports cars, walking our spaniel on Dartmoor, planning the next trip, managing the kitchen garden (especially the beans). *Address:* c/o Muscular Dystrophy Campaign, 7–11 Prescott Place, SW4 6BS; *e-mail:* p.butcher@muscular-dystrophy.org.

BUTCHER, Richard James; Under Secretary (Legal), Department of Health and Social Security, 1983–87, retired; *b* 5 Dec. 1926; *s* of late James Butcher, MBE and Kathleen Butcher; *m* 1954, Sheila Joan Windridge; one *s* two *d. Educ:* City of London Sch.; Peterhouse, Cambridge (BA 1948, MA 1961). Called to the Bar, Lincoln's Inn, 1950. Served Educn Br., RAF, 1948–50 (Flying Officer). Entered Legal Civil Service as Legal Asst, 1951; Sen. Legal Asst, 1960; Asst Solicitor, 1971. *Recreation:* gardening. *Address:* The Knoll, Park View Road, Woldingham, Surrey CR3 7DN. *T:* (01883) 652275.

BUTCHER, Willard Carlisle; Chairman and Chief Executive Officer, 1981–90, Chairman, Executive Committee, 1990–91, Chase Manhattan Bank (formerly Chase National Bank), New York City; *b* Bronxville, NY, 25 Oct. 1926; *s* of Willard F. Butcher and Helen Calhoun; *m* 1st, 1949, Sarah C. Payne (*d* 1955); two *d*; 2nd, 1956, Elizabeth Allen (*d* 1978); one *s* one *d*; 3rd, 1979, Carole E. McMahon; one *s. Educ:* Scarsdale High School, New York; Middlebury Coll., Vermont; Brown Univ., Rhode Island (BA; Fellow, 1981, now Emeritus). Served with USNR, 1944–45. Joined Chase National Bank, 1947; Asst Vice-Pres., 1956; Vice-Pres., 1958; Sen. Vice-Pres., 1961; assigned Internat. Dept, 1968; Exec. Vice-Pres. in charge of Dept, 1969; Vice-Chm. 1972; Pres. 1972–81; Chief Exec. Officer, 1979. Trustee, Amer. Enterprise Inst. (Chm., 1986–90). Director: Texaco Inc., 1981–98; Asarco Inc., 1974–98; International Paper Co., 1989–98. Hon. LLD: Brown Univ.; Pepperdine Univ.; Tulane Univ.; Hon. HLD Pace Univ. *Address:* 11 West 51st Street, 2nd Floor, New York, NY 10019, USA.

BUTE, 7th Marquess of, *cr* 1796; **John Colum Crichton-Stuart, (Johnny Bute);** Viscount Ayr, 1622; Bt (NS), 1627; Earl of Dumfries, Lord Crichton of Sanquhar and Cumnock, 1633; Earl of Bute, Viscount Kingarth, Lord Mountstuart, Cumrae and Inchmarnock, 1703; Baron Mountstuart, 1761, Baron Cardiff, 1776; Earl of Windsor, Viscount Mountjoy, 1796; Hereditary Sheriff of Bute; Hereditary Keeper of Rothesay Castle; *b* 26 April 1958; *s* of 6th Marquess of Bute, KBE and of his 1st wife, Nicola (*née* Weld-Forester); *S* father, 1993; *m* 1st, 1984, Carolyn E. R. M. (marr. diss. 1993), *d* of late Bryson Waddell; one *s* two *d*; 2nd, 1999, Serena Solitaire Wendell; one *d.* Motor racing career, 1980–92: British Formula Three Champion, 1984; FIA European Formula Three Championship runner-up, 1984 (15 wins); Formula One Ferrari test driver, 1985; JPS Team Lotus Formula One Driver, FIA Formula One World Championship, 1986; FIA World Sports Prototype Championship: 1 win, 1987; Team Silk Cut Jaguar Driver, 1988 (Jt Winner, 24 hr Le Mans sports car race, estd new outright lap record); Team Toyota GB Driver, 1989, 1990. Chairman: Mount Stuart Trust, 1993–; Bute Fabrics Ltd, 1993–. *Heir:* s Earl of Dumfries, *qv.*

BUTHELEZI, Mangosuthu Gatsha; Minister of Home Affairs, Republic of South Africa, 1994–2004; President, Inkatha Freedom Party; *b* 27 Aug. 1928; *s* of Chief Mathole Buthelezi and Princess Magogo; *m* 1952, Irene Audrey Thandekile Mzila; two *s* four *d* (and one *s* decd). *Educ:* Fort Hare Univ. (BA). Chief of Buthelezi Tribe, 1953–; involved in admin of Zulu people, 1953–68; Chief Minister, KwaZulu, 1976–94. Numerous foreign awards and orders. *Publication:* South Africa: my vision of the future, 1990. *Address:* c/o Inkatha Freedom Party, Albany House North, 4th Floor, Albany Grove, PO Box 4432, Durban 4000, S Africa.

BUTLER, family name of Earl of Carrick, Viscount Mountgarret, Baron Butler of Brockwell and Baron Dunboyne.

BUTLER OF BROCKWELL, Baron *cr* 1998 (Life Peer), of Herne Hill in the London Borough of Lambeth; **Frederick Edward Robin Butler,** KG 2003; GCB 1992 (KCB 1988); CVO 1986; PC 2004; Master, University College, Oxford, 1998–2008; Secretary of the Cabinet and Head of the Home Civil Service, 1988–98; *b* 3 Jan. 1938; *s* of late Bernard and Nora Butler; *m* 1962, Gillian Lois Galley; one *s* two *d. Educ:* Harrow Sch.; University Coll., Oxford (BA Lit. Hum., 1961). Joined HM Treasury, 1961; Private Sec. to Financial Sec. to Treasury, 1964–65; Sec., Budget Cttee, 1965–69; seconded to Cabinet Office as Mem., Central Policy Rev. Staff, 1971–72; Private Secretary: to Rt Hon. Edward Heath, 1972–74; to Rt Hon. Harold Wilson, 1974–75; returned to HM Treasury as Asst Sec. i/c Gen. Expenditure Intell. Div., 1975; Under Sec., Gen. Expenditure Policy Gp, 1977–80; Prin. Establishments Officer, 1980–82; Principal Private Sec. to Prime Minister, 1982–85; Second Perm. Sec., Public Expenditure, HM Treasury, 1985–87. Mem., Royal Commn on H of L reform, 1999; Chm., Review of Intelligence on Weapons of Mass Destruction, 2004. Non-executive Director: HSBC Hldgs, 1998–2008; ICI plc, 1998–2008. Governor, Harrow Sch., 1975–91 (Chm. of Govs, 1988–91); Chm. Govs, Dulwich Coll., 1997–2003. *Recreation:* competitive games. *Address:* House of Lords, SW1A 0PW. *Clubs:* Athenæum, Brooks's, Beefsteak, Royal Anglo-Belgian, MCC.

BUTLER, Alison Sarah; *see* Burns, A. S.

BUTLER, Allan Geoffrey Roy; HM Diplomatic Service, retired; *b* 25 Aug. 1933; *s* of Frederick William Butler and Florence May Butler; *m* 1965, Pauline Rosalind Birch, SRN; three *d. Educ:* Chatham House School, Ramsgate. RAF, 1952–54. Colonial Office, 1954–66; served in Aden and Washington; Asst Private Sec. to Colonial Sec., 1965–66; HM Diplomatic Service, 1966; Birmingham University, 1966; Consul, Athens, 1967; First Sec., Athens, 1969, Georgetown, 1972, FCO, 1975; Head of Chancery, Dakar, 1977; Nat. Defence Coll., Latimer, 1981; Head of Parly Relations, FCO, 1981; Ambassador to Mongolian People's Republic, 1984; Dep. Perm. Rep., UK Delegn to the Council of Europe, 1987–89. Director: Strategy, subseq. Saatchi & Saatchi Govt Communications, 1989–92; Park South Management, 1991–99; Hexagon Communications, 1991–93; Park South Ltd, 1996–2006. Chm., Anglo-Mongolian Soc., 1990–93. Chairman: Age Concern

Diss, 1999–2003; Age Concern St Albans, 2004–07. *Recreation:* listening to music. *Address:* 23 Farringford Close, Chiswell Green, St Albans AL2 3HS.

BUTLER, Anthony John; Director, Oxford University Careers Service, 1996–2006; Professorial Fellow, New College, Oxford, 1996–2006, now Emeritus Fellow; *b* 30 Jan. 1945; *s* of Martin Edward and Freda Alice Butler; *m* 1967, Margaret Ann, *d* of George and Margaret Randon; one *s* one *d. Educ:* Maidstone Grammar Sch.; University Coll., Oxford (Exhibnr, Mod. Hist.; MA); Inst. of Criminology and Trinity Hall, Cambridge (Dip. Crim.); Cambridge-Columbia Fellow, Columbia Law Sch., NY. FCIPD. Joined Home Office as Asst Principal, 1969; Police and Criminal Depts, 1969–72; Private Sec. to Minister of State, Home Office, 1972–74; Principal, Gen. Dept, Sex Discrimination and Race Relations Legislation Units and Broadcasting Dept, 1974–79; Private Sec. to Sec. of State for the Home Dept, 1979–80; Asst Sec., Broadcasting, Finance and Prisons Depts, 1980–88; Asst Under-Sec. of State, seconded to DoE, 1988 as Dir, Inner Cities; Principal Finance Officer, Home Office, 1990; Dir of Personnel and Finance, then of Personnel, later of Services, HM Prison Service, 1990–96. Ind. Assessor, DCMS, 2000–. Dir, 2000–06, Chm., 2005–06, CVs.ac.uk Ltd. Treas., 2002–04, Pres., 2004–06, Assoc. of Grad. Careers Adv. Services. Trustee, University Coll. Oxford Old Members' Trust, 1988–94 (Chm. Trustees, 1991–94). Foundn Gov., St Gregory the Great Sch., Oxford, 2007–. *Publication:* (ed with M. Dane) AGCAS: reflections on change 1967–2007, 2007. *Recreations:* solitary guitar music, virtual walking, under-gardening.

BUTLER, Hon. Sir Arlington Griffith, KCMG 1996; President, Bahamas Olympic Association; *b* 2 Jan. 1938; *s* of late James and Lovinia Butler; *m* 1965, Sheila Paulette Smith; two *s. Educ:* Loughborough Coll. (Dip. 1964). Teacher, 1957–67: Headmaster, Public Schs, Deep Creek, Eleuthera, West End, Grand Bahama, and Kemps Bay, Andros; Maths Master, Govt High Sch., Nassau; Dep. Head, Prince William High Sch., Nassau; Educn Trg Welfare Officer, Bahamas Electricity Corp., 1967. Formerly: Chm., Progressive Liberal Party, Bahamas; Dep. Speaker, House of Assembly; Minister for Public Safety and Immigration, 1992–94; Minister of Public Works, 1994; Bahamas Ambassador to USA, until 2000. Life Vice-Pres., Bahamas AAA. *Address:* Bahamas Olympic Association, PO Box SS-6250, 7th Terrace West, Collins Avenue, Bldg 10, Apt 4, Nassau, Bahamas.

BUTLER, Arthur William, ERD 1964; consultant on parliamentary relations; Secretary, Parliamentary & Scientific Committee, 1979–95, Hon. Life Member 1996; *b* 20 Jan. 1929; *s* of late F. Butler and E. Butler; *m* 1958, Evelyn Mary Luetchford; one *d. Educ:* Wanstead High Sch.; LSE (BSc (Econ)). Universities' Prize Essayist, RAS, 1950. Nat. Service, India Cadet Co., Queen's Royal Regt, RAOC, 1946–48, 2nd Lt; Lt, AER, RAOC, 1953, Capt., 1957–64. Trainee, Kemsley Newspapers Graduate Trng Course, Middlesbrough Evening Gazette, 1951–55; Political Correspondent, News Chronicle, 1956–60; Political Ed., Reynolds News, 1960–62; Political Correspondent, Daily Express, 1963–69; Political Ed., Daily Sketch, 1969–71; Man. Dir, Partnerplan Public Affairs, 1971–74; Dir, Public Affairs Div., John Addey Associates, 1974–77; Vice-Chm., Charles Barker Watney & Powell, 1988–89 (Jt. Man. Dir, 1978–87). Dir, CSM Parly Consultants Ltd, 1995–. Secretary: Roads Campaign Council, 1974–86; All-Party Roads Study Gp, 1974–86; Founder Secretary: Parly All-Party Motor Industry Gp, 1978–90; Parly IT Cttee, 1981–84; Associate Parly Gp on Meningitis, 1999–2001. Consultant on Parly Relns, McAvoy Wreford Bayley, 1989–92, GCI London, 1992–93. Jt Managing Editor, Science in Parliament, 1989–98; Editor, Free Romanian (English edn), 1985–95. Freeman, City of London, 1976; Liveryman, Co. of Tobacco Pipe Makers, 1977. Governor, Shelley Sch., Kennington, 1999–2003. *Publications:* No Feet to Drag (with Alfred Morris, MP), 1972; (with C. Powell) The First Forty Years: a history of the Parliamentary & Scientific Committee, 1980; (with D. Smith) Lobbying in the British Parliament, 1986; articles in newspapers and various pubns. *Recreations:* travel, collecting books and militaria, gardening. *Address:* 30 Chester Way, Kennington, SE11 4UR. *T:* (020) 7587 5170.

BUTLER, Mrs Audrey Maude Beman, MA; Headmistress, Queenswood (GSA), Hatfield, Herts, 1981–96; *b* 31 May 1936; *d* of Robert Beman Minchin and Vivien Florence Fraser Scott; *m* 1959, Anthony Michael Butler (marr. diss. 1981); two *d. Educ:* Queenswood, Hatfield; St Andrews Univ., Scotland (1st Cl. MA Hons, Geography and Polit. Economy; Scottish Univs Medal, RSGS, 1957–58). Asst Geography Teacher, Queenswood, 1958–59; part-time teacher, Raines Foundn Sch. for Girls, Stepney, 1959–61; Head of Geography, S Michael's, Burton Park, 1970–73, VI Form Tutor/ Geography asst, 1974–78; first House Mistress of Manor House, Lancing Coll., 1978–81. Chm., Boarding Schs Assoc., 1989–91 (Hon. Life Mem., 1996); Mem. Exec. Cttee, GSA, 1987–90 (Hon. Life Mem., GSA, 1996). Governor: Duncombe Sch., 1982–97; Tockington Manor Sch., 1984–97 (Chm., 1995–97); Aldenham Sch., 1987–2001; Maltman's Green Sch., 1988–98; St Mary's, Ascot, 1995–2002; St Leonard's, Mayfield, 1999–2004. Trustee, Bloxham Project, 1999–2003 (Vice-Chm., 1992–99). Dir, British Tennis Foundn, 1997–2007. Vice-Pres., Herts LTA, 1986–. Freeman, City of London, 1997. *Recreations:* golf (Sussex County Colours, 1970), travel, music. *Address:* Chandlers Cottage, Lodsworth Common, Petworth, W Sussex GU28 9DT. *T:* (01798) 861750.

BUTLER, Basil Richard Ryland, CBE 1997 (OBE 1976); FREng; FIMMM; Chairman, KS Biomedix plc, 1995–2001; Director, Murphy Oil Corp., Arkansas, 1991–2002; *b* 1 March 1930; *s* of Hugh Montagu Butler and Annie Isabel (*née* Wiltshire); *m* 1954, Lilian Joyce Haswell; one *s* two *d. Educ:* Denstone Coll., Staffs; St John's Coll., Cambridge (MA). Reservoir Engr, Trinidad Leaseholds Ltd, 1954; Petroleum Engr to Chief Petroleum Engr and Supt Prodn Planning Div., Kuwait Oil Co., 1958–68; transf. to BP, Operations Man., Colombia, 1968; Ops Man., BP Alaska Inc., Anchorage, 1970; seconded to Kuwait Oil Co. as Gen. Man. Ops, 1972; Manager: Ninian Develts, BP Petroleum Development Co. Ltd, London, 1975; Sullom Voe Terminal, Shetland Is, 1976; BP Petroleum Development Ltd: Gen. Man., Exploration and Prodn, Aberdeen, 1978; Chief Exec., London, 1980; Dir, BP Internat. Ltd; Chm., BP Exploration Co. Ltd, 1986–89 (Man. Dir and Chief Exec., 1986); Man. Dir, British Petroleum Co. plc, 1986–91; Dir, BP Solar Internat., 1991–98 (Chm., 1991–95). Chairman: Devonport Management, 1992–94; Brown and Root Ltd, 1993–98 (Dir, 1991–98). Chm., Europ. Council of Applied Scis and Engrg, 1992–97. Mem., Cttee for ME Trade, 1985–93. Pres., Inst. of Petroleum, 1990–92; Mem. Council, Royal Acad. of Engrg, 1994–2002 (Hon. Sec. for Internat. Affairs, 1995–98; Sen. Vice Pres., 1996–99). FInstPet 1965; Hon. FIChemE 1991. Liveryman, Shipwrights' Co., 1988. Cdre, Royal Western Yacht Club, 2004–08. *Recreations:* sailing, music. *Address:* Royal Academy of Engineering, SW1P 3LW.

BUTLER, Brian; Director of Communications, British Medical Association, since 2003; *b* 3 May 1949; *s* of Joseph and Alice Eileen Butler; *m* 1978, Margaret Ruth Anne Macdonald (marr. diss. 1990). *Educ:* Hunslet Carr Primary Sch., Leeds; Cockburn High Sch., Leeds; Univ. of Birmingham (BA). Journalist, Westminster Press, 1971–75; Central Office of Information: Information Officer, Newcastle upon Tyne, 1975–79; Sen. Information Officer, Birmingham, 1979–86; Sen. Information Officer, then Grade 7, DoH, 1986–88; Media and Govt Relns Manager, Lloyds Bank, 1988–94; Co-ordinator, Deregulation Task Forces, DTI, 1993–94; Head of Information Services, Benefits Agency, 1994–96; Head of News, 1996–98, Dir of Communication, 1998–2002, Home Office; Dir, Counter-Terrorism Communications, Cabinet Office, 2002–03. Pres., Westminster Players, 2001–. FRSA 2000. *Publications:* (ed jtly and contrib.) Oxford Dictionary of Finance, 1993; (ed jtly and contrib.) Oxford Dictionary of Finance and Banking, 1997. *Recreations:* acting, writing, singing, directing, the USA, the works of Stephen Sondheim. *Address:* (office) BMA House, Tavistock Square, WC1H 9JP. *T:* (020) 7383 6013. *Clubs:* Two Brydges; Meanwood Working Men's (Leeds) (Life Mem.).

BUTLER, Christine Margaret; *b* 14 Dec. 1943; *d* of late Cecil and Gertrude Smith; *m* 1964, Robert Patrick Butler; three *s. Educ:* Middlesex Univ. (BA Hons). MP (Lab) Castle Point, 1997–2001; contested (Lab) same seat, 2001. Mem., Envmt, Transport and Regl Affairs Select Cttee, 1997–2001. *Recreations:* walking, music, art.

BUTLER, (Christopher) David, CB 1995; Research Manager, 1999–2001, and Claims Process Manager, 2001–05, International Commission on Holocaust Era Insurance Claims; *b* 27 May 1942; *s* of Major B. D. Butler, MC (killed in action, 1944) and H. W. Butler (*née* Briggs); *m* 1967, Helen Christine, *d* of J. J. Cornwell and G. Cornwell (*née* Veysey); two *d. Educ:* Christ's Hospital; Jesus College, Oxford (BA); St Mary's Twickenham (TESOL Cert. 2006). Joined HM Treasury, 1964; Asst Private Sec. to Chancellor of Exchequer, 1967–69; Sec., Cttee to Review Nat. Savings (Page Cttee), 1970–72; Head of public expenditure divs, HM Treasury, 1978–82; Head of corporate planning div., Central Computer and Telecoms Agency, 1982–85; HM Treasury: Under-Sec., 1985–89; Head of running costs, manpower and superannuation group, 1985–86; Principal Estabt and Finance Officer, 1987–89; Dep. Dir, 1989–91, Dir, 1991–95, Dept for Nat. Savings; Chief Exec., The Princess Royal Trust for Carers, 1996–99. Governor, Sadler's Wells Foundn, 1989–94; Dir, Sadler's Wells Trust Ltd, 1989–95. *Recreations:* ballet, opera, reading, acting, teaching English as foreign language. *Club:* Civil Service (Chm., 1994–96).

BUTLER, Christopher John; Director, Butler Kelly Ltd, since 1998; *b* 12 Aug. 1950; *s* of late Dr John Lynn Butler and Eileen Patricia Butler; *m* 1989, Jacqueline Clair, *d* of Mr and Mrs R. O. F. Harper, Glos; one *s. Educ:* Emmanuel Coll., Cambridge (MA). Market Research Consultant, 1975–77; Cons. Res. Dept, 1977–80; Political Office, 10 Downing Street, 1980–83; Special Advr, Sec. of State for Wales, 1983–85; Market Res. Consultant, 1985–86; Special Advr, Minister for the Arts, and of the Civil Service, 1986–87; Consultant in Public Policy, Public Policy Unit, 1992–95; Dir, Grandfield Public Affairs, 1995–97. MP (C) Warrington South, 1987–92; contested (C) Warrington South, 1992; contested (C) Wales, Eur. Parly elecns, 1999. Mem., Select Cttee on Employment, 1990–92. Vice Chm., All Party Leasehold Reform Gp, 1989–92; Secretary: All Party Drugs Misuse Cttee, 1989–92; All Party Penal Affairs Cttee, 1990–92. Mem., Exec. Cttee, CPA, 1991–92. *Recreations:* writing, deltiology, book collecting. *Address:* Longwall House, Seven Mile Lane, Borough Green, Kent TN15 8QY.

BUTLER, Dr Colin Gasking, OBE 1970; FRS 1970; retired as Head of Entomology Department, Rothamsted Experimental Station, Harpenden, 1972–76 (Head of Bee Department, 1943–72); *b* 26 Oct. 1913; *s* of Rev. Walter Gasking Butler and Phyllis Pearce; *m* 1937, Jean March Innes; one *s* one *d. Educ:* Monkton Combe Sch., Bath; Queens' Coll., Cambridge. MA 1937, PhD 1938, Cantab. Min. of Agric. and Fisheries Research Schol., Cambridge, 1935–37; Supt Cambridge Univ. Entomological Field Stn, 1937–39; Asst Entomologist, Rothamsted Exper. Stn, 1939–43. Hon. Treas., Royal Entomological Soc., 1961–69, Pres., 1971–72, Hon. FRES, 1984; Pres., Internat. Union for Study of Social Insects, 1969–73; Mem., NT Regional Cttee for Devon and Cornwall, 1982–89. FRPS 1957; FIBiol. Hon. Fellow, British Beekeepers' Assoc., 1983. Silver Medal, RSA, 1945. *Publications:* The Honeybee: an introduction to her sense physiology and behaviour, 1949; The World of the Honeybee, 1954; (with J. B. Free) Bumblebees, 1959; scientific papers. *Recreations:* nature photography, fishing. *Address:* Hope Residential and Nursing Home, Brooklands Avenue, Cambridge CB2 2BQ. *T:* (01223) 359087.

BUTLER, Creon Adrian John Cotterell; HM Diplomatic Service; Minister and Deputy High Commissioner, New Delhi, since 2006; *b* 18 April 1960; *m* 1991, Wendy Joanne Niffikeer; one *s* one *d. Educ:* LSE (BSc, MSc). Bank of England, 1984–99: posts incl. Hd, Monetary Instruments and Markets Div.; Chief Economist, 1999–2007, Dir, Econ. Policy, 2004–06, FCO. *Address:* c/o Foreign and Commonwealth Office, King Charles Street, SW1A 2AH.

BUTLER, David; *see* Butler, C. D.

BUTLER, David; Chairman, The Executive Learning Alliance Ltd, since 2003; *b* 1 Feb. 1936; *s* of James Charles Butler and Ethel Violet (*née* Newell); *m* 1st, 1956, Catherine Anita Harry (marr. diss. 1974); one *s* two *d*; 2nd, 1975, Frances Mary McMahon; one *d. Educ:* Mill Hill Sch.; Keble Coll., Oxford (BA Lit. Hum.). Management Trainee, Herts CC, 1960–64; Computer Manager, NW Metropolitan Hosp. Bd, 1964–65; Management Consultant, Urwick Gp, 1965–72; Dir, Diebold Europe, 1972–76; Chm., Butler Cox plc and Butler Cox Foundn, 1977–92; Sen. Advr, Computer Scis Corp., 1994–2004. Dir, Istel, 1983–92; Investment Advr, United Bank of Kuwait, 1985–92. Mem., Fraud Trials Cttee, 1984–85; Vice Pres., BCS, 1981–83. *Publications:* The Convergence of Technologies, 1977; Britain and the Information Society, 1981; A Director's Guide to Information Technology, 1982; Trends in Information Technology, 1984; Information Technology and Realpolitik, 1986; The Men who Mastered Time (novel), 1986; Senior Management IT Education, 1987; Measuring Progress in IT, 1995; numerous press articles. *Recreations:* cricket, Rugby, ancient history. *Address:* 12 Laurel Road, SW13 0EE. *T:* (020) 8876 1810.

BUTLER, David Edgeworth, CBE 1991; FBA 1994; Fellow of Nuffield College, Oxford, since 1954; *b* 17 Oct. 1924; *yr s* of late Professor Harold Edgeworth Butler and Margaret, *d* of Prof. A. F. Pollard; *m* 1962, Marilyn Speers Evans (*see* M. S. Butler); two *s* (and one *s* decd). *Educ:* St Paul's; New Coll., Oxford (MA, DPhil). J. E. Procter Visiting Fellow, Princeton Univ., 1947–48; Student, Nuffield Coll., 1949–51; Research Fellow, 1951–54; Dean and Senior Tutor, 1956–64. Served as Personal Assistant to HM Ambassador in Washington, 1955–56. Co-editor, Electoral Studies, 1982–92. Chm., Hansard Soc., 1993–2001. DUniv Paris, 1978; Hon. DSSc QUB, 1985; Dr *hc* Essex, 1993; Hon. Dr: Plymouth, 1994; Teesside, 1999. OAM 2002. *Publications:* The British General Election of 1951, 1952; The Electoral System in Britain 1918–51, 1953; The British General Election of 1955, 1955; The Study of Political Behaviour, 1958; (ed) Elections Abroad, 1959; (with R. Rose) The British General Election of 1959, 1960; (with J. Freeman) British Political Facts, 1900–1960, 1963; (with A. King) The British General Election of 1964, 1965; The British General Election of 1966, 1966; (with D. Stokes) Political Change in Britain, 1969; (with M. Pinto-Duschinsky) The British General Election of 1970, 1971; The Canberra Model, 1973; (with D. Kavanagh) The British General Election of February 1974, 1974; (with D. Kavanagh) The British General Election of October 1974, 1975; (with U. Kitzinger) The 1975 Referendum, 1976; (ed) Coalitions in British Politics, 1978; (ed with A. H. Halsey) Policy and Politics, 1978; (with A. Ranney), Referendums, 1978; (with A. Sloman) British Political Facts 1900–79, 1980;

(with D. Kavanagh) The British General Election of 1979, 1980; (with D. Marquand) European Elections and British Politics, 1981; (with A. Ranney) Democracy at the Polls, 1981; (with V. Bogdanor) Democracy and Elections, 1983; Governing without a Majority, 1983; (with D. Kavanagh) The British General Election of 1983, 1984; A Compendium of Indian Elections, 1984; (with P. Jowett) Party Strategies in Britain, 1985; (with G. Butler) British Political Facts 1900–85, 1986; (with D. Kavanagh) The British General Election of 1987, 1988; British Elections since 1945, 1989; (with P. Roy) India Decides, 1989, 3rd edn as India Decides 1952–1991, 1995; (with A. Low) Sovereigns and Surrogates, 1991; (with B. Cain) Congressional Redistricting, 1991; (with D. Kavanagh) The British General Election 1992, 1992; (with A. Ranney) Electioneering, 1992; Failure in British Government, 1994; (with G. Butler) British Political Facts 1900–94, 1994; (with D. Kavanagh) The British General Election of 1997, 1997; (with M. Westlake) British Politics and European Elections 1994, 1999; (jtly) Law and Politics, 1999; (with G. Butler) British Political Facts 1900–2000, 2000; (with D. Kavanagh) The British General Election of 2001, 2001; (with M. Westlake) British Politics and European Elections 2004, 2005; (with D. Kavanagh) The British General Election of 2005, 2005. *Address:* Nuffield College, Oxford OX1 1NF. *T:* (01865) 278500.

BUTLER, Dawn; MP (Lab) Brent South, since 2005; an Assistant Government Whip, since 2008; *b* 3 Nov. 1969; *d* of Milo and Ambrozene Butler. *Educ:* Tom Hood Sch.; Waltham Forest Coll. Associate CIPD 1993. Systems analyst, Johnson Matthey, 1989–92; Exec. Officer, Employment Service, 1993–97; Union Officer and Race Audit Co-ordinator, GMB, 1997–2005. Voluntary work, incl. at African Caribbean Centre; mentor; fund-raising co-ordinator. PPS to Minister of State, Dept of Health, 2005–06. Chm., All Party Parly Gp on Youth Affairs, 2006–. Patron: W Indian Self Effort, Brent; Mathematics, Brent; Black Women's Mental Health Project, Brent. *Recreations:* salsa, mentoring. *Address:* House of Commons, SW1A 0AA. *T:* (020) 7219 4385; *e-mail:* butlerd@parliament.uk.

BUTLER, Eamonn Francis, PhD; Director, Adam Smith Institute, since 1978; *b* 3 Jan. 1952; *s* of Richard Henry Bland Butler and Janet Provan Butler (*née* MacDonald); *m* 1986, Christine Anna Pieroni; two *s*. *Educ:* Univ. of Aberdeen; Univ. of St Andrews (MA 1973, MA Hons 1974; PhD 1978). Research Associate, US House of Representatives, 1976–77; Asst Prof. of Philosophy, Hillsdale Coll., Michigan, 1977–78. Editor, The Broker, 1979–87. *Publications:* Hayek: his contribution to the social and economic thought of our time, 1983; Milton Friedman: a guide to his economic thought, 1985; Ludwig von Mises: fountainhead of the modern microeconomics revolution, 1989; Adam Smith: a primer, 2007; The Best Book on the Market, 2008; (with R. L. Schuettinger) Forty Centuries of Wage and Price Controls, 1979; with M. Pirie: Test Your IQ, 1983; Boost Your IQ, 1990; The Sherlock Holmes IQ Book, 1995; IQ Puzzlers, 1995; contrib. articles to various newspapers and jls. *Recreations:* archaeology, antiquarian books and prints. *Address:* The Adam Smith Institute, 23 Great Smith Street, SW1P 3BL; *e-mail:* eamonn.butler@adamsmith.org.

BUTLER, Georgina Susan; HM Diplomatic Service, retired; Consul, Tangier, since 2007; *b* 30 Nov. 1945; *d* of Alfred Norman Butler, LDS RCS and Joan Mary Butler (*née* Harrington); *m* 1st, 1970, Stephen John Leadbetter Wright (marr. diss. 2000); one *s* one *d*; 2nd, 2003, C. Robert D. Kelly. *Educ:* University Coll. London (LLB 1968; Fellow 2003). British Embassy, Paris, 1969–70; Southern European Dept, FCO, 1971–75; UN Secretariat, NY, 1975–77; Directorate Gen. Devel, EC, Brussels, 1982–84; Deputy Head: Information Dept, FCO, 1985–87; Latin American Dept, FCO, 1999–2001; Ambassador to Costa Rica and Nicaragua, 2002–06. *Recreations:* travel, riding, watersports, bird-watching. *Address:* British Consulate, Trafalgar House, 9 rue Amérique du Sud, Tangier, Morocco. *Club:* Lansdowne.

BUTLER, His Honour Gerald Norman; QC 1975; a Circuit Judge, 1982–97; Senior Judge at Southwark Crown Court, 1984–97; *b* 15 Sept. 1930; *s* of Joshua Butler and Esther Butler (*née* Lampel); *m* 1959, Stella, *d* of Harris and Leah Isaacs; one *s* two *d*. *Educ:* Ilford County High Sch.; London Sch. of Economics; Magdalen Coll., Oxford. LLB London 1952, BCL Oxon 1954. 2nd Lieut, RASC, 1956–57. Called to Bar, Middle Temple, 1955; a Recorder of the Crown Court, 1977–82. Inquiry and Reports into: English RFU, 1997; Central Casework at CPS, 1999; prosecution of Regina *v* Doran and others, 2000; Treasury Counsel instructed by CPS, 2000. *Recreations:* Rugby, opera, Japanese pottery, walking. *Address:* 1 Essex Court, Temple, EC4Y 9AR. *Clubs:* Garrick, MCC.

BUTLER, Sir James; *see* Butler, Sir P. J.

BUTLER, (James) Pearse; Director of Clinical Engagement, Computer Sciences Corporation, since 2007; *b* 27 Jan. 1957; *s* of James and Nancy Butler; *m* 1979, Deborah Veronica Downing; one *s* one *d*. *Educ:* St Mary's Coll., Crosby; Keble Coll., Oxford (BA). Community Worker, Liverpool CVS, 1979–80; Hosp. Admin, S Birmingham HA, 1980–83; Dep. Adminr, then Adminr, Bolton Gen. Hosp., 1983–85; Mgt Consultant, HAY-MSL Mgt Consultants, 1985–86; Gen. Manager, Obst. and Gyn. Service, Liverpool HA, 1986–88; Dist Gen. Manager, Chester HA, 1988–89; Chief Executive: Royal Liverpool Children's NHS Trust, 1990–93; Wirral HA, 1993–97; Wigan and Leigh NHS Trust, 1997–99; Royal Liverpool and Broadgreen Univ. Hosps NHS Trust, 1999–2002; Cumbria and Lancashire Strategic HA, 2002–06; Interim Chief Exec., E of England Strategic HA, 2006. *Recreations:* family, Everton FC, golf. *Address:* Computer Sciences Corporation, Royal Pavilion, Wellesley Road, Aldershot, Hants GU11 1PZ. *Clubs:* West Lancashire Golf, Campion Lawn Tennis.

BUTLER, James Walter, RA 1972 (ARA 1964); RWA; FRBS; *b* 25 July 1931; *m* (marr. diss.); one *d*; *m* 1975, Angela, *d* of Col Roger Berry, Johannesburg, South Africa; four *d*. *Educ:* Maidstone Grammar Sch.; Maidstone Coll. of Art; St Martin's Art Sch.; Royal Coll. of Art. National Diploma in Sculpture, 1950. Worked as Architectural Carver, 1950–53, 1955–60. Tutor, Sculpture and Drawing, City and Guilds of London Art School, 1960–75. Major commissions include: *portrait statues:* Pres. Kenyatta, Nairobi, 1973; Sir John Moore, Sir John Moore Barracks, Winchester, 1987; John Wilkes, New Fetter Lane, 1988, Wilkes Univ., USA, 1995; Thomas Cook, Leicester, 1994; Billy Wright, 1996, Stan Cullis, 2003, Molineux Stadium, Wolverhampton; James Brindley, Coventry Canal Basin, 1998; Duncan Edwards, Dudley, 1999; *portrait busts:* Sir Nicholas Bacon, St Albans Sch., 1994; Sir Frank Whittle, 1995, R. J. Mitchell, 2001, Roy Chadwick, 2003, RAF Club; Robert Beldam, Corpus Christi Coll., Cambridge, 2000; *memorial statues:* Richard III, Leicester, 1980; Field Marshal Earl Alexander of Tunis, Wellington Barracks, London, 1985; Reg Harris, Manchester, 1994; *other:* Monument to Freedom Fighters of Zambia, Lusaka, 1974; The Burton Cooper, Burton-on-Trent, 1977; Dolphin Fountain, Dolphin Square, London, 1988; Skipping girl, Harrow, 1988; The Leicester Seamstress, Leicester, 1990; James Henry Greathead, Cornhill, 1994; The Stratford Jester, Stratford-upon-Avon, 1995; D-day Memorial for Green Howards, Crépon, Normandy, 1996; Seagull Sculpture, Anchorpoint, Singapore, 1997; Memorial to Fleet Air Arm, Victoria Embankment Gdns, London, 2000; Great Seal of the Realm, 2001; 50p piece commemorating 50th anniv. of first sub 4 min. mile, 2004; crown piece commemorating 200th anniv. of death of Lord Nelson, 2005. Silver Medal, RBS, 1988. *Recreation:* interested in astronomy. *Address:* Valley Farm, Radway, Warwick CV35 0UJ. *T:* (01926) 641938. *Club:* Arts.

BUTLER, John Michael, CPFA, FCCA; consultant, since 2005; Director of Finance and Information Technology, East Riding of Yorkshire Council, 1995–2005; *b* 12 Sept. 1943; *s* of Reginald Butler and late Kathleen (*née* Garside); *m* 1964, Daphne Ann Head (*d* 1999); two *s*. *Educ:* Beckenham and Penge Grammar Sch. CPFA 1966; IRRV 1974; FCCA 1980. Audit Asst, Beckenham BC, 1960–61; Accountancy Assistant: Sevenoaks UDC, 1961–63; Caterham UDC, 1963–64; Sen. Accountant, Dorking UDC, 1964–66; Asst Treas., Esher UDC, 1966–70; Asst Borough Treas., Greenwich LBC, 1970–74; Chief Finance Officer, Lambeth LBC, 1974–79; City Treas., Swansea CC, 1979–95. National President: IRRV, 1989–90; Soc. of Dist Council Treasurers, 1992–93; CIPFA, 2007–08 (Mem. Council, 1994–). Treasurer: Welsh Orienteering Assoc., 2006–; Welsh Soc. of Kingston upon Hull, 2007–; Trustee, Age Concern E Yorks, 2007–. FCMI (FBIM 1969). *Recreations:* orienteering, ski-ing. *Address:* 33 Hambling Drive, Molescroft, Beverley HU17 9GD. *T:* (01482) 870312; *e-mail:* john@the-butlers.co.uk. *Clubs:* Swansea Bay Orienteering, Humberside and Lincolnshire Orienteering; Beverley Athletic; York Cross Country Ski.

BUTLER, Prof. John Nicholas, (Nick), OBE 1988; RDI 1981; FCSD; industrial designer; Chairman and Joint Managing Director, BIB Design Consultants, 1989–2003; *b* 21 March 1942; *s* of William and Mabel Butler; *m* 1st, 1967, Kari Ann Morrison (marr. diss. 1999); two *s*; 2nd, 2001, Mary Thompson. *Educ:* Leeds Coll. of Art (NDD); Royal Coll. of Art (DesRCA, 1st Cl. Hons). FCSD (FSIAD 1975). Founded BIB Design Consultants, 1967; Sen. Partner, 1967–89. Prof. of Industrial Design, RCA, 1987–90; Vis. Prof., Massey Univ., 1993–; Vis. Prof. and Chm., Industrial Adv. Bd, Univ. of Central Lancs, 2002– (Sen. Fellow, 2003); Chm., Faculty Adv. Bd, Cardiff Sch. of Creative and Cultural Industries, Glamorgan Univ., 2008–. Chm., British Design Export Gp, 1980–81; Member: Design Bd, RSA, 1987–; Design Council, 1988–93 (Mem., Chairman's Review Team, 1993–); Chairman's Design Bd, BAA, 1992–; Royal Fine Art Commn, 1998–99. Master, RDI, 1995–97. Chm., Creative Lancs Partnership, 2005–. Hon. Sec., SIAD, 1978–81, Treasurer 1981–84. FRSA 1983 (Vice Pres., 1995–). Sen. FRCA 1997. *Recreations:* reading, music, country pursuits, watching Rugby, drawing, watching cricket.

BUTLER, Keith Stephenson, CMG 1977; HM Diplomatic Service, retired; Appeal Director for various charities, since 1978; *b* 3 Sept. 1917; *s* of late Raymond R. Butler and Gertrude Stephenson; *m* 1st, 1952, Geraldine Marjorie Clark (*d* 1979); 2nd, 1979, Mrs Priscilla Wittels; no *c*. *Educ:* King Edward's Sch., Birmingham; Liverpool Coll.; St Peter's Coll., Oxford (MA). HM Forces, 1939–47 (despatches): served, RA, in Egypt, Greece and Crete; POW, Germany, 1941–45. Foreign Correspondent for Sunday Times and Kemsley Newspapers, 1947–50. Joined HM Foreign Service, 1950; served: First Sec., Ankara and Caracas; Canadian Nat. Defence Coll.; Paris; Montreal. HM Consul-General: Seville, 1968; Bordeaux, 1969; Naples, 1974–77. *Publications:* contrib. historical and political reviews. *Recreation:* historical research. *Address:* Sheilings, 10 Station Road, Kintbury, near Newbury, Berks RG17 9UP. *T:* (01488) 658350.

BUTLER, Prof. Marilyn Speers, DPhil; FBA 2002; Rector, Exeter College, 1993–2004, and Titular Professor of English Language and Literature, 1998–2004, University of Oxford; *b* 11 Feb. 1937; *d* of Sir Trevor Evans, CBE and Margaret (*née* Gribbin); *m* 1962, David Edgeworth Butler, *qv*; two *s* (and one *s* decd). *Educ:* Wimbledon High Sch.; St Hilda's Coll., Oxford (MA; DPhil). Trainee and talks producer, BBC, 1960–62; Oxford University: full-time res. and teaching, 1962–70, Jun. Res. Fellow, 1970–73, St Hilda's Coll.; Fellow and Tutor, St Hugh's Coll., 1973–85; Lectr, 1985–86; King Edward VII Prof. of English Lit., 1986–93, and Fellow of King's Coll., 1988–93, Univ. of Cambridge. Pt-time Lectr, ANU, 1967; British Academy Reader, 1982–85. Mem., HEFCE, 1997–2000. *Publications:* Maria Edgeworth: a literary biography, 1972; Jane Austen and the War of Ideas, 1975; Peacock Displayed, 1979; Romantics, Rebels and Reactionaries, 1981, 2nd edn 1985; (ed) Burke, Paine, Godwin and the Revolution Controversy, 1984; (ed with J. Todd) Works of Mary Wollstonecraft, 1989; (ed) Maria Edgeworth, Castle Rackrent, and Ennui, 1992; (ed) Frankenstein, the 1818 edition, 1993; (ed) Northanger Abbey, 1995; (ed) Works of Maria Edgeworth, 1999–2003. *Address:* 151 Woodstock Road, Oxford OX2 7NA.

BUTLER, Sir Michael; *see* Butler, Sir R. M. T.

BUTLER, Sir Michael (Dacres), GCMG 1984 (KCMG 1980 CMG 1975); HM Diplomatic Service, retired; Ambassador and Permanent UK Representative to European Communities, Brussels, 1979–85; *b* 27 Feb. 1927; *s* of T. D. Butler, Almer, Blandford, and Beryl May (*née* Lambert); *m* 1951, Ann, *d* of Rt Hon. Lord Clyde; two *s* two *d*. *Educ:* Winchester; Trinity Coll., Oxford. Joined HM Foreign Service, 1950; served in: UK Mission to UN, New York, 1952–56; Baghdad, 1956–58; FO, 1958–61 and 1965–68; Paris, 1961–65; Counsellor, UK Mission in Geneva, 1968–70; Fellow, Center for Internat. Affairs, Harvard, 1970–71; Counsellor, Washington, 1971–72; Head of European Integration Dept, FCO, 1972–74; Asst Under-Sec. in charge of European Community Affairs, FCO, 1974–76; Dep. Under-Sec. of State, FCO, 1976–79. Hambros PLC and Hambros Bank Ltd: Dir, 1986–94; non-executive Dir, 1994–97; Consultant, 1997–98; Chm., Internat. Adv. (formerly European Strategy) Bd, ICL, 1988–2001; Director: Eurosynergies (France), 1990–98; Homeport (UK and France), 2000–. Lab. Party's Special Envoy on EU Enlargement, 1996–97; Advr to Sec. of State for Foreign and Commonwealth Affairs, 1997–98. Advr, Govt of Ukraine, 1991–94. Chairman: City European Cttee, British Invisibles (formerly BIEC), 1988–93; Oriental Art Magazine, 1988–95; European Unification Bd, Hercules Europe, 1989–94; Honda Eur. Communication and Consultation Gp, 1994–; Business Link-Dorset, 1994–2000; Halo Ltd, 1994–96; Pathway Gp Ltd, 1995–2000; Guidephone Ltd, 1997–2002; Treasury Mgt Internat. Editl Adv. Panel, 1992–2006; Member: Standing Cttee on Internat. Relations, ACOST, 1987–90; Panel of Conciliators, Internat. Centre for the Settlement of Investment Disputes, 1987–94; Bank of Montreal Internat. Adv. Council, 1992–98; Adv. Council, Foreign Policy Centre, 1997–; Bd, Britain in Europe, 2001–06; Chm., European Senior Experts Gp, 2003–. Dir, Wellcome Foundn, 1986–95; Pro-Provost and Chm. Council, RCA, 1991–96 (Sen. Fellow, 1997); Mem. Council, Oriental Ceramic Soc., 1977–80, 1985–88 and 1995–98; Dep. Chm., Bd of Trustees, V&A Museum, 1985–97. Hon. DBA Bournemouth, 1998. Knight Grand Cross, Order of Merit (Portugal), 1998. *Publications:* Chinese Porcelain, The Transitional Period 1620–82: a selection from the Michael Butler Collection, 1986; Europe: More than a Continent, 1986; The Butler Family Collection, 17th Century Chinese Porcelain, 1990; Treasures from an Unknown Reign: the Shunzhi period, 2002; Seventeenth Century Jingdezhen Porcelain from the Shanghai Museum and the Butler Collections, 2006; contribs to Trans Oriental Ceramic Soc. *Recreation:* collecting Chinese porcelain. *Club:* Brooks's.

BUTLER, Michael Howard, OBE, FCA; Finance Director, British Coal (formerly National Coal Board), 1985–93, Member of the Board, 1986–93; *b* 13 Feb. 1936; *s* of Howard Butler and Constance Gertrude Butler; *m* 1961, Christine Elizabeth Killer; two *s* one *d*. *Educ:* Nottingham High School. Articled pupil, H. G. Ellis Kennewell & Co.,

Nottingham, 1952–58; Stewarts & Lloyds Gp, 1960–62; National Coal Board: various posts, NCB HQ, W Midlands Div. and NE Area, 1962–68; Chief Accountant, Coal Products Div., 1968; Dep. Treas., NCB HQ, 1970; Treas. and Dep. Dir Gen. of Finance, 1978; Dir Gen. of Finance, 1981; Chm., British Fuels Co., 1992–93. Director: British Coal Enterprises, 1988–96; Edinburgh Fund Managers, 1993–95; Chairman: CIN Management Ltd, 1993–96; British Investment Trust, 1993–97. Trustee, Mineworkers Pension Fund (formerly British Coal Pension Funds), 1981–2000 (Chm., 1995–2000). *Recreations:* gardening, listening to music, playing tennis. *Address:* Banstead Down, Chorleywood Road, Rickmansworth, Herts WD3 4EH. *T:* (01923) 778001.

BUTLER, Nick; *see* Butler, J. N.

BUTLER, Norman John Terence, (Terry), CBE 1993; Adviser in Public Services and Social Care, since 2005; Director of Social Services, Hampshire, 1988–2005; *b* 18 Feb. 1946; *s* of Arthur Reginald Butler and Lucy Mary Butler; *m*; one *s* two *d. Educ:* Peveril Bilateral Sch., Nottingham; Trent Polytechnic, Nottingham (Cert. in Social Work); Nat. Inst. of Social Work, London; Brunel Univ. (MA Public and Social Admin). Mental Welfare Officer, Nottingham, 1965–71; Sen. Social Worker, Nottingham, 1971–73; Area Man., Haringey, 1974–81; Asst Dir of Social Services, Royal Bor. of Kingston upon Thames, 1981–83; Dep. Dir of Social Services, E Sussex, 1983–88. Non-exec. Dir, NHS S Central Strategic HA, 2006–. Member: Firth Cttee, examining public expenditure on residential care, 1987; Algebra Gp, 1992–93; Inf. Tribunal (formerly Data Protection Tribunals Bd), 1996–; Standing Gp for Service Delivery and Orgn, NHS R & D Directorate, 1997–99; Co-Leader, Community Care Support Force, providing practical support to local and health authorities in implementation of NHS and Community Care Act, 1992–93; Mem. Adv. Bd for Restricted Patients, 1995–2001; Advr, Clinical Speciality (Social Care), to Nat. Patient Safety Agency, 2003–07; Ind. Mem., "No More Blame Game", Cons. Party Commn on Social Workers, 2007. Mem., Gen. Social Care Council, 2005–. Vice-Pres., Relatives and Residents Assoc., 1995–. Hon. Treas., 1997–2003, Co-Chm., Mental Health Cttee, 2003–05, Assoc. of Dirs of Social Services. *Publications:* articles in various jls, incl. Social Work Today, Insight and Community Care. *Recreations:* travel, tennis, swimming, entertaining, being entertained. *Address:* Edgar House, 17 Lansdowne Avenue, St Cross, Winchester, Hants SO23 9TU.

BUTLER, Patricia Josephine; *see* Ferguson, P. J.

BUTLER, Rt Rev. Paul Roger; *see* Southampton, Bishop Suffragan of.

BUTLER, Pearse; *see* Butler, J. P.

BUTLER, Sir (Percy) James, Kt 2001; CBE 1981; DL; FCA; Deputy Chairman, Camelot PLC, 1995–2002 (Director, 1994–2002); farmer, since 1974; *b* 15 March 1929; *s* of late Percy Ernest Butler and Phyllis Mary Butler (*née* Bartholomew); *m* 1954, Margaret Prudence Copland; one *s* two *d. Educ:* Marlborough Coll.; Clare Coll., Cambridge (MA). Joined Peat, Marwick, Mitchell & Co. (later KPMG Peat Marwick), 1952; qualified, 1955; Partner, 1965; Gen. Partner, 1971; Managing Partner, London Reg., 1981–85; Dep. Sen. Partner, 1985–86; Sen. Partner, 1986–93; Mem. of KPMG Exec. Cttee and Council, 1987–93; Chm., KPMG Internat., 1991–93. Director: Mersey Docks and Harbour Co., 1972–90 (Dep. Chm., 1987–90); Tompkins PLC, 1994–95; Wadworth and Co. Ltd, 1994–; Nicholson, Graham & Jones, 1994–2004; Chairman: European Passenger Services Ltd, 1994–96; Union Railways, 1995–96. Mem. (part time), BRB, 1994–95. Business Advr to Treasury and CS Cttee, 1980–82; Member: Cttee on review of Railway Finance, 1982; Cadbury Cttee on Financial Aspects of Corporate Governance, 1990–95. Member: Council, Business in the Community, 1988–90; ICAEW Council, 1992–94; Council, CBIs, 1989–94; Governing Body, City Res. Project, 1991–95; Adv. Council, Prince's Youth Business Trust, 1993–2001; Council, SCF, 1994–2000 (Chm., SCF Private Appeal, 1994–2000). Treasurer, Pilgrims Soc., 1982–97; Trustee, Royal Opera House Trust, 1991–99 (Chm., 1993–95; Vice Chm., 1995–99); Dir, Royal Opera House, 1994–98; Trustee: Winchester Cathedral Trust, 1991– (Chm., Cathedral Appeal, 1991–94); RA, 1997–2005 (Mem., Mgt Cttee, 1997–); Brendoncare Foundn Develt Trust, 1998–2005 (Chm., Brendoncare Foundn Appeal, 1998–2005); Chm. Trustees, Music at Winchester, 1999–; Chm., Lord Mayor's Appeal, 2002–03. Mem., Marlborough Coll. Council, 1975–2001 (Chm., 1992–2001). Liveryman: Worshipful Co. of Cutlers, 1965– (Mem. Court, 1985–; Master, 1995–96); Worshipful Co. of Chartered Accountants in England and Wales, 1977–. DL Hants, 1994. *Recreations:* bridge, shooting, opera, ballet, farming. *Club:* Boodle's.

BUTLER, Peter; Chief Executive, Flying Scotsman plc; *b* 10 June 1951; *s* of late Kenneth Jonathan Butler and Barbara Butler; *m* 1973, Peggy Mary, *d* of Richard Nott; three *d. Educ:* Adams Grammar Sch., Newport, Shropshire; St Edmund Hall, Oxford (MA English Lit.; PGCE 1974). Admitted Solicitor, 1978; Solicitor, Thames Valley Police, 1978–80; Partner, 1981–92, Consultant, 1992–2000, Linnells, solicitors, Oxford. Nat. Chm., Trainee Solicitors, England and Wales, 1976. Mem. (C) Oxfordshire CC, 1985–89. MP (C) Milton Keynes North East, 1992–97; contested (C) same seat, 1997. PPS to Minister of State, DoH, 1994–95, to Chancellor of Exchequer, 1995–97. Mem., Home Affairs Select Cttee, 1992. Non-exec. Dir, Continental Trustees Ltd. Non-exec. Dir, Milton Keynes Chamber of Commerce. Sch. Gov., 1985–92. *Recreations:* music, three energetic children, avoiding organised exercise. *Address:* Castle Farm, Lavendon, Olney, Bucks MK46 4JG. *T:* (01234) 240046. *Club:* Vintage Sports Car.

BUTLER, Sir (Reginald) Michael (Thomas), 3rd Bt *cr* 1922, of Old Park, Devizes; QC (Ont); Barrister and Solicitor, retired; sometime Partner of Butler, Angus, Victoria, BC; Hon. Director, Teck Cominco Ltd; *b* 22 April 1928; *s* of Sir Reginald Thomas, 2nd Bt, and Marjorie Brown Butler; *S* father, 1959; *m* Marja McLean (marr. diss.); three *s*; one *s* adopted; *m* Judith Ann Blackwell, LLB, *d* of Harold Blackwell. *Educ:* Brentwood Coll., Victoria, BC; Univ. of British Columbia (BA). Called to Bar (Hons) from Osgoode Hall Sch. of Law, Toronto, Canada, 1954. *Publication:* Milk Chronicles, 2007. *Heir: s* (Reginald) Richard (Michael) Butler [*b* 3 Oct. 1953; *m* 1st, 1982, Dale Karen Piner (marr. diss. 1998); three *s*; 2nd, 1999, Penelope Joy Lipsack]. *Address:* Old Park Cottage, 634 Avalon Road, Victoria, BC V8V 1N7, Canada; *e-mail:* blackbart@telus.net.

BUTLER, Hon. Sir Richard (Clive), Kt 1981; DL; Chairman, County Natwest Investment Management, 1989–96; Life Member, Council, National Farmers' Union, since 1962 (President, 1979–86); farmer since 1953; *b* 12 Jan. 1929; *e s* of late Baron Butler of Saffron Walden, KG, CH, PC and late Sydney, *o c* of late Samuel Courtauld; *m* 1952, Susan Anne Maud Walker; twin *s* one *d. Educ:* Eton Coll.; Pembroke Coll., Cambridge (MA). 2nd Lieut, Royal Horse Guards, 1947–49. Vice-Pres. 1970–71, Dep. Pres., 1971–79, NFU. Member: Agricultural Adv. Council, 1968–72; Central Council for Agricultural and Horticultural Co-operation, 1970–79. Director: NFU Mutual Insce Soc. Ltd, 1985–96; National Westminster Bank, 1986–96; Agroceres & Co. (formerly Ferruzzi Trading (UK)), 1986–98; Agricola (UK), 1986–92; Barton Bendish Farms, 1986–92; County Natwest Group (formerly Natwest Investment Bank), 1989–92; Avon Insurance, 1990–96. Chm., Kennedy Inst. for Rheumatology Trust, 1995–; Trustee, Arthritis Res. Campaign (formerly Arthritis and Rheumatism Council for Research), 1986–2005. Member, Court of Assistants: Farmers' Co. (Master, 1997–98); Skinners' Co. (Master, 1994–95). DL Essex, 1972. *Recreations:* hunting, shooting, DIY. *Address:* Gladfen Hall, Halstead, Essex CO9 1RN. *T:* (01787) 472828. *Club:* Farmers'.

BUTLER, Richard Edmund, AM 1988; telecommunication policy adviser; Secretary-General, International Telecommunication Union, United Nations, Specialised Agency, Geneva, 1983–89 (Deputy Secretary-General, 1968–82); *b* 25 March 1926; *m* 1951, Patricia Carmel Kelly; three *s* two *d. Educ:* A, DPA; AASA; CPA; FIPA. Posts in Australian Post Office, incl. Chief Industrial Officer, 1955–60; Exec. Officer, Dep. Asst Dir-Gen., 1960–68 (Ministerial and External Relations), 1960–68; apptd (in absentia) Sec., Aust. Telecommunications Commn, 1975 and later Dir, Corporate Planning Directorate. Formerly Member Australian delegations: for Internat. Telecommunication Satellite Consortium, Plenipotentiary Conf. 1965 (Dep. Leader; Mem. Administrative Council and Plan Cttees, 1962–68); to UN Conf. on Peaceful Uses of Outer Space, Vienna, 1968 (Dep. Leader). Mem., Admin. Cttee of Co-ordination for UN and Heads of Specialized Agencies; Chairman: Ad-Hoc UN Common System subsid. gps; ITU (Tripartite) Staff Pension Cttee, 1968–83; Member: Ministerial Adv. Cttee, Implementation of Australian Telecommns Reform decisions, 1990–91; Adv. Bd, Centre for Internat. Res. on Communication and ITs, Melbourne, 1991–2002; Associate Mem., Austr. Telecommn Authy), 1990–91. Chairman: Asiaspace Ltd, 1999– (Mem. Bd, 1995–); Sky Station Australia Pty Ltd, 1999– (Mem. Bd, 1996–); Mem. Internat. Adv. Bd, Sky Station Internat. Inc., 1995–. Member, Advisory Board: Pacific Telecommns Council, Hawaii, 1993–; Telematics, India, 1994–; Mem. Bd, Volunteers in Technical Assistance, 1993–. Governor, Internat. Computer Commns Conf., 1975–85; UN System co-ordinator, Develt of Commns Infrastructure prog., world commns year, 1983. Hon. Mem., Greek Soc. of Air and Space Law, 1984. FRIPA; Hon. Fellow, Instn of Electronic and Telecommunications Engrs, New Delhi, 1988. Fellow, Telecommns Soc. of Aust., 1995. Philipp Reis Medal, Germany, 1987. Grand Insignia, Order of Merit for Telecommunications, Spain, 1983. *Publications:* papers on changing telecommunication environment and on multi-dimensional consequences of telecommunications for economic development of nations. *Recreations:* golf, reading. *Address:* 40 Barrington Avenue, Kew, Vic 3101, Australia. *Clubs:* Royal Over-Seas League; CTA NSW (Sydney); Melbourne Cricket; Greenacres Golf (Kew).

BUTLER, Sir Richard (Pierce), 13th Bt *cr* 1628 (Ire.), of Cloughgrenan, Co. Carlow; *b* 22 July 1940; *s* of Col Sir Thomas Pierce Butler, 12th Bt, CVO, DSO, OBE and Rosemary Liège Woodgate Davidson-Houston (*d* 1997); *S* father, 1994; *m* 1965, Diana, *yr d* of Col S. J. Borg; three *s* one *d. Educ:* Eton; NY Univ. MBA. FCA 1963. Partner, Charles Wakeling & Co., 1964–66; Director: The First Boston Corp. (NY), 1967–78; PaineWebber Inc. (NY), 1978–88 (Management Council, 1985–88); PaineWebber International Bank, 1986–89; Emesco Industrial Equity Co. SA, 1987–2005; The Transportation Gp Ltd, 1989–94; RP&C Internat. (formerly Rauscher Pierce & Clark) Inc., 1992–2000. Mem. Council, Pestalozzi Children's Village Trust, 1983– (Chm., 1985–94); Founder, Pestalozzi Overseas Children's Trust, 1995. Treas., GAPAN, 1963–66. *Heir: s* Thomas Pierce [*b* 9 Oct. 1966; *m* 1993, Lucinda Pamela Murphy; two *s* two *d*].

BUTLER, Rosemary Jane; Director of Statistics, Department of Health, 1991–98; *b* 15 July 1946; *d* of Samuel Laight Medlar and Rosemary Peggy Medlar; *m* 1971, Anthony David Butler. *Educ:* Maynard School, Exeter; LSE (BSc Econ). Central Statistical Office, 1967–73; Unit for Manpower Studies, 1973–77; Dept of Employment, 1977–80; Statistician and Chief Statistician, MoD, 1980–85; Chief Statistician, HM Treasury, 1985–89; Asst Sec., DSS, 1989–91. FRSA 1993. *Recreations:* theatre, music, birdwatching.

BUTLER, Rosemary Janet Mair; Member (Lab) Newport West, National Assembly for Wales, since 1999; Deputy Presiding Officer, since 2007; *b* 21 Jan. 1943; *d* of Godfrey McGrath and late Gwyneth Jones; *m* 1966, Derek Richard Butler; two *d. Educ:* St Julian's High Sch., Newport. Qualified chiropodist, 1962; in practice, 1962–75. Dir, Tourism S and W Wales, 1993–99. Mem. (Lab) Newport BC, subseq. CBC, 1973–99 (Chm., Leisure Services, 1983–97); Mayor of Newport, 1989–90. National Assembly for Wales: Sec. for Educn and Children, 1999–2000; Chm., Culture, Sport and Welsh Lang. Cttee, 2004–07. Member: Sports Council for Wales, 1993–99; Museums and Galls Commn, 1996–2000; Broadcasting Council for Wales, 1997–99; Eur. Cttee of the Regions, 2002–07. Founder and Chair: Newport Internat. Comp. for Young Pianists, 1979–; Newport-Kutaisi (Republic of Georgia) Twinning Assoc., 1989–99; Chm., Bd, Nat. Industrial and Maritime Mus., Swansea, 2002–. Hon. Citizen, Kutaisi, Republic of Georgia, 1997. *Recreations:* museums, galleries, the arts, foreign travel. *Address:* National Assembly for Wales, Cardiff Bay, Cardiff CF99 1NA. *T:* (029) 2089 8470; (constituency office) 1 Transport House, Cardiff Road, Newport NP20 2EH. *T:* (01633) 222523.

BUTLER, Air Vice Marshal Stuart Denham; Capability Manager (Information Superiority), 2006–08, and Air Member for Equipment Capability, 2007–08, Ministry of Defence; *b* 15 Jan. 1956; *s* of Ralph and Melody Butler; *m* 1984, Linda Dorothy Ritchie; two *d. Educ:* Lafford Sch., Billingham, Lincs. Joined RAF, 1974; Nimrod pilot, 1979–84; Jet Provost flying instructor; Nimrod Sqdn Comdr; Stn Comdr, Kinloss; Dep. Dir, Underwater Battlespace, MoD; AO, Intelligence, Surveillance, Target Acquisition and Reconnaissance Equipment, HQ Strike Comd; Dir, Equipt Capability (ISTAR), MoD, 2005–06. *Recreations:* fanatical golfer - happy to take money off all comers!, DIY - a one year garden project now in its fourth year. *Address:* 8 Frank Whittle Close, Cranwell, Sleaford, Lincs NG34 8FH. *T:* (01400) 261831; *e-mail:* stu@frankwhittle.freeserve.co.uk. *Club:* South Kyme Golf (Lincs).

BUTLER, Terry; *see* Butler, N. J. T.

BUTLER, Rt Rev. Thomas Frederick; *see* Southwark, Bishop of.

BUTLER, Vincent Frederick, RSA 1977; RGI 1989; figurative sculptor; works in bronze; *b* Manchester, 27 Oct. 1933; *m* 1961, Camilla Luisa Meazza; two *s. Educ:* Acad. of Fine Art, Milan. Regular exhibitor at major exhibitions in Scotland; work in RA and several private galleries in Edinburgh, Glasgow and London. Prof. of Sculpture, Univ. of Northern Nigeria, 1960–63. *Publication:* Casting for Sculptors, 1997. *Address:* 17 Deanpark Crescent, Edinburgh EH4 1PH. *T:* (0131) 332 5884; *e-mail:* vincent.butler@talktalk.net.

BUTLER, Prof. William Elliott; John Edward Fowler Distinguished Professor of Law, Pennsylvania State University, since 2005; Professorial Research Associate, School of Oriental and African Studies, University of London, since 2006; Professor of Comparative Law in the University of London, 1976–2005, now Emeritus; Director, Vinogradoff Institute (formerly Centre for the Study of Socialist Legal Systems), University College London, since 1982; *b* 20 Oct. 1939; *s* of late William Elliott Butler and of Maxine Swan Elmberg; *m* 1st, 1961, Darlene Mae Johnson (*d* 1989); two *s*; 2nd, 1991, Maryann Elizabeth Gashi. *Educ:* The American Univ. (BA); Harvard Law School (JD); Acad. Law Sch., Russian Acad. of Scis (LLM); The Johns Hopkins Univ. (MA, PhD); London Univ.

(LLD). FSA 1989. Res. Asst, Washington Centre of Foreign Policy Res., Sch. of Advanced Internat. Studies, The Johns Hopkins Univ., 1966–68; Res. Associate in Law, and Associate, Russian Res. Centre, Harvard Univ., 1968–70; University of London: Reader in Comparative Law, 1970–76; Mem. Council, SSEES, 1973–93 (Vice-Chm., 1983–88); Dean of Faculty of Laws, UCL, 1977–79; Vice Dean, 1986–88, Dean, 1988–90, Faculty of Laws, London Univ; Mem., Cttee of Management, Inst. of Advanced Legal Studies, 1985–88. M. M. Speransky Prof. of Internat. and Comparative Law, 1993–2004, Dean, Faculty of Law, 1993–98, Moscow Higher Sch. of Social and Econ. Scis. Visiting Scholar: Faculty of Law, Moscow State Univ., 1972, 1980; Inst. of State and Law, USSR Acad. of Scis, 1976, 1981, 1983, 1984, 1988; Mongolian State Univ., 1979; Harvard Law Sch., 1982; Visiting Professor: NY Univ. Law Sch., 1978; Ritsumeikan Univ., 1985; Harvard Law Sch., 1986–87; Washington and Lee Univ. Law Sch., 2005; Lectr, Hague Acad. of Internat. Law, 1985. Associé, Internat. Acad. of Comparative Law, 1982–; Member, Bar: Dist of Columbia; US Supreme Court; Union of Jurists, 1990; Mem., Russian Ct of Internat. Commercial Arbitration, 1995–. Chm., Civil Rights in Russia Adv. Panel, Univ. of London, 1983–87; Co-ordinator, UCL-USSR Acad. of Sciences Protocol on Co-operation, 1981–; Special Counsel, Commn on Econ. Reform, USSR Council of Ministers, 1989–91; Of Counsel, Clifford Chance, London, Moscow and Almaty, 1992–94; Partner: White & Case, 1994–96; PricewaterhouseCoopers, 1997–2001; Sen. Partner, Phoenix Law Associates, Moscow, 2002–. Member: EC Joint Task Force on Law Reform in CIS, 1992–93; Working Gp on Commercial Law, Govt of Russian Fedn, 1992; Advr, State Property Fund, Rep. of Kyrgyzstan, 1992; Advr on Corporate Law Reform, Russian Min. of Econ. Develt and Trade, 2004–; Consultant, World Bank, 1992–. Mem., Secretariat, Internat. Assoc. of Mongolists (Ulan Bator), 1987–92; Hon. Member: All-Union Soc. of Bibliophiles, USSR, 1989; Soviet Assoc. of Maritime Law, 1990. Mem., Court of Governors, City of London Polytechnic, 1985–89. Sec., The Bookplate Soc., 1978–86 (Foreign Sec., 1988–94); Exec. Sec., Féd. Internat. des Sociétés d'Amateurs d'Ex-Libris, 1986– (Vice-Pres., 1984–86). Academician: Internat. Acad. of the Book and Art of the Book, Russia, 1992; Russian Acad. of Natural Scis (Russian Encyclopedia Section), 1992; Nat. Acad. of Scis of Ukraine, 1992; Russian Acad. of Legal Scis, 1999. Trustee, Hakluyt Soc., 2004–. Editor, Year Book on Socialist Legal Systems, 1985–90; Co-editor, The Bookplate Jl, 1989–91 (Editor, 1983–86); Editor: Bookplate Internat., 1994–; Sudebnik, 1996–; Russian Law, 2004–; Jl of Comparative Law, 2006–; E European and Russian Yearbook of Internat. and Comparative Law, 2007–; Mem., editorial bds of learned jls, incl. Marine Policy, 1988–2004, European Business Law Rev., 1990–2004, Internat. Law, 2002–; Comparative Law, 2006–; editor of looseleaf services and microfiche projects. FRSA 1986. Publications: more than 800 books, articles, translations, and reviews, including: The Soviet Union and the Law of the Sea, 1971; Russian Law, 1977; (with others) The Soviet Legal System, 3rd and 4th edns, 1977–84; A Source Book on Socialist International Organizations, 1978; Northeast Arctic Passage, 1978; International Law in Comparative Perspective, 1980; Basic Documents on Soviet Legal System, 1983, 3rd edn 1992; Chinese Soviet Republic 1931–1934, 1983; Soviet Law, 1983, 2nd edn 1988; Comparative Law and Legal System, 1985; The Law of the Sea and International Shipping, 1985; The Golden Era of American Bookplate Design, 1986; Justice and Comparative Law, 1987; International Law and the International System, 1987; The Non-Use of Force and International Law, 1989; Perestroika and International Law, 1990; The History of International Law in Russia 1647–1917, 1990; (with D. J. Butler) Modern British Bookplates, 1990; Sherlockian Bookplates, 1992; The Butler Commentaries: USSR Law on Ownership, 1991; USSR Fundamental Principles on Investment Activity, 1991; Foreign Investment Legislation in the Republic of the Former Soviet Union, 1993; (with M. E. Gashi-Butler) Doing Business in Russia, 1994; Russian-English Legal Dictionary, 1995, 2nd edn 2001; Russian Law, 1999, 2nd edn 2003; Tadzhikistan Legal Texts, 1999; Uzbekistan Legal Texts, 1999; American Bookplates, 2000; The Law of Treaties in Russia and Other Countries of the Commonwealth of Independent States, 2002; Russian Company and Commercial Law, 2003; Civil Code of the Russian Federation, 2003; Russian Foreign Relations and Investment Law, 2006; Russian Legal Biography, 2007; translations of: G. I. Tunkin, Theory of International Law, 1974, 2nd edn 2003; A. Kuznetsov, The Journey, 1984; Kazakhstan Civil Code, 1995, 2008; Uzbekistan Civil Code, 1998, 2007; Russian Civil Legislation, 1999; Foreign Investment Law in the Commonwealth of Independent States, 2002; A. Saidov, Comparative Law, 2003; A. A. Kovalev, Contemporary Issues of the Law of the Sea, 2004; A. N. Vylegzhaum and V. K. Zilanov, Spitzbergen, 2007. Recreations: book collecting, bookplate collecting. Address: 155 Mount Rock Road, Newville, PA 17241, USA. T: (717) 7767359. Clubs: Cosmos (Washington, DC); Grolier (New York).

BUTLER, William Gerard, Member (Lab) Glasgow Anniesland, Scottish Parliament, since Nov. 2000; b 30 March 1956; s of William Muir Butler and Mary Butler (née Watters); m 1988, Patricia Josephine Ferguson, qv. Educ: St Mungo's Acad., Glasgow; Univ. of Stirling (BA Hons); Notre Dame Coll. of Educn (PGCE 1980). Teacher of English: Greenock High Sch., 1980–83; Port Glasgow High Sch., 1983–84; Castlehead High Sch., 1984–85; John Street Secondary Sch., 1985–86; Stonelaw High Sch., 1986–2000. Member (Lab) Glasgow CC, 1987–2001 (Convener: Property Services, 1995–98, Policy Formulation, 1998–99; Vice-Convener, Policy and Resources, 1998–2000). Sec., Glasgow City Labour Gp, 1998–2000. Recreations: reading, theatre, film, visiting Italy, following Partick Thistle FC. Address: Scottish Parliament, Edinburgh EH99 1SP; Constituency Advice Office, 129 Dalsetter Avenue, Glasgow G15 8SZ. T: (0141) 944 9441.

BUTLER, William Gibson; Chief Operating Officer, Addaction, since 2005; b 11 May 1953; s of late William Gibson Butler and Anna Elizabeth Butler; m 1975, Jennifer Anne (née Dickson); two d. Educ: Ulster Poly. (CQSW 1975); Open Univ. (BA 1984; MBA 1993). Sen. Social Worker (community work), Eastern Health and Social Services Bd, 1979–86; Principal Community Services Develt Officer, Milton Keynes Develt Corp., 1986–92; Regl Dir, 1992–98, Ops Dir, 1998–2001, Nat. Schizophrenia Fellowship; Chief Exec., Arthritis Care, 2001–04. Recreation: going to meetings. Address: Addaction, 67–69 Cowcross Street, EC1M 6PU. T: (020) 7017 1666, Fax: (020) 7251 5890; e-mail: wbutler@addaction.org.uk.

BUTLER-BOWDON, Humphrey Anthony Erdeswick, (Humphrey Ocean), RA 2004; painter; b 22 June 1951; s of late Capt. Maurice Erdeswick Butler-Bowdon, OBE, RN, and Anne (née Darlington); m 1982, Miranda Argyle; two d. Educ: Ampleforth; Tunbridge Wells Art Sch.; Brighton Coll. of Art; Canterbury Coll. of Art. Bass player, Kilburn and the Highroads, 1971–73. Vis. Prof. of Painting and Drawing, Camberwell Coll. of Art, 2002–; Mem., Artistic Records Cttee, Imperial War Mus., 1985–98. Work includes: The First of England, Nat. Maritime Mus., 1999; portrait commissions for National Portrait Gallery: Tony Benn; William Whitelaw; A. J. Ayer; Philip Larkin; Paul McCartney; one-man exhibitions: Nat. Portrait Gall., 1984; Ferens Art Gall., Hull, 1986; Double-Portrait, Tate Gall., Liverpool, 1992; urbasuburba, Whitworth Art Gall., Manchester, 1997; The Painter's Eye, Nat. Portrait Gall., 1999; how's my driving, Dulwich Picture Gall., 2003; group exhibitions include: Das Automobil in der Kunst, Haus der Kunst, Munich, 1986; Martin Gropius Bau, Berlin, 1996; Treasures from NPG, British

Council, Japan, 1996; Best of British, NPG, Canberra, 2001; Royal Treasures, Queen's Gall., Buckingham Palace, 2002; Icons and Idols, NPG, 2006; work in collections: Ferens Art Gall., Hull; Imperial War Mus.; Christ Church, Oxford; Nat. Maritime Mus.; NPG; Royal Liby, Windsor Castle; Royal Opera House, Covent Gdn; Scottish NPG; Southwark Collection; Wellcome Trust; Wolverhampton Art Gall.; British Council; Whitworth Art Gall., Manchester; Goldsmiths Coll., Univ. of London; Port Authy, Bruges-Zeebrugge; V&A. Hon. Fellow, Kent Inst. of Art and Design, 2002. Imperial Tobacco Portrait Award, 1982; Wellcome Trust Sci-Art Award, 1998. Publications: The Ocean View, 1982; (with S. Nugent) Big Mouth: the Amazon speaks, 1990; Zeebrugge, 2001. Recreation: carrying binoculars. Address: 22 Marmora Road, SE22 0RX. T: (020) 8693 8387, T: and Fax: (studio) (020) 8761 7400.

BUTLER-SLOSS, family name of **Baroness Butler-Sloss.**

BUTLER-SLOSS, Baroness cr 2006 (Life Peer), of Marsh Green in the County of Devon; **Ann Elizabeth Oldfield Butler-Sloss,** GBE 2005 (DBE 1979); PC 1988; President of the Family Division, 1999–2005; b 10 Aug. 1933; d of late Sir Cecil Havers, QC, and late Enid Snelling; m 1958, Joseph William Alexander Butler-Sloss, qv, two s one d. Educ: Wycombe Abbey Sch. Called to Bar, Inner Temple, Feb. 1955, Bencher, 1979, Treasurer, 1998; practice at Bar, 1955–70; Registrar, Principal Registry of Probate, later Family, Division, 1970–79; a Judge of the High Court, Family Div., 1979–88; a Lord Justice of Appeal, 1988–99. Chairman: Cleveland Child Abuse Inquiry, 1987–88; Security Commn, 1993–2005; Adv. Council, St Paul's Cathedral, 2001–; Commn on Appointment of Archbishop of Canterbury, 2002. Contested (C), Lambeth, Vauxhall, 1959. Member: Medico-Legal Soc.; Judicial Studies Bd, 1985–89; former Pres., Commonwealth and England Bar Assoc. Pres., Honiton Agricultural Show, 1985–86; Chancellor, Univ. of West of England, 1993–; Visitor, St Hilda's Coll., Oxford. Hon. Mem., American Law Inst. Hon. Fellow: St Hilda's Coll., Oxford, 1988; Sarum Coll., 2004; Fellow, KCL, 1991. FRSocMed 1992, Hon. FRSocMed 1997; Hon. FRCP 1992; Hon. FRCPsych 1993; Hon. FRCPCH 1996 (Hon. Mem., BPA, 1988). Hon. LLD: Hull, 1988; Keele, Bristol, 1991; Exeter, Brunel, 1992; Manchester, 1995; Cantab, Greenwich, 2000; Liverpool, E Anglia, 2001; London, Ulster, 2004; Buckingham, 2006; Hon. DLitt Loughborough, 1992; DUniv: Central England, 1994; Bath, 2004; Open, 2005. Publications: Joint Editor: Phipson on Evidence (10th edn); Corpe on Road Haulage (2nd edn); a former Editor, Supreme Court Practice, 1976 and 1979. Clubs: Lansdowne, Royal Society of Medicine.

BUTLER-SLOSS, Joseph William Alexander; Chairman, 1992 Delimitation Commission, Botswana, 1992–93; b 16 Nov. 1926; 2nd and o surv. s of late Francis Alexander Sloss and Alice Mary Frances Violet Sloss (née Patchell); m 1958, Ann Elizabeth Oldfield Havers (see Baroness Butler-Sloss); two s one d. Educ: Bangor Grammar Sch., Co. Down; Hertford Coll., Oxford. Ordinary Seaman, RN, 1944; Midshipman 1945, Sub-Lieut 1946, RNVR. MA (Jurisprudence) Hertford Coll., Oxford, 1951. Called to Bar, Gray's Inn, 1952; joined Western Circuit, 1954; joined Inner Temple; a Recorder, 1972–84; a Judge of High Court, Kenya, 1984–90. Joint Master, East Devon Foxhounds, 1970–76. Hon. Editor, The Irish Genealogist, 1993–2001. Recreations: racing, the violin. Address: Higher Marsh Farm, Marsh Green, Rockbeare, Exeter EX5 2EX. Clubs: Carlton; Nairobi.

BUTLER-WHEELHOUSE, Keith Oliver; Chief Executive, Smiths Group (formerly Smiths Industries), 1996–2007; b 29 March 1946; s of late Kenneth Butler-Wheelhouse and May (née Page); m 1973, Pamela Anne Bosworth Smith; two s. Educ: Queen Mary's, Walsall; Grey Sch. and Technicon, Port Elizabeth; Witwatersrand Univ. (BCom); Cape Town Univ. Grad. Sch. Mfg, Product Develt, Finance and Mktg Depts, Ford Motor Co., 1965–85; General Motors, 1985–96 (led mgt buy-out of GMSA to form Delta, 1985–92); Pres., Saab Automobile, Sweden, 1992–96. Non-exec. Dir, J. Sainsbury plc, 1999–2004. Citizen of Year, Port Elizabeth, 1987. Recreations: golf, jogging, tennis, surfing. Clubs: Moor Park Golf, Wentworth Golf, Sunningdale Golf; Cumberland Lawn Tennis; Humewood Golf, St Francis Golf, Fancourt Golf, Johannesburg Country (S Africa).

BUTLIN, Martin Richard Fletcher, CBE 1990; FBA 1984; Keeper of Historic British Collection, Tate Gallery, 1967–89; Consultant, Christie's, since 1989; b 7 June 1929; s of late Kenneth Rupert Butlin and Helen Mary (née Fletcher), MBE, JP; m 1969, Frances Caroline Chodzko. Educ: Rendcomb Coll.; Trinity Coll., Cambridge (MA); Courtauld Inst. of Art, London Univ. (BA). DLit London 1984. Asst Keeper, Tate Gall., 1955–67. Publications: A Catalogue of the Works of William Blake in the Tate Gallery, 1957, 3rd edn 1990; Samuel Palmer's Sketchbook of 1824, 1962, 2nd edn as Samuel Palmer: the sketchbook of 1824, 2005; Turner Watercolours, 1962; (with Sir John Rothenstein) Turner, 1964; (with Mary Chamot and Dennis Farr) Tate Gallery Catalogues: The Modern British Paintings, Drawings and Sculpture, 1964; The Later Works of J. M. W. Turner, 1965; William Blake, 1966; The Blake-Varley Sketchbook of 1819, 1969; (with E. Joll) The Paintings of J. M. W. Turner, 1977, 2nd edn 1984 (jtly, Mitchell Prize for the History of Art, 1978); The Paintings and Drawings of William Blake, 1981; Aspects of British Painting 1550–1800, from the Collection of the Sarah Campbell Blaffer Foundation, 1988; (with Mollie Luther and Ian Warrell) Turner at Petworth, 1989; (with Ted Gott and Irena Zdanowicz) William Blake in the Collection of the National Gallery of Victoria, 1989; selected paintings and prepared catalogues for following exhibitions: (with Andrew Wilton and John Gage) Turner 1775–1851, 1974; William Blake, 1978; (with Gert Schiff) William Blake, Tokyo, 1990; (ed jtly) The Oxford Companion to J. M. W. Turner, 2001; articles and reviews in Burlington Mag., Connoisseur, Master Drawings, Blake Qly, Blake Studies, Turner Studies. Recreations: music, travel. Address: 74c Eccleston Square, SW1V 1PJ.

BUTLIN, Prof. Robin Alan, OBE 2004; DLitt; Professor of Historical Geography, University of Leeds, 2000–03, now Emeritus Professor of Geography (Leverhulme Emeritus Research Fellow, 2003–05); b 31 May 1938; s of late Rowland Henry Butlin and Mona Butlin; m 1961, Norma Coroneo; two s one d. Educ: Liverpool Univ. (BA, MA); DLitt Loughborough, 1987. Demonstrator, University Coll. of N Staffordshire, 1961–62; Lectr in Geography, UC Dublin, 1962–71; Queen Mary College, University of London: Lectr in Geography, 1971; Sen. Lectr, 1975; Reader in Historical Geography, 1977–79; Loughborough University: Prof. of Geography, 1979–95; Hd of Dept, 1979–91; Dean, Sch. of Human and Environmental Studies, 1983–86; Principal, and Prof. of Historical Geography, UC of Ripon and York St John, 1995–98. Vis. Associate Prof. of Geography, Univ. of Nebraska, 1969–70; Vis. Professorial Fellow and Leverhulme Res. Fellow, Wolfson Coll., Cambridge, 1986–87; Vis. Prof., Leeds Univ., 1998–2000. FRGS 1972 (Vice-Pres., RGS/IBG, 1995–98); CGeog 2002. Victoria Medal, RGS, 1999. Publications: (ed with A. R. H. Baker) Studies of Field Systems in the British Isles, 1973; (ed) The Development of the Irish Town, 1977; (ed with R. A. Dodgshon) An Historical Geography of England and Wales, 1978, 2nd edn 1990; (ed with H. S. A. Fox) Change in the Countryside: essays on rural England 1500–1900, 1979; The Transformation of Rural England c. 1580–1800, 1982; Historical Geography: through the gates of space and time, 1993; (ed jtly) Geography and Imperialism 1820–1940, 1995; (ed with N. Roberts) Ecological Relations in Historical Times, 1995; (ed with R. A. Dodgshon) Historical

Geography of Europe, 1999; (ed with I. S. Black) Place, Culture and Identity, 2001; (ed) Historical Atlas of North Yorkshire, 2003. *Recreations*: music, walking, reading. *Address*: 15 Lawnway, Stockton Lane, York YO31 1JD. *T*: (01904) 416544.

BUTROS, Prof. Albert Jamil; Istiqlal Order First Class, Jordan, 1987; Professor of English, University of Jordan, 1967–79 and 1985–2004, now Emeritus; *b* 25 March 1934; *s* of Jamil Issa and Virginie Antoine (Albina); *m* 1962, Ida Maria Albina; four *d*. *Educ*: Univ. of London (BA Hons English 1958); Univ. of Exeter (BA *ad eundem* 1958); Columbia Univ. (PhD English 1963). Teacher, Amman, 1950–55; Instructor in English, Teacher's Coll., Amman, 1958–60; Lectr, Hunter Coll., City Univ., NY, 1961; Instructor, Miami Univ., Oxford, Ohio, 1962–63; University of Jordan: Asst Prof., English, 1963–65; Associate Prof., 1965–67; Acting Chm., Dept of English, 1964–67; Chm., Dept of English, 1967–73, 1974–76; Dean, Research and Graduate Studies, 1973–76; Ambassador to UK, 1987–91, and (non-res.) to Ireland, 1988–91, and to Iceland, 1990–91. Special Advr to HRH Crown Prince Hassan of Jordan, 1984–85. Dir Gen./Pres., Royal Sci. Soc., Amman, 1976–84. Vis. Prof., Ohio Wesleyan Univ., 1971–72; Sen. Res. Fellow, Internat. Develt Res. Centre, Canada, 1983–84. Rapporteur, Cttee on Jordan Incentive State Prize in Translation, 2001; Member: Cttee on Selection for Shoman Foundn Prize for Young Arab Scholars in Humanities and Social Scis, 2002; Cttee on Selection of Outstanding Researchers in Jordan, 2004. Member: World Affairs Council, Amman, 1978–91; Arab Thought Forum, 1981–95. Gov., Internat. Develt Res. Centre, Canada, 1986–98; Mem., Bd of Trustees, Philadelphia Univ., Amman, 1995–. Mem., Adv. Bd, Jordanian Jl of Modern Langs and Lit., 2006–. Fellow, World Acad. of Art and Sci., 1986. KStJ 1991. Order of Merit, Italy, 1983. *Publications*: Tales of the Caliphs, 1965; Leaders of Arab Thought, 1969; The Translatability of Chaucer into Arabic: a test case, 1997; The English Language and Non-Native Writers of Fiction, 2004; articles and translations. *Recreations*: reading, writing, translation, art, world affairs, application of science and technology to development. *Address*: PO Box 309, Jubeiha, Amman 11941, Jordan.

BUTT, Amanda Jane; see Finlay, A. J.

BUTT, Geoffrey Frank; Principal Assistant Solicitor, Inland Revenue, 1993–96; *b* 5 May 1943; *s* of late Frank Thomas Woodman Butt and Dorothy Rosamond Butt; *m* 1972, Lee Anne Davey; two *s* one *d*. *Educ*: Royal Masonic Sch., Bushey; Univ. of Reading (BA). Solicitor 1970. Joined Solicitor's Office, HM Customs and Excise as Legal Asst, 1971; Sen. Legal Asst, 1974; Asst Solicitor, 1982; Prin. Asst Solicitor, 1986–93. *Recreations*: family life, classical music, literature and art, gardening. *Address*: 14 Richmond Close, Wellswood, Torquay, Devon TQ1 2PW.

BUTT, Prof. John Anthony, PhD; FBA 2006; FRSE; Gardiner Professor of Music, University of Glasgow, since 2001; *b* 17 Nov. 1960; *s* of late Wilfred Roger Butt and of Patricia Doreen Butt; *m* 1989, Sally Ann Cantlay; four *s* one *d*. *Educ*: Solihull Sch.; King's Coll., Cambridge (BA 1982; MPhil 1984; PhD 1987). FRCO(CHM); ADCM. Temp. Lectr, Univ. of Aberdeen, 1986–87; Res. Fellow, Magdalene Coll., Cambridge, 1987–89; Prof. of Music and Univ. Organist, Univ. of Calif, Berkeley, 1989–97; Lectr in Music and Fellow, King's Coll., Univ. of Cambridge, 1997–2001. FRSE 2003. *Publications*: Bach Interpretation, 1990; Bach Mass in B Minor, 1991; Music Education and the Art of Performance in the German Baroque, 1994; (ed) Cambridge Companion to Bach, 1997; Playing with History, 2002; (ed) Cambridge History of 17th Century Music, 2005. *Recreations*: reading, hill-walking. *Address*: Upper Culverden, 2 West Lennox Drive, Helensburgh G84 9AD. *T*: (01436) 673942.

BUTT, Michael Acton; Chairman, AXIS Capital Holdings Ltd, since 2002; *b* Thruxton, 25 May 1942; *s* of Leslie Acton Kingsford Butt and Mina Gascoigne Butt; *m* 1st, 1964, Diana Lorraine Brook; two *s*; 2nd, 1986, Zoé Benson. *Educ*: Rugby; Magdalen Coll., Oxford (MA History); INSEAD, France (MBA 1967). Bland Welch Gp, 1964; Dir, Bland Payne Holdings, 1970; Chm., Sedgwick Ltd, 1983–87; Dep. Chm., Sedgwick Gp plc, 1985–87; Chm. and Chief Exec., Eagle Star Hldgs, 1987–91; Dir, BAT, 1987–91; Pres. and CEO, Mid Ocean Ltd, 1993–98; Dir, XL Capital Ltd, 1998–2002. Director: Marceau Investissements, Paris, 1987–94; Phoenix International (Bermuda), 1992–97; INA, 1994–97; Bank of N. T. Butterfield & Son Ltd, 1996–2002. Board Mem., Internat. Adv. Council, INSEAD, 1982–. *Recreations*: travel, tennis, opera, reading, family, the European movement. *Address*: Leamington House, 50 Harrington Sound Road, Hamilton Parish CR 04, Bermuda. *T*: (441) 2931378, *Fax*: (441) 2938511. *Clubs*: Travellers; Royal Bermuda Yacht, Mid Ocean, Coral Beach (Bermuda).

BUTT, Richard Bevan; Chief Executive, Rural Development Commission, 1989–98; *b* 27 Feb. 1943; *s* of late Roger William Bevan and of Jean Mary (*née* Carter); *m* 1975, Amanda Jane Finlay, *qv*; two *s*. *Educ*: Magdalen Coll., Oxford (BA Hist.); Lancaster Univ. (MA Regional Econs). Asst Principal, Min. of Housing, 1965–68; Sen. Res. Associate, Birmingham Univ., 1969–72; Consultant, 1972; HM Treasury: Principal, 1973–78; Asst Sec., 1978–86; seconded as Financial Counsellor, UK Perm. Repn to EC, 1981–84; Head of Conservation, English Heritage, 1986–89. Specialist Advr to Agriculture Select Cttee, 1998–99. Trustee: Action for Market Towns, 1998–2003; Churches Conservation Trust, 1999–2008 (Dep. Chm., 2006–08); TCPA, 2004– (Mem., Policy Council, 1998–). *Recreations*: ceramics, architecture, gardening, travel. *Address*: 35 Gloucester Circus, SE10 8RY.

BUTT, Simon John; HM Diplomatic Service; Ambassador to Lithuania, since 2008; *b* 5 April 1958; *s* of William Hedley Butt and Joan Marion Newton Butt. *Educ*: New Coll., Oxford (BA 1st Cl. Hons PPE 1979; MA). Entered FCO, 1979; E Europe and Soviet Dept, FCO, 1979–80; lang. trng, 1980–82; Third Sec., Moscow, 1982–84; Second Secretary: Rangoon, 1984–86; Soviet Dept, FCO, 1986–88; ministerial speechwriter, 1988–90; First Sec., UK Perm. Representation to EC, 1990–94; Dep. Hd, Eastern Dept, FCO, 1994–97; Counsellor and Dep. Hd of Mission, Kiev, 1997–2000; Hd, Eastern Dept, FCO, 2001–04; Dep. High Comr, Islamabad, Pakistan, 2005–08. *Recreations*: travel, the company of friends, history, including a harmless obsession with Napoleon on St Helena. *Address*: c/o Foreign and Commonwealth Office, King Charles Street, SW1A 2AH; *e-mail*: simon.butt@fco.gov.uk.

BUTTER, Major Sir David (Henry), KCVO 1991; MC 1941; JP; landowner and farmer; company director; HM Lord-Lieutenant of Perth and Kinross, 1975–95; *b* 18 March 1920; *s* of late Col Charles Butter, OBE, DL, JP, Pitlochry, and Agnes Marguerite (Madge), *d* of late William Clark, Newark, NJ, USA; *m* 1946, Myra Alice (CVO 1992), *d* of Hon. Maj.-Gen. Sir Harold Wernher, 3rd Bt, GCVO, TD; one *s* four *d*. *Educ*: Eton; Oxford. Served War of 1939–45: 2nd Lieut Scots Guards, 1940, Western Desert and North Africa, Sicily (Staff), 1941–43; Italy (ADC to GOC 8th Army, Gen. Sir Oliver Leese, 1944); Temp. Major, 1946; retd Army, 1948. Captain, Queen's Body Guard for Scotland (Royal Company of Archers); Pres., Highland T&AVR, 1979–84. County Councillor, Perth, 1955–74; DL Perthshire, 1956, Vice-Lieutenant of Perth, 1960–71; HM Lieutenant of County of Perth, 1971–75, and County of Kinross, 1974–75. *Recreations*: shooting, golf, ski-ing, travel. *Address*: Cluniemore, Pitlochry, Scotland PH16 5NE. *T*: (01796) 472006; 64 Rutland Gate, SW7 1PJ. *T*: (020) 7589 6731. *Clubs*: Turf;

Royal and Ancient (St Andrews).
See also Earl of Dalhousie.

BUTTER, John Henry, CMG 1962; MBE 1946; Financial Director to Government of Abu Dhabi, 1970–83; *b* 20 April 1916; *s* of late Captain A. E. Butter, CMG, and late Mrs Baird; *m* 1950, Joyce Platt; three *s*. *Educ*: Charterhouse; Christ Church, Oxford. Indian Civil Service, 1939–47; Pakistan Admin. Service, 1947–50 (served in Punjab, except for period 1942–46 when was Asst to Political Agent, Imphal, Manipur State). HM Overseas Civil Service, Kenya, 1950–65 (Perm. Sec. to the Treasury, 1959–65); Financial Adviser, Kenya Treasury, 1965–69. *Publication*: Uncivil Servant, 1989. *Recreations*: golf, bridge. *Address*: Whitehill, Gordon, Berwickshire TD3 6LQ. *Club*: East India.

BUTTER, His Honour Neil (McLaren), CBE 2001; QC 1976; a Circuit Judge, 1982–2001; a Judge of Central London County Court, 1994–2001; Designated Civil Judge, London County Court Group, 1998–2001; Senior Circuit Judge, 1998–2001; *b* 10 May 1933; *y* *s* of late Andrew Butter, MA, MD and late Ena Butter, MB, ChB; *m* 1974, Claire Marianne Miskin, LLM. *Educ*: The Leys Sch.; Queens' Coll., Cambridge (MA). Called to Bar, Inner Temple, 1955, Bencher, 1994; an Asst and Dep. Recorder of Bournemouth, 1971; Recorder of the Crown Court, 1972–82; a Judge of Bow County Court, 1986–94; occasional Judge of Employment Appeal Tribunal, 1995–98. Member: Senate of the Inns of Court and the Bar, 1976–79; County Court Rule Cttee, 1993–99; Clinical Disputes Forum, 1997–2001; Chm., Court Mediation Scheme Cttee, 1996–2001. Inspector, for Dept of Trade, Ozalid Gp Hldgs Ltd, 1977–79. A Legal Assessor to GMC and GDC, 1979–82; Mem., Mental Health Review Tribunal, 1983–92. Chm., London County Court Assoc. of Circuit Judges, 1998–2001. Trustee, Kingdon-Ward Speech Therapy Trust, 1980–87. *Publication*: Doctor George and other short stories, 2007. *Recreations*: writing for amusement, browsing through Who's Who. *Club*: Royal Over-Seas League.

BUTTER, Peter Joseph Michael, CB 1992; Deputy Managing Director, Property Services Agency, Building Management, Department of the Environment, 1992, retired; *b* 9 Dec. 1932; *s* of Joseph Butter and Kathleen (*née* Woodward); *m* 1956, Pamela Frances Roberts; three *s*. *Educ*: Brighton, Hove and Sussex Grammar School. Served Royal Signals, 1951–53. BR, 1953–67; Principal, Min. of Transport, 1967–73; Private Sec. to Minister of Transport, 1973; joined PSA, 1974: Hd, Defence Secretariat (Navy), 1974–79; Asst Dir, Estate Surveying Services, 1979–84; Dir, SE Region, 1984–88; Dir, Home Regional Services, 1988–90; Dir. of Ops, PSA, Bldg Management, DoE, 1990–91. Sec., Sussex Cricket League, 1999–. *Recreations*: cricket administration, listening to music, exploring Britain. *Address*: 6 Scarletts Close, Uckfield, E Sussex TN22 2BA. *Club*: Sussex CC.

BUTTERFIELD, Hon. Sir (Alexander) Neil (Logie), Kt 1995; **Hon. Mr Justice Butterfield**; a Judge of the High Court of Justice, Queen's Bench Division, since 1995. *Educ*: Sidney Sussex Coll., Cambridge (BA 1964). Called to the Bar, Inner Temple, 1965; a Recorder, 1978–95; QC 1985. Leader, 1992–95, Presiding Judge, 1997–2000, Western Circuit. Mem., Parole Bd, 2003– (Vice Chm., 2005–). *Address*: Royal Courts of Justice, Strand, WC2A 2LL. *Club*: Athenæum.

BUTTERFIELD, Ven. David John; Archdeacon of East Riding, since 2007; *b* 1 Jan. 1952; *s* of John Alfred Butterfield and Agnes Butterfield (*née* Winn); *m* 1977, Irene Mary Abel; two *s*. *Educ*: Belle Vue Boys' Grammar Sch., Bradford; Royal Holloway Coll., London Univ. (BMus 1973); Nottingham Univ. (DipTh 1975); St John's Theol Coll., Nottingham. Ordained deacon, 1977, priest, 1978; Curate, Christ Church, Southport, 1977–81; Minister, St Thomas, Aldridge, 1981–91; Vicar, St Michael's, Lilleshall, St John's, Muxton, and St Mary's, Sheriffhales, 1991–2007; Rural Dean, Edgmond and Shifnal, 1997–2006. Mem., Crown Appts Commn, 2003. Mem., Gen. Synod, C of E, 1990–2005 (Chair, House of Clergy, Dio. of Lichfield, 2003–06). *Publication*: Getting Going, 1987. *Recreations*: piano (particularly Mozart's piano concertos), organ, a little composing, walking, swimming, reading, making marmalade. *Address*: Brimley Lodge, 27 Molescroft Road, Beverley HU17 7DX. *T*: and *Fax*: (01482) 881659; *e-mail*: archdeacon.of.eastriding@yorkdiocese.org.

BUTTERFIELD, Jeremy Nicholas, PhD; FBA 1996; Senior Research Fellow, Trinity College, Cambridge, since 2006; *b* 23 Dec. 1954; *s* of Baron Butterfield, OBE, DM, FRCP and of Isobel-Ann Foster Butterfield (*née* Kennedy); *m* 1978, Sally Damon Snell (marr. diss. 2007); one *s* one *d*; *m* 2008, Mari Hirano. *Educ*: Trinity Coll., Cambridge (BA 1976; PhD 1984). Cambridge University: Asst Lectr in Philosophy, 1981–85; Lectr, 1985–97; Reader in Philosophy, 1997; Fellow of Jesus Coll., 1981–97; Sen. Res. Fellow, All Souls Coll., Oxford, 1998–2006. Vis. Prof., Princeton Univ., 1989, 2004. *Publications*: articles in learned jls. *Recreation*: the Muppets. *Address*: Trinity College, Cambridge CB2 1TQ. *T*: (01223) 338400.

BUTTERFIELD, (John) Michael; Chief Executive, National Association of Youth Clubs, 1975–86; *b* 2 July 1926; *s* of late John Leslie Butterfield and Hilda Mary Butterfield (*née* Judson); *m* 1955, Mary Maureen (*d* 1998), *d* of John Martin; one *s* twin *d* (and one *s* decd). *Educ*: Leeds Modern Sch.; Leeds Univ. John Butterfield & Son, Leeds, 1949–60; John Atkinson & Sons (Sowerby Bridge) Ltd, 1960–61. Youth Officer, Coventry Cathedral, 1961–68; Liverpool Council of Social Service: Head of Youth and Community Dept, 1968–72; Operations Dir, 1972–75. Mem., BCC, 1954–73 (Mem., 1952–68); Chm., Exec. Cttee, 1962–67, Youth Dept); Vice-Chairman: Nat. Council for Voluntary Youth Services, 1977–83; UK Adv. Cttee, SCF, 1990–93; Chairman: Leics Council of Voluntary Youth Services, 1985–98; Youthaid, 1986–90; Youth Club Leics, 1987–99; UK Grants Cttee, Charity Projects later Comic Relief, 1992–98; Voluntary Action Hinckley and Bosworth (formerly Hinckley and Bosworth CVS), 1997–2005; Dark Horse Venture, 2001–. Merseyside Advr, Baring Foundn, 1987–96; UK Rep., Amer. Youth Work Center, 1987–98. *Recreations*: music, reading, walking, railways. *Address*: 2 Church Farm Court, Aston Flamville, near Hinckley, Leics LE10 3AF. *T*: (01455) 611027.

BUTTERFIELD, Leslie Paul, CBE 2007; brand strategy consultant; Chief Strategy Officer, Interbrand Group, since 2008; *b* Reading, 31 Aug. 1952; *s* of Leslie John and Ruth Butterfield; *m* 1988, Judy Tombleson (separated 2002); partner, Penny Harris; one *d*. *Educ*: North East London Poly. (BA 1st. Cl. Hons Business Studies 1974); Lancaster Univ. (MA Mktg 1975). Account Planner, BMP/DDB, 1975–80; Planning Dir, AMV/BBDO, 1980–87; Planning Dir and Chm., Butterfield Day Devito Hockney, subseq. Partners BDDH, 1987–2001; CEO, Butterfield 8, 2001–03; Partner, Ingram, 2003–07; CEO, ButterfieldPartners, 2007–08. *Publications*: Excellence in Advertising, 1997, 2nd edn 1999; Understanding the Financial Value of Brands, 1998; Advalue, 2003; Enduring Passion: the story of the Mercedes-Benz brand, 2005. *Recreations*: cars, ski-ing, railway archaeology, my daughter Alexa. *Address*: The Moat House, Smewins Road, White Waltham, Berks SL6 3SR. *T*: (0118) 932 1894.

BUTTERFIELD, Stewart David; Managing Director, Broadcasting, Granada plc (formerly Granada UK Broadcasting), 1997–2002; *b* 10 Sept. 1947; *s* of Bernard and

Moray Butterfield. *Educ:* Mount St Mary's Coll., Spinkhill, Derbys; London Sch. of Econs (BSc Econ). McCann-Erickson, 1973–91, European Media Dir, 1989–91; Dir of Advertising Sales and Mktg, Channel Four, 1991–97. Trustee, VSO, 2002–. *Club:* Royal Automobile.

BUTTERFILL, Sir John (Valentine), Kt 2004; MP (C) Bournemouth West, since 1983; *b* 14 Feb. 1941; *s* of George Thomas Butterfill and Elsie Amelia (*née* Watts); *m* 1965, Pamela Ross-Symons; one *s* three *d. Educ:* Caterham Sch.; Coll. of Estate Management. FRICS 1974. Valuer, Jones, Lang, Wootton, 1961–64; Sen. Exec., Hammerson Gp, 1964–69; Dir, Audley Properties Ltd (Bovis Gp), 1969–71; Man. Dir, St Paul's Securities Gp, 1971–76; Sen. Partner, Curchod & Co., 1977–91, Consultant, 1992–. Chm., Conservation Investments, 1978–2002; Director: Micro Business Systems, 1977–79; John Lelliott Developments, 1984–88; ISLEF Building and Construction, 1984–91; Pavilion Services Gp, 1992–94; Delphi Gp, 1996–99. Pres., European Property Associates, 1979–2003. Parliamentary Private Secretary: to Sec. of State for Energy, 1988–89; to Sec. of State for Transport, 1989–90; to Minister of State for NI, 1991–92. Member: Trade and Industry Select Cttee, 1992–2001; Select Cttee on Unopposed Bills, 1995–. Vice-Chairman: Backbench Tourism Cttee, 1986–88; Backbench Finance Cttee, 1992–2000; Sec., Backbench Trade and Industry Cttee, 1987–88, and 1991; Chm., Backbench European Affairs Cttee, 1995–97. Member: Parly Ct of Referees, 1995–; Speaker's Panel of Chairmen, 1996–. Chm., All Party Parly Gp on Occupational Pensions, 1992–; Vice-Chairman: All Party Parly Gp on Bldg Socs and Financial Mutual Instns, 1997– (Sec., 1996); All Party Parly Gp on ELT, 2008–; Jt Sec., All Party Parly Gp on Insurance and Financial Services, 1997–. Chm., Parly Members' Fund, 1997–2002; Trustee, 1997–, Chm. of Trustees, 2001–, Parly Contributory Pension Fund. 1922 Committee: Sec., 1996–97; Vice Chm., 1997–2001, 2005–06; Treas., 2001–05. Vice Pres., Cons. Gp for Europe, 1992–95 (Chm., 1989–92); Vice-Chm., Parly Gp, Cons. Friends of Israel, 1995–. Mem., Council of Management, PDSA, 1990–; Chm. of Trustees, PDSA Pension Fund, 2002–07. *Publications:* occasional contribs to property, insurance and financial publications. *Recreations:* ski-ing, tennis, bridge, music. *Address:* House of Commons, SW1A 0AA.

BUTTERSS, Rt Rev. Robert Leopold; Bishop of the Eastern Region (Assistant Bishop of the Diocese of Melbourne), 1985–94; *b* 17 Jan. 1931; *s* of A. L. Butterss; *m* 1956, Margaret (*née* Hayman); two *s* one *d. Educ:* Haileybury; Brighton and Ridley Coll., Melbourne. Ordained: deacon, 1955; priest, 1956; Curate, St Andrew's, Brighton, 1955–56; Vicar, Holy Trinity, Lara, 1956–60; Priest in charge, Popondetta, PNG, 1960–64; Vicar: Holy Trinity, Pascoe Vale, 1964–66; St Stephen's, Mt Waverley, 1970–76; Canon, St Peter and St Paul's Cathedral, PNG, 1976–83; Dean, St John's Cathedral, Brisbane, 1983–85. Chm., Australian Bd of Missions, Sydney, 1976–83 (Victorian Sec., 1966–70). *Recreation:* music. *Address:* Dayspring, Stroud, NSW 2425, Australia.

BUTTERWORTH, Anthony; *see* Butterworth, C. A.

BUTTERWORTH, Anthony Edward, PhD; FRS 1994; MRC External Scientific Staff, 1979–95, retired; Hon. Scientific Director, Biomedical Research and Training Institute, Harare, 2001–06; *b* 8 July 1945; *s* of late Edward Alexander Butterworth and Sylvia (*née* Hardy); *m* 1st, 1972, Margot Lois Hudson (marr. diss. 1999); one *s* one *d*; 2nd, 2001, Elizabeth Lucy Corbett; one *s* one *d. Educ:* Harrow Sch.; Trinity Hall, Cambridge (BA); St Mary's Hosp. Med. Sch., London (MB, BChir); Clare Coll., Cambridge (PhD). Wellcome Trust Research Fellow: Nairobi, Kenya, 1973–77; Harvard Med. Sch., Boston, 1977–79; University of Cambridge: Associate Lectr, 1980–89; Hon. Reader, 1989–93; Hon. Prof. of Med. Parasitology, 1993–95. Hon. Prof., LSHTM, 2001–. Frederick Murgatroyd Prize, RCP, 1979; Bernhard Nocht Medal, 1987; King Faisal Internat. Prize in Medicine, 1990; Chalmers Medal, RSTM&H, 1990. *Publications:* papers and book chapters on immunology and parasitology.

BUTTERWORTH, Prof. Brian Lewis, PhD; FBA 2002; CPsychol, FBPsS; Professor of Cognitive Neuropsychology, University College London, since 1992; *b* 3 Jan. 1944; *s* of Henry Lewis Butterworth and Cicely Rebecca (*née* Haringman); partner, Diana Margaret Laurillard; two *d. Educ:* Quintin Sch., London; Merton Coll., Oxford (BA); Univ. of Sussex (MA); PhD London 1972. CPsychol 1990; FBPsS 1990. Jun. Res. Fellow, MRC Speech and Communication Unit, Edinburgh, 1971–72; Lectr in Psychol., Dept of Exptl Psychol., Univ. of Cambridge, 1972–80; Lectr in Psychol., 1980–86, Reader, 1986–92, Dept of Psychol., UCL. Hon. and pt-time posts at Univ. of Tennessee, MIT, Univ. of Padova, Univ. of Trieste, Max Planck Inst. for Psycholinguistics, Nijmegen; Sen. Vis. Res. Fellow, 2000–03, Professorial Fellow, 2003–, Melbourne Univ. Ed.-in-Chief, Linguistics, 1978–83; Co-founding Ed., Lang. and Cognitive Processes, 1983–; Founding Ed., Mathematical Cognition, 1983–2000. Co-ordinator, Mathematics and the Brain, 1999–2003, Numeracy and Brain Develt, 2004–, Eur. Network. (Jtly) Babble to Babel (installation in Millennium Dome), 2000. *Publications:* (ed) Language Production, Vol. 1 1980, Vol. 2 1983; (ed jtly) Explanations for Language Universals, 1983; The Mathematical Brain, 1999; (ed) Mathematical Cognition, 2000; Dyscalculia Screener, 2003 (British Educn & Teaching with Technology Award for educnl software, 2004); (with Dorian Yeo) Dyscalculia Guidance, 2004; contrib. numerous acad. papers on speech production, aphasia, gestures, dyslexia, mathematical cognition and dyscalculia. *Recreations:* family holidays, rock art, archaeology and anthropology of numbers. *Address:* Institute of Cognitive Neuroscience, University College London, 17 Queen Square, WC1N 3AR. *T:* (020) 7679 1150, *Fax:* (020) 7813 2835; *e-mail:* b.butterworth@ucl.ac.uk.

BUTTERWORTH, Prof. (Charles) Anthony, CBE 1996; PhD; FRCN; Joint Director, Centre for Clinical and Academic Workforce Innovation, University of Lincoln, since 2005; *b* 14 March 1947; *s* of Norman Butterworth and Anne Alison Butterworth; *m* 1971, Jacqueline; one *s* one *d. Educ:* Univ. of Aston, Birmingham (MSc; PhD 1986); Storthes Hall Hosp., Huddersfield (RMN); Manchester Royal Infirmary (RGN); Univ. of Manchester (RNT). Clinical nurse, Yorks and Gtr Manchester, 1968–75; Lectr, then Sen. Lectr, 1975–80, Principal Lectr and Hd of Nursing, 1980–86, Manchester Poly; University of Manchester: Prof. of Community Nursing, Queen's Nursing Inst., 1987–2001; Pro-Vice-Chancellor, 1999–2001; Vis. Prof., 2001–; Chief Exec., Trent NHS Workforce Develt Confedn, 2001–05. FRCN 1996; Founder FMedSci 1998. Hon. FRCPsych 1999. FRSA 1996. *Publications:* Community Psychiatric Nursing, 1980; Caring for the Mentally Ill in the Community, 1981; Clinical Supervision and Mentorship in Nursing, 1992, 2nd edn 1999. *Recreations:* gardening, walking, travel, motor-cycling. *Address:* CCAWI, 3rd Floor, MHAC Building, University of Lincoln, Brayford Pool, Lincoln LN6 7TS.

BUTTERWORTH, Prof. Ian, CBE 1984; FRS 1981; Senior Research Fellow, Imperial College, since 1991; Professor of Physics, University of London, 1971–91, now Emeritus; *b* 3 Dec. 1930; *s* of Harry and Beatrice Butterworth; *m* 1964, Mary Therese (*née* Gough); one *d. Educ:* Bolton County Grammar Sch.; Univ. of Manchester. BSc 1951; PhD 1954. Sen. Scientific Officer, UK Atomic Energy Authority, 1954–58; Lectr, Imperial Coll., 1958–64; Vis. Physicist, Lawrence Radiation Laboratory, Univ. of California, 1964–65; Sen. Lectr, Imperial Coll., 1965–68; Group Leader, Bubble Chamber Research Gp, Rutherford High Energy Laboratory, 1968–71; Professor, 1971–86, Head of Dept, 1980–83, Dept of Physics, Imperial Coll.; on leave of absence as Res. Dir, CERN, 1983–86; Principal, QMC, then QMW, 1986–91; Pro Vice-Chancellor for Eur. Affairs, London Univ., 1989–91. Science and Engineering Research Council (formerly Science Research Council): Mem., 1979–83 (Mem., Nuclear Physics Bd, 1972–75 and 1978–83, Chm., 1979–83; Mem., Particle Physics Cttee, 1978–79; Chm., Film Analysis Grants Cttee, 1972–75); UK deleg. on Council, CERN, 1979–82 (Mem., Research Bd, 1976–82; Chm., Super Proton Synchroton Cttee, 1976–79). Member: Physics Res. Cttee, Deutsches Elektronen Synchroton, Hamburg, 1981–85; Sci. Policy Cttee, Stanford Linear Accelerator Center, Calif, 1984–88; Sci. Adv. Cttee, British Council, 1986–91; Science Cttee, 2000–03, Natural Sci. Cttee, 2005–06, UK Nat. Commn for UNESCO; Physical Scis and Engrg Standing Cttee, ESF, 2000–06; IUPAP deleg. to Internat. Council for Scientific and Technical Inf., 1999–2006. Council Member: Royal Soc., 1989–90; Inst. of Physics, 1989–92 (Vice Pres., 1993–97; Chm., IOP Publishing Ltd, 1993–97); MAE 1989 (Vice Pres., 1997–2003). Hon. Mem., Manchester Lit. and Phil. Soc., 1987. Fellow, Imperial Coll., 1988. Dr *hc* Soka Univ., 1989. Glazebrook Prize and Medal, Inst. of Physics, 1993. *Publications:* numerous papers in learned jls (on experimental particle physics). *Recreations:* reading, history of art. *Address:* Blackett Laboratory, Imperial College, Prince Consort Road, SW7 2AZ; 1 Paramount Court, University Street, WC1E 6JP.

BUTTERWORTH, Nicholas John; writer and illustrator of children's books, since 1980; *b* 24 May 1946; *s* of George and Nancy Butterworth; *m* 1975, Annette Fancourt; one *s* one *d. Educ:* Royal Liberty Grammar Sch., Romford. Left sch., aged 16; compositor and typographic designer, Printing Dept, NCH, Harpenden, 1962–65; graphic designer: Frank Overton Associates, 1965–67; with Crosby Fletcher Forbes, for Cunard Line, Southampton, then freelance, 1967–68; formed Baxter Butterworth Cope, 1968; worked in various graphic partnerships, 1968–80, incl. partnership with Mick Inkpen in graphics, illustration and writing; started writing for children, 1981 and went solo, 1988. Presenter, Rub-a-dub-tub (children's prog.), TV AM, 1982–83. *Publications:* books include: B B Blacksheep and Company, 1981, repr. as Nick Butterworth's Book of Nursery Rhymes, 1990; (with Mick Inkpen) The Nativity Play, 1985; (with Mick Inkpen) Just Like Jasper, 1989; One Snowy Night, 1989; Amanda's Butterfly, 1991; After the Storm, 1992; (with Mick Inkpen) Jasper's Beanstalk, 1992; Making Faces, 1993; The Rescue Party, 1993; The Secret Path, 1994; All Together Now, 1995; A Year in Percy's Park, 1995; (illus.) Jake, 1995; The Hedgehog's Balloon, 1996; The Treasure Hunt, 1996; THUD!, 1997; Four Feathers in Percy's Park, 1998; Jingle Bells, 1998; Percy's Bumpy Ride, 1999; Q Pootle 5, 2000; Everyone's Friend Percy, 2001; Albert Le Blanc, 2002; Q Pootle 5 In Space!, 2003; The Whisperer, 2004; Tiger!, 2006; Tiger in the Snow, 2006. *Recreations:* ski-ing, squash, tennis, pottering in the shed, gardening, woodworking, travel, music - listening - and playing piano badly! *Address:* HarperCollins Publishers, 77–85 Fulham Palace Road, Hammersmith, W6 8JB.

BUTTLE, Eileen, CBE 1995; PhD; FIBiol; Member, Scientific Committee, European Environment Agency, 1994–2002; *b* 19 Oct. 1937; *d* of late George Ernest Linford and Mary Stewart Linford; *m* 1970, Hugh Langley Buttle. *Educ:* Harrow Weald County Grammar Sch.; Univ. of Southampton (BSc (Hons); PhD). FIBiol 1990. Post-doctoral Res. Fellow, Univ. of Southampton, 1963–65; Research Scientist: Nat. Inst. of Res. in Dairying, 1965–71; Cattle Breeding Centre, MAFF, 1971–76; Policy Administrator, MAFF, 1976–89; Sec., NERC, 1989–94; Dir, World Humanity Action Trust, 1994–97. Dir, Shell Transport and Trading Co. plc, 1998–2005. Trustee: Buckland Foundn, 1994–2002; Horniman Mus. of Gdns, 1994–98; Onyx Envmtl Trust, 1997–2002; Earthwatch Europe, 1997–2003. Mem., 1999–2006, Dep. Chm., 2002–06, Council, ICSTM; Gov., Macaulay Inst., 2001–05. *Recreations:* golf, fly fishing. *Club:* Farmers'.

BUTTRESS, Donald Reeve, LVO 1997; OBE 2008; FSA; architect; Partner, Buttress Fuller Alsop Williams, Manchester, since 1974; Surveyor of the Fabric of Westminster Abbey, 1988–99, now Surveyor Emeritus; *b* 27 April 1932; *s* of Edward Crossley Buttress and Evelyn Edna Reeve-Whaley; *m* 1956, Elsa Mary Bardsley; two *s* three *d. Educ:* Stockport Sch.; Univ. of Manchester (MA, DipArch). ARIBA. Flying Officer, RAF, 1958–61. Lectr, Manchester Univ., 1964–78; Vis. Prof. and Fulbright Travelling Scholar, Univ. of Florida, 1967–68. Architect to: Bangor and Sheffield Cathedrals, 1978–88; Leeds (RC) Cathedral, 1983–95; Llandaff Cathedral, 1986–97; Surveyor to the Fabric, Chichester Cathedral, 1984–2007. Principal works: Stockport SS Community Centre, 1973; extn, St Matthew, Hayfield, 1978; St George's Chapel, Sheffield Cathedral, 1981; rebldg, St Matthew, Westminster, 1982; repair of spire, All Souls, Halifax, 1984; repair of nave, choir, North and South transepts and West front, Chichester Cath., 1985–2003; reconstruction, Tonbridge Sch. Chapel, 1992–95; restoration of West front and Henry VII Chapel, Westminster Abbey, 1989–95; design of London Memorial to Queen Elizabeth the Queen Mother, 2007. Member: Cathedrals and Churches Adv. Cttee (formerly Churches Sub-Cttee, English Heritage), 1988–94; Council for the Care of Churches, 1976–86, 1991–96; Council, Royal Archaeological Inst., 1991–94; Chester DAC, 1970–88; St Albans DAC, 1998–. President: Ecclesiol Soc., 1995– (Vice Pres., 1992–95); Surveyors' Club, 1994–95; ASCHB, 2006–07; Baconian Club, 2006–07. Gov., Sutton's Hosp. in Charterhouse, 2001–. Master, Art Workers' Guild, 2000 (Brother, 1989). Mem., Editl Bd, Church Building magazine, 1982–. DLitt Lambeth, 2001. *Publications:* Manchester Buildings, 1967; Gawthorpe Hall (NT guide), 1971; articles in learned jls. *Recreations:* ecclesiology, 18th Century furniture, stained glass, heraldry. *Address:* 95 Fishpool Street, St Albans AL3 4RU. *T:* (01727) 810753. *Club:* Royal Air Force.

BUTTREY, Prof. Theodore Vern, PhD; FSA; Keeper, Department of Coins, Fitzwilliam Museum, Cambridge, 1988–91, now Keeper Emeritus; *b* 29 Dec. 1929; *s* of Theodore Vern Buttrey and Ruth Jeanette Scoutt; *m* 1st, 1954, Marisa Macina (marr. diss. 1967); three *s* one *d*; 2nd, 1967, Ann Elizabeth Johnston. *Educ:* Phillips Exeter Acad.; Princeton Univ. (BA 1950; PhD 1953). Instr, 1954–58, Asst Prof., 1958–64, Yale Univ.; University of Michigan: Associate Professor, 1964–67; Prof. of Greek and Latin, 1967–85; Prof. Emeritus, 1985–; Chm., Dept of Classical Studies, 1968–71, 1983–84; Dir, Kelsey Mus. of Archaeology, 1969–71. Member: Clare Hall, Cambridge, 1971–; Faculty of Classics, Cambridge Univ., 1975–. Pres., RNS, 1989–94; Sec., UK Numismatic Trust, 1994–98. Corresp. Mem., Royal Danish Acad. of Scis and Letters, 1995. Medal, RNS, 1985; Medal, Amer. Numismatic Soc., 1996. *Publications:* (jtly) Greek, Roman and Islamic Coins from Sardis, 1981; (jtly) Morgantina Studies: the coins, 1989; numerous publications in ancient and modern numismatics. *Recreations:* Ernest Bramah, P. G. Wodehouse, travel. *Address:* 6 de Freville Avenue, Cambridge CB4 1HR. *T:* (01223) 351156; *e-mail:* tvb1@cam.ac.uk.

BUXTON, family name of **Barons Buxton of Alsa** and **Noel-Buxton**.

BUXTON OF ALSA, Baron *cr* 1978 (Life Peer), of Stiffkey in the County of Norfolk; **Aubrey Leland Oakes Buxton,** KCVO 1996; MC 1943; DL; Director, Anglia Television, since 1958 (Chairman, 1986–88); *b* 15 July 1918; *s* of Leland Wilberforce Buxton and Mary, *d* of Rev. Thomas Henry Oakes; *m* 1st, 1946, Pamela Mary (*d* 1983), *d* of Sir Henry Birkin, 3rd Bt; two *s* four *d*; 2nd, 1988, Mrs Kathleen Peterson, Maine,

USA. *Educ:* Ampleforth; Trinity Coll., Cambridge. Served 1939–45, RA; combined ops in Arakan, 1942–45 (despatches, 1944). Extra Equerry to Duke of Edinburgh. A Trustee of the British Museum (Natural History), 1971–73. Member: Countryside Commn, 1968–72; Royal Commission on Environmental Pollution, 1970–74; Nature Conservancy Council, 1988–92; British Vice Pres., World Wildlife Fund; Trustee, Wildfowl Trust; Treasurer, London Zoological Soc., 1978–83; Former Pres., Royal Television Soc.; Chairman: Independent Television Cos Assoc., 1972–75; UPITN Inc., USA, 1981–83; ITN, 1981–86. Wildlife Film Producer, Anglia TV. Golden Awards, Internat. TV Festival, 1963 and 1968; Silver Medal, Zoological Society of London, 1967; Silver Medal, Royal TV Society, 1968; Queen's Award to Industry, 1974; Gold Medal, Royal TV Soc., 1977. High Sheriff of Essex 1972; DL Essex, 1975–85. *Publications:* (with Sir Philip Christison) The Birds of Arakan, 1946; The King in his Country, 1955. *Recreations:* travel, natural history, painting, sport. *Address:* Old Hall Farm, Stiffkey, Norfolk NR23 1QJ. *Club:* White's.

BUXTON, Adrian Clarence, CMG 1978; HM Diplomatic Service, retired; Ambassador to Bolivia, 1977–81, and to Ecuador, 1981–85; *b* 12 June 1925; *s* of Clarence Buxton and Dorothy (*née* Lintott); *m* 1st, 1958, Leonora Mary Cherkas (*d* 1984); three *s*; 2nd, 1985, June Samson. *Educ:* Christ's Hosp., Horsham; Trinity Coll., Cambridge (Exhibnr). RNVR, 1944–46; FO, 1947; Bangkok, 1948–52; FO, 1952–53; Khartoum, 1953–55; Bonn, 1955–58; Bogota, 1958–62; FO, 1962–64; Saigon, 1964–67; Havana, 1967–69; Geneva, 1969–73; sabbatical, Univ. of Surrey, 1973–74; FCO, 1974–77. *Recreations:* golf, choral singing. *Address:* 89 Glenferness Avenue, Bournemouth BH3 7ES.

BUXTON, Andrew Robert Fowell, CMG 2003; *b* 5 April 1939; *m* 1965, Jane Margery Grant; two *d.* *Educ:* Winchester Coll.; Pembroke Coll., Oxford. Joined Barclays Bank, 1963; Man. Dir, 1988–92; Chief Exec., 1992–93; Chm., 1993–99. Director: Capitaland Ltd, Singapore, 2003–07; Development Bank of Singapore, 2006–. Mem. Court, Bank of England, 1997–2001. Pres., British Bankers' Assoc., 1997–2002. Patron, Nat. Educn Business Partnership Network, 2005–. *Club:* Royal Automobile.

BUXTON, Sir Jocelyn (Charles Roden), 7th Bt *cr* 1840, of Belfield, Dorset; VRD 1975; *b* 8 Aug. 1924; *er s* of Captain Roden H. V. Buxton, CBE, RN (*d* 1970) and Dorothy Alina St John Buxton (*d* 1956); *S* cousin, 1996; *m* 1960, Ann Frances, *d* of late Frank Smitherman, MBE; three *d.* *Educ:* Eton. Served RNVR, 1942–45 (despatches); Korea, 1952. *Heir: b* Lieut-Comdr Gerard St John Roden Buxton, RN [*b* 28 Sept. 1927; *m* 1954, Judith Averil, *d* of Hon. Angus Campbell, CBE; one *s* two *d*]. *Address:* Rodwell House, Loddon, Norfolk.

BUXTON, Prof. John Noel, FBCS; CEng; Chairman, Room Underwriting Systems Ltd, 1993–97; Professor of Information Technology, King's College, London, 1984–94; *b* 25 Dec. 1933; *s* of John William Buxton and Laura Frances Buxton; *m* 1958, Moira Jean O'Brien; two *s* two *d.* *Educ:* Bradford Grammar Sch.; Trinity Coll., Cambridge (BA 1955, MA 1959). FBCS 1968. Flight Trials Engr, De Havilland Propellers, 1955–59; Ops Res. Scientist, British Iron and Steel Res. Assoc., 1959–60; Applied Science Rep., IBM UK, 1960–62; Lectr, Inst. of Computer Science, Univ. of London, 1962–66; Chief Software Consultant, CEIR (now Scicon Ltd) 1966–68; Prof. of Computer Science, Univ. of Warwick, 1968–84. UNDP Proj. Manager, Internat. Computing Educn Centre, Budapest, 1975–77; Vis. Scholar, Harvard Univ., 1979–80; Dir of Systems Engrg, DTI, 1989–91 (on secondment). Hon. Vice-Pres. (Engrg), BCS, 1997–2000. *Publications:* (ed) Simulation Programming Languages, 1968; (ed jtly) Software Engineering Concepts and Techniques (Procs of NATO Confs 1968 and 1969), 1976; (jtly) The Craft of Software Engineering, 1987; three computer programming languages; papers in professional jls. *Recreations:* mountaineering, music, ancient houses, genealogy, local history. *Address:* The Guildhall, Church Street, Eye, Suffolk IP23 7BD.

BUXTON, Hon. Margaret Evelyn; *see* Aston, M. E.

BUXTON, Prof. Neil Keith; Vice-Chancellor, University of Hertfordshire, 1992–2003; *b* 2 May 1940; *s* of William F. A. Buxton and Janet A. Buxton; *m* 1962, Margaret G. Buxton (*née* Miller); two *s* one *d.* *Educ:* Aberdeen Univ. (MA Hons Political Econs); PhD Heriot-Watt. Asst Lectr, Dept of Political Econ., Aberdeen Univ., 1962–64; Lectr, Dept of Econ., Univ. of Hull, 1964–69; Lectr and Sen. Lectr, 1969–78, Prof., 1979–83, Heriot-Watt Univ.; Depute Dir, Glasgow Coll. of Technology, 1983–87; Dir, Hatfield Poly., 1987–92. Vis. Prof. in Econs and Public Admin, Lewis and Clark Coll., Oregon, 1982. Dir, Herts TEC, 1989–2001; Member: Board: Herts Business Centre (Businesslink), 1993–; Herts Learning and Skills Council, 2001–; Herts Prosperity Forum, 1998–. *Publications:* (with T. L. Johnston and D. Mair) Structure and Growth of the Scottish Economy, 1971; (with D. I. Mackay) British Employment Statistics, 1977; Economic Development of the British Coal Industry, 1978; (ed) British Industry Between the Wars, 1979; articles in professional jls. *Recreations:* sport, bridge, overseas travel, pipe smoking. *Address:* c/o University of Hertfordshire, College Lane, Hatfield, Herts AL10 9AB. *T:* (01707) 284000.

BUXTON, Paul William Jex; Northern Ireland Office, 1974–85 (Under Secretary, 1981–85); *b* 20 Sept. 1925; *s* of of late Denis Buxton and Emily Buxton (*née* Hollins); *m* 1st, 1950, Katharine Hull (marr. diss. 1971, she *d* 1977); two *s* one *d*; 2nd, 1971, Hon. Margaret Evelyn Aston (*née* Bridges) (*see* M. E. Aston); one *d* (and one *d* decd). *Educ:* Rugby Sch.; Balliol Coll., Oxford (MA). Coldstream Guards, 1944–47. HM Foreign, later Diplomatic, Service, 1950–71; served Delhi, UN, Guatemala and Washington, latterly as Counsellor. Investment banking, 1972–74; on staff of Monopolies and Mergers Commn, 1985–91. Treasurer: Anti-Slavery International (formerly Anti-Slavery Soc.), 1986–2002; Howard League for Penal Reform, 1991–97 (Mem. Council, 1985–99); Hon. Treas., Prisoners' Advice Service, 1991–96. *Recreation:* forestry. *Address:* Castle House, Chipping Ongar, Essex CM5 9JT. *T:* (01277) 362642. *Club:* Brooks's.

BUXTON, Rt Hon. Sir Richard (Joseph), Kt 1994; PC 1997; a Lord Justice of Appeal, 1997–2008; *b* 13 July 1938; *o s* of late Bernard Buxton, DSO, chartered mechanical engineer, and Sybil (*née* Hurley), formerly of Burton-upon-Trent; *m* 1987, Mary Tyerman, JP, *y d* of late Donald Tyerman, CBE and Margaret Tyerman. *Educ:* Brighton Coll. (Schol.); Exeter Coll., Oxford (Schol.; First Cl. Final Hon. Sch. of Jurisprudence 1961, First Cl. BCL 1962; Vinerian Schol. 1962; MA; Hon. Fellow, 1998). FCIArb 1992. Lectr, Christ Church, 1962–63; Lectr 1963–64, Fellow and Tutor 1964–73, Sub-Rector 1966–71, Exeter Coll., Oxford. Called to the Bar, Inner Temple, 1969; Bencher, 1992; in practice, 1972–88; QC 1983; a Recorder, 1987–93; a Law Comr, 1989–93; a Judge of the High Court, QBD, 1994–97; a Judge, Restrictive Practices Court, 1994–97. Second Lieut RAOC, 1957–58. Councillor, Oxford CC, 1966–69. Chm. of Governors, Penton I and JM Sch., London N1, 1986–91. Hon. LLD Nottingham, 2000. Médaille de la Ville de Paris (échelon argent), 1999. *Publications:* Local Government, 1970, 2nd edn 1973; articles in legal periodicals. *Recreation:* baseball. *Address:* c/o Royal Courts of Justice, Strand, WC2A 2LL.

BUXTON, Richard William; Head of Economic Development, City of Reutlingen, Germany, since 2005; *b* 11 Oct. 1956; *s* of Rev. William, (Paddy), and Pamela Buxton; *m* 1993, Christiane Regine Topf; two *s.* *Educ:* Downing Coll., Cambridge (MA); Univ. of Westminster (MBA). Coopers & Lybrand, 1989–91; Asst Dir (Housing and Social Services), Bexley BC, 1991–93; Dir, Local Govt Consultancy, Capita plc, 1993–95; Dir of Housing, City of Westminster, 1995–98; Dir of Ops, Legal Services Commn, 1998–2001; Chief Exec., Nat. Lottery Charities Bd, then Community Fund, 2001–04. Mem., ESRC Res. Grants Bd, 2002. Trustee, Langley House Trust, 1996–2003. *Recreations:* my two young children, learning German, Star Trek. *Address:* Marktplatz 22, 72764 Stadt Reutlingen, Germany.

BUXTON, Ronald Carlile, MA Cantab; *b* 20 Aug. 1923; *s* of Murray Barclay Buxton and Janet Mary Muriel Carlile; *m* 1959, Phyllida Dorothy Roden Buxton; two *s* two *d.* *Educ:* Eton; Trinity Coll., Cambridge. Chartered Structural Engineer (FIStructE). Director of H. Young & Co., London and associated companies. MP (C) Leyton, 1965–66. *Recreations:* travel, music, riding. *Address:* The Garden Cottage, Kimberley Hall, Wymondham, Norfolk NR18 0RT; 67 Ashley Gardens, SW1P 1QG. *Club:* Carlton.

BUYERS, Thomas Bartlett, OBE 1975; HM Chief Inspector of Prisons for Scotland, 1985–89, retired; *b* 21 March 1926; *s* of Charles Stuart Buyers and Bessie Heywood Buyers; *m* 1951, Agnes Lodge Alexander; three *d.* *Educ:* Glasgow Acad., Glasgow; Glasgow Univ. (BSc); BA Open Univ. 1998. MIChemE. Res. Chemist, Shell, 1947–50; professional and management posts, BP Chemicals, Grangemouth and Baglan Bay, 1951–73; Dir, Scottish Petroleum Office, 1973–74; Dir of Engrg, Offshore Supplies Office, Dept of Energy, 1974–75; BP Rep./Commissioning Man., Sullom Voe Terminal, Shetland, 1975–80; Special Projects Man., BP Chemicals, London, 1980–84. *Recreations:* gardening, hill walking, voluntary work.

BUZAN, Prof. Barry, PhD; FBA 1998; AcSS 2001; Professor of International Relations, London School of Economics, since 2002; *b* 28 April 1946; *s* of Gordon and Jean Buzan; *m* 1973, Deborah Skinner. *Educ:* Univ. of British Columbia (BA Hons 1968); London Sch. of Econs (PhD 1973). Res. Fellow, Inst. of Internat. Relns, Univ. of BC, 1973–75; University of Warwick: Lectr, 1976–83, Sen. Lectr, 1983–88, Reader, 1988–90, Dept of Internat. Studies; Prof., Dept of Politics and Internat. Studies, 1990–95; Res. Prof. of Internat. Studies, Univ. of Westminster, 1995–2002. Vis. Prof., Internat. Univ. of Japan, 1993; Olof Palme Vis. Prof., Sweden, 1997–98. Dir, project on European security, Copenhagen Peace Res. Inst., 1988–2002. Chm., British Internat. Studies Assoc., 1988–90; Internat. Vice-Pres., Internat. Studies Assoc., 1993–94. Ed., European Jl of Internat. Relns, 2004–07 (Mem., Internat. Adv. Bd, 1994–99). Francis Deak Prize, Amer. Jl of Internat. Law, 1982. *Publications:* Seabed Politics, 1976; (ed with R. J. Barry Jones) Change and the Study of International Relations: the evaded dimension, 1981; People, States and Fear: the national security problem in international relations, 1983, 2nd edn as An Agenda for International Security Studies in the Post-Cold War Era, 1991, 2007; (jtly) South Asian Insecurity and the Great Powers, 1986; An Introduction to Strategic Studies: military technology and international relations, 1987; (ed) The International Politics of Deterrence, 1987; (jtly) The European Security Order Recast: scenarios for the post-cold war era, 1990; (jtly) The Logic of Anarchy: neorealism to structural realism, 1993; (jtly) Identity, Migration and the New Security Agenda in Europe, 1993; (with T. Buzan) The Mind Map Book, 1993; (jtly) Security: a new framework for analysis, 1998; (with G. Segal) Anticipating the Future: twenty millennia of human progress, 1998; (with E. Herring) The Arms Dynamic in World Politics, 1998; (with R. Little) International Systems in World History: remaking the study of international relations, 2000; (with Ole Wæver) Regions and Powers, 2003; From International to World Society?, 2004; The United States and the Great Powers: world politics in the twenty-first century, 2004; contrib. numerous articles in learned jls incl. Survival, American Jl Internat. Law, Jl Peace Res., Internat. Orgn, Internat. Affairs, Rev. Internat. Studies, Internat. Pol Sci. Rev. and World Policy Jl. *Recreations:* chess, motorcycle touring, gardening. *Address:* Garden Flat, 17 Lambolle Road, NW3 4HS. *T:* (020) 7433 1431.

BUZEK, Dr Jerzy Karol; Member (European People's Party Group), European Parliament, since 2004; *b* 3 July 1940; *s* of Paweł Buzek and Bronisława Szczuka; *m* 1974, Ludgarda; one *d.* *Educ:* Silesian Poly.; Dr Tech. Scis Polish Acad. of Scis. Chemical Engineering Institute, Polish Academy of Sciences: scientific res.; Dir for Scientific Affairs, 1963–97; Lecturer: Silesian Technical Univ., 1975–80; Technical Univ., Opole, 1993–97; Researcher and Pro-Rector, Polonia Univ., Częstochowa, 2002. Prime Minister of Poland, 1997–2001. Chm., Cttee of European Integration, 1998. Mem., Solidarity, 1980–97: Chm., 1st, 4th, 5th and 6th Nat. Congress; Chm., Econ. Sub-Cttee, Election Cttee. Dr *hc*: Seoul, 1999; Dortmund, 2000; Isparta 2006. Golden Cross of Commitment (Poland), 1989. *Publications:* books, patents, numerous sci. articles, papers and speeches. *Recreations:* poetry, theatre, horse riding, tennis, sailing, canoeing. *Address:* European Parliament, Bâtiment Altiero Spinelli, 05F243, 60 rue Wiertz, 1047 Brussels, Belgium; *e-mail:* jbuzek@europarl.eu.int.

BUZZARD, Sir Anthony (Farquhar), 3rd Bt *cr* 1929; Lecturer in Theology, Atlanta Bible (formerly Oregon Bible) College, since 1982; *b* 28 June 1935; *s* of Rear-Admiral Sir Anthony Wass Buzzard, 2nd Bt, CB, DSO, OBE, and Margaret Elfreda (*d* 1989), *d* of Sir Arthur Knapp, KCIE, CSI, CBE; *S* father, 1972; *m* 1970, Barbara Jean Arnold, Mendon, Michigan, USA; three *d.* *Educ:* Charterhouse; Christ Church, Oxford (MA 1960); Ambassador Coll., Pasadena, USA (BA); MA Th Bethany Theol Seminary, 1990. ARCM. Lecturer in French, Ambassador Coll., Pasadena, 1962–65; Peripatetic Music Teacher for Surrey County Council, 1966–68; Lectr in French and Hebrew, Ambassador Coll., Bricket Wood, Herts, 1969–74; teacher of mod. langs, American Sch. in London, 1974–81. Founded Restoration Fellowship, 1981. *Publications:* The Coming Kingdom of the Messiah: a Solution to the Riddle of the New Testament, 1988; The Doctrine of the Trinity: Christianity's Self-Inflicted Wound, 1994; Our Fathers who Aren't in Heaven: the forgotten Christianity of Jesus the Jew, 1995; The Amazing Aims and Claims of Jesus: what you didn't learn in Church, 2006; Jesus was Not a Trinitarian: a call for a return to the creed of Jesus, 2007; articles on eschatology and Christology in various jls. *Recreations:* tennis, music. *Heir: b* Timothy Macdonnell Buzzard [*b* 28 Jan. 1939; *m* 1970, Jennifer Mary, *d* of late Peter Patching; one *s* one *d*]. *Address:* (home) 175 West Lake Drive, Fayetteville, GA 30214, USA. *T:* (770) 9641571; (office) Box 100,000, Morrow, GA 30260, USA. *T:* (404) 3620052.

BYAM SHAW, Nicholas Glencairn; Deputy Chairman, Macmillan Ltd, 1998–99 (Chairman, 1990–97); *b* 28 March 1934; *s* of Lieut. Comdr David Byam Shaw, RN, OBE (killed in action, 19 Dec. 1941) and Clarita Pamela Clarke; *m* 1st, 1956, Joan Elliott; two *s* one *d*; 2nd, 1974, Suzanne Filer (*née* Rastello); 3rd, 1987, Constance Wilson (*née* Clarke). *Educ:* Royal Naval Coll., Dartmouth. Commnd RN, 1955 (Lieut). Joined William Collins Sons & Co. Ltd, Glasgow, as salesman, 1956; Sales Manager, 1960; Macmillan and Co., subseq. Macmillan Publishers Ltd: Sales Manager, 1964; Sales Dir, 1965; Dep. Man. Dir, 1967; Man. Dir, 1969–90. Director: St Martins Press, 1980–99 (Dep. Chm., 1997–99); Pan Books, 1983–99 (Chm., 1986–99); Gruppe Georg von Holtzbrinck, Stuttgart,

1996–99. *Recreations:* gardening, travel. *Address:* 9 Kensington Park Gardens, W11 3HB. *T:* (020) 7221 4547.

BYATT, Antonia; *see* Byatt, H. A.

BYATT, Dame Antonia (Susan), (Dame Antonia Duffy), DBE 1999 (CBE 1990); FRSL 1983; writer; *b* 24 Aug. 1936; *d* of His Honour John Frederick Drabble, QC and late Kathleen Marie Bloor; *m* 1st, 1959, Ian Charles Rayner Byatt (*see* Sir I. C. R. Byatt) (marr. diss. 1969); one *d* (one *s* decd); 2nd, 1969, Peter John Duffy; two *d*. *Educ:* Sheffield High Sch.; The Mount Sch., York; Newnham Coll., Cambridge (BA Hons; Hon. Fellow 1999); Bryn Mawr Coll., Pa, USA; Somerville Coll., Oxford. Extra-Mural Lectr, Univ. of London, 1962–71; Lectr in Literature, Central Sch. of Art and Design, 1965–69; Lectr in English, 1972–81, Sen. Lectr, 1981–83, UCL (Hon. Fellow, 2004). Associate of Newnham Coll., Cambridge, 1977–82. Member: Social Effects of Television Adv. Gp, BBC, 1974–77; Bd of Communications and Cultural Studies, CNAA, 1978–84; Bd of Creative and Performing Arts, CNAA, 1985–87; Kingman Cttee on English Language, 1987–88; Management Cttee, Soc. of Authors, 1984–88 (Dep. Chm., 1986; Chm., 1986–88); Bd, British Council, 1993–98 (Mem., Literature Adv. Panel, 1990–98). Mem. Cttee, London Liby, 1989–92. Broadcaster, reviewer; judge of literary prizes (Hawthornden, Booker, David Higham, Betty Trask). FRSL. Hon. Fellow, London Inst., 2000. Hon. DLitt: Bradford, 1987; Durham, 1991; Nottingham, 1992; Liverpool, 1993; Portsmouth, 1994; London, 1995; Sheffield, 2000; Kent, 2004; Oxford, 2007; Winchester, 2007; Hon. LittD Cambridge, 1999; DUniv York, 1991; Hon. Dr Parma, 2007. Premio Malaparte, Capri, 1995; Shakespeare Prize, Hamburg, 2002. Chevalier de l'Ordre des Arts et des Lettres (France), 2003. *Publications:* Shadow of the Sun, 1964; Degrees of Freedom, 1965 (reprinted as Degrees of Freedom: the early novels of Iris Murdoch, 1994); The Game, 1967; Wordsworth and Coleridge in their Time, 1970 (reprinted as Unruly Times: Wordsworth and Coleridge in their Time, 1989); Iris Murdoch, 1976; The Virgin in the Garden, 1978; (ed) George Eliot, The Mill on the Floss, 1979; Still Life, 1985 (PEN/Macmillan Silver Pen of Fiction, 1986); Sugar and Other Stories, 1987; (ed) George Eliot: selected essays, 1989; Possession: a romance, 1990 (Booker Prize, 1990; Irish Times/Aer Lingus Internat. Fiction Prize, 1990; Eurasian section of Best Book in Commonwealth Prize, 1991) (filmed 2002); (ed) Robert Browning's Dramatic Monologues, 1990; Passions of the Mind (essays), 1991; Angels and Insects (novellae), 1992 (filmed, 1996); The Matisse Stories (short stories), 1993; The Djinn in the Nightingale's Eye: five fairy stories, 1994 (Mythopoeic Fantasy Award for Adult Lit., 1998); (jtly) Imagining Characters, 1995; (ed jtly) New Writing 4, 1995; Babel Tower, 1996; (ed jtly) New Writing 6, 1997; (ed) The Oxford Book of English Short Stories, 1998; Elementals: stories of fire and ice (short stories), 1998; The Biographer's Tale, 2000; On Histories and Stories (essays), 2000; Portraits in Fiction, 2001; (jtly) The Bird Hand Book, 2001; A Whistling Woman (novel), 2002; Little Black Book of Stories, 2003; (ed jtly) Memory: an anthology, 2008. *Address:* c/o Rogers, Coleridge & White Ltd, 20 Powis Mews, W11 1JN.

See also H. A. Byatt.

BYATT, Deirdre Anne, (Lady Byatt); *see* Kelly, D. A.

BYATT, (Helen) Antonia; Director, Literature Strategy, Arts Council England, since 2007; *b* 13 April 1960; *d* of Sir Ian Charles Rayner Byatt, *qv* and Dame Antonia Susan Byatt, *qv*; partner, Sampson Patrick Lincoln Collyns; one *s* two *d*. *Educ:* Mayfield Comprehensive Sch.; Putney High Sch.; Selwyn Coll., Cambridge (BA Hons). Gen. Sec., Fawcett Soc., 1987–88; Literature Officer, Arts Council of England, 1988–93; Hd of Literature, South Bank Centre, 1993–2000; Dir, The Women's Liby, London Metropolitan Univ., 2000–07. Mem., Children's Laureate Cttee, 2001. Bd Mem., Bishopsgate Inst., 2004–. Gov., Dog Kennel Hill Primary Sch., 2004–. *Publication:* (ed) The Chatto Book of Love Stories, 1993. *Recreations:* my family, swimming, walking. *Address:* Arts Council England, 14 Great Peter Street, SW1P 3NQ.

BYATT, Sir Hugh Campbell, KCVO 1985; CMG 1979; HM Diplomatic Service, retired; Director, EFM Japan Trust PLC, 1992–97; Chairman: EFM Java Trust, 1990–98; EFM Dragon Trust, 1992–98 (Director, 1987–98); *b* 27 Aug. 1927; *e s* of late Sir Horace Byatt, GCMG, and Lady Byatt (*née* Olga Margaret Campbell), MBE; *m* 1954, Fiona, *d* of Ian P. Coats, DL, and May Coats, MBE; two *s* one *d*. *Educ:* Gordonstoun; New College, Oxford (MA 1951). Served in Royal Navy, 1945–48 (Sub-Lieut RNVR); HMOCS Nigeria, 1952–57; Commonwealth Relations Office, 1958; Bombay, 1961–63; CRO, 1964–65; seconded to Cabinet Office, 1965–67; Head of Chancery, Lisbon, 1967–70; Asst Head, South Asian Dept, FCO, 1970–71; Consul-General, Mozambique, 1971–73; Inspector, HM Diplomatic Service, 1973–75; RCDS, 1976; Dep. High Comr, Nairobi, 1977–78; Ambassador to Angola, 1978–81, to São Tomé, 1980–81, to Portugal, 1981–86. Advr, RTZ, 1986–96; Special Advr, Scottish Financial Enterprise, 1986–92. Mem., Parole Bd for Scotland, 1990–92. Chm., Cttee for Scotland, Malcolm Sargent Cancer Fund for Children, 1991–96. Chm. of Govs, Centre for Inf. on Lang. Teaching and Res., 1986–90. FSAScot 1989. Hon. Sheriff, Campbeltown, 1994. Knight Grand Cross, Mil. Order of Christ (Portugal), 1985. *Recreation:* living in Argyll. *Address:* Leargnahension, Tarbert, Argyll PA29 6YB. *T:* (01880) 820644. *Clubs:* Royal Ocean Racing; New (Edinburgh); Royal Highland Yacht (Oban).

See also R. A. C. Byatt.

BYATT, Sir Ian (Charles Rayner), Kt 2000; Chairman, Water Industry Commission for Scotland, since 2005; Senior Associate, Frontier Economics, since 2001; Director General of Water Services, 1989–2000; *b* 11 March 1932; *s* of Charles Rayner Byatt and Enid Marjorie Annie Byatt (*née* Howat); *m* 1st, 1959, A. S. Byatt (*see* Dame A. S. Byatt) (marr. diss. 1969); one *d* (one *s* decd); 2nd, 1997, Prof. Deirdre Anne Kelly, *qv*; two step *s*. *Educ:* Kirkham Grammar Sch.; Oxford University. Commonwealth Fund Fellow, Harvard, 1957–58; Lectr in Economics, Durham Univ., 1958–62; Economic Consultant, HM Treasury, 1962–64; Lectr in Economics, LSE, 1964–67; Sen. Economic Adviser, Dept of Educn and Science, 1967–69; Dir of Econs and Stats, Min. of Housing and Local Govt, 1969–70; Dir Economics, DoE, 1970–72; Under Sec., 1972–78, Dep. Chief Econ. Advr, 1978–89, HM Treasury. Chm., Economic Policy Cttee of the European Communities, 1982–85 (Mem., 1978–89); Member: Central Council of Educn (England), 1965–66; Economics Cttee, CNAA, 1968–70; Urban Motorways Cttee, 1970; Cttee on Water Services: Econ. and Financial Objectives, 1970–73; ESRC, 1983–89; Public Services Productivity Panel, HM Treasury, 2000–02; Chief Sec.'s Adv. Panel on Better Public Services, 2002–06; Adv. Panel, Water Industry Comr for Scotland, 2002–04; Panel of Experts on Water Reforms in NI, 2003–06. Chm., Adv. Cttee to HM Treasury on Accounting for Econ. Costs and Changing Prices, 1986; Member: Bd, Public Finance Foundn, 1984–89; Bd of Mgt, Internat. Inst. of Public Finance, 1987–90, 2000–06; Council of Mgt, NIESR, 1996–2002; Council, Regulatory Policy Inst., 2001–. Member: Council, REconS, 1983–92 (Mem. Exec. Cttee, 1987–89); Governing Body, Birkbeck Coll., 1997–2005 (Chm., F and GP Cttee, 2001–05; Fellow, 2005); Bd of Advisors, St Edmund Hall, 1998–2003; Bd, Acad. of Youth, 2001–05; Council, Birmingham Cathedral, 2003–. Hon. Prof., Birmingham Univ., 2003–. President: Econs and Business Educn Assoc., 1998–2001; Human City Inst., 1999–2002; Vice-Pres., Strategic Planning Soc., 1993–; Co-Sec.-Gen., Foundn for Internat. Studies in Social Security, 2000–02. Treas., 1988–2002, Patron, 2006–, Holy Cross Centre Trust. Chm., Friends of Birmingham Cathedral, 1999–. CCMI (CIMgt 1993). Hon. Fellow, St Edmund Hall, 2007. DUniv: Brunel, 1994; Central England, 2000; Hon. DSc: Aston, 2005; Birmingham, 2007. *Publications:* The British Electrical Industry 1875–1914, 1979; Delivering Better Services for Citizens, 2001; (with Sir Michael Lyons) Role of External Review in Improving Performance, 2001; articles on economics in books and learned jls; official reports. *Recreations:* painting, family life. *Address:* Water Industry Commission for Scotland, Ochil House, Springkerse Business Park, Stirling FK7 7XE. *T:* (01786) 430200, *Fax:* (01786) 462018; *e-mail:* ian.byatt@watercommission.co.uk; Frontier Economics, 71 High Holborn, WC1V 6DA. *T:* (020) 7031 7067, *Fax:* (020) 7031 7001; *e-mail:* ian.byatt@frontier-economics.com; 34 Frederick Road, Birmingham B15 1JN. *T:* (0121) 689 7946, *Fax:* (0121) 454 6438; 17 Thanet Street, WC1H 9QL. *T:* (020) 7388 3888; *e-mail:* ianbyatt@blueyonder.co.uk. *Club:* Oxford and Cambridge.

See also H. A. Byatt.

BYATT, Ronald Archer Campbell, (Robin), CMG 1980; HM Diplomatic Service, retired; High Commissioner in New Zealand and concurrently to Western Samoa, and Governor (non-resident), Pitcairn Islands, 1987–90; *b* 14 Nov. 1930; *s* of late Sir Horace Byatt, GCMG and late Olga Margaret Campbell, MBE; *m* 1954, Ann Brereton Sharpe, *d* of C. B. Sharpe; one *s* one *d*. *Educ:* Gordonstoun; New Coll., Oxford; King's Coll., Cambridge. Served in RNVR, 1949–50. Colonial Admin. Service, Nyasaland, 1955–58; joined HM Foreign (now Diplomatic) Service, 1959; FO, 1959; Havana, 1961; FO, 1963; UK Mission to UN, NY, 1966; Kampala, 1970; Head of Rhodesia Dept, FCO, 1972–75; Vis. Fellow, Glasgow Univ., 1975–76; Counsellor and Head of Chancery, UK Mission to UN, NY, 1977–79; Asst Under Sec. of State, FCO, 1979–80; High Comr in Zimbabwe, 1980–83; Mem., Directing Staff, RCDS, 1983–84; Ambassador to Morocco, 1985–87. CSSB Panel Chm., 1992–95. Mem., HGTAC, 1993–98 (Chm., Envmt Sub-Cttee, 1993–98). Trustee: Beit Trust, 1987–; UK Antarctic Heritage Trust, 1992–2001. Alaouite Order, 1st cl. (Morocco), 1987. *Recreations:* sailing, gardening, watching and painting birds. *Address:* Drim-na-Vullin, Lochgilphead, Argyll PA31 8LE. *Club:* Oxford and Cambridge.

See also Sir H. C. Byatt.

BYCROFT, Prof. Barrie (Walsham), PhD; CChem, FRSC; Professor of Pharmaceutical Chemistry, University of Nottingham, 1979–2003, Emeritus Professor, 2004 (Head, Department of Pharmaceutical Sciences and School of Pharmacy, 1985–89 and 1995–2000); *b* 26 Jan. 1939; *s* of Henry Thomas Bycroft and Cissie Bycroft; *m* 1962, Jean Skinner (separated); one *s* one *d*. *Educ:* Univ. of Nottingham (BSc Chem.; PhD 1963). CChem 1982; FRSC 1982. NATO Fellow, Univ. of Zurich, 1963–65; University of Nottingham: Lectr, then Reader, Dept of Chemistry, 1965–79; Pro-Vice Chancellor (Research), 1990–94; Dean, Grad. Sch., 1994–96. Vis. Prof., Med. Sch., Federal Univ., Rio de Janeiro, 1973. Mem., Food Adv. Cttee, MAFF, 1988–92. Non-exec. Mem., Nottingham HA, 1990–94. Biotechnology and Biological Sciences Research Council: Mem., Sci. and Engrg Bd, 1993–96; Chm., Postgrad. Trng Award Panel, 1994–2000. Vice-Chm., UK Council for Grad. Educn, 1993–96. Hon. MPharmS 1990. *Publications:* numerous contribs to learned jls. *Recreations:* tennis, golf, good food and wine, travel. *Address:* 14 The Cloisters, Beeston, Nottingham NG9 2FR. *T:* (0115) 925 9415.

BYE, Christopher Harwood; Editor, Yorkshire Evening Post, 1987–98; Director, Yorkshire Post Newspapers Ltd, 1987–98; *b* 6 Feb. 1952; *s* of John Harwood Bye and Joan Alice (*née* Cushing). *Educ:* Tadcaster Grammar Sch.; Univ. of Leeds (Cert. Creative Writing 2005). News Editor, Yorkshire Post, 1980–82; Editor, Yorkshire Post Colour Magazine, 1981–83; Dep. Editor, Yorkshire Post, 1982–87. British Press award for investigative journalism, 1986. *Recreations:* classical music, antiques, wine, food, travel, walking, sport.

BYE, Ruby; *see* Wax, R.

BYERS, Hon. Charles William; His Honour Judge Byers; a Circuit Judge, since 1999; Resident Judge, Woolwich Crown Court, since 2007; *b* 24 March 1949; *o s* of Baron Byers, PC, OBE and Joan Elizabeth Byers (*née* Oliver); *m* 1972, Suzan Mary Stone (marr. diss. 1995); two *s*; *m* 2002, Mary Louise Elizabeth Ilett. *Educ:* Westminster Sch.; Christ Church, Oxford. Called to the Bar, Gray's Inn, 1973; Recorder, 1993–99. Dep. Chm., Gray's Inn Continuing Education Cttee, 1997–98; Mem., Adv. Panel, Coll. of Law, 1996–. Gov., Hurstpierpoint Coll., 1993–2003. *Recreations:* gardening, agriculture, sport, aquatics, acquiring practical skills. *Address:* Woolwich Crown Court, 2 Belmarsh Road, SRE28 0EY. *Club:* National Liberal.

BYERS, Dr Paul Duncan; Reader Emeritus in Morbid Anatomy, University of London; Head of Department of Morbid Anatomy, Institute of Orthopaedics, University of London, 1980–87, retired (Dean of Institute, 1971–79); *b* Montreal, 3 July 1922; *s* of A. F. Byers and Marion Taber; *m* 1959, Valery Garden (*d* 1999); *m* 1999, M. E. A. Brown. *Educ:* Bishops College Sch., PQ, Canada; McGill Univ. (BSc, MD, CM); Univ. of London (DCP, PhD). FRCPath. Alan Blair Memorial Fellow, Canadian Cancer Soc., 1955–57. Asst Morbid Anatomist, Inst. of Orthopaedics, 1960; Reader in Morbid Anatomy, Univ. of London, 1974. Hon. Consultant, Royal National Orthopaedic Hosp., 1965; Hon. Senior Lectr, Royal Postgrad. Med. Sch., 1969. Chm., Osteosarcoma Histopathol. Panel, MRC/EORTC, 1983–86; Member: Osteosarcoma Wkg Party, MRC, 1982–86; Soft Tissue Sarcoma Wkg Party, MRC, 1983–84. Mem., Management Cttee, Courtauld Inst. of Art, Univ. of London, 1979–82. *Publications:* (jtly) Diseases of Bones and Joints, 1994; articles in medical press on arthritis, metabolic bone disease, bone tumours, medical education. *Recreation:* arts. *Address:* 2 Manorside, Barnet, Herts EN5 2LD. *T:* (020) 8440 3376.

BYERS, Rt Hon. Stephen (John); PC 1998; MP (Lab) Tyneside North, since 1997 (Wallsend, 1992–97); *b* Wolverhampton, 13 April 1953; *s* of late Robert Byers. *Educ:* Chester City Grammar Sch.; Chester Coll. of Further Educn; Liverpool Polytechnic (LLB). Sen. Lectr in Law, Newcastle Polytechnic, 1977–92. Mem. (Lab) North Tyneside MBC, 1980–92 (Dep. Leader, 1985–92; Chm. Educn Cttee, 1982–85). Contested (Lab) Hexham, 1983. An Opposition Whip, 1994–95; frontbench spokesman on educn and employment, 1995–97; Minister of State, DfEE, 1997–98; Chief Sec. to HM Treasury, 1998; Sec. of State for Trade and Industry, 1998–2001; Sec. of State for Transport, Local Govt and the Regions, 2001–02. Mem., Select Cttee on Home Affairs, 1994. Chm., PLP Home Affairs Cttee, 1992–94. Leader, Council of Local Educn Authorities, 1990–92; Chairman: Nat. Employers' Orgn for Teachers, 1990–92; Educn Cttee, AMA, 1990–92; Mem., BTEC, 1985–89. FRSA 1991. *Address:* House of Commons, SW1A 0AA. *T:* (020) 7219 4085.

BYFORD, family name of **Baroness Byford**.

BYFORD, Baroness *cr* 1996 (Life Peer), of Rothley in the county of Leicestershire; **Hazel Byford,** DBE 1994; *b* 14 Jan. 1941; *d* of Sir Cyril Osborne, MP and Lady Osborne; *m* 1962, C. Barrie Byford, CBE; one *d* (one *s* decd). *Educ:* St Leonard's Sch., St Andrews; Moulton Agricl Coll., Northampton. WRVS Leics, 1961–93, County Organiser, 1972–76. House of Lords: an Opposition Whip, 1997–98; Opposition spokesman: on agriculture and rural affairs, 1998–2001; on envmt, 1998–2003; on food, farming and rural affairs, 2001–07. Chm., Nat. Cttee, Conservative Women, 1990–93; Vice Pres., 1993–96, Pres., 1996–97, Nat. Union of Cons. and Unionist Assocs. Member: Transport Users' Consultative Cttee, 1989–94; Rail Users' Consultative Cttee, 1994–95. President: Nat. Farm Attractions Network, 2002–08; Concordia, 2004–; Guild of Agricl Journalists, 2004–07; Pres., Leics Clubs for Young People, 2005–. Patron: Village Retail Services Assoc., 1998–2004; Inst. of Agricl Secs and Adminrs, 2000; Rural Stress Inf. Network, 2001–06; Women's Food and Farming Union, 2007–. Mem., Ct, Univ. of Leicester, 2002–08; Pres., St Leonard's Sch., St Andrews, 2003–. Hon. Canon, Leicester Cathedral, 2003–. Associate Mem., RASE, 2003. *Recreations:* golf, bridge, reading. *Club:* Farmers'.

BYFORD, Sir Lawrence, Kt 1984; CBE 1979; QPM 1973; DL; HM Chief Inspector of Constabulary, 1983–87; *b* 10 Aug. 1925; *s* of George Byford and Monica Irene Byford; *m* 1950, Muriel Campbell Massey; two *s* one *d*. *Educ:* Univ. of Leeds (LLB Hons). Served Royal Signals Special Commns Unit, 1944–45: in France, Belgium and Germany, SHAEF and on secondment to G2 Sect., US Army. Barrister-at-Law. Joined W Riding Police, 1947; served on Directing Staff of Wakefield Detective Sch., 1959–62, and Police Staff Coll., Bramshill, 1964–66; Divl Comdr, Huddersfield, 1966–68; Asst Chief Constable of Lincs, 1968, Dep. Chief Constable 1970, Chief Constable, 1973–77; HM Inspector of Constabulary for: SE Region, 1977–78; NE Region, 1978–82. Lecture tour of univs, USA and Canada, 1976; Headed: British Police Mission to Turkey, 1978–79; official review into Yorkshire Ripper case, 1981. DL: Lincs, 1987; N Yorks, 1998. Hon. LLD Leeds, 1987. *Recreations:* cricket, Pennine walking and travel. *Clubs:* Royal Over-Seas League (Chm., 1989–92, Vice-Pres., 1992–), MCC; Yorks County Cricket (Hon. Life Mem.; Chm., 1991–98; Pres., 1991–2000).

See also M. J. Byford.

BYFORD, Mark Julian; Deputy Director-General, BBC, and Head of BBC Journalism, since 2004; *b* 13 June 1958; *s* of Sir Lawrence Byford, *qv*; *m* 1980, Hilary Bleiker; two *s* three *d*. *Educ:* Lincoln Sch.; Univ. of Leeds (LLB 1979). BBC Television: Look North, Leeds, 1979–82; producer, South Today and Inquiry, Southampton, 1982–87; editor, Points West, Bristol, 1987–88; Home Editor, BBC News and Current Affairs, 1988–89; Head of Centre, Leeds, 1989–90; Asst Controller, 1991, Controller, 1991–94, Dep. Man. Dir, 1995–96, Dir, 1996–98, BBC Regl Broadcasting; Director: BBC World Service, 1998–2001; BBC World Service and Global News, 2002–04. Director: BARB, 1993–96; Radio Joint Audience Research Ltd, 1993–96. Trustee, BBC Children in Need Appeal, 1993–96. Fellow, Radio Acad., 2000. DUniv Winchester, 2006; Hon. LLD Leeds, 2008. *Recreations:* family, rock music, going to live gigs, football (Leeds United and Southampton), cricket, travel, the seaside, cathedrals, fell-walking, swimming. *Address:* Bolberry House, 1 Clifton Hill, Winchester, Hants SO22 5BL. *T:* (01962) 860197, *Fax:* (01962) 856873; BBC Media Centre, 201 Wood Lane, W12 7TQ. *T:* (020) 8008 5900, *Fax:* (020) 8008 5906; *e-mail:* mark.byford@bbc.co.uk. *Club:* Yorkshire County Cricket.

BYGRAVES, Max Walter, OBE 1983; entertainer; *b* 16 Oct. 1922; *s* of Henry and Lilian Bygraves, Rotherhithe, SE16; *m* 1942, Gladys Blossom Murray; one *s* two *d*. *Educ:* St Joseph's, Rotherhithe. Began in advertising agency, carrying copy to Fleet Street, 1936. Volunteered for RAF, 1940; served 5 years as fitter. Performed many shows for troops; became professional, 1946; has appeared in venues all over English-speaking world, incl. 19 Royal Command Performances; best selling record artist (31 Gold Discs). Host, Family Fortunes, TV, 1983–85. Freeman, City of London, 1994. *Publications:* I Wanna Tell You a Story (autobiog.), 1976; The Milkman's on his Way (novel), 1977; After Thoughts (autobiog.), 1988; I Wanna Tell You a Funny Story, 1992; In His Own Words (autobiog.), 1997; The Golden Years, 2004. *Recreations:* golf, painting, reading, writing. *Address:* c/o Johnny Mans Productions Ltd, PO Box 196, Hoddesdon, Herts EN10 7WG. *T:* (01992) 470907, *Fax:* (01992) 470516; *e-mail:* real@legend.co.uk. *Clubs:* St James's, East India.

BYLES, Timothy John, CBE 2006; Chief Executive, Partnerships for Schools, since 2006; *b* 7 Dec. 1958; *s* of Charles Humphrey Gilbert Byles and Pamela Beatrice Byles; *m* 1985, Shirley Elizabeth Rowland; three *s*. *Educ:* Univ. of Kent (BA Hons); Mid Kent Coll. of Further Educn (DMS London). British Gas, 1980–84: mgt trainee; Marketing Dept; Corporate Planning; English Tourist Board, 1984–88: Manager, Mgt Services, 1984–85; Asst Dir of Develt, 1985–88; Dir of Economic Develt, Kent CC, 1988–96; Chief Exec., Norfolk CC, 1996–2006. *Recreations:* music, swimming, church. *Address:* Partnerships for Schools, Fifth Floor, 8–10 Great George Street, SW1P 3AE.

BYNG, family name of **Earl of Strafford,** and of **Viscount Torrington**.

BYNG, Hon. James Edmund; Publisher, since 1994, and Managing Director, since 2006, Canongate Books Ltd; *b* 27 June 1969; *s* of 8th Earl of Strafford, *qv*; *m* 1st, 1994, Whitney Osborn McVeigh (marr. diss. 2004); one *s* one *d*; 2nd, 2005, Elizabeth Sheinkman. *Educ:* Winchester Coll.; Edinburgh Univ. (BA). FRSA. *Recreations:* cooking, deejaying, reading, tennis. *Address:* Canongate Books Ltd, 14 High Street, Edinburgh EH1 1TE. *T:* (0131) 524 9345, *Fax:* (0131) 557 5211; *e-mail:* jamie@canongate.co.uk. *Clubs:* Black's, Groucho, Union.

See also Viscount Enfield.

BYNOE, Dame Hilda Louisa, DBE 1969; in General Medical Practice, Port of Spain, Trinidad, 1974–89, retired; *b* Grenada, 18 Nov. 1921; *d* of late Thomas Joseph Gibbs, CBE, JP, Estate Proprietor, and Louisa Gibbs (*née* La Touche); *m* 1947, Peter Cecil Alexander Bynoe, ARIBA, Dip. Arch., former RAF Flying Officer; two *s*. *Educ:* St Joseph's Convent, St George's, Grenada; Royal Free Hospital Medical Sch., Univ. of London. MB, BS (London), 1951, MRCS, LRCP, 1951. Teacher, St Joseph's Convents, Trinidad and Grenada, 1939–44; hospital and private practice, London, 1951–53; public service with Govt of Trinidad and Tobago, 1954–55, with Govt of Guyana (then British Guiana), 1955–58, with Govt of Trinidad and Tobago, 1958–65; private practice, Trinidad, 1961–68; Governor of Associated State of Grenada, WI, 1968–74. Mem., Academic Bd, Sch. of Medicine, St George's Univ., Grenada. Mem. YWCA. Patron: Caribbean Women's Assoc., 1970–; John Hayes Meml Kidney Foundn, 1979–; Music Foundn of Trinidad and Tobago, 1986–; African Assoc. of Trinidad and Tobago. *Publication:* I Woke at Dawn, 1996. *Recreations:* swimming, music, reading, poetry-writing. *Club:* Soroptimist (Port of Spain).

BYNUM, Prof. William Frederick, MD; PhD; FRCP, FRCPE; Professor of History of Medicine, University College London, 1992–2003, now Professor Emeritus; *b* 20 May 1943; *s* of Raymond Tapley Bynum and Mary Catherine Adamson Bynum; *m* 1st, 1966, Annetta Boyett (marr. diss.); one *s*; 2nd, 2000, Dr Helen Joy Power. *Educ:* Swarthmore Coll. (BA 1964); Yale Univ. (MD 1969); King's Coll., Cambridge (PhD 1974). FRCP 1996; FRCPE 2000. Lectr, 1973–85, Reader, 1985–92, UCL; Hd, Jt Wellcome Inst./UCL Unit for Hist. of Medicine, 1973–96. Visiting Professor: Univ. of Minnesota, 1975; Union Coll., 1977; Johns Hopkins Univ., 1990, 1996. Co-Ed., Medical Hist., 1980–2002. *Publications:* Dictionary of the History of Science, 1981 (trans. Italian, Spanish and Chinese); Science and the Practice of Medicine in the Nineteenth Century, 1994 (trans. Chinese); Companion Encyclopedia of the History of Medicine, 2 vols, 1993; The Beast in the Mosquito: the correspondence of Ronald Ross and Patrick Manson, 1998; (ed with Roy Porter) Oxford Dictionary of Scientific Quotations, 2005; (ed with Helen Bynum) Dictionary of Medical Biography, 5 vols, 2007. *Recreations:* theatre, gardening, duck-keeping. *Address:* Wellcome Trust Centre for the History of Medicine at University College London, 183 Euston Road, NW1 2BE. *T:* (020) 7679 8164, *Fax:* (020) 7679 8194; *e-mail:* w.bynum@ucl.ac.uk. *Club:* MCC.

BYRAM-WIGFIELD, Timothy, FRCO; Director of Music, St George's Chapel, Windsor, since 2004; *b* 15 Sept. 1963; *s* of David and Morwen Byram-Wigfield. *Educ:* Oundle Sch. (Music Schol.); Royal Coll. of Music; Christ Church, Oxford (Organ Schol.; BA Hons). FRCO 1986. Chorister, King's Coll., Cambridge, 1972–76; Sub-organist, Winchester Cathedral, 1985–91; Master of the Music, St Mary's Episcopal Cathedral, Edinburgh, 1991–99; Dir of Music, Jesus Coll., Cambridge, 1999–2003. Has made numerous recordings. *Recreations:* cooking, gardening, keep fit (swimming, gym, running), reading. *Address:* 5 The Cloister, Windsor Castle, Windsor, Berks SL4 1NJ. *T:* (01753) 848747; *e-mail:* tim.byram-wigfield@stgeorges-windsor.org.

BYRNE, Colin; Chief Executive Officer, Weber Shandwick, UK and Ireland, since 2000; *b* 25 Feb. 1957; *s* of late Anthony Byrne and of Catherine Byrne; *m* (marr. diss.); one *s* one *d*. *Educ:* Kingston Polytech. (BA Hons English). Chief Press Officer, Labour Party, 1986–91; Communications Dir, Prince of Wales Business Leaders Forum, 1991–95; Man. Dir, Public Affairs, Shandwick, 1996–2000. *Recreations:* art, music, cooking, literature. *Address:* Weber Shandwick, Fox Court, 14 Gray's Inn Road, WC1X 8WS; *e-mail:* cbyrne@webershandwick.com.

BYRNE, Colin David; Regional Director, Government Office for the South East, since 2008; *b* 11 June 1957; *s* of Liam and Theresa Byrne; *m* 1986, Dr Mary Morrison; four *d*. *Educ:* Univ. of Edinburgh (BSc Hons Envmtl Chem.); Univ. of Pennsylvania. SO, MAFF, 1979–85; Department of the Environment, 1985–91: SSO, 1985–87; Nat. Expert, EC, 1988–91; Grade 6, DETR, 1991–97; Hd of Div., HSE, 1997–2000; Dir for Hampshire and IoW, Govt Office for South East, 2000–06; Dir, Town and Country Planning, 2006–07, Home Information Pack Implementation, 2007, DCLG. *Recreations:* walking, gardening, opera. *Address:* Government Office for the South East, Bridge House, 1 Walnut Tree Close, Guildford, Surrey GU1 4GA; *e-mail:* colin.byrne@gose.gsi.gov.uk.

BYRNE, David; Senior Counsel, European and International Law, Wilmer Cutler Pickering Hale and Dorr LLP, 2005; *b* 26 April 1947; *m* 1972, Geraldine Fortune; two *s* one *d*. *Educ:* University Coll. Dublin (BA; Hon. LLD). FCIArb 1998. Called to the Bar, King's Inns, Dublin, 1970; called to Inner Bar, 1985; Attorney General, Ireland, 1997–99; Mem., EC, 1999–2004. Member: Govt Review Body on Social Welfare Law, 1989; Constitution Review Gp, 1995–96. Member: Nat. Cttee, ICC, 1988–97; ICC Internat. Court of Arbitration, Paris, 1990–97. Special Envoy, WHO, 2004–05. Ext. Examr for arbitration and competition law, King's Inns, 1995–97. Adjunct Prof. of Law, UCD, 2005–06. Chancellor, Dublin City Univ., 2006–. Member: Bar Council, 1974–87 (Hon. Treas., 1982–83); Barristers' Professional Practices and Ethics Cttee, 1995–97. Non-exec. Director: Irish Life and Permanent Gp; Kingspan Gp. Hon. FRCPI 2000; Hon. FRCP. *Address:* (office) Pathwell Ltd, Park Lodge, 36 Booterstown Avenue, Blackrock, Co. Dublin. Ireland.

BYRNE, Dorothy; Head of News and Current Affairs, Channel 4 Television, since 2004; *d* of Charles and Agnes Byrne; one *d*. *Educ:* Manchester Univ. (BA Hons Philosophy); Sheffield Univ. (Dip. Business). Producer, World in Action, 1987–94; Ed., The Big Story, 1996–98; Commng Ed., Current Affairs, Channel 4 TV, 1998–2003. Vis. Prof., Sch. of Journalism, Lincoln Univ., 2005–. *Recreation:* being angry. *Address:* Channel 4 Television, 124 Horseferry Road, SW1P 2TX. *T:* (020) 7306 8664, *Fax:* (020) 7306 8359; *e-mail:* dbyrne@channel.4.co.uk.

BYRNE, Douglas Norman; Head of Marine Directorate, Department of Transport (formerly Marine Division, Department of Trade), 1980–84; *b* 30 Jan. 1924; *s* of Leonard William Byrne and Clarice Evelyn Byrne; *m* 1949, Noreen Thurlby Giles; one *s* one *d*. *Educ:* Portsmouth Grammar Sch.; St John's Coll., Cambridge (MA). RAF, 1942–46. Asst Principal, Min. of Supply, 1949; BoT, 1956; Cabinet Office, 1961–64; Asst Sec., 1964; on staff of Monopolies Commn, 1966–68; Under-Sec., Dept of Industry, 1974–77; Hd of Fair Trading Div., Dept of Prices and Consumer Protection, 1977–79; Under-Sec., Dept of Trade, 1979–83, Dept of Transport, 1983–84. *Recreations:* hill walking, natural history.

BYRNE, Prof. Edward, AO 2006; MD, DSc; FRACP, FRCPE; Executive Dean, Faculty of Biomedical Sciences, Head, Royal Free and University College Medical School, and Vice Provost, Health, University College London, since 2007; *b* 15 Feb. 1952; *s* of Henry Byrne and Marion Byrne (*née* Davis); *m* 1975, Melissa Elisabeth Youl; three *s* one *d*. *Educ:* Univ. of Tasmania (MB BS 1st Cl. Hons 1974; MD 1982); Univ. of Melbourne (DSc 1995); Univ. of Queensland (MBA 2005). FRACP 1980; FRCPE 1998. Hd of Neurol., St Vincent's Hosp., Melbourne, 1983–2000; University of Melbourne: Prof. of Neurol., 1992–2000; Prof. of Exptl Neurol. and Dir, Centre for Neurosci., 2000–03; Dean, Faculty of Medicine, Nursing and Health Scis, Monash Univ., 2003–07. Ed., Internal Medicine Jl, 1999–2005. *Publications:* over 200 articles on neuromuscular and metabolic disorders. *Recreation:* fly fishing. *Address:* Royal Free and University College Medical School, University College London, Gower Street, WC1E 6BT. *Clubs:* Athenæum; Melbourne.

BYRNE, John Anthony; teacher, lecturer and writer; Director of Ballet and Dance, Sydney Church of England Co-educational Grammar School (Redlands), 1997–2005; *b* Sydney, Australia, 14 Dec. 1945; *s* of Reginald Thomas Byrne and Mary Ida (*née* Sinclair). *Educ:* Scully-Borovansky Sch. of Ballet, Sydney; Univ. of Sydney (BA); Polytechnic of Central London (Dip. Arts Admin 1977); Royal Acad. of Dancing (ARAD; Dip. PDTC 1979; FRAD 2002). Professional dancer with various companies in ballet, opera-ballet and musicals, Australia, NZ, Germany, UK and Hong Kong, 1970–76; teaching dance in Australia, 1979–90; Royal Academy of Dance (formerly Dancing): Vocational Examr, 1987–; Tutor, Sydney and London HQ, 1990–91; Artistic Dir and Chm., Bd of Examrs, 1991–93. *Publications:* (jtly) Body Basics, 1992; Classical syllabus for boys, 1992; contrib. articles on dance criticism, etc to Dance Australia Mag., 1981–90. *Recreations:* walking, reading, gardens.

BYRNE, John Keyes; *see* Leonard, Hugh.

BYRNE, Rev. Canon John Victor; Vicar, All Saints', Branksome Park, since 2006; Chaplain to the Queen, since 2003; *b* 14 Nov. 1947; *s* of Frederick Albert Victor Byrne and Joan Blumer Byrne (*née* Robin); *m* 1970, Gillian Waveney Bannard-Smith; one *s* two *d*. *Educ:* John Lyon Sch., Harrow; St John's Coll., Nottingham (LTh 1973). FCA 1979. Chartered Accountant, Nevill, Hovey, Gardner & Co., London, 1965–70; ordained deacon, 1973, priest, 1974; Curate: St Mark's, Gillingham, 1973–76; St Luke's, Cranham Park, 1976–80; Vicar: St Mary's, Balderstone, Rochdale, 1980–87; St Jude's, Southsea, 1987–2006; Priest-in-charge, St Peter's, Southsea, 1995–2003. Hon. Canon, Portsmouth Cathedral, 1997–2006, now Canon Emeritus; Rural Dean of Portsmouth, 2001–06. Portsmouth Diocesan Stewardship Advr, 1994–97; Archbishops' Pastoral Advr, 1999–. *Recreations:* photography, reading, walking, arts, music. *Address:* 28 Western Road, Poole, Dorset BH13 7BP.

BYRNE, Lavinia; writer; *b* 10 March 1947; *d* of Basil James Byrne and (Edith Marion) Josephe Byrne. *Educ:* St Mary's Convent, Shaftesbury; Queen Mary College, London (BA Modern Langs); Hughes Hall, Cambridge (PGCE). Entered Inst. of Blessed Virgin Mary, 1964, resigned 2000; Tutor, Westcott House, Cambridge, 1997–2003. Associate Sec., CCBI, 1990–95. Co-Editor, The Way, 1985–90; internet columnist, The Tablet, 1999–2006; reporter, The Wells Jl, 2002–04. Hon. DD Birmingham, 1997. *Publications:* Women Before God, 1988; Sharing the Vision, 1989; (ed) The Hidden Tradition, 1990; (ed) The Hidden Journey, 1992; (ed) The Hidden Voice, 1994; Woman at the Altar, 1995; A Time to Receive, 1997; (ed) The Daily Service, 1997; The Dome of Heaven, 1999; The Journey is My Home, 2000; (ed) Pause for Thought, 2002; (ed) More Pause for Thought, 2004. *Recreations:* computers, cookery. *Address:* 38 South Street, Wells, Som BA5 1SL. *T:* (01749) 676117.

BYRNE, Rt Hon. Liam Dominic; PC 2008; MP (Lab) Birmingham, Hodge Hill, since July 2004; Chancellor of the Duchy of Lancaster and Minister for the Cabinet Office, since 2008; *b* 2 Oct. 1970; *s* of Dermot and Ruth Byrne; *m* 1998, Sarah; two *s* one *d*. *Educ:* Manchester Univ. (BA Hons); Harvard Business Sch. (Fulbright Schol.; MBA). Leader, Manchester Univ. Students' Union, 1992–93; Sen. Business Analyst, Strategic Services, Andersen Consulting, 1993–96; Advr on Reinventing Govt, then Dir, Business Liaison, Office of the Leader of the Labour Party, 1996–97; Exec., N. M. Rothschild & Sons Ltd, 1997–99; Co-Founder, EGS Gp Ltd, 2000–04. Associate Fellow, Social Market Foundn, 2001–05. Parly Under-Sec. of State, DoH, 2005–06; Minister of State, Home Office, 2006–08; Minister for the W Midlands, 2007–08. *Publications:* Local Government Transformed, 1996; Information Age Government, 1998; Cities of Enterprise: new strategies for full employment, 2002; Britain in 2020, 2003; Reinventing Government Again, 2004; contribs to Parly Affairs and Progress mag. *Recreation:* spending time with family. *Address:* House of Commons, SW1A 0AA. *T:* (020) 7219 3000.

BYRNE, Michael David; His Honour Judge Byrne; a Circuit Judge, since 2002; *b* 7 Dec. 1945; *s* of Gerard Robert Byrne and Margaret Doreen Byrne; *m* 1985, Felicity Jane Davies. *Educ:* St Edward's Coll., Liverpool; Liverpool Univ. (BA, LLB). Called to the Bar, Gray's Inn, 1971; in practice on Northern Circuit, 1971–2002; Asst Recorder, 1989–92; Recorder, 1992–2002. Mem., Lancs and Cumbria Courts Bd, 2007–. Chm., Managers Adv. Cttee, Ashworth Special Hosp., 1989–98 (non-exec. Dir, 1996–97); Vice-Chm., Ashworth SHA 1997–98. Legal Mem., Restricted Patients Panel, Mental Health Review Tribunal, 2006–. Gov., St Edward's Coll., Liverpool, 1993– (Chm. Govs, 1995–2004). KHS 2006. *Recreations:* music, literature, theatre, travel. *Address:* Preston Law Courts, Openshaw Place, The Ring Way, Preston PR1 2LL.

BYRNE, Rev. Father Paul Laurence, OMI; OBE 1976; Oblate Mission Procurator, since 2004; *b* 8 Aug. 1932; *s* of late John Byrne and Lavinia Byrne. *Educ:* Synge Street Christian Brothers' Sch. and Belcamp Coll., Dublin; University Coll., Dublin (BA, Hons Phil.); Oblate Coll., Piltown. Ordained, 1958. Teacher, Belcamp Coll., 1959–65; Dean of Belcamp Coll., 1961–65; Dir, Irish Centre, Birmingham, 1965–68; Dir, Catholic Housing Aid Soc. (Birmingham) and Family Housing Assoc., Birmingham, 1965–69; Nat. Dir, Catholic Housing Aid Soc., and Dir, Family Housing Assoc., London, 1969–70; Dir, SHAC (a housing aid centre), 1969–76; Sec. Gen., Conf. of Major Religious Superiors of Ire., 1980–87; Provincial Superior, Anglo-Irish Prov. of Missionary OMI, 1988–94; Dir, Irish Episcopal Commn for Emigrants, 1995–2004 (Bd Mem., 2004–). Bd Mem., Threshold Centre; Servite Houses; Housing Corp., 1974–77. Pres., St Stephen's Green Trust (Chm., 1994); Chm., Bd of Govs, Belcamp Coll., 2004–. Trustee, London Irish Centre, 2002–. Hon. Mem., Inst. of Housing, 1972. *Recreations:* golf, theatre-going. *Address:* House of Retreat, Tyrconnell Road, Inchicore, Dublin 8, Ireland; *e-mail:* procureomi@eircom.net. *Club:* Foxrock Golf.

BYRNE, Rosemary; Member for Scotland South, Scottish Parliament, 2003–07 (Scot Socialist, 2003–06, Solidarity, 2006–07); Co-Convenor, Solidarity (Scotland), since 2006. A principal teacher, Ardrossan Acad. Sec., Irvine and N Ayrshire Trades Union Council. Scot Socialist spokesman for educn and young people, Scottish Parlt, 2003–07. Contested (Scot Socialist) Cunninghame South, 2001. *Address:* Solidarity, PO Box 7565, Glasgow G42 2DN.

BYRNE, Terence Niall; HM Diplomatic Service, retired; Clerk/Adviser, House of Commons European Scrutiny Committee, 2002; *b* 28 April 1942; *e s* of late Denis Patrick Byrne and of Kathleen Byrne (*née* Carley); *m* 1st, 1966, Andrea Dennison (marr. diss. 1977); one *s* one *d*; 2nd, 1981, Susan Haddow Neill; two *d*. *Educ:* Finchley Catholic Grammar Sch.; Open Univ. (BA Hons). Min. of Housing and Local Govt, 1964–68; Prime Minister's Office, 1968–70; MAFF, 1971–78 (Private Sec. to Parly Sec., MAFF, 1974–75); First Sec. (Agriculture), The Hague, 1978–82; Commonwealth Co-ordination Dept, FCO, 1982–84; Asst Head, UN Dept, FCO, 1984–85; Head of Chancery and Consul, Quito, 1986–89; Counsellor and Dep. High Comr, Lusaka, 1990–93; Dir of Trade Promotion, Canberra, 1993–94; Dep. High Comr, Kuala Lumpur, 1994–98; Consul-Gen. and Dir of Trade Promotion, Auckland, 1999–2002. *Recreations:* running, golf, cinema. *Address:* (office) 7 Millbank, SW1P 3JA.

BYRNE, Terrance Dennis, CB 2003; a Commissioner, 1999–2004, and Director General, Law Enforcement, 2002–04, HM Customs and Excise; *b* 26 Nov. 1944; *s* of Thomas Edward Byrne and Sybil Elizabeth Byrne; *m* 1966, Pamela Ashley; one *s* one *d*. *Educ:* Downham Market Grammar Sch., Norfolk. Joined Civil Service, 1962; HM Customs and Excise, 1964–2004: specialist investigator, 1971–84; Mgt Consultant, 1984–88; Dep. Chief Investigation Officer, 1988–91; Head, Customs Enforcement Policy, 1991–99; Dir, Fraud and Intelligence, then Law Enforcement, 1999–2000. *Recreations:* horticulture, sport (mainly golf), reading.

BYRNE, Timothy Russell, FCA; Chairman: E-Travelmoney Ltd, 2005; Andrew Sumners Associates Ltd, 2005; Partner, Management Alliance LLP, 2004; *b* 16 March 1959; *s* of late Russell Vincent Byrne and of Barbara Ann Byrne; *m* 1986, Caroline Margaret Lander; three *d*. *Educ:* Stanney High Sch. FCA 1994. With Lowndes McLintock, 1980–84; Accountancy Tuition Centre, 1984–85; Granada TV Div., 1985–92; Airtours plc, subseq. Mytravel Group, 1993–2002: Group Financial Controller, 1993–97; Group Finance Dir, 1997–99; Group Chief Exec., 1999–2002. *Recreations:* country pursuits. *T:* (0161) 427 1797.

BYROM, Peter Craig, OBE 1987; self-employed textile consultant, since 1985; non-executive Director, Parry Murray & Co. Ltd, since 1992; *b* 4 Dec. 1927; *s* of Robert Hunter Byrom, Master Cotton Spinner and Winifred Agnes Byrom (*née* Goodwin); *m* 1st, 1952, Norma Frances Mawdesley Harris (marr. diss. 1984); three *s* three *d*; 2nd, 1984, Gillian Elizabeth Hoyte. *Educ:* Virginia Episcopal Sch., Lynchburg, USA; St Edward's Sch., Oxford; Univ. of Liverpool, Sch. of Architecture; Salford Royal Tech. Coll.; Admin. Staff Coll., Henley; Open Univ. (BA). CText; FTI 1986. RNVR, 1945–48. Asst Gen. Manager, Robert Byrom (Stalybridge), cotton spinners, 1951–59; Merchandising Manager, British Nylon Spinners, 1959–64; Marketing Manager and Adv. and Promotions Manager, ICI Fibres, 1964–71; Dir, Deryck Healey Internat., 1972–74; Man. Dir, Dartington Hall Tweeds, 1975–85. Lay Inspector of Schs, OFSTED, 1993–98. Consultant to: ODA, Nepal, 1980; Intermediate Tech. Gp, India, 1986; Chm., British Colour Council, 1971–73; Mem., Textile and Fashion Bd, CNAA, 1974–77; Chm. Council, RCA, 1981–86 (Mem., 1973–86; Sen. Fellow, 1983); Mem. Council, Textile Inst., 1986–96 (Service Medal, 1992); External Assessor, Manchester Metropolitan Univ., 1992–95. Governor: Dartington Coll. of Arts, 1979–89; Loughborough Coll. of Art and Design, 1993–98 (Vice-Chm., Govs, 1996–98). FRSA 1970 (Mem. Council, 1987–93; Mem. Design Bd, 1986–91; Chm., Textiles, Young Designers into Industry, 1985–90). Hon. Treas., Woodland PCC, 1995–. *Publications:* Textiles: product design and marketing, 1987; (foreword) Fancy Yarns: their manufacture and application, 2002; contrib. to Young Designers into the Textile Industry. *Recreations:* walking, swimming, theatre, music, books. *Address:* Barton House, Woodland, Ashburton, Devon TQ13 7LN. *T:* (01364) 653926.

BYRON, family name of **Baron Byron**.

BYRON, 13th Baron *cr* 1643, of Rochdale, Co. Lancaster; **Robert James Byron;** Partner, Holman Fenwick & Willan, since 1984; *b* 5 April 1950; *o* surv. *s* of 12th Baron Byron, DSO and Dorigen Margaret (*d* 1985), *o d* of Percival Kennedy Esdaile; *S* father, 1989; *m* 1979, Robyn Margaret, *d* of John McLean, Hamilton, NZ; one *s* three *d*. *Educ:* Wellington Coll.; Trinity Coll., Cambridge (MA). Called to the Bar, Inner Temple, 1974; admitted solicitor, 1978. *Heir:* *s* Hon. Charles Richard Gordon Byron, *b* 28 July 1990. *Address:* Marlow House, Lloyds Avenue, EC3N 3AL.

BYRON, Rt Hon. Sir (Charles Michael) Dennis, Kt 2000; PC 2005; Judge, since 2004, and President, since 2007, International Criminal Tribunal for Rwanda; *b* 4 July 1943; *s* of late Vincent Fitzgerald Byron, MBE and Pearl Eulalie Byron (*nee* O'Loughlin); *m* 1966, Monika Botfeldt (marr. diss.); four *s*; *m* Norma Theobalds. *Educ:* Fitzwilliam Coll., Cambridge (MA, LLB 1966). Called to the Bar, Inner Temple, 1965, Bencher, 2003; barrister-at-law, W Indies (Leeward Is), 1966–82; Eastern Caribbean Supreme Court: High Ct Judge, 1982–90; Justice of Appeal, 1990–96; Actg Chief Justice, 1996–99; Chief Justice, 1999–2008 (on leave of absence, 2004–08). Pres., Commonwealth Judicial Educn Inst., 1999–. *Recreations:* tennis, golf. *Address:* Arusha International Conference Centre, PO Box 6016, Arusha, Tanzania; *e-mail:* byrond@un.org.

BYRT, His Honour (Henry) John; QC 1976; a Circuit Judge, 1983–99; *b* 5 March 1929; *s* of Dorothy Muriel Byrt and Albert Henry Byrt, CBE; *m* 1957, Eve Hermione Bartlett; one *s* two *d*. *Educ:* Charterhouse; Merton Coll., Oxford (BA, MA). Called to the Bar, Middle Temple, 1953; called within the Bar, 1976; a Recorder of the Crown Court, 1976–83. First Pres., Social Security Appeal Tribunals and Medical Appeal Tribunals, 1983–90. Judge, Mayors and City of London Court, 1990–99 (Sen. Judge, 1994–99). Vice-Principal, Working Men's Coll., London, 1978–82, Principal, 1982–87; Mem. Council, Queen's Coll., London, 1982–99. Trustee, Cotswold Community Trust, 2003–. Patron, Jedidiah Foundn, 2005–. Freeman, City of London, 1999. *Recreations:* building, gardening, travel, music. *Address:* 13 Springalls Wharf, 25 Bermondsey Wall West, SE16 4TL. *T:* (020) 7740 1358. *Club:* Leander.

BYWATER, Air Cdre David Llewellyn, FRAeS; aviation consultant; Commandant, Aeroplane and Armament Experimental Establishment, Boscombe Down, 1988–92; *b* 16 July 1937; *s* of Stanley and Gertrude Bywater; *m* 1960, Shelagh May Gowling; one *s* one *d*. *Educ:* Liverpool Inst. High Sch.; RAF Coll., Cranwell. No XV Sqdn, 1958–63; Empire Test Pilots Sch., 1964; A&AEE Test Pilot, 1965–68; RAF Staff Coll., 1969; HQ Germany, 1970–73; Wing Comdr Flying, RAE Farnborough, 1974–78; MoD Operational Requirements, 1979–81; Gp Captain, Superintendent of Flying, A&AEE, 1982–85; RAF Staff Coll., Bracknell, 1985–88; Dir, Airport and Flight Ops, Marshall Aerospace, 1993–2002. Director: Royal Internat. Air Tattoo, 2005– (Vice-Pres., 1992); British Light Aircraft Centre, 2006–; Vice Pres., Aircraft Owners and Pilots Assoc., 2002–; Mem., Air League, 1994–. Hon. Mem., Airport Operators' Assoc., 2006. Liveryman, GAPAN, 2006. *Recreations:* sailing, ski-ing. *Club:* Royal Air Force.

C

CABALLÉ, Montserrat; Cross of Lazo de Dama of Order of Isabel the Catholic, Spain; opera and concert singer; *b* Barcelona, 12 April 1933; *d* of Carlos and Ana Caballé; *m* 1964, Bernabé Marti, tenor; one *s* one *d*. *Educ:* Conservatorio del Liceo, Barcelona. Continued to study singing under Mme Eugenia Kemeny. Carnegie Hall début as Lucrezia Borgia, 1965; London début in this role, with the London Opera Society, at the Royal Festival Hall, 1968. Has sung at Covent Garden, Glyndebourne, La Scala, Vienna, Metropolitan Opera, San Francisco and most major opera venues. Major roles include Maria Stuarda, Luisa Miller, Queen Elizabeth in Roberto Devereux, Imogene in Il Pirata, Violetta in La Traviata, Marguerite in Faust, Desdemona in Otello, Norma, Tosca, Turandot, Leonora in La Forza del Destino, Semiramide, Salome, Il Viaggio a Reims, Tristan und Isolde, and also those of contemporary opera. Over 120 roles sung and recorded. Numerous hon. degrees, awards and medals.

CABLE, Dr (John) Vincent; MP (Lib Dem) Twickenham, since 1997; Deputy Leader, Liberal Democrats, since 2006; *b* 9 May 1943; *s* of John Leonard Cable and Edith Cable; *m* 1st, 1968, Olympia Rebelo (*d* 2001); two *s* one *d*; 2nd, 2004, Rachel Wenban Smith. *Educ:* Fitzwilliam Coll., Cambridge (BA Hons; Pres., Cambridge Union); Glasgow Univ. (PhD). Finance Officer, Kenya Treasury, 1966–68; Lectr in Econs, Univ. of Glasgow, 1968–74; First Sec., FCO, 1974–76; Dep. Dir, ODI, 1976–83; Special Advr (Dir), Econs, Commonwealth Secretariat, 1983–90; Gp Planning Dept, Shell, 1990–93; Hd of Economic Prog., Chatham House, 1993–95; Chief Economist, Shell, 1995–97. Advr to Chm., World Commn on Envmt and Develt, UN, 1975–77; Special Advr to Sec. of State for Trade, 1979. Mem (Lab), Glasgow CC, 1971–74. Contested: (Lab) Glasgow, Hillhead, 1970; (SDP/L Alliance) York, 1983, 1987; (Lib Dem) Twickenham, 1992. Lib Dem spokesman on finance and EMU, 1997–99, on Trade and Industry, 1999–2003, on the economy, 2003–. Mem., Treasury Select Cttee, 1998–99. Visiting Fellow: Nuffield Coll., Oxford; LSE. *Publications:* Protectionism and Industrial Decline, 1983; (with B. Persaud) Foreign Investment and Development, 1985; Global Super Highways, 1994; The New Giants: China and India, 1994; The World's New Fissures, 1994; Globalisation and Global Governance, 2000; Public Services: reform with a purpose, 2005; Multiple Identities, 2005. *Recreations:* walking, riding, dancing. *Address:* 102 Whitton Road, Twickenham TW1 1BS. *T:* (020) 8892 3212.

CABLE, Prof. Margaret Ann, (Mrs J. R. W. Fletcher), FRCM; Professor of Singing, Royal College of Music, since 1964; *b* 3 June 1942; *d* of Sidney Frank Cable and Gladys Alfreda Cable (*née* Roberts); *m* 1967, John Richard William Fletcher; one *s* one *d*. *Educ:* Sawston Village Coll., Cambs; Royal Coll. of Music (Foundn Schol. and Exhibnr). FRCM 1985. Concert singer, 1963–2000; sang at major festivals incl. Lucerne, Edinburgh, Utrecht, Aldeburgh, Three Choirs and Henry Wood Promenade Concerts; roles at Kent Opera, 1974–80, include: Dorabella, in Così fan tutte; Marcellina, in Le nozze di Figaro; Mrs Grose, in The Turn of the Screw. Has made numerous recordings. Warden, Solo Performers' Section, ISM, 1985–86. *Recreations:* walking, theatre. *Address:* 17 Osten Mews, SW7 4HW. *T:* (020) 7341 9156; Royal College of Music, Prince Consort Road, SW7 2BS. *T:* (020) 7589 3643.

CABLE, Vincent; *see* Cable, J. V.

CABLE-ALEXANDER, Lt-Col Sir Patrick (Desmond William), 8th Bt *cr* 1809, of the City of Dublin; Chief Executive (Administration), Institute of Optometry, since 1999; *b* 19 April 1936; *s* of Sir Desmond William Lionel Cable-Alexander, 7th Bt and of Mary Jane, *d* of James O'Brien, Enniskillen; *S* father, 1988, but his name does not appear on the Official Roll of the Baronetage; *m* 1st, 1961, Diana Frances Rogers (marr. diss. 1976); two *d*; 2nd, 1976, Jane Mary Weekes (*née* Lewis); one *s*. *Educ:* Downside School; RMA Sandhurst. Commnd 3rd Carabiniers (POWDG), 1956; Lt-Col Royal Scots Dragoon Guards, 1976; comd Duke of Lancaster's Own Yeomanry, 1978–80; Chief of Staff, HQ North West District, 1980–83; retd, 1984. Sec. to the Council and Bursar, Lancing Coll., 1984–98. *Recreations:* cricket, visiting France, art. *Heir: s* Fergus William Antony Cable-Alexander, *b* 19 June 1981. *Address:* 15 Cambridge Road, Worthing, West Sussex BN11 1XD.

CABORN, Rt Hon. Richard (George); PC 1999; MP (Lab) Sheffield, Central, since 1983; *b* 6 Oct. 1943; *s* of late George and of Mary Caborn; *m* 1966, Margaret Caborn; one *s* one *d*. *Educ:* Hurlfield Comprehensive Sch.; Granville Coll. of Further Educn; Sheffield Polytechnic. Engrg apprentice, 1959–64; Convenor of Shop Stewards, Firth Brown Ltd, 1967–79. Mem. (Lab) Sheffield, European Parlt, 1979–84. Minister of State: (Minister for the Regions, Regeneration and Planning), DETR, 1997–99; DTI, 1999–2001; (Minister for Sport), 2001–07, (Minister for Tourism), 2003–05, DCMS; PM's Ambassador for the World Cup 2018, 2007–. Chm., Select Cttee on Trade and Industry, 1992–95. *Recreation:* amateur football. *Address:* House of Commons, SW1A 0AA; 29 Quarry Vale Road, Sheffield S12 3EB. *T:* (0114) 239 3802. *Club:* Carlton Working Men's (Sheffield).

CABRERA, Pablo; Ambassador of Chile to the Holy See, since 2006; *b* Santiago, 18 Jan. 1948; *m* 1973, Cecilia Pérez Walker; two *s* one *d*. *Educ:* Catholic Univ. of Chile (Lic. Juridical and Social Scis). Lawyer; entered Foreign Service, Chile, 1970: Consul, 1974, Second Sec., 1975–76, La Paz; Second Sec., Carácas, 1977–78; Consul Gen., Toronto, 1981–82; Chargé d'Affaires, Bucarest, 1983–85; Counsellor and Minister Counsellor, London, 1987–91; Minister Counsellor, Madrid, concurrent with Greece, 1991–93; Dep. Head, 1993, Head, 1994, Special Policy Dept, Min. of Foreign Affairs, Santiago; Under-Sec. of State for Navy, MoD, Santiago, 1995–99; Ambassador of Chile: to UK and Ireland, 1999–2000; to Russian Fedn, 2000–04, and concurrently to the Ukraine, 2001–04; to China, 2004–06. Formerly Head, Chilean Delegns to internat. confs. Vis. Prof., Nat. Acad. for Political and Strategic Studies, 1993–. Mem., Internat. Law Soc. of Chile, 1963–. Mem., Christian Democratic Party, 1963–. Official, 1980, and Great Cross, 1995, Order of Rio Branco (Brazil); Great Cross, Order of Civil Merit (Spain), 1996; Comdr First Cl., Polar Star Royal Order (Sweden), 1996. *Recreations:* golf, tennis, football. *Club:* Los Leones Golf (Santiago).

CACOYANNIS, Michael; director, stage and screen, since 1954; *b* 11 June 1922; *s* of late Sir Panayotis Cacoyannis and Angeliki, *d* of George M. Efthyvoulos and Zoe Constantinides, Limassol, Cyprus. *Educ:* Greek Gymnasium; Gray's Inn and Old Vic Sch., London. Radio Producer, BBC, Greek Service, 1941–50. Actor on English stage, 1946–51; parts included: Herod, in Salome, 1946; Caligula, in Caligula, 1949, etc. *Directed films:* Windfall in Athens, 1953; Stella, 1954; Girl in Black, 1956; A Matter of Dignity, 1958; Our Last Spring, 1960; The Wastrel, 1961; Electra, 1962; Zorba the Greek, 1964; The Day the Fish Came Out, 1967; The Trojan Women, 1971; Attila '74, 1975; Iphigenia, 1977; Sweet Country, 1986; Up, Down and Sideways, 1992; The Cherry Orchard, 2000; directed *plays:* produced several of these in Athens for Ellie Lambetti's Company, 1955–61; The Trojan Women, New York, 1963–65, Paris, 1965; Things That Go Bump in the Night, and The Devils, New York, 1965; Iphigenia in Aulis, New York, 1968; King Oedipus, Abbey Theatre, Dublin, 1973; Miss Margarita, Athens, 1975; The Bacchae, Comédie Française, 1977, New York, 1980; The Glass Menagerie, Nat. Theatre, Athens, 1978; Antony and Cleopatra, Athens, 1979; Zorba (musical), USA, 1983; Electra, Epidaurus, 1984; Naked, Athens, 1989; Henceforward, Athens, 1990; The Trojan Women, Epidaurus, 1995; Master Class, Athens, 1997; Medea, Epidaurus, 2001; Hamlet, Athens, 2003; Lysistrata, Delphi, Athens, 2005–06; Coriolanus, Athens, 2005; directed *operas:* Mourning Becomes Electra, Metropolitan Opera, NY, 1967; La Bohème, Juilliard, NY, 1972; La Traviata, Athens, 1983; Iphigenia in Aulis and in Tauris, Frankfurt State Opera, 1987; La Clemenza di Tito, Aix-en-Provence, 1988; Medea, Athens, 1995. Hon. DH Columbia Coll., Chicago, 1981; Hon. DLitt: Athens, 2002; Cyprus, 2003; Aristotelio Univ. of Thessaloniki, 2005. Silver Medal for Life Achievement, Greek Acad., 1995; Lifetime Achievement Awards: Fest. des Films du Monde, Montréal, 1999; Jerusalem Film Fest., 2000; Damascus Film Fest., 2004. Order of the Phœnix (Greece), 1965; Commandeur des Arts et des Lettres, 1987. *Publications:* Collected Writings, 1990; *translations:* (into English) The Bacchae, 1982; (into Greek) Antony and Cleopatra, 1980; Hamlet, 1985; Coriolanus, 1990; Othello, 2001; (into modern Greek) The Trojan Women, 1995. *Recreations:* walking, swimming. *Address:* 15 Mouson Street, Athens 117-41, Greece.

CADBURY, Sir Adrian; *see* Cadbury, Sir G. A. H.

CADBURY, Sir Dominic; *see* Cadbury, Sir N. D.

CADBURY, Sir (George) Adrian (Hayhurst), Kt 1977; DL; a Director of the Bank of England, 1970–94; *b* 15 April 1929; *s* of late Laurence John Cadbury, OBE and Joyce Cadbury, OBE, *d* of Lewis O. Mathews, Birmingham; *m* 1st, 1956, Gillian Mary (*d* 1992), *d* of late E. D. Skepper, Neuilly-sur-Seine; two *s* one *d*; 2nd, 1994, Susan Jacqueline, *d* of late D. B. Sinclair. *Educ:* Eton Coll.; King's Coll., Cambridge (MA Economics). Coldstream Guards, 1948–49; Cambridge, 1949–52. Cadbury Schweppes: Dep. Chm. and Man. Dir, 1969–74; Chm., 1975–89; Director: Cadbury Bros Ltd, 1958; IBM UK Ltd, 1975–94; Nat. Exhibition Centre, 1989–2001. Mem., Panel on Takeovers and Mergers, 1990–94. Chancellor, Univ. of Aston, 1979–2004. Chairman: West Midlands Economic Planning Council, 1967–70; CBI Econ. & Financial Policy Cttee, 1974–80; Food & Drink Industries Council, 1981–83; Promotion of Non-Exec. Dirs, 1984–95; Cttee on Financial Aspects of Corporate Governance, 1991–95; Pres., Birmingham Chamber of Industry and Commerce, 1988–89. High Sheriff, 1994–95, DL 1995, W Midlands. Freeman, City of Birmingham, 1982. Hon. DSc: Aston, 1973; Cranfield, 1985; Birmingham, 1996; Hon. LLD: Bristol, 1986; Birmingham, 1989; Lancaster, 1993; Cambridge, 1994; Hon. Dr Leuven and Gent, 2003; DUniv UCE, 2004; Hon. DLitt Aston, 2005. Albert Medal, RSA, 1995; Internat. Corporate Governance Network Award, 2001; Laureate Medal for Corporate Governance, Global Center for Leadership and Business Ethics, 2005. *Publications:* The Company Chairman, 1990, 2nd edn 1995; Corporate Governance and Chairmanship, 2002. *Fax:* (01564) 771130. *Clubs:* Boodle's; Hawks (Cambridge); Leander (Henley).

See also Sir N. D. Cadbury.

CADBURY, Sir (Nicholas) Dominic, Kt 1997; Chairman: The Wellcome Trust, since 2000 (a Governor, since 1999); Cadbury Schweppes plc, 1993–2000 (Chief Executive, 1984–93); *b* 12 May 1940; *s* of late Laurence John Cadbury, OBE and Joyce Cadbury, OBE; *m* 1972, Cecilia Sarah Symes; three *d*. *Educ:* Eton Coll.; Trinity Coll., Cambridge; Stanford Univ. (MBA). Chairman: Economist Gp, 1994–2003 (Dir, 1990–2003); Transense Technologies plc, 2000–03; Dep. Chm., Guinness PLC, 1994–97; Jt Dep. Chm., EMI Gp plc, 1999–2004 (Bd Mem., 1998–2004). Director: Misys plc, 2000– (Chm., 2005–); New Star Asset Mgt, 2005–07. Mem., President's Cttee, 1989–94 and 1998–2000, Chm., Educn and Trng Affairs Cttee, 1993–97, CBI; Dep. Chm., Qualifications and Curriculum Authority, 1997–2000; Member: Royal Mint Adv. Cttee, 1986–94; Stanford Adv. Council, 1989–95; Food Assoc., 1989–2000; NACETT, 1993–95; Marketing Council, 1997–2000; Council of Mgt, NIESR, 1998–2000. Pres., Food and Drink Fedn, 1998–99. Chancellor, Univ. of Birmingham, 2002–. Vice Pres., Edgbaston High Sch. for Girls, Birmingham, 1987–; Gov., Tudor Hall Sch., 1993–96. Fellow, Eton Coll., 1996–. CCMI (CBIM 1984); FCIM (Pres., 1996–97). *Recreations:* tennis, golf, shooting.

See also Sir G. A. H. Cadbury.

CADBURY, Nigel Robin; District Judge (Magistrates' Courts), Solihull and Sutton Coldfield, since 2005; *b* 6 July 1956; *s* of Robin Norman Cadbury, JP, and Rosemary Jayne Cadbury; *m* 1982, Julie Ann Dean; two *s* one *d*. *Educ:* Rugby Sch.; Kent Univ. (BA

Law 1978). Called to the Bar, Middle Temple, 1979; in practice at the Bar, 1979–97; Mem., Midland and Oxford Circuit, 1979–97; Stipendiary Magistrate, Leeds, 1997–2000; Dist Judge (Magistrates' Cts), Birmingham, 2000–05. Mem., Criminal Bar Assoc., 1990–97. Trustee, Edward Cadbury Charitable Trust, 1991–. *Recreations:* squash (Mem., Worcs Co. over-45 squash team), ski-ing, gardening, golf. *Address:* The Court House, Homer Road, Solihull, W Midlands B91 3RD. *T:* (0121) 705 8101. *Clubs:* Barnt Green Tennis & Squash; Blackwell Golf, Royal Cinque Ports Deal Golf.

CADBURY-BROWN, Henry Thomas, OBE 1967; TD; RA 1975 (ARA 1971); FRIBA; Professor of Architecture, Royal Academy, 1975–88; architect, in partnership with John F. Metcalfe and Elizabeth R. Cadbury-Brown, 1962–84; *b* 20 May 1913; *s* of Henry William Cadbury-Brown and Marion Ethel Sewell; *m* 1953, Elizabeth Romeyn (*d* 2002), *d* of Prof. A. Elwyn, Croton on Hudson, NY. *Educ:* Westminster Sch.; AA Sch. of Architecture (Hons Diploma). Architect in private practice since winning competition for British Railways Branch Offices, 1937. Work includes pavilions for "The Origins of the People", main concourse and fountain display at Festival of Britain; schools, housing, display and interiors. Architect for new civic centre at Gravesend and halls for residence for Birmingham Univ. and, with Sir Hugh Casson and Prof. Robert Goodden, for new premises for Royal College of Art; awarded London Architecture Bronze Medal, 1963; lecture halls for Univ. of Essex; for RBK & C: Tavistock Cres. housing; World's End redevelt (in gp partnership Eric Lyons, Cadbury-Brown, Metcalfe & Cunningham); interior alterations in Burlington House for RA. Taught at Architectural Association Sch., 1946–49; Tutor at Royal Coll. of Art, 1952–61. Invited as Visiting Critic to Sch. of Architecture, Harvard Univ., 1956. Retrospective exhibn, Elegant Variation, RA, 2006. Member: RIBA Council, 1951–53; MARS (Modern Architectural Research) group. Pres. Architectural Assoc., 1959–60. TA and military service, 1931–45; Major RA (TD). Hon. Fellow: RCA; Kent Inst. of Art and Design, 1992. DU Essex, 1989. *Recreations:* numerous, including work. *Address:* 3 Church Walk, Aldeburgh, Suffolk IP15 5DU. *T:* (01728) 452591.

CADDICK, David William; His Honour Judge Caddick; a Circuit Judge, since 2004; *b* 24 Dec. 1945; *s* of late William Caddick and Phyllis Caddick (*née* Brown, later Medhurst); *m* 1971, Susan Anne Wyton; two *s* two *d*. *Educ:* Simon Langton Grammar Sch., Canterbury; St John's Coll., Durham (BA 1967). Articled to D. L. Gulland, Solicitor, 1967–70; admitted solicitor, 1970; Partner, Gulland & Gulland, Solicitors, Maidstone, 1971–87; Dep. County Court Registrar, 1983–87; Registrar, then Dist Judge, 1987–2004; Nominated Dist Care Judge, Medway Care Centre, 1991–2004; a Recorder, Crown Court, 1998–2004. Chm. SE Circuit, Dist Judges' Assoc., 1995–98. *Recreations:* gardening, walking, all things connected with France. *Address:* Maidstone Combined Court, The Law Courts, Barker Road, Maidstone, Kent ME16 8EQ. *T:* (01622) 202000; *e-mail:* HHJudge.Caddick@judiciary.gsi.gov.uk.

CADELL, Patrick Moubray, CBE 2001; FSAScot; Keeper of the Records of Scotland, 1991–2000; *b* 17 March 1941; *s* of late Col Henry Moubray Cadell of Grange, OBE and Christina Rose Nimmo or Cadell; *m* 1st, 1968, Sarah Margaret Florence King (*d* 1996); two *s* one *d*; 2nd, 2001, Rachel Watson. *Educ:* Merchiston Castle Sch.; Trinity Coll., Cambridge (BA 1962); Toulouse Univ. FSAScot 1985. British Museum: guide lectr, Dept of Admin, 1964–66; Asst Keeper, Dept of Manuscripts, 1966–68; National Library of Scotland: Asst Keeper, Dept of Manuscripts, 1968–83; Keeper, Dept of Manuscripts, 1983–90. Bailie, Abbey Court of Holyrood, 1995–. Officier de l'Ordre des Arts et des Lettres (France), 2002. *Publications:* The Iron Mills at Cramond, 1973; (contrib.) The Water of Leith, 1984; The Abbey Court and High Constables of Holyrood, 1985; (contrib.) A Sense of Place: studies in Scottish Local history, 1988; (contrib.) For the Encouragement of Learning: Scotland's National Library 1689–1989, 1989; The Third Statistical Account of Scotland, Vol. for West Lothian, 1992; contribs on historical subjects to books and jls. *Recreations:* walking, the French language. *Address:* 5 Morham Park, Edinburgh EH10 5GF. *T:* (0131) 447 0635.
See also W. A. Cadell of Grange.

CADELL of Grange, William Archibald, RIBA; FRIAS; *b* 9 March 1933; *s* of late Col Henry Moubray Cadell of Grange, OBE, RE and Christina Rose Cadell (*née* Nimmo); *m* 1960, Mary-Jean Carmichael; three *s*. *Educ:* Merchiston Castle Sch.; Trinity Coll., Cambridge (BA 1956; MA); Regent St Poly., London (DipArch). RIBA 1961. Founded William A. Cadell Architects, 1968, retired, 1995; manager, Grange Estate, 1971–2000. Chm., Drum Housing Develt, 1991–. Comr, Royal Fine Art Commn for Scotland, 1992–2000; Trustee, Architectural Heritage Fund, 1997–2007. DL 1982–2000, Vice Lord-Lieutenant, 2000–01, West Lothian. *Recreations:* gardening, forestry, the Arts. *Address:* Swordie Mains, Linlithgow, West Lothian, EH49 7RQ. *T:* (01506) 842946.
See also P. M. Cadell.

CADMAN, family name of **Baron Cadman**.

CADMAN, 3rd Baron *cr* 1937, of Silverdale; **John Anthony Cadman;** farmer, 1964–85; *b* 3 July 1938; *s* of 2nd Baron Cadman and Marjorie Elizabeth Bunnis; *S* father, 1966; *m* 1975, Janet Hayes; two *s*. *Educ:* Harrow; Selwyn Coll., Cambridge; Royal Agricultural Coll., Cirencester. *Heir:* *s* Hon. Nicholas Anthony James Cadman, *b* 18 Nov. 1977. *Address:* 32 chemin de Labade, 11300 Pieusse, France.

CADMAN, Surg. Rear-Adm. (D) (Albert) Edward, CB 1977; Director of Naval Dental Services, 1974–77; *b* 14 Oct. 1918; *m* 1st, 1946, Margaret Henrietta Tomkins-Russell (*d* 1974); one *s* one *d*; 2nd, 1975, Mary Croil Macdonald (*d* 1987), Superintendent, WRNS; 3rd, 1988, Irene Davies (*née* Lowther). *Educ:* Dover Grammar Sch.; Guy's Hosp. Dental Sch. LDS RCS 1941. Surg. Lieut (D) RNVR, 1942; transf. to RN, 1947; served as Asst to Dir, Naval Dental Services, 1967–70; Comd Dental Surgeon on staff of Flag Officer, Naval Air Comd, 1970–74. QHDS 1974–77. *Address:* 28 Newton Lane, Romsey, Hampshire SO51 8GX. *T:* (01794) 522870.

CADMAN, Mark Robert; Chief Executive Officer, Euro RSCG London, since 2006; *b* Farnborough, 30 Dec. 1963; *s* of Colin and Jan Cadman; *m* 1998, Ayesha; two *d*. *Educ:* King's Sch., Canterbury; Queen Mary Coll., Univ. of London (LLB Hons). Managing Director: Lowe London, 2002–04; J. Walter Thomson, 2005. *Recreations:* tennis, golf, running. *Address:* c/o Euro RSCG London, Cupola House, Alfred Place, WC1E 7EB. *T:* (020) 7257 6002; *e-mail:* mark.cadman@eurorscg.com. *Club:* Harbour.

CADOGAN, family name of **Earl Cadogan**.

CADOGAN, 8th Earl *cr* 1800; **Charles Gerald John Cadogan;** DL; Baron Cadogan 1718; Viscount Chelsea 1800; Baron Oakley 1831; *b* 24 March 1937; *o s* of 7th Earl Cadogan, MC and his 1st wife, Hon. Primrose Lilian Yarde-Buller (*d* 1970), *yr d* of 3rd Baron Churston; *S* father, 1997; *m* 1st, 1963, Lady Philippa Wallop (*d* 1984), *d* of 9th Earl of Portsmouth; two *s* one *d*; 2nd, 1989, Jennifer Jane Greig Rae (marr. diss. 1994), *d* of J. E. K. Rae and Mrs S. Z. de Ferranti; 3rd, 1994, Dorothy Ann Shipsey, MVO, *yr d* of late Dr W. E. Shipsey. *Educ:* Eton. Chm., Leukaemia Research Fund, 1985–. Freeman, City of London, 1979; Liveryman, GAPAN. DL Greater London, 1996. *Heir:* *s* Viscount Chelsea, *qv*. *Clubs:* White's, Royal Automobile.

CADOGAN, Prof. Sir John (Ivan George), Kt 1991; CBE 1985; PhD, DSc London; FRS 1976; FRSE; CChem, FRSC; first Director General, Research Councils, 1994–98; Professorial Fellow, Swansea University (formerly University College of Swansea, University of Wales, then University of Wales, Swansea), since 1979; Chairman, Fusion Antibodies Ltd, since 2005; *b* Pembrey, Carmarthenshire, 8 Oct. 1930; *er s* of late Alfred Cadogan and Dilys Cadogan, MBE; *m* 1st, 1955, Margaret Jeanne (*née* Evans) (*d* 1992); one *s* (one *d* decd); 2nd, 1997, Elizabeth Purnell. *Educ:* Grammar Sch., Swansea; King's Coll., London (State Scholar, 1948; 1st cl. Hons Chem. 1951; Pres., Chem. Soc., 1951–52; soccer colours, 1952). Research at KCL, 1951–54. Civil Service Research Fellow, 1954–56; Lectr in Chemistry, King's Coll., London, 1956–63; Purdie Prof. of Chemistry and Head of Dept, St Salvator's Coll., Univ. of St Andrews, 1963–69; Forbes Prof. of Organic Chemistry, Edinburgh Univ., 1969–79; Chief Scientist, BP Res. Centre, 1979–81; Dir of Res., BP, 1981–92. Chm., BP Vencap, 1988–92; Director: BP Gas International, 1983–87; BP Ventures, 1981–90 (Chief Exec., 1988–90); BP Chemicals, 1983–92; BP Venezuela, 1985–92; BP Solar International, 1988–92 (Chm., 1988–90); Chairman: Kaldair Internat., 1988–90; DNA Res. Innovations Ltd, 1999–2004, acquired by Invitrogen Corp. Advr to EC Comr for Sci., R&D, 1993–94. Mem., Royal Commn on Criminal Justice, 1991–93. Chairman: Defence Sci. Adv. Council, 1985–91; Nuclear Weapons Safety Cttee, 1992–98; Nuclear Powered Warships Safety Cttee, 1992–98; Defence Nuclear Safety Cttee, 1998–2000. Member: Chemistry Cttee, SRC, 1967–71 (Chm. 1972–75); Council, SERC, 1981–85 (Chm., Science Bd, 1981–85; Mem., Science Bd, SRC, 1972–75); ACORD, Dept of Energy, 1987–89; HEFCW, 1992–95 (Chm., Res. Gp, 1992–94); HEFCE, 1994–98; Hong Kong Technol. Review Bd, 1992–95; Commn on New Policy, Irish Council for Sci. and Technol., 2002–03; Sci. Policy Advr, Sci. Foundn Ireland, 2000–05. Member: Council, Chem. Soc., 1966–69, 1973–76; Council, RIC, 1979–80; Chem. Soc.-RIC Unification Cttee, 1975–80; Council, RSC, 1980–85, 1989–92 (Pres. RSC, 1982–84); Council of Management, Macaulay Inst. for Soil Res., Aberdeen, 1969–79; Council, St George's Sch. for Girls, 1974–79; Council, RSE, 1975–80 (Vice-Pres., 1978–80); Council, Royal Soc., 1989–91, 1993–95 (Mem., Royal Soc. Sci. Inquiry, 1990–92); COPUS, 1994–97; Conseil d'Admin, Fondation de la Maison de la Chemie, 1994–; Vice-Pres., Royal Instn, 1986–87 (Mem. Council, 1984–87). Member: Bd of Trustees, Royal Observatory Trust, Edinburgh, 1979–86; Adv. Bd, RCDS, 1989–2001; Adv. Bd, Eur. Business Management Sch., UC Swansea, 1990–95; Adv. Council, RMCS, 1992–2002; Res. Cttee, Univ. of Newcastle upon Tyne, 1992–94; Ind. Adv. Cttee, Univ. of Durham, 1992–94; Trustee: Overseas Students Trust, UC Swansea, 1989–2000; RSE Scotland Foundn, 1998–2001. Governor: Jt Res. Centre, EC, 1994–2000; Salters' Inst. of Industrial Chem., 1999–. Pres., Chem. Sect., BAAS, 1981. Chemistry Advr, Carnegie Trust Univ. of Scotland, 1985–. Pres., Techniquest, 1997–99. Fellow: KCL, 1976 (Mem. Council, 1980–94; Vice-Chm., 1990–94); UC, Swansea, 1992; Cardiff Univ., 1998; FIC 1992. Hon. FREng (Hon. FEng 1992); Hon. FRSC 1999. Visiting Professor of Chemistry: Imperial Coll., London Univ., 1979–2002; Swansea Inst. Higher Educn, 2004. Lectures: Tilden, Chem. Soc., 1971; first RSE Schs Christmas, 1980; David Martin Royal Soc. BAYS, 1981; Humphry Davy, Royal Instn, 1982; Holroyd Meml, Soc. Chem. Ind., 1984; Salters' Co., Royal Instn, 1984; Philips, Royal Soc., 1985; Pedler, RSC, 1986; Dalton, RSC, 1989; BGS Dist., 1995; Irvine Meml, St Andrews, 1995; Salters' Millennium, 2000. Freeman, City of London; Liveryman, Salters' Co., 1993. Hon. DSc: St Andrews, 1983; Wales, 1984; Edinburgh, 1986; Aberdeen, 1991; Durham, 1992; Leicester, 1992; London, 1992; Sunderland, 1994; Cranfield, 1995; Glamorgan, 1996; Nottingham, 1999; Nottingham Trent, 1999; DUniv Stirling, 1984; Hon. Dr l'Univ Aix-Marseille, 1984. Samuel Smiles Prize, KCL, 1950; Millar Thomson Medallist, KCL, 1951; Meldola Medallist, Soc. of Maccabaeans and Royal Inst. of Chemistry, 1959; Corday-Morgan Medallist, Chem. Soc., 1965; SCI Medal, 2001. *Publications:* Principles of Free Radical Chemistry, 1971; Organophosphorus Reagents in Organic Synthesis, 1979; about 320 scientific papers, mainly in Jl RSC, and patents. *Recreations:* being in France, music, gardening, supporting Rugby football (Vice-Pres., Crawshay's Welsh RFC, London Welsh RFC; Patron, Swansea RFCC). *Address:* Department of Chemistry, Swansea University, Swansea SA2 8PP. *T:* (01792) 295506, *Fax:* (01792) 295747; *e-mail:* john@cadogan27.freeserve.co.uk. *Clubs:* Athenæum; Cardiff and County; Bristol Channel Yacht.

CADWALLADER, James Richard, CMG 2007; Counsellor, Foreign and Commonwealth Office, since 2001; *b* 1953; *s* of George Cadwallader and Kathleen Cadwallader; *m* 1975, Deborah Jane; two *s* one *d*. *Educ:* Ludlow Grammar Sch.; Keble Coll., Oxford (BA Engrg Sci., MA). FIET. Royal Corps of Signals, 1973–82; joined FCO, 1982. *Recreations:* hill walking, gardening, technology and people. *Address:* *e-mail:* jcadwallader@iee.org. *Club:* Army and Navy.

CÆSAR, Rev. Canon Anthony Douglass, CVO 1991 (LVO 1987); an Extra Chaplain to the Queen, since 1991; *b* 3 April 1924; *s* of Harold Douglass and Winifred Kathleen Cæsar. *Educ:* Cranleigh School; Magdalene Coll., Cambridge; St Stephen's House, Oxford. MA, MusB, FRCO. Served War with RAF, 1943–46. Assistant Music Master, Eton Coll., 1948–51; Precentor, Radley Coll., 1952–59; Asst Curate, St Mary Abbots, Kensington, 1961–65; Asst Sec., ACCM, 1965–70; Chaplain, Royal School of Church Music, 1965–70; Deputy Priest-in-Ordinary to the Queen, 1967–68, Priest-in-Ordinary, 1968–70; Resident Priest, St Stephen's Church, Bournemouth, 1970–73; Precentor and Sacrist, Winchester Cathedral, 1974–79; Sub-Dean of HM Chapels Royal, Dep. Clerk of the Closet, Sub-Almoner and Domestic Chaplain to the Queen, 1979–91; Hon. Canon of Winchester Cathedral, 1975–76 and 1979–91, Residentiary Canon, 1976–79, Canon Emeritus, 1991–; Chaplain, St Cross Hosp., Winchester, 1991–93. Hon. FGCM 2007. *Publications:* (jt ed.) The New English Hymnal, 1986; part songs, church music. *Recreation:* other people. *Address:* 26 Capel Court, The Burgage, Prestbury, Cheltenham, Glos GL52 3EL. *T:* (01242) 577541.

CAFFARI, Denise, (Dee), MBE 2007; professional sailor; Managing Director, Dee Caffari Ltd, since 2006; *b* 23 Jan. 1973; *d* of late Peter Caffari and of Barbara Caffari; partner, Harry Spedding. *Educ:* St Clement Danes Sch., Chorleywood; Leeds Metropolitan Univ. (BA Hons Sport Sci. 1994; PGCE Sec. Educn 1995). PE teacher, secondary sch.; Manager, Sports Coll. First woman to sail single-handed non-stop west around the world against the prevailing winds and currents, 2005–06. Mem., Inst. of Navigation. Hon. Dr Sport Sci. Leeds Metropolitan, 2006. *Publication:* Against the Flow, 2007. *Recreations:* outdoor activities, fitness, travel, reading, theatre. *Address:* Dee Caffari Ltd, 25 Barnes Wallis Road, Segensworth East, Fareham PO15 5TT. *Club:* Royal Southampton Yacht.

CAFFERTY, Michael Angelo; HM Diplomatic Service; Consul-General, Melbourne, Australia, 1983–87; *b* 3 March 1927; *m* 1950, Eileen E. Geer; two *s* three *d*. *Educ:* Univ. of London. BoT, 1951; Asst Trade Comr, Johannesburg, 1955, Pretoria, 1957; seconded to FO, Buenos Aires, 1958; Trade Comr, Singapore, 1964; FCO, 1968; Consul (Commercial), Milan, 1974; First Sec. and Head of Chancery, Rome (Holy See), 1977;

Ambassador and Consul-Gen., Santo Domingo, 1979–83. *Address:* 12 Brackendale Way, Earley, Reading RG6 1DZ.

CAGE, Nicolas; actor, director and producer; *b* Nicholas Kim Coppola, 7 Jan. 1964; *s* of Prof. August Coppola and Joy Vogelsang; one *s* by Kristina Fulton; *m* 1st, 1995, Patricia Arquette (marr. diss. 2001); 2nd, 2002, Lisa Marie Presley (marr. diss. 2004); 3rd, 2004, Alice Kim; one *s*. *Educ:* Beverly Hills High Sch. Co-owner, Saturn Films, prodn co. *Films include:* Valley Girl, Rumble Fish, 1983; The Cotton Club, Racing with the Moon, Birdy, 1984; Peggy Sue Got Married, 1986; Raising Arizona, Moonstruck, 1987; Vampire's Kiss, 1989; Wild at Heart, 1990; Honeymoon in Vegas, 1992; It Could Happen to You, 1994; Leaving Las Vegas, 1995 (Golden Globe and Acad. Awards for Best Actor, 1996); The Rock, 1996; Con Air, Face/Off, 1997; City of Angels, Snake Eyes, 1998; 8mm, 1999; Bringing Out the Dead, Gone in 60 Seconds, The Family Man, 2000; Captain Corelli's Mandolin, 2001; (also dir and prod.) Sonny, Windtalkers, Adaptation, 2002; Matchstick Men, 2003; National Treasure, 2004; (also prod.) Lord of War, 2005; The Weather Man, 2006; World Trade Center, 2006; The Wicker Man, 2006; Ghost Rider, 2007; Next, 2007; National Treasure: Book of Secrets, 2008; Bangkok Dangerous, 2008; producer: Shadow of the Vampire, 2000; The Life of David Gale, 2003; The Dresden Files (TV series), 2007. *Address:* c/o Creative Artists Agency, 2000 Avenue of the Stars, Los Angeles, CA 90067, USA; Saturn Films, Suite 911, 9000 Sunset Boulevard, Los Angeles, CA 90069, USA.

CAGIATI, Dr Andrea, Grand Cross, Italian Order of Merit, 1979; Hon. GCVO; Ambassador, retired 1988; *b* Rome, 11 July 1922; *m* 1968, Sigrid von Morgen; one *s* one *d*. *Educ:* University of Siena (Dr of Law). Entered Foreign Service, 1948. Served: Secretary, Paris, 1950; Principal Private Sec. to Minister of State, 1951; Vice-Consul-General, New York, 1953; Prin. Private Sec. to Minister of State and subsequently Dept of Political Affairs, 1955; Counsellor, Athens, 1957; Counsellor, Mexico City, 1960; Delegate, Disarmament Cttee, Geneva, March–Dec. 1962; Italian Delegation, UN, June 1962; Head, NATO Dept, Dec. 1962; Minister-Counsellor, Madrid, 1966; Ambassador, Bogotá, 1968; Inst. for Diplomatic Studies, 1971; Diplomatic Adviser to Prime Minister, 1972; Ambassador, Vienna, 1973; Ambassador, Court of St James's, 1980; Ambassador to the Holy See and to the Order of Malta, 1985. Vice Chm., 1989–94, Dir, 1987–94, Alitalia. President: Circolo di Studi Diplomatici, 1989–98 (now Hon. Pres.); Centro Conciliazione Internazionale, 1989–97; Fondazione Cagiati von Morgen, 1990–; Eurodéfence (Italia), 1994–99 (now Hon. Pres.); Fondazione Assistenza Sanitaria Melitense, 1995–; Vice-Pres., Fondazione De Gasperi, 1993–2003. Hon. GCVO during State Visit to Italy of HM The Queen, Oct. 1980; KM, 1953; Grand Cross: Order of Merit, Austria, 1980; Order of Merit, Malta, 1987; Order of Pius IX, Holy See, 1988. *Publications:* La Diplomazia dalle origini al XVII secolo, 1944; Verso quale avvenire?, 1958; I Sentieri della Vita, ricordi di un diplomatico, 1990; Scritti di Politica Estera, 4 vols 1991–2000; articles in quarterlies on foreign and defence affairs. *Recreations:* sculpture, golf, shooting. *Address:* Largo Olgiata, 15 (49D)–00123 Rome, Italy. *T:* and *Fax:* (6) 30888135. *Club:* Nuovo Circolo Scacchi (Rome).

CAHILL, Frances Rebecca; *see* Gibb, F. R.

CAHILL, Jeremy; *see* Cahill, P. J.

CAHILL, Kevin James Patrick, CBE 2007; Chief Executive, Comic Relief, since 1997 (Deputy Director, 1993–97); *b* 4 March 1952; *s* of James and Jean Cahill; *m* 1975, Shân Jones (marr. diss. 1982); one *s* one *d*; partner, Becky Webb; one *s*. *Educ:* Manchester Univ. (BA Hons English and Drama); PGCE Liberal Studies; RSA Dip. TEFL. Head of Educn, Nat. Theatre, later Royal Nat. Theatre, 1982–91; Dir of Educn, 1991–92, of Communications, 1992–93, Comic Relief. Patron, Nxt Theatre Co., 1999–. Chairman: Gate Theatre, 1988–; Review Bd, Nat. Professional Qualifications in Acting, Dance and Stage Mgt, 2001–02. Member: Council, Drama Centre, 1989–92; Bd, Young Vic Theatre, 1993–2001; Adv. Cttee, Active Community Unit, 2000–03. Chair, Trinity Coll. London, 1993–2002. Trustee: Internat. Broadcasting Trust, 1993–2002; Charity Projects Entertainment Fund, 2007–. *Recreations:* football (Manchester United supporter), France, food. *Address:* Comic Relief, 89 Albert Embankment, SE1 7TP. *Clubs:* Groucho, Soho House.

CAHILL, (Paul) Jeremy; QC 2002; *b* 28 Jan. 1952; *s* of Timothy Cahill and Mary (*née* O'Mahony); two *d*. *Educ:* Ratcliffe Coll., Leicester; Liverpool Univ. (LLB). Called to the Bar, Middle Temple, 1975 (Blackstone Schol.); in practice, 1976–, specialising in planning and environmental law. *Recreations:* conversation, theatre, golf, West Cork, wine, travel, music, reading. *Address:* No. 5 Chambers, Fountain Court, Steelhouse Lane, Birmingham B4 6DR. *T:* (0121) 606 0500; *e-mail:* jc@no5.com. *Clubs:* RAC; Copt Heath Golf.

CAHILL, Sally Elizabeth Mary; QC 2003; **Her Honour Judge Cahill;** a Circuit Judge, since 2004; *b* 12 Nov. 1955; *m* 1981, Patrick Cahill (*d* 2003); two *s* one *d*. *Educ:* Harrogate Ladies' Coll.; Leeds Univ. (LLB (Hons)). Called to the Bar, Gray's Inn, 1978; an Asst Recorder, 1997–2000; a Recorder, 2000–04. Chm. Leeds Reg., Family Law Bar Assoc., 1994–2004. Special Trustee, Leeds NHS Trust, 2001–. Gov., Richmond House Sch., 1994–2004. *Recreations:* sailing, ski-ing. *Address:* Leeds Combined Court Centre, 1 Oxford Row, Leeds LS1 3BG.

CAHILL, Teresa Mary; opera and concert singer; *b* 30 July 1944; *d* of Florence and Henry Cahill; *m* 1st, 1971, John Anthony Kiernander (marr. diss. 1978); 2nd, 2005, Robert Louis Alfred Saxton, *qv*. *Educ:* Notre Dame High Sch., Southwark; Guildhall School of Music and Drama; London Opera Centre (LRAM Singing, AGSM Piano). Glyndebourne début, 1969; Covent Garden début, 1970; La Scala Milan, 1976, Philadelphia Opera, 1981, specialising in Mozart, Strauss and Elgar; concerts: all London orchestras; Boston Symphony Orch., Chicago Symphony Orch., Rotterdam Philharmonic Orch., West Deutscher Rundfunk, Warsaw Philharmonic, RAI Turin, Frankfurt Radio Orch.; Promenade concerts; Festivals: Vienna, 1983; Berlin, 1987; Bath, 2000; BBC radio and TV; recordings, incl. Mozart, Strauss, Elgar and Mahler, for all major companies; master classes: Dartington Fest., 1984, 1986; Oxford Univ., 1995–; S'Hertogenbosch Vocal Concours, 1998 (Mem. Internat. Jury), 2000; Peabody Inst., Baltimore, 1999; Bowdoin Coll., Maine, 2004; recitals and concerts throughout Europe, USA, Far East. Prof., Trinity Coll. of Music, 1992–. Artistic Advr, Nat. Mozart Competition, 1994–2002. Mem. Jury, Kathleen Ferrier Comp., 1988; Adjudicator, 1988–, Music Advr, 2000–, Live Music Now; Adjudicator: Young Concert Artists' Trust, 1989–; annual music comp., Royal Over-Seas League, 1985–89, 1992, 1995, 2000. Gov., Royal Soc. of Musicians, 2000–. Silver Medal, Worshipful Co. of Musicians, 1966; John Christie Award 1970. *Recreations:* cinema, theatre, travel, reading, collecting things, sales from car boots to Sotheby's, photography. *Address:* 65 Leyland Road, SE12 8DW. *Club:* Royal Over-Seas League (Hon. Mem.).

CAHN, Sir Albert Jonas, 2nd Bt *cr* 1934; marital, sexual and hypno therapist; *b* 27 June 1924; *s* of Sir Julien Cahn, 1st Bt, and Phyllis Muriel, *d* of A. Wolfe, Bournemouth; *S* father, 1944; *m* 1948, Malka (*d* 2001), *d* of late R. Bluestone; two *s* two *d*. *Educ:* Headmaster's House, Harrow. Dir, Elm Therapy Centre, New Malden, 1983–93. *Recreations:* cricket, horse riding, photography. *Heir:* *s* Julien Michael Cahn [*b* 15 Jan. 1951; *m* 1987, Marilynne Janelle, *d* of Frank Owen Blyth; one *s* one *d*].

CAHN, Andrew Thomas, CMG 2001; Chief Executive, UK Trade and Investment, since 2006; *b* 1 April 1951; *s* of Prof. Robert Wolfgang Cahn, FRS and of Pat (*née* Hanson); *m* 1976, Virginia Beardshaw; two *s* one *d*. *Educ:* Bedales Sch.; Trinity Coll., Cambridge (BA 1st Cl. Hons). MAFF, 1973–77; FCO, 1977–78; Private Sec. to Perm Sec., MAFF, 1978–79; 1st Sec., Office of UK Perm. Repn to EC, FCO, 1982–84, Cabinet of Vice Pres., CEC, 1984–88; Asst Sec., MAFF, 1988–92; Principal Private Secretary to: Chancellor of Duchy of Lancaster, 1992–94; Minister of Agriculture, 1994–95; Dep. Head, European Secretariat, Cabinet Office, 1995–97; Chef de Cabinet to Rt Hon. Neil Kinnock, EC, Brussels, 1997–2000; Dir, Govt and Industry Affairs, British Airways plc, 2000–06. Non-exec. Dir, Cadbury Ltd, 1990–92. Gov., Bedales Sch., 1993–98. Trustee: Gatsby Charitable Foundn, 1996–; Royal Botanic Gardens, Kew, 2002– (Chm., Audit Cttee, 2004); Inst. for Govt, 2008–. FRSA 1979. *Recreations:* family, reading, long distance walks, golf. *Address:* UK Trade and Investment, Kingsgate House, 66–74 Victoria Street, SW1E 6SW. *T:* (020) 7215 4300; *e-mail:* andrew.cahn@ukti.gsi.gov.uk. *Clubs:* Royal Automobile; Hampstead Golf; St Cyr (Poitiers).

CAIE, Andrew John Forbes; HM Diplomatic Service, retired; Executive Director, CfBT Education Malaysia, since 2007; *b* 25 July 1947; *s* of Norman Forbes Caie and Joan Margaret Caie (*née* Wise); *m* 1976, Kathie-Anne Williams; one *s* one *d*. *Educ:* St Dunstan's Coll., Catford; Sidney Sussex Coll., Cambridge (MA). Joined FCO, 1969; Manila, 1976–80; FCO, 1980–84; Dep. Head of Mission, Bogotá, 1984–88; FCO, 1988–93; Dep. High Comr, Islamabad, 1993–96; FCO Resident Chair, CSSB, 1996–97; FCO, 1997–98; Ambassador to Guatemala, 1998–2001; High Comr, Brunei, 2002–05. Exec. Sen. Advr, SE Asia, CfBT Educn Trust, 2006. *Address:* Suite B306, Phileo Damansara 1, 9 Jalan 16/11, 46350 Petaling Jaya, Malaysia; *e-mail:* acaie@cfbt.com.my.

CAIE, Prof. Graham Douglas, PhD; FRSE; FEA; Professor of English Language, since 1990, and Clerk of Senate and Vice-Principal, since 2008, University of Glasgow; *b* Aberdeen, 3 Feb. 1945; *s* of William and Adeline Caie; *m* 1972, Ann Pringle Abbott; one *s* one *d*. *Educ:* Aberdeen Grammar Sch.; Aberdeen Univ. (MA Hons English); McMaster Univ. (MA, PhD 1973). Amanuensis and Lektor, English Dept, 1972–90, Chm., Medieval Centre, 1984–88, Univ. of Copenhagen; University of Glasgow: Hd, Dept of English Lang., 1992–96; Hd of Sch., 1994–98; Associate Dean (Res.), Arts Faculty, 2005–08. Lead Assessor, Teaching Quality Assessment (Scotland), 1996–98. Member, Panel: RAE (English) 2001 and 2008; AHRC, 2005–08. Mem., Lit. Cttee, Scottish Arts Council, 1998–. Vice Chm., Bd of Trustees, Nat. Liby of Scotland, 1998–. Chm., Christie's Jt Educn Bd, 2002–. Senate Assessor, Court, Univ. of Glasgow, 1998–2003. Vice-Pres., Scottish Text Soc., 1998–; Mem. Council, Dictionary of Older Scottish Tongue, 1990–2000. Founding FEA 2000; FRSE 2004. FRSA 1997. *Publications:* The Judgement Day Theme in Old English Poetry, 1976; Bibliography of Junius XI Manuscript, 1979; The Old English "Judgement Day II": a critical edition, 2000; (ed jtly) The Power of Words, 2007; (ed jtly) Medieval Texts in Context, 2008; contrib. articles on medieval lang., lit., manuscript studies. *Recreations:* reading, travel. *Address:* Senate Office, University of Glasgow, Glasgow G12 8QQ. *T:* (0141) 330 3292.

CAIGER-SMITH, Frances Mary; *see* Morris, F. M.

CAILLARD, Air Vice-Marshal (Hugh) Anthony, CB 1981; retired 1982; Director General, Britain-Australia Society, and Hon. Secretary, Cook Society, 1982–89; *b* 16 April 1927; *s* of late Col Felix Caillard, MC and Bar (mentioned in despatches), and Mrs Monica Y. Caillard; *m* 1957, Margaret-Ann Crawford, Holbrook, NSW, Australia; four *s*. *Educ:* Downside; Oriel Coll., Oxford. Cranwell, 1947–49; served, 1949–65: 13 Sqdn, Egypt; ADC to C-in-C MEAF, and to AOC-in-C Tech. Trng Comd; 101 Sqdn, Binbrook; RAAF No 2 Sqdn; 49 Sqdn (Sqdn Ldr) and 90 Sqdn; RN Staff Coll.; HQ Bomber Comd (Wg Cdr); OC 39 Sqdn, Malta, 1965–67; Jt Services Staff Coll., 1967; Planning Staffs, MoD, 1967–70; Asst Air Attaché, Washington (Gp Captain), 1970–73; OC Marham, 1974–75; Def. Intell. Staff (Air Cdre), 1975–79; Dep. Chief of Staff, Ops and Intelligence, HQ Allied Air Forces, Central Europe, 1979–82. Specialist Air Advr, H of C Defence Cttee, 1985–92. Chairman: Ex Forces Fellowship Centre, 1987–93; Ex Services Mental Welfare Soc., 1990–93; Member: Grants and Appeals Cttee, RAF Benevolent Fund, 1987–93; Britain-Australia Bicentennial Cttee, 1984–88; Council, British Atlantic Cttee, 1988–92; Lord Mayor of Sydney's Sister City Cttee, 1994–; Trustee, Australian Arts Foundn, 1985–89. *Address:* 58 Hilltop Road, Clareville, NSW 2107, Australia. *Clubs:* Royal Air Force; Union, University & Schools (Sydney).

CAIN; *see* Nall-Cain, family name of Baron Brocket.

CAIN, Sir Edney; *see* Cain, Sir H. E. C.

CAIN, Sir (Henry) Edney (Conrad), Kt 1986; OBE 1975 (MBE 1965); Order of Distinguished Service (Belize) 2006; FCCA; CA (Belize); first Governor, Central Bank of Belize, 1982–83, reappointed 1991; *b* 2 Dec. 1924; *s* of Henry Edney Conrad Cain I and Rhoda Cain (*née* Stamp); *m* 1951, Leonie (*née* Locke). *Educ:* St George's Coll., Belize; St Michael's Coll., Belize; Balham and Tooting Coll. of Commerce, London. FCCA 1977 (ACCA 1961); CA Belize 1984. Belize Government Service, 1940–: Examr of Accts, Audit Dept, 1954; Auditor, Audit Dept, 1959; Asst Accountant Gen., 1961; Accountant Gen., 1963; Man. Dir, Monetary Authority of Belize, 1976; Ambassador to USA, 1983; High Comr to Canada (resident in Washington, DC), 1984; Financial Sec., Ministry of Finance, Belize, 1985–87; High Comr to UK, 1987–90. Director: Belize Bank Ltd (Chm., 1995–2004); Carlisle Hldgs Ltd (formerly Belize Holdings Inc., then BHI Corp.), 1992–. *Publication:* When the Angel says 'Write' (verse), 1948, 2001. *Recreations:* music, reading, current affairs. *Address:* PO Box 238, 3 Amethyst Street, Orchid Gardens, Belmopan, Belize. *T:* (8) 222492.

CAIN, James Crookall, FCA; Speaker, House of Keys, Isle of Man, 1991–96; Deputy President of Tynwald, 1992–96; *b* Douglas, IOM, 19 March 1927; *s* of James Mylchreest Cain, OBE, JP, formerly MHK and Jean (*née* Crookall); *m* 1959, Muriel Duckworth; two *d*. *Educ:* King William's Coll., IOM. Nat. Service, 1945–48, SSC, E Lancs, 1946. Qualified as Chartered Accountant with W. H. Walker & Co. (Liverpool), 1953; returned to Douglas office, 1954; Partner, 1959–71; Pannell Kerr Forster, 1971–86: Sen. IOM Partner, 1974; retd 1986. Mem., House of Keys, 1986–96; Member: Treasury, 1986–88; Dept of Highways Posts & Properties, 1989; Minister for Health and Social Security, 1989–91. Pres., Hospice Care, 1990 (Chm., 1983–89). *Recreations:* walking, reading. *Address:* Maughold, Alexander Drive, Douglas, Isle of Man IM2 3QZ. *T:* (01624) 675068.

CAIN, Hon. John; MLA (Lab) for Bundoora, 1976–92; Premier of Victoria, 1982–90; Professorial Associate, Department of Political Science, University of Melbourne, since 1991; *b* 26 April 1931; *s* of late Hon. John Cain; *m* 1955, Nancye Williams; two *s* one *d*. *Educ:* Melbourne Univ. (LLB). Practised as barrister and solicitor. Mem., Law Reform

Commn, 1975–77. Pres., Law Inst. of Victoria, 1972–73 (Treasurer, 1969–70; Chm. of Council, 1971–72); Mem. Exec., Law Council of Australia, 1973–76. Vice-Chm., Vic Br., Australian Labor Party, 1973–75; Mem., Parly Labor Exec., 1977–90; Leader, State Labor Party, 1981–90; Leader of Opposition, 1981–82; Minister: for Fed. Affairs, 1982; for Women's Affairs, 1982–90; Attorney-General of Vic, 1982–83. Commonwealth Observer, S African elecns, Apr. 1994. Member: Academic Adv. Bd, Faculty of Business and Law, Deakin Univ., 2004–; Liby Bd of Victoria, 2005– (Pres., 2006–). Chm., Learning Adv. Bd, Hume Global Village, 2004–. Trustee, Melbourne Cricket Ground, 1982–98, 1999–; Mem., Melbourne and Olympic Parks Trust, 2005–. Pres., Grad. Union, Melbourne Univ., 2005–. *Publications:* John Cain's Years: power, parties and politics, 1994; On with the Show, 1998; (with John Hewitt) Off Course: from public place to marketplace at Melbourne University, 2004. *Address:* 9 Magnolia Road, Ivanhoe, Vic 3079, Australia.

CAIN, John Clifford; broadcasting research historian; Controller, Public Affairs, BBC, 1981–84; Hon. Vice-President, Broadcasting Support Services, since 1989 (Chairman, 1980–85; Trustee, 1985–89); *b* 2 April 1924; *s* of William John Cain and Florence Jessie (*née* Wood); *m* 1954, Shirley Jean Roberts; two *d*. *Educ:* Emanuel Sch.; Imperial Coll., Borough Road Coll., London Univ. (BSc); University Coll., London Univ. (MSc); Open Univ. (BA (Hons) 1988; PhD 1996). Served RAF (aircrew), 1944–47. Maths and science teacher in grammar, secondary modern and comprehensive schs and in polytechnic, 1950–59; Lectr, Science Museum, 1959–61; Asst Head of Sch. Broadcasting, Associated-Rediffusion, 1961–63; BBC Television: Producer, 1963–71; Asst Head of Further Educn Dept, 1971–72, Head, 1972–77; Asst Controller, Educn Br., BBC, 1977–80. Dir, Broadcasters' Audience Res. Bd, 1982–84. Mem., Health Educn Council, 1978–83. FRSA 1990. *Publications:* Talking Machines, 1961; (jtly) Mathematics Miscellany, 1966; (contrib.) Culture, Education and the State, 1988; The BBC: 70 years of broadcasting, 1992; (jtly) In a Class of its Own: BBC Education 1924–1994, 1994; articles in EBU Review, Adult Educn, etc. *Recreations:* reading, gardening, music, theatre.

CAIN, Steven Anthony; Co-Founder and Director, GoinGreen, since 2002; Director, Pacific Equity Partners, since 2005; *b* 30 Sept. 1964; *s* of Peter and Patricia Cain; *m* 1993; two *s* one *d*. *Educ:* Imperial Coll., London (MEng Chem. Engrg); Harvard; London Business Sch. Consultant, Bain & Co., 1987–89; Gp Develt Manager, Kingfisher plc, 1989–92; Asda plc: Mktg Controller, 1992–94; Grocery Trading Dir, 1994–95; Store Develt Dir, 1995–97; Mktg Dir, 1997–99; Chief Exec., Carlton Communications, 1999–2000; Gp Man. Dir, Coles Myer Ltd, 2003–05; non-executive Director: Godfreys, 2006–; ARW, 2007–; Borders (Australia), 2008–. Mem., Young Global Leaders, World Econ. Forum, 2005–. *Recreations:* golf, tennis, soccer. *Clubs:* Groucho; National Golf, Kooyong Tennis.

CAIN, His Honour Thomas William, CBE 2003; QC 1989; HM First Deemster and Clerk of the Rolls, Isle of Man, 1998–2003; *b* 1 June 1935; *s* of late James Arthur Cain and Mary Edith Cunningham (*née* Lamb); *m* 1961, Felicity Jane, *d* of late Rev. Arthur Stephen Gregory; two *s* one *d*. *Educ:* King's College Choir Sch., Cambridge; Marlborough Coll.; Worcester Coll., Oxford (BA 1958, MA 1961). National Service, 2nd Lieut RAC, 1953–55. Called to the Bar, Gray's Inn, 1959; Advocate, Manx Bar, 1961. Attorney-General, Isle of Man, 1980–93; Second Deemster, 1993–98. Pres., I of M Law Soc., 1985–89. Hon. Fellow, Soc. for Advanced Legal Studies, 2000. *Recreations:* sailing; Chairman, Manx Wildlife Trust. *Address:* Ivie Cottage, Kirk Michael, Isle of Man IM6 1AU. *T:* (01624) 878266.

CAINE, Sir Michael, Kt 2000; CBE 1992; actor; *b* Old Kent Road, London, 14 March 1933 (Maurice Joseph Micklewhite); *s* of late Maurice and of Ellen Frances Marie Micklewhite; *m* 1st, 1955, Patricia Haines (marr. diss.); one *d*; 2nd, 1973, Shakira Baksh; one *d*. *Educ:* Wilson's Grammar Sch., Peckham. Began acting in youth club drama gp. Served in Army, Berlin and Korea, 1951–53. Asst Stage Manager, Westminster Rep., Horsham, Sx, 1953; actor, Lowestoft Rep., 1953–55; Theatre Workshop, London, 1955; numerous TV appearances (over 100 plays), 1957–63; *play:* Next Time I'll Sing for You, Arts, 1963; *films:* A Hill in Korea, 1956; How to Murder a Rich Uncle, 1958; Zulu, 1964; The Ipcress File, 1965; Alfie, The Wrong Box, Gambit, 1966; Hurry Sundown, Woman Times Seven, Deadfall, 1967; The Magus, Battle of Britain, Play Dirty, 1968; The Italian Job, 1969; Too Late the Hero, 1970; The Last Valley, Get Carter, 1971; Zee & Co., Kidnapped, Pulp, 1972; Sleuth, 1973; The Black Windmill, Marseilles Contract, The Wilby Conspiracy, 1974; Fat Chance, The Romantic Englishwoman, The Man who would be King, Harry and Walter Go to New York, 1975; The Eagle has Landed, A Bridge Too Far, Silver Bears, 1976; The Swarm, 1977; California Suite, 1978; Ashanti, Beyond the Poseidon Adventure, The Island, Dressed to Kill, 1979; Escape to Victory, 1980; Death Trap, 1981; Jigsaw Man, Educating Rita, The Honorary Consul, 1982; Blame it on Rio, 1984; Water, The Holcroft Covenant, 1985; Hannah and Her Sisters (Academy Award), Half Moon Street, Mona Lisa, 1986; The Fourth Protocol, The Whistle Blower, Surrender, Jaws The Revenge, 1987; Without a Clue, Dirty Rotten Scoundrels, 1989; A Shock to the System, Bullseye, Mr Destiny, 1990; Noises Off, Blue Ice, The Muppet Christmas Carol, 1992; On Deadly Ground, 1993; Bullet to Beijing, 1994; Mandela and de Klerk, 1996; Blood & Wine, Curtain Call, Shadowrun, 1997; The Debtors, 1998; Little Voice, 1999; The Cider House Rules (Academy Award), Quills, Last Orders, Quick Sands, 2000; Miss Congeniality, Shiner, 2001; Last Orders, The Quiet American, Austin Powers in Goldmember, 2002; The Actors, Secondhand Lions, The Statement, 2003; Around the Bend, Batman Begins, Bewitched, 2005; The Weather Man, Children of Men, The Prestige, 2006; Sleuth, 2007; The Dark Knight, Is There Anybody There?, 2008; *films for TV:* Jack The Ripper, 1988; Jekyll and Hyde, 1989; World War II: When Lions Roared, 1994. Fellow, BAFTA, 2000. *Publications:* Not Many People Know That, 1985; Not Many People Know This Either, 1986; Moving Picture Show, 1988; Acting in Film, 1990; What's It All About (autobiog.), 1992. *Recreations:* cinema, theatre, travel, gardening. *Address:* c/o International Creative Management, Oxford House, 76 Oxford Street, W1N 0AX.

CAINES, Eric, CB 1993; Professor of Health Service Management, Nottingham University, 1993–96; *b* 27 Feb. 1936; *s* of Ernest and Doris Caines; *m* 1st, 1958 (marr. diss. 1984); three *s*; 2nd, 1984, Karen Higgs; two *s*. *Educ:* Rothwell Grammar School, Wakefield; Leeds Univ. (LLB Hons). Dip. Hist. Art, London Univ., 1984. Short Service Commission, RAEC, 1958–61. NCB, 1961–65; BBC, 1965–66; as Principal, Min. of Health, Management Side Sec., General Whitley Council, 1966–70; Sec., NHS Reorganisation Management Arrangements Study, 1970–73; Assistant Sec., DHSS, 1973–77; IMF/World Bank, Washington, 1977–79; Under Sec., DHSS, 1979, Dir, Regl Organisation, 1981–84; Dir, Personnel and Finance, Prison Dept, Home Office, 1984–87; Dir, Operational Strategy, DHSS, then DSS, 1987–90; Dir of Personnel, NHS, DoH, 1990–93. Mem., Sheehy Inquiry into Police Responsibilities and Rewards. Director: Trebor Ltd, 1985–90; Premier Prisons, 1994–. FIPM. *Recreation:* travelling on foot with a book. *Address:* Mill Farm, Church Road, Brasted, Westerham, Kent TN16 1HZ. *T:* (01959) 564478. *Club:* Athenæum.

CAINES, Sir John, KCB 1991 (CB 1983); Permanent Secretary, Department for Education (formerly of Education and Science), 1989–93; *b* 13 Jan. 1933; *s* of late John Swinburne Caines and Ethel May Stenlake; *m* 1963, Mary Large (*d* 2008); one *s* two *d*. *Educ:* Sherborne Prep. Sch.; Westminster Sch.; Christ Church, Oxford (MA). Asst Principal, Min. of Supply, 1957; Asst Private Sec., Min. of Aviation, 1960–61; Principal, Min. of Aviation, 1961–64; Civil Air Attaché in Middle East, 1964–66; Manchester Business Sch., 1967; Asst Sec., BoT, 1968; Sec., Commn on Third London Airport, 1968–71; Asst Sec., DTI, 1971–72; Principal Private Sec. to Sec. of State for Trade and Industry, 1972–74; Under-Sec., Dept of Trade, 1974–77; Sec., 1977–80, Mem. and Dep. Chief Exec., 1979–80, NEB; Dep. Sec., Dept of Trade, and Chief Exec., BOTB, 1980–82; Dep. Sec., Central Policy Review Staff, Cabinet Office, 1983; Dep. Sec., DTI, 1983–87; Permanent Sec., ODA, FCO, 1987–89. Director: Investors Compensation Scheme, 1993–2001 (Dep. Chm., 1997–2001); Norsk Hydro (UK) Ltd, 1994–2000; Medical Defence Union, 1998–2004; Chm., European Capital, 1995–2000. Mem., Gibraltar Financial Services Commn, 1995–2002. Ind. Reviewer for ASA, 1999–. Member of Council: Southampton Univ., 1993–2000; Open Univ., 1993–2001 (Chm., Audit Cttee, 1993–2001). Chm., Dr Busby's Trustees, Westminster Sch., 2002–. DUniv Open, 1993. *Address:* 13 Hambleden Place, SE21 7EY.

CAIO, Francesco; Vice-Chairman, Europe, 2006–08, and Chairman, European Advisory Board, 2007–08, Lehman Brothers; *b* 23 Aug. 1957; *m* 1986, Meryl Wakefield; two *s*. *Educ:* Politecnico of Milan (Master Computer Sci. 1980); Insead, France (Luca Braito Schol.; MBNA 1985). Product Manager, Telecom Systems, Olivetti SpA, 1982–84; McKinsey & Co., London, 1986–91; Olivetti SpA, 1991; founder and CEO, Omnitel Pronto Italia SpA, 1993–96; CEO, Olivetti SpA, Ivrea, 1996; CEO, Merloni Elettrodomestici SpA, 1997–2000; founder and CEO, Netscalibur Co., 2000–03; CEO, Cable and Wireless plc, 2003–06. *Recreations:* photography, Inter Milan FC, family.

CAIRD, Most Rev. Donald Arthur Richard; Archbishop of Dublin and Primate of Ireland, 1985–96; *b* Dublin, 11 Dec. 1925; *s* of George Robert Caird and Emily Florence Dreaper, Dublin; *m* 1963, Nancy Ballantyne, *d* of Prof. William Sharpe, MD, and Gwendolyn Hind, New York, USA; one *s* two *d*. *Educ:* Wesley Coll., Dublin, 1935–44; Trinity Coll., Dublin Univ., 1944–50. Sen. Exhibn, TCD, 1946; elected Schol. of the House, TCD, 1948; 1st cl. Moderatorship in Mental and Moral Science, 1949; Prizeman in Hebrew and Irish Language, 1946 and 1947; Lilian Mary Luce Memorial Prize for Philosophy, 1947; BA 1949; MA and BD 1955; HDipEd 1959. Curate Asst, St Mark's. Dundela, Belfast, 1950–53; Chaplain and Asst Master, Portora Royal Sch., Enniskillen, 1953–57; Lectr in Philosophy, University Coll. of St David's, Lampeter, 1957; Rector, Rathmichael Parish, Shankill, Co. Dublin, 1960–69; Asst Master, St Columba's Coll., Rathfarnham, Co. Dublin, 1960–67; Dept Lectr in Philosophy, Trinity Coll., Dublin, 1962–63; Lectr in the Philosophy of Religion, Church of Ireland Theol Coll., Dublin, 1964–70; Dean of Ossory, 1969–70; Bishop of Limerick, Ardfert and Aghadoe, 1970–76; Bishop of Meath and Kildare, 1976–85. Fellow of St Columba's Coll., Dublin, 1971. Vis. Prof., Gen. Theol Seminary of ECUSA, 1997. Mem., Bord na Gaeilge, 1974; Hon. Life Mem., Royal Dublin Soc., 1996. Hon. DD TCD, 1988; Hon. LLD: NCEA, 1993; NUI, 1995; Hon. PhD Pontifical Univ., St Patrick's Coll., Maynooth, 2002. *Publication:* The Predicament of Natural Theology since the Criticism of Kant, in Directions, 1970 (Dublin). *Recreations:* swimming, tennis, walking. *Address:* 3 Crofton Avenue, Dun Laoghaire, Co. Dublin, Ireland.

CAIRD, Prof. George, FRAM; oboist, since 1970; Principal: Birmingham Conservatoire, Birmingham City University (formerly University of Central England in Birmingham), since 1993; Birmingham School of Acting, since 2006; *b* 30 Aug. 1950; *s* of late Rev. Dr George Bradford Caird, FBA, and Viola Mary Caird (*née* Newport); *m* 1st, 1974, Sarah Dorothy Verney (marr. diss. 1999); three *s* one *d*; 2nd, 2001, Jane Amanda Salmon; one *d*. *Educ:* Magdalen Coll. Sch., Oxford; Royal Acad. of Music (LRAM, FRAM 1989); Peterhouse, Cambridge (MA). ARCM, FRCM 1999; FRNCM 2004. Hd, Woodwind and Orchestral Studies, RAM, 1987–93. Chamber musician, notably with Albion Ensemble, Caird Oboe Quartet. Has made recordings. Sec., Fedn of British Conservatoires, 1998–2003; Sec.-Gen., Assoc. of Eur. Conservatoires, 2004–. Chairman: Music Educn Council, 2001–04; Nat. Assoc. of Youth Orchestras, 2005–. Mem. Regl Cttee, Arts Council W Midlands, 2002–04. Pres., ISM, 2004–05. Trustee: Symphony Hall Birmingham, 2001–; Youth Music, 2004–; Countess of Munster Musical Trust, 2007–. Bd Mem., Culture W Midlands (formerly W Midlands Life), 2003–. Dir, New Generation Arts Fest., Birmingham, 2006–. Pres., Royal Acad. Music Club, 2007–08. FRSA 1994. Hon. FLCM 1999. *Publications:* contrib. articles to music and music educn jls. *Recreations:* reading, theatre, languages, travel, fell-walking. *Address:* Birmingham Conservatoire, Paradise Place, Birmingham B3 3HG. *T:* (0121) 331 5910; *e-mail:* george.caird@bcu.ac.uk; 77 Oxford Road, Moseley, Birmingham B13 9SG.

See also J. N. Caird.

CAIRD, John Newport; director, writer and producer of plays, opera and musical theatre; Hon. Associate Director, Royal Shakespeare Company, since 1990; *b* 22 Sept. 1948; *s* of late Rev. George Bradford Caird, DPhil, DD, FBA and Viola Mary Newport, MA; *m* 1st, 1972, Helen Frances Brammer (marr. diss. 1982); 2nd, 1982, Ann Dorszynski (marr. diss. 1990); two *s* one *d*; 3rd, 1990, Frances Ruffelle (marr. diss. 1997); one *s* one *d*; 4th, 1998, Maoko Imai; one *s* two *d*. *Educ:* Selwyn House Sch., Montreal; Magdalen Coll. Sch., Oxford; Bristol Old Vic Theatre Sch. Associate Dir, Contact Theatre, Manchester, 1974–76; directed, Contact: Games, After Liverpool, Krapp's Last Tape, Look Back in Anger, Downright Hooligan, Twelfth Night; Jt founder and Dir, Circle of Muses, touring music theatre troupe, 1976; Director: Regina v. Stephens, Avon Touring Th. Co.; Last Resort, Sidewalk Th. Co., 1976; Resident Dir, 1977–82, Associate Dir, 1983–90, RSC; directed, RSC: Dance of Death, 1977; Savage Amusement, Look Out, Here Comes Trouble, 1978; Caucasian Chalk Circle, 1979; (co-dir, with Trevor Nunn) Nicholas Nickleby, London, New York and Los Angeles, 1980, 1982, 1986 (SWET Award, 1980, Tony Award, 1982, for Best Dir; televised, 1981, Emmy Award, 1983); Naked Robots, Twin Rivals, 1981; Our Friends in the North, 1982; Peter Pan (adapted and co-dir with Trevor Nunn), 1982–84; Twelfth Night, Romeo and Juliet, 1983; The Merchant of Venice, Red Star, 1984; Philistines, 1985; Les Misérables (adapted and co-dir with Trevor Nunn), London, 1985 and worldwide, 1985–2008 (Tony Award for Best Dir, 1987); Every Man in his Humour, Misalliance, 1986; A Question of Geography, The New Inn, 1987; As You Like It, A Midsummer Night's Dream, 1989; Columbus and the Discovery of Japan, Antony and Cleopatra, 1992; directed, RNT: Trelawny of the 'Wells', 1993; The Seagull, 1994; Stanley, 1996, NY, 1997 (Outer Critics Circle Award for Best Dir); Peter Pan, 1997; Money, Candide (a new version with music by Leonard Bernstein), 1999 (Olivier Award, 2000); Hamlet, 2000 (world tour, 2001); Humble Boy, 2001, transf. Gielgud, 2002, NY, 2003, UK tour, 2003; Chain Play, 2001. Director: Song and Dance, London, 1982; As You Like It, Stockholm, 1984 (also for TV, 1985); Zaïdé by Mozart, Battignano, 1991; Life Sentences, NY, 1993; The Millionairess (UK tour), 1995; Murder in the Red Barn, Tiller-Clowes Marionettes, Theatre Mus., 1999; Midsummer Night's Dream, 2000, Twelfth Night, 2002, Stockholm; What the Night is For, 2002, Rattle of a Simple Man, 2004, Comedy Th.; Becket, Th. Royal, Haymarket, The Screams of Kitty

Genovese, NY, 2004; Macbeth, Almeida, 2005; Don Carlos, WNO, 2005; The Beggar's Opera, Tokyo and Osaka, 2006–08 (televised 2006); Dödsdansen, Stockholm, 2007 (televised 2007); A Midsummer Night's Dream, Tokyo, 2007; Don Carlos, Canadian Opera Co., Toronto, 2007; Aida, WNO, 2008. Devised and dir., Intimate Letters (a series of concerts for actors and string quartet); staged: WWF Religion and Interfaith Ceremony, Assisi, 1986; WWF Sacred Gifts for a Living Planet Ceremony, Bakhtapur, Nepal, 2000; wrote and directed: The Kingdom of the Spirit, London, 1986; Siegfried & Roy at the Mirage, Las Vegas, 1989; Children of Eden, a musical drama (with music and lyrics by Stephen Schwartz), London, 1991, and worldwide, 1991–2008; The Beggar's Opera (a new version with music by Ilona Sekacz), RSC and worldwide, 1992–2008; Jane Eyre, a musical drama (music by Paul Gordon), Canada and USA, 1995–2008; Twin Spirits, Royal Opera Hse Gala, 2005, New Victory Th., NY, Windsor Castle, Salisbury Cath., 2006; Kinshu (with Kiyomi Fujii), Tokyo, 2007 (Japan Maj. Theatres Award, 2008); wrote: Daddy Long Legs, a musical romance (music by Paul Gordon), 2004; Brief Encounter, opera (with music by André Previn), 2007; adapted and dir., Henry IV (BBC TV), 1995. Produced: (with Holly Kendrick) Fortnight of New Writing and Directing, Caird Co., Highgate, 2001; Observe the Sons of Ulster Marching Towards the Somme, Playing Soldiers, Pleasance Th., 2002; Disintegration, Arcola Th., 2002; New British Plays, Jerwood Space, 2002; Northern Lights, Soho Th., 2002; Robin Hood, NT, 2002; Five Corners, Jerwood Centre, 2003; Theatre Café, Arcola Th., 2004; Arab-Israeli Cookbook, Gate Th., 2004; Cancer Time, Theatre 503, New Directions, Th. Royal, Haymarket, 2004. Recordings: Beggar's Opera; Children of Eden; Jane Eyre; Candide. Trustee: G. B. Caird Meml Trust, 1990–; Friends of Highgate Cemetery Trust Ltd, 1999–. Hon. FRWCMD. Hon. Fellow, Mansfield Coll., Oxford, 2000. Hon. DLitt UEA, 2006. *Publications:* (with Trevor Nunn) Peter Pan, by J. M. Barrie (new versions), 1993, 1998; (with Stephen Schwartz) Children of Eden, 1996; The Beggar's Opera (new version, with Ilona Sekacz), 1999; Candide (new version, with music by Leonard Bernstein), 2003; (with Paul Gordon) Jane Eyre, 2003. *Recreations:* music, children. *Address:* Church House, 10 South Grove, Highgate, N6 6BS.

See also G. Caird.

CAIRNCROSS, Frances Anne, (Mrs Hamish McRae), CBE 2004; Rector, Exeter College, University of Oxford, since 2004; Chairman, Economic and Social Research Council, 2001–07; *b* 30 Aug. 1944; *d* of Sir Alexander Kirkland Cairncross, KCMG, FBA and late Mary Frances (*née* Glynn); *m* 1971, Hamish McRae, *qv*; two *d*. *Educ:* Laurel Bank Sch., Glasgow; St Anne's Coll., Oxford (MA History; Hon. Fellow 1993); Brown Univ., Rhode Island (MAEcon). On Staff of: The Times, 1967–69; The Banker, 1969; The Observer, 1970–73; Economics Correspondent, 1973–81, Women's Page Editor, 1981–84, The Guardian; The Economist: Britain Ed., 1984–89; Envmt Ed., 1989–94; Media Ed., 1994–97; Public Policy Ed., 1997–98; Mgt Ed., 1999–2004. Member: SSRC Economics Cttee, 1972–76; Newspaper Panel, Monopolies Commn, 1973–80; Council, Royal Economic Soc., 1980–85; Council, PSI, 1987–90; Cttee of Inquiry into Proposals to Amend the Shops Act, 1983–84; Inquiry into British Housing, 1984–85; School Teachers Review Body, 1991–94; Council, Inst. for Fiscal Studies, 1995–2001, 2007–; Scottish Council of Econ. Advrs, 2007–; Adv. Bd, Foundn for Effective Governance, Ukraine, 2007–. Director: Prolific Gp plc, 1988–89; Alliance & Leicester Gp plc (formerly Alliance & Leicester Building Soc.), 1990–2004; Stramongate Ltd, 2005–. Pres., BAAS, 2005–06 (Hon. Fellow, 2006). Gov., NIESR, 1995–2001. Vis. Fellow, Nuffield Coll., Oxford, 2001–04. Hon. Treas., Nat. Council for One Parent Families, 1980–83; Trustee, Kennedy Memorial Trust, 1974–90. High Sheriff, Greater London, 2004–05. Founding Fellow, Inst. of Contemporary Scotland, 2000; FRSE 2003. Hon. Fellow: St Peter's Coll., Oxford, 2003; Cardiff Univ., 2004. Hon. Life FRSA, 2006. Hon. DLitt: Glasgow, 2001; Loughborough, 2003; Hon. DSc: Birmingham, 2002; City, 2003; Bristol, 2004; TCD, 2005; Hon. DPhil London Metropolitan, 2004; Hon. DBA Kingston, 2005. European Women of Achievement Award, 2002 (Awards Pres., 2007–). *Publications:* Capital City (with Hamish McRae), 1971; The Second Great Crash (with Hamish McRae), 1973; The Guardian Guide to the Economy, 1981; Changing Perceptions of Economic Policy, 1981; The Second Guardian Guide to the Economy, 1983; Guide to the Economy, 1987; Costing the Earth, 1991; Green, Inc, 1995; The Death of Distance, 1997; The Company of the Future, 2002. *Recreation:* home life. *Address:* Exeter College, Oxford OX1 3DP.

CAIRNCROSS, Neil Francis, CB 1971; Deputy Under-Secretary of State, Home Office, 1972–80; *b* 29 July 1920; *s* of late James and Olive Hunter Cairncross; *m* 1947, Eleanor Elizabeth Leisten; two *s* one *d*. *Educ:* Charterhouse; Oriel Coll., Oxford. Royal Sussex Regt, 1940–45. Called to the Bar, 1948. Home Office, 1948; a Private Sec. to the Prime Minister, 1955–58; Sec., Royal Commn on the Press, 1961–62; Dep. Sec., Cabinet Office, 1970–72; Dep. Sec., NI Office, March–Nov. 1972. Member: Parole Bd, 1982–85; Home Grown Timber Adv. Cttee, 1981–90; (co-opted) Avon Probation Cttee, 1983–89. *Recreation:* painting. *Address:* Little Grange, The Green, Olveston, Bristol BS35 4EJ. *T:* (01454) 613060. *Club:* Oxford and Cambridge.

CAIRNS, family name of **Earl Cairns**.

CAIRNS, 6th Earl *cr* 1878; **Simon Dallas Cairns,** CVO 2000; CBE 1992; Baron Cairns 1867; Viscount Garmoyle 1878; Chairman, Charities Aid Foundation, since 2003; *b* 27 May 1939; *er s* of 5th Earl Cairns, GCVO, CB and Barbara Jeanne Harrisson, *y d* of Sydney H. Burgess; *S* father, 1989; *m* 1964, Amanda Mary, *d* of late Major E. F. Heathcoat Amory, and Mrs Roderick Heathcoat Amory; three *s*. *Educ:* Eton; Trinity Coll., Cambridge. Man. Dir, 1981–84, a Vice-Chm., 1984–86, Mercury Securities plc; S. G. Warburg & Co.: Man. Dir, 1979–85; Dir, 1985–95; a Vice-Chm., 1985–87; Jt Chm., 1987–91; Chief Exec. and Dep. Chm., 1991–95; Chairman: Commonwealth Develt Corp., subseq. CDC Gp plc, 1995–2004, subseq. Actis, 2004–05; BAT Industries, 1996–98 (Dir, 1990–); Allied Zurich, 1998–2000; Vice-Chairman: Zurich Financial Services, 1998–2000; Zurich Allied AG, 1998–2000; Dep. Chm., 2004–, Chm., 2007–, Celtel Internat. BV. Receiver-General, Duchy of Cornwall, 1990–2000. Mem., City Capital Markets Cttee, 1989–94. Chairman: VSO, 1981–92; ODI, 1995–2002; Commonwealth Business Council, 1997–2002 (Chm. Emeritus, 2003); Look Ahead Housing and Care, 2003–05. Curator, Oxford Univ. Chest, 1995–2000. Trustee, The Diana Princess of Wales Meml Fund, 1998–2006; Dir, M. Ibrahim Foundn, 2007–. *Heir:* *s* Viscount Garmoyle, *qv*. *Address:* (office) 78 Brook Street, W1K 5EF. *Club:* Turf.

CAIRNS, (Agnes Lawrie Addie) Shonaig; *see* Macpherson, A. L. A. S.

CAIRNS, Alun Hugh; Member (C) South Wales West, National Assembly for Wales, since 1999; *b* 30 July 1970; *s* of Hewitt and Margaret Cairns; *m* 1996, Emma Elizabeth Turner; one *s*. *Educ:* Ysgol Gyfun Ddwyieithog Ystalyfera; MBA Wales 2001. Joined Lloyds Bank Gp, 1989; Business Develt Consultant, Lloyds TSB (formerly Lloyds Bank), 1993–. Joined Conservative Party, 1987; economic spokesman, 1997–2007, educn spokesman, 2007–, Wales. Contested (C): Gower, 1997; Vale of Glamorgan, 2005. *Address:* National Assembly for Wales, Cardiff Bay, Cardiff CF99 1NA.

CAIRNS, Andrew Ruaraidh A.; *see* Adams-Cairns.

CAIRNS, David; MP (Lab) Inverclyde, since 2005 (Greenock and Inverclyde, 2001–05); *b* 7 Aug. 1966; *s* of John Cairns and Teresa Cairns (*née* Harkins). *Educ:* Gregorian Univ., Rome; Franciscan Study Centre, Canterbury. Priest, 1991–94; Dir, Christian Socialist Movement, 1994–97; Researcher to Siobhain McDonagh, MP, 1997–2001. Parly Under-Sec. of State: Scotland Office, 2005–07; NI Office, 2006–07; Minister of State, Scotland Office, 2007–08. *Recreations:* cinema, reading (US history). *Address:* House of Commons, SW1A 0AA.

CAIRNS, David Adam; Music Critic, Sunday Times, 1985–92; *b* 8 June 1926; *s* of Sir Hugh William Bell Cairns, KBE, FRCS and Barbara Cairns, *d* of A. L. Smith, sometime Master of Balliol; *m* 1959, Rosemary, *d* of Aubrey and Hilary Goodwin; three *s*. *Educ:* Trinity Coll., Oxford (1st Cl. Mod. History). Nat. Service, Intell. Corps, 1949–50. Co-Founder, Chelsea Opera Gp, 1950; Jane Eliza Procter Fellow, Princeton, 1950–51; Liby Clerk, H of C, 1951–53; TES, 1955–58; Music Critic, Evening Standard, and Spectator, 1958–62; Arts Editor, Spectator, 1961–62; Asst Music Critic, Financial Times, 1962–67; Music Critic, New Statesman, 1967–70; Classical Programme Co-ordinator, Philips Records, 1968–73; freelance music critic, 1973–85; founder and conductor, Thorington Players, 1983. Dist. Vis. Prof., Univ. of California, Davis, 1985; Vis. Scholar, Getty Center for History of Art and Humanities, 1992; Vis. Res. Fellow, Merton Coll., Oxford, 1993. FRSL 2001. Hon. RAM 2000. Hon. DLitt Southampton, 2001. CBE 1997; Officier de l'Ordre des Arts et des Lettres, 1991 (Chevalier, 1975). *Publications:* The Memoirs of Hector Berlioz (ed and trans.), 1969, 5th edn 2002; Responses: musical essays and reviews, 1973; Berlioz, vol. 1, The Making of an Artist 1803–1832, 1989 (Yorkshire Post Prize; Royal Phil. Soc. Award; Derek Allen Meml Prize, British Acad.; ASCAP Deems Taylor Award, 2001), vol. 2, Servitude and Greatness 1832–1869, 1999 (Whitbread Award for Biography, Royal Phil. Soc. Award, 1999; Samuel Johnson Non-fiction Prize, 2000; Prix de l'Academie Charles Croz, 2003); Mozart and His Operas, 2006; (jtly) English National Opera Guides: The Magic Flute, 1980; Falstaff, 1982. *Recreations:* conducting, Shakespeare, France and the French. *Address:* 49 Amerland Road, SW18 1QA. *T:* (020) 8870 4931.

CAIRNS, Air Vice-Marshal Geoffrey Crerar, CBE 1970; AFC 1960; FRAeS 1979; Chief of Staff No 18 Group, Strike Command, 1978–80; *b* 21 May 1926; *s* of late Dr J. W. Cairns, MD, MCh, DPH and Marion Cairns; *m* 1948, Carol (*d* 1985), *d* of H. I. F. Evernden, MBE; four *d*. *Educ:* Loretto School, Musselburgh; Cambridge Univ. Joined RAF, 1944; served: Sqdns 43 and 93, Italy; Sqdn 73, Malta, 1946–49; Sqdn 72, UK, 1949–51; Adjutant, Hong Kong Auxiliary Air Force; test pilot A&AEE, Boscombe Down, 1957–60; Jt Planning Staff, MoD, 1961; Chief Instructor, Helicopters, CFS, RAF Ternhill, 1963; JSSC 1966; Supt Flying A&AEE 1968; Dir, Defence Operational Requirements Staffs, MoD, 1970; Commandant, Boscombe Down, 1972–74; ACAS (Op. Requirements), MoD, 1974–76; Comdr, Southern Maritime Air Region, 1976–78. Dir, Trago Aircraft Ltd, 1982–87. Consultant: Marconi Avionics, 1980–81; FLS Aerospace (Lovaux) Ltd, 1992–94. *Recreations:* golf, railways. *Club:* Royal Air Force.

CAIRNS, Hugh John Forster, DM; FRS 1974; Professor of Microbiology, Harvard School of Public Health, 1980–91; *b* 21 Nov. 1922; *er s* of Prof. Sir Hugh Cairns, KBE, DM; *m* 1948, Elspeth Mary Foster; two *s* one *d*. *Educ:* Balliol Coll., Oxford Univ. (BA 1943; BM, BCh 1946; DM 1952). Surg. Registrar, Radcliffe Infirmary, Oxford, 1945; Med. Intern, Postgrad. Med. Sch., London, 1946; Paediatric Intern, Royal Victoria Infirmary, Newcastle, 1947; Chem. Pathologist, Radcliffe Infirmary, 1947–49; Virologist, Hall Inst., Melbourne, Aust., 1950–51; Virus Research Inst., Entebbe, Uganda, 1952–54; Research Fellow, then Reader, Aust. Nat. Univ., Canberra, 1955–63; Rockefeller Research Fellow, California Inst. of Technology, 1957; Nat. Insts of Health Fellow, Cold Spring Harbor, NY, 1960–61; Dir, Cold Spring Harbor Lab. of Quantitative Biology, 1963–68; Prof of Biology (Hon.), State Univ. of New York, Stony Brook, 1968–73, Amer. Cancer Soc. Prof. 1968–73; Head of Imperial Cancer Research Fund Mill Hill Laboratories, 1973–80. MacArthur Fellow, 1982. *Address:* 105 Alleyn Park, SE21 8AA. *T:* (020) 8693 3006; *e-mail:* j.cairns@ctsu.ox.ac.uk.

CAIRNS, Very Rev. John Ballantyne; Minister of Aberlady and Gullane Parish Churches, since 2001; Chaplain to the Queen, since 1997; Dean of the Chapel Royal in Scotland, since 2005; *b* 15 March 1942; *s* of William Cairns and Isobel Margaret (*née* Thom); *m* 1968, Elizabeth Emma Bradley; three *s*. *Educ:* Sutton Valence Sch., Kent; Bristol Univ. (LLB); Edinburgh Univ. (LTh). Messrs Richards, Butler & Co., Solicitors, 1964–68; E Lothian CC, 1968–69; Asst Minister, St Giles, Elgin, 1973–75; ordained, 1974; Minister: Langholm, Ewes and Westerkirk, 1975–85, also linked with Canonbie, 1981–85; Riverside, Dumbarton, 1985–2001. Moderator, Presbytery of Dumbarton, 1993–94. General Assembly of the Church of Scotland: Convener: Cttee on Maintenance of the Ministry and Bd of Ministry and Mission, 1984–88; Cttee on Chaplains to HM Forces, 1993–98; Chm., Judicial Commn, 1993–98; Chaplain to the Moderator, 1995–96; Moderator, 1999–2000; Chaplain to Lord High Comr (HRH the Duke of York), 2007. Gen. Trustee, Church of Scotland, 1996–. Chaplain, Queen's Body Guard for Scotland, Royal Co. of Archers, 2007–. Pres., Friends of St Andrew's, Jerusalem, 2005–. Hon. DD Aberdeen, 2003; Hon. LLD Bristol, 2004. *Publications:* Keeping Fit for Ministry, 1988; articles in various theol jls. *Recreations:* golf, gardening, Robert Burns. *Address:* The Manse, Hummel Road, Gullane EH31 2BG. *T:* (01620) 843192.

CAIRNS, Patricia Rose Marie R.; *see* Roberts Cairns.

CAIRNS, Robert; Chairman, East of Scotland Water, 1998–2002; *b* 16 July 1947; *s* of William and Mary Cairns; *m* 1st, 1972, Pauline Reidy (marr. diss. 1995); two *s*; 2nd, 2003, Jean Margaret Smith (*née* Dow). *Educ:* Morgan Acad., Dundee; Univ. of Edinburgh (MA Hons); Moray House Coll. (DipEd). Asst Ed., Scottish Nat. Dictionary, 1969–74; teacher, James Gillespie's High Sch., 1975–96. Mem. (Lab), Edinburgh CC, 1974–2007 (Convener, Planning Cttee, 1986; Exec. Mem. for Envmt and Streets, 2003–07). Contested (Lab) N Edinburgh, Nov. 1973, Feb. 1974. *Recreations:* theatre, food and drink, walking. *Address:* Eastergate Cottage, Harrietfield, Logiealmond, Perthshire PH1 3JD.

CAITHNESS, 20th Earl of, *cr* 1455; **Malcolm Ian Sinclair,** PC 1990; FRICS; Lord Berriedale, 1455; Bt 1631; consultant and trustee to various companies and trusts, since 1994; Chief Executive, Clan Sinclair Trust, since 1999; *b* 3 Nov. 1948; *s* of 19th Earl of Caithness, CVO, CBE, DSO, DL, JP; *S* father, 1965; *m* 1st, 1975, Diana Caroline (*d* 1994), *d* of Major Richard Coke, DSO, MC, DL; one *s* one *d*; 2nd, 2004, Leila Jenkins (marr. diss. 2007). *Educ:* Marlborough; Royal Agricl Coll., Cirencester. Savills, land and estate agents, 1972–78; Brown and Mumford, 1978–80; property developer and other small businesses, 1980–84. A Lord in Waiting (Govt Whip), 1984–85; parly spokesman on health and social security, 1984–85, on Scotland, 1984–86; Parly Under-Sec. of State, Dept of Transport, 1985–86; Minister of State: Home Office, 1986–88; DoE, 1988–89; Paymaster Gen. and Minister of State, HM Treasury, 1989–90; Minister of State: FCO, 1990–92; Dept of Transport, 1992–94; elected Mem., H of L, 1999. Dir, 1995–98, Consultant, 1998–2006, Victoria Soames, Residential Property Consultants; Consultant, Rickett-Tinne, 2006–. *Heir:* *s* Lord Berriedale, *qv*. *Address:* c/o House of Lords, SW1A 0PW.

CALATRAVA-VALLS, Dr Santiago; architect; *b* Valencia, 28 July 1951; *m* 1976, Robertina Calatrava-Maragoni; three *s*. *Educ:* art sch., Valencia; Escuela Technica Superior de Arquitectura de Valencia; Swiss Fed. Inst. of Technol., Zürich (studies in civil engrg; Dr Tech. Sci.). Asst, Inst. for Bldg Statics and Construction and for Aerodynamics and Light Weight Constructions, Zürich, 1979–81; Founder: architectural and civil engrg practice, Zürich, 1981; architectural practice, Paris, 1989, and Valencia, 1991. Major projects include: Stadelhofen Rly Stn, Zürich, 1983–90; Lucerne Stn Hall, 1983–89; BCE Place, Toronto, 1987–92; Alamillo Bridge and La Cartuja Viaduct, Seville, 1987–92; Lusitania Bridge, Merida, 1988–91; Montjuic Communication Tower, Barcelona, 1989–92; Lyon Airport Rly Stn, 1989–94; Campo Volantin Footbridge, Bilbao, 1990–97; Alameda Bridge and underground stn, Valencia, 1991–95; Kuwait Pavilion, Expo '92, Seville, 1991–92; Auditorio de Tenerife, 1991–2003; Oriente Rly Stn, Lisbon, 1993–98; Sondica Airport, Bilbao, 2000; Milwaukee Art Mus. expansion, 2001; Olympic Sports Complex, Athens, 2004; Zürich Univ. Law Faculty, 2004; Turning Torso Tower, Malmö, 2005. Exhibitions of work include: Mus. of Architecture, Basel, 1987; Design Mus., Zürich, 1991; Mus. of Modern Art, NY, 1993; retrospective, RIBA, London, 1992; Deutsches Mus., Munich, 1993; Valencia, Lübeck and Copenhagen, 1993; Florence, 2000. Member: Union of Swiss Architects, 1987; Internat. Acad. of Architecture, 1987; European Acad., 1992. Hon. FRIBA 1993. Hon. Mem., Union of German Architects, 1989. Hon. doctorates include Dr *hc*: Valencia, 1993; Seville, 1994. Numerous international prizes and awards including: Internat. Assoc. for Bridge and Structural Engrg Award, 1988; Gold Medal, IStructE, 1992. *Address:* Parkring 11, 8002 Zürich, Switzerland. *T:* (1) 204500, *Fax:* (1) 2045001.

CALDAS, Prof. Carlos, MD; FRCP, FACP, FMedSci; Professor of Cancer Medicine (formerly Clinical Oncology), University of Cambridge, since 2002; Hon. Consultant, Addenbrooke's Hospital, Cambridge, since 1996; *b* 27 June 1960; *s* of Carlos da Silva Caldas and Isilda de Jesus Catarino Simão; *m* 1988, Maria Isabel Rebelo de Andrade e Sousa; one *s* one *d*. *Educ:* Univ. of Lisbon (MD 1984). FACP 1999; FRCP 2002. Jun. House Officer, 1985–86, SHO, 1986–88, Santa Maria Univ. Hosp., Lisbon; Resident in Internal Medicine, Univ. of Texas Southwestern Med. Center, Dallas, 1988–91; Fellow in Med. Oncology, Johns Hopkins Univ. and Med. Instns, Baltimore, 1991–94; Sen. Res. Fellow, Chester Beatty Lab., Inst. of Cancer Res., London, 1994–96. FMedSci 2004. *Publications:* articles in New England Jl of Medicine, Nature Genetics, Cell, Cancer Res., Oncogene, Amer. Jl Pathology, Gastroenterol. *Recreations:* supporter of Benfica (the team of Eusebio), lover of Santa Cruz beach, Portugal. *Address:* Functional Breast Cancer Genomics Laboratory, Cancer Research UK Cambridge Research Institute and Department of Oncology, University of Cambridge, Li Ka Shing Centre, Robinson Way, Cambridge CB2 0RE. *T:* (01223) 404200, *Fax:* (01223) 404208; *e-mail:* cc234@cam.ac.uk.

CALDECOTE, 3rd Viscount *cr* 1939, of Bristol, co. Gloucester; **Piers James Hampden Inskip;** Chairman, Tangent Communications, since 2005; *b* 20 May 1947; *o s* of 2nd Viscount Caldecote, KBE, DSC and of Jean Hamilla, *d* of Rear-Adm. H. D. Hamilton; *S* father, 1999; *m* 1st, 1970, Susan Bridget (*née* Mellen); 2nd, 1984, Kristine Elizabeth, *d* of Harvey Holbrooke-Jackson; one *s*. *Educ:* Eton; Magdalene Coll., Cambridge. Gp Exec., Carlton Communications, 1989–2004. *Heir: s* Hon. Thomas James Inskip, *b* 22 March 1985. *Address:* 18 Langside Avenue, SW15 5QT.

CALDECOTT, Andrew Hilary; QC 1994; *b* 22 June 1952; *s* of Andrew Caldecott, CBE and Zita (*née* Belloc); *m* 1977, Rosamond Ashton Shuttleworth; two *s* two *d*. *Educ:* Eton Coll.; New Coll., Oxford (BA Hons Mod. Hist.). Called to the Bar, Inner Temple, 1975, Bencher, 2004. Play: Higher than Babel, Bridewell Theatre, 1999. *Address:* 1 Brick Court, Temple, EC4Y 9BY. *T:* (020) 7353 8845.

CALDER, Prof. Andrew Alexander, MD; FRCSE, FRCPGlas, FRCPE, FRCOG; Professor of Obstetrics and Gynaecology, University of Edinburgh, and Hon. Consultant Obstetrician and Gynaecologist, since 1987, Scientific Director, Jennifer Brown Research Laboratory, since 2004 and Tommy's Centre for Maternal and Fetal Health, since 2007, Queen's Medical Research Institute, Royal Infirmary of Edinburgh; *b* 17 Jan. 1945; *s* of Rev. Alastair Scott Calder and Aileen Calder (*née* Alexander); *m* 1972, Valerie Anne Dugard; one *s* two *d*. *Educ:* Glasgow Acad.; Glasgow Univ. Med. Sch. (MB ChB 1968; MD 1978). FRCOG 1984; FRCPGlas 1987; FRCPE 1993; FRCSE 1994. Res. Fellow, Nuffield Dept of Obstetrics and Gynaecology, Univ. of Oxford, 1972–75; Lectr, then Sen. Lectr in Obstetrics and Gynaecology, Univ. of Glasgow, 1975–86; University of Edinburgh: Vice Dean of Medicine, 1998–2003; Hd, Div. of Reproductive and Develtl Scis, 1999–; Dir of Quality Assce, Coll. of Medicine and Vet. Medicine, 2003–. Chm., Acad. of Royal Colls and Faculties in Scotland, 2001–04. British Exchange Prof., UCLA, 1992; Vis. Prof., Univ. of Pretoria, 2005. Hon. FCOG(SA) 2005. *Publications:* (with W. Dunlop) High Risk Pregnancy, 1992; (with J. O. Drife) Prostaglandins and the Uterus, 1992; (jtly) Munro Kerr's Operative Obstetrics, 11th (centenary) edn 2007; numerous scientific papers in Lancet, British Jl of Obstetrics and Gynaecology, Human Reproduction, etc. *Recreations:* music (especially organ), golf, curling, medical history. *Address:* Centre for Reproductive Biology, Queen's Medical Research Institute, Royal Infirmary of Edinburgh, 47 Little France Crescent, Edinburgh EH16 4TJ. *T:* (0131) 242 2694, *Fax:* (0131) 242 2686; *e-mail:* a.a.calder@ed.ac.uk. *Clubs:* New (Edinburgh); Honourable Company of Edinburgh Golfers (Muirfield).

CALDER, Elisabeth Nicole; Publisher (formerly Publishing Director), Bloomsbury Publishing, 1986–2008; *b* 20 Jan. 1938; *d* of Florence Mary Baber and Ivor George Baber; *m* 1st, 1958, Richard Henry Calder (marr. diss. 1972); one *d* one *s*; 2nd, 2000, Louis Baum. *Educ:* Broadfields, Edgware; Palmerston North Girls' High Sch., NZ; Canterbury Univ., NZ (BA 1958). Reader, Metro-Goldwyn-Mayer story dept, 1969–70; Publicity Manager, Victor Gollancz, 1971–74; Editorial Director: Victor Gollancz, 1975–78; Jonathan Cape, 1979–86. Co-founder, Internat. Fest. of Literature, Parati, Brazil, 2003. *Recreations:* reading, theatre, music - esp. Brazilian, thinking about gardening, junking. *Address:* Bloomsbury Publishing, 36 Soho Square, W1D 3QY. *T:* (020) 7494 2111.

CALDER, Dr Ian Maddison, TD 1973; MD; FRCPath; FFOM; Medical Director, Medico Legal Centre, London, since 2005; *s* of late Walter James Calder, MIMechE, and Alice (*née* Maddison); *m* 1964, Dorothy Joan Hubbard, MBE, RGN; one *s* one *d*. *Educ:* Norwich Sch.; Univ. of St Andrews (MB ChB 1962; State Scholar); Univ. of Dundee (MD 1977; DSc 1992). MRCPath 1981, FRCPath 1996; FFOM 1990; FCPath (HK) 1993; MRCP 1996. Served RA, 1955 (2nd Lieut); Hon. Col, 254 Field Ambulance, RAMC (V), 1991–; Mem., E Anglia TAVRA Cttee, 1990. Lectr in Forensic Medicine, St George's Hosp. Med. Sch., Univ. of London, 1972–76; Lectr, London Hosp. Med. Coll., 1976–81, then Hon. Lectr; Lectr in Forensic Science, Anglia Ruskin Univ., Cambridge, 2005–. Visiting Fellow: St Edmund's Coll., Cambridge, 1978–; Wellcome Inst. of Comparative Neurology, Univ. of Cambridge, 1978–; Travelling Scholar, UCLA, 1976; Advr to Nat. Undersea Res. Centre, Univ. of N Carolina. Ext. Examnr, Univ. of Hong Kong, 1985–90; Advr to Labour Dept, Hong Kong, 1991–94; Consultant advr on occupational medicine, MoD, 1994–2000; Advr to E and N Herts NHS Trust, 2000–04. Member: MoD Ethical Cttee, 1983–; DoH Dangerous Pathogens Working Party. Mem., Physicians for Human Rights. *Publications:* chapters in textbooks of pathology and occupational medicine; papers on diving and hyperbaric medicine research. *Recreations:* sailing, boat-building, antique furniture and cabinet making, rowing, church music, industrial archaeology. *Address:* Thorpe, Huntingdon Road, Girton, Cambridge CB3 0LG. *T:* (01223) 277220. *Club:* Athenæum.

CALDER, John Mackenzie; Managing Director, John Calder (Publishers) Ltd, 1950–91; Director, Calder Publications Ltd, 1991–2008 (Managing Director, 1991–2008); President, Riverrun Press Inc., New York, since 1978; *b* 25 Jan. 1927; *e s* of James Calder, Ardargie, Forgandenny, Perthshire, and Lucienne Wilson, Montreal, Canada; *m* 1st, 1949, Mary Ann Simmonds; one *d*; 2nd, 1960, Bettina Jonic (marr. diss. 1975); one *d*. *Educ:* Gilling Castle, Yorks; Bishops College Sch., Canada; McGill Univ.; Sir George Williams Coll.; Zürich Univ. Studied political economy; subseq. worked in Calders Ltd (timber co.), Director; founded John Calder (Publishers) Ltd, 1949; Man. Dir, Calder & Boyars, 1964–75; Chm., Calder Educnl Trust, 1975–; estab. Calder Bookshop, 2000. Organiser of literary confs for Edinburgh Festival, 1962 and 1963, and Harrogate Festival, 1969. Founded Ledlanet Nights, 1963, in Kinross-shire (music and opera festival, closed 1974). Active in fields related to the arts and on many cttees; Co-founder, Defence of Literature and the Arts Society; Chm., Fedn of Scottish Theatres, 1972–74; Administrator and Founder Mem., Godot Co., 2003. Contested (L): Kinross and W Perthshire, 1970; Hamilton, Oct. 1974; (European Parlt) Mid Scotland and Fife, 1979. FRSA 1974. Dr *hc* Edinburgh, 2002; Hon. DLitt Napier, 2008. Chevalier des Arts et des Lettres (France), 1975; Chevalier, 1983, Officier, 1997, de l'Ordre nationale de mérite (France). *Publications:* (ed) A Samuel Beckett Reader, 1967; (ed) Beckett at 60, 1967; (ed) William Burroughs Reader, 1982; (ed) New Samuel Beckett Reader, 1983; (ed) Henry Miller Reader, 1985; (ed) The Nouveau Roman Reader, 1986; (ed) As No Other Dare Fail: for Samuel Beckett on his 80th birthday, 1986; The Garden of Eros, 1997, 2003; The Philosophy of Samuel Beckett, 1997; What's Wrong, What's Right (poems), 1999; Pursuit (autobiog.), 2001; Solo (poems), 2008; (ed) Gambit International Drama Review, etc.; obituaries and reviews for newspapers; articles in many jls. *Recreations:* writing (several plays, stories; criticism, etc; translations); music, theatre, opera, reading, chess, lecturing, conversation; travelling, promoting good causes, fond of good food and wine. *Address:* c/o Calder Publications Ltd, 51 The Cut, SE1 8LF. *Clubs:* Caledonian; Scottish Arts (Edinburgh).

CALDER, Julian Richard; Director of Statistical Support Services (formerly Survey and Statistical Services) Group, Office for National Statistics, 1996–2000; *b* 6 Dec. 1941; *s* of Donald Alexander and Ivy O'Nora Calder; *m* 1965, Avril Tucker; two *s*. *Educ:* Dulwich College; Brasenose College, Oxford; Birkbeck College, London. Statistician, 1973, Chief Statistician, 1978, Central Statistical Office; Chief Statistician, 1981, Dir of Stats, 1985–94, Board of Inland Revenue; Hd of Div., Govt Statistical Service and Gen. Div., Central Statistical Office, 1994–96. *Recreations:* cycling, listening to music.

CALDER, Nigel David Ritchie, MA; science writer; *b* 2 Dec. 1931; *e s* of Baron Ritchie-Calder, CBE; *m* 1954, Elisabeth Palmer; two *s* three *d*. *Educ:* Merchant Taylors' Sch.; Sidney Sussex Coll., Cambridge. Physicist, Mullard Research Laboratories, 1954–56; Editorial staff, New Scientist, 1956–66; Science Editor, 1960–62; Editor, 1962–66. Science Correspondent, New Statesman, 1959–62 and 1966–71; Chairman, Assoc. of British Science Writers, 1962–64. Mem., Initiative Group, Foundn Scientific Europe, 1987–90; Consultant on public inf., ESA, 1994–. Vice-Pres., Cruising Assoc., 1981–84. FRAS. (Jtly) UNESCO Kalinga Prize for popularisation of science, 1972. *Publications:* Electricity Grows Up, 1958; Robots, 1958; Radio Astronomy, 1958; (ed) The World in 1984, 1965; The Environment Game, 1967; (ed) Unless Peace Comes, 1968; Technopolis: Social Control of the Uses of Science, 1969; Living Tomorrow, 1970; (ed) Nature in the Round: a Guide to Environmental Science, 1973; Timescale, 1983; 1984 and After, 1983; The English Channel, 1986; The Green Machines, 1986; (ed) Future Earth, 1988; (ed) Scientific Europe, 1990; Giotto to the Comets, 1992; Hubble Space Telescope, 1993; Beyond this World, 1995; The Manic Sun, 1997; Magic Universe: The Oxford Guide to Modern Science, 2003; (ed) Einstein, Relativity, 2006; (jtly) The Chilling Stars: a new theory of climate change, 2007; *books of own TV programmes:* The Violent Universe, 1969; The Mind of Man, 1970; The Restless Earth, 1972; The Life Game, 1973; The Weather Machine, 1974; The Human Conspiracy, 1975–76; The Key to the Universe, 1977; Spaceships of the Mind (TV series), 1978; Einstein's Universe, 1979, 2nd edn, 2005; Nuclear Nightmares, 1979; The Comet is Coming!, 1980; Spaceship Earth, 1991 (TV series). *Recreation:* painting. *Address:* 26 Boundary Road, Northgate, Crawley, W Sussex RH10 8BT. *T:* (01293) 549969. *Club:* Thames Sailing Barge Trust.
See also S. P. R. Calder.

CALDER, Simon Peter Ritchie; Senior Travel Editor, The Independent, since 2007; *b* Crawley, 25 Dec. 1955; *s* of Nigel David Ritchie Calder, *qv*; *m* 1997, Charlotte Hindle; two *d*. *Educ:* Univ. of Warwick (BSc Maths). Studio Manager, BBC Radio, 1979–94; Travel Editor, The Independent, 1994–2007; presenter: BBC TV, 1996–; LBC Radio, 2008–. *Publication:* No Frills: the truth behind the low-cost revolution in the skies, 2002, 3rd edn 2006. *Recreations:* walking, cycling. *Address:* The Independent, 191 Marsh Wall, E14 9RS. *T:* (020) 7005 2000, *Fax:* (020) 7005 2428; *e-mail:* simoncalder@hotmail.com; *web:* www.simoncalder.com.

CALDERWOOD, (Andrew) Bruce; Director, Disability and Carers Directorate, since 2004, Office for Disability Issues, since 2005, Department for Work and Pensions; *b* 14 March 1954; *s* of Bob and Betty Calderwood; *m* 1989, Vivienne Bennett; two *s* one *d*. *Educ:* York Univ. (BA Hons Philosophy and English). Chocolate packer, Rowntrees, 1978–79; computer programmer, CCTA, 1979–81; Policy Advr, DHSS, 1981–92; Policy Manager, DSS, 1993–95; Advr, Premier's Dept, Victoria, 1995–96; Business Architect, DSS, 1997–2002; Dir, Older People, DWP, 2003–04. *Recreations:* my allotment, hill walking, cooking, malt whisky, films. *Address:* c/o Department for Work and Pensions, The Adelphi, 1–11 John Adam Street, WC2N 6HT.

CALDICOTT, Dame Fiona, DBE 1996; FRCP, FRCPsych; Principal, Somerville College, Oxford, since 1996; Pro-Vice-Chancellor (Personnel and Equal Opportunities), Oxford University, since 2005 (a Pro-Vice-Chancellor, since 2001); *b* 12 Jan. 1941; *d* of Joseph Maurice Soesan and Elizabeth Jane (*née* Ransley); *m* 1965, Robert Gordon Woodruff Caldicott; one *d* (one *s* decd). *Educ:* City of London Sch. for Girls; St Hilda's Coll., Oxford (MA, BM, BCh; Hon. Fellow 1996). DPM; FRCPsych 1985; FRCP 1995; FRCPI 1996; FRCGP 1996. House Surgeon and Physician, Coventry Hosps, 1966–67; General Practice, Family Planning and Child Welfare, 1968–70; training in Psychiatry, Walsgrave Hosp., Coventry and Central Hosp., Warwick, 1970–76; Sen. Registrar in Psychiatry, W Midlands Regl Trng Scheme, 1977–79; Consultant Psychiatrist, Univ. of Warwick, 1979–85; Consultant Psychotherapist, Uffculme Clinic, Birmingham, 1979–96; Sen. Clinical Lectr in Psychotherapy, Univ. of Birmingham, 1982–96; Unit General Manager, Mental Health, Central Birmingham, 1989–91; Clin. Dir, Adult Psychiatric and Psychotherapy Service, Mental Health Unit, S Birmingham, 1991–94; Med. Dir, S

Birmingham Mental Health NHS Trust, 1994–96 (Hon. Consultant Psychiatrist, 1996–). Non-executive Director: Coventry Building Soc., 1997–2001; Oxford Radcliffe Hosps NHS Trust, 2002–. Chm., Cttee to Review Patient-Identifiable Information, reported 1997; Mem., Sec. of State's Standing Adv. Cttee, on Med. Workforce (formerly Manpower) Planning, 1991–2000; Mem., Broadcasting Standards Commn (formerly Council), 1996–2001. Pres., Section for Psychiatry, 1995–99 (Sec., 1991–95), Sec., European Bd of Psychiatry, 1992–96, Union of European Med. Specialists; Member: Council: BMA, 1996–2000 (Chm., Bd of Med. Educn, 1996–2000); RSocMed, 1996–99; Acad. Med. Sci., 1998–2001; GMC, 1999–2003; Mem., Hebdomadal Council, 1998–2000, Council, 2000–, Oxford Univ. Sub-Dean 1987–90, Dean 1990–93, Pres., 1993–96, RCPsych; Chm., Acad. of Med. Royal Colls, 1995–96. Pres., British Assoc. of Counselling, 2000–06. Consultant Advr to Commissioning Bd for High Security Psychiatric Care, 1996–2000. Trustee: Zito Trust, 1994–; Bethlem Art and History Collections Trust, 1995–99; Nuffield Trust, 1998–. Patron: Oxford Healthy Living Centre, 1996–2005; Family Nurturing Network, Oxford, 1997–; Hon. Pres., Guild of Health Writers, 1996–99. Founder FMedSci 1998; Fellow, Acad. of Medicine, Singapore, 1994; Mem., Czech Psychiatric Soc., 1994. Hon. DSc Warwick, 1997; Hon. MD Birmingham, 1997. Chevalier du Tastevin, 1991. *Publications:* contrib. Discussing Doctors' Careers (ed Isobel Allen), 1988; papers in Bull. RCPsych, Current Opinion in Psychiatry, Postgraduate Psychiatry. *Recreations:* family, friends, reading, wine. *Address:* Somerville College, Oxford OX2 6HD; The Old Rectory, Manor Farm Lane, Balscote, Banbury OX15 6JJ. *T:* (01295) 730293, *Fax:* (01295) 730549. *Clubs:* Reform, Royal Society of Medicine.

CALDWELL, Dr David Hepburn; Keeper, Department of Scotland and Europe, National Museums Scotland, since 2004; *b* 15 Dec. 1951; *s* of Alexander Caldwell and Dorothy (*née* Hepburn); *m* 1975, Margaret McGovern; one *s* two *d*. *Educ:* Ardrossan Acad.; Edinburgh Univ. (MA; PhD 1982). Curator, Nat. Mus. of Antiquities of Scotland, 1973–85; Asst Keeper, Scottish Medieval Collections, 1985–2001, Keeper, Hist. and Applied Art Dept, 2001–04, Nat. Mus of Scotland. *Publications:* The Scottish Armoury, 1979; Scottish Weapons and Fortifications, 1981; Scotland's Wars and Warriors, 1999; An Historical Guide to Islay, Jura and Colonsay, 2001. *Recreations:* travel, keeping fit (swimming and cycling). *Address:* National Museums Scotland, Chambers Street, Edinburgh EH1 1JF. *T:* (0131) 247 4068, *Fax:* (0131) 247 4070; *e-mail:* d.caldwell@nms.ac.uk.

CALDWELL, Sir Edward (George), KCB 2002 (CB 1990); Parliamentary Counsel, Law Commission, 2002–06; *b* 21 Aug. 1941; *s* of Arthur Francis Caldwell and Olive Caldwell (*née* Riddle); *m* 1st, 1965, Bronwen Crockett (marr. diss.); two *d*; 2nd, 1992, Dr Helen Janet Beynon (*see* H. J. Caldwell); two step *d*. *Educ:* St Andrew's, Singapore; Clifton College; Worcester College, Oxford. Law Commission, 1967–69, 1975–77, 1986–88; joined Office of Parly Counsel, 1969: Parly Counsel, 1981–99; First Parly Counsel, 1999–2002. Associate Sen. Res. Fellow, Inst. of Advanced Legal Studies, Univ. of London, 2004–07. Hon. QC 2002; Hon. Bencher, Inner Temple, 2005. Patron, Human Rights Lawyers' Assoc. *Address:* The Old School, School Lane, Chilson, Chipping Norton, Oxon OX7 3HT.

CALDWELL, Maj.-Gen. Frank Griffiths, OBE 1953 (MBE 1945); MC 1941 and Bar 1942; retired; *b* 26 Feb. 1921; *s* of William Charles Francis and Violet Marjorie Kathleen Caldwell; *m* 1945, Betty, *d* of Captain Charles Palmer Buesden; one *s* one *d*. *Educ:* Elizabeth Coll., Guernsey. Commnd Royal Engrs, 1940; served Western Desert RE, 1940–43 (MC and Bar; dispatches); Special Air Service NW Europe, 1944–45 (MBE); Malaya, 1951–53 (OBE); Comdr RE, 2 Div. BAOR, 1961–63; Corps Comdr RE, 1 (BR) Corps, 1967–68; Dir Defence Operational Plans, MoD, 1970; Engineer in Chief (Army), 1970–72; Asst CGS (Operational Requirements), 1972–74. Col Comdt, RE, 1975–80. Director: Scout Insurance (Guernsey) Ltd, 1990–2000; Guernsey Envmtl Services, 2001–04 (Man. Dir, 2004–07). Chm., Mines Awareness Trust Ltd, 2001–. President: RBL, Guernsey, 1986–2004; La Société Guernesiaise, 1994–96; Chm., Guernsey Scout Council, 1987–99. Belgian Croix de Guerre, 1940, and Croix Militaire, 1945. *Recreation:* ornithology. *Address:* Le Courtil Tomar, Rue des Pres, St Pierre du Bois, Guernsey GY7 9AQ.

CALDWELL, Dr Helen Janet, (Lady Caldwell), CB 2007; Parliamentary Counsel, since 2002; *b* 13 Sept. 1952; *d* of George Neville Burtenshaw and Margaret Deforel Burtenshaw (*née* Rose); *m* 1st, 1975, Gareth Wyn Beynon (marr. diss.); two *d*; 2nd, 1992, Sir Edward George Caldwell, *qv*; two step *d*. *Educ:* Dunottar Sch., Reigate; Reigate Co. Sch. for Girls; Girton Coll., Cambridge (Exhibnr; MA); Wolfson Coll., Oxford (DPhil). Called to the Bar, Lincoln's Inn, 1975 (Hardwick Schol.); Lectr in Law, Univ. of Reading, 1979–87; joined Parliamentary Counsel Office, 1987; at Law Commn, 1996–99; at Tax Law Rewrite Project, 1999–2001; at Law Commn, 2001–02. *Publications:* contrib. articles to Law Qly Rev., Modern Law Rev., Criminal Law Rev., etc. *Address:* Parliamentary Counsel Office, 36 Whitehall, SW1A 2AY; *e-mail:* helen.caldwell@cabinet-office.x.gsi.gov.uk.

CALDWELL, Prof. John, PhD, DSc; CBiol, FIBiol; Dean, Faculty of Medicine, since 2002, and Pro Vice-Chancellor, since 2007, University of Liverpool; *b* 4 April 1947; *s* of Reginald and Marian Caldwell; *m* 1969, Jill Gregory; two *s*. *Educ:* Chelsea Coll., Univ. of London (BPharm 1969); St Mary's Hosp. Med. Sch. (PhD Biochem. 1972); DSc Pharmacol. London, 1987. CBiol, FIBiol 1992. St Mary's Hospital Medical School: Lecturer: in Biochem., 1972–74; in Biochem. Pharmacol., 1974–78; Sen. Lectr, 1978–82; Reader in Drug Metabolism, 1982–88; Prof. of Biochem. Pharmacol., 1988–2002; Hd, Dept of Pharmacol. and Toxicol., 1992–97; Dean, ICSM at St Mary's, 1995–97; Hd, Div. of Biomed. Scis, 1998–2002, Hd, Undergrad. Medicine, 2000–02, Imperial Coll. London. Fondation Herbette Vis. Prof., Univ. of Lausanne, 1986; Sterling-Winthrop Dist. Prof., Univ. of Michigan Med. Center, 1995. Dir and Co-founder, Amedis Pharmaceuticals Ltd, 2000–02; non-exec. Dir, Eden Biopharma Gp Ltd, 2004–. Non-executive Director: St Mary's Hosp. NHS Trust, 1995–98; Cheshire and Merseyside Strategic HA, 2003–06; NW Strategic HA, 2006–. Chm., Scientific Cttee, NW Cancer Res., Fund, 2003–. Pres., Internat. Soc. for Study of Xenobiotics, 1994–95 (Hon. Mem., 2001). Hon. MRCP 1998; Hon. Mem., Canadian Soc. for Pharmaceutical Scis, 2002. Founder and Ed., Chirality, 1989– (Best New Jl in Sci., Technol. and Medicine Award, Assoc. Amer. Publishers, 1991). *Publications:* (ed) Amphetamines and Related Stimulants: chemical, biological, clinical and sociological aspects, 1980; *edited jointly:* Metabolic Basis of Detoxication, 1982; Sulfate Metabolism and Sulfate Conjugation, 1982; Biological Basis of Detoxication, 1983; Foreign Compound Metabolism, 1984; Microsomes and Drug Oxidations, 1985; Xenobiotic Conjugation Chemistry, 1986; Metabolism of Xenobiotics, 1988; Intermediary Xenobiotic Metabolism in Animals, 1989; Biochemistry and Redox Reactions, 1994; contribs on drug metabolism. *Recreations:* weekends in good hotels, some aspects of the Church of England, Venice. *Address:* Faculty of Medicine, University of Liverpool, Duncan Building, Daulby Street, Liverpool L69 3GA. *T:* (0151) 706 5668; *e-mail:* deanmed@liv.ac.uk. *Clubs:* Athenæum; Liverpool Medical Institution.

CALDWELL, Prof. John Anthony, DPhil; Titular Professor of Music, University of Oxford, 1999–2005; Senior Research Fellow, Jesus College, Oxford, 1999–2005, now Emeritus Fellow; *b* 6 July 1938; *s* of George Wilfrid Caldwell and Susannah Marion Caldwell (*née* Haywood); *m* 1967, Janet Susan Kellar; one *s* one *d*. *Educ:* Birkenhead Sch.; Keble Coll., Oxford (BA 1960; BMus 1961; MA 1964; DPhil 1965). FRCO 1957. Asst Lectr in Music, Bristol Univ., 1963–66; Oxford University: Lectr in Music, 1966–96, Reader in Music, 1996–99; Keble College: Lectr in Music, 1966–67; Res. Fellow, 1967–75; Official Fellow, 1975–92; Lecturer in Music: Balliol Coll., 1966–2005; Jesus Coll., 1970–2005; Lincoln Coll., 1972–2005. General Editor: Corpus of Early Keyboard Music, 1982–; Early English Church Music, 1995–2007; Co-editor, Plainsong and Medieval Music, 1992–96; Mem., Editl Bd and Trustee, Music and Letters, 1995– (Chm., 2005–). Organist: St Luke's, Tranmere, Birkenhead, 1955–57; St Giles', Oxford (also Choirmaster), 1966–67; SS Philip and James, Oxford, 1968–77. Hon. Fellow, Acad. St Cecilia, 2007. *Compositions:* Divertimento for orch., 1999; dramatic trilogy Paschale Mysterium (opera): Good Friday, prod 1998; The Word, prod 2001; Pascha Nostrum, prod 2002; The Story of Orpheus (opera), prod 2004; La Corona for soprano, chorus and strings, 2005; songs, motets, organ and chamber music. *Publications:* (ed) Early Tudor Organ Music I, 1966; English Keyboard Music before the Nineteenth Century, 1973; Medieval Music, 1978, rev. trans. as La música medieval, 1984; Editing Early Music, 1985, 2nd edn 1996; The Oxford History of English Music, Vol. i 1991, Vol. ii 1999; (ed) Tudor Keyboard Music, 1995. *Recreation:* visiting churches and archaeological sites. *Address:* Jesus College, Oxford OX1 3DW. *T:* (home) (01865) 310956.

CALDWELL, Prof. John Bernard, OBE 1979; PhD; FREng, FRINA; Emeritus Professor of Naval Architecture, University of Newcastle upon Tyne, since 1991; *b* 26 Sept. 1926; *s* of John Revie Caldwell and Doris (*née* Bolland); *m* 1955, Jean Muriel Frances Duddridge; two *s*. *Educ:* Bootham Sch., York; Liverpool Univ. (BEng); Bristol Univ. (PhD). CEng; FRINA 1963; FREng (FEng 1976). Res. Fellow, Civil Engrg, Bristol Univ., 1953; Sen. Scientific Officer 1955, Principal Sci. Off. 1958, Royal Naval Scientific Service; Asst Prof. of Applied Mechanics, RNC Greenwich, 1960–66; Newcastle upon Tyne University: Prof. of Naval Architecture, 1966–91; Hd of Dept of Naval Architecture, 1966–83; Hd, Sch. of Marine Technol., 1975–80, 1986–88; Dean of Faculty of Engrg, 1983–86. Director: Nat. Maritime Inst. Ltd, 1983–85; Marine Design Consultants Ltd, 1985–89; Newcastle Technology Centre, 1985–90; Northern Engrg Centre, 1989–92. Vis. Prof. of Naval Arch., MIT, 1962–63. President: N-E Coast Instn of Engrs and Shipbuilders, 1976–78; RINA, 1984–87 (Vice-Pres., 1977–84). Mem., Engineering Council, 1988–94 (Chm., Bd for Engrs' Registration, 1990–92). FRSA 1982. Hon. DSc Gdansk Tech. Univ., 1985. Froude Medal, RINA, 1984; David W. Taylor Medal, SNAME, 1987. *Publications:* numerous papers on research and educn in naval arch. *Address:* Barkbooth, Winster, Windermere, Cumbria LA23 3NZ. *T:* (01539) 568222.

CALDWELL, Marion Allan; QC (Scot.) 2000; *d* of late Henry Moffat Caldwell and of Elizabeth Bloomer Smith or Caldwell. *Educ:* Eastbank Acad., Glasgow; Aberdeen Univ. (LLB Hons); European Univ. Inst., Florence; Glasgow Univ. (DipLP). Journalist, 1970–77; trainee Solicitor, 1983–84; Solicitor, 1984–85; admitted to Faculty of Advocates, 1986; called to the Bar, Inner Temple, 1991; Standing Jun. Counsel to Accountant of Court and Accountant in Bankruptcy, Scotland, 1991–2000. Legal Chm., Pensions Appeal Tribunals for Scotland, 2001–. *Recreations:* swimming, ski-ing, walking, social tennis, reading. *Address:* Advocates Library, Parliament House, Edinburgh EH1 1RF. *T:* (0131) 226 5071.

CALDWELL, Philip; Chief Executive Officer, 1979–85, and Chairman of Board, 1980–85, Ford Motor Company; *b* Bourneville, Ohio, 27 Jan. 1920; *s* of Robert Clyde Caldwell and Wilhelmina (*née* Hemphill); *m* 1945, Betsey Chinn Clark; one *s* two *d*. *Educ:* Muskingum Coll. (BA Econs 1940); Harvard Univ. Graduate Sch. of Business (MBA Indust. Management, 1942). Served to Lieut, USNR, 1942–46. With Navy Dept, 1946–53, as civilian (Dep. Dir, Procurement Policy Div., 1948–53); joined Ford Motor Co., 1953: Vice Pres. and Gen. Man. Truck Ops, 1968–70; Pres. and Dir, Philco-Ford Corp. (subsid. of Ford Motor Co.), 1970–71; Vice Pres. Manufg Gp, N Amer. Automotive Ops, 1971–72; Chm. and Chief Exec. Officer, Ford of Europe, Inc., 1972–73; Dir, Ford Motor Co., 1973–90; Exec. Vice Pres., Internat. Automotive Ops, 1973–77; Vice Chm. of Bd, 1977–79; Dep. Chief Exec. Officer, 1978–79; Pres., 1978–79; Director: Ford of Europe, 1972–85; Ford Latin America, 1973–85; Ford Mid-East and Africa, 1973–85; Ford Asia-Pacific, 1973–85; Ford Motor Credit Co., 1977–85; Ford of Canada, 1977–85; Mem., Eur. Adv. Council, 1976–88 (Chm., 1987–88). Sen. Man. Dir, Lehman Brothers Inc., 1985–98. Director: Digital Equipment Corp., 1980–95; Chase Manhattan Corp., and Chase Manhattan Bank, NA, 1982–85 (Mem., Chase Manhattan Bank Internat. Adv. Cttee, 1979–85); Federated Dept Stores, 1984–88; Russell Reynolds Associates, Inc., 1984–2005; Kellogg Co., 1985–92; Shearson Lehman Brothers Hldgs Inc., 1985–93; Amer. Guarantee and Liability Insce Co., 1986–99; Zurich Reinsurance Co. of New York, 1987–90; Zurich-American Insurance Gp, 1989–99; Mexico Fund, 1991–2006; Specialty Coatings Internat., 1991–93; Zurich Reinsurance Centre Holdings, 1993–97; Waters Corp., 1994–; Castech Aluminium Gp, 1994–96; Mettler-Toledo Inc., 1996–2005 (Chm., 1996–98); Detroit Symphony Orch., 1974–85; Harvard Business Sch. Associates, 1977–93. Vice Chairperson, New Detroit, Inc., 1977–85; Vice Chm., Japan Soc., 1987–89 (Mem., 1983–89; Chm. Exec. Cttee, 1987–89); Member: US Chamber of Commerce Transportation Cttee, 1968–77; US Council, Internat. Chamber of Commerce, 1973–77; US Council for Internat. Business, 1977–85; Soc. of Automotive Engrs, 1969–85; Engrg Soc. of Detroit, 1970–85; Motor Vehicle Manufrs Assoc. of US, 1978–85 (Chm., 1978 and 1983; Mem., Motor Truck Cttee, 1964–70); Econ. Club of Detroit, 1977–86; Highway Users Fedn, 1977–85; INSEAD, 1978–81 (Chm., US Adv. Bd, 1979–84; Mem., Internat. Council, 1983–2002); Conf. Bd, 1979–; Cttee for Econ. Develt, 1979–; (Charter Mem.) Business Higher Educn Forum, 1979–83; Business Council, 1980–2001; Policy Cttee, Business Roundtable, 1980–85; Trilateral Commn, 1980–86; Citizens Res. Council of Mich, 1980–85; Adv. Council on Japan-US Econ. Relations, 1981–85; US Trade Representative Adv. Cttee for Trade Negotiations, 1983–85; President's Export Council, 1985–89; Council on Foreign Relations, 1985–; Mexico-US Bus. Com., 1985–. Bd of Advrs, Jerome Levy Econs Inst., 1988–2001. Trustee: Muskingum Coll., 1967–; Winterthur Mus. and Gdns, 1986–2000. Philip Caldwell Professorship of Business Admin, Harvard Business Sch., established 1989. Hon. HHD Muskingum, 1974; Hon. DBA Upper Iowa Univ., 1978; Hon. LLD: Boston Univ. and Eastern Mich Univ., 1979; Miami Univ., 1980; Davidson Coll., 1982; Univ. of Mich, 1984; Ohio Univ., 1984; Lawrence Inst. of Technol., 1984. 1st William A. Jump Meml Award, 1950; Meritorious Civilian Service Award, US Navy, 1953; Muskingum Coll. Alumni Dist. Service Award, 1978; Brigham Young Univ. Sch. of Management Internat. Exec. of the Year Award, 1983; Automotive Industry Leader of the Year, 1984; Club of Greater NY Business Statesman Award, 1984; Alumni Achievement Award, Harvard Business Sch., 1985; Club of Columbus Businessman of the Year, Columbus, Ohio, 1984; Automotive Hall of Fame, 1990; Statesman of the Year, Detroit, 1991. *Address:* Ford

Motor Co., 225 High Ridge Road, West Building, Stamford, CT 06905–3000, USA. *T:* (203) 3578880, *Fax:* (203) 3578241. *Clubs:* Links, River (New York).

CALDWELL, Sandra Mary, CB 2008; JP; Director, Field Operations, Health and Safety Executive, since 2004; *b* 20 June 1948; *m. Educ:* Imperial Coll., Univ. of London (BSc, MSc; dip. occupational health and safety). Joined HSE, 1976; Regl Dir, London and SE, HSC and Chief Inspector of Construction, HSE, 1998–99; Director: Health, then Health and Safety, 2000–03; Policy, 2003–04. JP W Herts, 2003. *Address:* Health and Safety Executive, Rose Court, 2 Southwark Bridge, SE1 9HS.

CALDWELL-MOORE, Sir Patrick Alfred; *see* Moore.

CALEDON, 7th Earl of, *cr* 1800; **Nicholas James Alexander;** Baron Caledon, 1790; Viscount Caledon, 1797; Lord Lieutenant of County Armagh, since 1989; *b* 6 May 1955; *s* of 6th Earl of Caledon, and Baroness Anne (*d* 1963), *d* of late Baron Nicolai de Graevenitz; *S* father, 1980; *m* 1st, 1979, Wendy (marr. diss. 1985), *d* of Spiro Coumantaros and Mrs Suzanne Dayton; 2nd, 1989, Henrietta (marr. diss. 2000), *d* of John Newman, Compton Chamberlayne, Wilts; one *s* one *d*; *m* 2008, Mrs Amanda Cayzer (*née* Squire). *Educ:* Sandroyd School; Gordonstoun School (Round-Square House). *Recreations:* ski-ing, tennis, swimming, photography, travel. *Heir: s* Viscount Alexander, *qv. Address:* Caledon Castle, Caledon, Co. Tyrone, Northern Ireland. *T:* (028) 3756 8232.

CALIGARI, Prof. Peter Douglas Savaria, PhD, DSc; CBiol, FIBiol; Titular Professor, Instituto de Biología Vegetal y Biotecnología, Universidad de Talca, Chile, since 2002 (Director, since 2004); Professor of Agricultural Botany, University of Reading, 1986–2006 (on leave of absence, 2002–06) (Head of Department, 1987–98); *b* 10 Nov. 1949; *s* of late Kenneth Vane Savaria Caligari, DFM, RAF , and of Mary Annetta (*née* Rock); *m* 1st, 1973 (marr. diss. 2004); two *d*; 2nd, 2007, Andrea Veronica Moreno Gonzalez; two step *d. Educ:* Hereford Cathedral Sch.; Univ. of Birmingham (BSc Biol Sci., 1971; PhD Genetics, 1974; DSc Genetics, 1989). CBiol 1997; FIBiol 1997. Res. Asst, 1971–74, Res. Fellow, 1974–81, Dept of Genetics, Univ. of Birmingham; SSO, 1981–84, PSO, 1984–86, Scottish Crop Res. Inst. Managing Director: BioHybrids International Ltd, 1996–; BioMarkers Ltd, 1997–2003. Dir, Genberries Ltd, 2008–. Member: Exec. Cttee, XVIIth Internat. Congress of Genetics, 1991–93; Governing Body, Plant Science Research Ltd, 1991–94; Governing Council, John Innes Centre, 1994–99; European Council, Volcani Centre, 1999–; Bd, Internat. Lupin Assoc., 1999–; Comité de Expertos, Beca Presidente de la República, Chile, 2006–07; Chm., Sci. Prog., Triennial EUCARPIA Congress, 1999–2001. Vice Pres., Inst. of Biology, 1999–2002 (Chm., Sci. Policy Bd, 1999–2002). FRSA 1990. Editor, Heredity, 1987–90 (Jun. Editor, 1985–87); Mem. Editl Bd, Euphytica, 1991–. *Publications:* (contrib.) The Potato Crop, 1991; (contrib.) Applications of Synthetic Seeds to Crop Improvement, 1992; (jtly) Selection Methods in Plant Breeding, 1995, 2nd edn 2008; (ed jtly) Compositae: biology and utilization, 1996; (contrib.) Lupins: production and utilization, 1998; (ed jtly) Cashew and Coconuts: trees for life, 1998; (jtly) Introduction to Plant Breeding, 2008; scientific papers and reports on genetics, plant breeding and biotechnology (*c* 300 papers, *c* 70 reports). *Address:* Instituto de Biología Vegetal y Biotecnología, Universidad de Talca, 2 Norte 685, Talca, Chile. *T:* (71) 200280, *Fax:* (71) 200276; *e-mail:* pcaligari@utalca.cl.

CALLADINE, Prof. Christopher Reuben, ScD; FRS 1984; FREng; Professor of Structural Mechanics, University of Cambridge, 1986–2002, now Emeritus; Fellow of Peterhouse, 1960–2002, now Emeritus; *b* 19 Jan. 1935; *s* of Reuben and Mabel Calladine (*née* Boam); *m* 1964, Mary R. H. Webb; two *s* one *d. Educ:* Nottingham High Sch.; Peterhouse, Cambridge; Massachusetts Inst. of Technology. Development engineer, English Electric Co., 1958; Demonstrator in Engrg, Univ. of Cambridge, 1960, Lectr, 1963; Reader, 1978. Vis. Research Associate, Brown Univ., 1963; Vis. Prof., Stanford Univ., 1969–70. Mem. Council, Royal Soc., 2000–02. Trustee, EMF Biol. Res. Trust, 2005– (Chm., 2007–). FREng (FEng 1994). Hon. DEng Univ. of Technol., Malaysia, 2002. James Alfred Ewing Medal, ICE, 1998. *Publications:* Engineering Plasticity, 1969; Theory of Shell Structures, 1983; (with H. R. Drew) Understanding DNA, 1992, 3rd edn 2004; papers in engrg and biological jls. *Recreations:* music, architecture, mending toys. *Address:* 25 Almoners Avenue, Cambridge CB1 8NZ. *T:* (01223) 246742.

CALLAGHAN, Rev. Brendan Alphonsus, SJ; Master of Campion Hall, Oxford, since 2008; *b* 29 July 1948; *s* of Dr Kathleen Callaghan (*née* Kavanagh) and Dr Alphonsus Callaghan. *Educ:* Stonyhurst; Heythrop, Oxon; Campion Hall, Oxford (MA 1977); Univ. of Glasgow (MPhil 1976); Heythrop Coll., Univ. of London (MTh 1979). AFBPsS; CPsychol. Joined Society of Jesus, 1967; Clinical Psychologist, Glasgow, 1974–76; Middx Hosp., 1976–79; ordained priest, 1978; curate, St Aloysius, Glasgow, 1979–80; Heythrop College, University of London: Lectr, 1980–2007, Sen. Lectr, 2007–08, in Psychol.; Principal, 1985–97; Acting Principal, 1998–99; Dir, Academic Standards Cttee, 2005–08; Dir of Academic Develt, 2007–08; Lectr in Psychol., Allen Hall, Chelsea, 1981–87. Superior: Brixton Jesuit Community, 1993–94; Merrivale Jesuit Community, KwaZulu-Natal, 1998; Wimbledon Jesuit Community, 1998–2005; Clapham Jesuit Community, 2007–08. Formation Asst to British Jesuit Provincial, 2001–07. University of London: Chm., Bd of Examrs, Theol and Religious Studies, 1987–89; Schools Examn Bd, 1987–97; Collegiate Council and Senate, 1989–94; Council, 1994–97; Institute of Medical Ethics: Hon. Asst/Associate Dir, 1976–89; Governing Body, 1989–2002; Gen. Sec., 1999–2002. Visiting Lecturer: St Joseph's Theol Inst., KwaZulu-Natal, 1987 and 1997–98; (in Med. Ethics), Imperial Coll., London, 1990–; KCL, 1991–94; Vis. Prof., Fordham Univ., NY, 1990; Vis. Scholar, Weston Sch. of Theol., Cambridge, Mass, 1992. Member: Conf. of Seminary Rectors, 1987–97; Cttee of Catholic Principals, 1985–97; Ethics Cttee, St Thomas' Hosp., 1990–2002; Higher Educn Cttee, RC Bps Conf. of England and Wales, 1986–97; Academic Bd, and Governing Body, Heythrop Coll., 1982–97; Academic Adv. Cttee, Jews' Coll., 1993–97. Chm. Govs, Digby Stuart Coll., 1998–2002, Mem. Council, 1998–2002, Univ. of Surrey Roehampton (formerly Roehampton Inst.); Member, Advisory Boards: Campion Hall, Oxford, 1985–95; Syon House, Angmering, 1985–97; Centre for the Study of Communication and Culture (Chm.), 1990–; Inst. of St Anselm, Westgate (Chm.), 1991–98. Vice Pres., Catholic Students Trust Appeal. Consultant Psychologist to Marriage Care (formerly Catholic Marriage Adv. Council), 1981–, and to religious congregations and orders. Hon. FCP 1996. Member: Catholic Inst. for Internat. Relations; British and Irish Assoc. for Practical Theol.; Soc. for Study of Religions; Amnesty; CND; Royal African Soc. FRSocMed. Broadcaster, BBC and World Service radio, Channel Four. Member, Editorial Board: Law and Justice, 1986–; Jl of Contemp. Religion, 1994–97; Mental Health, Religion and Culture, 1997–. *Publications:* Life Before Birth (with K. Boyd and E. Shotter), 1986; articles, reviews and verse in Br. Jl Psych., Jl Med. Ethics, Heythrop Jl, The Way and magazines. *Recreations:* photography, long distance walking, poetry. *Address:* Campion Hall, Oxford OX1 1QS. *T:* (01865) 286101.

CALLAGHAN, James; *b* 28 Jan. 1927. Lectr, Manchester Coll., 1959–74. Metropolitan Borough Councillor, 1971–74. MP (Lab) Middleton and Prestwich, Feb. 1974–1983, Heywood and Middleton, 1983–97. *Recreations:* sport and art. *Address:* 17 Towncroft Avenue, Middleton, Manchester M24 5DA.

CALLAGHAN, Prof. Paul Terence, PCNZM 2006; DPhil, DSc; FRS 2001; FRSNZ; Alan Macdiarmid Professor of Physical Sciences, Victoria University of Wellington, New Zealand, since 2001; *b* 19 Aug. 1947; *s* of Ernest Edward Callaghan and Mavis Eileen Callaghan; *m* 1st, 1969, Susan Audrey Roberts (marr. diss. 2005); one *s* one *d*; 2nd, 2006, Miang Hoong Lim. *Educ:* Victoria Univ. of Wellington (BSc Hons); Wolfson Coll., Oxford (DPhil 1974); DSc Oxon 1995. Massey University, NZ: Lectr in Physics, 1974–84; Prof. of Physics, 1984–2001; Sir Neil Waters Dist. Prof., 2001–. FRSNZ 1991. Cooper Medal, 1991, Hector Medal, 1998, Rutherford Medal, 2005, Royal Soc. of NZ; Mechaelis Medal, Otago Univ., 1995; Blake Medal, Sir Peter Blake Trust, 2007. *Publications:* Principles of Nuclear Magnetic Resonance Microscopy, 1991; contrib. numerous articles to learned jls. *Recreations:* music, walking. *Address:* School of Chemical and Physical Sciences, Victoria University of Wellington, Wellington, New Zealand. *T:* (4) 4721000.

CALLAGHAN, Sir William (Henry), Kt 2007; JP; Chairman, Legal Services Commission, since 2008; *b* 19 May 1948; *s* of Henry William Callaghan and Constance Callaghan; *m* 1st, 1977, Frances Sproat (marr. diss. 1981); 2nd, 2001, Pauline Ortiz (*d* 2002); one *s*; 3rd, 2007, Dr Josephine Glover. *Educ:* St John's Coll., Oxford (BA PPE); Univ. of Kent at Canterbury (MA Econs). Trades Union Congress: Asst, 1971–74, Asst Sec., 1974–77, Head, 1978–93, Econ. Dept; Head, Econ. and Social Affairs, and Chief Economist, 1994–99; Chm., HSC, 1999–2007. Member: Low Pay Commn, 1997–2000; Res. Priorities Bd, ESRC, 1994–99; Indep. Mem., Rev. of HE Finance and Pay Data for Univ. Employers and Trade Unions, 2007–08; Chair, Rev. of Regulatory Framework for Animal Pathogens, 2007. Member Board: BITC, 1991–99; Basic Skills Agency, 1996–99; DTI Innovation Gp, 2002–04; DTI Fair Markets Bd, 2004–07. Chair, British Occupational Health Res. Foundn, 2007–. JP, SW London, 2005. Vis. Fellow, Nuffield Coll., Oxford, 1999–2007. *Publications:* numerous TUC pubns on econ. and social affairs. *Recreations:* sailing, cycling, walking, listening to music.

CALLAN, Hilary Margaret West; Director, Royal Anthropological Institute of Great Britain and Ireland, since 2000; *b* 27 Oct. 1942; *d* of John Sydney Flashman and late Marion Louise Flashman (*née* Thornton) (Silver Laurel Leaf Emblem and King's Commendation for Brave Conduct in Civil Defence, 1941); *m* 1965, Ivan Roy Callan (marr. diss. 1987); one *d. Educ:* Marsden Sch., NZ; St Paul's Girls Sch.; Somerville Coll., Oxford (MA, MLitt, Dip. Social Anthropol.). Sen. Res. Associate, Birmingham Univ., 1968–70; Asst Prof., American Univ. of Beirut, Lebanon, 1971–75; Lecturer: Univ. of Kent at Canterbury, 1977–80; Trent Univ., Canada, 1981–84 (Harry Frank Guggenheim Res. Award, 1982–84); Oxford Poly., 1987–88; Brunel Univ., 1988–89; Asst Dir, UKCOSA: Council for Internat. Educn, 1989–93; Exec. Dir, Eur. Assoc. for Internat. Educn, 1993–2000 (Hon. Life Mem., 2000). Mem. Bd of Trustees, Gemini Action Internat., 2005–. Contested (SDP/Lib Alliance) Scarborough, 1987. *Publications:* Ethology and Society: towards an anthropological view, 1970; (ed jtly) The Incorporated Wife, 1984; (ed) International Education: towards a critical perspective, 2000; (contrib.) Engagements with Learning and Teaching in Higher Education: a view from anthropology, 2006; (contrib.) Identity and Networks, 2007; (contrib.) Professional Identities, 2007; (ed jtly) Early Human Kinship: from sex to social reproduction, 2008; numerous articles in books and jls in anthropology and internat. educn. *Recreations:* reading, music, family and friends. *Address:* Royal Anthropological Institute, 50 Fitzroy Street, W1T 5BT. *T:* (020) 7387 0455.

CALLAN, Sir Ivan, KCVO 1998; CMG 1990; HM Diplomatic Service, retired; Ambassador to Oman, 1999–2002; *b* 6 April 1942; *s* of Roy Ivan Callan and (Gladys) May Callan (*née* Coombe); *m* 1st, 1965, Hilary Flashman; one *d*; 2nd, 1987, Mary Catherine Helena Williams; two step *s* one step *d. Educ:* Reading Sch.; University Coll., Oxford. BA, Dip. Soc. Anthrop., BLitt, MA. Entered FCO, 1969; Middle East Centre for Arab Studies, 1970–71; Second, later First Sec., Beirut, 1971–75; FCO, 1975–80; First Sec. and Head of Chancery, Ottawa, 1980–83; Counsellor, Hd of Chancery and Consul-General, Baghdad, 1983–87; Consul-General, Jerusalem, 1987–90; Counsellor, FCO, 1991–94; High Comr, Brunei, 1994–98. Gt Commander, Orthodox Knights of the Holy Sepulchre, 1988. *Recreations:* fine arts, painting, craftsmanship. *Club:* Reform.

CALLAN, Maj.-Gen. Michael, CB 1979; President, and Chairman of Board of Trustees, Royal Army Ordnance Corps Charitable Trust, 1993–96; *b* 27 Nov. 1925; *s* of Major John Callan and Elsie Dorothy Callan (*née* Fordham); *m* 1948, Marie Evelyn Farthing; two *s. Educ:* Farnborough Grammar Sch., Hants. rcds, jssc, psc. Enlisted Hampshire Regt, 1943; commnd 1st (KGV's Own) Gurkha Rifles (The Malaun Regt), 1944; resigned commn, 1947; re-enlisted, 1948; re-commnd, RAOC, 1949; overseas service: India, Burma, French Indo China, Netherlands East Indies, 1944–47; Kenya, 1950–53; Malaya/Singapore, 1958–61; USA, 1966–68; Hong Kong, 1970–71; Comdr, Rhine Area, BAOR, 1975–76; Dir Gen., Ordnance Services, 1976–80. Col Comdt, RAOC, 1981–89; Hon. Col, SW London ACF, 1982–89. Registrar, Corporation of the Sons of the Clergy, 1982–83; consultant in defence logistics and admin, 1984–89. *Recreations:* sailing, DIY, gardening. *Address:* c/o Royal Bank of Scotland, Drummonds Branch, 49 Charing Cross, SW1A 2DX.

CALLANAN, Martin John; Member (C) North East Region, England, European Parliament, since 1999; *b* 8 Aug. 1961; *s* of John and Ada Callanan; *m* 1997, Jayne Burton; one *s. Educ:* Newcastle Poly. (BSc Electrical and Electronic Engrg). Project Engr, Scottish & Newcastle Breweries, 1986–99. *Recreations:* squash, football. *Address:* (office) Aston House, Redburn Road, Westerhope, Newcastle upon Tyne NE5 1NB. *T:* (0191) 214 6744; European Parliament, Rue Wiertz, 1047 Brussels, Belgium. *T:* (2) 2845701.

CALLANDER, Maj. (John) Henry; landowner and farmer; Vice Lord-Lieutenant, Midlothian, since 1996; *b* 9 May 1948; *s* of Maj. John David Callander, MC and Mary Callander (*née* Crampton-Roberts); *m* 1987, Jacqueline Hulda (*née* Crocker); two *s* one *d. Educ:* Eton Coll. Royal Scots Greys; Royal Scots Dragoon Guards; retd 1991. DL Midlothian. *Recreation:* field sports. *Address:* Prestonhall, Pathhead, Midlothian, EH37 5UG. *T:* (01875) 320949. *Club:* New (Edinburgh).

CALLAWAY, Anthony Leonard; a District Judge (Magistrates' Courts), since 2002; Designated District Judge, Croydon Magistrates' Court, since 2007; *b* 13 Oct. 1953; *s* of Leonard Cecil Callaway, CEng, MICE and Daphne Noreen Callaway (*née* Ibbett); *m* 2000, Heather Jean Foot, FIDM; one step *s* one step *d. Educ:* St Lawrence Coll.; KCL (BA Hons Pol Sci.; MA War Studies; MSc with Dist. War and Psychiatric Medicine). Called to the Bar, Middle Temple, 1978; in practice, S Eastern Circuit, 1978–2002; Actg Dep. Dist Judge, formerly Metropolitan Stipendiary Magistrate, 1997–2002. Mem., IISS, 2003–. *Recreations:* sailing, ski-ing, reading (military history). *Address:* 3rd Floor South, 2 Essex Court, Temple, EC4Y 9AP. *T:* (020) 7583 5427; Le Clos de Vallettes, 1145 Route de la Colle, Tourettes-sur-Loup, France. *Clubs:* Royal Automobile; Royal Solent Yacht, Bar Yacht.

CALLAWAY-FITTALL, Betty Daphne, (Betty Callaway), MBE 1984; trainer of skaters; skating consultant to Ice Arena, Slough, since 1986; *b* 22 March 1928; *d* of William

A. Roberts and Elizabeth T. Roberts; *m* 1st, 1949, E. Roy Callaway; 2nd, 1980, Captain W. Fittall (*d* 1990), British Airways, retd. *Educ:* Greycoat Sch., and St Paul's Convent, Westminster. Started teaching, Richmond Ice Rink, 1952; Nat. Trainer, W Germany, 1969–72; retired from full-time teaching, 1972. Commentator, ITV, 1984–. Pupils include: Angelika and Erich Buck (European Champions and 2nd in World Championship, 1972); Chrisztine Regoczy and Andras Sally (Hungarian and World Champions and Olympic silver medallists, 1980); Jayne Torvill and Christopher Dean (World Champions, 1981, 1982, 1983, 1984, European Champions, 1981, 1982, and Olympic gold medallists, 1984). Pres., British Ice Teachers Assoc., 1985–. Hon. Citizen, Ravensburg, Germany, 1972. Gold Medal, Nat. Skating Assoc., 1955; Hungarian Olympic Medal, 1980; Coach of the Year Award, Nat. Coaching Foundn, 1995. *Recreations:* music, water ski-ing, gardening. *Address:* 35 Long Grove, Seer Green, Beaconsfield, Bucks HP9 2YN.

CALLBECK, Hon. Catherine Sophia; Senator, Senate of Canada, since 1997; with Callbeck's Ltd, family business, 1978–88 and since 1996; *b* 25 July 1939; *d* of Ralph Callbeck and Ruth Callbeck (*née* Campbell), Central Bedeque, PEI. *Educ:* Mt Allison Univ. (BComm 1960); Dalhousie Univ. (BEd 1963); Syracuse Univ. Prince Edward Island: MLA (L) Fourth Dist, 1974–78; Minister of Health and Social Services and Minister responsible for Disabled, 1974–78; MP (L) Malpeque, 1988–93; Official Opposition Critic for Consumer and Corporate Affairs, Energy, Mines and Resources and Financial Instns, 1988–93; Associate Critic for Privatization and Regulatory Affairs; Vice-Chm., Caucus Cttee on sustainable develt; MLA (L) First Dist of Queens, and Premier of PEI, 1993–96; Member, Senate Standing Committees: on Agric. and Forestry; on Social Affairs, Sci. and Technol.; Vice-Chm., Task Force on Women Entrepreneurs, 2002–. Mem., Higher Educn Commn, Maritime Provinces. Leader, Liberal Party of PEI, 1993–96. Mem., Child Alliance Adv. Cttee, PEI, 1998–. Vice-Pres., Canada-Cuba Interparly Gp. Member: Bd of Regents, Mt Allison Univ.; Bd of Govs, Univ. of PEI; Bd, Inst. for Res. in Public Policy. Hon. Mem. Bd, Glaucoma Res. Soc. of Canada, 1998–. Hon. LLD Mt Allison, 1996. *Address:* Senate of Canada, Room 354, East Block, Ottawa, ON K1A 0A4, Canada.

CALLENDER, Dr Maurice Henry; Ministry of Defence, 1977–80; retired, 1980; *b* 18 Dec. 1916; *s* of Harry and Lizbeth Callender; *m* 1941, Anne Kassel; two *s*. *Educ:* Univ. of Durham (MA, PhD). Commissioned: Royal Northumberland Fusiliers, 1939–41; RAF, 1941–45. Lectr, Huddersfield Technical Coll., 1945–47; Research, Univ. of Durham, 1947–49; Lectr, Bristol Univ. Extra-Mural Dept, 1949–53; MoD, 1953–62; Joint Services Staff Coll., 1959–60; Cabinet Office, 1962–64; MoD, 1964–70; Cabinet Office, 1970–73; Counsellor, Canberra, 1973–77. *Publications:* Roman Amphorae, 1965; various articles in archaeological jls. *Recreations:* oil painting, golf, bridge. *Address:* 24 Glanleam Road, Stanmore, Middx HA7 4NW. *T:* (020) 8954 1435. *Club:* Aldenham Golf and Country.

CALLER, Maxwell Marshall, CBE 2005; Member, Electoral Commission, since 2007; Chair, Boundary Committee for England, since 2007; *b* 9 Feb. 1951; *s* of Abraham Leon Caller and Cynthia Rachel Caller; *m* 1972, Linda Ann Wohlberg; three *s* one *d*. *Educ:* Newport High Sch.; University Coll. London (BSc Hons Engrg). CEng, MICE; MCIWEM; CDipAF. GLC, 1972–74; Thames Water Authority, 1974–75; London Boroughs of: Hammersmith, 1975–78; Newham, 1978–81; Merton, 1981–85 (Asst Dir of Development); Barnet: Controller of Engrg Services, 1985–87; Dir of Technical Services, 1987–89; Chief Exec., 1989–2000; Man. Dir, subseq. Chief Exec., London Bor. of Hackney, 2000–04; Interim Chief Exec., London Bor. of Haringey, 2005–06. Technical Advr, N London Waste Authy, 1985–87; Adviser, Highways Cttee 1987–89, Public Works Cttee 1990–97, AMA. Founder Mem., 1990, and Vice Chm., Steering Cttee, 1990–2000, Barnet Crime Reduction Partnership; Director: Enfield Enterprise Agency, 1994–99; N London TEC, 1995–2000; Prospects Careers Services Ltd, 1999–2000; The Learning Trust, 2002–04; Bernie Grant Centre Ltd, 2005–06; Chm., Barfield Group Ltd, 1995–98. Trustee, Barnet War Memorials Initiative, 1994–. Mem., Adv. Council, Norwood, 2006–. Freeman, City of London, 1991. DUniv Middlesex, 2000. *Recreation:* watching Welsh Rugby Union. *Address:* Electoral Commission, Trevelyan House, Great Peter Street, SW1P 2HW; *e-mail:* mcaller@electoralcommission.org.uk.

CALLICOTT, Richard Kenneth; Founder and Managing Director, Reddenhill Consulting, since 2004; *b* 18 Sept. 1946; *s* of Ernest Victor Callicott and Joan Alfreda Callicott (*née* Furley); *m* 1st, 1972, Diane Lesley Kidd (marr. diss. 1984); two *s*; 2nd, 1985, Jacqueline Steele (marr. diss. 1995); one *s*; 3rd, 2003, Maroline Lasebikan. *Educ:* Colston's Sch., Bristol; City of Birmingham Coll. of Educn (Cert Ed); Univ. of Birmingham (BPhil Ed). Teacher, jun. schs, Smethwick and Warley, 1968–74; Warden, Churchbridge Teachers' Centre, 1974–80; Community Educn and Recreation Officer, Birmingham CC, 1980–83; Vice Principal, Central Inst., Birmingham, 1983–85; Area Manager, Recreation and Community, Birmingham CC, 1985; Co-ordinator, Birmingham's Olympic Bid, 1985–86; Develt Manager, Sport and Leisure, Birmingham CC, 1988–89; Dir of Sport, NEC Gp, 1989–99, and Hd of Sport, City of Birmingham, 1996–99; Chief Exec., UKSport, 1999–2004. Director: Saga Radio, 2001–; SBM (Sports) Ltd, 2007–. Dir, British Paralympic Assoc., 2005–; Mem., Nat. Olympic Cttee, 2006–. Pres., British Volleyball Fedn, 2005–. *Recreations:* golf, cycling, reading, gardening, theatre, insatiable appetite for sport. *Address:* Reddenhill Consulting, Stourbridge Road, Lloyd Hill, Penn, Wolverhampton WV4 5NF.

CALLIL, Carmen Thérèse; Founder, 1972, and Chairman, 1972–95, Virago Press; *b* 15 July 1938; *d* of Frederick Alfred Louis Callil and Lorraine Clare Allen. *Educ:* Star of the Sea Convent, Gardenvale, Melbourne; Loreto Convent, Mandeville Hall, Melbourne; Melbourne Univ. (BA). Buyer's Asst, Marks & Spencer, 1963–65; Editorial Assistant: Hutchinson Publishing Co., 1965–66; B. T. Batsford, 1966–67; Publicity Manager, Panther Books, later also of Granada Publishing, 1967–70; André Deutsch, 1971–72; publicity for Ink newspaper, 1972; founded Carmen Callil Ltd, book publicity co., 1972; founded Virago Press, 1972, incorp. as co., 1973, Man. Dir, 1972–82. Man. Dir, Chatto & Windus: The Hogarth Press, 1983–93; Publisher-at-Large, Random House UK, 1993–94; Ed.-at-Large, Knopf, NY, 1993–94. Mem. Bd, Channel 4, 1985–91. FRSA. Hon. LittD: Sheffield, 1994; Oxford Brookes, 1995; DUniv: York, 1995; Open, 1997. *Publications:* (ed with Craig Raine) New Writing 7, 1998; (with Colm Tóibín) The Modern Library: the 200 best novels in England since 1950, 1999; Bad Faith: a forgotten history of family and fatherland, 2006. *Recreations:* friends, reading, animals, television, sport, politics, films, gardening, France.

CALLINAN, Hon. Ian David Francis, AC 2003; Judge of the High Court of Australia, 1998–2007; *b* 1 Sept. 1937; *s* of William Peter Callinan and Lilian Rose Callinan; *m* 1960, Wendy Mary Ruth Hamon; one *s* one *d*. *Educ:* Univ. of Queensland (LLB). Admitted solicitor, 1960, called to the Bar, 1965, Qld; QC (Aust.) 1978. Hon. Dir, Barr Chambers Ltd, 1974–91. Chm., Qld Barrister Bd, 1987–88; Hon. President: Qld Bar Assoc., 1984–87; Australian Bar Assoc., 1984–85. Vis. Prof. of Law, Newcastle Univ., 1993. Chm., Australian Defence Force Acad., 2000–. Chm., Qld Totalizator Agency Bd, 1985–90; Director: QCT Ltd, 1988–97; Santos Ltd, 1996–97; ABC, 1997. Chm. Trustees, Qld Art Gallery, 1997–98; Dir, Nat. Gall. of Australia, 2007–. *Publications: plays:* Brazilian Blue, 1995; The Cellophane Ceiling, 1996; The Acquisition, 2000; *novels:* The Lawyer and the Libertine, 1997; The Coroner's Conscience, 1999; The Missing Masterpiece, 2001; Appointment at Amalfi, 2003; After the Monsoon, 2005; contrib. short stories to various anthologies. *Recreations:* history of Australian art, reading, tennis, cricket, Rugby. *Clubs:* Queensland, Tattersall's (Brisbane).

CALLMAN, His Honour Clive Vernon; a Circuit Judge, 1973–2000, assigned to South-Eastern Circuit; a Deputy Circuit Judge, 2000–02; a Deputy High Court Judge, 1976–2000; *b* 21 June 1927; *o s* of Felix Callman, DMD, LDS, RCS and Edith Callman, Walton-on-Thames, Surrey; *m* 1967, Judith Helen Hines, BA, DipSocStuds (Adelaide), *o d* of Gus Hines, OBE, JP, and Hilde Hines, St George's, Adelaide, S Aust.; one *s* one *d*. *Educ:* Ottershaw Coll.; St George's Coll., Weybridge; LSE, Univ. of London (BSc(Econ), Commercial Law); Univ. of Notre Dame (Mediator Dip. 2000). Called to the Bar, Middle Temple, 1951; Blackstone Pupillage Prizeman, 1951; practised as Barrister, London and Norwich, 1952–73 (Head of London chambers, 1963), South-Eastern Circuit; Hon. Mem., Central Criminal Court Bar Mess; Dep. Circuit Judge in Civil and Criminal Jurisdiction, 1971–73; Mediator, Ct of Appeal, 2004–. Legal Assessor: GMC, 2000–04; GDC, 2000–04. Dir, Woburn Press, Publishers, 1971–73; dir of finance cos, 1961–73; non-executive Director: Frank Cass & Co. Ltd, 2000–03; Vallentine Mitchell & Co. Ltd, 2000–. University of London: Fac. Mem., Standing Cttee of Convocation, 1954–79; Senator, 1978–94; Mem. Careers Adv. Bd, 1979–92; Mem., Commerce Degree Bureau Cttee, 1980; Mem., Adv. Cttee for Magistrates' Courses, 1979; Mem., Univ. Governing Council, 1994–2001; Vice-Pres., Graduates' Soc.; Governor: Birkbeck Coll., 1982–2000 (Fellow, 2000); LSE, 1990–; Hebrew Univ. of Jerusalem, 1992–; Mem. Court, City Univ., 1991–2001. Mem. Exec. Cttee, Soc. of Labour Lawyers, 1958; Chm., St Marylebone Constituency Labour Party, 1960–62. Mem. Council, Anglo-Jewish Assoc., 1956–; Trustee, Jewish Studies Foundn, 2004–. Editor, Clare Market Review, 1947; Member Editorial Board: Professional Negligence, 1985–95; Jl of Child Law, 1989–95; Child and Family Law Qly, 1995–2002. *Recreations:* reading, travelling, the arts. *Address:* 11 Constable Close, NW11 6UA. *T:* (020) 8458 3010. *Clubs:* Garrick, Bar Yacht.

CALLOW, Maj. Gen. Christopher George, CB 2001; OBE 1984; Chief Executive, Defence Secondary Care Agency, 1998–2000; *b* 12 July 1941; *s* of George Alexander Callow and Barbara Callow (*née* Tannahill); *m* 1967, Elizabeth Anne Macmillan Hynd; one *s* two *d*. *Educ:* Duke of York Sch., Nairobi; Univ. of Edinburgh (MB ChB 1966); DPhysMed 1971; MSc London 1984. MFCM 1987, FFPH (FFPHM 1996). RMO, 1st Bn, Green Howards, 1968–69; Army Staff Coll., 1976; Dep. Asst Dir Gen. AMS, MoD, 1977–79; CO, Armd Field Amb., 1979–83; Col, Med. Ops & Plans, MoD, 1985–88; Comdr Med., 1 Armd Div., 1988–90; Chief, Med. Plans & Policy, SHAPE, 1990–93; Comdr Med., BAOR, subseq. UKSC (Germany), 1993–96; Dir Gen., Defence Med. Trng, 1996–99. QHP 1995–2000. Consultant in Army Occupnl and Public Health Medicine, 1987–2000. OStJ 1995. *Publications:* articles on noise-induced hearing loss. *Recreations:* golf, music, travel, computing.

CALLOW, Prof. James Arthur, PhD; CBiol, FIBiol; Mason Professor of Botany, University of Birmingham, since 1983; *b* 17 Jan. 1945; *s* of James and Olive Callow; *m* 1968, Dr Maureen Elizabeth Wood; one *s*. *Educ:* Barrow-in-Furness Grammar Sch. for Boys; Univ. of Sheffield (BSc 1st cl. Hons Botany 1966; PhD 1969). Lectr in Botany, Univ. of Leeds, 1969–83. *Publications:* numerous, including books, professional academic jl articles. *Recreations:* golf, gardening, antiques, photography, travel. *Address:* School of Biosciences, University of Birmingham, Birmingham B15 2TT. *T:* (0121) 414 5559.

CALLOW, Simon Phillip Hugh, CBE 1999; actor and director; *b* 15 June 1949; *s* of Neil Callow and Yvonne Mary Callow. *Educ:* London Oratory Grammar Sch.; Queen's Univ. Belfast; Drama Centre. London productions include: Schippel, 1975; A Mad World My Masters, 1977; Arturo Ui, Mary Barnes, 1978; As You Like It, Amadeus, NT, 1979; The Beastly Beatitudes of Balthazar B, Total Eclipse, Restoration, 1981; The Relapse, 1983; On the Spot, 1984; Kiss of the Spider Woman, 1985; Faust I and II, Lyric, Hammersmith, 1988; Single Spies (double bill: A Question of Attribution (also dir); An Englishman Abroad), NT, 1988, Queen's, 1989; The Destiny of Me (also dir), Leicester Haymarket, 1994; The Alchemist, RNT, 1996; The Importance of Being Oscar, Savoy, 1997; In Defence of Fairies, Criterion, 1997; Chimes at Midnight, Chichester, 1998; The Mystery of Charles Dickens, Comedy, transf. Albery, 2000; Chicago, Albery, NY, Australia, 2002; Through the Leaves, Southwark, transf. Duchess, 2003; The Holy Terror, Duke of York's, 2004; The Woman in White, Palace, 2005; Aladdin, Richmond, 2005; Present Laughter, tour, 2006; Merry Wives: the Musical, RSC, 2006; Equus, tour, 2008; There Love Reigns, Stratford Ontario, 2008; *directed:* Loving Reno, Bush, 1984; The Passport, 1985, Nicolson Fights, Croydon, 1986, Offstage; Amadeus, Theatr Clwyd, 1986; The Infernal Machine, 1986; Così fan Tutte, Switzerland, 1987; Jacques and his Master, LA, 1987; Shirley Valentine, Vaudeville, 1988, NY, 1989; Die Fledermaus, Theatre Royal, Glasgow, 1988, 1989; Stevie Wants to Play the Blues, LA Theater Center, 1990; Carmen Jones, Old Vic, 1991; Ballad of the Sad Café (film), 1991; Shades, 1992; My Fair Lady, 1992; Les Enfants du Paradis, Barbican, 1996; Stephen Oliver Trilogy, 1996; Calisto, NY, 1996; Il Turco in Italia, Broomhill Opera, 1997; HRH, Playhouse, 1997; The Consul, Holland Park, 1999; The Pajama Game, Victoria Palace, 1999; Jus' Like That!, Garrick, 2003; Le Roi Malgré Lui, Grange Park, 2003; The Magic Flute, Opera Holland Park, 2008. *Films:* Amadeus, 1983; A Room with a View, The Good Father, 1986; Maurice, 1987; Manifesto, 1988; Mr & Mrs Bridge, Postcards from the Edge, Crucifer of Blood, 1991; Soft Top, Hard Shoulder, Don't Look Away, 1993; Four Weddings and a Funeral, 1994; Jefferson in Paris, 1995; Ace Ventura: when Nature calls, James and the Giant Peach, 1996; The Scarlet Tunic, 1998; Bedrooms and Hallways, Shakespeare in Love, 1999; Thunderpants, No Man's Land, George and the Dragon, 2002; Angels in America, Bright Young Things, 2003; Merci Docteur Rey, Phantom of the Opera, 2004; Bob the Butler, Ragtale, 2005; Surveillance, 2006; Chemical Wedding, 2008. *Television series:* Chance in a Million, 1983, 1985–86; David Copperfield, 1986; *other television includes:* Cariani and the Courtesans, 1987; Charles Laughton (documentary), 1987; Old Flames, 1989; Revolutionary Witness, 1989; Femme Fatale, 1993; The Purcell Film, 1995; An Audience with Charles Dickens, 1996; The Woman in White, 1997; A Christmas Dickens, 1997; The Mystery of Charles Dickens, 2002; Galileo's Daughter, 2003; Marple: The Body in the Library, 2004; Dr Who, Rome, 2005; Midsomer Murders, Roman Mysteries, 2006. *Publications:* Being an Actor, 1984, rev. edn 2004, trans. French as Dans la Peau d'un Acteur, 2006; A Difficult Actor: Charles Laughton, 1987; trans. Jacques et son Maître, by Kundera, 1986; Acting in Restoration Comedy, 1990; Shooting the Actor, 1990, rev. edn 2004; Orson Welles: The Road to Xanadu, 1995; Snowdon on Stage: with a personal view of the British theatre 1954–1996, 1997; The National, 1997; Love is Where it Falls, 1999; Shakespeare On Love, 2000; Oscar Wilde and his Circle, 2000; The Night of the Hunter, 2001; Dickens' Christmas, 2003; Actors on Shakespeare series: Henry IV Part One, 2002; Henry IV Part Two, 2003; Orson Welles: Hello Americans, 2006; Classical Destinations, 1, 2007, 2, 2008. *Address:* c/o Brebners, 180 Wardour Street, W1V 3AA.

CALLOWAY, Carol Elspeth Goodeve; *see* Brayne, C. E. G.

CALLUM, Ian Stuart, RDI 2007; Director of Design, Jaguar Cars, since 1999; *b* 30 July 1954; *s* of Stuart Callum and Sheila Callum; *m* 1977, Lesley Anne Watson; two *s*. *Educ:* Glasgow Sch. of Art (BA Product Design 1977); Royal Coll. of Art (MA Automotive Design 1979). Designer, Ford Motor Co., 1979–90, Manager, Ghia design studio, Turin, 1988–90; Manager, TWR Design, 1990–99. Hon. FRIBA 2006. Hon. DHL Acad. of Art, San Francisco, 2000; Hon. DDes De Montfort, 2002; Hon. DArts Abertay, 2006. Jim Clark Meml Award, Assoc. of Scottish Motoring Writers, 1995, 2006. *Recreations:* painting, designing, building hot rods, cycling. *T:* (024) 7620 6020, *Fax:* (024) 7620 6177; *e-mail:* icallum@jaguar.com.

CALLWAY, Eric Willi; HM Diplomatic Service, retired; Consul General, Frankfurt, 1997–2001; *b* 30 Jan. 1942; *s* of Edward and Auguste Callway; *m* 1965, Gudrun Viktoria Granström (*d* 2001); two *s*. Joined HM Foreign, later Diplomatic, Service, 1960: FO, 1960–61; CRO, 1961–63; New Delhi, 1963–66; Georgetown, Guyana, 1966–70; Second Sec., FCO, 1970–72; RAF Staff Coll., Bracknell, 1972; UK Mission, Geneva, 1973–77; First Secretary: FCO, 1977–79; on loan to MoD, 1979–80; FCO, 1980–81; (Commercial), E Berlin, 1981–84; (Labour), 1984–86, then (Commercial), Stockholm, 1986–88; on loan to ODA, 1988; FCO, 1989–94; Counsellor, and Dep. High Comr, Karachi, 1994–97. Vice Chm., Pakistan Soc., 2001–04. *Address:* 5 Bradbourne Street, SW6 3TF. *T:* (020) 7731 0432; *e-mail:* ericcallway@adslmail.newnet.co.uk.

CALMAN, Sir Kenneth (Charles), KCB 1996; DL; MD; FRCP, FRCS; FRSE; Chairman, National Cancer Research Institute, since 2008; Chancellor, University of Glasgow, since 2006; *b* 25 Dec. 1941; *s* of Arthur McIntosh Calman and Grace Douglas Don; *m* 1967, Ann Wilkie; one *s* two *d*. *Educ:* Allan Glen's Sch., Glasgow; Univ. of Glasgow (BSc, MD, PhD). FRCSGlas 1971; FRCP 1985, FRCPE 1989; FRCGP 1989; FFPH (FFCM 1989); FRSE 1979. Hall Fellow in Surgery, Western Infirmary, Glasgow, 1968; Lectr in Surgery, Univ. of Glasgow, 1969; MRC Clinical Res. Fellow, Inst. of Cancer Res., London, 1972; University of Glasgow: Prof. of Clinical Oncology, 1974; Dean of Postgrad. Medicine and Prof. of Postgrad. Med. Educn, 1984–88; Chief Medical Officer: Scottish Office Home and Health Dept, 1989–91; DES, later DFE, then DFEE, based at DoH, 1991–98; Vice-Chancellor and Warden, Univ. of Durham, 1998–2007. Mem., Statistics Commn, 2000–08. Lectures include: Honeyman Gillespie, Edinburgh Royal Infirmary, first annual Douglas, Liverpool Univ., Neil Wates Meml, RSocMed, Stanley Melville Meml, ICE, Wade, Keele Univ., 1993; Sir William Weipers Meml, Glasgow Univ., 1994; Frank Lowe, Liverpool Univ., 1995; Calman Muir Meml, RCPE, Brough, Paisley Univ., 1996; Dow Meml, Dundee Univ., 1997; Harben, RIPHH, 1998; Finlayson, RCPSGlas, Meriel, Academic Vet. Soc., first Hastings, Oxford, 1999; Henry Cohen, Hebrew Univ., Jerusalem, 2000. DL Durham, 2000. Hon. FRCR 1990; Hon. FRCSE 1991; Hon. FRCPath 1992; Hon. FFPM 1992; Hon. FFOM 1993; Hon. FRCS 1995; Hon. FRCOG 1996; Hon. FRCSI 1997; Hon. FRSocMed 1997; Founder FMedSci 1998; Hon. FRCOphth 1999; Hon. Fellow, Inst. of Cancer Res., 1999. DUniv: Stirling, 1992; Open, 1996; Paisley, 1997; Hon. DSc: Strathclyde, 1993; Westminster, 1995; Glasgow Caledonian, 1995; Glasgow, 1996; Brighton, 2000; Hon. MD: Nottingham, 1994; Newcastle, 1995; Birmingham, 1996; Hon. LLD Aberdeen, 2005. Medals include: Sir Thomas and Lady Dixon, Belfast, 1994; Francis Bissett Hawkins, RCP, 1995; Crookshanks, RCR, 1995; Alexander Hutchison, RSocMed, 1995; Gold, Macmillan Cancer Relief, 1996; Heberden (also Orator), British Soc. of Rheumatol., 1996; Silver, RCSI, 1997; Allwyn Smith, FPHM, 1998; Bradlaw, RCS Dental Faculty, 1999; Thomas Graham, Royal Philosophical Soc., Glasgow, 1999. *Publications:* Basic Skills for Clinical Housemen, 1971, 2nd edn 1983; Basic Principles of Cancer Chemotherapy, 1982; Invasion, 1984; Healthy Respect, 1987, 2nd edn 1994; The Potential for Health, 1998; Risk Communication and the Public Health, 1999; Storytelling, Humour and Learning in Medicine, 2001; Medical Education: past, present and future, 2006. *Recreations:* gardening, golf, collecting cartoons, Scottish literature. *Address:* University of Glasgow, Glasgow G12 8QQ.

CALNAN, Prof. Charles Dermod, MA, MB, BChir Cantab; FRCP; Director, Department of Occupational Dermatoses, St John's Hospital for Diseases of the Skin, 1974–82, retired; Honorary Consultant Dermatologist: Royal Free Hospital, 1958–82; St John's Hospital for Diseases of the Skin, London, 1958–82; *b* 14 Dec. 1917; *s* of James Calnan, Eastbourne, Sussex; *m* 1950, Josephine Gerard Keane, *d* of late Lt-Col Michael Keane, RAMC; three *s* one *d*. *Educ:* Stonyhurst Coll.; Corpus Christi Coll., Cambridge (BA 1939, MA 1943; MB BChir 1942); London Hospital. RAMC Specialist in Dermatology, Major, 1942–46; Marsden Prof., Royal Free Hosp., 1958; Visiting Research Associate, Univ. of Pennsylvania, 1959; Prof. of Dermatology, Inst. of Dermatology, 1960–74. WHO Cons. Adviser to Nat. Inst. of Dermatology of Thailand, 1971–82. Editor: Transactions of the St John's Hosp. Dermatological Soc., 1958–75; Contact Dermatitis, 1975–87. Hon. Fellow, Brit. Assoc. of Dermatology; Hon. FRSocMed (Mem. Dermatological Section). Order of the White Elephant (Thailand), 1986. *Publications:* Atlas of Dermatology, 1974; The Life and Times of Geoffrey Barrow Dowling, 1992; various papers in med. and dermatological jls. *Address:* 8 The Croft, Lewis Lane, Cirencester, Glos GL7 1EB.

CALNAN, Prof. James Stanislaus, FRCP; FRCS; Professor of Plastic and Reconstructive Surgery, University of London, at the Royal Postgraduate Medical School and Hammersmith Hospital, 1970–81, now Emeritus; *b* 12 March 1916; *e s* of James and Gertrude Calnan, Eastbourne, Sussex; *m* 1949, Joan (formerly County Councillor for Great Berkhamsted and Dacorum District Councillor, and Town Councillor, Berkhamsted), *e d* of George Frederick and Irene Maud Williams, Roath Park, Cardiff; one *d*. *Educ:* Stonyhurst Coll.; Univ. of London at London Hosp. Med. Sch. LDS RCS 1941; MRCS, LRCP 1943; DA 1944; DTM&H 1948; MRCP (London and Edinburgh) 1948; FRCS 1949; FRCP 1971. Served War of 1939–45, F/Lt RAF, UK, France, India. RMO, Hosp. for Tropical Diseases, 1948; Sen. Lectr, Nuffield Dept of Plastic Surgery, Oxford, 1954; Hammersmith Hospital and Royal Postgraduate Med. Sch.: Lectr in Surgery, 1960; Reader, 1965; Professor, 1970. Hunterian Prof. RCS, 1959. Vis. Prof. in Plastic Surgery, Univ. of Pennsylvania, 1959. Member: BMA, 1941–82; British Assoc. of Plastic Surgeons, 1949–71; Sen. Mem., Surgical Research Soc., 1962–. Fellow, Royal Soc. of Medicine, 1943; FCST 1966. Mem., Soc. of Authors, 1985–. Clemson Award for Bioengineering, 1980. *Publications:* Speaking at Medical Meetings, 1972, 2nd edn 1981; Writing Medical Papers, 1973; How to Speak and Write: a practical guide for nurses, 1975; One Way to do Research, 1976; Talking with Patients, 1983; Coping with Research: the complete guide for beginners, 1984; The Hammersmith 1935–1985: the first 50 years of the Royal Postgraduate Medical School, 1985; Principles of Surgical Research, 1989; contribs to medical and scientific jls and chapters in books, on cleft palate, wound healing, lymphatic diseases, venous thrombosis, research methods and organisation. *Recreations:* gardening, carpentry, reading and writing. *Address:* 4 Park House, Park Street, Berkhamsted, Herts HP4 1HY. *T:* (01442) 862320.

See also Prof. C. D. Calnan.

CALNE, Sir Roy (Yorke), Kt 1986; MA, MS; FRCS; FRS 1974; Professor of Surgery, University of Cambridge, 1965–98, now Emeritus; Fellow of Trinity Hall, Cambridge, 1965–98, now Emeritus; Visiting Professor, National University of Singapore, since 1998 (Yeoh Ghim Seng Professor of Surgery, 1998–2006); *b* 30 Dec. 1930; *s* of Joseph Robert and Eileen Calne; *m* 1956, Patricia Doreen Whelan; two *s* four *d*. *Educ:* Lancing Coll.; Guy's Hosp. Med. Sch. MB, BS London with Hons (Distinction in Medicine), 1953. House Appts, Guy's Hosp., 1953–54; RAMC, 1954–56 (RMO to KEO 2nd Gurkhas); Deptl Anatomy Demonstrator, Oxford Univ., 1957–58; SHO Nuffield Orthopædic Centre, Oxford, 1958; Surg. Registrar, Royal Free Hosp., 1958–60; Harkness Fellow in Surgery, Peter Bent Brigham Hosp., Harvard Med. Sch., 1960–61; Lectr in Surgery, St Mary's Hosp., London, 1961–62; Sen. Lectr and Cons. Surg., Westminster Hosp., 1962–65; Hon. Consulting Surgeon, Addenbrooke's Hosp., Cambridge, 1965–98. Royal Coll. of Surgeons: Hallet Prize, 1957; Jacksonian Prize, 1961; Hunterian Prof., 1962; Cecil Joll Prize, 1966; Mem. Ct of Examiners, 1970–76; Mem. Council, 1981–90; Vice-Pres., 1986–89; Hunterian Orator, 1989. Founder FMedSci 1998. Fellow Assoc. of Surgeons of GB; Mem. Surgical Research Soc.; Pres., European Soc. for Organ Transplantation, 1983–84; Corresp. Fellow, Amer. Surgical Assoc., 1972, Hon. Fellow 1981; Hon. FRCP 1989; Hon. FRCS Thailand, 1992; Hon. FRCSE 1993. Hon. MD: Oslo, 1986; Athens, 1990; Hanover, 1991; QUB, 1994; Karachi, 1994; Hon. DSc Edinburgh, 2001. Prix de la Société Internationale de Chirurgie, 1969; Faltin Medal, Finnish Surgical Soc., 1977; Lister Medal, 1984; Fothergill Gold Medal, Med. Soc. of London, 1989; Cameron Prize, Edinburgh Univ., 1990; Ellison-Cliffe Medal, 1990; Ernst Jung Preis, 1992; Medawar Prize, Transplantation Soc., 1992; Medal of Helsinki Univ., 1993; Gold Medal, Catalan Transplantation Soc., 1996; King Faisel Internat. Prize for Medicine, 2001; Prince Mahidal Internat. Award for Medicine, 2002. Grand Officer, Order of Merit (Republic of Italy), 2000. *Publications:* Renal Transplantations, 1963, 2nd edn 1967; (with H. Ellis) Lecture Notes in Surgery, 1965, 10th edn 2002; A Gift of Life, 1970; (ed and contrib.) Clinical Organ Transplantation, 1971; (ed and contrib.) Immunological Aspects of Transplantation Surgery, 1973; (ed and contrib.) Liver Transplantation, 1983; (ed and contrib.) Transplantation Immunology, 1984; Surgical Anatomy of the Abdomen in the Living Subject, 1988; (ed) Operative Surgery, 1992; Too Many People, 1994; Art Surgery and Transplantation, 1996; The Ultimate Gift, 1998; papers on tissue transplantation and general surgery; sections in several surgical text-books. *Recreations:* tennis, squash, painting, sculpture. *Address:* 22 Barrow Road, Cambridge CB2 2AS. *T:* (01223) 359831.

CALOW, Prof. Peter, OBE 2000; PhD, DSc; CBiol, FIBiol; FLS; Director, Environmental Assessment Institute, Denmark, 2004–06; Adjunct Professor, University of Roskilde, Denmark, since 2004; *b* 23 May 1947; *s* of late Harry Calow and Norah K. Calow; *m* 1971, Lesley Jane Chapman (marr. diss. 1991); one *s* one *d*. *Educ:* William Rhodes Sch., Chesterfield; Univ. of Leeds (BSc; PhD 1972; DSc 1984). CBiol, FIBiol 1985; FLS 1987. Lectr, then Reader, Univ. of Glasgow, 1972–84; Warden, Wolfson Hall of Residence, 1975–84; Prof. of Zoology, Univ. of Sheffield, 1984–2004. Founding Editor (with J. Grace), Functional Ecology, 1986–98; Editor, Integrated Environmental Management, 1991–95. Chairman: UK Govt Adv. Cttee on Hazardous Substances, 1991–2000; Jt Govt/Business Task Force on Application of Risk Benefit Analysis to Chemical Controls, 1993–95; Member: NE Regl Envmtl Adv. Cttee, Envmt Agency, 1996–2000; Adv. Cttee on Pesticides, 1997–2002 (Chm., Envmtl Panel, 1999–2002); Expert Panel, Res. Inst. for Fragrance Materials, 1999–; External Sci. Adv. Panel, European Chemical Industry Long-range Res. Initiative, 1999–2004 (Chm., 2003–04); Scientific Cttee on Toxicity, Ecotoxicity and Envmt, EC, 2000–04; Scientific Cttee, European Centre for Ecotoxicology and Toxicology of Chemicals, 2001–; Scientific Cttee on Health and Envmtl Risks, EU, 2004–. Vice-Pres., European Soc. of Evolutionary Biol., 1988–89; Pres., Soc. of Envmtl Toxicol. and Chemistry (UK), 1990–91, (Europe) 1991–92. Mem., Bd of Trustees, Health and Envmtl Scis Inst., 1996–2002; Member Council: Freshwater Biol Assoc., 1988–92 and 1995–99; Univ. of Buckingham, 1997–2002 (Chm., Acad. Adv. Council, 1999–2002). FRSA 1992. *Publications:* Biological Machines, 1976; Life Cycles, 1979; Invertebrate Biology, 1981; Evolutionary Principles, 1983; (with R. Sibly) Physiological Ecology of Animals, 1986; (with R. S. K. Barnes and P. J. W. Olive) The Invertebrates: a new synthesis, 1988, 3rd edn 2001; (ed) Handbook of Ecotoxicology, vol. 1 1993, vol. 2 1994; Controlling Environmental Risks from Chemicals, 1997; Handbook of Environmental Risk Assessment and Management, 1998; (Ed.-in-Chief) The Encyclopedia of Ecology & Environmental Management, 1998; numerous contribs to learned jls. *Recreations:* reading, writing, running. *Address:* Isafjordvej 66, 4000 Roskilde, Denmark.

CALTHORPE; *see* Anstruther-Gough-Calthorpe.

CALVER, Neil Richard; QC 2006; *b* 4 Sept. 1963; *s* of Richard George and Joyce Elizabeth Calver; one *d*. *Educ:* York Rd Co. Primary Sch., Kent; Dartford Grammar Sch.; Christ's Coll., Cambridge (BA 1st Cl. Hons Law 1986). Called to the Bar, Gray's Inn, 1987; in practice, 1995–, specialising in commercial and European law. *Recreations:* my daughter, Charlton Athletic FC, wine, occasional climbing of mountains, travelling. *Address:* Brick Court Chambers, 7–8 Essex Street, WC2R 3LD. *T:* (020) 7520 7895, *Fax:* (020) 7520 4137; *e-mail:* calver@brickcourt.co.uk. *Club:* Home House.

CALVERLEY, 3rd Baron *cr* 1945; **Charles Rodney Muff;** *b* 2 Oct. 1946; *s* of 2nd Baron Calverley and of Mary, *d* of Arthur Farrar, Halifax; *S* father, 1971; *m* 1972, Barbara Ann (marr. diss. 2000), *d* of Jonathan Brown, Kelbrook, near Colne; two *s*. *Educ:* Fulneck School for Boys. Police Officer, City of Bradford Police, 1963–74, W Yorks Police, 1974–97 (RUC secondment, 1979–80). *Heir:* *s* Hon. Jonathan Edward Muff, *b* 16 April 1975. *Address:* 72 West Street, Padiham, Lancs BB12 8JD.

CALVERLEY, Prof. Peter Martin Anthony, FRCP, FRCPE; Professor of Medicine (Pulmonary Rehabilitation), University of Liverpool, since 1995; *b* 27 Nov. 1949; *s* of Peter Calverley and Jennifer (*née* Taylor); *m* 1973, Margaret Tatam; four *s*. *Educ:* Univ. of Edinburgh (MB ChB). FRCP 1990; FRCPE 1990. Jun. physician posts in Edinburgh and Leicester, 1973–76; MRC Clinical Fellow, 1976–79, Sen. Registrar, 1979–85, Dept of Medicine, Royal Infirmary, Edinburgh; Consultant Physician, Aintree NHS Trust, Liverpool (later Aintree Univ. Hosps NHS Foundn Trust), 1988–95 (Hon. Consultant Physician, 1995–). Travelling Fellow, Meakin-Christie Labs, McGill Univ., Montreal, 1982–83. *Publications:* (ed jtly) Chronic Obstructive Pulmonary Disease, 1994; papers on pathophysiology and treatment of chronic obstructive pulmonary disease and sleep-related breathing disorders. *Recreations:* sailing, ski-ing, travel, family. *Address:* University Hospital Aintree, Aintree University Hospitals NHS Foundation Trust, Longmoor Lane, Liverpool L9 7AL. *T:* (0151) 529 5886.

CALVERT, Prof. (Alan) Hilary, MD; FRCP, FMedSci; Professor of Medical Oncology, University of Newcastle upon Tyne, since 1989 (Clinical Director, Northern Institute for Cancer Research, 1989); *b* 18 Feb. 1947; *s* of Norman Geoffrey Calvert and Mary Christine Calvert (*née* Whitehead); *m* 1969, Drusilla Dean; three *d*. *Educ:* Birkenhead Sch.; Peterhouse, Cambridge (BA Med. Sci. and Maths 1969; MB BChir 1972; MD 1981); University Coll. Hosp., London (Clinical Studies); Chelsea Coll., London (MSc Biochem. 1978). MRCP 1975, FRCP 1988; Accreditation Med. Oncol., RCP 1987. Clinical Res. Fellow, Royal Marsden Hosp., 1975–77; Institute of Cancer Research,

London: Lectr in Clinical Pharmacol., 1977–80; Sen. Lectr, 1980–85; Reader, 1985–89. Hon. Consultant: in Medicine, Royal Marsden Hosp., 1980–89; in Med. Oncol., Northern Centre for Cancer Treatment, Newcastle upon Tyne, 1989–. FMedSci 2002. Pfizer Award for Innovative Sci., 2005. *Publications:* (ed jtly) Handbook of Anticancer Drug Development, 2003; contribs on cancer research, esp. cancer therapy, incl. develt of platinum drugs and antifolates; also contribs on application of mathematical methods to cancer treatment. *Recreations:* ski-ing, hill-walking, music, opera, hi-fi circuit design and development, computer programming of MACREX indexing software (with Drusilla). *Address:* Northern Institute for Cancer Research, University of Newcastle upon Tyne, Medical School, Framlington Place, Newcastle upon Tyne NE2 4HH. *T:* (0191) 246 4300, *Fax:* (0191) 246 4301; *e-mail:* Hilary.Calvert@ncl.ac.uk; Northern Centre for Cancer Treatment, Newcastle General Hospital, Westgate Road, Newcastle upon Tyne NE4 6BE.

CALVERT, Barbara Adamson, (Lady Lowry); QC 1975; barrister-at-law; a Recorder of the Crown Court, 1980–98; *b* 30 April 1926; *d* of late Albert Parker, CBE; *m* 1st, 1948, John Thornton Calvert, CBE (*d* 1987); one *s* one *d*; 2nd, 1994, Baron Lowry, PC (*d* 1999). *Educ:* St Helen's, Northwood; London Sch. of Economics (BScEcon). Called to Bar: Middle Temple, 1959 (Bencher 1982); NI, 1978 (QC 1978; Hon. Bencher, 1995). Admin. Officer, City and Guilds of London Inst., 1961; practice at Bar, 1962–. Full-time Chm., Industrial Tribunals, London, 1986–96 (part-time Chm., 1974–86); Mem., Matrimonial Causes Rules Cttee, 1983–85. Freeman, City of London, 1989; Liveryman: Arbitrators' Co.; Water Conservators' Co. *Recreations:* crosswords, swimming, poetry. *Address:* (home) 32 Ashgrove House, Bessborough Gardens, Pimlico, SW1V 2HW; (chambers) 9–11 Fulwood Place, High Holborn, WC1V 6HG. *Clubs:* Royal Over-Seas League; Royal Fowey Yacht.

CALVERT, Denis; *see* Calvert, L. V. D.

CALVERT, Hilary; *see* Calvert, A. H.

CALVERT, John Raymond; Chairman, Worcestershire Partnership Mental Health NHS Trust, since 1999; *b* 14 June 1937; *s* of Matthew and Eva Mary Calvert; *m* 1962, Elspeth Sarah Naish; one *s* one *d*. *Educ:* Bootham, York; Manchester Univ. (BA Econs). FIPD (FIPM 1986). Cadbury Schweppes Ltd, 1961–70; Delta Metals Ltd, 1970–73; Pilkington Bros Ltd, 1973–84: Personnel Dir, Triplex Safety Glass Ltd, 1973–80; Dir, Chance Bros Ltd, 1973–80; Gp Employee Relations Manager, 1980–84; Dir, Industrial Relations, ITCA, 1984–88; Gp Personnel Dir, Yorkshire Tyne Tees TV Hldgs plc, 1988–93; Man. Dir, 1993–97, Dep. Chm., 1996–97, Tyne Tees TV. Director: Northern Sinfonia, 1993–; Newcastle Initiative, 1994–. Council Member: Industrial Soc., 1994–; NE Chamber of Commerce, 1995–. Chm., Newcastle Educn Business Partnership, 1995–. Trustee, Cleveland Community Foundn, 1995–. Gov., Newcastle Coll., 1994–. FRSA 1989. *Recreations:* church organist and choirmaster, fell walking, tennis. *Address:* (office) Isaac Maddox House, Shrub Hill Road, Worcester WR4 9RW. *T:* (01905) 681514; Strands, Droitwich Road, Feckenham, near Redditch, Worcs B96 6RT. *T:* (01527) 821607.

CALVERT, Hon. Lorne Albert; MLA (NDP) Saskatoon Riversdale, since 2001; Leader of the Opposition, Saskatchewan, since 2007; *b* Moose Jaw, Sask, 24 Dec. 1952; *s* of Albert Calvert and Beulah Awilda (*née* Phillips); *m* 1975, Betty Anne Sluzalo; one *s* one *d*. *Educ:* Univ. of Regina (BA 1973); Univ. of Saskatchewan (BD 1976). Ordained minister, United Ch of Canada, 1976; Minister: Gravelbourg United Ch, 1976–79; Zion United Ch, Moose Jaw, 1979–86. MLA (NDP) Moose Jaw South, 1986–91, Moose Jaw Wakamow, 1991–2001; Associate Minister of Health, and Minister resp. for Wakamow Valley Authy, 1992–95; Minister resp. for SaskPower and SaskEnergy, 1992–93; Minister: of Health, 1995; of Social Services, 1995–98 (also resp. for Seniors and Public Service Commn); Minister resp. for Disabilities Issues, 1997–98; Premier, and Pres., Exec. Council, 2001–07. Dep. Chm., Crown Corporations Cttee, 1991–92; Mem., Standing Cttee on the Envmt, 1991–92. Leader, NDP, 2001–. *Address:* Legislative Building, Regina, SK S4S 0B3, Canada.

CALVERT, (Louis Victor) Denis, CB 1985; Comptroller and Auditor General for Northern Ireland, 1980–89, retired; *b* 20 April 1924; *s* of Louis Victor Calvert, Belfast and Gertrude Cherry Hobson, Belfast; *m* 1949, Vivien Millicent Lawson; two *s* one *d*. *Educ:* Belfast Royal Academy; Queen's Univ., Belfast (BScEcon). Admin. Staff Coll., Henley-on-Thames. Served with RAF, 1943–47, navigator (F/O). Northern Ireland Civil Service, 1947–80: Min. of Agriculture, 1947–56; Dep. Principal 1951; Principal, Min. of Finance, 1956–63; Min. of Health and Local Govt, 1963–65; Asst Sec. 1964; Min. of Development, 1965–73; Sen. Asst Sec. 1970; Dep. Sec. 1971; Min. of Housing, Local Govt and Planning, 1973–76; DoE for NI, 1976–80. Mem. Bd, Internat. Fund for Ireland, 1989–92. *Recreations:* gardening, golf, reading.

CALVERT, Michael, OBE 1998; FRAgS; Chief Executive, Royal Agricultural Society of England, 2000–05; *b* 1950; *s* of Noel and Nancy Calvert; *m*; three *s*. *Educ:* Edinburgh Univ. (BSc Hons 1972). FRAgS 1998. Tech. Rep., ICI, 1972–74; Partner, Northwold Agricl Services, 1974–80; General Manager: Farmplan Pty, 1980–81; Sentry Farm Mgt, 1981–85; CWS Farms Gp, 1985–2000. Bd Mem., Rothamsted Exptl Stn, 2000–03. Mem., Council, BBSRC, 1998–2003; Chm., LINK Sustainable Livestock Prodn Prog., 1996–2004. *Recreations:* walking, tennis, gardening, in France.

CALVERT, Norman Hilton; retired; Deputy Secretary, Departments of the Environment and of Transport, 1978–80; *b* 27 July 1925; *s* of Clifford and Doris Calvert; *m* 1st, 1949, May Yates (*d* 1968); one *s* one *d*; 2nd, 1971, Vera Baker (*d* 1996). *Educ:* Leeds Modern Sch.; Leeds Univ.; King's Coll., Durham Univ. BA Hons 1st cl. Geography, 1950. Served Royal Signals, 1943–47: 81 (W African) Div., India, 1945–47. Min. of Housing and Local Govt: Asst Principal, 1950–55; Principal, 1956–64; Asst Sec., 1964–71; Sec., Water Resources Bd, 1964–68; Principal Regional Officer, Northern Region, 1969–71; Regional Dir, Northern Region, and Chm., Northern Econ. Planning Bd, 1971–73; Under Sec., DoE, 1971–78. *Recreations:* fell walking, listening to music, motoring. *Address:* 6 Monmouth Gardens, Beaminster, Dorset DT8 3BT. *T:* (01308) 863366.

CALVERT, Rev. Canon Peter Noel; House for Duty Priest-in-charge, Leven Valley Benefice, since 2007; Chaplain to the Queen, since 1998; *b* 20 Dec. 1941; *s* of Harry and Beatrice Annie Calvert; *m* 1980, Stella Christine Horrocks; two *s* one *d*. *Educ:* Queen Elizabeth GS, Wakefield; Arnold Sch., Blackpool; Christ's Coll., Cambridge (BA 1963; MA 1967). Ordained deacon, 1966, priest, 1967; Curate, Brighouse, 1966–71; Vicar, Heptonstall, 1971–82; Vicar of Todmorden, W Yorks, 1982–2007; Priest-in-charge, Cross Stone, 1983–93; Rural Dean, Calder Valley, 1984–2006; Hon. Canon, Wakefield Cathedral, 1992–2007. *Recreations:* photography, philately, walking, interest in transport. *Address:* The Vicarage, Haverthwaite, Ulverston, Cumbria LA12 8AJ. *T:* (01539) 531476.

CALVERT-SMITH, Hon. Sir David, Kt 2002; **Hon. Mr Justice Calvert-Smith;** a Judge of the High Court of Justice, Queen's Bench Division, since 2004; a Presiding Judge, South Eastern Circuit, since 2006; *b* 6 April 1945; *s* of late Arthur and Stella Calvert-Smith; *m* 1971, Marianthe Phoca; one *s* one *d*. *Educ:* Eton; King's Coll., Cambridge (MA). Called to the Bar, Middle Temple, 1969, Bencher, 1994; a Recorder, 1986–98; Jun. Treasury Counsel, 1986; Sen. Treasury Counsel, 1991; First Sen. Treasury Counsel, 1995; QC 1997; Dir of Public Prosecutions, 1998–2003. Mem., CRE, 2004–06. Vice-Chm., 1997–98, Chm., 1998, Criminal Bar Assoc.; Mem., Criminal Cttee, Judicial Studies Bd, 1997–98. *Recreations:* music, sports. *Address:* Royal Courts of Justice, Strand, WC2A 2LL.

CALVET, Jacques; President, Peugeot SA, 1984–97; Referendary Councillor, Cour des Comptes (Audit Office), since 1963; *b* 19 Sept. 1931; *s* of Prof. Louis Calvet and Yvonne Calvet (*née* Olmières); *m* 1956, Françoise Rondot; two *s* one *d*. *Educ:* Lycée Janson-de-Sailly; Law Faculty, Paris (Licencié en droit; Dipl. Inst. d'Etudes Politiques; Dipl. d'Etudes Supérieures d'Economie Politique et des Sciences Economiques). Trainee, l'Ecole Nationale d'Administration, 1955–57; Audit Office, 1957–59; Office of Sec. of State for Finance, 1959–62, of Minister of Finance, 1962–66; Dep. Dir, 1964, Head of Dept, 1967, Central Finance Admin; Head of Finance Dept, Paris Préfecture, 1967–69; Asst Dir, later Dir, Office of Minister of Economy and Finance, 1969–74; Dir in Ministry of Finance, 1973; Asst Dir Gen., 1974, Dir Gen., 1976, Pres., 1979–82, Banque Nationale de Paris; Vice-Prés. du Conseil d'Administration, 1984, Prés., 1990, Automobiles Peugeot; Président du Conseil d'Administration: Automobiles Citroën, 1983–97; Publicité Française, 1991–97. Vice Prés., Conseil de surveillance, Galeries Lafayette; Prés., Comité de surveillance, Bazar de l'hôtel de Ville; Administrateur: Icade Foncière des Pimonts; Cottin Frères; Société Foncière Lyonnaise. Consulting Advr, Banque de France. Commandeur, Légion d'Honneur, 1996; Officier: Ordre Nat. du Mérite, 1970; Ordre Nat. du Mérite Agricole, 1970; Chevalier des Palmes académiques, 1964; Grande Ufficiale, Ordine al Merito della Repubblica Italiana, 1995. *Address:* 31 avenue Victor Hugo, 75116 Paris, France.

CALVIN, Michael; Deputy Director, English Institute of Sport, 2002–06; *b* 3 Aug. 1957; *s* of Charles Calvin and Margaret Calvin (*née* Platts); *m* 1977, Lynn Goss; three *s* one *d*. *Educ:* Watford Grammar Sch. Reporter: Watford Observer, 1975–77; Hayters Sports Agency, 1977–79; writer and broadcaster, Thames TV, 1983–84; Chief Sports Writer, Westminster Press, 1979–83; Feature Writer, 1984–86, Chief Sports Writer, 1986–96, Daily Telegraph; Sen. Sports Writer, The Times, 1997–98; Chief Sports Feature Writer, Mail on Sunday, 1998–2002. Segrave Trophy for Outstanding Achievement, 1990; Sports Journalist of the Year, English Sports Council, 1992; Sports Reporter of the Year, British Press Awards, 1992, 1999; Award for Services to Yachting Journalism, RYA, 1993; led winning team for coverage of disabled sport, British Sports Assoc. for Disabled, 1994, 1995, 1996. *Publications:* Captaincy, 1977; Only Wind and Water, 1998. *Recreation:* long distance sailing. *Address:* Broomwood, Higher Rads End, Eversholt MK17 9ED. *T:* (01525) 280300. *Clubs:* Royal Ocean Racing; Cape Horners.

CALVOCORESSI, Peter (John Ambrose); author; *b* 17 Nov. 1912; *s* of Pandia Calvocoressi and Irene (Ralli); *m* 1st, 1938, Barbara Dorothy Eden (*d* 2005), *d* of 6th Baron Henley; two *s*; 2nd, 2006, Margaret Rachel, *d* of Hon. Ernest Scott, KCMG, MVO and Lady Scott. *Educ:* Eton (King's Scholar); Balliol Coll., Oxford. Called to Bar, 1935. RAF Intelligence, 1940–45; Wing Comdr. Trial of Major War Criminals, Nuremberg, 1945–46. Contested (L) Nuneaton, 1945. Staff of Royal Institute of International Affairs, 1949–54 (Mem. Council, 1955–70); Dir of Chatto & Windus Ltd and The Hogarth Press Ltd, 1954–65; Editorial Dir, 1972–76, Publisher and Chief Exec., 1973–76, Penguin Books. Chm., Open Univ. Educnl Enterprises Ltd, 1979–88. Reader (part time) in International Relations, Univ. of Sussex, 1965–71; Member: Council, Inst. for Strategic Studies, 1961–71; Council, Inst. of Race Relations, 1970–71; UN Sub-Commn on the Prevention of Discrimination and Protection of Minorities, 1962–71; Chm., The Africa Bureau, 1963–71; Mem., Internat. Exec., Amnesty International, 1969–71; Chm., The London Library, 1970–73; Dep. Chm., N Metropolitan Conciliation Cttee, 1967–71. DUniv Open, 1990. *Publications:* Nuremberg: The Facts, the Law and the Consequences, 1947; Surveys of International Affairs, vol. 1, 1947–48, 1950; vol. 2, 1949–50, 1951; vol. 3, 1951, 1952; vol. 4, 1952, 1953; vol. 5, 1953, 1954; (with Guy Wint) Middle East Crisis, 1957; South Africa and World Opinion, 1961; World Order and New States, 1962; World Politics since 1945, 1968, 8th edn as World Politics 1945–2000, 2000; (with Guy Wint) Total War, 1972, 2nd rev. edn (with John Pritchard) 1989; The British Experience 1945–75, 1978; Top Secret Ultra, 1980; Independent Africa and the World, 1985; A Time for Peace, 1987; Who's Who in the Bible, 1987; Resilient Europe 1870–2000, 1991; Threading My Way (memoirs), 1994; Fall Out: World War II and the shaping of Europe, 1997. *Address:* Old Mill Lane Farmhouse, Marnhull, Dorset DT10 1JY; Flat U, 12–18 Bloomsbury Street, WC1B 3GA. *Club:* Garrick.

CALVOCORESSI, Richard Edward Ion, CBE 2008; Director, Henry Moore Foundation, since 2007; *b* 5 May 1951; *s* of late Ion Melville Calvocoressi and of Katherine (*née* Kennedy); *m* 1976, Francesca Temple Roberts; one *s* two *d*. *Educ:* Eton; Brooke House, Market Harborough; Magdalen Coll., Oxford (Exhibnr; BA (Hons) English Lang. and Lit.); Courtauld Inst. of Art (MA Hist. of Art, 19th and 20th centuries). Research Assistant: Scottish Nat. Gall. of Modern Art, Edinburgh, 1977–79; Modern Collection, Tate Gall., 1979–82; Asst Keeper, Tate Gall., 1982–87; Keeper, then Dir, Scottish Nat. Gall. of Modern Art, 1987–2007. Art Advr, Chelmsford Mus., 1980–86; Member: Cttee, British Council, Scotland, 1989–98; Visual Arts Adv. Cttee, British Council, 1991–2006 (Chm., 1999–2006); Visual Arts Cttee, Scottish Arts Council, 1993–95. Dir, Grimsthorpe and Drummond Castle Trust, 1993–. Governor, Glasgow Sch. of Art, 1988–91; Expert Mem., Comité Magritte, 2001–; Mem., Francis Bacon catalogue raisonné Cttee, 2006–. Trustee, Edward James Foundn, 2007–. FRSA 2000. *Publications:* Magritte, 1979, rev. edn 1984; Lee Miller: portraits from a life, 2002; numerous exhibn catalogues, reviews and articles. *Address:* 20 Warriston Crescent, Edinburgh EH3 5LB.

CAMBRIDGE, Archdeacon of; *see* Beer, Ven. J. S.

CAMBRIDGE, Alan John; HM Diplomatic Service, retired; *b* 1 July 1925; *s* of Thomas David Cambridge and Winifred Elizabeth (*née* Jarrett); *m* 1947, Thelma Elliot; three *s* one *d*. *Educ:* Beckenham Grammar Sch. Served War, FAA and RAFVR, 1943–47 (Air Gunner, Bomber Comd). War Pensions Office and MPNI, 1948–55; entered CRO, 1955; Chief Clerk: Madras, 1956–58; Kuala Lumpur, 1959–62; 2nd Sec., Salisbury, Fedn of Rhodesia and Nyasaland, 1962–65; 1st Sec. (Political), Freetown, 1965–66; UN Dept, FCO, 1966–68; 1st Sec., Prague, 1969; 1st Sec. (Consular/Aid), Suva, 1970–72; HM Consul, Milan, 1972–74; Asst Head of Inf. Dept, FCO, 1974–78; 1st Sec., Ankara, 1978–81; Asst Head, 1981–82, Head and Counsellor, 1983–85, Migration and Visa Dept, FCO; Assessor, FCO, 1985–90. *Recreations:* photography, swimming. *Address:* 9 The Ferns, Carlton Road, Tunbridge Wells TN1 2JT. *T:* (01892) 531223. *Club:* Civil Service.

CAMBRIDGE, Sydney John Guy, CMG 1979; CVO 1979; HM Diplomatic Service, retired; *b* 5 Nov. 1928; *o s* of late Jack and Mona Cambridge; unmarried. *Educ:* Marlborough; King's Coll., Cambridge. Entered HM Diplomatic Service, Sept. 1952; Oriental Sec., British Embassy, Jedda, 1953–56; Foreign Office, 1956–60; First Sec., UK

Delegn to United Nations, at New York, 1960–64; Head of Chancery, British Embassy, Djakarta, 1964–66; FO, 1966–70; Counsellor, British Embassy, Rome, 1970–73; Head of Financial Relations Dept, FCO, 1973–75; Counsellor, British High Commn, Nicosia, 1975–77; Ambassador: to Kuwait, 1977–82; to Morocco, 1982–84. *Address:* Saint Peter's House, Filkins, Lechlade, Glos GL7 3JQ.

CAMDEN, 6th Marquess *cr* 1812; **David George Edward Henry Pratt;** Baron Camden, 1765; Earl Camden, Viscount Bayham, 1786; Earl of Brecknock, 1812; *b* 13 Aug. 1930; *o s* of 5th Marquess Camden and Marjorie, Countess of Brecknock, DBE (*d* 1989); *S* father, 1983; *m* 1961, Virginia Ann (marr. diss. 1984), *o d* of late F. H. H. Finlaison, Arklow Cottage, Windsor, Berks; one *s* one *d* (and one *s* decd). *Educ:* Eton. Late Lieutenant, Scots Guards. Dir, Clive Discount Co. Ltd, 1958–69. *Heir: s* Earl of Brecknock, *qv*. *Address:* Wherwell House, Andover, Hants SP11 7JP. *T:* (01264) 860020.

CAMDESSUS, Michel Jean, Hon. CBE 2007; Managing Director, International Monetary Fund, 1987–2000; *b* 1 May 1933; *s* of Alfred Camdessus and Madeleine Camdessus (*née* Cassembon); *m* 1957, Brigitte d'Arcy; two *s* four *d*. *Educ:* Inst. of Political Studies, Paris; Diploma, Nat. Sch. of Administration. Administrateur Civil, French Treasury, 1960; Financial Attaché, Permt French Delegn to European Communities, 1966–68; Asst Dir, Treasury, 1971, Dep. Dir, 1974, Dir, 1982; Dep. Governor, Bank of France, Aug. 1984, Governor, Nov. 1984. Chm., Paris Club, 1978–84. Commandeur de la Légion d'Honneur; Chevalier de l'Ordre National du Mérite; Croix de la valeur militaire. *Address:* 27 rue de Valois, 75001 Paris, France.

CAME, Nicholas John Gard, FICS; Director, Australian, New Zealand and Papua New Guinea Chambers of Commerce (UK), 1993–96; *b* Swansea, 10 March 1937; *s* of Victor Henry Thomas Came and Dorothy Edith Came (*née* Prestidge); *m* 1961, Edelgard Elise Irma Meyer; two *d*. *Educ:* Bromsgrove Sch. FICS 1964; MCIT 1988. Officer Cadet Trng Vessel, Rakaia, 1954–57; Bethell Gwyn & Co., 1958–59; Nat. Service, commnd RA, 1959–61; Exec., Dowie & Marwood Ltd, 1961–66; Manager: NZ Shipping Co. Ltd, London, 1967–71; P&OSN Co., 1971–78; Dir, Shipping Corp. of NZ (UK) Ltd, 1978–91. Director: Internat. Shipping Fedn, 1983–91; Shipowners Refrigerated Cargo Res. Assoc., 1984–91; Mem. Council, Internat. Chamber of Shipping, 1983–92. Dir, Aust. and NZ Trade Adv. Cttee, 1993–96; Leader, British Trade Missions to Australasia, 1992, 1993, 1994 and 1996. Pres., NZ Soc., 1990–91. Mem., Exec. Cttee, City of London Br., RNLI, 1996–99. Associate Mem., Master Mariners' Co., 2006. *Recreations:* walking, music, languages, travel. *Clubs:* Royal Over-Seas League, Little Ship; Bristol Channel Yacht (Mumbles).

CAMERON, family name of **Barons Cameron of Dillington** and **Cameron of Lochbroom**.

CAMERON OF DILLINGTON, Baron *cr* 2004 (Life Peer), of Dillington in the County of Somerset; **Ewen James Hanning Cameron,** Kt 2003; DL; FRICS; Chairman, Airports Direct Travel Ltd, since 2006; *b* 24 Nov. 1949; *s* of Maj. Allan John Cameron and Elizabeth Cameron (*née* Vaughan-Lee); *m* 1975, Caroline Anne Ripley; three *s* one *d*. *Educ:* Christ Church, Oxford (MA). FRICS 1992; FRAgS 1995. Owner/Manager, Dillington Estate, Somerset, 1971–. Founding Chm., Orchard Media Ltd, 1989–99; Chm., Lets Go Travel Ltd, 1998–2006. Mem., Minister of Agriculture's CAP rev. gp, 1995; Govt's Rural Advocate, 2000–04. Dir, Village Retail Services Assoc. for Village Shops, 1992–2000. Nat. Pres., CLA, 1995–97. Mem., UK Round Table for Sustainable Develt, 1997–2000. Chm., Countryside Agency, 1999–2004. Pres., Somerset Young Farmers, 1990–91; Mem., Mgt Bd, Nat. Fedn of Young Farmers, 1998–2000. Chm., Somerset Strategic Partnership, 2004–. Pres., Royal Bath and West Soc., 2006–07. FRSA 1996. High Sheriff, 1986–87, DL 1989, Somerset. Hon. LLD Exeter, 2004. *Recreations:* golf, shooting, windsurfing. *Address:* Dillington Farms, Ilminster, Som TA19 9EG.

CAMERON OF LOCHBROOM, Baron *cr* 1984 (Life Peer), of Lochbroom in the District of Ross and Cromarty; **Kenneth John Cameron;** PC 1984; a Senator of the College of Justice in Scotland, 1989–2003; *b* 11 June 1931; *s* of Hon. Lord Cameron, KT, DSC; *m* 1964, Jean Pamela Murray; two *d*. *Educ:* The Edinburgh Academy; Corpus Christi Coll., Oxford (MA 1955; Hon. Fellow, 1989); Edinburgh Univ. (LLB). Served RN, 1950–52; commissioned RNVR, 1951 (Lt). Admitted Faculty of Advocates, 1958; QC (Scot.) 1972; Standing Junior to Dept of Transport, 1964–71; to DoE, 1971–72; Chairman of Industrial Tribunals in Scotland, 1966–81; Advocate Depute, 1981–84; Lord Advocate, 1984–89. Chm. of Pensions Appeal Tribunal (Scotland), 1975, Pres. 1976–84. Chairman: Cttee for Investigation in Scotland of Agricultural Marketing Schemes, 1980–84; Scottish Civic Trust, 1989–95; Edinburgh New Town Conservation Cttee, 1991–94; Royal Fine Art Commn for Scotland, 1995–2005. Pres., Scottish Council for Voluntary Orgns, 1989–2001. Hon. Bencher, Lincoln's Inn, 1984. FRSE 1990. Hon. FRIAS 1994. *Recreations:* fishing, sailing, music. *Address:* Stoneyhill House, Musselburgh EH21 6RP. *T:* (0131) 665 1081. *Club:* New (Edinburgh).

CAMERON, Prof. Alan Douglas Edward, FBA 1975; Anthon Professor of Latin Language and Literature, Columbia University, New York, since 1977; *b* 13 March 1938; *er s* of A. D. Cameron, Egham; *m* 1st, 1962, Averil Sutton (*see* Dame A. M. Cameron) (marr. diss. 1980); one *s* one *d*; 2nd, 1987, Charlotte Innes (marr. diss. 1992); 3rd, 1998, Carla Asher. *Educ:* St Paul's Sch. (Schol.); New Coll., Oxford (Schol.). Craven Scholar 1958; 1st cl. Hon. Mods 1959; De Paravicini Scholar 1960; Chancellor's Prize for Latin Prose 1960; 1st cl. Lit. Hum. 1961; N. H. Baynes Prize 1967; John Conington Prize 1968. Asst Master, Brunswick Sch., Haywards Heath, 1956–57; Asst Lectr, then Lectr, in Humanity, Glasgow Univ., 1961–64; Lectr in Latin, 1964–71, Reader, 1971–72, Bedford Coll., London; Prof. of Latin, King's Coll., London, 1972–77. Visiting Professor: Columbia Univ., NY, 1967–68; UCLA, 1989; Visiting Fellow: Humanities Research Centre, ANU, 1985; Inst. for Advanced Study, Princeton, 1990; Guggenheim Fellow, 1986. Fellow: Amer. Acad. of Arts and Sciences, 1979; Amer. Philosophical Soc., 1992. Charles J. Goodwin Award, Amer. Philol Assoc., 1996; Lionel Trilling Award, Columbia Univ., 2005. *Publications:* Claudian: Poetry and Propaganda at the Court of Honorius, 1970; (contrib.) Prosopography of the Later Roman Empire, ed Jones, Morris and Martindale, i, 1971, ii, 1980; Porphyrius the Charioteer, 1973; Bread and Circuses, 1974; Circus Factions, 1976; Literature and Society in the Early Byzantine World, 1985; (jtly) The Consuls of the Later Roman Empire, 1985; (with J. Long) Barbarians and Politics at the Court of Arcadius, 1993; The Greek Anthology: from Meleager to Planudes, 1993; Callimachus and his Critics, 1995; Greek Mythography in the Roman World, 2004; The Last Pagans of Rome, 2009; articles and reviews in learned jls. *Recreation:* the cinema. *Address:* 450 Riverside Drive, New York, NY 10027, USA.

CAMERON, Alan John; Director, since 2001, Chairman, since 2005, NSW Growth Centres Commission; *b* 9 Feb. 1948; *s* of John and Norma Cameron; *m* 1971, Susan Patricia Sanders; two *s*. *Educ:* Sydney Univ. (BA, LLB, LLM). Principal Solicitor, NSW Aboriginal Legal Service, 1973–75; Lectr in Law, Univ. of N Sumatra, 1975–77; Dawson Waldron, Solicitors, later Blake Dawson Waldron: Partner, 1979–91; Man. Partner, 1982–85, 1989–91; Commonwealth Ombudsman (Australia), 1991–92; Chm., Australian Securities & Investments Commn, 1993–2000. Mem., Judicial Commn of NSW, 2001–. Director: Westpac Funds Management Ltd, 2006–; Multiplex Group, 2006–. *Recreations:* tennis, walking, reading. *Address:* 32 Hart Street, Balmain, NSW 2041, Australia.

CAMERON, Alexander, CBE 2000; Chairman, Parole Board for Scotland, since 2006; *b* 29 April 1950; *s* of Æneas and Ruby Cameron; *m* 1975, Linda J. T. Dobbie; two *s*. *Educ:* Duncanrig Sen. Secondary Sch.; Univ. of Strathclyde (BA); Univ. of Aberdeen (Cert. Applied Social Studies; CQSW 1973). Social worker, Clackmannan Co., 1973–75; Principal Officer, 1975–81, Asst Dir of Social Work, 1981–87, Central Reg.; Dir of Social Work, Borders Reg., 1987–95; Exec. Dir of Social Work, S Lanarks, 1995–2006. Vis. Prof., Strathclyde Univ., 1997–. Chair: Inst. for Res. and Innovation in Social Services (formerly Scottish Inst. for Excellence in Social Work Educn), 2003–; Scottish Inst. for Residential Child Care, 1996–2007. Non-exec. Dir, State Hosps Bd for Scotland, 2005–. Dir, Care Visions, 2006–. Pres., Assoc. of Dirs of Social Work, 1996–97. Fellow, British Amer. Project, 1988. *Recreations:* reading, architecture and design, cooking, dining out, travel, especially to USA. *Address:* Parole Board for Scotland, Saughton House, Edinburgh EH11 3XD. *T:* (0131) 244 8097, *Fax:* (0131) 244 6974; *e-mail:* cameronsathome@btinternet.com.

CAMERON, Alexander Allan; QC 2003; *b* 27 Aug. 1963; *s* of Ian Donald Cameron and Mary Fleur Cameron; *m* 1990, Sarah Louise Fearnley-Whittingstall; one *s* one *d*. *Educ:* Eton Coll.; Bristol Univ. (LLB Hons). Called to the Bar, Inner Temple, 1986; in practice, specialising in law of crime, incl. commercial crime, extradition and licensing. *Recreations:* various. *Address:* 3 Raymond Buildings, Gray's Inn, WC1R 5BH. *T:* (020) 7400 6400; *e-mail:* alexander.cameron@3raymondbuildings.com. *Clubs:* White's, Queen's, MCC.

See also Rt Hon. D. W. D. Cameron.

CAMERON, Major Allan John, MBE 1988; JP; Vice Lord-Lieutenant, Highland Region (Ross and Cromarty), 1977–92; *b* 25 March 1917; *s* of Col Sir Donald Cameron of Lochiel, KT, CMG (*d* 1951), and Lady Hermione Cameron (*d* 1978), *d* of 5th Duke of Montrose; *m* 1945, Mary Elizabeth Vaughan-Lee, Dillington, Somerset; two *s* two *d* (and one *s* decd). *Educ:* Harrow; RMC Sandhurst. Served QO Cameron Highlanders, 1936–48; Major, Retd (POW Middle East, 1942). County Councillor, Ross-shire, 1955–75 (Chm. Educn Cttee, 1962–75); Councillor, 1975–96, Convener, 1991–96, Ross and Cromarty DC. Former Member: Red Deer Commn; Countryside Commn for Scotland; Broadcasting Council for Scotland. *Recreations:* curling (Past Pres. Royal Caledonian Curling Club), gardening, golf. *Address:* Quarryfield Farmhouse, Munlochy, Ross-shire IV8 8NZ. *T:* (01463) 811249. *Club:* Naval and Military.

CAMERON, Rt Rev. Andrew Bruce; Bishop of Aberdeen and Orkney, 1992–2006 and Primus of the Episcopal Church in Scotland, 2000–06; *b* 2 May 1941; *s* of Andrew and Helen Cameron; *m* 1974, Elaine Gingles; two *s*. *Educ:* Eastwood Secondary Sch., Glasgow; Edinburgh Theol Coll.; Edinburgh Univ. (Cert. in Past. Studies); Urban Theology Unit, Sheffield (Dip. in Theology and Mission). Ordained deacon 1964, priest 1965; Assistant Curate: St Michael and All Angels, Helensburgh, 1964–67; Holy Cross, Edinburgh, 1967–70; Diocesan and Provincial Youth Chaplain and Chaplain, St Mary's Cathedral, Edinburgh, 1970–75; Rector, St Mary's, Dalmahoy and Anglican Chaplain, Heriot-Watt Univ., 1975–82; Churches Develt Officer in Livingston Ecumenical Parish, 1982–88; Rector, St John's, Perth and Convenor of Provincial Mission Bd, 1988–92. Resident Scholar, Bruton Parish Church, Williamsburg, Va, 2006–07. Interim Warden, Scottish Churches House, 2008. *Recreations:* golf, swimming, walking, singing, listening to music, theatre, reading. *Address:* 2 Newbigging Grange, Coupar Angus, Perthshire PH13 9GA. *T:* (01821) 650482; *e-mail:* bruce2541@gmail.com.

See also Rt Rev. D. M. Cameron.

CAMERON, Dame Averil (Millicent), DBE 2006 (CBE 1999); MA, PhD; FBA 1981; FSA 1982; Warden, Keble College, since 1994, Professor of Late Antique and Byzantine History, since 1998, Pro-Vice-Chancellor, since 2001, University of Oxford; *b* 8 Feb. 1940; *d* of T. R. Sutton, Leek, Staffs; *m* 1962, Alan Douglas Edward Cameron, *qv* (marr. diss. 1980); one *s* one *d*. *Educ:* Westwood Hall Girls' High Sch., Leek, Staffs; Somerville Coll., Oxford (Passmore Edwards Schol. 1960; Rosa Hovey Schol. 1962; MA); Univ. of Glasgow; University Coll. London (PhD; FKC 1987). King's College London: Asst Lectr, 1965; Lectr, 1968; Reader in Ancient History, 1970; Prof. of Ancient History, 1978–89; Head of Dept of Classics, 1984–89; Prof. of Late Antique and Byzantine Studies, and Dir, Centre for Hellenic Studies, 1989–94. Visiting Professor: Columbia Univ., 1967–68; Collège de France, 1987; Sather Prof., Univ. of Calif. at Berkeley, 1985–86; Vis. Member, Inst. of Advanced Study, Princeton, 1977–78; Summer Fellow, Dumbarton Oaks Center for Byzantine Studies, 1981; British Acad. Wolfson Res. Reader in Hist., 1990–92. Chm., British Nat. Byzantine Cttee, 1983–89; President: Roman Soc., 1995–98 (Vice-Pres., 1983–95, 1999–); Council for British Res. in the Levant, 2004–; Ecclesiastical History Soc., 2005–06; Vice-Pres., Fédn Internat. des Assocs d'Etudes Classiques, 2005–. Mem., British Acad. Council, 1983–86. Vice-Chm., then Chm., Cathedrals Fabric Commn for England, 1999–2005. Editor, Jl of Roman Studies, 1985–90. Corresp. mem., Akad. der Wiss. zu Göttingen, phil.-hist. Klasse, 2006. Hon. DLitt: Warwick, 1996; St Andrews, 1997; QUB, 2000; Aberdeen, 2003; London, 2005; DTheol Lund, 2001. *Publications:* Procopius, 1967; Agathias, 1970; Corippus: In laudem Iustini minoris, 1976; Change and Continuity in Sixth-Century Byzantium, 1981; (ed jtly) Images of Women in Antiquity, 1983, 2nd edn 1993; (ed jtly) Constantinople in the Eighth Century: the Parastaseis Syntomoi Chronikai, 1984; Procopius and the Sixth Century, 1985; (ed) History as Text: the writing of ancient history, 1989; Christianity and the Rhetoric of Empire, 1991; (ed jtly) The Byzantine and Early Islamic Near East, vol. I: Problems in the Literary Source Material, 1992, vol. II: Land Use and Settlement Patterns, 1994, vol. III: States, Resources and Armies, 1995; The Later Roman Empire, 1993; The Mediterranean World in Late Antiquity, AD 395–600, 1993; Changing Cultures in Early Byzantium, 1996; (ed with P. D. Gainsey) Cambridge Ancient History, vol. XIII, 1998; (ed with S. G. Hall) Eusebius, Life of Constantine, 1999; (ed jtly) Cambridge Ancient History, vol. XIV, 2001; (ed) Fifty Years of Prosopography, 2003; (ed jtly) Cambridge Ancient History, vol. XII, 2005; The Byzantines, 2006; numerous articles in learned jls. *Address:* Keble College, Oxford OX1 3PG.

CAMERON, Barbara Alexander; Her Honour Judge Cameron; a Circuit Judge, since 2007; *b* Totteridge, 3 June 1950; *d* of Thomas and Paula Alexander Cameron; *m* 1983; two *d*. *Educ:* Queen's Coll., Harley St; Lucy Cavendish Coll., Cambridge (BA Hons Law 1980). Called to the Bar, Lincoln's Inn, 1979; Mem., Inner Temple, 1983. Lectr in Law, City of London Poly., 1980–82; barrister, Henderson Chambers, Temple, 1982–2007; Recorder, 1999–2007; Dep. Dist Judge, 1999–2007. Family and Divorce Mediator, 1998–2007. Legal Assessor: to Nursing and Midwifery Council, 1993–2007; to GDC, GMC and Gen. Chiropractic Council, 2004–07. Mem., Appeals Cttee, Legal Services Commn, 1993–2007. Member: Family Law Bar Assoc., 1983–; Professional Negligence Bar Assoc., 1990–2008 (Mem., Exec. Cttee, 1993–95); Personal Injuries Bar Assoc., 1995–2008; Bar Disciplinary Tribunal, 1997–2007. Member: Assoc. of Women Lawyers, 2003–; Assoc. of Regulatory and Disciplinary Lawyers, 2004–. Panel Mem.,

Barristers' Complaints Adv. Service. *Recreations:* family life, opera, cooking and eating, walking the dog. *Address:* Medway County Court, Anchorage House, 47–67 High Street, Chatham, Kent ME4 4DW. *T:* (01634) 810720.

CAMERON, Colin Neil; freelance executive producer and media consultant; *b* 30 March 1950; *s* of late Hector MacDonald Cameron and of Frances (*née* Majury); *m* 1978, Christine Welsh Main; two *s*. *Educ:* Glasgow Acad.; Duke of York, Nairobi; Poly. of Central London (Dip. Communication Studies). Journalist, BBC Scotland, 1973–76; BBC TV: Film Dir, That's Life, 1976–77; Producer/Dir, Everyman and Heart of the Matter, 1977–85; Editor, Features and Documentaries, BBC North, 1985–88; Hd, Documentary Features, BBC TV, 1988–91; BBC Scotland: Hd of TV, 1991–96; Hd of Production, 1996–2000; Hd of Network Progs, 2000–01; Controller, Network Develt, BBC Nations and Regions, 2001–04; Man. Dir, Lion TV Scotland, 2004–07. Trustee, The Research Centre (Chm., 2004–07). Hon. Prof., Film and Media Studies, Univ. of Stirling, 2006–. Member: RTS, 1984–; BAFTA, 1984–. UNA Media Peace Prize, 1984. *Address:* 2 The Old Manse, Station Road, Balfron G63 0SX.

CAMERON, Rt Hon. David William Donald; PC 2005; MP (C) Witney, since 2001; Leader of the Conservative Party and Leader of the Opposition, since 2005; *b* 9 Oct. 1966; *s* of Ian Donald Cameron and Mary Fleur Cameron; *m* 1996, Samantha Gwendoline, *e d* of Sir Reginald Sheffield, Bt, *qv*; two *s* one *d*. *Educ:* Eton Coll.; Brasenose Coll., Oxford (BA 1st Cl. Hons PPE; Hon. Fellow, 2006). Cons. Res. Dept, 1988–92; Special Adviser: HM Treasury, 1992–93; Home Office, 1993–94; Hd, Corporate Affairs, Carlton Communications plc, 1994–2001. Shadow Sec. of State for Educn and Skills, 2005. Mem., Select Cttee on Home Affairs, 2001–05. Dep. Chm., Cons. Party, 2003–04. *Recreations:* tennis, bridge, cooking. *Address:* House of Commons, SW1A 0AA. *T:* (020) 7219 3000.
See also A. A. Cameron.

CAMERON, Rt Rev. Donald; *see* Cameron, Rt Rev. E. D.

CAMERON, Donald Allan, RDI 2004; Managing Director, Cameron Balloons Ltd, since 1970; *b* 16 July 1939; *s* of late David Stuart Cameron and Madge Kaye Cameron; *m* 1st, 1969, Dorothy Anne Golding (marr. diss. 1980); one *s* one *d*; 2nd, 1980, Margaret Louise Tobin; six *s* one *d*. *Educ:* Allan Glen's Sch.; Glasgow Univ. (BSc); Cornell Univ. (MS). Chm., Bristol Balloon Fiestas Ltd, 1992–. British Delegate to FAI (Ballooning), 1987–2002. Mem. Bd, Children's Hospice SW, 2003–. Mem., Bath Royal Literary and Scientific Instn, 2002– (Convenor, 2004–). Hon. Pres., 2494 Sqdn ATC, 2003–. Hon. Pres., City of Bristol Pipes & Drums, 2001–. Patron, IMechE, 2003–. Hon. Freeman, City of Bristol, 2007. Hon. MA Bristol, 1980; Hon. DEng Glasgow, 2000; Hon. DBA UWE, 2001. *Publications:* Ballooning Handbook, 1981; Purpose of Life, 2001. *Recreations:* ballooning, sailing, natural history. *Address:* c/o Cameron Balloons Ltd, St John Street, Bristol, BS3 4NH. *T:* (0117) 963 7216, *Fax:* (0117) 966 1168; *e-mail:* dcameron@cameronballoons.co.uk. *Clubs:* Royal Aero (Mem. Council, 1990–), British Balloon and Airship.

CAMERON of Lochiel, Donald Angus; 27th Chief of the Clan Cameron; Lord-Lieutenant of Inverness, since 2002; *b* 2 Aug. 1946; *s* of Col Sir Donald Hamish Cameron of Lochiel, KT, CVO, TD, 26th Chief of the Clan Cameron and Margaret (*née* Gathorne-Hardy); *S* father as 27th Chief, 2004; *m* 1974, Lady Cecil Kerr, OBE, *d* of 12th Marquess of Lothian, KCVO; one *s* three *d*. *Educ:* Harrow; Christ Church, Oxford (MA). FCA. Dir, J. Henry Schroder Wagg, subseq. J. Henry Schroder & Co., 1984–99. 2nd Lieutenant, Queen's Own Cameron Highlanders (TA), 1966–68. Pres., Highland Soc. of London, 1994–97. JP Highland, 2002–07. *Address:* Achnacarry, Spean Bridge, Inverness-shire PH34 4EJ. *T:* (01937) 712708.

CAMERON, Donald William; President, Maritime Steel and Foundries Ltd, since 2002; *b* 20 May 1946; *m* 1969, Rosemary Simpson; one *s* two *d*. *Educ:* East Pictou Rural High Sch.; Nova Scotia Agricl Coll.; McGill Univ. (BSc). Dairy farmer; MLA (PC) Pictou East, 1974–93; Minister of: Recreation, 1978–79; Fisheries, 1978–80; Industry, Trade and Technology, 1988–91; Leader, Nova Scotia Progressive Cons. Party, 1991; Premier of Nova Scotia, 1991–93; Canadian Consul Gen. to New England, 1993–97. *Recreations:* skiing, boating, hockey, tennis. *Address:* RR #1, New Glasgow, NS B2H 5C4, Canada.

CAMERON, Rt Rev. Douglas Maclean; Bishop of Argyll and the Isles, 1993–2003; *b* 23 March 1935; *s* of Andrew McIntyre Cameron and Helen Adam McKechnie; *m* 1969, Anne Patricia Purnell; two *d*. *Educ:* Eastwood Grammar Sch., Clarkston, Glasgow; Theol Coll., Edinburgh; Univ. of the South, Sewanee, Tennessee, USA. Bank of Scotland, 1951–59; RAF, 1953–55. Ordained: deacon, 1962; priest, 1963; curate, Christ Church, Falkirk, 1962–65; Anglican Church in Papua New Guinea: Mission Priest, 1966–67; priest in charge, Movi, 1967–72; Rector, St Francis, Goroka, 1972–74; Archdeacon of New Guinea Mainland, 1972–74; Priest in charge, St Fillan's, Edinburgh, 1974, Rector, 1978–88; Rector: St Hilda's, Edinburgh, 1977–88; St Mary's, Dalkeith and St Leonard's, Lasswade, 1988–93; Canon, St Mary's Cathedral, Edinburgh and Synod Clerk, 1990–91; Dean of Edinburgh, 1991–92. *Recreations:* hill-walking, listening to music. *Address:* 23 Craigs Way, Rumford, Falkirk FK2 0EU. *T:* (01324) 714137.
See also Rt Rev. A. B. Cameron.

CAMERON, Elizabeth; Member, Glasgow City Council, since 1992; Lord Provost and Lord-Lieutenant of Glasgow, 2003–07; *m* Duncan; one step *d*. *Educ:* Glasgow Univ. (MA Hons English Lang. and Lit.). Lectr, Further and Adult Educn. Glasgow City Council: Deputy Convener: Women's Cttee, 1993–95; Arts and Culture, 1995–98; Convener, Culture and Leisure Services, 1998–2003. Vice Chm., Glasgow City Mktg Bureau, 2007–; Chm., Culture and Sport Glasgow. Member: Scottish Arts Council, 2002–06; Bd of Trustees, Nat. Galls of Scotland, 2002–06; Board: Scottish Ensemble (Chm.); North Glasgow Coll.; Arches Th.; Glasgow Film Th.; Scottish Internat. Piano Comp.; Nat. Youth Choir Scotland; Royal Scottish Nat. Orch. Chorus Trust; Pres., Culture Commn Confedn of Cities of Atlantic Arc; Vice Chm., Les Rencontres Assoc. of European Cultural Cities. Patron, Glasgow Celtic Soc. DUniv: Glasgow, 2006; Caledonian; Strathclyde. Officier, Ordre des Arts et des Lettres (France). *Recreations:* music, choral singing, languages (French and Italian), reading, theatre. *Address:* 122 Earlbank Avenue, Glasgow G14 9DY; Glasgow City Council, City Chambers, Glasgow G2 1DU.

CAMERON, Rt Rev. (Ewen) Donald; Assistant Bishop, Diocese of Sydney, 1975–93; *b* 7 Nov. 1926; *s* of Ewen Cameron, Balranald, NSW, and Dulce M. Cameron, Sydney, NSW; *m* 1952, Joan R., *d* of T. Wilkins, Mosman, NSW; one *s* two *d*. *Educ:* Sydney C of E Grammar Sch., N Sydney; Moore Theological Coll., Sydney. CA; BD (London); ThSchol (Aust. Coll. of Theol.). Public Accountancy, 1945–57. Lectr, Moore Theological Coll., 1960–63; Rector, St Stephen's, Bellevue Hill, 1963–65; Federal Secretary, CMS of Aust., 1965–72; Archdeacon of Cumberland with Sydney, 1972–75; Bishop of North Sydney, 1983–90; Registrar, dio. of Sydney, 1990–93. Mem., ARCIC, 1983–90. *Address:* Unit 1, Gowrie Village, 10 Edward Street, Gordon, NSW 2072, Australia. *T:* (2) 94992493. *Club:* Union, University & Schools (Sydney).

CAMERON, Francis (Ernest), MA, DipEth (Oxon); FRCO(CHM), ARAM; organist and ethnomusicologist; Choirmaster and Organist, City Church of St Michael at the North Gate, Oxford, 1988–94; *b* London, 5 Dec. 1927; *er s* of Ernest and Doris Cameron; *m* 1952, Barbara Minns; three *d*. *Educ:* Mercers' Sch.; Caerphilly Boys' Secondary Sch.; Royal Acad. of Music; University Coll., Oxford. Henry Richards Prizewinner, RAM, 1946. Organist, St Peter's, Fulham, 1943; Pianist, Canadian Legion, 1944; Organist, St Luke's, Holloway, 1945; Sub-organist, St Peter's, Eaton Square, 1945; Organist, St James-the-Less, Westminster, 1946; commissioned RASC, 1948; Organ Scholar, University Coll., Oxford, 1950; Organist: St Anne's, Highgate, 1952; St Barnabas', Pimlico, 1953; St Mark's, Marylebone Road, 1957–58; Choirmaster, St Aloysius, Somers Town, 1959; Master of Music, Westminster Cathedral, 1959; Visiting Organist, Church of St Thomas of Canterbury, Rainham, Kent, 1961; Organist and Choirmaster, Church of Our Lady of the Assumption and St Gregory, Warwick Street, W1, 1962–68. Travel for UNESCO, 1952–55; Dep. Dir of Music, LCC (subsequently GLC), 1954–68; Asst-Dir of Music, Emanuel Sch., 1954; Music Master, Central Foundation Boys' Grammar Sch., 1956; Prof. of Organ and Composition, RAM, 1959–68; *locum tenens* Dir of Music, St Felix Sch., Southwold, 1963 and 1964; Asst Dir, 1968, Chm. of Musicology, 1974–79, NSW State Conservatorium of Music; Organist, Church of St Mary the Virgin, Iffley, 1980–88; Sen. Lectr, Musical Studies, Oxford Poly., 1982–86; Demonstrator: Oxford Univ. Computing Services, 1988–96; computing, Univ. of Oxford Dept for Continuing Educn, 1994–96, 2000–04; computer programming tutor, Oxford Centre for Adult Learning, 1992–96. Inaugural Conductor, Witan Operatic Soc., 1957–58; Conductor: "I Cantici", 1961–65; Francis Cameron Chorale, 1965–68; Singers of David, 1973–76; British Adjudicator, Fedn of Canadian Music Festivals, 1965; Examr Associated Bd of Royal Schools of Music, 1965–68; Dep. Chm., NSW Adv. Bd, Aust. Music Exams Bd, 1969–74. Field Officer, Deep Creek Aboriginal Monuments res. and recording prog., 1973; Mem., Lancefield Archaeol Expedn, 1975. President: "Open Score", 1946–68; Musicol Soc. of Aust., 1971–75 (jt leader, ethnomusicol expedn to New Hebrides, 1971–72); Sydney Univ. Anthropol Soc., 1974–75; Phoenix Photographic Circle, 1977–79; Conservatorium Professional Staff Assoc., 1978–79; Vice-Pres., Aust. Chapter, ISCM, 1970–77; Ed., INFO, European Seminar in Ethnomusicology, 1986–90. Beethoven Commemorative Medal, Fed. Repub. of Germany, 1970. *Publications:* editor (with John Steele) Musica Britannica vol. xiv (The Keyboard Music of John Bull, part I), 1960; Old Palace Yard, 1963; Eight dances from Benjamin Cosyn's Second Virginal Book, 1964; I Sing of a Maiden, 1966; John Bull, ausgewählte Werke, 1967; I Believe, 1969; incidental music for film The Voyage of the New Endeavour, 1970; songs and incidental music for Congreve's Love for Love, 1972; Alleluia, 1990; contributor to: Church Music; Composer; The Conductor; Liturgy; Musical Times; Australian Jl of Music Education; Studies in Music; Music in Tertiary Educn; Con Brio; Musicology IV; Aust. Nat. Hist.; Nation Review; Quanta; ICTM (UK) Bulletin; Eur. Studies in Ethnomusicol; Pagan Dawn; Pagan Times; Pentacle; Druids Voice. *Address:* 12 Norreys Avenue, Oxford OX1 4SS. *T:* (01865) 240058.

CAMERON, Sir (Hugh) Roy (Graham), Kt 1999; QPM 1994; DL; HM Chief Inspector of Constabulary, Scotland, 2002–04; *b* 14 April 1947; *s* of Angus and May Cameron; *m* 1969, Margaret Scott; two *s*. *Educ:* Bearsden Acad.; Univ. of Strathclyde (BA 1976; MPhil 1992). Cadet, Dunbartonshire Constabulary, 1964–66; Constable, 1966, Asst Chief Constable, 1990–94, Strathclyde Police; Chief Constable: Dumfries and Galloway Constabulary, 1994–96; Lothian and Borders Police, 1996–2002. DL East Lothian, 2004. *Recreations:* golf, music, cinema, reading.

CAMERON, Prof. Iain Thomas, MD; Professor of Obstetrics and Gynaecology, since 1999, and Head, School of Medicine, since 2004, University of Southampton; *b* 21 Feb. 1956; *s* of late James David Cameron and Stella (*née* Turner); *m* 1st, 1983 (marr. diss.); two *d*; 2nd, 1992, Heidi Wade; one *s* one *d*. *Educ:* Hutton Grammar Sch.; Univ. of Edinburgh (BSc Med. Sci. 1977; MB ChB 1980; MD 1988); MA Cantab 1992. MRCOG 1986, FRCOG 1999; MRACOG 1987; ILTM 2002. House Officer and Sen. House Officer, Western Infirmary, Glasgow, Royal Infirmary, Edinburgh and Simpson Meml Maternity Pavilion, Edinburgh, 1980–82; University of Edinburgh: Research Fellow, Dept of Obstetrics and Gynaecology, 1982–84; Lectr and Registrar, 1984–86; Monash University: Clinical Res. Fellow, 1986–88; Lectr, 1987–88; Sen. Registrar, Royal Women's Hosp., Melbourne, 1988–89; University of Cambridge: Lectr, 1989–92; Sen. Registrar, 1989–91; Consultant, 1991–92; Regius Prof. of Obstetrics and Gynaecology, Glasgow Univ., 1993–99; Mem., HFEA, 2001–06. Chm., Blair Bell Res. Soc., 1999–2002, Chm., Meetings Cttee, and Convenor, Postgrad. Meetings, 2000–03, Chm., Jt Wellbeing of Women Res. Adv. Cttee, RCOG, 2004–08. Specialist Advr, Menorrhagia, NICE, 2000; Member: Pharmaceuticals Panel, Health Tech. Assessment Prog., NHS Exec., 2001–04; Scientific and Ethical Rev. Gp, Special Prog. in Human Reproduction, WHO, 2003–; MRC Coll. of Experts, 2005–; Exec. Cttee, Council of Hds of Med. Schs, 2006–. Ed.-in-Chief, Reproductive Medicine Rev., 1999–2002. *Publications:* articles and other contribs on menstrual disorders, endometrium, and reproductive medicine. *Recreation:* solo piping. *Address:* Level B (801), South Academic Block, Southampton General Hospital, Tremona Road, Southampton SO16 6YD.

CAMERON, Ian Alexander; Sheriff of Grampian, Highland and Islands at Elgin, since 2001; *b* 5 Nov. 1938; *s* of late James Cameron and Isabella Cameron; *m* 1968, Dr Margaret Anne Innes; one *s*. *Educ:* Elgin Acad.; Edinburgh Univ. (MA); Aberdeen Univ. (LLB with dist.). Qualified as solicitor, 1961; Partner, Stewart & McIsaac, Solicitors, Elgin, 1962–87; Sheriff: of Lothian and Borders at Edinburgh, 1987–93; of Grampian, Highland and Is at Wick, Dornoch and Stornoway, 1993–2001. *Recreations:* travel, railway history. *Address:* Braemoray, Elgin, Moray IV30 4NJ. *T:* (01343) 542731; 19/4 Damside, Dean Village, Edinburgh EH4 3BB. *T:* (0131) 220 1548.

CAMERON, Prof. Ian Rennell, CBE 1999; DM; FRCP; Vice-Chancellor, University of Wales College of Medicine, 1994–2001; Chairman, Enfis Ltd, 2001–07; *b* 20 May 1936; *s* of James and Frances Mary Cameron; *m* 1st, 1964, Jayne Bustard (marr. diss.); one *s* one *d*; 2nd, 1980, Jennifer, *d* of Stewart and Josephine Cowin. *Educ:* Westminster Sch.; Corpus Christi Coll., Oxford (BA 1958 1st Cl. Hons Animal Physiol.; MA 1961; DM 1969; Hon. Fellow, 2000); St Thomas's Hosp. Med. Sch. (BM BCh 1961). FRCP 1976. Jun. med. appts, St Thomas' Hosp., 1961–64; Res. Asst, Dept of Physiol., UCL, 1966–68; Lectr 1967, Sen. Lectr 1969, Reader 1975, St Thomas's Hosp. Med. Sch.; Prof. of Medicine, UMDS of Guy's and St Thomas' Hosps, 1979–94 (Dean, St Thomas', 1986–89; Principal, UMDS, 1989–92, Hon. Fellow, 1997); Hon. Consultant Physician, St Thomas' Hosp., 1970–94. NIH Postdoctoral Fellowship at Cedars-Sinai Med. Center, LA, and Asst Prof., Dept of Physiol., UCLA, 1968–69. Mem., Medway HA, 1981–86; non-exec. Dir, Bro Taf HA, 1996–99; Dir, R&D, SE Thames RHA, 1993–94. Examiner, Univ. of London Final MB, 1980–94; Mem. Senate, Univ. of London, 1989–92. Member: Med. Res. Soc., 1966–; Physiol Soc., 1974–; Assoc. of Physicians of GB and Ire., 1979–; Council, RCP, 1992–95; GMC, 1994–2001 (Treas., 1997–2001); Univs UK (formerly CVCP), 1994–2001; Commn for Health Improvement, 1999–2004. Chm., UK Centre for Advancement of Inter-professional Educn, 1998–99. Mem. Council, KCL, 1993–99. Hon. FKC 1998; Hon. Fellow, Cardiff Univ., 2002; Founder FMedSci 1998. Hon. LLD

Wales, 2001; Hon. DSc Glamorgan, 2001; Hon. PhD: Kobe Gakuin Univ., Tokyo Women's Medical Univ., 2001. *Publications:* Respiratory Disorders (with N. T. Bateman), 1983; papers in various med. and physiol jls. *Recreation:* collecting (and selling) paintings. *Club:* Athenæum.

CAMERON, Ivor Gill S.; *see* Smith-Cameron.

CAMERON, James; *see* Cameron, J. J. O'G.

CAMERON, John Alastair; *see* Abernethy, Rt Hon. Lord.

CAMERON, John Bell, CBE 1982; Chairman, World Meats Group, International Federation of Agricultural Producers, since 1984; Director, South West Trains and Island Line, 1996–2007; *b* 14 June 1939; *s* of John and Margaret Cameron; *m* 1964, Margaret (*née* Clapperton). *Educ:* Dollar Academy. AIAgrE; FRAgS. Studied agriculture in various countries, Scandinavia, S America and Europe, 1956–61; farmed in Scotland, 1961–64. National Farmers' Union of Scotland: Mem. National Council, 1964; Vice-Pres., 1976; Pres., 1979–84 (first long-term Pres.). Mem., Agricultural Praesidium of EEC, 1979–89; Chairman: EEC Adv. Cttee for Sheep Meat, 1982–89; UK Sheep Consultative Cttee, 1986–87; Scottish Beef Council, 1997–2000; Standards Cttee, Quality Meat Scotland, 2005–. Pres., British Hereford Cattle Soc., 2003–05. Chm., BR (Scotland) and Scottish Mem., BRB, 1988–93. Chm. Governors, Dollar Acad., 1984–. Hon. DTech Napier, 1998. Winner: George Headley Award to the UK Sheep Industry, 1986; Sir William Young Award to the Scottish Livestock Industry, 1986. *Recreations:* flying, shooting, travelling. *Address:* Balbuthie Farm, By Leven, Fife, Scotland KY9 1EX. *T:* (01333) 730210.

CAMERON, John Charles Finlay; Member, London Transport Executive, 1975–84; *b* 8 Feb. 1928; *s* of Robert John and Nancy Angela Cameron; *m* 1st, Ruth Thompson, Sydney, Australia; two *s* two *d*; 2nd, Nancy Foy, author, Redlands, Calif. *Educ:* privately; University Coll., Southampton. CEng, MICE, FCILT, CCMI. Royal Marines, 1946–48. British Railways, Southern Region, Civil Engineering, 1948; BR Transport Commn, 1957; BR Rlys Workshops, 1962; Rank Organisation, 1968–75. Dir-Gen. and Sec., CIT, 1984–88 (Hon. Vice-Pres., 1988–91; Chm., Scot. Sect., 1995–96); Dir, BURA, 1989–93; Chm., Highland Perthshire Develt Co., 1990–94. Member: Management Cttee, Abbotstone, Ag. Prop. Unit Trust, 1982–91; Westminster Br., IMgt (Chm., 1985–88; Vice-Pres., 1988–91). Gov., Pitlochry Fest. Theatre, 1991–98. Major, Engr and Transport Staff Corps, RE (TA), 1985–98. Liveryman, Carmen's Co., 1984–2001. *Recreation:* book binding and restoration. *Address:* Clunemore Farm, Killiecrankie, Pitlochry, Perthshire PH16 5LS. *T:* (01796) 473470. *Club:* Oriental.

CAMERON, Prof. John Robinson; Regius Professor of Logic, University of Aberdeen, 1979–2001; *b* 24 June 1936; *s* of Rev. George Gordon Cameron and Mary Levering (*née* Robinson); *m* 1st, 1959, Mary Elizabeth Ranson (*d* 1984); one *s* two *d*; 2nd, 1987, Barbara Elizabeth Blair. *Educ:* Dundee High Sch.; Univ. of St Andrews (MA 1st Cl. Hons Maths, BPhil Philosophy); Univ. of Calif, Berkeley; Cornell Univ. Harkness Fellow, Berkeley and Cornell, USA, 1959–61; University of Dundee (formerly Queen's College): Asst in Phil., 1962–63; Lectr in Phil., 1963–73; Sen. Lectr in Phil., 1973–78. FRSA 2002. *Publications:* articles in phil jls. *Recreation:* bricolage. *Address:* 70 Cornhill Road, Aberdeen AB25 2EH. *T:* (01224) 486700.

CAMERON, John Taylor; *see* Coulsfield, Rt Hon. Lord.

CAMERON, (Jonathan) James (O'Grady); international lawyer, policy adviser and entrepreneur; Founder, Executive Director and Vice-Chairman, Climate Change Capital, specialist investment banking group, since 2003; *b* 28 Oct. 1961; *s* of John O'Grady Cameron and late Valerie Cameron (*née* Bromley); *m* 1988, Juliet Mary, *d* of Rt Hon. Sir John Douglas May, PC; three *d*. *Educ:* Windlesham House Sch., Sussex; Stowe Sch. Bucks; Univ. of Western Australia; University Coll. London (LLB); Queens' Coll., Cambridge (LLM 1st Cl.). Called to the Bar, Inner Temple, 1987; Res. Associate, Centre for Internat. Law, Cambridge, 1986–87; Dir of Studies in Law, Clare Hall, Cambridge, 1986–89; Lecturer in Law: KCL, 1989–92; SOAS, 1992–98; Prof., Coll. of Europe, Bruges, 1994–2002; Counsel, Baker & McKenzie, 1997–2003. Founder Director: Centre for Internat. Envmtl Law, 1989–99; Foundn for Internat. Envmtl Law and Develt (negotiated UN framework for Convention on Climate Change, 1992 and Kyoto Protocol, 1997 on behalf of Alliance of Small Island States). Visiting Professor: Australian Centre for Envmtl Law, Univ. of Sydney, 1996; Yale Center for Envmtl Law & Policy, 2005–. Chm., Cameron May Internat. Law Publisher, 1992–. Chm., Carbon Disclosure Project, 2002–; Treas., Renewable Energy and Energy Efficiency Partnership, 2004–. Trustee, Climate Gp, 2006–; Chm., Global Cool Foundn, 2006–. Mem., GE Ecoimagination Adv. Bd, 2006–. FRSA. *Publications:* (with M. Sheridan) EC Legal Systems: an introductory guide, 1992; (with M. Sheridan) EFTA Legal Systems, 1993; (with D. Gerardin) Trade and Environment: the search for balance, 1994; (with T. O'Riordan) Interpreting the Precautionary Principle, 1994; Improving Compliance with International Environmental Law, 1995; (with K. Campbell) Dispute Resolution in the WTO, 1998; (jtly) Trade and Environment: law and policy introduction, cases and materials, 2000; (jtly) Re-Interpreting the Precautionary Principle, 2001; articles in legal jls. *Recreations:* sport, music, journeys, clothes, conversation, family. *Clubs:* Savile, George; Wentworth.

CAMERON, Lewis; Sheriff of South Strathclyde, Dumfries and Galloway at Hamilton, 1994–2002; part-time Sheriff, 2002–05; *b* 12 Aug. 1935; *s* of James Aloysius Cameron and Marie Isobel McKenzie; *m* 1962, Sheila Colette Gallacher; two *s* two *d*. *Educ:* Blairs Coll., Aberdeen; St Sulpice, Paris; Glasgow Univ. (MA, LLB). Admitted Solicitor, 1962. RAF (Nat. Service), 1954–56. Chm., Social Security Appeal Tribunals, 1983–88; Mem., Legal Aid Central Cttee, 1970–80; Legal Aid Sec., Airdrie, 1978–87; Dean, Airdrie Soc. of Solicitors, 1984–85; Tutor, Strathclyde Univ., 1981–88; Sheriff of S Strathclyde, Dumfries and Galloway at Dumfries, 1988–94. Treas., Monklands Victim Support Scheme, 1983–88; Chairman: Dumfries and Galloway Family Conciliation Service, 1988–92; Dumfries and Galloway Scottish Assoc. for Study of Delinquency, 1989–92. Mem., Scotland Cttee, Nat. Children's Homes, 1991–94; Chm., Phew (Parental Help Evenings/Weekends, Mentally Handicapped), 1994–2000. Trustee, Oscar Marzaroli Trust, 1990–93. *Publications:* occasional articles and journalism. *Recreations:* cinema, theatre, tennis, travel. *Clubs:* Glasgow Art; Ross Priory (Gartocharn, Loch Lomond).

CAMERON, Sir Roy; *see* Cameron, Sir H. R. G.

CAMERON, Sheila Morag Clark, (Mrs G. C. Ryan), CBE 2004; QC 1983; Dean, Arches Court of Canterbury and Auditor, Chancery Court of York, since 2001; *b* 22 March 1934; *d* of Sir James Clark Cameron, CBE, TD, and Lady (Irene M.) Cameron; *m* 1960, Gerard Charles Ryan, *qv*; two *s*. *Educ:* Commonweal Lodge Sch., Purley; St Hugh's Coll., Oxford (MA). Called to the Bar, Middle Temple, 1957, Harmsworth Law Scholar, 1958, Bencher, 1988; Part-time Lectr in Law, Southampton Univ., 1960–64; part-time Tutor, Council of Legal Educn, 1966–71; a Recorder, 1985–99. Mem., Bar Council,

1967–70. Comr, Boundary Commn for England, 1989–96 (Asst Comr, 1981–89). Official Principal, Archdeaconry of Hampstead, 1968–86; Chancellor: Dio. of Chelmsford, 1969–2001; Dio. of London, 1992–2001; Vicar-Gen., Province of Canterbury, 1983–2005. Chairman: Archbishops' Group on the Episcopate, 1986–90; Ecclesiastical Judges Assoc., 1997–2004; Member: Legal Adv. Commn, Gen. Synod of C of E, 1975–; Gen. Synod Marriage Commn, 1975–78; Council on Tribunals, 1986–90. Mem. Council, Wycombe Abbey Sch., 1972–86. DCL Lambeth, 2002; LLM (Canon Law), Cardiff, 2008. *Address:* Bayleaves, Bepton, Midhurst, W Sussex GU29 9RB.

CAMERON, Stuart Gordon, MC 1943; Chairman and Chief Executive, Gallaher Ltd, 1980–89; *b* 8 Jan. 1924; *s* of late James Cameron and Dora Sylvia (*née* Godsell); *m* 1946, Joyce Alice, *d* of Roland Ashley Wood; three *s* one *d*. *Educ:* Chigwell School, Essex. Served War, 2nd Gurkha Rifles, 1942–46 (MC). Managing Dir, 1976–78, Dep. Chm., 1978–80, Gallaher Ltd. Director: American Brands Inc., 1980–89; Royal Mint, 1989–94; Saatchi & Saatchi Ltd, 1990–94. *Club:* Royal Thames Yacht.

CAMERON, Susan Ruth; Headmistress, North Foreland Lodge, 1996–2002; *b* Edinburgh; *e d* of James Norval Cameron and Ruth Scott Doig (*née* Nicolson). *Educ:* Wycombe Abbey Sch.; Westfield Coll., London (Exhibnr; BA Hons; Pres., Students' Union). VSO, Oguta, Eastern Nigeria; Housemistress, Godstowe Sch., High Wycombe; teacher, Housemistress, then Dep. Head, Woodford House, Hawkes Bay, NZ; Housemistress: Queenswood Sch., 1977–78; Sherborne Sch. for Girls, 1978–84; Headmistress: Cobham Hall, 1985–89; Downe House, 1989–96. Governor: Queen Margaret's Sch., York, 1986–95; Farlington Sch., Horsham, 1987–95; Repton Sch., 1995–2002; Gordonstoun Schs, 2000–02; Maynard Sch., Exeter, 2003–08; Bearwood Coll., 2004–; Marchant-Holliday Sch., 2005–. Vice-Pres., Seniors' Assoc., Wycombe Abbey Sch., 2004– (Pres., 1996–2004); Sec., Sherborne Abbey Fest. Cttee, 2004–. *Recreations:* music, sport (mostly non-active now), walking the dogs, language, creative thinking. *Address:* 5 Minterne House, Minterne Magna, Dorchester, Dorset DT2 7AX. *T:* (01300) 341616.

CAMERON, Thomas Anthony, (Tony), CB 2007; Chief Executive, Scottish Prison Service, 1999–2007; *b* 3 Feb. 1947; *o s* of late Thomas Alexander and Olive Cameron; *m* 1970, Elizabeth Christine Sutherland; two *s*. *Educ:* Stranraer High Sch. Dept of Agric. and Fisheries for Scotland, Scottish Office, 1966–72; Private Secretary: to Dep. Under Sec. of State, 1972; to Perm. Under Sec. of State, 1973–74; Department of Agriculture and Fisheries for Scotland: HEO(D), 1974–77; Principal, 1977–82; Asst Sec., 1982–87; Scottish Office Finance Div., 1987–92; Under Sec., 1992; Head of Food and Agric., Scottish Office, 1992–99. Mem., Duke of Edinburgh's Sixth Commonwealth Study Conf., Australia, 1986. Pres., Internat. Corrections and Prisons Assoc., 2003–. *Recreations:* reading, mountaineering, cycling. *Address:* 18 St Ninians Terrace, Edinburgh EH10 5NL.

CAMERON-RAMSAY-FAIRFAX-LUCY; *see* Fairfax-Lucy.

CAMERON WATT, Prof. Donald, FBA 1990; Stevenson Professor of International History in the University of London, 1981–93, now Professor Emeritus; *b* 17 May 1928; *s* of late Robert Cameron Watt and Barbara, *d* of late Rt Rev. E. J. Bidwell, former Bishop of Ontario; *m* 1st, 1951, Marianne Ruth Grau (*d* 1962); one *s*; 2nd, 1962, Felicia Cobb Stanley (*d* 1997); one step *d*. *Educ:* Rugby Sch.; Oriel Coll., Oxford (BA 1951; MA 1954; DLitt 1991; Hon. Fellow, 1998). FRHistS. Asst Editor, Documents on German Foreign Policy, 1918–1945, Foreign Office, 1951–54; Asst Lectr, Lectr, Sen. Lectr in Internat. History, LSE, 1954–66; Reader in Internat. History in Univ. of London, 1966; Titular Prof. of Internat. History, 1972–81. Editor, Survey of Internat. Affairs, Royal Inst. of Internat. Affairs, 1962–71; Rockefeller Research Fellow in Social Sciences, Inst. of Advanced Internat. Studies, Washington, 1960–61; Official Historian, Cabinet Office Historical Section, 1978–. Sec., 1967, Chm., 1970–77, Assoc. of Contemporary Historians; Mem. Bd, Inst. of Contemporary British History, 1987–2001; Chm., Greenwich Forum, 1974–84; Sec.-Treasurer, Internat. Commn for the Hist. of Internat. Relations, 1982–95 (Hon. Vice-Pres., 1995–). Member Editorial Board: Political Quarterly, 1969–2000; Marine Policy, 1978–94; Internat. History Rev., 1984–94; Intelligence and National Security, 1986–; Review of Internat. Studies, 1989–95; Gen. Ed. British Documents on Foreign Affairs, 1985–97; Ed., Amer. Studies in Europe newsletter, 1962–65. FRSA 1990. Foreign Mem., Polish Acad. of Arts and Scis, Krakow, 1993. *Publications:* (ed jtly) Oxford Poetry, 1950; Britain and the Suez Canal, 1956; (ed) Documents on the Suez Crisis, 1957; Britain looks to Germany, 1965; Personalities and Policies, 1965; (ed) Survey of International Affairs 1961, 1966; (ed) Documents on International Affairs 1961, 1966; (ed, with K. Bourne) Studies in International History, 1967; A History of the World in the Twentieth Century, Pt I, 1967; (ed) Contemporary History in Europe, 1969; (ed) Hitler's Mein Kampf, 1969, 2nd edn 1992; (ed) Survey of International Affairs 1962, 1969; (ed, with James Mayall): Current British Foreign Policy 1970, 1971; Current British Foreign Policy 1971, 1972; Current British Foreign Policy 1972, 1973; Too Serious a Business, 1975, 2nd edn 1993; (ed) Survey of International Affairs 1963, 1977; Succeeding John Bull: America in Britain's place 1900–1975, 1984; How War Came, 1989; (ed with Guido Di Tella) Argentina between the Great Powers, 1990. *Recreations:* exploring London, cats. *Address:* c/o London School of Economics and Political Science, Houghton Street, WC2A 2AE.

CAMILLERI, Victor; Ambassador and Permanent Representative for Malta to the United Nations, New York, since 2003; *b* 8 Oct. 1942; *s* of John Camilleri and Esther (*née* Casingena); *m* 1967, Elizabeth Bernadette Heaney; two *s*. *Educ:* Lyceum, Malta; Birmingham Univ. (BA Hons English). Joined Min. of Foreign Affairs, Malta, 1968: 2nd Sec., 1968–74; 1st Sec., 1974–86; Counsellor, 1986–90; 1st Counsellor, 1990; postings in Rome, Brussels, NY and London; Ambassador: to UNIDO and UNESCO, 1981–85; to CSCE, 1985–86; Actg Sec., Min. of Foreign Affairs, 1986–87; Dep. High Comr, 1987–90, High Comr, 1991 and 1996, London; Ambassador to UN, 1991–93; Ambassador and Perm. Rep. to Belgium, 1997–2003. *Recreations:* reading, swimming. *Address:* Maltese Permanent Mission to UN, 249 East 35th Street, New York, NY 10016, USA.

CAMLEY, Mark; Chief Executive, Royal Parks, since 2005; *b* 11 June 1964; *s* of Martin and Frances Camley; *m* 2002, Camilla Rosier. *Educ:* Lornshill Acad., Alloa; Univ. of Edinburgh (MA). Exec. Officer, Cabinet Office, 1986–88; Asst Statistician, CSO, 1988–90; Lord Chancellor's Department: Statistician, 1990–97; Hd, Estates Policy, 1997–98; Private Sec. to Perm. Sec., 1998–99; Dir, Crown Court, 1999–2001; Customer Service Dir, 2001–03; Dir, Supreme Court, 2003–05. Chm. of Govs, 2005–07, Dep. Chm., 2007–, Norwood Sch.; Chm. of Govs, Royal Docks Sch., 2007–. Hon. Crown Estate Paving Comr, 2005–. FRSA. *Publications:* contributor: Economic Trends, 1986; Social Trends and Regional Trends, 1988; Judicial Statistics, annually 1990–97; contribs to New Law Jl. *Recreations:* football, whites, reds, and Scottish single malts. *Address:* The Old Police House, Hyde Park, W2 2UH. *T:* (020) 7298 2123, *Fax:* (020) 7298 2005; *e-mail:* mcamley@royalparks.gsi.gov.uk.

CAMM, Prof. A(lan) John, MD; FRCP, FRCPE, FMedSci; FACC, FESC; QHP; St George's, University of London (formerly St George's Hospital Medical School): Prudential Professor of Clinical Cardiology (British Heart Foundation), since 1986; Chairman: Department of Medicine, 1991–94; Department of Cardiological Sciences, 1986–2002; Division of Cardiac and Vascular Sciences, since 2002; *b* 11 Jan. 1947; *s* of John Donald and Joan Camm; *m* 1987, Joy-Maria Frappell; one *s* one *d*. *Educ:* Guy's Hosp. Med. Sch., London Univ. (BSc 1968; MB BS 1971; MD 1981). LRCP, MRCS 1971; FACC 1981; FRCP 1984; FESC 1988; FRCPE 2003. Guy's Hospital: House Surgeon, 1971; House Physician, 1971–72; Jun. Registrar, 1972; Jun. Lectr in Medicine, 1972–73; Registrar in Cardiology, 1973–74; Clin. Fellow in Cardiology, Univ. of Vermont, USA, 1974–75; St Bartholomew's Hospital: British Heart Foundn Res. Registrar, 1975–76, Sen. Registrar 1977–79; Wellcome Sen. Lectr and Hon. Consultant Cardiologist, 1979–83; Sir Ronald Bodley Scott Prof. of Cardiovascular Medicine, 1983–86. Convener of Medicine, London Univ., 1994–. Ed. in Chief, Europace Jl, 2007. Dir, Eur. Soc. of Cardiol. Res. Foundn, 2008. Member, Council: RCP, 1994–97; British Cardiac Soc., 1997–98 (Pres. elect, 1998–2001, Pres., 2001–03); Pres., Arrhythmia Alliance, 2005. QHP 1992–. FCGC 1997; FAHA 2000; FMedSci 2005; FHRS 2006. Trustee: N American Soc. of Pacing and Electrophysiology, 1998–2001 (Dist. Teacher, 2001); Amer. Coll. of Cardiology, 2007–. Hon. Internat. Mem., Japanese Circulation Soc., 2006. Freeman, City of London, 1984. Gold Medal, European Soc. of Cardiology, 2006; Berzelius Medal, Swedish Soc. of Cardiology, 2006; Mackenzie Medal, British Cardiovascular Soc., 2008. CStJ 1990. *Publications:* First Aid, Step by Step, 1978; Pacing for Tachycardia Control, 1983; Heart Disease in the Elderly, 1984, 2nd edn 1994; Clinical Electrophysiology of the Heart, 1987; Heart Disease in Old Age, 1988, 2nd edn 1990; Clinical Aspects of Cardiac Arrhythmias, 1988; Diseases of the Heart, 1989, 2nd edn 1996; Geriatric Cardiology, 1994; Heart Rate Variability, 1998; Evidence Based Cardiology, 1998, 2nd edn 2003; Atrial Fibrillation, 2000, Hungarian edn 2002; Drug-induced Long QT Syndrome, 2002; Cardiovascular Risk Associated with Schizophrenia and its Treatment, 2003; Acquired Long QT Syndrome, 2004; Clinical Electrophysiology of the Heart, 2004; Dynamic Electrocardiography, 2004; European Society of Cardiology Textbook, 2005; approx. 1,000 papers in major jls. *Recreations:* collector of prints, watercolours and other antiques, model railway enthusiast. *Address:* St George's Hospital Medical School, Cranmer Terrace, Tooting, SW17 0RE. *Clubs:* Athenæum, Oriental, Royal Society of Medicine.

CAMM, Gillian Elizabeth; NHS Regional Appointments Commissioner for South West, 2001–03; *b* 31 Dec. 1959; *d* of Sir Robert Shields, *qv*; *m* 1987, Ian Sutcliffe Camm; one *s* one *d*. *Educ:* Birkenhead High Sch. for Girls; Univ. of Liverpool (BSc Hons Psychol.). Personnel Officer, Perkins Diesel Engines, 1981–84; Personnel Manager, Internat. Computers Ltd, 1984–87; Partner, Hay Mgt Consultants, 1987–94; Gen. Manager, Human Resources, 1994–97, Business Transformation Dir, 1997–2001, Clerical Medical Investments Gp. Non-exec. Dir, Supervisory Bd, Immigration and Nationality Directorate, Home Office, 2002–. Non-exec. Dir, Rok plc, 2002–. Mem., GMC, 2003–. Trustee: Gtr Bristol Foundn, 1998–; Council, St Monica Trust. *Recreations:* ski-ing, reading. *Address:* Oakleaze, Breadstone, Berkeley, Glos GL13 9HG. *T:* (01453) 810985, *Fax:* (01453) 511925; *e-mail:* gillian-camm@freeuk.com.

CAMMELL, John Ernest; Head, Manufacturing and Technology (formerly Mechanical Engineering and Manufacturing Technology) Division, Department of Trade and Industry, 1986–92; *b* 14 Nov. 1932; *s* of Ernest Alfred Cammell and Gladys Clara (*née* Burroughes); *m* 1976, Janis Linda Moody. *Educ:* Highfield Coll., Leigh-on-Sea, Essex. Mil. Service, Royal Signals. Joined Victualling Dept, Admiralty, 1952; DSIR, 1963; Min. of Technology, 1964; DTI, 1967; Dept of Industry, 1973; Dir, National Maritime Inst., 1981–84. British Standards Institution: a Dir, 1992–2000; Consultant, 2000–02. Part-time Lectr, Warwick Manufg Gp, Warwick Univ., 1993–2005. FIET (Companion, IProdE, 1988); FRSA. *Recreations:* amateur theatre, golf, cricket, eating. *Address:* 41 Cunnington Street, Chiswick, W4 5ER. *T:* (020) 8995 6937.

CAMOYS, 7th Baron *cr* 1264 (called out of abeyance, 1839); **Ralph Thomas Campion George Sherman Stonor,** GCVO 1998; PC 1997; DL; Lord Chamberlain of HM Household and Chancellor of Royal Victorian Order, 1998–2000; a Permanent Lord in Waiting to the Queen, since 2000; *b* 16 April 1940; *s* of 6th Baron Camoys and Mary Jeanne (*d* 1987), *d* of late Captain Herbert Marmaduke Joseph Stourton, OBE; *S* father, 1976; *m* 1966, Elisabeth Mary Hyde, *d* of Sir William Stephen Hyde Parker, 11th Bt; one *s* three *d*. *Educ:* Eton Coll.; Balliol Coll., Oxford (MA). Chm., Jacksons of Piccadilly, 1968–85; Gen. Manager and Director, National Provincial and Rothschild (London) Ltd, 1968; Man. Director, Rothschild Intercontinental Bank Ltd, 1969; Chief Exec. Officer and Man. Dir, 1975–77, Chm., 1977–78, Amex Bank Ltd; Man. Dir, 1978–84, Exec. Vice-Chm., 1984–86, Barclays Merchant Bank; Chief Exec., 1986–88, Dep. Chm., 1987–98, Barclays de Zoete Wedd (BZW); Dep. Chm., Sotheby's, 1993–97. Director: Barclays Bank Internat. Ltd, 1980–84; Barclays Bank PLC, 1984–94; Mercantile Credit Co. Ltd, 1980–84; National Provident Instn, 1982–93; Administrative Staff Coll., 1989–2000; 3i Group, 1991–2002; Perpetual, 1994–2000. A Lord in Waiting, 1992–97. Member: House of Lords EEC Select Cttee, 1979–81; Historic Bldgs and Monuments Commn for England, 1985–87; Royal Commn on Historical MSS, 1987–94. Pres., Mail Users' Assoc., 1977–84. Consultor, Extraordinary Section of Administration of Patrimony of Holy See, 1991–2006. Mem. Court of Assistants, Fishmongers' Co., 1980– (Prime Warden, 1992–93). DL Oxfordshire, 1993. Hon. DLitt Sheffield, 2001. Order of Gorkha Dakshina Bahu, 1st class (Nepal), 1981. GCSG 2006. *Recreations:* the arts, shooting. *Heir: s* Hon. (Ralph) William (Robert Thomas) Stonor [*b* 10 Sept. 1974; *m* 2004, Lady Ailsa Mackay, *d* of Earl of Inchcape, *qv*; one *s*]. *Address:* Stonor Park, Henley-on-Thames, Oxon RG9 6HF. *Clubs:* Boodle's; Leander (Henley-on-Thames).

See also Earl of Stair.

CAMP, Anthony John, MBE 1999; Director, Society of Genealogists, 1979–97; *b* 27 Nov. 1937; *s* of late Henry Victor Camp and Alice Emma Camp (*née* Doidge); *m* 1976, Deborah Mary (marr. diss. 1978), *d* of D. J. Jeavons; one *s*. *Educ:* Alleyne's Sch., Stevenage; University College London (BA Hons). Society of Genealogists: Res. Assistant, 1957; Librarian, 1959; Dir of Res., 1962; Hon. Fellow, 1982. Member Council: Assoc. of Genealogists and Record Agents, 1968–75 (Chm., 1973–75; Vice-Pres., 1980–); British Record Soc., 1967–71, 1983–2005; British Records Assoc. (Record Preservation Sect.), 1980–83, 1985–88; English Genealogical Congress, 1975–90 (Pres., 1991–92); Friends of Public Record Office, 1988–94; Marc Fitch Fund, 1991–2003; Fedn of Family History Socs, 1992–98 (Pres., 1998–2000); Pres., Herts Family and Population Hist. Soc., 1982–. Lecturer: yearly Nat. Geneal. Soc. Confs, USA, 1981–; Australasian Congress, Canberra, 1986; Sesquicentennial Conf., Auckland, 1990; First Irish Genealogical Congress, 1991. Fellow, Utah Geneal. Assoc., 1989. Freeman, City of London, 1984. Award of Merit, Nat. Geneal. Soc., USA, 1984. *Publications:* (with P. Spufford) Genealogists Handbook, 1961; Wills and their Whereabouts, 1963; Tracing Your Ancestors, 1964; Index to Wills proved in the Prerogative Court of Canterbury 1750–1800, 6 vols, 1976–92; Everyone has Roots, 1978; (contrib.) My Ancestor series, 1987–; (contrib.) The Records of the Nation, 1990; Royal Mistresses and Bastards: fact and fiction 1714–1936, 2007; articles to Family Tree and other jls. *Recreation:* genealogy. *Address:* 19 Tudor Rose Court, 35 Fann Street, EC2Y 8DY. *T:* (020) 7374 6836.

CAMP, Jeffery Bruce, RA 1984 (ARA 1974); artist; Lecturer, Slade School of Fine Art, 1963–88; *b* 1923. *Educ:* Edinburgh Coll. of Art. DA (Edin.). One-man exhibitions include: Galerie de Seine, 1958; Beaux Arts Gallery, 1959, 1961, 1963; New Art Centre, 1968; S London Art Gall., 1973 (retrospective); Serpentine Gall., 1978; Bradford City Art Gallery, 1979; Browse & Darby, 1984, 1993, 1997, 2001; Aldeburgh Fest., 1986; Nigel Greenwood Gall., 1986, 1990, 1993; Royal Acad., 1988 (retrospective); Flowers East, 1999; other exhibitions include: Hayward Annual, 1974, 1982, 1985; Serpentine Gall., 1974, 1987; Narrative Painting, ICA and Arts Council tour, 1979; British Council touring exhibns to China and Edinburgh, 1982, to India, 1985, to Kuala Lumpur, 1988; Chantrey Bicentenary, Tate Gall., 1981; The Hardwon Image, Tate Gall., 1984; group exhibn, Twining Gall., NY, 1985; Peter Moores exhibn, Liverpool, 1986; Athena Art Awards, 1987; represented in public collections including Arts Council, British Council, Tate Gall. and Royal Acad. *Publications:* Draw, 1981; Paint, 1996. *Address:* 27 Stirling Road, SW9 9EF; c/o Art Space Gallery, Michael Richardson Contemporary Art, 84 St Peter's Street, N1 8JS.

CAMPBELL, family name of **Duke of Argyll**, of **Earl Cawdor**, and of Barons **Campbell of Alloway**, **Colgrain** and **Stratheden**.

CAMPBELL OF ALLOWAY, Baron *cr* 1981 (Life Peer), of Ayr in the District of Kyle and Carrick; **Alan Robertson Campbell,** ERD 1996; QC 1965; a Recorder of the Crown Court, 1976–89; *b* 24 May 1917; *s* of late J. K. Campbell; *m* 1957, Vivien, *y d* of late Comdr A. H. de Kantzow, DSO, RN. *Educ:* Aldenham; Ecole des Sciences Politiques, Paris; Trinity Hall, Cambridge. Called to Bar, Inner Temple, 1939, Bencher, 1972; Western Circuit. Commissioned RA (Suppl. Res.), 1939; served France and Belgium, 1939–40; POW, 1940–45. Consultant to sub-cttee of Legal Cttee of Council of Europe on Industrial Espionage, 1965–74; Chm., Legal Res. Cttee, Soc. of Conservative Lawyers, 1968–80. Member: H of L Cttee for Privileges, 1982–2000; H of L Select Cttee on Murder and Life Imprisonment, 1988–89; Ecclesiastical Cttee, 2000–05; Jt Cttee on Human Rights, 2001–07; Jt Cttee on Statutory Instruments, 2008–. Member: Law Adv. Cttee, British Council, 1974–82; Management Cttee, UK Assoc. for European Law, 1975–90. Vice Pres., Assoc. de Juristes Franco-Britanniques, 1989–90. Pres., Colditz Assoc., 1998–2004. Patron, Inns of Court Sch. of Law Conservatives, 1996–2000. *Publications:* (with Lord Wilberforce) Restrictive Trade Practices and Monopolies, 1956, 2nd edn, 1966, Supplements 1 and 2, 1973; Restrictive Trading Agreements in the Common Market, 1964, Supplement, 1965; Common Market Law, vols 1 and 2, 1969, vol. 3, 1973 and Supplement, 1975; Industrial Relations Act, 1971; EC Competition Law, 1980; Trade Unions and the Individual, 1980. *Address:* House of Lords, SW1A 0PW. *Clubs:* Carlton (Mem., Political Cttee, 1967–79), Pratt's, Beefsteak.

CAMPBELL OF SURBITON, Baroness *cr* 2007 (Life Peer), of Surbiton in the London Borough of Kingston upon Thames; **Jane Susan Campbell,** DBE 2006 (MBE 2000); Member, Commission for Equality and Human Rights, since 2006; Chairman, Social Care Institute for Excellence, 2001–05; *b* 19 April 1959; *d* of Ron Campbell and Jessie Campbell; *m* Roger Symes. *Educ:* Hatfield Poly. (BA Hons Humanities (Hist. Major) 1979); Sussex Univ. (MA Political Hist. 1982). Admin Officer to REMAP, RADAR, 1983–84; Equal Opportunities Liaison Officer, GLC, 1984–86; Disability Training Develt Officer, London Boroughs Jt Disability Cttee, 1986–87; Prin. Disability Advr, Hounslow Council, 1987–88; Dir of Training, London Boroughs Disability Resource Team, 1988–94; freelance consultant, 1994–96; Co Dir, Nat. Centre for Independent Living, 1996–2001. Comr, Disability Rights Commn, 2000–07. Chm., British Council of Disabled People, 1991–95; Comr, Future of Voluntary Sector Commn, Joseph Rowntree Foundn and NCVO, 1994–96; Parly Rep. of Rights Now, 1995–; Vice Chm., Kingston Assoc. of Disabled People Exec., 1985–; Voluntary Sector Rep., Kingston LA Social Services Cttee, 1990–96; Trustee, Disability Awareness in Action, 1991–; Gov., NISW, 1995–. Hon. LLD Bristol, 2002; DUniv Sheffield Hallam, 2002. *Publications:* Good Guide to Disability Training, 1990; (with Mike Oliver) Disability Politics, 1996; (jtly) Direct Routes to Independence, 1999. *Recreations:* gardening, theatre, travel. *Address:* 116A Princes Avenue, Surbiton, Surrey KT6 7JW. *T:* (020) 8391 4160, *Fax:* (020) 8397 0678.

CAMPBELL, Aileen Elizabeth; Member (SNP) Scotland South, Scottish Parliament, since 2007; *b* 18 May 1980; *d* of Peter Campbell and Ann Campbell (*née* Webster). *Educ:* Collace Primary Sch.; Perth Acad.; Univ. of Glasgow (MA Hons Econ. and Soc. Hist. with Pols). Editor, Keystone (construction mag.), 2004–05; Editl Asst, Scottish Standard, 2005; Parly Asst to Nicola Sturgeon, MSP, 2005–06; Parly Researcher to Shona Robison, MSP, and Stewart Hosie, MP, 2006–07. *Recreations:* music, cinema, reading, football (St Johnstone FC). *Address:* Scottish Parliament, Holyrood, Edinburgh EH99 1SP. *T:* (0131) 348 6707, *Fax:* (0131) 348 6709; *e-mail:* aileen.campbell.msp@scottish.parliament.uk.

CAMPBELL, Alan; MP (Lab) Tynemouth, since 1997; Parliamentary Under-Secretary of State, Home Office, since 2008; *b* 8 July 1957; *s* of Albert Campbell and Marian Campbell (*née* Hewitt); *m* 1991, Jayne Lamont; one *s* one *d*. *Educ:* Univ. of Lancaster (BA Hons); Univ. of Leeds (PGCE); Newcastle Poly. (MA). Teacher: Whitley Bay High Sch., 1980–89; Hirst High Sch., Ashington, 1989–97. An Asst Govt Whip, 2005–06; a Lord Comr of HM Treasury (Govt Whip), 2006–08. *Address:* House of Commons, SW1A 0AA; (office) 99 Howard Street, North Shields NE30 1NA.

CAMPBELL, Alan Dermont; Managing Partner, Dundas & Wilson CS LLP, since 2006; *b* 17 Sept. 1960; *s* of late Dermont Campbell and of Doreen Catherine Campbell (*née* McCreath, now Morton); *m* 1986, Jane Porteous; two *d*. *Educ:* Fettes Coll.; Edinburgh Univ. (LLB Hons; DipLP). With Dundas & Wilson, Solicitors, 1984–, Partner, 1992–. *Recreations:* golf, ski-ing, walking, cooking. *Address:* Dundas & Wilson CS LLP, Saltire Court, 20 Castle Terrace, Edinburgh EH1 2EN. *Clubs:* Golf House (Elie); Gullane Golf.

CAMPBELL, Alan Grant, CBE 2002; Chief Executive, Aberdeenshire Council, since 1995; *b* 4 Dec. 1946; *s* of late Archie and Catherine Campbell; *m* 1974, Susan Marion Black; one *s* two *d*. *Educ:* Aberdeen GS; Aberdeen Univ. (LLB 1968). Admitted Solicitor, Scotland, 1970; legal appts, Aberdeen CC, 1968–75; Grampian Regional Council: Asst Dir, 1975–79, Depute Dir, 1979–84, Dir, 1984–91, of Law and Admin; Chief Exec., 1991–95. Chm., SOLACE (Scotland), 1997–99. Mem., Cttee of Inquiry into professional conditions of service for teachers, 2000. Hon. LLD Aberdeen, 2005. *Recreations:* competitive cycling and following the Tour de France, gardening, photography, the enjoyment of wine. *Address:* Woodhill House, Westburn Road, Aberdeen AB16 5GB. *T:* (01224) 665400.

CAMPBELL, Alastair John; Chairman of Fundraising, Leukaemia Research Fund, since 2004; freelance speaker and writer; *b* 25 May 1957; *s* of late Donald Campbell and of Elizabeth (*née* Caldwell); partner, Fiona Millar, *qv*; two *s* one *d*. *Educ:* City of Leicester Boys Sch.; Gonville and Caius Coll., Cambridge (MA). Trainee reporter, Tavistock Times and Sunday Independent, 1980–82; freelance reporter, London, 1982–83; reporter, Daily

Mirror, 1982–85; news editor, Sunday Today, 1985–86; reporter, Daily Mirror, 1986; Sunday Mirror: Political Corresp., 1986–87; Political Editor, 1987–89; Columnist, 1989–91; Daily Mirror: Political Editor, 1989–93; Columnist, 1991–93; Asst Editor and Columnist, Today, 1993–95; Press Sec. to Leader of Opposition, 1994–97; Prime Minister's official spokesman, 1997–2001; Dir of Communications and Strategy, Prime Minister's Office, 2001–03; Strategy and Commns Consultant, British and Irish Lions Tour to NZ, 2005; Dir, Election Communications, Labour Party, 2005. Freelance writer, The Times and elsewhere, 2003–. *Publication:* The Blair Years, 2007. *Recreations:* running, triathlon, bagpipes, Burnley Football Club.

CAMPBELL, Alastair Peter; *see* Bracadale, Hon. Lord.

CAMPBELL, Prof. Alastair Vincent; Chen Su Lan Centennial Professor of Medical Ethics, and Director, Centre for Biomedical Ethics, National University of Singapore, since 2006; *b* 16 April 1938; *s* of William Lee Campbell and Jean Graham Dow; *m* 1st, 1959, Paula Barker (marr. diss.); one *s* four *d*; 2nd, 1979, Sally Barbara Forbes; two *s. Educ:* Hamilton Acad.; Univ. of Edinburgh (MA, BD); San Francisco Theol Seminary (ThD). Ordained Minister, Church of Scotland, 1963. Associate Chaplain, Univ. of Edinburgh, 1964–69; Lectr in Ethics, RCN, Scotland, 1966–72; University of Edinburgh: Lectr and Sen. Lectr, Dept of Christian Ethics and Practical Theology, 1969–90; Head of Dept, 1987–90; Associate Dean, Faculty of Divinity, 1978–81; Prof. of Biomedical Ethics, Otago Med. Sch., and Dir, Bioethics Res. Centre, Dunedin, Univ. of Otago, NZ, 1990–96; Prof. of Ethics in Medicine, Univ. of Bristol, 1996–2003, now Emeritus. Foundn Editor, Jl of Medical Ethics, 1975–80. Milligan Soc. Medallion, 1980; H. K. Beecher Award, Hastings Center, NY, 1999. *Publications:* Moral Dilemmas in Medicine, 1972; Medicine, Health and Justice, 1978; Rediscovering Pastoral Care, 1981; (with R. Higgs) In That Case, 1982; Moderated Love, 1984; Paid to Care?, 1985; The Gospel of Anger, 1986; The Dictionary of Pastoral Care, 1987; (with G. R. Gillett and D. G. Jones) Practical Medical Ethics, 1992, 3rd edn, as Medical Ethics, 2001; Health as Liberation, 1995; articles in learned jls. *Recreations:* music, ski-ing, walking. *Address:* Yong Loo Lin School of Medicine, National University of Singapore, Centre for Biomedical Ethics, Blk MD 11, # 01–04, Clinical Research Centre, 10 Medical Drive, Singapore 117597.

CAMPBELL, Hon. Alexander Bradshaw; PC (Canada) 1967; Judge, Supreme Court of Prince Edward Island, 1978–94; *b* 1 Dec. 1933; *s* of Dr Thane A. Campbell and late Cecilia B. Campbell; *m* 1961, Marilyn Gilmour; two *s* one *d. Educ:* Dalhousie Univ. (BA, LLB). Called to Bar of Prince Edward Island, 1959; practised law with Campbell & Campbell, Summerside, PEI, 1959–66; QC (PEI) 1966. MLA, Prince Edward Island, 1965–78; Leader of Liberal Party, Dec. 1966–78; Premier, 1966–78; served (while Premier) as Attorney-Gen., 1966–69, Minister of Development, 1969–72, Minister of Agriculture, 1972–74, and Minister of Justice, 1974–78. Dir, Inst. of Man and Resources, 1976–80. Pres., Summerside YMCA, 1981–91; Founder Pres., Summerside Area Historical Soc., 1983; Founder Chm., PEI Council, Duke of Edinburgh Awards (Canada), 1984. Mem., Wyatt Foundn, 1993–. Mem., Heedless Hoarsemen Men's Chorus, Largo, Fla, 1996– (Manager, 2004–). Chm., PEI Day Cttee, Fla, 2000–. Elder of Trinity United Church, Summerside. Sigma Chi Fraternity. Hon. LLD: McGill 1967; PEI, 1978. *Recreations:* golf, boating, gardening. *Address:* Stanley Bridge, Kensington, RR #6, PE C0B 1M0, Canada. *T:* (902) 8862081. *Club:* Y's Men's (Summerside).

CAMPBELL, Alexander Buchanan, RSA 2005 (ARSA 1973); FRIBA, PPRIAS; architect; Senior Partner, A. Buchanan Campbell and Partners, Glasgow, 1949–90; *b* 14 June 1914; *s* of Hugh Campbell and Elizabeth Flett; *m* 1939, Sheila Neville Smith; one *s* one *d. Educ:* Royal Technical Coll., Glasgow; Glasgow School of Art; Univ. of Strathclyde (BArch). Assistant: Prof. T. Harold Hughes, 1937; G. Grey Wornum, 1938; City Architect, Glasgow, 1939; served War, Royal Engineers, 1940–46; Inspector, Inspectorate of Elect. and Mech. Equipment, 1947; Chief Technical Officer, Scottish Building Centre, 1948, Dep. Dir, 1949. Principal works include: Dollan Swimming Baths and Key Youth Centre, East Kilbride; Whittingehame Court, Ascot; Flats, Great Western Road, Glasgow; St Christopher's Church, Glasgow; Priesthill Church, Glasgow; St James Primary Sch., Renfrew; Callendar Park Coll. and Craigie College of Education at Falkirk and Ayr (Civic Trust Awards); High Rise Flats, Drumchapel. President: Glasgow Inst. of Architects, 1974–76; Royal Incorporation of Architects in Scotland, 1977–79. *Recreations:* music, art, golf. *Address:* 19 Lochan Avenue, Kirn, Dunoon, Argyll PA23 8HT. *T:* (01369) 703674. *Club:* Glasgow Art (President, 1972–74).

CAMPBELL, Sir Alexander Thomas C.; *see* Cockburn-Campbell.

CAMPBELL, Andrew Bruce; His Honour Judge Andrew Campbell; a Circuit Judge, since 2004; *b* 20 Feb. 1949; *s* of Keith Bruce Campbell and Betty Joan Campbell; *m* 1977, Felicity Jane (*née* Owen); two *d. Educ:* Harrow Sch.; Brasenose Coll., Oxford (MA Jurisprudence). Called to the Bar, Inner Temple, 1972; Asst Recorder, 1998–2000, Recorder, 2000–04. *Recreations:* long distance walking, theatre. *Address:* Kingston upon Thames Crown Court, 6–8 Penrhyn Road, Kingston upon Thames, Surrey KT1 2BB. *T:* (020) 8240 2500, *Fax:* (020) 8240 2675.

CAMPBELL, Andrew Neville; QC 1994; a Recorder, since 1989; *b* 17 June 1949; *s* of Archibald Campbell, CMG and of Peggie Campbell (*née* Hussey); *m* 1980, Rebecca Thornton; two *s* one *d. Educ:* Berkhamsted Sch.; New Coll., Oxford (BA Hons Jurisprudence). Called to the Bar, Middle Temple, 1972; Bencher, 2005. *Recreations:* fishing, shooting, cricket, squash, ski-ing, walking. *Address:* 10 Park Square, Leeds, W Yorks LS1 2LH. *T:* (0113) 245 5438. *Clubs:* Vincent's (Oxford); Harrogate Cricket (Pres.).

CAMPBELL, Andrew Simon; Director, Local Strategic Partnerships and Performance, Department for Communities and Local Government, since 2006; *b* 30 Sept. 1957; *s* of Brian Andrew Humphrey Campbell and Rita Audrey Campbell; *m* 1982, Jacqueline Fraser Craik; two *s* one *d. Educ:* St Andrews Univ. (MA); University Coll. London (MPhil). Joined Dept of Transport, 1983; DoE, 1988–96; seconded to EC, Brussels, 1990–93; Sec., Econ. and Domestic Secretariat, Cabinet Office, 1996–98; Area Dir, Kent, Govt Office for SE, 1998–2001; Private Secretary to Secretary of State: for Transport, Local Govt and the Regions, 2001–02; for Transport and Sec. of State for Scotland, 2002–03; Dir, Regl Co-ordination Unit, ODPM, subseq. DCLG, 2003–06. *Recreations:* tennis, golf, football, reading novels, listening to nearly all types of music. *Address:* (office) Eland House, Bressenden Place, SW1E 5DU. *Club:* Southampton FC.

CAMPBELL, Anne; *b* 6 April 1940; *d* of late Frank Lucas and Susan (*née* Chadwick); *m* 1963, Archibald MacRobert Campbell; one *s* two *d. Educ:* Newnham Coll., Cambridge (Maths Tripos Pt II, 1962; MA 1965). FSS 1985. Sen. Lectr in Statistics, Cambs Coll. of Arts and Technol., 1970–83; Head of Stats and Data Processing, Nat. Inst. of Agricl Botany, Cambridge, 1983–92. MP (Lab) Cambridge, 1992–2005; contested (Lab) same seat, 2005. PPS to Minister for E-commerce and Small Businesses, 1999–2001, to Sec. of State for Trade and Industry, 2001–03. Mem., Cambs CC, 1985–89. FRSA 1992.

Publication: Calculation for Commercial Students, 1972. *Recreations:* tennis, ski-ing, gardening, mountain walking. *Address:* 20 St Barnabas Road, Cambridge CB1 2BY.

CAMPBELL, Rt Hon. Sir Anthony; *see* Campbell, Rt Hon. Sir W. A.

CAMPBELL, Prof. Anthony Keith, PhD; Professor in Medical Biochemistry, Cardiff University (formerly University of Wales College of Medicine), since 1991; *b* 30 April 1945; *s* of Harold Keith Campbell and Jennet Mary Seth Campbell; *m* 1985, Dr Stephanie Beatrix Matthews; one *s* two *d*, and two *s* by previous marriage. *Educ:* City of London Sch.; Pembroke Coll., Cambridge (Exhibnr; Foundn Schol.; MA 1st cl. Natural Sci. 1967; PhD 1971). Lectr, 1970–78, Sen. Lectr, 1978–83, Welsh Nat. Sch. of Medicine; Reader, Univ. of Wales Coll. of Medicine, 1983–91. Founder, 1993, and Dir, Cardiff, 1993–2000, Pembs, 2000–, Darwin Centre. FLS 1995; FRSA 1995. Foreign Mem., Royal Soc. of Scis, Uppsala, 2001. *Publications:* Intracellular Calcium: its universal role as regulator, 1983; Chemiluminescence: principles and applications in biology and medicine, 1988; Rubicon: the fifth dimension of biology, 1994; (with S. B. Matthews) Lactose Intolerance and the MATHS Syndrome, 2001; Tony's Lactose-free Cookbook: the science of lactose intolerance and how to live without lactose, 2005; 7 patents; contrib. numerous scientific pubns, and papers to Nature, Proc. of NAS, Postgrad. Med. Jl. *Recreations:* music (singing/conducting), bridge, cooking, natural history. *Address:* Department of Medical Biochemistry and Immunology, Tenovus Building, Cardiff University, Heath Park, Cardiff CF14 4XN; *e-mail:* campbellak@cf.ac.uk.

CAMPBELL, Arthur McLure, CBE 1990; Principal Clerk of Session and Justiciary, Scotland, 1982–89, retired; *b* 15 Aug. 1932; *s* of late Hector Brownlie Campbell, MBE, AIPA and Catherine Smylie (*née* Renwick). *Educ:* Queen's Park Sch., Glasgow; Open Univ. (DipEurHum 1997; BA Hons 2001; BSc Hons 2008). Deptl Legal Qual., Scottish Court Service, 1956. National Service, FAA, 1950–52. Admiralty Supplies Directorate, 1953–54; entered Scottish Court Service (Sheriff Clerk Br.), 1954; Sheriff Clerk Depute, Kilmarnock, 1957–60; Sheriff Clerk of Orkney, 1961–65; seconded HM Treasury (O & M), 1965–69; Principal Sheriff Clerk Depute, Glasgow, 1969; Sheriff Clerk, Airdrie, 1969–72; Principal, Scottish Court Service Staff Trng Centre, 1973–74; Asst Sheriff Clerk of Glasgow, 1974–81. Clerk of Cttees, H of L (temp.), 1991. Secretary: Lord Chancellor's Cttee on Re-sealing of Probates and Confirmations, 1967–68; Scottish Office Cttee on Money Transfer Services, 1968–69; Chm., Simplified Divorce (Scotland) Implementation Gp, 1981–82 (Scottish Consumer Council's Consumer Champion Award, 1983); Mem., Review Body on Use of Judicial Time in Superior Courts in Scotland, 1985–86. Chm., Sheriff Clerks' Assoc., 1971–72. *Recreation:* opsimathy. *Address:* 1 West Hill, Lord Street West, Southport PR8 2BJ; Calle Maestro Nicolau 8, 07181 Palma Nova-Calvia, Mallorca. *Clubs:* National Liberal, Civil Service.

CAMPBELL, Rt Hon. Avril Phaedra; *see* Campbell, Rt Hon. Kim.

CAMPBELL, Bridget; Head, Police and Community Safety Group, Scottish Government (formerly Executive) Justice Department, since 2005; *b* 9 March 1959; *d* of Allan Walter Campbell and Margaret Campbell (*née* Brettell). *Educ:* St Anne's Coll., Oxford (BA Hons Lit. Hum.). Various posts in Depts of Envmt and Transport, dealing with housing, local govt and internat. envmtl policy, 1982–96; Cycle Internat. course, l'Ecole Nat. d'Admin, Paris, 1989–90; Head, Housing Policy and Home Ownership Div., DoE, 1996–98; Scottish Executive: Head: Envmt Protection Unit, 1997–99; Cabinet Secretariat, 2000–01; Public Service Delivery Gp, 2001–02. *Recreations:* reading, walking, looking at pictures. *Address:* Scottish Government Justice Department, St Andrew's House, Edinburgh EH1 3DD. *T:* (0131) 244 2127; *e-mail:* bridget.campbell@scotland.gsi.gov.uk.

CAMPBELL, Bruce; *see* Campbell, W. B.

CAMPBELL, Maj.-Gen. (Charles) Peter, CBE 1977; Director, Quicks (formerly H. & J. Quick) Group Plc, 1982–91; *b* 25 Aug. 1926; *s* of late Charles Alfred Campbell and Blanche Campbell; *m* 1st, 1949, Lucy Kitching (*d* 1986); two *s*; 2nd, 1986, Elizabeth Tristram. *Educ:* Gillingham Grammar Sch.; Emmanuel Coll., Cambridge. Commnd RE, 1945 (despatches, Palestine, 1948); psc 1957; DAA&QMG Trng Bde, RE, 1958–60; OC 11 Indep. Field Sqdn, RE, 1960–62; Jt Services Staff Coll., 1963; DAAG WO, 1963–65; Co. Comd, RMA Sandhurst, 1965–67; CO 21 Engr Regt, 1967–70; GSOI MoD, 1970–71; CRE 3 Div., 1971; Comd 12 Engr Bde, 1972–73; RCDS, 1974; COS HQ NI, 1975–77; Engineer-in-Chief (Army), 1977–80. Col Comdt, RE, 1981–86, Rep. Col Comdt, 1982; Hon. Colonel: RE (Vol.) (Explosive Ordnance Disposal), 1986–88; 101 (London) Engr Regt (Explosive Ordnance Disposal) (V), 1988–91. Chm., RE Assoc., 1983–89. Gov., Gordon's Sch., 1993–96; Mem., Foundn of Gordon's Sch., 1991–2001 (Vice-Chm., 1996–99). FCMI. *Recreations:* painting and collecting militaria.

CAMPBELL, Cheryl Anne; actress. *Educ:* London Acad. of Music and Dramatic Art (Rodney Millington Award). Acted at Glasgow Citizens Theatr, Watford Rep., Birmingham Rep., King's Head, National Theatre and Theatre Clwyd; Blanche Dubois in A Streetcar Named Desire (Best Actress, Regl Theatre Awards); Nora in A Doll's House (SWET Award, 1983, for best actress of 1982 in a revival), RSC; title rôle in Miss Julie, Lyric, Hammersmith, and Duke of York's, 1983; title rôle in Daughter-in-Law, Hampstead, 1985; The Sneeze, Aldwych, 1988; Betrayal, Almeida, 1991; The Changeling, RSC, 1992; Misha's Party, Macbeth, RSC, 1993; The Strip, Royal Court, 1995; Some Sunny Day, Hampstead, 1996; The Last Yankee, Mercury Th., Colchester, 1996; The Seagull, Donmar, 1997; What the Butler Saw, Sheffield Crucible, 1997; Passion Play, Donmar, 2000; Noises Off, Piccadilly and tour, 2003. *Television* serials: Pennies from Heaven, 1978; Testament of Youth (Best Actress Award, BAFTA, and British Broadcasting Press Guild Award, 1979); Malice Aforethought; Centrepoint; The Secret Agent, 1992; The Way We Live Now, 2001; series: William and Mary, 2003, 2004, 2005. *Films* include: Chariots of Fire, 1981; Greystoke, 1983; The Shooting Party, 1985. *Address:* c/o Amanda Howard Associates, 21 Berwick Street, W1F 0PZ. *T:* (020) 7287 9277.

CAMPBELL, Christopher James, CBE 1993; Chairman, British Shipbuilders, 1989–2002; *b* 2 Jan. 1936; *s* of David Heggie Campbell and Nettie Phyllis (*née* Burgess). *Educ:* Epsom College. FCA. Served RAPC, 1959–61. Debenhams and subsidiaries, 1966–86, incl. Man. Dir, Hardy Amies, 1978–79; former Director: Debenhams dept stores; Harvey Nichols; Lotus; Debenhams Finance; Debenhams (M & S). Mem., and chief negotiator, 1986–88, non-exec. Mem., 1988–91, National Bus Co.; Finance Dir, Nat. Rivers Authy Adv. Cttee, 1988–89; Director: Harrods Bank Ltd, 1991–2000; Crown Timber plc, 1996–2000; Riverside Mental Health NHS Trust, 1993–96; Mem., BRB, 1994–97 (Vice-Chm., 1994–96). Mem. Council, Specialist Schs and Academies Trust (formerly Technology Colls, then Specialist Schs, Trust), 2001–07. Gov., United World Coll. of the Atlantic, 1993–2002. Trustee: Cobbe collection of ancient keyboard instruments, 1998–2007; British Youth Opera, 2003–. Captain Paymaster, HAC Inf. Bn, 1960–63. *Recreations:* politics, opera, entertaining, visual arts. *Address:* 19 Morpeth Mansions, Morpeth Terrace, SW1P 1ER. *T:* (020) 7630 7527. *Club:* Garrick.

CAMPBELL, Colin Donald Norman; Master of the Supreme Court Costs (formerly Taxing) Office, since 1996; *b* 26 Nov. 1952; *s* of late Maj. Gregory Campbell, TD and Myra Campbell (*née* Robertson); *m* 1985, Jacqueline Merete Mollett; one *s* one *d*. *Educ:* Oundle; Univ. of London (BA). Admitted as solicitor, 1983; Partner, Brown Cooper Solicitors and Privy Council Agents, 1987–96; Dep. Taxing Master, 1993–96; Dep. Dist Judge, Midland Circuit, 2001–. *Recreations:* Rugby Union, ski-ing, fly-fishing. *Address:* The Old Vicarage, Syleham, near Eye, Suffolk IP21 4LN. *T:* (01379) 668306. *Club:* MCC.

CAMPBELL, Colin MacIver; Member (SNP) Scotland West, Scottish Parliament, 1999–2003; *b* 31 Aug. 1938; *s* of Archibald James Campbell, MB ChB, DPH, and Christina Ellen Campbell (*née* MacIver); *m* 1963, Evelyn Jean Marcella George; three *s* (and one *s* decd). *Educ:* Paisley Grammar Sch.; Glasgow Univ. (MA Hons); Jordanhill Coll. of Educn. Teacher: Hillhead High Sch., 1961–63; Paisley GS, 1963–67; Principal Teacher, Greenock Acad., 1967–73; Depute Head, Merksworth High Sch., 1973–77; Head, Westwood Secondary Sch., 1977–89; Tutor, Sen. Studies Inst., Strathclyde Univ., 1995–98. Mem., Renfrewshire Council, 1995–99. Nat. Sec., SNP, 1997–99 (Defence Spokesperson, 1995–2003). *Publication:* (jtly) Can't Shoot a Man with a Cold: Lt E. Alan Mackintosh, MC, 1893–1917, Poet of the Highland Division, 2004. *Recreation:* military history of the Great War. *Address:* Braeside, Shuttle Street, Kilbarchan, Renfrewshire PA10 2PR.

CAMPBELL, Colin Malcolm; *see* Malcolm, Hon. Lord.

CAMPBELL, Sir Colin (Murray), Kt 1994; DL; Vice-Chancellor, University of Nottingham, 1988–2008; Professor Emeritus, Queen's University, Belfast; First Commissioner for Judicial Appointments, 2001–06; *b* 26 Dec. 1944; *s* of late Donald Campbell and Isobel Campbell; divorced; one *s* one *d*. *Educ:* Robert Gordon's Coll., Aberdeen; Univ. of Aberdeen (LLB 1st Cl. Hons). Lecturer: Faculty of Law, Univ. of Dundee, 1967–69; Dept of Public Law, Univ. of Edinburgh, 1969–73; Prof. of Jurisprudence, 1974–88, Dean of Faculty of Law, 1977–80, Pro-Vice-Chancellor, 1983–87, QUB. Member: Council, Soc. for Computers and Law, 1973–88; Standing Adv. Commn on Human Rights, 1977–80; Legal Aid Adv. Cttee, NI, 1978–82; Mental Health Legislation Rev. Cttee, NI, 1978–82; UGC, 1987–88; Nottingham Develt Enterprise, 1988–91; UFC Scottish Cttee, 1989–93; HEFCE, 1992–97; Inquiry into Police Responsibilities and Rewards, 1992–93; Trent RHA, 1992–96. Chairman: QUBIS Ltd, 1983–88; Zeton Ltd, 1990; Ind. Adv. Gp on Consumers Protection in NI, 1984; NI Economic Council, 1987–94 (Mem., 1985–94); Lace Market Develt Co., 1989–97; Human Fertilisation and Embryology Authy, 1990–94; Med. Workforce Standing Adv. Cttee, 1991–2001; Food Adv. Cttee, 1994–2001; Human Genetics Adv. Commn, 1996–99. Non-exec. Dir, Swiss Re GB, 1999–2005. DL Notts, 1996. *Publications:* (ed jtly) Law and Society, 1979; (ed) Do We Need a Bill of Rights?, 1980; (ed) Data Processing and the Law, 1984; numerous articles in books and jls. *Recreations:* sport, walking, music, reading. *Club:* Athenæum.

CAMPBELL, Darren Andrew, MBE 2005; international athlete; *b* 12 Sept. 1973; *s* of Marva Campbell; *m* 2004, Clair Jacobs; two *s* one *d*. Athletic achievements include: Gold medals, 100m, 200m and 4 x 100m relay, Eur. Jun. Championships, 1991; Gold medal, 4 x 100m relay, Silver medals, 100m and 200m, World Jun. Championships, 1992; winner, 100m, National Championships, 1998; European Championships: Gold medals, 100m and 4 x 100m relay, 1998; Gold medal, 4 x 100m relay, 2002; World Championships: Bronze medal, 4 x 100m relay, 1997; Silver medal, 4 x 100m relay, 1999; Silver medal, 4 x 100m relay and Bronze medal, 100m, 2003; Commonwealth Games: Gold medal, 4 x 100m relay, Malaysia, 1998; Bronze medal, 200m, Gold medal, 4 x 100m relay, Manchester, 2002; Olympic Games: Silver medal, 200m, Sydney, 2000; Gold medal, 4 x 100m relay, Athens, 2004. *Recreation:* football. *Address:* c/o Nuff Respect, The Coach House, 107 Sherland Road, Twickenham, Middx TW1 4HB. *Club:* Sale Harriers.

CAMPBELL, David; Chief Executive Officer, Anschutz Entertainment Group UK, since 2005; *b* 4 Sept. 1959; *s* of Archibald and Jean Campbell; *m* 1995, Tracey; three *s* (incl. twin *s*) one *d*. *Educ:* Kelvinside Acad., Glasgow; Reeds Sch., Cobham; Washington Univ., St Louis (MBA, AB Media). Mktg, General Mills, 1981–92; Mktg Manager, Pepsi-Cola, 1982–86; various posts, Virgin Gp, 1986–90; Chief Executive Officer: Virgin TV (Europe), 1990–92; Virgin Radio, 1992–96; Virgin Media, 1997; Ginger Media Gp, 1997–2000; Vice Chm., Ministry of Sound, 2001–02; CEO, Visit London, 2003–05. *Recreations:* music, travel, family. *Address:* Anschutz Entertainment Group, 32nd Floor, 25 Canada Square, E14 5LQ. *T:* (020) 7536 2600, *Fax:* (020) 7536 2603; *e-mail:* david@anschutz-entertainment.com. *Clubs:* Soho House; Cowdray Polo (non-playing) (Midhurst).

CAMPBELL, David Arthur; Chief Executive, British Vita Plc, 2001–05; non-executive Director: Fenner plc, since 2005; Zotefoams plc, since 2007; *b* 5 March 1950; *s* of Arthur and Anne Campbell; *m* 1974, Sylvia; two *d*. *Educ:* BA Hons Business Studies. British Vita Plc, 1974–2005: Dir, 1999–2005; Man. Dir, 2000–01. Mem. Bd, Stahl BV, 2007–. FCIPD; CCMI. *Address:* c/o Fenner plc, Hesslewood Country Office Park, Ferriby Road, Hessle, E Yorks HU13 0PW.

CAMPBELL, David Ian; HM Diplomatic Service; Director, British Trade and Cultural Office, Taiwan, since 2009; *b* 9 July 1958; *s* of Ian Flett Campbell and Irene Joyce Campbell (*née* Cook). *Educ:* St Nicholas Grammar Sch., Northwood; Univ. of Bristol (LLB Hons 1980). Joined FCO, 1981; served: Budapest, 1984–85; Georgetown, 1985–87; FCO, 1987–89; First Sec., UK Mission to UN, Geneva, 1989–93; Belgrade, 1994; Human Rights Policy Dept, FCO, 1995–99; Dep. Hd of Mission, Manila, 2000–03; Deputy High Commissioner: Singapore, 2003–07; Canberra, 2008. *Recreations:* books, theatre, travel. *Address:* c/o Foreign and Commonwealth Office, King Charles Street, SW1A 2AH.

CAMPBELL, David Ross, CBE 2000; Chairman, NHS National Services Scotland, since 2004; *b* 27 Sept. 1943; *s* of William Pancost Clyde Campbell and Davidina (*née* Ross); *m* 1968, Moira Bagley Donald. *Educ:* Whitehill Sch.; James Watt Meml Coll. Radio Officer, MN, 1961–67; Sales Exec., Remington Rand, 1967–69; various posts, Glasgow Herald & Evening Times, 1969–75; Man. Dir, Scottish & Universal Newspapers, 1975–79; Exec. Dir, Scottish & Universal Investments, 1978–83; Dir, Clyde Cablevision Hldgs Ltd, 1983–87; Chm. and Chief Exec., West Independent Newspapers Ltd, 1984–94. Chairman: Saltire Hldgs Ltd, 1990–93; Clansman Leisure Ltd, 1990–93; Dep. Chm., Enterprise Ayrshire, 1991–2000. Scotland Bd Mem., New Opportunities Fund, 1998–2004, Big Lottery Fund, 2004–06; Chm., Health Educn Bd for Scotland, 1995–2001. Member: PPITB, 1976–78; Press Council, 1988–90. Pres., Glasgow Chamber of Commerce, 1988–90. Also holds various other public and private sector chm. and dir positions. FInstD 1980. Scottish Free Enterprise Award, Aims of Industry, 1990. *Recreations:* golf, theatre, travel, reading. *Address:* Summerlea, Summerlea Road, Seamill, W Kilbride KA23 9HP. *Club:* Western (Glasgow).

CAMPBELL, Donald le Strange, MC 1944; *b* 16 June 1919; *s* of late Donald Fraser Campbell and Caroline Campbell; *m* 1952, Hon. Shona Catherine Greig Macpherson (*d* 2004), *y d* of 1st Baron Macpherson of Drumochter; one *s* one *d*. *Educ:* Winchester Coll.; Clare Coll., Cambridge. Served War, 1939–45, Major RA (MC). EFCO Ltd, 1947–55; MEECO Ltd, 1955–61; Davy-Ashmore Ltd, 1961–67; Dep. Chm. and Man. Dir, Davy-Ashmore Internat., 1965–69; Dir, Hovair Ltd, 1970–78; farming, Berks and Devon, 1979–96. Chm., BNEC Latin America, 1967. *Recreations:* farming, sailing, field sports, music. *Address:* Flat 6, New Court, Sutton Manor, Sutton Scotney, Hants SO21 3JB. *Clubs:* Boodle's; Royal Yacht Squadron.

CAMPBELL, Duncan; Director of Communications, Scottish Natural Heritage, 1992–95; *b* 23 Sept. 1935; *s* of late Duncan Campbell, sometime Manager, Chartered Bank of India and Australasia, and Mary Beryl Campbell; *m* 1959, Morny Key; two *s*. *Educ:* Merchiston Castle Sch., Edinburgh; Edinburgh Univ.; Newcastle upon Tyne Univ. Nat. service, RHA, 1954–56. Forestry Commission: Forest Manager, 1960–73; Landscape Architect, 1973–80; Head of Design and Recreation Br., 1980–85; Head of Environment Br., 1985–88; Dir, Countryside Commission for Scotland, 1988–92. Director: Edinburgh & Lothians Greenspace Trust Ltd, 1997–2007; Colinton Community Conservation Trust Ltd, 2000–; Mavisbank Trust Ltd, 2002–; Chm., Colinton Amenity Assoc., 2002–05. Member Council: Scottish Council for Nat. Parks, 1997–2007; Edinburgh Civic Trust, 2003–. *Publications:* articles in Landscape Design and Jl of RASE. *Recreations:* landscape appreciation, fishing. *Address:* 62 Bonaly Wester, Edinburgh EH13 0RQ.

CAMPBELL, Francis Martin; HM Diplomatic Service; Ambassador to the Holy See, since 2005; *b* 20 April 1970; *s* of Daniel Joseph Campbell and Brigid Mary Campbell (*née* Cosgrove). *Educ:* Queen's Univ., Belfast (BA 1992); Katholieke Universiteit, Leuven (MA 1995); Univ. of Pennsylvania (MA). Joined HM Diplomatic Service, 1997; FCO, 1997; EC Delegn to the UN, NY, 1997–98; FCO, 1998–99; Policy Advr, 1999–2001, Private Sec., 2001–03, to the Prime Minister; First Sec. (External), Rome, 2003–05; Sen. Dir of Policy, Amnesty Internat., 2005. *Publication:* (contrib.) Federalism Doomed, 2002. *Recreations:* reading, walking, travelling. *Address:* British Embassy to the Holy See, Via XX Settembre 80a, Roma 00187, Italy. *T:* (06) 42204000, *Fax:* (06) 42204205.

CAMPBELL, Gordon Arden, CBE 2006; FREng, FIChemE; Chairman, British Nuclear Fuels plc, since 2004 (Director, since 2000); *b* 16 Oct. 1946; *s* of late Hugh Eric Campbell and Jessie Campbell; *m* 1970, Jennifer Vaughan; two *d*. *Educ:* Churchill Coll., Cambridge (MA). FIChemE 1987. Joined Courtaulds Research, 1968; Dir, British Celanese, 1976; Managing Director: Courtaulds Chemicals, 1980–85; SAICCOR, S Africa, 1985–87; Dir, 1987, Dep. Chief Exec., 1995, Chief Exec., 1996–98, Courtaulds. Chm., ITI Scotland, 2003–05. Mem., UKAEA, 1994–96; non-executive Director: AEA Technol., 1996–97; Argos plc, 1997–98; HSS Ltd, 2005–07; Accys Technologies, 2005–; non-executive Chairman: International Process Technologies, 1999–2001; Wade-Allied Hldgs, 1999–2003; Babcock International Gp, 2001–08; Jupiter Second Split Trust, 2004–. President: Comité Internat. de Rayon et Fibres Synthétiques, 1995–98; IChemE, 1998–99, 2004– (Vice-Pres., 1992–94). Member: President's Council, CBI, 1995–2000, 2004–; Council, British Heart Foundn, 1999–2005. Vis. Prof., Univ. of Strathclyde, 2003–. Mem. Court, Cranfield Univ., 1999–. FREng (FEng 1993; Vice-Pres., 2001–04). CCMI (CBIM 1990). *Recreations:* Rugby, golf, ski-ing. *Address:* c/o BNFL, 65 Buckingham Gate, SW1E 6AP.

CAMPBELL, Hon. Gordon Muir; MLA (L) Vancouver-Point Grey, since 1996 (Vancouver-Quilchene, 1994–96); Premier, British Columbia, Canada, since 2001; *b* 12 Jan. 1948; *s* of Charles Gordon Campbell and Margaret Janet Campbell (*née* Muir); *m* 1970, Nancy Jean Chipperfield; two *s*. *Educ:* Dartmouth Coll., New Hampshire; Simon Fraser Univ. (MBA). Secondary sch. teacher, and basketball and track coach, Yola, Nigeria, with Can. Univ. Students Overseas orgn, 1970–72; asst to Mayor of Vancouver, 1972–76; Marathon Realty, 1976–81 (Gen. Manager); Founder, Citycore Develt Corp., 1981. Mem., Vancouver CC, 1984–86, Mayor, 1986–93. Leader, Liberal Party of BC, 1993–. *Publication:* (for children) Tuaq: The Only One, 1995. *Address:* PO Box 9041 Stn Prov. Gov., Victoria, BC V8W 9E1, Canada. *T:* (250) 3871715, *Fax:* (250) 3870087; *e-mail:* premier@gov.bc.ca.

CAMPBELL, Graham Gordon, CB 1984; Under-Secretary, Department of Energy, 1974–84; *b* 12 Dec. 1924; *s* of late Lt-Col and Mrs P. H. Campbell; *m* 1955, Margaret Rosamond Busby; one *d*. *Educ:* Cheltenham Coll.; Caius Coll., Cambridge (BA Hist.). Served War, Royal Artillery, 1943–46. Asst Principal, Min. of Fuel and Power, 1949; Private Sec. to Parly Sec., Min. of Fuel and Power, 1953–54; Principal, 1954; Asst Sec., Min. of Power, 1965; Under-Sec., DTI, 1973. *Recreations:* watching birds, music, hill-walking, clearing scrub. *Address:* 3 Clovelly Avenue, Warlingham, Surrey CR6 9HZ. *T:* (01883) 624671.

CAMPBELL, Gregor Bruce Loudoun; Secretary-General, Institute of Actuaries, and Chief Executive (Joint Affairs), Faculty of Actuaries and Institute of Actuaries, 1997–2002; *b* 22 April 1942; *s* of Donald and Alison Campbell; *m* 1966, Suzanne Elizabeth Austin; one *s* two *d*. *Educ:* Glasgow Acad.; London Univ. (BScEng). Corps of Royal Engineers, 1962–92; retd as Brig.; Dep. Sec., Inst. of Actuaries, 1993–97. *Recreations:* family, travel, gardening, motor cycles.

CAMPBELL, Gregory Lloyd; MP (DemU) Londonderry East, since 2001; Member (DemU) Londonderry East, Northern Ireland Assembly, since 1998; *b* 15 Feb. 1953; *m* Frances; one *s* three *d*. *Educ:* Ebrington Primary Sch.; Londonderry Tech. Coll.; Magee Coll. Civil Servant, 1972–82 and 1986–94; businessman, 1994–. Mem. (DemU) Londonderry CC, 1981–. Mem. (DemU), NI Assembly, 1982–86; Mem., NI Forum for Political Dialogue, 1996–98. Minister for Regl Develt, NI, 2000–01. Contested (DemU): Foyle, 1992; E Londonderry, 1997. *Publications:* Discrimination: the truth, 1987; Discrimination: where now?, 1993; Ulster's Verdict on the Joint Declaration, 1994; Working Toward 2000, 1998. *Recreations:* soccer, music, reading. *Address:* (office) 25 Bushmills Road, Coleraine, Co. Londonderry, Northern Ireland BT52 2BP; 6–8 Catherine Street, Limavady BT49 9DB.

CAMPBELL, Dr Henrietta, CB 2000; FRCP, FRCPGlas, FFPH; Chief Medical Officer for Northern Ireland, 1995–2006; *b* 2 Nov. 1948; *d* of Thomas James Hanna and Jean Hanna; *m* 1972, William McBride Campbell; one *s* two *d*. *Educ:* Queen's Univ., Belfast (MD 1998). FFPH (FFPHM 1996); FRCP 1997; FRCPGlas 2000. GP, NI, 1974–79; civilian medical practitioner, BAOR, 1979–83; SMO, 1983–90, Dep. CMO, 1990–95, Dept of Health and Social Services, NI. Mem., UK Electoral Commn, 2007–. Trustee, Oxfam Ireland, 2006–. *Recreations:* gardening, water-colour painting, hill-walking. *Address:* 1A The Rookery, Killinchy, Co. Down, Northern Ireland BT23 6SY. *T:* (028) 9754 2800.

CAMPBELL, Hugh Hall; QC (Scot.) 1983; FCIArb; *b* 18 Feb. 1944; *s* of William Wright Campbell and Marianne Doris Stuart Hutchison or Campbell; *m* 1969, Eleanor Jane Hare; three *s*. *Educ:* Glasgow Acad.; Trinity Coll., Glenalmond (Alexander Cross Scholar);

Exeter Coll., Oxford (Open Scholar in Classics; BA Hons, MA); Edinburgh Univ. (LLB Hons). FCIArb 1986. Called to the Scottish Bar, 1969; Standing Jun. Counsel to Admiralty, 1976. *Recreations:* carnival, wine, music. *Address:* 12 Ainslie Place, Edinburgh EH3 6AS. *T:* (0131) 225 2067. *Club:* Hon. Company of Edinburgh Golfers.

CAMPBELL, Prof. Iain (Donald), PhD; FRS 1995; Professor of Structural Biology, University of Oxford, 1992–Sept. 2009; Tutorial Fellow in Biochemistry, St John's College, Oxford, 1989–Sept. 2009; *b* 24 April 1941; *s* of Daniel Campbell and Catherine Campbell (*née* Lauder); *m* 1967, Karin C. Wehle; one *s* two *d*. *Educ:* Perth Acad.; St Andrews Univ. (BSc 1963; PhD 1967); MA Oxon 1987. University Lectr, Dept of Biochem., Oxford, 1976–92. Croonian Lectr, Royal Soc., 2006. Member: Molecular and Cellular Medicine Bd, MRC, 1992–96; Wellcome Trust Molecular Cell Bd, 1997–2002. Mem., EMBO, 1990. Delegate, OUP, 1996–. Mem., various editl bds of scientific jls. Trustee: Edward P. Abraham Cephalosporin Fund, 2004–; EMF Biol Res. Trust, 2007–. Hon. DTech Lund, 2000; Hon. DSc Portsmouth, 2000. Education in Partnership with Industry Award, DTI, 1982; BDH Medal, 1990, Novartis Medal, 2003, Biochem. Soc. *Publications:* numerous scientific papers and reviews. *Address:* Department of Biochemistry, Oxford University, South Parks Road, Oxford OX1 3QU. *T:* (01865) 275346, *Fax:* (01865) 275253.

CAMPBELL, His Honour Ian Burns, CMG 2003; a Circuit Judge, 1984–2003; Deputy High Representative for Legal Affairs, and Head, Legal Affairs Department, Office of High Representative, Sarajevo, 2000–03 (on secondment from Lord Chancellor's Department); *b* 7 July 1938; *s* of late James Campbell and Laura Campbell; *m* 1967, Mary Elisabeth Poole, BArch, MCD Liverpool; two *s* one *d*. *Educ:* Tiffin Boys' Sch.; Cambridge Univ. (MA, LLM, PhD); Diplôme d'Etudes Supérieures de Droit Comparé, Strasbourg, 1964. Called to the Bar, Middle Temple, 1966. French Govt Scholar, Univ. of Paris, 1961–62; Asst Lectr in Law, Liverpool Univ., 1962–64, Lectr 1964–69; a Recorder, 1981–84; Liaison Judge, N and S Sefton Benches, 1988–2000; seconded to Legal Dept, Office of High Rep., Sarajevo, 1999–2000. Mem., Franco-British Judicial Co-operation Cttee, 1996–2000. Hon. Mem., Albanian Nat. Judicial Conf., 1999–2000. A Dep. Chm. Adv. Bd, CARDS Regl Project 2003, for estabt of an indep., reliable and functioning judiciary in Western Balkans, 2006–07. Vis. Prof., Sch. of Law, Liverpool Univ., 2002–06 (Hon. Vis. Prof., 1995–2002). Member, Editorial Board: Liverpool Law Review, 1996–2005; Judicial Studies Bd Jl, 1996–2000. Hon. LLD Liverpool, 2005. *Publications:* (contrib.) Legal Visions of the New Europe, 1993; contrib. legal jls. *Recreation:* journeying.

CAMPBELL, Ian Dugald, FRCPE, FFPH; Treasurer, Royal College of Physicians of Edinburgh, 1981–85; *b* Dornie, Kintail, 22 Feb. 1916; *s* of John Campbell and Margaret Campbell; *m* 1943, Joan Carnegie Osborn; one *s* two *d*. *Educ:* Dingwall Acad.; Edinburgh Univ. (MB, ChB 1939). FRCPE 1973, FFPH (FFCM 1974). Served War, 1941–46: UK, BAOR, MEF, RAMC; final appt OC Field Amb. (Lt-Col). Med. Supt, St Luke's Hosp., Bradford, 1946–49; Asst SMO, Leeds Reg. Hosp. Bd, 1949–57; Dep. Sen. Admin. MO, S-Eastern Reg. Hosp. Bd, Scotland, 1957–72, Sen. Admin. MO, 1972–73; Chief Admin. MO, Lothian Health Bd, 1973–80. QHP 1977–80. WHO assignments, SE Asia, 1969, 1971, 1975. *Publications:* various medical. *Recreations:* fishing, shooting, golf. *Address:* 5 Succoth Park, Edinburgh EH12 6BX. *T:* (0131) 539 5965. *Clubs:* New (Edinburgh); Hon. Company of Edinburgh Golfers (Muirfield); Royal Burgess Golfing Society (Barnton, Edinburgh).

CAMPBELL, Ian H.; *see* Hay-Campbell.

CAMPBELL, Ian James, FRAS; Director General Research Maritime, Ministry of Defence, 1978–81; *b* 9 June 1923; *s* of Allan and Elizabeth Campbell; *m* 1946, Stella Margaret Smith (*d* 2001). *Educ:* George Heriot's Sch.; Edinburgh Univ. (MA Hons, Maths and Natural Phil.). FRAS 2004. Op. Res. Sect., HQ Bomber Comd, 1943–46; Asst Lectr in Astronomy, St Andrews Univ., 1946–48; joined Royal Naval Scientific Service, 1948; Dept of Aeronaut. and Eng Res., Admiralty, 1948–49; Admiralty Res. Lab., 1949–59; Admiralty Underwater Weapons Estab., 1959–68 (leader of res. team which established concept and technol. base for Stingray torpedo, 1962–68); Chief Scientist, Naval Construction Res. Estab., 1969–73; Head of Weapons Dept, Admiralty Underwater Weapons Estab., 1973–76; Ministry of Defence: Dir of Res. (Ships), 1976–78; Scientific Advr to Ship Dept, 1976–81. Defence sci. consultant, 1982–92; Technical Dir, CAP Scientific, 1983–87; Dir of Studies, Centre for Operational Res. and Defence Analysis, 1987–88. Chm., Res. Adv. Cttee, Electronic Engrg Assoc., 1989–91. *Publications:* papers on fluid mechanics in scientific proceedings and jls. *Recreations:* astronomy, Scottish country dancing. *Address:* 6 Queens Avenue, Dorchester, Dorset DT1 2EW. *T:* (01305) 264270. *Club:* Sloane.

CAMPBELL, Sir Ian (Tofts), Kt 1988; CBE 1984; VRD 1961; JP; Director, Conservative Board of Finance, 1978–90; Director of Finance and Administration, Scottish Conservative Party, 1988–90; *b* 3 Feb. 1923; *o s* of John Walter Campbell and Mary Hardie Campbell (*née* Scott); *m* 1961, Marion Kirkhope Paterson (*née* Shiel); one *d*. *Educ:* Daniel Stewart's College, Edinburgh. FInstD 1964. RN 1942–46, RNR 1946–65 (Comdr). Man. Dir, MacGregor Wallcoverings, 1966–78. Chm., Select Assured Properties, Glasgow, 1989–96; Dep. Chm., Heath (Scotland) Ltd, 1988–95 (Dir, 1987–96; consultant, 1996–2000); Director: Travel System, 1987–89; Hermiston Securities, 1990–. Mem., Transport Users' Cons. Cttee for Scotland, 1981–87. Councillor, City of Edinburgh District Council, 1984–88. JP Edinburgh, 1987. Freeman, City of Glasgow, 1992. OStJ 1987. KLJ 1984. *Recreations:* golf, water colour painting, vintage cars. *Address:* Merleton, 10 Boswall Road, Edinburgh EH5 3RH. *T:* (0131) 552 4825. *Club:* New (Edinburgh).

CAMPBELL of Succoth, Sir Ilay (Mark), 7th Bt *cr* 1808, of Succoth, Dunbartonshire; *b* 29 May 1927; *o s* of Sir George Ilay Campbell, 6th Bt; *S* father, 1967; *m* 1961, Margaret Minette Rohais, *o d* of J. Alasdair Anderson; two *d*. *Educ:* Eton; Christ Church, Oxford. BA 1952; MA 1970. Chm., Christie's Scotland, 1978–96. Dir., High Craigton Farming Co. Member: Historic Buildings Council for Scotland, 1989–98; Gardens Cttee, Nat. Trust for Scotland, 1994–2001. Pres., Assoc. for Protection of Rural Scotland, 1978–90. Mem., C of S Cttee for Artistic Matters, 1984–91 (Convener, 1987–91); Convener, Church Bldgs Renewal Trust, Glasgow, 1995–98. Hon. Vice Pres., Scotland's Gardens Scheme, 1960–; Trustee, Crarae Gardens Charitable Trust, 1978–2002. *Publication:* (with Brian North Lee) Scottish Bookplates, 2006. *Recreations:* heraldry, collecting heraldic bookplates. *Heir:* none. *Address:* Crarae Lodge, Inveraray, Argyll PA32 8YA. *T:* (01546) 886274, *Fax:* (01546) 886262. *Club:* Turf.

CAMPBELL, James, FBA 1984; FSA 1971; Professor of Medieval History, University of Oxford, 1996–2002; Fellow of Worcester College, Oxford, since 1957; *b* 26 Jan. 1935; *m* 2006, Bärbel Brodt. *Educ:* Mill Road Mixed Infants, Clowne, Derbyshire and other primary schools; Lowestoft Grammar School; Magdalen College (Exhibitioner; BA 1955, MA). Oxford University: Junior Research Fellow, Merton College, 1956–57; Tutorial Fellow, 1957, Fellow Librarian, 1977–2002, Sen. Tutor, 1989–93, Worcester College; Lectr in Modern History, 1958–90; Reader in Medieval History, 1990–96; Senior Proctor, 1973–74. Visiting Professor: Univ. of South Carolina, 1969; Univ. of Rochester, 1986–87. Creighton Lectr, Univ. of London, 1995; Ford's Lectr, Univ. of Oxford, 1996. Hon. DLitt UEA, 2006. *Publications:* Norwich, 1975; (ed) The Anglo-Saxons, 1982; Essays in Anglo-Saxon History, 1986; The Anglo-Saxon State, 2000; articles in learned jls. *Recreation:* topography. *Address:* Worcester College, Oxford OX1 2HB; 9 The Willows, Newland Mill, Witney, Oxon OX28 3HN. *T:* (01993) 706019.

CAMPBELL, James Alastair G.; *see* Graham-Campbell.

CAMPBELL, Sir James (Alexander Moffat Bain), 9th Bt *cr* 1667, of Aberuchill, Perthshire; insurance broker, Lycetts Insurance Brokers, since 2007; *b* 23 Sept. 1956; *er s* of Sir Colin Campbell, 8th Bt and of Mary Campbell (*née* Bain); *S* father, 1997; *m* 1993, Carola Jane Denman; one *s* two *d*. *Educ:* Stowe. Scots Guards (Capt.), 1975–83. Motorcycle despatch rider, 1984; insurance broker: Bain Dawes Ltd, Bain Clarkson plc, Bain Hogg plc, Aon Corp., 1984–97; R. K. Harrison Ltd, 1997–2001; indep. insurance consultant, 2001–07. *Recreations:* shooting, trees, gardening. *Heir:* *s* Colin George Denman Bain Campbell, *b* 1 Oct. 1999. *Address:* Kilbryde Castle, Dunblane, Perthshire FK15 9NF. *T:* (01786) 824897.

CAMPBELL, James MacRae; Head of Energy Development (formerly Licensing and Consents, later Energy Resources and Development) Unit, Energy Group, Department of Energy and Climate Change (formerly Department of Trade and Industry, then Department for Business, Enterprise and Regulatory Reform), since 2003; *b* 17 June 1952; *s* of late Alistair Campbell and Flora MacKay Campbell (*née* MacRae); *m* 1975, Catherine Russell; one *s* one *d*. *Educ:* Strathclyde Univ. (BSc Hons (Physics) 1974). MInstP 1975; CPhys 1987. Res. Scientist, NEL, 1974–79; Offshore Supplies Office: Res. and Develt Assessor, 1979–82; Industrial Liaison, 1982–91; Asst Dir, and Hd UK Continental Shelf Develts, 1991–94; Asst Dir, Oil and Gas Projects and Supplies Office, 1994–96; Director: Industry and Downstream Exports, British Trade Internat., 1996–2000; Oil and Gas Envmt and Decommissioning, DTI, 2000–02. FRSA 2000. *Recreations:* hill walking, reading, running, cinema. *Address:* c/o Department of Energy and Climate Change, Atholl House, 86–88 Guild Street, Aberdeen AB11 6AR. *T:* (01224) 254093.

CAMPBELL, Jim; *see* Campbell, R. J.

CAMPBELL, John Davies, CVO 1980; CBE 1981 (MBE 1957); MC 1945, and bar 1945; HM Diplomatic Service, retired; Consul-General, Naples, 1977–81; *b* 11 Nov. 1921; *s* of late William Hastings Campbell and of late The Hon. Mrs Campbell (Eugenie Anne Westenra, subsequently Harbord), *d* of 14th Baron Louth; *m* 1959, Shirley Bouch; one *s* two *d*. *Educ:* Cheltenham Coll.; St Andrews Univ. Served War, HM Forces, Argyll and Sutherland Highlanders and Popski's Private Army, 1940–46. HM Colonial Service (subseq. HMOCS), 1949–61 (despatches, 1957); HM Foreign (subseq. HM Diplomatic) Service, 1961; First Secretary, 1961; Counsellor, 1972; Counsellor (Information) Ottawa, 1972–77. Commendatore dell'ordine al merito della Repubblica Italiana, 1980. *Recreations:* travel, music, theatre. *Address:* Townsend House, Luston, Leominster, Herefordshire HR6 0DZ. *T:* (01568) 612446. *Club:* Special Forces.

CAMPBELL, Prof. John Joseph, DPhil; Willis S. and Marion Slusser Professor of Philosophy, University of California at Berkeley, since 2004; *b* 2 Nov. 1956; *s* of Roderick Campbell and Catriona (*née* MacKinnon); *m* 1978, Patricia Carrol (marr. diss. 1986). *Educ:* Univ. of Stirling (BA); Univ. of Calgary (MA); Wolfson Coll., Oxford (BPhil, DPhil 1986). University of Oxford: Res. Lectr, Christ Church, 1983–86; Fellow and Tutor in Philosophy, New Coll., 1986–2001; British Acad. Res. Reader, 1995–97; Reader in Philosophy, 1997–2001; Wilde Prof. of Mental Philosophy, 2001–04; Fellow, Corpus Christi Coll., 2001–04. Visiting posts at: UCLA, 1988; Univ. of Cambridge, 1990–91; ANU 1991–92; Cornell Univ., 1998. *Publications:* Past, Space and Self, 1994; Reference and Consciousness, 2002. *Recreations:* gardening, country pubs. *Address:* University of California, Department of Philosophy, Berkeley, CA 94720–2390, USA.

CAMPBELL, (John) Quentin; His Honour Judge Quentin Campbell; a Circuit Judge, since 1996; *b* 5 March 1939; *s* of late John McKnight Campbell, OBE, MC, and late Katharine Margaret Campbell; *m* 1st, Penelope Jane Redman (marr. diss. 1976); three *s* one *d*; 2nd, 1977, Ann Rosemary Beeching, DL, a Circuit Judge; one *s* one *d*. *Educ:* Loretto Sch., Musselburgh, Scotland; Wadham Coll., Oxford (MA). Admitted as Solicitor, 1965; private practice, Linnell & Murphy, Oxford (Partner, 1968–80); Metropolitan Stipendiary Magistrate, 1981–96; a Recorder, 1989–96. A Pres., Mental Health Review Tribunals, 1996–; Mem., Parole Bd, 2000–07. Chairman, Bd of Governors, Bessels Leigh Sch., near Oxford, 1979–96. *Recreations:* opera, music, travel. *Address:* The Crown Court, Inner London Sessions House, Newington Causeway, SE1 6AZ. *T:* (020) 7234 3100. *Clubs:* Travellers; Frewen (Oxford).

CAMPBELL, Juliet Jeanne d'Auvergne, CMG 1988; HM Diplomatic Service, retired; Mistress of Girton College, Cambridge, 1992–98, now Life Fellow; *b* 23 May 1935; *d* of Maj.-Gen. Wilfred d'Auvergne Collings, CB, CBE and of Nancy Draper Bishop; *m* 1983, Prof. Alexander Elmslie Campbell (*d* 2002). *Educ:* a variety of schools; Lady Margaret Hall, Oxford (BA; Hon. Fellow, 1992). Joined Foreign Office 1957; Common Market Delegation, Brussels, 1961–63; FO, 1963–64; Second, later First Secretary, Bangkok, 1964–66; News Dept, FO, 1967–70; Head of Chancery, The Hague, 1970–74; European Integration Dept, FCO, 1974–77; Counsellor (Inf.), Paris, 1977–80; RCDS, 1981; Counsellor, Jakarta, 1982–83; Head of Training Dept, FCO, 1984–87; Ambassador to Luxembourg, 1988–91. Member: Cambridge Univ. Council of Senate (later Council), 1993–97; Wilton Park Academic Council, 1993–2000. Dep. Vice-Chancellor, Cambridge Univ., 1993–98. Mem. Council, RSAA, 2008–. Trustee: Changing Faces, 1992–2006; Cambridge European Trust, 1994–98; Kurt Hahn Trust, 1995–98; Cambridge Overseas Trust, 1995–98; Henry Fellowships, 1997–2005. Governor: Queen's Coll., Harley St, 1992–2002; Marlborough Coll., 1999–2007. *Address:* 3 Belbroughton Road, Oxford OX2 6UZ. *Club:* Oxford and Cambridge.

CAMPBELL, Air Vice-Marshal Kenneth Archibald, CB 1989; consulting engineer; Air Officer Maintenance, RAF Support Command, 1987–89; *b* 3 May 1936; *s* of John McLean and Christina Campbell; *m* 1959, Isobel Love Millar; two *d*. *Educ:* George Heriot's Sch.; Glasgow Univ. (BSc); College of Aeronautics, Cranfield (MSc). Various engrg appts, RAF, 1959–90; Air Officer, Wales, 1977–79; Dir, Engrg Policy (RAF), 1981–83; AO, Engrg and Supply, RAF Germany, 1983–85; DG Personal Services (RAF), 1985–87. *Recreations:* golf, ski-ing. *Club:* Royal Air Force.

CAMPBELL, Kenneth Ewen; Editor, Metro (UK), London, since 2001; *b* 20 Nov. 1967; *s* of Ewen and Christine Campbell; *m* 2005, Nina Helen Caplan. *Educ:* Caol Primary Sch., Caol; Lochaber High Sch., Fort William; Univ. of Aberdeen (MA Hons Politics and Econs). Trainee manager, Marks & Spencer, Perth, 1989–90; journalist: Press and Jl, Aberdeen, 1990–92; Evening News, Edinburgh, 1992–94; Chief Sub-Ed., Daily Mail, Glasgow, 1994–97; Night Ed., Daily Express, Glasgow, 1997–99; Deputy Editor: Metro, London, 1999–2000; Daily Mail, Glasgow, 2000–01. Board Member: Sci. Media Centre,

London, 2005–; Communications Cttee, RAEng, 2007–. Freeman, Co. of Stationers and Newspaper Makers, 2007. *Recreations:* a little wine and a little diving, with a dash of motor racing and a hint of PlayStation. *Address:* c/o Metro, Northcliffe House, 2 Derry Street, W8 5TT. *Club:* Ronnie Scott's.

CAMPBELL, Rt Hon. Kim, CC 2008; PC (Canada) 1989; QC (BC) 1990; Secretary General, Club of Madrid, 2004–07 (Member, Board of Directors, since 2002); *b* 10 March 1947; *m* 1997, Hershey Felder. *Educ:* Univ. of British Columbia (BA 1969; LLB 1983); LSE (Hon. Fellow, 1994). Called to the Bar of BC, 1984, Ont, 1990. Lectr in Pol Sci., Univ. of BC, 1975–78; Lectr in Pol Sci. and Hist., Vancouver Community Coll., 1978–81; Articled student, 1983–84, Associate, Gen. Litigation, 1984–85, Ladner Downs Vancouver; Exec. Dir, Office of Premier of BC, 1985–86; MLA Vancouver Point Grey, 1986–88; MP (PC) Vancouver Centre, 1988–93; Minister of State, Indian Affairs and Northern Develt, 1989–90; Minister of Justice and Attorney Gen., 1990–93; Minister of Nat. Defence and Minister of Veterans' Affairs, 1993; Prime Minister of Canada, 1993; Canadian Consul-Gen., LA, 1996–2000. Lectr, John F. Kennedy Sch. of Govt, Harvard Univ., 2003–04 (Vis. Prof. of Practice, 2001–04). Chair Emerita, Council of Women World Leaders, 2003 (Chair, 1999–2003); Pres., Internat. Women's Forum, 2003–05. Hon. LLD: Law Soc. of Upper Canada, 1991; Brock Univ., 1998; UBC, 2000; Mt Holyoke Coll., 2004; Chatham Coll.; Hon. DPS Northeastern, 1999; Hon. LHD Arizona State, 2005. *Publication:* Time and Chance: the political memoirs of Canada's first woman prime minister, 1996, 3rd edn 2008. *Web:* www.kimcampbell.net.

CAMPBELL, Sir Lachlan (Philip Kemeys), 6th Bt *cr* 1815; *b* 9 Oct. 1958; *e s* of Col Sir Guy Campbell, 5th Bt, OBE, MC and of Lizbeth Webb, *d* of late Frederick Holton; *S* father, 1993; *m* 1986, Harriet Jane Sarah, *o d* of F. E. J. Girling; two *s* one *d*. *Educ:* Temple Grove; Eton; RMA Sandhurst. The Royal Greenjackets (Lieut); served NI. *Recreations:* golf, Rugby, cricket, painting. *Heir: s* Archibald Edward FitzGerald Campbell, *b* 13 June 1990. *Address:* The Old School House, School Lane, Melbury Abbas, Shaftesbury, Dorset SP7 0DZ. *Clubs:* Army and Navy, Royal Greenjackets, MCC; London Scottish Golf and Rugby; Rushmore Golf.

CAMPBELL, Rev. Laurence Jamieson; Methodist Minister, Trinity Church, Newport, Gwent Circuit, 1987–94; Headmaster, Kingswood School, Bath, 1970–87; *b* 10 June 1927; *er s* of George S. Campbell and Mary P. Paterson; *m* 1954, Sheena E. Macdonald; two *s* one *d*. *Educ:* Hillhead High Sch., Glasgow; Aberdeen Univ., Edinburgh Univ. (MA). Lieut RA, 1945–48. Housemaster, Alliance High Sch., Kenya, 1952–56; Presbyterian Church of E Africa, 1957–61: Tumutumu Coll., 1957–60; Supervisor of Schs, 1960–61; Educn Sec., Christian Council of Kenya, 1962; Headmaster, Alliance High Sch., Kenya, 1963–70. Methodist minister, ordained 1988. Contested North Kenya Constituency, Kenya General Election, 1961. Mem. Council, Univ. of East Africa, 1963–69; Chm., Heads Assoc. of Kenya, 1965–69; Official of Kenya Commonwealth Games Team, 1970. Schoolmaster Fellow, Balliol Coll., Oxford, 1970. Chairman: Christians Abroad, 1977–81; Bloxham Project, 1981–84. *Recreations:* golf, travel, church. *Address:* 1A Edward VII Avenue, Newport, Gwent NP20 4NF.

CAMPBELL, Mark; Partner, Finance Practice, since 1991 and Head, Global Finance Practice, since 2002, Clifford Chance LLP; *b* Liverpool, 23 June 1960; *s* of George and Thelma Campbell; *m* 1994, Susan Gaye Carter; four *s* three *d*. *Educ:* St Wilfrid's High Sch., Litherland; Oriel Coll., Oxford (MA Juris. 1978); Coll. of Law, Guildford. Admitted solicitor, 1984; with Clifford Chance LLP, 1982–: Managing Partner, London Finance Practice, 1998–2002; Mem., Mgt Cttee, 2002–. Mem., Finance Law Cttee, City of London Solicitors' Co., 1996–. *Publications:* (jtly) Syndicated Lending: Documentation and Practice, 1993, 5th edn 2008. *Recreations:* music, novels, football, golf. *Address:* c/o Clifford Chance LLP, Canary Wharf, E14 5J.

CAMPBELL, Rt Hon. Sir Menzies; *see* Campbell, Rt Hon. Sir W. M.

CAMPBELL, Prof. Michael, OBE 2004; Director, Policy and Research, UK Commission for Employment and Skills, since 2008; *b* 31 Dec. 1948; *s* of Patrick Campbell and Phyllis Campbell (*née* Conn); partner, Prof. Janie Percy-Smith; two *d*. *Educ:* St Anselm's Grammar Sch., Birkenhead; Univ. of Sheffield (BA 1970); Univ. of Lancaster (MA 1972); Univ. of Leeds (MA 1985). Leeds Polytechnic, subseq. Leeds Metropolitan University: Lectr, Sen. Lectr, then Principal Lectr in Econs, 1972–90; Prof. of Policy Studies and Founding Dir, Policy Res. Inst., 1990–2002; Dir, Strategy and Res., Sector Skills Develt Agency, 2002–08. Expert: EC, 1989–2002; OECD, 1996–2002. British Council Dist. Vis. Fellow, Japan, 1993; Visiting Professor: Univ. of Hiroshima, 1993; Univ. of Durham, 2006–. FRSA. *Publications:* Capitalism in the UK, 1981; Capitalism and Public Policy in the UK, 1985; Controversy in Applied Economics, 1989; Local Economic Policy, 1990; Local Labour Markets, 1992; Learn to Succeed: the case for a skills revolution, 2002; Skills and Economic Performance, 2006; over 100 professional and tech. papers, book chapters and pubd reports on unemployment, skills and econ. performance. *Recreations:* cricket, Blackpool Football Club, travel, current affairs. *Address:* 3 Ashwood Villas, Leeds LS6 2EJ. *T:* (0113) 274 4290; *e-mail:* ProfMikeC@aol.com.

CAMPBELL, Niall Gordon; Under Secretary, Civil and Criminal Law Group, Scottish Executive Justice (formerly Scottish Office Home) Department, 1997–2001; *b* 9 Nov. 1941; *s* of Ian M. Campbell and Jean G. Sanderson; *m* 1975, Alison Margaret Rigg; three *s*. *Educ:* Edinburgh Academy; Merton College, Oxford (BA). Entered Scottish Office, 1964; Asst Sec., 1978; posts in Scottish Educn and Scottish Develt Depts; Under Sec., Social Work Services Gp, SHHD, then Scottish Office Home Dept, 1989–97. Mem., Parole Bd for Scotland, 2003–. Chairman: Scottish Assoc. for Study of Offending, 2001–06; SACRO, 2002–07. Mem. Council and Treas., British Trust for Ornithol., 2006–. *Address:* 15 Warriston Crescent, Edinburgh EH3 5LA. *T:* (0131) 556 2895.

CAMPBELL, Nicholas Charles Wilson; QC 2000; a Recorder, since 2000; *b* 8 May 1954; *s* of late Prof. Wilson William Campbell and Pearl Campbell (*née* Ackrill); *m* 1987, Hon. Nicole Montagu. *Educ:* King's Sch., Canterbury; Trinity Coll., Cambridge (BA). Called to the Bar, Inner Temple, 1978. *Address:* 3 Park Court, off Park Cross Street, Leeds LS1 2QH.

CAMPBELL, Maj.-Gen. Peter; *see* Campbell, Maj.-Gen. C. P.

CAMPBELL, Philip Henry Montgomery, PhD; Editor-in-Chief: Nature, since 1995; Nature Publications, since 1995; *b* 19 April 1951; *s* of Hugh and Mary Montgomery Campbell; *m* 1980, Judie Yelton (*d* 1992); two *s*. *Educ:* Shrewsbury Sch.; Bristol Univ. (BSc Aeronautical Engrg 1972); Queen Mary Coll., Univ. of London (MSc Astrophysics 1974); Leicester Univ. (PhD Ionospheric Physics 1978). FRAS 1979; FInstP 1995. Res., Leicester Univ., 1977–79; Asst Editor, 1979–82, Physical Scis Editor, 1982–88, Nature; Founding Editor, Physics World, 1988–95. Dir, Nature Publishing Gp, 1997–. Broadcasts on BBC. Trustee, Cancer Res. UK, 2003–. Hon. DSc Leicester, 1999. *Publications:* papers and articles in learned jls, magazines and newspapers. *Recreations:* music, art galleries. *Address:* Nature, 4 Crinan Street, N1 9XW. *T:* (020) 7833 4000.

CAMPBELL, Quentin; *see* Campbell, J. Q.

CAMPBELL, Prof. Robert James, (Jim); Professor of Education, University of Warwick, 1992–2007, now Emeritus; *b* 19 Dec. 1938; *s* of William Campbell and Elsie Campbell (*née* O'Connor); *m* 1st, 1964, Jennifer Rhodes (marr. diss. 1970); 2nd, 1972, Sarah Miranda Frankland (marr. diss. 2006); two *d*; 3rd, 2007, Wendy Robinson. *Educ:* Hull Univ. (BA Upper 2nd Cl. Classics 1959; PGCE 1960); Bradford Univ. (MSc Educnl Res. 1971). Teacher: Westgate Primary Sch., Newcastle upon Tyne, 1959; Nettleswell Comprehensive Sch., Harlow, 1960–62; Mkt Res. Officer, Mkt Res. Associates, London, 1962–63; Teacher, Latton Bush Comprehensive Sch., Harlow, 1963–64; Lectr, W Suffolk Coll. of Further Educn, Bury St Edmunds, 1964–67; Res. Student, Univ. of Bradford, 1967–68; Res. Officer, Curriculum Res. Unit, Inst. of Educn, Univ. of London, 1968–70; Lectr, Coventry Coll. of Educn, 1970–78; University of Warwick: Lectr, 1978–86; Sen. Lectr, 1986–89; Reader, 1989–92; Dir, Inst. of Educn, 1996–2001; Dir of Res., Nat. Acad. for Gifted and Talented Youth, Univ. of Warwick, 2004–07. FRSA 1998. Phi Delta Kappa, 1974. *Publications:* Developing the Primary School Curriculum, 1985; Humanities in the Primary School, 1989; Breadth and Balance in the Primary School Curriculum, 1991; Primary Teachers at Work, 1994; Secondary Teachers at Work, 1994; The Meaning of Infant Teachers' Work, 1994; Curriculum Reform at Key Stage 1: teacher commitment and policy failure, 1994; Assessing Teacher Effectiveness, 2004; contrib. numerous articles to jls. *Recreations:* wine, whisky, jazz. *Address:* Institute of Education, University of Warwick, Coventry CV4 7AL. *T:* (024) 7652 3850.

CAMPBELL, Sir Robin Auchinbreck, 15th Bt *cr* 1628 (NS); *b* 7 June 1922; *s* of Sir Louis Hamilton Campbell, 14th Bt and Margaret Elizabeth Patricia (*d* 1985), *d* of late Patrick Campbell; *S* father, 1970; *m* 1st, 1948, Rosemary, (Sally) (*d* 1978), *d* of Ashley Dean, Christchurch, NZ; one *s* two *d*; 2nd, 1978, Mrs Elizabeth Gunston (*d* 2005), *d* of Sir Arthur Colegate, Bembridge, IoW. Formerly Lieut (A) RNVR. *Heir: s* Louis Auchinbreck Campbell [*b* 17 Jan. 1953; *m* 1976, Fiona Mary St Clair, *d* of Gordon King; two *d*]. *Address:* 287A Waikawa Road, Picton, New Zealand.

CAMPBELL, Sir Roderick (Duncan Hamilton), 9th Bt *cr* 1831, of Barcaldine and Glenure, Argyllshire; Managing Partner, Barcaldine estates, since 2003; *b* 24 Feb. 1961; *s* of Sir Niall Campbell, 8th Bt and Norma Joyce Campbell (*née* Wiggin); *S* father, 2003; *m* 1989, Jean Caroline (*née* Bicknell); three *d*. *Educ:* Chiswick. Vardon plc, 1988–99; Nat. Trust for Scotland, 1999–2004. *Recreations:* talking to my wife, household maintenance, following sport, family history. *Heir: b* Angus Charles Dundas Campbell, *b* 27 Oct. 1967. *Address:* Barcaldine Castle, Benderloch, by Oban, Argyll PA37 1SA. *T:* (01631) 720598; *e-mail:* r.campbell@barcaldinecastle.co.uk. *Club:* West Bromwich Albion.

CAMPBELL, Ronald, (Ronnie); MP (Lab) Blyth Valley, since 1987; *b* 14 Aug. 1943; *m* 1967, Deirdre (*née* McHale); five *s* one *d*. *Educ:* Ridley High Sch., Blyth. Miner, 1958–86. Member: Blyth Borough Council, 1969–74; Blyth Valley Council, 1974–88 (Chm., Environmental Health Cttee; Vice-Chm., Housing Cttee). Mem., NUM. *Address:* 68 Broadway, Blyth, Northumberland NE24 2PR; House of Commons, SW1A 0AA.

CAMPBELL, Dr Simon Fraser, CBE 2006; FRS 1999; FRSC; FMedSci; Senior Vice-President, Worldwide Discovery and Medicinals R&D Europe, Pfizer Central Research, 1996–98; Director and Board Member, Pfizer Ltd, 1996–98, retired; *b* 27 March 1941; *s* of William Fraser Campbell and Ellen Mary Campbell; *m* 1966, Jill Lewis; two *s*. *Educ:* Birmingham Univ. (BSc 1st Cl. Hons 1962; PhD 1965). FRSC 1985. Postdoctoral Fellow: Univ. Tecnica Santa Maria, Valparaiso, 1966–67; Stanford Univ., Calif, 1968–70; Vis. Prof., Univ. do São Paulo, 1970–72; joined Pfizer Central Research, Sandwich, 1972: staff chemist, 1972–78; Manager, 1978–83, Dir, 1983–92, Discovery Chemistry; Gp Dir, 1992–93, Vice-Pres., 1993–96, Medicinals Discovery. Visiting Professor: Birkbeck Coll., Univ. of London, 1987–90; Univ. of Leeds, 1996–99. Chm., WHO Expert Scientific Adv. Cttee for Malaria, 1999–2003; Mem., BP Technology Council, 1999–2004. Pres., RSC, 2004–06 (Chm., Strategy Cttee, 2001–02). FMedSci 2003. Jt-Ed., Current Opinion in Drug Discovery and Develt, 1998–2004. Member: Acad. Adv. Bd, Dept of Chem., Bristol Univ., 1998–2001; Council, Univ. of Kent, 1999–. Award for Medicinal Chem., RSC, 1989; E. B. Hershberg Award, ACS, 1997; Achievement Award, Industrial Res. Inst. (US), 1997; Individual Achievement Award, CIA, 2006; Salen Medal, 2007. *Publications:* contribs to learned jls; patents. *Recreations:* gardening, travel, wine, active sports player.

CAMPBELL, Susan Catherine, CBE 2003 (MBE 1991); Chairman: UK Sport, since 2003; Youth Sport Trust, since 2005 (Chief Executive, 1995–2005); *b* 10 Oct. 1948. *Educ:* Long Eaton Grammar Sch.; Bedford Coll. of Physical Educn; Univ. of Leicester (Adv. DipEd; MEd). Teacher of Physical Educn, Whalley Range High Sch., Manchester, 1970–72; Dep. Dir of Physical Educn, Univ. of Leicester, 1972–76; Lectr, Dept of Physical Educn and Sports Sci., Univ. of Loughborough, 1976–80; Regl Officer, E Midlands, Sports Council, 1980–84; Dep. Chief Exec., 1984, Chief Exec., 1985–95, Nat. Coaching Foundn. Advr, DCMS and DFES, 2000–03. *Address:* UK Sport, 40 Bernard Street, WC1N 1ST.

[Created a Baroness (Life Peer) 2008 but title not gazetted at time of going to press.]

CAMPBELL, Rt Hon. Sir (Walter) Menzies, Kt 2004; CBE 1987; PC 1999; QC (Scot.) 1982; MP Fife North East, since 1987 (L 1987–88, Lib Dem since 1988); Leader, Liberal Democrats, 2006–07 (Deputy Leader, 2003–06); *b* 22 May 1941; *s* of George Alexander Campbell and Elizabeth Jean Adam Phillips; *m* 1970, Elspeth Mary Urquhart or Grant-Suttie, *d* of Maj.-Gen. R. E. Urquhart, CB, DSO. *Educ:* Hillhead High School, Glasgow; Glasgow Univ. (MA 1962, LLB 1965; President of the Union, 1964–65); Stanford Univ., Calif. Advocate, Scottish Bar, 1968; Advocate Depute, 1977–80; Standing Jun. Counsel to the Army, 1980–82. Member: Clayson Cttee on licensing reform, 1971; Legal Aid Central Cttee, 1983–87; Scottish Legal Aid Bd, 1987; Broadcasting Council for Scotland, 1984–87. Part-time Chairman: VAT Tribunal, 1984–87; Medical Appeal Tribunal, 1985–87. Chm., Scottish Liberal Party, 1975–77; contested (L): Greenock and Port Glasgow, Feb. 1974 and Oct. 1974; E Fife, 1979; NE Fife, 1983; Lib. spokesman on arts, broadcasting and sport, 1987–88; Lib Dem spokesman on arts, broadcasting and sport, 1988, on sport and defence, 1988–94, on foreign affairs and defence, 1994–97, chief spokesman on foreign affairs, 1997–2006, on Europe, 1997–2001, on defence, 1997–2001; Mem., Jt Cabinet Cttee on Constitutional Reform, 1997–2001. Member: Select Cttee on Members Interests, 1987–90; Select Cttee on Trade and Industry, 1990–92; Defence Select Cttee, 1992–99. Member: UK Delegn to N Atlantic Assembly, 1989–; UK Delegn to Parly Assembly, OSCE, 1992–97 and 1999–2006. Mem. Bd, British Council, 1998–2002; Gov., Ditchley Foundn, 1999–; Chancellor, Univ. of St Andrews, 2006–. Chm., Royal Lyceum Theatre Co., Edinburgh, 1984–87. Member: UK Sports Council, 1965–68; Scottish Sports Council, 1971–81. Governor, Scottish Sports Aid Foundn, 1981–90; Trustee: Scottish Internat. Educn Trust, 1984–; London Marathon, 1997–2000. AAA 220 Yards Champion, 1964 and 1967; UK 100 Metres Record Holder, 1967–74; competed at Olympic Games, 1964 and Commonwealth Games, 1966; Captain, UK Athletics Team, 1965 and 1966. *Publication:* Menzies Campbell: my autobiography, 2008. *Recreations:* all sports, reading, music, theatre. *Address:* c/o House of Commons, SW1A

0AA. *T:* (020) 7219 4446. *Club:* Reform.
See also Sir J. Grant-Suttie, Bt.

CAMPBELL, Rt Hon. Sir (William) Anthony, Kt 1988; PC 1999; a Lord Justice of Appeal, Supreme Court of Northern Ireland, 1998–2008; *b* 30 Oct. 1936; *s* of late H. E. Campbell and of Marion Wheeler; *m* 1960, Gail, *e d* of F. M. McKibbin; three *d. Educ:* Campbell Coll., Belfast; Queens' Coll., Cambridge. Called to the Bar, Gray's Inn, 1960, Hon. Bencher, 1995; called to the Bar of NI, 1960 (Bencher, 1983; Chm., Exec. Council, 1985–87). Jun. Counsel to Attorney-Gen. for NI, 1971–74; QC (NI) 1974; Senior Crown Counsel in NI, 1984–88; Judge of the High Ct of Justice, NI, 1988–98. Chairman: Council of Legal Educn in NI, 1994–2008; Judicial Studies Bd, NI, 1995–2008. Governor, Campbell Coll., 1976–98 (Chm., 1984–86). Hon. Fellow, Amer. Bar Foundn, 1997. *Recreations:* sailing, hill walking. *Clubs:* New (Edinburgh); Royal Ulster Yacht.

CAMPBELL, Prof. (William) Bruce, FRCS, FRCP; Consultant in Vascular and General Surgery, Royal Devon and Exeter Hospital, since 1986; Chairman, Interventional Procedures Advisory Committee, National Institute for Health and Clinical Excellence, since 2002; *b* London, 3 Dec. 1950; *s* of Dr William Campbell and Jill Campbell; *m* 2008, Janet Elizabeth Birch; one *s* one *d* from former marriage. *Educ:* Sherborne Sch.; Medical Coll. of St Bartholomew's Hosp., Univ. of London (MB BS Hons 1974; MS). FRCS 1978; FRCP 1996. Registrar, 1979–81, Res. Fellow, 1981–83, Bristol Royal Infirmary; Clin. Lectr in Surgery, Univ. of Oxford, 1983–86. Hon. Professor: Univ. of Exeter, 2000–02; Peninsula Med. Sch., Univs of Exeter and Plymouth, 2003–. Hon. Sec., Vascular Soc. of GB and Ireland, 1998–2002. *Publications:* Complications in Arterial Surgery, 1996; Understanding Varicose Veins, 2000; contrib. surgical and med. jls. *Recreations:* gardening, enjoying our home, walking, military history. *Address:* Royal Devon and Exeter Hospital, Exeter EX2 5DW. *T:* (01392) 410433, *Fax:* (01392) 421889.

CAMPBELL DAVIS, Trevor Fraser; Chief Executive, Oxford Radcliffe Hospitals NHS Trust, since 2003; *b* 16 July 1950; *o s* of Rev. Thomas Campbell Davis and Elizabeth Mary Evelyn, (Maeve), Davis (*née* Fraser); *m* 1978, Anne Eperon; partner, 1991, Dr Gwenda Elizabeth Porter; one *d. Educ:* Methodist Coll., Belfast; UMIST (BSc 1971). Accountant, Coopers and Lybrand, 1971–76; Financial Controller, Howard & Wyndham Gp, 1976–77; Financial Dir, W. H. Allen & Co. Ltd, 1977–80; Dir of Finance and Admin, McGraw-Hill Book Co. (UK) Ltd, 1980–84; Man. Dir, McGraw-Hill Internat. Trng Systems Ltd, 1984–87; Trustee, McGraw-Hill UK Pensions Schemes, 1980–87; Man. Dir, 1987–98, Chm., 1998–, European Communications Gp Ltd. Director: The Not So Silly Trng Co. Ltd, 1992–; Training Media and Copyright Assoc., 1992–2001; Future Health Network Ltd, 2002–. Chairman: Parkside NHS Trust, 1992–98; St Mary's Hosp. NHS Trust, Paddington, 1998–2000; Chief Exec., Whittington Hosp. NHS Trust, 2000–03. Member: London NHS Communications Gp, 1994–96; London Ambulance Service Communications Task Force, 1995–96; Consultant Workforce Review Gp, London, 2001–02; DoH Day Surgery Review Gp, 2001–02; Dr Foster Ethics Cttee, 2001–; Council, UCL Clin. Res. Network, 2001–03; Steering Gp, HFEA, 2002–03. Treasurer: MCB Assoc. in London, 1990– (Pres., 2002–04); Assoc. of UK Univ. Hosps, 2004–. Trustee, NHS Confedn, 2001– (Vice-Chm., 2001–03; Chm., Acute Services Policy Adv. Cttee, 1998–2000, 2001–). Special Trustee, St Mary's Hosp., Paddington, 1998–2000. Chm., British Amateur Radio Teledata Gp, 1978–83. Member Court: Middx Univ., 2000–03; Oxford Brookes Univ., 2004–. AIEE 1975; FInstD 1980; FIAA 1983; FCIM 1985; FRSA 1998. *Publications:* articles in jls on leadership, change mgt and communications. *Recreations:* helping organisations to change, opera, alpine sports, scuba diving, managing collections. *Address:* John Radcliffe Hospital, Headington, Oxford OX3 9DU. *T:* (01865) 221000; *e-mail:* tcd@orh.nhs.uk, tcd@eur.co.uk. *Club:* Downhill Only (Wengen).

CAMPBELL-GRAY, family name of **Lord Gray**.

CAMPBELL-JOHNSTON, Very Rev. Michael Alexander Ninian, SJ; Parish Priest, St Francis of Assisi, Barbados, since 2002; *b* 27 Sept. 1931; *s* of Ninian Campbell-Johnston and Marguerite Antoinette Shakespear. *Educ:* Beaumont College; Séminaire Les Fontaines, France (Lic Phil); LSE (BSc Econ, DipEd); Col. Max. Christi Regis, Mexico (STL). Dir, Guyana Inst. for Social Research and Action, 1967–75; Dir, Social Secretariat, Jesuit Generalate, Rome, 1975–84; Regional Co-ordinator, Jesuit Refugee Service for Mexico and Central America, El Salvador, 1984–87; Provincial, British Province, SJ, 1987–93; Dir, Servicio Jesuita para el Desarrollo, San Salvador, 1994–2002. Editor: Gisra; Promotio Justitiae. *Recreations:* reading, motorbike riding. *Address:* St Francis of Assisi, Mount Standfast, St James, Barbados, W Indies. *T:* 4222431; *e-mail:* sjbar@sunbeach.net.

CAMPBELL-JOHNSTON, Rachel, PhD; Chief Art Critic, The Times, since 2002; *b* 4 Oct. 1963; *d* of Christopher Campbell-Johnston and Mary Campbell-Johnston (*née* Symington); *m* 2007, William Nickerson. *Educ:* Convent of the Sacred Heart, Woldingham; Univ. of Edinburgh (MA 1st Cl. Hons Eng. Lit.; PhD Eng. Lit. 1991). The Times: Dep. Lit. Editor, 1995–97; Obituary Writer, 1997–99; Leader Writer, 1999–2002; Poetry Critic, 1998–. FRSA. *Recreations:* wildlife, wandering about. *Address:* The Times, 1 Pennington Street, E98 1TT. *T:* (020) 7782 5000; *e-mail:* rachel.johnston@thetimes.co.uk.

CAMPBELL-ORDE, Sir John (Alexander); *see* Orde.

CAMPBELL-PRESTON, Dame Frances (Olivia), DCVO 1990 (CVO 1977); Woman of the Bedchamber to HM Queen Elizabeth the Queen Mother, 1965–2002; *b* 2 Sept. 1918; *d* of Lt-Col Arthur Grenfell and Hilda Margaret Grenfell (*née* Lyttelton); *m* 1938, Lt-Col George Patrick Campbell-Preston (*d* 1960), The Black Watch; two *s* two *d. Educ:* St Paul's Girls' Sch. WRNS, 1941–43. Mem., Argyll CC, 1960–64; Chm., Children's Panel, Argyle and Argyll and Bute, 1970–80. *Publication:* (with Hugo Vickers) The Rich Spoils of Time (autobiog.), 2006. *Address:* 93 Whitelands House, Cheltenham Terrace, SW3 4RA.

CAMPBELL-SAVOURS, family name of **Baron Campbell-Savours**.

CAMPBELL-SAVOURS, Baron *cr* 2001 (Life Peer), of Allerdale in the County of Cumbria; **Dale Norman Campbell-Savours;** *b* 23 Aug. 1943; *s* of late John Lawrence and of Cynthia Lorraine Campbell-Savours; *m* 1970, Gudrun Kristin Runolfsdottir; two *s* (and one *s* decd). *Educ:* Keswick Sch.; Sorbonne, Paris. Technical and Export agent, 1964–69; Dir, manufacturing co., 1969–77. Member, Ramsbottom UDC, 1972–73. Mem., UNISON (formerly COHSE), 1970–. Contested (Lab): Darwen Division of Lancashire, Feb. 1974, Oct. 1974; Workington, Nov. 1976. MP (Lab) Workington, 1979–2001. Opposition front bench spokesman on overseas devlt, 1990–92, on agric., 1992–94. Member: Public Accounts Cttee, 1979–90; Select Committees: on Members Interests, 1983–91; on Procedure, 1984–90; on Agric., 1994–97; Intelligence and Security Cttee, 1997–2001; Standards and Privileges Cttee, 1996–2001. *Publications:* The Case for the Supplementary Vote (pamphlet), 1990; research into case for the University of the Lakes, 1996. *Address:* House of Lords, SW1A 0PW.

CAMPBELL-TIECH, Andrew; QC 2003; a Recorder, since 2000; *b* 5 Aug. 1955; *s* of Dr Paul Campbell-Tiech and Maureen (*née* Windsor, who *m* 1973, 3rd Baron Ponsonby of Shulbrede); *m* 1992, Sarah Rosemary Ann Lewis; one *d. Educ:* Highgate Sch.; College of Law. Called to the Bar, Inner Temple, 1978. *Recreations:* piano, violin, paying bills. *Address:* 2 Dyers Buildings, Holborn, EC1N 2JT. *T:* (020) 7404 1881, *Fax:* (020) 7404 1991; *e-mail:* andrew.campbell-tiech@2dyersbuildings.com.

CAMPBELL-WHITE, Martin Andrew; Joint Chief Executive, Askonas Holt Ltd, since 1999; *b* 11 July 1943; *s* of late John Vernon Campbell-White and Hilda Doris (*née* Ash); *m* 1969, Dr Margaret Mary Miles; three *s. Educ:* Dean Close Sch., Cheltenham; St John's Coll., Oxford; Univ. of Strasbourg. Thomas Skinner & Co. Ltd (Publishers), 1964–66; Ibbs & Tillett Ltd (Concert Agents), 1966–72, Dir, 1969–72; Harold Holt Ltd (Concert Agents), subseq. Askonas Holt Ltd, 1972–: Dir, 1973–; Dep. Chm., 1989–92; Chief Exec., 1992–99. Chm., Brit. Assoc. of Concert Agents, 1978–81. Council Mem., London Sinfonietta, 1973–86; Dir, Chamber Orchestra of Europe, 1983–93; Mem. Bd, Première Ensemble, 1991–. Asst Dir, Fest. of German Arts, 1987; Founding Dir, Japan Fest. 1991, 1991. Trustee: Abbado Trust for Young Musicians, 1987–2006; Salzburg Fest. Trust, 1996–2000; Exec. Trustee, Musicians Benevolent Fund, 2006–. Mem. Bd, Riverside Studios, 1988–2000. FRSA 1980. Sebetia Ter Prize for Culture, Naples, 1999. *Recreations:* golf, watching cricket, classical music, travel. *Address:* c/o Askonas Holt Ltd, Lincoln House, 300 High Holborn WC1V 7JH. *T:* (020) 7400 1700, *Fax:* (020) 7400 1799. *Clubs:* Arts, MCC.

CAMPDEN, Viscount; Anthony Baptist Noel; *b* 16 Jan. 1950; *s* and *heir* of 5th Earl of Gainsborough, *qv*; *m* 1972, Sarah Rose (LVO 1996, DL), *er d* of Col T. F. C. Winnington; one *s. Educ:* Ampleforth; Royal Agricultural Coll., Cirencester. *Heir: s* Hon. Henry Robert Anthony Noel [*b* 1 July 1977; *m* 2005, Zara, *yr d* of Geoffrey van Cutsem]. *Address:* Exton Park, Oakham, Rutland, Leics LE15 8AN. *T:* (01572) 812209. *Club:* White's.

CAMPEY, Rachael Elizabeth; freelance journalist and PR consultant; *b* 16 March 1955; *d* of Robert Wilson Campey and Ray Campey (*née* Sherwood). *Educ:* Liverpool Univ. (BA Hons (Medieval and Mod. Hist.) 1976). Reporter, Solihull News, 1978–80; Reporter and Asst News Ed., Coventry Evening Telegraph, 1980–85; Northern Echo: Dep. News Ed., News Ed., Asst Ed., 1985–90; Dep. Ed., 1990–91; Editor: Express and Echo, Exeter, 1991–96; Plymouth Evening Herald, 1996–2001; Dep. News Ed., The Times, 2001–03; Ed., Yorkshire Post, 2003–04; Press Officer, Bishop Burton Coll., 2005–06. *Recreations:* films, walking, history.

CAMPION, Peter James, DPhil; FInstP; physicist; *b* 7 April 1926; *s* of Frank Wallace Campion and Gertrude Alice (*née* Lambert); *m* 1st, 1950, Beryl Grace Stanton (*d* 1995), *e d* of John and Grace Stanton; one *s* one *d* (and one *s* decd); 2nd, 1997, Rev. Patricia Adele Houseman (*née* O'Brien); three step *d. Educ:* Westcliff High Sch., Essex; Exeter Coll., Oxford (MA, DPhil). FInstP 1964. RNVR, 1943. Nuffield Res. Fellow, Oxford, 1954; Chalk River Proj., Atomic Energy of Canada Ltd, 1955; National Physical Lab., Teddington, 1960–86: Supt, Div. of Radiation Science, 1964; Supt, Div. of Mech. and Optical Metrology, 1974; Dep. Dir, 1976. Mem., Comité Consultatif pour les Etalons de Mesure des Rayonnements Ionisante, 1963–79; Chm., Sect. II, reconstituted Comité Consultatif, Mesure des radionucléides, 1970–79; Mem., NACCB, 1984–86. Editor, Internat. Jl of Applied Radiation and Isotopes, 1968–71. *Publications:* A Code of Practice for the Detailed Statement of Accuracy (with A. Williams and J. E. Burns), 1973; A Campion Saga, 2000; Some Campion Wives, 2003; technical and rev. papers in learned jls on neutron capture gamma rays, measurement of radioactivity, and on metrology generally. *Recreations:* watercolour painting, genealogy.

CAMPLING, Very Rev. Christopher Russell; Dean of Ripon, 1984–95; *b* 4 July 1925; *s* of Canon William Charles Campling; *m* 1953, Juliet Marian Hughes; one *s* two *d. Educ:* Lancing Coll.; St Edmund Hall, Oxford (MA; Hons Theol. cl. 2); Cuddesdon Theol. Coll. RNVR, 1943–47. Deacon 1951, priest 1952; Curate of Basingstoke, 1951–55; Minor Canon of Ely Cathedral and Chaplain of King's School, Ely, 1955–60; Chaplain of Lancing Coll., 1960–67; Vicar of Pershore with Pinvin and Wick and Birlingham, 1968–76; RD of Pershore, 1970–76; Archdeacon of Dudley and Director of Religious Education, Diocese of Worcester, 1976–84. Mem., General Synod of Church of England, 1970–92; Chm., House of Clergy, Diocese of Worcester, 1981–84; Chm., Council for the Care of Churches, 1988–94. Lectr, Leeds Parish Church, 1988–. *Publications:* The Way, The Truth and The Life: Vol. 1, The Love of God in Action, 1964; Vol. 2, The People of God in Action, 1964; Vol. 3, The Word of God in Action, 1965; Vol. 4, God's Plan in Action, 1965; also two teachers' volumes; Words of Worship, 1969; The Fourth Lesson, Vol. 1 1973, Vol. 2 1974; The Food of Love, 1997; I Was Glad (memoirs), 2005. *Recreations:* music, drama, golf. *Address:* Pebble Ridge, Aglaia Road, Worthing, West Sussex BN11 5SW. *Club:* Naval.

CÁMPORA, Dr Mario; Argentine Ambassador to Belgium and Luxembourg, 1996–99; *b* 3 Aug. 1930; *m* 1972, Magdalena Teresa María Díaz Gavier; one *s* two *d. Educ:* Nat. Univ. of Rosario, Argentina (Dr in Diplomacy). Argentine Foreign Service, 1955–71 and 1973–75; Internat. Orgns Dept, Foreign Policy Bureau, and Legal Dept, Ministry for Foreign Affairs; has served in Geneva, Washington, The Hague, New Delhi, and as deleg. to UN and OAS; Mem., Justicialist Party, active in politics, 1971–73, 1975–; Ambassador Extraordinary, Argentine Special Mission for Disarmament, Geneva, 1985; Sec. of State, Ministry for Foreign Affairs, 1989–90; Argentine Ambassador to UK, 1990–94. *Publications:* articles on foreign policy and international relations.

CAMPOS, Prof. Christophe Lucien, OBE 1994; Director, British Institute in Paris, 1978–2003; *b* 27 April 1938; *s* of Lucien Antoine Campos and Margaret Lilian (*née* Dunn); *m* 1977, Lucy Elizabeth Mitchell; one *s* two *d*; two *d* by former marriage. *Educ:* Lycée Lamoricière, Oran; Lycée Français de Londres; Lycée Henri IV, Paris; Gonville and Caius Coll., Cambridge. LèsL (Paris), PhD (Cantab). Lector in French, Gonville and Caius Coll., 1959; Lecturer in French: Univ. of Maryland, 1963; Univ. of Sussex, 1964; Lectr in English, Univ. i Oslo, 1969; Prof. of French, University Coll., Dublin, 1974. Gen. Editor, Franco-British Studies, 1988–2004. Chevalier de l'Ordre des Arts et des Lettres (France), 1988. *Publications:* The View of France, 1964; L'Enseignement de la civilisation française, 1988; contribs to Th. Qly, TLS, Univs Qly, Franco-British Studies. *Recreations:* bees, football, gastronomy, navigation. *Address:* La Hocherie, 86230 Sossay, France.

CAMPRUBI, Catherine Jane; *see* Royle, C. J.

CAMRE, Henning Niels Juel; Knight Commander, Order of the Dannebrog, 2005; Chief Executive, Danish Film Institute, since 1998; *b* 15 Nov. 1938; *s* of Sigfred N. J. Camre and Carna (*née* Petersen); *m* 1st, 1967, Merete Friis (marr. diss.); one *d*; 2nd, 1978, Janne Giese (marr. diss.); one *d* and one adopted *d*; 3rd, 2005, Regitze Oppenhejm. *Educ:* Univ. of Copenhagen; Nat. Film Sch. of Denmark (Dip. in Cinematography). Dir of Photography (feature and documentary film), 1968–88; Director: Nat. Film Sch. of Denmark, 1975–92; Nat. Film and TV Sch., UK, 1992–98. Adjunct Prof., Copenhagen Business Sch., 2005. Chairman: Nordic Film Council, 1979–89; Danish State Film Studio,

1989–92; Centre International de Liaison des Ecoles de Cinéma et de Télévision: Mem., Exec. Council, 1980–86; Chm., Programme for Developing Countries, 1982–2002; Vice-Pres., 1986–2002; Hon. Mem., 2002. Founding Pres., European Film and Film Policy Think Tank, 2006. Chm., Cultural Area, Danish Nat. UNESCO Commn, 1999–. Chevalier de l'Ordre des Arts et des Lettres (France), 1990; Gloria Artis Medal (Poland), 2005. *Publications:* Bridging the Gap, 1982; Film and Television Training in Indonesia, 1985; Asia-Pacific Film and Television Schools, 1991. *Recreation:* cycling. *Address:* Callisensvej 25, 2900 Hellerup, Denmark; Danish Film Institute, Gothersgade 55, 1123 Copenhagen K, Denmark.

CAMROSE, 4th Viscount *cr* 1941, of Hackwood Park, Southampton; **Adrian Michael Berry;** Bt 1921; Baron 1929; *b* 15 June 1937; *er s* of Baron Hartwell (Life Peer), MBE, TD (who disclaimed his hereditary peerages for life, 1995); *S* father, 2001; *m* 1967, Marina Beatrice, *d* of Cyrus Sulzberger; one *s* one *d*. *Educ:* Eton; Christ Church, Oxford. Science Corresp., Daily Telegraph, 1977–96; Consulting Editor (Science), Daily Telegraph, 1996–. *Publications:* The Next Ten Thousand Years, 1974; The Iron Sun, 1977; From Apes to Astronauts, 1980; High Skies and Yellow Rain, 1983; The Super-Intelligent Machine, 1983; Koyama's Diamond, 1984; Ice With Your Evolution, 1986; Labyrinth of Lies, 1986; Harrap's Book of Scientific Anecdotes, 1989; (ed) Eureka!: The Book of Scientific Anecdotes, 1993; The Next 500 Years, 1995; Galileo and the Dolphins, 1996; The Giant Leap, 1999. *Heir: s* Hon. Jonathan William Berry [*b* 26 Feb. 1970; *m* 1996, Aurélie E. C. Molin; two *s* two *d*]. *Address:* Apt 3, 81 Holland Park, W11 3RZ. *T:* (020) 7792 2982.

See also N. W. Berry.

CANADA, Primate of; *see* Quebec, Archbishop of, (RC).

CANADA, Metropolitan of the Ecclesiastical Province of; *see* Quebec, Archbishop of.

CANAVAN, Dennis Andrew; Member (Ind.) Falkirk West, Scottish Parliament, 1999–2007; *b* 8 Aug. 1942; *s* of late Thomas and Agnes Canavan; one *s* one *d* (and three *s* decd). *Educ:* St Columba's High Sch., Cowdenbeath; Edinburgh Univ. (BSc Hons, DipEd). Head of Maths Dept, St Modan's High Sch., Stirling, 1970–74; Asst Head, Holy Rood High Sch., Edinburgh, 1974. District Councillor, 1973–74; Leader of Labour Gp, Stirling District Council, 1974; Member: Stirling Dist Educn Sub-cttee, 1973–74; Stirlingshire Youth Employment Adv. Cttee, 1972–74. Sec., W Stirlingshire Constituency Labour Party, 1972–74; Labour Party Agent, Feb. 1974; Treasurer, Scottish Parly Lab. Gp, 1976–79, Vice-Chm., 1979–80, Chm., 1980–81. MP (Lab 1974–99, Ind. 1999–2000) W Stirlingshire, Oct. 1974–1983, Falkirk W, 1983–2000. Member: H of C Select Cttee on For. Affairs, 1982–97, on Internat. Develt, 1997–99; Chair: PLP NI Cttee, 1989–97; Parly Br., EIS, 1983–2000; Vice-Chm., All-Party Hospice Gp, 1992–2000; Founder and Convener, All-Party Parly Scottish Sports Gp, 1987–99; Mem., British-Irish Inter-Parly Body, 1992–2000. Scottish Parliament: Mem., European and External Relns Cttee, 1999–2007; Founder and Convener, Sports Gp, 1999–2007. Pres., Ramblers Scotland. *Publications:* contribs to various jls on educn and politics. *Recreations:* hill walking, horse riding, running, swimming, reading, football (Scottish Univs football internationalist, 1966–67 and 1967–68; Hon. Pres., Milton Amateurs FC). *Address:* Ardsonas, Sauchieburn, Bannockburn, Stirlingshire FK7 9PZ. *T:* (01786) 812581.

CANAVAN, Vincent Joseph; Sheriff of North Strathclyde at Greenock, since 2001; *b* 13 Dec. 1946; *s* of James Canavan and Catherine Ludivine Brogan; *m* 1973, Mary Allison; three *s* three *d*. *Educ:* St Aloysius Coll., Glasgow; Univ. of Glasgow (LLB Hons 1968). Qualified as Solicitor, 1970; passed Advocate, 1980. Sheriff of S Strathclyde, Dumfries and Galloway at Hamilton, 1987–2001. Member: Victim Support (Scotland) Hamilton Court Project Working Party, 1990–94; Strathclyde Regl Council Cons. Cttee on Social Work in criminal justice system, 1991–96; Council, Sheriffs' Assoc., 1997–2000; Working Party on law of foreshore, 2000. Chm., Lanarks Br., Scottish Assoc. for Study of Delinquency, 1992–95 (Vice-Chm., 1991–92). *Recreations:* reading history, Italian cuisine, visiting art exhibitions. *Club:* Glasgow Art.

CANBERRA AND GOULBURN, Archbishop of, (RC), since 2006; **Most Rev. Mark Benedict Coleridge;** *b* 25 Sept. 1948; *s* of Bernard Coleridge. *Educ:* Rostrevor Coll., Adelaide; St Kevin's Coll., Melbourne; Melbourne Univ. (BA 1980); Corpus Christi Coll., Melbourne; Pontifical Biblical Inst., Rome (LSS 1984; DSS 1991). Ordained priest, 1974; Asst Priest, E Doncaster, Ashburton, Pascoe Vale, Melbourne, 1975–80; Catholic Theological College, Melbourne: Lectr in Biblical Studies, 1985–88 and 1991–97; Master, 1995–97; Official, First Section, Secretariat of State, Vatican, 1998–2002; Aux. Bishop of Melbourne, 2002–06. Member: Pontifical Council for Culture, 2004; Bishops' Commission: for Liturgy, 2006, for Doctrine and Morals, 2006. Chairman: Roman Missal Editl Commn, 2004–; Internat. Commn for the Preparation of an English-language Lectionary, 2005–. *Publication:* The Birth of the Lukan Narrative, 1993. *Address:* GPO Box 89, Canberra, ACT 2601, Australia.

CANDELAS, Prof. Philip, DPhil; Rouse Ball Professor of Mathematics, University of Oxford, and Fellow of Wadham College, Oxford since 1999; *b* 24 Oct. 1951; *m* Xenia de la Ossa. *Educ:* Christ's Coll., Cambridge (BA 1973); Wadham Coll., Oxford (DPhil 1977). Jun. Res. Fellow, Balliol Coll., Oxford, 1975–76; Res. Asst, 1976–77, Asst Prof., 1977–82, Associate Prof., 1982–89, Prof., 1989–99, Dept of Physics, Univ. of Texas, Austin. *Publications:* papers in learned jls. *Address:* Wadham College, Oxford OX1 3PN.

CANDLIN, Prof. Christopher Noel; Senior Research Professor in Linguistics, Macquarie University, Sydney, part-time 2002–06, full-time, since 2006; *b* 31 March 1940; *s* of late Edwin Frank Candlin, OBE and of Nora Candlin (*née* Letts); *m* 1964, Sally (*née* Carter); one *s* three *d*. *Educ:* Jesus Coll., Oxford (MA); Univ. of London (PGCE); Yale Univ. (MPhil). Research Associate, Univ. of Leeds, 1967–68; University of Lancaster: Lectr, 1968, later Sen. Lectr; Prof. of Linguistics and Modern English Language, 1981–87; Macquarie University, Sydney: Prof. and Chm., Linguistics Dept, 1987–98; Exec. Dir, Nat. Centre for Eng. Lang. Teaching and Res., 1988–98; Dir, Centre for Lang. in Social Life, 1993–98; Adjunct Prof. of Linguistics, 1998; Chair Prof. of Applied Linguistics and Dir, Centre for English Lang. Educn and Communication Res., City Univ. of Hong Kong, 1998–2002; Prof. of Applied Linguistics (pt-time), Open Univ., 2002–05. Visiting Professor: Univ. of Giessen, 1975; East-West Centre, Honolulu, 1978; Ontario Inst. for Studies in Educn, Toronto, 1983; Univ. of Hawaii at Manoa, 1984; Univ. of Melbourne, 1985; Jyväskylä Univ., Finland, 1993; Univ. of Wales, Cardiff, 1995 (Hon. Prof., 1995); Adjunct Prof., Univ. of Technol., Sydney, 1998. General Editor: Applied Linguistics and Language Study; Language in Social Life; Language Teacher Educn Scheme; Language Teaching Methodology Series; Applied Linguistics in Action; Advances in Applied Linguistics. Pres., Internat. Assoc. of Applied Linguistics, 1996–2002. FRSA. Hon. PhD Jyväskylä, 1996. *Publications:* Challenges, 1978; The Communicative Teaching of English, 1981; Computers in English Language Teaching and Research, 1985; Language Learning Tasks, 1986; Language, Learning and Community, 1989; English at Work, vol. 1, 1991, vol. 2, 1992; (ed jtly) Australian Learners' Dictionary, 1997; Writing: texts, processes and practices, 1999. *Recreations:* theatre, concerts, sailing, cooking. *Address:* Department of Linguistics, Macquarie University, Sydney, NSW 2109, Australia.

CANDLISH, Thomas Tait, FREng; Managing Director, George Wimpey PLC, 1978–85 (Director, 1973–85); *b* 26 Nov. 1926; *s* of John Candlish and Elizabeth (*née* Tait); *m* 1964, Mary Trinkwon; two *s*. *Educ:* Perth Acad.; Glasgow Univ. (BSc Eng). FICE 1971; FREng (FEng 1980). Served RE, 1946–49 (commnd). Student Engr, George Wimpey & Co. Ltd, 1944–46; rejoined Wimpey, 1951; served in: Borneo, 1951–54; Papua New Guinea, 1955–57; Arabian Gulf area, 1958–62; W Africa, 1962–65; Director: Wimpey Internat., 1973–85 (Chm., 1979–85); Wimpey ME & C, 1973–85; Wimpey Marine Ltd, 1975–85 (Chm., 1979–85); Brown & Root-Wimpey Highlands Fabricators, 1974–89 (Chm., 1981–86); British Smelter Constructions Ltd, 1977–83 (Chm., 1977–83); Hill Samuel Developments, 1978–85; A & P Appledore Holdings, 1979–85; Brown & Root (UK) Ltd, 1985–89; OGC Internat., 1993–97; Chairman: Howard Humphreys Gp Ltd, 1987–89; Historic Cars Ltd, 1989–97. Chm., Export Gp for Constructional Industries, 1983–85; Member: EDC for Civil Engrg, 1979–82; British Overseas Trade Bd, 1984–87. *Recreations:* motor sport, golf. *Address:* Tithe Cottage, Dorney Wood Road, Burnham, Bucks SL1 8EQ. *Clubs:* Royal Automobile; Denham Golf.

CANDY, Elizabeth Mary; Head Mistress, The Lady Eleanor Holles School, Hampton, 1981–2004; *b* 12 Oct. 1942; *d* of late Donald Glen Candy and Phyllis Mary Candy (*née* Denbury). *Educ:* Merrywood Grammar Sch., Bristol; Westfield Coll., London (BSc 1965). Chemistry Mistress then Jt Head of Science, Bromley High Sch., 1965–71; Head of Science then Second Mistress, Putney High Sch., 1971–81. Mem. Council, Royal Holloway, London Univ., 1995–2003. FRSA 1994. Gov., Old Vicarage Sch., Richmond, 2005–. Dame Chevalier, Ordre des Coteaux de Champagne, 1998. *Recreations:* opera, reading, France and French wine, photography, cycling, tennis, golf. *Address:* Miranda Cottage, 5 St John's Road, East Molesey, Surrey KT8 9JH. *T:* (020) 8941 3066. *Club:* Cripplegate Ward.

CANDY, Lorraine Ann; Editor, Elle, since 2004; *b* 8 July 1968; *d* of A. R. Butler and V. S. Butler; *m* 2000, C. James Candy. *Educ:* Liskeard Comprehensive Sch., Cornwall. Feature writer, Daily Mirror, 1990–93; Woman's Editor: Sun, 1993; Today, 1993–95; Associate Ed., Marie Claire mag., 1995–97; Dep. Ed., Times Saturday Mag., 1997–98; Ed., B mag., 1998–99; Features Ed., The Times, 1999–2000; Ed., Cosmopolitan, 2000–04. *Recreations:* riding, shopping. *Address:* Elle, Hachette Filipacchi UK, 64 North Row, W1K 7LL.

CANDY, Stuart Graham C.; *see* Cull-Candy.

CANE, Anthony Richard Godwin, FRICS; Senior Partner, Strutt & Parker, since 2003; *b* 4 Oct. 1948; *s* of Dr C. S. Cane, VRD, MRCP and Rachel Cane; *m* 1975, Susan Mary Mortimer; two *s*. *Educ:* Eton Coll.; RAC, Cirencester. FRICS 1986. With Strutt & Parker, 1973–, Partner, 1987. Dir, 2006–, Chm., 2008–, Epsom Downs Racecourse. Trustee, Childwick Trust, 2000–. *Recreations:* racing, shooting, Chelsea Football Club. *Address:* c/o Strutt & Parker, 37 Davies Street, W1K 4SP. *T:* (020) 7629 7282, *Fax:* (020) 7499 1657; *e-mail:* anthony.cane@struttandparker.co.uk. *Clubs:* Boodle's, Pratt's, Jockey.

CANE, Prof. Violet Rosina; Professor of Mathematical Statistics, University of Manchester, 1971–81, now Emeritus; *b* 31 Jan. 1916; *d* of Tubal George Cane and Annie Louisa Lansdell. *Educ:* Newnham Coll., Cambridge (MA, Dipl. in Math. Stats). BoT, 1940; Univ. of Aberdeen, 1941; FO, 1942; Min. of Town and Country Planning, 1946; Statistician to MRC Applied Psychol. Unit, 1948; Queen Mary Coll., London, 1955; Fellow, Newnham Coll., Cambridge, 1957; Lectr, Univ. of Cambridge, 1960. Mem., UGC, 1974–79. Mem., Cambridge CC, 1965–72, 1982–90 (Hon. Councillor, 1990). Hon. MSc Manchester, 1974. *Publications:* (contrib.) Current Problems in Animal Behaviour, 1961; (contrib.) Perspectives in Probability and Statistics, 1975; papers in Jl of Royal Stat. Soc., Animal Behaviour, and psychol jls. *Recreation:* supporting old houses.

CANHAM, Paul George, LVO 1991; JP; Official Secretary to Governor-General of New Zealand, 1985–90; *b* 25 Oct. 1933; *s* of George Ernest Canham and Ella Mary (*née* Mackenzie); *m* 1964, Diane Alderton; one *s* one *d*. *Educ:* Timaru Boys' High Sch.; Victoria Univ. of Wellington (BA, MA Hons History). Teacher: Pomfret Sch., Conn., 1957; Matamata Coll., NZ, 1960; Hauraki Plains Coll., 1967; Heretaunga Coll., 1969; Dep. Prin., Hutt Valley High Sch., 1973; Prin., Wanganui High Sch., 1979. Dist Manager, Baucau, Timor Leste, UN Population Fund Nat. Census, 2004. JP Hawkes Bay, 1991. *Publication:* The Return (novel), 1999. *Recreation:* bridge. *Address:* 106A Wharerangi Road, Greenmeadows, Napier 4112, New Zealand. *T:* (6) 8445823.

CANN, Anthony; *see* Cann, J. W. A.

CANN, Charles Richard, CB 1996; Deputy Secretary, Ministry of Agriculture, Fisheries and Food, 1991–96; *b* 3 Feb. 1937; *s* of Charles Alfred Cann and Grace Elizabeth Cann; *m* 1979, Denise Ann Margaret Love; two *s*. *Educ:* Merchant Taylors' Sch., Northwood, Middx; St John's Coll., Cambridge (MA). Asst Principal, MAFF, 1960, Principal 1965; Cabinet Office, 1969–71; Asst Sec., MAFF, 1971; Under Sec., 1981; Fisheries Sec., MAFF, 1987–91. Mem. Policy Cttee, CPRE, 1996–2002. *Address:* 50 St Peters Street, N1 8JT.

CANN, (John William) Anthony; Partner, 1978–2006, Senior Partner, 2001–06, Linklaters; *b* 21 July 1947; *s* of late Dr John Cann and Enid Grace Cann (*née* Long); *m* 1973, Anne Clausen; two *s* one *d*. *Educ:* Shrewsbury Sch.; Southampton Univ. (LLB Law 1969); Coll. of Law/Law Soc. (Hons). With Linklaters, 1970–2006: articled clerk, 1970–72; Associate Solicitor, 1972–78; NY Office, 1975–82; Hd of Corporate Dept, 1995–2000. Dir, Smiths News PLC, 2006–. Dir, Panmure Gordon & Co. plc, 2007–. Chm., Changing Faces, 2007–; Trustee, Adventure Capital Fund, 2006–. Governor, Haberdashers' Aske's Fedn, 2007–. *Publications:* Mergers and Acquisitions Handbook Part D, 1986; European Mergers and Acquisitions (United Kingdom), 1991. *Recreations:* sport, photography. *Address:* Langrick, 13 Murray Road, SW19 4PD. *T:* (020) 8946 6731; *e-mail:* anthony.cann@yahoo.com. *Clubs:* Athenæum, MCC; Wimbledon Racquet and Fitness.

CANN, Prof. Johnson Robin, ScD; FRS 1995; Professor of Earth Sciences, University of Leeds, 1989–2003, Senior Fellow, since 2003; *b* 18 Oct. 1937; *er s* of Johnson Ralph Cann and (Ethel) Mary (*née* Northmore); *m* 1st, 1963, Janet Hamson (*d* 1994); two *s*; 2nd, 2001, Helen Dunham. *Educ:* St Alban's Sch.; St John's Coll., Cambridge (MA, PhD, ScD). Research Fellow, St John's Coll., 1962–66; post-doctoral work in Depts of Mineralogy and Petrology, and Geodesy and Geophysics, Cambridge, 1962–66; Dept of Mineralogy, British Museum (Natural History), 1966–68; Lectr, then Reader, School of Environmental Sciences, Univ. of East Anglia, 1968–77; J. B. Simpson Prof. of Geology, Univ. of Newcastle upon Tyne, 1977–89; current research in hot springs of mid-ocean ridges, seafloor volcanoes, rocks of ocean floor, creation of oceanic crust, obsidian in archaeology. Member, then Chm., ocean crust panel, 1975–78, UK rep. on planning cttee, 1978–84, Jt Oceanographic Instns for Deep Earth Sampling; co-chief scientist on Glomar Challenger, 1976 and 1979; Adjunct Scientist, Woods Hole Oceanographic Instn, 1987–; Chief Scientist, British Mid-Ocean Ridge Initiative, 1992–2001. Chm., UK Ocean Drilling Program Grants Cttee, 1987–90. Mem., UGC physical sciences sub-cttee, 1982–88. Murchison Medal, Geol Soc. of London, 1990. *Publications:* papers in jls of earth science and archaeology. *Address:* Department of Earth Sciences, University of Leeds, Leeds LS2 9JT. *T:* (01931) 712429; *e-mail:* j.cann@see.leeds.ac.uk.

CANN, Paul Lewis; Director, Policy, Research and International Department, Help the Aged, since 2000; *b* 29 Aug. 1953; *s* of John Samuel Jones Cann and Eileen Dorothy Jean (*née* Daymond John); *m* 1981, Phillippa Terese Cook; one *s* one *d*. *Educ:* Tiffin Sch.; King's Coll., Cambridge (BA Hons 1975; MA 1979); Westminster Coll., Oxford (Cert Ed 1976). Schoolmaster: Christchurch Cathedral Sch., 1976–78; Abingdon Sch., 1978–81; Civil Service, 1981–88: Asst Private Secretary to: Lord Privy Seal, 1982–83; Minister for Arts, 1983–84; Principal, Cabinet Office, 1985–88; Sen. Consultant, Hay Mgt Consultants, 1988–90; Hd of Personnel, Newspaper Publishing plc, 1990–92; Exec. Dir, British Dyslexia Assoc., 1992–97; Chief Exec., Nat. Autistic Soc., 1997–2000. Vis. Fellow, Inst. of Ageing, Oxford Univ., 2004–07. Trustee: Contact a Family, 2001–06; Oxford Lieder, 2006–. Corporate Mem., Inst. Personnel and Develt, 1986. *Recreations:* singing, drinking wine, enjoying Hook Norton. *Address:* 7 Bell Hill, Hook Norton, Oxon OX15 5NG. *T:* (01608) 737282.

CANNADINE, Prof. David Nicholas, DPhil, LittD; FRHistS; FBA 1999; FSA; FRSL; Whitney J. Oates Senior Research Scholar, Humanities Council, Princeton University, since 2008; *b* 7 Sept. 1950; *s* of Sydney Douglas Cannadine and Dorothy Mary Cannadine (*née* Hughes); *m* 1982, Linda Jane Colley, *qv*; one *d* decd. *Educ:* King Edward's Five Ways Sch., Birmingham; Clare Coll., Cambridge (schol.; BA 1st cl. Hons 1972; MA 1975; LittD 1993); Princeton Univ. (Jane Eliza Procter Vis. Fellow); St John's Coll., Oxford (Sen. Schol.; DPhil 1975). FRHistS 1981; FSA 2005. Cambridge University: Res. Fellow, St John's Coll., 1975–77; Asst Lectr, 1976–80, Lectr, 1980–88, in Hist.; Christ's College: Fellow, 1977–88 (Hon. Fellow, 2005); Dir of Studies in Hist., 1977–83; Tutor, 1979–81; Prof. of History, 1988–92, Moore Collegiate Prof. of History, 1992–98, Columbia Univ.; Prof. of History and Dir, 1998–2003, Queen Elizabeth the Queen Mother Prof. of British History, 2003–08, Hon. Fellow, 2005, Inst. of Historical Res., Sch. of Advanced Study, Univ. of London. Dist. Sen. Fellow, Sch. of Advanced Study, Univ. of London, 2008; Hon. Prof., Univ. of London, 2008. Vis. Mem., Inst. for Advanced Study, Princeton, 1980–81; Vis. Prof., Birkbeck Coll., London Univ., 1995–97; Vis. Scholar, Pembroke Coll., Cambridge, 1997; Visiting Fellow: Whitney Humanities Center, Yale Univ., 1995–98; Council of the Humanities, Princeton Univ., 2003–05; ANU, 2005; Nat. Humanities Center, N Carolina, 2006; Adjunct Prof., ANU, 2006–. Lectures: Motitz, Kalamazoo, 1992; first Leonard Hastings Schoff, Columbia Univ., 1993; Hayes Robinson, RHC, 1994; Raleigh, British Acad., 1997; Charles Edmonson, Baylor Univ., 1997; George Orwell Meml, Sheffield Univ., 1997; Curtis, Univ. of Central Lancs, 1998; Earl, Keele, 1999; Beall-Russell, Baylor Univ., 1999; Esmée Fairbairn, Lancaster Univ., 1999; London Liby, 2001; Carnochan, Stanford Univ., 2001; Throckmorton, Lewis and Clark Coll., 2001; Burrows, Univ. of Essex, 2002; Rothschild Archive, 2002; Linbury, Nat. Gall., 2002; Golden Jubilee, Univ. of Newcastle, 2002; Dickinson, Newcomen Soc., 2003; T. S. Eliot, Washington Univ., St Louis, 2003; Roy Jenkins Meml, RSL, 2004; Thorpe, Princeton Univ., 2004; PSCP, Getty Res. Inst., 2006; Ramsay Murray, Selwyn Coll., Cambridge, 2006; History of Parlt, 2006; University, Carnegie-Mellon, 2006; George Macaulay Trevelyan, Cambridge Univ., 2007; John Hayes Meml, NPG, 2007; Eaton, Boston Athenaeum 2008. Fellow: Berkeley Coll., Yale Univ., 1985–; ACLS, 1990–91; J. P. Morgan Liby, NY, 1992–98. Regular broadcaster on wireless and television; presenter, A Point of View, BBC Radio 4, 2005–. Member: Eastern Regl Cttee, Nat. Trust, 2001–; Cttee of Mgt, Centre for Res. in the Arts, Social Scis and Humanities, Univ. of Cambridge, 2001–03; Archives Task Force, 2002–04; Royal Mint Adv. Cttee, 2004–; Rev. of 30 Year Rule, 2007–08. Historical Consultant, Cabinet War Rooms, 2002–04; Historical Advr, Ian Fleming Centenary Exhibn, Imperial War Mus., 2007–08. Comr, English Heritage, 2001– (Chm., Blue Plaques Panel, 2006–). Vice-President: British Records Soc., 1998–; RHistS, 1998–2002; Pres., Worcs Histl Soc., 1999–. Mem. Adv. Council, PRO, then Nat. Archives, 1999–2004; London University: Member Advisory Council: Warburg Inst. (formerly Adv. Bd), 1998–2003; Inst. of US Studies, 1999–2003; Inst. of English Studies, 2000–03; Inst. of Latin Amer. Studies, 2000–03; Inst. for Study of the Americas, 2004–08. Trustee: Kennedy Meml Trust, 2000–; Nat. Portrait Gall., 2000– (Vice-Chm., 2003–05; Chm., 2005–); British Empire and Commonwealth Mus., 2003–; Rothschild Archive Trust, 2005–. Patron, Attingham Trust, 2006–. Gov., Ipswich Sch., 1982–88. General Editor: Studies in Modern Hist., 1979–2002; Penguin Hist. of Britain, 1989–; Penguin Hist. of Europe, 1991–; Historical Res., 1998–2003; Reviews in History, 1998–2003; History Compass, 2000–03; Member, Editorial Board: Urban Hist. Yearbook, 1979–83; Past and Present, 1983– (Vice Chm., 2000–); Midland Hist., 1985–88; Twentieth Century British Hist., 1990–2007; Rural Hist., 1995–; Prospect, 1995–; Library Hist., 1998–; England's Landscape, 2000–06; History of Parliament, 2004–. FRSA 1998; FRSL 1999. Hon. DLitt: UEA, 2001; South Bank, 2001; Birmingham, 2002. T. S. Ashton Prize, Econ. Hist. Soc., 1977; Silver Jubilee Prize, Agricl Hist. Soc., 1977; Dean's Dist. Award in the Humanities, Columbia Univ., 1996; Dickinson Medal, Newcomen Soc., 2003; Tercentenary Medal, Soc. of Antiquaries, 2008. *Publications:* Lords and Landlords: the aristocracy and the towns 1774–1967, 1980; (ed and contrib.) Patricians, Power and Politics in Nineteenth-Century Towns, 1982; (ed jtly and contrib.) H. J. Dyos, Exploring the Urban Past, 1982; (ed jtly and contrib.) Rituals of Royalty: power and ceremonial in traditional societies, 1987; The Pleasures of the Past, 1989; (ed and contrib.) Winston Churchill's Famous Speeches, 1989; (ed jtly and contrib.) The First Modern Society: essays in English history in honour of Lawrence Stone, 1989; The Decline and Fall of the British Aristocracy (Lionel Trilling Prize), 1990; G. M. Trevelyan: a life in history, 1992; Aspects of Aristocracy: grandeur and decline in modern Britain, 1994; (ed jtly and contrib.) History and Biography: essays in honour of Derek Beales, 1996; Class in Britain, 1998; History in Our Time, 1998; Ornamentalism: how the British saw their Empire, 2001; In Churchill's Shadow: confronting the past in modern Britain, 2002; (ed and contrib.) What is History Now?, 2002; (ed and contrib.) History and the Media, 2004; (ed and contrib.) Admiral Lord Nelson: his context and legacy, 2005; (ed and contrib.) Trafalgar in History: a battle and its afterlife, 2006; Mellon: an American life, 2006; The National Portrait Gallery: a brief outline history, 2007; (ed and contrib.) Empire, the Sea and Global History: Britain's maritime world 1763–1833, 2007; (ed jtly and contrib.) History and Philanthropy: past, present, future, 2008; Making History Now and Then: discoveries, controversies and explorations, 2008; numerous contribs to other books and learned jls. *Recreations:* life, laughter. *Address:* Department of History, Dickinson Hall, Princeton University, NJ 08544, USA. *Clubs:* Athenæum; Norfolk (Norwich); Century (NY).

CANNAN, David; *see* Cannan, J. D. Q.

CANNAN, Denis; dramatist and script writer; *b* 14 May 1919; *s* of late Captain H. J. Pullein-Thompson, MC, and late Joanna Pullein-Thompson (*née* Cannan); *m* 1st, 1946, Joan Ross (marr. diss.); two *s* one *d*; 2nd, 1965, Rose Evansky; he changed name to Denis Cannan, by deed poll, 1964. *Educ:* Eton. A Repertory factotum, 1937–39. Served War of 1939–45, Queen's Royal Regt, Captain (despatches). Actor at Citizens' Theatre, Glasgow, 1946–48. *Publications: plays:* Max (prod. Malvern Festival), 1949; Captain Carvallo (Bristol Old Vic and St James's Theatres), 1950; Colombe (trans. from Anouilh), New Theatre, 1951; Misery Me!, Duchess, 1955; You and Your Wife, Bristol Old Vic, 1955; The Power and The Glory (adaptation from Graham Greene), Phoenix Theatre, 1956, and Phœnix Theatre, New York, 1958; Who's Your Father?, Cambridge Theatre, 1958; US (original text), Aldwych, 1966; adapted Ibsen's Ghosts, Aldwych, 1966; One at Night, Royal Court, 1971; The Ik (adaptation and collaboration), 1975; Dear Daddy, Oxford Festival and Ambassadors, 1976 (Play of the Year award, 1976); the screenplays of several films; plays for TV and radio, adaptations for TV series. *Address:* 30 Park Gate, Somerhill Road, Hove, Sussex BN3 1RL.

See also J. M. W. Pullein-Thompson.

CANNAN, (John) David (Qualtrough); Speaker, House of Keys, Isle of Man, 2000–01; MHK (Ind) Michael, since 1982; *b* 24 Aug. 1936; *s* of Rev. Canon Charles Alfred Cannan and Mary Eleanor Cannan (*née* Qualtrough); *m* 1966, Patricia Mary, *d* of Bernard and Jean Roberts, Taranaki, NZ; three *s* one *d*. *Educ:* King William's Coll., IOM. Martin's Bank, IOM, 1953–54; Nat. Service, RA, 1954–56; tea and rubber industries., Ceylon, 1956–61, Malaya, 1961–67; business interests, Berks, 1967–79. Mem. (C), Bradfield DC, 1970–74; returned to IOM, 1980; Minister for Treasury, 1986–89; Chm., Financial Supervision Commn, 1987–89; Vice-Chm., Public Accounts Commn, 1997–2000. *Recreations:* gardening, bee-keeping, Manx history. *Address:* Legislative Buildings, Douglas, Isle of Man IM1 3PW. *T:* (01624) 685500; *e-mail:* david.cannan@parliament.org.im; White Gables, Curragh Road, Ballaugh, Isle of Man IM7 5BG. *T:* and *Fax:* (01624) 897926.

CANNELL, Prof. Robert Quirk; Director, Virginia Agricultural Experiment Station and Associate Dean for Research, Virginia Polytechnic Institute and State University, 1994–99, now Emeritus; *b* 20 March 1937; *s* of William Watterson Cannell and Norah Isabel Corjeag; *m* 1962, Edwina Anne Thornborough; two *s*. *Educ:* King's Coll., Newcastle upon Tyne; Univ. of Durham (BSc, PhD). FIBiol 1986. Shell Chemical Co., London, 1959; School of Agriculture, Univ. of Newcastle upon Tyne, 1961; Dept of Agronomy and Plant Genetics, Univ. of Minnesota, 1968–69; Letcombe Lab., AFRC, Oxon, 1970; Dir, Welsh Plant Breeding Station, Aberystwyth, 1984–87; Head of Crop and Soil Envmtl Scis Dept, Virginia Polytech. Inst. and State Univ., 1987–94. *Publications:* papers in agricultural science jls. *Address:* Berk, Peel Road, Kirk Michael, Isle of Man IM6 1AP. *T:* (01624) 878039; *e-mail:* robertcannell@manx.net.

CANNELL, Sheila Elizabeth; Director, Library Services, since 2003, and Deputy Head, Information Services, since 2007, University of Edinburgh; *b* 2 Oct. 1951; *d* of Ernest and Sadie Best; *m* 1981, Peter Malcolm Cannell; one *s*. *Educ:* Univ. of Edinburgh (MA Hons); Univ. of Sheffield (MA Librarianship). Asst Librarian, Univ. of Glasgow, 1975–85; Medical Librarian, 1985–98, Dep. Librarian, 1998–2003, Univ. of Edinburgh. Member: Mgt Cttee, Scottish Liby and Inf. Council, 1994–97 and 2004–; Consortium of Univ. and Res. Libraries Bd, 2007–; Chair: Wkg Gp on Space, SCONUL, 2006–; Scottish Confedn of Univ. and Res. Libraries, 2007–. Trustee, Edinburgh City of Literature, 2005–. FRSA 2007. *Recreations:* gardening, music, family life. *Address:* Edinburgh University Library, George Square, Edinburgh EH8 9LX; *e-mail:* s.cannell@ed.ac.uk.

CANNING, family name of **Baron Garvagh.**

CANNING, Hugh Donaldson; Music Critic, The Sunday Times, since 1989; *b* 28 May 1954; *s* of David Donaldson Canning and Olga Mary Canning (*née* Simms). *Educ:* Oakham Sch.; Pembroke Coll., Oxford (BA). Freelance music critic, 1979–87; Music Critic: London Daily News, 1987; The Guardian, 1987–89; Opera Critic, The Listener. Critic of Year Award, Brit. Press Awards, 1994. *Recreations:* music, theatre, tennis, food, gossip. *Address:* c/o The Sunday Times, 1 Pennington Street, E1 9XN.

CANNING, Mark; HM Diplomatic Service; Ambassador to Burma, since 2006; *b* 15 Dec. 1954; *s* of late John Canning, OBE and of Paula Canning; *m* 2004, Cecilia Kenny; one *d*. *Educ:* Downside Sch.; University Coll. London (BA (Hons)); MBA 2003. First Sec., FCO, 1988–93; First Sec. (Commercial), Jakarta, 1993–97; First Sec., FCO, 1997–2001; Counsellor, FCO, 2001–02; Dep. High Comr, Kuala Lumpur, 2002–06. *Recreations:* tennis, sea fishing, reading. *Address:* c/o Foreign and Commonwealth Office, King Charles Street, SW1A 2AH. *T:* (01243) 263372.

CANNON, Prof. John Ashton, CBE 1985; PhD; Professor of Modern History, University of Newcastle upon Tyne, 1976–92, now Professor Emeritus; Pro-Vice Chancellor, 1983–86; *b* 8 Oct. 1926; *s* of George and Gladys Cannon; *m* 1st, 1948, Audrey Elizabeth, *d* of G. R. Caple (marr. diss. 1953); one *s* one *d*; 2nd, 1953, Minna, *d* of Frederick Pedersen, Denmark; one *s* two *d*. *Educ:* Hertford Grammar Sch.; Peterhouse, Cambridge (MA 1955). PhD Bristol, 1958. Served RAF, 1947–49 and 1952–55. History of Parlt Trust, 1960–61; Univ. of Bristol: Lectr, 1961; Sen. Lectr, 1967; Reader, 1970; Dean, Faculty of Arts, Univ. of Newcastle upon Tyne, 1979–82. Member: UGC, 1983–89 (Vice-Chm., 1986–89; Chm., Arts Sub-Cttee, 1983–89); Open Univ. Vis. Cttee, 1988–92. Lectures: Wiles, Queen's Univ. Belfast, 1982; Raleigh, British Acad., 1982; Prothero, RHistS, 1985; Stenton, Reading Univ., 1986; James Ford Special, Oxford, 1996. Chm., Radio Bristol, 1970–74. FRHistS 1980; FRSA 1990. *Publications:* The Fox-North Coalition: crisis of the constitution, 1970; Parliamentary Reform, 1640–1832, 1973; (ed with P. V. McGrath) Essays in Bristol and Gloucestershire History, 1976; (ed) The Letters of Junius, 1978; (ed) The Historian at Work, 1980; (ed) The Whig Ascendancy, 1981; Aristocratic Century, 1984; (ed jtly) The Blackwell Dictionary of Historians, 1988; (with R. Griffiths) The Oxford Illustrated History of the British Monarchy, 1988; Samuel Johnson and the politics of Hanoverian England, 1994; (ed) The Oxford Companion to British History, 1997; (ed) The Oxford Dictionary of British History, 2001; (with A. Hargreaves) The Kings and Queens of Britain, 2001. *Recreations:* music, losing at tennis. *Address:* 29 Lily Avenue, Jesmond, Newcastle upon Tyne NE2 2SQ. *T:* (0191) 281 4096.

CANNON, John Francis Michael; Keeper of Botany, Natural History Museum (formerly British Museum (Natural History)), 1978–90; *b* 22 April 1930; *s* of Francis Leslie Cannon and Aileen Flora Cannon; *m* 1954, Margaret Joy (*née* Herbert); two *s* one *d*. *Educ:* Whitgift Sch., South Croydon, Surrey; King's Coll., Newcastle upon Tyne, Univ. of Durham (BSc 1st Cl. Hons Botany). Dept of Botany, British Museum (Nat. History), 1952, Dep. Keeper 1972. President: Botanical Soc. of the British Isles, 1983–85; Ray Soc., 1986–88. *Publications:* papers in scientific periodicals and similar pubns. *Recreations:* travel, music, gardening.

CANNON, Mark Rennison Norris; QC 2008; *b* 9 June 1961; *s* of late Brian Norris Cannon and Ann Buckham Cannon (*née* Williams). *Educ:* St Dunstan's Coll., London; Lincoln Coll., Oxford (BA Mod. Hist. 1983); Robinson Coll., Cambridge (Pt 1B Law Tripos 1984). Called to the Bar, Middle Temple, 1985; in practice as a barrister, 1986–.

Publications: (ed) Jackson & Powell on Professional Liability, 3rd edn 1992, 6th edn 2006. *Recreations:* ski-ing, history, wine, Italy. *Address:* 95 Portland Road, W11 4LN; Brinshope House, Wigmore, Leominster, Herefordshire HR6 9UR; 4 New Square, Lincoln's Inn, WC2A 3RJ. *Clubs:* Buck's, Oxford and Cambridge.

CANNON, Richard, RIBA, FRIAS; RSA 2007; Partner, Elder & Cannon Architects, since 1980; *b* 18 Nov. 1943; *s* of Richard Cannon and Clara Cannon (*née* Benassi); *m* 1971, Angela Boyle; two *s* one *d*. *Educ:* Duncan of Jordanstone Coll. of Art. RIBA 1974; FRIAS 1986. Work on schs prog., Lanark Co. Architects, 1970–80. Major projects include: Ingram Sq. Develt, Glasgow, 1991 (Civic Trust Scotland Award); St Aloysius Jun. Sch., Glasgow, 1999 (RIBA and Glasgow Inst. of Archts Awards); Homes for the Future, Glasgow, 2000 (awards from RIBA, Glasgow Inst. of Archts, Civic Trust, Saltire Soc.; Regeneration of Scotland Supreme Award); Clavius Maths, Science and Technology Building, 2004 (Best Scottish Building Award, RIAS; awards from RIBA and Glasgow Inst. of Archts). Gold Medal for Architecture, Royal Scottish Acad., 1991. *Publications:* contribs to numerous architectural jls and books. *Recreation:* travel in Italy. *Address:* Elder & Cannon, 40 Berkeley Street, Glasgow G4 7DW. *T:* (0141) 204 1833, *Fax:* (0141) 204 1844; *e-mail:* d.cannon@elder-cannon.co.uk.

CANNON, Richard Walter, CEng, FIET; Joint Managing Director, 1977–83, Managing Director, 1983, Cable and Wireless plc; retired; *b* 7 Dec. 1923; *s* of Richard William Cannon and Lily Harriet Cannon (*née* Fewins); *m* 1949, Dorothy (formerly Jarvis); two *d*. *Educ:* Eltham Coll. Joined Cable and Wireless Ltd, 1941; Exec. Dir, 1973. Director: Batelco (Bahrain), 1981–90; Teletswana (Botswana), 1984–86. *Publications:* telecommunications papers for IEE and IERE.

CANNON, Thomas; Chief Executive: Ideopolis International Ltd, since 2004; MDE Services, since 1982; Managing Editor, New Academy Review, since 2001; *b* 20 Nov. 1945; *s* of Albert and Bridget Cannon; *m* 1971, Frances Cannon (*née* Constable); one *s* one *d*. *Educ:* St Francis Xavier's Grammar Sch., Liverpool; Borough Polytechnic. BSc (Hons) Sociology (London Univ. external degree). Res. Associate, Warwick Univ., 1969–71; Lectr, Middlesex Poly., 1971–72; Products Man., Imperial Gp, 1972–74; Lectr, Durham Univ., 1975–81; Prof., Univ. of Stirling, 1981–89; Dir, 1989–92, Vis. Prof., 1992–95, Manchester Business Sch.; Associate Rector, Hajioannion Univ., Cyprus, 1993–94. Visiting Professor: Kingston Univ., 1993–; Bradford Univ., 1997–2004; Middlesex Univ., 1997–; Mercers' Sch. Meml Prof. of Commerce, Gresham Coll., 1996–2000. Director: Stirling Gp, 1993–99; HIT Ltd, 2006–; Chief Executive: Mgt Charter Initiative, 1995–2001; Respect London Ltd, 2001. Member: ESRC; Industry, Environment and Economy R&D Gp, 1990–92; Jt Cttee, ESRC/SERC, 1990–94; Business Links Gp, 1993–94; Chairman: Jt Working Party, Scottish Examinations Bd, 1988–90; Rail Users Consultative Cttee for NW, 1996–97; Dep. Chm., Management Develt to the Millennium, Inst. of Management, 1992–95. Member: Quality Standard Cttee, NCVO, 1997–99; BBC Educn Council, 1998–2000. Trustee: CAPITB Trust, 2000–; ITB Pension Trust, 2004–. FCGI; FRSA. *Publications:* Advertising Research, 1972; Distribution Research, 1973; Advertising: the economic implications, 1974; Basic Marketing, 1976, 6th edn 1998; How to Win Profitable Business, 1983; How to Win Business Overseas, 1984; Enterprise, 1991; The World of Business, 1991; Women as Entrepreneurs, 1992; Corporate Responsibility, 1993; (ed jtly) The Times Good University Guide, 1994; How to Get Ahead in Business, 1994; The Guinness Book of Business Records, 1996; Welcome to the Revolution, 1998; The Good Sales Manager's Guide; The Ultimate Book of Business Breakthroughs, 2000; Football Finance After the Revolution, 2005; papers in learned jls. *Recreations:* soccer, supporting Everton FC, walking, writing. *Address:* 13 Old Broadway, Manchester M20 3DH. *T:* (0161) 434 2989.

CANNON-BROOKES, Peter, PhD; FMA, FIIC; international museum consultant; *b* 23 Aug. 1938; *s* of late Victor Montgomery Cannon Brookes and Nancy Margaret (*née* Markham Carter); *m* 1966, Caroline Aylmer, *d* of John Aylmer Christie-Miller; one *s* one *d*. *Educ:* Bryanston; Trinity Hall, Cambridge (MA); Courtauld Inst. of Art, Univ. of London (PhD). FMA 1975. Gooden and Fox Ltd, London, 1963–64; Keeper, Dept of Art, City Museums and Art Gall., Birmingham, 1965–78; Sessional Teacher in History of Art, Courtauld Inst. of Art, London, 1966–68; Keeper of Dept of Art, Nat. Mus. of Wales, Cardiff, 1978–86; Mus. Services Dir, STIPPLE Database Services, 1986–90. Internat. Council of Museums: Mem. Exec. Bd, UK Cttee, 1973–81; Pres., Internat. Art Exhibns Cttee, 1977–79 (Dir, 1974–80; Sec., 1975–77); Dir, Conservation Cttee, 1975–81 (Vice Pres., 1978–81). Member: Town Twinning Cttee, Birmingham Internat. Council, 1968–78; Birm. Diocesan Synod, 1970–78; Birm. DAC for Care of Churches, 1972–78; Edgbaston Deanery Synod, 1970–78 (Lay Jt Chm., 1975–78); Abingdon Deanery Synod, 2000–06; Oxford Dio. Synod, 2003–06; Oxford Dio. Bd of Educn, 2004–06. Member: Society of Authors, 1972–; Art and Design Adv. Panel, Welsh Jt Educn Cttee, 1978–86; Welsh Arts Council, 1979–84 (Member: Art Cttee, 1978–84; Craft Cttee, 1983–87); Projects and Orgns Cttee, Crafts Council, 1985–87. President: Welsh Fedn of Museums and Art Galleries, 1980–82; S Wales Art Soc., 1980–87. Trustee: Welsh Sculpture Trust, 1981–94; Bosnia-Herzegovina Heritage Rescue, 1992–99; Consultant Curator, Tabley House Collection, Manchester Univ., 1988–. Jt Editor, Museum Management and Curatorship, 1981–2003 (Founder Editor, 2003–). Freeman 1969, Liveryman 1974, Worshipful Co. of Goldsmiths. FRSA. JP Birmingham, 1973–78, Cardiff, 1978–82. Prize, Masaryk Acad. of Arts, Prague, 1998. *Publications:* (with H. D. Molesworth) European Sculpture, 1964; (with C. A. Cannon-Brookes) Baroque Churches, 1969; Omar Ramsden, 1973; Lombard Painting, 1974; After Gulbenkian, 1976; The Cornbury Park Bellini, 1977; Michael Ayrton, 1978; Emile Antoine Bourdelle, 1983; Ivor Roberts-Jones, 1983; Czech Sculpture 1800–1938, 1983; Paintings from Tabley, 1989; The Painted Word, 1991; William Redgrave, 1998; The Godolphin Arabian, 2004; contrib. Apollo, Art Bull., Arte Veneta, Burlington Mag., Connoisseur, Internat. Jl of Museum Management and Curatorship, and Museums Jl. *Recreations:* photography, growing vegetables, cooking. *Address:* Thrupp Farm, Abingdon, Oxon OX14 3NE. *T:* (01235) 520595, *Fax:* (01235) 534817. *Club:* Athenæum.

CANTACUZINO, Sherban, CBE 1988; FSA; FRIBA; Secretary, Royal Fine Art Commission, 1979–94; *b* 6 Sept. 1928; *s* of late Georges M. Cantacuzino and Sanda Stirbey; *m* 1954, Anne Mary Trafford; two *d* (one *s* decd). *Educ:* Winchester Coll.; Magdalene Coll., Cambridge (MA). Partner, Steane, Shipman & Cantacuzino, Chartered Architects, 1956–65; private practice, 1965–73; Asst Editor, Architectural Review, 1967–73, Exec. Editor, 1973–79. Sen. Lectr, Dept of Architecture, College of Art, Canterbury, 1967–70. Trustee: Thomas Cubitt Trust, 1978–98; Design Museum, 1981–98; Member: Arts Panel, Arts Council, 1977–80; Steering Cttee, Aga Khan Award for Architecture, 1980–83 (Mem., Master Jury, 1980); Council, RSA, 1980–85; Design Cttee, London Transport, 1981–82; Adv. Panel, Railway Heritage Trust, 1985–; Fabric Cttee, Canterbury Cathedral, 1987–; Adv. Cttee, Getty Grant Prog., 1993–98; Design Panel, Plymouth Develt Corp., 1994–98; Bd, Landscape Foundn, 1995–. Advr, Earth Centre, 1995–. Dir, Taylor Warren Ltd, 1995–2001. Pres., UK Cttee, ICOMOS, 1987–93 (Mem., Exec. Cttee, 1990–99). Chm., Princess Margarita of Roumania Trust, 1995–98; Trustee, Wallingford Arts Park Gallery Trust, 1995–98. FSA 1995. DUniv York, 1996. *Publications:* Modern Houses of the World, 1964, 3rd edn 1966; Great Modern Architecture, 1966, 2nd edn 1968; European Domestic Architecture, 1969; New Uses for Old Buildings, 1975; (ed) Architectural Conservation in Europe, 1975; Wells Coates, a monograph, 1978; (with Susan Brandt) Saving Old Buildings, 1980; The Architecture of Howell, Killick, Partridge and Amis, 1981; Charles Correa, 1984; (ed) Architecture in Continuity: building in the Islamic world today, 1985; Re/Architecture: old buildings/New uses, 1989; What makes a good building?: an inquiry by Royal Fine Art Commission, 1994; articles in Architectural Rev. *Recreations:* music, cooking. *Address:* 140 Iffley Road, W6 0PE. *T:* (020) 8748 0415. *Club:* Garrick.

CANTER, Prof. David Victor, PhD; FBPsS; Professor of Psychology, since 1994, and Director, Centre for Investigative Psychology, since 1996, University of Liverpool; *b* 5 Jan. 1944; *s* of late Hyman Victor Canter and Coralie Lilian Canter (*née* Hyam); *m* 1967, Sandra Lorraine Smith; one *s* two *d*. *Educ:* Liverpool Collegiate Grammar Sch.; Liverpool Univ. (BA Hons 1964; PhD 1969). Research Associate, Liverpool Univ., 1964–65; Strathclyde University: Res. Associate, 1966; Res. Fellow, Building Performance Res. Unit, 1967–70; Lectr, 1971–72; University of Surrey: Lectr, 1972–78; Reader, 1978–83; Prof. of Applied Psychology, 1983–87; Prof. of Psychology, 1987–94; Hd of Dept of Psychology, 1987–91. Writer and presenter, TV documentary series Mapping Murder, 2002. CPsychol 1988; FAPA; AcSS. Mem., Forensic Sci. Soc. Hon. Mem., Japanese Inst. of Architects, 1971. Man. Ed., Jl of Envmtl Psychology, 1981–. *Publications:* Architectural Psychology, 1970; Psychology for Architects, 1974; (ed jtly) Psychology and the Built Environment, 1974; Environmental Interaction, 1975; (with P. Stringer) Psychology of Place, 1977; (ed jtly) Designing for Therapeutic Environments, 1979; (ed) Fires and Human Behaviour, 1980, 2nd edn 1990; (ed jtly) Psychology in Practice, 1982; (ed) Facet Theory, 1985; (ed jtly) The Research Interview, 1985; (ed jtly) Environmental Perspectives, 1988; (ed jtly) Environmental Policy, Assessment and Communication, 1988; (ed jtly) New Directions in Environmental Participation, 1988; (ed jtly) Environmental Social Psychology, 1988; (with M. Comber and D. Uzzell) Football in its Place, 1989; (ed jtly) Empirical Approaches to Social Representations, 1992; Criminal Shadows: inside the mind of the serial killer (Golden Dagger Award, Anthony Award), 1994; (jtly) The Faces of Homelessness, 1995; Psychology in Action, 1996; (ed jtly) Criminal Detection and the Psychology of Crime, 1997; (ed jtly) Profiling in Policy and Practice, 1999; Interviewing and Deception, 1999; The Social Psychology of Crime, 2000; Profiling Property Crimes, 2000; Mapping Murder, 2003; (with G. Fairbairn) Becoming an Author, 2006; (with D. Youngs) Geographical Offender Profiling, vols 1 and 2, 2008; (with R. Zukauskiene) Psychology and Law, 2008; Criminal Psychology, 2008; The Faces of Terrorism, 2009; contribs to learned jls, newspapers, radio, TV. *Recreations:* clarinet, musical composition, horticulture. *Address:* Centre for Investigative Psychology, School of Psychology, University of Liverpool, Eleanor Rathbone Building, Bedford Street South, Liverpool L69 7ZA. *T:* (0151) 794 3910, *Fax:* (0151) 794 3938; *e-mail:* dcanter@liverpool.ac.uk.

CANTERBURY, Archbishop of, since 2002; **Most Rev. and Rt Hon. Rowan Douglas Williams;** PC 2002; FBA 1990; *b* 14 June 1950; *s* of Aneurin Williams and Nancy Delphine Williams; *m* 1981, Hilary Jane Paul; one *s* one *d*. *Educ:* Dynevor School, Swansea; Christ's College, Cambridge (BA 1971, MA 1975); Christ Church and Wadham College, Oxford (DPhil 1975; DD 1989). Lectr, College of the Resurrection, Mirfield, 1975–77; ordained deacon, 1977, priest, 1978; Chaplain, Tutor and Director of Studies, Westcott House, Cambridge, 1977–80; Cambridge University: Univ. Lectr in Divinity, 1980–86; Fellow and Dean of Clare Coll., 1984–86; Lady Margaret Prof. of Divinity, and Canon of Christ Church, Oxford, 1986–92; Bishop of Monmouth, 1992–2002; Archbishop of Wales, 2000–02. Hon. Asst Priest, St George's, Cambridge, 1980–83; Canon Theologian, Leicester Cathedral, 1981–92. Examining Chaplain to Bishop of Manchester, 1987–92. FRSL 2004. Hon. Fellow: UC, Swansea, 1993; Clare Coll., Cambridge, 1994; Univ. of Wales Coll., Newport, 2000; UC, Cardiff, 2002; UC, Aberystwyth, 2005. Hon. DTheol Erlangen, 1999; Hon. DD: Nashotah Hse, USA, 2000; Exeter, 2001; Aberdeen, 2002; Kent, 2003; Wales, 2003; Bonn, 2004; Cambridge, 2006; DUniv Open, 2004; Hon. DCL Oxford, 2005. *Publications:* The Wound of Knowledge, 1979; Resurrection, 1982; The Truce of God, 1983; (with Mark Collier) Beginning Now; peacemaking theology, 1984; Arius: heresy and tradition, 1987; (ed) The Making of Orthodoxy, 1989; Teresa of Avila, 1991; Open to Judgement, 1994; After Silent Centuries (poems), 1994; Sergii Bulgakov: towards a Russian political theology, 1999; On Christian Theology, 1999; Lost Icons, 2000; Christ on Trial, 2000; (ed jtly) Love's Redeeming Work: the Anglican quest for holiness, 2001; Remembering Jerusalem (poems), 2001; (ed jtly) The New Dictionary of Pastoral Studies, 2002; Ponder These Things: praying with icons of the Virgin, 2002; The Poems of Rowan Williams, 2002; The Dwelling of the Light, 2003; Silence and Honey Cakes, 2003; Anglican Identities, 2004; Why Study the Past?, 2005; Grace and Necessity, 2005; Tokens of Trust: an introduction to Christian belief, 2007; Wrestling with Angels: conversations in modern theology, 2007; Dostoevsky: language, fiction and faith, 2008; Headwaters (poems), 2008; contribs to Theologische Realencyklopädie, Jl of Theological Studies, Downside Review, Eastern Churches Review, Sobornost, New Blackfriars. *Recreations:* music, fiction, languages. *Address:* Lambeth Palace, SE1 7JU.

CANTERBURY, Dean of; *see* Willis, Very Rev. R. A.

CANTERBURY, Archdeacon of; *see* Watson, Ven. S. A.

CANTLE, Prof. Edward Francis, CBE 2004; DL; Professor, Institute of Community Cohesion (iCoCo), Coventry University, since 2005; Associate Director, Improvement and Development Agency, since 2001; *b* 12 Feb. 1950; *s* of John Victor Cantle and Isabel Ruth Cantle; *m* 1974, Heather Ann Welburn; two *d*. *Educ:* Shooters Hill Grammar Sch., London; Portsmouth Poly. (BSc Hons); Dip. Housing 1978. FCIH 1986 (Hon. Life Mem., 2005). Housing Advr, 1972–73, Area Improvement Officer, 1973–74, Manchester CC; Asst Chief Housing Officer, 1974–80, Chief Housing Officer, 1980–83, City of Wakefield; Under Sec., AMA, 1983–88; Dir of Housing, Leicester City, 1988–90; Chief Exec., City of Nottingham, 1990–2001. Chairman: DETR Local Govt Construction Task Force, 1999–2002; Community Cohesion Indep. Review Team, 2001–04 (reported on racial disturbances in northern towns and cities, 2001; final report, 2004); Integration of New and Renewable Energy in Buildings, Faraday Partnership, 200407. Mem. Bd, EA, 2000– (Dep. Chm., 2005–). Chm., Queen's Medical Centre, Nottingham Univ. Hosp. NHS Trust, 2001–06. Chm., Sustainability First (charity), 1999–. Vis. Prof., Business Sch., Nottingham Trent Univ., 2003–. DL Notts, 2004. Hon. LLD Portsmouth, 2006; DUniv. Oxford Brookes, 2006. *Publications:* Community Cohesion: a new framework for race and diversity, 2005; contrib. AMA studies, incl. Defects in Housing series; numerous contribs to local govt and construction press. *Recreations:* sports, including walking, tennis and golf. *Address:* Institute of Community Cohesion (iCoCo), 10 Coventry Innovation Centre, University Technology Park, Coventry CV1 2TL.

CANTOR, Anthony John James; HM Diplomatic Service, retired; Ambassador to Armenia, 2006–08; *b* 1 Feb. 1946; *s* of late John Stanley Frank Cantor and Olive Mary

Cantor (*née* McCartney); *m* 1968, Patricia Elizabeth Naughton; one *s* two *d*. *Educ:* Bournemouth Grammar Sch. Joined Diplomatic Service, 1965; FCO, 1965–68; Rangoon, 1968–71; Japanese lang. trng, Sheffield Univ., 1971–72, Tokyo, 1972–73; Third, then Second, Sec., Tokyo, 1973–76; Accra, 1977–80; Aid Policy Dept, 1980–82, W Indian and Atlantic Dept, 1982–83, FCO; Consul (Commercial), Osaka, 1983–89; Dep. Hd of Mission, Hanoi, 1990–92; Dep. Dir, Invest UK, 1992–94; First Sec., Tokyo, 1994–95; Dep. Consul-Gen., Osaka, 1995–98; EU Dept (Bilateral), FCO, 1999–2000; Dep. Comr-Gen., UK Pavilion, Hanover, 2000; Public Diplomacy Dept, FCO, 2000–01; Ambassador to Paraguay, 2001–05. Mem., Britain-Burma Soc. *Recreations:* travel, languages, horse-riding, World War II in Asia. *Club:* Kobe (Japan).

CANTOR, Prof. Brian, PhD; FREng; FIMMM; FInstP; FRMS; Vice-Chancellor, University of York, since 2002; *b* 11 Jan. 1948; *s* of Oliver Horace Cantor and Gertrude Mary Cantor (*née* Thompson); *m* 1st, 1967, Margaret Elaine Pretty (marr. diss. 1979); two *s*; 2nd, 1981, Anne Catherine Sharry (*d* 1993). *Educ:* Manchester Grammar Sch.; Christ's Coll., Cambridge (BA, MA, PhD 1972). CEng 1979, FREng (FEng 1998); FIMMM (FIM 1989); FRMS 1993; FInstP 1999. Res. Fellow, Sch. of Engrg, Sussex Univ., 1972–81; Oxford University: Lectr, 1981–91, Reader in Materials Processing, 1991–95, Head, 1995–2000, Dept of Materials; Cookson Prof. of Materials, 1995–2002; Head, Div. of Math. and Physical Scis, 2000–02; Sen. Res. Fellow, Jesus Coll., 1987–95; Fellow, St Catherine's Coll., 1995–2002; Dir, Oxford Centre for Advanced Materials and Composites, 1990–95; Academic Dir, Begbroke Sci. Park, 1998–2002. Industrial Fellow, GE Corporate Labs, Schenectady, NY, 1982. Chm. Bd, Amaethon, 2003–06; Dep. Chm. Bd, Yorkshire Science, 2005–; Member, Board: Isis Innovation, 2000–02; White Rose, 2002–; Worldwide University Network, 2002–; Yorkshire Univs, 2002–; Nat. Centre for Sci. Learning, 2003– (Chm., 2003–04) .Consultant: Alcan Internat., Banbury Labs, Oxon, 1986–94; Rolls-Royce, 1996–. Mem., World Technol. Forum, 2000–. Editl Advr, Inst. of Physics Press., 1983–2006; Jt Ed., Progress in Materials Science, 1988–. *Publications:* (ed) Rapidly Quenched Metals III, 1978; (ed with P. B. Hirsch) Tribute to J. W. Christian, 1992; (jtly) Stability of Microstructure in Metallic Systems, 1997; (ed jtly) Aerospace Materials, 2001; (ed jtly) Solidification and Casting, 2003; (ed jtly) Metal and Ceramic Matrix Composites, 2004; Novel Nanocrystalline Alloys & Magnetic Nanomaterials, 2005. *Recreations:* mountain walking, guitar. *Address:* University of York, Heslington, York YO10 5DD.

CANTOR, Deborah; *see* Klein, D.

CANTY, Brian George John, CBE 1993 (OBE 1988); HM Diplomatic Service, retired; Governor of Anguilla, 1989–92; *b* 23 Oct. 1931; *s* of George Robert Canty and Phœbe Charlotte Canty (*née* Cobb); *m* 1954, Maureen Kathleen Kenny; one *s* one *d*. *Educ:* South West Essex Technical College; external student, London University (Social Studies); RAF Staff College (psc 1970). RN 1950; Air Ministry, 1957; Financial Adviser's Office, Cyprus, 1960; MoD (Air), 1963; FCO, 1971; served Oslo, 1973, Kingston, 1977, Vienna, 1979; FCO, 1984; Dep. Governor, Bermuda, 1986. Director: A. S. Trust Ltd, 1993–; St Helena Transhipment Services Ltd, 2002–. JP Bermuda, 1986. *Publication:* (as Byron Casey) The Holy Loch Affair, 2006. *Recreations:* tennis, travel, writing.

CAPE, Donald Paul Montagu Stewart, CMG 1977; CBE 1998; HM Diplomatic Service, retired; Ambassador and UK Permanent Representative to the Council of Europe, Strasbourg, 1978–83; *b* 6 Jan. 1923; *s* of late John Scarvell and Olivia Millicent Cape; *m* 1948, Cathune Johnston; three *s* one *d* (and one *s* decd). *Educ:* Ampleforth Coll.; Brasenose Coll., Oxford. Scots Guards, 1942–45. Entered Foreign Service, 1946. Served: Belgrade, 1946–49; FO, 1949–51; Lisbon, 1951–55; Singapore, 1955–57; FO, 1957–60; Bogota, 1960–61; Holy See, 1962–67; Head of Information Administration Dept, FCO, 1968–70; Counsellor, Washington, 1970–73; Counsellor, Brasilia, 1973–75; Ambassador to Laos, 1976–78. Administrator, Anglo-Irish Encounter, 1983–98; Chm., Anglo-Portuguese Soc., 1988–91. *Recreations:* golf, walking, swimming. *Address:* Hilltop, Wonersh, Guildford, Surrey GU5 0QT.

CAPE TOWN, Archbishop of, and Metropolitan of Southern Africa, since 2008; **Most Rev. Thabo Cecil Makgoba;** *b* S Africa, 15 Dec. 1960; *s* of Masilo and Kedibome Makgoba; *m* 1991, Lungi Manona; one *s* one *d*. *Educ:* St Paul's Coll., Grahamstown (DipTh 1989); Univ. of Witwatersrand (MEd 1993). Asst Priest, St Mary's Cathedral, Johannesburg, 1990; Priest-in-charge, St Albans Parish, 1993; Lectr, Univ. of Witwatersrand, 1993–96; Dean, Knockando Residence and Sen. Lectr, Witwatersrand Coll. of Educn, 1996–98; Rector and Archdeacon, Sophiatown, 1998–2002; Suffragan Bishop of Grahamstown, 2002–04; Bishop of Grahamstown, 2004–08. *Publication:* Connectedness, 2006. *Recreations:* walking, music, reading. *Address:* 20 Bishopscourt Drive, Cape Town, 7708, South Africa; *e-mail:* archpa@anglicanchurchsa.org.za.

CAPELL, family name of **Earl of Essex**.

CAPELLA, Josephine Marie; *see* Durning, J. M.

CAPELLAS, Michael D.; Senior Advisor, Silver Lake Partners, since 2006; Director, Cisco Systems, Inc., since 2006; *m* Marie; two *c*. *Educ:* Kent State Univ. (BBA 1976). CPA. Systems analyst and manufg posts, Republic Steel Corp., 1976–81; Schlumberger Ltd, 1981–96: posts included Dir for Inf. Systems; Controller and Treas., Asia Pacific; Chief Financial Officer, Dowell Schlumberger Inc.; Ops Manager, Fairchild Semiconductor Unit; Founder, and Man. Partner, Benchmarking Partners, 1996; Dir of Supply Chain Mgt, SAP America, 1996–97; Sen. Vice-Pres. and Gen. Manager, Oracle Corp., 1997–98; Chief Inf. Officer, 1998–99, Chief Operating Officer, 1999, CEO, 1999–2002, Compaq Computer Corp.; Pres., Hewlett-Packard Co., 2002; CEO, 2002–06, Chm., 2002–04, and Pres., 2004–06, WorldCom, later MCI.

CAPEWELL, Maj. Gen. David Andrew, OBE 2002; Deputy Commander, NATO Rapid Reaction Corps (Italy), since 2008; *b* Huddersfield, 21 Aug. 1959; *s* of Dennis Capewell and Greta Capewell (*née* Rhodes); *m* 1981, Deborah Joy Snookes; two *d*. *Educ:* Holme Valley Grammar Sch.; Canadian Forces Command and Staff Coll. Commnd RM, 1979; COS 3 Cdo Bde, 1998–2000; CO 40 Cdo RM, 2000–02; COS UK Jt Force HQ, 2002–04; HCSC 2004; UK CDS LO to US Chm. of Jt Chiefs, 2005; ACOS J3 PJHQ, 2005–07; Comdr, 3 Cdo Bde, 2007–08. Pres., RM Rugby League Assoc., 2007–08. *Publication:* UK Approach to Amphibious Operations, 1997. *Recreations:* hill-walking, military history, kite surfing. *Address:* HQ NRDC Italy, BFPO 61.

CAPEWELL, Vasanti Emily Indrani; *see* Selvaratnam, V. E. I.

CAPLAN, Hon. Lord; Philip Isaac Caplan; a Senator of the College of Justice in Scotland, 1989–2000; *b* 24 Feb. 1929; *s* of Hyman and Rosalena Caplan; *m* 1st, 1953; two *s* one *d*; 2nd, 1974, Joyce Ethel Stone; one *d*. *Educ:* Eastwood Sch., Renfrewshire; Glasgow Univ. (MA, LLB). Solicitor, 1952–56; called to Bar, 1957; Standing Junior Counsel to Accountant of Court, 1964–70; QC (Scot.) 1970; Sheriff of Lothian and Borders, 1979–83; Sheriff-Principal of North Strathclyde, 1983–89. Member: Sheriff Court Rules Council, 1984–89; Adv. Council on Messengers-at-Arms and Sheriff Officers, 1987–89. Chairman: Plant Varieties and Seeds Tribunal, Scotland, 1977–79; Scottish Assoc. for Study of Offending (formerly Delinquency), 1985–89 (Hon. Vice-Pres., 1990–); Family Mediation Scotland (formerly Scottish Assoc. of Family Conciliation Services), 1989–94 (Hon. Pres., 1994–; Hon. Life Patron, 2006); Bd of Trustees, CommunicAbility (formerly James Powell UK Trust), 1992–. FRPS 1988; AFIAP 1985. Hon. LLD Glasgow, 1996. *Recreations:* photography, reading, music. *Club:* New (Edinburgh).

CAPLAN, Prof. (Ann) Patricia (Bailey), PhD; FRAI; Professor of Social Anthropology, Goldsmiths College, University of London, 1989–2003, now Emeritus; *b* 13 March 1942; *d* of Sylvester Launcelot Bailey and Marjorie Bailey (*née* Parr); *m* 1967, Prof. Lionel Caplan; one *s* one *d*. *Educ:* Sch. of Oriental and African Studies, Univ. of London (BA Hons African Studies 1963; MA Social Anthropology 1965; PhD 1968). Tutor: Birkbeck Coll., Univ. of London, 1964–65 and 1968–69; Open Univ., 1970–71 and 1974–75; Postdoctoral Fellow, SOAS, 1968–70 and 1974–76; Lectr, then Sen. Lectr, in Anthropology, Goldsmiths Coll., Univ. of London, 1977–89; Dir, Inst. of Commonwealth Studies, Univ. of London, 1998–2000. Chair, Assoc. of Social Anthropologists, 1997–2001. Trustee, Action Aid, 2006–. *Publications:* Priests and Cobblers: social change in a Hindu village in Western Nepal, 1972; Choice and Constraint in a Swahili Community: property, hierarchy and cognatic descent on the East African Coast, 1975; (ed with J. Bujra) Women United, Women Divided: cross cultural perspectives on female solidarity, 1978; Class and Gender in India: women and their organisations in a South Indian city, 1985; (ed) The Cultural Construction of Sexuality, 1987; (ed with F. le Guennec-Coppens) Les Swahili entre Afrique et Arabie, 1992; (ed jtly) Gendered Fields: women, men and ethnography 1993; (ed) Understanding Disputes: the politics of law, 1995; African Voices, African Lives: personal narratives from a Swahili village, 1997; (ed) Food, Health and Identity: approaches from the social sciences, 1997; (ed) Risk Revisited, 2000; (ed) The Ethics of Anthropology, 2003; (ed jtly) Swahili Modernities, 2004; numerous articles in learned jls. *Recreations:* swimming, walking, classical music, gardening. *Address:* Department of Anthropology, Goldsmiths, University of London, SE14 6NW. *T:* (020) 7919 7800, *Fax:* (020) 7919 7813; *e-mail:* p.caplan@gold.ac.uk.

CAPLAN, Jonathan Michael; QC 1991; a Recorder, since 1995; *b* 11 Jan. 1951; *s* of Dr Malcolm Denis Caplan and late Jean Hilary Caplan, JP; *m* 1993, Selena Lennard (*née* Peskin); one *s*, and one step *s* one step *d*. *Educ:* St Paul's Sch.; Downing Coll., Cambridge (MA). MCIArb. Called to Bar, Gray's Inn, 1973, Bencher, 2000; Asst Recorder, 1989–95. Mem., General Council of Bar, 1986–90; Chairman: Bar Council Report on Televising the Courts, 1989; Public Affairs Cttee, Bar Council, 1991–92. Mem., Broadcast and Publishing Standards Tribunal, Dubai, 2003–. Member: BBC Ind. Rev. Panel on documentaries, 1997; Develt Bd, Royal Court Theatre, 1997–. Chm., BAFTA Management Ltd, 2003–. Patron, Wiener Liby, 2006–. Mem. Editl Bd, Jl of Criminal Law, 1988–2005. *Publications:* The Confait Confessions, 1977; (contrib.) Disabling Professions, 1978. *Recreations:* writing, tennis, collecting historical newspapers and manuscripts, Khmer and Thai sculpture, cinema, ballet, books, flat horseracing. *Address:* 5 Paper Buildings, Temple, EC4Y 7HB. *T:* (020) 7583 6117. *Club:* Queen's.

CAPLAN, Michael Geoffrey; QC 2002; solicitor; Partner, Kingsley Napley, since 1982; a Recorder, since 2000; *b* 3 May 1953; *s* of late Alf and Hetty Caplan; *m* 1977, Jane Freedman; one *s* one *d*. *Educ:* Henry Thornton Sch., Clapham; King's Coll., London (LLB Hons, AKC 1974). Qualified solicitor, 1977. An Asst Recorder, 1994–2000. Chm., Solicitors' Assoc. of Higher Court Advocates, 2001–03. A Chm., Police Discipline Appeal Tribunal, 2003–. Mem., Law Soc., 1977–. *Recreations:* reading, writing, sport. *Address:* Kingsley Napley, Knights Quarter, 14 St John's Lane, EC1M 4AJ. *T:* (020) 7814 1200; *e-mail:* mcaplan@kingsleynapley.co.uk.

CAPLAN, Patricia; *see* Caplan, A. P. B.

CAPLAN, Philip Isaac; *see* Caplan, Hon. Lord.

CAPLIN, Dianne; *see* Hayter, D.

CAPLIN, Ivor Keith; Founder: Ostblut Productions Ltd, 2005; Ivor Caplin Consultancy Ltd, 2005; *b* 8 Nov. 1958; *s* of late Leonard Caplin and of Alma Caplin (*née* Silver); one *s* one *d*. *Educ:* King Edward's Sch., Witley; Brighton Coll. of Technol. (Nat. Cert. Business Studies 1979). Joined Legal & General Assurance Society, 1978: various mgt posts, 1989–94; Quality Manager, Sales Div., 1994–97. Nat. Sec., ASTMS, 1983–88. Hove Borough Council: Mem. (Lab), 1991–97; Leader, 1995–97; Mem., Brighton and Hove UA, 1996–98. MP (Lab) Hove, 1997–2005. PPS to Leader of H of C, 1998–2001; an Asst Govt Whip, 2001–03; Parly Under-Sec. of State, MoD, 2003–05. Treas., All Party Animal Welfare Gp, 1997–2001; Sec., Parly Lab. Local Govt Gp, 1997–99; Officer, All Party Football Gp, 1998–2001. Vice-Chm., Lab. Friends of Israel, 1997–2005. Trustee, Old Market Trust, Brunswick, Hove, 1997–2003. *Recreations:* supporter Brighton and Hove Albion FC and Sussex CCC, music, reading, film, theatre. *Address:* PO Box 43495, London SE17 3YZ.

CAPLIN, Maj. Gen. Nicholas J.; Kosovo Protection Corps Coordinator, 2008–09; General Officer Commanding UK Support Command (Germany), from Sept. 2009; *b* England, 4 Dec. 1958; *s* of John and Daphne Caplin; *m* 1983, Isobel McIntosh; one *s* one *d*. *Educ:* Broadstone Primary Sch.; Poole Grammar Sch.; Univ. of Surrey (BSc Hons Econ); RMA, Sandhurst; Army Staff Coll. CGIA. Commnd AAC, 1980; Infantry Attachment, 1 RGJ, 1981; Army Pilot Trng, 1981–82; Flight Comdr, 1982–85; Adjt, 1985–87; Indep. Flight Comdr, 1988 (Maj.); Army Staff Coll., 1989–90; MoD, 1991–93; Sqdn Comdr (incl. Bosnia) 1993–95; Directing Staff, Army Staff Coll., 1995–97 (Lt Col); CO, 3 Regt, AAC, 1997–2000; Private Office, 2000–01; Comdt, Sch. of Army Aviation, 2001–02 (Col); Dep. Comdr, Jt Helicopter Comd, 2003–05 (Brig.); Comdr, Collective Trng Gp, 2006–07. *Recreations:* enjoying the family, classical music (organ and piano), sailing (dinghy and offshore), walking far from the madding crowd. *Address:* c/o AAC Regimental Office, HQ Director Army Air Corps, Middle Wallop, Stockbridge, Hants SO20 8DY.

CAPP, Prof. Bernard Stuart, DPhil; FBA 2005; FRHistS; Professor of History, University of Warwick, since 1994; *b* 19 Nov. 1943; *s* of Walter Henry Capp and Marjorie Highwood Capp (*née* Coast); *m* 1966, Elizabeth Seal (marr. diss. 1980); one *s* one *d*. *Educ:* City of Leicester Boys' Sch.; Pembroke Coll., Oxford (Open Exhibnr 1962; BA 1st Cl. Hons Hist. 1965; Bryce Res. Student; MA; DPhil 1970). FRHistS 1975. University of Warwick: Asst Lectr in Hist., 1968–70; Lectr, 1970–80; Sen. Lectr, 1980–90; Reader, 1990–94; Chair, Hist. Dept, 1992–95. Mem., AHRB Panel 4, 2000–05. *Publications:* The Fifth Monarchy Men, 1972; Astrology and the Popular Press: English almanacs 1500–1800, 1979; Cromwell's Navy: the Fleet and the English Revolution 1648–60, 1989; The World of John Taylor, the Water Poet, 1578–1653, 1994; When Gossips Meet: women, family and neighbourhood in early modern England, 2003; (contrib. and Associate Ed.) Oxford DNB, 2004; contrib. to Past and Present, Seventeenth Century,

English Historical Rev. *Recreations:* mountain walking in the Alps, pottering in the garden. *Address:* Department of History, University of Warwick, Coventry CV4 7AL. *T:* (024) 7652 3410, *Fax:* (024) 7652 3437; *e-mail:* b.s.capp@warwick.ac.uk.

CAPPE, Melvin Samuel; President and Chief Executive Officer, Institute for Research on Public Policy, Montreal, since 2006; *b* 3 Dec. 1948; *s* of Dave and Patty Cappe; *m* 1971, Marni Pliskin; one *s* one *d*. *Educ:* Univ. of Toronto (BA); Univ. of Western Ontario (MA). Sen. official, Treasury Bd, Dept of Finance, and Consumer & Corporate Affairs, Canada, 1975–86; Asst Dep. Minister, Consumer & Corporate Affairs, 1986–90; Dep. Sec., Treasury Bd, 1990–94; Deputy Minister: of Envmt, 1994–96; of Human Resources Develt, 1996–99; Clerk of Privy Council, Sec. to Cabinet and Hd, Public Service of Canada, 1999–2002; High Comr of Canada in UK, 2002–06. *Recreations:* hiking, travel, family. *Address:* Institute for Research on Public Policy, 1470 Peel Street, Suite 200, Montreal, QC H3A 1T1, Canada; *e-mail:* mcappe@irpp.org.

CAPPER, Lynne; *see* Sedgmore, L.

CAPRON, (George) Christopher; independent television producer; Director, Capron Productions, 1987–99; *b* 17 Dec. 1935; *s* of late Lt-Col George Capron and Hon. Mrs (Edith) Christian Capron (*née* Hepburne-Scott); *m* 1958, Edna Naomi Goldrei; one *s* one *d*. *Educ:* Wellington Coll.; Trinity Hall, Cambridge (MA). Served Army, 12th Royal Lancers (Prince of Wales's), 1954–56. British Broadcasting Corporation: radio producer, 1963–67; television producer, 1967–76; Editor, Tonight, 1976–77; Editor, Panorama, 1977–79; Asst Head, 1979–81, Head, 1981–85, TV Current Affairs Programmes; Head of Parly Broadcasting, 1985–87. FRTS 1996. *Recreations:* tennis, golf. *Address:* Old Rectory, Church Lane, Stoke Doyle, Peterborough PE8 5TH. *Club:* MCC.

CAPSTICK, Charles William, CB 1992; CMG 1972; Deputy Secretary, Food Safety Directorate, Ministry of Agriculture, Fisheries and Food, 1989–94; *b* 18 Dec. 1934; *s* of late William Capstick and Janet Frankland; *m* 1962, Joyce Alma Dodsworth; two *s*. *Educ:* King's Coll., Univ. of Durham (BSc (Hons)); Univ. of Kentucky, USA (MS). MAFF: Asst Agricl Economist, 1961; Principal Agricl Economist, 1966; Senior Principal Agricl Economist, 1968; Sen. Econ. Advr and Head, Milk and Milk Products Div., 1976; Under Sec., 1977, Dir of Econs and Statistics, 1977. Pres., Agricultural Economics Soc., 1983. Pres., Old Clitheronians Assoc., 2001. *Recreations:* gardening, golf. *Address:* 18 Netherwood Gardens, Brockhall Village, Blackburn, Lancs BB6 8HR.

CARBERRY, Kay, CBE 2007; Assistant General Secretary, Trades Union Congress, since 2003; *b* 19 Oct. 1950; *d* of Sean and Sheila Carberry; one *s* by Peter Ashby. *Educ:* Royal Naval Sch., Malta; Sussex Univ. (BA Hons English); QTS. Secondary sch. teacher, 1972–75; Researcher, NUT, 1975–78; Trades Union Congress: Policy Officer, 1978–84; Sen. Policy Officer, 1984–88; Head, Equal Rights Dept, 1988–2003. Member: Women's Nat. Commn, 1987–92; EOC, 1999–2007; Commn for Equality and Human Rights, 2006–. Member: Nat. Adv. Body for Public Sector Higher Educn, 1984–87; Adv. Cttee for Women's Employment, Dept of Employment, 1987–90; Race Relations Employment Adv. Gp, Dept of Employment, then DfEE, 1990–96; Ministerial Adv. Cttee on Work-Life Balance Employment, DfEE, 2000–02; Ministerial Adv. Gp on Age, DTI, 2001–03; Work and Parents Taskforce, DTI, 2001; Steering Gp on Illegal Working, Home Office, 2003–06; Pensions Adv. Gp, DWP, 2003–04; Women and Work Commn, DTI, 2004–06. Trustee: NCOPF, 1990–; People's History Mus., 2003–; Work Foundn, 2005–. Mem., Franco-British Council, 2004–. *Recreations:* theatre, swimming. *Address:* Trades Union Congress, Congress House, Great Russell Street, WC1B 3LS. *T:* (020) 7467 1266.

CARBERY, 11th Baron *cr* 1715; **Peter Ralfe Harrington Evans-Freke;** Bt 1768; *b* 20 March 1920; *o s* of Major the Hon. Ralfe Evans-Freke, MBE (*yr s* of 9th Baron) (*d* 1969), and Vera (*d* 1984), *d* of late C. Harrington Moore; *S* uncle, 1970; *m* 1st, 1941, Joyzelle Mary (*d* 2006), *o d* of late Herbert Binnie; three *s* two *d*; 2nd, 2007, Mary Elisabeth Carew Hunt (*née* Kober), *widow* of Basil Carew Hunt. *Educ:* Downside School. MICE. Served War of 1939–45, Captain RE, India, Burmah. Member of London Stock Exchange, 1955–68. *Recreations:* hunting, tennis, winter sports. *Heir:* *e s* Hon. Michael Peter Evans-Freke [*b* 11 Oct. 1942; *m* 1967, Claudia Janet Elizabeth, *o d* of Captain P. L. C. Gurney; one *s* three *d*].

CARBERY, Prof. Thomas Francis, OBE 1983; Emeritus Professor, University of Strathclyde, since 1990; Consultant, Energy Action Scotland, since 2005 (Member of Board, 1996–2005; Deputy Chairman, 2002–03); *b* 18 Jan. 1925; *o c* of Thomas Albert Carbery and Jane Morrison; *m* 1954, Ellen Donnelly; one *s* two *d*. *Educ:* St Aloysius Coll., Glasgow; Univ. of Glasgow and Scottish Coll. of Commerce. Cadet Navigator and Meteorologist, RAFVR, 1943–47; Min. of Labour, 1947–61; Lectr, then Sen. Lectr, in Govt and Econs, Scottish College of Commerce, Glasgow, 1961–64; University of Strathclyde: Sen. Lectr in Govt-Business Relations, 1964–75; Head of Dept of Office Organisation, 1975–79, and Prof., 1979–85; Prof., Dept of Inf. Science, 1985–88, and Chm. of Dept, 1985–86; Prof. (part-time), Dept of Marketing, 1988–90. Chm., 1995–2005, Mem., Bd of Studies, 2005–07, Huron Univ. in London. Member: IBA (formerly ITA), 1970–79 (Chm., Scottish Cttee, 1970–79); Royal Commn on Gambling, 1976–78; Central Transport Users' Consultative Cttee, 1976–80 (Chm., Scottish Transport Users' Consultative Cttee, 1976–80); European (later International) Adv. Council, Salzburg Seminar, 1980–91; Broadcasting Complaints Commn, 1981–86; Data Protection Tribunal, 1984–98; Scottish Legal Aid Bd, 1986–92; Press Council, 1987–90. Dep. Chm., Scottish Consumer Council, 1980–84 (Mem. 1977–80); Chairman: S of Scotland Electricity Consumers' Cttee, 1990–95; Scottish Cttee, Information Technology, 1982–85; Ombudsman to Mirror Gp Newspapers Scottish titles, 1990–91; Special Adviser, H of C Select Cttee on Scottish Affairs, 1982. Academic Governor, Richmond Coll., 1983–95; Governor, 1984–2000, Trustee, 1991–, St Aloysius' Coll., Glasgow. Editor, Approaches to Information Technology (Plenum Press series), 1984–90. Hon. DBA Huron in London, 2007. KSG 1995. *Publications:* Consumers in Politics, 1969; (jtly) An Introduction to Office Management and Automation, 1991. *Recreations:* conversation, spectating at Association football, listening to Radio 4, watching television. *Address:* 24 Fairfax Avenue, Glasgow G44 5AL. *T:* (0141) 637 0514. *Clubs:* University of Strathclyde, Glasgow Art, Ross Priory (Glasgow).

CARDELLI, Luca, PhD; FRS 2005; Principal Researcher, Microsoft Research Ltd, since 2006. *Educ:* Univ. of Pisa; Univ. of Edinburgh (PhD 1982). Mem. of technical staff, AT&T Bell Labs, Murray Hill, 1982–85; mem. of res. staff, Digital Equipment Corp., Systems Res. Center, Palo Alto, 1985–97; Researcher, 1997–2000, Asst Dir, 2000–06, Microsoft Res. Ltd. *Publication:* (with Martin Abadi) A Theory of Objects, 1996. *Address:* Microsoft Research Ltd, St George House, 7 J J Thomson Avenue, Cambridge CB3 0FB.

CARDEN, (Sir) Christopher Robert, (5th Bt *cr* 1887, of Molesey, Surrey; but does not use the title); tropical forest management consultant; conservationist; *b* 24 Nov. 1946; *o s* of Sir Henry Carden, 4th Bt, OBE and of his 1st wife, Jane St Clare Daniell; *S* father, 1993, but his name does not appear on the Official Roll of the Baronetage; *m* 1st, 1972, Sainimere Rokotuibau (marr. diss. 1979), Suva, Fiji; 2nd, 1981, Clarita Eriksen (marr. diss. 1996), Manila, Philippines. *Educ:* Eton; Univ. of Aberdeen (BSc Forestry, 1970). Guide, Internat. Raëlian Movement. *Address:* Casilla 1341, Santa Cruz, Bolivia.

CARDEN, Sir John (Craven), 8th Bt *cr* 1787, of Templemore, Tipperary; *b* 17 Nov. 1953; *s* of Derrick Charles Carden, CMG and Elizabeth Anne, *d* of late Capt. Alfred Spalding Russell, DSO, RN; *S* cousin, 2008; *m* 1983, Celia Jane Cameron, *d* of late Angus Cameron Howitt; one *s*. *Educ:* Winchester Coll.; Sch. of Oriental and African Studies, London Univ.; Portsmouth Poly. (BA Arch.); Dept of Psychol., Univ. of Surrey. Sch. of Arch., Portsmouth Poly., 1980–82; Carden Publishing Services, 1982–88; Carden Publications Ltd, 1988–92; Fernhurst Books, 1995–98; John Wiley & Sons Ltd, 1999–2001; Tesco Stores Ltd, 2002–. *Recreations:* music of the romantic era, having my head in a book. *Heir:* *s* Patrick John Cameron Carden, *b* 7 March 1988. *Address:* 154 St Pancras, Chichester, W Sussex PO19 7SH. *T:* (01243) 784943.

CARDEN, Richard John Derek, CB 1998; consultant; Directorate-General for Trade, European Commission, 2003–05; *b* 12 June 1943; *s* of late John and Hilda Carden; *m* 1971, Pamela Haughton; one *s* one *d*. *Educ:* Merchant Taylors' Sch., Northwood; St John's Coll., Oxford (Craven Scholar, 1964; Derby Scholar, 1966; MA Lit. Hum. 1969; DPhil 1970); Freie Universität, Berlin. Research for Egypt Exploration Soc., 1969–70; entered Civil Service, MAFF, 1970; HM Treasury, 1977–79; MAFF, 1979–93 and 1994–2000: Chief Regional Officer, Midlands and Western Region, 1983–86; Under Sec., European Community and Ext. Trade Policy, 1987–91; Fisheries Sec., 1991–93; Dep. Hd, Eur. Secretariat, Cabinet Office, 1993–94; Dep. Sec., Food Safety Directorate, 1994–96; Hd, Food Safety and Envmt Directorate, 1996–2000; actg Perm. Sec., Feb.–May 2000; Dir-Gen., Trade Policy, subseq. Europe and World Trade, DTI, 2000–03. Dir (non-exec.), Golden Wonder Ltd, 1985–86; Associate, Mega Ace Consultancy (Mumbai and London), 2005–07. Vis. Fellow, Internat. Relations Dept, LSE, 2003–05. Member, Council: RSPB, 2003–08; World Pheasant Assoc., 2008–. *Publications:* The Papyrus Fragments of Sophocles, 1974; (contrib.) The Oxyrhynchus Papyri, vol. LIV, 1987; (contrib.) The New Economic Diplomacy, 2003; articles on Greek literature. *Address:* Rectory House, Brandon Road, Hilborough, Thetford, Norfolk IP26 5BW; *e-mail:* rcarden2@btinternet.com. *Club:* Travellers.

CARDEW, Anthony John; Chairman, Cardew Group (formerly Cardew & Co. Ltd), since 1991; *b* 8 Sept. 1949; *s* of Dr Martin Philip Cardew and Anne Elizabeth Cardew (*née* Foster); *m* 1971, Janice Frances Smallwood; one *s* one *d*. *Educ:* Marlborough. Work on local newspapers, 1967–70; United Press Internat., 1970–71; Financial Corresp., Reuters, 1971–74; Charles Barker City, 1974–83: Dir, 1976–83; Hd, Financial Public Relns, 1979–83; Dep. Chm., 1983–85, Chm., 1985–91, Grandfield Rork Collins Financial. Mem., London Library. *Recreations:* book collecting, walking, shooting. *Club:* Reform.

CARDIFF, Archbishop of, (RC), since 2001; **Most Rev. Peter David Smith;** *b* 21 Oct. 1943. *Educ:* Clapham Coll.; Univ. of Exeter (LLB 1966); St John's Seminary, Wonersh; Angelicum Univ., Rome (JCD *summa cum laude* 1977). Coutts Bank, London, 1962–63; ordained priest, 1972; Asst Priest, Larkhall Lane, London, 1972–74; Prof. of Canon Law, St John's Seminary, Wonersh, 1977–84; Parish Priest, St Andrew's, Thornton Heath, 1984–85; Rector, St John's Seminary, Wonersh, 1985–95; Bishop of E Anglia, 1995–2001. Vice-Officialis and Judge, Diocesan Marriage Tribunal, 1977; Officialis, Metropolitan Tribunal, 1980–85. Bishops' Conference: Mem., Cttee for Ministerial Formation, 1989–95; Chairman: Cttee for Marriage and Family Life, 1995–2001; Dept for Christian Responsibility and Citizenship, 1998–; Central Religious Adv. Cttee, 2001–04 (Dep. Chm., 1998–2001). Chairman: Catholic Truth Soc., 1993–; Catholic Assoc. Pilgrimage Trust, 1998–2001; Vice-Chm., Catholic Agency for Social Concern, 1996–2001. Mem. Mgt Cttee, Catholic Educn Service, 1998–2001. Hon. Fellow: Univ. of Wales, Lampeter, 2004; Cardiff Univ., 2006. *Address:* Archbishop's House, 41–43 Cathedral Road, Cardiff CF11 9HD.

CARDIFF, Jack, OBE 2000; film director and cameraman; *b* 18 Sept. 1914; *s* of John Joseph and Florence Cardiff; *m*; three *s*; *m* 1997, Angela Gray; one *s* and one adopted *s* one adopted *d*. *Educ:* various schools, incl. Medburn Sch., Herts. Started as child actor, 1918; switched to cameras, 1928. World travelogues, 1937–39. Photographed, MOI Crown Film Unit: Western Approaches, 1942; best known films include: A Matter of Life and Death, Black Narcissus, The Red Shoes, Scott of the Antarctic, Under Capricorn, Pandora and the Flying Dutchman, African Queen, War and Peace. Started as Director, 1958. *Films include: directed:* Sons and Lovers, My Geisha, The Lion, The Long Ships, Young Cassidy, The Mercenaries, The Liquidator, Girl on a Motorcycle, The Mutation; *photographed:* Ride a Wild Pony, The Prince and the Pauper, Behind the Iron Mask, Death on the Nile, Avalanche Express, The Awakening, The Dogs of War, Ghost Story, The Wicked Lady, Scandalous, The Far Pavilions, The Last Days of Pompeii, Conan II, First Blood II, Catseyes, Million Dollar Mystery, Showscan Hollywood, Journey into Space, Magic Balloon; *directed and photographed:* music documentaries, Delius, Vivaldi's Four Seasons. *Exhibitions:* Jack Cardiff: portraits from a Hollywood master, Regan Gall., Cardiff, 2003; Icons, RCA, 2004; Hallion Club, Edinburgh, 2004. FRPS 1945; Fellow, BFI, 2003. Hon. Member: Assoc. Française de Cameramen, 1971; BAFTA, 1995. Hon. Dr of Art: Rome, 1953; RCA, 2000; Hon. DLitt Bradford, 1996; Hon. PhD APU, 2001. Academy Award for photography, Black Narcissus, 1947; Golden Globe Award, 1947; Coup Ce Soir (France), 1951; Film Achievement Award, Look Magazine; British Acad. of Cinematographers Award, War and Peace; New York Critics Award for best film direction, Golden Globe Award, outstanding directorial award, Directors Guild of America (all for Sons and Lovers); Internat. Award for Outstanding Achievement, 1944, Hollywood Internat. Life Achievement Award, 1995, Amer. Soc. of Cinematographers; Contribn to Art of Photography award, British Acad. of Cinematographers, 1996; London Film Critics Life Achievement Award, 1997; Lumière Award, RPS, 1999; Academy Award for Lifetime Achievement, 2001; BAFTA Special Award, 2001; first Alexander Korda Award, 2004; Lifetime Achievement Award, Heritage Foundn, 2006. *Publication:* Magic Hour (autobiog.), 1996. *Recreations:* tennis, cricket, painting. *Clubs:* MCC, Groucho, Arts.

CARDIGAN, Earl of; David Michael James Brudenell-Bruce; Manager, since 1974, owner, and 31st Hereditary Warden, since 1987, Savernake Forest; *b* 12 Nov. 1952; *s* and *heir* of 8th Marquess of Ailesbury, *qv*; *m* 1980, Rosamond Jane, cookery author, *er d* of Captain W. R. M. Winkley, Wyke Champflower Manor, near Bruton, Somerset, and Mrs Jane Winkley; one *s* one *d*. *Educ:* Eton; Rannoch; Royal Agricultural Coll., Cirencester. Sec., Marlborough Conservatives, 1985–; Mem. Exec., Devizes Constituency Cons. Assoc., 1988–. *Heir:* *s* Viscount Savernake, *qv*. *Address:* Savernake Lodge, Savernake Forest, Marlborough, Wilts SN8 3HP.

CARDIN, Pierre; Commandeur de la Légion d'Honneur, 1997; couturier; *b* 2 July 1922. Designer: Paquin, Paris, 1945–46; Dior, Paris, 1946–50; founded own fashion house, 1950. Founder and Dir, Théâtre des Ambassadeurs, now Espace Pierre Cardin complex, 1970–; Chm., Maxim's Restaurant, 1981–. Designed costumes for films, including: Cocteau's La Belle et la Bête, 1946; The Yellow Rolls Royce, 1965. Retrospective exhibition, V&A, 1990. Dé d'Or, 1977, 1979, 1982; Fashion Oscar, 1985; prize of

Foundn for Advancement of Garment and Apparel Res., Japan, 1988. Grand Officer, Order of Merit (Italy), 1988. *Address:* (office) 27 avenue Mariguy, 75008 Paris, France; 59 rue du Faubourg Saint-Honoré, 75008 Paris, France.

CARDINAL, Martin John; His Honour Judge Cardinal; a Circuit Judge, since 2004; *b* 10 June 1952; *s* of Ralph William Cardinal and Ella Winifred Cardinal; *m* 1977, Janet Dorothy Allnutt; one *s* one *d*. *Educ:* King Edward's Sch., Birmingham; Magdalene Coll., Cambridge (BA 1974); Coll. of Law, Chester. Admitted solicitor, 1977; Partner: Wood Amphlet Wild & Co., 1978–85; Anthony Collins, 1985–94. Legal Chm., Mental Health Rev. Tribunal, 1987–94; Dep. Dist Judge, 1992–94, Dist Judge, 1994–2004; Asst Recorder, 1998–2000, Recorder, 2000–04. Chancellor, Dio. of Birmingham, 2005–. *Publication:* Matrimonial Costs, 2000, 2nd edn 2007. *Recreations:* gardening, walking, swimming, lay reader. *Address:* Birmingham County Court, 33 Bull Street, Birmingham B4 6DS. *T:* (0121) 681 4441.

CARDOSO E CUNHA, António José Baptista; Commissioner General, EXPO '98, 1993–98; Chairman: PARQUE EXPO '98 SA, 1993–98; TAP Air Portugal, 2003–05; *b* 28 Jan. 1934; *s* of Arnaldo and Maria Beatriz Cardoso e Cunha; *m* 1958, Dea Cardoso e Cunha; four *s*. *Educ:* Instituto Superior Tecnico; Lisbon Univ. MSc Chem. Engrg. Professional engineer, Lisbon, 1957–65; Man. Dir/Chief Exec. Officer of private cos, Sa da Bandeira, Angola, 1965–77; in business, director of private cos, Lisbon, 1977–78 and 1982–85. Mem. Portuguese Parlt, 1979–83 and 1985–89; Mem. Portuguese Government: Sec. of State for Foreign Trade, 1978, for Industry, 1979; Minister for Agriculture/ Fisheries, 1980–82; Mem., European Commn, 1986–92. Medalha de Honra, Lisbon, 2003. Grã-Cruz: Ordem Infant D. Henrique (Portugal), 1993; Ordem de Cristo (Portugal), 1999; Grand Croix, Leopold II (Belgium), 1980; Gran Cruz, Merito Agricola (Spain), 1981.

CARDOZO, Prof. Linda Dolores, MD; FRCOG; Professor of Urogynaecology, King's College London School of Medicine (formerly Guy's, King's and St Thomas' School of Medicine, King's College London), since 1994; Consultant Obstetrician and Gynaecologist, King's College Hospital, since 1985; *b* 15 Sept. 1950; *d* of Felix Cardozo and Olga Cardozo (*née* Watts); *m* 1974, Stuart Hutcheson; one *s* two *d*. *Educ:* Liverpool Univ. Med. Sch. (MB ChB 1974; MD 1979). MRCOG 1980, FRCOG 1991. Hse Officer, Liverpool, 1974–75; SHO, Mill Rd Maternity Hosp., Liverpool, 1975–76; Clin. Res. Fellow in Urodynamics, St George's Hosp., London, 1976–78; Registrar, 1979–81, Sen. Registrar, 1981–84, Obstetrics and Gynaecol., KCH. Co-Dir, WHO Internat. Consultation on Incontinence, 2001, 2004. Chairman: Continence Foundn UK, 1998–2006; British Menopause Soc., 2001–03; founder Chm., British Soc. of Urogynaecology, 2001–06; President: Assoc. of Chartered Physiotherapists in Women's Health, 1995–; Internat. Urogynaecol Assoc., 1998–2000; Sect. of Obstetrics and Gynaecol., RSocMed, 2001–02; Mem. Exec., 2001–, and Chm. Educn Cttee, 2001–, Internat. Continence Soc. *Publications:* Urogynaecology: the King's approach, 1997; (with D. Staskin) Female Urology and Urogynaecology, 2001, 2nd edn 2006; (ed jtly) Incontinence, 2nd edn 2002, 3rd edn 2005; contrib. over 200 papers and articles relating to lower urinary tract problems in women, incl. urinary incontinence, prolapse and reconstructive surgery. *Address:* King's College Hospital, Denmark Hill, SE5 9RS. *T:* (020) 3299 9000, *Fax:* (020) 7346 3449; 8 Devonshire Place, W1G 6HP. *T:* (020) 7935 2357, *Fax:* (020) 7224 2797; *e-mail:* lcardozo@compuserve.com. *Club:* Royal Society of Medicine.

CARDOZO, Lydia Helena L.; *see* Lopes Cardozo Kindersley.

CARDROSS, Lord; Henry Thomas Alexander Erskine; *b* 31 May 1960; *s* and *heir* of 17th Earl of Buchan, *qv*; *m* 1987, Charlotte, *d* of Hon. Matthew Beaumont and Mrs Alexander Maitland; two *s*.

CARDY, Prof. John Lawrence, PhD; FRS 1991; Professor of Physics, University of Oxford, since 1996; Senior Research Fellow, All Souls College, Oxford, since 1993; *b* 19 March 1947; *s* of late George Laurence Cardy and Sarah Cardy; *m* 1985, Mary Ann Gilreath. *Educ:* Downing Coll., Cambridge (BA 1968; PhD 1971). Research Associate: European Orgn for Nuclear Res., Geneva, 1971–73; Daresbury Lab., 1973–74; Res. Associate, 1974–76, Prof. of Physics, 1977–93, Univ. of California, Santa Barbara; Fellow: European Orgn for Nuclear Res., 1976–77; Alfred P. Sloan Foundn, 1978; Guggenheim Foundn, 1986. Paul Dirac Medal, Inst. of Physics, 2000; Lars Onsager Prize, APS, 2004. *Publications:* Finite-Size Scaling, 1988; Scaling and Renormalization in Statistical Physics, 1996; contrib. to learned jls. *Recreation:* mountaineering. *Address:* All Souls College, Oxford OX1 4AL.

CARDY, Peter John Stubbings; Chief Executive, Maritime and Coastguard Agency, since 2007; *b* 4 April 1947; *s* of Gordon Douglas Stubbings and Eva Stubbings (*née* Walker), assumed name of Cardy, 1987; *m* 1987, Christine Mary Cardy. *Educ:* University Coll., Durham (BA 1968); Cranfield Inst. of Technol. (MSc 1983). Adult Educn Principal, Cromwell Community Coll., Cambs, 1968–71; Dist Sec., WEA N of Scotland, 1971–77; Dep. Dir, Volunteer Centre, UK, 1977–87; Dir, Motor Neurone Disease Assoc., 1987–94; Chief Executive: Multiple Sclerosis Soc. of GB and NI, 1994–2001; Macmillan Cancer Relief, then Macmillan Cancer Support, 2001–07 (Vice Pres., 2007–). Chm., Nat. Assoc. of Volunteer Bureaux, 1988–91; Member: Charities Effectiveness Rev. Trust, 1990–93; HTA Pharmaceuticals Panel, 2002–04; Taskforce on Medicines Partnership, 2003–05; NHS Modernisation Bd, 2004; Bd, NCRI, 2003–06 (Chm., Lung Cancer Strategic Planning Gp); Sec.-Gen., Internat. Alliance of MND/ALS Assocs, 1991–94; Chairman: Neurological Alliance, 1998–2001; OST Foresight Healthcare Panel, 1999–2000; Brain and Spine Foundn, 2005–08; Disability Benefits Consortium, 2006; The Health Hotel, 2006; Comr, Medicines Commn, 1998–2003. Non-exec. Dir, Northampton NHS Community Health Trust, 1993–97. Patron, The Cancer Resource Centre, 2007–. Vis. Fellow, Cass Business Sch., City Univ., 2006–. Charcot Medal, Assoc. British Neurologists and MS Soc., 2001. *Publications:* numerous articles in voluntary sector and medical jls. *Recreations:* offshore sailing, conversation, travel, drawing, Georgian glass. *Address:* Maritime and Coastguard Agency, Spring Place, 105 Commercial Road, Southampton SO15 1EG. *T:* (023) 8032 9100. *Club:* Reform.

CAREW, 7th Baron (UK) *cr* 1838; **Patrick Thomas Conolly-Carew;** Baron Carew (Ire.) 1834; *b* 6 March 1938; *er s* of 6th Baron Carew, CBE and Lady Sylvia Maitland (*d* 1991), *o d* of 15th Earl of Lauderdale; *S* father, 1994; *m* 1962, Celia Mary, *d* of Col Hon. (Charles) Guy Cubitt, CBE, DSO, TD; one *s* three *d*. *Educ:* Harrow Sch.; RMA Sandhurst. RHG (The Blues), 1958–65 (Captain); served UK, Cyprus, Germany. Mem., Irish Olympic Three Day Event Team, Mexico 1968, Munich 1972, Montreal 1976. President: Equestrian Fedn of Ireland, 1979–84; Irish Horse Trials Soc., 1998–; Ground Jury, 3 Day Event, Olympic Games, 1992, 1996. Mem. Bureau, Fédération Equestre Internationale, 1989–97 (Hon. Mem., 1997; Chm., 3 Day Event Cttee, 1989–97). Trustee and Mem. Council, Internat. League for Protection of Horses, 2004–. Dir, Castletown Foundn, 1995–. Gold Medal, FEI. *Recreations:* all equestrian sports, cricket, shooting, bridge. *Heir:* *s* Hon. William Patrick Conolly-Carew [*b* 27 March 1973; *m* 2000, Jane Anne, *d* of Joseph Cunningham, Dublin; one *s* three *d*]. *Address:* The Garden House, Donadea, Naas, Co. Kildare, Ireland. *T:* (45) 868204, *Fax:* (45) 861105. *Club:* Kildare Street and University (Dublin).

See also Hon. G. E. I. Maitland-Carew.

CAREW, Hon. Gerald Edward Ian M.; *see* Maitland-Carew.

CAREW, Sir Rivers (Verain), 11th Bt *cr* 1661; journalist; *b* 17 Oct. 1935; *s* of Sir Thomas Palk Carew, 10th Bt, and Phyllis Evelyn (*d* 1976), *o c* of Neville Mayman; *S* father, 1976; *m* 1st, 1968, Susan Babington (marr. diss. 1991), *yr d* of late H. B. Hill, London; one *s* three *d* (and one *s* decd); 2nd, 1992, Siobhán (marr. diss. 2003), 2nd *d* of late C. MacCárthaigh, Cork. *Educ:* St Columba's Coll., Rathfarnham, Co. Dublin; Trinity Coll., Dublin. MA, BAgr (Hort.). Asst Editor, Ireland of the Welcomes (Irish Tourist Bd magazine), 1964–67; Joint Editor, The Dublin Magazine, 1964–69; Irish Television, 1967–87; BBC World Service, 1987–93. *Publication:* (with Timothy Brownlow) Figures out of Mist (verse). *Recreations:* reading, music, reflection. *Heir:* *s* Gerald de Redvers Carew, *b* 24 May 1975. *Address:* Cherry Bounds, 37 Hicks Lane, Girton, Cambridge CB3 0JS.

CAREW POLE, Sir (John) Richard (Walter Reginald), 13th Bt *cr* 1628, of Shute House, Devonshire; OBE 2000; DL; farmer and chartered surveyor; *b* 2 Dec. 1938; *s* of Sir John Gawen Carew Pole, 12th Bt, DSO, TD and Cynthia Mary (*d* 1977), OBE, *o d* of Walter Burns; *S* father, 1993; *m* 1st, 1966, Hon. Victoria Marion Ann Lever (marr. diss. 1974), *d* of 3rd Viscount Leverhulme, KG, TD; 2nd, 1974, Mary (CVO 2003), *d* of Lt-Col Ronald Dawnay; two *s*. *Educ:* Eton Coll.; Royal Agricultural Coll., Cirencester. MRICS (ARICS 1967). Lieut, Coldstream Guards, 1958–63. Asst Surveyor, Laws & Fiennes, Chartered Surveyors, 1967–72. Director: South West Venture Capital, 1985–87; Eden Project Ltd, 1999–2001; Mem. Regional Bd, West of England, subseq. Portman, Bldg Soc., 1989–91. Chm., Devon and Cornwall Police Authority, 1985–87 (Mem., 1973–89); Member: SW Area Electricity Bd, 1981–90; NT Cttee for Devon and Cornwall, 1979–83. President: Surf Life Saving Assoc. of GB, 1976–86; Royal Cornwall Agricultural Show, 1981; RHS, 2001–06 (Mem. Council, 1999–2006); Trustee: Nat. Heritage Meml Fund, 1991–2000; Countryside Commission, 1991–96; Tate Gall., 1993–2003. Chm., Steering Cttee, Combined Univs in Cornwall, 2000–03. Governor: Seale Hayne Agric. Coll., 1979–89; Plymouth Coll., 1985–96; Mem. Bd, Theatre Royal, Plymouth, 1985–97. Trustee: Eden Trust, 1996–2007; Trusthouse Charitable Foundn, 1999– (Chm., 2002–); Pilgrim Trust, 2000–; Royal Acad. of Arts Trust, 2007–. County Councillor, Cornwall, 1973–93 (Chairman: Planning Cttee, 1980–84; Finance Cttee, 1985–89; Property Cttee, 1989–93); High Sheriff of Cornwall, 1979; DL Cornwall, 1988. Liveryman, Fishmongers' Co., 1960 (Mem. Court of Assistants, 1993–). *Recreations:* gardening, daydreaming, contemporary art. *Heir:* *s* Tremayne John Carew Pole, *b* 22 Feb. 1974. *Address:* Antony House, Torpoint, Cornwall PL11 2QA. *T:* (01752) 814914.

CAREY, family name of **Baron Carey of Clifton**.

CAREY OF CLIFTON, Baron *cr* 2002 (Life Peer), of Clifton in the City and County of Bristol; **Rt Rev. and Rt Hon. George Leonard Carey;** Royal Victorian Chain, 2002; PC 1991; Archbishop of Canterbury, 1991–2002; Chancellor: University of Gloucestershire, since 2003; London School of Theology, since 2005; *b* 13 Nov. 1935; *s* of George and Ruby Carey; *m* 1960, Eileen Harmsworth Hood, Dagenham, Essex; two *s* two *d*. *Educ:* Bifrons Secondary Modern Sch., Barking; London College of Divinity; King's College, London. BD Hons, MTh; PhD London. National Service, RAF Wireless Operator, 1954–56. Deacon, 1962; Curate, St Mary's, Islington, 1962–66; Lecturer: Oak Hill Coll., Southgate, 1966–70; St John's Coll., Nottingham, 1970–75; Vicar, St Nicholas' Church, Durham, 1975–82; Principal, Trinity Coll., Stoke Hill, Bristol, 1982–87; Hon. Canon, Bristol Cathedral, 1983–87; Bishop of Bath and Wells, 1987–91; Hon. Asst Bp, Swansea and Brecon, 2004–. Freeman: City of Wells, 1990; City of Canterbury, 1992; City of London, 1997. FKC 1994; Fellow, Canterbury Christ Church UC, 1999. Hon. doctorates from UK and USA univs. *Publications:* I Believe in Man, 1975; God Incarnate, 1976; (jtly) The Great Acquittal, 1980; The Church in the Market Place, 1984; The Meeting of the Waters, 1985; The Gate of Glory, 1986, 2nd edn 1992; The Message of the Bible, 1988; The Great God Robbery, 1989; I Believe, 1991; (jtly) Planting New Churches, 1991; Sharing a Vision, 1993; Spiritual Journey, 1994; My Journey, Your Journey, 1996; Canterbury Letters to the Future, 1998; Jesus 2000, 1999; Know the Truth (autobiog.), 2004; contributor to numerous jls. *Recreations:* reading, writing, walking. *Address:* House of Lords, SW1A 0PW.

CAREY, Charles John, CMG 1993; Member, European Communities' Court of Auditors, 1983–92; *b* 11 Nov. 1933; *s* of Richard Mein Carey and Celia Herbert Amy (*née* Conway); *m* 1990, Elizabeth Dale (*née* Slade). *Educ:* Rugby; Balliol Coll., Oxford. Nat. Service, Russian interpreter, 1951–53. HM Treasury: Asst Principal, 1957; Principal, 1962; Asst Sec., 1971; seconded to HM Diplomatic Service as Counsellor (Econs and Finance), Office of UK Perm. Rep. to EEC, Brussels, 1974–77; Under Sec., HM Treasury, 1978–83. Chm., EC Conciliation Body for clearance of European Agricl Guidance and Guarantee Fund accounts, 1994–2001. Mem., CIPFA, 1988. Grand Croix de l'ordre de Merite (Luxembourg), 1992. *Publications:* (contrib.) Encyclopaedia of the European Union, 1998; articles on audit and financial mgt of EC funds in jls in UK, France and Netherlands. *Recreations:* Russian history and culture, Trollope novels. *Club:* Oxford and Cambridge.

CAREY, Prof. Christopher, PhD; Professor of Greek, since 2003, and Head of Department of Greek and Latin, 2004–Sept. 2009, University College London (Vice-Dean, Faculty of Arts and Humanities, 2005–06); *b* 14 Sept. 1950; *s* of Christopher and Alice Carey; *m* 1969, Pauline Hemmings; two *s* one *d*. *Educ:* Alsop High Sch., Liverpool; Jesus Coll., Cambridge (BA 1972, MA; PhD 1976). Res. Fellow, Jesus Coll., Cambridge, 1974–77; Lectr in Greek, St Andrews Univ., 1977–91; Prof. of Classics, RHUL (formerly RHBNC, Univ. of London), 1991–2003 (Dean of Arts, 1998–2000; acting Vice-Principal, 2001); Acting Dir, Inst. of Classical Studies, London Univ., 2003–04. Visiting Professor: Univ. of Minn, 1987–88; Carleton Coll., Minn, 1988; British Acad./ Leverhulme Sen. Res. Fellow, 1996–97. Arts and Humanities Research Board (later Council): Mem., 1998–2002, Chm., 2002–06, Postgrad. Panel (Classics); Member: Postgrad. Cttee, 2002–06; Bd of Mgt, 2002–04; Strategic Adv. Gp, 2004–06; Nominations Cttee, 2005–07. Chm., Classics, Ancient History, Byzantine and Modern Greek Panel, 2001 RAE. *Publications:* A Commentary on Five Odes of Pindar, 1981; (with R. A. Reid) Demosthenes: Selected Private Speeches, 1985; Lysias: Selected Speeches, 1989; Apollodoros Against Neaira: [Demosthenes] 59, 1992; Trials from Classical Athens, 1997; The Speeches of Aeschines, 2000; Democracy in Classical Athens, 2000; Lysiae orationes cum fragmentis, 2007; articles on Greek lyric, epic, drama, oratory and law. *Address:* Department of Greek and Latin, University College London, Gower Street, WC1E 6BT. *T:* (020) 7679 7522.

CAREY, Brig. Conan Jerome; Chief Executive (formerly Director General), The Home Farm Trust, 1988–2001; *b* 8 Aug. 1936; *s* of late Dr James J. Carey and Marion Carey; *m* 1966, Elizabeth Gay Docker, *d* of late Lt-Col L. R. Docker, OBE, MC, TD and Cynthia (*née* Washington); one *s* two *d*. *Educ:* Belvedere College, Dublin; RMA Sandhurst; RMCS Shrivenham; Staff Coll., Camberley (psc). FIPD. Enlisted Royal Hampshire Regt, 1954; Commissioned RASC, 1956; qualified aircraft pilot, 1960; seconded Army Air Corps, 1960–65; flying duties Malaya, Brunei, Borneo, Hong Kong, BAOR; transf. to RCT, 1965; Comdr 155 (Wessex) Regt RCT(V), 1976–78; Defence Staff, British Embassy, Washington DC, 1979–82; HQ BAOR, 1982; Dep. Dir-Gen., Transport and Movements, MoD, 1985; Comdr Training Gp, RCT, 1988. FRSA. *Recreations:* golf, walking, cooking, writing. *Address:* HFT, Merchants House, Bristol BS1 4RW. *Clubs:* Army and Navy; Gloucestershire Golf.

CAREY, Sir de Vic (Graham), Kt 2002; Bailiff of Guernsey, 1999–2005; a Judge of the Court of Appeal, Guernsey, since 2005; Commissioner, Royal Court of Jersey, since 2006 (Judge of the Court of Appeal, 1999–2005); *b* 15 June 1940; *s* of Victor Michael de Vic Carey and Jean Burnett (*née* Bullen); *m* 1968, Bridget Lindsay Smith; two *s* two *d*. *Educ:* Cheam Sch.; Bryanston Sch.; Trinity Hall, Cambridge (BA 1962; MA 1967); Univ. of Caen (Cert. des études juridiques françaises et normandes 1965). Admitted Solicitor, 1965; Advocate, Royal Court of Guernsey, 1966; QC (Guernsey) 1989. People's Dep., States of Guernsey, 1976; Solicitor-Gen. for Guernsey, 1977–82; Attorney-Gen., 1982–92; Receiver-Gen., 1985–92; Dep. Bailiff, 1992–99. Mem., Gen. Synod of C of E, 1982–98; Chm., House of Laity, Winchester Dio. Synod, 1993–97. *Address:* Les Padins, St Saviours, Guernsey GY7 9JJ. *T:* (01481) 264587, *Fax:* (01481) 263687.

CAREY, Godfrey Mohun Cecil; QC 1991; a Recorder of the Crown Court, since 1986; *b* 31 Oct. 1941; *s* of Dr Godfrey Fraser Carey, LVO and Prudence Loveday (*née* Webb); *m* 1st, 1965, Caroline Jane Riggall (marr. diss. 1975); one *s* one *d* (and one *s* decd); 2nd, 1978, Dorothy May Sturgeon (marr. diss. 1983); one *d*. *Educ:* Highfield, Liphook; Eton. Legal Advr, Small Engine Div., Rolls Royce Ltd, 1964–70. Called to the Bar, Inner Temple, 1969, Bencher, 2000; in practice at the Bar, 1971–. Legal Mem., Mental Health Review Tribunals, 2000–. *Recreations:* music, tennis, Aztec culture. *Address:* 5 Paper Buildings, EC4Y 7HB. *T:* (020) 7583 6117. *Club:* Boodle's.

CAREY, Hugh Leo; Partner, Harris Beach LLP; *b* Brooklyn, NY, 11 April 1919; *s* of Denis Carey and Margaret (*née* Collins); *m* 1947, Helen Owen Twohy (*d* 1974); seven *s* four *d*, and one step *d* (and two *s* decd). *Educ:* St Augustine's Academy and High School, Brooklyn; St John's Coll.; St John's Law School. JD 1951. Served War of 1939–45 (Bronze Star, Croix de Guerre with Silver Star); with US Army in Europe, 1939–46, rank of Lt-Col. Joined family business (petrochemicals), 1947. Called to Bar, 1951. Member US House of Reps, rep. 12th District of Brooklyn, 1960–75 (Democrat); Deputy Whip; Governor of New York State, 1974–83. Exec. Vice-Pres., W. R. Grace and Co., 1987–95. Dir, Triarc, 1994–.

CAREY, Jeremy Reynolds; His Honour Judge Carey; a Circuit Judge, since 2004; Liaison Judge for Kent Magistracy, since 2005; *b* 15 Jan. 1950; *s* of Edward Carey and Dr Audrey Carey (*née* Coghlan); *m* 1972, Alysoun Marshall; one *s* two *d*. *Educ:* King's Sch., Canterbury; Selwyn Coll., Cambridge (BA 1973). Called to the Bar, Inner Temple, 1974; Asst Recorder, 1998–2000, Recorder, 2000–04. Hon. Recorder, Maidstone, 2006–. Lay Assessor to GMC, 2000–04. Mem., Disciplinary Cttee, Bar Council, 2001–04. Mem., Inst. of Arbitrators, 2000–04. *Publication:* (sub-ed) Butterworth's Law of Limitation, 2003. *Recreations:* walking, golf, cricket, wine-tasting. *Address:* Maidstone Combined Court, Barker Road, Maidstone, Kent ME16 8EQ. *Clubs:* Royal St George's Golf (Sandwich), Rye Golf.

CAREY, Prof. John, FBA 1996; FRSL 1982; Merton Professor of English Literature, Oxford University, 1976–2001; Fellow of Merton College, Oxford, 1976–2001, now Emeritus; *b* 5 April 1934; *s* of Charles William Carey and Winifred Ethel Carey (*née* Cook); *m* 1960, Gillian Mary Florence Booth; two *s*. *Educ:* Richmond and East Sheen County Grammar Sch.; St John's Coll., Oxford (MA, DPhil; Hon. Fellow, 1991). 2nd Lieut, East Surrey Regt, 1953–54; Harmsworth Sen. Scholar, Merton Coll., Oxford, 1957–58; Lectr, Christ Church, Oxford, 1958–59; Andrew Bradley Jun. Research Fellow, Balliol, Oxford, 1959–60; Tutorial Fellow: Keble Coll., Oxford, 1960–64; St John's Coll., Oxford, 1964–75. Principal book reviewer, Sunday Times, 1977–. Chairman: Booker Prize Judges, 1982, 2003; Man Booker Internat. Prize Judges, 2005; W. H. Smith Prize Judge, 1990–2004; Irish Times Lit. Prize Judge, 1993. Mem. Council, RSL, 1989–95. Hon. Fellow, Balliol Coll., Oxford, 1992. *Publications:* The Poems of John Milton (ed with Alastair Fowler), 1968, 2nd edn 1997; Milton, 1969; (ed) Andrew Marvell, 1969; (ed) The Private Memoirs and Confessions of a Justified Sinner, by James Hogg, 1969, 2nd edn 1981; The Violent Effigy: a study of Dickens' imagination, 1973, 2nd edn 1991; (trans.) Milton, Christian Doctrine, 1973; Thackeray: Prodigal Genius, 1977; John Donne: Life, Mind and Art, 1981, 2nd edn 1990; (ed) William Golding—the Man and his Books: a tribute on his 75th birthday, 1986; Original Copy: selected journalism and reviews, 1987; (ed) The Faber Book of Reportage, 1987; (ed) Donne, 1990; The Intellectuals and the Masses, 1992; (ed) Saki, Short Stories, 1994; (ed) The Faber Book of Science, 1995; (ed) The Faber Book of Utopias, 1999; Pure Pleasure, 2000; What Good Are the Arts?, 2005; articles in Rev. of English Studies, Mod. Lang. Rev., etc. *Recreations:* swimming, gardening, bee-keeping. *Address:* Brasenose Cottage, Lyneham, Oxon OX7 6QL; 57 Stapleton Road, Headington, Oxford OX3 7LX. *T:* (01865) 764304.

CAREY, Dr Nicholas Anthony Dermot; Chairman, Alzheimer's Society, 2001–07; *b* 4 May 1939; *s* of Eustace Dermot Carey and Audrey Mabel Carey (*née* Grenfell); *m* 1964, Helen Margaret Askey; two *s*. *Educ:* Shrewsbury Sch.; Trinity Coll., Dublin (BA, MA); King's Coll., Cambridge (PhD). ICI, 1968–93: Gen. Manager, Chlorine and derivatives, 1980–87; Man. Dir, Petrochemicals and Plastics, 1987–92; Planning Manager, Millbank, 1992–93; Dir Gen., City and Guilds of London Inst., 1993–2001. Chm., Llandudno Dwellings Co., 1998–. Governor, Reaseheath Coll., 2001–. Liveryman: Vintners' Co., 1960–; Tallow Chandlers' Co., 1995–; Guild of Educators, 2001– (Master, 2004–05; Treas., 2008–). *Recreations:* opera, travel, an occasional game of golf. *Address: e-mail:* carey.nick@yahoo.co.uk. *Club:* Athenæum.

CAREY, Peter Philip, FRSL; writer; *b* 7 May 1943; *s* of Percival Stanley Carey and Helen Jean Carey; *m* 1st, 1964, Leigh Weetman; 2nd, 1985, Alison Margaret Summers; two *s*; 3rd, 2007, Frances Coady. *Educ:* Geelong Grammar Sch., Vic, Aust. FRSL 1988. Hon. DLitt: Queensland, 1989; Monash, 2000; Hon. DFA New School Univ., NY, 1998. *Publications:* Fat Man in History, 1980; Bliss, 1981; Illywhacker, 1985; Oscar and Lucinda, 1988 (Booker Prize, 1988; filmed, 1998); The Tax Inspector, 1991; The Unusual Life of Tristan Smith, 1994; Collected Stories, 1995; The Big Bazoohley, 1995; Jack Maggs, 1997; True History of the Kelly Gang, 2000 (Commonwealth Writers' Prize, Booker Prize, 2001); 30 Days in Sydney, 2001; My Life as a Fake, 2003; Wrong About Japan, 2004; Theft: a love story, 2006; His Illegal Self, 2008. *Recreation:* sleeping. *Address:* c/o Rogers, Coleridge & White, Powis Mews, W11 1JN.

CAREY, Sir Peter (Willoughby), GCB 1982 (KCB 1976; CB 1972); Senior Adviser, Morgan Grenfell Group, 1990–96; Chairman, Dalgety PLC, 1986–92 (Director, 1983–92); Director: BPB Industries PLC, 1983–95; NV Philips Electronics, 1984–95; *b* 26 July 1923; *s* of Jack Delves Carey and Sophie Carey; *m* 1946, Thelma Young; three *d*. *Educ:* Portsmouth Grammar Sch.; Oriel Coll., Oxford; Sch. of Slavonic Studies. Served War of 1939–45: Capt., Gen. List, 1943–45. Information Officer, British Embassy, Belgrade, 1945–46; FO (German Section), 1948–51; Bd of Trade, 1953; Prin. Private Sec. to successive Presidents, 1960–64; IDC, 1965; Asst Sec., 1963–67, Under-Sec., 1967–69, Bd of Trade; Under-Sec., Min. of Technology, 1969–71; Dep. Sec., Cabinet Office, 1971–72; Dep. Sec., 1972–73, Second Permanent Sec., 1973–74, DTI; Second Permanent Sec., 1974–76, Permanent Sec., 1976–83, DoI. Director: Morgan Grenfell Hldgs, then Morgan Grenfell Gp, 1983–90 (Chm., 1987–89); Cable and Wireless, 1984–94; Westland Gp, 1986–88. Hon. LLD Birmingham, 1983; Hon. DSc Cranfield Inst. of Tech., 1984; Hon. DCL City, 1991. *Recreations:* music, theatre, travel. *Address:* Knowle Park Nursing Home, Cranleigh, Surrey GU6 8JL.

CAREY EVANS, David Lloyd, OBE 1984; JP; DL; farmer; *b* 14 Aug. 1925; *s* of Sir Thomas Carey Evans, MC, FRCS and Lady Olwen Carey Evans, DBE; *m* 1959, Annwen Williams; three *s* one *d*. *Educ:* Rottingdean Sch.; Oundle Sch.; Univ. of Wales, Bangor. BSc (Agric.) 1950. Sub-Lieut, RNVR, 1943–46; farming 1947–; Chm., Welsh Council, NFU, 1976–79; Welsh Representative and Chm., Welsh Panel, CCAHC, 1974; Chm., WAOS. JP Portmadoc, Gwynedd, 1969. DL Gwynedd 1988. *Address:* Eisteddfa, Criccieth, Gwynedd LL52 0PT. *T:* (01766) 522104. *Club:* Sloane.

CAREY-HUGHES, Richard John; QC 2000; a Recorder, since 2000; *b* 18 Dec. 1948; *s* of John Carey-Hughes and Esme (*née* Klein); *m* 1st, 1972, Elizabeth Blackwood (marr. diss. 1976); one *d*; 2nd, 1987, Sophia Bayne-Powell (marr. diss. 1998); one *s* two *d*. *Educ:* Rugby Sch. Airline pilot with BOAC, then British Airways, 1969–76; called to the Bar, Gray's Inn, 1977, Bencher, 2007; specialist in crime cases. Member, Committee: Criminal Bar Assoc., 1991–98 (Hon. Sec., 1996–98); S Eastern Circuit, 1998–2001. *Recreations:* gardening, cycling, cinema. *Address:* 9 Bedford Row, WC1R 4AZ. *T:* (020) 7489 2727. *Club:* Chelsea Arts.

CARFRAE, Tristram George Allen, RDI 2006; FTSE; Chair, Arup Design and Technical Executive, since 2004; Deputy Chair, Arup Building Sector Board, since 2004; Principal Director, Arup Group Ltd, since 2005; *b* 1 April 1959; *s* of Lt Col Charles Cecil Allen Carfrae and June Beatrice de Warrenne Carfrae; *m* 1987, Jane Irving Burrows; one *s* one *d*. *Educ:* Dartington Primary Sch., Devon; King Edward VI Comprehensive Sch., Totnes; Clare Coll., Cambridge (BA Mech. Scis Tripos 1981). MIStructE 1989; MIE(Aust) 1992; FTSE 2004. Structural engr with Arup, in London and Sydney, 1981–; involved in design of: Lloyds of London, 1986; Schlumberger Res. Centre, Cambridge, 1984; Sydney Football Stadium, 1988; San Nicola Stadium, Bari, 1990; Pavilion of the Future, Seville, 1992; Brisbane Convention Exhibn Centre, 1994; Asian Games Stadium and Aquatic Centre, Bangkok, 1998; Sydney Olympic Velodrome, Tennis Centre and Sports Halls, 2000; Aurora Place, Sydney, 2000; City of Manchester Stadium, 2002; Khalifa Olympic Stadium, Doha, 2005; Northern Stand, Melbourne Cricket Ground, 2006; Beijing Olympic Aquatic Centre, 2008. Vis. Prof., Univ. of NSW, 2005–. Mem., Strategic Industry Leaders Gp: Built Envmt Design Professions Actions Agenda for Dept of Trade, Industry and Resources, 2007–. Dep. Chm., NSW Architects Registration Bd, 2004–. Arup Fellow, 2002–. Australian Professional Engr of Year, Instn of Engrs, Australia, 2001; Milne Medal, British Gp, IABSE, 2006. *Publications:* contribs to Australian Jl Structural Engrg, The Structural Engr. *Recreations:* sailing, travelling, eating and drinking. *Address:* (office) PO Box 76, Millers Point, NSW 2000, Australia. *T:* (2) 93209320, *Fax:* (2) 93209321; *e-mail:* tristram.carfrae@arup.com.au. *Club:* Royal Prince Alfred Yacht (Newport, NSW).

CARINE, Rear-Adm. James; Chief of Staff to Commander-in-Chief Naval Home Command, 1989–91; Registrar, Arab Horse Society, 1992–2000; *b* 14 Sept. 1934; *s* of Amos Carine and Kathleen Prudence Carine (*née* Kelly); *m* 1961, (Carolyn) Sally Taylor; three *s* one *d* (and two *s* decd). *Educ:* Victoria Road Sch., Castletown, IoM; King William's Coll., IoM. FCIS 1971. Joined Royal Navy 1951; Captain 1980; Sec., Second Sea Lord, 1979–82; SACLANT HQ, Norfolk, Va, 1982–85; Naval Home Staff, 1985–88; Commodore in Comd, HMS Drake, 1988–89. Pres., RN Assoc. (IOM), 1992–2000. Member: London Campaign Cttee for Multiple Sclerosis, 1993–95; Cttee, Ex-Services Mental Welfare Soc., 1997–2003; Copyright Tribunal, 1999–. Chairman: Age Concern Swindon, 2000–05; Wilts NHS Ambulance Service, 2002–06; Royal United Hosp. Bath NHS Trust, 2006–. Dir, United Services Trust, 1995–2005. Governor, St Antony's-Leweston Sch., 1996–2003. Chartered Secretaries' & Administrators' Co.: Liveryman, 1988; Mem., Court of Assistants, 1989; Jun. Warden, 1995–96; Sen. Warden, 1996–97; Master, 1997–98. KSG. *Recreations:* dinghy sailing, horse racing. *Address:* 5 Little Sands, Yatton Keynell, Chippenham, Wilts SN14 7BA.

CARINGTON, family name of **Baron Carrington**.

CARLAW, (David) Jackson; Member (C) Scotland West, Scottish Parliament, since 2007; *b* 12 April 1959; *s* of Ian Alexander Carlaw and Maureen Patricia Carlaw; *m* 1987, Wynne Stewart Martin; two *s*. *Educ:* Glasgow Acad. Man. Dir, Wylies Ltd, 1987–2000; Chm., First Ford (trading name of Eleander Ltd), 2000–02. Nat. Chm., Scottish Young Conservatives, 1984–86; Chm., Eastwood Conservatives, 1988–92; Scottish Conservative and Unionist Party: Vice Chm., 1992–97; Dep. Chm., 1997–98, 2005–06; Mem. Scottish Conservative Exec., 2003–07. Trustee, Glasgow Educnl and Marshall Trust, 2000–. Gov., Hutchesons' Grammar Sch., 2000–03. *Recreations:* theatre, film, reading, travel, family life. *Address:* Scottish Parliament, Edinburgh EH99 1SP. *T:* (0131) 348 6800, *Fax:* (0131) 348 6803; *e-mail:* jackson.carlaw.msp@scottish.parliament.uk.

CARLESS, Hugh Michael, CMG 1976; HM Diplomatic Service, retired; *b* 22 April 1925; *s* of late Henry Alfred Carless, CIE, and Gwendolen Pattullo; *m* 1956, Rosa Maria, *e d* of Martino and Ada Frontini, São Paulo; two *s*. *Educ:* Sherborne; Sch. of Oriental Studies, London; Trinity Hall, Cambridge. Served in Paiforce and BAOR, 1943–47; entered Foreign (subseq. Diplomatic) Service, 1950; 3rd Sec., Kabul, 1951; 2nd Sec., Rio de Janeiro, 1953; Tehran, 1956; 1st Sec., 1957; FO, 1958; Private Sec. to Minister of State, 1961; Budapest, 1963; Civil Service Fellow, Dept of Politics, Glasgow Univ., 1966; Counsellor and Consul-Gen., Luanda, 1967–70; Counsellor, Bonn, 1970–73; Head of Latin America Dept, FCO, 1973–77; Minister and Chargé d'Affaires, Buenos Aires, 1977–80; on secondment to Northern Engineering Industries International Ltd, 1980–82; Ambassador to Venezuela, 1982–85. Exec. Vice Pres., Hinduja Foundn (UK), 1986–97; Vice Chm., S Atlantic Council, 1987–97. Chm. British Cttee, Argentine-British Confs, 1994–96. Chm., GEECO International, 1997–2001. Cruise ship lectr, 2002–03. An Hon. Vice Pres., RSAA, 1992–95. *Recreations:* golf, history. *Address:* 15 Bryanston Square, W1H 2DN. *Clubs:* Travellers; Royal Mid Surrey Golf.

CARLETON, Air Vice-Marshal Geoffrey Wellesley, CB 1997; Director, Royal Air Force Legal Services, Ministry of Defence, 1992–97; Head of RAF Prosecuting Authority, 1997, retired; *b* 22 Sept. 1935; *s* of Gp Capt. Cyril Wellesley Carleton and Frances Beatrice (*née* Hensman); *m* 1985, Dianne Margaret Creswick; one *s*. *Educ:* Sherborne Sch. Admitted solicitor, 1959; commnd RAF, 1959, Pilot Officer, 1959–61; Asst Solicitor,

Herbert Smith & Co., 1961–65; re-joined RAF, 1965 as Flt Lieut; Legal Officer, HQ MEAF, Aden, HQ NEAF, Cyprus, HQ FEAF, Singapore, HQ RAF, Germany, 1965–78; Deputy Director of Legal Services: HQ RAF, Germany, 1978–82 and 1985–88; MoD, 1988–92. Non-exec. Dir, Poole Hospital NHS Trust, 1998–2006. *Publications:* articles in professional and service jls and pubns. *Recreations:* sailing, ski-ing, equitation, opera. *Address:* c/o National Westminster Bank, 5 Old Christchurch Road, Bournemouth BH1 1DU. *Clubs:* Royal Air Force, Royal Ocean Racing.

CARLETON-SMITH, Maj.-Gen. Sir Michael (Edward), Kt 1998; CBE 1980 (MBE 1966); DL; *b* 5 May 1931; *s* of late Lt-Col D. L. G. Carleton-Smith and Mrs B. L. C. Carleton-Smith (*née* Popham); *m* 1963, Helga Katja Stoss (*d* 1993); three *s*; partner, Lady Francis, (Penny), *widow* of Sir Richard Francis, KCMG. *Educ:* Radley Coll.; RMA, Sandhurst. Graduate: Army Staff Coll.; JSSC; NDC; RCDS. Commissioned into The Rifle Brigade, 1951; Rifle Bde, Germany, 1951–53; active service: Kenya, 1954–55; Malaya, 1957; Exchange PPCLI, Canada, 1958–60; GSO2 General Staff, HQ1(BR) Corps, 1962–63; Rifle Brigade: Cyprus, Hong Kong, active service, Borneo, 1965–66; Sch. of Infantry Staff, 1967–68; Comd Rifle Depot, 1970–72; Directing Staff NDC, 1972–74; Col General Staff, HQ BAOR, 1974–77; Commander Gurkha Field Force, Hong Kong, 1977–79; Dep. Director Army Staff Duties, MoD, 1981; Defence Advr and Head of British Defence Liaison Staff, Canberra, Australia, also Mil. Advr, Canberra, and Wellington, NZ, and Defence Advr, PNG, 1982–85, retd. Dir-Gen., Marie Curie Meml Foundn, then Marie Curie Cancer Care, 1985–96; Chm., Marie Curie Trading Co., 1990–95. Chm., Leicester Royal Infirmary NHS Trust, 1998–2000. Vice-Chm., Nat. Council for Hospice and Specialist Palliative Care Services, 1992–96. Chairman: Suzy Lamplugh Trust, 2000–01; Progressive Supra Nuclear Palsy Assoc. (Europe), 2001–. Gov., Royal Star and Garter Home, 1998–2002. Trustee, Britain Australia Soc., 1999–2003. DL Leics, 1992. *Recreations:* travel, current affairs, history. *Address:* Plough Cottage, Drayton, Market Harborough, Leics LE16 8SD.

CARLIER, Maj.-Gen. Anthony Neil, CB 1992; OBE 1982; Director, Haig Homes, 1992–2002; *b* 11 Jan. 1937; *s* of Geoffrey Anthony George and Sylvia Maude Carlier; *m* 1974, Daphne Kathleen Humphreys; one *s* one *d*. *Educ:* Highgate Sch.; RMA Sandhurst; RMCS. BSc(Eng) London. Troop Comdr, Cyprus, 1962–64; GSO3, 19 Inf. Bde, Borneo, 1965–66; Instructor, RMA Sandhurst, 1967–70; Staff Course: RMCS Shrivenham, 1971; BRNC Greenwich, 1972; GSO2, Staff of Flag Officer, Carriers and Amphibious Ships, 1973–74; Sqn Comdr, 1975–76; Regtl Comdr, 1977–80; Mil. Asst to Army Bd Mem., 1980–83; Engr Gp Comdr, 1983–85; rcds, 1986; Comdr British Forces, Falkland Is, 1987–88; Chief, Jt Services Liaison Organisation, Bonn, 1989–90; Team Leader, QMG's Logistic Support Review, 1991–92. Col Comdt, RE, 1993–2000. President: Officers' Christian Union, 1992–97; Mission to Mil. Garrisons, 1992–; Chm., UK Appeal Cttee for Christ Church Cathedral, Falkland Is, 1989–2000. Trustee: Cornelius Trust, 1992–2002; Royal Engineer Yacht Club, 1992–; Leadership and Ethics Centre, Ballycastle, Co. Antrim, 2001–. Gov., Monkton Combe Sch., 1996–2004; Chm., Clare Park Private Retirement Residences, 2007–. *Recreations:* offshore sailing, fishing, gardening, DIY. *Club:* International Association of Cape Horners (Faversham).

CARLILE, family name of **Baron Carlile of Berriew**.

CARLILE OF BERRIEW, Baron *cr* 1999 (Life Peer), of Berriew in the County of Powys; **Alexander Charles Carlile;** QC 1984; a Recorder, since 1986; a Deputy High Court Judge, since 1998; *b* 12 Feb. 1948; *m* Frances (marr. diss. 2007), *d* of Michael and Elizabeth Soley; three *d*; *m* Alison Frances Josephine Levitt, *qv*. *Educ:* Epsom Coll.; King's Coll., London (LLB; AKC; FKC 2003). Called to the Bar, Gray's Inn, 1970, Bencher, 1992. Hon. Recorder, City of Hereford, 1995–. Contested (L) Flint E, Feb. 1974, 1979. MP (L) 1983–88, (Lib Dem) 1988–97, Montgomery. Chm., Welsh Liberal Party, 1980–82; Leader, Welsh Lib Dems, 1992–97. Chm., Welsh Assembly Review on Safety of Children in the NHS, 2000–02; Ind. Reviewer of Terrorism Legislation, 2002–. Non-exec. Dir, Wynnstay Group (formerly Wynnstay & Clwyd Farmers) plc, 1998–. Member: Adv. Council on Public Records, 1989–95; GMC, 1989–99; Council, Justice, 1993–. Chm., Competition Appeals Tribunal, 2005–. Pres., Howard League for Penal Reform, 2006–. Director and Trustee: Nuffield Trust, 1997–2007; White Ensign Assoc. Ltd, 2002–; Trustee, Royal Med. Foundn of Epsom Coll., 2003–. Fellow, Industry and Parlt Trust, 1985. *Recreations:* reading, music. *Address:* 9–12 Bell Yard, WC2A 2JR.

CARLILE OF BERRIEW, Lady; *see* Levitt, A. F. J.

CARLILE, Thomas, CBE 1975; FREng; Chairman, Burnett and Hallamshire Holdings, 1985–88; *b* 9 Feb. 1924; *s* of late James Love Carlile and Isobel Scott Carlile; *m* 1955, Jessie Davidson Clarkson; three *d*. *Educ:* Minchenden County Sch.; City & Guilds Coll., London. Joined Babcock & Wilcox Ltd, 1944; Man. Dir, 1968–84, Dep. Chm., 1978–84, Babcock Internat. plc. Chm., Shipbuilding Industry Training Board, 1967–70; Dep. Chm., Police Negotiating Bd, 1987–95. Mem., Energy Commn, 1977–79. Pres., Engineering Employers' Fedn, 1972–74, a Vice-Pres., 1979–84. Director: Chubb & Son plc, 1976–84; French Kier Hldgs Plc, 1985–86. Chm., British Soc. of Master Glass Painters, 1995–2000. FCGI 1978; FREng (FEng 1979). *Address:* 8 Aldenham Grove, Radlett, Herts WD7 7BW. *T:* (01923) 857033.

CARLILL, Rear Adm. John Hildred, OBE 1969; DL; Royal Navy, retired 1982; *b* 24 Oct. 1925; *o s* of late Dr and Mrs H. B. Carlill; *m* 1955, (Elizabeth) Ann, *yr d* of late Lt Col and Mrs W. Southern; three *d*. *Educ:* RNC Dartmouth. psc 1961; jssc 1967. Served War 1939–45. Joined RN as Exec. Cadet 1939, transferred to Accountant Branch 1943; HMS Mauritius 1943–45. Comdr 1963, Captain 1972 (Sec. to FO Naval Air Comd, Dir Naval Manning and Training (S), Sec. to Second Sea Lord, Admty Interview Board, Cdre HMS Drake); Rear Admiral 1980; Adm. President, RNC Greenwich, 1980–82. Sec., Engineering Council, 1983–87. Chm., ABTA Appeal Bd, 1996–. President: Guildford Br., RN Assoc., 1989–; Guildford Sea Cadets, 1998–2007. Freeman: City of London, 1980; Drapers' Co., 1983. DL Surrey, 1994. Chevalier de la Légion d'Honneur (France), 2004. *Recreations:* walking, short story writing, water colour painting. *Address:* 1 Wonersh Court, The Street, Wonersh, Guildford, Surrey GU5 0PG. *T:* (01483) 893077.

CARLING, William David Charles, OBE 1991; Rugby football commentator, ITV, since 1997; *b* 12 Dec. 1965; *s* of Pamela and Bill Carling; *m* 1999, Lisa Cooke; two *c*. *Educ:* Sedbergh School; Durham Univ. (BA Psych.). Played for Harlequins, 1987–97 and 1999–2000; international career, 1988–97: 1st cap for England, 1988; 72 caps, 59 as Captain; Captain of England, 1988–96 (centre three-quarter); captained: three Grand Slam sides, 1991, 1992, 1995; World Cup final, 1991; Barbarians, in Hong Kong 7's, 1991; England tour, South Africa, 1994; World Cup, South Africa, 1995; Mem., British Lions, NZ tour, 1993. *Publications:* Captain's Diary, 1991; Rugby Skills, 1994; (with R. Heller) The Way to Win, 1995; (with P. Ackford) Will Carling: my autobiography, 1998. *Recreations:* theatre, sketching, golf. *Address:* WCM, 3000 Hillswood Drive, Chertsey, Surrey KT16 0RS. *Clubs:* Special Forces, Groucho; Harlequins, Harbour.

CARLISLE, 13th Earl of *cr* 1661; **George William Beaumont Howard;** Viscount Howard of Morpeth, Baron Dacre of Gillesland 1661; Lord Ruthven of Freeland 1651; *b* 15 Feb. 1949; *s* of 12th Earl of Carlisle, MC, and Hon. Ela Hilda Aline Beaumont, *o d* of 2nd Viscount Allendale, KG, CB, CBE, MC; *S* father, 1994. *Educ:* Eton Coll.; Balliol Coll., Oxford; Army Staff Coll., Camberley. 9th/12th Royal Lancers, 1967–87; Lieut 1970, Captain 1974, Major 1981. Lectr, Estonian Nat. Defence and Public Service Acad., 1995–96. Sec., British–Estonian All-Party Parly Gp, 1997–99. Contested: (L/Alliance) Easington, 1987; (Lib Dem): Northumbria, European parly elecn, 1989; Leeds West, 1992. Order of Marjamac, 1st class, 1998. *Recreations:* reading, travel, learning Estonian. *Heir:* *b* Hon. Philip Charles Wentworth Howard [*b* 25 March 1963; *m* 1992, Elizabeth Harrison (*née* Moore); one *s* one *d*]. *Clubs:* Beefsteak, Pratt's.

CARLISLE, Bishop of, since 2000; **Rt Rev. Geoffrey Graham Dow;** *b* 4 July 1942; *s* of Ronald Graham Dow and Dorothy May Dow (*née* Christie); *m* 1966, Molly Patricia (*née* Sturges); three *s* one *d*. *Educ:* St Alban's Sch.; Queen's Coll., Oxford (BA 1963; BSc 1965; MA 1968); Clifton Theol Coll.; Birmingham Univ. (Dip. Pastoral Studies 1974); Nottingham Univ. (MPhil 1982). Ordained deacon, 1967, priest, 1968; Asst Curate, Tonbridge Parish Church, 1967–72; Chaplain-Student, St John's Coll., Oxford, 1972–75; Lectr in Christian Doctrine, St John's Coll., Nottingham, 1975–81; Vicar, Holy Trinity, Coventry, 1981–92; Canon Theologian, Coventry Cathedral, 1988–92; Area Bp of Willesden, 1992–2000. *Publications:* Dark Satanic Mills? Shaftesbury Project, 1979; The Local Church's Political Responsibility, 1980; St John's College Extension Studies B1—God and the World, 1980; Whose Hand on the Tiller?, 1983; Those Tiresome Intruders, 1990; Explaining Deliverance, 1991; Christian Renewal in Europe, 1992; A Christian Understanding of Daily Work, 1994; Pathways of Prayer, 1996. *Recreations:* steam and narrow gauge railways, model railways, travel, music. *Address:* Rose Castle, Dalston, Carlisle CA5 7BZ. *T:* (016974) 76274, *Fax:* (016974) 76550; *e-mail:* bishop.carlisle@carlislediocese.org.uk.

CARLISLE, Dean of; *see* Boyling, Very Rev. M. C.

CARLISLE, Archdeacon of; *no new appointment at time of going to press.*

CARLISLE, Hugh Bernard Harwood; QC 1978; *b* 14 March 1937; *s* of late W. H. Carlisle, FRCS (Ed), FRCOG, and Joyce Carlisle; *m* 1964, Veronica Marjorie, *d* of late G. A. Worth, MBE; one *s* one *d*. *Educ:* Oundle Sch.; Downing Coll., Cambridge. Nat. Service, 2nd Lt, RA. Called to the Bar, Middle Temple, 1961, Bencher, 1985. Jun. Treasury Counsel for Personal Injuries Cases, 1975–78; a Recorder, 1983–2002; a Deputy High Court Judge, 1984–2002. Dept of Trade Inspector: Bryanston Finance Ltd, 1978–87; Milbury plc, 1985–87. Pres., Transport Tribunal, 1997–. Member: Criminal Injuries Compensation Bd, 1982–2000; Bar Council, 1989–92 (Chm., Professional Conduct Cttee, 1991–92). *Recreations:* fly fishing, woodworking, croquet. *Address:* 1 Temple Gardens, EC4Y 9BB. *T:* (020) 7583 1315. *Clubs:* Garrick, Hurlingham (Chm., 1982–85).

See also A. J. L. Worth.

CARLISLE, Sir James (Beethoven), GCMG 1993; Governor-General of Antigua and Barbuda, 1993–2007; *b* 5 Aug. 1937; *s* of late James Carlisle and of Jestina Jones; *m* 1st, 1963, Umilta Mercer (marr. diss. 1973); one *s* one *d*; 2nd, 1973, Anne Jenkins (marr. diss. 1984); one *d*; 3rd, 1984, Nalda Amelia Meade; one *s* one *d*. *Educ:* Univ. of Dundee (BDS). General Dentistry, 1972–92. Chief Scout of Antigua and Barbuda. Chm., Nat. Parks Authority, 1986–90. Member: BDA; Amer. Acad. of Laser Dentistry; Internat. Assoc. of Laser Dentistry. Hon. FDSRCSE 1995. Hon. LLD Andrews Univ., USA, 1995. Kt Grand Cross, Order of Queen of Sheba (Ethiopia), 1995. KStJ 2001. *Recreation:* gardening. *Address:* PO Box W1644, St John's, Antigua, West Indies.

CARLISLE, Sir (John) Michael, Kt 1985; DL; CEng, FIMechE, FIMarEST; Chairman, Trent Regional Health Authority, 1982–94; *b* 16 Dec. 1929; *s* of John Hugh Carlisle and Lilian Amy (*née* Smith); *m* 1957, Mary Scott Young; one *s* one *d*. *Educ:* King Edward VII Sch., Sheffield; Sheffield Univ. (BEng). Served Royal Navy (Lieut), 1952–54. Production Engr, Lockwood & Carlisle Ltd, 1954–57, Man. Dir, 1958–70, Chm. and Man. Dir, 1970–81; Dir of several overseas subsid. cos; Director: Eric Woodward (Electrical) Ltd, 1965–85; Diesel Marine Internat., 1981–89; Torday & Carlisle, 1981–94. Chairman: N Sheffield Univ. HMC, 1971–74; Sheffield AHA(T), 1974–82; Community Health Sheffield NHS Trust, 1994–99; Scarborough and NE Yorks Healthcare NHS Trust, 2007–; Member: Sheffield HMC, 1969–71; Bd of Governors, United Sheffield Hosps, 1972–74; MRC, 1991–95; NHS Policy Bd, 1993–94; Scarborough, Whitby and Ryedale Patient and Public Involvement Forum, 2003–07. Member Council: Sheffield Chamber of Commerce, 1967–78; Production Engrg Res. Assoc., 1968–73; Chm., Sheffield Productivity Assoc., 1970; Pres., Sheffield Jun. Chamber of Commerce, 1967–68; non-executive Director: Fenchurch Midlands Ltd, 1986–94; Norhomes plc, 1989–97; Welpac plc, 1991–95; Residences at York plc, 1992–97; York Science Park Ltd, 1992–; York Science Park (Innovation) Centre Ltd, 1995–2001; Headrow Northern plc, 1992–97; Headrow Western plc, 1993–97; Xceleron (formerly CBAMS) Ltd, 1997–2005; SE Sheffield Primary Care Gp, 1999–2001. Chm., Sheffield Macmillan Horizons Appeal, 1999–2002; Trustee, Age Concern (Scarborough and Dist.), 2004–. Governor: Sheffield City Polytechnic, 1979–82 (Hon. Fellow, 1977); Sheffield High Sch., 1977–87; Member: Sheffield Univ. Court, 1968–; Sheffield Univ. Careers Adv. Bd, 1974–82; Nottingham Univ. Court, 1982–94; Court, York Univ., 1991– (Mem. Council, 1991–2006; Pro-Chancellor, 1996–2006; Vice-Chm., 2001–06); Bd, Hull-York Med. Sch., 2002–07. CCMI. Freeman, City of London, 1989; Freeman, Co. of Cutlers in Hallamshire. DL S Yorks, 1996. Hon. LLD: Sheffield, 1988; Nottingham, 1992; DUniv York, 1998. *Recreations:* golf, country walking, water colour painting, genealogy. *Address:* St Ovin, Lastingham, N Yorks YO62 6TL. *T:* (01751) 417341; 4 Broad Elms Lane, Sheffield S11 9RQ. *T:* (0114) 236 5988. *Clubs:* Royal Society of Medicine; Sickleholme Golf; Kirkbymoorside Golf.

CARLISLE, John Russell; political and media consultant, since 2002; *b* 28 Aug. 1942; *s* of Andrew and Edith Carlisle; *m* 1964, Anthea Jane Lindsay May; two *d*. *Educ:* Bedford Sch.; St Lawrence Coll.; Coll. of Estate Management, London. Sidney C. Banks Ltd, Sandy, 1964–78; Consultant: Louis Dreyfus plc, 1982–87; Barry Simmons PR, 1987–97; non-executive Director: Bletchley Motor Gp, 1988–95; Charles Sidney plc, 1995–97; Member: London Corn Exchange, 1987–97; Baltic Exchange, 1991–97; Exec. Dir, Tobacco Manufrs' Assoc., 1997–2001. Chm., Mid Beds Cons. Assoc., 1974–76. MP (C) Luton West, 1979–83, Luton North, 1983–97. Chm., Cons Parly Cttee on Sport, 1981–82, 1983–84, 1985–97; Vice Chm., All-Party Football Cttee, 1987–97; Mem., Commons Select Cttee on Agriculture, 1985–88. Chm., British-S Africa Gp, 1987 (Sec., 1983–87); Treas., Anglo-Gibraltar Gp, 1981–82. Governor, Sports Aid Foundn (Eastern), 1985–96. President: Luton 100 Club; Luton Band; Bedfordshire CCC, 1993–97. *Recreations:* sport, music, shooting. *Address:* The Old Post House, Fairseat, Sevenoaks, Kent TN15 7LU. *Clubs:* Carlton, Farmers', MCC.

CARLISLE, Sir Kenneth (Melville), Kt 1994; *b* 25 March 1941; *s* of late Kenneth Ralph Malcolm Carlisle, TD and of Hon. Elizabeth Mary McLaren, *d* of 2nd Baron Aberconway; *m* 1986, Carla, *d* of A. W. Heffner, Md, USA; one *s*. *Educ:* Harrow; Magdalen Coll., Oxford (BA History). Called to Bar, Inner Temple, 1965. Brooke Bond Liebig, 1966–74; farming in Suffolk, 1974–. MP (C) Lincoln, 1979–97. PPS to: Minister of State for Energy, 1981–83; Minister of State for Home Office, 1983–84; Sec. of State for NI, 1984–85; Home Secretary, 1985–87; an Asst Govt Whip, 1987–88; a Lord Comr of HM Treasury, 1988–90; Parly Under-Sec. of State, MoD, 1990–92, Dept of Transport, 1992–93. Mem., Public Accts Cttee, 1994–97. Member Council: RSPB, 1985–87; RHS, 1996–2006; Suffolk Wildlife Trust, 2007–. *Recreations:* botany, gardening, history. *Address:* Wyken Hall, Stanton, Bury St Edmunds, Suffolk IP31 2DW.

CARLISLE, Sir Michael; *see* Carlisle, Sir J. M.

CARLOW, Viscount; Charles George Yuill Seymour Dawson-Damer; *b* 6 Oct. 1965; *s* and *heir* of 7th Earl of Portarlington, *qv*; *m* 2002, Clare, *y d* of Rodney Garside; three *d*. *Educ:* Eton College; Univ. of Edinburgh (MA Hons 1988). A Page of Honour to the Queen, 1979–80. *Address:* 7 Cambridge Avenue, Vaucluse, Sydney, NSW 2030, Australia. *Clubs:* Australian, Royal Sydney Golf (Sydney).

CARLOWAY, Rt Hon. Lord; Colin John MacLean Sutherland; PC 2008; a Senator of the College of Justice in Scotland, since 2000; *b* 20 May 1954; *s* of Eric Alexander Cruickshank Sutherland and Mary Macaulay or Sutherland; *m* 1988, Jane Alexander Turnbull; two *s*. *Educ:* Hurst Grange Prep. Sch., Stirling; Edinburgh Acad.; Edinburgh Univ. (LLB Hons). Advocate, 1977; Advocate Depute, 1986–89; QC (Scot.) 1990. Treas., Faculty of Advocates, 1994–2000. *Address:* Supreme Courts, Parliament House, Edinburgh EH1 1RQ. *T:* (0131) 225 2595. *Club:* Scottish Arts (Edinburgh).

CARLSSON, Prof. Arvid, MD; Professor of Pharmacology, University of Gothenburg, 1959–89, now Emeritus; *b* Uppsala, Sweden, 25 Jan. 1923. *Educ:* Univ. of Lund, Sweden (ML; MD 1951). Asst Prof., 1951–56, Associate Prof., 1956–59, Univ. of Lund. Vis. Scientist, Lab. of Chemical Pathol., Nat. Heart Inst., Bethesda, Md, 1955–56. Mem., Scientific Adv. Bd, Acadia Pharmaceuticals, 1999–. (Jtly) Nobel Prize for Physiol. or Medicine, 2000. *Publications:* articles in jls. *Address:* Department of Pharmacology, University of Gothenburg, Medicinaregatan 7, Box 431, 40530 Gothenburg, Sweden.

CARLTON, Viscount; Reed Montagu Stuart Wortley; *b* 5 Feb. 1980; *s* and *heir* of Earl of Wharncliffe, *qv*.

CARLUCCIO, Antonio Mario Gaetano, Hon. OBE 2007; restaurateur, broadcaster and author; *b* 19 April 1937; *s* of Giovanni Carluccio and Maria (*née* Trivellone); *m* 1981, Priscilla Marion Conran. *Educ:* Roland Matura Schule, Vienna. Reporter, Gazzetta del Popolo, and La Stampa, Turin, 1953–54; wine merchant, Germany, 1963–75, England, 1975–81; restaurateur, 1981–89, Proprietor, 1989–2007, The Neal Street Restaurant; Jt Proprietor, Carluccio's Italian Food Shop, 1991–. *Television:* various appearances, BBC2, 1986–; *series:* Italian Feast, BBC2, 1996; Southern Italian Feast, BBC2, 1998. Hon. Associate, Altagamma Internat. Hon. Council, 2005. Commendatore, Order of Merit (Italy), 1999. *Publications:* Invitation to Italian Cooking (Bejam Cookery Book of the Year), 1986; Passion for Mushrooms, 1989; Passion for Pasta, 1993; Italian Feast (Best Cookery Book, Good Food mag.), 1996; Carluccio's Complete Italian Food, 1997; Southern Italian Feast, 1998; The Carluccio Collection, 1999; Antonio Carluccio's Vegetables, 2000; The Complete Mushroom Book: the quiet hunt, 2003; Italia, 2005. *Address:* 34 Tavistock Street, WC2E 7BP.

CARLYLE, Joan Hildred; soprano; *b* 6 April 1931; *d* of late Edgar James and Margaret Mary Carlyle; *m*; two *d*. *Educ:* Howell's Sch., Denbigh, N Wales. Became Principal Lyric Soprano, Royal Opera House, Covent Garden, 1955; Oscar in Ballo in Maschera, 1957–58 season; Sophie in Rosenkavalier, 1958–59; Micaela in Carmen, 1958–59; Nedda in Pagliacci (new Zeffirelli production), Dec. 1959; Mimi in La Bohème, Dec. 1960; Titania in Gielgud production of Britten's Midsummer Night's Dream, London première, Dec. 1961; Pamina in Klemperer production of The Magic Flute, 1962; Countess in Figaro, 1963; Zdenko in Hartman production of Arabella, 1964; Sœur Angelica (new production), 1965; Desdemona in Otello, 1965, 1967; Sophie in Rosenkavalier (new production), 1966; Pamina in Magic Flute (new production), 1966; Arabella in Arabella, 1967; Marschallin in Rosenkavalier, 1968; Jenifer, Midsummer Marriage (new prod.), 1969; Donna Anna, 1970; Reiza, Oberon, 1970; Adrianna Lecouvreur, 1970; Rusalka, for BBC, 1969; Elizabeth in Don Carlos, 1975. Roles sung abroad include: Oscar, Nedda, Mimi, Pamina, Zdenko, Micaela, Desdemona, Donna Anna, Arabella, Elizabeth. Has sung in Buenos Aires, Belgium, Holland, France, Monaco, Naples, Milan, Berlin, Capetown, Munich. Has made numerous recordings; appeared BBC, TV (in film). Teaches at home and gives masterclasses. *Recreations:* gardening, cooking, interior decorating, countryside preservation. *Address:* Laundry Cottage, Hanmer, N Wales SY13 3DQ; *e-mail:* joan.carlyle@BTclick.com; *web:* www.joancarlyle.co.uk.

CARLYLE, Robert, OBE 1990; actor; *b* Glasgow, 14 April 1961; *s* of late Joseph Carlyle and of Elizabeth Carlyle; *m* 1997, Anastasia Shirley; two *s* one *d*. *Educ:* North Kelvinside Secondary Sch.; RSAMD. Founder, Rain Dog Theatre Co., 1990; dir of prodns incl. Wasted, One Flew Over the Cuckoo's Nest, Conquest of the South Pole, Macbeth. *Theatre includes:* Twelfth Night; Dead Dad Dog; Nae Problem; City; No Mean City; Cuttin' a Rug; Othello. *Television includes:* The Part of Valour, 1981; Hamish Macbeth, 1995; Cracker, 1993, 1997, 1999–2001; Safe, 1993; The Advocates; Arena; Byrne on Byrne; Taggart; Looking After Jo Jo, 1998; Hitler: the rise of evil, 2003; Gunpowder, Treason and Plot, 2004; Class of '76, 2005; The Last Enemy, 2008. *Films include:* Riff Raff, 1990; Silent Scream, 1990; Safe, 1993; Being Human, 1993; Priest, 1994; Go Now, 1995; Trainspotting, 1996; Carla's Song, 1996; Face, 1997; The Full Monty, 1997 (Best Actor, BAFTA, 1998); Ravenous, 1999; Plunkett & Macleane, 1999; The World is Not Enough, 1999; Angela's Ashes, 2000; The Beach, 2000; There's Only One Jimmy Grimble, 2000; To End All Wars, 2000; The 51st State, 2001; Once Upon a Time in the Midlands, 2002; Black and White, 2004; The Mighty Celt, Marilyn Hotchkiss' Ballroom Dancing and Charm School, 2005; 28 Weeks Later, 2007. Best Actor: Evening Standard Film Awards, 1998; Film Critics' Circle Awards, 1998; Bowmore Whisky/Scottish Screen Awards, 2001; Michael Elliott Awards, 2001; David Puttnam Patrons Award. *Address:* c/o Independent Talent Group Ltd, Oxford House, 76 Oxford Street, W1D 1BS.

CARMICHAEL, Alexander Morrison, (Alistair); MP (Lib Dem) Orkney and Shetland, since 2001; *b* 15 July 1965; *s* of Alexander C. Carmichael and Mina Neil McKay or Carmichael; *m* 1987, Kathryn Jane Eastham; two *s*. *Educ:* Port Ellen Primary Sch.; Islay High Sch.; Aberdeen Univ. (LLB 1992; DipLP 1993). Hotel Manager, Glasgow and Orkney, 1984–89; Procurator Fiscal Depute, Crown Office, Edinburgh and Aberdeen, 1993–96; solicitor in private practice, Aberdeen and Macduff, 1996–2001. *Recreations:* music, theatre. *Address:* House of Commons, SW1A 0AA. *T:* (020) 7219 8181; The Old Manse, Evie, Orkney KW17 2PH. *T:* (01856) 751343.

CARMICHAEL, Catherine McIntosh, (Kay); social worker; *b* 22 Nov. 1925; *d* of John D. and Mary Rankin; *m* 1948, Neil George Carmichael (later Baron Carmichael of Kelvingrove) (marr. diss.; he *d* 2001); one *d*; *m* 1987, David Vernon Donnison, *qv*. *Educ:* Glasgow and Edinburgh. Social worker, 1955–57; psychiatric social work, 1957–60; Dep. Dir, Scottish Probation Training Course, 1960–62; Lectr, 1962, Sen. Lectr, 1974–80, Dept of Social Administration and Social Work, Univ. of Glasgow. Mem., 1969–75, Dep. Chm., 1975–80, Supplementary Benefits Commn. Mem., Gareloch Horticulturalists; lifelong peace protester. *Publications:* Ceremony of Innocence, 1991; For Crying Out Loud, 1993; Sin and Forgiveness, 2003. *Recreation:* Alexander technique. *Address:* 23 Bank Street, Glasgow G12 8JQ. *T:* (0141) 334 5817.

CARMICHAEL, Sir David Peter William G. C.; *see* Gibson-Craig-Carmichael.

CARMICHAEL, Ian (Gillett), OBE 2003; actor; *b* 18 June 1920; *s* of Arthur Denholm Carmichael, Cottingham, E Yorks, and Kate Gillett, Hessle, E Yorks; *m* 1st, 1943, Jean Pyman Maclean (*d* 1983), Sleights, N Yorks; two *d*; 2nd, 1992, Kate Fenton, novelist. *Educ:* Scarborough Coll.; Bromsgrove Sch. Studied at RADA, 1938–39. Served War of 1939–45 (despatches). First professional appearance as a Robot in "RUR", by Karel and Josef Capek, The People's Palace, Stepney, 1939; *stage appearances* include: The Lyric Revue, Globe, 1951; The Globe Revue, Globe, 1952; High Spirits, Hippodrome, 1953; Going to Town, St Martin's, 1954; Simon and Laura, Apollo, 1954; The Tunnel of Love, Her Majesty's, 1958; The Gazebo, Savoy, 1960; Critic's Choice, Vaudeville, 1961; Devil May Care, Strand, 1963; Boeing-Boeing, Cort Theatre, New York, 1965; Say Who You Are, Her Majesty's, 1965; Getting Married, Strand, 1968; I Do! I Do!, Lyric, 1968; Birds on the Wing, O'Keefe Centre, Toronto, 1969; Darling I'm Home, S African tour, 1972; Out on a Limb, Vaudeville, 1976; Overheard, Theatre Royal, Haymarket, 1981; Pride and Prejudice, Theatre Royal, York and nat. tour, 1987; The Circle, nat. tour, 1990; The School for Scandal, Chichester, 1995. *Films* include: (from 1955) Simon and Laura; Private's Progress; Brothers in Law; Lucky Jim; Happy is the Bride; The Big Money; Left, Right and Centre; I'm All Right Jack; School for Scoundrels; Light Up The Sky; Double Bunk; The Amorous Prawn; Hide and Seek; Heavens Above!; Smashing Time; The Magnificent Seven Deadly Sins; From Beyond the Grave; The Lady Vanishes. *TV series* include: The World of Wooster; Bachelor Father; Lord Peter Wimsey; All For Love; Obituaries; Strathblair; Wives and Daughters, 1999; The Royal, 2002–. Hon. DLitt Hull, 1987. *Publication:* Will the Real Ian Carmichael… (autobiog.), 1979. *Recreations:* cricket, gardening, photography and reading. *Address:* c/o Diamond Management, 31 Percy Street, W1T 2DD. *Club:* MCC.

CARMICHAEL, Prof. Ian Stuart Edward, PhD; FRS 1999; Professor of Geology, University of California, Berkeley, 1967–2004, now Emeritus; *b* 29 March 1930; *s* of Edward Arnold Carmichael and Jeanette Carmichael; two *s* two *d* from former marriages. *Educ:* Trinity Hall, Cambridge (BA 1954); Imperial Coll., London Univ. (PhD 1958). Lectr in Geology, Imperial Coll., London Univ., 1958–63; NSF Fellow, Univ. of Chicago, 1964; University of California, Berkeley: Mem. Faculty, 1964–; Chm., Dept of Geology, 1972–76, 1980–82; Associate Dean, 1976–78, 1985–2000; Associate Provost for Res., 1986–2000; Director: Lawrence Hall of Sci., 1996–2003; Botanic Garden, 1997–99. Day Medal, Geol Soc. Amer., 1991; Schlumberger Medal, Mineralol Soc., 1992; Murchison Medal, Geol Soc., 1995; Roebling Medal, Mineralol Soc. Amer., 1997. *Publications:* Igneous Petrology, 1974; contribs to jls. *Address:* Department of Earth and Planetary Science, University of California, Berkeley, CA 94720, USA; *e-mail:* ian@eps.berkeley.edu.

CARMICHAEL, (Katharine) Jane, (Mrs A. Craxton); Director of Collections, National Museums of Scotland, since 2003; *b* 12 March 1952; *d* of Donald and Margaret Carmichael; *m* 1989, Adrian Craxton; two *d*, and one step *s* two step *d*. *Educ:* St Leonards, St Andrews; Edinburgh Univ. (MA Modern Hist.). Imperial War Museum, 1974–2003: Keeper, Photographic Archive, 1982–95; Dir of Collections, 1995–2003. Served various cttees of Nat. Museums Dirs Conf., 1995–. FRSA 2000. *Publications:* First World War Photographers, 1989; contrib. various jl articles. *Recreations:* the family, country walking, going to the ballet. *Address:* National Museums of Scotland, Chambers Street, Edinburgh EH1 1JF. *T:* (0131) 247 4415, *Fax:* (0131) 247 4308.

CARMICHAEL, Kay; *see* Carmichael, C. M.

CARMICHAEL, Keith Stanley, CBE 1981; FCA; chartered accountant in practice, 1969–81 and since 1990; *b* 5 Oct. 1929; *s* of Stanley and Ruby Dorothy Carmichael; *m* 1958, Cynthia Mary (née Jones); one *s*. *Educ:* Charlton House Sch.; Bristol Grammar Sch.; qualified as Chartered Accountant, 1951; FTII 1951, FCA 1961. Partner, Wilson Bigg & Co., 1957–69; Man. Partner, Longcrofts, 1981–90. Director: H. Foulks Lynch & Co. Ltd, 1957–69; Radio Rentals Ltd, 1967–69. Member: Monopolies and Mergers Commn, 1983–92; Council, Share and Business Valuers, 1995–; Soc. of Trust and Estate Practitioners, 1996–. Lloyd's Underwriter, 1976–90. Pres., Hertsmere Cons. Assoc. Chm. Bd of Governors, and Trustee, Rickmansworth Masonic Sch., 1984–. Freeman, City of London, 1960. FInstD. Mem., Editl Bd, Simon's Taxes, 1970–82. CStJ 2001. *Publications:* Spicer and Pegler's Income Tax (ed), 1965; Corporation Tax, 1966; Capital Gains Tax, 1968; Ranking Spicer and Pegler's Executorship Law and Accounts (ed), 1969, 1987; (with P. Wolstenholme) Taxation of Lloyd's Underwriters, 1980, 4th edn 1993; contribs to Accountancy. *Recreations:* gardening, reading, golf. *Address:* 117 Newberries Avenue, Radlett, Herts WD7 7EN. *T:* (01923) 855098. *Clubs:* Carlton (Dep. Chm., 1989–95; Trustee, 1999–), MCC, Lord's Taverners.

CARNAC, Sir Miles James R.; *see* Rivett-Carnac.

CARNALL, Ruth, CBE 2004; Chief Executive, Strategic Health Authority for London (NHS London), since 2007 (Interim Chief Executive, 2006–07); *b* 26 July 1956; *d* of Alan and Joan Taylor; *m* 1988, Colin Carnall; two *s*. *Educ:* Henley Coll. of Mgt (MBA). ACMA 1980; CPFA (IPFA 1984); IHSM 1988. Various posts in finance, St Thomas' Hosp., 1977–87; Dir of Finance, Hastings HA, 1987–89; Unit Gen. Manager, Hastings Acute Hosps, 1989–90; Dist Gen. Manager, then Chief Exec., Hastings and Rother HA, then NHS Trust, 1990–92; Dir of Perf. Mgt, 1992–93, Actg Regl Gen. Manager, 1993–94, SE Thames RHA; Chief Exec., W Kent HA, 1994–2000; Department of Health: Regl Dir, SE, NHS Exec., 2000–02; Regl Dir of Health and Social Care (S), 2002; Dir, Change Mgt Prog., 2003–04; freelance consultant to Govt depts and NHS, 2004–06. Non-exec. Dir, Care UK plc, 2004–06. *Recreations:* family, cooking, sport. *Address:* Eversleigh, London Road, Westerham, Kent TN16 1DS. *T:* (01959) 561211, *Fax:* (01959) 563999.

CARNARVON, 8th Earl of, *cr* 1793; **George Reginald Oliver Molyneux Herbert;** Baron Porchester 1780; *b* 10 Nov. 1956; *er s* of 7th Earl of Carnarvon, KCVO, KBE; *S* father, 2001; *m* 1st, 1989, Jayne (marr. diss. 1997), *d* of K. A. Wilby, Cheshire; one *s* one *d*; 2nd, 1999, Fiona, *e d* of late R. Aitken; one *s*. *Educ:* St John's Coll., Oxford (BA). A Page of Honour to the Queen, 1969–73. *Heir: s* Lord Porchester, *qv*. *Address:* The Field House, Highclere Park, Newbury RG15 9RN. *Club:* White's.

CARNE, Dr Stuart John, CBE 1986 (OBE 1977); FRCGP; Senior Partner, Grove Health Centre, 1967–91; *b* 19 June 1926; *s* of late Bernard Carne and Millicent Carne; *m* 1951, Yolande (*née* Cooper); two *s* two *d*. *Educ:* Willesden County Grammar Sch.; Middlesex Hosp. Med. Sch. MB BS; MRCS; LRCP; DCH. House Surgeon, Middlesex Hosp., 1950–51; House Physician, House Surgeon and Casualty Officer, Queen Elizabeth Hosp. for Children, 1951–52; Flight Lieut, Med. Branch, RAF, 1952–54; general practice in London, 1954–99; Sen. Tutor in General Practice, RPMS, 1970–91. DHSS appointments: Chm., Standing Med. Adv. Cttee, 1982–86 (Mem., 1974–86); Member: Central Health Services Council, 1976–79; Children's Cttee, 1978–81; Personal Social Services Council, 1976–80; Chm., Jt Cttee on Contraception, 1983–86 (Mem., 1975–86). Hon. Civil Consultant in Gen. Practice to RAF, 1974–. Royal College of General Practitioners: Mem. Council, 1961–91; Hon. Treasurer, 1964–81; Pres., 1988–91; Royal Society of Medicine: President: Section of General Practice, 1973–74; United Services Sect., 1985–87; Mem. Council, World Orgn of Nat. Colls and Acads of Gen. Practice and Family Medicine, 1970–80 (Pres., 1976–78); Mem. Exec. Council, British Diabetic Assoc., 1981–87. Examnr in medicine, Soc. of Apothecaries, 1980–88. Chm., St Mary Abbots Court Ltd, 1981–2004. Hon. MO, 1959–89, Vice-Pres., 1989–96, Queens Park Rangers FC. Hon. Fellow, Royal NZ Coll. of GPs, 1989; Hon. FRCPCH 1996; Hon. Mem., BPA, 1982. *Publications:* Paediatric Care, 1976; (jtly) DHSS Handbook on Contraceptive Practice, 3rd edn 1984, 4th edn 1988; numerous articles in Lancet, BMJ and other jls. *Recreations:* music, theatre, philately. *Address:* 5 St Mary Abbots Court, Warwick Gardens, W14 8RA. *T:* and *Fax:* (020) 7602 1970; *e-mail:* stuart@stuartcarne.com.

CARNEGIE, family name of **Duke of Fife** and **Earl of Northesk**.

CARNEGIE, Lord; Charles Duff Carnegie; *b* 1 July 1989; *s* and *heir* of Earl of Southesk, *qv*.

CARNEGIE, Lt-Gen. Sir Robin (Macdonald), KCB 1979; OBE 1968; DL; Director General of Army Training, 1981–82, retired; *b* 22 June 1926; *yr s* of late Sir Francis Carnegie, CBE; *m* 1955, Iona, *yr d* of late Maj.-Gen. Sir John Sinclair, KCMG, CB, OBE; one *s* two *d*. *Educ:* Rugby. Commnd 7th Queen's Own Hussars, 1946; comd The Queen's Own Hussars, 1967–69; Comdr 11th Armd Bde, 1971–72; Student, Royal Coll. of Defence Studies, 1973; GOC 3rd Div., 1974–76; Chief of Staff, BAOR, 1976–78; Military Secretary, 1978–80. Col, The Queen's Own Hussars, 1981–87. Non-Service Mem., Police, Prison and Fire Service Selection Bds, 1987–96. DL Wilts, 1990.
See also S. J. N. Heale.

CARNEGIE, Sir Roderick (Howard), AC 2003; Kt 1978; FTS; Executive Chairman, Pacific Edge Holdings Pty Ltd, since 1997; *b* 27 Nov. 1932; *s* of late Douglas H. Carnegie and Margaret F. Carnegie, AO; *m* 1959, Carmen, *d* of W. J. T. Clarke; three *s*. *Educ:* Geelong Church of England Grammar Sch.; Trinity Coll., Univ. of Melbourne (BSc 1954; Hon. Fellow, 1981); New Coll., Oxford Univ. (MA; Dip. Agricl Econs 1957); Harvard Business Sch., Boston (MBA 1959). FTSE (FTS 1985). McKinsey & Co., New York, 1958–70: Principal, 1964–68, Director, 1967–70; Exec. Dir, 1970–72, Man. Dir and Chief Exec., 1972–74, Chm. and Chief Exec., 1974–86, CRA Ltd; Chairman: Hudson Conway Ltd, 1987–2000; GIO Australia Hldgs Ltd, 1992–94; Newcrest Mining Ltd, 1993–98; Adacel Technologies Ltd, 1997–2003; World Competitive Practices Pty Ltd, 1997–2001; Director: ANZ Banking Gp, 1986–90; ANZ Executors & Trustee Co., 1990–92; John Fairfax Holdings, 1992–2004; Lexmark Internat. Inc., USA, 1994–98; Lexmark Internat. Gp Inc., 1994–98; AUSI Ltd, 1994–2002. Member: Internat. Council, J P Morgan & Co., 1986–95; Asia-Pacific Bd, IBM Corp., 1988–89; Internat. Adv. Bd, Internat. Finance Corp., 1991–92; Internat. Adv. Bd, World Bank, 1991–94. Director: Aust. Mining Industry Council, 1974 (a Sen. Vice-Pres., 1985); Macfarlane Burnet Centre for Med. Res., 1997–2000; Member: General Motors Aust. Adv. Council, 1979–2003; Aust.-China Council, 1979–82; Bd, CSIRO, 1986–91; Gp of Thirty, 1985–2001; Chm., Consultative Cttee on Relations with Japan, 1984–87; Chm., WA Energy Rev. Bd, 1992–93; President: German-Aust. Chamber of Industry and Commerce, 1985; Business Council of Aust., 1987–88; Consultant, Aust. Wool Corp., 1989–90; Patron, Australian Centre for Blood Diseases. Chm., Adv. Bd, Salvation Army, 1991–96 (Mem., 1990–91). Hon. DSc Newcastle, 1985. Centenary Medal, Australia, 2003. Comdr's Cross, Order of Merit (Germany), 1991. *Recreations:* surfing, tennis, reading. *Address:* Pacific Edge Holdings Pty Ltd, PO Box 7458, St Kilda Road, Melbourne, Vic 8004, Australia. *Clubs:* Melbourne (Vic); Australia (Vic and NSW); Harvard (New York).

CARNEGY OF LOUR, Baroness *cr* 1982 (Life Peer), of Lour in the District of Angus; **Elizabeth Patricia Carnegy of Lour;** formerly a farmer; *b* 28 April 1925; *e d* of late Lt Col U. E. C. Carnegy, DSO, MC, DL, JP, 12th of Lour, and Violet Carnegy, MBE. *Educ:* Downham Sch., Essex. Served Cavendish Lab., Cambridge, 1943–46. With Girl Guides Association, 1947–89: County Comr, Angus, 1956–63; Trng Adviser, Scotland, 1958–62; Trng Adviser, Commonwealth HQ, 1963–65; Pres. for Angus, 1971–79, for Scotland, 1979–89. Co-opted to Educn Cttee, Angus CC, 1967–75; Tayside Regional Council: Councillor, 1974–82; Convener: Recreation and Tourism Cttee, 1974–76; Educn Cttee, 1977–81. Chairman: Working Party on Prof. Trng for Community Education in Scotland, 1975–77; Scottish Council for Community Educn, 1981–88 (Mem., 1978–88); Tayside Cttee on Med. Res. Ethics, 1990–93. Member: MSC, 1979–82 (Chm., Cttee for Scotland, 1981–83); Council for Tertiary Educn in Scotland, 1979–84; Scottish Economic Council, 1981–93; Council, Open Univ., 1984–96; Admin. Council, Royal Jubilee Trusts, 1985–88; Court, St Andrews Univ., 1991–96. House of Lords: Mem., Scrutiny Cttees on European Community, 1983–97; Mem., Select Cttee on Delegated Powers and Regulatory Reform, 2002–05. Trustee, Nat. Museums of Scotland, 1987–91. Hon. Sheriff, 1969–84; DL Angus, 1988–2001. Hon. LLD: Dundee, 1991; St Andrews, 1997; DUniv Open, 1998. *Address:* Lour, by Forfar, Angus DD8 2LR. *T:* (01307) 820237; 33 Tufton Court, Tufton Street, SW1P 3QH. *Clubs:* Lansdowne; New (Edinburgh).

CARNELL, Rev. Canon Geoffrey Gordon; Chaplain to The Queen, 1981–88; Non-Residentiary Canon of Peterborough Cathedral, 1965–85, Canon Emeritus since 1985; *b* 5 July 1918; *m* 1945, Mary Elizabeth Boucher Smith; two *s*. *Educ:* City of Norwich Sch.; St John's Coll., Cambridge (Scholar, 1937; BA 1940; Naden Divinity Student, 1940; Lightfoot Scholar, 1940; MA 1944); Cuddesdon Coll., Oxford. Ordained deacon, Peterborough Cathedral, 1942; priest, 1943. Asst Curate, Abington, Northampton, 1942–49; Chaplain and Lectr in Divinity, St Gabriel's Coll., Camberwell, 1949–53; Rector of Isham with Great and Little Harrowden, Northants, 1953–71; Rector of Boughton, Northampton, 1971–85. Examining Chaplain to Bishop of Peterborough, 1962–86; Dir, Post-Ordination Trng and Ordinands, 1962–86; Peterborough Diocesan Librarian, 1968–93. Chaplain: to High Sheriff of Northants, 1972–73; to Mayor of Kettering, 1988–89. Member: Ecclesiastical History Soc., 1979–; Church of England Record Soc., 1992–; a Vice-Chm., Northants Record Soc., 1982–89. *Publication:* The Bishops of Peterborough 1541–1591, 1993. *Recreations:* walking, music, art history, local history. *Address:* 52 Walsingham Avenue, Barton Woods, Kettering, Northamptonshire NN15 5ER. *T:* (01536) 511415.

CARNELLEY, Ven. Desmond; Archdeacon of Doncaster, 1985–94, now Archdeacon Emeritus; *b* 28 Nov. 1929; *m* 1st, 1954, Dorothy Frith (*d* 1986); three *s* one *d*; 2nd, 1988, Marjorie Freeman. *Educ:* St John's Coll., York; St Luke's Coll., Exeter; William Temple Coll., Rugby; Ripon Hall, Oxford; BA (Open Univ.); Univ. of Wales, Cardiff (LLM Canon Law, 2002); Cert. Ed. (Leeds); Cert. Rel. Ed. (Exon). Curate of Aston, 1960–63; Priest-in-charge, St Paul, Ecclesfield, 1963–67; Vicar of Balby, Doncaster, 1967–72; Priest-in-charge, Mosborough, 1973; Vicar of Mosborough, 1974–85; RD of Attercliffe, 1979–84; acting Dir of Educn, dio. of Sheffield, 1991–92. *Recreations:* reading, theatre, walking in Derbyshire. *Address:* 7 Errwood Avenue, Buxton, Derbyshire SK17 9BD. *T:* (01298) 71460.

CARNEY, Michael; Secretary, Water Services Association (formerly Water Authorities Association), 1987–92; *b* 19 Oct. 1937; *s* of Bernard Patrick Carney and Gwyneth (*née* Ellis); *m* 1963, Mary Patricia (*née* Davies) (marr. diss. 2000); two *s* one *d*. *Educ:* University College of North Wales, Bangor (BA). Administrative Officer, NCB, 1962–65; Staff Officer to Dep. Chm., NCB, 1965–68; Electricity Council: Administrative Officer, 1968–71; Asst Sec. (Establishments), 1971–74; Sec., S Western Region, CEGB, 1974–80, Personnel Man., Midlands Region, 1980–82; Personnel Dir, Oxfam, 1982–87. *Publications:* Britain in Pictures: a history and bibliography, 1995; Stoker: the life of Hilda Matheson, OBE, 1888–1940, 1999. *Recreations:* reading, book collecting, music, theatre. *Address:* 16 Chester Street, Shrewsbury, Shropshire SY1 1NX. *T:* (01743) 369733; *e-mail:* michael.carney@care4free.net.

CARNLEY, Rt Rev. Peter Frederick, AC 2007 (AO 1998); PhD; Archbishop of Perth and Metropolitan of Western Australia, 1981–2005; Primate of Australia, 2000–05; *b* 17 Oct. 1937; *s* of Frederick Carnley and Gweyennetth Lilian Carnley (*née* Read); *m* 1966, Carol Ann Dunstan; one *s* one *d*. *Educ:* St John's Coll., Morpeth, NSW; Australian Coll. of Theol. (ThL 1st Cl., 1962); Univ. of Melbourne (BA, 1st Cl. Hons, 1966); Univ. of Cambridge (PhD 1970). Deacon 1962, priest 1964, Bath; Licence to Officiate, dio. Melbourne, 1963–65; Asst Curate of Parkes, 1966; Licence to Officiate, dio. Ely, 1966–69; Chaplain, Mitchell Coll. of Advanced Education, Bath, 1970–72; Research Fellow, St John's Coll., Cambridge, 1971–72 (Hon. Fellow, 2000); Warden, St John's College, St Lucia, Queensland, 1973–81; Residentiary Canon, St John's Cathedral, Brisbane, 1975–81; Examining Chaplain to Archbishop of Brisbane, 1975–81. Adjunct Prof. of Theol., Murdoch Univ., 2004–. Co-Chm., ARCIC, 2003–. Hon. Fellow, Trinity Coll., Univ. of Melbourne, 2000. DD *hc* Gen. Theological Seminary, NY, 1984; Hon. DLitt: Newcastle, 2000; W Australia, 2000; Queensland, 2002; DUniv Charles Sturt, 2001; Hon. Dr Sacred Theol. Melbourne Coll. of Divinity, 2004. ChStJ 1982 (Sub Prelate, 1991). *Publications:* The Structure of Resurrection Belief, 1987; The Yellow Wallpaper and Other Sermons, 2001; Faithfulness in Fellowship: reflections on homosexuality and the church, 2001; Reflections in Glass: trends and tensions in the Anglican church of Australia, 2004. *Recreations:* gardening, swimming. *Address:* PO Box 221, Nannup, WA 6275, Australia. *Clubs:* Western Australian, Weld (Perth); St John's (Brisbane).

CARNOCK, 4th Baron *cr* 1916, of Carnock; **David Henry Arthur Nicolson;** Bt (NS) of that Ilk and Lasswade 1629, of Carnock 1637; Chief of Clan Nicolson; solicitor; *b* 10 July 1920; *s* of 3rd Baron Carnock, DSO, and Hon. Katharine (*d* 1968), *e d* of 1st Baron Roborough; *S* father, 1982. *Educ:* Winchester; Balliol Coll., Oxford (MA). Admitted Solicitor, 1949; Partner, Clifford-Turner, 1953–86. Served War of 1939–45, Royal Devon Yeomanry and on staff, Major. *Recreations:* shooting, fishing, gardening. *Heir: cousin* Adam Nicolson [*b* 12 Sept. 1957; *m* 1st, 1982, Olivia Mary Rokeby Fane (marr. diss. 1992); three *s*; 2nd, 1993, Sarah Clare Raven; two *d*]. *Address:* 90 Whitehall Court, SW1A 2EL; Ermewood House, Harford, Ivybridge, S Devon PL21 0JE. *Clubs:* Travellers, Beefsteak.

CARNWATH, Alison Jane; Senior Advisor, Lexicon Partners, since 2005; Chairman, MF Global Inc., since 2007; *b* 18 Jan. 1953; *d* of Kenneth and Lois Tresise; partner, Peter Thomson. *Educ:* Howells Sch., Denbigh; Univ. of Reading (BA Econ/German 1975). ACA 1979. Peat Marwick Mitchell, later KPMG, 1975–79; J. Henry Schroder Wagg, 1983–93; Phoenix Partnership, 1993–97; Donaldson Lufkin Jenrette, 1997–2000. Non-executive Director: Man Group plc, 2001–; Land Securities plc, 2004–; Paccar Inc., 2005–. FRSA. *Recreations:* food and wine, ski-ing, music. *Address:* Lexicon Partners, 1 Paternoster Square, EC4M 7DX; MF Global Inc., 717 Fifth Avenue, 9th Floor, New York, NY 10022–8101, USA.

CARNWATH, Francis Anthony Armstrong, CBE 1997; Director, Greenwich Foundation for the Royal Naval College, 1997–2002; *b* 26 May 1940; *s* of Sir Andrew Hunter Carnwath, KCVO, DL and Kathleen Marianne (*née* Armstrong); *m* 1975, Penelope Clare Rose; one *s* one *d* (and one *d* decd). *Educ:* Eton (Oppidan Schol.); Cambridge (BA Econs). With Baring Brothers & Co., 1962–89: postings to S Africa, 1965–66, USA, 1969, France, 1972–73; Chief Exec. and Dir, Pertanian Baring Sanwa Multinational, Malaysia, 1977–79; Dir, 1979–89; Chm., Ravensbourne Registration Services Ltd, 1981–89. Dep. Dir, Tate Gall., 1990–94; Actg Dir, 1995, Advr, 1996–97, Nat. Heritage Meml Fund/Heritage Lottery Fund. English Heritage: Mem., London Adv. Cttee, 1990–99; Chm., Commemorative Plaques Panel, 1995–2002. Trustee and later Dep. Chm., Shelter, 1968–76; Treas., VSO, 1979–84. Chairman: Musgrave Kinley Outsider Trust, 1999–; Spitalfields Historic Buildings Trust, 1984–2000; Thames 21, 2003–; Architectural Panel, NT, 2004–; Trustee: Phillimore Estates, 1983–; Whitechapel Art Gall., 1994–2000 (Dep. Chm., 1996–2000); Royal Armouries, 2000–07; Spitalfields Fest., 2003–; Yorkshire Sculpture Park, 2003– (Chm., 2004–). Musicians' Co.: Master, 1995–96; Treas., 1993–97; Chm., various cttees, 1993–08. Hon. FTCL 2002; Hon. RCM 2003. *Recreations:* music, the arts, walking. *Address:* 26 Lansdowne Gardens, SW8 2EG. *T:* (020) 7627 2158. *Clubs:* Garrick, Beefsteak.
See also Rt Hon. Sir R. J. A. Carnwath.

CARNWATH, Rt Hon. Sir Robert (John Anderson), Kt 1994; CVO 1995; PC 2002; **Rt Hon. Lord Justice Carnwath;** a Lord Justice of Appeal, since 2002; Senior President of Tribunals, since 2004; *b* 15 March 1945; *s* of Sir Andrew Carnwath, KCVO; *m* 1974, Bambina D'Adda. *Educ:* Eton; Trinity Coll., Cambridge (MA, LLB). Called to the Bar, Middle Temple, 1968, Bencher 1991; QC 1985. Junior Counsel to Inland Revenue, 1980–85; Attorney Gen. to the Prince of Wales, 1988–94; a Judge of the High Court, Chancery Div., 1994–2002; Chm., Law Commn, 1999–2002. Jt Founder and Sec. Gen., EU Forum of Judges for Envmt, 2004–05. Chairman: Shepherds Bush Housing Assoc., 1988–93; Administrative Law Bar Assoc., 1993–94; Tabernacle Trust, 1996–99. Pres., UK Envmtl Law Assoc., 2006–. Governor, RAM, 1989–2002 (Hon. Fellow 1994). Trustee, 1996–, Chm., 2001–, Britten-Pears Foundn. *Publications:* Knight's Guide to Homeless Persons Act, 1977; (with Rt Hon. Sir Frederick Corfield) Compulsory Acquisition and Compensation, 1978; Enforcing Planning Control (report commnd for DoE), 1989; various legal texts and reports on envmtl and local govt law. *Recreations:* viola, singing (Bach Choir), tennis, golf, etc. *Address:* Royal Courts of Justice, Strand, WC2A 2LL.
See also F. A. A. Carnwath.

CARO, Sir Anthony (Alfred), OM 2000; Kt 1987; CBE 1969; RA 2004; sculptor; *b* 8 March 1924; *s* of late Alfred and Mary Caro; *m* 1949, Sheila May Girling; two *s*. *Educ:* Charterhouse; Christ's Coll., Cambridge (Hon. Fellow, 1981); Regent Street Polytechnic; Royal Acad. Schs, London (Landseer Schol., 1st Landseer Award). Served FAA, 1944–46. Asst to Henry Moore, 1951–53; taught part-time, St Martin's Sch. of Art, 1953–79; taught sculpture at Bennington Coll., Vermont, 1963–65. Initiated and taught at Triangle Workshop, Pine Plains, NY, 1982–89. Visiting Artist, 1989: Univ. of Alberta; Red Deer Coll., Alberta. *One-man exhibitions include:* Galleria del Naviglio, Milan, 1956; Gimpel Fils, London, 1957; Whitechapel Art Gall., 1963; Andre Emmerich Gall., NY, 1964, 1966, 1968, 1970, 1972, 1973, 1974, 1977, 1978, 1979, 1982, 1984, 1986, 1988, 1989; Washington Gall. of Modern Art, Washington, DC, 1965; Kasmin Ltd, London, 1965, 1967, 1971, 1972; David Mirvish Gall., Toronto, 1966, 1971, 1974; Galerie Bischofberger, Zürich, 1966; Rijksmuseum, Kröller-Müller, Holland, 1967; Hayward Gall., 1969; Norfolk and Norwich Triennial Fest., 1973; Kenwood House, Hampstead, 1974, 1981, 1994, 2004 (toured to Scripps Coll., Calif, Bentley Projects, Phoenix, and Garth Clark Gall., NY); Galleria dell'Ariete, Milan, 1974; Galerie Andre Emmerich, Zürich, 1974, 1978, 1985; Mus. of Modern Art, NY, 1975 (toured to Walker Art Center, Minn, Mus. of Fine Arts, Houston, Mus. of Fine Arts, Boston); Richard Gray Gall., Chicago, 1976, 1978, 1986, 1989; Watson/de Nagy Gall., Houston, 1976; Lefevre Gall., London, 1976; Galerie Wentzel, Hamburg, 1976, 1978, Cologne, 1982, 1984, 1985, 1988; Galerie Piltzer-Rheims, Paris, 1977; Waddington & Tooth Galls, London, 1977; Waddington Galls, London, 1983, 1986; Harkus Kracow Gall., Boston, 1978, 1981, 1985; Knoedler Gall., London, 1978, 1982, 1983, 1984, 1986, 1989, 1991; Ace Gall., Venice, Calif, 1978, Vancouver, 1979; Kunsthalle Mannheim, 1979; Kunstverein Braunschweig, 1979; Kunstverein Frankfurt, 1979; Städtische Galerie im Lenbachhaus, Munich, 1979; Gall. Kasahara, Osaka, Japan, 1979, 1990; York Sculptures, Christian Science Center, Boston, 1980; Acquavella Galls, NY, 1980, 1984, 1986; Galerie Andre, Berlin, 1980; Downstairs Gall., Edmonton, Alta, 1981; Storm King Art Center, Mountainville, NY, 1981; Städtische Galerie im Städel, Frankfurt, 1981; Saarland Mus., Saarbrücken, 1982; Gallery One, Toronto, 1982, 1985, 1987–88, 1990; Galerie de France, Paris, 1983; Martin Gerard Gall., Edmonton, 1984; Serpentine Gall., 1984; Whitworth Art Gall., Manchester, 1984; Leeds City Art Gall., 1984; Ordrupgaard Samlingen, Copenhagen, 1984; Kunstmuseum Düsseldorf, 1985; Joan Miró Foundn, Barcelona, 1985; C. Grimaldis Gall., Baltimore, 1985, 1987, 1989, 1994, 2004; Galerie Blanche, Stockholm, 1985; Galleri Lang, Malmö, 1985; Galerie Artek, Helsinki, 1985; Galleria Stendhal, Milan, 1985; Norrköpings Kunstmuseum, Sweden, 1985; Galerie Joan Prats, Barcelona, 1986, 2003; Comune di Bogliasco, Genoa, 1986; Iglesia de San Esteban, Spain, 1986; La Lonja, Spain, 1987; Soledad Lorenzo Galerie, Madrid, 1987; Northern Centre for Contemp. Art, Sunderland, 1987; Sylvia Cordish Fine Art, Baltimore, 1988; Elisabeth Franck Gall., Belgium, 1988; Galerie Renée Ziegler, Zürich, 1988; Annely Juda Fine Art, 1989, 1991, 1994 (retrospective), 1998, 2003, 2007; Walker Hill Art Center, Seoul, 1989; Galeria Fluxus, Porto, 1989; Galerie Lelong, Paris, 1990; Banque Paribas, Antwerp, 1990; Tate Gall., 1991, 2005; Yorkshire Sculpture Park, Wakefield, 1994, 2001; Kukje Gall., Seoul, 1994, 1998; Mus. of Contemp. Art, Tokyo, 1995; Galerie Josine Bokhoven, Amsterdam, 1995, 1998, 2004; Marlborough Gall., NY, 1997, 1998, 2001, Boca Raton, 1999; Nat. Gall., 1998; Garth Clark Gall., NY, 1998, 2004; Perimeter Gall., Chicago, 1998; Centrum Beeldende Kunst, Nijmegen, 1999; Museo des Bellas Artes, Bilbao, 2000; Galleri Weinberger, Copenhagen, 2000, 2007; Venice Design, Venice, 2000, 2007; Ameringer Howard, NY, 2000; Château-Musée, Dieppe, 2001; Kunsthalle Würth, Schwäbisch Hall, 2001, 2004; Centro Cultural Caixa Cataluña, Barcelona, 2002; Galeria Metta, Madrid, 2002, 2005; Galeria Altair, Palma, 2002, 2006; Galerie Besson, 2002; Mitchell Innes & Nash, NY, 2002, 2005, 2007; Frederik Meijer Sculpture Park, Grand Rapids, 2003; Meadows Mus., Dallas, 2003; Hubert Gall., NY, 2003; Artemis Greenberg van Doren, NY, 2003; Seoul Mus. of Art, 2004; Galerie Daniel Templon, Paris, 2005; Marc Selwyn/Daniel Weinberg, LA, 2005; Portland Art Mus., 2005; IVAM, Valencia, 2005, 2006; Joyas Grassy, 2006; Roche Ct, Salisbury, 2007; Mus. of Contemp. Art, Cleveland, 2007; NPG, 2007. British Council touring exhibitions: 1977–79, Tel Aviv, NZ and Australia; 1993–1995, Hungary, Romania, Turkey, Greece, Holland and Germany. *Group shows:* exhibited in over 200, many widely toured, in UK, USA, Canada, Europe, Australia and Far East, incl. Biennale in Venice, 1958, 1966, 1968, 1972, 1986, 1988 and 1999, Carrara, 1959, Paris, 1959 and 1977, Antwerp, 1959 and 1983, São Paolo, 1969, Arese, 1980, and Monte Carlo, 1989. Sculpture commnd by Nat. Gall. of Art, Washington, 1978. Co-Designer, Millennium Bridge, London, 1996–2000. Member: Council, RCA, 1981–83 (Hon. Fellow 1986); Council, Slade Sch. of Art, 1982–92; Trustee, Tate Gall., 1982–89. Sen. Academician, RA, 2004. Hon. Mem., Amer. Acad. and Inst. of Arts and Letters, 1979; For. Hon. Mem., Amer. Acad. of Arts and Sciences, 1988; Accademia di Belle Arte di Brera, 1992. Hon. FRIBA 1997; Hon. RBS 1997; Hon. Fellow: Alberta Univ., 1990; Wolfson Coll., Oxford, 1992; Southampton Univ., 1993; Glasgow Sch. of Art, 1998; Bretton Hall Coll., 1998; Univ. of the Arts London, 2004. Hon. DLitt: East Anglia, 1968; York Univ., Toronto, 1979; Brandeis Univ., Mass, 1981; Durham, 1997; Westminster, 1999; Hon. LittD Cambridge, 1985; DUniv Surrey, 1987; Hon. DFA: Yale, 1989; Florida, 1997; Hon. Dr RCA, 1994; Dr *hc* Charles de Gaulle, Lille, 1996, etc. Given key to City of New York, 1974. Henry Moore Grand Prize, 1991; Praemium Imperiale, 1992; Internat. Sculpture Centre Lifetime Achievement Award, 1997; Internat. Award for Visual Arts, Cristobal Gabarron Foundn, 2004; Julio Gonzales Award, Generalitat Valenciana, 2005. Chevalier des Arts et Lettres (France), 1996. *Relevant publications:* Anthony Caro, by R. Whelan *et al*, 1974; Anthony Caro, by W. S. Rubin, 1975; Anthony Caro, by D. Waldman, 1982; Anthony Caro, by Terry Fenton, 1986; Caro, by Karen Wilkin, 1991; Anthony Caro, by Giovanni Carandente, 1992; Caro, by Anzai, 1992; Anthony Caro and Twentieth Century Sculpture, by Giovanni Carandente, 1999; Anthony Caro, by Ian Barker, 2004; Anthony Caro, by Julius Bryant, 2004; Anthony Caro, by Paul Moorhouse, 2005; Interpreting Anthony Caro, by Paul Moorhouse, 2005. *Recreation:* his grandchildren.

CARO, Prof. David Edmund, AO 1986; OBE 1977; MSc, PhD; FInstP, FAIP, FACE; Chancellor, University of Ballarat, 1998–2004; Vice-Chancellor: University of Melbourne, 1982–87; (interim), Northern Territory University, 1988–89; *b* 29 June 1922; *s* of George Alfred Caro and Alice Lillian Caro; *m* 1954, Fiona Macleod; one *s* one *d*. *Educ:* Geelong Grammar Sch.; Univ. of Melbourne (MSc); Univ. of Birmingham (PhD). FInstP 1960, FAIP 1963, FACE 1982. Served War, RAAF, 1941–45. Demonstrator, Univ. of Melbourne, 1947–49; 1851 Overseas Res. Scholar, Birmingham, 1949–51; University of Melbourne: Lectr, 1952; Sen. Lectr, 1954; Reader, 1958; Foundn Prof. of Exper. Physics, 1961; Dean, Faculty of Science, 1970; Dep. Vice-Chancellor, 1972–77; Vice-Chancellor, Univ. of Tasmania, 1978–82. Chairman: Antarctic Res. Policy Adv. Cttee, 1979–85; Aust. Vice-Chancellors Cttee, 1982–83; Melbourne Theatre Co., 1982–87; Pres., Victorian Coll. of the Arts, 1989–91. Chairman: SSAU Nominees Ltd, 1984–89; UniSuper Ltd, 1990–94; Sarou Pty Ltd, 1991–. Member: Management Cttee, Royal Melbourne Hosp., 1982–92; Council, Univ. of South Australia, 1990–94; Council, Univ. of Ballarat, 1994–2004. Hon. LLD: Melbourne, 1978; Tasmania, 1982; Hon. DSc: Melbourne, 1987; Ballarat, 2004. *Publication:* (jtly) Modern Physics, 1961 (3rd edn 1978). *Recreations:* gardening, theatre. *Address:* 17 Fairbairn Road, Toorak, Vic 3142, Australia. *Clubs:* Melbourne (Melbourne); Peninsula Golf (Vic); Tasmanian (Hobart).

CAROL, Sister; *see* Griese, Sister Carol.

CAROLIN, Prof. Peter Burns, CBE 2000; ARIBA; Professor and Head of Department of Architecture, University of Cambridge, 1989–2000, now Professor Emeritus, and Fellow of Corpus Christi College, since 1989; *b* 11 Sept. 1936; *s* of late Joseph Sinclair Carolin and Jean Bell Carolin (*née* Burns); *m* 1964, Anne-Birgit Warning; three *d*. *Educ:* Radley Coll.; Corpus Christi Coll., Cambridge (MA); University Coll. London (MA Architecture). Served RNR, Lieut, 1955–61. Asst to John Voelcker, 1960–63; Architect: with Colin St John Wilson, 1965–70; with Sir John Burnet, Tait and Partners, 1970–71; Associate, 1971–73, and Partner, 1973–80, Colin St John Wilson and Partners; Partner, Cambridge Design, 1980–81; Technical Ed., 1981–84, Editor, 1984–89, Architects' Jl. Chm., Cambridge Futures, 1997–2001. Co-founder, Facilities Newsletter, 1983; Chm. Editl Bd, and Editor, arq (Architectural Res. Qly), 1995–2004. Magazine of Year Award (jtly), 1985; (jtly) numerous publishing awards, 1985–87; (jtly) Award for Innovation in Local Planning, RTPI, 2000; (jtly) Award for Learned Jls, ALPSP/Charlesworth, 2002. *Publications:* articles in professional jls. *Recreation:* sailing. *Address:* Orchard End, 15E Grange Road, Cambridge CB3 9AS. *T:* (01223) 352723; *e-mail:* pc207@hermes.cam.ac.uk.

CAROLUS, Cheryl Anne; Director: BDFM, since 2004; Investec, since 2005; *b* 27 May 1958; *m* 1990, Graeme Bloch. Former teacher; Dep. Sec. Gen., 1994–98, acting Sec.-Gen., March 1998, ANC; High Comr for S Africa in the UK, 1998–2001; CEO, SA Tourism, 2001–04; Chm., SA Parks Bd, 2004–.

CARON, Leslie (Claire Margaret); film and stage actress; *b* 1 July 1931; *d* of Claude Caron and Margaret Caron (*née* Petit); *m* 1st, 1951, George Hormel (marr. diss.); 2nd, 1956, Peter Reginald Frederick Hall (marr. diss. 1965); one *s* one *d*; 3rd, 1969, Michael Laughlin (marr. diss.). *Educ:* Convent of the Assumption, Paris. With Ballet des Champs Elysées, 1947–50, Ballet de Paris, 1954. *Films:* American in Paris, 1950; The Man With a Cloak, 1951; Lili, Story of Three Loves, 1953; Glory Alley, The Glass Slipper, 1954; Daddy Long Legs, 1955; Gaby, 1956; Gigi, The Doctor's Dilemma, 1958; The Man Who Understood Women, 1959; The Subterraneans, Austerlitz, 1960; Fanny, 1961; The L-Shaped Room, 1962; Guns of Darkness, 1963; Father Goose, A Very Special Favour, 1964; Les Quatres Vérités, Is Paris Burning?, 1965; Promise Her Anything, 1966; Head of the Family, 1968; Madron, 1970; Chandler, 1971; QB VII; Valentino, Sérail, 1975; L'homme qui aimait les femmes, 1976; Goldengirl, 1978; Tous Vedettes, 1979; The Contract, 1980; Imperatif, 1981; The Unapproachable, 1982; La Diagonale du Fou, 1983; Le Génie du Faux, 1984; Le Train de Lenine, 1987; Courage Mountain, Guerriers et Captives, 1988; Master of the Game; Damage, 1992; Funny Bones, Let it be Me, 1994; The Ring, 1995; The Reef, 1996; The Last of the Blonde Bombshells, 1999; Chocolat, 2001; Crime on the Orient Express, 2001; Le Divorce, 2003. *Plays:* Orvet, Paris, 1955; La Sauvage (TV), England; Gigi, (title rôle), New Th., 1956; 13 rue de l'Amour, USA and Australia; Ondine (title rôle), RSC, Aldwych, 1961; Carola (TV), USA; The Rehearsal, UK tour, 1983; On Your Toes, US tour, 1984; One for the Tango, USA tour, 1985; L'Inaccessible, Paris, 1985; George Sand, Greenwich Fest., 1995; Nocturne for Lovers, Chichester, 1997. *Musical:* Grand Hotel, Berlin, 1991. *Television:* Tales of the Unexpected, 1982. *Publication:* Vengeance (short stories), 1982. *Recreation:* collecting antiques. *Address:* c/o Maureen Vincent, United Agents, 12–26 Lexington Street, W1F 0LE.

CARPANINI, Prof. David Lawrence, RE 1982 (ARE 1979); RWA 1983 (ARWA 1977); RBA 1976; NEAC 1983; RCA 1992; painter and etcher; Professor of Art, University of Wolverhampton School of Education, 1992–2000, retired; *b* Abergwynfi, W Glam, 22 Oct. 1946; *o s* of Lorenzo Carpanini and Gwenllian (*née* Thomas); *m* 1972, Jane Allen, RWS, RBA, RWA; one *s*. *Educ:* Glanafan Grammar Sch., Port Talbot; Glos Coll. of Art & Design, Cheltenham (DipAD 1968); Royal Coll. of Art (MA 1971); Univ. of Reading (ATC 1972). Dir, Bankside Gall. Ltd, 1995–2003. Royal Society of British Artists: Hon. Treas., 1979–82; Vice-Pres., 1982–88; Mem. Council, 1993–95; Mem. Council, RWA, 1987–90; PRE, 1995–2003. Has exhibited at: RA, RBA, RWA, NEAC, Bankside Gall., Piccadilly Gall., Attic Gall., Agnews, Albany Gall., New Acad. Gall., Tegfryn; numerous one-man exhibitions, 1972–, including: Welsh Arts Council Gall., 1980; Warwick Arts Fest., 1986; Mostyn Gall., 1988; Rhondda Heritage Park, 1989, 1994; Walsall Mus., 1989; Swansea Arts Fest., 1994; Attic Gall., 1998, 2002, 2005, 2008; St David's Hall, 1999; Taliesin Gall., 2000. Work in collections, including: Nat. Mus. of Wales; Contemporary Art Soc. for Wales: Nat. Liby of Wales; Newport Mus. and Art Gall.; Govt Art Collection, DoE; Fitzwilliam Mus., Cambridge; BNOC; Univ. of Wales; Ashmolean Mus., Oxford. Gov., Fedn of British Artists, 1982–86. De Lazlo Medal, RBA, 1980; Agnews Drawing Prize, NEAC, 1992; Catto Gall. Award, 1993, First Prize, Daler Rowney Award, 1995, RWS Open. Hon. RWS 1996; Hon. RBSA 2002. *Publications:* Vehicles of Pictorial Expression, 1982; numerous articles and illustrations for instructional books and art periodicals. *Recreation:* opera. *Address:* Fernlea, 145 Rugby Road, Milverton, Leamington Spa, Warwicks CV32 6DJ. *T:* (01926) 430658.

CARPENTER; *see* Boyd-Carpenter.

CARPENTER, Harry Leonard, OBE 1991; sports commentator, BBC, 1949–94; *b* 17 Oct. 1925; *s* of Harry and Adelaide May Carpenter; *m* 1950, Phyllis Barbara Matthews; one *s*. *Educ:* Ashburton School, Shirley; Selhurst Grammar School, Croydon. Greyhound Express, 1941; RN, 1943–46; Greyhound Owner, 1946–48; Speedway Gazette, 1948–50; Sporting Record, 1950–54; Daily Mail, 1954–62; BBC TV, full-time 1962–94. Sports Personality of the Year, TV and Radio Industries, 1989; Internat. Award, Amer. Sportscasters' Assoc., 1989. *Publications:* Masters of Boxing, 1964; Illustrated History of Boxing, 1975; The Hardest Game, 1981; Where's Harry? My Story, 1992. *Recreations:* golf, chess, classical music. *Address:* Sommerfield Holdings plc, 35 Old Queen Street, SW1H 9JD.

CARPENTER, John; *see* Carpenter, V. H. J.

CARPENTER, Leslie Arthur; Chief Executive, 1982–86, Chairman, 1985–87, Reed International PLC; *b* 26 June 1927; *s* of William and Rose Carpenter; *m* 1st, 1952; one *d*; 2nd, 1989, (Elizabeth) Louise Botting, *qv*. *Educ:* Hackney Techn. Coll. Director: Country Life, 1965; George Newnes, 1966; Odhams Press Ltd (Managing), 1968; International Publishing Corp., 1972; Reed International Ltd, 1974; IPC (America) Inc., 1975; Chairman: Reed Hldgs Inc. (formerly Reed Publishing Hldgs Inc.), 1977; Reed Publishing Hldgs Ltd, 1981; Chm. and Chief Exec., IPC Ltd, 1974; Chief Exec., Publishing and Printing, Reed International Ltd, 1979. Dir, Watmoughs (Hldgs) plc, 1988–98. *Recreations:* racing, gardening. *Address:* Gable House, 75 High Street, Broadway, Worcs WR12 7DP.

CARPENTER, Louise, (Mrs L. A. Carpenter); *see* Botting, E. L.

CARPENTER, Michael Alan; Chairman, Southgate Alternative Investments, since 2007; *b* 24 March 1947; *s* of Walter and Kathleen Carpenter; *m* 1975, Mary A. Aughton; one *s* one *d*. *Educ:* Univ. of Nottingham (BSc 1968); Harvard Business Sch. (MBA 1973). Business analyst, Mond Div., ICI, Runcorn, 1968–71; Consultant, 1973–78, Vice-Pres., 1978–83, Boston Consulting Gp; joined General Electric Co., 1983: Vice-Pres., Corporate Business Develt and Planning, 1983–86; Exec. Vice-Pres., GE Capital Corp., 1986–89; Chm., Pres. and CEO, Kidder, Peabody Gp Inc., 1989–94; Chm. and CEO, Travelers Life and Annuity Co., and Vice-Chm., Travelers Gp, Inc., 1995–98; CEO, Global Corporate Investment Bank, and Chm. and CEO, Salomon Smith Barney, 1998–2002; Chm. and CEO, Citigroup Alternative Investments, 2002–06. Hon. LLD Nottingham, 2003. *Address:* Southgate Alternative Investments, 717 Fifth Avenue, Suite 1404, New York, NY 10022, USA.

CARPENTER, Michael Stephen Evans; Chairman, Alpha Common Investment Fund for Income and Reserves, since 2006; Deputy Chairman, Charity Trustee Network, since 2005; charity consultant, since 2003; *b* 7 Oct. 1942; *s* of Ernest Henry Carpenter and Eugenie Carpenter (*née* Evans); *m* 1968, Gabriel Marie Lucie Brain; one *s* one *d*. *Educ:* Eastbourne Coll.; Bristol Univ. (LLB). Admitted Solicitor, 1967; Slaughter and May, 1967–94 (Partner, 1974–94); Withers, 1994–97 (Partner, 1994–96; Consultant, 1997); Legal Comr, Charity Commn, 1998–2002. Sec., Garfield Weston Foundn, 1997. Trustee: Reach Out Projects, 2007–; Interactive Christian Extension Studies, 2007–. *Recreations:* hill-walking, golf, Scottish islands, the church.

CARPENTER, Maj.-Gen. (Victor Harry) John, CB 1975; MBE 1945; FCILT; Senior Traffic Commissioner, Western Traffic Area and Licensing Authority, 1990–91; *b* 21 June 1921; *s* of Harry and Amelia Carpenter; *m* 1946, Theresa McCulloch (*d* 2007); one *s* one *d*. *Educ:* Army schools; Apprentice Artificer RA; RMC Sandhurst. Joined the Army, Royal Artillery, 1936; commissioned into Royal Army Service Corps as 2nd Lieut, 1939. Served War of 1939–45 (Dunkirk evacuation, Western Desert, D-Day landings). Post-war appts included service in Palestine, Korea, Aden, and Singapore; also commanded a company at Sandhurst. Staff College, 1951; JSSC, 1960; served WO, BAOR, FARELF, 1962–71; Transport Officer-in-Chief (Army), MoD, 1971–73; Dir of Movements (Army), MoD, 1973–75; Chm., Traffic Comrs, NE Traffic Area (formerly Yorks Traffic Area), 1975–85; Traffic Comr, W Traffic Area, 1985–90. Col Comdt, 1975–87, Representative Col Comdt, 1976, 1978 and 1985, RCT. Nat. Pres., 1940 Dunkirk Veterans Assoc., 1991–2000; President: Artificers Royal Artillery Assoc., 1974–2001; RASC/RCT Assoc., 1977–87; Somerset Br., Normandy Veterans Assoc., 1994–2006. Chm., Yorkshire Section, CIT, 1980–81; Pres., Taunton Gp, IAM. Hon. FIRTE 1987. Commander, Order of Leopold II (Belgium), 1992. *Recreation:* gardening. *Club:* Royal Over-Seas League.

CARR, family name of **Baron Carr of Hadley**.

CARR OF HADLEY, Baron *cr* 1975 (Life Peer), of Monken Hadley; **(Leonard) Robert Carr;** PC 1963; FIC; *b* 11 Nov. 1916; *s* of late Ralph Edward and of Katie Elizabeth Carr; *m* 1943, Joan Kathleen, *d* of Dr E. W. Twining; two *d* (and one *s* decd). *Educ:* Westminster Sch. (Hon. Fellow, 1991); Gonville and Caius Coll., Cambridge (BA Nat. Sci Hons, 1938; MA 1942; Hon. Fellow, 2001). FIMMM (FIM 1957). Joined John Dale Ltd, 1938 (Dir, 1948–55; Chm., 1958–63); Director: Metal Closures Group Ltd, 1964–70 (Dep. Chm., 1960–63 and Jt Man. Dir, 1960–63); Carr, Day & Martin Ltd, 1947–55; Isotope Developments Ltd, 1950–55; Metal Closures Ltd, 1959–63; Scottish Union & National Insurance Co. (London Bd), 1958–63; S. Hoffnung & Co., 1963, 1965–70, 1974–80; Securicor Ltd and Security Services PLC, 1961–63, 1965–70, 1974–85; SGB Gp PLC, 1974–86; Prudential Assurance Co., 1976–85 (Dep. Chm., 1979–80, Chm., 1980–85); Prudential Corporation PLC, 1978–89 (Dep. Chm., 1979–80, Chm., 1980–85); Cadbury Schweppes PLC, 1979–87; Chm., Strategy Ventures, 1988–; Mem., London Adv. Bd, Norwich Union Insurance Gp, 1965–70, 1974–76; Member, Advisory Board: PA Strategy Partners, 1985–87; LEK Partnership, 1987–95. Mem. Council, CBI, 1976–87 (Chm., Educn and Trng Cttee, 1977–82); Chm., Business in the Community, 1984–87. MP (C) Mitcham, 1950–74, Sutton, Carshalton, 1974–76; PPS to Sec. of State for Foreign Affairs, Nov. 1951–April 1955, to Prime Minister, April–Dec. 1955; Parly Sec., Min. of Labour and Nat. Service, Dec. 1955–April 1958; Sec. for Technical Co-operation, 1963–64; Sec. of State for Employment, 1970–72; Lord President of the Council and Leader of the House of Commons, April–Nov. 1972; Home Secretary, 1972–74. Governor: St Mary's Hosp., Paddington, 1958–63; Imperial Coll. of Science and Technology, 1959–63 and 1976–87 (Fellow 1985); St Mary's Medical Sch. Council, 1958–63; Hon. Treas., Wright Fleming Inst. of Microbiology, 1960–63. Duke of Edinburgh Lectr, Inst. of Building, 1976. Pres., Surrey CCC, 1985–86. CCMI (CBIM 1982); CIPD (CIPM 1975). *Publications:* (jt) One Nation, 1950; (jt) Change is our Ally, 1954; (jt) The Responsible Society, 1958; (jt) One Europe, 1965; articles in technical jls. *Recreations:* lawn tennis, music, gardening. *Club:* Brooks's.

CARR, Alan Michael; Senior Partner, Simmons & Simmons, 1992–96; *b* 1 Sept. 1936; *m* 1963, Dalia Lebhar; two *s* one *d*. *Educ:* Gresham's Sch., Holt; King's Coll., Cambridge (MA). Articled Simmons & Simmons, 1957; admitted solicitor, 1961; Partner, 1966–96. FRGS 1989. *Recreation:* travel among remote people.

CARR, Sir (Albert) Raymond (Maillard), Kt 1987; DLitt (Oxon); FRHistS; FRSL; FBA 1978; Warden, 1968–87, Fellow, since 1964, St Antony's College, Oxford (Hon. Fellow, 1988); *b* 11 April 1919; *s* of Reginald and Marion Maillard Carr; *m* 1950, Sara Strickland; three *s* one *d*. *Educ:* Brockenhurst Sch.; Christ Church, Oxford (Hon. Student 1986). Gladstone Research Exhibnr, Christ Church, Oxford, 1941; Lectr, UCL, 1945–46; Oxford University: Fellow of All Souls' Coll., 1946–53; Fellow of New Coll., 1953–64; Director, Latin American Centre, 1964–68; Prof. of History of Latin America, 1967–68; Sub-Warden, St Antony's Coll., 1966–68. Distinguished Prof., Boston Univ., 1980; King Juan Carlos Prof. of Spanish History, NY Univ., 1992. Mem., Nat. Theatre Bd, 1968–77. Chm., Soc. for Latin American Studies, 1966–68. Corresp. Mem., Royal Acad. of History, Madrid. Hon. DLitt Madrid, 1999. Award of Merit, Soc. for Spanish Hist. Studies of the US, 1987; Leimer Award for Spanish Studies, Univ. of Augsburg, 1990; Prince of Asturias Award in Social Scis, Prince of Asturias Foundn, 1999. Grand Cross of the Order of Alfonso el Sabio (Spain), 1983; Order of Infante Dom Henrique (Portugal), 1989. *Publications:* Spain 1808–1939, 1966; Latin America (St Antony's Papers), 1969; (ed) The Republic and the Civil War in Spain, 1971; English Fox Hunting, 1976; The Spanish Tragedy: the Civil War in Perspective, 1977; (jtly) Spain: Dictatorship to Democracy, 1979; Modern Spain, 1980; (with Sara Carr) Fox-Hunting, 1982; Puerto Rico: a colonial experiment, 1984; (ed) The Spanish Civil War, 1986; (ed) The Chances of Death: a diary of the Spanish Civil War, 1995; Visiones de fin de siglio, 1999; (ed) Spain: a history, 2000; articles on Swedish, Spanish and Latin American history. *Recreation:* fox hunting. *Address:* 58 Fitzgeorge Avenue, W14 0SW. *T:* (020) 7603 6975. *Clubs:* Beefsteak, Oxford and Cambridge.

CARR, Andrew Jonathan, FRCS; Nuffield Professor of Orthopaedic Surgery, University of Oxford, and Fellow, Worcester College, Oxford, since 2001; *b* 18 June 1958; *s* of John Malcolm Carr and Patricia (*née* Hodgson); *m* 1985, Clare Robertson; one *s* three *d*. *Educ:* Bradford Grammar Sch.; Bristol Univ. (MB ChB 1982; ChM 1989). FRCS 1986. House surgeon and physician, 1982–83, anatomy demonstrator, 1983–84, Bristol Univ.; Surgical Lectr, Sheffield Univ., 1984–85; Metabolic Medicine Res. Fellow, Univ. of Oxford, 1985–87; Orthopaedic Registrar and Sen. Registrar, Nuffield Orthopaedic Centre and John Radcliffe Hosp., Oxford, 1988–92; Consultant Orthopaedic Surgeon, Nuffield Orthopaedic Centre, Oxford, 1993–2001. Research Fellow: Seattle, 1992; Melbourne, 1992; Hunterian Prof., RCS, 2000; Visiting Professor: Chinese Univ. of Hong Kong, 2004; Nat. Univ. of Singapore, 2005. Trustee: Arthritis Res. Campaign, 2004–; Jean Shanks Foundn, 2006–. Assoc. Ed., Jl of Bone and Joint Surgery, 2003–. Robert Jones Gold Medallist and British Orthopaedic Assoc. Prize Winner, 2000. *Publications:* (jtly) Outcomes in Orthopaedic Surgery, 1993; (jtly) Outcomes in Trauma, 1995; (jtly) Assessment Methodology in Orthopaedic Surgery, 1997; (jtly) Orthopaedics in Primary Care, 1999; (jtly) Classification in Trauma, 1999; (jtly) Oxford Textbook of Orthopaedic Surgery, 2001; contrib. to learned jls etc on shoulder and elbow surgery, genetics and osteoarthritis. *Recreations:* rowing, Real tennis, cooking. *Address:* Nuffield Department of Orthopaedic Surgery, Nuffield Orthopaedic Centre NHS Trust, Oxford OX3 7LD; Worcester College, Oxford OX1 2HB. *Club:* Leander (Henley-on-Thames).

CARR, Annabel; *see* Carr, E. A.

CARR, Anthony Paul; a District Judge (Magistrates' Courts), since 2003; *b* 30 March 1952; *s* of Alexander and June Carr; *m* 1983, Hilary (*née* Taylor); one *s* one *d*. *Educ:* Stockport Grammar Sch.; Selwyn Coll., Cambridge (BA 1974, MA 1975). Called to the Bar, Middle Temple, 1976; Dep. Clerk to Peterborough Justices, 1983–87; Clerk to SW Essex Justices, 1987–2000; Dir, Legal Services, and Clerk to Essex Justices, 2000–03. *Publications:* Criminal Procedure in Magistrates' Courts, 1982; (jtly) The Children Act in Practice, 3rd edn 2002; (ed) Stone's Justices Manual, 136th edn 2004, 138th edn 2006; (ed) Clarke Hall and Morrison on Children, 10th edn 2004. *Recreations:* reading, railways. *Address:* Croydon Magistrates' Court, Barclay Road, Croydon CR9 3NG. *T:* (020) 8603 0476.

CARR, Very Rev. (Arthur) Wesley, KCVO 2006; PhD; Dean of Westminster, 1997–2006; *b* 26 July 1941; *s* of Arthur and Irene Carr; *m* 1968, Natalie Gill; one *d*. *Educ:* Dulwich College; Jesus Coll., Oxford (MA); Jesus Coll., Cambridge (MA); Ridley Hall, Cambridge; Univ. of Sheffield (PhD). Curate, Luton Parish Church, 1967–71; Tutor, Ridley Hall, Cambridge, 1970–71, Chaplain 1971–72; Sir Henry Stephenson Fellow, Dept of Biblical Studies, Univ. of Sheffield, 1972–74; Hon. Curate, Ranmoor, 1972–74; Chaplain, Chelmsford Cathedral, 1974–78; Dep. Director, Chelmsford Cathedral Centre for Research and Training, 1974–82; Dir of Training, Diocese of Chelmsford, 1976–82; Canon Residentiary, Chelmsford Cathedral, 1978–87; Dean of Bristol, 1987–97. Mem., Gen. Synod of C of E, 1980–87, 1989–2000. Select Preacher, Univ. of Oxford, 1984–85; Hon. Fellow, New Coll., Edinburgh, 1986–94. Hon. DLitt: UWE, 1997; Sheffield, 2003. *Publications:* Angels and Principalities, 1977; The Priestlike Task, 1985; Brief Encounters, 1985; The Pastor as Theologian, 1989; Ministry and the Media, 1990; Lost in Familiar Places, 1991; (with E. R. Shapiro) Manifold Wisdom, 1991; (ed) Say One for Me, 1992; A Handbook of Pastoral Studies, 1997; (ed) The New Dictionary of Pastoral Studies, 2002; articles in Theology, etc. *Recreations:* music, reading, writing, gardening. *Address:* 56 Palmerston Street, Romsey, Hants SO51 8GG. *T:* (01794) 511969; *e-mail:* wesley@wesleycarr.wanadoo.co.uk.

CARR, Donald Bryce, OBE 1985; Secretary, Cricket Council and Test and County Cricket Board, 1974–86, retired; *b* 28 Dec. 1926; *s* of John Lillingston Carr and Constance Ruth Carr; *m* 1953, Stella Alice Vaughan Simpkinson; one *s* one *d*. *Educ:* Repton Sch.; Worcester Coll., Oxford (MA). Served Army, 1945–48 (Lieut Royal Berks Regt). Asst Sec., 1953–59, Sec., 1959–62, Derbyshire CCC; Asst Sec., MCC, 1962–74. *Recreations:* golf, following most sports. *Address:* 28 Aldenham Avenue, Radlett, Herts WD7 8HX. *T:* (01923) 855602. *Clubs:* MCC, British Sportsman's, Lord's Taverners; Vincent's, Oxford University Cricket (Oxford).

CARR, Edward Arthur John, CBE 1995; heritage and tourism consultant, since 1995; Chief Executive, CADW, Welsh Historic Monuments Executive Agency, 1991–95 (Director, 1985–91); *b* 31 Aug. 1938; *s* of Edward Arthur Carr, CMG and Margaret Alys Carr (*née* Willson); *m* 1st, 1960, Verity Martin (marr. diss.); two *d*; 2nd, 1980, Patrice Metro; one *s* one *d*. *Educ:* Leys Sch., Cambridge; Christ's Coll., Cambridge (BA 1960; MA 1963). Journalist: Thomson Regional Newspapers, 1960–65; Financial Times, 1965–67; Sunday Times, 1967–70; Manager, Times Newspapers, 1970–81; Chief Executive, Waterlow & Sons, 1981; Dir, Neath Develt Partnership, 1982–84. Vice-Chm., Bro Morgannwg NHS Trust, 1999–2005; Chairman: Swansea NHS Trust, 2005–07; NHS Wales Governance in Health Project, 2007–. Trustee, UK Buildings Preservation Trust, 1996–2007; Chm., Wales Cttee, Assoc. of Preservation Trusts, 1999–2007. *Recreations:* family, heritage, Rugby. *T:* (01792) 232800; *e-mail:* eajcarr@aol.com.

CARR, (Elizabeth) Annabel; QC 1997; **Her Honour Judge Annabel Carr;** a Circuit Judge, since 2001; *b* 14 Nov. 1954; *d* of William John Denys Carr and Norah Betty Carr; one *s* one *d*. *Educ:* Queenswood Sch., Hatfield; Sheffield Univ. (LLB Hons 1975). Called to the Bar, Gray's Inn, 1976; in practice at the Bar, 1977–2001; Recorder, 1995–2001. *Recreations:* travelling, family, theatre. *Address:* Sheffield Combined Court Centre, 50 West Bar, Sheffield S3 8PH.

CARR, Henry James; QC 1998; *b* 31 March 1958; *s* of Malcolm Carr and Dr Sara Carr; *m* 1988, Jan Dawson; three *s* one *d*. *Educ:* Hertford Coll., Oxford (BA 1st cl. Hons Jurisp.); Univ. of British Columbia (LLM). Called to the Bar, Gray's Inn, 1982, Bencher, 2005; in practice at the Bar, 1982–. Chm., Council of Experts, Intellectual Property Inst. *Publication:* Computer Software: legal protection in the United Kingdom, 1987, 2nd edn (jtly) 1992. *Recreations:* tennis, swimming, theatre. *Address:* 11 South Square, Gray's Inn, WC1R 5EU. *T:* (020) 7405 1222. *Clubs:* Royal Automobile, Hurlingham, Harbour.

CARR, Ian Henry Randell; freelance trumpeter, composer, author and broadcaster, since 1960; Associate Professor, Guildhall School of Music and Drama, since 1982; *b* 21 April 1933; *s* of late Thomas Randell Carr and Phyllis Harriet Carr; *m* 1963, Margaret Blackburn Bell (*d* 1967); one *d*; 2nd, 1972, Sandra Louise Major (marr. diss. 1993). *Educ:* Barnard Castle Sch.; King's Coll., Newcastle upon Tyne (BA Hons English Lang. and Lit. 1955). Nat. Service, 2nd Lieut, Royal Northumberland Fusiliers, 1956–58. Member: Emcee Five Quintet, 1960–62; Don Rendell/Ian Carr Quintet, 1963–69; Ian Carr's Nucleus, 1969–88 (toured world-wide); Founder Mem., United Jazz and Rock Ensemble, 1975–. Documentary, The Miles Davis Story, Channel 4 (Internat. Emmy Arts Documentary Award), 2001. Mem., Royal Soc. of Musicians of GB, 1982. Calabria Award for outstanding contrib. in the field of jazz (Italy), 1982. *Compositions:* Solar Plexus, 1970; Labyrinth, 1973; Will's Birthday Suite, 1974 (for Globe Theatre Trust); Out of the Long Dark, 1978; Old Heartland, 1988; Sounds and Sweet Airs, for trumpet and Cathedral organ, 1992; many broadcasts for BBC Radio 3. *Publications:* Music Outside, 1973; Miles Davis: a critical biography, 1982, 3rd edn 1998 (as Miles Davis: the definitive biography);

(jtly) Jazz: the essential companion, 1987; Keith Jarrett: the man and his music, 1991; (jtly) The Rough Guide to Jazz, 1995; contrib. BBC Music mag. *Recreations:* music, the visual arts, world literature, travel. *Club:* Ronnie Scott's.

CARR, John Roger, CBE 1991; Chairman, Countryside Commission for Scotland, 1986–92 (Member, 1979–84; Vice-Chairman, 1984–85); *b* 18 Jan. 1927; *s* of James Stanley Carr and Edith Carr (*née* Robinson); *m* 1951, Catherine Elise Dickson Smith; two *s*. *Educ:* Ackworth and Ayton (Quaker Schools). FRICS. Royal Marines, 1944–47; Gordon Highlanders (TA), 1950–54. Factor, Walker Scottish Estates Co., 1950–54; Factor, 1954–67, Dir and Gen. Man., 1967–88, Dir, 1988–90, Moray Estates Develt Co. Dir, Strathearn Tourism Develt Co., 1959–98. Mem., Wkg Party, Management Training for Leisure and Recreation in Scotland, 1986; Chm., Countryside around Towns Forum, 1991–95; Vice Pres., Farming and Wildlife Adv. Gp for Scotland, 1992–98; Director: Macaulay Land Use Res. Inst., 1987–97; UK 2000 Scotland, 1991–93. Mem., Moray DC, 1974–80. JP Moray, 1975–2007. *Recreations:* reading, photography, fishing, walking. *Address:* Goosehill, Invererne Road, Forres, Moray IV36 1DZ.

CARR, His Honour Maurice Chapman; a Circuit Judge, 1986–2005; *b* 14 Aug. 1937; *s* of John and Elizabeth Carr; *m* 1959, Caryl Olson; one *s* one *d*. *Educ:* Hookergate Grammar Sch.; LSE (LLB); Harvard Univ. (LLM). Lectr in Law, 1960–62, Asst Prof. of Law, 1963–64, Univ. of British Columbia; Lecturer in Law: UCW, 1964–65; Univ. of Newcastle upon Tyne, 1965–69. Called to the Bar, Middle Temple, 1966. *Recreations:* walking, music.

CARR, Michael; teacher; *b* 31 Jan. 1946; *s* of James and Sheila Mary Carr; *m* 1st (wife *d* 1979); one *s*; 2nd, 1980, Georgina Clare; four *s* two *d*. *Educ:* St Joseph's Coll., Blackpool; Catholic Coll., Preston; Margaret McMillan Coll. of Educn, Bradford (CertEd); Bradford and Ilkley Community Coll. (DPSE). Engrg apprentice, 1962–63; Local Govt Officer, 1964–68; partner in family retail newsagency, 1968–70; Teacher of Geography: Brookside Sec. Sch., Middlesbrough, 1973–74; Stainsby Sch., Middlesbrough, 1974–75; Head of Geog., St Thomas Aquinas RC High Sch., Darwen, Lancs, 1975–82; Head of Gen. Studies, Blackthorn County Sec. Sch. and Blackthorn Wing of Fearns CS Sch., Bacup, 1982–87; Mem., Lancs Educn Cttee Sch. Support Team (Disruptive Behaviour), 1988–91. Mem., Sabden Parish Council, 1976–78, 1979–83; Mem. (C 1979–81, SDP 1981–83), Ribble Valley BC, 1979–83. Joined SDP, 1981; contested (SDP/Lib Alliance) Ribble Valley, 1983, 1987; MP (Lib Dem) Ribble Valley, March 1991–1992; contested (Lib Dem) Ribble Valley, 1992, 1997, 2001. Mem., NAS/UWT (Dist Sec., Rossendale Assoc., 1983–87; Press Officer, Lancs Fedn, 1983–87, 1988–90). *Recreations:* hill walking, cooking, music.

CARR, Michael Douglas; Chief Science Officer, BT, since 2007; *b* Bletchley, 14 Sept. 1955; *s* of John Joseph Carr and Pamela Mary Carr; *m* 1981, Caroline Jane Daniels; two *d*. *Educ:* Plymouth Poly. (BScEng Hons Communication Engrg 1980). CEng, FIET 2004; FREng 2008. Joined BT as Technician Apprentice Field Engr, 1972; Researcher, Picture Compression, 1980–84, Hd, Video Conference Res. Gp, 1984–89, Gen. Manager, Video Res., 1989–94, BT Labs; Principal Advr, Multimedia, 1994–96; Hd, ICT Strategy Unit, 1996–99; Vice-Pres., Technology and Venturing USA, 1999–2001; Dir, Res. and Venturing, 2001–07. Mem. Bd, EPSRC, 2008–. *Publications:* articles in jls on video comparison and video transmission. *Recreations:* woodworking, gardening, playing the piano. *Address:* BT, Antares 3/23, Adastral Park, Martlesham Head, Ipswich, Suffolk IP5 3RE. *T:* (01473) 609083, *Fax:* (01473) 648860; *e-mail:* mike.d.carr@bt.com.

CARR, Peter; His Honour Judge Peter Carr; a Circuit Judge, since 2007; *b* Hamburg, 14 Nov. 1954; *s* of Derek and Anneliese Carr; *m* 1997, Julie Ann Campbell; one *d*. *Educ:* Dr Challoner's Grammar Sch., Amersham; Birmingham Univ. (LLB). Called to the Bar, Inner Temple, 1976; Recorder, 2001–07. *Recreations:* golf, bridge, cooking. *Address:* Birmingham Crown Court, 1 Newton Street, Birmingham B4 7NA. *T:* (0121) 681 3300. *Clubs:* Edgbaston Golf, Warwickshire County Cricket.

CARR, Sir Peter (Derek), Kt 2007; CBE 1989; DL; Chairman: North East Strategic Health Authority, since 2006; Peter Carr and Associates, since 2003; Durham County Waste Management Co., since 1993; *b* 12 July 1930; *s* of George William Carr and Marjorie (*née* Tailby); *m* 1958, Geraldine Pamela (*née* Ward); one *s* one *d*. *Educ:* Fircroft Coll., Birmingham; Ruskin Coll., Oxford; London Univ. National Service, RAF, 1951–53. Carpenter and joiner, construction industry, 1944–51 and 1953–56; college, 1956–60; Lectr, Percival Whitley Coll., Halifax, 1960–65; Sen. Lectr in Indust. Relations, Thurrock Coll., and part-time Adviser, NBPI, 1965–69; Director: Commn on Industrial Relations, 1969–74; ACAS, 1974–78; Diplomatic Service, Washington, 1978–83; Regl Dir, Northern Regl Office, Dept of Employment, and Leader, City Action Team, 1983–89; Chm., Co. Durham Develt Co., 1990–2001. Chairman: Northern Screen Commn, 1990–2002; Northern RHA, 1990–94; Occupational Pensions Bd, 1994–97; Newcastle and N Tyne HA, 1998–2002; Northumberland Tyne and Wear Strategic HA, 2002–06; Northern Regl Assembly Health Forum, 2002–06; Northern Adv. Cttee on Clinical Excellence Awards, 2003–. Chairman: Premier Waste Mgt, 1997–99; Acorn Energy Supplies Ltd, 1998–2000. Vis. Fellow, Durham Univ., 1989–. Mem. Ct, Univ. of Newcastle, 2006–. DL Durham, 1997. *Publications:* It Occurred to Me, 2004; directed study for CIR on worker participation and collective bargaining in Europe, and study for ACAS on industrial relations in national newspaper industry. *Recreations:* cycling, photography, cooking, furniture-making, American history. *Address:* 4 Corchester Towers, Corbridge, Northumberland NE45 5NP. *T:* (01434) 632841; *e-mail:* petercarr@aol.com.

CARR, Sir Raymond; *see* Carr, Sir A. R. M.

CARR, Reginald Philip; Director, University Library Services, and Bodley's Librarian, University of Oxford, 1997–2006, now Bodley's Librarian Emeritus; Fellow, Balliol College, Oxford, 1997–2006; *b* 20 Feb. 1946; *s* of Philip Henry Carr and Ida Bayley Carr; *m* 1968, Elizabeth Whittaker; one *s* three *d*. *Educ:* Manchester Grammar Sch.; Univ. of Leeds (BA 1968); Univ. of Manchester (MA 1971); MA Cantab 1983; MA Oxon 1997. English lang. teaching asst, Lycée Fontenelle, Rouen, 1966–67; Asst Librarian, John Rylands Univ. Liby, Manchester, 1970–72; Librarian-in-Charge, Sch. of Educn Liby, Univ. of Manchester, 1972–76; Sub-Librarian, Univ. of Surrey, 1976–78; Deputy Librarian: Univ. of Aston, 1978–80; Univ. of Cambridge, 1980–86; University of Leeds: Univ. Librarian and Keeper, Brotherton Collection, 1986–96; Dean, Information Strategy, 1996. Mem., Jt Information Systems Cttee, 1997–2005. Chm., Res. Libraries Gp Inc., 1999–2003. FRSA 1996. Hon. DLitt Leicester, 2000. Hon. Citizen, Toyota City, 1998. *Publications:* Anarchism in France: the case of Octave Mirbeau, 1977; (jtly) Spirit in the New Testament, 1985; The Mandrake Press, 1985; (jtly) An Introduction to University Library Administration, 1987; The Academic Research Library in a Decade of Change, 2007; contribs to professional and learned jls. *Recreations:* Bible study, book collecting. *Address:* c/o The Bodleian Library, Broad Street, Oxford OX1 3BG.

CARR, Hon. Robert John; Premier of New South Wales, 1995–2005; *b* 28 Sept. 1947; *s* of Edward and Phyllis Carr; *m* 1973, Helena. *Educ:* Univ. of NSW (BA Hons). Journalist, ABC Current Affairs Radio, 1969–72; Educn Officer, Labor Council, NSW, 1972–78; Journalist, The Bulletin, 1978–83. Government of New South Wales: MP (ALP) Maroubra, 1983–2005; Minister: for Planning and Envmt, 1984–88; for Consumer Affairs, 1986; for Heritage, 1986–88; Leader of the Opposition, 1988–95; Minister: for Ethnic Affairs, 1995–99; for the Arts, 1995–2005; for Citizenship, 1999–2005. Mem., Internat. Climate Change Taskforce, 2004. World Conservation Union Internat. Parks Award, 1998; Fulbright Dist. Fellow Award, 1999. *Publications:* Thoughtlines: reflections of a public man, 2002; What Australia Means to Me, 2003; My Reading Life: adventures in the world of books. *Address:* *e-mail:* bob.carr@bobcarr.com.au.

CARR, Rodney Paul, OBE 2005; yachtsman; Chief Executive, Royal Yachting Association, since 2000; *b* 10 March 1950; *s* of Capt. George Paul Carr and Alma Carr (*née* Walker); *m* 1971, Lynne Alison Ashwell; one *s* one *d*. *Educ:* Carlton Le Willows Grammar Sch., Nottingham; Univ. of Birmingham (BSc Geology 1972). Chief Sailing Instructor, London Bor. of Haringey, 1972–75; Instructor, 1975–79, Chief Instructor, 1979–81, Nat. Sailing Centre, Cowes, IoW; Mem., winning British Admiral's Cup team, 1981; joined RYA, 1984; Coach, GB Olympic Team: Los Angeles, 1984; Seoul, 1988; Barcelona, 1992; Overall GB Team Manager, Atlanta Olympic Games, 1996; Racing Manager and Performance Dir, RYA, 1997–2000; Dep. Chef de Mission, GB Olympic Team, Sydney, 2000. Mem., UK Sports Bd, 2005–. Trustee, John Merricks Sailing Trust, 1997–. Hon. MBA Southampton Inst., 2002. *Recreations:* played county level U19 Rugby for Nottinghamshire, keen interest in most sports, current affairs, music. *Address:* 14 Spring Way, Alresford, Hants SO24 9LN. *T:* (01962) 734148; (office) RYA House, Ensign Way, Hamble, Southampton SO31 4YA. *T:* (023) 8060 4102; *e-mail:* rod.carr@rya.org.uk. *Clubs:* Royal Thames Yacht; Hayling Island Sailing, Royal Southern Yacht, Royal Southampton Yacht.

CARR, Roger Martyn; Chairman: Centrica, since 2004 (non-executive Director, since 2000); Cadbury plc, since 2008 (Senior non-executive Director, 2000–03; Deputy Chairman, 2003–08); *b* 22 Dec. 1946; *s* of John and Kathleen Carr; *m* 1973, Stephanie Elizabeth; one *d*. *Educ:* Nottingham High Sch.; Nottingham Poly. Dir, Williams Hldgs plc, 1988–2000; Chief Exec., Williams plc, 1994–2000; Chm., Chubb plc, 2000–02. Dir, 1994–99, Chm., 1999–2000, Thames Water plc. Chm., Mitchells & Butlers, 2003–08; Sen. non-exec. Dir, Six Continents (formerly Bass) plc, 1996–2003. Non-exec. Dir, Bank of England, 2007–. Sen. Advr, Kohlberg, Kravis & Roberts & Co. Ltd, 2000–. Member: Industrial Adv. Bd, 2001–04; Council, CBI, 2001–04. CCMI (CIMgt 1997); FRSA 1996. *Recreations:* theatre, opera, golf, tennis. *Address:* Centrica plc, Millstream, Maidenhead Road, Windsor, Berks SL4 5GD. *Clubs:* London Capital, Royal Automobile; China (Hong Kong).

CARR, Sue Lascelles, (Mrs A. Birch); QC 2003; barrister; *b* 1 Sept. 1964; *d* of Richard Carr and Edda Harvey (*née* Armbrust); *m* 1993, Alexander Birch; two *s* one *d*. *Educ:* Trinity Coll., Cambridge (MA Law and Mod. Langs). Called to the Bar, Inner Temple, 1987, Bencher, 2006. Chm., Complaints Cttee, 2008–; Mem., Bar Standards Bd, 2008–. Gov., Wycombe Abbey Sch., 2007–. *Publication:* (ed) Professional Liability Precedents, 2000. *Recreations:* theatre, ski-ing, tennis. *Address:* 4 New Square, Lincoln's Inn, WC2A 3RJ. *T:* (020) 7822 2000, *Fax:* (020) 7822 2001; *e-mail:* s.carr@4newsquare.com.

CARR, Very Rev. Wesley; *see* Carr, Very Rev. A. W.

CARR, Prof. Wilfred; Professor, School of Education, University of Sheffield, since 1994; *b* 18 March 1943; *s* of Wilfred and Leah Carr; *m* 1976, Marisse Evans; three *d*. *Educ:* Xaverian Coll., Manchester; Shenstone Coll. of Educn, Worcs (DipEd); Warwick Univ. (BA, MA). History teacher, Oldbury Tech. Sch., Warley, Worcs, 1966–70; Lectr, Sch. of Educn, UCNW, 1974–88; University of Sheffield: Sen. Lectr, Dept of Educnl Studies, 1988–90, Reader 1990–94; Dean, Faculty of Educnl Studies, 1992–94; Head, Dept of Educnl Studies, then Sch. of Educn, 1996–2002 and 2005–06; Dean, Fac. of Soc. Scis, 2003–05. Hon. Prof., Faculty of Educn and Soc. Work, Univ. of Sydney, 2006–. Ed., Pedagogy, Culture and Society, 1993–. Chm., Philosophy of Educn Soc. of GB, 1996–99. *Publications:* (with S. Kemmis) Becoming Critical: education knowledge and action research, 1986 (trans. Spanish, 1988); For Education: towards critical educational inquiry, 1995 (trans. Spanish, 1996, Chinese, 1997). *Recreations:* cookery, reading, walking. *Address:* School of Education, Department of Educational Studies, University of Sheffield, 388 Glossop Road, Sheffield S10 2JA. *T:* (0114) 222 8085; *e-mail:* w.carr@sheffield.ac.uk.

CARR, William Compton; *b* 10 July 1918; *m*; two *s* one *d*. *Educ:* The Leys Sch., Cambridge. MP (C) Barons Court, 1959–64; PPS to Min. of State, Board of Trade, 1963; PPS to Financial Sec. to the Treasury, 1963–64. *Recreations:* reading, theatre-going, skin diving, eating, dieting.

CARR-ELLISON, Sir Ralph (Harry), KCVO 1999; Kt 1973; TD 1962; ED 1974; DL; Lord-Lieutenant of Tyne and Wear, 1984–2000; *b* 8 Dec. 1925; *s* of late Major John Campbell Carr-Ellison; *m* 1st, 1951, Mary Clare (*d* 1996), *d* of late Major Arthur McMorrough Kavanagh, MC; three *s* one *d*; 2nd, 1998, Louise Gay Dyer (*née* Walsh), *widow* of Simon Dyer, CBE. *Educ:* Eton. Served Royal Glos Hussars and 1st Royal Dragoons, 1944–49; Northumberland Hussars (TA), (Lt-Col Comdg), 1949–69; TAVR Col, Northumbrian Dist, 1969–72; Col, Dep. Comdr (TAVR), NE Dist, 1973; Chm., N of England TA&VRA, 1976–80 (Pres. 1987–90; Vice-Pres., 1990–2000); ADC (TAVR) to HM the Queen, 1970–75; Hon. Colonel: Northumbrian Univs OTC, 1982–86; QOY, 1988–90 (Northumberland Hussars Sqn, 1986–88); Col Comdt, Yeomanry RAC TA, 1990–94. Chairman: Northumbrian Water Authy, 1973–82; Tyne Tees Television Ltd, 1974–97 (Dir, 1966–97); Director: Newcastle & Gateshead Water Co., 1964–73; Trident Television, 1972–81 (Dep. Chm., 1976–81); Yorkshire-Tyne Tees Television Hldgs, 1992–97. Co. Comr, Northumberland Scouts, 1958–68; Mem. Cttee of Council, 1960–67, Mem. Council, 1982–2000, Scout Assoc. Chm., Berwick-on-Tweed Constituency Cons. Assoc., 1959–62, Pres., 1973–77; Northern Area Cons. Assocs: Treas., 1961–66, Chm., 1966–69; Pres., 1974–78; Vice-Chm., Nat Union of Cons. and Unionist Assocs, 1969–71. Chm., North Tyne Area, Manpower Bd, MSC, 1983–84. Vice Pres., Automobile Assoc., 1995–99 (Vice-Chm., 1985–86; Chm., 1986–95). Mem. Council, The Wildfowl Trust, 1981–88. Chm., Newcastle Univ. Develt Trust, 1978–81 (Mem., 1992–98); Mem. Ct, Newcastle Univ., 1979–2002; Governor, Swinton Conservative College, 1967–81. FRSA 1983. High Sheriff, 1972, JP 1953–75, DL 1981–85, Vice Lord-Lieut, 1984, Northumberland; DL Tyne and Wear, 2001. Hon. DCL Newcastle, 1989; Hon. LLD Sunderland, 1998. KStJ 1984. *Recreation:* Jt Master, West Percy Foxhounds, 1950–90. *Address:* Beanley Hall, Beanley, Alnwick, Northumberland NE66 2DX. *T:* (01665) 578273. *Clubs:* Cavalry and Guards, White's, Pratt's, MCC; Northern Counties (Newcastle upon Tyne).

CARR-GOMM, Richard Culling, OBE 1985; *b* 2 Jan. 1922; *s* of Mark Culling Carr-Gomm and Amicia Dorothy (*née* Heming); *m* 1957, Susan (*d* 2007), *d* of Ralph and Dorothy Gibbs; two *s* three *d*. *Educ:* Stowe School. Served War: commnd Coldstream

Guards, 1941; served 6th Guards Tank Bde, NW Europe (twice wounded, mentioned in despatches); Palestine, 1945; ME; resigned commn, 1955. Founded: Abbeyfield Soc., 1956; Carr-Gomm Soc., 1965; Morpeth Soc. (charity socs), 1972. Templeton UK Project Award, 1984; Beacon Lifetime Achievement Award, 2004; Pride of Britain Award, 2005. Croix de Guerre (Silver Star), France, 1944. KStJ. *Publications*: Push on the Door (autobiog.), 1979, 2nd edn as All Things Considered, 2004; Loneliness—the wider scene, 1987. *Recreations*: golf, backgammon, painting. *Address*: 9 The Batch, Batheaston, Somerset BA1 7DR. *T*: (01225) 858434.

CARR LINFORD, Alan; artist; *b* 15 Jan. 1926; *m* 1948, Margaret Dorothea Parish; two *s* one *d*. *Educ*: Royal College of Art (ARCA 1946), and in Rome. ARE 1946; ARWS 1949, RWS 1955. Prix de Rome, 1947. *Address*: 11 Walcot Buildings, Bath BA1 6AD.

CARR-SMITH, Maj.-Gen. Stephen Robert; Chairman, National Assembly for Property Search Standards; non-executive Director, Council for National Land and Property Information Service; *b* 3 Dec. 1941; *s* of Charles Carr-Smith and Elizabeth Carr-Smith (*née* Marsh); *m* 1967, Nicole Bould; two *s* one *d*. *Educ*: Welbeck College; RMA; RMCS; BA Open Univ., 1992. Commissioned Royal Signals, 1962; served in UK, Germany, Aden and Belgium; Mil. Sec., 1973–74, Operational Requirements, 1978–79, MoD; CO, 1st Armoured Div. HQ and Signal Regt, 1979–82; Instructor, Army Staff Coll., 1982–84; Comdt, Army Apprentices Coll., Harrogate, 1984–86; Col MGO Secretariat, MoD, 1986–88; Chief CIS Policy Branch, SHAPE, Mons, 1988–91; Dep. Dir Gen., NATO CIS Agency, Brussels, 1992–95; Dir of Special Projects, Defence Systems Ltd, 1995–98; Sen. Mil. Advr, CORDA, BAe and SEMA, 1995–99. Ombudsman for Estate Agents, 1999–2006; Chm., Applied Systems International plc, 1999–2001. Chm., Cancer Res. UK, Winchester, 2007–. Hon. Col, FANY, Princess Royal's Volunteer Corps, 1996–2006; Col Comdt, RCS, 1996–2002. Pres., Stragglers of Asia CC, 2003–. *Recreations*: cricket, golf, bridge. *Address*: c/o Cox's & King's, PO Box 1190, 7 Pall Mall, SW1Y 5NA.

CARRAGHER, Anna; Controller, BBC Northern Ireland, 2000–06; Member, Human Fertilisation and Embryology Authority, since 2006; *b* 9 July 1948; *d* of Thomas Carragher and Eileen Carragher; *m* 1974, Alain Le Garsmeur; two *s* one *d*. *Educ*: St Dominic's High Sch., Belfast; Queen's Univ., Belfast (BA Hons). BBC Radio: studio manager, 1970–73; Producer, Today prog., 1973–81; BBC Television: Producer: Television News progs, 1981–85; Question Time, 1985–89; Any Questions, 1989–92; Editor: Election Call, 1992; European progs, 1992–95; Hd of Programmes, BBC NI, 1995–2000. Dir, NI Film Commn, 1995–2003. Member: Radio Acad., 2000–02; Bd, BITC NI, 2001–06; Bd, Radio Jt Audience Res. Bd Ltd, 2002–06. Chm., Grand Opera House Trust, Belfast, 2006–. *Recreations*: hill-walking, opera, reading, listening to radio, watching television. *Address*: 24 College Park Avenue, Belfast BT7 1LR.

CARRAHER, Terezinha; *see* Nunes, T.

CARRELL, Prof. Robin Wayne, FRS 2002; FRSNZ 1980; FRCP; Professor of Haematology, University of Cambridge, 1986–2003; Fellow of Trinity College, Cambridge, since 1987; *b* 5 April 1936; *s* of Ruane George Carrell and Constance Gwendoline Carrell (*née* Rowe); *m* 1962, Susan Wyatt Rogers; two *s* two *d*. *Educ*: Christchurch Boys' High School, NZ; Univ. of Otago (MB ChB 1959); Univ. of Canterbury (BSc 1965); Univ. of Cambridge (MA, PhD 1968, ScD 2002). FRACP 1973; FRCPath 1976; MRCP 1985, FRCP 1990. Mem., MRC Abnormal Haemoglobin Unit, Cambridge, 1965–68; Dir, Clinical Biochemistry, Christchurch Hosp., NZ, 1968–75; Lectr and Consultant in Clinical Biochem., Addenbrooke's Hosp. and Univ. of Cambridge, 1976–78; Prof. of Clinical Biochem., Christchurch Sch. of Clinical Medicine, Univ. of Otago, 1978–86. Pres., British Soc. of Thrombosis and Haemostasis, 1999. Mem., Spongiform Encephalopathy Adv. Cttee, 2001–04. Member: Gen. Bd, Univ. of Cambridge, 1989–92; Court, Imperial Coll., London, 1997–2006. Commonwealth Fellow, St John's Coll. and Vis. Scientist, MRC Lab. of Molecular Biol., 1985. Founder FMedSci 1998. Hon. FRCPA 2005. Pharmacia Prize for biochem. res., NZ, 1984; Hector Medal, Royal Soc., NZ, 1986. *Publications*: articles in sci. jls, esp. on genetic abnormalities of human proteins. *Recreations*: gardening, walking. *Address*: 19 Madingley Road, Cambridge CB3 0EG. *T*: (01223) 312970.

CARRERAS, José; tenor; *b* 5 Dec. 1946; *s* of José and Antonia Carreras; *m*; one *s* one *d*. Opera début as Gennaro in Lucrezia Borgia, Barcelona, 1970; US début in Madama Butterfly, NY City Opera, 1972; Tosca, NY Met, 1974; Covent Garden début in La Traviata, 1974; Un Ballo In Maschera, La Scala, 1975; after break owing to illness, concerts in Barcelona, 1988, Covent Gdn, 1989; Music Dir, Barcelona Olympics, 1992; first UK perf., Stiffelio, Covent Gdn, 1993; appears at all major opera houses and festivals in Europe, USA and S America; has made many recordings. Films: Don Carlos, 1980; West Side Story (TV), 1985. Pres., José Carreras Internat. Leukaemia Foundn, 1988–. RAM 1990. Personality of the Year, Classical Music Awards, 1994. *Address*: c/o FIJC, Muntaner 383, 2°, 08021 Barcelona, Spain.

CARRICK, 10th Earl of *cr* 1748; **David James Theobald Somerset Butler;** Viscount Ikerrin 1629; Baron Butler (UK) 1912; *b* 9 Jan. 1953; *s* of 9th Earl of Carrick, and his 1st wife, (Mary) Belinda (*d* 1993), *e d* of Major David Constable-Maxwell, TD; *S* father, 1992; *m* 1975, Philippa J. V. (marr. diss. 2002), *yr d* of Wing Commander L. V. Craxton; three *s* (including twin *s*). *Educ*: Downside. *Heir*: *s* Viscount Ikerrin, *qv*.

CARRICK, Hon. Sir John (Leslie), AC 2008; KCMG 1982; Senator, Commonwealth Parliament of Australia, 1971–87; *b* 4 Sept. 1918; *s* of late A. J. Carrick and of E. E. Carrick (*née* Terry); *m* 1951, Diana Margaret Hunter; three *d*. *Educ*: Univ. of Sydney (BEc; Hon. DLitt 1988). Res. Officer, Liberal Party of Aust., NSW Div., 1946–48, Gen. Sec., 1948–71; Minister: for Housing and Construction, 1975; for Urban and Regional Develt, 1975; for Educn, 1975–79; Minister Assisting Prime Minister in Fed. Affairs, 1975–78; Minister for Nat. Develt and Energy, 1979–83; Dep. Leader, 1978, Leader, 1978–83, Govt in the Senate. Vice-Pres., Exec. Council, 1978–82. Chairman: NSW Govt Cttee of Review of Schs, 1988–89; Review of Report Implementation, 1990–95; Gas Council of NSW, 1990–95. Pres., Univ. of Sydney Dermatology Res. Foundn, 1989–2003; Mem. Adv. Bd, Macquarie Univ. Inst. of Early Childhood, 1992–2001 (Chm. Res. Foundn, 2001–); Chm., Adv. Cttee, GERRIC (Gifted Children), Univ. of NSW, 1998–. Carrick Nat. Inst. for Learning and Teaching in Higher Educn, estabd by Commonwealth Govt, 2004. Mem. Exec. Cttee, Foundn for Aged Care, 1989–2001. Mem., Commonwealth Roundtable (Indigenous), 2000–01. Hon. FACE 1994. Hon. DLitt: Macquarie, 2000; Western Sydney, 2006; Hon. DEd NSW, 2006. Centenary Medal, 2000. *Recreations*: swimming, reading. *Address*: 21 Cambridge Apartments, 162E Burwood Road, Concord, NSW 2137, Australia. *Club*: Australian (Sydney).

CARRICK, Mervyn; *see* Carrick, W. M.

CARRICK, Sir Roger (John), KCMG 1995 (CMG 1983); LVO 1972; HM Diplomatic Service, retired; international consultant; Chairman, Strategy International Ltd, since 2007 (non-executive Director, 2001–06); *b* 13 Oct. 1937; *s* of John H. and Florence M. Carrick; *m* 1962, Hilary Elizabeth Blinman; two *s*. *Educ*: Isleworth Grammar Sch.; Sch. of Slavonic and East European Studies, London Univ. Served RN, 1956–58. Joined HM Foreign (subseq. Diplomatic) Service, 1956; SSEES, 1961; Sofia, 1962; FO, 1965; Paris, 1967; Singapore, 1971; FCO, 1973; Counsellor and Dep. Head, Personnel Ops Dept, FCO, 1976; Vis. Fellow, Inst. of Internat. Studies, Univ. of Calif, Berkeley, 1977–78; Counsellor, Washington, 1978–82; Hd, Overseas Estate Dept, FCO, 1982–85; Consul-Gen., Chicago, 1985–88; Asst Under-Sec. of State (Economic), FCO, 1988–90; Ambassador, Republic of Indonesia, 1990–94; High Comr, Australia, 1994–97. Chm., CMB Ltd, 2001–03; Dep. Chm., The D Gp, 1999–2006. Churchill Fellow (Life), Westminster Coll., Fulton, Missouri, 1987. Member: RSAA; Britain-Australia Soc., 1998– (Dep. Chm., 1999; Chm., 1999–2001; Vice-Pres., 2002–; Mem. Educn Trust, 2001–); Pilgrims; Anglo-Indonesian Soc.; Chm., Cook Soc., 2002. Mem., Bd of Trustees, Chevening Estate, 1998–2003. Jt Founder, WADE. Freeman, City of London, 2002. *Publications*: East-West Technology Transfer in Perspective, 1978; Rolleround Oz, 1998; articles in jls. *Recreations*: travel, lecturing, reading, sailing, enjoying music and avoiding gardening. *Address*: Windhover, Wootton Courtenay, Minehead, Somerset TA24 8RD. *Clubs*: Royal Over-Seas League; Primary (Australia).

CARRICK, (William) Mervyn; Member (DemU) Upper Bann, Northern Ireland Assembly, 1998–2003; *b* 13 Feb. 1946; *s* of late William and of Margaret Carrick; *m* 1969, Ruth Cardwell; three *s* one *d*. *Educ*: Portadown Technical Coll. Accountant, 1961–. Mem., NI Forum for Political Dialogue, 1996–98. Mem. (DemU), Craigavon BC, 1990–2001 (Dep. Mayor, 1997–98, Mayor, 1998–99). *Recreation*: gardening. *Address*: 72 Dungannon Road, Portadown, Co. Armagh BT62 1LQ. *T*: (028) 3833 6392.

CARRIER, Dr John Woolfe; Chairman, Camden Primary Care Trust, since 2001; Senior Lecturer in Social Policy, 1974–2005, and Dean of Graduate Studies, 2002–05, London School of Economics and Political Science; *b* 26 Sept. 1938; *s* of Louis Carrier and Rachel Carrier; *m* 1964, Sarah Margaret Dawes; two *s* two *d*. *Educ*: Regent's Park Central Sch.; Chiswick Poly.; London Sch. of Econs (BSc (Soc) 1965; MPhil 1969; PhD 1983); Univ. of Westminster (LLB Hons. 1994). Principal Lectr, Goldsmiths' Coll., Univ. of London, 1967–74. Lectures: William Marsden, Royal Free Hosp., 1996; Richard Titmuss Meml, Hebrew Univ. of Jerusalem, 1997. Vis. Prof., Univ. of Greenwich, 2006–. Jt Ed., Internat. Jl Sociol. of Law, 1993–; Member, Editorial Board: Jl Social Policy, 1975–81; Ethnic and Racial Studies, 1990–96. Mem. (Lab) Camden BC, 1971–78. Mem. and Vice-Chm., Hampstead HA, 1982–91; Vice-Chm., 1991–97, Chm., 1997–2001, Royal Free Hampstead NHS Hosp. Trust. Vice-Chm. and Trustee, Centre for Advancement of Inter-professional Educn, 1990–99; Trustee, William Ellis and Birkbeck Schs Trust, 1996– (Chm. Trustees, 2005–). Mem. Council, Royal Free Hosp. Med. Sch., 1988–98; Trustee, RNTNEH, 1997–99; Special Trustee, Royal Free Hosp., 1999–; Member: London NE Sub-Cttee, Adv. Cttee on Clinical Excellence Awards, 2003– (Chm., 2008); Bar Standards Bd, 2005– (Chm., Educn and Trng Cttee, 2007). Chairman: Camden Victim Support Scheme, 1978–83; Highgate Cemetery Trust, 1983–97. Trustee, Hackney Youth Orch. Trust, 2002–. Governor: Gospel Oak Primary Sch., 1972–80 (Chm., 1977–80); Brookfield Primary Sch., 1974–89 (Chm., 1981–87); William Ellis Sch., 1971–96 (Chm., 1987–96). JP Highbury, 1983–90. Hon. FRSocMed 1999; FRSA 1999. *Publications*: with Ian Kendall: Medical Negligence: complaints and compensation, 1990; (ed) Socialism and the NHS, 1990; Health and the National Health Service, 1998; (ed jtly) Interprofessional Issues in Community and Primary Health Care, 1995; (ed jtly) Asylum in the Community, 1996; contrib. articles to learned jls. *Recreations*: running, tennis, walking, films, art galleries. *Address*: 37 Dartmouth Park Road, NW5 1SU. *T*: (020) 7267 1376.

CARRINGTON, 6th Baron (Ireland) *cr* 1796, (Great Britain) *cr* 1797; **Peter Alexander Rupert Carington,** KG 1985; GCMG 1988 (KCMG 1958); CH 1983; MC 1945; PC 1959; Baron Carington of Upton (Life Peer), 1999; Chairman, Christies International plc, 1988–93; Director, The Telegraph plc, 1990–2004; Chancellor, Order of the Garter, since 1994; *b* 6 June 1919; *s* of 5th Baron and Hon. Sibyl Marion (*d* 1946), *d* of 2nd Viscount Colville; *S* father, 1938; *m* 1942, Iona, *yr d* of late Sir Francis McClean; one *s* two *d*. *Educ*: Eton Coll.; RMC Sandhurst. Served NW Europe, Major Grenadier Guards. Parly Sec., Min. of Agriculture and Fisheries, 1951–54; Parly Sec., Min. of Defence, Oct. 1954–Nov. 1956; High Comr for the UK in Australia, Nov. 1956–Oct. 1959; First Lord of the Admiralty, 1959–63; Minister without Portfolio and Leader of the House of Lords, 1963–64; Leader of the Opposition, House of Lords, 1964–70 and 1974–79; Secretary of State: for Defence, 1970–74; for Energy, 1974; for For. and Commonwealth Affairs, 1979–82; Minister of Aviation Supply, 1971–74. Chm., Cons. Party Organisation, 1972–74. Chm., GEC, 1983–84; Sec.-Gen., NATO, 1984–88. Chm., EC Conf. on Yugoslavia, 1991–92. Sec. for Foreign Correspondence and Hon. Mem., Royal Acad. of Arts, 1982–; Chm., Bd of Trustees, V&A Museum, 1983–88. Chancellor, Univ. of Reading, 1992–2007. President: The Pilgrims, 1983–2002; VSO, 1993–99. Hon. Bencher, Middle Temple, 1983; Hon. Elder Brother of Trinity House, 1984. Chancellor, Order of St Michael and St George, 1984–94. JP 1948, DL Bucks. Fellow of Eton Coll., 1966–81; Hon. Fellow, St Antony's Coll., Oxford, 1982. Hon. LLD: Cambridge, 1981; Leeds, 1981; Aberdeen, 1985; Nottingham, 1993; Birmingham, 1993; Newcastle, 1998; Hon. Dr Laws: Univ. of Philippines, 1982; Univ. of S Carolina, 1983; Harvard, 1986; Reading, 1989; Sussex, 1989; DUniv: Essex, 1983; Buckingham, 1989; Hon. DSc Cranfield, 1988; Hon. DCL Oxford, 2003. *Publication*: Reflect on Things Past (autobiog.), 1988. *Heir*: *s* Hon. Rupert Francis John Carington [*b* 2 Dec. 1948; *m* 1989, Daniela, *d* of Mr and Mrs Flavio Diotallevi; one *s* two *d*]. *Address*: 32a Ovington Square, SW3 1LR. *T*: (020) 7584 1476; The Manor House, Bledlow, Princes Risborough, Bucks HP27 9PB. *T*: (01844) 343499. *Clubs*: Pratt's, White's.

CARRINGTON, Prof. Alan, CBE 1999; FRS 1971; Royal Society Research Professor, Southampton University, 1979–84 and 1987–99, Oxford University, 1984–87; *b* 6 Jan. 1934; *o s* of Albert Carrington and Constance (*née* Nelson); *m* 1959, Noreen Hilary Taylor; one *s* two *d*. *Educ*: Colfe's Grammar Sch.; Univ. of Southampton. BSc, PhD; MA Cantab, MA Oxon. FRSC 1989; FInstP 1993. University of Cambridge: Asst in Research, 1960; Fellow of Downing Coll., 1960, Hon. Fellow, 1999; Asst Dir of Res., 1963; Prof. of Chemistry, Univ. of Southampton, 1967; Fellow, Jesus Coll., Oxford, 1984–87. Sen. Fellowship, SRC, 1976. Tilden Lectr, Chem. Soc., 1972; George Pimental Meml Lectr, Univ. of Calif at Berkeley, 1996. Pres., Faraday Div., RSC, 1997–99. FRSA 1999. Foreign Hon. Mem., Amer. Acad. of Arts and Scis, 1987; Foreign Associate, Nat. Acad. of Scis, USA, 1994. Hon. DSc Southampton, 1985. Harrison Meml Prize, Chem. Soc., 1962; Meldola Medal, Royal Inst. of Chemistry, 1963; Marlow Medal, Faraday Soc., 1966; Corday Morgan Medal, Chem. Soc., 1967; Chem. Soc. Award in Structural Chemistry, 1970; Faraday Medal, 1985, Longstaff Medal, 2005, RSC; Davy Medal, Royal Soc., 1992. *Publications*: (with A. D. McLachlan) Introduction to Magnetic Resonance, 1967; Microwave Spectroscopy of Free Radicals, 1974; (with J. M. Brown) Rotational Spectroscopy of Diatomic Molecules, 2003; numerous papers on topics in chemical physics in various learned jls. *Recreations*: family, music, fishing. *Address*: 46 Lakewood Road, Chandler's Ford, Hants SO53 1EX. *T*: (023) 8026 5092.

CARRINGTON, Maj.-Gen. Colin Edward George, CB 1991; CBE 1983; Commander, Army Security Vetting Unit, 1991–2000; *b* 19 Jan. 1936; *s* of Edgar John Carrington and Ruth Carrington (*née* West); *m* 1967, Joy Bracknell; one *s* one *d*. *Educ:* Royal Liberty Sch.; RMA Sandhurst. FCILT (FCIT 1988). Troop Comdr, BAOR, 1956–59; Air Despatch duties, 1960–64; Instructor, RMA, 1964–68; Sqdn Comdr, BAOR, 1972–74; Directing Staff, Staff Coll., 1975–77; CO 1 Armd Div. Transport Regt, 1977–79; DCOS 1 Armd Div., 1979–82; RCDS 1983; Dir, Manning Policy (Army), 1984–86; Comd Transport 1 (BR) Corps, 1986–88; Dir Gen. Transport and Movements (Army), MoD, 1988–91, retd. Pres., RASC & RCT Assoc., 1992–. Freeman, City of London, 1988. *Recreations:* gardening, reading.

CARRINGTON, Matthew Hadrian Marshall; Director, Gatehouse Bank PLC, since 2007; Chief Executive, Retail Motor Industry Federation, 2002–06; *b* 19 Oct. 1947; *s* of late Walter Carrington and of Dilys Carrington; *m* 1975, Mary Lou Darrow (*d* 2008); one *d*. *Educ:* London Lycée; Imperial Coll. of Science and Technol., London (BSc Physics); London Business Sch. (MSc). Prodn Foreman, GKN Ltd, 1969–72; banker: with The First National Bank of Chicago, 1974–78; with Saudi Internat. Bank, 1978–87; Chm., Outdoor Advertising Assoc., 1998–2002. MP (C) Fulham, 1987–97; contested (C) Hammersmith and Fulham, 1997, 2001. PPS to Rt Hon. John Patten, MP, 1990–94; an Asst Govt Whip, 1996–97. Mem., Treasury and Civil Service Select Cttee, 1994–96; Chm., Treasury Select Cttee, 1996. *Recreations:* cooking, political history. *Address:* 34 Ladbroke Square, W11 3NB.

CARRINGTON, Ruth; *see* James, M. L.

CARROL, Charles Gordon; Director, Commonwealth Institute, Scotland, 1971–97; *b* 21 March 1935; *s* of Charles Muir Carrol and Catherine Gray Napier; *m* 1970, Frances Anne, *o d* of John A. and Flora McL. Sinclair; three *s*. *Educ:* Melville Coll., Edinburgh; Edinburgh Univ. (MA); Moray House Coll. (DipEd). Education Officer: Govt of Nigeria, 1959–65; Commonwealth Inst., Scotland, 1965–71. Lay Member, Press Council, 1978–82. *Recreations:* walking, reading, cooking. *Address:* 11 Dukehaugh, Peebles, Scotland EH45 9DN. *T:* (01721) 721296.

CARROLL, Ven. Charles William Desmond; Archdeacon of Blackburn, 1973–86, Archdeacon Emeritus since 1986; Vicar of Balderstone, 1973–86; *b* 27 Jan. 1919; *s* of Rev. William and Mrs L. Mary Carroll; *m* 1945, Doreen Daisy Ruskell; three *s* one *d*. *Educ:* St Columba Coll.; Trinity Coll., Dublin. BA 1943; Dip. Ed. Hons 1945; MA 1946. Asst Master: Kingstown Grammar Sch., 1943–45; Rickerby House Sch., 1945–50; Vicar of Stanwix, Carlisle, 1950–59; Hon. Canon of Blackburn, 1959; Dir of Religious Education, 1959; Hon. Chaplain to Bishop of Blackburn, 1961; Canon Residentiary of Blackburn Cathedral, 1964. *Publication:* Management for Managers, 1968. *Address:* 11 Assheton Road, Blackburn BB2 6SF. *T:* (01254) 51915. *Club:* Rotary (Blackburn).

CARROLL, Cynthia; Chief Executive, Anglo American plc, since 2007; *b* Philadelphia, 13 Nov. 1956; *m* 1988, David Carroll; one *s* three *d*. *Educ:* Skidmore Coll., NY (BS Geol.); Univ. of Kansas (MS Geol.); Harvard Univ. (MBA). Petroleum geologist, Amoco, 1981–87; Business Develt Gp, Rolled Products Div., Alcan Inc., 1989–91; Vice-Pres./Gen. Manager, Alcan Foil Products, 1991–96; Man. Dir, Aughinish Alumina Ltd, 1996–98; Pres., Bauxite, Alumina & Speciality Chemicals, 1998–2001, Pres. and CEO, Primary Metal Gp, 2002–06, Alcan Inc. *Recreations:* ski-ing, swimming, tennis, sailing, golf, sewing, family. *Address:* Anglo American plc, 20 Carlton House Terrace, SW1Y 5AN. *T:* (020) 7968 8888, *Fax:* (020) 7968 8500.

CARROLL, Eileen Philomena, (Mrs E. P. Carroll-Mackie); Deputy Chief Executive, Centre for Effective Dispute Resolution, since 1996; *b* 5 Dec. 1953; *d* of late Matthew Francis Carroll and of Mary Philomena Carroll; *m* 1st, Richard Peers-Jones (marr. diss.); one *d*; 2nd, 2001, Karl Joseph Mackie, *qv*. *Educ:* Holy Cross, Gerrards Cross; Univ. of Kent, Canterbury (LLB Hons (Law) 1979). Analyst, British Sulphur Corp., London, 1972–74; admitted as solicitor, 1981; Lawyer/Partner, then Internat. Strategy Partner, Turner Kenneth Brown, 1981–94; Vis. Partner, Thelen Reid Preist, San Francisco, 1988 and 1994; involved in foundn of CEDR, 1990 (Mem., Bd of Trustees, 1990–96); accredited CEDR mediator, 1993. Mem., Litigation Cttee, London Solicitors, 1987–90. Adv. Mem., Conflict Analysis Res. Centre, Univ. of Kent at Canterbury, 2006–; Mem., Forum UK, 2006–; Mem. Council, Distinguished Advisors, Straus Inst. for Dispute Resolution, 2007–. Gov., Surbiton High Sch., 2004–. Prize for Excellence in Dispute Resolution, Center for Public Resources Inst. for Dispute Resolution, NY, 1997; European Women of Achievement Award, EUW, 2005. *Publication:* (with Dr Karl Mackie) International Mediation: the art of business diplomacy, 2000, 2nd edn 2006. *Recreations:* spending time with family, ski-ing, photography, travel, the outdoor life. *Address:* Centre for Effective Dispute Resolution, International Dispute Resolution Centre, 70 Fleet Street, EC4Y 1EU. *Club:* Follett Group.

CARROLL, Most Rev. Francis Patrick; Archbishop of Canberra and Goulburn, (RC), 1983–2006; *b* 9 Sept. 1930; *s* of P. Carroll. *Educ:* De La Salle Coll., Marrickville; St Columba's Coll., Springwood; St Patrick's Coll., Manly; Pontifical Urban Univ. De Propaganda Fide. Ordained priest, 1954; Asst Priest, Griffith, NSW, 1955–59; Asst Inspector of Catholic Schs, dio. of Wagga, 1957–61; Asst Priest, Albury, 1959–61; Bishop's Sec., Diocesan Chancellor, Diocesan Dir of Catholic Educn, 1965–67; consecrated Co-Adjutor Bishop, 1967; Bishop of Wagga Wagga, 1968–83. Chm., Nat. Catholic Educn Commn, 1974–78; Mem., Internat. Catechetical Council, Rome, 1974–93; Pres., Australian Catholic Bishops' Conf., 2000–07. Hon. DLitt Charles Sturt Univ., NSW, 1994; DUniv Australian Catholic Univ., 2006. *Publication:* The Development of Episcopal Conferences, 1965. *Address:* PO Box 2396, Wagga Wagga, NSW 2650, Australia.

CARROLL, Prof. John Edward, FREng; Professor of Engineering, University of Cambridge, 1983–2001; Fellow of Queens' College, Cambridge, since 1967; *b* 15 Feb. 1934; *s* of Sydney Wentworth Carroll and May Doris Carroll; *m* 1958, Vera Mary Jordan; three *s*. *Educ:* Oundle Sch.; Queens' Coll., Cambridge (Wrangler; Foundn Schol., 1957). BA 1957; PhD 1961; ScD 1982. FIET; FREng (FEng 1985). Microwave Div., Services Electronic Res. Lab., 1961–67; Cambridge University: Lectr, 1967–76; Reader, 1976–83; Dep. Hd of Engrg Dept, 1986–90; Head of Electrical Div., 1992–99; Chm. Council, Sch. of Technol., 1996–99. Vis. Prof., Queensland Univ., 1982. Editor, IEE Jl of Solid State and Electron Devices, 1976–82. *Publications:* Hot Electron Microwave Generators, 1970; Physical Models of Semiconductor Devices, 1974; Solid State Devices (Inst. of Phys. vol. 57), 1980; Rate Equations in Semiconductor Electronics, 1986; Distributed Feedback Semiconductor Lasers, 1998; contribs on microwaves, semiconductor devices and optical systems to learned jls. *Recreations:* piano, walking, reading thrillers, carpentry. *Address:* Queens' College, Silver Street, Cambridge CB3 9ET. *T:* (01223) 332829; *e-mail:* jec1000@cam.ac.uk.

CARROLL, Mark Steven; Director, Race, Cohesion and Preventing Extremism, Department for Communities and Local Government, 2006; *b* 17 June 1962; *s* of Albert Carroll and Anne Carroll; *m* 1998, Randhirajpall Kaur Bilan; one *s* one *d*. *Educ:* Leicester Poly. (BA Hons Public Admin 1984); Univ. of Nottingham (MA Soc. Work 1988). Social worker, 1988–90; charity director, 1990–94; mgt consultant, 1994–2002; Home Office: Advr to Permanent Sec., 2002–03; Dir, Race and Cohesion, 2003–06. *Club:* West Ham United.

CARROLL, Michael John; His Honour Judge Carroll; a Circuit Judge, since 1996; *b* 26 Dec. 1948; *s* of Matthew Carroll and Gladys Carroll; *m* 1974, Stella Reilly; two *s* two *d* (and one *d* decd). *Educ:* Shebbear Coll., N Devon; City of London Business Sch. (BA Hons); Inns of Court Sch. of Law. Called to the Bar, Gray's Inn, 1973. Factory worker, 1964; shop asst, 1967; fastfood chef, 1968; public service vehicle conductor, 1968–72, and driver, 1973; part-time PO counter clerk, 1968–73. Asst Recorder, 1990–94; Recorder, 1994–96. Chairman: Abbeyfield Addiscombe Soc., 2002–07; Croydon Charitable Foundn, 2007–. *Recreations:* reading, antiques, football. *Address:* The Crown Court at Woolwich, 2 Belmarsh Road, SE28 0EY. *T:* (020) 8312 7000.

CARROLL, Rt Rev. Mgr Philip; Spiritual Director, Venerable English College, Rome, since 2006; *b* 30 Nov. 1946; *s* of Joseph Carroll and Jean Carroll (*née* Graham). *Educ:* Venerable English College, Rome (PhL, STL). Ordained 1971; Assistant Priest, Our Blessed Lady Immaculate, Washington, 1972–78; Hexham and Newcastle Diocesan Religious Educn Service, 1979–88; Asst Gen. Sec., 1988–91, Gen. Sec., 1992–96, Catholic Bishops' Conf.; Parish Priest, St Bede's Ch, Washington, 1996–2006; VG, then Episcopal Vicar, RC Dio. Hexham and Newcastle, 2001–06. *Recreations:* cricket, fell walking. *Address:* Venerabile Collegio Inglese, Via di Monserrato, 45, 00186 Roma, Italy. *T:* (06) 686 5808. *Clubs:* Ryton Cricket; Tyneside Golf.

CARROLL, Terence Patrick, (Terry); Head of Corporate Finance, Broadhead Peel Rhodes, since 2008; *b* 24 Nov. 1948; *s* of George Daniel Carroll and Betty Doreen Carroll (*née* Holmes); *m* 1st, 1971, Louise Mary (*née* Smith) (marr. diss. 1984); one *s*; 2nd, 1984, Penelope Julia, (Penny) (*née* Berry) (marr. diss. 1994); 3rd, 1994, Heather Carmen (*née* Summers). *Educ:* Gillingham Grammar Sch.; Univ. of Bradford (BSc Business Studies). FCA 1980; FCT 1990 (MCT 1985); FCIB (FCBSI 1986). Auditor and Computer Auditor, Armitage & Norton, 1970–76; Management Accountant, Bradford & Bingley Building Soc., 1976–80; Exec. and Mem. Stock Exchange, Sheppards & Chase, 1980–82; Treasurer, Halifax Building Soc., 1982–85; National & Provincial Building Society: Gen. Manager Finance, 1985–86; Acting Chief Exec., 1986–87; Finance Dir, 1987–90; Treasury Dir, 1990–91; Finance Dir, United Leeds Teaching Hosps NHS Trust, 1991–94; Managing Director: Hollins Consulting, later How To Be Your Best Ltd, 1994–2006; Portland Internat. HR Consultants Ltd, 1996–97; Gp Finance Dir, Eatonfield Gp plc, 2006–07; Chief Exec., Hadrian's Wall Heritage Ltd, 2006. Chairman: Bradford Breakthrough Ltd, 1989–91; Central Yorks Inst. of Mgt, 1996–98. *Publications:* The Role of the Finance Director, 1997, 3rd edn 2002; Moving Up, 1998; Understanding Swaps in a Day, 1999; NLP for Traders, 2000; The Risk Factor, 2001; Be Your Best with NLP, 2001. *Recreations:* golf, tennis, bridge. *Address:* Hollins House, Bishop Thornton, Harrogate, N Yorks HG3 3JZ. *Club:* Ilkley Golf.

CARROLL-MACKIE, Eileen Philomena; *see* Carroll, E. P.

CARRUTHERS, Alwyn Guy; Director of Statistics, Department of Employment, 1981–83 (Deputy Director, 1972–80); *b* 6 May 1925; *yr s* of late John Sendall and of Lily Eden Carruthers, Grimsby; *m* 1950, Edith Eileen (*d* 2007), *o d* of late William and Edith Addison Lumb; no *c*. *Educ:* Wintringham Grammar Sch., Grimsby; King's Coll., London Univ. BA First Cl. Hons in Mathematics, Drew Gold Medal and Prize, 1945. RAE, Farnborough, 1945–46; Instructor Lieut, RN, 1946–49; Rothamsted Experimental Station, 1949. Postgraduate Diploma in Mathematical Statistics, Christ's Coll., Cambridge, 1951. Bd of Trade and DTI Statistics Divisions, 1951–72. Lay Reader, Church of England, 1994–. *Publications:* articles in official publications and learned jls. *Recreations:* gardening, music. *Address:* 24 Red House Lane, Bexleyheath, Kent DA6 8JD. *T:* (020) 8303 4898.

CARRUTHERS, Sir Ian James, Kt 2003; OBE; Chief Executive, South West Strategic Health Authority (NHS South West), since 2006; *m*; one *s* one *d*. Dist Gen. Manager, W Dorset HA, 1987; Chief Executive: S and W RHA, until 1996; Dorset HA, then Dorset and Som Strategic HA, 1996–2006; Hants and IoW Strategic HA, 2005–06; on secondment as Transitional Dir, NHS Inst. for Innovation and Improvement, DoH, 2004–05; Actg Dir of Commissioning, then Actg Chief Exec. of NHS, DoH, 2006. Mem., NHS Modernisation Bd, then Nat. Leadership Network. *Address:* NHS South West, Wellsprings Road, Taunton, Somerset TA2 7PQ.

CARRUTHERS, James Edwin; Assistant Secretary, Royal Hospital Chelsea, 1988–94; *b* 19 March 1928; *er s* of James and Dollie Carruthers; *m* 1955, Phyllis Williams (*d* 1996); one *s*. *Educ:* George Heriot's Sch.; Edinburgh Univ. (MA; Medallist in Scottish Hist.). FSAScot. Lieut, The Queen's Own Cameron Highlanders, 1949–51, and TA, 1951–55. Air Ministry: Asst Principal, 1951; Private Sec. to DCAS, 1955; Asst Private Sec. to Sec. of State for Air, 1956; Principal, 1956; Min. of Aviation, 1960–62; Private Secretary: to Minister of Defence for RAF, 1965–67; to Parly Under Sec. of State for RAF, 1967; Asst Sec., 1967; Chief Officer, Sovereign Base Areas Admin, Cyprus, 1968–71; Dep. Chief of Public Relations, MoD, 1971–72; Private Sec. to Chancellor of Duchy of Lancaster, Cabinet Office, 1973–74; Sec., Organising Cttee for British Aerospace, DoI, 1975–77; Under-Sec., 1977; seconded as Asst to Chm., British Aerospace, 1977–79; Dir Gen., Royal Ordnance Factories (Finance and Procurement), 1980–83; Chm., CSSB, 1983–84; Asst Under Sec. of State, MoD, 1984–88. *Recreations:* painting, travel. *Address:* 11 John's Lee Close, Loughborough, Leics LE11 3LH.

CARRUTHERS, Hon. Norman Harry; Chief Justice of the Supreme Court of Prince Edward Island, 1985–2001 (Supernumerary Justice, part-time, 2001–02); *b* 25 Oct. 1935; *s* of Lorne C. H. Carruthers and Jean R. Webster; *m* 1970, Diana C. Rodd; one *s* two *d*. *Educ:* Prince of Wales Coll.; Mount Allison Univ. (BSc, BEd); Dalhousie Law Sch. (LLB). Canadian Industries Ltd, 1956–59; schoolteacher, 1961–64; Lawyer, Foster, MacDonald and Carruthers, 1968–80; Chief Judge, Provincial Court, PEI, 1980–85. Electoral Reform Comr, PEI, 2003. Co-founder and Pres., Community Foundn of PEI. *Address:* 16 Trafalgar Street, Charlottetown, PE C1A 3Z1, Canada. *T:* (902) 5663007.

CARRUTHERS, William Buttrick; part-time Chairman, Industrial Tribunals, then Employment Tribunals, 1995–99; *b* 1 Aug. 1929; *s* of Alexander Norman and Olive Carruthers; *m* 1961, Jennifer Stevens; one *s* two *d*. *Educ:* Middlesex School, Concord, Mass; Radley College; Clare College, Cambridge (BA Hons, LLB). Called to the Bar, Lincoln's Inn, 1954; practised in N Rhodesia (later Zambia), 1956–70; part-time Chm., Industrial Tribunals, 1970; Chm., 1975, Regl Chm., 1990–95, Industrial Tribunals, Bedford. *Recreation:* bridge. *Address:* Worlditch Hall, Kimbolton, Huntingdon, Cambs PE28 0LB. *T:* (01480) 860203.

CARRUTHERS-WATT, Miranda Lucy Mary, (Mrs P. Vercoe); Chief Executive, Lancashire Police Authority, since 2007; *b* 1 Sept. 1961; *d* of Calverley Vernon

Carruthers-Watt and late Pauline Mary Carruthers-Watt; *m* 1988, Philip Vercoe; two *s* (one *d* decd). *Educ:* Burnley High Sch. for Girls; Lancaster Univ. (LLB Hons Law 1983); Coll. of Law, Chester; Univ. of Hull (MBA 1998); Law Soc. Dip. in Local Govt Law 1991. Admitted Solicitor, 1987; private practice and local govt, 1986–97; Asst Dir, Rights, Advice and Entitlements, Blackburn with Darwen BC, 1997–2005; Dir, NW Centre of Excellence, 2005–07. *Recreations:* family, wine, walking. *Address:* Lancashire Police Authority, PO Box 653, Preston PR2 2WB.

CARSBERG, Sir Bryan (Victor), Kt 1989; Chairman, Pensions Compensation Board, 2001–05; *b* 3 Jan. 1939; *s* of Alfred Victor Carsberg and Maryllia (*née* Collins); *m* 1960, Margaret Linda Graham; two *d*. *Educ:* Berkhamsted Sch.; London Sch. of Econs and Polit. Science (MScEcon; Hon. Fellow, 1990). Chartered Accountant, 1960. Sole practice, chartered accountant, 1962–64; Lectr in Accounting, LSE, 1964–68; Vis. Lectr, Grad. Sch. of Business, Univ. of Chicago, 1968–69; Prof. of Accounting, Univ. of Manchester, 1969–81 (Dean, Faculty of Econ. and Social Studies, 1977–78); Arthur Andersen Prof. of Accounting, LSE, 1981–87; Dir of Res., ICA, 1981–87; Dir Gen. of Telecommunications, 1984–92; Dir Gen. of Fair Trading, 1992–95; Sec.-Gen., Internat. Accounting Standards Cttee, 1995–2001. Visiting Professor: of Business Admin, Univ. of Calif, Berkeley, 1974; of Accounting, LSE, 1988–89. Asst Dir of Res. and Technical Activities, Financial Accounting Standards Bd, USA, 1978–81; Mem., Accounting Standards Bd, 1990–94 (Vice-Chm., 1990–92). Mem. Council, ICA, 1975–79; Mem. Bd, Radiocommunications Agency, 1990–92. Director: Economists Adv. Gp, 1976–84; Economist Bookshop, 1981–91; Philip Allan (Publishers), 1981–92, 1995–2006; Cable & Wireless Communications, 1997–2000; RM plc, 2002–; SVB Hldgs plc, 2003–; Inmarsat plc, 2005–; Chm., MLL Telecom Ltd, 1999–2002; Advr on telecoms, KPMG, 2001–06; Mem., Equality of Access Bd, BT Gp plc, 2005–. Member, Council: Univ. of Surrey, 1990–92; Loughborough Univ., 1999– (Chm., 2001–). Mem., Royal Swedish Acad. of Engrg Scis, 1994. Hon. MA Econ Manchester, 1973; Hon. ScD UEA, 1992; Hon. DLitt Loughborough, 1994; DUniv Essex, 1995; Hon. LLD Bath, 1996. Chartered Accountants Founding Societies Centenary Award, 1988; Sempier Award, IFAC, 2002. *Publications:* An Introduction to Mathematical Programming for Accountants, 1969; (with H. C. Edey) Modern Financial Management, 1969; Analysis for Investment Decisions, 1974; (with E. V. Morgan and M. Parkin) Indexation and Inflation, 1975; Economics of Business Decisions, 1975; (with A. Hope) Investment Decisions under Inflation, 1976; (with A. Hope) Current Issues in Accountancy, 1977, 2nd edn 1984; (with J. Arnold and R. Scapens) Topics in Management Accounting, 1980; (with S. Lumby) The Evaluation of Financial Performance in the Water Industry, 1983; (with M. Page) Current Cost Accounting, 1984; (with M. Page *et al*) Small Company Financial Reporting, 1985. *Recreations:* gardening, theatre, music, opera. *Address: e-mail:* b.carsberg@ntlworld.com.

CARSON, Ciaran Gerard; Director, Seamus Heaney Centre for Poetry, Queen's University Belfast, since 2003; *b* 9 Oct. 1948; *s* of William and Mary Carson; *m* 1982, Deirdre Shannon; two *s* one *d*. *Educ:* QUB (BA Hons). Traditional Arts Officer, 1976–94, Literature Officer, 1994–98, Arts Council of NI; freelance writer, 1998–2003. *Publications: poetry:* The New Estate, 1976; The Irish for No, 1987; Belfast Confetti, 1989; First Language, 1993; Opera Et Cetera, 1996; The Twelfth of Never, 1998; The Alexandrine Plan, 1998; Breaking News, 2003; *prose:* The Pocket Guide to Irish Traditional Music, 1986; Last Night's Fun, 1996; The Star Factory, 1997; Fishing for Amber, 1999; Shamrock Tea, 2001; *translation:* The Inferno of Dante Alighieri: a new translation, 2002. *Recreation:* playing Irish traditional music. *Address: e-mail:* ciaran.carson@ntlworld.com.

CARSON, Hugh Christopher Kingsford; Headmaster, Malvern College, 1997–2006; *b* 29 Dec. 1945; *s* of late Lt-Col James Kingsford Carson and of Elsie Adeline Carson (*née* Cockersell); *m* 1972, Penelope Susan Elizabeth Hollingbury, PhD. *Educ:* Tonbridge Sch.; Royal Holloway Coll., London Univ. (BA Mod. Hist., Hist. of Econs and Politics, 1979); Reading Univ. (PGCE); RMA, Sandhurst. Commnd RTR, 1967–76. Asst Master, then Housemaster, Epsom Coll., 1980–90; Headmaster, Denstone Coll., 1990–96. Renter Warden, Skinners' Co., 2005–June 2009. *Recreations:* photography, historical research, hill-walking. *Address:* Hillside Farm, Back of Ecton, Wetton, Derbys DE6 2AH.

CARSON, Joan; *see* Carson, M. J.

CARSON, John, CBE 1981; draper; Member (OUP) for Belfast North, Northern Ireland Assembly, 1982–86; *b* 1934. Member, Belfast District Council, (formerly Belfast Corporation), 1971–97; Official Unionist Councillor for Duncairn; Lord Mayor of Belfast, 1980–81, 1985–86. MP (UU) Belfast North, Feb. 1974–1979. Dir, Laganside Corp., 1989; non-exec. Dir, Royal Gp of Hosps & Dental Hosp. HSS Trust, 1992–. Vice-Chm., NI Youth Council, 1985. Mem., Adv. Bd, Salvation Army. High Sheriff, Belfast, 1978. *Address:* 75 Donaghadee Road, Millisle, Co. Down, N Ireland BT22 2BZ.

CARSON, (Margaret) Joan; Member (UU) Fermanagh and South Tyrone, Northern Ireland Assembly, 1998–2003; *b* 29 Jan. 1935; *d* of Charles Patterson and Gladys Patterson (*née* Irvine); *m* 1957, James Carson; two *s* one *d*. *Educ:* Stranmillis Coll., Belfast. Teacher: Enniskillen Model Primary Sch., 1956–62; Granville Primary Sch., 1972–79; Dungannon Primary Sch., 1979–82; Principal, Tamnamore Primary Sch., 1982–88. Mem. (UU), Dungannon DC, 1997–2001. Constituency Sec., Fermanagh and S Tyrone, UUP; Party Officer, UUP. *Recreations:* ornithology, painting, reading. *Address:* Drumgold House, 115 Moy Road, Dungannon, Co. Tyrone BT71 7DX. *T:* (028) 8778 4285.

CARSON, Neil Andrew Patrick; Chief Executive Officer, Johnson Matthey plc, since 2004; *b* 15 April 1957; *s* of Patrick Carson and Sheila Margaret Rose; *m* 1988, Helen Barbara Huppler; two *s* one *d*. *Educ:* Emanuel Sch., Wandsworth; Coventry Univ. (BSc Combined Engrg). Joined Johnson Matthey plc, 1980: various sales and mktg roles, 1980–88; Mktg Dir, USA, 1988–90, Gen. Manager, London, 1990–93, Precious Metals Mktg; Sales and Mktg Dir, 1993–96, Man. Dir, 1996–97, Catalytic Systems Div., Europe; Dir, Catalysts Systems Div., 1997–99; Executive Director: Catalysts Div., 1999–2003; Catalysts and Precious Metals Div., 2003–04. Chm., Sustainable Consumption and Production Steering Gp, 2006–08. *Recreations:* watching Rugby, ski-ing, family. *Address:* Johnson Matthey plc, Orchard Road, Royston, Herts SG8 5HE. *T:* (01763) 253000; *e-mail:* carson@matthey.com.

CARSON, William Hunter Fisher, OBE 1983; jockey, retired 1997; racing pundit, BBC, since 1997; Manager, Thoroughbred Corp., Europe, since 1997; *b* 16 Nov. 1942; *s* of Thomas Whelan Carson and Mary Hay; *m* 1963, Carole Jane Sutton (marr. diss. 1979); three *s*; *m* 1982, Elaine Williams. *Educ:* Riverside, Stirling, Scotland. Apprenticed to Captain G. Armstrong, 1957; 1st winner, Pinkers Pond, Catterick, 1962; trans. to Fred Armstrong, 1963–66; First Jockey to Lord Derby, 1967; first classic win, High Top, 1972; Champion Jockey, 1972, 1973, 1978, 1980 and 1983; became First Jockey to W. R. Hern, 1977; also appointed Royal Jockey, riding Dunfermline to the Jubilee Oaks and St Leger wins in the colours of HM the Queen; won the 200th Derby on Troy, trained by W. R. Hern, 1979; the same combination won the 1980 Derby, with Henbit, and the 1980 Oaks, with Bireme; also won King George VI and Queen Elizabeth Stakes, on Troy, 1979, on Ela-Mana-Mou, 1980, on Petoski, 1985, on Nashwan, 1989; 1983 Oaks and St Leger, with Sun Princess; Ascot Gold Cup, on Little Wolf, 1983; St Leger, on Minster Son, 1988 (only jockey ever to breed and ride a Classic winner); Derby, on Nashwan, 1989; 1,000 Guineas, Oaks and Irish Derby, on Salsabil, 1990; 1,000 Guineas and Oaks, on Shadayid, 1991; Derby, on Erhaab, 1994. During the 1989 season rode 100th Group One winner in England; by 1997 had ridden 3,828 winners including 18 Classics. DUniv Stirling, 1998. *Address:* Minster House, Barnsley, Cirencester, Glos GL7 5DZ.

CARSS-FRISK, Monica Gunnel Constance; QC 2001. *Educ:* UCL (LLB); UC Oxford (BCL). Called to the Bar, Gray's Inn, 1985, Bencher, 2004; in practice at the Bar, 1986–. Part-time tutor in law, UCL, 1984–87. Mem., HM Treasury Solicitor's Supplementary Common Law Panel, 1997–99; Jun. Counsel to the Crown (A Panel), 1999–2001. Mem. Bd, Internat. Centre for Legal Protection of Human Rights. *Publications:* contributor: Human Rights Law and Practice, 1999; European Employment Law in the UK, 2001; Halsbury's Laws of England. *Recreation:* literature. *Address:* Blackstone Chambers, Blackstone House, Temple, EC4Y 9BW.

CARSTEN, Prof. Oliver Michael John, PhD; Professor of Transport Safety, Institute for Transport Studies, University of Leeds, since 2003; *b* 9 Aug. 1948; *s* of Francis and Ruth Carsten; *m* 1987, Svetlana; one *s* one *d*. *Educ:* Merton Coll., Oxford (BA Modern Hist. 1969); Univ. of Michigan (MA Hist. 1973; PhD Hist. 1981). University of Michigan Transportation Research Institute: Res. Asst, 1977–79; Res. Associate, 1979–85; Asst Res. Scientist, 1985–87; Institute for Transport Studies, University of Leeds: Res. Fellow, 1987–89; Sen. Res. Fellow, 1993–2003. Vis. Prof., Helsinki Univ. of Technol., 1999. Chm., Road Behaviour Wkg Party, Parly Adv. Council for Transport Safety, 1993–. *Publications:* contribs to learned jls. *Recreations:* walking, cycling, travel. *Fax:* (office) (0113) 343 5334; *e-mail:* o.m.j.carsten@its.leeds.ac.uk.

CARSWELL, family name of **Baron Carswell**.

CARSWELL, Baron *cr* 2004 (Life Peer), of Killeen in the county of Down; **Robert Douglas Carswell,** Kt 1988; PC 1993; a Lord of Appeal in Ordinary, 2004–June 2009; *b* 28 June 1934; *er s* of late Alan E. Carswell and Nance E. Carswell; *m* 1961, Romayne Winifred Ferris (*see* R. W. Carswell); two *d*. *Educ:* Royal Belfast Academical Instn; Pembroke Coll., Oxford (Schol.; 1st Cl. Honour Mods, 1st Cl. Jurisprudence, MA; Hon. Fellow, 1984); Univ. of Chicago Law Sch. (JD). Called to Bar of N Ireland, 1957 (Bencher, 1979), and to English Bar, Gray's Inn, 1972 (Hon. Bencher, 1993); Counsel to Attorney-General for N Ireland, 1970–71; QC (NI), 1971; Sen. Crown Counsel in NI, 1979–84; Judge of High Court of Justice, NI, 1984–93; Lord Justice of Appeal, Supreme Court of Judicature, NI, 1993–97; Lord Chief Justice of NI, 1997–2004. Chancellor, Dios of Armagh and of Down and Dromore, 1990–97. Chairman: Council of Law Reporting for NI, 1987–97; Law Reform Adv. Cttee for NI, 1989–97. Pres., NI Scout Council, 1993–. Pres., Royal Belfast Academical Instn, 2004– (Gov., 1967–2004; Chm. Bd of Govs, 1986–97); Pro-Chancellor and Chm. Council, Univ. of Ulster, 1984–94. Hon. Bencher, King's Inns, Dublin, 1997. Hon. DLitt Ulster, 1994. *Publications:* Trustee Acts (Northern Ireland), 1964; articles in legal periodicals. *Recreations:* golf, hill walking. *Address:* House of Lords, SW1A 0PW. *Club:* Ulster Reform (Belfast).

CARSWELL, Lady, (Romayne Winifred Carswell), OBE 1988; Lord-Lieutenant, County Borough of Belfast, since 2000; *d* of late James Ferris, JP, Greyabbey, Co. Down and of Eileen Ferris, JP; *m* 1961, Robert Douglas Carswell (*see* Baron Carswell); two *d*. *Educ:* Victoria Coll., Belfast; Queen's Univ., Belfast (BA, LLB). Asst Principal, NICS, 1959–61; Mem., 1977–83, Dep. Chm., 1983–94, Police Complaints Bd for NI, subseq. Ind. Commn for Police Complaints; Member: Standing Adv. Commn on Human Rights, 1984–86; Industrial Tribunals, 1987–97. Mem., Bd of Govs, Victoria Coll., Belfast, 1979–99 (Dep. Chm., 1995–99). Pres., Friends of Ulster Mus., 1996–; Trustee: Ulster Histl Foundn, 1991–2004 (Dep. Chm., 1997–2000); Winston Churchill Meml Trust, 2002–. Pres., RFCA for NI, 2005–; Hon. Captain, RNR, 2005–. DL Belfast, 1997; JP 2000. CStJ 2000. *Recreations:* heritage, conservation, hillwalking. *Address:* c/o Lord Carswell, Law Lords' Corridor, House of Lords, SW1A 0PW. *T:* (020) 7219 3202.

CARSWELL, (John) Douglas (Wilson); MP (C) Harwich, since 2005; *b* 3 May 1971; *s* of John Wilson Carswell, OBE, FRCS and Margaret Carswell (*née* Clark). *Educ:* Charterhouse; Univ. of E Anglia (BA Hons 1993); King's Coll. London (MA). Corporate Develt Manager, Orbit Television, Rome, 1997–99; Chief Project Officer, Invesco Continental Europe, 1999–2003. Mem., Cons. Party Policy Unit, 2004–05. Mem., Commons Select Cttee on Educn, 2006–; Jt Select Cttee on Human Rights. Founder, www.direct-democracy.co.uk. *Publications:* Direct Democracy, 2002; Paying for Localism, 2004; (jtly) Direct Democracy: an agenda for a new model party, 2005; Localist Papers, 2007. *Recreations:* keen swimmer, occasional rider. *Address:* House of Commons, SW1A 0AA. *T:* (020) 7219 3000; *e-mail:* carswelld@parliament.uk.

CARTER; *see* Bonham-Carter and Bonham Carter.

CARTER, family name of **Baron Carter of Coles**.

CARTER OF COLES, Baron *cr* 2004 (Life Peer), of Westmill in the County of Hertfordshire; **Patrick Robert Carter;** Chairman, Sport England, 2002–06; *b* 9 Feb. 1946; s of Robert Carter and Ann Carter (*née* Richards); *m* 1969, Julia Bourne; two *d*. *Educ:* Brentwood Sch.; Hatfield Coll., Univ. of Durham. Hambros Bank, 1967–70; Whitecross Equipment Ltd, 1970–75; Dir, MAI plc, 1975–85; founder and Dir, Westminster Health Care plc, 1985–99. Review Chairman: Commonwealth Games, 2001; Nat. Stadium, 2002; Payroll Services, 2003; Criminal Records, 2003; Offender Services, 2004; Legal Aid, 2005–06. *Recreations:* reading, opera, walking, ski-ing, gardening. *Address:* House of Lords, SW1A 0PW; *e-mail:* pippa.morgan@mckesson.co.uk.

CARTER, Andrew, CMG 1995; HM Diplomatic Service, retired; Warden, St George's House, Windsor Castle, since 2003; *b* 4 Dec. 1943; *s* of Eric and Margaret Carter; *m* 1st, 1973, Anne Caroline Morgan (marr. diss. 1986); one *d*; 2nd, 1988, Catherine Mary Tyler (marr. diss. 2003); one *s* one *d*. *Educ:* Latymer Upper Sch., Hammersmith; Royal Coll. of Music; Jesus Coll., Cambridge (Scholar 1962; MA). FRCO; LRAM; ARCM. Asst Master, Marlborough Coll., 1965–70. Joined HM Diplomatic Service, 1971; Warsaw, 1972; Geneva, 1975; Bonn, 1975; FCO, 1978; Brussels, 1986; Dep. Gov., Gibraltar, 1990–95; Minister, Moscow, 1995–97; UK Perm. Rep. to Council of Europe, Strasbourg, 1997–2003. *Recreation:* music. *Address:* c/o St George's House, Windsor Castle, Windsor, Berks SL4 1NJ.

CARTER, Bernard Thomas, Hon. RE 1975; full-time artist (painter and etcher), since 1977; *b* 6 April 1920; *s* of Cecil Carter and Ethel Carter (*née* Darby); *m* Eugenie Alexander, artist and writer; one *s*. *Educ:* Haberdashers' Aske's; Goldsmiths' College of Art, London Univ. NDD, ATD. RAF, 1939–46. Art lectr, critic and book reviewer, 1952–68; National Maritime Museum: Asst Keeper (prints and drawings), 1968; Dep. Keeper (Head of Picture Dept), 1970; Keeper (Head of Dept of Pictures and Conservation), 1972–77. One-man exhibns in London: Arthur Jeffress Gall., 1955; Portal Gall., 1963, 1965, 1967, 1969, 1974, 1978, 1979, 1981, 1984, 1987, 1990 and 1993; mixed exhibns: Royal

Academy, Arts Council, British Council and galleries in Europe and USA; works in public collections, galleries abroad and British educn authorities, etc. TV and radio include: Thames at Six, Pebble Mill at One, Kaleidoscope, London Radio, etc. *Publication:* Art for Young People (with Eugenie Alexander), 1958. *Recreations:* reading, listening to music, gardening, theatre. *Address:* 56 King George Street, Greenwich, SE10 8QD. *T:* (020) 8858 4281.

CARTER, Dr Brandon, FRS 1981; Directeur de Recherche (Centre National de la Recherche Scientifique), Observatoire de Paris-Meudon, since 1986; *b* Sydney, Australia, 26 May 1942; *s* of Harold Burnell Carter and Mary (*née* Brandon Jones); *m* 1969, Lucette Defrise; three *d. Educ:* George Watson's Coll., Edinburgh; Univ. of St Andrews; Pembroke Coll., Cambridge (MA, PhD 1968, DSc 1976). Res. Student, Dept of Applied Maths and Theoretical Physics, Cambridge, 1964–67; Res. Fellow, Pembroke Coll., Cambridge, 1967–68; Staff Mem., Inst. of Astronomy, Cambridge, 1968–73; Univ. Asst Lectr, 1973–74, Univ. Lectr, 1974–75, Dept of Applied Maths and Theoretical Physics, Cambridge; Maître de Recherche, co-responsable Groupe d'Astrophysique Relativiste (CNRS), Paris-Meudon, 1975–86. *Recreation:* wilderness. *Address:* 19 rue de la Borne au Diable, 92310 Sèvres, France. *T:* (1) 45344677.

CARTER, (Christopher) Peter, MBE 1971; Deputy Director-General, Office of Electricity Regulation, 1993–99; Chief Operating Officer, Office of Gas and Electricity Markets, 1999; *b* 10 Dec. 1945; *s* of Sir Charles Frederick Carter, FBA; *m* 1st, 1971, Pamela Joy Waddilove (marr. diss. 1985); two *s* one *d*; 2nd, 1986, Andrea Rigby; one *s* one *d. Educ:* Methodist Coll., Belfast; Manchester Grammar Sch.; St Catharine's Coll., Cambridge (BA Geography 1967). HM Diplomatic Service, 1967–78; served MECAS, Amman, Copenhagen and European Integration Dept, FCO; Department of Energy: Community and Internat. Policy Div., 1978–80; Energy Conservation Div., 1980–81; Coal Div., 1981–85; Gas Div., 1985–86; Dir, Res. and Develt, Offshore Supplies Office, 1986–93; Dep. Dir-Gen. (Scotland), Office of Electricity Regulation, 1993. Trustee, Quaker Study Centre, Woodbrooke, 2001–04. *Recreations:* playing the violin, gardening, podcasting (www.listen-to-english.com). *Address: e-mail:* cpetercarter@googlemail.com.

CARTER, David; *see* Carter, R. D.

CARTER, Dr David, CVO 1995; HM Diplomatic Service, retired; Bursar, Lucy Cavendish College, Cambridge University, since 2006; *b* 4 May 1945; *s* of John Carter and Kathleen Carter (*née* Oke); *m* 1968, Susan Victoria Wright; one *s* one *d. Educ:* Zambia; Univ. of Wales (BA Jt Hons); Univ. of Durham (PhD 1978). Joined HM Diplomatic Service, 1970; FCO, 1970–71; Accra, 1971–75; FCO, 1975–80; Hd of Chancery, Manila, 1980–83; 1st Sec., S Africa Desk, later Dep. Hd, SE Asia Dept, FCO, 1983–86; Dep. High Comr and Counsellor, Lusaka, 1986–90; Counsellor and Overseas Inspector, FCO, 1990–92; Counsellor and Dep. Hd of Mission, Cape Town/Pretoria, 1992–96; Minister and Dep. Head of Mission, New Delhi, 1996–99; High Comr, Bangladesh, 2000–04. Dep. Dir, Centre for Security and Diplomacy, Birmingham Univ., 2005–06. *Publications:* contrib. jls on Southern Africa. *Recreations:* distant travel, music, reading, walking, manual labour. *Address: e-mail:* dcarter@28scots.freeserve.co.uk. *Club:* Royal Commonwealth Society.

CARTER, Sir David (Craig), Kt 1996; FRCS, FRCSE, FRCSGlas, FRCPE, FFPH; FRSE; Chief Medical Officer, Scottish Executive (formerly Scottish Office) Department of Health, 1996–2000; *b* 1 Sept. 1940; *s* of Horace Ramsay Carter and Mary Florence Carter (*née* Lister); *m* 1967, Ilske Ursula Luth; two *s. Educ:* Cockermouth Grammar Sch.; St Andrews Univ. (MB ChB, MD). FRCSE 1967; FRCSGlas 1980; FRCPE 1993; FRCS 1995; FFPH (FFPHM 1998). FRSE 1995. British Empire Cancer Campaign Fellow, 1967; Lecturer in Surgery: Edinburgh Univ., 1969; Makerere Univ., Uganda, 1972; Wellcome Trust Sen. Lectr, Edinburgh Univ., 1974, seconded for 12 months to Center for Ulcer Res. and Educn, LA, 1976; Sen. Lectr in Surgery, Edinburgh Univ., 1974–79; St Mungo Prof. of Surgery, Glasgow Univ., 1979–88; Regius Prof. of Clinical Surgery, Edin. Univ., 1988–96. Hon. Consultant Surgeon, Royal Infirmary, Edin., 1988–96; Hon. Consultant Surgeon and Chm., Scottish Liver Transplantation Unit, 1992–96; Surgeon to the Queen in Scotland, 1993–97. External Examiner at univs incl. London, Oxford, Leeds, Dundee, Newcastle, Hong Kong, Nairobi, Penang and Kuwait. Chairman: Scottish Foundn for Surgery in Nepal, 1988–; Scottish Council for Postgrad. Med. Educn, 1990–96; Scientific Adv. Cttee, CRC, 2000–02; BMA Bd of Science, 2002–05; Queen's Nursing Inst., Scotland, 2002–; Scottish Stem Cell Network, 2003–05; Bd for Academic Med., Scotland, 2005–; Mem. Council, WMA, 2002–05; Dir, Scottish Cancer Foundn, 2000–; Member: Jt Med. Adv. Cttee, HEFC, 1993–96; Scientific Exec. Bd, Cancer Res. UK, 2002–04. President: Internat. Hepatobiliary-Pancreatic Assoc., 1988–89; Surgical Res. Soc., 1996–97; Assoc. of Surgeons of GB and Ire., 1996–97; BMA, 2001–02; Vice-Pres., RSE, 2000–03. Member: Council, RCSE, 1980–90; James IV Assoc. of Surgeons, 1981–; Internat. Surgical Gp, 1984–2005. Mem., Broadcasting Council, BBC Scotland, 1989–94. Non-exec. Dir, Lothian Health Bd, 1994–96. Company Sec., British Jl of Surgery Soc., 1991–95; Co-Editor, British Journal of Surgery, 1986–91; General Editor, Operative Surgery, 1983–96. Mem. Court, St Andrews Univ., 1997–2000; Vice-Principal, Edinburgh Univ., 2000–02; Governor: Beatson Inst. for Cancer Res., 1997–2000; The Health Foundn (formerly PPP Healthcare Med. Trust), 2001– (Chm., 2002–). Trustee, CRUK, 2004–07 (Chm. Council, Res. Strategy Gp, 2004–07; Vice Chm. Council, 2005–07). Mem., Amer. Surgical Assoc., 1997; Founder FMedSci 1998. Hon. FACS 1996; Hon. FRCSI 1996; Hon. FRACS 1998; Hon. FRCGP 1999; Hon. FRCPGlas 2003; Hon. FRCP 2005; Hon. Fellow: Deutsche Ges. für Chirurgie, 1994; Coll. of Surgeons of Hong Kong, 2003; Hon. Mem., Soc. of Surgeons of Nepal, 1994; For. Associate Mem., Inst. of Medicine, USA, 1998. Hon. DSc: St Andrews, 1997; Queen Margaret Coll., 1997; Aberdeen, 2000; Hon. LLD Dundee, 1997; Hon. MD Edinburgh, 2005. William Leslie Prize in Surgery, Univ. of Edinburgh, 1968; Moynihan Prize in Surgery, Assoc. of Surgeons of GB and Ire., 1973; Gold Medal, RCSE, 2000; G. B. Ong Medal, Hong Kong Univ., 2005; Gold Medal, BMA, 2006; Gold Medal, RSE, 2007. Gorka Dakshi Bahu (Nepal), 1999. *Publications:* Peptic Ulcer, 1983; Principles and Practice of Surgery, 1985; Pancreatitis, 1988; Surgery of the Pancreas, 1993, 2nd edn 1997; numerous contribs to surgical and gastroenterological jls. *Recreations:* music, gardening, philately. *Address:* 19 Buckingham Terrace, Edinburgh EH4 3AD. *T:* (0131) 332 5554. *Clubs:* New (Edinburgh); Luffness Golf.

CARTER, (Edward) Graydon; Editor in Chief, Vanity Fair, since 1992; *b* 14 July 1949; *s* of E. P. Carter and Margaret Ellen Carter; *m* 1st, 1982, Cynthia Williamson (marr. diss. 2003); three *s* one *d*; 2nd, 2005, Anna Scott, *d* of Sir Kenneth Bertram Adam Scott, *qv. Educ:* Carleton Univ. (incomplete); Univ. of Ottawa (incomplete). Editor, The Canadian Review, 1973–77; writer, Time, 1978–83; Writer, Life, 1983–86; Founder and Editor, Spy, 1986–91; Editor, New York Observer, 1991–92. Hon. Editor, Harvard Lampoon, 1989. Documentary producer: 9/11, 2002; The Kid Stays in the Picture, 2002. *Publications:* Vanity Fair's Hollywood, 2000; Vanity Fair's Oscar Nights, 2004; What We've Lost, 2004. *Recreation:* fly fishing. *Address:* Condé Nast Building, 4 Times Square, New York, NY 10036–6522, USA. *Club:* Washington (Washington, Connecticut).

CARTER, Elizabeth Angela; *see* Shaw, E. A.

CARTER, Elliott (Cook), DrMus; composer; *b* New York City, 11 Dec. 1908; *m* 1939, Helen Frost-Jones; one *s. Educ:* Harvard Univ. (MA); Ecole Normale, Paris (DrMus). Professor of Greek and Maths, St John's Coll., Annapolis, 1940–42; Professor of Music: Columbia Univ., 1948–50; Yale Univ., 1960–61; Juilliard Sch., 1967–84. *Compositions include:* First Symphony, 1942–43; Quartet for Four Saxophones, 1943; Holiday Overture, 1944; Piano Sonata, 1945; Ballet, The Minotaur, 1946–47; Woodwind Quintet, 1947; Sonata for Cello and Piano, 1948; First String Quartet, 1950–51; Sonata for Flute, Oboe, Cello and Harpsichord, 1952; Variations for Orchestra, 1953; Second String Quartet, 1960 (New York Critics' Circle Award; Pulitzer Prize; Unesco 1st Prize); Double Concerto for Harpsichord and Piano, 1961 (New York Critics' Circle Award); Piano Concerto, 1967; Concerto for Orchestra, 1970; Third String Quartet, 1971 (Pulitzer Prize); Duo for Violin and Piano, 1973–74; Brass Quintet, 1974; A Mirror on which to Dwell (song cycle), 1976; A Symphony of Three Orchestras, 1977; Syringa, 1979; Night Fantasies (for piano), 1980; In Sleep in Thunder, 1982; Triple Duo, 1983; Penthode, 1985; Fourth String Quartet, 1986; Oboe Concerto, 1988; Three Occasions for Orchestra, 1989; Violin Concerto, 1991; Partita, 1992; Adagio Tenebroso, 1993; Fifth String Quartet, 1995; Figment, 1996; Allegro Scorrevole, 1996; Clarinet Concerto, 1996; Luimen, 1997; What Next? (opera), 1998; Tempo e tempi, 1999; Statement, 1999; Fantasy, 1999; Asko Concerto, 2000; Cello Concerto, 2000; Oboe Quartet, 2001; Boston Concerto, 2002; Of Rewaking, 2002; Micomicon, 2003; Dialogue, 2003; Réflexions, 2004; Mosaic, 2004. Member: Nat. Inst. of Arts and Letters, 1956 (Gold Medal for Music, 1971); Amer. Acad. of Arts and Sciences (Boston), 1962; Amer. Acad. of Arts and Letters, 1971; Akad. der Kunste, Berlin, 1971. Hon. degrees incl. MusD Cantab, 1983. Sibelius Medal (Harriet Cohen Foundation), London, 1961; Premio delle Muse, City of Florence, 1969; Handel Medallion, New York City, 1978; Mayor of Los Angeles declared Elliott Carter Day, 27 April 1979; Ernst Von Siemens Prize, Munich, 1981; Gold Medal, MacDowell Colony, 1983; National Medal of Arts, USA, 1985. Commandeur, Ordre des Arts et des Lettres (France) 1987; Commander, Order of Merit (Italy), 1991. *Publications:* The Writings of Elliott Carter, 1977; Collected Essays and Lectures 1937–1995, 1997; *relevant publications:* The Music of Elliott Carter, by David Schiff, 1983; Elliott Carter ou le temps fertile, by Max Noubel, 2001. *Address:* c/o Boosey & Hawkes, 295 Regent Street, W1R 8JH.

CARTER, Maj. Gen. Sir Evelyn John W.; *see* Webb-Carter.

CARTER, His Honour Frederick Brian; QC 1980; a Circuit Judge, 1985–2001; *b* 11 May 1933; *s* of late Arthur and Minnie Carter; *m* 1960, Elizabeth Hughes, JP, *d* of late W. B. Hughes and Mrs B. M. Hughes; one *s* three *d* (and one *s* decd). *Educ:* Stretford Grammar Sch.; King's Coll., London (LLB). Called to Bar, Gray's Inn, 1955, practised Northern Circuit, 1957–85; Prosecuting Counsel for Inland Revenue, Northern Circuit, 1973–80; a Recorder, 1978–85. Acting Deemster, 2001–03. *Recreations:* golf, travel. *Address:* Croft Cottage, Start Lane, Whaley Bridge, High Peak SK23 7BR. *Clubs:* Big Four (Manchester); Chorlton-cum-Hardy Golf.

CARTER, George; *see* Carter, W. G. K.

CARTER, Rev. Graham; *see* Carter, Rev. R. G.

CARTER, Graydon; *see* Carter, E. G.

CARTER, Imelda Mary Philomena Bernadette; *see* Staunton, I. M. P. B.

CARTER, James Earl, Jr, (Jimmy); President of the United States of America, 1977–81; *b* Plains, Georgia, USA, 1 Oct. 1924; *s* of late James Earl Carter and Lillian (*née* Gordy); *m* 1946, Rosalynn Smith; three *s* one *d. Educ:* Plains High Sch.; Georgia Southwestern Coll.; Georgia Inst. of Technology; US Naval Acad. (BS); Union Coll., Schenectady, NY (post grad.). Served in US Navy submarines and battleships, 1946–53; Ensign (commissioned, 1947); Lieut (JG) 1950, (SG) 1952; retd from US Navy, 1953. Became farmer and warehouseman, 1953, farming peanuts at Plains, Georgia, until 1977. Member: Sumter Co. (Ga) School Bd, 1955–62 (Chm. 1960–62); Americus and Sumter Co. Hosp. Authority, 1956–70; Sumter Co. (Ga) Library Bd, 1961; President: Plains Develt Corp., 1963; Georgia Planning Assoc., 1968; Chm., W Central Georgia Area Planning and Develt Commn, 1964; Dir, Georgia Crop Improvement Assoc., 1957–63 (Pres., 1961). State Chm., March of Dimes, 1968–70; Dist Governor, Lions Club, 1968–69. State Senator (Democrat), Georgia, 1963–67; Governor of Georgia, 1971–75. Chm., Congressional Campaign Cttee, Democratic Nat. Cttee, 1974; Democratic Candidate for the Presidency of the USA, 1976. Founder, Carter Center, Emory Univ., 1982. Mem., Bd of Dirs, Habitat for Humanity, 1984–87; Chairman, Board of Trustees: Carter Center, Inc., 1986–; Carter-Menil Human Rights Foundn, 1986–; Global 2000 Inc., 1986–; Chairman: Council of Freely-Elected Heads of Government, 1986–; Council of Internat. Negotiation Network, 1991–. Distinguished Prof., Emory Univ., 1982–. Baptist. Hon. LLD: Morehouse Coll., and Morris Brown Coll., 1972; Notre Dame, 1977; Emory Univ., 1979; Kwansei Gakuim Univ., Japan, and Georgia Southwestern Coll., 1981; New York Law Sch., and Bates Coll., 1985; Centre Coll., and Creighton Univ., 1987; Hon. DE Georgia Inst. Tech., 1979; Hon. PhD: Weizmann Inst. of Science, 1980; Tel Aviv Univ., 1983; Haifa Univ., 1987; Hon. DHL Central; Connecticut State Univ., 1985. Awards include: Gold Medal, Internat. Inst. for Human Rights, 1979; Internat. Mediation Medal, American Arbitration Assoc., 1979; Harry S. Truman Public Service Award, 1981; Ansel Adams Conservation Award, Wilderness Soc., 1982; Distinguished Service Award, Southern Baptist Convention, 1982; Human Rights Award, Internat. League for Human Rights, 1983; Albert Schweitzer Prize for Humanitarianism, 1987; Jefferson Award, Amer. Inst. of Public Service, 1990; Nobel Peace Prize, 2002. *Publications:* Why Not the Best?, 1975; A Government as Good as its People, 1977; Keeping Faith: memoirs of a President, 1982; Negotiation: the alternative to hostility, 1984; The Blood of Abraham, 1985; (with Rosalynn Carter) Everything to Gain: making the most of the rest of your life, 1987; An Outdoor Journal, 1988; Turning Point: a candidate, a state and a nation come of age, 1992; Talking Peace: a vision for the next generation, 1993; Always a Reckoning (poetry), 1995; Living Faith, 1996; Sources of Strength, 1997; The Virtues of Ageing, 1998; An Hour Before Daylight: memoirs of a rural boyhood, 2001; Christmas in Plains, 2001; The Hornet's Nest (novel), 2003; Sharing Good Times, 2004; Our Endangered Values: America's moral crisis, 2005; Palestine: peace not apartheid, 2006. *Address:* (office) The Carter Center, One Copenhill, 453 Freedom Parkway, Atlanta, GA 30307, USA.

CARTER, Sir John (Alexander), Kt 1989; Chairman, Stock Land & Estates Ltd, 1987–2000; *b* 2 Nov. 1921; *s* of Allan Randolph Carter and Beatrice Alice Carter; *m* 1954; two *d. Educ:* Duke of York's Royal Military Sch., Dover, Kent. Served Territorial Army, 1939–45: Warwicks Yeo., RA and Loyal N Lancs Regt. Founder Chm., Carter Holdings PLC, 1964–89. Co-opted Mem., Conservative Central Bd of Finance, 1983–87; Conservative Party, East of England: Chm., Industrial Council, 1983–87; Chm., Property Adv. Bd, 1986–87. KStJ 1992; Chm. Council, Order of St John for Essex, 1988–94. *Recreations:* golf, swimming, reading. *Address:* Cobblers, Mill Road, Stock, near Ingatestone, Essex CM4 9RG. *T:* (01277) 840580. *Club:* Carlton.

CARTER, Sir John (Gordon Thomas), Kt 1998; FIA; Chief Executive, Commercial Union plc, 1994–98; *b* 28 Dec. 1937; *s* of Gordon Percival Carter and Mary Ann Carter (*née* Edgington); *m* 1961, Margaret Elizabeth Dobson; three *s*. *Educ:* City of Oxford High Sch.; Jesus Coll., Oxford (Lawrence Exhibnr; MA Maths; Hon. Fellow, 1998). FIA 1966. Nat. Service, MEAF, 1956–58. Joined Commercial Union, 1961: Life Manager, 1978–80; Dep. Gen. Manager, 1981–82; Gen. Manager, 1983–86; Dir, 1987–98. Director: Trade Indemnity plc, 1991–95; Credito Italiano Bank, 1994–99; NHBC, 1998– (Chm., 2002–); Canary Wharf Gp plc, 1999–2004; Mem., UK Bd Cttee, CGU plc, 1998–2000; Chm., St Paul Travelers Insce Co., 2007–. Mem., Council for Industry and Higher Educn, 1993–98. Chairman: Mgt Cttee, Motor Insurers Bureau, 1985–90; Loss Prevention Council, 1991–94; Assoc. of British Insurers, 1995–97; Policyholders Protection Bd, 2000–01. Adviser: HSBC Investment Bank, 1998–2001; Munich Reinsurance Co. Ltd, 1998–2002 and 2004–. Curator, Univ. Chest, 1998–2000, Mem. Investment Cttee, 2000–07, Oxford Univ.; Gov., London Guildhall Univ., 1998–2002 (Chm. Govs, 1999–2002); Chairman: London Metropolitan Univ., 2002–06; Cttee of Univ. Chairmen, 2004–06. *Recreations:* golf, ski-ing, hill walking, opera, theatre. *Address:* 42 Wolsey Road, Moor Park, Northwood, Middx HA6 2EN. *Club:* Moor Park Golf.

CARTER, Dr (John) Timothy, FRCP, FFOM; Chief Medical Adviser, Department for Transport (formerly Department of the Environment, Transport and the Regions, then Department for Transport, Local Government and the Regions), since 1999; Hon. Senior Clinical Lecturer, University of Birmingham, since 1995; *b* 12 Feb. 1944; *s* of Reginald John Carter and Linda Mary (*née* Briggs); *m* 1967, Judith Ann Lintott; one *s* two *d*. *Educ:* Dulwich Coll.; Corpus Christi Coll., Cambridge (MB, MA); University Coll. Hosp., London; Birmingham Univ. (PhD 2005). FFOM 1984; FRCP 1987. London Sch. of Hygiene, 1972–74 (MSc). MO, British Petroleum, 1974–78; SMO, BP Chemicals, 1978–83; Health and Safety Executive: Dir of Med. Services, 1983–92, and of Health Policy, 1989–92; Dir of Field Ops Div., 1992–96; Med. Advr, 1996–97. Member: MRC, 1983–96; Bd, Faculty of Occupnl Medicine, 1982–88 (Vice Dean, 1996–98); Hon. Sec., Occupnl Medicine Section, RSM, 1979–83; President: British Occupnl Hygiene Soc., 1987–88; Internat. Maritime Health Assoc., 2005–07. *Publications:* articles and books on transport safety and investigation and control of occupnl health hazards and med. history. *Recreation:* history—natural, medical and local. *Address:* Department for Transport, 2/09a Great Minster House, 76 Marsham Street, SW1P 4DR.

CARTER, Prof. Joy, PhD; Vice Chancellor, University of Winchester, since 2006; *b* 26 Dec. 1955; *d* of Douglas and Joyce; *m* Dr Martin Carter; four *s*. *Educ:* Univ. of Durham (BSc); Univ. of Lancaster (PhD). Reader in Geochem., Univ. of Reading; Dean of Sci., Univ. of Derby; Pro-Vice-Chancellor (Academic), Univ. of Glamorgan. *Publications:* (with T. Jickells) Biogeochemistry of Intertidal Sediments, 1997; (with A. Parker) Environmental Interactions of Clay Minerals, 1998; (with A. Stewart) Thematic Set on Environmental Geochemistry and Health, 2000; over 100 academic papers. *Recreations:* sports, antiques. *Address:* University of Winchester, Winchester, Hants SO22 4NR. *T:* (01962) 827222, *Fax:* (01962) 879033; *e-mail:* joy.carter@winchester.ac.uk.

CARTER, Matthew, RDI 1981; Principal, Carter & Cone Type Inc., Cambridge, Mass, since 1992; *b* London, 1 Oct. 1937; *s* of late Harry Graham Carter, OBE and Ella Mary Carter (*née* Garratt). Punch Cutter, Netherlands, 1956; freelance designer of lettering and type, London, 1957–63; typographical advr, Crosfield Electronics, 1963–65; type designer: Mergenthaler Linotype, NY, 1965–71; Linotype Cos, London, 1971–81; Co-founder, Sen. Vice Pres. and Dir, Bitstream Inc., 1981–92. Typographical Advr, HMSO, 1980–84; Consultant, Printer Planning Div., IBM, 1980–81. Typefaces designed include: Snell Roundhand, 1966; Olympian, 1970; Galliard, 1978; Bell Centennial, 1978; Bitstream Charter, 1987; Mantinia, 1993; Verdana, and Georgia, 1996; Miller, 1997. Hon. DFA Art Inst. of Boston, 1992. Middleton Award, Amer. Center for Design, 1995; Chrysler Award for Innovation in Design, 1996; Amer. Inst. of Graphic Arts Medal, 1996; Vadim Award, Moscow Acad. of Graphic Design, 1998; Special Commendation, Prince Philip Designers Prize, CSD, 2004. *Address:* 36–A Rice Street, Cambridge, MA 02140, USA.

CARTER, Matthew John; Managing Director, Penn, Schoen & Berland Associates, Inc., since 2006; *b* 22 March 1972; *s* of John Carter and Jill Tasker; *m* 1997, Erica Moffitt; three *s*. *Educ:* Univ. of Sheffield (BA Hons (Social and Pol Studies) 1993); Univ. of York (MA (Pol Philos.) 1994, DPhil (Politics) 1999). Tutor in Politics, Univ. of York, 1994–98; Labour Party: Regl Organiser, N and Yorks, 1998–99; Regl Dir, SW, 1999–2001; Asst Gen. Sec. (Policy and Pol Develt), 2001–03; Gen. Sec., 2004–05. *Publications:* The People's Party: the history of the Labour Party (with A. W. Wright), 1997; T. H. Green and the Development of Ethical Socialism, 2003. *Recreations:* enjoys hill walking in the Lake District, running, supporting Grimsby Town FC. *Address:* (office) 24–28 Bloomsbury Way, WC1A 2PX.

CARTER, Maj. Gen. Nicholas Patrick, CBE 2003 (MBE 1996; OBE 2001); General Officer Commanding 6 (UK) Division, from Jan. 2009; *b* Nairobi, 11 Feb. 1959; *s* of Gerald and Elspeth Carter; *m* 1984, Louise Anne Ewart; three *s* one *d*. *Educ:* Winchester Coll.; RMA Sandhurst. Commnd RGJ, 1978; Regtl duty, NI, Cyprus, Germany and GB, 1978–90; Staff Coll., 1991; Co. Comd, 3 RGJ, 1992–93; Mil. Asst CGS, 1994–95; DS Staff Coll., 1996–98; CO, 2 RGJ, 1998–2000; Comdr, 20 Armd Bde, 2004–05; Dir, Army Resources and Plans, 2006–08. Regtl Col, London Rifles, 2007–. *Recreations:* golf, cricket, field sports. *Club:* Berkshire Golf.

CARTER, Peter; *see* Carter, C. P.

CARTER, Peter; QC 1995; *b* 8 Aug. 1952. *Educ:* University Coll. London (LLB 1973). Called to the Bar, Gray's Inn, 1974, Bencher, 2002. *Publication:* (jtly) Offences of Violence, 1991, supplement 1994. *Recreations:* poetry, cricket, walking. *Address:* 18 Red Lion Court, EC4A 3EB. *T:* (020) 7520 6000.

CARTER, Dr Peter John, OBE 2006; Chief Executive and General Secretary, Royal College of Nursing, since 2007; *s* of Reginald and Mary Carter; *m* Lilian Yap; two *d*. *Educ:* Univ. of Birmingham (MBA 1992; PhD 1998). MCIPD 1986. Psychiatric nurse trng, Hill End Hosp., St Albans, 1971; gen. nurse trng, St Albans City Hosp. and Inst. of Urology, London, 1976; clinical and managerial posts in Herts and Bedfordshire; Chief Exec., Brent, Kensington, Chelsea and Westminster Mental Health Trust, then Central and NW London Mental Health NHS Trust, 1995–2007. *Recreations:* Rugby, cricket, scuba diving, cycling, music, literature. *Address:* Royal College of Nursing, 20 Cavendish Square, W1G 0RN.

CARTER, Peter Leslie; HM Diplomatic Service; Ambassador to Estonia, since 2007; *b* 19 Nov. 1956; *s* of late Leonard Arthur Carter and of Evelyn Joyce Carter; *m* 1985, Rachelle Rain Hays; one *d*. *Educ:* Skinners' Sch., Tunbridge Wells; New Coll., Oxford (BA Modern Langs). Trainee mgt consultant, Arthur Andersen, 1979–80; freelance lang. consultant, Italy, 1980–84; joined HM Diplomatic Service, 1984: Maritime, Aviation and Envmt Dept, FCO, 1984–85; Hindi language trng, 1985–86; Second, later First Sec., New Delhi, 1986–89; Hd of Indo-China Section, SE Asia Dept, FCO, 1989–92; Hd of Recruitment, Personnel Policy Dept, FCO, 1992–94; Principal Adminr, Common Foreign and Security Policy Unit, Gen. Secretariat, Council of EU, 1994–98; Hd, NE Asia and Pacific Dept, FCO, 1998–2001; Dep. Hd of Mission and Consul Gen., Tel Aviv, 2001–05; Consul Gen., Milan, 2006–07. *Recreations:* travel, reading, cinema, theatre. *Address:* c/o Foreign and Commonwealth Office, King Charles Street, SW1A 2AH. *T:* (020) 7008 1500.

CARTER, Sir Philip (David), Kt 1991; CBE 1982; Managing Director, Littlewoods Organisation, 1976–83; *b* 8 May 1927; *s* of Percival Carter and Isobell (*née* Stirrup); *m* 1946, Harriet Rita (*née* Evans); one *s* two *d*. *Educ:* Waterloo Grammar Sch., Liverpool. Volunteered for Fleet Air Arm, 1945. Professional career in Littlewoods Organisation, 1948–83. Chm., Forminster plc, 1995–. Chm., Mail Order Traders Assoc. of GB, 1979–83; Pres., European Mail Order Traders Assoc., 1983; Chm., Man Made Fibres Sector Wkg Party, 1980–82; Member: Jt Textile Cttee, NEDO, 1979–82; Distributive Trades EDC, 1980–83; Merseyside Develt Corp., 1981–91 (Chm., 1987–91); Merseyside Residuary Body, 1986–89. Chm., Merseyside Tourism Bd, 1986–93. Chairman: Empire Theatre Trust, Liverpool, 1986–; Liverpool John Moores Univ. Trust, 1993–; Pro-Chancellor, 1994–, and Chm. Bd of Govs, 1997–, Liverpool John Moores Univ. Chm., Liverpool Conservative Assoc., 1985–95. Dir, Everton FC, 1975– (Chm., 1978–91, 1998–2004; Life Pres., 2004); Pres., Football League, 1986–88. Chm., Roy Castle Lung Cancer Foundn, 1998–. *Recreations:* football, private flying, music, theatre. *Address:* Oak Cottage, Noctorum Road, Noctorum, Wirral, Cheshire CH43 9UQ. *T:* (0151) 652 4053.

CARTER, Rev. (Ralph) Graham; Chair, Darlington District of the Methodist Church, since 1997; President, Methodist Conference, 2006–07; *b* 11 July 1943; *s* of Thomas Wilfrid Carter and Eva Carter (*née* Williams); *m* 1967, Rosamond Catherine Shaw; one *s* one *d*. *Educ:* Bede Grammar Sch., Sunderland; Queens' Coll., Cambridge (MA); Hartley Victoria Coll., Manchester. Ordained Minister, 1970; served in: Newcastle-upon-Tyne, 1967–71; Cramlington, Northumberland, 1971–74; Birkenhead, 1974–81; Liverpool, 1981–92; Durham, 1992–97. Religious producer, BBC Radio Merseyside, 1987–92. *Recreations:* bird-watching, walking, model railways, supporting Sunderland FC and Durham CCC, listening to music, enjoying grandparenting. *Address:* 2 Edinburgh Drive, Darlington DL3 8AW. *T:* and *Fax:* (01325) 468119; *e-mail:* graham.carter@care4free.net.

CARTER, Raymond John, CBE 1991; Executive, 1980–2003, Director, 1983–2003, Marathon Oil Co.; *b* 17 Sept. 1935; *s* of late John Carter and Nellie Carter (*née* Woodcock); *m* 1959, Jeanette Hills; one *s* two *d*. *Educ:* Mortlake Co. Secondary Sch.; Reading Technical Coll.; Staffordshire Coll. of Technology. National Service, Army, 1953–55. Sperry Gyroscope Co.: Technical Asst, Research and Development Computer Studies, 1956–65. Electrical Engineer, Central Electricity Generating Bd, 1965–70, Mem., CEGB Management, 1979–80. Mem., Gen. Adv. Council, BBC, 1974–76. Mem., Interim Adv. Cttee (Teachers' Pay and Conditions), DES, 1987–91; Dep. Chm., School Teachers' Review Body, 1991–93. Mem. Easthampstead RDC, 1963–68. Contested: Wokingham, Gen. Elec., 1966; Warwick and Leamington, By-elec., March 1968; MP (Lab) Birmingham, Northfield, 1970–79; Parly Under-Sec. of State, Northern Ireland Office, 1976–79. Member: Public Accounts Cttee, 1973–74; Parly Science and Technology Cttee, 1974–76; author of Congenital Disabilities (Civil Liability) Act, 1976. Delegate: Council of Europe, 1974–76; WEU, 1974–76. Trustee: BM (Nat. Hist.), 1986–96; Guild of Handicraft Trust, 1991–. Mem., Develt Cttee, Arvon Foundn, 1995–. Co-cataloguer and exhibitor, works of Sir John Betjeman, 1983. *Recreations:* running, reading, book collecting. *Address:* 1 Lynwood Chase, Warfield Road, Bracknell, Berkshire RG12 2JT. *T:* (01344) 420237.

CARTER, Sir Richard (Henry Alwyn), Kt 1992; Chairman: Ports of Auckland Ltd, 1993–2000; Carter Holt Harvey Ltd, 1984–92; *b* 24 April 1935; *s* of Kenneth Clifford Alwyn Carter, OBE and Stella Grace (*née* Dedman); *m* 1960, June Doreen White; one *d*. *Educ:* Waitaki Boys' High Sch.; Auckland Univ. FCA. With Carter Consolidated, subseq. Carter Holt Hldgs, then Carter Holt Harvey Ltd, 1953–92: Gen. Manager, Admin, 1960; Associate Dir, 1961; Dir, 1966; Jt Man. Dir, 1974. Chm., Council, NZ Timber Industry, 1976–78; Member: NZ Timber Merchants Fedn Inc., 1960–78 (Pres., 1976–78); NZ Business Roundtable, 1974–92. *Recreations:* field shooting, farming. *Address:* Waytemore Farm, Ararimu Road, Drury RD 3, S Auckland, New Zealand. *T:* (9) 2925892.

CARTER, Prof. Richard Lawrance, CBE 1997; DM, DSc; Professorial Fellow and Visiting Professor, University of Surrey, 1994–2000; *b* 5 Sept. 1934; *o s* of Thomas Lawrance Carter and Rhoda Edith Carter (*née* Horton). *Educ:* St Lawrence Coll., Ramsgate; Corpus Christi Coll., Oxford (MA 1960; DM 1966); UCH, London (DSc 1978). FRCPath 1978; FFPM 1994; FRCP 2002. Med. posts, Radcliffe Infirmary, Oxford, Yale Univ., UCH; Reader in Pathology, Inst. of Cancer Research, and Consultant Histopathologist, Royal Marsden Hosp., Sutton, 1975–99. Former chm. or mem. of govt adv. cttees and wkg parties, DoH, DoE, MAFF, MoD; former examr, RCPath, RCS, RCSI; Fellow or Mem., RSocMed, UK Children's Cancer Study Gp. *Publications:* author, jt author or editor of books and papers on lab. and experimental aspects of human cancers, mainly of the head and neck, tumours in children, and human carcinogenesis. *Recreations:* gardening, birds, books, music. *Address:* Pine Cottage, Hascombe, Surrey GU8 4JN. *Club:* Athenæum.

CARTER, Air Cdre Robert Alfred Copsey, CB 1956; DSO 1942; DFC 1943; Royal Air Force, retired; *b* 15 Sept. 1910; *s* of S. H. Carter and S. Copsey; *m* 1947, Sally Ann Peters, Va, USA; two *s* one *d*. *Educ:* Portsmouth Grammar Sch.; RAF Coll., Cranwell. Cranwell Cadet, 1930–32; commissioned in RAF, 1932; served in India, 1933–36; grad. RAF School of Aeronautical Engineering, 1938; served in Bomber Command, 1940–45; commanded 103 and 150 Sqdns; Station Comdr, RAF, Grimsby; grad. RAF Staff Coll., 1945; attended US Armed Forces Staff Coll., Norfolk, Va, USA, 1947; attached to RNZAF, 1950–53; comd. RAF Station, Upwood, 1953–55; SASO, RAF Transport Command, 1956–58; Director of Personal Services, Air Ministry, 1958–61; AO i/c Admin, HQ, RAF Germany, 1961–64; retired 1964. MRAeS 1960; CEng, 1966. *Club:* Royal Air Force.

CARTER, Roland; HM Diplomatic Service, retired; *b* 29 Aug. 1924; *s* of Ralph Carter; *m* 1950, Elisabeth Mary Green; one *s* two *d*. *Educ:* Cockburn High Sch., Leeds; Leeds Univ. Served War of 1939–45: Queen's Royal Regt, 1944; 6th Gurkha Rifles, 1945; Frontier Corps (South Waziristan and Gilgit Scouts), 1946. Seconded to Indian Political Service, as Asst Political Agent, Chilas, Gilgit Agency, 1946–47; Lectr, Zurich Univ. and Finnish Sch. of Economics, 1950–53. Joined Foreign Service, 1953: FO, 1953–54; Third Sec., Moscow, 1955; Germany, 1956–58; Second Sec., Helsinki, 1959 (First Sec., 1962); FO, 1962–67; Kuala Lumpur, 1967–69; Ambassador to People's Republic of Mongolia, 1969–71; seconded to Cabinet Office, 1971–74; Counsellor: Pretoria, 1974–77; FCO, 1977–80, retired. Area Appeals Manager, N and NE England, Nat. Soc. for Cancer Relief, 1981–89. Vis. Fellow, 1990–91, Vis. Sen. Res. Fellow, 1991–92, Inst. for Res. in the Social Scis, York Univ. *Publication:* Näin Puhutaan Englantia (in Finnish; with Erik

Erämetsä), 1952. *Recreations:* music, linguistics, Iranian history and culture. *Address:* 4 Feversham Road, Helmsley, N Yorks YO62 5HN.

CARTER, (Ronald) David, CBE 1980; RDI 1975; Founder, DCA Design International Ltd, 1975 (Chairman, 1975–95; Director, 1995–99); Professor of Industrial Design Engineering, Royal College of Art, and Imperial College of Science, Technology and Medicine, 1991–95; *b* 30 Dec. 1927; *s* of H. Miles Carter and Margaret Carter; *m* 1953, Theo (Marjorie Elizabeth), *d* of Rev. L. T. Towers; two *s* two *d. Educ:* Wyggeston Sch., Leicester; Central Sch. of Art and Design, London. Served RN, 1946–48. Appts in industry, 1951–60; Principal, David Carter Associates, 1960–75. Visiting Lectr, Birmingham Coll. of Art and Design, 1960–65. Examnr, RCA, 1976–79 and 1987–90. Mem., Design Council, 1972–84 (Dep. Chm., 1975–84; Chm., Report on Industrial Design Educn in UK, 1977). Pres., Soc. of Industrial Artists and Designers, 1974–75; Chm., DATEC, 1977–82; Royal Fine Arts Comr, 1986–98. Vice-Chm., Design Mus. (formerly Conran Foundn), 1992– (Chm., 1986–92; Trustee, 1981–95); Moderator, Hong Kong Polytechnic, 1981–86; Mem., Prince of Wales Award for Indust. Innovation, 1981–85. Governor, London Inst., 1988–91. Design Awards, 1961, 1969, 1983; Duke of Edinburgh Prize for Elegant Design, 1967. FCSD (FSIA 1967); Sen. FRCA 1995. FRSA 1975. Hon. DDes: De Montfort, 1993; UCE, 2000. *Recreations:* dry stone walls, boats, County Cork. *Address:* The Old Parsonage, Compton Abdale, near Cheltenham, Glos GL54 4DS. *T:* (01242) 890340. *Club:* Reform.

CARTER, Ronald Louis, OBE 1999; DesRCA; RDI 1971; FCSD (FSIAD 1961); private consultancy design practice, 1974–96, then formed Ron Carter Design Ltd, 1996; *b* 3 June 1926; *s* of Harry Victor Carter and Ruth Allensen; *m* 1st (marr. diss.); three *d*; 2nd, 1985, Ann McNab; one step *s* two step *d. Educ:* Birmingham Central College of Art: studied Industrial and Interior Design (NDD; Louisa Anne Ryland Schol. for Silver Design), 1946–49; Royal College of Art: studied Furniture Design (1st Cl. Dip.; Silver Medal for work of special distinction; Travelling Schol. to USA), 1949–52; DesRCA 1952; Fellow, RCA, 1966; Hon. Fellow, 1974; Sen. Fellow, 1994. Staff Designer with Corning Glass, 5th Avenue, NY City, 1952–53; freelance design practice, Birmingham and London, 1954; Tutor, School of Furniture, RCA, 1956–74; Partner: Design Partners, 1960–68; Carter Freeman Associates, 1968–74; Dir, Miles-Carter, 1980–92. FRSA. *Recreations:* painting, walking, repairing old furniture. *Address:* 19 Denman Road, SE15 5NS. *T:* (020) 7708 1666.

CARTER, Sebastian; *see* Carter, T. S.

CARTER, Stephen Andrew, CBE 2007; Parliamentary Under-Secretary of State, Department for Business, Enterprise and Regulatory Reform and Department for Culture, Media and Sport, since 2008; *b* 12 Feb. 1964; *s* of Robert and Margaret Carter; *m* 1992, Anna Gorman; one *s* one *d. Educ:* Aberdeen Univ. (BA Hons Law); Harvard Business Sch. (AMP 1997). Man. Dir and Chief Exec., J. W. Thompson, 1992–2000; Chief Operating Officer and Man. Dir, ntl, UK and Ireland, 2000–02; CEO, OFCOM, 2003–06; Gp Chief Exec., Brunswick Gp LLP, 2007–08; Chief of Strategy and Principal Advr to the Prime Minister, 2008. Non-executive Director: Travis Perkins plc, 2006–08; Royal Mail Hldgs plc, 2007–08. Vice Pres., UNICEF, 2005–. Trustee, RSC, 2007–. Gov., Ashridge Business Mgt Sch., 2005– (Chm., 2007–); Mem., Sixth Century Campaign Bd, Aberdeen Univ., 2007–. *Address:* House of Lords, SW1A 0PW.

[Created a Baron (Life Peer) 2008 but title not gazetted at time of going to press.]

CARTER, (Thomas) Sebastian; designer and printer; Partner, since 1971, and owner, since 1991, Rampant Lions Press; *b* 20 Feb. 1941; *s* of late William Nicholas Carter, OBE and Barbara Ruth Carter (*née* Digby); *m* 1966, Penelope Ann Bowes Kerr; one *s* one *d. Educ:* Christ's Hosp.; King's Coll., Cambridge (MA). Designer: John Murray, 1962–63; The Trianon Press, Paris, 1963–65; Ruari McLean Associates, 1965–66; joined Rampant Lions Press, 1966. Mem., Internat. Acad. of the Book and Art of the Book, Russia, 1995. Ed., Parenthesis (jl of Fine Press Bk Assoc.), 2006–. Francis Minns Meml Prize (for Shades by David Piper), NBL, 1971. *Publications:* The Book Becomes, 1984; Twentieth Century Type Designers, 1987, 2nd edn 1995; contribs to Matrix. *Recreations:* gardening, food, listening to music. *Address:* Swan House, Over, Cambridge CB24 5ND. *T:* (01954) 231003.

CARTER, Timothy; *see* Carter, J. T.

CARTER, Prof. Timothy, PhD; David G. Frey Distinguished Professor of Music, University of North Carolina, since 2001; *b* 3 July 1954; *s* of Thomas Carter and Thais (*née* Epifantseff); *m* 1995, Annegret Fauser. *Educ:* Univ. of Durham (BA); Univ. of Birmingham (PhD 1980). Lectr in Music, Univ. of Lancaster, 1980–87; Lectr, 1987–92, Reader, 1992–95, Prof. of Music, 1995–2001, RHBNC, Univ. of London. Fellow, Harvard Center for Italian Renaissance Studies, Villa I Tatti, Florence, 1984–85. Ed., Music & Letters, 1992–99. Has made broadcasts. *Publications:* W. A. Mozart: Le Nozze di Figaro, 1987; Jacopo Peri (1561–1633): his life and works, 1989; Music in Late Renaissance and Early Baroque Italy, 1992; Monteverdi's Musical Theatre, 2002; Oklahoma!: the making of an American musical, 2006; articles and essays in Jl Royal Musical Assoc., Early Music Hist., Jl Amer. Musicological Soc. *Address:* Music Department, University of North Carolina, Chapel Hill, NC 27599–3320, USA.

CARTER, (William) George (Key), CBE 1994; DL; FCA; Chairman, Black Country Development Corporation, 1994–98; *b* 29 Jan. 1934; *s* of late William Tom Carter, OBE, JP and Georgina Margaret Carter (*née* Key); *m* 1965, Anne Rosalie Mary Flanagan; one *s* one *d. Educ:* Warwick School. FCA 1957. Articled with Loarridge Beaven & Co., 1951–56; joined Price Waterhouse, 1956; Nat. Service, 2nd Lieut, 16/5th Queen's Royal Lancers, 1958–60; returned to Price Waterhouse, 1960: Manager, 1963–66; Partner, London, 1966–82; Dir of Finance, 1966–70; Sen. Partner, W Midlands, 1982–94. Dir, W Midlands Develt Agency, 1989–95 (Chm., 1991–95); Mem., NW Worcs HA, 1994–96. Mem., Pharmacists Rev. Panel, 1981–97. Member: CBI W Midlands Regl Council, 1988–98; DTI Industry '96 Steering Gp, 1993–97. Pres., Birmingham Chamber of Industry and Commerce, 1993–94; Vice-Chm., Birmingham Mkting Partnership, 1993–95; Non-executive Director: Birmingham Econ. Develt Partnership, 1991–95; Birmingham Children's Hosp. NHS Trust, 1996–2003. Institute of Chartered Accountants: Member: Insce Industry Cttee (Chm., 1974–80); Parly and Law Cttee, 1978–83; Co-Chm., Auditors and Actuaries Cttee, 1975–80; Courses Cttee 1978–81. Member: Birmingham Univ. Business Sch. Adv. Bd, 1989–99; Council, Aston Univ., 1995–98. Pres., ESU, Worcs, 1998–2003. Gov. and Feoffee, Old Swinford Hosp. Sch., 1986–2000. FRSA 1993. DL W Midlands, 1996; High Sheriff, W Midlands, 1998–99. CStJ 1998 (Chm., Council, W Midlands, 1994–2001; Mem., Chapter Gen., 1996–99; Mem., Priory of England Chapter, 1999–2002). *Publication:* (jtly) Institute of Chartered Accountants Guide to Investigations, 1978. *Recreations:* gardening, golf, shooting. *Address:* The Old Rectory, Elmley Lovett, Droitwich, Worcs WR9 0PS. *T:* (01299) 851459; *e-mail:* wgkcarter@aol.com. *Club:* Cavalry and Guards.

CARTER, Prof. Yvonne Helen, (Mrs M. J. Bannon), OBE 2000; DL; MD; FRCGP; Dean, Warwick Medical School, since 2004, and Pro-Vice-Chancellor (Regional Engagement), since 2007, University of Warwick; *b* 16 April 1959; *d* of Percival Anthony Daniel Carter and Ellen Carter (*née* Bore); *m* 1988, Michael Joseph Bannon, *qv*; one *s. Educ:* Notre Dame High Sch., Liverpool; St Mary's Hosp. Med. Sch., Univ. of London (BSc, MB BS, MD 1994; DRCOG, DCH). FRCGP 1994. S Sefton Vocational Trng Scheme, Liverpool, 1984–87; General Practitioner: Liverpool, 1987–90; Newcastle-under-Lyme, 1990–93; Sen. Lectr, Dept of General Practice, Univ. of Birmingham, 1992–96; GP Tutor, Queen Elizabeth Postgrad. Med. Centre, Birmingham, 1994–96; Prof., and Hd of Dept of Gen. Practice and Primary Care, St Bartholomew's and Royal London Sch. of Medicine and Dentistry, QMW, subseq. Bart's and The London, Queen Mary's Sch. of Medicine and Dentistry, Univ. of London, 1996–2003 (Hon. Fellow, Queen Mary, Univ. of London, 2004–); Vice-Dean, Leicester Warwick Med. Schs, 2003–06. Hon. Res. Fellow, Keele Univ., 1990–92. Chm. of Res., RCGP, 1996–2000. DL W Midlands, 2008. Founder FMedSci 1998. *Publications:* (ed with C. Thomas) Research Methods in Primary Care, 1996; (ed jtly) Handbook of Palliative Care, 1998, 2nd edn 2005; (ed jtly) Handbook of Sexual Health in Primary Care, 1998, 2nd edn 2006; (ed jtly) Research Opportunities in Primary Care, 1999; papers in med. jls on injury prevention (accidents to children and older people; child protection and aggression and violence in general practice and primary care). *Recreations:* reading, theatre, interior design. *Address:* Warwick Medical School, University of Warwick, Coventry CV4 7AL. *T:* (024) 7657 3080. *Club:* Royal Society of Medicine.

CARTER-MANNING, Jeremy James; QC 1993; a Recorder, since 1993; *b* 25 Dec. 1947; *s* of Landon and Nancie Carter-Manning; *m* 1970, Bridget Mary Simpson; one *s* one *d. Educ:* St Paul's Sch. Solicitor, 1971; called to the Bar, Middle Temple, 1975, Bencher, 2002. Mem., Mental Health Rev. Tribunal, 1998–2003. Dir, Council for Registration of Forensic Practitioners, 1999–2006. *Recreations:* tennis, golf, food and wine. *Address:* 9–12 Bell Yard, WC2A 2JR. *T:* (020) 7400 1800. *Clubs:* Reform; Southampton Football.

CARTER-STEPHENSON, George Anthony; QC 1998; *b* 10 July 1952; *s* of Raymond M. Stephenson and Brenda S. Stephenson; *m* 1974, Christine Maria; one *s* one *d. Educ:* Leeds Univ. (LLB Hons). Called to the Bar, Inner Temple, 1975; in practice at the Bar, 1975–. *Recreations:* motorcycling, theatre, cinema, music. *Address:* 25 Bedford Row, WC1R 4HD. *T:* (020) 7067 1500.

CARTLEDGE, Sir Bryan (George), KCMG 1985 (CMG 1980); Principal of Linacre College, Oxford, 1988–96 (Hon. Fellow, 1996); *b* 10 June 1931; *s* of Eric Montague George Cartledge and Phyllis (*née* Shaw); *m* 1st, 1960, Ruth Hylton Gass (marr. diss. 1994; she *d* 1998), *d* of John Gass; one *s* one *d*; 2nd, 1994, Dr Freda Gladys Newcombe (*d* 2001); 3rd, 2005, Helen Manolatos (*née* Mostra). *Educ:* Hurstpierpoint; St John's Coll., Cambridge (Hon. Fellow, 1985). Queen's Royal Regt, 1950–51. Commonwealth Fund Fellow, Stanford Univ., 1956–57; Research Fellow, St Antony's Coll., Oxford, 1958–59 (Hon. Fellow, 1987). Entered HM Foreign (subseq. Diplomatic) Service, 1960; served in FO, 1960–61; Stockholm, 1961–63; Moscow, 1963–66; DSAO, 1966–68; Tehran, 1968–70; Harvard Univ., 1971–72; Counsellor, Moscow, 1972–75; Head of E European and Soviet Dept, FCO, 1975–77; Private Sec. (Overseas Affairs) to Prime Minister, 1977–79; Ambassador to Hungary, 1980–83; Asst Under-Sec. of State, FCO, 1983–84; Dep. Sec. of the Cabinet, 1984–85; Ambassador to the Soviet Union, 1985–88. *Publications:* (ed) Monitoring the Environment, 1992; (ed) Energy and the Environment, 1993; (ed) Health and the Environment, 1994; (ed) Population and the Environment, 1995; (ed) Transport and the Environment, 1996; (ed) Mind, Brain and Environment, 1997; The Will to Survive: a history of Hungary, 2006; Makers of the Modern World: Károlyi and Bethlen: Hungary, 2009. *Clubs:* Reform, Hurlingham.

CARTLEDGE, Prof. Paul Anthony, DPhil, PhD; FSA; A. G. Leventis Professor of Greek Culture, University of Cambridge, since 2008; Fellow, Clare College, Cambridge, since 1981; *b* 24 March 1947; *s* of Marcus Raymond and Margaret Christobel Cartledge; *m* 1976, Judith Portrait; one *d. Educ:* St Paul's Sch.; New Coll., Oxford (MA; DPhil 1975); MA TCD 1978; PhD Cantab 1979. FSA 1980. Craven Fellow, Oxford Univ., 1969–70; Harold Salvesen Jun. Fellow, University Coll., Oxford, 1970–72; Lecturer: in Classics, NUU, 1972–73, TCD, 1973–78; in Classical Civilization, Univ. of Warwick, 1978–79; University of Cambridge: Lectr in Classics, 1979–93; Reader in Greek History, 1993–99; Prof. of Greek History, 1999–2008; Chm., Faculty Bd of Classics, 2001–02. Visiting Professor: Centre Louis Gernet, Paris, 1990; Sorbonne, Univ. de Paris VII, 1998–99; Hellenic Parlt Global Dist. Prof., New York Univ., 2006–. Lectures: Lansdowne, Univ. of Victoria, BC, 1989, 1993; Crayenborgh Res. Seminar, Univ. of Leiden, 1999; T. B. L. Webster Meml, Stanford Univ., 1999. Syndic, Fitzwilliam Mus., 2002–. Gov., St Paul's Schs, 1991–2007. FRSA 2007. Hon. Citizen, Sparta, Greece, 2004. Golden Cross, Order of Honour (Greece), 2002. *Publications:* Sparta and Lakonia: a regional history 1300–362 BC, 1979, 2nd edn 2002; Agesilaos and the Crisis of Sparta, 1987; (with A. Spawforth) Hellenistic and Roman Sparta: a tale of two cities, 1989, rev. edn 2002; Aristophanes and his Theatre of the Absurd, 1990, rev. edn 1999; (ed jtly) Nomos: essays in Athenian law, politics and society, 1990; (ed and trans.) Religion in the Ancient Greek City, 1992; The Greeks: a portrait of self and others, 1993, 2nd edn 2002; (ed jtly) Hellenistic Constructs: essays in culture, history and historiography, 1997; (ed) The Cambridge Illustrated History of Ancient Greece, 1997, 2nd edn 2002; (with R. Waterfield) Xenophon: Hiero the Tyrant and other treatises, 1997; (ed jtly) Kosmos: essays in order, conflict and community in classical Athens, 1998; Democritus and Atomistic Politics, 1998; The Greeks: crucible of civilization, 2001; Spartan Reflections, 2001; (ed jtly) Money, Labour and Land: approaches to the economies of ancient Greece, 2001; The Spartans: an epic history, 2002, 2nd edn 2003; Alexander the Great: the hunt for a new past, 2004; Thermopylae: the battle that changed the world, 2006. *Recreations:* opera, ballet, theatre. *Address:* Clare College, Cambridge CB2 1TL. *T:* (01223) 333265, *Fax:* (01223) 333219.

CARTTISS, Michael Reginald Harry; Regional Organiser for Norfolk and Suffolk, SOS Children's Villages UK, since 1999; *b* Norwich, 11 March 1938; *s* of Reginald Carttiss and Doris Culling. *Educ:* Filby County Primary Sch.; Great Yarmouth Tech. High Sch.; Goldsmiths' Coll., London Univ. (DipEd); LSE (part time, 1961–64). Nat. Service, RAF, 1956–58. Teacher: Orpington, Kent, and Waltham Cross, Herts, 1961–64; Oriel Grammar Sch., 1964–69; Cons. Party Agent, Gt Yarmouth, 1969–82. Norfolk County Council: Mem., 1966–85, 2002–; Vice-Chm., 2006–07; Chm., 2007–; Vice-Chm., 1972, Chm., 1982–84, Educn Cttee; Mem., Gt Yarmouth BC, 1973–82 (Leader, 1980–82). MP (C) Great Yarmouth, 1983–97; contested (C) same seat, 1997. Chm., Norfolk Museums Service, 1981–85; Comr, Gt Yarmouth Port and Haven Commn, 1982–86. Mem., E Anglian RHA, 1981–85; Chairman: Gt Yarmouth and Waveney CHC, 2001–03; Norfolk Health Scrutiny Cttee, 2005–. *Recreations:* reading, writing, talking, walking, theatre. *Address:* Melrose, Main Road, Filby, Great Yarmouth, Norfolk NR29 3HN.

CARTWRIGHT, David Edgar, DSc; FRS 1984; Assistant Director, Institute of Oceanographic Sciences, Bidston Observatory, Birkenhead, 1973–86, retired; *b* 21 Oct. 1926; *s* of Edgar A. Cartwright and Lucienne Cartwright (*née* Tartanson); *m* 1952, Anne-

Marie Guerin; two *s* two *d*. *Educ:* St John's Coll., Cambridge (BA); King's Coll., London (BSc, DSc). Dept of Naval Construction, Admiralty, Bath, 1951–54; Nat. Inst. of Oceanography (later Inst. of Oceanographic Sciences), Wormley, Surrey: Sci. Officer, rising to Individual Merit SPSO, 1954–73; Research Associate, Univ. of California, La Jolla, 1964–65, 1993, 1994; Sen. Res. Associate, NASA-Goddard Space Flight Center, Greenbelt, Md, 1987–89; Consultant, NASA, 1990–92. Vis. Res. Fellow, Nat. Oceanographic Centre, Southampton, 1992–. Fellow: Royal Astronomical Soc., 1975; Amer. Geophysical Union, 1991. Dr (*hc*) Toulouse, 1992. *Publications:* Tides—a Scientific History, 1999; over 80 papers on marine sci. research; reviews, etc, in various learned jls. *Recreations:* music, walking. *Address:* 3 Borough House West, Borough Road, Petersfield, Hants GU32 3LF. *T:* (01730) 267195.

CARTWRIGHT, Harry, CBE 1979 (MBE 1946); MA, CEng, MIMechE, MIET; Director, Atomic Energy Establishment, Winfrith, 1973–83; *b* 16 Sept. 1919; *s* of Edwin Harry Cartwright and Agnes Alice Cartwright (*née* Gillibrand); *m* 1950, Catharine Margaret Carson Bradbury; two *s*. *Educ:* William Hulme's Grammar Sch., Manchester; St John's Coll., Cambridge (Schol.). 1st cl. Mechanical Sciences Tripos, 1940. Served War, RAF, 1940–46: Flt Lt, service on ground radar in Europe, India and Burma. Decca Navigator Co., 1946–47; English Electric Co., 1947–49; joined Dept of Atomic Energy, Risley, as a Design and Project Engr, 1949; Chief Engr, 1955; Dir in charge of UKAEA consultancy services on nuclear reactors, 1960–64; Dir, Water Reactors, 1964–70, and as such responsible for design and construction of Winfrith 100 MW(e) SGHWR prototype power station; Dir, Fast Reactor Systems, 1970–73. Pres., British Nuclear Energy Soc., 1979–82; Pres., European Nuclear Soc., 1983–85 (Vice-Pres., 1980–83). Chm. of Trustees, Corfe Castle Charities, 1991–98. Chm. of Govs, Purbeck Sch., 1985–88. *Publications:* various techn. papers. *Recreations:* walking, gardening. *Address:* Tabbit's Hill House, Corfe Castle, Wareham, Dorset BH20 5HZ. *T:* (01929) 480582. *Club:* Oxford and Cambridge.

CARTWRIGHT, John Cameron; JP; Deputy Chairman, Police Complaints Authority, 1993–99 (Member, 1992–99); *b* 29 Nov. 1933; *s* of Aubrey John Randolph Cartwright and Ivy Adeline Billie Cartwright; *m* 1959, Iris June Tant; one *s* one *d*. *Educ:* Woking County Grammar School. Exec. Officer, Home Civil Service, 1952–55; Labour Party Agent, 1955–67; Political Sec., RACS Ltd, 1967–72; Director, RACS Ltd, 1972–74. Leader, Greenwich Borough Council, 1971–74. Mem., Labour Party Nat. Exec. Cttee, 1971–75 and 1976–78. MP Greenwich, Woolwich East, Oct. 1974–1983, Woolwich, 1983–92 (Lab, 1974–81; SDP, 1981–90; Soc. Dem., 1990–92); contested (Soc. Dem.) Woolwich, 1992. PPS to Sec. of State for Education and Science, 1976–77; Chm., Parly Labour Party Defence Group, 1979–81; Mem., Select Cttee on Defence, 1979–82 and 1986–92; SDP party spokesman on environment, 1981–87, on defence and foreign affairs, 1983–87; SDP/Liberal Alliance spokesman on defence, 1987; SDP Parly Whip, 1983–92; Vice Pres., SDP, 1987–88, Pres., 1988–91. Jt Chm., Council for Advancement of Arab British Understanding, 1983–87; Vice-Chm., GB-USSR Assoc., 1983–91. Mem., Calcutt Cttee on Privacy and Related Matters, 1989–90. Non-executive Director: Lambeth, Southwark and Lewisham HA, 1995–2000; Maidstone and Tunbridge Wells NHS Trust, 2000–03. Vice-Pres., Assoc. of Metropolitan Authorities, 1974–. Trustee, Nat. Maritime Museum, 1976–83. Co. Sec., Maidstone Christian Care, 2002–. JP Inner London, 1970. *Publication:* (jtly) Cruise, Pershing and SS20, 1985. *Recreations:* do-it-yourself, listening to jazz, supporting Lincoln City FC. *Address:* 24 Juniper Close, Maidstone, Kent ME16 0XP. *T:* (01622) 691324.

CARTWRIGHT, Prof. Nancy Lynn Delaney, (Lady Hampshire), PhD; FBA 1996; Professor of Philosophy, Logic and Scientific Method, since 1991, and Chair, Centre for the Philosophy of Natural and Social Science, since 1993, London School of Economics and Political Science, London University; *b* 24 June 1944; *m* 1985, Sir Stuart Hampshire, FBA (*d* 2004); two *d*. *Educ:* Pittsburgh Univ. (BS Maths 1966); Illinois Univ. (PhD 1971). Asst Prof. of Philosophy, Maryland Univ., 1971–73; Stanford University: Asst Prof., 1973–77; Associate Prof., 1977–83; Prof. of Philosophy, 1983–91. Vis. Lectr, Cambridge Univ., 1974; Visiting Professor: UCLA, 1976; Princeton Univ., 1978; Pittsburgh Univ., 1984; Oslo Univ., 1993, 1994; Univ. of Calif, San Diego, 1995; Old Dominion Fellow, Princeton Univ., 1996; Prof. of Philosophy, Univ. of Calif, San Diego, 1997–. Assoc. Mem., Nuffield Coll., Oxford, 2001–05. Pres., Hist. of Sci., BAAS, 2001–02. Mem., Acad. Leopoldina, 1999; Hon. For. Mem., Amer. Acad. of Arts and Sci., 2001. *Publications:* How the Laws of Physics Lie, 1983; Nature's Capacities and their Measurement, 1989; (jtly) Otto Neurath: philosophy between science and politics, 1995; The Dappled World: a study of the boundaries of science, 1999; Measuring Causes: invariance, modularity and the Causal Markov Condition (monograph), 2000; Hunting Causes and Using Them: approaches to philosophy and economics, 2007. *Address:* Department of Philosophy, Logic and Scientific Method, London School of Economics and Political Science, Houghton Street, WC2A 2AE. *T:* (020) 7955 7330.

CARTWRIGHT, Rt Rev. Richard Fox; Assistant Bishop, Diocese of Exeter, since 1988; *b* 10 Nov. 1913; *s* of late Rev. George Frederick Cartwright, Vicar of Plumstead, and Constance Margaret Cartwright (*née* Clark); *m* 1947, Rosemary Magdalen (*d* 2003), *d* of Francis Evelyn Bray, Woodham Grange, Surrey; one *s* three *d*. *Educ:* The King's School, Canterbury; Pembroke Coll., Cambridge (BA 1935, MA 1939); Cuddesdon Theological Coll. Deacon, 1936; Priest, 1937; Curate, St Anselm, Kennington Cross, 1936–40; Priest-in-Charge, Lower Kingswood, 1940–45; Vicar, St Andrew, Surbiton, 1945–52; Proctor in Convocation, 1950–52; Vicar of St Mary Redcliffe, Bristol (with Temple from 1956 and St John Bedminster from 1965), 1952–72; Hon. Canon of Bristol, 1960–72; Suffragan Bishop of Plymouth, 1972–81; Asst Bishop, dio. of Truro, 1982–91. Sub-Chaplain, Order of St John, 1957–; Director: Ecclesiastical Insurance Office Ltd, 1964–85; Allchurches Trust Ltd, 1985–91. Chm. Governors, Kelly Coll., 1973–88. Hon. DD Univ. of the South, Tennessee, 1969. *Recreations:* fly-fishing, gardening, water-colour painting. *Address:* 5 Old Vicarage Close, Ide, Exeter, Devon EX2 9RE. *T:* (01392) 211270. *Club:* Army and Navy.

CARTWRIGHT, Lt-Col Robert Guy, LVO 2005; Secretary, Central Chancery of Orders of Knighthood, 1999–2005, and Assistant Comptroller, 1999–2004, Lord Chamberlain's Office; Extra Equerry to the Queen, since 2000; *b* 6 Aug. 1950; *s* of Major Robin Vivian Cartwright and Loveday Elizabeth Cartwright (*née* Leigh-Pemberton); *m* 1972, Caroline, *d* of late Gilbert Stephenson and Eleanor Stephenson; two *s*. *Educ:* Wellington Coll.; RMA Sandhurst; RMCS Shrivenham; RN Staff Coll. Commissioned Grenadier Guards, 1970; CO, 1st Bn Grenadier Guards, 1990–92; Directing Staff, RN Staff Coll., 1993–94; MoD, 1995–96; retired, 1996. Bursar, Ibstock Place Sch., Roehampton, 2005–. *Recreations:* running, reading, wine. *Address:* 151 Wakehurst Road, SW11 6BW. *Club:* HAC.

CARTWRIGHT, Hon. Dame Silvia (Rose), PCNZM 2001; DBE 1989; QSM 2006; Governor-General of New Zealand, 2001–06; Chairman, New Zealand National Commission, UNESCO, since 2006; *b* 7 Nov. 1943; *d* of Monteith Poulter and Eileen Jane Poulter, both of Dunedin, NZ; *m* 1969, Peter John Cartwright. *Educ:* Univ. of Otago, NZ (LLB). Partner, Harkness Henry & Co., Barristers and Solicitors, Hamilton, NZ, 1971–81; Dist Court and Family Court Judge, 1981–89; Chief Dist Court Judge, 1989–93; Judge of the High Court, NZ, 1993–2001; Judge, Extraordinary Chambers in the Courts of Cambodia, 2006–. Mem., Commn for the Future, 1975–80; conducted Inquiry into: Soc. Sci. Funding in NZ, 1986–87; Treatment of Cervical Cancer at Nat. Women's Hosp., Auckland, NZ, 1987–88. Mem. Cttee, UN Human Rights Convention to eliminate discrimination against women, 1992–2000. Hon. LLD: Otago, 1993; Waikato, 1994; Canterbury, 2004; Ewha, Seoul, 2006.

CARTWRIGHT, Sonia Rosemary Susan, (Mrs C. Cartwright); *see* Proudman, S. R. S.

CARTY, Hilary; Director, Cultural Leadership Programme, since 2006; *b* 26 May 1962; *d* of Solomon Carty and Catherine (*née* Bailey). *Educ:* Leicester Poly. (BA Hons Performing Arts, 1983); Cultural Trng Centre, Jamaica (Cert. in Dance Educn, 1984); Univ. of Westminster (MBA 1994). Community Arts Officer, Leics Expressive Arts, 1985; Community Arts Develt Officer, The Cave, Birmingham, 1985; Arts Officer (Dance and Mime), E Midlands Arts, 1986–90; Gen. Manager, Adzido Pan African Dance Ensemble, 1990–94; Dir of Dance, Arts Council, 1994–2003; Arts Council England: Dir, Performing Arts, 2003–06; on secondment as Dir, Culture and Educn, London 2012, 2004–06; Dir, London (Arts), 2006. Hon. DA De Montfort, 2001. *Publication:* Folk Dances of Jamaica, 1988. *Recreations:* squash, badminton, theatre, dance. *Address:* 296 Crystal Palace Road, Dulwich, SE22 9JJ. *T:* (020) 7973 6489.

CARUANA, Hon. Peter Richard; QC (Gibraltar) 1998; MP (GSD) Gibraltar, since 1991; Chief Minister of Gibraltar, since 1996; *b* 15 Oct. 1956; *s* of John Joseph Caruana and Maria Teresa Caruana (*née* Vasquez); *m* 1982, Cristina Maria Triay; three *s* three *d* (and one *s* decd). *Educ:* Ratcliffe Coll., Leicester; Queen Mary Coll., London Univ.; Council of Legal Educn, London. Called to the Bar, Inner Temple, 1979; with law firm Triay & Triay, Gibraltar, 1979–95, Partner specialising in commercial and shipping law, 1990–95. Joined GSD, 1990, Leader, 1991–; Leader of the Opposition, Gibraltar, 1992–96. *Recreation:* golf. *Address:* 10/3 Irish Town, Gibraltar; (home) 6 Convent Place, Gibraltar. *T:* 70071, *Fax:* 76396.

CARUS, Louis Revell, Hon. RAM, FRSAMD, FRCM, FBSM; Consultant to Benslow Musical Instrument Loan Scheme, Benslow Music Trust, since 1987; Principal, Birmingham School of Music, 1975–87; *b* Kasauli, India, 22 Oct. 1927; *s* of Lt-Col Martin and Enid Carus-Wilson; *m* 1951, Nancy Reade Noell (*d* 2005); two *s* one *d*. *Educ:* Rugby Sch.; Brussels Conservatoire; Peabody Conservatory, USA; Leeds Univ. (PGCA 2000). LRAM. Scottish National Orchestra, 1950; solo violinist and chamber music specialist, 1951–; Head of Strings, Royal Scottish Academy of Music, 1956; Scottish Trio and Piano Quartet, New Music Group of Scotland, 1956–75; Northern Sinfonia, Monteverdi Orchestras, 1963–73; Orchestra Da Camera, 1975; Artistic Dir, Internat. String Quartet Week, 1985–90. Adjudicator, 1960–; Examr, Associated Bd of Royal Schs of Music, 1976–96. Pres., ISM, 1986–87; FRSAMD 1976; Hon. RAM 1977; FRCM 1983; FBSM 1988. FUCEB. *Publications:* various musical journalism, eg, Strad Magazine, ISM Jl, Gulbenkian Report. *Recreations:* painting, gardening, travel. *Address:* Flat 3/12, GPO Building, 5 South Frederick Street, Glasgow G1 1JG. *T:* (0141) 248 9833. *Clubs:* Royal Society of Musicians, Incorporated Society of Musicians, European String Teachers Association; Rotary (Worcester).

CARUS, Roderick; QC 1990; a Recorder, since 1990; *b* 4 June 1944; *s* of Anthony and Kathleen Carus; *m* 1972, Hilary Mary (*née* Jones); two *s* two *d*. *Educ:* Wirral GS, Merseyside; University Coll., Oxford (BA Law); Manchester Business Sch. (Postgrad. Diploma in Advanced Business Studies). Called to the Bar, Gray's Inn, 1971. Merchant bank, investments, 1966–70. Asst Recorder, 1987–90. *Recreations:* chess, crosswords, fishing, gardening, sailing. *Address:* Higher House Farm, Ashley, Cheshire WA15 0RA.

CARUSO, Adam; Partner, Caruso St John Architects, since 1990; *b* 8 Feb. 1962; *s* of Irving and Naomi Caruso; *m* 1996, Helen Thomas; one *s*. *Educ:* McGill Univ., Montreal (BSc Arch 1984; BArch 1986). ARB 1990; RIBA 1991. Architectural asst, Florian Beigel, 1986–87; Architect, Arup Associates, 1987–90. Projects include: New Art Gall. and Public Sq., Walsall, 1996; Gagosian Galls, phases 1 and 2, 1999–2001, phase 3, 2004; Barbican concert hall refurbishment, 2001; Stortorget, Kalmar, Sweden, 2003; Bethnal Green Mus. of Childhood, phase 1, 2003, phase 2, 2006; Brick House, London, 2005; Hallfield Sch., London, 2005; West Range Project, Downing Coll., Cambridge, 2006; Tate Britain Masterplan, 2006; Centre for Contemporary Art, Nottingham, 2008. Taught, Univ. of North London, 1990–98; Prof., Univ. of Bath, 2002–04. Guest Professor: Acad. of Architecture, Mendrisio, Switzerland, 1999–2001; Sch. of Architecture, ETH Zurich, Switzerland, 2007–09; Design Critic, Graduate Sch. of Design, Harvard Univ., 2005; Vis. Prof., Cities Prog., LSE, 2006–08. *Publications:* contributor to: New Art Gallery Walsall, 2002; Caruso St John Architects: knitting, weaving, wrapping, pressing, 2002; As Built: Caruso St John Architects, 2005; Almost Everything, 2007. *Address:* Caruso St John Architects, 1 Coate Street, E2 9AG. *T:* (020) 7613 3161, *Fax:* (020) 7729 6188; *e-mail:* acaruso@carusostjohn.com.

CARVEL, John Douglas; Social Affairs Editor, The Guardian, since 2000; *b* 26 May 1947; *s* of late Robert Burns Carvel and of Florence Annie Carvel (*née* Wilson); marr. diss.; two *s*; partner, Alison Hargreaves. *Educ:* Merchant Taylors' Sch., Northwood; Exeter Coll., Oxford (BA Hons PPE). Reporter, Newcastle Jl, 1969–72; The Guardian, 1973–: Business Reporter, 1973–75; News Ed., Financial Guardian, 1975–76; Industrial Corresp., 1976–79; Dep. Features Ed., 1979–81; Local Govt Corresp., 1981–85; Political Corresp., 1985–89; Associate Ed., 1989–; Home Affairs Ed., 1989–92; Eur. Affairs Ed., 1992–95; Educn Ed., 1995–2000. Commendation, British Press Awards, 1984 and 1990; Local Govt Journalist of Year, Local Govt Inf. Services, 1985; Legal Affairs Journalist of Year, Bar Council, 1991; Freedom of Information Award, Campaign for Freedom of Inf., 1995; Medical Journalist of the Year, BMA, 2004. *Publications:* Citizen Ken, 1984, 2nd edn 1986; An Account of the Guardian Case, in Openness and Transparency in the EU, ed V. Deckmyn and I. Thomson, 1998; Turn Again Livingstone, 1999. *Recreations:* golf, gardening. *Address:* The Guardian, Kings Place, 90 York Way, N1 9AG.

CARVER, Prof. Martin Oswald Hugh; Professor of Archaeology, University of York, 1986–2008, now Emeritus; *b* 8 July 1941; *s* of John Hobart Carver and Jocelyn Louisa Grace Tweedie; *m* 1st, 1963, Carolyn Rose Haig (marr. diss. 1978); one *s* one *d*; 2nd, 1981, Madeleine Rose Hummler; three *s* one *d*. *Educ:* Ladycross Sch., Seaford; Wellington Coll., Crowthorne; RMA, Sandhurst; Royal Military Coll., Shrivenham (BSc London); Univ. of Durham (DipArch). Commnd RTR, 1961; Adjt, 4th RTR, 1969; retd in rank of Captain, 1972. Freelance archaeologist, researching and digging in England, Scotland, France, Italy and Algeria, 1973–86; Founder Dir, Birmingham Univ. Field Archaeol. Unit, 1978–86; Dir, Centre for Medieval Studies, Univ. of York, 2001–02. Ed., Antiquity, 2003–. Presenter/writer, BBC 2 progs on Sutton Hoo, 1985–88. Director: W Midlands Rescue Archaeol. Cttee, 1975–78; Tarbat Discovery Prog., 1994–. Sec., Inst. Field Archaeologists, 1983–88; Chm., Field Archaeol. Specialists, 1998–. Dir, Sutton Hoo

Res. Trust, 1983–. FSA 1981 (Vice Pres., 2001–06); FSAScot 1994. *Publications:* (ed) Medieval Worcester, 1980; (ed) Two Town Houses in Medieval Shrewsbury, 1983; Underneath English Towns, 1987; (ed) Prehistory in Lowland Shropshire, 1991; (ed) The Age of Sutton Hoo, 1992; (ed) In Search of Cult, 1993; Arguments in Stone, 1993; Sutton Hoo: burial ground of Kings?, 1998; Surviving in Symbols: a visit to the Pictish nation, 1999; (ed) The Cross Goes North, 2003; Archaeological Value and Evaluation, 2003; Sutton Hoo: a seventh century princely burial ground and its context, 2005; Portmahomack: monastery of the Picts, 2008; numerous contribs to archaeol jls and magazines. *Recreation:* playing the flute. *Address:* Ella House, Ellerton, York YO42 4PB; *e-mail:* martincarver@yahoo.co.uk.

CARVILL, Patrick, CB 1994; Permanent Secretary, Department of Finance and Personnel, Northern Ireland, 1998–2003; *b* 13 Oct. 1943; *s* of Bernard and Susan Carvill; *m* 1965, Vera Abbott; two *s*. *Educ:* St Mary's Christian Brothers Grammar School, Belfast; Queen's Univ., Belfast (BA Hons). Min. of Fuel and Power, Westminster, 1965; Min. of Development, Stormont, 1967; Min. of Community Relations, 1969; Asst Sec., Dept of Educn, 1975–83; Under-Secretary: Dept of Finance and Personnel, 1983–88; Dept of Econ. Develt, 1988–89; Dept of Finance and Personnel, 1989–90; Perm. Sec., Dept of Educn for NI, 1990–98. Chm., NI Clinical Excellence Awards Cttee. Non-exec. Dir, NI Guardian Ad Litem Agency. *Recreations:* reading, hill-walking, diving.

CARWARDINE, Prof. Richard John, DPhil; FRHistS, FBA 2006; Rhodes Professor of American History, and Fellow of St Catherine's College, University of Oxford, since 2002; *b* 12 Jan. 1947; *s* of John Francis Carwardine and Beryl Carwardine (*née* Jones); *m* 1975, Dr Linda Margaret Kirk. *Educ:* Corpus Christi Coll., Oxford (BA 1968, MA 1972); Queen's Coll., Oxford (Ochs-Oakes Sen. Schol.; DPhil 1976). FRHistS 1983. University of Sheffield: Lectr in American Hist., 1971–90; Sen. Lectr, 1990–94; Reader in Hist., 1994; Prof. of Hist., 1994–2002; Dean, Faculty of Arts, 1999–2001. Vis. Asst Prof., Syracuse Univ., 1974–75; Fulbright-ACLS Res. Fellow, Univ. of NC, Chapel Hill, 1989. Birkbeck Lectr, Trinity Coll., Cambridge, 2004; Stenton Lectr, Univ. of Reading, 2004; Harry Allen Lectr, Univ. of London, 2006; Burns Lectr, Univ. of Richmond, 2008. *Publications:* Transatlantic Revivalism: popular evangelicalism in Britain and America 1790–1865, 1978; Evangelicals and Politics in Antebellum America, 1993; Lincoln, 2003 (Lincoln Prize, 2004); Lincoln: a life of purpose and power, 2006; contrib. numerous articles and essays to learned jls, incl. Jl Amer. Hist., Jl Amer. Studies, Church Hist., Jl Ecclesiastical Hist. *Recreations:* acting, theatre-going. *Address:* St Catherine's College, Oxford OX1 3UJ. *T:* (01865) 271798, *Fax:* (01865) 271698.

CARWOOD, Andrew; tenor; conductor; Director of Music, St Paul's Cathedral, since 2007; *b* 30 April 1965; *s* of Thomas George Carwood and Daisy Ninnes. *Educ:* John Lyon Sch., Harrow; St John's Coll., Cambridge. Lay Clerk: Christ Ch, Oxford, 1987–90; Westminster Cathedral, 1990–95; Dir of Music, Brompton Oratory, 1995–2000. Director: Cardinall's Musick, 1989–; Edington Fest., 1992–97; Edington Schola Cantorum, 1998–; Jt Prin. Guest Conductor, BBC Singers, 2007–. Has made numerous recordings as singer and as conductor. ARSCM 2005. Hon. Fellow Royal Acad. of St Cecilia, 2003. *Recreations:* theatre, British comedy. *Address: e-mail:* a.carwood@cardinallsmusick.com, directorofmusic@stpaulscathedral.org.uk.

CARY, family name of **Viscount Falkland**.

CARY, Anthony Joyce, CMG 1997; HM Diplomatic Service; High Commissioner to Canada, since 2007; *b* 1 July 1951; *s* of Sir Michael Cary, GCB and Isabel Cary; *m* 1975, Clare Elworthy; three *s* one *d*. *Educ:* Eton; Trinity Coll., Oxford (MA English); Stanford Business Sch. (MBA). Joined FCO, 1973: BMG Berlin, 1974–77; Policy Planning Staff, FCO, 1978–80; Harkness Fellow, Stanford Business Sch., 1980–82; EC Dept, FCO, 1982–84; Private Sec. to Minister of State, FCO, 1984–86; Head of Chancery, Kuala Lumpur, 1986–88; on loan to Cabinet of Sir Leon Brittan, EC, Brussels, 1989–92; Head of EU Dept (Internal), FCO, 1993–96; Counsellor, Washington, 1997–99; on loan as Chef de Cabinet to Rt Hon. Christopher Patten, Mem. of EC, 1999–2003; Ambassador, Sweden, 2003–06. *Address:* c/o Foreign and Commonwealth Office, King Charles Street, SW1A 2AH.

CARY, Dr Nathaniel Roger Blair, FRCPath; Consultant Forensic Pathologist, Home Office Accredited, since 1992; Founder Member, Forensic Pathology Services, since 2001; *b* 13 Nov. 1957; 2nd *s* of Sir Roger Hugh Cary, *qv*; *m* 1st, 1978, Tesney Diane Vera Partington (marr. diss. 1994); two *s* one *d*; 2nd, 1994, Sally Ann Taylor; one *d*. *Educ:* St Paul's Sch., London (Foundn Schol.); Trinity Coll., Oxford (Open Schol.; MA 1982); Charing Cross Hosp. Med. Sch. (MB BS 1981; MD 1992). DMJ 1992; FRCPath 1997. Hse physician and hse surgeon, 1981–82, trainee pathologist, 1982–85, Charing Cross Hosp.; Charing Cross Trustees Res. Fellow, 1985–86; Lectr in Histopathol., Charing Cross and Westminster Med. Sch., 1986–89; Consultant Cardiac Histopathologist, Papworth Hosp., Cambs, 1989–98; Sen. Lectr in Forensic Medicine, 1998–2001, Dir, Guy's Campus, 1999–2001, GKT. *Publications:* contrib. chapters in books on pathology, and papers to med. scientific literature, mainly relating to heart pathol., incl. transplantation. *Recreations:* walking (uphill), ski-ing (downhill). *Address:* Forensic Pathology Services, F5 Culham Science Centre, Abingdon, Oxon OX14 3ED. *T:* (01235) 551662. *Club:* Royal Society of Medicine.

CARY, Sir Roger Hugh, 2nd Bt *cr* 1955; a consultant to BBC's Director-General, 1986–2002; *b* 8 Jan. 1926; *o s* of Sir Robert (Archibald) Cary, 1st Bt, and Hon. Rosamond Mary Curzon (*d* 1985), *d* of late Col Hon. Alfred Nathaniel Curzon; *S* father, 1979; *m* 1st, 1948, Marilda (marr. diss. 1951), *d* of Major Pearson-Gregory, MC; one *d*; 2nd, 1953, Ann Helen Katharine, *e d* of Hugh Blair Brenan, OBE (formerly Sec., Royal Hosp., Chelsea); two *s* one *d*. *Educ:* Ludgrove; Eton; New Coll., Oxford (BA Mod. Hist. 1949). Enlisted Grenadier Guards, 1943; Lieut 1945; Staff Captain and Instr, Sch. of Signals, Catterick, 1946; Signals Officer, Guards Trng Bn, 1946–47; R of O 1947. Sub-editor and Leader-writer, The Times, 1949–50; Archivist, St Paul's Cathedral, 1950; joined BBC, 1950: attached Home Talks, 1951; Producer, Overseas Talks, 1951–56; Asst, European Talks, 1956–58; Dep. Editor, The Listener, 1958–61; Man. Trng Organiser, 1961–66; Asst, Secretariat, 1966–72, Sen. Asst, 1972–74; Sec., Central Music Adv. Cttee, 1966–77, 1982–83; Special Asst (Public Affairs), 1974–77; Special Asst to Alasdair Milne, when Man. Dir, BBC TV, 1977–82; Chief Asst to Sec., BBC, 1982–83; Chief Asst to Dir of Progs, BBC TV, 1983–86; Research, Richard Cawston's documentary film, Royal Family, 1969; Secretary: Sims Cttee on portrayal of violence on TV, 1979, Wyatt Cttee revision 1983; Wenham Cttee on Subscription Television, 1980–81; Cotton Cttee on Sponsorship and BBC TV, 1981; British Deleg., Internat. Art-Historical Conf., Amsterdam, 1952; Salzburg Scholar in Amer. Studies, 1956. Associate, RHistS. Trustee, Kedleston, 1988–2002. *Recreation:* looking at pictures. *Heir: s* Nicolas Robert Hugh Cary [*b* 17 April 1955; *m* 1st, 1979, Pauline Jean (marr. diss. 1991), *d* of Dr Thomas Ian Boyd; three *s*; 2nd, 1994, Lesley Anne Gilham; one *s* one *d*]. *Address:* 36 Magnolia Road, Chiswick, W4 3QW. *Clubs:* Pratt's, First Guards.
See also N. R. B. Cary.

CASALE, Roger Mark; Managing Director: Roger Casale Associates Limited, since 2006; Chairman, The Portofino Dialogues, since 2004; *b* 22 May 1960; *s* of Edward Casale and Jean Casale (*née* Robins); *m* 1997, Fernanda Miucci; two *d*. *Educ:* King's Coll. Sch., Wimbledon; Hurstpierpoint Coll., Sussex (Scholar); Brasenose Coll., Oxford (BA Hons); Bologna Centre, Johns Hopkins Univ. (MA). Head, trng inst., Germany, 1986–92; Lectr in Politics, Greenwich Univ., 1994–97. MP (Lab) Wimbledon, 1997–2005; contested (Lab) same seat, 2005. PPS, FCO, 2002–05. Mem., Select Cttee on Eur. Legislation, 1997–2002; Chm., All Party British-Italian Gp, 1998–2005; Hon. Sec., PLP Foreign Affairs Cttee, 1999–2002. Hon. Pres., London and SE Direct Aid to Kosovo. Governor, Wimbledon Sch. of Art. *Recreations:* opera, languages, European history and history of art.

CASE, Anthea Fiendley, (Mrs D. C. Case), CBE 2003; Chairman, Heritage Link, since 2003; *b* 7 Feb. 1945; *d* of late Thomas Fiendley Stones and Bess Stones (*née* Mackie); *m* 1967, David Charles Case; one *d* (and one *d* decd). *Educ:* Christ's Hospital, Hertford; St Anne's Coll., Oxford (BA). HM Treasury: Asst Principal, 1966–70; Private Sec. to Financial Sec., 1970–71; Principal, 1971–79; Asst Sec., 1980–88; Under Sec., 1988–95 (with Fiscal Policy Gp, 1993–95); Asst Dir, Budget & Public Finances Directorate, 1995; Dir, Nat. Heritage Meml Fund (Heritage Lottery Fund), 1995–2003. Member: Bd, Living East (Regl Cultural Consortium), 2003–; East of England Regl Assembly, 2003–07; NT East of England Regl Cttee, 2003–; Comr, CABE, 2004–. Trustee: Lakeland Arts Trust, 2003–; Norwich Heritage and Econ. Regeneration Trust, 2005–; Inst. for Philanthropy, 2007–. *Address:* c/o Heritage Link, 89 Albert Embankment, SE1 7TP. *T:* (020) 7820 7796.

CASE, Humphrey John; Keeper, Department of Antiquities, Ashmolean Museum, 1973–82; *b* 26 May 1918; *s* of George Reginald Case and Margaret Helen (*née* Duckett); *m* 1st, 1942, Margaret Adelia (*née* Eaton); 2nd, 1949, Jean Alison (*née* Orr); two *s*; 3rd, 1979, Jocelyn (*née* Herickx). *Educ:* Charterhouse; St John's Coll., Cambridge (MA); Inst. of Archaeology, London Univ. Served War, 1939–46. Ashmolean Museum: Asst Keeper, 1949–57; Sen. Asst Keeper, 1957–69; Dep. Keeper, Dept of Antiquities, 1969–73. Vice-Pres., Prehistoric Soc., 1969–73; has directed excavations in England, Ireland and France. FSA 1954. *Publications:* in learned jls (British and foreign): principally on neolithic in Western Europe, prehistoric metallurgy and regional archaeology. *Recreations:* drawing, reading, music, gardening. *Address:* Pitt's Cottage, 187 Thame Road, Warborough, Wallingford, Oxon OX10 7DH.

CASE, Janet Ruth; Her Honour Judge Case; a Circuit Judge, since 2001; *b* 29 June 1943; *d* of James and Cathleen Simpson; *m* 1965, Jeremy David Michael Case (marr. diss. 1982); one *s* one *d*. *Educ:* Univ. of Durham (LLB 1965). Called to the Bar, Inner Temple, 1975; barrister, Wales and Chester Circuit, 1975–2001; Chm., Med. Appeals Tribunals, 1988–96; an Asst Recorder, 1992–95; a Recorder, 1995–2001; Designated Family Judge for Newport, S Wales, 2001–05. *Recreations:* gardening, opera, travel. *Address:* Warrington Combined Court, Legh Street, Warrington WA1 1UR. *Club:* Lansdowne.

CASE, Richard Ian, CBE 2002; FREng, FRAeS; DL; Managing Director, AgustaWestland and Chairman, Westland Helicopters, 2001–04; consultant to aerospace industry, since 2005; *b* 14 June 1945; *m* 1975, Denise Margaret Mills; one *s* one *d*. *Educ:* Cranfield Inst. of Technology (MSc Aircraft Propulsion). FRAeS 1985; FREng (FEng 1993). Technical Manager, Arab British Helicopters, Egypt, 1978–82; Westland Helicopters Ltd: Chief Designer, 1982–85; Engrg Dir, 1985–88; EH101 Project Dir and Engrg Dir, 1988–92; Man. Dir, 1992–95; Chief Exec., GKN Westland Helicopters Ltd, 1995–2001. Chm., William Fairey Engineering Ltd, 2007–; non-exec. Dir, FKI plc, 2006–. DL Somerset, 2005. RAeS Gold Medal, 1998. Cavaliere dell 'Ordine al Merito (Italy), 1995. *Recreations:* golf, opera.

CASE, Stephen M.; Chairman and Chief Executive Officer; Revolution LLC, since 2005; *b* Honolulu, 21 Aug. 1958; *s* of Dan and Carol Case; *m* 1st, 1985, Joanne (marr. diss.); three *d*; 2nd, Jean; two *c*. *Educ:* Punahou Sch., Honolulu; Williams Coll., Mass. (BA Pol Sci. 1980). Marketing Dept, Procter & Gamble, 1980–82; Manager, new pizza develt, Pizza Hut Div., PepsiCo, 1982–83; joined Control Video Corp., 1983, as mktg asst; co. renamed Quantum Computer Services, 1985, and became America Online, (AOL), 1991; CEO, 1991–2001, and Chm., 1995–2001, when merged with Time Warner; Chm., Time Warner Inc., 2001–03; Chm., Exclusive Resorts, 2004–07. Founder and Chm., Case Foundation, 1997–. *Address:* Case Foundation, 1717 Rhode Island Avenue NW, Washington, DC 20036, USA.

CASEBOURNE, Michael Victor, CEng, FICE, FASCE; private consultant; Project Director, ACTJV (Alstom and Carillion) Channel Tunnel Rail Link, since 2004; *b* 7 Oct. 1945; *s* of Eric Thomas Casebourne and Marjorie May Casebourne (*née* Chapman); *m* 1972, Margaret Dunlop (*d* 2002); one *s* one *d*. *Educ:* Harrow Co. Grammar Sch.; Nottingham Univ. (BSc). CEng 1967; FICE 1984. With Costain Civil Engrg, 1967–73; Trafalgar House Construction, 1973–90 (Dir, 1984–90); Managing Director: Wimpey Engrg & Construction UK, 1990–96; GT Railway Maintenance, 1996–99; Dir, Railtrack, 2001–02; Project Dir, Nottingham Tram, 2003–04. Chief Exec. and Sec., ICE, 1999–2001. FASCE. *Recreations:* sailing, motor boating. *Address:* The Boundary, Ballards Farm Road, S Croydon CR2 7JA.

CASEMENT, David John; QC 2008; a Recorder, since 2005; *b* Belfast, 19 Nov. 1969; *s* of late John Casement and of Helena Casement; *m* 1994, Ruth Ann Hadden; two *d*. *Educ:* Methodist Coll., Belfast; St Hugh's Coll., Oxford (MA). Called to the Bar, Middle Temple, 1992 (Astbury Schol.); in practice as barrister specialising in chancery and commercial litigation. Accredited Mediator. Pres., Oxford Univ. Law Soc., 1990. Mem., Exec. Bd, Anglo-Irish Encounter, 2000–06. *Address:* Exchange Chambers, 7 Ralli Courts, W Riverside, Manchester M3 5FT. *T:* (0161) 833 2722; Serle Court, 6 New Square, Lincoln's Inn, WC2A 3QS. *T:* (020) 7242 6105.

CASEY, Aprampar Apar Jot Kaur, (Joti); *see* Bopa Rai, A. A. J. K.

CASEY, Ben; *see* Casey, R. B.

CASEY, Derek Grant; international consultant; Chairman, World Leisure Organisation, since 2004 (Executive Member, since 2002); *b* 19 Feb. 1950; *s* of Andrew Casey and Jean Grant. *Educ:* St Aloysius' Coll., Glasgow; Univ. of Glasgow (MA Hons). Dir of Ops, Scottish Sports Council, 1979–88; GB Sports Council: Dir of Nat. Services, 1988–93; Chief Exec., 1993–96; Chief Exec., English Sports Council, subseq. Sport England, 1997–2001. Chairman: Cttee for Development of Sport, Council of Europe, 1993–95; UK Youth, 2003–. Bid Dir for Glasgow, 2014 Commonwealth Games, 2006–07; Interim Chief Exec., Glasgow 2014 Commonwealth Games, 2007–. Hon. Res. Fellow, Univ. of Stirling, 2003–. Hon. DSc Southampton, 1996. *Publications:* contribs on sport, recreation and physical activity, to jls and periodicals. *Recreations:* walking, theatre, American literature. *Address:* 42/5 Barnton Park Avenue, Edinburgh EH4 6EY.

CASEY, Most Rev. Eamonn, DD; RC Bishop of Galway and Kilmacduagh, 1976–92; Apostolic Administrator of Kilfenora, 1976–92; *b* Firies, Co. Kerry, 23 April 1927; *s* of late John Casey and late Helena (*née* Shanahan). *Educ:* St Munchin's Coll., Limerick; St

Patrick's Coll., Maynooth. LPh 1946; BA 1947. Priest, 1951; Curate, St John's Cath., Limerick, 1951–60; Chaplain to Irish in Slough, 1960–63; set up social framework to re-establish people into new environment; started social welfare scheme; set up lodgings bureau and savings scheme; invited by Cardinal Heenan to place Catholic Housing Aid Soc. on national basis; founded Family Housing Assoc., 1964; Dir, British Council of Churches Housing Trust; Trustee, Housing the Homeless Central Fund; Founder-Trustee of Shelter (Chm. 1968); Mem. Council, Nat. Fedn of Housing Socs; Founder Mem., Marian Employment Agency; Founder Trustee, Shelter Housing Aid Soc., 1963–69; Bishop of Kerry, 1969–76. Missionary work, Ecuador, 1992–98. Exec. Chm., Trocaire, 1973–92; Mem. Bd, Siamsa Tire, Nat. Folk Th. of Ireland. Launched Meitheal, 1982; estab. Galway Adult Educn Centre, 1985, Galway Family Guidance Inst., 1986. Chm., Nat. Youth Resource Gp, 1979–86. Member: Commn for Social Welfare, 1971–74; Maynooth Coll. Exec. Council, 1974–84; Episcopal Commn for Univs, 1976–92; Governing Body, University Coll., Galway, 1976–92. *Publications:* (with Adam Ferguson) A Home of Your Own; Housing—A Parish Solution; contribs to journals, etc. *Recreations:* music, theatre, concerts, films when time, conversation, motoring. *Address:* Priest's House, Shanaglish, Gort, Co. Galway, Ireland.

CASEY, Gavin Frank, FCA; Chairman: EDM Group Ltd, since 2004; Integrated Dental Holdings Ltd, since 2006; Credit Solutions Holdings Ltd, since 2006; *b* 18 Oct. 1946; *s* of Frank Frederick Casey and Diana Casey; *m* 1970, Lesley Riding; two *s* one *d*. Chartered Accountant, 1970; Harmood Banner & Co., 1965–70; Coopers & Lybrand, 1970–71; County Bank, later County NatWest, 1972–89; Smith New Court, later Merrill Lynch International, 1989–96; Chief Exec., London Stock Exchange plc, 1996–2000; Dep. Chm., Corporate Finance Adv. Bd, PricewaterhouseCoopers, 2001–05. Chairman: Tragus Hldgs Ltd, 2002–05; Knowledge Technology Solutions plc, 2003–05; Corporate Synergy plc, 2003–06; Director: Kinetic Inf. Systems Services Ltd, 2001–03; Mosaic Software Hldgs Ltd, 2002–03; Lawrence plc, 2002–07; Tellings Golden Miller Gp plc, 2003–05; Blue Oar (formerly Abingdon Capital, then Corporate Synergy Gp) plc, 2004–; VTB Bank Europe plc (formerly Moscow Narodny Bank Ltd), 2005–07; Baronsmead AiM VCT plc, 2006–; Member Advisory Board: Strathdon Investments Ltd, 2001–04; Warnborough Asset Mgt, 2002–04; Sen. Advr, The Policy Partnership Ltd, 2005–. Chm. of Treasurers, USPG, 1991–96. *Recreations:* theatre, horse racing. *Clubs:* Turf, City of London.

CASEY, Rt Hon. Sir Maurice (Eugene), Kt 1991; PC 1986; Judge of Court of Appeal of New Zealand, 1986–95; Judge of the Court of Appeal: Samoa and Cook Islands, 1995–2003; Fiji, 1995–2001; Niue, 1996–2001; Solomon Islands, 1996–98; *b* 28 Aug. 1923; *s* of Eugene Casey and Beatrice (*née* Nolan); *m* 1948, Stella Katherine Wright (Dame Stella Casey, DBE; she *d* 2000); three *s* six *d*. *Educ:* St Patrick's Coll., Wellington; Victoria Univ. (LLM Hons). Served War, Naval Officer, 1943–45. Barrister and Solicitor, 1946; Vice Pres., Auckland Dist Law Soc., 1974; Judge, Supreme (later High) Court, 1974. Chm., Penal Policy Review Cttee, 1981. Hon. CF (Fiji), 2003; Hon. CS (Samoa), 2005. *Publications:* Hire Purchase Law in New Zealand, 1961; Garrow and Casey's Principles of the Law of Evidence, 8th edn 1996; (contrib.) Laws of New Zealand, 1999. *Address:* 3A/5 The Promenade, Takapuna, Auckland, New Zealand. *T:* (9) 4864547. *Club:* Northern (Auckland).

CASEY, Michael Bernard; Chairman, Michael Casey & Associates, 1993–2000; *b* 1 Sept. 1928; *s* of late Joseph Bernard Casey, OBE, and Dorothy (*née* Love); *m*; two *s* two *d*. *Educ:* Colwyn Bay Grammar Sch.; LSE (Scholar in Laws, 1952; LLB 1954). RAF, 1947–49. Principal, MAFF, 1961; Office of the Minister for Science, 1963–64; Asst Sec., DEA, 1967; DTI (later Dept of Prices and Consumer Protection), 1970; Under Sec., DoI, 1975–77; a Dep. Chm. and Chief Exec., British Shipbuilders, 1977–80; Chm. and Man. Dir, Mather & Platt, 1980–81; Chm., Sallingbury Casey Ltd, later Rowland Sallingbury Casey, 1982–92. *Recreations:* golf, chess, bridge. *Address:* Correos Apartado 89, San Pedro de Alcantara, Málaga, Spain. *T:* (95) 2799029. *Club:* Reform.

CASEY, Michael Vince, OBE 1990; BSc(Eng); FREng, FIMechE; Chief Engineer, Channel Tunnel Rail Link, British Rail, 1989–90; *b* 25 May 1927; *s* of Charles John Casey and May Louise Casey; *m* 1954, Elinor Jane (*née* Harris) (*d* 1987); two *s* two *d*. *Educ:* Glossop Grammar Sch.; The College, Swindon. BSc(Eng) Hons London. Premium Apprentice, GWR Locomotive Works, Swindon, 1944–49; Univ. of London External Degree Course, 1949–52; British Rail Western Region: Locomotive Testing and Experimental Office, Swindon, 1952–58; Supplies and Contracts Dept, Swindon, 1958–61; Chief Mechanical and Electrical Engr's Dept, Paddington, 1961–63; Area Maintenance Engr, Old Oak Common, 1963–66; Chief Mech. and Elec. Engr's Dept, Paddington, 1966–71; Chief Mech. and Elec. Engineer: Scottish Region, Glasgow, 1971–76; Eastern Region, York, 1976–78; Engrg Dir, British Rail Engrg Ltd, 1978–82; Dir, Mechanical and Electrical Engrg, BRB, 1982–87; Project Dir (BR Engrg), 1987–89. FREng (FEng 1985). *Recreations:* gardening, philately.

CASEY, Dr Raymond, FRS 1970; retired; Senior Principal Scientific Officer (Special Merit), Institute of Geological Sciences, London, 1964–79; *b* 10 Oct. 1917; *s* of Samuel Gardiner Casey and Gladys Violet Helen Casey (*née* Garrett); *m* 1943, Norah Kathleen Pakeman (*d* 1974); two *s*. *Educ:* St Mary's, Folkestone; Univ. of Reading. PhD 1958; DSc 1963. Geological Survey and Museum: Asst 1939; Asst Exper. Officer 1946; Exper. Officer 1949; Sen. Geologist 1957; Principal Geologist 1960. *Publications:* A Monograph of the Ammonoidea of the Lower Greensand, 1960–80; (ed, with P. F. Rawson) The Boreal Lower Cretaceous, 1973; numerous articles on Mesozoic palaeontology and stratigraphy in scientific press. *Recreation:* research into early Russian postal and military history (Past Pres., British Soc. of Russian Philately). *Address:* 38 Reed Avenue, Orpington, Kent BR6 9RX. *T:* (01689) 851728.

CASEY, Prof. Robert Bernard, (Ben); Co-Founder and Executive Creative Director, Chase Creative Consultants Ltd, since 1986; Professor (part-time) of Visual Communication, University of Central Lancashire, since 1999; *b* 19 Oct. 1949; *s* of Thomas and Marie Casey; partner, Fiona Candy. *Educ:* Blackpool Coll. of Art. MCSD 1978. Typographer, Horniblow Cox-Freeman, London, 1969–72; Berkoff Associates, London, 1972–73; Designer: Conways, London, 1973–74; G&H, Manchester, 1974–77; Lecturer: Carlisle Coll. of Art, and Blackburn Coll. of Art, 1977–78; Harris Coll., Preston, 1978–83; Hd, Dept of Design, Lancs Poly., 1983–85; Sen. Lectr, Sch. of Communication Arts, London, 1985–86. Designer, Preston North End's Deepdale Stadium, 1995. Mem., Design Skills Panel, Design Council, 2005–. External Moderator: Staffs Univ., 1989–92; Manchester Metropolitan Univ., 1990–93 and 2002–05; Bretton Hall Coll., 1998–2001; Univ. of Northumbria, 2006–. Design and Art Directors Association: Chm., Educn Gp, 1991–95; Mem., Exec. Cttee, 1991–95; Chm., D&AD North, 2006–. *Publication:* How a Graphic Design Consultancy Thinks it Thinks, 1993. *Recreation:* watching Preston North End. *Address:* Woodbine Cottage, Dilworth Bottoms, Longridge, Preston PR3 2ZP; *e-mail:* ben.casey@thechase.co.uk.

CASH, Prof. John David, CBE 1998; PhD; FRCP, FRCPE, FRCPath, FRCSE, FRCPGlas; National Medical and Scientific Director, Scottish National Blood Transfusion Service, 1988–97; *b* 3 April 1936; *s* of John Henry Cash and May Annie Cash (*née* Taylor); *m* 1962, Angela Mary Thomson; one *s* one *d*. *Educ:* Ashville College, Harrogate; Edinburgh Univ. (BSc 1959, MB ChB 1961, PhD 1967). FRCPE 1970; FRCPath 1986; FRCPGlas 1994; FRCSE 1995; FRCP 1997. Regional Transfusion Centre Dir, Edinburgh and SE Scotland, 1974–79; Nat. Med. Dir, Scottish Nat. Blood Transfusion Service, 1979–88. Pres., RCPE, 1994–97 (Vice-Pres., 1992–94); Pres., British Blood Transfusion Soc., 1997–99. Chm., Govt Inquiry into Nat. Blood Authy, 1997–98; Member: Nat. Biol Standards Bd, 1997–2003; Internat. Review Panel, Irish Blood Transfusion Service, 2002. Hon. Prof., Edinburgh Univ., 1986. Governor, Fettes Coll., Edinburgh, 1988–2002. *Publication:* Progress in Transfusion Medicine, 1988. *Recreations:* fishing, gardening. *Address:* 1 Otterburn Park, Edinburgh EH14 1JX.

CASH, William Nigel Paul; MP (C) Stone, since 1997 (Stafford, 1984–97); *b* 10 May 1940; *s* of Paul Trevor Cash, MC (killed in action Normandy, July 13, 1944) and Moyra Roberts (*née* Morrison); *m* 1965, Bridget Mary Lee; two *s* one *d*. *Educ:* Stonyhurst Coll.; Lincoln Coll., Oxford (MA History). Qualified as Solicitor, 1967; William Cash & Co. (constitutional and administrative lawyer), 1979–. Shadow Attorney-General, 2001–03; Shadow Sec. of State for Constitutional Affairs, 2003. Mem., Select Cttee on European Legislation, 1985–; Chairman: Cons. Backbench Cttee on European Affairs, 1989–91; All Party Cttee on E Africa, (Uganda), 1988–; All Party Gp, Jubilee 2000, 1997–2003; All Party Cttee, Malaysia, 2006–; All Party Cttee, Sanitation and Water, 2007–; Jt Chm., All Party Jazz Gp, 1991–2000. Founder, and Chm., European Foundn, 1993–. Vice Pres., Cons. Small Business Bureau, 1986–2000. *Publications:* Against a Federal Europe—The Battle for Britain, 1991; Europe: the crunch, 1992. *Recreations:* history, cricket, jazz. *Address:* Upton Cressett Hall, near Bridgnorth, Shropshire WV16 6UH. *T:* (01746) 714307. *Clubs:* Garrick, Carlton, Beefsteak; Vincent's (Oxford).

CASHEL AND EMLY, Archbishop of, (RC), since 1988; **Most Rev. Dermot Clifford,** DD; *b* 25 Jan. 1939. *Educ:* St Brendan's Coll., Killarney, Co. Kerry; St Patrick's Coll., Maynooth (BSc 1960); Irish Coll., Rome; Lateran Coll., Rome (STL 1964); NUI (HDipE 1966); LSE (MSc 1974); Loughborough (PhD 1989). Ordained priest, Rome, 1964; Dean of Studies, St Brendan's Coll., Killarney, 1964–72; Diocesan Sec., Kerry, 1974–86; Lectr, Univ. Coll., Cork, 1975–81; Chaplain, St Mary of the Angels Home for Handicapped Children, Beaufort, Co. Kerry, 1976–86; ordained Archbishop, Thurles, 1986; Coadjutor Archbishop of Cashel and Emly, 1986–88. Chm., Council for R&D of Irish Episcopal Commn, 1991–. Mem. Governing Body, NUI, Cork, 2000–. Trustee: Mary Immaculate Teachers' Trng Coll., Limerick, 1987–; Bothar, Third World Aid Orgn, 1991–. Patron, Gaelic Athletic Assoc., 1989–. *Publication:* The Social Costs and Rewards of Caring, 1990. *Recreations:* reading, walking, sport. *Address:* Archbishop's House, Thurles, Co. Tipperary, Ireland. *T:* (504) 21512, *Fax:* (504) 22680.

CASHEL AND OSSORY, Bishop of, since 2006; **Rt Rev. Michael Andrew James Burrows;** *m* Claire; three *s* one *d*. *Educ:* Wesley Coll., Dublin; Trinity Coll. Dublin (MLitt). Ordained, 1987; Curate, Douglas Union with Frankfield, Cork; Dean of Residence, TCD, and Minor Canon, St Patrick's Cathedral, Dublin, 1991–94; Incumbent, Bandon Union, 1994–2002; Canon, Cork and Cloyne Cathedrals, 1996; Dean of Cork and Incumbent, St Fin Barre's Union, 2002–06. *Address:* The Bishop's House, Troysgate, Kilkenny, Co. Kilkenny, Republic of Ireland.

CASHMAN, John Prescott; Under-Secretary, Department of Health (formerly of Health and Social Security), 1973–88; *b* 19 May 1930; *s* of late John Patrick Cashman and late Mary Cashman (*née* Prescott). *Educ:* Balliol Coll., Oxford (MA (English Lang. and Lit.)). Army (Intell. Corps), 1948–49. Entered Min. of Health, 1951; Principal 1957; Private Sec. to Minister, 1962–65; Asst Sec. 1965; Nuffield Foundn Trav. Fellow, 1968–69; Private Sec. to Sec. of State, 1969. Trustee, Macfarlane Trust, 1989–97; Dir, Bd, Hospital Saving Assoc., 1999–2000 (Mem. Exec. Council, 1989–99). *Address:* 3 Paul Gardens, Croydon, Surrey CR0 5QL. *T:* (020) 8681 6578.

CASHMAN, Michael Maurice; Member (Lab) West Midlands Region, European Parliament, since 1999; *b* 17 Dec. 1950; *s* of John Cashman and Mary Cashman (*née* Clayton); partner, Paul Cottingham. *Educ:* St Mary's and St Joseph's Primary Sch.; Cardinal Griffin Secondary Modern Sch., London; Gladys Dare's Sch., Surrey; Borlands Tutorial, London. Actor, director and playwright, 1963–99; work includes: actor: *stage:* Oliver, Albery, 1963; Bent, RNT, 1990, transf. Garrick; Noises Off, Mobil Touring Theatre, nat. tour, 1995; Merchant of Venice, and Gypsy, W Yorks Playhouse, 1996; The Tempest, internat. tour, 1997; *television:* Eastenders, 1986–89; director: Kiss of the Spiderwoman, New Victoria Th., Newcastle-under-Lyme, 1998; playwright: Before your very Eyes; Bricks 'n' Mortar. Mem. Council and Hon. Treas., Equity, 1994–98; Mem., Labour Party NEC, 1998–2000 and 2001–. Founding Chm., Stonewall Gp, 1988–96. FRSA 1996. Hon. Dr Staffordshire, 2007. Special Service Award, Amer. Assoc. Physicians for Human Rights and Gay Med. Assoc., 1988; MEP of the Year Award, Justice and Human Rights, The House Mag., 2007. *Recreations:* travel, writing, photography, theatre. *Address:* West Midlands Labour European Office, Terry Duffy House, Thomas Street, West Bromwich B70 6NT. *T:* (0121) 569 1923; *e-mail:* michael.cashman@europarl.europa.eu.

CASHMORE, Prof. Roger John, CMG 2004; DPhil; FRS 1998; FInstP; Principal, Brasenose College, Oxford, since 2002; *b* 22 Aug. 1944; *e s* of C. J. C. and E. M. Cashmore; *m* 1971, Elizabeth Ann, *d* of Rev. S. J. C. Lindsay; one *s*. *Educ:* Dudley Grammar Sch.; St John's Coll., Cambridge (schol.; BA 1965; MA); Balliol Coll., Oxford (DPhil 1969). FInstP 1985. Weir Jun. Res. Fellow, University Coll., Oxford, 1967–69; 1851 Res. Fellow, 1968; Res. Associate, Stanford Linear Accelerator Centre, Calif, 1969–74; Oxford University: Res. Officer, 1974–79; Lectr, Christ Church, 1976–78; Fellow, Balliol Coll., 1979–2002 (Emeritus Fellow, 2003); Sen. Res. Fellow, Merton Coll., 1977–79; Tutor, Balliol Coll., and Univ. Lectr in Physics, 1979–90; Reader in Experimental Physics, 1990–91; Prof. of Experimental Physics, 1991–2003; Chm. of Physics, 1996–98; Res. Dir for Collider Progs, 1999–2003; Dep. Dir Gen., 2002–03, CERN. SERC Sen. Res. Fellow, 1982–87; Vis. Prof., Vrije Univ., Brussels, 1982; Guest Scientist, Fermilab, Chicago, 1986. Chairman: Sci. Cttee, Nat. Lab. of San Grasso, Italy, 2004–; Nuclear Res. Adv. Council, 2005–; Member: Sci. Adv. Cttee, Nat. Inst. for Nuclear Physics and High Energy Physics, Amsterdam, 2005–; policy and prog. cttees, CERN, Deutsches Electronen-Synchrotron, Hamburg, and SERC. Abdus Salam Meml Lect., Islamabad, 2001. Gov., Ludlow Coll., 1995–98. Trustee, Tanner Foundn, 2002–. MAE 1992. FRSA 1996. Hon. Doctor Jt Inst. for Nuclear Res., Dubna, 2004. C.V. Boys Prize, Inst. of Physics, 1983; Humboldt Res. Award, Alexander Von Humboldt Stiftung, 1995. *Publications:* contrib. Nuclear Physics, Physics Letters, Phys. Rev., Phys. Rev. Letters. *Recreations:* sports, wine. *Address:* Brasenose College, Oxford OX1 4AJ.

CASIDA, Prof. John Edward, PhD; William Muriece Hoskins Professor of Chemical and Molecular Entomology, University of California at Berkeley, since 1996; *b* 22 Dec. 1929; *s* of Lester Earl Casida and Ruth Casida (*née* Barnes); *m* 1956, Katherine Faustine Monson; two *s*. *Educ:* Univ. of Wisconsin (BS 1951; MS 1952; PhD 1954). Served USAF, 1953. University of Wisconsin: Res. Asst, 1951–53; Mem. Faculty, 1954–63; Prof. of

Entomology, 1959–63; University of California at Berkeley: Prof. of Entomology, 1964–; Dir, Envmtl Chemistry and Toxicology Lab., 1964–; Faculty Res. Lectr, 1998. Schol.-in-Res., Bellagio Study and Conf. Centre, Rockefeller Foundn, Lake Como, 1978; Sterling B. Hendricks Lectr, US Dept of Agric., and ACS, 1992–; Lectr, Third World Acad. of Sci., Univ. of Buenos Aires, 1997 (DUniv 1997). Mem., US Nat. Acad. of Sci., 1991; Foreign Mem., Royal Soc., 1998; Mem., Eur. Acad. of Sci., 2004. Hon. Mem., Pesticide Sci. Soc., Japan, 2005. Wolf Prize in Agriculture, 1993; Founder's Award, Soc. Envmt Toxicology and Chemistry, 1994; Kôrô-sho Prize, Pesticide Sci. Soc., Japan, 1995. *Address:* (office) University of California, Department of Environmental Science Policy Management, Wellman Hall, Berkeley, CA 94720–3112, USA.

CASKEN, Prof. John, DMus; composer; Professor of Music, University of Manchester, 1992–2008, now Emeritus; *b* 15 July 1949. *Educ:* Birmingham Univ. (BMus, MA); DMus Durham, 1992. FRNCM 1996. Polish Govt Scholarship, Warsaw, 1971–72. Lectr, Birmingham Univ., 1973–79; Res. Fellow, Huddersfield Poly., 1980–81; Lectr, Durham Univ., 1981–92. Northern Electric Performing Arts Award, 1990. *Compositions include: orchestral:* Tableaux des Trois Ages, 1977; Masque, 1982; Orion over Farne, 1984; Maharal Dreaming, 1989; Cello Concerto, 1991; Still Mine (baritone and orch.), 1992 (Prix de Composition Musicale, Prince Pierre de Monaco, 1993); Darting the Skiff, 1993; Violin Concerto, 1995; Sortilège, 1996; Distant Variations (saxophone quartet and wind orch.), 1997; Symphony (Broken Consort), 2004; Rest-ringing (string quartet and orch.), 2005; Farness - three poems of Carol Ann Duffy (soprano, solo viola and chamber orch.), 2006; Concerto for Orchestra, 2007; *ensemble and instrumental:* Amarantos, 1978; Firewhirl (soprano and ensemble), 1980; String Quartet No 1, 1982; Vaganza, 1985; Salamandra, 1986; Piano Quartet, 1990; String Quartet No 2, 1994; Infanta Marina, 1994; Après un silence, 1998; The Haunting Bough (solo piano), 1999; Nearly Distant (saxophone quartet), 2000; Piano Trio, 2002; Blue Medusa (bassoon and piano), 2003; *vocal and choral:* Ia Orana Gauguin, 1978; To Fields We Do Not Know, 1984; Three Choral Pieces, 1990–93; Sharp Thorne, 1992; To the Lovers' Well, 2001; The Dream of the Rood, 2008; *opera:* Golem, 1988 (first Britten Award, 1990; Gramophone Award for best contemp. recording, 1991); God's Liar, 2000; *electronic:* A Belle Pavine, 1980; Piper's Linn, 1984; Soul Catcher, 1988, 2004. *Address:* c/o Department of Music, University of Manchester, Oxford Road, Manchester M13 9PL.

CASLEY, Henry Roberts; non-executive Director, Scottish and Southern Energy plc, 1998–2005; *s* of Benjamin Rowe Casley and May Casley; *m* 1960, Sheila Laity; one *s* one *d.* MCIM. Eastern Electricity: Energy Mkting Manager, 1975–78; Supplies Manager, 1978–82; Mkting Dir, 1982–86; Southern Electric plc: Dep. Chm., 1986–89; Man. Dir, 1989–93; Chief Exec., 1993–96; non-exec. Dir, 1996–98. *Recreations:* sport, gardening. *Club:* Phyllis Court (Henley-on-Thames).

CASPI, Prof. Avshalom, PhD; FBA 2006; Edward M. Arnett Professor of Psychology and Neuroscience, Duke University, since 2008; *m* 1990, Prof. Terrie Edith Moffitt, *qv.* *Educ:* Univ. of Calif, Santa Cruz; Cornell Univ. (MA 1983; PhD 1986). Harvard Univ., 1986–89; joined Univ. of Wisconsin, 1989, Prof. of Psychol. until 2007; Prof. of Personality Develt, Inst. of Psychiatry, KCL, 1997–2007; Prof., Dept of Psychol. and Neurosci., Duke Univ., 2007–08. Mem. Council, Internat. Soc. for Study of Behavioural Develt, 2000–06. FMedSci 2002. *Publications:* (jtly) Persons in Context; (jtly) Sex Differences in Antisocial Behaviour, 2001; (jtly) Paths to Successful Development, 2002; (jtly) Causes of Conduct Disorder and Juvenile Delinquency, 2003; articles in learned jls. *Address:* Department of Psychology and Neuroscience, Duke University, Grey House, 2020 Main Street, Durham, NC 27708, USA.

CASS, Sir Geoffrey (Arthur), Kt 1992; MA; Chairman: Royal Shakespeare Company, 1985–2000; Royal Shakespeare Theatre Trust, since 1983; President, The Tennis Foundation (formerly British Tennis Foundation), since 2007 (Chairman, 2003–07); President, and Chairman of the Council, Lawn Tennis Association, 1997–99; Chief Executive, Cambridge University Press, 1972–92; Fellow of Clare Hall, Cambridge, since 1979; *b* 11 Aug. 1932; *o c* of late Arthur Cass and Jessie Cass (*née* Simpson), Darlington and Oxford; *m* 1957, Olwen Mary, JP, DL, *o c* of late William Leslie Richards and of Edith Louisa Richards, Llanelli and Brecon; four *d.* *Educ:* Queen Elizabeth Grammar Sch., Darlington (Head of Sch.); Jesus Coll., Nuffield Coll., and Dept of Social and Admin. Studies, Oxford Univ. (BA 1954; MA 1958; Hon. Fellow, Jesus Coll., 1998); MA Cantab, 1972. FInstD 1968; FIWM, FIIM 1979; CCMI (CBIM 1980). Commnd RAFVR, fighter control, 1954; served RAF, 1958–60: Air Min. Directorate of Work Study; Pilot Officer, 1958; Flying Officer, 1960. Consultant: PA Management Consultants Ltd, 1960–65; British Communications Corp., and Controls and Communications Ltd, 1965; Dir, Controls and Communications Ltd, 1966–69; Managing Director, George Allen and Unwin Ltd, 1967–71; Cambridge University Press: Sec., Press Syndicate, 1974–92; Univ. Printer, 1982–83, 1991–92; Consultant, 1992–; Director: Weidenfeld (Publishers) Ltd, 1972–74; Chicago Univ. Press (UK), 1971–86; Mem., Jesus Coll., Cambridge, 1972–. Member: Univ. of Cambridge Cttee of Management of Fenner's (and Exec. Cttee), 1976–; Univ. of Cambridge Careers Service Syndicate (formerly Appts Bd), 1977–2002 (Exec. Cttee, 1982–2002); Governing Syndicate, Fitzwilliam Mus., Cambridge, 1977–78; Chm., Univ. of Cambridge Sports Centre Appeal, 2001–; Chm. Governors, Perse Sch. for Girls, Cambridge, 1978–88 (Governor, 1977–); Trustee, Univ. of Cambridge Foundn, 1998– (Chm., Audit Cttee, 2006–); Chm., Univ. of Cambridge ADC Theatre Foundn, 2008– (Chm., Theatre Appeal, 2000–07). Founder Mem. Council, Royal Shakespeare Theatre Trust, 1967–; Gov., 1975–, Dep. Pres. of Govs, 2000–, RSC (Mem., Council, 1975–2000; Mem., 1976–2000, Chm. 1982–2000, Exec. Cttee, Council); Trustee and Guardian, Shakespeare Birthplace Trust, 1982– (Life Trustee, 1994); Founder Mem., Inigo Productions, 1996. Director: Newcastle Theatre Royal Trust, 1984–89; American Friends of the Royal Shakespeare Theatre, 1985–2000; Method & Madness (formerly Cambridge Theatre Co.), 1986–95; Theatres Trust, 1991–2000; Marc Sinden Productions, 2001–02; The All England LTC (Wimbledon) Ltd, 1997–2000; The All England Lawn Tennis Ground PLC, 1997–2000. Pres., Macmillan Cancer Support, Cambridgeshire (formerly Macmillan Cancer Relief Cambs and Peterborough Project), 1998–. Cambridgeshire LTA: Mem. Exec., 1974–84; Chm., F and GP Cttee 1982–84; Captain 1974–78; Pres., 1980–82; Hon. Life Vice-Pres., 1982–; The Lawn Tennis Association of GB: Dep. Pres., 1994–96; Member: Council, 1976–; Management Bd, 1985–90, 1993–2000; Nat. Trng and Internat. Match Cttee (Davis Cup, Fedn Cup, Wightman Cup, etc), 1982–90, 1992–93 (Chm., 1985–90); Internat. Events Cttee, 1991–93; Chm., Nat. Ranking Cttee, 1990–99; Wimbledon Championships: Member: Cttee of Management, 1990–2002; Jt Finance Bd, 1989–93; Jt Finance Cttee, 1993–2002 (Chm., 1997–99); British Jun. Championships Cttee of Management, 1983–90 (Chm., 1985–90); Nat. Championships Cttee of Management, 1988–89; Rules and Internat. Cttee, 1980–81; Re-orgn Wkg Party, 1984–85; Chm., Reconstruction Wkg Gp, 1994–99. Tennis singles champion: Durham County, 1951; Cambridgeshire, 1976; Oxford University: tennis Blue, 1953, 1954, 1955 (Sec., 1955); badminton, 1951, 1952 (Captain, 1952); Pres., Cambridge Univ. Lawn Tennis Club, 2007– (Chm., 1977–2007; Hon. Cambridge tennis Blue, 1980); Chm., Cambridge Univ. Cricket and Athletic Club, 2003–; played in Wimbledon Championships, 1954, 1955, 1956, 1959; played in inter-county lawn tennis championships for Durham County, then for Cambridgeshire, 1952–82; represented RAF, 1958–59; Brit. Veterans (over 45) singles champion, Wimbledon, 1978; Mem., Brit. Veterans' Internat. Dubler Cup Team, Barcelona, 1978, Milano Marittima, 1979 (Captain). Patron: Cambridge Rowing Trust, 2001–; Theatre Royal Bury St Edmunds Restoration Appeal Cttee, 2001–. FRSA 1991. Chevalier, Ordre des Arts et des Lettres (France), 1982. *Recreations:* lawn tennis, theatre. *Address:* Middlefield, Huntingdon Road, Girton, Cambridge CB3 0LH. *Clubs:* Garrick, Institute of Directors, All England Lawn Tennis and Croquet (Hon.), Queen's (Hon.), International Lawn Tennis of GB, The 45 (Hon.), Veterans' Lawn Tennis of GB; Hawks (Hon.) (Cambridge); Cambridge University Lawn Tennis; West Hants Lawn Tennis (Hon.).

CASS, John, QPM 1979; National Co-ordinator of Regional Crime Squads, 1981–84; Security Consultant; *b* 24 June 1925; *m* 1948, Dilys Margaret Hughes, SRN; three *d.* *Educ:* Nelson Sch., Wigton, Cumbria; UCW, Lampeter (DipTh 1997; BA Hons (Theol.) 1999). Served no 40 RM Commando, 1944–45. Joined Metropolitan Police, 1946; Comdt, Detective Training Sch., Hendon, 1974; Commander: CID, New Scotland Yard, 1975; Complaints Bureau, 1978; Serious Crime Squads, New Scotland Yard, 1980. UK Rep., Interpol Conf. on crime prediction, Paris, 1976. Student in Criminology, Cambridge Univ., 1966. Adviser, Police Staff Coll., on multi-Force major investigations, 1982–83; Chief Investigator, War Crimes Inquiry, Home Office, 1988–89. Mem., British Acad. of Forensic Scis, 1965. Member: Association of Chief Police Officers; Metropolitan Police Commanders' Assoc.; Internat. Police Assoc. Lay preacher; Asst Lay Chaplain, W Wales Hosp. Mem., Lampeter Soc. Freeman, City of London, 1979. *Recreations:* Lakeland, walking, wild life; and Janet (BA), Anne (BDS), Sarah (LLB), James (MB BS, MRCP), Gwilym, Bryn, Elizabeth, Ieuan Jack, Catherine Olivia and Joshua James. *Address:* Bryn Eryl, Peniel, Carmarthenshire SA32 7HT. *T:* (01267) 236948, (020) 8521 1580. *Club:* Special Forces.

CASS, Wilfred, CBE 2006; Co-Founder, Cass Sculpture Foundation, 1992; *b* Berlin, 11 Nov. 1924; *s* of Hans and Edith Cassirer; *m* 1983, Jeannette Futter; one *s* one *d.* *Educ:* Regent St Poly., London (HND Communication Technol. 1951). With Pye Ltd, Cambridge, 1951–57; Joint Founder (with brother, Eric): and Dep. Chm., Cass Electronics Ltd, 1955–85; Cass McLaren Ltd (Consultancy), 1959; Founder, and Man. Dir, 1965–71, non-exec. Dir, 1971–75, Gunson Sortex Ltd (Queen's Awards to Industry for export achievement and for tech. innovation, 1968); Managing Director: Hadfield Paints Ltd, 1972–75; Buck & Hickman Ltd, 1974–75; Chm. and Man. Dir, Reeves and Sons Ltd, subseq. Reeves Dryad Ltd, 1971–76; set up: Cass Arts & Crafts Ltd, 1976, sold 1985; Image Bank UK, 1979, sold 2001; Chm. and Chief Exec., Moss Bros plc, 1987–91. UK Founder and Chm., Kennedy Foundn, 1976–93. Hon. FRCA 1995. *Recreations:* films, reading, photography, travel, art. *Address:* Cass Sculpture Foundation, Goodwood, Chichester, W Sussex PO18 0QP. *T:* (01243) 538449; *e-mail:* wilfred@sculpture.org.uk. *Club:* Kennels (Goodwood).

CASSAM, Prof. Quassim, DPhil; Professor of Philosophy, University of Warwick, since 2009; *b* 31 Jan. 1961; *s* of Amir and Sultan Cassam. *Educ:* Keble Coll., Oxford (BA 1st Cl. Hons PPE; BPhil Philosophy; DPhil Philosophy 1985). Fellow and Lectr in Philosophy, Oriel Coll., Oxford, 1985–86; Fellow and Tutor in Philosophy, Wadham Coll., Oxford, 1986–2004; Prof. of Philosophy, UCL, 2005–06; Knightbridge Prof. of Philosophy, Univ. of Cambridge, 2007–08; Fellow, King's Coll., Cambridge, 2007–08. Vis. Associate Prof., Univ. of Calif, Berkeley, 1993; John Evans Dist. Vis. Prof., Northwestern Univ., 2004. *Publications:* Self and World, 1997; The Possibility of Knowledge, 2007. *Recreations:* films, music, eating out, watching cricket. *Address:* Department of Philosophy, University of Warwick, Coventry CV4 7AL.

CASSANI, Barbara Ann, Hon. CBE 2007; Chairman, Jurys Inns, Dublin, since 2008; *b* 22 July 1960; *d* of James and Noreen Cassani; *m* 1985, Guy Davis; one *s* one *d.* *Educ:* Mount Holyoke Coll., USA (BA Hons *magna cum laude* Internat. Relns); Woodrow Wilson Sch. of Public and Internat. Affairs, Princeton Univ. (MPA). Mgt Consultant, Coopers & Lybrand, in Washington and London, 1984–87; various mgt rôles with British Airways in UK and USA, 1987–97; CEO, Go Fly Ltd, 1997–2002; Chm., 2003–04, Vice-Chm., 2004–05, London 2012 Olympic Bid. *Publication:* (with K. Kemp) Go: an airline adventure, 2003. *Recreations:* reading, horse-riding, travel. *Address:* *e-mail:* bacassani@aol.com.

CASSAR, Francis Felix Anthony; Director, Omnirace Ltd, 1990–2000; *b* 10 May 1934; *s* of Carmelo and Filomena Cassar; *m* 1969, Doreen Marjorie; two *s.* *Educ:* Primary Sch., Malta; Lyceum, Malta. Emigrated to UK, 1953. Studied mech. engrg, 1953–58; Man. Dir of own motor engrg co., 1959–74; Co. Sec., Malta Drydocks (UK) Ltd, 1975–80. Represented Malta Labour Party in the UK, also at meetings of the Bureau of the Socialist International, 1960–80; Acting High Comr for Malta in London and Cyprus, 1981–85, High Comr, 1985–87; Chargé d'Affaires, Baghdad, 1988–90. Administrator, St Mark's Res. Foundn, 1991–2000; Financial Controller, St Mark's Educnl Trust, 1995–2000. Mem., Inst. of Management, 1977. JP: Brentford and Ealing, Tottenham, 1972–80; Enfield, 1990. *Recreations:* music, football, DIY, cooking.

CASSEL, family name of **Baroness Mallalieu.**

CASSEL, Sir Timothy (Felix Harold), 4th Bt *cr* 1920; QC 1988; *b* 30 April 1942; *s* of Sir Harold Cassel, 3rd Bt, TD, QC; *S* father, 2001; *m* 1st, 1971, Jenifer Puckle (marr. diss. 1976); one *s* one *d*; 2nd, 1979, Ann Mallalieu (marr. diss. 2007) (*see* Baroness Mallalieu); two *d.* *Educ:* Eton College. Called to the Bar, Lincoln's Inn, 1965, Bencher, 1994; Jun. Prosecuting Counsel at Central Criminal Court, 1978, Sen. Prosecuting Counsel, 1986–88; Asst Boundaries Comr, 1979–85. *Heir:* *s* Alexander James Felix Cassel, *b* 25 May 1974. *Address:* Kirtlington Park, Oxon OX5 3JN. *Clubs:* Garrick, Turf.

CASSELL, Frank, CB 1987; Chairman, Crown Agents Pension Scheme, 1997–2006 (Member, Board of Crown Agents, 1991–97); Economic Minister, Washington, and UK Executive Director, International Monetary Fund and World Bank, 1988–90; *b* 21 Aug. 1930; *s* of Francis Joseph Cassell and Ellen Blanche Cassell (*née* Adams); *m* 1957, Jean Seabrook; two *s* one *d.* *Educ:* Borden Grammar School; LSE (BSc Econ). Asst City Editor, News Chronicle, 1953–58; Dep. Editor, The Banker, 1958–65; HM Treasury: Economic Adviser, 1965; Senior Economic Adviser, 1968; Under Sec., 1974; Deputy Sec., 1983–88. Chm., Stats Cttee, Internat. Financial Services, London (formerly British Invisibles), 1994–2002. Vis. Scholar, Federal Reserve Bank of Minneapolis, 1970. *Publications:* Gold or Credit?, 1965; articles on economic policy, 1953–65. *Recreations:* walking, watching cricket, reading history.

CASSELL, Michael Robert; writer; *b* 2 June 1946; *s* of Donald and Joyce Cassell; *m* 1995, Linda Radway. *Educ:* Lode Heath High Sch.; Solihull Coll. Reporter, W Midlands Press, 1964–67; Business Reporter, Birmingham Post, 1967–69; City Reporter, Daily Express, 1969–70; Financial Times, 1970–2000: successively Property, Political, Industry, and Business Correspondent; Ed., Observer column, 1996–2000. *Publications:* One Hundred

Years of Co-operation, 1984; Readymixers, 1986; Dig it, Burn it, Sell it!, 1990; Long Lease, 1991. *Recreations:* horse riding, walking, watercolours. *Address:* Barnard Acres, Nazeing EN9 2LZ.

CASSELS, Sir John (Seton), Kt 1988; CB 1978; Chairman, UK SKILLS, 1990–2000; *b* 10 Oct. 1928; *s* of Alastair Macdonald Cassels and Ada White Cassels (*née* Scott); *m* 1956, Mary Whittington (*d* 2008); two *s* two *d*. *Educ:* Sedbergh Sch., Yorkshire; Trinity Coll., Cambridge (1st cl. Hons, Classics, 1951). Rome Scholar, Classical Archaeology, 1952–54. Entered Ministry of Labour, 1954; Secretary of the Royal Commission on Trade Unions and Employers' Associations, 1965–68; Under-Sec., NBPI, 1968–71; Managing Directors' Office, Dunlop Holdings Ltd, 1971–72; Chief Exec., Training Services Agency, 1972–75; Dir, Manpower Services Commn, 1975–81; Second Permanent Sec., MPO, 1981–83; Dir Gen., NEDO, 1983–88. Dir, Nat. Commn on Educn, 1991–97. Chm., Ind. Inquiry into the Role and Responsibilities of the Police, 1994–96. Member Council: Inst. of Manpower Studies, subseq. Inst. of Employment Studies, 1982– (Pres., 1989–95; Hon. Life Pres., 2001–); Policy Studies Inst., 1983–88; Industrial Soc., 1984–93; Assoc. for Consumer Res., 1989–94; NIESR, 1993–. Chm., Internat. Comparisons in Criminal Justice, 1990–95; Mem., Prince's Trust Volunteers Mgt Adv. Bd, 1998–2001; Chairman: Sussex Careers Services, 1995–98; Modern Apprenticeship Adv. Cttee, DfES, 2001; Mem., Apprenticeship Ambassadors Network, 2006–. Chm., Richmond Adult and Community Coll., 1996–2001. Dist. Vis. Fellow, 1989, Sen. Fellow, 1990, PSI. FIPD; FRSA. Hon. Dr: Sussex, 1995; Heriot-Watt, 1996; Brunel, 1997; Companion, De Montfort Univ., 1995. Hon. CGIA 1989. *Publication:* Britain's Real Skill Shortage—and what to do about it, 1990. *Address:* 10 Beverley Road, Barnes, SW13 0LX. *T:* (020) 8876 6270. *Club:* Reform.

CASSELS, Prof. John William Scott, FRS 1963; FRSE 1981; MA, PhD; Sadleirian Professor of Pure Mathematics, Cambridge University, 1967–84; Head of Department of Pure Mathematics and Mathematical Statistics, 1969–84; *b* 11 July 1922; *s* of late J. W. Cassels (latterly Dir of Agriculture in Co. Durham) and late Mrs M. S. Cassels (*née* Lobjoit); *m* 1949, Constance Mabel Merritt (*née* Senior) (*d* 2000); one *s* one *d*. *Educ:* Neville's Cross Council Sch., Durham; George Heriot's Sch., Edinburgh; Edinburgh and Cambridge Univs. MA Edinburgh, 1943; PhD Cantab, 1949. Fellow, Trinity, 1949–; Lecturer, Manchester Univ., 1949; Lecturer, Cambridge Univ., 1950; Reader in Arithmetic, 1963–67. Mem. Council, Royal Society, 1970, 1971 (Sylvester Medal, 1973); Vice Pres., 1974–78, Mem. Exec., 1978–82, Internat. Mathematical Union; Pres., London Mathematical Soc., 1976–78. Dr (*hc*) Lille Univ., 1965; Hon. ScD Edinburgh, 1977. De Morgan Medal, London Mathematical Soc., 1986. *Publications:* An Introduction to Diophantine Approximation, 1957; An Introduction to the Geometry of Numbers, 1959; Rational Quadratic Forms, 1978; Economics for Mathematicians, 1981; Local Fields, 1986; Lectures on Elliptic Curves, 1991; (with E. V. Flynn) Prolegomena to a Middlebrow Arithmetic of Curves of Genus 2, 1996; papers in diverse mathematical journals on arithmetical topics. *Recreations:* arithmetic (higher only), gardening (especially common vegetables). *Address:* 3 Luard Close, Cambridge CB2 8PL. *T:* (01223) 246108.

CASSELS, Adm. Sir Simon (Alastair Cassillis), KCB 1982; CBE 1976; *b* 5 March 1928; *o s* of late Comdr A. G. Cassels, RN, and Clarissa Cassels (*née* Motion); *m* 1962, Jillian Francies Kannreuther; one *s* one *d*. *Educ:* RNC, Dartmouth. Midshipman 1945; Commanding Officer: HM Ships Vigilant, Roebuck, and Tenby, 1962–63; HMS Eskimo, 1966–67; HMS Fearless, 1972–73; Principal Staff Officer to CDS, 1973–76; CO HMS Tiger, 1976–78; Asst Chief of Naval Staff (Op. Requirements), 1978–80; Flag Officer, Plymouth, Port Adm. Devonport, Comdr Central Sub Area Eastern Atlantic and Comdr Plymouth Sub Area Channel, 1981–82; Second Sea Lord, Chief of Naval Personnel and Adm. Pres., RNC, Greenwich, 1982–86. Dir Gen., TSB Foundn for Eng. and Wales, 1986–90. Younger Brother of Trinity House, 1963. Pres., Regular Forces Employment Assoc., 1990–93 (Chm., 1989). Freeman, City of London, 1983; Liveryman, Shipwrights' Co., 1984. FRGS 1947. *Publication:* Peninsular Portrait 1811–1814, 1963. *Recreations:* appreciation of archaeology, architecture and art, historical research. *Address:* c/o Lloyds TSB, Bishop's Waltham, Southampton SO32 1GS. *Club:* Army and Navy.

CASSELTON, Prof. Lorna Ann, (Mrs W. J. D. Tollett), PhD, DSc; FRS 1999; Professor of Fungal Genetics, University of Oxford, 1997–2003, now Emeritus; Fellow, St Cross College, Oxford, 1993–2003; Foreign Secretary and Vice-President, Royal Society, since 2006; *b* 18 July 1938; *d* of William Charles Henry Smith and Cecille Smith (*née* Bowman); *m* 1st, 1961, Peter John Casselton (marr. diss. 1978); 2nd, 1981, William Joseph Dennis Tollett. *Educ:* Southend High Sch. for Girls; University Coll. London (BSc; PhD 1964; DSc 1993); MA Oxon. Royal Commn for Exhibn of 1851 Sen. Student, 1963–65; Asst Lectr, RHC, 1966–67; Lectr, 1967–76, Reader, 1976–89, QMC; Prof. of Genetics, QMW, 1989–91; AFRC/BBSRC Postdoctoral Fellow, 1991–95, BBSRC Sen. Res. Fellow, 1995–2001, Univ. of Oxford. Vis. Prof. of Genetics, QMW, 1997–. Leverhulme Emeritus Fellow, 2003–05. Hon. Fellow, St Hilda's Coll., Oxford, 2000. Hon. Mem., British Mycological Soc., 2003–. *Publications:* numerous res. and rev. articles. *Recreations:* reading, classical music, dancing, walking. *Address:* 83 St Bernard's Road, Oxford OX2 6EJ. *T:* (01865) 559997.

CASSEN, Prof. Robert Harvey, OBE 2008; Visiting Professor, London School of Economics, since 1997; Professor of the Economics of Development, Queen Elizabeth House, International Development Centre, University of Oxford, 1986–97, and Professorial Fellow, St Antony's College, 1986–97, now Emeritus; *b* 24 March 1935; *s* of John and Liliane Cassen; *m* 1988, Sun Shuyun. *Educ:* Bedford School; New Coll., Oxford (BA LitHum, MA); Univ. of California, Berkeley; Harvard (PhD Econ). Dept of Economics, LSE, 1961–69; Sen. Economist, ODM, 1966–67; First Sec. (Econ.), New Delhi, 1967–68; Sen. Economist, World Bank, Washington, 1969–72 and 1980–81; Fellow, Inst. of Develt Studies, Sussex Univ., 1972–86; Sen. Res. Fellow, Centre for Population Studies, LSHTM, 1976–77; Dir, Queen Elizabeth House, Internat. Develt Centre, Oxford Univ., 1986–93. Special Adviser, H of C Select Cttee on Overseas Develt, 1973–74; Secretariat, Brandt Commn, 1978–79 and 1981–82; Mem., Bd of Trustees, Population Council, NY, 1978–87; UK Mem., UN Cttee for Develt Planning, 1982–84. *Publications:* India: Population, Economy, Society, 1978; (ed and contrib.) Planning for Growing Populations, 1979; (ed and contrib.) World Development Report, 1981; (ed and contrib.) Rich Country Interests and Third World Development, 1982; (ed) Soviet Interests in the Third World, 1985; Does Aid Work? (report), 1986, 2nd edn 1994; (ed) Poverty in India, 1992; (ed and contrib.) Population and Development: old debates, new conclusions, 1994; (ed) India: the future of economic reform, 1995; (ed and contrib.) 21st Century India: population, economy, human development and the environment, 2004; Tackling Low Educational Achievement (report), 2007; contribs to learned jls. *Recreations:* music, walking. *Address:* Centre for Analysis of Social Exclusion, LSE, Houghton Street, WC2A 2AE. *T:* (020) 7955 6003.

CASSERLEY, Dominic James Andrew; Managing Partner, UK and Ireland, McKinsey & Co., since 2003; *b* Gosport, 23 Dec. 1957; *s* of Christopher and Pamela Casserley; *m* 1986, Nancy Broadbent; two *s* one *d*. *Educ:* University Coll. Sch., London; Jesus Coll., Cambridge (BA Hons Hist. 1979). Exec., Investment Mgt, then Mergers & Acquisitions, Morgan Grenfell & Co., 1979–83; McKinsey & Co.: Associate, 1983–87; Principal, 1988–93; Dir, 1993–; Leader: Gtr China Practice, 1994–99; Eur. Banking and Securities Practice, 1999–2003. David Rockefeller Fellow, NY, 1991–92. Mem., US Presidential Taskforce on Mkt Mechanisms, 1987. Member: Bd, Manhattan Th. Club, 1991–94; Bd, Donmar Th., London, 2003–. Chm., Action on Addiction, 2007–. *Publications:* Facing up to the Risks: how financial institutions can survive and prosper, 1993, 4th edn 1997; (with G. Gibb) Banking in Asia, the End of Entitlement, 1999. *Recreations:* tennis, travelling. *Address:* McKinsey & Co., 1 Jermyn Street, SW1Y 4UH. *Clubs:* Reform, MCC; University (NY); Field (Greenwich, CT).

CASSIDI, Adm. Sir (Arthur) Desmond, GCB 1983 (KCB 1978); President, Royal Naval Association, 1987–96; Deputy Grand President, British Commonwealth Ex-Services League, 1986–96; *b* 26 Jan. 1925; *s* of late Comdr Robert A. Cassidi, RN and late Clare F. (*née* Alexander); *m* 1st, 1950, Dorothy Sheelagh Marie (*née* Scott) (*d* 1974); one *s* two *d*; 2nd, 1982, Dr Deborah Marion Pollock (*née* Bliss), FRCS. *Educ:* RNC Dartmouth. Qual. Pilot, 1946; CO, 820 Sqdn (Gannet aircraft), 1955; 1st Lieut HMS Protector, 1955–56; psc 1957; CO, HMS Whitby, 1959–61; Fleet Ops Officer Home Fleet, 1962–64; Asst Dir Naval Plans, 1964–67; Captain (D) Portland and CO HMS Undaunted, 1967–68; idc 1969; Dir of Naval Plans, 1970–72; CO, HMS Ark Royal, 1972–73; Flag Officer Carriers and Amphibious Ships, 1974–75; Dir-Gen., Naval Manpower and Training, 1975–77; Flag Officer, Naval Air Command, 1978–79; Chief of Naval Personnel and Second Sea Lord, 1979–82; C-in-C Naval Home Comd, 1982–85; Flag ADC to the Queen, 1982–85. Mem. Adv. Council, Science Museum, 1979–84, Trustee, 1984–92; Pres., FAA Museum, 1985–95. FRSA 1986. *Recreation:* country pursuits.

CASSIDY, Bryan Michael Deece; Founder, Cassidy and Associates International, EU Consultants, 1999; Member, European Economic and Social Committee, since 2002 (Chairman, Single Market Observatory, 2002–04); *s* of late William Francis Deece Cassidy and Kathleen Selina Patricia Cassidy (*née* Geraghty); *m* 1960, Gillian Mary Isobel Bohane; one *s* two *d*. *Educ:* Ratcliffe College; Sidney Sussex College, Cambridge. MA (Law). Commissioned RA, 1955–57 (Malta and Libya); HAC, 1957–62. With Ever Ready, Beecham's and Reed International (Dir, European associates). Mem. Council, CBI, 1981–84. Dir Gen., of a trade assoc., 1981–84. Contested (C) Wandsworth Central, 1966; Mem. GLC (Hendon North), 1977–86 (opposition spokesman on industry and employment, 1983–84). MEP (C), Dorset E and Hampshire W, 1984–94, Dorset and E Devon, 1994–99; contested (C) SW Reg., 1999. Assignments for BESO in Estonia, 2000, Mongolia, 2002. Dir of Studies, Hawksmere Brussels Briefings, 2001–04. Vis. Woodrow Wilson Fellow, American Univs, 2000, 2004. Mem., Adv. Bd, European Performance Inst., Brussels, 1999–2002. *Publication:* Hawksmere European Lobbying Guide, 2000; regular contribs to Industry Europe. *Recreations:* history, country sports, theatre. *Address:* 11 Esmond Court, Thackeray Street, W8 5HB. *T:* (020) 7937 3558, *Fax:* (020) 7937 3789; *e-mail:* bryan.cassidy@europundit.eu.

CASSIDY, His Eminence Cardinal Edward; *see* Cassidy, His Eminence Cardinal I. E.

CASSIDY, Elizabeth Grace; Command Secretary, Fleet, since 2007; *b* 6 July 1951; *er d* of late William Charles Cassidy and Mildred Joan Cassidy (*née* Ross); *m* 1984, Edward Roy Dolby. *Educ:* Girls' Grammar Sch., Prescot, Lancs; Girton Coll., Cambridge (MA); Wye Coll., Univ. of London (MSc). Ministry of Defence: Admin Trainee, 1978; Private Sec. to Chief of Defence Procurement, 1983; Principal, 1984; Private Sec. to CAS, 1990–93; Asst Sec., Hd, IT Business Systems, then IT Strategy, 1993–95; Advr to Jt Services Comd and Staff Coll. Project, 1995–97; Dir, Finance Policy, 1997–99; Command Sec. to Second Sea Lord and C-in-C Naval Home Command, and Asst Under-Sec. of State (Naval Personnel), 1999–2001; Review of Business Continuity for MoD HQ post-9/11, 2001–02; Comd Sec. to Adjt Gen., 2002–06. Dir, Regular Forces Employment Assoc. Ltd, 2006–. Mem., Royal Patriotic Fund Corp., 2003–06. Chm. Adv. Panel, Greenwich Hosp., 1999–2001 and 2007–; Comr, Royal Hosp. Chelsea, 2002–06. *Recreations:* music, reading, travel, sailing. *Address:* c/o HSBC, 9 Rose Lane, Canterbury, Kent CT1 2JP.

CASSIDY, Rt Rev. George Henry; *see* Southwell and Nottingham, Bishop of.

CASSIDY, Very Rev. Herbert; Dean of Armagh and Keeper of the Library, 1989–2006; *b* 25 July 1935; *s* of Herbert Cassidy and Frederica Jane Somerville; *m* 1961, Elizabeth Ann Egerton; one *s* two *d*. *Educ:* Cork Grammar Sch.; Trinity Coll., Dublin (BA 1957; MA 1965). Curate Assistant: Holy Trinity, Belfast, 1958–60; Christ Church, Londonderry, 1960–62; Rector: Aghavilly and Derrynoose, 1962–65; St Columba's, Portadown, 1965–85; Dean of Kilmore, 1985–89. Hon. Sec., Gen. Synod, Ch. of Ireland, 1990–2004. *Publications:* various pamphlets. *Recreations:* music, travel. *Address:* 2 Kilmore Meadows, Kilmore Road, Armagh BT61 8PA.

CASSIDY, His Eminence Cardinal Idris Edward, AC 1990; President, Pontifical Council for Promoting Christian Unity, and Commission for Religious Relations with the Jews, 1989–2001; *b* 5 July 1924; *s* of Harold George Cassidy and Dorothy May Phillips. *Educ:* Parramatta High Sch.; St Columba Seminary, Springwood; St Patrick's Coll., Manly; Lateran Univ., Rome (DCnL 1955); Diploma of Pontifical Eccl. Acad., Rome, 1955. Ordained priest, 1949; Asst Priest, Parish of Yenda, NSW, Australia, 1950–52; Secretary, Apostolic Nunciature, India, 1955–62 and Ireland, 1962–67; El Salvador, 1967–69; Counsellor, Apostolic Nunciature, Argentina, 1969–70; ordained Archbishop, Rome, 1970; Apostolic Pro-Nuncio: to Republic of China, 1970–79; to Bangladesh, 1973–79; to Lesotho, 1979–84, and Apostolic Delegate to Southern Africa; to the Netherlands, 1984–88; Substitute of Vatican Secretariat of State, 1988–89. Cardinal, 1991. Orders from El Salvador, China, Netherlands, Italy, France, Sweden and Germany. *Recreations:* tennis, golf. *Address:* 16 Coachwood Drive, Warabrook, NSW 2304, Australia.

CASSIDY, Most Rev. Joseph; Archbishop of Tuam, 1987–95; pastor, Moore; *b* 29 Oct. 1933; *s* of John Cassidy and Mary Gallagher. *Educ:* St Nathy's College, Maynooth; University College, Galway. Professor, Garbally College, Ballinasloe, 1959–77, President 1977–79; Coadjutor Bishop of Clonfert, 1979–82; Bishop of Clonfert, 1982–87; Spokesman for Irish Bishops' Conference, 1980–88. *Publications:* plays, articles and homilies. *Address:* Moore, Ballydangan, Athlone, Co. Roscommon, Ireland.

CASSIDY, Michael John, CBE 2004; Chairman: Board of Governors, Museum of London, since 2005; Homerton University Hospital Foundation Trust, since 2006; consultant: DLA Piper, since 2005; Colliers CRE, since 2007; *b* 14 Jan. 1947; *s* of Frank and Vera Cassidy; *m* 1st, 1974, Amanda (marr. diss. 1988); one *s* two *d*; 2nd, 1997, Amelia Simpson; two *d*. *Educ:* Downing Coll., Cambridge (BA); MBA (with distinction), City Univ. Business Sch., 1985. Qualified Solicitor, 1971; Partner: Maxwell Batley, 1971–2002 (Sen. Partner, 1991–2002); D. J. Freeman, 2002–03; Hammonds, 2003–04. Director: British Land Plc, 1996–2007; UBS Investment Bank (formerly UBS Warburg, then UBS Ltd), 2000–; Chairman: Askonas Holt Ltd, 2002–; Hemingway Properties Ltd, 2003–06; Gruppo Norman, 2004–05; Trikona Trinity Capital plc (formerly Trinity Property Co.), 2005–; Bulgarian Land Development plc, 2005–07. Corporation of London: Mem.,

Common Council, 1980–; Chairman: Planning Cttee, 1986–89; Policy and Resources Cttee, 1992–97; Chm., Barbican Arts Centre, 2000–03. Pres., London Chamber of Commerce and Industry, 2005–07 (Dep. Pres., 2004–05). Mem. Bd, London Pension Fund Authy, 2007–. Liveryman: Fletchers' Co.; Solicitors' Co. (Master, 2001–02). Hon. Fellow, London Business Sch., 1995; Hon. FRIBA 1995. Hon. LLD South Bank, 1995; Hon. DCL City, 1996. *Publications:* articles on City matters and pension fund investment. *Recreations:* boating, Barbican concerts. *Address:* 202 Cromwell Tower, Barbican EC2Y 8DD. *T:* (020) 7628 5687. *Club:* London Capital.

CASSIDY, Seamus John; television producer; Director, Happy Endings television production company, since 2001; *b* 20 Nov. 1958; *s* of late Michael Cassidy and of Patricia Cassidy. *Educ:* St Columb's Coll., Derry; Queen's Univ., Belfast (LLB Hons). Researcher, 1982–84; Asst Ed., 1984–87; Sen. Commissioning Ed., Comedy and Entertainment, Channel 4 TV, 1987–97; Sen. Producer, Comedy and Entertainment, Planet 24, 1997–99; Producer, The Panel, Saturday Night with Miriam, Podge and Rodge, all RTE, 2003–07. *Address:* Happy Endings Productions, 13 Merrion Square, Dublin 2, Eire.

CASSIDY, Dr Sheila Anne; lecturer and psychotherapist; Specialist in Psychosocial Oncology, Plymouth Oncology Centre, 1993–2002; *b* 18 Aug. 1937; *d* of late Air Vice-Marshal John Reginald Cassidy and Barbara Margaret Cassidy. *Educ:* Univ. of Sydney; Somerville Coll., Oxford (BM BCh 1963; MA). Worked in Oxford and Leicester to 1971; went to Chile to work, 1971; arrested for treating wounded revolutionary, 1975; tortured and imprisoned 2 months, released Dec. 1975; lectured on human rights; in monastic religious order, 1978–80; returned to medicine, 1980; Medical Dir, St Luke's Hospice, Plymouth, 1982–93; Palliative Care Physician, Plymouth Gen. Hosp., 1993; lecturer in UK and overseas, preacher, writer, broadcaster. Freedom, City of Plymouth, 1998. Hon. DSc Exeter, 1991; Hon. DLitt CNAA, 1992; Hon. DM Plymouth, 2001. Valiant for Truth Media Award, 1977. *Publications:* Audacity to Believe, 1977; Prayer for Pilgrims, 1979; Sharing the Darkness, 1988; Good Friday People, 1991 (Collins Religious Book Award Special Prize, 1991); Light from the Dark Valley, 1994; The Loneliest Journey, 1995; Made for Laughter, 2006. *Recreations:* writing, sewing, creative pursuits, reading, TV, walking her two Chows.

CASSIDY, Stuart; ballet dancer, ballet teacher and Pilates instructor; founder member, K. Ballet Co., since 1999; *b* 26 Sept. 1968; *s* of John and Jacqueline Cassidy; *m* 1993, Nicola Searchfield; two *s*. *Educ:* Royal Ballet Sch. (Hons 1987); RAD PDTDip (Dist.) 2003; Dreas Reyneke Pilates Instructor Course, 2004. Principal, Royal Ballet Co., 1991–99. *Principal rôles with Royal Ballet Company include:* Romeo and Mercutio, in Romeo and Juliet, Albrecht in Giselle, Siegfried in Swan Lake, Solor in La Bayadère, Jean de Brienne in Raymonda, Daphnis in Daphnis and Chloë, Florimund in Sleeping Beauty, Prince in Prince of the Pagodas, Prince in Nutcracker, Prince in Cinderella, Colas in La Fille Mal Gardée, Lescaut in Manon, Basilio in Don Quixote; Thaïs Pas de Deux, Tchaikovsky Pas de Deux. Nora Roche Award, 1986; Prix de Lausanne Prof. Prize, 1987. *Recreations:* golf, gardening, antiques.

CASSIRER, Nadine, (Mrs Reinhold Cassirer); *see* Gordimer, N.

CASSON, Prof. Andrew John, FRS 1998; Professor of Mathematics, Yale University, since 2000. *Educ:* Trinity Coll., Cambridge (BA 1965). Res. Fellow, 1967–71, Lectr in Maths, 1971–81, Trinity Coll., Cambridge; Professor of Mathematics: Univ. of Texas, Austin, 1981–86; Univ. of Calif, Berkeley, 1986–99. *Publication:* (with S. A. Bleiler) Automorphisms of Surfaces after Nielsen and Thurston, 1988. *Address:* Department of Mathematics, Yale University, New Haven, CT 06520, USA.

CASSON, Dinah Victoria, (Lady Moses), RDI 2006; FCSD; Co-founder and Director, Casson Mann Ltd, since 1983; *b* 8 Oct. 1946; *d* of Sir Hugh Maxwell Casson, CH, KCVO, RA, RDI and late Margaret MacDonald Casson; *m* 1992, Alan George Moses (*see* Rt Hon. Sir A. G. Moses); one *s* one *d* from previous marriage. *Educ:* Ravensbourne Coll. of Art (BA 1st Cl. Hons). Jun. designer, Conran Design Gp, 1968–70; freelance design practice, 1970–83. Casson Mann design practice has worked on interior, architectural, product develt, th. and mus. projects in USA, Italy, Russia and UK; major projects include: Grangelato ice cream shop, London, 1984; CSD HQ, London, 1988; The Garden, 1996, Wellcome Wing, 2000 and Energy Gall., 2005, Science Mus.; British Galls, 2001, Portrait Miniatures, 2005, V&A Mus.; Churchill Mus., Imperial War Mus., 2005. Teacher (pt-time), Kingston Poly. and RCA, 1974–94; Dir of Architecture and Interior Design, RCA, 1993–95. External Examiner: Chelsea Sch. of Art, 1985–92; Manchester Poly., 1989–91; Plymouth Sch. of Architecture, 1990–93; Newcastle Sch. of Architecture, 1994–98; Middx Univ., 1994–97; Bournemouth Univ., 1994–96; N London, 1995–99; Glasgow Sch. of Art, 1999–2003; Cardiff Sch. of Art, 2004–. Member: Design Council, 1978–82; Exec., D&AD, 2006–. Governor: Middx Poly., 1990–94; Sevenoaks Sch., 2005–. Hon. FRCA 1995. Hon. DDes UC for Creative Arts, Farnham, 2003. *Publications:* (contrib.) Creating the British Galleries at the V&A, ed C. Wilk and N. Humphrey, 2004; contrib. Blueprint, Architects' Jl, Designers' Jl, Building Design, Eye. *Address:* Casson Mann Ltd, 4 Northington Street, WC1N 2JG. *T:* (020) 7242 1112; *e-mail:* dinah.c@cassonmann.co.uk.

CASSON, Prof. Mark Christopher; Professor of Economics, University of Reading, since 1981; *b* 17 Dec. 1945; *s* of Stanley Christopher Casson and Dorothy Nowell Barlow; *m* 1975, Janet Penelope Close; one *d*. *Educ:* Manchester Grammar Sch.; Univ. of Bristol (BA 1st cl. hons 1966); Churchill Coll., Cambridge (graduate student). University of Reading: Lecturer in Economics, 1969; Reader, 1977; Head, Dept of Econs, 1987–94. Visiting Professor: of Internat. Business, Univ. of Leeds, 1995–; of Mgt, Queen Mary, Univ. of London, 2004–. Mem. Council, REconS, 1985–90. Vice-Pres., 2006–07, Pres., 2007–08, Assoc. of Business Historians. Chm., Business Enterprise Heritage Trust, 2000–. Fellow, Acad. of Internat. Business, 1993; FRSA 1996. *Publications:* Introduction to Mathematical Economics, 1973; (jtly) The Future of the Multinational Enterprise, 1976; Alternatives to the Multinational Enterprise, 1979; Youth Unemployment, 1979; Unemployment: a disequilibrium approach, 1981; The Entrepreneur: an economic theory, 1982; Economics of Unemployment: an historical perspective, 1983; (ed) The Growth of International Business, 1983; (jtly) The Economic Theory of the Multinational Enterprise: selected papers, 1985; (jtly) Multinationals and World Trade: vertical integration and the division of labour in world industries, 1986; The Firm and the Market: studies in multinational enterprise and the scope of the firm, 1987; Enterprise and Competitiveness: a systems view of international business, 1990; (ed) Entrepreneurship, 1990; (ed) Multinational Corporations, 1990; Economics of Business Culture: game theory, transaction costs and economic performance, 1991; (ed) Global Research Strategy and International Competitiveness, 1991; (ed) International Business and Global Integration, 1992; (ed jtly) Multinational Enterprise in the World Economy: essays in honour of John Dunning, 1992; (ed jtly) Industrial Concentration and Economic Inequality: essays in honour of Peter Hart, 1993; Entrepreneurship and Business Culture, 1995; The Organization of International Business, 1995; (ed) The Theory of the Firm, 1996; Information and Organization: a new perspective on the theory of the firm, 1997; (ed) Culture, Social Norms and Economic Performance, 1997; (ed jtly) Institutions and the Evolution of Modern Business, 1997; (ed jtly) The Economics of Marketing, 1998; (ed jtly) Cultural Factors in Economic Growth, 2000; Economics of International Business, 2000; Enterprise and Leadership, 2000; (ed jtly) Oxford Handbook of Entrepreneurship, 2005; Building the World's First Railway System, 2007. *Recreations:* collecting old books, studying old railways, visiting old churches. *Address:* 6 Wayside Green, Woodcote, Reading RG8 0QJ. *T:* (home) (01491) 681483; (office) (0118) 931 8227.

CASTALDI, Dr Peter; Chief Medical Officer, Scottish Equitable, since 2004 (Company Medical Officer, 1997–2004); *b* 13 Jan. 1942; *s* of Frank and Sarah Jane Castaldi; *m* 1967, Joan Sherratt; one *s* one *d*. *Educ:* Grammar Sch. for Boys, Neath; Welsh Nat. Sch. of Medicine (MB, BCh 1966). Resident hosp. posts, N Wales, 1966–69; Principal in General Practice, Bangor, Gwynedd, 1969–79; MO 1979–84, SMO 1984–86, DHSS; PMO, DSS, 1986–92. Chief Med. Advr, DSS, and Dir of Med. Services, Benefits Agency, 1992–95. Med. Dir, Mediprobe, 1997–; Company Medical Officer: UNUM UK, 1996–99; AEGON UK (formerly Guardian Royal Exchange), Lytham, 1997–; UNUM Ltd, 2001–04 (CMO, 1999–2001); Med. Mem., Indep. Tribunal Service, 1996–. CStJ 1993. *Recreations:* squash, swimming, armchair Rugby critic. *Address:* 24 Cavendish Road, Lytham St Annes, Lancs FY8 2PX.

CASTELL, Sir William (Martin), Kt 2000; LVO 2004; FCA; Chairman, Wellcome Trust, since 2006; External Director, General Electric, since 2006 (a Vice-Chairman, 2004–06); *b* 10 April 1947; *s* of William Gummer Castell and Gladys (*née* Doe); *m* 1971, Renice Mendelson; one *s* two *d*. *Educ:* St Dunstan's Sch.; City of London Coll. (BA). ACA 1974, FCA 1980. Various posts in marketing, finance and admin, Wellcome Foundn, 1975–86; Co-founding Dir, Biomedical Res. Centre, Vancouver, 1983; Man. Dir, Wellcome Biotech., 1984–87; Commercial Dir, Wellcome plc, 1987–89; Chief Exec., Amersham Internat., then Nycomed Amersham, subseq. Amersham plc, later Pres. and CEO, GE Healthcare, 1990–2006. Non-executive Director: Marconi (formerly GEC), 1997–2003; BP plc, 2006–. Chairman: Cttee on Design Bursaries Health and Envmt, RSA, 1986–88; Design Dimension, 1994–99 (Dep. Chm., 1988–94); Regeneration Through Heritage, BITC, 1997–2000; Prince's Trust, 1998–2003. Mem., MRC, 2001–04. Trustee, Natural Hist. Mus., 2004–08. Mem. Bd, Life Scis Inst., Michigan Univ., 2003–07; non-exec. Dir, Nat. Bureau of Asian Res., 2006–. Hon. Mem., Russian Academia Europaea, 1996. Hon. FMedSci 2004; Hon. Fellow: Green Coll., Oxford, 1993; Univ. of Cardiff, 2005; Hon. FKC 2006. Hon. DSSc Brunel, 2004; Hon. DCL Oxford, 2005. *Recreations:* international affairs, shooting, golf, tennis. *Address:* Wellcome Trust, 215 Euston Road, NW1 2BE. *T:* (020) 7611 8888. *Club:* Athenæum.

CASTILLO, Rudolph Innocent, MBE 1976; Secretary, National Advisory Commission on Belize-Guatemala Relations, 2000–03; Director, Secretariat of Relations with Guatemala, 2003; *b* 28 Dec. 1927; *s* of late Justo S. and Marcelina Castillo; *m* 1947, Gwen Frances Powery; three *s* four *d*. *Educ:* St John's Coll., Belize. Training assignments with BBC and COI, London. Lectr in Maths, Spanish and Hist., St John's Coll., 1946–52; Radio Belize: Announcer, 1952–53; Sen. Announcer, 1953–55; Asst Prog. Organizer, 1955–59; Govt Information Services: Information Officer, 1959–62; Chief Information Officer, 1962–74; Permanent Secretary: Agriculture, 1974–76; Education, 1976–79; Sec. to Cabinet, 1980–83; Chief of Protocol, 1981–83 and 2002; first High Comr for Belize in London, and first Belize Ambassador to France, Fed. Republic of Germany, Holy See, EEC and Unesco, 1983–85; retired from public service, 1985; first resident High Comr for Belize in Canada, 1990–93; Rep. to ICAO, 1991–93; business consultant, 1994–2000. Pres., Our Lady of Guadalupe Co-Cathedral Parish Council, Belmopan, 2002. ITV Commercial Productions (voicing commentary). Citation Award, Audubon Soc., 1994. *Publications:* The Rt Hon. George Price, PC: man of the people, 2002; Holy Redeemer Credit Union (HRCU): 60 years of growth, 2004. *Recreations:* photography, theatre, watercolour painting. *Address:* 29 Mahogany Street, Belmopan, Belize, Central America. *T:* (8) 220412; *e-mail:* ruincas@yahoo.com.

CASTLE, Rt Rev. Brian Colin; *see* Tonbridge, Bishop Suffragan of.

CASTLE, Enid, OBE 1997; JP; Principal, The Cheltenham Ladies' College, 1987–96; *b* 28 Jan. 1936; *d* of Bertram and Alice Castle. *Educ:* Hulme Grammar Sch. for Girls, Oldham; Royal Holloway Coll., Univ. of London. BA Hons History. Colne Valley High Sch., Yorks, 1958–62; Kenya High Sch., Nairobi, 1962–65; Queen's Coll., Nassau, Bahamas, 1965–68; Dep. Head, Roundhill High Sch., Leicester, 1968–72; Headmistress: High Sch. for Girls, Gloucester, 1973–81; Red Maids' Sch., Bristol, 1982–87. Pres., GSA, 1990–91. JP Glos, 1989. *Recreations:* travel, tennis, bridge, music.

CASTLE, John Christopher; Director, Farraxton Martlet Ltd, since 1998; *b* 4 Nov. 1944; *s* of George Frederick Castle and Winifred Mary Castle; *m* 1966, Susan Ann Neal; one *s* two *d*. *Educ:* Royal Grammar Sch., Guildford; Pembroke Coll., Cambridge (MA). With BP, 1963–68; Associated Industrial Consultants, 1968–73; Alcan Aluminium UK Ltd: Divl Dir of Industrial Relns, 1973–77; Chief Personnel Officer, 1977–80; Dir of Ops, 1980–82; Man. Dir, Base Internat. Ltd, 1982–86; Man. Dir, Thermalite, 1986–89, Gp Man. Dir, 1989–93, Marley plc; President: Avdel Textron, 1994–97; Textron Europe, 1995–97; Chief Exec., Taylor Woodrow plc, 1997. Non-executive Director: GKR Gp, 1993–99; ER Consultants Ltd, 1998–2000; Gibbs & Dandy plc, 2003–. Chm. Governing Council, Northampton Univ., 2005–. *Recreations:* tennis, bridge, restoration. *Address:* Farthingstone House, Farthingstone, Towcester, Northants NN12 8HB.

CASTLE, Rt Rev. Merwyn Edwin; *see* False Bay, Bishop of.

CASTLE STEWART, 8th Earl *cr* 1800 (Ireland); **Arthur Patrick Avondale Stuart;** Viscount Castle Stewart, 1793; Baron, 1619; Bt (NS) 1628, of Castle Stewart; retired farmer; *b* 18 Aug. 1928; 3rd but *e* surv. *s* of 7th Earl Castle Stewart, MC, and Eleanor May (*d* 1992), *er d* of late S. R. Guggenheim, New York; *S* father, 1961; *m* 1st, 1952, Edna Fowler (*d* 2003); one *s* one *d*; 2nd, 2004, Gillian Fitzwilliams, *d* of Frederick William Savill, Blaby, Leics; three step *d*. *Educ:* Brambletye; Eton; Trinity Coll., Cambridge (BA). Lieut Scots Guards, 1949. Vice-Pres., S. R. Guggenheim Mus., NY, 1967–97; Mem. Adv. Bd, Peggy Guggenheim Mus., Venice, 1980–. Trustee, Christian Community in UK, 1973–2003. FCMI. *Recreations:* woodland management, travel, walking, singing. *Heir: s* Viscount Stuart, *qv*. *Address:* Stuart Hall, Stewartstown, Co. Tyrone BT71 5AE. *T:* (028) 8773 8208; 539 Willoughby House, Barbican, EC2Y 8BN. *Club:* Carlton.

CASTLEMAINE, 8th Baron *cr* 1812; **Roland Thomas John Handcock,** MBE (mil.) 1981; *b* 22 April 1943; *s* of 7th Baron Castlemaine and Rebecca Ellen (*d* 1978), *o d* of William T. Soady, RN; *S* father, 1973; *m* 1st, 1969, Pauline Anne (marr. diss.), *e d* of John Taylor Bainbridge; 2nd, 1989, Lynne Christine, *e d* of Maj. Justin Michael Gurney, RAEC; one *s*. *Educ:* Campbell Coll., Belfast. psc, ph (cfs). Lt-Col, AAC, retd 1992. *Heir: s* Hon. Ronan Michael Edward Handcock, *b* 27 March 1989.

CASTLEREAGH, Viscount; Frederick Aubrey Vane-Tempest-Stewart; *b* 6 Sept. 1972; *s* and *heir* of 9th Marquess of Londonderry, *qv*.

CASTLES, Prof. Stephen, DPhil; Professor of Migration and Refugee Studies, since 2001 and Senior Research Fellow, International Migration Institute, James Martin 21st Century School, since 2006, University of Oxford (Director, Refugee Studies Centre, 2001–06); *b* Melbourne, 9 Nov. 1944; *s* of Heinz and Fay Castles; *m* 2000, Ellie Vasta. *Educ:* Oxted Co. Grammar Sch.; Univ. of Frankfurt am Main (Vor-Diplom); Univ. of Sussex (MA; DPhil). FASSA 1997. Res. Fellow, Res. Inst. Friedrich Ebert Foundn, Bonn, 1971–72; Lectr, 1972–75, Sen. Lectr, 1975–78, Prof. of Political Econ., 1978–79, Fachhochschule Frankfurt am Main; Co-ordinator, Totterdown Children's Community Workshop, Bristol, 1979–80; Lectr (pt-time) in Sociol., Bristol Poly., 1979–80; Co-ordinator, Design and Media, Foundn for Educn with Prodn, Botswana, 1981; Prof. of Political Econ. and Sociol., Fachhochschule Frankfurt am Main, 1982–86; Director: Centre for Multicultural Studies, Univ. of Wollongong, 1986–96; Centre for Asia Pacific Social Transformation Studies (jt venture of Univs of Wollongong and Newcastle), 1996–2001. Vis. Prof. of Migration Studies, Univ. of Sussex, 1998–2000; Vis. Fellow, Centre d'Etudes et Recherches Internat., Paris, 1995; Visiting Scholar: Cornell Univ., 1988; Eur. Univ. Inst., Florence, 1991–92. Dir Secretariat, UNESCO-MOST Asia Pacific Migration Res. Network, 1995–2000. Chm., UK Home Office Adv. Panel on Country Information, 2003–05. Member: Nat. Population Council, 1987–91; Multicultural and Population Res. Adv. Bd, Australian Bureau of Immigration, 1989–96. *Publications:* (with G. Kosack) Immigrant Workers and Class Structure in Western Europe, 1973 (Italian edn 1976, Spanish edn 1984); (with W. Wüstenberg) The Education of the Future, 1979 (Spanish edn 1982); Here for Good: Western Europe's new ethnic minorities, 1984 (German edn 1987); (jtly) Mistaken Identity: multiculturalism and the demise of nationalism in Australia, 1988, 3rd edn 1992; (with M. Miller) The Age of Migration: international population movements in the modern world, 1988, 4th edn 2008 (Japanese edn 1996, Spanish edn 2004); (jtly) A Shop Full of Dreams: ethnic small businesses in Australia, 1995; (jtly) Immigration and Australia, 1998; (with A. Davidson) Citizenship and Migration: globalization and the politics of belonging, 2000; Ethnicity and Globalization: from migrant worker to transnational citizen, 2000; (jtly) Migration, Citizenship and the European Welfare State: a European dilemma, 2006; *edited jointly:* Australia's Italians, 1992; The Teeth are Smiling… the persistence of racism in multicultural Australia, 1996; Migration in the Asia Pacific, 2003; Migration and Development: perspectives from the South, 2008 (Spanish edn 2007). *Recreations:* swimming, walking, photography. *Address:* International Migration Institute, Department of International Development, University of Oxford, Mansfield Road, Oxford OX1 3TB. *T:* (01865) 287305, *Fax:* (01865) 287435; *e-mail:* stephen.castles@qeh.ox.ac.uk.

CASTON, Geoffrey Kemp, CBE 1990; Vice-Chancellor, University of the South Pacific, 1983–92; *b* 17 May 1926; *s* of late Reginald and Lilian Caston, West Wickham, Kent; *m* 1st, Sonya Chassell; two *s* one *d*; 2nd, Judith Roizen, Berkeley, Calif; two step *s* one step *d*. *Educ:* St Dunstan's Coll.; (Major Open Scholar) Peterhouse, Cambridge (MA). First Cl. Pt 1 History; First Cl. Pt II Law (with distinction) and Geo. Long Prize for Jurisprudence, 1950; Harvard Univ. (Master of Public Admin. 1951; Frank Knox Fellow, 1950–51). Sub-Lt, RNVR, 1945–47. Colonial Office, 1951–58; UK Mission to UN, New York, 1958–61; Dept of Techn. Co-op., 1961–64; Asst Sec., Dept of Educn and Sci. (Univs and Sci. Branches), 1964–66; Jt Sec., Schools Council, 1966–70; Under-Secretary, UGC, 1970–72; Registrar of Oxford Univ. and Fellow of Merton Coll., Oxford, 1972–79; Sec.-Gen., Cttee of Vice-Chancellors and Principals, 1979–83. Project Manager, GAP, 1993–2001. Sec., Assoc. of First Div. Civil Servants, 1956–58; Adv. to UK Delegn to seven sessions of UN Gen. Assembly, 1953–63; UK Rep. on UN Cttee on Non-Self-Governing Territories, 1958–60; UN Techn. Assistance Cttee, 1962–64; Mem., UN Visiting Mission to Trust Territory of Pacific Islands, 1961; Consultant, Commonwealth Secretariat, 1992–2001. Chm., SE Surrey Assoc. for Advancement of State Educn, 1962–64; UK Delegn to Commonwealth Educn Confs, Ottawa, 1964, Gaborone, 1997. Ford Foundn travel grants for visits to schools and univs in USA, 1964, 1967, 1970. Vis. Associate, Center for Studies in Higher Educn, Univ. of Calif, Berkeley, 1978–2000. Chairman: Planning Cttee, 3rd and 4th Internat. Curriculum Confs, Oxford, 1967, New York, 1968; Ford Foundn Anglo-American Primary Educn Project, 1968–70; Library Adv. Council (England), 1973–78; Nat. Inst. for Careers Educn and Counselling, 1975–83; DES/DHSS Working Gp on Under 5s Res., 1980–82; Commonwealth Scholarship Commn in the UK, 1996–2002; Vice-Chm., Educnl Res. Bd, SSRC, 1973–77; Member: Steering Gp, OECD Workshops on Educnl Innovation, Cambridge 1969, W Germany, 1970, Illinois 1971; Exec. Cttee, Inter-Univ. Council for Higher Educn Overseas, 1977–83; Council, Univ. of Papua New Guinea, 1984–92; Council, ACU, 1987–88; Governor, Centre for Educnl Development Overseas, 1969–70; Dep., Admin. Bd, Internat. Assoc. of Univs, 1990–96. Trustee, Just World Partners, 1993–2005; Exeter CAB, 2004–. Bank of Hawaii Distinguished Lectr, Univ. of Hawaii, 1992; Dist. Fellow, Flinders Univ. Inst. of Internat. Educn, 1999–. Hon. Fellow, Univ. of Exeter, 2004. Hon. LLD Dundee, 1982; Hon. DLitt Deakin, 1991. Symons Medal, ACU, 2002. *Publications:* The Management of International Co-operation in Universities, 1996; contribs to educnl jls. *Address:* 3 Pennsylvania Park, Exeter EX4 6HB. *T:* (01392) 272986.

CASTRO, Rev. Emilio Enrique; Pastor, Methodist Church, Montevideo; *b* Uruguay, 2 May 1927; *s* of Ignacio Castro and Maria Pombo; *m* 1951, Gladys Nieves; one *s* one *d*. *Educ:* Union Theol Seminary, Buenos Aires (ThL); University of Basel (post graduate work, 1953–54); University of Lausanne (ThD 1984). Ordained, 1948; Pastor: Durazno and Trinidad (Uruguay), 1951–53; Central Methodist Church, La Paz, 1954–56; Central Methodist Church, Montevideo, 1957–65; concurrently Prof. of Contemp. Theol. Thought, Mennonite Seminary, Montevideo; Coordinator, Commn for Evangelical Unity in Latin America, 1965–72; Exec. Sec., S American Assoc. of Theol. Schools, 1966–69; Pres., Methodist Church in Uruguay, 1970–72; Dir, WCC Commn on World Mission and Evangelism, 1973–83; Gen. Sec., WCC, 1985–92. Chm., Fellowship of Christians and Jews in Uruguay, 1962–66; Moderator, Conf. on future of CCIA, Netherlands, 1967; Chm., WCC's Agency for Christian Literature Develt, 1970–72. Hon. DHL: Westmar Coll., USA, 1984; Holy Cross, Boston, 1988; Hon. DTh Geneva, 1992. *Publications:* Jesus the Conqueror, 1956; When Conscience Disturbs, 1959; Mission, Presence and Dialogue, 1963; A Pilgrim People, 1965; Reality and Faith, 1966; Amidst Evolution, 1975; Towards a Latin American Pastoral Perspective, 1973; Sent Free: Mission and Unity in the Perspective of the Kingdom, 1985; When we pray together, 1989; (ed and contrib.) Christian Century, 1971–75; (ed and contrib.) International Review of Mission, 1973–83; (ed) To the Wind of God's Spirit: Reflections on the Canberra Theme, 1990; A Passion for Unity, 1992; numerous articles in several languages. *Recreation:* basketball. *Address:* Chemin Briquet 22, 1209 Geneva, Switzerland. *Fax:* (22) 7333533.

CASTRO RUZ, Dr Fidel; Head of State, Cuba, 1976–2008; *b* 13 Aug. 1927; *s* of Angel Castro y Argiz and Lina Ruz de Castro (*née* González); *m* 1948, Mirta Diaz-Balart (marr. diss. 1955); one *s*. *Educ:* Colegio Lassalle; Colegio Dolores; Colegio Belén; Univ. of Havana (Pres., Students' Fedn; Dr Law 1950). Lawyer, Havana, 1950–53; imprisoned, 1953–55; C-in-C, Armed Forces, Cuba, 1959; Prime Minister of Cuba, 1959–76; Head, Nat. Defence Council, 1992–2008. Chm., Agrarian Reform Inst., 1965–2008. First Sec., Partido Comunista (formerly Partido Unido de la Revolución Socialista), 1963–2008. *Publications:* Ten Years of Revolution, 1964; History Will Absolve Me, 1968; Major Speeches, 1968; (jtly) Fidel, 1987; (jtly) How Far We Slaves Have Come, 1991; (jtly) My Life, 2007. *Address:* Palacio del Gobierno, Havana, Cuba.

CATCHPOLE, Nancy Mona, OBE 1987; Chairman, Board of Trustees, Bath Royal Literary and Scientific Institution, 2002–06 (a Trustee, since 1997); *b* 6 Aug. 1929; *d* of George William Page and Mona Dorothy Page (*née* Cowin), New Eltham; *m* 1959, Geoffrey David Arthur Catchpole; one *s* one *d*. *Educ:* Haberdashers' Aske's Hatcham Girls' Sch.; Bedford Coll., Univ. of London. BA Hons (History). Asst mistress, Gravesend Grammar Sch. for Girls, 1952–56; i/c History, Ipswich High Sch. GPDST, 1956–62; part time lectr in History and General Studies, Bath Tech. Coll., 1977–96. Sec., Bath Assoc. of University Women, 1970–75; Regional Rep. on Exec., BFUW, 1975–77, Vice-Pres., 1977–80, Pres., 1981–84. Women's National Commission: Co-Chairman, 1983–85; Immediate Past Co-Chairman, 1985–86; part-time Sec. with special responsibility for Women's Trng Roadshow prog., 1985–88; Actg Sec., March–Dec. 1988; Consultant for Women's Trng Roadshow prog. to RSA Women's Wkg Gp/Industry Matters, 1989–90; Vice-Chm., RSA Women's Adv. Gp (formerly Women's Working Group for Industry Year 1986), 1985–95; British Federation of Women Graduates Charitable Foundation (formerly Crosby Hall): Gov., 1992–98, 2002–04; Vice-Chm. of Govs, 1992–95, Chm., 1995–98; Chm., Grants Cttee, 1992–95. Chm., U3A, Bath, 2001–03. Chm., Bath Branch, Historical Assoc., 1993–96 (Sec., 1975–79; Hon. Treas., 2001–04). A Governor, Weston Infants' Sch., Bath, 1975–85 (Chm., 1981–83; Vice-Chm., 1983–86); Member: Managers, Eagle House Community Sch., Somerset CC, 1979–82; Case Cttee, Western Nat. Adoption Soc., 1975–77; Wessex RHA, 1986–90; Avon FHSA Service Cttee, 1990–96; Discipline Cttee, Avon HA, 1997–2003. FRSA 1986. *Recreations:* listening, viewing, talking, writing. *Address:* 66 Leighton Road, Weston, Bath BA1 4NG. *T:* (01225) 423338.

CATCHPOLE, Stuart Paul; QC 2002; a Recorder, since 2004; *b* 21 July 1964; *s* of Robert James Catchpole and Celia Catchpole; *m* 1995, Rebecca; one *s* two *d*. *Educ:* Univ. of Durham; Inns of Court Sch. of Law. Called to the Bar, Inner Temple, 1987, Bencher, 2008; in practice at the Bar, 1988–. Treasury Supplemental Panel (Common Law), 1992–98; Jun. Counsel to the Crown, 1998–2002. Part-time Legal Mem., Proscribed Orgns Appeal Commn, 2001–. *Publications:* (ed) Crown Proceedings, Halsbury's Laws, 4th edn, vol. 12 (1), 1998; (contrib.) Extradition, Halsbury's Laws, 4th edn, vol. 17 (2), 2000. *Recreations:* cinema, theatre, reading, wine. *Address:* 39 Essex Street, WC2R 3AT. *T:* (020) 7832 1111, *Fax:* (020) 7353 3978; *e-mail:* stuart.catchpole@39essex.com. *Club:* Royal Automobile.

CATER, Antony John E.; *see* Essex-Cater.

CATER, Dr John; Vice-Chancellor, Edge Hill University (formerly Principal, Edge Hill College of Higher Education), since 1993; *b* Northampton, 3 Feb. 1953; *s* of William Ernest and Frances Brenda Cater; *m* 1981, Sue Lawlor; one *s* one *d*. *Educ:* Univ. of Wales, Lampeter (BA Hons Geog. 1974); Council for Nat. Academic Awards (PhD 1984). Res. Asst, Lectr and Res. Fellow, Liverpool Poly., 1974–79; Edge Hill College of Higher Education: Lectr, Sen. Lectr, then Hd of Dept of Urban Policy and Race Relns, 1979–86; Dep. Dean, 1986–90; Hd, Policy Res. and Develt, 1990–92; Dir of Resources, 1992–93. Chair: Higher Educn NW, 1999–2001; Gtr Merseyside and W Lancs Lifelong Learning Network, 2006–. Director: Higher Educn Careers Service, 1994–; Standing Conf. of Principals, 1994–2004 (Vice-Chm., 1997–2001; Chm., 2001–03); TTA, 1999–2005 (Chairman: Audit Cttee, 2001–03; Accreditation Cttee, 2003–05); Trng and Develt Agency for Schs, 2005–06 (Chm., Accreditation Cttee, 2005–06). Mem., Adv. Cttee on Degree-Awarding Powers, QAA, 2006–. Mem., Health and Social Care Cttee, 2004–, Teacher Educn Adv. Gp, 2007–, Universities UK. Dir, 1994–, Chm., 2003–05, Liverpool City of Learning. *Publications:* (with T. P. Jones) Social Geography, 1989; contrib. articles and chapters on residential segregation, black and Asian business, housing and public policy. *Recreations:* most sports (Rugby, cricket, golf, squash), current affairs, reading, travel. *Address:* Edge Hill University, St Helens Road, Ormskirk, Lancs L39 4QP. *T:* (01695) 584234, *Fax:* (01695) 577137.

CATES, Prof. Michael Elmhirst, PhD; FRS 2007; FRSE; Professor of Natural Philosophy, School of Physics, University of Edinburgh, since 1995; *b* 5 May 1961. *Educ:* Trinity Coll., Cambridge (BA 1982, MA; PhD 1986). Cavendish Laboratory, Cambridge: Asst Lectr, 1989–92; Univ. Lectr, 1992–95. FRSE 2005. *Publications:* articles in learned jls. *Recreations:* hill-walking, painting, music. *Address:* School of Physics, University of Edinburgh, James Clerk Maxwell Building, The King's Buildings, Mayfield Road, Edinburgh EH9 3JZ. *T:* (0131) 650 5296, *Fax:* (0131) 650 5902.

CATESBY, (William) Peter; DL; Chairman, Real Hotel Company (formerly Choice Hotels Europe Group) plc, since 2002 (non-executive Director, since 2001); *b* 11 Sept. 1940; *s* of late Robert Cooper Catesby, MBE; *m* 1972, Cynthia Nixon (marr. diss. 2005); two *d*. *Educ:* Battersea Coll. of Advanced Technol. (ACT). Joined Grosvenor House Ltd, 1962; Hotel Manager, 1964–68; Hotels Trng Manager, Trust House Hotels Ltd, 1968–70; Dist Manager (SE), 1970–72, Asst Regl Dir (S), 1972–73, Trust House Forte Ltd; joined Swallow Hotels, 1973: Gen. Manager, Swallow Hotels Div., Vaux Breweries Ltd, 1973–75; Man. Dir, Swallow Hotels Ltd, 1975–77; Vaux Group plc: Main Bd Dir, 1977–2000; Gp Dep. Chm., 1990–99; Jt Man. Dir, 1992–99; Vaux Gp plc renamed Swallow Gp, 1999; Chm., Swallow Hotels Ltd, 1999–2000; Chief Exec., Swallow Gp plc, 1999–2000. FIH (FHCIMA 1974). Dir, BHA Ltd, 1998– (Chm., Finance Cttee). Hon. Dep. Col, D Rifles Co., 5 Bn RRF (formerly Hon. Col, 7 Bn DLI), 1994–. Vice Chm., N of England, RFCA, 1996–. DL Co. Durham, 1997. *Address:* Real Hotel Company plc, Premier House, 112–114 Station Road, Edgware, Middlesex HA8 7BI.

CATHCART, family name of **Earl Cathcart**.

CATHCART, 7th Earl, *cr* 1814; **Charles Alan Andrew Cathcart,** ACA; Lord Cathcart (Scot.) 1447; Viscount Cathcart, Baron Greenock 1807; *b* 30 Nov. 1952; *s* of 6th Earl Cathcart, CB, DSO, MC and Rosemary (*d* 1980), *yr d* of Air Cdre Sir Percy Smyth-Osbourne, CMG, CBE; *S* father, 1999; *m* 1981, Vivien Clare, *o d* of F. D. McInnes Skinner; one *s* one *d*. *Educ:* Eton. Commnd Scots Guards, 1972–75. Whinney Murray, 1976–79; Ernst & Whinney, 1979–83; Gardner Mountain and Capel-Cure Agencies Ltd, 1983–94; Director: Murray Lawrence Members Agencies Ltd, 1995–96; RGA Holdings Ltd, 1996–; RGA Capital Ltd, 1996–; RGA Reinsurance UK Ltd. Mem. (C) Breckland DC, 1997–2007. Elected Mem., H of L, 2007. Mem., Queen's Bodyguard for Scotland, Royal Co. of Archers. *Recreations:* ski-ing, sailing, country pursuits. *Heir:* *s* Lord Greenock, *qv*. *Address:* Gateley Hall, Norfolk. *Club:* Pratt's.

CATHCART, Samuel; Sheriff of Glasgow and Strathkelvin at Glasgow (formerly Floating Sheriff), since 2000; *b* 5 March 1950; *s* of Samuel Cathcart and Margaret Gordon or Cathcart; *m* 1985, Sandra Fullarton; one *s* one *d*. *Educ:* Dalry High Sch.; Edinburgh Univ. (LLB). Admitted Solicitor, 1974, in practice, 1974–77; Procurator Fiscal Depute, 1977–88; called to the Scottish Bar, 1989; Advocate, 1989–99; Advocate Depute, Crown

Office, 1996–99. *Recreations:* sailing, fishing. *Address:* 43 Douglas Street, Largs, Ayrshire KA30 8PT. *T:* (01475) 672478.

CATHERWOOD, Andrea Catherine, (Mrs R. G. Smith); International Correspondent and newscaster, ITV News, since 2001; *b* 27 Nov. 1967; *d* of late Henry Robert Courtney Catherwood and of Adrienne Catherwood; *m* 2002, Richard Gray Smith; three *s* (of whom two are twins). *Educ:* Strathearn Sch., Belfast; Manchester Univ. (LLB Hons). Reporter, Ulster TV, 1991–93; reporter, 1994–96, news anchor, 1996–98, CNBC Asia, in Hong Kong; corresp. and newscaster, ITV News, 1998–2000; evening newscaster, Channel 5 News, 2000–01. *Recreations:* sailing, scuba-diving, art and literature, travel, food. *Address:* c/o ITN, 200 Gray's Inn Road, WC1X 8XZ. *T:* (020) 7833 3000; *e-mail:* andrea.catherwood@itn.co.uk. *Clubs:* Home House; Royal North of Ireland Yacht.

CATHERWOOD, Sir (Henry) Frederick (Ross), Kt 1971; Vice President, Evangelical Alliance, since 2001 (President, 1992–2001); President, International Fellowship of Evangelical Students, 1995–2003 (Vice President, 2003); Member (C) Cambridge and North Bedfordshire, European Parliament, 1984–94 (Cambridgeshire, 1979–84); *b* 30 Jan. 1925; *s* of late Stuart and of Jean Catherwood, Co. Londonderry; *m* 1954, Elizabeth, *er d* of late Rev. Dr D. M. Lloyd Jones, Westminster Chapel, London; two *s* one *d*. *Educ:* Shrewsbury; Clare Coll., Cambridge (Hon. Fellow, 1992). Articled Price, Waterhouse & Co.; qualified as Chartered Accountant, 1951; Secretary, Laws Stores Ltd, Gateshead, 1952–54; Secretary and Controller, Richard Costain Ltd, 1954–55; Chief Executive, 1955–60; Asst Managing Director, British Aluminium Co. Ltd, 1960–62; Managing Director, 1962–64; Chief Industrial Adviser, DEA, 1964–66; Dir-Gen., NEDC, 1966–71; Managing Dir and Chief Executive, John Laing & Son Ltd, 1972–74. European Parliament: Chm., Cttee for External Economic Relations, 1979–84; a Vice-Pres., 1989–91; Vice Pres., Foreign Affairs Cttee, 1992–94. British Institute of Management, subseq. Institute of Management: Mem. Council, 1961–66, 1969–79; Vice-Chm., 1972; Chm., 1974–76. Member of Council: NI Development Council, 1963–64; RIIA, 1964–77; BNEC, 1965–71; NEDC, 1964–71; Chm., BOTB, 1975–79. Pres., Fellowship of Independent Evangelical Churches, 1977; Chm. of Council, 1971–77, Pres., 1983–84, Univs and Colls Christian Fellowship (formerly Inter-Varsity Fellowship); Mem., Central Religious Adv. Cttee to BBC and IBA, 1975–79. Hon. DSc Aston, 1972; Hon. DSc (Econ.) QUB, 1973; Hon. DUniv Surrey, 1979. *Publications:* The Christian in Industrial Society, 1964, rev. edn 1980 (On the Job, USA, 1983); Britain with the Brakes Off, 1966; The Christian Citizen, 1969; A Better Way, 1976; First Things First, 1979; God's Time God's Money, 1987; Pro Europe?, 1991; David: Poet, Warrior, King, 1993; At the Cutting Edge (memoirs), 1995; Jobs & Justice, Homes & Hope, 1997; It Can be Done, 2000; The Creation of Wealth, 2002. *Recreations:* music, gardening, reading. *Club:* Oxford and Cambridge.

CATHERWOOD, Herbert Sidney Elliott, CBE 1979; Chairman of Ulsterbus and Citybus, 1967–89; *b* 8 March 1929. *Educ:* Belfast Royal Academy, N Ireland. Chairman, Ulsterbus Ltd, from inception, 1967; Member, NI Transport Holding Co., 1968–73; Director of Merger of Belfast Corporation Transport with Ulsterbus, 1972. Director: Sea Ferry Parcels, 1972–99; RMC Catherwood, 1974–96; Chm., Lombard Ulster Bank Ltd, 1989–97. *Address:* Boulderstone House, 917 Antrim Road, Templepatrick, Co. Antrim, N Ireland BT39 0AT.

CATLIN, John Anthony, CB 2004; Director (Legal Services), Departments of Health and for Work and Pensions (formerly of Social Security), 1996–2007; *b* 25 Nov. 1947; *s* of John Vincent Catlin and Kathleen Glover Catlin (*née* Brand); *m* 1974, Caroline Jane Goodman; one *s* two *d*. *Educ:* Ampleforth Coll., York; Birmingham Univ. (LLB 1969). Solicitor of the Supreme Court, 1972. Articled Clerk, 1970–72, Asst Solicitor, 1972–75, Gregory Rowcliffe & Co.; Legal Asst, 1975–78, Sen. Legal Asst, 1978–84, Treasury Solicitor's Dept; Asst Solicitor, 1984–89, Dep. Solicitor, 1989–96, DoE. *Recreations:* history, music, computers.

CATLIN, Stephen John Oakley; Chief Executive and Deputy Chairman, Catlin Group Ltd, since 1995; *b* Aldershot, 25 June 1954; *s* of Robin John Oakley Catlin and Rita Fortune Catlin; *m* 1975, Helen Margaret Gill; two *d*. Dep. underwriter, B. L. Evens and Others, 1982–84; Founder and Chief Exec., Catlin Underwriting Agencies Ltd, 1984–95, Chm., 1987–95. Lloyd's Nominated Dir, Equitas Hldgs Ltd, 1996–2002. Chm., Lloyd's Market Assoc., 2002–03; Member: Council, Lloyd's, 2002–04; Lloyd's Franchise Bd, 2003–06. *Recreations:* fishing, shooting, ski-ing. *Address:* Catlin Group Ltd, 3 Minster Court, Mincing Lane, EC3R 7DD. *T:* (020) 7626 0486, *Fax:* (020) 7623 3667.

CATLING, Hector William, CBE 1989 (OBE 1980); MA, DPhil, FSA; Director of the British School at Athens, 1971–89, retired; *b* 26 June 1924; *s* of late Arthur William Catling and Phyllis Norah Catling (*née* Vyvyan); *m* 1948, Elizabeth Anne (*née* Salter) (*d* 2000); two *s* one *d*. *Educ:* The Grammar Sch., Bristol; St John's Coll., Oxford (Hon. Fellow 1986). Casberd Exhibnr, 1948, BA 1950, MA 1954, DPhil 1957. Served War, RNVR, 1942–46. At Univ.: undergrad. 1946–50, postgrad. 1950–54. Goldsmiths' Travelling Schol., 1951–53. Archaeological Survey Officer, Dept of Antiquities, Cyprus, 1955–59; Asst Keeper, Dept of Antiquities, Ashmolean Museum, Univ. of Oxford, 1959–64, Sen. Asst Keeper, 1964–71. Fellow, 1967–71, Supernumerary Fellow, 1991–, Linacre Coll., Oxford. Sanders Meml Lectr, Sheffield, 1979; Myres Meml Lectr, Oxford, 1987; Mitford Meml Lectr, St Andrews, 1989. Corresp. Mem., German Archaeological Inst., 1961; Hon. Mem., Greek Archaeological Soc., 1975 (Vice-Pres., 1998–). Hon. Dr Athens, 1987. *Publications:* Cypriot Bronzework in the Mycenaean World, 1964; (with J. N. Coldstream) Knossos, the North Cemetery: early Greek tombs, 4 vols, 1996; Sparta, Menelaion I: the bronze age, 2008; contribs to jls concerned with prehistoric and classical antiquity in Greek lands. *Recreation:* ornithology. *Address:* Dunford House, Langford, Lechlade, Glos GL7 3LN. *Club:* Athenæum.

CATLOW, Prof. (Charles) Richard (Arthur), DPhil; FRS 2004; FRSC, FInstP; Professor of Solid State Chemistry and Dean, Mathematics and Physical Sciences Faculty, University College London, since 2007 (Head, Department of Chemistry, 2007–08); *b* 24 April 1947; *s* of Rolf M. Catlow and Constance Catlow (*née* Aldred); *m* 1978, Carey Anne Chapman; one *s*; *m* 2000, Nora de Leeuw. *Educ:* Clitheroe Royal Grammar School; St John's College, Oxford (MA, DPhil). FRSC 1990; FInstP 1995. Research Fellow, Oxford Univ., 1973–76; Lectr, Dept of Chemistry, UCL, 1976–85; Prof. of Physical Chemistry, Univ. of Keele, 1985–89; Wolfson Prof. of Natural Philosophy, 1989–2007, Dir, Davy Faraday Lab., 1998–2007, Royal Instn of GB. Mem., CCLRC, 2006–07. Medal for Solid State Chem., 1992, Award for Interdisciplinary Science, 1998, RSC. *Publications:* (jtly) Point Defects in Materials, 1988; ed jtly and contrib. to works on computational and materials sciences; 700 papers in learned jls. *Recreations:* reading, music, walking. *Address:* Mathematics and Physical Sciences Faculty, University College London, Gower Street, WC1E 6BT; *e-mail:* c.r.a.catlow@ucl.ac.uk. *Club:* Athenæum.

CATO, Brian Hudson; Full-time Chairman of Industrial Tribunals, 1975–92, Regional Chairman, Newcastle upon Tyne, 1989–92; *b* 6 June 1928; *s* of Thomas and Edith Willis Cato; *m* 1963, Barbara Edith Myles; one *s*. *Educ:* LEA elem. and grammar schs; Trinity Coll., Oxford; RAF Padgate. MA Oxon, LLB London. RAF, 1952–54. Called to Bar, Gray's Inn, 1952; in practice NE Circuit, 1954–75; a Recorder of the Crown Court, 1974–75. Special Lectr (part-time) in Law of Town and Country Planning, King's Coll., now Univ. of Newcastle, 1956–75; Hon. Examnr, Inst. of Landscape Architects, 1960–75. Pres., N of England Medico-legal Soc., 1973–74. Corresp. Sec., Berwickshire Naturalists Club, 1992–96. Freeman of City of Newcastle upon Tyne by patrimony; Founder Mem. Scriveners' Co., Newcastle upon Tyne (Clerk, 1992–2006); Freeman, City of London, 1985. Hon. ALI. *Recreations:* bibliomania, antiquarian studies, family life. *Address:* 2 Croft Place, Newton-by-the-Sea, Alnwick, Northumberland NE66 3DL. *T:* (01665) 576334.

CATON, Martin Philip; MP (Lab) Gower, since 1997; *b* 15 June 1951; *s* of William John Caton and Pauline Joan Caton; *m* 1996, Bethan, *d* of late Hermus Evans and of Menai Evans; two step *d*. *Educ:* Newport Grammar Sch., Essex; Norfolk Sch. of Agriculture; Aberystwyth Coll. of FE (HNC). Scientific Officer, Welsh Plant Breeding Stn, Aberystwyth, 1974–84; Political Researcher, David Morris, MEP, 1984–97. Mem. (Lab) Swansea CC, 1988–97. *Address:* House of Commons, SW1A 0AA.

CATON, Dr Valerie, (Mrs D. M. Harrison); HM Diplomatic Service; Ambassador to Finland, since 2006; *b* 12 May 1952; *d* of Robert Caton and Florence Amy Caton (*née* Aspden); *m* 1987, David Mark Harrison; one *s* one *d*. *Educ:* Blackburn High Sch. for Girls; Bristol Univ. (BA, PhD); Grad. Sch. of European Studies, Univ. of Reading (MA). Lectrice, Univ. of Sorbonne, Paris, 1977–78; Tutor in French, Exeter Univ., 1978–80; joined HM Diplomatic Service, 1980: FCO, 1980–82; Second, later First Sec., EC Affairs, Brussels, 1982–84; First Sec. (Chancery), Paris, 1988–92; Dep. Head of Mission, Stockholm, 1993–96; Counsellor (Financial and Economic), Paris, 1997–2001; Sen. Associate Mem., St Antony's Coll., Oxford, 2001–02; Head: Envmt Policy Dept, FCO, 2002–04; Climate Change and Energy Gp, FCO, 2004–06. *Publications:* various articles in jls on EU issues and on works of French writer, Raymond Queneau. *Recreations:* reading, theatre, collecting humorous books, walking, riding. *Address:* c/o Foreign and Commonwealth Office, King Charles Street, SW1A 2AH.

CATOVSKY, Prof. Daniel, MD, DSc; FRCP, FRCPath, FMedSci; Professor of Haematology, and Head of Department of Haematology and Cytogenetics, Institute of Cancer Research, 1988–2004, now Professor Emeritus; Hon. Consultant, Royal Marsden Hospital, 1988–2004; *b* 19 Sept. 1937; *s* of Felix Catovsky and Ana Kabanchik; *m* 1960, Julia Margaret Polak (*see* Dame J. M. Polak); two *s* one *d*. *Educ:* Faculty of Medicine, Buenos Aires Univ. (MD 1961); London Univ. (DSc Med. 1985). FRCPath 1986; FRCP 1990. Royal Postgraduate Medical School: Fellow, 1967–76; Hon. Sen. Lectr in Haematol. and Medicine, 1976–87; Prof. of Haematol Oncology, 1987–88; Consultant, Hammersmith Hosp., 1976–88. Visiting Professor: Mount Sinai Med. Sch., NY, 1981; M. D. Anderson Cancer Center, Univ. of Texas, 2004–05. Ham-Wasserman Lecture (first annual), Amer. Soc. of Hematology, 1984. FMedSci 1999. British Soc. for Haematology Medal, 2000; Binet-Rai Medal, Internat. Workshop on Chronic Lymphocytic Leukaemia, 2005. *Publications:* The Leukemic Cell, 1981, 2nd edn 1991; (with A. Polliack) Chronic Lymphocytic Leukaemia, 1988; (with R. Foa) The Lymphoid Leukaemias, 1990; (ed with A. V. Hoffbrand and E. G. Tuddenham) Postgraduate Haematology, 5th edn 2005; 700 articles in learned jls. *Recreations:* walking, films, theatre. *Address:* Section of Haemato-Oncology, Institute of Cancer Research, 15 Cotswold Road, Sutton, Surrey SM2 5NG. *T:* (020) 8722 4114.

CATOVSKY, Dame Julia Margaret; *see* Polak, Dame J. M.

CATTANACH, Bruce Macintosh, PhD, DSc; FRS 1987; Senior Scientist, MRC, 1970–98; *b* 5 Nov. 1932; *s* of James and Margaretta Cattanach; *m* 1st, 1966, Margaret Bouchier Crewe (*d* 1996); two *d*; 2nd, 1999, Josephine Peters. *Educ:* King's Coll., Univ. of Durham (BSc, 1st Cl. Hons); Inst. of Animal Genetics, Univ. of Edinburgh (PhD, DSc). Scientific Staff, MRC Induced Mutagenesis Unit, Edinburgh, 1959–62, 1964–66; NIH Post Doctoral Res. Fellow, Biology Div., Oak Ridge Nat. Lab., Tenn, USA, 1962–64; Sen. Scientist, City of Hope Med. Centre, Duarte, Calif, 1966–69; Scientific Staff, 1969–86, Hd of Genetics Div., 1987–96, MRC Radiobiology Unit, Chilton, Oxon; Actg Dir, MRC Mammalian Genetics Unit, Harwell, 1996–97. *Publications:* contribs to several learned jls on X-chromosome inactivation, sex determination, mammalian chromosome imprinting, and genetics generally. *Recreations:* squash; breeding, showing and judging pedigree dogs; investigating inherited disease in dogs and devising control schemes for elimination. *Address:* Downs Edge, Reading Road, Harwell, Oxon OX11 0JJ. *T:* (01235) 835410.

CATTERALL, Dr John Ashley, OBE 1995; FIMMM, FInstP; Senior Executive, Engineering Council, 1997–99; *b* 26 May 1928; *s* of John William Catterall and Gladys Violet Catterall; *m* 1960, Jennifer Margaret Bradfield; two *s*. *Educ:* Imperial Coll. of Science and Technol., London (BSc, PhD, DIC). ARSM; FIMMM (FIM 1964); FInstP 1968; CPhys 1965; CEng 1978. National Physical Lab., 1952–74; Dept of Industry, 1974–81; Head, Energy Technology Div., and Dep. Chief Scientist, Dept of Energy, 1981–83; Sec., SERC, 1983–88; Sec., Inst. of Metals, 1988–91, then Sec. and Chief Exec., Inst. of Materials, 1991–97. Inst. of Metals Rosenhain Medal for Physical Metallurgy, 1970. *Publications:* (with O. Kubaschewski) Thermochemical Data of Alloys, 1956; contrib. Philos. Mag., Jl Inst. of Physics, Jl Inst. of Metals. *Recreation:* reading. *Address:* Hill House, The Doward, Whitchurch, Ross-on-Wye, Herefordshire HR9 6DU. *T:* (01600) 890341.

CATTERALL, John Stewart; Director, Agenda Planning Research Ltd, since 2001; *b* 13 Jan. 1939; *s* of John Bernard and Eliza Catterall; *m* 1965, Ann Beryl Hughes; two *s*. *Educ:* Blackpool Tech. Coll. and Sch. of Art. Mem. CIPFA. Posts in local authorities, 1961–70; Management Accountant, Cambridgeshire and Isle of Ely CC, 1970–72, Chief Accountant, 1972–73; Asst County Treasurer, Financial Planning and Accounting, Cambs CC, 1973–76; Dist. Treasurer, Southampton and SW Hants DHA, 1976–78, Area Treasurer, 1978–82; Regional Treasurer, NE Thames RHA, 1982–85; Dep. Dir, Finance, NHS Mgt Bd, 1985–89; Head of Health Services, 1985–89, Head of Health Adv. Services, 1989, CIPFA. Chm. and Chief Exec., C International Ltd, 1990–92; Dir, Capita PLC, 1992–93; Man. Dir, Conferences and Training Ltd, 1993–2001. *Publications:* contribs to professional jls. *Recreations:* golf, swimming, reading. *Address:* Le Moulin, Stock Lane, Landford Wood, Wilts SP5 2ER. *T:* (01794) 390719.

CATTERMOLE, Joan Eileen, (Mrs James Cattermole); *see* Mitchell, J. E.

CATTERSON, Marie Thérèse; Her Honour Judge Catterson; a Circuit Judge, since 2001; *b* 14 Oct. 1948; *e d* of James Joseph Catterson and Rosemary Catterson; *m* 1984; two *d*. *Educ:* Wyggeston Girls' Grammar Sch., Leicester; University Coll. London (LLB 1970). Called to the Bar, Gray's Inn, 1972; in practice as barrister, S Eastern Circuit, 1972–2001; a Recorder, 1996–2001. *Recreations:* gardening, travel. *Address:* The Crown Court, Bricket Road, St Albans, Herts AL1 3JW.

CATTO, family name of **Baron Catto**.

CATTO, 3rd Baron *cr* 1936, of Cairncatto, co. Aberdeen; **Innes Gordon Catto;** Bt 1921; *b* 7 Aug. 1950; *e s* of 2nd Baron Catto; *S* father, 2001. *Educ:* Grenville Coll.; Shuttleworth Agric. Coll. *Heir: b* Hon. Alexander Gordon Catto [*b* 22 June 1952; *m* 1981, Elizabeth Scott, twin *d* of Maj. T. P. Boyes; two *s* one *d*].

CATTO, Gay; *see* Catto, P. G. W.

CATTO, Sir Graeme (Robertson Dawson), Kt 2002; MD; DSc; FRCP, FRCPE, FRCPGlas, FMedSci; FRSE; Professor of Medicine, University of Aberdeen, since 2005; *b* 24 April 1945; *s* of William Dawson Catto and Dora Elizabeth (*née* Spiby); *m* 1967, Joan Sievewright; one *s* one *d*. *Educ:* Robert Gordon's Coll., Aberdeen; Univ. of Aberdeen (MB ChB Hons 1969; MD Hons 1975; DSc 1988). FRCPGlas 1982; FRCP 1984; FRCPE 1988; FRSE 1996. House Officer, Aberdeen Royal Infirmary, 1969–70; Res. Fellow, then Lectr, Univ. of Aberdeen, 1970–75; Harkness Fellow, Commonwealth Fund of NY; Fellow in Medicine, Harvard Univ., 1975–77; University of Aberdeen: Sen. Lectr, then Reader, 1977–88; Dean, Faculty of Medicine and Med. Scis, 1992–98; Prof. of Medicine and Therapeutics, 1988–2000; Vice Principal, 1995–2000; Hon. Consultant Physician and Nephrologist, Aberdeen Royal Infirmary, 1977–2000; Pro-Vice Chancellor (Medicine), Univ. of London, 2003–05; Vice Principal, KCL and Dean, GKT, 2000–05; Hon. Consultant Physician and Nephrologist, NHS Grampian, 2005–. Vice-Chm., Aberdeen Royal Hosps NHS Trust, 1992–99. Chief Scientist, Scottish Executive (formerly Scottish Office) Health Dept, 1997–2000. Member: GMC, 1994– (Pres., 2002–; Chm. Educn Cttee, 1999–2002); SHEFC, 1996–2002; Specialist Trng Authority, 1999–2002; Standing Medical Adv. Cttee, 2002–05; Council, Regulation of Healthcare Professionals, 2003–. Member: Lambeth, Southwark and Lewisham HA, 2000–02; SE London Strategic HA, 2003–05. Founder FMedSci 1998 (Treas., 1998–2001). Chm., Robert Gordon's Coll., Aberdeen, 1995–2005. Hon. FRCGP 2000; Hon. FRCSE 2002. FRSA 1996. FKC 2005. Hon. LLD Aberdeen, 2002; Hon. DSc: St Andrews, 2003; Robert Gordon's Univ., 2004; Kent, 2007; South Bank, 2007; Hon. MD Southampton, 2004. *Publications:* (ed) Clinical Transplantation: current practice and future prospects, 1987; (with D. A. Power) Nephrology, 1988; (ed) Calculus Disease, 1988; (ed) Chronic Renal Failure, 1988; (ed) Haemodialysis, 1988; (ed) Management of Renal Hypertension, 1988; (ed) Pregnancy and Renal Disorders, 1988; (ed) Drugs and the Kidney, 1989; (ed) Glomerulo-nephritis, 1989; Multisystem Diseases, 1989; Transplantation, 1989; (ed) Urinary Tract Infections, 1989; (with A. W. Thomson) Immunology of Renal Transplantation, 1993; contrib. to learned jls on aspects of renal disease. *Recreation:* hills and glens. *Address:* 4 Woodend Avenue, Aberdeen AB15 6YL. *T:* (01224) 310509; Maryfield, Glenbuchat, Aberdeenshire AB36 8TS. *T:* (01975) 641317. *Clubs:* Athenæum; Royal Northern and University (Aberdeen).

CATTO, Henry Edward; Chairman, Atlantic Council of the United States, 1999–2007; Partner, Catto & Catto, San Antonio, 1955–2003; *b* 6 Dec. 1930; *s* of Henry E. Catto and Maurine H. Catto; *m* 1958, Jessica Hobby; two *s* two *d*. *Educ:* Williams Coll. (BA). Businessman, San Antonio, Texas, 1952–69; Dep. US Rep., Orgn of American States, 1969–71; US Ambassador to El Salvador, 1971–73; US Chief of Protocol, 1974–76; Consultant, Washington DC, 1977–81; Asst Sec. of Defense, 1981–83; Vice-Chm., H & C Communications, 1983–89; US Ambassador to UK, 1989–91; Dir, US Inf. Agency, 1991–93. Diplomat-in-Residence, Univ. of Texas (San Antonio), 1993–. *Publication:* Ambassadors at Sea: the high and low adventures of a diplomat (memoirs), 1999. *Recreations:* tennis, hiking, running, ski-ing, golf.

CATTO, (Patricia) Gay (Warren), CVO 2005; Ceremonial Officer, Cabinet Office, 2000–05; *b* 16 Nov. 1940; *d* of late Rt Rev. (William) Warren Hunt and Mollie Hunt (*née* Green); *m* 1971, Alistair William Gillespie Catto (*d* 2006); one *s* one *d*. *Educ:* Sherborne Sch. for Girls; St Hugh's Coll., Oxford (BA). Asst Principal, Min. of Pensions and Nat. Insce, 1963–66; Private Sec. to Perm. Sec., Home Office, 1966–67; Principal: Home Office, 1967–73; Dept of Employment, 1978–83; Assistant Secretary: Resources and Planning Div., HSE, 1983–88; Police Dept, 1988–96, Constitutional Unit, 1996–2000, Home Office. *Address:* 7 Canonbury Lane, N1 2AS. *T:* (020) 7359 7232.

CAU, Antoine Emond André; Founding President, Antedman SA, Switzerland, since 2006; *b* 26 Aug. 1947; *s* of Henri and Laure Cau; *m* 1978, Patricia Stamm. *Educ:* Lycée Mignet, Aix-en-Provence; Institut d'Etudes Commerciales de Grenoble (diplôme de direction et de gestion des entreprises; maîtrise de gestion). Hertz: Station Manager, Avignon, 1970–75; station manager posts, 1975–77; District Manager: Nice, 1977; Côte d'Azur, 1978–80; Zone Manager, S of France, 1980–82; Ops Manager, Italy, 1982–84; Corporate Accounts Manager, Hertz Europe, 1984; Ops Manager, France, 1985–90; Vice Pres., Ops, Hertz Europe, 1990; Vice Pres., Hertz Corp., and Pres., Hertz International, 1990–97; Chief Executive: Forte Hotels, 1998–2001; W Eur. Div., Compass Gp, 2001–05. Chevalier: de l'Ordre National du Mérite (France), 1992; de la Légion d'Honneur (France), 2004. *Recreations:* motorsport, music. *Address:* Antedman, 6 Place des Perrières, 1296 Coppet, Switzerland; *e-mail:* antoine.cau@antedman.ch.

CAUDWELL, John David; Founder, Chairman and Chief Executive, Caudwell Group, since 1978; *b* 7 Oct. 1952; *s* of Walter and Beryl Caudwell; partner, Claire Johnson; two *s* two *d*. *Educ:* Berryhill Jun. High Sch.; Stoke-on-Trent Polytech. (HNC Mech. Engrg). With Michelin Tyre Co., 1970–80. *Recreations:* charity fundraising, cycling, flying, diving, motorcycling, antiques. *Address:* Caudwell Group, Shelton Old Road, Stoke-on-Trent, Staffs ST4 7RY. *T:* (01782) 600600, *Fax:* (01782) 600609; *e-mail:* h.q.@caudwell.com.

CAULCOTT, Thomas Holt; Chief Executive, Birmingham City Council, 1982–88; *b* 7 June 1927; *s* of late L. W. Caulcott and Doris Caulcott; *m* 1st, 1954, C. Evelyn Lowden (marr. diss. 1987); one *d* (and one *s* decd); 2nd, 1988, Jane Marguerite Allsopp. *Educ:* Solihull Sch.; Emmanuel Coll., Cambridge. Asst Principal, Central Land Bd and War Damage Commn, 1950–53; transferred to HM Treasury, 1953; Private Sec. to Economic Sec. to the Treasury, 1955; Principal, Treasury supply divs, 1956–60; Private Sec. to successive Chancellors of the Exchequer, Sept. 1961–Oct. 1964; Principal Private Sec. to First Sec. of State (DEA), 1964–65; Asst Sec., HM Treasury, 1965–66; Min. of Housing and Local Govt, 1967–69; Civil Service Dept, 1969–70; Under-Sec., Machinery of Govt Gp, 1970–73; Principal Finance Officer, Local Govt Finance Policy, DoE, 1973–76; Sec., AMA, 1976–82. Chm., Royal Shrewsbury Hosps NHS Trust, 1998–2003; non-exec. Dir, Heart of Birmingham PCT, 2006–. Mem., S Shropshire DC, 1991–95 (Chm., Policy and Resources Cttee, 1993–95). Mem. Cttee of Mgt, Hanover Housing Assoc., 1988–94. Mem. Bd, W Midlands Arts, 1996–97. Harkness Fellowship, Harvard and Brookings Instn, 1960–61; Vis. Fellow, Dept of Land Economy, Univ. of Cambridge, 1984–85; Hon. Fellow: Inst. of Local Govt Studies, Univ. of Birmingham, 1979–; Birmingham City Univ. (formerly Birmingham Polytechnic, later Univ. of Central England), 1990–. *Publication:* Management and the Politics of Power, 1996. *Address:* 12 Dinham, Ludlow, Shropshire SY8 1EJ. *T:* (01584) 875154.

CAULFEILD, family name of **Viscount Charlemont**.

CAULFIELD, Ian George, CBE 2000; DL; Clerk of the Council and Chief Executive, Warwickshire County Council, and Clerk to the Warwickshire Lieutenancy, 1986–2005; *b* 14 Dec. 1942; *s* of William and Elizabeth Caulfield; *m* 1967, Geraldine Mary Hind; three *s*. *Educ:* Liverpool Inst. High Schs for Boys; Univ. of Manchester (BA Hons Geography); Liverpool Poly. (DipTP). Jun. Planning Assistant, Liverpool City, 1964–65; Planning Assistant, Lancs CC, 1965–69; Sen. Planning Officer, Hants CC, 1969–74; Asst Hd, Res. and Intelligence Unit, 1974–76, Prin. Assistant to Chief Exec., 1976–78, Oxford CC; Asst Exec., 1978–83, Dep. Clerk and Asst Chief Exec., 1983–86, Warwicks CC. DL Warwicks, 2005. *Publication:* (jtly) Planning for Change: strategic planning and local government, 1989. *Recreation:* sport, particularly soccer.

CAUTE, (John) David; JP; MA, DPhil; writer; *b* 16 Dec. 1936; *m* 1st, 1961, Catherine Shuckburgh (marr. diss. 1970); two *s*; 2nd, 1973, Martha Bates; two *d*. *Educ:* Edinburgh Academy; Wellington; Wadham Coll., Oxford. Scholar of St Antony's Coll., 1959. Spent a year in the Army in the Gold Coast, 1955–56, and a year at Harvard Univ. on a Henry Fellowship, 1960–61. Fellow of All Souls Coll., Oxford, 1959–65; Visiting Professor, New York Univ. and Columbia Univ., 1966–67; Reader in Social and Political Theory, Brunel Univ., 1967–70. Regents' Lectr, Univ. of Calif., 1974; Vis. Prof., Bristol Univ., 1985. Literary Editor, New Statesman, 1979–80. Co-Chm., Writers' Guild, 1981–82; Chm., Sinclair Fiction Prize, 1984. FRSL 1998. JP Inner London, 1993. *Plays:* Songs for an Autumn Rifle, staged by Oxford Theatre Group at Edinburgh, 1961; The Demonstration, Nottingham Playhouse, 1969; The Fourth World, Royal Court, 1973; Brecht and Company, BBC TV, 1979; BBC Radio: Fallout, 1972; The Zimbabwe Tapes, 1983; Henry and the Dogs, 1986; Sanctions, 1988; Animal Fun Park, 1995. *Publications:* At Fever Pitch (novel), 1959 (Authors' Club Award and John Llewelyn Rhys Prize, 1960); Comrade Jacob (novel), 1961; Communism and the French Intellectuals, 1914–1960, 1964; The Left in Europe Since 1789, 1966; The Decline of the West (novel), 1966; Essential Writings of Karl Marx (ed), 1967; Fanon, 1970; The Confrontation: a trilogy, 1971 (consisting of The Demonstration (play), 1970; The Occupation (novel), 1971; The Illusion, 1971); The Fellow-Travellers, 1973, rev. edn 1988, as The Fellow-Travellers, Intellectual Friends of Communism; Collisions, 1974; Cuba, Yes?, 1974; The Great Fear: the anti-communist purge under Truman and Eisenhower, 1978; Under the Skin: the death of white Rhodesia, 1983; The K-Factor (novel), 1983; The Espionage of the Saints, 1986; News from Nowhere (novel), 1986; Sixty Eight: the year of the barricades, 1988; Veronica or the Two Nations (novel), 1989; The Women's Hour (novel), 1991; Joseph Losey: a revenge on life, 1994; Dr Orwell and Mr Blair (novel), 1994; Fatima's Scarf (novel), 1998; The Dancer Defects: the struggle for cultural supremacy during the cold war, 2003; *as John Salisbury: novels:* The Baby-Sitters, 1978; Moscow Gold, 1980. *Address:* 41 Westcroft Square, W6 0TA.

CAUTHEN, Stephen Mark; jockey; *b* Covington, Kentucky, 1 May 1960; *e s* of Ronald (Tex) Cauthen and Myra Cauthen; *m* Amy Kathrine Roth Fuss; three *d*. Apprentice jockey, 1976, Churchill Downs, Kentucky; first win, Red Pipe, 1976; raced at Aqueduct and Santa Anita; champion jockey, USA, 1977; won US Triple Crown on Affirmed, 1978; moved to Lambourn, 1979; champion jockey, UK, 1984, 1985, 1987; races won include: with Tap on Wood, 2,000 Guineas, 1979; with Slip Anchor, Derby, 1985; with Oh So Sharp, Oaks, 1,000 Guineas and St Leger, 1985; with Reference Point, Derby, St Leger and King George V and Queen Elizabeth Diamond Stakes, 1987; with Diminuendo, Oaks, 1988; with Michelozzo, St Leger, 1989; with Old Vic, French Derby and Irish Derby, 1989; Champion Stakes 3 times (Cormorant Wood, Indian Skimmer, In the Groove); Grand Prix de St Cloud (Atcatanango, Diamond Shoal); Prix de Diane (Indian Skimmer). *Address:* 167 S Main Street, Walton, KY 41094, USA.

CAUTLEY, (Edward) Paul (Ronald), CMG 2001; DL; Chief Executive and Founder Chairman, The D Group, since 1994; *b* 1 March 1940; *s* of Ronald Lockwood Cautley and Ena Lily Medwin; *m* 1966, Sandra Elizabeth Baker; two *d*. *Educ:* Downside Sch. Syndication Manager, Central Press Features, 1958–60; Retail Marketing Manager, ICI Paints, 1960–62; Finance Negotiator, GDM Finance, 1962–64; General Manager, Marling Industries, 1964–66; Account Dir, S. H. Benson, 1966–70; Dir, New Product Development, BRB, 1971–73; Chief Exec. and founder Chm., Strategy Ltd, 1974–94. HAC, 1958–61; RM Reserve, 1961–68. Hon. Col, RM Reserve, London, 1999–; Pres., Chatham Royal Marine Cadets, 2000–; Col, Royal Marine Cadets, 2004–. Trustee, Marine Soc. and Sea Cadets (formerly Sea Cadet Assoc.), 2001–. Freeman, City of London, 2008. DL Greater London, 2001. FRGS 1991; Member: Royal Philatelic Soc., 1992; RPS, 1992; Founder Mem., Foundn and Friends, Royal Botanic Gardens, Kew, 1989–; life mem., 15 railway preservation socs. *Publication:* The Cautley Chronicle, 1986. *Recreations:* philately (British Commonwealth), photography (mainly landscapes), 00 gauge model railway enthusiast, collector of Regency porcelain, silver and furniture. *Address:* 23 Grafton Street, W1S 4EY. *T:* (020) 7318 9200. *Clubs:* Army and Navy, Honourable Artillery Company, Special Forces.

CAVACO SILVA, Anibal; President of Portugal, since 2006; *b* 15 July 1939; *s* of Teodoro Silva and Maria do Nascimento Cavaco; *m* 1963, Maria Alves; one *s* one *d*. *Educ:* Superior Inst. Econs and Financial Scis, Lisbon; York Univ. (PhD 1973). Teacher of public economics and political economy: Inst. Econ. and Financial Studies, Lisbon, 1966–78; Catholic Univ., Lisbon, 1975–2006 (Prof., 1979–2006); New Univ. of Lisbon, 1978–2001 (Prof., 1979–2001); Res. Fellow, Calouste Gulbenkian Foundn, 1967–77; Dir, Res. and Statistical Dept, Bank of Portugal, 1977–80 and 1981–85; Minister of Finance and Planning, 1980–81; Pres., Council for Nat. Planning, 1981–84; Prime Minister of Portugal, 1985–95. Leader, PSD, 1985–95. Econ. Advr to Bank of Portugal, 1995–2004. Hon. Dr: York, 1993; Coruña, Spain, 1996. *Publications:* Budget Policy and Economic Stabilization, 1976; Economic Effects of Public Debt, 1977; The Macroeconomic Policy, 1992; A Decade of Reforms, 1995; Portugal and the Single Currency, 1997; European Monetary Union, 1999; Political Autobiography, 2002; numerous articles on financial mkts, public econs and Portuguese econ. policy. *Address:* Palácio de Belém, 1349–022 Lisbon, Portugal.

CAVADINO, Paul Francis; Chief Executive, Nacro, since 2002; *b* 5 Dec. 1948; *s* of John Joseph and Mary Patricia Cavadino; *m* 1970, Maria Claire Carrack; two *s*. *Educ:* St Michael's Coll., Leeds; Balliol Coll., Oxford (BA Jurisprudence). Univs and Colls Sec., Christian Aid, 1970–72; National Association for the Care and Resettlement of Offenders: NE Regl Orgnr, 1972–75; Sen. Inf. Officer, 1975–82; Sen. Press Officer, 1982–90; Principal Officer (Criminal Justice Policy), 1990–94; Director: of Communications, 1997–99; of Policy and Inf., 1999–2001; of Policy, Race and Resettlement, 2001–02. Chairman: Penal Affairs Consortium, 1989–2001 (full-time, 1994–97); Voluntary Sector Community Engagement Project, 2005–. Sec., New Approaches to Juvenile Crime, 1978–84; Clerk, Parly All-Party Penal Affairs Gp, 1980–2001. *Publications:* Bail: the law, best practice and the debate, 1993; Introduction to the Criminal Justice Process, 1995, 2nd edn, 2002; Children Who Kill, 1996. *Recreations:* cricket, jazz music, Italian food and drink. *Address:* (office) Park Place, 12 Lawn Lane, SW8 1UD. *T:* (020) 7840 7208, *Fax:* (020) 7840 7236; *e-mail:* paul.cavadino@nacro.org.uk; (home) 136 Onslow Gardens, Wallington, Surrey SM6 9QE.

CAVALIER-SMITH, Prof. Thomas, PhD; FRS 1998; FRSC 1997; Professor of Evolutionary Biology, Department of Zoology, University of Oxford, since 2000; *b* 21 Oct. 1942; *s* of Alan Hailes Spencer Cavalier-Smith and Mary Maude Cavalier-Smith; *m* 1st, 1964, Gillian Glaysher; one *s* one *d*; 2nd, 1991, Ema E-Yung Chao; one *d. Educ:* Kenninghall Primary Sch.; Norwich Sch.; Gonville and Caius Coll., Cambridge (MA 1967); King's Coll., London (PhD 1967); Open Univ. (BA). FLS; FIBiol. Tutorial Student, King's Coll., London, 1964–67; Guest Investigator, and Damon Runyon Meml Res. Fellow, Rockefeller Univ., NY, 1967–69; Lectr, 1969–82, Reader, 1982–89, in Biophysics, King's Coll., London; Prof. of Botany, Univ. of BC, 1989–99; NERC Professorial Fellow, Dept of Zool., Univ. of Oxford, 1999–2007. Vis. Fellow, Res. Sch. of Biol. Scis, ANU, 1981, 1985–86; Fellow, Canadian Inst. for Advanced Res. (Evolutionary Biol. Prog.), 1988–2007; Vis. Scientist, Univ. of Cape Town, 1995–96. Pres., British Soc. for Protist Biol., 2006–09. FRSA. Internat. Prize for Biol., Japan Soc. for Promotion of Sci., 2004; Linnean Medal for Zool., Linnean Soc. of London, 2007. *Publications:* (ed with J. P. Hudson) Biology, Society and Choice, 1982; (ed) The Evolution of Genome Size, 1985; over 180 scientific articles in jls, contribs to books. *Recreations:* reading, natural history, travel. *Address:* Department of Zoology, University of Oxford, South Parks Road, Oxford OX1 3PS. *T:* (01865) 281065.

CAVALIERO, Roderick; Deputy Director General, British Council, 1981–88 (Assistant Director General, 1977–81); *b* 21 March 1928; *s* of Eric Cavaliero and Valerie (*née* Logan); *m* 1957, Mary McDonnell (*d* 2007); one *s* four *d. Educ:* Tonbridge School; Hertford Coll., Oxford. Teaching in Britain, 1950–52; teaching in Malta, 1952–58; British Council Officer, 1958–88 (service in India, Brazil, Italy). Chm., Educnl and Trng Export Cttee, 1979–88; Dir, Open Univ. Educnl Enterprises, 1980–88; Pres., British Educnl Equipment Assoc., 1987–92. Mem., British Section, Franco-British Council, 1981–88. Trustee, Charles Wallace India Trust, 1981–2000. Mem. Council, British Sch. at Rome, 1989–96 (Chm., Management Cttee, 1991–95); Trustee, St George's English Sch., Rome, 1979–96. *Publications:* Olympia and the Angel, 1958; The Last of the Crusaders, 1960; The Independence of Brazil, 1993; Admiral Satan: the life and campaigns of Suffren, 1994; Strangers in the Land: the rise and decline of the British Indian Empire, 2002; Italia Romantica, English Romantics and Italian Freedom, 2005; Caverns of the Heart, 2007. *Address:* 10 Lansdowne Road, Tunbridge Wells, Kent TN1 2NJ. *T:* (01892) 533452.

CAVAN, 13th Earl of, *cr* 1647 (Ire.); **Roger Cavan Lambart;** Baron Cavan 1618; Baron Lambart 1618; Viscount Kilcoursie 1647; *b* 1 Sept. 1944; *s* of Frederick Cavan Lambart (*d* 1963) and Audrey May, *d* of Albert Charles Dunham. *Educ:* Wilson's School, Wallington, Surrey.

[Has not yet established his right to the peerage.]

CAVANAGH, Diana Lesley; Director of Educational Studies (formerly Strategic Director of Education), City of Bradford Metropolitan District Council, 1996–2001; *b* 19 Nov. 1944; *d* of Arthur and Nellie Eggleston; *m* 1973, Michael Cavanagh. *Educ:* Fairfield High Sch.; Westfield Coll., London (BA Hons 1966); Univ. of Liverpool (PGCE 1967); Univ. of Edinburgh (Dip. Applied Linguistics 1973); Sheffield Poly. (MSc 1982). German Teacher, Cumberland, 1967–70; English Teacher, Sulingen Gymnasium, W Germany, 1970–73; Lectr in English Lang./Educn, Univ. of Birmingham, 1973–75; British Council Project Co-ordinator, Medical Coll., Jeddah, 1975–77; Section Hd, ESOL, Abraham Moss Centre, Manchester, 1977–83; Professional Asst, and Dep. Area Educn Officer, Derbyshire, 1983–85; Asst Educn Officer (Reorgn and Curriculum), Rochdale, 1985–89; Institute of Citizenship Studies: Chief Asst Exec. Officer (Policy Develt), 1989–91; CEO, 1991–96. Chair, NW Reg., 1993, Council Mem., 1994, Soc. of Educn Officers; Mem. and Chair of the Board, NEAB, 1996; Chair, Assessment and Qualifications Alliance, 2003–07 (Dep. Chair, 1999–2003); Dir, Careers Bradford, 1996–2001. FRSA 1991. *Publications:* Introducing PET, 1980; Power Relations in the Further Education College, 1983; Staff Development in the Further Education College, 1984. *Recreations:* hill walking, polar travel, reading. *Address:* 4 Cross Cliffe, Glossop, Derbys SK13 8PZ.

CAVANAGH, John Patrick; QC 2001; a Recorder, since 2004; *b* 17 June 1960; *s* of Dr Gerry Cavanagh and Anne Cavanagh (*née* Kennedy); *m* 1989, Suzanne Tolley; one *s* three *d. Educ:* Mt Carmel Convent Sch., Stratford-on-Avon; Warwick Sch.; New Coll., Oxford (MA); Clare Coll., Cambridge (LLM); Univ. of Illinois Coll. of Law. Residential social worker, St Philip's Sch., Airdrie, 1979–80; Instructor in Law, Univ. of Illinois Coll. of Law, Urbana-Champaign, 1983–84; part-time Lectr in Law, New Coll., Oxford, 1984–87; called to the Bar, Middle Temple, 1985; in practice at the Bar, 1986–; Jun. Counsel to Crown, B Panel, 1997–2001. Chm., Employment Law Bar Assoc., 2005–07. *Publications:* (ed and contrib.) Tolley's Employment Handbook, 9th edn 1985 to 15th edn 2001; (contrib.) Butterworth's Local Government Law, 1998–2006; (ed jtly and contrib.) Harvey on Industrial Relations and Employment Law, annually 2000–04. *Recreations:* family, reading, football (Celtic from afar), avoiding gardening. *Address:* 11 King's Bench Walk, Temple, EC4Y 7EQ. *T:* (020) 7632 8500.

CAVE, Charles Anthony H.; *see* Haddon-Cave.

CAVE, Sir John (Charles), 5th Bt *cr* 1896, of Sidbury Manor, Sidbury, co. Devon; farmer and landowner; Vice Lord-Lieutenant of Devon, since 2007; *b* 8 Sept. 1958; *e s* of Sir Charles Cave, 4th Bt and of (Mary) Elizabeth, Lady Cave, *yr d* of late John Francis Gore, CVO, TD; *S* father, 1997; *m* 1984, Carey Diana (*née* Lloyd); two *s* one *d. Educ:* Eton; RAC, Cirencester. DL 2001, High Sheriff, 2005, Devon. *Heir: s* George Charles Cave, *b* 8 Sept. 1987. *Address:* Sidbury Manor, Sidmouth, Devon EX10 0QE. *Clubs:* Army and Navy, Farmers', MCC.

CAVE, Prof. Martin Edward, DPhil; Director, Centre for Management Under Regulation, Warwick Business School, University of Warwick, since 2001; *b* 13 Dec. 1948; *s* of D. T. and S. M. Cave; *m* 1972, Kathryn Wilson; one *s* two *d. Educ:* Balliol Coll., Oxford (BA 1969); Nuffield Coll., Oxford (BPhil 1971; DPhil 1977). Res. Fellow, Birmingham Univ., 1971–74; Brunel University: Lectr, 1974–81; Sen. Lectr, 1981–86; Prof. of Economics, 1986–2001; Vice-Principal, 1996–2001. Economic Consultant: HM Treasury, 1986–90; OFTEL, subseq., OFCOM, 1990–; Postal Services Commn, 2000–. Mem., Competition (formerly Monopolies and Mergers) Commn, 1996–2002; Dir, Payments Council, 2007–. *Publications:* Computers and Economic Planning: the Soviet experience, 1980; (with Paul Hare) Alternative Approaches to Economic Planning, 1981; (jtly) The Use of Performance Indicators in Higher Education, 1988, 3rd edn 1997; (ed jtly) Output and Performance Measurement in Government, 1990; (ed with Saul Estrin) Competition and Competition Policy: a comparative analysis of Central and Eastern Europe, 1993; (ed jtly) Reconstituting the Market: the political economy of microeconomic transformation, 1999; (with Robert Baldwin) Understanding Regulation, 1999; (ed jtly) Handbook of Telecommunications Economics, vol. 1, 2002, vol. 2, 2005; Every Tenant Matters, 2007; contrib. to jls on regulatory economics and other subjects. *Recreations:* tennis, cinema. *Address:* Warwick Business School, University of Warwick, Coventry CV4 7AL.

CAVE, Prof. Terence Christopher, FBA 1991; Professor of French Literature, Oxford University, 1989–2001, now Emeritus; Fellow and Tutor in French, St John's College, Oxford, 1972–2001, now Emeritus Research Fellow; *b* 1 Dec. 1938; *s* of Alfred Cyril Cave and Sylvia Norah (*née* Norman); *m* 1965, Helen Elizabeth Robb (marr. diss. 1990); one *s* one *d. Educ:* Winchester Coll.; Gonville and Caius Coll., Cambridge (MA; PhD; Hon. Fellow 1997). University of St Andrews: Assistant, 1962–63; Lectr, 1963–65; University of Warwick: Lectr, 1965–70; Sen. Lectr, 1970–72. Visiting Professor: Cornell Univ., 1967–68; Univ. of California, Santa Barbara, 1976; Univ. of Virginia, Charlottesville, 1979; Univ. of Toronto, 1991; Univ. of Alberta, 1992; Univ. of Paris VII, 1995; UCLA, 1997; RHUL, 2001–04; Visiting Fellow: All Souls Coll., Oxford, 1971; Princeton Univ., 1984; Royal Norwegian Soc. of Scis and Letters, Trondheim, 1991 (Mem., 1993); Hon. Sen. Res. Fellow, Inst. of Romance Studies, Univ. of London, 1990. MAE 1990. Hon. DLit London, 2007. Chevalier, l'Ordre Nat. du Mérite (France), 2001. *Publications:* Devotional Poetry in France, 1969; Ronsard the Poet, 1973; The Cornucopian Text: problems of writing in the French Renaissance, 1979; Recognitions: a study in poetics, 1988; (trans.) Madame de Lafayette, The Princesse de Clèves, 1992; (ed) George Eliot, Daniel Deronda, 1995; (ed) George Eliot, Silas Marner, 1996; Pré-histoires: textes troublés au seuil de la modernité, 1999; Pré-histoires II: langues étrangères et troubles économiques, 2001; (with S. Kay and M. Bowie) A Short History of French Literature, 2003; articles and essays in learned jls, collective vols, etc. *Recreations:* music, languages. *Address:* St John's College, Oxford OX1 3JP.

CAVE-BROWNE-CAVE, Sir Robert, 16th Bt *cr* 1641; *b* 8 June 1929; *s* of 15th Bt, and Dorothea Plewman, *d* of Robert Greene Dwen, Chicago, Ill; *S* father, 1945; *m* 1st, 1954, Lois Shirley (marr. diss. 1975), *d* of John Chalmers Huggard, Winnipeg, Manitoba; one *s* one *d*; 2nd, 1977, Joan Shirley, *d* of Dr Kenneth Ash Peacock, West Vancouver, BC. *Educ:* University of BC (BA 1951). KSJ 1986. *Heir: s* John Robert Charles Cave-Browne-Cave (*b* 22 June 1957; *m* 2001, Jennifer Angelica Fong]. *Address:* 7116–199 Street, Langley, BC V2Y 3H8, Canada.

CAVELL, John James; His Honour Judge Cavell; a Circuit Judge, since 1994; *b* 1 Oct. 1947; *s* of Eric Essery Cavell and Edith Emma Doreen (*née* Jose); *m* 1977, Philippa Julia Frances (*née* Kelly); one *s* one *d. Educ:* King Edward's Sch., Stourbridge; Churchill Coll., Cambridge (MA). Called to the Bar, Middle Temple, 1971. Practising Barrister on Midland and Oxford Circuit, 1971–94; a Recorder, 1991–94. *Recreations:* playing the piano, music generally, walking, bridge, gardening. *Address:* c/o Midland Circuit Secretariat Judicial Team, 6th Floor, The Priory Courts, 33 Bull Street, Birmingham B4 6DW.

CAVELL, Rt Rev. John Kingsmill; Assistant Bishop, Diocese of Salisbury, since 1988; Hon. Canon, Salisbury Cathedral, since 1988; *b* 4 Nov. 1916; *o s* of late William H. G. Cavell and Edith May (*née* Warner), Deal, Kent; *m* 1942, Mary Grossett (*née* Penman) (*d* 1988), Devizes, Wilts; one *d. Educ:* Sir Roger Manwood's Sch., Sandwich; Queens' Coll., Cambridge (MA; Ryle Reading Prize); Wycliffe Hall, Oxford. Ordained May 1940; Curate: Christ Church, Folkestone, 1940; Addington Parish Church, Croydon, 1940–44; CMS Area Secretary, dio. Oxford and Peterborough, and CMS Training Officer, 1944–52; Vicar: Christ Church, Cheltenham, 1952–62; St Andrew's, Plymouth, 1962–72; Rural Dean of Plymouth, 1967–72; Prebendary of Exeter Cathedral, 1967–72; Bishop Suffragan of Southampton, 1972–84; Bishop to HM Prisons and Borstals, 1975–85. Hon. Canon, Winchester Cathedral, 1972–84. Proctor in Convocation; Member of General Synod (Mem., Bd for Social Responsibility, 1982–84); Surrogate. Chm., Home Cttee, CMS London; Chm., Sarum Dio. Readers' Bd, 1984–88. Chaplain, Greenbank and Freedom Fields Hosps, Plymouth; Member: Plymouth City Educn Cttee, 1967–72; City Youth Cttee; Plymouth Exec. Council NHS, 1968–72; Chairman: Hants Assoc. for the Deaf, 1972–84; Salisbury Diocesan Assoc. for the Deaf, 1988–91; Pres., Hants Genealogical Soc., 1979–84; Vice-Pres., Soc. of Genealogists. Life Fellow, Pilgrim Soc., Massachusetts, 1974. Patron, Southampton RNLI Bd, 1976–84. Governor: Cheltenham Colls of Educn; King Alfred's College of Educn, 1973–84; Croft House Sch., Shillingstone, 1986–88; Chairman: St Mary's Coll., Cheltenham, Building Cttee, 1957–62; Talbot Heath Sch., Bournemouth, 1975–84; Queensmount Sch., Bournemouth, 1980–84. *Recreations:* historical research, genealogy, philately. *Address:* 143 The Close, Salisbury, Wilts SP1 2EY. *T:* (01722) 334782.

CAVENDISH, family name of **Duke of Devonshire** and **Barons Cavendish of Furness, Chesham,** and **Waterpark.**

CAVENDISH OF FURNESS, Baron *cr* 1990 (Life Peer), of Cartmel in the County of Cumbria; **Richard Hugh Cavendish;** Chairman, Holker Estate Group of Companies (interests including agricultural and urban property, leisure, mineral extraction, export, construction, national hunt racing and forestry), since 1971; *b* 2 Nov. 1941; *s* of late Richard Edward Osborne Cavendish and of Pamela J. Lloyd Thomas; *m* 1970, Grania Mary Caulfeild; one *s* two *d. Educ:* Eton. International banking, 1961–71. Dir, UK Nirex Ltd, 1993–99. A Lord in Waiting (Govt Whip), 1990–92. Member, House of Lords Select Committee: on Croydon Tramlink Bill, 1992–93; on EU Sub-Cttee B, 1999–2003; on EU, 2001–03. Mem., Hist. Buildings and Monuments Commn for England, 1992–98. Chm., Lancs & Cumbria Foundn for Med. Res., 1994–. Chm., Morecambe and Lonsdale Conservative Assoc., 1975–78. Chm. Governors, St Anne's Sch., Windermere, 1983–89. Mem., Cumbria CC, 1985–90. High Sheriff 1978, DL 1988, Cumbria. FRSA. *Recreations:* gardening, National Hunt racing, collecting drawings, reading, travel. *Address:* Holker Hall, Cark-in-Cartmel, Cumbria LA11 7PL. *T:* (015395) 58220. *Clubs:* Brooks's, Pratt's, White's, Beefsteak.

CAVENDISH, Lady Elizabeth (Georgiana Alice), CVO 1997 (LVO 1976); Extra Lady-in-Waiting to Princess Margaret, 1951–2002; Chairman, Cancer Research Campaign, 1981–96; Member, Press Complaints Commission, 1991–96; *b* 24 April 1926; *d* of 10th Duke of Devonshire, KG, and Lady Mary Cecil, GCVO, CBE (*d* 1988), *d* of 4th Marquess of Salisbury, KG, GCVO. *Educ:* private. Member: Advertising Standards Authority, 1981–91; Marre Cttee on Future of Legal Profession, 1986–89; Lay Mem., Disciplinary Cttee of Gen. Council of the Bar (formerly Senate of Inns of Court's Professional Conduct Cttee of Bar Council and Disciplinary Cttee Tribunal), 1983–. Chm., Bd of Visitors, Wandsworth Prison, 1970–73; Mem. Council, St Christopher's Hospice, Sydenham, 1991–. JP London, 1961; Chairman: N Westminster Magistrates' Court PSD, 1980–83; Inner London Juvenile Courts, 1983–86. *Address:* 19 Radnor Walk, SW3 4BP. *T:* (020) 7352 0774; Moor View, Edensor, Bakewell, Derbyshire DE45 1PH. *T:* (01246) 582204.

CAVENDISH, Maj.-Gen. Peter Boucher, CB 1981; OBE 1969; DL; retired; Chairman, Military Agency for Standardisation and Director, Armaments Standardisation and Interoperability Division, International Military Staff, HQ NATO, 1978–81; *b* 26 Aug. 1925; *s* of late Brig. R. V. C. Cavendish, OBE, MC (killed in action, 1943) and Helen Cavendish (*née* Boucher); *m* 1952, Marion Loudon (*née* Constantine); three *s. Educ:* Abberley Hall, Worcester; Winchester Coll.; New Coll., Oxford. Enlisted 1943; commnd The Royal Dragoons, 1945; transf. 3rd The King's Own Hussars, 1946; Staff Coll.,

Camberley, 1955; served Palestine, BAOR, Canada and N Africa to 1966; CO 14th/20th King's Hussars, 1966–69; HQ 1st British Corps, 1969–71; Comdt RAC Centre, 1971–74; Canadian Defence Coll., 1975; Sec. to Mil. Cttee and Internat. Mil. Staff, HQ NATO, 1975–78. Colonel, 14th/20th King's Hussars, 1976–81; Hon. Col, The Queen's Own Mercian Yeomanry, TAVR, 1982–87; Col Comdt, Yeomanry RAC TA, 1986–90. Mem., Peak Park Jt Planning Bd, 1982–91 (Vice-Chm., 1987–91). Chairman: SSAFA/FHS Derbyshire, 1987–96; Derbys Forces Link, 1990–2004. FCMI (FBIM 1979). High Sheriff, 1986–87, DL 1989, Derbys. *Recreations:* shooting, country pursuits, computers, DIY. *Address:* The Rakes End, Middleton, Bakewell, Derbys DE45 1LS. *T:* and *Fax:* (01629) 636225; *e-mail:* PBCav@aol.com.

CAVENDISH, Ruth; *see* Glucksmann, M. A.

CAWDOR, 7th Earl *cr* 1827; **Colin Robert Vaughan Campbell;** Baron Cawdor, 1796; Viscount Emlyn, 1827; DL; *b* 30 June 1962; *s* of 6th Earl and of his 1st wife, Cathryn, *d* of Maj.-Gen. Sir Robert Hinde, KBE, CB, DSO; *S* father, 1993; *m* 1994, Lady Isabella Stanhope, *y d* of Earl of Harrington, *qv*; one *s* three *d*. *Educ:* Eton; St Peter's College, Oxford. Member, James Bridal Meml Soc., London. DL Nairn, 1996. *Heir: s* Viscount Emlyn, *qv*. *Address:* Carnoch, The Streens, Nairn IV12 5RQ.

CAWLEY, family name of **Baron Cawley**.

CAWLEY, 4th Baron *cr* 1918; **John Francis Cawley;** Bt 1906; *b* 28 Sept. 1946; *s* of 3rd Baron Cawley and of Rosemary Joan (*née* Marsden); *S* father, 2001; *m* 1979, Regina Sarabia, *d* of late Marqués de Hazas, Madrid; three *s* one *d*. *Educ:* Eton. *Heir: s* Hon. William Robert Harold Cawley, *b* 2 July 1981. *Address:* Castle Ground, Ashton, Leominster, Herefordshire HR6 0DN. *T:* (01584) 711209.

CAWLEY, Stephen Ingleby, CVO 2007 (LVO 2003); FCA; Deputy Treasurer to the Queen, 2003–07; *b* 14 March 1947; *s* of Joe Cawley and Madge (*née* Ingleby); *m* 1971, Mariquet Scott; two *s*. *Educ:* Hull Grammar Sch.; Edinburgh Univ. (MA 1970). FCA 1973. Joined KPMG, 1970; Partner, 1984–94; Sen. Partner, Sussex, 1992–94; financial consultancy and Lectr, Univ. of Brighton, 1994–96; Dir of Finance, Property Services and Royal Travel, Royal Household, 1996–2003. *Recreations:* opera, wine, gardening, sports. *Address:* Robin Post, Firle Road, Seaford, E Sussex BN25 2HJ.

CAWSEY, Ian Arthur; MP (Lab) Brigg and Goole, since 1997; *b* 14 April 1960; *s* of Arthur Henry Cawsey and Edith Morrison Cawsey; *m* 1987, Linda Mary, *d* of Henry and Joy Kirman; one *s* two *d*. *Educ:* Wintringham Sch. Computer operator, 1977–78; computer programmer, 1978–82; systems analyst, 1982–85; IT consultant, 1985–87; PA to Elliot Morley, MP, 1987–97. Member (Lab): Humberside CC, 1989–96; N Lincs Unitary Council, 1995–97 (Leader, 1995–97); Chm., Humberside Police Authy, 1993–97. PPS to Leader of House of Lords, 2001–02; an Asst Govt Whip, 2005–07. Chm., All Party Gp on Animal Welfare, 1998–. *Address:* House of Commons, SW1A 0AA.

CAWSON, (Peter) Mark; QC 2001; a Recorder, since 2000; a Deputy High Court Judge, Chancery Division, since 2004; *b* 4 June 1959; *s* of Frederick Helenus Peter Cawson and Patricia Mary Cawson; *m* 1986, Julia Louise Hoe; two *s* one *d*. *Educ:* Wrekin Coll., Telford; Liverpool Univ. (LLB Hons). Called to the Bar, Lincoln's Inn, 1982; Junior, Northern Circuit, 1987; Asst Recorder, 1998–2000. *Recreations:* church affairs, armchair politics, travel, watching sports. *Address:* Exchange Chambers, 7 Ralli Courts, West Riverside, Manchester M3 5FT. *T:* (0161) 833 2722, *Fax:* (0161) 833 2789; *e-mail:* Cawsonqc@exchangechambers.co.uk. *Club:* Royal Birkdale Golf.

CAWTHRA, David Wilkinson, CBE 1997; FREng; FICE; Principal, Cawthra & Co., 1995–2005; *b* 5 March 1943; *s* of Jack and Dorothy Cawthra; *m* 1967, Maureen Williamson; one *s* one *d*. *Educ:* Heath Grammar Sch., Halifax; Univ. of Birmingham (BSc Hons). Mitchell Construction Co., 1963–73; Tarmac Construction, 1973–78; Balfour Beatty Ltd, 1979–91; Chief Executive: Balfour Beatty, 1988–91; Miller Group, 1992–94. Dir, BICC, 1988–91. Chm., Nat. Rail Contractors' Gp, 1999–2005. Vice-Pres., ICE, 1996–99. FREng (FEng 1990). *Recreation:* family history. *Address:* Willow House, Riverside Close, Oundle, Peterborough PE8 4DN.

CAYFORD, Philip John Berkeley; QC 2002; *b* 28 July 1952; *s* of Berkeley Cayford and late Christabel Cayford (*née* Robson); partner, Tanya; one *s*. *Educ:* Marlborough Coll.; University Coll., Cardiff (LLB). Called to the Bar, Middle Temple, 1975; in practice as barrister, 1978–. Photographer and conservation film maker: producer, African Hunters, 1984; producer/director: The Rhino War, 1987; Ivory Wars, 1989; The Last Show on Earth, 1992. FRGS; FZS. *Publication:* (contrib. illus.) The Percy Bass Book of Traditional Decoration, 2005. *Recreations:* country sports, cricket, flying, diving. *Address:* (chambers) 29 Bedford Row, WC1R 4HE; *e-mail:* pcayford@29bedfordrow.co.uk. *Clubs:* Royal Automobile, Chelsea Arts, MCC; Refreshers Cricket (Hon. Sec.), I Zingari.

CAYGILL, Hon. David Francis; Chairman, Education New Zealand Trust; *b* 15 Nov. 1948; *s* of Bruce Allott Caygill and Gwyneth Mary Caygill; *m* 1974, Eileen Ellen Boyd; one *s* three *d*. *Educ:* St Albans Primary Sch.; Christchurch Boys' High Sch.; Univ. of Canterbury (BA, LLB). Pres., Univ. of Canterbury Students' Assoc., 1971. Barrister and Solicitor, 1974–78; Partner, Buddle Findlay, 1996. Christchurch City Councillor, 1971–80; MP (Lab) St Albans, NZ, 1978–96; Minister of Trade and Industry, Minister of Nat. Develt, Associate Minister of Finance, 1984–87; Minister of Health, Dep. Minister of Finance, 1987–88; Minister of Finance, 1988–90; Dep. Leader of the Opposition, 1994–96. *Recreations:* collecting and listening to classical records, following American politics. *Address:* c/o Education New Zealand Trust, PO Box 10–500, Wellington, New Zealand.

CAYLEY, Sir Digby (William David), 11th Bt *cr* 1661; MA; Head of Classics, Pinewood School, Bourton, since 2003; *b* 3 June 1944; *s* of Lieut-Comdr W. A. S. Cayley, RN (*d* 1964) (*g g s* of 7th Bt), and Natalie Maud Cayley, BA (*d* 1994); *S* kinsman, 1967; *m* 1st, 1969, Christine Mary Gaunt (marr. diss. 1987); two *d*; 2nd, 1993, Cathryn Mary Russell, MA Cantab; two *s*. *Educ:* Malvern Coll.; Downing Coll., Cambridge (MA). Assistant Classics Master: Portsmouth Grammar Sch., 1968–73; Stonyhurst Coll., 1973–81; dealer in antiques, 1981–89; Assistant Classics Master: Marlborough Coll., 1989–90 and 1994–97; Abingdon Sch., 1990–94; Master i/c Shooting, Marlborough Coll., 1994–2000. *Recreations:* bridge, gardening. *Heir: s* Thomas Theodore William Cayley, *b* 17 Feb. 1997. *Address:* Meadowside, Hyde Lane, Marlborough, Wilts SN8 1JN. *T:* (01672) 513188, 07766 538478.

CAYLEY, Michael Forde; Director, Personnel and Support Services, Department of Social Security, 1998–2000; *b* 26 Feb. 1950; *s* of late Forde Everard De Wend Cayley and Eileen Lilian Cayley; *m* 1987, Jennifer Athalie Jeffcoate (*née* Lytle). *Educ:* Brighton Coll.; St John's Coll., Oxford (MA English). Admin Trainee, Inland Revenue, 1971–73; Private Sec. to Chm., Price Commn, 1973–75; Inland Revenue: Principal, 1975; Asst Sec., 1982; Under Sec., 1991; Dir, Financial Instns Div., 1994–98, Company Tax Div., 1995–98. *Publications: poems:* Moorings, 1971; (ed) Selected Poems of Richard Crashaw, 1972; The Spider's Touch, 1973; poems and articles on modern poets in various mags. *Recreations:* piano-playing, languages, walking, art, history, crosswords. *Address:* 7 The Strand, Hayling Island, Hants PO11 9UB.

CAYTON, William Henry Rymer, (Harry), OBE 2001; Chief Executive, Council for Healthcare Regulatory Excellence, since 2007; *b* 27 March 1950; *s* of late Dr Henry Rymer Cayton and Marion Cromie (*née* Young). *Educ:* Bristol Cathedral Sch.; New Univ. of Ulster (BA Hons 1971; Dist. Grad. Award, 2003); Univ. of Durham (Dip. Anth. 1973); Univ. of Newcastle upon Tyne (BPhil 1979). Teacher: King's Sch., Rochester, 1972; Dame Allan's Sch., Newcastle upon Tyne, 1973–76; Northern Counties Sch. for the Deaf, 1976–80; National Deaf Children's Society: Educn Officer, 1980–82; Dir, 1982–91; Exec. Dir, Alzheimer's Disease Soc., subseq. Chief Exec., Alzheimer's Soc., 1991–2003; Dir, Patients and the Public, DoH, 2003–07. Canadian Commonwealth Fellow, 1983. Member: Sec. of State for Health's Adv. Gp on Youth Treatment Service, 1991–96; Central R&D Cttee, NHS, 1999–; NHS Modernisation Bd, 2000–02; Human Genetics Commn Sub-Cttee, 2000–03; Vice Chm., Consumers in NHS Research, 1996–2003. Chm., Voluntary Council for Handicapped Children, 1986–91. Trustee: Hearing Res. Trust, 1985–2005; Nat. Children's Bureau, 1987–91; Age Concern England, 1992–94; Comic Relief, 2005–. Mem. Bd, Alzheimer Europe, 1998–2003. Pres. and Hon. Life Mem., European Fedn of Deaf Children's Assocs, 1990–91. Frequent broadcasts. FRSA 1995; FFPH (through distinction) 2007. Alzheimer Europe Award, 2003; Life-Time Achievement Award, RCPsych, 2007. *Publications:* Dementia: Alzheimer's and other dementias, 2002; numerous essays and articles. *Recreations:* modern British art, music, food. *Address:* 24 Barlby Gardens, North Kensington, W10 5LW. *T:* (office) (020) 7389 8030. *Club:* Athenæum.

CAYZER, family name of **Baron Rotherwick**.

CAYZER, Sir James Arthur, 5th Bt *cr* 1904; *b* 15 Nov. 1931; *s* of Sir Charles William Cayzer, 3rd Bt, MP (*d* 1940), and Beatrice Eileen (*d* 1981), *d* of late James Meakin and Emma Beatrice (later wife of 3rd Earl Sondes); *S* brother, 1943. *Educ:* Eton. Director: Caledonia Investments, 1958–88; Cayzer Trust Co., 1988–2001. *Heir: cousin* Baron Rotherwick, *qv*. *Address:* Kinpurnie Castle, Newtyle, Angus PH12 8TW. *T:* (01828) 650207. *Club:* Carlton.

CAZALET, Hon. Lady; Camilla Jane; *b* 12 July 1937; *d* of 6th Viscount Gage, KCVO, and Hon. Alexandra Imogen Clare Grenfell (*d* 1969); *m* 1965, Sir Edward Stephen Cazalet, *qv*; two *s* one *d*. *Educ:* Benenden Sch. Dir, Lumley Cazalet, 1967–2001. Trustee, Glyndebourne Arts Trust, 1978–2004; Member: Royal Nat. Theatre Bd, 1991–97; Exec. Cttee, Friends of Covent Garden, 1994–2000; Royal Nat. Theatre Develt Council, 1996–2008; Gov., Royal Ballet, 2000–08. *Recreations:* theatre, music, dance. *Address:* Shaw Farm, Plumpton Green, Lewes, Sussex BN7 3DG. *T:* (01273) 890207.

CAZALET, Sir Edward (Stephen), Kt 1988; DL; a Judge of the High Court of Justice, Family Division, 1988–2000; *b* 26 April 1936; *s* of late Peter Victor Ferdinand Cazalet and Leonora Cazalet (*née* Rowley); *m* 1965, Camilla Jane (*née* Gage) (*see* Hon. Lady Cazalet); two *s* one *d*. *Educ:* Eton Coll. (Fellow, 1989); Christ Church, Oxford (MA Jurisprudence). Called to the Bar, Inner Temple, 1960, Bencher, 1985. QC 1980; a Recorder, 1985–88; Family Division Liaison Judge for SE Circuit, 1990–96. Chairman: Horserace Betting Levy Appeal Tribunal, 1977–88; Sussex Assoc. for Rehabilitation of Offenders, 1991–98; CAB, Royal Courts of Justice, 1992–98; British Agencies for Adoption and Fostering, 2000–05; Jockey Club Appeal Bd, 2001–05; Injured Jockeys' Fund, 2002–06 (Trustee, 1987–2006). Chm. Trustees, Charles Douglas-Home Award, 1986–96; Trustee, Winston Churchill Meml Fund, 2004–. DL E Sussex, 1989. *Recreations:* riding, ball games, chess. *Address:* Shaw Farm, Plumpton Green, Lewes, East Sussex BN7 3DG. *Club:* Garrick.

CAZALET, Sir Peter (Grenville), Kt 1989; Chairman: Seascope Shipping Holdings plc, 2000–01 (Director, 1997–2000); Braemar Seascope Group plc, 2001–02; *b* 26 Feb. 1929; *e s* of Vice-Adm. Sir Peter (Grenville Lyon) Cazalet, KBE, CB, DSO, DSC, and Lady (Elise) Cazalet (*née* Winterbotham); *m* 1957, Jane Jennifer, *yr d* of Charles and Nancy Rew, Guernsey, CI; three *s*. *Educ:* Uppingham Sch., Uppingham, Rutland (schol.); Magdalene Coll., Cambridge (Schol.; MA Hons). General Manager, BP Tanker Co. Ltd, 1968; Regional Co-ordinator, Australasia and Far East, 1970; Pres., BP North America Inc., 1972–75; Director: Standard Oil Co. of Ohio, 1973–75; BP Trading Ltd, 1975–81; Peninsular & Oriental Steam Navigation Co., 1980–99; Man. Dir, 1981–89, Dep. Chm., 1986–89, BP; Chm., BP Oil International, 1981–89. Chm., APV plc, 1989–96; Dep. Chm., GKN, 1989–96; Chm., Hakluyt and Co., 1998–99 (Mem., Hakluyt Foundn, 1997–2000). Director: De La Rue Co., 1983–95; Energy Capital Investment Co. plc, 1994–98; General Maritime Corp., US, 2000–02. Chm., Armed Forces Pay Review Body, 1989–93; Mem., Top Salaries Review Body, 1989–94. Pres., China Britain Trade Gp, 1996–98 (Vice-Pres., 1993–96); a Vice-Pres., ME Assoc., 1982–; Hon. Sec., King George's Fund for Sailors, 1989–2000; Gov., Wellcome Trust Ltd, 1992–96 (Trustee, Wellcome Trust, 1989–92); Mem. Council, RIIA, 1995–98; Trustee, Uppingham Sch., 1976–95; Mem., Gen. Cttee, Lloyd's Register of Shipping, 1981–99 (Mem. Bd, 1981–86). CCMI (CBIM 1982). Liveryman: Tallow Chandlers' Co. (Master, 1991–92); Shipwrights' Co. *Recreations:* theatre, fishing. *Address:* c/o 53 Davies Street, W1K 5JH. *T:* (020) 7496 5821. *Clubs:* Brooks's, Hurlingham, Royal Wimbledon Golf, MCC.

CECIL; *see* Gascoyne-Cecil, family name of Marquess of Salisbury.

CECIL, family name of **Baron Amherst of Hackney, Marquess of Exeter** and **Baron Rockley**.

CECIL, Desmond Hugh, CMG 1995; international political and funding consultant, charity trustee; UK Representative, AREVA, since 2006; *b* 19 Oct. 1941; *s* of Dr Rupert Cecil, DFC, and Rosemary Cecil (*née* Luker); *m* 1964, Ruth Elizabeth Sachs; three *s* one *d*. *Educ:* Headington Co. Primary Sch.; Magdalen Coll. Sch., Oxford; Queen's Coll., Oxford (MA); studied violin/viola and oboe with Max Rostal, Berne and Joy Boughton, London. Violinist and oboist in Switzerland; Leader, Neuchâtel Chamber Orchestra, 1965–70; joined HM Diplomatic Service, 1970; Second Sec., FCO, 1970–73; First Secretary: Bonn, 1973–74; FCO, 1974–76; also Press Officer, Mission to UN, Geneva, 1976–80; FCO, 1980–85; Counsellor and Chargé d'Affaires, Vienna, 1985–89; FCO, 1989–92; on secondment with Board of P&O European Ferries, 1992; Under Sec., FCO, 1992–95. Senior Advisor: British Telecom, 1996–97; BNFL, 1996–2006; GEC/Marconi Communications, subseq. Marconi, 1998–2001. Chm., Arena Pal Ltd, 2002–03. Antiquarian book dealer, 1997–. Council Mem., Britain Russia Centre, 1998–2000; Member Board: Germany Project, Panel 2000, 1999–2000; Internat. Mendelssohn Foundn, Leipzig, 2001– (Chm., UK Friends, 2005–). Council Mem., Royal Philharmonic Soc., 1995–2005 (Chm., Sponsorship Cttee, 1998–2005; Hon. Co-Treas., 1999–2005); Dir and Trustee, Jupiter Orch., 1996–2002; Trustee, LPO, 2005–; Adviser: Russian Arts Help Charity, Moscow, 2000–; Menuhin Fest., Gstaad, 2001–; Nuclear Management Partners Ltd Bd, 2008– Trustee: Voices for Hospices, 2000–04; Norbert Brainin Foundn,

Asolo, 2003–; LPO, 2005–. Mem., Appeal Cttee, Queen's Coll., Oxford, 2005–. Member: Mensa, 1968–2005; Sherlock Holmes Soc. of London, 1970–; Kingston Chamber Music Soc., 1990–; British-German Assoc., 2001–05. *Recreations:* playing music and cricket, downhill ski-ing, chess, antiquarian travel books. *Address:* 38 Palace Road, East Molesey, Surrey KT8 9DL. *T:* (020) 8783 1998. *Clubs:* Athenæum (Chm., Wine Cttee, 1999–2001, Gen. Cttee, 2003–06; Trustee, 2008–), MCC (Eur. Cricket Advr, 1998–2002); Claygates Cricket (Life Vice Pres.).

CECIL, Henry Richard Amherst; trainer of racehorses; *b* 11 Jan. 1943; *s* of late Hon. Henry Kerr Auchmuty Cecil and of Elizabeth Rohays Mary (who *m* 2nd, Sir Cecil Boyd-Rochfort, KCVO), *d* of Sir James Burnett, 13th Bt, CB, CMG, DSO; *m* 1st, 1966, Julia (marr. diss. 1990), *d* of Sir Noel Murless; one *s* one *d*; 2nd, 1992, Natalie Payne (marr. diss. 2002); one *s*. *Educ:* Canford School. Commenced training under flat race rules, 1969; previously Assistant to Sir Cecil Boyd-Rochfort. Leading Trainer, 1976, 1978, 1979, 1982, 1984, 1985, 1987, 1988, 1990, 1993. *Publication:* On the Level (autobiog.), 1983. *Recreation:* gardening. *Address:* Warren Place, Newmarket, Suffolk CB8 8QQ. *T:* (01638) 662387.

CECIL, Rear-Adm. Sir (Oswald) Nigel (Amherst), KBE 1979; CB 1978; *b* 11 Nov. 1925; *s* of Comdr the Hon. Henry M. A. Cecil, OBE, RN, and the Hon. Mrs Henry Cecil; *m* 1961, Annette (CStJ 1980), *d* of Maj. Robert Barclay, TD, Bury Hill, near Dorking, Surrey; one *s*. *Educ:* Ludgrove; Royal Naval Coll., Dartmouth. Joined Navy, 1939; served World War II, Russian convoys, Western approaches and English Channel, 1943–45; HMS Swiftsure, British Pacific Fleet, 1945–46; in comd HM MTB 521, 1947–48; Flag Lieut to Admiral, BJSM, Washington, 1950–52; Comdr, 1959; Chief Staff Officer, London Div. RNR, 1959–61; in comd: HMS Corunna, 1961–63; HMS Royal Arthur, 1963–66; Captain 1966; Central Staff, MoD, 1966–69; Captain (D) Dartmouth Trng Sqdn and in comd HMS Tenby and HMS Scarborough, 1969–71; Senior British Naval Officer, S Africa, Naval Attaché, Capetown, and in command HMS Afrikander, as Cdre, 1971–73; Dir, Naval Operational Requirements, 1973–75; Naval ADC to the Queen, 1975; Rear-Adm., 1975; NATO Comdr SE Mediterranean, 1975–77; Comdr British Forces Malta, and Flag Officer Malta, 1975–79; Lieut Gov., Isle of Man, and Pres. of Tynwald, 1980–85. Pres., St John Council, IoM, 1980–85, IoW, 1996–2001; County Pres., IoW, St John Ambulance, 1991–96; Vice Pres., RUKBA (IndependentAge), 1991–; Vice Patron, Naval Officers Assoc. of Southern Africa, 1973–. FCMI (FBIM 1980). KStJ 1980 (OStJ 1971). *Address:* The Old Rectory, Shorwell, Isle of Wight PO30 3JL. *Clubs:* Lansdowne, MCC.

CEENEY, Natalie Anna; Chief Executive, National Archives and Keeper of the Public Records, since 2005; *b* 22 Aug. 1971; *d* of Anthony and Jacky Ceeney; partner, Simon Chaplin. *Educ:* Newnham Coll., Cambridge (MA 1st Cl. Maths/Social and Pol Sci.). NHS Manager: Northwick Park Hosp., 1992–94; Herts Health Agency, 1994–96; Gt Ormond St Hosp., 1996–98; Strategy Consultant, McKinsey, 1998–2001; Dir, Ops and Services, British Liby, 2001–05. Mem., Historical MSS Commn, 2005–. *Recreations:* reading, sports, music, theatre. *Address:* The National Archives, Kew, Richmond, Surrey TW9 4DU. *T:* (020) 8392 5220, *Fax:* (020) 8487 9207; *e-mail:* natalie.ceeney@nationalarchives.gov.uk.

CELAC, Sergiu; Chairman, EmC Emission Control Ltd, since 2000; President and Chief Executive Officer, Romanian Institute of International Studies, since 2002; *b* Bucharest, 26 May 1939; *s* of Nicolae and Elena Celac; *m* 1964, Rea-Silvia Casu. *Educ:* Bucharest Univ. Romanian Foreign Service, 1961–2000: Private Sec. to Dep. Foreign Minister, 1963–69; Dep. Dir, then Dir, Policy Planning, Min. of Foreign Affairs, 1969–74; interpreter at Presidency, 1974–78; reader, Scientific and Encyclopaedic Publishing House, 1978–89; Minister of Foreign Affairs, Dec. 1989–June 1990; Romanian Ambassador to the UK, 1990–96, and to Ireland, 1991–96. Member: Romanian Writers' Union, 1990–; Journalists' Soc. of Romania, 1991–2000; European Atlantic Gp, 1991–2000; Atlantic Council of UK, 1993–2000; IISS, 1994–2000. Vice-Pres., Black Sea Univ. Foundn, 2000–; Mem. Nat. Exec., Romanian Shooting and Fishing Sports Union, 1990– (Past Pres.). *Publications:* studies and essays on political sci.; trans. novels and poetry from and into Russian and English. *Recreation:* shooting. *Address:* Aleea Alexandru 10, 71273 Bucharest 1, Romania. *T:* (1) 2301935, *Fax:* (1) 2312068; *e-mail:* sergiu.celac@emcrom.ro.

CELLAN-JONES, Diane; *see* Coyle, D.

CERF, Vinton Gray, PhD; Vice-President and Chief Internet Evangelist, Google Inc., since 2005; *b* New Haven, Conn, 23 June 1943; *s* of Vinton Thruston Cerf and Muriel Cerf (*née* Gray); *m* 1966, Sigrid L. Thorstenberg; two *s*. *Educ:* Van Nuys High Sch., Calif; Stanford Univ. (BS 1965); UCLA (MS 1970; PhD 1972). Systems Engr, IBM Corp., 1965–67; Principal Programmer, Computer Sci. Dept, UCLA, 1967–72; Asst Prof. of Elec. Engrg and Computer Sci., Stanford Univ., 1972–76; Prog. Manager, 1976–81, Principal Scientist, 1981–82, Defense Advanced Res. Projects Agency; Vice-Pres. of Engrg, MCI Digital Inf. Services Co., 1982–86; Vice-Pres., Corp. for Nat. Res. Initiatives, 1986–94; Sen. Vice-Pres. for Data Architecture, MCI Telecoms Corp., 1994–95; Senior Vice-President: for Internet Architecture and Engrg, MCI Communications Corp., 1996–98; for Internet Architecture and Technol. Strategy, MCI WorldCom Corp., subseq. MCI, 1998–2005. Dist. Vis. Scientist, Jet Propulsion Lab., CIT, 1998–. Internet Society: Founder Mem., 1992; Founder Pres., 1992–95; Chm., 1998–99; Trustee, 1992–2002; Chm., Internet Societal Task Force, 1999–2000. FAAAS, 1990. Presidential Medal of Freedom (USA), 2005.

CESARANI, Prof. David, OBE 2006; DPhil; Research Professor of Jewish History, Royal Holloway, University of London, since 2004; *b* 13 Nov. 1956; *s* of Henry Cesarani and late Sylvia Cesarani (*née* Packman); *m* 1991, Dawn Waterman; one *s* one *d*. *Educ:* Latymer Upper Sch.; Queens' Coll., Cambridge (BA Hist.); Columbia Univ., NY (MA Jewish Hist.); St Antony's Coll., Oxford (DPhil 1986). Montague Burton Fellow in Modern Jewish Hist., Univ. of Leeds, 1983–86; part-time Lectr, Oxford Centre for Postgrad. Hebrew Studies, 1986–87; Barnett Shine Sen. Res. Fellow and Lectr in Politics, Dept of Political Studies, QMC, 1986–89; Dir of Studies and Educnl Activities, 1989–92, Dir, 1992–95 and 1996–2000, Inst. of Contemporary Hist. and Wiener Liby, London; Adjunct Lectr, Dept of Hebrew and Jewish Studies, UCL, 1990–95; Alliance Family Prof. of Modern Jewish Studies, Dept of Religions and Theol., Univ. of Manchester, 1995–96; Parkes-Wiener Prof. of Twentieth Century European Jewish Hist. and Culture, 1996–2000, Dir, AHRB Parkes Centre for the Study of Jewish/non-Jewish Relations and Prof. of Modern Jewish Hist., 2000–04, Southampton Univ. Trustee, Holocaust Meml Day, 2006–. *Publications:* (ed) The Making of Modern Anglo-Jewry, 1990; Justice Delayed: how Britain became a refuge for Nazi war criminals, 1992; (ed with T. Kushner) The Internment of Aliens in Twentieth Century Britain, 1993; (ed) The Final Solution: origins and implementation, 1994; The Jewish Chronicle and Anglo-Jewry 1841–1991, 1994; (ed with M. Fulbrook) Citizenship, Nationality and Migration in Europe, 1996; (ed) Genocide and Rescue: the Holocaust in Hungary 1944, 1997; (ed jtly) Belsen in History and Memory, 1997; Arthur Koestler: the homeless mind, 1998; (ed with Paul Levine) Bystanders to the Holocaust: a re-evaluation, 2002; (ed) Port Jews: Jewish communities in cosmopolitan maritime trading centres 1650–1950, 2002; Eichmann: his life and crimes, 2004; (ed) After Eichmann: collective memory and the Holocaust since 1961, 2005; (ed with G. Romain) Jews and Port Cities 1590–1990: commerce, community and cosmopolitanism, 2006. *Recreations:* running, food, films, friends and family. *Address:* Department of History, Royal Holloway, University of London, Egham, Surrey TW20 0EX.

CESCAU, Patrick Jean-Pierre; Chevalier, Légion d'Honneur, 2005; Group Chief Executive Officer, Unilever, 2005–08; *b* Paris, 27 Sept. 1948; *s* of Pierre and Louise Cescau; *m* 1974, Ursula Kadansky; one *s* one *d*. *Educ:* ESSEC Business Sch., Paris (business degree); INSEAD (MBA dist.). Unilever, 1973–2008: consultant, 1973–76, sen. consultant, 1976–77, Unilever France; Commercial Manager, Astra Calve, France, 1977–81; Chief Accountant, Union Deutsche Lebensmittelwerke GMbH, 1981; Germany, 1984; Commercial Mem., Unilever Edible Fats and Dairy Netherlands, 1984; Financial Dir, PT Unilever Indonesia, 1986–89; Nat. Manager, Unilever Portugal, 1989–91; Chm., PT Unilever Indonesia, 1991–95; Pres. and CEO, Van den Bergh Foods, USA, 1995–97; Mem. Bd Dirs, Unilever US, Inc., 1995–96; Pres., Lipton USA, 1997–98; Gp Financial Controller and Dep. Chief Financial Officer, 1998–99; Financial Dir, 1999–2000; Foods Dir, 2001–04; Chm., Unilever plc and Dep. Chm., Unilever NV, 2004–05. Non-exec. Dir, Pearson plc, 2002–. Conseiller du Commerce Extérieur de la France, Netherlands, 2002–. Chm., Nat. Assoc. of Margarine Manufacturers, USA, 1996–98; Mem. Bd and Exec. Cttee, Tea Council, USA, 1997–98. *Recreations:* arts, photography, reading, theatre. *Address:* c/o Unilever, Blackfriars, EC4P 4BQ.

CHADLINGTON, Baron *cr* 1996 (Life Peer), of Dean in the county of Oxfordshire; **Peter Selwyn Gummer;** Chief Executive, Huntsworth plc, since 2000; *b* 24 Aug. 1942; *s* of late Rev. Canon Selwyn Gummer and Sybille (*née* Mason); *m* 1982, Lucy Rachel, *er d* of A. Ponsonby Dudley-Hill; one *s* three *d*. *Educ:* King's Sch., Rochester, Kent; Selwyn Coll., Cambridge (BA, MA). Portsmouth and Sunderland Newspaper Gp, 1964–65; Viyella International, 1965–66; Hodgkinson & Partners, 1966–67; Industrial & Commercial Finance Corp., 1967–74; Chairman, Shandwick Internat. plc, 1974–2000; Internat. Public Relations, 1998–2000. Non-executive Director: CIA Group PLC, 1990–94; Halifax plc (formerly Halifax Building Soc.), 1994–2001 (non-exec. Mem., London Bd, 1990–94); Black Box Music Ltd, 1999–2001; Oxford Resources, 1999–2002; hotcourses.com, 2000–04; Britax Childcare Hldgs Ltd, 2005–; Chm., guideforlife.com, 2000–02. Marketing Gp of GB, 1993–95. Chm., Royal Opera House, Covent Gdn, 1996–97. Member: NHS Policy Bd, 1991–95; Arts Council of England (formerly of GB), 1991–96 (Chm., Nat. Lottery Adv. Bd for Arts and Film, 1994–96). Mem., EU Select Sub-Cttee B (Energy, Industry and Transport), H of L, 2000–03. Chm., Action on Addiction, 1999–2007. Chm., Understanding Industry Trust, 1991–96; Trustee, Atlantic Partnership, 1999–; Mem. Bd of Trustees, Amer. Univ., 1999–2001; Mem. Council, Cheltenham Ladies' Coll., 1998–2003. Gov., Ditchley Foundn, 2008–. FRSA. Hon. Fellow, Bournemouth Univ., 1999–. *Publications:* various articles and booklets on public relations and marketing. *Recreations:* opera, Rugby, cricket. *Address:* c/o House of Lords, SW1A 0PW. *T:* (020) 7408 2232. *Clubs:* Garrick, White's, Carlton, MCC, Walbrook (Dir, 1999–2004).

See also Rt Hon. J. S. Gummer.

CHADWICK, Charles McKenzie, CBE 1992 (OBE 1984); British Council Director (formerly Representative), Poland, 1989–92; *b* 31 July 1932; *s* of late Trevor McKenzie Chadwick and Marjory Baron; *m* 1st, 1965, Evelyn Ingeborg Ihlenfeldt (marr. diss.); one *s*; 2nd, 1999, Mary Christina Beatrice Teale; one *s*. *Educ:* Charterhouse School; Trinity Coll., Toronto (BA). Army service, 1950–52; HMOCS Provincial Administration, Northern Rhodesia, 1958–64; Lectr, 1964–66, and Head, Administrative Training, 1966–67, Staff Trng Coll., Lusaka; British Council Officer, 1967–92; service in Kenya, Nigeria, Brazil, London; British Election Supervisor, Zimbabwe, 1980; British Council Rep., Canada, 1981–88. Member: Commonwealth Observer Gp, Ghanaian Presidential elections, 1992, Pakistan National elections, 1993, Cameroon Parly elections, 1997; EU observer team, S African election, 1994; FCO Observer, Uganda elections, 1996; OSCE Supervisor, Bosnia elections, 1996. Gov., Hampstead Sch., 1992–2000. *Publications:* It's All Right Now, 2005; A Chance Acquaintance, 2009. *Address:* c/o United Agents Ltd, 12–26 Lexington Street, W1F 0LE.

CHADWICK, Derek James, DPhil; CChem, FRSC; Director, Novartis (formerly Ciba) Foundation, 1988–2008; *b* 9 Feb. 1948; *s* of Dennis Edmund and Ida Chadwick; *m* 1980, Susan Reid (*d* 2002); two *s*. *Educ:* St Joseph's Coll., Blackpool; Keble Coll., Oxford (BA, BSc, MA, DPhil). FRSC 1982; MACS 1989. ICI Fellow, Cambridge Univ., 1972–73; Prize Fellow, Magdalen Coll., Oxford, 1973–77; Lectr and Sen. Lectr, Liverpool Univ., 1977–88. Vis. Prof., Univ. of Trondheim, Norway, 1995–. Member: Sci. Cttee, Louis Jeantet Foundn, Geneva, 1989–98; Hague Club of European Foundn Dirs, 1989–2008 (Sec., 1993–97); Sci. Adv. Cttee, 1990–96, Exec. Council, 1991–2000 (Vice-Chm., 1994–2000), AMRC; CCLRC, 2002–07. Mem., Soc. of Apothecaries, 1990. *Publications:* chapters in: Aromatic and Heteroaromatic Chemistry, 1979; Comprehensive Heterocyclic Chemistry, 1984; The Research and Academic Users' Guide to the IBM PC, 1988; Pyrroles, Pt 1, 1990; ed many vols in Novartis (formerly Ciba) Foundn symposium series; many papers in chemistry jls, eg, Jl Chem. Soc., Tetrahedron, Tet. Letters, etc. *Recreations:* music, gardening. *Address:* 4 Bromley Avenue, Bromley, Kent BR1 4BQ. *T:* (020) 8460 3332; *e-mail:* derekchadwick@dsl.pipex.com.

CHADWICK, Fiona Jane; Ballet Administrator, Junior Royal Ballet School, 1996–99; *b* 13 May 1960; *d* of late William Chadwick and of Anne Chadwick; *m* 1st, 1990, Anthony Peter Dowson (marr. diss.); one *d*; 2nd, 1996, Robert Cave. *Educ:* Royal Ballet Sch. Joined Royal Ballet Co., 1978; Soloist, 1981–84; Principal, 1984–96. Leading rôles included: Swan Lake, Romeo and Juliet, Sleeping Beauty, Cinderella, La Fille Mal Gardée, Giselle, Prince of the Pagodas, La Bayadère, Pursuit, Firebird.

CHADWICK, Rear Adm. John, CB 2001; Director, Greenwich Hospital, 2003–07; *b* 26 March 1946; *s* of Alec and Elsie Chadwick; *m* 1970, Jacqueline Cosh; two *s*. *Educ:* Cheadle Hulme Sch. CEng 1973; FIET (FIEE 1996). BRNC Dartmouth, 1966; RNC Greenwich (electronic engrg), 1967–69; submarine service, 1970; served in HM Submarines Otter, Ocelot, Spartan, 1970–82; Sqdn Weapon Engr, 3rd Submarine Sqdn, 1984–86; Submarine Weapon System Manager, MoD(PE), 1987–89; Captain 1989; Asst Dir, Operational Requirements, MoD, 1990–93; Dir, Underwater Weapons, MoD(PE), 1993–96; i/c HMS Collingwood, 1996–98; Chief Naval Engr Officer, 1999–2001; FO Trng and Recruiting, 1998–2001. Pres., RN Rugby League, 1997–2001. *Recreations:* walking, gardening, house renovation.

CHADWICK, Rt Hon. Sir John (Murray), Kt 1991; ED; PC 1997; a Lord Justice of Appeal, 1997–2007; *b* 20 Jan. 1941; *s* of Hector George Chadwick and Margaret Corry Chadwick (*née* Laing); *m* 1975, Diana Mary Blunt; two *d*. *Educ:* Rugby School; Magdalene Coll., Cambridge (MA). Called to the Bar, Inner Temple, 1966 (Bencher, 1986; Treasurer, 2004). Standing Counsel to DTI, 1974–80; QC 1980; Judge of Courts of Appeal of Jersey and Guernsey, 1986–93; a Recorder, 1989–91; Judge of the High Court,

Chancery Div., 1991–97; Chancery Supervising Judge, Birmingham, Bristol and Cardiff, 1995–97. A Lieut Bailiff of Guernsey, 2008–; a Judge, Dubai Internat. Financial Centre Court, 2008–. Vice-Pres., Corp. of the Sons of the Clergy, 2004–. Dir, Utd Services Trust, 2005–. *Address:* Lower House Farm, East Meon, Hants GU32 1QJ. *Clubs:* Athenæum, Beefsteak; Royal Yacht Squadron (Cowes).

CHADWICK, Sir Joshua Kenneth B.; *see* Burton-Chadwick.

CHADWICK, Owen; *see* Chadwick, W. O.

CHADWICK, Peter, PhD, ScD; FRS 1977; Professor of Mathematics, University of East Anglia, 1965–91, now Emeritus; *b* 23 March 1931; *s* of late Jack Chadwick and Marjorie Chadwick (*née* Castle); *m* 1956, Sheila Gladys Salter (*d* 2004), *d* of late Clarence F. and Gladys I. Salter; two *d. Educ:* Huddersfield Coll.; Univ. of Manchester (BSc 1952); Pembroke Coll., Cambridge (PhD 1957, ScD 1973). Scientific Officer, then Sen. Scientific Officer, Atomic Weapons Res. Estabt, Aldermaston, 1955–59; Lectr, then Sen. Lectr, in Applied Maths, Univ. of Sheffield, 1959–65; Dean, Sch. of Maths and Physics, 1979–82, Leverhulme Emeritus Fellow, 1991–93, UEA. Vis. Prof., Univ. of Queensland, 1972. Hon. Mem., British Soc. of Rheology, 1991. Hon. DSc Glasgow, 1991. *Publications:* Continuum Mechanics: concise theory and problems, 1976, repr. 1999; numerous papers on theoretical solid mechanics and the mechanics of continua in various learned journals and books. *Address:* 8 Stratford Crescent, Cringleford, Norwich NR4 7SF. *T:* (01603) 451655.

CHADWICK, Dr Priscilla; Principal, Berkhamsted Collegiate School, 1996–2008; *b* 7 Nov. 1947; *d* of Prof. Henry Chadwick, KBE, FBA. *Educ:* Oxford High Sch.; Clarendon Sch., N Wales; Girton Coll., Cambridge (BA Theol Tripos 1970); Oxford Univ. (PGCE); London Univ. (MA Curriculum Studies 1983; PhD 1993). Head of Religious Education: St Helen's Sch., Northwood, 1971–73; Putney High Sch., 1973–78; St Bede's C of E/RC Comprehensive, Redhill, 1979–82; Dep. Head, Twyford C of E High Sch., Acton, 1982–85; Headteacher, Bishop Ramsey C of E Sch., Ruislip, 1986–91; Dean, Educnl Develt, South Bank Univ., 1992–96. Chm., HMC, 2005. Member: English Anglican/RC Cttee, 1981–2006; BBC/ITC Central Religious Adv. Cttee, 1983–93; Youth Crime Cttee, NACRO, 1988–94; Goldsmiths' Coll. Council, 1991–97. Chm., St Gabriel's Trust, 1987–. Gov., Westminster Sch., 1997–. FRSA 1992. Hon. DEd Herts 2006. *Publications:* Schools of Reconciliation, 1994; Shifting Alliances: the partnership of Church and State in English education, 1997; articles in various educnl jls. *Recreations:* music and the arts, world travel. *Club:* East India.

CHADWICK, (William) Owen, OM 1983; KBE 1982; FBA 1962; *b* 20 May 1916; 2nd *s* of John Chadwick and Edith (*née* Horrocks); *m* 1949, Ruth, *e d* of late Bertrand Leslie Hallward and Catherine Margaret Hallward; two *s* two *d. Educ:* Tonbridge; St John's Coll., Cambridge, and took holy orders. Fellow of Trinity Hall, Cambridge, 1947–56; Master of Selwyn Coll., Cambridge, 1956–83; Dixie Professor of Ecclesiastical History, 1958–68; Regius Prof. of Modern History, 1968–83; Vice-Chancellor, Cambridge Univ., 1969–71; Chancellor, UEA, 1985–94. Pres., British Academy, 1981–85. Chm., Archbishops' Commn on Church and State, 1966–70; Mem., Royal Commn on Historical MSS, 1984–91. Trustee, Nat. Portrait Gall., 1978–94 (Chm., 1988–94). Hon. Mem., American Acad. of Arts and Scis, 1977. Hon. Freeman, Skinners' Co., 2000. Hon. FRSE. Hon. DD: St Andrews; Oxford; Wales; Hon. DLitt: Kent; Bristol; London; Leeds; Hon. LittD: UEA; Cambridge; Hon. Dr of Letters, Columbia; Hon. LLD Aberdeen. *Publications include:* John Cassian, 1950; From Bossuet to Newman, 1957; Victorian Miniature, 1960; The Reformation, 1964; The Victorian Church, 1966, 1971; The Secularization of the European Mind in the 19th Century, 1976; The Popes and European Revolution, 1981; Britain and the Vatican during the Second World War, 1986; Michael Ramsey, 1990; The Spirit of the Oxford Movement, 1990; The Christian Church in the Cold War, 1992; A History of Christianity, 1995; A History of the Popes 1830–1914, 1998; The Early Reformation on the Continent, 2002. *Address:* 67 Grantchester Street, Cambridge CB3 9HZ.

CHADWICK-JONES, Prof. John Knighton, PhD, DSc(Econ); Research Professor, University of Fribourg, Switzerland, 1993–2002; *b* 26 July 1928; *s* of Thomas Chadwick-Jones and Cecilia Rachel (*née* Thomas); *m* 1965, Araceli Carceller y Bergillos, PhD; two *s* one *d. Educ:* Bromsgrove Sch.; St Edmund Hall, Oxford (MA). PhD Wales, 1960; DSc(Econ) Wales, 1981. CPsychol, FBPsS. Scientific Staff, Nat. Inst. of Industrial Psychol., London, 1957–60; Lectr, then Sen. Lectr, in Industrial Psychol., UC, Cardiff, 1960–66; Reader in Social Psychol., Flinders Univ. of South Australia, 1967–68; Dir, Occupational Psychol. Res. Unit, UC, Cardiff, 1968–74; Prof. of Psychology, Saint Mary's Univ., Halifax, Canada, 1974–93, now Emeritus (Mem., Exec. Cttee, Bd of Governors, 1975–78). Canada Soc. Scis and Humanities Res. Council Leave Fellow: Darwin Coll., Cambridge, 1980–81; MRC Unit on Develt and Integration of Behaviour, Cambridge, 1984–85; Visiting Fellow: Clare Hall, Cambridge, 1982; Wolfson Coll., Cambridge, 1984–85; Wolfson Coll., Oxford, 1988–89; St Edmund's Coll., Cambridge, 1990–91. Dir, Cambridge Canadian Trust (Toronto), 1988–94. Fellow, Amer. Psychol Assoc.; Hon. Fellow, Canadian Psychol Assoc. *Publications:* Automation and Behavior: a social psychological study, 1969; Social Exchange Theory: its structure and influence in social psychology, 1976; (jtly) Brain, Environment and Social Psychology, 1979; Absenteeism in the Canadian Context, 1979; (jtly) Social Psychology of Absenteeism, 1982; Developing a Social Psychology of Monkeys and Apes, 1998; articles in academic jls. *Address:* Clare Hall, Herschel Road, Cambridge CB3 9AL.

CHADWYCK-HEALEY, Sir Charles (Edward), 5th Bt *cr* 1919, of Wyphurst, Cranleigh, Co. Surrey and New Place, Luccombe, Somerset; DL; Chairman, Chadwyck-Healey Ltd, 1973–99; President, Chadwyck-Healey Inc., 1975–99; Director, openDemocracy Ltd, since 2001; *b* 13 May 1940; *s* of Sir Charles Arthur Chadwyck-Healey, 4th Bt, OBE, TD, and of Viola, *d* of late Cecil Lubbock; *S* father, 1986; *m* 1967, Angela Mary, *e d* of late John Metson; one *s* two *d. Educ:* Eton; Trinity Coll., Oxford (MA; Hon. Fellow, 2006). Member: Marshall Aid Commemoration Commn, 1994–2000; Liby and Inf. Commn, 1995–2000; Lord Chancellor's Adv. Council on Nat. Records and Archives (formerly Public Records), 2001–06. Mem., Ely Cathedral Council, 2001–07. High Sheriff, 2004–05, DL, 2004, Cambs. *Heir: s* Edward Alexander Chadwyck-Healey [*b* 2 June 1972; *m* 1999, Denise Suzanne, (Denny), *e d* of Caroline Osborne; two *d*]. *Address:* Manor Farm, Bassingbourn, Cambs SG8 5NX. *T:* (01763) 242447. *Clubs:* Athenæum, Brooks's.

CHAILLY, Riccardo; conductor; Kapellmeister, Gewandhaus Orchestra, Leipzig and General Music Director, Leipzig Opera, since 2005; *b* 20 Feb. 1953; *s* of late Luciano Chailly and of Anna Maria Chailly; *m* 1987, Gabriella Terragni; two *s. Educ:* Conservatory of Music, Perugia; St Cecilia, Rome; Giuseppe Verdi, Milan. Chief Conductor, Berlin Radio Symph. Orch., 1982–89; Principal Conductor and Music Dir, Teatro Comunale, Bologna, 1986–93; Principal Conductor: Royal Concertgebouw Orch., Amsterdam, 1988–2004; Orch. Giuseppe Verdi, Milan, 1999–2005, now Conductor Laureate; has conducted world's leading orchestras, including Vienna and Berlin Philharmonic, Chicago Symphony, Philadelphia and Cleveland; has performed in major opera houses, including: La Scala, Milan, Vienna State Opera, Covent Garden, Munich, Metropolitan Opera, NY. Hon. RAM 1996. Numerous recordings. Grand Prix du Disque, Acad. Charles Cros, 1984, 1985, 1987, 1992, and other recording awards. Grande Ufficiale, Italian Republic, 1994. *Address:* c/o Oper Leipzig, Opernhaus, Augustusplatz 12, 04109 Leipzig, Germany.

CHAISTY, Paul; QC 2001; a Recorder, since 2000; a Deputy High Court Judge, since 2006; *b* 12 March 1958; *s* of Dora Cranston (*née* Preston); *m* 1987, Margaret Judith Lewis; one *s* one *d. Educ:* Parrswood High Sch., Manchester; Nottingham Univ. (LLB); Exeter Coll., Oxford (BCL). Called to the Bar, Lincoln's Inn, 1982; in practice as barrister, Manchester, 1982–, London, 2006–, specialising in commercial and Chancery law. *Recreations:* fishing, family, football, friends. *Address:* Kings Chambers, 36 Young Street, Manchester M3 3FT. *T:* (0161) 832 9082; 3 Stone Buildings, Lincoln's Inn, WC2A 3XL. *T:* (020) 7242 4937.

CHAKRABARTI, Reeta; journalist; Political Correspondent, BBC, since 1999; *b* 12 Dec. 1964; *d* of Bidhan Kumar and Ruma Chakrabarti; *m* 1992, Paul Hamilton; two *s* one *d. Educ:* King Edward VI High Sch., Birmingham; Internat. Sch., Calcutta; Exeter Coll., Oxford (BA Hons English and French). BBC: current affairs producer, Today, The World at One and PM, Radio 4, 1992–94; reporter, Radio 5 Live Breakfast Prog., 1994–96; Community Affairs Corresp., 1997–99. Patron: Naz Project, 2001–; Nat. Mentoring Consortium, 2003–. Hon. Fellow, UEL, 2003. *Recreations:* reading, swimming, tennis, visiting beautiful European cities, enjoying my children! *Address:* c/o BBC Newsroom, 4 Millbank, SW1P 3UQ.

CHAKRABARTI, Shami, (Mrs M. J. Hopper), CBE 2007; Director, Liberty, since 2003; *b* 16 June 1969; *d* of Shyamalendou and Shyamali Chakrabarti; *m* 1995, Martyn John Hopper; one *s. Educ:* London Sch. of Econs and Pol Sci. (LLB). Called to the Bar, Middle Temple, 1994, Bencher, 2006; lawyer, Legal Advr's Br., Home Office, 1996–2001; In-house Counsel, Liberty, 2001–03. Vis. Fellow, Nuffield Coll., Oxford, 2006–. Mem., Tate Members Council, 2006–. Governor: LSE, 2005–; BFI, 2006–. *Publications:* contribs to Public Law and European Human Rights Law Review, and various newspapers and magazines. *Recreations:* friends, popular cinema, playing with my son. *Address:* Liberty, 21 Tabard Street, SE1 4LA. *T:* (020) 7403 3888, *Fax:* (020) 7607 5354; *e-mail:* info@liberty-human-rights.org.uk.

CHAKRABARTI, Sir Sumantra, KCB 2006; Permanent Secretary, Ministry of Justice, and Clerk of the Crown in Chancery, since 2007; *b* 12 Jan. 1959; *s* of Hirendranath Chakrabarti and Gayatri Chakrabarti (*née* Rudra); *m* 1983, Mari Sako, *qv*; one *d. Educ:* City of London Sch. for Boys; New Coll., Oxford (BA PPE 1981; Hon. Fellow 2004); Sussex Univ. (MA Econ 1984). ODI Fellow and Economist, Govt of Botswana, 1981–83; Sen. Economic Asst and Economic Advr, ODA, 1984–88; Asst to UK Exec. Dir, IMF and World Bank, Washington, 1988–90; Private Sec. to Rt Hon. Lynda Chalker, 1990–92; Assistant Secretary: Aid Policy and Resources Dept, ODA, 1992–96; Envmt, Transport, and Regions Team, Spending Directorate, HM Treasury, 1996–98; Dep. Dir, Budget and Public Finances, HM Treasury, 1998; Dir, Performance and Innovation Unit, 1998–2000, Head, Econ. and Domestic Affairs Secretariat, 2000–01, Cabinet Office; Dir Gen. for Regl Progs, 2001–02, Perm. Sec., 2002–07, DFID. Hon. LLD Sussex, 2004. *Recreations:* Indian history, soul music, football. *Address:* Ministry of Justice, Selborne House, 54–60 Victoria Street, SW1E 6QW.

CHALFONT, Baron, *cr* 1964 (Life Peer); **Alun Arthur Gwynne Jones;** PC 1964; OBE 1961; MC 1957; Chairman: Marlborough Stirling Group, 1994–99; Southern Mining Corp., 1997–99; *b* 5 Dec. 1919; *s* of Arthur Gwynne Jones and Eliza Alice Hardman; *m* 1948, Dr Mona Mitchell, MB ChB (*d* 2008); one *d* decd. *Educ:* West Monmouth Sch. Commissioned into South Wales Borderers (24th Foot), 1940; served in: Burma 1941–44; Malayan campaign 1955–57; Cyprus campaign 1958–59; various staff and intelligence appointments; Staff Coll., Camberley, 1950; Jt Services Staff Coll., 1958; Russian interpreter, 1951; resigned commission, 1961, on appt as Defence Correspondent, The Times; frequent television and sound broadcasts and consultant on foreign affairs to BBC Television, 1961–64; Minister of State, Foreign and Commonwealth Office, 1964–70; UK Permanent Rep. to WEU, 1969–70; Foreign Editor, New Statesman, 1970–71. Dep. Chm., IBA, 1989–90; Chm., Radio Authy, 1991–94. Director: W. S. Atkins International, 1979–83; IBM UK Ltd, 1973–90 (Mem. IBM Europe Adv. Council, 1973–90); Lazard Bros & Co. Ltd, 1983–90; Shandwick plc, 1985–95; Triangle Holdings, 1986–90; Dep. Chm., Television Corp. plc, 1996–2001; Chairman: Industrial Cleaning Papers, 1979–86; Peter Hamilton Security Consultants Ltd, 1984–86; VSEL Consortium, later VSEL, 1987–95; President: Abington Corp. (Consultants) Ltd, 1981–; Nottingham Bldg Soc., 1983–90. Pres., All Party Defence Gp, H of L, 1995– (Chm., 1980–94). President: Hispanic and Luso Brazilian Council, 1975–80; RNID, 1980–87; Llangollen Internat. Music Festival, 1979–90; Freedom in Sport, 1982–88; Chairman: UK Cttee for Free World, 1981–89; Eur. Atlantic Gp, 1983–; Member: Nat. Defence Industries Council, 1992–; IISS; Bd of Governors, Sandle Manor Sch. MRI; MInstD. FRSA. Hon. Fellow UCW Aberystwyth, 1974. Hon. Col, Univ. of Wales OTC, 1991–94. Liveryman, Worshipful Co. of Paviors. Freeman, City of London. *Publications:* The Sword and The Spirit, 1963; The Great Commanders, 1973; Montgomery of Alamein, 1976; (ed) Waterloo: battle of three armies, 1979; Star Wars: suicide or survival, 1985; Defence of the Realm, 1987; By God's Will: a portrait of the Sultan of Brunei, 1989; The Shadow of My Hand (autobiog.), 2000; contribs to The Times, and other national and professional journals. *Recreations:* formerly Rugby football, cricket, lawn tennis; now music and theatre. *Address:* House of Lords, SW1A 0PW. *Clubs:* Garrick, MCC, City Livery.

CHALK, Gerald Anthony; a District Judge (Magistrates' Courts), since 2004; *b* 26 Nov. 1950; *s* of William Pickering Chalk and Winifred Chalk (*née* James); one *s. Educ:* Univ. of Newcastle upon Tyne (LLB Hons 1973). Admitted as solicitor, 1978; articled to McKenzie Bell & Sons, (Solicitors), Sunderland, later Asst Solicitor, 1975–79; Asst Prosecutor to Prosecuting Solicitors' Dept, Northumbria Police, 1979–83; Asst Solicitor, then Partner, Hawley & Rodgers, (Solicitors), Nottingham, 1983–2001; Partner, Johnson Partnership, (Solicitors), Nottingham, 2001–04. Actg Stipendiary Magistrate, 1999. *Recreations:* sport, history, literature. *Address:* c/o Carlisle Magistrates' Court, Rickergate, Carlisle, Cumbria CA3 8OM. *T:* (01228) 518838.

CHALKE, Rev. Stephen John, MBE 2004; Baptist Minister; charity founder, writer and television and radio broadcaster; *b* 17 Nov. 1955; *s* of Victor Joseph Chalke and Ada Elizabeth (*née* Wroth); *m* 1980, Cornelia Maria Reeves; two *s* two *d. Educ:* Spurgeon's Coll., London (DipTh 1981). Ordained Minister, 1981; Minister, Tonbridge Baptist Ch, 1981–85; Founder, Oasis Trust, 1985–; Chm., Oasis Community Learning, 2005–; Founder, Faithworks, 2001–; Minister, church.co.uk, Waterloo, 2003–. Dir, Parentalk, 1998–. Mem., Adv. Bd, Soul in the City, 2003–; Vice Pres., Bible Soc., 1998–2007; Pres., Crusaders' Union, 1997–. Member: Boys' Bde, 1999–; Leadership Team, Spring Harvest, 2003–. Patron: Sean Internat.; Habitat for Humanity GB, 1995–; Arts Centre Gp Ltd, 1996–; Viva Network, 1997–; Christian Deaf Link UK, 1999–; Leeds Faith in Schs, 2000–. FRSA 1998. Hon. Fellow Sarum Coll., 2005. Templeton UK Award, 1997.

Publications: books include: More Than Meets the Eye, 1995, rev. edn 2003; The Parentalk Guide to Your Child and Sex, 2000; He Never Said, 2000; Faithworks, 2001; The Parentalk Guide to Great Days Out, 2001; Faithworks Stories of Hope, 2001; Faithworks Unpacked, 2002; Intimacy and Involvement, 2003; Faithworks 100 Proven Ways for Community Transformation, 2003; (jtly) The Lost Message of Jesus, 2003; Trust: a radical manifesto, 2004; Intelligent Church, 2006; Change Agents, 2007. *Recreations:* gym, running, football, Crystal Palace FC. *Address:* 1 Kennington Road, SE1 7QP. *T:* (020) 7921 4200, *Fax:* (020) 7921 4201; *e-mail:* steve.chalke@oasisuk.org. *Club:* Riverside.

CHALKER OF WALLASEY, Baroness *cr* 1992 (Life Peer), of Leigh-on-Sea in the County of Essex; **Lynda Chalker;** PC 1987; Chairman, Africa Matters Ltd, since 1998; independent consultant on Africa and development to business and governments; company director; *b* 29 April 1942; *d* of late Sidney Henry James Bates and Marjorie Kathleen Randell; *m* 1st, 1967, Eric Robert Chalker (marr. diss. 1973); no *c*; 2nd, 1981, Clive Landa (marr. diss. 2003). *Educ:* Heidelberg Univ.; London Univ.; Central London Polytechnic. Statistician with Research Bureau Ltd (Unilever), 1963–69; Dep. Market Research Man. with Shell Mex & BP Ltd, 1969–72; Chief Exec. of Internat. Div. of Louis Harris International, 1972–74. MP (C) Wallasey, Feb. 1974–1992; Opposition Spokesman on Social Services, 1976–79; Parly Under-Sec. of State, DHSS, 1979–82, Dept of Transport, 1982–83; Minister of State, Dept of Transport, 1983–86; Minister of State, 1986–97, and Minister for Overseas Develt, 1989–97, FCO. Non-executive Director: Freeplay Energy plc, 1997–2006; Capital Shopping Centres plc, 1997–2000; Develt Consultants Internat., 1999–2003; Ashanti Goldfields Co. Ltd, 2000–04; Group 5 (Pty) Ltd, 2001–; Unilever plc and Unilever NV, 2004–07 (Adv. Dir, 1998–2004); Member, International Advisory Board: Lafarge et Cie, 2004–; Merchant Bridge & Co., 2005–. Member: BBC Gen. Adv. Cttee, 1975–79; RIIA, 1977–. Pres., BESO, 1998–2005 (Chm., 1998–2004); Chm., Medicines for Malaria Venture, 2006–. Chm. Mgt Bd, LSHTM, 1998–2006. Hon. Col, 156(NW) Transport Regt, RLC(V), 1995–2000. *Publications:* (jtly) Police in Retreat (pamphlet), 1967; (jtly) Unhappy Families (pamphlet), 1971; (jtly) We are Richer than We Think, 1978; Africa: turning the tide, 1989. *Recreations:* music, cooking, theatre, driving. *Address:* House of Lords, SW1A 0PW.

CHALKLEY, Richard; a Senior Immigration Judge, Asylum and Immigration Tribunal (formerly a Vice President, Immigration Appeal Tribunal), since 2002; *b* 23 March 1949; *s* of late Kenneth Arthur Chalkley and Vera Chalkley; *m* 1973 (marr. diss. 2007); one *s* one *d*. *Educ:* College of Law. Articled to Ormsby Izzard-Davies, Woburn, 1969; admitted solicitor, 1974; Asst Solicitor, Graham Withers & Co., Solicitors, Shrewsbury, 1974–77; Partner: Bradfield & Howson, Solicitors, Maidstone, 1977–87; Thomson Snell & Passmore, Solicitors, Tunbridge Wells, 1987–99. Pt-time, 1995–99, full-time, 1999–2000, Immigration Adjudicator; pt-time Chm., Immigration Appeal Tribunal, 2000–02; Mem., Special Immigration Appeals Commn, 2005–. Chm., Kent Dental Services Cttee, 1985–95; Dep. Chm., Kent Medical Services Cttee, 1985–94; Member: Kent FPC, 1985–90; Bd, Kent Family Health Services Cttee, 1990–95. *Publications:* Professional Conduct: a hand book for chartered surveyors, 1990, 2nd edn 1994; contrib. various articles to Chartered Surveyor Weekly. *Recreations:* reading, opera, motorcycling, dining with friends. *Address:* Asylum and Immigration Tribunal, Field House, 15–25 Breams Buildings, EC4A 1DZ. *T:* (020) 7073 4200, *Fax:* (020) 7073 4004. *Clubs:* Royal Automobile; Bearsted and Thurnham (Bearsted).

CHALLACOMBE, Prof. Stephen James, PhD; FRCPath; FDSRCS, FDSRCSE; FMedSci; educator and medical researcher; Professor of Oral Medicine, King's College London, since 1988; Director of External Strategy, since 2004, and Vice Dean, since 2005, King's College London Dental Institute; Consultant in Diagnostic Microbiology, Guy's and St Thomas' NHS Foundation Trust, since 1984; *b* London, 5 April 1946; *s* of late Kenneth Vivian Challacombe, Sudbury, Suffolk, and Caryl Graydon (*née* Poore); *m* 1969, Christine Barbara, (Tina), *d* of Rt Rev. Francis William Cocks, CB; one *s* one *d*. *Educ:* Culford Sch.; Guy's Hosp. Dental Sch. (BDS 1969); PhD London 1976. LDSRCS 1968; FRCPath 1992; FDSRCSE 1994; FDSRCS 2004. Department of Immunology, Guy's Hospital Medical and Dental Schools: Res. Fellow, 1971–72; Lectr, 1972–76; Sen. Lectr, 1976–85; Reader in Oral Immunol., Univ. of London, 1985–88; King's College London Dental Institute: Sub-dean of Dental Studies, 1983–87; Hd, Dept of Oral Medicine and Pathol., 1986–2003; Postgrad. Sub-dean (Dental), 1992–2002. Sen. Res. Fellow, Dept of Immunol., Mayo Clinic, Rochester, Minn, 1978–79 (Edward C. Kendall Res. Fellow); Vis. Prof., Dept of Oral Biol., UCSF, 1995. Hon. Consultant in Oral Medicine to UK Armed Forces, 1998–. President: British Soc. for Oral Medicine, 1995–97; Odontological Section, RSM, 1996–97; Metropolitan Br., BDA, 1999; British Soc. for Dental Res. (British Div. of IADR), 2000–02; Internat. Assoc. Dental Res., 2003–04. FMedSci 1998. Mem., Hunterian Soc. Colgate Res. Prize, British Div., 1977, Basic Res. in Oral Sci. Award, 1981, Dist. Scientist Award for Exptl Pathol., 1997, IADR. *Publications: edited jointly:* Food Allergy and Intolerance, 1985, 2nd edn 2002; Practical and Theoretical Aspects of ELISA, 1988; Mucosal Immunology, 1990; Oral AIDS Research, 1997, 2nd edn 2006; Immunology of Oral Diseases, 1998; contrib. acad. papers on mucosal immunity, oral medicine, immunological, dermatological and microbiol aspects of oral diseases. *Recreations:* golf, tennis, ski-ing, sailing, theatre, formerly Rugby (Pres., Guy's Hosp. RFC, 1991–2001), water polo (Pres., Guy's Hosp. Swimming and Water Polo Club, 1985–98). *Address:* 101 Mycenae Road, Blackheath, SE3 7RX; King's College London Dental Institute, Guy's Hospital, SE1 9RT. *T:* (020) 7188 4373, (020) 7188 1159; *e-mail:* stephen.challacombe@kcl.ac.uk. *Clubs:* Savage, MCC; Nobody's Friends.

CHALLEN, Colin Robert; MP (Lab) Morley and Rothwell, since 2001; *b* 12 June 1953; *s* of late Grenfell Stephen William Challen and of Helen Mary Challen (*née* Swift). *Educ:* Hull Univ. (BA Hons Philosophy 1982). Served RAF, 1971–74. Postman, 1974–78; publisher and printer, Hull, 1983–94; Labour Party Organiser, Leeds and W Yorks, 1994–2000. Mem. (Lab) Hull CC, 1986–94. Mem., Envmtl Audit Select Cttee, 2001–; Chairman, All Party Parliamentary Group: on Climate Change, 2005–; on Intelligent Energy, 2005–. FRSA 2007. *Publication:* Price of Power: the secret funding of the Conservative Party, 1998. *Recreations:* rambling, art, music. *Address:* House of Commons, SW1A 0AA. *T:* (020) 7219 3000. *Clubs:* Rothwell Labour, Ackroyd Street Working Mens (Morley).

CHALLEN, David John, CBE 2002; Vice-Chairman, European Investment Bank, Citigroup (formerly Co-Chairman, Schroder Salomon Smith Barney), since 2000; *b* 11 March 1943; *s* of Sydney Albert Challen and Doris Ellen Challen (*née* Hardy); *m* 1967, Elizabeth McCartney; one *s* one *d*. *Educ:* The High Sch., Dublin; Trinity Coll., Dublin; Harvard Univ. (MBA). With J. Walter Thompson, 1964–72; J. Henry Schroder & Co. Ltd, 1972–2000: Dir, 1979–2000; Hd, Corporate Finance, 1990–94; Vice Chm., 1995–97; Chm., 1997–2000. Non-executive Director: Anglian Water PLC, 1993–2002; Thomson Travel Group plc, 1998–2000; Anglo American plc, 2002–; Amersham plc, 2003–04; Smiths Group plc, 2004–. Chm., Financial Services Practitioner Panel, 1998–2001; Member: Adv. Cttee on Business and the Envmt, 1991–92; Panel on Takeovers and Mergers, 1993–94, 1999– (Dep. Chm., 2006–); Financial Reporting Council, 1995–2003. Gov., Morley Coll., 1993–99. *Clubs:* Athenæum; Harvard (NYC).

CHALLEN, Rt Rev. Michael Boyd, AM 1988; Executive Director, Brotherhood of St Laurence, 1991–99; Adjunct Professor of Ethics, Curtin University of Technology, Perth, since 2000; *b* 27 May 1932; *s* of late B. Challen; *m* 1961, Judith, *d* of A. Kelly; two *d*. *Educ:* Mordialloc High School; Frankston High School; Univ. of Melbourne (BSc 1955); Ridley College, Melbourne (ThL 1956). Deacon 1957, priest 1958; Curate of Christ Church, Essendon, 1957–59; Member, Melbourne Dio. Centre 1959–63; Director, 1963–69; Priest-in-charge, St Luke, Fitzroy, 1959–61; St Alban's, N Melbourne, 1961–65; Flemington, 1965–69; Dir, Anglican Inner-City Ministry, 1969; Dir, Home Mission Dept, Perth, 1971–78; Priest-in-charge, Lockridge with Eden Hill, 1973; Archdeacon, Home Missions, Perth, 1975–78; Asst Bp, dio. of Perth, WA, 1978–91; Exec. Dir, Anglican Health and Welfare Service, Perth, 1977–78. *Address:* 8A John Street, North Fremantle, WA 6159, Australia. *T:* and *Fax:* (8) 94336784.

CHALLINOR, Robert Michael; His Honour Judge Challinor; a Circuit Judge, since 2004; *b* 10 July 1950; *s* of Henry Clive Challinor and Gladys Violet Challinor (*née* Chapman); *m* 1984, Jill; two *s*. *Educ:* St Peter's Sch., Bournemouth; Trent Polytech. (LLB London 1973). Called to the Bar, Gray's Inn, 1974; Asst Recorder, 1991–97; Recorder, 1997–2004. *Recreations:* art, walking, music, being with my family. *Address:* c/o Wolverhampton Crown Court, Pipers Row, Wolverhampton WV1 3LQ.

CHALLONER, Ven. Janet; see Henderson, Ven. J.

CHALMERS, Sir Iain (Geoffrey), Kt 2000; FRCP, FRCPE, FFPH, FCOG(SA); Editor, James Lind Library, since 2003; Director, UK Cochrane Centre, 1992–2002; *b* 3 June 1943; *s* of Hamish and Lois Chalmers; *m* 1972, Jan Skitmore; two *s*. *Educ:* Middlesex Hosp. Med. Sch., London Univ. (MB BS 1966; MSc Social Medicine 1975). MRCS 1966; LRCP 1966; DCH 1973; MRCOG 1973, FRCOG 1985; FFPH (FFPHM 1986); FRCPE 1996; FCOG(SA) 2001; FRCP 2002. House Physician, House Surgeon, Middlesex Hosp.; House Physician, Welsh Nat. Sch. of Medicine; House Surgeon, Raigmore Hosp., Inverness; MO, UNRWA for Palestinian Refugees, Gaza; Registrar, Dept of Obst. and Gynaecol., then MRC Fellow, Dept of Med. Stats, Welsh Nat. Sch. of Medicine, Cardiff; Oxford University: Dir, Nat. Perinatal Epidemiology Unit, 1978–92; Clin. Lectr in Obst. and Gynaecol., 1978–92; Archie Cochrane Res. Fellow, Green Coll., 1992–94; Hon. Consultant in Public Health Medicine, Oxfordshire HA, 1978–2002; Hon. Specialist in Public Health Medicine, Milton Keynes PCT, 2003–; Hon Mem., Sen. Scientific Staff, MRC Clin. Trials Unit, 2003–. Visiting Professor: Univ. of Liverpool, 1993–; Inst. of Child Health, 1997–2003, Sch. of Public Policy, 1998–2003, UCL; Exeter Univ., 2000–03. Hon. Professor: Cardiff Univ., 2006; Univ. of Edinburgh, 2008. Ed., Oxford Database of Perinatal Trials, 1988–92. FMedSci 1999. Hon. FRSocMed 2005; Hon. Fellow, Royal Statistical Soc. 2006. Hon. DSc: Aberdeen, 1999; London, 2004; Hon. MD Liverpool, 2001; DUniv York, 2001; Hon. Dr, Free Univ., Amsterdam, 2006. *Publications:* (ed jtly) Effectiveness and Satisfaction in Antenatal Care, 1982; (ed jtly) Effective Care in Pregnancy and Childbirth, 1989; (ed jtly) Systematic Reviews, 1995; (ed jtly) Non-random Reflections on Health Services Research, 1997; (jtly) Testing Treatments, 2006. *Address:* James Lind Initiative, Summertown Pavilion, Middle Way, Oxford OX2 7LG. *T:* (01865) 517636.

CHALMERS, Ian Pender, CMG 1993; OBE 1980; HM Diplomatic Service, retired; Counsellor, Foreign and Commonwealth Office, 1987–98; *b* 30 Jan. 1939; *s* of John William Pender Chalmers and Beatrice Miriam Emery; *m* 1962, Lisa Christine Hay; two *s* two *d* (and one *d* decd). *Educ:* Harrow; Trinity College Dublin. Joined HM Diplomatic Service, 1963; Second Sec., Beirut, 1966–68; FCO, 1968–70; First Sec., Warsaw, 1970–72; FCO, 1972–76; First Sec., Paris, 1976–80; FCO, 1980–84; Counsellor, UK Mission to UN, Geneva, 1984–87. *Recreations:* family, golf, watching sport, reading, dogs. *Address:* The Croft, Packhorse Lane, Marcham, Oxon OX13 6NT. *Clubs:* Army and Navy; Huntercombe Golf.

CHALMERS, Prof. John Philip, AC 1991; FAA; Professor of Medicine, since 1996, and Senior Director at the George Institute (formerly the Institute) for International Health, since 2000 (Professorial Fellow, 1999–2000), University of Sydney; *b* 12 Jan. 1937; *m* 1977, Dr Alexandra Bune; four *s* one *d*. *Educ:* King's Sch., Parramatta; St Paul's Coll., Univ. of Sydney (BSc, MB BS); Univ. of NSW (PhD). FRCP, FRCPG, FRCPE, FACP, FRACP, FRACMA. Medical appts, Royal Prince Alfred Hosp., to 1968; Research Fellow: Nat. Heart Foundn, Univ. of NSW, 1965–66; MIT, 1969–70; RPMS, 1970–71; University of Sydney: Sen. Lectr, 1971–72; Assoc. Prof. of Medicine, 1973–75; Prof. of Medicine, Flinders Univ., 1975–96. Hon. Physician, Royal Prince Alfred Hosp., 1971–75; Vis MO, Repatriation Gen. Hosp., Concord, 1972–75; Mem., Bd of Management, Flinders Med. Centre, 1977–; Dean, Sch. of Medicine, Flinders Univ., 1991–92; Res. Chm., Royal N Shore Hosp., 1996–2000; Chm., Res. Develt for Faculty of Medicine, Sydney Univ., 2000–02. Royal Australian College of Physicians: Chm., State Cttee for SA, 1982–86; Chm., Bd of Censors, 1984–88; Vice-Pres., 1988–90; Pres., 1990–92; Pres., Internat. Soc. of Hypertension, 1992–94; Chm., Scientific Adv. Bd, Internat. Soc. and Fedn of Cardiology, 1997–; former mem. and chm., numerous sci. adv. cttees and govt med. bodies. FAA 1987; Hon. FRACS. Hon. MD: Queensland, 1991; NSW, 1994; Flinders, 1999; Sydney, 2007. Wellcome Medal for contrib. to Med. Res., 1981; Volhard Award, Internat. Soc. of Hypertension, for contrib. to Hypertension Res., 1998. Mem., editl bds of learned jls. *Publications:* numerous contribs to medical jls, on pharmacology, physiology, blood pressure, hypertension and other medical research. *Recreations:* cricket, cooking, theatre, travel. *Address:* George Institute for International Health, University of Sydney, Royal Prince Alfred Campus (C39), PO Box M201, Missenden Road, Sydney, NSW 2050, Australia; 3A Dettmann Avenue, Longueville, NSW 2066, Australia.

CHALMERS, Sir Neil (Robert), Kt 2001; Warden, Wadham College, Oxford, since 2004; *b* 19 June 1942; *s* of William King and Irene Margaret Chalmers (*née* Pemberton); *m* 1970, Monica Elizabeth Byanjeru (*née* Rusoke); two *d*. *Educ:* King's College Sch., Wimbledon; Magdalen Coll., Oxford (BA); St John's Coll., Cambridge (PhD). Lectr in Zoology, Makerere University Coll., Kampala, 1966–69; Scientific Dir, Nat. Primate Res. Centre, Nairobi, 1969–70; Open University: Lectr, subseq. Sen. Lectr, then Reader in Biology, 1970–85; Dean of Science, 1985–88; Dir, British Mus. (Natural History), then Natural History Mus., 1988–2004. Chm., Nat. Biodiversity Network Trust, 2005–. President: Marine Biol Assoc. UK, 2002–07; Inst. of Biology, 2004–06. Fellow, Birkbeck Coll., Univ. of London, 2002. Hon. Fellow, King's College Sch., Wimbledon, 2003. Hon. DSc Plymouth, 2004. *Publications:* Social Behaviour in Primates, 1979; numerous papers on animal behaviour in Animal Behaviour and other learned jls. *Recreations:* music, squash. *Address:* Wadham College, Oxford OX1 3PN.

CHALMERS, Patrick Edward Bruce; JP; Chairman: Upper Deeside Access Trust, since 2003; Cairngorms Outdoor Access Trust, since 2008; *b* Chapel of Garioch, Aberdeenshire, 26 Oct. 1939; *s* of L. E. F. Chalmers, farmer, Lethenty, Inverurie, and Helen Morris Campbell; *m* 1963, Ailza Catherine Reid (*d* 2004), *d* of late William McGibbon, Advocate in Aberdeen; three *d*. *Educ:* Fettes Coll., Edinburgh; N of Scotland Coll. of Agriculture (NDA); Univ. of Durham (BScA). Joined BBC as radio talks producer, BBC Scotland,

1963; television producer, 1965; sen. producer, Aberdeen, 1970; Head of Television, Scotland, 1979–82; Gen. Man., Co-Productions, London, 1982; Controller, BBC Scotland, 1983–92; Dir, BBC World Service Television, Asia, 1992–93, retd 1994; Dir, Scottish Ensemble, 1995–2002. Director: Hutchvision News Ltd, 1992–93; Grampian Venture Capital Fund, 1996–. President: Edinburgh Television Fest., 1984–92; BAFTA, Scotland, 1990–92. Dir, Scottish Film Production Fund, 1988–91. Mem., Aberdeenshire Council, 1995–99 (Chm., Lib Dem Gp); Convenor, Grampian Police Bd, 1998–99. Chm., Marr Area Cttee, 1996–99. Mem., Grampian Region Children's Panel, 1974–79. FRSA 1990. Bailie of Bennachie, 1975. JP Aberdeenshire, 1996. *Recreations:* ski-ing, gardening. *Address:* Corblelack, Logie Coldstone, Aboyne, Aberdeenshire AB34 5PR. *T:* and *Fax:* (013398) 81439. *Clubs:* New (Edinburgh); Royal Northern (Aberdeen); Foreign Correspondents (Hong Kong); Kandahar Ski.

CHALONER, family name of **Baron Gisborough.**

CHALONER, Prof. William Gilbert, FRS 1976; Hildred Carlile Professor of Botany and Head of School of Life Sciences, Royal Holloway (formerly Royal Holloway and Bedford New College), University of London, 1985–94 (at Bedford College, 1979–85); Emeritus Professor, 1994, Hon. Fellow, 2002, and engaged in research, Department of Geology, since 1994; *b* London, 22 Nov. 1928; *s* of late Ernest J. and L. Chaloner; *m* 1955, Judith Carroll; one *s* two *d. Educ:* Kingston Grammar Sch.; Reading Univ. (BSc, PhD). 2nd Lt RA, 1955–56. Lectr and Reader, University Coll., London, 1956–72. Visiting Prof., Pennsylvania State Univ., USA, 1961–62; Prof. of Botany, Univ. of Nigeria, 1965–66; Prof. of Botany, Birkbeck Coll., Univ. of London, 1972–79. Wilmer D. Barrett Prof. of Botany, Univ. of Mass, 1988–91. Vis. Prof., UCL, 1995–. Member: Senate, Univ. of London, 1983–91; Bd of Trustees, Royal Botanic Gardens, Kew, 1983–96. Mem., NERC, 1991–94. President: Palaeontological Assoc., 1976–78; Internat. Orgn of Palaeobotany, 1981–87; Linnean Soc., 1985–88; Vice-Pres., Geol Soc. London, 1985–86. Corresponding Mem., Botanical Soc. of Amer., 1987–. Associé Etranger de l'Acad. des Scis, Inst de France, 1989. Linnean Medal (Botany), Linnean Soc., 1991; Lyell Medal, Geol. Soc., 1994; Lapworth Medal, Palaeontol Assoc., 2006. *Publications:* papers in Palaeontology and other scientific jls, dealing with fossil plants. *Recreations:* swimming, tennis. *Address:* 26 Warren Avenue, Richmond, Surrey TW10 5DZ. *T:* (020) 8878 2080.

CHALSTREY, Sir (Leonard) John, Kt 1996; MD; FRCS; JP; Lord Mayor of London, 1995–96; Consultant Surgeon, St Bartholomew's Hospital, 1969–96, Surgeon Emeritus, St Bartholomew's and the Royal London Hospitals, 1996; Senior Lecturer, St Bartholomew's Hospital Medical College, University of London, 1969–96; *b* 17 March 1931; *s* of late Leonard Chalstrey and Frances Mary (*née* Lakin); *m* 1958, Aileen Beatrice Bayes; one *s* one *d. Educ:* Dudley Sch., Worcs; Queens' Coll., Cambridge (BA Hons 1954; MA 1958); Med. Coll., St Bartholomew's Hosp. (MB, BChir 1957; MD 1967). MRCS, LRCP 1957; FRCS 1962. Nat. Service, RAEC, 1949–51. Jun. med. and surgical posts, St Bartholomew's Hosp., 1958–59; Lectr in Anatomy, Middx Hosp. Med. Sch., 1959–61; Jun. Surgical Registrar, St Bartholomew's Hosp., 1962; Registrar, then Sen. Surgical Registrar, Royal Free Hosp., 1963–69; Hon. Consultant Surgeon, St Luke's Hosp. for Clergy, 1975–93. Examiner in Surgery: Univ. of London, 1976–95; Univ. of Cambridge, 1989–94. Non-exec. Mem., City and Hackney HA, 1992–93. City University: Mem. Court, 1986–92; Mem. Council, 1992–2001; Chancellor, 1995–96. Maj., 357 Field Surgical Team, RAMC(V), TA, 1991–96; Hon. Col, 256 (City of London) Field Hosp., RAMC(V), 1996–2000; Member: City of London TAVRA, 1992–2000; Gtr London TAVRA, 1992–2000. Governor, Corp. of Sons of the Clergy, 1992–. Mem., Court of Common Council, City of London Corp., 1981–84; Alderman (Vintry Ward), City of London, 1984–2001; Sheriff, City of London, 1993–94; HM Lieut, City of London, 1995–2001; JP 1984. Member, Court of Assistants: Soc. of Apothecaries (Sen. Warden, 1992–93 and 1993–94; Master, 1994–95); Barbers' Co. (Master, 1998–99); Member: Parish Clerks' Co., 1993–2007; HAC, 1995– (Hon. Mem., Ct of Assts, 1984–2001). Vice-Pres., City of London Sect., BRCS, 1992–. Trustee, Morden Coll., 1995–2005; Special Trustee: St Bartholomew's Hosp., 1998–2001; Royal London Hosp., 1999–2001; Trustee, St Bartholomew's and The Royal London Hosps Charitable Foundn, 2001–08. Pres., Guildhall Historical Assoc., 2000–07. FRSocMed 1965; Fellow, Assoc. of Surgeons of GB and Ireland, 1969; FRSA 1996. Hon. GSM 1996; Hon. FRSH 1996; Hon. Fellow, QMW, 1996. Hon. DSc City, 1995. KStJ 1995 (Mem., Chapter-Gen., 1994–99); Surgeon-in-Chief, and Chm., Med. Bd, St John Ambulance, 1993–99; Hospitaller, Priory of England, 1999–2002 (Mem., Priory Council and Chapter, 1999–2002). Grand Officier, Ordre National du Merité (France), 1996. *Publications:* (with Coffman and Smith-Laing) Gastro-Intestinal Disorders, 1986; (contrib.) Cancer in the Elderly, 1990; (contrib.) Maingot's Abdominal Operations, 7th edn 1980, 8th edn 1986; papers on surgical subjects in Brit. Jl Surgery, Brit. Jl Cancer and Jl RSM. *Recreations:* painting in oils, history of City of London. *Address:* Danebury, 113 The Chine, N21 2EG. *T:* (020) 8360 8921. *Clubs:* Oxford and Cambridge, East India, Guildhall, City Pickwick (Pres., 2007–).

CHAMBERLAIN, Prof. Geoffrey Victor Price, RD 1974; MD; FRCS, FRCOG; Apothecaries' Lecturer in History of Medicine, School of Medicine, Swansea University (formerly Clinical Medical School, University of Wales, Swansea), since 2000; Professor and Chairman, Obstetrics and Gynaecology, St George's Hospital Medical School, 1982–95, now Emeritus Professor; *b* 21 April 1930; *s* of late Albert Chamberlain and Irene Chamberlain (*née* Price); *m* 1956, Jocelyn Olivia Kerley, *d* of late Sir Peter Kerley, KCVO, CBE; three *s* two *d. Educ:* Llandaff Cathedral Sch.; Cowbridge; University Coll. and UCH, London (Goldsmith Schol. 1948; MB 1954; Fellow, UCL, 1987); MD 1968; FRCS 1960; FRCOG 1978. Residencies at RPMS, Gt Ormond St, Queen Charlotte's and Chelsea Hosps, KCH, 1955–69; Tutor, George Washington Med. Sch., Washington DC, 1965–66; Consultant Obstetrician and Gynaecologist, Queen Charlotte's and Chelsea Hosps, 1970–82. RNR, 1955–74, Surgeon Comdr. Member: Council, RSocMed, 1977–84 (Council, Obst. Sect., 1970–93; Council, Open Sect., 1987–95); Council, RCOG, 1971–77, 1982–87, 1990–94 (Vice-Pres., 1984–87; Pres., 1993–94); Chairman: Med. Cttee, Nat. Birthday Trust, 1982–95; Blair Bell Res. Soc., 1977–80; Assoc. of Profs of Obstetrics and Gynaecology, 1989–92. Fulbright Fellow, 1966; Thomas Eden Fellow, RCOG, 1966; Visiting Professor: Beckman, USA, 1984; Daphne Chung, Hong Kong, 1985; Edwin Tooth, Brisbane, 1987; Peshwar, Pakistan, 1993; Chicago Univ., 1996. S African Representative Cttee, 1988. Hon. FACOG 1990; Hon. FSLCOG 1994; Hon. FFFP 1996; Hon. FMCOG, 2005. Hon. Mem., Polish Acad. of Medicine, 1992. Freeman, City of London, 1982; Liveryman, Apothecaries' Soc., 1981–. Foundn Prize, Amer. Assoc. of Obstetricians, 1967; James Simpson Gold Medal, RCSEd, 1993. Editor: Contemporary Reviews in Obstetrics and Gynaecology, 1987–2000; British Jl of Obstetrics and Gynaecology, 1992–95. *Publications:* Safety of the Unborn Child, 1969; Lecture Notes in Obstetrics, 1975, 8th edn 1999; British Births, 1970; Placental Transfer, 1979; Clinical Physiology in Obstetrics, 1980, 4th edn 1997; Tubal Infertility, 1982; Pregnant Women at Work, 1984; Prepregnancy Care, 1985; (ed) Obstetrics by Ten Teachers, 14th edn, 1985, to 16th edn, 1994; (ed) Gynaecology by Ten Teachers, 14th edn, 1985, to 16th edn, 1994; Birthplace, 1987; Lecture Notes in Gynaecology, 6th edn 1988 to 8th edn 1999; Manual of Obstetrics, 1988; Obstetrics, 1989, 3rd edn 1999; ABC of Antenatal Care, 1991, 4th edn 2002; Pregnancy in the 1990s, 1992; Relief of Pain in

Labour, 1993; Homebirth, 1997; ABC of Labour Care, 1999; A Practice of Obstetrics and Gynaecology, 1999; The Life of Victor Bonney, 2000; Life of W. C. W. Nixon, 2004; The History of British Obstetrics and Gynaecology, 2007; contribs to BMJ, Lancet, UK and overseas Jls of Obst. and Gyn. *Recreations:* music, lazing in wife's garden. *Address:* Sycamores, Llanmadoc, Gower, Glamorgan SA3 1DB.

CHAMBERLAIN, Very Rev. George Ford, (Leo), OSB; Parish Priest, St John the Evangelist, Easingwold, York, since 2008; *b* 13 Aug. 1940; *s* of Brig. Noel Joseph Chamberlain, CBE and Sarah (Sally) (*née* Ford). *Educ:* Ampleforth Coll.; University Coll., Oxford (BA 1961; MA 1965). Novitiate, Ampleforth Abbey, 1961, solemn profession, 1965; ordained priest, 1968; Ampleforth College: Housemaster, St Dunstan's House, 1972–92; Sen. History Master, 1973–92; Headmaster, 1992–2003; Master, St Benet's Hall, Oxford, 2004–07. Member: Council of Management, Keston Inst. (formerly Keston Coll.), 1985–2003; Catholic Bishops' Cttee for European Affairs, 1992–2000; HMC, 1993–2003; Catholic Ind. Schs Conf., 1993–2003 (Mem. Cttee, 1994–2000). Gov., St Gregory the Great Sch., Oxford, 2005–07. Titular Cathedral Prior of St Peter, Glos. Hon Fellow, St Benet's Hall, Oxford. *Address:* Ampleforth Abbey, York YO62 4EN. *Club:* Lansdowne.

CHAMBERLAIN, Kevin John, CMG 1992; barrister; Deputy Legal Adviser, Foreign and Commonwealth Office, 1990–99; *b* 31 Jan. 1942; *s* of late Arthur James Chamberlain and Gladys Mary (*née* Harris); *m* 1967, Pia Rosita Frauenlob; one *d. Educ:* Wimbledon Coll.; King's Coll., London (LLB). Called to the Bar, Inner Temple, 1965. HM Diplomatic Service, 1965–99: Asst Legal Adviser, FCO, 1965–74; Legal Adviser: British Mil. Govt, Berlin, 1974–76; British Embassy, Bonn, 1976–77; Asst Legal Adviser, FCO, 1977–79; Legal Counsellor, FCO, 1979–83; Counsellor (Legal Advr), Office of UK Perm. Rep. to EC, Brussels, 1983–87; Legal Counsellor, FCO, 1987–90. Mem., NATO Appeals Bd, 2004–. Legal Advr, Ministerial Adv. Panel on Illicit Trade in Cultural Objects, 2000–04. Dir and Co. Sec., Art Resolve, 2005–. Chm., Ind. Remuneration Panel, Reigate and Banstead BC, 2001–. Mem., Cultural Heritage Law Cttee, ILA, 2007–; Founder Mem., Internat. Foundn for Cultural Diplomacy, 2007–. CEDR Accredited Mediator, 2002, CEDR Registered Mediator, 2003. Vis. Sen. Lectr in Laws, KCL, 2006–. Hon. Sen. Lectr in Laws, UCL, 2004–05. Fellow, Soc. of Advanced Legal Studies, 2001–. *Publication:* War and Cultural Heritage, 2004. *Recreations:* opera, tennis, antiques, choral singing. *Address:* Fairfield, Warren Drive, Kingswood, Tadworth, Surrey KT20 6PY.

CHAMBERLAIN, Very Rev. Leo; *see* Chamberlain, Very Rev. G. F.

CHAMBERLAIN, (Leslie) Neville, CBE 1990; Chairman, The Northern Way, since 2006; Deputy Chairman, British Nuclear Fuels plc, 1995–99 (Chief Executive, 1986–96); *b* 3 Oct. 1939; *s* of Leslie Chamberlain and Doris Anne Chamberlain (*née* Thompson); *m* 1971, Joy Rachel Wellings; one *s* three *d. Educ:* King James Grammar School, Bishop Auckland; King's College, Univ. of Durham (BSc 1961; MSc 1962). FInstP. UKAEA, 1962–71; Urenco Ltd, 1971–77; British Nuclear Fuels: Fuel Production, 1977–81; Enrichment Business Manager, 1981–84; Dir, Enrichment Div., 1984–86. Dir, 1981–2005, Chm., 2002–05, Urenco Ltd; non-executive Director: Dennis Gp plc, 1994–98; Manchester 2002 Ltd, 1999–2002; New East Manchester Ltd, 1999–2002; RBG Resources plc, 2001–02; AMEC Nuclear Ltd, 2005–; Chm., Structure Vision Ltd, 2007–. Chm., Nat Council, TEC, 1999–2001; Mem., NACETT, 1999–2001. Mem. Bd, NW Develt Agency, 2001–04. Chairman: British Energy Assoc., 1999–2001; Internat. Nuclear Energy Acad., 2001–04; Manufg Inst., 2002–; Cheshire and Warrington Econ. Alliance, 2005–; Co-Chm., Trans-Atlantic Nuclear Energy Forum, 2005–. Trustee, N of England Zool Soc., 2004–. Mem., Council, Salford Univ., 2000–. Freeman, Fuellers' Co., 1997–. FInstE; CCMI; FRSA. Hon. FINucE 1994; Hon. Fellow, European Nuclear Soc., 1994. Hon. DSc Salford, 1989. Melchett Lectr and Medal, Inst. of Energy, 1989. *Recreations:* horse racing, swimming, music, endangered animals. *Address:* Oaklands, 2 The Paddock, Hinderton Road, Neston, South Wirral, Cheshire CH64 9PH. *T:* (0151) 353 1980. *Club:* Athenæum.

CHAMBERLAIN, Prof. Mary Christina, FRHistS; Professor of Modern History, Oxford Brookes University, since 1995; *b* 3 Sept. 1947; *d* of Arthur James Chamberlain and Gladys Mary Chamberlain (*née* Harris); *m* 1st, 1971, Carey Harrison (marr. diss. 1977); one *d*; 2nd, 1980, Peter Lane (marr. diss. 1997); two *d*; 3rd, 2002, Prof. Stein Ringen, *qv. Educ:* Univ. of Edinburgh (MA Hons); London Sch. of Econs and Pol Sci. (MSc). Researcher, Arms Control and Disarmament Res. Unit, FCO, 1970–71; Lecturer: Norfolk Coll. of Art and Technol., 1973–74; London Coll. of Fashion, 1974–75; Ipswich Civic Coll., 1975–77; Sen. Lectr, London Coll. of Printing (London Inst.), 1977–87; Lectr (pt-time), Univ. of WI (Cave Hill, Barbados), 1988–91; Fellow, Univ. of Essex, 1991–93; Sen. Lectr, Oxford Brookes Univ., 1993–95. Visiting Professor: Univ. of WI, 2004, 2006; NY Univ., 2004. Founding Ed., Studies in Memory and Narrative, 1997–. Mem., Adv. Gp, Virago Press, 1976–91. Member: UK Govt Caribbean Adv. Gp, 1998–2002; Panel of Assessors, Big Lottery Fund, 2001–. Consultant, Barbados Nat. Oral Hist. Project, 1999; Trustee, Nat. Life Story Collection, Nat. Sound Archive, BL, 1991–2004. FRHistS 2002. Mem., Adv. Gp, Raphael Samuel History Centre, 2002–. *Publications:* Fenwomen, 1975, 2nd edn 1983; Old Wives' Tales, 1981, 2nd edn 2006; (ed) Writing Lives, 1988; Growing Up in Lambeth, 1989; Narratives of Exile and Return, 1997, 2nd edn 2004; (ed with P. Thompson) Narrative and Genre, 1998, 2nd edn 2004; (ed) Caribbean Migration: globalised identities, 1998; (ed with H. Goulbourne) Caribbean Families in Britain and the Atlantic World, 2001; Family Love in the Diaspora: migration and the Anglo-Caribbean experience, 2006. *Recreations:* walking, swimming, travel, cooking, grandchildren, gardening, cinema. *Address:* School of Arts and Humanities, Oxford Brookes University, Gipsy Lane, Oxford OX3 0BP. *T:* (01865) 484130, *Fax:* (01865) 484082; *e-mail:* mcchamberlain@brookes.ac.uk.

CHAMBERLAIN, Michael Aubrey, OBE 2007; FCA; Consultant, KPMG, Leicester, since 1994; *b* 16 April 1939; *s* of George Thomas Everard Chamberlain and Doris (*née* Arden). *Educ:* Repton Sch., Derbys. FCA 1963. Sen. Partner, KPMG Peat Marwick, 1974–93. Pres., Inst. of Chartered Accountants in England and Wales, 1993–94 (Vice-Pres., 1991–92; Dep. Pres., 1992–93); Chm., Chartered Accountants Compensation Scheme, 1998–. Chm., Leicester Diocesan Bd of Finance, 1983–98; Member: Archbishops' Council, 1999– (Chm. Finance Cttee, 1999–); Adv. Bd, RSCM, 2000–. Dir, Allchurches Trust Ltd, 2006–. Mem. Council, Univ. of Leicester, 1996– (Treas., 1999–). Hon. LLD Leicester, 1993. *Address:* 1 Waterloo Way, Leicester LE1 6LP. *T:* (0116) 256 6221.

CHAMBERLAIN, Rt Rev. Neville; Master, Hugh Sexey's Hospital, Bruton, since 2005; *b* 24 Oct. 1939; *s* of Albert Victor Chamberlain and Miriam Chamberlain; *m* 1964, Diana Hammill; three *s* one *d. Educ:* Salford Grammar Sch.; Nottingham Univ. (BA Theol.); MA Applied Social Studies; CQSW); Ripon Hall, Oxford (DPSA 1962). Ordained deacon, 1963, priest, 1964; Asst Curate, St Paul's, Birmingham, 1963–64; Priest-in-charge, St Michael's, Birmingham, 1964–69; Rector, Deer Creek Parish, USA, 1967–68; Vicar, St Michael's Anglican/Methodist Church, Birmingham, 1969–72; Probation Officer, Grimsby, 1972–74; Exec. Sec., Lincoln Diocesan Social Responsibility Cttee, 1974–82;

Rector, St John the Evangelist, Edinburgh, 1982–97; Bishop of Brechin, 1997–2005. Prebend and Canon, Lincoln Cathedral, 1979–. *Recreations:* golf, cycling, cinema. *Address:* The Master's House, Hugh Sexey's Hospital, High Street, Bruton, Som BA10 0AS. *T:* (01749) 813369.

CHAMBERLAIN, Neville; see Chamberlain, L. N.

CHAMBERLAIN, Paul Arthur; Headmaster, Cheltenham College, 1997–2004; *b* 10 June 1948; *s* of Arthur and Lilian Amy Chamberlain; *m* 1970, Kathleen Eleanor Hopley; one *s* one *d. Educ:* Verdin Grammar Sch., Winsford, Cheshire; Univ. of Durham (BSc Hons Zoology 1969; PGCE 1970). Haileybury College: Asst Master, 1970–83; Housemaster, 1983–88; Headmaster, St Bees Sch., Cumbria, 1988–97. *Recreations:* fell walking, fly-fishing, music, photography. *Address:* Drumlins, Lowick Green, Ulverston, Cumbria LA12 8DY. *T:* (01229) 885424.

CHAMBERLAIN, Peter Edwin, FREng; FRINA; Director, Pai Faena Srl, since 2003; *b* 25 July 1939; *s* of late Dr Eric Alfred Charles Chamberlain, OBE, FRSE, and Winifred Louise, (Susan) (*née* Bone); *m* 1963, Irene May Frew; two *s* one *d. Educ:* Royal High Sch.; Edinburgh Univ. (Keasby Schol., BSc); RN Colls Manadon and Greenwich. RCNC. Asst Constructor, ship and submarine design, ME and Bath, 1963–68; Constructor: submarine design, Bath, 1968–69; submarine construction, Birkenhead, 1969–72; ship structures R&D, Dunfermline, 1972–74; postgrad. programmes in Naval Architecture, UCL, 1974–77; ship design, Bath, 1977–78; Chief Constructor: Hd of Secretariat, Bath, 1978–80; Surface Ship Forward Design, Bath, 1980–82; RCDS 1983; Asst Sec., Hd of Secretariat to Master Gen. of Ordnance, London, 1984–85; Under Sec., Dir Gen. Future Material Programmes (Naval), London, 1985–87; Dep. Controller Warship Equipments, MoD, 1987–88; Chief Underwater Systems Exec., MoD, 1988–89; creation of Defence Res. Agency, MoD, 1989–92; Engr Dir, System and Services Div., BAe, 1992–98; Dir, ANZAC WIP Project, BAe Australia, 1999. Director: Timely Solutions Ltd, 2000–06; Xienta, 2001–03. Mem., Internat. Council on Systems Engrg, 1995–. FREng (FEng 1988); FRINA 1988. *Recreations:* music, visual arts, poetry, computing. *Address:* Coste Faena 112, 06057 Monte Castello di Vibio (PG), Italy; *e-mail:* peter_e_chamberlain@compuserve.com.

CHAMBERLEN, Nicholas Hugh; Chairman, Clive Discount Company, 1977–93; *b* 18 April 1939; *s* of late Rev. Leonard Saunders Chamberlen, MC, and Lillian Margaret (*née* Webley); *m* 1st, 1962, Jane Mary Lindo (*d* 1998); three *s* one *d*; 2nd, 2001, Christine Mary Lacy. *Educ:* Sherborne Sch.; Lincoln Coll., Oxford (BA Hons). Nat. Cash Register Co., 1962–67; Clive Discount Co. Ltd, 1967–93. *Recreations:* shooting, golf, cricket. *Address:* Lampool, Fairwarp, East Sussex TN22 3DS. *Clubs:* Turf; Royal and Ancient Golf (St Andrews).

CHAMBERS, Aidan; writer; *b* 27 Dec. 1934; *m* 1968, Nancy Lockwood. Teacher, 1957–68; Jt Founder, Thimble Press, 1969, publisher of Signal: Approaches to Children's Books, 1970–2003. Pres., Sch. Library Assoc., 2003–06. Hon. PhD Umeå, 2003. Children's Lit. Assoc. award, USA, 1979; Eleanor Farjeon Award, Children's Book Circle, 1982; Hans Andersen Award, Internat. Bd on Books for Young People, 2002. *Publications:* The Reluctant Reader, 1969; Introducing Books to Children, 1973; Booktalk, 1985; The Reading Environment, 1991; Tell Me: children, reading and talk, 1993; Reading Talk, 2001; *novels:* Breaktime, 1978; Dance on my Grave, 1982; Now I Know, 1987; The Toll Bridge, 1992; Postcards from No Man's Land, 1999 (Carnegie Medal, LA, 1999); Michael Printz Award, USA, 2003); This Is All: the pillow book of Cordelia Kenn, 2005; *for children:* Seal Secret, 1980; The Present Takers, 1983; *plays for young people:* Johnny Salter, 1966; The Car, 1967; The Chicken Run, 1968; The Dream Cage, 1981; Only Once, 1998; The Toll Bridge, 1998; ed. of anthologies etc. *Address:* Lockwood, Station Road, South Woodchester, Stroud, Glos GL5 5EQ.

CHAMBERS, Prof. Andrew David; Member, Management Audit LLP (formerly Director, Management Audit Ltd), since 1991; Professor of Internal Auditing, London South Bank University, since 2004; *b* 7 April 1943; *s* of Lewis Harold and Florence Lilian Chambers; *m* 1st, 1969, Mary Elizabeth Ann Kilbey (marr. diss. 1984); two *s*; 2nd, 1987, Celia Barrington (*née* Pruen); two *s* two *d* (incl. twin *s* and *d*), and one step *s. Educ:* St Albans Sch.; Hatfield Coll., Univ. of Durham (BA Hons). CEng; FCA, FBCS, FCCA, FIIA. Arthur Andersen & Co., 1965–69; Barker & Dobson, 1969–70; United Biscuits, 1970–71; City University Business School: Lectr in Computer Applications in Accountancy, 1971–74; Leverhulme Sen. Res. Fellow in Internal Auditing, 1974–78; Sen. Lectr in Audit and Management Control, 1978–83; Prof. of Internal Auditing, 1983–93, then Emeritus; Administrative Sub-Dean, 1983–86; Acting Dean, 1985–86; Dean, 1986–91; Head of Dept of Business Studies, 1986–89; Warden, Northampton Hall, City Univ., 1983–86 (Dep. Warden, 1972–76); Prof. of Audit and Control, Univ. of Hull, 1994–98; Academic Dir, FTMS, 1999–2001. Vis. Professor: in Computer Auditing, Univ. of Leuven, Belgium, 1980–81, 1992–93; of Internal Auditing, Birmingham City Univ. (formerly Univ. of Central England), 2006–; Chm., Harlequin IT Services Ltd, 1998–99. Consultant: MacIntyre Hudson, Chartered Accountants, 1987–89; BBHW, Chartered Accountants, 1990–92; Director: Paragon Gp of Cos (formerly Nat. Home Loans Hldgs), 1991–2003 (Chm., Remuneration Cttee, 1992–95, Audit Cttee, 1995–2003); Nat. Mortgage Bank, 1991–92; IIA Inc., 1993–96 (Mem. Internat. Standards Bd, 1992–95, 2008–); Pilgrim Health NHS Trust, 1996–99; FTMS Online, 1999–2002. Mem. Auditing Practices Bd, 2006–. Institute of Internal Auditors–UK: Mem. Council, 1985–86; Mem., Professional Standards and Guidelines Cttee (Chm., 1991–95); Association of Chartered Certified Accountants: Mem., Auditing Cttee, 1994–; Chm., Internal Auditing Cttee, 2002–06; Chm., Corporate Governance and Risk Mgt Cttee, 2006–. Member: Council, BCS, 1979–82 (Mem., Tech. Bd; Chm., Meetings Cttee); IT Cttee, 1986–91, Internal Audit Cttee, 1998–2003, Corporate Governance Cttee, 2004–, ICAEW; Educn, Training and Technol. Transfer Cttee, British Malaysian Soc., 1987–90; MBA Adv. Bd, Ashridge Management Coll., 1986–92; Council, Tavistock Inst., 2004–; Director: Council of Univ. Management Schs, 1988–92; Med. Defence Union, 2004–06 (Chm., Audit Cttee, 2004–06); Hon. Auditor, RSAA, 1986–91. External Examr, Dundee Univ., 1998–2002. MInstD 1986; CITP; FRSA. Gov., Islington Green Comprehensive Sch., 1989–91. Liveryman, Loriners' Co., 2003–. Member, Editorial Board: Computer Fraud and Security, 1981–87; Managerial Auditing Jl, 1986–94; Asian Acad. of Mgt Jl, 2003–; Gen. Editor, Internat. Jl of Auditing, 1995–2003; Editor: Internal Control, 1997–2005; Corporate Governance, 1998–2004; Fraud, 2000–01. *Publications:* (with O. J. Hanson) Keeping Computers Under Control, 1975; (ed) Internal Auditing: developments and horizons, 1979; Internal Auditing: theory and practice, 1981, 2nd edn (with G. M. Selim and G. Vinten) 1987; Computer Auditing, 1981, 3rd edn (with J. M. Court) 1991; Effective Internal Audits: how to plan and implement, 1992; (with G. Rand) Auditing the IT Environment, 1994; (with G. Rand) Auditing Contracts, 1994; (ed) Internal Auditing, 1996; (with G. Rand) The Operational Auditing Handbook: auditing business processes, 1997; (with J. Ridley) Leading Edge Internal Auditing, 1998; Tolley's Corporate Governance Handbook, 2002, 4th edn 2008 as Corporate Governance Handbook; Tolley's Internal Auditor's Handbook, 2005, 2nd edn 2009; papers in learned jls.

Recreation: family. *Address:* Management Audit LLP, Moat Lane, Old Bolingbroke, Spilsby, Lincs PE23 4ES. *T:* (01790) 763350; *e-mail:* Profadc@aol.com. *Clubs:* Reform, Travellers.

CHAMBERS, Daniel; Joint Company Director, Blink Films Ltd, since 2007; *b* 13 Sept. 1968; *s* of Michael Earnest Chambers and Florence Ruth Cooper; partner, Rebecca Claire Eisig Cotton. *Educ:* William Ellis Sch.; University Coll. Sch.; Brasenose Coll., Oxford (BA Hons). Career journalist, Evening Standard, 1991–92; researcher/asst producer, Panorama, Dispatches and Equinox, 1992–96; Director: Equinox Sun Storm, 1996; Equinox Russian Roulette, 1997; Science Department, Channel 4: Dep. Commng Ed., 1998–99; Editor, 1999–2001: devised Secrets of the Dead; commnd Private Lives of the Pharaohs, Better by Design, Accident Blackspot, Escape from Colditz, Cannibal, Extinct and Salvage Squad; responsible for Scrapheap Challenge; jtly responsible for Big Brother; Controller of Factual Progs, Channel 5, subseq. Five, 2001–03: devised History Strand Revealed; commnd World War I in Colour, Kings & Queens, Britain's Finest, Dream Holiday Home, Britain's Worst Driver, Fifth Gear and Be a Grand Prix Driver; Dir of Programmes, Five, 2003–06. Gov., London Film Sch., 2006–. Author of play, Selling Out (first dir. by Alan Ayckbourn, Scarborough, 1992). *Recreations:* ski-ing, scuba diving, cinema. *Address:* Blink Films Ltd, Biscuit Building, 10 Redchurch Street, E2 7DD. *T:* (020) 7749 3160. *Club:* Shoreditch House.

CHAMBERS, Dominic Kern; QC 2008; *b* Solihull, 28 Feb. 1963; *s* of Martin Royston Chambers and Marcia Parsons Chambers; *m* 1992, Georgina Kent; one *s* two *d. Educ:* Sandroyd Sch.; Harrow Sch.; King's Coll. London (LLB Hons). Called to the Bar, Gray's Inn, 1987; in practice as barrister, 1988–, specialising in internat. and commercial litigation and arbitration. Freeman, City of London, 1983; Liveryman, Co. of Pewterers, 1992. *Recreations:* horology, wine, shooting, Brazil rainforest. *Address:* Maitland Chambers, 7 Stone Buildings, Lincoln's Inn, WC2A 3SZ. *T:* (020) 7406 1200, *Fax:* (020) 7406 1300; *e-mail:* dchambers@maitlandchambers.com.

CHAMBERS, Dr Douglas Robert; HM Coroner, City of London, 1994–2002; *b* 2 Nov. 1929; *s* of Douglas Henry Chambers and Elizabeth Paterson; *m* 1955, Barbara June Rowe; one *s* two *d. Educ:* Shene Grammar Sch.; King's College, London (MB BS; AKC 1953); LLB London Univ. (ext.) 1960; MA Univ. of Wales, 1989. FIBiol 1992. Called to the Bar, Lincoln's Inn, 1965. RAF Med. Br., 1955–58; Med. Advr, Parke Davis, 1959–61, Nicholas Laboratories, 1961–63; Pharmacia, 1964–65; Med. Dir, Hoechst Pharmaceuticals, 1965–70; Dep. Coroner, West London, 1969–70; HM Coroner, Inner North London, 1970–94. Hon. Sen. Clin. Lectr in med. law, UCL, 1978–96; Hon. Sen. Lectr, medical law, Royal Free Hosp., 1978–2002. Chairman: Richmond Div., BMA, 1969–70; Animal Research and Welfare Panel, Biological Council, 1986–92; Animal Welfare in Res. and Educn Cttee, Inst. of Biology, 1992–95; Pres., Library (sci. research) section, RSocMed, 1979–80; Pres., British sect., Anglo-German Med. Soc., 1980–84; Pres., Coroners' Soc., 1985–86. Hon. Mem., British Micro-circulation Soc., 1986 (Hon. Treas., 1968–86). Dist Comr, Richmond & Barnes Dist Scouts, 1976–85 (Silver Acorn 1984). Pres., Kensington Rowing Club, 1973–78. Baron C. ver Heyden de Lancey Prize for services to law and medicine, RSocMed, 1990. *Publications:* (jtly) Coroners' Inquiries, 1985; (consultant ed.) Jervis on Coroners, (with Dr J. Burton) 11th edn 1993, (with Dr J. Burton and M. J. C. Burgess) 12th edn 2002; papers on medico-legal subjects. *Recreation:* local history of coroners and of scouting. *Address:* 4 Ormond Avenue, Richmond, Surrey TW10 6TN. *T:* (020) 8940 7745. *Club:* Auriol-Kensington Rowing.

CHAMBERS, Ernest George Wilkie; Managing Director, Beattie Communications Group (formerly Beattie Media), since 2001; *b* 10 May 1947; *s* of Ernest and Ada Chambers; *m* 1971, Jeanette; one *s* one *d. Educ:* Harris Acad., Dundee; Dundee Univ. (BSc 1st Cl. Hons Applied Sci. 1969); Strathclyde Univ. (MBA 1987). Graduate civil engr, E of Scotland Water Bd, 1969–73; Asst Engr, Lower Clyde Water Bd, 1973–75; Area Engr (Renfrew), 1975–78; Lower Clyde Division: Divl Ops Engr, 1978–84; Asst Divl Manager, 1984–86; Asst Dir (Ops and Maintenance), 1986–88; Dir of Water, 1988–94; Dir, Water Services, Strathclyde Regl Council, 1994–95; Chief Exec., West of Scotland Water, 1995–2001. *Recreations:* DIY, gardening. *Address:* (office) 118 North Main Street, Carronshore, Falkirk FK2 8HU.

CHAMBERS, Fredrick Rignold H.; see Hyde-Chambers.

CHAMBERS, John T.; President and Chief Executive Officer, Cisco Systems Inc., since 1995; *m* Elaine; two *c. Educ:* West Virginia Univ. (BS/BA business; JD); Indiana Univ. (MBA). Formerly posts with IBM (incl. Exec. Vice-Pres.), and Wang Labs (latterly Sen. Vice-Pres. of US Ops); Sen. Vice-Pres. for Worldwide Ops, 1991–94, Exec. Vice-Pres., 1994–95, Cisco Systems Inc. Formerly Mem., US President's Cttee for Trade Policy. *Address:* Cisco Systems Inc., 170 West Tasman Drive, San Jose, CA 95134, USA.

CHAMBERS, Michael Laurence; QC 2003; a Recorder, since 2000; *b* 3 Dec. 1956; *s* of late Lawrence Chambers, CEng and Maureen Chambers; *m* 1989, Verity Susan Stowell Hunt; one *s* one *d. Educ:* Cheltenham Coll.; St Peter's Coll., Oxford (MA). Called to the Bar, Lincoln's Inn, 1980; in practice, Wales and Chester Circuit, 1981–; Circuit Jun., 2002. An Asst Recorder, 1997–2000; Standing Counsel to HM Customs and Excise, 2001. Legal Assessor, GMC, 2002–. *Address:* 9–12 Bell Yard, WC2A 2JR. *T:* (020) 7400 1800. *Club:* Chester City.

CHAMBERS, Nicholas Mordaunt; QC 1985; **His Honour Judge Chambers;** a Circuit Judge, since 1999; Mercantile Judge for Wales, since 2007 (Mercantile Judge for Wales and Chester, 1999–2007); *b* 25 Feb. 1944; *s* of Marcus Mordaunt Bertrand Chambers and Lona Margit Chambers (*née* Gross); *m* 1966, Sally Elizabeth, *er d* of T. H. F. (Tony) Banks; two *s* one *d. Educ:* King's School, Worcester; Hertford College, Oxford (BA 1965). Called to the Bar, Gray's Inn, 1966, Bencher, 1994; a Recorder, 1987–99; a Dep. High Court Judge, 1994–99. Member: Civil Procedure Rule Cttee, 1997–99; Civil Cttee, Judicial Studies Bd, 2002–. Chm., Incorporated Council of Law Reporting, 2001–. *Recreation:* sketching. *Address:* Civil Justice Centre, 2 Park Street, Cardiff CF10 1ET. *Clubs:* Garrick, Lansdowne.

CHAMBERS, Maj.-Gen. Peter Antony, CB 2002; MBE 1982; Interim Chief Executive Officer, Richmond upon Thames Council for Voluntary Service, 2006–07; *b* 23 April 1947; *s* of Mary Eugenie Chambers and Vincent Gerard Chambers; *m* 1968, Valerie Anne Straker; two *d. Educ:* De La Salle Grammar Sch.; Liverpool Univ. (BA Hons). FCIPS; FCILT (FCIT, FILT). Commissioned RAOC, 1969; Staff Coll., 1979 (psc); OC 51 Ordnance Co., 1980–83; CO 1 Ordnance Bn, 1985–88; Col Ordnance 1, 1988–90; Higher Comd and Staff Course, 1990; Comdr Supply, 1st (BR) Corps, 1990–93; Sen. Army Mem., RCDS, 1993; Dir, Logistic Support Policy, 1995–97; Mem., RCDS, 1997–98; DCS, HQ Land Command, 1998–2002. Dir, Hill Homes, 2002–06. Rep. Col Comdt, RLC, 2003–04, 2006–07. FCMI. *Recreations:* walking, dinghy sailing, family. *Address:* RHQ the RLC, Dettingen House, The Princess Royal Barracks, Deepcut, Camberley, Surrey GU16 6RW.

CHAMBERS, Prof. Richard Dickinson, PhD, DSc; FRS 1997; Professor of Chemistry, University of Durham, 1976–2000, now Emeritus; *b* 16 March 1935; *s* of Alfred and Elizabeth Chambers; *m* 1959, Anne Boyd; one *s* one *d*. *Educ:* Stanley Grammar Sch.; Univ. of Durham (BSc; PhD 1959; DSc 1968). Research Fellow, UBC, Vancouver, 1959–60; University of Durham: Lectr, 1960–69; Reader, 1969–76; Head of Dept, 1983–86; Sir Derman Christopherson Res. Fellow, 1988–89. Vis. Lectr and Fulbright Fellow, Case-Western Reserve Univ., Cleveland, Ohio, 1966–67; Tarrant Vis. Prof., Univ. of Florida, Gainesville, 1999. Non-exec. Dir, F2 Chemicals Ltd, 1995–2000. Internat. Award for Creative Work in Fluorine Chemistry, ACS, 1991; Moissan Internat. Prize, 2003. *Publications:* Fluorine in Organic Chemistry, 1973, 2nd edn 2004; contribs to jls on many aspects of organo-fluorine compounds. *Recreations:* opera, golf, soccer. *Address:* Department of Chemistry, University of Durham, South Road, Durham DH1 3LE. *T:* (0191) 374 3120; *e-mail:* R.D.Chambers@durham.ac.uk; 5 Aykley Green, Whitesmocks, Durham DH1 4LN. *T:* (0191) 386 5791.

CHAMBERS, Robert Alexander H.; *see* Hammond-Chambers.

CHAMBERS, Prof. Robert Guy; Professor of Physics, University of Bristol, 1964–90, Emeritus 1990; *b* 8 Sept. 1924; *s* of A. G. P. Chambers; *m* 1st, 1950, Joan Brislee (marr. diss. 1981); one *d*; 2nd, 1988, Susan Eden. *Educ:* King Edward VI Sch., Southampton; Peterhouse, Cambridge. Work on tank armament (Ministry of Supply), 1944–46; Electrical Research Association, 1946–47; Royal Society Mond Laboratory, Cambridge, 1947–57; Stokes Student, Pembroke Coll., 1950–53; PhD 1952; ICI Fellow, 1953–54; NRC Post-doctoral Fellow, Ottawa, 1954–55; University Demonstrator, Cambridge, 1955–57; Bristol University: Sen. Lectr, 1958–61; Reader in Physics, 1961–64; Dean of Science, 1973–76, 1985–88; Pro-Vice-Chancellor, 1978–81. Member: Physics Cttee, 1967–71, Nuclear Physics Bd, 1971–74, Sci. Bd, 1975–78, SRC; Physical Sci. Sub-Cttee, UGC, 1974–81. Institute of Physics: Mem., Publications Cttee, 1969–81 (Chm., 1977–81); Vice-Pres., 1977–81. Chm., Standing Conf. of Physics Profs, 1987–89. Chairman: SLS (Information Systems) Ltd, 1986–89; Track Analysis Systems Ltd, 1986–92. Hon. Fellow, Univ. of Bristol, 1994. Hughes Medal, Royal Soc., 1994. *Publications:* Electrons in Metals and Semiconductors, 1990; various papers in learned journals on the behaviour of metals at low temperatures. *Recreation:* hill-walking. *Address:* 9 Apsley Road, Clifton, Bristol BS8 2SH. *T:* (0117) 973 9833.

CHAMBERS, Sarah Penelope; Chief Executive, Postal Services Commission, 2004–08; *b* 8 Nov. 1958; *d* of Sir (Stanley) Paul Chambers, KBE, CB, CIE and of Edith Chambers; *m* 1985, Andrew Hearn; three *s*. *Educ:* Channing Sch., N London; Somerville Coll., Oxford (BA Hons PPE). Department of Trade and Industry, 1979–2004: on loan to OFT, 1980–81; on loan to Oftel as Dir, Licensing, 1994–98; Dir, Strategy and Competitiveness Unit, 1999–2001; Dir, Automotive Unit, 2001–04. *Recreations:* tennis, fantasy football.

CHAMBERS, Stephen Lyon, RA 2005; artist; *b* 20 July 1960; *s* of John Tangye Chambers and Gillian Mure Chambers; *m* 1991, Denise de Cordova; three *s*. *Educ:* Winchester Sch. of Art (Fellow 1986); St Martin's Sch. of Art (BA 1st Cl. Hons 1982); Chelsea Sch. of Art (MA 1983). Rome Schol., 1983–84; Fellow, Downing Coll./Kettle's Yard, Cambridge, 1998–99. Trustee, Bryan Robertson Trust, 2003–. *Solo exhibitions* include: Flowers East Gall., London, 1989, 1992, 1995, 1998, 2000, 2003, 2006; Flowers Graphics, London, 1995, 1997, 2003, 2005; Flowers West, Santa Monica, 1998, 2000; Ikon Gall., Birmingham, 1993; Kettle's Yard, Cambridge, 1998, 1999; Gal. Kemper, Munich, 2000, 2001; Frissiras Mus., Athens, 2002; Gal. Frank Pages, Baden-Baden, 2005; *group exhibitions* include: Flowers East Gall.; RCA; Winchester Gall.; Plymouth Arts Centre; Riverside Studios; London Inst.; Flowers, NY; Nigel Greenwood Gall., London; Eagle Gall., London. Set designs for Royal Ballet, 2001. *Publications:* Long Pig, 1994; Four Heads, 1994; Healing Poems for the Great Ape, 1997; (with Marina Warner) Lullabye for an Insomniac Princess, 2006; A Year of Ranting Hopelessly, 2007. *Recreations:* cryptic crosswords, avoiding listening to speeches, Middle Eastern cooking, growing vegetables, Liverpool Football Club, contemplating revenge. *Address:* 31 Sotheby Road, N5 2UP. *T:* (020) 8985 3003; *e-mail:* stephenlyonchambers@btinternet.com.

CHAMBERS, Stuart John; Group Chief Executive, NSG Group, since 2008 (Director, since 2006; Chief Operating Officer, 2007–08); Chief Executive, Pilkington Group Ltd, since 2006; *b* 25 May 1956; *s* of Reginald and Eileen Chambers; *m* 1984, Nicolette Horrocks; one *s* two *d*. *Educ:* Friends Sch., Great Ayton; UCL (BSc Hons). Shell, 1977–88; Mars Corp., 1988–96; Pilkington: Gp Vice Pres. Marketing, Building Products, 1996–97; Gen. Manager, Pilkington UK Ltd, 1997–98; Man. Dir, Primary Products Europe, 1998–2000; Pres., Building Products Worldwide, 2000–07; Gp Chief Exec., Pilkington plc, 2002–06. Non-exec. Director: ABP Hldgs plc, 2002–06 (Chm., Remuneration Cttee, 2005–06); Smiths Gp plc, 2006– (Chm., Remuneration Cttee, 2006–). Mem., NorthWest Business Leadership Team, 1997– (Chm., 2006–). *Recreations:* tennis, supporting Rugby Union. *Address:* Pilkington Group Ltd, Prescot Road, St Helens WA10 3TT. *T:* (01744) 28882, *Fax:* (01744) 20038.

CHAMBERS, Timothy Lachlan; JP; FRCP; Physician (general and renal medicine), Bristol Royal Hospital for Children (formerly Royal Hospital for Sick Children, Bristol) and paediatric departments, Southmead Hospital, Bristol, and Weston-super-Mare General Hospital, since 1979; *b* 11 Feb. 1946; *né* Seamus Rory Dorrington; *s* of late Mary Teresa Dorrington, Moate, Co. Westmeath, and adopted *s* of late Victor Lachlan Chambers and Elsie Ruth (*née* Reynolds); *m* 1971, (Elizabeth) Joanna Ward, DL, FRCP; one *s* one *d* (and one *d* decd). *Educ:* Wallington County Grammar Sch.; King's College London; King's Coll. Hosp. Med. Sch. (MB BS 1969). FRCP 1983; FRCPE 1985; FRCPI 1995; FRCPCH 1997. Jun. med. posts, London and SE England, 1969–73; Tutor in paed. and child health, Univ. of Leeds, 1973–76 (Sen. Registrar in medicine, St James's Hosp., Leeds, 1974–75); Physician and nephrologist, Derbyshire Children's Hosp. and other Derby and Nottingham Hosps, 1976–79; University of Bristol: Sen. Clinical Lectr in Child Health, 1979–; Clinical Dean, Southmead Hosp., 1983–90; Member: Governing Body, Inst. of Child Health, 1987–97 (Mem. Court, 1994–99); Hosps for Sick Children (London) SHA, 1993–94. Dep. Med. Dir, Southmead Health Services NHS Trust, 1994–96. Consultant in paediatrics: MoD, 1985–; RN, 1993–. Medicines and Healthcare Products Regulatory Agency (formerly Medicines Control Agency): Member: Cttee on Safety of Medicines, 1999–2005; Paediatric Medicines Working Gp, 2000–05; Adv. Bd on Registration of Homoeopathic Products, 2000– (Chm., 2003–); Adv. Cttee on Clinical Excellence Awards (Med. Vice Chm., SW subcttee, 2007–). UK Delegate, Paediatric Cttee, EMEA. Royal College of Physicians: Mem. Council, 1990–92; Censor, 1992–94. Regl (SW England) Advr, RCPE, 1996–2001; Mem., BMA 1979 (Chm., Paed. Sub-Cttee, Central Consultants and Specialists Cttee, 1989–94); Hon. Sec., Internat. Bd, RCPCH, 1998–2000 (Mem., 1976–97, Hon. Sec., 1984–89, BPA); FRSocMed 1977 (a Vice-Pres., 2001–03; Mem. Council, 1995–2003; Pres., Sect. of Paediatrics, 1994–95; Hon. Editor, 1997–2001; Pres., United Services Section, 2001–03); President: Union of Nat. Eur. Paed. Socs and Assocs, 1990–94; Bristol Medico-Chirurgical Soc., 1996–97; Bristol Div., BMA, 1999–2000; SW Paediatric Club, 2004–06; Bristol Medico-Legal Soc., 2007–May 2009. Sometime examnr to med. bodies and univs at home and abroad; chm.

and mem., prof. and govtl cttees and adv. bodies in UK and Europe. Sometime Member: Philosophical Soc., Oxford; British Assoc. for Paed. Nephrology; Corresp. Mem., Société Française de Pédiatrie, 1994. Mem., Editl Bd, Sri Lanka Jl of Child Health. Trustee: St John's Home, Bristol, 1985–93; Royal Med. Benevolent Fund, 1988–2004; Educn and Resources for Improving Childhood Continence, 2006–. Lt Col, RAMC(V), (commnd Captain, 1984); Clin. Dir 243 (The Wessex) Field Hosp., 2006–08; MO Somerset Cadet Bn The Rifles (formerly Light Infantry) (ACF), 2002–. Eucharistic Minister and Reader, RC Cathedral Church of SS Peter and Paul, Clifton, 1991–. Master, Bristol Br., Guild of Catholic Doctors, 2006–08. Freeman: City of London; Barbers' Co., 2004; Liveryman, Apothecaries' Soc., 1985– (Member: Court of Assts, 2000–; Examinations Cttee, 2002–; Chm., Academic and Resources Cttee, 2003–08). JP Bristol, 1993. Hon. FSLCPaed 2002. *Publications:* Fluid Therapy in Childhood, 1987; contribs to med. and lay jls and collective works. *Recreation:* ocean sunsets. *Address:* 4 Clyde Park, Bristol BS6 6RR. *T:* (0117) 974 2814. *Clubs:* Athenæum, Army and Navy, MCC (Associate Mem.); Clifton (Bristol); Galle Face Hotel (Colombo).

CHAMIER, Anthony Edward Deschamps; Under Secretary, Department of Education and Science, 1980–92; *b* 16 Aug. 1935; *s* of Brig. George Chamier, OBE and Marion (*née* Gascoigne); *m* 1962, Anne-Carole Tweeddale Dalling, *d* of William and Kathleen Dalling, Transvaal, S Africa; one *s* one *d*. *Educ:* Stowe, Buckingham; Trinity Hall, Cambridge; Yale Univ. (Henry Fellow). Military service, 1st Bn Seaforth Highlanders, 1953–55. HM Foreign (later Diplomatic) Service, 1960; Third Secretary, Foreign Office, 1960–62; Second Sec., Rome, 1962–64; Asst Political Adviser, HQ Middle East Comd, Aden, 1964–66; First Sec., FCO, 1966–71; Head of Chancery, Helsinki, 1971–72; seconded, later transf. to Dept of Educn and Science; Principal, 1972–73; Principal Private Sec. to Sec. of State for Educn and Science, 1973–74; Asst Sec., 1974–79; Prin. Estabt Officer, 1980–84. Director, Clan Munro Heritage Ltd, 1994–. *Recreations:* shooting, gardening, family history. *Address:* Achandunie House, Ardross, by Alness, Ross-shire IV17 0YB. *T:* and *Fax:* (01349) 883255.

CHAMIER, Michael Edward Deschamps, FCA; Director of Finance, European Parliament, 1983–2002; *b* 4 Feb. 1941; *s* of late Saunders Edward Chamier and Mary Frances (*née* Chapman); *m* 1977, Deborah Mary Unwin; one *s* two *d*. *Educ:* Ampleforth Coll., York. FCA 1975. Sen. Audit Mgr, Arthur Young, Paris, 1965–68; Dep. Dir, Finance and Admin, Reckitt & Coleman, France, 1968–72; Asst Financial Controller for Europe, Squibb Europe, 1972–77; Dep. Dir of Financial Admin, Europe, CABOT Europe, 1977–83. *Publication:* Property Purchasing in France, 1981. *Recreations:* travel, music. *Address:* 1 rue de Limpach, Reckange-sur-Mess, 4980 Luxembourg; *e-mail:* chamier@europe.com.

CHAMP, Andrea Helen; *see* Quinn, A. H.

CHAMPION, Prof. Justin Adrian Ivan, PhD; FRHistS; Professor of History of Early Modern Ideas, since 2003, Head, Department of History, since 2005, Royal Holloway, University of London; *b* 22 Dec. 1960; *s* of Ivan Champion and Ann (*née* Davies); partner, Sylvia Carter; one *d*. *Educ:* Churchill Coll., Cambridge (BA 1983; MA 1985; PhD 1989). FRHistS 1995. Lectr in Early Modern Hist., La Sainte Union, Southampton, 1990–92; Lectr, 1992–95, Sen. Lectr, 1995–99, Reader, 1999–2003, Royal Holloway, Univ. of London. John Hinkley Chair of British Hist., Johns Hopkins Univ., 2003. FRSA 2005. Presenter, television programmes: The Great Plague of London, 1999; Secrets of the Palace, 2002; Kings and Queens, 2003; also radio broadcasts. *Publications:* The Pillars of Priestcraft Shaken, 1992; (ed) Epidemic Disease in London, 1993; London's Dreaded Visitation, 1995; John Toland's Nazarenus, 1999; Republican Learning, 2003; contrib. learned jls. *Recreations:* squash, cricket, walking the line, fine cheese. *Address:* Department of History, Royal Holloway, University of London, Egham Hill, Egham TW20 0EX. *T:* (01784) 443749. *Club:* Royal Ascot Cricket.

CHAN, Cho-chak John, GBS 1999; CBE 1993 (OBE 1985); LVO 1986; JP; Director, Transport International Holdings Ltd (formerly Kowloon Motor Bus Holdings Ltd), since 1997 (Managing Director, Kowloon Motor Bus Co. (1933) Ltd, 1993); *b* 8 April 1943; *s* of late Kai Kit Chan and Yuk Ying Wong; *m* 1965, Wai-chun Agnes Wong; one *s* one *d*. *Educ:* St Rose of Lima's Sch.; Wah Yan Coll., Kowloon; La Salle Coll., Univ. of Hong Kong (BA (Hons), DMS). Commerce and Industry Dept, 1964; Economic Br., Govt Secretariat, 1970; Private Sec. to Gov., 1973; City Dist Comr (Hong Kong), 1975; Asst Dir of Home Affairs, 1976; Dep. Dir of Trade, 1977; Exec. Dir and Gen. Man., Sun Hung Kai Finance Co. Ltd, 1978; Principal Assistant Secretary: for Security, Govt Secretariat, 1980; for CS, 1982; Dep. Dir of Trade, 1983; Dep. Sec. (Gen. Duties), 1984; Dir of Inf. Services, 1986; Dep. Chief Sec., 1987; Sec. for Trade and Industry, 1989; Sec. for Educn and Manpower, 1991. Chm. Council, Hong Kong Univ. of Sci. and Technol., 2002–08. JP Hong Kong, 1984. Hon. Fellow, Univ. of Hong Kong, 2000. Hon. DBA Internat. Management Centres, 1997. *Recreations:* swimming, ten-pin bowling, music, reading. *Address:* Transport International Holdings Ltd, 9 Po Lun Street, Lai Chi Kok, Kowloon, Hong Kong. *T:* 27868833. *Clubs:* Hong Kong Jockey (Chm., 2006–); Hong Kong (Chm., 2007–08).

CHAN FANG, Anson Maria Elizabeth, (Mrs Anson Chan), GBM 1999; Hon. GCMG 2002; CBE 1992; JP; Member (Hong Kong Island), Legislative Council of Hong Kong, since 2007; *b* 17 Jan. 1940; *d* of Howard Fang and Fang Zhao Ling; *m* 1963, Archibald John Chan Tai-wing, MBE, QPM, CPM; one *s* one *d*. *Educ:* Univ. of Hong Kong (BA Hons). Admin. Officer, Hong Kong Govt, 1962–70; Asst Financial Sec., 1970–72; Asst Sec. for New Territories, 1972–75; Principal Asst Sec. for Social Services, 1975–79; Dep. Dir, 1979–84, Dir, 1984–87, Social Welfare; Sec. for Econ. Services, 1987–93; Sec. for CS, April–Nov. 1993; Chief Sec., 1993–97; Chief Sec. for Admin, Govt Secretariat, HKSAR, 1997–2001. JP Hong Kong, 1975. *Recreation:* music. *Address:* E2, 11th Floor, Villa Monte Rosa, 41A Stubbs Road, Hong Kong. *Clubs:* Zonta (Hong Kong East); Hong Kong, Hong Kong Jockey, Hong Kong Country (Hong Kong).

CHAN, Rt Hon. Sir Julius, GCMG 1994; KBE 1980 (CBE 1975); PC 1981; MP (People's Progress), Papua New Guinea, 1968–97 and since 2007; *b* 29 Aug. 1939; *s* of Chin Pak and Tingoris Chan; *m* 1966, Stella Ahmat. *Educ:* Marist Brothers Coll., Ashgrove, Qld; Univ. of Queensland, Australia (Agricl Science). Co-operative Officer, Papua New Guinea Admin, 1960–62; private business, coastal shipping and merchandise, 1963–70. Minister for Finance, 1972–77; Dep. Prime Minister and Minister for Primary Industry, 1977–78; Prime Minister, 1980–82; Minister for Finance and Planning, 1985–86; Dep. Prime Minister, 1985–88; Minister for Trade and Industry, 1986–88; Dep. Opposition Leader, 1988–92; Dep. Prime Minister and Minister for Finance and Planning, 1992–94; Prime Minister and Minister for Foreign Affairs, 1994–97; Parly Leader, People's Progress Party, 1970–97. Hon. Dr Technol., Univ. of Technol., PNG, 1983. *Recreations:* swimming, walking, boating. *Address:* Parliament House, Waigani, NCD, Papua New Guinea.

CHAN SEK KEONG, Hon.; Chief Justice, Supreme Court of Singapore, since 2006; *b* Ipoh, Perak, 5 Nov. 1937; *m* 1965, Elisabeth Albyn Eber; three *d*. *Educ:* Univ. of Malaya in Singapore (LLB Hons). Legal Asst, Bannon & Bailey, Malaya, 1962; Legal Asst, 1963–66, Partner, 1966–69, Braddell Bros, Singapore; Partner, Shook Lin & Bok, Singapore and Malaya, 1969–86; Judicial Comr of the Supreme Court, 1986–88; Judge of the Supreme Court, 1988–92; Attorney-Gen. of Singapore, 1992–2006; Sen. Counsel 1996. Pres., Legal Service Commn, 2006–. Chm., Presidential Council for Minority Rights, 2006–. Pres., Singapore Acad. of Law, 2006–. DSO, Darjah Utama Bakti Cemerlang (Singapore), 1999; Seri Paduka Mahkota Perak (Perak), 1999. *Recreation:* reading. *Address:* Supreme Court of Singapore, 1 Supreme Court Lane, Singapore 178879. *T:* 63323901, *Fax:* 63379450.

CHAN, Siu-Oi, Patrick; Hon. Mr Justice Chan; Permanent Judge, Court of Final Appeal, Hong Kong, since 2000; *b* 21 Oct. 1948; *s* of late Chan Chu-Yau and of Li Man-Yee; *m* 1990, Lisa Chiang Miu-Chu. *Educ:* Univ. of Hong Kong (LLB 1974; Postgrad. Cert. in Laws, 1975; Hon. Fellow 2003). Barrister in private practice, Hong Kong, 1977–87; Judge of District Court, 1987–91; Dep. Registrar of Supreme Court, 1991–92; Judge, 1992–97, Chief Judge, 1997–2000, High Court of Hong Kong. Hon. Bencher, Inner Temple, 2001. *Address:* Court of Final Appeal, 1 Battery Path, Central, Hong Kong. *T:* 21230033.

CHAN, Dr Stephen Ming Tak; HM Coroner, Inner North London, 1995–2002; *b* 16 Oct. 1948; *s* of late Kwok Kong Chan and Fun Ching Cheung; *m* 1972, Margaret Ann Small, *y d* of Francis Shadrack Small and Edith May Small. *Educ:* Bishop Hall Jubilee Sch., Hong Kong; RMN 1970; Kent Univ.; Charing Cross Hosp. Med. Sch., Univ. of London (MB, BS 1978; DMJ 1988); Cardiff Law Sch., Univ. of Wales (LLM 1992). Psychiatric nurse, St Augustine's Hosp., near Canterbury, 1967–70; jun. med. posts, Radcliffe Infirmary and John Radcliffe Hosp., Oxford and Charing Cross Hosp., 1979–80; postgrad. medical trng, Hammersmith Hosp., RPMS, Univ. of London, 1980–83; Principal in general practice, Epsom, 1983–86; Forensic Medical Examnr, 1984–90, Sen. Forensic Medical Examnr, 1990–94, Metropolitan Police; Forensic Medical Consultant in private practice, 1986–94; Asst Dep. Coroner, 1989–93, Dep. Coroner, 1993–94, Southern Dist, Gtr London; Asst Dep. Coroner, City of London, 1990–93. Member: Coroners' Soc. for England & Wales, 1989–2002; Council, Medico-Legal Soc., 1994–2002 (Hon. Treas., 1990–94); British Acad. Forensic Sci., 1988–2002; RSAA, 1992– (Trustee and Mem. Council, 2006–); RIIA, 1993– (Founder Mem. and Donor, Life Membership Legacy Fund, 2005–). Mem., Pugin Soc., 2002–. Patron, NACF, 2000–. *Publications:* Suicide Verdict: the coroner's dilemma, 1992; papers on medico-legal subjects. *Recreations:* Italian opera, Victorian antiques, Chinese history, song writing. *Address:* 6 Albion Place, Ramsgate, Kent CT11 8HQ. *Clubs:* Lansdowne, Royal Over-Seas League.

CHANCE, Sqdn Ldr Dudley Raymond, FRGS; a Recorder of the Crown Court, 1980–86; *b* 9 July 1916; *s* of Captain Arthur Chance, Sherwood Foresters, and Byzie Chance; *m* 1958, Jessie Maidstone, widow, *d* of John and Alice Dewing. *Educ:* Nottingham High Sch.; London Univ. (BA Oriental Religions and Philosophies, LLB 1969); BA Hons Internat. Politics and For. Policy, Open Univ., 1980. Called to Bar, Middle Temple, 1955; Dep. Circuit Judge, 1973–80. Commissioned in Royal Air Force, 1936; served Egypt, Transjordan, 1936–37; Bomber Comd (4 Gp), 1938; served in Bomber Comd Nos 97 and 77 Sqdns; took part in first raids on Norway; crashed off Trondheim; picked up later from sea by HMS Basilisk, later sunk at Dunkirk; Air Ministry, Whitehall, 1941–42, later in 2 Group, Norfolk, 21 Sqdn; also served in SEAC, Bengal/Burma. Sqdn Ldr, RAFO, until March 1961; gazetted to retain rank of Sqdn Ldr from that date. Member: panel of Chairmen of Medical Appeal Tribunals (DHSS), 1978–88; panel of Independent Inspectors for motorway and trunk road inquiries for DoE, 1978–83. Contested (C) Norwich North, 1959. FRGS 1979. *Recreations:* violin, painting. *Address:* Lamb Buildings, Temple, EC4Y 7AS; Fenners Chambers, 4 Madingley Road, Cambridge CB3 0EE. *Club:* Goldfish (RAF aircrew rescued from sea).

CHANCE, Sir (George) Jeremy (ffolliott), 4th Bt *cr* 1900, of Grand Avenue, Hove; retired; *b* 24 Feb. 1926; *s* of Sir Roger James Ferguson Chance, 3rd Bt, MC and Mary Georgina (*d* 1984), *d* of Col William Rowney; *S* father, 1987; *m* 1950, (cousin) Cecilia Mary Elizabeth, *d* of Sir William Hugh Stobart Chance, CBE; two *s* two *d*. *Educ:* Gordonstoun School; Christ Church, Oxford (MA). Sub-Lieut RNVR, 1944–47. Harry Ferguson Ltd, 1950–53; Massey-Ferguson, 1953–78; Director, Massey-Ferguson (UK) Ltd, 1973–78; farmer, 1978–87. *Recreations:* choral singing, painting. *Heir:* *s* (John) Sebastian Chance [*b* 2 Oct. 1954; *m* 1977, Victoria Mary, *d* of Denis McClean; two *s* one *d*]. *Address:* Ty'n-y-Berllan, Criccieth, Gwynedd LL52 0AH.

CHANCE, Michael Edward Ferguson; counter-tenor; *b* Penn, Bucks, 7 March 1955; *s* of John Wybergh Chance and Wendy Muriel (*née* Chance); *m* 1991, Irene, *d* of Hon. Francis Edward Noel-Baker, *qv*; one *s* one *d*. *Educ:* St George's Sch., Windsor; Eton Coll.; King's Coll., Cambridge (MA English 1977; Mem., King's Coll. Choir, 1974–77). Stockbroker, Mullens & Co., 1977–80. Founder Mem., The Light Blues, 1977–83; Mem., Monteverdi Choir, 1980–83; solo career, 1983–: operatic débuts: Buxton Fest., 1983; Kent Opera, Opéra de Lyon, Göttingen Handel Fest., 1985; Paris Opera, 1988; Glyndebourne Fest., 1989; ENO, Netherlands Opera, 1991; Covent Garden, Scottish Opera, 1992; Australian Opera, 1993; Buenos Aires, 1996; WNO, 1997; San Francisco Opera, 1998; Maggio Musicale, Florence, 1999; Leipzig Opera, 2000; Munich State Opera, 2003; rôles include: Oberon in A Midsummer Night's Dream; Apollo in Death in Venice; Julius Caesar; Andronico in Tamerlano; Bertarido in Rodelinda; Orfeo in Orfeo ed Euridice; Ottone in Agrippina; Ottone in L'incoronazione di Poppea; Military Governor in A Night at the Chinese Opera; Orpheus in The Second Mrs Kong; concert performances in Europe, USA and Japan. Visiting Professor: RCM, 1996–; Scuola di Musica di Fiesole, 1997. Numerous recordings of oratorio, opera and recitals. *Recreations:* racquet sports, hill-walking, olive cultivation. *Address:* c/o Ingpen & Williams, 7 St George's Court, 131 Putney Bridge Road, SW15 2PA. *T:* (020) 8874 3222, *Fax:* (020) 8877 3113. *Club:* Garrick.

CHANCE, Michael Spencer; Executive Counsel, Joint Disciplinary Scheme, 1993–97; *b* 14 May 1938; *s* of Florence and Ernest Horace Chance; *m* 1962, Enid Mabel Carter; three *d*. *Educ:* Rossall School. Solicitor. With Challinor & Roberts, Warley, 1962–70; Senior Asst Prosecuting Solicitor, Sussex Police Authy, 1970–72; Office of Director of Public Prosecutions, 1972–86: Asst Dir, 1981–86; Chief Crown Prosecutor, North London, 1986–87; Asst Head of Legal Services, Crown Prosecution Service, 1987; Dep. Dir, Serious Fraud Office, 1987–90; Consultant, Cameron Markby Hewitt, 1991–93. *Address:* Box Tree Cottage, Arkesden, Saffron Walden, Essex CB11 4EX.

CHANCELLOR, Alexander Surtees; columnist, The Guardian, since 1996; *b* 4 Jan. 1940; *s* of Sir Christopher Chancellor, CMG and Sylvia Mary, OBE, *e d* of Sir Richard Paget, 2nd Bt and Lady Muriel Finch-Hatton, *d* of 12th Earl of Winchilsea and Nottingham; *m* 1964, Susanna Elisabeth Debenham; two *d*. *Educ:* Eton College; Trinity Hall, Cambridge. Reuters News Agency, 1964–74; ITN, 1974–75; Editor: The Spectator, 1975–84; Time and Tide, 1984–86; Dep. Editor, Sunday Telegraph, 1986; US Editor, The Independent, 1986–88; Editor: The Independent Magazine, 1988–92; The New Yorker's Talk of the Town, 1992–93; columnist, The Times, 1992–93; Associate Ed., Sunday Telegraph, 1994–95; Founding Ed., Sunday Telegraph Mag., 1995; columnist, Daily Telegraph, 1998–2004. Comr, English Heritage, 1990–92. *Publication:* Some Times in America, 1999. *Address:* Stoke Park, Stoke Bruerne, Towcester, Northamptonshire NN12 7RZ. *T:* (01604) 862329. *Clubs:* Garrick, Beefsteak.

CHAND, Ravi Parkash, QPM 2002; Director, Group Human Resources, Home Office; *b* Bedford, 23 Dec. 1969; *s* of Mehar Chand and Charan Kaur; *m* 2002, Elizabeth Mary Rose White; two *s* one *d*. MCIPD 2008. With Police Service, 1989–2003, incl. Head of Equality, Bedfordshire Police, 1999; Man. Consultant, Veredus Exec. Resourcing, 2003–06; estabd small financial services co.; Hd, Gp Equality and Diversity, and Dir, Strategic Diversity Action Team, Home Office, 2006–07. Mem., Home Sec.'s Stephen Lawrence Steering Gp, 2000–03. Comr, Formal Investigation into Police Service in England and Wales under Race Relns Act, 2004–05. Pres., Nat. Black Police Assoc., 2001–03. Advr on equality issues, nationally and internationally. *Publication:* (jtly) The Police Service in England and Wales, 2005. *Recreations:* golf, travelling, DIY, entertaining my children. *Address:* Home Office, 2 Marsham Street, SW1P 4DF. *T:* (020) 7035 4455; *e-mail:* Ravi.chand2@homeoffice.gsi.gov.uk.

CHANDE, Jayantilal Keshavji, Hon. KBE 2003; Chairman, Kioo Ltd, since 1972; *b* 27 Aug. 1929; *s* of Keshavji Jethabhai and Kankuben Chande; *m* 1955, Jayalaxmi Madhvani; three *s*. Chairman: Air Tanzania Corp., 1977–89; Tanzania Harbours Authy, 1987–95; Tanzania Rlys Corp., 1995–; Barclays Bank Tanzania Ltd, 2000–; Alexander Forbes Tanzania Ltd, 2002–. Director: World Business Acad., 1996–2003; Internat. Inst. for Peace through Tourism, 2002–; Chm., Inst. for Envmtl Innovation, 2005–. Chm., Muhimbili Orthopaedic Inst., Dar es Salaam, 2004–. FAIM; Fellow, World Innovation Foundn, 2002. Chm., Rotary Foundn of UK, 2003–; Trustee: Rotary Foundn of Rotary Internat., 2003–; Muhimbili Nat. Hosp., Dar es Salaam, 2001–; Founder Trustee, Tanzania Soc. for Deaf, 1970–. Hon. Rep., Royal Commonwealth Soc.; Chm., Nat. Museums of Tanzania, 1963–84, 1989–92; Vice-Chm., Governing Body, Coll. of Business Educn, 1965–90 (Chm., Bd of Examiners, 1966–). *Publications:* Whither Directing Your Course, 1995, 4th edn 2006; A Knight in Africa: journey from Bukene, 2005. *Recreations:* reading, walking. *Address:* PO Box 9251, Dar es Salaam, Tanzania. *T:* (22) 2863196, *Fax:* (22) 2863822; *e-mail:* andychande@yahoo.com. *Clubs:* Commonwealth; Upanga Sports (Trustee), Dar es Salaam Gymkhana (Hon. Mem.) (Dar es Salaam); Cricket of India (Mumbai) (Hon. Mem.).

See also M. J. Chande.

CHANDE, Manish Jayantilal; Chief Executive and Co-Founder, Mountgrange Capital plc, since 2002; *b* 23 Feb. 1956; *s* of Jayantilal Keshavji Chande, *qv*; one *s* one *d*. *Educ:* City Univ. (Dip. Accountancy). Chief Exec. and Finance Dir, Imry Plc, 1985–97; Chief Exec., Trillium plc, then Land Securities Trillium, 1997–2002. Non-exec. Chm., Nat. Car Parks Ltd, 2003–05; non-exec. Dir, Mitie plc, 2003–06. Comr, English Heritage, 2004–. Trustee, Windsor Leadership Trust, 2005–. *Address:* Mountgrange Capital plc, 13 Albemarle Street, W1S 4HJ. *T:* (020) 7297 4960, *Fax:* (020) 7297 4969; *e-mail:* manish@mountgrange.net. *Club:* Lansdowne.

CHANDLER, Sir Colin (Michael), Kt 1988; FRAeS; Chairman, easyJet plc, since 2002; *b* 7 Oct. 1939; *s* of Henry John Chandler and Mary Martha (*née* Bowles); *m* 1964, Jennifer Mary Crawford; one *s* one *d*. *Educ:* St Joseph's Acad.; Hatfield Polytechnic. FCMA; FRAeS 1994. Commercial Apprentice, De Havilland Aircraft Co., 1956; Hawker Siddeley Aviation, later British Aerospace, Kingston: Commercial Manager, 1967–72; Exec. Dir, Commercial, 1973–78; Divl Man. Dir., 1978–82; Gp Marketing Dir, 1983–85; Hd of Defence Export Services, MoD, 1985–89; Vickers plc: Man. Dir, 1990–92; Chief Exec., 1992–98; Chm., 1997–2000; Chm., Vickers Defence Systems Ltd, 2000–02. Chairman: TI Automovie Ltd, 2003–07; Automotive Technik Ltd, 2004–08; Dep. Chm., Clarity Commerce Solutions, 2007–. Non-executive Director: Siemens Plessey Electronic Systems, 1990–95; TI Group, subseq. Smiths Group, 1992– (Dep. Chm., 1999–2004); Guardian Royal Exchange, 1995–99; Racal Electronics plc, 1999–2000 (Chm., 2000–); Thales plc, 2000–02. Vice Pres., EEF, 1991; Member: NDIC, 1992–2002; Cttee, DTI Priority Japan Campaign, 1992–2001. Pro-Chancellor, Cranfield Univ., 2001–07. Commander, Order of the Lion of Finland, 1982. *Recreations:* playing tennis, reading, gardening, listening to music. *Address:* c/o easyJet plc, Hangar 89, London Luton Airport, Luton, Beds LU2 9PF. *Clubs:* Reform, Mark's; Harbour.

CHANDLER, Sir Geoffrey, Kt 1983; CBE 1976; Chairman Emeritus, Business Group, Amnesty International UK (Founder Chairman, 1991–2001); *b* 15 Nov. 1922; *s* of Frederick George Chandler, MD, FRCP, and Marjorie Chandler; *m* 1955, Lucy Bertha Buxton; four *d*. *Educ:* Sherborne; Trinity Coll., Cambridge (MA History). Military Service, 1942–46: Captain 60th Rifles; Political Warfare Exec., Cairo; Special Ops Exec. (Force 133), Greece; Anglo-Greek Information Service, W Macedonia, 1945; Press Officer, Volos and Salonika, 1946. Cambridge Univ., 1947–49; Captain, Univ. Lawn Tennis, 1949. BBC Foreign News Service, 1949–51; Leader Writer and Features Editor, Financial Times, 1951–56; Commonwealth Fund Fellow, Columbia Univ., New York, 1953–54; Shell Internat. Petroleum Co.: Manager, Econs Div., 1957–61; Area Co-ordinator, W Africa, 1961–64; Chm. and Man. Dir, Shell Trinidad Ltd, 1964–69; Shell Internat. Petroleum Co.: Public Affairs Co-ordinator, 1969–78; Dir, 1971–78; Dir, Shell Petroleum Co., and Shell Petroleum NV, 1976–78; initiator, Shell's first Statement of Gen. Business Principles, 1976; Dir Gen., NEDO, and Mem., NEDC, 1978–83; Dir, Industry Year 1986, 1984–86; Leader, RSA Industry Matters team, 1987–89; Industry Advr, RSA, 1987–92. Pres., Inst. of Petroleum, 1972–74. Member: Council and Exec. Cttee, Overseas Develt Inst., 1969–78; British Overseas Trade Adv. Council, 1978–82; Council and Exec. Cttee, VSO, 1980–96; Chm., NCVO, 1989–96. Chm., BBC Consultative Group on Industrial and Business Affairs, and Mem. BBC Gen. Adv. Council, 1983–88; Chm., Consultative Council, Soc. of Educn Officers Schools Curriculum Award, 1984–96; Member: Wilton Park Academic Council, 1983–87; Council for Charitable Support, 1990–96; Council, SustainAbility Ltd, 2000–; Associate, Ashridge Management Coll., 1983–89; Pres., Assoc. for Management & Business Educn, 1986–90. Trustee: Charities Aid Foundn, 1990–96; The Environment Foundation, 2001–; UK Trustee, Council on Economic Priorities (Europe), 1997–99. FRSA. Hon. Mem., CGLI, 1988. Hon. Fellow: Sheffield City Polytechnic, 1981; Girton Coll., Cambridge, 1986; Hon. FInstPet 1982. Hon. DBA Internat. Management Centre from Buckingham, 1986; Hon. DSc: CNAA, 1986; Bradford, 1987; Aston, 1987; Hon. CGIA 1987. *Publications:* The Divided Land: an Anglo-Greek Tragedy, 1959, 2nd edn 1994; (jtly) The State of the Nation: Trinidad & Tobago in the later 1960s, 1969; Industry Year 1986: an attempt to change a culture, its allies and obstacles, 2003; contributed to: Britain's Economic Performance, 1994, 2nd edn 1998; Corporate Citizenship, 1998; Human Rights Standards and the Responsibility of Transnational Corporations, 1999; Human Rights and the Oil Industry, 2000; Business and Human Rights: dilemmas and solutions, 2003; Business Ethics and the 21st Century Organisation, 2006; articles on oil, energy, trans-national corporations, human rights and corporate responsibility; numerous speeches and articles, urging employee participation, coherent British indust. policy and the need for clearly articulated business principles. *Recreations:* working in woodland, gardening, music, observing butterflies. *Address:* Little Gaterounds, Parkgate Road, Newdigate, Dorking, Surrey RH5 5AJ. *T:* (01306) 631612. *Club:* Hawks (Cambridge).

CHANDLER, Very Rev. Michael John; Dean of Ely, since 2003; *b* 27 May 1945; *s* of late John Godfrey Chandler and Ena Doris (*née* Holdstock); *m* 1966, Janet Mary (*née* Raines); one *s* one *d. Educ:* Brasted Place Coll.; Lincoln Theol Coll.; KCL (PhD 1987); Dip. Theol. London Univ. (ext.) 1975; Dip. Theol. (STh) Lambeth (ext.) 1980. Ordained deacon, 1972, priest, 1973; Curate: St Dunstan's, Canterbury, 1972–75; St John the Baptist, Margate, 1975–78; Vicar of Newington, 1978–88 (with Bobbing and Iwade, 1978–80, with Hartlip and Stockbury, 1980–88); Rector, St Stephen's, Hackington, 1988–95; Canon Res., Canterbury Cathedral, 1995–2003. Rural Dean: Sittingbourne, 1984–88; Canterbury, 1994–95. *Publications:* The Life and Work of John Mason Neale, 1995; The Life and Work of Henry Parry Liddon, 2000; An Introduction to the Oxford Movement, 2003; contrib. Oxford DNB. *Recreations:* walking, birdwatching, reading, sailing. *Address:* The Deanery, Ely, Cambs CB7 4DN. *T:* (01353) 667735, *Fax:* (01353) 665658; *e-mail:* Dean@cathedral.ely.anglican.org. *Club:* Athenæum.

CHANDLER, Paul Geoffrey; Chief Executive, Traidcraft, since 2001; *b* 13 Oct. 1961; *s* of late Dr David Geoffrey Chandler and of Gillian Chandler; *m* 1993, Sarah Gillian Munro-Faure; three *d. Educ:* Wellington Coll., Berks; St John's Coll., Oxford (Stanhope Histl Essay Prize, 1983; BA Mod. Hist. 1983; MA 1987); Henley Mgt Coll. (MBA 1987). ACIB 1985. Joined Barclays Bank, 1983: Manager, Moorgate Br., 1986–87; on secondment to Church Urban Fund, 1987; Manager, Gp Strategic Planning, 1987–89; Asst Personal Sector Dir, London Western Reg., 1990–92; Gen. Sec., SPCK, 1992–2001 (Vice-Pres., 2001–). Tutor, St Chad's Coll., Durham Univ., 2005–. Member: Council, Overseas Bishoprics Fund, 1992–2001; Bd of Mission, C of E, 1994–2001; Exec. Cttee, Feed the Minds, 1996–2001; Trustee, C of E Pensions Bd, 1998–2001. Trustee, SPCK-USA, 1992–2001; Member: Cttee of Mgt, Assoc. for Promoting Christian Knowledge (Ireland), 1995–2001; Exec. Cttee, Indian SPCK, 1998–2001; Exec. Cttee, European Fair Trade Assoc., 2002– (Pres., 2007–); Gen. Council, S American Mission Soc., 2002–06; IPPR North, 2005–; NE Regl Council, CBI, 2008–; Durham Cathedral Council, 2008–. Churchwarden, St Stephen's, S Lambeth, 2000–01 (Mem. PCC, 1984–94, 1996–2001); Mem. PCC, St Nicholas, Durham, 2002–05, St John's, Neville's Cross, 2007–. Gov., St Martin-in-the-Fields High Sch. for Girls, 1992–2001 (Vice-Chm., 1993–2001); Lay Adv. Gov., Chorister Sch., Durham, 2005–. Trustee, All Saints Educnl Trust, 1992–2005. Dir, William Leech Foundn, 2001– (Mem., Professorial Fellowship Mgt Cttee, 2006–). Dir, Cafédirect Guardian Share Co., 2006– (Chm., 2007–). *Recreations:* time with my family, reading, history, walking on Yorkshire Moors, collecting works of John Buchan, keeping chickens. *Address:* The Hermitage, Sunderland Bridge Village, Durham DH6 5HD.

CHANDLER, Tony John; Hon. Research Fellow, University College London, since 1989; Visiting Professor, King's College, London, since 1989; *b* 7 Nov. 1928; *s* of Harold William and Florence Ellen Chandler; *m* 1954, Margaret Joyce Weston; one *s* one *d. Educ:* King's Coll., London. MSc. PhD, AKC, MA. Lectr, Birkbeck Coll., Univ. of London, 1952–56; University Coll. London: Lectr, 1956–65; Reader in Geography, 1965–69; Prof. of Geography, 1969–73; Prof. of Geography, Manchester Univ., 1973–77; Master of Birkbeck Coll., Univ. of London, 1977–79. Sec., Royal Meteorological Soc., 1969–73, Vice-Pres., 1973–75. Member: Council, NERC; Health and Safety Commn; Cttee of Experts on Major Hazards; Royal Soc. Study Gp on Pollution in the Atmosphere, 1974–77; Clean Air Council; Royal Commn on Environmental Pollution, 1973–77; Standing Commn on Energy and the Environment 1978. *Publications:* The Climate of London, 1965; Modern Meteorology and Climatology, 1972, 2nd edn 1981; contribs to: Geographical Jl, Geography, Weather, Meteorological Magazine, Bulletin of Amer. Meteorological Soc., etc. *Recreations:* horology, music, reading, travel. *Address:* 15 Durrell Close, Langney, Eastbourne, East Sussex BN23 7AN.

CHANDLER, Victor William; Chairman, Victor Chandler International Ltd, since 1996; *b* 18 April 1951; *s* of late Victor and Elizabeth Chandler; *m* 2004, Susan Kim; two *s. Educ:* Millfield Sch. Chm. and Man. Dir, Victor Chandler Ltd, 1974–96. *Recreation:* equestrian pursuits. *Address:* Victor Chandler International Ltd, Leanse Place, 50 Town Range, Gibraltar. *T:* 41313, *Fax:* 44066; *e-mail:* victor.chandler@vcint.com.

CHANDLER, Wendy; *see* Hall, W.

CHANDOS, 3rd Viscount *cr* 1954, of Aldershot; **Thomas Orlando Lyttelton;** Baron Lyttelton of Aldershot (Life Peer) 2000; Chairman, The Television Corporation, since 2004; *b* 12 Feb. 1953; *s* of 2nd Viscount Chandos and of Caroline Mary (who *m* 1985, Hon. David Hervey Erskine), *d* of Rt Hon. Sir Alan Lascelles, GCB, GCVO, CMG, MC; *S* father, 1980; *m* 1985, Arabella Sarah, *d* of Adrian Bailey and Lady Mary Russell; two *s* one *d. Educ:* Eton; Worcester College, Oxford (BA). Banker, 1974–93, Dir, 1985–93, Kleinwort Benson. Opposition spokesman on Treasury matters, 1995–97. Chief Exec., Northbridge Ventures Ltd; Chairman: Lopex plc, 1997–99; Capital & Regional plc, 2000–; Director: Botts Co. Ltd, 1993–97; Cine-UK Ltd, 1995–; Middlesex Hldgs; Global Natural Energy plc, 2000–. Director: ENO; Nat. Film and Television Sch.; Education 2000. *Heir: s* Hon. Oliver Antony Lyttelton, *b* 21 Feb. 1986. *Address:* 149 Gloucester Avenue, NW1 8LA. *T:* (020) 7722 8329.

CHANDRACHUD, Hon. Yeshwant Vishnu; Chief Justice of India, 1978–85; *b* Poona (Maharashtra), 12 July 1920; *s* of Vishnu Balkrishna Chandrachud and Indira; *m* Prabha; one *s* one *d. Educ:* Bombay Univ. (BA, LLB). Advocate of Bombay High Court, 1943, civil and criminal work; part-time Prof. of Law, Government Law Coll., Bombay, 1949–52; Asst Govt Pleader, 1952; Govt Pleader, 1958; Judge, Bombay High Court, 1961–72; one-man Pay Commn for Bombay Municipal Corporation officers, later Arbitrator in dispute between Electricity Supply and Transport Undertaking and its employees' union; one-man Commn to inquire into circumstances leading to death of Deen Dayal Upadhyaya; Judge, Supreme Court of India, 1972–78. President: Internat. Law Assoc. (India Branch), 1978; Indian Law Inst., 1978–85. *Address:* (official) 7–B Samata, General Bhosale Marg, Mumbai 400021, India. *T:* (22) 2042474.

CHANEY, Prof. Edward Paul de Gruyter, PhD; FSA, FRHistS; Professor of Fine and Decorative Arts, and Chair, History of Collecting Research Centre, Southampton Solent University (formerly Southampton Institute), since 1998; *b* 11 April 1951; *s* of Edward Robert Dell Chaney and Maaike Louise Chaney (*née* de Gruyter); *m* 1973, Lisa Maria Jacka (marr. diss. 2002); two *d. Educ:* Leighton Park Sch., Reading; Ealing Sch. of Art; Reading Univ. (BA Hist. of Art); Warburg Inst. (MPhil 1977; PhD 1982); Eur. Univ. Inst., Florence. Lectr, Univ. of Pisa, 1979–85; Adjunct Asst Prof., Georgetown Univ. in Florence, Villa Le Balze, 1982–83; Associate, Harvard Univ. Center for Italian Renaissance Studies, Villa I Tatti, Florence, 1984–85; Shuffrey Res. Fellow in Architectural Hist., Lincoln Coll., Oxford, 1985–90; Lectr in Hist. of Art (pt-time), Oxford Poly., 1990–91; Historian to London Div., English Heritage, 1991–93; Lectr in Hist. of Art (pt-time), Oxford Brookes Univ., 1993–; Sen. Lectr in Fine Arts Valuation, Southampton Inst., 1996. Res. Fellow, Huntington Liby, San Marino, Calif, 1994. FSA 1993; FRHistS 2006. Commendatore, Stella della Solidarietà (Italy), 2003. *Publications:* (ed with N. Ritchie) Oxford, China and Italy: writings in honour of Sir Harold Acton, 1984; The Grand Tour and the Great Rebellion: Richard Lassels and "The Voyage of Italy" in the Seventeenth Century, 1985; A Traveller's Companion to Florence, 1986, rev. edn 2002; (ed with P. Mack) England and the Continental Renaissance: essays in honour of J. B. Trapp, 1990; (ed with J. Bold) English Architecture Public and Private: essays for Kerry Downes, 1993; The Evolution of the Grand Tour: Anglo-Italian cultural relations since the Renaissance, 1998, rev. edn 2000; (with G. Worsdale) The Stuart Portrait: status and legacy, 2001; (with C. Clearkin) Richard Eurich (1903–1992): visionary artist, 2003; The Evolution of English Collecting: receptions of Italian art in the Tudor and Stuart periods, 2003; Inigo Jones's 'Roman Sketchbook', 2 vols, 2006; contribs to books, jls, newspapers, exhibition catalogues, etc. *Address:* Faculty of Media, Arts and Society, Southampton Solent University, East Park Terrace, Southampton SO14 0RF; *e-mail:* edward.chaney@solent.ac.uk.

CHANG-HIM, Rt Rev. French Kitchener; *see* Seychelles, Bishop of.

CHANNER, Jillian; Heritage Policy Adviser, English Partnerships, since 2007 (on secondment from Prince's Regeneration Trust); *b* 2 July 1949; *d* of Eric David Kerr, MC and Betty (*née* Knight); *m* 1998, Donal Gilbert O'Connell Channer. *Educ:* Univ. of York (BA Hons 1970, MA 1971). Dept of MSS and Early Printed Books, TCD, 1971–72; Photo-Archives, Courtauld Inst. of Art, Univ. of London, 1973–75; Sec., Corpus Vitrearum Medii Aevii, GB, 1975–84; English Heritage: Inspector, Ancient Monuments and Historic Buildings, 1984–88; Head of SW and W Midlands, Historic Buildings Div., 1988–91; Head of SW Team, 1991–98; Project Dir, 1998–2002; Dir, Prince of Wales's Regeneration Trust (formerly Phoenix Trust), 2002–. Mem., Stained Glass Adv. Cttee, Council for Care of Churches, 1984–91; Mem., Inst. of Historic Buildings Conservation, 1997–. Member: Council, British Soc. of Master Glass Painters, 1969–86 (Jt Ed., Jl, 1983–86); British Archaeol Assoc., 1972–85 (Mem. Council, 1981–85); Assoc. for Studies in Conservation of Historic Buildings, 1984– (Mem. Council, 1988–2002); Wells Cathedral Fabric Adv. Cttee, 2007–. FRSA 2002; FSA 2003. Hon. Sec. to Trustees, Ely Stained Glass Mus., 1978–84; Trustee: Ancient Monuments Soc., 2002–; Woodchester Mansion Trust, 2007–. Freeman, City of London, 1984; Liveryman, Co. of Glaziers, Painters and Stainers of Glass, 1984–. *Publications:* various contribs to specialist pubns on historic buildings conservation and stained glass. *Recreations:* fly-fishing, gardening, talking. *Address:* 110 Buckingham Palace Road, SW1W 9SA. *T:* (020) 7881 1621, 07825 403177, *Fax:* (020) 7881 1678; *e-mail:* jillchanner@englishpartnerships.co.uk.

CHANNING, Alastair; *see* Channing, R. A.

CHANNING, Jeffrey Paul; consultant, since 2006; Director, Thames Gateway, Department for Communities and Local Government (formerly Office of the Deputy Prime Minister), 2003–06; *b* 8 Aug. 1950; *s* of Leonard Herbert Channing and Joy Channing; *m* 1994, Kate Munson. *Educ:* Aylesbury Grammar Sch.; University Coll. London (BSc Geog.). Joined Civil Service as trainee, 1974; Hd of Central Policy, 1989–92, Hd of Urban Develt Corps, 1992–94, DoE; Cabinet Office, 1994–95; Hd of Construction Policy, DoE, 1995–98; Hd of Planning Policy, DETR, 1998–2003. Mem. of Bd, First Wessex Housing Gp Ltd, 2007–. *Recreations:* yoga, horse-riding, pottery. *Address: e-mail:* jning01-mail@yahoo.co.uk.

CHANNING, (Raymond) Alastair, FCILT; Managing Director, Associated British Ports, 1995–97; *b* 2 May 1943; *s* of late Geoffrey Channing, FRCS and Kathleen Channing; *m* 1976, Victoria Margaret Nish. *Educ:* Clifton Coll.; Clare Coll., Cambridge (MA; athletics Blue, 1965, and competed for Oxford and Cambridge against various American Univs, 1965). Various posts in Depts of Transport and Envmt, incl. Asst Private Sec. to successive Ministers of Transport; British Transport Docks Board, later Associated British Ports: Sec., 1979–84; Dir, 1984; Dep. Man. Dir, 1991–95; Dir, ABP Hldgs plc, 1992–97. FCILT (FCIT 1994 (Chm., 1996–98)). *Recreations:* listening to music, making furniture, the countryside, athletics (now vicarious). *Address:* The Old Manor House, Hampnett, Cheltenham, Glos GL54 3NW. *T:* (01451) 860795. *Club:* Reform.

CHANT, Ann; *see* Chant, E. A.

CHANT, Christopher Marc; Chief Information Officer, Department for Environment, Food and Rural Affairs, since 2005; *b* 3 July 1955; *s* of Frank and Olive Chant; *m* 1977, Beryl; one *s* one *d. Educ:* Dane Court Tech. High Sch. Inland Revenue: Ops and Investigation, 1976–99; E Service Delivery Dir, 1999–2002; Hd of Service Delivery, Cabinet Office, 2002–05. *Recreations:* ski-ing, photography, cooking. *Address:* Department for Environment, Food and Rural Affairs, Government Buildings, Epsom Road, Guildford, Surrey GU1 2LD. *T:* (01483) 404521, *Fax:* (01483) 404366; *e-mail:* chris.chant@defra.gsi.gov.uk.

CHANT, (Elizabeth) Ann, CB 1997; Deputy Director of Charities to TRH the Prince of Wales and the Duchess of Cornwall, since 2005; *b* 16 Aug. 1945; *d* of late Capt. Harry Charles Chant and Gertrude Chant (*née* Poel). *Educ:* Blackpool Collegiate Sch. for Girls. Nat. Assistance Bd, Lincoln, 1963–66; Min. of Social Security, Lincoln, 1966–70; NHS Whitley Council, DHSS London, 1970–72; DHSS, Lincoln, 1972–74; DHSS Regl Office, Nottingham, 1974–82; Manager, DHSS Sutton-in-Ashfield, 1982–83; DHSS HQ, London, 1983–85; Prin. Private Sec. to Permanent Sec., DHSS, 1985–87; Head: Records Br., DSS, Newcastle upon Tyne, 1987–89; Contribns Unit, 1990–91; Chief Executive: Contributions Agency, DSS, 1991–94; Child Support Agency, DSS, 1994–97; Man. Dir for Corporate Social Responsibility, BITC, 1997–99; Reviews of Public Trust Office and Legal Services Ombudsman's Office for Lord Chancellor's Dept, 1999; a Comr and Dep. Chm., Bd of Inland Revenue, 2000–04; acting Chm., Bd of Inland Revenue, 2004; Dir Gen., HM Revenue and Customs, 2005. Exec. Council Mem., Industrial Soc., 1993–2000. Trustee, Citizens Advice, 2005–07. Lay Gov., London South Bank (formerly S Bank) Univ., 2001–. FRSA 1991. *Recreations:* friends, music (especially opera), theatre. *Address:* Clarence House, SW1A 1BA. *Club:* Athenæum.

CHANTLER, Sir Cyril, Kt 1996; MD; FRCP; Chairman: Great Ormond Street Hospital for Sick Children NHS Trust, since 2000; King Edward VII Hospital Fund for London, since 2004 (Senior Associate, 2001–04); Children Nationwide Medical Research Fund Professor of Paediatric Nephrology, London University, 1990–2000, Emeritus Professor, since 2001; *b* 12 May 1939; *s* of Fred Chantler and Marjorie Chantler (*née* Clark); *m* 1963, Shireen Saleh; two *s* one *d. Educ:* Wrekin Coll.; St Catharine's Coll., Cambridge (BA 1960; MB BChir 1963; MD 1973); Guy's Hosp. Med. Sch. FKC 1998. MRC Travelling Fellow, Univ. of California, 1971; Guy's Hospital: Sen. Lectr and Consultant Paediatrician, 1972–80; Prof. of Paediatric Nephrology, 1980–2000; General Manager, 1985–88; Clinical Dean, Principal, 1989–92, 1992–98, UMDS, Guy's and St Thomas' Hosps; Vice Principal, KCL, and Dean, GKT Hosps' Med. and Dental Sch. of KCL, 1998–2000; Pro-Vice-Chancellor, London Univ., 1997–2000. Mem., NHS Policy Bd, 1989–95. Chairman: Sci. Adv. Cttee, Foundn for the Study of Infant Deaths, 1988–90; Standards Cttee, GMC, 1997–2002; Council of Heads of UK Med. Schs, 1998–99. Non-executive Director: Guy's and Lewisham NHS Trust, 1991–92; Guy's and St Thomas'

NHS Trust, 1993–97; Lambeth, Southwark, Lewisham HA, 1998–2000; Pres., British Assoc. of Medical Managers, 1991–97. Teale Lectr, 1987, Censor, 1989–90, Harveian Orator, 2002, RCP. Founder FMedSci 1998. Mem., Inst. of Medicine, Nat. Acad. of Scis, USA, 1999; Hon. Mem., Amer. Paed. Assoc., 1992. James Spence Medal, RCPCH, 2005. Co-Editor, Pediatric Nephrology Jl, 1986–96. Dr *hc* Lille, 1998; Hon. DSc London South Bank, 1999; Hon. DSc(Med) London Univ., 2005. *Recreations:* golf, opera, reading. *Address:* 6 Charlton Park House, Charlton Park, near Malmesbury, Wilts SN16 9DG; 22 Benbow House, 24 New Globe Walk, Bankside, SE1 9DS. *T:* (020) 7401 3246, *Fax:* (020) 7401 3250. *Club:* Athenæum.

CHANTRY, Dr George William, CEng, FIET; CPhys, FInstP; Director, European Operations, 1990–93, Senior Vice-President Europe, 1994–99, Carnahan & Associates; Consultant to Ministry of Defence on Strategic Defence Initiative Technology Transfer, 1990–98; *b* 13 April 1933; *s* of George William Chantry and Sophia Veronica (*née* Johnston); *m* 1956, Diana Margaret Rhodes (*née* Martin); two *s* one *d. Educ:* Christ Church, Oxford (DPhil 1959, MA 1960). CEng, FIET (FIEE 1976); FInstP 1974. Res. Associate, Cornell Univ., 1958; National Physical Lab., Dept of Industry: Sen. Res. Fellow, 1960; Sen. Scientific Officer, 1962; Principal Sci. Officer, 1967; Sen. Principal Sci. Officer, 1973; Dep. Chief Sci. Officer, DoI HQ, 1982, seconded to FCO; Counsellor (Sci. and Tech.), Bonn and Berne, 1982; Res. and Technol. Policy Div., DTI, 1985; seconded to MoD as Asst Dir for Industry in SDI Participation Office, 1985. Past Chm., European Molecular Liquids Gp; Mem., Science Educn and Technol. Bd, IEE, 1980–82. Editor, Proc. IEE, Science, Measurement and Technology (formerly Part A), 1981–2001 (Guest Editor, 2001–02). *Publications:* Submillimetre Spectroscopy, 1971; High-Frequency Dielectric Measurement, 1972; Submillimetre Waves and their Applications, 1978; Modern Aspects of Microwave Spectroscopy, 1980; Long-Wave Optics, 1983; papers in learned literature. *Recreations:* philately, bridge, gardening, music.

CHAPLIN, Edward Graham Mellish, CMG 2004; OBE 1988; HM Diplomatic Service; Ambassador to Italy, since 2006; *b* 21 Feb. 1951; *s* of late James and Joan Chaplin; *m* 1983, Nicola Helen Fisher; one *s* two *d. Educ:* Queens' Coll., Cambridge (BA 1st Cl. Hons Oriental Studies 1973). Entered FCO, 1973; Muscat, 1975–77; Brussels, 1977–78; Ecole Nat. d'Admin, Paris, 1978–79; on secondment to CSD as Private Sec. to Lord Pres. of the Council and Leader of H of L, 1979–81; FCO, 1981–84; Head of Chancery, Tehran, 1985–87; FCO, 1987–89; on secondment to Price Waterhouse Management Consultants, 1990–92; Dep. Perm. Rep., UKMIS Geneva, 1992–96; Hd, ME Dept, FCO, 1997–99; Ambassador to the Hashemite Kingdom of Jordan, 2000–02; Dir, Middle East and N Africa, FCO, 2002–04; Ambassador to Iraq, 2004–05; Vis. Fellow, Centre of Internat. Studies, Univ. of Cambridge, 2005–06. *Recreations:* music, tennis, hill/mountain walking. *Address:* c/o Foreign and Commonwealth Office, SW1A 2AH.

CHAPLIN, John Cyril, CBE 1988; FREng; FRAeS; Member, Civil Aviation Authority and Group Director, Safety Regulation (formerly Safety Services), 1983–88; *b* 13 Aug. 1926; *s* of late Ernest Stanley Chaplin and Isabel Chaplin; *m* 1st, 1949, Ruth Marianne Livingstone (*d* 2004); two *s* two *d*; 2nd, 2005, Margaret Bronwen Nelson (*née* Evans), *widow* of William Nelson. *Educ:* Keswick School. Miles Aircraft, 1946; Vickers-Supermarine, 1948; Handley Page, 1950; Somers-Kendall Aircraft, 1952; Heston Aircraft, 1956; Air Registration Board, 1958; Civil Aviation Authority, 1972, Dir-Gen. Airworthiness, 1979. FREng (FEng 1987). *Publications:* papers to RAeS. *Recreations:* sailing, photography, travel. *Club:* Cruising Association (Vice-Pres., 1995–98; Pres., 2003–04).

CHAPLIN, Laura Susan; *see* McGillivray, L. S.

CHAPLIN, Sir Malcolm (Hilbery), Kt 1991; CBE 1984; FRICS; Chairman, Hilbery Chaplin, chartered surveyors, Romford and Essex (formerly Senior Partner, Hilbery Chaplin & Hilbery Chaplin Porter, chartered surveyors, Romford and London, W1); *b* 17 Jan. 1934; *s* of Sir George Chaplin, CBE, FRICS and Lady Chaplin, (Doris Evelyn, *née* Lee); *m* 1959, Janet Gaydon; three *s. Educ:* Summerfields, Oxford; Rugby Sch.; Trinity Hall, Cambridge (MA Est. Man. 1961; Athletics Blue, 440 yds). Former Member: Barking, Havering and Brentwood DHA; Essex AHA. Treasurer: Billericay Cons. Assoc., 1970–73; Brentwood and Ongar Cons. Assoc., 1973–79 (Pres., 1988–92); Eastern Area Cons. Assocs, 1980–88 (Vice Pres., 1988–98); Mem., Nat. Union Exec. and Gen. Purposes Cttees, 1980–98; Chm., Cons. Bd of Finance, 1993 (Dep. Chm., 1988–93); Conservative Party: Mem. Bd of Mgt, 1993–98; Treasurer, 1993; Association Chm., 1994; Trustee, Cons. Agents Superannuation and Benevolent Funds, 1992–. Former Governor: Brentwood Sch.; St Martins Schs, Hutton. Trustee, Romford War Meml Old Folks Club and other trusts. Freeman, City of London. Liveryman: Innholders' Co. (Master, 1992–93); Chartered Surveyors' Co. *Recreations:* dairy farming (retired), golf, watching cricket and Rugby. *Address:* c/o 84 Market Place, Romford, Essex RM1 3JE. *Clubs:* Carlton, Bucks, Oxford and Cambridge, MCC; Hawks (Cambridge); Gentlemen of Essex CC.

CHAPMAN, family name of **Baron Northfield**.

CHAPMAN, Baroness *cr* 2004 (Life Peer), of Leeds in the County of West Yorkshire; **Nicola Jane Chapman;** Chair, Leeds Centre for Integrated Living, since 2004 (Member, since 1993); *b* 3 Aug. 1961; *d* of Peter Leslie Chapman and late Marlene Chapman. *Educ:* John Jamieson Sch. for Physically Disabled Children; Park Lane Coll. of Further Educn, Leeds; Trinity and All Saints Coll., Leeds. Volunteer Tutor, Apex Trust, 1985–86; Leeds City Council: Finance Clerk, 1986–89; IT Tutor, 1989–92; IT Tutor, E Leeds Women's Workshops, 1992–93. Member: Cttee, Habinteg Housing Assoc., 1993–; Leeds Utd Disabled Orgn, 1994–2004 (Chm., 1997–). *Recreations:* Leeds Utd FC, reading. *Address:* House of Lords, SW1A 0PW; *e-mail:* chapmann@parliament.uk.

CHAPMAN, Angela Mary, (Mrs I. M. Chapman); Headmistress, Central Newcastle High School (GDST), 1985–99; *b* 2 Jan. 1940; *d* of Frank Dyson and Mary Rowe; *m* 1959, Ian Michael Chapman; two *s. Educ:* Queen Victoria High Sch., Stockton; Univ. of Bristol (BA Hons French); Sorbonne (Dip. de Civilisation Française). Teacher of French, Bede Sch., Sunderland, 1970–80; Dep. Headmistress, Newcastle upon Tyne Church High Sch., 1980–84. *Recreations:* military history, walking, tennis. *Address:* 14 Alpine Way, Sunderland, Tyne and Wear SR3 1TN.

CHAPMAN, Prof. Antony John, PhD; CPsychol, FBPsS; AcSS; Vice-Chancellor and Principal, University of Wales Institute, Cardiff, since 1998; Professor, University of Wales, since 1998 (Senior Vice-Chancellor and Chief Executive, 2004–07); *b* 21 April 1947; *s* of Arthur Charles Chapman and Joan Muriel Chapman (*née* Brown); *m* 1985, Dr Siriol David; two *s* two *d. Educ:* Milford Haven Grammar Sch.; Bexley Grammar Sch.; Univ. of Leicester (BSc 1968; PhD 1972). FBPsS 1978; CPsychol 1988. University of Wales Institute of Science and Technology, Cardiff: Lectr, 1971–78; Sen. Lectr, 1978–83; University of Leeds: Prof. of Psychol., 1983–98 (on secondment, pt-time, to CVCP Acad. Audit Unit, 1990–94); Dir, Centre for Applied Psychol Studies, 1987–90; Dean of Sci., 1992–94; Pro-Vice-Chancellor, 1994–98; Vis. Prof., 1998–2003. Ed.-in-Chief, Current Psychol., 1985–89; Ed., British Jl Psychol., 1989–95; Senior Editor, book series: Psychol. for Professional Gps, 1981–88; Psychol. in Action, 1985–89; Internat. Liby of Critical Writings in Psychol., 1991–95; Mem. Bd, BPS Communications, 1979–; Founding Co-Dir, Sound Alert Ltd, 1994 (winner, Prince of Wales Award for Innovation, 1997); Member: Council, CBI Wales, 1999–2004, 2006–; Bd, Cardiff Business Technol. Centre, 2000–; Council, Cardiff Chamber of Commerce, 2004–07. Economic and Social Research Council: Vice-Chm., Trng Bd, 1995–96; Chairman: Res. Recognition Exercise, 1993–96; Policy Rev. Gp, 1994–96; Psychol Subject Panel, 1996–2001. Chairman: Assoc. of UK Heads of Psychol. Depts, 1990–92; UK Deans of Sci. Cttee, 1992–94; Mem., Cttee Eur. Assoc. Deans of Sci., 1993–94; a Vice-Pres., UUK, 2002–04 (Mem. Bd, 2002–); Chm., Higher Educn Wales Charitable Trust, 2002–04. Member: RAE Psychol. Panel, HEFCE, 1992, 1996; Northern Exams and Assessment Bd, 1994–98; Bd, QAA, 2000–06 (Chairman: Access Recognition and Licensing Cttee, 2003–06; Adv. Cttee for Wales, 2004–06); Council for Ind. and Higher Educn, 2002–; Bd, Univs and Colls Employers' Assoc., 2002–05; Bd, Leadership Foundn for Higher Educn, 2003–07; Council, All Party Parly Gp on Higher Educn, 2004–; Bd, Univs and Colls Admissions Service, 2007–; Adv. Bd, London Sch. of Commerce, 2007–. British Psychological Society: Chm., Bd of Examrs, Qualifying Exam, 1986–90; Pres., 1988–89; Chm., Jls Cttee, 1995–98; Hon. Fellow, 1999; President: Psychol. Section, BAAS, 1993–94; Assoc. of Learned Socs for the Social Scis, 1995–98. Vice-Pres., Cardiff Business Club, 2007–. Fellow, Inst. of Welsh Affairs, 2007–. AcSS 1999; FRSA 1997. Hon. DSc Leicester, 2008. *Publications:* jointly: Humour and Laughter: theory, research and applications, 1976, 2nd edn 1995; It's a Funny Thing, Humour, 1977; Friendship and Social Relationships in Children, 1980, 2nd edn 1995; Models of Man, 1980; Children's Humour, 1980; Road Safety: research and practice, 1981; Pedestrian Accidents, 1982; Psychology and People, 1983; Psychology and Social Problems, 1984; Elements of Applied Psychology, 1984; Psychology and Law, 1984; Noise and Society, 1984; Cognitive Processes in the Perception of Art, 1984; Cognitive Science, Vols I, II and III, 1995; Biographical Dictionary of Psychology, 1997; guest co-ed., collections of papers in various jls; contrib. articles to jls and chapters in books. *Recreations:* family, music, cricket, soccer. *Address:* University of Wales Institute, Cardiff, Llandaff Campus, Western Avenue, Cardiff CF5 2SG. *T:* (029) 2041 6101, *Fax:* (029) 2041 6910; *e-mail:* ajchapman@uwic.ac.uk.

CHAPMAN, Ben; *see* Chapman, J. K.

CHAPMAN, Charles Cyril Staplee; corporate development consultant; Member for Corporate Development and Finance, UK Atomic Energy Authority, 1988–90; *b* 9 Aug. 1936; *s* of Thomas John Chapman and Gertrude Gosden Chapman; *m* 1963, Lorraine Dorothy Wenborn; two *s. Educ:* St Peter's Sch., York; Univ. of Sheffield (BSc Hons). British Petroleum Co., 1958, Manager, Chemicals, Corporate Planning, Minerals, 1962–85; Senior Strategy Advisor, British Telecom, 1986–88. *Recreation:* growing rhododendrons.

CHAPMAN, Christine; Member (Lab) Cynon Valley, National Assembly for Wales, since 1999; *b* 7 April 1956; *d* of late John Price and Edith Jean Price; *m* 1981, Dr Michael Chapman; one *s* one *d. Educ:* Porth County Girls' Sch.; UCW, Aberystwyth (BA Hons); South Bank Poly. (Dip. Careers Guidance 1989); UWCC (MSc Econ 1992; MPhil 2001); Univ. of Wales Swansea (PGCE 1995). Mid Glamorgan County Council: Community Services Agency, 1979–80; Mid Glamorgan Careers, 1980–93; Educn Business Partnership (on secondment), 1993–94; teaching and consultancy posts, 1995–96; Co-ordinator, Torfaen Educn Business Partnership, 1996–99. Mem. (Lab) Rhondda Cynon Taff Council, 1995–99. Dep. Minister for Educn and Lifelong Learning and for Local Govt, Welsh Assembly Govt, 2005–07. *Recreations:* keeping fit, playing the piano, women's history. *Address:* National Assembly for Wales, Cardiff Bay, Cardiff CF99 1NA. *T:* (029) 2089 8364; (constituency office) Midland Bank Chambers, 28a Oxford Street, Mountain Ash, Rhondda Cynon Taff CF45 3EU. *T:* (01443) 478098.

CHAPMAN, Prof. Christopher Hugh; Scientific Consultant, Schlumberger Cambridge Research, since 2005 (Scientific Adviser, 1991–2005); *b* 5 May 1945; *s* of late John Harold Chapman and Margaret Joan Weeks; *m* 1974, Lillian Tarapaski; one *s* one *d. Educ:* Latymer Upper School; Christ's College, Cambridge (MA); Dept of Geodesy and Geophysics, Cambridge (PhD). Asst Prof., Univ. of Alberta, 1969–72, Associate Prof., 1973–74; Asst Prof., Univ. of California, Berkeley, 1972–73; University of Toronto: Associate Prof., 1974–80; Prof., 1980–84; Killam Research Fellow, 1981–83; Adjunct Prof., 1984–88; Prof. of Physics, 1988–90; Prof. of Geophysics, Dept of Earth Scis, and Fellow, Christ's Coll., Cambridge, 1984–88. Hon. Prof. of Theoretical Seismology, Univ. of Cambridge, 2005–. Green Scholar, Univ. of California, San Diego, 1978–79, 1986. *Publications:* Fundamentals of Seismic Wave Propagation, 2004; research papers in sci. jls. *Recreations:* sailing, photography, woodwork. *Address:* Schlumberger Cambridge Research, High Cross, Madingley Road, Cambridge CB3 0EL. *T:* (01223) 315576.

CHAPMAN, His Honour Cyril Donald; QC 1965; a Circuit Judge, 1972–86; *b* 17 Sept. 1920; *s* of Cyril Henry Chapman and Frances Elizabeth Chapman (*née* Braithwaite); *m* 1st, 1950, Audrey Margaret Fraser (*née* Gough) (marr. diss. 1959); one *s*; 2nd, 1960, Muriel Falconer Bristow; one *s. Educ:* Roundhay Sch., Leeds; Brasenose Coll., Oxford (MA). Served RNVR, 1939–45. Called to Bar, 1947; Harmsworth Scholar, 1947; North Eastern Circuit, 1947; Recorder of Huddersfield, 1965–69, of Bradford, 1969–71. Contested (C) East Leeds 1955, Goole 1964, Brighouse and Spenborough, 1966. *Address:* Hill Top, Collingham, Wetherby, W Yorks LS22 5BB. *T:* (01937) 572813.

CHAPMAN, Sir David (Robert Macgowan), 3rd Bt *cr* 1958, of Cleadon, Co. Durham; DL; Consultant, UBS Wealth Management (UK) (formerly Laing & Cruickshank Investment Management, later UBS Laing & Cruickshank) Ltd, since 2002; *b* 16 Dec. 1941; *s* of Sir Robert Macgowan Chapman, 2nd Bt, CBE, TD and Barbara May, *d* of Hubert Tonks; *S* father, 1987; *m* 1965, Maria Elizabeth de Gosztonyi-Zsolnay, *o d* of late Dr N. de Mattyasovsky-Zsolnay; one *s* one *d. Educ:* Marlborough; McGill Univ., Montreal (BCom). Wise Speke Ltd, then Wise Speke Div., Brewin Dolphin Securities Ltd, stock and share brokers, Newcastle upon Tyne: Partner, 1971–87; Dir, 1987–99; First Vice-Pres. and Sen. Relationship Manager for NE England, Merrill Lynch Internat. Bank, 1999–2002. Chairman: Team General Partner Ltd, 1994–; Northern Enterprise General Partner Ltd, 2000–; Director: Northern Rock plc, then Northern Rock Building Soc. (formerly North of England Building Soc.), 1974–2004 (Chm., Trustees, Northern Rock Pension Scheme, 2004–); Breathe North Appeal Ltd, 1988–2001; British Lung Foundation Ltd, 1989–95; Gordon Durham & Co. Ltd, 1994–98; High Gosforth Park Ltd, 1999–2004; NE Regl Investment Fund Ltd, 1999–; NES General Partner Ltd, 1999–; Zytronic plc, 2000–; Salle Farms Ltd, 2000–; Guestwick Farms Ltd, 2000–; NE Regl Investment Fund Two Ltd, 2001–, Three Ltd, 2002–; CNE General Partner Ltd, 2001–; Farmstar Polska Sp.zo.o Co., 2006–; NE Regl Investment Fund Partner Ltd, 2006–. Stock Exchange: Mem. Council, 1979–88; Chairman: Northern Unit, 1988–91; NE Reg. Adv Gp, 1991–98. MSI 1991 (NE Pres., 1993–). Mem. Council, CBI, 2001–03; Chm., 2001–03, Dep. Chm., 2003–05, NE Reg., CBI. Chm., Northumbria Coalition Against Crime, 1995–2000. Mem., Greenbury Cttee, 1995. Dir, Shrievalty Assoc. Ltd,

1999–2001. Trustee: Northern Rock Foundn, 2002–; Industrial Trust, 2004–. Governor: St Aidan's Coll., Durham, 1987–97; UC, Durham, 1998–2000 (Chm., Graduates' Soc., 2001–04); Mem. Council, Univ. of Durham, 1997–2003. Tyne and Wear: High Sheriff, 1993–94; DL 1997. *Heir: s* Michael Nicholas Chapman [*b* 21 May 1969; *m* 1998, Eszter, *y d* of Dr Attila Perlényi]. *Address:* The Hawthorns, Marsden Road, Cleadon, Sunderland, Tyne and Wear SR6 7RA; UBS Wealth Management (UK) Ltd, 2 St James' Gate, Newcastle upon Tyne NE4 7JH.

CHAPMAN, (Francis) Ian, CBE 1988; Chairman, Radiotrust PLC, 1997–2001; Chairman, 1991–96, Deputy Chairman, 1997–99, Guinness Publishers Ltd; Chairman, Scottish Radio Holdings (formerly Radio Clyde) PLC, 1972–96 (Hon. President, 1996–2001); *b* 26 Oct. 1925; *s* of late Rev. Peter Chapman and Frances Burdett; *m* 1953, Marjory Stewart Swinton; one *s* one *d. Educ:* Shawlands Academy, Glasgow; Ommer Sch. of Music, Glasgow. Served RAF, 1943–44; worked in coal mines as part of national service, 1945–47. Joined Wm Collins Sons & Co. Ltd, 1947 as management trainee; Sales Manager, 1955; Gp Sales Dir, 1960; Jt Man. Dir, 1968–76; Dep. Chm., William Collins Hldgs, 1976–81; Chm., William Collins Publishers Ltd, 1979–81; Chm. and Gp Chief Exec., William Collins Hldgs plc, 1981–89. Chairman: Harvill Press Ltd, 1976–89; Hatchards Ltd, 1976–89; Ancient House Bookshop (Ipswich) Ltd, 1976–89; Co-Chm. and Actg Chief Exec., Harper & Row, NY, 1987–89; Chm. and Man. Dir, Chapmans Publishers, 1989–94. Chm., The Listener Publications PLC, 1988–93; Dep. Chm., Orion Publishing Gp, 1993–94; Director: Independent Radio News, 1984–85; Pan Books Ltd, 1962–84 (Chm., 1974–76); Book Tokens Ltd, 1981–94; Stanley Botes Ltd, 1985–89; (non-exec.) Guinness PLC, 1986–91; (non-exec.) United Distillers PLC, 1987–91; Pres.-Dir Gen., Guinness Media SAS, Paris, 1996–99. Publishers' Association: Mem. Council, 1963–76, 1977–82; Vice Pres., 1978–79 and 1981–82; Pres., 1979–81; Trustee, 1993–97. Chm., Nat. Acad. of Writing, 2000–03; Member: Bd, Book Develt Council, 1967–73; Governing Council, Scottish Business in the Community, 1983–98; Dir, Scottish Opera, Theatre Royal Ltd, 1974–79; Trustee, Book Trade Benevolent Soc., 1982–2003. Chm. Council, Strathclyde Univ. Business School, 1985–88. FRSA 1985; CCMI (CBIM 1982). Hon. DLitt Strathclyde, 1990. Scottish Free Enterprise Award, 1985. *Publications:* various articles on publishing in trade jls. *Recreations:* music, golf, reading, grandchildren. *Address:* Kenmore, 46 The Avenue, Cheam, Surrey SM2 7QE. *T:* (020) 8642 1820, *Fax:* (020) 8642 7439; *e-mail:* fic@onetel.com. *Clubs:* Garrick, MCC; Royal Wimbledon Golf; Walton Heath Golf.

See also I. S. Chapman.

CHAPMAN, Frank Arthur; His Honour Judge Chapman; a Senior Circuit Judge, since 2003 (a Circuit Judge, since 1992); *b* 28 May 1946; *s* of Dennis Arthur Chapman and Joan Chapman; *m* 1968, Mary Kathleen Jones; one *s* one *d. Educ:* Newton-le-Willows Grammar School; University College London (LLB, LLM; Brigid Cotter Prize). Called to the Bar, Gray's Inn, 1968; practice at Birmingham. Resident Judge, Wolverhampton, 1997–2007; Hon. Recorder, Birmingham, 2007. Practising Anglican. *Recreations:* travel, mountaineering, antiques, theatre, good food, wine and company.

CHAPMAN, Frank Joseph, CEng, FIMechE; Chief Executive, BG Group plc, since 2000; *b* 17 June 1953; *s* of Frank William Chapman and Clara Minnie Chapman; *m* 1st, 1975, Evelyn Mary Hill (marr. diss. 1995); two *d*; 2nd, 1996, Kari Elin Theodorsen; one *s* one *d. Educ:* East Ham Tech. Coll. (OND (Dist.) 1971); Queen Mary Coll., London Univ. (BSc 1st Cl. Hons Mech. Engrg 1974). CEng 1999; FIMechE 1999. Engr, BP, 1974–78; various engrg and mgt appts, Shell, 1978–96; joined British Gas, 1996; Man. Dir, BG Exploration and Production, 1996–99; Dir, BG Gp (formerly BG) plc, 1997–; Pres., BG Internat., 1999–2000. FRSA 2000. CCMI (CIMgt 2001). *Recreations:* yachting, ski-ing, music. *Address:* BG Group plc, 100 Thames Valley Park Drive, Reading, Berks RG6 1PT. *T:* (0118) 929 2006.

CHAPMAN, Frederick John; Group Treasurer, LucasVarity, 1996–98; *b* 24 June 1939; *s* of late Reginald John Chapman and Elizabeth Chapman; *m* 1964, Paula Brenda Waller; one *s* two *d. Educ:* Sutton County Grammar Sch. Joined ECGD, 1958; Principal, 1969; Asst Sec., 1977; Under Sec., 1982; Principal Estabt and Finance Officer, 1985–88; Varity Corporation: Treas. (Europe), 1988–89; Treas. and Vice-Pres., 1990–96. *Recreations:* reading, music. *Address:* 14511 Grande Cay Circle, Apt 2806, Fort Myers, FL 33908, USA.

CHAPMAN, Sir George (Alan), Kt 1982; FCA; FCIS; Senior Partner, Chapman Upchurch, Chartered Accountants, 1958–2000; *b* 13 April 1927; *s* of late Thomas George Chapman and Winifred Jordan Chapman; *m* 1950, Jacqueline Sidney (*née* Irvine); two *s* five *d. Educ:* Trentham Sch.; Hutt Valley High Sch.; Victoria University. Fellow, Chartered Inst. of Secretaries, 1969 (Mem., 1948–); Fellow, Inst. of Chartered Accountants of NZ (formerly NZ Soc. of Accountants), 1969 (Mem., 1948–). Joined Chapman Ross & Co., subseq. Chapman Upchurch, 1948. Chairman: Norwich Union General Insurance (formerly Norwich Winterthur) (NZ), 1985–92 (Dir, 1982–92); BNZ Finance, 1979–88 (Dir, 1977–88); Mitel Telecommunications, 1984–91; Pilkington (formerly Pilkington Brothers) (NZ), 1989–94 (Dir, 1982–94); Director: Bank of New Zealand, 1968–86 (Dep. Chm., 1976–86); Maui Developments Ltd, 1979–85; Offshore Mining Co. Ltd, 1979–85; Liquigas Ltd, 1981–85 (Chm., 1982–84); NZ Bd, Norwich Union Life Insurance Soc., 1982–92; Skellerup Industries Ltd, 1982–90 (Dep. Chm., 1984–87); Skellerup Industries, Malaysia, 1986–90; State Insurance Ltd, 1990–99 (Vice Chm., 1992–99); Norwich Union Holdings (NZ) Ltd, 1990–99 (Vice Chm., 1992–99); Vice Chm., Norwich Union Life Insurance (NZ) Ltd, 1993–98. Chairman: NZ Building Industry Authority, 1992–2000; Housing New Zealand Ltd, 1992–95 (Chm. Housing Corp. of NZ and Housing NZ Estabt Bd, April–July 1992). NZ National Party: Member, 1948–; Vice-Pres., 1966–73; Pres., 1973–82. Councillor, Upper Hutt Bor. Council, 1952–53, Deputy Mayor, Upper Hutt, 1953–55; Member: Hutt Valley Drainage Bd, 1953–55; Heretaunga Bd of Governors, 1953–55; Pres., Upper Hutt Chamber of Commerce, 1956–57. FInstD 1979. *Publication:* The Years of Lightning, 1980. *Recreations:* golf, reading, tennis. *Address:* 53 Barton Avenue, Heretaunga, Wellington, New Zealand. *T:* (4) 5283512. *Clubs:* Wellington Golf, Wellington Racing.

CHAPMAN, Honor Mary Ruth, CBE 1997; FRICS; Executive Chairman, Future London, since 2004; *b* 29 July 1942; *d* of Alan Harry Woodland and Frances Evelyn (*née* Ball); *m* 1966, David Edwin Harold Chapman (marr. diss. 1997). *Educ:* Coll. of Estate Mgt, London Univ. (BSc Estate Mgt 1963); University Coll. London (MPhil Town Planning 1966). MRTPI 1971; FRICS 1979. Surveyor, Valuation Dept, LCC, 1963–64; with Nathaniel Lichfield & Partners (Econ. and Planning Consultants), 1966–76 (Partner, 1971–76); freelance Consultant, 1976–79; Sloan Fellow, London Business Sch., 1977; Chm., Research, then Internat. Partner, Jones Lang Wootton, 1979–2000; Consultant, Jones Lang LaSalle, 2000–03; Chief Exec. (on secondment half-time), London First Centre, 1993–95 (Dir, 1993–99). Dir, Legal and General plc, 1993–2001. Vice-Chm., 2000–03, Chm., 2003–04, London Develt Agency; Board Member: English Estates, 1984–92; Cardiff Bay Urban Develt Corp., 1987–94; a Crown Estate Comr, 1997–2004. Gov. and Mem., Exec. Cttee, Centre for Economic Policy Res., 1988–96. Chm., Burlington Gardens Client Cttee, Royal Academy, 2001–. FRSA 1992. *Recreations:* dairy farming, watching people do things well. *Address:* Future London, c/o Visit London, 2 More London Riverside, SE1 2RR. *Club:* University Women's.

CHAPMAN, Ian; *see* Chapman, F. I.

CHAPMAN, Ian Stewart; Managing Director and Chief Executive Officer, Simon and Schuster UK Ltd, since 2000; *b* 15 Jan. 1955; *s* of (Francis) Ian Chapman, *qv*; *m* 1978, Maria Samper; one *s* two *d. Educ:* Cranleigh Sch., Surrey; Univ. of Durham (BA (French and Spanish) 1980). Bookseller: Hatchards, Oxford St, 1973–74; WH Smith, Paris, 1974–75; trainee: Doubleday and Co. Inc., NY, 1980–81; Berkley Publishers, Putnam Gp, NY, 1981; editl asst, William Morrow Inc. NY, 1981–82; Ed., then Editl Dir, Hodder and Stoughton Ltd, 1983–88; Pan Macmillan: Publishing Dir, 1988–94; Man. Dir, 1994–2000. *Recreations:* cricket, golf, walking, ski-ing. *Address:* Benedict House, Staplecross Road, Northiam, E Sussex TN31 6JJ. *T:* (01580) 830222, *Fax:* (01580) 830027; Simon and Schuster UK Ltd, Africa House, 64–78 Kingsway, WC2B 6AH. *T:* (020) 7316 1910, *Fax:* (020) 7316 0331; *e-mail:* ian.chapman@simonandschuster.co.uk. *Clubs:* Garrick; Rye Golf.

CHAPMAN, James Keith, (Ben); MP (Lab) Wirral South, since Feb. 1997; *b* 8 July 1940; *s* of John Hartley and Elsie Vera Chapman; *m* 1st (marr. diss); three *d*; 2nd, 1999, Maureen Ann (*née* Byrne), pharmacist; one step *s. Educ:* Appleby Grammar Sch., Appleby in Westmorland. Pilot Officer, RAFVR, 1959–61. Min. of Pensions and Nat. Insce, 1958–62; Min. of Aviation/BAA, 1962–67; Rochdale Cttee of Inquiry into Shipping, 1967–70; BoT, 1970–74; First Sec. (Commercial), Dar es Salaam, 1974–78; First Sec. (Econ.), Accra, 1978–81; Asst Sec., DTI, 1981–87; Commercial Counsellor, Peking, 1987–90; Dep. Regl Dir, NW, and Dir, Merseyside, 1991–93, Regl Dir, Northwest, 1993–94, DTI; Dir, Trade and Industry, Govt Office for NW, 1994–95. Founder Consultant, Ben Chapman Associates, 1995–97. PPS to Minister of State, DETR, 1997–99, DTI, 1999–2001, DCMS, 2001–05. Member: Intelligence and Security Cttee, 2005–; Ecclesiastical Cttee, 2005–. All-Party Parliamentary Groups: Chairman: China, 1997–; Britain-Turkey, 1998–2001; Soap and Detergents Industry, 1999–2001; Cleaning and Hygiene Products Industry, 2001–; Vietnam, 2003–; Vice-Chair, Turkish Northern Cyprus, 2006–; Sec., Chile, 2005–. Mem., Commonwealth Parly Assoc. Exec. Cttee, 2005–. Fellow, Industry and Parlt Trust, 2006–. Dir, Wirral Chamber of Commerce, 1995–96; Chm., Adv. Bd, China Gateway-North West, 1996–97; Pres., Wirral Investment Network, 2007– (Hon. Vice-Pres., 1997–2007). Dep. Patron, BESO, 2003–05. Hon. Ambassador: for Cumbria, 1995–; for Merseyside, 1997–. Fellow, 48 Gp Club. *Recreations:* opera, music, walking. *Address:* House of Commons, SW1A 0AA.

CHAPMAN, Prof. John Newton, PhD; Professor of Physics, University of Glasgow, since 1988; *b* 21 Nov. 1947; *s* of John Avi Chapman and Nora Chapman; *m* 1972, Judith Margaret Brown; one *s* one *d. Educ:* St John's Coll., Cambridge (BA 1st Cl. Hons Natural Scis 1969); Fitzwilliam Coll., Cambridge (PhD 1973). Res. Fellow, Fitzwilliam Coll., Cambridge, 1971–74; Lectr, 1974–84, Reader, 1984–88, Univ. of Glasgow. Mem., EPSRC, 2003–08. *Recreations:* tennis, hill walking, photography, music. *Address:* Department of Physics and Astronomy, Kelvin Building, University of Glasgow, Glasgow G12 8QQ. *T:* (0141) 330 4462, *Fax:* (0141) 330 4464; *e-mail:* j.chapman@physics.gla.ac.uk.

CHAPMAN, Jonathan; *see* Chapman, S. J.

CHAPMAN, Keith; Co-Founder and Creative Director, Chapman Entertainment, since 2001; *b* 12 Dec. 1958; *s* of Roy Kenneth Chapman and Patricia Margaret Chapman (*née* Rose); *m* 1984, Kirsty Jane Asher; three *s. Educ:* St Nicholas Comp. Sch., Basildon; Great Yarmouth Art Coll. (Graphics Distn and Coll. Award). Art Dir, Garrat Baulcombe Advertising Agency, 1980–82; Creative Dir, McCarthy Oswin Advertising, 1982–85; Art Dir, Jim Henson Entertainment, 1985–88; Art Dir, Bastable Daley, 1988–95; freelance art dir/illustrator, 1995–2000. Children's television shows: Creator: Bob the Builder, 1999; Fifi and the Flowertots, 2005; Co-Creator, Roary the Racing Car, 2007. *Recreations:* writing, painting, football, golf. *Address:* Chapman Entertainment, 90 Point Pleasant, Wandsworth, SW18 1PP. *T:* 07885 765674, (office) 0870 403 0556, *Fax:* 0870 403 0557; *e-mail:* keith@chapmanentertainment.co.uk. *Clubs:* Coombe Hill Golf, Nairn Golf; Bank of England Veterans Football.

CHAPMAN, Leslie Charles; Founder and Chairman, Campaign to Stop Waste in Public Expenditure, since 1981; *b* 14 Sept. 1919; *e s* of Charles Richard Chapman and Lilian Elizabeth Chapman; *m* 1947, Beryl Edith England; (one *s* decd). *Educ:* Bishopshalt Sch. Served War, Army, 1939–45. Civil Service, 1939 and 1945–74; Regional Dir, Southern Region, MPBW and PSA, 1967–74. Chm. and mem., various cttees; Mem. (pt-time), LTE, 1979–80. *Publications:* Your Disobedient Servant, 1978, 2nd revised edn 1979; Waste Away, 1982. *Recreations:* reading, music, spoiling our granddaughter Siobhan. *Address:* Cae Caradog, Ffarmers, Llanwrda, Dyfed SA19 8NQ. *T:* (01558) 650504.

CHAPMAN, Mark Fenger, CVO 1979; HM Diplomatic Service, retired; Member, Police Complaints Authority, 1991–95; *b* 12 Sept. 1934; *er s* of late Geoffrey Walter Chapman and Esther Marie Fenger; *m* 1959, Patricia Mary Long; three *s* (and one *s* decd). *Educ:* Cranbrook Sch.; St Catharine's Coll., Cambridge. Entered HM Foreign Service, 1958; served in: Bangkok, 1959–63; FO, 1963–67; Head of Chancery, Maseru, 1967–71; Asst Head of Dept, FCO, 1971–74; Head of Chancery, Vienna, 1975–76; Dep. High Comr and Counsellor (Econ. and Comm.), Lusaka, 1976–79; Diplomatic Service Inspector, 1979–82; Counsellor, The Hague, 1982–86; Ambassador to Iceland, 1986–89. *Club:* Norfolk (Norwich).

CHAPMAN, Mary Madeline, (Mrs A. R. Pears); Chief Executive, Chartered Management Institute (formerly Director General, Institute of Management), 1998–2008; *b* 9 March 1949; *d* of Kenneth F. Chapman, MBE and Agnes G. B. Chapman (*née* Thompson); *m* 1st, 1976, Robert Henry Lomas (marr. diss. 1986); 2nd, 1990, Andrew Roger Pears; one *d. Educ:* Sutton High Sch.; Univ. of Bristol (BA Hons). Dip CIM 1975; CDir 2005. Mkting Exec., BTA, 1971–76; Mkting Manager, L'OREAL (Golden Ltd), 1976–82; General Manager: Nicholas Labs Ltd, 1982–86; Biotherm, 1986–88; Man. Dir, Helena Rubinstein, 1988–90; Dir, Personnel Ops, L'OREAL (UK), 1990–93; Chief Exec., Investors in People UK, 1993–98. Non-exec. Dir, Royal Mint, 2008–. Mem., Nat. Lottery Commn, 2008–. *Recreations:* walking, sailing, theatre, church and community projects.

CHAPMAN, Ven. Michael Robin; Archdeacon of Northampton, 1991–2004; *b* 29 Sept. 1939; *s* of Frankland and Kathleen Chapman; *m* 1973, Bernadette Taylor; one *s* one *d. Educ:* Lichfield Cathedral Sch.; Ellesmere Coll.; Leeds Univ. (BA 1961); Coll. of the Resurrection, Mirfield. Ordained, dio. of Durham, deacon, 1963, priest, 1964; curate, St Columba, Sunderland, 1963–68; Chaplain, RN, 1968–84; Vicar, St John the Evangelist, Farnham, 1984–91; Rural Dean of Farnham, 1988–91. *Recreations:* flying light aircraft, music, hill walking. *Address:* Dolphin House, High Street, Caenby, Market Basen, Lincs LN8 2HL. *T:* (01673) 876190.

CHAPMAN, Nicholas John; Managing Director, The Irish Times Ltd, 1999–2001; *b* 17 June 1947; *s* of Frank and Elizabeth Chapman; *m* 1995, Louise Shaxson; two *d. Educ:* Merchant Taylors' Sch.; Clare Coll., Cambridge (MA). With Hodder and Stoughton: Graduate Trainee, 1969; European Sales, 1970; Editor, 1973; Publishing Dir, Associated Business Press, 1975; Editor-in-Chief, Futura Paperbacks, 1979; Publishing Director: Macdonald Futura, 1980; Macmillan London, 1983; Head of BBC Books and Educn, 1986–89, Dir, Consumer Products Gp, 1989–94, BBC Enterprises; Man. Dir, BBC Worldwide Publishing, 1994–97; Director: BBC Worldwide Ltd, 1994–97; BBC Americas Inc., 1994–97; Mem., BBC Bd of Management, 1994–96; Man. Dir & Publisher, Orion Military, subseq. Cassell Mil. Publishing, Orion Publishing Gp, 1998–99. Pres., Publishers Assoc., 1994–96. Gov., Norwood Sch., 1998–99. *Recreations:* walking, natural history, reading. *Address:* Ferncroft House, Walton Elm, Marnhull, Dorset DT10 1QG.

CHAPMAN, Nigel Conrad, CMG 2008; Director, BBC World Service, since 2004 (Deputy Director, 2000–04); Chairman, Plan UK, since 2003; *b* 14 Dec. 1955; *s* of late Prof. Norman Bellamy Chapman; *m* 1984, Margaret Farrar; two *d. Educ:* Hymers Coll., Hull; Magdalene Coll., Cambridge (MA Hons English Lit.). Joined BBC, 1977: researcher and producer, BBC News and Current Affairs, incl. Nationwide, Newsnight and Breakfast News, 1979–89; Editor, Public Eye, 1989–92; Head: Regl and Local Progs, SE, 1992–94; Broadcasting, Midlands and East, 1994–96; Controller, English Regions, 1996–98; Dir, BBC Online, 1999–2000. *Recreations:* sport (football and cricket), music, walking, reading, charity work. *Address:* BBC World Service, Bush House, PO Box 76, WC2B 4PH.

CHAPMAN, Patricia Maud; journalist; *b* 3 May 1948; *d* of Arthur and Elizabeth Chapman; *m* 1970, David Clark; one *s. Educ:* Rochford Secondary Sch., Essex. Tea-girl, sub-ed. and columnist, Boyfriend mag., 1964–67; reporter, Romford Times and Havering Express, then sub-ed., Western Daily Press, Bristol, 1967–71; sub-ed., The Sun, 1971–79; sub-ed., Daily Mirror, 1979–82; Asst Night Ed., 1982–86, Dep. Ed., 1986–88, The Sun; Ed., News of the World, 1988–94. A Founder Mem., Press Complaints Commn, 1991–93 (Chm., Code of Practice Cttee, 1991). *Recreations:* painting, ephemera, cooking and eating! *Address:* c/o News International plc, 1 Virginia Street, E98 1EX.

CHAPMAN, Rev. Canon Rex Anthony; Residentiary Canon of Carlisle Cathedral, 1978–2004, now Canon Emeritus; Diocesan Director of Education, 1985–2004; Chaplain to the Queen, 1997–2008; *b* 2 Sept. 1938; *s* of Charles Arthur Chapman and Doris Chapman (*née* Eldred); *m* 1964, Margaret Anne (*née* Young); one *s* one *d. Educ:* Leeds Grammar Sch.; UCL (BA Classics 1962); St Edmund Hall, Oxford (BA Theol. 1964; MA 1968); Wells Theol Coll.; Univ. of Birmingham (DPS 1967). National Service, RAF, 1957–59. Ordained deacon, 1965, priest, 1966; Asst Curate, St Thomas', Stourbridge, 1965–68; Associate Chaplain, Univ. of Aberdeen, 1968–78; Hon. Canon, St Andrew's Cathedral, Aberdeen, 1976–78; Vice-Dean, Carlisle Cathedral, 1980, 1982, 1984, 1989, 1994, 1998, 2002; Bishop's Advr for Educn, dio. of Carlisle, 1978–85; Bishops' Selector for Ministry in C of E, 1985–2004 (Sen. Selector, 1997–2004); warrant, dio. of Aberdeen and Orkney, 2006–. Chm., Vacancy-in-See Cttee, dio. of Carlisle, 1997–2003; Mem., Crown Appts Commn for See of Carlisle, 1988, 2000. Member: Gen. Synod of C of E, 1985–2000 (Mem., Bd of Educn, 1985–96; Chm., Schs Cttee, 1990–96); Carlisle Diocesan Synod, 1978–2003; Chm., House of Clergy, dio. of Carlisle, 1996–2003. Member: Cumbria Educn Cttee, 1978–98; Cumbria Educn Forum, 1999–2004; Standing Adv. Council for Religious Educn, Cumbria, 1978–2003 (Chm., 1989–2003); Cumbria Learning and Recreation Scrutiny Panel, 2001–04; Standing Cttee, Nat. Soc. for Promoting Religious Educn, 1982–97; Chm. Orgn Cttee, Cumbria Schs, 2001–04 (Vice-Chm., 1999–2001). Governor: Trinity Sch., Carlisle, 1978–2003 (Chm., 1989–2003); Carlisle and Blackburn (formerly Carlisle) Dio. Trng Inst., 1979–2004 (Vice-Chm., 2001–04); St Martin's Coll. (formerly UC of St Martin), Lancaster, 1985–2004; St Chad's Coll., Durham, 1989–94. Trustee, Carlisle Educnl Charity, 1978–2004 (Chm. of Trustees, 1998–99). Chm., Carlisle and Eden Valley Marriage Guidance Council, 1984–87; Mem., Cumbria Cttee, Royal Jubilee and Prince's Trust, 1985–87. *Publications:* A Kind of Praying, 1970; Out of the Whirlwind, 1971; A Glimpse of God, 1973; The Cry of the Spirit, 1974; The Glory of God, 1978; contrib. to A Dictionary of Christian Spirituality, 1983. *Recreations:* travel, photography, hill-walking, chess problem solving, malt whisky. *Address:* Myreside, Finzean, Banchory, Aberdeenshire AB31 6NB. *T:* (01330) 850485. *Club:* Royal Over-Seas League.

CHAPMAN, Hon. Rhiannon Elizabeth, FCIPD; Managing Director, Plaudit, since 1994; *b* 21 Sept. 1946; *d* of 2nd Viscount St Davids and Doreen Guinness Jowett; *m* 1974, Donald Hudson Chapman (marr. diss. 1992); two step *s. Educ:* Tormead Sch., Guildford; King's Coll., London Univ. (LLB Hons 1967; AKC). FCIPD (FIPM 1972). Industrial Soc., 1968; LWT, 1968–70; Philips Electronics Industries, 1970–77; CPI Data Peripherals Ltd, 1977–80; Personnel Dir, London Stock Exchange, 1980–90; business consultant, 1990–91; Dir, Industrial Soc., 1991–93; Mem., WDA, 1994–98. Chairman: National Australia CIF Trustee Ltd, 1994–96; Fleming Managed Growth plc, 1999–2002; Visions Consulting, 2004–; non-executive Director: S. R. Gent plc, 1994–97; Bibby Financial Services, 2002–03. Dir, South West of England Urban Regeneration Fund, 2003–. Member: UFC, 1989–93; Employment Appeal Tribunal, 1991–; Council, PSI, 1993–98; Technical Mem., BUPA, 1997–. External Reviewer of Complaints, TTA, 1998–2004; Advr, People and Skills Agenda, SBAC, 2005–07. CCMI. *Recreations:* circuit training, handcrafts, opera, travel. *Address:* 3 Church Green, Great Wymondley, Hitchin, Herts SG4 7HA. *T:* (01438) 759102.

CHAPMAN, Roger Ralph, CBE 2007; Vice Chairman, James Fisher Defence Ltd, since 2003; *b* 29 July 1945; *s* of Ralph Aubrey Hector Chapman and Hilda Bisset Chapman; *m* 1971, Patricia June Nelson Sansom; two *s. Educ:* Chesterton Sch., Seaford; Bedford Sch.; BRNC, Dartmouth. Royal Navy Submarines, 1963–71: 2nd i/c conventional submarine (Long (N) Specialist); invalided out due to poor eyesight; submersible pilot and Survey Manager, Vickers Oceanics Ltd, 1971–76 (with co-pilot, rescued from submersible at 1575ft in Atlantic, 1973); Managing Director: Subsea Surveys Ltd, 1976–84 (pioneering robotics in North Sea and worldwide); James Fisher Rumic Ltd (specialising in submarine rescue services for RN, incl. rescue of 7 Russian sailors trapped in submarine in Russian Far East, 2005), 1984–2003. Fellow, Soc. for Underwater Technol., 1985. Pres., Barrow Br., RNLI, 1998–2003. Founder, with wife, Rumic Foundn Trust (helping young disadvantaged people in Cumbria), 2003. Gov., Chetwynde Sch., Barrow., 2005–. *Publication:* No Time on Our Side, 1975. *Recreations:* golf, sailing (Clipper Round World Race, 1998–99), rock-climbing, music, Italian food and red wine at lunchtime, laughing and having fun with my family, ski-ing. *Address:* Rumic Foundation Trust, 38½ The Gill, Ulverston, Cumbria LA12 7BP. *T:* (01229) 586426; *e-mail:* chapman_roger@hotmail.com. *Club:* Sloane.

CHAPMAN, Roy de Courcy; Headmaster of Malvern College, 1983–96; *b* 1 Oct. 1936; *s* of Edward Frederic Gilbert Chapman and Aline de Courcy Ireland; *m* 1959, Valerie Rosemary Small; two *s* one *d. Educ:* Dollar Academy; St Andrews Univ. (Harkness Schol.: MA 1959); Moray House Coll. of Educn, Edinburgh. Asst Master, Trinity Coll., Glenalmond, 1960–64; Marlborough College: Asst Master, 1964–68; Head of Mod. Langs, 1968–75; OC CCF, 1969–75; Rector of Glasgow Acad., 1975–82. Chairman: Common Entrance Bd, 1988–93; HMC, 1994. *Publications:* Le Français Contemporain, 1971; (with D. Whiting) Le Français Contemporain: Passages for translation and comprehension, 1975. *Recreations:* France, snorkelling, cruising. *Address:* 41 North Castle Street, St Andrews, Fife KY16 9BG.

CHAPMAN, Roy John, FCA; Chairman: Royal Mail (formerly Post Office, then Consignia) Pension Fund, 1995–2004; AEA Technology Pension Fund, 1996–2004; Director, Eurotunnel plc, 1995–2004; *b* 30 Nov. 1936; *s* of William George Chapman and Frances Harriet (*née* Yeomans); *m* 1961, Janet Gibbeson Taylor; two *s* one *d. Educ:* Kettering Grammar Sch.; St Catharine's Coll., Cambridge (Athletics Blue; MA). Joined Arthur Andersen & Co., Chartered Accountants, 1958; consulting, UK and abroad, incl. France, USA, Algeria, Greece, Turkey, Thailand and Switzerland, 1964–84; admitted to Partnership, 1970; Hd of Financial Services Practice, 1970–84; Man. Partner, London, 1984–89; Sen. Partner, 1989–93; Mem., Internat. Bd, 1988–93. Director: Halifax Bldg Soc., then Halifax plc, 1994–2001; Westminster Forum Ltd, 1989–99. Member: Adv. Council, London Enterprise Agency, 1985–88; Jt Disciplinary Scheme for Accounting Profession, 1994–. Mem. Governing Body, SOAS, London, 1990–2000. Council Mem., BITC, 1991–93. London Marathon, 1983 (Save the Children). St Catharine's College, Cambridge: Pres., St Catharine's Coll. Cambridge Soc., 1994–95; Chm., Develt Campaign, 1994–2000; Fellow Commoner, 2006–. Liveryman, Farriers' Co., 1992–. CCMI; FRSA. *Publications:* contribs to professional jls. *Recreations:* walking, reading, travel. *Address:* 9 Chislehurst Road, Bickley, Kent BR1 2NN. *T:* (020) 8467 3749. *Clubs:* Athenæum, Oxford and Cambridge, MCC; Hawks (Cambridge); Chislehurst Golf.

CHAPMAN, Prof. (Stephen) Jonathan, DPhil; Professor of Mathematics and its Applications, and Fellow of Mansfield College, University of Oxford, since 1999; *b* 31 Aug. 1968; *s* of Stephen Cyril Chapman and Pauline Mary Chapman; *m* 1996, Aarti Chand; one *s* one *d. Educ:* Merton Coll., Oxford (BA Maths 1989); St Catherine's Coll., Oxford (DPhil Applied Maths 1991). Research Fellow: Stanford Univ., Calif, 1992–93; St Catherine's Coll., Oxford, 1993–95; Royal Soc. Res. Fellow, Univ. of Oxford, 1995–99. Richard C. Diprima Prize, 1994, Julian Cole Prize, 2002, SIAM; Whitehead Prize, London Mathematical Society, 1998. *Publications:* papers in learned jls. *Recreations:* squash, golf, drinking with Paul. *Address:* Mathematical Institute, 24–29 St Giles, Oxford OX1 3LB. *T:* (01865) 270507.

CHAPMAN, Sir Sydney (Brookes), Kt 1995; RIBA; FRTPI; Chartered Architect and Chartered Town and Country Planner; private planning consultant (non-practising); freelance writer; *b* 17 Oct. 1935; *m* 1st, 1976, Claire Lesley McNab (*née* Davies) (marr. diss. 1987); two *s* one *d*; 2nd, 2005, Teresa Munoz Ernest. *Educ:* Rugby Sch.; Manchester University. DipArch 1958; ARIBA 1960; DipTP 1961; AMTPI 1962; FFB 1980. Nat. Chm., Young Conservatives, 1964–66 (has been Chm. and Vice-Chm. at every level of Movt); Sen. Elected Vice-Chm., NW Area of Nat. Union of C and U Assocs, 1966–70. Contested (C) Stalybridge and Hyde, 1964; MP (C): Birmingham, Handsworth, 1970–Feb. 1974; Chipping Barnet, 1979–2005; PPS to Sec. of State for Transport, 1979–81, to Sec. of State for Social Services, 1981–83; an Asst Govt Whip, 1988–90; a Lord Comr of HM Treasury (Govt Whip), 1990–92; Vice-Chamberlain of HM Household, 1992–95; PPS to Shadow Foreign and Commonwealth Sec., and Dep. Leader, Cons. Party, 2004–05. Member, Select Committee: on Environment, 1983–87; on Public Service, 1995–97; on Accommodation and Works, 1995–2001 (Chm., 1997–2001); on Public Admin, 2002–05; Member: House of Commons Services Cttee, 1983–87; Jt Cttee on Private Bill Procedure, 1987–88; Co-Chairman: Parly Road Transport Study Gp, 1997–2005; All Party Built Envmt Gp, 1997–2005. Chm., Parly Consultants Gp, British Consultants Bureau, 1980–88. Mem., Council of Europe and WEU Assembly, 1997–2005; Chm., Council of Europe Sustainable Develt Cttee, 2001–04. Lectr in Arch. and Planning at techn. coll., 1964–70; Dir (Information), British Property Fedn, 1976–79; Dir (non-exec.), Capital and Counties plc, 1980–88; consultant to YJ Lovell (Holdings) plc, 1982–88. Originator of nat. tree planting year, 1973; President: Arboricultural Assoc., 1983–89; London Green Belt Council, 1985–89; Chm., Queen's Silver Jubilee London Tree Group, 1977; Vice-Chm., Wildlife Link, 1985–89; Patron, Tree Council. RIBA: Vice-Pres., 1974–75; Chm., Public Affairs Bd, 1974–75; Mem. Council, 1972–77. President: Friends of Barnet Hosps, 1981–2006; Friends of Tamarisk Trust (formerly Peter Pan Homes), 1981–2005; Barnet Soc., 1990–2006. Hon. Life Pres., Chipping Barnet Cons. Assoc., 2005. Hon. Mem. BVA, 2006– (Hon. Assoc. Mem., 1983–2005); Hon. ALI; FRSA; Hon. FBEng (Hon. FIAAS 1987); Hon. FFB 1989 (Pres., 1999–2000); Hon. FSVA 1997; Hon. RICS 2000. *Publications:* Town and Countryside: future planning policies for Britain, 1978; regular contributor to bldg and property jls and to political booklets. *Recreation:* tree spotting. *Address:* 88 Lexham Gardens, Kensington, W8 5JB.

CHAPMAN, Gen. Sir Timothy John G.; *see* Granville-Chapman.

CHAPMAN, William Edward, CVO 2008; Director of Policy, Tony Blair Faith Foundation, since 2008; *b* 20 March 1952; *s* of late Philip Chapman and Pam Chapman. *Educ:* High Wych Primary Sch.; Bishop's Stortford Coll.; St Peter's Coll., Oxford (MA); Hertford Coll., Oxford (MLitt). Joined DoE (subseq. DETR), 1976; Information Directorate and speech writer for two Secs of State, 1988–91; Private Sec. for Home Affairs, then Parly Affairs, to the Prime Minister, 1991–94; Head: Planning Policies Div., 1994–98; Regeneration Div., 1998–99; Sec. for Appts to the Prime Minister and Ecclesiastical Sec. to the Lord Chancellor, 1999–2008; PM's Advr on Sen. Church and Lord-Lieut Appts, 2008. Mem., Adv. Council, McDonald Centre for Theology, Ethics and Public Life, 2008–. Trustee: Mitzvah Trust, 1998–2008; S Hackney Parochial Sch. Charity. *Recreations:* books, pictures, music, liming. *Address:* PO Box 60519, London, W2 7JU.

CHAPPATTE, Hon. Victoria Madeleine; *see* Sharp, Hon. V. M.

CHAPPELOW, Peter Raymond; company chairman; *b* 23 March 1947; *s* of Raymond and Stella Chappelow and step *s* of James Tillett; *m* 1990, Tina Margaret Jones; two *d. Educ:* Hanson Grammar Sch., Bradford. Mktg Dir, Grattan, 1969–89; CEO, The Marketing Co., 1989–91; Dir, Racing Green, 1991–96; Man. Dir, Country Holidays, 1992–94; Dir, Thomson Travel Gp, 1994–2001. Chairman: School-Safe, 2004–; Graphic-Inline, 2005–; Kingswood, 2006–; Travelsphere, 2006–; Hotter, 2007. Member: Bd, English Tourism Council, 1995–2003; Economy sub-cttee, Cabinet Office Honours Cttee, 2005–. *Recreations:* squash, tennis, golf, real music. *Address: e-mail:* chappelow@hotmail.com. *Clubs:* Lansdowne; Carnegie (Skibo); Key Royale (Florida); Otley Golf, Ilkley Lawn Tennis and Squash.

CHAPPLE, Field Marshal Sir John, GCB 1988 (KCB 1985); CBE 1980 (MBE 1969); DL; Vice Lord-Lieutenant of Greater London, 1997–2005; *b* 27 May 1931; *s* of C. H.

Chapple; *m* 1959, Annabel Hill; one *s* three *d*. *Educ:* Haileybury; Trinity Coll., Cambridge (MA). Joined 2nd KEO Goorkhas, 1954; served Malaya, Hong Kong, Borneo; Staff Coll., 1962; jssc 1969; Commanded 1st Bn 2nd Goorkhas, 1970–72; Directing Staff, Staff Coll., 1972–73; Services Fellow, Fitzwilliam Coll., Cambridge, 1973; Commanded 48 Gurkha Infantry Bde, 1976; Gurkha Field Force, 1977; Principal Staff Officer to Chief of Defence Staff, 1978–79; Comdr, British Forces Hong Kong, and Maj.-Gen., Brigade of Gurkhas, 1980–82; Dir of Military Operations, 1982–84; Dep. Chief of Defence Staff (Progs and Personnel), 1985–87; C-in-C, UKLF, 1987–88; CGS, 1988–92; Gov. and C-in-C, Gibraltar, 1993–95. ADC Gen. to the Queen, 1987–92. Col, 2nd Goorkhas, 1986–94. Hon. Col, Oxford Univ. OTC, 1988–95. Chm., UK Trust for Nature Conservation in Nepal, 1993–; Trustee, King Mahendra Trust, Nepal, 1993–2006. Mem. Council, WWF UK, 1984–99 (Trustee, 1988–93; Amb., 1999– (Chm. of Ambs, 2003–)). Vice Patron: Army Mus. Ogilby Trust, 1995–; Gurkha Mus., 2003– (Trustee, 1973–2003); Nat. Army Mus., 2003– (Trustee, 1981–2003); President: Indian Mil. Hist. Soc., 1991–; Mil. Hist. Soc., 1992–; Soc. for Army Histl Res., 1993–; Trekforce, 1998–2006; Sir Oswald Stoll Foundn, 1998–; BSES Expeditions, 1999–; Bilimoria Foundn, 2005–. Pres., Combined Services Polo Assoc., 1991–2006. FZS (Pres., 1992–94), FLS, FRGS, FSA, FRSA. DL Greater London, 1996. KStJ. *Club:* Beefsteak.

CHAPPLE, Keith, FIET; Chairman, Alliance for Electronic Business, 2001–02; *b* 11 Aug. 1935; *s* of Reginald Chapple and Gladys Evelyn (*née* Foster); *m* 1962, Patricia Margaret Aitchison; one *s* two *d*. *Educ:* City of Bath Boys' Sch.; Rugby Coll. of Technol. FIET (FIEE 1984). Engrg Manager, Gen. Precision Systems Ltd, 1961–66; Sales Engr, SGS-Fairchild Ltd, 1966–69; Mktg Manager, SGS-Fairchild SpA (Italy), 1969–70; Sales Manager, Intel Corp. (Belgium), 1970–72; Chm. and Man. Dir, Intel Corp. (UK) Ltd, 1972–2000. President: Fedn of Electronics Industry, 1996–97 (Vice-Pres., 1997–99); Swindon Chamber of Commerce, 1996–98; Chm., EU Cttee, American Chamber of Commerce in Belgium, 1998–2001. Mem., Oxford Isis Br., Rotary Club. MCMI (MIMgt 1976); FRSA 1999. Hon. DTech Loughborough, 1986. *Recreations:* music, family. *Club:* Clarendon (Oxford) (Pres., 2003–04).

CHAPPLE, Air Vice-Marshal Robert, CB 1994; Principal Medical Officer, Royal Air Force Support Command, 1991–94, retired; *b* 2 May 1934; *s* of Kevin Chapple and Florence Elsie (*née* Cann); *m* 1960, Barbara Ann (*née* Webster); one *s* one *d*. *Educ:* Finchley Catholic Grammar Sch.; St Mary's Hosp. Med. Sch. (MB, BS 1958). MRCS, LRCP 1958; DPH 1973; MFPHM 1978; MFOM 1980. Joined RAF Med. Br., 1960; served in UK, Singapore, Gibraltar, Germany and Cyprus; Officer Commanding: Princess Mary Hosp., Cyprus, 1982–85; Princess Mary's RAF Hosp., Halton, 1987–89; Princess Alexandra Hosp., Wroughton, 1989–91; Commandant, RAF Central Med. Estabt, 1991. QHP, 1992–94. MCMI (MBIM 1974). *Recreations:* golf, watching most sports, archaeology, visiting old churches, matters of general interest. *Address:* Hazel House, Withington, Cheltenham, Glos GL54 4DA.

CHAPPLE, Roger Graham; His Honour Judge Chapple; a Circuit Judge, since 2004, a Senior Circuit Judge, since 2007; Resident Judge, Inner London Crown Court, since 2007; *b* 28 Aug. 1951; *s* of Robert William Chapple and Elsie Mary Chapple (*née* Hubbard). *Educ:* Univ. of Leeds (LLB Hons). Called to the Bar, Gray's Inn, 1974; in practice as a barrister, specialising in common law, 1974–94; Dep. JA, 1994–95; an Asst JAG, 1995–2004; Asst Recorder, 1999–2000, Recorder, 2000–04; Resident Judge, Middlesex Guildhall Crown Court, 2005–07; Sen. Judge, Sovereign Base Areas, Cyprus, 2007–. *Recreations:* travel, music (particularly opera), combining the two. *Address:* Crown Court at Inner London, Sessions House, Newington Causeway, SE1 6AZ.

CHAREST, Hon. Jean; Member (PC, then Quebec L) for Sherbrooke, National Assembly of Quebec, since 1984; Premier of Quebec, since 2003; *b* 24 June 1958; *s* of Claude Charest and Rita Charest (*née* Leonard); *m* 1980, Michèle Dionne; one *s* two *d*. *Educ:* Univ. of Sherbrooke (LLB 1980). Called to the Bar, Quebec, 1981; Lawyer: Legal Aid Office, 1980–81; Beauchemin, Dussault, 1981–84. National Assembly of Quebec: Asst Dep. Speaker, 1984–86; Minister of State for Youth, 1986–90; Dep. Govt Leader; Minister: for Fitness and Amateur Sport, 1988–90; of Envmt, 1991–93; Dep. Prime Minister, 1993; Minister: for Industry, Sci. and Technol., 1993; responsible for Federal Business Develt Bank, 1993; Leader: Progressive Conservative Party, 1993–98; Quebec Liberal Party, 1998; Leader of Official Opposition, 1998–2003. Member: Quebec Bar Assoc.; Canadian Bar Assoc. *Address:* Office of the Premier, Edifice Honoré-Mercier, 3e étage, 835 boulevard René-Lévesque Est, Québec, QC G1A 1B4, Canada. *T:* (418) 6435321, *Fax:* (418) 6461854; *e-mail:* commentairespm@mce.gouv.qc.ca.

CHARING CROSS, Archdeacon of; *see* Jacob, Ven. W. M.

CHARKIN, Richard Denis Paul; Executive Director, Bloomsbury Publishing plc, since 2007; *b* 17 June 1949; *s* of Frank Charkin and Mabel Doreen Charkin (*née* Rosen); *m* 1972, Susan Mary Poole; one *s* two *d*. *Educ:* Haileybury and ISC; Trinity College, Cambridge (MA); Harvard Bus. Sch. (AMP). Science Editor, Harrap & Co., 1972; Sen. Publishing Manager, Pergamon Press, 1973; Oxford University Press: Medical Editor, 1974; Head of Science and Medicine, 1976; Head of Reference, 1980; Managing Dir, Academic and General, 1984; Octopus Publishing Group (Reed International Books), 1988; Chief Exec., Reed Consumer Books, 1989–94; Exec. Dir, 1988–96 and Chief Exec., 1994–96, Reed Internat. Books; CEO, Current Science Gp, 1996–97; Chief Exec., Macmillan Ltd, 1998–2007. Mem., Bd of Mgt, John Wisden & Son, 1995–; non-executive Director: Scoot.com plc, 2000–02; Xrefer Ltd, 2000–04 (Chm., 2003–04); Melbourne University Publishing, 2006–; Chm., Macmillan India Ltd, 2004–07. Vice-Pres., 2004–05, 2006–07, Pres., 2005–06, Publishers Assoc. Vis. Fellow, Green College, Oxford, 1987; Vis. Prof., Univ. of the Arts, London (formerly London Inst.), 2003–. Chm. Trustees, Whitechapel Art Gall., 1997–2000; Chm., Common Purpose UK, 1998–2007; Mem. Strategy Adv. Cttee, BL, 2004–. *Recreations:* music, cricket. *Address:* *e-mail:* richard.charkin@bloomsbury.com.

CHARLEMONT, 15th Viscount *cr* 1665 (Ire.); **John Dodd Caulfeild;** Baron Caulfeild of Charlemont 1620 (Ire.); *b* 15 May 1966; *o s* of 14th Viscount Charlemont and Judith Ann (*née* Dodd); *S* father, 2001; *m* 1991, Nadea Stella, *d* of Wilson Fortin; two *s*. *Heir:* *s* Hon. Shane Andrew Caulfeild, *b* 19 May 1996. *Address:* 3749 Densbury Drive, Mississauga, ON L5N 6Z2, Canada.

CHARLES, Rt Rev. Adrian Owen, AM 1994; RFD 1983; ED 1976; Bishop of Western Region (Assistant Bishop of Diocese of Brisbane), 1984–92; Bishop to Australian Defence Force, 1989–94; *b* 31 July 1926; *s* of Robert Charles and Alice (*née* Donovan); *m* 1955, Leonie Olive (*née* Robinson); one *s* one *d*. *Educ:* Slade Sch., Warwick, Qld; St Francis Coll., Univ. of Qld; Anglican Central Coll., Canterbury (ThL, Diploma in Divinity). Ordained priest, 1952; Royal Australian Army Chaplains Dept, 1955–83; Rector: Christ Church, St Lucia, Brisbane, 1958–66; St Paul's, Ipswich, 1966–71; Dir, Religious Studies, Christ Church Grammar Sch., Perth, 1971–72; Dean, St James' Cathedral, Townsville, 1972–77; Rector, St David's, Chelmer, Brisbane, 1977–83; Sen. Chaplain, 1st Mil. Dist, 1981–83; Archdeacon and Chaplain to Archbishop of Brisbane, 1981–83; Bishop of Southern Region, 1983–84. Mem., Brisbane Cricket Ground Trust. *Recreations:* reading, cricket, golf, theatre. *Address:* 16 Sandalwood Street, Sinnamon Park, Qld 4073, Australia. *Club:* Brisbane Golf.

CHARLES, Hon. Sir (Arthur) William (Hessin), Kt 1998; **Hon. Mr Justice Charles;** a Judge of the High Court of Justice, Family Division, since 1998; *b* 25 March 1948; *s* of late Arthur Attwood Sinclair Charles and May Davies Charles (*née* Westerman); *m* 1974, Lydia Margaret Ainscow; one *s* one *d*. *Educ:* Malvern College; Christ's College, Cambridge (MA Hons). Called to the Bar, Lincoln's Inn, 1971; Junior Counsel to the Crown (Chancery), 1986; First Junior Counsel to HM Treasury on Chancery Matters, 1989–98. *Recreations:* golf, tennis. *Address:* Royal Courts of Justice, Strand, WC2A 2LL. *Clubs:* Hawks (Cambridge); Denham Golf.

CHARLES, His Honour (Bernard) Leopold; QC 1980; a Circuit Judge, 1990–2002; a Senior Circuit Judge, 1998–2002; a Deputy Circuit Judge, 2002–04; *b* 16 May 1929; *s* of Chaskiel Charles and Mary Harris; *m* 1st, 1958, Margaret Daphne Abel (marr. diss. 1993); one *s* two *d*; 2nd, 1994, Judith Lynda Orus. *Educ:* King's Coll., Taunton. Called to the Bar, Gray's Inn, 1955. Practised in London and on South Eastern Circuit, 1956–90; a Recorder, 1985–90. Legal Assessor to GMC and GDC, 1985–90. *Recreations:* music, politics. *Address:* Lamb Building, Temple, EC4Y 7AS. *T:* (020) 7797 8300.

CHARLES, Caroline, (Mrs Malcolm Valentine), OBE 2002; fashion designer; Founder, Caroline Charles, 1963; *b* 18 May 1942; *m* 1966, Malcolm Valentine; one *s* one *d*. *Educ:* Sacred Heart Convent, Woldingham; Swindon Art Sch. *Recreations:* gardening, tennis, theatre, travel. *Address:* 56/57 Beauchamp Place, SW3 1NY. *T:* (020) 7225 3197.

CHARLES, Hampton; *see* Martin, R. P.

CHARLES, James Anthony, ScD; FREng; Reader in Process Metallurgy, University of Cambridge, 1978–90, now Emeritus; Fellow, St John's College, Cambridge, since 1963; *b* 23 Aug. 1926; *s* of John and Winifred Charles; *m* 1st, 1951, Valerie E. King (*d* 2001); two *s*; 2nd, 2003, Dr Marcia Edwards. *Educ:* Imperial College of Science and Technology, Royal School of Mines (BScEng, ARSM); MA, ScD Cantab. J. Stone & Co. Ltd, 1947–50; British Oxygen Ltd, 1950–60; Dept of Metallurgy and Materials Science, Univ. of Cambridge, 1960–90. Vis. Prof., UCL (Inst. of Archaeology), 1991–; Special Prof., Univ. of Nottingham, 1993–99. Hon. Keeper of Metalwork, Fitzwilliam Museum, 1996– (Syndic., 1986–96). FREng (FEng 1983); Hon. FIMMM 2002. Sir George Beilby Medal and Prize, RIC, Soc. Chem. Ind. and Inst. of Metals, 1965; Sir Robert Hadfield Medal, Metals Soc., 1977; Kroll Medal, Inst. of Metals, 1989; Elegant Work Prize, Inst. of Materials, 1992. *Publications:* Oxygen in Iron and Steel Making, 1956; Selection and Use of Engineering Materials, 1984, 3rd edn 1997; Out of the Fiery Furnace: recollections and meditations of a metallurgist, 2000; Light Blue Materials, 2005; One Man's Cambridge, 2006; numerous papers on the science and technology of metals and archaeometallurgy. *Recreations:* philately, listening to music, archaeology. *Address:* 2A Buristead, Great Shelford, Cambridge CB22 5EJ. *T:* (01223) 843812.

See also R. A. Charles.

CHARLES, Jonathan James; District Judge (Magistrates' Courts), South Wales, since 2003; *b* 4 Sept. 1946; *s* of William Robert Charles and Elizabeth Charles; *m* 1970, Linda Ann Llewellyn; two *s* one *d*. *Educ:* Bridgend Boys' Grammar Sch.; Bristol Poly. Admitted Solicitor, 1980; Justices' Clerk: Merthyr Tydfil, 1981–85; Lower Rhymney Valley, 1985–88; Bridgend, 1988–97; Consultant Solicitor, Keith Evans & Co., Newport, 1997–2001; District Judge (Magistrates' Courts), Wolverhampton, 2001–03. Sec., Lord Chancellor's Adv. Cttee for Mid-Glamorgan, 1995–97. *Recreations:* travel, Rugby football, cricket. *Address:* Magistrates' Court, Fitzalan Place, Cardiff CF24 0RZ. *T:* (029) 2046 3040.

CHARLES, Leopold; *see* Charles, His Honour B. L.

CHARLES, Michael Geoffrey A.; *see* Audley-Charles.

CHARLES, Nicola; *see* Perry, J. A.

CHARLES, Air Vice-Marshal Richard Anthony, CB 2005; Director of Legal Services (Royal Air Force), since 2002; *b* 24 Feb. 1954; *s* of James Anthony Charles, *qv*; *m* 1979, Anne Moreland; two *s*. *Educ:* Perse Sch., Cambridge; Nottingham Univ. (LLB); Coll. of Law. Admitted solicitor, 1978; commnd Legal Branch, RAF, 1978; Legal Services: RAF Germany, 1979–83; MoD, 1983–85; RAF Hong Kong, 1985–87; MoD, 1987–89; Dep. Dir, Legal Services, RAF Germany, 1989–92; Legal Services: MoD, 1993–94; PTC, 1994–97; Dep. Dir, Legal Services, 1997–2002; Dir of Legal Services, RAF Prosecuting Authy, 2002–07. Adjudicator, Traffic Penalty Tribunal, 2001–. FRAeS 2008. *Recreations:* watching Rugby Union, walking the Cotswold Way, the Avro Lancaster. *Club:* Royal Air Force.

CHARLES, Sir Robert (James), KNZM 1999; CBE 1992 (OBE 1972); golf professional, since 1960; *b* 14 March 1936; *s* of Albert Ivor Charles and Phyllis Irene Charles; *m* 1962, Verity Joan Aldridge; one *s* one *d*. *Educ:* Wairarapa Coll. Nat. Bank of NZ, 1954–60. Golf tournament victories include: NZ Open, 1954 (amateur), 1966, 1970, 1973; NZ PGA, 1961, 1979, 1980; Swiss Open, 1962, 1974; British Open, 1963; Atlanta Classic, USA, 1967; Canadian Open, 1968; Piccadilly World Match Play, England, 1969; John Player Classic and Dunlop Masters, England, 1972; S African Open, 1973; joined Senior Tour, 1986: 75 victories incl. Sen. British Open, 1989 and 1993. *Publications:* Left Handed Golf, 1965; The Bob Charles Left Handers Golf Book, 1985, 2nd edn 1993; Golf for Seniors, 1994. *Recreations:* farming, golf course architecture, tennis, boating. *Address:* Lytham, Burnt Hill Road, Oxford 8253, New Zealand. *Club:* Christchurch Golf (New Zealand).

CHARLES, Hon. Sir William; *see* Charles, Hon. Sir A. W. H.

CHARLES-EDWARDS, Prof. Thomas Mowbray, DPhil; FBA 2001; Jesus Professor of Celtic, and Fellow of Jesus College, University of Oxford, since 1997; *b* 11 Nov. 1943; *s* of Thomas Charles-Edwards and Imelda Charles-Edwards (*née* Bailey); *m* 1975, Davina Gifford Lewis (pen name Gifford Lewis); two *s*. *Educ:* Ampleforth Coll.; Corpus Christi Coll., Oxford (BA, MA, DPhil, Dip. Celtic Studies). Scholar, Dublin Inst. for Advanced Studies, 1967–69; P. S. Allen Jun. Res. Fellow in History, 1969–71, Fellow and Tutor in Modern Hist., 1971–96, Corpus Christi Coll., Oxford. *Publications:* Bechbretha (with Fergus Kelly), 1983; The Welsh Laws, 1989; Early Irish and Welsh Kinship, 1993; Early Christian Ireland, 2000. *Recreations:* sailing, dog-walking. *Address:* 32 Harbord Road, Oxford OX2 8LJ. *T:* (01865) 552839; Jesus College, Oxford OX1 3DW. *T:* (01865) 279739; *e-mail:* thomas.charles-edwards@jesus.ox.ac.uk.

CHARLESWORTH, Anita Rose; Director, Department for Culture, Media and Sport, since 2006; *b* 17 Jan. 1967; *d* of Terry and Jean Bird; *m* 1998, Nick Charlesworth; three *d*. *Educ:* PCL (BA Hons Social Sci.); Univ. of York (MSc Health Econs). Economist: DoH, 1990–95; HM Treasury, 1995–96; Associate Dir, SmithKline Beecham, 1996–98; Team

Leader, Welfare to Work and various public services, 1998–2003, Dir, Public Services, 2003–06, HM Treasury. Non-exec. Dir, Islington PCT. Trustee, Tommy's. *Recreations:* spending time with my husband and children, camping, scuba diving, running, swimming. *T:* (020) 7211 6459; *e-mail:* anita.charlesworth@culture.gov.uk.

CHARLESWORTH, Prof. Brian, PhD; FRS 1991; FRSE; Professor, Institute of Evolutionary Biology (formerly Institute of Cell, Animal and Population Biology), University of Edinburgh, since 2007 (Royal Society Research Professor, 1997–2007); *b* 29 April 1945; *s* of Francis Gustave Charlesworth and Mary (*née* Ryan); *m* 1967, Deborah Maltby (*see* D. Charlesworth); one *d. Educ:* Queens' Coll., Cambridge (BA Natural Scis; PhD Genetics). FRSE 2000. Post-Doctoral Fellow, Univ. of Chicago, 1969–71; Lectr in Genetics, Univ. of Liverpool, 1971–74; Lectr, 1974–82, Reader, 1982–84, in Biology, Univ. of Sussex; Prof., 1985–92, Chm., 1986–91, G. W. Beadle Distinguished Service Prof., 1992–97, Dept of Ecology and Evolution, Univ. of Chicago. President: Soc. for Study of Evolution, 1999; Genetics Soc., 2006–March 2009. Fellow, Amer. Acad. of Arts and Scis, 1996. Darwin Medal, Royal Soc., 2000. *Publications:* Evolution in Age-Structured Populations, 1980, 2nd edn 1994; (with Deborah Charlesworth) Evolution: a very short introduction, 2003; papers in Nature, Science, Genetics, Genetical Res., Evolution, Amer. Naturalist, Procs Roy. Soc. *Recreations:* reading, listening to classical music, walking. *Address:* Institute of Evolutionary Biology, University of Edinburgh, West Mains Road, Edinburgh EH9 3JT.

CHARLESWORTH, Prof. Deborah, PhD; FRS 2005; FRSE; Professorial Research Fellow, Institute of Evolutionary Biology (formerly Institute of Cell, Animal and Population Biology), University of Edinburgh, since 1997; *née* Maltby; *m* 1967, Brian Charlesworth, *qv*; one *d. Educ:* Newnham Coll., Cambridge (BA 1965; PhD 1968). FRSE 2001. MRC Jun. Res. Fellow, Univ. of Cambridge, 1968–69; Postdoctoral Fellow, Univ. of Chicago, 1969–71; Hon. Res. Fellow, Univ. of Liverpool, 1971–74; temp. Lectr, Univ. of Sussex, 1974–84; Res. Associate, 1984–88, Asst Prof., 1988–92, Prof., 1992–97, Univ. of Chicago. *Publications:* (with Jonathan Silvertown) Introduction to Plant Population Biology, 2001; (with Brian Charlesworth) Evolution: a very short introduction, 2003. *Address:* Institute of Evolutionary Biology, University of Edinburgh, West Mains Road, Edinburgh EH9 3JT.

CHARLESWORTH, His Honour Peter James; a Circuit Judge, 1989–2004; *b* 24 Aug. 1944; *s* of late Joseph William Charlesworth and Florence Mary Charlesworth; *m* 1967, Elizabeth Mary Postill; one *s* one *d. Educ:* Hull Grammar Sch.; Leeds Univ. (LLB 1965, LLM 1966). Called to the Bar, Inner Temple, 1966. In practice on North-Eastern Circuit, 1966–89; a Recorder, 1982–89. Judicial Mem., Parole Bd, 2005–. Rugby Football League: Mem., Adv. Panel, 1994–2004; Sen. Mem., Judiciary Panel, 2004–07; Chairman: Disciplinary Cttee, 1998–; Operational Rules Tribunal, 2007–. Member: Council, Bodington Hall, Univ. of Leeds, 2001–; Council of Mgt, Yorkshire Dales Soc., 2005–. Trustee, Yorks Dales Millennium Trust, 2003– (Chm., 2006–). *Recreations:* tennis, reading, Rugby League football (spectating), walking in the Yorkshire dales. *Address:* Daleswood, Creskeld Gardens, Bramhope, Leeds LS16 9EN. *Club:* Leeds Adel Tennis.

CHARLIER, Rear Adm. Simon Boyce; Chief of Staff (Aviation and Carriers) to Commander-in-Chief Fleet, and Rear Admiral, Fleet Air Arm, since 2008; Aide-de-Camp to the Queen, since 2006; *b* Pembury, Kent, 15 March 1958; *s* of Wing Cdr Dennis Claude Charlier, MC and Mary P. Charlier; *m* 1990, Margaret Anna Johns; two *s* one *d. Educ:* Dover Coll. Royal Navy, 1978–: CO HMS Sheraton, 1990–91; Sen. Pilot, 815 Sqdn, 1992–95; CO HMS Northumberland, 1996–98; MoD DN Plans, then MoD NATO and EU Policy Directorate, 1998–2002; CO HMS Cornwall, 2002–04. Pres., RN Equestrian Soc., 2008–. *Recreations:* eventing, golf, mountain biking, ski-ing, clarinet. *Address:* Sydling St Nicholas, Dorset. *Club:* Naval.

CHARLTON, Alan, CMG 1996; CVO 2007; HM Diplomatic Service; Ambassador to Brazil, since 2008; *b* 21 June 1952; *s* of Henry and Eva Charlton; *m* 1974, Judith Angela Carryer; two *s* one *d. Educ:* Nottingham High Sch.; Gonville and Caius Coll., Cambridge (MA); Leicester Univ. (PGCE); Manchester Univ. (BLing). Teacher, Gesamtschule, Gelsenkirchen, Germany, 1975–77; West Africa Dept, FCO, 1978–79; Amman, 1981–84; Near East and North Africa Dept, FCO, 1984–86; BMG Berlin, 1986–90; Dep. Chief, Assessments Staff, Cabinet Office, 1991–93; Head, Eastern Adriatic Unit, FCO, 1993–95; Bosnia Contact Group Rep., 1995–96; Political Counsellor, 1996–98, Dep. Hd of Mission, 1998–99, Bonn; Dep. Hd of Mission, Berlin, 1999–2000; Dir, SE Europe, FCO, 2001; Dir, Personnel, then HR Dir, FCO, 2002–04; Dep. Hd of Mission, Washington, 2004–07, and Ambassador to Orgn of American States, 2006–07. FRSA. *Recreations:* history, films, football, cricket, dancing. *Address:* c/o Foreign and Commonwealth Office, SW1A 2AH.

CHARLTON, Alexander Murray; QC 2008; *b* Herts, 13 March 1958; *s* of Murray Anthony Charlton and Pamela Charlton; *m* 1989, Emma Marie Clezy; one *s* two *d. Educ:* Tonbridge Sch.; St Andrews Univ. (MA Hons English); City Univ. (Dip. Law). Called to the Bar, Middle Temple, 1983. Contributing Ed., Professional Negligence and Liability, 1st edn 2000, updated annually. *Recreations:* sailing, ski-ing, Rugby. *Address:* 4 Pump Court, EC4Y 7AN. *T:* (020) 7842 5555, *Fax:* (020) 7583 2036; *e-mail:* acharlton@4pumpcourt.com. *Clubs:* Brooks's; Sea View Yacht (Seaview, IoW).

CHARLTON, Sir Bobby; *see* Charlton, Sir Robert.

CHARLTON, Celia Anne; *see* Dawson, C. A.

CHARLTON, Graham; *see* Charlton, T. A. G.

CHARLTON, Prof. Graham, MDS; FDSRCSE; Professor of Conservative Dentistry, University of Edinburgh, 1978–91, now Emeritus Professor (Dean of Dental Studies, 1978–83); *b* 15 Oct. 1928; *s* of Simpson R. Charlton and Georgina (*née* Graham); *m* 1956, Stella Dobson; two *s* one *d. Educ:* Bedlington Grammar Sch., Northumberland; St John's Coll., York (Teaching Cert.); King's Coll., Univ. of Durham (BDS); Univ. of Bristol (MDS). Teacher, Northumberland, 1948–52; National Service, 1948–50; Dental School, 1952–58; General Dental Practice, Torquay, 1958–64; University of Bristol: Lecturer, 1964–72; Cons. Sen. Lectr, 1972–78; Dental Clinical Dean, 1975–78. *Address:* 10 Pear Tree Court, Aldwark, York YO1 7DF. *T:* (01904) 655619.

CHARLTON, Henry Marshall, DPhil; FRS 1994; Reader in Neuroendocrinology, University of Oxford, 1990–2006, now Emeritus; Fellow of Linacre College, Oxford, 1970–2006, now Emeritus; *b* 10 March 1939; *s* of Joseph Douglass Charlton and Lilian Charlton; *m* 1965, Margaret Jeffrey; one *s* one *d. Educ:* Corpus Christi Coll., Oxford (MA, DPhil). Mem., MRC Neuroendocrinology Unit, Oxford, 1964–68; Lectr, Oxford Univ., 1968–90. Founder FMedSci 1998. *Publications:* contrib. scientific jls. *Recreations:* Real tennis, hill walking, gardening. *Address:* 61 Plantation Road, Oxford OX2 6JE. *T:* (01865) 554248.

CHARLTON, John, (Jack), OBE 1974; DL; Manager, Republic of Ireland Football Team, 1986–95; broadcaster; *b* 8 May 1935; *s* of late Robert and Elizabeth Charlton; *m* 1958, Patricia; two *s* one *d. Educ:* Hirst Park Sch., Ashington. Professional footballer, Leeds United, 1952–73; 35 England caps, 1965–70; Manager: Middlesbrough, 1973–77; Sheffield Wednesday FC, 1977–83; Newcastle United FC, 1984–85. Mem., Sports Council, 1977–82. DL Northumberland, 1997. *Publications:* Jack Charlton's American World Cup Diary, 1994; The Autobiography, 1996. *Recreations:* shooting, fishing, gardening.

See also Sir Robert Charlton.

CHARLTON, John, CBE 2007; JP; Director and Chairman, JCC Consultancy Ltd, since 1996; Chairman, University Hospital Birmingham NHS Foundation Trust (formerly NHS Trust), 1998–2006; *b* 11 Oct. 1940; *s* of late F. E. Charlton and Esther (*née* Lakin); *m* 1965, Carol Rosemary Shaw; two *s. Educ:* King Edward's Grammar Sch., Five Ways; Birmingham Univ. (BDS, LDS). DDH, DDPH 1970. Area Dental Officer, Oldbury, 1964–66; Dep. Chief Dental Officer, 1966, Chief Dental Officer, 1966–74, Warley; Area Dental Officer, Sandwell, 1974–82; Sandwell Health Authority: Dist Dental Officer, 1982–92; Consultant in Dental Public Health, 1992–96; Exec. Dir, 1993–96. Mem., Birmingham AHA, 1974–82; Dental Advr, W Midlands RHA, 1977–80; Chm., S Birmingham HA, 1981–91. Chm., Arden Gp Sec., Weoley Ward Lab. Party, 1967–83. Birmingham District Council: Mem. (Lab), Weoley Ward, 1980–82, Bartley Gn Ward, 1982–90; Hon. Alderman, 1990. Dir, British Fluoridation Soc., 1993–. Founder Member: Bournville Village Lessees Assoc.; SW Birmingham Assoc. for Advancement of State Educn; Lunar Soc., 1990. Trustee, University Hosp. Birmingham Charities, 1999–. JP Birmingham, 1992–2000. *Recreations:* squash, travelling, politics. *Address:* 48 Middle Park Road, Selly Oak, Birmingham B29 4BJ. *T:* (0121) 475 7700.

CHARLTON, Prof. Kenneth; Emeritus Professor of History of Education, King's College, University of London, since 1983; *b* 11 July 1925; 2nd *s* of late George and Lottie Charlton; *m* 1953, Maud Tulloch Brown, *d* of late P. R. Brown, MBE and M. B. Brown; one *s* one *d. Educ:* City Grammar Sch., Chester; Univ. of Glasgow. MA 1949, MEd 1953, Glasgow. RNVR, 1943–46. History Master, Dalziel High Sch., Motherwell, and Uddingston Grammar Sch., 1950–54; Lectr in Educn, UC N Staffs, 1954–64; Sen. Lectr in Educn, Keele Univ., 1964–66; Prof. of History and Philosophy of Educn, Birmingham Univ., 1966–72; Prof. of History of Educn and Head of Dept of Educn, King's Coll., Univ. of London, 1972–83. *Publications:* Recent Historical Fiction for Children, 1960, 2nd edn 1969; Education in Renaissance England, 1965; Women, Religion and Education in Early Modern England, 1999; (contrib.) Cambridge History of Early Modern English Literature 1530–1675, 2002; (contrib.) A Companion to Early Modern Women's Writing, 2002; contrib. Oxford DNB; contribs to Educnl Rev., Brit. Jl Educnl Psych., Year Bk of Educn, Jl Hist. of Ideas, Brit. Jl Educnl Studies, Internat. Rev. of Educn, Trans Hist. Soc. Lancs and Cheshire, Irish Hist. Studies, Northern Hist., Hist. of Educn, Hist. of Educn Quarterly. *Recreations:* gardening, listening to music. *Address:* 128 Ridge Langley, Sanderstead, Croydon CR2 0AS.

See also P. Charlton.

CHARLTON, Louise; Co-founder, 1987, and Group Senior Partner, since 2004, Brunswick Group LLP; *b* Wakefield, 25 May 1960; *d* of John Charlton and Patricia Crawford (*née* Hulme); *m* 1985, Andrew Durant; two *s* one *d. Educ:* Univ. of Reading (BA Hons French). Non-exec. Dir, RPS Gp, 2008–. Dir and Trustee, Natural Hist. Mus., 2006–. *Recreations:* family, fishing, cinema, travel, reading. *Address:* c/o Brunswick Group LLP, 16 Lincoln's Inn Fields, WC2A 3ED. *T:* (020) 7396 7437; *e-mail:* lcharlton@brunswickgroup.com.

CHARLTON, Philip, OBE 1987; FCIB; Co-Founder, and Chairman, 1991–96, Charlton Associates; *b* 31 July 1930; *s* of George and Lottie Charlton; *m* 1953, Jessie Boulton; one *s* one *d. Educ:* Chester Grammar School. Entered service of Chester Savings Bank, 1947; Gen. Manager, Chester, Wrexham and N Wales Savings Bank, 1966–75; Gen. Manager, TSB Wales & Border Counties, 1975–81; TSB Group Central Executive: Dep. Chief Gen. Manager, 1981–82; Chief Gen. Manager, 1982–85; Gp Man. Dir, 1986–88; Chief Exec., 1988–89; Dep. Chm., 1990–91; Mem., TSB Central Bd, 1976–77, 1981–90; Director: TSB Computer Services (Wythenshawe) Ltd, 1976–81; TSB Trust Co. Ltd, 1979–82; TSB Gp Computer Services Ltd, 1981–86; Central Trustee Savings Bank, later TSB Bank, 1982–89; TSB (Holdings) Ltd, 1982–86; Hill Samuel Gp, 1987–89. Council Mem., 1968–71, Hon. Treasurer, 1975–77, Savings Bank Inst.; Vice Pres., Internat. Savings Banks Inst. (Geneva), 1988–91; Mem., Bd of Admin, European Savings Banks Gp, Brussels, 1989–91. Chm., TSB Nat. Sports Council, 1979–82. FCIB (FIB 1977; Mem. Council, 1982–; Dep. Chm., 1989–91; Pres., 1990–92); CCMI (CBIM 1983). *Recreations:* music, swimming, sport. *Address:* 62 Quinta Drive, Arkley, near Barnet, Herts EN5 3BE. *T:* (020) 8440 4477. *Clubs:* Royal Automobile; City (Chester).

See also Prof. K. Charlton.

CHARLTON, Richard McKenzie, AM 1996; FTS; FInstPet; Chairman, South East Water Ltd, 1995–2002; *b* 20 March 1935; *s* of Richard Rutherford Charlton and Yvonne Gladys Charlton (*née* McKenzie); *m*; two *s* two *d. Educ:* Sydney Univ. (BE Mining 1957; MESc 1959). Joined Shell as trainee petroleum engr, 1959: various posts in The Hague, UK, Nigeria, Kuwait, Trinidad and Brunei, 1959–75; Shell Australia: Gen. Manager, Exploration & Prodn, 1975–76; Exec. Dir, NW Shelf Project, 1976–80; Dir Ops, Shell UK Exploration & Prodn, Aberdeen, 1980–83; Chm., Shell Cos in Malaysia, 1983–86; Hd, Exploration & Prodn Ops & Liaison, The Hague, 1986–91; Chm. and Chief Exec. Officer, Shell Gp of Cos in Australia, 1991–95, retd. Director: Fujitsu Australia Ltd, 1994–97; Coles-Myer Ltd, 1995–2003; Hongkong Bank of Australia, 1996–2001; Chm., Adcorp Australia Ltd, 1999–. Chancellor, Univ. of Newcastle, NSW, 1994–. Chairman: Art Foundn, Victoria, 1994–97 (Dep. Chm., 1992–94); Hunter Symphony Orch., 1995–97; Australia-Malaysia Soc., 1995–. Chm., Nat. Basketball League, 1997–2000. Mem., Soc. Petroleum Engrs, 1971; FAICD; FInstD; FAIM. *Publications:* papers on petroleum industry. *Recreations:* horse racing, Rugby, snow ski-ing, surfing, tennis. *Address:* Milton House, 25 Flinders Lane, Melbourne, Vic 3000, Australia. *T:* (3) 96668850. *Clubs:* Melbourne, Australia (Melbourne); Victoria Racing, Moonee Valley Racing.

CHARLTON, Sir Robert, (Sir Bobby), Kt 1994; CBE 1974 (OBE 1969); Director, Manchester United Football Club, since 1984; *b* 11 Oct. 1937; *s* of late Robert and Elizabeth Charlton; *m* 1961, Norma Ball; two *d. Educ:* Bedlington Grammar Sch., Northumberland. Professional Footballer with Manchester United, 1954–73, for whom he played 751 games and scored 245 goals; FA Cup Winners Medal, 1963; FA Championship Medals, 1956–57, 1964–65 and 1966–67; World Cup Winners Medal (International), 1966; European Cup Winners medal, 1968. 100th England cap, 21 April 1970; 106 appearances for England, 1957–73. Manager, Preston North End, 1973–75. Mem., Cttee, FIFA. Hon. Fellow, Manchester Polytechnic, 1979. Hon. MA Manchester Univ. Sir Stanley Matthews Award, 2000. *Publications:* My Soccer Life, 1965; Forward for England, 1967; This Game of Soccer, 1967; Book of European Football, Books 1–4,

1969–72; My Manchester United Years: the autobiography, 2007. *Recreation:* golf. *Address:* 4 Cranford Court, King Street, Knutsford, Cheshire WA16 8BW.
See also John Charlton.

CHARLTON, (Thomas Alfred) Graham, CB 1970; Secretary, Trade Marks, Patents and Designs Federation, 1973–84; *b* 29 Aug. 1913; 3rd *s* of late Frederick William and Marian Charlton; *m* 1940, Margaret Ethel, *yr d* of A. E. Furst; three *d. Educ:* Rugby School; Corpus Christi Coll., Cambridge. Asst Principal, War Office, 1936; Asst Private Secretary to Secretary of State for War, 1937–39; Principal, 1939; Cabinet Office, 1947–49; Asst Secretary, 1949; International Staff, NATO, 1950–52; War Office, later MoD, 1952–73; Asst Under-Sec. of State, 1960–73. Coronation Medal, 1953. *Recreation:* gardening. *Address:* Room 14, Bradbury House, Windsor End, Beaconsfield, Bucks HP9 2JW.

CHARLTON-WEEDY, Maj. Gen. Michael Anthony, CBE 1997 (OBE 1993); Director, Emergency Planning College, Cabinet Office, since 2003; *b* 11 June 1950; *s* of late Kenneth Charlton Weedy and of Valerie (*née* Reed); *m* 1979, Julia Redfern; two *s* one *d. Educ:* Millfield; Sandhurst. Commnd RA, 1971; sc 1982; CO 4th Regt RA, 1990–92 (despatches 1992); rcds 1995; Chief Faction Liaison Officer, Bosnia, 1995–96; Dir, OR (Land CIS), MoD, 1997–2000; Sen. Directing Staff (Army), RCDS, 2001–02; Dep. Adjt Gen., MoD, 2002–03. *Recreations:* country sports. *Address:* c/o HSBC, Kingsbridge, Devon TQ7 1PB.

CHARMLEY, Prof. John Denis, DPhil; FRHistS; Professor of Modern History, since 1998, Dean, School of History, since 2002, and Associate Dean, Research, Faculty of Arts and Humanities, since 2005, University of East Anglia; *b* 9 Nov. 1955; *s* of John Charmley and Doris Charmley; *m* 1st, 1977, Ann Dorothea Bartlett (marr. diss. 1992); three *s* (incl. twins); 2nd, 1992, Lorraine Fegan (marr. diss. 2003); 3rd, 2004, Rachael Heap. *Educ:* Rock Ferry High Sch., Birkenhead; Pembroke Coll., Oxford (BA 1977; MA 1982; DPhil 1982). FRHistS 1987. University of East Anglia: Lectr in English Hist., Sch. of English and American Studies, 1979–92; Sen. Lectr in Hist., Sch. of Hist., 1992–96; Reader in Hist., 1996–98. Fulbright Prof., Westminster Coll., Fulton, Mo, 1992–93. Chm., Mid-Norfolk Cons. Assoc., 2000–03; Election Agent: Mid Norfolk, 2000–02; S Norfolk, 2005–. Pres., Norfolk and Norwich Br., Historical Assoc., 2000–; Vice Chm., Cons. Hist. Gp, 2003–. *Publications:* Duff Cooper, 1986; Lord Lloyd and the Decline of the British Empire, 1987; (ed) Descent to Suez: the diaries of Sir Evelyn Shuckburgh, 1987; Chamberlain and the Lost Peace, 1989; Churchill: the end of glory, 1993; Churchill's Grand Alliance, 1995; A History of Conservative Politics 1990–1996, 1996; Splendid Isolation?: Britain and the balance of power 1874–1914, 1999; The Princess and the Politicians, 2005; A History of Conservative Politics since 1830, 2008. *Recreations:* reading, walking, dining out. *Address:* School of History, University of East Anglia, Norwich NR4 7TJ. *T:* (01603) 592790. *Club:* Norfolk (Norwich).

CHARNLEY, Helen; *see* Dunmore, H.

CHARNLEY, Sir (William) John, Kt 1981; CB 1973; MEng, FREng, FRAeS, FRIN; *b* 4 Sept. 1922; *s* of George and Catherine Charnley; *m* 1945, Mary Paden (*d* 2007); one *s* one *d. Educ:* Oulton High Sch., Liverpool; Liverpool Univ. MEng 1945; FREng (FEng 1982); FRIN 1963; FRAeS 1966. Aerodynamics Dept, RAE Farnborough, 1943–55; Supt. Blind Landing Experimental Unit, 1955–61; Imperial Defence Coll., 1962; Head of Instruments and Electrical Engineering Dept, 1963–65, Head of Weapons Dept, 1965–68, RAE Farnborough; Head of Research Planning, 1968–69, Dep. Controller, Guided Weapons, Min. of Technology, later MoD, 1969–72; Controller, Guided Weapons and Electronics, MoD (PE), 1972–73; Chief Scientist (RAF), 1973–77, and Dep. Controller, R&D Establishments and Res. C, MoD, 1975–77; Controller, R&D Establishments and Res., MoD, 1977–82. Director: Fairey Holdings Ltd, 1983–86; Winsdale Investments Ltd, 1985–88. Technical Advr, Monopolies and Mergers Commn, 1982; Specialist Advr to House of Lords Select Cttee on Science and Technology, 1986. Chm., Civil Aviation Res. and Develt Programme Bd, 1984–92; Mem., Air Traffic Control Bd, 1985–96. President: Royal Inst. of Navigation, 1987–90; European Orgn for Civil Aviation Equipment, 1993–97. Trustee, Richard Ormonde Shuttleworth Remembrance Trust, 1987–98. Hon. FRAeS 1992. Hon. DEng Liverpool, 1988. Bronze Medal, 1960, Gold Medal, 2001, RIN, Silver Medal, 1973, Gold Medal, 1980, RAeS. *Publications:* papers on subjects in aerodynamics, aircraft all weather operation, aircraft navigation, defence R&D. *Address:* Kirkstones, 29 Brackendale Close, Camberley, Surrey GU15 1HP. *T:* (01276) 22547. *Club:* Royal Air Force.

CHARONE, Barbara; Director, MBC PR, since 2000; *b* Chicago, 22 March 1952; *d* of Rose Charone. *Educ:* New Trier High Sch.; Northwestern Univ. (BA Hons). Journalist, Sounds mag., 1974–77, Dep. Ed., until 1977; freelance journalist, Daily Mail, Rolling Stone, Cream, Crawdaddy, 1979–81; with Warner Bros Records, 1981–2000, Dir of Press, until 2000. *Publication:* Late as a Rolling Stone: authorised biography of Keith Richards, 1978 (also German, Japanese and US edns). *Recreations:* tennis, Chelsea Football Club (season ticket holder, since 1980), music, theatre. *Address:* MBC PR, The Wellington Building, 28–32 Wellington Road, NW8 9SP. *T:* (020) 7483 9205; *e-mail:* bc@mbcpr.com. *Clubs:* Groucho, Home House, Ivy.

CHARPAK, Georges; Physicist, Organisation européenne pour la recherche nucléaire (CERN); *b* Poland, 1 Aug. 1924; *s* of Anne Szapiro and Maurice Charpak; *m* 1953, Dominique Vidal; three *c. Educ:* Ecole des Mines de Paris. Went to France at age 7; served in French Resistance; imprisoned for 1 year in Dachau. Centre national de la recherche scientifique (CNRS), 1948; CERN, Geneva, 1959; in 1968 invented multiwire proportional chamber (linked to computers) for detecting particles in atom smashers. Mem., Acad des Sciences, France, 1985; Foreign Associate of Nat. Acad. of Sciences, USA, 1986. Nobel Prize for Physics, 1992. *Recreations:* ski-ing, travel, music. *Address:* CERN, 1211 Geneva 23, Switzerland. *T:* (22) 7672144, *Fax:* (22) 7677555.

CHART, Jennifer Ann, CBE 2004; Head Teacher, Portland School, Sunderland, since 1996; *b* 23 April 1951; *d* of John and Edna Hunt; *m*; one *s* one *d. Educ:* Univ. of Newcastle upon Tyne (Cert Ed SEN; Dip. Adv. Educnl Studies SEN; BPhil). Teacher, 1972–75; class teacher, 1980–89, Dep. Head Teacher, 1989–96, Ashleigh Sch., N Tyneside. Asst Sec., Thompson Hall (Tyneside MENCAP), 1968–72; Chm., N Tyneside Toy Liby, 1977–89. Trustee, Adventure Holidays (for disabled/disadvantaged children in Tyneside), 2001–. *Recreations:* outdoor activities, including walking, cycling and golf; needlecraft, painting. *Address:* Portland School, Weymouth Road, Chapelgarth, Sunderland, Tyne and Wear SR3 2NQ. *T:* (0191) 553 6050, *Fax:* (0191) 553 6048; *e-mail:* Jennifer.Chart@schools.sunderland.gov.uk.

CHARTER, Joseph Stephen; High Commissioner for Grenada to the Court of St James's, since 2005; *b* 26 Dec. 1943; *s* of late Vivian Charter and Daphne (later Mrs Daphne Johnson); *m* 1968, Aileen Valerie Cox; three *s* one *d. Educ:* Avery Hill Coll., Univ. of London (BEd Hons). Perm. Sec., Min. of Educn, Grenada, 1981; Ambassador, Libya, 1982–84; Permanent Secretary: Min. of Communication and Works, 1996–2001; Min. of Health and Envmt, 2001–04. Vice Pres., Chamber of Commerce, 1992–95; Chairman: Grenada Broadcasting Corp., 1998–2001; Nat. Water and Sewerage Authy, 1999–2002; Hosp. Governance Bd, 2003–05; Nat. Insce Bd, 2003–05. *Recreations:* music, theatre, sport. *Address:* Grenada High Commission, The Chapel, Archel Road, West Kensington, W14 9QH. *T:* (020) 7385 4415; *e-mail:* grenada@high-commission.demon.co.uk. *Clubs:* Royal Commonwealth Society, Royal Over-Seas League.

CHARTERIS, family name of **Earl of Wemyss.**

CHARTRES, Rt Rev. and Rt Hon. Richard John Carew; *see* London, Bishop of.

CHARVET, Richard Christopher Larkins, RD 1972; Consultant: Tyser & Co., 1999; Johnson Stevens Agencies, 1999–2000; General Manager, Morline Ltd (formerly Associate Director, Anglo Soviet Shipping Co. Ltd), 1988–94; *b* 12 Dec. 1936; *s* of late Patrice and Eleanor Charvet; *m* 1990; two *s* one *d* by a previous marriage. *Educ:* Rugby. FITT, ACIArb; FCIS; FCMI; MIFF; MIEx. FRSA 1985. National Service, Royal Navy, 1955–57; Mem., London Div., RNR, 1955–. Union Castle Line, 1957–58; Killick Martin & Co. Ltd, Shipbrokers, 1958–81; Vogt and Maguire Ltd, Shipbrokers, 1981–88. Consultant, Howden Marine Ltd, then AON Gp, 1994–99. Mem., Court of Common Council for Aldgate Ward, City of London, 1970–76; Alderman, Aldgate Ward, 1976–85; Sheriff, 1983–84. Prime Warden, Worshipful Co. of Shipwrights, 1985–86 (Renter Warden, 1984–85); Master, Guild of World Traders, 1991. Pres., City of London Sea Cadet Unit, 1994; Area Pres., N and E London, 1994–2000, New Forest, 2000, St John Ambulance, POW Dist; Chairman: City Br., St John Ambulance Appeal, 1985–92; City Br., RNLI, 1986–98. JP 1976–2001. KStJ 2001 (CStJ 1989). Hon. JSM, Malaysia, 1974. *Publication:* Peter and Tom in the Lord Mayor's Show, 1982. *Recreations:* gardening, travel, sailing. *Clubs:* Aldgate Ward, Lime Street Ward.

CHASE, Graham Frank; Chairman, Chase and Partners, since 1995; President, Royal Institution of Chartered Surveyors, 2006–07; *b* 5 Jan. 1954; *s* of late Frank Augustus Chase, FSVA and of Joan Lynette Chase (*née* Hibbert); *m* 1980, Fiona Anderson Batley; two *d. Educ:* Mill Hill Sch.; Willesden Coll. of Professional Building (DipEstMan 1976). FRICS 1988; FCIArb 1999; FICPD 2005. Estates Surveyor, BBC, 1976–79; Estates Manager, Ladbroke Racing Ltd, 1978–79; Clive Lewis and Partners: Shops Surveyor, 1980–84; Partner, 1984–86; Dir, 1986–93; Dir, Colliers Erdman Lewis, 1993–94. Non-exec. Dir, Assura Gp Ltd, 2003–. Royal Institution of Chartered Surveyors: Chairman: Internat. Cttee, 1991–94; Metrication Cttee, 1993–94; Commercial Mkt Panel, 1995–99; Commercial Property Fac., 2000–04; Review Cttee, Code of Practice for Commercial Leases, 2004; Representative: on H of C Select Cttee on future of shopping, 1993; Retail Property, 1996–99; on Modernising Stamp Duty Cttee, HM Treasury, 2003–04; to H of L Select Cttee on property taxation reform, 2004; Member: Code of Measuring Practice, 1993–94; Commercial Property Policy Panel, 1996–99; President's Arbitrators Panel, 1998–; President's Ind. Experts Panel, 2000–; Leadership Team, 2004–; Gen. Council, 1999–2000; Governing Council, 2001–03, 2004–; Gen. Practice Divl Pres., 2000; Vice Pres., 2004–05; Sen. Vice Pres., 2005–06. Member: Shops Agents Soc., 1980–; Accessible Retail, 1987–; Investment Property Forum, 1995–; British Council of Shopping Centres, 1995–; Property Industry Forum, 1996–99, Property Adv. Gp, 1999–2004, DETR; Property Forum, Bank of England, 2000–04; Empty Property Gp, ODPM, 2003–06. Jt Chm., Property Mktg Awards. Governor: Woodhouse VI Form Coll., 1996–2000; Mill Hill Sch., 2000–08; Trustee: Alford House Youth Club, Lambeth, 1999–; Bd, Coll. of Estate Mgt, 2005–. Freeman, City of London, 1991; Liveryman and Mem. Court, Co. of Chartered Surveyors, 1991–. Mem., Old Millhillians Club, 1972–. *Publication:* Business Tenancy Renewal Handbook, 2006. *Recreations:* Rugby, cricket, hockey, wine, food, disc jockey (as Fat Boy Fat), cycling, reading, sailing, UK history, UK geography, walking, curry. *Address:* 146 Green Dragon Lane, Winchmore Hill, N21 1ET. *T:* (020) 8364 0738; *e-mail:* gfc@chaseandpartners.co.uk. *Clubs:* Old Millhillians Rugby Football (player, 1972–97); Saracens; Arsenal Football; Winchmore Hill and Enfield Hockey (player, 1997–); Hazelwood Lawn Tennis and Squash.

CHASE, Prof. Howard Allaker, PhD, ScD; FREng, CEng; CSci; CChem, FIChemE; Fellow and Director of Studies in Chemical Engineering, Magdalene College, Cambridge, since 1984; Professor of Biochemical Engineering, University of Cambridge, since 2000; Founding Director and Chairman, Enval Ltd, since 2005; *b* 17 Nov. 1954; *s* of Peter Howard Chase and Phoebe Farrar Chase (*née* Winn); *m* 1st, 1982, Penelope Jane Lewis (marr. diss. 2003); one *s* one *d*; 2nd, 2003, Dawn Christine Leeder. *Educ:* Westminster Sch., London; Magdalene Coll., Cambridge (Exhibnr; BA 1975, MA 1978); PhD 1979, ScD 2001, Cantab. CChem, MRSC 1987; FIChemE 1998; CEng 1998, FREng 2005; CSci 2005. Hirst Res. Centre, GEC, Wembley, 1971–72; University of Cambridge: Bye Fellow, Magdalene Coll., 1977; Res. Fellow, St John's Coll., 1978; post-doctoral res. asst, Dept of Biochem., 1978–81; Department of Chemical Engineering: Res. Associate, 1982–83; Royal Soc. Res. Fellow, 1983–84; Asst Lectr in Chem. Engrg, 1984–86; Lectr, 1986–96; Reader in Biochem. Engrg, 1996–2000; Hd of Dept, 1998–2006; Magdalene College: Lectr in Natural Sci., 1984–2000; Tutor for Grad. Students, 1987–93; Sen. Tutor, 1993–96; Tutor, 1996–98. University College London: Vis. Prof., Dept of Chem. and Biochem. Engrg, 1991–92; Hon. Res. Fellow, 1993–. Mem. editl cttees and bds of scientific jls. External Examiner: Dept of Chem. Engrg, Univ. of Bradford, 2001–05; Dept of Chem. Engrg, Univ. of Newcastle upon Tyne, 2003–05; Dept of Biochem. Engrg, UCL, 2007–; Dept of Chem. Engrg, Univ. of Manchester, 2008–. Sir George Beilby Medal and Prize, Soc. Chem. Ind., RSC and Inst. Metals, 1993; BOC Envmtl Award, IChemE Awards, 2001. *Publications:* contribs to scientific jls specialising in biotechnol., biochem. engrg, microbiol., etc. *Recreations:* food and drink, public transport, hot beaches. *Address:* Department of Chemical Engineering, University of Cambridge, Pembroke Street, Cambridge CB2 3RA. *T:* (01223) 334781, *Fax:* (01223) 334796; *e-mail:* hac1000@cam.ac.uk.

CHASE, Prof. Mark Wayne, PhD; FRS 2003; Keeper of the Jodrell Laboratory, Royal Botanic Gardens, Kew, since 2006 (Head of Molecular Systematics, 1992–2006); *b* 17 Jan. 1951; *s* of Wayne Marshall Chase and Helen Louise Chase (*née* Andrews). *Educ:* Paw Paw High Sch., Mich.; Albion Coll., Albion, Mich. (BA Hons Hist. 1973); Univ. of Michigan, Ann Arbor (MS Biology 1980; PhD Botany 1985). Postdoctoral Res. Fellow, Dept of Biol., 1986–88, Lectr, Botany (Plant Systematics), 1987, Univ. of Mich., Ann Arbor; Asst Prof., 1988–92, Dir, Univ. Herbarium, 1990–92, Univ. of N Carolina, Chapel Hill. *Publications:* (ed jtly) Genera Orchidacearum: vol. 1, Introduction, Apostasioideae, and Cypripedioideae, 1999; vol. 2, Orchidoideae I, 2001; vol. 3, Orchidoideae II and Vanilloideae, 2003; contribs to books and many articles in professional jls. *Recreation:* gardening. *Address:* Jodrell Laboratory, Royal Botanic Gardens, Kew, Richmond, Surrey TW9 3AB.

CHASE, Robert John; HM Diplomatic Service, retired; Secretary General, International Aluminium Institute (formerly International Primary Aluminium Institute), since 1997; *b* 13 March 1943; *s* of late Herbert Chase and of Evelyn Chase; *m* 1966, Gillian Ann Chase (*née* Shelton); one *s* two *d. Educ:* Sevenoaks Sch.; St John's Coll., Oxford. MA (Mod.

Hist.). Entered HM Diplomatic Service, 1965; Third, later Second Sec., Rangoon, 1966–69; UN Dept, FCO, 1970–72; First Sec. (Press Attaché), Brasilia, 1972–76; Hd Caribbean Section, Mexico and Caribbean Dept, FCO, 1976–80; on secondment as a manager to Imperial Chemical Industries PLC, 1980–82; Asst Hd, S American Dept, FCO, 1982–83; Asst Hd, Maritime, Aviation and Environment Dept, FCO, 1983–84; Counsellor (Commercial), Moscow, 1985–88; Overseas Inspector, FCO, 1988–89; Hd, Resource Mgt Dept, FCO, 1989–92; Consul-Gen., Chicago, 1993–96; Dir Gen. of Trade and Investment, and Consul-Gen., Milan, 1996–97. MInstD. *Recreations:* military history, politics, visiting historic sites, swimming. *Address:* IAI, New Zealand House, Haymarket, SW1Y 4TE. *T:* (020) 7930 0528.

CHASE, Rodney Frank, CBE 2000; Chairman, Petrofac, since 2005; *b* 12 May 1943; *s* of late Norman Maxwell Chase, MBE and of Barbara Chase (*née* Marshall). *Educ:* Liverpool Univ. (BA Hons Hist.). Joined British Petroleum, 1964: various posts in marketing, oil trading and shipping distribn, 1964–81; Dir (Exploration and Prodn), BP Australia, 1982–85; Gp Treas., BP, 1986–89; Chief Exec. Officer, BP Exploration (USA), 1989–92; a Man. Dir, BP, 1992–98; Chm. and Chief Exec. Officer, BP America, 1992–94; Dep. Gp Chief Exec., BP, 1998–2003. Dep. Chm. and Sen. non-exec. Dir, Tesco plc, 2004– (non-exec. Dir, 2002–); non-executive Director: BOC, 1995–2001; Diageo, 1999–2004; Computer Scis Corp., 2001–; Nalco Co., 2005–; Sen. Advr, Lehman Brothers, 2003–08. Chm., UK Emissions Trading Gp, 1998–2002; Mem., Adv. Cttee on Business and the Envmt, 1993–2000. Mem., Amer. Petroleum Inst., 2000–02. *Recreations:* golf, ski-ing. *Address: e-mail:* rodney@rfchase.com.

CHASE, Roger Robert; Director of Personnel, BBC, 1989–91; *b* 19 Sept. 1928; *s* of Robert Joseph Chase and Lillian Ada (*née* Meredith); *m* 1958, Geraldine Joan Whitlamsmith; three *d*. *Educ:* Gosport Grammar Sch. Served RN, 1947–49. Joined BBC, 1944; Engrg Div., 1944–47 and 1949–67; Television Personnel Dept, 1967–74; Head, Central Services Dept, 1974–76; Controller, Personnel, Television, 1976–82; Dep. Dir of Personnel, 1982–89. Chm., BBC Club, 1979–91. *Recreation:* sailing. *Address:* Vernons, Vernons Road, Chappel, Colchester, Essex CO6 2AQ. *T:* (01206) 240143. *Club:* Royal Naval Sailing Association.

CHASKALSON, Hon. Arthur, SCOB 2002; Chief Justice of South Africa and of the Constitutional Court of South Africa, 2001–05 (President, Constitutional Court of South Africa, 1994–2001); *b* Johannesburg, 24 Nov. 1931; *s* of Harry and Mary Chaskalson; *m* 1961, Lorraine Dianne Ginsberg; two *s*. *Educ:* Hilton Coll., Natal; Univ. of Witwatersrand (BCom 1952; LLB *cum laude* 1955). Called to Johannesburg Bar, 1956; SC 1971; in practice as barrister, 1956–94: defence counsel for mems of liberation movements at several major political trials, incl. that of Nelson Mandela, 1963–64. Jt Founder, 1978, and Dir, 1978–93, Legal Resources Centre. Member: Legal Aid Bd, 1992–2000; Judicial Service Commn, 1994–2005; Comr, Internat. Commn of Jurists, 1995– (Pres., 2002). Consultant to Namibian Constituent Assembly on drafting of Constitution of Namibia, 1989–90. Mem., Johannesburg Bar Council, 1967–71 and 1973–84 (Chm., 1976, 1982); Vice-Chm., Gen. Council of Bar of S Africa, 1982–87 (Jt Hon. Pres., 1994–); Vice-Chm., Internat. Legal Aid Div., Internat. Bar Assoc., 1983–93. Mem., Nat. Council of Lawyers for Human Rights, 1980–91. Hon. Prof. of Law, Univ. of Witwatersrand, 1981–95. Hon. LLD: Natal, 1986; Witwatersrand, 1990; Rhodes, 1997; Amsterdam, 2002; Port Elizabeth, 2002. Numerous awards, incl. (jtly) Human Rights Award, Foundn for Freedom and Human Rights, Berne, 1990. *Address:* c/o Constitutional Court, Private Bag X32, Braamfontein 2017, S Africa.

CHATAWAY, Rt Hon. Sir Christopher (John), Kt 1995; PC 1970; Chairman, Bletchley Park Trust, 2000–07; *b* 31 Jan. 1931; *m* 1st, 1959, Anna Lett (marr. diss. 1975); two *s* one *d*; 2nd, 1976, Carola Walker; two *s*. *Educ:* Sherborne Sch.; Magdalen Coll., Oxford (BA Hons PPE). Rep. Great Britain, Olympic Games, 1952 and 1956; briefly held world 5,000 metres track record in 1954. Arthur Guinness Son & Co., 1953–55; Independent Television News, 1955–56; BBC Television, 1956–59. Elected for N Lewisham to LCC, 1958–61; Leader, Educn Cttee, ILEA, 1967–69. MP (C): Lewisham North, 1959–66; Chichester, May 1969–Sept. 1974; PPS to Minister of Power, 1961–62; Joint Parly Under-Secretary of State, Dept of Education and Science, 1962–64; Minister of Posts and Telecommunications, 1970–72; Minister for Industrial Develt, DTI, 1972–74. Chairman: LBC, 1981–93; CAA, 1991–96. Man. Dir, Orion Royal Bank, 1974–88; Director: BET, 1974–96; Credito Italiano Internat., 1992–96; Macquarie Securities Ltd, 1994–2001; 1975–92: Chm., United Med. Enterprises, Isola 2000, Kitcat & Aitken, RBC CI, Crown Communications; Dir, Fisons, Plessey Telecommunications, Dorchester Hotel, UK subsids of Honeywell, GE of America and Petrofina. Treasurer, Nat. Cttee for Electoral Reform, 1976–84. Chairman: Groundwork Foundn, 1985–90; UK Athletics, 1998–2000. Pres., Commonwealth Games Council for England, 1986–; Treas., 1976–86, Chm., 1986–92, Action Aid. Trustee, Foundn for Sport and the Arts, 1993–. Hon. DLitt: Loughborough, 1985; Macquarie, 2000; Hon. DSc Cranfield, 1994. Nansen Medal, 1960. *Club:* Garrick.

See also C. A. R. Walker.

CHATELIER, Trevor Mansel; a District Judge (Magistrates' Courts), Liverpool, since 2001; a Recorder, since 2006; *b* 5 Oct. 1950; *s* of Dr Mansel Frederick Chatelier and Barbara Winifred Chatelier; *m* (marr diss.); twin *s*. *Educ:* Uxbridge Tech. Coll.; Mid-Essex Tech. Coll. (LLB); Coll. of Law. Admitted solicitor, 1974; asst solicitor posts, 1974–79; Solicitor, Messrs Wilson Houlder & Co., Southall, 1979–2001; Actg Stipendiary Magistrate, Leeds Magistrates' Court, 1998–2001. Member: YHA; NT. *Publications:* Criminal Advocacy in the Magistrates' Court, 1981; article in Law Soc. Gazette. *Recreations:* coastal sailing, angling, cycle touring, camping, motor-cycling, classical guitar, languages, good food, good company and going out. *T:* (0151) 708 9114; *e-mail:* smart.alec@virgin.net. *Clubs:* Liverpool Yacht; Moulton Bicycle; Iver Flyfishing.

CHATER, Dr Anthony Philip John; Editor, Morning Star, 1974–95; parents both shoe factory workers; *m* 1954, Janice (*née* Smith); three *s*. *Educ:* Northampton Grammar Sch. for Boys; Queen Mary Coll., London. BSc (1st cl. hons Chem.) 1951, PhD (Phys. Chem.) 1954. Fellow in Biochem., Ottawa Exper. Farm, 1954–56; studied biochem. at Brussels Univ., 1956–57; Teacher, Northampton Techn. High Sch., 1957–59; Teacher, Blyth Grammar Sch., Norwich, 1959–60; Lectr, subseq. Sen. Lectr in Phys. Chem., Luton Coll. of Technology, 1960–69; Head of Press and Publicity of Communist Party, 1969–74; Nat. Chm. of Communist Party, 1967–69. Contested (Com) Luton, Nov. 1963, 1964, 1966, 1970. Mem. Presidential Cttee, World Peace Council, 1969–74. *Publications:* Race Relations in Britain, 1966; numerous articles. *Recreations:* walking, swimming, music, camping.

CHATER, Prof. Keith Frederick, PhD; FRS 1995; Head, Department of Molecular Microbiology, John Innes Centre, 2001–04, now Emeritus Fellow; *b* 23 April 1944; *s* of Frederick Ernest Chater and Marjorie Inez Chater (*née* Palmer); *m* 1966, Jean Wallbridge; three *s* one *d*. *Educ:* Trinity Sch. of John Whitgift, Croydon; Univ. of Birmingham (BSc 1st Cl. Hons Bacteriol. 1966; PhD Genetics 1969). John Innes Institute, later John Innes Centre: research scientist in Streptomyces genetics, 1969–; Dep. Head, 1989–98, Head, 1998–2001, Dept. of Genetics. Fulbright Scholar, Harvard Univ., 1983; Hon. Professor: UEA, 1988–; Chinese Acad. of Scis, Inst. of Microbiology, 1999; Huazhong Agricl Univ., Wuhan, 2000; Univ. of Newcastle upon Tyne, 2006–. *Publications:* (jtly) Genetic Manipulation of Streptomyces: a laboratory manual, 1985; (ed jtly) Genetics of Bacterial Diversity, 1989; (jtly) Practical Streptomyces Genetics, 2000. *Recreations:* painting, gardening, bird-watching. *Address:* John Innes Centre, Norwich Research Park, Colney, Norwich NR4 7UH. *T:* (01603) 450297, *Fax:* (01603) 450045; *e-mail:* keith.chater@bbsrc.ac.uk.

CHATFIELD, Sir John (Freeman), Kt 1993; CBE 1982; DL; Chairman, Association of County Councils, 1989–92; Consultant Solicitor in private practice, 1989–95; *b* 28 Oct. 1929; *s* of Cecil Freeman Chatfield and Florence Dorothy Chatfield; *m* 1954, Barbara Elizabeth Trickett. *Educ:* Southdown Coll., Eastbourne; Roborough Sch., Eastbourne; Lawrence Sheriff Sch., Rugby; Lewes Grammar Sch.; Law Soc. Sch. (Final, 1951). Solicitor, 1952; Sen. Partner, Hart Reade & Co., Eastbourne, 1976–89; Dep. Registrar, County Court, 1965–78. Mem., E Sussex CC, 1972–93 (Leader, 1981–85; Chm., 1985–87); Chairman: Sussex Police Authy, 1982–85; Police Cttee, ACC, 1982–85; Official Side, Police Negotiating Bd, 1982–85; Mem., Police Adv. Bd, England and Wales, 1980–85; Vice-Chm., ACC, 1986–89; Chm., UK Local Authorities Internat. Bureau, 1989–92; first Chm., Internat. Council for Local Envmt Initiatives, 1990–93; Pres., Consultative Council of Local and Regional Authorities in Europe, 1990–93; a Vice-President: CEMR, 1989–93; British Section, IULA/CEMR, 1993–97; Leader, UK Delegn, 1989–92, Mem., Standing Cttee, 1990–93, CLRAE. Mem. Ct and Council, Sussex Univ., 1981–85 and 1991–2001 (Vice-Chm. Council, 1996–99); Gov., Ravensbourne Coll. of Design and Communication, 1999–2004. President: Eastbourne Law Soc., 1972–73; Eastbourne Symphony Orch., 2002–08 (Patron, 2008–). Freeman, City of London, 1994; Liveryman, Co. of Basketmakers, 1995–2005. DL E Sussex, 1986. *Recreations:* music, theatre, travel, watercolour painting. *Address:* 74 Linkswood, Compton Place Road, Eastbourne, E Sussex BN21 1EF. *T:* (01323) 638733.

CHATTERJEE, Krishna; *see* Chatterjee, V. K. K.

CHATTERJEE, Dr Satya Saran, OBE 1971; JP; FRCP, FRCPE; Consultant Chest Physician and Physician in Charge, Department of Respiratory Physiology, Wythenshawe Hospital, Manchester, 1959–88; *b* 16 July 1922; *m* 1948, Enid May (*née* Adlington); one *s* two *d*. *Educ:* India, UK, Sweden and USA. MB, BS; FCCP (USA). Asst Lectr, Dept of Medicine, Albany Med. Coll. Hosp., NY, 1953–54; Med. Registrar, Sen. Registrar, Dept of Thoracic Medicine, Wythenshawe Hosp., Manchester, 1954–59. Mem., NW RHA, 1976–. Chairman: NW Conciliation Cttee, Race Relations Board, 1972–77; Overseas Doctors Assoc., 1975–81 (Pres., 1981–87); Manchester Area Cttee on Ethnic Minority Health, 1993–94; Member: Standing Adv. Council on Race Relations, 1977–86; GMC, 1979–92; NW Adv. Council, BBC, 1987–92; Vice-Pres., Manchester Council for Community Relations, 1974–. Chm., ODA News Review, 1986–99. President: Rotary Club, Wythenshawe, 1975–76; Indian Assoc., Manchester, 1962–71. Mem. Bd and Trustee, Community Technical Aid Centre, Manchester, 1998–99 (Dir, 1992–97). *Publications:* research papers in various projects related to cardio/pulmonary disorders. *Address:* 15 Hunters Mews, Macclesfield Road, Wilmslow, Cheshire SK9 2AR. *T:* (01625) 522559.

CHATTERJEE, Prof. (Vengalil) Krishna (Kumar), FRCP, FMedSci; Professor of Endocrinology, University of Cambridge, since 1998; Fellow of Churchill College, Cambridge, since 1990; *b* 23 April 1958. *Educ:* Wolfson Coll., Oxford (BA, BM BCh). FRCP 1996. SHO, Hammersmith, Brompton and St Thomas' Hosps., 1983–85; Registrar, Hammersmith Hosp., 1985–87; Res. Fellow, Massachusetts Gen. Hosp., 1987–90; Wellcome Sen. Fellow and Hon. Cons. Physician, Addenbrooke's Hosp., 1994–. FMedSci 2000. *Recreations:* travel, music. *Address:* Department of Medicine, University of Cambridge, Addenbrooke's Hospital, Hills Road, Cambridge CB2 2QQ.

CHATTERTON DICKSON, Robert Maurice French; HM Diplomatic Service; Head of Counter-Terrorism Policy Department, since 2007; *b* 1 Feb. 1962; *s* of Capt. W. W. F. Chatterton Dickson, RN and Judith Chatterton Dickson (*née* French); *m* 1995, Teresa Bargielska Albor; two *d* and one step *s* one step *d*. *Educ:* Wellington Coll.; Magdalene Coll., Cambridge (Exhibnr; BA 1984, MA 1988). Investment analyst, subseq. instnl and internat. portfolio manager, Morgan Grenfell Asset Mgt Ltd, 1984–90; entered FCO, 1990; 2nd Sec. (Chancery/Inf.), Manila, 1991–94; First Secretary: FCO, 1994–97; Washington, 1997–2000; FCO, 2000–03; Counsellor, FCO, 2003–04; Ambassador to Republic of Macedonia, 2004–07. Chm., Diplomatic Service Assoc., 2002–04. *Recreations:* history, recreational running, messing about in boats. *Address:* c/o Foreign and Commonwealth Office, King Charles Street, SW1A 2AH. *Club:* Bosham Sailing (W Sussex).

CHATTO, Beth, OBE 2002; VMH 1988; Creator and Managing Director of The Beth Chatto Gardens; *b* 27 June 1923; *d* of William George and Bessie Beatrice Little; *m* 1943, Andrew Edward Chatto (*d* 1999); two *d*. *Educ:* Colchester County High Sch.; Hockerill Training Coll. for Teachers. No formal horticultural educn; parents enthusiastic gardeners; husband's lifelong study of natural associations of plants was original inspiration in use of species plants in more natural groupings, thus introducing ecology into garden design; Sir Cedric Morris' knowledge and generosity with many rare plants from his rich collection at Benton End, Suffolk, became basis for gdns at Elmstead Market; began career demonstrating flower arranging; Beth Chatto Gardens, 1960–, Nursery, 1967–; a keen advocate of organic gardening and diet for over 40 yrs. Founder Mem., Colchester Flower Club (2nd Flower Club in England). Lectures throughout UK; lecture tours and talks: USA, 1983, 1984 and 1986; Holland and Germany, 1987; Australia and Toronto, 1989. DUniv Essex, 1988. Lawrence Meml Medal, RHS, 1988. *Publications:* The Dry Garden, 1978; The Damp Garden, 1982, rev. edn 2005; Plant Portraits, 1985; The Beth Chatto Garden Notebook, 1988; The Green Tapestry, 1989 (also USA); (with Christopher Lloyd) Dear Friend and Gardener: letters exchanged between Beth Chatto and Christopher Lloyd, 1998; The Gravel Garden, 2000; The Woodland Garden, 2002; articles in The Garden, The English Garden, Horticulture, Amer. Jl of Hort., Sunday Telegraph, and Hortus. *Recreations:* family, cooking, entertaining, music, reading—and always creating the garden. *Address:* The Beth Chatto Gardens, Elmstead Market, Colchester, Essex CO7 7DB. *T:* (01206) 822007.

CHATWANI, Jaswanti; Legal Chairman, Immigration Appeal Tribunal, 2000–03 (Vice President, 1992–2000); *b* 23 Nov. 1933; *d* of Keshavji Ramji Tanna and Shantaben Tanna; *m* 1953, Rajnikant Popatlal Chatwani; one *s* one *d*. *Educ:* Government Sch., Dar-es-Salaam, Tanzania. Called to the Bar, Lincoln's Inn, 1959; attached to Chopra & Chopra, Legal Practice, Mwanza, Tanzania, 1959–60; in private practice, Zanzibar, 1960–65; Sec. and Legal Aid Counsel, Tanganyika Law Soc., 1965–68; in private practice, Dar-es-Salaam, Tanzania, 1968–70; Sen. Immigration Counsellor, UKIAS, 1971–78; Legal Officer, then Sen. Complaints Officer, CRE, 1979–87; part-time Adjudicator, Immigration Appeals, 1980–87, full-time Adjudicator 1987–92. Mem., Judicial Studies Bd, Ethnic Minorities Adv. Cttee, 1991–94. *Recreations:* walking, travel, reading.

CHATWIN, (John) Malcolm, CEng, FIET; Chairman, Warrington Homes, since 2003; *b* 19 July 1945; *s* of John Edward Chatwin and Louie Valerie Chatwin; *m* 1969, Elizabeth Joy West; one *s* two *d. Educ:* City of London Sch.; University College London (BSc(Eng) Elect. Eng.). Operations Engr, LEB, 1969–73; Commercial Economist, Seeboard, 1973–77; Pricing Policy Manager, Electricity Council, 1977–79; Dep. Commercial Dir and Commercial Dir, N of Scotland Hydro-Electric Bd, 1980–87; Yorkshire Electricity: Dir, Business Planning, 1987–90; Commercial Dir, 1990–92; Chief Exec., 1992–97. Dir, Electricity Assoc., 1992–97; Chm., Regional Power Generators, 1992–94, 1996–97. Dir, Century Inns, 1995–99. *Recreations:* ski-ing, sailing.

CHAUDHRY, Mahendra Pal; MP, Fiji, 1987, 1992–99 and since 2001; Minister of Finance, National Planning, Sugar Industry and Public Utilities (Water and Energy) in the Interim Administration, Fiji, 2007; Prime Minister of Fiji, 1999–2000; *b* 2 Sept. 1942; *m* Virmati Frank; two *s* one *d. Educ:* Tavua Indian Sch.; Shri Vivekananda High Sch. Assistant, Res. Lab., Emperor Gold Mines, 1959–60; Office of the Auditor Gen., 1960–75 (Sen. Auditor, 1973–75); General Secretary: Fiji Public Service Assoc., 1970–99; Nat. Farmers' Union, 1978–. Asst Nat. Sec., 1975–87, Nat. Sec., 1988–92, Fiji TUC. Minister: of Finance, April–May 1987; of Finance, Public Enterprises, Sugar Industry and Information, 1999–2000. Fiji Labour Party: Founder Mem., 1985; Asst Sec.-Gen., 1985–94; Sec.-Gen. and Parly Leader, 1994–.

CHAUDHURI, Prof. Kirti Narayan, PhD; FBA 1990; FRHistS; External Professor of History, European University Institute, Florence; *b* 8 Sept. 1934; *s* of late Nirad C. Chaudhuri, CBE, FRSL, FRAS; *m* 1961, Surang Chaudhuri; one *s. Educ:* privately in India; London Univ. (BA Hons Hist., 1959; PhD 1961). Derby Postgrad. Schol., London Univ., 1959–61; School of Oriental and African Studies, London University: Res. Fellow in Econ. Hist., 1961–63; Lectr in Econ. Hist. of Asia, 1963–74; Reader, 1974–81; Prof. of Econ. Hist. of Asia, 1981–91; Chairman: S Asia Area Studies Centre, 1982–85; History Exam. Bd, 1982–87; Vasco da Gama Prof. of Hist. of European Expansion, European Univ. Inst., Florence, 1991–99; Director: Centre for Comparative Studies, Provence, 1999; Gallery Schifanoia, Mas de San Vitale, 1999. FRHistS 1993; MAE 1994. D. João de Castro Internat. History Prize. *Publications:* The English East India Company: the study of an early joint-stock company 1600–1640, 1965; The Economic Development of India under the East India Company 1814–58: a selection of contemporary writings, 1971; The Trading World of Asia and the English East India Company 1660–1760, 1978; Trade and Civilisation in the Indian Ocean: an economic history from the rise of Islam to 1750, 1985; Asia before Europe: the economy and civilisation in the Indian Ocean from the rise of Islam to 1750, 1990; From the Atlantic to the Arabian Sea, 1995; The Dream of the Unicorn in the Year of Geneviève, 1996; A Mediterranean Triptych, 1998; The Landscape of the Corvo, 1998; (ed jtly) Historia Expansão Portuguesa, 5 vols, 1998–99; The Sacrifice, 2000; Venezia, the Vision of the Blind Gladiator, 2000; Interlace, Variations on Ornamental Space, 2001; Polyphony, 2002; Notre Dame sous la Neige, 2002; Sea & Civilisation: a visual archive, 3 vols, 2003; Veneto, 2003; Capri: resurrection of the drowned Aphrodite, 2003; Avignon in July: a midnight and two afternoons in the life of Lady Georgina Saville, 2004; Form in an Arid Land: Sahara and the Maghreb, 2004; Tango in San Telmo, 2005; A Purple Land, 2005; Tree of Blood, 2005; Cleopatra in Tripolitania: an imaginary text in images, 2005; Islam and Space: a transcontinental visual narrative of space and architectonics, 3 vols, 2005; Roman Mediterranean and the Passion of Perpetua, 2006; Forms of Perception: point, straight line, curve, solid, monochrome, and colour, 2006; Garden of the Tuareg, 2006; Bodas de Sangre, 2006; Jaguar of Chaco, 2007; Entre Primavera y Invierno, 2007; Bailarinas del Camba, 2007; Jane and Idle Days in Patagonia, 2007; El Asesino del Rio Grande, 2007; contribs to Econ. Hist. Rev., Eng. Histl Rev., Jl of European Econ. Hist., Jl of RAS, Modern Asian Studies, TLS. *Recreations:* exploration, collecting modern prints, photography, wine tasting, designing typography and books, and hand-printing limited-edition books and prints. *Address:* Flat 8, 155 Arlington Road, NW1 7ET. *Club:* Athenæum.

CHAUNY de PORTURAS-HOYLE, Gilbert; Ambassador of Peru to the Kingdom of the Netherlands, Permanent Representative of Peru to Organisation for the Prohibition of Chemical Weapons, and Governor of Peru to Common Fund for Commodities, since 2007; *b* Lima, 8 March 1944; *m* 1971, Carmen Loreto; two *s* one *d. Educ:* UNI (BA Arch 1966); Pontificia Universidad Católica, Peru (BA Arts 1967). Peruvian Diplomatic Acad. (Dip. and Licentiate Internat. Relns 1969). Joined Peruvian Diplomatic Service, 1970: Third Secretary: Under-Secretariat for Political and Diplomatic Affairs, Dept of Europe, Africa, Asia and Oceania, Min. of Foreign Affairs, Lima, 1970–72; Bogotá, 1972–75; Second Sec., Perm. Representation to Internat. Orgns, Geneva, and Consul Gen., Geneva and Vaud, 1975–78; First Secretary: Head: of Ceremonials, Protocol Dept, 1978–79; OAS Dept, Dept for Internat. Orgns and Confs, 1979–80; Counsellor, Hd of Political Dept, Washington, 1980–84; Minister Counsellor: and Consul Gen., Toronto, 1984–86; Asst Dir for America, Min. of Foreign Affairs, 1986–88; Minister, Dir of Aeronautical and Space Affairs, Min. of Foreign Affairs, 1988–89 (Delegate to Internat. Civil Aviation Orgn, Montreal); Minister and Hd of Chancery, London, and Perm. Rep. to IMO, 1989–93 (Chargé d'Affaires, March–June 1989 and March–Nov. 1993); Ambassador: Dir Gen. of Special Pol Affairs, Min. of Foreign Affairs, 1993–95; to Austria, and concurrently to Slovenia, Slovakia and Turkey, 1995–2000; Perm. Rep. of Peru to UN Office, Vienna, UNIDO, IAEA and Comp. Nuclear Test-Ban Treaty Orgn, 1995–2000; Ambassador to UK and to Ireland, 2000–01; Nat. Dir. for Frontier Develt, Min. of Foreign Affairs, 2002–03; Under-Sec. for Internat. Cultural Affairs, Min. of Foreign Affairs, 2003–05; Ambassador to Hungary, and concurrently to Croatia and Bosnia-Herzegovina, 2005–07. President, National Commission: for Antarctic Affairs, 1993–95; for Biol Diversity, 1993–95; for Climatic Changes and Ozone, 1993–95. Member: Peruvian Inst. for Genealogical Res., 1962–; Peruvian Inst. Aerospace Law, 1994–2000. Mem., Confrérie des Chevaliers du Tastevin. Dir (Chancellor), Peruvian Assoc. of Kts of SMO, Malta. Kt 1988, Grand Cross of Merit, 2001, SMO Malta; Kt Comdr with Star, Constantinian Order of St George, 2000. Kt Comdr, Orden de Bogotá (Colombia), 1974; Official: Order of San Carlos (Colombia), 1975; Orden de Isabel la Católica (Spain), 1978; Grand Cross, Orden del Condor de los Andes (Bolivia), 1995; Gold Grand Cross, Honour Badge for Merit (Austria), 2000; Grand Cross, Orden al Mérito por Servicios Distinguidos (Peru), 2005. *Publications:* contrib. books and periodicals on internat. diplomatic relns, protocol, hist. of art, hist., and genealogy. *Recreations:* art and old map collecting, historical and genealogical research, tennis, bridge. *Address:* Lima Los Cedros 475, San Isidro, Lima 27, Peru; Embassy of Peru, Nassauplein 4, 2585 EA The Hague, The Netherlands. *Clubs:* Nacional, Regatas, Lima Golf (Lima); St Johanns (Vienna); Haagsche Club-Plaats Royaal (The Hague).

CHAUVIN, Yves; Research Director, Institut Français du Pétrole, 1991–95, now Honorary; *b* Menin, Belgium, 10 Oct. 1930; *m* 1960 (*d* 2004); two *s. Educ:* Ecole supérieure de chimie industrielle de Lyon. Research Engineer: Société Progil, 1958–60; Inst Français du Pétrole, 1960–95. Emeritus Dir of Res., Lab. de Chimie Organométallique de Surface, Ecole supérieure de chimie physique electronique de Lyon. Mem., Acad. des Scis, France, 2005. (Jtly) Nobel Prize for Chemistry, 2005. *Publications:*

articles in jls. *Address:* M Yves Chauvin, c/o Institut Français du Pétrole, 1 & 4 avenue de Bois-Préau, 92852 Rueil-Malmaison Cedex, France.

CHAUVIRÉ, Yvette; Commandeur de la Légion d'Honneur, 1988 (Officier, 1974); Commandeur des Arts et des Lettres, 1975; Grand Croix, Ordre National du Mérite, 1998 (Officier, 1972; Commandeur, 1981); ballerina assoluta, since 1950; *b* Paris, 22 April 1917. *Educ:* Ecole de la Danse de l'Opéra, Paris. Paris Opera Ballet, 1931; first major rôles in David Triomphant and Les Créatures de Prométhée; Danseuse étoile 1942; danced Istar, 1941; Monte Carlo Opera Ballet, 1946–47; returned to Paris Opera Ballet, 1947–49. Has appeared at Covent Garden, London; also danced in the USA, and in cities of Rome, Moscow, Leningrad, Berlin, Buenos Aires, Johannesburg, Milan, etc; official tours: USA 1948; USSR 1958, 1966, 1969; Canada 1967; Australia. Leading rôles in following ballets: Les Mirages, Lac des Cygnes, Sleeping Beauty, Giselle, Roméo et Juliette, Suite en Blanc, Le Cygne (St Saens), La Dame aux Camélias, etc; Giselle, Moscow, 1966 (guest for 125th anniversary celebration); acting rôle, Reine Léda, Amphitryon 38, Paris, 1976–77; La Comtessa de Doris in Raymonda, Paris, 1983. Choreographer: La Péri, Roméo et Juliette, Le Cygne; farewell performances: Paris Opera, Giselle, Nov. 1972, Petrouchka and The Swan, Dec. 1972; Berlin Opera, Giselle, 1973; Artistic and Tech. Adviser, Paris Opera, 1963–72, teacher of dance for style and perfection, 1970–; Acad. Internat. de la Danse, Paris, 1972–76; Artistic Dir, Acad. ARIMA, Kyoto, Japan, 1980–81. *Films:* La Mort du Cygne, 1937 (Paris); Carrousel Napolitain, 1953 (Rome); Dominique Delouche présente un grand portrait sur Yvette Chauviré, une Etoile pour l'exemple, 1988. *Publication:* Je suis Ballerine. *Recreations:* painting and drawing, collections of swans. *Address:* 21 Place du Commerce, Paris 75015, France.

CHAVASSE, Christopher Patrick Grant; *b* 14 March 1928; *s* of late Grant Chavasse and Maureen Shingler (*née* Whalley); *m* 1st, 1955, Audrey Mary Leonard (*d* 2003); two *s* one *d;* 2nd, 2004, Rosamund Ann Viney, *widow* of Elliott Viney. *Educ:* Bedford Sch.; Clare Coll., Cambridge (Exhibitioner; MA). Commissioned The Rifle Brigade, 1947; served in Palestine (despatches), 1948; RAFVR 1949. Admitted Solicitor, 1955; Partner: Jacobs & Greenwood, 1960–70; Woodham Smith, 1970–80; President, Holborn Law Soc., 1977–78. Hon. Liveryman, Worshipful Co. of Grocers, 1988– (Clerk, 1981–88). Chairman: NADFAS Tours Ltd, 1986–92; Totnes DFAS, 1993–96; Vice-President: NADFAS, 1992–97; Chiltern DFAS, 1986–. Hon. Steward of Westminster Abbey, 1950–; Treasurer, St Mary-le-Bow Church, 1981–88. Secretary: Governing Body of Oundle and Laxton Schs, 1981–88; The Grocers' Charity, 1981–88. Mem. Ct, Corp. of Sons of the Clergy, 1985–2003. *Publications:* Conveyancing Costs, 1971; Non-Contentious Costs, 1975; The Discretionary Items in Contentious Costs, 1980; various articles in Law Society's Gazette, New Law Jl, Solicitors Jl, and others. *Address:* Whistler's View, 5 Oving Road, Whitchurch, Bucks HP22 4JF. *Clubs:* Royal Air Force; Leander.

CHÁVEZ FRÍAS, Hugo Rafael; President of Venezuela, since 1999; *b* 28 July 1954; *s* of Hugo de los Reyes Chávez and Elena de Chávez; *m* Maria Isabel Rodriguez; two *s* three *d. Educ:* Liceo O'Leary, Barinas State; Venezuelan Military Acad., Caracas (grad. 1975); Univ. Simón Bolívar, Caracas. Paratrooper, Venezuelan Army (Lt-Col). Jt Founder, Movimiento Revolucionario Bolivariano 200, 1982; led failed mil. coup against Pres. Carlos Pérez, 1992 (imprisoned); Founder, Movimiento Quinta República, 1997. *Address:* Central Information Office of the Presidency, Torre Oeste 18°, Parque Central, Caracas 1010, Venezuela.

CHAYTOR, Sir Bruce Gordon, 9th Bt *cr* 1831, of Croft, Yorkshire and Witton Castle, Durham; *b* 31 July 1949; *s* of Herbert Gordon Chaytor and Mary Alice Chaytor (*née* Craven); *S* kinsman, Sir George Reginald Chaytor, 8th Bt, 1999, but his name does not appear on the Official Roll of the Baronetage; *m* 1969, Rosemary Lea Stephen (marr. diss. 1978); one *s* one *d. Heir:* *s* John Gordon Chaytor, *b* 17 Jan. 1973. *Address:* 2785 Sooke Road, Victoria, BC V9B 1Y8, Canada.

CHAYTOR, David Michael; MP (Lab) Bury North, since 1997; *b* 3 Aug. 1949; *m;* one *s* two *d. Educ:* Bury Grammar Sch.; Royal Holloway Coll., London (BA Hons 1970); Leeds Univ. (PGCE 1976); London Univ. (MPhil 1979). Sen. Staff Tutor, Manchester Coll. of Adult Educn, 1983–90; Hd, Dept of Continuing Educn, Manchester Coll. of Arts and Technology, 1993–97. Mem., Calderdale MBC, 1982–97. Contested (Lab) Calder Valley, 1987, 1992. *Address:* House of Commons, SW1A 0AA.

CHAZOT, Georges-Christian; international consultant; *b* 19 March 1939; *s* of late Raymond Chazot, banker and Suzanne Monnet; *m* 1962, Marie-Dominique Tremois, painter; one *s* two *d. Educ:* Lycée Gauthier; Lycée Bugeaud Algiers; Ecole Polytechnique, Paris; Univ. of Florida (MSEE 1964); Internat. Marketing Inst., Harvard, 1972. Joined Schlumberger Group, 1962; Electro-Mechanical Research, USA, 1962–65; Schlumberger Instrument and Systems, 1965–76; Alcatel Alsthom, 1977–92; Saft, 1977–88; Chairman and Chief Executive: Saft, 1984–88; Alcatel Business Systems, 1989–92; ADIA France, 1992–93; Gp Man. Dir, Eurotunnel, 1994–2000; Chairman: Prosegur France, 2003–05; Eurotunnel Development Ltd, 2002–04. Mem. Adv. Council, X-PM Transition Partners, 2001–; Mem. Bd, Giat Industries, 2002–. Dir, Actim, Paris, 1988–92. Treas., Fondn Franco Japonaise Sasakawa, 1990–; Vice-Chm., FM Radio Notre-Dame, 2001–; Dir and former Dir, internat. cos. Mem., Adv. Council, World Economic Forum, Switzerland, 1983–87; Vice-Pres., French Chamber of Commerce in London, 1995–2002. Vice-Chm., Hôpital Paris St Joseph, 2008–. Chevalier: Légion d'honneur, 1990; Ordre de St Gregoire Le Grand; Officier, Ordre National du Mérite (France), 1996. *Recreations:* sailing, ski-ing. *Address:* 24 rue des Réservoirs, Versailles 78000, France; *e-mail:* georgeschazot@ orange.fr. *Club:* UNCL (Union Nationale pour la Course au Large) (Paris).

CHEADLE, Rear Adm. Richard Frank, CB 2005; DL; Director, Atkins, since 2006; *b* 27 Jan. 1950; *s* of Marcus and Marion Cheadle; *m* 1972, Sonja Arntzen; one *s* one *d. Educ:* Peter Symonds Sch.; RNEC (MSc Marine Engrg). Joined RN, 1968; engrg appts in nuclear submarines, Renown, Dreadnought and Splendid, 1975–85; Dep. Sqn Engr, 1985–87; Hd, In Service Submarine Propulsion Systems, 1987–90; jsdc 1991–92; CSO (Nuclear), Rosyth, 1992–95; Director: Naval Manpower Develt, 1995–97; Nuclear Propulsion, 1997–2000; Comdr, Devonport Naval Base, 2000–02; COS, Second Sea Lord and Chief Naval Engrg Officer, 2003; Controller of the Navy and Dir, Land Maritime, 2003–06. Advr, Defence Cttee, H of C. Pres., Devon, RBL. DL Devon, 2008. *Recreations:* painting, golf, repairing broken machinery.

CHECKETTS, Sir David (John), KCVO 1979 (CVO 1969; MVO 1966); Squadron Leader, retired; an Extra Equerry to the Prince of Wales, since 1979; *b* 23 Aug. 1930; 3rd *s* of late Reginald Ernest George Checketts and late Frances Mary Checketts; *m* 1958, Rachel Leila Warren Herrick; one *s* three *d.* Flying Training, Bulawayo, Rhodesia, 1948–50; 14 Sqdn, Germany, 1950–54; Instructor, Fighter Weapons Sch., 1954–57; Air ADC to C-in-C Malta, 1958–59; 3 Sqdn, Germany, 1960–61; Equerry to Duke of Edinburgh, 1961–66, to the Prince of Wales, 1967–70; Private Sec. to the Prince of Wales, 1970–79. *Recreation:* ornithology. *Address:* Forges, Fulford Barnyard, Cullompton, Devon EX15 1TJ. *T:* (01884) 839779.

CHECKETTS, Guy Tresham, CBE 1982; Deputy Chairman and Managing Director, Hawker Siddeley International, 1975–90, retired; *b* 11 May 1927; *s* of John Albert and Norah Maud Checketts; *m* 1957, Valerie Cynthia Stanley; four *s*. *Educ:* Warwick Sch.; Birmingham Univ. (BScEng Hons). British Thompson Houston Co., Rugby, 1948–51; Brush Group, 1951–57; Hawker Siddeley International, 1957–90. Chm., SE Asia Trade Adv. Gp, 1979–83; Mem., BOTB, 1981–84. *Recreation:* sailing. *Club:* Royal Over-Seas League.

CHECKLAND, Sir Michael, Kt 1992; Director-General, BBC, 1987–92; Chairman, Higher Education Funding Council for England, 1997–2001; *b* 13 March 1936; *s* of Leslie and Ivy Florence Checkland; *m* 1st, 1960, Shirley Frances Corbett (marr. diss. 1983); two *s* one *d*; 2nd, 1987, Sue Zetter. *Educ:* King Edward's Grammar Sch., Fiveways, Birmingham; Wadham Coll., Oxford (BA Modern History; Hon. Fellow, 1989). FCMA; CCMI. Accountant: Parkinson Cowan Ltd, 1959–62; Thorn Electronics Ltd, 1962–64; BBC: Senior Cost Accountant, 1964; Head of Central Finance Unit, 1967; Chief Accountant, Central Finance Services, 1969; Chief Accountant, Television, 1971; Controller, Finance, 1976; Controller, Planning and Resource Management, Television, 1977; Director of Resources, Television, 1982; Dep. Dir-Gen., 1985; Director: BBC Enterprises, 1979–92 (Chm., 1986–87); Visnews, 1980–85; Nynex Cable Communications, 1995–97. President: Commonwealth Broadcasting Assoc., 1987–88; Birmingham & Midland Inst., 1994; Vice-President: RTS, 1985–94 (FRTS 1987); EBU, 1991–92; Methodist Conf., 1997; Mem., ITC, 1997–2003. Chairman: NCH, 1991–2001; Brighton Internat. Fest., 1993–2002; CBSO, 1995–2001; Director: Nat. Youth Music Theatre, 1992–2002; Wales Millennium Centre, 2003–. Chm., Horsham YMCA, 2005–. Trustee, Reuters, 1994–. Governor: Westminster Coll., Oxford, 1993–97; Birkbeck Coll., 1993–97; Brighton Univ., 1996–97 and 2001–07 (Chm., 2002–06); Wesley House, 2002–08. *Recreations:* sport, music, travel. *Address:* Orchard Cottage, Park Lane, Maplehurst, near Horsham, West Sussex RH13 6LL.

CHECKLEY, Prof. Stuart Arthur, FRCPsych; Consultant Psychiatrist, Maudsley Hospital, 1981–2001; Dean, 1989–2001, and Professor of Psychoneuroendocrinology, 1994–2001, now Emeritus, Institute of Psychiatry; *b* 15 Dec. 1945; *s* of Arthur William George Checkley and Hilda Dorothy Checkley; *m* 1970, Marilyn Jane Evans, BA; one *s* one *d*. *Educ:* St Albans Sch.; Brasenose Coll., Oxford (BA, BM BCh). FRCP, FRCPsych. House appts, London Hosp. and St Charles Hosp., 1970–73; Registrar in Psych., London Hosp., 1973–74; Maudsley Hospital: Registrar, 1974–76; Hon. Sen. Registrar, 1977–78; Hon. Consultant, 1980–81; research worker, supported by Wellcome Trust, 1978–81; Mapother Travelling Fellow, USA, 1979; Institute of Psychiatry: Sen. Lectr, 1979–81; Sen. Lectr, Metabolic Unit, 1985–94. Non-exec. Dir, S London and Maudsley NHS Trust, 1999–2001. FKC 2001. *Publications:* (ed) The Management of Depression, 1998; papers on treatment of depression and hormones in relation to depression. *Recreation:* bird watching.

CHEESEMAN, Prof. Ian Clifford, PhD; ARCS; CEng, FRAeS; Professor of Helicopter Engineering, University of Southampton, 1970–82, now Emeritus; consultant in aeronautical, acoustic and general engineering matters; *b* 12 June 1926; *s* of Richard Charles Cheeseman and Emily Ethel Clifford; *m* 1957, Margaret Edith Pither; one *s* two *d*. *Educ:* Andover Grammar Sch.; Imperial Coll. of Science and Technology. Vickers Supermarine Ltd, 1951–53; Aeroplane and Armament Estab., 1953–56; Atomic Weapons Res. Estab., 1956–58; Nat. Gas Turbine Estab., 1958–70. Res. Dir, 1983–87, Dir and Consultant, 1987–88, Stewart Hughes Ltd, Southampton. Pres., Airship Assoc., 1986–94. *Publications:* (contrib.) Airship Technology, 1999; contribs to Jl RAeS, Jl CIT, Jl Sound and Vibration, Procs Phys. Soc. 'A', Vertica. *Recreations:* dog breeding, gardening, photography, historical research. *Address:* Abbey View, Tarrant Keynston, Blandford Forum, Dorset DT11 9JE. *T:* (01258) 456877.

CHEESMAN, Colin; Chief Executive, Cheshire County Council, 1998–2002; *b* 8 Nov. 1946; *s* of John Hamilton Cheesman and Elsie Louisa Cheesman; *m* 1969, Judith Mary Tait; one *s* three *d*. *Educ:* Alleyn's Sch., Dulwich; Liverpool Univ. (LLB Hons). Admitted Solicitor, 1971. Portsmouth County BC, 1969–71; Notts CC, 1971–73; joined Cheshire CC, 1973; Group Director: Support Services, 1991–94; Information and Leisure Services, 1994–97. Clerk, Cheshire Lieutenancy and Sec. to Cheshire Adv. Cttee, 1998–2002; Sec. and Solicitor, Cheshire Fire Authy, 1998–2002; Sec., Cheshire Probation Bd, 1998–2002. Mem. Court, Univ. of Liverpool, 1999–2002. Hon. Sec., Parkinson's Disease Soc., 2007–. *Recreations:* reading, hill walking, keeping fit, theatre. *Address:* 7 Radnor Drive, Westminster Park, Chester CH4 7PS. *T:* (01244) 678866.

CHEETHAM, Anthony John Valerian; Co-Founder, and Chairman, Quercus Publishing plc, since 2005; *b* 12 April 1943; *s* of Sir Nicolas John Alexander Cheetham, KCMG; *m* 1st, 1969, Julia Rollason (marr. diss.); two *s* one *d*; 2nd, 1979, Rosemary de Courcy (marr. diss.); two *d*; 3rd, 1997, Georgina Capel. *Educ:* Eton Coll.; Balliol Coll., Oxford (BA). Editorial Dir, Sphere Books, 1968; Managing Director: Futura Publications, 1973; Macdonald Futura, 1979; Chm., Century Publishing, 1982–85; Man. Dir, Century Hutchinson, 1985; Chm. and Chief Exec., Random Century Gp, 1989–91; Chief Exec., Orion Books, subseq. Orion Publishing Gp Ltd, 1991–2003. *Publication:* Richard III, 1972. *Recreations:* walking, tennis, gardening. *Address:* 8 Morpeth Mansions, Morpeth Terrace, SW1P 1ER. *T:* (020) 7834 3684.

CHEETHAM, Prof. Anthony Kevin, FRS 1994; FRSC; Goldsmiths' Professor of Materials Science, University of Cambridge, since 2008 (Professor of Materials Science, 2007–08); Professor of Solid State Chemistry, Royal Institution, since 1986; Emeritus Student, Christ Church, Oxford, since 1991; *b* 16 Nov. 1946; *s* of Norman James Cheetham and Lilian Cheetham; *m* 1984, Janet Clare (*née* Stockwell); one *s* one *d*, and one *s* one *d* from a previous marriage. *Educ:* Stockport Grammar Sch.; St Catherine's Coll., Oxford (Hon. Scholar); Wadham Coll., Oxford (Sen. Scholar). BA (Chem.) 1968; DPhil 1971. University of Oxford: Cephalosporin Fellow, Lincoln Coll., 1971–74; Lectr in Inorganic Chem., St Hilda's Coll., 1971–85; Lectr in Chemical Crystallography, 1974–90; Tutor in Inorganic Chem., Christ Church, 1974–91; Reader in Inorganic Materials, 1990–91; University of California at Santa Barbara: Prof. of Materials, 1991–2007; Prof. of Chemistry, 1992–2007; Dir, Materials Res. Lab., 1992–2004; Dir, Internat. Center for Materials Res., 2004–07. Visiting Professor: Arizona State Univ., 1977; Univ. of California, Berkeley, 1979; Blaise Pascal Internat. Res. Prof., Paris, 1997–99; Vis. Foreign Scientist, Amer. Chem. Soc., 1981; Francqui Internat. Chair, Brussels, 2001–02. Humphry Davy Lectr, Royal Soc., 2003. Mem. Scientific Council, Institut Laue-Langevin, Grenoble, 1988–90. Dir, Gen. Funds Investment Trust plc, 1984–87; Founder, NGEN Enabling Technologies Fund, 2001. Foreign Mem., Indian Nat. Acad. of Scis, 1998; Foreign Fellow, Pakistan Acad. of Scis, 1997; Distinguished Fellow, Nehru Center for Advanced Scientific Res., Bangalore, 1999; Associate Fellow, Acad. of Scis for the Developing World (formerly Third World Acad. of Scis), 1999. Dr *hc* Versailles Saint-Quentin-en-Yvelines, 2006. Corday-Morgan Medal and Prize, 1982, Solid State Chemistry Award, 1988, Structural Chemistry Award, 1996, RSC; Bonner Chemiepreis, Univ. of Bonn, 2001; (jtly) Somiya Award, Internat. Union of Materials Res. Socs, 2004. *Publications:* Solid State Chemistry: techniques (with P. Day), 1986; Solid State Chemistry: compounds (with P. Day), 1992; contribs to sci. jls. *Recreations:* international affairs, golf. *Address:* Department of Materials Science and Metallurgy, University of Cambridge, Pembroke Street, Cambridge CB2 3QZ. *T:* (01223) 767061; *e-mail:* akc30@cam.ac.uk; (home) 1695 East Valley Road, Montecito, CA 93108, USA. *T:* (805) 5651211.

CHEETHAM, Prof. Juliet, OBE 1995; Member, Mental Health Tribunal for Scotland, since 2005; Sessional Inspector, Social Work Inspection Agency, since 2006; *b* 12 Oct. 1939; *d* of Harold Neville Blair and Isabel (*née* Sanders); *m* 1965, Christopher Paul Cheetham; one *s* two *d*. *Educ:* St Andrews Univ. (MA); Oxford Univ. (Dip. in Social and Admin. Studies). Qual. social worker. Probation Officer, Inner London, 1960–65; Lectr in Applied Social Studies, and Fellow of Green Coll., Oxford Univ., 1965–85; Prof. and Dir, Social Work Res. Centre, Stirling Univ., 1986–95, now Prof. Emeritus; Contract Res. Co-ordinator, SHEFC, 1996–97; Develt Officer, E Lothian Council, 1998; Social Work Comr, Mental Welfare Commn for Scotland, 1998–2005. Member: Cttee of Enquiry into Immigration and Youth Service, 1966–68; Cttee of Enquiry into Working of Abortion Act, 1971–74; NI Standing Adv. Commn on Human Rights, 1974–77; Central Council for Educn and Trng in Social Work, 1973–89; Commn for Racial Equality, 1977–84; Social Security Adv. Cttee, 1983–88; CNAA Social Scis Cttee, 1989–91; ESRC Res. Resources Bd, 1993–96. Vice-Chm., Social Policy and Social Work Panel, HEFCE Res. Assessment Exercise, 1996. *Publications:* Social Work with Immigrants, 1972; Unwanted Pregnancy and Counselling, 1977; Social Work and Ethnicity, 1982; Social Work with Black Children and their Families, 1986; (jtly) Evaluating Social Work Effectiveness, 1992; (jtly) The Working of Social Work, 1998; contrib. collected papers and prof. jls. *Recreation:* canal boats. *Address:* Peffermill House, 91 Peffermill Road, Edinburgh EH16 5UX. *T:* (0131) 661 0948.

CHEETHAM, Rt Rev. Richard Ian; *see* Kingston-upon-Thames, Area Bishop of.

CHEFFINS, Prof. Brian Robert; S. J. Berwin Professor of Corporate Law, and Fellow of Trinity Hall, University of Cambridge, since 1998; *b* 21 Jan. 1961; *s* of Ronald Ian Cheffins and Sylvia Joy Cheffins; *m* 1992, Joanna Hilary Thurstans; two *d*. *Educ:* Univ. of Victoria, BC (BA, LLB); Trinity Hall, Cambridge (LLM). Faculty of Law, University of British Columbia, Vancouver: Asst Prof., 1986–91; Associate Prof., 1991–97; Prof., 1997. Vis. Prof., Harvard Law Sch., 2002; Visiting Fellow: Duke Univ., 2000; (also Lectr) Stanford Law Sch., 2003. John S. Guggenheim Meml Fellow, 2002–03. *Publications:* Company Law: theory, structure and operation, 1997 (SPTL Prize, 1998); The Trajectory of (Corporate Law) Scholarship, 2004. *Address:* Faculty of Law, University of Cambridge, 10 West Road, Cambridge CB3 9DZ. *T:* (01223) 330084; *e-mail:* brc21@cam.ac.uk.

CHELMSFORD, 4th Viscount *cr* 1921, of Chelmsford, co. Essex; **Frederic Corin Piers Thesiger;** Baron Chelmsford 1858; *b* 6 March 1962; *o s* of 3rd Viscount Chelmsford and of Clare Rendle, *d* of Dr G. R. Rolston; *S* father, 1999; *m* 2002, Charlotte, *d* of Patrick Robin and Madeleine de Gerault de Langalarie; one *s*. *Heir: s* Hon. Frederic Thesiger, *b* 9 Feb. 2006. *Address:* 4/4 Hampstead Hill Gardens, NW3 2PL.

CHELMSFORD, Bishop of, since 2003; **Rt. Rev. John Warren Gladwin;** *b* 30 May 1942; *s* of Thomas Valentine and Muriel Joan Gladwin; *m* 1981, Lydia Elizabeth Adam. *Educ:* Hertford Grammar School; Churchill Coll., Cambridge (BA History and Theology, MA 1969); St John's Coll., Durham (Dip. Theol). Asst Curate, St John the Baptist Parish Church, Kirkheaton, Huddersfield, 1967–71; Tutor, St John's Coll., Durham and Hon. Chaplain to Students, St Nicholas Church, Durham, 1971–77; Director, Shaftesbury Project on Christian Involvement in Society, 1977–82; Secretary, Gen. Synod Board for Social Responsibility, 1982–88; Prebendary, St Paul's Cathedral, 1984–88; Provost of Sheffield, 1988–94; Bishop of Guildford, 1994–2003. Mem., Gen. Synod of C of E, 1990–. Jt Pres., Church Nat. Housing Coalition, 1997–; Chm. Bd, Christian Aid, 1998–2008. *Publications:* God's People in God's World, 1979; The Good of the People, 1988; Love and Liberty, 1998. *Recreations:* gardening, travel, beekeeping. *Address:* Bishopscourt, Margaretting, Ingatestone, Essex CM4 0HD. *T:* (01277) 352001, *Fax:* (01277) 355374; *e-mail:* bishopscourt@chelmsford.anglican.org.

CHELMSFORD, Dean of; *see* Judd, Very Rev. P. S. M.

CHELSEA, Viscount; Edward Charles Cadogan; *b* 10 May 1966; *s* and *heir* of 8th Earl Cadogan, *qv*; *m* 1990, Katharina Johanna Ingeborg, *d* of Rear-Adm. D. P. A. Hülsemann; two *s* one *d*. *Educ:* St David's Coll., Llandudno. Joined RAF, 1987; served Germany, UK and Cyprus; Flt Lt. Gulf War Medal with Clasp, 1991. *Recreations:* country pursuits, skiing, rock climbing, hill walking. *Heir: s* Hon. George Edward Charles Diether Cadogan, *b* 24 Sept. 1995. *Club:* Royal Air Force.

CHELTENHAM, Archdeacon of; *see* Ringrose, Ven. H. S.

CHELTON, Captain Lewis William Leonard, RN; Secretary, Engineering Council, 1987–97; *b* 19 Dec. 1934; *s* of Lewis Walter Chelton and Doris May Chelton (*née* Gamblin); *m* 1957, Daphne Joan Landon; three *s*. *Educ:* Royal Naval College, Dartmouth. Called to the Bar, Inner Temple, 1966. Entered RN as Cadet, 1951; served in ships and shore estabts, home and abroad; Fleet Supply Officer, 1979–81; Captain, 1981; Chief Naval Judge Advocate, 1982–84; retired (voluntarily), 1987. Sec., 1997–2007, Treas., 1997–, Hatch Beauchamp and Dist Cons. Assoc.; Dep. Chm., Taunton Constituency Cons. Assoc., 1999–2004. Vice-Chm., R. S. Surtees Soc. Gov., Bruton Sch. for Girls, 1999–. Mem., Hatch Beauchamp PCC, 1997–. *Recreations:* shooting, gardening, country life. *Address:* Palmers Green House, Hatch Beauchamp, near Taunton, Som TA3 6AE. *T:* (01823) 480221. *Club:* Farmers'.

CHENERY, Peter James; General Manager, Royal Anniversary Trust, since 2007; *b* 24 Oct. 1946; *s* of late Dudley James Chenery and Brenda Dorothy (*née* Redford); *m* 1979, Alice Blanche Faulder; three *d*. *Educ:* Forest Sch.; Christ Church, Oxford (MA); SOAS, London Univ. (Cert. in Arabic and Islamic Studies). Teacher, Ghana Teaching Service, 1967–70; joined British Council, 1970: Amman, 1971–73; Middle East Dept, 1973–76; Iran, 1976; Riyadh, 1977; Freetown, 1978–80; Jedda, 1981–84; Representative, Sana'a, 1984–88; Munich, 1988–90; Sec. of the Council and Hd of Public Affairs, 1990–97; Director and Cultural Counsellor: Greece, 1997–2000; Canada, 2000–06. Mem. British Cttee and Hon. Treas., UK-Canada Colloquia, 2006–. Associate Mem., St Antony's Coll., Oxford, 2000. FRSA 1996. *Publication:* (contrib.) The International Encyclopaedia of Cheese, 2007. *Recreations:* amusing conversation, beers of the world, early Greek and English coins, the works of Lord Byron. *Address:* c/o Royal Anniversary Trust, Caxton House, Tothill Street, SW1H 9NA. *Club:* Leander.

CHENEVIX-TRENCH, Jonathan Charles Stewart; Chief Operating Officer, Institutional Securities Group, since 2007; *b* 24 March 1961; *s* of Anthony Chenevix-Trench and Elizabeth (*née* Spicer); *m* 1998, Lucy Ward; two *s* two *d*. *Educ:* Eton Coll.; Merton Coll., Oxford (BA Lit.Hum. 1984). Morgan Stanley International, 1984–: Vice Pres., Financial Engrg, 1990–92; Exec. Dir, Overall Risk Manager for Eur. Derivative Products, 1992–94; Man. Dir, 1994–99; Hd, Fixed Income in Europe, 1999–2004; Global

Hd, Interest Rates and Foreign Exchange, 2000–05; Chm., 2006–07. *Recreations:* reading, outdoor activities, gardening, natural history. *Address:* Morgan Stanley International, 25 Cabot Square, Canary Wharf, E14 4QA. *Clubs:* Pratt's, Walbrook.

CHENEY, Richard Bruce; Vice-President of the United States of America, 2001–09; *b* 30 Jan. 1941; *s* of Richard H. Cheney and Marjorie Dickey Cheney; *m* 1964, Lynne Ann Vincent; two *d. Educ:* Casper Elementary Sch.; Natrona County High Sch.; Univ. of Wyoming (BA 1965; MA 1966); Univ. of Wisconsin. Public service, Wyoming, 1965–69; Federal service, 1969–73; Vice-Pres., Bradley Woods, 1973–74; Dep. Asst to Pres. Ford, 1974–75; Asst to Pres. Ford and White House Chief of Staff, 1975–77; Mem. (Republican) for Wyoming House of Representatives, 1978–89; Chm., Repub. Policy Cttee, 1981, Repub. House Conf., 1987; Repub. House Whip, 1988; Sec. of Defense, USA, 1989–93; Mem., Cttees on Interior and Insular Affairs, Intelligence, Iran Arms Deals. Sen. Fellow, Amer. Enterprise Inst., 1993–95. Chm. Bd, and CEO, Halliburton Co., 1995–2000. *Publication:* (with Lynne V. Cheney) Kings of the Hill, 1983. *Address:* c/o The White House, Washington, DC 20501, USA.

CHÉRIF, Taïeb, PhD; Secretary General, International Civil Aviation Organization, since 2003; *b* 29 Dec. 1941; *m* 1971, Meryem Elkaouakibi; three *s. Educ:* Univ. d'Alger, Algiers (BMaths); École nationale de l'aviation civile, Toulouse (Dip. Aeronautical Engrg); Cranfield Inst. of Technology (MSc Air Transport; PhD Air Transport Econs). Various positions of responsibility, Civil Aviation Authy, Algeria, 1971–92; State Sec. for Higher Educn, Algeria, 1992–94; civil aviation consultant, 1995–97; Rep. of Algeria, Council, ICAO, 1998–2003. *Address:* International Civil Aviation Organization, 999 University Street, Montreal, QC H3C 5H7, Canada. *T:* (514) 9548041, *Fax:* (514) 9546077; *e-mail:* secgen@icao.int.

CHERNAIK, Judith Sheffield, Hon. OBE 2002; PhD; writer; Founder and Co-Editor, Poems on the Underground, since 1986; *b* 24 Oct. 1934; *d* of Reuben Sheffield and Gertrude Lapidus; *m* 1956, Warren Lewis Chernaik; one *s* two *d. Educ:* Cornell Univ. (BA); Yale Univ. (PhD). Instr in English, Columbia Univ., 1963–65; Asst Prof. of English, Tufts Univ., 1965–69 (Scholar, Radcliffe Inst., 1966–68); Lectr, QMW, Univ. of London, 1975–88. Writer: features and documentaries for BBC Radio; The Two Marys (play), perf. in London and Bologna, 1997. Fellow, Amer. Council of Learned Socs, 1972. *Publications:* The Lyrics of Shelley, 1972; *novels:* Double Fault, 1975; The Daughter, 1979; Leah, 1987; Mab's Daughters, 1991 (US title, Love's Children, 1992; trans Italian, 1997); *poetry anthologies:* (ed jtly) 100 Poems on the Underground, 1991, (ed) 10th edn, Poems on the Underground, 2001; (ed) Reflecting Families, 1995; (ed jtly) New Poems on the Underground, 2004, new edn 2006; (ed) Carnival of the Animals, 2005; reviews and essays in TLS, The Times, New York Times, Guardian, etc. *Recreations:* chamber music, travel. *Address:* 124 Mansfield Road, NW3 2JB.

CHERRY, Alan Herbert, CBE 2003 (MBE 1984); DL; FRICS; Founder Director, 1971, and Chairman, since 1981, Countryside Properties plc; *b* 4 Aug. 1933; *s* of William Alfred Cherry and Helen Grace (*née* Parrish); *m* 1976, Fay Angela Robbins; two *s. Educ:* Mayfield Sch. Founder Partner, Bairstow Eves, 1958–81; Dep. Chm., Workspace Gp plc, 1987–2004. Non-exec. Dir, MEPC Ltd, 2006–. Member: Inquiry into British Housing, 1985–87; Urban Task Force, 1998–99. Dir, E of England Investment Agency, 1997–2002; Mem. Bd, E of England Develt Agency, 1998–2002; Chm., E of England, CBI, 2001–03. Nat. Pres., Home Builders' Fedn, 1988. Chm. Govs, Anglia Poly. Univ., 1988–2002. Hon. MRTPI 1991. DL Essex, 2002. *Recreations:* ski-ing, walking, swimming. *Address:* (office) Countryside House, The Drive, Brentwood, Essex CM13 3AT. *T:* (01277) 260000.

CHERRY, Bridget Katherine, OBE 2003; FSA; Editor: Buildings of England, 1983–2002; Buildings of Scotland, Ireland and Wales, 1991–2002; *b* 17 May 1941; *d* of Norman Stayner Marsh, *qv*; *m* 1966, John Cherry, *qv*; one *s* one *d. Educ:* Oxford High Sch. for Girls; Lady Margaret Hall, Oxford (BA Modern Hist.); Courtauld Inst. of Art, Univ. of London (Dip. Hist. of Art). FSA 1980. Asst Librarian, Conway Library, Courtauld Inst., 1964–68; Res. Asst to Sir Nikolaus Pevsner, Buildings of England, 1968–83. Mem., Royal Commn on Historical Monuments of England, 1987–94; English Heritage: Comr, 1992–2001; Mem., Adv. Cttee, 2003–; Mem., London Adv. Cttee, 1985–99; Mem., Historic Built Environment (formerly Buildings) Adv. Cttee, 1986–2003. Trustee: Sir John Soane's Mus., 1994–; Historic Royal Palaces, 2003–. Hon. FRIBA 1993. *Publications:* reviser or part author, 2nd edns, Buildings of England series, incl. Wiltshire, 1975, Hertfordshire, 1977, London 2: South, 1983, Devon, 1989, London 3: North West, 1991, London 4: North, 1998, London 5: East, 2005; articles and reviews on arch. subjects in learned jls. *Recreation:* walking. *Address:* 58 Lancaster Road, N4 4PT.

CHERRY, Colin; Director of Operations, Inland Revenue, 1985–90; *b* 20 Nov. 1931; *s* of late Reginald Cherry and Dorothy (*née* Brooks); *m* 1958, Marjorie Rose Harman; two *d. Educ:* Hymers Coll., Hull. Joined Inland Revenue, 1950; HM Inspector of Taxes, 1960; Under Sec., 1985. Fiscal Advr, IMF, 1994–99. Chm., CS Retirement Fellowship, 1992–94. *Recreations:* music, chrysanthemums, photography.

CHERRY, John, FSA, FRHistS; Keeper, Department of Medieval and Modern Europe, British Museum, 1998–2002; *b* 5 Aug. 1942; *s* of Edwin Lewis Cherry and Vera Edith Blanche (*née* Bunn); *m* 1966, Bridget Katherine Marsh (*see* B. K. Cherry); one *s* one *d. Educ:* Portsmouth Grammar Sch.; Christ Church, Oxford (Open Scholar 1960, MA). British Museum: Asst Keeper, Dept of British and Medieval Antiquities, 1964–69; Asst Keeper, 1969–81, Dep. Keeper, 1981–98, Dept of Medieval and Later Antiquities. Dir, British Archaeological Assoc., 1977–82; Vice Pres., Soc. of Antiquaries of London, 1996–2000 (Sec., 1986–96); Pres., Soc. of Jewellery Historians, 2006–. Vis. Fellow, All Souls Coll., Oxford, 2003. Mem., Treasure Valuations Cttee, DCMS, 2006–. Chm., Emery Walker Trust, 2007– (Trustee, 1999–); Trustee, York Museums Trust, 2002–. *Publications:* (jtly) The Ring from Antiquity to the 20th Century, 1981; (ed with I. H. Longworth) Archaeology in Britain since 1945, 1986; Medieval Decorative Art, 1991; Goldsmiths, 1992; The Middleham Jewel and Ring, 1994; (ed) Mythical Beasts, 1995; (ed with M. Caygill) Sir Augustus Wollaston Franks: Collecting and the British Museum, 1997; Medieval Love Poetry, 2005; articles in learned jls on topics of archaeology and collecting. *Address:* 58 Lancaster Road, N4 4PT. *T:* (020) 7272 0578.

CHERRY, John Mitchell; QC 1988; a Recorder, 1987–2003; *b* 10 Sept. 1937; *s* of John William and Dorothy Mary Cherry; *m* 1972, Eunice Ann Westmoreland; one *s* two *d* (and one *s* decd). *Educ:* Cheshunt Grammar Sch.; Council of Legal Education. Called to the Bar, Gray's Inn, 1961. Mem., Criminal Injuries Compensation Bd, 1989–2002; Legal Mem., Mental Health Review Tribunals, 2002–. *Recreations:* cricket, Rugby, food, wine. *Address:* Winterton, Turkey Street, Bulls Cross, Enfield, Middx EN1 4RJ. *T:* (01992) 719018.

CHERRYMAN, John Richard; QC 1982; *b* 7 Dec. 1932; *s* of Albert James and Mabel Cherryman; *m* 1963, Anna Greenleaf Collis; three *s* one *d. Educ:* Farnham Grammar Sch.; London School of Economics (LLB Hons); Harvard Law Sch. Called to Bar, Gray's Inn, 1955, Bencher, 1988. *Recreations:* restoring old houses in Italy, music, theatre. *Club:* Travellers.

CHESHAM, 6th Baron, *cr* 1858; **Nicholas Charles Cavendish;** *b* 7 Nov. 1941; *s* of 5th Baron Chesham, TD, PC and Mary Edmunds, *d* of late David G. Marshall; *S* father, 1989; *m* 1st, 1965, Susan Donne Beauchamp (marr. diss. 1969); 2nd, 1973, Suzanne Adrienne, *d* of late Alan Gray Byrne; two *s. Educ:* Eton. Chartered Accountant. Capt. of the Yeoman of the Guard (Dep. Govt Chief Whip in H of L), 1995–97. *Recreations:* tennis, ski-ing, shooting. *Heir: s* Hon. Charles Gray Compton Cavendish [*b* 11 Nov. 1974; *m* 2002, Sarah Elizabeth, *d* of Bruce Dawson; one *s* one *d*]. *Address:* The Old Post House, Church Street, Ropley, Alresford, Hants SO24 0DR. *Clubs:* Pratt's; Australian (Sydney); Royal Sydney Golf.

CHESHER, Prof. Andrew Douglas, FBA 2001; Professor of Economics, University College London, since 1999; *b* 21 Dec. 1948; *s* of late Douglas George Chesher and of Eileen Jessie Chesher (*née* Arnott); *m* 1st, 1971, Janice Margaret Elizabeth Duffield (marr. diss.); two *s*; 2nd, 2000, Valérie Marie Rose Jeanne Lechene; two *d. Educ:* Whitgift Sch.; Univ. of Birmingham (BSocSc Maths, Econs and Stats). Res. Associate, Acton Soc., 1970–71; Lectr in Econometrics, Univ. of Birmingham, 1972–83; Prof. of Econometrics, 1984–99, Hd, Dept of Econs, 1987–90 and 1996–98, Univ. of Bristol; Dir, Centre for Microdata Methods and Practice, Inst. for Fiscal Studies and Dept of Econs, UCL, 2000–. Vis. Prof., Univ. of Bristol, 2000–; Res. Fellow, Inst. for Fiscal Studies, 2001–. Mem. Council, ESRC, 2001–05 (Mem., 1996–2000, Vice-Chm., 1997–2000, Res. Resources Bd; Chm., Res. Grants Bd, 2001–05). Mem. Cttee, Nat. Food Survey, 1987–. Mem. Council, REconS, 1998–2004. Governor, NIESR, 2002–. Fellow, Econometric Soc., 1999. Associate Editor: Econometrica, 1990–96 and 2000–03; Jl Econometrics, 1995–2003; Econ. Jl, 1997–2000; Jl Royal Statistical Soc., Series A, 1999–2001; Co-Ed., Econometric Soc. Monograph Series, 2001–. *Publications:* (with R. Harrison) Vehicle Operating Costs in Developing Countries, 1987; contribs to learned jls in econs and stats. *Address:* Woodcroft, Foxcombe Lane, Boars Hill, Oxford OX1 5DH.

CHESHIRE, Dr (Christopher) Michael, FRCP; Consultant Physician, Manchester Royal Infirmary, since 1983; Clinical Vice-President, Royal College of Physicians, since 2007 (Censor, 2006–07); *b* 18 July 1946; *s* of Gordon Sydney Cheshire and Vera Cheshire; *m* 1970, Jane Mary Cordle; one *s* one *d. Educ:* Manchester Univ. (BSc Hons 1969; MB ChB Hons 1976). DCH 1979; FRCP 1990. House Officer, Medicine and Surgery, Manchester Royal Infirmary, 1976–77; Senior House Officer: Cardiothoracic Medicine, Wythenshawe, 1977–78; Paediatrics, Univ. Hosp., S Manchester, 1978–79; Medicine, Manchester Royal Infirmary, 1979–80; Lectr in Geriatric Medicine, Univ. Hosp., S Manchester, 1980–83; Med. Dir, 1993–97, Dir of Educn, 1997–2005, Central Manchester Healthcare NHS Trust; Clinical Dir of Service Redesign, 2005–06, Clinical Head of Intermediate Care, 2006–07, Central Manchester PCT. Chairman: NW, British Geriatrics Soc., 1998–2001; Educn Gp, British Assoc. of Med. Managers, 1998–2001. *Publications:* contribs on topics of medicine and management. *Recreations:* swimming, reading novels, garden, family. *Address:* 38 The Crescent, Davenport, Stockport SK3 8SN. *T:* (0161) 483 2972.

CHESHIRE, Lt Col Colin Charles Chance, OBE 1993; Secretary General, International Confederation of Fullbore Rifle Associations, since 2003; *b* 23 Aug. 1941; *s* of Air Chief Marshal Sir Walter Graemes Cheshire, GBE, KCB and Mary Cheshire (*née* Chance), DL; *m* 1st, 1968, Cherida Evelyn (marr. diss. 1975), *d* of Air Chief Marshal Sir Wallace Hart Kyle, GCB, KCVO, CBE, DSO, DFC; one *s* one *d*; 2nd, 1976, Angela, *d* of D. Fulcher. *Educ:* Worksop Coll. Royal Tank Regiment: served Borneo, Singapore, Malaysia, BAOR, NI, UK; Armour Sch., Bovington Camp, 1968; RMCS, 1972–73; Staff Coll., Camberley, psc† 1974; Bde Major, RAC, HQI (BR) Corps, 1978–80; Lt Col, 1980; retd 1981. Sales and Marketing Manager: Vickers Instruments Ltd, 1981–83; Army Systems, Ferranti Computer Systems, 1983–85; Sales and Mktg Dir, Wallop Gp, and Man. Dir, Walloptronics Ltd, 1985–87; Bursar, Oundle Sch., 1987–95; Chief Exec., NRA, 1995–2002. Mem., Exec. Cttee, Independent Schs Bursars Assoc., 1992–95. Chm., GB Target Shooting Fedn, 1994–97; Mem., British Rifle Team, 1971– (Captain, 1991, 1992, 1994, 1995, Vice Captain, 1982, 1999); Winner, World Long Range Rifle Team Championships, Palma Match, 1992, 1995. Mem., HAC, 1960–. Mem., Guild of Sports Internationalists, 1998–2002 (Middle Warden, 2001). FCMI (FIMgt 1985). *Publication:* History and Records of the World Long Range Rifle Championships - the Palma Match 1876 to date, 1992. *Recreations:* rifle shooting, golf, Freemasonry. *Address:* Santa Marina No 22, PO Box 91, 7743 Psematismenos Village, Larnaca, Cyprus. *T:* (24) 333380.

See also Sir J. A. Cheshire.

CHESHIRE, Ian Michael; Chief Executive, Kingfisher plc, since 2008; *b* 6 Aug. 1959; *s* of Donald and Pamela Cheshire; *m* 1984, Kate Atherton; two *s* one *d. Educ:* King's Sch., Canterbury; Christ's Coll., Cambridge (Schol.; BA 1st Cl. Hons Law and Econs 1980). Partner, Piper Trust Ltd, 1992–95; Gp Commercial Dir, Sears plc, 1995–98; Kingfisher plc, 1998–: Strategy Dir, 1998–2000; Dir, 2000–; Chief Executive Officer, eKingfisher, 2000–03; Internat. and Develt, 2003–05; Chief Exec., B&Q plc, 2005–08. Chm., Skillsmart Retail, 2004–06; non-executive Director: HIT Entertainment, 1998–2000; Bradford & Bingley plc, 2003–. Chm. Trustees, Medicinema (charity), 2003–. Chm., Govs, Ernest Bevin Coll., 2000–. FRSA 1999; MInstD 1992. *Recreations:* reading, arts, music, sailing, ski-ing. *Address:* *e-mail:* iancheshire@kingfisher.com. *Clubs:* Reform; Bembridge Sailing.

CHESHIRE, Prof. Jennifer Lilian, PhD; Professor of Linguistics, Queen Mary, University of London, since 1996; *b* 26 Feb. 1946; *d* of Sydney Harold Russell and Elsie Millicent Russell; *m* 1970, Paul Charles Cheshire; one *s* one *d. Educ:* London Sch. of Econs (BA Hons 1st cl. French and Linguistics 1971); Univ. of Reading (PhD 1979). Lectr, Univ. of Bath, 1980–83; Lectr, then Sen. Lectr, Birkbeck Coll., London, 1983–91; Prof. of English Linguistics, Univ. of Fribourg, 1991–96. Member: ESRC Bd of Examiners, 1999–2003; ESRC Recognition Exercise, Linguistics, 2001, 2005; Linguistics Panel, 2001 and 2008 RAEs; NZ Peer-based Review Funding Exercise, Humanities and Law Panel, 2003 and 2006. Gov., Raines Foundn Sch., 1998–. *Publications:* Variation in an English Dialect, 1982; English Around the World: sociolinguistic perspectives, 1991; (with P. Trudgill) A Reader in Sociolinguistics, 1998; (with D. Britain) Social Dialectology, 2003; articles in Jl of Sociolinguistics, Language and Educn, Language in Society, etc. *Recreations:* mountain walking, cinema. *Address:* Department of Linguistics, School of Modern Languages, Queen Mary, University of London, Mile End Road, E1 4NS. *T:* (020) 7882 8923, *Fax:* (020) 8980 5400; *e-mail:* J.L.Cheshire@qmul.ac.uk.

CHESHIRE, Air Chief Marshal Sir John (Anthony), KBE 1995 (CBE 1991; OBE 1982); CB 1994; FRAeS; Lieutenant-Governor and Commander-in-Chief, Jersey, 2001–06; *b* 4 Sept. 1942; *s* of Air Chief Marshal Sir Walter Cheshire, GBE, KCB and Lady Cheshire; *m* 1964, Shirley Ann Stevens; one *s* one *d. Educ:* Ipswich Sch.; Worksop Coll.; RAF Coll., Cranwell. Operational Flying Duties, UK and Singapore, 1964–70; Air Ops Officer, Special Forces, 1971–73; Canadian Forces Staff Coll., 1973–74; Operational Flying Duties, Special Forces, 1975–76; Air Plans, MoD, 1976–79; Commander: Air

Wing, Brunei, 1980–82; RAF Lyneham, 1983–85; Plans Br., HQ Strike Command, 1986–87; Defence and Air Attaché, Moscow, 1988–90; Dep. Comdt, RAF Staff Coll., 1991–92; ACOS (Policy), SHAPE, 1992–94; UK Mil. Rep., HQ NATO, 1995–97; C-in-C, Allied Forces NW Europe, 1997–2000. KStJ 2002. *Recreations:* squash, tennis, golf, field shooting. *Address:* Little Court, Batcombe, Som BA4 6HF. *Club:* Royal Air Force.
See also C. C. C. Cheshire.

CHESHIRE, Michael; *see* Cheshire, C. M.

CHESSELLS, Sir Arthur David, (Sir Tim), Kt 1993; Chairman of Trustees, British Telecommunications Pension Scheme, 1999–2007; *b* 15 June 1941; *s* of late Brig. Arthur Chessells and Carmel Mary (*née* McGinnis); *m* 1966, Katharine, *d* of Dick and Rachel Goodwin; two *s* two *d. Educ:* Stonyhurst Coll. CA 1965. Partner, Arthur Young, 1972–89; Mem., Kent AHA, 1979–82; Vice-Chm., Tunbridge Wells HA, 1982–88; Mem., SE Thames RHA, 1988–90; Chairman: NE Thames RHA, 1990–92; London Implementation Gp, 1992–95; Legal Aid Bd, 1995–2000. Non-exec. Mem., NHS Policy Bd, 1992–95. Director: Odgers and Co. Ltd, 1989–95; Price and Pierce Inc., 1993–97; Dixons Gp, 1995–2001; Care UK, 1995–2005; Hermes Pension Mgt, 1999–2007 (Chm., 1999–2004), and other cos. Chm., Nat. Approval Council for Security Systems, 1995–99. Mem. Council, St Christopher's Hospice, 1989–92. Trustee: Kent Community Housing Trust, 1990–95; Stonyhurst Charitable Fund, 1980–93; Chatham Historic Dockyard, 1992–97; Charities Aid Foundn, 1998–2005; Chm. Trustees, Horder Centre for Arthritis, 2000–; Chm. Trustees, Guy's and St Thomas' Charitable Foundn, 1996–2006. *Recreations:* reading, shooting, gardening. *Address:* Oakleigh, Catts Hill, Mark Cross, Crowborough TN6 3NQ. *Club:* Carlton.
See also J. M. Chessells.

CHESSELLS, Prof. Judith Mary, OBE 2004; MD; FRCP, FRCPath; Leukaemia Research Fund Professor of Haematology and Oncology, Institute of Child Health, London University, 1988–2002; *b* 30 Dec. 1938; *d* of late Brig. Arthur Edgar Chessells and Carmel Mary Chessells (*née* McGinnis); *m* 1969, Dr Gerald McEnery; one *d. Educ:* Sacred Heart Convent, Brighton; London Hosp. Med. Coll., London Univ. (MB BS Hons; MD). Lectr in Haematology, Inst. of Child Health, 1972–73; Consultant Haematologist, Hosp. for Sick Children, Great Ormond St, 1973–87, Hon. Consultant, 1988–2002. FRCPCH 1997. *Publications:* contrib. to learned jls. *Recreations:* theatre, literature.
See also Sir A. D. Chessells.

CHESSELLS, Sir Tim; *see* Chessells, Sir A. D.

CHESSHYRE, (David) Hubert (Boothby), CVO 2004 (LVO 1988); FSA; Clarenceux King of Arms, since 1997; Secretary, Most Noble Order of the Garter, 1988–2003; Registrar of the College of Arms, 1992–2000; *b* 22 June 1940; *e s* of late Col Hubert Layard Chesshyre and Katharine Anne (*née* Boothby), Canterbury, Kent. *Educ:* King's Sch., Canterbury; Trinity Coll., Cambridge (Choral Clerk; MA); Christ Church, Oxford (DipEd 1967). FSA 1977; FHS 1990. Taught French in England and English in France, at intervals 1962–67; wine merchant (Moët et Chandon and Harvey's of Bristol), 1962–65; Hon. Artillery Co., 1964–65 (fired salute at funeral of Sir Winston Churchill, 1965); Green Staff Officer at Investiture of the Prince of Wales, 1969; Rouge Croix Pursuivant, 1970–78, and on staff of Sir Anthony Wagner, Garter King of Arms, 1971–78; Chester Herald of Arms, 1978–95; Norroy and Ulster King of Arms, 1995–97. Mem., Westminster Abbey Fabric Commn (formerly Architectural Adv. Panel), 1985–2003. Member: Council, Heraldry Soc., 1973–85; Bach Choir, 1979–93; Madrigal Soc., 1980–; London Docklands Singers, 2002–. Hon. Genealogist to Royal Victorian Order, 1987–. Lectr, NADFAS, 1982–2002. Lay Clerk, Southwark Cathedral, 1971–2003. Freeman: City of London, 1975; Musicians' Co., 1994 (Liveryman, 1995–). *Publications:* (Eng. lang. editor) C. A. von Volborth, Heraldry of the World, 1973; The Identification of Coats of Arms on British Silver, 1978; (with A. J. Robinson) The Green: a history of the heart of Bethnal Green, 1978; (with Adrian Ailes) Heralds of Today, 1986, 2nd edn 2001; (ed with T. Woodcock) Dictionary of British Arms, vol. I, 1992; Garter Banners of the Nineties, 1998; (with P. J. Begent) The Most Noble Order of the Garter, 650 Years, 1999; genealogical and heraldic articles in British Heritage and elsewhere. *Recreations:* singing, gardening, mountain walking, motorcycling. *Address:* Hawthorn Cottage, 1 Flamborough Walk, E14 7LY. *T:* (020) 7790 7923; College of Arms, Queen Victoria Street, EC4V 4BT. *T:* (020) 7248 1137.

CHESSUN, Rt Rev. Christopher Thomas James; *see* Woolwich, Area Bishop of.

CHESTER, Bishop of, since 1996; **Rt Rev. Peter Robert Forster;** *b* 16 March 1950; *s* of Thomas and Edna Forster; *m* 1978, Elisabeth Anne Stevenson; two *s* two *d. Educ:* Merton Coll., Oxford (MA 1973); Edinburgh Univ. (BD 1977; PhD 1985); Edinburgh Theol Coll. Ordained deacon, 1980, priest, 1981; Asst Curate, St Matthew and St James, Mossley Hill, Liverpool, 1980–82; Senior Tutor, St John's Coll., Durham, 1983–91; Vicar, Beverley Minster and Asst Curate, Routh, 1991–96. Introduced to H of L, 2001. *Recreations:* tennis, woodcrafts, family. *Address:* Bishop's House, Abbey Square, Chester CH1 2JD. *T:* (01244) 350864, *Fax:* (01244) 314187.

CHESTER, Dean of; *see* McPhate, Very Rev. G. F.

CHESTER, Archdeacon of; *see* Allister, Ven. D. S.

CHESTER, Maj.-Gen. John Shane, OBE 1982; Chief Executive (formerly Secretary), Chartered Institute of Management Accountants, 1995–2001; *b* 21 April 1944; *s* of late Hugh Chester and Stella Florence Mary Chester (*née* Turner); *m* 1970, Amanda Gay, *d* of late Wing Comdr Stanley Graham Pritchard; two *s. Educ:* St Joseph's Coll., Ipswich; Southampton Solent Univ. (BA Hons 2007). 2nd Lieut, RM, 1963; served 40, 41, 43 and 45 Commandos RM (Borneo, Norway, NI), 1964–88 (despatches 1981); BM, 3 Commando Brigade, 1981–83 (incl. Falklands Campaign); CO 40 Commando RM, 1987–89 (despatches 1988); COS, HQ Special Forces, 1989–91; Brig. Comdg Training and Reserve Forces, RM, 1991–92; Sen. Directing Staff (Navy), RCDS, 1993–95. Gov., Royal Naval Scholarship Fund, 1996–2002. Lay Member: Special Immigration Appeals Commn, 2002–; Hants CC Standards Cttee, 2002–06. FCIPD (FIPD 1992). *Recreations:* sailing, golf, ski-ing, military history. *Address:* c/o Lloyds TSB, Budleigh Salterton, Devon EX9 6NQ. *Clubs:* Army and Navy; Royal Marines Sailing.

CHESTER, Dr Peter Francis, FREng; FInstP; FIET; Chairman, National Wind Power Ltd, 1991–95; *b* 8 Feb. 1929; *s* of late Herbert and of Edith Maud Chester (*née* Pullen); *m* 1953, Barbara Ann Collin; one *s* four *d. Educ:* Gunnersbury Grammar Sch.; Queen Mary College, London (BSc 1st Physics 1950); PhD London 1953. Post-doctoral Fellow, Nat. Research Council, Ottawa, 1953–54; Adv. Physicist, Westinghouse Res. Labs, Pittsburgh, 1954–60; Head of Solid State Physics Section, CERL, 1960–65; Head of Fundamental Studies Section, CERL, 1965–66; Res. Man., Electricity Council Res. Centre, 1966–70; Controller of Scientific Services, CEGB NW Region, 1970–73; Dir, Central Electricity Res. Labs, 1973–82; a Dir, Technol. Planning and Res., Div., CEGB, 1982–86; Dir, Environment, CEGB, 1986–89; Exec. Dir, Technology and Environment, Nat. Power, 1990–92. Science Research Council: Mem., 1976–80; Mem., Science Bd, 1972–75; Chm., Energy Round Table and Energy Cttee, 1975–80. Mem., ACORD, DTI, 1992–93. Vice-Pres., Inst. of Physics, 1972–76. A Dir, Fulmer Res. Inst., 1976–83. Faraday Lectr, IEE, 1984–85. Robens Coal Science Medal, 1985. *Publications:* original papers in solid state and low temperature physics, reports on energy and the environment, acid rain, clean technology, renewable energy and windpower.

CHESTERFIELD, Archdeacon of; *see* Garnett, Ven. D. C.

CHESTERMAN, Rev. Canon (George) Anthony, PhD; Chaplain to the Queen, 1998–2008; Continuing Ministerial Education Adviser to Bishop of Derby and Residentiary Canon (later Canon Theologian), Derby Cathedral, 1989–2003; *b* 22 Aug. 1938; *s* of late Francis John Chesterman and Frances Annie Chesterman; *m* 1964, Sheila Valerie Wilkinson; one *s* one *d. Educ:* Lancaster Royal Grammar Sch.; Univ. of Manchester (BSc); Nottingham Univ. (DipAE 1974; PhD 1989); Coll. of the Resurrection, Mirfield. Ordained deacon, 1964, priest, 1965; Curate, St John the Evangelist, Newbold, Chesterfield, 1964–67; Litchurch Gp Ministry, Derby (youth and adult educn specialist), 1967–70; Rector, All Saints, Mugginton and Kedleston, 1970–89; Diocesan Adult Educn Officer, Derby, 1970–79; Vice-Principal, E Midlands Ministry Trng Course, 1979–88. Mem., Gen. Synod, 1990–95. *Publications:* occasional articles and book reviews. *Recreations:* cooking, gardening, fishing, natural history, music, the visual arts, golf. *Address:* 7 Hillside, Lesbury, Alnwick, Northumberland NE66 3NR.

CHESTERMAN, Gordon; Director, Careers Service, University of Cambridge, since 2002; *b* 14 March 1957; *s* of Frederick and Marie Chesterman; *m* 1984, Deirdre McCormack; two *s* one *d. Educ:* University College Sch., Hampstead; London Coll. of Printing (HND Printing). Graduate trainee, then Personnel Officer, De La Rue Company, 1978–83; Graduate Recruitment Manager, Deloitte Haskins & Sells, 1983–86; Account Manager, Publishing Resources Ltd, Cambridge, 1986–90; self employed, 1990–95; Careers Advr, then Dep. Dir, Careers Service, Univ. of Cambridge, 1995–2002. Member: Steam Boat Assoc.; Ely Choral Soc. *Recreations:* choral singing, historic ship preservation, visiting Colombia, oil painting. *Address:* Cambridge University Careers Service, Stuart House, Mill Lane, Cambridge CB2 1XE. *T:* (01223) 338288; *e-mail:* gc214@cam.ac.uk. *Club:* Oxford and Cambridge.

CHESTERS, Rt Rev. Alan David, CBE 2007; Bishop of Blackburn, 1989–2003; Hon. Assistant Bishop: of Chester, since 2003; of Europe, since 2005; *b* 26 Aug. 1937; *s* of Herbert and Catherine Rebecca Chesters; *m* 1975, Jennie Garrett; one *s. Educ:* Elland Grammar Sch., W Yorks; St Chad's Coll., Univ. of Durham (BA Mod. History); St Catherine's Coll., Oxford (BA Theol., MA); St Stephen's House, Oxford. Curate of St Anne, Wandsworth, 1962–66; Chaplain and Head of Religious Education, Tiffin School, Kingston-upon-Thames, 1966–72; Director of Education and Rector of Brancepeth, Diocese of Durham, 1972–84; Hon. Canon of Durham Cathedral, 1975–84; Archdeacon of Halifax, 1985–89. A Church Comr, 1982–98 (Mem., Bd of Governors, 1984–89, 1992–98). Mem., General Synod, 1975–2003 (Mem., Standing Cttee, 1985–89, 1990–95); Chm., C of E Bd of Educn, and Council, Nat. Soc., 1999–2003. Mem. Cathedral Chapter, Chester, and Hon. Rural Life Consultant to Dio. of Chester, 2003–. Member: Countryside Commn, 1995–99; Countryside Agency, 1999–2001; Chm., NW Rural Affairs Forum, 2002–06. Pres., Cheshire Assoc. of Local Councils, 2005–. Chairman: Govs, St Martin's Coll. of Higher Educn, Lancaster, 1990–2002; Council, St Stephen's House, Oxford, 1995–2003; Mem. Council, Univ. of Chester, 2005–. House of Lords, 1995–2003. Hon. Fellow: Univ. of Central Lancs, 2001; St Martin's Coll. of HE, 2003; Blackburn Coll., 2004; Myerscough Coll., 2004; Univ. of Cumbria, 2007. *Recreations:* railways, walking, reading. *Address:* 64 Hallfields Road, Tarvin, Chester CH3 8ET.

CHESTERS, Pamela Joy; Chair, Royal Free Hampstead NHS Trust, since 2001; *b* 28 April 1956; *d* of Ian Storrie Beveridge and late Kathleen Mary Beveridge; *m* 1991, Alan Chesters. *Educ:* St Andrews Univ. (MA Hons Mediaeval Hist.). British Petroleum: various posts in UK and USA, latterly CEO, Duckhams Oils, 1979–98. Contested (C) Bristol W, 2001. Mem. (C) London Borough of Camden, 1990–2000 (Leader of Opposition, 1998–2000). Mem., Nat. Educn Exec., LGA, 1997–2000. Chair, English Churches Housing Gp, 2003–. Dir, Opera della Luna, 1994–2004. Trustee: Common Purpose, 2005–; NCH, 2006– (Chm., 2007–). *Recreations:* theatre, travel. *Address:* 62 Redington Road, NW3 7RS. *T:* (020) 7435 4190.

CHESTERTON, David, CB 1999; Chief Executive, UK Sports Council, 1998–99 (on secondment); *b* 30 Nov. 1939; *s* of Raymond and Joyce Chesterton; *m* 1st, 1965, Ursula Morgan; one *s* three *d*; 2nd, 1977, Lindsay Fellows; three step *d. Educ:* Reading Sch.; St Catherine's Coll., Oxford (BA). Editorial Assistant: Financial World, 1961–62; Fleet Street Letter, 1962–65; Producer, BBC External Services, 1965–68, Exec. Producer, 1968–74; Northern Ireland Office: Principal, 1974–80; Asst Sec., 1980–85; Under Sec., 1985–92; Hd of Heritage and Tourism Gp, DNH, 1992–96; Head of Sport, Tourism, Millennium and Nat. Lotteries Charities Bd Gp, DNH, then DCMS, 1996–98. *Recreations:* walking, food and drink.

CHESWORTH, Air Vice-Marshal George Arthur, CB 1982; OBE 1972; DFC 1954; JP; Lord-Lieutenant of Moray, 1994–2005; Chairman, Moray, Badenoch and Strathspey Enterprise Co., 1996–2000 (Deputy Chairman, 1991–96); *b* 4 June 1930; *s* of Alfred Matthew Chesworth and Grace Edith Chesworth; *m* 1951, Betty Joan Hopkins; two *d* (one *s* decd). *Educ:* Carshalton and Wimbledon. Joined RAF, 1948; commissioned, 1950; 205 Flying boat Sqdn, FEAF, 1951–53 (DFC 1954); RAF Germany, RAF Kinloss, RAF St Mawgan, 1956–61; RN Staff Coll., 1963; MoD, 1964–67; OC 201 Nimrod Sqdn, 1968–71 (OBE); OC RAF Kinloss, 1972–75; Air Officer in Charge, Central Tactics & Trials Orgn, 1975–77; Director, RAF Quartering, 1977–80; C of S to Air Comdr CTF 317 during Falkland Campaign, Apr.–June 1982 (CB); C of S, HQ 18 Gp, RAF, 1980–84. Chief Exec., Glasgow Garden Fest. (1988), 1985–89; Dir, SEC Ltd, 1989–95. Hon. Col, 76 Engr Regt (Vols), 1992–97. Chm., ATC Council for Scotland and NI, 1989–95; Pres., Highland RFCA (formerly TAVR), 1998–2005 (Vice-Chm. (Air), 1990–98). Develt Dir, Military and Aerospace Mus. (Aldershot) Trust, 1990–91; Trustee, MacRobert Trusts, 1994–2000; Mem. Management Bd, RAF Benevolent Fund Home, Alastrean House, Tarland, Aberdeenshire, 1990– (Chm., 1994–2001). Hon. Air Cdre, No 2622 (Highland) Sqdn, RAuxAF Regt, 2000–08. DL Moray, 1992; JP Moray, 1994. *Address:* Pindlers Croft, Lower Califer, Forres, Moray IV36 2RQ. *T:* (01309) 674136. *Club:* Royal Air Force.

CHESWORTH, John, FCA; Managing Director, 1980–2002, Chairman, 2002, Bodycote International plc; *b* 8 June 1937; *m* Elizabeth Ann; two *s* three *d. Educ:* Burnage Grammar Sch., Manchester. FCA 1964. Articled clerk, Burne Phillips & Co., 1958–63; Chartered Accountant, Deloitte & Co., 1964–67; Financial Accountant, Kellog Co. of GB Ltd, 1967–68; Gp Accountant, Nemo Heat Treatments Ltd, 1968–71; Chief Exec., Bodycote (UK) Gp, 1972. Harold Moore Meml Lectr, Royal Soc., 1995. Member: ICAEW; Adv. Gp, Dept of Materials and Metallurgy, Univ. of Birmingham, 1995–. *Publications:* papers on metallurgical heat treatment in jls. *Recreations:* sailing, swimming, soccer (represented Lancashire). *Address:* Oulton Manor, Rushton Spencer, Macclesfield, Cheshire SK11 0RS. *T:* (01260) 226314. *Clubs:* Tytherington; Royal Yacht.

CHETWODE, family name of **Baron Chetwode**.

CHETWODE, 2nd Baron *cr* 1945, of Chetwode; **Philip Chetwode;** Bt, 1700; *b* 26 March 1937; *s* of Capt. Roger Charles George Chetwode (*d* 1940; *o s* of Field Marshal Lord Chetwode, GCB, OM, GCSI, KCMG, DSO) and Hon. Molly Patricia Berry, *d* of 1st Viscount Camrose (she *m* 2nd, 1942, 1st Baron Sherwood, from whom she obtained a divorce, 1948, and *m* 3rd, 1958, Sir Richard Cotterell, 5th Bt, CBE); *S* grandfather, 1950; *m* 1st, 1967, Mrs Susan Dudley Smith (marr. diss. 1979); two *s* one *d*; 2nd, 1990, Mrs Fiona Holt. *Educ:* Eton. Commissioned Royal Horse Guards, 1956–66. *Heir: s* Hon. Roger Chetwode [*b* 29 May 1968; *m* 1998, Miranda, *d* of Comdr Graeme Rowan-Thomson; two *s* one *d*]. *Address:* 6 Alexandra Avenue, SW11 4DZ. *Club:* White's.

CHETWYN, Robert; *b* 7 Sept. 1933; *s* of Frederick Reuben Suckling and Eleanor Lavinia (*née* Boffee). *Educ:* Rutlish, Merton, SW; Central Sch. of Speech and Drama. First appeared as actor with Dundee Repertory Co., 1952; subseq. in repertory at Hull, Alexandra Theatre, Birmingham, 1954; Birmingham Repertory Theatre, 1954–56; various TV plays, 1956–59; 1st prodn, Five Finger Exercise, Salisbury Playhouse, 1960; Dir of Prodns, Opera Hse, Harrogate, 1961–62; Artistic Dir, Ipswich Arts, 1962–64; Midsummer Night's Dream, transf. Comedy (London), 1964; Resident Dir, Belgrade (Coventry), 1964–66; Assoc. Dir, Mermaid, 1966, The Beaver Coat, three one-act plays by Shaw; There's a Girl in My Soup, Globe, 1966 and Music Box (NY), 1967; A Present for the Past, Edinburgh Fest., 1966; The Flip Side, Apollo, 1967; The Importance of Being Earnest, Haymarket, 1968; The Real Inspector Hound, Criterion, 1968; What the Butler Saw, Queens, 1968; The Country Wife, Chichester Fest., 1968; The Bandwaggon, Mermaid, 1968 and Sydney, 1970; Cannibal Crackers, Hampstead, 1969; When We are Married, Strand, 1970; Hamlet, in Rome, Zurich, Vienna, Antwerp, Cologne, then Cambridge (London), 1971; Parents Day, Globe, 1972; Restez Donc Jusqu'au Petit Déjeuner, Belgium, 1973; Who's Who, Fortune, 1973; At the End of the Day, Savoy, 1973; Chez Nous, Globe, 1974; Qui est Qui, Belgium, 1974; The Doctor's Dilemma, Mermaid, 1975; Getting Away with Murder, Comedy, 1976; Private Lives, Melbourne, 1976; It's All Right If I Do It, Mermaid, 1977; A Murder is Announced, Vaudeville, 1977; Arms and The Man, Greenwich, 1978; LUV, Amsterdam, 1978; Brimstone and Treacle, Open Space, 1979; Bent, Royal Court and Criterion, 1979; Pygmalion, National Theatre of Belgium, 1979; Moving, Queen's, 1980; Eastward Ho!, Mermaid, 1981; Beethoven's 10th, Vaudeville, 1983 (also Broadway, New York); Number One, Queen's, 1984; Why Me?, Strand, 1985; Selling The Sizzle, Hampstead, 1988; Independent State, Sydney Opera House, 1995. Has produced and directed for BBC (incl. series Private Shultz, by Jack Pullman, film, That Uncertain Feeling, Born In the Gardens) and ITV (Irish RM first series, Small World, Case of the Late Pig). Trustee, Dirs' Guild of GB, 1984–. *Publication:* (jtly) Theatre on Merseyside (Arts Council report), 1973. *Recreations:* tennis, films, gardening. *Address:* 1 Wilton Court, Eccleston Square, SW1V 1PH.

CHETWYND, family name of **Viscount Chetwynd**.

CHETWYND, 10th Viscount *cr* 1717 (Ireland); **Adam Richard John Casson Chetwynd;** Baron Rathdown, 1717 (Ireland); Life Assurance Agent, Liberty Life Association of Africa Ltd, Sandton Branch, Johannesburg; *b* 2 Feb. 1935; *o s* of 9th Viscount and Joan Gilbert (*d* 1979), *o c* of late Herbert Alexander Casson, CSI, Ty'n-y-coed, Arthog, Merioneth; *S* father, 1965; *m* 1st, 1966, Celia Grace (marr. diss. 1974), *er d* of Comdr Alexander Robert Ramsay, DSC, RNVR, Fasque, Borrowdale, Salisbury, Rhodesia; twin *s* one *d*; 2nd, 1975, Angela May, *o d* of Jack Payne McCarthy, 21 Llanberis Grove, Nottingham. *Educ:* Eton. Fellow, Inst. of Life and Pension Advrs, 1982. 2nd Lieut Cameron Highlanders, 1954–56. With Colonial Mutual Life Assurance Soc. Ltd, Salisbury, Rhodesia, then Johannesburg, 1968–78; Liberty Life Assoc. of Africa (formerly Prudential Assurance Co. of South Africa), 1978–. Liveryman, GAPAN. Qualifying Mem., Million Dollar Round Table, 1979–; qualified Top of the Table, 1984–; Holder, Internat. Quality Award, 1979–. *Recreations:* astronomy, travel. *Heir: s* Hon. Adam Douglas Chetwynd [*b* 26 Feb. 1969; *m* 2000, Johanna Marie Karatau; one *s*]. *Address:* PO Box 69062, Bryanston 2021, Republic of South Africa. *Club:* Rotary (Morningside).

CHETWYND, Sir Robin John Talbot, 9th Bt *cr* 1795, of Brocton Hall, Staffordshire; *b* 21 Aug. 1941; *s* of Sir Arthur Chetwynd, 8th Bt and of Marjory May McDonald Chetwynd (*née* Lang); *S* father, 2004, but his name does not appear on the Official Roll of the Baronetage; *m* 1st, 1967, Heather Helen (marr. diss. 1986), *d* of George Bayliss Lothian; one *s* one *d*; 2nd, 1986, Donna Davey. *Heir: s* Peter James Talbot Chetwynd, *b* 21 Sept. 1973.

CHETWYND-TALBOT, family name of **Earl of Shrewsbury and Waterford**.

CHEWTON, Viscount; Edward Robert Waldegrave; *b* 10 Oct. 1986; *e s* of 13th Earl Waldegrave, *qv*. *Educ:* Eton Coll.; Christ Church, Oxford. *Address:* Chewton House, Chewton Mendip, Radstock, Som BA3 4LL.

CHEYNE, David Watson; Senior Partner, Linklaters, since 2006; *b* 30 Dec. 1948; *s* of Brig. W. W. Cheyne, DSO, OBE and L. A. Cheyne; *m* 1978, J. Gay Passey; three *s*. *Educ:* Stowe Sch.; Trinity Coll., Cambridge (BA Law 1971). Admitted solicitor, 1974; Linklaters: Asst Solicitor, 1974–80; Partner, 1980–; Hd of Corporate, 2000–05. *Recreations:* shooting, fishing, collecting antiques. *Address:* 19 Ladbroke Gardens, W11 2PT. *T:* (020) 7456 3174; *e-mail:* david_cheyne@linklaters.com.

CHEYNE, Iain Donald, CBE 1995; Director, Habib Bank, Pakistan, since 2004; Vice Chairman, Habib and Allied Bank, UK, since 2004; *b* 29 March 1942; *s* of Andres Delporte Gordon Cheyne and Florence Muriel Cheyne; *m* 1969, Amelia Martinez Arriola; two *s* one *d*. *Educ:* Hertford Coll., Oxford (MA English Lit. 1963); London Univ. (MPhil Archaeol. 1994). Articled Clerk, Droogleever and Co., Solicitors, 1964–68; admitted solicitor, 1967; Partner, Alfille and Co., Solicitors, 1968–72; Lloyds Bank, subseq. Lloyds TSB, plc: Legal Advr, 1972–86; General Manager: Corporate Communications, 1986–88; Strategic Planning, 1988–91; Corporate and Instnl Banking, 1991–97; Man. Dir, Internat. Banking, 1997–2000; Dir of Private Affairs to HH the Aga Khan, 2000–05. *Recreations:* archaeology, game shooting, vintage car racing. *Address:* 39 Quai d'Anjou, 75004 Paris, France.

CHEYNE, Sir Patrick (John Lister), 4th Bt *cr* 1908, of Leagarth, Fetlar; *b* 2 July 1941; *s* of Sir Joseph Lister Watson Cheyne, 3rd Bt, OBE and Mary Mort Allen; *S* father, 2007; *m* 1968, Helen Louise Trevor (*née* Smith); one *s* three *d*. *Educ:* Lancing Coll. FRICS 1997 (ISVA 1973). Cadet Seaman, British India Steam Navigation Co. Ltd, 1959; Seaman Cadet, RN, 1963; completed Commn as Lt Torpedo Anti-Submarine Officer, 1973. *Recreations:* fell walking, photography, gardening, croquet. *Heir: s* Louis Richard Patrick Lister Cheyne, *b* 25 March 1971. *Address:* Laurel Bank, 34 Stamford Road, Bowdon, Altrincham, Cheshire WA14 2JX. *T:* (0161) 928 0448, *Fax:* (0161) 941 4879; *e-mail:* patrickcheyne@aol.com.

CHEYSSON, Claude; Commander Legion of Honour; Croix de Guerre (5 times); Hon. GCMG 1984; Member, European Parliament, 1989–94; Town Councillor, Bargemon, 1983–89 and since 1995; *b* 13 April 1920; *s* of Pierre Cheysson and Sophie Funck-Brentano; *m* 1969, Danièle Schwarz; one *s* two *d* (and two *s* one *d* by former marrs). *Educ:* Coll. Stanislas, Paris; Ecole Polytechnique; Ecole Nationale d'Administration. Escaped from occupied France, 1943; Tank Officer, Free French Forces, France and Germany, 1943–45. Liaison Officer with German authorities, Bonn, 1948–52; Political Adviser to Viet Nam Govt, Saigon, 1952–53; Personal Adviser: to Prime Minister of France, Paris, 1954–55; to French Minister of Moroccan and Tunisian Affairs, 1956; Sec.-Gen., Commn for Techn. Cooperation in Africa, Lagos, Nairobi, 1957–62; Dir-Gen., Sahara Authority, Algiers, 1962–66; French Ambassador in Indonesia, 1966–69; Pres., Entreprise Minière et Chimique, 1970–73; European Comr (relations with Third World), 1973–81, 1985–89; Minister for External Relations, 1981–84. Bd Mem., Le Monde, 1970–81, 1985–92. President: Institut Pierre Mendès-France, 1987–89; Arche de la Fraternité, 1989–93. Grand Cross, Grand Officer and Comdr of many national orders; US Presidential Citation. Dr *hc* Univ. of Louvain; Joseph Bech Prize, 1978; Luderitz Prize, 1983. *Publications:* Une idée qui s'incarne, 1978; articles on Europe, and develt policies. *Address:* 52 rue de Vaugirard, 75006 Paris, France. *T:* and *Fax:* 143264665.

CHIBNALL, Marjorie McCallum, OBE 2004; MA, DPhil; FSA; FBA 1978; Fellow of Clare Hall, Cambridge, since 1975; *b* 27 Sept. 1915; *d* of J. C. Morgan, MBE; *m* 1947, Prof. Albert Charles Chibnall, FRS (*d* 1988); one *s* one *d* and two step *d*. *Educ:* Shrewsbury Priory County Girls' Sch.; Lady Margaret Hall, Oxford; Sorbonne, Paris. BLitt, MA, DPhil (Oxon); PhD (Cantab). Amy Mary Preston Read Scholar, Oxford, 1937–38; Goldsmiths' Sen. Student, 1937–39; Nursing Auxiliary, 1939; Susette Taylor Research Fellow, Lady Margaret Hall, Oxford, 1940–41; Asst Lectr, University Coll., Southampton, 1941–43; Asst Lectr, 1943–45, Lectr, 1945–47, in Medieval History, Univ. of Aberdeen; Lectr in History, later Fellow of Girton Coll., Cambridge, 1947–65; Research Fellow, Clare Hall, Cambridge, 1969–75; Leverhulme Emeritus Fellowship, 1982. Dir, Battle Conf. on Anglo-Norman Studies, 1989–93. Prothero Lectr, RHistS, 1987. Vice-Pres., Selden Soc., 1987–90. Corresp. Fellow, Medieval Acad. of America, 1983. Hon. Fellow, Girton Coll., Cambridge, 1988. Hon. DLitt Birmingham, 1979; Hon. LittD Cambridge, 2002. *Publications:* The English Lands of the Abbey of Bec, 1946; Select Documents of the English Lands of the Abbey of Bec, 1951; The *Historia Pontificalis* of John of Salisbury, 1956; The Ecclesiastical History of Orderic Vitalis, 6 vols, 1969–80; Charters and Custumals of the Abbey of Holy Trinity Caen, 1982; The World of Orderic Vitalis, 1984; Anglo-Norman England 1066–1166, 1986; (ed) Anglo-Norman Studies, XII, 1990, XIII, 1991, XIV, 1992, XV, 1993, XVI, 1994; The Empress Matilda, 1991; (ed with Leslie Watkiss) The Waltham Chronicle, 1994; (ed with R. H. C. Davis) The *Gesta Guillelmi* of William of Poitiers, 1998; The Debate on the Norman Conquest, 1999; Piety, Power and History in Medieval England and Normandy, 2000; The Normans, 2000; numerous articles and reviews, principally in English and French historical jls. *Address:* Clare Hall, Cambridge CB3 9AL. *T:* (01223) 353923. *Club:* University Women's.

CHIBWA, Anderson Kaseba; High Commissioner for Zambia in the United Kingdom, since 2003; *b* 24 March 1950; *s* of Chulu and Sarah Chibwa; *m* 1990, Grace Mwewa Kasese; three *s* three *d*. *Educ:* Univ. of Zambia (BA 1974); Univ. of Miami (MA 1979). Sen. Researcher, Nat. Council for Scientific Res., Zambia, 1974–82; Sen. Lectr, Pan African Inst. for Develt, 1982–99; Project Manager, CARE Internat., Zambia, 1999–2003. *Publications:* Population Atlas of Zambia, 1974; Internal Migrations in the Commonwealth of the Bahamas 1970–75, 1980. *Recreations:* reading, meeting people. *Address:* High Commission for Zambia, 2 Palace Gate, Kensington, W8 5NG. *T:* (020) 7589 6655, *Fax:* (020) 7581 1353; *e-mail:* zhcl@btconnect.com.

CHICHESTER, family name of **Marquess of Donegall**.

CHICHESTER, 9th Earl of, *cr* 1801; **John Nicholas Pelham;** Bt 1611; Baron Pelham of Stanmer, 1762; *b* (posthumous) 14 April 1944; *s* of 8th Earl of Chichester (killed on active service, 1944) and Ursula (*d* 1989) (she *m* 2nd, 1957, Ralph Gunning Henderson; marr. diss. 1971), *o d* of late Walter de Pannwitz, de Hartekamp, Bennebroek, Holland; *S* father, 1944; *m* 1975, Mrs June Marijke Hall; one *d*. *Recreations:* music, flying. *Heir: kinsman* Richard Anthony Henry Pelham [*b* 1 Aug. 1952; *m* 1987, Georgina, *d* of David Gilmour; two *s*]. *Address:* Little Durnford Manor, Salisbury, Wilts SP4 6AH.

CHICHESTER, Bishop of, since 2001; **Rt Rev. John William Hind;** *b* 19 June 1945; *s* of late Harold Hind and Joan Mary Hind; *m* 1966, Janet Helen McLintock; three *s*. *Educ:* Watford Grammar Sch.; Leeds Univ. (BA 1966). Asst Master, Leeds Modern Sch., 1966–69; Asst Lectr, King Alfred's Coll., Winchester, 1969–70; Cuddesdon Theol Coll.; Deacon 1972, Priest 1973; Asst Curate, St John's, Catford, 1972–76; Vicar, Christ Church, Forest Hill, 1976–82 and Priest-in-Charge, St Paul's, Forest Hill, 1981–82; Principal, Chichester Theol Coll., 1982–91; Area Bishop of Horsham, 1991–93; Bishop of Gibraltar in Europe, 1993–2001. Canon Residentiary and Bursalis Preb., Chichester Cathedral, 1982–90. Chm., Faith and Order Adv. Gp, C of E, 1991–; Mem., Faith and Order Commn, WCC, 1999– (Vice-Moderator, 2006–). *Recreations:* cooking, languages. *Address:* The Palace, Chichester, W Sussex PO19 1PY.

CHICHESTER, Dean of; *see* Frayling, Very Rev. N. A.

CHICHESTER, Archdeacon of; *see* McKittrick, Ven. D. H.

CHICHESTER, Giles Bryan; Member (C) South West England and Gibraltar, European Parliament, since 2004 (Devon and East Plymouth, 1994–99; South West Region, England, 1999–2004); *b* 29 July 1946; *s* of Sir Francis Chichester, KBE and Sheila Mary (*née* Craven); *m* 1979, Virginia Ansell; two *s* one *d*. *Educ:* Westminster Sch.; Christ Church, Oxford (BA Hons Geography; MA). FRGS 1972. Trainee, Univ. of London Press and Hodder & Stoughton, publishers, 1968–69; Francis Chichester Ltd: Production Manager, 1969–71; Co. Sec., 1970–89; Dir, 1971–; Man. Dir, 1983–; Chm., 1989–. Chm., Foreign Affairs Forum, 1987–90. European Parliament: Cons. spokesman: on Research, Technol Develt and Energy Cttee, 1994–99; on Industry, External Trade, Res. and Energy Cttee, 1999–2004; Chm., Industry, Research and Energy Cttee, 2004–07; Leader, Cons. MEPs, 2007–08; Pres., Delegn for Relns with Australia and NZ, 2007–08. Pres., European Energy Forum (formerly Foundn), 2004– (Vice Pres., 1995–2004). Mem. Council, Air League, 1995–99. *Publications:* pamphlets on nuclear energy, small business, opportunities for young people in Europe, sustainable energy. *Recreations:* rowing, sailing, snooker, vegetarian cooking. *Address:* (office) 9 St James's Place, SW1A 1PE. *T:* (020) 7493 0932; Longridge, West Hill, Ottery St Mary, Devon EX11 1UX. *T:* (01404) 851106; *e-mail:* giles@gileschichestermep.org.uk. *Clubs:* Pratt's, United and Cecil; London Rowing; Royal Western Yacht (Plymouth); Royal Yacht Squadron (Cowes).

CHICHESTER, Sir James (Henry Edward), 12th Bt cr 1641, of Raleigh, Devonshire; founder and Chairman, Chichester Trees and Shrubs Ltd; b 15 Oct. 1951; s of Sir (Edward) John Chichester, 11th Bt and of Hon. Anne, d of 2nd Baron Montagu of Beaulieu; S father, 2007; m 1990, Margaret Anne, o d of late Major John Walkelyne Chandos-Pole, Radbourne Hall, Derbys; two s. Educ: Eton. Recreations: dendrology, stalking, shooting, ornithology. Heir: s Edward John Chandos-Pole Chichester, b 27 July 1991. Address: The Mill Studio, Beaulieu, Hampshire SO42 7YG. T: (01590) 612198, Fax: (01590) 612194. Clubs: Pratt's, Shikar.

CHICHESTER CLARK, Emma; freelance illustrator and author, since 1983; b 15 Oct. 1955; d of Sir Robin Chichester-Clark, qv, and Jane Helen Goddard; m 2008, C. Rupert Wace. Educ: Chelsea Sch. of Art (BA Hons); Royal Coll. of Art (MA Hons). Teacher, 1983–85: foundn students, City & Guilds Sch. of Art; Middx Poly. Publications: author and illustrator: Catch that Hat!, 1986; The Story of Horrible Hilda and Henry, 1988; Myrtle, Tertle and Gertle; The Bouncing Dinosaur, 1990; Tea with Aunt Augusta, 1991; Miss Bilberry's New House, 1993; Piper; Little Miss Muffet counts to Ten, 1997; More!, 1998; I Love you, Blue Kangaroo!, 1998; Follow my Leader, 1999; Where are you, Blue Kangaroo?, 2000; It was you, Blue Kangaroo!, 2001; No more kissing!, 2001; I'll show you, Blue Kangaroo!, 2003; Up in Heaven, 2003; No more teasing!, 2004; Just for you, Blue Kangaroo!, 2004; Will and Squill, 2005; Melrose and Croc, 2005; Amazing Mr Zooty!, 2006; Melrose and Croc Find a Smile, 2006; Melrose and Croc Friends for Life, 2006; Happy Birthday to You, Blue Kangaroo!, 2006; Eliza and The Moonchild, 2007; Melrose and Croc By the Sea, 2007; Melrose and Croc Go to Town, 2007; Minty and Tink, 2008; Melrose and Croc: a hero's birthday, 2008; illustrated books include: Laura Cecil: Listen to this!, 1987; Stuff and Nonsense, 1989; Boo!, 1990; A Thousand Yards of Sea, 1992; Preposterous Pets, 1994; The Frog Princess, 1994; Noah and the Space Ark, 1998; The Kingfisher Book of Toy Stories, 2000; Cunning Cat Tales, 2001; Wicked Wolf Tales, 2001; Geraldine McCaughren: The Orchard Book of Greek Myths, 1992; The Orchard Book of Greek Gods and Goddesses, 1997; The Orchard Book of Roman Myths, 1999; Adele Geras: Sleeping Beauty, 2000; Giselle, 2000; Swan Lake, 2000; The Nutcracker, 2000; Primrose Lockwood, Cissy Lavender, 1989; Margaret Ryan, Fat Witch Rides Again, 1990; James Reeves, Ragged Robin, 1990; Pat Thomson, Beware of the Aunts!, 1991; Margaret Mahy, The Queen's Goat, 1991; Roald Dahl, James and the Giant Peach, 1991; Ben Frankel, Tertius and Pliny, 1992; D. J. Enright, The Way of the Cat, 1992; Peter Dickinson, Time and the Clockmice, 1993; Ann Turnbull, Too Tired, 1993; Anne Fine, The Haunting of Pip Parker, 1994; Gina Pollinger, Something Rich and Strange, 1995; Allan Ahlberg, Mrs Vole the Vet, 1996; Sam McBratney, Little Red Riding Hood, 1996; John Yeoman, The Glove Puppet Man, 1997; Jane Falloon, Thumbelina, 1997; Adrian Mitchell, The Adventures of Robin Hood and Marian, 1998; Naomi Lewis, Elf Hill, 1999; Kevin Crossley-Holland, Enchantment, 2001; Rosemary Sutcliff, The Minstrel and the Dragon Pup, 2001; Diana Wynne Jones, Wild Robert, 2001; Oxford First Illustrated Dictionary, 2004; Michael Morpurgo, Aesop's Fables, 2004; Reinhardt Jung, Bambert's Book of Missing Stories; Michael Morpurgo, Hansel and Gretel, 2008. Recreations: walking, cinema, music, friends. Address: c/o Laura Cecil, 17 Alwyne Villas, N1 2HG. Club: Chelsea Arts.

CHICHESTER-CLARK, Sir Robert, (Sir Robin), Kt 1974; b 10 Jan. 1928; s of late Capt. J. L. C. Chichester-Clark, DSO and Bar, DL, MP, and Mrs C. E. Brackenbury; m 1st, 1953, Jane Helen Goddard (marr. diss. 1972); one s two d; 2nd, 1974, Caroline, d of late Anthony Bull, CBE; two s. Educ: Royal Naval Coll.; Magdalene Coll., Cambridge (BA Hons Hist. and Law). Journalist, 1950; Public Relations Officer, Glyndebourne Opera, 1952; Asst to Sales Manager, Oxford Univ. Press, 1953–55. MP (UU) Londonderry City and Co., 1955–Feb. 1974; PPS to Financial Secretary to the Treasury, 1958; Asst Government Whip (unpaid), 1958–60; a Lord Comr of the Treasury, 1960–61; Comptroller of HM Household, 1961–64; Chief Opposition Spokesman on N Ireland, 1964–70, on Public Building and Works and the Arts, 1965–70; Minister of State, Dept of Employment, 1972–74. Mem. Council of Europe and Delegate to WEU, 1959–61. Dir, Instn of Works Managers, 1968–72. Chairman: Restoration of Appearance and Function Trust, 1988–2000; Arvon Develt Cttee, 1995–; Arvon Foundn, 1997–2001 (Jt Pres., 2001–); Trustee: Royal Philharmonic Orchestra Develt Trust, 1993–95; Mus. of Illustration, 2002–. Hon. FIWM 1972. Recreations: fishing, reading. Club: Brooks's.

See also E. Chichester Clark, P. Hobhouse.

CHICK, John Stephen; educational consultant; HM Diplomatic Service, retired; b 5 Aug. 1935; m 1966, Margarita Alvarez de Sotomayor; one s three d. Educ: St John's Coll., Cambridge (BA 1959); Univ. of Pennsylvania (MA 1960). Entered FO, 1961; Madrid, 1963–66; First Sec., Mexico City, 1966–69; FCO, 1969–73; First Sec. and Head of Chancery, Rangoon, 1973–76; Head of Chancery, Luxembourg, 1976–78; Commercial Counsellor and Consul-Gen., Buenos Aires, 1978–81; Head of Arms Control Dept, FCO, 1981–83; Head of S Pacific Dept, FCO, 1983–85. Consul-Gen., Geneva, 1985–89. Dir of Internat. Affairs, Sallingbury Casey Ltd, 1990–91; Associate Dir, Rowland Public Affairs, 1991. Address: 21 Ranelagh Avenue, SW13 0BL. T: (020) 8876 5916.

CHIDDICK, Prof. David Martin, FRICS; Vice Chancellor, University of Lincoln, since 2000; b 26 Oct. 1948; s of Derek and Jeanette Chiddick; m 1973, Jane Elizabeth Sills; one s two d. Educ: Poly. of Central London; Cranfield Univ. (MSc). FRICS 1975; MRTPI 1979. Sen. Planning Officer, Herts CC, 1977–79; Prof. of Land Econ., 1985–87, Sen. Dean, 1987–89, Dep. Dir, 1989–93, Leicester Poly., then De Montfort Univ.; Pro-Vice Chancellor, De Montfort Univ., 1993–2000. Non-executive Director: Leicester Royal Infirmary, 1993–2000; NHS E Midlands; Chm., HEFCE Space Mgt Gp. Founding Ed., Jl of Property Mgt, 1984–95. Liveryman, Merchant Taylors' Co. FRSA 1992. Publications: (ed with A. Millington) Land Management: new directions, 1983; Lincoln 2020, 2006. Recreations: mountain walking, watching Rugby Union, golf, reading, music. Address: University of Lincoln, Brayford Pool, Lincoln LN6 7TS. T: (01522) 886100, Fax: (01522) 886200; e-mail: dchiddick@lincoln.ac.uk.

CHIDGEY, family name of Baron Chidgey.

CHIDGEY, Baron cr 2005 (Life Peer), of Hamble-le-Rice in the county of Hampshire; **David William George Chidgey,** CEng, FICE, FIHT, FIEI; b 9 July 1942; s of Cyril Cecil Chidgey and Winifred Hilda Doris Chidgey (née Weston); m 1965, April Carolyn Idris-Jones; one s two d. Educ: Royal Naval Coll., Portsmouth; Portsmouth Poly. CEng 1971; MCIT 1985; FIHT 1990; FIEI 1990; FICE 1993; MConsEI 1993. Mech. and aeronautical engr, Admiralty, 1958–64; Highways and Civil Engr, Hants CC, 1965–72; Brian Colquhoun and Partners: Chartered Engr and Project Manager, UK, ME and W Africa, 1973–85; Associate Partner and Man. Dir, Ireland, 1981–88; Associate Partner, Central Southern England, 1988–93; Thorburn Colquhoun: Associate Dir, Southern England and Project Dir, Engrg Facilities Management, mil. estabts in Hants, 1994–. Contested: (SLD) Hampshire Central, Eur. Parlt, Dec. 1988 and 1989; (Lib Dem) Eastleigh, 1992. MP (Lib Dem) Eastleigh, June 1994–2005. Lib Dem spokesman for: employment, 1994–95; transport, 1995–97; trade and industry, 1997–99; Lib Dem dep. spokesman for defence, 2006–. Member: Foreign Affairs Cttee, 1999–2005; Chairmen's Panel, 2001–05; Jt Cttee on Human Rights, 2003–05; EU Sub Cttee C, Foreign Affairs, Defence and Develt, H of L, 2006–. CRAeS. Publications: papers in technical jl, Traffic Engineering and Control. Recreations: walking, reading. Address: House of Lords, SW1A 0PW. Club: National Liberal.

CH'IEN Kuo Fung, Dr Raymond, GBS 1999; CBE 1994; JP; Chairman: CDC Corporation (formerly chinadotcom corporation), since 1999; MTR Corporation Ltd, since 2003; Hang Seng Bank Ltd, since 2007; b 26 Jan. 1952; s of James Ch'ien and Ellen Ma; m Whang Hwee Leng; one s two d. Educ: Rockford Coll., Illinois (BA 1973); Univ. of Pennsylvania (PhD Econs 1978). Gp Man. Dir, Lam Soon Hong Kong Gp, 1984–97. MEC, Hong Kong, then HKSAR, 1992–2002. JP Hong Kong, 1993. Young Industrialist Award, Hong Kong, 1988. Recreation: scuba diving. Address: 22/F Citicorp Centre, 18 Whitfield Road, North Point, Hong Kong. T: 28801328. Clubs: Hong Kong, Hong Kong Jockey.

CHIENE, John; b 27 Jan. 1937; s of John and Muriel Chiene; m 1st, 1965, Anne; one s one d; 2nd, 1986, Carol; one d. Educ: Rugby; Queens' Coll., Cambridge (BA). Wood Mackenzie: joined, 1962; Man. Partner, 1969; Sen. Partner, 1974; Jt Chief Exec., Hill Samuel & Co. Ltd (who had merged with Wood Mackenzie), 1987; Chm., County NatWest Securities, on their merger with Wood Mackenzie, 1988–89; Dep. Chm., County NatWest Ltd, 1989–90; Chm., Gartmore Capital Strategy Fund, 1996–2002. Recreations: golf, opera, ski-ing. Address: 7 St Leonard's Terrace, SW3 4QB. Clubs: City of London; New (Edinburgh).

CHIEPE, Hon. Gaositwe Keagakwa Tibe, PH 1996; PMS 1975; MBE 1962; FRSA; Minister for Education, Botswana, 1995–99; b 20 Oct. 1922; d of late T. Chiepe. Educ: Fort Hare, South Africa (BSc, EdDip); Bristol Univ., UK (MA (Ed)). Asst Educn Officer, 1948–53; Educn Officer and Schools Inspector, 1953–62; Sen. Educn Officer, 1962–65; Dep. Dir of Educn, 1965–67; Dir of Educn, 1968–70; High Comr to UK and Nigeria, 1970–74; Ambassador: Denmark, Norway, Sweden, France and Germany, 1970–74; Belgium and EEC, 1973–74; Minister of Commerce and Industry, 1974–77; Minister for Mineral Resources and Water Affairs, 1977–84; Minister for External Affairs, 1984–95. Chairman: Africa Region, CPA, 1981–83; Botswana Branch, CPA, 1981–. Member: Botswana Society; Botswana Girl Guide Assoc.; Internat. Fedn of University Women. Hon. Pres., Kalahari Conservation Soc.; Patron, Botswana Forestry Assoc. Hon. LLD Bristol, 1972; Hon. DLitt de Paul Univ., Chicago, 1994; Hon. DEd Fort Hare Univ., SA, 1996. FRSA 1973. Recreations: gardening, a bit of swimming (in Botswana), reading. Address: PO Box 186, Gaborone, Botswana.

CHIGNELL, Anthony Hugh, FRCS; Consulting Ophthalmic Surgeon: St Thomas' Hospital, 1973–99; King Edward VII Hospital, 1985–2000; Hospitaller, St John of Jerusalem, 2002–08; b 14 April 1939; s of Thomas Hugh Chignell and Phyllis Una (née Green); m 1962, Phillippa Price Brayne-Nicholls; one s two d. Educ: Worth Sch.; Downside Sch.; St Thomas' Hosp. (MB BS 1962). DO 1966; FRCS 1968. Registrar, Moorfields Eye Hosp., 1966–69; Sen. Registrar, Retinal Unit, Moorfields Eye Hosp. and St Thomas' Hosp., 1969–73; Teacher in Ophthalmology, London Univ., 1980–99. Civilian Consultant in Ophthalmology to Army, 1983–99; Consultant Advr in Ophthalmology to Metropolitan Police, 1988–99. Scientific Advr, Nat. Eye Inst., 1991–99. Gov., Royal Nat. Coll. for Blind, 1987–97; Mem. Council, GDBA, 1989–2002 (Dep. Chm., 2001–02). Mem., Jules Gonin Club, 1972. Trustee: Ridley Foundn, 1988– (Chm., 2001–04); Fight for Sight, 1992–95. Hon. FRCOphth 2006. Mem. Court, Spectacle Makers' Co., 1988– (Master, 1999–2000). GCStJ 2008. Publications: Retinal Detachment Surgery, 1979, 2nd edn 1988; Vitreo-Retinal Surgery, 1998; numerous articles related to retinal detachment surgery. Recreations: fly-fishing, golf, the theatre, Herefordshire. Address: 3 Tedworth Square, SW3 4DU. Clubs: MCC; New Zealand Golf (Weybridge); Seniors Golfing Soc.

CHIKETA, Stephen Cletus; Ambassador of Zimbabwe to Australia, since 2007; b 16 Sept. 1942; s of Mangwiro S. Chiketa and Mary Magdalene (née Chivero); m 1976, Juliet Joalane; one s two d. Educ: Univ. of South Africa (BA Hons); Univ. of Basutoland, Botswana and Swaziland (BA, PGCE). Asst Teacher, Swaziland schs, 1967–73; part-time Lectr, Univ. of Botswana, Lesotho and Swaziland, 1972–73; Principal, High School in Lesotho, 1974–80; Under Sec., Min. of Foreign Affairs, 1982; Dep. Perm. Rep., UN, 1982–86; Dep. Sec., Min. of Foreign Affairs, 1986–87; Ambassador to Romania and Bulgaria, 1987–90; High Comr for Zimbabwe in London, 1990–93; Dep. Sec., Ministry of Foreign Affairs, Harare, 1993–95; Ambassador to Kuwait, Bahrain, Oman, Qatar and UAE, 1995–2002; Ambassador to Iran, 2002–07. Publications: history articles in Swaziland weekly newspapers. Recreations: photography, tennis, reading, table tennis, cards. Address: c/o Embassy of Zimbabwe, 11 Culgoa Circuit, O'Malley, ACT 2606, Australia.

CHILCOT, Rt Hon. Sir John (Anthony), GCB 1998 (KCB 1994; CB 1990); PC 2004; Chairman: B & CE Group, since 1999; Police Foundation, since 2001; b 22 April 1939; s of Henry William Chilcot and Catherine Chilcot (née Ashall); m 1964, Rosalind Mary Forster. Educ: Brighton Coll. (Lyon Scholar); Pembroke Coll., Cambridge (Open Scholar; MA; Hon. Fellow, 1999). Joined Home Office, 1963; Asst Private Sec. to Home Secretary (Rt Hon. Roy Jenkins), 1966; Private Sec. to Head of Civil Service (late Baron Armstrong of Sanderstead), 1971–73; Principal Private Secretary to Home Secretary (Rt Hon. Merlyn Rees; Rt Hon. William Whitelaw), 1978–80; Asst Under-Sec. of State, Dir of Personnel and Finance, Prison Dept, 1980–84; Under-Sec., Cabinet Office (MPO), 1984–86; Asst Under Sec. of State, 1986 (seconded to Schroders, 1986–87), Dep. Under Sec. of State, 1987–90, Home Office; Permanent Under Sec. of State, NI Office, 1990–97. Staff Counsellor: Security and Intelligence Agencies, 1999–2004; Nat. Criminal Intelligence Service, 2002–06. Member: Indep. Commn on the Voting System, 1997–98; Lord Chancellor's Adv. Council on Public Records, 1999–2003; Nat. Archives Council, 2003–04; Review of Intelligence on Weapons of Mass Destruction, 2004; Chm., Privy Council Cttee on Intercept as Evidence, 2007–08. Director: RTZ Pillar, 1986–90; Abraxa Ltd, 1998–; NBW Ltd, 2002–. Pres., First Div. Pensioners' Gp, 1998–2002. Trustee, The Police Rehabilitation Trust, 2002–. Mem., Awards Council, Royal Anniversary Trust, 2003–. Vice-Pres. and Fellow, Brighton Coll., 2005–. Recreations: reading, music and opera, travel. Address: c/o Police Foundation, 1st Floor, Park Place, 12 Lawn Lane, SW8 1UD. Club: Travellers.

CHILCOTT, Dominick John, CMG 2003; HM Diplomatic Service; High Commissioner, Sri Lanka, 2006–08; b 17 Nov. 1959; s of Michael and Rosemary Chilcott; m 1983, Jane Elizabeth Bromage; three s one d. Educ: St Joseph's Coll., Ipswich; Greyfriars Hall, Oxford (BA Hons (Philosophy and Theol.) 1982). Midshipman, RN, 1978–79; entered FCO, 1982; Southern African Dept, FCO, 1982–83; Turkish lang. trng, 1984; Third, later Second, Sec., Ankara, 1985–88; First Sec., Central African Dept, then EC Dept (Internal), FCO, 1988–92; Hd, Political Section, Lisbon, 1993–95; Private Sec. to Foreign Sec., 1996–98; Counsellor, Ext. Relns, UK Perm. Repn to EU, Brussels, 1998–2002; Dir, Iraq Policy Unit, 2002–03; Dir, EU Directorate, FCO, 2003–06. Recreations: walking, reading, attending my children's school matches, renovating an old bakery in the Dordogne. Address: c/o Foreign and Commonwealth Office, King Charles

Street, SW1A 2AH; *e-mail:* dominick.chilcott@fco.gov.uk; 145 Jerningham Road, SE14 5NJ.

CHILCOTT, Robert Lionel; tenor; conductor; full-time composer, since 1997; *b* Plymouth, 9 April 1955; *m* 1st, Polly (marr. diss.); one *s* three *d*; 2nd, 2005, Kate. *Educ:* King's Coll., Cambridge (choral scholar; BA 1976). Mem., King's Singers, 1986–97. Principal Guest Conductor, BBC Singers; former Conductor, Royal Coll. of Music Chorus; conductor of choirs worldwide incl. World Youth Choir, RIAS Kammerchor, Orphei Drangar, Jauna Musika, Taipei Chamber Singers and Tower NZ Youth Choir. Composer of choral music, esp. for youth choirs. *Compositions include:* Can you hear me?, 1998; The Making of the Drum, 1999; Jubilate, 1999; Canticles of Light, 2000; A Little Jazz Mass, 2004; Advent Antiphons, 2005; Weather Report, 2006; Missa Cantate, 2006; This Day, 2007. *Address:* c/o Choral Connections, 14 Stevens Close, Prestwood, Great Missenden, Bucks HP16 0SQ; *web:* www.bobchilcott.com.

CHILD, Sir (Coles John) Jeremy, 3rd Bt *cr* 1919; actor; *b* 20 Sept. 1944; *s* of Sir Coles John Child, 2nd Bt, and Sheila (*d* 1964), *e d* of Hugh Mathewson; *S* father, 1971; *m* 1971, Deborah Jane (*née* Snelling) (marr. diss. 1976); one *d*; *m* 1978, Jan (marr. diss. 1986), *y d* of B. Todd, Kingston upon Thames; one *s* one *d*; *m* 1987, Libby, *y d* of Rev. Grenville Morgan, Canterbury, Kent; one *s* one *d*. *Educ:* Eton; Univ. of Poitiers (Dip. in French). Trained at Bristol Old Vic Theatre Sch., 1963–65; Bristol Old Vic, 1965–66; repertory at Windsor, Canterbury and Colchester; Conduct Unbecoming, Queen's, 1970; appeared at Royal Court, Mermaid and Bankside Globe, 1973; Oh Kay, Westminster, 1974; Donkey's Years, Globe, 1977; Hay Fever, Lyric, Hammersmith, 1980; Out of Order, Far and Middle East tour, 1995; Plenty, Albery, 1999; Pride and Prejudice, UK tour, 2000; The Circle, UK tour, 2002; Ying Tong, New Ambassadors, 2005; An English Tragedy, Palace Th., Watford, 2008; *films include:* Privilege, 1967; Oh What a Lovely War!, 1967; The Breaking of Bumbo, 1970; Young Winston, 1971; The Stud, 1976; Quadrophenia, 1978; Sir Henry at Rawlinson's End, 1979; Chanel Solitaire, 1980; High Road to China, 1982; Give my Regards to Broad Street, 1983; Taffin, 1987; A Fish called Wanda, 1989; The Madness of King George, 1994; Regeneration, 1996; Don't Go Breaking My Heart, 1997; Whatever Happened to Harold Smith?, 1999; Lagaan, 2000; Laisser Passer, South Kensington, 2001; Wimbledon, Separate Lies, 2003; *television includes:* 'Tis Pity She's a Whore; Diana, Her True Story; Falklands Play, 2002; *series:* Father, Dear Father, Edward and Mrs Simpson, The Jewel in the Crown, Bergerac, The Glittering Prizes, Wings, Fairly Secret Army, Oxbridge Blues, Edge of Darkness, First Among Equals, Game, Set and Match, Lovejoy, Perfect Scoundrels, Gravy Train Goes East, Headhunters, Harnessing Peacocks, Sharpe's Enemy, Frank Stubbs Promotes, A Dance to the Music of Time, Mosley, A Touch of Frost, Love in a Cold Climate, Doc Marten, Midsomer Murders, Judge John Deed, Amnesia, East Enders. *Heir: s* Coles John Alexander Child, *b* 10 May 1982. *Club:* Garrick.

CHILD, Denis Marsden, CBE 1987; Director, Eurotunnel plc, 1985–98; *b* 1 Nov. 1926; *s* of late Percival Snowden Child and Alice Child (*née* Jackson); *m* 1973, Patricia Charlton; two *s* one *d* by previous marr. *Educ:* Woodhouse Grove Sch., Bradford. Joined Westminster Bank, Leeds, 1942; RN, 1944–48; rejoined Westminster Bank; National Westminster Bank: Asst Area Manager, Leeds, 1970; Area Manager, Wembley, 1972; Chief Manager, Planning and Marketing, 1975; Head, Management Inf. and Control, 1977; Gen. Manager, Financial Control Div., 1979; Dir, NatWest Bank, 1982–96; Dep. Gp Chief Exec., 1982–87; Dir, Coutts & Co., 1982–97; Chm., Lombard North Central, 1991–96. Chairman: Exec. Cttee, BBA, 1986–87; Council, Assoc. for Payment Clearing Services, 1985–86; Financial Markets Cttee, Fedn Bancaire, EC, 1985–87; Director: Internat. Commodities Clearing House, 1982–86 (Chm., 1990–93); Investors Compensation Scheme Ltd, 1988–92. Bd Mem., CAA, 1986–90. Mem., IBM UK Pensions Trust, 1984–97 (Chm., 1994–97). Member: Accounting Standards Cttee, 1985–90; Securities and Investments Bd, 1986–92. FCIB; FCT; FCIS. *Recreations:* golf, gardening. *Address:* Fairways, Park Road, Farnham Royal, Bucks SL2 3BQ. *T:* (01753) 648096. *Club:* Stoke Poges Golf.

CHILD, Sir Jeremy; *see* Child, Sir C. J. J.

CHILD, Prof. John, FBA 2006; Professor of Commerce, University of Birmingham, since 2000; *b* 10 Nov. 1940; *s* of late Clifton James Child, OBE and Hilde Child (*née* Hurwitz); *m* 1965, Elizabeth Anne Mitchiner; one *s* one *d*. *Educ:* St John's College, Cambridge (scholar; MA, PhD, ScD). Rolls-Royce, 1965–66; Aston Univ., 1966–68; London Business Sch., 1968–73; Prof. of Organizational Behaviour, Aston Univ., 1973–91 (Dean, Aston Business Sch., 1986–89); Dean and Dir, China-Europe Management Inst., Beijing, 1989–90; Diageo Prof. of Mgt Studies, Univ. of Cambridge, and Fellow of St John's Coll., Cambridge, 1991–2000. Vis. Fellow, Nuffield Coll., Oxford, 1973–78; Vis. Prof., Univ. of Hong Kong, 1998–2000. Editor-in-Chief, Organization Studies, 1992–96. *Publications include:* British Management Thought, 1969; The Business Enterprise in Modern Industrial Society, 1969; Organization, 1977; (jtly) Lost Managers, 1982; (ed) Reform Policy and the Chinese Enterprise, 1990; (jtly) Reshaping Work, 1990; (jtly) New Technology in European Services, 1990; Management in China, 1994; (jtly) Co-operative Strategy, 1998, 2nd edn 2005; (jtly) The Management of International Acquisitions, 2001; Organization, 2005; (jtly) Corporate Co-evolution, 2008; numerous contribs to learned jls. *Recreations:* sailing, mountain walking, bridge. *Address:* Birmingham Business School, University House, University of Birmingham, Birmingham B15 2TT. *T:* (0121) 414 6701; *e-mail:* J.Child@bham.ac.uk. *Club:* Earlswood Sailing.

CHILD, Prof. Mark Sheard, PhD; FRS 1989; Coulson Professor of Theoretical Chemistry, University of Oxford, 1994–2004, and Fellow of University College, Oxford, since 1994; *b* 17 Aug. 1937; *s* of George Child and Kathleen (*née* Stevenson); *m* 1964, Daphne Hall; one *s* two *d*. *Educ:* Pocklington Sch., Yorks; Clare Coll., Cambridge (BA, PhD). Vis. Scientist, Berkeley, California, 1962–63; Lectr in Theoretical Chem., Glasgow Univ., 1963–66; Oxford University: Lectr in Theoretical Chem., 1966–89; Aldrichian Praelector in Chemistry, Oxford Univ., 1989–92; Prof. of Chemical Dynamics, 1992–94; Fellow, St Edmund Hall, 1966–94, Emeritus Fellow, 1994–. *Publications:* Molecular Collision Theory, 1974; Semiclassical Methods with Molecular Applications, 1991. *Recreations:* gardening, walking. *Address:* Physical and Theoretical Chemistry Laboratory, South Parks Road, Oxford OX1 3QZ.

CHILD VILLIERS, family name of **Earl of Jersey**.

CHILDS, David Robert; Managing Partner, Clifford Chance, since 2006; *b* 28 June 1951; *s* of Robert and Gwenifer Childs; *m* 1993, Julie Meyer; two *s* one *d*. *Educ:* Sheffield Univ. (LLB); University Coll. London (LLM). Admitted solicitor, 1976; Clifford Chance: Partner, 1981–; Hd, Global Corporate Practice Area, 2000–05; Chief Operating Officer, 2003–06. *Recreations:* wining and dining, woodland, travel. *Address:* Clifford Chance, 10 Upper Bank Street, E14 5JJ. *T:* (020) 7006 1000; *e-mail:* david.childs@cliffordchance.com.

CHILLINGWORTH, Rt Rev. David Robert; *see* St Andrews, Dunkeld and Dunblane, Bishop of.

CHILSTON, 4th Viscount *cr* 1911, of Boughton Malherbe; **Alastair George Akers-Douglas;** Baron Douglas of Baads, 1911; film producer; *b* 5 Sept. 1946; *s* of Ian Stanley Akers-Douglas (*d* 1952) (*g s* of 1st Viscount) and of Phyllis Rosemary (who *m* 2nd, John Anthony Cobham Shaw, MC), *d* of late Arthur David Clere Parsons; *S* cousin, 1982; *m* 1971, Juliet Anne, *d* of Lt-Col Nigel Lovett, Glos Regt; three *s*. *Educ:* Eton College; Madrid Univ. *Recreation:* sailing. *Heir: s* Hon. Oliver Ian Akers-Douglas [*b* 13 Oct. 1973; *m* 2005, Camilla Elizabeth Haldane; one *s*]. *Address:* Tichborne Cottage, Tichborne, Alresford, Hants SO24 0NA. *T:* (01962) 734010.

CHILTON, John James; jazz musician and author; *b* 16 July 1932; *s* of Thomas William Chilton and Eileen Florence (*née* Burke); *m* 1963, Teresa McDonald; two *s* one *d*. *Educ:* Yardley Gobion Sch., Northants; Claremont Sch., Kenton, Middx. Nat. Service, RAF, 1950–52. Worked in an advertising agency and for nat. newspaper before becoming professional musician, leading own band, 1958; played in a ship's orchestra, 1960; with Bruce Turner's Jump Band, 1960–63; jt-leader with Wally Fawkes, 1969–72; formed The Feetwarmers, 1972, regular accompanists for George Melly, 1972–2002. Recording, composing and arranging, 1972–. Grammy Award, USA, for best album notes, 1983; ARSC Award, USA, for best researched jazz or blues book, 1992; Jazz Writer of the Year, British Jazz award, 2000. *Publications:* Who's Who of Jazz, 1970, 5th edn 1989; Billie's Blues, 1974, 5th edn 1990; McKinney's Music, 1978; Teach Yourself Jazz, 1979, 2nd edn 1980; A Jazz Nursery, 1980; Stomp Off, Let's Go, 1983; Sidney Bechet: the wizard of jazz, 1987, 2nd edn 1996; The Song of the Hawk, 1990; Let the Good Times Roll, 1992; Who's Who of British Jazz, 1996, 2nd edn 2004; Ride, Red, Ride, 1999; Roy Eldridge: little jazz giant, 2002; Hot Jazz, Warm Feet (autobiog.), 2007; articles on jazz in books and newspapers. *Recreations:* watching cricket, soccer, collecting modern first editions.

CHILVER, family name of **Baron Chilver**.

CHILVER, Baron *cr* 1987 (Life Peer), of Cranfield in the County of Bedfordshire; **Henry Chilver,** Kt 1978; FRS 1982; FREng; Chairman, Chiroscience Group plc, 1995–98; *b* 30 Oct. 1926; *e s* of A. H. Chilver and A. E. Mack; *m* 1959, Claudia M. B. Grigson, MA, MB, BCh, *o d* of Sir Wilfrid Grigson; three *s* two *d*. *Educ:* Southend High Sch.; Bristol Univ. (Albert Fry Prize 1947). Structural Engineering Asst, British Railways, 1947; Asst Lecturer, 1950, Lecturer, 1952, in Civil Engineering, Bristol Univ.; Demonstrator, 1954, Lectr, 1956, in Engineering, Cambridge Univ.; Fellow of Corpus Christi Coll., Cambridge, 1958–61 (Hon. Fellow, 1981); Chadwick Prof. of Civil Engineering, UCL, 1961–69; Vice-Chancellor, Cranfield Inst. of Technology, 1970–89; Director: Centre for Environmental Studies, 1967–69; Node Course (for civil service and industry), 1974–75. Chairman: English China Clays, 1989–95 (Dir, 1973–95); RJB Mining plc, 1993–97; Director: SKF (UK), 1972–80; De La Rue Co., 1973–81; SE Reg., Nat. Westminster Bank, 1975–83; Delta Gp, 1977–84; Powell Duffryn, 1979–89; TR Technology Investment Trust, 1982–88; Hill Samuel Gp, 1983–87; Britoil, 1986–88; ICI, 1990–93; Zeneca Group, 1993–95. Chairman: Milton Keynes Develt Corp., 1983–92; Plymouth Develt Corp., 1996–98. Chairman: PO, 1980–81; Higher Educn Review Body, NI, 1978–81; Univs' Computer Bd, 1975–78; RAF Trng and Educn Adv. Cttee, 1976–80; Adv. Council, RMCS, Shrivenham, 1978–83; Working Gp on Advanced Ground Transport, 1978–81; Electronics EDC, 1980–85; ACARD, 1982–85; Interim Adv. Cttee on Teachers' Pay, 1987–91; UFC, 1988–91; Innovation Adv. Bd, DTI, 1989–93. Member: Ferrybridge Enquiry Cttee, 1965; Management Cttee, Inst. of Child Health, 1965–69; ARC, 1967–70 and 1972–75; SRC, 1970–74; Beds Educn Cttee, 1970–74; Planning and Transport Res. Adv. Council, 1972–79; Cttee for Ind. Technologies, 1972–76; ICE Special Cttee on Educn and Trng, 1973 (Chm.); CNAA, 1973–76; Royal Commn on Environmental Pollution, 1976–81; Standing Commn on Energy and the Environment, 1978–81; Adv. Bd for Res. Councils, 1982–85; Bd, Nat. Adv. Body for Local Authority Higher Educn, 1983–85. Dep. Pres., Standing Conf. on Schools Sci. and Technol.; Assessor, Inquiry on Lorries, People and the Envt, 1979–80. President: Inst. of Management Services, 1982–2000; Inst. of Logistics, 1993–95; Vice-Pres., ICE, 1981–83; Mem., Smeatonian Soc. of Civil Engrs (Pres., 1997). Member Council: Birkbeck Coll., 1980–82; Cheltenham Coll., 1980–88. Lectures: STC Communications, 1981; O'Sullivan, Imperial Coll., 1984; Lady Margaret Beaufort, Bedford, 1985; Fawley, Southampton Univ., 1985; Lubbock, Oxford, 1990. Telford Gold Medal, ICE, 1962; Coopers Hill War Meml Prize, ICE, 1977. FREng (FEng 1977). CCMI. Hon. DSc: Leeds, 1982; Bristol, 1983; Salford, 1983; Strathclyde, 1986; Bath, 1986; Cranfield, 1989; Buckingham, 1990; Compiègne, 1990. *Publications:* Problems in Engineering Structures (with R. J. Ashby), 1958; Strength of Materials (with J. Case), 1959, 3rd edn as Strength of Materials and Structures (with J. Case and C. T. Ross), 1993, 4th edn 1999; Thin-walled Structures (ed), 1967; papers on structural theory in engineering journals. *Clubs:* Athenæum, Oxford and Cambridge.

CHILVER, Elizabeth Millicent, (Mrs R. C. Chilver); Principal of Lady Margaret Hall, Oxford, 1971–79, Honorary Fellow, 1979; *b* 3 Aug. 1914; *o d* of late Philip Perceval Graves and late Millicent Graves (*née* Gilchrist); *m* 1937, Richard Clementson Chilver, CB (*d* 1985). *Educ:* Benenden Sch., Cranbrook; Somerville Coll., Oxford (Hon. Fellow, 1977). Journalist, 1937–39; temp. Civil Servant, 1939–45; Daily News Ltd, 1945–47; temp. Principal and Secretary, Colonial Social Science Research Council and Colonial Economic Research Cttee, Colonial Office, 1948–57; Director, Univ. of Oxford Inst. of Commonwealth Studies, 1957–61; Senior Research Fellow, Univ. of London Inst. of Commonwealth Studies, 1961–64; Principal, Bedford Coll., Univ. of London, 1964–71, Fellow, 1974. Mem. Royal Commn on Medical Education, 1965–68. Trustee, British Museum, 1970–75; Mem. Governing Body, SOAS, Univ. of London, 1975–80. Médaille de la Reconnaissance française, 1945. *Publications:* (with U. Röshenthaler) Cameroon's Tycoon, 2001; articles on African historical subjects. *Address:* 47 Kingston Road, Oxford OX2 6RH. *T:* (01865) 553082.

CHILVERS, Prof. Clair Evelyn Druce; DL; Chair, Nottinghamshire Healthcare NHS Trust, since 2007; *b* 8 Feb. 1946; *d* of Air Cdre Stanley Edwin Druce Mills, CB, CBE and Joan Mary Mills (*née* James); *m* 1st, 1965, Antony Stuart Chilvers, MA, MChir, FRCS (marr. diss. 1995); one *s* one *d*; 2nd, 1998, Bill Crampin (marr. diss. 2007). *Educ:* Cheltenham Ladies' Coll.; LSE (BSc Econ); LSHTM (MSc); DSc Nottingham 1995. Scientist, Inst. of Cancer Res., 1979–90; Prof. of Epidemiology, Med. Sch., 1990–99, now Emeritus, and Dean of Grad. Sch., 1996–99, Nottingham Univ.; Department of Health: Dir of R & D, Trent Region, NHS Exec., 1999–2002; Head of R & D, Directorate of Health and Social Care, Midlands and E of England, 2002–04; Dir, NHS R & D, Mental Health, 2004–06; Research Director: Nat. Inst. for Mental Health, 2004–06; Care Services Improvement Partnership, DoH, 2006–07; Mental Health Act Commission, 2006. Mem., Royal Commn on Envmtl Pollution, 1994–98. Mem., Cttee on Carcinogenicity of Chemicals in Food, Consumer Products and Envmt, DoH, 1993–2000. Non-executive Director: Nottingham Community Health NHS Trust, 1991–96; Learning and Skills (formerly Further Education) Develt Agency, 1998–2001. Trustee, Lloyds TSB Foundn, 2005–. Mem. Council, Nottingham Univ., 1994–99; Chm. Council, Southwell Cathedral, 2000–06. DL Notts, 2007. *Publications:* numerous in learned jls, mainly in field of cancer epidemiology. *Recreations:* music, cinema, food and wine. *Club:* Royal Automobile.

CHILVERS, Prof. Edwin Roy, PhD; FRCP, FRCPE; FMedSci; Professor of Respiratory Medicine, University of Cambridge, since 1998, and Fellow of St Edmund's College, Cambridge, since 1999; *b* 17 March 1959; *s* of Derek John Chilvers and Marjorie Grace Chilvers; *m* 1982, Rowena Joy Tyssen; two *s* one *d.* *Educ:* Univ. of Nottingham Med. Sch. (BMedSci 1980; BM BS Hons 1982); PhD London 1991; MA Cantab 2002. MRCP 1985, FRCP 1999; FRCPE 1995. Registrar, Ealing and Hammersmith Hosps, 1985–87; MRC Clinical Trng Fellow, 1987–90; Edinburgh University: Lectr in Respiratory Medicine, 1990–92; Wellcome Trust Sen. Res. Fellow in Clinical Sci., 1992–98; Reader in Medicine, 1997–98. Hon. Consultant Physician: Royal Infirmary, Edinburgh, 1992–98; Addenbrooke's and Papworth Hosps, 1998–. Non-exec. Dir, Papworth Hosp. NHS Trust, 2002–06. FMedSci 2007; FHEA 2007. *Publications:* (ed jtly) Davidson's Principles and Practice of Medicine, 17th edn 1995 to 19th edn 2002; contrib. scientific papers on inflammatory cell biol. and intracellular signalling. *Recreations:* modern literature, spectator sport. *Address:* 4 Mallows Close, Comberton, Cambridge CB3 7GN. *T:* (01223) 762007.

CHILWELL, Hon. Sir Muir Fitzherbert, Kt 1989; Judge of the Court of Appeal, Cook Islands, 1990–2005; Judge of the High Court, Cook Islands, 1991–94; *b* 12 April 1924; *s* of Benjamin Charles Chilwell and Loris Madeleine Chilwell; *m* 1947, Lynette Erica Frances Cox; two *d* (one *s* decd). *Educ:* Auckland University Coll., Univ. of New Zealand (LLB 1949; LLM Hons 1950). Law Clerk, 1941–49; admitted Barrister and Solicitor, 1949; Partner, Haddow, Haddow & Chilwell, later Haddow Chilwell Pain & Palmer, 1949–65; QC 1965; admitted Victorian Bar (Aust.) and QC Vict. 1970; Judge of the Supreme, later High, Court of NZ, 1973–91; Admin. Div., High Court, 1982–91. Lectr, Univ. of Auckland, 1950 and 1953–60. Member: Contracts and Commercial Law Reform Cttee, 1966–68 (Chm., 1968–73); Law Revision Commn, 1968–73; Disciplinary Cttee, NZ Law Soc., 1971–73; Council, Legal Educn, NZ, 1985–91 (Assessor in Law of Contract, 1964–67); Chm., Legal Res. Foundn, 1977–81; Mem. Council, Auckland Dist Law Soc., 1960–67, Pres., 1967–68; Pres., Auckland Medico-Legal Soc., 1969–70, Life Mem., 1989. Silver Jubilee Medal, 1977; Commemoration Medal, NZ, 1990. *Recreation:* bowling. *Address:* 29A The Parade, St Heliers, Auckland 1071, New Zealand. *T:* (9) 5757999. *Clubs:* Royal New Zealand Yacht Squadron; St Heliers Bowling.

CHINERY, David John; District Judge (Magistrates' Courts) (formerly Stipendiary Magistrate), West Midlands, since 1998; a Recorder, since 2002; *b* 10 Aug. 1950; *s* of Oliver John Chinery and Gladys Alberta Chinery; *m* 1973, Jeannette Elizabeth Owens; two *d.* *Educ:* Alleyne's Sch., Stevenage; Coll. of Law. Justices' Clerk's Asst, Hitchin Magistrates' Court, 1969–75; Asst Clerk to Justices, Northampton Magistrates' Court, 1975–79; admitted solicitor, 1979; Asst Solicitor, 1979–82, Partner, 1982–90, Borneo, Martell & Partners, Northampton; sole practitioner, 1990–98. Deputy Stipendiary Magistrate: Nottingham, 1993–98; Doncaster, 1996–98; Birmingham, 1997–98. *Recreations:* Rugby Union football, cricket, music, Victorian poetry. *Address:* Victoria Law Courts, Corporation Street, Birmingham B4 6QA.

CHING, Henry, CBE 1982; Secretary General, Caritas-Hong Kong, 1990–91; *b* 2 Nov. 1933; *s* of Henry Ching, OBE and Ruby Irene Ching; *m* 1963, Eileen Frances Peters; two *d.* *Educ:* Diocesan Boys' School, Hong Kong; Hong Kong Univ. (BA Hons); Wadham Coll., Oxford (MA, DipEd). Schoolmaster, 1958–61; Hong Kong Civil Service: various appts, 1961–73; Principal Asst Financial Sec., 1973–76; Dep. Financial Sec., 1976–83; Sec. for Health and Welfare and MLC, Hong Kong, 1983–85, retired. Chief Administrator, Hong Kong Foundn, 1989. Chm., Hong Kong Volunteer and ex-POW Assoc. of NSW, 2006–. *Recreations:* cricket, rowing. *Address:* 39 Saiala Road, East Killara, NSW 2071, Australia.

CHINN, Antony Nigel Caton; QC 2003; a Recorder, since 2000; *b* 20 May 1949; *s* of Edward William Chinn and Barbara Ursula Neene Chinn (*née* Tilbury); *m* 1973, Margot Susan Elizabeth Emery; two *s.* *Educ:* Ardingly Coll.; Inns of Court Sch. of Law. Called to the Bar, Middle Temple, 1972; in practice, specialising in criminal law; Asst Recorder, 1996–2000. *Recreations:* motor sport, football, music. *Address:* 9 Bedford Row, WC1R 4AZ. *T:* (020) 7489 2727, *Fax:* (020) 7489 2828. *Club:* Goodwood Road Racing.

CHINN, Susan Avril, (Lady Chinn); JP; *b* Cobham, 4 April 1943; *d* of late Louis Speelman and of Meryl Speelman; *m* 1965, Sir Trevor Edwin Chinn, *qv*; two *s.* *Educ:* The Warren, Worthing. PR Consultant, 1983–95. Mem. Bd, 2003–, and Chm., Develt Council, 2003–, RNT. Vice Chm., Royal Marsden Cancer Appeal, 1990–93. Special Trustee, Gt Ormond St Hosp. for Sick Children, 1990–2000; Trustee, Child Psychotherapy Trust, 1993–96. JP Inner London, 1980. *Recreations:* theatre, gardening, fly fishing. *Address:* *e-mail:* susan@chinn.com.

CHINN, Sir Trevor (Edwin), Kt 1990; CVO 1989; Chairman, Automobile Association, 2004–07; *b* 24 July 1935; *s* of late Rosser and Susie Chinn; *m* 1965, Susan Avril Speelman (*see* S. A. Chinn); two *s.* *Educ:* Clifton Coll.; King's Coll., Cambridge. Lex Service, subseq. RAC plc: Dir, 1959–2002; Man. Dir, 1968–73; Chief Exec., 1973–96; Chm., 1973–2003; Chm., Kwik-Fit, 2002–05. Chairman: ITIS, 2000–; Vigilant Technology Ltd, 2005–; Aurora Russia Ltd, 2006–; Streetcar Ltd, 2007–. Vice-Chm., Commn for Integrated Transport, 1999–2004; Chm., Motorists' Forum, 2000–. Sen. Advr, CVC Capital Partners, 2002–. President: United Jewish Israel Appeal, 1993–; Norwood Ravenswood, subseq. Norwood, 1996–2006; Vice Chm., Wishing Well Appeal, Gt Ormond St Hosp. for Sick Children, 1985–89. Trustee, Royal Acad. Trust, 1989–2004 (Dep. Chm., 1996–2004). Trustee, Duke of Edinburgh's Award, 1978–88. Freeman of the City of London. Chief Barker, Variety Club of GB, 1977, 1978. *Address:* Marble Arch Tower, 55 Bryanston Street, W1H 7AJ. *T:* (020) 7868 8836.

CHINNERY, (Charles) Derek; Controller, Radio 1, BBC, 1978–85; *b* 27 April 1925; *s* of Percy Herbert and Frances Dorothy Chinnery; *m* 1953, Doreen Grace Clarke. *Educ:* Gosforth Grammar School. Youth in training, BBC, 1941; RAF Cadet Pilot, 1943. BBC: Technical Asst, 1947; Programme Engineer, 1948; Studio Manager, 1950; Producer, 1952; Executive Producer, 1967; Head of Radio 1, 1972. *Recreations:* DIY, travelling. *Address:* 19 South Ridge, Brunton Park, Newcastle upon Tyne NE3 2EJ.

CHIONA, Most Rev. James; Archbishop of Blantyre, (RC), 1967–2001; *b* 12 Sept. 1924. *Educ:* Nankhunda Minor Seminary, Malaŵi; Kachebere Major Seminary, Malaŵi. Priest, 1954; Asst Parish Priest, 1954–57; Prof., Nankhunda Minor Seminary, 1957–60; study of Pastoral Sociology, Rome, 1961–62; Asst Parish Priest, 1962–65; Auxiliary Bishop of Blantyre and Titular Bishop of Bacanaria, 1965; Vicar Capitular of Archdiocese of Blantyre, 1967. *Recreation:* music. *Address:* c/o Archdiocese of Blantyre, PO Box 385, Blantyre, Malaŵi.

CHIPIMO, Elias Marko Chisha; Ambassador of Zambia to Japan, also accredited to Indonesia, Korea and the Philippines, and as High Commissioner, Australia and New Zealand, 2000; *b* 23 Feb. 1931; *s* of Marko Chipimo, Zambia (then Northern Rhodesia); *m* 1959, Anna Joyce Nkole Konie; four *s* three *d.* *Educ:* St Canisius, Chikuni, Zambia; Munali; Fort Hare Univ. Coll., SA; University Coll. of Rhodesia and Nyasaland; Univ. of Zambia (LLB 1985). Schoolmaster, 1959–63; Sen. Govt Administrator, 1964–67; High Comr for Zambia in London, and Zambian Ambassador to the Holy See, 1968–69; Perm. Sec., Min. of Foreign Affairs, 1969; Hon. Minister, Lusaka Province, 1991–96; MP (MMD) Kantanshi, 1991–96; Nat. Chm., 1991–96, and Mem., Nat. Exec. Cttee, until 1996, MMD; Ambassador to Germany, 1997–2000. Chairman: Zambia Stock Exchange Council, 1970–72; Zambia Nat. Bldg Soc., 1970–71; Dep. Chm., Development Bank of Zambia Ltd, 1973–75; Dep. Chm., 1975, Chm., 1976–80, Standard Bank Zambia Ltd; Director: Zambia Airways Corp., 1975–81; Zambia Bata Shoe Co. Ltd, 1977–92. Mem., Nat Council for Sci. Res., 1977–80. Pres., Zambia Red Cross, 1990–95 (Vice-Pres., 1976–90; Life Mem., 1995; Pres., Lusaka Br., 1970–75); Mem., Zambia Univ. Council, 1970–76; Dir, Internat. Sch. of Lusaka, 1970–76. Cllr, Lusaka City Council, 1974–80. Rep., Commonwealth Soc., 1979–88. *Publications:* Our Land and People, 1966; Tied Loans and the Role of Banks (vol. 2 of International Financing of Economic Development), 1978; articles in Univ. of Zambia Jl. *Recreations:* gardening, reading, general literature, linguistics, philosophy, politics, economics, discussions, chess. *Address:* c/o Ministry of Foreign Affairs, PO Box 50069, Lusaka, Zambia.

CHIPMAN, Dr John Miguel Warwick, CMG 1999; Director General and Chief Executive, The International Institute for Strategic Studies, since 1993; Director: IISS-US and IISS-Asia, since 2001; Arundel House Enterprises, since 1999; *b* 10 Feb. 1957; *s* of Lawrence Carroll Chipman and Maria Isabel (*née* Prados); *m* 1997, Lady Theresa Helen Margaret Manners, *yr d* of 10th Duke of Rutland, CBE; twin *s.* *Educ:* Harvard Coll. (BA Hons); London Sch. of Economics (MA Dist.); Balliol Coll., Oxford (MPhil, DPhil). Research Associate: IISS, 1983–84; Atlantic Inst. for Internat. Affairs, Paris, 1985–87; The International Institute for Strategic Studies: Asst Dir for Regl Security, 1987–91; Dir of Studies, 1991–93. Member, International Advisory Board: Reliance Industries Ltd (Mumbai), 2006–; Nat. Bank of Kuwait, 2008–. Mem. Bd, Aspen Inst., Italy, 1995–. Founder, Strategic Comments jl, 1995. *Publications:* V ième République et Défense de l'Afrique, 1986; (ed and jt author) NATO's Southern Allies, 1988; French Power in Africa, 1989; numerous contribs to edited vols, learned jls and newspapers. *Recreations:* tennis, ski-ing, scuba diving, riding, collecting travel books. *Address:* The International Institute for Strategic Studies, Arundel House, 13–15 Arundel Street, Temple Place, WC2R 3DX. *T:* (020) 7379 7676. *Clubs:* Brooks's, Beefsteak, Garrick, White's; Harvard (New York).

CHIPPERFIELD, David Alan, CBE 2004; RDI 2006; RIBA; Principal, David Chipperfield Architects, since 1984; *b* 18 Dec. 1953; *s* of Alan John Chipperfield and Peggy Chipperfield (*née* Singleton); partner, Dr Evelyn Stern; two *s* one *d*, and one *s* from previous relationship. *Educ:* Wellington Sch., Somerset; Kingston Poly.; Architectural Assoc. (AA Dip). RIBA 1982. Designer, Douglas Stephens & Partners, 1977–78; Architect, Richard Rogers & Partners, 1978–79; Project Architect, Foster Associates, 1981–84. Projects include: private museum, Japan, 1987; TAK Design Centre, Kyoto, Japan, 1989; Matsumoto Corp. HQ, Okayama, Japan, 1990; Landeszentralbank HQ, Gera, Germany, and Joseph, Sloane Avenue, London, 1996; River and Rowing Mus., Henley-on-Thames, 1996–97 (Best Building in England, RFAC Trust/BSkyB Building of the Year Award, 1999); Neues Mus., Berlin, Kaistrasse Office Building, Düsseldorf, and Shore Club Hotel, Miami, 1997; Ernsting Service Centre, Munster, Berlin Museum Is Masterplan, San Michele Cemetery, Venice, and Bryant Park Hotel, NY, 1998; Palace of Justice, Salerno, Davenport Mus. of Art, Iowa, and New Entrance Mus., Berlin, 1999; Ansaldo City of Cultures Mus., Milan, 2000; BFI, London, and Polo Culturale, Verona, 2001; City of Justice, Barcelona, 2002; Housing Villaverde, Madrid, Pantaenius House, Hamburg, Hotel Beaumont, Maastricht, Figge Art Mus., Davenport, Iowa and Hotel Puerta America, Madrid, 2005; Mus. of Modern Lit., Marbach am Neckar (RIBA Stirling Prize, 2007), Rena Lange shop, Munich, Des Moines Public Liby, Iowa, BBC Scotland Pacific Quay, Glasgow and America's Cup Bldg, Valencia, 2006; Freshfields Bruckhaus Deringer office bldg, Amsterdam, Liangzhu Culture Mus., China, Empire Riverside Hotel, Hamburg and Gall. 'Hinter dem Giesshaus 1', Berlin, 2007. Founder and Dir, 9H Gall., London. Design Tutor, RCA, 1988–89; Prof. of Architecture, Staatliche Akad. der Bildenden Künste, Stuttgart, 1995–2000; Mies van der Rohe Chair, Escuela Técnica, Barcelona, 2001; Visiting Professor: Harvard Univ., 1987–88; Graz Univ., 1992; Naples Univ., 1992; Ecole Polytechnique, Lausanne, 1993–94. Trustee, Architecture Foundn, 1992–97. Special Mention, Financial Times Award, 1991; Andrea Palladio Prize, 1993; Regl Award, RIBA, 1996, 1998; RIBA Award, 1998, 2002, 2003, 2004; Tessenow Gold Medal, 1999; Civic Trust Award, 1999. *Publication:* Theoretical Practice, 1994; *relevant publications:* El Croquis (monograph), 1998, 2001, 2004, 2006; David Chipperfield, Architectural Works 1990–2002, 2003; David Chipperfield, Idea e Realta, 2005. *Recreations:* reading, drawing, swimming. *Address:* (office) 1A Cobham Mews, Agar Grove, NW1 9SB. *T:* (020) 7267 9422. *Club:* Royal Automobile.

CHIPPERFIELD, Sir Geoffrey (Howes), KCB 1992 (CB 1985); Deputy Chairman, 2000–03, and Director, 1993–2003, Pennon Group (formerly South West Water plc); *b* 20 April 1933; *s* of Nelson Chipperfield and Eleanor Chipperfield; *m* 1959, Gillian James; two *s.* *Educ:* Cranleigh; New Coll., Oxford. Called to the Bar, Gray's Inn, 1955. Joined Min. of Housing and Local Govt, 1956; Harkness Fellow, Inst. of Govtl Studies, Univ. of Calif, Berkeley, 1962–63; Principal Private Sec., Minister of Housing, 1968–70; Sec., Greater London Develt Plan Inquiry, 1970–73; Under Sec., 1976, Dep. Sec., 1982–87, DoE; Dep. Sec., Dept of Energy, 1987–89; Perm. Under-Sec. of State, Dept of Energy, 1989–91; Perm. Sec. and Chief Exec., PSA Services, 1991–93. Chm., Heliodynamics Ltd, 2000–. Chairman: DTI Energy Adv. Panel, 1996–2001; British Cement Assoc., 1996–2001. Pro-Chancellor, Univ. of Kent, 1998–2005. Mem. Council, Foundn of Sci. and Technol., 2005–. *Recreations:* reading, gardening. *Clubs:* Oxford and Cambridge, Athenæum.

CHIPPINDALE, Christopher Ralph, PhD; Reader in Archaeology, University of Cambridge, at University Museum of Archaeology and Anthropology, since 2001; *b* 13 Oct. 1951; *s* of Keith and Ruth Chippindale; *m* 1976, Anne Lowe (marr. diss. 2008); two *s* two *d.* *Educ:* Sedbergh School; St John's College, Cambridge (BA Hons); Girton Coll., Cambridge (PhD). MIFA; FSA. Editor, freelance, Penguin Books, Hutchinson Publishing Group, 1974–82; Res. Fellow in Archaeology, 1985–88, Bye-Fellow, 1988–91, Girton Coll., Cambridge; Asst Curator, 1988–93, Sen. Asst Curator, 1993–, Cambridge Univ. Mus. of Archaeol. Vis. Prof., Univ. of Witwatersrand, 2002–. Editor, Antiquity, 1987–97. *Publications:* Stonehenge Complete, 1983, 2nd edn 1994; (ed jtly) The Pastmasters, 1989; (jtly) Who owns Stonehenge?, 1990; A High Way to Heaven, 1998; (ed jtly) The Archaeology of Rock Art, 1999; (ed jtly) Landscapes of European Rock-art, 2002; articles in jls. *Recreations:* work, worrying. *Address:* 46 High Street, Chesterton, Cambridge CB4 1NG.

CHIPPING, Hilary Jane; Director, Network Strategy, Highways Agency, since 2001; *b* 31 Jan. 1955; *d* of late Clarence John Watts and Alice Mary Watts; *m* 1975, Richard Frank

Chipping; one *s* one *d.* *Educ:* Bletchley Grammar Sch.; Univ. of Manchester (BA (Econ) 1975, MA (Econ) 1977). Joined Civil Service, 1977; Head: Local Govt Finance Div., 1990–94, Water Services Div., 1994–95, DoE; Local Authy Housing Div., DETR, 1995–2000; Roads Policy Div., DTLR, 2000–01. *Recreations:* walking, cookery. *Address:* Highways Agency, 123 Buckingham Palace Road, SW1W 9HA. *T:* (020) 7153 4764; *e-mail:* hilary.chipping@highways.gsi.gov.uk.

CHIRAC, Jacques René; President of the French Republic, 1995–2007; *b* Paris, 29 Nov. 1932; *s* of François Chirac, company manager and Marie-Louise (*née* Valette); *m* 1956, Bernadette Chodron de Courcel; two *d.* *Educ:* Lycée Carnot and Lycée Louis-le-Grand, Paris; Diploma of Inst. of Polit. Studies, Paris, and of Summer Sch., Harvard Univ., USA. Served Army in Algeria. Ecole Nat. d'Admin, 1957–59; Auditor, Cour des Comptes, 1959; Head Dept: Sec.-Gen. of Govt, 1962; Private Office of Georges Pompidou, 1962–67; Counsellor, Cour des Comptes, 1965; State Secretary: Employment Problems, 1967–68; Economy and Finance, 1968–71; Minister for Parly Relations, 1971–72; Minister for Agriculture and Rural Development, 1972–74; Home Minister, March-May 1974; Prime Minister, 1974–76 and 1986–88. Deputy from Corrèze, elected 1967, 1968, 1973, 1976 (UDR), 1978 (RPR), 1981, 1986, 1988 and 1993; Sec.-Gen., UDR, Dec. 1974–June 1975; Pres., Rassemblement pour la République, 1976–81 and 1982–94. Mayor of Paris, 1977–95. Member from Meymac, Conseil Général of Corrèze, 1968–, Pres. 1970–79. Mem., European Parlt, 1979–80. Treasurer, Claude Pompidou Foundn (charity for elderly and for handicapped children), 1969–. Grand-Croix, Ordre national du Mérite; Croix de la valeur militaire; Chevalier du Mérite agricole, des Arts et des Lettres, de l'Etoile noire, du Mérite sportif, du Mérite touristique; Médaille de l'Aéronautique. *Publications:* a thesis on development of Port of New Orleans, 1954; Discours pour la France à l'heure du choix, 1978; La lueur d'espérance: réflexion du soir pour le matin, 1978; Une Nouvelle France, 1994; La France pour Tous, 1995. *Address:* c/o Palais de l'Elysée, 75008 Paris, France.

CHISHOLM, Prof. Alexander William John; Professor Emeritus, University of Salford, since 1994; *b* 18 April 1922; *s* of Thomas Alexander Chisholm and Maude Mary Chisholm (*née* Robinson); *m* 1945, Aline Mary (*née* Eastwood) (*d* 1995); one *s* (one *d* decd). *Educ:* Brentwood Sch., Essex; Northampton Polytechnic; Manchester Coll. of Science and Technology; Royal Technical Coll., Salford (BSc(Eng) London). CEng, FIMechE, FIET. Section Leader, Res. Dept, Metropolitan Vickers Electrical Co. Ltd, 1944–49; Sen. Scientific Officer, then Principal Scientific Officer, Nat. Engrg Lab., 1949–57; UK Scientific Mission, British Embassy, USA, 1952–54; Head of Dept of Mechanical Engrg, then Prof. of Mechanical Engrg, Royal Coll. of Advanced Technology, Salford, 1957–67; University of Salford: Prof. of Mech. Engineering, 1967–82; Research Prof. in Engrg., 1982–87; Professorial Fellow, 1987–94; Chm., Salford Univ. Industrial Centre, subseq. Salford Univ. Industrial Centre Ltd, 1968–82. Visitor, Cambridge Univ. Engrg Dept and Vis. Fellow, Wolfson Coll., 1973–74. Chm., Engrg Profs' Conf., 1976–80; Dir, Prog. for Improvement of Quality of Engrg Educn, 1990–95 (Hon. Chm., 1995–96). Chm., Industrial Admin and Engrg Prodn Gp, IMechE, 1960–62. Nat. Council for Technological Awards: Chm., Mechanical/Prodn Engrg Cttee, 1960–63; Vice-Chm., Bd of Studies in Engrg and Governor, 1963–65. Member: Technology Cttee, UGC, 1969–74; Engrg Processes Cttee, SERC, 1980–83. Pres., CIRP, 1983–84 (Hon. Life Mem. 1987; Chm., UK Bd, 1977–88). Mem., Court, Cranfield Inst. of Technology, 1974–91. Whitworth Prize, IMechE, 1965. *Publications:* numerous on production process technology, manufacturing systems, industrial research, educn and training of engineers, human factors in manufacturing. *Recreations:* hill walking, sailing, tree planting. *Address:* 12 Legh Road, Prestbury, Macclesfield, Cheshire SK10 4HX. *T:* (01625) 829412. *Club:* Athenæum.

CHISHOLM, Catherine Alexandra, (Kitty), (Lady Chisholm); Consultant and coach, since 2007; *b* 19 April 1946; *d* of Gregory Panas and Aleca Panas, Athens; *m* 1969, Sir John Alexander Raymond Chisholm, *qv*; one *s* one *d.* *Educ:* Girton Coll., Cambridge (BA 1969); Open Univ. (MSc 2001). Open University: Res. Asst in Classics, 1976–82; Course Co-ordinator in Contg Educn, 1982–83; Adminr, Sci. and Technol. Updating, 1983–89; Business Develt Manager, 1989–91; Dir of Develt, 1991–2002; Dir of Develt, Brunel Univ., 2003–07. Member: Bd, British Telecom Acad., 2000–02; Borderless Educn Observatory Bd, 2001–; Adv. Bd, Vosper Thorneycroft Educn Services, 2003–06. Trustee: CASE Europe, 1995–2001 (Chm., 1998–2001); Reach, 2003–; Nat. Mus of Sci. and Industry, 2007–. FRSA 2000. *Publications:* Political and Social Life in the Great Age of Athens, 1978; Rome, the Augustan Age, 1981. *Recreations:* pink roses, reading, walking, watching husband race classic cars. *Club:* Reform.

CHISHOLM, Sir John (Alexander Raymond), Kt 1999; FREng; Chairman: Medical Research Council, since 2006; QinetiQ Group plc, since 2005; *b* 27 Aug. 1946; *s* of Ruari Ian Lambert Chisholm and Pamela Harland Chisholm; *m* 1969, Catherine Alexandra (*née* Pana) (*see* C. A. Chisholm); one *s* one *d.* *Educ:* Queens' Coll., Cambridge (BA 1968). CEng 1974, FREng (FEng 1996); FIET (FIEE 1995); FRAeS 1996; FInstP 1999. Vauxhall Motors, 1964–69; Scicon Ltd, 1969–79; Cap Scientific Ltd, 1979–91: Man. Dir, 1981–86; Chm., 1986–91; Chm., Yard Ltd, 1986–91; UK Man. Dir, Sema Group plc, 1988–91; Chief Executive: DRA, subseq. DERA, 1991–2001; QinetiQ plc, 2001–05. Non-executive Director: Expro Internat. plc, 1994–2003; Bespak plc, 1999–2005. Mem., UK Foresight Steering Gp, 1993–2000. President: Electronic and Business Equipment Assoc., 1989–90; IEE, 2005–06; IET, 2006. Mem. Council, Cranfield Univ., 1995–2002. *Recreations:* participative sports, old cars. *Address:* Batchworth Hill House, London Road, Rickmansworth WD3 1JS.

CHISHOLM, John William, CBE 2000; FRCGP; Medical Director, Concordia Health Ltd, since 2006; Adviser, NHS Working in Partnership Programme, since 2005; Consultant, Dr Foster, since 2005; *b* 29 Dec. 1950; *s* of late William Chisholm and of Olive Chisholm (*née* Tomlinson); *m* 1977, Caroline Mary Colyer (*née* Davis) (marr. diss. 2006); two *d,* and one step *s*; partner, Prof. Ann Marie Sommerville (*née* Pryal). *Educ:* Clifton Coll. Prep. Sch.; Clifton Coll.; Peterhouse, Cambridge (BA 1971, BChir 1974, MB 1975); Westminster Med. Sch. DRCOG 1977; MRCGP, 1978, FRCGP 1995. House surgeon, 1974–75, house physician, 1975, Croydon Gen. Hosp.; GP trainee, Reading Vocational Trng Scheme, 1976–79; GP, Twyford, 1979–2004. Member Board: DPP 2000, 2004–; BMJ Pubns Gp, 2002–04. Member: Jt Cttee on Postgrad. Trng for Gen. Practice, 1980–90, 1995–2005; Supervisory Bd, NHS Centre for Coding and Classification, 1990–97; Standing Med. Adv. Cttee, 1998–2005; Partners' Council, NICE, 1998–2001; Expert Patients Task Force, 1999–2000; Patient Care (Empowerment) Modernisation Action Team, 2000; NHS IT Task Force, 2002–04; Primary Care Task Gp, 2003; Nat. Primary Care Develt Team Adv. Bd, 2004–06. Observer, Clinical Standards Adv. Gp, 1993–96. Mem., GMC, 1999–2003 (Mem., Standards Cttee, 1999–2002); British Medical Association: Chm., Junior Members Forum, 1981–82; Mem. Council, 1981–82, 1988–; Member: Finance Cttee, 2002–06; Med. Ethics Cttee, 2004–; Gen. Med. Services Cttee, subseq. GPs Cttee, 1977– (Negotiator, 1990–97; Jt Dep. Chm., 1991–97; Chm., 1997–2004; Chairman: Trainees Subcttee, 1978–80; Jt (with RCGP) Computing Gp, 1984–86; Practice Orgn Subcttee, 1986–90; Nurse Prescribing Wkg Gp, 1988–89); Mem. Council, RCGP, 2005– (Observer, 2004–05). Chairman: Gen. Med. Services Defence Fund, 1997–2001; Gen. Practitioners Defence Fund, 2001–04. Observer, Acad. of Med. Royal Colls, 2002–04. Rep., European Union of GPs (UEMO), 1988–2004. Patron, Men's Health Forum, 2004–. *Publications:* (ed jtly) Micros in Practice: report of an appraisal of GP microcomputer systems, 1986; (ed) Making Sense of the Red Book, 1989, (with N. D. Ellis) 2nd edn 1993, 3rd edn 1997; (ed) Making Sense of the New Contract, 1990; (ed) Making Sense of the Cost Rent Scheme, 1992; articles esp. concerning gen. practice orgn. *Recreations:* reading, art, photography, music (former amateur flautist, singer, conductor). *Address:* 5 Elmers End Road, Anerley, SE20 7ST. *T:* (020) 8778 2550; *e-mail:* john.chisholm@john-chisholm.demon.co.uk, john.chisholm@concordiahealth.co.uk.

CHISHOLM, Kitty; *see* Chisholm, C. A.

CHISHOLM, Malcolm George Richardson; Member (Lab) Edinburgh North and Leith, Scottish Parliament, since 1999; *b* 7 March 1949; *s* of late George and Olive Chisholm; *m* 1975, Janet Broomfield, writer; two *s* one *d.* *Educ:* George Watson's Coll.; Edinburgh Univ. (MA Hons, Dip Ed). Formerly Teacher of English, Castlebrae High School and Broughton High School. MP (Lab) Edinburgh, Leith, 1992–97, Edinburgh North and Leith, 1997–2001. Parly Under-Sec. of State, Scottish Office, 1997. Scottish Executive: Dep. Minister, 2000–01, Minister, 2001–04, for Health and Community Care; Minister for Communities, 2004–07. *Recreations:* reading, cinema. *Address:* Scottish Parliament, George IV Bridge, Edinburgh EH99 1SP. *T:* (020) 7219 4613.

CHISHOLM, Prof. Malcolm Harold, FRS 1990; Distinguished University Professor and Chair, Department of Chemistry, Ohio State University, since 2000; *b* 15 Oct. 1945; *s* of Angus and Gweneth Chisholm; *m* 1st, 1969, Susan Sage (marr. diss.); one *s*; 2nd, 1982, Cynthia Brown; two *s.* *Educ:* London Univ. (BSc 1966; PhD 1969). Sessional Lectr, Univ. of W Ontario, 1970–72; Asst Prof. of Chemistry, Princeton Univ., 1972–78; Indiana University: Associate Prof., 1978–80; Prof., 1980–85; Distinguished Prof. of Chemistry, 1985–99. Guggenheim Fellow, 1985–86. Editor, Polyhedron, 1983–98; Associate Editor: Dalton Trans., 1988–2003; Chemical Communications, 1995–99. FAAAS 1987; FRSE 2005; Fellow: Amer. Acad. Arts and Scis, 2004; German Acad. of Scis Leopoldina, 2004; MNAS, 2005. Hon. DSc: London, 1980; Western Ontario, 2008. RSC Award for Chem. and Electrochem. of Transition Elements, 1987; Alexander von Humboldt Sen. Scientist Award, 1988; (jtly) ACS Nobel Laureate Signature Award, 1988; ACS Award in Inorganic Chm., 1989; Centenary Medal and Lectr, RSC, 1995; ACS Distinguished Service to Inorganic Chemistry, 1999; Davy Medal, Royal Soc., 1999; Ludwig Mond Medal and Lectr., RSC, 2000; Basolo Medal, Northwestern Univ., Chicago, 2004; Bailar Medal, 2006. *Publications:* Reactivity of Metal-Metal Bonds, 1982; Inorganic Chemistry: towards the 21st century, 1983; Early Transition Metal Clusters with π-Donor Ligands, 1995; numerous articles, mostly in chem. jls. *Recreations:* squash, gardening. *Address:* 100 Kenyon Brook Drive, Worthington, OH 43085, USA. *T:* (614) 9850942; 38 Norwich Street, Cambridge CB2 1NE. *T:* (01223) 312392.

CHISHOLM, Prof. Michael Donald Inglis, FBA 2002; Professor of Geography, University of Cambridge, 1976–96, now Emeritus; Professorial Fellow, St Catharine's College, Cambridge, 1976–96; *b* 10 June 1931; *s* of M. S. and A. W. Chisholm; *m* 1st, 1959, Edith Gretchen Emma (*née* Hoof) (marr. diss. 1981); one *s* two *d*; 2nd, 1986, Judith Carola Shackleton (*née* Murray). *Educ:* St Christopher Sch., Letchworth; St Catharine's Coll., Cambridge (MA; ScD 1996). Nat. Service Commn, RE, 1950–51. Deptl Demonstrator, Inst. for Agric. Econs, Oxford, 1954–59; Asst Lectr, then Lectr in Geog., Bedford Coll., London, 1960–64; Vis. Sen. Lectr in Geog., Univ. of Ibadan, 1964–65; Lectr, then Reader in Geog., Univ. of Bristol, 1965–72; Prof. of Economic and Social Geography, Univ. of Bristol, 1972–76. Associate, Economic Associates Ltd, consultants, 1965–77. Geography Editor for Hutchinson Univ. Lib., 1973–82. Mem. SSRC, and Chm. of Cttees for Human Geography and Planning, 1967–72; Member: Local Govt Boundary Commn for England, 1971–78; Rural Develt Commn, 1981–90; English Adv. Cttee on Telecommunications, 1990–92; Local Govt Commn for England, 1992–95. Mem. Council, IBG, 1961 and 1962 (Jun. Vice-Pres., 1977; Sen. Vice-Pres., 1978; Pres. 1979). Conservator of River Cam, 1979– (Chm., 1991–); Bd Mem., Cambridge Preservation Soc., 2000–; Vice-Chm., Cambs ACRE, 2001–02. Gill Memorial Prize, RGS, 1969. *Publications:* Rural Settlement and Land Use: an essay in location, 1962; Geography and Economics, 1966; (ed jtly) Regional Forecasting, 1971; (ed jtly) Spatial Policy Problems of the British Economy, 1971; Research in Human Geography, 1971; (ed) Resources for Britain's Future, 1972; (jtly) Freight Flows and Spatial Aspects of the British Economy, 1973; (jtly) The Changing Pattern of Employment, 1973; (ed jtly) Studies in Human Geography, 1973; (ed jtly) Processes in Physical and Human Geography: Bristol Essays, 1975; Human Geography: Evolution or Revolution?, 1975; Modern World Development, 1982; Regions in Recession and Resurgence, 1990; (ed jtly) Shared Space: Divided Space, 1990; Britain on the Edge of Europe, 1995; (ed jtly) A Fresh Start for Local Government, 1997; Structural Reform of British Local Government: rhetoric and reality, 2000; papers in Farm Economist, Oxford Econ. Papers, Trans Inst. British Geographers, Geography, Geographical Jl, Applied Statistics, Area, Envmt and Planning, Jl of Local Govt Law, Jl of Histl Geography, Proceedings of Cambridge Antiquarian Soc., etc. *Recreations:* gardening, theatre, opera, interior design. *Address:* 5 Clarendon Road, Cambridge CB2 8BH.

CHISHOLM, (Peter) Nicolas; Headmaster, Yehudi Menuhin School, since 1988; *b* 7 Dec. 1949; *s* of David Whitridge Chisholm and Marjorie Chisholm; *m* 1977, Auriol Mary Oakeley. *Educ:* Christ's Hospital, Horsham; St John's Coll., Cambridge (MA). Tenor Lay Vicar, Chichester Cathedral, 1972–76; Asst Master, Prebendal Sch., Chichester, 1972–76; Hurstpierpoint College: Hd Classics, 1976–88; Housemaster, Eagle Hse, 1982–88. Chairman: Sussex Assoc. of Classical Teachers, 1982–88; Trustees, SE Music Schemes, 1996–; Nat. Assoc. of Music and Dance Schools, 2001–. Member: Performing Arts Panel, SE Arts Bd, 1990–96; Educn Cttee, 1996–2003, Sports, Arts, Recreation Cttee, 2008–, SHMIS; Music and Dance Scheme Expert Panel, DCSF, 2007– (Chm., Excellent! Gala Steering Cttee, 2007–). Pres., Surrey Philharmonic Orch., 2000–01. Gov., Royal Ballet Sch., 1997–. FRSA. *Recreations:* music, classic cars, walking, photography, archaeology. *Address:* Yehudi Menuhin School, Stoke D'Abernon, Cobham, Surrey KT11 3QQ. *T:* (01932) 584418.

CHISLETT, Derek Victor; Warden, Sackville College, 1988–96; *b* 18 April 1929; *s* of Archibald Lynn Chislett and Eva Jessie Chislett (*née* Collins); *m* 1954, Joan Robson; two *d.* *Educ:* Christ's Hospital. Admiralty, 1946–53; HM Forces, 1947–49; Nat. Assistance Board, 1953–66; Min. of Social Security, 1966–68; Department of Health and Social Security, 1968–88: Under Sec., 1983; Controller, Newcastle Central Office, 1983–86; Dir of Finance (Social Security), 1986–88. Mem. Exec. Cttee, Nat. Assoc. of Almshouses, 1989–2001 (Vice-Chm., 1995–2001). Trustee, Motability Tenth Anniversary Trust, 1989–2000. Freeman, City of London, 1998; Mem., Guild of Freemen, City of London, 1999. *Publication:* Sackville College: a short history and guide, 1995. *Recreations:* opera, playing and listening to the 'cello. *Address:* Greensands, Ripe, Lewes, East Sussex BN8 3AX. *T:* (01323) 811525.

CHISNALL, Air Vice-Marshal Steven, CB 2008; Chief Operating Officer, Simulstrat Ltd, since 2008; *b* Urmston, Manchester, 12 June 1954; *s* of Eric and Muriel Chisnall; *m* 1980, Elizabeth Ennis; three *s*. *Educ:* Urmston Grammar Sch.; Univ. of Sheffield (BA English 1976; PGCE 1977); St John's Coll., Cambridge (MPhil Internat. Relns 1989). English Teacher, Hinde House, Sheffield, 1977–79; RAF, 1980–2008: tours incl. Germany, 1981–84, NI, 1991–93; Cabinet Office, 1993–95; Dep. Dir, Defence Policy, MoD, 1996–98; Station Comdr, RAF Halton, 1998–99; Liaison Officer, Islamabad, 2002; Sen. Directing Staff (Air), RCDS, 2004–08. Patron, RAF Holmpton, 2006–. *Recreations:* sport, reading and writing—history, international relations, fiction, jazz. *Address:* 11 Bulback, Halton, Aylesbury HP22 5NZ. *T:* (01296) 620316; *e-mail:* chisnall@ chisnalls.fsnet.co.uk. *Club:* Royal Air Force (Chm., 2005–08).

CHISWELL, Rt Rev. Peter; Bishop of Armidale, 1976–99; *b* 18 Feb. 1934; *s* of Ernest and Florence Ruth Chiswell; *m* 1960, Betty Marie Craik; two *s* one *d*. *Educ:* Univ. of New South Wales (BE); Moore Theological College (BD London, Th. Schol.). Vicar of Bingara, 1961–68; Vicar of Gunnedah, 1968–76; Archdeacon of Tamworth, 1971–76. Chm., Fed. Exec., CMS, Australia, 1999–2003. *Address:* 93 Trelawney Road, Armidale, NSW 2350, Australia. *T:* (2) 67713919.

CHISWELL, Maj.-Gen. Peter Irvine, CB 1985; CBE 1976 (OBE 1972; MBE 1965); Chairman, Buckland Leadership Development Centre, 1996–2004 (Director, 1989–2004); *b* 19 April 1930; *s* of late Col Henry Thomas Chiswell, OBE (late RAMC) and Gladys Beatrice Chiswell; *m* 1958, Felicity Philippa, *d* of R. F. Martin; two *s*. *Educ:* Allhallows School; RMA Sandhurst. Commissioned Devonshire Regt, 1951; transf. Parachute Regt, 1958; DAAG HQ Berlin Inf. Bde, 1963–65; Brigade Major, 16 Para Bde, 1967–68; GSO1 (DS), Staff Coll., 1968–69; CO 3 PARA, 1969–71; Col GS (Army Training), 1971–74; Comd British Contingent DCOS UN Force Cyprus, 1974–76; Comd, 44 Para Bde, 1976–78; ACOS (Operations), HQ Northern Army Gp, 1978–81; Comd, Land Forces NI, 1982–83; GOC Wales, 1983–85. Dep. Chm., Leadership Cttee, MODEM, 2005–. Gov., Christ Coll., Brecon, 1987–. FRSA 1994. DL Powys, 1994–2005. *Recreation:* travel.

CHISWICK, Prof. Malcolm Leon, MD; FRCP, FRCPCH; Hon. Consultant Paediatrician, St Mary's Hospital for Women and Children, Manchester, since 2006 (Consultant Paediatrician, 1975–2006); Hon. Professor of Child Health, University of Manchester, since 2006 (Professor, 1992–2006); *b* 26 July 1940; *s* of Samuel and Polly Chiswick; *m* 1964, Claire Dodds; one *s* one *d*. *Educ:* Univ. of Newcastle upon Tyne (MB BS; MD 1974). FRCP 1980; FRCPCH 1997. Registrar in Paediatrics: Southampton Children's and General Hosps, 1969–70; St George's Hosp., London, 1970–71; Med. Dir, Central Manchester and Manchester Children's Univ. Hosps NHS Trust, 2002–06. Pres., British Assoc. of Perinatal Medicine, 2002–05. Member: Manchester Medico-Legal Soc., 1992–; Manchester Literary and Philosophical Soc., 1999–. Ed., Archives of Diseases in Childhood, 1987–99. *Publications:* Neonatal Medicine, 1978; The Complete Book of Baby Care, 1978, 2nd edn 1988; Birth Asphyxia and the Brain, 2002; papers in learned jls on disorders of the newborn and birth injury. *Recreations:* Coronation Street, writing. *Address:* Highclere, Parkfield Road, Altrincham, Cheshire WA14 2BT; *e-mail:* malcolm.chiswick@manchester.ac.uk. *Club:* Athenæum.

CHITNIS, family name of **Baron Chitnis.**

CHITNIS, Baron *cr* 1977 (Life Peer), of Ryedale, N Yorks; **Pratap Chidamber Chitnis;** Chairman, British Refugee Council, 1986–89; *b* 1 May 1936; *s* of late Chidamber N. Chitnis and Lucia Mallik; *m* 1964, Anne Brand; one *s* decd. *Educ:* Penryn Sch.; Stonyhurst Coll.; Univs of Birmingham (BA) and Kansas (MA). Admin. Asst, Nat. Coal Board, 1958–59; Liberal Party Organisation: Local Govt Officer, 1960–62; Agent, Orpington Liberal Campaign, 1962; Trng Officer, 1962–64; Press Officer, 1964–66; Head of Liberal Party Organisation, 1966–69. Sec., 1969–75, Chief Exec. and Dir, 1975–88, Joseph Rowntree Social Service Trust. Mem., Community Relations Commn, 1970–77; Chm., BBC Immigrants Programme Adv. Cttee, 1979–83 (Mem., 1972–77). Chm., Refugee Action, 1981–86. Reported on elections in: Zimbabwe, 1979; (jtly) Guyana, 1980; El Salvador, 1982, 1984, 1988 and 1989; Nicaragua, 1984. *Address:* Quartier des Trois Fontaines, 84490 Vaucluse, France.

CHITTENDEN, Rear Adm. Timothy Clive, CEng, FIMechE; Safety Assurance Director, BAE Systems Submarines Solutions, since 2007; *b* 25 May 1951; *s* of late Frederick William John Chittenden and Pauline Beryl (*née* Cockle); *m* 1974, Anne Clare Style; three *d*. *Educ:* Chatham House Grammar Sch.; Churchill Coll., Cambridge (MA Engrg Sci.); MSc Marine Engrg RNEC; Royal Naval Coll., Greenwich (Dip. Nuclear Technol.). MINucE 1982; CEng 1988; MIMechE 1988, FIMechE 2001; FINucE 2005. Marine Engineer Officer: HMS Warspite, 1982–85; HMS Talent, 1988–90; Asst Dir, Nuclear Safety, MoD (PE), 1990–93; Prodn Manager, Clyde Submarine Base, 1993–94; Captain 1994; Assistant Director: Business and Safety, Chief Strategic Systems Exec., MoD (PE), 1995–97; Swiftsure & Trafalgar Update, Defence Procurement Agency, MoD, 1997–99; Dir, Inservice Submarines, Ship Support Agency, MoD, Naval Support Comd, 1999–2000; Submarine Support Integrated Project Team Leader and Dir, Warship Support Agency, 2000–03; COS (Support) to C-in-C Fleet, 2003–05; Prog. Dir, ASTUTE, BAE Systems Submarines Solutions, 2005–07. Freeman, Co. of Carmen, 2004–. *Recreations:* sailing and dinghy racing, hill-walking, 0.22 target rifle shooting, reading, listening to music. *Address:* BAE Systems Submarines Solutions Ltd, Barrow-in-Furness, Cumbria LA14 1AF. *T:* (01229) 874000. *Clubs:* Hawks (Cambridge); Bassenthwaite Sailing.

CHITTICK, Carolyn Julie; *see* Fairbairn, C. J.

CHITTY, Alison Jill, OBE 2004; theatre designer; *b* 16 Oct. 1948; *d* of late Ernest Hedley Chitty, Prebendary of St Paul's Cathedral and of Irene Joan Waldron. *Educ:* King Alfred School, London; St Martin's School of Art; Central School of Art and Design (Degree in Theatre Design); Arts Council Scholarship. Victoria Theatre, Stoke-on-Trent, 1970–79 (designed over 40 productions; Head of Design 4 years); designer, 1970–, for *theatre:* Hampstead Theatre, Riverside studios, RSC (Hamlet, 2000), Haymarket, Stratford East, Playhouse (Rose Tattoo, 1991); RNT (Cardiff East, 1997; Remembrance of Things Past, 2000 (Best Costume Designer, Laurence Olivier Awards, 2001); Luther, 2001; Bacchai, 2002; Scenes from the Big Picture, 2003; Two Thousand Years, 2005; The Voysey Inheritance, 2006 (Best Costume Designer, Laurence Olivier Awards, 2007)); Sheffield (Original Sin, 2002); Chichester (Merchant of Venice, The Seagull, 2003; A Midsummer Night's Dream, The Master and Margherita, 2004; King Lear, 2005); Donmar Th. (Days of Wine and Roses, 2005); Rose Th., Kingston, and UK tour (Uncle Vanya, 2007–08); Apollo, and UK tour (The Vortex, 2008); for *opera:* Opera North, Houston Grand Opera, Royal Opera House (Gawain, 1991; Billy Budd, Arianna, 1995; The Bartered Bride, 1998; The Minotaur, 2008); Opera Theatre, St Louis (The Vanishing Bridegroom, 1991);

Gotenborg Music Theatre (Falstaff, 1993); Dallas Opera (Jenufa, 1993); ENO (Khovanshchina, 1994; La Vestale, 2002; Così Fan Tutti, 2003); Geneva Opera (Billy Budd, 1994; Aida, 1999); Santa Fe Opera (Blond Eckbert, 1994; Modern Painters, 1995; Dialogues of the Carmelites, 1999); Danish Royal Opera (Die Meistersinger, 1996); Bastille Opera, Paris (Turandot, 1997); Bordeaux Opera (Julius Caesar, 1999); Bavarian State Opera (Otello, 1999); Glyndebourne Touring Opera (The Last Supper, 2000; Tangier Tattoo, 2005); Almeida Opera (Ion, 2000; The Io Passion, also at Aldeburgh and Bregenz, 2004); Seattle Opera, and Tel Aviv Opera (Billy Budd, 2001); San Francisco Opera (Jenufa, 2001); Royal Albert Hall (Cavalleria Rusticana and Pagliacci, 2002); Opera Zuid (L'Enfant et les Sortilèges, L'Heure Espagnole, 2003); Chicago Opera (Midsummer Marriage, 2005); Greek Nat. Opera (Carmen, 2007); Bergen, Norway (The Flying Dutchman, 2008); Cologne (Adriana's Fall, 2008); for *films:* Blue Jean, Aria, Life is Sweet, 1991; A Sense of History, 1992; Naked, 1993; Secrets & Lies, 1995 (Palme d'Or, 1996); The Turn of the Screw, 2004. Co-Dir, 1992–2000, Dir, 2000–, Motley Theatre Design Sch. Associate, NT, 2003–. Hon. Dr Staffordshire, 2005. Misha Black Medal, CSD, 2007; Young Vic Award, 2007. *Publication:* (contrib.) Theatre in a Cool Climate. *Address:* c/o Allied Artists, 42 Montpellier Square, SW7 1JZ.

CHITTY, Dr Anthony; retired; Director of Corporate Engineering, Rolls-Royce Power Engineering Ltd (formerly Northern Engineering Industries, R-R Industrial Power Group), 1989–93 (Deputy Director, 1988–89); *b* 29 May 1931; *s* of Ashley George Chitty and Doris Ellen Mary Buck; *m* 1956, Audrey Munro; two *s* one *d*. *Educ:* Glynn Grammar Sch., Epsom; Imperial Coll., London. BSc, PhD, DIC; CEng. GEC Res. Labs, 1955; Hd, Creep of Steels Lab., ERA, 1959; GEC Power Gp, 1963; Chief Metallurgist (Applications), C. A. Parsons, 1966; Dir, Advanced Technol. Div., Clarke Chapman-John Thompson, 1973; Internat. Res. and Develt, 1978; Gen. Manager, Engrg Products, N.E.I. Parsons, 1979; Regional Industrial Adviser, NE Region, DTI, 1984–88. Vis. Prof., Univ. of Aston in Birmingham, 1977–84. Chairman: Bd of Newcastle Technol. Centre, 1988–90 (Dep. Chm., 1985–88); Centre for Adhesive Technol., 1990–93; Member, Board: Newcastle Univ. New Ventures Ltd, 1989–93; Newcastle Polytechnic Products Ltd, 1989–93. *Publications:* research publications in the fields of materials and welding for power generation. *Recreations:* hill walking, gardening. *Address:* 1 Willow Way, Darras Hall, Ponteland, Northumberland NE20 9RJ.

CHITTY, (Margaret) Beryl, (Mrs Henry Fowler), CMG 1977; HM Diplomatic Service, retired; *b* 2 Dec. 1917; *d* of Wilfrid and Eleanor Holdgate; *m* 1st, 1949, Keith Chitty, FRCS (*d* 1958); 2nd, 1989, Henry Fowler, CD (*d* 2007), Kingston, Jamaica. *Educ:* Belvedere Sch. (GPDST), Liverpool; St Hugh's Coll., Oxford (BA, MA; Hon. Fellow, 1982). Dominions Office, 1940; Private Sec. to Parly Under-Sec. of State, 1943–45; Principal, 1945; CRO, 1947–52; First Sec., Commonwealth Office, 1958; Jt Sec., First Commonwealth Educn Conf., 1959; UK Mission to UN, New York, 1968–70; FCO, 1970–71; Dep. (and Acting) British High Comr in Jamaica, 1971–75; Head of Commonwealth Co-ord. Dept, FCO, 1975–77. Appeal Sec., St Hugh's Coll., Oxford, 1978–81; Appeal Dir, St Peter's Coll., Oxford, 1982–88. Non-Press Mem., Press Council, 1978–80. Mem., Governing Body, Queen Elizabeth House, Oxford, 1977–80. *Address:* 79 Bainton Road, Oxford OX2 7AG. *T:* (01865) 553384.

CHITTY, Susan Elspeth, (Lady Chitty); author; *b* 18 Aug. 1929; *d* of Rudolph Glossop and Mrs E. A. Hopkinson (writer, as Antonia White); *m* 1951, Sir Thomas Willes Chitty, Bt, *qv*; one *s* three *d*. *Educ:* Godolphin Sch., Salisbury; Somerville Coll., Oxford. Mem. editorial staff, Vogue, 1952–53; subseq. journalist, reviewer, broadcaster and lecturer. *Publications: novels:* Diary of a Fashion Model, 1958; White Huntress, 1963; My Life and Horses, 1966; *biographies:* The Woman who wrote Black Beauty: a life of Anna Sewell, 1972; The Beast and the Monk: a life of Charles Kingsley, 1975; Charles Kingsley and North Devon, 1976; Gwen John 1876–1939, 1981; Now to My Mother, 1985; That Singular Person Called Lear, 1988; Playing the Game: a biography of Sir Henry Newbolt, 1997; *non-fiction:* (with Thomas Hinde) On Next to Nothing, 1976; (with Thomas Hinde) The Great Donkey Walk, 1977; The Young Rider, 1979; *edited:* The Intelligent Woman's Guide to Good Taste, 1958; The Puffin Book of Horses, 1975; As Once in May, by Antonia White, 1983; Antonia White: Diaries 1926–1957, vol. I, 1991, vol. II, 1992. *Recreations:* riding, travel. *Address:* Bow Cottage, West Hoathly, Sussex RH19 4QF. *T:* (01342) 810269.

CHITTY, Sir Thomas Willes, 3rd Bt *cr* 1924; author (as Thomas Hinde); *b* 2 March 1926; *e s* of Sir (Thomas) Henry Willes Chitty, 2nd Bt, and Ethel Constance (*d* 1971), *d* of S. H. Gladstone, Darley Ash, Bovingdon, Herts; *S* father, 1955; *m* 1951, Susan Elspeth (*see* S. E. Chitty); one *s* three *d*. *Educ:* Winchester; University Coll., Oxford. Royal Navy, 1944–47. Shell Petroleum Co., 1953–60. Granada Arts Fellow, Univ. of York, 1964–65; Visiting Lectr, Univ. of Illinois, 1965–67; Vis. Prof., Boston Univ., 1969–70. *Publications: novels:* Mr Nicholas, 1952; Happy as Larry, 1957; For the Good of the Company, 1961; A Place Like Home, 1962; The Cage, 1962; Ninety Double Martinis, 1963; The Day the Call Came, 1964; Games of Chance, 1965; The Village, 1966; High, 1968; Bird, 1970; Generally a Virgin, 1972; Agent, 1974; Our Father, 1975; Daymare, 1980; *non-fiction:* (with wife, as Susan Hinde) On Next to Nothing, 1976; (with Susan Chitty) The Great Donkey Walk, 1977; The Cottage Book, 1979; Stately Gardens of Britain, 1983; Forests of Britain, 1985; (ed) The Domesday Book: England's heritage, then and now, 1986; Courtiers: 900 years of court life, 1986; Tales from the Pumproom: an informal history of Bath, 1988; Imps of Promise: a history of the King's School, Canterbury, 1990; Looking Glass Letters, 1991; Paths of Progress: a history of Marlborough College, 1993; A History of Highgate School, 1993; A History of King's College School, 1994; Carpenter's Children: a history of the City of London School, 1995; The University of Greenwich, 1996; The Martlet and the Griffen: a history of Abingdon School, 1997; *autobiography:* Sir Henry and Sons, 1980; *biography:* A Field Guide to the English Country Parson, 1983; Capability Brown, 1986; *anthology:* Spain, 1963. Heir: *s* Andrew Edward Willes Chitty, *b* 20 Nov. 1953. *Address:* Bow Cottage, West Hoathly, Sussex RH19 4QF. *T:* (01342) 810269.

CHIVERS, (Tom) David; QC 2002; *b* 17 Nov. 1960; *s* of Tom Alan Chivers and Anneliese Chivers (*née* Ungar); *m* 1996, Helen Lorraine Searle; one *s* one *d*. *Educ:* Millfield Sch.; Downing Coll., Cambridge (BA Hons Law). Called to the Bar, Lincoln's Inn, 1983. *Publications:* (contrib.) Co-operatives That Work, 1988; (contrib.) Practice and Procedure in the Companies Court, 1997. *Address:* Erskine Chambers, 33 Chancery Lane, WC2A 1EN. *T:* (020) 7242 5532; *Fax:* (020) 7831 0125. *Club:* Athenæum.

CHO, Yoon-Je; Ambassador of Republic of Korea to the Court of St James's, 2004–08; *b* 22 Feb. 1952; *s* of Yong-Chan Cho and Kwi-Ju Chung; *m* 1980, Sun-Ae Woo; one *s* two *d*. *Educ:* Seoul Nat. Univ. (BA Econs); Stanford Univ. (MA; PhD Econs 1984). Sen. Economist, World Bank, 1984–88 and 1992–93; Economist, IMF, 1989–92; Vice Pres., Korea Inst. of Public Finance, 1994–95; Sen. Advr to Minister of Finance and Dep. Prime Minister, Republic of Korea, 1995–97; Prof. of Econs, Sogang Univ., 1997–2003; Chief Econ. Advr to Pres. of Republic, 2003–05. *Publications:* Lessons of Financial Liberalization from Asia and Latin America, 1987; Industrialization of Korea, 1992; contrib. numerous articles to Jl Money, Credit Banking, Jl Develt Econs, World Econ., World Develt, World Bank Econ. Rev., World Bank Res. Observer, etc. *Address:* c/o Embassy of Republic of Korea, 60 Buckingham Gate, SW1E 6AJ. *Clubs:* Athenæum, Travellers.

CHOI SUNG-HONG; Minister of Foreign Affairs and Trade, Republic of Korea, 2002–04; *b* 24 Dec. 1938; *m* 1968, Wha-boo; one *s* two *d. Educ:* Coll. of Law, Seoul Nat. Univ. (degree in Law). Entered Diplomatic Service, 1970: Third Sec., Bonn, 1970–74; First Sec., Rome, 1974–78; Dir for Legal Affairs, Office of Planning and Mgt, Seoul, 1978–80; Dir, Treaties Div. 1, Treaties Bureau, Min. of Foreign Affairs, 1980–81; Counsellor, Abu Dhabi, 1981–84; Dir, Internat. Econ. Orgns Div., Internat. Econ. Affairs Bureau, Min. of Foreign Affairs, 1984–85; Protocol Sec. to Pres., 1985–89; Consul-Gen., Montreal, 1989–93; Dir-Gen., Eur. Affairs Bureau, Min. of Foreign Affairs, 1992–93; Ambassador to Hungary, 1993–96; Ambassador and Dep. Perm. Rep., Korean Perm. Mission to UN, 1996–98; Dep. Minister for Foreign Affairs, Min. of Foreign Affairs and Trade, 1998–99; Ambassador to UK, 1999–2001. Service Medal, 1986, Meritorious Service Medal, 1988 (Korea); Diplomatic Medal (Hungary), 1995. *Recreations:* painting, golf. *Address:* c/o Ministry of Foreign Affairs and Trade, 77, 1-ka, Sejong-no, Chongno-ku, Seoul, Republic of Korea. *Clubs:* Athenæum, Travellers; Coombe Hill Golf, Wentworth Golf.

CHOLMELEY, Sir (Hugh John) Frederick (Sebastian), 7th Bt *cr* 1806, of Easton, Lincolnshire; *b* 3 Jan. 1968; *o s* of Sir Montague Cholmeley, 6th Bt and of Juliet Auriol Sally (*née* Nelson); *S* father, 1998; *m* 1993, Ursula Anne, *d* of Hon. Sir H. P. D. Bennett, *qv*; one *s* one *d. Educ:* Eton Coll.; RAC Cirencester. MRICS (ARICS 1992). *Recreation:* the countryside. *Heir: s* Montague Hugh Peter Cholmeley, *b* 19 May 1997.

CHOLMONDELEY, family name of **Marquess of Cholmondeley,** and of **Baron Delamere**.

CHOLMONDELEY, 7th Marquess of, *cr* 1815; **David George Philip Cholmondeley,** KCVO 2007; Bt 1611; Viscount Cholmondeley (Ire.), 1661; Baron Cholmondeley of Namptwich (Eng.), 1689; Earl of Cholmondeley, Viscount Malpas, 1706; Baron Newborough (Ire.), 1715; Baron Newburgh (Gt Brit.), 1716; Earl of Rocksavage, 1815; Joint Hereditary Lord Great Chamberlain of England (acting for the reign of Queen Elizabeth II); *b* 27 June 1960; *s* of 6th Marquess of Cholmondeley, GCVO, MC and of Lavinia Margaret (DL Cheshire), *d* of late Col John Leslie, DSO, MC; *S* father, 1990. *Heir: cousin* Charles George Cholmondeley, *b* 18 March 1959. *Address:* Cholmondeley Castle, Malpas, Cheshire.

CHOMSKY, Prof. (Avram) Noam, PhD; Institute Professor, Massachusetts Institute of Technology, 1976–2002, now Emeritus (Ferrari P. Ward Professor of Modern Languages and Linguistics, 1966–76); *b* Philadelphia, 7 Dec. 1928; *s* of late William Chomsky and of Elsie Simonofsky; *m* 1949, Carol Doris Schatz; one *s* two *d. Educ:* Central High Sch., Philadelphia; Univ. of Pennsylvania (BA 1949; MA 1951; PhD 1955); Society of Fellows, Harvard, 1951–55. Massachusetts Institute of Technology: Asst Prof., 1955–58; Associate Prof., 1958–61; Prof. of Modern Langs, 1961–66. Res. Fellow, Harvard Cognitive Studies Center, 1964–65. Vis. Prof., Columbia Univ., 1957–58; Nat. Sci. Foundn Fellow, Inst. for Advanced Study, Princeton, 1958–59; Linguistics Soc. of America Prof., Univ. of Calif, LA, 1966; Beckman Prof., Univ. of Calif, Berkeley, 1966–67; Vis. Watson Prof., Syracuse Univ., 1982; Lectures: Shearman, UCL, 1969; John Locke, Oxford, 1969; Bertrand Russell Meml, Cambridge 1971; Nehru Meml, New Delhi, 1972; Whidden, McMaster Univ., 1975; Huizinga Meml, Leiden, 1977; Woodbridge, Columbia, 1978; Kant, Stanford, 1979. Member: Nat. Acad. of Scis; Amer. Acad. of Arts and Scis; Linguistic Soc. of America; Amer. Philosophical Assoc.; Bertrand Russell Peace Foundn; Utrecht Soc. of Arts and Scis; Deutsche Akademie der Naturforscher Leopoldina; Corresp. Mem., British Acad., 1974; Hon. Mem., Ges. für Sprachwissenschaft, Germany, 1990. Fellow, Amer. Assoc. for Advancement of Science; William James Fellow, Amer. Psychological Assoc., 1990. Hon. FBPsS; Hon. FRAI 1990. Hon. DLitt: London, 1967; Visva-Bharati, West Bengal, 1980; Cambridge, 1995; Harvard, 2000; Calcutta, 2001; Hon. DHL: Chicago, 1967; Loyola Univ., Chicago, 1970; Swarthmore Coll., 1970; Bard Coll., 1971; Delhi, 1972; Massachusetts, 1973; Pennsylvania, 1985; Maine, 1992; Gettysburg Coll., 1992; Amherst Coll., 1995; Buenos Aires, 1996; Rovira i Virgili, Tarragona, 1998; Guelph, 1999; Columbia, 1999; Connecticut, 1999; Scuola Normale Superiore, Pisa, 1999; Toronto, 2000; Western Ontario, 2000; Free Univ. of Brussels, 2003; Central Conn. State, 2003; Athens, 2004; Florence, 2004; Bologna, 2005; Ljubljana, 2005; Santa Domingo Inst. of Technol., 2006; Dr *hc* Univ. Nacional del Comahue, Argentina, 2002; Univ. Nacional de Colombia, 2002; Univ. of Cyprus, 2006; Univ. de Chile, Santiago, 2006; Univ. de la Frontera, Temuco, 2006. Distinguished Scientific Contribution Award, Amer. Psychological Assoc., 1984; Kyoto Prize in Basic Science, Inamori Foundn, 1988; Orwell Award, Nat. Council of Teachers of English, 1987, 1989; Killian Award, MIT, 1992; Lannan Literary Award, for non-fiction, 1992; Homer Smith Award, New York Univ. Sch. of Medicine, 1994; Loyola Mellon Humanities Award, Loyola Univ., Chicago, 1994; Helmholtz Medal, Berlin-Brandenburgische Akad. Wissenschaften, 1996; Rabindranath Tagore Centenary Award, Asiatic Soc., Calcutta, 2000. *Publications:* Syntactic Structures, 1957; Current Issues in Linguistic Theory, 1964; Aspects of the Theory of Syntax, 1965; Cartesian Linguistics, 1966; Topics in the Theory of Generative Grammar, 1966; Language and Mind, 1968; (with Morris Halle) Sound Pattern of English, 1968; American Power and the New Mandarins, 1969; At War with Asia, 1970; Problems of Knowledge and Freedom, 1971; Studies on Semantics in Generative Grammar, 1972; For Reasons of State, 1973; The Backroom Boys, 1973; Peace in the Middle East?, 1974; (with Edward Herman) Bains de Sang, 1974; Reflections on Language, 1975; The Logical Structure of Linguistic Theory, 1975; Essays on Form and Interpretation, 1977; Human Rights and American Foreign Policy, 1978; Language and Responsibility, 1979; (with Edward Herman) Political Economy of Human Rights, 1979; Rules and Representations, 1980; Radical Priorities, 1981; Lectures on Government and Binding, 1981; Towards a New Cold War, 1982; Some Concepts and Consequences of the Theory of Government and Binding, 1982; Fateful Triangle: the United States, Israel and the Palestinians, 1983; Modular Approaches to the Study of the Mind, 1984; Turning the Tide, 1985; Barriers, 1986; Pirates and Emperors, 1986; Knowledge of Language: its nature, origin and use, 1986; Generative Grammar: its basis, development and prospects, 1987; On Power and Ideology, 1987; Language in a Psychological Setting, 1987; Language and Problems of Knowledge, 1987; The Chomsky Reader, 1987; The Culture of Terrorism, 1988; (with Edward Herman) Manufacturing Consent, 1988; Necessary Illusions, 1989; Deterring Democracy, 1991; Chronicles of Dissent, 1992; Year 501: the conquest continues, 1993; Rethinking Camelot: JFK, the Vietnam war, and US political culture, 1993; Letters from Lexington: reflections on propaganda, 1993; World Orders, Old and New, 1994; The Minimalist Program, 1995; Powers and Prospects, 1996; Class Warfare (interviews), 1996; The Common Good (interviews), 1998; Profit Over People, 1998; The New Military Humanism, 1999; New Horizons in the Study of Language and Mind, 2000; Rogue States, 2000; A New Generation Draws the Line, 2000; 9–11, 2001; Understanding Power, 2002; On Nature and Language, 2002; Hegemony or Survival, 2003; Middle East Illusions, 2003; Imperial Ambitions, 2005; Failed States, 2006; (with Gilbert Achcar) Perilous Power, 2006; What We Say Goes, 2008. *Address:* Department of Linguistics and Philosophy, Massachusetts Institute of Technology, 32–D808, 77 Massachusetts Avenue, Cambridge, MA 02139–4307, USA. *T:* (617) 2537819.

CHOPE, Christopher Robert, OBE 1982; MP (C) Christchurch, since 1997; barrister; *b* 19 May 1947; *s* of late His Honour Robert Charles Chope and Pamela Durell; *m* 1987, Christo Hutchinson; one *s* one *d. Educ:* St Andrew's Sch., Eastbourne; Marlborough Coll.; St Andrews Univ. (LLB Hons). Called to the Bar, Inner Temple, 1972. Mem., Wandsworth Borough Council, 1974–83; Chm., Housing Cttee, 1978–79; Leader of Council, 1979–83. Consultant, Ernst & Young, 1992–98. MP (C) Southampton, Itchen, 1983–92; contested (C) Southampton, Itchen, 1992. PPS to Minister of State, HM Treasury, 1986; Parly Under-Sec. of State, DoE, 1986–90; Parly Under-Sec. of State (Minister for Roads and Traffic), Dept of Transport, 1990–92; front bench spokesman on trade and industry, 1998–99, on Treasury, 2001–02, on Transport, 2002–05. Jt Sec., Cons. Backbench Environment Cttee, 1983–86; Member: Select Cttee on Procedure, 1984–86, 2005–; Select Cttee on Trade and Industry, 1999–2001. Member: Exec., 1922 Cttee, 2005–; Delegn, Council of Europe, 2005–. Chm., Cons. Parly Candidates Assoc., 1995–97. A Vice Chm., Cons. Party, 1997–98. Chm., Cons. Way Forward, 2002–. Member: HSC, 1993–97; Local Govt Commn for England, 1994–95; Vice-Pres., LGA, 2000. Mem. Exec. Cttee, Soc. of Cons. Lawyers, 1983–86. *Address:* House of Commons, SW1A 0AA. *T:* (020) 7219 5808. *Clubs:* Royal Southampton Yacht; Christchurch Conservative.

CHORLEY, family name of **Baron Chorley**.

CHORLEY, 2nd Baron *cr* 1945, of Kendal; **Roger Richard Edward Chorley,** FCA; Chairman, National Trust, 1991–96; *b* 14 Aug. 1930; *er s* of 1st Baron Chorley, QC, and Katharine Campbell (*d* 1986), *d* of late Edward Hopkinson, DSc; *S* father, 1978; *m* 1964, Ann, *d* of late A. S. Debenham; two *s. Educ:* Stowe Sch.; Gonville and Caius Coll., Cambridge (BA). Pres., CU Mountaineering Club. Expedns to Himalayas, 1954 (Rakaposhi), 1957 (Nepal); joined Cooper Brothers & Co. (later Coopers & Lybrand), 1955; New York office, 1959–60; Pakistan (Indus Basin Project), 1961; Partner, 1967–89; seconded to Nat. Bd for Prices and Incomes as accounting adviser, 1965–68; Visiting Prof., Dept of Management Sciences, Imperial Coll. of Science and Technology, Univ. of London, 1979–82. National Trust: Member: Finance Cttee, 1970–90; Exec. Cttee, 1989–96; Council, 1989–98; British Council: Mem. Rev. Cttee, 1979–80; Bd Mem., 1981–99; Dep. Chm., 1990–99. Mem., H of L Select Cttee on Sci. and Technology, 1983, 1987, 1988, 1989, 1993, 1994, 2007, and Select Cttee on Sustainable Develt, 1994–95; elected Mem., H of L, 2001–. Member: Royal Commn on the Press, 1974–77; Finance Act 1960 Tribunal, 1974–79; Ordnance Survey Rev. Cttee, 1978–79; Nat. Theatre Bd, 1980–91; Top Salaries Review Body, 1981–90; Ordnance Survey Adv. Bd, 1983–85; NERC, 1988–94; Council, City and Guilds of London Inst., 1977–90; Council, RGS, 1984–93 (Pres., 1987–90); Council, RSA, 1987–89; Chm., Cttee into Handling of Geographic Information, 1985–87; Vice Pres., Council for Nat. Parks, 1997–. Hon. Sec., Climbers Club, 1963–67; Mem. Management Cttee, Mount Everest Foundn, 1968–70; Pres., Alpine Club, 1983–85; Hon. Pres., Assoc. for Geographic Inf., 1993–. Hon. Fellow, Central Lancs Univ., 1993; Hon. FRICS 1995. Hon. DSc: Reading, 1990; Kingston, 1992; Hon. LLD Lancaster, 1995. *Recreation:* mountains. *Heir: s* Hon. Nicholas Rupert Debenham Chorley, *b* 15 July 1966. *Address:* 50 Kensington Place, W8 7PW. *Club:* Alpine.

CHOTE, Robert William; Director, Institute for Fiscal Studies, since 2002; *b* 24 Jan. 1968; *s* of Morville Vincent William Chote and Mary Isabel Chote (*née* Davis); *m* 1997, Sharon Michele White, *qv*; one *s. Educ:* Queens' Coll., Cambridge (MA Econs). Econs corresp. and commentator, The Independent and Independent on Sunday, 1990–94; Econs Ed., FT, 1995–99; Advr and speechwriter to First Dep. Man. Dir, IMF, Washington, 1999–2002. Gov., NIESR, 1997–. Member: Stats Adv. Cttee, ONS, 1998–99; Adv. Bd, UK Centre for Measurement of Govt Activity, ONS, 2006–; Acad. and Policy Bd, Oxford Inst. for Econ. Policy; Tax Policy Sub-cttee, Chartered Inst. of Taxation. *Publications:* (with J. Cremona) Exploring Nature in the Wilds of Europe, 1988; (with J. Cremona) Exploring Nature in North Africa, 1989; (contrib.) Insight Guide to Tunisia, 1990; An Expensive Lunch: the political economy of Britain's new monetary framework, 1997; (ed jtly) IFS Green Budget (annual report), 2003–. *Address:* Institute for Fiscal Studies, 7 Ridgmount Street, WC1E 7AE. *T:* (020) 7291 4800, *Fax:* (020) 7323 4780; *e-mail:* mailbox@ifs.org.uk.

CHOTE, Sharon Michele; *see* White, S. M.

CHOTHIA, Cyrus Homi, PhD; FRS 2000; Member of Scientific Staff, MRC Laboratory of Molecular Biology, Cambridge, since 1990; Senior Research Fellow, Wolfson College, Cambridge, since 2003; *b* 19 Feb. 1942; *s* of Homi and Betty Chothia; *m* 1967, Jean Sandham; one *s* one *d. Educ:* Alleyn's Sch., London; Univ. of Durham (BSc 1965); Birkbeck Coll., London Univ. (MSc 1967); UCL (PhD 1970). Mem., Scientific Staff, MRC Lab. of Molecular Biology, Cambridge, 1970–73; EMBO Fellow, Dept of Molecular Biochemistry and Biophysics, Yale Univ., and Dept of Chemical Physics, Weizmann Inst. of Science, Israel, 1974; Chargé de Recherche, Service du Biochimie Cellulaire, Institut Pasteur, Paris, 1974–76; Res. Associate, Dept of Chemistry, UCL, 1976–80; Royal Soc. EPA Cephalosporin Fund Sen. Res. Fellow, MRC Lab. of Molecular Biology, Cambridge, and Dept of Chemistry, UCL, 1980–90; Mem., Scientific Staff, Cambridge Centre for Protein Engrg, 1990–93. Mem., EMBO, 1988. *Publications:* papers on molecular biology in scientific jls. *Recreations:* cinema, books, conversation. *Address:* MRC Laboratory of Molecular Biology, Hills Road, Cambridge CB2 0QH. *T:* (01223) 402221; 26 Clarendon Street, Cambridge CB1 1JX.

CHOUDHURY, Anwar; HM Diplomatic Service; High Commissioner, Bangladesh, 2004–08; *b* 15 June 1959; *s* of Afruz Bokth Choudhury and Ashrafun Nessa Choudhury; *m* 2001, Momina Laskar; one *s* two *d. Educ:* Salford Univ. (BSc Engrg); Durham Univ. (MBA). Principal Design Engr, Siemens and Plessey Radar, 1985–90; Design Engr/Strategist, RAF, 1990–93; Asst Dir, MoD, 1994–99; Dir, Policy, Cabinet Office, 2000–03; Dir, Policy/Strategy, FCO, 2003–04. Hon. DSc Salford. *Recreations:* cricket, bridge, addiction to Bangladeshi cuisine. *Address:* c/o Foreign and Commonwealth Office, King Charles Street, SW1A 2AH. *Club:* Travellers.

CHOW, Sir Chung Kong, Kt 2000; FREng; FIChemE; FHKEng, FCILT; Chief Executive Officer, Mass Transit Railway Corporation, Hong Kong, since 2003; *b* 9 Sept. 1950. *Educ:* Univ. of Wisconsin (BS Chem. Engrg 1972); Univ. of California (MS Chem. Engrg 1974); Chinese Univ. of Hong Kong (MBA 1981); Harvard (AMP 1991). CEng; FIChemE 1997; FREng 2001. Res. Engr, Climax Chemical Co., New Mexico, 1974–76; Process Engr, Sybron Asia Ltd, Hong Kong, 1976–77; with BOC Group, 1977–96: Hong Kong Oxygen, Hong Kong and BOC, Australia, 1977–84; Man. Dir, Hong Kong Oxygen, 1984–86; Pres., BOC Japan, 1986–89; Gp Manager, Gases Business Develt, BOC Gp plc, England and USA, 1989–91; Regl Dir, N Pacific, based in Tokyo and Hong Kong, 1991–93; Chief Exec., Gases, 1993–96; joined Main Bd, 1994; Man. Dir, 1994–97;

Chief Exec., GKN plc, 1997–2001; CEO, Brambles Industries, 2001–03. Non-exec. Dir, Standard Chartered plc, 1997–2008; Chm., Standard Chartered Bank (Hong Kong) Ltd, 2004–. Pres., 1999–2000, Dep. Pres., 2000–01, SBAC. FCGI 2000; FCILT 2004; FHKEng 2005. Hon. FHKIE 2004. Hon. DEng Bath, 2001. *Address:* Mass Transit Railway Corporation, GPO Box 9916, Hong Kong.

CHOWDHURY, Ajay; Chief Executive Officer, EnQii Holdings plc, since 2007; *b* 29 April 1962; *s* of Micky and Indira Chowdhury; *m* 1995, Liz McDonnell; two *d*. *Educ:* Sydenham Coll., Bombay (BCom 1st Cl.); Wharton Sch., Univ. of Penn (MBA); Central Sch. of Speech and Drama; Metropolitan Film Sch. Manager, Bain & Co., 1986–91; Gp Develt Manager, MAI PLC, 1991–92; Develt Dir, MAI Media, 1993–94; Man. Dir, United Interactive, 1994–99; Chief Executive Officer: Lineone, 1999–2000; NBC Internet Europe, 2000; Man. Partner, IDG Ventures Europe, 2000–06; Gen. Partner, Acacia Capital, 2006–07. Chm., Shazam Entertainment, 2001–; Director: Empower Interactive, 2002–06; Lionhead Games, 2004–06. Dir, MLA (formerly Resource: Council for Mus, Archives and Libraries), 2000–06; Trustee, 24 Hour Museum, 2002–06. Artistic Dir, Rented Space Th. Co., 1988–. *Recreations:* directing plays, theatre, films, music, bridge, diving. *Address:* 16 Harman Drive, NW2 2EB.

CHRÉTIEN, Rt Hon. Jean; PC (Canada) 1967; QC (Canada) 1980; Prime Minister of Canada, 1993–2003; Counsel, Heenan Blaikie, since 2004; *b* 11 Jan. 1934; *s* of Wellie Chrétien and Marie Boisvert Chrétien; *m* 1957, Aline Chaîné; two *s* one *d*. *Educ:* Trois-Rivières; Joliette; Shawinigan; Laval Univ. (BA, LLL). Called to the Bar, and entered Shawinigan law firm of Chrétien, Landry, Deschênes, Trudel and Normand, 1958; Counsel, Lang Michener Lawrence and Shaw, 1986–90; Director: Shawinigan Sen. Chamber of Commerce, 1962; Bar of Trois-Rivières, 1962–63. Government of Canada: MP (L): St Maurice, 1963–86; Beauséjour, New Brunswick, 1990–93; St Maurice, 1993–2003; Parly Sec. to Prime Minister, 1965, and to Minister of Finance, 1966; Minister of State, 1967; Minister of National Revenue, Jan. 1968; Minister of Indian and Northern Affairs, July 1968; Pres., Treasury Bd, 1974; Minister of Industry, Trade and Commerce, 1976; Minister of Finance, 1977–79; Minister of Justice, responsible for constitutional negotiations, Attorney General, Minister of State for Social Develt, 1980–82; Minister of Energy, Mines and Resources, 1982–84; Deputy Prime Minister and External Affairs Minister, 1984; External Affairs Critic for official Opposition, 1984–86; Leader of the Opposition, 1990–93. Elected Leader, Liberal Party of Canada, June 1990. Hon LLD: Wilfred Laurier, 1981; Laurentian, 1982; W Ontario, 1982; York, Ont., 1986; Alberta, 1987; Lakehead, 1988; Ottawa, 1994; Meiji, Tokyo, 1996; Warsaw Sch. of Econs, Michigan State, 1999; Hebrew Univ. of Jerusalem, Meml, St Johns, 2000. *Recreations:* skiing, fishing, golf, reading, classical music. *Address:* (office) 55 Metcalfe Street, Suite 300, Ottawa, ON K1P 6L5, Canada.

CHRIMES, Neil Roy; Head of Programmes, Lord Mayor's Office, City of London, since 2006; *b* 10 June 1954; *er s* of Geoffrey Richard Chrimes and Dorothy Enid Chrimes (*née* Wyatt); *m* 1982, Anne Margery, (Henny), Barnes; one *s* one *d*. *Educ:* Queen Mary's Grammar Sch., Basingstoke; Univ. of Exeter (BA 1975); MIT (SM 1979). Economic Assistant, MAFF, 1975–77; Harkness Fellow, MIT, 1977–79; Sen Economic Assistant, MAFF, 1979–81; HM Diplomatic Service, 1981–2006: Economic Advr, FCO, 1981–87; Economist, Res. Dept, IMF, Washington, 1987–89; Sen. Econ. Advr, FCO, 1989–94; Dep. UK Perm. Rep. and Counsellor (Econ. and Financial), OECD, Paris, 1994–98; Economic Counsellor, Jakarta, 1998; Hd, African Dept (Southern), FCO, 1999–2001; Counsellor (Econ., Sci. and Trade), Ottawa, 2001–06. Liveryman, Horners' Co., 1980. FRSA 2006. *Recreations:* travel, wine, music (especially mediaeval), gardening, cricket. *Address:* c/o Mansion House, EC4N 8BH. *Club:* MCC.

CHRIST CHURCH, Dublin, Dean of; *see* Dunne, Very Rev. D. P. M.

CHRIST CHURCH, Oxford, Dean of; *see* Lewis, Very Rev. C. A.

CHRISTCHURCH, Bishop of, since 2008; **Rt Rev. Victoria Matthews;** *b* 1954; *d* of late Beverley Matthews and Pauline Ritchie Matthews. *Educ:* Trinity Coll., Univ. of Toronto (BA (Hons) 1976; ThM 1987); Yale Univ. Divinity Sch. (MDiv 1979). Ordained deacon, 1979, priest, 1980; Asst Curate, St Andrew, Scarborough, 1979–83; Incumbent: Parish of Georgina, York-Simcoe, 1983–87; All Souls, Lansing, York-Scarborough, 1987–94; Suffragan Bishop of Toronto (Bishop of the Credit Valley), 1994–97; Bishop of Edmonton (Alberta), 1997–2007; Bishop-in-residence, Wycliffe Coll., Toronto, 2008. N Amer. Theol Fellow, 1976–79. *Recreations:* reading, hiking, swimming, travel. *Address:* The Anglican Centre, PO Box 4438, Christchurch 8140, New Zealand.

CHRISTENSEN, Jayne, (Mrs P. L. Christensen); *see* Torvill, J.

CHRISTENSEN, Jens; Commander First Class, Order of the Dannebrog; Hon. GCVO; Ambassador of Denmark to Organization for Economic Co-operation and Development, 1989–91; *b* 30 July 1921; *s* of Christian Christensen and Sophie Dorthea Christensen; *m* 1st, 1950, Tove (*née* Jessen) (*d* 1982); one *s* two *d*; 2nd, 1983, Vibeke Pagh. *Educ:* Copenhagen Univ. (MPolSc 1945). Joined Danish Foreign Service, 1945; Head of Section, Econ. Secretariat of Govt, 1947; Sec. to OEEC Delegn in Paris, 1949 and to NATO Delegn, 1952; Hd of Sect., Min. of Foreign Affairs, 1952, Actg Hd of Div., 1954; Chargé d'Affaires *a.i.* and Counsellor of Legation, Vienna, 1957; Asst Hd of Econ.-Polit. Dept, Min. of For. Affairs, 1960; Dep. Under-Sec., 1961; Under-Sec. and Hd of Econ.-Polit. Dept, 1964–71; Hd of Secretariat for Europ. Integration, 1966; Ambassador Extraord. and Plenipotentiary, 1967; State Sec. for Foreign Econ. Affairs, 1971; Ambassador to the Court of St James's, 1977–81; Pres., Danish Oil and Natural Gas Co., 1980–84; Ambassador to Austria, 1984–89. Governor for Denmark, The Asian Development Bank, 1967–73. Chm., Cross Cultures Project Assoc., 1999–2006. Knight Grand Cross: Order of Icelandic Falcon; Order of Northern Star, Sweden; Order of St Olav, Norway; Royal Victorian Order; Austrian Order of Honour. *Address:* Strandvejen 647, 2930 Klampenborg, Denmark.

CHRISTIAN, Louise; Co-Founder and Senior Partner, Christian Khan (formerly Christian Fisher), Solicitors, since 1985; *b* Oxford, 22 May 1952; *d* of John, (Jack) and Maureen Christian. *Educ:* St Anne's Coll., Oxford (BA Hons Hist. 1973). Solicitor: Lovell White & King, 1976–79; Plumstead Law Centre, 1979–81; Legal Advr to Police Cttee, GLC, 1981–84. Chair: Inquest, 1998–2007 (Mem. Bd, 2007–); Liberty, 2007–; Member Board: Centre for Corporate Accountability, 2002–; Article 19, 2006–; Mem., Adv. Bd, Kurdish Human Rights Project, 1997–. Has undertaken human rights missions to ME, Turkey, etc. Hon. Dr Staffs, 2003. Legal Aid Personality of Year Award, Legal Aid Practitioners Gp, 2004; Human Rights Award, Liberty/Law Soc./Justice, 2004. *Publication:* (jtly) Inquests: a practitioner's guide, 2002. *Address:* Christian Khan, 42 Museum Street, WC1A 1LY. *T:* (020) 7831 1750, *Fax:* (020) 7831 1726; *e-mail:* louisec@christiankhan.co.uk.

CHRISTIAN, Prof. Reginald Frank; Professor of Russian, St Andrews University, 1966–92, Emeritus Professor 1992; *b* Liverpool, 9 Aug. 1924; *s* of late H. A. Christian and late Jessie Gower (*née* Scott); *m* 1952, Rosalind Iris Napier; one *s* one *d*. *Educ:* Liverpool Inst.; Queen's Coll., Oxford (Open Scholar; MA). Hon. Mods Class. (Oxon), 1943; 1st cl. hons Russian (Oxon), 1949. Flying Officer, RAF, 1944; flying with Atlantic Ferry Unit and 231 Sqdn, 1943–46. FO, British Embassy, Moscow, 1949–50; Lectr and Head of Russian Dept, Liverpool Univ., 1950–55; Sen. Lectr and Head of Russian Dept, Birmingham Univ., 1956–63; Vis. Prof. of Russian, McGill Univ., Canada, 1961–62; Prof. of Russian, Birmingham Univ., 1963–66; Exchange Lectr, Moscow, 1964–65. Mem. Univ. Ct, 1971–73 and 1981–85, Associate Dean, Fac. of Arts, 1972–73, Dean, Fac. of Arts, 1975–78, St Andrews Univ. Pres., British Univs Assoc. of Slavists, 1967–70; Member: Internat. Cttee of Slavists, 1970–75; UGC Atkinson Cttee, 1978–81. *Publications:* Korolenko's Siberia, 1954; (with F. M. Borras) Russian Syntax, 1959, 2nd rev. edn, 1971; Tolstoy's War and Peace: a study, 1962; (with F. M. Borras) Russian Prose Composition, 1964, 2nd rev. edn, 1974; Tolstoy: a critical introduction, 1969; (ed and trans.) Tolstoy's Letters, 2 vols, 1978; (ed and trans.) Tolstoy's Diaries, 2 vols, 1985, abridged edn, Tolstoy's Diaries, 1994; Alexis Aladin: the tragedy of exile, 1999; numerous articles and reviews in Slavonic and E European Review, Slavonic and E European Jl, Mod. Languages Review, Survey, Forum, Birmingham Post, Times Lit. Supp., Oxford Slavonic Papers, etc. *Recreations:* reading, violin. *Address:* 48 Lade Braes, St Andrews KY16 9DA. *T:* (01334) 474407; 7 Knockard Road, Pitlochry, Perthshire PH16 5HJ. *T:* (01796) 472993.

CHRISTIANI, Alexander, Dr jur; Ambassador of Austria to the Court of St James's, 2000–05; *b* 31 May 1940; *s* of Dr Alfred Christiani-Kronwald, (Baron von Christiani-Kronwald), and Rose Christiani-Kronwald; *m* 1968, Renate Sedlmayer, PhD; one *s* one *d*. *Educ:* Univ. of Vienna (Dr jur 1964); Diplomatic Acad., Vienna. Federal Ministry for Foreign Affairs, Austria: Political Dept, 1966–69; Asst to Sec.-Gen. for Foreign Affairs, 1969; UN Mission, NY, 1970–75; Alternate Rep. of Austria to Security Council, 1973–74; Dir, Div. i/c of Vienna Internat. Centre, 1976–81; Consul Gen., Austrian Delegn, Berlin, 1981–86; Ambassador to South Africa, 1986–90; Dir, Dept for ME and Africa, 1990–96; Ambassador to the Netherlands, 1996–2000. Mem., Austrian Delegns to UN Gen. Assemblies, 1967–81. Cross, KM. Grand Cross: Order of Oranje-Nassau (Netherlands), 2000; Al-Istiglal Order (Jordan); Grand Officer, Order of Merit (Syria); Comdr, Order of Oak Crown (Luxembourg); Grand Decoration of Honour in Gold (Austria). *Recreations:* music, travelling, theatre. *Address:* Reithlegasse 1–3, 1190 Vienna, Austria. *T:* and *Fax:* (1) 3681525; *e-mail:* achristiani@hotmail.com. *Clubs:* Rotary, St Johann's (Vienna).

CHRISTIANSON, Rev. Canon Rodney John, (Bill); Secretary General, The Mission to Seafarers, since 2001; *b* S Africa, 19 March 1947; *s* of late Kenneth Alfred John Christianson and Jessie Winifred Nelson (*née* Kelly). *Educ:* Glenwood High Sch., Durban; Officer Trng Sch., S Africa; St Paul's Theol Coll., Grahamstown (DipTh); Open Univ. Ordained deacon 1972, priest 1973; Curate, Pietermaritzburg, SA, 1972–75; Missions to Seamen, subseq. Mission to Seafarers: Asst Chaplain, Gravesend, 1976–81; Sen. Chaplain, Port of London, 1981–82; Port Chaplain, Richards Bay, SA, 1982–91; also Parish Priest, St Andrew, Richards Bay and St Aidan, Kwambonambi, 1982–91; Trng Chaplain, Hull, 1991–93; Ministry Sec., 1993–2000. Mem., Archbp of Cape Town's Commn to conduct investigation into work amongst young people in the Church of SA, 1974. Guild Chaplain, St Bride's Ch, London, 1990; Chaplain, Innholders' Co., 2002–. Hon. Canon, Bloemfontein Cathedral, SA, 1993. Hon. Master Mariner, SA, 1988. *Recreations:* painting/art, music, theatre, photography. *Address:* The Mission to Seafarers, St Michael Paternoster Royal, College Hill, EC4R 2RL. *T:* (020) 7248 5202.

CHRISTIE, Aidan Patrick; QC 2008; *b* Edinburgh, 26 Oct. 1962; *s* of William James Christie, *qv*; *m* 1991, Claire Elliott; one *s* one *d*. *Educ:* Edinburgh Acad.; Hertford Coll., Oxford (BA Lit.Hum 1985); Downing Coll., Cambridge (MA Law 1987). Called to the Bar, Middle Temple, 1988. *Recreation:* reading. *Address:* 4 Pump Court, Temple, EC4Y 7AN. *T:* (020) 7842 5555; *e-mail:* achristie@4pumpcourt.com. *Club:* New (Edinburgh).

CHRISTIE, Augustus Jack; Executive Chairman, Glyndebourne Productions Ltd, since 2000 (Director, since 1989); *b* 4 Dec. 1963; *s* of Sir George William Langham Christie, *qv*; *m* 1993, Imogen Lycett Green (marr. diss. 2006); four *s*. *Educ:* St Aubyns, Rottingdean; Eton Coll.; King's Coll., London (2nd Cl. Hons Zool.). Worked in various theatres, incl. Tricycle, NT, Batignano Opera, Robert Fox Associates, 1987; asst ed. and asst cameraman, Partridge Films, 1989–91; freelance cameraman, 1991–; documentaries include: A Puffin's Tale, Halloween, 1991; A New Fox in Town, 1993; The Lion's Share, Lions, 1994; Hugo's Diary, 1995; Red Monkeys of Zanzibar, 1996; The Battle of the Sexes, The Tale of Two Families, 1998; Buffalo: the African boss, Triumph of Life, 1999. *Recreations:* sport, music, nature. *Address:* Glyndebourne, Lewes, E Sussex BN8 5UU.

CHRISTIE, Campbell, CBE 1997; General Secretary, Scottish Trades Union Congress, 1986–98; *b* 23 Aug. 1937; *s* of Thomas Christie and Johnina Rolling; *m* 1962, Elizabeth Brown Cameron; two *s*. *Educ:* Albert Sen. Secondary Sch., Glasgow. Civil Service, 1954–72: Admiralty, 1954–59; DHSS, 1959–72; Society of Civil and Public Servants, 1972–85: Asst Sec., 1972–73; Asst Gen. Sec., 1973–75; Dep. Gen. Sec., 1975–85. Mem., EU Economic and Social Cttee, 1986–2002. Alternate Mem., Takeover Panel, 2006–. Board Member: Scottish Enterprise, 1998–2004; British Waterways, 1998–; South West Trains Ltd, 1998–. Mem., Scotland's Futures Forum, 2005–. Trustee, Forth Valley Acute Hosps NHS Trust, 1993–2001; Mem. Bd, NHS Forth Valley, 2001–. Chm., Falkirk FC, 1993–94, 2002– (Mem. Bd, 1996–2002). FEIS; FSQA. Hon. DLitt: Napier, 1992; Stirling, 2000; St Andrews, 2001; Hon. DLit: Queen Margaret Coll., Edinburgh, 1998; Glasgow Caledonian, 1999. *Address:* 31 Dumyat Drive, Falkirk, Stirlingshire FK1 5PA. *T:* (01324) 624555.

CHRISTIE, David; Warden, St Edward's School, Oxford, 1988–2004; *b* 22 Feb. 1942; *s* of William and Jean Christie, Bannockburn; *m* 1969, Elsa Margaret Shearer; one *s* two *d*. *Educ:* Dollar Acad.; Univ. of Strathclyde; Univ. of Glasgow. Lektor, British Centre, Folkuniversity of Sweden, 1965–66; Asst Master, George Watson's Coll., 1966–71; Lectr in Economics, Moray House Coll., Edinburgh, 1971–77; Res. Associate (part-time), Esmée Fairbairn Research Centre, Heriot-Watt Univ., 1972–77; Teacher, European Sch., Luxembourg, 1977–83; pt-time Faculty Mem., Miami Univ. European Center, Luxembourg, 1980–83; Head of Econs, Winchester Coll., 1983–88. Member: Econs and Business Studies Panel, Scottish Cert. of Educn Exam. Bd, 1973–77 (Convenor, 1975–77); Scottish Cttee, IBA, 1973–77; Dep. Chm., HMC Wkg Party on Inspection, 1993–97; Chm., Oxford Conf. in Educn, 1997–2002. Educn Adviser, Haberdashers' Co., 2004–. Governor: Loretto Sch., 2004–; St Clare's, Oxford, 2007–. Dir, Ecclesiastical Insurance Gp plc, 2002–. Mem., Council of Mgt, Hebridean Trust, 1998–. Editor, Educn Sect., Economics, 1973–80. FRSA 1994. *Publications:* (contrib.) Curriculum Development in Economics, 1973; (contrib.) Teaching Economics, 1975; (with Prof. A. Scott) Economics in Action, 1976; articles, reviews and entries in jls and in Cambridge Guide to Literature, Golfers' Handbook. *Recreations:* books, golf, hills. *Address:* 26 Yarnells Hill, Oxford OX2 9BD. *Club:* Royal & Ancient (St Andrews).

CHRISTIE, Elizabeth Mary, (Mrs Stuart Christie); *see* Steel, E. M.

CHRISTIE, Sir George (William Langham), CH 2002; Kt 1984; DL; Director, Glyndebourne Productions Ltd (Chairman, 1956–99); *b* 31 Dec. 1934; *o s* of John Christie, CH, MC, and Audrey Mildmay Christie; *m* 1958, Patricia Mary Nicholson; three *s* one *d*. *Educ:* Eton. Asst to Sec. of Calouste Gulbenkian Foundation, 1957–62. Chm. of various family companies. Mem., Arts Council of GB, 1988–92 (Chm., Adv. Panel on Music, 1988–92). Founder Chm., The London Sinfonietta, 1968–88. DL E Sussex, 1983. Hon. FRCM 1986; Hon. FRNCM 1986; Hon. GSM 1991. DUniv Sussex, 1990; Hon. DMus: Keele, 1993; Exeter, 1994. Cavaliere al Merito della Repubblica Italiana, 1977; Commandeur, l'Ordre des Arts et des Lettres (France), 2006. *Address:* Old House, Moor Lane, Ringmer, E Sussex BN8 5UR. *T:* (01273) 813706.

See also A. J. Christie.

CHRISTIE, Herbert; Director General, European Investment Bank, 1995–99, now Hon. Director General (Director, Research Department, 1983–95); *b* 26 Sept. 1933; *s* of Brig.-Gen. H. W. A. Christie, CB, CMG, and Mary Ann Christie; *m* 1982, Gilberte F. M. V. Desbois; one *s*. *Educ:* Methodist Coll., Belfast; Univ. of St Andrews (MA). Asst Lectr, Univ. of Leeds, 1958–60; Econ. Asst, HM Treasury, 1960–63; First Sec., Washington, DC, 1963–66; Econ. Adviser, J. Henry Schroder Wagg and Co. Ltd, 1966–71, with secondment as Econ. Adviser, NBPI, 1967–71; Sen. Econ. Adviser, Min. of Posts and Telecommunications, 1971–74, and Dept of Prices and Consumer Protection, 1974–76; Econ. Adviser, EEC Commn, Brussels, 1976–78; Under Sec., HM Treasury, 1978–83. Hon. Vis. Prof., Middlesex Univ., 1990–95. Order of European Merit, 2005. *Publications:* contrib. to books and learned jls. *Recreations:* languages, foreign travel. *Address:* 47 Rue J-B Esch, 1473 Luxembourg. *Club:* Reform.

CHRISTIE, Prof. Ian Leslie, FBA 1994; Anniversary Professor of Film and Media History, Birkbeck College, University of London, since 1999; *b* 23 Feb. 1945; *s* of late Robert Christie and Ethel Christie; *m* 1989, Patsy Nightingale; one *s* three *d*. *Educ:* Belfast Royal Acad.; Queen's Univ., Belfast (BA 1966). Lectr in Complementary Studies, Derby Coll. of Art, 1969–73; Sen. Lectr in Art Hist. and Film Studies, Derby Coll. of Higher Educn, 1973–75; British Film Institute: Regl Prog. Advr, then Hd of Programming, 1976–84; Hd of Distbn, 1984–92; Head of Special Projects, 1993–94; Associate Ed., Sight and Sound, 1995–97; Prof. of Film Studies, Univ. of Kent at Canterbury, 1997–99. Vis. Dir, Film Centre, Art Inst. of Chicago, 1985–86; Vis. Prof., Univ. of S Florida, 1989; Dist. Vis. Fellow, European Humanities Res. Centre, 1995–98, Vis. Lectr in Film, and Fellow, Magdalen Coll., 1995–98, Oxford Univ.; Slade Prof. of Fine Art, Cambridge Univ., 2005–06. Dir, Connoisseur Video, 1990–97. Vice-Pres., Europa Cinemas, 1993–. Mem. Exec. Cttee, GB-USSR Assoc., 1983–89. Jt Ed., Film Studies jl, 1999–. Co-curator of exhibitions: Eisenstein: his life and art, MOMA, Oxford, and Hayward Gall., 1988; Spellbound: art and film, Hayward Gall., 1996; The Director's Eye, MOMA, Oxford, 1996; Modernism: designing a new world, V&A Mus., 2006. Frequent radio and television broadcaster on cinema. *Publications:* Powell, Pressburger and Others, 1978; Arrows of Desire: the films of Michael Powell and Emeric Pressburger, 1985, 2nd edn 1994; (ed) The Life and Death of Col Blimp, 1994; The Last Machine, 1995; (ed) Gilliam on Gilliam, 1999; A Matter of Life and Death, 2000; The Art of Film: John Box and production design, 2008; *edited jointly:* FEKS, Formalism, Futurism, 1978; The Film Factory, 1988, 2nd edn 1994; Eisenstein at 90, 1988; Scorsese on Scorsese, 1989, 3rd edn 2003; Inside the Film Factory, 1991; Eisenstein Rediscovered, 1993; Protazanov and the Continuity of Russian Cinema, 1993; Spellbound: art and film, 1996; Law's Moving Image, 2004; The Cinema of Michael Powell: international perspectives on an English film-maker, 2005. *Recreations:* running, ski-ing, coarse carpentry, affordable wine, unaffordable opera. *Address:* 131 Mount View Road, N4 4JH. *T:* (020) 8348 3656.

CHRISTIE, Julie (Frances); actress; *b* 14 April 1940; *d* of Frank St John Christie and Rosemary Christie (*née* Ramsden). *Educ:* Convent; Brighton Coll. of Technology; Central Sch. of Speech and Drama. *Films:* Crooks Anonymous, 1962; The Fast Lady, 1962; Billy Liar, 1963; Darling, 1964 (Oscar, NY Film Critics Award, Br. Film Academy Award, etc); Young Cassidy, 1964; Dr Zhivago, 1965 (Donatello Award); Fahrenheit 451, 1966; Far from the Madding Crowd, 1966; Petulia, 1967; In Search of Gregory, 1969; The Go-Between, 1971; McCabe and Mrs Miller, 1972; Don't Look Now, 1973; Shampoo, 1974; Heaven Can Wait, 1978; Memoirs of a Survivor, 1981; The Animals Film, 1982; Return of the Soldier, 1982; Heat and Dust, 1983; The Gold Diggers, 1984; Power, 1987; Miss Mary, 1987; The Railway Station Man, 1992; Hamlet, 1997; Afterglow, 1998; Troy, Finding Neverland, 2004; Away From Her, 2007; *stage:* Old Times, Wyndham's, 1995; Suzanna Andler, Chichester, 1997. Fellow, BAFTA, 1997. Motion Picture Laurel Award, Best Dramatic Actress, 1967; Motion Picture Herald Award, Best Dramatic Actress, 1967.

CHRISTIE, Linford, OBE 1998 (MBE 1990); athlete; athletics coach; Managing Director, Nuff Respect, sports management company; *b* Jamaica, 2 April 1960; *s* of James and late Mabel Christie. *Educ:* Wandsworth Tech. Coll. Competed as a runner over 50 times for Great Britain, 1980–97. *European indoor championships:* Gold medal (200 m), 1986; Gold medal (60 m), 1988 and 1990; *European championships:* Gold medal (100 m), 1986 and 1990; *Commonwealth Games:* Silver medal (100 m), 1986; Gold medal (100 m), 1990 and 1994; *European Cup:* Gold medals (100 and 200 m), 1987; Gold medal (100 m), 1991, 1992 and 1994; Gold medals (100 and 200 m), 1997 (Men's Team Captain); *Olympic Games:* Silver medal (100 m), 1988; Gold medal (100 m), 1992 (British Men's Team Captain); *World indoor championships:* Silver medals (60 and 200 m), 1991; *World Cup:* Silver medal (200 m), 1992; Gold medal (100 m), 1989 and 1992; *World championships:* Gold medal (100 m), 1993; Silver medal (100 m relay), 1993. British and European 100 m record (9.87 seconds), and British 200 m record (20.09 seconds), 1988; British 100 yards record (9.30 seconds), Edinburgh, 1994; European 60 m record (6.47 seconds) and World indoor 200 m record (20.25 seconds), 1995. British Athletics Writers' Assoc., Male Athlete of the Year, 1988 and 1992. Hon. MSc Portsmouth Univ., 1993. *Publications:* Linford Christie (autobiog.), 1989; To Be Honest With You (autobiog.), 1995. *Address:* Nuff Respect, The Coach House, 107 Sherland Road, Twickenham, Middlesex TW1 4HB. *T:* (020) 8891 4145; *e-mail:* nuff_respect@msn.com. *Club:* Thames Valley Harriers (Pres., 1997).

CHRISTIE, Richard Hamish; QC 2006; *b* 17 April 1963; *s* of Martin and Phoebe Christie; *m* 1989, Jane; three *d*. *Educ:* Clifton Coll.; Manchester Univ. (LLB 1984). Called to the Bar, Inner Temple, 1986; Head of Chambers, 2 Pump Court. *Recreations:* cinema, Scotland, walking. *Address:* 2 Pump Court, Temple, EC4Y 7AH.

CHRISTIE, Prof. Thomas; Director, The Aga Khan University Examination Board, since 2003; Professor of Educational Assessment and Evaluation, University of Manchester, 1994–2003, now Professor Emeritus; *b* 12 May 1939; *s* of John Frew Christie and Margaret Watson Christie; *m* 1962, Patricia Ray Bozie; two *s* one *d*. *Educ:* Univ. of Edinburgh (MA, BEd). Res. Associate, 1963–66, Lectr in Educn, 1966–73, Sen. Lectr, 1973–76 and 1978–86, Dept of Educn, Univ. of Manchester; Sen. Lectr in Educnl Res., Dept of Educn, Univ. of Guyana, and Commonwealth Fund for Tech. Co-operation Consultant to Caribbean Exams Council, Barbados, 1976–78; University of Manchester: Dir, Centre for Formative Assessment Studies, Sch. of Educn, 1986–96; Dean, Fac. of Educn and Dir, Sch. of Educn, 1997–2002. Hon. DSc National Univ. of Mongolia, 1998. *Publications:* (jtly) Creativity: a selective review of research, 1968, 2nd edn 1971; (with G. M. Forrest) Standards at GCE A Level: 1963 and 1973, 1980; (with G. M. Forrest) Defining Public Examination Standards, 1981; A Guide to Teacher Assessment (3 vols), 1990; (ed with B. Boyle) Issues in Setting Standards: establishing comparabilities, 1996. *Recreations:* reading, crossword puzzles, desert travel. *Address:* 284 Bramhall Lane South, Bramhall, Stockport SK7 3DJ. *T:* (0161) 439 1518.

CHRISTIE, Sir William, Kt 1975; MBE 1970; JP; Lord Mayor of Belfast, 1972–75; a Company Director; *b* 1 June 1913; *s* of Richard and Ellen Christie, Belfast; *m* 1935, Selina Pattison (*d* 2000); one *s* two *d* (and one *s* decd). *Educ:* Ward Sch., Bangor, Northern Ireland. Belfast City Councillor, 1961; High Sheriff of Belfast, 1964–65; Deputy Lord Mayor, 1969; Alderman, 1973–77. JP Belfast, 1951; DL Belfast, 1977. Freeman, City of London, 1975. Salvation Army Order of Distinguished Auxiliary Service, 1973. *Recreations:* travel, walking, boating, gardening.

CHRISTIE, William James; Sheriff of Tayside, Central and Fife at Kirkaldy, 1979–97; *b* 1 Nov. 1932; *s* of William David Christie and Mrs Anne Christie; *m* 1957, Maeve Patricia Gallacher; three *s*. *Educ:* Holy Cross Acad., Edinburgh; Edinburgh Univ. (LLB). Nat. Service, 1954–56; commnd Royal Scots. Private Practice, 1956–79. Mem. Council, Law Soc. of Scotland, 1975–79; President: Soc. of Procurators of Midlothian, 1977–79; Soc. of Solicitors in the Supreme Court, 1979. *Recreations:* music, reading, shooting. *Address:* 63/6 Canaan Lane, Edinburgh EH10 4SG. *Club:* New (Edinburgh).

See also A. P. Christie.

CHRISTIE, William Lincoln; harpsichord player, organist and conductor; Founder and Director, Les Arts Florissants, since 1979; *b* New York, 19 Dec. 1944; *s* of William Lincoln Christie and Ida Jones Christie; adopted French citizenship. *Educ:* Harvard Coll. (BA 1966); Yale Univ. (MusM 1969). Student of piano and harpsichord in US, 1957–70; Asst in Hist. of Music and Dir, Collegium Musicum, Dartmouth Coll., USA, 1970–71; moved to France, 1971; Collaborator, Soc. de musique d'autrefois, Paris, 1972–75; Visiting Professor: Conservatoires of Paris, Lyon and The Hague, and GSMD, 1977–81; Sommer Akademie für Musik, Innsbrück, 1978–83; Prof., Paris Conservatoire, 1982–95. Musical Dir, Hippolyte et Aricie, L'Opéra de Paris, 1985; regularly conducts orchs in France, Switzerland, UK and USA; Glyndebourne début, Handel's Theodora, 1996. Mem., Vis. Cttee for Music, Harvard Univ., 1993–96. Has made numerous recordings, 1976–, esp. works for harpsichord, and vocal works of 17th and 18th centuries with Les Arts Florissants. Hon. DMus NY at Buffalo, 1997. Prix Georges Pompidou, 2005. Officier des Arts et des Lettres (France); Chevalier de la Légion d'Honneur (France), 1993. *Publications:* Sonate Baroque, 1989; Purcell au Coeur du Baroque, 1995. *Recreation:* gardening. *Address:* Les Arts Florissants, 46 rue Fortuny, 75017 Paris, France. *T:* (1) 43879888; Le Logis, 85210 Thiré, France.

CHRISTMAS, Timothy John, MD; FRCS; Consultant Urological Surgeon, Charing Cross Hospital, since 1992 and Royal Marsden Hospital, since 2000; *b* 2 Feb. 1956; *s* of Leslie George Christmas and Lydia Valerie (*née* Brown); *m* 2003, Dr Ethna Mannion; one *s*. *Educ:* Bournemouth Sch.; Middlesex Hosp. Med. Sch., London Univ. (MB BS 1980, MD 1992). FRCS 1984, FRCS (Urol) 1991. Surgical Registrar, London Hosp., 1986–88; Res. Fellow, UCL, 1988–91; Sen. Registrar, St Bartholomew's Hosp., 1991–92; Res. Fellow, Univ. of S California, LA, 1992; Consultant Urological Surgeon, Chelsea and Westminster Hosp., 1993–99. Fellow, European Bd of Urology, 1992. *Publications:* Benign Prostatic Hyperplasia, 1993, 2nd edn 1997; Prostate Cancer, 1996, 2nd edn 2001; Diseases of the Testis, 1997; Clinical Progress in Renal Cancer, 2006; numerous articles on genito-urinary cancer surgery. *Recreations:* travel, ornithology, photography. *Address:* 15th Floor, Charing Cross Hospital, Fulham Palace Road, W6 8RF. *T:* (020) 8846 7669, *Fax:* (020) 8846 7696; *e-mail:* Timothychristmas@aol.com, timothy.christmas@rmh.nhs.uk.

CHRISTO AND JEANNE-CLAUDE; artists; Christo Javacheff, *b* Gabrovo, Bulgaria, 13 June 1935 and Jeanne-Claude (*née* de Guillebon), *b* Casablanca, 13 June 1935; *m*; one *s*. Emigrated to USA 1964. Completed works include: Wrapped Objects, 1958; Stacked Oil Barrels and Dockside Packages, Cologne Harbour, 1961; Iron Curtain-Wall of Oil Barrels, blocking Rue Visconti, Paris, 1962; Store Fronts, NYC, 1964; Wrapped Kunsthalle, Berne, and Wrapped Fountain and Wrapped Medieval Tower, Spoleto, Italy, 1968; 5,600 Cubicmeter Package, Documenta 4, Kassel, 1968; Wrapped Floor and Stairway, Mus. of Contemporary Art, Chicago, 1969; Wrapped Coast, Little Bay, Sydney, Australia, 1969; Wrapped Monuments, Milan, 1970; Wrapped Floors and Covered Windows and Wrapped Walk Way, Krefeld, Germany, 1971; Valley Curtain, Grand Hogback, Rifle, Colo, 1970–72; The Wall, Wrapped Roman Wall, Via V. Veneto and Villa Borghese, Rome, 1974; Ocean Front, Newport, RI, 1974; Running Fence, Sonoma and Marin Counties, Calif, 1972–76; Wrapped Walk Ways, Kansas City, Mo, 1977–78; Surrounded Islands, Biscayne Bay, Miami, Fla, 1980–83; The Pont Neuf Wrapped, Paris, 1975–85; The Umbrellas, Japan-USA, 1984–91; Wrapped Floors and Stairways and Covered Windows, Mus. Würth, Künzelsau, Germany, 1995; Wrapped Reichstag, Berlin, 1971–95; Wrapped Trees, Switzerland, 1997–98; The Gates, Central Pk, NYC, 2005. *Fax:* (212) 9662891; *web:* www.christojeanneclaude.net.

CHRISTOPHER, Baron *cr* 1998 (Life Peer), of Leckhampton in the co. of Gloucestershire; **Anthony Martin Grosvenor Christopher,** CBE 1984; Chairman, TU Fund Managers Ltd (formerly Trades Union Unit Trust), since 1983 (Director, since 1981); public and political affairs consultant, since 1989; General Secretary, Inland Revenue Staff Federation, 1976–88; *b* 25 April 1925; *s* of George Russell Christopher and Helen Kathleen Milford Christopher (*née* Rowley); *m* 1962, Adela Joy Thompson. *Educ:* Cheltenham Grammar Sch.; Westminster Coll. of Commerce. Articled Pupil, Agric. Valuers, Gloucester, 1941–44; RAF, 1944–48; Inland Revenue, 1948–57; Asst Sec. 1957–60, Asst Gen. Sec. 1960–74, Jt Gen. Sec. 1975, Inland Revenue Staff Fedn. Member: TUC General Council, 1976–89 (Chm., 1988–89); TUC Economic Cttee, 1977–89; TUC Education Cttee, 1977–85; TUC Educn and Training Cttee, 1985–86; TUC Employment Policy and Orgn Cttees, 1985–89; TUC International Cttee, 1982–89; TUC Finance and General Purposes Cttee, 1983–89; TUC Media Working Group, 1979–89 (Chm., 1985–89); TUC Employment Policy and Orgn Cttee, 1979–85; TUC Social Insurance Cttee, 1986–89; Mems Auditor, ICFTU, 1984–. House of Lords: Member, Select Committees: Audit, 2003–; Consolidation of Bills, 2003–; Mem., European Cttee on Envmt and Agric., 2000–03, 2005–. Member: Tax Reform Cttee, 1974–80; Tax Consultative Cttee, 1980–88; Royal Commn on Distribution of Income and Wealth, 1978–79; IBA, 1978–83; Council, Inst. of Manpower Studies, 1984–89; ESRC, 1985–88; GMC, 1989–94. Chm., Tyre Industry EDC, 1983–86; Vice Pres., Building Socs Assoc., 1985–90; Director: Civil Service Building Soc., 1958–87 (Chm., 1978–87); Birmingham Midshires Building Soc., 1987–88; Policy Studies Inst. Council, 1983–91; Member: Bd, Civil Service Housing Assoc., 1958–96 (Vice-Chm., 1988–96); Council, NACRO, 1956–98 (Chm., 1973–98); Home Sec.'s Adv. Council for Probation and After-care, 1967–77; Inner London Probation and After-care Cttee, 1966–79; Audit

Commn, 1989–95; Broadcasting Complaints Commn, 1989–97; Council, 1985–90, Assembly, 1990–, SCF; Chm., Alcoholics Recovery Project, 1970–76; Member: Home Sec.'s Working Party on Treatment of Habitual Drunken Offenders, 1969–71; Inquiry into Rover Cowley Works Closure, 1990; Trustee: Commonwealth Trades Union Council Charitable Trust, 1985–89; Inst. for Public Policy Res., 1989–94 (Treas., 1990–94). Vis. Fellow, Univ. of Bath, 1981–; Mem. Council, Royal Holloway and Bedford New Coll., 1985–89. FRSA 1989. *Publications:* (jtly) Policy for Poverty, 1970; (jtly) The Wealth Report, 1979; (jtly) The Wealth Report 2, 1982. *Recreations:* gardening, reading, walking dogs. *Address:* c/o TU Fund Managers Ltd, Congress House, Great Russell Street, WC1B 3LQ. *Clubs:* Beefsteak, Royal Automobile.

CHRISTOPHER, Ann, RA 1989 (ARA 1980); RWA; FRBS; sculptor; *b* 4 Dec. 1947; *d* of William and Phyllis Christopher; *m* 1969, Kenneth Cook. *Educ:* Harrow School of Art (pre-Diploma); West of England College of Art (DipAD Sculpture). RWA 1983; FRBS 1992. Prizewinner, Daily Telegraph Young Sculptors Competition, 1971; Arts Council grants, 1973–76; Silver Medal for Sculpture of Outstanding Merit, RBS, 1994. *Exhibitions include:* RA Summer Exhibns, 1971–; Oxford Gallery, Oxford, 1973, 1974, 1978; Dorset County Mus. and Art Gall. (retrospective), 1989; Victoria Art Gall., Bath, 1992; Courcoux & Courcoux, 1991, 1999; Sculpture 93, London, 1993; Summer Exhibns, Redfern Gall., 1995, 1996; solo exhibitions: Redfern Gall., 1997; Jubilee Park, Canary Wharf, 2004; The Power of Place, RA, 2008. *Work in Collections:* Bristol City Art Gallery; Contemporary Arts Soc.; Chantrey, London; Glynn Vivian Art Gall., Swansea; RWA. *Commissions:* 3½m bronze, Tower Bridge Rd, London, 1990; 4½m bronze, Castle Park, Bristol, 1993; 2·3m bronze, Washington, USA, 1994; 4·8m corten steel, Plymouth, 1996; 2·3m bronze, Linklaters & Paines, London, 1997; 3m bronze, Great Barrington, Mass, USA, 1998; 5·5m corten steel, Portmarine, 2001; medal for British Art Medal Soc., 2004. *Recreation:* cinema.

CHRISTOPHER, Sir (Duncan) Robin (Carmichael), KBE 2000; CMG 1997; HM Diplomatic Service, retired; Secretary General, Global Leadership Foundation, since 2007; *b* 13 Oct. 1944; *m* 1980, Merril Stevenson; two *d. Educ:* Keble Coll., Oxford (BA); Fletcher Sch., Tufts Univ., USA (MA). FCO, 1970; Second, then First, Sec., New Delhi, 1972; First Sec., FCO, 1976; Dep. Hd of Mission, Lusaka, 1980; FCO, 1983; on secondment to Cabinet Office, 1985; Counsellor: Madrid, 1987; FCO, 1991; Ambassador: to Ethiopia, 1994–97; to Indonesia, 1997–2000; to Argentina, 2000–04. Dir, Rurelec plc, 2005–. Trustee: The Brooke Hosp., 2005–; St Matthew's Children's Fund, Ethiopia, 2005–; Prospect Burma, 2005–; Redress, 2005–. Fellow, Inst. for the Study of the Americas, 2006–. *Recreations:* ski-ing, music, motorcycling. *Address:* e-mail: rchristopher2@yahoo.co.uk.

CHRISTOPHER, John; *see* Youd, S.

CHRISTOPHER, John Anthony, CB 1983; BSc; FRICS; Chief Valuer, Valuation Office, Inland Revenue, 1981–84, retired; *b* 19 June 1924; *s* of John William and Dorothy Christopher; *m* 1947, Pamela Evelyn Hardy; one *s* one *d* (and one *s* decd). *Educ:* Sir George Monoux Grammar Sch., Walthamstow; BSc Estate Management (London). Chartered Surveyor; LCC Valuation Dept, 1941. Served War, RAF, 1943–47. Joined Valuation Office, 1952; District Valuer and Valuation Officer, Lincoln, 1965; Superintending Valuer, Darlington, 1972; Asst Chief Valuer, 1974; Dep. Chief Valuer, Valuation Office, Inland Revenue, 1978. *Recreation:* golf. *Address:* 40 Svenskaby, Orton Wistow, Peterborough, Cambs PE2 6YZ. *T:* (01733) 238199.

CHRISTOPHER, Sir Robin; *see* Christopher, Sir D. R. C.

CHRISTOPHER, Warren; lawyer; Senior Partner, O'Melveny and Myers, since 1997; Secretary of State, United States of America, 1993–97; *b* 27 Oct. 1925; *s* of Ernest and Catharine Christopher; *m* 1956, Marie Wyllis; three *s* one *d. Educ:* Univ. of Southern California; Stanford Law Sch. USNR, 1943–45. Joined O'Melveny and Myers, LA, 1950, partner, 1958–67, 1969–76, 1981–92. Dep. Attorney-Gen., USA, 1967–69; Dep. Sec. of State, 1977–81. US Medal of Freedom, 1981. *Publications:* In the Stream of History: shaping foreign policy for a new era, 1998; Chances of a Lifetime (memoirs), 2001. *Address:* (office) Suite 700, 1999 Avenue of the Stars, Los Angeles, CA 90067–6035, USA.

CHRISTOPHERS, Richard Henry Tudor, (Harry); conductor; *b* 26 Dec. 1953; *s* of Richard Henry Christophers and Constance Clavering Christophers (*née* Thorp); *m* 1979, Veronica Mary Hayward; two *s* two *d. Educ:* Canterbury Cathedral Choir Sch.; King's Sch., Canterbury; Magdalen Coll., Oxford (Mods Classics, BA Music, MA). Founder and Conductor, The Sixteen Choir and Orchestra, then The Sixteen and the Symphony of Harmony and Invention, 1977–; débuts: BBC Prom. concert, 1990; Salzburg Fest., 1989; Lisbon Opera, 1994; ENO, 2000; freelance conductor: BBC Philharmonic, City of London Sinfonia, Acad. of St Martin in the Fields, Hallé, London Symphony, San Francisco Symphony, Handel and Haydn Society (Boston), Orquesta Comunidad de Madrid, etc. Numerous recordings. Grand Prix du Disque, 1988; Deutschen Schallplattenkritik, 1992 and 1993; Gramophone Award, 1992; Diapason d'or, 1995 and 1996; Classical Brit Award, 2005. *Recreations:* cooking, Arsenal FC. *Address:* The Sixteen, Raine House, Raine Street, E1W 3RJ.

CHRISTOPHERSEN, Henning; Senior Partner, Kreab, Brussels, since 2002; *b* Copenhagen, 8 Nov. 1939; *m* Jytte Risbjerg Christophersen; one *s* two *d. Educ:* Copenhagen University (MA Econs, 1965). Head, Economic Div., Danish Fedn of Crafts and Smaller Industries, 1965–70; economics reporter for periodical NB, 1970–71, for weekly Weekendavisen, 1971–78. MP (L) for Hillerød, 1971–84; Nat. Auditor, 1976–78; Minister for Foreign Affairs, 1978–79; Pres., Liberal Party Parly Gp, 1979–82; Dep. Prime Minister and Minister for Finance, 1982–84; a Vice-Pres., EC (formerly CEC), 1985–95. Mem., parly finance and budget cttee, 1972–76 (Vice-Chm., 1975); Chm., parly foreign affairs cttee, 1979–81; Mem., Nordic Council, 1981–82. Dep. Leader, Danish Liberal Party, Venstre, 1972–77; Political spokesman of Liberal MPs, 1973–78; Acting Leader, Liberal Party, 1977, Party Leader, 1978–84. Vice-Pres., Fedn of European Liberals and Democrats, 1980–84. Man. Dir, Epsilon SPRL, 1995–2001; Sen. Advr to Czech Govt, 1996–99; Chm., Örestad Develt Co., 1999–; Vice-Chm., Scania Danmark AS, 2000–06. Director: Danish Central Bank, 1979–82; Scancem AB, 1998–99; Den Danske Bank, 1995–; Mem. Bd, KS Consult AS, 1999–2002. Member: Danish Council for Eur. Policy, 1995–98; Prime Minister's Adv. Council for Baltic Sea Co-operation, Sweden, 1996–2000; European Convention and Presidium, 2002–03; Pres., Energy Charter Conf., Brussels, 1998–2006. Pres., Rockwool Foundn (Mem. Bd, 1995–). Chm., Eur. Inst. of Public Admin, Maastricht, 1996–. *Publications:* books and articles on political and economic subjects. *Address:* Kreab, Avenue de Tervueren 2, 1040 Brussels, Belgium.

CHRISTOPHERSON, Harald Fairbairn, CMG 1978; Commissioner of Customs and Excise, 1970–80, retired; *b* 12 Jan. 1920; *s* of late Captain Harald and Mrs Laura Christopherson; *m* 1947, Joyce Winifred Emmett (*d* 1979); one *s* two *d. Educ:* Heaton Grammar Sch., Newcastle upon Tyne; King's Coll., Univ. of Durham (BSc and DipEd). Served in RA, 1941–46, Captain 1945. Teacher and lecturer in mathematics, 1947–48.

Entered administrative class, Home CS, Customs and Excise, 1948; seconded to Trade and Tariffs Commn, W Indies, 1956–58; Asst Sec., 1959; seconded to Treasury, 1965–66; Under Sec., 1969. Senior Clerk, Committee Office: House of Commons, 1980–85; House of Lords, 1985–86. Mem. Cttee for Southern Region, Nat. Trust, 1986–94. *Recreations:* music, museums and galleries, books, travel. *Address:* 57a York Road, Sutton, Surrey SM2 6HN. *T:* (020) 8642 2444. *Club:* Reform (Chm., 1998–99).

CHRUSZCZ, Charles Francis; QC 1992; a Recorder, since 1990; *b* 19 Nov. 1950; *s* of Janick Francis Chruszcz and Kathleen Whitehurst Chruszcz; *m* 1972, Margaret Olivia Chapman; three *s. Educ:* Queen Mary Coll., London (LLB Hons). Called to the Bar, Middle Temple, 1973; Asst Recorder, 1985–90. *Recreations:* reading, music, building renovation, the outdoors. *Address:* Exchange Chambers, Pearl Assurance House, Derby Square, Liverpool L2 9XX. *T:* (0151) 236 7747; Exchange Chambers, Ralli Courts, West Riverside, Manchester M3 5FT. *T:* (0161) 833 2722.

CHU, Prof. Steven, PhD; Professor of Physics and of Molecular and Cell Biology, University of California, Berkeley; Director, Lawrence Berkeley National Laboratory, since 2004; *b* 28 Feb. 1948; *s* of Ju Chin Chu and Ching Chen Li; two *s. Educ:* Univ. of Rochester (AB Maths 1970, BS Physics 1970); Univ. of Calif, Berkeley (PhD Physics 1976). Postdoctoral Res. Fellow, Univ. of Calif, Berkeley, 1976–78; Mem., Technical Staff, Bell Labs, Murray Hill, 1978–83; Hd, Quantum Electronics Res. Dept, AT&T Bell Labs, Holmdel, 1983–87; Prof. of Physics and Applied Physics, 1987–, Theodore and Frances Geballe Prof. of Physics and Applied Physics, 1990–2007, Chm., Physics Dept, 1990–93, 1999–2001, Stanford Univ. Vis. Prof., Collège de France, 1990. Fellow: APS, 1987; Optical Soc. of America, 1988; Amer. Acad. Arts and Scis, 1992. Member: NAS, 1993; Academica Sinica, 1994; Amer. Philosophical Soc., 1998; Foreign Member: Chinese Acad. Scis, 1998; Korean Acad. Scis and Technol., 1998. Broida Prize for Laser Spectroscopy, 1987; Schawlow Prize for Laser Sci., 1994, APS; King Faisal Internat. Prize for Sci., 1993; Meggers Award for Spectroscopy, Optical Soc. of America, 1994; Humboldt Sen. Scientist Award, 1995; Science for Art Prize, LVMH, 1995; (jtly) Nobel Prize for Physics, 1997. *Recreations:* swimming, cycling, tennis. *Address:* Lawrence Berkeley National Laboratory, 1 Cyclotron Road, Berkeley, CA 94720, USA; 6231 Contra Costa Road, Oakland, CA 94618, USA.

CHUA, Nam-Hai, FRS 1988; Andrew W. Mellon Professor and Head of Laboratory of Plant Molecular Biology, Rockefeller University, since 1981; *b* 8 April 1944; *m* 1970, Suat Choo Pearl; two *d. Educ:* Univ. of Singapore (BSc Botany and Biochem.); Harvard Univ. (AM, PhD Biol.). Lectr, Biochem. Dept, Univ. of Singapore, 1969–71; Rockefeller University, Cell Biology Department: Res. Associate, 1971–73; Asst Prof., 1973–77; Associate Prof., 1977–81. Chm., Management Bd, 1995–, Scientific Adv. Bd, 1995–, Inst. of Molecular Agrobiology, Nat. Univ. of Singapore. Fellow, Acad. Sinica, Taipei, 1988; Associate Fellow, Third World Acad. of Scis, 1988; Hon. Mem., Japanese Biochemical Soc., 1992. Nat. Sci. and Technol. Medal, Singapore, 1998. *Publications:* Methods in Chloroplast Molecular Biology, 1982; Plant Molecular Biology, 1987; Methods in Arabidopsis Research, 1992; 317 pubns in professional jls. *Recreations:* squash, ski-ing. *Address:* Rockefeller University, 1230 York Avenue, New York, NY 10021–6399, USA. *T:* (212) 3278126, *Fax:* (212) 3278327; *e-mail:* chua@mail.rockefeller.edu.

CHUAN LEEKPAI; MHR, Trang Province, Thailand, since 1969; Leader of the Opposition, 1995–97 and 2001–03; *b* 28 July 1938. *Educ:* Trang Wittaya Sch.; Silpakorn Pre-Univ.; Thammasat Univ. (LLB 1962). Barrister-at-Law, Thai Bar, 1964; lawyer. Thailand; Dep. Minister of Justice, 1975; Minister to Prime Minister's Office, 1976; Minister: of Justice, 1976 and 1980–81; of Commerce, 1981; of Agric. and Co-operatives, 1982–83; of Educn, 1983–86; Speaker, House of Reps, 1986–88; Minister of Public Health, 1988–89; Dep. Prime Minister and Minister of Agric. and Co-operatives, 1990–92; Prime Minister, 1992–95; Prime Minister and Minister of Defence, 1997–2001. Leader, Democrat Party. Vis. Lectr, Forensic Medicine Dept, Faculty of Medicine, Chulalongkorn Univ. Hon. Dr Political Science: Srinakharinwirot, 1985; Ramkhamhaeng, 1987; Hon. LLD: Philippines, 1993; Vongchavalitkul, 1998; Hon. LitD: (Painting) Silpakorn, 1994; Nat. Univ. of San Marcos, Lima, 1999. Kt Grand Cross (First Cl.), 1979, Kt Grand Cordon, 1981, Order of Crown (Thailand); Kt Grand Cross (First Cl.), 1980, Kt Grand Cordon (Special Cl.), 1982, Order of White Elephant (Thailand). *Address:* Parliament House, Bangkok 10300, Thailand.

CHUBB, family name of **Baron Hayter**.

CHUBB, Anthony Gerald Trelawny, FCA; Chairman, Foseco (formerly Foseco Minsep) PLC, 1986–90; *b* 6 April 1928; *s* of Ernest Gerald Trelawny Chubb and Eunice Chubb; *m* 1951, Beryl Joyce (*née* Cross); two *s. Educ:* Wylde Green Coll., Sutton Coldfield. FCA 1962 (ACA 1951); ACMA 1956. CBIM 1981. Joined Foundry Services Ltd, 1951; Man. Dir, Foseco UK, 1964–69; Dir, Foseco Ltd, 1966; Man. Dir, Foseco International, 1969–78; Dep. Gp Man. Dir, 1974–79, Gp Man. Dir, 1979–86, Foseco Minsep PLC; Chm., Electrocomponents PLC, 1986–90 (Dep. Chm., 1983–86; Dir, 1980–90). *Recreations:* golf, gardening, reading.

CHUBB, Prof. Ian William, AC 2006 (AO 1999); DPhil; Vice Chancellor, Australian National University, since 2000; *b* 17 Oct. 1943; *s* of Ian and Lillian Chubb; *m* 1971, Claudette Maes; three *d. Educ:* Christ Church, Oxford (MSc, DPhil 1975). Heyman's Res. Fellow, Univ. of Ghent, 1969–71; Wellcome Schol., Christ Church, Oxford, 1971–73; Res. Fellow, St John's Coll., Oxford, 1973–77; Lectr, Sen. Lectr, then Associate Prof., Flinders Univ., 1977–85; Dep. Vice-Chancellor, 1986–90, Emeritus Prof., 1990, Univ. of Wollongong; Chair, Commonwealth Higher Educn Council, 1990–95; Dep. Vice-Chancellor, Monash Univ., 1993–94; Vice Chancellor, Flinders Univ., 1995–2000. Chm., Australian Vice-Chancellors' Cttee, 2000–01; Pres., Gp of Eight Univs, 2004–05. Hon. DSc Flinders, 2000. *Address:* Australian National University, Canberra, ACT 0200, Australia.

CHUNG, Kyung-Wha, Korean Order of Merit; concert violinist; *b* 26 March 1948; *d* of Chun-Chai Chung and Won-Sook (Lee) Chung; *m;* two *s. Educ:* Juilliard Sch. of Music, New York. Moved from Korea to New York, 1960; 7 years' study with Ivan Galamian, 1960–67; New York début with New York Philharmonic Orch., 1967; European début with London Symphony Orch., Royal Festival Hall, London, 1970. First prize, Leventritt Internat. Violin Competition, NY, 1967. *Address:* c/o Independent Artists Ltd, 4–6 Soho Square, W1D 3PZ.

CHUNG, Sir Sze-yuen, GBE 1989 (CBE 1975; OBE 1968); Kt 1978; PhD; FREng; JP; Pro-Chancellor, Hong Kong University of Science and Technology, since 1999 (Founding Chairman, 1988–99); Chairman, Transport International Holdings (formerly Kowloon Motor Bus Holdings) Ltd, since 1999; *b* 3 Nov. 1917; *m* 1942, Nancy Cheung (*d* 1977); one *s* two *d. Educ:* Hong Kong Univ. (BScEng 1st Cl. Hons, 1941); Sheffield Univ. (PhD 1951). FREng (FEng 1983); FIMechE 1957, Hon. FIMechE 1983; Hon. FHKIE 1976; FIET (FIProdE 1958); CCMI (FBIM 1978). Consulting engr, 1952–56; Gen. Man., Sonca Industries (now Sonca Products), 1956–60, Man. Dir 1960–77, Chm.

1977–88. Director: CLP Hldgs (formerly China Light & Power Co.), 1968–; Sun Hung Kai Properties Ltd, 2001–. Mem., Hong Kong Legislative Council, 1965–74, Sen. Mem., 1974–78; Mem., Hong Kong Exec. Council, 1972–80, Sen. Mem., 1980–88; Advr to Govt of People's Republic of China on Hong Kong affairs, 1992–97; Mem., Chinese Govt's Preparatory Cttee for establishment of HKSAR, 1996–97; Convenor, HKSAR Exec. Council, 1997–99. Chairman: Standing Commn on CS Salaries and Conditions of Service, 1980–88; Hong Kong Productivity Council, 1974–76; Asian Product. Orgn, 1969–70; Hong Kong Industrial Design Council, 1969–75; Fedn of Hong Kong Industries, 1966–70 (Hon. Life Pres. 1974); Hong Kong Metrication Cttee, 1969–73; Hong Kong-Japan Business Co-operation Cttee, 1983–88; Hong Kong-US Econ. Co-operation Cttee, 1984–88. Founding Chairman: Hong Kong Polytechnic, 1972–86; City Polytechnic of Hong Kong, 1984 (Founding Fellow, 1986); Hong Kong Hosp. Authy, 1991–95 (Chm., Provisional Hosp. Authy, 1988–90). Founding Pres., Hong Kong Acad. of Engrg Scis, 1994–97; Pres., Engrg Soc. of Hong Kong, 1960–61. LLD (*hc*): Chinese Univ. of Hong Kong, 1983; Sheffield, 1985; DSc (*hc*) Hong Kong Univ., 1976; DEng (*hc*) Hong Kong Polytechnic, 1989; DBA (*hc*) City Polytechnic of Hong Kong, 1989. JP Hong Kong, 1964. Man of the Year, Hong Kong Business Today magazine, 1985. Defence Medal, 1948; Silver Jubilee Medal, 1977; Gold Medal, Asian Productivity Orgn, 1980; HKSAR Grand Bauhinia Medal, 1997. Japanese Order of Sacred Treasure (3rd cl.), 1983. *Publications:* Hong Kong's Journey to Reunification (memoirs), 2001; contrib. Proc. IMechE, Jl Iron and Steel Inst., Jl Hong Kong Instn of Engrs, and Jl Engrg Soc. of Hong Kong. *Recreation:* swimming. *Address:* House 25, Bella Vista, Silver Terrace Road, Clear Water Bay, Kowloon, Hong Kong. *T:* 27610281, 27192857, *Fax:* 27607493, 23580689. *Clubs:* Hong Kong, Hong Kong Jockey, Kowloon Cricket, Pacific (Hong Kong).

CHURCH, Ian David, CBE 2002; Editor, Official Report (Hansard), House of Commons, 1989–2002; *b* 18 Oct. 1941; *s* of John Jasper and Violet Kathleen Church; *m* 1964, Christine Stevenson; one *d*. *Educ:* Roan School. Journalist with: Dundee Courier and Advertiser, 1958–64; Press Association, 1964; The Scotsman, 1966; The Times, 1968; joined Hansard, 1972; Dep. Editor, 1988. Sec., Commonwealth Hansard Editors Assoc., 1990–2002 (Pres., 1996–99). Ind. Mem., Standards Cttee, Mid-Sussex DC 2007.

CHURCH, John Carver, CMG 1986; CVO 1988; MBE 1970; HM Diplomatic Service, retired; *b* 8 Dec. 1929; *s* of Richard Church, CBE, FRSL, and Catherina Church; *m* 1953, Marie-Geneviève Vallette; two *s* two *d*. *Educ:* Cranbrook Sch., Kent; Ecole Alsacienne, Paris; Christ's Coll., Cambridge (MA 1953). Reuters News Agency, 1953–59; Central Office of Information, 1959–61; Commonwealth Relations Office: Information Officer, Calcutta, 1961–65; Foreign and Commonwealth Office: Second Secretary (Commercial) Rio de Janeiro, 1966–69; First Sec. (Information) Tel Aviv, 1969–74; First Sec., News Dept, FCO, 1974–77; Consul (Commercial) Milan, 1977–78; Consul-General: São Paulo, 1978–81; Naples, 1981–86; Barcelona, 1986–89. *Address:* 41 rue de Rochechouart, 75009 Paris, France; La Métairie, Le Maine, 24510 Ste Alvère, France.

CHURCH, John George, CBE 1998; DL; FCA; President, Church & Co. plc, since 2002 (Chairman, 1991–2001); *b* 14 May 1936; *s* of Dudley Ross Church and Louise Elizabeth Church; *m* 1965, Rhona Elizabeth Gibson; one *s* one *d*. *Educ:* Stowe Sch. FCA 1959. Mgt Consultant, Annan Impey Morrish, 1961–64; joined Church & Co. plc, 1964: Asst Co. Sec., 1964–67; Co. Sec., 1967–76; Dir, 1968–2001; Man. Dir, 1976–97. Non-executive Director: Babers Ltd, 1972– (Chm., 1996–); James Southall and Co. Ltd, 1985–98 and 2000–06 (Dep. Chm., 2002–06); Start Rite Ltd, 1985–98 and 2000–06; Kingsley Park Properties (formerly St Matthew's Hosp.) Ltd, 1981–2003. President: British Footwear Mfrs Fedn, 1988–89; Boot Trade Benevolent Soc., 1984–85. St Andrew's Group of Hospitals, Northampton: Gov., 1995–; Mem. Bd Mgt, 1999–; non-exec. Dir, 2004–. Member: Ct, Univ. of Northampton (formerly Nene Coll., Northampton, subseq. UC of Northampton), 1994–; Bd of Mgt, Cordwainers' Coll., 1976–2000. Liveryman, Cordwainers' Co., 1958– (Mem. of Ct, 1992–; Master, 1998–99). High Sheriff, Northants, 1993–94; DL Northants, 1997. FRSA 1995. Hon. Fellow, UC of Northampton, 2002. *Recreation:* country pursuits. *Club:* Royal Automobile.

CHURCH, Judith Ann; *b* 19 Sept. 1953; *d* of late Edmund Church and of Helen Church; two *s*. *Educ:* Leeds Univ. (BA Hons Maths and Phil.); Huddersfield Poly. (PGCE Technical); Aston Univ. (Postgrad. Dip. Occupational Health and Safety); Thames Valley Coll. (DMS). Teacher, VSO, 1975–77; Process Research, Mars UK, 1979–80; HM Inspector of Factories, HSE, 1980–86; Nat. Health and Safety Officer, MSF, 1986–94. Contested (Lab) Stevenage, 1992; MP (Lab) Dagenham, June 1994–2001. *Recreation:* keeping fit.

CHURCHHOUSE, Prof. Robert Francis, CBE 1982; PhD; Professor of Computing Mathematics, University of Wales, College of Cardiff (formerly University College, Cardiff), 1971–95; *b* 30 Dec. 1927; *s* of Robert Francis Churchhouse and Agnes Howard; *m* 1954, Julia McCarthy; three *s*. *Educ:* St Bede's Coll., Manchester; Manchester Univ. (BSc 1949); Trinity Hall, Cambridge (PhD 1952). Royal Naval Scientific Service, 1952–63; Head of Programming Gp, Atlas Computer Lab., SRC, 1963–71. Vis. Fellow, St Cross Coll., Oxford, 1972–90. Chm., Computer Bd for Univs and Res. Councils, 1979–82; Mem., Welsh Cttee, UFC, 1989–93. Pres., IMA, 1986–87. Hon. DSc South Bank, 1993. KSG 1988. *Publications:* (ed jtly) Computers in Mathematical Research, 1968; (ed jtly) The Computer in Literary and Linguistic Studies, 1976; Numerical Analysis, 1978; Codes and Ciphers, Julius Caesar, the Enigma and the Internet, 2002; papers in math. and other jls. *Recreations:* cricket, astronomy. *Address:* 15 Holly Grove, Lisvane, Cardiff CF14 0UJ. *T:* (029) 2075 0250.

CHURCHILL; *see* Spencer-Churchill.

CHURCHILL, 3rd Viscount *cr* 1902; **Victor George Spencer,** OBE 2001; Baron Churchill of Wychwood 1815; Managing Director, CCLA Investment Management Ltd, 1988–99; *b* 31 July 1934; *s* of 1st Viscount Churchill, GCVO, and late Christine Sinclair (who *m* 3rd, Sir Lancelot Oliphant, KCMG, CB); *S* half-brother, 1973. *Educ:* Eton; New Coll., Oxford (MA). Lieut, Scots Guards, 1953–55. Morgan Grenfell & Co. Ltd, 1958–74; Investment Manager: Central Bd of Finance, C of E, 1974–99; Charities Official Investments Fund, 1974–95. A Church Comr, 2001–04. Director: Local Authorities' Mutual Investment Fund, 1974–99; Charter Pan-European Trust, 1992–2004; F & C Income and Growth Investment Trust, 1994–2005; Allchurches Trust, 1994–2006; Schroder Split Fund, 1995–2002. *Heir* (to Barony only): Richard Harry Ramsay Spencer [*b* 11 Oct. 1926; *m* 1st, 1958, Antoinette Rose-Marie de Charrière (*d* 1994); two *s*; 2nd, 1999, Cressida Josephine Alice Sykes (*née* Van Halle)]. *Address:* 6 Cumberland Mansions, George Street, W1H 5TE. *T:* (020) 7262 6223.

CHURCHILL, Caryl, (Mrs David Harter); playwright; *b* 3 Sept. 1938; *d* of Robert Churchill and Jan (*née* Brown); *m* 1961, David Harter; three *s*. *Educ:* Trafalgar Sch., Montreal; Lady Margaret Hall, Oxford (BA 1960). Student prodns of early plays, 1958–61; *radio plays:* The Ants, 1962; Lovesick, 1966; Identical Twins, 1968; Abortive, 1971; Not… not… not… not… not enough oxygen, 1971; Schreiber's Nervous Illness, 1972; Henry's Past, 1972; Perfect Happiness, 1973; *television plays:* The Judge's Wife, 1972; Turkish Delight, 1973; The After Dinner Joke, 1978; The Legion Hall Bombing, 1978; Crimes, 1981; (with Ian Spink) Fugue, 1987; *stage plays:* Owners, 1972; Moving Clocks Go Slow, 1975; Objections to Sex and Violence, 1975; Light Shining in Buckinghamshire, 1976; Vinegar Tom, 1976; Traps, 1977; (contrib.) Floorshow, 1977; Cloud Nine, 1979; Three More Sleepless Nights, 1980; Top Girls, 1982; Fen, 1983; Softcops, 1984; (collaborator) Midday Sun, 1984; (with David Lan and Ian Spink) A Mouthful of Birds, 1986; Serious Money, 1987; Ice cream, 1989; Hot Fudge, 1989; Mad Forest, 1990; (with Ian Spink and Orlando Gough) Lives of the Great Poisoners, 1991; The Skriker, 1994; (trans.) Seneca's Thyestes, 1994; Blue Heart, 1997; This is a Chair, 1997, Far Away, 2000; A Number, 2002; Drunk Enough to Say I Love You?, 2006. *Publications:* Owners, 1973; Light Shining, 1976; Traps, 1977; Vinegar Tom, 1978; Cloud Nine, 1979; Top Girls, 1982; Fen, 1983; Fen and Softcops, 1984; A Mouthful of Birds, 1986; Serious Money, 1987; Plays I, 1985; Plays II, 1988; Objections to Sex and Violence in Plays by Women, vol. 4, 1985; Light Shining, 1989; Traps, 1989; Cloud Nine, 1989; Ice cream, 1989; Mad Forest, 1990; Lives of the Great Poisoners, 1992; The Skriker, 1994; Thyestes, 1994; Blue Heart, 1997; This is a Chair, 1999; Far Away, 2000; A Number, 2002; Drunk Enough to Say I Love You?, 2006; anthologies. *Address:* c/o Casarotto Ramsay Ltd, Waverley House, 7–12 Noel Street, W1F 8GQ. *T:* (020) 7287 4450.

CHURCHILL, Lawrence; Chairman, Pension Protection Fund, since 2004; *b* 5 Aug. 1946; *s* of Austin and Kathleen Churchill; *m* 1991, Karen Darcy; twin *d*, and one *s* one *d* from previous marriage. *Educ:* Birkenhead Sch.; St John's Coll., Oxford (MA). Systems Analyst, Proctor & Gamble, 1969–73; Sen. Systems Designer, then Exec. Dir, Hambro Life Assce, 1973–85; Exec. Dir, Allied Dunbar Assce, 1985–91; Chief Exec., NatWest Life, 1991–95; Man. Dir, NatWest Life Investments, 1995–98; Chm., Unum Ltd, 1998–2002; CEO, Zurich Financial Services, 2002–04. Non-executive Director: Good Energy (formerly Monkton) plc, 2004–; Huntswood, 2005–06; Children's Mutual, 2005–. Non-executive Director: PIA, 1994–98; ABI, 1995–98; Employers' Forum on Disability, 2000–03; Financial Ombudsman Service, 2002–05. Chm., Raising Standards Quality Mark Scheme, 2000–02; Mem., Bd for Actuarial Standards, 2006–. Vice Pres., Employment Opportunities, 2004–. Trustee, RSA, 2000–02; Internat. Longevity Centre - UK, 2007–. *Publications:* (jtly) A Changing Nation, 1997; (jtly) New Beginnings, 2000. *Recreations:* Rugby, theatre, opera, family. *T:* (01373) 830325, *Fax:* (01373) 831277; *e-mail:* lawrence.churchill@tiscali.co.uk. *Club:* Oxford and Cambridge.

CHURCHILL, Neil Gareth; Chief Executive, Asthma UK, since 2007; *b* Carshalton, 6 Sept. 1966; *s* of Ronald and Shirley Churchill; *m* 1996, Anna Barlow; two *d*. *Educ:* Fitzwilliam Coll., Cambridge (BA Hist. 1988); London South Bank Univ. (MBA 2000). Head of Communications: Barnado's, 1991–96; PSI, 1996–98; Dep. Chief Exec., Crisis, 1998–2001; Ext. Affairs Dir, Age Concern, 2001–07. Mem., Edtl Bd, Cultural Trends, 2000–. *Recreations:* reading, 40s cinema, medieval history, China and Japan, philosophy, live music and theatre. *Address:* Asthma UK, Summit House, 70 Wilson Street, EC2A 2DB. *T:* (020) 7786 4902; *e-mail:* nchurchill@asthma.org.uk.

CHURCHILL, Winston Spencer; author; journalist; parliamentarian; *b* 10 Oct. 1940; *s* of late Hon. Randolph Frederick Edward Spencer Churchill, MBE and Hon. Mrs Averell Harriman, US Ambassador to France, 1993–97; *m* 1st, 1964, Mary Caroline, (Minnie), d'Erlanger (marr. diss. 1997); two *s* two *d*; 2nd, 1997, Luce Engelen. *Educ:* Eton; Christ Church, Oxford (MA). War correspondent in Yemen, Congo and Angola, 1963; Correspondent: Borneo and Vietnam, 1966; Middle East, 1967; Chicago, Czechoslovakia, 1968; Nigeria, Biafra and Middle East, for The Times, 1969–70; Special Correspondent: China, for The Observer, 1972; Portugal, for The Daily Telegraph, 1975. Presenter, This Time of Day, BBC Radio, 1964–65. Lecture tours of the US and Canada, 1965–2005. Contested Gorton Div. of Manchester, Nov. 1967. MP (C) Stretford, 1970–83, Davyhulme, Manchester, 1983–97. PPS to Minister of Housing and Construction, 1970–72, to Minister of State, FCO, 1972–73; Sec., Cons. Foreign and Commonwealth Affairs Cttee, 1973–76; Conservative Party front-bench spokesman on Defence, 1976–78. Member: Select Cttee on Defence, 1983–97; Select Cttee on H of C (Services), 1985–86. Vice-Chm., Cons. Defence Cttee, 1979–83; Cons. Party Co-ordinator for Defence and Multilateral Disarmament, 1982–84; Mem. Exec., 1922 Cttee, 1979–85, Treas., 1987–88. Sponsored Motor Vehicles (Passenger Insce) Act 1972, Crown Proceedings (Armed Forces) Act 1987. Pres., Trafford Park Indust. Council, 1971–97. Member, Council: Consumers' Assoc., 1990–93; British Kidney Patients Assoc., 1990–2004. President: Friends of Airborne Forces, 1996–2004; War Memls Trust (formerly Friends of War Memls), 1997–; Chairman: Nat. Benevolent Fund for the Aged, 1994– (Trustee, 1974–); Winston Churchill Meml Trust, 2002– (Trustee, 1965–); Trustee, Sandy Gall's Afghanistan Appeal, 1995–. Governor, English-Speaking Union, 1975–80; Vice-Pres., British Technion Soc., 1976–. Hon. Fellow, Churchill Coll., Cambridge, 1969. Hon. FSE 1989. Hon. LLD Westminster Coll., Fulton, Mo, USA, 1972; Hon. DSc Technion, Israel, 1997. *Publications:* First Journey, 1964; Six Day War, 1967; Defending the West, 1981; Memories and Adventures, 1989; His Father's Son, 1996; The Great Republic, 1999; (ed) Never Give In!: the best of Winston Churchill's speeches, 2003. *Recreations:* tennis, sailing, ski-ing, golf, trekking in the Himalayas. *Clubs:* White's, Buck's, Press; Air Squadron; St Moritz Tobogganing; Queenwood Golf (Everglades, USA).

CHURSTON, 5th Baron *cr* 1858; **John Francis Yarde-Buller;** Bt 1790; *b* 29 Dec. 1934; *s* of 4th Baron Churston, VRD and Elizabeth Mary (*d* 1951), *d* of late W. B. du Pre; *S* father, 1991; *m* 1973, Alexandra Joanna, *d* of A. G. Contomichalos; one *s* two *d*. *Educ:* Eton Coll. 2nd Lt RHG, 1954. A Freemason. *Heir:* *s* Hon. Benjamin Anthony Francis Yarde-Buller [*b* 13 Sept. 1974; *m* 2000, Sophie Frances, *e d* of Brian Duncan]. *Address:* Yowlestone House, Puddington, Tiverton, Devon EX16 8LN. *T:* (01884) 860328. *Clubs:* Buck's, White's.

CHYNOWETH, David Boyd; Chief Executive, Universities Superannuation Scheme Ltd, 1994–2003; *b* 26 Dec. 1940; *s* of Ernest and Blodwen Chynoweth; *m* 1968, Margaret Slater; one *s* two *d*. *Educ:* Simon Langton Sch., Canterbury; Univ. of Nottingham (BA). CPFA (IPFA 1966); FCCA 1983. Public Finance posts with Derbs CC, 1962 and London Borough of Ealing, 1965; Asst County Treas., Flints CC, 1968; Dep. County Treas., West Suffolk CC, 1970; County Treasurer, S Yorks CC, 1973; Dir of Finance, Lothian Regl Council, 1985–94. Vice-Chairman: UK-American Properties Inc., 1980–86; American Properties Unit Trust, 1980–86; Mem. Bd, Lazards Small Cos Exempt Unit Trust, 1979–97. Mem. Council, CIPFA, 1983–99 (Vice Pres., 1991–92; Pres., 1992–93); Mem. Investment Protection Cttee, 1976–80, 1982–86 and 1999–2004, Council Mem., 1998–2004, Nat. Assoc. of Pension Funds; Mem. Bd, Foundn for Regulation of Accountancy Profession, 1999–2004. Pres., Assoc. of Public Service Finance Officers, 1981–82. *Recreations:* walking, photography. *Address:* 27 Whitehall Road, Rhos on Sea, Colwyn Bay LL28 4HW. *T:* (01492) 545867. *Club:* Royal Over-Seas League.

CHYNOWETH, Rt Rev. Neville James, AM 1996; ED 1966; *b* 3 Oct. 1922; *s* of Percy James and Lilian Chynoweth; *m* 1951, Joan Laurice Wilson; two *s* two *d*. *Educ:* Manly High School; Sydney Univ. (MA); Melbourne Coll. of Divinity (BD); Moore Theological Coll. (ThL). ARSCM 1993. Assistant, St Michael's, Sydney, 1950; Rector, Kangaroo

Valley, 1951–52; Chaplain, Royal Prince Alfred Hospital, 1952–54; Rector: St John's, Deewhy, 1954–63; St Anne's, Strathfield, 1963–66; All Saints, Canberra, 1966–71; St Paul's, Canberra, 1971–74; Archdeacon of Canberra, 1973–74; Assistant Bishop of Canberra and Goulburn, 1974–80; Bishop of Gippsland, 1980–87. *Recreations:* music, biography. *Address:* 10 Fortitude Street, Red Hill, Canberra, ACT 2603, Australia. *T:* (2) 62397056.

CIAMPI, Dr Carlo Azeglio; President of the Republic of Italy, 1999–2006; *b* Livorno, 9 Dec. 1920; *s* of Pietro and Maria Ciampi; *m* 1946, Franca Pilla; one *s* one *d*. *Educ:* Scuola Normale Superiore, Pisa; Univ. of Pisa (BA, LLB 1946). Served Italian Army, 1941–44 (MC). Joined Bank of Italy, Rome, 1946: work in various branches, 1946–60; Economist and Hd, Res. Dept, 1960–73; Sec.-Gen., 1973–76; Dep. Dir Gen., 1976–78; Dir Gen., 1978; Gov., and Chm., Ufficio Italiano dei Cambi, 1979–83 (Hon. Gov., 1993–); Gov. for Italy, IBRD, IDA, IFC, Washington, and ADB, Manila, 1979–93; Pres., Council of Ministers, Rome, 1993–94; Vice-Pres., BIS, Basle, 1994–96 (Dir, 1979–93); Chm., Competitiveness Adv. Gp, EU, 1995–96; Minister of the Treasury, Budget and Econ. Programming, 1996–99; Chm., Interim Cttee, IMF, Washington, 1998–99. Pres., Venice Internat. Univ., 1996–99. *Publications:* Un Metodo per Governare, 1996; contrib. numerous reports and articles. *Address:* c/o Palazzo del Quirinale, 00187 Rome, Italy.

CICCONE, Madonna Louise Veronica, (Madonna); singer and actress; *b* 16 Aug. 1958; *d* of Sylvio, (Tony), Ciccone and late Madonna Ciccone; *m* 1st, 1985, Sean Penn (marr. diss. 1989); one *d* by Carlos Leon; 2nd, 2000, Guy Ritchie; one *s*. *Educ:* Adams High Sch.; Univ. of Michigan (dance scholarship); Alvin Alley Studios, NY. Formed Maverick Records Co., 1992; *recordings* include: first hit single, Holiday, 1983; albums: Madonna, 1983; Like a Virgin, 1984; True Blue, 1986; Like a Prayer, 1989; Erotica, 1992; Bedtime Stories, 1994; Ray of Light, 1998; Music, 2000; American Life, 2003; Confessions on a Dance Floor, 2005; I'm Going to Tell You a Secret, 2006; The Confessions Tour, 2007; Hard Candy, 2008. *Films:* A certain Sacrifice, 1979; Vision Quest, 1985; Desperately seeking Susan, 1985; Shanghai Surprise, 1986; Who's that Girl?, 1987; Bloodhounds of Broadway, 1989; Dick Tracy, 1989; Soap-Dish, 1990; Shadows and Fog, 1991; A League of their Own, 1991; In Bed with Madonna, 1991; Truth or Dare, 1991; Body of Evidence, 1992; Snake Eyes, 1994; Dangerous Game, 1994; Blue in the Face, 1995; Girl 6, 1996; Evita (Golden Globe Award for best actress), 1996; Four Rooms, 1996; The Next Best Thing, 2000; Swept Away, 2002; Die Another Day, 2002; dir, Filth and Wisdom, 2008; writer and exec. prod., I Am Because We Are, 2008; *theatre:* Up For Grabs, Wyndham's, 2002. *Publications:* Sex, 1992; *for children:* The English Roses, 2003; Mr Peabody's Apples, 2003; Yakov and the Seven Thieves, 2004; The Adventures of Abdi, 2004.

CICUTTO, Francis John; Chairman: ORIX Australia, 2004–08; Run Corporation, since 2005; *b* 9 Nov. 1950; *s* of Francesco Cicutto and Ultima (*née* Margaritta); *m* 1982, Christine Bates; one *s*. *Educ:* Univ. of NSW. Chief Manager, Central Business Dist, Victoria Nat. Australia Bank Ltd, 1986–88; Exec. Vice Pres., Americas, NAB, USA, 1988–89; NAB Australia: Gen. Manager, Credit Bureau, 1989–92; State Manager, NSW and ACT, 1992–94; Dir and Chief Exec., Clydesdale Bank PLC, 1994–96; Chief Gen. Manager, 1996–99, Man. Dir and CEO, 1999–2004, Nat. Australia Bank Ltd. *Recreations:* Rugby, golf, cricket, theatre. *Clubs:* Union, Killara Golf (Sydney); Australian (Melbourne).

CIECHANOVER, Prof. Aaron J., MD, DSc; Professor, since 1992, and Distinguished Research Professor, since 2002, Faculty of Medicine, Technion-Israel Institute of Technology, Haifa, Israel; *b* 1 Oct. 1947; *s* of Yitzhak and Bluma Ciechanover; *m* 1975, Dr Menucha Siletzky; one *s*. *Educ:* Hebrew Univ., Jerusalem (MSc 1970; MD 1974); Technion-Israel Inst. of Technol., Haifa (DSc 1982). Nat. Compulsory Service, Israel Defence Forces, 1974–77: Mil. Physician, Israeli Navy and Unit for R&D, Surgeon-Gen. HQ. Department of Biochemistry, Faculty of Medicine, Technion-Israel Institute of Technology: Res. Fellow, 1977–79; Lectr, 1979–81; Sen. Lectr, 1984–87; Associate Prof., 1987–92; Dir, Rappaport Family Inst. for Res. in Med. Scis, 1993–2000. Vis. Scientist, Inst. for Cancer Res., Fox Chase Cancer Center, Philadelphia, 1978, 1979, 1980, 1981; Postdoctoral Fellow, Dept of Biol., MIT and Whitehead Inst. for Biomed. Res., Cambridge, Mass, 1981–84; Visiting Professor: Dana Farber Cancer Inst. and Harvard Med. Sch., 1985, 1986; Div. of Haematol.-Oncology, Dept of Pediatrics, Children's Hosp., Washington Univ. Sch. of Medicine, St Louis, annually, 1987–99 and 2001; Univ. of Kyoto Sch. of Medicine, 2000; Northwestern Univ. Sch. of Medicine, 2002, 2003; Microbiol. and Tumor Biol. Center, Karolinska Inst., Stockholm, 2003; City Univ. of Osaka Sch. of Medicine, 2003–04, 2005; Rockefeller Univ., NY, 2004; Amer. Cancer Soc. Eleanor Roosevelt Meml Fellow, 1988–89. Mem., EMBO, 1996. Hon. FRSC 2005. Hon. PhD: Tel Aviv, 2002; Ben Gurion, 2004; City Univ. of Osaka, 2005. Holds numerous awards and prizes, including: (jtly) Albert and Mary Lasker Award for Basic Med. Res., 2000; (jtly) Nobel Prize in Chemistry, 2004. *Publications:* contrib. numerous original articles, book chapters and review articles on intracellular proteolysis. *Address:* Faculty of Medicine, Technion-Israel Institute of Technology, Haifa 31096, Israel. *T:* 48295379, *Fax:* 48513922; *e-mail:* c_tzachy@netvision.net.il.

CIMA, Maj. Gen. Keith Harington, CB 2007; CEng; Resident Governor and Keeper of the Jewel House, HM Tower of London, since 2006; *b* 28 May 1951; *s* of Peter Harington Cima and late Ivy Rose Cima; *m* 1985, Susan Diane Rook; three *s* one *d* (and one *d* decd). *Educ:* Brasenose Coll., Oxford (MA); Open Univ. (MBA); RMA Sandhurst. CEng, MIMechE 1992. Grad. trainee, Babcock and Wilcox Ltd, 1973–74. Troop Commander: 1 Trng Regt, RE, 1975–76; 20 Field Sqn, 1977–78; Intelligence Officer, HQ RE, 2nd Div., 1978; Adjt 25 Engr Regt, 1979–80; psc(a)† 1981; SO2 MoD, 1982–83; OC 3 Field Sqn, 1984–85; SO2 RE, HQ UK Mobile Force, 1986–87; SO1 Directing Staff, RMCS, 1988–90; CO 38 Engr Regt, 1991–93; Project Manager, Mines and Demolitions, 1994, Gen. Engrg Equipt, 1995, Procurement Exec.; Col Personnel Br. 7, Mil. Sec., 1995; rcds 1996; Director: Engr Support (Army), 1997–99; Manning (Army), 1999–2000; COS, Adjt Gen., 2001–02; Sen. Army Mem., RCDS, 2002–05; Team Leader, Project Hyperion - the co-location and integration of HQ Land and Adjt Gen., MoD, 2005–06. Trustee: Ulysses Trust, 2006–; St Katharine & Shadwell Trust, 2006–; Constables' Fund, HM Tower of London, 2006–; Overseas Cemeteries Trust, 2007– (Chm., 2007–). Pres., Instn of RE, 2007–. Col Comdt, RE, 2003–; Hon. Col, Royal Monmouthshire RE (Militia), 2006– (Chm., Regtl Trust, 2006–). Operational Volunteer, Thames Lifeboat, RNLI. FCMI 2004. *Publication:* Reflections from the Bridge, 1994. *Recreations:* dinghy sailing, marathons, gardening, DIY, building a $^1/_8$ scale steam railway. *Address:* c/o RHQ Royal Engineers, Brompton Barracks, Chatham, Kent ME4 4UG.

CITARELLA, Victor Thomas; social care and management consultant; Director and Trustee, Skills for Care, since 2000; *b* 8 May 1951; *s* of Thomas and Evelyn R. M. Citarella; *m* 1975, Jacqueline Hopley; three *s* one *d*. *Educ:* Sweyne Grammar Sch., Essex; University Coll., Cardiff (BSc Hons Econs 1973, Cert. Social Work 1978). Residential Child Care Officer, S Glamorgan, 1974–80; Team Manager, Hillingdon Social Services, 1980–82; Day and Residential Care Officer, W Sussex, 1982–85; Area Manager, Bristol, Avon, 1985–88; Dep. Dir of Social Services, 1988–91, Dir of Social Services, 1991–2000, City of Liverpool. Pres., Social Care Assoc., 1992. *Address:* 5 New Acres, Newburgh, Wigan, Lancs WN8 7TU. *T:* (01257) 462698; *e-mail:* citarella@supanet.com.

CLAES, Willy; Secretary General, NATO, 1994–95; *b* Hasselt, Belgium, 24 Nov. 1938; *m* 1965, Suzanne Meynen; one *s* one *d*. *Educ:* Free Univ., Brussels. Asst Sec., then Provincial Sec., De Voorzorg, 1962–65; Local Councillor, Hasselt, 1964–94; MHR (Socialist), Hasselt, 1968–94; Minister of: Nat. Educn, Flemish Reg., 1972–73; Econ. Affairs, 1973–74 and 1977–79; Deputy Prime Minister and Minister of: Econ. Affairs, 1979–81; Econ. Affairs and Planning and Nat. Educn, 1987; Foreign Affairs, 1992–94. Belgian Socialist Party: Mem., Exec. Cttee, 1965–94; Co-Pres., 1975–77. Numerous decorations from Europe, Mexico and Bolivia. *Publications:* Tussen droom en werkelijkheid: bouwstenen voor en ander Europa, 1979; La Chine et l'Europe, 1980; Livre Blanc de l'Energie, 1980; Quatre Années aux Affaires Economiques, 1980; Elementen voor een nieuw energiebeleid, 1980; Belgie … quo vadis?: un conte moderne, 1980; De Derde Weg: beschouwingen over de Wereldcrisis, 1987. *Recreations:* piano music, conducting orchestras. *Address:* Berkenlaan 62, 3500 Hasselt, Belgium.

CLAGUE, Joan; Director of Nursing Services, Marie Curie Memorial Foundation, 1986–90; *b* 17 April 1931; *d* of James Henry Clague and Violet May Clague (*née* Johnson). *Educ:* Malvern Girls' Coll.; Guy's Hosp.; Hampstead Gen. Hosp.; Simpson Meml Maternity Pavilion. Asst Regional Nursing Officer, Oxford Regional Hosp. Bd, 1965–67; Principal, then Chief Nursing Officer, St George's Hosp. Bd of Governors, 1967–73; Area Nursing Officer, Merton, Sutton and Wandsworth AHA, 1973–81; Regl Nursing Officer, NE Thames RHA, 1981–86. Pres., Assoc. of Nurse Administrators, 1983–85. Trustee, WRVS Trustees Ltd, 1991–96. WHO Fellow, 1969; Smith and Nephew EEC Scholar, 1981. *Recreations:* walking, domestic pursuits. *Address:* 7 Tylney Avenue, SE19 1LN. *T:* (020) 8670 5171.

CLANCARTY, 9th Earl of, *cr* 1803; **Nicholas Power Richard Le Poer Trench;** Baron Kilconnel 1797; Viscount Dunlo 1801; Baron Trench (UK) 1815; Viscount Clancarty (UK) 1823; Marquess of Heusden (Kingdom of the Netherlands) 1818; *b* 1 May 1952; *o s* of Hon. Power Edward Ford Le Poer Trench (*d* 1975), *y s* of 5th Earl of Clancarty, and Jocelyn Louise Courtney (*d* 1962); *S* uncle, 1995; *m* 2005, Victoria Frances Lambert; one *d*. *Educ:* Westminster Sch.; Ashford Grammar Sch.; Plymouth Polytech.; Univ. of Colorado; Sheffield Poly.

CLANCHY, Joan Lesley, (Mrs Michael Clanchy); Headmistress, North London Collegiate School, 1986–97; *b* 26 Aug. 1939; *d* of Leslie and Mary Milne; *m* 1962, Dr Michael Clanchy; one *s* one *d*. *Educ:* St Leonard's Sch., St Andrews; St Hilda's Coll., Oxford. MA; DipEd. Schoolteacher: Woodberry Down Sch., London, 1962–63; The Park Sch., Glasgow, 1967–76; Headmistress, St George's Sch., Edinburgh, 1976–85.

CLANCY, Claire Elizabeth; Chief Executive and Clerk, National Assembly for Wales, since 2007; *b* 14 March 1958; *d* of Douglas and Teresa Coates; *m* 1994, Michael John Clancy, *qv*. *Educ:* Dartford Grammar Sch. for Girls; Open Univ. (BA 1st Cl. Psychol.). Manpower Services Commn, 1977–88; Dept of Employment, 1988–90; Chief Exec., Powys TEC, 1990–92; Govt Office for SW, 1992–96; Dir of Policy and Planning, Companies House, 1996–97; Dir, Patent Office, 1999–2002; Registrar of Companies and Chief Exec., Companies House, 2002–07. *Recreation:* horse-riding. *Address:* National Assembly for Wales, Cardiff Bay, Cardiff CF99 1NA. *T:* (029) 2089 8233; *e-mail:* claire.clancy@wales.gsi.gov.uk.

CLANCY, Deirdre V., (Mrs M. M. Steer); set and costume designer; portrait painter; *b* 31 March 1943; adopted *d* of Julie M. Clancy; *m* 1975, Michael Maxwell Steer; one *s* two *d*. *Educ:* Convent of Sacred Heart, Tunbridge Wells; Birmingham Coll. of Art (NDD 1st Cl. Hons). Arts Council Asst, Lincoln Rep., 1965; House Designer, Royal Court Theatre, 1966–68: productions include costumes for D. H. Lawrence Trilogy, 1966; sets and costumes for: Early Morning, 1967; The Sea, 1973; has designed for RNT, RSC, ENO, Scottish Opera, New Sadlers Wells Opera, Chichester Fest. Theatre; costumes for Oliver, Tivoli, 2007; numerous prodns in Europe, N America, Japan and Australia, incl. Marriage of Figaro, LA Opera, 2004, Così fan Tutte, 2006 and Marriage of Figaro, 2007, Opéra Lyon. Founder dir, Cherubim Music Trust, 2001–. *Films* include: The Virgin and The Gypsy, 1969; Mrs Brown, 1997 (Best Film Costumes, BAFTA Award, 1998); Tom's Midnight Garden, 1998; *television:* Wives and Daughters, 1999. Has exhibited designs. DUniv UCE, 2003. Green Room Award, Vic, Australia, for Best Costume (opera), 1990 and 1991; Olivier Award for Best Costume Design (for A Month in the Country, Triumph Prodns, and Loves Labours Lost, RSC), 1997, (for All's Well That Ends Well, RSC), 2005. *Publication:* Costume since 1945, 1996. *Recreations:* infrequent domesticity, family pursuits, more painting. *Address:* 125 Duck Street, Tisbury, Wilts SP3 6LJ; *e-mail:* d@clancy.uk.com.

CLANCY, His Eminence Cardinal Edward Bede, AC 1992 (AO 1984); Archbishop of Sydney, (RC), 1983–2001; *b* 13 Dec. 1923; *s* of John Bede Clancy and Ellen Lucy Clancy (*née* Edwards). *Educ:* Marist Brothers Coll., Parramatta, NSW; St Patrick's Coll., Manly, NSW; Biblical Inst., Rome (LSS); Propaganda Fide Univ., Rome (DD). Ordained to priesthood, 1949; parish ministry, 1950–51; studies in Rome, 1952–54; parish ministry, 1955–57; seminary staff, 1958–61; studies in Rome, 1962–64; seminary staff, Manly, 1966–73; Auxiliary Bishop, Sydney, 1974–78; Archbishop of Canberra and Goulburn, 1979–82. Cardinal, 1988. Chancellor, Aust. Catholic Univ., 1990–2001. Hon. DHum Ateneo de Manila, Philippines, 2001; DUniv Aust. Catholic Univ., 2002. *Publications:* The Bible—The Church's Book, 1974; Come Back—the Church Loves You, 2002; Walk Worthy of Your Vocation—a Spiritual Journey with St Paul, 2004; God's Early Trailblazers—Great Figures in the Early Church, 2005; contribs to Australian Catholic Record. *Recreation:* golf. *Address:* 54 Cranbrook Road, Bellevue Hill, NSW 2023, Australia.

CLANCY, Michael John; HM Diplomatic Service; Governor and Commander-in-Chief, St Helena and Dependencies, 2004–07; *b* 31 March 1949; *s* of William John Clancy and Chrissie Melinda Clancy (*née* Clarke); *m* 1994, Claire Elizabeth Coates (*see* C. E. Clancy); one *s* one *d*. *Educ:* Lewis Sch., Pengam; Trinity Coll., Cambridge (BA Econs Tripos 1970). Trainee and Private Sec. to Sec. of State, Welsh Office, 1972–81; Principal, Hong Kong Govt, 1981–86; Hd, Personnel Mgt, Welsh Office, 1986–90; Sen. Consultant, Hay Mgt Consultants, 1990–92; Dir for Wales, Dept of Employment, 1992–95; Housing, Welsh Office, 1995–97; Chief Sec., St Helena Govt, 1997–2000; Hd of Investment, Nat. Assembly for Wales, 2001–04. *Recreations:* horse-riding, sailing, hill-walking, cycling. *Address:* c/o Foreign and Commonwealth Office, SW1A 2AH. *Club:* St Helena Yacht.

CLANCY, Richard Francis Stephen; District Judge (Magistrates' Courts), Liverpool, since 2005; *b* 2 Sept. 1948; *s* of Francis Gerrard Clancy and Evaline Margaret Clancy; *m* 1976, Anne Margaret Lawless; one *s* one *d*. *Educ:* St Ambrose Coll., Altrincham; Coll. of Law, Guildford. Articled to John Arthur Wheeler, OBE, Solicitor, Warrington, 1969–74; admitted solicitor, 1974; prosecuted, W Midlands and Merseyside, 1974–83; in private practice as partner, Ridgway Greenall, Warrington, and E. Rexmakin & Co., Liverpool, 1983–2000; Acting Stipendiary Magistrate for Staffs, 1998–2000; District Judge (Magistrates' Cts), Birmingham, 2001–05. Member: Risley Prison Visitors' Centre Cttee, 1990–2000 (Chm., 1998–2000); Merseyside Criminal Justices Strategy Cttee, 1997–2000; Merseyside Justices' Issues Cttee, 2005–. Mem., Warrington Sports Council (Chm., 1996–99); former Auditor, Warrington Athletic Club. *Recreations:* sport, piano, accordion, history, literature.

CLANCY, Thomas Leo, Jr, (Tom); writer; *b* 12 March 1947; *m* 1969, Wanda Thomas (marr. diss. 1998); one *s* three *d*; *m* 1999, Alexandra Marie Llewellyn. *Educ:* Loyola Coll., Baltimore, Md. Served USAR OTC. Former insurance agent, Baltimore, Md and Hartford, Conn; joined O. F. Bowen Agency, insurance firm, Owings, Md, 1973, owner (with wife), 1980; co-owner and Vice-Chm., Community Projects and Public Affairs, Baltimore Orioles. Co-founder, Red Storm Entertainment, 1996. *Publications:* (as Tom Clancy): *novels:* The Hunt for Red October, 1984 (filmed); Red Storm Rising, 1986; Patriot Games, 1987 (filmed); Cardinal of the Kremlin, 1988; Clear and Present Danger, 1989 (filmed); The Sum of all Fears, 1991 (filmed); Without Remorse, 1993; Debt of Honor, 1994; Reality Check, 1995; Executive Orders, 1996; Balance of Power, 1998; Rainbow Six, 1998; Carrier, 1999; The Bear and the Dragon, 2000; Red Rabbit, 2002; The Teeth of the Tiger, 2003; Net Force series (with Steve Pieczevik): Net Force; The Deadliest Game; End Game; The Great Race; One is the Loneliest Number; The Ultimate Escape; Cyberspy; Hidden Agendas; Gameprey; Deathworld; Night Moves; Breaking Point; Private Lives; Virtual Vandals; Springboard; Op Centre series (with Steve Pieczevik): Op Centre, 1995; Mirror Image, 1995; Games of State, 1996; Acts of War, 1997; State of Siege; Balance of Power; Divide and Conquer; Line of Control, 2003; Call to Treason, 2004; War of Eagles, 2005; Power Plays series (with M. H. Greenberg): Politika; Ruthless.com; Shadow Watch; Bio-Strike, 2000; Cutting Edge; Wild Card; *non-fiction:* Submarine, 1993; Fighter Wing, 1995; Armored Warfare, 1996; Marine, 1996; Airborne, 1997; Carrier; (with Fred Franks Jr) Into the Storm, 1997; (with J. B. Alexander) Future War; War in the Boats; Every Man a Tiger, 1999; (jtly) Battle Ready, 2004.

CLANFIELD, Viscount; Ashton Robert Gerard Peel; *b* 16 Sept. 1976; *s* and *heir* of 3rd Earl Peel, *qv*; *m* 2004, Matilda Rose Aykroyd; two *d*. *Educ:* Ampleforth; Durham Univ. (BA Hons 1999); Univ. of Buckingham (MBA 2004). With Cazenove Fund Management, 2000–02, Panmure Gordon and Co., 2006–.

CLANMORRIS, 8th Baron *cr* 1800 (Ire.); **Simon John Ward Bingham,** MA; FCA; *b* 25 Oct. 1937; *s* of 7th Baron Clanmorris and of Madeleine Mary, *d* of late Clement Ebel; *S* father, 1988; *m* 1971, Gizella Maria, *d* of Sandor Zverkó; one *d*. *Educ:* Downside; Queens' College, Cambridge (MA). ACA 1965, FCA 1975. Director: Pyreco Ltd; The Original Smoothie Co. Ltd. *Heir: cousin* Robert Derek de Burgh Bingham [*b* 29 Oct. 1942; *m* 1969, Victoria Mary, *yr d* of P. A. Pennant-Rea; three *d*]. *Address:* c/o Child & Co., 1 Fleet Street, EC4Y 1BD.
See also Hon. C. M. T. Bingham.

CLANWILLIAM, 7th Earl of, *cr* 1776 (Ire.); **John Herbert Meade;** Bt 1703; Viscount Clanwilliam, Baron Gillford 1766; Baron Clanwilliam (UK) 1828; *b* 27 Sept. 1919; 2nd *s* of Adm. Hon. Sir Herbert Meade Fetherstonhaugh, GCVO, CB, DSO (*d* 1964) (3rd *s* of 4th Earl) and Margaret Ishbel Frances (*d* 1977), *d* of Rt. Rev. Hon. Edward Carr Glyn, DD; *S* cousin, 1989; *m* 1956, Maxine (*d* 2004), *o d* of late J. A. Hayden-Scott; one *s* two *d*. *Educ:* RNC Dartmouth. *Heir: s* Lord Gillford, *qv*. *Address:* Blundells House, Tisbury, Wilts SP3 6JP. *Club:* Turf.

CLAPHAM, Michael; MP (Lab) Barnsley West and Penistone, since 1992; *b* 15 May 1943; *s* of late Thomas Clapham and of Eva Clapham; *m* 1965, Yvonne Hallsworth; one *s* one *d*. *Educ:* Leeds Polytechnic (BSc); Leeds Univ. (PGCE); Bradford Univ. (MPhil). Miner, 1958–70; Lectr, 1974–77; Dep. Head, Yorks NUM Compensation Dept, 1977–83; Head of Industrial Relations, NUM, 1983–92. PPS to Minister of State for Health, 1997. Mem., Trade and Industry Cttee, 1992–97, 2003–05; Vice Chm., back-bench Trade and Industry Gp, 1996–97; Chairman, All-Party Group: on Occupational Safety and Health, 1996–; on Coalfield Communities, 1997–; on NATO Parly Assembly, 2000; Jt Chm., All-Party Gp on Fire Safety, 2001–; Hon. Sec., All-Party Gp on Energy Studies, 1997–. Chair, NATO Civil Dimensions and Security, 2004–. Chairman: Barnsley Community Safety Partnership (formerly Barnsley Crime Prevention Partnership), 1995–; Multi Agency Panel, 1999–. *Recreations:* reading, walking, gardening, squash. *Address:* (office) 18 Regent Street, Barnsley, Yorks S70 2HG. *T:* (01226) 731244.

CLAPHAM, Peter Brian, CB 1996; PhD; CEng, FInstP; Consultant on technology and public administration reform, since 1996; Director, National Physical Laboratory, 1990–95; *b* 3 Nov. 1940; *s* of Wilfred Clapham and Una Frances (*née* Murray); *m* 1965, Jean Margaret (*née* Vigil); two *s*. *Educ:* Ashville Coll., Harrogate; University Coll. London (BSc, PhD; Fellow, 1996). Research in optics and metrology, NPL, 1960–70; Sec., Adv. Cttee on Res. on Measurements and Standards, 1970–71; res. management and head of marketing, NPL, 1972–81; Res. and Technology Policy, DoI, 1981–82; Supt of Div. of Mech. and Optical Metrology, NPL, 1982–84; Dir 1985, Chief Exec. 1989, Nat. Weights and Measures Lab. Chm., W European Legal Metrology Cooperation, 1989–90; Member: Presidential Council of Internat. Orgn of Legal Metrology, 1985–90; Internat. Cttee of Weights and Measures, 1991–96; British Hallmarking Council, 2001–. Dir, Bushy Park Water Gardens Trust, 1997–2002. *Publications:* numerous sci. contribs to learned jls. *Recreations:* peregrination, crafts, Catenians.

CLAPP, Captain Michael Cecil, CB 1982; RN retired; *b* 22 Feb. 1932; *s* of Brig. Cecil Douglas Clapp, CBE and Mary Elizabeth Emmeline Palmer Clapp; *m* 1975, Sarah Jane Alexander; one *s* two *d*. *Educ:* Chafyn Grove Sch., Salisbury; Marlborough College. Joined Royal Navy, 1950; commanded HM Ships Puncheston, Jaguar and Leander, and 801 Sqdn; Commander, Falklands Amphibious Task Gp, 1982. Mem., Stock Exchange, 1987–95. Gov., Kelly Coll., 1985–. *Publication:* Amphibious Assault, Falklands, 1996. *Recreations:* sailing, shooting, fishing, country life. *Club:* Royal Cruising.

CLAPP, Susannah; Theatre Critic, The Observer, since 1997; *b* 9 Feb. 1949; *d* of Ralph James Clapp and Marion (*née* Heeremans). *Educ:* Ashford Co. Grammar Sch.; Univ. of Bristol (BA Hons). Sub-editor, The Listener, 1970–74; reader and ed., Jonathan Cape, 1974–79; radio critic, Sunday Times, 1978–80; Asst Ed., London Rev. of Books, 1979–92; Theatre Critic: Nightwaves, Radio 3, 1994–; New Statesman, 1996–97. *Publication:* With Chatwin: portrait of a writer, 1997. *Address:* 37 Granville Square, WC1X 9PD. *T:* (020) 7837 1686.

CLAPPISON, (William) James; MP (C) Hertsmere, since 1992; *b* 14 Sept. 1956; *m* 1984, Helen Margherita Carter; one *s* three *d*. *Educ:* St Peter's Sch., York; Queen's Coll., Oxford (Schol.; PPE). Called to the Bar, Gray's Inn, 1981. Contested (C): Barnsley E, 1987; Bootle, May and Nov. 1990. Parly Under-Sec. of State, DoE, 1995–97; Opposition frontbench spokesman on home affairs, 1997–2001; Shadow Minister for Work, 2001–02; Opposition front bench spokesman, Treasury affairs, 2002. Mem., Home Affairs Select Cttee, 2002–. *Recreations:* bridge, walking. *Address:* House of Commons, SW1A 0AA. *Club:* Carlton.

CLAPTON, Eric Patrick, CBE 2004 (OBE 1995); singer, guitarist and songwriter; *b* 30 March 1945; *s* of Patricia Clapton; *m* 1979, Patricia Ann Harrison (*née* Boyd) (marr. diss. 1988); (one *s* decd by Lori Del Santo); one *d* by Yvonne Kelly; *m* 2002, Melia McEnery; three *d*. *Educ:* St Bede's Sch., Surrey; Kingston Coll. of Art. Guitarist with: Roosters, 1963; Yardbirds, 1963–65; John Mayall's Bluesbreakers, 1965–66; Cream, 1966–68; Blind Faith, 1969; Delaney and Bonnie, 1970; Derek and the Dominoes, 1970; solo performer, 1972–. Albums include: (with Yardbirds): Five Live Yardbirds, 1964; For Your Love, 1965; (with Bluesbreakers) Blues Breakers, 1966; (with Cream): Fresh Cream, 1967; Disraeli Gears, 1967; Wheels of Fire, 1968; Goodbye, 1969; (with Blind Faith) Blind Faith, 1969; (with Derek and the Dominoes) Layla and Other Assorted Love Songs, 1970; *solo:* Eric Clapton, 1970; 461 Ocean Boulevard, 1974; There's One in Every Crowd, 1975; E. C. Was Here, 1975; No Reason to Cry, 1976; Slowhand, 1977; Backless, 1978; Just One Night, 1980; Another Ticket, 1981; Money and Cigarettes, 1983; Behind the Sun, 1985; August, 1986; Journeyman, 1989; 24 Nights, 1992; Unplugged, 1992; From the Cradle, 1994; Pilgrim, 1998; Blues, 1999; (with B. B. King) Riding with the King, 2000; Reptile, 2001; One More Car One More Rider, 2002; Me and Mr Johnson, 2004; Back Home, 2005; (with J. J. Cale) The Road to Escondido, 2006. Co-owner and Design Dir, Cordings of Piccadilly, 2003–; Co-owner, Le Charlot, NY, 1997–. Founder, Crossroads Centre, Antigua, 1997. Numerous awards. *Publication:* Eric Clapton: the autobiography, 2007.

CLARE, James Paley S.; *see* Sabben-Clare.

CLARE, John Charles, CBE 2005; Chief Executive, DSG International (formerly Dixons Group) plc, 1994–2007; *b* 2 Aug. 1950; *s* of Sidney Charles and Joan Mildred Clare; *m* 1974, Anne Ross; two *s*. *Educ:* Edinburgh Univ. (BSc Hons Applied Maths). Sales and marketing roles in UK, Switzerland, Denmark, Sweden, Mars Ltd, 1972–82; Business Develt Dir and Marketing Dir, Racing Div., Ladbroke Gp plc, 1982–85; Dixons Group plc: Marketing Dir 1985–86, Man. Dir 1986–88, Dixons Ltd; Gp Dir, 1988–92; Man. Dir, Dixons Stores Gp, 1988–92; Gp Man. Dir, 1992–94. *Recreations:* cricket, music, family, Tottenham Hotspur supporter.

CLARE, John Robert; Education Editor, Daily Telegraph, 1988–2006; *b* 19 Aug. 1941; *s* of late John Arnold Clare and of Ludmilla Clare (*née* Nossoff); two *s* one *d* from former marriages. *Educ:* St George's Grammar Sch., Cape Town; Univ. of Cape Town. Reporter: Post, Johannesburg, 1963–64; The Journal, Newcastle upon Tyne, 1965–66; sub-editor, Daily Mirror, 1966–67; sub-editor, then reporter, The Times, 1967–72; reporter, ITN, 1972–73; Dep. Ed., LBC, 1973–74; Labour Corresp., The Observer, 1974–76; Social Services Corresp., Evening Standard, 1976–77; Community Relns Corresp., then Educn Corresp., BBC, 1977–86; Educn Corresp., The Times, 1986–88. Reporter of Year, BPA, 1971. *Recreation:* daydreaming. *Address:* 11 Blackmore's Grove, Teddington, Middx TW11 9AE; *e-mail:* clarej@msn.com.
See also Rear Adm. R. A. G. Clare.

CLARE, Michael George; Founder, and President, since 2008, Dreams plc (Executive Chairman and Managing Director, 1987–2008); Chairman, Clarenco Ltd; *b* 8 Feb. 1955; *s* of late Thomas Isaac Clare and Betty Clare (*née* Jeffries); *m* 1979, Carol Ann Ballingall; two *s* two *d*. *Educ:* Davenies Sch.; High Wycombe Coll. Br. Manager, Williams Furniture, 1976–78; Area Manager: Hardys Furniture, then Queensway, 1978–80; Perrings Furniture, 1980–83; Sales Dir, Deanes Furniture, 1983–85; Proprietor, Sofa Bed Centres, 1985–87. Dir, British Retail Consortium, 2006–. Pres., Furniture Trade Benevolent Assoc., 2006–07; Patron, Retail Trust, 2007–. FInstD 1990. Freeman, City of London, 2001; Liveryman, Co. of Furniture Makers, 2001–. Trustee, Buckinghamshire Foundn, 2003–. Gov., Bucks Chiltern UC, 2006–; Patron, Chalfonts Community Coll., 2008–. Bucks Ambassador, 2007–. Regl Entrepreneur of Year, Ernst & Young, 2002. *Recreations:* travelling the world, making dreams a reality. *Address:* c/o Dreams plc, Knaves Beech, High Wycombe HP10 9YU. *T:* (01628) 535363; *e-mail:* mike@clarenco.co.uk. *Clubs:* Home House; Cliveden.

CLARE, Pauline Ann, CBE 2002; QPM 1996; DL; executive coach, since 2002; Chief Constable of Lancashire, 1995–2002; *b* 26 July 1947; *d* of Kathleen and Thomas Rostron; *m* 1983, Reginald Stuart Clare; two step *d*. *Educ:* St Mary's Secondary Modern Sch., Leyland, Lancs; Open Univ. (BA Hons). CCMI (CIMgt 1996). Lancashire Constabulary: Police Cadet, 1964; Constable to Inspector, Policewomen's Dept, Juvenile Liaison, 1966; Merseyside Police: Inspector Uniform Patrol and Computer Project Team, 1973; Chief Inspector, Uniform Patrol, Community Services Dept, 1983; Supt, Community Services Dept, Sub Divl and Dep. Divl Comd, Sefton, 1987; Chief Supt, Divl Comd, Sefton, 1991; Asst Chief Constable, Crime and Ops, 1992–94; Dep. Chief Constable, Cheshire Constabulary, 1994–95. Hon. Col, Lancs ACF, 1996–2002. Pres., Lancs Assoc. of Clubs for Young People (formerly Lancs Assoc. of Boys' Clubs), 1995–2002. Comdr, St John Ambulance, Lancs, 2004–07. DL Lancs 1998. FRSA 2002. Hon. Fellow, Univ. of Central Lancashire, 1994. DUniv Open, 1999. Police Long Service and Good Conduct Medal, 1988; Lancashire Woman of the Year, 1993. SSStJ 1985 (Mem. Council, Lancs, 1998–). *Recreations:* gardening, horse riding, tapestry, reading novels, entertaining at home. *Address:* Dalton, Wigan, Lancs.

CLARE, Roy Alexander George, CBE 2007; Chief Executive, Museums, Libraries and Archives Council, since 2007; *b* 30 Sept. 1950; *s* of late John Arnold Clare and Ludmilla Clare (*née* Nossoff); *m* 1st, 1979, Leonie (Mimi) Hutchings (*d* 1979); 2nd, 1981, Sarah Catherine Jane Parkin; one *s* two *d*. *Educ:* St George's Grammar Sch., Cape Town; BRNC, Dartmouth (Queen's Sword, 1972). Joined Royal Navy, 1966; jun. rating, HMS Ganges and HMS Decoy, 1966–68; Upperyardman Cadet, Dartmouth, 1968; Midshipman, HMS Ashanti, 1970–71; Sub-Lieut, Yacht Adventure, Whitbread Round The World Race, 1973–74; Lieut, HMS Diomede, 1974–75; First Lieut, HMS Bronington (HRH The Prince of Wales), 1975–77; Principal Warfare Officer, HMS Juno, 1978–80; CO, HMS Bronington, 1980–81; Ops Officer, HMS Glamorgan (Lt Comdr), 1982–83; Staff of Flag Officer Sea Trng, 1984–85; rnsc, Greenwich (Comdr), 1985–86; CO, HMS Birmingham, 1987–89; MA to Minister of State for Armed Forces, 1989–91; CO, HMS York and Capt., Third Destroyer Sqdn, 1991–92; rcds, 1993; Asst Dir, Naval Plans and Programmes Div., MoD, 1993–96; CO, HMS Invincible, 1996–97; Commodore, BRNC, 1998–99; Rear-Adm. 1999; Dir Operational Mgt, NATO Regl Comd North, 1999–2000; Dir, Nat. Maritime Mus., 2000–07. Member, Board: Creative and Cultural Skills, 2005–07; MLA, 2006–07. Trustee: Bronington Trust, 1990–99 (Vice Pres., 1999–2002); Naval Review, 2000–; Britannia Assoc., 2001–04. Chm., Midland Naval Officers' Assoc., 2000–02; Member: Greenwich Forum, 2000–07; Univ. of Greenwich Assembly, 2000–07; RNSA. Freeman: City of London, 2001; Clockmakers' Co., 2004; Shipwrights' Co., 2005– (Liveryman, 2002–05). CCMI (CIMgt 2001); FRSA 2005–08; MInstD 2006. Hon. DLitt Greenwich, 2007. *Publications:* (ed) HMS Bronington: a tribute to one of Britain's last wooden walls, 1996; contrib. to Naval Rev. *Recreations:* family, sailing, walking. *Address:* Museums, Libraries and Archives Council, Wellcome Wolfson Building, 165 Queen's Gate, SW7 5HD; *e-mail:* roy.clare@

mla.gov.uk. *Clubs:* Anchorites, Royal Navy of 1765 and 1785, City Naval; Royal Yacht Squadron (Naval Mem.).

See also J. R. Clare.

CLARENDON, 7th Earl of, 2nd *cr* 1776; **George Frederick Laurence Hyde Villiers;** Baron Hyde 1756; Managing Director, 1962–93, and Chairman, 1985–93, Seccombe Marshall and Campion plc; *b* 2 Feb. 1933; *o s* of Lord Hyde (*d* 1935) and Hon. Marion Féodorovna Louise Glyn, Lady Hyde (*d* 1970), *er d* of 4th Baron Wolverton; *S* grandfather, 1955; *m* 1974, Jane Diana, DL, *d* of late E. W. Dawson; one *s* one *d*. Page of Honour to King George VI, 1948–49; Lieut RHG, 1951–53. Mem. Ct of Assts, Fishmongers' Co., 1988– (Prime Warden, 1999–2000). *Heir: s* Lord Hyde, *qv*. *Address:* Holywell House, Swanmore, Hants SO32 2QE. *T:* (01489) 896090.

CLARFELT, Jack Gerald; Chairman, Heathcourt Properties Ltd, since 1987; *b* 7 Feb. 1914; *s* of Barnett Clarfelt and Rene (*née* Frankel); *m* 1948, Baba Fredman; one *s* one *d*. *Educ:* Grocers' Co. Sch.; Sorbonne. Qualified as Solicitor, 1937; Man. Dir, Home Killed Meat Assoc., 1940–43 and 1945–54; Queen's Royal Surreys, 1943–45; Man. Dir, Fatstock Marketing Corp., 1954–60; Chm., Smithfield & Zwanenberg Gp Ltd, 1960–75; Exec. Dep. Chm., 1975–79, Dir, 1979–83, FMC Ltd. Dir, S. and W. Berisford Ltd, 1973–75; Chm., Linhay Frizzell Insurance Brokers Ltd, 1984–88. Farming, Hampshire. Master, Worshipful Co. of Butchers, 1978. *Recreations:* golf, swimming. *Address:* 76 Hamilton Terrace, NW8 9UL. *T:* (020) 7289 7143. *Club:* Farmers'.

See also R. E. Rhodes.

CLARIDGE, Prof. Michael Frederick; Emeritus Professor of Entomology, Cardiff University; *b* 2 June 1934; *s* of Frederick William Claridge and Eva Alice (*née* Jeffery); *m* 1967, Lindsey Clare Hellings; two *s* one *d*. *Educ:* Lawrence Sheriff Sch., Rugby; Keble Coll., Oxford (MA, DPhil). Lectr in Zoology 1959–74, Sen. Lectr in Zoology 1974–77, Univ. Coll., Cardiff; Reader in Entomology 1977–83, Prof. of Entomology, 1983–99, Head of Sch. of Biol., 1989–94, Univ. of Wales, Cardiff. President: Linnean Soc. of London, 1988–91; Systematics Assoc., 1991–94; Royal Entomol Soc., 2000–02 (Hon. Fellow, 2006). Linnean Medal for Zool., Linnean Soc., 2000. *Publications:* Handbook for the Identification of Leafhoppers and Planthoppers of Rice, 1991; chapters in: The Leafhoppers and Planthoppers, 1985; Organization of Communities—Past and Present, 1987; Prospects in Systematics, 1988; The Biodiversity of Micro-organisms and Invertebrates, 1991; Evolutionary Patterns and Processes, 1993; Planthoppers: their ecology and management, 1993; Identification of Pest Organisms, 1994; Species—the Units of Biodiversity, 1997; Insect Sounds and Communication: physiology, behaviour, ecology and evolution, 2006; papers in Biol Jl of Linnean Soc., Ecological Entomology, Amer. Naturalist. *Recreations:* classical music, cricket, natural history. *Address:* School of Biosciences, Cardiff University, Cardiff CF10 3TL; *e-mail:* claridge@cardiff.ac.uk.

CLARK; *see* Chichester Clark and Chichester-Clark.

CLARK, family name of **Baron Clark of Windermere**.

CLARK OF CALTON, Baroness *cr* 2005 (Life Peer), of Calton in the City of Edinburgh; **Lynda Margaret Clark,** PhD; a Senator of the College of Justice in Scotland, since 2006; *b* 26 Feb. 1949. *Educ:* St Andrews Univ. (LLB Hons); Edinburgh Univ. (PhD). Lectr, Univ. of Dundee, 1973–76; admitted Advocate, Scots Bar, 1977; QC (Scot.) 1989; called to the English Bar, Inner Temple, 1988, Bencher, 2000. Advocate Gen. for Scotland, 1999–2006. Contested (Lab) Fife North East, 1992. MP (Lab) Edinburgh Pentlands, 1997–2005. Mem. Court, Edinburgh Univ., 1995–97. *Address:* House of Lords, SW1A 0PW.

CLARK OF WINDERMERE, Baron *cr* 2001 (Life Peer), of Windermere in the County of Cumbria; **David George Clark;** PC 1997; DL; Chairman, Forestry Commission, since 2001; *b* 19 Oct. 1939; *s* of George and Janet Clark; *m* 1970, Christine Kirkby; one *d*. *Educ:* Manchester Univ. (BA(Econ), MSc); Sheffield Univ. (PhD 1978). Forester, 1956–57; Laboratory Asst in Textile Mill, 1957–59; Student Teacher, 1959–60; Student, 1960–63; Pres., Univ. of Manchester Union, 1963–64; Trainee Manager in USA, 1964; University Lecturer, 1965–70. Non-executive Director: Homeowners Friendly Soc., 1987–97, 1999–; Thales plc, 1999–; Carlisle Utd Ltd, 2001–; Sellafield Ltd, 2007–. Contested Manchester (Withington), 1966; MP (Lab) Colne Valley, 1970–Feb. 1974; contested same seat, Oct. 1974; MP (Lab) South Shields, 1979–2001. Opposition spokesman on Agriculture and Food, 1973–74, on Defence, 1980–81, on the Environment, 1981–86; Opposition front bench spokesman on: environmental protection and develt, 1986–87; food, agriculture and rural affairs, 1987–92; defence, disarmament and arms control, 1992–97; Chancellor, Duchy of Lancaster, 1997–98. Mem., Parly Assembly, NATO, 1981–2005 (Leader, UK delegn, 2001–05); Chm., Atlantic Council of UK, 1998–2003. Pres., Open Spaces Soc., 1979–88. DL Cumbria, 2007. Freedom, Borough of S Tyneside, 1989. *Publications:* The Industrial Manager, 1966; Colne Valley: Radicalism to Socialism, 1981; Victor Grayson, Labour's Lost Leader, 1985; We Do Not Want The Earth, 1992; various articles on Management and Labour History. *Recreations:* fell-walking, ornithology, watching football, gardening. *Address:* House of Lords, SW1A 0PW.

CLARK, Alan Richard; HM Diplomatic Service, retired; *b* 4 Sept. 1939; *s* of George Edward Clark and Norah Ivy Maria Clark (*née* Hope); *m* 1961, Ann Rosemary (*née* Hosford); one *s*. *Educ:* Chatham House Grammar Sch., Ramsgate. Foreign Office, 1958; HM Forces, 1960–62; FO 1962; served Tehran, 1964–66; Jedda, 1966–68; Second Sec. (Economic), later First Sec., Paris, 1969–71; FCO, 1972–76; Dep. Hd of Mission, Freetown, 1976–80; FCO, 1980–84; secondment (with rank of Counsellor) to Vickers Shipbuilding and Engineering Ltd, 1984–86; Counsellor and Head of Chancery, Bucharest, 1986–89; Consul-Gen., Montreal, 1990–93; Sen. Overseas Inspector, FCO, 1994–96. Vice-Chm., Thanet Community Housing Assoc., 1999–2003. Complaint Convenor, Kent and Medway HA, 2002–05; Perf. Assessor, GMC, 2002–. Non-exec. Dir, E Kent Hosps NHS Trust, 2003–; Interim Chm., Shepway PCT, 2004–05. Trustee, Michael Yoakley's Charity, 2000– (Chm. of Trustees, 2005–). *Recreations:* swimming, walking, reading. *Address:* Dane End, 103 Sea Road, Westgate-on-Sea, Kent CT8 8QE. *Club:* Royal Commonwealth Society.

CLARK, Alistair Campbell; Consultant, Blackadder Reid Johnston (formerly Reid Johnston Bell & Henderson), Solicitors, Dundee, 1995–99 (Partner, 1961–95); *b* 4 March 1933; *s* of Peter Campbell Clark and Janet Mitchell Scott or Clark; *m* 1960, Evelyn M. Johnston; three *s*. *Educ:* St Andrews Univ. Admitted solicitor, 1957. WS 1991. Hon. Sheriff, Tayside Central and Fife, 1986–. Mem. Council, Law Soc. of Scotland, 1982–91 (Pres., 1989–90); Dean, Faculty of Procurators and Solicitors, Dundee, 1979–81 (Hon. Mem., 1991). Chm., Scottish Conveyancing and Executry Services Bd, 1996–2003. Chm., Dovetail Enterprises. Founder Chm., Broughty Ferry Round Table; Founder Pres., Claverhouse Rotary Club, Dundee. *Recreations:* family, travel, erratic golf. *Address:* Blythe Lodge, 85a Dundee Road, West Ferry, Dundee DD5 1LZ. *T:* (01382) 477989. *Club:* Royal and Ancient (St Andrews).

CLARK, Alistair MacDonald, PhD; QC (Scot.) 2007; *b* Glasgow, 3 Dec. 1955; *s* of John and Matilda Clark; *m* 1980, Jacqueline Wright; one *s* two *d*. *Educ:* Univ. of Glasgow (LLB); Univ. of Strathclyde (PhD). Lectr, Glasgow Coll. of Technol., 1978; Lectr, Sen. Lectr, then pt-time Lectr and Tutor, Univ. of Strathclyde, 1978–96; Advocate, 1994. *Publications:* Product Liability, 1989; contrib. legal jls. *Recreations:* reading, hill-walking, music, football, golf. *Address:* 56 Southbrae Drive, Glasgow G13 1QD. *T:* (0141) 954 7951; *e-mail:* alistair.clark@advocates.org.uk.

CLARK, Andrew George; Chief Music Critic, Financial Times, since 1996; *b* 30 Nov. 1952; *s* of George Clark and Georgina Brenda Clark (*née* Gibson); *m* 1987, Alison Gibson; one *s*. *Educ:* Sedbergh Sch.; Durham Univ. (BA Hons Modern Hist.). Eur. Arts Corresp., Financial Times, 1981–95. Mem., Editl Bd, Opera mag., 1992–. Critic Prize, Cultural Foundn of City of Salzburg, 1998; Special Prize, Anglo-German Foundn, 2000. *Address:* c/o Financial Times, Number One Southwark Bridge, SE1 9HL.

CLARK, Antony Roy; Headmaster, Malvern College, since 2008; *b* 7 Nov. 1956; *s* of Roger and Betty Clark; *m* 1981, Dr Brigitte Jennifer Lang; one *s* two *d*. *Educ:* St Andrew's Coll., S Africa; Rhodes Univ. (BA; HDE); Downing Coll., Cambridge (Douglas Smith Scholar, MA 1981). Teacher, Westerford High Sch., Cape Town, 1984–90; investment business, 1990–91; Headmaster: St Joseph's Marist Coll., Cape Town, 1992–93; St Andrew's Coll., Grahamstown, 1994–2002; Gresham's Sch., Holt, 2002–08. Mem., Old Andrean Club. *Recreations:* cricket, squash, chess, reading, hiking. *Address:* Malvern College, College Road, Malvern, Worcs WR14 3DF. *Clubs:* Quidnuncs; Hawks.

CLARK, Sir Arnold; *see* Clark, Sir J. A.

CLARK, Brian Robert, FRSL 1985; playwright; *b* 3 June 1932; *s* of Leonard and Selina Clark; *m* (marr. diss.); two *s*; *m* 1990, Cherry Potter. *Educ:* Merrywood Grammar Sch., Bristol; Redland Coll. of Educn, Bristol; Central Sch. of Speech and Drama, London; Nottingham Univ. BA Hons English. Teacher, 1955–61, and 1964–66; Staff Tutor in Drama, Univ. of Hull, 1966–70. Since 1971 has written some thirty television plays, incl. Whose Life Is It Anyway? and The Saturday Party; television film, (with Cherry Potter) House Games; also series: Telford's Change; Late Starter. Stage plays: Whose Life Is It Anyway? (SWET award for Best Play, 1977; filmed, 1982); Can You Hear Me At the Back?, 1978; Campions Interview; Post Mortem; Kipling, London and NY, 1985; The Petition, NY and Nat. Theatre, 1986; (with Kathy Levin) Hopping to Byzantium, Germany 1989, Sydney, Aust., 1990; In Pursuit of Eve (also acted), London, 2001. Founded Amber Lane Press, publishing plays and books on the theatre, 1978. *Publications:* Group Theatre, 1971; Whose Life Is It Anyway?, 1978; Can You Hear Me At the Back?, 1979; Post Mortem, 1979; The Petition, 1986; In Pursuit of Eve, 2001. *Address:* c/o Judy Daish Associates, 2 St Charles Place, W10 6EG. *T:* (020) 8964 8811.

CLARK, Rt Rev. Bruce Quinton; Bishop of Riverina, 1993–2004; *b* Brisbane, Qld, 22 May 1939; *s* of Quinton Clark; *m* 1965, Elizabeth Shufflebotham. *Educ:* Brisbane Boys Coll.; St Francis Theol Coll., Brisbane (ThL). Ordained deacon and priest, 1963; Assistant Curate: All Saints, Chermside, 1963–65; St Matthew's, Groveley, 1965–67; Vicar, St Luke's, Miles, 1967–70; Rector: St Matthew's, Gayndah, 1970–76; St Peter's, Gympie, 1976–83; St Paul's, Maryborough, 1983–89; Surfers Paradise Parish, 1989–93. Archdeacon: Wide Bay, Burnett, 1985–89; Moreton, 1989–91; Gold Coast and Hinterland, 1991–93. *Recreations:* restoring furniture, music, photography.

CLARK, Charles Anthony, (Tony), CB 1994; higher education consultant; Director, Student Support, Department for Education and Employment, 1999–2000; *b* 13 June 1940; *s* of late Stephen and Winifred Clark; *m* 1968, Penelope Margaret (*née* Brett); one *s* two *d*. *Educ:* King's Coll. Sch., Wimbledon; Pembroke Coll., Oxford (MA Nat. Sci.). Pressed Steel Co., 1961; Hilger & Watts Ltd, 1962–65; DES, subseq. DFE, later DFEE, 1965–2000; seconded to UGC, 1971–73; Under Sec., 1982; Hd of Finance Br. and Prin. Finance Officer, 1987–89; Dir (formerly Under Sec.), Higher Educn, 1989–99. Mem., Effingham Parish Council, 2003–. Mem. Council, Surrey Univ., 1999–2006; Gov., Southampton Solent Univ. (formerly Southampton Inst.), 2000–. Hon. LLD Nottingham Trent, 2000. *Recreations:* gardening, golf, travel. *Address:* The Paddock, Guildford Road, Effingham, Surrey KT24 5QA.

CLARK, Rt Hon. Charles Joseph, (Joe), CC 1995; PC (Canada) 1979; President, Joe Clark & Associates (Principal Partner, 1994); Executive Chairman, Clark Sustainable Resource Developments Ltd; *b* 5 June 1939; *s* of Charles and Grace Clark; *m* 1973, Maureen Anne McTeer (she retained her maiden name); one *d*. *Educ:* High River High Sch.; Univ. of Alberta (BA History; MA Polit. Sci.). Journalist, Canadian Press, Calgary Herald, Edmonton Jl, High River Times, 1964–66; Lectr in Political Science, Univ. of Alberta, Edmonton, 1966–67; Exec. Asst to Hon. Robert L. Stanfield, Leader of the Opposition, 1967–70. MP (Progressive C): Rocky Mountain, later Yellowhead, 1972–93; Kings-Hants, 2000; Calgary Centre, 2000–04; Leader of the Opposition, Canada, 1976–79; Prime Minister of Canada, 1979–80; Leader of the Opposition, 1980–83; Sec. of State for External Affairs, 1984–91; Minister for Constitutional Affairs, 1991–93. Leader, Progressive Cons. Party of Canada, 1976–83 and 1998–2002. UN Special Rep. for Cyprus, 1993–95. Pres., Queen's Privy Council for Canada, 1991–93. Hon. LLD: New Brunswick, 1976; Calgary, 1984; Alberta, 1985; King's Coll., Halifax, 1994; Concordia, 1994; St Thomas, Minn, 1999. Alberta Order of Excellence, 1983. *Recreations:* riding, reading, walking, film going.

CLARK, Christopher Harvey; QC 1989; **His Honour Judge Christopher Harvey Clark;** a Circuit Judge, since 2005; *b* 20 Dec. 1946; *s* of Harvey Frederick Beckford Clark and Winifred Julia Clark; *m* 1st, 1972, Gillian Elizabeth Ann Mullen (marr. diss. 2004); one *s* two *d*; 2nd, 2004, Mrs Wendy Gay Keith. *Educ:* Taunton's Grammar Sch., Southampton; The Queen's Coll., Oxford (BA 1968; MA 1987). Called to the Bar, Gray's Inn, 1969, Bencher, 2000; Mem., Western Circuit, 1969–2005; an Asst Recorder, 1982–86; a Recorder, 1986–2005. Head of Pump Court Chambers, 2001–05. Chancellor: dio. of Winchester, 1993–; dio. of Portsmouth, 2003– (Dep. Chancellor, 1994–2003); Deputy Chancellor: dio. of Chichester, 1995–; dio. of Salisbury, 1997–. Lay Reader, C of E, 1998–. *Recreations:* amateur dramatics, golf, cricket, gardening, youth club work, fishing, ski-ing. *Address:* c/o 31 Southgate Street, Winchester, Hants SO23 9EE. *T:* (01962) 868161. *Club:* Athenæum.

CLARK, Christopher Richard Nigel; Chairman: Associated British Ports Holdings Ltd, since 2004; Wagon plc, since 2005; Urenco Ltd, since 2006; JSC Severstal, since 2007; *b* 29 Jan. 1942; *s* of late Rev. Vivian George Clark and Aileen Myfanwy Clark (*née* Thompson); *m* 1964, Catherine Ann Mather; two *s* one *d* (and one *s* decd). *Educ:* Marlborough Coll.; Trinity Coll., Cambridge; Brunel Univ. MIMMM (MIM 1967). Johnson Matthey plc, 1962–2004: Mem. Bd, 1990–2004; Chief Operating Officer, 1996–98; Chief Exec., 1998–2004. Non-executive Director: Trinity Holdings (Dennis), 1993–98; FKI plc, 2000–06; Rexam plc, 2003–06 (Dep. Chm., 2003–06). MInstD 1990; CCMI 2001. Centenary Medal, SCI, 2002. *Recreations:* shooting, golf, opera, ballet, watching Rugby and cricket. *Address:* 30 Marryat Road, SW19 5BD. *T:* (020) 8946 5887. *Clubs:* Travellers; Jesters.

CLARK, Prof. Colin Whitcomb, PhD; FRS 1997; FRSC 1988; Professor of Mathematics, University of British Columbia, 1969–94, Professor Emeritus, since 1994; *b* 18 June 1931; *s* of George Savage Clark and Irene (Stewart) Clark; *m* 1955, Janet Arlene Davidson; one *s* two *d. Educ:* Univ. of BC (BA 1953); Univ. of Washington (PhD 1958). Instructor, Univ. of Calif, Berkeley, 1958–60; Asst Prof., then Associate Prof. of Maths, Univ. of BC, 1960–69. Regent's Lectr in Maths, Univ. of Calif, Davis, 1986; Visiting Professor: of Ecology and Systematics, Cornell Univ., 1987; of Ecology and Evolutionary Biol., Princeton Univ., 1997. Hon. DSc Victoria, BC, 2000. *Publications:* Mathematical Bioeconomics, 1976, 2nd edn 1990; Bioeconomic Modelling and Fisheries Management, 1985; (with M. Mangel) Dynamic Modelling in Behavioral Ecology, 1988; (with M. Mangel) Dynamic State Variable Models in Ecology, 2000; The Worldwide Crisis in Fisheries, 2007. *Recreations:* natural history, ski-ing, hiking. *Address:* Institute of Applied Mathematics, University of British Columbia, Vancouver, BC V6T 1Z2, Canada. *T:* (604) 2745379.

CLARK, Dr Cynthia Zang Facer; international statistical consultant, since 2007; Executive Director for Methodology, Office for National Statistics, 2004–07; *b* 1 April 1942; *d* of Joseph Elmer Facer and Flora Burnell Zang Facer (*née* Zang); *m* 1963, Glenn Willet Clark; three *s* three *d. Educ:* Mills Coll. (BA Maths 1963); Univ. of Denver (MA Maths 1964); Iowa State Univ. (MS 1974; PhD Stats 1977). Mathematical Statistician, Statistical Res. Div., US Census Bureau, 1977–79; Econ. Statistician, Statistical Policy Office, Office of Mgt and Budget, 1979–83; Asst Div. Chief for Res. and Methodology, Agric. Div., US Census Bureau, 1983–90; Dir, Survey Methods Div., Nat. Agricl Stats Service, US Dept of Agriculture, 1990–96; Associate Dir for Methodology and Standards, Census Bureau, US Dept of Commerce, 1996–2004. Fellow, Amer. Statistical Assoc., 1997. Mem., ISI, 1987–. *Publications:* (ed jtly) Computer Assisted Survey Information Collection, 1998; Training for the Future: addressing tomorrow's survey tasks, 1998. *Recreations:* genealogy, ice-skating, travel, family activities. *Address:* 6628 McLean Court, McLean, VA 22101, USA. *T:* (703) 6638746; *e-mail:* czfclark@cox.net.

CLARK, David Beatson, CBE 1986; TD 1966; DL; Chairman, Rotherham District Health Authority, 1993–96 (Member, 1985–96); *b* 5 May 1933; *s* of late Alec Wilson Clark, OBE, JP, DSc(Tech) and Phyllis Mary Clark; *m* 1959, Ann Morgan Mudford; two *s* one *d. Educ:* Wrekin College; Keele Univ. (BA Hons Physics and Econs). Beatson Clark: joined 1958; Managing Dir, 1971; Chm. and Managing Dir, 1979; Exec. Chm., 1984–88. Non-Executive Director: Royal Bank of Scotland, 1988–91; Yorkshire Electricity Gp, 1990–94 (Mem., Yorkshire Electricity Bd, 1980–90); Rotherham TEC, 1990–92. President: Rotherham Chamber of Commerce, 1975–76; Sheffield Br., BIM, 1983–86; Glass Manufacturers' Fedn, 1982–83; Mem. Council, Univ. of Sheffield, 1984–2000. Liveryman, Glass Sellers' Co., 1967; Freeman, Cutlers' Co. in Hallamshire, 1980. DL S Yorks, 1990; High Sheriff, S Yorks, 1992. Hon. Fellow, Sheffield City Polytechnic, 1988. *Address:* 19 Beech Avenue, Rotherham, South Yorks S65 3HN. *T:* (01709) 546495.

CLARK, David John; Director of Corporate Development, Commission for Social Care Inspection, 2004 (Transition Director, 2003–04); *b* 20 Sept. 1947; *m* 1970, Caroline Russell; two *s* three *d. Educ:* Univ. of Kent at Canterbury (MA). Department of Health and Social Security, later Departments of Health and of Social Security: Asst Principal, 1969; Principal, 1973; Asst Sec., 1983; Under Sec., 1990; Department of Health: Dir of Personnel, Personnel Services Div., 1994–99; Hd of Resource Mgt Div., 1999–2001; Hd of Corporate Change Gp, 2001–03.

CLARK, Prof. David Millar, DPhil; FMedSci; FBA 2003; Professor of Psychology, Institute of Psychiatry, King's College London, since 2000 (Head, Department of Psychology, 2000–06); *b* 20 Aug. 1954; *s* of Herbert Clark and Doris Alice Millar; *m* 1994, Prof. Anke Ehlers; two *s. Educ:* Christ's Hosp.; Oxford Univ. (MA Exptl Psychol.; DPhil); London Univ. (MPhil Clinical Psychol.). Lectr, 1983–93, Prof., 1996–2000, Dept of Psychiatry, Univ. of Oxford; Wellcome Principal Res. Fellow, 1993–2000; Fellow, University Coll., Oxford, 1987–2000. President: British Assoc. of Behavioural and Cognitive Psychotherapies, 1992–93; Internat. Assoc. of Cognitive Psychotherapy, 1992–95. FMedSci 1999. *Publications:* Cognitive Behaviour Therapy for Psychiatric Problems, 1989; Science and Practice of Cognitive Behaviour Therapy, 1996; contrib. numerous articles on causes and treatment of anxiety disorders to learned jls. *Recreations:* travel, wine, modern art. *Address:* Department of Psychology, PO Box 77, Institute of Psychiatry, De Crespigny Park, SE5 8AF. *T:* (020) 7848 0245, *Fax:* (020) 7848 0763; *e-mail:* d.clark@iop.kcl.ac.uk.

CLARK, Prof. (David) Stuart (Thorburn), PhD; FBA 2000; FRHistS; Professor of Early Modern History, Swansea University (formerly University of Wales, Swansea), 1998–2008; *b* 22 Nov. 1942; *m* 1965, Janet Stephanie Gaze; one *s* two *d. Educ:* UC Swansea (BA 1964); Trinity Hall, Cambridge (PhD 1971). Lectr, 1967–95, Sen. Lectr, 1995–98, Dept of History, UC Swansea, subseq. Univ. of Wales, Swansea. Fellow: IAS, Princeton, 1988–89; Nat. Humanities Centre, NC, 1999–2000; British Acad. Reader, 1998–2000; Vis. Prof., Univ. of Richmond, Va, 2003; Vis. Fellow, 2004–05, Vis. Prof., 2008, Princeton Univ. FRHistS 1985. *Publications:* Thinking with Demons: the idea of witchcraft in early modern Europe, 1997; (ed) Annales School: critical assessments in history, 4 vols, 1999; (ed) The Athlone History of Witchcraft and Magic in Europe, 6 vols, 1999–2002; (ed) Languages of Witchcraft: narrative, ideology and meaning in early modern culture, 2001; Vanities of the Eye: vision in early modern European culture, 2007. *Recreations:* music, Arsenal FC. *Address:* 44 Manselfield Road, Murton, Swansea SA3 3AR.

CLARK, His Honour Denis; a Circuit Judge, 1988–2007; *b* 2 Aug. 1943; twin *s* of John and Mary Clark; *m* 1967, Frances Mary (*née* Corcoran); four *d. Educ:* St Anne's RC Primary, Rock Ferry, Birkenhead; St Anselm's Coll., Birkenhead; Sheffield Univ. LLB. Called to the Bar, Inner Temple, 1966; practised Northern Circuit, 1966–88; a Recorder, 1984–88. *Recreations:* medieval history, cricket, theatre.

CLARK, Derek John, FCIS; Principal, DJC Services, since 1994; *b* 17 June 1929; *s* of Robert Clark and Florence Mary (*née* Wise); *m* 1949, Edna Doris Coome; one *s* one *d. Educ:* Selhurst Grammar Sch., Croydon; SE London Technical Coll. FCIS 1982 (ACIS 1961). National Service, RAF, 1948–49. Corp. of Trinity House, 1949–66; RICS, 1966–71; ICMA, 1971–82; Sec., IStructE, 1982–94. Secretary and Director: Detecnicks (Property) Ltd, 1999–; Detecnicks (Finance) Ltd, 2000–; Sec., Detecnicks Ltd, 1999. Hon. FIStructE 1994. *Recreations:* athletics (until 1961), squash (until 1994). *Address:* 24 North Way, Felpham, Bognor Regis, W Sussex PO22 7BT. *T:* (01243) 822585.

CLARK, Derek Roland; Member (UK Ind) East Midlands, European Parliament, since 2004; *b* 10 Oct. 1933; *m* 1973, (Rosemary) Jane Purser. *Educ:* Univ. of Bristol (Teaching Cert.); Univ. of Exeter (Dip. Sci.). ACP 1971. Teacher of Sci., Air Balloon Hill Secondary Sch., Bristol, 1954–62; Hd of Sci. Dept, 1962–74, Sen. Master, 1970–74, Cherry Orchard Sch., Northampton; Sen. Hd of House, Lings Upper Sch., Northampton, 1974–85; Teacher of Sci., Falcon Manor Sch., Northants, 1985–93. Chm., Physics Subject Panel, CSE, E Midlands, 1970–76. UK Independence Party: Chm., Northants Br., 1995–2004; Chm., E Midlands Regl Cttee, 1996–2003; Mem., NEC, 2001–04; Party Sec., 2002–04. *Address:* (office) Rowan House, 23 Billing Road, Northampton NN1 5AT; European Parliament, Rue Wiertz, 1047 Brussels, Belgium.

CLARK, (Elizabeth) Jane G.; *see* Gordon Clark.

CLARK, Sir Francis (Drake), 5th Bt *cr* 1886, of Melville Crescent, Edinburgh; *b* 16 July 1924; *yr s* of Sir Thomas Clark, 3rd Bt and Ellen Mercy (*d* 1987), *d* of late Francis Drake; *S* brother, 1991; *m* 1958, Mary (*d* 1994), *yr d* of late John Alban Andrews, MC, FRCS; one *s. Educ:* Edinburgh Acad. RN 1943–46. Dir, Clark Travel Service Ltd, London, 1948–80. *Recreations:* tennis, cricket, music, gardening. *Heir: s* Edward Drake Clark, *b* 27 April 1966. *Address:* Woodend Cottages, Burgh-next-Aylsham, Norfolk NR11 6TS.

CLARK, Frank, CBE 1991; Convenor, Scottish Commission for the Regulation of Care, since 2006; *b* 17 Oct. 1946; *m*; two *d.* MHSM 1974; DipHSM 1974. Clerical Trainee, Bd of Mgt for Royal Cornhill and Associated Hosps, 1965–67; Higher Clerical Officer, Kingseat Hosp., 1967–69; Dep. Hosp. Sec., 1969–70, Hosp. Sec., 1970–71, Canniesburn and Schaw Hosps; Dep. Hosp. Sec., Glasgow Royal Infirmary and Sub-Gp, 1971–74; Administrator, Glasgow Royal Infirmary, 1974–77; Greater Glasgow Health Board Eastern District: Asst Dist Administrator, 1977–81; Dist Gen. Administrator, 1981–83; Hamilton and E Kilbride Unit, Lanarkshire Health Board: Dist Administrator, 1983–84; Dir of Admin. Services, June–Sept. 1984; Sec. to Bd, Lanarks Health Bd, 1984–85; General Manager: Lanarks Health Bd, 1985–96; Lothian Health Bd, May–Dec. 1990; Dir, Strathcarron Hospice, 1996–2006. Vis. Prof., Health Fac., Glasgow Caledonian Univ., 1993–; Hon. Prof., Dept of Nursing and Midwifery, Univ. of Stirling, 1997–. Chairman: W of Scotland Health Service Res. Network, 1990–95; Scottish Health Bd Gen. Managers Gp, 1993–95 (Vice Chm., 1995–96); Lanarks Drugs Action Team, 1995–96; Scottish Hospices Forum, 1998–2001; Central Scotland Health Care NHS Trust, Jan.–March 1999; Forth Valley Primary Care Trust, April–Sept. 1999; Ministerial Task Force, NHS Tayside, 2000; Bd, NHS Forth Valley, 2001–02; Scottish Partnership for Palliative Care, 2003–06; Vice Chm., Scottish Partnership Agency for Palliative and Cancer Care, 1998–2001; Member: Chief Scientist's Health Service Res. Cttee, 1989–93; Scottish Health Service Adv. Council, 1990–93; Scottish Overseas Health Support Policy Bd, 1990–96; Jt Wkg Gp on Purchasing, 1992–96; Scottish Implementation Gp, Jun. Doctors' and Dentists' Hours of Work, 1992–96; Scottish Council for Postgrad. Med. and Dental Educn, 1993–96; Implementation Gp, Scottish Health Services Mgt Centre, 1993–96; Strategy Gp, R&D Strategy for NHS in Scotland, 1994–96; Indep. Hospices Representative Cttee, Help the Hospices, 1998–2001; Scottish Social Services Council, 2006–. Mem. Bd, New Lanarkshire Ltd, 1992–98. Non-exec. Dir, Voluntary Assoc. for Mental Welfare, 1997–2006. Mem. Editl Adv. Bd, Health Bulletin, 1993–96. Pres., Cumbernauld Rotary Club, 2000–01, 2005–06. *Address:* 7 Heatherdale Gardens, Head of Muir, Stirlingshire FK6 5JN.

CLARK, Gerald, CBE 1990; Inspector of Companies, Head of Companies Investigation Branches, Department of Trade and Industry, 1984–90; *b* 18 Sept. 1933; *s* of John George and Elizabeth Clark (*née* Shaw); *m* 1958, Elizabeth McDermott; one *s. Educ:* St Cuthbert's Grammar School, Newcastle upon Tyne. Chartered Secretary. National Health Service, Northumberland Exec. Council, 1949–55; National Coal Board 1955–60; Board of Trade, Official Receiver's Service, 1960–71; Companies Investigation Branch, 1971–79; Official Receiver, High Court of Justice, 1981–83; Principal Examiner, Companies Investigation Branch, 1983–84. Mem., Herts Area Cttee, Sanctuary Housing Assoc., 1990–2001 (Chm., 1992–2000). *Recreations:* music, photography. *Clubs:* Civil Service, MCC.

CLARK, Gerald Edmondson, CMG 1989; Secretary, International Nuclear Energy Academy, since 2000; General Secretary, Energy Strategists Consultancy Ltd, since 2001; International Energy Adviser, 33 St James's, since 2004; Consultant, Pell Frischmann, since 2006; *b* 26 Dec. 1935; *s* of Edward John Clark and Irene Elizabeth Ada Clark (*née* Edmondson); *m* 1967, Mary Rose Organ; two *d. Educ:* Johnston Grammar School, Durham; Jt Services Sch. for Linguists; New College, Oxford (MA). FEI (FInstE 1998). HM Diplomatic Service, 1960–93: Foreign Office, 1960; Hong Kong, 1961; Peking, 1962–63; FO, 1964–68; Moscow, 1968–70; FCO, 1970–73; Head of Chancery, Lisbon, 1973–77; Asst Sec., Cabinet Office, 1977–79; seconded to Barclays Bank International, 1979–81; Commercial Counsellor, Peking, 1981–83; FCO, 1984–87; UK Perm. Rep to IAEA, UNIDO, and to UN in Vienna, 1987–92; Sen. DS, RCDS, 1993; Sec. Gen., Uranium Inst., 1994–2000. Patron, New London Orchestra, 1993–2006. Chm., London Gp, Henley Alumni Assoc., 1997–2007. *Publications:* articles and speeches on the civil nuclear fuel cycle and related subjects. *Recreations:* conversation with my wife and friends, gardening, long distance walking. *Address:* Lew Hollow, Beer Hill, Seaton, Devon EX12 2PY. *T:* (01297) 22001; *e-mail:* geraldeclark@aol.com. *Club:* Athenæum.

CLARK, Hon. Glen David; President, News Group Canada, and Executive Vice-President, since 2005, Jim Pattison Group; Premier of British Columbia, 1996–99; *b* 22 Nov. 1957; *m* 1980, Dale Babish; one *s* one *d. Educ:* Simon Fraser Univ. (BA Pol Sci. & Canadian Studies); Univ. of BC (MA Community & Regl Planning). MLA (NDP) Vancouver East, 1986–91, Vancouver-Kingsway, 1991–2001. Minister of: Finance and Corporate Relns, 1991–93; Employment and Investment, 1993–96; Leader, NDP, BC, 1996–2001. Pacific NW Manager, 2001, then Vice-Pres., later Gen. Manager, Jim Pattison Sign Gp. *Recreation:* spending time with family. *Address:* Jim Pattison Group, Suite 1800-1067 West Cordova Street, Vancouver, BC V6C 1C7, Canada.

CLARK, Prof. Gordon Leslie, DSc; FBA 2005; Halford Mackinder Professor of Geography, University of Oxford, since 1995; Professorial Fellow, St Peter's College, Oxford, since 1995; Research Fellow, Institute of Ageing, University of Oxford, since 2001; *b* 10 Sept. 1950; *s* of Bryan Clark and Florence Lesley Clark (*née* Cowling); *m* 1972, Shirley Anne Spratling; one *s. Educ:* Monash Univ. (BEcon, MA); McMaster Univ. (PhD 1978; Dist. Alumni Award, 1998); MA, DSc 2002, Oxon. Asst Prof., Harvard Univ., 1978–83; Associate Prof., Univ. of Chicago, 1983–85; Prof., Carnegie Mellon Univ., 1985–91; Monash University: Prof., 1989–95; Hd of Dept, 1990–93; Associate Dean, 1991–94; Actg Dean, 1993–94; Dir, Inst. of Ethics and Public Policy, 1991–95; University of Oxford: Chm., Faculty Bd of Anthropology and Geography, 1999–2001; Professorial Fellow, Saïd Business Sch., 2000–03; Head, Centre for the Envmt (incl. Sch. of Geog. and the Envmt), 2003–08. Nat. Research Council Fellow, US Nat. Acad. of Sci., 1981–82; Fellow, Lincoln Land Inst., 1981–82. FASSA 1993. Chancellor's Medal, UCSB, 2000. *Publications:* Interregional Migration, National Policy and Social Justice, 1983; (jtly) State Apparatus, 1984; Judges and the Cities, 1985; (jtly) Regional Dynamics, 1986; Unions and Communities Under Siege, 1989; Pensions and Corporate Restructuring in American Industry, 1993; (ed jtly) Multiculturalism, Difference and Postmodernism, 1993; (ed jtly) Management Ethics, 1995; (ed jtly) Asian Newly Industrialised Economies in the Global Economy, 1996; (ed jtly) Accountability and Corruption: public sector ethics, 1997; Pension Fund Capitalism, 2000; (ed jtly) Oxford Handbook of Economic Geography,

2000; European Pensions & Global Finance, 2003; (ed jtly) Pension Security in the 21st Century, 2003; (jtly) Global Competitiveness and Innovation, 2004; (ed jtly) The Oxford Handbook of Pensions and Retirement Income, 2006; (jtly) The Geography of Finance, 2007. *Recreations:* walking, reading, holidays. *Address:* Oxford University Centre for the Environment, South Parks Road, Oxford OX1 3QY.

CLARK, Prof. Graeme Milbourne, AC 2004 (AO); PhD; FRS 2004; Founder and Director, the Bionic Ear Institute, Melbourne, since 1984; *b* 16 Aug. 1935; *s* of Colin and Dorothy Clark; *m* 1961, Margaret Burtenshaw; one *s* four *d*. *Educ:* Univ. of Sydney (MB BS 1957; MS 1968; PhD 1969). FRCSE 1961; FRCS 1962 (Hon. FRCS 2004); FRACS 1966. University of Melbourne: Foundn Prof. of Otolaryngology and Chm., 1970–2004; Laureate Prof., 1999–2004; Laureate Professorial Fellow, 2004; Hd and Founder, Cochlear Implant Clinic, Royal Victorian Eye and Ear Hosp., 1985–2004. FAA 1998; FTSE 1998. Hon. FRSocMed 2003. Hon. MD: Medizinische Hochschule, Hannover, 1988; Sydney, 1989; Hon. DSc Wollongong, 2002; Hon. DEng Chung Yuan Christian Univ., Taiwan, 2003; Hon. LLD Monash, 2004. *Publications:* Sounds from Silence, 2000; Cochlear Implants: fundamentals and applications, 2003; 52 book chapters, more than 355 refereed contribs to scientific jls, 1 monograph and 5 edited books and jl supplements. *Recreations:* surfing, reading the Bible. *Address:* Clinical Neurosciences, St Vincent's Hospital Melbourne, PO Box 2900, Fitzroy, Vic 3065, Australia. *T:* (3) 92883564, *Fax:* (3) 92883350; *e-mail:* gclark@bionicear.org. *Club:* Melbourne (Melbourne).

CLARK, Gregor Munro, CB 2006; Parliamentary Counsel to the Scottish Law Commission, 1995–2000 and since 2006; *b* 18 April 1946; *s* of late Ian Munro Clark and Norah Isobel Joss; *m* 1st, 1974, Jane Maralyn Palmer (*d* 1999); one *s* two *d*; 2nd, 2000, Alexandra Plumtree (*née* Miller). *Educ:* Queen's Park Senior Secondary Sch., Glasgow; St Andrews Univ. (LLB Hons). Admitted Faculty of Advocates, 1972; entered Lord Advocate's Dept, London, 1974; Asst Parly Draftsman, then Dep. Parly Draftsman, 1974–79; Asst Legal Sec. to Lord Advocate, and Scottish Parly Counsel, 1979–99; Scottish Exec., 1999–2002 and 2004–06; Scottish Parly Counsel (UK), Scotland Office, 2002–04. *Recreations:* piano, opera, Scandinavian languages and literature. *Address:* 18 Rocheid Park, Inverleith, Edinburgh EH4 1RU. *T:* (0131) 3154634.

CLARK, Greg(ory David), PhD; MP (C) Tunbridge Wells, since 2005; *b* 28 Aug. 1967; *s* of John and Patricia Clark; *m* 1999, Helen Fillingham; one *s* two *d*. *Educ:* St Peter's Comprehensive Sch., S Bank, Middlesbrough; Magdalene Coll., Cambridge (MA Econs); LSE (PhD 1992). Consultant, Boston Consulting Gp, 1991–94; res. and teaching, LSE and Open Univ. Business Sch., 1994–96; Special Advr to Sec. of State for Trade and Industry, 1996–97; Chief Advr, 1997–99, Controller, 1999–2001, Commercial Policy, BBC; Dir of Policy, 2001–03, of Policy and Res., 2003–05, Cons. Party. Shadow Minister: for Charities, Social Enterprise and Volunteering, 2006–08; for Cabinet Office, 2007–08; Shadow Energy and Climate Change Sec., 2008–. Mem. (C) Westminster CC, 2002– (Cabinet Mem., 2003–). Vis. Fellow, Nuffield Coll., Oxford, 2007–. *Address:* House of Commons, SW1A 0AA. *Club:* Reform.

CLARK, Guy Wyndham Nial Hamilton, FSI; JP; Lord-Lieutenant, Renfrewshire, since 2007 (Vice Lord-Lieutenant, 2002–07); Senior Divisional Director, Bell Lawrie, since 2006; Managing Director, Aberdeen Private Investors Ltd, since 2001; *b* 28 March 1944; *s* of late Capt. George Hubert Wyndham Clark and Lavinia Mariquita Smith (*née* Shaw Stewart); *m* 1967, Brighid Lovell Greene; two *s* one *d*. *Educ:* Eton Coll.; Mons Officer Cadet Sch. Commnd Coldstream Guards, 1962–67; Investment Manager, Murray Johnstone, 1973–77; Partner, R. C. Greig & Co. (Glasgow), 1977–86; Dir, Greig, Middleton & Co. Ltd, 1986–97; Man. Dir, Murray Johnstone Private Investors Ltd, 1997–2001. Mem., Internat. Stock Exchange, 1983; MSI 1992, FSI 2005. Mem. Exec. Cttee, Erskine Hosp. for Ex Servicemen, 1981–97. Inverclyde: JP 1981; DL 1987. Vice Chm., JP Adv. Cttee for Inverclyde, 1990–2003. *Recreations:* country sports, gardening. *Address:* (home) Braeton House, Inverkip, Renfrewshire PA16 0DU. *T:* (01475) 520619, *Fax:* (01475) 521030; *e-mail:* g.clark282@btinternet.com. *Clubs:* Turf, MCC; Western (Glasgow).

CLARK, Rt Hon. Helen Elizabeth; PC 1990; MP (Lab) Mount Albert, New Zealand, 1981–96 and since 1999 (Owairaka, 1996–99); Prime Minister of New Zealand, since 1999 and Minister of Arts, Culture and Heritage, since 2002; *b* 26 Feb. 1950; *d* of George and Margaret Clark; *m* 1981, Dr Peter Byard Davis. *Educ:* Epsom Girls' Grammar School; Auckland Univ. (BA 1971; MA Hons 1974). Junior Lectr in Political Studies, Auckland Univ., 1973–75; UGC Post Graduate Scholar, 1976; Lectr, Political Studies Dept, Auckland Univ., 1977–81. Minister: of Housing, of Conservation, 1987–89; of Health, of Labour, 1989–90; Dep. Prime Minister, 1989–90; Dep. Leader of the Opposition, 1990–93, Leader, 1993–99; Minister of Arts and Culture, 1999–2002. *Recreations:* theatre, music, ski-ing, trekking, reading. *Address:* Parliament House, Wellington, New Zealand. *T:* (4) 4719999.

CLARK, Helen Rosemary; writer, since 2005; policy adviser and consultant specialising in climate change, since 2007; *b* 23 Dec. 1954; *d* of George Henry Dyche and Phyllis May Dyche (*née* James); *m* (marr. diss.); two *c*; *m* 2001, Alan Clark. *Educ:* Spondon Park Grammar Sch.; Bristol Univ. (BA Hons Eng Lit. 1976; MA Medieval Lit. 1978; PGCE 1979). English Teacher, 1979–97. Examr, English Lit. and Lang., London, Cambridge, Southern and Northern Exam. Bds, 1985–97. MP (Lab) Peterborough, 1997–2005; contested (Lab) same seat, 2005. *Publications:* contrib. to various political jls, national newspapers and specialist mags. *Recreations:* reading novels and political biography, modern films and theatre.

CLARK, Henry Maitland; journalist with Avon Advertiser, 1989–97; *b* 11 April 1929; *s* of Major H. F. Clark, Rockwood, Upperlands, Co. Londonderry; *m* 1972, Penelope Winifred Tindal (*d* 1994); one *s* two *d*. *Educ:* Shrewsbury Sch.; Trinity Coll., Dublin; Trinity Hall, Cambridge. Entered Colonial Service and appointed District Officer, Tanganyika, 1951; served in various Districts of Tanganyika, 1951–59; resigned from Colonial Service, 1959 (to stand for Parlt). Wine merchant, IDV Ltd and Cock Russell Vintners, 1972–76; Hd of Information, CoSIRA, 1977–89. MP (UU) Antrim North (UK Parliament), Oct. 1959–1970; Chm. Conservative Trade and Overseas Develt Sub-Cttee; Member: British Delegation to Council of Europe and WEU, 1962–65; Select Cttee on Overseas Aid and Develt, 1969–70. Grand Jury, Co. Londonderry, 1970. A Commonwealth Observer, Mauritius General Election, 1967. Mem., Exec. Cttee, Lepra (British Leprosy Relief Assoc.). Vice-Pres., Dublin Univ. Boat Club. *Recreations:* rowing coach, sailing, shooting, golf, collecting old furniture. *Address:* Staddles, Hindon Lane, Tisbury, Wilts SP3 6PU. *T:* (01747) 870330. *Club:* Royal Portrush Golf.

See also H. W. S. Clark.

CLARK, (Henry) Wallace (Stuart), MBE 1970; DL; Vice Lord-Lieutenant of County Londonderry, 1993–2001; Director, Wm Clark & Sons, Linen Manufacturers, 1972–87 (non-executive Director, 1987–2002); *b* 20 Nov. 1926; *s* of Major H. F. Clark, MBE, JP, RA, Rockwood, Upperlands, and Sybil Emily (*née* Stuart); *m* 1957, June Elisabeth Lester Deane; two *s*. *Educ:* Shrewsbury School. Lieut, RNVR, 1945–47 (bomb and mine disposal); Cattleman, Merchant Navy, 1947–48. District Comdt, Ulster Special Constabulary, 1955–70; Major, Ulster Defence Regt, 1970–81. Chm., Bolson Investments Ltd, 1999–. Foyle's Lectr, USA tour, 1964. Led Church of Ireland St Columba commemorative curragh voyage, Derry to Iona, 1963; Dir and Skipper, Lord of the Isles Voyage, Galway to Stornaway in 16th century galley, 1991. FRSAI 2005. DL 1962, High Sheriff 1969, Co. Londonderry. *Publications:* (jtly) North and East Coasts of Ireland, 1957; (jtly) South and West Coasts of Ireland, 1962, 2nd edn 1970; Guns in Ulster, 1967; Rathlin Disputed Island, 1972; Sailing Round Ireland, 1976; Linen on the Green, 1982; Lord of the Isles Voyage, 1993; Upperlands History and Visitors Guide, 1998; Sailing Round Europe, 1998; Sailing Round Russia: the story of Miles Clark's unique voyage, 1999; Brave Men and True: early days in the Ulster Defence Regiment, 2002; Sailing the Donegal Islands, 2003; Sailing the Connaught Islands, 2005; Five Years on Full Alert: diaries of Ulster anti-aircraft gunners, 2007; Growing up in Upperlands, 2007. *Recreation:* yacht cruising. *Address:* Gorteade Cottage, Upperlands, Co. Londonderry, N Ireland BT46 5SB. *T:* (028) 7964 2737. *Clubs:* Royal Cruising, Irish Cruising (Cdre 1962).

See also H. M. Clark.

CLARK, Prof. Ian, PhD; FBA 1999; Professor of International Politics, Aberystwyth University (formerly University of Wales, Aberystwyth), since 1998; *b* 14 March 1949; *m* 1970, Janice (*née* Cochrane); one *s* one *d*. *Educ:* Glasgow Univ. (MA); Australian National Univ. (PhD 1975). Lectr, 1974–81, Sen. Lectr, 1981–84, Univ. of Western Australia; Fellow, Selwyn Coll., Cambridge, 1985–97, Hon. Fellow, 2000; Dep. Dir, Centre of Internat. Studies, Cambridge, 1993–97. Leverhulme Major Res. Fellow, 2002–04; Vis. Fellow, ANU, 2003; Professorial Fellow, ESRC, 2007–. British Academy: Mem. Council, 2001–04; Chair, Political Studies, 2005–08, Posts, 2005–. *Publications* include: The Hierarchy of States, 1989; Nuclear Diplomacy and the Special Relationship, 1994; Globalization and Fragmentation: international relations in the twentieth century, 1997; Globalization and International Relations Theory, 1999; The Post-Cold War Order, 2001; Legitimacy in International Society, 2005; International Legitimacy and World Society, 2007. *Recreations:* hill walking, grandfather. *Address:* Department of International Politics, Aberystwyth University, Penglais, Aberystwyth SY23 3FE. *T:* (01970) 621767.

CLARK, Ian Robertson, CBE 1979; Chairman, Dalzell Consulting Ltd, 2002–08; *b* 18 Jan. 1939; *s* of Alexander Clark and Annie Dundas Watson; *m* 1961, Jean Scott Waddell Lang; one *s* one *d*. *Educ:* Dalziel High Sch., Motherwell. FCCA, CPFA. Trained with Glasgow Chartered Accountant; served in local govt, 1962–76, this service culminating in the post of Chief Executive, Shetland Islands Council; full-time Mem., BNOC, from 1976 until privatisation in 1982; Jt Man. Dir, Britoil plc, 1982–85; Chm., Ventures Div., Costain Gp, subseq. Urban Enterprises Ltd, 1987–93; former Chairman: Clark & Associates Ltd; C & M (Hydraulics) Ltd. Hon. LLD Glasgow, 1979. *Publications:* Reservoir of Power, 1980; contribs to professional and religious periodicals. *Recreations:* theology, general reading, walking. *Address:* Bellfield House, High Askomil, Campbeltown, Argyll PA28 6EN. *T:* (01586) 553905.

CLARK, Jacqueline; *see* Davies, J.

CLARK, James Frame; HM Diplomatic Service; Consul General, Chicago, since 2007; *b* 12 March 1963; *s* of James F. Clark and Anne Clark (*née* Wilson); partner, Anthony J. Stewart. *Educ:* Edinburgh Univ. (BSc Hons Geog.). Teacher, W Berlin, 1985–87; entered FCO, 1988; Mexico and Central America Dept, 1988–89; Arabic lang. trng, 1989; Cairo, 1990; ME Dept, FCO, 1990–91; UK Rep., Brussels, 1991–93; First Secretary: Econ. Relns Dept, FCO, 1994–95; Press Office, FCO, 1995–97; on loan to German Foreign Min., Bonn, 1997–98; EU, Bonn, 1998–99; Hd, Conf. and Visits Gp, FCO, 1999–2003; Commercial Dir, FCO Services, 2003–04; Ambassador to Luxembourg, 2004–07. *Recreations:* friends, food, fitness, reading, ski-ing, travel. *Address:* c/o Foreign and Commonwealth Office, King Charles Street, SW1A 2AH.

CLARK, James Leonard; Under Secretary, Establishment Personnel Division, Departments of Industry and Trade Common Services, 1980–83 (Under Secretary, Department of Trade, 1978–80); *b* 8 Jan. 1923; *s* of James Alfred and Grace Clark; *m* 1st, 1954, Joan Pauline Richards (*d* 1992); 2nd, 1997, Helga Thomas. *Educ:* Mercers' School. Lieut (A), Fleet Air Arm, 1942–46. Clerical Officer, HM Treasury, 1939; Private Sec. to successive First Secs of State, 1964–67; Cabinet Office, 1969–71; Asst Sec., Price Commn, 1973–75; Dept of Industry, 1975–78. CBI, 1983–85; Hd of Administration, SIB, 1985–89. *Address:* 4 Westcott Way, Cheam, Surrey SM2 7JY. *T:* (020) 8393 2622.

CLARK, Dame Jill M.; *see* Macleod Clark.

CLARK, Rt Hon. Joe; *see* Clark, Rt Hon. C. J.

CLARK, Sir (John) Arnold, Kt 2004; Chairman and Chief Executive, Arnold Clark Automobiles Ltd; *b* 27 Nov. 1927; *m* Philomena, (Mena); five *s* four *d* (and one *s* decd). Served RAF. Founded Arnold Clark Automobiles Ltd, 1956. Trustee, Kelvingrove Halls, Glasgow. FIMI. DUniv Glasgow, 2005. *Address:* Arnold Clark Automobiles Ltd, 134 Nithsdale Drive, Glasgow G41 2PP. *Club:* Rotary (Glasgow).

CLARK, Prof. John Benjamin; Professor of Neurochemistry, Institute of Neurology, University of London, at University College London (formerly at British Postgraduate Medical Federation), 1990–2006, now Emeritus (Academic Vice Dean, 1996–2002); Hon. Consultant Neurochemist, National Hospital of Neurology and Neurosurgery, 1990–2006; *b* 30 Jan. 1941; *e s* of P. B. Clark and J. E. Clark (*née* Smith); *m* 1965, Joan Gibbons; one *s* one *d* (and one *s* decd). *Educ:* Southend High Sch. for Boys; University College London (BSc 1962; PhD 1964; DSc 1982). St Bartholomew's Hospital Medical College, University of London: Lectr, Sen. Lectr and Reader in Biochemistry, 1965–86; Prof. of Cell Biochemistry, 1986–90. MRC Travelling Fellow, Johnson Res. Foundn, Univ. of Pennsylvania, 1969–70; Vis. Prof., Dept of Biochem. and Molecular Biol., UCL, 1991–2006. *Publications:* numerous contribs to sci. jls on mitochondrial metabolism and brain development. *Recreations:* walking, fine wines, reading. *Address:* c/o Miriam Marks Department of Neurochemistry, Institute of Neurology, Queen Square, WC1N 3BG. *T:* (020) 7829 8722.

CLARK, John Edward, OBE 1995; Secretary, National Association of Local Councils, 1978–95; *b* 18 Oct. 1932; *s* of Albert Edward Clark and Edith (*née* Brown); *m* 1969, Judith Rosemary Lester; one *s* (one *d* decd). *Educ:* Royal Grammar Sch., Clitheroe; Keble Coll., Oxford (MA, BCL). Called to the Bar, Gray's Inn, 1957; practised at the Bar, 1957–61. Dep. Sec., National Assoc. of Local (formerly Parish) Councils, (part-time) 1959–61, (full-time) 1961–78. Hon. Consultant, Assoc. of Burial Authorities, 1998–. Publicity Asst, Dulwich Fest., annually, 1999–2004. Archivist, All Saints, W Dulwich, 2003–. *Publications:* chapters on local govt, public health, and theatres, in Encyclopaedia of Court Forms, 2nd edn 1964 to 1975. *Recreations:* walking, indoor games, collecting detective fiction, fortifications, rough ecclesiastical carpentry. *Address:* 14 Idmiston Road, West Norwood, SE27 9HG.

CLARK, John Mullin; Director, Mission and Public Affairs, Archbishops' Council, Church of England, 2002–07; *b* 19 April 1946; *s* of James and Margaret Clark; *m* 1975, Jenny Brown; one *s. Educ:* St Peter's Coll., Oxford (MA); Inst. of Educn, London Univ. (PGCE 1974); King's Coll., London (MA 1999). Operation Mobilisation, Iran, 1967–73; Iran Literature Assoc., Tehran, 1976–80; Church Missionary Society: Regl Sec., ME and Pakistan, 1980–86; Communications Sec., 1987–91; Sec., Overseas Bishoprics' Fund, and Partnership Sec., Partnership for World Mission, Bd of Mission, C of E, 1992–2000; Chief Sec. for Mission, Archbishops' Council, C of E, 2000–02. *Recreations:* walking, church history, T. E. Lawrence, Iran. *Address:* 32 Weigall Road, Lee, SE12 8HE. *T:* (020) 8852 2741.

CLARK, Sir John S.; *see* Stewart-Clark.

CLARK, Prof. Jonathan Charles Douglas, PhD; Hall Distinguished Professor of British History, University of Kansas, since 1995; *b* 28 Feb. 1951; *s* of Ronald James Clark and Dorothy Margaret Clark; *m* 1996, Katherine Redwood Penovich. *Educ:* Downing Coll., Cambridge (BA 1972); Corpus Christi Coll., Cambridge (MA 1976); Peterhouse, Cambridge (PhD 1981). Research Fellow: Peterhouse, Cambridge, 1977–81; Leverhulme Trust, 1983; All Souls Coll., Oxford, 1986–95 (Sen. Res. Fellow, 1995). Vis. Prof., Cttee on Social Thought, Univ. of Chicago, 1993; Dist. Vis. Lectr, Univ. of Manitoba, 1999; Vis. Fellow, Forschungszentrum Europäische Aufklärung, Potsdam, 2000; Vis. Prof., Univ. of Northumbria, 2001–03. Initiated Oxford American Inst. (now Rothermere Amer. Inst.), 1990. Gov., Pusey House, Oxford, 1991–98. *Publications:* The Dynamics of Change, 1982; English Society 1688–1832, 1985, 2nd edn, as English Society 1660–1832, 2000; Revolution and Rebellion, 1986; (ed) The Memoirs and Speeches of James, 2nd Earl Waldegrave, 1988; (ed) Ideas and Politics in Modern Britain, 1990; The Language of Liberty 1660–1832, 1994; Samuel Johnson, 1994; (ed) Edmund Burke, Reflections on the Revolution in France, 2001; (ed jtly) Samuel Johnson in Historical Context, 2002; Our Shadowed Present, 2003; articles in learned jls. *Recreation:* more history. *Address:* Department of History, University of Kansas, 1445 Jayhawk Boulevard, Lawrence, KS 66045–7590, USA. *T:* (785) 8643569. *Club:* Beefsteak.

CLARK, Sir Jonathan (George), 5th Bt *cr* 1917, of Dunlambert, City of Belfast; Managing Director, DC Training and Recruitment Solutions, since 2002; *b* 9 Oct. 1947; *o s* of Sir Colin Douglas Clark, 4th Bt and of Margaret Coleman Clark (*née* Spinks); *S* father, 1995; *m* 1971, Susan Joy, *d* of Brig. T. I. G. Gray; one *s* two *d. Educ:* Eton. Royal Green Jackets, 1966–78. Various appts within private health care industry, 1978–2001. *Recreations:* horse trials, hunting. *Heir: s* Simon George Gray Clark, *b* 3 Oct. 1975. *Address:* Somerset House, Threapwood, Malpas, Cheshire SY14 7AW. *T:* (01948) 770205.

CLARK, Judy Anne M.; *see* MacArthur Clark.

CLARK, Dame June; *see* Clark, Dame M. J.

CLARK, Kathryn Sloan, (Katy); MP (Lab) Ayrshire North and Arran, since 2005; *b* 3 July 1967. Admitted solicitor, 1992. Contested (Lab) Galloway and Upper Nithsdale, 2001. *Address:* (office) 53 Main Street, Kilbirnie KA25 7BX; House of Commons, SW1A 0AA.

CLARK, Keith; International General Counsel, Morgan Stanley, since 2002; *b* 25 Oct. 1944; *s* of Douglas William Clark and Evelyn Lucy (*née* Longlands); *m* 2001, Helen Paterson; one *s* one *d* by a previous marriage. *Educ:* Chichester High Sch. for Boys; St Catherine's Coll., Oxford (MA Jurisprudence; BCL). Joined Clifford Chance, 1971; Partner, 1976; Sen. Partner, 1993; Chm., 2000–02. *Publications:* (jtly) Syndicated Lending Practice Documentation, 1993; articles on banking and financial topics. *Recreations:* walking, ballet, theatre, novels. *Address:* Morgan Stanley, 25 Cabot Square, Canary Wharf, E14 4QA.

CLARK, Ven. Kenneth James, DSC 1944; Archdeacon of Swindon, 1982–92; *b* 31 May 1922; *er s* of Francis James Clark and Winifred Adelaide Clark (*née* Martin); *m* 1948, Elisabeth Mary Monica Helen Huggett (*d* 2005); three *s* three *d. Educ:* Watford Grammar School; St Catherine's Coll., Oxford (MA); Cuddesdon Theological Coll. Midshipman RN, 1940; Lieutenant RN, 1942; served in submarines, 1942–46. Baptist Minister, Forest Row, Sussex, 1950–52; Curate of Brinkworth, 1952–53; Curate of Cricklade with Latton, 1953–56; Priest-in-Charge, then Vicar (1959), of Holy Cross, Inns Court, Bristol, 1956–61; Vicar: Westbury-on-Trym, 1961–72; St Mary Redcliffe, Bristol, 1972–82; Hon. Canon of Bristol Cathedral, 1974. Member, Gen. Synod of C of E, 1980–92. *Recreations:* music, travel. *Address:* 25 Emmanuel Court, Guthrie Road, Clifton, Bristol BS8 3EP. *T:* (0117) 923 9083.

CLARK, Luther Johnson, (L. John Clark); Founding Partner, Compass Partners International LLC Ltd, 1997–2005; Chairman, Steamboat Capital Group; *b* 27 Aug. 1941; *s* of E. T. Clark and Mary Opal Clark; *m* 1965, Judith Dooley; one *s* one *d. Educ:* Wharton Sch. of Finance & Commerce, Univ. of Pennsylvania (BS Econs/Finance 1963); Wharton Graduate Sch. of Finance & Commerce (MBA Marketing/Finance 1968). Captain, US Marine Corps, 1963–66. Singer Co.: joined 1968; Corp. Vice-Pres., 1978–81; Pres. and Chief Exec., Europe, Africa and Middle East, 1982–85; Exec. Vice-Pres., V. F. Corp., 1986–87; Chm. and Chief Exec., Coremark Internat. Inc., 1988–91; Chief Exec. and Man. Dir, BET PLC, 1991–96. Non-executive Director: Yale and Nutone, 1988–91; Rolls-Royce PLC, 1993–96; Kvaerner ASA, 1997–2001. Overseer, Wharton Sch., 1989–; Trustee, Exec. Cttee, Univ. of Pennsylvania, 1996– (Chm., Budget and Finance, 1996–).

CLARK, Malcolm, CB 1990; Inspector General, Insolvency Service, Department of Trade and Industry, 1984–89, retired; *b* 13 Feb. 1931; *s* of late Percy Clark and Gladys Helena Clark; *m* 1956, Beryl Patricia Dale; two *s. Educ:* Wheelwright Grammar Sch., Dewsbury, Yorks. FCCA 1980. Department of Trade and Industry Insolvency Service: Examiner, 1953–62; Sen. Examiner, 1962–66; Asst Official Receiver, Rochester, 1966–70; Official Receiver, Lytham St Annes, 1970–79; Principal Inspector of Official Receivers, 1979–81; Dep. Inspector Gen., 1981–84. *Recreations:* theatre, gardening, reading. *Address:* 7 Sea Point, Martello Park, Canford Cliffs, Poole BH13 7BA.

CLARK, Dr Malcolm Brian, OBE 2001; Chairman, Grant & Cutler, since 2000; Director, Queen Elizabeth's Foundation for Disabled People, 1980–2001; *b* 17 May 1934; *s* of Herbert Clark and Doris May Clark (*née* Waples); *m* 1st, 1960, Jennifer Anne Thonger (*d* 1985); one *s* one *d*; 2nd, 1988, Lorna Stephanie Killick (marr. diss. 1995). *Educ:* Univ. of Birmingham (BSc Chem. Engrg; PhD 1958). Chemical Engineer: Albright & Wilson, 1958–62; A. Boake Roberts, 1962–66; Marketing Manager, Bush Boake Allen, 1966–68; Albright & Wilson: Res. Manager, 1968–70; Personnel Dir, 1970–72; Personnel and Prodn Dir, 1972–74; Man. Dir, Bush Boake Allen, 1975–80. Mem. Council, Grange Centre, 2001–. *Recreations:* books, walking, theatre, music, wine. *Address:* 2 Howard Close, Leatherhead, Surrey KT22 8PH.

CLARK, Dame (Margaret) June, DBE 1995; FRCN; Professor of Community Nursing, University of Wales, Swansea, 1997–2003, now Emeritus; *b* 31 May 1941; *d* of Ernest Harold Hickery and Marion Louise Hickery (*née* Walters); *m* 1966, Roger Michael Geoffrey Clark; one *s* one *d. Educ:* Pontywaun Grammar Sch.; University College London (BA Hons Classics 1962); University College Hosp. (SRN 1965); Royal College of Nursing (RHV 1967); Univ. of Reading (MPhil 1972); PhD South Bank Polytechnic 1985. FRCN 1982. Nurse, 1965; health visitor, 1967; clinical nursing appts, combined with teaching and research while bringing up a family; resumed as health visitor, Berks, 1981; Senior Nurse (Research), 1983; Health Authority posts: Special Projects Co-ordinator, Lewisham and N Southwark, 1985–86; Dir, Community Nursing Services, W Lambeth, 1986–88; Chief Nursing Adviser, Harrow, 1988–90; Prof. of Nursing, Middlesex Poly., later Univ., 1990–96. Mem., Royal Commn on Long Term Care of the Elderly, 1997–98. Pres., RCN, 1990–94. Council of Europe Fellow, 1981; Churchill Fellow, 1996. *Publications:* A Family Visitor, 1973; (with R. Hiller) Community Care, 1975; What Do Health Visitors Do?, 1981; (with S. Parsonage) Infant Feeding and Family Nutrition, 1981; (with J. Henderson) Community Health, 1983; (with M. Baly) District Nursing, 1981; many papers in med. and nursing jls. *Recreations:* travel, gardening, grandchildren.

CLARK, Maxwell Robert Guthrie Stewart S.; *see* Stafford-Clark.

CLARK, Dr Michael; Chairman, MAT Group, 2002–04 (Director, 1993–2004); *b* 8 Aug. 1935; *s* of late Mervyn Clark and of Sybilla Norma Clark (*née* Winscott); *m* 1958, Valerie Ethel, *d* of C. S. Harbord; one *s* one *d. Educ:* King Edward VI Grammar School, East Retford; King's College London (BSc (1st cl. Hons) Chemistry, 1956; FKC 1987); Univ. of Minnesota (Fulbright Scholar, 1956–57); St John's College, Cambridge (PhD 1960). FRSC 1988. Research Scientist, later Factory Manager, ICI, 1960–66; Smith's Industries Ltd, 1966–69; PA International Management Consultants, 1969–73; Marketing Manager, St Regis Paper Co., 1973–78; Dir, Courtenay Stewart International, 1978–81; PA International Management Consultants, 1981–93 (Trustee, 1994–2000). Treasurer, 1975–78, Chm., 1980–83, Cambs Cons. Assoc.; Cons. Eastern Area Exec., 1980–83. Contested (C) Ilkeston, 1979; MP (C) Rochford, 1983–97, Rayleigh, 1997–2001. Chm., Sci. and Technol. Select Cttee, 1997–2001; Member: Select Cttee for Energy, 1983–92 (Chm., 1989–92); Select Cttee on Trade and Industry, 1992–94; Council, Parly IT Cttee, 1984–90; Speaker's Panel of Chairmen, 1997–2001; Chairman: All Party Gp for the Chemical Industry, 1994–97 (Hon. Sec. 1985–90; Vice-Chm., 1990–94); Parly Gp for Energy Studies, 1992–97; Bd, Parly Office of Sci. and Technol., 1993–97; Parly British-Russian Gp, 1994–2001; Parly British-Venezuelan Gp, 1995–2001; Hon. Secretary: Parly and Scientific Cttee, 1985–88; Parly Anglo-Nepalese Soc., 1985–90; Parly Anglo-Malawi Gp, 1987–90; Parly Space Cttee, 1989–91; Cons. Backbench Energy Cttee, 1986–87 (Vice-Chm., 1987–90); Mem., 1922 Exec. Cttee, 1997–2001; Chm., IPU, 1990–93 (Mem. Exec., 1987–94). Mem., Adv. Panel, Conservation Foundn, 1995–2000. Mem., Adv. Bd, Fulbright Commn, 1995–2001. Governor, Melbourn Village Coll., 1974–83 (Chm., 1977–80). *Publications:* The History of Rochford Hall, 1990; Clark of the House, 2005. *Recreations:* gadding about, golf, grandchildren. *Address:* 7 Leeward Court, Exmouth Quay, Devon EX8 1FD. *T:* (01395) 279846.

CLARK, Michael Duncan; choreographer; Artistic Director, Michael Clark Company; *b* 2 June 1962; *s* of late William Clark and Elizabeth Duncan. *Educ:* Kintore Primary Sch.; Rubislaw Acad., Aberdeen; Royal Ballet Sch. Resident choreographer, Riverside Studios, London, 1982; launched the Michael Clark Company, 1984. Key works: New Puritan, 1984; Do You Me? I Did, 1984; not H.air, 1985; Because We Must, 1987; I am curious, Orange, 1988; Mmm…, 1992; "O", 1994; current/SEE, 1998; Oh My Goddess, 2003; I Do, 2007. *Address:* c/o Barbican Centre, Silk Street, EC2Y 8DS.

CLARK, Michael William, CBE 1977; DL; Deputy Chairman and Deputy Chief Executive, Plessey Co. plc, 1970–87; *b* 7 May 1927; *yr s* of late Sir Allen Clark and late Jocelyn Anina Maria Louise Clark (*née* Emerson Culverhouse); *m* 1st, 1955, Shirley (*née* MacPhadyen) (*d* 1974); two *s* one *d* (and one *d* decd); 2nd, 1985, Virginia, Marchioness Camden. *Educ:* Harrow. 1st Foot Guards, Subaltern, 1945–48. Plessey Co. plc, 1950–87: founded and built Electronics Div., 1951; Main Bd Dir, 1953; Dir, Corporate Planning, 1965, Man. Dir, Telecommunications Gp, 1967; Chief. Exec., Defence Electronics, 1970–87. Member: Electronics EDC, 1975–80; Council, Inst. of Dirs; Nat. Electronics Council; Ct of Univ. of Essex. President: Essex Br., SSAFA, 1988–99; Essex Br., Grenadier Guards Assoc., 1988–99. FIET (CompIEE, 1964); CompIERE, 1965. FCMI (FBIM 1974). DL Essex, 1988, High Sheriff, 1991–92. *Recreations:* fishing, shooting, forestry. *Address:* Braxted Park, Witham, Essex CM8 3EN. *Clubs:* Boodle's, Pratt's.

CLARK, Oswald William Hugh, CBE 1978; Assistant Director-General, Greater London Council, 1973–79; *b* 26 Nov. 1917; *s* of late Rev. Hugh M. A. Clark and Mabel Bessie Clark (*née* Dance); *m* 1966, Diana Mary (*née* Hine); one *d. Educ:* Rutlish Sch., Merton; Univ. of London (BA; BD Hons); Univ. of Wales (LLM). Local Govt Official, LCC (later GLC), 1937–79. Served War, HM Forces, 1940–46: Major, 2nd Derbyshire Yeo., Eighth Army, Middle East, NW Europe. Member: Church Assembly (later General Synod), 1948–90; Standing and Legislative Cttees, 1950–90; Standing Orders Cttee (Chm.), 1950–90; Crown Appts Commn, 1987–90; Chm., House of Laity, 1979–85 (Vice-Chm., 1970–79); a Church Commissioner, 1958–88 (Mem. Bd of Governors, 1966–68, 1969–73, 1977–88); a Reader, 1951–96. Vice-Pres., Corp. of Church House, 1981–98. Principal, Soc. of the Faith, 1987–92. Parish Clerk, 1992–2008, and Churchwarden, 1990–2000, St Andrew by the Wardrobe. Co. of Parish Clerks, 1986– (Master, 1997–98); Liveryman, Upholders' Co., 1999–. Life Fellow, Guild of Guide Lectrs, 1982. *Recreations:* London's history and development, Goss china, heraldry. *Address:* 5 Seaview Road, Highcliffe, Christchurch, Dorset BH23 5QJ. *T:* (01425) 280823. *Clubs:* Cavalry and Guards, Pratt's.

CLARK, Paul Anthony Mason; a District Judge (Magistrates' Courts) (formerly Metropolitan Stipendiary Magistrate), since 1996; Designated District Judge for West London, since 2007; a Recorder, since 2003; *b* 19 Aug. 1952; *s* of Thomas James, (Tony), Clark and Winifred Mary Clark (*née* Mason); *m* 1979, Jane Ann; one *s* two *d. Educ:* John Leggott GS, Scunthorpe; Jesus Coll., Oxford (MA). Called to the Bar, Middle Temple, 1975 (Astbury Schol.); in practice, 1975–96. Chm., Inner London Youth Courts, 1997–2000. Mem., Council of Dist Judges for England and Wales, 2001–. Lectr, Gen. Council of the Bar, 1998–2004. Mem. Bd, Internat. Inst. on Special Needs Offenders, 2003–07. Pres., David Isaacs Fund, 2004– (Vice Pres., 1998–2004). *Recreations:* cricket, painting, gardening, book and china collecting. *Address:* Office of the Senior District Judge, City of Westminster Magistrates' Court, 70 Horseferry Road, SW1P 2AX. *Club:* Oxford and Cambridge.

CLARK, Air Vice-Marshal Paul Derek, CB 1993; CEng, FRAeS; Vice President, Homeland Security, BAE SYSTEMS North America, Arlington, Virginia, 2003–05, retired 2006; *b* 19 March 1939; *s* of John Hayes Clark and Kathleen Clark; *m* 1963, Mary Elizabeth Morgan; two *d. Educ:* Orange Hill Grammar Sch.; RAF Henlow Technical Coll.; BA Open Univ., 1985. CEng 1970; FRAeS 1987. Commnd Engr Br., RAF, 1961;

RAF Wittering, 1961–63, Topcliffe, 1963, Wittering, 1964–69, Cranwell, 1969–70; RAF Staff Coll., Bracknell, 1971; HQ Logistics Comd, USAF, 1972–74; HQ Strike Comd, 1974–76; Nat. Defence Coll., 1977; OC Engrg Wing, RAF Leuchars, 1977–79; HQ No 1 Gp, RAF Bawtry, 1980–81; Stn Comdr No 30 Maintenance Unit, RAF Sealand, 1981–83; RCDS, 1984; MoD, 1985–86; Directorate Electronics Radar Air, MoD (PE), 1986–87; Dir, European Helicopter 101 Project, MoD (PE), 1987–89; Comdt RAF Signals Engrg Estabt, 1990–91; AO, Engrg and Supply, HQ Strike Comd, 1991–93; retd, 1994; Dir of Mil. Support, Support Div., GEC-Marconi Avionics, 1994–95; RMPA Prog. Dir, GEC-Marconi Aerospace Systems Ltd, 1995–97; Pres. and CEO, GEC-Marconi Avionics Inc., Atlanta, 1997–98; Vice President: GEC Account Dir for Lockheed Martin, 1998–99; C–130 Avionics Modernization Prog., BAE SYSTEMS Aerospace Sector, Austin, Texas, 2000–01; Inf. and Electronics System Integration Sector, BAE SYSTEMS Nashua, New Hampshire, 2001–03. *Recreations:* theatre, art, high handicap golfing. *Club:* Royal Air Force.

See also Prof. T. J. H. Clark.

CLARK, Paul Gordon; MP (Lab) Gillingham, since 1997; Parliamentary Under-Secretary of State, Department for Transport, since 2008; *b* 29 April 1957; *s* of Gordon Thomas Clark and Sheila Gladys Clark; *m* 1980, Julie Hendrick; one *s* one *d*. *Educ:* Gillingham Grammar Sch.; Keele Univ. (BA Hons 1980; Sec., Students' Union, 1977–78); Univ. of Derby (DMS 1996). Res. Assistant to Pres., then Educn Adminr, AEU, 1980–86; Admin. Asst Sec., then Manager, Nat. Educn Centre, TUC, 1986–97. Mem., Gillingham BC, 1982–90 (Leader, Lab. Gp, 1989–90). Contested (Lab) Gillingham, 1992. PPS, LCD, 1999–2001, to Minister for Housing and Planning, 2001–02, to Minister for Criminal Justice, 2002–03, to Dep. Prime Minister, 2005–07; an Asst Govt Whip, 2003–05. Mem. Bd, Thames Gateway Kent Partnership, 2000–. Mem. Bd, Groundwork Medway/Swale, 2001–. *Address:* House of Commons, SW1A 0AA.

CLARK, His Honour Paul Nicholas Rowntree; a Circuit Judge, 1985–2003; *b* 17 Aug. 1940; *s* of late Henry Rowntree Clark and Gwendoline Victoria Clark; *m* 1st, 1967; two *s* one *d*; 2nd, 1997, Jacqueline Davies, *qv*. *Educ:* Bristol Grammar Sch.; New Coll., Oxford (Open Schol.; MA (Lit. Hum.)). Called to the Bar, Middle Temple, 1966 (Harmsworth Schol.), Bencher 1982, Reader 2005; in practice on Midland and Oxford (formerly Oxford) Circuit, 1966–85; a Recorder, 1981–85. Pres., Council of HM Circuit Judges, 1998. Chm., Disciplinary Court, Oxford Univ., 2002–04. Chm., Friends of the Ashmolean Mus., 1996–2005. Pres., Old Bristolians' Soc., 1999–2000. *Address:* 2 Harcourt Buildings, Temple, EC4Y 9DB. *T:* (020) 7353 6961. *Club:* Garrick.

CLARK, Peter Charles Lister; His Honour Judge Peter Clark; a Circuit Judge, since 1995; a Senior Circuit Judge, Employment Appeal Tribunal, since 2006; *b* 16 June 1948; *s* of Charles Lister Clark and Mary Isobel Clark; *m* 1973, Josephine Neilson Hogg; one *s* one *d*. *Educ:* Repton Sch.; Southampton Univ. (LLB). Called to the Bar, Gray's Inn, 1970; in practice at the Bar, 1971–95; a Recorder, Midland and Oxford Circuit, 1994–95. *Recreations:* various. *Address:* Devereux Chambers, Devereux Court, WC2R 3JJ. *T:* (020) 7353 7534. *Club:* Reform.

CLARK, Petula, (Sally Olwen), CBE 1998; singer, actress; *b* 15 Nov. 1932; *d* of Leslie Clark; *m* 1961, Claude Wolff; one *s* two *d*. Own BBC radio series, Pet's Parlour, 1943; early British films include: Medal for the General, 1944; I Know Where I'm Going, 1945; Here Come the Huggetts, 1948; Dance Hall, 1950; White Corridors, 1951; The Card, 1951; Made in Heaven, 1952; The Runaway Bus, 1953; That Woman Opposite, 1957. Began career as singer in France, 1959. Top female vocalist, France, 1962; Bravos du Music Hall award for outstanding woman in show business, France, 1965; Grammy awards for records Downtown and I Know A Place. Numerous concert and television appearances in Europe and USA including her own BBC TV series; world concert tour, 1997. *Films:* Finian's Rainbow, 1968; Goodbye Mr Chips, 1969; Second to the Right and Straight on till Morning, 1982; *musicals:* The Sound of Music, Apollo Victoria, 1981; (also composer and creator) Someone Like You, Strand, 1990; Blood Brothers, NY, 1993, nat. tour, 1994–95; Sunset Boulevard, Adelphi, 1995, 1996, NY, 1998, nat. US tour, 1998–2000. *Address:* c/o John Ashby, PO Box 288, Woking, Surrey GU22 0YN.

CLARK, Ramsey; lawyer in private practice, New York City, since 1969; *b* Dallas, Texas, 18 Dec. 1927; *s* of late Thomas Clark, and of Mary Ramsey; *m* 1949, Georgia Welch, Corpus Christi, Texas; one *s* one *d*. *Educ:* Public Schs, Dallas, Los Angeles, Washington; Univ. of Texas (BA); Univ. of Chicago (MA, JD). US Marine Corps, 1945–46. Engaged private practice of law, Dallas, 1951–61; Asst Attorney Gen., Dept of Justice, 1961–65; Dep. Attorney Gen., 1965–67, Attorney Gen., 1967–69. *Address:* 37 West 12th Street, New York, NY 10011-8503, USA.

CLARK, Reginald Blythe; Chief Executive, Rhino Rugby, since 2006; Director, London & Oxford Group, since 1993 (Director, London & Oxford Securities, since 1988); *b* 15 March 1958; *s* of Thomas Harold Clark and Catherine Clark; *m* 1983, Judith Anne Brown; one *s* one *d*. *Educ:* Brinkburn Comprehensive Sch., Hartlepool; Christ Church, Oxford (MA). Capital markets career with Yamaichi Internat., Swiss Bank Corp. and J P Morgan, then European Finance Dir, Kobe Steel, Japan, 1988–97; Man. Dir, Loxko Venture Managers Ltd, 1991–2005; Dir, Darwin Rhodes Gp, 2005–07. Party Treasurer, Liberal Democrats, 2000–05. *Recreations:* cycling, jogging, Rugby (Oxford Blue 1978, 1979). *Clubs:* Garrick, National Liberal; Vincent's (Pres., 1979–80).

CLARK, Richard David; Clerk to Devon and Cornwall Police Authority, 1993–97 (Associate Clerk, 1989–93); *b* 2 Sept. 1934; *s* of David and Enid Clark; *m* 1958, Pamela Mary (*née* Burgess); two *d*. *Educ:* Keele Univ. (BA, DipEd); Univ. de Paris, Sorbonne. Teaching, Woodberry Down Comprehensive School, 1957–61; Education Admin, Herts CC, 1961–69; Asst Educn Officer, Lancs CC, 1969–71; Second Dep. County Educn Officer, Hants CC, 1972–76; Chief Educn Officer, Glos CC, 1976–83; County Educn Officer, Hants CC, 1983–88; Chief Exec., and Clerk to the Lieutenancy, Devon CC, 1989–95. Dir, Devon and Cornwall TEC, 1989–95. Mem., Adv. Cttee on Supply and Educn of Teachers. Adviser to: Burnham Cttee, 1982–87; Educn Cttee, ACC, 1982–89, 1990–95; Council of Local Educn Authorities, 1983–89. Governor: Plymouth Univ., 1995–2000; Sidmouth Coll., 1995–2000. Fellow Commoner, Churchill Coll., Cambridge, 1983; Vis. Fellow, Southampton Univ., 1986–88; Hon. Fellow, Exeter Univ., 1992–98. FRSA 1977. *Recreations:* books, gardening, wood turning, croquet. *Address:* Glendale House, Rannoch Road, Crowborough, East Sussex TN6 1RB.

CLARK, Sir Robert (Anthony), Kt 1976; DSC 1944; Chairman, RP & C International (formerly Rauscher Pierce & Clark), since 1992; *b* 6 Jan. 1924; *yr s* of John Clark and Gladys Clark (*née* Dyer); *m* 1949, Andolyn Marjorie Lewis; two *s* one *d*. *Educ:* Highgate Sch.; King's Coll., Cambridge. Served War, Royal Navy, 1942–46. Partner with Slaughter and May, Solicitors, 1953–61; Director: Alfred McAlpine plc (formerly Marchwiel plc), 1957–96; Hill Samuel Bank Ltd, merchant bankers (formerly Philip Hill, Higginson, Erlangers Ltd, then Hill Samuel & Co. Ltd), 1961–91 (Chm., 1974–87); Bank of England, 1976–85; Eagle Star Holdings Ltd, 1976–87; BL, subseq. Rover Gp plc, 1977–88; Shell Transport and Trading Co., plc, 1982–94; SmithKline Beecham plc, 1987–95 (Vice-Chm.); Vodafone Group plc (formerly Racal Telecom PLC), 1988–98; Chairman: Hill Samuel Gp plc, 1980–88 (Chief Exec., 1976–80); IMI plc, 1981–89; Marley plc, 1985–89; Mirror Group (formerly Mirror Group Newspapers) plc, 1992–98; Lambert Fenchurch Gp (formerly Lowndes Lambert Group Hldgs) plc, 1995–98 (Dep. Chm., 1992–95); Dep. Chm., TSB Gp, 1989–91 (Dir, 1987–91). Chairman: Industrial Development Adv. Bd, 1973–80; Review Body on Doctors' and Dentists' Remuneration, 1979–86; Council, Charing Cross and Westminster Med. Sch., 1982–96; Dir, ENO, 1983–87. Hon. DSc Cranfield Inst. of Technol., 1982. *Recreations:* reading, music, collecting antiquarian books, the garden at Munstead Wood. *Address:* Munstead Wood, Godalming, Surrey GU7 1UN. *T:* (01483) 417867; RP & C International, 31A St James's Square, SW1Y 4JR. *Clubs:* Pratt's, Special Forces.

See also T. N. Clark.

CLARK, Prof. Robert Bernard, DSc, PhD; FIBiol, FRSE; Professor of Zoology, University of Newcastle upon Tyne, 1966–89, now Emeritus; *b* 13 Oct. 1923; *s* of Joseph Lawrence Clark and Dorothy (*née* Halden); *m* 1st, 1956, Mary Eleanor (*née* Laurence) (marr. diss.); 2nd, 1970, Susan Diana (*née* Smith); one *s* one *d*. *Educ:* St Marylebone Grammar Sch.; Chelsea Polytechnic (BSc London 1944); University Coll., Exeter (BSc 1950); Univ. of Glasgow (PhD 1956); DSc London 1965. FIBiol 1966, FLS 1969, FRSE 1970. Asst Experimental Officer, DSIR Road Research Laboratory, 1944; Asst to Prof. of Zoology, Univ. of Glasgow, 1950; Asst Prof., Univ. of California (Berkeley), 1953; Lectr in Zoology, Univ. of Bristol, 1956; Head of Dept of Zoology and Dir of Dove Marine Laboratory, Univ. of Newcastle upon Tyne, 1966–77, Dir of Research Unit on Rehabilitation of Oiled Seabirds, 1967–76; Dir of NERC Research Unit on Rocky Shore Biology, 1981–87. Member: NERC, 1971–77 and 1983–86; Royal Commn on Environmental Pollution, 1979–83; Adv. Cttee on Pesticides, 1986–90; Mem. Council, Nature Conservancy, 1975. *Publications:* Neurosecretion (ed jtly), 1962; Dynamics in Metazoan Evolution, 1964, corrected repr. 1967; Practical Course in Experimental Zoology, 1966; (jtly) Invertebrate Panorama, 1971; (jtly) Synopsis of Animal Classification, 1971; (ed jtly) Essays in Hydrobiology, 1972; (ed) The Long-Term Effects of Oil Pollution on Marine Populations, Communities and Ecosystems, 1982; Marine Pollution, 1986, 5th edn 2001; The Waters Around the British Isles: their conflicting uses, 1987; (ed jtly) Environmental Effects of North Sea Oil and Gas Development, 1987; Founder, 1968, and ed, Marine Pollution Bulletin; numerous papers in learned jls. *Recreations:* architecture, music, unambitious gardening, cooking. *Address:* Highbury House, 53 Highbury, Newcastle upon Tyne NE2 3LN. *T:* (0191) 281 4672.

CLARK, Robert Joseph, CBE 2000; international court management consultant, British Council, European Union and others, since 2001; Circuit Administrator, South Eastern Circuit, Lord Chancellor's Department, 1997–2001; *b* 29 March 1942; *s* of late Edward Clark and Elsie Clark (*née* Bush); *m* 1970, Elke Agnes, *d* of late Hans Schmidt and Herma Schmidt; two *d*. *Educ:* state schools in London. Lord Chancellor's Department: Official Solicitor's Dept, 1960–70; Nat. Industrial Relns Court, 1970–74; HQ, 1974–77; Trng Centre, 1977–79; Chief Clerk, Court of Protection, 1979–83; S Eastern Circuit Office, 1983–88; Head: Civil Business Div., 1988–91; Judicial Appointments Div. II, 1991–93; Circuit Administrator, Western Circuit, 1993–97. *Recreations:* theatre, walking. *Address:* 36 Kayemoor Road, Sutton, Surrey SM2 5HT. *Club:* Civil Service.

CLARK, Prof. Robin Jon Hawes, CNZM 2004; FRS 1990; Sir William Ramsay Professor of Chemistry, University College London, since 1989; *b* 16 Feb. 1935; *s* of Reginald Hawes Clark, JP, BCom and Marjorie Alice Clark (*née* Thomas); *m* 1964, Beatrice Rawdin Brown, JP; one *s* one *d*. *Educ:* Christ's Coll., NZ; Canterbury University Coll., Univ. of NZ (BSc 1956; MSc (1st cl. hons) 1958); Univ. of Otago; University Coll. London (British Titan Products Scholar and Fellow; PhD 1961); DSc London 1969. FRSC 1969. University College London: Asst Lectr in Chemistry, 1962; Lectr 1963–71; Reader 1972–81; Prof., 1982–89; Dean of Faculty of Science, 1988–89; Hd, Dept of Chemistry, 1989–99; Mem. Council, 1991–94; Fellow, 1992. Mem., Senate and Academic Council, Univ. of London, 1988–93. Visiting Professor: Columbia, 1965; Padua, 1967; Western Ontario, 1968; Texas A&M, 1978; Bern, 1979; Fribourg, 1979; Auckland, 1981; Odense, 1983; Sydney, 1985; Bordeaux, 1988; Pretoria, 1991; Würzburg, 1996; Indiana, 1998; Thessaloniki, 1999; Lectures: Kresge-Hooker, Wayne State, 1965; Frontiers, Case Western Reserve Univ., Cleveland, 1967; John van Geuns, Amsterdam, 1979; Firth, Sheffield, 1991; Carman, SA Chemical Inst., 1994; Moissan, Paris, 1998; Leermakers, Wesleyan Univ., 2000; Hassel, Oslo, 2000; Ralph Anderson, Horners' Co., 2003. Mem. Council, Royal Soc., 1993–94; Royal Society of Chemistry: Mem., Dalton Divl Council, 1985–88, Vice-Pres., 1988–90; Lectures: Tilden, 1983–84; Nyholm, 1989–90; Thomas Graham, 1991; Harry Hallam, 1993, 2000; Liversidge, 2003–04; UK-Canada Rutherford, 2000, Bakerian, 2008, Royal Soc. Member: SRC Inorganic Chem. Panel, 1977–80; SERC Post-doctoral Fellowships Cttee, 1983; SERC Inorganic Chem. Sub-Cttee, 1993–94; Chairman: XI Internat. Conf. on Raman Spectroscopy, London, 1988; Steering Cttee, Internat. Confs on Raman Spectroscopy, 1990–92 (Mem., 1988–). Mem. Council, Royal Instn of GB, 1996– (Vice-Pres., 1997–; Sec., 1998–2004; Hon. Life Fellow, 2004). Trustee, Ramsay Meml Fellowships Trust, 1993– (Chm. Adv. Council, 1989–); Chm., Univ. of Canterbury Trust, 2004–. MAE 1990; FRSA 1992. Hon. FRSNZ, 1989. Hon. DSc Canterbury, 2001. Joannes Marcus Marci Medal, Czech Spectroscopy Soc., 1998; T. K. Sidey Medal, Royal Soc. of NZ, 2001; Lifetime Achievement Award, NZ Soc., London, 2004. *Publications:* The Chemistry of Titanium and Vanadium, 1968; (jtly) The Chemistry of Titanium, Zirconium and Hafnium, 1973; (jtly) The Chemistry of Vanadium, Niobium and Tantalum, 1973; (ed jtly) Advances in Spectroscopy, vols 1–26, 1975–98; (ed jtly) Raman Spectroscopy, 1988; (ed) nine monographs on Inorganic Chemistry, 1978–; about 500 contribs to learned jls, in fields of transition metal chem. and spectroscopy. *Recreations:* golf, long distance walking, travel, bridge, music, theatre, wine. *Address:* Christopher Ingold Laboratories, University College London, 20 Gordon Street, WC1H 0AJ. *T:* (020) 7679 7457, *Fax:* (020) 7679 7463; 3a Loom Lane, Radlett, Herts WD7 8AA. *T:* (01923) 857899. *Clubs:* Athenæum, Porters Park Golf (Radlett).

CLARK, Roderick David; Director General Strategy, Ministry of Justice (formerly Department for Constitutional Affairs), since 2005; *b* 10 May 1961; *s* of Sydney Clark and Mary Anne Clark (*née* Kellas); *m* 1995, Kate Paul; one *d*. *Educ:* Corpus Christi Coll., Oxford (BA Lit.Hum). Civil Servant, 1984–, posts mainly in field of social security. *Recreations:* cooking, walking, bridge. *Address:* Ministry of Justice, Selborne House, 54/60 Victoria Street, SW1F 6QW.

CLARK, Prof. Ronald George, FRCSE, FRCS; Professor of Surgery, 1972–93, now Emeritus, and Pro-Vice-Chancellor, 1988–93, University of Sheffield; Consultant Surgeon: Northern General Hospital, 1966–93; Royal Hallamshire Hospital, since 1966; *b* 9 Aug. 1928; *s* of late George Clark and of Gladys Clark; *m* 1960, Tamar Welsh Harvie; two *d*. *Educ:* Aberdeen Acad.; Univ. of Aberdeen (MB, ChB); MD Sheffield 1996. FRCSE 1960; FRCS 1980. House appts, Aberdeen Royal Infirmary, 1956–57; Registrar, Western Infirmary, Glasgow, 1958–60; Surgical Res. Fellow, Harvard, USA, 1960–61; Lectr in Surgery, Univ. of Glasgow, 1961–65; Sheffield University: Sen. Lectr in Surgery,

1966–72; Dean, Faculty of Medicine and Dentistry, 1982–85. Examiner, Universities of: Aberdeen, Glasgow, Edinburgh, Liverpool, Newcastle, Leicester, London, Southampton, Malta, Ibadan, Jos. Chm., European Soc. for Parenteral and Enteral Nutrition, 1982–87; Council Mem., Nutrition Soc., 1982–85; Scientific Governor, British Nutrition Foundn, 1982–98; Member: GMC, 1983–93; GDC, 1990–93; Assoc. of Surgeons of GB and Ireland, 1968–; Surgical Res. Soc., 1969–. Mem., Editorial Bd, Scottish Medical Jl, 1962–65; Editor-in-Chief, Clinical Nutrition, 1980–82. *Publications:* contribs to books and jls on surgical topics and metabolic aspects of acute disease. *Recreation:* golf. *Address:* Brookline, 15 Comerton Place, Drumoig, Leuchars, St Andrews, Fife KY16 0NQ. *T:* and *Fax:* (01382) 540058.

CLARK, Stuart; *see* Clark, D. S. T.

CLARK, Sir Terence (Joseph), KBE 1990; CMG 1985; CVO 1978; HM Diplomatic Service, retired; Senior Consultant, MEC, since 1995; *b* 19 June 1934; *s* of Joseph Clark and Mary Clark; *m* 1960, Lieselotte Rosa Marie Müller; two *s* one *d*. *Educ:* Thomas Parmiter's, London. RAF (attached to Sch. of Slavonic Studies, Cambridge), 1953–55; Pilot Officer, RAFVR, 1955. HM Foreign Service, 1955; ME Centre for Arab Studies, 1956–57; Bahrain, 1957–58; Amman, 1958–60; Casablanca, 1961–62; FO, 1962–65; Asst Polit. Agent, Dubai, 1965–68; Belgrade, 1969–71; Hd of Chancery, Muscat, 1972–73; Asst Hd of ME Dept, FCO, 1974–76; Counsellor (Press and Information), Bonn, 1976–79; Chargé d'Affaires, Tripoli, Feb.-March 1981; Counsellor, Belgrade, 1979–82. Dep. Leader, UK Delegn, Conf. on Security and Co-operation in Europe, Madrid, 1982–83; Hd of Information Dept, FCO, 1983–85; Ambassador to Iraq, 1985–89; Ambassador to Oman, 1990–94. Dir, Internat. Crisis Gp Bosnia Project, Sarajevo, 1996. Chm., Anglo-Omani Soc., 1995–2004; Mem., Exec. Cttee of Mgt, ME Assoc., 1998–2004. Mem. Council, British Sch. of Archaeology in Iraq, 2003–. Member: RSAA, 1991 (Mem. Council, 2001–07); RIIA, 1995–2007; FRGS 1993. Chm., Saluki Coursing Club, 2000–05; Sec. Gen., British Iraqi Friendship Soc., 2008–. Commander's Cross, Order of Merit (Fed. Republic of Germany), 1978. *Publications:* (jtly) The Saluqi: coursing hound of the East, 1995; (jtly) Oman in Time, 2001; (jtly) Al-Mansur's Book on Hunting, 2001; (jtly) Dogs in Antiquity, 2001; Underground to Overseas: the story of petroleum development Oman, 2007; articles on Salukis and coursing in magazines. *Recreations:* Salukis, walking. *Club:* Hurlingham.

CLARK, Thomas Alastair; Adviser to Governor, Bank of England, since 2003; *b* 27 Feb. 1949; *s* of late Andrew Evans Clark and Freda (*née* Seal); *m* 1986, Shirley Anne Barker; one *s* (one *d* decd). *Educ:* Stockport Grammar Sch.; Emmanuel Coll., Cambridge (MA Maths); London Sch. of Econs (MSc Econs); Stanford Business Sch. (SEP). Bank of England, 1971–2007: PA to Dep. Governor, 1980–81; UK Alternate Exec. Dir, IMF, 1983–85; UK Alternate Dir, EIB, 1986–88; Head: Financial Markets and Instns Div., 1987–93; European Div., 1993–94; Dep. Dir, 1994–97; Exec. Dir, 1997–2003. Director: International Financial Services, London (formerly British Invisibles), 1997–2007; Crestco, 1998–2002; LIFFE, 2007–. Hon. Vis. Prof., Cass Business Sch., City Univ., 2007–. Gov., King's Coll. Sch., Wimbledon, 2007–; Mem. Adv. Council, City Univ., 2006–. Hon. Fellow, ACT, 2007–. *Recreations:* joinery, hill-walking. *Address:* 54 Forest Road, Richmond, Surrey TW9 3BZ.

CLARK, Prof. Timothy John Hayes, FRCP; Professor of Pulmonary Medicine, Imperial College Faculty of Medicine at the National Heart and Lung Institute, since 1990; *b* 18 Oct. 1935; *s* of John and Kathleen Clark; *m* 1961, Elizabeth Ann Day; two *s* two *d*. *Educ:* Christ's Hospital; Guy's Hospital Medical Sch. BSc 1958; MB BS (Hons) 1961, MD 1967 London. FRCP 1973 (LRCP 1960, MRCP 1962); MRCS 1960. Fellow, Johns Hopkins Hosp., Baltimore USA, 1963; Registrar, Hammersmith Hosp., 1964; Lecturer and Sen. Lectr, Guy's Hospital Med. Sch., 1966; Consultant Physician: Guy's Hosp., 1968–90; Royal Brompton Hosp., 1970–98; Prof. of Thoracic Med., Guy's Hosp. Med. Sch., later UMDS, 1977–89; Dean: Guy's Hosp., 1984–89; UMDS, 1986–89; Pro-Vice-Chancellor for Medicine and Dentistry, Univ. of London, 1987–89; Dean, Nat. Heart and Lung Inst., 1990–97; Pro-Rector (Medicine), 1995–97, (Educnl Qly), 1997–2000, Imperial Coll.; Pro-Rector and Provost, Imperial Coll. at Wye, 2000–01; Pro-Rector (Admission), Imperial Coll., 2001–02. Mem., Council of Governors, UMDS, 1982–89, 1990–95. Specialist Adviser to Social Services Cttee, 1981 and 1985. Special Trustee, Guy's Hosp., 1982–86. Pres., British Thoracic Soc., 1990–91; Chm., Global Initiative for Asthma, 2000–04; Vice-Chairman: Nat. Asthma Campaign, 1993–2000; ICRF, 1997–2002; Trustee and Mem. Council, Stroke Assoc., 2002–. FKC 1995. *Publications:* (jtly) Asthma, 1977, 4th edn 2000; (ed) Small Airways in Health and Disease, 1979; (jtly) Topical Steroid Treatment of Asthma and Rhinitis, 1980; (ed) Clinical Investigation of Respiratory Disease, 1981; (jtly) Practical Management of Asthma, 1985, 3rd edn 1998; articles in British Medical Jl, Lancet, and other specialist scientific jls. *Recreation:* cricket. *Address:* 8 Lawrence Court, NW7 3QP. *T:* (020) 8959 4411. *Club:* MCC.

See also Air Vice-Marshal P. D. Clark.

CLARK, Timothy Nicholas; Senior Partner, Slaughter and May, 2001–08; *b* 9 Jan. 1951; *s* of Sir Robert Anthony Clark, *qv*; *m* 1974, Caroline Moffat; two *s*. *Educ:* Sherborne Sch.; Pembroke Coll., Cambridge (MA Hist.). Admitted solicitor, 1976; with Slaughter and May (Solicitors), 1974–2008, Partner, 1983–2008. Non-executive Director: Big Yellow Gp plc, 2008–; COIF Funds, 2008–. *Recreations:* flying, football, cricket, theatre. *Address:* *e-mail:* timnclark@googlemail.com. *Clubs:* Air Squadron, Lowtonians.

CLARK, Tony; *see* Clark, C. A.

CLARK, Wallace; *see* Clark, H. W. S.

CLARK, Gen. Wesley K., Hon. KBE 2000; Supreme Allied Commander, Europe, 1997–2000; Commander-in-Chief, United States European Command, 1997–2000. *Educ:* US Military Acad.; Univ. of Oxford (Rhodes Schol.). Served in Vietnam (Silver and Bronze Stars); Sen. Military Asst to Gen. Alexander Haig; Head, Nat. Army Trng Centre; Dir of Strategy, Dept of Defense; Mem., American negotiating team, Bosnian peace negotiations, Dayton, Ohio, 1995; Head, US Southern Comd, Panama. *Publications:* Waging Modern War, 2001; Winning Modern Wars, 2003. *Address:* Wesley K. Clark & Associates, PO Box 3276, Little Rock, AR 72203, USA. *T:* (501) 2449522, *Fax:* (501) 2442203.

CLARK, William P.; Senior Counsel, Clark, Cali and Negranti, since 1997; *b* 23 Oct. 1931; *s* of William and Bernice Clark; *m* 1955, Joan Brauner; three *s* two *d*. *Educ:* Stanford Univ., California; Loyola Law Sch., Los Angeles, California. Admitted to practice of law, California, 1958; Sen. Member, law firm, Clark, Cole & Fairfield, Oxnard, Calif, 1958–67. Served on Cabinet of California, Governor Ronald Reagan, first as Cabinet Secretary, later as Executive Secretary, 1967–69; Judge, Superior Court, State of California, County of San Luis Obispo, 1969–71; Associate Justice: California Court of Appeal, Second District, Los Angeles, 1971–73; California Supreme Court, San Francisco, 1973–81; Dep. Secretary, Dept of State, Washington, DC, 1981–82; Assistant to Pres. of USA for Nat. Security Affairs, 1982–83; Sec. of the Interior, 1983–85. Chairman: Presidential Task Force on Nuclear Weapons Program Management, 1985; USA-ROC (Taiwan) Business Council; Member: Commn on Defense Management, 1985–86; Commn on Integrated Long-Term Strategy, 1987. Counselor, Standing Cttee on Law and Nat. Security, American Bar Assoc. Dir, Mus. of Flying, Santa Monica, California. *Publications:* judicial opinions in California Reports, 9 Cal. 3d through 29 Cal. 3d. *Recreations:* ranching, horseback riding, outdoor sports, flying. *Address:* Clark Company, Clark Building, 1031 Pine Street, Paso Robles, CA 93446, USA. *Clubs:* Bohemia (San Francisco); California Cattleman's Association; Rancheros Visitadores (California).

CLARKE, family name of **Baron Clarke of Hampstead**.

CLARKE, Hon. Lord; Matthew Gerard Clarke; a Senator of the College of Justice in Scotland, since 2000; *s* of Thomas Clarke and Ann (*née* Duddy). *Educ:* Holy Cross High Sch., Hamilton; Univ. of Glasgow (MA; LLB; Francis T. Hunter Scholar; Cunninghame Bursar). Solicitor, 1972. Lectr, Dept of Scots Law, Edinburgh Univ., 1972–78; admitted to Faculty of Advocates, 1978; Standing Junior Counsel to Scottish Home and Health Dept, 1983–89; QC (Scot.) 1989; a Judge of the Courts of Appeal of Jersey and Guernsey, 1995–2000. Member: Consumer Credit Licensing Appeal Tribunal, 1976–2000; Estate Agents Tribunals, 1980–2000; Trademarks Tribunal, 1995–2000; Chm. (part-time), Industrial Tribunals, 1987–2000. Leader, UK Delegn, Council of the Bars and Laws Socs of EC, 1992–96 (Mem., 1989–99). British Council: Mem., Scottish Cttee, 2001–; Chm., Scottish Law Cttee, 2001–07. Hon. Fellow, Europa Inst., Univ. of Edinburgh, 1995–. *Publications:* (Scottish Editor) Sweet & Maxwell's Encyclopaedia of Consumer Law, 1980; (contrib.) Corporate Law: the European dimension, 1991; (contrib.) Butterworth's EC Legal Systems, 1992; (contrib.) Green's Guide to European Laws in Scotland, 1995; (contrib.) McPhail, Sheriff Court Practice, 1999; (contrib.) A True European: essays for Judge David Edward, 2004; (contrib.) Court of Session Practice, 2005. *Recreations:* opera, chamber music, the music of Schubert, travel. *Address:* Parliament House, Parliament Square, Edinburgh EH1 1RQ.

CLARKE OF HAMPSTEAD, Baron *cr* 1998 (Life Peer), of Hampstead in the London Borough of Camden; **Anthony James Clarke,** CBE 1998; *b* 17 April 1932; *s* of Henry Walter and Elizabeth Clarke; *m* 1954, Josephine Ena (*née* Turner); one *s* one *d*. *Educ:* New End Primary Sch., Hampstead; St Dominic's RC Sch., Kentish Town; Ruskin Coll., Oxford (TU educn course, 1954). Nat. Service, Royal Signals, 1950–52; TA and AER, 1952–68. Joined PO as Telegraph Boy at 14; worked as Postman until elected full-time officer, Union of Post Office Workers, 1979; Nat. Editor, The Post, UPW jl, 1979–82; Dep. Gen. Sec., UPW, later CWU, 1982–93. Member: Hampstead Lab Party, 1954–86; St Albans Lab Party, 1986–; Lab Party NEC, 1983–93; Chm., Lab Party, 1992–93. Mem. (Lab) Camden LBC, 1971–78. Contested (Lab) Camden, Hampstead, Feb. and Oct. 1974. Member: Exec. Cttee, Camden Cttee for Community Relns, 1974–81; Camden Council of Social Services, 1978–87. Mem., Labour Friends of Israel, 1972–. Governor, Westminster Foundn for Democracy, 1992–98. Trustee, RAF Mus., 2001–. Trustee, Wells and Campden Charitable Trust; Founder Mem., and Trustee, One World Action (formerly One World), 1984–. KSG 1994. *Recreations:* Arsenal FC, The Archers, reading. *Address:* 83 Orchard Drive, St Albans, Herts AL2 2QH. *T:* (01727) 874276; House of Lords, SW1A 0PW.

CLARKE, Prof. Adrienne Elizabeth, AC 2004 (AO 1991); PhD; FTSE, FAA; Laureate Professor, Personal Chair in Botany, University of Melbourne, since 1985; Victoria's first Ambassador for Biotechnology, 2001–03; *b* 6 Jan. 1938; *d* of A. L. Petty; *m* (marr. diss.); two *d* one *s*. *Educ:* Ruyton Grammar Sch.; Univ. of Melbourne (PhD). Melbourne University: Reader in Botany, 1981–85; Dir, Plant Cell Biol. Res. Centre, 1982–99; Dep. Head, Sch. of Botany, 1992–2000. Chm., CSIRO, 1991–96; Mem., Sci. Adv. Bd, Friedrich Meischer Inst., 1991. Director: Alcoa of Australia, 1993–96; AMP Soc., 1994–99; Woolworths Ltd, 1994–2007; WMC Ltd, 1996–2002; WMC Resources Ltd, 2002–05. Dir, Fisher & Paykel Healthcare, 2002–08. Lt-Governor, Victoria, 1997–2001. Pres., Internat. Soc. for Plant Molecular Biology, 1997–98. Foreign Associate, Nat. Acad. of Scis, USA; Comp., Inst. of Engrs, Australia. *Publications:* (ed with I. Wilson) Carbohydrate-Protein Recognition, 1988; (with B. A. Stone) Chemistry and Biology of Glucans, 1992; chapters in numerous books; contribs to learned jls. *Recreations:* swimming, bush walking. *Address:* School of Botany, University of Melbourne, Vic 3010, Australia. *T:* (3) 83445568.

CLARKE, Alan; Chief Executive, One NorthEast Regional Development Agency, since 2003; *b* 18 Aug. 1953; *s* of Neville Clarke and late Jean Clarke; *m* 1977, Deborah Anne Hayes; one *s* two *d*. *Educ:* Univ. of Lancaster (BA Hons Econs 1974); Univ. of Liverpool (MCD 1977). MRTPI 1980. Policy Officer, South Ribble BC, 1974–75; Planning Asst, S Tyneside Council, 1977–79; Newcastle City Council: Planning Asst, 1979–83; Sen. Econ. Devélt Asst, 1983–86; Hd, Econ. Develt, 1986–91; Chief Econ. Develt Officer, 1991–95; Asst Chief Exec., Sunderland CC, 1995–2000; Chief Exec., Northumberland CC, 2000–03. *Recreations:* cycling, football, hill-walking. *Address:* (office) Stella House, Goldcrest Way, Newburn Riverside, Newcastle upon Tyne NE15 8NY.

CLARKE, Prof. Alan Douglas Benson, CBE 1974; Professor of Psychology, University of Hull, 1962–84, now Emeritus; *b* 21 March 1922; *s* of late Robert Benson Clarke and Mary Lizars Clarke; *m* 1950, Prof. Ann Margaret (*née* Gravely); two *s*. *Educ:* Lancing Coll.; Univs of Reading and London. 1st cl. hons BA Reading 1948; PhD London 1950; FBPsS. Reading Univ., 1940–41 and 1946–48. Sen. Psychol., 1951–57 and Cons. Psychol., 1957–62, Manor Hosp., Epsom. Dean of Faculty of Science, 1966–68, and Pro-Vice-Chancellor 1968–71, Univ. of Hull. Vis. Prof., Univ. of Hertfordshire, 1992–98. Rapporteur, WHO Expert Cttee on Organization of Services for Mentally Retarded, 1967; Mem. WHO Expert Adv. Panel on Mental Health, 1968–85; Chm., Trng Council for Teachers of Mentally Handicapped, 1969–74; Hon. Vice-Pres., Nat. Assoc. for Mental Health, 1970–; President: Internat. Assoc. for Sci. Study of Mental Deficiency, 1973–76 (Hon. Past-Pres., 1976–88; Hon. Life Pres., 1988–); BPsS, 1977–78. Member: Personal Social Services Council, 1973–77; DHSS/SSRC Organizing Gp Transmitted Deprivation, 1974–83 (Chm. 1978–83); Cons., OECD/NZ Conf. on Early Childhood Care and Educn, 1978; Chairman: Sec. of State's Adv. Cttee on Top Grade Clinical Psychologist Posts and Appts, NHS, 1981–82; Adv. Cttee, Thomas Coram Res. Unit, Univ. of London Inst. of Educn, 1981–98. Lectures: Maudsley, RMPA, 1967; Stolz, Guy's Hosp., 1972; Tizard Meml, Assoc. for Child Psychol. and Psychiatry, 1983. Hon. Life Mem., Amer. Assoc. on Mental Deficiency, 1975 (Research award, 1977, with Ann M. Clarke). Hon. FRCPsych 1989; Hon. FBPsS 2007. Hon. DSc Hull, 1986. (With Ann M. Clarke) Distinguished Achievement Award for Scientific Lit., Internat. Assoc. for Scientific Study of Mental Deficiency, 1982. Editor, Brit. Jl Psychol., 1973–79; Mem., Editorial Bds of other jls. *Publications:* with Ann M. Clarke: Mental Deficiency: the Changing Outlook, 1958, 4th edn 1985; Mental Retardation and Behavioural Research, 1973; Early Experience: myth and evidence, 1976; Early Experience and the Life Path, 2000; Human Resilience: a fifty year quest, 2003; (with B. Tizard) Child Development and Social Policy: the life and work of Jack Tizard, 1983; (with P. Evans) Combating

Mental Handicap, 1991; numerous in psychol and med. jls. *Address:* 109 Meadway, Barnet, Herts EN5 5JZ. *T:* (020) 8441 9690.

CLARKE, Andrew Bertram; QC 1997; *b* 23 Aug. 1956; *s* of Arthur Bertram Clarke and Violet Doris Clarke; *m* 1981, Victoria Clare Thomas; one *s* two *d. Educ:* Crewe Grammar Sch.; King's Coll., London (LLB; AKC); Lincoln Coll., Oxford (BCL). Called to the Bar, Middle Temple, 1980; in practice at the Bar, 1981–. Gov., Goffs Foundn Sch., Cheshunt, 1996–. Chm., Friends of St Mary's Church, Cheshunt, 1994–. *Recreations:* supporter of Crewe Alexandra FC, Gloucestershire CCC; collector of European ceramics and modern prints. *Address:* 38 Albury Ride, Cheshunt, Herts EN8 8XF. *T:* (020) 7797 8600.

CLARKE, Rt Hon. Sir Anthony (Peter), Kt 1993; PC 1998; Master of the Rolls, since 2005; Head of Civil Justice, since 2005; *b* 13 May 1943; *s* of late Harry Alston Clarke and Isobel Corsan Clarke (*née* Kay); *m* 1968, Rosemary (*née* Adam); two *s* one *d. Educ:* Oakham Sch.; King's Coll., Cambridge (Econs Pt I, Law Pt II; MA). Called to the Bar, Middle Temple, 1965, Bencher, 1987; QC 1979; a Recorder, 1985–92; a Judge of the High Court of Justice, QBD, 1993–98; Admiralty Judge, 1993–98; a Lord Justice of Appeal, 1998–2005. *Recreations:* golf, tennis, holidays. *Address:* Royal Courts of Justice, Strand, WC2A 2LL.

See also C. A. Clarke.

CLARKE, Anthony Richard; *b* 6 Sept. 1963; *s* of Walter Arthur Clarke and Joan Ada Iris Clarke; *m* Carole Chalmers; one *s* one *d. Educ:* Lings Upper Sch., Northampton. Social Work Trainer, Northamptonshire CC; Disability Trng Officer. MP (Lab) Northampton South, 1997–2005; contested (Lab) same seat, 2005. Mem. (Ind) Northampton BC, 2007–.

CLARKE, Dr Arthur S.; Keeper, Department of Natural History, Royal Scottish Museum, 1980–83, retired; *b* 11 Feb. 1923; *yr s* of late Albert Clarke and Doris Clarke (*née* Elliott); *m* 1951, Joan, *er d* of Walter Andrassy; one *s* one *d. Educ:* Leeds Boys' Modern School; Aireborough Grammar School; Leeds Univ. (BSc 1948, PhD 1951). Pilot, RAF, 1943–46. Asst Lecturer, Glasgow Univ., 1951; Asst Keeper, Royal Scottish Museum, 1954; Deputy Keeper, 1973. *Address:* Rose Cottage, Yarrow, Selkirk TD7 5LB.

CLARKE, Rt Rev. Barry Bryan; *see* Montreal, Bishop of.

CLARKE, Brian; *see* Clarke, J. B.

CLARKE, Brian; artist; *b* 2 July 1953; *s* of late Edward Ord Clarke and of Lilian Clarke (*née* Whitehead); *m* 1972, Elizabeth Cecilia (marr. diss. 1996), *d* of Rev. John Finch; one *s. Educ:* Clarksfield Sch., Oldham; Oldham Sch. of Arts and Crafts (Jr Schol.); Burnley Sch. of Art; North Devon Coll. of Art and Design (Dip. Art and Design). Vis. Prof., Archtl Art, UCL, 1993. Executor, Estate of Francis Bacon, 1998. Trustee and Mem. Cttee, Robert Fraser Foundn, 1990–; Trustee: Ely Stained Glass Mus.; Lowe Educnl Charitable Foundn, 2001; Winston Churchill Meml Trust, 2007– (Mem. Council, 1985–); Chm., Architecture Foundn, 2007–. *Major exhibitions* include: Glass/Light Exhibn, Fest. of City of London, 1979; New Paintings, Constructions and Prints, RIBA, 1981; Paintings, Robert Fraser Gall., 1983; 1976–86, Seibu Mus. of Art, Tokyo, 1987; Malerei und Farbfenster 1977–88, Hessisches Landesmuseum, 1988; Intimations of Mortality, Galerie Karsten Greve, Köln; Into and Out of Architecture, 1990, New Paintings, 1993, Mayor Gall., London; Architecture and Stained Glass, Sezon Mus. of Art, Tokyo, 1990; Paintings and Stained Glass Works in Architecture, 1995, The Glass Wall, 1998, Transillumination, 2003, Tony Shafrazi Gall., NY; Brian Clarke Linda McCartney, Musée Suisse du Vitrail au Château de Romont and German Mus. for Stained Glass, Linnich, 1997–98; 80 Artistes autour du Mondial, Galerie Enrico Navarra, Paris, 1998; Fleurs de Lys, Faggionato Fine Arts, London, 1999; Flowers for New York, Corning Gall., Steuben, NY, 2002; Lamina, Gagosian Gall., London, 2005; *major stained glass works* include: St Gabriel's Ch, Blackburn, 1976; All Saints Ch, Habergham, 1976; Queen's Med. Centre, Nottingham, 1978; Olympus Optical Europa GmbH HQ Building, Hamburg, 1981; King Kahled Internat. Airport, Riyadh, 1982; Buxton Thermal Baths, 1987; Lake Sagami Country Club, Yamanishi, 1988; New Synagogue, Darmstadt, 1988; Victoria Quarter, Leeds, 1989; Cibreo Restaurant, Tokyo, 1990; Glaxo Pharmaceuticals, Uxbridge, 1990; Stansted Airport, 1991; Spindles Shopping Centre, Oldham, 1991–93; España Telefonica, Barcelona, 1991; Carmelite, London, 1992; (with Will Alsop) facade of Hotel de Ville des Bouches-du-Rhone, Marseille, 1992–94; Glass Dune, Hamburg, 1992; New Synagogue, Heidelberg, 1993; Crossrail Paddington, London, 1994; Cliveden Hotel, 1994; (with Linda McCartney) Rye Hosp., 1995; Valentino Village, Noci, 1996; Center Villa-Lobos (design), São Paulo, 1997; Offenbach Synagogue, 1997; New Catholic Church, Obersalbach, 1997; Pfizer Pharmaceuticals, NY, 1997, 2001, 2003; Warburg Dillon Read (stained glass cone), Stamford, Conn, 1998; (with Lord Foster) Al Faisaliah Centre, Riyadh, 2000; West Winter Garden (design), Heron Quays, London, 2001; Hotel and Thalassotherapy Centre, Nova Yardinia, Italy, 2002; Ascot Racecourse (stained glass façade), 2003; Linköping Cathedral (design), Sweden, 2005; (with Lord Foster) Pyramid of Peace (stained glass apex), Astana, Kazakhstan, 2006; stage designs for Paul McCartney World Tour, 1989; designed: stadia sets for Paul McCartney New World Tour, 1993; stage sets for The Ruins of Time (ballet), Dutch Nat. Ballet, 1993. FRSA 1988. Hon. FRIBA 1993; Hon. DLitt Huddersfield. Churchill Fellow in archtl art, 1974; special commendation award, Art and Work, Arts Council, 1989; Europa Nostra award, 1990; Special Award for Stained Glass, Leeds Award for Architecture, 1990; special commendation award, Working for Cities, British Gas, 1992; Europ. Shopping Centre Award, 1995; BDA Auszeichnung guter Bauten, Heidelberg, 1996. *Recreations:* reading, hoarding. *Address:* c/o Eastman & Eastman, 39 West 54th Street, New York, NY 10019, USA; *web:* www.brianclarke.co.uk.

CLARKE, Prof. Bryan Campbell, DPhil; FRS 1982; Foundation Professor of Genetics, 1971–93, Research Professor, 1993–97, University of Nottingham, now Professor Emeritus; *b* 24 June 1932; *s* of Robert Campbell Clarke and Gladys Mary (*née* Carter); *m* 1960, Ann Gillian, *d* of late Prof. John Jewkes, CBE; one *s* one *d. Educ:* Fay Sch., Southborough, Mass, USA; Magdalen Coll. Sch., Oxford; Magdalen Coll., Oxford (MA, DPhil). FLS 1980. National Service, 1950–52 (Pilot Officer, RAF). Asst 1959, Lectr 1963, Reader 1969, Dept of Zoology, Univ. of Edinburgh. Res. Fellow, Stanford Univ., 1973; SRC Sen. Res. Fellow, 1976–81; Hon. Res. Fellow, Natural Hist. Mus., 1993–. Joint Founder, Population Genetics Gp, 1967; Pres., Section D (Biology), BAAS, 1989; Vice-President: Genetical Soc., 1981; Linnean Soc., 1985–87; Soc. for Study of Evolution, USA, 1990–91; Zool Soc. of London, 1998–99; Chairman: Terrestrial Life Sciences Cttee, NERC, 1984–87; Biol Scis Sub-Cttee, HEFCE, 1992–97. Mem., Council, Royal Soc., 1994–96. Chm. Trustees, Charles Darwin Trust, 2000–04; Co-Founder and Trustee, Frozen Ark Project, 2004–. Scientific expeditions to: Morocco, 1955; Polynesia, 1962, 1967, 1968, 1980, 1982, 1986, 1991, 1994, 2000. Editor: Heredity, 1978–85; Proceedings of the Royal Society, Series B, 1989–93. Foreign Mem., Amer. Philosophical Soc., 2003; Foreign Hon. Mem., Amer. Acad. of Arts and Scis, 2004. Linnean Medal for Zoology, 2003. *Publications:* Berber Village, 1959; contrib. scientific jls, mostly on ecological genetics and evolution. *Recreations:* sporadic painting, archaeology, computing. *Address:* Linden Cottage, School Lane, Colston Bassett, Nottingham NG12 3FD. *T:* (01949) 81243. *Club:* Royal Air Force.

CLARKE, Sir (Charles Mansfield) Tobias, 6th Bt *cr* 1831; *b* Santa Barbara, California, 8 Sept. 1939; *e s* of Sir Humphrey Orme Clarke, 5th Bt, and Elisabeth (*d* 1967), *d* of Dr William Albert Cook; *S* father, 1973; *m* 1971, Charlotte (marr. diss. 1979), *e d* of Roderick Walter; *m* 1984, Teresa L. A. de Chair, *d* of late Somerset de Chair; one *s* two *d. Educ:* Eton; Christ Church, Oxford (MA); Univ. of Paris; New York Univ. Graduate Business Sch. Bankers Trust Co., NY, 1963–80 (Vice-Pres., 1974–80). Associate Dir, Swiss Bank Corp., London, 1992–94. Underwriting Mem., Lloyds, 1984–; MSI 1993. Chm., Standing Council of the Baronetage, 1993–96 (Vice-Chm., 1990–92; Hon. Treas., 1980–92); Editor and founder, The Baronets Journal, 1987–99; Chm. Trustees, Baronets Trust, 1996– (Trustee, 1989–); Publisher, The Official Roll of the Baronetage, 1997. Lord of the Manor of Bibury. *Recreations:* accidental happenings, riding, gardening, photography, stimulating conversation; Pres., Bibury Cricket Club. *Heir: s* (Charles Somerset) Lawrence Clarke, *b* 12 March 1990. *Address:* South Lodge, 80 Campden Hill Road, W8 7AA. *T:* (020) 7938 2955; The Church House, Bibury, Cirencester, Glos GL7 5NR. *T:* (01285) 740293. *Clubs:* White's, Boodle's, Beefsteak, Pratt's, Pilgrims', MCC; Jockey (Paris); The Brook, Racquet & Tennis (New York).

CLARKE, Rt Hon. Charles (Rodway); PC 2001; MP (Lab) Norwich South, since 1997; *b* 21 Sept. 1950; *s* of Sir Richard Clarke, KCB, OBE and Brenda Clarke (*née* Skinner); *m* 1984, Carol Marika Pearson; two *s. Educ:* Highgate Sch.; King's Coll., Cambridge (BA Hons 1973). Pres., NUS, 1975–77; various admin. posts, 1977–80; Head, Office of Rt Hon. Neil Kinnock, MP, 1981–92; Chief Exec., Quality Public Affairs, 1992–97. Mem. (Lab) Hackney LBC, 1980–86. Parly Under-Sec. of State, DfEE, 1998–99; Minister of State, Home Office, 1999–2001; Minister without Portfolio and Chm., Labour Party, 2001–02; Sec. of State for Educn and Skills, 2002–04, for the Home Dept, 2004–06. Mem., Treasury Select Cttee, 1997–98. *Recreations:* chess, reading, walking. *Address:* House of Commons, SW1A 0AA. *T:* (020) 7219 3000. *Club:* Norwich Labour.

CLARKE, Christopher Alan; Member, since 2001, a Deputy Chairman, since 2004, Competition Commission; *b* 14 May 1945; *s* of late Harry Alston Clarke and of Isobel Corsan Clarke (*née* Kay); *m* 1978, Charlotte Jenkins; one *s* one *d. Educ:* Oakham Sch.; Selwyn Coll., Cambridge (BA Econs 1967, MA); London Business Sch. (MSc/MBA 1972). With Shell Internat. Petroleum Co. Ltd, 1967–73; IDJ Ltd, 1973–74; Man. Dir, Arbuthnot Latham Asia Ltd, 1979–82; Arbuthnot Latham & Co. Ltd, 1974–82 (Dir, 1978–82); Director: Samuel Montagu & Co. Ltd, 1982–96; HSBC Investment Banking, 1996–98. Non-executive Director: Weir Gp, 1999–; Omega Underwriting Hldgs, 2005–. *Recreations:* golf, fishing, books. *Address:* Competition Commission, Victoria House, Southampton Row, WC1B 4AD. *Club:* Berkshire Golf.

See also Rt Hon. Sir A. P. Clarke.

CLARKE, Sir Chris(topher James), Kt 2005; OBE 2000; business and communications consultant; Chairman, South Gloucestershire Primary Care Trust, since 2006; Managing Director, Word on the Street Ltd, since 2006; *b* 24 March 1941; *s* of Thomas Edward Clarke and Theresa Margaret Clarke (*née* Kiernan); *m* 1st, 1964, Sheila Ann Ridgway (marr. diss. 1995); one *s* one *d*; 2nd, 2006, Elizabeth Boait. *Educ:* Westcliff-on-Sea Grammar Sch.; City of London Coll. Commercial apprentice, 1959–62, mkt res. exec., 1962–65, Rank Orgn; retail merchandise and mktg manager, G. J. Keddie & Sons, 1965–71; retail consultant, then sen. consultant, then gen. manager, C. & J. Clark Ltd, 1971–90; business journalist, then business consultant, later implementation manager: self-employed, 1990–2005; with Improvement and Develt Agency, 2005–. Mem. Council, Arts Council England SW, 2005–. Member (Lib Dem): Richmondshire (N Yorks) DC, 1983–84; Somerset CC, 1985–2005 (Leader, 1993–2001); Mendip DC, 1991–95 (Leader, 1992–93); founder Chm., SW Regl Assembly, 1998–2000. Lib Dem Dep. Leader, 1999–2001, Lib Dem Leader and Dep. Chm., 2001–05, LGA. Member: Inst. Business Counsellors, 1992–; Inst. Journalists, 1991–. FRSA 2006. *Recreations:* cycling, swimming, reading, music, arts. *Address:* Old School House, Tibberton, Glos GL19 3AQ. *T:* (01452) 790369; *e-mail:* chrisclarke001@tesco.net.

CLARKE, (Christopher) Michael; Director, National Gallery of Scotland, since 2001; *b* 29 Aug. 1952; *s* of Patrick Reginald Clarke and Margaret Catherine Clarke (*née* Waugh); *m* 1978, Deborah Clare Cowling; two *s* one *d. Educ:* Felsted; Manchester Univ. (BA (Hons) History of Art). Art Asst, York City Art Gall., 1973–76; Res. Asst, British Mus., 1976–78; Asst Keeper in Charge of Prints, Whitworth Art Gall., Manchester Univ., 1978–84; Asst Keeper, 1984–87, Keeper, 1987–2000, Nat. Gall. of Scotland. Vis. Fellow: Yale Center for British Art, 1985; Clark Art Inst., 2004. Chevalier, Ordre des Arts et des Lettres (France), 2004. *Publications:* Pollaiuolo to Picasso: Old Master prints in the Whitworth Art Gallery, 1980; The Tempting Prospect: a social history of English watercolours, 1981; (ed with N. Penny) The Arrogant Connoisseur: Richard Payne Knight, 1982; The Draughtsman's Art: Master Drawings in the Whitworth Art Gallery, 1983; Lighting up the Landscape: French Impressionism and its origins, 1986; Corot and the Art of Landscape, 1991; Eyewitness Art: watercolour, 1993; (ed jtly) Corot, Courbet und die Maler von Barbizon, 1996; Oxford Concise Dictionary of Art Terms, 2001; The Playfair Project, 2004; articles, reviews, etc, in Apollo, Art Internat., Burlington Magazine, Museums Jl. *Recreations:* golf, travel, cycling slowly. *Address:* c/o National Gallery of Scotland, Edinburgh EH2 2EL. *Club:* Royal and Ancient (St Andrews).

CLARKE, Hon. Sir Christopher (Simon Courtenay Stephenson), Kt 2005; **Hon. Mr Justice Christopher Clarke;** a Judge of the High Court of Justice, Queen's Bench Division, since 2005; *b* 14 March 1947; *s* of late Rev. John Stephenson Clarke and S of Enid Courtenay Clarke; *m* 1974, Caroline Anne Fletcher; one *s* two *d. Educ:* Marlborough College; Gonville and Caius College, Cambridge (MA). Called to the Bar, Middle Temple, 1969, Bencher, 1991; Attorney of Supreme Court of Turks and Caicos Islands, 1975; QC 1984; a Recorder, 1990–2004; a Deputy High Ct Judge, 1993–2004; a Judge of the Cts of Appeal of Jersey and Guernsey, 1998–2004. Counsel to Bloody Sunday Inquiry, 1998–2004. Councillor, Internat. Bar Assoc., 1988–90; Chm., Commercial Bar Assoc., 1993–95; Mem., Bar Council, 1993–99. FRSA 1995. *Address:* Royal Courts of Justice, Strand, WC2A 2LL. *Clubs:* Brooks's, Hurlingham.

CLARKE, Darren Christopher; professional golfer, since 1990; *b* 14 Aug. 1968; *m* Heather (*d* 2006); two *s.* Amateur wins include: Spanish, Irish, N of Ireland and S of Ireland Championships, 1990; has played on European Tour, 1991–, PGA Tour, 2005–; wins include: Alfred Dunhill Open, 1993; Benson and Hedges Internat., Volvo Masters, 1998; Compass Gp Eur. Open, 1999; Compass Gp English Open, 1999, 2000, 2002; World Golf Championships (WGC) Accenture Match Play, 2000 (first European to win a WGC event); Smurfit Eur. Open, Chunichi Crowns, Japan, 2001; WGC NEC-Invitational, NI Masters, 2003; Mitsui Sumitomo VISA Taiheijo Masters, Japan, 2004, 2005; Member: Alfred Dunhill Cup team, 1994, 1995, 1996, 1997, 1998, 1999; World Cup team, 1994, 1995, 1996; Ryder Cup team, 1997, 1999, 2002, 2004, 2006; Seve Trophy team, 2000, 2002; Royal Trophy team, 2007. Founder, Darren Clarke Foundn,

2002. *Publications:* The Mind Factor, 2005; Darren Clarke: my Ryder Cup story, 2006. *Recreations:* films, reading, cars, fishing, Liverpool FC. *Address:* c/o ISM Ltd, Cherry Tree Farm, Cherry Tree Lane, Rostherne, Cheshire WA14 3RZ. *T:* (01565) 832100, *Fax:* (01565) 832200; *e-mail:* ism@sportism.net.

CLARKE, Hon. Sir David (Clive), Kt 2003; **Hon. Mr Justice David Clarke;** a Judge of the High Court of Justice, Queen's Bench Division, since 2003; a Presiding Judge, Northern Circuit, since 2006; *b* 16 July 1942; *s* of Philip George Clarke and José Margaret Clarke; *m* 1969, Alison Claire, *d* of Rt Rev. Percy James Brazier; two *s* (and one *s* decd). *Educ:* Winchester Coll.; Magdalene Coll., Cambridge (BA 1964, MA 1968). Called to the Bar, Inner Temple, 1965, Bencher, 1992; in practice, Northern Circuit, 1965–93 (Treas., 1988–92); a Recorder, 1981–93; QC 1983; a Circuit Judge, 1993–97; a Sen. Circuit Judge, and Hon. Recorder of Liverpool, 1997–2003. Mem., Criminal Justice Consultative Council, 1999–2003. Chm., Merseyside Area Criminal Justice Strategy Cttee, 1997–2003. Hon. Fellow, Liverpool John Moores Univ., 2007. Hon. LLD Liverpool, 2004. *Recreations:* walking, sailing, swimming, canals. *Address:* Royal Courts of Justice, Strand, WC2A 2LL. *Club:* Trearddur Bay Sailing (Anglesey).

CLARKE, David Stuart, AO 1992; Chairman: Macquarie Group (formerly Macquarie Bank) Ltd, since 2007 (Executive Chairman, 1985–2007); Goodman International Ltd (formerly Macquarie Goodman Group), since 2000; Australian Vintage (formerly Brian McGuigan Wines, then McGuigan Simeon Wines) Ltd, since 1991; *b* 3 Jan. 1942; *s* of Stuart Richardson Clarke and Ailsie Jean Talbot Clarke; *m* 1st, 1964, Margaret Maclean Partridge (marr. diss. 1994); two *s*; 2nd, 1995, Jane Graves. *Educ:* Knox Grammar Sch.; Sydney Univ. (BEcon Hons); Harvard Univ. (MBA). Hill Samuel Australia Ltd: Jt Man. Dir, 1971–77; Man. Dir, 1977–84; Exec. Chm., 1984–85; Director: Darling & Co. Ltd (now Schroder Australia Ltd), 1966–71; Babcock Aust. Holdings Ltd, 1972–81; Chairman: Accepting Houses Assoc. of Aust., 1974–76; Sceggs Darlinghurst Ltd, 1976–78; Barlile Corp. Ltd, 1986–93; Goodman Fielder Ltd, 1995–2000; Director: Hill Samuel & Co. Ltd (London), 1978–84; Hooker Corp. Ltd, 1984–86; Reil Corp. Ltd, 1986–87. Member: Lloyds of London, 1983–97; Fed. Govt Cttee under Financial Corporations Act, 1975–85; Exec. Cttee, Cttee for Econ. Devlt of Australia, 1982–98; Affiliate, Aust. Stock Exch. Ltd, 1987–2004. Mem. Adv. Bd, Bloomberg Asia Pacific, 2006–. Chairman: Australian Opera, 1986–95; Aust. Wool Realisation Commn, 1991–93. Member: Council, Royal Agricl Soc. of NSW, 1986– (Chm., Wine Cttee, 1990–); Harvard Business Sch. Alumni Council, 1986–89; Investment Adv. Cttee, Australian Olympic Foundn, 1996–; Stage II Project, Nat. Inst. for Dramatic Art, 1996–2003; Asia Adv. Cttee, Harvard Business Sch., 1997–; Seoul Internat. Business Adv. Council, 2003–; Corporate Governance Cttee, Aust. Inst. of Co. Dirs, 2005–. Hon. Fed. Treas., Liberal Party of Aust., 1987–89. Member: Bd Trustees, Financial Markets Foundn for Children, 1989–2000 (Hon. Life Mem.); Sydney Adv. Bd, Salvation Army, 1990–2006 (Chm., 1999–2006); Corporate Citizens Cttee, Children's Cancer Inst. of Australia, 1992–; Chairman: Salvation Army Red Shield Appeal, 1990–92 (Cttee Mem., 1985–88; Dep. Chm., 1989–90); Menzies Res. Centre, 1994–97; George Gregan Foundn, 2005–; Nat. Leadership Council, Social Ventures Australia; Campaign Chm., (NSW), Salvation Army Educn Foundn, 1996–98; Dir, Clayton Utz Foundn Pty Ltd, 2003–; Advocate, Macfarlane Burnet Centre for Med. Res., 1999–. Gov., Aust. Ireland Fund, 1998–. Mem., Cook Soc., 1979– (Co-Convener, 1988–97). President: Nat. Council, Opera Australia, 1996–2000 (Chm., Opera Australia Capital Fund, 1996–); Winemakers' Fedn of Australia, 2007–. Chairman: NSW Rugby Union, 1989–95 (Treas., 1989); Australian Rugby Union, 1998–2001 (Dir, 1990–97; Dep. Chm., 1997–98); Council Rep., Mem. Games Regulation Cttee and Mem. Bd Policy Cttee, Internat. Rugby Bd, 1998–2001; Vice-Pres., Sydney Univ. CC, 2000–; Chm., Sydney Univ. FC Foundn, 2003–. Chm., Business Club Australia Beijing, 2008, Australian Trade Commn. Confrère des Chevaliers du Tastevin. Hon. DScEcon Sydney, 2000. Centenary Medal, Aust., 2001; Richard Pratt Business Leadership Award, Australia Business Arts Foundn, 2006. *Recreations:* opera, skiing, golf, bridge, philately, ballet, wine. *Clubs:* Australian, Harvard of Australia (Pres. 1977–79), Royal Sydney Golf, Elanora Country, Cabbage Tree, Vintage Golf (Sydney).

CLARKE, Prof. David William, DPhil; FRS 1998; FREng, FIET; Professor of Control Engineering, Oxford University, since 1992; Fellow, New College, Oxford, since 1969; *b* 31 May 1943; *s* of Norman William Clarke and Laura (*née* Dewhurst); *m* 1967, Lynda Ann Weatherhead; two *s*. *Educ:* Balliol Coll., Oxford. MA, DPhil Oxon. FIET (FIEE 1984); FREng (FEng 1989). Oxford University: Astor Res. Fellow, New Coll., 1966–69; Lectr, 1969–86; Reader in Information Engrg, 1986–92; Hd, Dept of Engrg Sci., 1994–99. Dir, Invensys UTC for Advanced Instrumentation. Sir Harold Hartley Silver Medal, Inst. of Measurement and Control, 1983. *Publications:* Advances in Model-Based Predictive Control, 1994; papers in learned jls. *Recreation:* gardening. *Address:* New College, Oxford OX1 3BN. *T:* (01865) 279507.

CLARKE, Donald Roberts; Finance Director, 3i (formerly Investors in Industry) Group plc, 1988–91; *b* 14 May 1933; *s* of Harold Leslie Clarke and Mary Clarke; *m* 1959, Susan Charlotte Cotton; one *s* three *d*. *Educ:* Ealing Grammar Sch.; The Queen's Coll., Oxford (MA). Articled Peat Marwick Mitchell & Co., 1957–62; Accountant, The Collingwood Group, 1962–64; Industrial and Commercial Finance Corporation: Investigating Accountant, 1964; Controller, 1964–67; Br. Manager, 1967–68; Co. Sec., 1968–73; Investors in Industry Gp (formerly Finance for Industry): Sec./Treasurer, 1973–76; Asst Gen. Manager, 1976–79; Gen. Manager, Finance, 1979–88. Dir, Consumers' Assoc. Ltd, 1990–92. Member: UGC, 1982–85; Industrial, Commercial and Prof. Liaison Gp, National Adv. Body for Local Authority Higher Educn, 1983–85; Continuing Educn Standing Cttee, Nat. Adv. Body for Local Authority Higher Educn and UGC, 1985–89; Council, Royal Holloway, Univ. of London (formerly RHBNC), 1987–2002 (Hon. Fellow, 2005). Trustee, Hestercombe Gardens Trust, 2001–. *Publication:* (jtly) 3i: 50 years investing in industry, 1995. *Recreations:* music, gardening, photography. *Club:* Oxford and Cambridge.

CLARKE, Most Rev. E(dwin) Kent, DD; *b* 21 Jan. 1932. *Educ:* Bishop's Univ., Lennoxville (BA 1954, LST 1956); Union Seminary, NY (MRE 1960); Huron Coll., Ontario (DD). Deacon 1956, priest 1957, Ottawa. Curate of All Saints, Westboro, 1956–59; Director of Christian Education, Diocese of Ottawa, 1960–66; Rector of St Lambert, Montreal, 1966–73; Diocesan Sec., Diocese of Niagara, 1973–76; Archdeacon of Niagara, 1973–76; Bishop Suffragan of Niagara, 1976–79; Bishop of Edmonton, 1980; Archbishop of Edmonton and Metropolitan of Rupert's Land, 1986–87. *Address:* RR3 Stn Main, Pembroke, ON K8A 6W4, Canada.

CLARKE, Elaine Denise; *see* Watson, E. D.

CLARKE, Sir Ellis (Emmanuel Innocent), TC 1969; GCMG 1972 (CMG 1960); Kt 1963 (but does not use the title within Republic of Trinidad and Tobago); President of Trinidad and Tobago, 1976–86 (Governor General and C-in-C, 1973–76); *b* 28 Dec. 1917; *o c* of late Cecil Clarke and Elma Clarke; *m* 1952, Eyrmyntrude (*née* Hagley) (*d* 2002); one *s* one *d*. *Educ:* St Mary's Coll., Trinidad (Jerningham Gold Medal, 1936, and other prizes); London Univ. (LLB 1940). Called to the Bar, Gray's Inn, 1940. Private practice at Bar of Trinidad and Tobago, 1941–54; Solicitor-Gen., Oct. 1954; Dep. Colonial Sec., Dec. 1956; Attorney-Gen., 1957–62; Actg Governor, 1960; Chief Justice designate, 1961; Trinidad and Tobago Perm. Rep. to UN, 1962–66; Ambassador: to United States, 1962–73; to Mexico, 1966–73; Rep. on Council of OAS, 1967–73. Chm. of Bd, British West Indian Airways, 1968–72. KStJ 1973. *Address:* (office) 16 Frederick Street, Port of Spain, Trinidad, West Indies. *T:* 6272150. *Clubs:* Queen's Park Cricket (Port of Spain); Trinidad Turf, Arima Race (Trinidad); Tobago Golf (President, 1969–75).

CLARKE, Prof. Eric Fillenz, PhD; Heather Professor of Music, University of Oxford, since 2007; *b* 31 July 1955; *s* of John Clarke and Marianne (*née* Fillenz); *m* Catherine Ferreira; one *s* one *d*. *Educ:* Univ. of Sussex (BA Music 1977, MA Music 1978); Univ. of Exeter (PhD Psychol. 1984). Lectr, 1981–88, Sen. Lectr, 1988–91, Reader, 1991–93, in Music, City Univ., London; James Rossiter Hoyle Prof. of Music, Univ. of Sheffield, 1993–2007. *Publications:* Empirical Musicology (ed with Nicholas Cook), 2004; Ways of Listening, 2005; contrib. numerous papers to jls of Music Perception, Psychology of Music, Musicae Scientiae, Music Analysis, Popular Music. *Recreations:* cycling, doing up old bikes, gardening, walking, playing music with friends. *Address:* Music Faculty, University of Oxford, St Aldate's, Oxford OX1 1DB. *T:* (01865) 276125, *Fax:* (01865) 276128; *e-mail:* eric.clarke@music.ox.ac.uk.

CLARKE, Eric Lionel; *b* 9 April 1933; *s* of late Ernest and Annie Clarke; *m* 1955, June Hewat; two *s* one *d*. *Educ:* St Cuthbert's Holy Cross Acad.; W. M. Ramsey Tech. Coll.; Esk Valley Tech. Coll. Coalminer: Roslin Colliery, 1949–51; Lingerwood Colliery, 1951–69; Bilston Glen Colliery, 1969–77; Trade Union Official, 1977–89; Gen. Sec., NUM Scotland; redundant, unemployed, 1989–92. Mem., Midlothian CC and then Lothian Regl Council, 1962–78. MP (Lab) Midlothian, 1992–2001. An Opposition Whip, 1994–97. *Recreations:* fly fishing, gardening, carpentry, football spectator. *Address:* 32 Mortonhall Park Crescent, Edinburgh EH17 8SY. *T:* (0131) 664 8214. *Clubs:* Mayfield Labour; Morris Working Men's; Danderhall Miners' Welfare.

CLARKE, Frederick, BSc; FBCS; Director: DS Information Systems, since 1991; DS Group Holdings Ltd; *b* 8 Dec. 1928; *s* of George and Edna Clarke; *m* 1955, Doris Thompson (marr. diss. 1987); two *d*; *m* 1988, Dorothy Sugrue. *Educ:* King James I Grammar Sch., Bishop Auckland; King's Coll., Durham Univ. (BSc 1951). FBCS 1972. Served RAF, 1951–54. Schoolmaster, 1954–57; IBM, 1957–82 (final appts, Gen. Manager and Dir); Chm., Royal Ordnance plc (formerly Royal Ordnance Factories), 1982–85. Chm., Lingfield Park Racecourse, 1988–90; Dir, Leisure Investments, 1985–90. Freeman, City of London, 1987. *Recreations:* golf, cricket, racing, reading. *Address:* Arran, Bute Avenue, Petersham, Richmond, Surrey TW10 7AX.

CLARKE, Garth Martin; Chief Executive, Transport Research Laboratory, 1997–2001; *b* 1 Feb. 1944; *s* of Peter Oakley Clarke and Ella Audrey (*née* Jenner); *m* 1966, Carol Marian Trimble; three *d*. *Educ:* Duke's Grammar Sch., Alnwick, Northumberland; Liverpool Univ. (BSc Hons). FIHT 1996. Research Physicist, 1966–73, Ops Dir, 1983–87, Plessey Research (Caswell) Ltd; Dir, Commercial Ops, Plessey Res. and Technology Ltd, 1987–89; Business Devélt Dir, Business Systems Gp, GPT Ltd, 1990–93; Business Dir, TRL, 1993–97. Chief Exec., Transport Res. Foundn, 1997–2001; Chm., Viridis, 1999–2001. Dir, Parly Adv. Council for Transport Safety, 2001–05. Fellow, Transport Res. Foundn, 1998. CCMI. *Recreations:* birdwatching, water colour painting, photography.

CLARKE, Geoffrey, RA 1976 (ARA 1970); ARCA; artist and sculptor; *b* 28 Nov. 1924; *s* of John Moulding Clarke and Janet Petts; two *s*. *Educ:* Royal College of Art (Hons). Exhibitions: Gimpel Fils Gallery, 1952, 1955; Redfern Gallery, 1965; Taranman Gallery, 1975, 1976, 1982; Yorkshire Sculpture Park, Chappel Gall., Colchester, and Friends Room, Royal Acad., 1994; Fine Art Soc., 2000, 2006; touring exhibitions: Christchurch Mansions, Ipswich, 1994; Herbert Art Gall., Coventry, and Pallant House, Chichester, 1995; Bury St Edmunds Art Gall., 2003; Derby Mus. and Art Gall., 2004. Works in public collections: Victoria and Albert Museum; Tate Gallery; Arts Council; Museum of Modern Art, NY; BM; Leeds Art Gall.; etc. Prizes for engraving: Triennial, 1951; London, 1953, Tokyo, 1957. Commissioned work includes: mosaics, Liverpool Univ. Physics Block; stained glass windows for Treasury, Lincoln Cathedral; bronze sculpture, Thorn Electric Building, Upper St Martin's Lane; 3 stained glass windows, high altar, cross and candlesticks, the flying cross and crown of thorns, all in Coventry Cathedral; sculpture, Nottingham Civic Theatre; UKAEA Culham; Univs of Liverpool, Exeter, Cambridge, Manchester, Loughborough and Warwick; screens in Royal Military Chapel, Birdcage Walk. Further work at Chichester, Newcastle, Manchester, Plymouth, Ipswich, Taunton, Winchester, St Paul, Minnesota, Lincoln, Nebraska, Newcastle Civic Centre, Leicester, Churchill Coll., Aldershot, Suffolk Police HQ, All Souls, W1, The Majlis, Abu Dhabi, York House, N1.

CLARKE, Giles Colin Scott, PhD; museums and heritage consultant; Head, Department of Exhibitions and Education, Natural History Museum, 1994–2001; *b* 9 Jan. 1944; *s* of Colin Richard Clarke and Vera Joan, (Georgie), Clarke (*née* Scott); *m* 1967, Helen Parker (*see* Helen Clarke); one *s*. *Educ:* Sevenoaks Sch.; Keble Coll., Oxford (MA 1970); Birmingham Univ. (PhD 1970). VSO, Gambia, 1963; Mem., Internat. Biological Prog. Bipolar Expeditions, 1967–68; Asst Keeper of Botany, Manchester Mus., 1970–73; Head, Pollen Section, 1973–79, Dep. Head, Dept of Public Services, 1979–94, British Mus. (Natural History), later Natural History Mus. Member: Council, British Bryological Soc., 1971–2001 (Pres., 1998–99; Hon. Mem., 2005); Cttee, Wildlife Photographer of the Year, 1984–2001; Cttee, Trends in Leisure and Entertainment Conf. and Exhibn, 1993–2005 (Chair, 1998). Trustee, Eureka! Children's Mus., 1999–. FLS 1971; FMA 1996; FRSA 1997. *Publications:* numerous papers in prof. jls on botany and museums. *Recreations:* opera, organ music, art galleries, reading, making things. *Address:* Kynance, Clarence Road, Tunbridge Wells, Kent TN1 1HE.

CLARKE, Graham Neil; Chairman, Hamdene Horticultural Publishing Services Ltd, since 2006; *b* 23 July 1956; *s* of late Henry Charles Owen Clarke, RVM and Doris May Clarke; *m* 1980, Denise Carole (*née* Anderson); two *d*. *Educ:* Rutherford Sch., N London; Wisley School of Horticulture (WisCertHort). Staff gardener, Buckingham Palace, 1975–76; Nurseryman, Hyde Park, 1976; Amateur Gardening: Sub-Editor, 1976–79; Chief Sub-Editor, 1979–81; Dep. Editor, 1981–86; Editor, 1986–98; Editor, Home Plus Magazine, 1984–85; IPC gardening titles: Gp Editor, 1993–95; Special Projects Editor, 1995–98; Editor-at-Large, 1998–99; Editor: Exotic & Greenhouse Gardening, 2000–01; Garden Calendar, 2000–01; Devélt Ed., 1999–2001, Man. Ed., 2000–02, Guild of Master Craftsman Pubns; Editor: Water Gardening, 1999–2002; Business Matters, 2002–03; Guild News, 2003–04, 2007–; Horticulture Week, 2004–05; publishing and horticulture consultant, 2002–04 and 2005–06. FLS 1990; MIHort 1995 (AIHort 1991). *Publications:* Step by Step Pruning, 1985; Autumn and Winter Colour in the Garden, 1986; Complete Book of Plant Propagation, 1990; The Ultimate House Plant Handbook, 1997; Beginner's Guide to Water Gardening, 2002; Collins Practical Guide: Water Gardening, 2004; Collins Practical Guide: Pruning, 2005; Success with Roses, 2007; Success with Shade-Loving Plants, 2007; Success with Sun-Loving Plants, 2007; Success with Water Gardens,

2007; Success with Water-Saving Gardens, 2007; Success with Acid-Loving Plants, 2008; Success with Alkaline-Loving Plants, 2008; The Organic Gardener's Year, 2008. *Recreations:* writing, genealogy, philately, gardening. *Address:* Hamdene Horticultural Publishing Services Ltd, Hamdene House, 127 Magna Road, Bournemouth, Dorset BH11 9NE. *Club:* Royal Horticultural Society Garden (Surrey).

CLARKE, Gregory; Chief Executive Officer, Lend Lease Corporation, since 2002; *b* 27 Oct. 1957; *s* of George and Mary Clarke; *m* 1984, Anne Wilson; four *d*. *Educ:* Gateway Grammar Sch., Leicester; Wolverhampton Poly (BA Hons 1980); City Univ. Business Sch. (MBA 1983). Vice Pres., Global Cellular, Nortel, 1992–95; Chief Exec., Cable & Wireless Mobile, 1995–97; Chief Operating Officer, 1997–99, Chief Exec., 1999–2000, Cable & Wireless Communications plc; CEO, ICO Teledisc, 2000–02. Chm., Eteach UK Ltd, 2000–02; non-executive Director: BUPA Ltd, 2001–07; Leicester City plc, 2002–07. *Recreations:* family, Leicester City FC, opera, Rugby, reading. *Address:* Lend Lease Corporation, Level 4, 30 The Bond, 30 Hickson Road, Millers Point, Sydney, NSW 2000, Australia.

CLARKE, Dr Helen, FSA; Director, Society of Antiquaries, 1990–94; *b* 25 Aug. 1939; *d* of George Parker and Helen (*née* Teare); *m* 1967, Giles Colin Scott Clarke, *qv*; one *s*. *Educ:* Univ. of Birmingham (BA; PhD); Univ. of Lund, Sweden. FSA 1972. Dir of Excavations, King's Lynn, 1963–67; Res. Fellow, Sch. of History, Birmingham Univ., 1965–67; Lecturer in Medieval Archaeology: Glasgow Univ., 1967–69; UCL, 1976–90. Visiting Professor in Medieval Archaeology: Lund Univ., Sweden, 1991; Århus Univ., Denmark, 1992; Kiel Univ., Germany, 1993. Editor and Translator: Royal Swedish Acad. of History and Antiquities, 1975–; Bd of National Antiquities, Sweden (also Consultant), 1990–95; Consultant, English Heritage, 1987–94. Trustee, Council for British Archaeol., 2004–07. Member: Svenska Arkeologiska Samfundet, 1988; Vetenskapssocieten i Lund, 1988. Hon. Fil Dr Lund, 1991. *Publications:* Regional Archaeologies: East Anglia, 1971; Excavations in King's Lynn, 1963–1970, 1977; The Archaeology of Medieval England, 1984, 2nd edn 1986; Towns in the Viking Age, 1991, 2nd edn 1995. *Recreations:* attending opera, watching cricket, looking at the landscape.

CLARKE, Henry Benwell; Board Member, Rail Estate Consultancy, since 1998; *b* 30 Jan. 1950; *yr s* of late Stephen Lampard Clarke and Elinor Wade Clarke (*née* Benwell); *m* 1973, Verena Angela Lodge; four *s* one *d*. *Educ:* St John's Sch., Leatherhead; South Bank Polytechnic (BSc Estate Management 1972); Imperial College London (MSc Management Science 1977; DIC 1977). ARICS 1973, FRICS 1986; ACIArb 1979. British Rail Property Board: S Region, 1972–78; NW Region, 1978–82; E Region, 1982–85; Regional Estate Surveyor and Manager, Midland Region, 1985–86; Chief Estate Surveyor, HQ, 1986–87; Nat. Develt Manager, 1987–88; Dep. Chief Exec., Crown Estate Comrs, 1988–92, Acting Chief Exec. and Accounting Officer, 1989. Mem., Gen. Council, British Property Fedn, 1989–92. Member, Board: People and Places Internat., 1993–2004; Telecom Property Ltd, 1999–; Crownmead Properties Ltd, 2001–; Kings Yard Developments, 2003–04; Intelligent Business Space Ltd, 2004–; The Model Bus Co., 2006–; Jackson Green Ltd, 2006–. Mem. Council, Christian Union for Estate Profession, 1983–88; Member, Board: Youth with a Mission (England), 1990–; Mercy Ships (UK), 1995–; Moggerhanger House Preservation Trust, 1997–2005; Railway Children Trust, 2002–; advisor to various Christian trusts. *Recreations:* reading, walking, transport, architecture, Church. *Address:* 42 Wordsworth Road, Harpenden, Herts AL5 4AF.

CLARKE, (James) Brian; author and journalist; Fishing Correspondent, The Times, since 1991; *b* 28 May 1938; *s* of Thomas Clarke and Annette Clarke (*née* Vickers); *m* 1968, (Edith Isobel) Anne Farley; three *d*. *Educ:* St Mary's Grammar Sch., Darlington; Darlington Tech. Coll. Reporter and sub-ed., Northern Echo, Darlington, 1955–59; Dep. Features Ed., Evening Gazette, Middlesbrough, 1959–61; home news sub-ed., Scottish Daily Mail, Edinburgh, 1961–62; home news and Parly sub-ed., The Guardian, 1962–67; Nat. Press Officer, IBM UK, 1967–68; Public Affairs Advr, Nat. Computing Centre, 1968–69; indep. mgt consultant, 1969–74; various corporate communications and envmtl mgt posts, IBM UK, 1974–91 (on secondment to BBC, 1988–90: series producer, In the Name of the Law (television), 1988–89; Consultant, BBC Bd of Mgt, 1989–90); consultant, envmtl progs, IBM UK, 1990–91; Fishing Corresp., Sunday Times, 1975–96. Pres., Wild Trout Trust, 2003–. *Publications:* The Pursuit of Stillwater Trout, 1975, 7th edn 2001; (contrib.) The Masters on the Nymph (US), 1976; (contrib.) Stillwater Trout Fisheries, 1976; (contrib.) The Complete Salmon and Trout Fisherman, 1978; The Trout and the Fly, 1980, 7th edn 2005; (contrib.) West Country Fly Fishing, 1983; (contrib.) The Fly-Fishers, 1984; (contrib.) The One That Got Away, 1991; Flyfishing for Trout (US), 1993; Trout etcetera: selected writings 1982–1996, 1996; (contrib.) Lessons from the Fish, 1996; (contrib.) Trout and Salmon, 1999; (contrib.) Fly-Fishers' Progress, 2000; The Stream (novel), 2000 (BP Natural World Book Prize, 2000; Authors' Club Best First Novel Award, 2000); Understanding Trout Behaviour (US), 2002; (contrib.) The World of Fly-Fishing, 2003; (contrib.) The Literary Non-Fiction Collection, 2005; On Fishing: journalism and essays 1996–2007, 2007. *Recreations:* fishing, walking, photography, sitting still in the countryside watching and listening. *Address:* c/o Watson, Little Ltd, Capo di Monte, Windmill Hill, NW3 6RJ. *Clubs:* Arts (Hon. Mem.), Flyfishers.

CLARKE, Jane; Head of Communications, Kent County Council, since 2008; *d* of Michael David Hilborne-Clarke and Margaret Lythell; one *d* by Howard Austin Trevette. *Educ:* Norwich High Sch. for Girls; University College London (BA Hons English Lang. and Lit. 1975); Slade Sch. of Fine Art. Film Programmer, BFI, 1980–82; Features Prod., TV-am, 1982–88: Ed., Henry Kelly Saturday Show, 1984–85; Features Ed., Good Morning Britain, 1985–87; Ed., After Nine, 1987–88; Independent Prod., Pithers, Clarke and Ferguson, 1988–89 (prod., Children First, 1989); Series Ed., New Living for British Satellite Broadcasting, 1990–91; Controller, Features, West Country TV, 1992–95; Dep. Dir, BFI, 1995–97; Chief Exec., BAFTA, 1998; Foreign and Commonwealth Office: Head: Broadcast and Allied Media, subseq. TV and Radio, Public Diplomacy Dept, 1999–2002; Strategy and Progs, then Strategy and Campaigns, Public Diplomacy Team, 2002–05; Internal Communications, 2005–06; Hd of Communications, Sport England, 2006–08. Bd Mem., London Fest. of Literature, 2000–01. *Publication:* Move Over Misconceptions: Doris Day reappraised, 1981. *Recreations:* football, air rifle shooting, reading, music. *Address:* c/o Kent County Council, County Hall, Maidstone, Kent ME14 1XQ.

CLARKE, Prof. John, FRS 1986; Professor of Physics, since 1973, and Luis W. Alvarez Memorial Chair for Experimental Physics, since 1994, University of California, Berkeley; *b* 10 Feb. 1942; *s* of Victor Patrick and Ethel May Clarke; *m* 1979, Grethe F. Pedersen; one *d*. *Educ:* Christ's Coll., Cambridge (BA, MA 1968; Hon. Fellow, 1997); Darwin Coll., Cambridge (PhD 1968; ScD 2003). Postdoctoral Scholar, 1968, Asst Prof., 1969, Associate Prof., 1971–73, Univ. of California, Berkeley. Alfred P. Sloan Foundn Fellow, 1970; Adolph C. and Mary Sprague Miller Inst. for Basic Research into Science Prof., 1975, 1994; John Simon Guggenheim Fellow, 1977; Vis. Fellow, Clare Hall, Cambridge, 1989; By-Fellow, Churchill Coll., Cambridge, 1998; Faculty Res. Lectr, Univ. of California,

Berkeley, 2005. For. Mem., Royal Soc. of Arts and Scis, Sweden. FAAAS 1982; Fellow, Amer. Phys. Soc., 1985; FInstP 1999. Charles Vernon Boys Prize, Inst. of Physics, 1977; Calif. Scientist of the Year, 1987; Fritz London Meml Award for Low Temperature Physics, 1987; Joseph F. Keithley Award, APS, 1998; Comstock Prize for Physics, NAS, 1999; IEEE Council on Superconductivity Award, 2002; Scientific American 50 Award, 2002; Lounasmaa Prize, Finnish Acad. of Arts and Scis, 2004; Hughes Medal, Royal Soc., 2004. *Publications:* numerous contribs to learned jls. *Address:* Department of Physics, University of California, Berkeley, CA 94720–7300, USA. *T:* (510) 6423069.

CLARKE, John Francis; Chief Executive, Welsh European Funding Office, National Assembly for Wales, 2000–03; *b* 10 June 1947; *s* of Francis William Clarke and Joan Margaret Clarke; *m* 1969, Lynda Mary Hudson; three *s*. *Educ:* Windermere Grammar Sch.; Manchester Univ. (BA Hons). ACIB. Sen. Vice Pres., Barclays USA, 1984–86; Barclays: Corporate Finance Dir, 1986–91; Regl Dir, 1991–99. Chm., Greater Nottingham TEC, 1997–98; Mem., East Midlands Regl IDB, 1992–97. Chairman: The Stables Theatre, Wavendon, 1977–91; St Donats Arts Centre Ltd, 2006–. Pres., Llantwit Major Rotary Club, 2002–03 (Mem., 1999–); Vice-Pres., Cardiff Business Club, 1998–. Mem., Audit Cttee, Univ. of Wales Inst., Cardiff, 2006–; Gov., Llantwit Major Comprehensive Sch., 2005–. *Recreations:* golf, gardening, philately. *Address:* The Old Vicarage, St Donats, Llantwit Major, Vale of Glamorgan CF61 1ZB. *T:* (01446) 793180. *Club:* Cottrell Park Golf.

CLARKE, Prof. John Frederick, FRS 1987; Professor of Theoretical Gas Dynamics, Cranfield Institute of Technology, 1972–91, Professor Emeritus, since 1992; *b* 1 May 1927; *s* of Frederick William Clarke and Clara Auguste Antonie (*née* Nauen); *m* 1953, Jean Ruth Gentle; two *d*. *Educ:* Warwick School; Queen Mary Coll., Univ. of London (BSc Eng 1st Cl. Hons, David Allan Low Prize, PhD; Hon. Fellow, 1992). FIMA 1965; FRAeS 1969; FInstP 1999. Qualified Service Pilot, RN, 1946–48; Aerodynamicist, English Electric Co., 1956–57; Lectr, Coll. of Aeronautics, 1958–65 (Vis. Associate Prof. and Fulbright Scholar, Stanford Univ., 1961–62); Reader, Cranfield Inst. of Technology, 1965–72. Vis. Prof. at univs in USA, Australia and Europe; Vis. Res. Fellow, Centre for Non-linear Studies, Univ. of Leeds, 1987–; Benjamin Meaker Vis. Prof., Univ. of Bristol, 1988–89; first G. C. Steward Vis. Fellow, Gonville and Caius Coll., Cambridge, 1992. Member: NATO Collaborative Research Grants Panel, 1987–90; Esso Energy Award Cttee, 1988–93; Maths Cttee, SERC, 1990–91. Member, Editorial Board: Qly Jl Mech. Appl. Math., 1982–2003; Combustion Theory & Modelling, 1997–2003; Philosophical Trans A, Royal Soc., 1997–2002. *Publications:* (with M. McChesney) The Dynamics of Real Gases, 1964; (with M. McChesney) Dynamics of Relaxing Gases, 1976; contribs to professional jls on gas dynamics and combustion theory. *Recreation:* Sunday painter. *Address:* Field House, Green Lane, Aspley Guise MK17 8EN. *T:* (01908) 582234.

CLARKE, Prof. John Innes, OBE 2003; DL; Chairman, NE Regional Awards Committee, National Lottery Charities Board, 1997–2002; *b* 7 Jan. 1929; *s* of late Bernard Griffith Clarke and Edith Louie (*née* Mott); *m* 1955, Dorothy Anne Watkinson (*d* 2008); three *d*. *Educ:* Bournemouth Sch.; Univ. of Aberdeen (MA 1st cl., PhD); Univ. of Paris (French Govt scholar). FRGS 1963. RAF 1952–54 (Sword of Merit, 1953). Asst Lectr in Geog., Univ. of Aberdeen, 1954–55; Prof. of Geog., Univ. Coll. of Sierra Leone, 1963–65; University of Durham: Lectr in Geog., 1955–63; Reader in Geog., 1965–68; Prof. of Geog., 1968–90, now Emeritus; Acting Principal, Trevelyan Coll., 1979–80; Pro-Vice-Chancellor and Sub-Warden, 1984–90; Leverhulme Emeritus Fellow, 1990–92. Visiting Professor: Univ. of Wisconsin, 1967–68; Cameroon, 1965, 1966, 1967; Clermont-Ferrand, 1974; Cairo, 1982; Shanghai, 1986. Acting Chm., Human Geog. Cttee, SSRC, 1975; RGS rep. on British Nat. Cttee for Geography, 1976–81, 1988–89; Chairman: IGU Commn on Population Geography, 1980–88; Higher Educn Support for Industry in the North, 1987–89; Cttee on Population and Environment, Internat. Union for Scientific Study of Population, 1990–95; Durham, then N Durham DHA, 1990–96. Bd Mem., Co. Durham Foundn, 1995–. Vice-President: Eugenics Soc., 1981–84; RGS, 1991–95. DL Durham, 1990. FRSA 1990. Silver Medal, RSGS, 1947; Victoria Medal, RGS, 1991. *Publications:* Iranian City of Shiraz, 1963; (jtly) Africa and the Islands, 1964, 4th edn 1977; Population Geography, 1965, 2nd edn 1972; (with B. D. Clark) Kermanshah: an Iranian Provincial City, 1969; Population Geography and the Developing Countries, 1971; (jtly) People in Britain: a census atlas, 1980; The Future of Population, 1997; The Human Dichotomy, 2000; *edited:* Sierra Leone in Maps, 1966, 2nd edn 1969; An Advanced Geography of Africa, 1975; Geography and Population: approaches and applications, 1984; *co-edited:* Field Studies in Libya, 1960; Populations of the Middle East and North Africa: a geographical approach, 1972; Human Geography in France and Britain, 1976; Régions Géographiques et Régions d'Aménagements, 1978; Change and Development in the Middle East, 1981; Redistribution of Population in Africa, 1982; Population and Development Projects in Africa, 1985; Population and Disaster, 1989; Mountain Population Pressure, 1990; Environment and Population Change, 1994; Population-Environment-Development Interactions, 1995; Population and Environment in Arid Regions, 1997; Arid Land Resources and their Management, 1998; author of many learned articles. *Recreations:* travel, sports (now vicariously), countryside, family history. *Address:* Tower Cottage, The Avenue, Durham DH1 4EB. *T:* (0191) 384 8350.

CLARKE, Very Rev. John Martin; Dean of Wells, since 2004; *b* 20 Feb. 1952; *s* of Roland Ernest Clarke and Edna Lucy Hay; *m* 1985, Constance Elizabeth Cressida Nash; two *s* one *d*. *Educ:* West Buckland Sch.; Hertford Coll., Oxford (MA); Edinburgh Theol Coll. (BD). Ordained deacon, 1976, priest, 1977; Asst Curate, The Ascension, Kenton, Newcastle, 1976–79; Precentor, St Ninian's Cathedral, Perth, 1979–82; Information Officer and Communications Advr to the Gen. Synod of the Scottish Episcopal Church, 1982–87; Philip Usher Scholarship, Greece, 1987–88; Vicar, St Mary, Battersea, 1989–96; Principal, Ripon Coll., Cuddesdon, 1997–2004; Canon and Preb., Lincoln Cathedral, 2000–04. *Recreations:* walking, reading, music, cricket. *Address:* The Dean's Lodging, 25 The Liberty, Wells, Somerset BA5 2SZ.

CLARKE, (John) Neil; Chairman, British Coal, 1991–97; *b* 7 Aug. 1934; *s* of late George Philip Clarke and Norah Marie Clarke (*née* Bailey); *m* 1958, Sonia Heather Beckett; three *s*. *Educ:* Rugby School; King's College London (LLB). FICA 1959. Partner, Rowley, Pemberton, Roberts & Co., 1960–69; Charter Consolidated, 1969–88: Dir, 1973; Exec. Dir, 1974; Man. Dir, 1979; Chief Exec., 1980; Dep. Chm. and Chief Exec., 1982–88; Chairman: Johnson Matthey, 1984–89; Molins, 1989–91 (Dir, 1987–91); Genchem Holdings, 1989–2006; Director: Anglo American Corp. of SA, 1976–90; Consolidated Gold Fields, 1982–89; Travis Perkins, 1990–2002. Chm., ESCP-EAP, London, 1986–2006. Trustee, King George VI and Queen Elizabeth Foundn of St Catharine's, 1974–. Chevalier, Ordre Nat. du Mérite (France), 2002. *Recreations:* music, tennis, golf. *Address:* High Willows, 18 Park Avenue, Farnborough Park, Orpington, Kent BR6 8LL. *T:* (01689) 851651. *Clubs:* MCC; Royal West Norfolk Golf, Addington Golf.

CLARKE, Rear-Adm. John Patrick, CB 1996; LVO 1986; MBE 1978; Chief Executive, British Marine Federation, 2001–06; Hydrographer of the Navy and Chief Executive, United Kingdom Hydrographic Office (formerly Hydrographic Agency),

1996–2001; *b* 12 Dec. 1944; *s* of Frank and Christine Clarke; *m* 1st, 1969, Ann Parham (marr. diss. 1997); one *s* two *d*; 2nd, 1998, Mrs Jeffy J. Salt. *Educ:* Epsom Coll.; BRNC. Commanding Officer, HM Ships: Finwhale, 1976; Oberon, 1977; Dreadnought, 1979–80; CO, Submarine CO's Qualifying Course, 1983–84; Exec. Officer, HM Yacht Britannia, 1985–86; Captain: Submarine Sea Training, 1986–89; Seventh Frigate Squadron, 1989–90; Asst Dir, Naval Staff Duties, 1990–92; Dir, Naval Warfare, 1992; Dir, Naval Management, Communications and Inf. Systems, 1993–94; Flag Officer Trng and Recruiting, 1994–96. Younger Brother, Trinity House, 1997. FCMI. Hon. Mem., RICS. *Recreations:* golf, sailing. *Address:* c/o British Marine Federation, Marine House, Thorpe Lea Road, Egham, Surrey TW20 8BF. *Clubs:* Lansdowne; Liphook Golf; Royal Yacht Squadron.

CLARKE, Most Rev. John Robert; *see* Athabasca, Archbishop of.

CLARKE, His Honour Sir Jonathan (Dennis), Kt 1981; a Circuit Judge, 1982–93; *b* 19 Jan. 1930; *e s* of late Dennis Robert Clarke, Master of Supreme Court, and of Caroline Alice (*née* Hill); *m* 1956, Susan Margaret Elizabeth (*née* Ashworth); one *s* three *d*. *Educ:* Kidstones Sch.; University Coll. London. Admitted Solicitor, 1956; partner in Townsends, solicitors, 1959–82; a Recorder of the Crown Court, 1972–82. Mem. Council, Law Soc., 1964–82, Pres., 1980–81; Sec., Nat. Cttee of Young Solicitors, 1962–64; Member: Matrimonial Causes Rule Cttee, 1967–78; Legal Studies Bd, CNAA, 1968–75; Judicial Studies Bd, 1979–82; Criminal Injuries Compensation Bd, 1993–2004; Criminal Injuries Compensation Appeals Panel, 1996–2004. Governor, College of Law, 1970–90, Chm. of Governors, 1982. *Recreations:* sailing, ski-ing. *Address:* c/o HSBC, The Forum, Marlborough Road, Swindon, Wilts SN3 1QT. *Clubs:* Garrick, Farmers'; Royal Western Yacht.

CLARKE, Rt Hon. Kenneth Harry; PC 1984; QC 1980; MP (C) Rushcliffe, since 1970; *b* 2 July 1940; *e c* of Kenneth Clarke and Doris (*née* Smith), Nottingham; *m* 1964, Gillian Mary Edwards; one *s* one *d*. *Educ:* Nottingham High Sch.; Gonville and Caius Coll., Cambridge (BA, LLB; Hon. Fellow, 1997). Chm., Cambridge Univ. Conservative Assoc., 1961; Pres., Cambridge Union, 1963; Chm., Fedn Conservative Students, 1963. Called to Bar, Gray's Inn 1963, Hon. Bencher, 1989, Bencher, 1998; Mem., Midland Circuit. Director: Independent News & Media (UK) Ltd, 1999–; Independent News & Media plc. Research Sec., Birmingham Bow Group, 1965–66. Contested Mansfield, 1964 and 1966. PPS to Solicitor General, 1971–72; an Asst Govt Whip, 1972–74 (Govt Whip for Europe, 1973–74); a Lord Comr, HM Treasury, 1974; Parly Sec., DoT, later Parly Under Sec. of State for Transport, 1979–82; Minister of State (Minister for Health), DHSS, 1982–85; entered Cabinet as Paymaster General and Minister for Employment, 1985–87; Chancellor of Duchy of Lancaster and Minister for Trade and Industry (with additl responsibility to co-ordinate Govt policy on Inner Cities), 1987–88; Secretary of State: for Health, 1988–90; for Educn and Science, 1990–92; for the Home Dept, 1992–93; Chancellor of the Exchequer, 1993–97. Mem., Parly delegn to Council of Europe and WEU, 1973–74; Sec., Cons. Parly Health and Social Security Cttee, 1974; Opposition Spokesman on: Social Services, 1974–76; Industry, 1976–79. Liveryman, Clockmakers' Co., 2001–. Hon. LLD: Nottingham, 1989; Huddersfield, 1993; DUniv Nottingham Trent, 1996. *Publications:* New Hope for the Regions, 1969; pamphlets published by Bow Group, 1964–. *Recreations:* modern jazz music; watching Association Football and cricket, bird-watching. *Address:* House of Commons, SW1A 0AA. *Clubs:* Garrick; Nottinghamshire CC (Pres., 2002–04).

CLARKE, Rt Rev. Kenneth Herbert; *see* Kilmore, Elphin and Ardagh, Bishop of.

CLARKE, Prof. Malcolm Alistair, PhD; Professor of Commercial Contract Law, Cambridge University, since 1999; Fellow, St John's College, Cambridge, since 1970; *b* 1 April 1943; *s* of Kenneth Alfred William Clarke and Marian Florence Clarke (*née* Rich); *m* 1968, Eva Olga Bergman; two *s*. *Educ:* Kingswood Sch., Bath; L'Ecole des Roches, Verneuil-sur-Avre, France; St John's Coll., Cambridge (LLB 1965; MA 1968; PhD 1973). Asst, Institut de Droit Comparé, Paris, 1965–66; Research Fellow, Fitzwilliam Coll., Cambridge, 1966–68; Lectr, Univ. of Singapore, 1968–70; Cambridge University: Asst Lectr in Law, 1970–75; Lectr, 1975–93; Reader in Commercial Contract Law, 1993–99; Dir of Studies, St John's Coll., Cambridge, 1972–92. *Publications:* Aspects of the Hague Rules, 1976; (jtly) Shipbuilding Contracts, 1981, 2nd edn 1992; The International Carriage of Goods by Road: CMR, 1982, 4th edn 2003; The Law of Insurance Contracts, 1989, 5th edn 2006, and bi-annually, 1999–; Policies and Perceptions of Insurance, 1997; Contracts of Carriage by Air, 2002; (jtly) Butterworths Law of Contract, 2nd edn 2003, 3rd edn pt 4 2007; Contracts of Carriage by Land and Air, 2004; Policies and Perceptions of Insurance in the Twenty-First Century, 2005. *Recreations:* cycling, music, photography, more or less concurrently. *Address:* St John's College, Cambridge CB2 1TP. *T:* (01223) 338600, *Fax:* (01223) 337720.

CLARKE, Prof. Malcolm Roy, FRS 1981; Senior Principal Scientific Officer, Marine Biological Association of the UK, 1978–87; *b* 24 Oct. 1930; *s* of Cecil Dutfield Clarke and Edith Ellen Woodward; *m* 1958, Dorothy Clara Knight; three *s* one *d*. *Educ:* eleven schools and finally Wallingford County Grammar Sch.; Hull Univ. BSc 1955, PhD 1958, DSc 1978. National Service, Private, RAMC, 1949–50. Teacher, 1951; Hull Univ., 1951–58; Whaling Inspector in Antarctic, 1955–56; Scientific Officer, later PSO, Nat. Inst. of Oceanography, 1958–71; led Oceanographic Expedns on RRS Discovery, RRS Challenger, RRS Frederick Russell and RV Sarsia; PSO, Marine Biol Assoc. of UK, 1972–78. Visiting Professor: in Zoology, Liverpool Univ., 1987–2003; in Marine Biol., Azores Univ., 1994–. Involved in construction and curation of Cochalotes and Lulas mus. (private museum on sperm whales and squids), São João, 2003–. *Publications:* (ed jtly) Deep Oceans, 1971; Identification of Cephalopod Beaks, 1986; (ed jtly) Evolution, vol. 10, The Mollusca, 1986, vol. 11, Form and Function, 1987, vol. 12, Palaeontology and Neontology of the Cephalopoda, 1987; (ed jtly) Identification of "Larval" Cephalopods, 1987; (ed jtly) Cephalopod Diversity, Ecology and Evolution, 1998; papers on squids and whales in Jl of Marine Biol Assoc., Nature etc, and a Discovery Report, 1980. *Recreations:* boating, painting, wood carving, writing. *Address:* Rua do Porto 18, São João, 9960 Lajes do Pico, Azores, Portugal.

CLARKE, Mark Galbraith, FCA; Director General, Finance and Strategy, Department for Business, Enterprise and Regulatory Reform (formerly Department of Trade and Industry), since 2006; *b* 19 June 1953; *s* of Sir Richard William Barnes Clarke, KCB, OBE and Brenda Clarke; *m* 1982, Dr Alexandra Macleod; one *s* two *d*. *Educ:* Jesus Coll., Oxford (MA PPE). Arthur Andersen & Co., 1975–82; TSB Gp plc, 1982–89; Coopers & Lybrand, then PricewaterhouseCoopers, mgt consultants, 1989–2000; Barclays plc, 2000–03; Abbey National plc, 2003–05; Bank of Ireland, 2005–06. Mem., Exchequer Funds Audit Cttee, HM Treasury, 2007–. Gov., Highgate Sch., 2007–.

CLARKE, Prof. Martin Lowther; *b* 2 Oct. 1909; *s* of late Rev. William Kemp Lowther Clarke; *m* 1942, Emilie de Rontenay Moon (*d* 1991), *d* of late Dr R. O. Moon; two *s*. *Educ:* Haileybury Coll.; King's Coll., Cambridge. Asst, Dept of Humanity, Edinburgh Univ., 1933–34; Fellow of King's Coll., Cambridge, 1934–40; Asst Lecturer in Greek and Latin, University Coll., London, 1935–37. Foreign Office, 1940–45. Lecturer, 1946–47, and Reader, 1947–48, in Greek and Latin, University Coll., London; Prof. of Latin, University Coll. of North Wales, 1948–74, Vice-Principal, 1963–65, 1967–74. *Publications:* Richard Porson, 1937; Greek Studies in England, 1700 to 1830, 1945; Rhetoric at Rome, 1953; The Roman Mind, 1956; Classical Education in Britain, 1500–1900, 1959; George Grote, 1962; Bangor Cathedral, 1969; Higher Education in the Ancient World, 1971; Paley, 1974; The Noblest Roman, 1981. *Address:* 61 Ilges Lane, Cholsey, Wallingford OX10 9PA. *T:* (01491) 651389.

CLARKE, Martin Peter; Associate Editor, The Daily Mail, since 2005; *b* 26 Aug. 1964; *s* of Robert William Clarke and Doris May (*née* Snowden); *m* 1998, Veronica (*née* Gilfedder); one *s*. *Educ:* Gravesend Grammar Sch. for Boys; Bristol Univ. (BA Hons). Daily Mail Executive, 1988–94; News Ed., Daily Mirror, 1995; Editor: Scottish Daily Mail, 1995–97; The Scotsman, 1997–98; Editor-in-Chief: Daily Record and Sunday Mail Ltd, 1998–2000; Ireland on Sunday, 2001–04; Exec. Ed., Mail on Sunday, 2004–05. *Address:* The Daily Mail, Northcliffe House, 2 Derry Street, W8 5TS. *T:* (020) 7938 6000.

CLARKE, Mary; Editor, Dancing Times, 1963–2008, now Emeritus; *b* 23 Aug. 1923; *d* of Frederick Clarke and Ethel Kate (*née* Reynolds); unmarried. *Educ:* Mary Datchelor Girls' School. London Corresp., Dance Magazine, NY, 1943–55; London Editor, Dance News, NY, 1955–70; Asst Editor and Contributor, Ballet Annual, 1952–63; joined Dancing Times as Asst Editor, 1954. Dance critic, The Guardian, 1977–94, retired. Queen Elizabeth II Coronation Award, Royal Acad. of Dancing, 1990; Nijinsky Medal, Poland, 1996. Kt, Order of Dannebrog (Denmark), 1992. *Publications:* The Sadler's Wells Ballet: a history and an appreciation, 1955; Six Great Dancers, 1957; Dancers of Mercury: the story of Ballet Rambert, 1962; ed (with David Vaughan) Encyclopedia of Dance and Ballet, 1977; (with Clement Crisp): Ballet, an Illustrated History, 1973, 2nd edn 1992; Making a Ballet, 1974; Introducing Ballet, 1976; Design for Ballet, 1978; Ballet in Art, 1978; The History of Dance, 1981; Dancer, Men in Dance, 1984; Ballerina, 1987; contrib. Encycl. Britannica, Oxford DNB. *Address:* 54 Ripplevale Grove, N1 1HT. *T:* (020) 7607 3422. *Club:* Gautier.

CLARKE, Matthew Gerard; *see* Clarke, Hon. Lord.

CLARKE, Michael; *see* Clarke, C. M.

CLARKE, Prof. Michael, CBE 2003; FRCP, FRCPE, FFPH, FMedSci; Professor of Epidemiology, University of Leicester, 1981–2002; Hon. Consultant, Leicestershire Health, 1974–2002; *b* 2 Nov. 1940; *s* of late Leslie Frederick Clarke and Gertrude Mary Clarke (*née* Dring); *m* 1966, Susan Jenkins Thompson (marr. diss. 1994); one *s* one *d*. *Educ:* Middlesex Hosp. Med. Sch., Univ. of London (MB BS 1965). MRCS, LRCP 1965; DPH 1968; MFPHM 1974, FFPH (FFPHM 1979); FRCP 1991; FRCPE 1996. Lectr, St Thomas' Hosp., London, 1968–74; Vis. Scientist, R&D, Nat. Centre for Health Services, 1972–73; Sen. Lectr, Dept of Community Health, Univ. of Leicester, 1974–80. Dir, Trent Inst. for Health Services Res., 1993–2002. Member: MRC Public Health & Health Services Res. Bd, 1990–94; Chair, Strategic Review of the NHS R&D Levy, 1998–2000. Vice Pres., FPHM, 1995–2000. FMedSci 2002. *Publications:* articles on epidemiology and health services res., particularly in relation to reproduction, care of the elderly and urinary incontinence. *Recreations:* cooking, interior design. *Address:* 106 Albert Dock, 17 New Wharf Road, N1 9RB.

CLARKE, Canon Prof. Michael Gilbert, CBE 2000; DL; Professor, School of Public Policy, 1993–2008, now Emeritus, Pro-Vice-Chancellor, 1998–2003, and Vice-Principal, 2003–08, University of Birmingham; *b* 21 May 1944; *s* of Rev. Canon Reginald Gilbert Clarke and Marjorie Kathleen Clarke; *m* 1967, Angela Mary Cook; one *s* two *d*. *Educ:* Queen Elizabeth Grammar Sch., Wakefield; Sussex Univ. (BA 1966; MA 1967). Teaching Assistant, Essex Univ., 1967–69; Lectr and Dir of Studies in Politics, Edinburgh Univ., 1969–75; Asst Dir and Depute Dir, Policy Planning, Lothian Regl Council, 1975–81; Dir, LGTB, 1981–90; Chief Exec., Local Govt Mgt Bd, 1990–93; Head, Sch. of Public Policy, Univ. of Birmingham, 1993–98. Member: Council, Queen's Foundn, Birmingham, 1997–; W Midlands Regl Assembly, 1999–. Chairman: Worcs Partnership Bd, 2002–; Visit Worcester, 2006–; West Midlands Regl Marketing Bd, 2008–; Dir, Govt Office for W Midlands, 2003–. Chm., Central Technology Belt, 2003–. Trustee: Worcs Community Foundn, 2004–; Elgar Foundn, 2008–; Barber Inst., 2008–; Pres., Herefordshire and Worcs Community First, 2005–; Governor: King's Sch., Worcester, 2006–; Univ. of Worcester, 2007–. Mem., Gen. Synod of C of E, 1990–93, 1995–; Lay Canon and Mem. Chapter, Worcester Cathedral, 2001–. DL Worcs, 2000. *Publications:* Getting the Balance Right, 1990; Choices for Local Government: the 1990s and beyond, 1991; How Others See Us, 1995; Breaking Down the Barriers, 1995; Renewing Public Management, 1996; articles on UK public policy and management issues esp. local govt and central-local relns. *Recreations:* reading, grandchildren, gardening. *Address:* Millington House, 15 Lansdowne Crescent, Worcester WR3 8JE. *T:* (01905) 617634. *Club:* Reform.

CLARKE, Maj.-Gen. Michael Hugo Friend; Immigration Appeals Adjudicator, 1993–2004; *b* 22 Sept. 1936; *s* of Patrick Joseph Clarke and Catherine Amy Clarke (*née* Friend); *m* 1962, Gerritje van der Horst; one *s* one *d*. *Educ:* Rutland House Sch.; Allhallows Sch. Called to the Bar, Lincoln's Inn, 1959; enlisted RASC, 1959; commissioned 2nd Lieut RASC, 1960; Captain, Army Legal Services, 1961; served BAOR, Singapore, Nairobi, Hong Kong, Cyprus, N Ireland; HQ Army Legal Aid, 1981; MoD, 1983; Army Legal Aid, BAOR, 1986; Army Legal Group UK, 1987; Brig., Legal HQ BAOR, 1989; Dir, Army Legal Services, 1992–94. Trustee, Inst. of Obs and Gyn., 1995–2003. *Recreations:* gardening, walking, sport.

CLARKE, Neil; *see* Clarke, J. N.

CLARKE, Nicholas Stephen; QC 2006; a Recorder, since 2000; *b* Rochdale, 30 Dec. 1959; *s* of Thomas Clarke and Marjorie Clarke; *m* 1986, Gillian Mary Slator; one *s* one *d*. *Educ:* Sheffield Univ. (LLB Hons 1980). Called to the Bar, Middle Temple, 1981; Asst Recorder, 1999–2000. *Recreations:* keeping marine fish, growing orchids, playing golf and snooker, Chairman of 3rd Hazel Grove Scout Group, Manchester United season ticket holder. *Address:* 9 St John Street, Manchester M3 4DN. *T:* (0161) 955 9000, *Fax:* (0161) 955 9001; *e-mail:* clerks@9stjohnstreet.co.uk. *Club:* Disley Golf.

CLARKE, Nicky, OBE 2007; hair stylist; Co-Founder and Co-Director, Nicky Clarke Salon, Mayfair, and Nicky Clarke Haircare Products; *b* 17 June 1958; *m* 1982, Lesley Anne Gale; one *s* one *d*. Director: Southern Tropics Ltd; Nicky Clarke Products Ltd. Has made numerous TV appearances as expert and spokesperson on matters related to hair. Numerous awards, including: British Hairdresser of Year Award; London Hairdresser of Year Award. *Publications:* Hair Power, 1999; contribs to newspapers and magazines, incl. Vogue, Tatler, Marie Claire and Harpers Bazaar. *Recreations:* ski-ing, water ski-ing, contemporary music. *Address:* 130 Mount Street, W1K 3NY. *T:* (020) 7491 4700.

CLARKE, Prof. Patricia Hannah, DSc; FRS 1976; Emeritus Professor, University of London, since 1984; *b* 29 July 1919; *d* of David Samuel Green and Daisy Lilian Amy

Willoughby; *m* 1940, Michael Clarke; two *s*. *Educ:* Howells Sch., Llandaff; Girton Coll., Cambridge (BA). DSc London. Armament Res. Dept, 1940–44; Wellcome Res. Labs, 1944–47; National Collection of Type Cultures, 1951–53; University College London: Lectr, Dept of Biochemistry, 1953; Reader in Microbial Biochemistry, 1966; Prof. of Microbial Biochemistry, 1974–84; Hon. Fellow, 1995. Leverhulme Emer. Fellow, 1984–87; Hon. Professorial Fellow, UWIST, Univ. of Wales, 1984–90; Kan Tong-Po Prof., Chinese Univ. of Hong Kong, 1986. Chm., Inst. for Biotechnological Studies, 1986–87. Hon. Gen. Sec., Soc. for General Microbiology, 1965–70 (Hon. Mem., 1996); Mem., CNAA, 1973–79. Gov., Cirencester Deer Park Comprehensive Sch., 1988–99. Lectures: Royal Soc. Leeuwenhoek, 1979; Marjory Stephenson, Soc. for Gen. Microbiology, 1981; A. J. Kluyver, Netherlands Soc. for Microbiology, 1981. A Vice-Pres., Royal Soc., 1981–82. Hon. DSc: Kent, 1984; CNAA, 1990. *Publications:* Genetics and Biochemistry of Pseudomonas (ed with M. H. Richmond), 1975; papers on genetics, biochemistry and enzyme evolution in Jl of Gen. Microbiol. and other jls. *Recreations:* walking, gardening, travelling. *Address:* 7 Corinium Gate, Cirencester, Glos GL7 2PX.

CLARKE, Paul Robert Virgo, FRICS; Chief Executive, Clerk of the Council, Keeper of the Records and Surveyor General, Duchy of Lancaster, since 2000; *b* 13 Aug. 1953; *s* of Robert Charles Houghton Clarke and Joan Clarke (*née* Stanton); *m* 1978, Vanessa Carol Pike; two *d*. *Educ:* Abingdon Sch.; W London Coll. FRICS 1988. Valuation Surveyor and Tech. Asst to Exec. Trustee, Grosvenor Estate, 1974–82; Equity Partner, Clarke & Green, Chartered Surveyors, 1982–96; Property Investment Manager, Wellcome Trust, 1996–2000. Property Adv. Mem., Greenwich Hosp. Adv. Panel, 2002–; Chm., Adv. Panel, ING UK Property Income Fund. *Recreations:* ski-ing, walking, horse riding, painting, travel. *Address:* Duchy of Lancaster Office, 1 Lancaster Place, Strand, WC2E 7ED. *T:* (020) 7269 1700.

CLARKE, Peter, CBE 1983; PhD; CChem, FRSC; Principal, Robert Gordon's Institute of Technology, Aberdeen, 1970–85, retired; Chairman, Scottish Vocational Education Council, 1985–91; *b* 18 March 1922; *er s* of Frederick John and Gladys May Clarke; *m* 1947, Ethel Jones; two *s*. *Educ:* Queen Elizabeth's Grammar Sch., Mansfield; University Coll., Nottingham (BSc). Industrial Chemist, 1942; Sen. Chemistry Master, Buxton Coll., 1947; Lectr, Huddersfield Technl Coll., 1949; British Enka Ltd, Liverpool, 1956; Sen. Lectr, Royal Coll. of Advanced Tech., Salford, 1962; Head of Dept of Chemistry and Biology, Nottingham Regional Coll. of Technology, 1963; Vice-Principal, Huddersfield Coll. of Technology, 1965–70. Member: SERC (formerly SRC), 1978–82; Council for Professions Supplementary to Medicine, 1977–85; Scottish Technical Educn Council, 1982–85; CNAA, 1982–87 (Chm., Cttee for Scotland, 1983). Chm., Assoc. of Principals of Colleges (Scotland), 1976–78; President: Assoc. of Principals of Colleges, 1980–81; Assoc. for Educnl and Trng Technol., 1993–95. Chairman: Aberdeen Enterprise Trust, 1984–92; Industrial Trng Centre Aberdeen Ltd, 1989–95; Gordon Cook Foundn, 1997–99 (Trustee, 1989–2005). Burgess of Guild, City of Aberdeen, 1973. Hon. LLD Aberdeen, 1985; Hon. DEd: CNAA, 1992; Robert Gordon, 1999. *Recreation:* walking. *Address:* 108 Whinhill Gate, Aberdeen AB11 7WF.

CLARKE, Prof. Peter Frederick, LittD; FBA 1989; Master of Trinity Hall, Cambridge, 2000–04 (Hon. Fellow, 2005); Professor of Modern British History, Cambridge University, 1991–2004; *b* 21 July 1942; *s* of late John William Clarke and Winifred Clarke (*née* Hadfield); *m* 1st, 1969, Dillon Cheetham (marr. diss. 1990); two *d*; 2nd, 1991, Dr Maria Tippett, FRS(Can), British Columbia. *Educ:* Eastbourne Grammar Sch.; St John's Coll., Cambridge (BA 1963; MA 1967; PhD 1967; LittD 1989). FRHistS 1972. Asst Lectr and Lectr in History, 1966–78, Reader in Modern Hist., 1978–80, UCL; Cambridge University: Fellow, St John's Coll., 1980–2000 (Tutor, 1982–87); Lectr in History, 1980–87; Reader in Modern History, 1987–91; Sec., Faculty Bd of Hist., 1985–86. Vis. Prof. of Modern British Hist., Harvard Univ., 1974; Vis. Fellow, Res. Sch. of Social Scis, ANU, 1983. Creighton Lectr, London Univ., 1998; Ford's Lectr, Univ. of Oxford, 2002. Member: Council, RHistS, 1979–83; Adv. Council on Public Records, 1995–2000; Royal Commn on Historical MSS, 2000–03; Adv. Council on Nat. Records and Archives, 2003–05. Chm., S Cambs Area Party, SDP, 1981–82. Jt Review Ed., History, 1967–73; Chm., Editl Bd, Twentieth Century British History, 1988–98. *Publications:* Lancashire and the New Liberalism, 1971, 2nd edn 1993; Liberals and Social Democrats, 1978, 3rd edn 1993; The Keynesian Revolution in the Making, 1988, 2nd edn 1990; A Question of Leadership: from Gladstone to Thatcher, 1991, 2nd edn 1992, new edn, from Gladstone to Blair, 1999; Hope and Glory: Britain 1900–1990, 1996, 2nd edn as Hope and Glory: Britain 1900–2000, 2004; The Keynesian Revolution and its Economic Consequences, 1998; The Cripps Version: the life of Sir Stafford Cripps, 2002; The Last Thousand Days of the British Empire, 2007; articles in learned jls; contribs to TLS, London Rev. of Books, etc. *Recreations:* walking, cooking. *Address:* Brick Cottage, Back Lane, Kettlebaston, Suffolk IP7 7QA; PO Box 100, Pender Island, BC V0N 2M0, Canada. *Clubs:* Royal Over-Seas League; Union (Victoria, BC).

CLARKE, Peter Henry, FRICS; Member of the Lands Tribunal, part time, 1993–96, full time, 1996–2005; *b* 22 Sept. 1935; *s* of late Henry George Clarke and Winifred Eva Clarke (*née* Sharp); *m* 1964, May Connell; one *d*. *Educ:* Ealing Technical Coll.; Coll. of Estate Management; LLB 1972, MPhil 1993, London. ARICS 1957, FRICS 1973; ACIArb 1976. With G. L. Hearn & Partners, 1952–57, 1959–60; Cubitt Estates, 1960–64; Eldonwall Ltd, 1964–69; Donaldsons, 1969–96 (Partner, 1972–96). *Publications:* (jtly) Land Values, 1965; (jtly) Valuation: Principles into Practice, 1980, 5th edn 2000; The Surveyor in Court, 1985; articles on compensation and rent reviews in various jls. *Recreations:* music, opera, reading, walking, dogs. *Address:* 65 Brittains Lane, Sevenoaks, Kent TN13 2JS. *T:* (01732) 456437.

CLARKE, Peter James, CBE 1993; Secretary of the Forestry Commission, 1976–94, retired; *b* 16 Jan. 1934; *s* of Stanley Ernest Clarke and Elsie May (*née* Scales); *m* 1966, Roberta Anne, *y d* of Robert and Ada Browne; one *s* one *d*. *Educ:* Enfield Grammar Sch.; St John's Coll., Cambridge (MA). Exec. Officer, WO, 1952–62 (univ., 1957–60), Higher Exec. Officer, 1962; Sen. Exec. Officer, Forestry Commn, 1967, Principal 1972; Principal, Dept of Energy, 1975. *Recreations:* gardening, walking, travel. *Address:* 5 Murrayfield Gardens, Edinburgh EH12 6DG. *T:* (0131) 337 3145.

CLARKE, Peter John Michael, CVO 2001; OBE 2006; QPM 2002; Deputy Assistant Commissioner, Head of Anti-Terrorist Branch and National Co-ordinator of Terrorist Investigations, Metropolitan Police, 2002–08; *b* Epsom, Surrey, 27 July 1955; *s* of Ernest John Wallace Clarke and Doris Louisa Emma Clarke (*née* Wakeham); *m* 1983, Deborah Ann Bazalgette; two *s* one *d*. *Educ:* Glyn Grammar Sch., Epsom; Univ. of Bristol (LLB Hons 1977); Cabinet Office Top Mgt Prog., 1998. Joined Metropolitan Police, 1977; Inspector, 1984–89; Chief Inspector, 1989–92; Superintendent, 1992–94; Staff Officer to Comr, 1993–94; Divl Comdr, Brixton Div., 1994–96; Comdr, Royalty and Diplomatic Protection Dept, 1997–2000; Dep. Asst Comr, HR, 2001; rcds 2002. Fellow, Center for Law and Security, NY Univ., 2008–. Pres., Metropolitan and City Police Relief Bd, 1997–2008. Chm., Metropolitan Police Cricket Club, 2002–08. Hon. LLD Bristol, 2008. *Recreations:* watching cricket, walking, cycling. *Address:* e-mail: peterjmclarke@aol.com. *Clubs:* Special Forces, MCC.

CLARKE, Peter William; QC 1997; a Recorder, since 1991; *b* 29 May 1950; *s* of His Honour Edward Clarke, QC, and Dorothy May Clarke (*née* Leask); *m* 1978, Victoria Mary, *d* of Michael Francis Gilbert, CBE, TD; one *s* one *d*. *Educ:* Sherborne Sch.; Inns of Court Sch. of Law. Called to the Bar, Lincoln's Inn, 1973, Bencher, 2003; in practice at the Bar, specialising in criminal law, 1974–; Asst Recorder, 1987–91. *Recreations:* losing at tennis to my children, ski-ing, golf (winner, Bar golfing tournament, 1985), digital photography, enjoying my wife's paintings. *Address:* 3rd Floor, Queen Elizabeth Building, Temple, EC4Y 9BS. *T:* (020) 7583 5766. *Club:* Garrick.

CLARKE, Rachel Emma; *see* Cusk, R. E.

CLARKE, Richard Ian; HM Diplomatic Service; High Commissioner to Tanzania, 2001–03; *b* 7 Sept. 1955; *s* of Sydney Thomas Reginald Clarke and Joan Clarke; *m* 1st, 1978, Anne Elizabeth Menzies (marr. diss. 1993); one *s*; 2nd, 1993, Sheenagh Marie O'Connor; two *s* one *d*. *Educ:* Market Harborough Upper Sch.; Univ. of E Anglia (BSc). Joined FCO, 1977: 3rd, later 2nd, Sec., Caracas, 1978–83; 2nd, later 1st, Sec., FCO, 1983–87; 1st Sec., Washington, 1987–91; Asst Hd, Planning Staff, FCO, 1991–93; Dep. Hd, UN Dept, FCO, 1993–96; Counsellor and Dep. Hd of Mission, Dublin, 1996–98; Hd, Policy Planning Staff, FCO, 1998–2001. Ian St James Award for short fiction, 1991. *Publication:* (contrib.) Midnight Oil, 1991. *Recreations:* Leicester City, reading, Wars of the Roses, American Civil War, Glamrock, crisps, early 20th century art.

CLARKE, Most Rev. Richard Lionel; *see* Meath and Kildare, Bishop of.

CLARKE, Sir Robert (Cyril), Kt 1993; Chairman, Thames Water Plc, 1994–99 (non-executive Director, since 1988); *b* 28 March 1929; *s* of Robert Henry Clarke and Rose Lilian (*née* Bratton); *m* 1952, Evelyn (Lynne) Mary, *d* of Cyrus Harper and Ann Ellen (*née* Jones); three *s* (incl. twin *s*) one *d*. *Educ:* Dulwich Coll.; Pembroke Coll., Oxford (MA Hist.; Hon. Fellow, 1993). Served Royal West Kent Regt, 1947–49. Joined Cadbury Bros, as trainee, 1952; Gen. Manager, John Forrest, 1954; Marketing Dir, Cadbury Confectionery, 1957; Man. Dir, 1962–69, Chm., 1969–71, Cadbury Cakes; Dir, Cadbury Schweppes Foods, 1969–71; Man. Dir, McVitie & Cadbury Cakes, 1971–74; Dir, 1974–95, Chm. and Man. Dir, 1984–95, United Biscuits UK Ltd; Man. Dir, UB Biscuits, 1977–84; Dir, 1984–95, Gp Chief Exec., 1986–90, Chm., 1990–95, United Biscuits (Holdings). Member: Council, Cake and Biscuit Alliance, 1965–83; Council, ISBA, 1977–84; Resources Cttee, Food and Drink Fedn, 1984–86; Bd of Dirs, Grocery Manufrs of America, 1991–95. Gov., World Economic Forum, 1990–. Special Trustee, Gt Ormond St Hosp. for Children NHS Trust, 1991–99 (Chm., Special Trustees, 1994–99; non-exec. Mem., Trust Bd, 1994–99). Fellow, Dulwich Coll., 2003. Hon. Fellow, Inst. of Child Health, 1997. FIGD; CCMI. *Recreations:* reading, walking, renovating old buildings, planting trees.

CLARKE, Rev. Robert Sydney, OBE 2000; Secretary and Director of Training, Hospital Chaplaincies Council, 1994–2000; Chaplain to HM the Queen, 1987–2005; *b* 31 Oct. 1935; *s* of George Sydney and Elizabeth Clarke. *Educ:* St Dunstan's College; King's Coll., Univ. of London (AKC 1964; MA 1965). Chaplain: New Cross Hospital, Wolverhampton, 1970–74; Herrison and West Dorset County Hosp., Dorchester, 1974–79; Westminster Hosp. and Westminster Medical School, Univ. of London, 1979–85; Winchester HA, 1985–94. Sen. Hon. Chaplain, Winchester and Eastleigh NHS Trust, 1994–2000. *Recreations:* breeding and showing dogs, music, travel, DIY. *Address:* c/o 3 Brook Court, Middlebridge Street, Romsey, Hants SO51 8HR; *e-mail:* robertsclarke@tiscali.co.uk. *Club:* Kennel.

CLARKE, Roger Eric; literary translator; Director of Shipping and Ports, Department of the Environment, Transport and the Regions, 1997–99; *b* 13 June 1939; *s* of late Frederick Cuérel Clarke and Hilda Josephine Clarke; *m* 1983, Elizabeth Jane, *d* of late Gordon W. Pingstone and Anne Ellen Pingstone; one *d*. *Educ:* UCS, Hampstead; Corpus Christi Coll., Cambridge (MA). Various posts in civil aviation divs of Min. of Aviation, BoT and Depts of Trade and Transport, 1961–72 and 1980–85; Air Traffic Rights Advr to Govt of Fiji, 1972–74; Asst Sec., Insce and Overseas Trade Divs, Dept of Trade, 1975–80; Under Sec., Civil Aviation Policy Directorate, 1985–89, Public Transport Directorate, 1989–91, Shipping Policy Directorate, 1991–97, Dept of Transport. *Publications:* (trans.) Pushkin, Eugene Onegin, 1999; (trans.) Pushkin, Boris Godunov, 1999; The Trawler Gaul: why was no search made for the wreck?, 2000; The Trawler Gaul: the search for bodies of the crew in northern Russia, 2000; (trans.) Pushkin, Ruslan and Lyudmila, 2005; (trans.) Pushkin, Eugene Onegin and other works, 2005; (trans.) Erasmus, Praise of Folly and Pope Julius Barred from Heaven, 2008; (trans.) M. Benoît, Prisoner of God, 2008. *Recreations:* family, friends, church, philately, garden, walking, theatre, music, languages, travel. *Address:* 64 Scotts Lane, Shortlands, Bromley, Kent BR2 0LX. *Club:* Reform.

CLARKE, Roger Howard, CBE 2005; PhD; Director, National Radiological Protection Board, 1987–2003; *b* 22 Aug. 1943; *s* of late Harold Pardoe and Laurie Gwyneth Clarke; *m* 1966, Sandra Ann (*née* Buckley); one *s* one *d*. *Educ:* King Edward VI Sch., Stourbridge; Univ. of Birmingham (BSc, MSc); Polytechnic of Central London (PhD). Res. Officer, Berkeley Nuclear Laboratories, CEGB, 1965–77; Hd of Nuclear Power Assessments, NRPB, 1978–83; Bd Sec., 1983–87. Deleg. to UN Sci. Cttee on the Effects of Atomic Radiation, 1979–2004; Chairman: OECD Nuclear Energy Agency Cttee on Radiation Protection and Public Health, 1987–92; Internat. Commn on Radiol Protection, 1993–2005 (Mem., 1989–93; Emeritus Mem., 2005); Mem., Gp of Experts, Article 31, Euratom, 1988–2004. Visiting Professor: Imperial Coll. of Science, Technol. and Medicine, 1993–2002; Univ. of Surrey, 1994–. Lindell Lectr, Swedish Risk Kollegiat, 1999. Hon. FRCR 1994; Hon. FSRP 1995; Hon. FINucE 2002. DUniv Surrey, 2004. G. William Morgan Award, US Health Physics Soc., 1994; Ellison-Cliffe Medal, RSocMed, 1996; Hanns Langendorff Medal, Voreinigung deutscher Strahlenschutzärtze, 2002; Medal, French Nat. Assembly, 2005. *Publications:* Carcinogenesis and Radiation Risk (with W. V. Mayneord), 1975; numerous papers in sci. and technical literature. *Recreations:* gardening, theatre, travel. *Address:* Corner Cottage, Woolton Hill, Newbury, Berks RG20 9XJ. *T:* (01635) 253957.

CLARKE, Roy, OBE 2002; writer, since 1965; *b* 28 Jan. 1930; *s* of Austin and Alice Clarke; *m* 1953, Enid Kitching; one *s* one *d*. *Educ:* badly during World War II. Soldier, salesman, policeman and teacher until I was able to persuade people I was actually a writer. *Television series:* The Misfit, 1970–72; Last of the Summer Wine, 1972–; Open All Hours, 1975–82; Potter, 1979–83; Pulaski, 1987; Single Voices, 1990; The World of Eddie Weary, 1990; Keeping Up Appearances, 1990–96; Ain't Misbehaving, 1994; *films:* Hawks, 1988; A Foreign Field, 1993; *stage:* Mr Wesley, Lincoln Cathedral, Southwell Minster etc, 2003. Freeman of Doncaster, 1994. Hon. DLitt: Bradford, 1988; Huddersfield, 1997; DUniv Sheffield Hallam, 2001. Best Series Award, Writers' Guild, 1970; Pye TV Award, 1982, Denis Potter Award, 1996, BAFTA. *Publications:* Summer Wine Chronicles, 1986; The Moonbather, 1987; Summer Wine Country, 1995; (with J. Rice) Hyacinth Bucket's

Hectic Social Calendar, 1995. *Recreations:* walking, reading, hiding. *Address:* c/o The Agency, 24 Pottery Lane, Holland Park, W11 4LZ. *T:* (020) 7727 1346.

CLARKE, Sir Rupert (Grant Alexander), 4th Bt *cr* 1882, of Rupertswood, Colony of Victoria; *b* 12 Dec. 1947; *s* of Major Sir Rupert Clarke, 3rd Bt, AM, MBE and Kathleen Clarke (*née* Hay); *S* father, 2005; *m* 1978, Susannah, *d* of Sir Robert Law-Smith, CBE, AFC; one *s* two *d*. *Educ:* Melbourne Univ. (LLB). *Heir: s* Rupert Robert William Clarke, *b* 24 June 1981. *Address:* Bolinda Vale, Clarkefield, Vic 3430, Australia.

CLARKE, Samuel Laurence Harrison, CBE 1988; CEng, FIET; Assistant Technical Director, GEC plc, 1981–91; Director: Sira Ltd, 1989–95; Filtronic Ltd, 1989–93; *b* 16 Dec. 1929; *s* of late Samuel Harrison Clarke, CBE; *m* 1952, Ruth Joan Godwin, *yr d* of Oscar and Muriel Godwin; one *s* three *d*. *Educ:* Westminster Sch.; Trinity Coll., Cambridge (BA). Technical Dir, GEC-Elliott Automation Ltd, 1970–74; Technical Dir (Automation), GEC-Marconi Electronics Ltd, 1974–81; Director, GEC Computers Ltd, 1971–83. Dep. Dir, 1983–87, Dir, 1987, Alvey Programme, DTI. *Publications:* various papers in learned and technical jls. *Recreations:* tapestry, church finance. *Address:* Sarum End, Salisbury Road, Southwold, Suffolk IP18 6LG. *T:* (01502) 725116.

CLARKE, Mrs Stella Rosemary, CBE 1997; JP; Chairman, Community Self Build Agency, since 1989; Vice Lord-Lieutenant, County of Bristol, 2004–07; *b* 16 Feb. 1932; *d* of John Herbert and Molly Isabel Bruce King; *m* 1952, Charles Nigel Clarke; four *s* one *d*. *Educ:* Cheltenham Ladies' Coll.; Trinity Coll. Dublin. Long Ashton RDC: Councillor, Chm. Council, Housing and Public Health Cttees, 1955–73; Mem., Woodspring Dist Council, 1973–76; co-opted Mem., Somerset CC, Social Services and Children's Cttee, 1957–73. A Governor, BBC, 1974–81. Purchased and restored Theatre Royal, Bath, with husband, 1974–76. Dir, Fosters Rooms Ltd, 1975–96. Member: Housing Corp., 1988–95; Bristol Develt Corp., 1989–96; Lord Chancellor's Lay Interviewers Panel for Judges, 1994–2001; Nat. Lottery Charities Bd, 1995–99 (Chm., England Cttee, 1997–99). Member, Board: Knightstone Housing Assoc., 1976–2000 (Chm., 1997–2000); At-Bristol, 2000–. Pro-Chancellor, Bristol Univ., 1997–2007 (Chm. Council, 1987–97). JP Bristol, 1968 (Chm., Bench, 1991–95); DL Bristol (formerly Avon), 1986. *Recreations:* family and the variety of life. *Address:* Gatcombe Court, Flax Bourton, Bristol BS48 3QT. *T:* (01275) 393141, *Fax:* (01275) 394274.

CLARKE, Stephen Patrick; His Honour Judge Stephen Clarke; a Circuit Judge, since 1995; *b* 23 March 1948; *s* of Leslie Clarke and Anne Mary Clarke; *m* 1974, Margaret Roberta Millar; two *s*. *Educ:* Rostrevor Coll., Adelaide, SA; Univ. of Hull (LLB Hons). Called to the Bar, Inner Temple, 1971; practised as barrister on Wales and Chester Circuit, 1971–95; Circuit Junior, 1988–89; Asst Recorder, 1988–92; Recorder, 1992–95; Liaison Judge, Chester and Ellesmere Port Magistrates, and Vale Royal Magistrates, 2007–. Asst Parly Boundary Comr for Wales, 1994–95. Member: Probation Bd, Cheshire, 2001–; HM Council of Circuit Judges, 2005–. *Recreations:* rambling, watching cricket, theatre. *Address:* The Crown Court, The Castle, Chester CH1 2AN. *T:* (01244) 317606. *Clubs:* City (Chester); Lancs County Cricket.

CLARKE, Rt Hon. Thomas, CBE 1980; PC 1997; JP; MP (Lab) Coatbridge, Chryston and Bellshill, since 2005 (Coatbridge and Airdrie, June 1982–1983, Monklands West, 1983–97, Coatbridge and Chryston, 1997–2005); *b* 10 Jan. 1941; *s* of James Clarke and Mary (*née* Gordon). *Educ:* All Saints Primary Sch., Airdrie; Columba High Sch., Coatbridge; Scottish College of Commerce. Started working life as office boy with Glasgow Accountants' firm; Asst Director, Scottish Council for Educational Technology, before going to Parliament. Councillor: (former) Coatbridge Council, 1964; (reorganised) Monklands District Council, 1974; Provost of Monklands, 1975–77, 1977–80, 1980–82. Vice-President, Convention of Scottish Local Authorities, 1976–78, President, 1978–80. Opposition front bench spokesman on: Scottish Affairs, 1987; health and social security (personal social services), 1987–90; Scotland, 1992–93; overseas aid, 1993–94; disabled people's rights, 1994–97; Minister of State (Minister for Film and Tourism), Dept of Culture, Media and Sport, 1997–98. Chm., PLP Foreign Affairs Cttee, 1983–86. Author and main sponsor: Disabled Persons (Consultation, Representation and Services) Act, 1986; Internat. Develt (Reporting and Transparency) Act, 2006. Director, award winning amateur film, Give Us a Goal, 1972; former President, British Amateur Cinematographers' Central Council. JP County of Lanark, 1972. *Recreations:* films, reading, walking. *Address:* 37 Blair Road, Coatbridge, Lanarkshire ML5 1JQ. *T:* (01236) 600800.

CLARKE, Timothy; Chief Executive, Mitchells & Butlers plc, since 2003; *b* 24 March 1957; *s* of David Clarke and Molly Clarke; *m* 1986, Fiona Haigh; two *s*. *Educ:* Corpus Christi Coll., Oxford (BA 1978, MA). Panmure Gordon & Co., 1979–90; Bass plc, subseq. Six Continents plc, 1990–2003 (Chief Exec., Bass Retail, 1995–2000; Chief Exec., 2000–03). Non-exec. Dir, Associated British Foods plc, 2004–. Dir, British Beer and Pub Assoc., 1995– (Chm., 2002). Trustee, Drinkaware Trust, 2007–. Trustee Dir, Birmingham Royal Ballet, 2006–. *Address:* Mitchells & Butlers plc, 27 Fleet Street, Birmingham B3 1JP.

CLARKE, Sir Tobias; *see* Clarke, Sir C. M. T.

CLARKE, William Malpas, CBE 1976; Chairman, Central Banking Publications Ltd, 1990–2007; *b* 5 June 1922; *o s* of late Ernest and Florence Clarke; *m* 1st, 1946, Margaret Braithwaite; two *d*; 2nd, 1973, Faith Elizabeth Dawson. *Educ:* Audenshaw Grammar Sch.; Univ. of Manchester (BA Hons Econ). Served Royal Air Force, 1941–46; Flying Instructor, Canada, 1942–44; Flight-Lieut, 1945. Editorial Staff, Manchester Guardian, 1948–55; The Times, 1955–66: City Editor, 1957–62; Financial and Industrial Editor, 1962–66; Editor, The Banker, March–Sept. 1966, Consultant 1966–76. Dir, 1968–76, Dep. Chm. and Dir Gen., 1976–87, British Invisible Exports Council (formerly Cttee on Invisible Exports); Deputy Chairman: City Communications Centre, 1976–87; Trade Indemnity Co. Ltd, 1980–86; Chairman: Grindlays Bank (Jersey), 1981–92; ANZ Merchant Bank, 1987–91 (Dir, 1985–91); Transatlantic Capital (Biosciences) Ltd, 1989–92; Director: ANZ Grindlays Bank (formerly Grindlays Bank), 1966–85, 1987–92; Euromoney Ltd, 1969–84; Trade Indemnity plc, 1971–87; Swiss Reinsurance Co. (UK) plc, 1977–93; ANZ Holdings, 1985–87. Chm., Harold Wincott Financial Journalist Press Award Panel, 1971–92. Governor, The Hospitals for Sick Children, 1984–90; Chm., Great Ormond Street Wishing Well Redevelt Appeal Trust, 1985–94. Hon. DLitt London Guildhall Univ., 1992. *Publications:* The City's Invisible Earnings, 1958; The City in the World Economy, 1965; Private Enterprise in Developing Countries, 1966; (ed, as Director of Studies) Britain's Invisible Earnings, 1967; (with George Pulay) The World's Money, 1970; Inside the City, 1979, rev. edn 1983; How the City of London Works, 1986, 6th edn 2004; The Secret Life of Wilkie Collins, 1988, rev. edn 2004; Planning for Europe: 1992, 1989; The Lost Fortune of the Tsars, 1994 (US and German edns, 1995; Argentine edn, 1996; Polish and Romanian edns, 1998), 4th edn as Romanoff Gold 2007; (ed) Letters of Wilkie Collins, 1999; The Golden Thread, 2001; The White Pimpernel, 2008. *Recreations:* books, theatre. *Address:* 37 Park Vista, Greenwich, SE10 9LZ. *T:* (020) 8858 0979. *Club:* Reform.

CLARKE, William Michael; Member (SF) South Down, Northern Ireland Assembly, since 2003; *b* 13 Oct. 1966; *s* of Patrick and Margaret Clarke; *m* 2001, Paula Sloan; one *d*. *Educ:* St Malachy's High Sch., Castlewellan, Co. Down. Mem. (SF), Down DC, 2001– (Chm., 2006–07). *Recreations:* hill walking, reading, cycling. *Address:* 37 King Street, Newcastle, Co. Down BT33 0HD. *T:* (028) 4377 0185, *Fax:* (028) 4377 1826.

CLARKE-HACKSTON, Fiona; Director, British Screen Advisory Council, since 1990 (Secretary, 1987–90); *b* 30 April 1954; *d* of Donald Gordon Hackston and Muriel Lesley Hackston (*née* Glover); *m* 1984, Norman Malcolm Clarke; one *s* one *d*. *Educ:* UC of S Wales and Monmouthshire, Cardiff (BA Hons); Univ. of Southampton (MA 1977). Sec. to Marketing Dir, Grants of St James, 1978–79; Editor, and Head of Book Dept, Truman & Knightley, 1979–81; Personnel Advr, Ernst & Whinney, Middle East, 1981–84; Asst, Film, TV and Video, British Council, 1986. *Recreations:* film, walking, music, family. *Address:* 353 Wimbledon Park Road, SW19 6NS.

CLARKSON, Rt Hon. Adrienne; PC (Can.) 1999; CC 1999 (OC 1992); CMM; CD; Governor General of Canada, 1999–2005; *b* Hong Kong, 10 Feb. 1939; naturalised Canadian citizen; *m* John Ralston Saul, writer. *Educ:* Univ. of Toronto (BA Hons English Lit.; MA 1961); Sorbonne, Univ. of Paris. Agent-Gen. for Ontario, Paris, 1982–87; Pres. and Publisher, McClelland & Stewart, 1987–88; Presenter, Writer and Producer: Take Thirty, Adrienne at Large, The Fifth Estate, CBC TV, 1965–82; Adrienne Clarkson's Summer Festival, 1988–98; Adrienne Clarkson Presents, 1988–98; Exec. Prod. and Presenter, Something Special. Chair, Bd of Trustees, Canadian Mus. of Civilization, Quebec, 1995–99; formerly Pres., Exec. Bd, IMZ, Vienna. Lay Bencher, Law Soc. of Upper Canada, 1999. Sen. Fellow, Massey Coll., 1993. Hon. Fellow: Royal Conservatory of Music, Toronto, 1993; Univ. of Trinity Coll., Toronto, 1996. Hon. LLD: Dalhousie, 1991; Acadia, 1994; PEI, 1996; Victoria, 2000; Laval, 2002; York, Queen's, Western Ontario, Ottawa, Law Soc. of Upper Canada, 2003; Hon. DCL Lakehead, 1992; Hon. DLitt: Manitoba, 2001; Bishop's, 2003; Dr *hc* Siena, 2002. *Publications:* three books; numerous articles in newspapers and jls.

CLARKSON, Ven. Alan Geoffrey; Archdeacon of Winchester, 1984–99, Archdeacon Emeritus, since 1999; Vicar of Burley, Ringwood, 1984–99; *b* 14 Feb. 1934; *s* of Instructor Captain Geoffrey Archibald Clarkson, OBE, RN and Essie Isabel Bruce Clarkson; *m* 1959, Monica Ruth (*née* Lightburne); two *s* one *d*. *Educ:* Sherborne School; Christ's Coll., Cambridge (BA 1957, MA 1961); Wycliffe Hall, Oxford. Nat. Service Commn, RA, 1952–54. Curate: Penn, Wolverhampton, 1959–60; St Oswald's, Oswestry, 1960–63; Wrington with Redhill, 1963–65; Vicar, Chewton Mendip with Emborough, 1965–74; Vicar of St John Baptist, Glastonbury with Godney, 1974–84; Priest in Charge: West Pennard, 1981–84; Meare, 1981–84; St Benedict, Glastonbury, 1982–84. Proctor in Convocation, 1970–75, 1990–95. Hon. Canon, Winchester Cathedral, 1984–99. *Recreations:* music, gardening, carpentry, wood-turning. *Address:* 4 Harefield Rise, Linton, Cambridge CB21 4LS. *T:* (01223) 892988; *e-mail:* a.clarkson@talktalk.net.

CLARKSON, Prof. Brian Leonard, DSc; FREng; Principal, University College of Swansea, 1982–94; Vice-Chancellor, University of Wales, 1987–89; *b* 28 July 1930; *s* of L. C. Clarkson; *m* 1953, Margaret Elaine Wilby; three *s* one *d*. *Educ:* Univ. of Leeds (BSc, PhD). FREng (FEng 1986); FRAeS; Hon. FInst Acoustics. George Taylor Gold Medal, RAeS, 1963. Dynamics Engineer, de Havilland Aircraft Co., Hatfield, Herts, 1953–57; Southampton University: Sir Alan Cobham Research Fellow, Dept of Aeronautics, 1957–58; Lectr, Dept of Aeronautics and Astronautics, 1958–66; Prof. of Vibration Studies, 1966–82; Dir, Inst. of Sound and Vibration Res., 1967–78; Dean, Faculty of Engrg and Applied Science, 1978–80; Deputy Vice-Chancellor, 1980–82. Sen. Post Doctoral Research Fellow, Nat. Academy of Sciences, USA, 1970–71 (one year's leave of absence from Southampton). Chm., ACU, 1992–93 (Vice-Chm., 1990–92). Sec., Internat. Commn on Acoustics, 1975–81. Pres., Fedn of Acoustical Socs of Europe, 1982–84. Member: SERC, 1984–88; CNAA, 1988–91. Hon. DSc: Leeds, 1984; Southampton, 1987; Universiti Sains Malaysia, 1990; Hon. LLD Wales, 1996. *Publications:* author of sections of three books: Technical Acoustics, vol. 3 (ed Richardson) 1959; Noise and Acoustic Fatigue in Aeronautics (ed Mead and Richards), 1967; Noise and Vibration (ed White and Walker), 1982; (ed) Stochastic Problems in Dynamics, 1977; technical papers on Jet Noise and its effect on Aircraft Structures, Jl of Royal Aeronautical Soc., etc. *Recreations:* walking, gardening, travelling, golf. *Address:* 17 Southgate Road, Southgate, Swansea SA3 2BT.

CLARKSON, His Honour Derek Joshua; QC 1969; a Circuit Judge, 1977–95; Middlesex Liaison Judge, 1985–95; *b* 10 Dec. 1929; *o s* of Albert and Winifred Charlotte Clarkson (*née* James); *m* 1960, Peternella Marie-Luise Ilse Canenbley; one *s* one *d*. *Educ:* Pudsey Grammar Sch.; King's Coll., Univ. of London. LLB (1st cl. Hons) 1950. Called to Bar, Inner Temple, 1951; Nat. Service, RAF, 1952–54 (Flt Lt). In practice as Barrister, 1954–77; Prosecuting Counsel to Post Office on North-Eastern Circuit, 1961–65; Prosecuting Counsel to Inland Revenue on North-Eastern Circuit, 1965–69; Recorder of Rotherham, 1967–71; Recorder of Huddersfield, 1971; a Recorder of the Crown Court, 1972–77. Mem., Gen. Council of the Bar, 1971–73. Inspector of companies for the Department of Trade, 1972–73, 1975–76. Pres., Middlesex Magistrates' Assoc., 1994–95. *Recreations:* theatre-going, walking, book collecting. *Address:* 2 Harlow Oval Court, Harlow Oval, Harrogate HG2 0DT.

CLARKSON, Prof. Geoffrey Peniston Elliott, PhD; Chairman, Circle L Ltd, since 1990; Professor of Business Administration, Touro University International, since 2003; *b* 30 May 1934; *s* of George Elliott Clarkson and Alice Helene (*née* Manneberg); *m* 1960, Eleanor M. (*née* Micenko); two *d*. *Educ:* Carnegie-Mellon Univ., Pittsburgh, Pa (BSc, MSc, PhD). Asst Prof., Sloan Sch. of Management, MIT, 1961–65, Associate Prof., 1965–67, Vis. Prof., 1975–77. Vis. Ford Foundn Fellow, Carnegie-Mellon Univ., 1965–66; Vis. Prof., LSE, 1966–67; Nat. Westminster Bank Prof. of Business Finance, Manchester Business Sch., Univ. of Manchester, 1967–77; Prof. of Business Admin, 1977–89, and Dean, Coll. of Business Admin, 1977–79, Northeastern Univ., Boston. Dir of and consultant to public and private manufng and financial services cos, 1969–; Chairman: Polymerics Inc., 1983–89; Sealcorp Ltd, 1990–94. MInstD 1973. *Publications:* Portfolio Selection: a simulation of trust investment, USA 1962 (Ford Dissertation Prize, 1961); The Theory of Consumer Demand: a critical appraisal, USA 1963; Managerial Economics, 1968; (with B. J. Elliott) Managing Money and Finance, 1969 (3rd edn 1982); Jihad, 1981; Day Trader, 2000. *Recreations:* fishing, sailing, reading. *Address:* 2805 Oakland Park Blvd, #122, Fort Lauderdale, FL 33306, USA.

CLARKSON, Gerald Dawson, CBE 1990; QFSM 1983; Chief Fire Officer and Chief Executive, London Fire and Civil Defence Authority, 1987–91, retired; Chairman, Dawson Usher International Ltd, 1994–2002; *b* 4 June 1939; *s* of Alexander Dickie Clarkson and Agnes Tierney Price; *m* 1959, Rose Lilian Hodgson; one *s* one *d*. *Educ:* Westminster Technical Coll.; Polytechnic of Central London (BA Hons). FIMS, FCMI, FRSH. Served Royal Engineers, 1960–61. Joined London Fire Bde, 1961; Dep. Chief Officer, 1983; Reg. Fire Comdr No 5, Greater London Region, 1987–91. Member: Central Fire Bdes Adv. Council, 1987–91; Fire Service Central Examinations Bd, 1987–;

Ind. Mem., Kent Police Authy, 1995–2003; Adviser: Nat. Jt Council for Local Authorities Fire Bdes, 1987–91; Assoc. of Metropolitan Authorities, 1987–91; Chairman: Fedn of British Fire Orgns, 1990–91; London Fire Brigade Retired Members Association, 1991–; President: London Fire Brigade Widows' and Orphans' Friendly Soc., 1987–91; Commonwealth and Overseas Fire Service Assoc., 1990–2000; Dir, Nat. Fire Protection Assoc., USA, 1990–93. Founder Chm., Firefighters Meml Charitable Trust, 1990–. Mem. (C), Ashford BC, 2006– (Member: Planning Cttee, 2006–; Audit Cttee, 2007–). Chm., Charing Rd Safety and Traffic Mgt Cttee, 2005–; Vice Chm., Charing Playing Fields Cttee, 2005–. Freeman, City of London, 1985; Founder Master, Guild of Firefighters, 1988; Founder Mem., Worshipful Co. of Firefighters (formerly Co. of Firefighters), 1995– (Sen. Past Master); Mem., HAC, 2004–. OStJ 1989. Hon. FIFireE 1989. *Recreations:* reading, golf, sailing, fishing. *Address:* Charing House, Station Road, Charing, Kent TN27 0JA. *Club:* East India.

CLARKSON, Harriet; *see* Green, H.

CLARKSON, Jeremy Charles Robert; journalist and broadcaster, since 1978; *b* 11 April 1960; *m* 1993, Frances Catherine Cain, *d* of Major Robert Henry Cain, VC and Mary Denise Addison; one *s* two *d*. *Educ:* Repton Sch. Rotherham Advertiser, 1978–81; family co., selling Paddington Bears, 1981–84; established Motoring Press Agency, 1984–94; columnist: Performance Car magazine, 1986–93; Top Gear magazine, 1993–; Esquire magazine, 1992–93; Sunday Times, 1993–; The Sun, 1996–; *television:* presenter: Top Gear, 1989–99, and 2002–; Jeremy Clarkson's Motorworld, 1995, 1996; Extreme Machines, 1998; Robot Wars, 1998; Clarkson, 1998, 1999, 2000; Clarkson's Car Years, 2000; Speed, 2001; Meet the Neighbours, 2002; Great Britons: Brunel, 2003; The Victoria Cross: For Valour, 2003; Inventions That Changed the World, 2004; The Greatest Raid of All Time, 2006. *Publications:* Clarkson on Cars, 1996; Clarkson Hot 100, 1997; Planet Dagenham, 1998; Born to be Riled, 1999; Jeremy Clarkson on Ferrari, 2000; The World According to Jeremy Clarkson, 2004; I Know You Got Soul, 2004; And Another Thing: the world according to Clarkson, vol. 2, 2006; Don't Stop Me Now, 2007; For Crying Out Loud!: the world according to Clarkson, vol. 3, 2008.

CLARKSON, Patrick Robert James; QC 1991; a Recorder, since 1996; *b* 1 Aug. 1949; *s* of Commander Robert Anthony Clarkson, LVO, RN and Sheila Clarissa Neale; *m* 1975, Bridget Cecilia Doyne; two *s* one *d*. *Educ:* Winchester. Called to the Bar, Lincoln's Inn, 1972. *Recreation:* country. *Address:* Landmark Chambers, 180 Fleet Street, EC4A 2HG. *T:* (020) 7430 1221. *Clubs:* Boodle's, MCC.

CLARKSON, Dr Peter David; Executive Secretary, Scientific Committee on Antarctic Research, 1989–2005; Emeritus Associate, Scott Polar Research Institute, since 2005; *b* 19 June 1945; *s* of late Maurice Roland Clarkson and of Jessie Yoxall (*née* Baker); *m* 1974, Rita Margaret Skinner; one *d*. *Educ:* Epsom Coll.; Univ. of Durham (BSc 1967); Univ. of Birmingham (PhD 1977). FGS 1980. Geologist with British Antarctic Survey, 1967–89: wintered in Antarctica, Halley Bay, 1968 and 1969; Base Comdr, 1969; Antarctic field seasons in Shackleton Range (leader 3 times), 1968–78; in S Shetland Is, 1974–75; in Antarctic Peninsula, 1985–86 (leader). UK adviser to PROANTAR, Brazil, 1982. Chm., Trans-Antarctic Assoc., 2006– (Hon. Sec., 1980–93; Grants Sec., 1993–96; Trustee, 1996–). Polar Medal, 1976. *Publications:* (jtly) Natural Wonders of the World: 100 spectacular wonders of the natural world, 1995; Volcanoes, 2000; articles on Antarctic geology. *Recreations:* walking, woodwork, photography, music, lecturing on Antarctic cruise ships, all matters Antarctic. *Address:* Scott Polar Research Institute, Lensfield Road, Cambridge CB2 1ER. *T:* (01223) 336531; 35 King's Grove, Barton, Cambridge CB23 7AZ. *T:* (01223) 263417. *Club:* Antarctic.

CLARRICOATS, Prof. Peter John Bell, CBE 1996; FRS 1990; FREng; Professor of Electronic Engineering, Queen Mary and Westfield (formerly Queen Mary) College, University of London, 1968–97, now Emeritus Professor, Queen Mary, University of London (Head of Department, 1979–97); *b* 6 April 1932; *s* of John Clarricoats and Cecilia (*née* Bell); *m* 1st, 1955, Gillian (*née* Hall) (marr. diss. 1962); one *s* one *d*; 2nd, 1968, Phyllis Joan (*née* Lloyd); two *d*, and one step *s* one step *d*. *Educ:* Minchenden Grammar Sch.; Imperial College. BSc (Eng), PhD, DSc (Eng) 1968; FInstP 1964; FIET (FIEE 1967); FIEEE 1967; FCGI 1980; FREng (FEng 1983). Scientific Staff, GEC, 1953–58; Lectr, Queen's Univ. Belfast, 1959–62; Sheffield Univ., 1962–63; Prof. of Electronic Engineering, Univ. of Leeds, 1963–67; Mem., Governing Body, QMC, 1976–79, Dean of Engineering, 1977–80; Fellow, QMW, 1999. Founder Editor, Electronics Letters (IEE Jl), 1964–. Chm., Defence Scientific Adv. Council, MoD, 1997–2000. Chm., British Nat. Cttee for Radio Sci., subseq. UK Panel for URSI, 1985–93; Vice-Pres., URSI, 1993–99. Chairman: 1st Internat. Conf. on Antennas and Propagation, IEE, 1978; European Microwave Conf., 1979; Mil. Microwaves Conf., 1988; Microwaves and RF Conf., 1994. Distinguished Lectr, IEEE, 1987–88. Institution of Electrical Engineers: Vice-Pres., 1989–91; Mem. Council, 1964–67, 1977–80; Chm., Electronics Div., 1978–79; Hon. Fellow, 1993; awards: Premia, Electronics Section, 1960, 1961; Marconi, 1974; Measurement Prize, 1989; J. J. Thomson Medal, 1989; Oliver Lodge, 1992. Hon DSc: Kent, 1993; Aston, 1995. Coopers Hill Meml Prize, ICE, 1964; European Microwave Prize, 1989, Dist. Achievement Medal, 2005, European Microwave Assoc.; Cert. of Appreciation, 1989, Millennium Medal, 2000, Distinguished Achievement Award, 2001, IEEE. *Publications:* Microwave Ferrites, 1960; (with A. D. Olver) Corrugated Horns for Microwave Antennas, 1984; (with A. D. Olver) Microwave Horns and Feeds, 1994; papers on antennas and waveguides. *Recreations:* music, history. *Address:* The Red House, Grange Meadows, Elmswell, Suffolk IP30 9GE. *T:* (01359) 240585, *Fax:* (01359) 242665.

CLARY, Prof. David Charles, FRS 1997; President, Magdalen College, Oxford, since 2005; Professor of Chemistry, University of Oxford, since 2002; *b* Halesworth, Suffolk, 14 Jan. 1953; *s* of late Cecil Raymond Clary and of Mary Mildred Clary (*née* Hill); *m* 1975, Heather Ann Vinson; three *s*. *Educ:* Colchester Royal Grammar Sch.; Sussex Univ. (BSc 1974); Corpus Christi Coll., Cambridge (PhD 1977); ScD Cantab 1998. CChem, FRSC 1997; CPhys, FInstP 1997. IBM World-Trade Postdoctoral Fellow, San Jose, Calif, 1977–78; Postdoctoral Fellow, Manchester Univ., 1978–80; Research Lectr in Chemistry, UMIST, 1980–83; Department of Chemistry, Cambridge University: Demonstrator, 1983–87; Lectr, 1987–93; Reader in Theoretical Chem., 1993–96; Magdalene College, Cambridge: Fellow, 1983–96 (Hon. Fellow, 2005); Dir of Studies in Natural Scis, 1988–96; Sen. Tutor, 1989–93; Fellow Commoner, 1996–2002; Prof. of Chem. and Dir, Centre for Theoretical and Computational Chem., UCL, 1996–2002; Hd, Div. of Mathematical and Physical Scis, Univ. of Oxford, and Fellow, St John's Coll., Oxford, 2002–05. Visiting Fellow: Univ. of Colo, 1987–88; Canterbury Univ., NZ, 1992; Univ. of Sydney, Australia, 1994; Hebrew Univ. of Jerusalem, 1994; Université de Paris Sud, 1995; Miller Vis. Prof., Univ. of Calif at Berkeley, 2001; Vis. Prof., Nat. Univ. of Singapore, 2002. Lectures: George B. Kistiakowsky, Harvard Univ., 2002; Kenneth Pitzer, Univ. of Calif at Berkeley, 2004; Burton Meml, Imperial Coll., London, 2004; Paul Grandpierre, Columbia Univ., 2004; Thomas Graham, UCL and RSC, 2004. Trustee, Henry Fund, 2007–. Mem. Council, Royal Soc., 2003–05; Royal Society of Chemistry: Mem. Council, 1990–93 and 1994–2001, Vice-Pres., 1997–2001, Pres., 2006–, Faraday

Div.; Meldola Medal, 1981; Marlow Medal, Faraday Div., 1986; Corday-Morgan Medal, 1989; Tilden Medal and Lectr, 1998; Chemical Dynamics Prize, 1998; Polanyi Medal, 2004. Fellow: AAAS, 2003; APS, 2003; FRSA 2005; Foreign Hon. Mem., Amer. Acad. of Arts and Scis, 2003. Annual Medal, Internat. Acad. of Quantum Molecular Scis, 1989 (Mem., 1998–). Editor, Chemical Physics Letters, 2000–. *Publications:* papers on chemical physics and theoretical chemistry in learned jls. *Recreations:* family, football, foreign travel. *Address:* Magdalen College, Oxford OX1 4AU. *T:* (01865) 276101.

CLASPER, Michael, CBE 1995; Chairman, HM Revenue and Customs, since 2008; Member, Investor Board, EMI, since 2007; *b* 21 April 1953; *s* of Douglas and Hilda Clasper; *m* 1975, Susan Rosemary Shore; two *s* one *d*. *Educ:* Bede Sch., Sunderland; St John's Coll., Cambridge (1st cl. Hons Engineering). British Rail, 1974–78; joined Procter & Gamble 1978, Advertising Dir, 1985–88; Gen. Manager, Procter & Gamble Holland, 1988–91; Man. Dir and Vice-Pres., Procter & Gamble UK, 1991–95; Regl Vice-Pres., Laundry Products, Procter & Gamble Europe, 1995–99; Pres., Global Home Care and New Business Develt, Procter & Gamble, 1999–2001; Dep. Chief Exec., 2001–03, Chief Exec., 2003–06, BAA plc; Operating Man. Dir, Terra Firma, 2007–08. Non-exec. Dir, ITV plc, 2006–. Member: Adv. Council on Business and the Envmt, 1993–99; Mgt Cttee, Business and Envmt Prog., Univ. of Cambridge Prog. for Industry, 2000–; Nat. Employment Panel, 2006–; Chair, BITC Marketplace Taskforce, 2005–07. *Recreations:* cycling, ski-ing, tennis, golf.

CLATWORTHY, Robert, RA 1973 (ARA 1968); sculptor; *b* 31 Jan. 1928; *s* of E. W. and G. Clatworthy; *m* 1954, Pamela Gordon (marr. diss.); two *s* one *d*. *Educ:* Dr Morgan's Grammar Sch., Bridgwater. Studied West of England Coll. of Art, Chelsea Sch. of Art, The Slade. Teacher, West of England Coll. of Art, 1967–71. Visiting Tutor, RCA, 1960–72; Mem., Fine Art Panel of Nat. Council for Diplomas in Art and Design, 1961–72; Governor, St Martin's Sch. of Art, 1970–71; Head of Dept of Fine Art, Central Sch. of Art and Design, 1971–75. Exhibited: Hanover Gall., 1954, 1956; Waddington Galls, 1965; Holland Park Open Air Sculpture, 1957; Battersea Park Open Air Sculpture, 1960, 1963; Tate Gallery, British Sculpture in the Sixties, 1965; British Sculptors 1972, Burlington House; Basil Jacobs Fine Art Ltd, 1972; Diploma Galls, Burlington House, 1977; Photographers Gall., 1980; Quinton Green Fine Art, London, 1986; British Sculpture 1950–65, New Art Centre, 1986; Chapman Gall., 1988, 1989; Keith H. Chapman Gall., 1988, 1992, 1994, 1996; Keith Chapman Fine Art, 2008; Austin Desmond Fine Art, 1991, 1998. Work in Collections: Arts Council, Contemporary Art Soc., Tate Gallery, Victoria and Albert Museum, Greater London Council, Nat. Portrait Gall. (portrait of Dame Elisabeth Frink, 1985). Public sculptures include: Large Bull, Roehampton, SW15, 1956; Monumental Horse and Rider, Finsbury Avenue, London, 1984, subseq. moved to Charing Cross Hosp., London. *Address:* Moelfre, Cynghordy, Llandovery, Carms SA20 0UW. *T:* (01550) 720201. *Clubs:* Chelsea Arts, Arts.

CLAUGHTON, John Alan; Chief Master, King Edward's School, Birmingham, since 2006; *b* 17 Sept. 1956; *s* of Ronald Claughton and Patricia Claughton (*née* Dobell); *m* 1993, Alexandra Dyer; three *s*. *Educ:* King Edward's Sch., Birmingham; Merton Coll., Oxford (MA 1st Cl. Lit. Hum.). Professional cricketer, Warwickshire CCC, 1979–80; corp. finance advr, N. M. Rothschild & Sons, 1980–82; schoolmaster: Bradfield Coll., 1982–84; Eton Coll., 1984–2001; Headmaster, Solihull Sch., 2001–05. Chm., Cricket Cttee, Warwicks CCC, 2005–. *Recreations:* sport, travel, ballet, reading. *Address:* Vince House, 341 Bristol Road, Edgbaston, Birmingham B5 7SW. *T:* (0121) 472 0652; *e-mail:* claughtonj@kes.bham.sch.uk.

CLAUSEN, Alden Winship, (Tom); Chairman, and Chief Executive Officer, Bank of America, 1986–90; *b* 17 Feb. 1923; *s* of Morton and Elsie Clausen; *m* 1st, 1950, Mary Margaret Crassweller (*d* 2001); two *s*; 2nd, 2002, Helen T. Higgins. *Educ:* Carthage Coll. (BA 1944); Univ. of Minnesota (LLB 1949); Grad. Harvard Advanced Management Program, 1966. Admitted to Minnesota Bar, 1949, to California Bar, 1950. Joined Bank of America, 1949: Vice-Pres., 1961–65; Sen. Vice-Pres., 1965–68; Exec. Vice-Pres., 1968–69; Vice-Chm. of Bd, 1969; Pres. and Chief Exec. Officer, 1970–81; Pres., The World Bank, 1981–86. President: Fed. Adv. Council, 1972; Internat. Monetary Conf., Amer. Bankers' Assoc., 1977. Former Director: US-USSR Trade and Econ. Council, 1974–81; Nat. Council for US-China Trade, 1974–81; Co-Chm., Japan-California Assoc., 1973–80; Chm., World Affairs Council of Northern California, 1995–98. Hon. LLD: Carthage, 1970; Lewis and Clark, 1978; Gonzaga Univ., 1978; Univ. of Notre Dame, 1981; Univ. of the Pacific, 1987; Hon. DPS Univ. Santa Clara, 1981. *Address:* c/o Bank of America, 555 California Street, San Francisco, CA 94104, USA.

CLAY, Sir Edward, KCMG 2005 (CMG 1994); HM Diplomatic Service, retired; High Commissioner, Kenya, 2001–05; *b* 21 July 1945; *m* 1969, Anne Stroud; three *d*. FO, later FCO, 1968; Nairobi, 1970; Second, later First, Sec., Sofia, 1973; FCO, 1975; First Secretary: Budapest, 1979; FCO, 1982; Counsellor: Nicosia, 1985; FCO, 1989; Ambassador (non-resident) to Rwanda, 1994–95, to Burundi, 1994–96; High Comr to Uganda, 1993–97; Dir, Public Diplomacy and Public Services, FCO, 1997–99; High Comr to Cyprus, 1999–2001.

CLAY, John Martin; Deputy Chairman: Hambros plc, 1986–90; Hambros Bank Ltd, 1972–84 (Director, 1961–84); *b* 20 Aug. 1927; *s* of late Sir Henry Clay and Gladys Priestman Clay; *m* 1st, 1952, Susan Jennifer (*d* 1997), *d* of Lt-Gen. Sir Euan Miller, KCB, KBE, DSO, MC; four *s*; 2nd, 2001, Ann Monica (*d* 2005), *widow* of Martin Beale, OBE, JP and *d* of Eric Barnard, CB, CBE, DSO. *Educ:* Eton; Magdalen Coll., Oxford. Chairman: Johnson & Firth Brown Ltd, 1973–93; Hambro Life Assurance Ltd, 1978–84. Dir, Bank of England, 1973–83. Mem., Commonwealth Develt Corp., 1970–88. FCMI (FBIM 1971). *Recreation:* sailing. *Club:* Royal Thames Yacht.

CLAY, Sir Richard (Henry), 7th Bt *cr* 1841, of Fulwell Lodge, Middlesex; *b* 2 June 1940; *s* of Sir Henry Felix Clay, 6th Bt, and Phyllis Mary (*d* 1997), *yr d* of late R. H. Paramore, MD, FRCS; *S* father, 1985; *m* 1963, Alison Mary, *d* of late Dr James Gordon Fife; three *s* two *d*. *Educ:* Eton. FCA 1966. *Recreation:* sailing. *Heir: s* Charles Richard Clay [*b* 18 Dec. 1965; *m* 2000, Janette Maria, *o d* of Steve Carothers, USA]. *Address:* The Copse, Shiplate Road, Bleadon, N Somerset BS24 0NX.

CLAY, Robert Alan; Partner, Roots Music, since 1993; *b* 2 Oct. 1946; *s* of Albert Arthur Clay, OBE and Joyce Doris (*née* Astins); *m* 1980, Uta Christa. *Educ:* Bedford Sch.; Gonville and Caius Coll., Cambridge. Busdriver, Tyne and Wear PTE, 1975–83. Branch Chm., GMBATU, 1977–83. MP (Lab) Sunderland North, 1983–92. Treas., 1983–86, Sec., 1986–87, Campaign Gp of Labour MPs. Chief Exec., Pallion Engrg Ltd, 1992–93. *Recreations:* walking, reading.

CLAYDON, Geoffrey Bernard, CB 1990; Member, Legal Directorate, Department of Transport, 1990–95; *b* 14 Sept. 1930; *s* of Bernard Claydon and Edith Mary (*née* Lucas); unmarried. *Educ:* Leeds Modern; King Edward's, Birmingham; Birmingham Univ. (LLB). Articled at Pinsent & Co., Birmingham, 1950; admitted Solicitor, 1954. Legal Asst, 1959, Sen. Legal Asst, 1965, Treasury Solicitor's Dept; Asst Solicitor, DTI, 1973; Asst Treasury

Solicitor, 1974; Principal Asst Treasury Solicitor and Legal Advr, Dept of Energy, 1980. Mem., Editorial Bd, Jl of Energy and Natural Resources Law, 1983–90. National Tramway Museum: Sec., 1958–84; Vice-Chm., 1969–99; Vice-Pres., 1998–2005; Pres., 2005–06. Vice-Pres., Light Rail Transit Assoc. (formerly Light Railway Transport League), 1968– (Chm. of League, 1963–68); Pres., Tramway and Light Railway Soc., 1996–2001 (Chm., 1967–93; Vice-Pres., 1993–96); Dir, Heritage Railway Assoc., 2003– (Mem., Legislation Cttee, 1995–2002; Chm., Legal Services Cttee, 2002–). Chm., Consultative Panel for Preservation of British Transport Relics, 1982–; Member: Inst. of Transport Admin, 1972–; Fixed Track Section, Confedn of Passenger Transport, 1996–; CIT Working Party on transport legislation, 1996–98. CMILT (MCIT 1997; MILT 1999). *Publications:* (contrib. on tramways) Halsbury's Laws of England, 2000; (ed) British Tramway Accidents, 2006. *Recreations:* rail transport, travel. *Address:* 3 The Park, Duffield, Derbys DE56 4ER. *T:* (01332) 841007. *Club:* Royal Automobile.

CLAYMAN, David, CEng, FIChemE; Managing Director, Esso UK plc, 1986–95; *b* 28 May 1934; *s* of Maurice and Nancy Clayman; *m* 1956, Patricia Moore; two *s*. *Educ:* Purley Grammar Sch.; University College London (BSc Chem. Engrg). Joined Esso Petroleum Co., 1956; Supply Manager, London, 1966–67, Esso Europe Inc., 1970–71; Marketing Div. Dir, 1971–79; Exec. Asst to Chm., Exxon Corp., 1979–80; Dir, Esso Petroleum Co., 1982–83; Pres., Esso Africa Inc., 1983–86; Director: Esso Europe Inc., 1983–86; Esso Exploration and Production UK, 1986–95; Esso Pension Trust, 1986–95; Chm., Mainline Pipeline, 1986–95. Mem., Sen. Salaries Review Body, 1997–2006 (Chm., Judicial Sub-cttee, 2002–06). Council Member: GCBS, 1986–87; Foundn for Management Educn, 1986–95; Pres., UKPIA, 1988–90 and 1992–94 (Vice Pres., 1986–88); Vice-Pres., Oil Industries Club, 1988–95. *Clubs:* Royal Automobile; Burhill Golf.

CLAYSON, Timothy; His Honour Judge Clayson; a Circuit Judge, since 2004; *b* 19 Aug. 1952; *s* of Victor Clayson and Elsie Clayson (*née* Cryer); *m* 1st, 1976, Anita Morton (marr. diss. 1995); two *s* one *d*; 2nd, 1997, Heidi Svensgaard (marr. diss. 2002); partner, Joanne Lowe. *Educ:* Christ's Hosp.; University Coll. London (LLB 1973). Called to the Bar, Gray's Inn, 1974; a Recorder, 1996–2004; International Judge, UN, Kosovo, 2001–03: Dist Court, Gjilan, 2001, Mitrovica, 2002; Supreme Court, 2003. *Recreations:* sailing, classical music. *Address:* Northern Circuit Administrator, Young Street Chambers, 76 Quay Street, Manchester M3 4PR.

CLAYTON, Prof. Dame Barbara (Evelyn), (Dame Barbara Klyne), DBE 1988 (CBE 1983); MD, PhD; FRCP, FRCPath; CBiol; Hon. Research Professor in Metabolism, Faculty of Medicine, University of Southampton, since 1987 (Professor of Chemical Pathology and Human Metabolism, 1979–87, and Dean of the Faculty of Medicine, 1983–86); *b* 2 Sept. 1922; *m* 1949, William Klyne (*d* 1977); one *s* one *d*. *Educ:* Univ. of Edinburgh (MD, PhD). FRCP 1972; FRCPath 1971; FRCPE 1985; CBiol 2000. Consultant in Chem. Pathology, Hosp. for Sick Children, London, 1959–70; Prof. of Chem. Pathology, Inst. of Child Health, Univ. of London, 1970–78. Leverhulme Emeritus Fellow, 1988–90. Hon. Consultant, 1979–92, Mem., 1983–87, Southampton and SW Hants HA. Member: Commonwealth Scholarship Commn, 1977–93; Royal Commn on Environmental Pollution, 1981–96. Chm., Task Force on Nutrition, DoH, 1992–95; Member: Study Gp on Long Term Toxicity, Royal Soc., 1976–78; Standing Med. Adv. Cttee (DHSS), 1981–87; Cttee on Toxicity of Chemicals in Food, Consumer Products and the Environment, DoH (formerly DHSS), 1977–93; Systems Bd, MRC, 1974–77; British Nat. Cttees on Chemistry and Biochemistry, 1977–78; British Nat. Cttee on Problems of the Environment, 1988–89; COMA Panel on Dietary Reference Values, 1987–91; WHO Expert Adv. Panel on Nutrition, 1989–97; DoH Steering Gp on Undergrad. Med. and Dental Educn and Res., 1989–; Adv. Gp on Medical Educn, Trng and Service, DoH, 1995–2003; Chairman: Adv. Cttee on Borderline Substances, 1971–83; MRC Adv. Gp on Lead and Neuropsychol Effects in Children, 1983–88; Cttee on Med. Aspects of Contaminants in Air, Soil and Water, 1984–90; Standing Cttee on Postgrad. Med. and Dental (formerly Med.) Educn, 1988–99; Med. and Scientific Panel, Leukaemia Res. Fund, 1989–2003; MRC Cttee on Toxic Hazards in the Workplace and the Environment, 1989–95. Council, RCPath, 1974–77 and 1982– (Pres., 1984–87); GMC, 1983–87. President: Assoc. of Clinical Biochemists, 1977, 1978; Soc. for Study of Inborn Errors of Metabolism, 1981–82; Biomedical Scis Sect., BAAS, 1989–90; British Dietetic Assoc., 1989–; Nat. Soc. for Clean Air and Envmtl Protection, 1995–97 (Vice Pres., 1999–); Hon. President: British Dietetic Assoc., 1989–; British Nutrition Foundn, 1999– (Gov., 1987–99). Member: Bd of Govs, Hosps for Sick Children, London, 1968–78; Scientific Adv. Cttee, Assoc. of Med. Res. Charities, 1990–97. Lectures: Stanley Davidson, RCPE, 1973; Harben, RIPH&H, 1988; Wellcome, Assoc. of Clinical Biochemists, 1988; Osler, 1989; Ireland, Liverpool, 1990; Hartley, Southampton Univ., 1990; G. H. Foote Meml, Southampton Med. Soc., 1991; Wilfred Fish Meml, GDC, 1993; British Nutrition Foundn Annual, 1997; Osler Annual Oration, 1997. Sen. Mem., Soc. for Endocrinol., 1951. Hon. Member: Soc. for Study of Inborn Errors of Metabolism, 1988; Assoc. of Clinical Biochemists, 1990; Corresponding Member: Société Française Pédiatric, 1975; Gesellschaft für Laboratoriumsmedizin, 1990. Member, Editorial Board: Archives of Diseases in Childhood; Clin. Sci.; Jl Endocrinol.; Clin. Endocrinol. Hon. Mem., British Dietetic Assoc., 1976; Hon. Fellow: Faculty of Pathology, RCPI, 1986; Amer. Soc. of Clin. Pathologists, 1987; Hon. FIBiol 2000; Hon. FRCPCH 1997 (Hon. Mem., BPA, 1963); FMedSci 2000. Hon. DSc: Edinburgh, 1985; Southampton, 1989; Hon. DSc (Med) London, 2000. Jessie MacGregor Prize for Med. Sci., RCPE, 1955 and 1985; Wellcome Prize, Assoc. of Clin. Biochemists, 1988; BMA Gold Medal for Distinguished Merit, 1999. *Publications:* contrib. learned jls, incl. Jl Endocrinol., Arch. Dis. Childhood, and BMJ. *Recreations:* natural history, walking. *Address:* Bay View, The Glebe, Studland, Dorset BH19 3AS.

CLAYTON, Rear Adm. Christopher Hugh Trevor; Assistant Director Intelligence, NATO International Military Staff, 2004–07; *b* 21 May 1951; *s* of Arthur Henry Trevor Clayton and Patricia June Norma Clayton; *m* 1997, Deirdre Hannah; one *s* two *d*, and two step *s*. *Educ:* Bishop McKenzie's Sch., Lilongwe, Nyasaland; Wells House, Malvern Wells, Worcs; St John's Sch., Leatherhead. Entered BRNC as naval aviator, 1970; Commanding Officer: HMS Beaver (T22 Frigate), 1993–94; HMS Chatham (T22 Frigate), 1996–97; Commodore Naval Aviation, i/c Naval Air Comd, 2000–02; HCSC 2003; CO, HMS Ocean (Helicopter Carrier), 2003–04; Rear Adm. 2004. Chairman: RN Winter Sports Assoc., 1997–2004, Pres., 2004–; Combined Services Winter Sports Assoc., 2003–. *Recreations:* squash, golf, winter sports, modern history, carpentry and cabinet making, tending 6 acres. *Address:* c/o Naval Secretary, Fleet Headquarters, Whale Island, Portsmouth PO2 8BY. *Club:* Naval and Military.

CLAYTON, Captain Sir David (Robert), 12th Bt *cr* 1732, of Marden; Shipmaster since 1970; Director, Oceanic Lines (UK) Ltd, since 1989; *b* 12 Dec. 1936; *s* of Sir Arthur Harold Clayton, 11th Bt, DSC, and of Alexandra, Lady Clayton, *d* of late Sergei Andreevsky; *S* father, 1985; *m* 1971, Julia Louise, *d* of late Charles Henry Redfearn; two *s*. *Educ:* HMS Conway. Joined Merchant Service, 1953; promoted to first command as Captain, 1970. *Recreations:* shooting, sailing. *Heir:* *s* Robert Philip Clayton [*b* 8 July 1975; *m* 2004, Rachel Kathleen Hughes; one *d*]. *Address:* Rock House, Kingswear, Dartmouth, Devon TQ6 0BX. *T:* (01803) 752433. *Club:* Royal Dart Yacht (Kingswear).

CLAYTON, Jeremy Paul; Deputy Head, Government Office for Science, Department for Innovation, Universities and Skills, since 2007; *b* 3 Feb. 1956; *s* of Giles Conrad Clayton and Anne Margaret Clayton (*née* Crennell); *m* 1990, Mary Lucille Hindmarch. *Educ:* Bedales Sch.; Christ Church, Oxford (MA Physics). Department of Energy, 1978–91: Private Sec. to Norman Lamont, MP, David Mellor, MP, and Rt Hon. Nigel Lawson, MP, 1981–83; Secretariat, Sizewell B Public Inquiry, 1984–87; electricity privatisation, 1989–91; Dir, Building Mgt Privatisation Unit, PSA Services, 1991–94; Department of Trade and Industry: Director: Prog. Finance and Public Expenditure Survey, 1994–97; Radiocommunications Agency Third Generation Mobile Communications Auction Team, 1997–2000; Export Control, 2000–03; Gp Dir, Transdeptl Sci. and Technol., OST, subseq. Office of Sci. and Innovation, 2003–07. Member: Glyndebourne Fest. Soc.; Wagner Soc.; Benslow Music Trust; Ramblers Assoc.; London Wildlife Trust; Woodland Trust; RSPB; Friend: Covent Gdn; Aldeburgh Fest.; Wigmore Hall; RA; Lake Dist. *Recreations:* cello, piano, singing, walking, cricket (Gloucestershire supporter), wife and cats. *Address:* Department for Innovation, Universities and Skills, Kingsgate House, 66–74 Victoria Street, SW1E 6SW. *T:* (020) 3300 8531; *e-mail:* jeremy.clayton@dius.gsi.gov.uk.

CLAYTON, John Pilkington, CVO 1986 (LVO 1975); MA, MB, BChir; Apothecary to HM Household at Windsor, 1965–86; Surgeon Apothecary to HM Queen Elizabeth the Queen Mother's Household at the Royal Lodge, Windsor, 1965–86; Senior Medical Officer, Eton College, 1965–86 (MO, 1962–65); *b* 13 Feb. 1921; *s* of late Brig.-Gen. Sir Gilbert Clayton, KCMG, KBE, CB, and Enid, *d* of late F. N. Thorowgood. *Educ:* Wellington Coll.; Gonville and Caius Coll., Cambridge; King's Coll. Hospital. RAFVR, 1947–49; Sqdn Ldr 1949. Senior Resident, Nottingham Children's Hosp., 1950. MO, Black and Decker Ltd, 1955–70; MO, 1953–62, SMO 1962–81, Royal Holloway Coll. *Address:* Knapp House, Market Lavington, near Devizes, Wilts SN10 4DP.

CLAYTON, Prof. Keith Martin, CBE 1984; Professor of Environmental Sciences, University of East Anglia, 1967–93, now Emeritus; *b* 25 Sept. 1928; *s* of Edgar Francis Clayton and Constance Annie (*née* Clark); *m* 1st, 1950 (marr. diss. 1976); three *s* one *d*; 2nd, 1976. *Educ:* Bedales Sch.; Univ. of Sheffield (MSc). PhD London. Demonstrator, Univ. of Nottingham, 1949–51. Served RE, 1951–53. Lectr, 1953–63, Reader in Geography, 1963–67, LSE; University of East Anglia: Founding Dean, Sch. of Environmental Scis, 1967–71 and 1987–93; Pro-Vice-Chancellor, 1971–73; Dir, Centre of E Anglian Studies, 1974–81. Vis. Professor, State Univ. of New York at Binghamton, 1960–62. Chm., Adv. Cttee, Document Supply Centre, British Library, 1986–93; Member: NERC, 1970–73; UGC, 1973–84; Nat. Radiological Protection Bd, 1980–85; Nat. Adv. Bd for Local Authority Higher Educn, 1982–84; Cttee on Med. Aspects of Radiation in Environment, DHSS, 1985–2001; Ministerial Adv. Cttee on Envmt and Energy, MoD, 1990–; Broads Authy, 1994–98; Dounreay Particles Adv. Gp, SEPA, 2000–06. Chm., Broadland Housing Assoc., 1995–2001. Councillor, Broadland DC, 1994–98. Pres., IBG, 1984. Hon. DSc Lancaster, 1995. Patron's Medal, RGS, 1989. *Publications:* Editor and publisher, Geo Abstracts, 1960–85. *Recreation:* gardening. *Address:* Well Close, Pound Lane, Thorpe, Norwich NR7 0UA. *T:* (01603) 433780.

CLAYTON, Margaret Ann; Chairman, Farriers Registration Council, 2001–06; *b* 7 May 1941; *d* of late Percy Thomas Clayton and of Kathleen Clayton (*née* Payne). *Educ:* Christ's Hospital, Hertford; Birkbeck Coll., London (BA, MSc). Entered Home Office, 1960; Executive Officer/Asst Principal, 1960–67; Asst Private Secretary to Home Secretary, 1967–68; Principal, 1968–75 (seconded to Cabinet Office, 1972–73); Asst Sec., 1975–82; Asst Under Sec. of State, 1983–96; Resident Chm., CSSB, 1983; Dir of Services, Prison Service, 1986–90; Police Dept, 1990–93; Personnel Dept, 1994. Dir, Butler Trust, 1996–99; Chm., Mental Health Act Commn, 1999–2002. Mem., Lambeth, Southwark and Lewisham HA, 1995–99. Freeman, City of London, 1984; Liveryman, Farriers' Co., 1984–. *Recreations:* equitation, gardening, theatre. *Club:* Civil Service.

CLAYTON, Michael Aylwin; Editor of Horse and Hound, 1973–96; Editor-in-Chief, IPC country titles, 1994–97; *b* 20 Nov. 1934; *s* of late Aylwin Goff Clayton and Norah (*née* Banfield); *m* 1988, Marilyn Crowhurst (*née* Orrin); one *s* one *d* from a previous marriage. *Educ:* Bournemouth Grammar School. National Service, RAF, 1954–56. Reporter: Lymington Times and New Milton Advertiser, 1951–54; Portsmouth Evening News, 1956–57; London Evening News, 1957–61; reporter/feature writer, New Zealand Herald, 1961; reporter, London Evening Standard, 1961, Dep. News Editor, 1962–64; News Editor, Southern Ind. Television, 1964–65; staff correspondent, BBC TV and radio (incl. Vietnam, Cambodia, India, Pakistan and Middle East), 1965–73; Presenter, Today, BBC Radio 4, 1973–75. Dir, IPC Magazines, 1994–97. Chm., British Soc. of Magazine Editors, 1986. Mem., Press Complaints Commn, 1991–93. Chairman: BHS, 1998–2001; British Horse Industry Confedn, 1999–2004. *Publications:* A Hunting We Will Go, 1967; (with Dick Tracey) Hickstead—the First Twelve Years, 1972; (ed) The Complete Book of Showjumping, 1975; (ed) Cross-Country Riding, 1977; The Hunter, 1980; The Golden Thread, 1984; Prince Charles: horseman, 1987; The Chase: a modern guide to foxhunting, 1987; Foxhunting in Paradise, 1993; Endangered Species, 2004; The Glorious Chase, 2005; Peterborough Royal Foxhound Show - a history, 2006. *Recreations:* foxhunting, music.

CLAYTON, Prof. Nicola Susan, PhD; Professor of Comparative Cognition, University of Cambridge, since 2005; Fellow of Clare College, Cambridge, since 2000; *b* 22 Nov. 1962; *d* of Colin and Angela Clayton; *m* 2001, Dr Nathan Jon Emery. *Educ:* Pembroke Coll., Oxford (BA Hons Zoology 1984; Domus Scholarship); Univ. of St Andrews (PhD Bird Song 1987). University of California, Davis: Asst Prof., 1995–98; Associate Prof., 1998–2000; Chair, Animal Behavior Grad. Gp, 1999–2000; Full Prof., 2000; University of Cambridge: Univ. Lectr, 2000–02, Reader in Comparative Cognition, 2002–05, Dept of Experimental Psychol.; Tutor and Dir of Studies, Clare Coll., Cambridge, 2000–. Member: Cognitive Neurosci. Section, Fac. of 1000 Biology, 2002–; Animal Scis Cttee, BBSRC, 2003–05; Adv. Bd, Culture and Mind Proj., AHRC, 2004–. Member: Assoc. for Study of Animal Behaviour; British Neurosci. Assoc. (Mem., Organizing Cttee, 2002–03); Europ. Psychological Soc. Internat. Affiliate: Amer. Psychol Assoc.; Assoc. for Psychol Scis. Consulting Editor: Behavioural Neuroscience, 1999–2002; Learning and Behavior, 2007–; Associate Editor: Learning and Motivation, 2000–03; Qly Jl of Experimental Psychology, 2001–04; Animal Behaviour, 2001–04; Mem., Editl Cttee, Biological Reviews, 2003–06; Member, Editorial Board: Public Library of Science One, 2006–; Procs of Royal Soc. B, 2007–. Frank Beach Award, Amer. Psychol Assoc., 2000; Klaus Immelmann prize in animal behaviour, Bielefeld Univ., 2003. *Publications:* (jtly) Social Intelligence: from brain to culture, 2007; 155 articles in scientific jls incl. Nature and Science. *Recreations:* ballet, jazz, salsa and tango dancing, bird watching, playing clarinet and saxophone. *Address:* Department of Experimental Psychology, University of Cambridge, Downing Street, Cambridge CB2 3EB. *T:* (01223) 333559, *Fax:* (01223) 333564; *e-mail:* nsc22@cam.ac.uk.

CLAYTON, Richard Anthony; QC 2002; a Recorder, since 2006; *b* 25 May 1954; *s* of Dennis Lloyd and Patricia Estelle Clayton; *m* 1st, 1980, Isabel Glen Japp; one *s*; 2nd, 1992, Anne Bernadette Burns; one *s*. *Educ:* New Coll., Oxford (BA PPE). Called to the Bar, Middle Temple, 1977; South Islington Law Centre, 1980–82; Osler, Hoskin Harcourt, Toronto, 1982–83; in Chambers, 1984–. Vis. Fellow, Centre for Public Law, Univ. of Cambridge, 2001–. *Publications:* Practice and Procedure at Industrial Tribunals, 1987; (jtly) Civil Actions Against the Police, 1987, 3rd edn 2004; Judicial Review Procedure, 1993, 2nd edn 1996; Police Actions, 1993, 2nd edn 1996; The Law of Human Rights, 2000. *Recreations:* theatre, reading, ski-ing. *Address:* 39 Essex Street, WC2R 3AT. *T:* (020) 7832 1111, *Fax:* (020) 7353 3978; *e-mail:* richard.clayton@39essex.com.

CLAYTON, Prof. Robert Norman, FRS 1981; Professor, Departments of Chemistry and of the Geophysical Sciences, University of Chicago, 1966–2001, now Emeritus; *b* 20 March 1930; *s* of Norman and Gwenda Clayton; *m* 1971, Cathleen Shelburne Clayton; one *d*. *Educ:* Queen's Univ., Canada (BSc, MSc); California Inst. of Technol. (PhD). Res. Fellow, Calif. Inst. of Technol., 1955–56; Asst Prof., Pennsylvania State Univ., 1956–58; University of Chicago: Asst Prof., 1958–62; Associate Prof., 1962–66. *Publications:* over 200 papers in geochemical journals. *Address:* 5201 South Cornell, Chicago, IL 60615, USA. *T:* (773) 6432450; Enrico Fermi Institute, University of Chicago, 5640 South Ellis Avenue, Chicago, IL 60637, USA.

CLAYTON, Stanley James; Town Clerk of the City of London, 1974–82; *b* 10 Dec. 1919; *s* of late James John Clayton and late Florence Clayton; *m* 1955, Jean Winifred, *d* of late Frederick Etheridge; one *s* one *d*. *Educ:* Ensham Sch.; King's Coll., London (LLB). Served War of 1939–45, commnd RAF. Admitted Solicitor 1958. City of Westminster, 1938–52; Camberwell, 1952–60; Asst Solicitor, Holborn, 1960–63; Deputy Town Clerk: Greenwich, 1963–65; Islington, 1964–69; City of London, 1969–74. Comdr, Order of Dannebrog (Denmark); holds other foreign orders. *Address:* Fairfield, Purston Lane, High Ackworth, W Yorks WF7 7EQ. *Club:* Royal Air Force.

CLEALL, Charles; author; *b* 1 June 1927; *s* of Sydney Cleal and Dorothy (*née* Bound); *m* 1953, Mary (*d* 2005), *yr d* of G. L. Turner, Archery Lodge, Ashford, Middx; two *d*. *Educ:* Hampton Sch.; Univ. of London (BMus); Univ. of Wales (MA); Jordanhill Coll. of Educn, Glasgow (Scottish Teacher's Cert.). ADCM, GTCL, FRCO(CHM), LRAM, Hon. TSC. Organist and Choirmaster, St Luke's, Chelsea, 1945–46; Command Music Adviser, RN, Plymouth Command, 1946–48; Prof. of Solo Singing and Voice Production, TCL, 1949–52; Conductor, Morley Coll. Orch., 1949–51; Choral Scholar, Westminster Abbey, 1949–52; Organist and Choirmaster, Wesley's Chapel, City Road, EC4, 1950–52; Conductor, Glasgow Choral Union, 1952–54; BBC Music Asst, Midland Region, 1954–55; Music Master, Glyn County Sch., Ewell, 1955–66; Conductor, Aldeburgh Festival Choir, 1957–60; Organist and Choirmaster: St Paul's, Portman Sq., W1, 1957–61; Holy Trinity, Guildford, 1961–65; Lectr in Music, Froebel Inst., 1967–68; Adviser in Music, London Borough of Harrow, 1968–72; Warden, Education Section, ISM, 1971–72; music specialist, N Div., HM Inspectorate of Schs in Scotland, 1972–87; Tutor in Speech-Training, Scottish Congregational Coll. and Scottish Churches' Open Coll., Napier Univ., 1996–2000. Regd Teacher, Sch. of Sinus Tone, 1985–. Lay Minister (formerly Reader), Salisbury Dio., 2000–. Editor: Jl of Ernest George White Soc., 1983–88; Shaston Key-Ring, 2001–07. Presented papers at: study-conf. of teachers of singing, The Maltings, Snape, 1976; Nat. Course on Develt of Young Children's Musical Skills, Univ. of Reading Sch. of Educn, 1979; annual conf., Scottish Fedn of Organists, 1980; Nat. Conf., Assoc. of Music Advisers in Scotland, 1987; Edinburgh Centre of ISM, 1993. Internat. Composition Prizeman of Cathedral of St John the Divine, NY; Limpus Fellowship Prizeman of RCO. *Publications:* Voice Production in Choral Technique, 1955, rev. edn 1970; The Selection and Training of Mixed Choirs in Churches, 1960; Sixty Songs from Sankey, 1960; (ed) John Merbecke's Music for the Congregation at Holy Communion, 1963; Music and Holiness, 1964; Plainsong for Pleasure, 1969; Authentic Chanting, 1969; Guide to Vanity Fair, 1982; Walking round the Church of St James the Great, Stonehaven, 1993; A Jewel of a Church: Laleham-All Saints', 2001. *Recreations:* reading, writing, walking. *Address:* 14 Heathfields Way, Shaftesbury, Dorset SP7 9JZ.

CLEARY, Anthony Simon Lissant; His Honour Judge Cleary; a Circuit Judge, since 2006; *b* 21 Jan. 1946; *s* of Bruce and Patricia Cleary; *m* 1st, 1968, Georgina Clark (marr. diss. 1973); one *s* two *d*; 2nd, 1974, Carmel Briddon; one *s*. *Educ:* Fettes Coll.; Sheffield Univ. (LLB Hons). Account Exec., Benton & Bowles Advertising Agency, 1968–70; admitted solicitor, 1971; Registrar, then Dist Judge, 1986–2006; Asst Recorder, 1989–92, Recorder, 1992–2006. Civil Tutor Judge, 2001–, IT Liaison Judge, 2003–, Judicial Studies Bd. Member: Lord Chancellor's Matrimonial Causes Rules Cttee, 1984–86; Lord Chancellor's Children Act Procedure Adv. Gp, 1989–91; Lord Chancellor's Children Act Adv. Cttee, 1991–93; Judicial Liaison Panel, CAFCASS, 2004–06. Chm., Sheffield Family Conciliation Service, 1984–86 (Chm., Steering Cttee); Mem. Cttee, Birmingham Family Mediation Service, 1987–89. Mem., Family Law Cttee, Law Soc., 1984–86. Lecturer in Family Law: for Jordans (publishers of Family Law Jl), Birmingham Law Soc. and FLBA, 1987–; for Judicial Studies Bd, 1999–. Contributing Ed., Butterworth's County Court Precedents and Pleadings, 1988–; Gen. Ed., Family Court Practice, annually, 1993–. *Recreations:* music (choral clerk, Coventry Cathedral; Mem., Armonico Consort), rifle shooting, planning, usually without success, return trips to homeland, NZ.

CLEARY, Jon Stephen; novelist; *b* 22 Nov. 1917; *s* of Matthew Cleary and Ida (*née* Brown); *m* 1946, Constantine Lucas (*d* 2003); one *d* (and one *d* decd). *Educ:* Marist Brothers' Sch., Randwick, NSW. Variety of jobs, 1932–40; served with AIF, 1940–45; freelance writer, 1945–48; journalist with Australian News and Information Bureau: London, 1948–49; New York, 1949–51; subseq. full-time writer. Jt winner, Nat. Radio Play Contest, ABC, 1945; second prize, Sydney Morning Herald Novel Comp., 1946; Australian Lit. Soc. Gold Medal, 1950; regional winner, NY Herald Tribune World Short Story Contest, 1950; First Lifetime Award, Aust. Crime Writers' Soc., 1998. *Publications:* These Small Glories (short stories), 1946; You Can't See Round Corners, 1947 (2nd Prize, Novel Contest, Sydney Morning Herald); The Long Shadow, 1949; Just Let Me Be, 1950 (Crouch Gold Medal for best Australian novel); The Sundowners, 1952; The Climate of Courage, 1953; Justin Bayard, 1955; The Green Helmet, 1957; Back of Sunset, 1959; North from Thursday, 1960; The Country of Marriage, 1962; Forests of the Night, 1963; A Flight of Chariots, 1964; The Fall of an Eagle, 1964; The Pulse of Danger, 1966; The High Commissioner, 1967; The Long Pursuit, 1967; Season of Doubt, 1968; Remember Jack Hoxie, 1969; Helga's Web, 1970; Mask of the Andes, 1971; Man's Estate, 1972; Ransom, 1973; Peter's Pence (Edgar Award for best crime novel; Mystery Writers of America, Best Crime Novel), 1974; The Safe House, 1975; A Sound of Lightning, 1976; High Road to China, 1977; Vortex, 1977; The Beaufort Sisters, 1979; A Very Private War, 1980; The Golden Sabre, 1981; The Faraway Drums, 1981; Spearfield's Daughter, 1982; The Phoenix Tree, 1984; The City of Fading Light, 1985; Dragons at the Party, 1987; Now and Then, Amen, 1988; Babylon South, 1989; Murder Song, 1990; Pride's Harvest, 1991; Dark Summer, 1992; Bleak Spring, 1993; Autumn Maze, 1994; Winter Chill, 1995; Endpeace, 1996; A Different Turf, 1997; Five Ring Circus, 1998; Dilemma, 1999; Bear Pit, 2000; Yesterday's Shadow, 2001; The Easy Sin, 2002; Degrees of Connection, 2003; Miss Amber Regrets, 2004; Morning's Gone, 2006. *Recreation:* reading. *Address:* c/o HarperCollins, 77–85 Fulham Palace Road, W6 8JB.

CLEARY, Dr Mark Christopher; Vice Chancellor and Principal, University of Bradford, since 2007; *b* Birmingham, 27 Dec. 1954; *s* of Michael and Dorothy Cleary; *m* 1980, Marie Frances Brophy; two *s*. *Educ:* Jesus Coll., Cambridge (BA Hons Geog. 1977; PhD 1983). Lectr, Univ. of Exeter, 1980–89; Senior Lecturer: Univ. of Brunei, 1989–92; Univ. of Waikato, NZ, 1992–93; University of Plymouth: Reader, 1995–99; Prof. of Geog., 1999–2003; Dean of Social Sci. and Business, 2003–04; Dep. Vice-Chancellor, 2005–07. *Publications:* Peasants, Politicians and Producers: the organisation of agriculture in France since 1918, 1989, repr. 2006; (with P. Eaton) Borneo: change and development, 1992; (with S. Y. Wong) Oil, Economic Development and Diversification in Brunei Darussalam, 1994; (with P. Eaton) Tradition and Reform: land tenure and rural development in Southeast Asia, 1996; (with Goh Kim Chuan) Environment and Development in the Straits of Malacca, 2000. *Recreations:* cycling, walking. *Address:* University of Bradford, Bradford BD7 1DP. *T:* (01274) 233011, *Fax:* (01274) 233003; *e-mail:* m.c.cleary@bradford.ac.uk.

CLEASBY, Very Rev. Thomas Wood Ingram; Dean of Chester, 1978–86, Dean Emeritus, since 1986; *b* 27 March 1920; *s* of T. W. Cleasby, Oakdene, Sedbergh, Yorks, and Jessie Brown Cleasby; *m* 1st, 1956, Olga Elizabeth Vibert Douglas (*d* 1967); one *s* one *d* (and one *d* decd); 2nd, 1970, Monica, *e d* of Rt Rev. O. S. Tomkins; one *d*. *Educ:* Sedbergh Sch., Yorks; Magdalen Coll., Oxford; Cuddesdon Coll., Oxford. BA, MA (Hons Mod. History) 1947. Commissioned, 1st Bn Border Regt, 1940; served 1st Airborne Div., 1941–45, Actg Major. Ordained, Dio. Wakefield, 1949 (Huddersfield Parish Church). Domestic Chaplain to Archbishop of York, 1952–56; Anglican Chaplain to Univ. of Nottingham, 1956–63; Archdeacon of Chesterfield, 1963–78; Vicar of St Mary and All Saints, Chesterfield, 1963–70; Rector of Morton, Derby, 1970–78. *Recreations:* fell-walking, bird-watching, gardening, fishing, local history. *Address:* Low Barth, Dent, Cumbria LA10 5SZ. *T:* (01539) 625476.

CLEAVE, Brian Elseley, CB 1995; Solicitor of Inland Revenue, 1990–99; *b* 3 Sept. 1939; *s* of Walter Edward Cleave and Hilda Lillian Cleave (*née* Newman); *m* 1979, Celia Valentine Williams. *Educ:* Eastbourne Coll. (Duke of Devonshire's schol.); Exeter Univ. (LLB 1961); Kansas Univ.; Manchester Univ. Admitted Solicitor, 1966; called to the Bar, Gray's Inn, 1999. Asst Solicitor, Wilkinson Howlett and Durham, 1966–67; Inland Revenue Solicitor's Office, 1967–99: Asst Solicitor, 1978; Prin. Asst Solicitor, 1986. Senior Consultant: EU/Tacis Taxation Reform Project, Moscow, 2000–05; EU/Tacis Assistance to the State Tax Admininstration, Ukraine Project, 2006–07. Hon. QC 1999. FRSA 1995. *Recreations:* theatre, travel, walking. *Address:* Gray's Inn Tax Chambers, Third Floor, Gray's Inn Chambers, Gray's Inn, WC1R 5JA.

CLEAVER, Sir Anthony (Brian), Kt 1992; FBCS; Chairman, Engineering and Technology Board, since 2007; Chairman: SThree plc, since 2000; Working Links (Employment) Ltd, since 2003; Novia Financial Holdings Ltd, since 2008; *b* 10 April 1938; *s* of late William Brian Cleaver and Dorothea Early Cleaver (*née* Peeks); *m* 1st, 1962, Mary Teresa Cotter (*d* 1999); one *s* one *d*; 2nd, 2000, Mrs Jennifer Guise Lloyd Graham, widow. *Educ:* Berkhamsted Sch.; Trinity Coll., Oxford (Schol.; MA; Hon. Fellow 1989). FRCM 2008. Joined IBM United Kingdom, 1962; IBM World Trade Corp., USA, 1973–74; Dir, DP Div., IBM UK, 1977; Vice-Pres. of Marketing, IBM Europe, Paris, 1981–82; Gen. Man., 1984, Chief Exec., 1986–91, Chm., 1990–94, IBM United Kingdom Holdings Ltd; Chairman: General Cable PLC, 1995–98 (Dir, 1994–98); IX Europe plc, 1999–2007. Chairman: UKAEA, 1993–96; AEA Technology plc, 1996–2001; MRC, 1998–2006; Nuclear Decommissioning Authy, 2004–07. Chairman: The Strategic Partnership Ltd, 1997–2000; Baxi Partnership, 1999–2000; UK eUnivs Worldwide Ltd, 2001–04; Asia Pacific Advisers (UK Trade & Investment, formerly Trade Partners UK), 2000–03. Director: General Accident plc (formerly General Accident, Fire & Life Assurance Corp.), 1988–98; Smith & Nephew PLC, 1993–2002; Loral Europe Ltd, 1995–96; Cable Corp., 1995–96; Lockheed Martin Tactical Systems UK Ltd, 1996–99; Lockheed Martin UK Ltd, 1999–2006. Dir, Nat. Computing Centre, 1976–80. Member Board: UK Centre for Econ. and Environmental Develt, 1985–98 (Dep. Chm., 1992–98); BITC, 1985–2000 (Chm., Business in the Envmt Target Team, 1988–99; Mem., President's Cttee, 1988–91; Dep. Chm., 1991–2000); RIPA, 1985–90; Mem., Council, ABSA, 1985–97 (Dir, 1991–97); Pres., Involvement and Participation Assoc., 1997–2002. Chairman: Industrial Develt Adv. Bd, DTI, 1993–99; TEC Ind. Assessors Cttee, 1994–98; Council for Excellence in Mgt and Leadership, 2000–02; Member: Nat. Adv. Council for Educn and Trng Targets, 1993–98; Electronics EDC, NEDO, 1986–92; CBI, 1986–97 (Mem., President's Cttee, 1988–92); BOTB, 1988–91; Nat. Trng Task Force, 1989–92; Adv. Council, Centre for Dispute Resolution, 1996–2007; Partnership Korea, 1997–99; PPARC Appointments Cttee, 1996–2000; Cttee on Standards in Public Life, 1997–2003; British Government Panel on Sustainable Develt, 1998–2000; Singapore British Business Council, 1999–2000, 2003–04. Dir, American Chamber of Commerce, 1989–91. Member: HRH Duke of Edinburgh's Seventh Commonwealth Study Conf. Council, 1990–92; Council for Industry and Higher Educn, 1991–94; Carnegie Inquiry into Third Age, 1991–93. Chm., Portsmouth Univ. Business Adv. Bd, 1992–99; Member: Oxford Univ. Adv. Council on Continuing Educn, 1993–99; Oxford Univ. Develt Prog. Adv. Bd, 1999–; President's Cttee, Oxford Univ. Appeal, 1988; Appeal Chm., Trinity Coll., Oxford, 1989–98; Chm., RCM, 1999–2007 (Mem. Council, 1998–99; Vice-Pres., 2008–); Member Council: Templeton Coll., Oxford, 1982–93; PSI, 1985–88; Pres., Inst. of Mgt, 1999–2000; Chm. Govs, Birkbeck Coll., 1989–98; Mem., Cttee of Chm. of Univ. Councils, 1992–98; Trustee, Oxford Univ. Higher Studies Fund, 1994–. Dep. Chm., ENO, 1998–2000 (Dir, 1988–2000). Pres., Classical Assoc., 1995–96. Pres., Business Commitment to the Envmt, 2000–. Freeman, City of London, 1987; Co. of Information Technologists, 1985– (Liveryman, 1994); Co. of Musicians, 2003– (Liveryman, 2005). FCGI 2004. Hon. FCIM 1989 (Hon. Vice-Pres., 1991–; Pres., London Br., 1993–2000); Hon. FCIPS 1996; FRSA 1987 (Chm., RSA Inquiry into Tomorrow's Co., 1993–95). Mem. Council, WWF, 1988–92. Patron, Friends of Classics, 1991–. Hon. Fellow: Birkbeck Coll., London, 1999; Univ. of Central Lancashire, 2007. Hon. LLD: Nottingham, 1991; Portsmouth, 1996; Hon. DSc: Cranfield, 1995; Hull, 2002; City, 2002; Hon. DTech London Metropolitan, 2003; DUniv Middx, 2003. UN Envmt Program Global 500 Roll of Honour, 1989. *Recreations:* music, especially opera; sport, especially cricket, golf. *Address:* Engineering and Technology Board, 2nd Floor, Weston House, 246 High Holborn, WC1V 7EX. *Clubs:* Athenæum, Royal Automobile, MCC, Serpentine Swimmers.

CLEERE, Henry Forester, OBE 1992; FSA; Director, Council for British Archaeology, 1974–91 (Hon. Vice-President, 1994); World Heritage Co-ordinator, International Council on Monuments and Sites, 1991–2002; *b* 2 Dec. 1926; *s* of late Christopher Henry John Cleere and Frances Eleanor (*née* King); *m* 1st, 1950, Dorothy Percy (marr. diss.); one *s* one *d*; 2nd, 1975, Pamela Joan Vertue; two *d*. *Educ:* Beckenham County Sch.; University Coll. London (BA Hons 1951; Fellow 1992); Univ. of London Inst. of Archaeology (PhD 1981). FSA 1967. Commissioned Royal Artillery, 1946–48. Successively, Production

Editor, Asst Sec., Man. Editor, Dep. Sec., Iron and Steel Inst., 1952–71; Industrial Development Officer, UN Industrial Develt Org., Vienna, 1972–73. Archaeol Advr, GLC Historic Buildings Panel, 1979–84; World Heritage Advr, State Admin for Cultural Heritage, People's Republic of China, 2002–05. Member: Exec. Cttee, ICOMOS, 1981–90; Duchy of Cornwall Archaeol Adv. Panel, 1983–90; Scientific Cttee, Centro Universitario Europeo per i Beni Culturali, 1985–95; NT Archaeol. Panel, 1990–94. President: Sussex Archaeol Soc., 1987–91 (Vice Pres., 1994); Europ. Forum of Heritage Assocs, 1991–93; Sec., Europ. Assoc. of Archaeologists, 1991–96. Editor, Antiquity, 1992. MIFA 1982, Hon. MIFA 1991; FCMI; Hon. Foreign Mem., Archaeol Inst. of America, 1995. Winston Churchill Fellow, 1979; Hon. Vis. Fellow, Univ. of York, 1988–92; Vis. Res. Fellow, Univ. de Paris I (Sorbonne), 1989; UK Trust Sen. Fellow, Indian Nat. Trust for Art and Cultural Heritage, 1990. Hon. Prof., Inst. of Archaeology, UCL, 1998–. Hon. DLitt Sussex, 1993. European Archaeological Heritage Prize, 2002. *Publications:* Approaches to the Archaeological Heritage, 1984; (with D. W. Crossley) The Iron Industry of the Weald, 1985; Archaeological Heritage Management in the Modern World, 1989; Oxford Archaeological Guide to Southern France, 2001; papers in British and foreign jls on heritage mgt, early ironmaking, Roman fleets, etc. *Recreations:* gardening, cookery. *Address:* Acres Rise, Acres Rise, Ticehurst, Wadhurst, East Sussex TN5 7DD. *T:* (01580) 200752; *e-mail:* henry.cleere@btinternet.com.

CLEESE, John Marwood; writer and actor; *b* 27 Oct. 1939; *s* of late Reginald and Muriel Cleese; *m* 1st, 1968, Connie Booth (marr. diss. 1978); one *d*; 2nd, 1981, Barbara Trentham (marr. diss. 1990); one *d*; 3rd, 1993, Alyce Faye Eichelberger. *Educ:* Clifton Sports Acad.; Downing College, Cambridge (MA). Founder and former Dir, Video Arts Ltd. Started making jokes professionally, 1963; started on British television, 1966; TV series have included: The Frost Report, At Last the 1948 Show, Monty Python's Flying Circus, Fawlty Towers, The Human Face (documentary). Films include: Interlude, 1968; And Now For Something Completely Different, 1970; The Magic Christian, 1971; Monty Python and the Holy Grail, 1974; Romance with a Double Bass, 1974; Life of Brian, 1978; Privates on Parade, 1982; The Meaning of Life, 1982; Yellowbeard, 1983; Silverado, 1985; Clockwise, 1986; A Fish Called Wanda, 1988; Erik the Viking, 1989; Splitting Heirs, 1993; Mary Shelley's Frankenstein, 1994; Rudyard Kipling's The Jungle Book, 1995; Fierce Creatures, 1997; The Out of Towners, 1998; Isn't She Great, 1998; The World Is Not Enough, 1999; Rat Race, 2002; Die Another Day, 2002; Harry Potter and the Chamber of Secrets, 2002; Scorched, 2005. Andrew D. White Prof.-at-Large, Cornell Univ., 1999–. Hon. LLD St Andrews. *Publications:* (with Robin Skynner) Families and How to Survive Them, 1983; The Golden Skits of Wing Commander Muriel Volestrangler FRHS and Bar, 1984; The Complete Fawlty Towers, 1989; (with Robin Skynner) Life and How to Survive It, 1993; (with Brian Bates) The Human Face, 2001; (jtly) The Pythons Autobiography by the Pythons, 2004. *Recreations:* gluttony, sloth. *Address:* c/o David Wilkinson, 115 Hazlebury Road, SW6 2LX.

CLEGG, Prof. Edward John, MD, PhD; FIBiol; Regius Professor of Anatomy, University of Aberdeen, 1976–89; Professor of Biological Anthropology, University of Aberdeen, 1990–91, now Emeritus; *b* 29 Oct. 1925; *s* of Edward Clegg and Emily Armistead; *m* 1958, Sheila Douglas Walls; two *d* (and one *d* decd). *Educ:* High Storrs Grammar Sch., Sheffield; Univ. of Sheffield (MB, ChB Hons 1948, MD 1964). PhD Liverpool, 1957; FIBiol 1974. RAMC, 1948–50 and RAMC (TA), 1950–61; late Major, RAMC (RARO). Demonstr, Asst Lectr and Lectr in Anatomy, Univ. of Liverpool, 1952–63; Lectr, Sen. Lectr and Reader in Human Biology and Anatomy, Univ. of Sheffield, 1963–77. MO, British Kangchenjunga Expedn, 1955; Sci. Mem., Chogolungma Glacier Expedn, 1959; Leader, WHO/IBP Expedn, Simien Mountains, Ethiopia, 1967. Pres., Anat. Soc. of GB and Ire., 1988–89; Chm., Soc. for the Study of Human Biology, 1988–92. *Publications:* The Study of Man: an introduction to human biology, 1968 (2nd edn 1978); papers on anatomy, endocrinology and human biology. *Recreations:* mountaineering, music. *Address:* 22 Woodburn Avenue, Aberdeen AB15 8JQ; c/o School of Biomedical Sciences, Marischal College, Aberdeen AB9 1AS. *T:* (01224) 274324. *Clubs:* Alpine; Wayfarers (Liverpool).

CLEGG, Prof. John Brian, PhD; FRS 1999; Professor of Molecular Medicine, University of Oxford, 1996–2001, now Emeritus; *b* 9 April 1936; *s* of John Richard and Phyllis Clegg. *Educ:* Arnold Sch., Blackpool; Fitzwilliam House, Cambridge (MA 1963; PhD 1963). Univ. of Washington, Seattle, 1963; Johns Hopkins Univ., 1964–65; MRC Lab. of Molecular Biology, 1965; Department of Medicine, University of Liverpool: Lectr, 1966–68; Sen. Lectr, 1969–74; University of Oxford: Lectr, Dept of Medicine, 1974–79; Reader in Molecular Haematology, 1987–96; Asst Dir, Inst. of Molecular Medicine, 1989–2001; MRC Sen. Scientific Staff, 1979–2001. Hon. MRCP 1986, Hon. FRCP 1999. *Publications:* (with D. J. Weatherall) The Thalassaemia Syndromes, 1965, 4th edn 2001; scientific contribs to learned jls. *Recreations:* gardening, travel in France. *Address:* Institute of Molecular Medicine, John Radcliffe Hospital, Oxford OX3 9DS. *T:* (01865) 222398.

CLEGG, Rt Hon. Nicholas (William Peter); PC 2008; MP (Lib Dem) Sheffield Hallam, since 2005; Leader, Liberal Democrats, since 2007; *b* 7 Jan. 1967; *s* of Nicholas P. Clegg and Hermance Eulalie Van den Wall Bake; *m* 2000, Miriam Gonzalez Durantez; two *s*. *Educ:* Westminster Sch.; Robinson Coll., Cambridge (MA Anthropol.); Univ. of Minnesota (post grad. res., Political Theory); Coll. of Europe, Bruges (MA European Studies). Trainee journalist, The Nation mag., NY, 1990; Consultant, GJW Govt Relns, London, 1992–93; Official, Relns with New Independent States, EC, 1994–96; Mem. of Cabinet, Office of Sir Leon Brittan, EC, 1996–99; MEP (Lib Dem) E Midlands, 1999–2004. Lib Dem Home Affairs spokesman, 2006–07. Political Columnist, Guardian Unlimited, 2000–05. Pt-time Lectr, Sheffield Univ., 2004–05. David Thomas Prize, Financial Times, 1993. *Recreations:* ski-ing, theatre. *Address:* (office) 85 Nethergreen Road, Sheffield S11 7EH. *T:* (0114) 230 9002. *Club:* National Liberal.

CLEGG, Peter Alexander; Senior Partner, Feilden Clegg Bradley Architects, since 1978; *b* 29 Aug. 1950; *s* of Alexander Bradshaw Clegg and Jessie Coverdale Clegg (*née* Phillips); *m* 1975, Elizabeth Derry Watkins; two *s*. *Educ:* Tadcaster Grammar Sch.; Clare Coll., Cambridge (BA 1972, MA); Yale Univ. Sch. of Architecture (MED1974). Worked for Herbert Newmann Associates, New Haven, Conn, 1974–75; Cambridge Design Architects, 1975–78. Vis. Prof., Bath Univ., 1998–. Major projects include: envmtl office, BRE; gall. and visitor facilities, Yorks Sculpture Park; central office, Nat. Trust, Swindon. *Publications:* (with D. Watkins) The Complete Greenhouse Book, 1975; (with D. Watkins) Sunspaces, 1978; contribs to UK-based architectural jls. *Recreations:* walking, music, gardening, work. *Address:* Hill Farm Barn, Cold Ashton, Chippenham, Wilts SN14 8LA; Feilden Clegg Bradley Architects, Bath Brewery, Tollbridge Road, Bath BA1 7DE.

CLEGG, Philip Charles; His Honour Judge Clegg; a Circuit Judge, since 1987; *b* 17 Oct. 1942; *s* of Charles and Patricia Clegg; *m* 1st, 1965, Caroline Frances Peall (marr. diss. 1996); one *s* two *d*; 2nd, 1997, Fiona Cameron. *Educ:* Rossall; Bristol Univ. (LLB Hons). Called to the Bar, Middle Temple, 1966; in practice on Northern Circuit; Asst Recorder,

1980–83; Recorder, 1983–87; Resident Judge, Basildon Combined Crown Court, 1996–2007. Mem., Sentencing Adv. Panel, 2005–. *Recreations:* sailing, model engineering.

CLEGG, Richard Ninian Barwick; QC 1979; a Recorder of the Crown Court, 1978–93; *b* 28 June 1938; *o s* of Sir Cuthbert Clegg, TD; *m* 1963, Katherine Veronica, *d* of A. A. H. Douglas; two *s* one *d*. *Educ:* Aysgarth; Charterhouse; Trinity Coll., Oxford (MA). Captain of Oxford Pentathlon Team, 1959. Called to Bar, Inner Temple, 1960, Bencher, 1985. Chm., NW section of Bow Group, 1964–66; Vice-Chm., Bow Group, 1965–66; Chm., Winston Circle, 1965–66; Pres., Heywood and Royton Conservative Assoc., 1965–68. *Publication:* (jtly) Bow Group pamphlet, Towards a New North West, 1964. *Recreations:* sport, music, travel. *Address:* Ford Farm, Wootton Courtenay, Minehead, Somerset TA24 8RW. *T:* (01643) 841669. *Club:* Lansdowne.

CLEGG, Simon Paul, CBE 2006 (OBE 2001); Chief Executive, British Olympic Association, since 1997; Director, London Organising Committee for the Olympic Games, since 2005 (Director, London Olympic Bid, 2003–05); *b* 11 Aug. 1959; *s* of Peter Vernon Clegg and Patricia Anne Clegg (*née* Long); *m* 1985, Hilary Anne Davis; one *s* one *d*. *Educ:* Stowe Sch. Commnd RA, 1981; OC Battery, 7th Parachute Regt, RHA, 1989. Manager, British Biathlon Team, 1984–85; British Olympic Association, 1989–: Asst Gen. Sec., 1989–91; Dep. Gen. Sec., 1991–96; Olympic Quartermaster, Summer and Winter Olympic Games, 1988 (on secondment); Great Britain Team: Dep. Chef de Mission, Olympic Games, 1992 and 1996, Olympic Winter Games, 1994; Chef de Mission: Olympic Winter Games, 1998, 2002 and 2006; Olympic Games, 2000, 2004 and 2008; Chief Exec., European Youth Olympic Games, Bath, 1995. Royal Artillery Charitable Fund, 2006–. *Address:* British Olympic Association, 1 Wandsworth Plain, SW18 1EH. *T:* (020) 8871 2677. *Club:* Cavalry and Guards.

CLEGG, William; QC 1991; a Recorder, since 1992; *b* 5 Sept. 1949; *s* of Peter Hepworth Clegg and Sheila Clegg; *m* 1974, Wendy Doreen Chard (marr. diss. 2002); one *s* one *d*; *m* 2008, Judith Gay Matthews. *Educ:* St Thomas More High School; Bristol Univ. (LLB). Called to the Bar, Gray's Inn, 1972; in practice, SE Circuit. Head of Chambers, 1995–. *Recreations:* squash, cricket. *Address:* 2 Bedford Row, WC1R 4BU. *T:* (020) 7440 8888. *Clubs:* Garrick, MCC.

CLEGG-HILL, family name of **Viscount Hill.**

CLEGHORN, Bruce Elliot, CMG 2002; HM Diplomatic Service, retired; High Commissioner, Malaysia, 2001–06; *b* 19 Nov. 1946; *s* of Ivan Robert Cleghorn and Margaret (*née* Kemplen); *m* 1976, Sally Ann Robinson; three *s*. *Educ:* Sutton Valence Sch., Kent; St John's Coll., Cambridge (BA Hons). Commonwealth Fellow, Panjab Univ., 1970–72; Jun. Res. Fellow, Inst. of Commonwealth Studies, Univ. of London, 1972–74; joined HM Diplomatic Service, 1974; Delegn to CSCE, 1974–75; FCO, 1975–76; First Secretary: Delegn to NATO, 1976–79; New Delhi, 1980–83; FCO, 1983–87; Counsellor, CSCE Delegn, Vienna, 1987–89; Dep. Hd, UK Delegn to negotiations on conventional arms control, Vienna, 1989–91; Dep. High Comr and Counsellor (Econ. and Commercial), Kuala Lumpur, 1992–94; Head of Non-Proliferation Dept, FCO, 1995–97; Minister and Dep. Perm. Rep., UK Delegn to NATO, Brussels, 1997–2001. *Publication:* (with V. N. Datta) A Nationalist Muslim and Indian Politics, 1974. *Recreations:* swimming, walking, studying British 20th century painters.

CLEIN, Natalie; solo cellist; *b* 25 March 1977; *d* of Peter Clein and Channa Clein (*née* Salomonson). *Educ:* Royal Coll. of Music; Hochschule Vienna (with Heinrich Schiff). Artist in Association, RCM, 2005–. Young Musician of Year, BBC, 1994; Eurovision Young Musician, 1994; Ingrid zu Zolms Kultur Preis, 2003; Young Artist Brit Award, 2005. *Address:* c/o Askonas Holt, Lincoln House, 300 High Holborn, WC1V 7JH.

CLELAND, Helen Isabel; Headteacher, Woodford County High School, since 1991; *b* 3 July 1950; *d* of John Douglas Cleland and Hilda Malvina Cleland; *m* 1973, Dr Robin Hoult (*d* 2001); one *s* one *d*. *Educ:* King Edward VI High Sch. for Girls, Birmingham; Exeter Univ. (BA Hons English); Homerton Coll., Cambridge (PGCE). English Teacher, Dame Alice Owen's Sch., London, 1972–76; English Teacher, 1976–79, Sen. Teacher, 1979–86, Haverstock Sch., London; Dep. Head, Edmonton Sch., Enfield, 1986–91. *Recreations:* reading, theatre, hill walking, horse-riding, travel. *Address:* Woodford County High School, High Road, Woodford Green, Essex IG8 9LA. *T:* (020) 8504 0611.

CLELAND, Prof. John Goodhart, CBE 2008; FBA 2003; Professor of Medical Demography, London School of Hygiene and Tropical Medicine, since 1993; *b* 9 March 1942; *s* of late William Paton Cleland; *m* 1st, 1969, Susan Gilbert Harman (marr. diss. 1990); one *s* one *d*; 2nd, 2004, Sandra Carr. *Educ:* Charterhouse Sch.; Selwyn Coll., Cambridge (MA). Res. Officer, LSE, 1966–69; Sociologist, Population Bureau, ODA, 1969–72; Demographer, Med. Dept, Fiji, 1972–74; Demographic Analyst, World Fertility Survey, ISI, 1975–87; Sen. Res. Fellow, LSHTM, 1988–92. Mem., Scientific and Adv. Gp, Dept of Reproductive Health and Res., WHO, 1999–2005; Chm., Population Investigation Cttee, 2003–. President: British Soc. for Population Studies, 1997–99; Internat. Union for Scientific Study of Population, 2006–. *Publications:* (with J. Hobcraft) Reproductive Change in Developing Countries: insights from the World Fertility Survey, 1985; (with C. Scott) The World Fertility Survey: an assessment, 1987; (with A. Hill) The Health Transition: methods and measures, 1991; (jtly) The Determinants of Reproductive Change in Bangladesh, 1994; (with B. Ferry) Sexual Behaviour and AIDS in the Developing World, 1995. *Recreations:* fishing, woodland management. *Address:* The Manor House, Silver Street, Barton St David, Somerset TA11 6DB. *T:* and *Fax:* (01458) 851266; *e-mail:* John.Cleland@lshtm.ac.uk.

CLELLAND, David Gordon; MP (Lab) Tyne Bridge, since Dec. 1985; *b* 27 June 1943; *s* of Archibald and Ellen Clelland; *m* 2004, Brenda; two *d* from former marr. *Educ:* Kelvin Grove Boys' School, Gateshead; Gateshead and Hebburn Technical Colleges. Apprentice electrical fitter, 1959–64; electrical tester, 1964–81. Gateshead Borough Council: Councillor, 1972–86; Recreation Chm., 1976–84; Leader of Council, 1984–86. Nat. Sec., Assoc. of Councillors, 1981–85. An Asst Govt Whip, 1997–2000; a Lord Comr of HM Treasury (Govt Whip), 2000–01. Member: Home Affairs Select Cttee, 1986–88; Energy Select Cttee, 1989–90; OPDM Select Cttee, 2001–05; Transport Select Cttee, 2005–. Chairman, All Party Group: on non-profit-making Members' Clubs; on Turks and Caicos Is, 2005–; Chairman: Backbench Envmt Cttee, 1990–97; PLP Regl Govt Gp, 1992–97; PLP Trade Union Gp, 1994–97; Vice-Chm., Northern Gp of Lab MPs (Sec.), 1990–98). *Recreation:* golf, music, reading. *Address:* (office) 19 Ravensworth Road, Dunston, Gateshead NE11 9AB. *T:* (0191) 420 0300.

CLEMENS, Clive Carruthers, CMG 1983; MC 1946; HM Diplomatic Service, retired; High Commissioner in Lesotho, 1981–84; *b* 22 Jan. 1924; British; *s* of late M. B. Clemens, Imperial Bank of India, and late Margaret Jane (*née* Carruthers); *m* 1947, Philippa Jane Bailey; two *s* (and one *s* decd). *Educ:* Blundell's Sch.; St Catharine's Coll., Cambridge. War Service 1943–46: commissioned in Duke of Cornwall's Light Infantry; served in India and Burma, 1944–45. Entered HM Foreign Service and apptd to FO, 1947; Third Sec.,

Rangoon, 1948; Third (later Second) Sec., Lisbon, 1950; FO, 1953; First Sec., Budapest, 1954; Brussels, 1956; Seoul, 1959; FO, 1961; Strasbourg (UK Delegn to Council of Europe), 1964; Counsellor, Paris, 1967; Principal British Trade Comr, Vancouver, 1970–74; Dep. Consul-Gen., Johannesburg, 1974–78; Consul-Gen., Istanbul, 1978–81. *Recreations:* birdwatching, photography. *Address:* 9 Saxonhurst, Downton, Salisbury, Wilts SP5 3JN.

CLEMENT, David James, OBE 2006; Chairman, Systems Network, since 1997; *b* 29 Sept. 1930; *s* of James and Constance Clement; *m* 1958, Margaret Stone; two *s* one *d. Educ:* Chipping Sodbury Grammar Sch.; Univ. of Bristol (BA). CPFA 1957. Internal Audit Asst, City of Bristol, 1953–56; Accountancy/Audit Asst, 1956–60, Chief Accountancy Asst, 1960–65, City of Worcester; Dep. Chief Finance Officer, Runcorn Develt Corp., 1965–68; Chief Finance Officer, Antrim and Ballymena Develt Commn, 1968–72; Asst Sec., Dept of Finance, NI, 1972–75, Dep. Sec., 1975–80; Under Sec., DoE, NI, 1980–84. Financial consultant, 1985–90; Chm., HELM Corp., 1990–98. Mem., Investigations Cttee, CIPFA, 2001–. Chm. Trustees, Ulster Historical Foundn, 2000–. Hon. Treas., NI Council for Voluntary Action, 2000–05. *Recreations:* lawn tennis, Association football, contract bridge, philately.

CLEMENT, John; Chairman: Culpho Consultants, since 1991; Tuddenham Hall Foods, since 1991; *b* 18 May 1932; *s* of Frederick and Alice Eleanor Clement; *m* 1956, Elisabeth Anne (*née* Emery); two *s* one *d. Educ:* Bishop's Stortford College. Howards Dairies, Westcliff on Sea, 1949–64; United Dairies London Ltd, 1964–69; Asst Managing Director, Rank Leisure Services Ltd, 1969–73; Chairman, Unigate Foods Div., 1973; Chief Executive, 1976–90, Chm., 1977–91, Unigate Group. Non-executive Chairman: The Littlewoods Organisation, 1982–90; Nat. Car Auctions Ltd, 1995–98; Director: NV Verenigde Bedrijven Nutricia, 1981–92; Eagle Star Holdings plc, 1981–86; Eagle Star Insce Co., 1981–84; Anglo American Insce Co., 1991–94 (Chm., 1993–94); Ransomes plc, 1991–98 (Chm., 1993–98); Dresdner RCM Second Endowment Policy Trust plc (formerly Kleinwort Second Endowment Trust plc), 1993– (Chm., 1998–); Jarvis Hotels Ltd, 1994–2004. Mem., Securities and Investments Bd, 1986–89. Chairman: King's Coll., Cambridge I-IV (business expansion scheme), 1993–98; Govs, Framlingham Coll., 1991–2001 (Gov., 1982–2001). Chairman: Children's Liver Disease Foundn, 1979–95; British Liver Trust, 1992–99. High Sheriff, Suffolk, 2000–01. CCMI (FBIM 1977); FIGD 1979. *Recreations:* shooting, sailing, bridge, Rugby, tennis. *Address:* Tuddenham Hall, Tuddenham, Ipswich, Suffolk IP6 9DD. *T:* (01473) 785217. *Clubs:* Farmers'; Cumberland Lawn Tennis; Royal Harwich Yacht.

See also R. Clement.

CLEMENT, Marc; *see* Clement, R. M.

CLEMENT, Richard, (Dick), OBE 2007; freelance writer, director and producer; *b* 5 Sept. 1937; *s* of Frederick and Alice Eleanor Clement; *m* 1st, Jennifer F. Sheppard (marr. diss. 1981); three *s* one *d*; 2nd, 1982, Nancy S. Campbell; one *d. Educ:* Bishop's Stortford Coll.; Westminster Sch., Conn, USA. Co-writer (with Ian La Frenais): *television:* The Likely Lads, 1964–66; Whatever Happened to the Likely Lads, 1972–73; Porridge, 1974–76; Thick as Thieves, 1974; Going Straight, 1978; Auf Wiedersehen, Pet, 1983–84, 2002–04; Freddie and Max, 1990; Full Stretch, 1993; The Rotters' Club (adaptation), 2005; Archangel (adaptation), 2005; *films:* The Jokers, 1967; Otley, 1968; Hannibal Brooks, 1968; Villain, 1971; Porridge, 1979; Water, 1984; Vice Versa, 1987; The Commitments, 1991; Still Crazy, 1998; Honest, 2000; Goal, 2005; Flushed Away, 2006; Across the Universe, 2007; The Bank Job, 2008. Director: *films:* Otley, 1968; A Severed Head, 1969; Porridge, 1979; Bullshot, 1983; Water, 1984; co-producer (with Ian La Frenais) Vice Versa, 1987; The Commitments, 1991 (jtly, Evening Standard Peter Sellers Award, 1992); *stage:* Billy, 1974; Anyone for Denis?, 1981. *Recreations:* work, tennis, dinner; supporting Essex CCC, Chelsea FC and Los Angeles Dodgers. *Address:* 9700 Yoakum Drive, Beverly Hills, CA 90210, USA. *Clubs:* Garrick; Mulholland Tennis (LA).

See also John Clement.

CLEMENT, Prof. (Robert) Marc, PhD; CPhys, FIET; Vice-Chancellor and Chief Executive, University of Wales, since 2007; *b* Llwynhendy, Llanelli, 19 Nov. 1953; *s* of Gerald Edmund Clement and Eira Mary Clement; one *d. Educ:* Univ. of Wales, Swansea (BSc 1st cl. Hons Physics 1976; Postgrad. Dip. Ionisation Physics 1977); Univ. of Wales (PhD Laser Physics 1979). CPhys, MInstP 1984; FIET 2002. Teacher of Maths and Physics, Ystalyfera Sch., 1980; Royal Soc. Scholarship for Postdoctoral Study, Centre d'Etudes Nucleaire de Saclay, Paris, 1981–82; West Glamorgan Institute of Higher Education: Temp. Lectr, 1982, Lectr I, 1983, Lectr II, 1984, in Maths; transfer to Fac. of Electronic Engrg, 1985; Sen. Lectr in Microelectronics, 1986; Principal Lectr and Hd, Sch. of Electrical Engrg, 1987; Dean, Fac. of Electronic Engrg, 1988; University of Wales, Swansea: Chair of Innovation, Sch. of Engrg, 2000; Sen. Exec. to Vice Chancellor's Office, 2004. P. M. Davidson Prize for Theoretical Physics, Univ. of Wales, Swansea, 1976; Business Award, HTV/Western Mail, 1990. *Publications:* books and articles in academic jls. *Recreations:* ski-ing, squash, weight training, choral singing, Sunday school teacher, adjudicator at many National and Urdd Eisteddfodau. *Address:* University of Wales Registry, King Edward II Avenue, Cardiff CF10 3NS. *T:* (029) 2037 6965, *Fax:* (029) 2037 6982; *e-mail:* r.m.clement@wales.ac.uk.

CLEMENT-JONES, family name of **Baron Clement-Jones.**

CLEMENT-JONES, Baron *cr* 1998 (Life Peer), of Clapham in the London Borough of Lambeth; **Timothy Francis Clement-Jones,** CBE 1988; Chairman: Global Government Relations (formerly Upstream), government and media relations practice of DLA Piper (formerly Dibb Lupton Alsop, subseq. DLA Piper Rudwick Gray Cary), since 1999; Context Group (formerly Environmental Context) Ltd, since 1997; Federal Treasurer, Liberal Democrats, since 2005; *b* 26 Oct. 1949; *s* of late Maurice Llewelyn Clement-Jones and of Margaret Jean Clement-Jones (*née* Hudson); *m* 1st, 1973, Dr Vicky Veronica Yip (*d* 1987); 2nd, 1994, Jean Roberta Whiteside; one *s. Educ:* Haileybury; Trinity Coll., Cambridge (Economics Pt I, Law Tripos Pt II; MA). Admitted Solicitor, 1974. Articled Clerk, Coward Chance, 1972–74; Associate, Joynson-Hicks, 1974–76; Corporate Lawyer, Letraset Internat. Ltd, 1976–80; Hd Legal Services, LWT, 1980–83; Legal Dir, Grand Metropolitan Retailing, 1984–86; Gp Co. Sec. and Legal Advr, Woolworth Hldgs, then Kingfisher plc, 1986–95; Director: Political Context Ltd, 1996–99; British American Business Inc., 2006–. Lib Dem spokesman on health, H of L, 1998–2004, on culture, media and sport, 2004–. Vice-Chairman: All-Party China Gp; All-Party Autism Gp. Chm., Assoc. of Liberal Lawyers, 1982–86. Chairman: Liberal Party, 1986–88; Lib Dem Finance Cttee, 1991–98; Dir, Lib Dem EP election campaign, 1994; Chm., Lib Dem Mayoral and Assembly campaign, London, 2000, 2004. Trustee and Dir, Cancer BACUP, subseq. Cancerbackup (founded by Dr V. V. Clement-Jones), 1986–2008. Chairman: Crime Concern, 1991–95; Lambeth Crime Prevention Trust, 2004–; Mem. Bd, Centre for Reform, 1998–. Chm. Council, Sch. of Pharmacy, Univ. of London, 2008–. Chm. Trustees, Treehouse, educnl charity for autistic children, 2001–; Gov., Haileybury, 2001–. FRSA. *Recreations:* reading, eating, talking, diving, travelling, walking. *Address:* 10 Northbourne Road, SW4 7DJ. *T:* (020) 7622 4205; *e-mail:* clementjonest@parliament.uk.

CLEMENTI, Sir David (Cecil), Kt 2004; Chairman, Prudential plc, 2002–08; *b* 25 Feb. 1949; *s* of Air Vice-Marshal Cresswell Montagu Clementi, CB, CBE and Susan (*née* Pelham); *m* 1972, Sarah Louise, (Sally), Cowley; one *s* one *d. Educ:* Winchester Coll.; Lincoln Coll., Oxford; Harvard Business Sch. (MBA 1975). With Arthur Andersen & Co., 1970–73; qualified as CA 1973; with Kleinwort Benson Ltd, 1975–97: Dir, 1981–97; Man. Dir, KB Securities, 1987–89; Head, Corporate Finance, 1989–94; Chief Exec., 1994–97; Vice Chm., 1997; Dep. Gov., Bank of England, 1997–2002. Non-exec. Dir, Rio Tinto plc, 2003–. Trustee, Royal Opera House, 2006–. Warden, Winchester Coll., 2008–. *Recreation:* sailing. *Clubs:* Royal Ocean Racing; Royal Yacht Squadron.

CLEMENTS, Alan William, CBE 1990; Director, Capital Value Brokers Ltd, 1999–2006; *b* 12 Dec. 1928; *s* of William and Kathleen Clements; *m* 1953, Pearl Dorling (*d* 1993); two *s* one *d. Educ:* Culford School, Bury St Edmunds; Magdalen College, Oxford (BA Hons). HM Inspector of Taxes, Inland Revenue, 1952–56; ICI: Asst Treasurer, 1966; Dep. Treasurer, 1971; Treasurer, 1976; Finance Director, 1979–90. Chairman: David S. Smith (Hldgs), 1991–99; Cementone, 1994–97; Non-executive Director: Trafalgar House, 1980–95 (Chm., 1992–93); Cable & Wireless, 1985–91; Guinness Mahon Hldgs, 1988–92; Granada Gp, 1990–94; Mirror Gp (formerly Mirror Gp Newspapers), 1991–99 (Dep. Chm., 1992–99); Brent Walker Gp, 1991–93. Lay Mem., Internat. Stock Exchange, 1984–88. Founder Pres., Assoc. of Corp. Treasurers, 1979–82 (Hon. Fellow). *Publications:* articles on finance in jls. *Recreations:* golf, music, reading.

CLEMENTS, Andrew; *see* Clements, F. A.

CLEMENTS, Andrew Joseph; Music Critic, Guardian, since 1993; *b* 15 Sept. 1950; *s* of Joseph George Clements and Linda Helen Clements; *m* 1977, Kathryn Denise Coltman (marr. diss. 2007); two *d. Educ:* Crypt Sch., Gloucester; Emmanuel Coll., Cambridge (BA). Music Critic: New Statesman, 1977–88; Financial Times, 1979–93; Editor, Musical Times, 1987–88. Dir, Holst Foundn, 1992–. *Publication:* Mark-Anthony Turnage, 2000. *Recreation:* birding. *Address:* c/o Guardian, Kings Place, 90 York Way, N1 9AG.

CLEMENTS, Dr (Frederick) Andrew; Director, British Trust for Ornithology, since 2007; *b* Morecambe, Lancs, 25 Oct. 1954; *s* of Frederick George Clements and Clarice Clements (*née* Hartley); *m* 1997, Susannah Burton (marr. diss. 2008); one *s* one *d. Educ:* Haberdashers' Aske's Sch.; University Coll. of Wales, Bangor (BSc Hons Zool.); Univ. of Wales (PhD Zool. 1980). Conservation Officer, NCC, 1982–87; Chief Wildlife Inspector, DoE, 1987–91; Manager, 1991–2000, Dir, Protected Areas, 2000–06, English Nature; Dir, Ferrypath Consulting Ltd (own co.), 2006–08. Wildlife Tour Leader (pt-time), Himalayas, Ethiopia, Namibia, 1990–2002. *Publications:* (contrib.) AA Field Guide to the Birds of Britain and Europe, 1998; (contrib.) Silent Summer, 2009; contrib. scientific papers to New Scientist, Animal Behaviour, Behaviour, Zeitschrift fur Tierpsychologie. *Recreations:* birding, watching wildlife round the world, rowing on an Ergo, veggie cooking. *Address:* c/o British Trust for Ornithology, The Nunnery, Thetford, Norfolk IP24 2PU. *T:* (01842) 750050, (01842) 750030; *e-mail:* andy.clements@bto.org, andy.clements@ferrypath.co.uk.

CLEMENTS, John Rodney, FCA; Finance Manager, People & Planet Ltd, since 2006; *b* 19 Jan. 1947; *s* of late Peter Larby Clements and of Ethel Blanche Lillian Clements (*née* Steele); *m* 1st, 1969, Janet Sylvia Mallender (marr. diss. 1992); two *d*; 2nd, 1999, Georgina Margaret Eckles (marr. diss. 2005). *Educ:* Univ. of Manchester (BA Hons Mod. Hist. with Econs and Politics 1968). ACA 1973, FCA 1978. Auditor, KPMG Peat Marwick, Accountants, 1968–73; Financial Accountant, Co-operative Bank, 1973–74; Asst to Chief Accountant, Stock Exchange, 1974–79; Dep. Finance Officer, UCL, 1979–85; Dep. Dir of Finance, Univ. of Sheffield, 1985–92; Dir of Finance, Univ. of Leeds, 1992–94; independent consultant, 1994–95; Sec. of the Chest, then Dir of Finance and Sec. of the Chest, Univ. of Oxford, 1995–2004; Fellow, Merton Coll., Oxford, 1995–2004. *Recreations:* history, literature, hill walking, model railways. *Address:* 19 Raleigh Park Road, Oxford OX2 9AZ.

CLEMENTS, Judith M.; independent consultant, since 2001; Chief Executive, National Association for Mental Health, 1992–2001; *b* 27 June 1953; *d* of Robert and Margaret Dunn; *m* 1st, 1975, Paul Clements (marr. diss. 1979); 2nd, 1998, Rex Hewitt. *Educ:* Birmingham Univ. (LLB Hons 1974); Brunel Univ. (MA Public and Social Admin 1979). Dip. Inst. Housing 1976. London Borough of Camden: Estate Manager, 1974–76; Sen. Estate Manager, 1976–79; Tenancy Services Officer, 1979–81; Business System Analyst, 1981–82; Asst Dir of Housing, 1982–87; Dep. Chief Housing Officer, Brighton BC, 1987–91; Hd of Management Practice, Local Govt Management Bd, 1991–92. Trustee, Mentality, 2001–03; Mem., UK Grants Cttee, Comic Relief, 2003–. Mem. Bd of Govs, Brighton Univ., 2000–. FRSA 1999. Hon. DSocSci Brunel, 1997. *Recreations:* reading, especially crime fiction and feminist fiction, yoga. *Address:* Studio 1, Limehouse Cut, 46 Morris Road, E14 6NQ. *T:* (020) 7987 9487; *e-mail:* Judi@studione.info.

CLEMENTS, Julia; *see* Seton, Lady, (Julia).

CLEMENTS, Rev. Keith Winston, PhD; General Secretary, Conference of European Churches, 1997–2005; *b* China, 7 May 1943; *s* of Harry Clements and Alfreda (*née* Yarwood); *m* 1967, Margaret Hirst; two *s. Educ:* King Edward VII Sch., Lytham; King's Coll., Cambridge (MA 1969); Regent's Park Coll., Oxford (MA 1972, BD 1980); PhD Bristol 1997. Ordained to Baptist Ministry, 1967; Associate Minister, Mid-Cheshire Fellowship of Baptist Chs, 1967–71; Minister, Downend Baptist Ch, Bristol, 1971–77; Tutor, Bristol Baptist Coll., 1977–90; Sec. for Internat. Affairs, CCBI, 1990–97. Part-time Lectr, Dept of Theol. and Religious Studies, Univ. of Bristol, 1984–90; Select Preacher, Univ. of Cambridge, 1993. Hon. Fellow, New Coll., Edinburgh, 1990–99. Ed., Baptist Historical Soc., 1980–85. *Publications:* Faith, 1981; A Patriotism for Today: dialogue with Dietrich Bonhoeffer, 1984; The Theology of Ronald Gregor Smith, 1986; Friedrich Schleiermacher, 1987; Lovers of Discord, 1988; What Freedom?: the persistent challenge of Dietrich Bonhoeffer, 1990; Learning to Speak: the Church's voice in public affairs, 1995; Faith on the Frontier: a life of J. H. Oldham, 1999; The Churches in Europe as Witnesses to Healing, 2003; Bonhoeffer and Britain, 2006; numerous articles in learned jls on theol. and religion. *Recreations:* ornithology, reading, listening to music, walking, jogging. *Address:* 67 Hillcrest Road, Portishead, N Somerset BS20 8HN. *T:* (01275) 845242.

CLEMENTS, Kirsty Anne; *see* Wark, K. A.

CLEMENTS, Michael Alan; Resident Senior Immigration Judge, Asylum and Immigration Tribunal, since 2007; *b* 25 Nov. 1954; *s* of Philip and Gwendoline Clements; *m* 1978, Carol Mary; three *s. Educ:* King Edward VI Sch., Bath. Admitted solicitor, 1983; NP; articled clerk, solicitor, then Partner, Giffin Couch & Archer, Leighton Buzzard, 1979–90; Solicitor, Horwood & James, Aylesbury, 1990–2001; Immigration Adjudicator, 2001–; Sen. Immigration Judge, 2006. Legal Mem., Tribunals Service, 1993–. Pres.,

Allotment Soc. *Recreations:* collection of broken clocks, curing and smoking of meat and fish, gardening, walking in desolate places. *Address:* York House, 2/3 Dukes Green Avenue, Feltham, Middx TW14 0LR. *T:* (020) 8831 3522, *Fax:* (020) 8890 7647.

CLEMENTS, Prof. Ronald Ernest; Samuel Davidson Professor of Old Testament Studies, King's College, University of London, 1983–92, now Professor Emeritus; *b* 27 May 1929; *m* 1955, Valerie Winifred (*née* Suffield); two *d. Educ:* Buckhurst Hill County High Sch.; Spurgeon's Coll.; Christ's Coll., Cambridge; Univ. of Sheffield. MA, DD Cantab. Asst Lectr 1960–64, Lectr 1960–67, Univ. of Edinburgh; Lectr, Univ. of Cambridge, 1967–83. Hon. For. Sec., SOTS, 1973–83 (Pres., 1985–); Hon. Mem., OTWSA, 1979–. Hon. DLitt Acadia, Nova Scotia, 1982. *Publications:* God and Temple, 1965; Prophecy and Covenant, 1965; Old Testament Theology, 1978; Isaiah 1–39, 1979; A Century of Old Testament Study, 1976, 2nd edn 1983; Prayers of the Bible, 1986; Jeremiah, 1988; (ed) The World of Ancient Israel, 1989; Wisdom in Theology, 1993; Old Testament Prophecy: from oracles to canon, 1996; contrib. Vetus Testamentum, Jl of Semitic Studies. *Recreations:* reading, travel, photography, aeromodelling. *Address:* 8 Brookfield Road, Coton, Cambridge CB23 7PT.

CLEMINSON, Sir James (Arnold Stacey), KBE 1990; Kt 1982; MC 1945; DL; Deputy Chairman, J. H. Fenner plc, 1993–97 (Director, 1989–97); *b* 31 Aug. 1921; *s* of Arnold Russel Cleminson and Florence Stacey; *m* 1950, Helen Juliet Measor; one *s* two *d. Educ:* Rugby Sch. Served War, 1940–46, mainly in Parachute Regt. Reckitt & Colman, 1946–86: Chief Exec., 1973–80; Chm., 1977–86; Chairman: Jeyes Hygiene, 1986–89; Riggs A P Bank, 1987–91 (Dir, 1985–2002); Director: Norwich Union, 1979–92 (Vice-Chm., 1981–92); United Biscuits, 1982–89; Eastern Counties Newspaper Gp, 1987–93; Riggs Nat. Bank of Washington, 1991–93; Member: Council, CBI, 1978–86 (Dep. Pres., 1983; Pres., 1984–86); London Cttee, Toronto Dominion Bank, 1982–90; NEDC, 1984–86. Jt Chm., Netherlands British Chamber of Commerce Council, 1978–84; Chairman: Food and Drink Industries Council, 1983–84; Nurses' Independent Pay Review Body, 1986–90; BOTB, 1986–90. Pres., Endeavour Trng, 1984–98; Trustee, Airborne Forces Security Fund, 1972–2006. Chm., Theatre Royal Norwich Trust, 1991–98. Pro-Chancellor, Hull Univ., 1985–94. Hon. LLD Hull, 1985. DL Norfolk, 1983. *Recreations:* field sports, golf. *Address:* Loddon Hall, Hales, Norfolk NR14 6TB. *Club:* Norfolk (Norwich).

CLEMITS, John Henry, RIBA; Managing Director, PSA Projects Cardiff, 1990–92; *b* 16 Feb. 1934; *s* of late Cyril Thomas Clemits and Minnie Alberta Clemits; *m* 1958, Elizabeth Angela Moon; one *s* one *d. Educ:* Sutton High Sch.; Plymouth College of Art. ARIBA 1962 (Dist. in Thesis). National Service, RAF, 1959–61; Captain, RE (TA), 43 Wessex Div. and Royal Monmouthshire RE (Militia), 1964–69. Plymouth City Architects Dept, 1954–59; Watkins Gray & Partners, Architects, Bristol, 1961–63; SW RHB, 1963–65; Architect, MPBW, Bristol, 1965–69; Sen. Architect, MPBW, Regional HQ, Rheindahlen, Germany, 1969–71; Naval Base Planning Officer, MPBW, Portsmouth, 1971–73; Suptg Architect, PSA, Directorate of Bldg Develt, 1973–75; Suptg Planning Officer, PSA, Rheindahlen, 1975–79; Dir of Works (Army), PSA, Chessington, 1979–85; Dir for Wales, PSA, Central Office for Wales, DoE, 1985–90. Chairman: Cowbridge Choral Soc., 1988–90; Vale of Glamorgan Buildings Preservation Trust, 1994–97; Chm., 1995–2001, Vice-Chm., 2001–, Dewi Sant Housing Assoc. Mem. Nat. Council, Welsh Fedn of Housing Assocs, 1996–99. Chm., S Wales Art Soc., 2005–06 (Prog. Sec., 2002–05). *Recreations:* music, DIY, painting, travel. *Address:* The Lodge, Hendrescythan, Creigiau, Cardiff CF15 9NN. *T:* (029) 2089 1786.

CLEMMOW, Jana Eve; *see* Bennett, J. E.

CLEMMOW, Simon Phillip; Founder, CHI & Partners (formerly Clemmow Hornby Inge Ltd), advertising agency, 2001; *b* Cambridge, 30 June 1956; *s* of Dr Phillip Charles and Joan Alicia Clemmow; *m* 1987, Elizabeth Danuta Kaminska; one *s* and one step *d. Educ:* Univ. of Reading (BA Hons Typography and Graphic Communication). Trainee, Benton & Bowles, 1982; Account Planner, Gold Greenlees Trott, 1983–88; Founder, Simons Palmer Denton Clemmow & Johnson, 1988–97; CEO, TBWA, 1997–2001. *Recreations:* books, crosswords, music, cycling, golf, ski-ing, walking, watching Arsenal FC and the England cricket team. *Address:* CHI & Partners, 7 Rathbone Street, W1T 1LY. *T:* (020) 7462 8580, *Fax:* (020) 7462 8501; *e-mail:* simon.clemmow@chiandpartners.com. *Clubs:* Home House, Union; Brocket Hall Golf.

CLEOBURY, Nicholas Randall, MA; FRCO; conductor; *b* 23 June 1950; *s* of John and Brenda Cleobury; *m* 1978, Heather Kay; one *s* one *d. Educ:* King's Sch., Worcester; Worcester Coll., Oxford (MA Hons). Assistant Organist: Chichester Cathedral, 1971–72; Christ Church, Oxford, 1972–76; Chorus Master, Glyndebourne Opera, 1977–79; Asst Director, BBC Singers, 1977–79; Conductor: main BBC, provincial and London orchestras and opera houses, also in Albania, Australia, Austria, Belgium, Canada, Denmark, France, Germany, Holland, Italy, Lithuania, Norway, Poland, Singapore, Slovenia, S Africa, Spain, Sweden, Switzerland, USA; regular BBC TV appearances; numerous CD recordings. Principal Opera Conductor, Royal Academy of Music, 1981–88; Artistic Director: Aquarius, 1983–92; Cambridge Symphony Soloists, 1990–92; Britten Sinfonia, 1992–2005; Music Dir, Oxford Bach Choir, 1997–; Founder and Artistic Dir, 1997–2006, Principal Conductor, 2006–, Sounds New; Associate Dir, Orchestra of the Swan, 2004–; Principal Guest Conductor, Gävle, Sweden, 1989–91; Guest Conductor, Zürich Opera, 1993–. Music Dir, Broomhill Arts, 1990–94; Artistic Director: Cambridge Fest., 1992; Mozart Now, 2004–06; Artistic Advr, Berks Choral Fest., USA, 2002–. Hon. RAM 1985. *Recreations:* reading, food, wine, theatre, walking, cricket. *Address:* 20 Denbigh Street, SW1V 2ER. *T:* 07831 148637; *e-mail:* NicholasCleobury@btinternet.com. *Clubs:* Savage, MCC, Lord's Taverners.

See also S. J. Cleobury.

CLEOBURY, Stephen John, FRCM; FRCO; Fellow, Director of Music and Organist, King's College, Cambridge, since 1982; Conductor, Cambridge University Musical Society, since 1983; Organist, Cambridge University, since 1991; *b* 31 Dec. 1948; *s* of John Frank Cleobury and Brenda Julie (*née* Randall); *m*; two *d*; *m* 2004, Emma Sian, *d* of John Ivor Disley, *qv*; one *d. Educ:* King's Sch., Worcester; St John's Coll., Cambridge (MA, MusB). FRCO 1968; FRCM 1993. Organist, St Matthew's, Northampton, 1971–74; Sub-Organist, Westminster Abbey, 1974–78; Master of Music, Westminster Cathedral, 1979–82. Chief Conductor, 1995–2007, Conductor Laureate, 2007–, BBC Singers. President: IAO, 1985–87; Cathedral Organists' Assoc., 1988–90; RCO, 1990–92, 2008– (Hon. Sec., 1981–90); Mem. Council, RSCM, 1982–. Hon. DMus Anglia Poly., 2001. *Recreation:* reading. *Address:* King's College, Cambridge CB2 1ST. *T:* (01223) 331224.

See also N. R. Cleobury.

CLERIDES, Glafcos John; President of Cyprus, 1993–2003; *b* Nicosia, 24 April 1919; *s* of Yiannis Clerides, CBE, QC and Elli Clerides; *m* 1946, Lilla Erulkar; one *d. Educ:* Pancyprium Gymnasium, Nicosia; King's Coll., London (LLB 1948). Served in RAF, 1939–45; shot down and taken prisoner, 1942–45 (mentioned in despatches). Called to the Bar, Gray's Inn, 1951; practised in Cyprus, 1951–60; Head, Greek Cypriot Delegn, Jt Constitutional Cttee, 1959–60; Minister of Justice, 1959–60; Mem. for Nicosia, House of Representatives, 1960–76, 1981–93; First Pres. of House, 1960–76; Leader, Greek Cypriot Delegn to London Conf., 1964; Rep. of Greek Cypriots to intercommunal talks, 1968–76; Actg Pres., July–Dec. 1974 (after Turkish invasion of Cyprus). Founder and Leader: Unified Party, 1969–76; Democratic Rally Party, 1976–93. Cert. of Honour and Life Mem., Cyprus Red Cross (Pres., 1961–63). Gold Medal, Order of the Holy Sepulchre, 1961. Grand Cross of the Redeemer (Greece), 1993. *Publication:* My Deposition, 4 vols. *Address:* 5 Ioannis Clerides Street, Nicosia, Cyprus.

CLERK, Sir Robert (Maxwell), 11th Bt *cr* 1679, of Penicuik (NS); OBE 1995; DL; *b* 3 April 1945; *er s* of Sir John Dutton Clerk, 10th Bt, CBE, VRD and Evelyn Elizabeth Clerk (*née* Robertson); *S* father, 2002; *m* 1970, Felicity Faye Collins; two *s* one *d. Educ:* Winchester Coll.; Wye Coll., London Univ. (BScAgric). FRICS. Partner, Smiths Gore, Chartered Surveyors, 1980–2003. Chm., Atlantic Salmon Trust, 2005–; Vice-Pres., Assoc. of Salmon Fishery Bds, 1996–. Brig., Queen's Body Guard for Scotland (Royal Company of Archers). DL Midlothian, 1995. *Recreations:* bee-keeping, landscape gardening, field sports. *Heir: s* George Napier Clerk, *b* 27 May 1975. *Club:* New (Edinburgh).

CLERKE, Sir John Edward Longueville, 12th Bt *cr* 1660; Captain Royal Wilts Yeomanry, RAC, TA; *b* 29 Oct. 1913; *er s* of Francis William Talbot Clerke (killed in action, 1916), *e s* of 11th Bt, and late Albinia Mary, *er d* of Edward Henry Evans-Lombe (who *m* 3rd, 1923, Air Chief Marshal Sir Edgar Rainey Ludlow-Hewitt, GCB, GBE, CMG, DSO, MC); *S* grandfather, 1930; *m* 1948, Mary (marr. diss. 1987; she *d* 1998), *d* of late Lt-Col I. R. Beviss Bond, OBE, MC; one *s* two *d. Heir: s* Francis Ludlow Longueville Clerke [*b* 25 Jan. 1953; *m* 1982, Vanessa Anne, *o d* of late Charles Cosman Citron and of Mrs Olga May Citron, Mouille Point, Cape Town; one *s* one *d*].

CLEVELAND, Archdeacon of; *see* Ferguson, Ven. P. J.

CLEVELAND, Alexis Jane, CB 2004; Director General, Transformational Government and Cabinet Office Management, Cabinet Office, since 2007; *b* 28 Jan. 1954; *d* of Arthur and Peggy Cleveland. *Educ:* Brighton and Hove High Sch.; Univ. of Salford. Business Develt Dir, IT Services Agency, 1989–93; Benefits Agency, Department of Social Security, subseq. Department for Work and Pensions: Territorial and Jobseekers Allowance Dir, 1993–97; Ops Support Dir, 1997–2000; Chief Exec., 2000–02; Chief Exec., Pension Service, 2002–07. *Recreations:* travel, walking, swimming, cinema, theatre. *Address:* Cabinet Office, Admiralty Arch, The Mall, SW1A 2WH.

CLEVELAND, Harlan; President, World Academy of Art and Science, 1991–2000, now President Emeritus; Professor, 1980–88 and Dean, 1980–87, Hubert H. Humphrey Institute of Public Affairs, University of Minnesota, now Professor Emeritus; *b* 19 Jan. 1918; *s* of Stanley Matthews Cleveland and Marian Phelps (*née* Van Buren); *m* 1941, Lois W. Burton; one *s* two *d. Educ:* Phillips Acad., Andover, Mass; Princeton Univ.; Oxford Univ. (Rhodes Scholar). Farm Security Admin, Dept of Agric., 1940–42; Bd of Econ. Warfare (subseq. Foreign Econ. Admin), 1942–44; Exec. Dir Econ. Sect., 1944–45, Actg Vice-Pres., 1945–46, Allied Control Commn, Rome; Mem. US Delegn, UNRRA Council, London, 1945; Dept Chief of Mission, UNRRA Italian Mission, Rome, 1946–47; Dir, UNRRA China Office, Shanghai, 1947–48; Dir, China Program, Econ. Coop. Admin., Washington, 1948–49; Dept Asst Adminstr, 1949–51; Asst Dir for Europe, Mutual Security Agency, 1952–53; Exec. Editor, The Reporter, NYC, 1953–56, Publisher, 1955–56; Dean, Maxwell Sch. of Citizenship and Pub. Affairs, Syracuse Univ., 1956–61; Asst Sec. for Internat. Orgn Affairs, State Dept, 1961–65; US Ambassador to NATO, 1965–69; Pres., Univ. of Hawaii, 1969–74; Dir, Program in Internat. Affairs, Aspen Inst. for Humanistic Studies, 1974–80. Distinguished Vis. Tom Slick Prof. of World Peace, Univ. of Texas at Austin, 1979. Delegate, Democratic National Convention, 1960. Chairman: Weather Modification Adv. Bd, US Dept of Commerce, 1977–78; Nat. Retiree Volunteer Coalition, 1989–92; Volunteers in Technical Assistance, 1994–96. Holds hon. degrees. Woodrow Wilson Award, Princeton Univ., 1968; Prix de Talloires, Groupe de Talloires, 1981; Elmer Staats Lifetime Public Service Award, Amer. Soc. for Public Admin, 2003. US Medal of Freedom, 1946; foreign orders. *Publications:* Next Step in Asia (jtly), 1949; (ed jtly) The Art of Overseasmanship, 1957; (jtly) The Overseas Americans, 1960; (ed) The Promise of World Tensions, 1961; (ed jtly) The Ethic of Power, 1962; (ed jtly) Ethics and Bigness, 1962; The Obligations of Power, 1966; NATO: the Transatlantic Bargain, 1970; The Future Executive, 1972; China Diary, 1976; The Third Try at World Order, 1977; (jtly) Humangrowth: an essay on growth, values and the quality of life, 1978; (ed) Energy Futures of Developing Countries, 1980; (ed jtly) Bioresources for Development, 1980; (ed) The Management of Sustainable Growth, 1981; The Knowledge Executive, 1985; The Global Commons, 1990; Birth of a New World, 1993; Leadership and the Information Revolution, 1997; Nobody in Charge, 2002. *Address:* 46891 Grissom Street, Sterling, VA 20165, USA. *T:* and *Fax:* (703) 4500428. *Club:* Century (NY).

CLEVERDON, Dame Julia (Charity), (Dame Julia Garnett), DCVO 2008 (CVO 2003); CBE 1996; Vice President, Business in the Community, since 2008 (Chief Executive, 1992–2008); *b* 19 April 1950; *d* of late Thomas Douglas James Cleverdon, BBC producer and Elinor Nest Lewis; *m* 1st, 1973, Martin Christopher Ollard (marr. diss. 1978); 2nd, 1985, (William) John (Poulton Maxwell) Garnett, CBE (*d* 1997); two *d. Educ:* Newnham Coll., Cambridge (BA Hons History). Communication Adviser, British Leyland and Anglo-American Mining Corp., S Africa, 1972–75; Industrial Society: Head, Eastern and Public Services Dept, 1975–77; Head, Common Purpose Campaign, 1977–79; Dir, Communication and Publicity Div., 1979–81; founded Pepperell Dept for Inner Cities and Educn work, 1981–88; Man. Dir, Develt, BITC, 1988–92. Dir, In Kind Direct. Ambassador for WWF; Trustee, Timebank; Patron: Helena Kennedy Bursary Scheme; Volunteer Reading Help. Gov., Henley Mgt Coll. *Publication:* Why Industry Matters, 1978. *Recreations:* children, gardening, collecting pink lustre. *Address:* (office) 137 Shepherdess Walk, N1 7RQ. *T:* 0870 600 2482; 8 Alwyne Road, Islington, N1 2HH.

CLEVERLY, James Spencer; Member (C) Bexley and Bromley, London Assembly, Greater London Authority, since 2008; *b* Lewisham, 4 Sept. 1969; *s* of James Philip Cleverly and Evelyn Suna Cleverly; *m* 2000, Susannah Janet Temple Sparks; two *s. Educ:* Colfe's Sch. for Boys; Thames Valley Univ. (BA Hons Hospitality Mgt). Sales Manager, VNU, 1996–2002; Internat. Advertising Manager, Informa, 2002–04; mobilised service, British Army, 2004; Gp Advertising Manager, Crimson Publishing, 2005–06; Online Commercial Manager, Caspian Publishing, 2006–07; Dir, Point & Fire Media Ltd, 2007–. Served TA, 1989–. *Recreations:* Rugby, triathlon, spending time with my family. *Address:* Greater London Authority, City Hall, The Queen's Walk, SE1 2AA. *T:* (020) 7983 6571; *e-mail:* james.cleverly@london.gov.uk. *Club:* Carlton.

CLEWS, Michael Arthur; Master of the Supreme Court Taxing Office, 1970–87; *b* Caudebec, France, 16 Sept. 1919; *s* of late Roland Trevor Clews and late Marjorie (*née* Baily); *m* 1947, Kathleen Edith Hollingworth; one *s* two *d. Educ:* Epworth Coll., Rhyl; Clare Coll., Cambridge (MA). Served in Indian Army (Major, RA and V Force),

1940–46. Solicitor, 1953; Partner, W. H. House & Son, and Knocker & Foskett, Sevenoaks, 1957–70. Mem., Lord Chancellor's Adv. Cttee on Legal Aid, 1977–84. *Address:* Hameau de Coriolan 9, 83120 Plan de la Tour, Var, France.

CLIBBORN, John Donovan Nelson dalla Rosa, CMG 1997; HM Diplomatic Service; Foreign and Commonwealth Office, since 1995; *b* 24 Nov. 1941; *s* of Donovan Harold Clibborn, CMG, and Margaret Mercedes Edwige (*née* Nelson); *m* 1968, Juliet Elizabeth Pagden; one *s* two *d*. *Educ:* Downside Sch., Stratton-on-the-Fosse, Bath; Oriel Coll., Oxford (1st Cl. Hon. Mods and Lit.Hum. BA, MA). Joined HM Diplomatic Service, 1965; FCO, 1965–67; 3rd, subseq. 2nd Sec., Nicosia, 1967–69; FCO, 1970–72; 1st Secretary: Bonn, 1972–75; UK Mission to EC, Brussels, 1975–78; Jt Res. Centre, EEC, 1978–81; FCO, 1981–88; Counsellor, Washington, 1988–91; FCO, 1991–93; Counsellor, Washington, 1994–95. Member: Soc. for the Promotion of Roman Studies, 1963–; Soc. for the Promotion of Hellenic Studies, 1964–; Palestine Exploration Fund, 1965–. *Recreations:* classical literature, ancient history. *Address:* c/o Foreign and Commonwealth Office, SW1A 2AH. *Club:* Athenæum.

CLIBURN, Van, (Harvey Lavan Cliburn Jr); pianist; Artistic Adviser, Van Cliburn International Piano Competition, since 1962; *b* Shreveport, La, 12 July 1934; *o c* of Harvey Lavan Cliburn and late Rildia Bee (*née* O'Bryan). *Educ:* Kilgore High Sch., Texas; Juilliard Sch. of Music, New York. Made début in Houston, Texas, 1947; subsequently has toured extensively in N and S America, Europe and Asia. Awards include first International Tchaikovsky Piano Competition, Moscow, 1958, and every US prize, for pianistic ability. US Presidential Medal of Freedom, 2003. *Recreation:* swimming. *Address:* c/o McClain Asset Management, PO Box 470217, Fort Worth, TX 76147, USA.

CLIFF, Prof. Andrew David, FBA 1996; FSS; CGeog; Professor of Theoretical Geography, since 1997 and Pro-Vice-Chancellor, since 2004, University of Cambridge; Fellow, Christ's College, Cambridge, since 1974; *b* 26 Oct. 1943; *s* of Alfred Cliff and Annabel Cliff (*née* McQuade); *m* 1964, Margaret Blyton; three *s*. *Educ:* King's Coll. London (BA 1964); Northwestern Univ. (MA 1966); Univ. of Bristol (PhD 1969; DSc 1982); MA Cantab 1973. FSS 1968; CGeog 2002. Teaching Asst in Geog., Northwestern Univ., 1964–66; Res. Associate in Geog., 1968–69, Lectr, 1969–72, Bristol Univ.; Lectr in Geog., 1973–91, Reader in Theoretical Geog., 1991–97, Univ. of Cambridge. MAE 2002. *Publications:* jointly: Spatial Autocorrelation, 1973; Elements of Spatial Structure: a quantitative approach, 1975; Locational Analysis in Human Geography, 2nd edn 1977; Locational Models, 1977; Locational Methods, 1977; Spatial Processes: models and applications, 1981; Spatial Diffusion: an historical geography of epidemics in an island community, 1981; Spatial Components in the Transmission of Epidemic Waves through Island Communities: the spread of measles in Fiji and the Pacific, 1985; Spatial Aspects of Influenza Epidemics, 1986; Atlas of Disease Distributions: analytical approaches to epidemiological data, 1988; London International Atlas of AIDS, 1992; Measles: an historical geography of a major human viral disease from global expansion to local retreat 1840–1990, 1993; Deciphering Global Epidemics: analytical approaches to the disease records of world cities 1888–1912, 1998; Island Epidemics, 2000; War and Disease, 2004; World Atlas of Epidemic Diseases, 2004; Poliomyelitis: a world geography - emergence to eradication, 2006. *Recreations:* watching Grimsby Town FC, old roses, theatre. *Address:* University of Cambridge, The Old Schools, Trinity Lane, Cambridge CB2 1TN. *T:* (01223) 765692.

CLIFF, Ian Cameron, OBE 1991; HM Diplomatic Service; UK Permanent Representative to the Organisation for Security and Co-operation in Europe, Vienna (with personal rank of Ambassador), since 2007; *b* 11 Sept. 1952; *s* of late Gerald Shaw Cliff and Dorothy Cliff; *m* 1988, Caroline Mary Redman; one *s* two *d*. *Educ:* Hampton Grammar Sch.; Magdalen Coll., Oxford (MA Modern Hist.). Asst Master (Hist.), Dr Challoner's GS, Amersham, 1975–79; joined HM Diplomatic Service, 1979: SE Asia Dept, 1979–80; Arabic lang. trng, St Andrews Univ. and Damascus, 1980–82; First Sec., Khartoum, 1982–85; Head, Arabian Peninsula Section, ME Dept, FCO, 1985–87; Perm. Under Sec.'s Dept, FCO, 1987–89; First Sec., UK Mission to UN, NY, 1989–93; Counsellor, on loan to DTI as Dir, Exports to ME, Near East and N Africa, 1993–96; Deputy Hd of Mission, Consul-Gen. and Dir of Trade Promotion, Vienna, 1996–2001; Ambassador to: Bosnia and Herzegovina, 2001–05; Sudan, 2005–07. *Publications:* occasional articles in railway magazines. *Recreations:* railways, philately, music. *Address:* c/o Foreign and Commonwealth Office, King Charles Street, SW1A 2AH.

CLIFFE, Air Vice-Marshal John Alfred, CB 2008; OBE 1994; Director, Warfare Training, Cobham Aviation Services, since 2008; *b* Hyde, Cheshire, 14 June 1953; *s* of Kenneth Cliffe and Mary Vickerman Cliffe (*née* Ellor); *m* 1975, Amanda Penelope Barr. *Educ:* Hyde Co. Grammar Sch. Commnd RAF, 1972; flying trng, 1972–74; Pilot, XI, 19, 23 and 43 Sqdns and Lightning Trng Flight, 1974–88; RNSC, 1988; Personal Staff Officer to AOC II Gp, 1989–90; OC XI Sqdn, 1991–94; Air Plans, MoD, 1994–95; Plans, HQ RAF Stike Comd, 1995–97; rcds, 1998; OC RAF Leeming, 1999–2000; Comdr, British Forces, Falkland Is, 2001; Dir, Flying Trng, 2002–03; COS, HQ RAF Strike Comd, 2003–05; Dir Gen., Trng and Educn, MoD, 2005–07. *Recreations:* flying, ornithology, hill walking, golf. *Address:* *e-mail:* john.cliffe@cobham.com. *Club:* Royal Air Force.

CLIFFORD, family name of **Baron Clifford of Chudleigh**.

CLIFFORD OF CHUDLEIGH, 14th Baron *cr* 1672; **Thomas Hugh Clifford;** Count of The Holy Roman Empire; *b* 17 March 1948; *s* of 13th Baron Clifford of Chudleigh, OBE and Hon. Katharine Vavasseur Fisher, 2nd *d* of 2nd Baron Fisher; *S* father, 1988; *m* 1st, 1980, (Muriel) Suzanne (marr. diss. 1993), *d* of Major Campbell Austin and Mrs Campbell Austin; two *s* one *d*; 2nd, 1994, Clarissa, *er d* of His Honour A. C. Goodall, MC. *Educ:* Downside Abbey. Commnd Coldstream Guards, 1967; stationed British Honduras, 1967–68; Instructor, Guards Depot, 1968–69; Northern Ireland, 1969, 1971, 1972; ADC to Chief of Defence Staff, 1972–73; served with ACE Mobile Force, 1973; Adjutant, Guards Depot, 1973–75. Royal Agricultural College, Cirencester, 1976–78. *Recreations:* fishing, croquet. *Heir:* *s* Hon. Alexander Thomas Hugh Clifford, *b* 24 Sept. 1985. *Address:* Ugbrooke Park, Chudleigh, South Devon TQ13 0AD. *T:* (office) (01626) 852179.

CLIFFORD, Most Rev. Dermot; *see* Cashel and Emly, Archbishop of, (RC).

CLIFFORD, Maxwell; Founder and Proprietor, Max Clifford Associates Ltd, press and public relations consultants, since 1968; *b* 6 April 1943; *s* of Frank and Lilian Clifford; *m* Elizabeth (*d* 2003); one *d*. Formerly: jun. reporter, Merton and Morden News; Jun. Publicity Officer, EMI Records (promoter of The Beatles); asst to Syd Gillingham (promoter of Tom Jones, Jimi Hendrix, Bee Gees, Cream). Clients of Max Clifford Associates have included: Muhammad Ali, Shane Warne, Simon Cowell, David Copperfield, Diana Ross, O. J. Simpson, Mohammed Al Fayed, Simon Jordan (Chm., Crystal Palace FC), Peter Jones (owner, Phones Internat.), Shilpa Shetty. Media advisor/commentator for TV, radio, newspapers on major news stories; public speaker. *Publication:* Max Clifford: Read All About It (autobiog.), 2005. *Address:* Max Clifford Associates Ltd, Moss House, 15–16 Brooks Mews, Mayfair, W1K 4DS.

CLIFFORD, Nigel Richard; Chief Executive, Symbian, since 2005; *b* 22 June 1959; *s* of Dr John Clifford and Barbara Dorothy Clifford; *m* 1989, Jeanette Floyd; two *s* one *d*. *Educ:* Portsmouth Grammar Sch.; Downing Coll., Cambridge (MA 1983); Strathclyde Univ. (MBA 1994); DipCAM 1986; Dip. Inst. Mkting 1984. British Telecom, 1981–92: Head, Internat. Operator Services, 1987–90; Sen. Strategy Advr, Chm's Office, 1990; Head, Business Strategy and Develt, Mobile Communications, 1990–92; Chief Exec., Glasgow Royal Infirmary Univ. NHS Trust, 1992–98; Sen. Vice Pres., Service Delivery, Cable & Wireless Communications, 1998–2000; Chief Exec., Tertio Ltd, 2000–05. Founding Dir, Herald Foundn for Women's Health, 1994. FCMI (FIMgt 1995); FRSA 1996. *Recreations:* family life, walking, running. *Address:* Symbian, 2–6 Boundary Row, SE1 8HP. *Club:* Morpeth Comrades Social (Morpeth).

CLIFFORD, Sir Roger (Joseph), 7th Bt *cr* 1887; *b* 5 June 1936; *s* of Sir Roger Charles Joseph Gerard Clifford, 6th Bt and Henrietta Millicent Kiver (*d* 1971); *S* father, 1982; *m* 1968, Joanna Theresa, *d* of C. J. Ward, Christchurch, NZ; two *d*. *Educ:* Beaumont College, England. *Recreations:* golf, Rugby football. *Heir:* *b* Charles Joseph Clifford [*b* 5 June 1936; *m* 1983, Sally Green]. *Clubs:* Blenheim (Blenheim, NZ); Christchurch, Christchurch Golf.

CLIFFORD, Susan Merlyn, MBE 1994; Founder Director, 1983, and Joint Co-ordinator (formerly Joint Executive Director), since 1988, Common Ground; *b* 16 April 1944; *d* of Bernard Clifford and Hilda Clifford (*née* Moorley). *Educ:* Brincliffe Grammar Sch., Nottingham; Univ. of Hull (BSc Hons); Edinburgh Coll. of Art (DipTP). Work in planning consultancy, Edinburgh, 1966–68; landscape architecture practice, 1968–69; Lectr in Extra-Mural Studies, Edinburgh Univ., 1968–69; Lectr, then Sen. Lectr in Planning and Natural Resource Mgt, PCL, 1970–74; Lectr, Bartlett Sch. of Architecture and Planning, UCL, 1975–90. Hon. Dir, Friends of the Earth (UK), 1971–82; Founder Trustee, Earth Resources Res., 1972; Hon. Dir, Common Ground, 1983–88 (initiated Apple Day annual fest., 21 Oct.); Hon. Mem., Culture SW (Regl Cultural Consortium), 2000–03; Mem., Design Review Cttee, CABE, 2000–02. Has initiated and toured exhibns, including: The Tree of Life, with S Bank Centre, 1989–90; Out of the Wood, with Crafts Council, 1989–90; Leaves by Andy Goldsworthy, Natural Hist. Mus., 1989; from place to PLACE, Barbican Centre, 1996. *Publications:* (ed jtly) Second Nature, 1984; (ed jtly) Pulp!, 1989; Places: the city and the invisible, 1993; with Angela King: Holding Your Ground: an action guide to local conservation, 1985; The Apple Source Book, 1991, enlarged edn 2007; Celebrating Local Distinctiveness, 1994; A Manifesto for Fields, 1997; Rivers, Rhynes and Running Brooks, 2000; England in Particular: a celebration of the commonplace, the local, the vernacular and the distinctive, 2006; (with Angela King) Community Orchards Handbook, 2008; edited with Angela King: Trees Be Company: an anthology of tree poetry, 1989, 2nd edn 2001; Local Distinctiveness: place particularity and identity, 1993; from place to PLACE: maps and parish maps, 1996; Field Days: an anthology of poetry about fields, 1998; The River's Voice: an anthology of poetry about rivers, 2000; The Common Ground Book of Orchards, 2000. *Recreation:* looking at the land. *Address:* c/o Common Ground, Gold Hill House, 21 High Street, Shaftesbury, Dorset SP7 8JE. *T:* (01747) 850820.

CLIFFORD, Sir Timothy (Peter Plint), Kt 2002; Director-General, National Galleries of Scotland, 2001–06 (Director, 1984–2000); *b* 26 Jan. 1946; *s* of late Derek Plint Clifford and Anne (*née* Pierson); *m* 1968, Jane Olivia, *yr d* of Sir George Paterson, OBE, QC; one *d*. *Educ:* Sherborne, Dorset; Perugia Univ. (Dip. Italian); Courtauld Inst., Univ. of London (BA Hons, History of Art). Dip. Fine Art, Museums Assoc., 1972; AMA. Asst Keeper, Dept of Paintings, Manchester City Art Galleries, 1968–72, Acting Keeper, 1972; Asst Keeper, Dept of Ceramics, Victoria and Albert Mus., London, 1972–76; Asst Keeper, Dept of Prints and Drawings, British Mus., London, 1976–78; Dir, Manchester City Art Galls, 1978–84. Member: Manchester Diocesan Adv. Cttee for Care of Churches, 1978–84; NACF Cttee (Cheshire and Gtr Manchester Br.), 1978–84; North Western Museum and Art Gall. Service Jt Adv. Panel, 1978–84; Cttee, ICOM (UK), 1980–82; Chm., Internat. Cttee for Museums of Fine Art, ICOM, 1980–83 (Mem., Exec. Cttee, 1983–88); Board Member: Museums and Galleries Commn, 1983–88; British Council, 1987–92 (Fine Arts Adv. Cttee, 1988–92); Founder and Committee Member: Friends of Manchester City Art Galls, 1978–84; Patrons and Associates, Manchester City Art Galls, 1979–; Mem. Exec. Cttee, Scottish Museums Council, 1984–2006; Mem. Adv. Council, Friends of Courtauld Inst. Cttee Mem., Derby Internat. Porcelain Soc., 1983–86; Vice-Pres., Turner Soc., 1984–86, and 1989–; Pres., NADFAS, 1996–2006; Mem., Adv. Cttee, Come and See Scotland's Churches, 1989–90. Member Consultative Committee: Sculpture Jl, 1998–; Gazette des Beaux-Arts, 1999–. Vice-Pres., Frigate Unicorn Preservation Soc., 1987–2003. Trustee: Lake Dist Art Gall. and Mus. Trust, 1989–97; Royal Yacht Britannia, 1998–; Hermitage Develt Trust, 1999–2003; Stichting Hermitage aan de Amstel, 1999–; Wallace Collection, 2003–. Patron, Friends of Sherborne House, 1997–. Member: Accademia Italiana delle Arti Applicate, 1988; Ateneo Veneto, Italy, 1997. FRSA; FRSE 2001; FSAScot 1986. Freeman: Goldsmiths' Co., 1989; City of London, 1989. Hon. LLD St Andrews, 1996; Hon. DLitt Glasgow, 2001. Special Award, BIM, 1991. Commendatore al Ordine della Repubblica Italiana, 1999 (Cavaliere, 1988). *Publications:* (with Derek Clifford) John Crome, 1968; (with Dr Ivan Hall) Heaton Hall, 1972; (with Dr T. Friedmann) The Man at Hyde Park Corner: sculpture by John Cheere, 1974; Vues Pittoresques de Luxembourg … par J. M. W. Turner, (Luxembourg) 1977; Ceramics of Derbyshire 1750–1975 (ed, H. G. Bradley), 1978; J. M. W. Turner, Acquerelli e incisioni, (Rome) 1980; Turner at Manchester, 1982; (with Ian Gow) The National Gallery of Scotland: an architectural and decorative history, 1988; (jtly) Raphael: the pursuit of perfection, 1994; (with Ian Gow) Duff House, 1995; (with A. Weston-Lewis) Effigies and Ecstasies: Roman Baroque sculpture and design in the age of Bernini, 1998; Designs of Desire: architectural and ornament prints and drawings 1500–1850, 2000; (with Nicholas Barker and Hugh Brigstocke) A Poet in Paradise: Lord Lindsay and Christian Art, 2000; contrib. Burlington Magazine, Apollo, etc. *Recreations:* bird watching, entomology. *Address:* c/o National Galleries of Scotland, The Mound, Edinburgh EH2 2EL. *Clubs:* Turf, Beefsteak; New (Edinburgh).

CLIFT, Richard Dennis, CMG 1984; HM Diplomatic Service, retired; *b* 18 May 1933; *s* of late Dennis Victor Clift and Helen Wilmot Clift (*née* Evans); *m* 1st, 1957, Barbara Mary Travis (marr. diss. 1982); three *d*; 2nd, 1982, Jane Rosamund Barker (*née* Homfray). *Educ:* St Edward's Sch., Oxford; Pembroke Coll., Cambridge. BA 1956. FO, 1956–57; Office of British Chargé d'Affaires, Peking, 1958–60; British Embassy, Berne, 1961–62; UK Delegn to NATO, Paris, 1962–64; FO, 1964–68; Head of Chancery, British High Commn, Kuala Lumpur, 1969–71; FCO, 1971–73; Counsellor (Commercial), Peking, 1974–76; Canadian Nat. Defence Coll., 1976–77; seconded to NI Office, 1977–79; Hd of Hong Kong Dept, FCO, 1979–84; High Comr in Freetown, 1984–86; Political Advr, Hong Kong Govt, 1987–89. Student, London Coll. of Furniture, 1989–91. *Recreations:* sailing, walking. *Address:* 18 Langwood Chase, Teddington, Middx TW11 9PH.

CLIFT, Prof. Roland, CBE 2006 (OBE 1994); FREng, FIChemE; Professor of Environmental Technology (formerly Environmental Strategy), University of Surrey, since 1992; *b* 19 Nov. 1942; *s* of Leslie William Clift and Ivy Florence Gertrude Clift (*née*

Wheeler); *m* 1st, 1968, Rosena Valory (*née* Davison); one *d*; 2nd, 1979, Diana Helen (*née* Manning); one *s* (and one *s* decd). *Educ:* Trinity Coll., Cambridge (BA 1963; MA 1967); PhD McGill 1970. CEng, FIChemE 1984; FREng (FEng 1986). Technical Officer (Chem. Engr), ICI, 1964–67; Lectr, Asst Prof. and Associate Prof., McGill Univ., 1967–75; Lectr, Imperial Coll., London, 1975–76; Lectr, Univ. of Cambridge, 1976–81; Fellow, Trinity Coll., Cambridge, 1976–81 (Praelector, 1980–81); University of Surrey: Prof. of Chem. Engrg, 1981–92; Dir, Centre for Envmtl Strategy, 1992–2005. Visiting Professor: Univ. di Napoli, 1973–74; Chalmers Univ. of Technol., Gothenburg, 1989–. Editor in Chief, Powder Technology, 1987–95. Director: ClifMar Associates, 1986–; Merrill Lynch New Energy Technologies, 1999–. Chairman: Clean Technology Management Cttee, SERC, 1990–94; Engrg Bd, AFRC, 1992–94; Member: UK Ecolabelling Bd, 1992–98; Royal Commn on Envmtl Pollution, 1996–2005; Sci. Adv. Council, DEFRA, 2006–; specialist advr to H of L on energy efficiency, 2004–05. Mem., Governing Body, Charterhouse Sch., 1982–91. Hon. Citizen of Augusta, Georgia, 1987. FRSA 1986. Hon. FCIWEM 2001. Sir Frank Whittle Medal, Royal Acad. of Engrg, 2003. *Publications:* (jtly) Bubbles, Drops and Particles, 1978, repr. 2005; (ed jtly) Fluidization, 1985; (jtly) Slurry Transport using Centrifugal Pumps, 1992, 3rd edn 2005; (jtly) Processing of Particulate Solids, 1997; (ed jtly) Sustainable Development in Practice, 2004. *Recreation:* arguing and thinking. *Address:* Centre for Environmental Strategy, University of Surrey, Guildford, Surrey GU2 5XH. *T:* (01483) 259271, *Fax:* (01483) 259394. *Club:* Athenæum.

CLIFTON, Lord; Ivo Donald Stuart Bligh; *b* 17 April 1968; *s* and *heir* of 11th Earl of Darnley, *qv*; *m* 1997, Peta, *d* of A. R. Beard; three *s*. *Educ:* Marlborough Coll.; Edinburgh Univ. *Heir:* *s* Hon. Henry Robert Stuart Bligh, *b* 23 April 1999.

CLIFTON, Bishop of, (RC), since 2001; **Rt Rev. Declan Lang;** *b* 15 April 1950; *s* of Francis and Mai Lang. *Educ:* Ryde Sch., IoW; Allen Hall, St Edmund's Coll., Ware; Royal Holloway Coll., Univ. of London (BA Hons). Ordained priest, 1975; Asst Priest, St John's Cathedral, Portsmouth, 1975–79; Sec. to Bishop of Portsmouth, 1979–82; Diocesan Advr for Adult Religious Educn, 1982–90; Parish Priest: Our Lady of the Apostles, Bishop's Waltham, Hants, 1982–86; Sacred Heart, Bournemouth, 1986–90; Administrator, St John's Cathedral, Portsmouth, 1990–96; VG, Dio. Portsmouth and Parish Priest, St Edmund, Abingdon, 1996–2001. *Publication:* (jtly) Parish Project: a resource book for parishes to review mission, 1992. *Recreations:* walking, travel, cinema, theatre. *Address:* St Ambrose, North Road, Leigh Woods, Bristol BS8 3PW. *T:* (0117) 973 3072.

CLIFTON, Gerald Michael; His Honour Judge Clifton; a Circuit Judge, since 1992; *b* 3 July 1947; *s* of Frederick Maurice Clifton and Jane Clifton; *m* 1973, Rosemary Anne Vera Jackson; two *s*. *Educ:* Liverpool Coll.; Brasenose Coll., Oxford (Open Classical Schol., MA). Called to the Bar, Middle Temple, 1970, Bencher, 2006; joined Northern Circuit, 1970; Asst Recorder, 1982; Recorder, 1988; Mem., Manx Bar, 1992. Pres., NW Area, Mental Health Review Tribunal, 1997–2004; Mem., Parole Bd, 2004–. Foundn Mem., 1992–, and Vice-Pres., 2001–, Liverpool Coll. *Recreations:* walking, philately, sailing, tennis. *Address:* c/o Circuit Administrator, Northern Circuit, Young Street Chambers, 76 Quay Street, Manchester M3 4PR. *Clubs:* Bar Yacht; Athenæum (Liverpool).

CLIFTON, Richard Francis; Head, UK Delegation, Channel Tunnel Safety Authority, since 2003; *b* 18 Sept. 1946; *s* of Joseph Walter Clifton and Georgina Clifton (*née* Naughton); *m* 1970, Gloria Christine Hugill; two *d*. *Educ:* Univ. of Warwick (BA Econs 1969; MA Industrial Relns 1970). Policy Advr, Dept of Employment, 1974–86; Health and Safety Executive, 1986–2006: Head of Med. Admin, 1986–90; Head of Finance and Planning, 1990–96; Head of Policy Unit, 1996–2001; Dir, Railway Policy, 2001–03. Chm. Bd, European Agency for Safety and Health at Work, Bilbao, 2000–01. Chm., wkg party on Obstruction of the Railway by Road Vehicles, reported 2002. *Recreation:* Mem., Phoenix Windband, Sutton. *Address:* Office of Rail Regulation, 1 Kemble Street, WC2B 4AN. *T:* (020) 7282 2137; *e-mail:* richard.clifton@orr.gsi.gov.uk; 55 The Ridgway, Sutton, Surrey SM2 5JX. *Club:* Highfields Lawn Tennis (Sutton).

CLIFTON, Rita Ann; Chairman, Interbrand, since 2002; *b* 30 Jan. 1958; *d* of late Arthur Leonard Clifton and Iris Mona Clifton (*née* Hill); *m* Brian Martin Astley; two *d*. *Educ:* Newnham Coll., Cambridge (MA Hons Classics). Sen. Account Rep., J. Walter Thompson, 1983–86; Strategic Planning Dir, then Vice Chm. and Exec. Planning Dir, Saatchi & Saatchi, 1986–97; CEO, Interbrand, 1997–2001. Non-exec. Chm., Populus Ltd, 2004–; non-executive Director: DSG Internat. (formerly Dixons Gp) plc, 2003–; EMAP plc, 2005–08. Vis. Prof., Henley Mgt Coll., 2006–. Mem., Sustainable Develt Commn, 1999–2005. Pres., WACL, 1997–98; Mem., Mktg Gp of GB, 1999–. Mem., Adv. Bd, Judge Inst. of Mgt Studies, Cambridge, 2000–. Trustee, WWF-UK, 2007–. FRSA 1997; Fellow, Mktg Soc., 2004. *Publications:* How to Plan Advertising, 1997; The Future of Brands, 2000; Brands and Branding, 2004. *Recreations:* dance, environment, fashion, media. *Address:* c/o Interbrand, 85 Strand, WC2R 0DW. *T:* (020) 7554 1000, *Fax:* (020) 7554 1020.

CLIFTON, Gen. Shaw, PhD; General of The Salvation Army, since 2006; *b* 21 Sept. 1945; *s* of Albert Clifton and Alice Jane Clifton (*née* Shaw); *m* 1967, Helen Ashman; two *s* one *d*. *Educ:* Latymer Sch., Edmonton; King's Coll., London (LLB Hons, BD 1st Cl. Hons, AKC 1968; Relton Prize for Histl and Biblical Theol.; PhD1988). Lecturer in Law: Inns of Court Sch. of Law, 1968–70; Univ. of Bristol, 1970–71; commnd and ordained Officer of The Salvation Army, 1973; Salvation Army appointments: Burnt Oak, London, 1973; Mazoe, 1975, Bulawayo, 1978, Rhodesia; Enfield, London, 1979; Legal and Parly Sec., Internat. HQ, London, 1982–89; Bromley, Kent, 1989–92; Divisional Commander: Durham and Tees, 1992–95; Mass, USA, 1995–97; Territorial Commander: Pakistan, 1997–2002; NZ, Fiji and Tonga, 2002–04; UK with Republic of Ireland, 2004–06. Principal Lectr, Samuel Logan Brengle Insts, UK, Pakistan, India, Australia, NZ; Frederick Coutts Meml Lectr, Sydney, 2003. Member: Vis. Faculty, Internat. Coll. for Officers, London, 1982–; Internat. Doctrine Council, 1980–83; Internat. Moral and Social Issues Council, 1983–93. *Publications:* What Does the Salvationist Say?, 1977; Growing Together, 1984; Strong Doctrine, Strong Mercy, 1985; Never the Same Again, 1997; Who Are These Salvationists?, 1999; New Love - Thinking Aloud About Practical Holiness, 2004. *Recreations:* music, reading, walking, family. *Address:* The Salvation Army, 101 Queen Victoria Street, EC4P 4EP. *T:* (020) 7332 8001; *e-mail:* shaw_clifton@salvationarmy.org.

CLIFTON-BROWN, Geoffrey Robert; MP (C) Cotswold, since 1997 (Cirencester and Tewkesbury, 1992–97); chartered surveyor and farmer; *b* 23 March 1953; *s* of Robert and late Elizabeth Clifton-Brown; *m* 1979, Alexandra Peto-Shepherd (marr. diss. 2004); one *s* one *d*. *Educ:* Tormore Sch., Kent; Eton Coll.; RAC, Cirencester. FRICS 2002. Chm., N Norfolk Cons. Assoc., 1986–91 (Mem., Eastern Area Exec., 1986–91); Vice Chm., Norfolk Eur. Constituency Council, 1990–91. PPS to Minister of Agric., Fisheries and Food, 1995–97; an Opposition Whip, 1999–2001, 2004, Opposition Asst Chief Whip, 2005; Opposition front bench spokesman on local and devolved govt, 2003–04; Shadow Minister: for Foreign Affairs and Trade, 2005–07; for Internat. Develt and Trade, 2007–. Member: Envmt Select Cttee, 1992–95; Public Accounts Commn, 1997–99; Public Accounts Cttee, 1997–99. Chm., All Party Gp on Population, Develt and Reproductive Health, 1995–97; Vice Chairman: Cons. Backbench Cttee on Eur. Affairs, 1997–99 (Sec., 1992–95); Euro Atlantic Gp, 1996–. Vice Chairman: Charities Property Assoc., 1993–2003; Small Business Bureau, 1995–. Freeman, City of London, 1981; Liveryman, Farmers' Co., 1984. *Recreations:* fishing, all country pursuits. *Address:* House of Commons, SW1A 0AA. *T:* (020) 7219 3000. *Clubs:* Carlton, Farmers'.

CLINCH, David John, (Joe), OBE 1997; Consultant, Milton Keynes Economy and Learning Partnership, since 2001; Secretary, Open University, 1981–98; *b* 14 Feb. 1937; *s* of Thomas Charles Clinch and Madge Isabel Clinch (*née* Saker); *m* 1963, Hilary Jacques; one *s* one *d*. *Educ:* Nautical Coll., Pangbourne; St Cuthbert's Soc., Univ. of Durham (BA); Indiana Univ. (MBA). National Service, Royal Navy (Sub-Lieut), Supply and Secretariat, 1955–57. Administrator, Univ. of Sussex, 1963–69; Deputy Secretary and Registrar, Open University, 1969–81; Registrar Counterpart, Allama Iqbal Open Univ., Pakistan, 1976–77. Consultant: Univ. for Industry, 2000–02; UNESCO, 2003–04. Member: Conf. of Univ. Administrators, 1973–99; British Fulbright Scholars Assoc., 1978–; Conf. of Registrars and Secs, 1981–98 (Chm., 1990–91); Council of Foundn, Internat. Baccalaureate Orgn, 1999–2005 (Treas., 2000–05; Sec., 2003–05; Hon. Mem., 2005); Trustee and Secretary: Internat. Baccalaureate Fund Inc., USA, 2004–07; Internat. Baccalaureate Fund, Canada, 2004–07; Internat. Baccalaureate Fund UK, 2006–07; Internat. Baccalaureate Bd of Trustees, 2007–. Dir, Nat. Educnl Resources Information Service Trust, 1989–93; Bd Mem., COUNTEC, 2005–. Trustee, Open Univ. Superannuation Scheme, 1989–97; Hon. Vice Pres., Open Univ. Students Assoc., 2000–05 (Hon. Life Mem., 2005). Mem. Ct, Univ. of Surrey, Roehampton, 2000–04. Dir, Milton Keynes City Orch., 2001–08. FRSA 1997. DUniv Open, 2000. *Recreations:* music, natural history, reading, walking. *Address:* 39 Tudor Gardens, Stony Stratford, Milton Keynes MK11 1HX. *T:* (01908) 562475.

CLINES, Prof. David John Alfred; Professor of Biblical Studies, University of Sheffield, 1985–2003, now Emeritus; Director: Dictionary of Classical Hebrew Ltd, since 2001; Sheffield Phoenix Press, since 2004; *b* 21 Nov. 1938; *s* of Alfred William and Ruby Coral Clines; *m* 1st, 1963, Dawn Naomi Joseph; one *s* one *d*; 2nd, 1989, Heather Ann McKay. *Educ:* Univ. of Sydney (BA Hons 1960); St John's Coll., Cambridge (BA 1963; MA 1967). University of Sheffield: Asst Lectr in Biblical History and Literature, 1964–67; Lectr, 1967–73, Sen. Lectr, 1973–79, Reader, 1979–85, in Biblical Studies. Co-Founder and Partner, JSOT Press, 1976–87; Dir, Sheffield Acad. Press, 1987–2001 (Chm., 1987–92). Pres., SOTS, 1996. Hon. PhD Amsterdam, 2001. *Publications:* I, He, We and They: a literary approach to Isaiah 53, 1976; The Theme of the Pentateuch, 1978, 2nd edn 1997; Ezra, Nehemiah, Esther, 1984; The Esther Scroll; the story of the story, 1984; Job 1–20, 1990; What Does Eve Do to Help? and Other Readerly Questions to the Old Testament, 1990; Interested Parties: the ideology of writers and readers of the Hebrew Bible, 1995; The Bible and the Modern World, 1997; The Sheffield Manual for Authors and Editors in Biblical Studies, 1997; On the Way to the Postmodern: Old Testament essays 1967–1998, 1998; Job 21–37, 2006; Job 38–42, 2008; The Unfolding Drama of the Book of Job; *edited:* The Dictionary of Classical Hebrew: vol. 1, 1993, vol. 2, 1995, vol. 3, 1996, vol. 4, 1998, vol. 5, 2001, vol. 6, 2006; The Poetical Books: a Sheffield reader, 1997; *edited jointly:* Art and Meaning: rhetoric in biblical literature, 1982; Midian, Moab and Edom: the history and archaeology of late Bronze and Iron Age Jordan and North-West Arabia, 1983; The Bible in Three Dimensions (essays), 1990; Telling Queen Michal's Story: an experiment in comparative interpretation, 1991; Among the Prophets: imagery, language and structure in the prophetic writings, 1993; Of Prophets' Visions and the Wisdom of Sages (essays), 1993; The New Literary Criticism and the Hebrew Bible, 1993; The Bible in Human Society (essays), 1995; The World of Genesis: persons, places, perspectives, 1998; Auguries: the Jubilee volume of the Department of Biblical Studies, 1998; Weisheit in Israel, 2003; articles in learned jls. *Recreations:* congresses, spreadsheets. *Address:* Department of Biblical Studies, University of Sheffield, Sheffield S10 2TN. *T:* (0114) 255 0562; *e-mail:* d.clines@shef.ac.uk.

CLINTON; *see* Fiennes-Clinton, family name of Earl of Lincoln.

CLINTON, 22nd Baron *cr* 1299 (title abeyant 1957–65); **Gerard Nevile Mark Fane Trefusis;** DL; landowner; *b* 7 Oct. 1934; *s* of Capt. Charles Fane (killed in action, 1940); assumed by deed poll, 1958, surname of Trefusis in addition to patronymic; *m* 1959, Nicola Harriette Purdon Coote; one *s* two *d*. *Educ:* Gordonstoun. Took seat in House of Lords, 1965. Mem., Prince of Wales's Councils, 1968–79. JP Bideford, 1963–83; DL Devon, 1977. *Recreations:* shooting, fishing, forestry. *Heir:* *s* Hon. Charles Patrick Rolle Fane Trefusis [*b* 21 March 1962; *m* 1992, Rosanna, *yr d* of John Izat; three *s*]. *Address:* Heanton Satchville, near Okehampton, North Devon EX20 3QE. *T:* (01805) 804224. *Club:* Boodle's.

CLINTON, Alan; *see* Clinton, R. A.

CLINTON, Bill; *see* Clinton, W. J.

CLINTON, Hillary Diane Rodham, JD; US Senator from New York State, since 2001; *b* Chicago, 26 Oct. 1947; *d* of Hugh Ellsworth and Dorothy Howell Rodham; *m* 1975, William Jefferson, (Bill), Clinton, *qv*; one *d*. *Educ:* Wellesley Coll.; Yale Univ. Law Sch. (JD 1973). Attorney, Children's Defense Fund, Cambridge, Mass and Washington, 1973–74; legal consultant, Carnegie Counsel on Children, New Haven, 1973–74; legal counsel, Nixon impeachment inquiry, Judiciary Cttee, US House of Reps, 1974; Asst Prof. of Law and Dir, Legal Aid Clinic, Univ. of Arkansas, Fayetteville, 1974–77; Partner, Rose Law Firm, 1977–92; Asst Prof. of Law, Univ. of Arkansas, Little Rock, 1979–80. Hd, Presidential Task Force on Nat. Health Care Reform, 1993. Numerous awards for humanitarian work. *Publications:* It Takes a Village, 1996; Dear Socks, Dear Buddy, 1998; Living History, 2003; contribs to professional jls. *Address:* US Senate, Washington, DC 20510, USA.

CLINTON, (Robert) Alan; Director, 1986–95, Managing Director, 1987–95, Picton House Group of Companies, property development cos; *b* 12 July 1931; *s* of John and Leah Clinton; *m* 1956, Valerie Joy Falconer. *Educ:* George Dixon Grammar Sch., Edgbaston, Birmingham; Manchester Business Sch. On leaving school, joined the Post Office, 1948; Member, North Western Postal Board, 1970; Asst Director (Personnel), London, 1975; Asst Director (Operations), London, 1976; Director of Eastern Postal Region, Colchester, 1978; Director of Postal Operations, London, 1979; Member Post Office Board, 1981–85: for Mails Network and Develt, 1981; for Mails Ops and Estates, 1982; for Corporate Services, 1984–85; Man. Dir, Counter Services, 1984–85. Mem. Mgt Cttee, Royal Assoc. in Aid of Deaf People, 1994–97. Pres., Clacton and NE Essex Arts and Literary Soc., 1992–97; Mem. Cttee, St Osyth Historical Soc., 1995–2006. Chm., St Osyth Almshouse Charity, 1995–; Consultant, Hampton Discretionary Trust, 1997–2002. FCILT (FCIT 1982). Mem., Worshipful Company of Carmen, 1981; Freeman of City of London, 1979. *Recreations:* music, walking, cooking. *Address:* Summer Cottage, The

Quay, St Osyth, Clacton-on-Sea, Essex CO16 8EZ. *T:* (01255) 820368; *e-mail:* alanclinton@uwclub.net. *Club:* City of London.

CLINTON, Robert George, CVO 2008; Consultant, Farrer & Co., since 2008 (Partner, 1979–2008; Senior Partner, 2002–08); *b* 19 Aug. 1948; *s* of George Thomas and Mary Josephine Clinton; *m* 1981, Annita Louise Bennett; one *s* one *d*. *Educ:* Beaumont Coll.; Brasenose Coll., Oxford (MA 1975). Admitted solicitor, 1975. *Recreations:* sailing, travel. *Address:* Farrer & Co., 66 Lincoln's Inn Fields, WC2A 3LH. *T:* (020) 7242 2022, *Fax:* (020) 7917 7569. *Club:* Garrick.

CLINTON, William Jefferson, (Bill), JD; President of the United States of America, 1993–2001; *b* 19 Aug. 1946; *s* of late Virginia Kelly; *m* 1975, Hillary Diane Rodham (*see* H. D. R. Clinton); one *d*. *Educ:* Georgetown Univ. (BS 1968); University Coll., Oxford (Rhodes Schol.). Hon. Fellow, 1993; DCL by Diploma, 1994); Yale Univ. Law Sch. (JD 1973). Prof., Univ. of Arkansas Law Sch., 1974–76; Attorney Gen., Arkansas, 1977–79; with Wright, Lindsey & Jennings, law firm, 1981–83; Governor of Arkansas, 1979–81 and 1983–92. Chairman: Educn Commn of the States, 1986–87; Nat. Governors' Assoc., 1986–87 (Co-Chm., Task Force on Educn, 1990–91); Democratic Governors' Assoc., 1989–90 (Vice Chm., 1987–88); Democratic Leadership Council, 1990–91. Democrat. Hon. DCL Oxford, 1994. *Publications:* Between Hope and History, 1996; My Life, 2004; Giving: how each of us can change the world, 2007. *Address:* (office) 55 West 125th Street, New York, NY 10027, USA.

CLINTON-DAVIS, family name of **Baron Clinton-Davis**.

CLINTON-DAVIS, Baron *cr* 1990 (Life Peer), of Hackney in the London Borough of Hackney; **Stanley Clinton Clinton-Davis;** PC 1998; *b* 6 Dec. 1928; *s* of Sidney Davis; name changed to Clinton-Davis by deed poll, 1990; *m* 1954, Frances Jane Lucas; one *s* three *d*. *Educ:* Hackney Downs Sch.; Mercers' Sch.; King's Coll., London University (LLB 1950; FKC 1996). Admitted Solicitor, 1953; in practice, 1953–70; consultant, S. J. Berwin & Co., 1989–97, 1998–. Mem. Exec. Council, Nat. Assoc. of Labour Student Organisations, 1949–50. Councillor, London Borough of Hackney, 1959; Mayor of Hackney, 1968. Contested (Lab): Langstone Div. of Portsmouth, 1955; Yarmouth, 1959 and 1964. MP (Lab) Hackney Central, 1970–83; Parly Under-Sec. of State, Dept of Trade, 1974–79; Opposition spokesman on trade, prices and consumer protection, 1979–81, on foreign affairs, 1981–83; Opposition frontbench spokesman on transport, H of L, 1990–97; Minister of State, DTI, 1997–98. Vice Chm., Parly Envmt Gp. Mem., Commn of EC, 1985–89. Chm., Adv. Cttee on Protection of the Sea, 1984–85, 1989–97; Pres., Refugee Council, 1989–97; Pres., AMA, 1992–97. Vice Pres., Lab. Finance and Industry Gp, 1993–. Member: RIIA; Council and Exec. Cttee, Justice; UN Selection Cttee for Sasakawa, Envmt Project; Adv. Bd, Centre of European Law, KCL; formerly Mem., Bd of Deputies of British Jews; Parly Relations Sub-Cttee of the Law Soc.; Hon. Mem., London Criminal Courts Solicitors' Assoc. Mem. Council, British Maritime League, 1989–97. Jt Pres., Soc. of Labour Lawyers, 1991–; President: UK Pilots Assoc. (Marine), 1991–; BALPA, 1994–; Inst. of Travel Management; Aviation Envmt Fedn; Vice-Pres., Chartered Instn of Envmtl Health Officers, 1991–. Pres., Hackney Br., Multiple Sclerosis Soc.; Vice-Pres., Hackney Assoc. for Disabled; Hon. Mem. Rotary Club, Hackney. Hon. Mem., 1979, and former Trustee, NUMAST (formerly Merchant Navy and Airline Officers' Assoc.); Hon. Fellow, QMW, 1993; Hon. FCIWEM; FRSA 1992 (Mem. Acad. Bd for Internat. Trade). Hon. Dr *hc* Polytechnical Inst., Bucharest, 1993. First Medal for Outstanding Services to Animal Welfare in Europe, Eurogroup for Animal Welfare, 1988. Grand Cross, Order of Leopold II, Belgium (for services to EC), 1990. *Recreations:* golf, Association football, reading biographical histories. *Address:* House of Lords, SW1A 0PW.

CLITHEROE, 2nd Baron *cr* 1955, of Downham; **Ralph John Assheton;** Bt 1945; Chairman, Yorkshire Bank, 1990–99; Vice Lord-Lieutenant of Lancashire, 1995–99; *b* 3 Nov. 1929; *s* of 1st Baron Clitheroe, KCVO, PC, FSA, and Sylvia Benita Frances, Lady Clitheroe, FRICS, FLAS, (*d* 1991), *d* of 6th Baron Hotham; *S* father, 1984; *m* 1961, Juliet, *d* of Lt-Col Christopher Lionel Hanbury, MBE, TD; two *s* one *d*. *Educ:* Eton; Christ Church, Oxford (Scholar, MA). FCIB 1991. Served as 2nd Lieut Life Guards, 1948–49. Chairman: RTZ Chemicals Ltd, 1973–87; RTZ Borax Ltd, 1979–89; US Borax and Chemical Corp., 1980–89; RTZ Oil & Gas Ltd, 1983–88; Director: Borax Consolidated, 1960–89; RTZ Corp., 1968–89; First Interstate Bank of California, 1981–89; TR Natural Resources Investment Trust, 1982–87; American Mining Congress, 1982–89; Halliburton Co., Texas, 1987–2002. Mem., Council, Chemical Industries Assoc., 1984–88. Liveryman, Skinners' Co. DL Lancs, 1986. *Heir: s* Hon. Ralph Christopher Assheton [*b* 19 March 1962; *m* 1996, Olivia, *o d* of Anthony Warrington]. *Address:* Downham Hall, Clitheroe, Lancs BB7 4DN. *Clubs:* Boodle's, Royal Automobile.

See also Hon. N. Assheton.

CLITHEROW, Rev. Canon Andrew; Priest in Charge: St Cuthbert's, Lytham, since 2007; St John's, Lytham, since 2008; Chaplain to the Queen, since 2007; *b* Guildford, 18 Nov. 1950; *s* of late Rt Rev. Richard George Clitherow and of Diana Clitherow; *m* 2002, Rebekah Clare Eames; two *s* two *d*. *Educ:* Ellesmere Coll., Shropshire; St Chad's Coll., Durham Univ. (BA Hons 1972); Salisbury and Wells Theol Coll.; Exeter Univ. (MPhil 1987). Ordained deacon, 1979, priest, 1980; Hon. Curate, Christ Church, Bedford, 1979–84; Asst Chaplain, Bedford Sch., 1979–84; Chaplain, Caldicott Sch., 1984–85; Res. Minister, St James, Acton Trussell and All Saints', Bednall, and Curate, St Michael and All Angels, Penkridge, 1985–88; Chaplain and Hd of Religious Studies, Rossall Sch., 1989–94; Vicar, St Paul's, Scotforth, 1994–2000; Res. Canon, Blackburn Cathedral, 2000–07; Dir of Trng, Dio. of Blackburn, 2000–07. *Publications:* Into Your Hands: prayer and the call to holiness in everyday ministry and life, 2001; Renewing Faith in Ordained Ministry, 2004; Creative Love in Tough Times, 2007; Desire, Love and the Rule of St Benedict, 2008. *Recreations:* walking, cycling, music, reading, fishing, cooking. *Address:* The Vicarage, Church Road, Lytham, Lancs FY8 5PX. *T:* (01253) 736168; *e-mail:* clitherow814@btinternet.com.

CLIVE, Viscount; Jonathan Nicholas William Herbert; *b* 5 Dec. 1979; *s* and *heir of* Earl of Powis, *qv*.

CLIVE, Eric McCredie, CBE 1999; FRSE; Visiting Professor, University of Edinburgh, since 1999; *b* 24 July 1938; *s* of Robert M. Clive and Mary L. D. Clive; *m* 1962, Kay M. McLeman; one *s* two *d* (and one *d* decd). *Educ:* Univs of Edinburgh (MA, LLB with dist.); Michigan (LLM); Virginia (SJD). Solicitor. Lecturer 1962–69, Sen. Lectr 1969–75, Reader 1975–77, Professor of Scots Law 1977–81, Univ. of Edinburgh; a Scottish Law Comr, 1981–99. FRSE 1999. *Publications:* Law of Husband and Wife in Scotland, 1974, 4th edn 1997; articles and notes in legal jls. *Address:* 14 York Road, Edinburgh EH5 3EH. *T:* (0131) 552 2875.

CLOAKE, John Cecil, CMG 1977; FSA; HM Diplomatic Service, retired; *b* 2 Dec. 1924; *s* of late Dr Cecil Stedman Cloake, Wimbledon, and Maude Osborne Newling; *m* 1956, Margaret Thomure Morris (*d* 2008), Washington, DC, USA; one *s*. *Educ:* King's Coll. Sch., Wimbledon; Peterhouse, Cambridge. Served in Army, 1943–46 (Lieut RE). Foreign

Office, 1948; 3rd Sec., Baghdad, 1949, and Saigon, 1951; 2nd Sec., 1952; FO, 1954; Private Sec. to Permanent Under-Sec., 1956, and to Parly Under-Sec., 1957; 1st Sec., 1957; Consul (Commercial), New York, 1958; 1st Sec., Moscow, 1962; FO, 1963; DSAO, 1965; Counsellor, 1966; Head of Accommodation Dept, 1967; Counsellor (Commercial), Tehran, 1968–72; Fellow, Centre for International Studies, LSE, 1972–73; Head of Trade Relations and Exports Dept, FCO, 1973–76; Ambassador to Bulgaria, 1976–80. Member: Council, British Inst. of Persian Studies, 1981–95 (Hon. Treas., 1982–90); Cttee of Honour for Bulgarian 1300th Anniv., 1981. Chairman: Richmond Soc. History Section, 1975–76, 1984–85; Richmond Local Hist. Soc., 1985–90 (Pres., 1990–); Richmond Museum Project, 1983–86; Mus. of Richmond, 1986–95; Pres., Richmond upon Thames Soc. of Voluntary Guides, 1997–2007. FSA 1998. Hon. DLitt Kingston, 2004. *Publications:* Templer: Tiger of Malaya, 1985; Richmond Past, 1991; Royal Bounty, 1992; Palaces and Parks of Richmond and Kew, Vol. 1, 1995, Vol. 2, 1996; Richmond Past and Present, 1999; Cottages and Common Fields of Richmond and Kew, 2001; monographs and articles on local history. *Recreations:* gardening, painting, architecture, local history, genealogy. *Address:* 4 The Terrace, Richmond Hill, Richmond, Surrey TW10 6RN.

CLOGHER, Bishop of, since 2002; **Rt Rev. Michael Geoffrey St Aubyn Jackson,** PhD, DPhil; *b* 24 May 1956; *s* of late Robert Stewart Jackson and of Margaret Jane Frances Jackson (*née* Sloan); *m* 1987, Inez Elizabeth (*née* Cooke); one *d*. *Educ:* Trinity Coll. Dublin (BA Classics 1979, MA 1982); St John's Coll., Cambridge (BA Theol. and Religious Studies 1981, MA 1985; PhD 1986); C of I Theol Coll.; Christ Church, Oxford (MA, DPhil 1989, by incorporation). Ordained deacon, 1986, priest, 1987; Curate-asst, Zion Parish, Rathgar, 1986–89; Minor Canon, Treasurer's Vicar and Chancellor's Vicar, St Patrick's Cathedral, Dublin, 1987–89; Asst Lectr, Dept of Hebrew, Biblical and Theol Studies, TCD, and in C of I Theol Coll., 1987–89; Chaplain, Christ Church, Oxford, 1989–97; Asst Lectr, Theology Faculty, Oxford Univ., 1991–97; Dir of Studies in Theol., St Anne's Coll., Oxford, 1995–97; Incumbent, St Fin Barre's Union, Cork and Dean of Cork, 1997–2002; Chaplain to UC, Cork and Cork Inst. of Technol., and Asst Lectr, Sch. of Classics and Sch. of Educn, UC, Cork, 1997–2002. Examining Chaplain to Bp of Cork, Cloyne and Ross, 1999–2002. Chm., Network of Inter-Faith Concerns of Anglican Communion 2004–; Mem., Anglican/Oriental Orthodox Internat. Commn, 2002–. Chm., St Fin Barre's Beyond 2000, 1998–2002. *Publications:* A History of the Vaughan Charity (with Claire Jackson), 1980; articles, papers and reviews. *Address:* The See House, Fivemiletown, Co. Tyrone BT75 0QP. *T:* and *Fax:* (028) 8952 2475; *e-mail:* bishop@ clogher.anglican.org.

CLOGHER, Bishop of, (RC), since 1979; **Most Rev. Joseph Duffy,** DD; *b* 3 Feb. 1934; *s* of Edward Duffy and Brigid MacEntee. *Educ:* St Macartan's College, Monaghan; Maynooth College. MA, BD, HDipEd. Ordained priest, 1958; Teacher, 1960–72; Curate, 1972–79. *Publications:* Patrick in his own words, 1972, 2nd edn 2000; Lough Derg Guide, 1980; Monaghan Cathedral, 1992. *Recreations:* local history, travel. *Address:* Tigh an Easpaig, Monaghan, Ireland. *T:* (47) 81019, *Fax:* (47) 84773.

CLOKE, Prof. (Frederick) Geoffrey (Nethersole), DPhil; FRS 2007; Professor of Chemistry, University of Sussex, since 1994; *b* 12 April 1953; *s* of late Frederick and Cecelia Cloke; partner, Siobhan Mehaffy. *Educ:* Balliol Coll., Oxford (BA Hons 1975; DPhil 1978; MA 1981). SERC Postdoctoral Fellow, Inorganic Chemistry Lab., Oxford, 1978–79; Jun. Res. Fellow, Balliol Coll., Oxford, 1979–83; Postdoctoral Associate, MIT, Cambridge, 1981–82; University of Sussex: SERC Advanced Fellowship, 1983–84; New Blood Lectr in Inorganic Chem., 1984–89; Sen. Lectr in Chem., 1989–90; Reader in Chem., 1990–94. *Publications:* over 150 res. papers in learned jls inc. Science, Jl of Amer. Chemical Soc., Angewandte Chemie, Chemical Communications. *Recreations:* sport— golf (playing), cricket (now only watching!), mountain walking/scrambling, woodworking, movies, jazz and 70s music. *Address:* Department of Chemistry, Chichester Building, University of Sussex, Brighton BN1 9QJ. *T:* (01273) 678735, *Fax:* (01273) 677196; *e-mail:* f.g.cloke@sussex.ac.uk.

CLOKE, Prof. Paul John, PhD; DSc; Professor of Geography, University of Exeter, since 2006; *b* 17 Feb. 1953; *s* of William and Iris Cloke (*née* Tinton); *m* 1974, Vivien Jane Hewitt; one *s* one *d*. *Educ:* Southampton Univ. (BA); Wye Coll., London (PhD); Bristol Univ. (DSc). Lectr, Reader, then Prof. of Geog., Univ. of Wales, Lampeter, 1977–92; Reader, 1992–93, Prof. of Geog., 1993–2005, Univ. of Bristol. *Publications:* Key Settlements in Rural Areas, 1979; Introduction to Rural Settlement Planning, 1983; (with C. Park) Rural Resource Management, 1985; Rural Planning, 1987; Policies and Plans for Rural People, 1988; Rural Land Use Planning, 1989; (with P. Bell) Deregulation and Transport, 1990; (with J. Little) The Rural State, 1990; (with C. Philo and D. Sadler) Approaching Human Geography, 1991; Policy and Change in Thatcher's Britain, 1992; (jtly) Writing the Rural, 1994; (ed jtly) Contested Countryside Cultures, 1997; Rural Wales, 1997; (ed jtly) Introducing Human Geographies, 1999; (with P. Milbourne and R. Widdowfield) Rural Homelessness, 2002; (with O. Jones) The Culture of Trees, 2002; Country Visions, 2003; (jtly) Practising Human Geography, 2004; (ed jtly) Envisioning Human Geographies, 2004; (ed jtly) Spaces of Geographic Thought, 2005; (ed jtly) Handbook of Rural Studies, 2006; (ed jtly) International Perspectives on Rural Homelessness, 2006. *Recreations:* Christian music, countryside walking, Tottenham Hotspur Football Club. *Address:* School of Geography, University of Exeter, Amory Building, Rennes Drive, Exeter EX4 4QE. *T:* (01392) 264522, *Fax:* (01392) 263342; *e-mail:* p.cloke@exeter.ac.uk.

CLOONEY, George Timothy; actor, director and producer; *b* 6 May 1961; *s* of Nicholas Clooney and Nina Bruce Clooney (*née* Warren); *m* 1989, Talia Balsam (marr. diss. 1993). *Educ:* Northern Kentucky Univ. *Television series: actor:* E/R, 1984–85; The Facts of Life, 1985–86; Roseanne, 1988–89; Sunset Beat, 1990; Baby Talk, 1991; Bodies of Evidence, 1992; Sisters, 1992–94; ER, 1994–99; *director and producer:* K Street, 2003; Unscripted, 2005; *actor in television films:* Combat High, 1986; Fail Safe (also prod.), 2000. *Films: actor:* Return of the Killer Tomatoes, 1988; Red Surf, 1990; Unbecoming Age, 1993; From Dusk Till Dawn, One Fine Day, 1996; Batman and Robin, 1997; The Peacemaker, Out of Sight, The Thin Red Line, 1998; Three Kings, 1999; The Perfect Storm, O Brother, Where Art Thou? (Best Actor, Golden Globe Awards, 2001), 2000; Spy Kids, Ocean's Eleven, 2001; Welcome to Collinwood (also prod.), 2002; Solaris, Confessions of a Dangerous Mind (also dir), Intolerable Cruelty, 2003; Ocean's Twelve, 2005; Syriana (also prod.) (Best Supporting Actor, Golden Globe and Academy Awards, 2006), Good Night, and Good Luck (also writer and dir), 2006; The Good German (also prod.), Ocean's Thirteen, Michael Clayton, 2007; Leatherheads (also dir), 2008; *producer:* Rock Star, 2001; Insomnia, Far From Heaven, 2002; Criminal, 2004; The Jacket, The Big Empty, Rumour Has It, 2005; PU-239, A Scanner Darkly, 2006. *Address:* c/o Creative Artists Agency, 2000 Avenue of the Stars, Los Angeles, CA 90067, USA.

CLORE, Melanie; Co-Chairman Worldwide, Impressionist and Modern Art Department, Sotheby's, since 2000; Deputy Chairman, Sotheby's Europe, since 1997; *b* 28 Jan. 1960; *d* of Martin and Cynthia Clore; *m* 1992, Yaron Meshoulam; one *s* one *d*. *Educ:* Channing

Sch., Highgate; Univ. of Manchester (BA Hons Hist. of Art 1981). Became an auctioneer, 1985; Sotheby's: Hd, Impressionist and Modern Art Dept, 1991–; Member: European Bd, 1995–; Exec. Mgt Cttee, 1995–. Trustee, Tate, 2004–08. *Recreations:* going to the movies, pottering in the garden. *Address:* Sotheby's, 34–35 New Bond Street, W1A 2AA. *T:* (020) 7293 5394, *Fax:* (020) 7293 5932.

CLOSE, Anthony Stephen, CBE 1997; Chairman, Health Education Authority, 1994–99; *b* 9 Aug. 1931; *s* of Steven John Henry Close and Marion Lily Close (*née* Matthews); *m* 1961, Josephine Oakey; one *d*. *Educ:* Colston's Sch.; Queen's Coll., Oxford (MA); Birkbeck Coll., London (MSc). AFBPsS. Shell International Petroleum Co.; BOAC; Beecham Group; Grand Metropolitan, 1973–83; Group Dir of Personnel, Trusthouse Forte, 1983–93. Director: BIOSS Internat., 1993–; EAR Ltd, 1997–2001. Member: FEFC, 1992–95; Adv. Bd, Public Concern at Work, 1993–; Adv. Bd, QMC Public Policy Seminars, 1995–2002; Adv. Bd, Centre for Public Policy Seminars, 2002–06. MInstD (Mem. Council, 1985–2001). *Recreations:* walking, opera, golf, cooking. *Address:* Danes, Cox Green Lane, Maidenhead SL6 3EY. *T:* (01628) 622910. *Club:* Savile.

CLOSE, Prof. Francis Edwin, OBE 2000; FInstP; Professor of Theoretical Physics, University of Oxford, since 2001; Fellow, Exeter College, Oxford, since 2001; *b* 24 July 1945; *s* of Frederick Archibald Close and Frances Moreton Close; *m* 1969, Gillian Matilda Boyce; two *d*. *Educ:* King's Sch., Peterborough; St Andrews Univ. (BSc 1967); Magdalen Coll., Oxford (DPhil 1970). FInstP 1991. Research Fellow: Stanford Linear Accelerator, Calif, 1970–72; Daresbury Lab., 1973; CERN, Geneva, 1973–75; Res. Scientist, 1975–2000, and Head of Theoretical Physics Div., 1991–2000, Rutherford Appleton Lab. Dist. Scientist, Oak Ridge Nat. Lab. and Univ. of Tennessee, 1988–90; Vis. Prof., Birmingham Univ., 1996–2002; Sen. Scientist, CERN, 1997–2000; Gresham Prof. of Astronomy, 2000–03. Mem. Council, Royal Instn, 1997–99 (Christmas Lectr, 1993); Vice-Pres., BAAS, 1993–99. Chm., British Physics Olympiad, 2003–. Fellow, APS, 1992; Fellow in Public Understanding of Physics, Inst. Physics, 1995–97. Kelvin Medal, Inst. Physics, 1996. *Publications:* Introduction to Quarks and Partons, 1979; The Cosmic Onion, 1983; The Particle Explosion, 1987; End, 1988; Too Hot to Handle, 1991; Lucifer's Legacy, 2000; The Particle Odyssey, 2002; numerous res. papers on theoretical physics, and articles on science in The Guardian. *Recreations:* writing, singing, travel, squash, Real tennis. *Address:* Department of Theoretical Physics, Keble Road, Oxford OX1 3NP. *Club:* Harwell Squash.

CLOSE, Glenn; actress; *b* 19 March 1947; *d* of William and Bettine Close; *m* 1st, 1969, Cabot Wade (marr. diss.); 2nd, 1984, James Marlas (marr. diss.); 3rd, 2006, David Shaw; one *d* by John Starke. *Educ:* William and Mary Coll. (BA 1974). With New Phoenix Repertory Co., 1974–75; *theatre* includes: New York: Love for Love, 1974; A Streetcar Named Desire; The Crucifer of Blood, 1978–79; Barnum, 1980–81; The Real Thing, 1984 (Tony Award); Benefactors, 1986; Death and the Maiden, 1992 (Tony Award); Sunset Boulevard, LA, 1993–94, NY, 1994–95 (Tony Award); A Streetcar Named Desire, NT, 2002; *films* include: The World According to Garp, 1982; The Natural, 1984; Fatal Attraction, 1987; Dangerous Liaisons, 1989; Hamlet, 1991; The House of Spirits, 1994; Serving in Silence: the Margarethe Cammermeyer story, 1995; Air Force One, 1997; Paradise Road, 1997; Cookie's Fortune, 1999; Things You Can Just Tell by Looking at Her, 2000; 102 Dalmatians, 2000; The Safety of Objects, 2003; The Stepford Wives, 2004; The Chumscrubber, Evening, 2007; numerous TV appearances incl. Damages (series), 2007. *Address:* c/o CAA, 2000 Avenue of the Stars, Los Angeles, CA 90067, USA.

CLOSE, Roy Edwin, CBE 1973; Director General, British Institute of Management, 1976–85; *b* 11 March 1920; *s* of Bruce Edwin and Minnie Louise Close; *m* 1947, Olive Joan Forty; two *s*. *Educ:* Trinity County Sch., N London; MSc Aston 1973. Served Army, 1939–46; RASC; Para Regt; SAS, 1943–46 (Captain). Editorial Staff, The Times; Asst Editor, The Times Review of Industry, 1949–56; Executive, Booker McConnell GP; Dir, Bookers Sugar Estates, 1957–65; Directing Staff, Admin. Staff Coll., Henley, 1965; Industrial Adviser, NEDO, 1966–69; Industrial Dir, NEDO, 1969–73; Chm., Univ. of Aston Management Centre, and Dean of Faculty of Management, 1973–76; Proprietor, Management Adv. Services, 1986–92. Director: Davies and Perfect, 1985–87; Flextech plc, 1985–87; Kepner Tregoe Ltd, 1986–89; Broad Street Group, 1986–91 (Chm., 1986–88); Equity Development Ltd, 1996–2000 (Chm., 1996–99); Equity I (formerly Equity Develt) Ltd, 2000–06. Chm., Open Univ. Mgt Educn Sector Bd, Open Business Sch., 1984–87; Mem., Open Univ. Business Sch. Industrial and Professional Adv. Cttee, 1988–93 (Chm., 1988–90). Chm., Conservation Foundn, 1987–98 (Dir, 1986–98). Mem. Council, Farm-Africa, 1987–92. CCMI (FBIM 1979); FIIM (FIWM 1979); FRSA 1980. DUniv Open, 1987. *Publications:* The Cruellest of Tests (novel), 2005; In Action with the SAS: a soldier's odyssey from Dunkirk to Berlin (war memoirs), 2005; various articles on industrial, economic subjects. *Recreations:* swimming, walking, reading, listening to music. *Address:* Cathedral Cottage, Church Lane, North Elmham, Dereham, Norfolk NR20 5JU. *Clubs:* Reform, Special Forces.

CLOSE, Seamus Anthony, OBE 1996; Member (Alliance) Lagan Valley, Northern Ireland Assembly, 1998–2007; *b* 12 Aug. 1947; *s* of late James and of Kathleen Close; *m* 1978, Deirdre McCann; three *s* one *d*. *Educ:* St Malachy's Coll.; Belfast Coll. of Business Studies. Company Sec., 1970–85; Financial Dir, 1985–. Mem. (Alliance), Lisburn CC (formerly Lisburn BC), 1973– (Mayor, 1993–94); Mem. (Alliance) NI Assembly, 1982–86; Negotiator: Brooke/Mayhew Talks, 1991–92; Good Friday Agreement, 1998. Dep. Leader, Alliance Party, 1991–2001. Contested (Alliance): Fermanagh and S Tyrone, Aug. 1981; S Antrim, 1983; Lagan Valley, 1987, 1992, 1997, 2001, 2005. Chm., Lisburn City Dist Policing Partnership, 2005–06. *Recreations:* sports, family, current affairs. *Address:* 123 Moira Road, Lisburn, Northern Ireland BT28 1RJ. *T:* (028) 9267 0639.

CLOTHIER, Sir Cecil (Montacute), KCB 1982; QC 1965; Chairman, Council on Tribunals, 1989–92; *b* 28 Aug. 1919; *s* of Hugh Montacute Clothier, Liverpool; *m* 1st, 1943, Mary Elizabeth (*d* 1984), *o d* of late Ernest Glover Bush; one *s* two *d*; 2nd, 1992, Diana Stevenson (*née* Durrant). *Educ:* Stonyhurst Coll.; Lincoln Coll., Oxford (BCL, MA; Hon. Fellow 1984). Served 1939–46, 51 (Highland) Div.; British Army Staff, Washington, DC; Hon. Lt-Col Royal Signals. Called to Bar, Inner Temple, 1950, Bencher, 1973. Recorder of Blackpool, later of the Crown Court, 1965–78; Judge of Appeal, IoM, 1972–78. A Legal Assessor to Gen. Medical and Gen. Dental Councils, 1972–78; Mem., Royal Commn on NHS, 1976–78; Parly Comr for Admin, and Health Service Comr for England, Wales and Scotland, 1979–84; Chm., Police Complaints Authority, 1985–89; Mem., Sen. (formerly Top) Salaries Rev. Body, 1989–95; Vice-Pres., Interception of Communications Tribunal, 1986–96; Chairman: Cttee on Ethics of Gene Therapy, 1990–92; Inquiry into Deaths in Devonport Hosp., 1972; Allitt Inquiry, 1993–94; Review Body on Police Services in Jersey, 1996–97; Review Panel on Machinery of Govt in Jersey, 1999–2001. Mem., Adv. Council, British Library, 1993–98. Chm., Harefield Res. Foundn, 2001–03. Hon. Life Pres., Magdi Yacoub Inst., 2005. John Snow Meml Lectr (Assoc. of Anaesthetists of GB and Ireland/Amer. Assoc. of Anaesthesiologists), 1981. Hon. Mem., Assoc. of Anaesthetists of GB and Ireland, 1987; Hon. FRPharmS 1990; Hon. FRCP 1998. Rock Carling Fellow, Nuffield Provincial Hosps Trust, 1987. Hon. LLD Hull, 1982. *Address:* 1 Temple Gardens, Temple, EC4Y 9BB.

CLOTHIER, Richard John; Chairman: Robinson plc, since 2004; Spearhead International Ltd, since 2005; Aqua Bounty Technologies plc, since 2006; *b* 4 July 1945; *s* of J. Neil Clothier and Barbara Clothier; *m* 1st, 1972, Ingrid Hafner (*d* 1994); two *s*; 2nd, 1995, Sarah (*née* Riley). *Educ:* Peterhouse, Zimbabwe; Univ. of Natal (BSc Agric.); Harvard (AMP). Milk Marketing Board, 1971–77; Dalgety Agriculture, 1977–88; Chief Executive: Pig Improvement Co., 1988–92; Dalgety plc, 1993–97; Plantation & Gen. Investments, later PGI Gp, 1998–2005; Director: Granada Gp, 1996–2004; PGI Gp, 2005–06. *Publication:* The Bundu Book, 1969. *Recreations:* yacht racing, field sports. *Address:* c/o 81 Carter Lane, EC4V 5EP. *T:* (020) 7246 0207. *Clubs:* Farmers, Royal Thames Yacht, Royal Ocean Racing.

CLOUDSLEY-THOMPSON, Prof. John Leonard, MA, PhD (Cantab), DSc (London); FRES, FLS, FZS, CBiol, FIBiol, FWAAS; Professor of Zoology, Birkbeck College, University of London, 1972–86, now Emeritus (Reader 1971–72); *b* Murree, India, 23 May 1921; *s* of Dr Ashley George Gyton Thompson, MA, MD (Cantab), DPH, and Muriel Elaine (*née* Griffiths); *m* 1944, Jessie Anne Cloudsley, MCSP, DipBS, LCAD; three *s*. *Educ:* Marlborough Coll.; Pembroke Coll., Univ. of Cambridge. War of 1939–45: commissioned into 4th Queen's Own Hussars, 1941; transf. 4th Co. of Lond. Yeo. (Sharpshooters); N Africa, 7th Armoured Div., 1941–42 (severely wounded); Instructor (Capt.), Sandhurst, 1943; rejoined regt for D Day (escaped from Villers-Bocage), Caen Offensive, etc, 1944 (Hon. rank of Capt. on resignation). Lectr in Zoology, King's Coll., Univ. of London, 1950–60; Prof. of Zoology, Univ. of Khartoum, and Keeper, Sudan Nat. Hist. Museum, 1960–71. Nat. Science Foundn Sen. Res. Fellow, Univ. of New Mexico, Albuquerque, USA, 1969; Visiting Professor: Arizona State Univ., 1969; Univ. of Kuwait, 1978 and 1983; Univ. of Nigeria, Nsukka, 1981; Univ. of Qatar, 1986; Sultan Qaboos Univ., Muscat, 1988; Leverhulme Emeritus Fellow at UCL, 1987–89; Visiting Research Fellow: ANU, 1987; Desert Ecol. Res. Unit of Namibia, 1989. Hon. Consultant: Univ. of Malaya, 1969; Arabian Gulf Univ., Bahrain, 1986; Univ. of Kuwait, 1990; Indo-British Workshop on Biodiversity, 1993. Took part in: Cambridge Iceland Expedn, 1947; Expedn to Southern Tunisia, 1954; univ. expedns with his wife to various parts of Africa, 1960–73, incl. trans-Sahara crossing, 1967. Chairman: British Naturalists' Assoc., 1974–83 (Vice-Pres., 1985–; Hon. FBNA 2007); Biological Council, 1977–82 (Medal, 1985). President: British Arachnological Soc., 1982–85 (Vice-Pres., 1985–86); British Soc. for Chronobiology, 1985–87; Vice-President: Linnean Soc., 1975–76 and 1977–78; 1st World Congress of Herpetology, 1989. Hon. FLS 1997; Hon. Member: Royal African Soc., 1969 (Medal, 1969); British Herpetological Soc., 1983 (Pres., 1991–96); Centre Internat. de Documentation Arachnologique, Paris, 1995. Liveryman, Worshipful Co. of Skinners, 1952. Silver Jubilee Gold Medal and Hon. DSc, Khartoum, 1981. Inst. of Biology K. S. S. Charter Award, 1981; J. H. Grundy Meml Medal, Royal Army Med. Coll., 1987; Foundn for Envmtl Conservation Prize, Geneva, 1989; Peter Scott Meml Award, British Naturalists' Assoc., 1993. Editor-in-Chief (formerly Founding Editor) (assisted by wife), Jl of Arid Environments Vol. 1, 1978–Vol. 37, 1997, now Editor Emeritus; Editor: (with wife) Natural History of the Arabian Gulf (book series), 1981–82; Adaptations of Desert Organisms (book series), 1989–2000 (25 vols). *Publications:* Biology of Deserts (ed), 1954; Spiders, Scorpions, Centipedes and Mites, 1958 (2nd edn 1968); Animal Behaviour, 1960; Rhythmic Activity in Animal Physiology and Behaviour, 1961; Land Invertebrates (with John Sankey), 1961; Life in Deserts (with M. J. Chadwick), 1964; Desert Life, 1965; Animal Conflict and Adaptation, 1965; Animal Twilight: man and game in eastern Africa, 1967; Microecology, 1967; Zoology of Tropical Africa, 1969; The Temperature and Water Relations of Reptiles, 1971; Desert Life, 1974; Terrestrial Environments, 1975; Insects and History, 1976; Evolutionary Trends in the Mating of Arthropoda, 1976; (ed jtly) Environmental Physiology of Animals, 1976; Man and the Biology of Arid Zones, 1977; The Water and Temperature Relations of Woodlice, 1977; The Desert, 1977; Animal Migration, 1978; Why the Dinosaurs Became Extinct, 1978; Wildlife of the Desert, 1979; Biological Clocks: their functions in nature, 1980; Tooth and Claw: defensive strategies in the animal world, 1980; (ed) Sahara Desert, 1984; Guide to Woodlands, 1985; Evolution and Adaptation of Terrestrial Arthropods, 1988; Ecophysiology of Desert Arthropods and Reptiles, 1991; The Diversity of Desert Life, 1993; (novel) The Nile Quest, 1994; Predation and Defence Amongst Reptiles, 1994; Biotic Interactions in Arid Lands, 1996; Teach Yourself Ecology, 1998; The Diversity of Amphibians and Reptiles: an introduction, 1999; Ecology and Behaviour of Mesozoic Reptiles, 2005; Sharpshooter: memories of armoured warfare 1939–45, 2006; contribs to Encyclopædia Britannica, Encyclopedia Americana; shorter monographs and eleven children's books; many scientific articles in learned jls, etc. *Recreations:* music (especially opera), photography, travel. *Address:* 10 Battishill Street, N1 1TE.

CLOUGH, Alan; *see* Clough, J. A.

CLOUGH, Christopher George, FRCP; Director, Royal Colleges of Physicians Training Board (formerly Joint Committee on Higher Medical Training, Royal College of Physicians), since 2005; Consultant Neurologist, King's College Hospital, since 1995; *b* 30 Aug. 1953; *s* of George and Daisy Clough; *m* 1979, Lyn Sylvia Griffiths; two *s* one *d*. *Educ:* Manchester Univ. (MB ChB). FRCP 1992. Royal Alexandra Hosp., Rhyl, 1975–76; Hull Royal Infirmary, 1976–79; Leeds Gen. Infirmary, 1979–80; Mount Sinai Med. Centre, 1980–81; Queen Elizabeth Med. Centre, Birmingham, and Midlands Centre for Neurology and Neurosurgery, Smethwick, 1981–89; Cons. Neurologist, Brook Regl Neuroscience Centre and Bromley Hosps, 1989–95; Dir, Regl Neuroscis Centre, 1991–98; Med. Dir, KCH, 1998–2003; Chief Med. Advr, SE London Strategic HA, 2003–06. Member: Fabian Soc.; Labour Party. *Publications:* pubns on Parkinson's Disease, headache and restless legs. *Recreations:* tennis, music, lifelong Spurs fan. *Address:* 17 Blenheim Road, Bickley BR1 2EX.

CLOUGH, (John) Alan, CBE 1972; MC 1945; Chairman, British Mohair Holdings plc (formerly British Mohair Spinners Ltd), 1980–84 (Deputy Chairman, 1970–80, Chief Executive, 1977–80, Joint Managing Director, 1980–83); *b* 20 March 1924; *s* of late John Clough and Yvonne (*née* Dollfus); *m* 1st, 1949, Margaret Joy Catton (marr. diss.); one *s* two *d*; 2nd, 1961, Mary Cowan Catherwood; one *s* one *d*. *Educ:* Marlborough Coll.; Leeds Univ. HM Forces, Queen's Bays, 1942–47, N Africa and Italy (Captain); TA Major, Yorkshire Hussars, 1947–55. Mayor, Co. of Merchants of Staple of England, 1969–70. Chairman: Wool Industries Res. Assoc., 1967–69; Wool Textile Delegn, 1969–72; Textile Res. Council, 1984–89; Member: Wool Textile EDC, 1967–72; Jt Textile Cttee, NEDO, 1972–74; President: Comitextil (Co-ordinating Cttee for Textile Industries in EEC), Brussels, 1975–77; British Textile Confedn, 1974–77; Textile Inst., 1979–81; Confedn of British Wool Textiles, 1982–84. Chm., Instant Muscle Ltd, 1989–94. CompTI 1975. Hon. DSc Bradford, 1987. *Recreations:* fishing, gardening, travel. *Club:* Boodle's.

CLOUGH, Mark Gerard; QC 1999; Partner, Addleshaw Goddard, since 2006; *b* 13 May 1953; *s* of Philip Gerard Clough, *qv* and Mary Elizabeth Clough (*née* Carter); one *d*; *m*

1989, Joanne Elizabeth Dishington; two *s. Educ:* Ampleforth Coll.; St Andrews Univ. (MA 1976). Called to the Bar, Gray's Inn, 1978; admitted Solicitor, 1995; Solicitor Advocate, 1996; Partner, Ashurst Morris Crisp, then Ashurst, 1995–2006. Chm., Solicitors Assoc. of Higher Ct Advocates, 2003–06; Member: Adv. Bd, British Inst. of Internat. and Comparative Law Competition Law Forum, 2003–; Bd, European Maritime Law Orgn, 2004–. Mem., Editl Bd, Internat. Trade Law and Regulation Jl, 1996–. *Publications:* EC Competition Law and Shipping, 1990; EC Merger Regulation, 1995; (contrib.) Vaughan's Laws of the European Communities, 1997; Trade and Telecoms, 2002; (ed) Collective Dominance: the contribution of the Community Courts, 2003; (contrib.) A True European—essays for Judge David Edward, 2004; articles on EC Law and competition law. *Recreations:* theatre, poetry, tennis, golf. *Address:* Addleshaw Goddard, 150 Aldersgate Street, EC1A 4EJ. *Club:* Travellers.

CLOUGH, Philip Gerard; Justice of Appeal: Hong Kong, 1986–92; Bermuda, 1998–2004; Gibraltar, 1998–2004; *b* 11 March 1924; *s* of Gerard Duncombe Clough and Grace Margaret (*née* Phillips); *m* 1st, Mary Elizabeth Carter (marr. diss.); one *s*; 2nd, Margaret Joy Davies; one *s* one *d. Educ:* Dauntsey's Sch.; King's Coll., Cambridge (Exhibnr; MA). War service, Sub Lieut (A) RNVR, 1942–46. Called to the Bar, Inner Temple, 1949; Colonial Legal Service: Federal Counsel, Malaya, 1951–58; Chancery Bar, Lincoln's Inn, 1958–78; Legal Affairs Advr, Brunei, 1978–81; Dist Judge, 1981–83, High Court Judge, 1983–86, Hong Kong. Non permanent Mem., Court of Final Appeal, Hong Kong, 1997–2006. *Address:* 2 Adlam Buildings, Harcourt Terrace, Salisbury, Wilts SP2 7SA. *T:* (01722) 415750. *Clubs:* Garrick; Hong Kong.
See also M. G. Clough.

CLOUGH, Susanna Patricia; *see* FitzGerald, S. P.

CLOUT, Prof. Hugh Donald, PhD, DLit; FBA 1997; Professor of Geography, University College London, 1987–2007, now Emeritus; *b* 29 April 1944; *s* of Donald Clout and Florence (*née* Allwood). *Educ:* University College London (BA, MPhil, PhD 1979, DLit 2000); Univ. de Paris I (Dde l'Univ 1983). Lectr, 1967–81, Reader, 1981–87, in Geography, UCL. *Publications:* (ed) Regional Development in Western Europe, 1975, 3rd edn 1987; (ed) Themes in the Historical Geography of France, 1977; Agriculture in France on the Eve of the Railway Age, 1980; The Land of France 1815–1914, 1982; (ed) Western Europe: geographical perspectives, 1985, 3rd edn 1994; (ed) Times London History Atlas, 1991, 5th edn, as The Times History of London, 2007; After the Ruins: restoring the countryside of northern France after the Great War, 1996. *Address:* Department of Geography, University College London, Gower Street, WC1E 6BT.

CLOWES, Alfred William; General Secretary, Ceramic and Allied Trades Union, 1980–95; *b* 17 Dec. 1931. Joined the Industry on leaving school; Asst Gen. Sec., Ceramic and Allied Trades Union, 1975–80. Hon. Freeman, City of Stoke-on-Trent, 1995. *Address:* 22 Meadow Avenue, Wetley Rocks, Stoke-on-Trent ST9 0BD.

CLUCAS, Sir Kenneth (Henry), KCB 1976 (CB 1969); Permanent Secretary, Department of Trade, 1979–82; Chairman, Nuffield Foundation Committee of Inquiry into Pharmacy, 1983–86; *b* 18 Nov. 1921; *o s* of late Rev. J. H. Clucas and Ethel Clucas (*née* Sim); *m* 1960, Barbara (*d* 1993), *e d* of late Rear-Adm. R. P. Hunter, USN, Washington; two *d. Educ:* Kingswood Sch.; Emmanuel Coll., Cambridge. Royal Signals, 1941–46 (despatches). Joined Min. of Labour as Asst Principal, 1948; 2nd Sec. (Labour), British Embassy, Cairo, 1950; Principal, HM Treasury, 1952; Min. of Labour, 1954; Private Sec. to Minister, 1960–62; Asst Sec., 1962; Under-Sec., 1966–68; Sec., Nat. Bd for Prices and Incomes, 1968–71; First Civil Service Comr, and Dep. Sec., CSD, 1971–73; Dep. Sec., DTI, 1974; Permanent Sec., Dept of Prices and Consumer Protection, 1974–79. Member: Council on Tribunals, 1983–89; Adv. Panel, Freedom of Information Campaign, 1984–; RIPA Wkg Gp on Politics and the Civil Service, 1985–86; Chairman: Cttee of Inquiry into Advertising Controls, 1986–87; Monitoring Cttee, ABI Code of Practice, 1989–93; FIMBRA, 1993–98 (Mem. Council, 1986–); Dep. Chm., CIBA Foundn Media Resource Steering Cttee, 1984–93; Chm., Lloyd's Wkg Pty on Consumer Guarantees, 1985; Lloyd's Members Ombudsman, 1988–94. Chm., Nat. Assoc. of Citizens' Advice Bureaux, 1984–89 (Vice Chm., 1983–84; Chm. Surrey and W Sussex Area Cttee, 1982–84); Mem. Management Cttee, Godalming CAB, 1982–85; Vice Pres., and Chm. of Trustees, Friends of CAB, 1991–95. FRSA. Hon. FRPharmS, 1989. *Recreations:* walking, theatre, opera, composing and solving puzzles. *Address:* Cariad, Knoll Road, Godalming, Surrey GU7 2EL. *T:* (01483) 416430.

CLUCKIE, Prof. Ian David, FREng, FCIWEM; FICE; Professor of Hydrology and Water Management, and Director, Water and Environmental Management Research Centre, Bristol University, since 1997; *b* Edinburgh, 20 July 1949; *m* 1972; one *s* one *d. Educ:* Univ. of Surrey (BSc); Univ. of Birmingham (MSc, PhD). CEng, FREng (FEng 1997); FIWEM 1983; FICE 1988; FRMetS 1979. W. S. Atkins, Swansea, 1966–72; Central Water Planning Unit, Reading, 1974–76; Lectr, Univ. of Birmingham, 1976–88; Salford University: Prof. of Water Resources, 1988–97; Chm., Dept of Civil Engrg, 1991–96; Dir, Telford Res. Inst., 1993–94, 1996–97; Acad. Dir, Salford Civil Engineering Ltd, 1989–97. Natural Environment Research Council: Mem., AAPS Res. Grants and Trng Awards Cttee, 1988–91; Chm., AAPS Cttee, 1991–94; Mem., Terrestrial and Freshwater Scis, Marine Scis, Atmospheric Scis and Higher Educn Affairs Cttees, 1991–94. Chm., UK IAHS Cttee, 2006–; Pres.-elect, IAHS ICR5, 2008–. FRSA 1993. *Publications:* (with C. G. Collier) Hydrological Applications of Weather Radar, 1991; (jtly) Radar Hydrology for Real-time Flood Forecasting, 2001; contribs to learned jls. *Recreations:* sailing, hill walking.

CLUFF, John Gordon, (Algy); Chairman and Chief Executive, Cluff Gold, since 2004; Chairman, The Spectator, 1985–2005 (Proprietor, 1981–85); *b* 19 April 1940; *o s* of late Harold Cluff and Freda Cluff, Waldeshare House, Waldeshare, Kent; *m* 1993, Blondel Hodge, Anguilla, WI; three *s. Educ:* Stowe Sch. 2/Lieut, Grenadier Guards, 1959; Captain, Guards Independent Parachute Co., 1963; served W Africa, Cyprus, Malaysia, retd 1965. Founded Cluff Oil, subseq. Cluff Resources, 1971, Chief Exec., 1971, Chm., 1979; founded Cluff Mining, 1996, Chm., 1996–2004, Chief Exec., 1996–2003. Contested (C) Ardwick Div. of Manchester, 1966. Chm., Cons. Commn on the Commonwealth, 2000. A Dir, Centre for Policy Studies, 1998–2005. Governor: Commonwealth Inst., 1994–; Stowe Sch., 1998–. Pres., ATC, Kent, 2007–; Vice Pres., Army Benevolent Fund, Kent, 2007–. Trustee, Stowe House Preservation Trust, 1999–; Chm. Trustees, War Memorials Trust, 2003–. *Address:* 24 Queen Anne's Gate, SW1H 9AA. *Clubs:* White's, Beefsteak, Brooks's, Pratt's, City of London, Special Forces; Royal Yacht Squadron; Brook, Racquet and Tennis (New York).

CLUNAS, Prof. Craig, PhD; FBA 2004; Professor of the History of Art, and Fellow of Trinity College, University of Oxford, since 2007; *b* 1 Dec. 1954; *s* of Charles Clunas and Elizabeth Clunas (*née* Robertson); one *s. Educ:* Aberdeen Grammar Sch.; King's Coll., Cambridge (BA 1st cl. (Chinese Studies) 1977); SOAS, Univ. of London (PhD 1983). Res. Asst, Far Eastern Dept, 1979–93, Sen. Res. Fellow in Chinese Studies, 1993–94, V&A Mus.; Sen. Lectr in Hist. of Art, 1994–97, Prof. of Hist. of Art, 1997–2003, Univ. of Sussex; Percival David Prof. of Chinese and East Asian Art, SOAS, Univ. of London, 2003–07. *Publications:* Chinese Export Watercolours, 1984; Chinese Furniture, 1989; Superfluous Things: social status and material culture in Early Modern China, 1991; Fruitful Sites: garden culture in Ming Dynasty China, 1996; Art in China, 1997; Pictures and Visuality in Early Modern China, 1997; Elegant Debts: the social art of Wen Zhengming, 2004; Empire of Great Brightness: visual and material cultures of Ming China, 2007; numerous articles in learned jls. *Address:* History of Art Department, Littlegate House, St Ebbe's, Oxford OX1 1PT; *e-mail:* craig.clunas@hoa.ox.ac.uk.

CLUNES, Martin Alexander; actor; *b* 28 Nov. 1961; *s* of late Alec Sheriff de Moro Clunes and Daphne (*née* Acott); *m* 1st, Lucy Aston (marr. diss. 1993); 2nd, 1997, Philippa Braithwaite; one *d.* Founder: Big Arts, 1990; Buffalo, prodn co. *Theatre includes:* The Henrys, ESC; The Admirable Crichton, Th. Royal, Haymarket; Much Ado About Nothing, Julius Caesar, Open Air Th., Regent's Park; Party Tricks, Nottingham Playhouse (dir), 1995; Tartuffe, NT, 2002. *Television includes:* No Place Like Home, 1983; All At Number 20, 1986; Men Behaving Badly, 1991–98; Jeeves and Wooster, 1991; If You See God, Tell Him, 1993; Demob, 1993; Harry Enfield and Chums, 1994; An Evening with Gary Lineker, 1994; Born to Be Wild, 1999; Gormenghast, 2000; Men Down Under, 2000; Lorna Doone, 2000; William and Mary, 2003; Doc Martin, 2004, 2005, 2007; *television films:* Over Here, 1996; Neville's Island, 1998; Touch and Go, 1998; Hunting Venus (also dir), 1999; Sex 'n' Death, 1999; Dirty Tricks, 2000; A is for Acid, 2002; Goodbye Mr Chips, 2002; Beauty, 2004. *Films:* The Russia House, 1990; Carry on Columbus, 1992; Swing Kids, 1993; Staggered (also dir), 1994; Sweet Revenge, 1998; Shakespeare in Love, 1998; The Acid House, 1998; Saving Grace, 2000; Global Heresy, 2002.

CLUNIES ROSS, Prof. Margaret Beryl, (Mrs J. R. Green); McCaughey Professor of English Language and Early English Literature, University of Sydney, since 1990; Director, Centre for Medieval Studies, since 1997; President, National Academies Forum, 1998; *b* 24 April 1942; *d* of Ernest Phillips Tidemann and Beryl Chudleigh Tidemann (*née* Birch); *m* 1st, 1964, Bruce Axel Clunies Ross; 2nd, 1971, Lester Richard Hiatt; one *s* one *d*; 3rd, 1990, John Richard Green. *Educ:* Walford Girls' Grammar Sch., Adelaide; Univ. of Adelaide (BA Hons 1963); Somerville Coll., Oxford (MA 1970; BLitt 1973). George Murray Overseas Scholar, Univ. of Adelaide at Somerville Coll., Oxford, 1963–65; Lectr in Medieval English Lang. and Lit., St Hilda's Coll. and LMH, Oxford, 1965–68; Alice B. Horsman Travelling Fellow, Somerville Coll., Oxford, at Arnamagnaean Inst. for Icelandic Studies, Copenhagen Univ., 1968–69; University of Sydney: Lectr, Dept of Early Eng. Lit. and Lang., 1969–73; Sen. Lectr, English Dept, 1974–83; Associate Prof., 1984–90; Head, Dept of English, 1993–94. Vis. Mem., Linacre Coll., Oxford and Hon. Res. Associate, UCL, 1979–80; Guest researcher, Univ. of Munich, 1986–87; Vis. Scholar, Univ. of N Carolina, Chapel Hill, 1991–92; Vis. Prof., McMaster Univ., Ont and Vis. Scholar, Pontifical Inst. of Mediaeval Studies, Toronto, 1995; Exchange scholar, Kungl. Vitterhetsakademien, Sweden 1996; Quatercentenary Vis. Fellow, Emmanuel Coll., Cambridge, 1997; Vis. Scholar, Humboldt Univ., Berlin, 2002–03; Vis. Fellow, All Souls Coll., Oxford, 2003. Mem., Australian Res. Council, 1995–97. Mem., Nat. Bd of Employment, Educn and Trng, 1995–97. Pres., Aust. Acad. of Humanities, 1995–98. Fellow, Royal Gustavus Adolphus Acad., Uppsala, 2001. Hon. DPhil Göteborg Univ., 2000. Centenary Medal, Commonwealth of Australia, 2003. *Film:* (jtly) Waiting for Harry, 1980 (1st Prize, RAI film comp., 1982). *Publications:* (with S. A. Wild) Djambidj: an Aboriginal song series from Northern Australia, 1982; (ed jtly) Songs of Aboriginal Australia, 1987; Skáldskaparmál: Snorri Sturluson's ars poetica and medieval theories of language, 1987; (with J. Mundrugmundrug) Goyulan the Morning Star: an Aboriginal clan song series from North Central Arnhem Land, 1988; Prolonged Echoes: Old Norse myths in Medieval northern society, Vol. 1: The Myths, 1994; Vol. 2: The Reception of Myth in Medieval Iceland, 1998; (ed jtly) Old Norse Studies in the New World, 1994; The Norse Muse in Britain 1750–1820, 1998; (ed) Old Icelandic Literature and Society, 2000; (ed jtly) Skaldic Poetry of the Scandinavian Middle Ages, 2000, 2nd edn 2002; The Old Norse Poetic Translations of Thomas Percy, 2001; (ed) Old Norse Myths, Literature and Society, 2003; (ed jtly) The Correspondence of Edward Lye, 2004; A History of Old Norse Poetry and Poetics, 2005; contrib. numerous articles in learned jls and chapters in books of essays. *Recreations:* gardening, staying at home and on my country property. *Address:* Department of English, University of Sydney, NSW 2006, Australia. *T:* (2) 93516832.

CLUTTERBUCK, Vice-Adm. Sir David Granville, KBE 1968; CB 1965; *b* Gloucester, 25 Jan. 1913; *m* 1937, Rose Mere Vaile, Auckland, NZ; two *d.* Joined RN, 1929. Served War of 1939–45 (despatches twice): navigating officer of cruisers HMS Ajax, 1940–42, HMS Newfoundland, 1942–46 (present Japanese surrender at Tokyo). Subsequently commanded destroyers Sluys and Cadiz, 1952–53; Naval Attaché at British Embassy, Bonn; Capt. (D) of Third Training Squadron in HMS Zest, Londonderry, 1956–58; commanded cruiser HMS Blake, 1960–62; Chief of Staff to C-in-C Home Fleet and C-in-C Allied Forces Eastern Atlantic, 1963–66; Rear-Adm., 1963; Vice-Adm. 1966; Dep. Supreme Allied Comdr, Atlantic, 1966–68.

CLUTTON, Rafe Henry, CBE 1992; FRICS; Partner, Cluttons, Chartered Surveyors, London, 1955–92 (Senior Partner, 1982–92); *b* 13 June 1929; *s* of late Robin John Clutton and Rosalie Muriel (*née* Birch); *m* 1954, Jill Olwyn Evans; four *s* one *d. Educ:* Tonbridge Sch., Kent. FRICS 1959. Director: Legal & General Group PLC (formerly Legal & General Assurance Soc. Ltd), 1972–93; Rodamco (UK) BV (formerly Haslemere Estates), 1990–96. Member: Royal National Theatre Bd, 1976–93; Salvation Army London Adv. Bd, 1971–93; Royal Commn for Exhibn of 1851, 1988–99. Governor, Royal Foundn of Grey Coat Hosp., 1967–2002 (Chm., 1981–2001). *Publication:* Take One Surveyor (autobiog.), 2004. *Recreations:* grandchildren, books, admiring the view. *Address:* Providence Cottage, Church Road, Barcombe, East Sussex BN8 5TP. *T:* (01273) 400763. *Club:* Royal Thames Yacht.

CLUTTON-BROCK, Prof. Timothy Hugh, PhD; ScD; FRS 1993; Prince Philip Professor of Ecology and Evolutionary Biology, University of Cambridge, since 2007 (Professor of Animal Ecology, 1994–2007); *b* 13 Aug. 1946; *s* of Hugh Alan Clutton-Brock and Eileen Mary Stableforth; *m* 1980, Dafila Kathleen Scott; one *s* one *d. Educ:* Rugby Sch.; Magdalene Coll., Cambridge (BA, MA, PhD, ScD). NERC res. fellowship, Animal Behaviour Res. Gp, Oxford, 1972; Lectr in Ethology, Univ. of Sussex, 1973; Cambridge University: Sen. Res. Fellow in Behavioural Ecology, King's Coll., 1976; SERC Advanced Fellow, Dept of Zoology, 1981; Royal Soc. Res. Fellow in Biology, 1983; Lectr in Zoology, 1987–91; Reader in Animal Ecology, 1991–94. Chm., IUCN Deer Specialist Gp, 1980–90. Jt Editor, Princeton Monographs in Behavioral Ecology, 1982–. Scientific Medal, 1984, Frink Medal, 1998, Zoological Soc. of London; Hart Merriam Award, Mammal Soc. of America, 1991; Marsh Award, British Ecol Soc., 1998. *Publications:* (ed) Primate Ecology, 1977; (ed) Readings in Sociobiology, 1978; Red Deer: the behaviour and ecology of two sexes, 1982; (ed) Rhum, Natural History of an Island, 1987; (ed) Reproductive Success, 1988; Red Deer in the Highlands, 1989; The Evolution of Parental Care, 1991; Meerkat Manor: flower of the Kalahari, 2007; approx. 250 sci.

papers on animal behaviour, ecology and evolution in Nature, Jl Animal Ecol., Evolution, Amer. Naturalist, Jl of Zoology, Animal Behaviour, Behaviour, Behavioral Ecol. and Sociobiol., Folia Primatologica and other jls. *Recreations:* bird watching, fish watching, fishing. *Address:* Department of Zoology, Downing Street, Cambridge CB2 3EJ. *T:* (01223) 336618.

CLWYD, 4th Baron *cr* 1919, of Abergele, co. Denbigh; **John Murray Roberts;** Bt 1908; *b* 27 Aug. 1971; *e s* of 3rd Baron Clwyd and of Geraldine (*née* Cannons); *S* father, 2006; *m* 2004, Lea-Anne Margaret Henry; one *s* one *d. Heir: s* Hon. John David Roberts, *b* 16 June 2006.

CLWYD, Rt Hon. Ann; PC 2004; MP (Lab) Cynon Valley, since May 1984; journalist and broadcaster; *b* 21 March 1937; *d* of Gwilym Henri Lewis and Elizabeth Ann Lewis; *m* 1963, Owen Dryhurst Roberts, TV director and producer. *Educ:* Halkyn Primary Sch.; Holywell Grammar Sch.; The Queen's Sch., Chester; University Coll., Bangor. Former: Student-teacher, Hope Sch., Flintshire; BBC Studio Manager; freelance reporter, producer; Welsh corresp., The Guardian and The Observer, 1964–79; Vice-Chm., Welsh Arts Council, 1975–79. Member: Welsh Hospital Board, 1970–74; Cardiff Community Health Council, 1975–79; Royal Commn on NHS, 1976–79; Working Party, report, Organisation of Out-Patient Care, for Welsh Hosp. Bd; Working Party, Bilingualism in the Hospital Service; Labour Party Study Gp, People and the Media; Arts Council of Gt Britain, 1975–80; Labour Party NEC, 1983–84; PLP Exec., 1997– (Vice Chm., 2001–05; Chm., 2005–06); Chm., Cardiff Anti-Racialism Cttee, 1978–80. Chm., Labour back bench cttee on Health and Social Security, 1985–87; Vice-Chm., Labour back bench cttee on Defence, 1985–87; Opposition front bench spokesperson on women, 1987–88, on educn, 1987–88, on overseas develt and co-operation, 1989–92, on Wales, 1992, on Nat. Heritage, 1992–93, on employment, 1993–94, on foreign affairs, 1994–95. Member: Shadow Cabinet, 1989–93; Internat. Develt Select Cttee, 1997–. Chm., All Party Gp on Human Rights, 1997–; Special Envoy to the Prime Minister on Human Rights in Iraq, 2003–. Member: NUJ; TGWU. Contested (Lab): Denbigh, 1970; Gloucester, Oct. 1974; Mem. (Lab) Mid and West Wales, European Parlt, 1979–84. Backbencher of the Year, House Magazine and Spectator Parly Awards, 2003; Campaigning MP of the Year, Channel 4 Political Awards, 2003. *Address:* (office) 6 Deans Court, Dean Street, Aberdare, Mid Glam CF44 7BN. *T:* (01685) 871394.

CLYDE, family name of **Baron Clyde**.

CLYDE, Baron *cr* 1996 (Life Peer), of Briglands in Perthshire and Kinross; **James John Clyde;** PC 1996; a Lord of Appeal in Ordinary, 1996–2001; *b* 29 Jan. 1932; *s* of Rt Hon. Lord Clyde; *m* 1963, Ann Clunie Hoblyn; two *s. Educ:* Edinburgh Academy; Corpus Christi Coll., Oxford (BA; Hon. Fellow, 1996); Edinburgh Univ. (LLB). Called to Scottish Bar, 1959; QC (Scot.) 1971; Advocate-Depute, 1973–74. Chancellor to Bishop of Argyll and the Isles, 1972–85; a Judge of the Courts of Appeal of Jersey and Guernsey, 1979–85; a Senator of the College of Justice in Scotland, 1985–96; Justice Oversight Comr, NI, 2003–06. Chairman: Med. Appeal Tribunal, 1974–85; Cttee of Investigation for Scotland on Agricl Mktg, 1984–85; Scottish Valuation Adv. Council, 1987–96 (Mem., 1972–96); Faculty of Advocates' Disciplinary Tribunal, 2004–07; Orkney Children Inquiry, 1991–92; Children in Scotland, 2003–06. Mem., UK Delegn to CCBE, 1978–84 (Leader, 1981–84). Assessor to Chancellor, 1989–97, Vice-Chm., 1993–96, Court of Edinburgh Univ.; Chm., Europa Inst., Edinburgh Univ., 1990–97; Pres., Scottish Univs Law Inst., 1991–98. Dir, Edinburgh Acad., 1979–88; Trustee: St Mary's Music Sch., 1976–92; Nat. Library of Scotland, 1977–93; Chm. of Govs, St George's Sch. for Girls, 1989–97; Gov., Napier Polytechnic, 1989–93. Chm. Special Trustees, St Mary's Hosp., Paddington, 1997–99; Pres., Dumfries Burns Club, 1996–97. Vice-Pres., Royal Blind Asylum and Sch., 1987–; Pres., SSAFA, Edinburgh & Lothians Br., 2007–. Hon. Pres., Scottish Young Lawyers' Assoc., 1988–97. Hon. Bencher, Middle Temple, 1996. DUniv Heriot-Watt, 1991; Dr *hc* Edinburgh, 1997; Hon. DLitt Napier, 1995. *Publications:* (ed jtly) Armour on Valuation, 3rd edn, 1961, 5th edn, 1985; (jtly) Judicial Review, 2000. *Recreations:* music, gardening. *Address:* House of Lords, SW1A 0PW. *Club:* New (Edinburgh).

CLYDE, (Samuel) Wilson; Member (DUP) Antrim South, Northern Ireland Assembly, 1998–2007; *b* 8 April 1934; *m* 1970, Margaret Evelyn; one *s. Educ:* Shane's Castle Primary Sch. Farmer, 1948–98. Mem. (DUP), Antrim BC, 1981–2005. *Recreations:* go-karting, motor cycling. *Address:* 21 Groggan Road, Randalstown, Antrim BT41 3HA. *T:* (028) 9447 8370.

CLYDESMUIR, 3rd Baron *cr* 1948, of Braidwood, co. Lanark; **David Ronald Colville;** *b* 8 April 1949; *e s* of 2nd Baron Clydesmuir, KT, CB, MBE, TD and of Joan Marguerita, *d* of late Lt-Col E. B. Booth, DSO; *S* father, 1996; *m* 1978, Aline Frances, *er d* of Peter Merriam; two *s* two *d. Educ:* Charterhouse. *Heir: s* Hon. Richard Colville, *b* 21 Oct. 1980. *Address:* Langlees House, Biggar, Lanarkshire ML12 6NP.

COADY, Frances Rachel; Vice-President and Publisher, Picador USA, since 2000; *b* 16 June 1958; *d* of Matthew and Patricia Coady. *Educ:* Streatham Hill and Clapham High Sch.; Bromley High Sch.; Univ. of Sussex (BA Hons English Lit. 1980); Univ. of Essex (MA English Lit. 1981). Faber and Faber, 1982–86, Sen. Non-Fiction Commng Editor, 1983–86; Researcher for Alan Yentob, Head of Dept of Music and Arts, BBC TV, 1986; Random House, 1986–95: Editl Dir, Jonathan Cape, 1986–89; Founder Publisher, Vintage Paperbacks, 1989–93; Publisher, overseeing Jonathan Cape, Chatto & Windus, Pimlico and Vintage, 1993–95; Publisher, Granta Books, 1995–99. *Recreations:* theatre, cinema, reading. *Address:* Picador, 19th floor,175 Fifth Avenue, New York, NY 10010, USA.

COAKER, Vernon Rodney; MP (Lab) Gedling, since 1997; Minister of State, Home Office, since 2008; *b* 17 June 1953; *s* of Edwin Coaker; *m* 1978, Jacqueline Heaton; one *s* one *d. Educ:* Drayton Manor Grammar Sch., London; Warwick Univ. (BA Hons); Trent Poly. (PGCE). Hist. Teacher, Manvers Pierrepont Sch., 1976–82; Hd of Dept, Arnold Hill Sch., 1982–88; Sen. Teacher, Bramcote Pk Sch., 1989–95; Dep. Headteacher, Big Wood Sch., 1995–97. Mem., Rushcliffe BC, 1983–97 (Leader, 1987–97). PPS to Minister of State for Social Security, 1999, to Financial Sec. to HM Treasury, 1999–2001, to Minister of State (Minister for School Standards), DfES, 2001–02, to Sec. of State for Culture, Media and Sport, 2002–03; an Asst Govt Whip, 2003–05; a Lord Comr of HM Treasury (Govt Whip), 2005–06; Parly Under-Sec. of State, Home Office, 2006–08. Contested (Lab): Rushcliffe, 1983; Gedling, 1987, 1992. *Address:* House of Commons, SW1A 0AA.

COAKLEY, Rev. Prof. Sarah Anne; Norris-Hulse Professor of Divinity, University of Cambridge, since 2007; Fellow, Murray Edwards College (formerly New Hall), since 2007; *b* 10 Sept. 1951; *d* of (Frank) Robert Furber, *qv* and Anne Wilson Furber; *m* 1975, Dr James Farwell Coakley; two *d. Educ:* Blackheath High Sch.; New Hall, Cambridge (BA 1973; MA, PhD 1982); Harvard Divinity Sch. (ThM 1975). Harkness Fellow, 1973–75; Univ. Lectr in Religious Studies, 1976–90, Sen. Lectr, 1990–91, Lancaster Univ.; Tutorial Fellow in Theology, Oriel Coll., and Univ. Lectr in Theology, Oxford, 1991–93; Prof. of Christian Theology, 1993–95, Edward Mallinckrodt, Jr, Prof. of Divinity, 1995–2007, Vis. Prof. of Systematic and Philosophical Theology, 2007–08, Harvard Univ. Vis. Professorial Fellow, Princeton Univ., 2003–04. Select Preacher, Oxford Univ., 1991; Hulsean Lectr, Cambridge Univ., 1991–92; Henry Luce III Fellow, 1994–95; Hulsean Preacher, Cambridge Univ., 1996; Mulligan Preacher, Gray's Inn, 2003. Lectures: Samuel Ferguson, Manchester Univ., 1997; Riddell, Newcastle Univ., 1999; Tate-Willson, Southern Methodist Univ., 1999; Prideaux, Exeter Univ., 2000; Jellema, Calvin Coll., Mich, 2001; Stone, Princeton Theol Seminary, 2002; Cheney, Berkeley Divinity Sch. at Yale, 2002; Hensley Henson, Oxford Univ., 2005; J. A. Hall, Univ. of Victoria, BC, 2007. Ordained deacon, 2000, priest, 2001; Asst Curate, SS Mary and Nicholas, Littlemore, 2000–07; Assoc. Priest, The Good Shepherd, Waban, MA, 2001–08. Consultant to C of E Doctrine Commn, 1982–84, Mem., 1984–92. ThD *hc* Lund, 2006; DD *hc* Gen. Theol Seminary, NY, 2008. *Publications:* Christ Without Absolutes: a study of the Christology of Ernst Troeltsch, 1988; (ed with David A. Pailin) The Making and Remaking of Christian Doctrine, 1993; (ed) Religion and the Body, 1997; Powers and Submissions: spirituality, philosophy and gender, 2002; (ed) Re-thinking Gregory of Nyssa, 2003; (ed with Kay Kaufman Shelemay) Pain and Its Transformations: the interface of biology and culture, 2007; (ed with Samuel Wells) Praying for England: priestly presence in contemporary culture, 2008; (ed with Charles M. Stang) Re-thinking Dionysius the Areopagite, 2009; contrib. to C of E reports and to theol. jls. *Recreations:* musical activities, thinking about the garden. *Address:* Faculty of Divinity, University of Cambridge, West Road, Cambridge CB3 9BS.

See also R. J. Furber, W. J. Furber.

COASE, Prof. Ronald Harry, DSc; Professor Emeritus and Senior Fellow in Law and Economics, University of Chicago, since 1982; *b* 29 Dec. 1910; *s* of Henry Joseph Coase and Rosalie Elizabeth (*née* Giles); *m* 1937, Marian Ruth Hartung. *Educ:* Kilburn Grammar Sch.; LSE (BCom 1932; DSc Econ 1951). Assistant Lecturer: Dundee Sch. of Econs, 1932–34; Univ. of Liverpool, 1934–35; later Lectr, then Reader, LSE, 1935–40, 1946–51; War service: Hd of Statistical Div., Forestry Commn, 1940–41; Statistician, later Chief Statistician, Central Statistical Office, Offices of War Cabinet, 1941–46; Professor: Univ. of Buffalo, 1951–58; Univ. of Virginia, 1958–64; Clifford R. Musser Prof., Univ. of Chicago Law Sch., 1964–82. Fellow, Amer. Acad. of Arts and Scis, 1978; Dist. Fellow, Amer. Econ. Assoc., 1980; Membre Titulaire, European Acad., 1992; Corresp. Fellow, British Acad., 1985; Hon. Fellow, LSE. Hon. doctorates: Dr rer. pol. Cologne, 1988; DSocSc Yale, 1989; LLD Washington, St Louis, 1991; LLD Dundee, 1992; DSc Buckingham, 1995; DHL Beloit Coll., 1996; Dr *hc* Paris, 1996; DHum Clemson, 2003. Nobel Prize for Economics, 1991; Innovations Award, The Economist, 2003. *Publications:* British Broadcasting: a study in monopoly, 1950; The Firm, the Market and the Law, 1988; Essays on Economics and Economists, 1994. *Address:* University of Chicago Law School, 1111 East 60th Street, Chicago, IL 60637, USA; The Hallmark, 2960 N Lake Shore Drive, Chicago, IL 60657, USA.

COATES, Sir Anthony Robert M.; *see* Milnes Coates.

COATES, David; HM Diplomatic Service, retired; Director, British Bankers' Association, since 2006; *b* 13 Nov. 1947; *s* of late Matthew Coates and Margaret Ann Davies Coates (*née* Ross); *m* 1974, Joanna Kay Weil; two *d. Educ:* Dame Allan's Boys' Sch., Newcastle; Univ. of Bristol (BA Hist.); Univ. of Hawaii; Joint Univ. Centre, Taiwan. FCO, 1974–77; language training, Hong Kong, 1977–78; First Sec., Peking, 1978–81; Iran Desk, FCO, 1981–83; Asst Head, S America Dept, 1983–86; First Sec., UKMIS, Geneva, 1986–89; Counsellor and Head, Political Section, Peking, 1989–92; Head, Jt Assistance Unit, Central and E Europe, FCO, 1993–95; Head, Far Eastern and Pacific Dept, FCO, 1995–98; Dir Gen., British Trade and Cultural Office, Taipei, 1999–2002; Estate Modernisation Man., FCO, 2002–04; Ambassador to Côte d'Ivoire, 2004–06. *Recreations:* ski-ing, theatre, hill-walking, leeks. *Address:* British Bankers' Association, Pinners Hall, 105–108 Old Broad Street, EC2N 1EX.

COATES, Sir David (Charlton Frederick), 3rd Bt *cr* 1921, of Haypark, City of Belfast; *b* 16 Feb. 1948; *o s* of Sir Frederick Gregory Lindsay Coates, 2nd Bt and Joan Nugent, *d* of Maj.-Gen. Sir Charlton Spinks, KBE, DSO; *S* father, 1994; *m* 1973, Christine Helen, *d* of Lewis F. Marshall; two *s. Educ:* Millfield. *Heir: s* James Gregory David Coates [*b* 12 March 1977; *m* 2004, Laura Claire, *er d* of Gordon and Margaret Bennett]. *Address:* Launchfield House, Briantspuddle, Dorchester, Dorset DT2 7HN.

COATES, David Randall, CB 2000; consulting economist; Chairman, North West Economic Forecasting Panel, since 2003; *b* 22 March 1942; *m* Julia Hagedorn (*d* 1995); one *s* one *d. Educ:* Leeds Grammar Sch.; Queen's Coll., Oxford; LSE. Res. Assistant, Univ. of Manchester and Manchester Business Sch., 1966–68; Economic Advr, Min. of Technology and DTI, 1968–74; Sen. Economic Advr, Dept of Trade and DTI, 1974–82; Department of Trade and Industry: Asst Sec., 1982–89; Grade 3, 1989; Chief Economic Advr, and Hd of Econs Profession, 1990–2002. *Recreations:* family, gardening, travel, music. *Address: e-mail:* david.r.coates@btopenworld.com.

COATES, Dudley James; consultant and writer; Head of Environment Group, Ministry of Agriculture, Fisheries and Food, 1996–2001; Vice President, Methodist Conference, 2006; *b* 15 Sept. 1946; *o s* of late Edward and Margot Coates; *m* 1969, Rev. Canon Dr Jean Walsingham; two *d. Educ:* Westcliff High School for Boys; Univ. of Sussex (BA (Hons)). Joined MAFF as Asst Principal, 1968; Second Sec., UK Delegn to the EC, Brussels, 1970–72; Principal, MAFF, 1973; Lectr, Civil Service Coll., 1978–81; Head of Animal Health Div. II, 1981–83, Head of Financial Management Team, 1983–87, MAFF; Dir Gen. of Corporate Services, Intervention Bd for Agricultural Produce, 1987–89; Dir, Regl Services, MAFF, 1989–96. Public Mem., Network Rail, 2002–. Methodist local preacher, 1970–; Member: Methodist Conf., 1988, 1989, 1993–2004, 2006–08; Methodist Council, 2004–; Chair, Methodist Publishing House, 1996–2004; Methodist ecumenical rep., Gen. Synod of C of E, 2001–07. Gov., STETS, 2002–. *Publications:* (contrib.) Policies into Practice (ed David Lewis and Helen Wallace), 1984; Shades of Grey, 2006. *Recreations:* Christian activities, cycling, singing. *Address:* 15 Lewcos House, 57–63 Regency Street, SW1P 4AF; *e-mail:* dudley@coates.ctlconnect.co.uk.

COATES, Prof. Geoffrey Edward, MA, DSc; Professor of Chemistry, University of Wyoming, 1968–79, now Emeritus; *b* 14 May 1917; *er s* of Prof. Joseph Edward Coates, OBE; *m* 1951, Winifred Jean Hobbs; one *s* one *d. Educ:* Clifton Coll.; Queen's Coll., Oxford. Research Chemist, Magnesium Metal Corp., 1940–45; Univ. of Bristol: Lecturer in Chemistry, 1945–53; Sub-Warden of Wills Hall, 1946–51; Prof. of Chemistry, Univ. of Durham, 1953–68. *Publications:* Organo-metallic Compounds (monograph), 1956, 3rd edn (2 vols), 1967–68; Principles of Organometallic Chemistry, 1968; papers in scientific journals. *Club:* Royal Commonwealth Society.

See also J. F. Coates.

COATES, James Richard, CB 1992; FCILT; Under Secretary, Urban and Local Transport Directorate, Department of Transport, 1994; *b* 18 Oct. 1935; *s* of William

Richard Coates and Doris Coral (*née* Richmond); *m* 1969, Helen Rosamund Rimington; one *s* one *d*. *Educ:* Nottingham High Sch.; Clare Coll., Cambridge (MA). Joined Ministry of Transport, 1959; Private Sec. to Permanent Sec., 1962–63; Principal, 1963; Private Sec. to Secretary of State for Local Govt and Regional Planning, 1969, and to Minister of Transport, 1970–71; Asst Sec., DoE, 1971; Under Secretary, 1977; Dir, London Reg., PSA, 1979–83; Department of Transport: Highways Policy and Prog. Directorate, 1983–85; Rlys Directorate, 1985–91; Urban and Gen. Directorate, 1991–93. FCILT (FCIT 1996; Mem., Policies Cttee). *Recreations:* reading, listening to music, looking at buildings, gardening. *Address:* 10 Alwyne Road, N1 2HH.

COATES, John Dowling, AC 2006 (AO 1995; AM 1989); President, Australian Olympic Committee, since 1990; Member, International Olympic Committee, since 2001; Partner, Kemp Strang Lawyers, since 2001; *b* 7 May 1950; *s* of Sidney Dowling Coates and Valerie Irene Coates; *m* 1981, Pauline Frances Kahl (marr. diss. 2005); five *s* one *d*. *Educ:* Homebush Boys' High Sch.; Sydney Univ. (LLB). Joined Greaves Wannan & Williams, 1971: Partner, 1977–87 and 1991–2001; Consultant, 1987–91. Man. Dir, Austus Properties Ltd, 1987–90 (Dir, 1990–91); Chairman: Reef Casino Trust, 1993–97; Triplecee Retail Investment Trust, 1994–99; Accord Pacific Hldgs Ltd, 1994–2002; Australian Olympic Foundn Ltd, 1996–; Burson-Marsteller Australia, 2000–04; William Inglis & Son Ltd; Dep. Chm., Kengfu Properties Pte Ltd, 1997–2002; Dir, 1995–, Dep. Chm., 2003–, David Jones Ltd; Member: Grant Samuel Adv. Bd, 2002– (Dir, managers, Grant Samuel Laundy Pub Fund, 2005–07); Sydney Olympic Park Authy, 2005–; Director: United Customer Solutions Pty Ltd, 2004–06; Grosvenor Australia Properties Pty Ltd, 2005– (Consultant, 2004–); Grosvenor Australia Investments Ltd, 2005–; Events NSW Pty Ltd, 2007–. Dir, Australian Inst. of Sport, 1985–86 (Dep. Chm., 1986–89); Dep. Chm., Australian Sports Commn, 1989–98 (Mem., 1987–89); Mem. Council, Internat. Rowing Fedn, 1992–; Vice-Pres., Internat. Council of Arbitration for Sport, 1994–. Australian Olympic Committee: Mem., Exec. Bd, 1982–85; Vice-Pres., 1985–90; Exec. Dir, 1992 Olympic Games Bid, Brisbane CC, 1985–86; Vice Pres., Sydney Olympics 2000 Bid Ltd, 1991–93; Sen. Vice Pres., Sydney Organising Cttee for Olympic Games, 1999–2000. Dir, Roseville Coll. Foundn Ltd, 1997–2003; Vice Patron, Sydney Cancer Foundn, 2003–. Rowing Manager, Australian Team, Montreal Olympics, 1976; Admin Dir., Australian Team, Moscow Olympics, 1980; Asst Gen. Manager, Australian Team, Los Angeles Olympics, 1984; Chef de Mission and Gen. Manager, Australian Olympic Team: Seoul, 1988; Barcelona, 1992; Atlanta, 1996; Sydney, 2000; Athens, 2004; Beijing, 2008. Hon. Life Member: NSW Olympic Council Inc., 1990; Australian Rowing Council Inc., 1993; NSW Rowing Assoc. Inc., 1994; Australian Olympic Cttee, 1997. IOC Centennial Trophy, 1994; Olympic Order in Gold, 2000; FISA Medal of Honour, 2000. Centenary Medal, Australia, 2003. *Recreations:* golf, swimming, rowing, other sports, the Olympic movement. *Address:* c/o Australian Olympic Committee Inc., Level 27, The Chifley Tower, 2 Chifley Square, Sydney, NSW 2000, Australia. *Clubs:* Commonwealth (Canberra); Sydney Rowing (Hon. Life Mem.), Royal Sydney Yacht, Sydney Turf, Carbine (past Chm.), Australian Jockey; Drummoyne Sailing, Drummoyne Rowing, Concord Golf.

COATES, John Francis, OBE 1955; Deputy Director, Ship Design, Ministry of Defence, 1977–79, retired; *b* 30 March 1922; *s* of Joseph Edward Coates and Ada Maria Coates; *m* 1954, Jane Waymouth; two *s*. *Educ:* Clifton Coll.; Queen's Coll., Oxford (MA 1946). Entered RCNC, 1943; RCDS, 1971; Supt, Naval Construction Res. Estabt, Dunfermline, 1974. Dir, The Trireme Trust, 1985–. Hon. DSc Bath, 1989. *Publications:* (with J. S. Morrison): The Athenian Trireme, 1986, 2nd edn (with N. B. Rankov) 2000; The Age of the Galley, 1995; Greek and Roman Oared Warships, 1996; papers on naval architecture of ancient ships. *Recreation:* nautical research. *Address:* Sabinal, Lucklands Road, Bath BA1 4AU. *T:* (01225) 423696.

See also Prof. G. E. Coates.

COATES, Prof. John Henry, FRS 1985; Sadleirian Professor of Pure Mathematics, Cambridge University, since 1986; Professorial Fellow of Emmanuel College, Cambridge, since 1986; *b* 26 Jan. 1945; *s* of J. R. Coates and Beryl (*née* Lee); *m* 1966, Julie Turner; three *s*. *Educ:* Australian National Univ. (BSc); Trinity Coll., Cambridge (PhD). Assistant Prof., Harvard Univ., 1969–72; Associate Prof., Stanford Univ., 1972–74; Univ. Lectr, Cambridge, and Fellow, Emmanuel Coll., 1974–77; Prof., ANU, 1977–78; Prof. of Maths, Univ. de Paris, Orsay, 1978–86, Ecole Normale Supérieure, Paris, 1985–86; Hd of Dept of Pure Maths and Math. Stats, Cambridge Univ., 1991–97. Pres., London Math. Soc., 1988–90; Vice-Pres., Internat. Mathematical Union, 1991–95; Mem. Council, Royal Soc., 1992–94. Dr *hc* Ecole Normale Supérieure, 1997. *Address:* Emmanuel College, Cambridge CB1 2EA; 104 Mawson Road, Cambridge CB1 2EA. *T:* (01223) 740260.

COATES, Kenneth Sidney; Special Professor in Continuing Education, University of Nottingham, 1990–2004 (Reader, 1980–89); *b* 16 Sept. 1930; *s* of Eric Arthur Coates and Mary Coates; *m* 1969, Tamara Tura; three *s* three *d* (and one *d* decd). *Educ:* Nottingham Univ. (Mature State Scholar, 1956; BA 1st Cl. Hons Sociology, 1959). Coal miner, Notts Coalfield, 1948–56; student, 1956–60; Asst Tutor, Tutor, and Sen. Tutor in Adult Educn, Univ. of Nottingham, 1960–80. MEP (Lab 1989–98, Ind. Lab 1998–99), Nottingham, 1989–94, Notts N and Chesterfield, 1994–99. Chm., Human Rights Subcttee, 1989–94, Rapporteur, Temp. Cttee on Employment, 1994–95, EP. Member: Bertrand Russell Peace Foundn, 1965–; Inst. of Workers' Control, 1968–; Jt Sec., European Nuclear Disarmament Liaison Cttee, 1981–89. Ed., The Spokesman, 1970–. *Publications:* (with A. J. Topham) Industrial Democracy in Great Britain, 1967, 3rd edn 1976; (with R. L. Silburn) Poverty, the Forgotten Englishmen, 1970, 4th edn 1983; (with A. J. Topham) The New Unionism, 1972, 2nd edn 1974; (with A. J. Topham) Trade Unions in Britain, 1980, 3rd edn 1988; Heresies, 1982; The Most Dangerous Decade, 1984; (with A. J. Topham) Trade Unions and Politics, 1986; Think Globally, Act Locally, 1988; (with A. J. Topham) The Making of the Transport and General Workers' Union, 1991; Clause IV: common ownership and the Labour Party, 1995; The Right to Work, 1995; (with S. Holland) Full Employment for Europe, 1995; (jtly) Dear Commissioner, 1996; (with M. Barratt Brown) The Blair Revelation, 1996; Community Under Attack, 1998; Worker's Control, 2003; Empire No More!, 2004. *Recreations:* walking, reading. *Address:* Russell House, Bulwell Lane, Nottingham NG6 0BT. *T:* (0115) 978 4504.

COATES, Marten Frank; His Honour Judge Coates; a Circuit Judge, since 1997; *b* 26 March 1947; *s* of Frank and Violet Coates; *m* 1973, Susan Anton-Stephens; three *d*. *Educ:* Pocklington Sch., York; Durham Univ. (BA Hons 1972); Cert. Biblical Studies. Called to the Bar, Inner Temple, 1972; Asst Recorder, Midland and Oxford Circuit, 1989–93; Recorder, 1993–97. Chancellor, Dio. Lichfield, 2006–. *Address:* c/o Midland and Oxford Circuit Office, The Priory Court, 33 Bull Street, Birmingham B4 6DW.

COATES, Prof. Nigel Martin; Professor of Architectural Design and Head of Department of Architecture, Royal College of Art, since 1995; Joint Founder and Co-director, Branson Coates Architecture Ltd, 1985; *b* 2 March 1949; *s* of Douglas Coates and Margaret Coates (*née* Trigg). *Educ:* Hanley Castle Grammar Sch., Malvern; Univ. of Nottingham (BA Arch Hons); Architectural Assoc. (AA Dip (Year Prize)); Univ. of Rome (Italian Govt Scholar). Unit Master, AA, 1979–89. Course Master, Bennington Coll., Vt, 1980–81. Founder Mem., Narrative Architecture Today, 1979–89. Mem., Adv. Bd, ICA, 1987–89. Architecture columnist, Independent on Sunday, 2003–05. Trustee, Architecture Foundn, 2000–. External Examiner: Bartlett Sch. of Architecture and AA, 1993–94; Dept of Architecture, Univ. of Cambridge, 2000–02. Presenter, 1989, advr and subject, 1992, TV documentaries. Lectures world-wide. Branson Coates' projects include: Katharine Hamnett shop, London, 1988; Café Bongo 1985, Arca di Noe 1988, Hotel Otaru Marittimo 1989, Nishi Azabu Wall 1990 and Art Silo 1993, in Japan; (built projects) Taxim Nightpark 1991 and Key fihan 1999, in Turkey; shops for Jigsaw in UK, Ireland and Japan, 1988–96; new depts for Liberty, Regent St, branches and airport shops, 1992–96; La Forêt and Nautilus Restaurants, Schiphol Airport, Amsterdam, 1993; Bargo Bar, Bass Taverns, 1996; Oyster House and Powerhouse::uk, London, 1998; New Gall. Bldg, Geffrye Mus., 1998; Nat. Centre for Popular Music, Sheffield, 1998; British Expo Pavilion, Lisbon 98; Body Zone, Millennium Dome, London, 2000; Inside Out, travelling exhibn, British Council, 2001; Mktg Suite and Roman Amphitheatre display, Guildhall, London, 2002; House to Home, Houses of Parliament, 2004; (shop design) Charles Fish, London, 2006. Branson Coates' exhibition design projects include: (contrib.) Living Bridges Exhibn, RA, 1996; (contrib.) Erotic Design Exhibn, Design Mus., 1997; Look Inside! New British Public Interiors, internat. tour, 1997; Colani Exhibn, Design Mus., 2007. Nigel Coates designs include: Metropole and Jazz furniture collections, 1986; Noah collection, 1988; Female, He-man and She-woman mannequins, 1988; Tongue chair, 1989; Carpet collection, 1990; Gallo collection, Poltronova, 1991; Slipper chair, 1994; glass vase collection, Simon Moore, 1996; Oxo furniture, Hitch Mylius; Oyster furniture, Lloyd Loom; Fiesolani vases, Salviati; Slamp:ville, Slamp; Big Shoom, Alessi; Tête-a-Tête collection, Fornasetti; G-love chair, Contempo, 2006; Bodypark Tiles, Bardelli, 2006. Exhibitions: Gamma City, Air Gall., 1985; (one-person) Ark Albion, AA, 1984; Ecstacity, AA, 1992; Latent Utopias, Graz, 2002; Micro Utopias, Valencia Biannual, 2003; Vextacity, Fabbrica Europa, Florence, 2003; Greetings from London, Selfridges and Architecture Foundn, 2004; Babylon:don, 10th Internat. Architecture Exhibn, Venice Biennale, 2006; FutureCities, Barbican Art Gall., 2006; work in collections of V&A Mus. and Cooper Hewitt Mus., NY; work exhibited in UK, Europe, US and Japan. Mem., Soc. of Authors. Inter-Design Award for Contribution to Japanese cities, Japan Inter-Design Forum, 1990. *Publications:* Ecstacity, 1992; Guide to Ecstacity, 2003; Collidoscope, 2004. *Recreations:* contemporary art, video-making, Italian culture, riding. *Address:* Department of Architecture, Royal College of Art, Kensington Gore, SW7 2EU. *T:* (020) 7590 4567; *e-mail:* architecture@rca.ac.uk. *Clubs:* Groucho, Blacks.

COATES, Suzanne; Her Honour Judge Suzanne Coates; a Circuit Judge, since 1998; *b* 2 Aug. 1949; *d* of late Jack Coates and of Elsie Coates (now Brown); *m* 1980, John Brian Camille Tanzer, *qv*; two *s*. *Educ:* Skipton Girls' High Sch.; Guy's Hosp.; South Bank Poly. (HVCert 1972); Queen Mary Coll., London Univ. (LLB 1977). SRN, Guy's Hosp., 1968–71; Health Visitor, Bromley LBC, 1972–74; called to the Bar, Gray's Inn, 1978; Asst Recorder, 1992–96; a Recorder, 1996–98. *Recreations:* music, reading, walking, football (watching), gardening, travel, cooking. *Address:* Brighton County Court, John Street, Brighton, Sussex. *T:* (01273) 674421.

COATS, Sir Alastair Francis Stuart, 4th Bt *cr* 1905; *b* 18 Nov. 1921; *s* of Lieut-Col Sir James Stuart Coats, MC, 3rd Bt and Lady Amy Coats (*d* 1975), *er d* of 8th Duke of Richmond and Gordon; *S* father, 1966; *m* 1947, Lukyn, *d* of Capt. Charles Gordon; one *s* one *d*. *Educ:* Eton. Served War of 1939–45, Coldstream Guards (Capt.). *Heir: s* Alexander James Coats [*b* 6 July 1951; *m* 1999, Clara, *d* of Ernesto Abril de Vivero]. *Address:* Birchwood House, Durford Wood, Petersfield, Hants GU31 5AW. *T:* (01730) 892254.

COATS, David Richard Graham; Associate Director - Policy, The Work Foundation, since 2004; *b* 28 Aug. 1962; *s* of Frank Alexander Coats and Doreen Coats. *Educ:* Portway Sch., Bristol; University Coll. London (LLB 1983; LLM 1986); Inns of Court Sch. of Law. Called to the Bar, Inner Temple, 1985; Trades Union Congress: Policy Officer, Orgn and Industrial Relns Dept, 1989–94; Sen. Policy Officer, 1994–99, Head, 1999–2004, Econ. and Social Affairs Dept. Mem., Low Pay Commn, 2000–04. Member: Partnership Fund Assessment Panel, DTI, 2000–04; Central Arbitration Cttee, 2005–; Nat. Stakeholder Council on Health, Work and Well-Being, DWP, 2006–. Member, Advisory Board: ESRC Future of Work Prog., 2000–05; Industrial Relns Res. Unit, Univ. of Warwick, 2000–. Mem. (Lab) Haringey BC, 1990–98. *Recreations:* cycling, travel, reading, cooking. *Address:* The Work Foundation, 21 Palmer Street, SW1H 0AD. *T:* (020) 7976 3603; *e-mail:* dcoats@theworkfoundation.com.

COATS, Sir William David, Kt 1985; DL; Chairman, Coats Patons PLC, 1981–86 (Deputy Chairman, 1979–81); Deputy Chairman, Clydesdale Bank, 1985–93 (Director, since 1962); *b* 25 July 1924; *s* of Thomas Heywood Coats and Olivia Violet Pitman; *m* 1950, Hon. Elizabeth Lilian Graham MacAndrew; two *s* one *d*. *Educ:* Eton Coll. Entered service of J. & P. Coats Ltd, later Coats Patons PLC, 1948: Director: The Central Agency Ltd (subsid. co.), 1953–55; Coats Patons PLC, 1960–86; Murray Caledonian Trust Co. Ltd, 1961–81; Weir Group Ltd, 1970–83; Murray Investment Trusts, 1986–92. Mem., S of Scotland Electricity Bd, 1972–81. Hon. LLD Strathclyde, 1977. DL Ayr and Arran, 1986. *Recreation:* golf. *Club:* Western (Glasgow).

COBB, Henry Nichols; Partner, Pei Cobb Freed & Partners, Architects, since 1960; *b* 8 April 1926; *s* of Charles Kane Cobb and Elsie Quincy Cobb; *m* 1953, Joan Stewart Spaulding; three *d*. *Educ:* Harvard College (AB 1947); Harvard Graduate Sch. of Design (MArch 1949). Architectural Div., Webb & Knapp, 1950–60; Pei Cobb Freed & Partners (formerly I. M. Pei & Partners), 1960–. Sch. of Architecture, Yale University: William Henry Bishop Vis. Prof., 1973, 1978; Charlotte Sheperd Davenport Vis. Prof., 1975; Graduate School of Design, Harvard: Studio Prof. and Chm., Dept of Architecture, 1980–85; Adjunct Prof. of Architecture and Urban Design, 1985–88. Hon. DFA Bowdoin Coll., 1985; Dr Technical Scis *hc*, Swiss Fed. Inst. of Technol., 1990. Topaz Medallion for Excellence in Architectural Educn, Assoc. of Collegiate Schs of Architecture/AIA, 1995. *Publications:* Where I Stand, 1980; Architecture and the University, 1985. *Address:* Pei Cobb Freed & Partners, 88 Pine Street, New York, NY 10005–1801, USA. *T:* (212) 8724020.

COBB, Henry Stephen, CBE 1991; FSA; FRHistS; Clerk of the Records, House of Lords, 1981–91; *b* 17 Nov. 1926; *y s* of Ernest Cobb and Violet Kate Cobb (*née* Sleath), Wallasey; *m* 1969, Eileen Margaret Downer. *Educ:* Birkenhead Sch.; London School of Economics (BA, MA); Liverpool Univ. (Dip. Archive Admin). Archivist, Church Missionary Soc., 1951–53; Asst Archivist, House of Lords, 1953–59, Asst Clerk of the Records, 1959–73, Dep. Clerk, 1973–81. Lecturer in Palaeography, School of Librarianship, North London Polytechnic, 1973–77. Pres., Soc. of Archivists, 1992–96 (Mem. Council, 1970–82; Chm., 1982–84); Mem. Council, British Records Assoc., 1978–81; Chm., London Record Soc., 1984–2005. Mem. Cttee of Management, Inst. of Historical Research, 1986–90. FSA 1967; FRHistS 1970. *Publications:* (ed) The Local Port Book of Southampton 1439–40, 1961; (ed with D. J. Johnson) Guide to the Parliament and the Glorious Revolution Exhibition, 1988; (ed) The Overseas Trade of London: Exchequer Customs Accounts 1480–1, 1990; contribs to Economic History Rev., Jl of Soc. of Archivists, Archives, etc. *Recreations:* music, historical research. *Address:* 1 Child's Way, Hampstead Garden Suburb, NW11 6XU. *T:* (020) 8458 3688.

COBB, Prof. Justin Peter, FRCS; Professor of Orthopaedics, Imperial College London, since 2005; Orthopaedic Surgeon to the Queen, since 2008; *b* 15 March 1958; *s* of Capt. Peter Cobb, OBE and Jennifer Cobb (*née* Martin); *m* 1985, Iona Stormonth Darling; three *s* one *d*. *Educ:* Sherborne Sch.; Magdalen Coll., Oxford (BM BCh 1982; MCh 1991). FRCS 1986. Registrar, St Thomas' Hosp., 1985–87; Sen. Registrar, Middlesex Hosp. and Royal Nat. Orthopaedic Hosp., 1987–91; Consultant Orthopaedic Surgeon: UCL Hosps NHS Trust, 1991–2005; King Edward VII's Hosp. Sister Agnes (formerly King Edward VII's Hosp. for Officers), 1995–. Dir, Stanmore Implants Worldwide, 1997–; Founder, 1999, Dir, 2001–, Acrobot Co. Ltd. *Publications:* pubns in musculoskeletal oncology and computer-assisted surgery. *Recreations:* sailing, ski-ing, golf, but mainly work. *Address:* St Johns House, Chiswick Mall, W4 2PS; *e-mail:* j.cobb@imperial.ac.uk. *Clubs:* Hurlingham; St Albans Medical.

COBB, Stephen William Scott; QC 2003; a Recorder, since 2004; *b* 12 April 1962; *s* of Hon. Sir John Francis Scott Cobb and of Lady (Joan Mary) Cobb; *m* 1989, Samantha Cowling; two *s* one *d*. *Educ:* Winchester Coll.; Liverpool Univ. (LLB Hons 1984). Called to the Bar, Inner Temple, 1985; Head of Chambers, One Garden Court, 2007–. Mem., Family Justice Council, 2004–. Vice-Chm., Family Law Bar Assoc., 2008–. *Publications:* (ed) Essential Family Practice, 2000; (ed) Clarke, Hall and Morrison, On Children, 2004–. *Recreations:* music, sailing, wine, family. *Address:* One Garden Court, Temple, EC4Y 9BJ. *T:* (020) 7797 7900, *Fax:* (020) 7797 7929. *Clubs:* Hurlingham; Bembridge Sailing.

COBBETT, David John, TD 1973; ERD 1962; railway and transportation management consultant; *b* 9 Dec. 1928; *m* 1952, Beatrix Jane Ogilvie Cockburn; three *s*. *Educ:* Royal Masonic Sch. FCILT (FILT). Gen. Railway admin. and managerial positions, 1949–67; Divl Movements Manager, Liverpool Street, 1967; Divl Manager, Norwich (British Railways Bd), 1968–70; Asst Managing Dir, Freightliners Ltd, 1970–73; Dep. Gen. Manager, British Railways Bd Scottish Region, 1973; Gen. Manager, British Railways Scottish Region, 1974–76; Chm., British Transport Ship Management, Scotland, 1974–76; Gen. Manager, BR Eastern Region, 1976–77; British Railways Board: Export Dir (Special Projects), 1977–78; Dir, Strategic Studies, 1978–83; Dir, Information Systems and Technology, 1983–85. Dir, Transmark, 1978. Mem. Bd, Railway Benevolent Instn, 1974–99 (Dep. Chm., 1981–84; Chm., 1984–98; Vice Pres., 2000–). Dir, Sec. and Treas., Dachaidh Respite Care, Aviemore, 1996–. Bt Col, Royal Corps of Transport (RARO), 1974. *Recreations:* military matters, historical reading, games. *Address:* Ballytruim, Newtonmore, Inverness-shire PH20 1DS. *T:* and *Fax:* (01540) 673269. *Clubs:* Army and Navy, MCC.

COBBOLD; *see* Lytton Cobbold, family name of Baron Cobbold.

COBBOLD, 2nd Baron *cr* 1960, of Knebworth; **David Antony Fromanteel Lytton Cobbold;** DL; Chairman and Managing Director, Lytton Enterprises Ltd, Knebworth House, since 1971; *b* 14 July 1937; *s* of 1st Baron Cobbold, KG, GCVO, PC, and Lady Hermione Bulwer-Lytton, *er d* of 2nd Earl of Lytton, KG, GCSI, GCIE, PC; assumed by deed poll, 1960, additional surname of Lytton; *S* father, 1987; *m* 1961, Christine Elizabeth, 3rd *d* of Major Sir Dennis Frederic Bankes Stucley, 5th Bt; three *s* one *d*. *Educ:* Eton College; Trinity Coll., Cambridge (BA Hons Moral Sciences). Fellow, Assoc. of Corporate Treasurers. PO, RAF, 1955–57. NATO Flying Training Scheme, Canada 1956–57. Morgan Guaranty Trust Co., New York, 1961–62; Bank of London and South America Ltd, London, Zürich, Barcelona, 1962–72; Treasurer, Finance for Industry Ltd, 1974–79; Manager Treasury Div., BP Finance International, The British Petroleum Co. plc, 1979–87; Gen. Manager Financial Markets, TSB England & Wales plc, 1987–88; Dir, Hill Samuel Bank Ltd, and Head of TSB-Hill Samuel Treasury Div., 1988–89; Man. Dir, Gaiacorp Currency Managers, 1991–94 (Dir, 1989–94); Director: Close Brothers Gp plc, 1993–2000; Stevenage Leisure Ltd, 1999–2002. Mem., Assoc. for Monetary Union in Europe, 1992–2002. Mem., Develt Cttee, 1991–2005, Bd of Govs, 1993–2005, Fellow, 2006–, Univ. of Hertfordshire (formerly Hatfield Poly.). Mem., Finance and Policy Cttee, HHA, 1973–97 (Hon. Treas., 1988–97); Gov., Union of European HHAs, 1993–97. Chm., Stevenage Community Trust, 1990–2006; Trustee, Pilgrim Trust, 1993–; Director: Shuttleworth Trust, 1998–2002; English Sinfonia Orch. Ltd, 1998–2002. Elected Mem., H of L, 2000–, crossbencher. Contested (L): Bishop Auckland, Oct. 1974; Hertfordshire, European Parly Election, 1979. DL Herts, 1993. *Recreation:* travel. *Heir:* *s* Hon. Henry Fromanteel Lytton Cobbold [*b* 12 May 1962; *m* 1987, Martha Frances, *d* of James Buford Boone, Jr; one *s* one *d*]. *Address:* 2d Park Place Villas, W2 1SP. *T:* (020) 7724 3734.

COBBOLD, Rear-Adm. Richard Francis, CB 1994; Vice President, Strategic Development, Duos Technologies International Inc., since 2007; *b* 25 June 1942; *s* of Geoffrey Francis and Elizabeth Mary Cobbold; *m* 1975, Anne Marika Hjörne (marr. diss. 1995); one *s* one *d*. *Educ:* Bryanston Sch.; BRNC Dartmouth. Early service, RN: HMS Kent; Staff of FO Naval Flying Training; HMS Juno; HMS Hermes; loan to RAN; RN Staff College 1973; Arctic Flight in comd, 1973–74; 820 Sqdn, Sen. Observer, 1974–75; MoD, 1975–77; HMS Mohawk in comd, 1977–79; MoD, 1979–83; RCDS 1984; HMS Brazen in comd, 1985–86; Dir of Defence Concepts, MoD, 1987–88; Captain 2nd Frigate Sqdn, 1989–90; ACDS Op. Requirements (Sea), 1991–94, and for Jt Systems, 1992–94; Dir, RUSI, 1994–2007. Specialist Adviser: H of C Defence Cttee, 1997–2007; H of C Foreign Affairs Cttee, 2003; Sen. Policy Advr, Ocean Security Initiative, 2005–. FRAeS 1994. Governor, London Nautical Sch., 1997–. *Recreations:* ski-ing, running marathons, gardening, naval and military history. *Address:* Duos Technologies International, Suite 414, Trafalgar House, 11 Waterloo Place, SW1Y 4AU. *Club:* Army and Navy.

COBHAM, 12th Viscount *cr* 1718; **Christopher Charles Lyttelton;** Bt 1618; Baron Cobham 1718; Lord Lyttelton, Baron of Frankley 1756 (renewed 1794); Baron Westcote (Ire.) 1776; *b* 23 Oct. 1947; 2nd *s* of 10th Viscount Cobham, KG, GCMG, GCVO, TD, PC and Elizabeth Alison, *d* of J. R. Makeig-Jones, CBE; *S* brother, 2006; *m* 1973, Tessa Mary, *d* of late Col A. G. Readman, DSO; one *s* one *d*. *Educ:* Eton. *Heir:* *s* Hon. Oliver Christopher Lyttelton, *b* 24 Feb. 1976.

COBHAM, Penelope, Viscountess; Penelope Ann Lyttelton; Deputy Chairman, VisitBritain, since 2005 (Director, since 2003); *b* 2 Jan. 1954; *d* of late Roy and Dorothy Cooper; *m* 1974, 11th Viscount Cobham (marr. diss. 1995; he *d* 2006). *Educ:* St James's Sch., Malvern. Chairman: British Casino Assoc., 1999–; Civic Trust, 1999–2003. Comr, Museums and Galls Commn, 1993–2000; Trustee, V&A, 1993–2003; Member: LDDC, 1993–98; Historic Royal Palaces Ministerial Adv. Bd, 1990–98; Exec. Council, HHA, 1985–; Council, Nat. Trust, 2004–. Co. Dir and Consultant incl. Chm., Heart of England Radio Ltd, subseq. Chrysalis Radio Midlands, 1993–2007. Consultant: Ernst & Young, 1997–; GI Partners (UK) Ltd, 2007–; aAIM Infrastructure, 2007–. Guardian, Birmingham Assay Office, 1990–. Chm., The Art Fund (formerly Gulbenkian) Prize for Museums and Galleries, 2001–. Pres., governor and patron, numerous civic, charitable and educnl bodies. Freeman: City of London; Goldsmiths' Co. DL West Midlands, 1994–95. FRSA. *Address:* (office) Canal House, 200 Hagley Road, Stourbridge, W Midlands DY8 2JN. *T:* (01384) 377517. *Club:* Birmingham Press (Pres.).

COCHRANE, family name of **Earl of Dundonald** and **Baron Cochrane of Cults.**

COCHRANE, Lord; Archie Iain Thomas Blair Cochrane; *b* 14 March 1991; *s* and *heir* of Earl of Dundonald, *qv*.

COCHRANE OF CULTS, 4th Baron *cr* 1919; **(Ralph Henry) Vere Cochrane;** DL; Chairman, Craigtoun Meadows Ltd, since 1972; *b* 20 Sept. 1926; 2nd *s* of 2nd Baron Cochrane of Cults, DSO and Hon. Elin Douglas-Pennant (*d* 1934), *y d* of 2nd Baron Penrhyn; *S* brother, 1990; *m* 1956, Janet Mary Watson, *d* of late William Hunter Watson Cheyne, MB, MRCS, LRCP; two *s*. *Educ:* Eton; King's Coll., Cambridge (MA). Served RE, 1945–48 (Lieut). Formerly: Vice-Chm., Cupar-Fife Savings Bank; Dir for Fife, Tayside Savings Bank. Underwriting Mem. of Lloyds, 1965–96. Gen. Comr for Income Tax. Mem., Queen's Body Guard for Scotland (Royal Co. of Archers), 1962–. DL Fife 1976. *Heir:* *s* Hon. Thomas Hunter Vere Cochrane, LLB, ACII, *b* 7 Sept. 1957. *Club:* New (Edinburgh).

COCHRANE, (Alexander John) Cameron, MBE 1987; MA; education consultant, since 1996; *b* 19 July 1933; *s* of late Dr Alexander Younger Cochrane and Jenny Johnstone Cochrane; *m* 1958, Rosemary Aline, *d* of late Robert Alexander Ogg and Aline Mary Ogg; one *s* two *d*. *Educ:* The Edinburgh Academy; University Coll., Oxford. National Service in RA, 1952–54. Asst Master, St Edward's Sch., Oxford, 1957–66; Warden, Brathay Hall, Ambleside, Cumbria, 1966–70; Asst Dir of Educn, City of Edinburgh, 1970–74; Headmaster, Arnold Sch., Blackpool, 1974–79; Headmaster, Fettes Coll., Edinburgh, 1979–88; first Principal, Prince Willem-Alexander Coll., Holland, 1988–91; Principal, British Internat. Sch., Cairo, 1992–95. Member: Lancashire CC Educn Cttee, 1976–79; Council, Outward Bound Trust, 1979–88; Admiralty Interview Bd, 1979–88; Scottish Cttee, Duke of Edinburgh's Award, 1981–86; Chairman: Outward Bound Ullswater, 1979–84; Outward Bound Loch Eil, 1984–88; Lothian Fedn of Boys' Clubs, 1981–84; HMC Services Cttee, 1982–88. Nat. Educn Officer, Atlantic Council of UK, 2001–03. Commandant, XIII Commonwealth Games Village, Edinburgh, 1986. Governor: Aiglon Coll., 1985–94; Pocklington Sch., 1985–2002. Session Clerk, Auchtertool Kirk, 1998–2004. CFM 1988. *Recreations:* games, the countryside, photography, friends, family, France. *Address:* 26 Buckstone Avenue, Edinburgh EH10 6QN. *T:* (0131) 445 1437. *Clubs:* East India, MCC; Vincent's (Oxford).

COCHRANE, Sir (Henry) Marc (Sursock), 4th Bt *cr* 1903; *b* 23 Oct. 1946; *s* of Sir Desmond Oriel Alastair George Weston Cochrane, 3rd Bt, and of Yvonne Lady Cochrane (*née* Sursock); *S* father, 1979; *m* 1969, Hala (*née* Es-Said); two *s* one *d*. *Educ:* Eton; Trinity Coll., Dublin (BBS, MA). Director: Hambros Bank Ltd, 1979–85; GT Management PLC, subseq. LGT Asset Management, 1985–98; INVESCO, 1998–99; Henderson Global Investors, 2000–05. Hon. Consul General of Ireland in Beirut, 1979–84. Trustee, Chester Beatty Library and Gall. of Oriental Art, Dublin. *Recreations:* ski-ing, target shooting, electronics. *Heir:* *s* Alexander Desmond Cochrane, *b* 7 May 1973. *Address:* Woodbrook, Bray, Co. Wicklow, Ireland. *T:* (1) 2821421; Palais Sursock, PO Box 154, Beirut, Lebanon. *T:* (1) 331607.

COCHRANE, Keith Robertson; Group Finance Director, Weir Group PLC, since 2006; *b* 11 Feb. 1965; *m* 1998, Fiona Margaret Armstrong; one *s* one *d*. *Educ:* Dunblane High Sch.; Univ. of Glasgow (BAcc 1st Cl. Hons). CA 1989; Audit Manager, Arthur Andersen, 1990–93; Gp Financial Controller and Co. Sec., 1993–96, Gp Financial Dir, 1996–2000, Stagecoach Holdings plc; Chief Exec., Stagecoach Gp, 2000–02; Dir of Gp Financial Reporting, 2003–04, Gp Controller, 2004–05, Gp Dir of Finance, 2005–06, Scottish Power plc. *Recreations:* golf, music, travel, reading. *Address:* Weir Group PLC, 20 Waterloo Street, Glasgow G2 6DB.

COCHRANE, Malcolm Ralph; Vice Lord-Lieutenant of Oxfordshire, since 1999; *b* 8 Aug. 1938; *s* of Air Chief Marshal Hon. Sir Ralph Cochrane, GBE, KCB, AFC and Hilda (*née* Wiggin); *m* 1972, Mary Anne Scrope, *d* of Ralph Scrope and Lady Beatrice Scrope, *d* of 6th Earl of Mexborough; one *s* two *d*. *Educ:* Eton Coll.; Balliol Coll., Oxford. Nat. Service, Scots Guards, 1957–58. Design Research Unit, 1962–65; Design Panel, BRB, 1965–72; Director: Cochranes of Oxford Ltd, 1972–; Cults Lime Ltd, 1976–. High Sheriff, 1996, DL 1998, Oxon. *Recreations:* arts, gardening, watching sport. *Address:* Grove Farmhouse, Shipton-under-Wychwood, Oxon OX7 6DG. *T:* (01993) 830742.

COCHRANE, Sir Marc; *see* Cochrane, Sir H. M. S.

COCHRANE, Prof. Peter, OBE 1999; PhD, DSc; FREng, FIET, FIEEE; Co-Founder and Chairman, Cochrane Associates, since 2006; consultant to government and international companies; *b* 11 July 1946; *s* of Colin Cochrane and Gladys Cochrane; *m* 1971, Brenda Cheetham (*d* 2003); two *s* two *d*; *m* 2005, Jane Tromans. *Educ:* Trent Poly. (BSc Electrical Engrg 1973); Essex Univ. (MSc Telecommunications 1976; PhD Transmission Systems 1979; DSc Systems Design 1991). CGIA 1975; CEng 1977; FIET (FIEE 1987; MIEE 1977); FIEEE 1992 (MIEEE 1983); FREng (FEng 1994). General Post Office: Technician, System Maintenance, 1962–69; Student Engr, 1969–73; Exec. Engr, GPO Res. Labs, 1973–79; BT Laboratories: Head of Gp, 1979–83; Head of Section, 1983–87; Head, Optical Networks Div., 1987–91; Head, Systems Res., 1991–93; Head, Advance Res., 1993–94; Head of Res., 1994–99; Chief Technologist, BT, 1999–2000; Co-Founder and CEO, ConceptLabs, Calif., 2000–06. Mem. Adv. Bd, Computer Scis Corp. Vanguard Prog., 1996–98. Visiting Professor: CNET, Lannion Univ., France, 1978; NE London Poly., 1980–90; Essex Univ., 1988–; Southampton Univ., 1991–94; Kent Univ., 1991–96; UCL, 1994–. Mem., NY Acad. of Scis, 1995. FRSA. Hon. DTech Stafford, 1996. Holds 14 original patents. *Publications:* (with J. E. Flood) Transmission Systems, 1991; (with D. J. T. Heatley) Modelling Telecommunication Systems, 1995; Tips for Time Travellers, 1997; Uncommon Sense, 2004; numerous professional papers and articles in IEE, IEEE, and other jls. *Recreations:* music, running, mathematics, philosophy, my family, fly fishing, reading. *Address:* Cochrane Associates, c/o Blick Rothenberg, 12 York Gate, NW1 4QS.

COCHRANE-DYET, Fergus John; HM Diplomatic Service; High Commissioner to Seychelles, since 2007; *b* 16 Jan. 1965; *s* of Lt-Col Iain Cochrane-Dyet and Rosemary Cochrane-Dyet; *m* 1987, Susie Emma Jane Aram; three *s*. *Educ:* Felsted Sch.; Jesus Coll., Oxford; Durham Univ. (BA Hons). Joined HM Diplomatic Service, 1987; Third Sec. (Political), Lagos, 1990–93; Second Sec. (Political), Abuja, 1993–94; First Secretary: Hd, N Africa Section, FCO, 1994–96; Hd, British Interests Section, Tripoli, 1996–97; (Commercial), Jakarta, 1998; Dir, Trade and Investment Promotion for Australia, and Dep. Consul Gen., Sydney, 1998–2001; Chargé d'Affaires, Conakry, 2001–02; Dep. Hd of Mission, Kabul, 2002; Dep. Hd, Africa Dept (Southern), FCO, 2002–04; Dep. High Comr, Lusaka, 2004–07; Dep. Hd, Helmand Provincial Reconstruction Team, Lashkar

Gah, Afghanistan, 2007. *Recreations:* running, scuba diving, films. *Address:* c/o Foreign and Commonwealth Office, King Charles Street, SW1A 2AH. *Club:* Lansdowne.

COCKAYNE, Prof. David John Hugh, DPhil; FRS 1999; Professor of the Physical Examination of Materials, University of Oxford, 2000–Sept. 2009; Fellow, Linacre College, Oxford, since 2000; *b* 19 March 1942; *s* of John Henry Cockayne and Ivy Cockayne; *m* 1967, Jean Mary Kerr; one *s* two *d. Educ:* Geelong C of E Grammar Sch., Australia; Trinity Coll., Univ. of Melbourne (BSc 1964; MSc 1966); Magdalen Coll., Oxford (DPhil 1970). Res. Lectr and Jun. Res. Fellow, Christ Church, and Res. Fellow, Dept of Materials, Univ. of Oxford, 1969–74; Dir, Electron Microscope Unit, 1974–2000, Prof. of Physics, 1992–2000, Hon. Prof., 2001–, Univ. of Sydney; Dir, Aust. Key Centre for Microscopy and Microanalysis, 1996–2000. Visiting Research Scientist: Atomic Energy of Canada, 1970; Univ. of Calif at Berkeley, 1979; Royal Soc. Anglo-Australasian Vis. Fellow, Univ. of Oxford, 1982; Hon. Professor: Univ. of Sci. and Tech., Beijing, 2005–; Lanzhou Univ. of Tech., 2006–07; Vis. Prof., Univ. of Paris, 1993. General Secretary: Cttee, Asia Pacific Socs, Electron Microscopy, 1984–96; Internat. Fedn of Socs for Electron Microscopy, 1995–2002 (Pres., 2003–06); Chm., Nat. Cttee, Electron Microscopy, Australian Acad. of Sci., 1986–94. FAIP; FInstP 1999. *Publications:* over 200 scientific articles. *Recreation:* walking. *Address:* Department of Materials, University of Oxford, Parks Road, Oxford OX1 3PH.

COCKBURN, David; The Certification Officer for Trade Unions and Employers' Associations, since 2001; (part-time) Employment Judge (formerly Chairman, Employment Tribunals), since 2001; *b* 30 Nov. 1948; *s* of John William Cockburn and Nora Cockburn (*née* Carr); *m* 1976, Polly Dickey; one *s* two *d. Educ:* King's Sch., Pontefract; LSE (LLB 1970; MSc (Econ) 1972). Admitted solicitor, 1975; Partner, Pattinson & Brewer, solicitors, 1978–2001. Chm., Compliance Panel, PhonepayPlus, 2008–. Chairman: Industrial Law Soc., 1983–86 (Vice-Pres., 1986–); Employment Lawyers' Assoc., 1994–96; Employment Law Cttee, Law Soc., 1995–99; Treas., Inst. of Employment Rights, 1995–2001. Vis. Prof., Middlesex Univ., 2002–. Member, Editorial Committee: Industrial Law Jl, 1986–; Encyclopaedia of Employment Law, 1990–. *Publications:* (contrib.) Justice for a Generation, 1985; (contrib.) Labour Law in Britain, 1986; (jtly) Know-how in Employment Law, 1995; (contrib.) The Changing Institutional Face of British Employment Relations, 2006; articles on labour law in learned jls. *Recreations:* jogging, cycling, sailing, ski-ing, jazz, theatre. *Address:* Certification Officer for Trade Unions and Employers' Associations, Brandon House, 180 Borough High Street, SE1 1LW. *T:* (020) 7210 3734, *Fax:* (020) 7210 3612; *e-mail:* david.cockburn@certoffice.org.

COCKBURN, Prof. Forrester, CBE 1996; MD; FRCPE, FRCPGlas; FRSE; Samson Gemmell Professor of Child Health, University of Glasgow, 1977–96, now Emeritus Professor; Chairman, Yorkhill NHS Trust, 1997–2001; *b* 13 Oct. 1934; *s* of Forrester Cockburn and Violet E. Bunce; *m* 1960, Alison Fisher Grieve; two *s. Educ:* Leith Acad.; Univ. of Edinburgh (MB ChB 1959; MD *cum laude* 1966); DCH Glasgow 1961. FRCPE 1971; FRCPGlas 1978; FRSE 1999. Med. trng, Royal Infirmary of Edinburgh, Royal Hosp. for Sick Children, and Simpson Memorial Maternity Pavilion, Edinburgh, 1959–63; Huntingdon Hertford Foundn Res. Fellow, Boston Univ., Mass, 1963–65; Nuffield Sen. Res. Fellow, Univ. of Oxford, 1965–66; Wellcome Trust Sen. Med. Res. Fellow, Univ. of Edin. and Simpson Meml Maternity Pavilion, 1966–71; Sen. Lectr, Dept of Child Life and Health, Univ. of Edin., 1971–77. Chm., Panel on Child Nutrition and Wkg Gp on Weaning Diet, Cttee on Med. Aspects of Food Policy (Report, 1994). Hon. FRCPCH 1996; Hon. FRCSE 2000. James Spence Medal, RCPCH, 1998. *Publications:* Neonatal Medicine, 1974; The Cultured Cell in Inherited Metabolic Disease, 1977; Inborn Errors of Metabolism in Humans, 1980; (with O. P. Gray) Children—A Handbook for Children's Doctors, 1984; (with J. H. Hutchison) Practical Paediatric Problems, 6th edn 1986; (with T. L. Turner and J. Douglas) Craig's Care of the Newly Born Infant, 8th edn 1988; Fetal and Neonatal Growth, 1988; (ed jtly and contrib.) Diseases of the Fetus and Newborn, 1989, 2nd edn 1995; (jtly) Children's Medicine and Surgery, 1996; around 200 articles mainly on fetal and neonatal nutrition and inherited metabolic disease. *Recreation:* sailing. *Address:* University Department of Child Health, Royal Hospital for Sick Children, Yorkhill, Glasgow G3 8SJ. *T:* (0141) 201 0000.

COCKBURN, Sir John (Elliot), 12th Bt of that Ilk, *cr* 1671; *b* 7 Dec. 1925; *s* of Lieut-Col Sir John Cockburn, 11th Bt of that Ilk, DSO and Isabel Hunter (*d* 1978), *y d* of late James McQueen, Crofts, Kirkcudbrightshire; *S* father, 1949; *m* 1949, Glory Patricia, *er d* of Nigel Tudway Mullings; three *s* two *d* (of whom one *s* one *d* are twins). *Educ:* RNC Dartmouth; Royal Agricultural Coll., Cirencester. Served War of 1939–45, joined RAFVR, July 1943. *Recreation:* reading. *Heir: s* Charles Christopher Cockburn [*b* 19 Nov. 1950; *m* 1985, Ruth, *d* of Samuel Bell; two *s* one *d* (of whom one *s* one *d* are twins)]. *Address:* 48 Frewin Road, SW18 3LP.

COCKBURN, William, CBE 1989; TD 1980; Deputy Chairman, Business Post plc, since 2002; *b* 28 Feb. 1943. Entered Post Office, 1961; held various junior and middle management positions; apptd Mem., PO Board, 1981, Mem. for Finance, Counter Services and Planning, 1982–84; Mem. for Royal Mail Operations, 1984–86; Man. Dir, Royal Mail, 1986–92; Chief Executive: The Post Office, 1992–95; W. H. Smith Gp PLC, 1996–97; Gp Man. Dir, BT UK, 1997–2001; Chm., Parity Gp plc, 2001–03; Dep. Chm., AWG, 2003–06. Chm., Internat. Post Corp., 1994–95; non-executive Director: Lex Service plc, 1993–2002; Centrica plc, 1997–99; Army Bd, 2008–. Member: Bd, BITC, 1990–2003; Council, Industrial Soc., 1992–2002; Chairman: Sch. Teachers' Review Body, 2002–; Senior Salaries Review Body, 2008–. Pres., Inst. of Direct Marketing, 2001–06. Col, RE Postal and Courier Service (V), 1986–91; Hon. Col, RE Postal and Courier Service, 1992–94; Hon. Col Comdt, RLC, 1996–2006. FCIT 1993; FRSA; CCMI (CIMgt 1993). Freeman, City of London.

COCKBURN-CAMPBELL, Sir Alexander (Thomas), 7th Bt *cr* 1821, of Gartsford, Ross-shire; Building Operations Supervisor, Knight Frank Facilities Managers, Perth, WA, since 2000; *b* 16 March 1945; *o s* of Sir Thomas Cockburn-Campbell, 6th Bt and of Josephine Zoi Cockburn-Campbell (*née* Forward); *S* father, 1999; *m* 1969, Kerry Ann, *e d* of Sgt K. Johnson; one *s* one *d. Educ:* Edwards Business Coll. (Adv. Cert. Mkting/Mgt). Prodn Mgr, 1980–90; Maintenance Manager, Uniting Church Homes, 1995–2000. Protestant Lay Minister, 1980– (Dip. Ministry). *Recreation:* surf-board riding. *Heir: s* Thomas Justin Cockburn-Campbell, *b* 10 Feb. 1974. *Address:* 103 Waterperry Drive, Canning Vale, WA 6155, Australia. *T:* (8) 92562049.

COCKCROFT, Barry Michael; Chief Dental Officer for England, Department of Health, since 2006; *b* 6 Nov. 1950; *s* of late Harry and Margaret Cockcroft; *m* 1973, Diane Lay; one *s* two *d. Educ:* De La Salle Coll., Salford; Univ. of Birmingham (BDS 1973; Charles Greene Prize, 1973). Sen. House Officer, Coventry & Warwickshire Hosp., 1974; general dental practitioner: Coventry, 1975–79; Rugby, 1979–2002; Dep. Chief Dental Officer, DoH, 2002–06. JP Rugby, 1992–2000. Hon. FDS RCS 2007. *Recreations:* getting home at weekends, live music and theatre, watching Rugby RFC, supporting Bolton Wanderers FC. *Address:* Department of Health, New Kings Beam House, 22 Upper Ground, SE1 9BW. *T:* (020) 7633 4144, *Fax:* (020) 7633 4127; *e-mail:* Barry.cockcroft@dh.gsi.gov.uk.

COCKCROFT, John Hoyle; author and journalist; Director, International Conflict Resolution, 1990–2006; writer and political and corporate adviser; various electronics directorships, since 1977; *b* 6 July 1934; *s* of late Lionel Fielden Cockcroft and Jenny Hoyle; *m* 1971, Tessa Fay Shepley; three *d. Educ:* Primary, Trearddur House; Oundle; St John's Coll., Cambridge (Sen. Maj. Scholar (History), 1953). MA Hons History and Econs 1958; Pres., Cambridge Union, 1958. Royal Artillery, 2nd Lieut, 1953–55. Feature writer, Financial Times, 1959–61; Economist, GKN, 1962–67; seconded to Treasury, Public Enterprises Div. (transport), 1965–66; Econ. Leader-writer, Daily Telegraph, 1967–74. MP (C) Nantwich, Feb. 1974–1979; Mem. Select Cttee on Nationalised Industries (transport), 1975–79; Company Secretaries Bill (Private Member's), 1978. Duff Stoop & Co., stockbrokers (corporate finance), 1978–86; Laurence Prust, stockbrokers (corporate finance), 1986–90; Dir, BR (Eastern Region), 1984–89; Consultant: GKN, 1971–76; Mail Users' Assoc., 1976–79; Inst. of Chartered Secretaries, 1977–79; BR, 1979–84; Cray Electronics, 1982–84; Dowty, 1983–86; Wedgwood, 1983–84; Crystalate, 1983–86; Commed Ltd, 1983–93; MAP Securities (corporate finance), 1992–95; Heathmere (UK), 1996–; ESL & N, 2006–. Consultant: NEI History Archives, 1980–85; GKN History Archives, 2002–. Member Council: European Movement, 1973–74, 1983–84; Conservative Gp for Europe, 1980–87. Member: RUSI; UNA/European-Atlantic Gp. Trustee, Sanderson Trust (Oundle), 1992–. Leader-writer, Sunday Telegraph, 1981–86; Columnist: Microscope, 1982–85; electronic money transmission, Banking World, 1984–86; Westminster Watch, Electronics Times, 1985–90. *Publications:* (jtly) Reforming the Constitution, 1968; (jtly) Self-Help Reborn, 1969; Why England Sleeps, 1971; (jtly) An Internal History of Guest Keen and Nettlefolds, 1976; Microelectronics, 1982; Microtechnology in Banking, 1984; articles in The European, The Scotsman, Jl of Contemp. British Hist., Essex Chronicle, 1979–. *Recreations:* walking, reading, writing, entertaining. *Address:* 315 Broomfield Road, Chelmsford CM1 4DU.

COCKELL, Merrick Richard; Member (C), since 1986, and Leader of the Council, since 2000, Royal Borough of Kensington and Chelsea; *b* 16 June 1957; *s* of late Peter Colvile Cockell and of Hildegard Christina Gaskell (*née* Kern); *m* 1986, Karen Libby; two *d. Educ:* Pierrepont Sch. Trader, F. M. Barshall Ltd, Ghana, Togo, Sierra Leone, The Gambia, then in China, 1977–82; Founder Dir, Abingdon Cockell Ltd, 1982–2006; Dir, Localis Research Ltd, 2008–. Royal Borough of Kensington and Chelsea: Chm., Educn Authy, 1992–95; Chief Whip, 1995–2000. Mem., London Governance Commn, 2004–06. Chm., London Councils (formerly Assoc. of London Govt), 2006–. Chairman: Cons. Councillors' Assoc., 2008– (Dep. Chm., 2005–08); Bd, Cons. Party, 2008–. Trustee, Public Services Res. Gp, 2008–. *Recreations:* opera, travel. *Address:* Royal Borough of Kensington and Chelsea, The Town Hall, Hornton Street, W8 7NX. *T:* (020) 7361 2114, *Fax:* (020) 7361 3105; *e-mail:* leader@rbkc.gov.uk. *Club:* Chelsea Arts.

COCKELL, Michael Henry; a Deputy Chairman of Lloyd's, 1986; *b* 30 Aug. 1933; *s* of Charles and Elise Seaton; *m* 1961, Elizabeth Janet Meikle; one *s* three *d. Educ:* Harrow School. Survey officer, 1st Regt HAC (RHA), 1955–59. Underwriter for G. N. Rouse Syndicate 570, 1968–90; Chm., M. H. Cockell & Co., 1978; Senior Partner, M. H. Cockell & Partners, 1986; Chm., Atrium Cockell Underwriting Ltd, 1997–98; Dir, Medway plc, 1997–2000. Dep. Chm., Lloyd's Non-Marine Assoc., 1982, Chm., 1983–; Mem. Council, Lloyd's, 1984–87, 1990–93 and 1995–96. *Recreations:* all sport (especially cricket), ornithology, melodic music, gardening, countryside. *Address:* Court Horeham, Cowbeech, Herstmonceaux, E Sussex BN27 4JN. *T:* (01323) 833171. *Clubs:* City of London, MCC; IZ.

COCKER, Victor, CBE 2000; Chairman, Aga Foodservice Group, 2004–08; *b* 30 Oct. 1940; *s* of Harold Nathan Cocker and Marjorie Cocker; *m* 1963, Jennifer Nicholls; two *d. Educ:* King Edward VII Sch., Sheffield; Nottingham Univ. (BA Econ Hons); Harvard Business Sch. (Internat. SMP 1990). FCIWEM. NW Gas Board, 1962–68; West Midlands Gas, 1968–74; Severn Trent Water Authy, 1974–89; Man. Dir, Severn Trent Water Ltd, 1991–95; Gp Chief Exec., Severn Trent plc (formerly Chief Exec., Severn Trent Water), 1995–2000. Non-executive Director: Aquafin NV, 1993–2000; Railtrack Gp, 1999–2002; Aga Foodservice Gp (formerly Glynwed Internat.), 2000–08; Modern Waste, 2008–. Founder Chm., Waste and Resources Action Prog., 2000–08. Water Aid: Trustee, 1996–2007; Vice Chm., 1998–2001; Chm., 2001–07; Chm., Severn Trent Region, 1997–2000. Dir, Midlands Excellence, 1996–2000. Member: Adv. Cttee on Business in Environment, 1996–2003; World Business Council for Sustainable Develt, 1997–2000. Chm., Forward Birmingham RNLI Lifeboat Campaign, 1994–96; Member: RNLI Cttee of Mgt, 1996–2002; RNLI Council, 2003–; RSA Council, 2004–. CCMI. Hon. FCIWM 2004. DUniv Central England, 2006. *Recreations:* hill walking, National Hunt. *Address:* Tredington Manor, Tredington, Shipston on Stour CV36 4NJ. *T:* (01608) 663779. *Club:* Royal Automobile.

COCKERAM, Eric (Paul); JP; *b* 4 July 1924; *er s* of Mr and Mrs J. W. Cockeram; *m* 1949, Frances Irving; two *s* two *d. Educ:* The Leys Sch., Cambridge. Served War, 1942–46: Captain The Gloucestershire Regt; "D Day" landings (wounded and later discharged). MP (C): Bebington, 1970–Feb. 1974; Ludlow, 1979–87. PPS: to Minister for Industry, 1970–72; to Minister for Posts and Telecommunications, 1972; to Chancellor of Exchequer, 1972–74. Mem., Select Cttee on Corporation Tax, 1971, on Industry and Trade, 1979–87; Mem., Public Accounts Cttee, 1983–87. Pres., Menswear Assoc. of Britain, 1964–65. Mem., Bd of Governors, United Liverpool Hosps, 1965–74; Chm., Liverpool NHS Exec. Council, 1970. Chairman: Watson Prickard Ltd, 1966–2001; Johnson Fry (Northern) Ltd, 1988–94; Director: TSB (NW), 1968–83; TSB (Wales & Border Counties), 1983–88; Liverpool Building Soc., 1975–82 (Vice-Chm., 1981–82); Midshires Building Soc., 1982–88; Muller Group (UK) Ltd, 1983–94. Member of Lloyd's. Liveryman, Worshipful Co. of Glovers, 1969–, Mem. Court, 1979–89. Freeman: City of London; City of Springfield, Ill. JP, City of Liverpool, 1960. *Recreations:* bridge, golf, shooting, country walking. *Address:* Fairway Lodge, Caldy, Wirral, Cheshire CH48 1NB. *T:* (0151) 625 1100. *Clubs:* Carlton, Army and Navy.

COCKERELL, Michael Roger Lewis; political documentary maker, author, broadcaster; *b* 26 Aug. 1940; *s* of Prof. Hugh Cockerell and Fanny Cockerell (*née* Jochelman); *m* 1st, 1970, Anne Faber (marr. diss. 1980); one *s* one *d*; 2nd, 1984, Bridget Heathcoat-Amory (marr. diss. 1990); two *d*; partner, Anna Lloyd; three *d. Educ:* Kilburn Grammar Sch.; Heidelberg Univ.; Corpus Christi Coll., Oxford (MA PPE). Magazine journalist, 1962–66; Producer, BBC African Service, 1966–68; Current Affairs, BBC TV, 1968–87: Producer, 24 Hours, 1968–72; reporter: Midweek, 1972–75; Panorama, 1975–87; freelance TV reporter and documentary maker, 1987–: *programmes* include: investigations into political lobbying, the Honours system, the Whips, and the Cabinet; How to Be series; profiles of Alan Clark, James Callaghan, Edward Heath, Enoch Powell, Barbara Castle, Roy Jenkins, Betty Boothroyd, Stella Rimington, The Rivals (Gordon Brown and Michael Portillo); Tony Blair's Thousand Days, 2000; News from Number Ten: Alastair Campbell and the media, 2000; Trust Me, I'm a Politician, 2003; With

Friends Like These: Britain's relations with France, Germany and US, 2003; The Downing Street Patient: Health of PMs, 2004; Do You Still Believe in Tony?, 2004; The Brown-Blair Affair, 2004; Michael Howard: No More Mr Nasty, 2005; How We Fell for Europe, 2005; How to be Tory Leader, 2005; Tony's Tight Spot, 2006; Blair: the inside story (three-part series), How to be ex-Prime Minister, 2007; Dave Cameron's Incredible Journey, 2007; The Making of the Iron Lady, 2008; BBC Radio 4 documentaries: The Trial of David Irving, 2004; Tales from the Cutting Room, 2006; Profile: Conrad Black, 2007; Speaker Michael Martin, 2008. Vis. Lectr, LSE, 1998–, Nuffield Coll., Oxford, 2001–04. Huw Wheldon Lect., BBC2, 2000. Consultant, Oxford DNB, 2000–. Hon. DCL UEA, 2007. Emmy Award, 1980; Best Documentary Award, RTS, 1982; Golden Nymph Award, Monte Carlo, 1988; Judges' Award for Special Contrib. to Politics, Pol Studies Assoc., 2008. *Publications:* (jtly) Sources Close to the Prime Minister, 1984; Live from Number Ten: the inside story of Prime Ministers and TV, 1988; (contrib.) The Blair Effect, 2001; (contrib.) Where the Truth Lies, 2006; articles in newspapers. *Recreations:* cricket, tennis, merry-making. *Address:* 27 Arundel Gardens, W11 2LW. *T:* (020) 7727 8035, 07747 031940; *e-mail:* michael.cockerell@gmail.com. *Clubs:* MCC (playing mem.), Lord's Taverners, Bushmen.

COCKERHAM, David, CBE 1995; HM Diplomatic Service, retired; International Director, Invest.UK (formerly Invest in Britain Bureau), 1999–2001; *b* 14 May 1944; *s* of late Henry Cockerham and Eleanor Cockerham (*née* Nicholls); *m* 1967, Ann Lesley Smith; two *s*. *Educ:* Leeds Central High Sch. Joined FO, 1962; Saigon, 1967–68; Japanese studies, Tokyo, 1969–71; Vice-Consul: Yokohama, 1971–72; Tokyo, 1972–75; FCO, 1975–79; Vice-Consul (Commercial Inf.), British Inf. Services, NY, 1979–81; Consul (Commercial) and Exec. Asst to Dir-Gen. of Trade Develt, USA, British Trade Develt Office, NY, 1981–83; First Sec. (Commercial), Tokyo, 1983–87; Hd, Exports to Japan Unit, DTI, 1987–90 (on secondment); Dir of Ops, Migration and Visa Dept, FCO, 1990–91; Dep. High Comr, Madras, 1991–94; Consul-Gen. and Dir of Trade Promotion, Osaka, 1994–98. Member: FCO Assoc., 2000–; Bearsted and Thurnham Soc. (Vice-Chm. and Sec., 2005–07). *Recreation:* golf.

COCKERILL, Geoffrey Fairfax, CB 1980; Secretary, University Grants Committee, 1978–82; *b* 14 May 1922; *e s* of late Walter B. Cockerill and Mary W. Cockerill (*née* Buffery); *m* 1959, Janet Agnes Walters, JP, MA (*d* 2006); two *s*. *Educ:* Humberstone Foundation Sch.; UC Nottingham. BA London 1947. Royal Artillery, 1941–45 (Captain). Min. of Labour, 1947; Min. of Educn, 1952; Private Sec. to last Minister of Educn and Secs of State for Educn and Science, 1963–65; Asst Sec., 1964; Sec., Public Schools Commn, 1966–68; Jt Sec., Schools Council for Curriculum and Examinations, 1970–72; Under-Sec., DES, 1972–77; Dep. Sec., 1978. Chairman: Anglo-Amer. Primary Educ. Project, 1970–72; Working Party on Nutritional Aspects of School Meals, 1973–75; Kingston-upon-Thames CAB, 1985–88; Member: Adv. Gp on London Health Services, 1980–81; RCN Commn on Nursing Educn, 1984–85; RCN Strategy Gp, 1985–87; UGC, Univ. of S Pacific, 1984–87; Vice-Pres., Experiment in Internat. Living, 1989–98. Reviewed for Government: Central Bureau for Educational Visits and Exchanges, 1982; Youth Exchanges, 1983; Nat. Youth Bureau, 1983; Consultant to Cttee of Vice-Chancellors and Principals, 1984–85. Hon. Senior Research Fellow, KCL, 1982–86. *Recreations:* gardening, photography. *Address:* 29 Lovelace Road, Surbiton, Surrey KT6 6NS. *T:* (020) 8399 0125. *Clubs:* Athenæum, Royal Commonwealth Society.

COCKERTON, Rev. Canon John Clifford Penn; Rector of Wheldrake with Thorganby, 1985–92 (Rector of Wheldrake, 1978–85); Canon of York (Prebend of Dunnington), 1987–92, Canon Emeritus 1992; *b* 27 June 1927; *s* of late William Penn Cockerton and Eleanor Cockerton; *m* 1974, Diana Margaret Smith (*d* 1987), *d* of Mr and Mrs W. Smith, Upper Poppleton, York. *Educ:* Wirral Grammar Sch.; Univ. of Liverpool; St Catherine's Society, Oxford; Wycliffe Hall, Oxford. Deacon 1954; Priest 1955; Asst Curate, St Helens Parish Church, 1954–58; Tutor 1958–60, Chaplain 1960–63, Cranmer Hall, Durham; Vice-Principal, St John's Coll., Durham, 1963–70; Principal, St John's College and Cranmer Hall, Durham, 1970–78. Examining Chaplain to Bishop of Durham, 1971–73; Proctor in Convocation, 1980–85. *Recreation:* music.

COCKETT, Ven. Elwin Wesley; Archdeacon of West Ham, since 2007; *b* Kotagiri, Tamil Nadu, India, 24 May 1959; *s* of late Dr Norman Cockett and of Janet Cockett (*née* Graham, now Slade); *m* 1977, Susan Mary Jones; one *s* two *d*. *Educ:* St Paul's Cath. Choir Sch.; Forest Sch., Snaresbrook; Oak Hill Theological Coll. (BA Theol. and Pastoral Studies 1991). Practice Manager, Bethnal Green Med. Mission, 1983–88; ordained deacon, 1991, priest, 1992; Curate, St Chad's, Chadwell Heath, 1991–94; Curate i/c, 1994–95, Priest i/c, 1995–97, Vicar, 1997–2000, St Paul's, Harold Hill; Team Rector, Billericay and Little Burstead, 2000–07; Rural Dean, Basildon, 2004–07. Club Chaplain, West Ham UFC, 1992–. *Recreations:* music, motorcycling, sailing. *Address:* 86 Aldersbrook Road, E12 5DH. *T:* (020) 8989 8557, *Fax:* (020) 8530 1311; *e-mail:* a.westham@chelmsford.anglican.org.

COCKETT, Frank Bernard, MS, FRCS; Consulting Surgeon to: St Thomas' Hospital; King Edward VII Hospital for Officers, London; *b* Rockhampton, Australia, 22 April 1916; *s* of late Rev. Charles Bernard Cockett, MA, DD; *m* 1945, Felicity Ann (*d* 1958), *d* of Col James Thackeray Fisher, DSO, Frieston, near Grantham, Lincs; one *s* two *d*; *m* 1960, Dorothea Anne Newman (MBE 1999); twin *s*. *Educ:* Bedford Sch.; St Thomas's Hosp. Med. Sch. BSc (1st Cl. Hons), 1936; MRCS, LRCP 1939; MB, BS (London) 1940; FRCS Eng 1947; MS (London) 1953. Sqdn Ldr (Surgical Specialist) RAFVR, 1942–46; Surgical Registrar, St Thomas' Hosp., 1947–48; Resident Asst Surg., St Thomas' Hosp., 1948–50, Consultant, 1954–81; Senior Lecturer in Surgery, St Thomas's Hosp. Med. Sch., 1950–54; Consultant, King Edward VII Hosp. for Officers, 1974–81. Fellow Assoc. of Surgs of Gt Brit.; Mem. European Soc. of Cardiovascular Surgery; Pres., Vascular Surgical Soc. of GB and Ireland, 1980; Chm., Venous Forum, RSM, 1986–87. *Publications:* The Pathology and Surgery of the Veins of the Lower Limb, 1956, 2nd edn 1976; several contribs to Operative Surgery (ed C. G. Rob and Rodney Smith), 1956; The War Diary of St Thomas' Hospital 1939–1945, 1991; Early Sea Painters, 1995; Peter Monamy, 2000; various papers in medical and surgical journals. *Recreations:* sailing, tennis, gardening, marine paintings. *Address:* 14 Essex Villas, Kensington, W8 7BN. *T:* (020) 7937 9883.

See also R. D. Hull.

COCKETT, Geoffrey Howard; consultant; Chief Scientific Officer, Ministry of Defence, and Deputy Director, Royal Armament Research and Development Establishment, 1983–86; *b* 18 March 1926; *s* of late William Cockett and Edith (*née* Dinham); *m* 1951, Elizabeth Bagshaw; two *d*. *Educ:* King Edward VI Sch., Southampton; Univ. of Southampton (BSc, Hons Maths, and Hons Physics). MRI; FInstP; CPhys. Royal Aircraft Establishment, 1948–52; Armament Research Estabt, Woolwich, 1952–62; RARDE, 1962–68; Supt of Physics Div., Chemical Defence Estabt, 1968–71; RARDE: Supt, Optics and Surveillance Systems Div., 1971–76; Head, Applied Physics Group, 1976–83. Chm., Sci. Recruitment Bds, CS Commn, 1985–94; Consultant, Directorate of Sci. (Land), MoD, 1986–98. (Jtly) Gold Medal, Congrès des Materiaux Résistant à Chaud, Paris, 1951. *Publications:* official reports; scientific and technical papers in various learned jls. *Recreations:* computing, photography, under gardening. *Address: e-mail:* ghc1uk@yahoo.co.uk. *Club:* Civil Service.

COCKING, Prof. Edward Charles Daniel, FRS 1983; Professor of Botany, University of Nottingham, 1969–97, now Professor Emeritus; *b* 26 Sept. 1931; *y s* of late Charles Cocking and Mary (*née* Murray); *m* 1960, Bernadette Keane; one *s* one *d*. *Educ:* Buckhurst Hill County High Sch., Essex; Univ. of Bristol (BSc, PhD, DSc). FIBiol. Civil Service Commission Research Fellow, 1956–59; Nottingham University: Lectr in Plant Physiology, 1959–66; Reader, 1966–69; Head of Dept of Botany, 1969. Leverhulme Trust Res. Fellow, 1995–97. S. Yoshida Meml Lecture, Hangzhou Univ., China, 1987. Member: Lawes Agricl Trust Cttee, Rothamsted Experimental Stn, 1987–91 (Mem., Governing Body, 1991–; Chm., 1999–2003); Adv. Cttee on Forest Res., Forestry Commn, 1987–95; Council, Royal Soc., 1986–88; AFRC, 1990–94 (Royal Soc. Assessor, 1988–90); Lawes Agriculture Trust Co., 2000–. Mem., Bd of Trustees, Royal Botanic Gardens, Kew, 1983–93; Member, Governing Body: Glasshouse Crops Res. Inst., 1983–87; British Soc. Horticultural Res., 1987–89. Pres., Sect. K, BAAS, 1983. Royal Soc. Trustee, Uppingham Sch., 1997–2007. MAE 1993. Hon. Mem., Hungarian Acad. Scis, 1995; Fellow: Indian Acad. of Agricl Scis, 2000; World Innovation Foundn, 2003. Lifetime Achievement Award, Univ. of Toledo, USA, 2004. *Publications:* Introduction to the Principles of Plant Physiology (with W. Stiles, FRS), 3rd edn 1969; numerous scientific papers in botanical/genetics jls on plant genetic manipulations and nitrogen fixation. *Recreations:* walking, travelling, especially by train, occasional chess. *Address:* Centre for Crop Nitrogen Fixation, Plant Sciences Division, School of Biology, and School of Biosciences, University of Nottingham, University Park, Nottingham NG7 2RD. *T:* (0115) 951 3056, *Fax:* (0115) 951 3240; 30 Patterdale Road, Woodthorpe, Nottingham NG5 4LQ. *T:* (0115) 926 2452.

COCKRILL, Prof. Maurice, RA 1999; PRCA (RCA 2001); artist; Keeper of the Royal Academy of Arts, since 2004; President, Royal Cambrian Academy, since 2006; *b* Hartlepool, 8 Oct. 1935; *s* of William and Edith Cockrill; *m* 1st, 1957, Pauline Hinds (marr. diss. 1963); one *s*; 2nd, 1963, Elizabeth Ashworth (marr. diss. 1968); one *s*; partner 1974, Helen Moslin; one *s*. *Educ:* Wrexham Sch. of Art (NDD 1960); Univ. of Reading (ATD 1964). Numerous exhibns in UK, Paris, Düsseldorf, Frankfurt, Stavelot, NY, Sydney 1960–, including: Edward Totah Gall., London, annually 1982–86; Kunstmus., Düsseldorf, 1985; Bernard Jacobson Gall., annually 1986–96; Retrospectives, Walker Art Gall., Liverpool, 1994; RWA, 1998; work in many collections, including: BM; Arts Council; Contemporary Arts Soc.; Walker Art Gall.; Kunstmus., Düsseldorf; Deutsche Bank; Unilever; RA. Hon. Prof. of Contemporary Fine Art, Liverpool John Moores Univ., 2005–. *Publications:* Paintings and Drawings, 2002; various exhibn catalogues and bibliography. *Recreations:* walking esp. in Snowdonia (where has a small studio), reading esp. modern poetry, contemporary classical music, jazz, nature. *Address:* 78B Park Hall Road, SE21 8BW; *e-mail:* admin@cockrill.co.uk. *Clubs:* Chelsea Arts, Arts, Lansdowne.

COCKROFT, Peter John; His Honour Judge Cockroft; a Circuit Judge, since 1993; *b* 24 Sept. 1947; *s* of late Walter Philip Barron Cockroft and Nora (*née* Collett); *m* 1975, Maria Eugenia Coromina Perandones; one *s* two *d*. *Educ:* Queen Elizabeth I Grammar Sch., Darlington; Queens' Coll., Cambridge (BA, LLB). Called to the Bar, Middle Temple, 1970 (Astbury Scholar); practised NE Circuit; Asst Recorder, 1985–89; Recorder, 1989–93. *Recreations:* visiting Spain, gardening. *Address:* Brackenwell Cottage, North Rigton, N Yorks LS17 0DG. *T:* (01423) 734585. *Clubs:* Yorkshire County Cricket; Yorkshire Rugby Football Union.

COCKS, family name of **Baron Somers**.

COCKS, Hon. Anna Gwenllian S.; *see* Somers Cocks.

COCKS, Freda Mary, CBE 1999 (OBE 1972); JP; Deputy Leader, Birmingham City Council, 1982–86; *b* 30 July 1915; *d* of Frank and Mary Wood; *m* 1942, Donald Francis Melvin, *s* of Melvin J. Cocks; one *d* (and one *d* decd). *Educ:* St Peter's Sch., Harborne; Queen's Coll., Birmingham. Birmingham Council, 1953–78: Alderman, 1965–74; Lord Mayor of Birmingham, 1977–78; Dep. Chm., Housing Cttee, 1968–70, Chm. 1970–72. Founder Sec., Birmingham Sanatoria League of Friends, 1950–68; Founder and Chm., Birm. Hosps Broadcasting Assoc., 1952–78; Member: Little Bromwich Hosp. Management Cttee, 1953–68; West Birmingham Health Authority, 1981–92; Vice-Pres. and Mem., Nat. Careers Assoc., 1985–. Conservative Women's Central Council: Chm., 1968–71; Chm., Gen. Purposes Cttee, 1978; service on housing, finance, policies, and land cttees; Vice Pres., Edgbaston Conservative Assoc., 1992– (Pres., 1980–92). Member: Focus Housing Assoc.; Civic Housing Assoc.; Birmingham Blind Action Forum; Council Mem., Birmingham Rathbone Soc. (Patron, 1998). Pres., Missions to Seamen, subseq. Mission to Seafarers, Birmingham, 1981–2003 (Patron, 2003–). Patron, Pulse Trust, 1997–. JP Birmingham, 1968. Hon. Freeman: City of Birmingham, 1986; Du-Panne, Belgium, 1978. *Recreations:* hospitals and housing. *Address:* 49 Timber Mill Court, Serpentine Road, Harborne, Birmingham B17 9RD. *T:* (0121) 427 9123.

COCKS, Dr Leonard Robert Morrison, (Dr Robin Cocks), OBE 1999; TD 1979; Keeper of Palaeontology, Natural History Museum (formerly British Museum (Natural History)), 1986–98; *b* 17 June 1938; *s* of late Ralph Morrison Cocks and Lucille Mary Cocks (*née* Blackler); *m* 1963, Elaine Margaret Sturdy; one *s* two *d*. *Educ:* Felsted School; Hertford College, Oxford (BA, MA, DPhil, DSc). FGS; CGeol. Commissioned Royal Artillery 1958; active service Malaya, 1958–59; DSIR Research Student, Oxford Univ., 1962–65; British Museum (Nat. Hist.), 1965–; Dep. Keeper of Palaeontology, 1980–86. Geologist, Royal Engineers, 1970–83. President: Palaeontographical Soc., 1994–98; GA, 2004–06 (Vice-Pres., 2003–04, 2006–07); Member: Council, Palaeontological Assoc., 1969–82, 1986–88 (Editor, 1971–82, Pres., 1986–88); Council, Geological Soc., 1982–89, 1997–2000 (Sec., 1985–89; Pres., 1998–2000; Coke Medal, 1995); NERC Geological Res. Grants Cttee, 1978–81, 1984. Comr, Internat. Commn on Zoological Nomenclature, 1982–2000. Vis. Fellow, Southampton Univ., 1988–95; Vis. Prof., Imperial Coll., London, 1997–2001. Visitor, Oxford Univ. Mus. of Natural Hist., 1997–. Dumont Medal, Belgian Geol Soc., 2003. *Publications:* The Evolving Earth, 1979; (ed) Encyclopedia of Geology, 5 vols, 2005; papers in sci. jls, on Ordovician-Silurian biostratigraphy and brachiopods, esp. from Britain, Canada, Norway, Sweden, China. *Recreations:* country pursuits. *Address:* Department of Palaeontology, Natural History Museum, Cromwell Road, SW7 5BD. *T:* (020) 7942 5140; *e-mail:* r.cocks@nhm.ac.uk.

COCKS, Robin; *see* Cocks, L. R. M.

COCKSHAW, Sir Alan, Kt 1992; FREng; FICE; FIHT; Chairman: Shawbridge Management Ltd, since 1996; Cibitas Investments Ltd, since 2003; English Partnerships (formerly English Partnerships, and Commission for New Towns), 1998–2001; *b* 14 July 1937; *s* of John and Maud Cockshaw; *m* 1960, Brenda Payne; one *s* three *d*. *Educ:* Farnworth Grammar Sch.; Leeds Univ. (BSc). FIHT 1968; FICE 1985; FREng (FEng 1986). Chief Executive: Fairclough Civil Engrg, 1978–85; Fairclough Parkinson-Mining, 1982–85; Fairclough Engrg, 1983–84; Gp Chief Exec., 1984–88, Chm., 1988–97, AMEC plc; Chairman: Manchester Millennium Ltd, 1996–2003; Roxboro Gp, 1997–2005; British Airways Regl, 2000–03; New East Manchester Ltd, 2000–02; HPR Hldgs Ltd, 2003–. Non-exec. Dep. Chm., Norweb plc, 1992–95; non-executive Director: New Millennium Experience Co., 1997–2000; Pidemco Land, then CapitaLand, Singapore, 1999–2005. Chairman: Overseas Projects Bd, DTI, 1992–95; Oil and Gas Projects and Supplies Office, DTI, 1994–97; Mem., BOTB, 1992–95; Dep. Chm., NW Business Leadership Team, 1990–97. Chm., Major Projects Assoc., 1998–2004. Pres., ICE, 1997–98. Hon. DEng UMIST, 1997; Hon. DSc Salford, 1998. *Recreations:* Rugby (both codes), cricket, walking, gardening. *Address:* Century House, 11 St Peter's Square, Manchester M2 3DN. *T:* (0161) 237 3919.

COCKSHUT, Gillian Elise, (Mrs A. O. J. Cockshut); *see* Avery, G. E.

COCKSWORTH, Rt Rev. Christopher John; *see* Coventry, Bishop of.

CODD, Michael Henry, AC 1991; Chancellor, University of Wollongong, since 1997; *b* 26 Dec. 1939; *s* of Ernest Applebee Codd and Nell Gregory (*née* Pavy). *Educ:* Univ. of Adelaide (BEc Hons). Statistician, 1962–69; joined Dept of Prime Minister, Australia, 1969; Under-Sec., Dept of Prime Minister and Cabinet, 1979–81; Sec., Dept of Employment and Ind. Relns, 1981–83; Chm., Industries Assistance Commn, 1983–85; Sec., Dept of Community Services, 1985–86; Head, Dept of Prime Minister and Cabinet and Sec. to Cabinet, 1986–91. Non-executive Director: Qantas, 1992–; MLC, 1996–; Australian Nuclear Science and Technol. Orgn, 1996–2001; CitiPower, 1999–2002; Ingeus, 2003–. *Address:* 586 Williamsdale Road, Williamsdale, NSW 2620, Australia. *T:* (2) 62350160.

CODD, Ronald Geoffrey, CEng; CITP; Managing Partner, InterChange Associates, since 1990; *b* 20 Aug. 1932; *s* of Thomas Reuben Codd and Betty Leyster Codd (*née* Sturt); *m* 1960, Christine Ellen Léone Robertson; one *s* two *d*. *Educ:* Cathedral Sch., Llandaff; The College, Llandovery. FBCS; CEng 1990. Dip. in Company Direction, 1989. Served RAF, Transport Comd, 1952–57. Rolls Royce, Aero-Engine Div., 1957–58; International Computers, 1958–61; Marconi Co., 1961–70; J. Bibby & Sons, Liverpool, 1970–74; Weir Gp, Glasgow, 1974–80; Brooke Bond Gp, 1981–86; Under Sec. and Dir., Information and Risks Management, ECGD, 1986–90. Dir, Randolph Enterprise, 1992–98. Advr to Bd, HM Customs and Excise, 1992–96. Associate, Wentworth Res., 1992–. Mem., ELITE Forum, BCS, 1991–. FInstD. Freeman, City of London, 1990; Liveryman, Co. of Inf. Technologists, 1990. *Publications:* The Drowning Director, 2007; contributor to business magazines. *Recreations:* competitive and leisure sailing, theatre, practical pastimes. *Address:* The White House, Church Lane, Osmington, Dorset DT3 6EJ. *Clubs:* City Livery; Royal Dorset Yacht.

CODRINGTON, Sir Christopher (George Wayne), 4th Bt *cr* 1876, of Dodington, Gloucestershire; *b* 20 Feb. 1960; *s* of Sir Simon Codrington, 3rd Bt and of Pamela Joy Halliday Codrington (*née* Wise); *S* father, 2005; *m* 1991, Noelle Lynne, *d* of Dale Leverson; two *s* one *d*. *Educ:* Millfield; RAC Cirencester. *Heir: s* Alexander Edward Kristoffer Codrington, *b* 9 Nov. 1993. *Address:* Springfield House, Fordwells, Witney, Oxon OX29 9PP.

CODRINGTON, Sir Giles Peter, 9th Bt *cr* 1721, of Dodington, Gloucestershire; *b* 28 Oct. 1943; *s* of Sir William Richard Codrington, 7th Bt, and Joan Kathleen Birelli, *e d* of Percy E. Nicholas; *S* brother, 2006; *m* 1989, Shirley Linda Duke; two *s* one *d*.

CODRINGTON, John Ernest Fleetwood, CMG 1968; *b* 1919; *s* of late Stewart Codrington; *m* 1951, Margaret, *d* of late Sir Herbert Hall Hall, KCMG; three *d*. *Educ:* Haileybury; Trinity Coll., Cambridge. Served RNVR, 1940–42: HMS Enchantress, HMS Vanity; Royal Marines, 1942–46: 42 (RM) Commando; Colonial Administrative Service, 1946: Gold Coast (later Ghana), 1947–58; Nyasaland, 1958–64; Financial Sec., Bahamas, 1964–70; Bahamas Comr in London, 1970–73, acting High Comr, 1973–74; Financial Sec., Bermuda, 1974–77. Consultant, FCO, 1991–94. *Recreation:* sailing. *Address:* 2 Bryn Road, St Davids, Pembs SA62 6SG. *Club:* Army and Navy.

CODRINGTON, Richard John; HM Diplomatic Service; Head, Afghanistan Group, Foreign and Commonwealth Office, since 2005; *b* 18 Dec. 1953; *s* of Capt. Christopher Thomas Codrington, RN and Anna Maria (*née* Hanscomb); *m* 1985, Julia Elizabeth Nolan; two *s*. *Educ:* Ampleforth; Lincoln Coll., Oxford (BA). MoD, 1975–78; entered HM Diplomatic Service, 1978: FCO, 1978–79; 2nd, later 1st, Sec., Dar es Salaam, 1980–82; FCO, 1983–85; 1st Sec., New Delhi, 1985–88; Asst Hd, S Asian Dept, FCO, 1989–92; on loan to S. G. Warburg & Co. Ltd, 1992–94; on loan, as Hd, Cross-media ownership review team, DNH, 1994; Dir of Trade Promotion and Investment, Paris, 1995–99; Dep. High Comr, Ottawa, 1999–2003; Head, Online Communications Dept, FCO, 2003–04; RCDS, 2004. *Recreations:* photography, family history. *Address:* c/o Foreign and Commonwealth Office, SW1A 2AH.

CODRON, Michael Victor, CBE 1989; theatrical producer; *b* 8 June 1930; *s* of I. A. Codron and Lily (*née* Morgenstern). *Educ:* St Paul's Sch.; Worcester Coll., Oxford (MA). Director: Aldwych Theatre; Cameron Mackintosh Prof. of Contemporary Theatre, Oxford Univ., 1993. Emeritus Fellow, St Catherine's Coll., Oxford, 2003. Productions include: Share My Lettuce, Breath of Spring, 1957; Dock Brief and What Shall We Tell Caroline?, The Birthday Party, Valmouth, 1958; Pieces of Eight, 1959; The Wrong Side of the Park, The Caretaker, 1960; Three, Stop It Whoever You Are, One Over the Eight, The Tenth Man, Big Soft Nellie, 1961; Two Stars for Comfort, Everything in the Garden, Rattle of a Simple Man, 1962; Next Time I'll sing to You, Private Lives (revival), The Lovers and the Dwarfs, Cockade, 1963; Poor Bitos, The Formation Dancers, Entertaining Mr Sloane, 1964; Loot, The Killing of Sister George, Ride a Cock Horse, 1965; Little Malcolm and his Struggle against the Eunuchs, The Anniversary, There's a Girl in my Soup, Big Bad Mouse, 1966; The Judge, The Flip Side, Wise Child, The Boy Friend (revival), 1967; Not Now Darling, The Real Inspector Hound, 1968; The Contractor, Slag, The Two of Us, The Philanthropist, 1970; The Foursome, Butley, A Voyage Round my Father, The Changing Room, 1971; Veterans, Time and Time Again, Crown Matrimonial, My Fat Friend, 1972; Collaborators, Savages, Habeas Corpus, Absurd Person Singular, 1973; Knuckle, Flowers, Golden Pathway Annual, The Norman Conquests, John Paul George Ringo… and Bert, 1974; A Family and A Fortune, Alphabetical Order, A Far Better Husband, Ashes, Absent Friends, Otherwise Engaged, Stripwell, 1975; Funny Peculiar, Treats, Donkey's Years, Confusions, Teeth 'n' Smiles, Yahoo, 1976; Dusa, Stas, Fish & Vi, Just Between Ourselves, Oh, Mr Porter, Breezeblock Park, The Bells of Hell, The Old Country, 1977; The Rear Column, Ten Times Table, The Unvarnished Truth, The Homecoming (revival), Alice's Boys, Night and Day, 1978; Joking Apart, Tishoo, Stage Struck, 1979; Dr Faustus, Make and Break, The Dresser, Taking Steps, Enjoy, 1980; Hinge and Bracket at the Globe, Rowan Atkinson in Revue, House Guest, Quartermaine's Terms, 1981; Season's Greetings, Noises Off, Funny Turns, The Real Thing, 1982; The Hard Shoulder, 1983; Benefactors, 1984; Why Me?, Jumpers, Who Plays Wins, Look, No Hans!, 1985; Made in Bangkok, Woman in Mind, 1986; Three Sisters, A View from the Bridge, 1987; Hapgood, Uncle Vanya, Re: Joyce, The Sneeze, Henceforward, 1988; The Cherry Orchard, 1989; Man of the Moment, Look Look, Hidden Laughter, Private Lives, 1990; What the Butler Saw, 70 Girls 70, The Revengers' Comedies, 1991; The Rise and Fall of Little Voice, 1992; Time of My Life, Jamais Vu, 1993; Kit and the Widow, Dead Funny, Arcadia, The Sisters Rosensweig, 1994; Indian Ink, Dealer's Choice, 1995; The Shakespeare Revue, A Talent to Amuse, 1996; Tom and Clem, Silhouette, Heritage, 1997; Things We Do for Love, Alarms and Excursions, The Invention of Love, 1998; Copenhagen, Comic Potential, 1999; Peggy for You, 2000; Blue/Orange, 2001; Life After George, Bedroom Farce, Damsels in Distress, 2002; My Brilliant Divorce, Dinner, 2003; Democracy, 2004; Ying Tong, Losing Louis, 2005; Glorious!, 2006; Entertaining Angels, 2006; The Bargain, 2006; *film:* Clockwise, 1986. *Recreation:* collecting Caroline of Brunswick memorabilia. *Address:* Aldwych Theatre Offices, Aldwych, WC2B 4DF. *Club:* Garrick.

COE, family name of **Baron Coe**.

COE, Baron *cr* 2000 (Life Peer), of Ranmore in the co. of Surrey; **Sebastian Newbold Coe,** KBE 2006 (OBE 1990; MBE 1982); Chairman, London Organising Committee for the Olympic Games, since 2005; Global Adviser, Nike International, since 2001; *b* 29 Sept. 1956; *s* of late Peter and Angela Coe; *m* 1990, Nicola McIrvine (separated); two *s* two *d*. *Educ:* Loughborough University (BSc Hons Economics and Social History). Won gold medal for running 1500m and silver medal for 800m at Moscow Olympics, 1980; gold medal for 1500m and silver medal for 800m at Los Angeles Olympics, 1984; European Champion for 800m, Stuttgart, 1986; set world records at 800m, 1000m and mile, 1981. Research Assistant, Loughborough Univ., 1981–84. Sports Council: Mem., 1983–89; Vice-Chm., 1986–89; Chm., Olympic Review Gp, 1984–85. Member: HEA, 1987–92; Olympic Cttee, Medical Commn, 1987–93; Athletes Commn, IOC, Lausanne (first Chm., 1981–92); Olympic Cttee, Sport for All Commn, 1997–. Chm., London 2012 Olympic Bid, 2004–05 (Vice-Chm., 2003–04). Steward, BBBC, 1995–97; Chm., FIFA Ethics Cttee, 2006–. Chm., Diadora (UK), 1987–94. Sebastian Coe Health Clubs, Jarvis Hotel Group, 1994–. MP (C) Falmouth and Camborne, 1992–97; contested (C) same seat, 1997. PPS to Ministers of State for Defence Procurement and for Armed Forces, MoD, 1994–95, to Dep. Prime Minister, 1995–96; a Govt Whip, 1996–97. Dep. Chief of Staff, 1997, Private Sec., 1997–2001, to Leader of Conservative Party. Pres., AAA of England, 2000–; Founder Mem., Laureus World Sports Acad., 2000–; Vice Pres., IAAF, 2007– (Mem. Council, 2003–); Assoc. Mem., Académie des Sports, France. Sports columnist, The Daily Telegraph, 2000–. Hon. DTech Loughborough, 1985; Hon. DSc Hull, 1988. Principe de Asturias award (Spain), 1987. *Publications:* (with David Miller) Running Free, 1981; (with Peter Coe) Running for Fitness, 1983; (with Nicholas Mason) The Olympians, 1984, 2nd edn 1996. *Recreations:* listening to recorded or preferably live jazz, theatre. *Address:* House of Lords, SW1A 0PW. *Clubs:* East India, Sportsman's.

COE, Albert Henry, (Harry); Chairman: Travelsphere Holdings Ltd, 2000–06; Jaycare Holdings Ltd, 2000–04; Leisure Ventures plc, 2002–04; *b* 28 May 1944; *m* Beryl Margaret; two *d*. Supervisor, Coopers & Lybrand, 1967–70; Gp Financial Controller, Aerialite Ltd, 1970–72; Gp Finance Dir, London Scottish Bank, 1972–75; Finance Director: (print and packaging), Smurfit Ltd, 1975–81; Granada TV, 1981–88; Airtours plc: Gp Finance Dir, 1988–96; Dep. Chief Exec., 1996–97; Gp Man. Dir, 1997–99; non-exec. Dir, 1999–2001. Non-executive Director: Britannia Bldg Soc., 2000–03; Capital Ideas plc, 2004–07. *Recreations:* cricket, tennis, golf, ski-ing, stock market, current affairs. *Address:* Finvara, Wilmslow Road, Mottram St Andrew, Cheshire SK10 4QT.

COE, Denis Walter; Founder, 1987 and Executive Chairman, 1987–97, British Youth Opera; *b* 5 June 1929; *s* of James and Lily Coe, Whitley Bay, Northumberland; *m* 1953, Margaret Rae Chambers (marr. diss. 1979); three *s* one *d*; *m* 1979, Diana Rosemary, *d* of Maxwell and Flora Barr. *Educ:* Bede Trng Coll., Durham; London Sch. of Economics. Teacher's Certificate, 1952; BSc (Econ.) 1960; MSc (Econ.) 1966. National Service in RAF, 1947–50; Junior and Secondary Schoolmaster, 1952–59; Dep. Headmaster, Secondary Sch., 1959–61; Lectr in Govt, Manchester Coll. of Commerce, 1961–66. Contested (Lab) Macclesfield, 1964; MP (Lab) Middleton, Prestwich and Whitefield, 1966–70; Parly deleg. to Council of Europe and WEU, 1968–70. Dean of Students, NE London Polytechnic, 1970–74; Asst Dir, Middx Polytechnic, 1974–82; Dir of Cleveland Arts, 1986–89; Founder/Dir, Cleveland Music Fest., 1985–89. Member: Archbishops Cttee, Church and State, 1966–69; Warnock Cttee of Enquiry on Special Educational Needs, 1974–78; Planning Cttee, Arts Council, 1987–90. Vice Pres., NYT, 1989– (Mem., Governing Council, 1968–89); Founder Chm., Nat. Bureau for Handicapped Students, 1975–83. FRSA 1992; Hon. Fellow, South Bank Univ., 1993; Hon. GSM 1993; Hon. FRAM 1998. DUniv Middlesex, 1994. *Publication:* Variety Certainly Adds Spice: a memoir of my life in education, politics and the arts, 2008. *Recreations:* music, drama, walking, painting.

COE, Harry; *see* Coe, A. H.

COE, Jonathan, PhD; writer, since 1987; *b* 19 Aug. 1961; *s* of Roger and Janet Coe; *m* 1989, Janine McKeown; two *d*. *Educ:* Trinity Coll., Cambridge (BA); Warwick Univ. (MA, PhD 1986). Hon. Dr UCE, 2002. Chevalier, Ordre des Arts et des Lettres (France), 2004. *Publications:* The Accidental Woman, 1987; A Touch of Love, 1989; The Dwarves of Death, 1990; Humphrey Bogart: take it and like it, 1991; James Stewart: leading man, 1994; What a Carve Up!, 1994; The House of Sleep, 1997; The Rotters' Club, 2001 (televised 2005); Like a Fiery Elephant: the story of B. S. Johnson, 2004 (Samuel Johnson Prize, 2005); The Closed Circle, 2004; The Rain Before It Falls, 2007. *Recreations:* music, cycling. *Address:* c/o Peake Associates, 14 Grafton Crescent, NW1 8SL. *T:* (020) 7267 8033.

COE, Rosalind; QC 2008; a Recorder, since 2003; *b* Nottingham, 2 Sept. 1959; *d* of James Thompson, *qv*; *m* 1980, David Lockhart Coe; one *s* one *d*. *Educ:* Nottingham Univ. (LLB 1981); Inns of Court Sch. of Law. Called to the Bar, Middle Temple, 1983. *Recreations:* family, films, holidays. *Address:* 7 Bedford Row, WC1R 4BS. *T:* (020) 7242 3555, *Fax:* (020) 7242 2511; *e-mail:* clerks@7br.co.uk.

COEN, Prof. Enrico Sandro, CBE 2003; PhD; FRS 1998; John Innes Professor, John Innes Centre and School of Biology, University of East Anglia, since 1999; *b* 29 Sept. 1957; *s* of Ernesto Coen and Dorothea Coen (*née* Cattani); *m* 1984, Lucinda Poliakoff; two *s* one *d*. *Educ:* King's Coll., Cambridge (BA 1979; PhD Genetics 1982). SERC Postdoctoral Fellow, Cambridge, 1982–84; Res. Fellow, St John's Coll., Cambridge, 1982–85; Res. Scientist, John Innes Centre, BBSRC, 1984–99. Foreign Associate, US Nat. Acad. of Scis, 2001. EMBO Medal, Rome, 1996; Science for Art Prize, LVMH, Moët Hennessy, Paris, 1996; Linnean Medal, 1997; Darwin Medal, Royal Soc., 2004. *Publications:* papers in Nature, Cell, Science. *Recreation:* painting. *Address:* Department of Cell and Developmental Biology, John Innes Centre, Colney Lane, Norwich NR4 7UH. *T:* (01603) 450274.

COEN, Paul; Chief Executive, Local Government Association, since 2006; *b* 21 Dec. 1953; *s* of Patrick Coen and Anne Coen (*née* O'Neil); *m* 1974, Kate Knox; two *s* two *d*.

Educ: Manchester Univ. (BA Econ Hons Govt). NCB, later British Coal, 1977–89; Hertfordshire County Council, 1990–95: Dir, Commercial Services, 1990–91; Dir, Business Services, 1991–94; Dep. Chief Exec., 1995; Chief Executive: Surrey CC, 1995–2004; Essex CC, 2005–06. *Recreations:* reading, cycling, walking, cooking. *Address:* (office) Local Government House, Smith Square, SW1P 3HZ.

COEN, Yvonne Anne, (Mrs John Pini); QC 2000; a Recorder, since 2000; *d* of John and Bernadette Coen; *m* 1991, John Peter Julian Pini, *qv;* one *s* one *d. Educ:* Loreto Coll., St Albans; St Catherine's Coll., Oxford (MA Hons Jurisp.). Called to the Bar, Lincoln's Inn, 1982 (Hardwicke Schol. and Eastham Schol.), Bencher, 2008; criminal practitioner, Midland and Oxford Circuit, 1982–; an Asst Recorder, 1997–2000. Mem., Bar Council, 1987–90. *Recreation:* Stamford Shoestring Theatre. *Address:* 7 Bedford Row, WC1R 4BS. *T:* (020) 7242 3555.

COETZEE, Prof. John M.; writer; Research Fellow, University of Adelaide, since 2002; *b* 9 Feb. 1940; one *d* (one *s* decd). *Educ:* Univ. of Cape Town (MA); Univ. of Texas (PhD). FRSL 1988. Assistant Professor of English, State University of New York at Buffalo, 1968–71; Lectr in English, 1972–82, Prof. of Gen. Lit., 1983–98, Dist. Prof. of Lit., 1999–2001, Univ. of Cape Town. Butler Prof. of English, State Univ. of New York at Buffalo, 1984; Hinkley Prof. of English, Johns Hopkins Univ., 1986, 1989; Visiting Professor of English: Harvard Univ., 1991; Univ. of Texas, 1995; Dist. Service Prof. of Social Thought, Univ. of Chicago, 1996–2003. Hon. Fellow, MLA, 1989. Hon. DLitt: Strathclyde, 1985; SUNY, 1989; Cape Town, 1995; Natal, 1996; Rhodes, 1999; Oxford, 2002; La Trobe, 2004; Adelaide, 2005. Nobel Prize for Literature, 2003. Order of Mapungubwe (Gold) (S Africa), 2005. *Publications:* Dusklands, 1974; In the Heart of the Country, 1977 (CNA Literary Award, 1977; filmed as Dust, 1986); Waiting for the Barbarians, 1980 (CNA Literary Award, 1980); James Tait Black Prize, 1980; Geoffrey Faber Award, 1980); Life and Times of Michael K, 1983 (CNA Literary Award, 1983; Booker-McConnell Prize, 1983; Prix Femina Etranger, 1985); Foe, 1986 (Jerusalem Prize, 1987); (ed with André Brink) A Land Apart, 1986; White Writing, 1988; Age of Iron, 1990 (Sunday Express Award, 1990); Doubling the Point, 1992; The Master of Petersburg, 1994 (Irish Times Internat. Fiction Award, 1995); Giving Offence, 1996; Boyhood, 1997; The Lives of Animals, 1999; Disgrace, 1999 (Booker Prize, 1999); Stranger Shores, 2001; Youth, 2002; Elizabeth Costello, 2003 (Qld Premier's Literary Award, 2004); Slow Man, 2005; Inner Workings: essays, 2007; Diary of a Bad Year, 2007; essays in Comp. Lit., Jl of Mod. Lit., Linguistics, Mod. Lang. Notes, Pubns of MLA, etc. *Address:* PO Box 3045, Newton, SA 5074, Australia.

COEY, Prof. (John) Michael (David), PhD; FRS 2003; Erasmus Smith's Professor of Natural and Experimental Philosophy, since 2007, and Fellow, since 1982, Trinity College, Dublin (Professor of Experimental Physics, 1987–2007); *b* 24 Feb. 1945; *s* of David Stuart Coey and Joan Elizabeth Coey (*née* Newsam); *m* 1973, Wong May; two *s. Educ:* Jesus Coll., Cambridge (BA 1966); Univ. of Manitoba (PhD 1971). Chargé de Recherche, CNRS, Grenoble, 1971–78; Trinity College, Dublin: Lectr, 1978–84; Associate Prof., 1984–87. Visiting Scientist: IBM, Yorktown Heights, 1979; CEN Grenoble, 1985; Applied Physics Lab., Johns Hopkins, 1986; Visiting Professor: Inst. of Physics, Peking, 1980; McGill Univ., 1982; Univ. of Bordeaux, 1984; Univ. of Paris VI, 1992; UCSD, 1997; Florida State Univ., 1998; Univ. of Paris XI, 1998; Le Mans Univ., 1999, 2001, 2003. Fulbright Fellow, 1997. Founder/Dir, Magnetic Solutions Ltd, 1994–2006. Chm., Magnetism Commn, Internat. Union of Pure and Applied Physics, 2002–05. Co-ordinator, Concerted European Action on Magnets, 1985–94. MRIA 1982 (Vice-Pres., 1989–90; Gold Medal, 2005); FInstP 1984 (Charles Chree Medal and Prize, 1997). Fellow: American Mineralog. Soc., 1995; APS, 2000. Foreign Associate, Nat. Acad. of Scis, USA, 2005. Dr *hc* Inst. Nat. Poly., Grenoble, 1994. Advisory Editor: Jl of Magnetism and Magnetic Materials, 1990–; Materials Sci. and Engrg B, 1992–; Physical Rev. Letters, 1999–2005. *Publications:* (with K. Moorjani) Magnetic Glasses, 1984; Rare Earth Iron Permanent Magnets, 1996; (with R. Skomski) Permanent Magnetism, 1999; numerous articles on magnetism and electronic properties of solids in learned jls. *Recreation:* gardening. *Address:* Physics Department, Trinity College, Dublin 2, Ireland. *T:* (1) 6081470; *e-mail:* jcoey@tcd.ie.

COFFEY, Ann; see Coffey, M. A.

COFFEY, Rev. David Roy, OBE 2008; General Secretary, Baptist Union of Great Britain, 1991–2006; President, Baptist World Alliance, since 2005; *b* 13 Nov. 1941; *s* of Arthur Coffey and Elsie Maud Willis; *m* 1966, Janet Anne Dunbar; one *s* one *d. Educ:* Spurgeon's Coll., London (BA). Ordained, 1967; Minister: Whetstone Baptist Church, Leicester, 1967–72; North Cheam Baptist Ch., London, 1972–80; Sen. Minister, Upton Vale Baptist Ch, Torquay, 1980–88; Sec. for Evangelism, BUGB, 1988–91. President: BUGB, 1986–87; European Baptist Fedn, 1997–99; Vice-Pres., Baptist World Alliance, 2000–05; Free Churches Moderator and a co-Pres., Churches Together in England, 2003–07. Hon. DD: Dallas Baptist Univ., Texas, 2007; Palmer Seminary, Philadelphia, 2008. *Publications:* Build that Bridge—a Study in Conflict and Reconciliation, 1986; Discovering Romans, 2000; Joy to the World, 2008. *Recreations:* Elgar Society, Chelsea FC, grandchildren, music, walking. *Address:* 129 Broadway, Didcot, Oxon OX11 8XD. *T:* (01235) 517601.

COFFEY, John Joseph; QC 1996; a Recorder, since 1989; *b* 29 July 1948; *s* of John and Hannah Coffey; *m* 1970, Patricia Anne Long; three *s* (and one *s* decd). *Educ:* Bishop Ward Secondary Modern Sch., Dagenham; Mid-Essex Coll. of Technology (LLB Hons London). Called to the Bar, Middle Temple, 1970; Asst Recorder, 1985. *Recreation:* supporting West Ham United. *Address:* 3 Temple Gardens, Temple, EC4Y 9AU. *T:* (020) 7353 3102.

COFFEY, (Margaret) Ann; MP (Lab) Stockport, since 1992; *b* 31 Aug. 1946; *d* of late John Brown, MBE, and of Marie Brown; *m* 1973 (marr. diss. 1989); one *d. Educ:* Poly. of South Bank (BSc); Manchester Univ. (MSc). Trainee Social Worker, Walsall Social Services Dept, 1971–72; Social Worker: Birmingham, 1972–73; Gwynedd, 1973–74; Wolverhampton, 1974–75; Stockport, 1977–82; Cheshire, 1982–88; Team Leader, Fostering, Oldham Social Services Dept, 1988–92. Mem. (Lab) Stockport MBC, 1984–92 (Leader, Labour Group, 1988–92). Contested (Lab) Cheadle, 1987. An Opposition Whip, 1995–96; Opposition spokeswoman on health, 1996–97; PPS to Prime Minister, 1997–98, to Sec. of State for Work and Pensions, 1998–2001, to Sec. of State for Transport, 2001–05, to Sec. of State for Trade and Industry, 2005–07, to Chancellor of the Exchequer, 2007–. Mem., Trade and Industry Select Cttee, 1993–95. *Address:* House of Commons, SW1A 0AA.

COFFIN, Rt Rev. Peter Robert; Bishop of Ottawa, 1999–2007; Bishop Ordinary (Anglican) to Canadian Forces, since 2004; *b* 31 May 1946; *s* of Gerald R. A. Coffin and Jean Mary Thorburn Coffin (*née* Edwards); *m* 1972, Deborah Creighton; one *d. Educ:* Univ. of King's Coll., Halifax, NS (BA); Trinity Coll., Toronto (STB); Carleton Univ., Ottawa (MA Internat. Affairs). Ordained deacon, 1971, priest 1971; Asst Curate, St Matthew's, Ottawa, 1971–73; Lectr, House of the Epiphany, Kuching, Sarawak, E Malaysia, 1973–76; Incumbent, Parish of Hull, Quebec, 1976–84; Archdeacon of W Quebec, 1978–84; Incumbent, Christ Church, Bell's Corners, Ottawa (Nepean), 1984–90; Archdeacon of Carleton, 1986–90; Rector of Christ Church Cathedral, Ottawa and Dean of Ottawa, 1990–99. Hon. DD: Trinity Coll., Toronto, 1997; Univ. of King's Coll., Halifax, NS, 1998. *Address:* 42 Bridle Park Drive, Kanata, Ottawa, ON K2M 2E2, Canada.

COGBILL, Vivienne Margaret; *see* Dews, V. M.

COGDELL, Prof. Richard John, PhD; FRS 2007; FRSE; Hooker Professor of Botany, University of Glasgow, since 1989; *b* 4 Feb. 1949; *s* of Harry William Frank Cogdell and Evelyn Cogdell; *m* 1970, Barbara Lippold; one *s* one *d. Educ:* Royal Grammar Sch., Guildford; Univ. of Bristol (BSc Hons Biochem. 1970; PhD Biochem. 1973). Postdoctoral res., Cornell Univ., Ithaca, and Univ. of Washington, Seattle, 1973–75; Lectr, Dept of Botany, Univ. of Glasgow, 1975–89. Visiting Professor: UCLA, 1979; Univ. of Paris-Sud, 2004; Adjunct Prof., Chinese Nat. Acad. of Scis Inst. of Biophysics, Beijing, 2005–07. FRSE 1991. Alexander von Humboldt Res. Prize, 1995; Daiwa-Adrian Prize for Anglo-Japanese Res., 2002. *Publications:* over 250 scientific papers in learned jls. *Recreations:* playing cricket, going to opera and theatre, Scottish country dancing. *Address:* 152 Hyndland Road, Glasgow G12 9PN. *T:* (0141) 330 4232, *Fax:* (0141) 330 4620; *e-mail:* R.Cogdell@bio.gla.ac.uk.

COGGINS, Prof. John Richard, OBE 2008; PhD; FRSE; Professor of Molecular Enzymology, since 1995, and Vice-Principal, Life Sciences, Medicine and Veterinary Medicine, since 2006, University of Glasgow; *b* 15 Jan. 1944; *s* of Cecil Rex Coggins and Pamela Mary Coggins (*née* Burnet); *m* 1970, Lesley Frances Watson; one *s* one *d. Educ:* Bristol GS; Queen's Coll., Oxford (MA); Univ. of Ottawa (PhD). FRSE 1988. Research Fellow: Brookhaven Nat. Lab., USA, 1970–72; Cambridge Univ., 1972–74; Glasgow University: Lectr, 1974–78; Sen. Lectr, 1978–86; Prof. of Biochemistry, 1986–95; Dir, Grad. Sch. of Biomedical and Life Scis, 1995–97; Hd, Div. of Biochemistry and Molecular Biology, 1997–98; Res. Dir, 1998–2000, Dir and Dean, 2000–05, Inst. of Biomed. and Life Scis; Chm., Hds of Univ. Biol Sci. Depts, 2003–07. Chm., Biochem. and Biophys. Cttee, 1985–88, Mem., Biotechnol. Directorate Management Cttee, 1987–90, SERC; Member: Liby and Inf. Services Cttee, Scotland, 1982–88; Biotechnol. Jt Adv. Bd, 1989–94; Wkg Party on Biotechnol., NEDO, 1990–92; AFRC, 1991–94; Council, Hannah Res. Inst., 1994–2005; Scottish Sci. Adv. Cttee, 2002–07; BBSRC, 2008–; Governing Mem., 1994–2007, Chm., 2007–, Caledonian Res. Foundn; Advr for Biochem., UFC, 1989–92; Chm., HEFCE RAE Panel for Biochemistry, 1995–96; Vice-Pres. (Life Scis), RSE, 2003–06 (Res. Awards Convener, 1999–2002). Chm., Molecular Enzymol. Gp, 1981–85, Chem. Policy Cttee, 2004–08, Biochemical Soc. Trustee, Glasgow Sci. Centre, 2004–. Mem. Adv. Bd, Research Inf. Network, 2005–. *Publications:* Multidomain Proteins: structure and evolution, 1986; contribs on enzymes and on plant and microbial biochem. to Biochem. Jl, Jl of Biol Chem., Jl Molecular Biol., etc. *Recreations:* sailing, travel, good food, reading. *Address:* University of Glasgow, 11 The Square, Glasgow G12 8QQ. *T:* (0141) 330 8137. *Club:* New (Edinburgh).

COGGON, Prof. David Noel Murray, OBE 2002; PhD; DM; FRCP, FFOM, FFPH, FMedSci; Professor of Occupational and Environmental Medicine, MRC Epidemiology Resource Centre (formerly Environmental Epidemiology Unit), University of Southampton, since 1997; *b* 25 Dec. 1950; *s* of Frederick and Annette Coggon; *m* 1976, Sarah (*née* Cole); one *s* four *d. Educ:* New Coll., Oxford (BM BCh 1976; DM 1993); Clare Coll., Cambridge (MA 1976); Univ. of Southampton (PhD 1984). MRCP 1978, FRCP 1992; FFOM 1993; FFPH 2005. Clinical Scientist, MRC Envmtl Epidemiol. Unit, Univ. of Southampton, 1980–97. Chairman: Depleted Uranium Oversight Bd, 2001–07; Mobile Telecommns and Health Res. Prog. Mgt Cttee, 2008–; Member: Industrial Injuries Adv. Council, 1988–2003; Adv. Cttee on Pesticides, 1997–2000 (Chm., 2000–05); Ind. Expert Gp on Mobile Phones, 1999–2000; Adv. Gp on Non-ionising Radiation, 2001–; Plant Protection Products and Residues Panel, Europ. Food Safety Authy, 2006–; Cttee on Toxicity of Chemicals in Food, Consumer Products and the Envmt, 2007–. Pres., Faculty of Occupational Medicines, RCP, 2008–. FMedSci 1998. *Publications:* Statistics in Clinical Practice, 1995, 2nd edn 2002; (jtly) Epidemiology for the Uninitiated, 3rd edn 1993 to 5th edn 2003. *Recreations:* rambling, gardening, cabinet making, choral singing. *Address:* MRC Epidemiology Resource Centre, Southampton General Hospital, Southampton SO16 6YD. *T:* (023) 8077 7624, *Fax:* (023) 8070 4021; *e-mail:* dnc@mrc.soton.ac.uk.

COGHILL, Sir Patrick Kendal Farley, 9th Bt *cr* 1778, of Coghill, Yorkshire; *b* 3 Nov. 1960; *o s* of Sir Toby Coghill, 8th Bt; *S* father, 2000. *Heir: cousin* John Kendal Plunket Coghill, OBE [*b* 17 July 1929; *m* 1951, Diana Mary Callen; three *d*].

COGHLAN, Terence Augustine; QC 1993; a Recorder, since 1989; *b* 17 Aug. 1945; *s* of late Austin Frances Coghlan and of Ruby Coghlan (*née* Comrie); *m* 1973, Angela Agatha Westmacott; one *s* two *d. Educ:* Downside; Perugia; New Coll., Oxford; Inns of Court. Called to the Bar, Inner Temple, 1968 (Scholar; Bencher, 2004). Pres., Mental Health Review Tribunal, 2000–. Film extra, 1968; Director: City of London Sinfonia, 1975–; Temple Music Foundn, 2004–. Chm., St Endellion Fests Trust, 2007–. *Publications:* Meningitis, 1998; medico-legal articles. *Recreations:* wandering around buildings with Pevsner, wine, walking, cycling, singing in choirs. *Address:* 1 Crown Office Row, Temple, EC4Y 7HH. *T:* (020) 7797 7500. *Clubs:* Omar Khayyam, Les Six, MCC.

COGHLIN, Hon. Sir Patrick, Kt 1997; **Hon. Mr Justice Coghlin;** a Judge of the High Court of Justice, Northern Ireland, since 1997; President, Lands Tribunal, Northern Ireland, since 1999; *b* 7 Nov. 1945; *s* of late James Edwin Coghlin and Margaret Van Hovenberg Coghlin; *m* 1971, Patricia Ann Elizabeth Young; one *s* three *d. Educ:* Royal Belfast Academical Instn; Queen's Univ., Belfast (LLB Hons); Christ's Coll., Cambridge (Dip. Criminology). Called to the Bar: NI, 1970; Gray's Inn, 1975 (Hon. Bencher 2000); NSW, 1992; Republic of Ireland, 1995; Jun. Crown Counsel for NI, 1983–85; QC (NI) 1985; Dep. County Court Judge, 1983–94; Sen. Crown Counsel, NI, 1993–97. Vice-Chm., Mental Health Review Tribunal, 1987–97; Mem., Law Reform Adv. Cttee, NI, 1988–93; Vice-Pres., VAT Tribunal, NI, 1990–93; Dep. Chm., Boundary Commn, NI, 1999–2002. Chm., NI Bar Council, 1991–93. *Recreations:* Rugby, soccer, squash, reading, music, travel. *Address:* Royal Courts of Justice, Belfast, N Ireland BT1 3JY. *Clubs:* Royal Ulster Yacht, Ballyholme Yacht; Bangor Rugby, Perennials Rugby; Ballyholme Bombers FC.

COHAN, Robert Paul, CBE 1989; Founder Artistic Director, Contemporary Dance Trust; *b* 27 March 1925; *s* of Walter and Billie Cohan; British citizen, 1989. *Educ:* Martha Graham Sch., NYC. Joined Martha Graham Co., 1946; Partner, 1950; Co-Dir, Martha Graham Co., 1966; Artistic Dir, Contemporary Dance Trust Ltd, 1967; Artistic Dir and Principal Choreographer, 1969–87, Dir, 1987–89, London Contemporary Dance Theatre; Artistic Advr, Batsheva Co., Israel, 1980–90; Director: York Univ., Toronto Choreographic Summer Sch., 1977; Gulbenkian Choreographic Summer Sch., Univ. of Surrey, 1978, 1979, 1982; Banff Sch. of Fine Arts Choreographic Seminar, Canada, 1980;

New Zealand Choreographic Seminar, 1982; Choreographic Seminar, Simon Fraser Univ., Vancouver, 1985; Internat. Dance Course for Professional Choreographers and Composers, Surrey Univ., 1985, 1989. With London Contemporary Dance Theatre toured Britain, E and W Europe, S America, N Africa and USA; major works created: Cell, 1969 (recorded for BBC TV, 1982); Stages, 1971; Waterless Method of Swimming Instruction, 1974 (recorded for BBC TV); Class, 1975; Stabat Mater, 1975 (recorded for BBC TV); Masque of Separation, 1975; Khamsin, 1976; Nympheas, 1976 (recorded for BBC TV, 1983); Forest, 1977 (recorded for BBC TV); Eos, 1978; Songs, Lamentations and Praises, 1979; Dances of Love and Death, 1981; Agora, 1984; A Mass for Man, 1985 (recorded for BBC TV); Ceremony, 1986; Interrogations, 1986; Video Life, 1986; Phantasmagoria, 1987; A Midsummer Night's Dream, 1993; The Four Seasons, 1996; Aladdin, 2000. Editor, Choreography and Dance, 1988–2000. Hon. Fellow, York Univ., Toronto. Hon. DLitt: Exeter, 1993; Kent, 1996; DUniv: Middlesex, 1994; Winchester, 2006. Evening Standard Award for most outstanding achievement in ballet, 1975; Soc. of West End Theatres Award for most outstanding achievement in ballet, 1978; UK Dance Critics' Circle Cttee Award for Lifetime Achievement, 2005. *Publication:* The Dance Workshop, 1986. *Recreation:* dancing. *Address:* The Place, 17 Dukes Road, WC1H 9AB. *T:* (020) 7387 0161.

COHEN; *see* Waley-Cohen.

COHEN, family name of **Baroness Cohen of Pimlico**.

COHEN OF PIMLICO, Baroness *cr* 2000 (Life Peer), of Pimlico in the City of Westminster; **Janet Cohen;** Director: London Stock Exchange, since 2001; MCG plc, since 2003; Chairman: InviseoMedia Holdings Ltd, since 2007; Trillium Holdings, since 2008; *b* 4 July 1940; *d* of late George Edric Neel and Mary Isabel Neel (*née* Budge); *m* 1971, James Lionel Cohen; two *s* one *d*. *Educ:* Newnham Coll., Cambridge (BA Hons Law 1962; Associate Fellow, 1988–91). Articled clerk, Frere Cholmeley, 1963–65; admitted solicitor, 1965; Consultant: ABT Associates, USA, 1965–67; John Laing Construction, 1968–69; Department of Trade and Industry: Principal, 1969–78; Asst Sec., 1978–82; Asst Dir, 1982–88, Dir, 1988–2000, Charterhouse Bank Ltd. Chm., Café Pelican Ltd, 1984–90; Vice Chm., Yorks Building Soc., 1994–99 (Dir, 1991–94); non-executive Director: Waddington plc (formerly John Waddington), 1994–97; London & Manchester Gp plc, 1997–98; United Assce Gp, 1998–99; BPP Hldgs, 1994–2006 (Chm., 2002–06). Mem., Schools Exam. and Assessment Council, 1990–93. Mem. Bd, Sheffield Develt Corp., 1993–97. Pres., BPP Coll. of Professional Studies, 2008–. A Governor, BBC, 1994–99. Mem., EU Scrutiny Cttee, H of L, 2006– (Chm., Sub Cttee A). Chairman: Parlt Choir, 2006–08; Cambridge Arts Th., 2007–. Hon. Fellow: St Edmund's Coll., Cambridge, 2000; Lucy Cavendish Coll., Cambridge, 2007. Hon. DLitt Humberside, 1995. *Publications:* as Janet Neel: Death's Bright Angel, 1988; Death on Site, 1989; Death of a Partner, 1991; Death among the Dons, 1993; A Timely Death, 1996; To Die For, 1998; O Gentle Death, 2000; Ticket to Ride, 2005; as Janet Cohen: The Highest Bidder, 1992; Children of a Harsh Winter, 1994. *Recreations:* hill walking, singing.

COHEN, Prof. Anthony Paul, CBE 2008; PhD; FRSE; Principal and Vice-Chancellor, Queen Margaret University (formerly Queen Margaret University College), since 2003; *b* 3 Aug. 1946; *s* of Mark Cohen and Mary Cohen (*née* Nissenbaum); *m* 1968, Dr Bronwen J. Steel, OBE; three *s*. *Educ:* Univ. of Southampton (BA Hons; MSc Social Sci; PhD 1973). Res. Fellow, Meml Univ. of Newfoundland, 1968–70; Asst Prof., Queen's Univ. at Kingston, Ont., 1970–71; Lectr, then Sen. Lectr in Social Anthropol., Univ. of Manchester, 1971–89; University of Edinburgh: Prof. of Social Anthropol., 1989–2003; Provost of Law and Social Scis, and Dean of Social Scis, 1997–2002; Hon. Prof. of Social Anthropol., 2003–. FRSE 1995. Hon. DSc Edinburgh, 2005. *Publications:* The Management of Myths: the politics of legitimation in a Newfoundland community, 1975; (ed) Belonging: identity and social organisation in British rural cultures, 1982; The Symbolic Construction of Community (CHOICE Award for Outstanding Book of the Year), 1985 (trans. Turkish and Japanese); (ed) Symbolising Boundaries: identity and diversity in British cultures, 1982; Whalsay: symbol, segment and boundary in a Shetland Island community, 1987; (ed with K. Fukui) Humanising the City?: social contexts of urban life at the turn of the Millennium, 1993 (trans. Japanese); (jtly) Villages Anglais, Ecossaises, Irlandaises, 1993; Self Consciousness: an alternative anthropology of identity, 1994 (trans. Danish); (ed with N. J. Rapport) Questions of Consciousness, 1995; (ed) Signifying Identities: anthropological perspectives on boundaries and contested values, 2000; papers and chapters in books. *Recreations:* music, reading, occasional thinking. *Address:* Queen Margaret University, Musselburgh EH21 6UU. *T:* (0131) 474 0000. *Club:* New (Edinburgh).

COHEN, Prof. Bernard Woolf; Slade Professor, and Chair of Fine Art, University of London, 1988–2000, now Emeritus Slade Professor; *b* 28 July 1933; *s* of Victor and Leah Cohen; *m* 1959, Jean Britton; one *s* one *d*. *Educ:* Slade School of Fine Art, University Coll. London (Dip. Fine Art). Head of Painting, Wimbledon Sch. of Art, 1980–87. Vis. Prof., Univ. of New Mexico, USA, 1969–70. Fellow: UCL, 1992; Kent Inst. of Art and Design, 1998. First one man exhibn, Gimpel Fils Gall., 1958, again in 1960; other exhibitions: Molton Gall., 1962; Kasmin Gall., Bond Street, 1963, 1964, 1967; Waddington Gall., 1974, 1977, 1979, 1990; First New York exhibn, Betty Parsons Gall., 1967; major retrospective, Hayward Gall., 1972; print retrospective, Tate Gall., 1976; drawing retrospective, Ben Uri Gall., 1994; paintings, Tate Gall., 1995; paintings of the 90s, Flowers East Gall., London, 1998, Flowers West Gall., Santa Monica, 1999; Flowers Central, London, 2001, 2004; paintings, Flowers Gall., NY, 2006; paintings from the 60s, Flowers East Gall., 2007; represented GB at Venice Biennale, 1966. Work in collections of Tate Gall., Mus. of Modern Art, New York; Fogg Mus., Mass; Minneapolis Walker Art Centre; Carnegie Inst., Pittsburgh, and others. *Recreations:* travel, music. *Address:* 80 Camberwell Grove, SE5 8RF.

COHEN, Betty; *see* Jackson, B.

COHEN, Ven. Clive Ronald Franklin; Archdeacon of Bodmin, since 2000; *b* 30 Jan. 1946; *s* of Ronald Arthur Wilfred Cohen, MBE, and Janet Ruth Lindsay Cohen (*née* Macdonald); *m* 1969, (Elizabeth) June Kingsley Kefford; three *s* one *d* (and one *s* decd). *Educ:* Salisbury and Wells Theol Coll. ACIB 1971. Asst Master, Edinburgh House Sch., 1965–67; Midland Bank plc, 1967–79; ordained deacon, 1981, priest, 1982; Asst Curate, Esher, Surrey, 1981–85; Rector, Winterslow, Wilts, 1985–2000; Rural Dean, Alderbury, Wilts, 1989–93; Non-Residentiary Canon and Prebendary, Salisbury Cathedral, 1992–2000. *Publications:* Crying in the Wilderness, 1994; So Great a Cloud, 1995. *Recreation:* local history. *Address:* Archdeacon's House, Cardinham, Bodmin, Cornwall PL30 4BL. *T:* (01208) 821614.

COHEN, Daniel; Controller, BBC Three, since 2007; *b* London, 15 Jan. 1974; *s* of Ernie and Rosalind Cohen; partner, Dr Noreena Hertz. *Educ:* City of London Sch.; Lady Margaret Hall, Oxford (BA Hons Double First English Lit.). Channel 4: Commissioning Ed., Documentaries, 2001–04; Head of Documentaries, 2004–06; Head of Factual Entertainment and of E4, 2006–07. *Recreations:* football, cricket, English literature, TV and new media, pickle, current affairs, meditation, giraffes, contemporary art. *Address:* c/o BBC Three, BBC TV Centre, Wood Lane, W12 7RJ; *e-mail:* danny.cohen@bbc.co.uk. *Club:* Groucho.

COHEN, Sir Edward, Kt 1970; company director; solicitor; *b* 9 Nov. 1912; *s* of Brig. Hon. H. E. Cohen; *m* 1939, Meryl D., *d* of D. G. Fink; one *s*. *Educ:* Scotch Coll., Melbourne (Exhibnr in Greek and Roman History); Ormond Coll., Univ. of Melbourne (LLB; Aust. Blue Athletics, Hockey). Served, 1940–45: AIF, 2/12 Fd Regt, 9th Div. Artillery, Captain 1942. Partner, Pavey, Wilson, Cohen & Carter, 1945–76, then, following amalgamation, Consultant, Corrs Chambers Westgarth, solicitors, Melbourne, 1976–98; Director: Carlton and United Breweries, 1947–84 (Chm., 1967–84); Swan Brewery, 1947–57; Associated Pulp & Paper Mills Ltd, 1951–83 (Dep. Chm. 1981–83); Electrolytic Zinc Co., A'asia, 1951–84 (Chm., 1960–84); Glazebrooks Paints and Chemicals Ltd, 1951–61; Standard Mutual Bldg Soc., 1951–64; E. Z. Industries, 1956–84 (Chm., 1960–84, Pres., 1984–); Pelaco Ltd, 1959–68; Commercial Union Assurance, 1960–82 (Chm., 1964–82); Union Assce Soc. of Aust., 1960–75 (Local Advisor, 1951–60); Michaelis Bayley Ltd, 1964–80; Qld Brewery (later CUB Qld), 1968–84; Herald and Weekly Times Ltd, 1974–77 (Vice-Chm., 1976–77); Chairman: Derwent Metals, 1957–84; CUB Fibre Containers, 1963–84; Emu Bay Railway Co., 1967–84; Manufrs Bottle Co., Vic, 1967–84; Northern Aust. Breweries (CUB (N Qld)), 1967–84; Nat. Commercial Union, 1982–84. Past Member: Faculty of Law of Melbourne Univ.; Internat. Hse Council, Melbourne Univ.; Council of Legal Education and Bd of Examiners. Mem. Council Law Inst. of Victoria, 1959–68, Pres. 1965–66. Chairman: Pensions Cttee, Melbourne Legacy, 1961–84 (Mem., 1955–84); Royal Women's Hosp. 1968 Million Dollar Bldg Appeal; Eileen Patricia Goulding Meml Fund Appeal, 1983; Life Governor: Austin, Prince Henry's, Royal Children's, Royal Melbourne, Royal Women's Hosps; Corps of Commissionaires; Adult Deaf and Dumb Soc. of Victoria. Hon. Solicitor, Queens Fund, 1951–94. Twelfth Leonard Ball Orator, Victorian Foundn on Alcoholism and Drug Dependence, 1980. *Address:* 722 Orrong Road, Toorak, Victoria 3142, Australia. *Clubs:* Naval and Military, Victoria Racing, Royal Automobile, Melbourne Cricket, Kooyong Lawn Tennis (Melbourne).

COHEN, Gabrielle Ann; an Assistant Auditor General, National Audit Office, since 2005; *b* 25 May 1961; *d* of David Michael Cowell and Gloria Ethel Cowell; three *s*. *Educ:* Univ. of Kent (BA Hons Hist. and Pols). CPFA. National Audit Office, 1987–: Head of Press Office, 1996–2000; Dir, Communications and Corporate Affairs, 2000–05. *Recreations:* current affairs, reading, theatre, cinema, football. *Address:* National Audit Office, 197 Buckingham Palace Road, SW1W 9SP. *T:* (020) 7798 7782; *e-mail:* Gabrielle.Cohen@nao.gsi.gov.uk.

COHEN, Prof. Gerald Allan, FBA 1985; Chichele Professor of Social and Political Theory, Oxford University, 1985–2008, now Professor Emeritus; Fellow of All Souls College, Oxford, 1985–2008; *b* 14 April 1941; *s* of Morrie Cohen and Bella Lipkin; *m* 1st, 1965, Margaret Florence Pearce (marr. diss. 1996); one *s* two *d*; 2nd, 1999, Michèle Jacottet. *Educ:* Morris Winchevsky Jewish School, Montreal; Strathcona Academy, Montreal; Outremont High School, Montreal; McGill University (BA 1961); New College, Oxford (BPhil 1963). Lectr in Philosophy, University College London, 1963, Reader, 1978–84. Vis. Asst Prof. of Political Science, McGill Univ., 1965; Vis. Associate Prof. of Philosophy, Princeton Univ., 1975; Vis. Prof., McGill Univ., 2000–. *Publications:* Karl Marx's Theory of History: a defence, 1978, expanded edn 2000; History, Labour and Freedom: themes from Marx, 1988; Self-ownership, Freedom and Equality, 1995; If You're An Egalitarian, How Come You're So Rich?, 2000; articles in anthologies, philosophical and social-scientific jls. *Recreations:* Guardian crosswords, the visual arts, patience, travel. *Address:* All Souls College, Oxford OX1 4AL. *T:* (01865) 279379.

COHEN, Harry Michael; MP (Lab) Leyton and Wanstead, since 1997 (Leyton, 1983–97); accountant; *b* 10 Dec. 1949; *m* 1978, Ellen Hussain; one step *s* one step *d*. Mem., Waltham Forest Borough Council, 1972–83 (formerly Chm., Planning Cttee and Sec., Labour Group). Mem., Select Cttee on Defence, 1997–2001; Sec., All-Party Parly Gp on Race and Community. Mem., N Atlantic Assembly, 1992– (Rapporteur; Chm. sub-cttee for Economic Co-operation and Convergence with Central & Eastern Europe, 1996–2000). Mem., UNISON. Vice Pres., Royal Coll. of Midwives. *Address:* House of Commons, SW1A 0AA.

COHEN, Sir Ivor (Harold), Kt 1992; CBE 1985; TD 1968; Chairman: Remploy Ltd, 1987–93; Japan Electronics Business Association, 1991–2002; *b* 28 April 1931; *s* of Jack Cohen and Anne (*née* Victor); *m* 1963, Betty Edith, *yr d* of Reginald George and Mabel Appleby; one *d*. *Educ:* Central Foundation Sch., EC2; University Coll. London (BA (Hons) Mod. Hist.; Fellow, 1987). Nat. Service, Royal Signals, 1952–54 (2nd Lieut); TA, Royal Signals, 1954–69 (Major 1964). Engrg industry, 1954–57; range of managerial posts, Mullard Ltd (subsid. of Philips (UK)), 1957–77; Dir, Philips Lighting, 1977–79; Man. Dir, Mullard Ltd, 1979–87; Dir, Philips Electronics (UK) Ltd, 1984–87. Non-executive Director: AB Electronic Products Gp plc, 1987–93; Océ (UK) Ltd, 1988–2001; PA Holdings Ltd, 1989–2001; Redifon Holdings Ltd, 1989–94; Magnetic Materials Gp plc, 1992; Electron Technologies Ltd, 1994–97; Deltron Electronics, 1995–2003; Russell Partnership Ltd, 1996–97; Chairman: Optima Group Ltd, 1995–96; Sira Ltd, 1998–2001; Cons., Comet Gp plc, 1987–90; Advr, Apax & Co. Ventures (formerly Alan Patricof Associates), 1987–93; Mem., Adv. Cttee, Mitsubishi Electric Europe BV (formerly Mitsubishi Electric (UK) Ltd), 1991–2002. Member: IT Adv. Panel, 1981–86; Teletext and Viewdata Steering Gp, DTI, 1981–86; Electronic Components EDC, NEDO, 1980–88; Electronics Ind. EDC, NEDO, 1982–86; Steering Cttee, Telecom. Infrastructure, DTI, 1987–88; Computing Software and Communications Requirements Bd, DTI, 1984–88; Steering Bd, Radiocommunications Agency, DTI, 1990–95; Electronics Ind. Sector Gp, NEDO, 1988–92 (Chm., 1990–92); Chairman: Electronic Applications Sector Gp, NEDO, 1988–90; Measurement Adv. Cttee, DTI, 1994–97; Member Council: Electronic Components Ind. Fedn, 1980–87; European Electronic Components Assoc., 1985–87; Dir, Radio Industries Council, 1980–87. Mem., Schs Examinations and Assessment Council, 1988–90; British Schools Technology: Mem. Council of Management, 1984–87, Trustee Dir, 1987–89; Mem., Management Adv. Gp IT Res. Inst., Brighton Poly., 1987–90. FIET (CompIEE 1988); CompInstMC 1997; Hon. Mem. CGLI, 1989; FInstD 1988–2003; FRSA 1984; Hon. FREng (Hon. FEng 1992). Freeman, City of London, 1982; Liveryman, Sci. Instrument Makers' Co., 1982– (Master, 1997). Hon. DSc City, 1998. Mem., Editl Bd, Nat. Electronics Review, 1987–90. *Publications:* articles on electronics policy and marketing and use of inf. technology in the technical press. *Recreations:* opera, reading, occasional sculpting, walking in towns, video film making. *Address:* 24 Selborne Road, Croydon, Surrey CR0 5JQ. *Clubs:* East India, Reform.

COHEN, Janet; *see* Baroness Cohen of Pimlico.

COHEN, Prof. Jonathan, FRCP, FRCPath; FMedSci; Dean, Brighton and Sussex Medical School, University of Sussex, since 2002; *b* 11 Oct. 1949; *s* of Norman and Ruth Cohen; *m* 1973, Noëmi Weingarten; one *s* one *d*. *Educ:* William Ellis Grammar Sch.,

London; Charing Cross Hosp. Med. Sch. (MB, BS). FRCP 1987; FRCPath 1992. Jun. trng appts at Whittington Hosp., LSHTM, and Duke Univ. Med. Center, NC, USA, 1975–85; Wellcome Sen. Lectr in Infectious Diseases, RPMS, 1985–92; Prof. and Hd of Dept of Infectious Diseases, RPMS, later Imperial Coll., London, 1992–2002. Member: Jt Commn on Vaccination and Immunisation, 2000–05; Nat. Expert Panel on New and Emerging Infections, 2004–07. Member: SE England Sci. and Technol. Adv. Council, 2003–08; Infections and Immunity Bd, MRC, 2004–07; Council, Internat. Soc. Infectious Diseases, 2006–. Academy of Medical Sciences: Fellow, 2000; Mem. Council, 2002–05. Chair, Clin. Trials Adv. and Awards Cttee, CRUK, 2006–. Member Editorial Board: Lancet Infectious Diseases, 2000–; PLoS Medicine, 2004–; Ed.-in-Chief, Internat. Jl Infectious Diseases, 2001–06. *Publications:* (ed jtly) Infectious Diseases, 1999, 2nd edn 2004; contrib. scientific papers on infection, immunity and sepsis. *Recreations:* family, photography, ski-ing, pipe-smoking. *Address:* Brighton and Sussex Medical School, University of Sussex, Falmer, Sussex BN1 9PX. *T:* (01273) 877577; *e-mail:* j.cohen@bsms.ac.uk.

COHEN, Jonathan Lionel; QC 1997; a Recorder, since 1997; a Deputy High Court Judge (Family Division), since 2005; *b* 8 May 1951; *s* of late Hon. Leonard Harold Lionel Cohen, OBE and of Eleanor Lucy Quixano Cohen (*née* Henriques); *m* 1983, Bryony Frances Carfrae; two *s* one *d. Educ:* Eton Coll.; Univ. of Kent at Canterbury (BA Hons). Called to the Bar, Lincoln's Inn, 1974, Bencher, 2004; SE Circuit. Mem., Mental Health Review Tribunal, 2000–. Liveryman, Skinners' Co., 1978– (Master, 2005–06). Governor: Skinners' Co.'s Sch. for Girls, Hackney, 1994–2002; Judd Sch., Tonbridge, 2002–06; Tonbridge Sch., 2006– (Chm., 2007–); Mem., Develt Bd, LAMDA, 2004–07. *Address:* 4 Paper Buildings, Temple, EC4Y 7EX.

COHEN, Leonard, CC 2002 (OC 1991); writer and composer; *b* Montreal, 21 Sept. 1934. *Educ:* McGill Univ. Composer and singer: Songs of Leonard Cohen, 1967; Songs from a Room, 1969; Songs of Love and Hate, 1971; Live Songs, 1972; New Skin for the Old Ceremony, 1973; The Best of Leonard Cohen, 1975; Death of a Ladies' Man, 1977; Recent Songs, 1979; Various Positions, 1985; I'm Your Man, 1987; The Future, 1992; Cohen Live, 1994; More Best Of, 1997; Field Commander Cohen: tour of 1979, 2001; Ten New Songs, 2001; The Essential Leonard Cohen, 2002; Dear Heather, 2004; Blue Alert, 2006; composer, lyrics, for Night Magic, the musical, 1985. *Publications: poetry:* Let us Compare Mythologies, 1956; The Spice Box of Earth, 1961; Flowers for Hitler, 1964; Parasites of Heaven, 1966; Selected Poems 1965–68, 1968; The Energy of Slaves, 1972; Stranger Music: selected poems and songs, 1993; The Book of Longing, 2006; *novels:* The Favourite Game, 1963; Beautiful Losers, 1966; Death of a Lady's Man, 1978; Book of Mercy, 1984. *Address:* c/o S. L. Feldman & Associates, 200–1505 West 2nd Avenue, Vancouver, BC V6H 3Y4, Canada.

COHEN, Lt-Col Mordaunt, TD 1954; DL; Regional Chairman of Industrial Tribunals, 1976–89 (Chairman, 1974–76); *b* 6 Aug. 1916; *s* of Israel Ellis Cohen and Sophie Cohen; *m* 1953, Myrella Cohen (Her Honour Myrella Cohen, QC) (*d* 2002); one *s* one *d. Educ:* Bede Collegiate Sch. for Boys, Sunderland. Admitted solicitor, 1938. Served War, RA, 1940–46: seconded RWAFF; despatches, Burma campaign; served TA, 1947–55: CO 463(M) HAA Regt, RA(TA), 1954–55. Alderman, Sunderland Co. Bor. Council, 1967–74; Chm., Sunderland Educn Cttee, 1970–72; Chm., NE Council of Educn Cttees, 1971; Councillor, Tyne and Wear CC, 1973–74; Dep. Chm., Northern Traffic Comrs, 1973–74. Chm., Mental Health Review Tribunal, 1967–76. Chm. of Governors, Sunderland Polytechnic, 1969–72; Mem. Court, Univ. of Newcastle upon Tyne, 1968–72. Pres., Sunderland Law Soc., 1970; Hon. Life Pres., Sunderland Hebrew Congregation, 1988; Mem., Bd of Deputies of British Jews, 1964–2006 (Chm., Provincial Cttee, 1985–91; Dir, Central Enquiry Desk, 1990–2000); former Mem., Chief Rabbinate Council; Vice Pres., AJEX, 1995– (Chm., 1993–95); Life Pres., Sunderland Br., AJEX, 1970; Trustee: AJEX Charitable Trust, 1978–; AJEX Charitable Foundn, 2000–; Trustee, Colwyn Bay Synagogue Trust, 1978–. Chm. of Govs, Edgware Sch., 1991–96. FRSA 1998. DL Tyne and Wear, 1986. *Recreations:* watching sport; communal service, promoting inter-faith understanding. *Address:* Flat 1, Peters Lodge, 2 Stonegrove, Edgware, Middlesex HA8 7TY. *Clubs:* Ashbrooke Cricket and Rugby Football (Sunderland); Durham County Cricket (Life Mem.).

COHEN, Sir Philip, Kt 1998; PhD; FRS 1984; FRSE 1984; Royal Society Research Professor, since 1984, Director, Medical Research Council Protein Phosphorylation Unit, since 1990, and Director, Scottish Institute for Cell Signalling, since 2008, University of Dundee; *b* 22 July 1945; *s* of Jacob Davis Cohen and Fanny (*née* Bragman); *m* 1969, Patricia Townsend Wade; one *s* one *d. Educ:* Hendon County Grammar Sch.; University Coll. London (BSc 1st Cl. Hons (Biochemistry Special), 1966; PhD Biochem., 1969; Fellow, 1993). SRC/NATO Postdoctoral Res. Fellow, Dept of Biochem., Univ. of Washington, Seattle, USA, 1969–71; Univ. of Dundee: Lectr in Biochem., 1971–78; Reader in Biochem., 1978–81; Prof. of Enzymology, 1981–84; Dir, Wellcome Trust Biocentre, 1997–2007. Croonian Lectr, Royal Soc., 1998. Pres., British Biochemical Soc., 2006– (Hon. Mem., 2003). Mem., Eur. Molecular Biology Orgn, 1982–; MAE 1990. Founder FMedSci 1998. Hon. FRCPath 1998. Foreign Associate, US NAS, 2008. Hon. DSc: Abertay, 1998; Strathclyde, 1999; Debrecen, 2004; St Andrews, 2005; Hon. MD Linköping, 2004; Hon. LLD Dundee, 2007. Anniversary Prize, Fedn of Eur. Biochemical Socs, 1977; Colworth Medal, 1978, CIBA medal and prize, 1992, British Biochem. Soc.; Prix van Gysel, Belgian Royal Acads of Medicine, 1992; Dundee City of Discovery Rosebowl Award, 1993; Bruce Preller Prize, RSE, 1993; Special Achievement Award, 1996, Dist. Service Award, 2005, Miami Biotech. Winter Symposium; Louis-Jeantet Prize for Medicine, 1997; Pfizer Award for Innovative Sci., 1999; Sir Hans Krebs Medal, Fedn of Eur. Biochem. Socs, 2001; Bristol Myers Squibb Dist. Achievement Award in Metabolic Res., 2002; Royal Medal, RSE, 2004; Debrecen Award for Molecular Medicine, 2004; Rolf Luft Prize, Karolinska Inst., Stockholm, 2006; Royal Medal, Royal Soc., 2008; Achievement Award, Soc. for Biomolecular Sci., 2009. Hon. Mem., Dundee Rotary Club, 2006. Man. Editor, Biochimica et Biophysica Acta, 1981–92. *Publications:* Control of Enzyme Activity, 1976, 2nd edn 1983; (ed series) Molecular Aspects of Cellular Regulation: vol. 1, 1980; vol. 2, 1982; vol. 3, 1984; vol. 4, 1985; vol. 5, 1988; vol. 6, 1991; over 450 original papers and revs in scientific jls. *Recreations:* chess, bridge, golf, natural history. *Address:* MRC Protein Phosphorylation Unit, College of Life Sciences, University of Dundee, MSI/WTB Complex, Dow Street, Dundee DD1 5EH; Inverbay II, Invergowrie, Dundee DD2 5DQ. *T:* (01382) 562328. *Clubs:* Downfield Golf; Isle of Harris Golf; Dundee Bridge.

COHEN, Robert; cellist and conductor; *b* London, 15 June 1959; *s* of Raymond Cohen and Anthya Cohen (*née* Rael); *m* 1987, Rachel Smith; four *s. Educ:* Purcell Sch.; Guildhall Sch. of Music; cello studies with William Pleeth, André Navarra, Jacqueline du Pré and Mstislav Rostropovich. Started playing cello, aged 5; début at RFH (Boccherini Concerto), aged 12; London recital début, Wigmore Hall, aged 17; Tanglewood Fest., USA, 1978; recording début, 1979; concerts with major orchestras in USA, Europe and worldwide, 1979–. Conductor: various chamber orchestras, 1990–; symphony orchestras, 1997–. Dir, Charleston Manor Fest., E Sussex, 1989–. Vis. Prof., Royal Acad. of Music, 1998–; Prof. of Advanced Cello Studies, Conservatorio della Svizzera Italiana di Lugano, 2000–; Fellow, Purcell Sch. for Young Musicians, 1992–. Has made numerous recordings; internat. radio broadcasts and TV appearances. Winner: Young Concert Artists Internat. Comp., NY, 1978; Piatigorsky Prize, Tanglewood Fest., 1978; UNESCO Internat. Comp., Czechoslovakia, 1981. *Recreations:* photography, computers, playing sports with my children. *T:* (Jo Carpenter, Music Management and PR) (020) 7737 5994, 07771 538868, *Fax:* 0870 912 5965; *e-mail:* jo@jocarpenter.com.

COHEN, Prof. Robert Donald, CBE 1997; MD; FRCP, FMedSci; Professor of Medicine and Director, Academic Medical Unit (Whitechapel), St Bartholomew's and the Royal London School of Medicine and Dentistry, Queen Mary and Westfield College, (formerly London Hospital Medical College), University of London, 1981–99, now Professor Emeritus; *b* 11 Oct. 1933; *s* of Dr Harry H. and Ruby Cohen; *m* 1961, Dr Barbara Joan Boucher; one *s* one *d. Educ:* Clifton Coll.; Trinity Coll., Cambridge. MA, MD (Cantab). Hon. Cons. Physician, London Hosp., 1967–99; Dir, Academic Unit of Metabolism and Endocrinology, 1974, Prof. of Metabolic Medicine, 1974–81, London Hosp. Med. Coll. Chairman: Adv. Cttee on the Application of Computing Science to Medicine and the Nat. Health Service, 1976–77; DHSS Computer R&D Cttee, 1977–80; DHSS/MRC Monitoring Cttee on Magnetic Resonance Imaging, 1986–89; Review Body, British Diabetic Assoc., 1990–95; Member: Jt Cttee on Higher Med. Trng, 1983–90, 1996–97 (Chm., Special Adv. Cttee on Gen. Internal Medicine, 1983–90); GMC, 1988–96; Physiological Systems Bd, MRC, 1990–92; Health Services Res. Cttee, MRC, 1990–92; Physiological Medicine and Infections Bd, MRC, 1992–94; Health Services and Public Health Bd, MRC, 1992–94; Innovation Grants Cttee, MRC, 1998–2000; Cttee, Nat. Kidney Res. Fund, 1992–98; Council, King Edward VII Hosp., Midhurst, 1997–2000. Chm., ICRF, 1994–2003 (Mem. Council, 1989–2002; Vice-Chm., 1991–94); Mem. Council, Cancer Res. UK, 2002–03. Sen. Censor and First Vice-Pres., RCP, 1991–93. Founder FMedSci 1998. Hon. Fellow, QMW, 2001. Chm., Editorial Bd, Clinical Science and Molecular Medicine, 1973–74. External Reviewer, Canada Foundn for Innovation, 2000–. *Publications:* Clinical and Biochemical Aspects of Lactic Acidosis (with H. F. Woods), 1976; (jtly) The Metabolic and Molecular Basis of Acquired Disease, 1990; papers in Clin. Sci. and Molecular Med., Jl of Clin. Investigation, Lancet, Biochemical Journal. *Address:* Long Meadow, East Dean, Chichester, W Sussex PO18 0JB. *T:* (01243) 811230; *e-mail:* rcohen@doctors.org.uk.

COHEN, Sir Ronald (Mourad), Kt 2001; Chairman: The Portland Trust, since 2005; Portland Capital LLP, since 2006; Founder, 1972, Chairman, 1972–2005, Apax Partners Worldwide LLP (formerly Apax Partners Holdings Ltd); *b* 1 Aug. 1945; *s* of late Michel Mourad Cohen and of Sonia Sophie Cohen (*née* Douek); *m* 1st, 1972, Carol Marylene Belmont (marr. diss. 1975); 2nd, 1983, Claire Whitmore Enders (marr. diss. 1986); 3rd, 1987, Sharon Ruth Harel; one *s* one *d. Educ:* Orange Hill GS; Exeter Coll., Oxford (Exhibnr, MA; Hon. Fellow, 2000; Pres., Oxford Union Soc.); Harvard Business Sch. (MBA; Henry Fellowship). Consultant, McKinsey & Co. (UK and Italy), 1969–71; Chargé de mission, Institut de Développement Industriel France, 1971–72. Founder Director: British Venture Capital Assoc., 1983 (Chm., 1985–86); Eur. Venture Capital Assoc., 1985; City Gp for Smaller Cos, 1992; a Founder and Vice-Chm., Eur. Assoc. Securities Dealers Automated Quotation, 1995–2001; Dir, NASDAQ Europe, 2001–03. Chairman: Tech. Stars Steering Cttee, DTI, 1997–2000; Social Investment Task Force, 2000–; Bridges Ventures Ltd, 2002–; Commn on Unclaimed Assets, 2005–; Member: Finance and Industry Cttee, NEDC, 1988–90; Wider Share Ownership Cttee, 1988–90, City Adv. Gp, 1993–99, CBI; Wkg Party on Smaller Cos, Stock Exchange, 1993; UK Competitiveness Cttee, DTI, 1998–2000. Member: Exec. Cttee, Centre for Econ. Policy Res., 1996–99; Finance Cttee, Inst. for Social and Econ. Policy in ME, Kennedy Sch., Harvard Univ., 1997–98; Adv. Bd, Fulbright Commn, 1997–99; Franco-British Council, 1997–99; Dean's Adv. Bd, Harvard Business Sch., 2005; Bd of Overseers, Harvard Univ., 2007–; Investment Cttee, Oxford Univ., 2007–; RIIA; Trustee Mem., Exec. Cttee, IISS, 2005–. Mem., Internat. Council, Tate Gall., 2004–; Trustee, BM, 2005–. Mem., Adv. Bd, InterAction, 1986–; Hon. Pres., Community Develt Finance Assoc., 2005–07. Contested (L): Kensington N, 1974; London W, EP elecn, 1979. Vice-Chm., Ben-Gurion Univ. *Publication:* The Second Bounce of the Ball: turning risk into opportunity, 2007. *Recreations:* music, art, theatre, cinema, tennis. *Address:* The Portland Trust, 42 Portland Place, W1B 1NB. *T:* (020) 7182 7800, *Fax:* (020) 7182 7897. *Clubs:* Athenæum, Royal Automobile, Queen's.

COHEN, Prof. Stanley, PhD; FBA 1997; Martin White Professor of Sociology, London School of Economics, 1995–2005, now Professor Emeritus; *b* 23 Feb. 1942; *s* of Ray and Sie Cohen; *m* 1963, Ruth Kretzmer; two *d. Educ:* Univ. of Witwatersrand, Johannesburg (BA); LSE, Univ. of London (PhD). Psychiatric social worker, 1963–64; Lectr in Sociology: Enfield Coll., 1965–67; Univ. of Durham, 1967–72; Sen. Lectr in Sociol., 1972–74, Prof. of Sociol., 1974–81, Univ. of Essex; Prof. of Criminology, Hebrew Univ., Jerusalem, 1981–95. Vis. Centennial Prof., LSE, 1994–95. DU Essex, 2003. Sellin-Glueck Award, Amer. Soc. of Criminology, 1985. *Publications:* Images of Deviance, 1971; Folk Devils and Moral Panics, 1972; Psychological Survival, 1972; The Manufacture of News, 1973; Escape Attempts, 1976; Prison Secrets, 1978; Social Control and the State, 1984; Visions of Social Control: crime, punishment and classification, 1985; Against Criminology, 1988; States of Denial: knowing about atrocities and suffering, 2000 (British Acad. Book Prize, 2002). *Address:* Department of Sociology, London School of Economics, Houghton Street, WC2A 2AE.

COHEN, Prof. Stanley; Distinguished Professor, Department of Biochemistry, Vanderbilt University School of Medicine, 1986–2000, now Emeritus; *b* 17 Nov. 1922; *s* of Louis Cohen and Fruma Feitel; *m* 1st, 1951, Olivia Larson; three *s*; 2nd, 1981, Jan Elizabeth Jordan. *Educ:* Brooklyn Coll., NY; Oberlin Coll., Ohio; Univ. of Michigan (BA, PhD). Teaching Fellow, Dept of Biochem., Univ. of Michigan, 1946–48; Instructor, Depts of Biochem. and Pediatrics, Univ. of Colorado Sch. of Medicine, 1948–52; Fellow, Amer. Cancer Soc., Dept of Radiology, Washington Univ., St Louis, 1952–53; Associate Prof., Dept of Zoology, Washington Univ., 1953–59; Vanderbilt University School of Medicine, Nashville: Asst Prof. of Biochem., 1959–62; Associate Prof., 1962; Prof. 1967–86. Mem., Editl Bds of learned jls. Mem., Nat. Acad. of Science, and other sci. bodies. Hon. DSc Chicago, 1985. Nobel Prize for Physiology or Medicine, 1986 (jtly); other prizes and awards. *Publications:* papers in learned jls on biochemistry, cell biology, human developmental biology, embryology. *Address:* 4308 Lone Oak Road, Nashville, TN 37215, USA; *e-mail:* stancohen@earthlink.net.

COHEN, Prof. Sydney, CBE 1978; FRS 1978; Professor of Chemical Pathology, Guy's Hospital Medical School, 1965–86, now Emeritus Professor, University of London; *b* Johannesburg, SA, 18 Sept. 1921; *s* of Morris and Pauline Cohen; *m* 1st, 1950, June Bernice Adler (*d* 1999); one *s* one *d*; 2nd, 1999, Deirdre Maureen Ann Boyd. *Educ:* King Edward VIIth Sch., Johannesburg; Witwatersrand and London Univs. MD, PhD. EMS, UK, 1944–45. Lectr, Dept of Physiology, Witwatersrand Univ., 1947–53; Scientific Staff, Nat. Inst. for Med. Research, London, 1954–60; Reader, Dept of Immunology, St Mary's Hosp. Med. Sch., 1960–65. Mem., MRC, 1974–76; Chm., Tropical Med. Research Bd,

MRC, 1974–76; Chm., WHO Scientific Gp on Immunity to Malaria, 1976–81; Mem., WHO expert adv. panel on malaria, 1977–89; Mem. Council, Royal Soc., 1981–83; Royal Soc. Assessor, MRC, 1982–84. Nuffield Dominion Fellow in Medicine, 1954; Founder Fellow, RCPath, 1964. Hon. DSc Witwatersrand, 1987. *Publications:* papers on immunology and parasitic diseases in sci. jls. *Recreations:* golf, gardening, forestry. *Address:* 8 Gibson Place, St Andrews, Fife KY16 9JE; Hafodfraith, Llangurig, Powys SY18 6QG. *Club:* Royal and Ancient (St Andrews).

COHEN, Hon. William S(ebastian); Chairman and Chief Executive Officer, Cohen Group, since 2001; *b* 28 Aug. 1940; *s* of Reuben Cohen and Clara (*née* Hartley); *m*; two *s*. *Educ:* Bangor High Sch.; Bowdoin Coll. (AB 1962); Boston Univ. Law Sch. (LLB 1965). Admitted: Maine Bar; Massachusetts Bar; Dist of Columbia Bar; Partner, Prairie, Cohen, Lynch, Weatherbee and Kobritz, 1966–72; Asst Attorney, Penobscot County, Maine, 1968–70; Instr., Univ. of Maine at Orono, 1968–72; Mem., US Congress, 1972–79; US Senator from Maine, 1979–97; Sec. of Defense, USA, 1996–2001. Fellow, John F. Kennedy Inst. of Politics, Harvard, 1972. Mem., Bangor City Council, 1969–72 (Mayor, 1971–72). *Publications:* Of Sons and Seasons, 1978; Roll Call, 1981; (jtly) Getting the Most Out of Washington, 1982; (jtly) The Double Man, 1985; A Baker's Nickel, 1986; (jtly) Men of Zeal, 1988; One-Eyed Kings, 1991; (jtly) Murder in the Senate, 1993. *Address:* Cohen Group, 500 8th Street NW, Suite 200, Washington, DC 20004, USA.

COHEN-TANNOUDJI, Prof. Claude, PhD; Officier, Légion d'Honneur; Commandeur, Ordre National du Mérite; Professor of Atomic and Molecular Physics, Collège de France, Paris, since 1973; *b* 1 April 1933; *s* of Abraham Cohen-Tannoudji and Sarah Sebbah; *m* 1958, Jacqueline Veyrat; one *s* one *d* (and one *s* decd). *Educ:* Ecole Normale Supérieure, Paris; Univ. of Paris (PhD Physics 1962). Researcher, CNRS, 1960–64; Associate Prof., 1964–67, Prof., 1967–73, Univ. of Paris. Member: Académie des Sciences, Paris, 1981; NAS, USA, 1994. (Jtly) Nobel Prize for Physics, 1997. *Publications:* (jtly) Quantum Mechanics, Vols I and II, 1977; Atoms in Electromagnetic Fields, 1994; with J. Dupont-Roc and G. Grynberg: Photons and Atoms: introduction to Q.E.D., 1989; Atom-photon Interactions, 1992. *Recreation:* music. *Address:* Laboratoire Kastler Brossel, Département de Physique de l'ENS, 24 rue Lhomond, 75231 Paris Cedex 05, France. *T:* (1) 47077783.

COHN-SHERBOK, Rabbi Prof. Dan; Professor of Judaism, University of Wales, Lampeter, since 1997; *b* 1 Feb. 1945; *s* of Dr Bernard Sherbok and Ruth Sherbok (*née* Goldstein), Denver, Colo; *m* 1976, Lavinia Charlotte Heath. *Educ:* Williams Coll., Mass (BA); Hebrew Union Coll., Ohio (BHL, MAHL); Wolfson Coll., Cambridge (MLitt, PhD). Served as rabbi in US, Australia, SA and England, 1970–75; Chaplain, Colorado Hse of Representatives, 1971; Lectr in Jewish Theology, Univ. of Kent, 1975–97; Dir, Centre for Study of Religion and Society, Univ. of Kent, 1982–90. Mem., AHRC Peer Review Coll., 2007–. Visiting Professor: Univ. of Essex, 1993–94; of Inter-Faith Dialogue, Univ. of Middx, 1995–; of Judaism, Univ. of Wales at Lampeter, 1995–97; Univ. of St Andrews, 1995; Univ. of Wales, Bangor, 1998; Vilnius Univ., 2000; Univ. of Durham, 2002; Trinity Coll., Carmarthen, 2007–; Visiting Scholar: Sarum Coll., 2005–; St Mary's University Coll., 2007–. FRAS. Hon. DD Hebrew Union Coll., 1996. *Publications:* On Earth as it is in Heaven, 1987; The Jewish Heritage, 1988; Holocaust Theology, 1989; Jewish Petitionary Prayer, 1989; Rabbinic Perspectives on the New Testament, 1990; (ed) The Canterbury Papers, 1990; (ed) The Salman Rushdie Controversy, 1990; (ed) Using the Bible Today, 1991; (ed) A Traditional Quest, 1991; (ed) The Sayings of Moses, 1991; (ed) Tradition and Unity, 1991; (ed) Problems in Contemporary Jewish Philosophy, 1991; A Dictionary of Judaism and Christianity, 1991; Issues in Contemporary Judaism, 1991; The Blackwell Dictionary of Judaica, 1992; The Crucified Jew, 1992; Israel: the history of an idea, 1992; Exodus, 1992; (ed) Many Mansions, 1992; (ed) World Religions and Human Liberation, 1992; (ed) Religion in Public Life, 1992; (ed) Torah and Revelation, 1992; Atlas of Jewish History, 1993; The Jewish Faith, 1993; Judaism and Other Faiths, 1994; The Future of Judaism, 1994; Jewish and Christian Mysticism, 1994; The American Jew, 1994; Jewish Mysticism, 1995; (ed) Divine Interventions and Miracles, 1996; Medieval Jewish Philosophy, 1996; The Hebrew Bible, 1996; Modern Judaism, 1996; Biblical Hebrew for Beginners, 1996; God and the Holocaust, 1996; Fifty Key Jewish Thinkers, 1997; (ed) Islam in a World of Diverse Faiths, 1997; The Jewish Messiah, 1997; After Noah, 1997; (ed) Theodicy, 1997; Concise Encyclopedia of Judaism, 1998; Understanding the Holocaust, 1999; (ed) The Future of Jewish Christian Dialogue, 1999; (ed) The Future of Religion, 1999; Judaism, 1999; Jews, Christians and Religious Pluralism, 1999; Messianic Judaism, 2000; Holocaust Theology: a Reader, 2001; Interfaith Theology, 2001; (jtly) The Palestine-Israeli Conflict, 2001; (ed jtly) Religious Diversity in the Graeco-Roman World, 2001; (ed) Voices of Messianic Judaism, 2001; Anti-Semitism, 2002; Judaism: history, belief and practice, 2003; What's a Nice Jewish Boy Like You Doing in a Place Like This?, 2003; The Vision of Judaism: wrestling with God, 2004; (jtly) An Encyclopedia of Judaism and Christianity, 2004; Dictionary of Jewish Biography, 2005; (jtly) Pursuing the Dream: a Jewish-Christian conversation, 2005; The Paradox of Antisemitism, 2006; The Politics of Apocalypse, 2006; Kabbalah and Jewish Mysticism, 2006; What Do You Do When Your Parents Live Forever?, 2007; numerous articles to learned jls. *Recreations:* keeping cats, walking, drawing cartoons. *Address:* Department of Theology and Religious Studies, University of Wales, Lampeter SA48 7ED. *T:* (01570) 424968; *e-mail:* cohn-sherbok@ukonline.co.uk. *Clubs:* Athenæum, Lansdowne; Williams (New York).

COID, Dr Donald Routledge; Executive Director of Medical Services, Wide Bay Health Service District, Queensland, since 2006; *b* 13 June 1953; *s* of Charles Routledge Coid and late Marjory Macdonald Coid (*née* Keay); *m* 1985, Susan Kathleen Ramus (*née* Crocker); three *d*. *Educ:* Bromley Grammar Sch. for Boys; Harrow County Sch. for Boys; Univ. of Nottingham (BMedSci; BM, BS); LSHTM (MSc 1981). MRCP 1979; MFCM 1985, MFPHM 1989, FFPH (FFPHM 1996); FRACMA 1985; FAFPHM 1991; FRCPE 1998; FRIPH (FRIPHH 1998). Hse Physician, Nottingham City Hosp., 1976; Hse Surgeon, Nottingham Gen. Hosp., 1977; Sen. Hse Officer, Brook Gen. Hosp., London, 1977–78; Res. Asst, Middlesex Hosp. Med. Sch., 1979; Field Med. Officer, Royal Flying Doctor Service, Australia, Eastern Goldfields Sect., 1979–80; MO, Community Health Services, WA, 1981–82; Regl Dir of Public Health, Eastern Goldfields, WA, 1982–85; Med. Supt, Kalgoorlie Reg. Hosp., WA, 1984–85; Fife Health Board: Cons. in Public Health, 1985–92; Asst Gen. Manager, 1992–93; Chief Admin. MO, Dir of Public Health and Exec. Dir, Tayside Health Bd, 1994–98; Consultant in Health Services Res., Ninewells Hosp. and Med. Sch., Dundee, 1998–2000; Public Health Consultant, Grampian Health Bd, 2000–01; Dir of Med. Services, Armadale Health Service, WA, 2001–06. Consultant to: Govt of Qatar, 1999; WHO, 2000; overseas projects, Corp. of Victoria, 2003. Hon. Sen. Lectr, Dundee Univ., 1994–2001. *Publications:* on public health and related topics in learned jls. *Recreations:* golf, singing, cricket, piano, freemasonry. *Address:* 5 Judith Street, Bargara, Qld 4670, Australia. *Clubs:* Royal & Ancient Golf, New Golf (St Andrews); Lakelands Country (WA); Bargara Golf (Qld).

COJOCARU, Alina; ballet dancer; Principal, Royal Ballet, since 2001; *b* Bucharest, 27 May 1981; *d* of Gheorge Cojocaru and Nina Cojocaru. *Educ:* Ukrainian State Ballet Sch.; Royal Ballet Sch. With Kiev Ballet, 1998; joined Royal Ballet, 1999. Guest dancer with Mariinsky Ballet, American Ballet Th., Royal Danish Ballet, Hungarian Nat. Ballet, Paris Opera Ballet, Romanian Nat. Ballet, Bolshoi Ballet. Performances include main rôles in The Nutcracker, Romeo and Juliet, Giselle, Don Quixote, Swan Lake, Sleeping Beauty, Cinderella, Onegin, Manon, Coppelia and Mayerling. Trustee, Hospices of Hope, 2008–. Prix de Lausanne, 1997; Best Female Dancer, Critics' Circle Dance Award, 2002. *Address:* c/o Royal Ballet, Royal Opera House, Covent Garden, WC2E 9DD.

COKAYNE, family name of **Baron Cullen of Ashbourne**.

COKE, family name of **Earl of Leicester**.

COKE, Viscount; Thomas Edward Coke; *b* 6 July 1965; *er s* and *heir* of Earl of Leicester, *qv*; *m* 1996, Polly, *y d* of David Whately; one *s* three *d*. *Educ:* Eton; Univ. of Manchester (BA). Scots Guards, 1987–93. Pres., Caravan Club, 2006–. *Heir:* *s* Hon. Edward Horatio Coke, *b* 11 June 2003. *Address:* Holkham, Wells-next-the-Sea, Norfolk NR23 1AB. *Club:* White's.

COKER, Naaz; Chair, St George's Healthcare NHS Trust, since 2003; *b* 14 Oct. 1948; *d* of Rahemtula and Shirin Suleman; *m* 1973, Raymond Coker. *Educ:* Portsmouth Univ. (BSc Pharm.); Chelsea Coll., London Univ. (MSc); Open Univ. (MBA). Chief Pharmacist, Royal Marsden Hosp., Sutton, 1973–76; Principal Pharmacist, Bromley & Beckenham Hosps, 1976–79; Dist Pharmaceutical Officer, Lewisham Health Dist, 1979–87; Guy's and Lewisham NHS Trust: Dir, Pharmacy and Med. Supplies, 1988–90; Clinical Dir, Clinical Support Services, 1990–92; Actg Unit Gen. Manager, 1992; King's Fund: Fellow, Leadership Develt, 1992–2002; Dir, Race and Diversity, 1998–2002. Hon. Clinical Lectr, Dept of Pharmacy, Univ. of Brighton, 1992–96. Chair: British Refugee Council, 1998–2005; Shelter, 2007–; Mem., Race Equality Adv. Panel, Home Office, 2003–. Chm., Aga Khan Health Bd UK (for Ismaili Muslim community), 1990–93; Mem., Ismaili Council for EU, 1999–2005. Chm., First Steps Nursery Sch., Streatham and London, 1985–87. Mem., Mgt Cttee, St Cecilia's Leonard Cheshire Foundn Home, Bromley, 1996–2000. Trustee: Media Trust, 2001–05; Ashoka Trust, 2002–03; RSA, 2005–. Hon. DSc Leeds Metropolitan, 2005; DUniv UCE, 2007. Asian Woman of Year: Asia Mktg Gp, 2000; Asian Guild, 2003; Asian Women of Achievement Award, 2004. *Publications:* (ed) Racism in Medicine, 2001; interviews and book reviews; numerous articles, chapters and reports in med., pharmaceutical and mgt jls. *Recreations:* reading, gardening, walking, cooking.

COKER, Paul, FCA; Managing Director, Ranks Hovis McDougall, 1992–93; *b* 27 July 1938; *s* of Leslie and Mabel Coker; *m* 1965, Delphine Rostron Baden; twin *s* one *d*. *Educ:* Merchant Taylors' Sch. Joined Ranks Hovis McDougall (Cerebos Group), 1964: Man. Dir, General Products, 1982–87; Planning Dir, 1987–89; Dep. Man. Dir, 1989–91; Finance Dir, 1991–92. *Recreations:* golf, cricket, gardening, theatre. *Address:* Courtlands, Nightingales Lane, Chalfont St Giles, Bucks HP8 4SL. *T:* (01494) 762040.

COKER, William John; QC 1994; *b* 19 July 1950; *s* of Edgar and Peggy Coker; *m* 1977, Ruth Elaine Pull; one *s* one *d*. *Educ:* Bedford Sch.; Manchester Univ. (LLB). Called to the Bar, Gray's Inn, 1973. *Recreations:* golf, fishing. *Address:* 7 Bedford Row, WC1R 4BS. *T:* (020) 7242 3555.

COLCHESTER, Area Bishop of, since 2001; **Rt Rev. Christopher Heudebourck Morgan;** *b* 23 March 1947; *m* 1975, Anne Musgrave; one *s* one *d*. *Educ:* City of Bath Boys' Sch.; Kelham Theol Coll.; Lancaster Univ. (BA 1973); Heythrop Coll., London (MTh 1991). Ordained deacon, 1973, priest, 1974; Curate, St James the Great, Birstall, 1973–76; Chaplain to EC staff, and Asst Chaplain, Holy Trinity Ch, Brussels, 1976–80; Team Vicar, St George, Redditch, and part-time Industrial Chaplain, 1980–85; Vicar, Sonning, 1985–96; Gloucester Diocesan Officer for Ministry, and a Residentiary Canon, Gloucester Cathedral, 1996–2001. Principal, Berks Christian Trng Scheme, 1985–89; Dir, Pastoral Studies, St Albans and Oxford Diocesan Ministry Course, 1992–96. *Recreations:* hill walking, amateur dramatics, improving at golf, music. *Address:* 1 Fitzwalter Road, Lexden, Colchester, Essex CO3 3SS.

COLCHESTER, Archdeacon of; *see* Cooper, Ven. A. J.

COLCLOUGH, Prof. Christopher Louis, PhD; Professor of the Economics of Education, and Director, Centre for Commonwealth Education, University of Cambridge, since 2005; Fellow, Corpus Christi College, Cambridge, since 2006; *b* 10 July 1946; *s* of Frederick and Margaret Colclough; *m* 1992, Sarah Elizabeth Butler; one *s*. *Educ:* Univ. of Bristol (BA Philosophy and Econs 1967); PhD Econs Cambridge 1971. Econ. Advr, Min. of Finance and Develt Planning, Botswana Govt, 1971–75; Fellow, 1975–94, Professorial Fellow, 1994–2004, Inst. of Develt Studies, Univ. of Sussex; Dir, Educn for All Global Monitoring Report, UNESCO, Paris, 2002–04. Advisor: to UK Parly Select Cttee on Overseas Aid and Develt, 1980–81; to govts of PNG and Botswana on wages and incomes policy, 1981–83; to UNICEF on educn financing, 1989–90; to S African Govt on educn policy, 1994–2000; Chief, UNDP Tech. Co-operation Mission to Zambia, 1986. Pres., British Assoc. for Internat. and Comparative Educn, 2004–05. Man. Ed., Jl of Develt Studies, 1989–2002. AcSS 2005. FRSA 2004. *Publications:* (jtly) The Political Economy of Botswana: a study of growth and distribution, 1980; (ed jtly) States or Markets, 1991; (jtly) Educating All the Children: strategies for primary schooling in the South, 1993; (ed) Public Sector Pay and Adjustment, 1997; (ed) Marketizing Education and Health in Developing Countries, 1997; (jtly) Achieving Schooling for All in Africa: costs, commitment and gender, 2003. *Recreations:* playing the piano and 'cello, opera, walking in the Pennines. *Address:* Little Hallands, Norton, Seaford, E Sussex BN25 2UN. *T:* (01323) 896101; *e-mail:* c.colclough@educ.cam.ac.uk.

COLCLOUGH, Rt Rev. Michael John; a Residentiary Canon, St Paul's Cathedral, since 2008; *b* 29 Dec. 1944; *s* of Joseph and Beryl Colclough; *m* 1983, Cynthia Flora Mary De Sousa; two *s*. *Educ:* Leeds Univ. (BA Hons English and Religious Studies); Cuddesdon Coll., Oxford. Ordained deacon, 1971, priest, 1972; Curate: St Werburgh, Burslem, 1971–75; St Mary, S Ruislip, 1975–79; Vicar, St Anselm, Hayes, 1979–86; Area Dean of Hillingdon, 1985–92; Team Rector, Uxbridge, 1986–92; Archdeacon of Northolt, 1992–94; personal asst to Bp of London (Archdeacon at London House), 1994–96; Priest-in-Charge: St Vedast-alias-Foster, 1994–96; St Magnus the Martyr, London Bridge, 1995–96; Dep. Priest in Ordinary to the Queen, 1995–96; Area Bishop of Kensington, 1996–2008. Chm. Mission, Evangelism and Renewal in England Cttee, C of E, 1999–2003. Patron: Micro Loan Foundn, 1999–2008; London Care Connections, 2003–08; Shooting Star Trust, 2005–08; W London Action for Children, 2005–08; Hoffman Foundn for Autism, 2005–. *Recreations:* travel, walking in the English countryside, reading, people. *Address:* 2 Amen Court, EC4M 7BU. *T:* (020) 7236 0199; *e-mail:* canonpastor@stpaulscathedral.org.uk.

COLDSTREAM, John Richard Francis; writer; Literary Editor, The Daily Telegraph, 1991–99; *b* 19 Dec. 1947; *s* of Gerald Coldstream and Marian Gatehouse; *m* 1977, Susan Elizabeth Pealing. *Educ:* Bradfield Coll.; Univ. of Nice; Univ. of Sussex. Evening Echo,

Hemel Hempstead, 1971–74; joined Daily Telegraph, Peterborough column, 1974; Dep. Literary Editor, Daily Telegraph, 1984–91 and Sunday Telegraph, 1989–91. Member: Arts Council Literature Adv. Panel, 1992–97; Man Booker (formerly Booker) Prize Adv. Cttee, 1996–2004. *Publications:* (ed) The Daily Telegraph Book of Contemporary Short Stories, 1995; Dirk Bogarde: the authorised biography, 2004; (ed) Ever, Dirk: the Bogarde letters, 2008. *Recreations:* theatre, being walked by the dog. *Address: e-mail:* jcoldstream@ dial.pipex.com. *Club:* Garrick.

COLE, family name of **Earl of Enniskillen.**

COLE, Allan Gordon Halliwell, FRCA; Medical Director, University Hospitals of Leicester NHS Trust, since 2000; Consultant Anaesthetist, Glenfield Hospital and Leicester Royal Infirmary, since 1985; *b* 20 Feb. 1949; *s* of late Robert Randle Cole and Anne Dorothy Cole; *m* Penelope Gaye Cole (marr. diss.); one *s* one *d*; *m* Jennifer. *Educ:* Marlborough Coll.; St Bartholomew's Hosp. (MB BS 1973). MRCS, LRCP 1973; FRCA (FFARCS 1979). SHO, then Registrar in Anaesthesia, St Bartholomew's Hosp., 1976–80; Sen. Registrar in Anaesthesia, John Radcliffe Hosp., Oxford, 1980–85; Med. Dir, Glenfield Hosp., Leicester, 1993–2000. Chm., British Assoc. of Med. Managers, 2003–05. *Publications:* papers in peer-reviewed jls of anaesthesia and med. mgt. *Recreations:* golf, singing (choir). *Address:* 42 Groby Lane, Newtown, Linford, Leics LE6 0HH. *T:* (0116) 256 3871; *e-mail:* coleallan@doctors.org.uk.

COLE, Babette S.; author and illustrator of children's books; *b* Jersey, 10 Sept. 1950. *Educ:* convent, Jersey; Canterbury Coll. of Educn (BA 1st Cl. Hons Illustration and Audio Visual 1973). Worked for BBC Children's TV. Member: BSJA; SSA. Side Saddle Rider of the Year, 1998; Side Saddle Nat. Champion (Working Hunter), 2002, 2003. Fellow, Kent Inst. of Art and Design, 2003. DVD, Writing and Illustrating a Children's Picture Book, 2008. *Publications:* include: Hairy Book, 1984; Slimy Book, 1985; Smelly Book, 1987; Silly Book, 1989; Trouble with Grandad, 1989; Cupid, 1989; Three Cheers for Errol, 1992; Princess Smartypants, 1992; Mummy Laid an Egg (BRIT Award Best Illustrated Children's Bk of Year), 1993 (trans. 73 languages); Prince Cinders, 1993; Hurrah for Ethelyn, 1993; Tarzanna, 1993; Trouble with Mum, 1993; Trouble with Uncle, 1994; Dr Dog, 1994 (TV series); Trouble with Dad, 1995; Winni Allfours, 1995; Drop Dead, 1996; Trouble with Gran, 1997; Two of Everything, 1997; Bad Good Manners Book, 1997; King Change-a-lot, 1998; Hair in Funny Places, 1999; Bad Habits!, 1999; Animals Scare Me Stiff, 2000; Truelove, 2001; Lady Lupin's Book of Etiquette, 2002; Mummy Never Told Me, 2003; The Sprog Owner's Manual, 2004; Long Live Princess Smartypants, 2004; That's Why, 2006; A Dose of Dr Dog, 2007; *illustrated:* Richard Hamilton, If I Were You, 2008. *Recreations:* breeding and showing show hunters, sailing. *Address:* c/o Rosemary Sandberg Ltd, 6 Bayley Street, WC1B 3HB. *T:* (020) 7304 4110; *web:* www.babette-cole.com.

COLE, Caroline Louise; *see* Flint, C. L.

COLE, Frank; *see* Cole, G. F.

COLE, George, OBE 1992; actor on stage, screen, radio and television; *b* 22 April 1925; *m* 1st, 1954, Eileen Moore (marr. diss. 1966); one *s* one *d*; 2nd, 1967, Penelope Morrell; one *s* one *d*. *Educ:* Surrey County Council Secondary Sch., Morden. Made first stage appearance in White Horse Inn, tour and London Coliseum, 1939; Cottage to Let, Birmingham, 1940; West End and on tour, 1940–41; subseq. West End plays included Goodnight Children, New, 1942; Mr Bolfry, Playhouse, 1943. Served in RAF, 1943–47. Returned to stage in Dr Angelus, Phoenix, 1947; The Anatomist, Westminster, 1948; Mr Gillie, Garrick, 1950; A Phoenix too Frequent and Thor with Angels, Lyric, Hammersmith, 1951; Misery Me, Duchess, 1955; Mr Bolfry, Aldwych, 1956; Brass Butterfly, Strand, 1958; The Bargain, St Martin's, 1961; The Sponge Room and Squat Betty, Royal Court, 1962; Meet Me on the Fence (tour), 1963; Hedda Gabler, St Martin's, 1964; A Public Mischief, St Martin's, 1965; Too True To Be Good, Strand, 1965; The Waiting Game, Arts, 1966; The Three Sisters, Royal Court, 1967; Doubtful Haunts, Hampstead, 1968; The Passionate Husband, 1969; The Philanthropist, Mayfair, 1971; Country Life, Hampstead, 1973; Déjà Revue, New London, 1974; Motive (tour), 1976; Banana Ridge, Savoy, 1976; The Case of the Oily Levantine, Guildford, 1977; Something Afoot, Hong Kong, 1978; Brimstone and Treacle, Open Space, 1979; Liberty Hall, Greenwich, 1980; The Pirates of Penzance, Drury Lane, 1982; A Month of Sundays, Duchess, 1986; A Piece of My Mind, Apollo, 1987; Peter Pan, Cambridge, 1987; The Breadwinner (tour), 1989; Natural Causes (tour), 1993; Theft (tour), 1995; Lock Up Your Daughters, Chichester, 1996; Heritage, Hampstead, 1997; The Play What I Wrote, Wyndhams, 2001; Party Piece (tour), 2004–05. *Films include:* Cottage to Let, 1941; Morning Departure, Laughter in Paradise, Scrooge, Top Secret, 1949–51; Will Any Gentleman?, The Intruder, 1952; Happy Ever After, Our Girl Friday, 1953; Belles of St Trinian's, 1954; Quentin Durward, 1955; The Weapon, It's a Wonderful World, The Green Man, 1956; Blue Murder at St Trinian's, Too Many Crooks, Don't Panic Chaps, The Bridal Path, 1957–59; The Pure Hell of St Trinian's, Cleopatra, Dr Syn, 1961–62; One Way Pendulum, Legend of Dick Turpin, 1964; Great St Trinian's Train Robbery, 1965; The Green Shoes, 1969; Vampire Lovers, 1970; Girl in the Dark, 1971; The Blue Bird, 1975; Minder on the Orient Express (TV film), 1985; Mary Reilly, 1996; The Ghost of Greville Lodge, 2000. *Television:* The Sleeper, Station Jim, Life after Life, Single Voices, Bodily Harm, A Class Apart, Diamond Geezer, Miss Marple, New Tricks, The Dinner Party, Midsomer Murders; series include Life of Bliss (also radio), A Man of our Times, Don't Forget to Write, Minder (9 series), The Bounder (2 series), Blott on the Landscape, Comrade Dad, My Good Friend (2 series), An Independent Man, Dad (2 series), Family Business. *Address:* c/o Joy Jameson, 21 Uxbridge Street, Kensington, W8 7TQ.

COLE, George Francis, (Frank); Founder Director, Frank Cole (Consultancy) Ltd, since 1979; *b* 3 Nov. 1918; *m* Gwendoline Mary Laver (decd); two *s* one *d*; *m* Barbara Mary Booth (*née* Gornall). *Educ:* Manchester Grammar Sch. Dir and Gen. Manager, Clarkson Engineers Ltd, 1944–53; Gen. Man., Ariel Motors Ltd (BSA Group), 1953–55; Dir, then Man. Dir, Vono Ltd, 1955–67. Past Chairman: Grovewood Products Ltd; Portways Ltd; R. & W. H. Symington Holdings Ltd; National Exhibition Centre Ltd; Crane's Screw (Hldgs); Stokes Bomford (Holdings) Ltd; Debenholt Ltd; Stokes Bomford (Foods) Ltd; James Cooke (Birmingham) Ltd; Franklin Medical Ltd; Aero Needles Gp plc; Needle Industries Gp Ltd; F. J. Neve & Co. Ltd; Wild Barnsley Engrg Gp Ltd; Past Director: Duport Ltd; Shipping Industrial Holdings Ltd; G. Clancey Ltd; Armstrong Equipment PLC (retd as Dep. Chm., 1989); William Mitchell (Sinkers) Ltd (Chm., 1982–89); Director: Alexander Stenhouse (formerly Reed Stenhouse) UK Ltd, 1981–91; Mitchell-Grieve Ltd, 1989–91. Pres., Birmingham Chamber of Commerce and Industry, 1968–69. Leader of Trade Missions to West Germany, Yugoslavia, Romania and Hungary. CCMI; Life Governor, Birmingham Univ.; Liveryman of City of London. Radio and Television appearances. *Publications:* press articles on economics, exports, etc. *Recreations:* tennis (competes regularly in Nat. Veteran Championships of GB), oil painting, snooker, gardening. *Address:* 2 Woodcote Drive, Dorridge, Solihull, West Midlands B93 8JR. *T:* (01564) 777795.

COLE, Gordon Stewart; QC 2006; *b* 25 March 1956; *s* of Dermott and Jean Cole; *m* 1989, Sarah, (Sally), Cooper; one *s* one *d*. *Educ:* John Moores Univ., Liverpool (BA Hons Law); Inns of Court Sch. of Law. Called to the Bar, Inner Temple, 1979; in practice as barrister, 1979–, specialising in criminal law. *Recreations:* fly fishing, tennis, golf, Liverpool FC, taxi-driving the children. *Address:* c/o Exchange Chambers, Pearl Assurance House, Derby Square, Liverpool L2 9XX. *T:* (0151) 236 7747; *e-mail:* coleqc@ exchangechambers.co.uk.

COLE, John Morrison; Political Editor, BBC, 1981–92; *b* 23 Nov. 1927; *s* of George Cole and Alice Jane Cole, Belfast; *m* 1956, Margaret Isobel, *d* of Mr and Mrs John S. Williamson, Belfast; four *s*. *Educ:* Fortwilliam and Skegoneill Primary Schs, Belfast; Belfast Royal Acad.; London Univ. (BA External). Belfast Telegraph, 1945–56: successively reporter, industrial, municipal and political correspondent; The Guardian: reporter, 1956–57; Labour Correspondent, 1957–63; News Editor, 1963–69; Dep. Editor, 1969–75; The Observer: Asst Editor, 1975; Dep. Editor, 1976–81. DUniv Open, 1992; Hon. DSSc QUB, 1992; Hon. DLitt Ulster, 1992; Hon. LLD St Andrews, 1993. Granada TV Scoop of the Year Award, 1960; Television Journalist of the Year, RTS, 1990; Richard Dimbleby Award, BAFTA, 1992. *Publications:* The Poor of the Earth, 1976; The Thatcher Years: a decade of revolution in British politics, 1987; As It Seemed To Me: political memoirs, 1995; A Clouded Peace (novel), 2001; contrib. to books on British and Irish politics. *Recreations:* reading, travel. *Address:* c/o BBC Office, House of Commons, Westminster, SW1A 0AA. *T:* (020) 7219 4765. *Club:* Athenæum.

COLE, Prof. John Peter; Professor of Human and Regional Geography (formerly of Regional Geography), University of Nottingham, 1975–94, Emeritus since 1994; *b* Sydney, Australia, 9 Dec. 1928; *s* of Philip and Marjorie Cecelia Cole; *m* 1952, Isabel Jesús Cole (*née* Urrunaga); two *s*. *Educ:* Bromley Grammar Sch.; Univ. of Nottingham (State Schol., BA, MA, PhD, DLitt); Collegio Borromeo, Pavia Univ., Italy (British Council Schol.). Demonstrator, Univ. of Nottingham, 1951–52; Nat. Service with RN, Jt Services Sch. for Linguists, Russian Language Interpreter, 1952–54 (Lt Comdr RNR, retired); Oficina Nacional de Planeamiento y Urbanismo, Lima, Peru, 1954–55; Lectr in Geography, Univ. of Reading, 1955–56; Lectr in Geography, Univ. of Nottingham, 1956–69. Reader, 1969–75; Vis. Lectr or Prof., Univs of Washington, Columbia, Mexico, Valparaíso, Nanjing, Beijing. *Publications:* Geography of World Affairs, 1959, 6th edn 1983; (with F. C. German) Geography of the USSR, 1961, 2nd edn 1970; Italy, 1964; Latin America, 1965, 2nd edn 1975; (with C. A. M. King) Quantitative Geography, 1968; (with N. J. Beynon) New Ways in Geography, 1968, 2nd edn 1982; Situations in Human Geography, 1975; The Development Gap, 1981; Geography of the Soviet Union, 1984; China 1950–2000 Performance and Prospects, 1985; The Poverty of Marxism in Contemporary Geographical Applications and Research, 1986; Development and Underdevelopment, 1987; (with T. Buck) Modern Soviet Economic Performance, 1987; (with F. J. Cole) The Geography of the European Community, 1993, 2nd edn 1997; Geography of the World's Major Regions, 1996; Global 2050: a basis for speculation, 1999; Geography at Nottingham 1922–1970: a record, 2000; contribs to learned jls, UK and overseas. *Recreations:* travel, languages, pen drawing and painting, gardening. *Address:* 10 Ranmore Close, Beeston, Nottingham NG9 3FR. *T:* (0115) 925 0409.

COLE, Margaret Rose, (Mrs Graeme Cooke); Director of Enforcement, Financial Services Authority, since 2005; *b* Preston, Lancs, 17 June 1961; *d* of late Herbert and Patricia Cole; *m* 1998, Graeme Cooke. *Educ:* Winkley Sq. Convent Sch., Preston; New Hall, Cambridge (BA 1982); Coll. of Law, Lancaster Gate. Admitted solicitor, 1985. Stephenson Harwood: articled clerk, 1983; Asst Solicitor, 1985–90; Partner, 1990–95; Partner, White & Case, 1995–2005. *Publication:* (contrib.) A Practitioner's Guide to FSA Investigations and Enforcement, 2nd edn 2007. *Recreations:* horse riding, travel, opera. *Address:* Financial Services Authority, 25 The North Colonnade, Canary Wharf, E14 5HS. *T:* (020) 7066 3700, *Fax:* (020) 7066 3701; *e-mail:* margaret.cole@fsa.gov.uk.

COLE, Prof. Peter Geoffrey; journalist; Professor of Journalism, University of Sheffield, since 2000; *b* 16 Dec. 1945; *s* of Arthur and Elizabeth Cole; *m* 1982, Jane Ellison; three *s* one *d*. *Educ:* Tonbridge Sch.; Queens' Coll., Cambridge. Reporter, Evening News, 1968–72; Diary Editor, Evening Standard, 1976–78; News Editor, Deputy Editor, The Guardian, 1978–88; Editor, Sunday Correspondent, 1988–90; News Review Editor, The Sunday Times, 1990–93; Prof. of Journalism, Univ. of Central Lancs, 1993–2000. *Publication:* Can You Positively Identify This Man? (with Peter Pringle), 1975. *Address:* Department of Journalism Studies, University of Sheffield, Minalloy House, Regent Street, Sheffield S1 3NJ. *Clubs:* Garrick; Plymouth Argyle Supporters' (London Branch); Lancashire County Cricket.

COLE, His Honour Richard Raymond Buxton; DL; a Circuit Judge, 1984–2007; *b* 11 June 1937; *s* of late Raymond Buxton Cole, DSO, TD, DL, and Edith Mary Cole; *m* 1962, Sheila Joy Rumbold; one *s* one *d*. *Educ:* Dragon School; St Edward's, Oxford. Admitted as Solicitor 1960; Partner in Cole & Cole Solicitors, Oxford, 1962–84; Recorder, 1976–84; Hon. Recorder, City of Coventry, 1999–2007. Mem., Parole Bd, 1981–83. President: Berks, Bucks and Oxon Law Soc., 1981–82; Council of HM Circuit Judges, 2001. Mem. Governing Body, Dragon Sch., 1975–92, Chm., 1986–92. Chm., Burford Parish Council, 1976–79, first Town Mayor, 1979. Master, Upholders' Co., 1992–93. Hon. Pres., Assoc. of Master Upholsterers, 1993–. DL Warwickshire, 2001. *Recreations:* sport, gardening. *Clubs:* MCC; Frewen (Oxford).

COLE, Robert Templeman, CBE 1981; FREng; DL; Chairman, Conder Group plc, 1979–87; *b* 14 Dec. 1918; *s* of Percival P. Cole and Amy Gladys Cole (*née* Templeman); *m* 1947, Elspeth Lawson; one *s* one *d*. *Educ:* Harrow; Cambridge Univ. (MA). FIStructE; FREng (FEng 1982). Served RAF, 1940–46. Hampshire County Council, 1946–47; Founder Partner, Conder Engineering, 1947; Chairman: Conder Engineering Co. Ltd, 1950; Conder International Ltd, 1964. DL Hants 1988. Hon. DSc Southampton, 1980. *Recreations:* contemplation, travel. *Address:* Chilland Rise, Martyr Worthy, Winchester, Hampshire SO21 1AS. *T:* (01962) 779264.

COLE, Sir (Robert) William, Kt 1981; Director, Legal and General, Australia, 1987–91; *b* 16 Sept. 1926; *s* of James Henry and Rita Sarah Cole; *m* 1956, Margaret Noleen Martin; one *s* one *d*. *Educ:* Univ. of Melbourne (BCom). Joined Australian Public Service, 1952; Res. Officer, Treasury, 1952–57; Technical Asst, IMF, Washington, 1957–59; various positions, Treasury, 1959–70; Dir, Bureau of Transport Econs, Dept of Shipping and Transport, 1970–72; First Asst Sec., Gen. Financial and Economic Policy Div., Treasury, 1972–76; Australian Statistician, 1976; Sec., Dept of Finance, 1977–78; Chm., Public Service Bd, 1978–83; Sec., Defence Dept, 1983–86. Hon. Treas., Winston Churchill Meml Trust. *Recreations:* reading, fishing, wine. *Address:* 14 Macarthur Street, Cottesloe, WA 6011, Australia.

COLE, Stephanie, (Mrs Peter Birrel), OBE 2005; actress; *b* 5 Oct. 1941; *d* of June Sheldon; *m* 1st, 1973, Henry Marshall (marr. diss.); one *d*; 2nd, 1998, Peter Birrel. *Educ:* Clifton High Sch., Bristol; Bristol Old Vic Sch. Work in repertory theatre, and with Old Vic, etc; *television:* Soldiering On (Alan Bennett Talking Heads monologue), 1988; *series:*

Tenko, 1980–84; Waiting for God, 1989–94; Keeping Mum, 1997–99; Life As We Know It, 2001; Doc Martin, 2004; *theatre* includes: A Passionate Woman, Comedy, 1995; Quartet, Albery, 1999; So Long Life, Th. Royal, Bath, 2001; The Shell Seekers, tour, 2003–04; Blithe Spirit, Savoy, 2005; The Rivals, Th. Royal, Bath, 2005; Born in the Gardens, Th. Royal, Bath, 2008; *films* include: Grey Owl, 2000. Best TV Comedy Actress, 1992; Best TV Comedy Performance, 1999. *Publication:* A Passionate Life, 1998. *Recreations:* reading, gardening, painting, walking, theatre-going. *Address:* c/o John Grant, Conway van Gelder Grant Ltd, 18–21 Jermyn Street, SW1Y 6HP. *T:* (020) 7287 0077.

COLE, Prof. Stewart Thomas, PhD; FRS 2007; Director, Global Health Institute, Ecole Polytechnique Fédérale de Lausanne, Switzerland, since 2007; *b* 14 Jan. 1955; *s* of Leonard Thomas Cole and Jean Margaret Cole; *m* 1980, Lesley Curnick; one *s* one *d*. *Educ:* University Coll., Cardiff (BSc Hons 1976); Univ. of Sheffield (PhD 1979). Res. Asst, Max-Planck Institut for Biology, Tübingen, 1980–83; Institut Pasteur, Paris: staff scientist, 1984–89; Hd, Unité de Génétique Moléculaire Bactérienne, 1989–2007; Dir, Strategic Technol., 2000–04; Scientific Dir, 2004–05. Chevalier de la Légion d'Honneur (France), 2004. *Publications:* (ed jtly) Tuberculosis and the Tubercle Bacillus, 2005; over 250 scientific articles. *Recreations:* fly fishing, ski-ing, opera, Rugby. *Address:* Global Health Institute, Ecole Polytechnique Fédérale de Lausanne, Station 15, 1015 Lausanne, Switzerland. *T:* (21) 6931851, *Fax:* (21) 6931790; *e-mail:* stewart.cole@epfl.ch.

COLE, Sir William; *see* Cole, Sir R. W.

COLE-HAMILTON, (Arthur) Richard, CBE 1993; BA; CA; FCIBS; Chairman, Stakis PLC, 1995–98 (Deputy Chairman, 1994–95); Chief Executive, Clydesdale Bank PLC, 1982–92; *b* 8 May 1935; *s* of late John Cole-Hamilton, CBE; *m* 1963, Prudence Ann; one *s* two *d*. *Educ:* Ardrossan Academy; Loretto School; Cambridge Univ. (BA). Commissioned Argyll and Sutherland Highlanders, 1960–62. Brechin Cole-Hamilton & Co. (Chartered Accountants), 1962–67; Clydesdale Bank, 1967–92: Manager, Finance Corp. and Money Market, 1971; Asst Manager, Chief London Office, 1971; Supt of Branches, 1974; Head Office Manager, 1976; Asst Gen. Manager, 1978; Gen. Manager, 1979; Dep. Chief Gen. Manager, Feb. 1982; Dir, 1984–92. Chm., Cttee of Scottish Clearing Bankers, 1985–87, and 1991–92; Vice-Pres., Scottish Council for Develt and Industry, 1992–96; Dir, Glasgow Chamber of Commerce, 1985–91; Pres., Ayrshire Chamber of Commerce and Industry, 1992–96. Pres., Inst. of Bankers in Scotland, 1988–90. Mem. Council, Inst. of Chartered Accts of Scotland, 1981–85. Trustee: Nat. Galls of Scotland, 1986–96; Princess Royal Trust for Carers, 1991–98; Mem. Exec. Cttee, Erskine Hosp., 1976–2004. *Recreation:* golf. *Address:* 28 South Beach, Troon, Ayrshire KA10 6EF. *T:* (01292) 310603. *Clubs:* Western (Glasgow); Highland Brigade; Royal and Ancient Golf (Capt., 2004–05), Prestwick Golf.

COLEBROOK, Philip Victor Charles, CEng; retired 1984; Managing Director, Imperial Continental Gas Association, 1973–84 (Director, 1971; Director, CompAir Ltd, 1980–84); Director: Calor Group Ltd, 1969–84; Century Power & Light Ltd, 1980–84; Contibel SA (Belgium), 1978–84; *b* 8 March 1924; *s* of Frederick Charles Colebrook and Florence Margaret (*née* Cooper); *m* 1946, Dorothy Ursula Kemp; one *s* three *d*. *Educ:* Andover Grammar Sch.; Guildford Technical Coll.; Battersea Polytechnic, London. Served War of 1939–45, RNVR. Joined Pfizer as Works and Production Manager, 1952; Dir, 1956, Man. Dir, 1958–69, Pfizer Ltd; Chm. and Man. Dir, Pfizer Gp, 1961–69; Vice-Pres., Pfizer Internat., 1967–69; Man. Dir, Calor Gas Holding Co., 1969–80. Member: NHS Affairs Cttee, Assoc. of the British Pharmaceutical Industry, 1963–67; CBI Cttee on State Intervention in Private Business, 1975–78. Trustee and Mem. of Steering Cttee, Univ. of Kent at Canterbury, 1964–65. *Publication:* Going International, 1972. *Recreations:* sailing, ski-ing, golf, painting (exhib. RA, 2001).

COLEBY, Anthony Laurie; Executive Director, Bank of England, 1990–94; *b* 27 April 1935; *s* of Dr Leslie James Moger Coleby and Laurie Coleby (*née* Shuttleworth); *m* 1966, Rosemary Melian Elisabeth, *d* of Sir Peter Garran, KCMG; one *s* two *d*. *Educ:* Winchester; Corpus Christi, Cambridge (BAEcon, MA). Bank of England: joined, 1961; Personal Asst to Man. Dir, IMF, 1964–67; Assistant Chief, Overseas Dept, 1969; Adviser, Overseas Dept, 1972; Dep. Chief Cashier, 1973; Asst Dir, 1980–86; Chief Monetary Advr to the Governor, 1986–90; Exec. Dir, 1990–94. Non-executive Director: Halifax Building Soc., subseq. Halifax plc, 1994–2001; Anglo Irish Bank Corp., 1994–2001; Italian Internat. Bank, 1994–99. *Recreations:* choral singing, railways and transport. *Address:* Woodruff Farm, Debden Green, Saffron Walden, Essex CB11 3LZ.

COLEGATE, Isabel Diana, (Mrs Michael Briggs); writer; *b* 10 Sept. 1931; *d* of Sir Arthur Colegate, sometime MP, and Winifred Mary, *d* of Sir William Worsley, 3rd Bt; *m* 1953, Michael Briggs; two *s* one *d*. *Educ:* Runton Hill Sch., Norfolk. Worked as literary agent at Anthony Blond (London) Ltd, 1952–57. FRSL 1981. Hon. MA Bath, 1988. *Publications:* The Blackmailer, 1958; A Man of Power, 1960; The Great Occasion, 1962 (re-issued as Three Novels, 1983); Statues in a Garden, 1964; Orlando King, 1968; Orlando at the Brazen Threshold, 1971; Agatha, 1973 (re-issued as The Orlando Trilogy, 1984); News from the City of the Sun, 1979; The Shooting Party, 1980 (W. H. Smith Literary Award, 1980; filmed, 1985); A Glimpse of Sion's Glory, 1985; Deceits of Time, 1988; The Summer of the Royal Visit, 1991; Winter Journey, 1995; A Pelican in the Wilderness: hermits, solitaries and recluses, 2002. *Recreation:* walking the dog. *Address:* c/o Society of Authors, 84 Drayton Gardens, SW10 9SD.

COLELLA, Anton; Chief Executive, Institute of Chartered Accountants of Scotland, since 2006; *b* 25 May 1961; *s* of Dominic Colella and Anna Colella (*née* Bruno); *m* 1988, Angela Cooney; two *s* two *d*. *Educ:* St Mungo's Acad., Glasgow; Stirling Univ. (BA Hons 1983; DipEd). Teacher of RE, Holyrood Secondary Sch., Glasgow, 1983–87; Principal Teacher of RE, St Columba's High Sch., Gourock, 1987–92; Principal Teacher of RE, 1992–96, Asst Hd Teacher, 1996–99, Holyrood Secondary Sch.; Depute Hd Teacher, St Margaret Mary's Secondary Sch., Glasgow, 1999–2001, seconded to SQA, 2001; Dir of Qualifications, 2002–03, Chief Exec., 2003–06, SQA. Mem., QAA Scotland Cttee, 2001–; Mem. Bd, Scottish Further Educn Unit, 2001–07. Member: Bd, Glasgow Coll. of Nautical Studies, 1998–2007; Bd of Trustees, Columba 1400, 2007–. *Recreations:* family, walking, listening to music, playing guitar, Rugby, eating out. *Address:* Institute of Chartered Accountants of Scotland, CA House, 21 Haymarket Yards, Edinburgh EH12 5BH.

COLEMAN, Prof. Alice Mary; Professor of Geography, King's College, London, 1987–96, now Emeritus; *b* 8 June 1923; *d* of Bertie Coleman and Elizabeth Mary (*née* White). *Educ:* Clarendon House Sch.; Furzedown Training Coll. (Cert. of Educn); Birkbeck Coll., Univ. of London (BA Hons 1st Cl.); King's Coll., Univ. of London (MA with Mark of Distinction). FKC 1980. Geography Teacher, Northfleet Central Sch. for Girls, 1943–48; Geography Dept, King's Coll., London: Asst Lectr, 1948; Lectr, 1951; Sen. Lectr, 1963; Reader, 1965. Vis. Prof. for Distinguished Women Social Scientists, Univ. of Western Ontario, 1976; BC/Mombusho Prof. of Geog., Hokkaido Univ. of Educn at Asahikawa, 1985. Initiated and directed Second Land Utilisation Survey of Britain, 1960–; Dir, Design Improvement Controlled Experiment, 1988–94. Editor, Graphological Magazine, 1995–. Gill Meml Award, RGS, 1963; The Times-Veuve Clicquot Award, 1974; Busk Award, RGS, 1987. *Publications:* The Planning Challenge of the Ottawa Area, 1969; Utopia on Trial, 1985; PACE Graphological Thesaurus, 1985; Scapes and Fringes: environmental territories of England and Wales, 2000; (English lang. ed. and designer) Graphology Across Cultures, 2003; (with Mona McNee) The Great Reading Disaster, 2007; 120 land-use maps in eleven colours at the scale of 1:25,000; over 300 academic papers. *Recreations:* reading, graphology. *Address:* 19–20 Giles Coppice, SE19 1XF. *T:* (020) 8244 6733.

COLEMAN, Bernard, CMG 1986; HM Diplomatic Service, retired; Ambassador to Paraguay, 1984–86; *b* 3 Sept. 1928; *s* of William Coleman and Ettie Coleman; *m* 1st, 1950, Sonia Dinah Walters (*d* 1995); two *d*; 2nd, 1996, Georgina Edith Dorndorf; three step *d*. *Educ:* Alsop High Sch., Liverpool. HM Forces (RAEC), 1946–48. Entered Foreign (later Diplomatic) Service, 1950; FO, 1950–53; Lima, 1953–56; Detroit, 1956–59; Second Secretary (Information): Montevideo, 1959–62; Caracas, 1962–64; First Sec. (Inf.), Caracas, 1964–66; FCO, 1967–69; First Sec. (Inf.), Ottawa, 1969–73; FCO, 1973–74; seconded to DTI, 1974–75; Consul-Gen., Bilbao, 1976–78; First Sec. (Commercial), Dublin, 1979–80; High Commissioner, Tonga, 1980–83. *Recreations:* golf, bowls, bridge, reading, walking, travel.

COLEMAN, Brian John; Member (C) Barnet and Camden, since 2000, and Deputy Chairman, 2005–06 and 2007–May 2008, London Assembly, Greater London Authority (Chairman, 2004–05 and 2006–07); *b* 25 June 1961; *s* of John Francis Coleman and Gladys Coleman (*née* Cramp). *Educ:* Queen Elizabeth Boys' Sch., Barnet. Mills Allen Ltd, advertising co., 1989–99. Mem., Barnet CHC, 1991–94. Mem. (C) Barnet BC, 1998– (Cabinet Mem. for Envmt, 2002–04, for Community Safety and Community Engagement, 2006–; Dep. Mayor, 2004–05). Dep. Leader, Cons. Gp, GLA, 2002–04; Conservative Group Leader: London Fire and Emergency Planning Authy, 2000– (Dep. Chair, 2000–05; Vice Chair, 2005–08; Chair, 2008–); N London Waste Authy, 2002–08 (Chm., 2006–08). Hon. Pres., London Home and Water Safety Council, 2001–. Vice President: Chipping Barnet Cons. Assoc., 2002–; Hendon Cons. Assoc., 2002–. Governor: Christchurch Secondary Sch., 1993–2005 (Chm., 1999–2000); Ravenscroft Sch., 1996–; Queen Elizabeth's Boys' Sch., 2005–. Vice Pres., Friern Barnet Summer Show (Chm., 1995–99); Trustee, Finchley Charities, 2000–. Pres., Hendon and Edgware Dist Scouts, 2004–. FRSA 2004. Freeman: City of London, 2003; Farriers' Co., 2008. Paul Harris Fellow, Rotary Internat., 2006. Hon. Dr Middlesex, 2008. *Recreations:* opera, theatre. *Address:* 1 Essex Park, Finchley, N3 1ND. *T:* (020) 8349 2024. *Club:* Finchley Rotary.

COLEMAN, David Frederick, QPM 2004; DL; Chief Constable, Derbyshire Constabulary, 2001–07; *b* 4 Oct. 1952; *s* of Frederick and Margaret Elizabeth Coleman; *m* 1974, Hilary Grace Taylor; two *s*. *Educ:* Univ. of Manchester (BA Hons Geog.). Joined Derbyshire Constabulary, 1975; Divl Comdr, Derby, 1994–95; Asst Chief Constable, Leics Constabulary, 1996–2000. DL Derbys, 2007. *Recreations:* golf, reading, watching football, gardening.

COLEMAN, Dr Dena; Headteacher, Yavneh College, since 2005; *b* 7 Sept. 1952; *d* of Norman and Muriel Friedman; *m* 1974, Gordon David Coleman; one *s* one *d*. *Educ:* Copthall Co. Grammar Sch.; Manchester Univ. (BSc Hons Botany and Zool.; PGCE); Chelsea Coll., London (MA); King's Coll. London (PhD 1991). Sci. teacher, various London schools, 1974–86; Head of Sci., Queenswood Sch., 1986–90; Dep. Headteacher, 1990–95, Headteacher, 1995–98, Hasmonean High Sch; Headteacher, Bushey Meads Sch., 1998–2005. Member: Exec. Cttee, Assoc. Foundn and Vol. Aided (formerly Grant Maintained and Aided) Schools, 1997–2005; Herts Sch. Orgn Cttee, 1999–2005; Salters' Inst. Teachers' Prize Cttee, 2001–05; Adv. Gp, Nat. Network of Science Learning Centres, 2003–05; Bd, Herts Learning and Skills Council, 2003–; Exec. Cttee, Foundn and Aided Schs Nat. Assoc., 2005–. Consultant, York Univ. Nat. Curriculum Sci. QCA Proj., 2000–01. *Publications:* (with R. Gold) Running a School, 2002; contrib. to Hist. of Educn Jl. *Recreations:* foreign travel, piano, clothes shopping. *Address:* Yavneh College, Hillside Avenue, Borehamwood, Herts WD6 1HL.

COLEMAN, Prof. Dulcie Vivien, MD; FRCPath; Professor Emeritus of Cell Pathology, Imperial College School of Medicine, London University, since 1998 (Head of Department of Cytopathology and Cytogenetics, St Mary's Hospital, London, 1972–98; Professor of Cell Pathology, St Mary's Hospital Medical School, 1988–98); *b* 19 Oct. 1932; *d* of Dr Frank Stuart Coleman and Celia Coleman (*née* Walsman); *m* 1957, Jacob Benjamin Poznansky; three *s* one *d*. *Educ:* Bournemouth Sch. for Girls; Roedean Sch.; St Bartholomew's Hosp. Med. Sch. (MB, BS 1956; MD 1972). MRCPath 1980, FRCPath 1992. Hse Surgeon, Churchill Hosp., Oxford, 1956–57; Hse Physician, Plaistow Hosp., Essex, 1957–58; GP locums, 1959–64; Med. Asst (part-time), RPMS, 1967–70; Clin. Asst (part-time) (Cytopathol. and Cytogenetics), St Mary's Hosp., London, 1964–72; St Mary's Hospital Medical School: Sen. Lectr and Hon. Consultant in Cytopathol. and Cytogenetics, 1972–83; Reader in Cell Pathology, 1983–88; Hon. Consultant Cytopathologist, Hammersmith Hosps NHS Trust, 1998–. Member: Wkg Party on Safety of Chronic Villus sampling, MRC, 1987–90; Jt Wkg Party on Cytology Trng, DHSS, Inst. of Med. Lab. Scis and British Soc. for Clin. Cytol., 1988–90; Panel of Advrs, ACU, 1991–; Chairman: Wkg Party on Cervical Cancer Screening, Europe Against Cancer, 1990–; Wkg Party on Eur. Guidelines for Quality Assce in Cervical Screening (report pubd 1993); Cttee for Quality Assce, European Fedn of Cytology Socs, 1993–. Chm., Brit. Soc. for Clinical Cytology, 1989–92; Pres., Oncology section, RSM, 1988. Editor-in-Chief, Cytopathology, 1989–; Member, Editorial Board: Analytical Cellular Pathol.; Prenatal Diagnosis. Examr in Cytopathol. and Cytogenetics, Univs of London and Brunel, and RCPath. Hon. Member: Greek Cytology Soc.; CERDEC, France. Fellow, Internat. Acad. of Cytology. Morgani Medal, Italian Soc. of Pathology and Cytology, 1998. *Publications:* (with L. G. Koss) Advances in Clinical Cytology, Vol. 1 1981, Vol. 2 1984; (with D. M. D. Evans) Biopsy Pathology and Cytology of the Cervix, 1988, 2nd edn, 1999; (with P. C. Chapman) Clinical Cytotechnology, 1989; numerous papers, chapters, reviews on human polyomaviruses, human papillomaviruses, and other virus cytopathol. and prenatal diagnosis, incl. new techniques for cytodiagnosis of malignant disease, also on automated analysis of cervical smears. *Recreations:* gardening, swimming, nature walks. *Address:* Flat 12, 24 Hyde Park Square, W2 2NN. *T:* (020) 7262 0240.

COLEMAN, Iain; *b* 18 Jan. 1958; *m* 1996, Sally Powell (*see* Dame S. A. V. Powell); one *s*. *Educ:* Tonbridge Sch. Former Local Govt Officer. Mem., Hammersmith and Fulham BC, 1986–97 (Leader, 1991–96; Mayor, 1996–97). MP (Lab) Hammersmith and Fulham, 1997–2005.

COLEMAN, Isobel Mary; *see* Plumstead, I. M.

COLEMAN, Jeremy Barrington; a District Judge (Magistrates' Courts) (formerly Metropolitan Stipendiary Magistrate), since 1995; *b* 9 June 1951; *s* of late Neville Coleman and Pauline Coleman; *m* 1975, Margot; one *s* one *d*. *Educ:* Coll. of Law, London. LRPS

1982. Admitted solicitor, 1976; Partner in family firm, Samuel Coleman, 1976–. Mem., Law Soc. Children's Panel, 1990. Mem., RPS. *Publication:* (contributing ed.) Archbold Magistrates' Court Criminal Practice, 2004. *Recreations:* photography, cricket, archaeology. *Address:* West London Magistrates' Court, 181 Talgarth Road, W6 8DN. *Club:* Middlesex CC.

COLEMAN, John Ennis, CB 1990; Legal Adviser, Department of Education and Science, 1983–90, retired; *b* 12 Nov. 1930; *o s* of late Donald Stafford Coleman and Dorothy Jean Balieff (*née* Ennis); *m* 1958, Doreen Gwendoline Hellinger; one *s* one *d*. *Educ:* Dean Close Sch., Cheltenham; Dulwich Coll.; Worcester Coll., Oxford (MA). Solicitor (Hons), 1957. Legal Asst, Treasury Solicitor's Dept, 1958; Senior Legal Asst, 1964; Asst Solicitor, 1971; Under Sec. (Legal), Depts of Industry and Trade, 1980–83. Jt Editor, The Law of Education, 1993–2008. *Publication:* (jtly) Butterworth's Education Law, 1997.

COLEMAN, Katharine; glass engraver; *b* 30 Jan. 1949; *d* of Hector Colin Beardmore Mackenzie and Frances Mackenzie; *m* 1974, David Edward Coleman; one *s* one *d*. *Educ:* Roedean Sch.; Girton Coll., Cambridge (BA Geog 1970; MA 1974). Regd Artist/Maker, Crafts Council. Solo exhibn, Scottish Gall., Edinburgh, 2008. Work in public collections: Cheltenham Art Gall. and Mus.; Nat. Mus of Scotland, Edinburgh; Shipley at Gateshead; Birmingham City; Lybster, Caithness; Kamenicky Šenov; V&A; Broadfield House Glass Mus.; Kunstsammlungen Veste Coburg; Alexander Tutsek Collection, Munich. Chm., Guild of Glass Engravers, 2002–05; FGE (FGGE 1992). Member: Contemp. Applied Arts, 2004; Art Workers Guild, 2004. Mem., Samuel Pepys Club. Adrian Sassoon Prize for Arts of the Kiln, 2004; Hon. Mention Prize, Coburg Glass Prize, 2006; (first) Glass Sellers' Prize for Engraving on Glass, 2007. *Recreations:* other people's gardens, opera, antique glass. *Address:* 261 Cromwell Tower, Barbican, EC2Y 8DD. *T:* (020) 7628 6552; *e-mail:* katharine@katharinecoleman.co.uk.

COLEMAN, Lucille Madeline; *see* Stone, L. M.

COLEMAN, Nicholas John; His Honour Judge Coleman; a Circuit Judge, since 1998; Resident Judge, Peterborough Combined Court, since 2001; *b* 12 Aug. 1947; *s* of late Leslie Ernest Coleman and Joyce Coleman; *m* 1971, Isobel Mary Plumstead, *qv*; one *s* two *d*. *Educ:* Royal Pinner Sch.; Liverpool Univ. (LLB Hons). Called to the Bar, Inner Temple, 1970, Bencher, 2005; practised SE Circuit, 1972–98; a Recorder, 1989–98. Lectr, 1970–72, Examr, 1972–76, Inns of Court Sch. of Law. Judicial Mem., Parole Bd, 2004–. *Recreations:* sport, travel, theatre, cinema. *Address:* c/o Peterborough Combined Court, Crown Building, Rivergate, Peterborough PE1 1EJ. *T:* (01733) 349161. *Clubs:* MCC; Hampstead and Westminster Hockey; Hunstanton Golf, Aldeburgh Golf.

COLEMAN, Peter Anthony; Secretary General, European Parliamentary Labour Party, 1997–2004; *b* 10 Oct. 1945; *s* of late William and of Maggie Coleman; *m* 1966, Dorothy Edith Lawrence; two *d*. *Educ:* Avenue Primary Sch., Wellingborough; Park Road Junior Sch., Kettering; Kettering Sch. for Boys; Kettering Boot and Shoe Tech. Coll. (ABBSI). Progress chaser: Holyoake Footwear, 1961–64; Wilson & Watsons, 1964–66; Labour Party: organiser: Peterborough, 1967–71; Nottingham, 1972–76; SE Derbys, 1976–78; Asst Regl Organiser, E Midland, 1978–83, Regl Dir, 1983–93; Nat. Dir of Orgn and Develt, 1993–97. Nat. Vice-Pres., Nat. Union of Labour Organisers, 1977–78; Nat. Chair, Computing for Labour, 2003–06. Member: Exec. Cttee, Fabian Soc., 1994–95; Mgt Cttee, H. S. Chapman Soc., 2000–04. *Publications:* (ed) Labour's Fundraising Guide, 1984; pamphlets on electoral law, Labour Party regeneration and polling-day systems. *Recreations:* theatre, travel, watching cricket and football. *Club:* Hampshire CC.

COLEMAN, Sir Robert John, KCMG 2005; Visiting Research Fellow, Institute of Governance, Queen's University, Belfast, since 2004 (Senior Practitioner Fellow, 2003–04); *b* 8 Sept. 1943; *s* of Frederick and Kathleen Coleman; *m* 1966, Malinda Tigay Cutler; two *d*. *Educ:* Univ. of Oxford (MA); Univ. of Chicago (JD). Called to the Bar, Inner Temple, 1969. Lectr in Law, Univ. of Birmingham, 1967–70; Barrister at Law, 1970–73; European Commission: Administrator, subseq. Principal Administrator, 1974–82; Dep. Head of Div., safeguard measures and removal of non-tariff barriers, 1983; Head of Div., Intellectual Property and Unfair Competition, 1984–87; Dir, Public Procurement, 1987–90; Dir, Approximation of Laws, Freedom of Estabt, and Freedom to Provide Services, 1990–91; Director General: Transport, 1991–99; Health and Consumer Protection, 1999–2003. Vis. Prof., Univ. of East London, 1997–. Mem. Adv. Bd, Sch. of Mgt, Univ. of Bath, 2001–. *Publications:* contribs and articles on legal and policy issues, concerning corporate accounting, employee participation, intellectual property and transport. *Recreations:* cycling, music. *Address:* Institute of Governance, Queen's University, Belfast BT7 1NN.

COLEMAN, Roger, FRCA; Co-Director, Helen Hamlyn Centre (formerly Research Centre), since 1999, and Professor of Inclusive Design, since 2002, Royal College of Art; *b* 20 March 1943; *s* of Ronald Charles Coleman and Margaret Grace Coleman (*née* Thomas); *m* 1st, 1965, Alison Fell (marr. diss. 1967); one *s*; 2nd, 1995, Sally Reilly. *Educ:* Ealing Grammar Sch. for Boys; Edinburgh Sch. of Art and Edinburgh Univ. (Andrew Grant Schol.; MA Hons Fine Art). Lectr, Leeds Sch. of Art and Design, and Vis. Lectr, Bradford Sch. of Art and Design, 1967–70; Sen. Lectr, St Martin's Sch. of Art and Design, 1970–72; Partner, Community Press, London, 1972–73; freelance designer and maker, 1973–84; Director: Community, Construction and Design Ltd, 1984–91; London Innovation Ltd, 1985–2003; Dir, DesignAge prog., RCA, 1991–98. Co-ordinator, Eur. Design for Ageing Network, 1994–98. Jury Chm., RSA Student Design Awards, 1992–. Founder and Mem. Council, Welfare State Internat. (perf. community arts gp), 1968–. Exhibitions: One Rock, Lanternhouse, Ulverston, 2003; Flat Earth, Old Fire Engine House, Ely, 2006; Flat Earth 2007, EXHIBIT, London, 2007. FRCA 1996; FRSA 2000. Sir Misha Black Award for Innovation in Design Educn, 2001. *Publications:* The Art of Work: an epitaph to skill, 1988, rev. Japanese edn 1998; Designing for our Future Selves, 1993; Design Research for our Future Selves, 1994; Working Together: a new approach to design, 1997; (jtly, also ed) Design für die Zukunft, 1997; Living Longer: the new context for design, 2001; (jtly) Inclusive Design: design for the whole population, 2003; (jtly) Design for Patient Safety: a system-wide design-led approach to tackling patient safety in the NHS, 2003; (jtly) Design for Patient Safety: future ambulances, 2007. *Recreations:* fen watching and imaginary punt-gunning - waiting for the seas to rise. *Address:* Helen Hamlyn Centre, Royal College of Art, Kensington Gore, SW7 2EU. *T:* (020) 7590 4242, *Fax:* (020) 7590 4244; *e-mail:* roger.coleman@rca.ac.uk; *web:* www.rogercolemanphotography.com.

COLEMAN, Terry, (Terence Francis Frank); reporter and author; *b* 13 Feb. 1931; *s* of J. and D. I. B. Coleman; *m* 1st, 1954, Lesley Fox-Strangeways Vane (marr. diss.); two *d*; 2nd, 1981, Vivien Rosemary Lumsdaine Wallace; one *s* one *d*. *Educ:* 14 schs. LLB London. Formerly: Reporter, Poole Herald; Editor, Savoir Faire; Sub-editor, Sunday Mercury, and Birmingham Post; Reporter and then Arts Corresp., The Guardian, 1961–70, Chief Feature Writer, 1970–74; Special Writer with Daily Mail, 1974–76; The Guardian: Chief Feature Writer, 1976–79, writing mainly political interviews, incl. last eight British Prime Ministers; NY Correspondent, 1981; special corresp., 1982–89; Associate Editor, The Independent, 1989–91. FRSA. Feature Writer of the Year, British Press Awards, 1982; Journalist of the Year, Granada Awards, 1987. *Publications:* The Railway Navvies, 1965 (Yorkshire Post prize for best first book of year), rev. edn 2000; A Girl for the Afternoons, 1965; (with Lois Deacon) Providence and Mr Hardy, 1966; The Only True History: collected journalism, 1969; Passage to America, 1972, rev. edn 2000; (ed) An Indiscretion in the Life of an Heiress (Hardy's first novel), 1976; The Liners, 1976; The Scented Brawl: collected journalism, 1978; Southern Cross, 1979; Thanksgiving, 1981; Movers and Shakers: collected interviews, 1987; Thatcher's Britain, 1987; Empire, 1993; Nelson: the man and the legend, 2001, US edn as The Nelson Touch, 2002; Olivier: the authorised biography, 2005. *Recreations:* cricket, opera, circumnavigation. *Address:* c/o Peters, Fraser & Dunlop, Drury House, 34–43 Russell Street, WC2B 5HA. *T:* (020) 7720 2651. *Club:* MCC.

COLEMAN, Victor Paul; Deputy Director, Corporate Science and Analytical Services, Health and Safety Executive, since 2006; *b* 28 Feb. 1952; *s* of Richard William Coleman and Edna Grace Coleman; *m* 1978, Eleanor Jane Kirkwood. *Educ:* Greenford Co. Grammar Sch.; King's Coll., Cambridge (MA); Univ. of Aston in Birmingham (Dip. Occupational Safety and Health). HM Inspector of Factories, 1973–83; Health and Safety Executive: Principal Inspector of Factories, 1983–92; Hd, Railway Safety Policy, 1992–94; Dep. Chief Inspector of Railways, 1995–98; Chief Inspector of Railways, 1998–2002; Hd of Policy for Hazardous Industries, 2002–03; Hd of Finance and Planning, 2003–06. Chm., Railways Industry Adv. Cttee, HSC, 1998–2001; Mem., Channel Tunnel Safety Authy, 1995–98. *Recreations:* theatre, walking. *Address:* (office) Rose Court, 2 Southwark Bridge, SE1 9HS. *T:* (020) 7717 6204.

COLENSO-JONES, Maj. (Gilmore) Mervyn (Boyce); one of HM Body Guard, Honourable Corps of Gentlemen-at-Arms, 1982–2000 (Harbinger, 1997–2000); *b* 4 Sept. 1930; *s* of late Dr Gilmore Leonard Colenso Colenso-Jones and Kathleen Edwina Colenso-Jones (*née* Macartney); *m* 1968, Rosamond Anne Bowen. *Educ:* Rugby Sch. Commnd Royal Welch Fusiliers, 1950: served at home and abroad; jssc, Latimer, 1968–69; Brit. Exchange Officer, US Continental Army Comd, Va, 1969–70; retd 1972, in rank of Maj.; Regtl Sec., RWF, 1972–81. Mem., S Glamorgan HA, 1981–84. CStJ 1981 (Priory Sec. for Wales, 1981–84). *Recreations:* country pursuits, water-colour painting. *Address:* 18 Bearwater, Hungerford, Berks RG17 0NN. *T:* (01488) 683250.

COLERAINE, 2nd Baron *cr* 1954, of Haltemprice; **James Martin Bonar Law;** *b* 8 Aug. 1931; *s* of 1st Baron Coleraine, PC, *y s* of Rt Hon. Andrew Bonar Law, and Mary Virginia (*d* 1978), *d* of A. F. Nellis, Rochester, NY; *S* father, 1980; *m* 1st, 1958, Emma Elizabeth Richards (marr. diss.); two *d*; 2nd, 1966, Anne Patricia, (Tomt) (*d* 1993), *yr d* of Major-Gen. R. H. Farrant, CB; one *s* one *d* (and one *d* decd); 3rd, 1998, Marion Robina, (Bobbie), *d* of Sir Thomas Ferens, CBE and *widow* of Peter Smyth. *Educ:* Eton; Trinity College, Oxford. Formerly in practice as a solicitor. Hon. Consultant, Fedn of Private Residents' Assocs, 1994–. *Heir: s* Hon. James Peter Bonar Law, *b* 23 Feb. 1975. *Address:* 4 Ashdown Lodge, Chepstow Villas, W11 3EE. *T:* (020) 7221 4148; The Dower House, Sunderlandwick, Driffield, E Yorks YO25 9AD. *T:* (01377) 253535.

See also Baron Ironside.

COLERIDGE, family name of **Baron Coleridge**.

COLERIDGE, 5th Baron *cr* 1873, of Ottery St Mary; **William Duke Coleridge;** *b* 18 June 1937; *s* of 4th Baron Coleridge, KBE, and Cecilia Rosamund (*d* 1991), *d* of Adm. Sir William Wordsworth Fisher, GCB, GCVO; *S* father, 1984; *m* 1st, 1962, Everild Tania (marr. diss. 1977), *d* of Lt-Col Beauchamp Hambrough, OBE; one *s* two *d*; 2nd, 1977, Pamela, *d* of late G. W. Baker, CBE, VRD; two *d*. *Educ:* Eton; RMA Sandhurst. Commissioned into Coldstream Guards, 1958; served King's African Rifles, 1962–64; commanded Guards Independent Parachute Company, 1970–72. Director: Abercrombie & Kent, 1978–90; Larchpark Properties Ltd, 1987–92; Chairman: Universal Energy Ltd, 1984–90; European Leisure Estates plc, 1988–90; Advr, Nat. Marine Aquarium, 1990–. Gov., Royal West of England Residential Sch. for the Deaf, 1984–. *Heir: s* Hon. James Duke Coleridge, *b* 5 June 1967. *Address:* The Manor House, Ottery St Mary, Devon EX11 1DR. *T:* (01404) 812564.

COLERIDGE, David Ean; Chairman of Lloyd's, 1991, 1992 (Deputy Chairman, 1985, 1988, 1989); *b* 7 June 1932; *s* of Guy Cecil Richard Coleridge, MC and Katherine Cicely Stewart Smith; *m* 1955, Susan Senior; three *s*. *Educ:* Eton. Glanvill Enthoven, 1950–57; R. W. Sturge & Co., 1957–95: Dir, 1966–95; Chm., A. L. Sturge (Holdings) Ltd (now Sturge Holdings PLC), 1978–95. Chm., Oxford Agency Hldgs Ltd, 1987–90; Director: R. A. Edwards (Holdings) Ltd, 1985–90; Wise Speke Hldgs Ltd, 1987–94; Ockham Hldgs, subseq. Highway Insurance, 1995–2006 (Chm., 1995). Mem., Council and Cttee of Lloyd's, 1983–92. *Recreations:* golf, racing, gardening, family. *Address:* Spring Pond House, Wispers, near Midhurst, W Sussex GU29 0QH. *T:* (01730) 813277; 37 Egerton Terrace, SW3 2BU. *T:* (020) 7581 1756.

See also N. D. Coleridge.

COLERIDGE, Geraldine Margaret, (Gill), (Mrs D. R. Leeming); Director, Rogers Coleridge and White, Literary Agency, since 1988; *b* 26 May 1948; *d* of Antony Duke Coleridge and June Marian Caswell; *m* 1974, David Roger Leeming; two *s*. *Educ:* Queen Anne's School, Caversham; Marlborough Secretarial College, Oxford. BPC Partworks, Sidgwick & Jackson, Bedford Square Book Bang, to 1971; Publicity Manager, Chatto & Windus, 1971–72; Dir and Literary Agent, Anthony Sheil Associates, 1973–88. Pres., Assoc. of Authors' Agents, 1988–91. *Recreations:* entertaining, reading, music, gardening. *Address:* 113 Calabria Road, N5 1HS. *T:* (020) 7226 5875.

COLERIDGE, Most Rev. Mark Benedict; *see* Canberra and Goulburn, Archbishop of, (RC).

COLERIDGE, Nicholas David; Managing Director: Condé Nast Publications, since 1992 (Editorial Director, 1989–91); CondéNet Ltd, since 1999; Vice-President, Condé Nast International Inc., since 1999; Director: Les Publications Condé Nast, since 1994; Condé Nast India, since 2006; *b* 4 March 1957; *s* of David Ean Coleridge, *qv*; *m* 1989, Georgia Metcalfe; three *s* one *d*. *Educ:* Eton; Trinity Coll., Cambridge. Associate Editor, Tatler, 1979–81; Columnist, Evening Standard, 1981–84; Features Editor, Harpers and Queen, 1985–86, Editor, 1986–89. Chm., Periodical Publishers Assoc., 2004–06; Dir, Press Bd of Finance, 2006–. Chairman: British Fashion Council, 2000–03; Fashion Rocks for the Prince's Trust, RAH, 2003; Director: Prince's Trust Trading Bd, 2004–07; Adv. Bd, Concert for Diana, Wembley Stadium, 2007. Council Mem., RCA, 1995–2000. Young Journalist of the Year, British Press Awards, 1983; Mark Boxer Award, BSME, 2001. *Publications:* Tunnel Vision, collected journalism, 1982; Around the World in 78 Days, 1984; Shooting Stars, 1984; The Fashion Conspiracy, 1988; How I Met My Wife and other stories, 1991; Paper Tigers, 1993; With Friends Like These, 1997; Streetsmart, 1999; Godchildren, 2002; A Much Married Man, 2006. *Address:* Wolverton Hall, Pershore, Worcs WR10 2AU. *T:* (01905) 841697; 29 Royal Avenue, SW3 4QE. *T:* (020) 7730 5998.

COLERIDGE, Hon. Sir Paul (James Duke), Kt 2000; **Hon. Mr Justice Coleridge**; a Judge of the High Court, Family Division, since 2000; *b* 30 May 1949; *s* of late James Bernard and Jane Evelina Coleridge; *m* 1973, Judith Elizabeth Rossiter; two *s* one *d*. *Educ*: Cranleigh Sch., Surrey; College of Law, London. Called to the Bar, Middle Temple, 1970, Bencher, 2000; in practice at the Bar, 1970–85; Internat. Legal Advr to Baron Hans Heinrich Thyssen-Bornemisza, Switzerland, 1985–89; private practice, 1989–2000; QC 1993; a Recorder, 1996–2000; Family Div. Liaison Judge, Western Circuit, 2002–. *Recreations*: Dorset, gardening, motor-bikes. *Address*: Royal Courts of Justice, Strand WC2A 2LL. *Club*: MCC.

COLES, Adrian Michael; Director-General, Building Societies Association, since 1993; *b* 19 April 1954; *s* of Kenneth Ernest Coles and Constance Mary (*née* Sykes); *m* 1981, Marion Alma Hoare; one *s* one *d*. *Educ* Holly Lodge Grammar Sch., Smethwick; Univ. of Nottingham (BA Hons); Univ. of Sheffield (MA). Economist, Electricity Council, 1976–79; Building Societies Association: Economist, 1979–81; Head: Econs and Stats, 1981–86; External Relns, 1986–93; Dir-Gen., Council of Mortgage Lenders, 1993–96. Chm., Thames Valley Housing Assoc., 1990–93; Director: Housing Securities Ltd, 1994–; Banking Code Standards Bd Ltd, 1999–; Parsons Mead Educnl Trust Ltd, 2000–07; Communicate Mutuality Ltd, 2001–; Independent Housing Ombudsman, 2001–04; Sec. Gen., Internat. Union for Housing Finance, 2001–. Trustee, Money Advice Trust, 1994–2004. *Publications*: (with Mark Boleat) The Mortgage Market, 1987; numerous articles in housing and housing finance jls. *Recreations*: gym, walking, reading, family. *Address*: The Building Societies Association, 6th Floor, York House, 23 Kingsway, WC2B 6UJ. *T*: (020) 7437 0655.

COLES, Alec; Director, Tyne & Wear Museums, since 2002; *b* Wolverhampton, 3 Jan. 1959; *s* of William John and Kathleen Audrey Coles; *m* 1981, Nicola Jill Wren; two *s*. *Educ*: Univ. of Leicester (BSc Hons Biol Scis); Univ. of Newcastle upon Tyne (Post Grad. Cert. Cultural Mgt); Univ. of E Anglia (Mus. Leadership Prog.). AMA 1986. Asst Curator, 1980–86, Dep. Curator, 1986–88, Woodspring Mus.; Sen. Museums Officer, Tyne & Wear Museums, 1988–92; Curator, Hancock Mus., Newcastle upon Tyne, 1992–96; Sen. Curator, Tyne & Wear Museums, 1996–2000; Chief Exec., Northumberland Wildlife Trust, 2000–02. Hon. Treas., Museums Assoc., 2006–. FLS 1990. *Recreations*: natural history (botany), music. *Address*: Discovery Museum, Blandford Square, Newcastle upon Tyne NE1 4JA. *T*: (0191) 232 6789, *Fax*: (0191) 230 2614; *e-mail*: alec.coles@twmuseums.org.uk.

COLES, Sir (Arthur) John, GCMG 1997 (KCMG 1989; CMG 1984); HM Diplomatic Service, retired; Permanent Under-Secretary of State, Foreign and Commonwealth Office, and Head of the Diplomatic Service, 1994–97; *b* 13 Nov. 1937; *s* of Arthur Strixton Coles and Doris Gwendoline Coles; *m* 1965, Anne Mary Sutherland Graham; two *s* one *d*. *Educ*: Magdalen Coll. Sch., Brackley; Magdalen Coll., Oxford (BA 1960, MA). Served HM Forces, 1955–57. Joined HM Diplomatic Service, 1960; Middle Eastern Centre for Arabic Studies, Lebanon, 1960–62; Third Sec., Khartoum, 1962–64; FO (later FCO), 1964–68; Asst Political Agent, Trucial States (Dubai), 1968–71; FCO, 1971–75; Head of Chancery, Cairo, 1975–77; Counsellor (Developing Countries), UK Perm. Mission to EEC, 1977–80; Head of S Asian Dept, FCO, 1980–81; Private Sec. to Prime Minister, 1981–84; Ambassador to Jordan, 1984–88; High Commissioner to Australia, 1988–91; Dep. Under-Sec. of State, FCO, 1991–94. Non-exec. Dir, BG plc, 1998–. Chm., Sight Savers Internat., 2001–07. Trustee, Imperial War Mus., 1999–2004. Vis. Fellow, All Souls Coll., Oxford, 1998–99. Gov., Ditchley Foundn, 1997–; Mem. Council, Atlantic Coll., 2001–03. President, FCO Assoc., 2000–02. Gov., Sutton's Hosp. in Charterhouse, 2003–05. *Publications*: British Influence and the Euro, 1999; Making Foreign Policy: a certain idea of Britain, 2000; Blindness and The Visionary: the life and work of John Wilson, 2006. *Recreations*: walking, cricket, bird-watching, reading, music. *Address*: Kelham, Dock Lane, Beaulieu, Hants SO42 7YH. *Club*: Oxford and Cambridge.

COLES, Bruce; *see* Coles, N. B. C.

COLES, Prof. Bryony Jean, FBA 2007; FSA; Professor of Prehistoric Archaeology, University of Exeter, 1996–2008, now Emeritus; *b* 12 Aug. 1946; *d* of John Samuel Orme, CB, OBE, and Jean Esther Orme (*née* Harris); *m* 1985, John Morton Coles, *qv*. *Educ*: High Wycombe High Sch.; Univ. of Bristol (BA Hist. 1968); Inst. of Archaeology, Univ. of London (Postgrad. Dip. Archaeol. 1970); University Coll. London (MPhil Anthropol. 1972). FSA 1975. University of Exeter: Lectr, 1972–89; Sen. Lectr, 1989; Reader, 1990; British Acad. Res. Readership, 1991–94. Co-Dir (with J. M. Coles), Somerset Levels Proj., 1973–89; Dir, Wetland Archaeol. Res. Proj., 1989–. Editor, Jl of Wetland Archaeol., 2000–. Mem., Archaeol. Adv. Panel, Nat. Mus. and Galls of Wales, 1991–2003; Vice Pres., Prehistoric Soc., 1994–97; Chm., NW Wetland Survey, 1994–98. Mem., Scientific Adv. Council, Netherlands Archaeol. Res. Sch., 1997–. Pres., Devon Archaeol. Soc., 2006–08. Baguley Award, Prehistoric Soc., 1990, 1999; George Stephenson Medal, ICE, 1995; (jtly) British Archaeol Award, 1986, 1988, 1998. *Publications*: Anthropology for Archaeologists, 1981; Beavers in Britain's Past, 2006; with J. M. Coles: Prehistory of the Somerset Levels, 1980; Sweet Track to Glastonbury: the Somerset Levels in prehistory, 1986; People of the Wetlands, 1989; Enlarging the Past: the contribution of wetland archaeology (Rhind Lects 1994–95), 1996; contribs to Wetland Archaeol. Res. Proj. occasional papers, British and Europ. conf. procs and learned jls. *Recreations*: walking, wildlife and wetlands, gardening, reading. *Address*: c/o Department of Archaeology, University of Exeter, Laver Building, North Park Road, Exeter EX4 4QE. *T*: (01392) 264350.
See also J. D. Orme.

COLES, Rt Rev. Dr David John; Vicar of Wakatipu, Queenstown, since 2008; Bishop of Christchurch, 1990–2008; *b* 23 March 1943; *s* of Samuel Arthur and Evelyn Ann Coles; *m* 1st, 1970, Ceridwyn Mary Parr (marr. diss.); one *s* one *d*; 2nd, 2001, Joy Woodley. *Educ*: Auckland Grammar Sch.; Univ. of Auckland (MA Hons 1967); Univ. of Otago (BD 1969; MTh 1971); Univ. of Manchester (PhD 1974); Melbourne Coll. of Divinity (Dip. Religious Educn). Deacon 1968, priest 1969; Curate, St Mark, Remuera, Auckland, 1968–70; Asst Chaplain, Selwyn Coll., Dunedin, 1970–71; Curate, Fallowfield, 1972–73; Chaplain, Hulme Hall, Univ. of Manchester, 1973–74; Vicar of: Glenfield, 1974–76; Takapuna, 1976–80; Examining Chaplain to Bp of Auckland, 1974–80; Dean and Vicar of St John's Cathedral, Napier, dio. Waiapu, 1980–84; Dean of Christchurch and Vicar-General, dio. Christchurch, 1984–90. Pres., Conf. of Churches of Aotearoa-NZ, 1991. *Recreations*: music, ski-ing, tramping. *Address*: 5 Poolburn Court, Lake Hayes Estate, Queenstown 9304, New Zealand.

COLES, Prof. Harry James, PhD, DSc; FInstP; Professor of Photonics of Molecular Materials, and Director, Centre of Molecular Materials for Photonics and Electronics, University of Cambridge, since 2002; Fellow of St Catharine's College, Cambridge, since 2006; *b* 28 Aug. 1946; *s* of William and Audrey Joan Coles; *m* 1st, 1968, Janet Phillips (marr. diss. 2008); one *s*; 2nd, 2008, Leona Marie Hope (*née* Averis). *Educ*: Tal Handaq Grammar Sch., Malta; Trowbridge Boys' High Sch.; Queen Elizabeth Coll., Univ. of London (BSc Hons); Brunel Univ. (PhD 1975); Victoria Univ. of Manchester (DSc 1985).

FInstP 1985. Maître de Recherche, Univ. Louis Pasteur, Strasbourg, 1975–79; Victoria University of Manchester: Lectr, 1980–85; Sen. Lectr, 1985–87; Reader, 1988–90; Prof., 1991–95; Prof., Univ. of Southampton, and Dir, Southampton Liquid Crystal Inst., 1995–2002. Visiting Professor: Berlin, 1990; Tokyo, 1990; Directeur de Recherche, Strasbourg, 1991. George Gray Medal, British Liquid Crystal Soc., 2003. *Publications*: (jtly) Liquid Crystal Handbook, Vol. IIB, 1998; contrib. numerous papers to learned jls; 23 internat. patents; numerous presentations to scientific confs. *Recreations*: running, gardening, oil painting, Charlton Athletic FC, fast cars. *Address*: CMMPE, Electrical Engineering Division, Department of Engineering, University of Cambridge, 9 JJ Thompson Avenue, Cambridge CB3 0FA. *T*: (01223) 748344, *Fax*: (01223) 748310; *e-mail*: hjc37@cam.ac.uk.

COLES, Jenny; *see* Joseph, J.

COLES, Sir John; *see* Coles, Sir A. J.

COLES, John David, CB 2005; FREng; RCNC; Carrier Vehicle Future Integrated Project Team Leader, Defence Procurement Agency, Ministry of Defence, 2005–07; *b* 10 May 1945; *s* of William Frederick Coles and Alice Marie Coles; *m* 1967, Judith Ann Baker (*d* 1992); two *d*. *Educ*: University Coll. London (BSc 1969; MSc 1970). FRINA 1998; FREng 2004. RCNC 1971–2005; Staff Constructor to Flag Officer Submarines, 1978–82; Head of British Admiralty Office, USA, 1982–85; Assistant Director: Future Projects, 1985–88; Dir Gen. Submarines, 1988–92; Dir of Works, Strategic Systems, 1992–94; rcds, 1994; Supt Ships, Devonport, MoD, 1995–97; Dir Gen., Equipment Support (Sea), Chief Exec., Ships, then Warship, Support Agency, and Head of RCNC, 1998–2007. Hon. DEng Bath. *Address*: c/o Ministry of Defence Abbey Wood, Filton, Bristol BS34 8JH.

COLES, John Morton, ScD, PhD; FBA 1978; Professor of European Prehistory, University of Cambridge, 1980–86; Fellow of Fitzwilliam College, since 1963, Hon. Fellow, 1987; *b* 25 March 1930; *s* of Edward John Langdon Coles and Alice Margaret (*née* Brown); *m* 1985, Bryony Jean Orme (see B. J. Coles); two *s* two *d* of previous marr. *Educ*: Woodstock, Ontario; Univ. of Toronto (BA; tennis colours 1952); Univ. of Cambridge (MA, ScD); Univ. of Edinburgh (PhD; Scottish Tennis Cup 1957). Carnegie Scholar and Research Fellow, Univ. of Edinburgh, 1959–60; Asst Lectr, 1960–65, Lectr, 1965–76, Reader, 1976–80, Univ. of Cambridge. Fellow, McDonald Inst. for Archaeological Res., Univ. of Cambridge, 1992–96; Hon. Res. Prof., Univ. of Exeter, 1993–2003. President, Prehistoric Soc., 1978–82. Member: Royal Commn on Ancient and Historical Monuments of Scotland, 1992–2002; Directorate, Discovery Prog. Ireland, 2001–06. MAE 1989; Hon. Corresp. Mem., Deutsches Archäologisches Institut, 1979; Hon. Member: Inst. of Field Archaeologists, 1991; RIA, 2005. FSA 1963 (Vice-Pres., 1982–86); Hon. FSAScot 2000. Hon. FilDr Uppsala Univ., 1997. Grahame Clark Medal, British Acad., 1995; ICI Medal, British Archaeol Awards, 1998; Europa Prize for Prehistory, Prehistoric Soc., 2000; Gold Medal, Soc. of Antiquaries of London, 2002; European Archaeol Heritage Prize, 2006; Rajewski Medal, Warsaw, 2007. *Publications*: The Archaeology of Early Man (with E. Higgs), 1969; Field Archaeology in Britain, 1972; Archaeology by Experiment, 1973; (with A. Harding) The Bronze Age in Europe, 1979; Experimental Archaeology, 1979; (with B. Orme) Prehistory of the Somerset Levels, 1980; The Archaeology of Wetlands, 1984; (with B. J. Coles) Sweet Track to Glastonbury: the Somerset Levels in prehistory, 1986; (ed with A. Lawson) European Wetlands in Prehistory, 1987; Meare Village East, 1987; (with B. J. Coles) People of the Wetlands, 1989; Images of the Past, 1990; From the Waters of Oblivion, 1991; (with A. Goodall and S. Minnitt) Arthur Bulleid and the Glastonbury Lake Village 1892–1992, 1992; (with D. Hall) Fenland Survey, 1994; Rock Carvings of Uppland, 1994; (with S. Minnitt) Industrious and Fairly Civilised: the Glastonbury lake village, 1995; (with B. Coles) Enlarging the Past: the contribution of wetland archaeology, 1996; (with S. Minnitt) The Lake Villages of Somerset, 1996; (with D. Hall) Changing Landscapes: the ancient Fenland, 1998; (ed jtly) World Prehistory: studies in memory of Grahame Clark, 1999; (ed jtly) Bog Bodies, Sacred Sites and Wetland Archaeology, 1999; Patterns in a Rocky Land: rock carvings in South West Uppland, Sweden, 2000; (jtly) Ceremony and Display: the South Cadbury Bronze Age shield, 2000; Shadows of a Northern Past: rock carvings of Bohuslän and Østfold, 2005; contrib. Proc. Prehist. Soc., Antiquaries Jl, Antiquity, Somerset Levels Papers, etc. *Recreations*: music, ancient art, wetlands, woodlands. *Address*: Fursdon Mill Cottage, Cadbury, Devon EX5 5JS. *T*: (01392) 860125.

COLES, Jonathan Andrew; Director, 14–19 Reform, Department for Children, Schools and Families (formerly Department for Education and Skills), since 2005; *b* 5 May 1972; *s* of Robert and Josephine Coles; *m* 1995, Rachel Brooks; two *d*. *Educ*: Judd Sch., Tonbridge; Mansfield Coll., Oxford (BA); St Catharine's Coll., Cambridge (PGCE); York Univ. (MA). Head, Class Size Unit, DfES, 1998–99; Perf. and Innovation Unit, Cabinet Office, 1999–2000; Head, Educn Green Paper, White Paper and Bill, 2000–02, Dir, London Challenge, 2002–05, DfES. *Address*: Department for Children, Schools and Families, Sanctuary Buildings, Great Smith Street, SW1P 3BT; *e-mail*: jon.coles@dcsf.gsi.gov.uk.

COLES, Kenneth George, AM 2000; BE; FIEAust; CEng, FIMechE, FAIM; Chairman, Conveyor Co. of Australia Pty Ltd, 1957–91; *b* Melbourne, 30 June 1926; *s* of Sir Kenneth Coles; *m* 1st, 1950, Thalia Helen Goddard (marr. diss. 1980); one *s* two *d*; 2nd, 1985, Rowena Danziger. *Educ*: The King's Sch., Parramatta, NSW; Sydney Univ. (BE 1948). FIE(Aust) 1986; FIMechE 1969; FAIM 1959. Gained engrg experience in appliance manufacturing and automotive industries Nuffield Aust. Pty Ltd, Gen. Motors Holdens Pty Ltd and Frigidaire, before commencing own business manufacturing conveyors, 1955; Chm. and Man. Dir, K. G. Coles & Co. Pty Ltd, 1955–76, Chm. 1976–95; Chm. and Man. Dir, KGC Magnetic Tape Pty Ltd, 1973–80. Director: Australian Oil & Gas Corp. Ltd, 1969–89 (Dep. Chm., 1984–89); A. O. G. Minerals Ltd, 1969–87 (Dep. Chm., 1984–87); Coles Myer Ltd (formerly G. J. Coles & Coy Ltd), 1976–94; Electrical Equipment Ltd, 1976–84; Permanent Trustee Co. Ltd, 1978–94 (Vice Chm., 1990–91; Chm., 1991–94); Centre for Industrial Technol. Ltd, 1985–87; Chatham Investment Co. Ltd, 1987–94; NRMA Insurance Ltd, 1989–90; Stockland Trust Group, 1990–95; Chairman: Innovation Council of NSW Ltd, 1984–89 (Dir, 1982–89); Nat. Engrg (now Metal and Engrg) Training Bd, 1988–99. Metal Trades Industry Association: Gen. Councillor, NSW Br., 1976–94; Nat. Councillor, 1988–94; Mem. Bd, Sir William Tyree MTIA Foundn, 1995–2002. Chm., Lizard Island Reef Res. Foundn, 1994– (Dir, 1992–). Member: Internat. Solar Energy Soc., 1957–97; Science & Industry Forum, Australian Academy of Science, 1983–94; Mem. and Employers' Rep., NSW Bd of Secondary Educn, 1987–90. Mem. Council, Nat. Roads and Motorists Assoc., NSW, 1986–90. Councillor and Mem. Bd of Governors, Ascham Sch., 1972–82; Employers' Rep., NSW Secondary Schs Bd, 1979–83. Sydney University: Fellow, Senate, 1983–97; Chairman: Internat. House, 2001–03 (Mem. Council 1993–2003); Save Sight Inst., 2001– (Mem. Council, 1998–). Hon. Dr Univ. Sydney, 1999. *Publication*: Branching Out: the George Coles family tree, 2001. *Address*: 501/170 Ocean Street, Edgecliff, NSW 2027, Australia. *T*: (2) 93286084, *Fax*: (2) 93274010. *Clubs*: Union, Australian, Sydney Rotary (Sydney); Royal Sydney Golf; Rose Bay Surf.

COLES, His Honour (Norman) Bruce (Cameron); QC 1984; a Circuit Judge, 1997–2006; *b* 28 Feb. 1937; *s* of Sir Norman Coles and of Dorothy Verna (*née* Deague); *m* 1961, Sally Fenella Freeman; one *s* three *d*. *Educ:* Melbourne Grammar Sch.; Univ. of Melbourne (LLB); Magdalen Coll., Oxford Univ. (BCL). 2nd Lieut, 6th Bn Royal Melbourne Regt, 1956–59. Associate to Sir Owen Dixon, Chief Justice of High Court of Australia, 1959–60; called to English Bar, Middle Temple, 1963, Bencher, 1991; admitted to Bar of Supreme Court of Victoria, 1964. Assistant Recorder, 1982–86; Recorder, 1986–97; Dep. Official Referee, 1992–97. Chm., Bar Race Relations Cttee, 1994–97; Mem., Equal Treatment Adv. Cttee, Judicial Studies Bd, 1999–. Mem. Council, Oxfam, 1985–98. Chm. of Govs, Enstone Co. Primary Sch., 1993–2000. *Recreations:* mountaineering, cycling, theatre, music. *Clubs:* Cyclist Touring (Surrey); Gentian Mountaineering (Glos).

COLES, Sir Sherard (Louis) C.; *see* Cowper-Coles.

COLEY, Dr Graham Douglas; Group Director Compliance, QinetiQ Ltd, 2006–08 (Business Continuity Director, 2001–06); *b* 16 Nov. 1946; *s* of late Douglas Leonard Coley and of Phyllis Adeline Coley (*née* Hughes); *m* 1972, Susan Elizabeth Thackery. *Educ:* Halesowen Grammar Sch.; Birmingham Univ. (BSc 1st Cl. Hons); Darwin Coll., Cambridge (PhD 1971). FIET (FIEE 1994); FInstP 1998. Midlands Res. Station, Gas Council, 1967–68; Atomic Weapons Research Establishment, Aldermaston, 1968–87: Supt, Explosives Technol. Br., 1982–85; Head, Chemical Technol. Div., 1985–87; Dir, Nuclear Resources, MoD PE, 1987–90; Dep. Head, Efficiency Unit, Prime Minister's Office, 1990–92; Asst Chief Scientific Advr (Projects), MoD, 1992–94; Man. Dir, Protection and Life Scis Div., 1994–97, Man. Dir, Science, 1997–2000, Business Continuity Dir, 2000–01, DERA. Trustee, Wild Trout Trust, 2003–. *Publications:* papers in technical jls and internat. conf. proc. *Recreations:* flyfishing, shooting, gardening (auriculas). *Club:* Flyfishers'.

COLFER, Eoin; author; *b* 14 May 1965; *s* of Billy and Noreen Colfer; *m* 1991, Jacqueline Power. *Educ:* Carysfort Coll. of Educn (BEd). Teacher: Scoil Mhuire Primary Sch., Wexford, 1986–94; Jeddah Private Acad., Saudi Arabia, 1994–95; Internat. Sch. of Martina Franca, Italy, 1995–96; Sfat Internat. Sch., Tunisia, 1996–98; Scoil Mhuire Primary Sch., 1998–2002. *Publications:* Benny and Omar, 1998; Benny and Babe, 1999; Going Potty, 1999; The Wish List, 2000; Ed's Funny Feet, 2000; Ed's Bed, 2001; Artemis Fowl, 2001; Artemis Fowl and the Arctic Incident, 2002; Artemis Fowl and the Eternity Code, 2003; Spud Murphy, 2004; The Supernaturalist, 2004; Artemis Fowl and the Opal Deception, 2005; Half Moon Investigations, 2006; Captain Crow's Teeth, 2006; Artemis Fowl and the Lost Colony, 2006; The Worst Boy in the World, 2007; Airman, 2008; Artemis Fowl and the Time Paradox, 2008. *Address:* c/o Ed Victor Ltd, 6 Bayley Street, Bedford Square, WC1B 3HB.

COLFOX, Sir (William) John, 2nd Bt *cr* 1939; JP; DL; *b* 25 April 1924; *yr* and *o* surv. *s* of Sir (William) Philip Colfox, 1st Bt, MC, and Mary (Frances) Lady Colfox (*d* 1973); *S* father, 1966; *m* 1962, Frederica Loveday, *d* of Adm. Sir Victor Crutchley, VC, KCB, DSC; two *s* three *d*. *Educ:* Eton. Served in RNVR, 1942–46 (Battle of North Cape, 1943), leaving as Lieut. Qualified Land Agent, 1950. Chm., Land Settlement Assoc., 1980–81. Vice-Chm., TSW plc, 1981–92. Mem. Council, Royal Bath and West Show, 1950– (Chm., Sheep Shearing Cttee); Chairman: Dorset Agricl Exec. Cttee, 1960–73; Golden Shears World Championship Cttee, 1977–2005; Jt Founder, World Fedn of Golden Shears; President: W Dorset Scouts, 1960–80; Dorset Young Farmers, 1964. Mem., W Dorset DC, 1953–74. JP Dorset, 1962, High Sheriff of Dorset, 1969, DL Dorset, 1977. Chm. Govs, Colfox Comp. Sch., 1970–97. *Heir: s* Philip John Colfox [*b* 27 Dec. 1962; *m* 1993, Julia, *yr d* of G. St G. Schomberg; one *s* three *d* (incl. twins)]. *Address:* Symondsbury House, Bridport, Dorset DT6 6HB. *T:* (01308) 422956.

COLGAN, Michael Anthony; Artistic Director and Member Board, Gate Theatre, Dublin, since 1983; *b* 17 July 1950; *s* of James Colgan and Josephine Colgan (*née* Geoghegan); *m* 1975, Susan Fitzgerald (separated); one *s* two *d*. *Educ:* Trinity Coll., Dublin (BA). Dir, Abbey Th., Dublin, 1974–78; Co-Manager, Irish Th. Co., 1977–78; Dublin Theatre Festival: Manager, 1978–80; Artistic Dir, 1981–83; Mem., Bd of Dirs, 1983–. Exec. Dir, Little Bird Films, 1986–; Co-Founder, Blue Angel Films Co., 1999. Artistic Dir, Parma Fest., 1982; Chm., St Patrick's Fest., 1996–99; Mem. Bd, Millennium Festivals Ltd, Laura Pels Foundn, NY, 2000–04. Mem., Irish Arts Council, 1989–94. Mem., Gov. Authy, Dublin City Univ. Theatre productions include: I'll Go On; Juno and the Paycock; Salomé; four Beckett Fests, Dublin, NY and London; four Pinter Fests, Dublin and NY. World premières incl. Molly Sweeney, Port Authority, Afterplay, See You Next Tuesday, Shining City, The Home Place. Prod., TV drama, Two Lives, 1986. Hon. LLD TCD. Sunday Independent Arts Award, 1985, 1987; Nat. Entertainment Award, 1996; People of the Year Award, 1999; Irish Times Theatre Lifetime Achievement Award, 2006. *Recreations:* middle distance running, chamber music. *Address:* Gate Theatre, 1 Cavendish Row, Dublin 1, Ireland. *T:* (1) 8744368, *Fax:* (1) 8745373; *e-mail:* info@gate-theatre.ie. *Club:* Groucho.

COLGAN, Samuel Hezlett; His Honour Judge Colgan; a Circuit Judge, since 1990; *b* 10 June 1945; *s* of late Henry George Colgan and of Jane Swan Hezlett. *Educ:* Foyle College, Londonderry; Trinity College Dublin (MA, LLB). Called to the Bar, Middle Temple, 1969; a Recorder, SE Circuit, 1987. *Recreations:* travelling, the arts, reading, tennis. *Address:* SE Circuit, 2 Southwark Bridge, SE1 9HS.

COLGRAIN, 4th Baron *cr* 1946, of Everlands, co. Kent; **Alastair Colin Leckie Campbell;** *b* 16 Sept. 1951; *s* of 3rd Baron Colgrain and of Veronica Margaret, *d* of late Lt-Col William Leckie Webster, RAMC; *S* father, 2008; *m* 1979, Annabel Rose, *yr d* of late Hon. Robin Hugh Warrender; two *s*. *Educ:* Eton; Trinity Coll., Cambridge (BA 1973). *Heir: s* Hon. Thomas Colin Donald Campbell, *b* 9 Feb. 1984.

COLIN-THOMÉ, David Geoffrey, OBE 1997; FRCGP, FFPH; General Practitioner, Castlefields, Runcorn, 1971–2007; National Director for Primary Care Commissioning and System Management Directorate (formerly National Clinical Director of Primary Care), Department of Health, since 2001; *b* 5 Oct. 1943; *s* of William James Charles Colin-Thomé and Pearl Erin Colin-Thomé; *m* 1969, Christine Mary Simpson; one *s* one *d*. *Educ:* Hutton Grammar Sch., Preston; Newcastle upon Tyne Medical Sch. (MB BS 1966). FRCGP 1990; MHSM 1998; FFPH (FFPHM 2002). Dir Primary Care, NW Regl Office, NHS Exec., DoH, 1994–96; SMO, Scottish Office, 1997–98; Dir Primary Care, London Region, DoH, 1998–2001. Hon. Visiting Professor: Centre for Public Policy and Mgt, Manchester Univ., 2002–; Sch. of Health, Durham Univ., 2004–. Hon. FFGDP(UK) 2005. *Recreations:* eclectic interests in theatre, dance, books and sport; devoted grandfather to Amber, Jacob, Luca, Ryan, Beth and Zachary; supporter of Everton FC. *Address:* Hunter House, Bainbridge Lane, Eshott, Northumberland NE65 9FD.

COLL, Dame Elizabeth Anne Loosemore E.; *see* Esteve-Coll.

COLLARBONE, Dame Patricia, DBE 1998; EdD; Director, Education Change Associates Ltd, since 2006; Executive Director for Development, Training and Development Agency, 2006–07 (on secondment from Institute of Education). *Educ:* MBA 1995; EdD Lincolnshire and Humberside Univ. 1999. Headteacher, Haggerston Sch., Hackney, 1990–96; Founding Dir, London Leadership Centre, Inst. of Education, Univ. of London, 1997–2002; Dir of Leadership Progs, Nat. Coll. for Sch. Leadership, Nottingham, 2002–04; Dir, Nat. Remodelling Team, Nat. Coll. for Sch. Leadership, then TTA, 2003–06. Manager, London Regl Assessment Centre, 1996–98, London Regl Trng and Development Centre, 1998–99, NPQH. Advr, on rôle of the Headteacher, Govt 9th Select Cttee, 1998; Special Advr, on headship and leadership issues, DfEE, 1999–2001. Former Member: SCAA Key Stage 3 Adv. Gp; DfEE Adv. Cttee on Improving Schs; Educn Summit. Member: DfEE Sch. Improvement Team; NPQH Mgt Develt Gp, TTA. London Pres., NAHT. Fellow: Univ. of Lincolnshire and Humberside; Hull Univ., 2000. FRSA.

COLLARD, Paul Anthony Carthew; National Director, Creative Partnerships, since 2005; *b* 17 Aug. 1954; *s* of late Douglas Reginald Collard, OBE and Eleni Cubitt; *m* 1983, Hilary Porter; three *s* one *d*. *Educ:* Ampleforth Coll., York; Trinity Coll., Cambridge (BA Hons). Exec. Sec., Friends of Cyprus, 1976–80; Administrator, Aga Khan Award for Architecture, 1980–82; Gen. Manager, ICA, 1983–87; Dep. Controller, BFI, South Bank, 1988–92; Director: UK Year of Visual Arts, 1993–97; Internat. Fest. of Arts and Ideas, New Haven, CT, 1997–2001; Hd, Programme Develt, Newcastle Gateshead Initiative, 2001–04. Programme Co-ordinator, Newcastle Gateshead Bid for European Capital of Culture, 2001–03. David Goldman Prof. of Business Innovation, Univ. of Newcastle upon Tyne, 2003–04. Mem., Arts Council of England, subseq. Arts Council England, 2002–04 (Chm., NE Regl Arts Council, 2002–04). *Recreation:* arguing with the children. *Address:* Arts Council England, 14 Great Peter Street, SW1P 3NQ.

COLLAS, Richard John; Deputy Bailiff, Guernsey, since 2005; *b* 27 May 1953; *s* of Peter Renouf Collas and Nora Kathleen Collas (*née* Turner); *m* 1986, Amanda Judith Kenmir; two *s* one *d*. *Educ:* Jesus Coll., Oxford (BA Engrg Sci. 1975); City Univ., London (Dip. Law 1981). Lever Brothers Ltd, 1975–80. Called to the Bar, Gray's Inn, 1982, Guernsey, 1983; Collas Day Advocates, 1983–2005. *Recreations:* family, boating. *Address:* Bailiff's Chambers, St Peter Port, Guernsey GY1 2PB. *T:* (01481) 726161, *Fax:* (01481) 713861; *e-mail:* richard.collas@gov.gg. *Clubs:* United (Guernsey); Guernsey Yacht, Royal Channel Islands Yacht.

COLLECOTT, Dr Peter Salmon, CMG 2002; HM Diplomatic Service; Ambassador to Brazil, 2004–08; *b* 8 Oct. 1950; *s* of George William Collecott and Nancie Alice Collecott (*née* Salmon); *m* 1982, Judith Patricia Pead. *Educ:* Chigwell Sch., Essex; St John's Coll., Cambridge (MA 1976; PhD 1976); MIT (Kennedy Schol. 1972). Royal Soc. Fellow, Max Planck Inst. for Physics and Astrophysics, Munich, 1976–77; joined HM Diplomatic Service, 1977: FCO, 1977–78; MECAS, Lebanon, later London, 1978–80; 1st Secretary: (Political), Khartoum, 1980–82; (Econ., Commercial, Agricl), Canberra, 1982–86; Head, Iran/Iraq Section, ME Dept, FCO, 1986–88; Asst Head, EC Dept (Ext.), FCO, 1988–89; Counsellor, Head of Chancery and Consul Gen., later Dep. Head of Mission, Jakarta, 1989–93; Counsellor (EU and Econ.), Bonn, 1994–98; Hd, Admin Restructuring Rev. Team, FCO, 1998–99; Dir, Resources, FCO, 1999–2001; Dep. Under-Sec. of State and Chief Clerk, subseq. Dir Gen., Corporate Affairs, FCO, 2001–03. *Publications:* papers on theoretical physics in learned jls. *Recreations:* walking, reading. *Address:* c/o Foreign and Commonwealth Office, King Charles Street, SW1A 2AH.

COLLEE, Prof. (John) Gerald, CBE 1991; MD; FRCPath; FRCPE; FRSE; Robert Irvine Professor of Bacteriology and Head of Department of Medical Microbiology (formerly Department of Bacteriology), University of Edinburgh, 1979–91, now Emeritus Professor; Chief Bacteriologist to Edinburgh Royal Infirmary and Consultant Bacteriologist, Lothian Health Board, 1979–91; Consultant Adviser in Microbiology to Scottish Home and Health Department, 1986–91; *b* 10 May 1929; *s* of John Gerald Collee and Mary Hay Wilson Kirsopp Cassels; *m* 1st, 1952, Isobel McNay Galbraith (marr. diss. 1995); two *s* one *d*; 2nd, 1995, Anne Ferguson (*d* 1998). *Educ:* Bo'ness Acad.; Edinburgh Acad.; Edinburgh Univ. MB ChB, MD (Gold Medal). Ho. Phys., 1951–52. AMS (Captain RAMC), 1952–54. Lectr in Bacteriology, Edinburgh, 1955–63; WHO Vis. Prof. of Bacteriol., Baroda, 1963–64; Sen. Lectr, Edinburgh, and Hon. Cons. Bacteriologist, 1964–70; Reader in Bacteriol. 1970–74, Personal Prof. of Bacteriol. 1974–79, Edinburgh. Member: Scottish Health Service Planning Council Adv. Gp on Infection, 1981–90; Jt Cttee on Vaccination and Immunisation, 1982–95; Cttee on Safety of Medicines, 1987–92; Cttee on Vaccination and Immunisation Procedures, MRC, 1988–95; Medicines Commn, 1992–95. *Publications:* Applied Medical Microbiology, 1976, 2nd edn 1981; contrib. and ed several textbooks, incl. Mackie and McCartney's Practical Medical Microbiology, 1996; many sci. papers on aspects of infection, anaerobes of clin. importance, antimicrobial drugs and immunization, BSE and VCJD. *Recreations:* woodwork, poetry, fishing, music, painting. *Address:* 27B Drummond Place, Edinburgh EH3 6PN. *T:* (0131) 557 5234. *Clubs:* Scottish Arts, New (Edinburgh).

COLLENDER, Andrew Robert; QC 1991; **His Honour Judge Collender;** a Circuit Judge, since 2006; *b* 11 Aug. 1946; *s* of John and Kathleen Collender; *m* 1974, Titia Tybout; two *s*. *Educ:* Mt Pleasant Boys High Sch., Zimbabwe; Univ. of Bristol (LLB Hons). Called to the Bar, Lincoln's Inn, 1969, Bencher, 2000; a Recorder, 1993–2006; a Dep. High Ct Judge, 1998–; Head of Chambers, 2 Temple Gardens, 2002–05. *Recreations:* playing the violin, sailing. *Address:* c/o Central London Civil Justice Centre, 26 Park Crescent W1N 4NT. *Club:* Bosham Sailing.

COLLENETTE, Hon. David (Michael); PC (Canada) 1983; Distinguished Fellow, Glendon College, York University, Toronto, since 2004; *b* 24 June 1946; *s* of David Henry and Sarah Margaret Collenette; *m* 1975, Penny Hossack; one *s*. *Educ:* Glendon Coll., York Univ. (BA Hons; MA). Admin. Officer, Marketing Div., Internat. Life Assurance Co., UK, 1970–72; Exec. Vice-Pres., Mandrake Management Consultants, Canada, 1987–93. Advr, Intergraph Corp., 2005–. MP (L): York East, 1974–79 and 1980–84; Don Valley East, 1993–2004; Minister of State for Multiculturalism, 1983–84; Minister of Nat. Defence and of Veterans' Affairs, 1993–96; Minister of Transport, 1997–2003. Sec.-Gen., Liberal Party of Canada, 1985–87 (Exec. Dir, Toronto, 1969–70, Ontario, 1972–74). Mem., Internat. Adv. Council, Inst. for Internat. Studies, Stanford Univ., 1999–2005. *Recreations:* swimming, theatre, classical music. *Address:* C-110, York Hall, Glendon College, York University, 2275 Bayview Avenue, Toronto, ON M4N 3M6, Canada; *e-mail:* dcollenette@glendon.yorku.ca. *Club:* University (Toronto).

COLLENS, Rupert; *see* Mackeson, Sir R. H.

COLLETT, Sir Christopher, GBE 1988; JP; Partner in Ernst & Young, Chartered Accountants, London, retired 1993; Lord Mayor of London, 1988–89; *b* 10 June 1931; 2nd *s* of Sir Henry Seymour Collett, 2nd Bt, and Lady (Ruth Mildred) Collett (*née* Hatch) (*d* 1994); *m* 1959, Christine Anne, *d* of Oswald Hardy Griffiths, Nunthorpe, Yorks; two *s* one *d*. *Educ:* Harrow; Emmanuel Coll., Cambridge. MA; FCA. Nat. Service, RA and

Surrey Yeomanry; Captain TA (RA). Articled with Cassleton Elliott & Co., Chartered Accountants, 1954; qualified, 1958; Partner, Ghana 1960, London 1963; firm merged to become Josolyne Miles and Cassleton Elliott, Josolyne Layton Bennett & Co., Arthur Young, and then Ernst & Young. Mem., Court of Common Council (Broad Street Ward), City of London, 1973–79; Alderman, 1979–2001; Sheriff, City of London, 1985–86; HM Lieut, 1988–2001; Trustee, Temple Bar Trust, 1992– (Chm., 1993–); Chm., Lord Mayor's 800th Anniversary Awards Trust, 1989–. Liveryman: Glovers' Co., 1965 (Master, 1981); Chartered Accts in Eng. and Wales' Co., 1984 (Asst, 1986–93); Haberdashers' Company: Hon. Liveryman, 1990; Asst, 1991; Third Warden, 1993; Hon. Asst, 1994–2006; Member: Guild of Freemen, 1983–2000; City of London TAVR Cttee, 1980–92. Non-exec. Mem., Dumfries and Galloway Health Bd, 1997–2001. Council Mem., Action Research for the Crippled Child, 1984–93; Mem., Scottish Appeals Cttee, Police Dependants' Trust, 2001–04 (Mem., 1996, Chm., 2001–04, Dumfries & Galloway Appeals Cttee); Chm., South of Scotland Youth Awards Trust, 1999–. Governor: Haberdashers' Aske's Schs, Elstree, 1982–94; King Edward's Sch., Witley, 1983–94; Music Therapy Gp Ltd, 1986–94; Bridewell Royal Hosp., 1987–94; Hon. Treas., Lee House, Wimbledon, 1950–2002; Trustee, Morden Coll., 1993–2004; Chm., Eskdale Foundn, 1996–2006. Pres., Broad Street Ward Club, 1979–2001. JP City of London, 1979. Hon. DSc City, 1988. KStJ 1988. Order of Merit (cl. II), State of Qatar, 1985; Orden del Merito Civil (cl. II), Spain, 1986; Commander, Order of Merit, Federal Republic of Germany, 1986; CON, 1st cl. (Nigeria), 1989. *Recreations:* gardening, fishing. *Address:* Altnaharrie, Lodsworth, Petworth, West Sussex GU28 9DG. *T:* (01798) 861792.

COLLETT, Sir Ian (Seymour), 3rd Bt *cr* 1934; *b* 5 Oct. 1953; *s* of David Seymour Collett (*d* 1962), and of Sheila Joan Collett (who *m* 1980, Sir James William Miskin, QC), *o d* of late Harold Scott; *S* grandfather, 1971; *m* 1982, Philippa, *o d* of late James R. I. Hawkins, Preston St Mary, Suffolk; one *s* one *d. Educ:* Lancing College, Sussex. Mem., Internat. Inst. of Marine Surveyors, 1998. *Recreations:* golf, fishing, cricket, shooting. *Heir: s* Anthony Seymour Collett, *b* 27 Feb. 1984. *Clubs:* MCC; Aldeburgh Golf; Aldeburgh Yacht.

COLLEY, Maj.-Gen. (David) Bryan (Hall), CB 1988; CBE 1982 (OBE 1977; MBE 1968); FCILT; Director-General, Road Haulage Association, 1988–97; *b* 5 June 1934; *s* of Lawson and Alice Colley; *m* 1957, Marie Thérèse (*née* Préfontaine); one *s* one *d. Educ:* King Edward's Sch., Birmingham; RMA, Sandhurst. Commissioned: RASC, 1954; RCT, 1965; regimental appts in Germany, Belgium, UK, Hong Kong and Singapore; Student, Staff Coll., Camberley, 1964; JSSC Latimer, 1970; CO Gurkha Transport Regt and 31 Regt, RCT, 1971–74; Staff HQ 1st (British) Corps, 1974–77; Comd Logistic Support Gp, 1977–80; Col AQ (Ops and Plans) and Dir Admin. Planning, MoD (Army), 1980–82; Comd Transport 1st (British) Corps and Comdr Bielefeld Garrison, 1983–86; Dir Gen., Transport and Movts (Army), 1986–88, retired. Col Comdt, RCT, 1988–93; Col Comdt, Royal Logistic Corps, 1993–2000. Pres., RASC and RCT Benevolent Fund, 2006–. Freeman, City of London, 1986; Hon. Liveryman, Worshipful Co. of Carmen, 1986. *Recreations:* travel, information technology, military history. *Address:* c/o HSBC, Redditch, Worcs B97 4EA. *Club:* Army and Navy.

COLLEY, Surg. Rear-Adm. Ian Harris, OBE 1963; Member, Committee of Management, Royal National Lifeboat Institution, since 1982; *b* 14 Oct. 1922; *s* of Aubrey James Colley and Violet Fulford Colley; *m* 1952, Joy Kathleen (*née* Goodacre). *Educ:* Hanley Castle Grammar Sch.; King's Coll., London and King's Coll. Hosp. MB, BS 1948; DPH; MFOM; FFCM. Royal Naval Medical Service, 1948–80: MO HMS Cardigan Bay and HMS Consort, 1949–52; service with Fleet Air Arm, 1955–78: as PMO HMS Centaur; MO i/c Air Med. Sch.; Pres., Central Air Med. Bd; Comd MO to Flag Officer, Naval Air Comd; Surg. Rear Adm. (Ships and Estabs), 1978–80, retired. QHP 1978–80. Consultant in Aviation Medicine; former Examr to Conjoint Bd, Royal College of Surgeons and Royal College of Physicians for DAvMed. Life Vice-Pres., RNLI, 1997 (Vice-Pres., 1989–97; Chm., Med. and Survival Cttee, 1984–88). CStJ 1980. *Publications:* papers in field of aviation medicine. *Address:* c/o Royal Bank of Scotland, Inveraray, Argyll PA32 8TY.

COLLEY, Kitty; *see* Ussher, K.

COLLEY, Prof. Linda Jane, PhD; FRHistS; FBA 1999; FRSL; Shelby M. C. Davis 1958 Professor of History, Princeton University, since 2003; *b* 13 Sept. 1949; *d* of Roy Colley and Marjorie (*née* Hughes); *m* 1982, David Nicholas Cannadine, *qv*; one *d* decd. *Educ:* Bristol Univ. (BA); Cambridge Univ. (MA, PhD). University of Cambridge: Eugenie Strong Research Fellow, Girton Coll., 1975–78; Fellow: Newnham Coll., 1978–79; Christ's Coll., 1979–81 (Hon. Fellow, 2006); Yale University: Dir, Lewis Walpole Liby, 1982–96; Asst Prof., History, 1982–85; Associate Prof., 1985–90; Prof., History, 1990–92; Richard M. Colgate Prof. of History, 1992–98. Sch. Prof. in History and Leverhulme Personal Res. Prof., European Inst., LSE, 1998–2003. Hooker Distinguished Vis. Prof., McMaster Univ., 1999; Glaxo Smith Kline Sen. Fellow, Nat. Humanities Center, NC, 2006; Adjunct Prof., Humanities Res. Centre, ANU, 2006–. Journalism and work on radio and TV. Lectures: Anstey, Univ. of Kent, 1994; William Church Meml, Brown Univ., 1994; Dist. (in British Hist.), Univ. of Texas at Austin, 1995; Trevelyan, Cambridge Univ., 1997; Wiles, QUB, 1997; Hayes Robinson, Royal Holloway, Univ. of London, 1998; Ford Special, Oxford Univ., 1998; Bliss Carnochan, Stanford Humanities Center, 1998; Prime Minister's Millennium, 1999; Ena H. Thompson, Pomona Coll., Calif, 2001; Raleigh, British Acad., 2002; Nehru, London, 2003; Bateson, Oxford Univ., 2003; Chancellor Dunning Trust, Queen's Univ., Ont., 2004; Byrn, Vanderbilt Univ., 2005; Annual Internat. Hist., LSE, 2006; C. P. Snow, Christ's Coll., Cambridge, 2007; Political Sci. Quarterly, 2007; Victoria County Hist., 2007; President's, Princeton Univ., 2007. Member: Council, Tate Gall. of British Art, 1999–2003; BL Bd, 1999–2003; Adv. Council, Paul Mellon Centre for British Art, 1998–2003; Bd, Princeton Univ. Press, 2007–. FRHistS 1988; FRSL 2004. Hon. DLitt: South Bank, 1998; UEA, 2005; Bristol, 2006; DUniv Essex, 2004. *Publications:* In Defiance of Oligarchy: The Tory Party 1714–60, 1982; Namier, 1989; Crown Pictorial: art and the British monarchy, 1990; Britons: forging the nation 1707–1837, 1992 (Wolfson Prize, 1993); Captives: Britain, Empire and the world 1600–1850, 2002; The Ordeal of Elizabeth Marsh, 2007; numerous articles and reviews in UK and USA jls. *Recreations:* travel, looking at art. *Address:* Department of History, Princeton University, 129 Dickinson Hall, Princeton, NJ 08544–1017, USA; c/o Gill Coleridge, 20 Powis Mews, W11 1JN.

COLLIER, family name of **Baron Monkswell**.

COLLIER, Andrew James, CB 1976; Deputy Secretary, Department of Health and Social Security, 1973–82; *b* 12 July 1923; *s* of Joseph Veasy Collier and Dorothy Murray; *m* 1950, Bridget, *d* of George and Edith Eberstadt, London; two *d. Educ:* Harrow; Christ Church, Oxford. Served Army, RHA, 1943–46. Entered HM Treasury, 1948; Private Sec. to successive Chancellors of the Exchequer, 1956–59; Asst Sec., 1961; Under-Sec., 1967; Under-Secretary: Civil Service Dept, 1968–71; DHSS, 1971–73. *Address:* 12 Oxford House, 52 Parkside, Wimbledon, SW19 5NE. *T:* (020) 8946 4220. *Club:* Athenæum.

COLLIER, Andrew John, CBE 1995; Schools Adjudicator, 1999–2005; General Secretary, Society of Education Officers, 1996–99 (Treasurer, 1987–92; President, 1990); *b* 29 Oct. 1939; *s* of Francis George Collier and Margaret Nancy (*née* Nockles); *m* 1964, Gillian Ann (*née* Churchill); two *d. Educ:* University College Sch.; St John's Coll., Cambridge (MA). Assistant Master, Winchester Coll., 1962–68; Hampshire County Educn Dept, 1968–71; Buckinghamshire County Educn Dept, 1971–77; Dep. Chief Educn Officer, 1977–80, Chief Educn Officer, 1980–96, Lancashire CC. Member: Open Univ. Vis. Cttee, 1982–88; Council for Accreditation of Teacher Educn, 1984–89; Nat. Training Task Force, 1989–92; Gen. Synod Bd of Educn, 1993–2001; Educn Cttee, Royal Soc., 1995–2000; Chm., County Educn Officers' Soc., 1987–88; Treas., Schools Curriculum Award, 1987–92. Liveryman, Worshipful Company of Wheelwrights, 1972–2002. Mem. Council, Univ. of Lancaster, 1981–86, 1988–94, 1996–99; Governor: Myerscough Coll., 1996–2003; St Martin's Coll., Lancaster, 2001–07; Whitechapel Primary Sch., 2002–05 (Chm. of Govs, 2003–04); Univ. of Cumbria, 2007–. Pres., Lancs Fedn of Young Farmers' Clubs, 1985–88. *Publications:* (contrib.) New Directions for County Government, 1989; articles in jls. *Recreations:* music, walking, boating. *Clubs:* Athenæum; Leander (Henley-on-Thames); Salcombe Yacht.

COLLIER, Air Vice-Marshal Andy; *see* Collier, Air Vice-Marshal J. A.

COLLIER, Prof. Christopher George, PhD; CMet, CEnv; Professor of Environmental Remote Sensing, University of Salford, since 1995; *b* 10 Sept. 1946; *s* of George and Barbara Collier; *m* 1969, Cynthia Dawson; two *s. Educ:* Hyde County Grammar Sch.; Imperial Coll., London (BSc Hons Physics 1968; ARCS); Univ. of Salford (PhD 1999). CMet 1995; CEnv 2005. Meteorological Office, 1968–95; University of Salford, 1995–: Dir, Telford Res. Inst., 1997–98; Dean, Fac. of Sci., Engrg and Envmt, 1999–2003. Chm., EU COST-73 Internat. Radar Networking Mgt Cttee, 1986–91. Member: RMetS, 1967– (Pres., 2004–06); British Hydrological Soc.; CIWEM; Amer. Meteorological Soc. Hon. DSc Salford, 2008. Robert Hugh Mill Medal, RMetS, 1982; L. G. Groves Prize, Met. Office, 1984; first Vaisala Prize, WMO, 1986. *Publications:* Applications of Weather Radar Systems, 1996; 80 refereed scientific pubns and over 200 conf. papers and reports. *Recreations:* swimming, reading, gardening, writing, Church of England. *Address:* School of Environment and Life Sciences, Peel Building, University of Salford, Salford, Greater Manchester M5 4WT. *T:* (0161) 295 5465, *Fax:* (0161) 295 5015; *e-mail:* c.g.collier@salford.ac.uk.

COLLIER, David Gordon; Chief Executive, England and Wales Cricket Board, since 2005; *b* 22 April 1955; *s* of John and Pat Collier; *m* 1980, Jennifer Pendleton; two *s* one *d. Educ:* Loughborough Grammar Sch.; Loughborough Univ. (BSc Hons Sports Sci. and Recreation Mgt). Dep. Manager, Adams Sports Centre, Wem, 1979–80; Dep. Sec. Gen. and Manager, Essex CCC, 1980–83; Chief Exec., Glos CCC, 1983–86; Mktg Manager, Sema Gp plc, 1986–88; Sen. Vice-Pres., American Airlines, 1988–92; Man. Dir, Servisair plc, 1992–93; Chief Executive: Leics CCC, 1993–99; Notts CCC, 1999–2004. Internat. hockey umpire, 1985–. Member: European Hockey Fedn, 2000–; Fedn of Internat. Hockey, 2002–. Sydney Friskin Award, Hockey Writers, 2003. *Recreations:* cricket, hockey, golf. *Address:* England and Wales Cricket Board, Lord's Cricket Ground, St John's Wood, NW8 8QZ. *T:* (020) 7432 1200, *Fax:* (020) 7289 5619; *e-mail:* david.collier@ecb.co.uk.

COLLIER, Air Vice-Marshal James Andrew, (Andy), CB 2005; CBE 1995; Deputy Commander-in-Chief Personnel and Training Command and Chief of Staff to Air Member for Personnel, 2003–05; *b* 6 July 1951; *s* of late Charles Robert Collier and of Cynthia Collier (*née* Walsh), and step *s* of late Paul Scott; *m* 1972, Judith Arnold; one *d. Educ:* Headlands Sch., Swindon; Univ. of Durham (BSc 1972). Commnd RAF 1972; Sqn Ldr 1980; Wing Comdr 1987; Gp Capt. 1991; Air Cdre 1998; Air Vice-Marshal 2003. *Recreations:* golf, cross-country ski-ing, watching sport (especially Rugby), reading about science. *Club:* Royal Air Force.

COLLIER, John Spencer, FCA; Director, Clive & Stokes International, since 2004; Secretary General, Institute of Chartered Accountants in England and Wales, 1997–2002; *b* 4 March 1945; *s* of James Bradburn Collier and Phyllis Mary Collier; *m* 1972, Theresa Mary Peers; two *s* one *d. Educ:* Trinity Coll., Cambridge (BA Geography 1967). FCA 1973. Joined Price Waterhouse, 1969: various posts, incl. Sen. Manager, 1969–81; Partner, 1981–92; Chief Executive: Newcastle Initiative, 1992–95; Lowes Gp plc, 1995–96; Finance Dir, Earth Centre, 1996–97. Chm., Friends of Richmond Park, 2004–07; Treas., Wordsworth Trust, 2004–. *Publication:* The Corporate Environment: the financial consequences for business, 1995. *Recreations:* mountains, marathons. *Address:* 147 Queens Road, Richmond, Surrey TW10 6HF. *T:* (020) 8940 1921. *Club:* Travellers.

COLLIER, Lesley Faye, CBE 1993; Répétiteur, Royal Ballet, since 2000; Principal Dancer with the Royal Ballet, 1972–95; *b* 13 March 1947; *d* of Roy and Mavis Collier; twin *s. Educ:* The Royal Ballet School, White Lodge, Richmond. Joined Royal Ballet, 1965; has danced most principal roles in the Royal repertory; Ballet Mistress, 1995–99, Mem., Classical Ballet Staff, 1999–2000, Royal Ballet Sch. Evening Standard Ballet Award, 1987. *Address:* Royal Ballet, Royal Opera House, Covent Garden, WC2E 9DD.

COLLIER, Prof. Leslie Harold, MD, DSc; FRCP, FRCPath; Professor of Virology, University of London, 1966–86, now Emeritus; Consulting Pathologist, Royal London Hospital (formerly London Hospital), since 1987; *b* 9 Feb. 1921; *s* of late Maurice Leonard Collier and Ruth (*née* Phillips); *m* 1942, Adeline Barnett; one *s. Educ:* Brighton Coll.; UCH Med. Sch. MD London 1953; DSc London 1968; MRCP 1969; FRCPath 1975; FRCP 1980. House Phys., UCH, 1943; served RAMC, 1944–47; Asst Pathologist, St Helier Hosp., Carshalton, 1947; Lister Inst. of Preventive Medicine, 1948–78: Head, Dept of Virology, 1955–74; Dep. Dir, 1968–74; Dir, Vaccines and Sera Laboratories, 1974–78; Hon. Dir, MRC Trachoma Unit, 1957–73; Prof. of Virology and Sen. Lectr, Jt Dept of Virology, London Hosp. Med. Coll. and St Bartholomew's Hosp. Med. Coll., 1978–86; Hd, Dept of Virology, London Hosp. Med. Coll., 1982–86. Hon. Consultant in Virology, Tower Hamlets HA, 1978–86. Pres., Sect. of Pathology, RSM, 1986–88, Hon. Mem., 1994. Chibret Gold Medal, Ligue contre le Trachome, 1959; Luys Prize, Soc. de Médecine de Paris, 1963. *Publications:* (ed jtly) Topley and Wilson's Principles of Bacteriology, Virology and Immunity, 8th edn, 1990, 9th edn, as Topley and Wilson's Microbiology and Microbial Infections (Editor in Chief), 1997 (Soc. of Authors and Med. Soc. of London award, 1998); (jtly) Human Virology, 1993, 3rd edn 2006; papers in med. and scientific jls. *Recreations:* various. *Address:* 8 Peto Place, Regent's Park, NW1 4DT. *T:* (020) 7487 4848.

COLLIER, Prof. Melvyn William; Director, Leuven University Library, Belgium, since 2004; *b* 31 July 1947; *s* of late James Collier and Jessie Collier (*née* Siddall); *m* 1968, Anne Nightingale (*d* 2004); one *s* one *d. Educ:* Bolton Sch.; Univ. of St Andrews (MA); Strathclyde Univ. (DipLib). FCLIP (ALA 1981; MIInfSc 1990, FIInfSc 1997). Academic Librarian posts at St Andrews Univ., UC, Cardiff and Hatfield Poly., 1970–79; Dep. Hd, Liby Services, PCL, 1980–84; Librarian, Leicester Poly., 1985–89; Hd, Div. of Learning Devełt, and Prof. of Information Mgt, De Montfort Univ., 1989–97; Director: Strategic and Operational Planning, Dawson Hldgs, 1997–2000; Tilburg Univ. Liby, Netherlands, 2001–03. Vis. Prof., De Montfort Univ., 1997–2001; part-time Prof., Univ. of Northumbria, 2000–06. Mem., Liby and Inf. Commn, 1996–2000 (Chm., Res. Cttee, 1996–2000); Chairman: Liby and Inf. Adv. Cttee, British Council, 1995–2001; UK Office for Liby Networking, 1995–97; Mem., Jt Inf. Systems Cttee, HEFCs, 1996–97. Director: Open Learning Foundn, 1995–97; Information For All, 1997–99. Hon. DLitt Strathclyde, 2006. Medal, Hungarian Liby Assoc., 1992. *Publications:* Local Area Networks: the implications for library and information science, 1984; (ed) Case Studies in Software for Information Management, 1986; (ed) Telecommunications for Information Management and Transfer, 1987; (jtly) Decision Support Systems in Academic Libraries, 1991; (jtly) Decision Support Systems and Performance Assessment in Academic Libraries, 1993; (ed) Electronic Library and Visual Information Research: ELVIRA 1, 1995, ELVIRA 2, 1996; numerous jl articles and res. reports. *Recreations:* golf, hill-walking. *Address:* Central Library, Leuven University, Mgr Ladeuzeplein 21, 3000 Leuven, Belgium. *Club:* Leicestershire Golf.

COLLIER, Prof. Paul, CBE 2008; DPhil; Professor of Economics, since 1993 and Director, Centre for Study of African Economies, since 1991, Oxford University (on leave of absence, 1998–2003); Fellow, St Antony's College, Oxford, since 1986; *b* 23 April 1949; *s* of Charles and Doris Collier; *m* 1998, Pauline Boerma; one *s*. *Educ:* King Edward VII Grammar Sch., Sheffield; Trinity Coll., Oxford (MA 1970); Nuffield Coll., Oxford (DPhil 1975). Oxford University: Fellow, Keble Coll. and Research Officer, Inst. of Econs and Stats, 1976–86; Univ. Lectr in Econs, 1986–89; Reader in Econs, 1989–92; Dir, Res. Dept, World Bank, Washington, 1998–2003. Prof. Invité, Centre d'Études et de Recherches sur le Développement Internat., Univ. d'Auvergne, 1989–; Vis. Prof., Kennedy Sch. of Govt, Harvard, 1992–96; Fellow, Centre for Economic Policy Res., 1993–; Associate, Tinbergen Inst., 1994–95. Lectures: Rausig, Moscow, 2000; Summers, Pa, 2001. Member: Overseas Develt Council, Program Associates Gp, Washington, 1994–96; Africa Panel, SSRC, NY, 1993–96; ESCOR Cttee, ODA then DFID, 1996–98. Man. Editor, Jl of African Economies, 1992–. Edgar Graham Prize, SOAS, 1988; Distinction Award, 1996, 1998. *Publications:* Labour and Poverty in Kenya, 1986; Labour and Poverty in Rural Tanzania, 1986, 2nd edn 1991; Peasants and Governments, 1989; Controlled Open Economies, 1990, 2nd edn 1994. *Address:* Centre for the Study of African Economies, Department of Economics, University of Oxford, Manor Road, Oxford OX1 3UQ.

COLLIER, Peter Neville; QC 1992; **His Honour Judge Collier;** a Senior Circuit Judge, since 2007; Resident Judge, Leeds Combined Court Centre, since 2007; *b* 1 June 1948; *s* of late Arthur Neville Collier and of Joan Audrey Collier (*née* Brewer); *m* 1972, Susan Margaret Williamson; two *s*. *Educ:* Hymer's Coll., Hull; Selwyn Coll., Cambridge (MA). Called to the Bar, Inner Temple, 1970, Bencher, 2002; Leader, NE Circuit, 2002–05. A Recorder, 1988–2007; a Dep. High Court Judge (Family Div.), 1998–2007; Hon. Recorder of Leeds, 2007. Chancellor: dio. of Wakefield, 1992–2006; dio. of Lincoln, 1998–2006; dio. of York, 2006–. Mem., Bar Council, 2000–07. Lay Canon, York Minster, 2001–; Chm., York Minster Council, 2005–. *Recreations:* walking, reading, music. *Address:* Leeds Combined Court Centre, 1 Oxford Row, Leeds LS1 3BG.

COLLIN, Maj.-Gen. Geoffrey de Egglesfield, CB 1975; MC 1944; DL; *b* 18 July 1921; *s* of late Peter Charles de Egglesfield Collin and Catherine Mary Collin; *m* 1949, Angela Stella (*née* Young); one *s* three *d*. *Educ:* Wellington Coll., Berks. Served War of 1939–45: commissioned as 2nd Lt, RA, 1941; in India and Burma, 1942–45. Qualified as Army Pilot, 1946; attended Staff Coll., Camberley, 1951; Instructor at RMA, Sandhurst, 1954–56; served Kenya, 1956–58; JSSC, 1958; Instructor at Staff Coll., Camberley, 1960–62; comd 50 Missile Regt, RA, 1962–64; GSO 1 Sch. of Artillery, 1965; CRA, 4th Div., 1966–67; attended Imperial Defence College, London, 1968; Comdt, Royal School of Artillery, 1969–71; Maj.-Gen. RA, HQ BAOR, 1971–73; GOC North East District, York, 1973–76; retired 1976. Col Comdt, RA, 1976–83 (Rep. Col Comdt, 1982). Chairman: CS Selection Bd, 1981–91 (Mem., 1978); Retired Officer Selection Bd, 1979–2001. Hon. Dir, Great Yorks Show, 1976–87; Pres., Yorks Agricl Soc., 1988–89. Guide, Ripon Cathedral, 1981–. DL N Yorks, 1977. *Recreations:* fishing, ornithology, music, keeping gun dog and garden under control. *Address:* c/o Lloyds TSB, 8 Cambridge Crescent, Harrogate HG1 1PQ. *Club:* Army and Navy.

COLLIN, Jack, MA, MD; FRCS; Consultant Surgeon, John Radcliffe Hospital, Oxford and Fellow of Trinity College, Oxford, since 1980; *b* 23 April 1945; *s* of John Collin and Amy Maud Collin; *m* 1971, Christine Frances Proud; three *s* one *d*. *Educ:* Univ. of Newcastle (MB BS, MD); Mayo Clinic, Minn. University of Newcastle: Demonstrator in Anatomy, 1969–70; Sen. Res. Associate, 1973–75; Registrar in Surgery, Royal Victoria Infirmary, Newcastle, 1971–80; Chm., Faculty of Clin. Medicine, Univ. of Oxford, 1990–92. Mayo Foundn Fellow, Mayo Clinic, Minn, 1977. Moynihan Fellow, Assoc. of Surgeons of GB and Ire., 1980; James IV Fellow, James IV Assoc. of Surgeons Inc., NY, 1993. Royal College of Surgeons: Arris and Gale Lectr, 1976; Jacksonian Prize, 1977; Hunterian Prof., 1988–89. Non-exec. Dir, Nuffield Orthopaedic Centre NHS Trust, 1990–93. Member: Internat. Soc. of Surgery, 1994–; European Surgical Assoc., 1994–. Jobst Prize, Vascular Surgical Soc. of GB and Ireland, 1990. *Publications:* papers on vascular surgery, intestinal myoelectrical activity and absorption, parenteral nutrition and pancreatic and intestinal transplantation. *Recreations:* gardening, walking. *Address:* Nuffield Department of Surgery, John Radcliffe Hospital, Oxford OX3 9DU. *T:* (01865) 221282, 221286.

COLLIN, (John) Richard (Olaf), FRCS; Consultant Surgeon: Moorfields Eye Hospital, since 1981; King Edward VII's Hospital, Sister Agnes (formerly King Edward VII Hospital for Officers), since 1993; Hon. Consultant Ophthalmic Surgeon, Great Ormond Street Hospital for Sick Children, since 1983; *b* 1 May 1943; *s* of late John Olaf Collin and Ellen Vera (*née* Knudsen); *m* 1st, 1979, Theresa Pedemonte (marr. diss. 1982); 2nd, 1993, Geraldine O'Sullivan; two *d*. *Educ:* Charterhouse; Sidney Sussex Coll., Cambridge (MA); Westminster Med. Sch. (MB BChir). FRCS 1972. House surgeon and house physician, Westminster Hosp., 1967–68; ship's surgeon, P&O, 1969–70; Ophthalmology Registrar, Moorfields Eye Hosp., 1972–75; Fellow in Ophthalmic Plastic and Reconstructive Surgery, Univ. of Calif, San Francisco, 1976–77; Lectr, then Sen. Lectr, Professorial Unit, Moorfields Eye Hosp., 1978–81. Master, Oxford Ophthalmol Congress, 1997–98. Mem., representing oculoplastic surgery, Adv. Cttee to Internat. Council of Ophthalmol., 2000–. President: British Ocular Plastic Surgery Soc., 2002–05; European Soc. Oculo Plastic and Reconstructive Surgery, 2003–05. *Publications:* A Manual of Systematic Eyelid Surgery, 1983, 3rd edn 2006; (with A. G. Tyers) A Colour Atlas of Ophthalmic Plastic Surgery, 1995, 2nd edn 2001; articles on ophthalmic, plastic and reconstructive surgery topics. *Recreations:* sailing, shooting, tennis, hunting, fishing, theatre, opera. *Address:* 67 Harley Street, W1G 8QZ. *T:* (020) 7486 2699; 48 South Eaton Place, SW1W 9JJ. *T:* (020) 7730 9794. *Clubs:* Royal Ocean Racing, Hurlingham; Beaulieu River Sailing (Beaulieu).

COLLING, Rev. Canon James Oliver, MBE 1995; Rector of Warrington, 1973–97; Canon Diocesan of Liverpool Cathedral, 1976–97, now Canon Emeritus; Chaplain to The Queen, 1990–2000; *b* 3 Jan. 1930; *e s* of late Leonard Colling and Dorothy Colling (*née* Atherton); *m* 1957, Jean Wright; one *s* one *d* (one twin *s* decd). *Educ:* Leigh Grammar Sch.; Univ. of Manchester (BA 1950); Cuddesdon Coll., Oxford. Commissioned RAF, 1950–52 (Nat. Service). Deacon 1954; priest 1955; Asst Curate, Wigan Parish Church, 1954–59; Vicar of Padgate, 1959–71, Rector, 1971–73; Rural Dean of Warrington, 1970–82 and 1987–89, Area Dean, 1989–95. Chairman: Warrington CHC, 1974–82; Warrington Community Council, 1974–87; Warrington Jt Consultative Cttee, 1987–89; Vice-Chm., Warrington HA, 1982–89; Member: Cheshire Family Practitioner Cttee, 1983–85; Cheshire FHSA, 1990–94 (Chm., Pharmaceutical Develt Gp). Chairman: Warrington C of E Educnl Trust, 1973–97; Warrington and Dist Soc. for the Deaf, 1974–93 (Vice-Pres., 1993–); Warrington Charities Trust, 1989–91 (Patron, 1992–); Vice-Pres., Cheshire Deaf Soc. (operating as Deafness Support Network), 1980–. Chairman: Governors, Sir Thomas Boteler High Sch., Warrington, 1988–97; Boteler Educnl Trust, 1995–97. *Recreations:* looking at buildings and places, local history. *Address:* 19 King Street, Chester CH1 2AH. *T:* (01244) 317557.

COLLINGE, Prof. John, CBE 2004; MD; FRS 2005; Professor of Neurology and Head, Department of Neurodegenerative Disease, Institute of Neurology, University College London, since 2001; *b* 25 Jan. 1958; *s* of late Robert Collinge and of Edna Collinge; *m* 1986, Donna Anne Keel (marr. diss. 1990). *Educ:* Burnley Grammar Sch.; St John's Coll., Cambridge; Univ. of Bristol (BSc Hons 1981; MB ChB 1984; MD 1992). MRCP 1988, FRCP 1998; FRCPath 1999. Bristol Royal Infirmary: House Surg., 1984–85; House Physician, 1985; Hon. Sen. House Officer in Pathology, 1985–86; Demonstrator in Pathology, Univ. of Bristol, 1985–86; Med. Rotation, Westminster Hosp., 1986–87; Senior House Officer: in Medicine, Hammersmith Hosp., 1987; in Neurology, Nat. Hosp. for Neurology and Neurosurgery, 1987–88; Merck, Sharp and Dohme Fellow, 1988, Clin. Scientific Staff, 1988–90, MRC Div. of Psychiatry, Clin. Res. Centre, Harrow; Hon. Registrar in Psychiatry, Northwick Park Hosp., 1988–90; Clin. Res. Fellow, Dept of Biochemistry and Molecular Genetics, St Mary's Hosp. Med Sch., 1990–91; St Mary's Hospital: Hon. Registrar, 1990–91, Hon. Sen. Registrar, 1991–94, in Neurology; Hon. Consultant in Neurology and Molecular Genetics, 1994–; Imperial College School of Medicine at St Mary's (formerly St Mary's Hospital Medical School): Wellcome Sen. Res. Fellow, 1992–96, Prin. Res. Fellow, 1996–2000, in Clin. Scis; Prof. of Molecular Neurogenetics and Hd, Dept of Neurogenetics, 1994–; Hon. Consultant Neurologist, Nat. Hosp. for Neurology and Neurosurgery, 1996–; Hon. Dir, MRC Prion Unit, 1998–. Member: Neuroscis Panel, Wellcome Trust, 1994–97; Spongiform Encephalopathy Adv. Cttee, 1996–2001; Dep. Chm., High-level Gp on BSE, EU, 1996–97; Chm., Res. Adv. Panel, MND Assoc., 1997– (Mem., 1994–97). Member: Amer. Acad. of Neurology, 1993; Clin. Genetics Soc., 1993; Assoc. of British Neurologists, 1995. Founder FMedSci 1998. Linacre Medal, 1992, Graham Bull Prize in Clin. Sci., 1993, RCP; Alfred Meyer Medal, British Neuropathol Soc., 1997; Howard Taylor Ricketts Medal, Univ. of Chicago, 2001. *Publications:* (ed jtly) Prion Diseases of Humans and Animals, 1992; (ed jtly) Prion Diseases, 1997; papers on prion diseases and neurogenetics. *Recreations:* mountain walking, flying. *Address:* MRC Prion Unit, Department of Neurodegenerative Disease, National Hospital for Neurology and Neurosurgery, Queen Square, WC1N 3BG. *T:* (020) 7837 4888.

COLLINGE, John Gregory; High Commissioner for New Zealand in the United Kingdom, 1994–97, and concurrently High Commissioner in Nigeria and Ambassador to the Republic of Ireland; *b* 10 May 1939; *s* of Norman Gregory Collinge and Hilary Winifred Fendall; *m* 2003, Margaret Elaine Postlethwaite; two *d* by a previous marriage. *Educ:* Auckland Univ. (LLB); University Coll., Oxford (MLitt). Called to the Bar, 1963, and admitted Solicitor, 1963, High Court of NZ; called to the Bar, 1966, and admitted Solicitor, 1966, High Court of Australia. Sen. Lectr in Law, Melbourne Univ., 1967–70; Partner, law firm, Melbourne, Wellington and Auckland, 1969–2005. Pres., NZ National Party, 1989–94. Chairman: Policy and Finance Cttee, Auckland Regl Authy, 1983–86; Commerce Commn, 1984–89; Alcohol Adv. Council of NZ, 1991–94; Nat. Civil Defence Energy Planning Cttee, 1992–94. Member: Auckland Electric Power Bd, 1977–80, 1992–93 (Chm., 1980–92); Electrical Develt Assoc. of NZ, 1990–91 (Pres., 1991–94); Council, Electricity Supply Assoc. of NZ, 1991–92. Chairman: New Zealand Pelagic Fisheries Ltd, 1975–81; United Distillers (NZ) Ltd, 1991 (Dir, 1986–91); Director: Mercury Energy Ltd, 1998–99; Vector Ltd, 2002–04 (Dep. Chm., 2002–04). Pres., Auckland Citizens and Ratepayers Inc., 1999–2004; Trustee, Auckland Energy Consumer Trust, 2000–06 (Dep. Chm., 2001–04). Alternate Gov., EBRD, 1994–97. Comr, Commonwealth War Graves Commn, 1994–97; Gov., Commonwealth Foundn, 1994–97; Mem. Bd of Govs, Commonwealth Inst., 1994–97. Vice-Pres., Royal Over-Seas League, 1994–97; Trustee, Waitangi Foundn, 1994–97; Patron: Captain Cook Birthplace Trust, 1994–97; Shakespeare Globe Trust, 1994–97; British/NZ Trade Council, 1994–97. Commemoration Medal, NZ, 1990. *Publications:* Restrictive Trade Practices and Monopolies in New Zealand, 1969, 2nd edn 1982; Tutorials in Contract, 1985, 4th edn 1989; The Law of Marketing in Australia and New Zealand, 1989, 2nd edn 1990. *Recreations:* New Zealand history, restoring colonial houses and colonial antiques, Rugby, cricket. *Address:* 10 London Street, St Mary's Bay, Auckland, New Zealand. *T:* 93608951; Frog Pond Farm, Ansty, Wilts SP3 5PY. *Clubs:* Vincent's (Oxford); Wellington (NZ).

COLLINGRIDGE, Prof. Graham Leon, PhD; FRS 2001; Professor of Neuroscience, Department of Anatomy, since 1994, and Director, MRC Centre for Synaptic Plasticity, since 1999, University of Bristol; *b* 1 Feb. 1955; *s* of Cyril Leon Collingridge and Marjorie May Caesar; *m* 1992, Catherine Rose; one *s* two *d*. *Educ:* Enfield GS; Univ. of Bristol (BSc 1977); Sch. of Pharmacy, London Univ. (PhD 1980). CBiol, FIBiol 1997. Res. Fellow in Physiology, Univ. of British Columbia, 1980–82; Sen. Res. Officer, Dept of Physiology and Pharmacology, Univ. of NSW, 1983; Lectr, 1983–90, Reader, 1990, Dept of Pharmacology, Univ. of Bristol; Prof., and Head of Dept of Pharmacology, Univ. of Birmingham, 1990–94; Head of Dept of Anatomy, Univ. of Bristol, 1996–98. Member: Neurosci. Bd, 1995–99, LINK Panel, 1995–99, MRC; Internat. Interest Gp, Wellcome Trust, 1996–2001. Founder, European Dana Alliance for the Brain, 1997. Founder FMedSci 1998. Editor-in-Chief, Neuropharmacology, 1993–. *Publications:* numerous papers in scientific jls, such as Nature, Neuropharmacology, on the neural basis of learning and memory and other aspects of neuroscience. *Recreations:* ski-ing, travel. *Address:* Department of Anatomy, University of Bristol, Bristol BS8 1TD. *T:* (0117) 928 7420.

COLLINGRIDGE, Jean Mary; see King, J. M.

COLLINGS, Juliet Jeanne d'Auvergne; see Campbell, J. J. d'A.

COLLINGS, Matthew Glynn Burkinshaw; QC 2006; *b* 13 Aug. 1961; *s* of Frederick, (Burke), Collings and Beryl Collings; *m* 1984, Amanda Maine-Tucker; two *s*. *Educ:* Colston's Sch., Bristol; London Sch. of Econs (LLB). Called to the Bar, Lincoln's Inn, 1985; in practice as barrister, 1986–, specialising in company, insolvency and commercial law. Former Mem., Insolvency Rules Adv. Cttee. Chm., Oxfordshire and Bucks Cons. Party, 2006–. Contested (C) Newport E, 2005. *Recreations:* vintage cars, opera, ski-ing.

Address: Maitland Chambers, 7 Stone Buildings, Lincoln's Inn, WC2A 3SZ. *T:* (020) 7406 1200, *Fax:* (020) 7406 1300; *e-mail:* mcollings@maitlandchambers.com.

COLLINGS, Very Rev. Neil; Dean of St Edmundsbury, since 2006; *b* 26 Aug. 1946; *s* of James Philip Sanford Collings and Edith Lilian Collings (*née* Neill). *Educ:* Torquay Grammar Sch.; King's Coll. London (BD, AKC); St Augustine's Coll., Canterbury. Ordained deacon, 1970, priest 1971; Curate, 1970–72, Team Vicar, 1972–74, Littleham cum Exmouth; Chaplain, Westminster Abbey, 1974–79; Dir of Ordinands and Post-ordination Trng, Dio. Hereford, and Preb., Hereford Cathedral, 1979–86; Chaplain to the Bishop of Hereford, 1982–86; Rector: St Nicholas, Hereford, 1979–86; St Nicholas, Harpenden, 1986–99; Hon. Canon, St Alban's Cathedral, 1996–99; Canon Residentiary and Treas., Exeter Cathedral, 1999–2006. Chaplain, Devon and Cornwall Constabulary, 1999–2006. *Publication:* Young Person's Guide to Westminster Abbey, 1979. *Recreations:* swimming, cats, Queen Victoria, 'The Archers', travel. *Address:* The Cathedral Office, Abbey House, Angel Hill, Bury St Edmunds IP33 1LS. *T:* (01284) 754933, *Fax:* (01284) 768655; *e-mail:* dean@stedscathedral.co.uk. *Club:* National.

COLLINGWOOD, John Gildas, FREng, FIChemE; Director: Unilever Ltd, 1965–77; Unilever NV, 1965–77; Head of Research Division of Unilever Ltd, 1961–77; *b* 15 June 1917; *s* of Stanley Ernest Collingwood and Kathleen Muriel (*née* Smalley); *m* 1942, Pauline Winifred Jones (*d* 1998); one *s* one *d*. *Educ:* Wycliffe Coll., Stonehouse, Glos; University Coll. London (BSc; Fellow, 1970). English Charcoal, 1940–41; British Ropeway Engrg Co., 1941–44; De Havilland Engines, 1944–46; Olympia Oil and Cake Mills Ltd, 1946–49; British Oil and Cake Mills Ltd, 1949–51; Mem., UK Milling Group of Unilever Ltd, 1951–60; Dir, Advita Ltd, 1951–60; Dir, British Oil & Cake Mills Ltd, 1955–60. Mem. Research Cttee, 1963–68, Mem. Council, 1964–67, IChemE. Member: Council, Univ. of Aston, 1971–83 (Chm., Academic Advisory Cttee, 1964–71); Research Cttee, CBI, 1970–71; Council for Scientific Policy, 1971–72; Exec. Cttee, British Nutrition Foundn, 1978–82 (Council, 1970–85); Food Standards Cttee, 1972–80; Royal Commn on Environmental Pollution, 1973–79; Standing Commn on Energy and the Environment, 1978–81. A Gen. Sec., BAAS, 1978–83, 1986–88. Vice Pres., Nat. Children's Home, 1989– (Chm., F and GP Cttee, 1983–89); Pres., Wycliffe Coll., Stonehouse, Glos, 1997–2006 (Mem. Council, 1967–2006; Chm., 1985–89; Vice-Pres., 1989–97). Hon. DSc Aston, 1966. *Recreations:* sailing, music. *Address:* 54 Downs Road, Coulsdon, Surrey CR5 1AA. *T:* (01737) 554817. *Club:* Athenæum.

COLLINI, Prof. Stefan Anthony, PhD; FRHistS; FBA 2000; Professor of Intellectual History and English Literature, Cambridge University, since 2000; Fellow, Clare Hall, Cambridge, since 1986; *b* 6 Sept. 1947; *s* of Raymond Collini and Hilda May (*née* Brown); *m* 1971, Ruth Karen Morse. *Educ:* St Joseph's Coll., Beulah Hill; Jesus Coll., Cambridge (BA 1969, MA 1973; Thirlwall Prize and Seeley Medal 1973; PhD 1977); Yale Univ. (MA 1970). FRHistS 1981. Res. Fellow, St John's Coll., Cambridge, 1973–74; University of Sussex: Lectr in Intellectual Hist., 1974–82; Reader, 1982–86; Cambridge University: Asst Lectr in English, 1986–90; Lectr, 1990–94; Reader, 1994–2000. Visiting Fellow: History of Ideas Unit, ANU, 1982–83 and 1987; Clare Hall, Cambridge, 1986; Vis. Prof., Inst. Internacional de Estudios Avanzados, Caracas, 1983; Dir d'études associé, Ecole des Hautes Etudes en Scis Sociales, Paris, 1986 and 1991; Mem., Inst. for Advanced Study, Princeton, 1994–95; British Studies Fellow, Ransom Humanities Res. Center, Austin, Tex., 1995; Sen. Res. Fellowship, British Acad., 1999–2000; Leverhulme Major Res. Fellowship, 2007–. Lectures: Mary Parker Yates, Tulane, 2000; Bateson, Oxford, 2002; Sir D. Owen Evans Meml, Aberystwyth, 2002; Gauss Seminars, Princeton, 2002; Prothero, RHistS, 2003; George Orwell, London, 2003; Bristol Inst. for Res. in Humanities and Arts, 2005; Kent Inst. of Advanced Studies in Humanities, 2007; Jacques Berthoud, York, 2008. Co-ed., Cambridge Rev., 1986–93. *Publications:* Liberalism and Sociology, 1979; (jtly) That Noble Science of Politics, 1983; Arnold, 1988, 2nd edn 1994; (ed) On Liberty, by J. S. Mill, 1989; Public Moralists, 1991; (ed) Interpretation and Overinterpretation, by Umberto Eco, 1992; (ed) Culture and Anarchy, by Matthew Arnold, 1993; (ed) The Two Cultures, by C. P. Snow, 1993; English Pasts: essays in history and culture, 1999; (ed jtly) Economy, Polity, and Society, 2000; (ed jtly) History, Religion, and Culture: British Intellectual History 1750–1950, 2000; Absent Minds: intellectuals in Britain, 2006; Common Reading: critics, historians, publics, 2008; contrib. essays and reviews in jls, incl. TLS, London Rev. of Books, etc. *Address:* Faculty of English, Cambridge University, 9 West Road, Cambridge CB3 9DP. *T:* (01223) 335082.

COLLINS, Sir Alan (Stanley), KCVO 2005; CMG 1998; HM Diplomatic Service; Consul-General, New York and Director-General, Trade and Investment in the US, since 2007; *b* 1 April 1948; *s* of Stanley Arthur Collins and Rose Elizabeth Collins; *m* 1971, Ann Dorothy Roberts; two *s* one *d*. *Educ:* Strand GS; London School of Economics and Political Science (BSc Econs). Joined MoD, 1970; Private Sec. to Vice Chief of Air Staff, 1973–75; joined FCO, 1981; Deputy Head of Mission: Addis Ababa, 1986–90; Manila, 1990–93; Counsellor, FCO, 1993–95; Dir-Gen., British Trade and Cultural Office, Taipei, 1995–98; Ambassador, Philippines, 1998–2002; (on secondment) Vice-Pres. for Internat. Relns, Shell, 2002–07; High Comr, Singapore, 2003–07. *Recreations:* sport, antiques, reading, walking. *Address:* c/o Foreign and Commonwealth Office, King Charles Street, SW1A 2AH. *Club:* Royal Commonwealth Society.

COLLINS, Hon. Sir Andrew (David), Kt 1994; **Hon. Mr Justice Collins;** a Judge of the High Court of Justice, Queen's Bench Division, since 1994; *b* 19 July 1942; *s* of late Rev. Canon Lewis John Collins, MA, and Dame Diana Clavering Collins, DBE; *m* 1970, Nicolette Anne Sandford-Saville; one *s* one *d*. *Educ:* Eton; King's Coll., Cambridge (BA, MA). Called to the Bar, Middle Temple, 1965, Bencher, 1992; QC 1985; a Recorder, 1986–94. Pres., Immigration Appeal Tribunal, 1999–2002; Lead Judge, Administrative Court, 2004–07. *Address:* Royal Courts of Justice, Strand, WC2A 2LL.

COLLINS, Arthur John, OBE 1973; HM Diplomatic Service, retired; Representative of the Secretary of State, Foreign and Commonwealth Office, 1988–2006; *b* 17 May 1931; *s* of Reginald and Margery Collins; *m* 1952, Enid Maureen, *d* of Charles Stableford, FRIBA and Sarah Stableford; one *s* one *d*. *Educ:* Purley Grammar Sch. Served RAF, 1949–51. Min. of Health, 1951–68 (Private Sec. to Perm. Sec., 1960–61, and to Parly Sec., 1962–63); transf. to HM Diplomatic Service, 1968; FCO, 1968–69; First Secretary and Head of Chancery: Dhaka, 1970–71; Brasilia, 1972–74; Asst Head of Latin America and Caribbean Depts, FCO, 1974–77; Counsellor, UK Del. to OECD, Paris, 1978–81; High Comr, Papua New Guinea, 1982–85; adviser on management, FCO, 1986–88; Consultant, EBRD, 1991; Assessor, VSO, 1993–99. Pres., Brighton and Hove Archaeol Soc., 1996–99. Chm., Brighton, Hove and Dist, ESU, 1998–2004. *Publications:* papers on early colonialism in New Guinea. *Address:* 60 Dean Court Road, Rottingdean, Sussex BN2 7DJ. *Club:* Hove (Hove).

COLLINS, Basil Eugene Sinclair, CBE 1983; Chairman, Nabisco Group, 1984–89; *b* 21 Dec. 1923; *s* of Albert Collins and Pauline Alicia (*née* Wright); *m* 1942, Doris Slott (*d* 2004); two *d*. *Educ:* Great Yarmouth Grammar School. Sales Manager, L. Rose & Co. Ltd, 1945; Export Dir, Schweppes (Overseas) Ltd, 1958; Group Admin Dir, Schweppes Ltd, 1964, Chm. of Overseas Gp 1968; Chm. of Overseas Gp, Cadbury Schweppes Ltd, 1969, Dep. Man. Dir 1972, Man. Dir 1974, Dep. Chm. and Group Chief Exec., Cadbury Schweppes plc, 1980–83; Director: Thomas Cook Gp, 1980–85; British Airways Bd, 1982–88; Royal Mint, 1984–88. Royal College of Nursing: Chm., Finance and General Purposes Cttee, 1970–86; Hon. Treasurer, 1970–86; Vice-Pres., 1972, Life Vice-Pres., 1986. Fellow Inst. of Dirs, 1974, Council Mem., 1982–89; Managing Trustee, Inst. of Economic Affairs, 1987–91; Mem. Council, UEA, 1987–94. FZS 1975; CCMI (FBIM 1976); Fellow, Amer. Chamber of Commerce, 1979, Dir, 1984–89. FRSA 1984. Hon. Fellow, UEA, 1995. *Recreations:* music, languages, travel, English countryside. *Address:* Wyddial Parva, Buntingford, Herts SG9 0EL.

COLLINS, Prof. Brian Stanley, DPhil; CEng, FIET; FBCS; Professor of Information Systems, Cranfield University, since 2003; Chief Scientific Adviser: Department for Transport, since 2006; Department for Business, Enterprise and Regulatory Reform, since 2008; *b* 3 Oct. 1945; *s* of James and Maud Collins; *m* 1st (marr. diss.); one *s* one *d*; *m* 2nd (marr. diss.); partner, Gillian Sowerby. *Educ:* Chislehurst and Sidcup Grammar Sch.; St Peter's Coll., Oxford (Open Schol.; BA Physics 1967, MA); DPhil Astrophysics Oxon 1971. FInstP 1984; CEng 1988; FIET (FIEE 1988); FBCS 2000; CITP 2000. Res. Scientist, 1973–85, Dep. Dir, 1987, RSRE; rcds 1986; Chief Scientist and Dir, Technol. (Grade 3), GCHQ, 1987–91; Partner, KPMG, 1991–92; IT Dir, Wellcome Trust, 1994–97; Global Chief Inf. Officer, Clifford Chance, 1999–2001. Vice President: IEE, 1999–2002; BCS, 2003–06. Mem., Court of Assts, Co. of Information Technologists, 2004–. FRSA 1997. *Publication:* (ed with Prof. R. Mansell) Trust and Crime in Information Societies, 2004. *Recreations:* golf (learning), cricket and Rugby (watching), country walks, ballet, music, reading. *Address:* c/o Department of Transport, Great Minster House, 76 Marsham Street, SW1P 4DR; *e-mail:* b.s.collins@cranfield.ac.uk.

COLLINS, Sir Bryan (Thomas Alfred), Kt 1997; OBE 1989; QFSM 1983; HM Chief Inspector of Fire Services, 1994–98; *b* 4 June 1933; *m* 1959, Terry Skuce; one *s* one *d*. *Educ:* Queen Mary's Sch. RAF, 1951–53; with Fire Service, 1954–98; Chief Fire Officer, Humberside, 1979–89; Inspector of Fire Services: Northern Area, 1989–93; Midlands and Wales, 1993–94. *Address:* Gwelo, Thatcher Stanfords Close, Melbourn, S Cambs SG8 6DT.

COLLINS, Christopher Douglas; Chairman, Old Mutual plc, since 2005 (non-executive Director, since 1999); *b* 19 Jan. 1940; *s* of Douglas and Patricia Collins; *m* 1976, Susan Anne Lumb; one *s* one *d*. *Educ:* Eton. Chartered Accountant. Articled clerk, Peat Marwick Mitchell, 1958–64; Goya Ltd: Man. Dir, 1968–75; Dir, 1975–80; joined Hanson, 1989: Dir, 1991–2005; Vice Chm., 1995–97; Chm., 1998–2005. Chm., Forth Ports PLC, 2000–. Amateur steeplechase jockey, 1965–75; represented GB in 3-day equestrian events, 1974–80; Chm., British Team Selection Cttee, 1981–84; Jockey Club Steward, 1980–81; Mem., Horse Race Betting Levy Bd, 1982–84. Chairman: Aintree Racecourse Ltd, 1983–88; National Stud, 1986–88; Jockey Club Racecourses (formerly Racecourse Hldgs Trust), 2005–08. *Recreation:* ski-ing. *Address:* Old Mutual plc, Old Mutual Place, 2 Lambeth Hill, EC4V 4GG. *T:* (020) 7002 7000. *Clubs:* Jockey, White's, Pratt's.

COLLINS, Crispian Hilary Vincent; Chairman: ING Global Real Estate Securities Ltd, since 2006; Matrix European Real Estate Investment Trust Ltd, since 2007; *b* 22 Jan. 1948; *s* of late Bernard John Collins, CBE, and Gretel Elisabeth Collins (*née* Piehler); *m* 1974, Diane Barbara Bromley; one *s* two *d*. *Educ:* Ampleforth Coll.; University Coll., Oxford (BA Hons Modern History). Joined Phillips & Drew, 1969; Fund Manager, Pension Funds, 1975–98; Partner, 1981–85; Chief Exec., 1998–2000; Chm., 1999–2002; Dir, 1985–2002, Mem., Mgt Cttee, 1994–2000, Phillips & Drew Fund Mgt. Vice Chm., UBS (later UBS Global) Asset Management, 2000–03. Director: Salvation Army Trustee Co., 2003–; The Children's Mutual, 2003–. Chm. of Govs, St Leonards-Mayfield Sch., 2003–. *Recreations:* golf, watching sport, opera, gardens. *Address:* *e-mail:* crispiancollins@btinternet.com.

COLLINS, Prof. David John, PhD; Performance Director, UK Athletics, 2005–08; *b* 31 Dec. 1953; *s* of Arthur and Ivy Collins; *m* 2003, Helen Brooker; two *d*, and one *s* two *d* from previous marriage. *Educ:* Borough Rd Coll. (CertEd, BEd Hons); Pennsylvania State Univ. (MSc); Univ. of Surrey (PhD 1990); BASES accredited Sport Psychologist; BOA registered Sport Psychologist. Commn RM, 1972–76. Teacher: Stowe Sch., 1978–79; Bucks CC, 1979–80 and 1981–85; Sen. Lectr, St Mary's Coll., Twickenham, 1985–93; Reader, then Prof., Manchester Metropolitan Univ., 1993–98; Prof. of Physical Educn and Sport Performance, 1998–2005, Adjunct Prof., 2005–, Univ. of Edinburgh. Sport Psychologist: RFU, 1990–91; Olympic Weightlifting, 1992–97; Short Track Speed Skating, 1993–99; Scottish Judo, 1999–2004; Scottish Curling, 1999–2004; UK Athletics, 1999–2005. *Publications:* The Use of Physiological Measures in Sport Psychology: a handbook, 1982; (jtly) Working with Teams, 1990; (jtly) Get Ready for Squash, 1990; Sport Psychology and Motor Control, 1992; Applying Psychological Research for Coaching and Performance Enhancement, 1993; (jtly) Talent Identification and Development: an academic review, 2002; (jtly) Rugby Tough, 2002; Performance Psychology: a guide for practitioners, 2008; chapters in books; contrib. learned jls. *Recreations:* scuba-diving, martial arts, motor-cycling, outdoor pursuits, curry consumption. *Clubs:* Romford Rugby, Saracens, Bedford Rugby, Northampton and Brackley Rugby; Royal Canoe (Teddington).

COLLINS, Dr David John, CBE 2005; Principal and Chief Executive, South Cheshire College, since 1993; *b* 13 Nov. 1949; *s* of Leslie Reginald Collins and Vera Collins (*née* Harvey); *m* 1972, Linda Patterson; two *s*. *Educ:* Humphry Davy Grammar Sch., Penzance; Univ. of Edinburgh (MA Hons; PhD). Res. Asst, Univ. of Edinburgh, 1972–73; Educn Co-ordinator, HM YOI and HM Prison Edinburgh, 1973–75; Hd of Dept, 1975–85, Coll. Develt Officer, 1985–88, Redditch Coll.; Vice-Principal, Sandwell Coll., 1988–92; on secondment as Principal and Chief Exec., Bolton Coll., 1999–2000. Vis. Professorial Fellow, Univ. of Lancaster, 2005–. Member, Board: Cheshire and Warrington LSC, 2004–07; Assoc. of Colls, 2006– (Pres., 2008–July 2009); Learning and Skills Network 2006–08. FRSA 2005. Hon. DBA Chester, 2008. *Publications:* A Survival Guide for College Leaders and Managers, 2006; The Role of the Principal, 2008. *Recreations:* travel, writing, sport, hill-walking. *Address:* South Cheshire College, Dane Bank Avenue, Crewe, Cheshire CW2 8AB. *T:* (01270) 654601, *Fax:* (01270) 651515; *e-mail:* d-collins@s-cheshire.ac.uk.

COLLINS, Deborah; Director, Legal and Democratic Services, Southwark Council, since 2007; *b* 18 April 1963; *d* of Brig. Kenelm John and Angela Charlotte Hathaway; *m* 1991, Tim Collins; one *s* one *d*. *Educ:* Worcester Coll., Oxford (BA (Jurisprudence) 1984). Articled Clerk, Coward Chance, 1985–87, Solicitor, Clifford Chance, 1987–88; merchant banker, J. Henry Schroder Wagg & Co. Ltd, 1988–91; Govt Legal Service: DTI, 1991–97; European Secretariat, Cabinet Office Legal Advrs, 1997–99; Divl Manager, DFEE Legal, 1999–2002; Legal Advr to Highways Agency, 2002–03; Dir, Legal Services Gp, DTI, 2003–06; Dir, Legal (Ops), HMRC, 2006–07. *Recreations:* shoes, ski-ing, walking, cooking, watching plants grow in my garden. *Address:* Southwark Town Hall, Peckham Road, SE5 8UB. *T:* (020) 7525 7630; *e-mail:* deborah.collins@southwark.gov.uk.

COLLINS, Francis Sellers, MD; PhD; Director, National Human Genome Research Institute, Bethesda, Maryland, since 1993; *b* 14 April 1950; *s* of Fletcher and Margaret Collins; *m* 1998, Diane Lynn Baker; two *d*. *Educ:* Univ. of Virginia, Charlottesville (BS Highest Hons 1970); Yale Univ. (MPhil, PhD Physical Chem. 1974); Univ. of N Carolina Sch. of Medicine (MD Hons 1977). University of Michigan: Asst Prof. of Internal Medicine and Human Genetics, Med. Sch., Ann Arbor, 1984–88; Chief, Div. of Med. Genetics, Dept of Internal Medicine and Human Genetics, 1988–91; Prof. of Internal Medicine and Human Genetics, 1991–93 (on leave, 1993–2003). Asst Investigator, 1987–88, Investigator, 1991–93, Howard Hughes Med. Inst., Ann Arbor, Mich. Presidential Medal of Freedom (USA), 2007. *Address:* National Human Genome Research Institute, 31 Center Drive, MSC 2152, Building 31, Room 4B09, Bethesda, MD 20892–2152, USA. *T:* (301) 4960844, *Fax:* (301) 4020837; *e-mail:* fc23a@nih.gov.

COLLINS, Gerard; *see* Collins, James G.

COLLINS, Prof. Hugh Graham, FBA 2006; Professor of English Law, since 1991, Head, Department of Law, 1994–97 and since 2006, London School of Economics; *b* 21 June 1953; *s* of Richard and Joan Collins; *m* 1983, Prof. Emily Simonoff; two *d*. *Educ:* Pembroke Coll., Oxford (MA, BCL); Harvard Law Sch. (LLM). Fellow, Brasenose Coll., Oxford, 1976–91. Mem., Adv. Forum on Impact of Employment Policies, DTI, 2006–. Member, Editorial Committee: Industrial Law Jl, 1982–; Modern Law Rev., 1992–; Eur. Rev. of Contract Law, 2005–. *Publications:* Marxism and Law, 1982; The Law of Contract, 1986, 4th edn 2003; Justice in Dismissal, 1992; Regulating Contracts, 1999; Employment Law, 2003; Labour Law: texts and materials, 2001, 2nd edn 2005. *Recreations:* opera, theatre, modern art, painting, sailing, building walls. *Address:* Department of Law, London School of Economics, Houghton Street, WC2A 2AE. *T:* (020) 7955 7246, *Fax:* (020) 7955 7366; *e-mail:* h.collins@lse.ac.uk.

COLLINS, Jacqueline Jill, (Jackie); writer; *b* London, 4 Oct.; *d* of late Joseph Collins and Elsa (*née* Bessant); *m* Wallace Austin (marr. diss.); one *d*; *m* 1966, Oscar Lerman (*d* 1992); two *d*. Formerly TV and film actress. *Publications:* The World is Full of Married Men, 1968; The Stud, 1969 (filmed, 1978); Sunday Simmons and Charlie Brick, 1971 (new edn as Sinners, 1984); Lovehead, 1974; The World is Full of Divorced Women, 1975; Lovers and Gamblers, 1977; The Bitch, 1979 (filmed, 1979); Chances, 1981 (televised, 1990); Hollywood Wives, 1983 (televised); Lucky, 1985 (televised); Hollywood Husbands, 1986; Rock Star, 1988; Love Killers, 1989; Lady Boss, 1990 (televised); American Star, 1993; Hollywood Kids, 1994; Vendetta: Lucky's revenge, 1996; Thrill, 1998; LA Connections (four parts), 1998; Dangerous Kiss, 1999; Lethal Seduction, 2000; Hollywood Wives: the new generation, 2001; Hollywood Divorces, 2003; Lovers and Players, 2005; Drop Dead Beautiful, 2007; Married Lovers, 2008. *Address:* c/o Simon and Schuster, 1230 Avenue of the Americas, New York, NY 10020, USA.

See also Joan H. Collins.

COLLINS, (James) Gerard; Member, European Parliament, 1994–2004; *b* Abbeyfeale, Co. Limerick, 16 Oct. 1938; *s* of late James J. Collins, TD and Margaret Collins; *m* 1969, Hilary Tattan. *Educ:* University Coll., Dublin (BA). Teacher. Asst Gen. Sec., Fianna Fáil, 1965–67. TD (FF) Limerick W, 1967–97; Parly Sec. to Ministers for Industry and Commerce and for the Gaeltacht, 1969–70; Minister for Posts and Telegraphs, 1970–73; opposition front-bench spokesman on agriculture, 1973–75; spokesman on justice, 1975–77; Minister for Justice, 1977–81; Minister for Foreign Affairs, March–Dec. 1982; opposition front-bench spokesman on foreign affairs, 1983–87; Minister for Justice, 1987–89; Minister for Foreign Affairs, 1989–92. Mem., Consultative Assembly, Council of Europe, 1973–77; Chm., Parly Cttee on Secondary Legislation of European Communities, 1983–87. Mem., Limerick CC, 1974–77. *Address:* The Hill, Abbeyfeale, Co. Limerick, Ireland.

COLLINS, Dr Jane Elizabeth, (Mrs David Evans), FRCP, FRCPCH; Chief Executive, Great Ormond Street Hospital NHS Trust, since 2001; Consultant in Metabolic Medicine, Great Ormond Street Hospital, since 1996; *b* 19 Oct. 1954; *d* of Thomas and Betsy Collins; *m* 1978, David Evans; one *s* one *d*. *Educ:* Portsmouth High Sch.; Univ. of Birmingham (MSc, MD 1988). FRCP 1994; FRCPCH 1996. Consultant Paediatric Neurologist: Guy's Hosp., 1991–94; Gt Ormond St Hosp., 1994–96; Med. Dir, Gt Ormond St Hosp. NHS Trust, 1999–2001. Paediatric consultant (formerly Children's Doctor columnist), The Times, 1999–. *Address:* Great Ormond Street Hospital, WC1N 3JH. *T:* (020) 7813 8330.

COLLINS, Prof. Jeffrey Hamilton, FRSE; FREng; Professor and Specialist Advisor to Vice-Chancellor, Napier University, 1994–97; *b* 22 April 1930; *s* of Ernest Frederick and Dora Gladys Collins; *m* 1956, Sally Parfitt; two *s*. *Educ:* London Univ. (BSc, MSc, DSc). FIET (FIEE 1973), CPhys 1974, FInstP 1974, FIEEE 1980; CEng 1973, FREng (FEng 1981), FRSE 1983. GEC Research Laboratories, London, 1951–56; Ferranti Ltd, Edinburgh, 1956–57; Univ. of Glasgow, 1957–66; Research Engr, Stanford Univ., Calif, 1966–68; Dir of Physical Electronics, Rockwell International, Calif, 1968–70; University of Edinburgh: Research Prof., 1970–73; Prof. of Industrial Electronics, 1973–77; Prof. of Electrical Engrg and Hd of Dept, 1977–84; Emeritus Prof., 1984; Chm., Parallel Computing Centre, 1991–94. Dir, Automation and Robotics Res. Inst., and Prof. of Electrical Engrg, Univ. of Texas at Arlington, 1976–77 and 1987–90; Sen. Technical Specialist, Lothian Regl Council, 1991–93. Member: Electronics Res. Council, 1979; Computer Bd for Univs and Res. Councils, 1985–86; Information Systems Cttee, UFC, 1992–93; Jt Information Systems Cttee, HEFCs, 1993–94. Director: MESL, 1970–79; Racal-MESL, 1979–81; Advent Technology, 1981–86; Filtronics Components, 1981–85; Burr-Brown Ltd, 1985; River Bend Bank, Fort Worth, 1987–90. Member Honour Societies: Eta Kappa Nu; Tau Beta Pi; Upsilon Pi Epsilon; Phi Beta Delta. Hon. DEng Napier, 1997. *Publications:* Computer-Aided Design of Surface Acoustic Wave Devices, 1976; 197 articles in learned soc. electrical engrg jls. *Recreations:* music, DIY, tennis.

COLLINS, Joan Henrietta, OBE 1997; actress; *b* 23 May 1933; *er d* of late Joseph Collins and Elsa (*née* Bessant); *m* 1st, 1954, Maxwell Reed (marr. diss. 1957; he *d* 1974); 2nd, 1963, (George) Anthony Newley (marr. diss. 1970; he *d* 1999); one *s* one *d*; 3rd, 1972, Ronald S. Kass (marr. diss. 1983); one *d*; 4th, 1985, Peter Holm (marr. diss. 1987); 5th, 2002, Percy Gibson. *Educ:* Francis Holland Sch.; RADA. *Films include:* Lady Godiva Rides Again, I Believe in You, 1952; Our Girl Friday, The Square Ring, 1953; The Good Die Young, Turn the Key Softly, 1954; Land of the Pharaohs, The Virgin Queen, The Girl in the Red Velvet Swing, 1955; The Opposite Sex, 1956; The Wayward Bus, Island in the Sun, Sea Wife, 1957; The Bravados, 1958; Rally Round the Flag, Boys, 1959; Esther and the King, Seven Thieves, 1960; Road to Hong Kong, 1962; Warning Shot, The Subterfuge, 1967; Can Hieronymous Merkin Ever Forget Mercy Humppe and Find True Happiness?, Drive Hard Drive Fast, 1969; Up in the Cellar, The Executioner, 1970; Quest for Love, Revenge, 1971; Tales from the Crypt, Fear in the Night, 1972; Tales that witness Madness, 1973; Dark Places, Alfie Darling, 1974; The Call of the Wolf, I don't want to be born, 1975; The Devil within Her, 1976; Empire of the Ants, 1977; The Big Sleep, 1978; Sunburn, The Stud, 1979; The Bitch, 1980; The Nutcracker, 1984; The Cartier Affair, 1985; Decadence, 1994; In the Bleak Midwinter, 1995; The Clandestine Marriage, 1998; Joseph and the Amazing Technicolor Dreamcoat, 1999; The Flintstones in Viva Rock Vegas, 2000; Those Old Broads, 2000; Ellis in Glamourland, 2005; *stage includes:* The Last of Mrs Cheyney, Cambridge Th., 1980; Private Lives, Aldwych, 1990, US tour and NY, 1992; Love Letters, US, 2000; Over the Moon, Old Vic, 2001; Full Circle, UK tour, 2004; An Evening with Joan Collins, UK tour, 2006; Legends, US tour, 2006–07; *television includes:* serials: Dynasty, 1981–89; Sins, 1986; Monte Carlo, 1986; Guiding Light, 2002; Footballers' Wives, 2006; series: Tonight at 8.30, 1991; film: Annie: A Royal Adventure, 1995; also appearances in plays and series. Awards: Best TV Actress, Golden Globe, 1982; Hollywood Women's Press Club, 1982; Favourite TV Performer, People's Choice, 1985. *Publications:* Past Imperfect (autobiog.), 1978; The Joan Collins Beauty Book, 1980; Katy: a fight for life, 1982; My Secrets, 1994; Second Act (autobiog.), 1996; My Friends' Secrets, 2000; Joan's Way, 2002; *novels:* Prime Time, 1988; Love and Desire and Hate, 1990; Too Damn Famous, 1995; Star Quality, 2002; Misfortune's Daughter, 2004. *Address:* c/o Paul Keylock, 16 Bulbecks Walk, South Woodham Ferrers, Essex CM3 5ZN. *T:* (01245) 328367, *Fax:* (01245) 328625.

See also J. J. Collins.

COLLINS, Sir John (Alexander), Kt 1993; Chairman, DSG international (formerly Dixons Group) plc, since 2002 (Deputy Chairman, 2001–02); *b* 10 Dec. 1941; *s* of John Constantine Collins and Nancy Isobel Mitchell; *m* 1965, Susan Mary Hooper. *Educ:* Campbell Coll., Belfast; Reading Univ. Joined Shell, 1964; various appointments in Shell in Kenya, Nigeria, Colombia and UK; Chm. and Chief Exec., Shell UK, 1990–93; Chief Exec., Vestey Gp, 1994–2001; Chm., National Power, 1997–2000. Director: BSkyB, 1994–97; N. M. Rothschild & Sons, 1995–2005; LSO, 1997–2000; P&O, 1998–2006; Rothschild Continuation Hldgs AG, 1999–; Stoll Moss Theatres Ltd, 1999–2000. Chm., Cantab Pharmaceuticals plc, 1996–99. Chairman: Adv. Cttee on Business and Envmt, 1991–93; Energy Adv. Panel, DTI, 2001–03; Sustainable Energy Policy Adv. Bd, DTI/DEFRA, 2004–07; Pres., The Energy Institute, 2005–07. Gov., Wellington Coll., 1995–99. *Recreations:* theatre, sailing. *Address:* DSG international plc, Maylands Avenue, Hemel Hempstead HP2 7TG. *Clubs:* Royal Yacht Squadron (Cowes); Muthaiga Country (Nairobi).

COLLINS, John Ernest Harley, MBE 1944; DSC 1945 and Bar 1945; Chairman: Morgan Grenfell Holdings Ltd, 1974–80; Guardian Royal Exchange Assurance, 1974–88; *b* 24 April 1923; *o s* of late G. W. Collins, Taynton, Glos; *m* 1st, 1946, Gillian (*d* 1981), *e d* of 2nd Baron Bicester; one *s* one *d*; 2nd, 1986, Jennifer Faith, *widow* of Capt. A. J. A. Cubitt, and *yr d* of Lt Gen. W. H. E. Gott, CB, CBE, DSO, MC. *Educ:* King Edward's Sch., Birmingham; Birmingham Univ. Royal Navy, 1941–46. Morgan Grenfell & Co. Ltd, 1946, Dir 1957. Director: Royal Exchange Assce, 1957; Rank Hovis McDougall Ltd, 1965–91; Charter Consolidated Ltd, 1966–83; Hudson's Bay Co., 1957–74. Chm. United Services Trustee, 1968–76. DL Oxon, 1975–96; High Sheriff, Oxon, 1975. KStJ 1983. *Recreation:* fishing. *Address:* Chetwode Manor, Buckingham MK18 4BB. *T:* (01280) 848333.

COLLINS, (John) Martin; QC 1972; Commissioner, Royal Court, Jersey, 2000–02; a Judge of the Courts of Appeal of Jersey, 1984–99, and of Guernsey, 1984–2000; *b* 24 Jan. 1929; *s* of John Lissant Collins and Marjorie Mary Collins; *m* 1957, Daphne Mary, *d* of George Martyn Swindells, Prestbury; two *s* one *d*. *Educ:* Uppingham Sch.; Manchester Univ. (LLB). Called to Bar, Gray's Inn, 1952 (Bencher, 1981; Chm., Mgt Cttee, 1990; Vice-Treas., 1998; Treas., 1999); called to the Bar of Gibraltar, 1990. Dep. Chm., Cumberland QS, 1969–72; a Recorder, 1972–88. Member: Senate of Inns of Court and Bar, 1981–84; Gen. Council of the Bar, 1991. *Address:* Les Grandes Masses, 50580 Denneville, France. *Club:* Athenæum.

COLLINS, John Morris; a Recorder of the Crown Court, 1980–98; *b* 25 June 1931; *s* of late Emmanuel Cohen, MBE, and Ruby Cohen; *m* 1968, Sheila Brummer; one *d*. *Educ:* Leeds Grammar Sch.; The Queen's Coll., Oxford (MA LitHum). Called to Bar, Middle Temple, 1956, Member of North Eastern Circuit; Hd of Chambers, 1966–2001, Jt Hd of Chambers, 2001–02; a Deputy Circuit Judge, 1970–80. Pres., Leeds Jewish Representative Council, 1986–89. *Publications:* Summary Justice, 1963; various articles in legal periodicals, etc. *Recreation:* walking. *Address:* (home) 14 Sandhill Oval, Leeds LS17 8EA. *T:* (0113) 268 6008; (chambers) Zenith Chambers, 10 Park Square, Leeds LS1 2LH. *T:* (0113) 245 5438, *Fax:* (0113) 242 3515.

COLLINS, John Vincent, MD; FRCP; Consultant Physician, since 1976; Senior Medical Adviser, Benenden Healthcare Society, since 1979; Group Medical Adviser, Smith & Nephew plc, since 1987; Consultant Physician and Director of Education and Professional Development, Benenden Hospital, Kent; *b* 16 July 1938; *s* of Thomas Ernest Vincent Collins and Zillah Phoebe Collins; *m* 1963, Helen Eluned Cash; one *s* one *d*. *Educ:* Guy's Hosp. Med. and Dental Sch. (BDS 1961; MD 1974). FRCP 1981. Dental and Medical Schs, Guy's Hosp., 1956–66; Guy's, St Mary's, Royal Brompton and Westminster Hosps, 1967–72; Hon. Consultant Physician and Sen. Lectr, St Bartholomew's Hosp. Med. Sch., London, 1973–76; Consultant Physician: Royal Brompton Hosp., 1976–2003; Chelsea & Westminster Hosp., 1976–2003 (Med. Dir, 1994–2003); St Stephen's Hosp., 1979–89; Hon. Consultant, In Pensioners, Royal Hosp., Chelsea, 1980–2003. Chm., Clinical Standards Cttee, RCP, 2000–03. Mem., Soc. of Apothecaries. *Publications:* more than 150 papers, two monographs, and contribs to books. *Recreations:* painting, travel, tennis. *Address:* Royal Brompton Hospital, Fulham Road, SW3 6NP; The Lister Hospital, Chelsea Bridge Road, SW1W 8RH.

COLLINS, Judith, (Mrs R. J. H. Collins); *see* McClure, J.

COLLINS, Kathleen Joyce, (Kate), (Mrs D. A. L. Cooke); Director, Career Development and Assessment, Home Office, 2006–07; *b* 12 March 1952; *d* of Norman Jeffrey Collins and Phyllis Laura Collins (*née* Yardley); *m* 1984, David Arthur Lawrence Cooke, *qv*. *Educ:* Lady Margaret Hall, Oxford (BA Mod. Langs 1973; MA 1974). Joined Home Office as Immigration Officer, 1975; Admin Trainee, 1977; Principal, 1982; Dep. Chief Insp., 1988–91, Dir (Ports), 1991–94, Immigration Service; Cabinet Office, 1994–96; Home Office: Police Dept, 1997; Dep. Dir Gen., Immigration and Nationality Directorate, 1998–2000; Director: Organised Crime, 2000–03; Adelphi Prog., 2003–06. *Recreations:* music, reading, countryside.

COLLINS, Sir Kenneth Darlingston, (Sir Ken), Kt 2003; Chairman, Scottish Environment Protection Agency, 1999–2007; *b* 12 Aug. 1939; *s* of Nicholas Collins and Ellen Williamson; *m* 1966, Georgina Frances Pollard; one *s* one *d*. *Educ:* St John's Grammar Sch.; Hamilton Acad.; Glasgow Univ. (BSc Hons); Strathclyde Univ. (MSc). FRSGS 1993. Left school, 1956; steelworks apprentice, 1956–59; univ., 1960–65; planning officer, 1965–66; WEA Tutor-Organiser, 1966–67; Lecturer: Glasgow Coll. of Bldg, 1967–69; Paisley Coll. of Technol., 1969–79. MEP (Lab) Strathclyde E, 1979–99. European Parliament: Dep. Leader, Labour Gp, 1979–84; Socialist spokesman on envmt, public health and consumer protection, 1984–89; Chm., Cttee on Envmt, Public Health and Consumer Protection, 1979–84 and 1989–99 (Vice Chm., 1984–87); Chm., Conf. of

Cttee Chairmen, 1993–99. Dir, Inst. for Eur. Envmt Policy, London, 1991–99 (Bd Mem., 1999–2006). Member: Adv. Bd, ESRC Genomics Policy and Res. Forum, 2006–; Professional Practices Panel, Eur. Public Affairs Consultancies' Assoc., 2006–; EU High-Level Gp on Competitiveness, Energy and the Envmt, 2006–. Member: East Kilbride Town and Dist Council, 1973–79; Lanark CC, 1973–75; East Kilbride Develt Corp., 1976–79; Bd, Forward Scotland, 1996–2003; Bd, EEA, 2000–05; Chairman: NE Glasgow Children's Panel, 1974–76; Central Scotland Forest (formerly Countryside) Trust, 1998–2001; Adv. Cttee, Scottish Alliance for Geoscis, Envmt and Society, 2008–. Hon. Sen. Res. Fellow, Dept of Geography, Lancaster Univ., 1991–98; Associate Fellow, Eur. Centre for Public Affairs, 1999–. Vice-Pres., Assoc. of Drainage Authorities. Hon. Mem., Landscape Inst. Member: Fabian Soc.; Amnesty Internat.; Labour Movement in Europe; Hon. Pres., Scottish Assoc. of Geography Teachers, 2003–06; Hon. Vice-President: Royal Envmtl Health Inst. of Scotland, 1983; Internat. Fedn on Envmtl Health, 1987; Inst. of Trading Standards Admin; Inst. of Environmental Health Officers; Nat. Soc. for Clean Air; Town and Country Planning Assoc. Chm., Tak Tent Cancer Support Charity, 1999–2002; Ambassador, Nat. Asthma Campaign Scotland, 2002. Fellow, Industry and Parlt Trust, 1984. Hon. FCIWEM 1994; Hon. FCIWM 2001. Mem. Adv. Bd, Jl Water Law. DUniv Paisley, 2004. *Publications:* contributed to European Parliament reports; various articles on European envmt policy. *Recreations:* music, boxer dogs, gardening. *Address:* 11 Stuarton Park, East Kilbride, Lanarkshire G74 4LA. *T:* and *Fax:* (01355) 237282.

COLLINS, Rt Hon. Sir Lawrence (Antony), Kt 2000; PC 2007; LLD; FBA 1994; **Rt Hon. Lord Justice Lawrence Collins;** a Lord Justice of Appeal, since 2007; Fellow of Wolfson College, Cambridge, since 1975; *b* 7 May 1941; *s* of late Sol Collins and Phoebe (*née* Barnett); *m* 1982, Sara Shamni (marr. diss. 2003); one *s* one *d*. *Educ:* City of London Sch.; Downing Coll., Cambridge (BA, George Long Prize, McNair Schol., 1963; LLB, Whewell Schol., 1964; LLD 1994; Hon. Fellow, 2000); Columbia Univ. (LLM 1965). Mem. Inst de Droit Internat., 1989. Admitted solicitor, 1968; Partner, Herbert Smith, solicitors, 1971–2000 (Hd, Litigation and Arbitration Dept, 1995–98); QC 1997; a Dep. High Court Judge, 1997–2000; a Judge of High Court of Justice, Chancery Div., 2000–07. Bencher, Inner Temple, 2001. Vis. Prof., QMC, then QMW, 1982–; Lectr, Hague Acad. of Internat. Law, 1991, 1998, 2007; Graveson Meml Lectr, KCL, 1995; F. A. Mann Lectr, British Inst. of Internat. and Comparative Law, 2001; Lionel Cohen Lectr, Hebrew Univ., Jerusalem, 2007. Member: Lord Chancellor's Wkg Party on Foreign Judgments, 1979–81; Bar and Law Soc. Jt Wkg Party on UK-US Judgments Convention, 1980–82; Law Commn Jt Wkg Party on Torts in Private Internat. Law, 1982–84; Ministry of Justice (formerly DCA) Adv. Cttee on Private Internat. Law, 2004–. Hon. Sec., British Br., 1983–88, Chm., Cttee on Internat. Securities Regulation, 1988–94, Internat. Law Assoc. Member: Adv. Council, Centre for Commercial Law Studies, QMW, 1989–; Adv. Bd, Cambridge Univ. Centre for European Legal Studies, 1993–97; Adv. Council, British Inst. of Internat. and Comparative Law, 2006– (Mem., Council of Mgt, 1992–2006). Hon. Mem., SPTL, 1993; Hon. Life Mem., Law Soc., 2000. Member: Editl Adv. Cttee, Law Qly Rev., 1988–; Bd of Eds, Internat. and Comparative Law Qly, 1988–; Editl Cttee, British Yearbook of Internat. Law, 1991–; Editl Bd, Civil Justice Qly, 2005–; Adv. Ed., Civil Procedure, 2002–. *Publications:* European Community Law in the United Kingdom, 1975, 4th edn 1990; Civil Jurisdiction and Judgments Act 1982, 1983; Essays in International Litigation and the Conflict of Laws, 1994; (Gen. Ed.) Dicey & Morris (now Dicey, Morris & Collins), Conflict of Laws, 11th edn 1987, 14th edn 2006. *Address:* Royal Courts of Justice, Strand, WC2A 2LL.

COLLINS, Lesley Elizabeth; *see* Appleby, L. E.

COLLINS, Margaret Elizabeth, CBE 1983; RRC; Matron-in-Chief, Queen Alexandra's Royal Naval Nursing Service, 1980–83; *b* 13 Feb. 1927; *d* of James Henry Collins and Amy Collins. *Educ:* St Anne's Convent Grammar Sch., Southampton. RRC 1978 (ARRC 1965). Royal Victoria Hosp., Bournemouth, SRN 1949; West Middlesex Hosp., CMB Part 1; entered QARNNS as Nursing Sister, 1953; accepted for permanent service, 1958; Matron, 1972; Principal Matron, 1976. SSStJ 1978. QHNS, 1980–83. *Recreations:* gardening, theatre-going. *Address:* Lancastria, 5 First Marine Avenue, Barton-on-Sea, Hants BH25 6DP. *T:* (01425) 612374.

COLLINS, Mark; *see* Collins, N. M.

COLLINS, Martin; *see* Collins, J. M.

COLLINS, Michael; aerospace consultant; Vice President, LTV Aerospace and Defense Company (formerly Vought Corporation), 1980–85; former NASA Astronaut; Command Module Pilot, Apollo 11 rocket flight to the Moon, July 1969; *b* Rome, Italy, 31 Oct. 1930; *s* of Maj.-Gen. and Mrs James L. Collins, Washington, DC, USA; *m* 1957, Patricia M. Finnegan, Boston, Mass; one *s* two *d*. *Educ:* St Albans Sch., Washington, DC (grad.). US Mil. Academy, West Point, NY (BSc); advanced through grades to Colonel; Harvard Business Sch. (AMP), 1974. Served as an experimental flight test officer, Air Force Flight Test Center, Edwards Air Force Base, Calif; he was one of the third group of astronauts named by NASA in Oct. 1963; served as backup pilot for Gemini 7 mission; as pilot with John Young on the 3-day 44-revolution Gemini 10 mission, launched 18 July 1966, he shared record-setting flight (successful rendezvous and docking with a separately launched Agena target vehicle; completed two periods of extravehicular activity); Command Module Pilot for Apollo flight, first lunar landing, in orbit 20 July 1969, when Neil Armstrong and Edwin Aldrin landed on the Moon. Asst Sec. of State for Public Affairs, US, 1970–71; Dir, Nat. Air and Space Museum, Smithsonian Institution, 1971–78; Under Sec., Smithsonian Inst., 1978–80. Maj. Gen. Air Force Reserve, retired. Member: Bd of Trustees, Nat. Geographic Soc.; Soc. of Experimental Test Pilots; Fellow, Amer. Astronautical Soc. Member, Order of Daedalians. Hon. degrees from: Stonehill Coll.; St Michael's Coll.; Northeastern Univ.; Southeastern Univ. Presidential Medal of Freedom, NASA; FAI Gold Space Medal; DSM (NASA); DSM (AF); Exceptional Service Medal (NASA); Astronaut Wings; DFC. *Publications:* Carrying the Fire (autobiog.), 1974; Flying to the Moon and Other Strange Places (for children), 1976; Liftoff, 1988; Mission to Mars, 1990. *Recreations:* fishing, painting. *Clubs:* Alfalfa, Alibi (Washington, DC).

COLLINS, Michael Brendan, OBE 1983 (MBE 1969); HM Diplomatic Service, retired; HM Consul-General, Istanbul, 1988–92; *b* 9 Sept. 1932; *s* of Daniel James Collins, GM and Mary Bridget Collins (*née* Kennedy); *m* 1959, Maria Elena Lozar. *Educ:* St Illtyd's College, Cardiff; University College London. HM Forces, 1953–55. FO 1956; Santiago, Chile, 1959; Consul, Santiago, Cuba, 1962; FO, 1964; Second, later First, Sec. (Admin.) and Consul, Prague, 1967; Dep. High Comr, Bathurst, The Gambia, 1970; Head of Chancery, Algiers, 1972; First Sec., FCO, 1975; Consul Commercial, Montreal, 1978; Consul for Atlantic Provinces of Canada, Halifax, 1981; Counsellor (Economic and Commercial), Brussels, 1983. *Recreations:* fishing, golf, walking, reading, music. *Club:* Army and Navy.

COLLINS, Michael Geoffrey; QC 1988; barrister, arbitrator and mediator; *b* 4 March 1948; *s* of late Francis Geoffrey Collins and Margaret Isabelle Collins; *m* 1985, Bonnie Gayle Bird. *Educ:* Peterhouse, Rhodesia (now Zimbabwe); Exeter Univ. (LLB). Called to the Bar, Gray's Inn, 1971, Bencher, 1999. A Recorder, 1997–2001. Special Legal Consultant: Fulbright & Jaworski LLP, Washington, 2002–06; Crandall, Hanscom & Collins PA, Rockland, ME, 2006–. *Publication:* contributor, Private International Litigation, 1988. *Recreations:* golf, tennis, watercolours, amateur dramatics. *Address:* PO Box 1156, Islesboro, ME 04848, USA. *T:* (207) 7346781; Essex Court Chambers, 24 Lincoln's Inn Fields, WC2A 3EG. *T:* (020) 7813 8000.

COLLINS, Michael John; clarinettist; Professor, Royal College of Music, since 1983; *b* 27 Jan. 1962; *s* of Gwendoline Violet and Fred Allenby Collins; *m* 1997, Isabelle van Keulen; one *s* one *d*. *Educ:* Royal Coll. of Music (ARCM, Clarinet and Piano with Hons). BBC Young Musician of the Year, 1978. Principal clarinet: London Sinfonietta, 1982–; Nash Ensemble, 1982–88; Philharmonia Orchestra, 1988–95; Dir, London Winds Ensemble, 1988–. Many solo recordings. Hon. RAM 1997. Musicians' Co. Medal, 1980; competition winner: Leeds, 1980; Concert Artists' Guild, NY, 1982 (Amcon Award); Internat Rostrum of Young Performers, Unesco, 1985; Tagore Gold Medal, 1982. *Recreations:* walking, driving, wildlife.

COLLINS, Neil Adam; Columnist, Evening Standard, since 2005; *s* of Clive and Joan Collins; *m* 1981, Vivien Goldsmith (marr. diss. 1994); one *d*; *m* 1999, Julia Frances Barnes; one *s* one *d*. *Educ:* Uppingham School; Selwyn College, Cambridge (MA). City Editor: Evening Standard, 1979–84; Sunday Times, 1984–86; Daily Telegraph, 1986–2005; Flyfishing correspondent, The Spectator, 2002–04. Director: Templeton Emerging Markets Investment Trust plc, 2006–; Dyson James Ltd, 2006–07; Finsbury Growth & Income Trust, 2008–. Gov., St Andrew's School, Eastbourne, 1999–2003. Financial Journalist of the Year, British Press Awards, 2002. *Recreations:* walking, wine, fly fishing, opera. *Address:* 12 Gertrude Street, SW10 0JN. *T:* (home) (020) 7352 9595, 07836 256674; *e-mail:* n.collins413@ntlworld.com.

COLLINS, (Nicholas) Mark, PhD; Director, Commonwealth Foundation, since 2005; *b* 23 April 1952; *s* of late John Anthony Collins and of Mary Collins (*née* Humphries); *m* 1982, Melanie Margaret Stephens; one *s* one *d*. *Educ:* Wadham Coll., Oxford (BA 1973, MA 1974); Imperial Coll., London (DIC 1977; PhD 1977); MBA Open Univ. 1999. Centre for Overseas Pest Res., Nigeria and Sarawak, 1974–80; Internat. Centre for Insect Physiol. and Ecol., Kenya, 1980–82; IUCN, 1982–88; World Conservation Monitoring Centre, 1988–2000 (Dir, 1994–2000); UNEP, Cambridge and Kenya, 2000–05. HM Inspector of Zoos, 1990–2000. Trustee: FFI, 1989–98; Wildscreen Trust, 1997–2004; Galapagos Conservation Trust, 2006–; Total Foundn, 2003–06; Mem., Darwin Initiative Adv. Cttee, 2001–06. Chairman: Cambridge Sustainable City, 1996–2002; Cambridge and Peterborough Sustainable Develt Round Table, 2003–04. Mem., Commonwealth Scholarship Commn, 2008–. Gov., Meridian Co. Primary Sch., 1996–99. Member: Royal Entomolog. Soc.; RGS. Busk Medal, RGS, 2000. *Publications:* (jtly) The IUCN Invertebrate Red Data Book, 1983; (with M. G. Morris) Threatened Swallowtail Butterflies of the World, 1985; (ed jtly) Kora: an ecological inventory of the Kora National Reserve, Kenya, 1986; (ed jtly) Insect-Fungus Interactions, 1988; (ed) The Management and Welfare of Invertebrates in Captivity, 1989; The Last Rainforests, 1990; (ed jtly) The Conservation of Insects and their Habitats, 1991; The Conservation Atlas of Tropical Forests: (ed jtly) Asia, 1991, (ed jtly) Africa, 1992; (editl advr and co-ordinator) Encyclopedia of the Biosphere, Vol. II, Tropical Rainforests, 2000; numerous contribs to learned jls. *Recreations:* tennis, golf, countryside. *Address:* Commonwealth Foundation, Marlborough House, Pall Mall, SW1Y 5HY. *T:* (020) 7747 6578; *e-mail:* m.collins@commonwealth.int. *Clubs:* Royal Commonwealth Society, Royal Over-Seas League, Travellers.

COLLINS, Nina; *see* Lowry, Noreen Margaret.

COLLINS, Patrick Michael; Chief Sports Writer, Mail on Sunday, since 1982; *b* 23 Nov. 1943; *s* of Patrick and Julia Collins (*née* Canty); *m* 1969, Julie Kathleen Grundon; three *s* one *d*. *Educ:* St Joseph's Acad., Blackheath, London. Reporter, Kentish Mercury, 1962–65; sports writer: Sunday Citizen, 1965–67; News of the World, 1967–78; sports columnist: London Evening News, 1978–80; London Evening Standard, 1980–82; Punch, 1990–92. Mem., English Sports Council, 1999–2002. British Sports Journalism Awards: British Sports Journalist of the Year, 1989, 1990, 1997, 2002; Sports Feature Writer of the Year, 1993, 2002; Sport Columnist of the Year, 1999, 2000, 2004, 2006. *Publications:* (with Pat Pocock) Percy, 1987; The Sportswriter, 1996. *Recreations:* watching cricket, reading, family. *Address:* Mail on Sunday, Northcliffe House, 2 Derry Street, W8 5TS. *T:* (020) 7938 6000, *Fax:* (020) 7937 4115; *e-mail:* patrick.collins@mailonsunday.co.uk.

COLLINS, Paul Howard, CBE 1999; **His Honour Judge Collins;** a Circuit Judge, since 1992; Senior Circuit Judge, Central London Civil Justice Centre, since 2001; *b* 31 Jan. 1944; *s* of Michael and Madie Collins; *m* 1987, Sue Fallows; one step *s*. *Educ:* Orange Hill Grammar Sch.; St Catherine's Coll., Oxford (MA). Called to the Bar, Lincoln's Inn, 1966 (Bencher, 2000); a Recorder, 1989. Designated Civil Judge for London Gp of County Cts, 2001–08. Dir of Studies, Judicial Studies Bd, 1997–99. *Address:* Central London Civil Justice Centre, 26 Park Crescent, W1B 1HT. *Club:* Questors.

COLLINS, Pauline, OBE 2001; actress (stage and television); *b* Exmouth, Devon, 3 Sept. 1940; *d* of William Henry Collins and Mary Honora Callanan; *m* John Alderton, *qv*; two *s* one *d*. *Educ:* Convent of the Sacred Heart, Hammersmith, London; Central Sch. of Speech and Drama. *Stage:* 1st appearance in A Gazelle in Park Lane, Theatre Royal, Windsor, 1962; 1st London appearance in Passion Flower Hotel, Prince of Wales, 1965; The Erpingham Camp, Royal Court, 1967; The Happy Apple, Hampstead, 1967, and Apollo, 1970; Importance of Being Earnest, Haymarket, 1968; The Night I chased the Women with an Eel, 1969; Come As You Are (3 parts), New, 1970; Judies, Comedy, 1974; Engaged, National Theatre, Old Vic, 1975; Confusions, Apollo, 1976; Rattle of a Simple Man, Savoy, 1980; Romantic Comedy, Apollo, 1983; Shirley Valentine, Vaudeville, 1988, NY, 1989 (Tony Award, Best Actress, 1989); Shades, Albery, 1992; *television*, 1962–: series: Upstairs Downstairs; No Honestly; P. G. Wodehouse; Thomas and Sarah; The Black Tower; Forever Green; The Ambassador; plays: Long Distance Information, 1979; Knockback, 1984; Man and Boy, 2002; Sparkling Cyanide, 2003; *films:* Shirley Valentine, 1989 (Evening Standard Film Actress of the Year, 1989; BAFTA Best Actress Award, 1990); City of Joy, 1992; My Mother's Courage, 1997; Paradise Road, 1997; Mrs Caldicott's Cabbage War, 2002. Dr *hc* Liverpool Poly., 1991. *Publication:* Letter to Louise, 1992. *Address:* c/o Independent Talent Group Ltd, Oxford House, 76 Oxford Street, W1D 1BS.

COLLINS, Peter; *see* Collins, V. P.

COLLINS, Peter G., RSA 1974 (ARSA 1966); painter in oil; *b* Inverness, 21 June 1935; *s* of E. G. Collins, FRCSE; *m* 1959, Myra Mackintosh (marr. diss. 1978); one *s* one *d*. *Educ:* Fettes Coll., Edinburgh; Edinburgh Coll. of Art. Studied in Italy, on Andrew Grant Major Travelling Scholarship, 1957–58. Work in permanent collections: Aberdeen Civic;

Glasgow Civic; Scottish Arts Council. *Recreations:* music, art-historical research. *Address:* Royal Scottish Academy, The Mound, Edinburgh EH2 2EL; The Cottage, Hilltown of Ballindean, Inchture, Perthshire PH14 9QS.

COLLINS, Air Vice-Marshal Peter Spencer, CB 1985; AFC 1961; *b* 19 March 1930; *s* of Frederick Wildbore Collins and Mary (*née* Spencer); *m* 1953, Sheila Mary (*née* Perks) (*d* 2000); three *s* one *d*. *Educ:* Royal Grammar Sch., High Wycombe; Univ. of Birmingham (BA (Hons) History). Joined RAF, 1951; flying tours incl. service on squadron nos: 63, 141, 41, AWDS, AFDS; RAF Handling Sqdn, nos 23 and 11; commanded: 111 Sqdn, 1970–72; RAF Gütersloh, 1974–76; staff tours include: Air Ministry, 1962–64; Strike Comd HQ, 1968–70 and 1972–74; Dir of Forward Policy (RAF), 1978–81; SASO, HQ 11 Gp, 1981–83; DG, Communications, Inf. Systems and Orgn (RAF), 1983–85; psc 1965, rcds 1977; retired 1985. Marconi Radar Systems: Dir, Business Develt, 1986–88; Consultant Dir, 1988–95; Consultant, GEC-Marconi Res. Centre, 1989–95. Hon. Pres., Essex Wing, ATC, 2001–; Vice-Pres., Chelmsford Br., RAFA, 1998–; Pres., United Services Assoc., Chelmsford & Dist., 2000–. CCMI (FBIM 1979). *Publications:* contribs to service jls and to Seaford House Papers, 1978. *Recreations:* golf, music, gardening. *Address:* 2 Doubleday Gardens, Braintree, Essex CM7 9SW. *Club:* Royal Air Force.

COLLINS, Philip, LVO 1994; singer, drummer, songwriter, actor and record producer; Trustee, Prince's Trust, since 1983; patron of numerous charities; *b* 30 Jan. 1951; *s* of Greville and June Collins; *m* 1st, 1976 (marr. diss.); one *s* one *d*; 2nd, 1984, Jill Tavelman (marr. diss. 1995); one *d*; 3rd, 1999, Orianne Cevey (marr. diss. 2008); two *s*. *Educ:* primary and secondary schs; Barbara Speake Stage Sch. Played parts in various television, film and stage productions, 1965–67; mem. of various rock groups, 1967–70; drummer, 1970–96, lead singer, 1975–96, Genesis; started writing songs, 1976; toured Japan, USA and Europe, 1978, 1987; reunion tour, Europe and N America, 2007; first solo album, 1981; solo world tours, 1985, 1990; started producing records for other artists, 1981. *Albums* include: *with Genesis:* Nursery Cryme, 1971; Foxtrot, 1972; Genesis Live, 1973; Selling England by the Pound, 1973; The Lamb Lies Down on Broadway, 1974; A Trick of the Tail, 1976; Genesis Rock Roots, 1976; Wind and Wuthering, 1977; Genesis Seconds Out, 1977; And Then There Were Three, 1978; Duke, 1980; Abacab, 1981; Three Sides Live, 1982; Genesis, 1983; Invisible Touch, 1986; We Can't Dance, 1991; *solo:* Face Value, 1981; Hello … I must be Going, 1982; No Jacket Required, 1985; But Seriously, 1989; Both Sides, 1993; Dance into the Light, 1996; Hits, 1998; Testify, 2002. *Films:* Buster (lead role), 1988; Frauds, 1993. Numerous awards, incl. Grammy (eight), Ivor Novello (six), Brit (four), Variety Club of GB (two), Silver Clef (two), Academy Award, and Elvis awards.

COLLINS, Philip James; Senior Visiting Fellow, London School of Economics, since 2007; *b* 16 May 1967; *s* of Frederick John Collins and Jennifer Anne Collins (*née* Taylor, now Dawson); *m* 2002, Geeta Guru-Murthy; two *s*. *Educ:* Birmingham Univ. (BA Hons 1988); Birkbeck Coll., London (MSc Dist. 1991); St John's Coll., Cambridge. Res. Officer, London Weekend TV, 1988–89; Political Asst to Frank Field, MP, 1989–92; Research Officer: Inst. of Educn, London Univ., 1992; Fleming Investment Mgt, 1995–97; Equity Strategist: HSBC James Capel, 1997–99; Dresdner Kleinwort Benson, 1999–2000; Dir, Social Mkt Foundn, 2000–05; Chief Speech Writer, Prime Minister's Policy Directorate, 2005–07. FRSA. *Publications:* (ed) An Authority in Education, 2001; The Men from the Boys, 2002; (ed) Culture or Anarchy?, 2002; Bobby Dazzler, 2003; (ed) Reinventing Government Again, 2004. *Recreations:* music, cricket, football, poetry, television, philosophy. *Address:* Department of Government, London School of Economics, Houghton Street, WC2A 2AE; *e-mail:* p.j.collins@lse.ac.uk.

COLLINS, Terence Bernard; Chairman, 1984–87, Vice Chairman, 1976–84, Group Managing Director, 1975–86, Berger Jenson Nicholson; *b* 3 March 1927; *s* of George Bernard Collins and Helen Theresa Collins; *m* 1956, Barbara (*née* Lowday); two *s* two *d*. *Educ:* Marist Coll., Hull; Univ. of St Andrews (MA Hons). Trainee, Ideal Standard, 1951–52; Blundell Spence: Area Manager, 1953–55; Regl Manager, 1955–57; UK Sales Manager, 1957–59; Berger Jenson Nicholson: Sales Manager, 1959–62; Man. Dir, Caribbean, 1962–69; Overseas Regl Exec., 1969–70; Gp Dir UK, 1970–74. Chairman: Cranfield Conf. Services Ltd, 1987–93; Cranfield Ventures Ltd, 1990–93; CIT Hldgs Ltd, 1991–92 (Dir, 1989–93); Interact Design and Print Ltd (formerly Interact Ltd), 1994–2001; Director: A. G. Stanley Hldgs, 1977–87; Hoechst UK, 1979–87; Hoechst Australia Investments, 1980–87; Mayborn Gp PLC, 1986–91; Phoenix Develts Ltd, 1987–94, 1995–2001 (Chm., 2000–01); Aldehurst Consultants Ltd, 1987–94; Cranfield Precision Engineering Ltd, 1990–95; Chm., Management Bd, Kingline Consultants Ltd, 1989–90. Mem., Duke of Edinburgh's Award Internat. Panel, 1978–86; Trustee, Atlas Econ. Foundn UK, 1986–93. Cranfield University (formerly Institute of Technology): Mem. Court, 1977–98; Mem. Council, 1981–93; Treasurer, 1991–92; Chm., Finance Cttee, 1991–92; University of Buckingham: Vice-Chm. Council, 1987–95; Chm., F and GP Cttee, 1987–94. DUniv Buckingham, 1994. *Recreations:* music, gardening. *Address:* Woodbridge, Suffolk.

COLLINS, Most Rev. Thomas; *see* Toronto, Archbishop of, (RC).

COLLINS, Timothy William George, CBE 1996; *b* 7 May 1964; *s* of late William and of Diana Collins; *m* 1997, Clare, *d* of Geoffrey and Auriel Benson; one *s*. *Educ:* Chigwell Sch., Essex; LSE (BSc); KCL (MA). Cons. Res. Dept, 1986–89; Advr to Secs of State for the Envmt, 1989–90, for Employment, 1990–92; Press Sec. to Prime Minister, 1992; Dir of Communications, Cons. Party, 1992–95; Mem., Prime Minister's Policy Unit, 1995; Sen. Strategy Consultant, WCT Ltd, 1995–97. MP (C) Westmorland and Lonsdale, 1997–2005; contested (C) same seat, 2005. An Opposition Whip, 1998–99; Shadow Minister for the Cabinet Office, 2001–02; Shadow Secretary of State: for Transport, 2002–03; for Educn, 2003–05. Vice-Chm., Cons. Party, 1999–2001.

COLLINS, Prof. (Vincent) Peter, MD; FRCPath, FMedSci; Professor of Histopathology, University of Cambridge, since 1997; Hon. Consultant Pathologist, Addenbrooke's Hospital, since 1997; *b* 3 Dec. 1947; *s* of James Vincent Collins and Mary Ann Collins (*née* Blanche). *Educ:* University Coll., Dublin (MB, BCh, BAO 1971); Karolinska Inst., Stockholm (MD 1978). MRCPath 1988, FRCPath 1996. House appts, Mater Hosp., Dublin, 1972–73; junior appts, 1974–82, Cons. Pathologist, 1982–90, Sen. Cons. Pathologist, 1994–97, Karolinska Inst.; Head of Clin. Res., Ludwig Inst. for Cancer Res., Stockholm Br., 1986–98; Prof. of Neuropathology, Univ. of Gothenburg, 1990–94; Sen. Cons. Pathologist, Sahlgrenska Univ. Hosp., Gothenburg, 1990–94; Prof. of Tumour Pathology, Karolinska Inst., 1994–97. Foreign Adjunct Prof., Karolinska Inst., 1998–. FMedSci 2002. *Publications:* over 250 papers on human brain tumours. *Recreations:* sailing, ski-ing, music. *Address:* Department of Histopathology, Box 235, Addenbrooke's Hospital, Cambridge CB2 2QQ. *T:* (01223) 336072.

COLLINS, William Janson; Chairman, William Collins Sons & Co. (Holdings) Ltd, 1976–81; *b* 10 June 1929; *s* of late Sir William Alexander Roy Collins, CBE, and Lady Collins (Priscilla Marian, *d* of late S. J. Lloyd); *m* 1951, Lady Sara Elena Hely-Hutchinson, *d* of 7th Earl of Donoughmore; one *s* three *d*. *Educ:* Magdalen Coll., Oxford (BA). Joined William Collins Sons & Co. Ltd, 1952; Dir, then Man. Dir, 1967; Vice-Chm., 1971; Chm., 1976. *Recreations:* Royal tennis, shooting, fishing, tennis, golf. *Address:* High Coodham, Symington, Kilmarnock, Ayrshire KA1 5SJ. *T:* (01563) 830253, *Fax:* (01563) 830673. *Club:* All England Lawn Tennis and Croquet.

COLLINS RICE, Rowena; Director General, Democracy, Constitution and Law, and Chief Legal Officer, Ministry of Justice, since 2008; *b* 24 April 1960; *d* of John Frederick, (Jack), Collins and Hilda Collins (*née* Campbell); *m* 1986, Hugh Robert Collins Rice; two *s*. *Educ:* Westbourne Sch., Glasgow; Hertford Coll., Oxford (BA 1st Cl. Hons Jurisprudence 1981). Home Office, 1985–91; Treasury Solicitor's Dept, 1992–95; admitted solicitor, 1995; Home Office, 1995–2003; DCA, 2003–05; HMRC, 2005–07, Dir, Legal (Tax Law); Legal Dir, DCA, subseq. Min. of Justice, 2007–08. *Address:* Ministry of Justice, Selborne House, 54 Victoria Street, SW1E 6QW.

COLLINSON, Rev. Nigel Thomas; Methodist Minister; Secretary, Methodist Conference, 1999–2003 (President, 1996–97); *b* 14 March 1941; *s* of Tom and Agnes Collinson; *m* 1964, Lorna Ebrill; two *d*. *Educ:* Forster Street Sch., Tunstall; Hanley High Sch., Stoke on Trent; Hull Univ. (BA Theol 1962); Wesley House, Cambridge (MA Theol 1964). Ordained 1967; Methodist Minister: Clifton and Redland Circuit, Bristol, 1964–67; Stroud and Cirencester Circuit, 1967–72; Wolverhampton Trinity Circuit, 1972–80; Supt, Oxford Circuit and Methodist Chaplain to Univ. students, 1980–88; Chm., Southampton Dist, 1988–98. Hon. Chaplain, British and Internat. Sailors' Soc., 2005. Hon. DD Hull, 1997. *Publications:* The Opening Door, 1986; (with David Matthews) Facing Illness, 1986; The Land of Unlikeness, 1996. *Recreations:* golf, fishing, gardening, the arts. *Address:* 15 Stockmeadow Gardens, Bishopsteignton, Devon TQ14 9QJ.

COLLINSON, Prof. Patrick, CBE 1993; PhD; FBA 1982; FRHistS, FAHA; Regius Professor of Modern History, University of Cambridge, 1988–96, now Emeritus; Fellow of Trinity College, Cambridge, since 1988; *b* 10 Aug. 1929; *s* of William Cecil Collinson and Belle Hay (*née* Patrick); *m* 1960, Elizabeth Albinia Susan Selwyn; two *s* two *d*. *Educ:* King's Sch., Ely; Pembroke Coll., Cambridge (Exhibnr 1949, Foundn Scholar 1952; BA 1952, 1st Cl. Hons Hist. Tripos Pt II; Hadley Prize for Hist., 1952); PhD London, 1957. University of London: Postgrad. Student, Royal Holloway Coll., 1952–54; Res. Fellow, Inst. of Hist. Res., 1954–55; Res. Asst, UCL, 1955–56; Lectr in Hist., Univ. of Khartoum, 1956–61; Asst Lectr in Eccles. Hist., King's Coll., Univ. of London, 1961–62, Lectr, 1962–69 (Fellow 1976); Professor of History: Univ. of Sydney, 1969–75; Univ. of Kent at Canterbury, 1976–84; Prof. of Modern Hist., Sheffield Univ., 1984–88. Vis. Fellow, All Souls Coll., Oxford, 1981; Andrew W. Mellon Fellow, Huntington Library, California, 1984; Douglas S. Freeman Vis. Prof., Richmond Univ., Va, 1999; Vis. Hon. Prof., Univ. of Warwick, 2000–03. Lectures: Ford's, in Eng. Hist., Univ. of Oxford, 1978–79; Birkbeck, Univ. of Cambridge, 1981; Stenton Meml, Univ. of Reading, 1985; Neale Meml, Univ. of Manchester, 1986; Anstey Meml, Univ. of Kent, 1986; Neale Meml, UCL, 1987; F. D. Maurice, KCL, 1990; Homer J. Crotty, Huntington Liby, 1990; Sir D. Owen Evans Meml, UCW Aberystwyth, 1992; A. H. Dodd Meml, UCNW Bangor, 1992; Raleigh, British Academy, 1993; S. T. Bindoff Meml, QMW, 1995; Douglas S. Freeman, Richmond Univ., Va, 1999; Eberhard L. Faber, Princeton Univ., 1999; Creighton, Univ. of London, 2002; St Robert Southwell, Fordham, 2007. Chm., Adv. Editorial Bd, Jl of Ecclesiastical History, 1982–93. President: Ecclesiastical Hist. Soc., 1985–86; C of E Record Soc., 1991–2001 (Vice-Pres., 2001–); Mem. Council, British Acad., 1986–89. FRHistS 1967 (Mem. Council, 1977–81, Vice-Pres., 1983–87 and 1994–98, Hon. Vice-Pres., 2001–); FAHA 1974. MAE 1989; Corresp. Mem., Massachusetts Historical Soc., 1990. DUniv York, 1988; Hon. DLitt: Kent at Canterbury, 1989; Oxford, 1997; Essex, 2000; Warwick, 2003; Hon. LittD: TCD, 1992; Sheffield, 1995. Medlicott Medal, Histl Assoc., 1998. *Publications:* The Elizabethan Puritan Movement, 1967 (USA 1967; repr. 1982); Archbishop Grindal 1519–1583: the struggle for a Reformed Church, 1979 (USA 1979); The Religion of Protestants: the Church in English Society 1559–1625 (Ford Lectures, 1979), 1982; Godly People: essays on English Protestantism and Puritanism, 1983; English Puritanism, 1983; The Birthpangs of Protestant England: religious and cultural change in the 16th and 17th centuries, 1988; Elizabethan Essays, 1994; (jtly) A History of Canterbury Cathedral, 1995; (ed jtly) The Reformation in English Towns 1500–1640, 1998; (jtly) A History of Emmanuel College, Cambridge, 1999; (ed) Short Oxford History of the British Isles: The Sixteenth Century, 2002; Elizabethans, 2002; The Reformation, 2003 (Portuguese edn 2004; Slovak edn 2005; Brazilian edn 2006); (jtly) Conferences and Combination Lectures in the Elizabethan Church: Dedham and Bury St Edmunds, 1582–1590, 2003; From Cranmer to Sancroft: more essays on English Protestantism and Puritanism, 2005; Elizabeth I, 2007; articles and revs in Bull. Inst. Hist. Res., Eng. Hist. Rev., Jl of Eccles. Hist., Studies in Church Hist., TLS, London Rev. of Books. *Recreations:* hills, music, grandchildren. *Address:* New House, Crown Square, Shaldon, Teignmouth, Devon TQ14 0DS; Trinity College, Cambridge CB2 1TQ.

COLLIS, Ian; His Honour Judge Collis; a Circuit Judge, since 2000; *b* 21 Feb. 1946; *s* of late Harold Collis and Florence Collis; *m* 1968, Julia Georgina Cure; three *s*. *Educ:* Dartford Grammar Sch.; LLB (Hons) London. Admitted Solicitor, 1970; District Judge, 1987–2000; a Recorder, 1996–2000. *Recreations:* gardening, walking dog.

COLLIS, Peter George, CB 2005; Chief Land Registrar and Chief Executive, HM Land Registry, since 1999; *b* 13 Oct. 1953; *s* of Martin Arthur Collis and Margaret Sophie Collis; *m* 1978, Linda Jean Worssam (marr. diss. 1999); one *s* one *d*; *m* 2000, Jan Morgan; one step *s*. *Educ:* Univ. of Aston in Birmingham (BSc 1st Cl. Hons Communication Sci. and Linguistics 1975). Joined Civil Service, 1975; admin trainee, Depts of Trade, Industry and Prices and Consumer Protection, 1975–78; Personal Asst to Chm. and Dep. Chm., NEB, 1978–80; Principal, Dept of Trade, 1980–83; Mktg Exec., Balfour Beatty, 1983–85 (on secondment); Principal, Dept of Transport, 1985–88; Head, Driver Licensing Div., DVLA, 1988–91; Head, Finance Exec. Agencies 2 Div., 1991–92, Highways Resource Mgt Div., 1992–94, Dept of Transport; Strategy and Private Finance Dir, Highways Agency, 1994–97; Business Develt Dir, Dept of Transport, 1997; Finance and Commercial Policy Dir, Employment Service, 1997–99. *Recreations:* family, travelling, enjoying the countryside. *Address:* HM Land Registry, 32 Lincoln's Inn Fields, WC2A 3PH. *T:* (020) 7166 4497.

COLLIS, Simon Paul; HM Diplomatic Service; Ambassador to Syria, since 2007; *b* 23 Feb. 1956. *Educ:* King Edward VII Sch., Sheffield; Christ's Coll., Cambridge (BA Hons). Joined HM Diplomatic Service, 1978: FCO, 1978–80; Arabic lang. trng, 1980–81; 3rd, later 2nd, Sec., Bahrain, 1981–83; 1st Secretary: FCO, 1984–85; UK Mission to UN, NY, 1986; Head, India Section, S Asia Dept, FCO, 1987–88; Head of Chancery, Tunis, 1988–90; Gulf War Emergency Unit, FCO, 1990–91; New Delhi, 1991–94; Asst Head, Near East and N Africa Dept, FCO, 1994–96; Dep. Hd of Mission, Amman, 1996–99; on secondment to BP, 1999–2000; Consul General: Dubai, 2000–04; Basra, 2004–05;

Ambassador to Qatar, 2005–07. *Address:* c/o Foreign and Commonwealth Office, King Charles Street, SW1A 2AH.

COLLYEAR, Sir John (Gowen), Kt 1986; FREng; Chairman, USM Texon Ltd (formerly United Machinery Group), 1987–95; *b* 19 Feb. 1927; *s* of John Robert Collyear and late Amy Elizabeth Collyear (*née* Gowen); *m* 1953, Catherine Barbara Newman; one *s* two *d*. *Educ:* Leeds Univ. (BSc). FIMechE (Hon. FIMechE 1995); FIMMM (Hon. FIMMM 2002), FIET; FREng (FEng 1979). Graduate apprentice and Production Engr, Joseph Lucas Industries, 1951; Glacier Metal Company Ltd: Production Engr, 1953; Production Manager, 1956; Chief Production Engr, 1956; Factory Gen. Manager, 1959; Managing Director, 1969; Bearings Div. Man. Dir, Associated Engineering Ltd, 1972; Group Man. Dir, AE plc, 1975, Chm., 1981–86. Chairman: MK Electric Gp PLC, 1987–88; Fulmer Ltd, 1987–91. Chm., Technology Requirements Bd, DTI, 1985–88. President: Motor Industry's Res. Assoc., 1987–97; Inst. of Materials, 1992–94. Hon. Bencher, Gray's Inn, 2000. *Publications:* Management Precepts, 1975; The Practice of First Level Management, 1976. *Recreations:* golf, bridge, piano music. *Address:* Donnington House, Cotswold Heights, Lower Swell Road, Stow-on-the-Wold, Cheltenham, Glos GL54 1LT. *T:* (01451) 830565. *Club:* Athenæum.

COLMAN, Hon. Sir Anthony (David), Kt 1992; a Judge of the High Court of Justice, Queen's Bench Division, Commercial Court, 1992–2007; *b* 27 May 1938; *s* of late Solomon and Helen Colman, Manchester; *m* 1964, Angela Glynn; two *d*. *Educ:* Harrogate Grammar Sch.; Trinity Hall, Cambridge (Aldis Schol.; Double First in Law Tripos; MA). FCIArb 1978. Called to the Bar, Gray's Inn, 1962, Master of the Bench, 1986; QC 1977; a Recorder, 1986–92; Judge in charge of Commercial Court List, 1996–97. Mem., Bar Council, 1990–92 (Chm., Central and E European Sub-Cttee, 1991–92); Chairman: Commercial Bar Assoc., 1991–92 (Treasurer, 1989–91); Lloyd's Disciplinary Cttee for PCW and Minet, 1984; Mem., Cttee of Enquiry into Fidentia at Lloyd's, 1982–83; conducted Investigation into loss of MV Derbyshire, 1999–2000. Special Advr to Govt of Czech Republic on civil litigation procedure, 2000–01; accession advr to EC for Czech Republic, 2002, and for Slovakia, 2003. Co-Founder and Consultant, Eur. Commercial Judges Forum, 2003–07. Principal, Faculty of Mediation, Acad. of Experts, 2004–. Hon. Pres., Italian Soc. of Mediation and Conciliation, 2002–. Gratias Agit Award from Czech Republic for services to judicial reform, 2006. *Publications:* Mathew's Practice of the Commercial Court (1902), 2nd edn, 1967; The Practice and Procedure of the Commercial Court, 1983, 5th edn 2000; (Gen. Editor and contrib.) Encyclopedia of International Commercial Litigation, 1991. *Recreations:* tennis, music, gardening, the 17th Century, Sifnos, the River Chess. *Address:* c/o Royal Courts of Justice, Strand, WC2A 2LL.

COLMAN, Anthony John; Director (formerly Associate Director), Africa Practice Ltd, since 2005; *b* 24 July 1943; *s* of late William Benjamin Colman and Beatrice (*née* Hudson); *m* Juliet Annabelle, *d* of Alec and June Owen; two *s*, and four *s* two *d* by prev. marriages. *Educ:* Paston Grammar Sch.; Magdalene Coll., Cambridge (MA); Univ. of E Africa, 1964–66; LSE, 1966. Unilever (United Africa Co.), 1964–69; Burton Group, 1969–90: Merchandise Manager, 1971–74, Buying and Merchandising Dir, 1974–76, Top Shop; Asst Man. Dir, Womenswear Sector, 1976–81; Director: Burton Menswear, 1976–81; Top Man, 1976–81; Dorothy Perkins, 1979–81; Dir, 1981–90. Director: GLE, 1990–97 (Chm., GLE Development Capital, 1990–97); Aztec, 1990–98; London First Centre Ltd, 1994–2002. Mem. (Lab) Merton LBC, 1990–98 (Leader of Council, 1991–97). Chair, Local Govt Superannuation Funds Cttee (incl. Police, Fire Bde and Teachers), 1992–98. Vice-Chm., ALA, 1991–95. Contested (Lab), SW Herts, 1979. MP (Lab) Putney, 1997–2005; contested (Lab) same seat, 2005. PPS to Minister of State, NI Office, 1998–2000. Member: Treasury Select Cttee, 1997–98; Internat. Develt Select Cttee, 2000–05; Chairman: All Party Gp on Socially Responsible Investment, 1998–2005; All Party Gp on Mgt, 2001–05; All Party UN Gp, 2002–05; PLP Trade and Industry Cttee, 1997–99. Chairman: Low Pay Unit, 1990–98; London Res. Centre, 1994–97; Dir, Public Private Partnerships Prog. Ltd, 1998–2001 (Chm., 1996–98); Member: Price Commn, 1977–79; Labour Finance & Industry Gp, 1973–; Labour Party Enquiry into Educn & Trng in Europe, 1991–93; Exec. Cttee, UNED, subseq. Stakeholder Forum for Our Common Future, 1995–2005; African Venture Capital Assoc., 2005–08. Pres., UNA UK SE Reg., 2005–07 (Deleg. to UN Gen. Assembly Millennium Develt Goals, 2005); Smart Partner, Commonwealth Partnership for Technology Mgt, 2008–. Member of Council: VSO, 2000–07; Chatham House, 2001–07; ODI, 2006–; World Future Council, 2007–. Chm., One World Trust, 2007–; Trustee, New Economics Foundn, 2005–. One People Oration, Westminster Abbey, 2006. Chm., Wimbledon Theatre Trust, 1991–96; Dir, London Arts Bd, 1994–98. Patron: Friends of Africa, 2004–07; Friends of Ahmadiyya Muslim Assoc., 2005–07. Local preacher, Methodist Ch, 2005–. Industrial Fellow, Kingston Univ. (formerly Poly.), 1983–; Fellow, Southlands Coll., Roehampton Univ., 2003. Liveryman, Horners' Co. FRSA 1983; FRGS 2003; CCMI 2003. *Clubs:* Reform, Royal Commonwealth Society; Cromer and Sheringham Rotary.

COLMAN, Jeremy Gye; Auditor General for Wales, since 2005; *b* 9 April 1948; *s* of Philip Colman and Georgina Maude Colman (*née* Gye); *m* 1st, 1978, Patricia Ann Stewart, *qv* (marr. diss. 1996); 2nd, 1997, Gillian Margaret Carless. *Educ:* John Lyon Sch., Harrow; Peterhouse, Cambridge (BA Mathematical Tripos 1969, MA 1973); Imperial Coll., London (MSc; DIC 1972); Open Univ. (PGDCCI 2001). Home Civil Service, 1971–88: CSD, 1971–75, Private Sec. to Second Perm. Sec., 1973–74; Principal, Industrial Policy: HM Treasury, 1975–78; CSD, 1978–81; Private Sec. to successive heads of Home Civil Service, 1980–82; Principal, Health Finance, 1982–84, Asst Sec., Public Enterprises, 1984–88, HM Treasury; Dir, Co. NatWest Ltd, 1988–90; Partner, Privatisation Services, London, 1991, Head of Corp. Finance practice, Prague, 1992–93, Price Waterhouse; Dir, 1993–98, Asst Auditor Gen., 1999–2005, National Audit Office. Freeman, Ironmongers' Co., 1991. *Recreations:* cookery, fine furniture-making. *Address:* Wales Audit Office, 24 Cathedral Road, Cardiff CF11 9LJ. *T:* (029) 2032 0510. *Club:* Oxford and Cambridge (Chm., 1992–94).

COLMAN, Sir Michael (Jeremiah), 3rd Bt *cr* 1907; Chairman, Reckitt and Colman plc, 1986–95; First Church Estates Commissioner, 1993–99; *b* 7 July 1928; *s* of Sir Jeremiah Colman, 2nd Bt, and Edith Gwendolyn Tritton; *S* father, 1961; *m* 1955, Judith Jean Wallop, JP, DL, *d* of Vice-Adm. Sir Peveril William-Powlett, KCB, KCMG, CBE, DSO; two *s* three *d*. *Educ:* Eton. Director: Reckitt & Colman plc, 1970–95; Foreign and Colonial Ventures Advisors Ltd, 1988–99; Foreign and Colonial Private Equity Trust, 1995–2002. Member: Council of Royal Warrant Holders, 1977–, Pres., 1984–85; Trinity House Lighthouse Bd, 1985–94 (Younger Brother, 1994). Member: Council, Chemical Industries Assoc., 1982–84; Bd, UK Centre for Econ. and Environmental Develt, 1985–99 (Chm., 1996–99). Mem., Council, Scout Assoc., 1985–2000. Mem. Gen. Council and Mem. Finance Cttee, King Edward's Hosp. Fund for London, 1978–2004; Special Trustee, St Mary's Hosp., 1988–99; Trustee: Royal Foundn of Grey Coat Hosp., 1989–2004; Allchurches Trust Ltd, 1994. Capt., Yorks Yeomanry, RARO, 1967. Mem. Ct, Skinners' Co., 1985– (Master, 1991–92). Hon. LLD Hull, 1993. Cross of St Augustine, 1999. *Recreations:* farming, shooting. *Heir:* *s* Jeremiah Michael Powlett Colman [*b* 23 Jan. 1958; *m* 1981, Susan Elizabeth, *yr d* of John Henry Britland, York; two *s* one *d*]. *Address:* Malshanger, Basingstoke, Hants RG23 7EY. *T:* (01256) 780241; 40 Chester Square, SW1W 9HT; Tarvie, Bridge of Cally, Blairgowrie, Perthshire PH10 7PJ. *Clubs:* Cavalry and Guards, Boodle's.

COLMAN, Dr Peter Malcolm, FAA, FTSE; Head, Structural Biology Division, Walter and Eliza Hall Institute of Medical Research, Melbourne, since 2001; *b* 3 April 1944; *s* of Clement Colman and Kathleen Colman (*née* Malcolm); *m* 1967, Anne Elizabeth Smith; two *s*. *Educ:* University of Adelaide (BSc 1st Cl. Hons 1966; PhD 1970). FAA 1989; FTSE 1997. Postdoctoral Fellow: Univ. of Oregon, 1969–72; Max Planck Inst., Munich, 1972–75; Queen Elizabeth II Fellow, 1975–77, Principal Investigator, NH&MRC, 1977–78, Univ. of Sydney; Scientist, 1978–89, Chief, Div. of Biomolecular Engrg, 1989–97, CSIRO; Dir, Biomolecular Res. Inst., Melbourne, 1991–2000. Involved in res. which determined the 3-dimensional structure of influenza virus neuraminidase and established and led the group which subsequently discovered Relenza, the first neuraminidase inhibitor to be approved for use in treatment of influenza. Professorial Associate, 1988–98, Professorial Fellow, 1998–2004, Univ. of Melbourne; Adjunct Prof., La Trobe Univ., 1998–. Mem., Asia-Pacific Internat. Molecular Biol. Network, 1998–. Hon. DSc Sydney, 2000. (Jtly) Australia Prize, 1996. *Publications:* contribs to scientific jls on structural biol., influenza virus and drug discovery. *Recreation:* music. *Address:* 74 Hotham Street, E Melbourne, Vic 3002, Australia. *T:* (3) 94161969.

COLMAN, Sir Timothy (James Alan), KG 1996; Lord-Lieutenant for Norfolk, 1978–2004; *b* 19 Sept. 1929; 2nd but *o* surv. *s* of late Captain Geoffrey Russell Rees Colman and Lettice Elizabeth Evelyn Colman, Norwich; *m* 1951, Lady Mary Cecilia (Extra Lady in Waiting to Princess Alexandra), twin *d* of late Lt-Col Hon. Michael Claude Hamilton Bowes Lyon and Elizabeth Margaret, Glamis; two *s* three *d*. *Educ:* RNC, Dartmouth and Greenwich. Lieut RN, 1950, retd 1953. Chm., Eastern Counties Newspapers Group Ltd, 1969–96; Director: Reckitt & Colman plc, 1978–89; Whitbread & Co. PLC, 1980–86; Anglia Television Group PLC, 1987–94; Life Trustee, Carnegie UK Trust, 1966–2000 (Chm., 1982–87). Member: Countryside Commn, 1971–76; Water Space Amenity Commn, 1973–76; Adv. Cttee for England, Nature Conservancy Council, 1974–80; Eastern Regional Cttee, National Trust, 1967–71. Pro-Chancellor, Univ. of E Anglia, 1974–2000 (Chm. Council, 1973–86). Chairman: Trustees, Norfolk and Norwich Festival, 1974–2002; Royal Norfolk Agricl Assoc., 1985–96 (Pres., 1982, 1997); Trustees, E Anglia Art Foundn, 1993–2005; Trustees, Norwich Cathedral Trust, 1998–. President: Norfolk Naturalists Trust, 1962–78; Friends of Norwich Museums, 1978–. Pres., E. Anglian TAVRA, 1989–95. FRSA 1995. JP 1958, DL 1968, High Sheriff, 1970, Norfolk. Hon. Fellow, UEA, 2004. Hon. DCL UEA, 1973; DUniv Anglia Poly., 1999. KStJ 1979. *Address:* Bixley Manor, Norwich, Norfolk NR14 8SJ. *T:* (01603) 625298. *Clubs:* Turf, Pratt's; Norfolk (Norwich); Royal Yacht Squadron.

See also P. J. C. Troughton.

COLMER, Ven. Malcolm John; Archdeacon of Hereford, since 2005; *b* 15 Feb. 1945; *s* of Frederick and Gladys Colmer; *m* 1966, Kathleen Elizabeth Colmer (*née* Wade); one *s* three *d*. *Educ:* Sussex Univ. (BSc (Maths); MSc (Fluid Mechs)); Nottingham Univ. (BA (Theol.)). Scientific Officer, RAE, 1967–71; ordained deacon, 1973, priest, 1974; Assistant Curate: St John the Baptist, Egham, 1973–76; St Mary, Chadwell, 1976–79; Vicar: St Michael, S Malling, Lewes, 1979–85; St Mary, Hornsey Rise, 1985–87; Team Rector, Hornsey Rise, Whitehall Park Team, 1987–96; Archdeacon of Middx, 1996–2005. Area Dean of Islington, 1990–95. *Recreations:* music, painting, natural history, gardening. *Address:* 3 St John Street, Hereford HR1 2NB. *T:* (01432) 272873; *e-mail:* archdeacon@hereford.anglican.org.

COLOMBO, Emilio; Minister of Foreign Affairs, Italy, 1980–83 and 1992–93; Life Senator, Italy, since 2003; *b* Potenza, Italy, 11 April 1920. *Educ:* Rome Univ. Deputy: Constituent Assembly, 1946–48; (Christian Democrat), Italian Parlt, 1948–94; Under-Secretary: of Agriculture, 1948–51; of Public Works, 1953–55; Minister: of Agriculture, 1955–58; of Foreign Trade, 1958–59; of Industry and Commerce, 1959–60, March–April 1960, July 1960–63; of the Treasury, 1963–70, Feb.–May 1972, 1974–76; Prime Minister, 1970–72; Minister of State for UN Affairs, 1972–73; Minister of Finance, 1973–74. European Parliament: Mem., 1976–80, 1989–92; Chm., Political Affairs Cttee, 1976–77; Pres., 1977–79. Pres., Atlantic Cttee, 1990–; Formerly Vice-Pres., Italian Catholic Youth Assoc. Charlemagne Prize, 1979. *Address:* Via Vittorio Veneto 146, Rome, Italy.

COLQUHOUN, Prof. Alan Harold; architect; Professor, School of Architecture, Princeton University, 1981–91, now Emeritus; *b* 27 June 1927; *s* of John Sydney Plumptree Colquhoun and Clariss Thelma Colquhoun (*née* Soden). *Educ:* Edinburgh Coll. of Art; AA Dip 1949. Architects' Dept, LCC, 1949–55; Candilis and Woods, Paris, 1955–56; Lyons Israel and Ellis, London, 1956–61; own practice, Colquhoun & Miller, Architects, 1961–88. Lectr, PCL, 1974–78; many short-term or part-time teaching posts in UK, Switzerland, Ireland and USA, 1957–; lectures and seminars in UK, France, Germany, Spain, Holland, Switzerland, Portugal, USA, Canada, Brazil, Argentina, Chile, India and Singapore, 1960–. Guggenheim Fellowship, 1996; Centre for Advanced Study in the Visual Arts Fellowship, Nat. Gall. of Art, Washington, 1996. *Publications:* Modern Architecture and Historical Change, 1982 (trans. French, Italian, Spanish and Turkish); Modernity and the Classical Tradition, 1987 (trans. Spanish and Portuguese); Modern Architecture 1890–1965, 2002 (trans. French and Spanish); contrib. learned jls in UK, USA and Europe. *Recreations:* music (as listener), painting (as occasional practitioner and enjoyer), literature. *Address:* 96 Regent's Park Road, NW1 8UG.

COLQUHOUN, Andrew John, PhD; Chairman, National Horticultural Forum, since 2002; Director General, Royal Horticultural Society, 1999–2006; *b* 21 Sept. 1949; *s* of late Kenneth James Colquhoun, MC, and of Christine Mary Colquhoun (*née* Morris); *m* 1975, Patricia Beardall; one *s* one *d*. *Educ:* Tiffin Sch.; Nottingham Univ. (BSc 1st Cl. Hons 1971); Glasgow Univ. (PhD 1974); City Univ. Business Sch. (MBA Dist. 1987). Joined HM Diplomatic Service, 1974; Third Sec., FCO, 1974–75; Second Sec., MECAS, 1975–77; Second, later First, Sec., Damascus, 1977–79; First Sec., Tel Aviv, 1979–81; Principal, Cabinet Office, 1981–83; Planning Staff, FCO, 1983–84; Shandwick Consultants (on secondment to ICA), 1984–86; Dir of Educn and Trng, 1987–90; Sec. and Chief Exec., 1990–97, ICAEW. Sec., Consultative Cttee of Accountancy Bodies, 1990–97. Non-exec. Dir, NERC, 2007–. Member: Audit Cttee, Edexcel Foundn, 1997–2002; BITC Headteacher Mentoring Prog., 1998–; Mid Sussex Literacy Project, 1998–2004; Rail Passengers (formerly Rail Users Consultative) Cttee for Southern England, 1999–2003; Chm., SEEDA Horticulture Wkg Gp, 2006–. Mem. Council, Nottingham Univ., 1999–2006. *Publications:* various articles on accountancy, professions, educn, horticulture and recruitment in nat., educnl and professional press. *Recreations:* bird watching, gardening, country life, reading. *Address:* Studio House, 64 Croft Road, Hastings, Sussex TN34 3HE. *Club:* Reform.

COLQUHOUN, Prof. David, FRS 1985; Professor of Pharmacology, since 1983 (A. J. Clark Professor of Pharmacology, 1983–2004), Director, Wellcome Laboratory for Molecular Pharmacology, 1993–2004, and Hon. Fellow, 2004, University College

London; *b* 19 July 1936; *s* of Gilbert Colquhoun and Kathleen Mary (*née* Chambers); *m* 1976, Margaret Ann Boultwood; one *s*. *Educ:* Birkenhead Sch.; Liverpool Technical Coll.; Leeds Univ. (BSc); Edinburgh Univ. (PhD). Lectr, Dept of Pharmacol., UCL, 1964–70; Vis. Asst, then Associate Prof., Dept of Pharmacol., Yale Univ. Med. Sch., 1970–72; Sen. Lectr, Dept of Pharmacol., Univ. of Southampton Med. Sch., 1972–75; Sen. Lectr, Dept of Pharmacol., St George's Hosp. Med. Sch., 1975–79; Reader, Dept of Pharmacol., UCL, 1979–83. Guest Prof., Max-Planck-Institut für Medizinische Forschung, Heidelberg, 1990–91. Krantz Lectr, Univ. of Maryland, 1987. Trustee, Sir Ronald Fisher Meml Cttee, 1975–. Alexander von Humboldt Prize, 1990. Member Editorial Board: Jl of Physiology, 1974–81; Jl Gen. Physiology, 1998–; Series B, Proceedings of Royal Soc. *Publications:* Lectures on Biostatistics, 1971; articles in Jl of Physiology, British Jl of Pharmacology, Proc. of Royal Soc., etc. *Recreations:* walking, running, sailing, linear algebra. *Address:* Chiddingstone, Common Lane, Kings Langley, Herts WD4 8BL. *T:* (01923) 266154.

COLQUHOUN of Luss, Sir Malcom (Rory), 9th Bt *cr* 1786, of Luss, Dumbarton; Joint Principal, Broomwood Hall and Northcote Lodge Schools, since 1984; Chairman, Luss Estates Co., since 2008; *b* 20 Dec. 1947; s of Sir Ivar Iain Colquhoun, 8th Bt and Kathleen Colquhoun (*née* Duncan); *S* father, 2008; *m* 1st, 1978, Susan Timmerman (marr. diss. 1983); one *s*; 2nd, 1989, Katharine Mears; one *s* one *d*. *Educ:* Eton; Univ. of Reading (BSc Est. Man.). *Recreations:* opera, travel, piano. *Heir: s* Patrick John Colquhoun, *b* 17 Dec. 1980. *Address:* 74 Nightingale Lane, SW12 8NR. *T:* (020) 8682 8899; Camstraddan, Luss, Argyllshire G83 8NX. *T:* (01436) 860245; *e-mail:* m.colquhoun@lussestates.co.uk. *Clubs:* White's, Turf.

COLQUHOUN, Ms Maureen Morfydd; political researcher and writer; Chief Executive, North West Government Relations, since 1994; *b* 12 Aug. 1928; *m* 1949, Keith Colquhoun (marr. diss. 1980); two *s* one *d*; partner, 1975–, Ms Barbara Todd; extended family, two *d*. Mem. Labour Party, 1945–; Member: Shoreham UDC, 1965–74; Adur District Council, 1973–74; West Sussex CC, 1971–74; Hackney BC, 1982–90; Lakes Parish Council, 1994–98, 2006–. MP (Lab) Northampton North, Feb. 1974–1979. Information Officer, Gingerbread, 1980–82. Hon. Sec., All-Party Parly Gp on AIDS, 1987–88; Chm., Secretaries and Assistants' Council, H of C, 1992–93. Mem., Assoc. of Former MPs, 2005– (Mem., Exec. Cttee, 2006–). Founder and Chairman: Historic Ambleside Trust, 1992–; Pensions Lobbying, 1996–; Co-Founder, Lakes Vision Gp, 1997; Mem. Exec. Cttee, Ambleside Civic Trust, 1993–99; Sec. of State Appointee, Lake Dist Nat. Park Authy, 1998–2006. Co-Founder and Chairperson to Trustees, Harriet Martineau Foundn, 2000. *Publications:* A Woman In the House, 1980; Inside the Westminster Parliament, 1992; New Labour–New Lobbying, 1998. *Recreations:* fell-walking, jazz, opera, theatre. *Address:* South Knoll, Rydal Road, Ambleside, Cumbria LA22 9AY. *Club:* University Women's.

COLSTON, His Honour Colin Charles; QC 1980; a Circuit Judge, 1983–2003; *b* 2 Oct. 1937; *yr s* of late Eric Colston, JP, and Catherine Colston; *m* 1963, Edith Helga, *d* of late Med. Rat Dr Wilhelm and Frau Gisela Hille, St Oswald/Freistadt, Austria; two *s* one *d*. *Educ:* Rugby Sch.; The Gunnery, Washington, Conn, USA; Trinity Hall, Cambridge (MA). National Service, RN, 1956–58; commissioned, RNR, 1958–64. Called to the Bar, Gray's Inn, 1962; Midland and Oxford Circuit (formerly Midland Circuit); Recorder of Midland Circuit, 1968–69; Member, Senate of Inns of Court and Bar, 1977–80; Recorder of the Crown Court, 1978–83; Resident Judge, St Albans, 1989–2000. Lay Judge, Court of Arches, Canterbury, 1992–. Member: Criminal Cttee, Judicial Studies Bd, 1989–92; Parole Bd for England & Wales, 2004–. Chm., St Albans Diocesan Bd of Patronage, 1987–2000. Hon. Canon, St Albans Cathedral, 2002–07, Canon Emeritus, 2007–. *Address:* c/o The Crown Court, Bricket Road, St Albans, Herts AL1 3JW.

COLSTON, Michael; Chairman, Ewelme Park Farm Ltd, since 1996; *b* 24 July 1932; *s* of Sir Charles Blampied Colston, CBE, MC, DCM, FCGI and Lady (Eliza Foster) Colston, MBE; *m* 1st, 1956, Jane Olivia Kilham Roberts (marr. diss.); three *d*; 2nd, 1977, Judith Angela Briggs. *Educ:* Ridley Coll., Canada; Stowe; Gonville and Caius Coll., Cambridge. Joined 17th/21st Lancers, 1952; later seconded to 1st Royal Tank Regt for service in Korea. Founder Dir, Charles Colston Group Ltd (formerly Colston Appliances Ltd) together with late Sir Charles Colston, 1955, Chm. and Man. Dir, 1969–89; Chm. and Man. Dir, Colston Domestic Appliances Ltd, 1969–79. Chairman: Colston Consultants Ltd, 1989–93; Tallent Engineering Ltd, 1969–89; Tallent Holdings plc, 1989–90; ITS Rubber Ltd, 1969–85; Quit Ltd, 1989–93; Dishwasher Council, 1970–75. Dir, Farming and Wildlife Adv. Gp, 1991–2002. Chm., Assoc. Manufrs of Domestic Electrical Appliances, 1976–79. Member Council: Inst. of Directors, 1977–93 (Pres., Thames Valley Br., 1983–93); CBI, 1984–90 (Chm., S Regl Council, 1986–88); British Electrotechnical Approvals Bd, 1976–79; SMMT, 1987–90. Trustee, Hawk and Owl Trust, 1991–96. *Recreations:* fishing, shooting, tennis; founder Cambridge Univ. Water Ski Club. *Address:* C6 Albany, Piccadilly, W1J 0AW. *T:* (020) 7734 2452.

COLT, Sir Edward (William Dutton), 10th Bt *cr* 1694; MB, FRCP, FACP; Attending Physician, St Luke's-Roosevelt Hospital, New York; Associate Professor of Clinical Medicine (part-time), Columbia University, New York; *b* 22 Sept. 1936; *s* of Major John Rochfort Colt, North Staffs Regt (*d* 1944), and of Angela Miriam Phyllis (*née* Kyan; she *m* 1946, Capt. Robert Leslie Cock); *S* uncle, 1951; *m* 1st, 1966, Jane Caroline (marr. diss. 1972), *d* of James Histed Lewis, Geneva and Washington, DC; 2nd, 1979, Suzanne Nelson (*née* Knickerbocker); one *d* (one *s* decd). *Educ:* Stoke House, Seaford; Douai Sch.; University Coll., London. Lately: Medical Registrar, UCH; House Physician, Brompton Hosp. *Publications:* contribs, especially on sports medicine, particularly running, to British and American med. jls. *Recreations:* golf, ski-ing. *Heir:* none.

COLTART, Simon Stewart; His Honour Judge Coltart; a Circuit Judge, since 1991; *b* 3 Sept. 1946; *s* of late Gilbert McCallum Coltart and of Mary Louise (*née* Kemp); *m* 1973, Sarah Victoria Birts; three *s*. *Educ:* Epsom Coll.; Leeds Univ. (LLB). Called to the Bar, Lincoln's Inn, 1969 (Eastham Scholar); a Recorder, 1987–91. Mem., Parole Bd, 1997–2003. Mem., Court of Assts, Grocers' Co., 1991– (Master, 1999). Governor: Stoke Brunswick Sch., 1991–2006; Oundle Sch., 2003–. *Recreations:* sailing, golf, shooting, fishing. *Address:* Lewes Combined Court, Lewes, East Sussex BN7 1YB. *Clubs:* Boodle's; Sussex; Bar Yacht, Royal Yacht Squadron; Rye Golf.

COLTHURST, Sir Charles (St John), 10th Bt *cr* 1744, of Ardrum, co. Cork; *b* 21 May 1955; *s* of Sir Richard La Touche Colthurst, 9th Bt and Janet Georgina (*née* Wilson-Wright) (*d* 2007); *S* father, 2003; *m* 1987, Nora Mary, *d* of Mortimer Kelleher; one *s* three *d*. *Educ:* Eton; Magdalene Coll., Cambridge (MA); University Coll., Dublin. Solicitor. *Heir: s* John Conway La Touche Colthurst, *b* 13 Oct. 1988. *Address:* Blarney Castle, Blarney, Co. Cork, Ireland. *Clubs:* MCC; Royal Irish Automobile, Kildare Street (Dublin).

COLTMAN, Anne Clare, (Mrs T. C. Coltman); *see* Riches, A. C.

COLTON, Rt Rev. (William) Paul; *see* Cork, Cloyne and Ross, Bishop of.

COLTRANE, Robbie, OBE 2006; actor and director; *b* Glasgow, 31 March 1950; *m* 1999, Rhona Irene Gemmell; one *s* one *d*. *Educ:* Trinity Coll., Glenalmond; Glasgow Sch. of Art (DA Drawing and Painting). *Television* includes: Laugh? I nearly paid my licence fee!, 1985; Hooray for Holyrood, 1986; Tutti Frutti, 1986; The Miners' Strike, 1987; Mistero Buffo, 1990; Coltrane in a Cadillac, 1992; Cracker (3 series), 1993, 1994, 1995, (TV films) White Ghost, 1996, Cracker, 2006; The Ebb Tide, 1997; Coltrane's Planes and Automobiles, 1997; The Plan Man, 2003; Frazier, 2004; Robbie Coltrane: B-Road Britain, 2007; *films* include: Absolute Beginners, 1985; Mona Lisa, 1985; Danny Champion of the World, 1988; Henry V, 1988; Nuns on the Run, 1989; The Pope Must Die, 1990; Oh, What a Night, 1991; Huck Finn, 1992; Goldeneye, 1995; Buddy, 1996; Montana, 1997; Frogs for Snakes, 1997; Message in a Bottle, 1999; The World Is Not Enough, 1999; Harry Potter and the Philosopher's Stone, 2001; From Hell, 2002; Harry Potter and The Chamber of Secrets, 2002; Harry Potter and the Prisoner of Azkaban, 2004; Ocean's Twelve, 2005; Harry Potter and the Goblet of Fire, 2005; Harry Potter and the Order of the Phoenix, 2006; Provoked, 2007; Bloom Brothers, 2007; *theatre:* has appeared and toured with Traverse Theatre Co. and Borderline Theatre Co., 1976–, incl. Mistero Buffo, 1990; Yr Obedient Servant, Lyric, 1987. Silver Rose Award, Montreux TV Fest., 1987; Evening Standard Peter Sellers Award, 1991; TV Best Actor Awards: BAFTA, 1994, 1995, 1996; Silver Nymph, Monte Carlo, 1994; BPG, 1994; RTS, 1994; FIPA (French Acad.), 1994; Cable Ace, 1994; Cannes TV Fest., 1994. *Publications:* Coltrane in a Cadillac, 1993; (with John Binias) Planes and Automobiles, 1997; newspaper and magazine articles. *Recreations:* politics, drawing, vintage cars, reading, sailing, piano, fishing, film, ships. *Address:* c/o CDA, 125 Gloucester Road, SW7 4TE. *T:* (020) 7373 3323. *Clubs:* Groucho, Soho House, Chelsea Arts, Marzipan; Glasgow Arts.

COLVER, Hugh Bernard, CBE 1991; public affairs consultant; Group Communications Director, BAE SYSTEMS, 2000–05; *b* 22 Aug. 1945; *s* of late Rev. Canon John Lawrence Colver and Diana Irene (*née* Bartlett); *m* 1970, Gillian Ogilvie (marr. diss. 2001), *y d* of late Morris and Dorothy Graham, Christchurch, NZ; one *s* one *d*; partner, Penny Studholme; one *s*. *Educ:* King Edward VI Grammar Sch., Louth, Lincs. Reporter: Market Rasen Mail, 1961–63; Hereford Times and Hereford Evening News, 1963–67; Asst Editor, Helicopter World and Hovercraft World, 1967–68; Journalist, FT Surveys, Financial Times, 1968–71; freelance journalist, writer and PR consultant, 1971–75; Press Officer, MoD, 1975–78; PRO, RAE, 1978–79; Staff PRO to Flag Officer, Scotland and NI, 1979–81; Press Officer, Prime Minister's Office, 1981–82; Chief Press Officer, Dept of Employment, 1982–84; Dep. Dir of Information, Metropolitan Police, 1984–85; Ministry of Defence: Dep. Chief of PR, 1985–87; Chief of PR, 1987–92; Public Affairs Dir, British Aerospace Defence Ltd, 1992–95; Dir of Communications, Cons. Central Office, 1995. Non-executive Chairman: Europac Gp Ltd, 2000– (Dir, 1997–); Defence Public Affairs Consultants, 2000– (Dir, 1997–). Hon. Col, Media Ops Gp (Vols), TA, 2002–06. FRAeS 1998; FRSA. Liveryman, Bowyers' Co., 2005. *Publication:* This is the Hovercraft, 1972. *Recreations:* motoring, motor racing, walking. *Club:* Reform.

COLVILLE, family name of **Viscount Colville of Culross** and of **Baron Clydesmuir**.

COLVILLE OF CULROSS, 4th Viscount *cr* 1902; **John Mark Alexander Colville;** QC; 14th Baron (Scot.) *cr* 1604; 4th Baron (UK) *cr* 1885; a Circuit Judge, 1993–99; *b* 19 July 1933; *e s* of 3rd Viscount and Kathleen Myrtle (*d* 1986), OBE 1961, *e d* of late Brig.-Gen. H. R. Gale, CMG, RE, Bardsey, Saanichton, Vancouver Island; *S* father, 1945; *m* 1st, 1958, Mary Elizabeth Webb-Bowen (marr. diss. 1973); four *s*; 2nd, 1974, Margaret Birgitta, Viscountess Davidson, LLB, JP, Barrister, *o d* of Maj.-Gen. C. H. Norton, CB, CBE, DSO; one *s*. *Educ:* Rugby (Scholar); New Coll., Oxford (Scholar) (MA; Hon. Fellow, 1997). Lieut Grenadier Guards Reserve. Barrister-at-law, Lincoln's Inn, 1960 (Buchanan prizeman), Bencher, 1986; QC 1978; a Recorder, 1990–93. Minister of State, Home Office, 1972–74; elected Mem., H of L, 1999. Dir, Securities and Futures Authy (formerly Securities Assoc.), 1987–93. Chm., Norwich Information and Technology Centre, 1983–85; Director: Rediffusion Television Ltd, 1961–68; British Electric Traction Co. Ltd, 1968–72, 1974–84 (Dep. Chm., 1980–81); Mem., CBI Council, 1982–84. Chairman: Mental Health Act Commn, 1983–88; Alcohol Educn and Res. Council, 1984–90; Parole Bd, 1988–92; UK rep., UN Human Rights Commn, 1980–83; Mem., UN Working Gp on Disappeared Persons, 1980–84 (Chm., 1981–84); Special Rapporteur on Human Rights in Guatemala, 1983–86; Mem., UN Human Rights Cttee, 1995–2000; Asst Surveillance Comr, 2001–. Reports on Prevention of Terrorism Act and NI Emergency Powers Act, for HM Govt, 1986–93. Mem. Council, Univ. of E Anglia, 1968–72. Mem., Royal Company of Archers (Queen's Body Guard for Scotland). Governor, BUPA, 1990–93. Hon. DCL UEA, 1998. *Heir: s* Master of Colville, *qv*. *Address:* House of Lords, SW1A 0PW.

See also Baron Carrington.

COLVILLE, Master of; Hon. Charles Mark Townshend Colville; *b* 5 Sept. 1959; *s* and *heir* of 4th Viscount Colville of Culross, *qv*. *Educ:* Rugby; Univ. of Durham.

COLVIN, Andrew James; Comptroller and City Solicitor, City of London Corporation (formerly Corporation of London), since 1989; *b* 28 April 1947; *s* of Gilbert Russell Colvin, OBE, MA, and Dr Beatrice Colvin, MRCS, LRCP, DPH; *m* 1971, Helen Mary Ryan; one *s* three *d*. *Educ:* qualified Solicitor, 1975; LLM Leicester Univ., 1996. Articled to Borough Solicitor, subseq. Asst Town Clerk, London Borough of Ealing, 1971–82; Dep. Town Clerk and Borough Solicitor, Royal Borough of Kensington and Chelsea, 1982–89. Legal Advr, Assoc. of London Govt, subseq. London Councils, 1996– (London Boroughs' Assoc., 1984–96); Advr, English Nat. Stadium Trust, 1997–. Governor: St Gregory's RC Sch., 1989–93; Cardinal Wiseman RC Sch., 1992–99 (Chm., 1994–99). Freeman: City of London, 1989; City of London Solicitors' Co., 1996. *Recreations:* sailing, music, cycling. *Address:* Guildhall, EC2P 2EJ.

COLVIN, David, CBE 1991; Chief Adviser in Social Work, The Scottish Office, 1980–91; Scottish Secretary, British Association of Social Workers, 1992–97; *b* 31 Jan. 1931; *s* of James Colvin and Mrs Crawford Colvin; *m* 1957, Elma Findlay, artist; two *s* three *d*. *Educ:* Whitehill Sch., Glasgow; Glasgow and Edinburgh Univs. Probation Officer, Glasgow City, 1955–60; Psychiatric Social Worker, Scottish Prison and Borstal Service, 1960–61; Sen. Psychiatric Social Worker, Crichton Royal Hosp., Child Psychiatric Unit, 1961–65; Director, Family Casework Unit, Paisley, 1965; Social Work Adviser, Scottish Office, 1966, and subseq.; Interim Dir of Social Work, Shetland Islands Council, 1991. At various times held office in Howard League for Penal Reform, Assoc. of Social Workers and Inst. for Study and Treatment of Delinquency. Sen. Associate Research Fellow, Brunel Univ., 1978. Chm., Dumfries Constituency Labour Party, 1963–65. Chairman: Scotland Cttee, Nat. Children's Homes, 1991–97; Marriage Council, Scotland, 1991–95; SACRO, 1997–2003 (Mem., Exec. Cttee, 1992–94); Vice-Chm., Scottish Consortium on Criminal Justice, 1998–2003; Vice-Pres., Scottish Carers Assoc., 1998–2001. Governor, Nat. Inst. for Social Work, 1986–89; Hon. Adviser, British Red Cross, 1982–90. Gov., St Columba's Hospice, 1998–2004; Trustee, Scottish Disability Foundn, 1998–2004. Chm., Exhibiting Socs of Scottish Artists, 1999–2008. Member: Labour Party, 1949–2001; SNP, 2007–. Hon. Mem., Soc. of Scottish Artists. DUniv Stirling,

1998. *Recreations:* collector; swimming, climbing, the arts, social affairs. *Address:* Kinloch, 19 Glamis Road, Kirriemuir DD8 5BN; *e-mail:* davidcolvin@gmail.com.

COLVIN, David Hugh, CMG 1993; HM Diplomatic Service, retired; Executive Director, Jordan International Bank plc, since 2005; *b* 23 Jan. 1941; 3rd *s* of late Major Leslie Hubert Boyd Colvin, MC, and of Edna Mary (*née* Parrott); *m* 1971, (Diana) Caroline Carew, *y d* of Gordon MacPherson Lang Smith and Mildred (*née* Carew-Gibson); one *s* one *d. Educ:* Lincoln Sch.; Trinity Coll., Oxford (MA). Assistant Principal, Board of Trade, 1966. Joined HM Foreign (later Diplomatic) Service, 1967; Central Dept, FO, 1967; Second Secretary, Bangkok, 1968–71; European Integration Dept, FCO, 1971–75; First Sec., Paris, 1975–77; First Sec. (Press and Inf.), UK Permanent Representation to the European Community, 1977–82; Asst Sec., Cabinet Office, 1982–85; Counsellor and Hd of Chancery, Budapest, 1985–88; Hd, SE Asian Dept, FCO, 1988–91; Minister, Rome, 1992–96; Ambassador to Belgium, 1996–2001. Diplomatic Communications Consultant, Adam Smith Inst., 2001–03. Consultant, SCS Ltd, 2003–. Mem., New Europe Adv. Council, 2001–06; Vice-Pres., European-Atlantic Gp, 2001–06. Chairman: British-Italian Soc., 2001–06; Anglo-Belgian Soc., 2001–; Patron, Drones Club of Belgium (P. G. Wodehouse Soc.), 1997–2001. Trustee, Prospect Burma, 2001–. Freeman, City of London, 2002. Commendatore, Ordine della Stella della Solidarieta Italiana (Italy), 2003. *Recreations:* military history, tennis, shooting, rallying old cars. *Address:* 15 Westmoreland Terrace, SW1V 4AG. *T:* (020) 7630 8349. *Clubs:* Travellers, Royal Anglo-Belgian (Dir, 2001–).

COLVIN, Kathryn Frances, CVO 2002; FCIL; HM Diplomatic Service, retired; Ambassador to the Holy See, 2002–05; *b* 11 Sept. 1945; *d* of Ernest Osborne and Frances Joy Osborne (*née* Perman); *m* 1971, Brian Colvin. *Educ:* Walthamstow Hall, Sevenoaks; Bristol Univ. (BA Hons 1967); Bordeaux Univ. (Diplome d'Etudes Supérieures 1965). FCIL (FIL 1968). Joined FO (later FCO), 1968; Res. Analyst, Western and Central Europe, 1968–94: Inf. Res. Dept, 1968–77; Res. Dept, 1977–94; Mem., UK Delegn to UN Commn on Human Rights, 1980–90; Temp. Duty as 1st Sec., Political, Rome, 1988 and 1991, and Paris, 1992; Deputy Head: OSCE Dept, 1994–95; Western Eur. Dept, 1995–98; Whitehall Liaison Dept, 1998–99; Vice-Marshal of the Diplomatic Corps, and Head, Protocol Div., FCO, 1999–2002. Officier, Légion d'Honneur (France), 1996. *Recreations:* art, design, opera, theatre, cinema, swimming.

COLWYN, 3rd Baron, *cr* 1917; **Ian Anthony Hamilton-Smith,** CBE 1989; Bt 1912; dental surgeon, 1966–2006; *b* 1 Jan. 1942; *s* of 2nd Baron Colwyn and Miriam Gwendoline (*d* 1996), *d* of Victor Ferguson; *S* father 1966; *m* 1st, 1964, Sonia Jane (marr. diss. 1977; she *d* 2006), *d* of P. H. G. Morgan; one *s* one *d*; 2nd, 1977, Nicola Jeanne, *d* of Arthur Tyers, The Avenue, Sunbury-on-Thames; two *d. Educ:* Cheltenham Coll.; Univ. of London. BDS London 1966; LDS, RCS 1966. Dir, Dental Protection Ltd, 1990–2001 (Chm., 1996–2001). Non-exec. Dir, Project Hope UK, 1998–2001; Chm., Campbell Montague Internat., 2005–08; Dir, London Sedation Services Ltd, 2007–. President: Natural Medicines Soc., 1989–2005; Huntington's Disease Assoc., 1991–98; Arterial Health Foundn, 1992–2004; Soc. for Advancement of Anaesthesia in Dentistry, 1994–97; Mem. Council, Med. Protection Soc., 1994–2001. Mem., H of L Sci. and Technol. Select Cttee, 2006–; Pres., All Party Parly Gp for Complementary and Integrated Healthcare (formerly Alternative and Complementary Medicine), 1989–; Co-Chm., All Party Parly Jazz Gp, 1994–; Chm., Refreshment Cttee, H of L, 1997–2004; a Dep. Chm. of Cttees, 2007–; elected Mem., H of L, 1999. Patron: Res. Council for Complementary Medicine; Blackie Foundn. *Recreations:* riparian activities, music, dance band, golf. *Heir: s* Hon. Craig Peter Hamilton-Smith [*b* 13 Oct. 1968; *m* 2003, Louise Vanessa, *d* of Callum Barney; one *s*]. *Address:* House of Lords, SW1A 0PW. *T:* (020) 7219 3000.

COLYER, His Honour John Stuart; QC 1976; a Circuit Judge, 1991–2000; *b* 25 April 1935; *s* of late Stanley Herbert Colyer, MBE, and Louisa (*née* Randle); *m* 1961, Emily Warner, *o d* of late Stanley Leland Dutrow and Mrs Dutrow, Blue Ridge Summit, Pa, USA; two *d. Educ:* Dudley Grammar Sch.; Shrewsbury; Worcester Coll., Oxford (Open History Scholarship; BA 1958, MA 1961). 2nd Lieut RA, 1954–55. Called to the Bar, Middle Temple, 1959 (Bencher, 1983); Instructor, Univ. of Pennsylvania, Philadelphia, 1959–60, Asst Prof., 1960–61; practised English Bar, Midland and Oxford Circuit (formerly Oxford Circuit), 1961–91; a Recorder, 1986–91. Hon. Reader, 1985–91, and Mem. Council, 1985–91, Council of Legal Educn (Lectr (Law of Landlord and Tenant), 1970–89); Vice-Pres., Lawyers' Christian Fellowship, 1993– (Chm., 1981–89); Mem., Anglo-American Real Property Inst., 1980– (Treasurer, 1984). Blundell Meml Lectr, 1977, 1982, 1986. Trustee and Gov., Royal Sch. for Deaf Children, Margate, 2000– (Chm., 2005–). *Publications:* (ed jtly) Encyclopaedia of Forms and Precedents (Landlord and Tenant), vol. XI, 1965, vol. XII, 1966; A Modern View of the Law of Torts, 1966; Landlord and Tenant, in Halsbury's Laws of England, 4th edn, 1981, new edn, 1994; Gen. Ed., Megarry's The Rent Acts, 11th edn, 1988; articles in Conveyancer and other professional jls. *Recreations:* entertaining my family, opera, cultivation of cacti and of succulents (esp. Lithops), gardening generally, travel, education and welfare of the profoundly deaf. *Address:* c/o Falcon Chambers, Falcon Court, EC4Y 1AA. *T:* (020) 7353 2484, *Fax:* (020) 7353 1261.

COLYER, Peter John, DPhil; Fellow, Centre for Christianity and Culture, Regent's Park College, Oxford; Secretary, UK Science and Religion Forum, since 2007; *b* 24 March 1943; *s* of Sydney Colyer and Beryl Colyer; *m* 1968, Kay Holloway; three *s. Educ:* Hertford Coll., Oxford (MA 1969); Regent's Park Coll., Oxford (MSt 2003; DPhil 2007). Research Scientist, Hydraulics Res., Wallingford, Oxon, 1966–83; Scientific Advr, Laboratorio de Hidraulica Aplicada, Buenos Aires, 1972–74; Science Policy Unit, Dept of Transport, 1983–86 and 1990; Sen. Principal, Sci. and Technol. Secretariat, Cabinet Office, 1986–90; Co-ordinator of Scientific Networks, ESF, Strasbourg, 1991–95; Exec. Sec., Academia Europaea, 1995–2001. *Publications:* numerous scientific reports and papers. *Recreations:* sport, arts, travel. *Address:* 29 Marlborough Place, Charlbury, Oxon OX7 3SH.

COLYTON, 2nd Baron *cr* 1956, of Farway, Devon and of Taunton, Somerset; **Alisdair John Munro Hopkinson;** *b* 7 May 1958; *s* of Hon. Nicholas Henry Eno Hopkinson (*d* 1991), *o s* of 1st Baron Colyton, PC, CMG and Fiona Margaret (*d* 1996), *o d* of Sir Thomas Torquil Alphonso Munro, 5th Bt; *S* grandfather, 1996; *m* 1980, Philippa, *d* of P. J. Bell; two *s* one *d. Heir: s* Hon. James Patrick Munro Hopkinson, *b* 8 May 1983. *Address:* Lindertis, by Kirriemuir, Angus DD8 5NT.

COMBER, Ven. Anthony James; Archdeacon of Leeds, 1982–92, now Archdeacon Emeritus; *b* 20 April 1927; *s* of late Norman Mederson Comber and Nellie Comber. *Educ:* Leeds Grammar School; Leeds Univ. (MSc Mining); St Chad's Coll., Durham (DipTh); Munich Univ. Colliery underground official, 1951–53. Vicar: Oulton, 1960–69; Hunslet, 1969–77; Rector of Farnley, 1977–82. *Publication:* (contrib.) Today's Church and Today's World, 1977. *Recreations:* politics; walking in Bavaria. *Address:* 10 Tavistock Park, Leeds LS12 4DD. *T:* (0113) 263 0311.

COMBERMERE, 6th Viscount *cr* 1827; **Thomas Robert Wellington Stapleton-Cotton;** Bt 1677; Baron 1814; *b* 30 Aug. 1969; *o s* of 5th Viscount Combermere; *S* father, 2000; *m* 2005, Caroline Sarah, *o d* of Charles Leonard Anthony Irby, *qv. Heir: uncle* Hon. David Peter Dudley Stapleton-Cotton [*b* 6 March 1932; *m* 1955, Susan Nomakepu, *d* of Sir George Werner Albu, 2nd Bt; two *s* two *d*].

COMBES, Ven. Roger Matthew; Archdeacon of Horsham, since 2003; *b* 12 June 1947; *m* 1983, Christine Mary Keiller; two *d. Educ:* King's Coll., London (LLB 1969); Ridley Hall, Cambridge. Ordained deacon, 1974, priest, 1975; Curate: St Paul's, Onslow Square, 1974–77; Holy Trinity, Brompton, 1976–77; Holy Sepulchre with All Saints, Cambridge, 1977–86; Rector, St Matthew's, Silverhill, 1986–2003; RD, Hastings, 1998–2002. *Address:* 3 Danehurst Crescent, Horsham, W Sussex RH13 5HS.

COMFORT, Anthony Francis; HM Diplomatic Service, retired; *b* Plymouth, 12 Oct. 1920; *s* of Francis Harold Comfort and Elsie Grace (*née* Martin); *m* 1948, Joy Margaret Midson (*d* 2003); two *s* one *d. Educ:* Bristol Grammar Sch.; Oriel Coll., Oxford. Entered Foreign Service, 1947; 2nd Sec. (Commercial), Athens, 1948–51; Consul, Alexandria, 1951–53; 1st Sec. (Commercial), Amman, 1953–54; Foreign Office, 1954–57; seconded to Colonial Office, 1957–59; 1st Sec. (Commercial), Belgrade, 1959–60; 1st Sec. and Consul, Reykjavik, 1961–65; Inspector, 1965–68, retired 1969. *Recreations:* walking, looking at churches. *Address:* 4 Charles Ponsonby House, Osberton Road, Oxford OX2 7PQ. *T:* (01865) 552677.

COMINS, David; Rector, Glasgow Academy, 1994–2005; *b* 1 March 1948; *s* of Jack Comins and Marjorie Mabel (*née* Rowbotham); *m* 1972, Christine Anne Speak; one *s* two *d. Educ:* Scarborough Boys' High Sch.; Downing Coll., Cambridge (BA, MA, PGCE). Assistant Mathematics Teacher: Mill Hill Sch., 1971–75; Strathallan Sch., Perthshire, 1975–76; Glenalmond College, Perthshire: Asst Maths Teacher, 1976–80; Head of Maths, 1980–85; Dir of Studies, 1985–89; Dep. Head, Queen's Coll., Taunton, 1989–94. Teacher of Maths, Shenzhen Coll. of Internat. Educn, Shenzhen, 2005–07. Churchill Fellow, 1981. *Recreations:* mountaineering, ballet, music, crosswords, sudoku. *Address:* Flat 6, Block 8, Kirklee Gate, Glasgow G12 0SZ. *Clubs:* East India, Alpine.

COMNINOS, Sophie Henrietta; *see* Turner Laing, S. H.

COMPAGNONI, Marco; Partner, Weil Gotshal & Manges, since 2006; *b* Haltwhistle, Northumberland, 3 May 1962; *s* of Peter Compagnoni and Santina Margherita Compagnoni. *Educ:* Queen Elizabeth Grammar Sch., Hexham; Univ. of Newcastle upon Tyne (LLB Hons). Admitted solicitor, 1987; Partner, Lovell White Durrant, subseq. Lovells, 1993–2006 (Hd, Internat. Private Equity Practice, 2002–06; Mem., Partnership Bd, 1996–99 and 2001–04). Trustee: Serpentine Gall., 2000–; Royal Opera Hse, Covent Gdn, 2000–07; Royal Opera Hse Benevolent Fund, 2000–07; Mem., London Adv. Bd, Morphoses, Christopher Wheeldon Co., 2007–; Gov., Royal Ballet Co., 2001–07; Mem. Council, Friends of Covent Gdn, 1995– (Chm., 2000–07). Mem., Law Panel, The Times. *Recreations:* opera, dance, contemporary art, shooting, Parson Jack Russell terriers, eating. *Address:* c/o Weil, Gotshal & Manges, One South Place, EC2M 2WG.

COMPSTON, Alastair; *see* Compston, D. A. S.

COMPSTON, Christopher Dean, MA; **His Honour Judge Compston;** a Circuit Judge, since 1986; *b* 5 May 1940; *s* of Vice Adm. Sir Peter Maxwell Compston, KCB and Valerie Bocquet; *m* 1st, 1968, Bronwen Henniker Gotley (marr. diss. 1982); one *d* (and two *s* decd); 2nd, 1983, Caroline Philippa, *d* of Paul Odgers, CB, MBE, TD; two *s* one *d. Educ:* Epsom Coll. (Prae Sum.); Magdalen Coll., Oxford (MA). Called to the Bar, Middle Temple, 1965, Bencher, 2006; a Recorder, 1982–86. Mem. Senate, Inns of Court, 1983–86. Trustee: Fund for Epilepsy, 2000–05; Prison Fellowship, 2001–07. *Publications:* Recovery from Divorce: a practical guide, 1993; (contrib.) Relational Justice, 1994; Cracking up without Breaking up, 1998. *Recreations:* the arts, writing, family, gardening. *Address:* c/o Royal Courts of Justice, Strand, WC2A 2LL. *Club:* Seaview Yacht.

COMPSTON, Prof. (David) Alastair (Standish), FRCP, FMedSci, FIBiol; Professor of Neurology, University of Cambridge, since 1989; Fellow of Jesus College, Cambridge, since 1990; *b* 23 Jan. 1948; *s* of late Nigel Dean Compston and of Diana Mary Compston (*née* Standish); *m* 1973, Juliet Elizabeth Page (*see* J. E. Compston); one *d. Educ:* Rugby Sch.; Middlesex Hospital Med. Sch., London Univ. (MB BS (Hons); PhD). FRCP 1986. Jun. Hosp. appts, Nat. Hosp. for Nervous Diseases, 1972–82; Cons. Neurologist, University Hosp. of Wales, 1982–87; Prof. of Neurology, Univ. of Wales Coll. of Medicine, 1987–88. Editor, Brain, 2004–. Pres., Assoc. of British Neurologists, April 2009–. Founder FMedSci 1998; FIBiol 2000. FRSA 1997. *Publications:* (ed) McAlpine's Multiple Sclerosis, 4th edn 2005; contribs to human and experimental demyelinating diseases, in learned jls. *Recreations:* being outside, antiquarian books. *Address:* Pembroke House, Mill Lane, Linton, Cambridge CB1 6JY. *T:* (01223) 893414. *Club:* Garrick.

COMPSTON, Prof. Juliet Elizabeth, MD; FRCP, FRCPath, FMedSci; Professor of Bone Medicine, University of Cambridge, since 2003; *b* 18 Dec. 1945; *d* of Sir Denys Lionel Page, FBA and Katharine Elizabeth Page; *m* 1976, (David) Alastair (Standish) Compston, *qv*; one *d. Educ:* Middlesex Hosp. Med. Sch., London Univ. (BSc 1967; MB BS 1970; MD 1979). FRCP 1988; FRCPath 1996. Sen. Lectr and Hon. Consultant, Univ. Hosp. of Wales; Med. Registrar, St Thomas' Hosp., London; SHO, Brompton Hosp.; Lectr in Medicine, then Reader in Metabolic Bone Disease, 1999–2003, Univ. of Cambridge. Hon. Consultant Physician, Addenbrooke's Hospital, Cambridge. FMedSci 1999. Kohn Foundn Award, Nat. Osteoporosis Soc., 2006. *Publications:* (ed) Osteoporosis: new perspectives on causes, prevention and treatment, 1996; (with Clifford Rosen) Osteoporosis, 1997, 2nd edn 2001; Understanding Osteoporosis, 1998; (with Ignac Fogelman) Key Advances in the Effective Management of Osteoporosis, 1999; (ed jtly) HRT and the Menopause: current therapy, 2002; (jtly) Osteoporosis: best medicine for osteoporosis, 2005; (ed jtly) Bone Disease of Organ Transplantation, 2005. *Address:* Department of Medicine, University of Cambridge Clinical School, Addenbrooke's Hospital, Hills Road, Cambridge CB2 2QQ; 24 Mill Lane, Linton, Cambridge CB1 6JY.

COMPSTON, Prof. William, PhD; FRS 1987; FAA; FTSE; Australian National University: Professor in Isotope Geochemistry, 1987–96, now Emeritus; Consultant, Research School of Earth Sciences, 1997–99 and since 2002; University Fellow, 2000–01, Visiting Fellow, since 2002; *b* 19 Feb. 1931; *s* of late J. A. Compston; *m* 1952, Elizabeth Blair; three *s* one *d. Educ:* Christian Brothers' Coll., Fremantle; Univ. of WA (BSc (Hons); PhD). Res. Fellow, CIT, 1956–58; Res. Fellow, Dept of Terrestrial Magnetism, Carnegie Inst. of Washington, 1958; Lectr, Univ. of WA, 1959–60; Australian National University: Fellow, then Sen. Fellow, 1961–74; Professorial Fellow, 1974–87. Lectures: Mawson, 1988, Flinders, 1998, Australian Acad. of Sci.; Hallimond, Mineralogical Soc., 1998. Hon. DSc Western Australia, 1988. Stillwell Award, Geol Soc. of Australia, 1990; Clunies Ross Award, Clunies Ross Meml Foundn, 1995. *Address:* Research School of Earth Sciences, Australian National University, Canberra, ACT 0200, Australia; 8 Wells Gardens, Manuka, ACT 2603, Australia.

COMPTON, family name of **Marquess of Northampton**.

COMPTON, Earl; Daniel Bingham Compton; *b* 16 Jan. 1973; *s* and *heir* of Marquess of Northampton, *qv*; *m* 2001, Lucy (marr. diss. 2008), 5th *d* of Lt-Col Benedict Cardozo; two *d*. *Address:* Castle Ashby, Northants NN7 1LF.

COMPTON, Michael Graeme, CBE 1987; Keeper of Museum Services, Tate Gallery, 1970–87, retired; *b* 29 Sept. 1927; *s* of Joseph Neild Compton, OBE, and Dorothy Margaret Townsend Compton; *m* 1952, Susan Paschal Benn; two *d*. *Educ:* Courtauld Institute, London (BA Hons History of Art). Asst to Director, Leeds City Art Gallery and Templenewsam, 1954–57; Keeper of Foreign Schools, Walker Art Gallery, Liverpool, 1957–59; Dir, Ferens Art Gall., Hull, 1960–65; Asst Keeper, Modern Collection, Tate Gall., 1965–70. Frederick R. Weisman Art Foundn Award, 1991. *Publications:* Optical and Kinetic Art, 1967; Pop Art, 1970; (jtly) Catalogue of Foreign Schools, Walker Art Gallery, 1963; Marcel Broodthaers, 1989; articles in art jls, exhibn catalogues.

COMPTON, Robert Edward John; DL; Chairman: Time-Life International Ltd, 1979–90 (Chief Executive Officer, 1985–88); Time SARL, 1985–90; *b* 11 July 1922; *yr s* of late Major Edward Robert Francis Compton, JP, DL, and Sylvia Farquharson; *m* 1951, Ursula Jane Kenyon-Slaney; two *s*. *Educ:* Eton; Magdalen Coll., Oxford, 1940–41. Served War, Coldstream Guards, 1941–46 (wounded); Mil. Asst to British Ambassador, Vienna, 1946. Studied fruit growing and horticulture (Diploma), 1946–48; with W. S. Crawford Ltd, Advertising Agency, 1951–54; joined Time International, 1954; advertising sales, 1954–58, UK Advtsg Dir, 1958–62; also Dir, Time-Life Internat. Ltd, 1958–79. Pres., Highline Finances Services, SA, and Dir, Highline Leasing Ltd, 1985–94; Bd Dir, Extel Corp., Chicago, 1973–80; Dir, Transtel Communications Ltd, Slough, 1974–83. Vice-Chm., Yorks, Nat. Trust, 1970–85. President: Nat. Council for the Conservation of Plants and Gardens, 1994– (Chm., 1988–94); N of England Horticultural Soc., 1984–86; Northern Horticultural Soc., 1986–96; Yorks Agricl Soc., 1995–96; Vice Pres., RHS, 1996. High Sheriff, 1978–79, DL 1981, N Yorks. VMH 1994. *Recreations:* gardening, music. *Address:* The Manor House, Marton Le Moor, Ripon, N Yorks HG4 5AT. *T:* (01423) 323315; Newby Hall Estate Office, Ripon, Yorkshire HG4 5AE. *T:* (01423) 322583. *Club:* White's.

See also Captain A. A. C. Farquharson of Invercauld.

COMRIE, Rear-Adm. (Alexander) Peter, CB 1982; defence equipment consultant; Director, A. Comrie & Sons Ltd, since 1983; *b* 27 March 1924; *s* of Robert Duncan Comrie and Phyllis Dorothy Comrie; *m* 1945, Madeleine Irene (*née* Bullock) (*d* 1983); one *s* one *d*. *Educ:* Sutton Valence Sch., Kent; County Technical Coll., Wednesbury, Staffs, and in the Royal Navy. Joined Royal Navy, 1945; served in cruisers, frigates, minesweepers and RN air stations; RCDS 1973; Captain HMS Daedalus, 1974; Director of Weapons Coordination and Acceptance (Naval), 1975; Deputy Controller Aircraft, MoD, 1978–81; Dir-Gen. Aircraft (Navy), 1981–83, retired. Vice Pres., IEE, 1988–91 (Mem. Council, 1981–84); Member: IEE Electronics Divisional Bd, 1976–77; IEE Qualifications Bd, 1981–88; Chairman: IEE International (formerly Overseas) Bd, 1988–91; Executive Gp Cttee 3, Engrg Council, 1986–94. FIET (FIEE 1975); FRAeS 1978; Eur Ing 1987. *Recreations:* sailing, swimming, DIY. *Club:* Royal Commonwealth Society.

COMYNS, Jacqueline Roberta; a District Judge (Magistrates' Courts) (formerly a Metropolitan Stipendiary Magistrate), since 1982; *b* 27 April 1943; *d* of late Jack and Belle Fisher; *m* 1963, Malcolm John Comyns, medical practitioner; one *s*. *Educ:* Hendon County Grammar Sch.; London Sch. of Econs and Pol Science (LLB Hons 1964). Called to the Bar, Inner Temple, 1969; practised on South Eastern Circuit; a Recorder, 1991–2002. *Recreations:* theatre, travel, swimming. *Address:* Thames Magistrates' Court, 58 Bow Road, E3 4DJ. *T:* (020) 8271 1222.

CONANT, Sir John (Ernest Michael), 2nd Bt *cr* 1954; farmer and landowner, since 1949; *b* 24 April 1923; *s* of Sir Roger Conant, 1st Bt, CVO, and Daphne, Lady Conant, *d* of A. E. Learoyd; *S* father, 1973; *m* 1st, 1950, Periwinkle Elizabeth (*d* 1985), *d* of late Dudley Thorp, Kimbolton, Hunts; two *s* two *d* (and one *s* decd); 2nd, 1992, Mrs Clare Attwater, *yr d* of W. E. Madden. *Educ:* Eton; Corpus Christi Coll., Cambridge (BA Agric). Served in Grenadier Guards, 1942–45; at CCC Cambridge, 1946–49. Farming in Rutland, 1950–; High Sheriff of Rutland, 1960. *Recreations:* fishing, shooting, tennis. *Heir:* *s* Simon Edward Christopher Conant, *b* 13 Oct. 1958. *Address:* Periwinkle Cottage, Lyndon, Oakham, Rutland LE15 8TU. *T:* (01572) 737275.

CONCANNON, Dr Harcourt Martin Grant; President, Pensions Appeal Tribunals for England and Wales, since 1998; *s* of Edwin Martin Joseph Concannon and Caroline Elizabeth Margaret Concannon (*née* Grant); *m* 1978, Elaine Baldwin; one *s* one *d*. *Educ:* University Coll. Sch.; University College London (LLB, LLM, PhD). Solicitor. Articled to Town Clerk, London Borough of Bexley, 1960–64; Lectr in Law, Nottingham Poly., 1964–68; Senior Lecturer: Sheffield City Poly., 1968–71; Univ. of Salford, 1972–93; Full-time Chm., Independent Tribunal Service, 1993–98. *Recreations:* languages, garden design, walking. *Address:* Pensions Appeal Tribunals, Procession House, 55 Ludgate Hill, EC4M 7JW.

CONDON, family name of **Baron Condon**.

CONDON, Baron *cr* 2001 (Life Peer), of Langton Green in the County of Kent; **Paul Leslie Condon,** Kt 1994; QPM 1989; DL; Commissioner, Metropolitan Police, 1993–2000; Chairman, Anti-Corruption and Security (formerly Anti-Corruption) Unit, International Cricket Council, since 2003 (Director, 2000–03); *m*; two *s* one *d*. *Educ:* St Peter's Coll., Oxford (Bramshill Scholar; MA; Hon. Fellow). Joined Metropolitan Police, 1967; Inspector, 1975–78; Chief Inspector, 1978–81; Superintendent, Bethnal Green, 1981–82; Staff Officer to Comr as Superintendent, then as Chief Superintendent, 1982–84; Asst Chief Constable, Kent Constabulary, 1984–87; Dep. Asst Comr, 1987–88, Asst Comr, 1988–89, Metropolitan Police; Chief Constable, Kent Constabulary, 1989–92. Pres., BSIA, 2003–06. Non-exec. Dir, Group 4 Securicor (formerly Securicor), 2000– (Dep. Chm., 2006–). CCMI (CIMgt 1991); FRSA 1992. DL Kent, 2001. *Address:* c/o Group 4 Securicor, The Manor, Manor Royal, Gatwick, W Sussex RH10 9UN.

CONDRY, Rev. Canon Dr Edward Francis; Canon Treasurer, Canterbury Cathedral, since 2002; *b* 25 April 1953; *s* of Roy and Muriel Condry; *m* 1977, Sarah Louise Long; two *s* two *d*. *Educ:* Latymer Upper Sch.; Univ. of E Anglia (BA 1974); Exeter Coll., Oxford (BLitt 1977); DPhil Oxon 1980; Lincoln Theol Coll.; Univ. of Nottingham (DipTh 1981); MBA Open Univ. 2002. Ordained deacon, 1982, priest, 1983; Asst Curate, Weston Favell, Northampton, 1982–85; Vicar, Bloxham with Milcombe and S Newington, 1985–93; Rector, Rugby Team Ministry, 1993–2002. *Recreations:* running, cycling, canoeing, rowing, walking, laughing at my own jokes, planning adventures. *Address:* 15 The Precincts, Canterbury, Kent CT1 2EL. *T:* (01227) 865228; *e-mail:* edwardc@canterbury-cathedral.org. *Club:* Canterbury Harriers.

CONGDON, David Leonard; Head of Campaigns and Policies (formerly Director of Public Affairs, then Head of External Relations), MENCAP, since 1998; *b* 16 Oct. 1949; *s* of Archibald George Congdon and late Marjorie Congdon; *m* 1972, Teresa Winifred Hill; one *d*. *Educ:* Alleyn's Sch.; Thames Polytechnic (BSc Hons Econ.). Graduate Systems Analyst, ICL, 1970; Philips Electronics: Systems Analyst, 1973–85; Computer Consultant, 1985–92. London Borough of Croydon: Councillor, 1976–92; Vice-Chm., Educn Cttee, 1979–83; Chm., Social Services, 1983–86, 1990–91; Dep. Leader, 1986–92; Chm., Finance Sub-Cttee. Vice-Chm., local Cons. Assocs, 1979–82. MP (C) Croydon North East, 1992–97; contested (C) Croydon Central, 1997, 2001. PPS to Minister of State for Social Security, 1995–97. Mem., Select Cttee on Health, 1992–95. Governor, Croydon Coll., 1979–92. *Recreations:* tennis, badminton, reading political biographies, listening to music; lapsed Fulham fan. *Address:* MENCAP, 123 Golden Lane, EC1Y 0RT.

CONGDON, Timothy George, CBE 1997; Chief Economist, Lombard Street Research, 2001–05 (Managing Director, 1989–2001); *b* 28 April 1951; *s* of D. G. Congdon and Olive Emma Congdon (*née* Good); *m* 1988, Dorianne Preston-Lowe; one *d*. *Educ:* Univ. of Oxford (BA 1st cl. Hons Mod. Hist. and Econs). MSI. On economics staff, The Times, 1973–76; Chief Economist, L. Messel & Co., 1976–86 (Partner, 1980–86); Chief London Economist, Shearson Lehman, 1986–88. Non-exec. Chm., SBW Insurance Research, 1994–97. Mem., Treasury Panel of Independent Forecasters, 1993–97. Hon. Prof., Cardiff Business Sch., 1990–2006; Vis. Prof., Sir John Cass Business Sch., City of London (formerly City Univ. Business Sch.), 1998–2004; Vis. Fellow, LSE, 2005–. Hon. Sec., Political Economy Club, 1999–. FRSA 1991; Fellow, Soc. of Business Economists, 2000. Hon. FIA 2002. *Publications:* Monetary Control in Britain, 1982; The Debt Threat, 1988; Reflections on Monetarism, 1992; Money and Asset Prices in Boom and Bust, 2005; Keynes, the Keynesians and Monetarism, 2007. *Recreations:* reading, walking, chess, opera. *Address:* Huntley Manor, Huntley, Glos GL19 3HQ. *Club:* Royal Automobile.

CONGLETON, 8th Baron *cr* 1841; **Christopher Patrick Parnell;** Bt 1766; *b* 11 March 1930; 3rd *s* of 6th Baron Congleton (*d* 1932) and Hon. Edith Mary Palmer Howard (MBE 1941) (she *m* 2nd, 1946, Flight Lieut A. E. R. Aldridge, who died 1950), *d* of late R. J. B. Howard and late Lady Strathcona and Mount Royal; *S* brother, 1967; *m* 1955, Anna Hedvig, *d* of G. A. Sommerfelt, Oslo, Norway; two *s* three *d*. *Educ:* Eton; New Coll., Oxford (MA). Mem., Salisbury and Wilton RDC, 1964–74; Vice-President: RDCA, 1973–74; Assoc. of District Councils, 1974–79. Chm., Salisbury and S Wilts Museum, 1972–77; Mem., Adv. Bd for Redundant Churches, 1981–87. President: Nat. Ski Fedn of GB, 1976–81; Ski Club of GB, 1991–97; Mem., Eligibility Cttee, Internat. Ski Fedn, 1976–88. Trustee: Sandroyd Sch. Trust, 1975–92 (Chm., 1980–84); Wessex Med. Trust, 1984–90 (Chm., 1996–2000); Southampton Univ. Develt Trust, 1986–95. Hon. LLD Southampton, 1990. *Recreations:* music, fishing. *Heir:* *s* Hon. John Patrick Christian Parnell [*b* 17 March 1959; *m* 1985, Marjorie-Anne, *o d* of John Hobdell, Cobham, Surrey; two *s* one *d*]. *Address:* West End Lodge, Ebbesbourne Wake, Salisbury, Wilts SP5 5JR.

CONGO, Sonia, (Mrs C. W. Congo); *see* Lawson, S.

CONGREVE, Ambrose, CBE 1965; *b* London, 4 April 1907; *s* of John Congreve, DL, JP, and Lady (Helena Blanche) Irene Ponsonby, *d* of 8th Earl of Bessborough; *m* 1935, Marjorie (*d* 1995), *d* of Dr Arthur Graham Glasgow, London, and Richmond, Virginia, and Margaret, *d* of John P. Branch, President of Virginia's Merchants National Bank. *Educ:* Lockers Park; Eton; Trinity Coll., Cambridge. Employed by Unilever Ltd, in England and China, 1927–36; joined Humphreys & Glasgow Ltd (London), as Director, 1936; responsible for the company, 1939–83, in succession to Dr Glasgow who founded the firm in 1892. Served War of 1939–45: Air Intelligence, working for Plans and Bomber Command, then Min. of Supply under Sir Vyvyan Board. A Vice-Pres., RHS; First Patron, RHS Ireland; Patron, Tree Council of Southern Ireland. Hon. FIChemE 1967; Hon. Fellow, Royal Dublin Soc., 2003; Hon. Mem., An Taisce, Ireland, 2007. Hon. Dr Iur Dublin, 2002. Veitch Meml Medal, RHS, 1987; Gold Medal (for A Great Garden of the World), Botanic Gardens, Boston, Mass, 2001; Special Award, City of Waterford, 2006. *Recreation:* large-scale outdoor cultivation in Ireland of plant species and hybrids from all over the world, incl. Asiatic magnolias and camellias. *Address:* Mount Congreve, Waterford, Ireland. *T:* (51) 384103, *Fax:* (51) 384299; Warwick House, Stable Yard, St James's, SW1A 1BD. *T:* (020) 7839 3301, *Fax:* (020) 7839 2132. *Club:* Beefsteak.

CONINGSBY, His Honour Thomas Arthur Charles; QC 1986; a Circuit Judge, 1992–2006; Designated Civil Judge, 1999–2006; Vicar General of the Province of York, since 1980; *b* 21 April 1933; *s* of Francis Charles and Eilleen Rowena Coningsby; *m* 1959, Elaine Mary Coningsby; two *s* three *d*. *Educ:* Epsom; Queens' Coll., Cambridge (MA). Called to the Bar, Gray's Inn, 1957; Mem., Inner Temple, 1988. A Recorder, 1986–92; Head of Chambers, 3 Dr Johnson's Building, Temple, 1988–92; Dep. High Court Judge, 1992–2006; Liaison Judge, 1995–2005. Chancellor: Dio. of York, 1977–2006; Dio. of Peterborough, 1989–2006. Member: Lord Chancellor's Matrimonial Causes Rule Cttee, 1986–89; Gen. Council of the Bar, 1988–90; Supreme Court Procedure Cttee, 1988–92; Chm., Family Law Bar Assoc., 1988–90 (Sec., 1986–88); Pres., SE London Magistrates' Assoc., 1996–2006. Member, General Synod, 1970– (Member: Legal Adv. Commn, 1975–; Fees Adv. Commn, 1979–92). Mem. Governing Body, SPCK, 1990–92. *Recreation:* lawn tennis. *Address:* Leyfields, Chipstead, Surrey CR5 3SG. *T:* (01737) 553304. *Club:* Athenæum.

CONLAN, Bernard; engineer; *b* 24 Oct. 1923; *m*; one *d*. *Educ:* Manchester Primary and Secondary Schs. Mem., AEU (now AEEU), 1940–, Officer, 1943–87. City Councillor, Manchester, 1954–66. Joined Labour Party, 1942; contested (Lab) High Peak, 1959. MP (Lab) Gateshead East, 1964–87. A Vice-Chm., Parly Lab. Party Trade Union Gp, 1974–. Member: House of Commons Expenditure Cttee (from inception), 1971–79; Trade and Industry Select Cttee, 1983–86; Select Cttee on Defence, 1979–83. *Address:* 33 Beccles Road, Sale, Cheshire M33 3RP. *T:* (0161) 973 3991.

CONLEY, Rosemary Jean Neil, CBE 2004; DL; diet and fitness expert; Partner, Rosemary Conley Enterprises, since 1986; Co-Founder and Chairman: Rosemary Conley Diet and Fitness Clubs Ltd, since 1993; Quorn House Publishing Ltd, since 1995; Rosemary Conley Licences Ltd, since 2003; *b* 19 Dec. 1946; *d* of Oswald Neil Weston and Edith Cecilia Weston; *m* 1st, 1968, Philip Conley (marr. diss. 1983); one *d*; 2nd, 1986, Michael John Rimmington. *Educ:* Bushloe High Sch., Wigston. RSA Exercise to Music. Secretary, then founded own slimming club business, Slimming and Good Grooming, 1971; sold business to IPC Magazines, 1981; Man. Dir, Successful Slimming and Good Grooming Clubs Ltd, subsid. of IPC, 1981–85; (with Mike Rimmington): founded: Rosemary Conley Enterprises, 1986; Rosemary Conley Diet and Fitness Clubs Ltd, 1993; Rosemary Conley Diet and Fitness magazine, Quorn House Publishing Ltd, 1996–; launched online slimming programme, slimwithRosemary.com, 2003. Patron: Breast Cancer Campaign; Shaftesbury Soc.; Mildmay; Send a Cow; Laura Centre, Leicester; STEPS Conductive Educn Sch., Shepshed, Leics. DL Leics, 1999. Hon. Freeman, City of Leicester, 2001. *Publications:* Eat Yourself Slim, 1982; Eat and Stay Slim, 1983; Positive Living, 1984; Rosemary Conley's Hip and Thigh Diet, 1988, 2nd edn 1992; Rosemary Conley's Complete Hip and Thigh Diet, 1989, 2nd edn 2002; Looking Good, Feeling Great, 1989; Rosemary Conley's Inch Loss Plan, 1990, 2nd edn 1998; Whole Body

Programme, 1992; Rosemary Conley's Metabolism Booster Diet, 1991; (with Patricia Bourne) Rosemary Conley's New Hip and Thigh Diet Cookbook, 1993; Shape Up For Summer, 1993; Rosemary Conley's Flat Stomach Plan, 1994; Rosemary Conley's Beach Body Plan, 1994; Be Slim, Be Fit, 1995; Rosemary Conley's Complete Flat Stomach Plan, 1996, 2nd edn 2002; Rosemary Conley's New Body Plan, 1997, 2nd edn 2002; Rosemary Conley's Low Fat Cookbook, 1999; Rosemary Conley's Low Fat Cookbook 2, 2000; Rosemary Conley's Red Wine Diet, 2000; Eat Yourself Slim, 2001; Rosemary Conley's GI Jeans Diet, 2006; Rosemary Conley's Ultimate GI Jeans Diet, 2007; GI Hip and Thigh Diet, 2008; presented over 29 fitness videos. *Recreations:* ski-ing, ice skating, walking our dogs, home making, cooking, flower arranging, writing, speaking about and sharing my Christian testimony. *Address:* Quorn House, Meeting Street, Quorn, Leics LE12 8EX. *T:* (01509) 620222, *Fax:* (01509) 621046; *e-mail:* rosemary@rosemaryconley.com.

CONLON, Michael Anthony; QC 2002; *b* 26 Nov. 1951; *s* of Thomas Reginald Conlon and Barbara (*née* Capper); *m* 1974, Pamela Carter; one *s* one *d. Educ:* Enfield Grammar Sch.; Queens' Coll., Cambridge (BA 1973, MA 1977). Called to the Bar, Inner Temple, 1974; in practice at the Bar, 1974–76; government lawyer, 1976–86; tax partner in accounting firms, 1986–91; solicitor, 1992–97; Partner, Allen & Overy, 1993–97; returned to the Bar, 1997. Mem., Tax Law Rev. Cttee, 1994–. Nat. Pres., VAT Practitioners Gp, 1998–; Pres., Inst. of Indirect Taxation, 1999– (Fellow, 1998). FTII 1997; Fellow, Soc. of Advanced Legal Studies, 1999. Liveryman: Co. of Tax Advisers, 2006– (Mem. Court of Assts, 1999–); Co. of Spectacle Makers, 2006–. Exec. Ed., VAT Intelligence, 1993–2006; Member Editorial Board: De Voil Indirect Tax Service, 1999–; Tax Jl, 2000–. *Publications:* numerous technical articles. *Recreations:* art, music, literature, badminton. *Address:* Pump Court Tax Chambers, 16 Bedford Row, WC1R 4EB. *T:* (020) 7414 8080, *Fax:* (020) 7414 8099; *e-mail:* clerks@pumptax.com.

CONN, Edward, CBE 1979; FRCVS; Technical Consultant, Norbrook Laboratories Ltd, Newry, Northern Ireland, 1983–90, retired; *b* 25 March 1918; *s* of late Edward and Elizabeth Conn; *m* 1st, 1943, Kathleen Victoria Sandford (*d* 1974); three *d;* 2nd, 1975, Lilian Frances Miley. *Educ:* Coleraine Academical Instn; Royal (Dick) Veterinary Sch., Edinburgh Univ. Qual. Vet. Surgeon, 1940; Diploma; MRCVS 1940; FRCVS 1984. Gen. practice, Coleraine, 1940–43; Chief Vet. Officer, Hampshire Cattle Breeders, 1943–47; Dept of Agriculture, NI, 1947–83, Chief Vet. Officer, 1958–83. Pres., Coleraine Old Boys Assoc., 1979–80 (Pres., Belfast Br., 1991–92). Governor, Coleraine Academical Instn, 1972–. *Recreations:* golf, walking; watching all sports, particularly Rugby and athletics. *Address:* Ardeena, 23 The Brae, Groomsport, Co. Down BT19 2JQ. *Clubs:* Clandeboye Golf; Bangor Rugby and Athletic (Pres., 1974–75).

CONNAGHAN, John; Director of Delivery, Scottish Government (formerly Scottish Executive), since 2004; *b* Glasgow, 2 Sept. 1954; *s* of John Connaghan and Mary Connaghan; *m* 1983, Evelyn Joyce Steven; three *s* one *d. Educ:* Glasgow Caledonian Univ. (BA Business Studies 1976); Univ. of Strathclyde (DMS 1980; MBA 1984). Gen. Manager, Charles Letts & Co. Ltd, 1979–87; Chief Executive: Victoria Infirmary NHS Trust, 1987–94; Western General NHS Trust, 1995–2000; Fife Acute Hosps Trust, 2000–04. Dir, OPEX Ltd, 1998–. Dir, Maggie's Centres, 1994–2005. Mem., Scotch Malt Whisky Soc. *Recreations:* golf, walking, hockey (current Scottish Veterans' Internat. Team), fine wine. *Address:* 54A St Albans Road, Edinburgh EH9 2LX. *T:* 07836 704107; *e-mail:* connaghan2000@yahoo.com. *Clubs:* Blairgowrie Golf, Prestonfield Golf; Waverley & Inveresk Hockey.

CONNAL, (Robert) Craig; QC (Scot.) 2002; Partner, since 1980, Senior Litigation Partner and Head of Advocacy, since 2007, McGrigors (formerly McGrigor Donald) (Head, Commercial Litigation, 2002–07); *b* 7 July 1954; *s* of James Brownlee Connal and Jean Elizabeth Polley or Connal; *m* 1976, Mary Ferguson Bowie; two *d. Educ:* Hamilton Acad.; Glasgow Univ. (LLB 1st Cl. Hons). Admitted Solicitor, Scotland, 1977, England and Wales, 2006; Solicitor Advocate: (civil), 1996, (criminal), 2004, Scotland; (all courts), England and Wales, 2006. Ext. Examr in Law, Dept of Land Econ., Aberdeen Univ., 2001–05. Mem., Wkg Party on Partnership Law, Scottish Law Commn, 2000–03. Member Council: Royal Faculty of Procurators in Glasgow, 1995–98; SSC, 1999–. Convenor, Rights of Audience Course (Civil), Law Soc. of Scotland, 2004–. *Publications:* (contrib.) Stair Memorial Encyclopaedia of Scots Law, 1986; contrib. articles to learned jls incl. Jl Law Soc. of Scotland, Jl Planning & Envmtl Law, Estates Gazette, Scottish Planning and Envmt Law; contribs to general press. *Recreations:* Rugby referee, food and wine, gardens (but not gardening). *Address:* McGrigors, Pacific House, 70 Wellington Street, Glasgow G2 6SB. *T:* (0141) 248 6677, *Fax:* (0141) 221 5178; *e-mail:* craig.connal@mcgrigors.com. *Club:* Whitecraigs Rugby.

CONNARTY, Michael; MP (Lab) Linlithgow and East Falkirk, since 2005 (Falkirk East, 1992–2005); *b* 3 Sept. 1947; *m* 1969, Margaret Doran; one *s* one *d. Educ:* St Patrick's High Sch., Coatbridge; Stirling and Glasgow Univs (Student Pres., Stirling Univ., 1970–71); Jordanhill Coll. of Educn (BA; DCE). Teacher of econs and modern studies (secondary and special needs), 1976–92. Exec. Mem., Central region, EIS, 1978–84 (Pres., 1982–83). Rector, Stirling Univ., 1983–84. Mem. (Lab) Stirling DC, 1977–90 (Leader of Council, 1980–90); Chm., Lab. Party Scottish Local Govt Cttee, 1988–90. Mem., Lab. Party Scottish Exec., 1981, 1983–92. Contested (Lab) Stirling, 1983, 1987. PPS to Minister of State for Film and Tourism, 1997–98. Member: Information Select Cttee, 1997–2001; European Scrutiny Select Cttee, 1998– (Chm., 2006–). Chairman: Parly Gp on Haemophilia, 2000–; Parly Jazz Appreciation Gp, 2001–; Vice-Chm., All Party Parly Gp on Pharmaceutical Industry; Secretary: Offshore Oil & Gas Industry Gp, 1998–; All Party Parly Gp on Nuclear Energy; Mem., All-Party Parly Gp on Chemical Industries (Treas., 1994–97; Chm., 1997–2000; Sec., 2000–06); Sec., PLP Sci. and Technol. Cttee, 1992–97; Co-ordinator, PLP Scottish Task Force, Skills and Trng, Youths and Students, 1994–97; Vice Chm., Scottish PLP Gp, 1996–98 (Chm., 1998–99). Mem. Bd, POST, 1997–. JP 1977–90. *Address:* House of Commons, SW1A 0AA.

CONNELL, His Eminence Cardinal Desmond, DD; Archbishop of Dublin, and Primate of Ireland, (RC), 1988–2004; *b* 24 March 1926; *s* of John Connell and Maisie Connell (*née* Lacy). *Educ:* St Peter's National School, Phibsborough; Belvedere College; Clonliffe College; University Coll., Dublin (MA); St Patrick's Coll., Maynooth; Louvain Univ., Belgium (DPhil); DLitt NUI, 1981. University College, Dublin: Dept of Metaphysics, 1953–72; Prof. of General Metaphysics, 1972–88; Dean, Faculty of Philosophy and Sociology, 1983–88. Chaplain: Poor Clares, Donnybrook, 1953–55; Carmelites, Drumcondra, 1955–66; Carmelites, Blackrock, 1966–88. Prelate of Honour, 1984; Cardinal, 2001. *Publications:* The Vision in God, 1967; articles in reviews. *Address:* 29 Iona Road, Drumcondra, Dublin 9, Ireland. *T:* (1) 83004388.

CONNELL, George Edward, OC 1987; PhD; FCIC; FRSC; President, University of Toronto, 1984–90; *b* 20 June 1930; *m* 1955, Sheila Horan; two *s* two *d. Educ:* Univ. of Toronto (BA, PhD Biochemistry). FCIC 1971; FRSC 1975. Post-doctoral Fellow, Div. of Applied Biol., National Res. Council, Ottawa, Ont, 1955–56; Fellow, National Science Foundn (US), Dept of Biochem., New York University Coll. of Medicine, 1956–57; University of Toronto: Asst Prof. of Biochem., 1957–62; Associate Prof. of

Biochem., 1962–65; Prof. and Chm. Dept of Biochem., 1965–70; Associate Dean, Faculty of Med., 1972–74; Vice-Pres., Res. and Planning, 1974–77; Pres. and Vice-Chancellor, Univ. of Western Ontario, 1977–84. Prin. Advr, Commn of Enquiry on Blood System of Canada, 1993–95; Sen. Policy Advr, Canada Foundn for Innovation, 1997; Mem., Res. Adv. Panel, Walkerton Inquiry, 2000–01. Chairman: Exec. Cttee, Internat. Congress of Biochem., 1979; Nat. Round Table on the Envmt and Economy, 1991–95; Technical Cttee 207 (Envmtl Management), ISO, 1993–96; Task Force on Funding and Delivery of Med. Care in Ontario, 1995–96; Canadian Prostate Cancer Res. Initiative, 2000–; Vice-Chairman: Envmtl Assessment Bd, Ontario, 1990–93; Sustainable Cities Foundn, 1993–98; Protein Engrg Nat. Centre of Excellence, 1995–97; Mem. Bd of Dirs, Lake Simcoe Region Conservation Foundn, 2001–. Member: MRC of Canada, 1966–70; Ont Council of Health, 1978–84; Bd of Dirs and Nat. Exec. Cttee, Canadian Arthritis and Rheumatism Soc., 1965–75; Bd of Dirs, Nat. Inst. of Nutrition, 1984–91; Bd of Res. Inst., Toronto Hosp., 1994–96; Council, Ont Univs, 1977–90 (Chm., 1981–83); Bd of Governors, Upper Canada Coll., 1982–90; Bd of Trustees, Royal Ont Mus., 1984–90; Trustee, R. Samuel McLaughlin Foundn, 1996–2001. Mem., Ontario Press Council, 1996–. Member, Board of Directors: Southam Inc., 1985–93; Allelix Biopharmaceuticals Inc., 1995–99. Hon. LLD: Trent, 1984; Univ. of Western Ont, 1985; McGill, 1987; Hon. DSc Toronto, 1993. *Publications:* scientific papers in jls incl. Canadian Jl of Biochem., Biochemical Jl (UK), and Jl of Immunol. *Recreations:* ski-ing, tennis, wilderness canoe trips. *Address:* 904–130 Carlton Street, Toronto, ON M5A 4K3, Canada; *e-mail:* george.connell@synpatico.ca. *Club:* Badminton and Racquet (Toronto).

CONNELL, Prof. John Jeffrey, CBE 1985; PhD; FRSE; FIFST; Director, Torry Research Station, Aberdeen (Ministry of Agriculture, Fisheries and Food), 1979–87 (Assistant Director, 1969–79); Emeritus Professor, Aberdeen University, 1987; *b* 2 July 1927; *s* of John Edward Connell and Margaret Connell; *m* 1950, Margaret Parsons; one *s* two *d* (and one *d* decd). *Educ:* Burnage High Sch.; Univ. of Manchester (BSc 1947); Univ. of Edinburgh (PhD 1950). FIFST 1970; FRSE 1984. Torry Research Station: Scientific Officer, 1950; Sen. Sci. Officer, 1955; Principal Sci. Officer, 1961; Dep. Chief Sci. Officer, 1979; Officer i/c Humber Lab., Hull (Sen. Principal Sci. Officer), 1968–69. Res. Associate, 1969–79 and Hon. Res. Lectr, 1979–83, Aberdeen Univ. Mem., Fisheries Res. and Develt Bd, 1979–84. *Publications:* Control of Fish Quality, 1975, 4th edn 1995 (Spanish edn 1978); Trends in Fish Utilisation, 1982; scientific and technical papers related to use of fish as food. *Recreations:* music, hill walking. *Address:* 61 Burnieboozle Crescent, Aberdeen AB15 8NR. *T:* (01224) 315852.

CONNELL, John MacFarlane; Chairman, The Distillers Company plc, 1983–86; *b* 29 Dec. 1924; *s* of late John Maclean Connell and late Mollie Isobel MacFarlane; *m* 1949, Jean Matheson Sutherland Mackay, *d* of late Major George Sutherland Mackay and late Christine Bourne; two *s. Educ:* Stowe; Christ Church, Oxford. Joined Tanqueray, Gordon & Co. Ltd, 1946, Export Dir 1954, Man. Dir 1962–70; Dir, Distillers Co. Ltd, 1965, Mem., Management Cttee, 1971–86; Chm., United Glass Holdings plc, 1979–83. Chm., Gin Rectifiers and Distillers Assoc., 1968–71. Pres., Royal Warrant Holders Assoc., 1975. *Recreations:* golf, shooting, fishing. *Club:* Royal and Ancient (St Andrews).

CONNELL, Prof. John Muir Cochrane, MD; FRCPGlas, FMedSci; FRSE; Professor of Endocrinology, University of Glasgow, since 1995; *b* 10 Oct. 1954; *s* of William and Betty Connell; *m* 1978, Lesley Elizabeth Armstrong; three *s* one *d. Educ:* Speirs Sch., Beith, Ayrshire; Hutchesons' Grammar Sch., Glasgow; Univ. of Glasgow (MB ChB 1977; MD 1986). MRCP 1979; FRCPGlas 1989. Clin. Scientist, 1983–87, Sen. Clin. Scientist, 1987–94, MRC Blood Pressure Unit, Western Infirmary, Glasgow; MRC Travelling Fellow, Howard Florey Inst., Melbourne, 1986–87; Hon. Prof. in Medicine, Univ. of Glasgow, 1994–95. Sec., 2000–03, Treas., 2003–07, Assoc. of Physicians of GB and Ireland. Gov., Hutchesons' GS, 2001–04. FMedSci 1999; FRSE 2002. *Publications:* (contrib. with A. F. Dominiczak) Handbook of Hypertension, Vol. 44, 2007; contrib. learned articles on aspects of endocrinology and genetics of cardiovascular disease. *Recreations:* family, golf, travel. *Address:* BHF Glasgow Cardiovascular Research Centre, University of Glasgow, 126 University Place, Glasgow G12 8TA. *T:* (0141) 330 2228, *Fax:* (0141) 330 6997; *e-mail:* Jmcc1m@clinmed.gla.ac.uk. *Clubs:* Glasgow Golf; New Golf (St Andrews).

CONNELL, Margaret Mary, MA; Principal, Queen's College, London, since 1999; *b* 3 Jan. 1949; *d* of late Leo Connell and Margaret Isobel Connell. *Educ:* Lady Margaret Hall, Oxford (MA). Physics teacher, Headington Sch., Oxford, 1970–76; maths teacher, North London Collegiate Sch., 1976–86; Dep. Headmistress, Bromley High Sch. (GPDST), 1986–91; Headmistress, More House Sch., 1991–99. *Recreations:* music, travel, reading. *Address:* Apartment 8, 15 Sundridge Avenue, Bromley, Kent BR1 2PU. *T:* (020) 8460 1577. *Club:* University Women's.

CONNELL, Hon. Sir Michael (Bryan), Kt 1991; a Judge of the High Court of Justice, Family Division, 1991–2002; *b* 6 Aug. 1939; *s* of late Lorraine Connell and Joan Connell; *m* 1965, Anne Joan Pulham; three *s* one *d. Educ:* Harrow; Brasenose Coll., Oxford (MA Jurisprudence). Called to the Bar, Inner Temple, 1962, Bencher, 1988; QC 1981; a Recorder, 1980–91. Governor, Harrow Sch., 1983–2002 (Chm., 1997–2002). Mem., 1988–, Dep. Sen. Steward, 2004–, Jockey Club; Dir, Horseracing Regulatory Authy, 2006–07; Mem. Regulatory Cttee, British Horseracing Authy, 2007–. *Recreations:* steeplechasing, cricket, foxhunting. *Clubs:* Garrick, Buck's; MCC.
See also S. A. O'Sullivan.

CONNELL-SMITH, Prof. Gordon Edward, PhD; FRHistS; Professor of Contemporary History, University of Hull, 1973–85; *b* 23 Nov. 1917; 2nd *s* of George Frederick Smith and Margaret Smith (*née* Woolerton); surname changed to Connell-Smith by deed-poll, 1942; *m* 1954, Wendy Ann (*d* 1987), *o d* of John Bertram and Kathleen Tomlinson; one *s* one *d. Educ:* Richmond County Sch., Surrey; University Coll. of SW of England, Exeter (BA); Birkbeck Coll., London (PhD). FRHistS 1959. Served War, RA and Staff, 1940–46 (Staff Major). Julian Corbett Prize, Inst. of Historical Res., 1949; University of Hull: Staff Tutor/Lectr in Adult Educn and History Depts, 1952–63; Sen. Lectr, 1963–69; Reader in Contemp. Internat. History, 1969–73. Mem., Cttee of Management, Univ. of London Inst. of Latin Amer. Studies, 1973–85. Chm., Latin American Newsletters, Ltd, London, 1969–72. *Publications:* Forerunners of Drake, 1954; Pattern of the Post-War World, 1957; The Inter-American System, 1966 (Spanish edn 1971); (co-author) The Relevance of History, 1972; The United States and Latin America, 1974 (Spanish edn 1977); The Future of History, 1975; Latin American Relations with the World 1826–1976, 1976; contrib. to Bull. Inst. of Historical Res., Contemp. Rev., Econ. History Rev., Eng. Historical Rev., History, Internat. Affairs, Jl of Latin Amer. Studies, World Today, etc. *Recreations:* travel, sport. *Address:* 7 Braids Walk, Kirk Ella, Hull HU10 7PA. *T:* (01482) 652624.

CONNELLY, Brian Norman, OBE 2002; HM Diplomatic Service, retired; High Commissioner, Kingdom of Tonga, and Consul for Pacific Islands under American sovereignty South of the Equator, 1999–2001; *b* 25 Dec. 1941; *s* of late Bernard and Julia Murphy; *m* 1965, Theresa, (Terrie), Hughes; one *s* one *d. Educ:* Holycross Acad.,

Edinburgh. Joined FO, 1967; Budapest, 1969–71; Montevideo, 1971–74; FCO, 1974–76; Kuwait, 1976–80; Seoul, 1980–84; First Sec., FCO, 1984–86; First Sec. (Commercial), Dhaka, 1987–90; Adminr, Ascension Island, 1991–95; High Comr, Solomon Is, 1996–98. *Recreations:* golf, tennis, snorkelling. *Address:* 24 Latimer, Stony Stratford, Bucks MK11 1HY. *Club:* Royal Air Force.

CONNER, Rt Rev. David John; Dean of Windsor, since 1998; Register, Order of the Garter, since 1998; Domestic Chaplain to the Queen, since 1998; Bishop to the Forces, since 2001; *b* 6 April 1947; *s* of late William Ernest Conner and Joan Millington Conner; *m* 1969, Jayne Maria Evans; two *s*. *Educ:* Erith Grammar School; Exeter College, Oxford (Symes Exhibnr; MA); St Stephen's House, Oxford. Asst Chaplain, St Edward's School, Oxford, 1971–73, Chaplain, 1973–80; Team Vicar, Wolvercote with Summertown, Oxford, 1976–80; Senior Chaplain, Winchester College, 1980–86; Vicar, St Mary the Great with St Michael, Cambridge, 1987–94; RD of Cambridge, 1989–94; Bishop Suffragan of Lynn, 1994–98. Hon. Fellow, Girton Coll., Cambridge, 1995. Hon. Chaplain, The Pilgrims, 2002–. *Address:* The Deanery, Windsor Castle, Berks SL4 1NJ. *T:* (01753) 865561, *Fax:* (01753) 819002.

CONNERY, Sir Sean, Kt 2000; actor; *b* 25 Aug. 1930; *s* of Joseph and Euphamia Connery; named Thomas; adopted stage name of Sean, 1953; *m* 1st, 1962, Diane Cilento (marr. diss. 1974); one *s*; 2nd, 1975, Micheline Roquebrune; two step *s* one step *d*. Served Royal Navy. Has appeared in films: No Road Back, 1956; Action of the Tiger, 1957; Another Time, Another Place, 1957; Hell Drivers, 1958; Tarzan's Greatest Adventure, 1959; Darby O'Gill and the Little People, 1959; On the Fiddle, 1961; The Longest Day, 1962; The Frightened City, 1962; Woman of Straw, 1964; The Hill, 1965; A Fine Madness, 1966; Shalako, 1968; The Molly Maguires, 1968; The Red Tent (1st Russian co-production), 1969; The Anderson Tapes, 1970; The Offence, 1973; Zardoz, 1973; Ransom, 1974; Murder on the Orient Express, 1974; The Wind and the Lion, 1975; The Man Who Would Be King, 1975; Robin and Marian, 1976; The First Great Train Robbery, 1978; Cuba, 1978; Meteor, 1979; Outland, 1981; The Man with the Deadly Lens, 1982; Wrong is Right, 1982; Five Days One Summer, 1982; Highlander, 1986; The Name of the Rose, 1987 (BAFTA Award for Best Actor, 1988); The Untouchables, 1987 (Best Supporting Actor, Academy Awards, 1988; Golden Globe Award); The Presidio, 1989; Indiana Jones and the Last Crusade, 1989; Family Business, 1990; The Hunt for Red October, 1990; The Russia House, 1991; Highlander II–The Quickening, 1991; Medicine Man, 1992; Rising Sun, 1993; A Good Man in Africa, 1994; First Knight, 1995; Just Cause, 1995; The Rock, 1996; Dragonheart, 1996; The Avengers, 1998; Entrapment, 1999; Playing by Heart, 1999; Finding Forrester, 2001; League of Extraordinary Gentlemen, 2003; as James Bond: Dr No, 1963; From Russia With Love, 1964; Goldfinger, 1965; Thunderball, 1965; You Only Live Twice, 1967; Diamonds are Forever, 1971; Never Say Never Again, 1983. Producer, Art, Wyndhams, 1996 (Tony Award, 1998). FRSAMD 1984. Fellow, BAFTA, 1998. Freedom of City of Edinburgh, 1991. Hon. DLitt: Heriot-Watt, 1981; St Andrews, 1988. BAFTA Life Time Achievement Award, 1990; Man of Culture Award, 1990; Scot of the Year Award, BBC Scotland, 1991; American Cinematique Award, 1992; Rudolph Valentino Award, 1992; Nat. Board of Review Award, 1994; Golden Globe Cecil B. De Mille Award, 1996; Lifetime Achievement Award, European Film Awards, 2005. Commander, Order of Arts and Literature (France), 1987; Légion d'Honneur. *Publication:* (with Murray Grigor) Being A Scot, 2008. *Recreations:* golf, tennis, reading.

CONNING, David Michael, OBE 1994; FRCPath; FIBiol; Director-General, British Nutrition Foundation, 1985–94; *b* 27 Aug. 1932; *s* of Walter Henry Conning and Phyllis Elsie Conning (*née* Lovell); *m* 1st, 1956, Betty Sleightholme (marr. diss. 1991); three *s* one *d*; 2nd, 1991, Lesley Myra Yeomans (*née* Beresford). *Educ:* Dame Allan's Boys' Sch., Newcastle upon Tyne; Med. Sch., King's Coll., Univ. of Durham (MB, BS). FRCPath 1982; FIBiol 1984; FIFST 1988. RAMC, 1956–59. SMO Pathology, Middlesbrough Gen. Hosp., 1959–61; Lectr in Pathology, Royal Victoria Infirmary, 1961–65; Hon. Consultant Pathologist, Newcastle and Dist Hosps, 1963–65; Dep. Dir, Central Toxicol. Lab., ICI plc, 1966–78; Dir, BIBRA, 1978–85. Chm., Brit. Toxicol Soc., 1981. Hon. Mem., European Toxicol Soc. (Pres., 1983–86). Hon. Prof. of Toxicology, Surrey Univ., 1977–86. *Publications:* Toxic Hazards in Foods, 1983; Experimental Toxicology, 1988, 2nd edn 1993; contrib. book chapters and articles in jls of toxicol. and nutrition. *Recreation:* mending things. *Address:* Blacksmith's Cottage, Totnor, Brockhampton, Hereford HR1 4TJ. *T:* (01989) 740303.

CONNOCK, Alexander; Co-Founder and Chief Executive, Ten Alps plc, factual media company, since 1999; *b* June 1965; *s* of Michael and Caroline Connock; *m* 1998, Sumitra; one *d*. *Educ:* Manchester Grammar Sch.; St John's Coll., Oxford (BA Hons Politics and Econs); Columbia Univ. (MA Journalism); INSEAD (MBA). Researcher, Granada TV, 1989–90; asst producer, BBC, 1990–92; Planet TV: producer: The Word, 1992–93; The Big Breakfast, 1993–96; Man. Dir, Planet TV Radio, 1996–99. Mem., RTS 2007. *Recreations:* orienteering, piano, photography, Lake District. *Address:* c/o Ten Alps plc, 9 Savoy Street, WC2E 7HR. *T:* (020) 7878 2311; *e-mail:* moira@tenalps.com. *Clubs:* Groucho, Soho House.

CONNOLLY, Billy, CBE 2003; stand-up comedian, actor; *b* 24 Nov. 1942; *m* 1st, Iris (marr. diss. 1985); one *s* one *d*; 2nd, 1990, Pamela Stephenson; three *d*. Welder, Clyde shipyards; (with Gerry Rafferty) formed folk duo, Humblebums; first solo concert, 1971; *theatre* includes: writer, The Red Runner, Edinburgh, 1979; performer: Die Fledermaus, Scottish Opera, 1978; The Pick of Billy Connolly, Cambridge, 1981; The Beastly Beatitudes of Balthazar B, Duke of York's, 1982; one-man show, London Palladium, 1985; Rebel Without a Clue, world tour, 1987; Billy Connolly Live In New York, 2005; Was it Something I Said?, world tour, 2006–07; *films* include: Big Banana Feet; Absolution, 1979; Bullshot, 1984; Water, 1985; The Big Man, 1990; Muppet Treasure Island, 1996; Mrs Brown, Ship of Fools, Paws, 1997; Still Crazy, The Changeling, Boon Dock Saints, 1998; The Debt Collector, The Imposters, 1999; Beautiful Joe, 2000; An Everlasting Piece, Gabriel and Me, 2001; The Man Who Sued God, Timeline, 2003; The Last Samurai, Lemony Snicket's A Series of Unfortunate Events, 2004; Fido, Open Season, Garfield 2, 2006; The X-Files: I Want to Believe, 2008; *television* includes: Head of the Class (series, USA), 1990–92; Billy (series, USA), 1992; Billy Connolly's World Tour of Scotland (series), 1994; A Scot in the Arctic, 1995; Billy Connolly's World Tour of Australia (series), 1996; Erect for 30 Years, 1998; Gentlemen's Relish, 2000; Billy Connolly's World Tour of England, Ireland and Wales, 2002; Billy Connolly's World Tour of New Zealand (series), 2004; presenter, The Bigger Picture, 1994; *plays:* Androcles and the Lion, 1984; Down Among the Big Boys, 1993; Deacon Brodie, 1997. Numerous recordings. *Publications:* Gullible's Travels, 1982; Billy Connolly's World Tour of Australia, 1996. *Address:* c/o Tickety-boo Ltd, 2 Triq Il-Barriera, Balzan BZN 06, Malta. *T:* 21556166.

CONNOLLY, Edward Thomas; Regional Chairman of Industrial Tribunals, Manchester, 1988–98; *b* 5 Sept. 1935; *s* of Edward Connolly and Alice Joyce; *m* 1962, Dr Pamela Marie Hagan; one *s* one *d*. *Educ:* St Mary's Coll., Crosby; Prior Park Coll.; Liverpool Univ. (LLB). Qualified as solicitor, 1960. Asst Solicitor, Lancs CC, 1960–63 Asst Prosecuting Solicitor, Liverpool City Council, 1963–65; Dep. Chief Legal Officer Skelmersdale Develt Corp., 1965–68; Asst Clerk of the Peace, Lancs CC, 1968–71; Dep Circuit Administrator, Northern Circuit, 1971–76; Chm. of Industrial Tribunals 1976–88.

CONNOLLY, John Patrick, FCA; Chief Executive and Senior Partner, Deloitte, since 1999; Global Managing Director, Deloitte Touche Tohmatsu, since 2003; *b* 29 Aug. 1950; *s* of John Connolly and Mary Connolly (*née* Morrison); *m* 1992, Odile Lesley Griffith; one *s* one *d* (and one *s* decd) from former marriage. *Educ:* St Bede's Coll., Manchester. FCA 1971. Partner: Mann Judd, Chartered Accountants, 1977; Touche Ross, 1980: Regl Partner i/c North, 1983–87; Managing Partner: Regl Offices, 1987–90; London and South, 1990–95; Managing Partner, Deloitte & Touche, 1995–99. *Recreations:* opera, horseracing, country pursuits, wine, sport. *Address:* Deloitte, Stonecutter Court, 1 Stonecutter Street, EC1A 4TR. *T:* (020) 7936 3000.

CONNOLLY, Joseph; novelist and author; *b* 23 March 1950; *s* of Joseph and Lena Connolly; *m* 1970, Patricia Quinn; one *s* one *d*. *Educ:* Oratory Sch. Apprentice, then Ed., Hutchinson Publishers, 1969–71; owner, Flask Bookshop, Hampstead, 1975–88; columnist, The Times, 1984–88; regular contributor, The Times, Daily Telegraph and other nat. newspapers, 1984–; occasional writer, Spectator, Independent and others. Founder Mem., Useless Inf. Soc., 1994–. Member: Soc. of Authors; RSL. Hon. Life Mem., Wodehouse Soc. *Publications:* Collecting Modern First Editions, 1977; P. G. Wodehouse: an illustrated biography, 1979; Jerome K. Jerome: a critical biography, 1981; Modern First Editions: their value to collectors, 1984; The Penguin Book Quiz Book, 1985; Children's Modern First Editions, 1988; Beside the Seaside, 1999; All Shook Up: a flash of the Fifties, 2000; Christmas and How to Survive It, 2003; Wodehouse, 2004; Faber and Faber: 80 years of book design, 2009; *novels:* Poor Souls, 1995; This Is It, 1996; Stuff, 1997; Summer Things, 1998 (filmed as Embrassez qui vous voudrez, and, in English, as Summer Things, 2002); Winter Breaks, 1999; It Can't Go On, 2000; SOS, 2001; The Works, 2003; Love is Strange, 2005; Jack the Lad and Bloody Mary, 2007; Boys and Girls, 2009; *contributor:* Jerome K. Jerome: my life and times, 1992; Booker 30: a celebration of 30 years of the Booker Prize for Fiction 1969–1998, 1998; British Greats, 2000; The Book of Useless Information, 2002; The Man Booker Prize: 35 years of the best in contemporary fiction 1969–2003, 2003; British Comedy Greats, 2003; Icons in the Fire: the decline and fall of almost everybody in the British film industry 1984–2000, by Alexander Walker, 2004; Private Passions, by Michael Berkeley, 2005; Folio 60: a bibliography of the Folio Society 1947–2006, 2007; A Hedonist's Guide to Life, 2007. *Recreations:* books, Times crossword, wine, lunching and loafing. *Address:* c/o A. M. Heath & Company Ltd, 6 Warwick Court, WC1R 5DJ. *T:* (020) 7242 2811, *Fax:* (020) 7242 2711; *e-mail:* evan.thorneycroft@amheath.com. *Clubs:* Chelsea Arts, Groucho.

CONNOLLY, Sarah Patricia; opera singer; mezzo-soprano; *b* 13 June 1963; *d* of Gerald J. I. Connolly and Jane Connolly (*née* Widdowson); *m* Carl Randolph Talbot; one *d*. *Educ:* Raventhorpe Sch., Darlington; Queen Margaret's Sch., Escrick; Royal Coll. of Music (Dip RCM Piano; Dip RCM Singing). Rôles include: English National Opera: Dido in The Trojans, 2004; Sesto in La clemenza di Tito, 2005; title rôle in Agrippina, 2007; title rôle in Giulio Cesare, Glyndebourne, 2005; début, Metropolitan Opera, as Annio in La clemenza di Tito; début, La Scala, Milan as Dido; Octavian in Der Rosenkavalier, Scottish Opera, 2006; concert appearances include: Salzburg Fest., Tanglewood Fest., Vienna Konzerthaus, Berlin Philharmonie, Zanket Hall, NY and Concertgebouw, Amsterdam. *Recreations:* reading, teaching, cooking, gardening. *Address:* c/o Askonas Holt Ltd, Lincoln House, 300 High Holborn, WC1V 7JH; *e-mail:* keiron.cooke@askonasholt.co.uk.

CONNOR, Bishop of, since 2007; **Rt Rev. Alan Francis Abernethy;** *b* 12 April 1957; *s* of Walter Abernethy and Margaret (*née* Sloan); *m* 1983, Liz Forster; one *s* one *d*. *Educ:* Harding Meml Primary, Belfast; Grosvenor High Sch., Belfast; Queen's Univ., Belfast (BA 1978; BD 1989); Trinity Coll., Dublin (DipTh 1981). Ordained deacon, 1981, priest, 1982; Assistant Curate: St Elizabeth's, Dundonald, 1981–84; Lecale Gp of Parishes, 1984–87; Officiating Chaplain, RAF Bishopscourt, 1984–87; Rector: St John's, Helen's Bay, 1987–90; St Columbanus, Ballyholme, 1990–2007. Canon, Down Cath., 2000–07. Religious Advr, Downtown Radio, 1985–90. *Publication:* Fulfilment and Frustration, 2002. *Recreations:* tennis, cycling, family holidays, reading, cooking. *Address:* Bishop's House, 113 Upper Road, Greenisland, Carrickfergus, Co. Antrim BT38 8RR. *T:* (home) (028) 9086 3165, (office) (028) 9032 3188, *Fax:* (028) 9023 7802; *e-mail:* bishop@connor.anglican.org.

CONNOR, Rt Rev. George Howard Douglas; *see* Dunedin, Bishop of.

CONNOR, Prof. James Michael, MD, DSc; FRCPGlas, FRCPE; Burton Professor of Medical Genetics, Glasgow University, since 1987; *b* 18 June 1951; *s* of James Connor and Mona Connor (*née* Hall); *m* 1979, Dr Rachel Alyson Clare Brooks; two *d*. *Educ:* Liverpool Univ. (BSc (Hons); MB ChB (Hons); MD; DSc). MRCP 1977; FRCPGlas 1988; FRCPE 1990. Gen. med. professional trng in various Liverpool hosps, 1975–77; Resident in Internal Medicine, Johns Hopkins Hosp., Baltimore, 1977–78; Univ. Res. Fellow, Dept of Medicine, Liverpool Univ., 1978–81; Instr in Med. Genetics, John Hopkins Hosp., 1981–82; Cons. in Med. Genetics, 1982–84, Wellcome Trust Sen. Lectr in Med. Genetics, 1984–87, Duncan Guthrie Inst. of Med. Genetics, Glasgow. *Publications:* Essential Medical Genetics, 1984, 6th edn 2008; Prenatal Diagnosis in Obstetric Practice, 1989, 2nd edn 1995; (ed jtly) Emery and Rimoin's Principles and Practice of Medical Genetics, 3rd edn 1996 to 5th edn 2007; articles on pathophysiology and prevention of genetic disease. *Recreations:* mountain biking, cycle touring, sea kayaking.

CONNOR, His Honour Jeremy George; a Circuit Judge, 1996–2004; *b* 14 Dec. 1938; *s* of Joseph Connor and Mabel Emmeline (*née* Adams), ARCA. *Educ:* Beaumont; University Coll., London (LLB; DRS); Heythrop Coll., Univ. of London (MA 2005). Called to the Bar, Middle Temple, 1961, Bencher, 2003; S Eastern Circuit. Apptd to Treasury List, Central Criminal Court, 1973; Metropolitan Stipendiary Magistrate, 1979–96; a Recorder, 1986–96; a Chm., Inner London Youth Cts (formerly Juvenile Cts), 1980–96; Chairman: Family Proceedings Court, 1991–94; Inner London and City Probation Cttee, 1989–96; Member: Exec. Cttee, Central Council of Probation for England and Wales, 1982–89; Parole Bd, 1998–2004; Lord Chancellor's Adv. Cttee on Legal Educn and Conduct, 1996–99. Referee, Mental Health Foundn, 1993–2004. Mem., Judicial Studies Bd, 1990–95. Pres., British Acad. of Forensic Scis, 1989–90 (Chm., Exec. Council, 1983–86; Mem. Council, 1982–93); Chm., Inst. for Study of Treatment of Delinquency, 1992–93. Trustee: Grubb Inst. of Social Studies, 1995–2004; Stapleford Trust for Drug Treatment and Res., 1995–98; London Action Trust, 1996–2005; Assoc. of Blind Catholics, 1996–2004; Rainer Foundn, 1997–98 (Mem. Council, 1996–97); New Lease Trust, 1997–99; Royal Philanthropic Soc., 1998–99. Vice-Patron, Blind in Business, 1999–. Fellow, Soc. of Advanced Legal Studies, 1999. Freeman, City of London, 1980; Liveryman, Fanmakers' Co., 1981 (Mem., Livery Cttee, 1987–90; Master, 2007–08). *Publications:* chapter in Archbold, Criminal Pleading, Evidence and Practice,

38th and 39th edns. *Recreations:* travel, theatre, occasional broadcasting. *Clubs:* Garrick, Royal Society of Medicine.

CONNOR, Michael Henry; HM Diplomatic Service, retired; Director of Trade Promotion, and Commercial Counsellor, Madrid, 1995–2000; *b* 5 Aug. 1942; *s* of late Henry Connor and Agnes Cecilia Connor (*née* Lindsey); *m* 1964, Valerie Jannita Cunningham; three *s. Educ:* St John's Coll., Portsmouth. Joined HM Diplomatic Service, 1964; FO, 1964–68; Attaché, Cairo, 1968–70; Commercial Officer, Vienna, 1970–73; Second Sec. (Commercial/Aid), Kathmandu, 1973–76; FCO, 1976–81; First Sec., 1979; Havana: First Sec. (Commercial) and Consul, 1981–82; First Sec. and Hd of Chancery, 1982–83; Hd of Chancery, Ottawa, 1983–88; First Sec., FCO, 1988–91; Ambassador, El Salvador, 1991–95. *Recreations:* swimming, photography, trekking, theatre.

CONNOR, His Honour Roger David; DL; a Circuit Judge, 1991–2005; *b* 8 June 1939; *s* of Thomas Bernard Connor and Susie Violet Connor (*née* Spittlehouse); *m* 1967, Sandra Home Holmes; two *s. Educ:* Merchant Taylors' School; Brunel College of Advanced Science and Technology; The College of Law. Solicitor; articled to J. R. Hodder, 1963–68; Asst Solicitor, 1968–70; Partner, Hodders, 1970–83; Metropolitan Stipendiary Magistrate, 1983–91; a Recorder, 1987–91. DL Bucks, 2005. *Recreations:* music, golf, gardening. *Address:* Bourn's Meadow, Little Missenden, Amersham, Bucks HP7 0RF. *Club:* Beaconsfield Golf.

CONNOR, Sir William Joseph, (Sir Bill), Kt 2003; General Secretary, Union of Shop Distributive and Allied Workers, 1997–2004; *b* 21 May 1941; *s* of William and Mary Connor; *m* 1962, Carol Ann Beattie; one *s* one *d.* Union of Shop Distributive and Allied Workers: Area Organiser, 1971–78; Nat. Officer, 1978–89; Dep. Gen. Sec., 1989–97. Member: TUC Gen. Council and Exec. Cttee, 1997–2004; Partnership Fund Assessment Panel, 1998–2004; Central Arbitration Cttee, 2000–. Dir, Unity Bank, 1997–2004. Chairman: Nat. Register of Hypnotherapists and Psychotherapists, 2004–; Supervisory Bd, Union Modernisation Fund, 2005–. *Recreations:* music, reading, computers. *Address:* 25 Abington Drive, Banks, Southport, Merseyside PR9 8FL.

CONNORS, James Scott, (Jimmy); tennis player; tennis commentator, CBS television; *b* 2 Sept. 1952; *s* of late James Scott Connors and of Gloria Thompson Connors; *m*; one *s. Educ:* Univ. of California at Los Angeles. Amateur tennis player, 1970–72, professional, 1972; major Championships won: Australia, 1974; Wimbledon, 1974, 1982; USA, 1974, 1976, 1978, 1982, 1983; South Africa, 1973, 1974; WCT, 1977, 1980; Grand Prix, 1978; played for USA, Davis Cup, 1976, 1981. Champions Tour, 1993–99. BBC Overseas Sports Personality, 1982.

CONOLLY, Mrs Yvonne Cecile; consultant in primary education; Head of Inspection and Monitoring, London Borough of Islington, 1995–99 (Senior Inspector for Primary Education, 1989–95); *b* 12 June 1939; *d* of Hugh Augustus and Blanche Foster; *m* 1965, Michael Patrick Conolly (marr. diss. 1996); one *d. Educ:* Westwood High Sch., Jamaica; Shortwood Coll., Jamaica (Teachers' CertEd); Polytechnic, N London (BEd Hons Primary Educn). Primary school teacher: Jamaica, 1960–63; London, 1963–68; Head Teacher, London, 1969–78; ILEA Inspector, Multi-ethnic Education, 1978–81; Inspector of Primary Schools, 1981–90, Dist Primary Inspector, 1988–90, ILEA. Member: Home Secretary's Adv. Council on Race Relations, 1977–86; IBA, 1982–86; Consumer Protection Adv. Cttee, 1974–75. Governor, former Centre for Information and Advice on Educnl Disadvantage, 1975–80; (first) Chm., Caribbean Teachers' Assoc., 1974–76. Registered Inspector, OFSTED, 1993–2000. Governor: Stroud Green Primary Sch., 1992–2004; Park View Community Coll. (formerly Langham Sch.), 1997–2004. Chaplaincy Visitor, Whittington Hosp., 2007–. Mem., Soroptimist Internat. of Gtr London, 2001– (Hon. Sec., 2003–04; Pres., 2005–06). *Publications:* (contrib.) Mango Spice, book of 44 Caribbean songs for schools, 1981; (contrib.) Against the Tide—Black Experience in the ILEA, 1990. *Recreations:* special interest in the activities of ethnic minority groups; travelling, conversing.

CONOLLY-CAREW, family name of **Baron Carew.**

CONQUEST, (George) Robert (Acworth), CMG 1996; OBE 1955; writer; *b* 15 July 1917; *s* of late Robert Folger Westcott Conquest and Rosamund, *d* of H. A. Acworth, CIE; *m* 1st, 1942, Joan Watkins (marr. diss. 1948); two *s*; 2nd, 1948, Tatiana Mihailova (marr. diss. 1962); 3rd, 1964, Caroleen Macfarlane (marr. diss. 1978); 4th, 1979, Elizabeth, *d* of late Col Richard D. Neece, USAF. *Educ:* Winchester; Magdalen Coll., Oxford. MA Oxon 1972; DLitt 1975. Oxf. and Bucks LI, 1939–46; Foreign Service, 1946–56; Fellow, LSE, 1956–58; Vis. Poet, Univ. of Buffalo, 1959–60; Literary Editor, The Spectator, 1962–63; Fellow: Columbia Univ., 1964–65; Woodrow Wilson International Center, 1976–77; Hoover Instn, 1977–79 and 1981–; Distinguished Vis. Scholar, Heritage Foundn, 1980–81; Research Associate, Harvard Univ., 1982–83; Adjunct Fellow, Center for Strategic and Internat. Studies, 1983–. Jefferson Lecture in Humanities, 1993. FRSL 1972; Corresp. FBA 1994. Presidential Medal of Freedom (USA), 2005. *Publications:* Poems, 1955; A World of Difference, 1955; (ed) New Lines, 1956; Common Sense About Russia, 1960; Power and Policy in the USSR, 1961; Courage of Genius, 1962; Between Mars and Venus, 1962; (ed) New Lines II, 1963; (with Kingsley Amis) The Egyptologists, 1965; Russia after Khrushchev, 1965; The Great Terror, 1968; Arias from a Love Opera, 1969; The Nation Killers, 1970; Lenin, 1972; Kolyma, 1978; The Abomination of Moab, 1979; Present Danger, 1979; Forays, 1979; We and They, 1980; (with Jon Manchip White) What to do when the Russians Come, 1984; Inside Stalin's Secret Police, 1985; The Harvest of Sorrow, 1986; New and Collected Poems, 1988; Tyrants and Typewriters, 1989; Stalin and the Kirov Murder, 1989; The Great Terror Reassessed, 1990; Stalin: breaker of nations, 1991; Demons Don't, 1998; Reflections on a Ravaged Century, 1999; The Dragons of Expectation: reality and delusion in the course of history, 2005. *Address:* 52 Peter Coutts Circle, Stanford, CA 94305, USA. *Club:* Travellers.

CONRAD, Alan David; QC 1999; a Recorder, since 1997; *b* 10 Dec. 1953; *s* of Maurice and Peggy Conrad; *m* 1st, 1982, Andrea Williams (marr. diss. 1998); one *s* one *d*; 2nd, 2002, Julie Thompson. *Educ:* Bury Grammar Sch.; Brasenose Coll., Oxford (BA Hons Jurisp.). Called to the Bar, Middle Temple, 1976; Asst Recorder, 1993–97. *Recreations:* travel, reading, music, motor cars, food and drink, cricket. *Address:* Lincoln House Chambers, 1 Brazennose Street, Manchester M2 5EL. *T:* (0161) 832 5701. *Club:* Lancashire County Cricket.

CONRAD, Peter John; writer; Student, and Tutor in English Literature, Christ Church, Oxford, since 1973; *b* 11 Feb. 1948; *s* of Eric and Pearl Conrad. *Educ:* Hobart High Sch.; Univ. of Tasmania (BA); New Coll., Oxford (MA). Fellow, All Souls Coll., Oxford, 1970–73. Boyer Lectr, ABC, 2004. Hon. DLitt Tasmania, 1993. *Publications:* The Victorian Treasure-House, 1973; Romantic Opera and Literary Form, 1977; Shandyism, 1978; Imagining America, 1980; Television: the medium and its manners, 1982; The Art of the City: views and versions of New York, 1984; The Everyman History of English Literature, 1985; A Song of Love and Death: the meaning of opera, 1987; Down Home: revisiting Tasmania, 1988; Where I Fell to Earth, 1990; Underworld, 1992; Feasting with Panthers, 1994; To Be Continued, 1995; Modern Times, Modern Places, 1998; The Hitchcock Murders, 2000; Orson Welles: the stories of his life, 2003; At Home in Australia, 2003; Tales of Two Hemispheres, 2004; Creation: artists, gods and origins 2007. *Address:* Christ Church, Oxford OX1 1DP. *T:* (01865) 276194.

CONRAN, Elizabeth Margaret, OBE 1994; MA, FMA; Curator, The Bowes Museum, Barnard Castle, 1979–2001; *b* 5 May 1939; *d* of James Johnston and Elizabeth Russell Wilson; *m* 1970, George Loraine Conran (*d* 1986); one *d. Educ:* Falkirk High Sch.; Glasgow Univ. (MA). FMA 1969. Res. Asst, Dept of History of Fine Art, Glasgow Univ., 1959–60; Asst Curator, The Iveagh Bequest, Kenwood, 1960–63; Keeper of Paintings, City Art Galls, Manchester, 1963–74; Arts Adviser, Greater Manchester Council, 1974–79. FRSA 1987. *Publications:* exhibn catalogues; articles in art and museum jls. *Recreations:* gardens, ballet. *Address:* 31 Thorngate, Barnard Castle, Co. Durham DL12 8QB. *T:* and *Fax:* (01833) 631055.

CONRAN, Jasper Alexander Thirlby, OBE 2008; Designer (clothing, accessories and bridalwear, ceramics, crystal, furniture, theatre), Chairman and Chief Executive Officer, Jasper Conran Holdings Ltd; *b* 12 Dec. 1959; *s* of Sir Terence Conran, *qv* and Shirley Conran, *qv. Educ:* Bryanston School, Dorset; Parsons School of Art and Design, New York. First womenswear collection, 1978; menswear introd 1985; J by Jasper Conran collection at Debenhams, launched 1996. Costumes for: Anouilh's The Rehearsal, 1990 (Laurence Olivier Award, 1991); My Fair Lady, 1992; (also sets), Bintley's Tombeaux, Royal Opera House, 1993; Sleeping Beauty, Scottish Ballet, 1994; The Nutcracker Sweeties, 1996, Edward II, 1997, Arthur, 2000, Birmingham Royal Ballet. Vis. Prof., Univ. of the Arts London, 2007–. Trustee, Wallace Collection, 2007–. Gov., Bryanston Sch., 2007–. Hon. DLitt Heriot-Watt, 2004; Hon. DCL East Anglia, 2006. Fil d'Or (Internat. Linen Award), 1982 and 1983; British Fashion Council Designer of the Year Award, 1986–87; Fashion Group of America Award, 1987; British Collections Award, 1991; Prince's Medal, Homes and Gardens Classic Design Awards, 2003. *Address:* 1–7 Rostrevor Mews, Fulham, SW6 5AZ. *T:* (020) 7384 0800; *e-mail:* info@jasperconran.com.

CONRAN, Shirley Ida, OBE 2004; writer; Founder President, Work-Life Balance Trust (formerly Mothers in Management), 1998–2005; *b* 21 Sept. 1932; *d* of W. Thirlby Pearce and Ida Pearce; *m* 1955, Sir Terence Conran (marr. diss. 1962); two *s. Educ:* St Paul's Girls' Sch.; Southern College of Art, Portsmouth. Fabric Designer and Director of Conran Fabrics, 1956–62; Member, Selection Cttee, Design Centre, 1961–69. Journalist; (first) Woman's Editor, Observer Colour Magazine, 1964; Woman's Editor, Daily Mail, 1969; Life and Style Editor, Over 21, 1972–74. *Publications:* Superwoman, 1975, revd edn as Down with Superwoman, 1990; Superwoman Year Book, 1976; Superwoman in Action, 1977; (with E. Sidney) Futurewoman, 1979; The Magic Garden, 1983; The Amazing Umbrella Shop, 1990; *novels:* Lace, 1982; Lace 2, 1985; Savages, 1987; Crimson, 1991; Tiger Eyes, 1994; The Revenge, 1997. *Recreations:* reading, swimming, Yoga.

See also J. A. T. Conran.

CONRAN, Sir Terence (Orby), Kt 1983; Chairman: The Conran Shop Ltd, since 1976; Conran Ltd, since 1990; Conran Holdings Ltd, since 1993; Conran & Partners (formerly C. D. Partnership), since 1993; Conran Restaurants Ltd, since 1994; *b* 4 Oct. 1931; *m*; two *s*; *m* 1963, Caroline Herbert (marr. diss. 1996); two *s* one *d*; *m* 2000, Vicki Davis. *Educ:* Bryanston, Dorset. Chm., Conran Holdings Ltd, 1965–68; Jt Chm., Ryman Conran Ltd, 1968–71; Chairman: Habitat Group Ltd, 1971–88; RSCG Conran Design (formerly Conran Design Group/Conran Associates), 1971–92; Habitat France SA, 1973–88; Conran Stores Inc., 1977–88; J. Hepworth & Son Ltd, 1981–83 (Dir, 1979–83); Habitat Mothercare Ltd, 1982–88; Jasper Conran Ltd, 1982–; Heal & Sons Ltd, 1983–87; Richard Shops, 1983–87; Storehouse plc, 1986–90 (Chief Exec., 1986–88; non-exec. Dir, 1990); Butlers Wharf Ltd, 1984–90; Bibendum Restaurant Ltd, 1986–; Benchmark Woodworking Ltd, 1989–; Blue Print Café Ltd, 1989–; Conran Shop Holdings Ltd, 1990–; Le Pont de La Tour Ltd, 1991–; Conran Shop SA, 1991–; Butlers Wharf Chop House Ltd, 1993–; Quaglino's Restaurant Ltd, 1991–; Bluebird Store Ltd, 1994–; Mezzo Ltd, 1995–; Conran Shop Marylebone, 1995–; Gustavino's Inc., 1997–; Conran Collection Ltd, 1997–; Conran Shop Manhattan Inc., 1997–; Coq d'Argent Ltd, 1997–; Orrery Restaurant Ltd, 1997–; The Great Eastern Hotel Co. Ltd, 1997–; Sartoria Restaurant Ltd, 1997–; Zinc Bar & Grill Ltd, 1997–; Atlantic Blue SNC, 1998–; Conran Finance Ltd, 1998–; Almeida Restaurant Ltd, 2001–; Director: Conran Ink Ltd, 1969–; The Neal Street Restaurant, 1972–89; Conran Octopus, 1983–; BhS plc, 1986–88; Savacentre Ltd, 1986–88; Michelin House Investment Co. Ltd, 1989–; Vice-Pres., FNAC, 1985–89. Estabd Conran Foundn for Design Educn and Research, 1981–. Mem., Royal Commn on Environmental Pollution, 1973–76. Member: Council, RCA, 1978–81, 1986–; Adv. Council, V&A Mus., 1979–83; Trustee: V&A Museum, 1984–90; Internat. Design (formerly Design) Museum, 1989– (Chm., 1992). Gov., Bryanston Sch. RSA Presidential Medal for Design Management to Conran Group; RSA Presidential Award for Design Management to Habitat Designs Ltd, 1975; SIAD Medal, 1981; Assoc. for Business Sponsorship of the Arts and Daily Telegraph Award to Habitat Mothercare, 1982; RSA Bicentenary Medal, 1982; President's Award, D&AD, 1989. Hon. FRIBA 1984. Commandeur de l'Ordre des Arts et des Lettres (France), 1991. *Publications:* The House Book, 1974; The Kitchen Book, 1977; The Bedroom & Bathroom Book, 1978; (with Caroline Conran) The Cook Book, 1980, rev. edn as The Conran Cookbook, 1997; The New House Book, 1985; Conran Directory of Design, 1985; Plants at Home, 1986; The Soft Furnishings Book, 1986; Terence Conran's France, 1987; Terence Conran's DIY by Design, 1989; Terence Conran's Garden DIY, 1990; Toys and Children's Furniture, 1992; Terence Conran's Kitchen Book, 1993; Terence Conran's DIY Book, 1994; The Essential House Book, 1994; Terence Conran on Design, 1996; (with Dan Pearson) The Essential Garden Book, 1998; Easy Living, 1999; Chef's Garden, 1999; Terence Conran on Restaurants, 2000; Terence Conran on London, 2000; Terence Conran on Small Spaces, 2001; Q & A: a sort of autobiography, 2001; Kitchens: the hub of the home, 2002; Classic Conran, 2003. *Recreations:* gardening, cooking, cigar smoking. *Address:* 22 Shad Thames, SE1 2YU. *T:* (020) 7378 1161, *Fax:* (020) 7403 4309.

See also J. A. T. Conran.

CONROY, Harry; author, financial journalist; Proprietor, Conroy Associates, public relations consultants, since 1992; Editor, Scottish Catholic Observer, 2000–07 (Managing Editor, 2001–05); *b* Scotland, 6 April 1943; *s* of Michael Conroy and Sarah (*née* Mullan); *m* 1965, Margaret Craig (*née* Campbell); twin *s* one *d.* Trainee Lab. Technician, Southern Gen. Hosp., 1961–62; Night Messenger (copy boy), 1962–63, Jun. Features Sub-Editor, 1963–64, Scottish Daily Express; Daily Record: Reporter, 1964–66 and 1967–69; Financial Correspondent, 1969–85; Reporter, Scottish Daily Mail, 1966–67. Campaign Dir, Scottish Constitutional Convention, 1990–92. Mem., ASTMS, 1961–62. National Union of Journalists: Mem., 1963– (Hon. Mem., 2000); Mem., Nat. Exec. Council, 1976–85; Vice-Pres., 1980–81; Pres., 1981–82; Gen. Sec., 1985–90. Bureau Mem., Internat. Fedn of Journalists, 1986–90; Founding Mem., Inst. of Employment Rights, 1989. Associate Mem., GMBATU, 1984–85. Trustee, Share Charity, 1993–; Dir, Consumer Credit Counselling (Glasgow) Ltd, 1996–99; Chm., TACT Scotland, 2008–.

Publications: (with Jimmy Allison) Guilty By Suspicion, 1995; (with Allan Stewart) The Long March of the Market Men, 1996; Off The Record: a life in journalism, 1997; (ed) The People Say Yes: the making of Scotland's Parliament, 1997; (ed) They Rose Again, 2003; Callaghan, 2006. *Recreations:* stamp and post-card collecting, supporting Glasgow Celtic FC. *Address:* 44 Redwood Crescent, Cambuslang, Glasgow G72 7FZ. *T:* (0141) 641 9071; *e-mail:* harry@conroy.co.uk.

CONROY, Paul Martin; Chief Executive Officer, Adventures in Music Ltd, since 2002; *b* Surbiton, 14 June 1949; *s* of D. and M. Conroy; *m* 1st, 1980, Maxine Felstead (marr. diss. 1989); one *s*; 2nd, 1993, Katie Rennie; one *d*. *Educ:* John Fisher Sch., Purley. Has worked in various areas of music business, 1971–: agent: Terry King Associates, 1971–73; Charisma Artistes, 1973–75; Manager, Kursaal Flyers, 1975–77; Gen. Manager, Stiff Records, 1977–83; Man. Dir, US Div., WEA Records, 1983–89; President: Chrysalis Records, 1989–92; Virgin Records UK Ltd, 1992–2002. Chm., BRIT Awards, 1998, 1999, 2000. Trustee, Mus. of Childhood, Bethnal Green, 2004–. President's Award, Country Music Assoc. of USA, 1987. *Recreations:* cycling, supporting Chelsea, cricket, antique collecting. *Address:* e-mail: paul@adventuresin-music.com.

CONRY, Rt Rev. Kieran Thomas; see Arundel and Brighton, Bishop of, (RC).

CONS, Sir Derek, Kt 1990; SPMB; President, Court of Appeal, Brunei, 2003–06; *b* 15 July 1928; *s* of Alfred Henry Cons and Elsie Margaret (*née* Neville); *m* 1952, Mary Roberta Upton Wilkes. *Educ:* Rutlish; Birmingham Univ. (LLB (Hons)). Called to Bar, Gray's Inn, 1953. RASC (2nd Lieut), 1946–48. Hong Kong: Magistrate, 1955–62, Principal Magistrate, 1962–66; District Judge, 1966–72; Judge of Supreme Court, 1972–80, Justice of Appeal, 1980–86, Vice Pres., Court of Appeal, 1986–93; Comr of the Supreme Court, Brunei, 1974–2003; Justice of Appeal, Bermuda, 1994–2002; Mem., Court of Final Appeal, Hong Kong, 1997–2006. SPMB (Negara Brunei Darussalam), 2003. *Recreations:* walking, ski-ing. *Address:* Mulberry Mews, Church Street, Fordingbridge, Hants SP6 1BE; RS2, Rosalp, 1972 Anzere, Switzerland. *Club:* Bramshaw Golf (Hants).

CONSTABLE, (Charles) John, DBA; management educator and consultant; Director-General, British Institute of Management, 1985–86; *b* 20 Jan. 1936; *s* of late Charles and Gladys Constable; *m* 1960, Elisabeth Mary Light; three *s* one *d*. *Educ:* Durham Sch.; St John's Coll., Cambridge (MA); Royal Sch. of Mines, Imperial Coll. London (BSc); Harvard Grad. Sch. of Bus. Admin. (DBA). NCB, 1959–60; Wallis & Linnel Ltd, 1960–63; Arthur Young & Co., 1963–64; Lectr and Sen. Lectr, Durham Univ. Business Sch., 1964–71; Prof. of Operations Management, Business Policy, 1971–82, Dir 1982–85, Cranfield Sch. of Management. Chairman: Bright Tech Develts, 1989–98; LTB Ltd, 2001–03; Internetcamerasdirect Ltd, 2001–04; non-executive Director: IMS Ltd, 1984–91; Lloyds Abbey Life (formerly Abbey Life), 1987–97; Sage Gp plc, 1996–2005; NMBZ Holdings Ltd, 1997–03. Member: Heavy Electrical EDC, NEDO, 1977–87; N Beds HA, 1987–90; Res. Grants Bd, ESRC, 1989–90. Chm. of Govs, Harpur Trust, 1995–2003 (Governor, 1979–2003); Trustee, Pensions Trust, 1996–2003. *Publications:* (jtly) Group Assessment Programmes, 1966; (jtly) Operations Management Text and Cases, 1976; (jtly) Cases in Strategic Management, 1980; The Making of British Managers (BIM/CBI report), 1987. *Recreations:* golf, family. *Address:* 12 Mount Street, Taunton TA1 3QB.

CONSTABLE, Sir Frederic S.; see Strickland-Constable.

CONSTABLE, John Robert; Principal Pianist, London Sinfonietta, since 1968; Principal Harpsichordist, Academy of St Martin in the Fields, since 1984; Professor, Royal College of Music, since 1984; *b* 5 Oct. 1934; *s* of Ernest Charles William Constable and May Jane Constable (*née* Rippin); *m* 1956, Kate Ingham; two *d*. *Educ:* Leighton Park Sch., Reading; Royal Acad. of Music (pupil of Harold Craxton; LRAM and Recital Dip.; FRAM 1986). Pianist, piano accompanist and harpsichordist, music from medieval and baroque to modern; repetiteur, Royal Opera House, 1960–72; concerts at Wigmore Hall, Queen Elizabeth Hall, Royal Opera House and in major European, USA and Japanese cities; numerous TV and radio appearances; many records incl. lieder, chansons, Spanish songs, Victorian ballads, song cycles, chamber music, harpsichord concertos and harpsichord continuo in operas. *Recreations:* travel, looking at paintings, watching cricket. *Address:* 13 Denbigh Terrace, W11 2QJ. *T:* (020) 7229 4603.

CONSTABLE, Paule; lighting designer; Technical Associate, Royal National Theatre; *b* 9 Nov. 1966; *d* of Paul and Lyn Constable; partner, Ian Richards; one *s* one *d*. *Educ:* Stamford High Sch.; Goldsmiths' Coll., Univ. of London (BA Drama and English). Productions for: RNT; Glyndebourne; Royal Opera House; ENO; RSC; Donmar Th.; productions include: Street of Crocodiles, 1993, The 3 Lives of Lucie Cabrol, 1995, Théâtre de Complicité; His Dark Materials, RNT, 2005 (Olivier Award for Best Lighting Design, 2005); Don Carlos, Gielgud, 2005 (Olivier Award for Best Lighting Design, 2006); Evita, Adelphi, 2006; St Matthew Passion, Glyndebourne, 2007; Vernon God Little, Young Vic, 2007; Satyagraha, ENO, 2007; 7 Deadly Sins, Royal Ballet, 2007; Das Rheingold, Strasbourg, 2007; Attempts on her Life, St Joan, Warhorse, RNT, 2007; Othello, Donmar Warehouse, 2007; for BBC: Carmen, 2003; Magic Flute, 2003; Giulio Cesare, 2005; Marriage of Figaro, 2006; Così Fan Tutti, 2006. Mem., Assoc. Lighting Designers. Hon. Fellow, Goldsmiths' Coll., Univ. of London. Hospital Award for Contribn to Theatre, Hosp. Club, 2006. *Recreations:* surfing, cycling, walking, digging the allotment, being with the kids. *Address:* c/o David Watson, Simpson Fox Associates, 52 Shaftesbury Avenue, W1D 6LP. *T:* (020) 7434 9167.

CONSTANCE, Angela; Member (SNP) Livingston, Scottish Parliament, since 2007; *b* 15 July 1970; *d* of Sonny Constance and Mary (*née* Colquhoun); *m* 2000, Garry Knox; one *s*. *Educ:* Univ. of Glasgow (MA Soc. Sci.); Univ. of Stirling (MSocSc Soc. Work). Social Worker (Criminal Justice): Clackmannanshire Council, 1998; Perth and Kinross Council, 1999; Social Worker (Mental Health), S Lanarks Council, 2001–07. Mem. (SNP), W Lothian Council, 1997–2007. *Recreations:* jogging, eating out, cinema. *Address:* Scottish Parliament, Edinburgh EH99 1SP. *T:* (0131) 348 6751; *e-mail:* angela.constance.msp@scottish.parliament.uk.

CONSTANT, Charles Kenvyn ff.; see ffrench-Constant.

CONSTANTINE, David Peter; Co-Founder, 1990 and Executive Officer, since 1992, Motivation Charitable Trust; *b* 14 July 1960; *s* of William Geoffrey Constantine and Jean Virginia Constantine. *Educ:* Writtle Agricl Coll. (DipAgr 1982); Oxford Brookes Univ. (BSc Hons 1986); Royal Coll. of Art (MDes 1990; Hon. FRCA 1999; Sen. FRCA 2008). Programmer, IBM, 1986–88. Founded Motivation to help people with mobility disabilities, creating sustainable projects in low-income, countries. Mem., Internat. Cttee, Leonard Cheshire, 1997–2006; Trustee and Director: Design Mus., 1999–; Calvert Trust, Exmoor, 2004–. Hon. MA Bristol, 2003; DUniv Oxford Brookes, 2006. *Recreations:* photography, hand-cycling, cinema, modern history, kite flying. *Address:* Motivation, Brockley Academy, Brockley Lane, Backwell, Bristol BS48 4AQ. *T:* (01275) 464012; *e-mail:* info@motivation.org.uk.

CONSTANTINOU, Sir Georgkios, (Sir George), Kt 1997; OBE 1992; Chairman, Constantinou Group of Companies; *b* 11 May 1930; *s* of Costas Savva Constantinou and Eleni Lazarou; *m* 1955, Maria (separated); two *s* two *d*; Cecelia; three *s* three *d*. *Educ:* in Cyprus. Established companies which form Constantinou Group: Papuan Welders, 1954; Papuan Transport Contractors/Roadmakers, 1955; Rouna Quarries Pty Ltd, 1960; Hebou Constructions (PNG) Pty Ltd, 1973; Airways Hotel & Apartments Pty Ltd, 1986; Yodda Resources Pty Ltd, 1996; Kidu Kidu Pty Ltd, 1996. Hon. Consul of Cyprus in PNG, 1986–. *Recreations:* fishing, walking. *Address:* PO Box 120, Port Moresby, Papua New Guinea. *T:* 3253077. *Clubs:* Royal Papua Yacht (Port Moresby); Queensland Turf.

CONTE-HELM, Marie Theresa, (Mrs A. W. Purdue); Director General, Daiwa Anglo-Japanese Foundation, since 2000; *b* 13 Nov. 1949; *d* of Angelo and Santa Conte; *m* 1979, Arthur William Purdue; one *d*. *Educ:* CUNY (BA Art History 1971); East-West Center, Univ. of Hawaii (MA Asian Art 1973). Cultural Officer, Embassy of Japan, 1975–79; Lectr in Art History, Sunderland Poly., 1979–86; Head of Japanese Studies Div., and Reader in Japanese Studies, Sunderland Poly., subseq. Univ. of Sunderland, 1986–94; Reader in Japanese Studies and Dir, East Asian Affairs, Univ. of Northumbria at Newcastle, 1994–99. Vis. Prof., Univ. of Northumbria at Newcastle, 1999–. *Publications:* Japan and the North East of England: from 1862 to the present day, 1989 (trans. Japanese 1991); The Japanese and Europe: economic and cultural encounters, 1996; academic papers, articles and book reviews. *Recreations:* theatre, film, swimming, walking. *Address:* Daiwa Anglo-Japanese Foundation, 13/14 Cornwall Terrace, NW1 4QP. *T:* (020) 7486 4348; *e-mail:* marie.conte-helm@dajf.org.uk; The Old Rectory, Allendale, near Hexham, Northumberland NE47 9DA. *T:* (01434) 683350.

CONTI, Most Rev. Mario Joseph; see Glasgow, Archbishop of, (RC).

CONTI, Tom; actor, since 1960; director; *b* Scotland, 1942; *m* Kara Wilson; one *d*. London appearances include: Savages, Royal Court and Comedy, 1973; Other People, The Black and White Minstrels, Hampstead; The Devil's Disciple, RSC Aldwych, 1976; Whose Life is it Anyway?, Mermaid and Savoy, 1978, NY 1979 (SWET Award for Best Actor in a new play, Variety Club of GB Award for Best Stage Actor, 1978, Tony Award for Best Actor, 1979); They're Playing Our Song, Shaftesbury, 1980; Romantic Comedy, Apollo, 1983; An Italian Straw Hat, Shaftesbury, 1986; Otherwise Engaged (also dir), Theatre Royal, Windsor, 1990; The Ride Down Mount Morgan, Wyndham's, 1991; Present Laughter (also dir), Globe, 1993; Chapter Two, Gielgud, 1996; Jesus, My Boy, Apollo, 1998; Jeffrey Bernard is Unwell, Garrick, 2006; Romantic Comedy (also dir), UK tour, 2007; *directed:* Last Licks, Broadway, 1979; Before the Party, Oxford Playhouse and Queen's, 1980; The Housekeeper, Apollo, 1982; Treats, Hampstead, 1989; *films include:* Galileo, Flame, 1974; Eclipse, 1975; Full Circle, The Duellists, 1977; The Wall, 1980; Merry Christmas, Mr Lawrence, 1983; Reuben, Reuben, 1983; American Dreamer, 1985; Miracles, 1985; Saving Grace, 1986; Heavenly Pursuits, 1987; Beyond Therapy, 1987; The Dumb Waiter (USA); White Roses; Shirley Valentine, 1989; Two Brothers Running; Someone Else's America, 1997; Sub Down, 1997; Out of Control, 1997; Something To Believe In, 1997; Don't Go Breaking My Heart, 1998; *television appearances include:* Madame Bovary, The Norman Conquests, Glittering Prizes, The Beate Klarsfeld Story, Fatal Dosage, The Quick and the Dead, Blade on the Feather, Wright Verdicts, Friends, The Cosby Show, I Was a Rat, Deadline, Donovan. *Publication:* The Doctor (novel), 2004. *Address:* Finch & Partners, 4 Heddon Street, W1B 4BS. *Club:* Garrick.

CONTOGEORGIS, George; Member, Commission of the European Communities, 1981–85; *b* 21 Nov. 1912; *s* of Leonidas and Angeliki Contogeorgis; *m* 1949, Mary Lazopoulou. *Educ:* Athens Sch. (now University) of Economic and Commercial Sciences. Ministry of Trade, Greece: Administrator, 1937; Chief of Section, 1945; Dir, 1952; Dir Gen., 1964–67, resigned. Gen. Sec., Tourism, Govt of Nea Dimokratia, 1974; Dep. Minister of Co-ordination (Econs), 1974–77; Minister for EEC Affairs, 1977–81; Minister of Nat. Economy, 1989–90. MP, 1977–81. Grand Comdr, Order of the Phoenix (Greece), 1966; Grand Croix de l'Ordre de Leopold II (Belgium), 1984; Grand Comdr, Order of Lion (Finland), 1962; Comdr, OM (Germany, 1956, Italy, 1964 and France, 1977). *Publications:* Greece's Association Agreement with the EEC, 1962; Greece in Europe, 1985; Problems and issues in EEC–USA relations, 1989; European Union and the Balkan States, 1993; The European Idea, 1995; The European Union, 1995; Greece, 1995. *Address:* Rue Anagnostopoulou 26–28, Athens 10673, Greece. *T:* (1) 3616844.

CONTRERAS, Dame (Carmen) Marcela, DBE 2007; MD; FRCP, FRCPE, FRCPath; Professor of Transfusion Medicine, Royal Free and University College Medical School of University College London, since 1998; Director, Diagnostics, Development and Research, National Blood Service, 1999–2007; *b* 4 Jan. 1942; *d* of Dr Juan Eduardo Contreras and Elena Mireya (*née* Arriagada); *m* 1968, Dr Roberto Jaime Guiloff (marr. diss. 1997); one *s* one *d*. *Educ:* Dunalastair British Sch. for Girls, Santiago; Sch. of Medicine, Univ. of Chile (BSc 1963; LMed 1967; MD 1972). MRCPath 1988, FRCPath 1997; FRCPE 1992; FRCP 1998. British Council Schol., RPMS and MRC Blood Gp Unit, London, 1972–74; SSO, 1974–76, Med. Asst in Blood Transfusion, 1976–78, N London Blood Transfusion Centre, Edgware; Sen. Registrar in Haematology, St Mary's Hosp., London, 1978–80; Dep. Dir, 1980–84, Chief Exec. and Med. Dir, 1984–95, N London Blood Transfusion Centre; Exec. Dir, London and SE Zone, Nat. Blood Service, 1995–99. Vis. Prof., Faculty of Applied Scis, UWE, 2004–. Hon. Mem., MRC Blood Gp Unit, 1987–95. President: Internat. Soc. of Blood Transfusion, 1996–98; British Blood Transfusion Soc., 2001–03. Review Editor, Vox Sanguinis, 1989–96, 2003– (Ed.-in-Chief, 1996–2003); Member, Editorial Board: Transfusion Medicine, 1990–; Transfusion Medicine Reviews, 1993–; Blood Reviews, 1995–; Transfusion Alternatives in Transfusion Medicine, 1999–. FMedSci 2003. *Publications:* (jtly) Blood Transfusion in Clinical Medicine, 8th edn 1987, 10th edn 1997; ABC of Transfusion, 1990, 3rd edn 1998; Blood Transfusion: the impact of new technologies, 1990; contrib. numerous papers and chapters in the field of transfusion medicine. *Recreations:* theatre, travelling, opera, horse riding, walking, training in developing countries.

CONVILLE, David Henry, OBE 1983; theatre director and producer; *b* 4 June 1929; *s* of Lt Col Leopold Henry George Conville, CBE and Katherine Mary Conville; *m* 1st, 1956, Jean Margaret Bury (*d* 1967); one *d*; 2nd, 1970, Philippa Falcke (*d* 1999); one *s*. *Educ:* Marlborough Coll.; St John's Coll., Oxford; RADA (Dip.). Commnd Royal W African Frontier Force, Royal Welch Fusiliers, 1948–49. *Actor:* Ipswich Rep. Co., 1952; Colchester Rep. Co., 1953; Dial M for Murder, Dundee Rep. Co. (tour), 1954; King Lear and Much Ado About Nothing (European, London and provincial tour), 1955, Titus Andronicus (European and London tour), 1957, Stratford Meml Theatre Co.; Folkestone and Richmond Rep. Cos, and TV, 1956; Dry Rot, Brian Rix Co. (London and tour), 1957; The Reluctant Débutante, 1957, Not in the Book, 1959, tours with Jack Hulbert; Surgical Spirit, Granada TV, 1988–95; *producer:* provincial tours, then several West End prodns, 1959–61; Toad of Toad Hall, London, Dec.–Jan., 1960–84; founded New Shakespeare Co., Open Air Theatre, Regent's Park, 1962 (Chm., 1987–); prod./dir of more than 100 classical prodns, 1962–87; *writer:* plays: Chetwode, Sandy and Co., Orange Tree Theatre, 1985; Wind in the Willows, London, 1986–87, Chichester, 1989; Look

Here Old Son, BBC Radio, 1987; Obituaries, King's Head Theatre and BBC 1, 1989; Births, King's Head Theatre, 1990. Pres., SWET, 1975–76, 1982. Coronation Medal, 1953. *Publication:* The Park: the story of the Open Air Theatre, 2007. *Recreations:* Real tennis, walking, travel. *Address:* The Old Farmhouse, Okeford Fitzpaine, Blandford, Dorset DT11 0RP. *T:* (01258) 860034. *Clubs:* Garrick; Royal Tennis Court, Canford Tennis.

CONWAY, Christopher John; Chief Executive, 1993–98, Chairman, 1994–98, Digital Equipment Co. Ltd; *b* 3 Nov. 1944; *s* of John Francis Conway and Monica Conway (*née* Hawksworth); *m* 1969, Gillian May Burrow; two *s* one *d*. *Educ:* Univ. of S Africa (BA Hons 1967). IBM (UK) Ltd, 1969–93: Dir, Financial Services, 1992–93. Non-executive Director: Brammer plc, 1997–; Detica plc, 2000–; DICOM plc, 2004–. *Recreations:* golf, tennis, music.

CONWAY, (David) Martin; President, Selly Oak Colleges, Birmingham, 1986–97; *b* 22 Aug. 1935; *s* of Geoffrey S. and Dr Elsie Conway; *m* 1962, Ruth, *d* of Rev. Richard Daniel; one *s* two *d*. *Educ:* Sedbergh Sch.; Gonville and Caius Coll., Cambridge (BA, MA); and by friends and fellow Christians in many different cultures. Internat. Sec., SCM of GB and Ire., 1958–61; Study Sec., World Student Christian Fedn, Geneva, 1961–67; Sec. for Chaplaincies in Higher Educn, Gen. Synod of C of E, 1967–70; Publications Sec., WCC, 1970–74; Asst Gen. Sec. for Ecumenical Affairs, BCC, 1974–83; Dir, Oxford Inst. for Church and Society, and Tutor, Ripon Coll., Cuddesdon, Oxford, 1983–86. Simultaneous interpreter at assemblies and major world confs of WCC, 1961–; Consultant, Faith and Order Commn, WCC, 1971–82; Consultant, 1974–83, and Mem., 1986–91, C of E Bd for Mission and Unity. DLitt Lambeth, 1994. Editor: The Ecumenical Review, 1972–74; Christians Together, 1983–91; Oxford Papers on Contemporary Society, 1984–86. *Publications:* The Undivided Vision, 1966; (ed) University Chaplain?, 1969; The Christian Enterprise in Higher Education, 1971; Seeing Education Whole, 1971; Look Listen Care, 1983; That's When the Body Works, 1991; Journeying Together Towards Jubilee, 1999; Introducing the World Council of Churches, 2001; World Christianity in the 20th Century, 2 vols, 2008; contribs to Student World, New Christian, Audenshaw Papers, Internat. Rev. of Mission, etc. *Recreations:* other people—family, friends, colleagues; travel, music. *Address:* 303 Cowley Road, Oxford OX4 2AQ. *T:* (01865) 723085.

CONWAY, Derek Leslie, TD 1990; MP Old Bexley and Sidcup, since 2001 (C, 2001–08; Ind C, since 2008); *b* 15 Feb. 1953; *s* of Leslie and Florence Conway; *m* 1980, Colette Elizabeth Mary (*née* Lamb); two *s* one *d*. *Educ:* Beacon Hill Boys' School. Principal Organiser, Action Research for the Crippled Child, 1974–83; Chief Exec., Cats Protection League, 1998–2003. Borough Councillor and Dep. Leader of the Opposition, Gateshead Metropolitan Borough Council, 1974–78; Mem., Tyne and Wear Metropolitan County Council, 1977–83 (Leader, 1979–82); Member Board: Washington Develt Corp., 1979–83; North of England Develt Council, 1979–83; Newcastle Airport, 1980–83; Northern Arts, 1980–83. Non-exec. Dir, Foreign & Colonial Gp Investment Fund, 1997–2001. MP (C) Shrewsbury and Atcham, 1983–97; contested (C) same seat, 1997. PPS to Minister of State: Welsh Office, 1988–91; Dept of Employment, 1992–93; an Asst Govt Whip, 1993–94; a Lord Comr of HM Treasury (Govt Whip), 1994–96; Vice Chamberlain of HM Household, 1996–97. Mem., Speaker's Panel of Chairmen, 2001–08; Member, Select Committee: on Agric., 1987; on Transport, 1987–88; on Armed Forces Discipline, 1991; Liaison, 2001–08; Finance and Services, 2001–08; Chm., Select Cttee on Accommodation and Works, 2001–08. Chairman: British-Morocco Parly Gp, 1988–97; British-Venezuelan Gp, 1987–93; Mem. Exec., British American Parly Gp, 2001–08; Vice Chm., Cons. backbench Defence Cttee, 1991–97. Treas., IPU, 2001–08 (Mem. Exec. Cttee, 1986–97; Vice-Chm., British Gp, 1992–93); Vice-Chm., CPA, 2004–08. Member, Conservative Party Committees: Nat. Exec. Cttee, 1971–81; Nat. Gen. Purposes Cttee, 1972–74; Nat. Local Govt Cttee, 1979–83; Nat. Vice-Chm., Young Conservatives, 1972–74. Mem. Exec. Cttee, British Venezuela Soc., 1987–93. Commnd RMA Sandhurst into Royal Regt of Fusiliers; Major, 5th Bn (TA) Light Infantry. MInstD. *Recreation:* historical fiction. *Address:* House of Commons, SW1A 0AA.

CONWAY, Sir Gordon (Richard), KCMG 2005; DL; FRS 2004; FIBiol; Chief Scientific Adviser, Department for International Development, since 2005; Professor of International Development, Imperial College, London, since 2005; President, Royal Geographical Society, since 2006; *b* 6 July 1938; *s* of Cyril Conway and Thelma (*née* Goodwin); *m* 1965, Susan Mary Mumford; one *s* two *d*. *Educ:* Kingston Grammar Sch.; Kingston Polytechnic; University Coll. of North Wales, Bangor (BSc 1959). DipAgricSci, Cambridge, 1960; DTA University Coll. of West Indies, Trinidad, 1961; PhD Univ. of California, Davis, 1969; FIBiol 1978 (Hon. FIBiol 2001). Research Officer (Entomology), Agric. Res. Centre, State of Sabah, Malaysia, 1961–66; Statistician, Inst. Ecology, Univ. of California, Davis, 1966–69; Imperial College, London: Res. Fellow and Lectr, Dept of Zoology and Applied Entomology, 1970–76; Dir, 1977–80, Chm., 1980–86, Centre for Envtl Technol.; Reader in Environmental Management, Univ. of London, 1976–80; Prof. of Environmental Technol., 1980–88; Rep. for India, Nepal and Sri Lanka, Ford Foundn, 1989–92; Vice-Chancellor, 1992–98, Emeritus Prof., 2003–, Univ. of Sussex. Pres., Rockefeller Foundn, 1998–2004. Vis. Prof., Imperial Coll., 1989–2004. Director: Sustainable Agric. Prog., Internat. Inst. for Envmt and Develt, 1986–88; BOC Foundn, 1994–97; Sussex Enterprise, 1995–98; RSA, 2005–06. Mem., Royal Commn on Environmental Pollution, 1984–88. Chm. Bd, Inst. Develt Studies, 1992–98; Member: Internat. Inst. for Envmt and Develt, 1993–97; Bd, Internat. Food Policy Res. Inst., Washington, 1994–97. Chairman: Runnymede Trust Commn on Muslims in Britain, 1996–97; Living Cities (formerly Nat. Community Develt Initiative), 2000–04; Visiting Arts, 2004–; UK Collaborative on Develt Scis, 2007–. DL E Sussex, 2006. FCGI 2006; Fellow, Amer. Acad. of Arts and Scis, 2000. Hon. Fellow, Univ. of Wales, Bangor, 1997. Hon. LLD Sussex, 1998; Hon. DSc: W Indies, 1999; Brighton, 2001; DUniv Open, 2004. *Publications:* Pest and Pathogen Control, 1984; (jtly) After the Green Revolution, 1990; (jtly) Unwelcome Harvest, 1991; Doubly Green Revolution: food for all in the 21st century, 1997; papers and reports on agricl ecology. *Recreations:* travel, movies, music. *Address:* Department for International Development, 1 Palace Street, SW1E 5HE. *Club:* Reform.

CONWAY, Prof. John Horton, FRS 1981; John von Neumann Professor of Mathematics, Princeton University, USA, since 1986. *Educ:* Gonville and Caius Coll., Cambridge (BA 1959; MA 1963; PhD 1964). Cambridge University: Lectr in Pure Maths, to 1973; Reader in Pure Mathematics and Mathematical Statistics, 1973–83; Prof. of Maths, 1983–87; Fellow: Sidney Sussex Coll., 1964–70; Gonville and Caius Coll., 1970–87. Hon. DSc Liverpool, 2001. Polya Prize, London Mathematical Soc., 1987; Frederic Esser Nemmers Prize, Northwestern Univ., 1999; Steele Prize, AMS, 1999; Joseph Priestley Award, 2001. *Publications:* Regular Algebra and Finite Machines, 1971; On Numbers and Games, 1976; Atlas of Finite Groups, 1985; The Book of Numbers, 1996; The Sensual Quadratic Form, 1997. *Address:* Department of Mathematics, Princeton University, Fine Hall, Washington Road, Princeton, NJ 08544–1000, USA.

CONWAY, Martin; *see* Conway, D. M.

CONWAY, Peter; *see* Gautier-Smith, P. C.

CONWAY, Rt Rev. Stephen David; *see* Ramsbury, Area Bishop of.

CONWAY MORRIS, Prof. Simon, PhD; FRS 1990; Professor of Evolutionary Palaeobiology, since 1995, and Fellow of St John's College, since 1987, Cambridge University; *b* 6 Nov. 1951; *s* of Richard Conway Morris and Barbara Louise Maxwell; *m* 1975, Zoë Helen James; two *s*. *Educ:* Univ. of Bristol (BSc Hons); Univ. of Cambridge (PhD). Research Fellow, St John's Coll., Cambridge, 1975–79; Lectr, Open Univ., 1979–83; Lectr in Palaeontology, 1983–91, Reader in Evolutionary Palaeobiology, 1991–95, Cambridge Univ. Gallagher Vis. Scientist, Univ. of Calgary, 1981; Nuffield Sci. Res. Fellowship, 1987–88; Merrill W. Haas Vis. Dist. Prof., Univ. of Kansas, 1988; Selby Fellow, Aust. Acad. of Scis, 1992. Member Council: Systematics Assoc., 1981–85; NERC, 1996–2002. Royal Instn Christmas Lectr, 1996; Gifford Lectr, Univ. of Edinburgh, 2007. Hon. Fellow, Eur. Union of Geoscis, 1997. Hon. DPhil Uppsala, 1993. Walcott Medal, Nat. Acad. of Scis, 1987; Charles Schuchert Award, Paleontol. Soc., 1989; George Gaylord Simpson Prize, Yale Univ., 1992; Lyell Medal, Geol Soc. of London, 1998; Kelvin Medal, Royal Philosophical Soc. of Glasgow, 2007; Ide and Luella Prize, Coll. of Sci., A&M Univ., Texas, 2007. *Publications:* The Crucible of Creation, 1998; Life's Solution, 2003; contribs to professional jls. *Recreations:* G. K. Chesterton, wine, punting. *Address:* Department of Earth Sciences, Downing Street, Cambridge CB2 3EQ. *T:* (01223) 333400.

CONYNGHAM, family name of **Marquess Conyngham**.

CONYNGHAM, 7th Marquess *cr* 1816; **Frederick William Henry Francis Conyngham;** Baron Conyngham, 1781; Viscount Conyngham, 1789; Earl Conyngham, Viscount Mount Charles, 1797; Earl of Mount Charles, Viscount Slane, 1816; Baron Minster (UK), 1821; late Captain Irish Guards; *b* 13 March 1924; *e s* of 6th Marquess Conyngham and Antoinette Winifred (*d* 1966), *er d* of late J. W. H. Thompson; *S* father, 1974; *m* 1st, 1950, Eileen Wren (marr. diss. 1970), *o d* of Capt. C. W. Newsam, Ashfield, Beauparc, Co. Meath; three *s*; 2nd, 1971, Mrs Elizabeth Anne Rudd; 3rd, 1980, Mrs D. G. A. Walker (*d* 1986); 4th, 1987, Annabelle Agnew. *Educ:* Eton. *Heir: s* Earl of Mount Charles, *qv*. *Address:* Myrtle Hill, Andreas Road, Ramsey, Isle of Man IM8 3UA. *T:* (01624) 815532. *Club:* Royal St George Yacht.

COOGAN, Ven. Robert Arthur William; Archdeacon of Hampstead, 1985–94, now Archdeacon Emeritus; *b* 11 July 1929; *s* of Ronald Dudley Coogan and Joyce Elizabeth Coogan (*née* Roberts). *Educ:* Univ. of Tasmania (BA); Univ. of Durham (DipTheol). Asst Curate, St Andrew, Plaistow, 1953–56; Rector of Bothwell, Tasmania, 1956–62; Vicar: North Woolwich, 1962–73; St Stephen, Hampstead, 1973–77; Priest in Charge, All Hallows, Gospel Oak, 1974–77; Vicar of St Stephen with All Hallows, Hampstead, 1977–85; Priest in Charge: Old St Pancras with St Matthew, 1976–80; St Martin with St Andrew, Gospel Oak, 1978–81; Area Dean, South Camden 1975–81, North Camden 1978–83; Prebendary of St Paul's Cathedral, 1982–85. Commissary for Bishop of Tasmania, 1968–88; Exam. Chaplain to Bishop of Edmonton, 1985–94. *Recreations:* reading, gardening, travel. *Address:* Salters Hall West, Stour Street, Sudbury, Suffolk CO10 2AX. *T:* (01787) 370026. *Club:* Oriental.

COOGAN, Steve; actor, writer and producer; *b* 14 Oct. 1965; one *d* by Anna Cole; *m* 2002, Caroline Hickman (marr. diss. 2005). *Educ:* Manchester Poly. Sch. of Theatre. Partner, Baby Cow Prodns Ltd, 1999–. *Radio:* On The Hour, 1992; Knowing Me, Knowing You, with Alan Partridge, 1992; *television* includes: Spitting Image, 1984; The Day Today (also writer), 1994; Knowing Me, Knowing You, with Alan Partridge (also writer), 1995; Coogan's Run (also writer), 1995; I'm Alan Partridge (also writer), 1997, 2002; The Fix, 1997; Alice Through the Looking Glass, 1998; Dr Terrible's House of Horrible (also writer and prod.), 2001; The Private Life of Samuel Pepys (also prod.), 2003; Saxondale (also writer and prod.), 2006, 2007; *films:* The Wind in the Willows, 1996; The Parole Officer (also writer), 2001; 24 Hour Party People, 2002; Coffee and Cigarettes, 2003; Around the World in 80 Days, 2004; Happy Endings, A Cock and Bull Story, 2005; The Alibi, Marie Antoinette, 2006; Night at the Museum, 2006; Hot Fuzz, 2007; *theatre:* The Man Who Thinks He's It (tour), 1998. *Address:* Baby Cow Productions Ltd, 77 Oxford Street, W1D 2ES; c/o Independent Talent Group Ltd, Oxford House, 76 Oxford Street, W1D 1BS.

COOK, Alan Ronald, CBE 2006; FCII; Managing Director, Post Office Ltd, since 2006 (non-executive Director, 2005–06); *b* 23 Sept. 1953; *s* of Ronald Joseph Cook and Dorothy May Cook; *m* 1975, Anita Patricia Kelleher; two *s* one *d*. *Educ:* Ealing Grammar Sch. for Boys. FCII 1975. Prudential Assce Co. Ltd, 1970–93; Sen. Vice Pres., Jackson Nat. Life, USA, 1993–96; Prudential Assurance Co. Ltd: Acquisitions Dir, 1996–97; Man. Dir, Gen. Insce, 1997–99; Man. Dir, Retail Insce Ops, 1999–2000; Chief Exec., Insce Services, 2000–01; Chief Operating Officer, UK and Europe, 2001–02; CEO, Nat. Savings & Investments, 2002–06. Gov., Inst. of Financial Services, 2005. Vice-Chm. Govs, Luton Univ., 2003–05. FRSA 2000; FCMI 2005. Freeman, City of London, 2003; Mem., Co. of Insurers, 2005–. *Recreations:* fell-walking, swimming. *Address:* Post Office Ltd, 80 Old Street, EC1V 9NN. *T:* (020) 7320 7400, *Fax:* (020) 7320 7601; *e-mail:* alan.cook@postoffice.co.uk.

COOK, Allan Edward, CBE 2008; Chief Executive, Cobham plc, since 2001; *b* 27 Sept. 1949; *s* of late Stanley Livingston Porter and of Sarah Neve; *m* 1970, Kathleen Pegg; two *d*. *Educ:* Sunderland Coll. of FE; Sunderland Poly. (DMS; Full Technol. Cert); Sunderland Univ. (BSc Hons Electronics). Chief Exec., Hughes Aircraft (Europe), 1995; Man. Dir, GEC-Marconi Avionics, 1998–2000; Gp Man. Dir Progs and Man. Dir Eurofighter, BAE Systems, 2000–01. Director: Manufg Forum; Ministerial Adv. Gp for Manufg, 2006; Chm., Nat. Skills Acad. for Manufg, 2008–. Pres., SBAC, 2007–Sept. 2009. *Recreations:* squash, music, walking, theatre, wine. *Address:* Cobham plc, Brook Road, Wimborne BH21 2BJ. *T:* (01202) 882020, *Fax:* (01202) 840523; *e-mail:* cooka@cobham.com. *Club:* Royal Air Force.

COOK, Andrew John, CBE 1996; Chairman and Chief Executive, William Cook Holdings Ltd, since 1982; *b* 11 Oct. 1949; *s* of late Andrew McTurk Cook and Barbara Jean (*née* Gale); *m* 1987, Alison Jane Lincoln; one *s* three *d*. *Educ:* High Storrs Grammar Sch., Sheffield; University Coll. London (LLB). Called to the Bar, Gray's Inn, 1972. Dir, William Cook & Sons (Sheffield) Ltd, 1974–82. *Publication:* Thrice Through the Fire: the history of the William Cook company 1985–1998, 1999. *Recreations:* boats, mountains, my children, history, trains, planes, bikes. *Address:* Reduit, Le Variouf, Forest, Guernsey GY8 0BH. *Clubs:* Royal Thames Yacht; Sheffield Sports Cycling.

COOK, Ann; *see* Christopher, A.

COOK, Brian Francis, FSA; classical archaeologist; Keeper of Greek and Roman Antiquities, British Museum, 1976–93; *b* 13 Feb. 1933; *yr s* of late Harry Cook and Renia

Cook; *m* 1962, Veronica Dewhirst. *Educ:* St Bede's Grammar Sch., Bradford; Univ. of Manchester (BA); Downing Coll. and St Edmund's House, Cambridge (MA); British Sch. at Athens. FSA 1971. NCO 16/5 Lancers, 1956–58. Dept of Greek and Roman Art, Metropolitan Museum of Art, New York: Curatorial Asst, 1960; Asst Curator, 1961; Associate Curator, 1965–69; Asst Keeper, Dept of Greek and Roman Antiquities, BM, 1969–76. Corr. Mem., German Archaeol. Inst., 1977. Hon. Member: Anglo-Hellenic League, 1981; Caryatids, 1992. *Publications:* Inscribed Hadra Vases in the Metropolitan Museum of Art, 1966; Greek and Roman Art in the British Museum, 1976; The Elgin Marbles, 1984 (Spanish edn 2000), 2nd edn 1997; The Townley Marbles, 1985; Greek Inscriptions, 1987 (Dutch edn 1990, French edn 1994, Japanese edn 1996); (ed) The Rogozen Treasure, 1989; (jtly) Relief Sculpture of the Mausoleum at Halicarnassus, 2005; articles and revs on Greek, Etruscan and Roman antiquities in Brit. and foreign periodicals. *Recreations:* reading, gardening. *Address:* 4 Belmont Avenue, Barnet, Herts EN4 9LJ. *T:* (020) 8440 6590.

COOK, Sir Christopher Wymondham Rayner Herbert, 5th Bt *cr* 1886; company director, since 1979; Director, Diamond Guarantees Ltd, 1980–91; *b* 24 March 1938; *s* of Sir Francis Ferdinand Maurice Cook, 4th Bt and Joan Loraine, *d* of John Aloysius Ashton-Case; *S* father, 1978; *m* 1st, 1958, Mrs Malina Gunasekera (from whom he obtained a divorce, 1975); one *s* one *d*; 2nd, 1975, Mrs Margaret Miller, *d* of late John Murray; one *s* one *d*. *Educ:* King's School, Canterbury. *Recreations:* reading, philately, painting. *Heir:* *s* Richard Herbert Aster Maurice Cook, *b* 30 June 1959. *Address:* La Fosse Equierre, Bouillon Road, St Andrew's, Guernsey GY6 8YN.

COOK, David Julian; Second Parliamentary Counsel, since 2007; *b* 15 July 1962; *s* of Stanley and Dorothy Mary Cook; *m* 1988, Christine Margaret Alice Barnard; two *s* one *d*. *Educ:* Merton Coll., Oxford (BA Classics 1985, MA); Coll. of Law (CPE 1986; Law Finals 1987). Articled Clerk, then Solicitor, Freshfields, 1988–91; Office of Parliamentary Counsel: Asst Parly Counsel, 1991–95; Sen. Asst Parly Counsel, 1995–99; Dep. Parly Counsel, 1999–2003; Parly Counsel, 2003–; Hd of Drafting Team, Tax Law Rewrite Project, Bd of Inland Revenue, 2003–05 (on secondment). *Recreations:* archaeology, walking, Victorian novels.

COOK, David Somerville; solicitor; Senior Partner, Messrs Sheldon & Stewart, Solicitors, Belfast; Chairman, Police Authority for Northern Ireland, 1994–96; Lord Mayor of Belfast, 1978–79; *b* 25 Jan. 1944; *s* of late Francis John Granville Cook and Jocelyn McKay (*née* Stewart); *m* 1972, Mary Fionnuala Ann Deeny (*see* M. F. A. Cook); four *s* one *d*. *Educ:* Campbell Coll., Belfast; Pembroke Coll., Cambridge (MA). Alliance Party of Northern Ireland: Founder Member, 1970; Hon. Treasurer, 1972–75; Central Executive Cttee, 1970–78, 1980–85; Dep. Leader, 1980–84; Pres., 1992–93. Chm., NI Voluntary Trust, 1979–99. Mem., Belfast City Council, 1973–85; Mem. (Alliance) for Belfast S, NI Assembly, 1982–86; contested (Alliance): Belfast South, Feb. 1974, by-elections March 1982 and Jan. 1986, gen. election, 1987; N Ireland, European Parly elecn, 1984. Trustee: Ulster Museum, 1974–85; The Buttle Trust, 1991–2001; Vice Pres., NI Council on Alcohol, 1978–83; Member: NI Council, European Movement, 1980–84; Cttee, Charity Know How Fund, 1991–94; Exec. Cttee, Assoc. of Community Trusts and Foundns, 1992–98 (Chm., 1994–95); Exec. Cttee, Clanmil Housing Assoc. (formerly RBL Housing Assoc. Ltd), 1994–99; Chm., Craigavon and Banbridge Community Health and Social Services Trust, 1994–2001. Director: Ulster Actors' Co. Ltd, 1981–85; Crescent Arts Centre, Belfast, 1994–96. Mem., Royal Naval Assoc. Gov., Brownlow Coll. (Integrated Secondary Sch.), 1994–98. Obtained Orders of Mandamus and fines for contempt of court against Belfast City Council, following its unlawful protest against the Anglo-Irish Agreement, 1986, 1987. Chm., West Down Beagles Hunt Club, 2003–. *Publications:* Blocking the Slippery Slope, 1997; (contrib.) The Republican Ideal, ed Norman Porter, 1998. *Recreations:* pamphleteering, fieldsports, marmalade making, observing politicians, hunting on foot. *Address:* Sheldon & Stewart, 70 Donegall Pass, Belfast BT7 1BU. *Club:* Ulster Reform (Belfast).

COOK, Derek Edward, TD 1967; Deputy Chairman, 1987–92, and Group Managing Director, 1990–92, Pilkington plc (Director, 1984–92); *b* 7 Dec. 1931; 2nd *s* of late Hubert Edward Cook and Doris Ann Cook (*née* Appleyard); *m* 1968, Prudence Carolyn Wilson; one *s* one *d*. *Educ:* Fyling Hall; Denstone Coll.; Corpus Christi Coll., Oxford (MA); Salford Univ.; Huddersfield Tech. Coll. FSS; CText, FTI. Commissioned Z Battery, BAOR, 1951; W Riding Artillery, 1952–68. Tootal Ltd, 1955–61; John Emsley Ltd, 1961–63; Man. Dir, A. & S. Henry & Co. Ltd (Bradford), 1963–70; Man. Dir, 1971–75, Chm., 1976–79, Fibreglass Pilkington Ltd, India; Chm. and Man. Dir, Hindusthan-Pilkington Glass Works Ltd, India, 1976–79; Director: R. H. Windsor Ltd, India, 1976–79; Killick Halco Ltd, India, 1977–79; Chm. and Man. Dir, Pilkington Cos, S Africa and Zimbabwe, 1979–84, incl. Pilkington Bros S Africa Pty, Armour Plate Safety Glass Pty, and Glass S Africa Pty; Director: Pilkington Glass Ltd, 1982–85 (Chm., 1984–85); Pilkington Holdings Inc., 1984–89; Triplex Safety Glass Co. Ltd, 1984–85 (Chm.); Pilkington Floatglas AB, 1985–87; Flachglas AG, 1985–89. Chm., Pilkington Superannuation Scheme, 1987–2003; Director: Rowntree plc, 1987–88; Libby-Owens-Ford Co., USA, 1987–92; Charter Consolidated plc, 1988–93; Charter plc, 1993–97; Powell Duffryn plc, 1989–98; Leeds Permanent Building Soc., 1991–95; MFI (Furniture Group) plc, 1992–99; Littlewoods Organisation plc, 1992–99; D. E. Cook (Consultants), 1992–2008 (Sen. Consultant, 1992–2008); Kwik Save Gp plc, 1993–98; Halifax Bldg Soc., 1995–97; Halifax plc, 1996–98; Somerfield plc, 1998–99; Hobart Pension Trustee Ltd, 1993–97; Littlewoods Pension Trust Ltd, 1994–2001; Trustee: MFI Pension Plan, 1994–99; Halifax plc (formerly Bldg Soc.) Retirement Fund, 1995–98; Kwik Save Retirement Fund, 1997–2000 (Chm., 1998–2000). Member: Council of Industry and Parlt Trust, 1987–92; Council, CBI, 1988–92; Council, Textile Inst., 1994–99; Court, Univ. of Leeds, 1989–2001; Dir, Leeds Univ. Foundn Ltd, 1989–2002. Gov., Cathedral Sch., Bombay, 1974–79; Dir, Breach Candy Hosp. Trust, 1974–79. Trustee, W Riding Artillery Trust, 2001–. Mem., Cook Soc., 1985–2002. Holder of Royal Warrant of Appointment, 1984–85. FInstD; CCMI; FRSA. Freeman, City of London; Liveryman, Glass Sellers' Co., 1991–. *Recreations:* sailing (British Admirals Cup team, 1967), general sporting and country life interests. *Address:* Snaplock, 3 Abbey Mill, Prestbury, Cheshire SK10 4XY. *T:* (01625) 827985. *Clubs:* Oriental, Cavalry and Guards, East India, Royal Thames, Royal Automobile, Royal Ocean Racing; New (Edinburgh); Royal Yorkshire Yacht (Bridlington); Leander (Henley); Racquets (Manchester); Rand (Johannesburg); Royal Bombay Yacht (Cdre, 1977–78).

COOK, Fionnuala; *see* Cook, M. F. A.

COOK, Francis; MP (Lab) Stockton North, since 1983; *b* 3 Nov. 1935; *s* of James Cook and Elizabeth May Cook; *m* 1959, Patricia (marr. diss. 1998), *d* of Thomas and Evelyn Lundrigan; one *s* three *d*. *Educ:* Corby School, Sunderland; De La Salle College, Manchester; Institute of Education, Leeds. Schoolmaster, 9½ years; Construction Project Manager with Capper-Neill International. Vice-Pres., NATO Parly Assembly, 1998–; a Dep. Speaker in Westminster Hall, 1999–. *Recreations:* climbing, fell walking, singing, swimming. *Address:* 128 Oxbridge Lane, Stockton-on-Tees TS18 4HW.

COOK, Gordon Charles, DSc, MD; FRCP; physician with special interest in tropical and infectious diseases, and medical historian; President, Fellowship of Postgraduate Medicine, 2000–07; Visiting Professor, University College London, since 2002; *b* Wimbledon, 17 Feb. 1932; *e s* of late Charles Francis Cook and Kate Cook (*née* Kraninger, then Grainger); *m* 1963, Elizabeth Jane, *d* of late Rev. Stephen Noel Agg-Large; one *s* three *d*. *Educ:* Wellingborough, Kingston-upon-Thames and Raynes Park Grammar Schs; Royal Free Hosp. Sch. of Medicine, London Univ. (BSc Physiol 1955; MB BS 1957; MD 1965; Charlotte Brown Prize, 1965; Cunning Award, 1967; Legg Award, 1969; DSc 1976). MRCS; LRCP 1957, MRCP 1960, FRCP 1972; FRACP 1978; FLS 1989; FRCPE 2002. Commissioned RAMC, seconded to Royal Nigerian Army, 1960–62. Hosp. appts, Royal Free, Hampstead Gen., Royal Northern, Brompton, St George's, 1958–63; Lectr, Royal Free Hosp Sch. of Medicine and Makerere Univ. Coll., Uganda, 1963–69; Prof. of Medicine and Cons. Physician, Univs of Zambia, 1969–74, Riyadh, 1974–75, Papua New Guinea, 1978–81; Sen. MO, MRC, 1975–76; Sen. Lectr in Clinical Scis, LSHTM, 1976–97; University College London: Hon. Sen. Lectr in Medicine (Infectious Diseases), 1981–2002; Sen. Res. Fellow, Wellcome Trust Centre for History of Medicine, 1997–2002. Hon. Consultant Physician: Hosp. for Trop. Diseases and UCL Hosps, 1976–97; St Luke's Hosp. for the Clergy, 1988–; Hon. Lectr in Clinical Parasitology, St Bart's Hosp. Med. Coll., 1992–. Vis. Prof., Univs of Basrah, Mosul, Doha. Consultant, advr and mem., professional and learned bodies; Mem., Jt Cttee on Higher Med. Trng, 1987–93. Member: Assoc. of Physicians of GB and Ireland, 1973–; Exec. Council, Med. Writers Gp, Soc. of Authors, 1994–99 (Chm., 1997–99); Mem. Exec. Cttee and Examiner, Faculty of Hist. and Philosophy of Medicine and Pharmacy, Soc. of Apothecaries, 1997–; Examiner for membership of RCP, 1977–84. Lectures: Ahmed Hafez Moussa Meml, 1994; Stanley Browne Meml, 1995; Monckton Copeman, Soc. of Apothecaries, 2000; Denny, Barber-Surgeons' Co., 2003. President: RSTM&H, 1993–95; Osler Club, London, 1993–95; Baconian Club of St Albans, 1995–96; History of Medicine Sect., RSM, 2003–04 (Vice-Pres., 1994–96); Chm., Erasmus Darwin Foundn, Lichfield, 1994–; Trustee, Bookpower (formerly Educnl Low-priced Sponsored Texts), 1996–; Member: Council, Galton Inst., 2005–; Cttee, Friends of Florence Nightingale Mus., 2005– (Vice-Chm., 2006–). Hon. Archivist, Seamen's Hosp. Soc., 2002– (Hon. Life Gov., 2007–); Hon. Res. Associate, Greenwich Maritime Inst., 2003–. Mem. Council, Cathedral and Abbey Church of St Alban, 1983–88. Liveryman, Apothecaries' Co., 1981. Editor, Jl of Infection, 1995–97; mem., editl bds, med. jls. Frederick Murgatroyd Meml Prize, RCP, 1973; Hugh L'Etang Prize, RSM, 1999. *Publications:* (ed jtly) Acute Renal Failure, 1964; Tropical Gastroenterology, 1980; (jtly) 100 Clinical Problems in Tropical Medicine, 1987, 2nd edn 1998; Communicable and Tropical Diseases, 1988; Parasitic Disease in Clinical Practice, 1990; From the Greenwich Hulks to Old St Pancras: a history of tropical disease in London, 1992; (ed) Gastroenterological Problems from the Tropics, 1995; (ed) Travel-associated disease, 1995; (ed) Manson's Tropical Diseases, 20th edn, 1996 to 22nd edn, 2008; Victorian Incurables: a history of the Royal Hospital for Neuro-Disability, Putney, 2004; John MacAlister's Other Vision: a history of the Fellowship of Postgraduate Medicine, 2005; The Incurables Movement: an illustrated history of the British home, 2006; Tropical Medicine: an illustrated history of the pioneers, 2007; Disease in the Merchant Navy: a history of the Seamen's Hospital Society, 2007; Health Care for All: a history of a third-world dilemma, 2008; numerous research papers, chapters, reviews and editorials. *Recreations:* cricket, walking, listening to baroque and classical music, medical/scientific history. *Address:* 11 Old London Road, St Albans, Herts AL1 1QE. *T:* (01727) 869000. *Clubs:* Athenæum, MCC.

COOK, Jeremy Laurence C.; *see* Curnock Cook.

COOK, John, FRCSEd; FRSE 1970; Consultant Surgeon, Eastern General Hospital, Edinburgh, 1964–87; *b* 9 May 1926; *s* of George Cook and Katherine Ferncroft (*née* Gauss); *m* 1st, 1953, Patricia Mary Bligh (*d* 1998); one *s* four *d*; 2nd, 2005, Judith Mary Strangward Hill. *Educ:* Fettes Coll., Edinburgh; Edinburgh Univ. (MB 1949, ChM 1963). FRCSEd 1954. Served Med. Br., RAF, 1950–52 (Flt Lieut). House Surgeon, Royal Infirmary, Edinburgh, 1949; Res. Asst, Radcliffe Infirm., Oxford, 1954–55; First Asst, Dept of Surg., Makerere University Coll., Uganda, 1955–64 (Reader in Surg., 1962–64). Royal Coll. of Surgeons of Edinburgh: Hon. Sec., 1969–72; Mem. Council, 1974–84. Representative Mem., GMC, 1982–86; Hon. Sec., Internat. Fedn of Surgical Colls, 1974–84. *Publications:* contrib. surgical jls. *Recreation:* music.

COOK, Dr John Barry; Headmaster, Epsom College, 1982–92; *b* 9 May 1940; *er s* of late Albert Edward and Beatrice Irene Cook, Gloucester; *m* 1964, Vivien Margaret Roxana Lamb, *o d* of late Victor and Marjorie Lamb, St Albans; two *s* one *d*. *Educ:* Sir Thomas Rich's Sch., Gloucester; King's Coll., Univ. of London (BSc 1961, AKC 1961); Guy's Hosp. Med. Sch. (PhD 1965). Guy's Hospital Medical School: Biophysics research, 1961–64; Lectr in Physics, 1964–65; Haileybury College: Asst Master, 1965–72; Senior Science Master and Head of Physics Dept, 1967–72; Headmaster, Christ Coll., Brecon, 1973–82. Dir, Inner Cities Young People's Project, 1992–95; Principal, King George VI & Queen Elizabeth Foundn of St Catharine's at Cumberland Lodge, 1995–2000; educnl consultant, 2000–. Church in Wales: Mem. Governing Body, 1976–83; Coll. of Episcopal Electors, 1980–83. Chairman: S Wales ISIS, 1978–82; Academic Policy Cttee, HMC, 1985–88. Children's Hospice Association for South-East: Chm., 1995–97; Trustee, 1995–2002. Chm. Governors, Royal School, Great Park, Windsor, 1998–2000. Liveryman, Barbers' Co., 1999– (Chm., 700th Anniv. Appeal, 2008). *Publications:* (jtly) Solid State Biophysics, 1969; Multiple Choice Questions in A-level Physics, 1969; Multiple Choice Questions in O-level Physics, 1970; papers in Nature, Molecular Physics, Internat. Jl of Radiation Biology, Jl of Scientific Instruments, Educn in Science, Conference and Trends in Education. *Recreations:* sports, photography, philately. *Address:* 6 Chantry Road, Bagshot, Surrey GU19 5DB. *T:* (01276) 475843.

COOK, Leonard Warren, CBE 2005; CRSNZ 2005; National Statistician and Registrar General for England and Wales, 2000–05; *b* 13 April 1949; *s* of late Archie Cook and of Jean (*née* Paterson). *Educ:* Univ. of Otago, New Zealand (BA Hons Maths and Stats). Department of Statistics, New Zealand: Res. Officer, 1971–79; Dir, Statistical Methods, 1979–82; Asst Govt Statistician, 1982–86; Dep. Govt Statistician, 1986–91; Govt Statistician, 1992–2000. Secretariat, Task Force on Tax Reform, NZ, 1981; Mem., Royal Commn on Social Policy, NZ, 1987–88; Chm., Medical Training Bd. Vis. Prof., UCL, 2005–. *Publications:* contribs to NZ Population Review, Proceedings of ISI. *Recreations:* fly fishing, travel. *Address:* 59 Ponsonby Road, Karori, Wellington, New Zealand.

COOK, Prof. Malcolm Charles, PhD; Professor of French Eighteenth-Century Studies, University of Exeter, 1994–2008; *b* 19 May 1947; *s* of Francis H. Cook and Betty J. G. Cook; *m* 1974, Odile Jaffré; two *s* one *d*. *Educ:* Univ. of Warwick (BA 1969; PhD 1974). Assistant associé, Université de Paris X, Nanterre, 1972–76; Lectr in French, Westfield Coll., London, 1977–78; Exeter University: Lectr in French, 1978–88; Sen. Lectr, 1988–93; Reader, 1993–94; Dep. Vice-Chancellor, 2001–04. Chm., MHRA, 1999–. Gen. Editor, MLR, 1994–2001 (French Ed., 1987–93). Chevalier, Ordre des Palmes Académiques (France), 1998. *Publications:* Fictional France, 1993; (ed) French Culture since 1945, 1993; (ed) Journalisme et Fiction au 18e siècle, 1999; (ed) Modern France: society in transition, 1999; (ed) Anecdotes, Faits-Divers, Contes, Nouvelles, 1700–1820, 2000; Critical Inventory of the Correspondence of Bernardin de Saint-Pierre, 2001; (ed) Réécritures 1700–1820, 2002; Bernardin de Saint-Pierre: a life of culture, 2006; (ed) Critique, Critiques, 2006; La Correspondance de Bernardin de Saint-Pierre, édition critique, 2007. *Recreations:* golf, walking, watching soccer and cricket. *Address:* Myrtle Cottage, 10 East Terrace, Budleigh Salterton, Devon EX9 6PG. *T:* (01395) 446854.

COOK, Margaret Stella; *see* Singh, M. S.

COOK, (Mary) Fionnuala (Ann), OBE 2002; Chairwoman, Southern Health and Social Services Board, Northern Ireland, since 2003; *b* 3 May 1946; *d* of late Dr Donnell McLarnon Deeny and Annie Deeny (*née* McGinley); *m* 1972, David Somerville Cook, *qv*; four *s* one *d*. *Educ:* Loreto Abbey, Rathfarnham, Dublin; University Coll., Dublin (BA 1968). Member: Gen. Adv. Council, BBC, 1979–85; Bd, NI Housing Exec., 1985–91; Gen. Consumer Council, NI, 2002–. Chairwoman, Southern HSS Council, NI, 1991–2001. Actg Chair, Gen. Osteopathic Council of UK, 2001–. Founding Gov., Integrated Educn Fund, 1992–97. Chairwoman, Bd of Govs, Bridge Integrated Primary Sch., 2003–. High Sheriff, Co. Down, 2006. Mem., Loughbrickland WI. *Recreations:* gardening, gossip. *Address:* 8 Main Street, Loughbrickland, Banbridge, Co. Down BT32 3NQ. *T:* (028) 4066 9669.

See also Hon. Sir D. J. P. Deeny, M. E. McL. Deeny.

COOK, Michael Edgar, CMG 2000; HM Diplomatic Service, retired; High Commissioner, Kampala, 1997–2000; *b* 13 May 1941; *s* of FO Aubrey Edgar Cook, RAFVR (killed in action, 1944) and late Muriel Constance Molly Bateman (*née* Wemyss); *m* 1st, 1970, Astri Edel Wiborg (marr. diss. 1983); one *s* one *d*; 2nd, 1983, Annebritt Maria Aslund; two step *d*. *Educ:* Bishops Stortford Coll.; Fitzwilliam Coll., Cambridge (MA Hons); Regent St Poly. (Dip. Mgt Studies). Export Manager, Young's Sea Foods, 1964–66; joined FCO, 1966; 3rd Sec., Commercial, Oslo, 1967–70; FCO, 1970–73; 1st Sec. then Head of Chancery, Accra, 1973–77; 1st Sec., Commercial, Stockholm, 1977–81; Head of Chancery and Dep. High Comr, Port of Spain, 1981–84; Counsellor and Dep. High Comr, Dar es Salaam, 1984–87; FCO, 1987–92; Consul Gen., Istanbul, 1992–97. Area Dir for Brighton and Hove, Sussex Enterprise, 2001–03; non-exec. Chm., Orient Bank Ltd, Uganda, 2006–; Dir/Trustee, Concordia (YSV) Ltd, 2006–. Mem., Conservative Party Globalisation and Global Poverty Gp, 2006–07. *Recreations:* squash, tennis, wine and cooking, jazz. *Address:* 17 Denmark Villas, Hove, E Sussex BN3 3TD.

COOK, His Honour Michael John; a Circuit Judge, 1986–2003; consultant solicitor, since 2005; *b* 20 June 1930; *s* of George Henry Cook and Nora Wilson Cook (*née* Mackman); *m* 1st, 1958, Anne Margaret Vaughan; three *s* one *d*; 2nd, 1974, Patricia Anne Sturdy; one *d*. *Educ:* Leeds Grammar Sch.; Worksop Coll.; Univ. of Leeds (LLB 2(1) Cl. Hons). Admitted Solicitor, 1953. National Service, commnd Royal Artillery, 1954. Willey Hargrave & Co., Solicitors, to 1957; Ward Bowie, Solicitors, 1957–86 (Senior Partner, 1965–86); a Recorder, 1980–86; Designated Family Judge for Surrey (formerly Designated Child Care Judge), Guildford County Ct, 1995–2003. Founder Mem., Holborn and City of Westminster Law Socs, 1962–; Past Hon. Sec. and Pres., London Solicitors' Litigation Assoc.; Hon. Pres., Assoc. of Law Costs Draftsmen, 1997–2003; Member: Solicitors Disciplinary Tribunal, 1975–86; Law Society sub-cttees and working parties. Royal Med. Foundn, 2000–. Gov., Epsom Coll., 1990–2007. Patron: Assoc. for Families who have Adopted from Abroad, 1995–; Surrey Family Mediation Service, 2003–. Freeman, City of London, 1990. General Editor: The Litigation Letter, 1981–; Butterworths Costs Service, 1991–. *Publications:* The Courts and You, 1976; The Taxation of Contentious Costs, 1979; The Taxation of Solicitors Costs, 1986; Cook on Costs, 1991, annually, 2000–; (jtly) The New Civil Costs Regime, 1999; contrib. to Cordery on Solicitors, 1995–; contrib. Civil Justice Qly. *Recreations:* tennis, gardening, theatre, sitting on moving horses. *Clubs:* Law Society; St George's Hill Tennis.

COOK, Prof. Nicholas (John), PhD; FBA 2001; Professorial Research Fellow in Music, Royal Holloway, University of London, since 2005 (Professor of Music, 2004–05); Director, AHRC (formerly AHRB) Research Centre for the History and Analysis of Recorded Music, since 2004; *b* Athens, 5 June 1950; *s* of late Prof. John Manuel Cook, FBA and Enid May Cook (*née* Robertson); *m* 1975, Catherine Bridget Louise Elgie; one *s* one *d*. *Educ:* King's Coll., Cambridge (BA 1971, MA 1976; PhD 1983); Univ. of Southampton (BA 1977). Lectr in Music, Univ. of Hong Kong, 1982–90; Prof. of Music, 1990–99, Dean of Arts, 1996–98, Res. Prof. of Music, 1999–2003, Univ. of Southampton. Chair, Music Panel, HEFC RAE 2001. Ed., Jl Royal Musical Assoc., 1999–2004. *Publications:* A Guide to Musical Analysis, 1987; Music, Imagination and Culture, 1990; Beethoven: Symphony No 9, 1993; Analysis Through Composition: principles of the classical style, 1996; Analysing Musical Multimedia, 1998; Music: a very short introduction, 1998; (ed jtly) The Cambridge History of Twentieth-Century Music, 2004; (ed jtly) Empirical Musicology: aims, methods, prospects, 2004; The Schenker Project: culture, race, and music theory in fin-de-siècle Vienna, 2007; contrib. articles in most major musicological jls. *Address:* Old School House, School Hill, Alderbury, Salisbury SP5 3DR. *T:* (01722) 710012.

COOK, Prof. Paul Derek, MBE 1985; PhD; CEng; Chairman and Managing Director, Scientifica-Cook Ltd, since 1962; Professor of Laser Science, Brunel University, 1986–97; *b* 12 March 1934; *s* of James Walter Cook and Florence Jefferay; *m* 1954, Frances Ann James; four *d*. *Educ:* Queen Mary Coll., London (BSc Hons; PhD 1963; Sir John Johnson Scholar, 1959). Res. Scientist: MRC, 1960–62; Middlesex Hosp. Med. Sch., 1962–65. Prof. of Laser Physics, Brunel Univ., 1986–91. Scientific Adviser to: Minister for the Envmt and Countryside, DoE, 1990–92; British Gas, 1990–92; Laser Consultant, BAe, 1986–; former Consultant, W Midlands Police, 1991–92; Scientific Advr to Lady Olga Maitland, 1992–96. Responsible for design and develt of numerous laser systems used in med. and mil. estabts throughout world, incl. ophthalmic LaserSpec; originator and inventor of Laser Guidance Systems for weapon alignment in each Tornado; major contrib. to Europe's first laser gyroscope in 1970s; invention of laser instrument that improves safety of motorists by detecting and correcting night myopia; estab. world's first Night Vision Clinic for treating night blindness disorders. Dep. Chm., Conserve, 1990–93; Founder/President: British Science and Technol. Trust, 1985–96; Science and Technol. Trust, 2002–; UK Pres., Japanese Zen Nippon Airinkai, 1978–81. *Recreations:* breeding and rearing exotic Japanese carp, cultivating Japanese bonzai, inventing, experimenting with ideas, especially those related to improving safety on the roads, passion for early automobile number plates. *Address:* Carlton House, 78 Bollo Bridge Road, W3 8AU.

COOK, Sir Peter Frederic Chester, Kt 2007; RA 2003; RIBA; Bartlett Professor of Architecture, University College London, since 1990 (Chairman, Bartlett School of Architecture, 1990–2004); Joint Professor of Architecture, Royal Academy, since 2005; Design Principal, HOK International, since 2004; *b* 22 Oct. 1936; *s* of Major Frederick William Cook and Ada Cook (*née* Shaw); *m* 1st, 1960, Hazel Aimee Fennell (marr. diss. 1989); 2nd, 1989, Yael Reisner; one *s*. *Educ:* Bournemouth Coll. of Art; Architectural Assoc. (AA Dip. 1960). Tutor, Architectural Assoc., 1964–90; Prof. of Arch., HBK Städelschule, Frankfurt am Main, 1984–2002. Director: ICA, 1969–71; Art Net, 1972–79. Visiting Professor: UCLA, 1968–69; Southern Calif Inst. of Arch., 1980, 1983, 1992; Oslo Sch. of Arch., 1982; Univ. of Qld, 1993; Nihon Univ., Tokyo, 1994; Tech. Univ., Vienna, 1997, 1999, 2001, 2002. Founder Mem., Archigram, 1961–76. Mem., European Acad. of Sci. and Art; Bund Deutscher Architekten. Sen. FRCA; FRSA. Royal Gold Medal in Arch., RIBA, 2002; Gustav Eiffel Prize, Ecole Spéciale d'architecture, Paris, 2005. Commandeur, Ordre des Arts et des Lettres (France), 2002. *Publications:* Architecture: action and plan, 1972; Experimental Architecture, 1982; (with R. Llewellyn-Jones) New Spirit in Architecture, 1992; Peter Cook: six conversations, 1993; Primer, 1996; (with N. Spiller) The Power of Contemporary Architecture, 1999; (with N. Spiller) The Paradox of Contemporary Architecture, 2001; The City: as a garden of ideas, 2003. *Recreations:* music, observing towns. *Address:* 54 Compayne Gardens, NW6 3RY. *T:* and *Fax:* (020) 7372 3784; *e-mail:* peter.cook@ucl.ac.uk; Bartlett School of Architecture, 22 Gordon Street, WC1H 0QB. *T:* (020) 7679 7504.

COOK, Dr Peter John, CBE 1996; FTSE; Chief Executive, Co-operative Research Centre for Greenhouse Gas Technologies, since 2003; Director: PJC International, since 1998; MineXchange, since 1999; *b* 15 Oct. 1938; *s* of John and Rose Cook; *m* 1961, Norma Irene Walker; two *s*. *Educ:* Durham Univ. (BSc Hons, DSc); ANU (MSc); Univ. of Colorado (PhD). FTSE 1998. Geologist to Sen. Geologist, BMR, Canberra, 1961–76; Sen. Res. Fellow, ANU Res. Sch. of Earth Sci., 1976–82 (Vis. Fellow, 1982–90); Chief of Div./Chief Res. Scientist, BMR, 1982–90 (Prof., Univ. Louis Pasteur, Strasbourg, 1989); Dir, British Geol Survey, 1990–98; Dir, Australian Petroleum Co-op. Res. Centre, 1998–2003. Adrian Fellow, Univ. of Leicester, 1992–98. Chairman: Consortium for Ocean Geosci., 1980–82; Commonwealth/State Hydrogeol. Cttee, 1983–88; Intergovtl Oceanographic Commn, Prog. Ocean Sci. and Non-Living Resources, 1984–2001; Member: Adv. Cttee, Aust. Nuclear Sci. and Tech. Orgn, 1984–90; Geolog. Adv. Panel, BM (Nat. Hist.), 1990–98; Earth Scis Cttee, 1990–94, Earth Scis Tech. Bd, 1995–98, NERC; Chm., Forum of European Geol Surveys, 1996–97. President: EuroGeoSurveys, 1995–96; Aust.-French Assoc. of Scientists, 2000–03; Member: Council, MIRO, 1991–98; Adv. Cttee for Protection of the Seas, 1997–99. Fellow, Geol Soc. of Aust., 2007. Major John Coke Medal, Geol Soc., London, 1997; Lewis G. Weeks Gold Medal, Australian Petroleum and Exploration Assoc., 2004; Leopold von Buch Medal, Geol Soc., Germany, 2004. Centenary Medal, Australia, 2001. *Publications:* more than 130 contribs to books and learned jls, on energy and sustainability, greenhouse gas technologies, phosphate deposits, marine mineral resources, coastal zone studies, palaeogeography, science management and science policy. *Recreations:* ski-ing, hiking, travel, history. *Address:* 21 Empire Circuit, Forrest, Canberra, ACT 2603, Australia. *T:* (2) 62396504, *Fax:* (2) 62396049; *e-mail:* pjcook@co2crc.com.au. *Club:* Commonwealth (Canberra).

COOK, Roger James; investigative journalist; broadcaster: The Cook Report, ITV, 1985–97; Cook Report Specials, ITV, 1998–2004; *b* 6 April 1943; *s* of Alfred and Linda Cook; *m* 1st, 1966, Madeline Koh (marr. diss. 1974); 2nd, 1982, Frances Alice Knox; one *d*. *Educ:* Hurlstone Agricl Coll.; Sydney Univ. TV and radio reporter, ABC (Australia), 1960–66; TV and radio dir, Warnock Sandford Advertising (Aust.), 1966–68; reporter, BBC Radio 4, World at One, World This Weekend, PM, 1968–76; freelance documentary dir, 1968–72; creator and presenter, Checkpoint, Radio 4, 1973–85; presenter and reporter, Radio 4 documentary series: Time for Action; Real Evidence; investigative reporter, BBC TV: Nationwide; Newsnight, 1972–84. Vis. Prof., Centre for Broadcast Journalism, Nottingham Trent Univ., 1997–. Hon. DLitt Nottingham Trent, 2004. BPG Award, for outstanding contrib. to radio, 1978; Pye (now Sony) Radio Personality of the Year, 1979; Ross McWhirter Foundn Award, for courageous reporting, 1980; Valiant for Truth Award, 1988; TV and Radio Industries Award, for best ITV prog., 1993, and Special Award, for outstanding contrib. to broadcasting, 1998; RTS (Midlands) Best On-Screen Personality, 1996; Houston Worldfest Silver Award, for best interview, 1997; Charleston Worldfest Gold Award, for best investigative prog., 1997; Brigitte Bardot Internat. Award (Genesis Awards), for best campaigning wildlife prog., 1997; British Acad. Special Award, for outstanding investigative reporting, 1998. *Publications:* (with Tim Tate) What's Wrong With Your Rights?, 1988; (with Howard Foster) Dangerous Ground, 1999. *Recreations:* walking, music, motor sport. *Address:* c/o The Roseman Organisation, 51 Queen Anne Street, W1G 9HS. *T:* (020) 7486 4500.

COOK, Prof. Stephen Arthur, PhD; FRS 1998; FRSC 1984; University Professor, Department of Computer Science, University of Toronto, since 1985; *b* 14 Dec. 1939; *s* of Gerhard A. Cook and Lura Cook; *m* 1968, Linda Craddock; two *s*. *Educ:* Univ. of Michigan (BSc Math. 1961); Harvard Univ. (SM Math. 1962; PhD Math. 1966). Asst Prof., Math. and Computer Science, Univ. of Calif at Berkeley, 1966–70; University of Toronto: Associate Prof., 1970–75, Prof., 1975–85, Dept of Computer Science. Member: Nat. Acad. of Scis (US), 1985; Amer. Acad. of Arts and Scis, 1986. A. M. Turing Award, ACM, 1982. *Publications:* numerous papers in jls. *Recreation:* sailing. *Address:* Department of Computer Science, University of Toronto, Toronto, ON M5S 3G4, Canada. *T:* (416) 9785183. *Club:* Royal Canadian Yacht.

COOK, Timothy, OBE 1997; Clerk to the Trustees, City Parochial Foundation, 1986–98; *b* 25 April 1938; *s* of late Stephen Cook and Kathleen (*née* Henwood); *m* 1967, Margaret Taylor; one *s* one *d*. *Educ:* Loughborough Grammar Sch.; Trinity Hall, Cambridge (BA); Brunel Univ. (MA). Called to the Bar, Middle Temple, 1961. Asst Lectr in Law, Sheffield Univ., 1960–61; Asst Warden, Norman House, 1962–64; Prison Welfare Officer, HM Prison, Blundeston, 1964–66; Dir, Alcoholics Recovery Project, 1966–74; Hd, Cambridge House and Talbot, 1975–77; Dir, Family Service Units, 1978–85. *Publications:* Vagrant Alcoholics, 1975; (ed jtly) The Drunkenness Offence, 1969; (ed) Vagrancy, 1979; Merfyn Turner: practical compassion, 1999; (jtly) A Management Companion for the Voluntary Sector, 2000; Reflections on Good Grant Making, 2000; History of the Carers' Movement, 2007. *Recreations:* cinema, reading, theatre. *Address:* 26 Criffel Avenue, SW2 4AZ. *T:* (020) 8674 3141.

COOK, William Birkett, MA; Master of Magdalen College School, Oxford, 1972–91; *b* 30 Aug. 1931; *e s* of late William James and Mildred Elizabeth Cook, Headington, Oxford; *m* 1958, Marianne Ruth, *yr d* of late A. E. Taylor, The Schools, Shrewsbury; one *s* one *d* (and one *d* decd). *Educ:* Dragon Sch.; Eton (King's Schol.); Trinity Coll., Cambridge (Schol.). National Service, 1950–51 (commnd in RA). Porson Prizeman, 1953; 1st cl. Classical Tripos Pt I, 1953, Pt II, 1954; Henry Arthur Thomas Student, 1954; MA Oxon by incorporation, 1972. Asst Master, Shrewsbury Sch., 1955–67, and Head of Classical Faculty, 1960–67; Headmaster of Durham Sch., 1967–72. Governor: Oxford High Sch., 1979–2000; Bedford Modern Sch., 1992–2001. Administrator, Choir Schools' Assoc. Bursary Trust, 1987–92; Dir, Thomas Wall Trust, 1992–2002; Gov., Ewelme Exhibn Endowment, 1993–2008 (Chm., 1999–2008). *Recreations:* music, gardening, Scottish country dancing. *Address:* 2 Cannon's Field, Old Marston, Oxford OX3 0QR. *T:* (01865) 250882.

COOKE, Alistair Basil, OBE 1988; PhD; Consultant and Editor in Chief, Conservative Research Department, since 2004; official historian and archivist, Carlton Club, since 2007; *b* 20 April 1945; 2nd *s* of Dr Basil Cooke and Nancy Irene Cooke (*née* Neal). *Educ:* Framlingham Coll., Suffolk; Peterhouse, Cambridge (MA 1970); Queen's Univ., Belfast (PhD 1979). Lectr and Tutor in Modern History, Queen's Univ., Belfast, 1971–77; Conservative Research Department: Desk Officer, 1977–83; Political Advr to Shadow Minister for NI, 1977–79; Asst Dir, 1983–85; Dep. Dir, 1985–97. Dir, Conservative Political Centre, 1988–97. Gen. Sec., ISC, 1997–2004. Chm. of Trustees, Friends of the Union, 1995–2003; Founder, 1997, Mem., 2005–, Cons. Party Archive Trust; Sen. Trustee, T. E. Utley Meml Fund, 2000–. Gov., John Lyon Sch., Harrow, 1999–2005. Patron, NI Schs Debating Comp., 2001–. *Publications:* (ed jtly) Lord Carlingford's Journal, 1971; (jtly) The Governing Passion; cabinet government and party politics in Britain 1885–86, 1974; (ed) The Ashbourne Papers 1869–1913, 1974; (ed) The Conservative Party's Campaign Guides, 7 vols, 1987–2005; (ed) The Conservative Party: seven historical studies, 1997; (ed) The Conservative Research Department 1929–2004, 2004; (jtly) The Carlton Club 1832–2007, 2007; An Unsung Tory Heroine: a memoir of Dorothy Brant, 2008; A Party of Change: a brief history of the Conservatives, 2008; (contrib.) Between the Thin Blue Lines, 2008; pamphlets on Northern Ireland and constitutional issues; articles in historical jls and educnl pubns. *Recreations:* writing letters to the press (and getting them published), collecting royal and political memorabilia, music, walking briskly. *Address:* Flat 1, 68 St George's Square, SW1V 3QT. *T:* (020) 7821 9520. *Clubs:* Carlton, St Stephen's.

COOKE, Rear-Adm. Anthony John, CB 1980; Private Secretary to Lord Mayor of London, 1981–92; *b* 21 Sept. 1927; *s* of Rear-Adm. John Ernest Cooke, CB and late Kathleen Mary Cooke; *m* 1st, 1951, Margaret Anne (marr. diss. 1994), *d* of late Frederick Charles Hynard; two *s* three *d*; 2nd, 1995, Patricia Sinclair Stewart, *d* of late William Sinclair Stewart and of Margaret Jane Stewart; one step *s* two step *d*. *Educ:* St Edward's Sch., Oxford. Entered RN 1945; specialised in navigation, 1953; Army Staff Coll., 1958; Sqdn Navigating Officer, HMS Daring, Second Destroyer Sqdn, 1959–61; Staff Navigating Officer to Flag Officer, Sea Trng, 1961; Comdr 1961; Directorate of Naval Ops and Trade, 1961–63; i/c HMS Brighton, 1964–66; Directorate of Navigation and Tactical Control, 1966; Captain 1966; Captain of Dockyard and Queen's Harbourmaster, Singapore, 1967–69; Captain 1st Destroyer Sqdn, Far East, later Divnl Comdr 3rd Div. Western Fleet, i/c HMS Galatea, 1969–71; Dir, Royal Naval Staff Coll., 1971–73; Cdre Clyde i/c Clyde Submarine Base, 1973–75; Rear-Adm. 1976; Senior Naval Mem., Directing Staff, RCDS, 1975–78; Adm. Pres., RNC Greenwich, 1978–80, retd. Police Foundn, 1980–81. A Younger Brother, Trinity House, 1974. Freeman: City of London, 1979; Shipwrights' Co., 1980. OStJ 1990. *Recreation:* keeping my wife in champagne and out of the red. *Address:* Sinclair House, 4 Amherst Road, Ealing, W13 8ND. *T:* (020) 8997 2620.

See also Rear-Adm. D. J. Cooke.

COOKE, Anthony Roderick Chichester Bancroft; Director, 1999–2007, and Chairman, 2005–07, Baltic Exchange Ltd; *b* 24 July 1941; *s* of Maj.-Gen. Ronald Basil Brown Bancroft Cooke, CB, CBE, DSO and Joan, *d* of Maj. Claude O. Chichester; *m* 1972, Daryll, *d* of David Aird Ross; two *s* one *d*. *Educ:* Ampleforth Coll.; London Business Sch. (MSc 1970). FCA 1964; MICS 2005. With Binder Hamlyn & Co., 1960–68; Manager, Jessel Securities plc, 1970–72; Man. Dir, London Australian & Gen. Exploration Co., 1972–75; Ellerman Lines plc, 1975–91: Chief Exec., Investment Services, 1975–78; Chief Exec., City Liners, 1978–85; Chief Executive and Chairman: Ellerman Lines plc, 1985–87; Cunard Ellerman, 1987–91; Gp Chief Exec., Andrew Weir & Co. Ltd, 1991–99. Director: James Fisher & Sons plc, 2002–; West of England Shipowners Insce Assoc. Ltd, 2002–; Oikos Storage Develts, 2007–. President: Chamber of Shipping, 1996–97; Inst. of Chartered Shipbrokers, 2002–04. High Sheriff, Hampshire, 2001–02. FRSA 1980. *Recreation:* active sports. *Address:* Poland Court, Odiham, Hampshire RG29 1JL. *T:* (01256) 702060, *Fax:* (01256) 701477. *Club:* Boodle's.

COOKE, Brian; Circuit Administrator, South Eastern Circuit, 1989–95; *b* 16 Jan. 1935; *s* of Norman and Edith Cooke; *m* 1958, Edith Mary Palmer; two *s* one *d*. *Educ:* Manchester Grammar Sch.; University Coll. London (LLB). Served Royal Air Force, 1956–59. Called to Bar, Lincoln's Inn, 1959; Dept of Director of Public Prosecutions, 1960–68; Deputy Clerk of the Peace, Inner London Quarter Sessions, 1968–71; Dep. Circuit Administrator, North Eastern Circuit, 1971–81, Circuit Administrator 1981–82; Sec. of Commissions, 1982–88, Hd of Judicial Appointments Gp, 1987–88, Lord Chancellor's Dept. Part-time Pres., Mental Health Rev. Tribunals, 1996–2003. JP Middx, 1985–99. *Recreations:* golf, walking, theatre, music, the arts. *Address:* 12 The Pryors, East Heath Road, NW3 1BS. *Club:* Hampstead Golf.

COOKE, Colin Ivor; non-executive Chairman: Fenner PLC, since 1993; Dowlis Corporate Solutions plc, since 2005; Energybuild Group plc, since 2007; *b* 17 Dec. 1939; *m* 1983, Sheila Handley; four *s* one *d*. *Educ:* Cardiff High Sch.; Advanced Coll. of Technology, Newport (HND Metallurgy). GKN, 1956–63; Hepworth Ceramic, 1963–71; RTZ, 1971–72; Du-Port, 1972–80, Main Bd Dir, 1982–86; Dir, WDA, 1987–89; Dir, 1989–98, Chm., 1991–98, Triplex Lloyd. Dir, Dynacast Internat., 1999–2003; non-executive Director: Ash & Lacy, 1987–97; British Dredging, 1990–93; Yorkshire Water, 1995–97; Oystertec plc, 2002–. Chm., Tipton City Challenge, 1993–98. FIMMM (FIM 1996). Freeman, City of London, 1996; Liveryman, Founders' Co., 1996–. *Recreations:* golf, swimming, military history. *Clubs:* Royal Porthcawl Golf; Cardiff County.

COOKE, Cynthia Felicity Joan, CBE 1975; RRC 1969; Matron-in-Chief, Queen Alexandra's Royal Naval Nursing Service, 1973–76; *b* 11 June 1919; *d* of late Frank Alexander Cooke, MBE, DCM, and of Ethel May (*née* Buckle). *Educ:* Streatham Secondary Sch. for Girls; Victoria Hosp. for Children, Tite Street, Chelsea; RSCN, 1940; University Coll. Hosp., London, SRN, 1942; Univ. of London, Sister Tutor Diploma, 1949. Joined QARNNS, 1943; served in: Australia, 1944–45; Hong Kong, 1956–58; Malta, 1964–66. HMS: Collingwood, Gosling, Goldcrest; RN Hospitals: Chatham, Plymouth, Haslar. Principal Tutor, Royal Naval School of Nursing, 1967–70; Principal Matron, RN Hosp., Haslar, 1970–73. QHNS 1973–76. CStJ 1975. *Address:* The Banquet House, Kings Head Mews, The Pightle, Needham Market, Suffolk IP6 8AQ.

COOKE, David Arthur Lawrence; Director, British Board of Film Classification, since 2004; *b* 11 March 1956; *s* of James Robert Cooke and Verity Cooke (*née* Brandrick); *m* 1984, Kathleen Joyce Collins, *qv*. *Educ:* University Coll., Oxford (BA 1st Cl. Hons Mod Hist.; MA). Home Office: admin trainee, 1977–81; Private Sec. to Patrick Mayhew, MP (Minister of State), 1981–82; Principal, Prisons, Drugs and Broadcasting Depts, 1982–89; G5, Broadcasting Dept, 1990; on loan to other govt depts, 1990–93; Dir, Asylum, and Immigration Service Enforcement, Home Office, 1994–97; G3, Constitution Secretariat, Cabinet Office, 1997; Director: Central Inf. Technol. Unit, Cabinet Office, 1997–2000; Criminal Policy Gp, Home Office, 2000–02; Associate Pol Dir, NI Office, 2002–04. *Recreations:* film, music, sport, cooking. *Address:* British Board of Film Classification, 3 Soho Square, W1D 3HD. *Club:* Athenæum.

COOKE, David Charles; Consultant, Pinsent Masons (formerly Pinsents), Solicitors, since 2002; *b* 22 March 1938; *s* of F. J. E. Cooke and Hilda Cooke. *Educ:* Bolton Sch.; Accrington Grammar Sch.; Manchester Univ. (LLB). Hall Brydon & Co., Manchester, 1961–64; King & Partridge, Madras, 1964–67; Pinsent & Co., Birmingham, then Pinsent Curtis, subseq. Pinsent Curtis Biddle, solicitors: Asst Solicitor, 1967; Partner, 1969–86; Sen. Partner, 1986–94. *Recreations:* classical music, fell walking, theatre, reading. *Address:* Pinsent Masons, 3 Colmore Circus, Birmingham B4 6BH. *T:* (0121) 200 1050. *Club:* Oriental.

COOKE, David John, OBE 1995; Director, British Council, Brazil, 2002–05; *b* 4 Jan. 1947; *s* of late Dennis and of Bessie Cooke; *m* 1970, Lindsey Ram; two *d*. *Educ:* Oxford Coll. of Technology (ONC 1967, HNC Applied Biology 1968); Univ. of Leicester (BSc Biological Sci. 1971; PhD Genetics 1974). Jun. Technician, Dept of Biochemistry, Oxford Univ., 1963–65; Site Services Operator, UKAEA Culham, 1965–66; Scientific Asst, UKAEA Harwell, 1966–68; SRC/NATO Res. Fellow, Univ. of Tromsø, Norway, 1974–76; Res. Fellow and Lectr in Genetics, Univ. of Sheffield, 1976–78; British Council: Sci. Advr, London, 1978–81; Sci. Officer, Belgrade, 1981–84; First Sec. (Sci.), British High Commn, New Delhi, 1984–87; Dir, Project Develt Dept, 1989–91; Educn Attaché, British Embassy, Washington, 1991–94; Dep. Dir, Manchester, 1994–99; Dir, Develt and Training Services, and Mem., Sen. Mgt Strategy Team, 1999–2002. *Recreations:* walking, cycling, cross-country ski-ing, gardening. *Address:* *e-mail:* cooke.dave@gmail.com.

COOKE, Rear-Adm. David John, MBE 1989; Commander (Operations) to Commander-in-Chief Fleet, Commander Allied Submarines North and Rear Admiral Submarines, 2006–09; *b* 15 Aug. 1955; *s* of Rear-Adm. Anthony John Cooke, *qv*; *m* 1980, Sarah Jane Keeble; two *s* one *d*. *Educ:* Tonbridge Sch. Entered RN, 1973; specialised in submarines and navigation; served HM Ships: Lowestoft, 1975; Oberon, 1976–80; Warspite, 1980–84; Trafalgar, 1984–86; CO, HMS Onslaught, 1986–88; SWO to Captain Submarine Sea Trng, 1989; Comdr 1989; CNOCS, 1990–91; USS Cincinnati, 1991; CO, HMS Torbay, 1992–94; Navy Plans, MoD, 1994–96; Captain 1995; DOR (Sea), 1996–98; Cdre, Strategic Defence Review Implementation Team, 1999; HCSC 2000; CO, HMS Cumberland, 2000–01; Dir, Equipment Plan, MoD, 2001–04; Dep. Comdr, Strike Force NATO, 2004–06. Younger Brother, Trinity House, 1988. Freeman, City of London, 2008; Liveryman, Shipwrights' Co., 2008. *Recreations:* reading, history, maintaining an old house, travel. *Address:* c/o Naval Secretary, Fleet Headquarters, Whale Island, Portsmouth PO2 8BY.

COOKE, David John; His Honour Judge David Cooke; Specialist Chancery Judge, since 2008; *b* Rugby, 23 Aug. 1956; *s* of Matthew and Margaret Cooke; *m* 1979, Susan George; one *s* one *d*. *Educ:* Lawrence Sheriff Sch., Rugby; Trinity Coll., Cambridge (BA 1978). Admitted Solicitor, 1981; Partner, Pinsent & Co., Solicitors, 1983–2001; Dep. Dist Judge, 1997–2001; Dist Judge, 2001–08. *Recreations:* competitive swimming, sailing, golf. *Address:* Birmingham Civil Justice Centre, Bull Street, Birmingham B4 6DS.

COOKE, Col Sir David (William Perceval), 12th Bt *cr* 1661; freelance consultant/researcher; *b* 28 April 1935; *s* of Sir Charles Arthur John Cooke, 11th Bt, and Diana (*d* 1989), *o d* of late Maj.-Gen. Sir Edward Maxwell Perceval, KCB, DSO; *S* father, 1978; *m* 1959, Margaret Frances, *o d* of Herbert Skinner, Knutsford, Cheshire; three *d*. *Educ:* Wellington College; RMA Sandhurst; Open Univ. (BA). FCILT; FCMI; Associate, Internat. Inst. of Risk and Safety Management. Commissioned 4/7 Royal Dragoon Guards, 1955; served BAOR, 1955–58; transferred to RASC, 1958; served: BAOR, 1958–60; France, 1960–62; Far East, 1962–65; UK. Transferred to RCT on formation, 1965, and served UK, 1965–76, and BAOR, 1976–80; AQMG, MoD, 1980–82; Comdr, Transport and Movements, HQ British Forces, Hong Kong, 1982–84; Comdr, Transport and Movts, NW Dist, Western Dist and Wales, 1984–87; Col, Movements 1 (Army), MoD, 1987–90. Operational service: Brunei, 1962; Malay Peninsula, 1964–65; N Ireland, 1971–72. Attended Staff Coll., Camberley, 1968 and Advanced Transport Course, 1973–74. Col 1984. Dir of Finance and Resources, Bradford City Technol. Coll., 1990–92. Silver Jubilee Medal, 1977. *Recreations:* fishing, ornithology, military history. *Heir:* *cousin* Edmund Harry Cooke-Yarborough [*b* 25 Dec. 1918; *m* 1952, Anthea Katharine (*d* 2007), *er d* of J. A. Dixon; one *s* one *d*]. *Address:* c/o HSBC, Knutsford, Cheshire WA16 6BZ.

COOKE, Dominic; Artistic Director, Royal Court Theatre, since 2007; *b* 1966; *s* of Malcolm Cooke and Gloria Solomon (*née* Turower). *Educ:* Westminster City Sch.; Univ. of Warwick (BA Hons Eng. and Theatre Studies 1988). Associate Dir, Royal Court Th., 1998–2002; Associate Dir, RSC, 2002–07; productions include: *Royal Court:* Other People, Fireface, 2000; Spinning into Butter, Redundant, Fucking Games, 2001; Plasticine, The People are Friendly, This is a Chair (co-dir), Identical Twins, 2002; Rhinoceros, The Pain and the Itch, 2007; *Royal Shakespeare Co.:* The Malcontent, 2002; Cymbeline, 2003; Macbeth, 2004; As You Like It, Postcards From America, 2005; The Crucible, The Winter's Tale, Pericles, 2006; Noughts and Crosses, 2007. *Publication:* Arabian Nights (adaptation), 1998; Noughts and Crosses (adaptation), 2007. *Address:* Royal Court Theatre, Sloane Square, SW1W 8AS. *T:* (020) 7565 5050, *Fax:* (020) 7565 5001; *e-mail:* info@royalcourttheatre.com.

COOKE, Prof. Elizabeth Jane; a Law Commissioner, since 2008; Professor of Law, University of Reading, since 2003; *b* Uxbridge, 29 April 1962; *d* of Gerald Coppin and Mary Coppin (*née* Netherwood); *m* 1985, John Cooke; one *s* one *d* (and one *s* one *d* decd). *Educ:* Magdalen Coll., Oxford (BA); Univ. of Reading (LLM). Admitted solicitor, 1988; Assistant Solicitor: Withers, 1988; Barrett & Thomson, 1989–91; University of Reading: Lectr, 1992–2001; Reader, 2001–03. *Publications:* (jtly) The Family, Law and Society, 4th edn 1996 to 6th edn 2008; The Modern Law of Estoppel, 2000; The New Law of Land Registration, 2003; Land Law, 2006; Modern Studies in Property Law, 2001, 4th edn 2007. *Recreations:* friendship, making music (organ, recorders, piano, singing), walking, watching the garden grow. *Address:* c/o The Law Commission, Steel House, 11 Tothill Street, SW1H.

COOKE, George Venables, CBE 1978; *b* 8 Sept. 1918; *s* of William Geoffrey Cooke and Constance Eva (*née* Venables); *m* 1941, Doreen (*née* Cooke); one *s* two *d*. *Educ:* Sandbach Sch., Cheshire; Lincoln Coll., Oxford, 1936–39 and 1946. MA, DipEd (Oxon). Served Army, 1939–46 (Major). Teacher, Manchester Grammar Sch., 1947–51; Professional Asst (Educn), W Riding of Yorkshire CC, 1951–53; Asst Dir of Educn, Liverpool, 1953–58; Dep. Dir of Educn, Sheffield, 1958–64; Dir of Educn, Lindsey (Lincs) CC, 1965–74; County Educn Officer, Lincolnshire CC, 1974–78; Gen. Sec., Soc. of Education Officers, 1978–84. Chm., Secretary of State's Adv. Cttee on Handicapped Children, 1973–74; Vice-Chm., Nat. Cttee of Enquiry into Special Educn (Warnock Cttee), 1974–78; Member: Jt Adv. Cttee on Agricultural Educn (Hudson Cttee), 1971–74; Parole Bd, 1984–87. Pres., Soc. of Educn Officers, 1975–76; Chm., County Educn Officers' Soc.,

1976–77. Chm., Lincs and Humberside Arts, 1987–92. Hon. LLD Hull, 1991. *Club:* Royal Over-Seas League.

COOKE, Gilbert Andrew, FCA; Chairman and Chief Executive, C. T. Bowring & Co. Ltd, 1982–88; Director, Marsh & McLennan Companies Inc., 1980–88; *b* 7 March 1923; *s* of Gilbert N. Cooke and Laurie Cooke; *m* 1949, Katherine Margaret Mary McGovern; one *s* one *d. Educ:* Bournemouth Sch. FCA 1950. Sen. Clerk, chartered accountants, 1950–54; Bowmaker Ltd: Chief Accountant, 1955; Dir, 1968; Man. Dir, 1968; Dep. Chm. and Chief Exec., 1972; C. T. Bowring & Co. Ltd: Dir, 1969; Gp Man. Dir, 1976–82. Chm., Bowring UK, 1984–88. Chm., Finance Houses Assoc., 1972–74. *Recreations:* music, reading. *Address:* Kilmarth, 66 Onslow Road, Burwood Park, Walton-on-Thames, Surrey KT12 5AY. *T:* (01932) 240451.

COOKE, Gregory Alan; Chairman, Atisreal (formerly ATIS Real Weatheralls), since 2001 (Senior Partner, Weatherall Green & Smith, 1998–2001); *b* 28 April 1949; *m* Elizabeth; one *s* two *d. Educ:* Trent Coll. (BSc). MRICS. Henley Sch. of Business Studies. Capital & Counties Property Co. Ltd, 1972–73; with Weatherall Green & Smith, subseq. ATIS Real Weatheralls, then Atisreal, 1973–. *Recreations:* ski-ing, sailing, tennis. *Address:* Atisreal, Norfolk House, 31 St James's Square, SW1Y 4JR. *Club:* Royal Automobile.

COOKE, Helen Jane; Head of Information and Research, Penny Brohn Cancer Care (formerly Bristol Cancer Help Centre), since 2005; *b* 20 Sept. 1963; *d* of Dr Michael Cooke and Mary Cooke (now Brash). *Educ:* Orme Girls' Sch., Newcastle, Staffs; St Bartholomew's Hosp., London (RGN Cert.); Univ. of Exeter (MA Complementary Health Studies 2001). Staff Nurse, St Bartholomew's Hosp., London, 1987; Hd of Nursing, Promis Recovery Centre, 1988–90; Sister, Abbotsleigh Nursing Home, 1990–92; Bristol Cancer Help Centre: Therapy Manager, then Patient Services Manager, 1992–2000; Dir of Therapy, 2000–05. *Publications:* The Bristol Approach to Living with Cancer, 2003; contrib. Complementary Therapies in Nursing and Midwifery jl. *Recreations:* stained glass design, art, travel, walking, laughing. *Address:* Penny Brohn Cancer Care, Chapel Pill Lane, Pill, Bristol BS20 0HH. *T:* (01275) 370100.

COOKE, Sir Howard (Felix Hanlan), ON 1991; GCMG 1991; GCVO 1994; CD 1978; Governor-General of Jamaica, 1991–2006; *b* 13 Nov. 1915; *s* of David Brown Cooke and Mary Jane Minto; *m* 1939, Ivy Sylvia Lucille Tai; two *s* one *d.* Teacher, Mico Trng Coll., 1936–38; Headmaster, Belle Castle All-Age Sch., 1939–50; Teacher: Port Antonio Upper Sch., 1951; Montego Bay Boys' Sch., 1952–58; Br. Manager, Standard Life Insce Co., 1960–71; Unit Manager, Jamaica Mutual Life Assce Co., 1971–81; Br. Manager, Alico Jamaica, 1982–91. Member: WI Federal Parlt, 1958–62; Senate, 1962–67; House of Representatives, 1967–80; Govt Minister, 1972–80. Sen. Elder, United Church of Jamaica and Grand Cayman; lay pastor and former Chm., Cornwall Council of Churches. Mem., Ancient and Accepted Order of Masons. Special Plaque for Distinguished Service, CPA, 1980. *Recreations:* cricket, football, gardening, reading. *Address:* c/o Office of Governor General, King's House, Hope Road, Kingston 6, Jamaica, WI.

COOKE, Hon. Sir Jeremy (Lionel), Kt 2001; **Hon. Mr Justice Cooke;** a Judge of the High Court, Queen's Bench Division, and of the Commercial Court, since 2001; a Presiding Judge, South Eastern Circuit, since 2007; *b* 28 April 1949; *s* of late Eric Edwin Cooke and of Margaret Lilian Cooke; *m* 1972, Barbara Helen Willey; one *s* two *d. Educ:* Whitgift Sch., Croydon; St Edmund Hall, Oxford (Open Exhibn, 1967; MA Jurisprudence, 1st cl. Hons 1970; Rugby blue, 1968, 1969). Harlequins RFC, 1970–75. Admitted Solicitor, 1973; with Coward Chance, 1973–76; called to the Bar, Lincoln's Inn (Droop Schol.), 1976, Bencher, 2001; QC 1990; an Asst Recorder, 1994–98; a Recorder, 1998–2001; Hd of Chambers, 7 King's Bench Walk, 1999–2001. Mem. Council, LICC Ltd (formerly London Inst. for Contemporary Christianity), 1997–. Vice-Pres., Lawyers' Christian Fellowship, 2003–. Reader, C of E, 2001–. *Recreation:* golf. *Address:* Royal Courts of Justice, Strand, WC2A 2LL. *Clubs:* National (Vice Pres., 2007–); Vincent's (Oxford).

COOKE, John Arthur; international economic relations consultant, since 2003; *b* 13 April 1943; *er s* of late Dr Arthur Hafford Cooke, MBE and Ilse Cooke (*née* Sachs); *m* 1970, Tania Frances, 2nd *d* of A. C. Crichton; one *s* two *d. Educ:* Dragon Sch.; Magdalen Coll. Sch., Oxford; Univ. of Heidelberg; King's Coll., Cambridge (Exhibnr, Sen. Scholar, BA History 1964, MA 1968); LSE. Mem., Cambridge Univ. expedition to Seistan, 1966. Asst Principal, Board of Trade, 1966; Second, later First, Sec., UK Delegn to European Communities, 1969–73; DTI, 1973–76; Office of UK Perm. Rep. to European Communities, 1976–77; Dept of Trade, 1977–80 (at Inst. Internat. d'Administration Publique, Paris, 1979); Asst Sec., Dept of Trade, 1980–84; seconded to Morgan Grenfell & Co. as Asst Dir, 1984–85; Department of Trade and Industry, 1985–97: Under Sec., Overseas Trade Div. 2, 1987–89; Head of Central Unit, 1989–92; Dir, Deregulation Unit, 1990–92; Head of Internat. Trade Policy Div., 1992–96; Dir and Advr on Trade Policy, 1996–97; Leader, UK delegn to 9th UN Conf. on Trade and Devel, 1996; Chm., OECD Trade Cttee, 1996–97; Hd of Internat. Relations, ABI, 1997–2003. Non-executive Director: RTZ Pillar Ltd, 1990–93; W Middx Univ. Hosp. NHS Trust, 1996–98; Bd Sec., ENO, 1996–. Chairman: Financial Leaders' Wkg Gp Insurance Evaluation Team, 2002–; Liberalisation of Trade in Services Cttee, Internat. Financial Services, London, 2006–; European Co-Chm., Financial Leaders' Wkg Gp, 2006–; Dep. Chm., SITPRO Ltd, 2006–. Member: Exec. Bd, Anglo-Irish Encounter, 2004–08; Adv. Council, Federal Trust, 2004–; Adv. Bd, Eur. Centre for Internat. Political Economy, 2008–. Trustee, St Luke's Community Trust, 1983–93 and 1996–2000 (Vice-Chm., 1991–93; Patron, 2000–); Member: Council, Marie Curie Cancer Care (formerly Marie Curie Meml Foundn), 1992–2008 (Vice Pres., 2008–); Bd, Marie Curie Trading Ltd, 1999–2002. Trustee, ENO Benevolent Fund, 2001–. Mem. Editl Bd, Internat. Trade Law Reports, 1997–. *Publications:* articles and contribs to seminars, mainly on internat. trade in financial services. *Recreations:* reading, travelling, looking at buildings. *Address:* 29 The Avenue, Kew, Richmond, Surrey TW9 2AL. *T:* (020) 8940 6712, *Fax:* (020) 8332 7447. *Clubs:* Oxford and Cambridge; Cambridge Union.

COOKE, Air Vice-Marshal John Nigel Carlyle, CB 1984; OBE 1954; Consultant Physician: Civil Aviation Authority, 1985–2003; King Edward VII Hospital, Midhurst, 1988–93; *b* 16 Jan. 1922; *s* of Air Marshal Sir Cyril Bertram Cooke, KCB, CBE and Phyllis Amelia Elizabeth Cooke; *m* 1958, Elizabeth Helena Murray Johnstone; two *s* one *d. Educ:* Felsted Sch.; St Mary's Hosp., Paddington (MD, BS (London)). FRCP, FRCPEd, MRCS, MFOM. House Physician, St Mary's, Paddington, 1945; RAF medical Br., 1945–85; Sen. Registrar, St George's, London, 1956–58; Consultant Physician, RAF, 1958–85; overseas service in Germany, Singapore, Aden; Prof. of Aviation Medicine, 1974–79; Dean of Air Force Medicine, 1979–83; Senior Consultant, RAF, 1983–85. UK Mem., Medical Adv. Bd, European Space Agency, 1978–84; Consultant to CAA, UK, 1972–; Consultant Advr to Sultan of Oman's Air Force, 1985–91. Chairman: Defence Med. Services Postgrad. Council, 1980–82; Ethics Cttee, RAF Inst. of Aviation Medicine, 1987–89; Pres., Assoc. of Aviation Med. Examiners, 1986–94. QHP 1979–85. *Publications:* articles on metabolic and aviation medicine subjects in numerous medical jls. *Recreations:* gliding, fly fishing. *Address:* 4 Lincoln Close, Stoke Mandeville, Bucks HP22 5YS. *Cl* Royal Air Force.

COOKE, Joseph; *see* Cooke, P. J. D.

COOKE, Kathleen Joyce; *see* Collins, K. J.

COOKE, Margaret Rose; *see* Cole, M. R.

COOKE, Nicholas Orton; QC 1998; **His Honour Judge Cooke;** a Senior Circ Judge, since 2007; Recorder of Cardiff, since 2008; *b* 1 July 1955; 2nd and *o* surv. *s* of O. Cooke and V. Cooke; *m* 1979, Jean Ann Tucker; two *d. Educ:* King Edward's Sc Birmingham; UC Wales, Aberystwyth (Sweet and Maxwell Prize; LLB 1st Cl. Ho 1976). Called to the Bar, Middle Temple, 1977 (Blackstone Entrance Exhibn 1976); practice at the Bar, 1978–2007; Asst Recorder, 1994–97; Recorder, 1997–2007; Lead Wales and Chester Circuit, 2007. Dep. Pres., Mental Health Review Tribunal, Wal 1999–. Judge of the Provincial Court of the Church in Wales, 2004–; Chancellor, Dio. St Davids, 2005–. *Recreations:* hockey, theatre. *Address:* Cardiff Crown Court, Ki Edward VII Avenue, Cathays Park, Cardiff CF10 3PG.

COOKE, (Patrick) Joseph (Dominic), FCMC; Vice-Chairman, Daily Telegrap 1994–96 (Managing Director, 1987–94); *s* of Patrick Cooke and Mary (*née* Naughton); 1960, Margaret Mary Brown; two *s* four *d. Educ:* St Joseph's Coll.; University Co Galway (BE). CEng, MICE, MIMechE; FCMC (FIMC 1968); AIIRA. United Steel Co 1952–54; Workington Iron & Steel Co., 1954–61; Urwick, Orr and Partners Lt 1961–73: Sen. Partner, 1967; Principal Partner, 1970; founded Cooke Manageme Consultants Ltd, 1973; non-exec. Dir, EMAP plc, 1984–96; Consultant, Daily Telegrap 1985–87; non-executive Director: IFRA, 1990–94 (Senator, 1994–); Hollinger, 1992–9 Sandford Smith Award, Inst. Management Consultants, 1967. *Recreations:* golf, gardenin *Address:* Apartment 305, Bâtiment les Terrasses, Parc Saint Roman, 7 Avenue Sai Roman, MC 98000, Monaco. *Club:* Monte-Carlo (Pres., 2003–04).

COOKE, Peter; *see* Cooke, W. P.

COOKE, Prof. Richard William Ingram, MD; FRCP, FRCPH, FMedSci; Profess of Neonatal Medicine, University of Liverpool, 1988–90 and since 1998; *b* 23 May 194 *s* of Edward Ingram Cooke and Pauline Ellen Ross Cooke (*née* Foster); *m* 1977, There Elizabeth Reardon Garside; one *s* three *d. Educ:* Colfe's Sch.; Charing Cross Hosp. Me Sch. (qual. 1971; MD 1979). DCH 1973; FRCP 1986; FRCPCH 1997. Research Fellow then Lectr, Oxford Univ., 1976–78; Staff Paediatrician, Sophia Kinderziekenhu Rotterdam, 1978–79; University of Liverpool: Sen. Lectr in Child Health, 1980–8 Reader, 1983–87; Prof. of Paediatric Medicine, 1991–98. President: British Asso Perinatal Paediatrics, 1990–92; Neonatal Soc., 1997–2000; Vice-Pres., RCPCH, 199 (Actg Pres., 1999–2000). Founder FMedSci 1998. *Publications:* (ed jtly) Chemical Tra Names and Synonyms, 1978; (jtly) The Very Immature Infant, 1989; (ed jtly) The Ba under 1000 grams, 1989; (ed jtly) Practical Perinatal Care, 1999; numerous articles an papers on neonatal medicine. *Recreations:* jazz, contemporary painting. *Address:* Neonat Unit, Liverpool Women's Hospital, Liverpool L8 7SS. *T:* (0151) 702 4093; 11 Weste Drive, Liverpool L19 0LX.

COOKE, His Honour Roger Arnold; a Circuit Judge, 1989–2005; Deputy Circu Judge, 2005–07; *b* 30 Nov. 1939; *s* of late Stanley Gordon and Frances Mabel Cooke; 1970, Hilary Robertson; two *s* two *d. Educ:* Repton; Magdalen Coll., Oxford (BA 196 MA 1966). Astbury Scholar, Middle Temple, 1962; called to the Bar, Middle Templ 1962, *ad eund* Lincoln's Inn, 1967 (Bencher, 1994); in practice, Chancery Bar, 1963–8 Asst Recorder, 1982–87; Recorder, 1987–89; authorised to sit as a Judge of the Hig Court, Chancery Div., 1993, QBD, 1995. Sec., Chancery Bar Assoc., 1979–89; Membe Bar Disciplinary Tribunal, 1988–89; Inns of Court Advocacy Trng Cttee, 1995–200 Advocacy Studies Bd, 1996–2000. Mem., Inst. of Conveyancers, 1983–; MRI 196 *Publication:* (contrib.) A Portrait of Lincoln's Inn, 2007. *Recreations:* gardenin photography, history, old buildings, travel. *Address:* c/o Radcliffe Chambers, 11 Ne Square, Lincoln's Inn, WC2A 3QB. *Club:* Athenæum.

COOKE, Roger Malcolm; Partner in charge, Administration, Arthur Anderse 1995–98; *b* 12 March 1945; *s* of Sidney and Elsie Cooke; *m* 1968, Antoinette; one *s* on *d.* FCA, FTII. Qualified Chartered Accountant, 1968; Arthur Andersen & Co.: joine 1968, Tax Div.; Partner, 1976; Head, London Tax Div., 1979–89; area co-ordinator, ta practice, Europe, Middle East, Africa and India, 1989–93; Dep. Man. Partner, UK, an Area Co-Ordinator, Tax Europe, 1989–93; Man. Partner-Chief Financial Office Chicago, 1993–95. Mem., Exec. Bd, 2006–, Hon. Treas., 2007–, Glos CCC. Hon. Treas Wooden Spoon Soc., 1999–2006. *Publication:* Establishing a Business in the Unite Kingdom, 1978. *Recreations:* playing tennis, travel, ski-ing, cricket, football, good foo *Address:* Madoreen, Larch Avenue, Sunninghill SL5 0AP. *Club:* Royal Berkshire Racque and Health.

COOKE, Prof. Sir Ronald Urwick, Kt 2002; DL; PhD, DSc; AcSS; Vice-Chancello University of York, 1993–2002; *b* 1 Sept. 1941; *y s* of Ernest Cooke and Lillian (*n* Mount), Maidstone, Kent; *m* 1968, Barbara Anne, *d* of A. Baldwin; one *s* one *d. Edu* Ashford Grammar Sch.; University College London, Univ. of London (BSc 1st Cl. Hon MSc, PhD, DSc; Fellow, 1994). Lectr, UCL, 1961–75; Prof. of Geography, 1975–8 Dean of Science, 1978–80, and Vice-Principal, 1979–80, Bedford Coll., Univ. of London Prof. and Hd of Dept of Geography, 1981–93, Dean of Arts, 1991–92, and Vice-Provos 1991–93, UCL. Dir, UCL Press, 1990–95. Amer. Council of Learned Societies Fellow UCLA, 1964–65 and 1973; Visiting Professor: UCLA, 1968; Univ. of Arizona, Tucsor 1970; Arizona State Univ., Tempe, 1988. Desert research in N and S America, N Afric and ME. Chm. and co-Founder, Geomorphological Services Ltd, 1986–90. Member: US UK Fulbright Commn, 1995–2000; HEFCE, 1996–2003; Chm., Jt Informations Systen Cttee, 2003–. Chm., British Geomorphological Res. Group, 1979; Pres., RGS, 2000–0 (Mem. Council, 1980–83; Back Grant, 1977; Founder's Medal, 1994); Mem. Counci Inst. of British Geographers, 1973–75 (Pres., 1991–92). Hon. Sec., York Archaeologica Trust, 1994–96; Chairman: Castle Howard Arboretum Trust, 2002–; York Local Strateg Partnership, 2007–; Trustee: Laurence Sterne Trust, 1994–2006; Nat. Mus. of Science an Industry, 2002–; York Museums Trust, 2002–08; York Civic Trust, 2002–; St Leonard Hospice, York, 2003–. Patron: York Early Music Fest., 1995–; Elvington Air Mus 1999–. Mem., Co. of Merchant Adventurers of City of York. DL N Yorks, 2002. Hon Freeman, City of York, 2006. Fellow, RHBNC, 1993. Hon. DCL Kent, 2004; Hon DPhil Glos, 2004; DUniv York, 2005. *Publications:* (ed with J. H. Johnson) Trends i Geography, 1969; (with A. Warren) Geomorphology in Deserts, 1973; (with J. C Doornkamp) Geomorphology in Environmental Management, 1974, 2nd edn 1990; (wit R. W. Reeves) Arroyos and Environmental Change in the American Southwest, 197 (contrib.) Geology, Geomorphology and Pedology of Bahrain, 1980; (contrib.) Urba Geomorphology in Drylands, 1982; Geomorphological Hazards in Los Angeles, 198 (with A. Warren and A. S. Goudie) Desert Geomorphology, 1993; (with G. B. Gibb

Crumbling Heritage?, 1993; Why York is Special, 2006; contribs mainly on desert and applied geomorphology in prof. jls. *Address:* 31 New Walk Terrace, York YO10 4BG.

COOKE, (William) Peter, CBE 1997; *b* 1 Feb. 1932; *s* of late Douglas Edgar Cooke, MC and Florence May (*née* Mills); *m* 1st, 1957, Maureen Elizabeth (*d* 1999), *er d* of late Dr E. A. Haslam-Fox; two *s* two *d*; 2nd, 2005, Mrs Julia Mary Bain (*née* Warrack). *Educ:* Royal Grammar Sch., High Wycombe; Kingswood Sch., Bath; Merton Coll., Oxford (MA; Hon. Fellow 1997). Entered Bank of England, 1955; Bank for Internat. Settlements, Basel, 1958–59; Personal Asst to Man. Dir, IMF, Washington, DC, 1961–65; Sec., City Panel on Takeovers and Mergers, 1968–69; First Dep. Chief Cashier, Bank of England, 1970–73; Adviser to Governors, 1973–76; Hd of Banking Supervision, 1976–85; Associate Dir, 1982–88; Chm., Price Waterhouse Regulatory Adv. Practice, 1989–96; Advr, Price Waterhouse, subseq. PricewaterhouseCoopers, 1997–2002. Housing Corporation: Mem. Bd, 1988–97; Dep. Chm., 1994–97; Chm., 1997. Chairman: City EEC Cttee, 1973–80; Group of Ten Cttee on Banking Regulations and Supervisory Practices at BIS, Basel, 1977–88. Director: Safra Republic Holdings SA, 1989–99; FSA (UK), 1994–; Alexander & Alexander Services Inc., 1994–96; Bank of China Internat. Hldgs Ltd, 1997–98; Housing Finance Corp., 1997–2003; State Street Bank (Europe) Ltd, 1998–2006; Bank of China Internat. UK Ltd, 1999–; HSBC Republic Holdings SA, 2000–01; Bank of China Ltd, 2004–07; Medi Capital Hldgs, 2006–. Dir, Church Housing Trust, 1984–2006. Member: Nat. Cttee, English Churches Housing Group, 1977–94; Council, RIIA, 1992–2005 (Dep. Chm., 1998–2005). Governor: Pangbourne Coll., 1982–2002; Kingswood Sch., 1991–2002. Pres., Merton Soc., 1995–98. *Recreations:* music, golf, travel. *Address:* Oak Lodge, Maltmans Lane, Gerrards Cross, Bucks SL9 8RP. *Clubs:* Reform; Denham Golf.

COOKE-PRIEST, Rear Adm. Colin Herbert Dickinson, CB 1993; Chief Executive, The Trident Trust, 1994–99; a Gentleman Usher to the Queen, since 1994; *b* 17 March 1939; *s* of Dr William Hereward Dickinson Priest and Harriet Lesley Josephine Priest (*née* Cooke); *m* 1965, Susan Mary Diana Hobler; two *s* two *d*. *Educ:* St Pirans, Maidenhead; Marlborough Coll.; BRNC, Dartmouth. Entered RN, 1957; Lieut, 1960; exchange service with RAN, 1968–70; commanded: HMS Plymouth, 1975–76; HMS Berwick, 1976; Airwarfare Directorate, Naval Staff, MoD, 1977–79; Naval Asst to C-in-C Fleet, 1979–81; Asst Dir, Naval Air Warfare, 1981–82; CO, HMS Boxer, 1983–85; Dir, Maritime Tactical Sch., 1985–87; CO, HMS Brilliant and Capt. Second Frigate Sqn, 1987–89; Dep. Asst Chief of Staff (Ops) to Supreme Allied Comdr Europe, 1989–90; Flag Officer, Naval Aviation, 1990–93. Chm., FAA Officers' Assoc., 1998–2005. FRAeS 1992. Freeman, City of London, 1985; Hon. Liveryman, Coachmakers' and Coachharness Makers' Co., 1985; Liveryman, GAPAN, 1999– (Master, March 2009–). *Address:* Northwood Farmhouse, Northwood Lane, Hayling Island, Hants PO11 0LR. *Club:* Army and Navy.

COOKSEY, Sir David (James Scott), GBE 2007; Kt 1993; Chairman: London & Continental Railways Ltd, since 2006; Eurasian Natural Resources Corp. plc, since 2007; a Director, Bank of England, 1994–2005 (Chairman, non-executive Directors Committee, 2001–05); *b* 14 May 1940; *s* of Dr Frank S. Cooksey, CBE, and Muriel M. Cooksey; *m* 1973, Janet Wardell-Yerburgh (marr. diss. 2003); one *s* one *d*. *Educ:* Westminster Sch.; St Edmund Hall, Oxford Univ. (MA; Hon. Fellow 1995). Dir of Manufacturing, Formica International, 1969–71; Man. Dir, Intercobra Ltd, 1971–80; Man. Dir, 1981–87, Chm., 1987–2006, Advent Venture Partners; Director: Advent International Corp., 1985–90; Electra Risk Capital, 1981–90; Bespak plc, 1993–2004 (Chm., 1995–2004); William Baird plc, 1995–2002; Establishment Investment Trust plc, 2002–; Diamond Light Source Ltd, 2002–08 (Chm.); Resolution plc (formerly Resolution Life Gp), 2004–08; Chm., Quadrille Publishing Ltd, 2007–. Chairman: Audit Commn, 1986–95; Local Govt Commn for England, 1995–96. Member: Council, CBI, 1976–88; Scottish Economic Council, 1980–87; Council, British Venture Capital Assoc., 1983–89 (Chm., 1983–84); Innovation Adv. Bd, DTI, 1988–93; Dir, Eur. Venture Capital Assoc., 2004–07 (Chm., 2005–06); Chairman: MRC/DoH Jt Health Res. Delivery Gp, 2004–06; DoH UK Clinical Res. Collaboration Industry Reference Gp, 2004–; HM Treasury Cooksey Review of UK Health Res., 2006. Chairman: Small Business Investment Taskforce, DTI, 2000–04; Biosci. Innovation Growth Taskforce, DoH/DTI, 2003–08; Steering Gp, UK Centre for Med. Res. and Innovation, 2008–. Chm., State Honours Cttee, 2005–. Mem. Council, 1993–2003, Pro Chancellor, 2007–, Southampton Univ. Trustee: Mary Rose Trust, 1994–2001 (Chm., 1996–2001); Gov., Wellcome Trust, 1995–99. Hon. FMedSci 2004; Hon. Fellow, BAAS, 2004. Hon. Fellow: Univ. of Wales, Cardiff, 1998; Imperial Coll. London, 2007. Hon. DBA Kingston, 1996; Hon. DSc Southampton, 2008. *Recreations:* sailing, music, theatre. *Address:* c/o Eurasian Natural Resources Corp. plc, 16 St James's Street, SW1A 1ER. *Clubs:* Boodle's, Royal Thames Yacht; Royal Yacht Squadron.

COOKSEY, Janet Clouston Bewley, (Poppy), (Lady Cooksey), OBE 2004; PhD; art historian and picture restorer, since 1978; *b* 15 Feb. 1940; *d* of late Dr Ian Aysgarth Bewley Cathie and Dr Marian Josephine Cunning; *m* 1966, Hugh Arthur Wardell-Yerburgh (*d* 1970); one *d*; *m* 1973, Sir David Cooksey, *qv* (marr. diss. 2003); one *s* one *d*. *Educ:* Cheltenham Ladies' Coll.; Univ. of London (BSc ext.); Univ. of St Andrews (PhD Fine Arts). Amateur fencer, 1956–72, 1998–: Jun. Schs Champion, 1954 and 1955; Sen. Schs and under-20 Champion, 1956; British Ladies Foil Champion, 1965, 1967 and 1969–72; winner: De Beaumont International, 1967, 1971 and 1972; Desprez Cup, 1964–67, 1969 and 1972; Jubilee Bowl, 1964–67, 1970–72; double gold medallist, Commonwealth Games, 1966 and 1970; repr. GB in Olympic fencing teams, 1964, 1968, 1972 and in World Championships, 1963–72; veteran competitions include: double gold medallist (foil and epée individual and team) Commonwealth Games, Johannesburg, 1999, Wales, 2001; double gold medallist (foil and epée), World Championships, Budapest, 2000, Martinique, 2001, Tampa, Fla, 2002; double gold medallist (foil and epée), European Champs, Cologne, 2001. Lectr, extra-mural studies, Univ. of St Andrews, 1975–78, and Dir, Alexander Nasmyth exhibn, 1979; Dir, Special Projects, Univ. of Southampton, 1993–96. Mem., Bd of Trustees, Royal Armouries, 1993–99 (Mem., Design Cttee, 1994–99). Chairman: RNLI Crew Training Appeal, 1996–2000; Countess Mountbatten Hospice Appeal, 1996–2000; Gift of Sight Appeal, Southampton Gen. Hosp., 1998–2001; Area Chm., Children's Hospice Appeal, 1994–96. Member: Corporate Develt Bd, NSPCC, 1997–2008; Bd Trustees, Mental Health Foundn, 1997–2000; Nat. Appeal Bd, Marie Curie Cancer Care, 1997–2000; Scrutiny Panel for N and Mid Hants HA, 2000. Trustee, British Fencing Assoc., 2000–. FRSA 1986. Freeman, City of London, 2004; Mem. Court, Guild of Freemen, 2005–. DL Hants, 1998–2005. *Publications:* The Pleasure of Antiques, 1973; Alexander Nasmyth 1758–1840 (exhibn catalogue), 1979; Alexander Nasmyth: a man of the Scottish Renaissance, 1991; contributed to: The Dictionary of Art, 1996; Oxford DNB, 2004. *Recreations:* entertaining, reading, gardens, the arts, travel, tennis, sailing, fencing. *Address:* Uplands House, Upton, Banbury, Oxon OX15 6HJ. *Clubs:* Royal Thames Yacht, Salle Paul Fencing.

COOKSLEY, Nigel James; QC 2002; *b* 2 April 1953; *s* of Norman Cooksley and Diana Margaret Barnes Cooksley; *m* 1980, Stephanie Jupe; one *s* one *d*. *Educ:* Felsted Sch.; Queens' Coll., Cambridge (MA Law). Called to the Bar, Inner Temple, 1975; in practice, specialising in personal injury, clinical negligence, professional negligence, health and safety work and matters relating to conditional fees. Bar Council: Mem., Conditional Fee Agreements Panel; Mem., Civil Justice Council, 2002–04; Chm., Personal Injuries Bar Assoc. *Recreations:* travel, golf, football, cricket, Rugby, horse racing. *Address:* Old Square Chambers, 10–11 Bedford Row, WC1R 4BU. *T:* (020) 7269 0300, *Fax:* (020) 7405 1387; *e-mail:* cooksley@oldsquare.co.uk; 3 Orchard Court, St Augustine's Yard, Bristol BS1 5DP. *Clubs:* Chesfield Downs Golf, Letchworth Golf, Weston Cricket.

COOKSON, Clive Michael; Science Editor, Financial Times, since 1991; *b* London, 13 Feb. 1952; *s* of Prof. Richard Clive Cookson, *qv*; *m* 1978, Caroline Davidson; one *s* one *d*. *Educ:* Winchester Coll.; Brasenose Coll., Oxford (BSc 1st Cl. Hons Chem.). Trainee journalist, Luton Evening Post, 1974–76; Sci. corresp., THES, 1976–77; American Ed., Times supplements, 1977–81; Technol. corresp., The Times, 1981–83; Sci. corresp., BBC Radio, 1983–87; Technol. Ed., 1987–90, Pharmaceuticals corresp., 1990–91, FT. *Address:* Financial Times, 1 Southwark Bridge, SE1 9HL; *e-mail:* clive.cookson@ft.com.

COOKSON, Prof. Richard Clive, MA, PhD; FRS 1968; FRSC; Research Professor of Chemistry in the University of Southampton, 1983–85, now Emeritus Professor (Professor of Chemistry, 1957–83); *b* 27 Aug. 1922; *s* of late Clive Cookson; *m* 1948, Ellen Fawaz (*d* 2002); two *s*. *Educ:* Harrow Sch.; Trinity Coll., Cambridge. BA 1944; MA, PhD Cantab 1947. Research Fellow, Harvard Univ., 1948; Research Div. of Glaxo Laboratories Ltd, 1949–51; Lectr, Birkbeck Coll., London Univ., 1951–57. *Publications:* papers, mainly in Jl Chem. Soc. *Address:* Northfield House, Coombe Bissett, Salisbury, Wilts SP5 4JZ.

See also C. M. Cookson.

COOKSON, Thomas Richard, MA; Headmaster, Winchester College, 2003–05; *b* 7 July 1942; *s* of Samuel Harold Cookson, MD, FRCP and Elizabeth Mary Cookson; *m* 1972, Carol Hayley; three *d*. *Educ:* Winchester Coll.; Balliol Coll., Oxford (MA Eng.Lit.). Assistant Master: Winchester, 1964–65; Hopkins Grammar Sch., New Haven, USA, 1965–67; Winchester, 1967–72; Manchester Grammar Sch., 1972–74; Head of English, Winchester, 1974–83, Housemaster, 1983–90; Headmaster: King Edward VI Sch., Southampton, 1990–96; Sevenoaks School, 1996–2001; Principal, British Sch. in Colombo, 2002–03. Governor: Rugby Sch., 2005–; English Coll. in Prague, 2005–; New Sch. at W Heath, 2006–. *Publications:* John Keats, 1972; Bernard Shaw, 1972. *Recreation:* golf. *Address:* Chapel Cottage, Kemsing Road, Wrotham, Kent TN15 7BU.

COOLING, Rear Adm. Robert George; Assistant Chief of the Naval Staff, Ministry of Defence, since 2008; *b* 11 July 1957; *s* of Edwin and Rosalind Cooling; *m* 1984, Helen Smith; two *s*. *Educ:* Christchurch Cathedral Sch., Oxford; King's Sch., Canterbury; Keele Univ. (BA Hons Internat. Relns 1978); BRNC, Dartmouth, 1978. Commnd RN, 1978; comd, HMS Sandpiper, 1985–86; Instructor in Navigation, US Naval Acad., Annapolis, 1990–92; comd HMS Battleaxe, 1992–93; jssc 1993; CoS to Comdr UK Task Gp, 1997–98; comd HMS Montrose and 6th Frigate Sqn, 1998–2000; Dir Naval Staff, MoD, 2002–03; hcsc 2004; comd HMS Illustrious, 2004–06 (Carrier Strike Gp Comdr); has served in ops in Arctic Circle, ME and Gulf reg., Indian Ocean, Mediterranean, S China Sea and Atlantic; comd UK Task Gp evacuation operation from Beirut, 2006; Dep. Comdr, Striking and Support Force, NATO, 2006–08. Freeman, City of London, 2007; Hon. Mem., Co. of Lightermongers, 2004. *Recreations:* travel, country pursuits. *Address:* Ministry of Defence, Main Building, Whitehall, SW1A 2HB. *Clubs:* Liberal; Royal Navy of 1765 and 1785.

COOMBE, His Honour Gerald Hugh; a Circuit Judge, 1986–98; *b* 16 Dec. 1925; *s* of William Stafford Coombe and Mabel Florence Coombe; *m* 1957, Zoë Margaret Richards; one *s* one *d*. *Educ:* Alleyn's School, Dulwich; Hele's School, Exeter; Exeter College, Oxford. MA 1950. RAF (Navigator), 1944–48; Solicitor, 1953; Partner, Whitehead Monckton, Maidstone, 1956–86; HM Coroner, Maidstone, 1962–86; a Recorder, 1983–86. *Club:* Royal Air Force.

COOMBES, Charles; *see* Coombes, R. C. D. S.

COOMBES, Keva Christopher; formerly with R. M. Broudie & Co., solicitors; *b* 23 Dec. 1949; *s* of Arthur Edward Coombes and Beatrice Claire Coombes; *m* 1970, Kathy Gannon; two *s* one *d*. *Educ:* Chatham House Grammar Sch.; Univ. of East Anglia (BA). Admitted Solicitor, 1977; Consultant, David Phillips Harris & Whalley, 1986. Member: Liverpool CC, 1976–80, 1986–92 (Leader, 1987–90); Merseyside CC, 1981–86 (Leader, 1982–86). Contested (Lab) Hyndburn, 1987. *Address:* c/o R. M. Broudie & Co., 1–3 Sir Thomas Street, Liverpool L1 8BW. *T:* (0151) 227 1429.

COOMBES, Prof. (Raoul) Charles (Dalmedo Stuart), MD; PhD; FRCP, FMedSci; Professor of Medical Oncology and Head of Department of Cancer Medicine, since 1997, and Director of Cancer Research UK (formerly Imperial College Cancer Research (UK)) Laboratories, since 1999, Imperial College Faculty of Medicine, Hammersmith Hospital; Director of Cancer Services, Hammersmith Hospitals NHS Trust, 1995–2006; *b* 20 April 1949; *s* of late Raoul Coombes and Doreen Coombes; *m* 1984, Caroline Sarah Oakes; two *s* two *d*. *Educ:* Douai Sch.; St George's Hosp. Med. Sch. (MB BS); Inst. of Cancer Res., London (PhD 1978; MD 1981). MRCP 1973, FRCP 1990. MRC Clinical Res. Fellow, 1974–77; Sen. Registrar, 1977–80, Hon. Consultant, 1980–83, Royal Marsden Hosp.; Sen. Clinical Scientist, Ludwig Inst. for Cancer Res., 1980–83; Consultant Physician, St George's Hosp., 1983–90; Prof. and Hd of Dept of Med. Oncology, 1990–97, Dean of Res., 1993–97, Charing Cross and Westminster Med. Sch. Civilian Consultant, RAF, 1993–. FMedSci 2001. *Publications:* Breast Cancer Management, 1981; The New Endocrinology of Cancer, 1987; New Targets in Cancer Therapy, 1994; numerous papers and articles in professional jls. *Recreations:* painting, walking. *Address:* 13 Dorlcote Road, SW18 3RT. *Club:* Chelsea Arts.

COOMBS, Anthony Michael Vincent; Chairman, S & U plc, since 2008 (Managing Director, 1999–2008); Director, Grevayne Properties Ltd, since 1972; *b* 18 Nov. 1952; *s* of Clifford Keith Coombs and Celia Mary Gostling (*née* Vincent); *m* 1984, Andrea Caroline (*née* Pritchard); one *s*. *Educ:* Bilton Grange Sch.; Charterhouse; Worcester Coll., Oxford (MA). Birmingham City Council: Mem., 1978–88: Deputy Chairman: Educn Cttee, 1982–84; Social Services Cttee, 1982–84; Cons. spokesman on educn, Birmingham MDC, 1984–86. MP (C) Wyre Forest, 1987–97; contested (C) same seat, 1997. PPS to Rt Hon. David Mellor, MP, 1989–92, to Rt Hon. Gillian Shephard, MP, 1995–96; an Asst Govt Whip, 1996–97. Vice-Chairman: Cons. Back-Bench Educn Cttee, 1993–97 (Sec., 1987–93); Cons Parly Educn Cttee, 1993–97; All Party Parly Sports Cttee, 1993–97; Parly Human Rights Gp, 1993–97 (Sec., 1987–93); Parly Social Scis Gp, 1994–97; Sec., Cons. Parly Finance Cttee, 1994–96. Mem., Exec. Cttee, Conservative Team 1000, 1997–2001; Treas., Cons Party, 2004–05. Chairman: Businessesforsale.com plc, 2000–02; Cubana Restaurants Ltd, 2002–. Member: Bd, Develt Cttee, Worcester Coll., Oxford, 1996–98; Bd, Birmingham Royal Ballet Develt Trust, 1998–. Dir, Schools Outreach, 1997–. Pres., Wyre Forest "Solidarity" Campaign, 1987–97; Mem., One Nation Gp.

Vice-Chm., Friends of Cyprus, 1992–97. Chm. of Governors, Perry Common Sch., Birmingham, 1978–93; Governor: King Edward Foundn, 1982–88; Birmingham Coll. of Tourism, 1982–88; Ind. Primary and Secondary Educn Trust, 1997–. Chm. of Trustees, Nat. Inst. for Conductive Educn, 2001– (Trustee, 1998–). *Publications:* Bow Group papers, numerous articles in newspapers and jls. *Recreations:* golf, tennis, occasional football, music, theatre, ballet. *Address:* 18 Cheyne Walk, SW3 5RA. *Clubs:* Royal Automobile, Annabel's; Little Aston Golf.

COOMBS, Derek Michael; *b* 12 Aug. 1937; *m* 1986, Jennifer Lonsdale; two *s*, and one *s* one *d* by previous marriage. *Educ:* Rydal Prep. Sch.; Bromsgrove. Dir, Metalrax Gp plc, 1975–2002; Chairman: S & U plc, 1976–2008; Co-Founder, Chm., 1995–2007, Chief Exec., 1999–2007, President, 2007–, Prospect Publishing Ltd. Political journalist. MP (C) Yardley, 1970–Feb. 1974. Successfully introduced unsupported Private Member's Bill for relaxation of Earnings Rule, 1972, establishing parly record for a measure of its kind; specialist on economic affairs. Lectured on foreign affairs at Cons. weekend confs. Active pro-European. Governor, Royal Hosp. and Home for Incurables. *Publications:* numerous articles on home, economic and European affairs. *Recreations:* friends, reading, painting. *Address:* Cheyne Row, SW3. *T:* (020) 7352 6709.

COOMBS, Douglas Stafford, PhD; Controller, Books Division, British Council, 1980–83, retired; *b* 23 Aug. 1924; *s* of Alexander John Coombs and Rosina May (*née* Stafford); *m* 1950, Valerie Nyman; one *s* three *d*. *Educ:* Royal Liberty Sch., Romford; University College of Southampton; University College London (BA Hons, PhD). Served Royal Air Force, 1943–47. Lecturer in History, University College of the Gold Coast (subseq. Univ. of Ghana), 1952–60; British Council, 1960–: Nigeria, 1960–62; Overseas Student Centre, London, 1962–67; Bombay, 1967–73; Representative: Zambia, 1973–76; Yugoslavia, 1976–79; Visiting Fellow, Postgrad. School of Librarianship and Information Science, Univ. of Sheffield, 1979–80. Consultant, Byways and Bridleways Trust, 1984–; Chm., Wootton Rivers Village Soc., 1985–88. Election Agent, Devizes CLP, 1996–97. Jt Editor, Rights of Way Law Review, 1998–2001. *Publications:* The Conduct of the Dutch, 1958; The Gold Coast, Britain and The Netherlands, 1963; Spreading the Word: the library work of the British Council, 1988; articles in historical jls. *Recreations:* travel, walking, watching cricket. *Address:* 33 Whiteledges, Ealing, W13 8JB. *T:* (020) 8998 6311. *Club:* Royal Commonwealth Society.

COOMBS, Kay, OBE 2005; HM Diplomatic Service, retired; Ambassador to Honduras, 2002–04; *b* 8 July 1945; *d* of late William Tom Coombs and Beatrice Mabel Coombs (*née* Angel). *Educ:* Univ. of Newcastle upon Tyne (BA Hons). Joined FCO, 1967; Bonn, 1971–73; Latin American floater, 1974–75; Zagreb, 1976–79; FCO, 1979–82; La Paz, 1982–86; Rome, 1987–91; FCO, 1991–95; Beijing, 1995–98; Ambassador to Mongolia, 1999–2001. *Recreations:* listening to classical music, reading, flora, cooking, languages, Museum of Garden History, enjoying the arts generally.

COOMBS, Ven. Peter Bertram; Archdeacon of Reigate, 1988–95, now Emeritus; *b* 30 Nov. 1928; *s* of Bertram Robert and Margaret Ann Coombs; *m* 1953, Catherine Ann (*née* Buckwell); one *s* one *d*. *Educ:* Reading Sch.; Bristol Univ. (MA 1960); Clifton Theological Coll. Curate, Christ Church, Beckenham, 1960–64; Rector, St Nicholas, Nottingham, 1964–68; Vicar, Christ Church, New Malden, 1968–75; Rural Dean of Kingston upon Thames, 1970–75; Archdeacon of Wandsworth, 1975–88. *Recreations:* walking, sketching. *Address:* 92 Locks Heath Park Road, Locks Heath, Southampton SO31 6LZ. *T:* (01489) 577288.

COOMBS, Simon Christopher; Managing Agent, South Swindon Conservative Association, 2001–04; *b* 21 Feb. 1947; *s* of late Ian Peter Coombs and of Rachel Robins Coombs; *m* 1983, Kathryn Lee Coe Royce (marr. diss. 2003). *Educ:* Reading University (BA, MPhil); Wycliffe College. Marketing Executive, British Telecom and Post Office, Data and Telex, 1970–82; Marketing Manager, Telex Networks, British Telecom, 1982–83; Business Develt Advr, Inst. of Customer Service, 1997–2001. Mem., Southern Electricity Consultative Council, 1981–84. Reading Borough Council: Mem., 1969–84; Chm., Transportation Cttee, 1976–83; Vice-Chm., Policy Cttee, 1976–83; Dep. Leader, 1976–81; Chief Whip, 1983. MP (C) Swindon, 1983–97; contested (C) Swindon South, 1997, 2001. PPS to Minister of State for Industry and IT, 1984–85, to Parly Under-Sec. of State DoE, and Minister of State for the Environment, 1985, to Sec. of State for Scotland, 1993–95, to Pres. of BoT, 1995–97. Member: Select Cttee on Employment, 1987–92; British-American Parly Gp, 1983–; CPA, 1983–97; Chairman: Cable TV Gp, 1987–97 (Sec., 1986–87); British Malaŵi Parly Gp, 1985–93 (Sec., 1985–89); Pres., Parly Food and Health Forum, 1993–97 (Chm., 1989–93; Sec., 1985–89); Treasurer: Parly IT Cttee, 1987–97; Anglo-Malta Parly Gp, 1994–97; Sec., Anglo-Tunisia Parly Gp, 1994–97. Vice-Chairman: Cons. Tourism Cttee, 1988–92 (Chm., 1992–97); All Party Tourism Cttee, 1992–97; All Party Manuf. Gp, 1993–97; All Party Exports Gp, 1993–97; Sec., Cons. Employment Cttee, 1991; Chm., Cons. Party, Wessex Area, 1980–83; Chm., Wessex Area Young Conservatives, 1973–76; Pres., Wilts Young Conservatives, 1984–97. Pres., Swindon Music Fest., 1987–2004; Mem. Cttee, English Music Fest., 2002–05. Gov., Wycliffe Coll., 1995–2006. *Recreations:* music, cricket, philately, reading. *Address:* 24 Wellsworth Lane, Rowlands Castle, Hants PO9 6BY. *Club:* Hampshire Cricket.

COONEY, David John; Ambassador of Ireland to the Court of St James's, since 2007; *b* London, 29 April 1954; *m* Geraldine O'Kelly; one *s* three *d*. *Educ:* Univ. of Keele (BA Hons Politics and Hist.). Exec. Officer, Dept of Agric., Ireland, 1976–78; Admin. Officer, Dept of Public Service, 1978–79; Department of Foreign Affairs: Third Secretary: Inf. Sect., 1979–80; Develt Cooperation Div., 1980–81; Sec., Embassy to the Holy See, 1981–85; Third Sec., Political Div., 1985–86; Private Sec. to Sec.-Gen., 1986–88; Sec., Embassy of Ireland, Vienna, 1988–89; First Secretary: Econ. Div., 1989–90; (Antici), Perm. Repn to EU, Brussels, 1990–93; Counsellor, Eur. Corresp., 1994; Coordinator of White Paper on Irish For. Policy, 1994–95; Counsellor: Hd, Political Sect., Anglo-Irish Div. (participated in negotiation of Good Friday Agreement), 1995–98; Dep. Perm. Rep. to OECD, Paris, 1998–2000; Minister-Counsellor, Paris, 2000; Ambassador, Dep. Perm. Rep. to UN, NY, 2000–01; Political Dir, Asst Sec.-Gen., 2001–05; Perm. Rep. to UN, NY, 2005–07. *Address:* Embassy of Ireland, 17 Grosvenor Place, SW1X 7HR. *T:* (020) 7235 8483, *Fax:* (020) 7235 2851.

COONEY, Lorna; *see* Fitzsimons, L.

COONEY, Raymond George Alfred, (Ray), OBE 2005; actor, author, director, theatrical producer; created Theatre of Comedy at Shaftesbury Theatre, and Little Theatre of Comedy at Ambassadors Theatre, 1983; purchased The Playhouse, London, 1992; *b* 30 May 1932; *s* of Gerard Cooney and Olive (*née* Clarke); *m* 1962, Linda Dixon; two *s*. *Educ:* Alleyn's Sch., Dulwich. First appeared in Song of Norway, Palace, 1946; toured in Wales, 1954–56; subseq. played in: Dry Rot and Simple Spymen, Whitehall; Mousetrap, Ambassador; Charlie Girl, Adelphi; Not Now Darling, Savoy (also film); Not Now Comrade (film); Run for your Wife, Guildford; Two into One, Leicester and Guildford; Caught in the Net, Windsor; (and dir) It Runs in the Family, Playhouse, 1992; (and dir) Funny Money, Playhouse, 1995; The Chiltern Hundreds, Vaudeville, 1999. Producti (some jointly) include: Thark (revival); Doctor at Sea; The Queen's Highland Servant; Giddy Aunt; Move Over Mrs Markham; The Mating Game; Lloyd George Knew Father; That's No Lady-That's My Husband; Say Goodnight to Grandma; Two and T Make Sex; At the End of the Day; Why Not Stay for Breakfast?; A Ghost on Tiptoe; Son's Father; The Sacking of Norman Banks; The Bedwinner; The Little Hut; Springti for Henry; Saint Joan; The Trials of Oscar Wilde; The Dame of Sark; Jack the Ripp There Goes the Bride (and played leading role, Ambassadors, 1974); Ipi Tombi; What Nice Country Like US Doing In a State Like This?; Some of My Best Friends Husbands; Banana Ridge; Fire Angel; Elvis; Whose Life is it Anyway? (London and N Clouds; Chicago; Bodies; Beatlemania; Not Now Darling (revival); Hello Dolly (reviv Duet for One (London and NY); They're Playing Our Song; Children of a Lesser G Run for your Wife; Aladdin; See How They Run; Pygmalion; Two Into One; Passi Play; Loot (revival); Intimate Exchanges; Wife Begins at Forty; An Italian Straw (revival); It Runs in the Family; Out of Order; Fools Rush In; Run for your Wife Caught in the Net; Over the Moon; Twice Upon a Time. *Publications:* (with H. and Williams) Charlie Girl, 1965; *plays:* (with Tony Hilton) One for the Pot, 1961; Chase Comrade, 1964; (with Tony Hilton) Stand by your Bedouin, 1966; (with John Chapm Not Now Darling, 1967; (with John Chapman) My Giddy Aunt, 1968; (with Jo Chapman) Move Over Mrs Markham, 1969; (with Gene Stone) Why Not Stay Breakfast?, 1970; (with John Chapman) There Goes the Bride, 1973; Run for Your Wi 1981; Two into One, 1983; Wife Begins at Forty, 1986; It Runs in the Family, 1989; C of Order, 1990; Funny Money, 1996; Caught in the Net, 2000; (with Michael Coon Tom, Dick and Harry, 2003. *Recreations:* tennis, swimming, golf. *Address:* Ridge Hou Forest Side, Epping, Essex CM16 4ED.

COOPER; *see* Ashley-Cooper, family name of Earl of Shaftesbury.

COOPER, family name of **Viscount Norwich**.

COOPER, Adam; dancer, choreographer and actor; *b* 1971; *m* 2000, Sarah Wildor, *Educ:* Arts Educational Sch.; Royal Ballet Sch. Royal Ballet, 1989–97: Principal Danc 1994; main rôles include: Prince Rudolf, in Mayerling; Kings of the North and South, Prince of the Pagodas; Romeo, and Tybalt, in Romeo and Juliet; Lescaut, in Man Espada, in Don Quixote; created rôles in Bloodlines, Ebony Concerto, Tombea Firstext, Room of Cooks; with Adventures in Motion Pictures: The Swan, in Swan La 1995; The Pilot, in Cinderella, 1998; On Your Toes (also choreog.), Leicester Haymark 2002, RFH, 2003; Singin' in the Rain, Sadler's Wells, 2004; Sky Masterson, in Guys a Dolls, Piccadilly, 2006; The Wizard of Oz, RFH, 2008; with Adam Cooper Productio Les Liaisons Dangereuses (also choreog.), Japan, then Sadler's Wells, 2005; *choreograp* includes, Grand Hotel, Donmar Warehouse, 2004; for Scottish Ballet: Elegy for T Reflections for Images of Dance; *television:* Madame Bovary, 2000. Dir of Boys, Lond Studio Theatre. *Address:* c/o Jean Diamond, Diamond Management, 31 Percy Stre W1T 2DD.

COOPER, Sir Adrian; *see* Cooper, Sir R. A.

COOPER, Sir Alexander (Paston Astley), 7th Bt *cr* 1821, of Gadebridge, Hertfordshi *b* 1 Feb. 1943; *o s* of Sir Patrick Graham Astley Cooper, 6th Bt and Audrey Anne Jervoi *d* of Major D.P. J. Collas; *S* father, 2002; *m* 1974, Minnie Margaret, *d* of Charles Harris *Heir: kinsman* Gerald Nigel Astley Cooper [*b* 8 June 1916; *m* 1st, 1941, Mary Constan Piercy (marr. diss. 1945); one *d*; 2nd, 1951, Joan Ryland, *d* of Dr Bernard Wall; one *s* o *d*]. *Address:* 8 Berkshire Close, Leigh-on-Sea, Essex SS9 4RT.

COOPER, Ven. Annette Joy; Archdeacon of Colchester, since 2004; *b* 15 Nov. 1953 of Harry Whitaker and Grace Mary Whitaker (*née* Parnham, now James); *m* 1972, Andre John Cooper; two *s*. *Educ:* Lilley and Stone Newark Girls' High Sch.; Open Univ. (E 1980); London Univ. (CQSW, DipSW 1985, ext.); Dip. Religious Studies, Southwa Ordination Course, 1988. Local Authority social worker, 1979–88. Ordained deac 1988, priest, 1994; NSM, St Peter, Pembury, and full-time Asst Chaplain, Tunbrid Wells HA, 1988–91; full-time Chaplain, Bassetlaw Hosp. and Community Services NI Trust, 1991–96; Priest i/c Edwinstowe St Mary, 1996–2004. Chaplain: Center Par Sherwood, 1996–2000; Southwell Diocesan Mothers' Union, 1996–99; Area Dea Worksop, 1999–2004. Hon. Canon: Southwell Minster, 2002–04; Chelmsford Cathedr 2004–. *Publication:* It's Hard to Say Goodbye, 1994. *Recreations:* sailing, singir entertaining family and friends. *Address:* 63 Powers Hall End, Witham, Essex CM8 1N *T:* (01376) 513130, *Fax:* (01376) 500789; *e-mail:* a.colchester@chelmsford.anglican.org

COOPER, Anthony; *see* Cooper, D. A.

COOPER, Anthony William, CBE 2003; Principal, Aldercar Community Langua College, since 1995; *b* 22 Sept. 1952; *s* of Lawrence and Mary Cooper; *m* 1985, Sus Margaret Howard; four *d*. *Educ:* Leeds Univ. (BEd Hons 1975); Nottingham Univ. (M 1982). Teacher of Geog., 1975–81, Hd of Humanities, 1981–89, Western Mere Sc Derbys; Hd of Humanities, High View Community Tech. Sch., Derbys, 1989–90; De Hd, Aldercar Sch., Derbys, 1990–95. Mem., E Midlands Judging Panel, The Teachi Awards, 2001–. FRSA 2003. Nat. Award for Secondary Sch. Leadership, The Teachi Awards, 2000. *Recreations:* reading, antique collections, theatre and concerts, holidays wi 5 girls (including Sue). *Address:* Aldercar Community Language College, Daltons Clo Langley Mill, Derbys NG16 4HL.

COOPER, Beryl Phyllis; QC 1977; a Recorder of the Crown Court, 1977–98; Depu High Court Judge, 1980–98; *b* 24 Nov. 1927; *o c* of late Charles Augustus Cooper a Phyllis Lillie Cooper (*née* Burrows). *Educ:* Surbiton High Sch. (Head Girl, 1945–4 Univ. of Birmingham (BCom 1950; Hon. Sec., Guild of Undergrads, 1949–50). Call to the Bar, Gray's Inn, 1960, Bencher, 1988; barrister, 1960–98; Dep. Circuit Judg 1972–77. Hosp. Sec., Gray's Inn Rd and Liverpool Rd branches, Royal Free Hos 1951–57. Councillor, St Pancras MBC, 1959–62. Formerly: Mem., Homeopathic Hos Cttee; Mem., Bd of Visitors, Wandsworth Prison. Conservative Parly Candidate, Stepne 1966; Founder Mem., Bow Gp (former Sec. and Council Mem.); Mem. Exec. Cttee, Sc of Cons. Lawyers, 1981–87. Chm., Justice Report on Fraud Trials, 1985–86. Former Member: Cripps Cttee, Women and the Law; Home Office Cttee on Criminal Statisti (Perks Cttee); Member: Housing Corp., 1976–79; Lambeth, Southwark and Lewisha AHA (Teaching), 1980–82; Criminal Injuries Compensation Bd, 1978–98; Review Bo for Nursing Staff, Midwives, Health Visitors, and Professions Allied to Medicin 1983–90; Council of Justice, 1986–96; Family Law Bar Assoc. Cttee, 1986–88. FRH 1951; FRSA 1992. *Publications:* pamphlets for CPC, Justice, Bow Gp, etc.; articles social, legal, criminal and local govt matters. *Recreations:* travel, swimming. *Address:* 8 South Cliff Tower, Bolsover Road, Eastbourne, Sussex BN20 7JN. *T:* (01323) 73288 *Clubs:* English-Speaking Union; Devonshire (Eastbourne); Royal Eastbourne Golf.

COOPER, Rt Rev. Carl Norman; Chief Executive Officer, Powys Association Voluntary Organisations, since 2008; *b* 4 Aug. 1960; *s* of Joseph and Kathleen Ma

Cooper; *m* 1982, Joy Erica Bowyer; one *s* two *d*. *Educ:* St David's University Coll., Lampeter (BA Hons French 1982); Wycliffe Hall, Oxford; Trinity Coll., Carmarthen (MPhil Wales 1999). Ordained deacon, 1985, priest, 1986; Curate, Llanelli, 1985–87; Priest i/c, 1987–88, Rector, 1988–93, Ciliau Aeron, Llannerch Aeron, Dihewyd and Mydroilyn; Rector, Rectorial Benefice of Dolgellau, 1993–2002; Diocesan Warden of Ordinands, Bangor, 1999–2001; Archdeacon of Meirionnydd, 2000–02; Bishop of St Davids, 2002–08. *Address:* c/o Powys Association of Voluntary Organisations, Marlow, South Crescent, Llandrindod Wells, Powys LD1 5DH.

COOPER, Prof. Cary Lynn, CBE 2001; Professor of Organizational Psychology and Health, Lancaster University Management School, since 2003; Pro Vice-Chancellor, Lancaster University, since 2004; *b* 28 April 1940; adopted British nationality, 1993; *s* of Harry and Caroline Cooper; *m* 1984, Rachel Faith Cooper; two *d*; one *s* one *d* from previous marr. *Educ:* Univ. of California (BS, MBA); Univ. of Leeds (PhD). FBPsS 1982. Lectr in Psychology, Univ. of Southampton, 1967–73; University of Manchester Institute of Science and Technology: Prof. of Organizational Psychol., subseq. BUPA Prof. of Organizational Psychol. and Health, 1975–2003; Pro-Vice-Chancellor, 1995–2000; Dep. Vice-Chancellor, 2000–02. Advr to WHO and ILO, 1982–84. Founding Editor, Jl of Organizational Behavior, 1980–; Co-Editor: Stress and Health (formerly Stress Medicine), 1992– (Associate Ed., 1987–92); Internat. Jl Mgt Reviews, 1999–2001. Member: Bd of Trustees, Amer. Inst. of Stress, 1984–; Adv. Council, Nat. Inst. of Clin. Applications of Behavioral Medicine, USA; ESRC Research Priorities Bd, 1998–2000; Pres., British Acad. of Management, 1987–90, 1997–2004 (Fellow, 1995). President: Inst. of Welfare Officers, 1998–; Internat. Stress Mgt Assoc. (UK), 2000–; Vice Pres., 2000–06, Pres., 2007–, British Assoc. of Counselling and Psychotherapy. Ambassador, The Samaritans, 2000–. Myers Lectr, BPsS, 1986; Apothecaries Lect., Soc. of Occupational Medicine, 2001. FRSA 1990; FRSocMed 1995; FRSH 1997; Fellow, Amer. Acad. of Mgt, 1997 (Mem. Bd of Govs, 2000–03; Dist. Service Award, 1998); CCMI (CIMgt 1997); AcSS 2001. Hon. Mem., Soc. of Psychosom. Res.; Hon. FFOM 2005; Hon. FRCP 2006. MSc Manchester, 1979; Hon. DLitt Heriot-Watt, 1998; Hon. DBA Wolverhampton, 1999; Hon. DSc Aston, 2002; DUniv Middx, 2003. Lifetime Achievement Award, Div. of Occupational Psychol., BPsS, 2007. *Publications:* (jtly) T-Groups, 1971; Group Training for Individual and Organizational Development, 1973; Theories of Group Processes, 1975; Developing Social Skills in Managers, 1976; OD in the US and UK, 1977; (jtly) Understanding Executive Stress, 1978; Advances in Experiential Social Processes, vol. 1, 1978, vol. 2, 1980; (jtly) Stress at Work, 1978; (jtly) Executives under Pressure, 1978; Behavioural Problems in Organizations, 1979; (jtly) The Quality of Working Life in Western and Eastern Europe, 1979; Learning from Others in Groups, 1979; The Executive Gypsy, 1979; Current Concerns in Occupational Stress, 1980; Developing Managers for the 1980's, 1980; (jtly) Combating Managerial Obsolescence, 1980; The Stress Check, 1980; White Collar and Professional Stress, 1981; Improving Interpersonal Relations, 1981; (jtly) Groups at Work, 1981; Executive Families Under Stress, 1981; (jtly) After Forty, 1981; Coping with Stress at Work, 1982; Psychology and Management, 1982; (jtly) Management Education, 1982; (jtly) Introducing Organization Behaviour, 1982; (jtly) High Pressure, 1982; Stress Research, 1983; (jtly) Human Behaviour in Organizations, 1983; (jtly) Stress and the Woman Manager, 1983; Public Faces, Private Lives, 1984; (jtly) Working Women, 1984; (jtly) Psychology for Managers, 1984; Psychosocial Stress and Cancer, 1984; (jtly) Women in Management, 1984; (jtly) The Change Makers, 1985; (jtly) Job Stress and Blue Collar Work, 1985; (jtly) International Review of Industrial and Organizational Psychology, annually 1986–2004; (jtly) Man and Accidents Offshore, 1986; (jtly) Stress and the Nurse Manager, 1986; (jtly) Pilots under Stress, 1986; (jtly) Psycho-social Factors at Work, 1987; (jtly) Retirement in Industrialized Societies, 1987; Living with Stress, 1988; Stress and Breast Cancer, 1988; (jtly) High Fliers, 1988; (jtly) Early Retirement, 1989; (jtly) Career Couples: contemporary lifestyles and how to manage them, 1989; (jtly) Understanding Stress: health care professionals, 1990; (jtly) Managing People at Work, 1990; Industrial and Organizational Psychology: critical writings, 1991; (jtly) Stress Survivors, 1991; (jtly) Cancer and Stress, 1991; (jtly) Work Psychology, 1991, 2nd edn 1997; (jtly) Stress and Accidents in the Offshore Oil and Gas Industry, 1991; Managing Organizations in 1992, 1991; (jtly) On the Move: the psychology of change and transitions, 1991; Personality and Stress, 1991; (jtly) Mergers and Acquisitions: the human factor, 1992; (jtly) Shattering the Glass Ceiling: the woman manager, 1992; (jtly) Relax: dealing with stress, 1992; (jtly) Women's Career Development, 1992; (jtly) Total Quality and Human Resources, 1992; (jtly) Successful Stress Management, 1993; (jtly) Stress in the Dealing Room, 1993; (jtly) The Workplace Revolution, 1993; (jtly) No Hassle: taking the stress out of work, 1994; (jtly) Business Elites, 1994; Handbook on Stress Medicine and Health, 1995; Trends in Organizational Behaviour, 1995; (jtly) Stress and Employer Liability, 1996, 2nd edn 2001; (jtly) Organizations and the Psychological Contract, 1996; (ed jtly) Blackwell Encyclopedia of Management, 1997; (jtly) Creating Tomorrow's Organizations, 1997; (jtly) Balancing Work, Life and Family, 1998; (ed jtly) Concise Encyclopedia of Management, 1998; (ed) Theories of Organizational Stress, 1998; (jtly) Stress and Strain, 1999; (ed) Who's Who in the Management Sciences, 2000; (ed jtly) Cancer and the Family, 2000; (jtly) Conquer your Stress, 2000; (ed) Classics in Management Thought, 2000; (jtly) Strategic Stress Management, 2000; (jtly) Organizational Stress, 2001; (jtly) Occupational Health Psychology, 2001; (jtly) New World of Work, 2001; (jtly) Emotions at Work, 2001; (ed jtly) International Handbook of Organizational Culture and Climate, 2001; Fundamentals of Organizational Behaviour (4 vols), 2002; (jtly) FT Guide to Executive Health, 2002; (jtly) Workplace Bullying, 2002; (ed jtly) Advances in Mergers and Acquisitions, 2003; (ed jtly) Bullying and Emotional Abuse in the Workplace, 2003; (jtly) Creating a Balance, 2003; (jtly) Destressing Doctors, 2003; (jtly) The Employment Relationship, 2003; (jtly) Managing the Risk of Workplace Stress, 2004; (jtly) Stress: a brief history, 2004; (jtly) Work-Life Integration, 2005; (ed) Leadership and Management in the 21st Century, 2005; (ed) Handbook of Stress Medicine and Health, 2005; (ed jtly) Work, 6 vols, 2005; (ed jtly) Workplace Violence, 2005; (ed jtly) Reinventing Human Resource Management, 2005; (ed jtly) Inspiring Leaders, 2006; Managing Emotions in Mergers and Acquisitions, 2005; (jtly) Managing Value-based Organizations, 2006; (jtly) Happy Performing Managers, 2006; (ed jtly) Positive Organizational Behavior, 2007; (jtly) How to Deal with Stress, 2007; (jtly) Detox Your Desk, 2007; (ed jtly) Building More Effective Organizations, 2007; articles on social science and medicine, stress medicine. *Recreations:* reading 19th century Russian fiction, living in hope with Manchester City football, enjoying my four children. *Address:* Lancaster University Management School, Bailrigg, Lancaster LA1 4YX; 25 Lostock Hall Road, Poynton, Cheshire SK12 1DP. *T:* (01625) 871450. *Club:* St James's.

COOPER, Prof. Cyrus, DM; FRCP, FFPH; Norman Collisson Professor of Musculoskeletal Sciences, University of Oxford, since 2007; Fellow of St Peter's College, Oxford, since 2007; *b* 14 Feb. 1957; *s* of Dr Sarosh Cooper and Khorshed Cooper; *m* 1984, Margaret O'Donovan; two *s*. *Educ:* Gonville and Caius Coll., Cambridge (BA 1977); St Bartholomew's Hosp., London (MB BS 1980); DM Soton 1985. FRCP 1996; FFPH 2005. Sen. Registrar, Bristol Royal Infirmary, 1988–90; Asst Prof., Mayo Clinic, Minn, 1990–92; University of Southampton: Sen. Lectr in Rheumatol., 1992–97; Prof. of Rheumatol., 1997–2007; Dir, MRC Epidemiol. Resource Centre, 2003–07. Chm., Bd of Trustees, Nat. Osteoporosis Soc., 2004–. FMedSci 2000. *Publications:* (jtly) Prevention and Treatment of Osteoporosis: a clinician's guide, 2005; original res. contribs to learned jls on epidemiology of osteoporosis, osteoarthritis and other rheumatic disorders, studies into develt origins of coronary heart disease and metabolic syndrome. *Recreation:* cricket. *Address:* Nuffield Department of Orthopaedic Surgery, University of Oxford, Nuffield Orthopaedic Centre, Windmill Road, Oxford OX3 7LD. *Club:* Hampshire County Cricket.

COOPER, David Antony; a District Judge (Magistrates' Courts) (formerly Metropolitan Stipendiary Magistrate), since 1991; *b* 12 June 1945; *s* of Rev. Stanley Francis Cooper and Jane Anne Cooper; *m* 1968, Françoise Armandine Henriette Fourré; three *s*. *Educ:* Sandown Grammar Sch., IoW; Exeter Univ. (LLB); College of Law. Articled to David Rule Pyott, Freshfields, London, 1966–69; admitted Solicitor, 1969; with Heppenstalls, Lymington, 1969–71; Solicitor and Partner in charge of criminal litigation, Ellison & Co., Colchester, 1971–91. *Recreation:* undisturbed reading.

COOPER, Prof. David Edward; Professor of Philosophy, University of Durham, 1986–2008; *b* 1 Oct. 1942; *s* of late Edward Cooper and Lilian Doris Cooper (*née* Turner); *m* 1st, 1971, Patricia Patterson; 2nd, 1980, Sheila Ann Armstrong, *qv* (marr. diss. 1998); 3rd, 2000, Joy Palmer. *Educ:* Highgate Sch.; St Edmund Hall, Oxford; Nuffield Coll., Oxford (MA, BPhil). Lectr in Philosophy, Pembroke and Jesus Colls, Oxford, 1966–69; Asst Prof. of Philosophy, Univ. of Miami, 1969–72; Lectr in Phil. of Educn, Univ. of London Inst. of Educn, 1972–74; Reader in Phil., Univ. of Surrey, 1974–85. Visiting Professor, Universities of: Khartoum, 1975; Minnesota, 1977; Capetown, 1979; Heidelberg and Tübingen, 1985; Trinity (Texas), 1986; Alberta, 1987; Vanderbilt, 1990; Malta, 1994; Ruhuna, Sri Lanka, 2006–; Rivers Distinguished Vis. Prof. of the Humanities, E Carolina Univ., 1998; Vis. Sen. Res. Fellow, KCL, 1991–94; Leverhulme Res. Fellow, 1996–97; AHRB Res. Fellow, 1999–2000; Leverhulme res. grant, 2002–03, 2006–07. Fellow, Internat. Soc. for Intercultural Studies and Res., India, 1993–. Chairman: Phil. of Educn Soc., 1987–90; Friedrich Nietzsche Soc., 1991–94; President: Mind Assoc., 1991; Aristotelian Soc., 1993–94; Member: Council, Royal Inst. of Philosophy, 1995–; Exec. Cttee, Royal Inst. of Phil., 1997–. Trustee, Philosophy in Britain, 1995–. Patron, Earthkind, 1991–. Hon. Diploma, Univ. Nacional de Educación a Distancia, Madrid, 1992. *Publications:* Philosophy and the Nature of Language, 1973; Presupposition, 1974; Knowledge of Language, 1975; (ed) The Manson Murders, 1975; Illusions of Equality, 1980; Authenticity and Learning, 1983; Metaphor, 1986; (ed) Education, Values and Mind, 1986; Existentialism: a reconstruction, 1990, 2nd rev. edn 1999; (ed jtly) The Environment in Question, 1992; (ed) Blackwell's Companion to Aesthetics, 1993; (ed jtly) Just Environments, 1995; World Philosophies: an historical introduction, 1995, 2nd edn 2002; Heidegger, 1996; (ed) Aesthetics: the classic readings, 1997; (ed) Ethics: the classic readings, 1998; (ed) Epistemology: the classic readings, 1998; (ed jtly) Spirit of the Environment, 1998; (ed) Metaphysics: the classic readings, 1999; The Measure of Things: humanism, humility and mystery, 2002; Meaning, 2003; (with S. P. James) Buddhism, Virtue and Environment, 2005; A Philosophy of Gardens, 2006; (ed jtly) Philosophy: the classic readings, 2009. *Recreations:* music, walking, wildlife. *Address:* c/o Department of Philosophy, University of Durham, 50 Old Elvet, Durham DH1 3HN. *T:* (0191) 334 6550; *e-mail:* D.E.Cooper@durham.ac.uk.

COOPER, (Derek) Anthony; Member, Nuclear Decommissioning Authority, since 2005; *b* 11 Dec. 1943; *s* of Donald Cooper and Freda Cooper (*née* Sheridan); *m* 1967, June Iley; one *s* two *d*; one *s*. *Educ:* Whitehaven Grammar Sch.; Edinburgh Univ. (BSc Forestry and Wild Life Mgt). Forest Officer, Forestry Commn, 1967–76; Institution of Professionals, Managers and Specialists: Negotiations Officer, 1976–79; Asst Sec., 1979–82; Asst Gen. Sec., 1982–87; Dep. Gen. Sec., 1987–91; Gen. Sec., Engrs and Managers Assoc., 1991–2001; Jt Gen. Sec., Prospect, 2001–02; Chm., Nuclear Industry Assoc. (formerly British Nuclear Industry Forum), 2002–05. Chairman: Aid Tspt Ltd, 1993–98; 4U@work Ltd, 2000–03; PPP Consultancy Ltd, 2002–06; Nuclear Industry Pension Trustees Ltd, 2006–; Dir, Way Ahead Training Ltd, 1999–2003. Commissioner: Postal Services Commn, 2000–; Forestry Commn, 2001–06. Member: Govt Energy Adv. Panel, 1993–2003; EU Energy Consultative Cttee, 1998–2001; Strategy Bd, 2002–04, Investment Cttee, 2003–04, Nuclear Decommissioning Agency Prog. Bd, 2003–04, DTI. Mem., Gen. Council, TUC, 1997–2000. Trustee: Power Aid Logistics, 1993–98; Royal Hosp. for Neuro-disability, Putney, 1995–97. *Recreations:* reading, sailing, climbing. *Address:* 91 Anstey Lane, Alton, Hants GU34 2NJ.

See also Rt Hon. Y. Cooper.

COOPER, Derek Macdonald, OBE 1997; author, broadcaster and journalist; *b* 25 May 1925; *s* of George Stephen Cooper and Jessie Margaret Macdonald; *m* 1953, Janet Marian Feaster; one *s* one *d*. *Educ:* Raynes Park Grammar Sch.; Portree High Sch.; University Coll., Cardiff; Wadham Coll., Oxford (MA Hons). Served RN, 1943–47. Joined Radio Malaya as producer, 1950, retired as Controller of Progs, 1960; Producer, Roving Report, ITN, 1960–61; has worked widely as presenter, interviewer and writer in both television and radio. Columnist: The Listener; Guardian; Observer magazine; Sunday Standard (House of Fraser Press Award, 1984); Homes & Gardens; Saga magazine; Woman's Journal; Scotland on Sunday. Founder Mem. and first Chm., 1985–88, Pres., 1988–95, Guild of Food Writers. Hon. DLitt Queen Margaret UC, Edinburgh, 1999. Glenfiddich Trophy as Wine and Food Writer, 1973, 1980; Broadcaster of the Year, 1984. *Publications:* The Bad Food Guide, 1967; Skye, 1970, 4th edn 1995; The Beverage Report, 1970; The Gullibility Gap, 1974; Hebridean Connection, 1977, 2nd edn 1991; Guide to the Whiskies of Scotland, 1978; Road to the Isles, 1979 (Scottish Arts Council Award, 1980), 4th edn 2002; (with Dione Pattullo) Enjoying Scotch, 1980; Wine With Food, 1982, 2nd edn 1986; (with Fay Godwin) The Whisky Roads of Scotland, 1982; The Century Companion to Whiskies, 1983; Skye Remembered, 1983, 2nd edn 1993; The World Of Cooking, 1983; The Road to Mingulay, 1985, 2nd edn 1989; The Gunge File, 1986; A Taste of Scotch, 1989; The Little Book of Malt Whiskies, 1992; The Balvenie, 1993; Snail Eggs and Samphire, 2000, 2nd edn 2002. *Address:* 3 Richmond Bridge Mansions, Willoughby Road, Twickenham, Middx TW1 2QJ. *T:* (020) 8892 9195.

COOPER, Wing Comdr Donald Arthur, CBE 1990; AFC 1961; Chief Inspector, Air Accidents Investigation Branch, Department of Transport, 1986–90; *b* 27 Sept. 1930; *s* of A. A. Cooper and E. B. Cooper (*née* Edmonds); *m* 1958, Belinda, 3rd *d* of Adm. Sir Charles Woodhouse, KCB and Lady Woodhouse; three *s*. *Educ:* Queen's Coll., British Guiana; RAF Coll., Cranwell; BA Open. ATPL (H) 1961, ATPL (A) 1972. FRAeS. Served on fighter and trng sqdns, 1952–56; Empire Test Pilot's Sch., 1957; RAE Farnborough, 1958–60; RAF sc 1961; Sqdn Comdr CFS Helicopter Wing, 1962–64; HQ FTC, 1964–66; Defence Operational Requirements Staff, MoD, 1966–70; joined Accidents Investigation Br., BoT, on retirement, 1970. *Recreations:* walking, ballroom dancing, amateur dramatics. *Address:* 7 Lynch Road, Farnham, Surrey GU9 8BZ.

COOPER, (Edward) John; Chief Executive, Hammersmith Hospitals NHS Trust, 1994–2001; *b* 21 April 1943; *s* of John and Rosalind Cooper; *m* 1977, Susan Hitchin. *Educ:*

Malvern Coll.; Nottingham Univ. (BA); Manchester Business Sch. (MBA 1971). AHSM 1969. Nat. Admin. Trng Scheme, NHS, 1965–66; United Liverpool Hosps, 1966–67; Univ. Hosp., S Manchester, 1967–69; various posts, Llewelyn-Davies Internat., 1971–78; S Australian Health Commn, 1978–85 (Dep. Chm. and Comr, 1983–85); Dist Gen. Manager, Hampstead HA, 1985–91; Chief Exec., Royal Free Hampstead NHS Trust, 1991–94. Mem. Council, RCP, 2004–08. Hon. FRCP 2008. *Recreations:* performing arts, travel. *Address:* 74 High Street, Hemingford Grey, Cambs PE28 9BN. *T:* (01480) 461164.

COOPER, Eileen, RA 2001; RE 2002; career artist; *b* 10 June 1953; *d* of John Lawrence and Marjorie Cooper; *m* 1983, David Malcolm Southward; two *s*. *Educ:* Goldsmiths' Coll., London (DipAD); RCA (MA Painting; FRCA 2006). Has taught widely, always pt-time; part-time Tutor, Printmaking: RCA, 1994–; Royal Acad. Schs, 2005–; Artist in Residence, Dulwich Picture Gall., 1998–99. Solo exhibitions include: at Art First, London: Open Secrets, 1998; Raw Material Part II, 2000; Works on Paper, 2002; Eileen Cooper 50 New Works, 2003; Time of Your Life, 2005; Deeper Water, 2007; Second Skin: Eileen Cooper in the 80's and 90's, touring show, 1999; Raw Material Part I, Dulwich Picture Gall., 2000; Passions: new work on paper, Art First, NY, 2002; A Celebration, Art First Projects, NY, 2003. Numerous gp exhibns in Britain, Europe, USA and Asia; works in public and private collections worldwide. *Publications:* (cover) Women who Run with the Wolves, by Clarissa Pinkola Estés, 1998; (cover and illus.) Meeting Midnight, by Carol Ann Duffy, 1999. *Recreations:* family, reading, walking the dog. *Address:* Art First, First Floor Gallery, 9 Cork Street, W1S 3LL. *T:* (020) 7734 0386, *Fax:* (020) 7734 3964; *e-mail:* info@artfirst.co.uk.

COOPER, Prof. (Elizabeth) Helen, PhD, DLitt; FBA 2006; Professor of Medieval and Renaissance English, University of Cambridge, since 2004; Fellow, Magdalene College, Cambridge, since 2004; *b* 6 Feb. 1947; *d* of Sir Percy Edward, (Sir Peter), Kent, FRS and late (Margaret) Betty Kent; *m* 1970, Michael George Cooper (*d* 2007); two *d*. *Educ:* New Hall, Cambridge (BA 1968, MA; PhD 1972); DLitt Oxford 1996. Jun. Res. Fellow, New Hall, Cambridge, 1971–74; Beaverbrook Tutorial Fellow in English and Univ. CUF Lectr, University Coll., Oxford, 1978–2004. Editor for Old and Middle English, Medium Ævum, 1989–2002. Pres., New Chaucer Soc., 2000–02. Hon. DLitt Washington and Lee, 2001. *Publications:* Pastoral: Mediaeval into Renaissance, 1978; Great-Grandmother Goose, 1978; The Structure of the Canterbury Tales, 1983; Oxford Guides to Chaucer: The Canterbury Tales, 1989, 2nd edn 1996; (ed) Sir Thomas Malory: Le Morte Darthur, 1998; The English Romance in Time, 2004; numerous articles in books and periodicals. *Address:* Magdalene College, Cambridge CB3 0AG. *T:* (01223) 767293; *e-mail:* ehc31@cam.ac.uk.

COOPER, Emmanuel, OBE 2002; PhD; artist potter; Editor, Ceramic Review, since 1997; Art Critic, Tribune, since 1990; *b* 12 Dec. 1938; *s* of Fred Cooper and Kate Elizabeth (*née* Cooke). *Educ:* Dudley Trng Coll.; Bournemouth Coll. of Art; Hornsey Coll. of Art; PhD Middlesex 1996. Art teacher, Downs View Central Sch., 1961–63; asst art master (pt-time), Harrow Sch., 1963–65; art teacher (pt-time), Central Foundn Girls' Sch., Spitalfields, 1965–70; Lectr (pt-time), Hornsey Sch. of Art, 1971–75; Sen. Lectr (pt-time), Middx Poly., later Middx Univ., 1975–96. Vis. Prof. of Ceramics and Glass, RCA, 2000–; Visiting Lecturer: Camberwell Sch. of Art, 1976–80; Goldsmiths' Coll., 1995–. Co.-Ed. and publisher, Ceramic Rev., 1970–97; Series Ed., The Complete Potter, 1985–95. External Assessor: Glasgow Sch. of Art, 1988–92; Buckingham Coll. of Higher Educn, 1990–94; Cardiff Sch. of Art, UWIC, 1992–96; Bath Spa UC, 1997–2002; Univ. of Westminster, 2005–. Numerous one-man exhibns in UK and Germany; work in mixed exhibns and in public collections in UK and USA. Arts Council England (formerly Arts Council of England): Mem., 2000–02; Mem., London Regl Council, 2002–. Fellow: Craft Potters' Assoc.; Soc. of Designer Craftsmen; FRSA 1998. Mem., Internat. Acad. Ceramics, 2006. Trustee, Craft Potters Charitable Trust, 1995–. Writers' Guild Award, 1997; Crafts Council Award, 1997; Silver Medal, Soc. of Designer Craftsmen, 2002. Hon. MA, Surrey Inst. of Art and Design UC, 2003. *Publications:* Handbook of Pottery, 1970; History of Pottery, 1972; (with E. Lewenstein) Potters, 1972, 8th edn 1989; (with E. Lewenstein) New Ceramics, 1974; Taking Up Pottery, 1974; Pottery, 1976; Ceramic Review Book of Glaze Recipes, 1977, 7th edn 1995; (with D. Royle) Glazes for the Studio Potter, 1978; World History of Pottery, 1982; Electric Kiln Pottery, 1982; Baron Von Gloeden: photographer (monograph), 1982; Interiors: paintings by Cornelius McCarthy, 1984; The Sexual Perspective: homosexuality and art in the last 100 years in the West, 1986, 2nd edn 1994; Cooper's Book of Glaze Recipes, 1987; The Life and Work of Henry Scott Tuke, 1987; Machinations: photographs by Arthur Tress, 1989; Fully Exposed: the male nude in photography, 1990, 2nd edn 1995; People's Art: working class art from 1750 to the present day, 1994; Ten Thousand Years of Pottery, 2000; (ed) Lucie Rie, 2002; David Leach, 2003; Bernard Leach, Life and Work, 2003; Male Bodies: male nude in photography, 2004; Janet Leach: a potter's life, 2006; contribs to numerous books and catalogues. *Recreations:* theatre, fine craft, the South coast, modern dance. *Address:* 38 Chalcot Road, NW1 8LP. *T:* (020) 7722 9090; *e-mail:* emmanuelcooper@lineone.net.

COOPER, Sir (Frederick Howard) Michael C.; *see* Craig-Cooper.

COOPER, Gareth; *see* Cooper, W. G.

COOPER, George A.; marketing and business consultant; Chairman, Independent Television Publications Ltd, 1971–89; *b* 9 Oct. 1915; *s* of late Joseph Cooper; *m* 1944, Irene Burns; one *d*. Exec. with internat. publishing gp; served War of 1939–45, Royal Artillery (Captain); Exec., Hulton Press, 1949–55; Director: ABC Television Ltd, 1955–77; Thames Television Ltd, 1968 (Man. Dir, 1974–77); Independent Television News, 1976–77; Chm., Network Programme Cttee of Independent Television, 1975–77. FRTS 1987. *Address:* 43 Rivermill, 151 Grosvenor Road, SW1V 3JN. *T:* (020) 7821 9305. *Clubs:* Royal Automobile, Thirty.

COOPER, Gen. Sir George (Leslie Conroy), GCB 1984 (KCB 1979); MC 1953; DL; Chief Royal Engineer, 1987–93; *b* 10 Aug. 1925; *s* of late Lt-Col G. C. Cooper and Mrs Y. V. Cooper, Bulmer Tye House, Sudbury; *m* 1957, Cynthia Mary Hume; one *s* one *d*. *Educ:* Downside Sch.; Trinity Coll., Cambridge. Commnd 1945; served with Bengal Sappers and Miners, 1945–48; Korea, 1952–53; psc 1956; jssc 1959; Instructor, RMA Sandhurst, 1959–62 and Staff Coll., Camberley, 1964; Brevet Lt-Col, 1964; GSO1, 1st Div., 1964–66; CRE, 4th Div., 1966–68; MoD, 1968–69; Comdr, 19th Airportable Bde, 1969–71; Royal Coll. of Defence Studies, 1972; Dep. Dir Army Trng, 1973–74; GOC SW District, 1974–75; Dir, Army Staff Duties, 1976–79; GOC SE District, 1979–81; Adjt-Gen., 1981–84, retd. ADC General to the Queen, 1982–84. Mem., UK Bd of Management, and Dir of Management Develt, GEC, 1985–86. Colonel Commandant: RE, 1980–93; RPC, 1981–85; Col, Queen's Gurkha Engineers, 1981–91. Mem. Council, Nat. Army Mus., 1981–95. Chm., Knightstone Syndicate Management (formerly HGP Managing Agency), 1991–93 (Dir, 1990–91). Lay Rep., Senate and Bar Council Disciplinary Bodies, 1984–90. Chm., 1980–95, Jt Pres., 1995–2002, Jt Patron, 2002–, Infantile Hypercalcæmia Foundn, later Williams Syndrome Foundation; Chm., Princess Alexandra's NHS Hosp. Trust, 1994–96; Mem. Council, Action Research (formerly Nat. Fund for Res. into Crippling Diseases), 1982–95; Trustee, Harlow War Meml Inst., 1990–; Patron, Pahar Trust, 1993–. DL Essex, 1990. *Publications:* (with D. A. Alexander) The Bengal Sappers 1803–2003, 2003; articles and book reviews. *Recreations:* writing, going round bookshops, gardening. *Address:* 37 Mulberry Green, Old Harlow, Essex CM17 0EY. *T:* (01279) 427214. *Clubs:* Army and Navy, MCC; Essex.

COOPER, Gilead Patrick; QC 2006; *b* 24 April 1955; *s* of Lionel and Lily Cooper. *Educ:* Haileybury; Christ Church, Oxford (MA); City Univ. (Dip. Law). Called to the Bar, Middle Temple, 1983; in practice specialising in Chancery law. *Recreation:* anything other than sport. *Address:* 3 Stone Buildings, Lincoln's Inn, WC2A 3XL. *T:* (020) 7242 4937, *Fax:* (020) 7405 3896; *e-mail:* sibyl@cumae.demon.co.uk.

COOPER, Helen; *see* Cooper, E. H.

COOPER, Sir Henry, Kt 2000; OBE 1969; professional boxer, 1954–71; *b* 3 May 1934; *s* of late Henry William Cooper and Lily Nutkins; *m* 1960, Albina Genepri; two *s*. *Educ:* Athelney Street Sch., Bellingham. Presenter, Be Your Own Boss (series), Channel 4, 1983. KSG 1978. *Film:* Royal Flash, 1975. *Publications:* Henry Cooper: an autobiography, 1972; The Great Heavyweights, 1978; Henry Cooper's Book of Boxing, 1982; Henry Cooper's 100 Greatest Boxers, 1990. *Recreation:* golf. *Address:* 15 Barley House, Hildenbrook Farm, Riding Lane, Hildenborough, Kent TN11 9JN.

COOPER, Imogen, CBE 2007; concert pianist; *b* 28 Aug. 1949; *d* of late Martin Du Pré Cooper, CBE; *m* 1982, John Alexander Batten (marr. diss. 2002). *Educ:* Paris Conservatoire, with Jacques Février and Yvonne Lefébure, 1961–67 (Premier Prix, 1967); Vienna, with Alfred Brendel, 1970. Plays regularly with all major British orchestras; regular appearances at Proms, 1975–; first British pianist, and woman, to have appeared in South Bank Piano Series, 1975; British festivals include Bath, Cheltenham, Harrogate, Brighton, Edinburgh and Aldeburgh. Overseas engagements incl. concerts with Berlin, Vienna, New York and Los Angeles Philharmonic Orchestras, and regular tours to Australasia, Holland, France, Scandinavia, USA and Japan. Recordings include: Schubert's late works; Schubert lieder (with Wolfgang Holzmair), Brahms and Schumann; Mozart's Concerti for Two and Three Pianos, with Alfred Brendel and Acad. of St Martin-in-the-Fields. Mozart Meml Prize, 1969. *Recreations:* architecture, cooking. *Address:* c/o Askonas Holt, Lincoln House, 300 High Holborn, WC1V 7JH. *T:* (020) 7400 1700.

COOPER, Jilly, (Mrs Leo Cooper), OBE 2004; author; *b* 21 Feb. 1937; *d* of Brig. W. B. Sallitt, OBE, and Mary Elaine Whincup; *m* 1961, Leo Cooper; one *s* one *d*. *Educ:* Godolphin Sch., Salisbury. Reporter, Middlesex Independent, Brentford, 1957–59; followed by numerous short-lived jobs as account executive, copy writer, publisher's reader, receptionist, puppy fat model, switchboard wrecker, and very temporary typist. Columnist: Sunday Times, 1969–82; Mail on Sunday, 1982–87. *Publications:* How to Stay Married, 1969; How to Survive from Nine to Five, 1970 (new edn as Work and Wedlock, 1978); Jolly Super, 1971; Men and Super Men, 1972; Jolly Super Too, 1973; Women and Super Women, 1974 (new edn as Super Men and Super Women, 1977); Jolly Superlative, 1975; Super Jilly, 1977; Class, 1979; The British in Love, 1980; (with Tom Hartman) Violets and Vinegar, 1980; Supercooper, 1980; Intelligent and Loyal, 1981, re-issued as Mongrel Magic, 1981; Jolly Marsupial, 1982; (with Imperial War Museum) Animals in War, 1983; The Common Years, 1984; Leo and Jilly Cooper on Cricket, 1985; (with Patrick Lichfield) Hot Foot to Zabrieskie Point, the Unipart Calendar Book, 1985; How to Survive Christmas, 1986; Leo and Jilly Cooper on Horse Mania, 1986; Turn Right at the Spotted Dog, 1987; Angels Rush In, 1990; *novels:* Emily, 1975; Bella, 1976; Harriet, 1976; Octavia, 1977; Prudence, 1978; Imogen, 1978; Riders, 1985 (televised, 1993); Rivals, 1988; Polo, 1991; The Man who made Husbands Jealous, 1993 (televised, 1995); Araminta's Wedding, 1993; Appassionata, 1996; Score, 1999; Pandora, 2002; Wicked!, 2006; *short stories:* Love and Other Heartaches, 1981, re-printed as Lisa and Co., 1982; *for children:* Little Mabel, 1980; Little Mabel's Great Escape, 1981; Little Mabel Wins, 1982; Little Mabel Saves the Day, 1985. *Recreations:* merry-making, wild flowers, music, mongrels, greyhounds. *Address:* c/o Curtis Brown, Haymarket House, 28–29 Haymarket, SW1Y 4SP.

COOPER, John; *see* Cooper, E. J.

COOPER, Rev. Canon John Leslie; Archdeacon of Coleshill, 1990–93; *b* 16 Dec. 1933; *s* of Iris and Leslie Cooper; *m* 1959, Gillian Mary Dodds; two *s* one *d*. *Educ:* Tiffin School, Kingston, Surrey; Chichester Theological Coll. BD 1965, MPhil 1978, London Univ. (External Student). National Service, RA; commissioned, 1952–54. General Electric Co. management trainee, 1954–59; Chichester Theolog. Coll., 1959–62; Asst Curate, All Saints, Kings Heath, Birmingham, 1962–65; Asst Chaplain, HM Prison, Wandsworth, 1965–66; Chaplain: HM Borstal, Portland, Dorset, 1966–68; HM Prison, Bristol, 1968–72; Research Fellow, Queen's Coll., Birmingham, 1972–73; Priest-in-Charge 1973–81, Vicar 1981–82, St Paul's, Balsall Heath, Birmingham. Examining Chaplain to Bishop of Birmingham, 1981–82; Archdeacon of Aston, and Canon Residentiary, St Philip's Cathedral, Birmingham, 1982–90; Asst Curate, Holy Trinity, Sutton Coldfield, 1993–96. Hon. Canon, Birmingham Cathedral, 1993–97, now Canon Emeritus. *Recreations:* music, reading, walking, travel, carpentry, photography. *Address:* 4 Ireton Court, Kirk Ireton, Ashbourne, Derbys DE6 3JP. *T:* (01335) 370459.

COOPER, Prof. John Philip, CBE 1983; DSc; FRS 1977; FIBiol; Emeritus Professor of Agricultural Botany, University of Wales, 1984; *b* Buxton, Derbyshire, 16 Dec. 1923; *o s* of Frank Edward and Nora Goodwin Cooper; *m* 1951, Christine Mary Palmer; one *s* three *d*. *Educ:* Stockport Grammar Sch.; Univ. of Reading (BSc 1945, PhD 1953, DSc 1964); FitzWilliam House, Cambridge (DipAgrSc 1946). Scientific Officer, Welsh Plant Breeding Station, 1946–50; Lectr, Univ. of Reading, 1950–54; Welsh Plant Breeding Station, University College of Wales, Aberystwyth: Plant Geneticist, 1950–59; Head, Dept of Develtl Genetics, 1959–75; Dir, and Prof. of Agricl Botany, 1975–83. Consultant, FAO Headquarters, Rome, 1956; Nuffield Royal Society Bursary, CSIRO, Canberra, 1962; Visiting Professor: Univ. of Kentucky, 1965; Univ. of Khartoum, 1975; Univ. of Reading, 1984–89; Hon. Fellow, BBSRC (formerly AFRC) Inst. for Grassland and Envmtl Res., 1992–. Member: UK Seeds Exec., 1979–86; Internat. Bd for Plant Genetics Resources, 1981–86. *Publications:* (ed with P. F. Wareing) Potential Crop Production, 1971; (ed) Photosynthesis and Productivity in Different Environments, 1975; various papers on crop physiology and genetics in sci. jls. *Recreation:* gentle gardening. *Address:* 31 West End, Minchinhampton, Glos GL6 9JA. *T:* (01453) 882533.

COOPER, Rear-Adm. John Spencer, OBE 1974; *b* 5 April 1933; *s* of Harold Spencer Cooper and Barbara (*née* Highet); *m* 1966, Jacqueline Street (*née* Taylor); two *d*. *Educ:* St Edward's Sch., Oxford; Clare Coll., Cambridge (MA 1959). Joined RN, 1951; served as Lieut on HM Ships Ceylon and Ark Royal; joined Submarines 1966, Polaris Systems Officer in HMS Renown; Comdr 1969; MoD, 1970–73; Flag Officer, Submarines Staff, 1974–76; Captain 1976; Director, Trials, Chevaline programme, 1976–78; Special Proj., RN, Washington, 1978–80; Cdre 1981; Dir, Weapons (Strategic Systems), 1981–83; Dir Gen., Strategic Weapon Systems, 1983–85; Chief Strategic Systems Exec., MoD,

1985–88. Operations Manager: Naval Command and Control Div., Ferranti International, 1988–90; Ferranti Naval Systems, 1990–93.

COOPER, Kenneth Reginald, CB 1991; Chief Executive, The British Library, 1984–91; *b* 28 June 1931; *s* of Reginald and Louisa May Cooper; *m* 1955, Olga Ruth (*née* Harvey); two *s* two *d*. *Educ:* Queen Elizabeth's Grammar Sch., Barnet; New Coll., Oxford (MA). FIPM; FITD (Pres., 1981–83); FIInfSc (Pres., 1988–89). Various appointments, Min. of Labour, 1954–62; Principal, HM Treasury, 1962–65; Principal Private Secretary to Minister of Labour, 1966–67; Asst Sec. for Industrial Training, Min. of Labour, 1967–70; Chief Executive: Employment Services Agency, 1971–75; Training Services Agency, 1975–79; Dir Gen., Nat. Fedn of Building Trades Employers, 1979–84. Vis. Prof., Strathclyde Univ., 1987–91. Dep. Chm., CICI, 1988–92; Dir, Book Trust, 1988–93. CCMI (CBIM 1989); FRSA 1987. Hon. Fellow, Brighton Poly., 1991. Hon. FCLIP 2002. *Recreations:* music, Rugby football.

COOPER, Prof. Leon N., PhD; Thomas J. Watson, Sr, Professor of Science, Brown University, Providence, RI, since 1974; Director, Institute for Brain and Neural Systems, since 1991, and Director, Brain Science Program, since 2000, Brown University; *b* NYC, 28 Feb. 1930; *s* of Irving Cooper and Anna Cooper (*née* Zola); *m* 1969, Kay Anne Allard; two *d*. *Educ:* Columbia Univ. (AB 1951, AM 1953, PhD 1954). Nat. Sci. Foundn post-doctoral Fellow, and Mem., Inst. for Advanced Study, 1954–55; Res. Associate, Univ. of Illinois, 1955–57; Asst Prof., Ohio State Univ., 1957–58; Associate Prof., Brown Univ., 1958–62, Prof., 1962–66, Henry Ledyard Goddard Prof., 1966–74. Consultant, various governmental agencies, industrial and educational organizations. Lectr, Summer Sch., Varenna, Italy, 1955; Visiting Professor: Brandeis Summer Inst., 1959; Bergen Internat. Sch. Physics, Norway, 1961; Scuola Internazionale di Fisica, Erice, Italy, 1965; Ecole Normale Supérieure, Centre Universitaire Internat., Paris, 1966; Cargèse Summer Sch., 1966; Radiation Lab., Univ. of Calif at Berkeley, 1969; Faculty of Scis, Quai St Bernard, Paris, 1970, 1971; Brookhaven Nat. Lab., 1972; Chair of Math. Models of Nervous System, Fondation de France, 1977–83; Mem., Conseil Supérieur de la Recherche, l'Université René Descartes, Paris, 1981–87. Alfred P. Sloan Foundn Res. Fellow, 1959–66; John Simon Guggenheim Meml Foundn Fellow, 1965–66. Co-Chm., Bd of Dirs, Nestor Inc. Fellow: Amer. Physical Soc.; Amer. Acad. of Arts and Sciences. Member: Amer. Philosoph. Soc.; National Acad. of Sciences; Sponsor Fedn of Amer. Scientists; Soc. for Neuroscience, Amer. Assoc. for Advancement of Science; Defense Science Bd, 1989–93. Mem. Bd of Govs, Internat. Neural Network Soc., 1989–94. (Jtly) Comstock Prize, Nat. Acad. of Scis, 1968; (jtly) Nobel Prize for Physics, 1972; Award of Excellence, Grad. Fac. Alumni, Columbia Univ., 1974; Déscartes Medal, Acad. de Paris, Univ. René Déscartes, 1977; Yrjö Reenpää Medal, Finnish Cultural Foundn, 1982; John Jay Award, 1985, Award for Distinguished Achievement, 1989, Columbia Univ.; Alexander Hamilton Award, Columbia Coll., 1996. Hon. DSc: Columbia, 1973; Sussex, 1973; Illinois, 1974; Brown, 1974; Gustavus Adolphus Coll., 1975; Ohio State Univ., 1976; Univ. Pierre et Marie Curie, Paris, 1977. Public lectures, internat. confs, symposia. *Publications:* Introduction to the Meaning and Structure of Physics, 1968; (contrib.) The Physicist's Conception of Nature, 1973; How We Learn, How We Remember: toward an understanding of brain and neural systems, 1995; contrib. The Many Body Problem, 1963; contrib. to numerous jls incl. Physics Rev., Amer. Jl Physics, Biological Cybernetics, Jl of Neurosci., Jl of Neurophysiol., Procs of the US Nat. Acad. of Scis. *Recreations:* music, theatre, ski-ing. *Address:* Physics Department, Brown University, Providence, RI 02912, USA. *T:* (401) 8632172. *Clubs:* University, Faculty (Providence, RI).

COOPER, Sir Louis Jacques B.; *see* Blom-Cooper.

COOPER, Margaret Jean Drummond, OBE 1980; Chief Education Officer, General Nursing Council for England and Wales, 1974–82; *b* 24 March 1922; *d* of Canon Bernard R. Cooper and A. Jean Cooper (*née* Drackley). *Educ:* School of St Mary and St Anne, Abbots Bromley; Royal College of Nursing; Open Univ. (BA 1987). SRN, SCM, RNT. Nursing trng and early posts, Leicester Royal Infirmary, 1941–47; Midwifery trng, General Lying-in Hosp., SW1 and Coventry and Warwicks Hosp.; Nurse Tutor, Middlesex Hosp., 1953–55; Principal Tutor: General Hosp., Northampton, 1956–63; Addenbrooke's Hosp., Cambridge, 1963–68; Principal, Queen Elizabeth Sch. of Nursing, Birmingham, 1968–74. Chm., General Nursing Council for England and Wales, 1971–74 (Mem., 1965–74). *Recreations:* birds, books, buildings. *Address:* Howard House, 8 Vicarage Way, Gerrards Cross, Bucks SL9 8AT.

COOPER, Michael John; Director General, British Diabetic Association, 1991–98; *b* 24 July 1937; *s* of Frederick Walton Cooper and Ivy Kathleen (*née* Harris); *m* 1961, Kathy Cockett; two *s* one *d*. *Educ:* King's Sch., Rochester; Univ. of Exeter (BA 1960); Oberlin Coll., Ohio; Internat. Management Develt Inst., Switzerland (MBA 1970). RAF, 1955–57. Shell Internat. Petroleum Co. Ltd, 1961–69; Man. Dir, Panocean-Anco Ltd, 1970–82; Dir, Burmah Castrol PLC, 1982–91. Vice-Chm., E Sussex HA, 1996–2000 (Dir, 1992–2000). Vis. Prof., Univ. of Westminster, 1992–2001. Chm., Care for the Carers, 2000–07. Vice-Chm., Queen's Nursing Inst., 2004– (Trustee, 2002–); Trustee: Diabetes Network Internat., 2002–; Council for Music in Hosps, 2003–. Member: Exec. Cttee, Lib Dem Wealden Constituency, 2004– (Vice Chm., 2004–06); Exec. Cttee, Lib Dem European Gp, 2006–. Chm. Govs, High Hurstwood C of E Primary Sch., 1998–2007. *Recreations:* music, walking, cricket, tennis, travel. *Address:* Old Hall Cottage, High Hurstwood, Uckfield, E Sussex TN22 4AD. *T:* (01825) 733268; Flat 5, 130 Belgrave Road, SW1V 2BL; Le Gouttat, 71520 Clermain, France. *Club:* Oriental.

COOPER, Michael John, OBE 1997; CBiol; Staff Development Adviser and Trainer, Voluntary Service Overseas, 2005–07; *b* 5 April 1949; *s* of Stanley and Evelyn Cooper; *m* 1975, Gillian Isted; two *s*. *Educ:* Sutton High Sch., Plymouth; York Univ. (BA). CBiol, MIBiol 1971. VSO, Chassa Secondary Sch., Zambia, 1972; Mill Hill Sch., London, 1973–78 (Dir of Biol., 1974–78); Dep. Head, Upper Sch., Moulsham High Sch., Chelmsford, 1978–81; Dep. Headteacher, Valley Sch., Worksop, 1982–85; Headmaster, Hillcrest Sch., Hastings, 1985–90; Principal, British Sch. in the Netherlands, 1990–99; Headmaster, Latymer Sch., 1999–2005. Selector, VSO, 1975–90. Governor: Middx Univ., 2003–06; Enfield Coll., 2003–06. FRSA 1991. *Recreations:* walking, gardening, swimming, reading. *Address:* Blue Ocean, Chapel Point Lane, Cornwall PL26 6PP. *T:* (01726) 842955. *Club:* East India.

COOPER, Morris; a District Judge (Magistrates' Court), since 2004; *b* 10 Oct. 1948; *s* of Arthur Cooper and Elsie Cooper; *m* 1989, Vivien Joy Hallam; one *s* two *d*. Called to the Bar, Gray's Inn, 1979; Clerk to the Justices: for Burton-on-Trent and Uttoxeter, 1980–88; for N Staffs, 1988–89; in practice as a barrister, 1991–2004; actg Stipendiary Magistrate, 1999, subseq. Dep. Dist Judge (Magistrates' Court), 2000–04. *Recreation:* enjoying life. *Address:* Nottingham Magistrates' Court, Carrington Street, Nottingham NG2 1EE. *T:* (0115) 955 8111.

COOPER, Nigel Cookson; Co-ordinator, Wimbledon Tennis Championships, 1988–95; *b* 7 May 1929; *s* of Richard and Violet Sarah Cooper; *m* 1972, Elizabeth Gillian Smith; two *s* one *d*. *Educ:* Leeds Training Coll., Leeds Univ. (LLB); State Univ. of Iowa, USA (MA). Teacher, primary and secondary schools, 1950–59; Lecturer: Trent Park Training Coll., 1959–61; Loughborough Training Coll., 1961–64; Provincial Supervisor (Schools and Community) for Nova Scotia, Canada, 1964–65; County Organiser of Schools for Norfolk, 1965–68; Asst Education Officer for Oldham, 1970–72; Asst Director of Educn for British Families Educn Service in Europe, 1972–78; Registrar, Kelvin Grove College of Advanced Education, Brisbane, Australia, 1978–82; Gen. Sec., BAAB, 1982–87. Mem., Elmbridge BC, 1999– (Dep. Mayor, 2007–08). *Recreations:* playing the trumpet, squash, jogging. *Address:* 24 Southfields, East Molesey, Surrey KT8 0BP. *T:* and *Fax:* (020) 8224 0712.

COOPER, Philip John, CB 1989; Comptroller-General of Patents, Designs and Trade Marks, Department of Trade and Industry, 1986–89; *b* 15 Sept. 1929; *s* of Charles Cooper and Mildred Annie Marlow; *m* 1st, 1953, Dorothy Joan Chapman (*d* 1982); two *d*; 2nd, 1986, Pamela Mary Pysden (*d* 1988); 3rd, 1993, Antoinette Erasmus. *Educ:* Deacon's Sch., Peterborough; University Coll., Leicester. BSc (Chem. 1st Cl. Hons). CChem, FRSC. Joined Dept (later Laboratory) of Govt Chemist, 1952; Nat. Service, 2nd Lt, R Signals, 1953–55; Dept of Scientific and Ind. Res., 1956–67; Principal, Min. of Technology, 1967; Prin. Private Sec. to Minister for Industrial Develt, 1972–73; Asst Sec., 1973–79, Under Sec., 1979–89, DoI and DTI; Dir, Warren Spring Lab., DTI, 1984–85. *Publications:* various papers on analytical and chemical matters. *Address:* 12 The Lye, Tadworth, Surrey KT20 5RS.

COOPER, Sir (Richard) Adrian, 6th Bt *cr* 1905, of Shenstone Court, co. Stafford; *b* 21 Aug. 1960; *o s* of Sir Richard Powell Cooper, 5th Bt and Angela Marjorie (*née* Wilson); *S* father, 2006; *m* 1994, Belinda Potter. *Educ:* Millfield Sch. *Heir:* none. *Address:* Hill Farm, Swalcliffe, Banbury, Oxon OX15 5EN.

COOPER, Rev. Canon Richard Thomas; Rector of Richmond, North Yorkshire, since 1998; Chaplain to the Queen, since 2003; *b* 7 March 1946; *s* of Frank and Margaret Cooper; *m* 1978, Janet Johnston; one *s* one *d*. *Educ:* Ripon Grammar Sch.; Leeds Univ. (BA 1969); Coll. of the Resurrection, Mirfield. Ordained deacon, 1971, priest, 1972; Assistant Curate: Rothwell, 1971–75; Adel, Leeds, 1975–78; Priest i/c, Holy Trinity, Knaresborough, 1978–81; Vicar: Middleton Tyas, Croft and Eryholme, 1981–90; Aldborough with Boroughbridge and Roecliffe, 1990–98. RD, Richmond, 1986–90; Area Dean, Ripon, 1990–93; Chaplain, The Green Howards, 2002–; Regtl Chaplain, Yorks Regt, 2007–. Hon. Canon, Ripon Cathedral, 1997–. Proctor in Convocation and Mem., Gen. Synod of C of E, 1986–90; Chm., House of Clergy, dio. Ripon, 1993–2001. Freeman and Chaplain: Mercers', Grocers' and Haberdashers' Co., Richmond, 1991– (Warden, 2007); Fellmongers' Co., Richmond, 1998–. *Recreations:* choral singing, cycling, fishing. *Address:* The Rectory, Church Wynd, Richmond, N Yorks DL10 7AQ. *T:* (01748) 823398.

COOPER, Robert Francis, CMG 1997; MVO 1975; HM Diplomatic Service; Director General for External Affairs, Council Secretariat of the European Union, since 2002; *b* 28 Aug. 1947; *s* of late Norman and Frances Cooper. *Educ:* Delamere Sch., Nairobi; Worcester Coll., Oxford (BA); Univ. of Pennsylvania (MA). Joined FCO 1970; Tokyo 1972; London 1977; seconded to Bank of England, 1982; UK Rep. to EC, 1984; Head of Management Review Staff, FCO, 1987; Head of Far Eastern Dept, FCO, 1987; Hd of Policy Planning Staff, FCO, 1989; Counsellor, 1993, Minister and Dep. Hd of Mission, 1996–98, Bonn; Dir, Asia, FCO, 1998–99; Hd, Defence and Overseas Secretariat, Cabinet Office (on secondment), 1999–2001; Govt's special rep. for Afghanistan, 2001–02. *Publications:* The Postmodern State and the World Order, 1996; The Breaking of Nations, 2003. *Recreations:* Shakespeare, ballroom dancing, bicycling. *Address:* Council Secretariat, European Union, Rue de la Loi 175, 1048 Brussels, Belgium.

COOPER, Prof. Robin Hayes, PhD; FBA 1993; Professor of Computational Linguistics, University of Gothenburg, since 1995; Director, Swedish National Graduate School of Language Technology, since 2001; *b* 23 Dec. 1947; *s* of Dennis J. Cooper and Marjorie (*née* Wilding); *m* 1985, Elisabet B. Engdahl; two *d*. *Educ:* Corpus Christi Coll., Cambridge (MA); Univ. of Massachusetts at Amherst (PhD). Lektor, Universität Freiburg, 1969–71; Assistant Professor: Univ. of Texas at Austin, 1975–76; Univ. of Massachusetts at Amherst, 1976–77; Univ. of Wisconsin, Madison, 1977–81, Associate Prof., 1981–87; Docent, Lund Univ., 1984–87; University of Edinburgh: Lectr, 1986–89; Reader in Cognitive Sci., 1989–96. Mellon Fellow, Stanford Univ., 1980–81; Fellow, Center for Advanced Study in Behavioral Scis, Stanford, 1981–82; Guggenheim Fellow, Edinburgh and Stanford, 1986–87. Fellow, Royal Soc. of Arts and Scis, Göteborg, 1996. FilDr *hc* Uppsala, 2006. *Publications:* Quantification and Syntactic Theory, 1983; (ed jtly) Situation Theory and its Applications, Vol. 1, 1990; contribs to numerous books, contrib. Computational Intelligence, Ethnomusicology, Jl Logic, Lang. and Information, Jl Logic and Computation, Lang., Linguistics and Philosophy, Musique en Jeu, Nordic Jl Linguistics, Res. on Lang. and Computation. *Recreations:* yoga, music. *Address:* Department of Linguistics, University of Gothenburg, Box 200, 40530 Göteborg, Sweden; Bigatan 1, 43139 Mölndal, Sweden.

COOPER, Ronald Cecil Macleod, CB 1981; Deputy Secretary, Department of Transport, 1986–90; *b* 8 May 1931; *s* of Cecil Redvers Cooper and Norah Agnes Louise Cooper (*née* Macleod); *m* 1st, 1953, June Bicknell (marr. diss. 1967); 2nd, 1967, Christine Savage; one *s* two *d*. *Educ:* Royal Grammar Sch., Newcastle upon Tyne; St Edmund Hall, Oxford (MA). Asst Principal, Min. of Supply, 1954–59; Principal, Min. of Aviation, 1959–62; on loan to European Launcher Develt Org., Paris, 1962–67; Asst Sec., Min. of Technology, 1968–70, DTI, 1970–73; Under Sec., Dept of Trade, 1973–78; Sec., Price Commn, 1979; Dep. Sec. and Principal Estabt and Finance Officer, DTI, 1979–85. *Recreations:* music, reading. *Address:* 18 Rignall Road, Great Missenden, Bucks HP16 9AN.

COOPER, Rosemary Elizabeth; MP (Lab) Lancashire West, since 2005; *b* 5 Sept. 1950; *d* of William and Rose Cooper. *Educ:* Bellerive Convent GS; Liverpool Univ. W. Cooper Ltd, 1973–80; Littlewoods Organisation: merchandiser, 1980–92; PR Manager, Littlewoods Internat., 1994–95; Gp Corporate Communications Manager, 1995–2001; Project Co-ordinator, 1999–2000. Mem. and Vice-Chm., Liverpool HA, 1994–96; Chm., Liverpool Women's Hosp. NHS Trust, 1996–2005. Mem. (Lib Dem, then Lab), Liverpool CC, 1973–2000; Lord Mayor of Liverpool, 1992–93. Contested (Lib Dem): Knowsley N, Nov. 1986, 1987; Liverpool Garston, 1983; Liverpool Broadgreen, 1992; contested (Lab) NW Reg., EP elecns, 2004. Former Director: Merseyside Centre for Deaf People; Roy Castle Foundn. *Address:* House of Commons, SW1A 0AA.

COOPER, Russell; *see* Cooper, T. R.

COOPER, Sidney Pool; Head of Public Services, British Museum, 1973–76; *b* 29 March 1919; *s* of late Sidney Charles Henry Cooper and Emily Lilian Baptie; *m* 1940, Denise Marjorie Peverett (*d* 2003); two *s* one *d*. *Educ:* Finchley County Sch.; Northern Polytechnic (BSc); University Coll. London (MSc). Laboratory of the Government Chemist, 1947; Asst Keeper, National Reference Library of Science and Invention, British

Museum, 1963; Dep. Keeper, NRLSI, 1969. *Address:* 11 Bridgewater Hill, Northchurch, Berkhamsted, Herts HP4 1LW. *T:* (01442) 864145.

COOPER, Maj.-Gen. Sir Simon (Christie), GCVO 2000 (KCVO 1991); Master of HM's Household, 1992–2000; *b* 5 Feb. 1936; *s* of Maj.-Gen. Kenneth Christie Cooper, CB, DSO, OBE and Barbara Harding-Newman; *m* 1967, Juliet Elizabeth Palmer; one *s* one *d*. *Educ:* Winchester College; rcds, psc. Commissioned Life Guards, 1956; served Aden, London, BAOR, 1957–63; Captain-Adjt, Household Cavalry Regt, 1963–65; ADC to CDS Earl Mountbatten of Burma, 1965–66; Borneo, Malaya, 1966–67; Staff Coll., 1968; BAOR, 1969–75; CO Life Guards, 1974–76; GSO1, Staff Coll., 1976–78; OC Household Cavalry and Silver Stick in Waiting, 1978–81; Commander, RAC Centre, 1981–82; RCDS, 1983; Dir, RAC, 1984–87; Comdt, RMA, Sandhurst, 1987–89; GOC London Dist and Maj.-Gen. Commanding Household Div., 1989–91. Hon. Colonel: Westminster Dragoons, 1987–97; Royal Yeomanry, 1987–97. *Recreations:* cricket, ski-ing, sailing, shooting. *Clubs:* Army and Navy, MCC.

COOPER, Simon Nicholas; a District Judge (Magistrates' Courts), since 2002; a Recorder, since 2002; *b* 2 Sept. 1953; *s* of Lt Comdr Alan Geoffrey Cooper and Wendy Anne Cooper (*née* Mcleod); *m* 1998, Philippa Mason. *Educ:* Kelly Coll.; Bristol Univ. (LLB Hons); RNC Dartmouth; Inns of Court Sch. of Law. Joined RN, 1972; served HMS Wilton, Rhyl, Intrepid, Hecate and Yarmouth; called to the Bar, Middle Temple, 1982; RN Judge Advocate, 1988; Comdr 1994; Dep. Chief Naval Judge Advocate, 1994–97 and 2001–02; retd from RN, 2002. *Recreations:* fly fishing, golf, choral singing. *Address:* North West Wiltshire Magistrates' Court, The Court House, Pewsham Way, Chippenham, Wilts SN15 3BF. *T:* (01249) 466203. *Club:* Naval and Military.

COOPER, Prof. Susan, PhD; Professor of Experimental Physics, and Fellow of St Catherine's College, University of Oxford, since 1995; *b* USA, 1949. *Educ:* Colby Coll., USA (BA); Univ. of California at Berkeley (PhD). Guest Physicist, Deutsches Electronen Synchrotron, Germany, 1980–83; Research Associate, Stanford Linear Accelerator Center, USA, 1984–86; Asst Prof., MIT, 1987–89; Group leader, Max Planck Inst. of Physics, Munich, 1989–96. *Publications:* numerous papers in sci. jls. *Address:* Denys Wilkinson Building, Oxford University, Keble Road, Oxford OX1 3RH.

COOPER, (Theo) Russell; MLA (National Party) Crows Nest, Queensland, 1992–2001 (Roma, Queensland, 1983–92); *b* 4 Feb. 1941; *s* of Theo Beverley Cooper and Muriel Frances Cooper; *m* 1965, Penelope Anne Parkinson; one *s* three *d*. *Educ:* Surfers Paradise State Sch.; Correspondence Sch.; Toowoomba Prep. Sch.; King's Sch., Parramatta. Councillor, 1976–88, Dep. Chm., 1982–86, Bendemere Shire Council; Dep. Chm., Roma Electorate NP Council, 1980–83; Chm., Wallumbilla-Yuleba Branch, NP, 1974–83. Minister for: Corrective Services and Admin. Services, 1987–89; Police and Emergency Services, 1989; Premier of Qld, Sept.–Dec. 1989; Leader of the Opposition, 1989–91; Opposition spokesman for police and corrective services, 1992–96; Minister for Police and Corrective Services and for Racing, 1996–98; Opposition spokesman on Primary Industries, 1998–2000. Vice-Pres., Maranoa Graziers Assoc., 1979–80 (Chm., Wallumbilla Br.); Pres., Roma and Dist Amateur Race Club, 1981–83. *Recreations:* golf, tennis (active), Rugby League, Rugby Union, cricket. *Address:* 10 Somerset Drive, Buderim, Qld 4556, Australia. *Clubs:* Queensland; Headland Golf.

COOPER, Hon. Warren Ernest, CNZM 1997; MP (National Party) Otago, 1975–96; Minister of Defence and Minister responsible for War Pensions, New Zealand, 1990–96, also Minister of Civil Defence and of Internal Affairs, 1993–96; *b* Dunedin, 21 Feb. 1933; *s* of William Cooper; *m* 1959, Lorraine Margaret, *d* of Angus T. Rees; three *s* two *d*. *Educ:* Musselburgh Sch.; King's High Sch., Dunedin. Formerly Minister of Tourism, Minister of Regional Develt, Minister in charge of Publicity and in charge of Govt Printing Office; Postmaster Gen., 1980; Minister of Broadcasting and Assoc. Minister of Finance, 1981; Minister of Foreign Affairs and Overseas Trade, 1981–84; Minister of Local Govt and of Radio and Television, 1990–93. Mem., Cabinet Cttees on Expenditure Control and Revenue, State Sector, Appts and Honours, Social and Family Policy, Treaty of Waitangi Issues, 1990–96. Member Executive: S Island Publicity Assoc., 1971; NZ Municipal Assoc. Life Mem. and former Pres., Queenstown Jaycees. Mayor of Queenstown, 1968–75 and 1995–2001. JP Queenstown. Silver Jubilee Medal, 1977. *Address:* 8 Park Street, Queenstown, New Zealand.

COOPER, Sir William (Daniel Charles), 6th Bt *cr* 1863, of Woollahra; Company Director of The Garden Maintenance Service and G.M.S. Vehicles; *b* 5 March 1955; *s* of Sir Charles Eric Daniel Cooper, 5th Bt, and Mary Elisabeth (*d* 1999), *e d* of Captain J. Graham Clarke; *S* father, 1984; *m* 1988, Julia Nicholson. *Educ:* Northease Manor, Lewes, Sussex. *Heir: b* George John Cooper, *b* 28 June 1956.

COOPER, (William) Gareth, FCILT; Chairman, Stena Line, since 1997; *b* 19 Aug. 1943; *s* of William Alderson Cooper and Florence Morwen Cooper (*née* Matthews); *m* 1966, Carole Roberta Davies; one *s* one *d*. *Educ:* University Coll., Swansea (BScEng). Managing Director: Wallington Weston Co. Ltd, 1977–83; Weston Hyde Products Ltd, 1983–87; Crown Berger Ltd, 1987–91; Stena Line UK Ltd, 1991–97; Chairman: White Young Green plc, 1997–2004; Arriva plc, 1999–2004. *Recreations:* opera, travel, photography. *Address:* 1 Lady Place, Sutton Courtenay, Oxfordshire OX14 4FB.

COOPER, William Robert Patrick W.; *see* White-Cooper.

COOPER, Rt Hon. Yvette; PC 2007; MP (Lab) Pontefract and Castleford, since 1997; Chief Secretary to HM Treasury, since 2008; *b* 20 March 1969; *d* of (Derek) Anthony Cooper, *qv* and June Cooper (*née* Iley); *m* 1998, Rt Hon. Edward Michael Balls, *qv*; one *s* two *d*. *Educ:* Eggars Comprehensive Sch., Hants; Balliol Coll., Oxford (BA 1st Cl. Hons PPE 1990); Harvard Univ.; London Sch. of Econs (MSc Econs 1995). Economic researcher for Rt Hon. John Smith, MP, 1991–92; Domestic Policy specialist, Clinton Presidential Campaign, Arkansas, 1992; Policy Advr to Labour's Treasury Team, 1992–95; leader writer and economic columnist, The Independent, 1995–97. Parliamentary Under-Secretary of State: for Public Health, DoH, 1999–2002; Lord Chancellor's Dept, 2002–03; (Social Exclusion Minister), ODPM, 2003–05; Minister of State (Minister for Housing and Planning), ODPM, later DCLG, 2005–07; Minister for Housing, DCLG, 2007–08. Member: Select Cttee on Educn and Employment, 1997–99; Intelligence and Security Cttee, 1997–99. *Recreations:* swimming, watching Disney videos. *Address:* House of Commons, SW1A 0AA. *T:* (020) 7219 5080.

COORAY, His Honour (Bulathsinhalage) Anura (Siri); a Circuit Judge, 1991–97; *b* 20 Jan. 1936; *s* of (Bulathsinhalage) Vincent Cooray, accountant, and Dolly Perera Manchanayake, Etul Kotte, Sri Lanka; *m* 1957, Manel Therese, *d* of late George Perera, planter, and late Myrtle Perera, Kandy, Sri Lanka; two *s* three *d*. *Educ:* Christian Coll., Kotte, Sri Lanka; London Univ. Called to the Bar, Lincoln's Inn, 1968. Served RAF, Cranwell and Locking, 1952–55 (RAF Boxing Assoc. Sigrist Trophy, 1953–54); served Royal Ceylon Air Force, 1955–60. Practised in Common Law Chambers at Middle Temple; later, Dep. Head of Chambers at No 1 Gray's Inn Sq.; Mem., South Eastern Circuit; Prosecuting Counsel for DPP and Met. Police Solicitors, 1969–82; a Metropolitan Stipendiary Magistrate, 1982–91; a Recorder, 1989–91. Mem., Cttee of Magistrates, 1989. *Recreations:* wine making (and tasting too!), gardening. *Address:* 1 Gray's Inn Square, WC1R 5AA; Kingsland, Etul Kotte, Kotte, Sri Lanka.

COOTE, Anna; policy analyst and writer; Commissioner for Health, UK Sustainable Development Commission, since 2000; *b* 1 April 1947; *d* of Capt. J. O. Coote and Sylvia Coote; one *d*. *Educ:* Edinburgh Univ. (MA). FFPH (FFPHM 2001). Feature Writer, Observer, 1968–72; Dep. Editor, New Statesman, 1978–82; Editor, Diverse Reports, Channel 4, 1982–86; Res. Fellow, IPPR, 1989–91; Sen. Lectr, Goldsmiths' Coll., London Univ., 1991–93; Dep. Dir, IPPR, 1993–98; Dir of Health Policy, King's Fund, 1998–2005; Hd of Patient and Public Involvement, Healthcare Commn, 2005–08. Mem., London Health Commn, 2000–05. Trustee, Help the Aged, 2001–06. Hon. DLitt Bath, 1999. *Publications* include: (jtly) Civil Liberty: the NCCL guide, 1972; (jtly) Women's Rights: a practical guide, 1974; (jtly) Sweet Freedom, 1987; (jtly) Power and Prejudice, 1990; (ed) The Welfare of Citizens, 1992; (jtly) Citizens' Juries, 1994; New Gender Agenda, 2000; (ed) Claiming the Health Dividend, 2002; Finding Out What Works, 2004. *Recreations:* cycling, walking, cinema, theatre. *Address:* 8/51 Surrey Row, SE1 0BZ.

COOTE, Sir Christopher (John), 15th Bt *cr* 1621; Senior Baronetcy of Ireland in use; *b* 22 Sept. 1928; *s* of Rear Adm. Sir John Ralph Coote, 14th Bt, CB, CBE, DSC, and Noreen Una (*d* 1996), *o d* of late Wilfred Tighe; *S* father, 1978; *m* 1952, Anne Georgiana, *d* of Lt-Col Donald Handford; one *s* one *d*. *Educ:* Winchester; Christ Church, Oxford (MA 1957). Coffee and tea merchant. *Heir: s* Nicholas Patrick Coote [*b* 28 July 1953; *m* 1980, Mona, *d* of late Moushegh Bedelian; one *s* one *d*].

COOTE, Prof. John Haven; Bowman Professor, 1987–2003, and Head of Department of Physiology, 1984–2003, Birmingham University, now Professor Emeritus; *b* 5 Jan. 1937; *m* 1976, Susan Hylton; one *s* two *d*. *Educ:* Royal Free Hosp. Sch. of Medicine (BSc (Hons) Physiol.; PhD London); DSc Birmingham 1980. CBiol, FIBiol 1988. Birmingham University: Prof. of Physiology, 1984–2003; Hd of Sch. of Basic Med. Scis, 1988–91. Vis. Scientist, Inst. de Medicina Experimental, Univ. of Caracas, Venezuela, 1971; Visiting Professor: Inst. of Gerontology, Tokyo, 1974–75; Inst. of Physiological Scis, Warsaw, 1977–78; Shanghai Univ., 1988; Chicago Univ., 1988; Leicester Univ., 2003; Warwick Univ., 2003; Nankai and Tiansin Univs, China, 2004. Carl Ludwig Dist. Lectr, Fedn of Amer. Socs for Experimental Biol., 2003; Paton Lectr, Physiol. Soc., 2005. Chm., Human Scis Ethics Cttee, DERA/QinetiQ, 1998–; Member: Internat. Adv. Bd, Acta Physiologica Sinica, 2002–; Defence Sci. Adv. Council, 2003–. Member: AAAS, 1989; NY Acad. of Scis, 1991. Mem. Council, BHF, 1998–2003. Civil Consultant, Applied Physiol., RAF Centre for Aviation Medicine, 2002–. Hon. Mem., Physiol Soc., 2004. Chm. Editorial Bd, Experimental Physiology, 2000–06. FRGS 2004. Hon. DipMed Krakow, 1995. *Publications:* contribs to Jl of Physiol., Jl of the Autonomic Nervous System, Brain Res., Exptl Physiol., Neurosci., Ann. Thoracic Surgery, Circ. Cardiovascular Res., British Jl Pharmacol. *Recreation:* mountaineering. *Address:* Division of Neuroscience, Medical School, University of Birmingham, Birmingham B15 2TT.

COPE, family name of **Baron Cope of Berkeley**.

COPE OF BERKELEY, Baron *cr* 1997 (Life Peer), of Berkeley in the co. of Gloucestershire; **John Ambrose Cope,** Kt 1991; PC 1988; *b* 13 May 1937; *s* of George Cope, MC, FRIBA, Leicester; *m* 1969, Djemila Lovell Payne, *d* of late Col P. V. L. Payne, Martinstown, Dorset and Mrs Tanetta Blackden, Amer. Colony of Jerusalem; two *d*. *Educ:* Oakham, Rutland. Chartered Accountant; Company Director. Commnd RA and RE, Nat Service and TA. Contested (C) Woolwich East, 1970; MP (C) South Gloucestershire, Feb. 1974–1983, Northavon, 1983–97; contested (C) Northavon, 1997. A Govt Whip, 1979–87, and Lord Comr of HM Treasury, 1981–83; Treas. of HM Household and Dep. Chief Whip, 1983–87; Minister of State: Dept of Employment and Minister for Small Businesses, 1987–89; NI Office, 1989–90; Dep. Chm. and Jt Treas., Cons. Party, 1990–92; HM Paymaster Gen., 1992–94; Opposition spokesman on NI, 1997–98, on home affairs, 1998–2001, H of L; Opposition Chief Whip, H of L, 2001–07. Sen. Comr, Royal Hospital Chelsea, 1992–94. Pres., Inst. of Business Counsellors, 1988–90; Dep. Chm., Small Business Bureau, 1995–2001; Pres., S Glos Chamber of Commerce, 1993–2001. Chm., Horse and Pony Taxation Cttee, 1994–2000. Vice Pres., Royal Soc. of St George, 1998–. Trustee, War Memls Trust (formerly Friends of War Memls), 1997–. Patron: Avon Riding for the Disabled, 1985–; Vigilant Trust, 1993–. *Publications:* (with Bernard Weatherill) Acorns to Oaks (Policy for Small Business), 1967; (ed) A Funny Thing Happened, 1991; I'm sorry you were in when I called, 1992. *Recreation:* woodwork. *Address:* House of Lords, SW1A 0PW. *Clubs:* Carlton, Pratt's, Beefsteak; Tudor House (Chipping Sodbury).

COPE, Alan, CPFA, FCCA; County Treasurer, Cheshire County Council, 1997–2001; *b* 8 Oct. 1946; *s* of John William Cope and Bertha Cope; *m* 1969, Gillian Mary Kirk; two *s*. *Educ:* Swanwick Hall Grammar Sch.; Univ. of Liverpool (MA 2004). CPFA 1968; FCCA 1981. Accountant, Derbyshire CC, 1963–69; Cheshire County Council: Sen. Auditor, 1969–72; Technical Accountant, 1972–74; Gp Accountant, 1974–78; Chief Accountant, 1978–85; Asst Dir, Policy Unit, 1985–87; Asst Co. Treas., 1987–89; Co. Finance Officer, 1989–97. Treasurer: Cheshire Fire Authy, 1997–2001; Cheshire Probation Service, 1997–2001; Cheshire Police Authy, 1998–2001. Non-exec. Mem., Finance Cttee, Royal Mencap Soc., 2004–. *Address:* The Meadows, 19 Dee Crescent, Farndon, Chester CH3 6QJ. *T:* (01829) 270602.

COPE, David Robert, MA; education and recruitment consultant; *b* 24 Oct. 1944; *yr s* of late Dr Cuthbert Cope, FRCP and Eileen Cope (*née* Putt); *m* 1st, 1966, Gillian Margaret Peck (marr. diss. 1994); one *s* two *d*; 2nd, 1996, Juliet Caroline, *e d* of Prof. Richard Swinburne, *qv*; two *s*. *Educ:* Winchester Coll. (Scholar); Clare Coll., Cambridge (Scholar). 1st Cl. Hons Hist. Tripos Part II, 1965; BA 1965; MA 1972. Asst Master, Eton Coll., 1965–67; Asst British Council Rep. (Cultural Attaché), Mexico City, 1968–70; Asst Master, Bryanston Sch., 1970–73; Headmaster: Dover College, 1973–81; British Sch. of Paris, 1981–86; Master of Marlborough Coll., 1986–93; Field Dir, Zambia, VSO, 1994–97. Director: Ashoka (UK) Trust, 1998–2001; Application Research Ltd, 2002–; Sen. Associate, Search Associates, 2002–. FRSA. *Recreations:* music, running, books, travel. *Address:* Berry House, 41 High Street, Over, Cambridge CB24 5NB. *T:* (01954) 232170. *Clubs:* Athenæum, Royal Commonwealth Society.

COPE, David Robert; Director, Parliamentary Office of Science and Technology, since 1998; *b* 7 July 1946; *s* of Lawrence William and Ethel Anne Cope; *m* 1992, Reiko Takashina. *Educ:* Fitzwilliam Coll., Cambridge Univ. (MA); London School of Economics (MScEcon, with dist.). Res. Officer, University Coll. London, 1969–70; Lectr, Nottingham Univ., 1970–81; Environment Team Leader, Internat. Energy Agency Coal Unit, 1981–86; Exec. Dir, UK CEED, 1986–97; Prof. of Energy Econs, Doshisha Univ., Kyoto, Japan, 1997–98. Special Lectr in Energy and Environment Studies, Nottingham Univ., 1985–94; Vis. Lectr, Cambridge Univ., 1988–95; First Caltex Green Fund Fellow, 1992, and Ext. Examiner, 1992–, Centre of Urban Planning and Envmtl Mgt, Univ. of

Hong Kong; Associate, Clare Hall, Cambridge Univ., 2005–. Member: Council, Nat. Soc. for Clean Air, 1990–98; Standing Cttee on the Envmt, ACOST, 1990–92; Climate Change Wkg Gp, 1993; Packaging Standards Council (formerly Packaging Council), 1992–96; Envmtl Stats Adv. Cttee, DoE, later DETR, 1994–98. Chm., Europe-Japan Experts' Assoc., 2002–. Hon. PhD N London, 2001. *Publications:* (with P. Hills and P. James) Energy Policy and Land Use Planning, 1984; (with S. Owens) Land Use Planning Policy and Climate Change, 1992; numerous papers on energy and environmental policy topics. *Recreations:* amateur volcanology, hill walking, woodworking. *Address:* Parliamentary Office of Science and Technology, Westminster House, 7 Millbank, SW1P 3JA. *T:* (020) 7219 2848, *Fax:* (020) 7219 2849; *e-mail:* coped@parliament.uk.

COPE, Jeremy Ewart; Managing Director, UK, Royal Mail Group, 2002–03; *b* 30 Nov. 1951; *s* of Michael Ewart Cope and Maureen Ann Cope (*née* Casey); *m* 1985, Dianne Elizabeth Gilmour; one *s*. *Educ:* St Paul's Sch.; Jesus Coll., Cambridge (MA); Warwick Univ. (MSc). MCIPD. Joined Post Office as management trainee, 1973; Asst Head Postmaster, Southend, 1980; Dir of Personnel, Royal Mail, 1986; Gen. Manager, London, 1988; Dir of Strategy, Royal Mail, 1989; Dir of Strategy and Commercial Develt, Post Office, 1992; Man. Dir, Strategy and Personnel, Post Office, 1995; Mem. for Strategy and Personnel, Post Office Bd, 1996–99; Gp Man. Dir, Post Office, subseq. Consignia, then Royal Mail Gp, 1999–2003. Dir, Camelot plc, 2000–03; Chm., T-Three Ltd (formerly HRS Ltd), 2004–; non-exec. Dir, GCDA, 2007–. Chm., Prison Service Pay Review Body, 2005–. Chm., London Regl Cttee, FEFC, 2000–01. Gov., Kingston Univ., 1999–2007 (Chm., 2002–07). *Recreations:* bridge, supporting Fulham FC, cooking, theatre, avoiding the gardening. *Address:* 24 Auckland Road, SE19 2DJ. *Club:* Hurlingham.

COPE, Jonathan, CBE 2003; Répétiteur, Royal Ballet Company, since 2005 (Principal, 1987–90 and 1992–2006); *b* 1963; *m* Maria Almeida; one *s* one *d*. *Educ:* Royal Ballet Sch. Joined Royal Ballet Co., 1982; Soloist, 1985–86; property business, 1990–92. Leading rôles include: Cinderella, Pursuit, Giselle, Swan Lake, Prince of the Pagodas, Fearful Symmetries, The Sons of Horus, Romeo and Juliet, Sleeping Beauty, La Bayadère, Different Drummer, Frankenstein, Fleeting Figures, The Modern Prometheus, Words Apart, Manon, The Nutcracker, Ondine, Mayerling, The Judas Tree, Aminta, in Sylvia. *Address:* c/o Royal Ballet Company, Royal Opera House, Covent Garden, WC2E 9DD.

COPE, Wendy Mary, FRSL; writer, freelance since 1986; *b* 21 July 1945; *d* of Fred Stanley Cope and Alice Mary (*née* Hand). *Educ:* Farringtons Sch.; St Hilda's Coll., Oxford (MA); Westminster College of Education, Oxford (DipEd). Teacher in London primary schs, 1967–81 and 1984–86; Arts editor, ILEA Contact, 1982–84; Television columnist, The Spectator, 1986–90. FRSL 1992. Hon. DLitt: Southampton, 1999; Oxford Brookes, 2003. Cholmondeley Award for Poetry, 1987; Michael Braude Award, Amer. Acad. of Arts and Letters, 1995. *Publications:* Making Cocoa for Kingsley Amis (poems), 1986; Twiddling Your Thumbs (rhymes for children), 1988; (ed) Is That The New Moon?, 1989; The River Girl, 1991; Serious Concerns, 1992; (ed) The Orchard Book of Funny Poems, 1993; (ed) The Funny Side, 1998; (ed) The Faber Book of Bedtime Stories, 2000; If I Don't Know, 2001; (ed) Heaven on Earth: 101 happy poems, 2001; (ed) George Herbert, Verse and Prose, 2002; Two Cures for Love: selected poems 1979–2006, 2008. *Recreations:* playing the piano, shopping. *Address:* c/o Faber and Faber, 3 Queen Square, WC1N 3AU.

COPISAROW, Sir Alcon (Charles), Kt 1988; DUP; FInstP; FIET; Chairman of Trustees, Eden Project, 1996–2000; *b* 25 June 1920; *o s* of late Dr Maurice Copisarow, Manchester; *m* 1953, Diana (OBE 2004), *y d* of Ellis James Castello, MC, Bucklebury, Berks; two *s* two *d*. *Educ:* Manchester Central Grammar Sch.; University of Manchester; Imperial Coll. of Science and Technology; Sorbonne, Paris (DUP 1960). Council of Europe Research Fellow. Served War, 1942–47; Lieut RN, 1943–47; British Admiralty Delegn, Washington, 1945. Home Civil Service, 1946–66; Office of Minister of Defence, 1947–54. Scientific Counsellor, British Embassy, Paris, 1954–60. Dir, Forest Products Research Laboratory, Dept of Scientific and Industrial Research, 1960–62; Chief Technical Officer, Nat. Economic Development Council, 1962–64; Chief Scientific Officer, Min. of Technology, 1964–66. Dir, McKinsey & Co. Inc., 1966–76; non-exec. Dir, British Leyland, 1976–77; Mem., BNOC, 1980–83; Chm., APAX Venture Capital Funds, 1981–94; Dir, Touche Remnant Holdings and portfolio cos, 1985–96. Special Advr, Ernst & Young, 1993–99; Chm., ARINSO Internat., 2000–03. By-Fellow, Churchill Coll., Cambridge, 2005. Chairman: Commonwealth Forest Products Pre-Conf., Nairobi, 1962; CENTO Conf. on Investment in Science, Teheran, 1963; Member: Scientific Manpower Cttee, Advisory Council on Scientific Policy, 1963–64; Econ. Develt Cttees for Electronics Industry and for Heavy Electrical Industry; Trop. Prod. Adv. Cttee, 1965–66; Press Council, 1975–81. A Chm., Gen. Comrs for Income Tax, 1975–95. External Mem., Council of Lloyd's, 1982–90; Dep. Chm., Lloyd's Tercentenary Trust, 1989– (Chm., 1988 and 2007; Hon. Lloyd's Fellow 2008). Dep. Chm., Bd of Governors, English-Speaking Union, 1976–83; Chm., Youth Business Initiative, subseq. The Prince's Youth Business Trust, 1982–87. Dir, Windsor Fest., 1983–2000. Trustee: Duke of Edinburgh's Award, 1978–84; FMI, 1995–2001; Member Council: Royal Jubilee Trusts, 1981–87; Zoological Soc., 1990–91. Patron, Société des Ingénieurs et des Scientifiques de France, 1992–. Governor, Benenden Sch., 1976–86. Freeman, City of London, 1981. Hon. FTCL. *Address:* 7 Southwell Gardens, SW7 4SB. *Clubs:* Athenæum (Sen. Trustee), Beefsteak.

COPLAND, Rev. Canon Charles McAlester; Provost of St John's Cathedral, Oban, 1959–79, and Dean of Diocese of Argyll and The Isles, 1977–79; *b* 5 April 1910; *s* of Canon Alexander Copland and of Violet Williamina Somerville McAlester; *m* 1946, Gwendoline Lorimer Williamson (*d* 2001); two *d*. *Educ:* Forfar Academy; Denstone Coll.; Corpus Christi Coll., Cambridge (MA); Cuddesdon College. Reserve of Officers, 1933–38. Curate, Peterborough Parish Church, 1934–38; Mission Priest, Chanda, CP, India, 1938–53 (Head of Mission, 1942–53); Canon of Nagpur, 1952; Rector, St Mary's, Arbroath, 1953–59; Canon of Dundee, 1953; Hon. Canon of Oban, 1979. *Publications:* Chanda: history of a mission, 1988; India: past glimpses of country life, 2007. *Recreations:* formerly Rugby football, athletics; rifle shooting (shot for Cambridge, for Scotland 1932–84). *Address:* 3 West Hill Road, Kirriemuir, Angus DD8 4PR. *T:* (01575) 575415.

COPLAND, Geoffrey Malcolm, CBE 2007; DPhil; CPhys, FInstP; Rector and Vice-Chancellor, University of Westminster, 1996–2007; *b* 28 June 1942; *s* of late Cyril Charles Copland and Jessie Palmer Copland; *m* 1st, 1967, Janet Mary Todd (marr. diss. 1985); one *s* one *d*; 2nd, 1985, Dorothy Joy Harrison. *Educ:* Fitzmaurice Grammar Sch., Bradford-on-Avon; Merton Coll., Oxford (MA, DPhil 1967). MInstP 1973; CPhys 1973; FInstP 2003. Post-doctoral scientist, Yale Univ., 1967–69; University of London: Researcher and Lectr in Physics, QMC, 1969–71; Lectr in Physics, Queen Elizabeth Coll., 1971–80; Dean of Studies, Goldsmiths' Coll., 1981–87; Dep. Rector, Poly. of Central London, later Univ. of Westminster, 1987–95. Mem. Council, UUK (formerly CVCP), 1998–2007 (Vice-Pres. and Chm., England and NI Council, 2003–07). Member Board: Edexcel Foundn, 1998–2003; PSI, 1998–2007; Central London Partnership, 2001–07; Central London LSC, 2005–07; Chm. Bd, Univs and Colls Employers Assoc., 2002–06. Pres., Assoc. of ASET, 2006–. Mem., Council for Industry and Higher Educn, 1999–2007 (Trustee, 2001–07); Chm., Thomas Wall Trust, 1999–; Trustee: Regent St Polytechnic Trust, 1996–; Quintin Hogg Trust, 1996–; Quintin Hogg Meml Fund, 1996–; Internat. Student House, 2000–; Learning from Experience Trust, 2000–. Governor: Trinity Laban, 2007–; Univ. of Bedfordshire, 2008–. FRSA 1991; FGCL 2000; Hon. FTCL 2000. *Publications:* research papers in physics and higher educn in various jls. *Recreations:* walking, cricket, gardening. *Address:* 24 The Broadway, Wheathampstead, St Albans AL4 8LN. *T:* (01438) 833663. *Club:* Oxford and Cambridge.

COPLEY, John (Michael Harold); opera director; *b* 12 June 1933; *s* of Ernest Harold Copley and Lilian Forbes; civil partnership 2006, John Hugh Chadwyck-Healey. *Educ:* King Edward's, Five Ways, Birmingham; Sadler's Wells Ballet Sch.; Central Sch. of Arts and Crafts, London (Dip. with Hons in Theatre Design). Appeared as the apprentice in Britten's Peter Grimes for Covent Garden Opera Co., 1950; stage managed: both opera and ballet companies at Sadler's Wells, in Rosebery Avenue, 1953–57; also various musicals, plays, etc, in London's West End, incl. The World of Paul Slickey and My Fair Lady. Joined Covent Garden Opera Co.: Dep. Stage Manager, 1960; Asst Resident Producer, 1963; Associate Resident Producer, 1966; Resident Producer, 1972; Prin. Resident Producer, 1975–88. *Productions include: at Covent Garden:* Suor Angelica, 1965; Così fan Tutte, 1968, 1981; Orpheo ed Euridice, 1969; Le Nozze di Figaro, 1971, 1985; Don Giovanni, 1973; La Bohème, 1974, 1985; Faust, 1974; L'elisir d'amore, 1975, 1981, 1985; Benvenuto Cellini, 1976; Ariadne auf Naxos, 1976; Maria Stuarda; Royal Silver Jubilee Gala, 1977; Werther, 1979; La Traviata, Lucrezia Borgia, 1980; Alceste, 1981; Semele, 1982, 1988, 1996; Norma, 1987; L'elisir d'amore, 1992; *at London Coliseum (for Sadler's Wells, subseq. ENO):* Carmen, Il Seraglio, Il Trovatore, La Traviata, Mary Stuart; Rosenkavalier, La Belle Hélène, 1975; Werther, 1977; Manon, Aida, Julius Caesar, Les Mamelles de Tirésias, 1979; The Merry Widow, 2008; *Athens Festival:* Macbeth; *Netherlands Opera:* Lucia; *Opera National de Belge:* Lucia; *Wexford Festival:* La Clemenza di Tito; L'Infedelta delusa; *Dallas Civic Opera:* Lucia; Hansel and Gretel, 1991; Elektra, Il Trovatore, 1996; Ariodante, 1998; *Chicago Lyric Opera:* Lucia; La Bohème, 1983; Orlando, 1986; Tancredi, 1989; The Barber of Seville, 1989; Peter Grimes, Idomeneo, 1997; Gioconda, 1998; Die Fledermaus, 1999; *Canadian Opera, Toronto:* Lucia; Falstaff; La Bohème, 1984; Adriana Lecouvreur, La Forza del Destino, 1987; *Greek Nat. Opera:* Madame Butterfly; Otello; *Australian Opera:* Fidelio, Nozze di Figaro, Rigoletto, Magic Flute, Jenufa, Ariadne auf Naxos, Madame Butterfly, Fra Diavolo, Macbeth, La Traviata, Manon Lescaut, Lucia di Lammermoor, Tosca, Manon; Adriana Lecouvreur, 1984; Peter Grimes, 1986; Carmen, 1987; La Forza del Destino, 1988; *Victoria State Opera:* Don Carlos, 1984; La Bohème, 1985; *WNO:* La Traviata, Falstaff, Peter Grimes, Tosca; Peter Grimes, 1983; *Opera North:* Les Mamelles de Tirésias, Madama Butterfly; *Scottish Opera:* Lucia, Ballo in Maschera, Dido and Aeneas; Acis and Galatea for English Opera Group in Stockholm, Paris, Aldeburgh Fest.; *New York City Opera:* Le Nozze di Figaro; Der Freischutz; Don Quichotte; *Santa Fé Opera:* Ariodanie, 1987; Così fan tutte, 1988; Der Rosenkavalier, La Traviata, 1989; La Bohème, 1990; Tosca, 1994; Semele, 1997; Idomeneo, 1999; *Ottawa Festival:* Midsummer Night's Dream; Eugene Onegin, 1983; *Vancouver Opera:* Carmen; *San Francisco Opera:* Julius Caesar; The Midsummer Marriage, 1983; Don Giovanni, 1984; Orlando, 1985; Le Nozze di Figaro, Eugene Onegin, 1986; La Traviata, 1987; Idomeneo, 1989; Midsummer Night's Dream, 1992; Pique Dame, 1993; Peter Grimes, 1998; *San Diego Opera:* Eugene Onegin, 1985; Le Nozze di Figaro, 1986; Così fan tutte, 1991; *Staatsoper Munich:* Adriana Lecouvreur, 1984; *Teatro La Fenice, Venice:* Semele, 1991 and 1992; *Deutsche Oper, Berlin:* L'Elisir d'amore, 1988; *Metropolitan Opera, NY:* Julius Caesar, 1988; Semiramide, 1990; L'Elisir d'amore, 1991; Norma, 2001; Le Pirata, 2002; *Opera Theatre of St Louis:* La Rondine, 1996. Sang as soloist in Bach's St John Passion, Bremen, Germany, 1965; appeared as Ferdy in John Osborne's play, A Patriot for Me, at Royal Court Theatre, 1965. Co-directed (with Patrick Garland): Fanfare for Europe Gala, Covent Garden, 3 Jan. 1973; Fanfare for Elizabeth gala, Covent Garden, 21 April 1986. Hon. RAM 1999; Hon. RCM 2002. *Recreation:* cooking. *Address:* 9D Thistle Grove, SW10 9RR.

COPLEY, Peter Edward; His Honour Judge Copley; a Circuit Judge, since 1995; *b* 15 Feb. 1943; *s* of Edward Thomas Copley and Florence Hilda Copley; *m* 1st; one *s* one *d*; 2nd, 1986, Janice Patricia Webster; one *d*. *Educ:* College of Law. Qualified Solicitor, 1966. *Recreation:* sailing. *Address:* c/o Circuit Administrator, 2nd Floor, Rose Court, 2 Southwark Bridge, SE1 9HS.

COPP, Prof. Andrew John, DPhil; FRCPath; Professor of Developmental Neurobiology, since 1996, and Dean/Director, Institute of Child Health, since 2003, University College London; *b* 27 Feb. 1954; *s* of Frederick John Copp and Doreen Ann Copp (*née* Crouch). *Educ:* St Peter's Coll., Oxford (BA 1st Cl. Hons (Zool.) 1975); Wolfson Coll., Oxford (DPhil (Exptl Embryol.) 1978); Guy's Hosp. Med. Sch., London Univ. (MB BS 1983). FRCPath 2003. Fogarty Internat. Res. Fellow, Dept of Paediatrics, Stanford Univ. Med. Sch., Calif, 1984–86; Res. Scientist, ICRF, Univ. of Oxford, 1986–92; Sen. Lectr, then Reader, Inst. of Child Health, UCL, and Wellcome Sen. Res. Fellow in Clin. Sci., 1992–96. Mem., Neuroscis & Mental Health Bd, MRC, 2003–. Non-exec. Dir, Gt Ormond St Hosp. NHS Trust, 2003–. Mem., Med. Adv. Bd, SPARKS, 1999–2004. Pres., Develtl Pathol. Soc., UK, 1993–97. Mem. Bd of Advrs, Foulkes Foundn, 2000–. FMedSci 2000. Man. Ed., Anatomy and Embryology, 1998–; Associate Ed., Birth Defects Res. A: Clinical and Molecular Teratology, 2002–. *Publications:* (with D. L. Cockcroft) Postimplantation Mammalian Embryos: a practical approach, 1990; peer-reviewed articles in acad. jls on birth defects, esp. neural tube defects such as spina bifida, develtl biol., genetics. *Address:* Institute of Child Health, University College London, 30 Guilford Street, WC1N 1EH. *T:* (020) 7905 2189, *Fax:* (020) 7242 8437; *e-mail:* dean@ich.ucl.ac.uk.

COPP, Darrell John Barkwell, OBE 1981; General Secretary, Institute of Biology, 1951–82; *b* 25 April 1922; *s* of J. J. H. Copp and L. A. Hoad; *m* 1944, Margaret Henderson; two *s* one *d*. *Educ:* Taunton's Sch., Southampton; Southampton Univ. (BSc). Scientific Officer, Admty Signals Estabt, 1942–45; Asst Sec., British Assoc. for Advancement of Science, 1947–51. Sec., Council for Nature, 1958–63; originator and co-ordinator of first National Nature Week, 1963. Hon. Treas., Parly and Scientific Cttee, 1980–83; Sec., European Community Biologists' Assoc., 1975–85. Trustee, Rye Art Gall., 1985–90. Hon. MTech Bradford, 1975; Hon. FIBiol 1984. *Publications:* reports and reviews in scientific jls. *Recreations:* walking, renovating farm buildings. *Address:* Underhill Farmhouse, Wittersham, Tenterden, Kent TN30 7EU. *T:* (01797) 270633.

COPPEL, Andrew Maxwell, CBE 2008; FCA; Chief Executive, Jockey Club Racecourses (formerly Racecourse Holdings Trust), 2004–07; Chairman, Tourism Ireland Ltd, 2001–07; *b* 22 Aug. 1950; *s* of Isaac Coppel and Marjorie Coppel; *m* 1974, June Vanessa Gillespie; one *s* one *d*. *Educ:* Belfast Royal Acad.; Queen's Univ., Belfast (LLB Hons). FCA 1982. With Coopers & Lybrand, 1973–77; Asst Dir, Morgan Grenfell & Co. Ltd, 1977–86; Finance Dir, Ratners Gp plc, 1986–90; Chief Executive: Sale Tilney plc, 1990–92; Queens Moat Houses plc, 1993–2003. Vice Pres., Queen's Univ. Assoc.,

London, 2000–. *Recreations:* tennis, golf, Rugby, cinema, reading. *Clubs:* Claygate Tennis, St George's Hill Tennis, Burhill Golf (Surrey); Malone Golf (Belfast).

COPPEL, Yvonne Ruth; Her Honour Judge Coppel; a Circuit Judge, since 2007; *b* Salford, 24 July 1954; *d* of Hyman and Hilda Coppel; *m* 1988; one *s* one *d*. *Educ:* N Manchester High Sch. for Girls; Univ. of Birmingham (LLB Hons). Called to the Bar, Inner Temple, 1976; Asst Recorder, 1996–2000; Recorder, 2000–07. *Recreations:* cinema, fell walking, theatre. *Address:* Liverpool Civil and Family Courts, 35 Vernon Street, Liverpool L2 2BX. *T:* (0151) 296 2200.

COPPEN, Dr Alec James, MD, DSc; FRCP, FRCPsych; Director, Medical Research Council Neuropsychiatry Laboratory, and Emeritus Consultant Psychiatrist, West Park Hospital, Epsom, Surrey, 1974–89, retired; *b* 29 Jan. 1923; *y s* of late Herbert John Wardle Coppen and Marguerite Mary Annie Coppen; *m* 1952, Gunhild Margareta (*d* 2007), *y d* of late Albert and Sigrid Andersson, Båstad, Sweden; one *s*. *Educ:* Dulwich Coll.; Univ. of Bristol (MB, ChB 1953; MD 1958; DSc 1978); Maudsley Hosp.; Univ. of London (DPM 1957); MRCP 1975, FRCP 1980, FRCPsych 1971 (Hon. FRCPsych 1995). Registrar, then Sen. Registrar, Maudsley Hosp., 1954–59; MRC Neuropsychiatry Research Unit, 1959–74, MRC External Staff, 1974–89; Consultant Psychiatrist: St Ebba's Hosp., 1959–64; West Park Hosp., 1964–89; Hon. Cons. Psychiatrist, St George's Hosp., 1965–70. Head of WHO designated Centre for Biological Psychiatry in UK, 1974–89; Consultant, WHO, 1977–89; Examiner, Royal Coll. of Psychiatry, 1973–77; Andrew Woods Vis. Prof., Univ. of Iowa, 1981; Lectr to learned socs and univs in Europe, N and S America, Asia and Africa. Mem. Council, RMPA (Chm., Research and Clinical Section), 1965–70; Chairman, Biolog. Psychiatry Section, World Psychiatric Assoc., 1972; President, British Assoc. of Psychopharmacology, 1975; Member: Internat. Coll. Neuropsychopharm., 1960– (Mem. Council, 1979; Pres., 1988–90); RSM, 1960–; British Pharmacol. Soc., 1977–; Special Health Auth., Bethlem Royal and Maudsley Hosp., 1982–87; Hon. Member: Mexican Soc. for Biolog. Psychiatry, 1973–; Mexican Inst. of Culture, 1974–; Swedish Psychiatric Assoc., 1977–; European Collegium Neuro-Psychopharmacologicum, 1987–; Corresponding Member: Amer. Coll. of Neuropsychopharm., 1977–; Deutsche Gesellschaft für Psychiatrie und Nervenheilkunde; Distinguished Fellow, APA, 1981. Freeman, City of London, 1980; Soc. of Apothecaries: Yeoman, 1980; Liveryman 1985. Anna Monika Prize, 1969; European Prize for Psychopharmacology, 1991; Lifetime Achievement Gold Medal, British Assoc. of Psychopharmacology, 1998; Pioneer in Psychopharmacology Award, Collegium Internat. Neuro-Psychopharmacologicum, 2000; Award, American Assoc. for Suicide Prevention, 2004. *Publications:* (jtly) Recent Developments in Schizophrenia, 1967; (jtly) Recent Developments in Affective Disorders, 1968; (jtly) Psychopharmacology of Affective Disorders, 1979; contribs to text books; papers in Nature, Lancet, BMJ, etc (Current Contents Citation Classic, 1978, Biochemistry of the Affective Disorders). *Recreations:* golf, opera. *Address:* 5 Walnut Close, Epsom, Surrey KT18 5JL. *T:* (01372) 720800. *Clubs:* Athenæum, Royal Automobile.

COPPEN, Luke Benjamin Edward; Editor, The Catholic Herald, since 2004; *b* 8 Feb. 1976; *s* of Rev. Canon Martin Coppen and Christine Coppen (*née* Stevens); *m* 2004, Marlena Marciniszyn; one *d*. *Educ:* Testbourne Community Sch., Whitchurch, Hants; Cricklade Coll., Andover; Sch. of Oriental and African Studies, Univ. of London (BA Study of Religions and Politics); Univ. of Wales, Cardiff (Postgrad. Dip. Journalism Studies). Film Ed., London Student mag., 1996–97; reporter, 1998–2000, Dep. Ed., 2000–04, Catholic Herald; Faith in Brief columnist, The Times, 2001–05. *Recreations:* cinema, cycling, rabbit-keeping. *Address:* The Catholic Herald, Herald House, Lambs Passage, Bunhill Row, EC1Y 8TQ. *T:* (020) 7448 3606, *Fax:* (020) 7256 9728; *e-mail:* luke@catholicherald.co.uk.

COPPIN, Alan Charles; Chairman, Redstone plc, since 2006; *b* 4 June 1950; *s* of Charles and Vera Coppin; *m* 1975, Gaynor Hilary Wareham; one *s*. *Educ:* Westlain Grammar Sch., Brighton; Brighton Poly. Mgt posts with cos incl. Strutt & Parker, THF Leisure, Associated Leisure and Bembom Group, 1971–86; Sen. Mgt Consultant, KPMG, 1986–88; Chief Exec., Wembley Stadium Ltd, 1988–95, Wembley plc, 1995–98; Chief Exec., Historic Royal Palaces, 1999–2003. Associate, Prime Minister's Delivery Unit, Cabinet Office, 2002–04. Chm., Danoptra Hldgs, 2002–06; Mem. Exec. Bd, Compass Gp plc, 1998–99; non-executive Director: Metroline plc, 1997–2000; Carillion plc, 1999–2002; Expocentric plc, 2000–02; Protocol n. v., 2002–04; Capital & Regional plc, 2004–; Berkeley Gp Hldgs plc, 2006–. Non-exec. Dir, Air Comd, RAF, 2007–. Chairman: NW London TEC, 1990–92; Stadium and Arena Mgt Project, 1994–95. Chairman: Include, nat. children's charity, 1997–2000; Robinia Care Gp, 2003–04; Prince's Foundn for Built Envmt, 2004–06 (Trustee, 2003–04); Trustee, Greenwich Foundn, 2003–04. Mem., Adv. Forum, Saïd Business Sch., Oxford Univ., 2002–07. Patron, Windsor Leadership Trust, 2003–. Hon. Vis. Prof., Business Sch., Univ. of N London, 1998–2003. CCMI (CIMgt 1997). FRSA 2003. *Publication:* (jtly) Timeless Management, 2002. *Recreations:* family activities, cinema, writing. *Address:* Briar Hedge, The Drive, Abbotsbrook, Bourne End, Bucks SL8 5RE. *T:* (01628) 850142. *Club:* Arts.

COPPOCK, Surgeon Rear-Adm. (D) David Arthur, CB 1990; Director, Defence Dental Services, 1988–90; *b* 19 April 1931; *s* of Oswald John Coppock and Ada Katherine Beaven; *m* 1st, 1956, Maria Averil Ferreira (*d* 1985); two *d*; 2nd, 1990, Sally Annette Arnold. *Educ:* Bishop Wordsworth School; Guy's Hosp. (BDS); George Washington Univ. (MSc). Entered RN 1955; HM Ships Eagle, 1956, Tamar, Hong Kong, 1959, Hermes, 1963, Rooke, Gibraltar, 1965; US Navy exchange, 1972; Dep. Dir, Naval Dental Services, 1980; Comd Dental Surgeon to C-in-C Naval Home Command, 1983; Dir, Naval Dental Services, 1985–88. QHDS, 1983–90. Mem., Assoc. of Professional Game Angling Instructors, 1991–. OStJ 1983. *Recreation:* fishing. *Address:* 12 Fitzhamon House, Idsworth Down, Petersfield, Hants GU31 4EB. *T:* (01730) 710618.

COPPOLA, Francis Ford; Artistic Director, Zoetrope Studios, since 1969; *b* 7 April 1939; *s* of late Carmine Coppola and of Italia Pennino; *m* 1963, Eleanor Neil; one *s* one *d* (and one *s* decd). *Educ:* Hofstra Univ. (BA); Univ. of Calif, LA (MFA). Films directed: Dementia 13, 1963; You're a Big Boy Now, 1967; Finian's Rainbow, 1968; The Rain People, 1969; The Godfather, 1972; The Conversation, 1974; The Godfather Part II, 1974; Apocalypse Now, 1979; One From the Heart, 1981; The Outsiders, 1983; Rumble Fish, 1983; The Cotton Club, 1984; Peggy Sue Got Married, 1987; Gardens of Stone, 1988; Tucker: The Man and his Dream, 1988; New York Stories (Life Without Zoe), 1989; The Godfather Part III, 1991; Bram Stoker's Dracula, 1993; Jack, 1996; John Grisham's The Rainmaker, 1998; Apocalypse Now Redux, 2001; Youth Without Youth, 2007; executive producer: Black Stallion, 1979; Hammett, 1983; Lionhart, 1987; The Secret Garden, 1993; Mary Shelley's Frankenstein, 1994. Commandeur, Ordre des Arts et des Lettres, 1983. *Recreations:* reading, writing, scientific discovery. *Address:* Zoetrope Studios, 916 Kearny Street, San Francisco, CA 94133–5138, USA. *T:* (415) 7887500.

COPPS, Hon. Sheila Maureen; PC (Can.) 1993; radio and television presenter; newspaper columnist; actress; *b* 27 Nov. 1952; *d* of Vic Copps and Geraldine (*née* Guthro); one *d*. *Educ:* Univ. of Western Ontario (BA Hons English and French); Univ. of Rouen; McMaster Univ. Journalist, 1974–77. MPP (L) Ontario, 1981–84; MP (L) Hamilton E, Canada, 1984–2004. Official Opposition Critic for: Housing and Labour, 1984–87; Health and Welfare and Fitness and Amateur Sport, 1987–89; Envmt and Co-Critic for Social Policy, 1989–90; Industry, 1990–91; Dep. Leader of Opposition, 1991–93; Minister of the Envmt, 1993–96; Dep. Prime Minister, 1993–97; Minister of Canadian Heritage, 1996–2003. *Publications:* Nobody's Baby, 1986; Worth Fighting For, 2004.

CORBEN, Albert Edward; Assistant Under Secretary of State, Radio Regulatory Department, Home Office (and subsequently with Department of Trade and Industry), 1980–83, retired; *b* 25 Nov. 1923; *s* of Ebenezer Joseph James Corben and Frances Flora (*née* Orchard); *m* 1953, Doris Dodd; two *s*. *Educ:* Portsmouth Grammar Sch.; Sir John Cass Technical Inst. Served Royal Artillery, 1943–47. Entered Home Office, as Executive Officer, 1947; Higher Executive Officer, 1955–62; Sen. Executive Officer, 1962–66; Principal, 1966–72; Secretary to Advisory Council on Penal System, 1966–68; Sen. Principal, 1972–73; Asst Sec., 1973–80. *Recreations:* swimming, golf, walking. *Address:* The Gables, 30 Kingswood Road, Bromley, Kent BR2 0NF. *T:* (020) 8460 4106.

CORBET, Dr Gordon Barclay; zoologist; *b* 4 March 1933; *s* of George and Mary Corbet; *m* 1959, Elizabeth Urquhart; one *s* one *d*. *Educ:* Morgan Acad., Dundee; Univ. of St Andrews. BSc, PhD. Asst Lectr in Biology, Sir John Cass Coll., London, 1958–59; British Museum (Natural History): Sen., later Principal, Scientific Officer, Dept of Zoology, 1960–71; Dep. Keeper of Zoology, 1971–76; Hd, Dept of Central Services, 1976–88. *Publications:* The Terrestrial Mammals of Western Europe, 1966; Finding and Identifying Mammals in Britain, 1975; The Handbook of British Mammals, 2nd edn (with H. N. Southern), 1977, 3rd edn (with S. Harris), 1991; The Mammals of the Palaearctic Region, 1978; The Mammals of Britain and Europe, 1980; A World List of Mammalian Species (with J. E. Hill), 1980, 3rd edn 1991; The Mammals of the Indomalayan Region (with J. E. Hill), 1992; The Nature of Fife, 1998. *Recreation:* natural history. *Address:* Little Dumbarnie, Newburn, Upper Largo, Fife KY8 6JG. *T:* (01333) 340634.

CORBETT, family name of **Barons Corbett of Castle Vale** and **Rowallan**.

CORBETT OF CASTLE VALE, Baron *cr* 2001 (Life Peer), of Erdington in the County of West Midlands; **Robin Corbett;** journalist; *b* 22 Dec. 1933; *s* of Thomas Corbett and Marguerite Adele Mainwaring; *m* 1970, Val Hudson; one *s* two *d*. *Educ:* Holly Lodge Grammar Sch., Smethwick. Newspaper and magazine journalist, 1950–69; Editorial Staff Develt Exec., IPC Magazines, 1969–72; Sen. Lab. Adviser, IPC Magazines, 1972–74. Mem. Nat. Union of Journalists Nat. Exec. Council, 1965–69. MP (Lab): Hemel Hempstead, Oct. 1974–1979; Birmingham, Erdington, 1983–2001. Opposition front bench spokesman on home affairs, 1985–92, on broadcasting, the media and nat. heritage 1992–94, on disabled people's rights, 1994–95. Member: Select Cttee on Agriculture 1996–97; Select Cttee on Home Affairs, 1997–2001 (Chm., 1999–2001); Expenditure Cttee, 1976–79; Commons Home Affairs Cttee, 1984–86; Vice Chm., All Party Animal Welfare Gp, 1976–79; Jt Vice-Chm., All Party Motor Gp, 1987–; Treas., All Party Anzac Gp, 1992– (Chm., 1997–2001; Jt Sec., 1985); Chm., All Party MS Gp, 1997–2001; Vice Chm., Indo-British Parly Gp, 1997–2001; Chairman: PLP Agric. Gp, 1977–78; PLP Home Affairs Cttee, 1984–86; Sec., PLP Civil Liberties Gp, 1974–79; Mem., PLP Campaign Unit, 1985–86. Mem., Sub-cttee F, EU Select Cttee, H of L, 2002–07. Chm. Lab Peers Gp, 2005–. Chm., Friends of Cyprus, 2001– (Jt Vice-Chm., 1987). Mem., Food and Agriculture Sub-Cttee, Labour Party Nat. Exec. Cttee, 1974–79; Chm., farm animal welfare co-ordinating exec., 1977–92. Member, Council: RCVS, 1989–92; SCF 1987–90; Mem. Bd, Rehab UK, 1996–; sponsor, Terrence Higgins Trust, 1987–99 Mem., Wilton Park Acad. Council, 1995–2006. Chm., Mgt Bd, Castle Vale HAT 2002–04, Partnership Bd, Castle Vale Neighbourhood, 2004–. Pres., Josiah Mason Sixth Form Coll., Erdington, 2002–. Fellow, Industry and Parlt Trust, 1979. *Publications:* (jtly) Can I Count on your Support?, 1986; On the Campaign Trail, 1987. *Recreations:* walking reading, pottering. *Address:* House of Lords, SW1A 0PW. *Clubs:* Castle Vale Resident Association; Forget-Me-Not (Erdington).

CORBETT, Dame Antoinette; *see* Sibley, Dame A.

CORBETT, Gerald Michael Nolan; Chairman: SSL International PLC, since 2005 Britvic PLC, since 2005; Moneysupermarket.com plc, since 2007; *b* 7 Sept. 1951; *s* of lat John Michael Nolan Corbett and of Pamela Muriel Corbett (*née* Gay); *m* 1976, Virgini Moore Newsum; one *s* three *d*. *Educ:* Tonbridge Sch.; Pembroke Coll., Cambridg (Foundn Schol.; MA); London Business Sch. (MSc with Dist.); Harvard Business Sch (Exchange Schol.). Boston Consulting Gp, 1975–82; Dixons Group plc: Gp Financ Controller, 1982–85; Corporate Finance Dir, 1985–87; Group Finance Director: Redlan plc, 1987–94; Grand Metropolitan plc, 1994–97; Chief Exec., Railtrack Gp pl 1997–2000. Chairman: Woolworths Gp plc, 2001–07; Holmes Place plc, 2003–06; non executive Director: MEPC Plc, 1995–98; Burmah Castrol Plc, 1998–2000; Greencore G plc, 2004–. Chm., RNID, 2007–. Chm. Govs, Abbot's Hill Sch., 1997–2002; Gov Luton Univ., 2002–05. Freeman, City of London. FRSA 2006. *Recreations:* countr pursuits, golf, ski-ing, bridge. *Address:* Holtsmere End Farm, Redbourn, Herts AL3 7AW *Clubs:* Oxford and Cambridge, MCC.

CORBETT, Graham; *see* Corbett, P. G.

CORBETT, Prof. Greville George, PhD; FBA 1997; AcSS; Distinguished Professo (formerly Professor) of Linguistics and of Russian Language, University of Surrey, sinc 1988; *b* 23 Dec. 1947; *s* of George Pilsbury Corbett and Elsie Mary Bates; *m* 1974, Judit Mary Baird; three *s*. *Educ:* Univ. of Birmingham (BA 1970; MA 1971; PhD 1976). Lect 1974–85, Reader, 1985–88, Univ. of Surrey. Pres., Linguistics Assoc. of GB, 1994–9 AcSS 2000. *Publications:* Predicate Agreement in Russian, 1979; Hierarchies, Targets an Controllers: agreement patterns in Slavic, 1983; (jtly) Computers, Language Learning an Language Teaching, 1985; Gender, 1991; (ed jtly) Heads in Grammatical Theory, 199 (ed jtly) The Slavonic Languages, 1993; Number, 2000; (jtly) The Syntax-Morpholog Interface: a study of syncretism, 2005; Agreement, 2006; (ed jtly) Deponency an Morphological Mismatches, 2007. *Recreation:* music. *Address:* Surrey Morphology Grou Faculty of Arts and Human Sciences, University of Surrey, Guildford, Surrey GU2 7XH

CORBETT, Captain Hugh Askew, CBE 1968; DSO 1945; DSC 1943; RN (retired); 25 June 1916; *s* of late Rev. F. St John Corbett, MA, FRSL, FRHistS and Elsie L. V. (*n* Askew); *m* 1945, Patricia Nancy, *d* of late Thomas Patrick Spens, OBE, MC, LLD; thr *s*. *Educ:* St Edmund's Sch., Canterbury. Joined Royal Navy, 1933; HMS Cæsar as Cap (D), 8th Destroyer Sqdn, 1961–63; HMS Fearless, 1965–67 (Capt.). *Address:* Hol Cottage, 3 Clare Road, Cambridge CB3 9HN. *T:* (01223) 357735.

CORBETT, James Patrick; QC 1999; FCIArb; a Recorder, since 2000; Trust and Esta Practitioner, since 2005; *b* 10 May 1952; *s* of late Patrick Francis Corbett and of Kathlee Mary Corbett (*née* O'Callaghan); *m* 1979, Barbara Janet Willett; one *s* four *d*. *Educ:* Sloan Sch., Chelsea; Univ. of Exeter (LLB 1973; LLM European Legal Studies 1975); Inns Court Sch. of Law. FCIArb 1997; Chartered Arbitrator, 2001. Called to the Bar, Inn

Temple, 1975, Lincoln's Inn, *ad eundem*, 1998; Lectr in Law, Univ. of Leicester, 1975–77; in practice at the Bar, 1977–; joined Midland and Oxford Circuit, 1979; called to Irish Bar, 1981, Northern Irish Bar, 1994, NSW Bar, 2002, Anguilla Bar, 2002, St Kitts and Nevis Bar, 2004, BVI Bar, 2004. Asst Recorder, 1996–2000. CEDR Registered Mediator, 2000. Mem., Soc. of Trust and Estate Practitioners. Contested (SDP): Erewash, Derbys, 1983; Cheshire E, 1984; Staffs Moorlands, 1987. Liveryman: Arbitrators' Co., 2000–; Bowyers' Co., 2003–. *Publications:* articles in legal and arbitration jls. *Recreations:* jazz, the cinema, Rugby League. *Address:* Serle Court, 6 New Square, Lincoln's Inn, WC2A 3QS. *Club:* Athenæum.

CORBETT, (Peter) Graham, CBE 1994; Chairman: Postal Services Commission, 2000–04; Ricability (Research and Information for Consumers with Disabilities), since 1998; *b* 6 Nov. 1934; *s* of John and Greta Corbett; *m* 1964, Anne (*née* James), PhD, journalist; two *s*. *Educ:* Stowe Sch. ACA 1957, FCA 1962. Peat Marwick, London, 1959–75; Sen. Partner, Peat Marwick Continental Europe, 1975–87; Chief Financial Officer, Eurotunnel plc and Eurotunnel SA, 1987–96; Dep. Chm., Monopolies and Mergers, then Competition Commn, 1997–2000. Non-executive Director: Kier Gp plc, 1996–2000; Remploy Ltd, 2004–. Trustee, Franco-British Council, 1995–99. CCMI (CIMgt 1994); FRSA 1999. DUniv Brunel 1995. *Address:* 95 Coleherne Court, Old Brompton Road, SW5 0ED. *T:* (020) 7373 9878.

CORBETT, Dr Richard Graham; Member (Lab) Yorkshire and the Humber Region, European Parliament, since 1999 (Merseyside West, Dec. 1996–99); *b* 6 Jan. 1955; *s* of Harry Graham Corbett and Kathleen Zita Corbett (*née* Bryant); *m* 1st, 1984, Inge van Gaal (marr. diss.); one *s*; 2nd, 1989, Anne de Malsche; two *d*. *Educ:* Farnborough Rd Sch., Southport; Internat. Sch., Geneva; Trinity Coll., Oxford (BA Hons PPE); Univ. of Hull (Extra Mural Doctorate 1995). Stagiare, Socialist Gp, European Parlt, 1976; UK Labour Delegn, 1977; Commn (Regl Policy), 1977; Sec. Gen., European Co-ordination Bureau, Internat. Youth Orgns, 1977–81; European civil servant, 1981–89; European Parliament: political advr, 1989–94, Dep. Gen. Sec., 1995–96, Socialist Gp; Vice Pres., Cttee on Instnl Affairs, 1997–99; Labour Party and Socialist Gp spokesman on constitutional affairs, 1999–; Dep. Leader, Labour MEPs, 2006–; Mem. Bd, Britain in Europe, 2001–05. Mem. Regl Bd, Yorks, Labour Party, 1999–2001 and 2007–. *Publications:* A Socialist Policy for Europe, 1985; The European Parliament, 1990, 7th edn 2007; The Treaty of Maastricht: from conception to ratification, 1993; The European Parliament's Role in closer EU integration, 1998; contrib. Annual Rev. on Instnl Develts in EU for Jl Common Mkt Studies. *Recreations:* cycling, squash, ski-ing, watching football, reading. *Address:* European Parliament, Rue Wiertz, 1047 Brussels, Belgium. *T:* (2) 2845504.

CORBETT, Maj.-Gen. Sir Robert (John Swan), KCVO 1994; CB 1991; Director, Dulverton Trust, 1994–2003; *b* 16 May 1940; *s* of Robert Hugh Swan Corbett and Patricia Elizabeth Cavan Corbett (*née* Lambart); *m* 1966, Susan Margaret Anne O'Cock; three *s*. *Educ:* Woodcote House; Shrewsbury School; Army Staff Coll., 1973; US Armed Forces Staff Coll., 1980. Commissioned Irish Guards, 1959; served UK, Cyprus, Hong Kong, Falkland Is, Belize, BAOR; Brigade Major, HQ Household Div., 1980–81; CO, 1st Bn Irish Guards (4 Armoured Brigade, BAOR), 1981–84; Chief of Staff, British Forces Falkland Is, 1984–85; Comdr, 5th Airborne Brigade, 1985–87; Mem., RCDS, 1987; Dir, Defence Programme, MoD, 1987–89; GOC Berlin (British Sector) and British Comdt, Berlin, 1989–3 Oct. 1990 (German re-unification); attached HQ BAOR, 1990–91; GOC London Dist, and Maj. Gen. Comdg Household Div., 1991–94. Mem. Adv. Bd, Deutsche Bank Berlin AG, 1991–2000. Chairman: Guards Chapel Adv. Cttee, 1993–; Berlin Infantry Bde Meml Trust Fund, 1992–99. Regtl Lt-Col, Irish Guards, 1988–91. Hon. Col, London Irish Rifles, 1993–2000. Liveryman, Vintners' Co., 1968. Hon. Citizen, 1993, Mem., Conseil Municipal, 2000–04, Pierrefeu, France. Order of Merit, Berlin, 1990; Hon. Grand Officier, Ordre de Mérite (Luxembourg), 1994; Hon. Grande Oficial, Ordem do Infante Dom Henrique (Portugal), 1994; Hon. Dato Paduka, Order of Crown of Brunei, 1993. *Publication:* Berlin and the British Ally 1945–1990, 1993. *Recreations:* travel, reading, walking, English church history and architecture. *Address:* c/o RHQ Irish Guards, Wellington Barracks, SW1E 6HQ. *Clubs:* Pratt's, Buck's.

CORBETT, Ronald Balfour, OBE 1978; comedian/character actor; *b* 4 Dec. 1930; *s* of William Balfour Corbett and Anne Elizabeth Corbett; *m* 1965, Anne Hart; two *d*. *Educ:* James Gillespie Sch., Edinburgh; Royal High Sch., Edinburgh. *Films:* Top of the Form; You're Only Young Once; Casino Royale, 1966; No Sex Please, We're British, 1974; Fierce Creatures, 1997; *television:* Frost Report, 1966–67; Frost on Sunday, 1968–69; The Two Ronnies (12 in series), 1971–85, 2005; The Two Ronnies Christmas Special, 1982, 1987; Variety Specials, 1977; Sorry! (8 in series), 1981–88; Small Talk (3 series), 1994–96; *theatre:* Twang (Lionel Bart musical), 1965; Cinderella, London Palladium, Christmas 1971–72; two seasons at London Palladium, 1978, 1983; The Dressmaker (Feydeau), 1990; Out of Order, UK and Australian tour, 1992–93. *Publications:* Small Man's Guide to Life; Armchair Golf, 1986; High Hopes (autobiog.), 2000; And It's Goodnight from Him: the autobiography of the two Ronnies, 2006. *Recreations:* golf, racing, soccer, cooking. *Clubs:* Saints and Sinners; Addington Golf (Surrey); Gullane Golf (East Lothian); Hon. Company of Edinburgh Golfers (Muirfield).

CORBIN, Christopher John; restaurateur; *b* 1 March 1952; *s* of Frederick Christopher Corbin and Vera Corbin (*née* Copperwaite); *m* 1982, Francine Checinski; one *s* one *d* (twins). *Educ:* St Christopher's, Bournemouth; Westminster Tech. Coll. Co-founder and Director (with Jeremy King): Caprice Hldgs Ltd, 1982–; Caprice Events Ltd, 1995–; co-proprietor (with Jeremy King), restaurants: Le Caprice, 1981–2004; The Ivy, 1990–2004; J. Sheekey, 1998–; The Wolseley, 2003–; St Alban, 2006–. Restaurateur of Year, Caterer and Hotelkeeper, 1993. *Recreations:* eating, tennis, British modern art, meditation. *Clubs:* Queen's, Royal Automobile, Groucho, Hurlingham.

CORBIN, Maurice Haig Alleyne; Justice of Appeal, Supreme Court, Trinidad and Tobago, 1972–81; *b* 26 May 1916; *s* of L. A. Corbin; *m* 1943, Helen Jocelyn Child (decd); one *s* two *d*; *m* 1968, Jean Barcant (decd). *Educ:* Harrison Coll., Barbados; Queen's Royal Coll., Trinidad. Solicitor, 1941; appointed Magistrate, Trinidad, 1945; called to the Bar, Middle Temple, 1949; Crown Counsel, 1953; Registrar, Supreme Court, 1954; Puisne Judge, Supreme Court, 1957–72. *Address:* 77 Brook Road, Goodwood Park, Pt Cumana, Trinidad. *Club:* Queen's Park Cricket (Port of Spain, Trinidad).

CORBITT, Air Vice Marshal Ian Stafford; Chief Executive, RAF Training Group Defence Agency, and Air Officer Commanding, RAF Training Group, 1999–2002; *b* 30 July 1947; *s* of John Kellock Corbitt and Hilda Mary Corbitt; *m* 1976, Anne Lucille Worthy; two *d*. *Educ:* Simon Langton Grammar Sch., Canterbury; Quaid-i-Azam Univ., Islamabad (MSc Defence and Strategic Studies 1993). ACCA; CDipAF 1999. No 48 Sqdn, RAF Changi, Singapore, 1970–72; qualified Flying Instructor, RAF Leeming, 1973; ADC to AOC 46 Gp, RAF Upavon, 1973–75; Flt Comdr, No 30 Sqdn, 1976–77, OC Hercules Conversion Sqdn, 1977–79, RAF Lyneham; Staff Coll., Bracknell, 1980; HQ British Forces, Hong Kong, 1981–83; OC 242 OCU, RAF Lyneham, 1983–86; Flt Examr, USAF, Scott AFB, Ill, 1986–88; OC RAF Lyneham, 1989–91; HCSC, 1992; Nat. Defence Coll., Rawalpindi, 1992–93; Contingency Plans, HQ STC, 1993–95; Air Cdre, Policy and Plans, HQ PTC, 1995–99. *Club:* Royal Air Force.

CORBY, Sir (Frederick) Brian, Kt 1989; FIA; Chairman, Prudential Corporation plc, 1990–95; *b* 10 May 1929; *s* of Charles Walter and Millicent Corby; *m* 1952, Elizabeth Mairi McInnes; one *s* two *d*. *Educ:* Kimbolton Sch.; St John's Coll., Cambridge (MA). Joined Prudential Assce Co. Ltd, 1952; Dep. Gen. Manager, 1974; Gen. Manager, 1976–79; Gp Gen. Manager, Prudential Corp. Ltd, 1979–82; Dir, 1981–89, Chief Gen. Manager, 1982–85, Chm., 1985–89, Prudential Assce Co. Ltd; Chief Exec., Prudential Corp., 1982–90. Dir, 1982–90, Chm., 1985–90, Mercantile & General Reinsce Co. Chm., South Bank Bd, 1990–98; a Dir, Bank of England, 1985–93; Member Board of Governors: NASD Inc., 2001–07; FINRA Inc., 2007–. Vice-President, Inst. of Actuaries, 1979–82; Chm., Assoc. of British Insurers, 1985–87; President: CBI, 1990–92; NIESR, 1994–2003. Chancellor, Univ. of Hertfordshire, 1992–96. Hon. DSc: City, 1989; Hertfordshire, 1996; Hon. DLitt CNAA, 1991. *Publications:* contribs to Jl of Inst. of Actuaries. *Recreations:* reading, golf.

CORBY, Mary Margaret; *see* Reilly, M. M.

CORBYN, Jeremy Bernard; MP (Lab) Islington North, since 1983; *b* 26 May 1949; *s* of David Benjamin Corbyn. *Educ:* Adams Grammar Sch., Newport, Shropshire. NUPE Official, 1975–83; sponsored NUPE, then UNISON, MP. Mem., Haringey Borough Council, 1974–84 (Chm., Community Develt Cttee 1975–78, Public Works 1978–79, Planning Cttee 1980–81, 1982–83). Mem., Select Cttee on Social Security, 1990–97; Chair, London Gp of Lab MPs, 1993–96 (Vice-Chair, 1985–93); Vice Chair, Parly Human Rights Gp. Chair of Liberation, Nat. Council CND. *Address:* House of Commons, SW1A 0AA. *T:* (020) 7219 3545.

CORCORAN, Prof. Neil, FEA; King Alfred Professor of English Literature, University of Liverpool, since 2004; *b* 23 Sept. 1948; *s* of John Patrick Corcoran and Angela (*née* Attwood); *m* 1979, Gillian Anne Jeffs; three *s*. *Educ:* Austin Friars Sch., Carlisle; St Edmund Hall, and Wolfson Coll., Oxford (MA, MLitt). Lectr, then Sen. Lectr in English, Sheffield Univ., 1974–94; Professor of English: Univ. of Wales, Swansea, 1994–96; Univ. of St Andrews, 1996–2004. FEA 2001. *Publications:* The Song of Deeds: a study of The Anathemata of David Jones, 1982; Seamus Heaney, 1986; (ed) The Chosen Ground: essays on the contemporary poetry of Northern Ireland, 1992; English Poetry since 1940, 1993; After Yeats and Joyce, 1997; The Poetry of Seamus Heaney: a critical study, 1998; Poets of Modern Ireland: text, context, intertext, 1999; (ed) Do You, Mr Jones?: Bob Dylan with the poets and professors, 2002; Elizabeth Bowen: the enforced return, 2004; (ed) Cambridge Companion to Twentieth-Century English Poetry, 2007. *Recreations:* swimming, listening to various kinds of music, looking at paintings. *Address:* School of English, University of Liverpool, Liverpool L69 7ZR. *T:* (0151) 794 2720; *e-mail:* nc23@liverpool.ac.uk.

CORDARA, Roderick Charles; QC 1994; *b* 26 March 1953; *s* of Carlo and Sylvia Cordara; *m* 1997, Tsambika Anastasas; one *d*. *Educ:* City of London Sch.; Trinity Hall, Cambridge. Called to the Bar, Middle Temple, 1975; SC (NSW) 2000. *Address:* Essex Court Chambers, 24 Lincoln's Inn Fields, WC2A 3ED. *Club:* Oxford and Cambridge.

CORDER, Rear Adm. Ian Fergus; Deputy Commander Striking Force NATO, since 2009; *b* Nuneaton, 6 Aug. 1960; *s* of William and Colleen Corder; *m* 1984, Kathryn Alison Snoad; two *s*. *Educ:* Rugby Sch.; Peterhouse, Cambridge (BA Maths 1981). Joined RN, 1978; various operational submarine appts, 1982–88; Submarine Comd Course, 1989; EO, HMS Sceptre, 1990–91; Commanding Officer: HMS Oracle, 1991–92; HMS Splendid, 1996–98; Naval Asst to First Sea Lord, 1999–2001; CO, HMS Cumberland, 2001–02; Dep. Dir, Policy on Internat. Orgns, MoD, 2002–03; Chief of Strategic Systems Exec., 2004–06; Dir, Naval Personnel Strategy, 2006–08. *Recreations:* reading, music, running, travel. *Address:* c/o Naval Secretary, Leach Building, Navy Headquarters, Whale Island, Portsmouth PO2 8BY.

CORDEROY, Rev. Graham Thomas; Minister, Hutton and Shenfield Union Church, 1987–96; *b* 15 April 1931; *s* of Thomas and Gladys Corderoy; *m* 1957, Edna Marian Barnes; six *d*. *Educ:* Emanuel Sch., London; Manchester Univ. (BA Theology 1957). Ordained 1957; King's Lynn, 1957–62; commissioned RAF Chaplain, 1962; Principal Chaplain, Church of Scotland and Free Churches, and Hon. Chaplain to the Queen, 1984–87. Inst. of Alcohol Studies Bd, 1986–2006. *Recreations:* Rugby referee 1964–87, Gilbert and Sullivan buff. *Address:* Longmead, 66 Hardwick Lane, Bury St Edmunds, Suffolk IP33 2RB. *Club:* Royal Air Force.

CORDERY, Margaret Patricia Joyce; *see* Haines, M. P. J.

CORDINER, William Lawson, OBE 1995; HM Diplomatic Service, retired; High Commissioner, Kingdom of Tonga, and Consul for Pacific Islands under American sovereignty South of the Equator, 1990–94; *b* 9 March 1935; *s* of late Alexander Lamb Cordiner and Jessie Cordiner; *m* 1958, Anne Milton; one *s*. *Educ:* Peterhead Acad.; Boroughmuir, Edinburgh. Inland Revenue, 1952–60; E African Common Services Orgn, 1960–67; HM Diplomatic Service: London, 1967–68; Saigon, 1968–70; Addis Ababa, 1971–74; Kuwait, 1974–75; Baghdad, 1975–77; on secondment to Export Div., DHSS, 1977–79; Rhodesia Dept, FCO, 1979–80; Govt Rep., Antigua and Barbuda, and St Kitts Nevis, 1980–83; Consul for Pacific NW of USA, Seattle, 1983–87; Asst, Commonwealth Co-ordination Dept, FCO, 1988–90. British Delegn Sec., Commonwealth Heads of Govt Meeting, Kuala Lumpur, 1989. Hon. Citizen of Washington State, 1987; Hon. Ambassador of Goodwill, Washington State, 1987. *Publication:* Diplomatic Wanderings: from Saigon to the South Seas, 2003. *Recreations:* golf, gardening, writing, oil painting, travel, music. *Address:* Les Mulots, 47120 Loubès-Bernac, France. *T:* and *Fax:* (33) 553942951; *e-mail:* bill.cordiner@wanadoo.fr. *Clubs:* St Francis Bay Golf (South Africa); Château des Vigiers (Monestier, France).

CORDINGLEY, David; Director Brazil, British Council, since 2005; *b* 27 Oct. 1952; *s* of Robert and Annie Burrell Cordingley; *m* 1992, Patricia Lobo; one *s*. *Educ:* Lancaster Royal Grammar Sch.; St Peter's Coll., Oxford (BA Physics 1973, MA 1977; PGCE 1974); Univ. of E Anglia (MA Develt Studies 1993). VSO, St Kitts, WI, 1974–76; teacher, Tonbridge Sch., 1977–79; Hd of Sci., Navrongo Secondary Sch., Ghana, 1979–81; teacher, Island Sch., Hong Kong, 1981–86; joined British Council, 1986: Asst Rep., Malaŵi, 1987–88; First Sec. (Sci. and Health), British Council Div., High Commn, New Delhi, 1988–92; Contract Dir, Manchester, 1993–97; Project Manager, Nairobi, 1997–2000; Dir, Vietnam, 2000–04; Regl Dir, Americas and Australasia, 2004–05. *Recreations:* transport (railways, motoring, aviation), sport (walking, cycling, soccer), travel, photography. *Address:* c/o Foreign and Commonwealth Office, King Charles Street, SW1A 2AH; *e-mail:* david.cordingley@britishcouncil.org.br.

CORDINGLEY, Maj.-Gen. John Edward, OBE 1959; *b* 1 Sept. 1916; *s* of Air Vice-Marshal Sir John Cordingley, KCB, KCVO, CBE, and late Elizabeth Ruth Carpenter; *m* 1st, 1940, Ruth Pamela (marr. diss. 1961), *d* of late Major S. A. Boddam-Whetham; two *s*; 2nd, 1961, Audrey Helen Anne, *d* of late Maj-Gen. F. G. Beaumont-Nesbitt, CVO, CBE, MC; two step *d*. *Educ:* Sherborne; RMA, Woolwich. 2nd Lieut RA, 1936; served War of 1939–45, Europe and India. Brigade Comdr, 1961–62; Imperial Defence Coll., 1963; Dir of Work Study, Min. of Defence (Army), 1964–66; Dep. Dir, RA, 1967–68; Maj.-Gen., RA, BAOR, 1968–71, retired. Controller, Royal Artillery Instn, 1975–82; Chm. Bd of Management, RA Charitable Fund, 1977–82. Col Comdt, RA, 1973–82. Bursar, Sherborne Sch., 1971–74; Chm., J. W. Carpenter Ltd, 1984–87. Fellow, Inst. of Work Study Practitioners, 1965; MCMI (MBIM 1966); FInstD 1985. *Recreations:* golf and gardening. *Address:* 15 High Street, Ramsbury, Marlborough, Wilts SN8 2PA. *T:* (01672) 520056. *Clubs:* Army and Navy; Senior Golfers.

See also Maj.-Gen. P. A. J. Cordingley.

CORDINGLEY, Maj.-Gen. Patrick Anthony John, DSO 1991; Chairman, MMI Research, since 2001; *b* 6 Oct. 1944; *s* of Maj.-Gen. John Edward Cordingley, *qv* and Ruth Pamela St John Carpendale; *m* 1968, Melissa Crawley; two *d*. *Educ:* Sherborne School. Commissioned into 5th Royal Inniskilling Dragoon Guards, 1965; commanded, 1984–87; commanded 7th Armoured Brigade, 1988–91; served Libya, Cyprus, UK, BAOR, Gulf; Comdr, Combined Arms Trng Centre, 1991–92; GOC Eastern Dist, 1992–95; GOC 2nd Div., 1995–96; Sen. British Loan Service Officer, Sultanate of Oman, 1996–2000. Col, Royal Dragoon Guards, 2000–05; Hon. Col, Bristol Univ. OTC, 2000–05. Chm., Defence and Security Forum, 2002–. Chm. Trustees, Gilbert White House and Oates Mus., 2002–; Chm., Nat. Meml Arboretum Future Foundns Appeal, 2007–. Gov., Sherborne Sch., 2001– (Chm., Internat. Coll., 2007–). Mem. Ct, Ironmongers' Co., 2000–. FRGS 1986. Hon. DSc Hull, 2007. OStJ 1993. USA Bronze Star, 1991; Order of Oman, 2000. *Publications:* Captain Oates: soldier and explorer, 1984, 3rd edn 1985; In the Eye of the Storm, 1996. *Recreations:* country pursuits, whale-watching. *Club:* Cavalry and Guards (Chm., 2002–04).

CORDINGLY, David Michael Bradley, DPhil; writer; *b* 5 Dec. 1938; *s* of late Rt Rev. Eric Cordingly, MBE, sometime Bishop of Thetford, and of Mary Mathews; *m* 1971, Shirley Elizabeth Robin; one *s* one *d*. *Educ:* Christ's Hosp., Horsham; Oriel Coll., Oxford; (MA); Univ. of Sussex (DPhil). Graphic designer, 1960–68; Exhibn designer at BM, 1968–71; Keeper of Art Gall., Royal Pavilion and Museums, Brighton, 1971–78; Asst Dir, Mus. of London, 1978–80; National Maritime Museum: Asst Keeper, 1980–82; Dep. Keeper, 1982–86; Keeper of Pictures, 1986–88; Head of Exhibns, 1988–93. Adjunct Curator, South Street Seaport Mus., NY, 1995–; Guest Curator, Mariners' Mus., Va, 2000–01. Exhibns organised include: Looking at London, 1980; Sea Finland, 1986; Captain Cook, Brisbane Expo, 1988; Mutiny on the Bounty, 1989; Henry VIII at Greenwich, 1991; Pirates: Fact and Fiction, 1992. FRSA 1974. Order of the White Rose of Finland, 1986. *Publications:* Marine Painting in England, 1974; Painters of the Sea, 1979; (with W. Percival Prescott) The Art of the Van de Veldes, 1982; Nicholas Pocock, 1986; Captain James Cook, Navigator, 1988; Pirates: fact and fiction, 1992; Life Among the Pirates, 1995; Pirates: an illustrated history, 1996; Ships and Seascapes, 1997; Heroines and Harlots: women at sea in the great age of sail, 2001; Billy Ruffian: the Bellerophon and the downfall of Napoleon, 2003; Cochrane the Dauntless: the life and adventures of Thomas Cochrane, 2007. *Recreations:* sailing, carpentry. *Address:* 2 Vine Place, Brighton, Sussex BN1 3HE.

CORDY, Timothy Soames; Director, Global to Local Ltd, since 2006 (Consultant, 2000–05); *b* 17 May 1949; *s* of John Knutt Cordy and Margaret Winifred Cordy (*née* Sheward); *m* 1974, Dr Jill Margaret Tattersall; one *s* one *d*. *Educ:* Dragon Sch., Oxford; Sherborne Sch.; Durham Univ. (BA); Glasgow Univ. (MPhil). MRTPI 1976. Leicester City Council, 1974–85 (Asst City Planning Officer, 1980–85); Communauté Urbaine de Strasbourg, 1978–79; Asst Chief Exec., Bolton MBC, 1985–87; Chief Exec., RSNC, 1987–94. Director: UK 2000, 1987–95; Volunteer Centre UK, 1989–95; TCPA, 1995–97; Envmtl Trng Orgn, 1996–98. *Publications:* Planning and Environmental Protection, 2002; articles on housing renewal, local economic develt, biodiversity, sustainability. *Recreations:* music, France, food. *Address:* 20 Harrowby Lane, Grantham, NG31 9HX. *T:* (01476) 410904.

CORDY-SIMPSON, Lt-Gen. Sir Roderick (Alexander), KBE 1998 (OBE 1984); CB 1993; DL; President, Royal British Legion, 2000–04; *b* 29 Feb. 1944; *s* of late Col John Roger Cordy-Simpson, CBE, MC and Mrs Ursula Margaret Wadham; *m* 1974, Virginia Rosemary Lewis; one *s* one *d*. *Educ:* Radley College. Commissioned 1963, commanded, 1983–86, 13th/18th Royal Hussars (QMO); Comd 4th Armoured Brigade, 1988–90; COS, UN Bosnia Hercegovina, 1992–93; COS BAOR, 1993–94; GOC 1st (UK) Armd Div., 1994–96; Dep. Force Comdr, Bosnia Hercegovina, 1996–97; retd 1998. Lieut, HM Tower of London, 2001–04. Hon. Col, Light Dragoons, 2000–08. Pres., Regular Forces Employment Assoc., 2002–07 (Chm., 1999–2002); Chm., Services Sound and Vision Corp., 2004–. DL Wilts, 2004. *Recreations:* ski-ing, shooting, reading. *Address:* c/o Coutts & Co., 440 Strand, WC2R 0QS. *Club:* Cavalry and Guards.

COREN, Giles Robin Patrick; opinion columnist, since 1999, Restaurant Critic, since 2002, The Times; *b* 29 July 1969; *s* of late Alan Coren, writer and broadcaster, and of Anne Coren (*née* Kasriel). *Educ:* Westminster Sch.; Keble Coll., Oxford (BA Hons English Lit.). The Times: feature writer, 1993–96; Ed., Times Diary, 2000–01; columnist, Tatler, and Ed., Tatler About Town, 1998–99; columnist: Match of the Day mag., 1996–99; Mail on Sunday, 1997–98; Sunday Times, 2002–06; GQ mag., 2004–; restaurant critic, Independent on Sunday, 1999–2000; television: co-presenter, The F-word, 2005; presenter: Movie Lounge, 2006; Animal Farm, 2007; Edwardian Supersize Me, 2007; The Supersizers Go…, 2008; writer and presenter, Tax the Fat, 2006. *Publications:* Against the Odds: James Dyson, an autobiography, 1997; Winkler, 2005. *Recreations:* Eton fives, cricket, writing fiction, daily afternoon naps. *Address:* The Times, 1 Pennington Street, E98 1TT. *T:* (020) 7782 5000. *Clubs:* Old Westminster Fives; Queen's Park Rangers.

COREY, Prof. Elias James, PhD; Professor of Chemistry, Harvard University, since 1959; *b* 12 July 1928; *s* of Elias Corey and Tina Corey (*née* Hasham); *m* 1961, Claire Higham; two *s* one *d*. *Educ:* MIT (BS 1948; PhD 1951). University of Illinois, Urbana-Champaign: Instructor, 1951; Asst Prof., 1953–55; Prof. of Chemistry, 1955–59. Former Member: Bd of Dirs, physical sciences, Alfred P. Sloan Foundn; Sci. Adv. Bd, Robert A. Welch Foundn. Foreign Mem., Royal Soc., 1998. Hon. DSc: Chicago, 1968; Hofstra, 1974; Oxford, 1982; Liège, 1985; Illinois, 1985; Hon. ScD Cantab, 2000; Hon. AM Harvard, 1959. Numerous awards, medals and prizes from univs and learned bodies in USA, Europe and Asia, incl. US Nat. Medal of Science, 1988 and Nobel Prize for Chemistry, 1990. *Publications:* numerous papers in learned jls on pure and synthetic chemistry, esp. on development of methods of organic synthesis, making possible mass production of medicinal and other products, based on natural materials. *Address:* Department of Chemistry, Harvard University, 12 Oxford Street, Cambridge, MA 02138, USA. *T:* (617) 4954033.

CORFIELD, Sir Kenneth (George), Kt 1980; FREng; Chairman, 1979–85, and Managing Director, 1969–85, STC PLC (formerly Standard Telephones & Cables plc); Chairman, Tanks Consolidated Investments, since 1990; *b* 27 Jan. 1924; *s* of Stanley Corfield and Dorothy Elizabeth (*née* Mason); *m* 1960; one *d*. *Educ:* South Staffs Coll. of Advanced Technology. FREng (FEng 1979); FIMechE. Management Develt, ICI Metals Div., 1946–50; Man. Dir, K. G. Corfield Ltd, 1950–60; Exec. Dir, Parkinson Cowan, 1960–66; Dep. Chm., STC Ltd, 1969–79; Sen. Officer, ITT Corp. (UK), 1974–84. Chairman: Standard Telephones and Cables (NI), 1974–85; Distributed Information Processing Ltd, 1987–; Vice-Pres., ITT Europe Inc., 1967–85; Director: Midland Bank Ltd, 1979–91; Britoil PLC, 1982–88; Octagon Investment Management, 1987–95. Chairman: EDC for Ferrous Foundries Industry, 1975–78; British Engrg Council, 1981–85; Defence Spectrum Review, 1985–88; Radio Spectrum Review, 1990–93; Mem., ACARD, 1981–84. President: TEMA, 1974–80; BAIE, 1975–79; Vice-Pres., Engineering Employers' Fedn, 1979–85; Member Council: CBI, 1971–85; Inst. of Dirs, 1981– (Pres. 1984–85); BIM, 1978– (Vice-Pres. 1978–83). Trustee, Science Museum, 1984–92 (Mem. Adv. Council, 1975–83). CCMI; FIEE (CompIEE 1974), Hon. FIET (Hon. FIEE 1985). Hon. Fellow: Sheffield Polytechnic, 1983; Wolverhampton Polytechnic, 1986. DUniv: Surrey, 1976; Open, 1985; Hon. DSc: City, 1981; Bath, 1982; Aston in Birmingham, 1985; Hon. DScEng London, 1982; Hon. DSc (Engrg) QUB, 1982; Hon. LLD Strathclyde, 1982; Hon. DTech Loughborough, 1983; Hon. DEngrg Bradford, 1984. Bicentennial Medal for design, RSA, 1985. *Publications:* Product Design, Report for NEDO, 1979; No Man An Island, 1982 (SIAD Award). *Recreations:* photography, music. *Address:* 10 Chapel Place, Rivington Street, EC2A 3DQ.

CORK AND ORRERY, 15th Earl of, *cr* 1620; **John Richard Boyle, (Jonathan);** Baron Boyle of Youghal, 1616; Viscount Dungarvan, 1620; Baron Boyle of Broghill, 1621; Viscount Boyle of Kinalmeaky and Baron of Bandon Bridge, 1627; Earl of Orrery 1660 (all Ire.); Baron Boyle of Marston (GB) 1711; Chairman, Maritime Investment Holdings Pte Ltd, Singapore, since 1986; *b* 3 Nov. 1945; *e s* of 14th Earl of Cork and Orrery, DSC, VRD; S father, 2003; *m* 1973, Hon. Rebecca Juliet Noble, *y d* of Baron Glenkinglas (Life Peer), PC; one *s* two *d* (of whom one *s* one *d* are twins). *Educ:* Harrow; RNC Dartmouth. Lt-Comdr RN, retd. Dir, E. D. & F. Man Sugar Ltd, London 1994–2006. Life Governor, Soc. for the Advancement of the Christian Faith. Mem Council, Internat. Dendrol. Soc. Trustee: Chichester Cathedral Restoration and Devel Trust; Map Action. *Recreations:* country pursuits, sailing, ski-ing, classic cars, cathedrals. *Heir: s* Viscount Dungarvan, *qv*. *Address:* Lickfold House, Petworth, West Sussex GU28 9EY. *Clubs:* Boodle's; Royal Yacht Squadron, Royal Northern and Clyde Yacht; Castaways.

CORK, CLOYNE, AND ROSS, Bishop of, since 1999; **Rt Rev. (William) Paul Colton;** *b* 13 March 1960; *s* of George Henry Colton and Kathleen Mary Colton (*née* Jenkins); *m* 1986, Susan Margaret Good; two *s*. *Educ:* Ashton Sch., Cork; Lester B; Pearson Coll. of the Pacific, BC, Canada; University Coll., Cork (BCL Hons); Trinity Coll. Dublin (DipTh, MPhil); Univ. of Wales, Cardiff (LLM 2006). Curate, St Paul, Lisburn dio. Connor, 1984–87; Domestic Chaplain to Bp of Connor, 1985–90; Vicar Choral Belfast Cathedral, 1987–90, Minor Canon, 1989–90; Priest Vicar, Registrar and Chapter Clerk, Christ Church Cathedral, Dublin, 1990–95; Co-ordinator of Religious Programmes (Protestant), RTE, 1993–99; Incumbent of Castleknock and Mulhuddart with Clonsilla, dio. Dublin, 1990–99; Canon, Christ Church Cathedral, Dublin, 1997–99. Associate, Centre for Law and Religion, Cardiff Univ., 2006–. Clerical Hon. Sec., Gen Synod of C of I, 1999. *Recreations:* piano, organ, music, walking, reading, computers, Manchester United Football Club. *Address:* The Palace, Bishop Street, Cork, Ireland. *T:* (21) 5005080. *Club:* Kildare Street and University (Dublin).

CORK, Richard Graham; art critic, art historian, broadcaster and exhibition organiser; *b* 25 March 1947; *s* of Hubert Henry Cork and Beatrice Hester Cork; *m* 1970, Vena Jackson; two *s* two *d*. *Educ:* Kingswood Sch., Bath; Trinity Hall, Cambridge (MA, PhD). Art critic, Evening Standard, 1969–77, 1980–83; Editor, Studio International, 1975–79; art critic, The Listener, 1984–90; Chief Art Critic, The Times, 1991–2002; Art Critic, New Statesman, 2003–06. Slade Prof. of Fine Art, Cambridge, 1989–90; Lethaby Lectr, RCA, 1974; Durning-Lawrence Lectr, UCL, 1987; Henry Moore Foundn Sen. Fellow, Courtauld Inst. of Art, 1992–95. Former Member: Hayward Gall. Advisory Panel; Fine Arts Advisory Cttee, British Council; Cttee, Contemp. Art Soc.; Mem., Arts Council of England, 1995–98 (Chm., Visual Art Panel, 1995–98). Selector: Critic's Choice, 1973; Vorticism and its Allies, 1974; Beyond Painting and Sculpture, 1974; Sculpture Now: Dissolution or Redefinition?, 1974; Arte Inglese Oggi, 1976; Art for Whom?, 1978; Art for Society, 1978; Un Certain Art Anglais, 1979; British Art in the 20th Century, 1987; David Bomberg retrospective, 1988; Turner Prize, 1988; British Art Show, 1995; Citibank Photography Prize, 1997; Natwest Art Prize, 1998; North Meadow Millennium Dome Sculpture Project, 1998–2000; Sunderland Gateway Commn, 1999–; John Moores Painting Prize, 1999; Times/Artangel Open, 1999–2000; Jerwood Drawing Prize, 2001; Elector, Slade Professorship of Fine Art, Univ. of Cambridge, 1999–; Member: Trafalgar Sq. Plinth Adv. Gp, 1999–2000; Selection Cttee, New St Paul's Cathedral Font, 1999; Adv. Council, Paul Mellon Centre for British Art, 1999–2005; Design Cttee, Diana Princess of Wales Meml Fountain, 2000–02; BBC Churchill Commn, 2003–; St Martin-in-the-Fields Crib Sculpture, 2004; Chm. of Judges, Rouse Kent Public Art Award, 2004 and 2007; Judge: BlindArt, 2006; St Martin-in-the-Fields East Window, 2006; Chichester Open Art Exhibn, 2007; Curator, A Life of Their Own, Lismore Castle, 2008. Syndic, Fitzwilliam Mus., Cambridge, 2002–. Trustee, Public Art Develt Trust, 1988–95. Organiser of many exhibns, incl. shows in Milan, Paris, Berlin and at Hayward Gall., Tate Gall. and RA. Frequent broadcaster on radio and television. John Llewellyn Rhys Mem. Prize, 1976; Sir Banister Fletcher Award, 1986; NACF Award, 1995. *Publications:* Vorticism and Abstract Art in the First Machine Age, vol. I: Origins and Development, 1975, vol. II: Synthesis and Decline, 1976; The Social Role of Art, 1979; Art Beyond the Gallery in Early Twentieth Century England, 1985; David Bomberg, 1987; Architect's Choice, 1992; A Bitter Truth: Avant-Garde Art and the Great War, 1994; Bottle of Notes: Claes Oldenburg and Coosje van Bruggen, 1997; Jacob Epstein, 1999; Everything Seemed Possible: art in the 1970s, 2003; New Spirit, New Sculpture, New Money: art in the 1980s, 2003; Breaking Down the Barriers: art in the 1990s, 2003; Annus Mirabilis?: art in the year 2000, 2003; Michael Craig-Martin, 2006; contribs to art magazines and exhibn catalogues. *Recreations:* enjoying family, looking at art, walking. *Address:* 24 Milman Road, NW6 6EG. *T:* (020) 8960 2671.

CORKERY, Michael; QC 1981; *b* 20 May 1926; *o s* of late Charles Timothy Corkery and of Nellie Marie Corkery; *m* 1967, Juliet Shore Foulkes, *o d* of late Harold Glyn Foulkes; one *s* one *d*. *Educ:* The King's Sch., Canterbury. Grenadier Guards, 1944; Commissioned in Welsh Guards, 1945; served until 1948. Called to Bar, Lincoln's Inn, 1949 (Bencher 1973, Master of the Library, 1991, Treasurer, 1992). Mem., South Eastern Circuit; 3rd Junior Prosecuting Counsel to the Crown at the Central Criminal Court, 1959; 1st Junior Prosecuting Counsel to the Crown, 1964; 5th Senior Prosecuting Counsel to the Crown, 1970; 3rd Sen. Prosecuting Counsel, 1971; 2nd Sen. Prosecuting Counsel, 1974; 1st Sen. Prosecuting Counsel, 1977–81. *Recreations:* shooting, sailing, gardening, music. *Address:* 5 Paper Buildings, Temple, EC4Y 7HB. *Clubs:* Cavalry and Guards, Garrick, Hurlingham, Itchenor Sailing; Friends of Arundel Castle Cricket.

CORKUM, Paul Bruce, PhD; FRSC 1996; FRS 2005; Leader, Atomic, Molecular and Optical Science Group, National Research Council of Canada; *b* 30 Oct. 1943. *Educ:* Acadia Univ., Nova Scotia (BSc 1965); Lehigh Univ., Penn (MS 1967; PhD 1972). Joined Nat. Research Council of Canada, 1973. Gold Medal, Canadian Assoc. of Physicists, 1996; Killam Prize, 2006. Golden Jubilee Medal, 2002. *Publications:* articles in learned jls. *Address:* Steacie Institute for Molecular Sciences, National Research Council of Canada, 100 Sussex Drive, Ottawa, ON K1A 0R6, Canada; 15 Rothwell Drive, Ottawa, ON K1J 7G3, Canada.

CORLETT, Clive William, CB 1995; Deputy Chairman, Board of Inland Revenue, 1994–98 (Under Secretary, 1985–92; Director General, 1992–94); *b* 14 June 1938; *s* of F. William and Hanna Corlett; *m* 1964, Margaret Catherine Jones; one *s*. *Educ:* Birkenhead Sch.; Brasenose Coll., Oxford (BA PPE). Merchant Navy, 1957. Joined Inland Revenue, 1960; seconded to: Civil Service Selection Bd, 1970; HM Treasury, 1972–74 (as Private Sec. to Chancellor of Exchequer) and 1979–81. Hon. Treas., Old Colfeians RFC, 2000–.

CORLETT, Gerald Lingham; Chairman, Higsons Brewery plc, 1980–88; *b* 8 May 1925; *s* of Alfred Lingham Corlett and Nancy Eileen Bremner; *m* 1957, Helen Bromfield Williamson; three *s* one *d*. *Educ:* Rossall School; Aberdeen University (short war-time course). RA, 1943–47 (Lieut, Royal Indian Artillery). Higsons Brewery, 1947–88. Director: Westminster (Liverpool) Trust Co., 1960–2001 (Chm., 1995–2001); Midshires Building Soc. (Northern Bd), 1977–87; Radio City (Sound of Merseyside), 1982–88 (Chm., 1985–88); Boddington Gp, 1985–88; Watson Prickard, 1991–96 (Chm., 1991–96). Member, Council: Brewers' Soc., 1964–88; Rossall Sch., 1956–95. Mem., Brewers' Co., 1983–2006. *Recreation:* family. *Address:* Kirk House, 4 Abbey Road, West Kirby, Wirral CH48 7EW. *T:* (0151) 625 5425. *Club:* Royal Liverpool Golf.

CORLETT, William John Howarth; QC (I of M) 1999; Attorney General, Isle of Man, since 1998; *b* 25 March 1950; *s* of William Thomas Kaneen Corlett and Jean Mary Corlett; *m* 1974, Janice Mary Crowe; one *s*. *Educ:* King William's Coll., Isle of Man; Univ. of Nottingham (LLB). Called to the Bar, Gray's Inn, 1972; admitted to Manx Bar, 1974; Partner, Dickinson Cruickshank & Co., Advocates, 1975–92; Sen. Partner, Corlett Bolton & Co., Advocates, 1992–98. *Recreations:* golf, salmon fishing. *Address:* Close Jairg, Old Church Road, Crosby, Isle of Man IM4 2HA. *T:* (01624) 852119. *Club:* Royal Over-Seas League.

CORLEY, Paul John; Managing Director, GMTV, 2001–07; *b* 23 Dec. 1950; *s* of Robert Charles Corley and Margaret Dorothy Corley. *Educ:* Worcester Coll., Oxford (BA Hons Modern Hist.). Journalist, Westminster Press, 1972–76; News and Current Affairs, BBC TV, 1976–81; Producer, The Tube, Tyne Tees TV, 1982–84; Director of Programmes: Border TV, 1984–91; Granada Gp, NE TV, 1991–92; Controller: Factual Progs, Carlton TV, and Man. Dir, Carlton Broadcasting, 1992–96; Network Factual Progs, ITV Network Centre, 1996–98; Chief Exec., Border TV, 1998–2000. *Recreations:* television, music, ski-ing. *Clubs:* Groucho, Soho House.

CORLEY, Peter Maurice Sinclair; Under Secretary, Department of Trade and Industry, 1981–93; *b* 15 June 1933; *s* of Rev. James Maurice Corley, MLitt and Mrs Barbara Shearer Corley; *m* 1961, Dr Marjorie Constance Doddridge; two *d*. *Educ:* Marlborough Coll.; King's Coll., Cambridge (MA). Min. of Power, 1957–61; Min. of Transport, 1961–65; BoT, 1965–69; Commercial Sec., Brussels, 1969–71; Asst Sec., DTI, 1972–75; Dir Gen., Econ. Co-operation Office, Riyadh, 1976–78; Dept of Industry, 1978–81. Consultant, Year of Engineering Success, 1993–96. *Recreation:* bookbinding. *Club:* Oxford and Cambridge.

CORLEY, Roger David, CBE 1993; Director, Clerical, Medical and General Life Assurance Society, 1975–97 (Managing Director, 1982–95); *b* 13 April 1933; *s* of Thomas Arthur and Erica Trent Corley; *m* 1964, Brigitte (*née* Roeder), PhD, FSA, FRSA; three *s*. *Educ:* Hymers College, Hull; Univ. of Manchester (BSc). FIA 1960. Joined Clerical Medical, 1956: Investment Manager, 1961–72; Actuary, 1972–80; Dep. Gen. Manager and Actuary, 1980–82. Chairman: Pharos SA, 1995–2006; St Andrew's Gp, 1995–2003; Director: Korea Asia Fund Ltd, 1990–2000; Nat. Westminster Life Assce Ltd, 1992–95; Lands Improvement Hldgs, 1994–99; City of Westminster Arts Council, 1994–2003; British Heart Foundn, 1995–2004; Medical Defence Union Ltd, 1996–2004; Fidelity Investments Life Insurance Ltd, 1997–; RGA Reinsurance UK Ltd, 1999–. Mem., Financial Services Commn of Gibraltar, 1995–2000. Pres., Inst. of Actuaries, 1988–90 (Mem. Council, 1976–94; Hon. Sec., 1980–82; Vice-Pres., 1985–88); Vice Pres., Internat. Actuarial Assoc., 1990–98 (Mem. Council, 1983–98; Nat. Correspondent for England, 1984–90); Mem., Deutsche Gesellschaft für Versicherungsmathematik, 1975–. Master, Actuaries' Co., 1992–93 (Mem. Court, 1985–). FRSA 1990. *Recreations:* theatre, travel, music.

CORMACK, Dr Douglas; independent consultant on environment and management; *b* 10 Jan. 1939; *s* of Douglas Cormack and Mary Hutton (*née* Bain); *m* 1966, Barbara Ann Jones (*d* 2004); two *s*. *Educ:* Gourock High Sch.; Greenock High Sch.; Univ. of Glasgow (BSc 1961; PhD Physical Chemistry 1964). Res. Associate, Chemical Oceanography, Woods Hole Oceanographic Instn, Mass, USA, 1964–67; Warren Spring Laboratory, Department of Trade and Industry: SSO, 1967–72; PSO, 1972–74; Sen. Principal and Hd, Oil Pollution Div., 1974–79; Scientific Advr, Marine Pollution Control Unit, Depts of Trade and Industry and Transport, 1979–86; Warren Spring Laboratory, Department of Trade and Industry: Dep. Dir with responsibility for Envmtl Res. and Personnel, 1986–89; Dep. Dir and Business Manager, 1989–92; Chief Exec., 1992–94; Dir, Envmt, British Maritime Technology, 1994–96. Chm., British Oil Spill Control Assoc., 2000–04; Mem., UK Accreditation Exec. Gp, 2003–04; Chm., ISAA, 2003–. Mem. Bd, Soc. of Maritime Industries (formerly British Marine Equipment Council), 2000–04. Vice-Chm., Adv. Cttee on Protection of the Sea, 1992–95. Associate, Paragon Associates, Envmntl Consultants, 1994–97; Ind. Consultant, Cormack Associates, 1997–. Mem., Council, RNLI, 2003–. FRSA 1988; Founding Fellow, Inst. of Contemp. Scotland, 2001. Editor, Jl of Oil and Chem. Pollution, 1985–91. *Publications:* Response to Oil and Chemical Marine Pollution, Applied Science, 1983; Response to Marine Oil Pollution—Review and Assessment, 1999; numerous scientific papers and reports on atmospheric pollution abatement, catalytic processes, marine pollution prevention and response, waste recycling and final disposal. *Recreations:* sailing, beagling, reading philosophy, history. *Address:* 1 Flint Copse, Redbourn, Herts AL3 7QE. *Clubs:* Civil Service; Royal Gourock Yacht.

CORMACK, John, CB 1982; Director, Parliamentary and Law, Institute of Chartered Accountants of Scotland, 1987–88 (Assistant Director, 1984–87); Fisheries Secretary, Department of Agriculture and Fisheries for Scotland, 1976–82; *b* 27 Aug. 1922; *yr s* of late Donald Cormack and Anne Hunter Cormack (*née* Gair); *m* 1947, Jessie Margaret Bain; one *s* one *d* (and one *d* decd). *Educ:* Royal High Sch., Edinburgh. Served RAPC, 1941–46; Captain and Command Cashier, CMF, 1946. Entered Department of Agriculture for Scotland, 1939: Principal, 1959; Private Sec. to Sec. of State for Scotland, 1967–69; Asst Sec., 1969; Under Sec., 1976. *Recreations:* golf, music. *Address:* 9/1 Murrayfield Road, Edinburgh EH12 6EW.

CORMACK, Sir Patrick (Thomas), Kt 1995; MP (C) Staffordshire South, since 1983 (Cannock, 1970–74; Staffordshire South West, 1974–83); *b* 18 May 1939; *s* of Thomas Charles and Kathleen Mary Cormack, Grimsby; *m* 1967, Kathleen Mary McDonald; two *s*. *Educ:* St James' Choir School and Havelock School, Grimsby; Univ. of Hull. Second Master, St James' Choir School, Grimsby, 1961–66; Company Education and Training Officer, Ross Group Ltd, Grimsby, 1966–67; Assistant Housemaster, Wrekin College, Shropshire, 1967–69; Head of History, Brewood Grammar School, Stafford, 1969–70. Vis. Lectr, Univ. of Texas, 1984. Dir, Historic House Hotels Ltd, 1981–89; Chm., Aitken Dott Ltd (The Scottish Gallery), 1983–89. Trustee, Tradescant Trust, 1980–2001; President: Staffs Historic Buildings Trust, 1983–; Staffs Historic Churches Trust, 1997–; Staffs Parks and Gdns Trust, 2006–; Vice-President: Lincs Old Churches Trust, 1997–; Nat. Churches Trust (formerly Historic Churches Preservation Trust, 2005– (Trustee, 1972–2006); Member: Historic Buildings Council, 1979–84; Faculty Jurisdiction Commn, 1979–84; Heritage in Danger (Vice-Chm., 1974–2000); Council for British Archaeology, 1979–89; Royal Commn on Historical Manuscripts, 1981–2003; Council for Independent Educn (Chm., 1979–97); Lord Chancellor's Adv. Cttee on Public Records, 1979–84; Council, Georgian Gp, 1985–; Council, Winston Churchill Meml Trust, 1983–93; Adv. Council on Nat. Records and Archives, 2003–06. Chairman: William Morris Craft Fellowship, 1988–; Adv. Council, Nat. Fisheries Mus., 1997–2000; Ambassador, Nat. Forest, 2005–. Dep. Shadow Leader of H of C, 1997–2000. Member: Select Cttee on Educn, Science and Arts, 1979–84; Select Cttee on Foreign Affairs, 2001–03; Chairman's Panel, H of C, 1983–97; Chm., NI Affairs Select Cttee, 2005–; Chm., H of C Works of Art Cttee, 1987–2001; Mem., H of C Commn, 2001–05. Member: All Party Arts and Heritage Gp (Chm. 1979–); Cons. Party Arts and Heritage Cttee, 1979–84 (Chm.); Chm., Cons. Party Adv. Cttee on Arts and Heritage, 1988–99; Treas., CPA, 2000–03; Mem. Exec., 1922 Cttee, 2002–05; Dir, Parly Broadcasting Unit, 2002–. Chairman: British-Finnish Parly Gp, 1992–; British-Bosnian Parly Gp, 1992–97, 2001–; British-Croatian Parly Gp, 1992–97. Sen. Associate Mem., St Antony's Coll., Oxford, 1996– (Vis. Parly Fellow, 1994–95); Vis. Schol., Hull Univ., 1995–. Trustee, 1983–, Chm., 2001–, History of Parlt Trust. Chm. Editorial Bd, Parliamentary Publications, 1983–; Ed., The House Magazine, 1983–2005 (Chm. Editl Bd, 1978–; Life Pres., 2005); Internat. Pres., First mag., 1994–. FSA 1978 (Vice Pres., 1994–98). Rector's Warden, 1978–90, Parly Warden, 1990–92, St Margaret's Church, Westminster; Mem., Gen. Synod of C of E, 1995–2005. Governor, ESU, 1999–2006. Mem., Worshipful Co. of Glaziers, 1979–; Freeman, City of London, 1979. Hon. Citizen of Texas, 1985. Commander, Order of the Lion (Finland), 1998. *Publications:* Heritage in Danger, 1976; Right Turn, 1978; Westminster: Palace and Parliament, 1981; Castles of Britain, 1982; Wilberforce—the Nation's Conscience, 1983; Cathedrals of England, 1984. *Recreations:* fighting philistines, walking, visiting old churches, avoiding sitting on fences. *Address:* House of Commons, SW1A 0AA. *Clubs:* Athenæum, Arts (Hon. Mem.).

CORMACK, Robert Linklater Burke, CMG 1988; DL; HM Diplomatic Service, retired; *b* 29 Aug. 1935; *s* of late Frederick Eunson Cormack, CIE, and Elspeth Mary (*née* Linklater), Dounby, Orkney; *m* 1962, Eivor Dorotea Kumlin; one *s* two *d*. *Educ:* Trinity Coll., Glenalmond; Trinity Hall, Cambridge (BA Agric.). National Service, 2nd Lieut, The Black Watch, 1954–56. Dist Officer, Kenya (HMOCS), 1960–64; entered CRO (subseq. Diplomatic Service), 1964: Private Sec. to Minister of State, 1964–66; 1st Secretary: Saigon, 1966–68; Bombay, 1969–70; Delhi, 1970–72; FCO, 1972–77; Counsellor and Consul-Gen., Kinshasa, 1977–79; RCDS, 1980; Counsellor (Economic and Commercial), Stockholm, 1981–85; Hd of Information Technology Dept, FCO, 1985–87; Ambassador, Zaire and (non-resident) Rwanda and Burundi, 1987–91; Ambassador, Sweden, 1991–95. Hon. Consul for Sweden in Orkney, 1996–2006. Mem. (Ind.), Orkney Is Council, 1997–2003. DL Orkney, 1996; JP Orkney, 2002–07. Comdr, Order of North Star (Sweden), 1983. *Address:* Westness, Rousay, Orkney KW17 2PT.

CORMACK, Prof. Robin Sinclair, PhD; FSA; Professor in the History of Art, Courtauld Institute of Art, London University, 1991–2004, now Emeritus; Special Professor in Classics, University of Nottingham, since 2005; *b* 27 Sept. 1938; *s* of James Menzies Cormack and Meryl Joyce Cormack (*née* Pendred); *m* 1st, 1961, Annabel Shackleton (marr. diss. 1985); one *s* one *d*; 2nd, 1985, (Winifred) Mary Beard, *qv*; one *s* one *d*. *Educ:* Bristol Grammar Sch.; Exeter Coll., Oxford (BA Lit.Hum. 1961; MA 1965); Courtauld Inst. of Art, London Univ. (AcDip 1964; PhD 1968). FSA 1975. Gall. Manager, ICA, 1961–62; Lectr in History of Slavonic and E European Art, SSEES and Courtauld Inst. of Art, London Univ., 1966–73; Vis. Fellow, Dumbarton Oaks, Center for Byzantine Studies, Harvard Univ., 1972–73; Lectr in History of Art, Courtauld Inst., London Univ., 1973–82; British Academy Reader, Warburg Inst., London Univ., 1982–85; Bye Fellow, Robinson Coll., Cambridge, 1984–85 (Sen. Mem., 1985–); Reader in History of Art, 1986–90, Dep. Dir, 1999–2002, Courtauld Inst., London Univ. Geddes-Harrower Prof. of Greek Art and Archaeology, Aberdeen Univ., 2001–02; Leverhulme Emeritus Fellow, 2004–06; Getty Scholar, Res. Inst., The Getty, Los Angeles, 2005–06. Consultant to RA for Byzantium 330–1453 exhibn, 2008–09. *Publications:* Writing in Gold, 1985 (trans. French, Icones et Société à Byzance, 1993); The Church of S Demetrios of Thessaloniki, 1985; The Byzantine Eye, 1989; Painting the Soul, 1998 (Runciman Award, Anglo-Hellenic League and Onassis Foundn); Byzantine Art, 2000; Icons, 2007. *Address:* 120 Huntingdon Road, Cambridge CB3 0HL. *T:* (01223) 312734.

CORMACK, (Winifred) Mary; *see* Beard, W. M.

CORNBERG, Catherine, (Mrs Sol Cornberg); *see* Gaskin, C.

CORNELIUS, David Frederick, FIHT; transport and research consultant; *b* 7 May 1932; *s* of Frederick M. N. and Florence K. Cornelius; *m* 1956, Susan (*née* Austin); two *s* two *d*. *Educ:* Teignmouth Grammar Sch.; Exeter University Coll. (BSc (Hons) Physics). Royal Naval Scientific Service, 1953–58; UKAEA, 1958–64; Research Manager, Road Research Laboratory, 1964–72; Asst Director, Building Research Estabt, 1973–78; Head, Research, Transport and Special Programmes, 1978–80, Transport Science Policy Unit, 1980–82, Dept of Transport; Asst Dir, 1982–84, Dep. Dir, 1984–88, Actg Dir, 1988–89, Dir, 1989–91, Transport and Road Res. Lab. FRSA. *Publications:* Path of Duty (biog.), 2000; scientific papers to nat. and internat. confs and in jls of various professional instns on range of topics in tribology, highway transportation and internat. collaboration in res. *Recreations:* European touring by motorhome, swimming, cycling, world travel by container ships, antiques. *Address:* White Poplars, 40 Webb Lane, Hayling Island, Hants PO11 9JE. *T:* (023) 9246 7212.

CORNELL, Eric Allin, PhD; Adjoint Professor, Department of Physics, University of Colorado, Boulder, since 1995 (Assistant Adjoint Professor, 1992–95); Fellow, Joint Institute for Laboratory Astrophysics and National Institute of Standards and Technology, since 1994; *b* Palo Alto, Calif, 1961; *s* of Prof. Allin Cornell and Elizabeth Cornell (*née* Greenberg); *m* 1995, Celeste Landry; two *d*. *Educ:* Stanford Univ. (BS 1985); MIT (PhD 1990). Postdoctoral res. asst, Jt Inst. for Lab. Astrophysics, Boulder, 1990–92; Sen. Scientist, Nat. Inst. of Standards and Technol., Boulder, 1992–. (Jtly) Nobel Prize for

Physics, 2001. *Publications:* articles in jls. *Address:* Joint Institute for Laboratory Astrophysics, University of Colorado, Campus Box 440, Boulder, CO 80309–0440, USA.

CORNELL, Jim Scott, CEng, FREng; FICE; FCILT; Executive Director, Railway Heritage Trust, since 1996; *b* 3 Aug. 1939; *s* of James William Cornell and Annie Cornell (*née* Scott); *m* 1962, Winifred Eileen Rayner; one *s* one *d*. *Educ:* Thirsk Grammar Sch.; Bradford Inst. of Technol. CEng 1967; FICE 1983; FCILT (FCIT 1986); FREng (FEng 1992). With British Rail, 1959–96: jun. and middle mgt civil engrg posts, 1959–76; Divisional Civil Engineer: King's Cross, 1976–78; Newcastle, 1978–81; Asst Regl Civil Engr, York, 1981–83; Regl Civil Engr, Scotland, 1983–84; Dep. Gen. Manager, 1984–86, Gen. Manager, 1986–87, ScotRail; Dir, Civil Engrg, 1987–92; Man. Dir, Regl Railways, 1992–93; Man. Dir, BR Infrastructure Services, 1993–96. Non-exec. Dir, Railtrack plc, subseq. Network Rail, 2002–. FCMI (FIMgt 1987). *Recreations:* tennis, gardening. *T:* (01525) 851070.

CORNELL, Peter; Managing Director, Stakeholder Relationships, Terra Firma Capital Partners Ltd, since 2007; Founder, Cornell Institute, 2007; *b* 5 Oct. 1952; *s* of Dr Sydney Page Cornell and Marjorie Joan Cornell; *m* 1981, Bernadette Conway; one *s* three *d*. *Educ:* Tonbridge Sch., Kent; Exeter Univ.; Chester Law Coll. SSC. Admitted solicitor, 1975; joined Clifford Chance, 1975: on secondment to Philip Morris, Lausanne, 1978–79; opened Singapore office, 1981; returned to London office, 1986; Man. Partner, Madrid office, 1989–2001; opened Barcelona office, 1993; Eur. Man. Partner, 1996–2001; Global Managing Partner, 2001–07. *Recreations:* family, sport, tennis, golf, squash, ski-ing, surfing. *Address:* Terra Firma Capital Partners Ltd, 2 More London Riverside, SE1 2AP. *Clubs:* Roehampton; La Moraleja, de Campo (Madrid).

CORNER, Diane Louise; HM Diplomatic Service; Director of Shared Services Programme, Foreign and Commonwealth Office, since 2006; *b* 29 Sept. 1959; *d* of Captain Alaric John Corner and Marjorie Corner (*née* Ashcroft); *m* 1986, Peter Timothy Stocker; four *d*. *Educ:* Winchester Co. High Sch. for Girls; Peter Symonds' Coll.; Univ. of Bristol (BA Hons French and Politics). Entered FCO, 1982; Second Sec. (Chancery), Kuala Lumpur, 1985–88; First Sec., FCO, 1989–91; Cabinet Office (on secondment), 1991–93; Dep. Hd of Mission, Berlin, 1994–98; Dep. Hd, OSCE/Council of Europe Dept, FCO, 1998–2000; NATO Defence Coll., Rome, 2000; Counsellor and Dep. High Comr, Harare, 2001–03; Counsellor, FCO, 2003–04; on loan to Cabinet Office as Chief Assessor, CSSB, 2004–05; Dir, Prism Change Prog., FCO, 2005–06. *Recreation:* reading. *Address:* c/o Foreign and Commonwealth Office, King Charles Street, SW1A 2AH.

CORNER, Frank Henry, CMG 1980; retired New Zealand Civil Servant and Diplomat; *b* 17 May 1920; *y s* of Charles William Corner, Napier, NZ, and Sybil Corner (*née* Smith); *m* 1943, Lynette Robinson; two *d*. *Educ:* Napier Boys' High Sch.; Victoria Univ. of Wellington. MA, 1st cl. History; James Macintosh and Post-graduate Scholar. External Affairs Dept, NZ, and War Cabinet Secretariat, 1943; 1st Sec., NZ Embassy, Washington, 1948–51; Sen. Counsellor, NZ High Commn, London, 1952–58; Dep. Sec. NZ Dept of External Affairs, 1958–62; Perm. Rep. (Ambassador) to UN, 1962–67; Ambassador of NZ to USA, 1967–72; Permanent Head of Prime Minister's Dept, 1973–75; Secretary of Foreign Affairs, 1973–80; Administrator of Tokelau, 1976–85. Chm., NZ Defence Cttee of Enquiry, 1985–86. Mem., NZ Delegn to Commonwealth Prime Ministers' Meetings, 1944, 1946, 1951–57, 1973, 1975, 1977, 1979; Deleg. to UN Gen. Assembly, 1949–52, 1955, 1960–68, 1973, 1974; NZ Rep. on UN Trusteeship Council, 1962–66 (Pres., 1965–66; Chm., UN Vis. Mission to Micronesia, 1964); NZ Rep. on UN Security Coun., 1966; Adviser, NZ Delegn: Paris Peace Conf., 1946; Geneva Conf. on Korea, 1954; numerous other internat. confs as adviser or delegate. Mem., Bd of NZ-US Educnl Foundn, 1980–88 (Chm., 1983–88); Patron, Assoc. of NZ Art Socs, 1973–88; Mem. Council, Victoria Univ. of Wellington, 1981–87. FRSA. Hon. LLD Victoria Univ. of Wellington, 2005. *Publications:* contrib. to: New Zealand's External Relations, 1962; The Feel of Truth, 1969; An Eye, an Ear and a Voice, 1993; Unofficial Channels, 1999; Three Labour Leaders, 2001; Celebrating New Zealand's Emergence, 2005. *Address:* 26 Burnell Avenue, Wellington 6011, New Zealand. *T:* (4) 4737022; 29 Kakariki Grove, Waikanae 5036, New Zealand. *T:* (4) 2936235.

CORNER, Prof. Jessica Lois, PhD; Head, School of Health Sciences, University of Southampton, since 2008; Chief Clinician, Macmillan Cancer Support, since 2008 (Director for Improving Cancer Services, 2005–08); *b* 22 March 1961; *d* of Rodney, (Bunny), Corner and Judith Corner; *m* 1st, 1985, Cameron Findlay (marr. diss. 1998); one *d*; 2nd, 1999, Christopher Bailey; one *d*. *Educ:* Chelsea Coll., London (BSc Hons Nursing Studies 1983); King's Coll., London (PhD 1990). RN 1983; Oncology Nurse Cert. 1985; Mem. Inst. for Learning and Teaching. 2002. Staff Nurse: Cardiothoracic Unit, St George's Hosp., London, 1983–84; Royal Marsden Hosp., London, 1984–85; Nursing Studies Department, King's College, London: Res. Asst, 1985; Postgrad. Researcher, 1985–87; Macmillan Lectr in Cancer and Palliative Care, 1987–90; Sen. Macmillan Lectr and Hd, Academic Nursing Unit, Inst. of Cancer Res. and Royal Marsden Hosp., 1990–94; Institute of Cancer Research, London: Dir and Dep. Dean (Nursing), Centre for Cancer and Palliative Care Studies, 1994–2002; Prof. of Cancer Nursing, 1996–2002; Prof. of Cancer and Palliative Care, Univ. of Southampton, 2002–08. *Publications:* Becoming a Staff Nurse, 1991; Cancer Nursing: care in context, 2001, 2nd edn 2007; Researching Palliative Care, 2001; over 80 acad. papers in books and jls. *Recreations:* a very amateur gardener and flautist, walking in the Lake District, chaotic family life with two daughters born 12 years apart. *Address:* Macmillan Cancer Support, 89 Albert Embankment, SE1 7UQ. *T:* (020) 7840 4669; *e-mail:* jcorner@macmillan.org.uk.

CORNER, Philip; Director General of Quality Assurance, Ministry of Defence Procurement Executive, 1975–84, retired; Chairman, Institute of Quality Assurance's Management Board (for qualification and registration scheme for lead assessors of quality assurance management system), 1984–92; *b* 7 Aug. 1924; *s* of late William Henry Corner and Dora (*née* Smailes); *m* 1948, Nora Pipes (*d* 1984); no *c*; *m* 1985, Paula Mason. *Educ:* Dame Allan's Boys' Sch., Newcastle upon Tyne; Bradford Technical Coll.; RNEC Manadon; Battersea Polytechnic. BScEng (London); CEng 1966; MIMechE 1952; MIET (MIEE 1957); Hon. FCQI (Hon. FIQA 1985). Short Bros (Aeronautical Engrs), 1942–43; Air Br., RN, Sub-Lieut RNVR, 1944–46; LNER Co., 1946–47; Min. of Works, 1947–50; Min. of Supply, 1950; Ministry of Defence: Dir of Guided Weapons Prodn, 1968–72; Dir of Quality Assurance (Technical), 1972–75. Member: Metrology and Standards Requirements Bd, DoI, 1974–84; Adv. Council for Calibration and Measurement, DoI, 1975–84; BSI Quality Assurance Council, 1979–84; BSI Bd, 1980–84. *Recreations:* reading, listening to music. *Address:* 3 The Green, Dyke Road, Hove, E Sussex BN3 6TH.

CORNER, Timothy Frank; QC 2002; a Recorder, since 2004; *b* 25 July 1958; *s* of Frank and June Corner. *Educ:* Bolton Sch.; Magdalen Coll., Oxford (Demy (Open Scholar); BCL; MA Jurisprudence). Called to the Bar, Gray's Inn, 1981, Bencher, 2008; Attorney General's Supplementary Panel of Counsel, Common Law, 1995–99; Junior Counsel to the Crown, A Panel, 1999–2002. Chm., Adv. Panel on Standards for the Planning Inspectorate, 2006– (Mem., 2001–). Vice-Chm., Planning and Envmt Bar Assoc., 2004–. *Publications:* contrib. Jl of Planning and Envmt Law. *Recreations:* singing, walking, books, travel. *Address:* 4–5 Gray's Inn Square, WC1R 5AH. *T:* (020) 7404 5252, *Fax:* (020) 7242 7803; *e-mail:* tcorner@4-5.co.uk. *Club:* Athenæum.

CORNESS, Sir Colin (Ross), Kt 1986; Chairman, Glaxo Wellcome plc, 1995–97; *b* 9 Oct. 1931; *s* of late Thomas Corness and Mary Evlyne Corness. *Educ:* Uppingham Sch.; Magdalene Coll., Cambridge (BA 1954, MA 1958; Hon. Fellow, 2001); Graduate Sch. of Business Admin, Harvard, USA (Advanced Management Program Dip. 1970). Called to the Bar, Inner Temple, 1956. Dir, Taylor Woodrow Construction Ltd, 1961–64; Man. Dir, Redland Tiles Ltd, 1965–70; Redland PLC: Man. Dir, 1967–82; Chief Exec., 1977–91; Chm., 1977–95. Chm., Nationwide Building Soc., 1991–96. Director: Chubb & Son PLC, 1974–84 (Dep. Chm., 1984); W. H. Smith & Son (Holdings) PLC, 1980–87; Gordon Russell PLC, 1985–89; Courtaulds PLC, 1986–91; S. G. Warburg Gp, 1987–95; Unitech, 1987–95; Union Camp Corp., 1991–99; Chubb Security, 1992–97; Taylor Woodrow plc, 1997–2001. A Dir, Bank of England, 1987–95. Chm., Building Centre, 1974–77; Pres., Nat. Council of Building Material Producers, 1985–87; Member: EDC for Building, 1980–84; Industrial Develt Adv. Bd, 1982–84. Trustee, Uppingham Sch., 1996–99. Hon. DBA Kingston, 1994. *Recreations:* gardening, travel, music.

CORNFORD, James Peters; *b* 25 Jan. 1935; *s* of John Cornford and Rachel Peters; *m* 1960, Avery Amanda Goodfellow; one *s* three *d*. *Educ:* Winchester Coll.; Trinity Coll., Cambridge (MA). Fellow, Trinity Coll., Cambridge, 1960–64; Harkness Fellow, 1961–62; Univ. of Edinburgh: Lectr in Politics, 1964–68; Prof. of Politics, 1968–76; Dir, Outer Circle Policy Unit, 1976–80; Director: Nuffield Foundn, 1980–88; Inst. for Public Policy Res., 1989–94; Paul Hamlyn Foundn, 1994–97; Special Adviser to Chancellor of Duchy of Lancaster, 1997–98; Dep. Dir, Inst. of Community Studies, 1998–2000. Chm. Constitution Unit, UCL, 1995–97. Vis. Fellow, All Souls Coll., Oxford, 1975–76; Vis Prof., Birkbeck Coll., Univ. of London, 1977–80. Mem., Cttee of Inquiry into Educn o Children from Ethnic Minority Gps (DES), 1981–85. Dir, 1979–97, Chm., 1999–2002 Job Ownership Ltd. Mem. Bd, Co-op. Develt Agency, 1987–90. Chairman of Council RIPA, 1984–85; Campaign for Freedom of Information, 1984–97, 1998–. Chm. o Trustees, Southern African Advanced Educn Project, 1990–99; Trustee: Elm Farm Res Centre, 1997–2005; Dartington Hall Trust, 1998– (Chm., 2002–07); Sch. for Socia Entrepreneurs, 2000– (Chm., 2000); Foundn for Social Entrepreneurs, 2001–05; Inst. o Community Studies, 2001–05; The Young Foundn, 2005–. Chm., The Politica Quarterly, 1993–99 (Lit. Ed., 1976–93). *Publications:* contribs to books and jls. *Address* Osborne House, High Street, Stoke Ferry, King's Lynn, Norfolk PE33 9SF. *T:* (01366 500808.

CORNFORTH, Sir John (Warcup), AC 1991; Kt 1977; CBE 1972; DPhil; FRS 1953 Royal Society Research Professor, University of Sussex, 1975–82, now Emeritus; *b* 7 Sept 1917; *er s* of J. W. Cornforth, Sydney, Aust.; *m* 1941, Rita, *d* of W. C. Harradence; one two *d*. *Educ:* Sydney High Sch.; Universities of Sydney and Oxford. BSc Sydney 1937 MSc Sydney, 1938; 1851 Exhibition Overseas Scholarship, 1939–42; DPhil Oxford, 1941 scientific staff of Med. Research Coun., 1946–62; Dir, Shell Research, Milstead Lab. o Chem. Enzymology, 1962–75. Assoc. Prof. in Molecular Sciences, Univ. of Warwick 1965–71; Vis. Prof., Univ. of Sussex, 1971–75; Hon. Prof., Beijing Med. Univ., 1986– Lectures: Pedler, Chem. Soc., 1968–69; Max Tishler, Harvard Univ., 1970; Rober Robinson, Chem. Soc., 1971–72; Sandin, Univ. of Alberta, 1977. For. Hon. Mem Amer. Acad., 1973; Corresp. Mem., Aust. Acad., 1977; For. Associate, US Nat. Acad. o Scis, 1978; For. Mem., Royal Netherlands Acad. of Scis, 1978. Hon. Fellow, S Catherine's Coll., Oxford, 1976; Hon. DSc: ETH Zürich, 1975; Oxford, Warwick Dublin, Liverpool, 1976; Aberdeen, Hull, Sussex, Sydney, 1977; Kent, 1995. Corday Morgan Medal and Prize, Chem. Soc., 1953; (with G. J. Popjak) CIBA Medal, Biochem Soc., 1965; Flintoff Medal, Chem. Soc., 1966; Stouffer Prize, 1967; Ernest Guenthe Award, Amer. Chem. Soc., 1969; (with G. J. Popjak) Davy Medal, Royal Soc., 1968; Pri Roussel, 1972; (jtly) Nobel Prize for Chemistry, 1975; Royal Medal, Royal Soc., 1976 Copley Medal, Royal Soc., 1982. Has been deaf since boyhood. *Publications:* numerou papers on organic chemical and biochemical subjects. *Recreations:* chess, gardening *Address:* Saxon Down, Cuilfail, Lewes, East Sussex BN7 2BE.

CORNICK, Rev. Dr David George; General Secretary, Churches Together in Englanc since 2008; Fellow of Robinson College, Cambridge, since 1997; *b* 12 Sept. 1954; *s* o Cecil George Cornick and Thelma (*née* Le Brun); *m* 1977, Mary Hammond; two *s*. *Edu* Hertford and Mansfield Colls, Oxford (MA); King's Coll., London (BD; PhD 1982 Open Univ. (MBA 2008). United Reformed Church: Minister, Radlett an Borehamwood, 1981–84; Chaplain, Robinson Coll., Cambridge, 1984–87; Trng Office South-Western Province, 1987–92; Dir of Studies in Church Hist., 1992–2001, Principa 1996–2001, Westminster Coll., Cambridge; Gen. Sec., URC, 2001–08. Select Preache Univ. of Cambridge, 2003. *Publications:* Under God's Good Hand, 1998; (contrib. and ec jtly) From Cambridge to Sinai: the worlds of Agnes Smith Lewis and Margaret Dunlo Gibson, 2006; Letting God be God: the reformed tradition, 2008. *Recreations:* musi walking, embroidery. *Address:* Churches Together in England, 27 Tavistock Squar WC1H 9HH. *T:* (020) 7529 8131; Robinson College, Grange Road, Cambridge CB 9AN.

CORNISH, Prof. Alan Richard Henry, PhD; CEng, FIChemE; Ramsay Memori Professor of Chemical Engineering and Head of Department of Chemical an Biochemical Engineering, University College London, 1990–96, now Professor Emeritu *b* 14 March 1931; *s* of late Richard Heard Cornish and Evelyn Jennie Cornish (*n* Hatton); *m* 1957, Rita Ellen Wright; one *s* one *d*. *Educ:* Emanuel Sch.; Illinois Inst. Technology (PhD 1962). CEng; MIChemE 1965, FIChemE 1986; MIGEM; MEI; CS 2004. King George VI Meml Fellow, ESU, 1956–57; Shell Oil Fellow, 1959–61; Imperi College, London: Asst Lectr, Lectr, Sen. Lectr, 1962–88; Dir of Studies, Dept of Chen Engrg, 1982–88; Prof. of Chemical Engineering, Univ. of Bradford, 1988–90. Draper Co. Vis. Lectr, Univ. of Sydney, 1974; Vis. Prof., Univ. de Pau et des Pays de l'Adou 1994, 1997, 1998. Pres., Ramsay Soc., 1990–96; Hon. Treas., IChemE, 1997–200 FRSA. Freeman, City of London, 1996; Liveryman, Engineers' Co., 1996–. Dr L'Institut Nat. Polytechnique de Toulouse, 1999. *Publications:* contribs to professional jl *Club:* Athenæum.

CORNISH, Francis; *see* Cornish, R. F.

CORNISH, Iain Charles Andrew; Chief Executive, Yorkshire Building Society, sinc 2003; *m* Josette; two *d*. *Educ:* Univ. of Southampton (BSc 1982). Statistician, DTI; Se Consultant, Strategy Services Consultancy Practice, KPMG; Corporate Planner, Bradfo & Bingley Bldg Soc.; Corporate Develt Manager, 1992, later Gen. Mktg Manager, Yor Bldg Soc. Dep. Chm., 2006–07, Chm., 2007–08, Building Societies' Assoc. *Addres* Yorkshire Building Society, Yorkshire House, Yorkshire Drive, Bradford, West Yor BD5 8LJ.

CORNISH, James Easton; Director and European Market Strategist, BT Alex. Brow (formerly NatWest Securities), 1990–99; *b* 5 Aug. 1939; *s* of Eric Easton Cornish and Iv

Hedworth (née McCulloch); m 1968, Ursula Pink; one s. Educ: Eton Coll.; Wadham Coll., Oxford (BA); Harvard. Joined FO, 1961; Bonn, 1963; British Mil. Govt, Berlin, 1965; FCO, 1968; Washington, 1973; Dep. Head of Planning Staff, FCO, 1977; Central Policy Rev. Staff, 1980; seconded to Phillips & Drew, 1982; resigned HM Diplomatic Service, 1985; Manager, Internat. Dept, Phillips & Drew, 1982–87; Asst Dir, subseq. Associate Dir, County Securities Ltd, 1987–90.

CORNISH, (Robert) Francis, CMG 1994; LVO 1978; HM Diplomatic Service, retired; Chairman, South West Tourism Ltd, since 2003; b 18 May 1942; s of late Charles Derrick Cornish and of Catherine Cornish; m 1964, Alison Jane Dundas; three d. Educ: Charterhouse; RMA Sandhurst. Commissioned 14th/20th King's Hussars, 1962–68; HM Diplomatic Service 1968; served Kuala Lumpur, Jakarta and FCO, 1969–76; First Sec., Bonn, 1976–80; Asst Private Sec. to HRH the Prince of Wales, 1980–83; High Comr, Brunei, 1983–86; Counsellor (Inf.), Washington, and Dir, British Inf. Service, NY, 1986–90; Head of News Dept, and Spokesman, FCO, 1990–93; Sen. British Trade Comr, Hong Kong, 1993–97; Consul-Gen., HKSAR, 1997; Sen. Directing Staff, RCDS, 1998; Ambassador to Israel, 1998–2001. FRSA 2003. Director: Gross Hill Properties Ltd, 2002–; Sydney & London Properties Ltd, 2003–. Club: Cavalry and Guards.

CORNISH, Prof. William Rodolph, FBA 1984; Herchel Smith Professor of Intellectual Property Law, Cambridge University, 1995–2004 (Professor of Law, 1990–95); Fellow, Magdalene College, Cambridge, since 1990 (President, 1998–2001); b 9 Aug. 1937; s of Jack R. and Elizabeth E. Cornish, Adelaide, S Australia; m 1964, Lovedy E. Moule; one s two d. Educ: Univs of Adelaide (LLB) and Oxford (BCL); LLD Cantab. 1996. Lectr in Law, LSE, 1962–68; Reader in Law, Queen Mary Coll., London, 1969–70; Prof. of English Law, LSE, 1970–90. Ext. Acad. Mem., Max Planck Inst. for Intellectual Property, Competition and Tax Law (formerly for Patent, Copyright and Competition Law), Munich, 1989–. Hon. QC 1997; Bencher, Gray's Inn, 1998. MAE 2001. Hon. Mem., Chartered Inst. of Patent Agents, 2005. Publications: The Jury, 1968; (Jt Editor) Sutton and Shannon on Contracts, 1970; (jtly) Encyclopedia of United Kingdom and European Patent Law, 1977; Intellectual Property, 1981, 6th edn 2007; Law and Society in England 1750–1950, 1989; articles etc in legal periodicals. Address: Magdalene College, Cambridge CB3 0AG.

CORNOCK, Maj.-Gen. Archibald Rae, CB 1975; OBE 1968; FIMgt; Chairman, London Electricity Consultative Council, 1980; b 4 May 1920; s of Matthew Cornock and Mrs Mary Munro MacRae; m 1951, Dorothy Margaret Cecilia; two d. Educ: Coatbridge. NW Frontier, 1940–42; Burma, 1942–43; transf. Royal Indian Navy, 1943; Burma (Arakan), 1944–46; Gordon Highlanders, 1947–50; transf. RAOC, 1950; psc 1954; GSO2 Intelligence, 1955–57; DAQMG Northern Army Gp, 1959–61; comd 16 Bn RAOC, 1961–64; SEATO Planning Staff, Bangkok, 1964; Defence Attaché, Budapest, 1965–67; Comdt 15 Base Ordnance Depot, 1967; DDOS Strategic Comd, 1968–70; Brig. Q (Maint.), MoD, 1970–72; Dir of Clothing Procurement, 1972; Dir of Army Quartering, 1973–75. Col Comdt, RAOC, 1976–80. Pres., Mahratta LI Regtl Assoc., 2000–. Chm., Army Athletic Assoc., 1968–75; Mem. Council, Back Pain Assoc., 1979–. FCMI (MBIM 1965). Recreations: sailing, opera, golf. Clubs: Royal Thames Yacht, Roehampton; Royal Scots (Edinburgh); Highland Brigade.

CORNOCK, Maj.-Gen. Charles Gordon, (Bill), CB 1988; MBE 1974; Bursar, Cranleigh School, 1989–95; b 25 April 1935; s of Gordon Wallace Cornock and Edith Mary (née Keeley); m 1963, Kay Smith; two s. Educ: King Alfred Sch., Plön, Germany; RMA, Sandhurst. Commnd RA, 1956; served, 1957–71: 33 Para Lt Regt; 1 RHA; RMA, Sandhurst; Staff Coll., Camberley; BMRA; Armed Forces Staff Coll., Norfolk, Va; Second in Comd, 1972–74 and CO 1974–76, 7 Para RHA; GSO1 DS Staff Coll., Camberley, 1977–78; Col GS HQ UKLF, 1979; CRA 3rd Armoured Div., 1980–81; RCDS, 1982; Dep. Comdt, Staff Coll., Camberley, 1983; Dir, RA, 1984–86; C of S and Head of UK Delegn, Live Oak, SHAPE, 1986–89. Col Comdt RA, 1986–94; Rep. Col Comdt, RA, 1991–92. Chm., Confedn of British Service and Ex-Service Orgns, 1996–99. Comdr, St John Ambulance (Jersey), 1999–2004. Mem., Police Complaints Authy (Jersey), 2001–05. President: RA Golfing Soc., 1989–98; Jersey Scout Assoc., 2005–; Mem. Cttee, Jersey Blind Soc., 2006–; Vice-Pres., Combined Services and Army Hockey Assoc. Mem., Sen. Golfers' Soc. FCMI. Recreations: hockey, tennis, golf, ski-ing, water ski-ing. Address: Upton, Trinity, Jersey JE3 5DT. Clubs: Army and Navy; La Moye Golf (Jersey).

CORNWALL, Archdeacon of; see Bush, Ven. R. C.

CORNWALL, Christopher John; His Honour Judge Cornwall; a Circuit Judge, since 2002; b 20 Dec. 1950; s of Geoffrey and Joan Cornwall; m 1977, Elizabeth Dunbar Cliff; two s one d. Educ: Shrewsbury Sch.; St Catherine's Coll., Oxford (BA Hons). Called to the Bar, Lincoln's Inn, 1975; Asst Recorder, 1990–94; a Recorder, 1994–2002. Recreations: hill-walking, gardening, European literature, classical music, the visual arts. Address: Preston Combined Court Centre, Openshaw Place, Ring Way, Preston PR1 2LL. T: (01772) 844700, Fax: (01772) 844759; e-mail: HHJudge.Cornwall@judiciary.gsi.gov.uk.

CORNWALL, Hugo; see Sommer, P. M.

CORNWALL-LEGH, family name of **Baron Grey of Codnor.**

CORNWALLIS, family name of **Baron Cornwallis.**

CORNWALLIS, 3rd Baron cr 1927, of Linton, Kent; **Fiennes Neil Wykeham Cornwallis,** OBE 1963; DL; b 29 June 1921; s of 2nd Baron Cornwallis, KCVO, KBE, MC, and Cecily Etha Mary (d 1943), d of Sir James Walker, 3rd Bt; S father, 1982; m 1st, 1942, Judith Lacy Scott (marr. diss. 1948); one s (one d decd); 2nd, 1951, Agnes Jean Russell Landale (d 2001); one s three d; 3rd, 2002, Stephanie Coleman. Educ: Eton. Served War, Coldstream Guards, 1940–44. Pres., British Agricultural Contractors Assoc., 1952–54; Pres., Nat. Assoc. of Agricultural Contractors, 1957–63 and 1986–98; Vice-Pres., Fedn of Agricl Co-operatives, 1984–86; Chm., Smaller Firms Council, CBI, 1978–81. Representative, Horticultural Co-operatives in the EEC, 1974–87. Chm., English Apples & Pears Ltd, 1990–94; Dir, Town & Country Building Soc. (formerly Planet, then Magnet & Planet, Bldg Soc.) 1967–92 (Chm., 1973–75; Dep. Chm., 1975–77; Chm., 1978–81 and 1991–92). Dep. Chm. and Exec. Gov., Cobham Hall Sch., 1969–72; Mem., Bd of Trustees, Chevening Estate, 1979–98. Fellow, Inst. of Horticulture, 1986; FRPSL 1998. Pro Grand Master, United Grand Lodge of England, 1982–91. DL Kent, 1976. Recreations: fishing, philately. Heir: s Hon. (Fiennes Wykeham) Jeremy Cornwallis [b 25 May 1946; m 1969, Sara Gray de Neufville, d of Lt-Col Nigel Stockwell, Benenden, Kent; one s two d]. Address: Old Parsonage Cottage, Goudhurst, Cranbrook, Kent TN17 1AN. T: (01580) 211226. Clubs: Brooks's, Flyfishers'.

CORNWELL, Bernard, OBE 2006; novelist, since 1980; b 23 Feb. 1944; s of William Oughtred and Dorothy Rose Cornwell and adopted s of late Joseph and Margery Wiggins; m 1st, 1967, Lindsay Leworthy (marr. diss. 1976); one d; 2nd, 1980, Judy Cashdollar. Educ: Monkton Combe Sch.; London Univ. (BA ext.). Producer, BBC TV, 1970–76; Hd,

Current Affairs TV, BBC NI, 1976–78; Ed., Thames TV News, 1978–80. Dir, Amer. Associates of Nat. Army Mus. Publications: Sharpe's Eagle, 1981; Sharpe's Gold, 1981; Sharpe's Company, 1982; Sharpe's Sword, 1983; Sharpe's Enemy, 1984; Sharpe's Honour, 1985; Sharpe's Regiment, 1986; Sharpe's Siege, 1987; Redcoat, 1987; Sharpe's Rifles, 1988; Wildtrack, 1988; Sharpe's Revenge, 1989; Sea Lord, 1989; Sharpe's Waterloo, 1990; Crackdown, 1990; Stormchild, 1991; Sharpe's Devil, 1992; Scoundrel, 1992; Rebel, 1993; Copperhead, 1994; Sharpe's Battle, 1995; Battle Flag, 1995; The Winter King, 1995; The Bloody Ground, 1996; Enemy of God, 1996; Sharpe's Tiger, 1997; Excalibur, 1997; Sharpe's Triumph, 1998; Sharpe's Fortress, 1999; Stonehenge, 2000 BC, 1999; Sharpe's Trafalgar, 2000; Harlequin, 2000; Sharpe's Prey, 2001; Gallows Thief, 2001; Vagabond, 2002; Sharpe's Havoc, 2003; Heretic, 2003; Sharpe's Escape, 2004; The Last Kingdom, 2004; The Pale Horseman, 2005; Sharpe's Fury, 2006; Lords of the North, 2006; Sword Song, 2007. Recreation: sailing. Address: PO Box 168, West Chatham, MA 02669, USA. Club: Stage Harbor Yacht (Chatham, Mass).

CORNWELL, David John Moore, (John le Carré); writer; b 19 Oct. 1931; s of late Ronald Thomas Archibald Cornwell and Olive (née Glassy); m 1954, Alison Ann Veronica Sharp (marr. diss. 1971); three s; m 1972, Valerie Jane Eustace; one s. Educ: Sherborne; Berne Univ.; Lincoln Coll., Oxford (1st cl. Modern Languages; Hon. Fellow 1984). Taught at Eton, 1956–58. Mem. of HM Foreign Service, 1960–64. Hon. DLitt: Exeter, 1990; St Andrews, 1996; Southampton, 1997; Bath, 1998. Cartier Diamond Dagger, CWA, 1988. Comdr, Ordre des Arts et des Lettres (France), 2005. Publications: Call for the Dead, 1961 (filmed as The Deadly Affair, 1967); A Murder of Quality, 1962; The Spy Who Came in from the Cold, 1963 (Somerset Maugham Award; Crime Writers' Assoc. Gold Dagger, 1963, Dagger of Daggers, 2005) (filmed); The Looking-Glass War, 1965 (filmed); A Small Town in Germany, 1968; The Naïve and Sentimental Lover, 1971; Tinker, Tailor, Soldier, Spy, 1974 (televised 1979); The Honourable Schoolboy, 1977 (James Tait Black Meml Prize; Crime Writers' Assoc. Gold Dagger); Smiley's People, 1980 (televised 1982); The Little Drummer Girl, 1983 (filmed 1985); A Perfect Spy, 1986 (televised 1987); The Russia House, 1989 (filmed 1991); The Secret Pilgrim, 1991; The Night Manager, 1993; Our Game, 1995; The Tailor of Panama, 1996 (filmed 2001); Single & Single, 1999; The Constant Gardener, 2001 (filmed 2005); Absolute Friends, 2003; The Mission Song, 2006. Address: c/o Jonny Geller, Curtis Brown Group Ltd, Haymarket House, 28–29 Haymarket, SW1Y 4SP.

CORNWELL, Patricia D(aniels); American crime novelist; b 9 June 1956; d of Sam and Marilyn Daniels; m 1980, Charles Cornwell (marr. diss. 1990). Educ: Davidson Coll., N Carolina (BA English 1979). Crime Reporter, Charlotte Observer, 1979–81 (N Carolina Press Assoc. Award, 1980); Technical Writer, then Computer Analyst, Office of Chief Med. Examr, Richmond, Va, 1984–90; Volunteer Police Officer. Publications: non-fiction: A Time For Remembering: the story of Ruth Bell Graham, 1983, re-issued as Ruth—a Portrait, 1997; Portrait of a Killer: Jack the Ripper—case closed, 2002; fiction: Hornet's Nest, 1997; Southern Cross, 1999; Isle of Dogs, 2001; Dr Kay Scarpetta novels: Postmortem, 1990 (John Creasey Meml Award, CWA; Edgar Award, MWA; Anthony Award, Boucheron Award, World Mystery Convention; MacAvity Award, Mystery Readers Internat.); Body of Evidence, 1991; All That Remains, 1992; Cruel and Unusual, 1993; The Body Farm, 1994; From Potter's Field, 1995; Cause of Death, 1996; Unnatural Exposure, 1997; Point of Origin, 1998; Black Notice, 1999; The Last Precinct, 2000; Blow Fly, 2003; Predator, 2005; At Risk, 2006; Book of the Dead, 2007; The Front, 2008. Address: c/o Little, Brown & Co., Brettenham House, Lancaster Place, WC2E 7EN; c/o Don Congdon Associates Inc., 156 5th Avenue, Suite 625, New York, NY 10010–7002, USA.

COROB, Sidney, CBE 1993; Chairman: Corob Consolidated Ltd, 1984–2004; Corob Holdings Ltd, 1959–2004; b 2 May 1928; s of Wolf and Rachel Corob; m 1949, Elizabeth Springer; three d. Educ: Tree of Life Coll. Chief Exec., W. Corob & Son, 1951–59; Chairman: Corob Construction Co. Ltd, 1952–2001; Western & Northern Investments Ltd, 1964–68; Corob Intercity Ltd, 1968–77; Mayfair & City Properties plc, 1984–87. Lloyds Underwriter, 1978–85. Chairman: British Technion Soc., 1984–2000 (Hon. Pres., 2000–); Internat. Centre for Enhancement of Learning Potential, 1991–. Director: Eur. Jewish Publication Soc., 1995–; Jewish Assoc. for Business Ethics, 1994–. Vice President: CCJ, 1995– (Vice-Chm., 1978–95); British ORT, 1996–; Central Council for Jewish Social Services, 1989–99; Westmount Housing Assoc., 1974–. Life Pres., The HOPE Charity, 1998–. Hon. DSc Technion, Israel Inst. of Engrg and Technology, 1986. Recreations: foreign travel, hiking, Bible studies, opera, reading. Address: 62 Grosvenor Street, W1K 3JF. T: (020) 7499 4301.

CORP, Maj.-Gen. Philip James Gladstone, CB 1996; CEng, FIMechE; b 23 June 1942; s of Wilfred James Corp and Janet Maude Corp (née Gladstone); m 1st, 1965, Penelope Joan Smith (marr. diss.); two s; 2nd, 1978, Dawn Phyllis Durrant (née Holder); one step s two step d. Educ: Warwick Sch.; Queen Elizabeth GS, Crediton; Pembroke Coll., Cambridge (MA Mech. Scis and Law). Commissioned REME from RMA Sandhurst, 1962; RMCS and Staff Coll., 1973–74; Op. Requirements, MoD, 1975–76; Comd 3 Field Workshop, 1977–78; REME Combat Develt, 1979–80; Dep. Project Manager, MoD (PE), 1981–83; Comd 7 Armd Workshop, BAOR, 1984–86; QMG Staff, MoD, 1987–89; Comdt, REME Officers' Sch., 1990; Dir, Equipment Engrg, MoD, 1990–93; Dir-Gen. Equipment Support (Army), 1993–97; Chief Exec., IRTE, subseq. Soc. of Ops Engrs, 1998–2002. Col Comdt, REME, 1996–2000. Mem. Bd, Engrg Council (UK), 2002–08. Vice-Pres., C&G, 2008–. Trustee: Army Rifle Assoc., 1996–; Council for Cadet Rifle Shooting, 1998–. Hon. FSOE 2001. Recreations: music, furniture restoration, idleness. Address: RHQ REME (Box H075), Arborfield, Reading RG2 9NJ.

CORP, Rev. Ronald Geoffrey, SSC; freelance conductor and composer; b 4 Jan. 1951; s of Geoffrey Charles Corp and Elsie Grace (née Kinchin). Educ: Blue Sch., Wells; Christ Church, Oxford (MA); Southern Theol Educn and Trng Scheme (DipTheol). Librarian, producer and presenter, BBC Radio 3, 1973–87; freelance, 1987–: Conductor: Highgate Choral Soc., 1984–; London Chorus (formerly London Choral Soc.), 1985–; New London Orch., 1988–; New London Children's Choir, 1991–; has conducted: BBC Singers, BBC Concert Orch., Leipzig Philharmonic Orch., Brussels Radio and TV Orch., Royal Scottish Nat. Orch., BBC Scottish SO and at BBC Promenade concerts. Numerous recordings. Trustee, Musicians Benevolent Fund, 2000– (Chm., Educn Cttee, 2002); Vice-Pres., Sullivan Soc., 2001. Ordained deacon, 1998, priest, 1999; NSM, St James, Hampstead and St Mary with All Souls, Kilburn, 1998–2002; Assistant Curate (non-stipendiary): Christ Church, Hendon, 2002–07; St Alban's, Holborn, 2007–. Freeman, City of London, 2007; Freeman, Musicians' Co., 2007. Compositions: choral works including: And All The Trumpets Sounded (cantata), 1989; Laudamus, 1994; Four Elizabethan Lyrics, 1994; Cornucopia, 1997; Piano Concerto, 1997; A New Song (cantata), 1999; Mary's Song, 2001; Adonai Echad, 2001; Kaleidoscope, 2002; Missa San Marco, 2002; Dover Beach, 2003; Forever Child, 2004; Waters of Time, 2006; String Quartet, 2007; Jubilate Deo, 2008. Publication: The Choral Singer's Companion, 1987, 2nd edn 2000. Recreation: reading. Address: Bulford Mill, Bulford Mill Lane, Cressing, Essex CM77 8NS.

CORRALL, Prof. Sheila Mary, (Mrs R. G. Lester), FCLIP; Professor of Librarianship and Information Management, since 2004, and Head, Department of Information Studies, since 2006, University of Sheffield; *b* 11 Sept. 1950; *d* of Baron Lowry, PC, PC (NI) and Mary Audrey Lowry (*née* Martin); *m* 1st, 1974, Jonathan Austyn Corrall (marr. diss. 1995); 2nd, 1996, Raymond George Lester. *Educ:* Richmond Lodge Sch., Belfast; Girton Coll., Cambridge (BA Classical Tripos 1974, MA 1977); Poly of N London (Postgrad. DipLib (CNAA) 1976); Roffey Park Mgt Inst. (MBA Sussex 1992); Univ. of Southampton (MSc Inf. Systems 2002). ALA 1977, FLA 1999, MIInfSc 1986, FCLIP 2002. Hd, Inf. Services, Sci. Ref. and Inf. Service, BL, 1988–90; Dir, Liby and Inf. Services, Aston Univ., 1991–95; Librarian, Univ. of Reading, 1995–2001; Dir, Acad. Services, Univ. of Southampton, 2001–03. Chairman: Adv. Cttee, UKOLN, 1995–98; Inf. Services NTO, 1999–2001; Mgt Bd, Manchester Inf. and Associated Services, 2006–; Hds of Schs and Depts Cttee, British Assoc. for Inf. and Liby Educn and Res., 2006–; Member: Cttee on Electronic Inf., 1994–98, Learning and Teaching Cttee, 2005–08, JISC; Libraries and Inf. Adv. Cttee, British Council, 1995–98. Mem., Presidential Cttee for Internat. Agenda on Lifelong Literacy, IFLA, 2005. Pres., Chartered Inst. of Liby and Inf. Professionals, 2002–03. FRSA 1996; MIMgt 1998; FCMI 2003. Lifetime Achievement Award, Internat. Inf. Industries, 2003. *Publications:* (ed) Collection Development: options for effective management, 1988; Strategic Planning for Library and Information Services, 1994; (with A. Brewerton) The New Professional's Handbook: your guide to information services management, 1999; Strategic Management of Information Services: a planning handbook, 2000; contrib. numerous articles and book chapters on liby and inf. mgt. *Recreations:* walking, theatre. *Address:* Department of Information Studies, University of Sheffield, Regent Court, 211 Portobello Street, Sheffield S1 4DP. *T:* (0114) 222 2632, *Fax:* (0114) 278 0300; *e-mail:* s.m.corrall@sheffield.ac.uk.

CORRAN, Anne Jane; *see* Mills, A. J.

CORREA, Charles Mark; Padma Shri, 1972; architect; *b* 1 Sept. 1930; *s* of Carlos M. Correa and Ana Florinda de Heredia; *m* 1961, Monika Sequeira; one *s* one *d*. *Educ:* Univ. of Michigan (BArch); MIT (MArch). Private practice, Bombay, 1958–; work includes: Mahatma Gandhi Memorial, Sabarmati Ashram; State Assembly for Madhya Pradesh; low cost housing projects in Delhi, Bombay, Ahmedabad and other cities in India; Jawahar Kala Kendra, Jaipur; Nat. Crafts Mus., and British Council HQ, Delhi; Chief Architect for planning of New Bombay. Jawaharlal Nehru Vis. Prof. and Fellow of Churchill Coll., Cambridge, 1985–86. Chm., Nat. Commn on Urbanisation, 1985–88. Founder Mem., Steering Cttee, Aga Khan Award for Architecture, 1977–86; Jury Mem., Pritzker Prize, 1993–98. Hon. Vis. Prof., Tonji Univ., Shanghai. Member: French Acad., 1985; Internat. Acad. of Architects, Bulgaria, 1987; Finnish Assoc. of Architects, 1992; Foreign Hon. Mem., Amer. Acad. of Arts and Scis, 1993; Hon. MRIAI, 1997; Amer. Acad. of Arts and Letters, 1998. Hon. Fellow: United Architects of Philippines, 1990; RIBA 1993. Hon. FAIA 1979. Hon. Dr Univ. of Michigan, 1980. Royal Gold Medal for Architecture, RIBA, 1984; Gold Medal, Indian Inst. of Architects, 1987; Gold Medal, IUA, 1990; Praemium Imperiale Prize, Japan Art Assoc., 1994; Aga Khan Award for Architecture, 1998. *Publication:* The New Landscape, 1984; *relevant publications:* S. Cantacuzino, Charles Correa, 1984; Kenneth Frampton, Charles Correa, 1996. *Recreations:* tennis, model trains, chess. *Address:* 9 Mathew Road, Bombay 400004, India. *T:* (22) 3633307. *Clubs:* Bombay Gymkhana, Willingdon Sports, Royal Bombay Yacht (Bombay).

CORRIE, John Alexander; consultant on African affairs and development, and financial advisor to developing countries, since 2004; Chairman, Polymer Training Ltd, since 2008; Member (C) West Midlands Region, European Parliament, 1999–2004 (Worcestershire and South Warwickshire, 1994–99); *b* 29 July 1935; *s* of John Corrie and Helen Brown; *m* 1965, Sandra Hardie; one *s* two *d*. *Educ:* Kirkcudbright Acad.; George Watson's Coll.; Lincoln Agric. Coll., NZ. Farming in NZ, 1955–59, in Selkirk, 1959–65 and in Kirkcudbright, 1965–. Lectr for British Wool Marketing Bd and Agric. Trng Bd, 1966–74; Mem. Cttee, NFU, SW Scotland, 1964–74 (Vice-Chm. Apprenticeship Council, 1971–74); Nuffield Scholar in Agriculture, 1972. Dist Officer, Rotary Internat., 1973–74 (Community service). Nat. Chm., Scottish Young Conservatives, 1964. Contested (C): North Lanark, 1964; Central Ayr, 1966; Cunninghame N, 1987; Argyll and Bute, 1992. MP (C): Bute and N Ayr, Feb. 1974–1983; Cunninghame N, 1983–87. Opposition spokesman on educn in Scotland, Oct. 1974–75; an Opposition Scottish Whip, 1975–76 (resigned over Devolution); PPS to Sec. of State for Scotland, 1979–81; Mem., Council of Europe and WEU, 1982–87. Treas., Scottish Cons. Back Bench Cttee, 1980, Chm. 1981–82; Leader, Cons. Gp on Scottish Affairs, 1982–84; Sec., Cons. Back Bench Fish-farming Cttee, 1982–86; brought in Pvte Mem.'s Bill, Diseases of Fish, 1983. Mem. European Parlt, 1975–76 and 1977–79 (Mem. Cttees of Agriculture, Reg. Develt and Transport, 1977–79). Vice-President: EEC-Turkey Cttee, 1975–76; EEC Fisheries Cttee, 1977–79; EEC Mediterranean Agricl Cttee, 1977–79; Rapporteur for EEC Fisheries Policy, 1977–78. European Parliament: Chief Whip of Cons. Gp, 1997–99; Member: Employment and Social Affairs, 1998–99; Agric. and Budgets Cttees, 1999; Chm., 1979 Back Bench Cttee; Dir, Human Rights Cttee, 1994–99; Dir, Animal Rights and Sustainable Develt Intergp, 1994–99; Chm., Pensions Cttee, 1999–2004; Co-ordinator, Develt Cttee, 1999–2004; Co-Pres., ACP/EU Jt Parly Assembly, 1999–2002 (Vice-Pres. and Hon. Life Pres., 2002–04). Pres., European Sustainable Develt Gp, 2004–; Mem., Council, AWEPA European Parliamentarians for Africa, 2004–. Mem., N/S Cttee, Council of Europe. Chm., Transport Users' Consultative Cttee for Scotland, 1989–94; Mem., Central Transport Consultative Cttee, 1989–94 (Vice Chm., 1992–94; Mem., Railways Industry Adv. Cttee, 1993–94; Mem., Health Safety Cttee, 1993–94). Member: Council, Scottish Landowners Fedn, 1990–94 (Vice Chm., SW Reg., 1992–94); Judges Panel for Belted Galloway Soc., 1991– (Council Mem., 2004–); Timber Growers UK (SW), 1991–94; Dir, Ayr Agricl Soc., 1990–95. Industry and Parlt Trust Fellowship with Conoco (UK) Ltd, 1986–87. *Publications:* (jtly) Towards a European Rural Policy, 1978; Towards a Community Forestry Policy, 1979; Fish Farming in Europe, 1979; The Importance of Forestry in the World Economy, 1980. *Recreations:* shooting, fishing. *Address:* Park House, Tongland, Kirkcudbright DG6 4NE. *T:* (01557) 820232, *Fax:* (01557) 820211; *e-mail:* johncorrie@btconnect.com.

CORRIE, Thomas Graham Edgar; His Honour Judge Corrie; a Circuit Judge, since 1994; *b* 18 Dec. 1946; *s* of late John Alexander Galloway Corrie, OBE, MC and Barbara Phyllis Corrie (*née* Turner); *m* 1971, Anna Cathinca Logsdail; one *s* two *d*. *Educ:* Eton; Brasenose Coll., Oxford (MA). Called to the Bar, Gray's Inn, 1969; Midland and Oxford Circuit, 1971–94; a Recorder, 1988–94. *Recreations:* cycling, canal boating. *Address:* 2 Harcourt Buildings, Temple, EC4Y 9DB. *T:* (020) 7353 6961. *Club:* Frewen (Oxford).

CORRIGAN, Prof. (Francis) Edward, PhD; FRS 1995; Professor of Mathematics and Principal, Collingwood College, Durham University, since 2008; *b* 10 Aug. 1946; *s* of late Anthony Corrigan and of Eileen Corrigan (*née* Ryan); *m* 1970, Jane Mary Halton; two *s* two *d*. *Educ:* St Bede's Coll., Manchester; Christ's Coll., Cambridge (MA, PhD). A. J. Wheeler Fellow, Durham, 1972–74; CERN Fellow, Geneva, 1974–76; Durham University: Lectr, Sen. Lectr and Reader, 1976–92; Prof. of Maths, 1992–99; Hd, Dept of Math. Scis, 1996–98; University of York: Prof. of Maths, 1999–2007; Hd, Dept of Maths, 1999–2004, 2005–07. Joliot-Curie Fellow, ENS Paris, 1977–78; Vis. Associate, C 1978–79; Vis. Fellow, Dept of Applied Maths and Theoretical Physics, Cambridge, 1 Derman Christopherson Fellow, Durham Univ., 1983–84; Visiting Professor: Centre Particle Theory, Durham Univ., 1999–2002; Kyoto Univ., 2005. Life Mem., Clare H Cambridge. Hon. Ed., Jl of Physics A, 1999–2003. *Publications:* articles on elemen particle theory and mathematical physics in learned jls. *Recreations:* playing and listenin music, squash. *Address:* Collingwood College, Durham University, South Road, Durh DH1 3LT. *T:* (0191) 334 5011; *e-mail:* edward.corrigan@durham.ac.uk.

CORRIGAN, Margaret Mary; Teacher of children with special needs, Beechw School, Aberdeen, 2007–08; *d* of Joseph Hamilton and Mary Anna (*née* Monaghan 1979, Gerard Michael Corrigan; one *s* two *d*. *Educ:* Univ. of Strathclyde (BA H English); Edinburgh Univ. (PGCE 2005). Trainee journalist with newspaper/magaz publishers D. C. Thomson, Dundee, 1977–78; Advertising Copywriter and Acct Ex Austin Knight Advertising, Glasgow, 1978–81; Depute Dir of Public Relns, Cumberna Develt Corp., 1981–83; Mktg and Communications Officer/Lectr, Falkirk Coll. Further and Higher Educn, 1999–2004; Teacher of English, Mearns Ac Aberdeenshire, 2005–07. Mem., Radio Authority, 1990–95. *Recreations:* swimmi music, theatre.

CORRIGAN, Thomas Stephen, OBE 1999; Chairman, 2change, since 2003; *b* 2 J 1932; *s* of late Thomas Corrigan and Renée Victorine Chaborel; *m* 1963, Sally Marg Everitt; two *d*. *Educ:* Beulah Hill; Chartered Accountant (Scottish Inst.). Nat. Serv Army (2nd Lieut), 1955–57. Chief Accountant, Lobitos Oilfields, 1957–62; Exec., Ke Ullmann, 1962–64; Inveresk Group: Finance Dir, 1964–71; Man. Dir, 1971–74; Ch 1974–83. Chairman: Havelock Europa, 1983–89; Rex Stewart Gp Ltd, 1987–90; di other cos. Pres., British Paper and Board Industry Fedn, 1975–77; Vice-Pres., Europ Confedn of Pulp, Paper and Board Industries, 1982–83; Mem., NEDC (Tripartite Sec Working Party on paper industry), 1976–77. Chairman: POUNC, 1984–94; Direct M Accreditation and Recognition Centre, 1995–97. Advr and Chief Assessor, 1994–20 Mem. Ind. Panel of Judges, 2001–03, Charter Mark Awards, Cabinet Office; Me London Award Panel, Prince's Trust, 2002–; Mem., Investment Cttee, Print Charitable Corp., 2006–. Master: Makers of Playing Cards Co., 1978–79; Stationers Newspaper Makers' Co., 1990–91; Marketors' Co., 1995. FRSA. *Recreations:* golf, brid tennis, travel. *Address:* 57 Marsham Court, Marsham Street, SW1P 4JZ. *T:* (020) 7 2078. *Clubs:* MCC, Royal Automobile, City Livery; Royal & Ancient Golf (St Andrew Walton Heath Golf.

CORRIGAN-MAGUIRE, Mairead; Co-Founder, Northern Ireland Peace Movem later Community of the Peace People, 1976 (Hon. Life President); *b* 27 Jan. 1944; Andrew and Margaret Corrigan; *m* 1981, Jackie Maguire; two *s* and three step *c*. *Educ* Vincent's Primary Sch., Falls Road, Belfast; Miss Gordon's Commercial Coll., Belf Secretarial qualification. Confidential Sec. to Managing Director, A. Guinness Son & (Belfast) Ltd, Brewers, Belfast. Initiator of Peace Movement in Northern Ireland, A 1976; Chm., Peace People Organisation, 1980–81. Hon. Dr of Law, Yale Univ., 19 Nobel Prize for Peace (jtly), 1976; Carl-Von-Ossietzky Medaille for Courage, Ber 1976. *Address:* 224 Lisburn Road, Belfast, N Ireland BT9 6GE. *T:* (business) (028) 9 3465, *Fax:* (028) 9068 3947; *e-mail:* info@peacepeople.com.

CORRIN, Prof. Bryan, MD; FRCPath; Professor of Thoracic Pathology, National H and Lung Institute, London University, 1979–98, now Emeritus; *b* 27 May 1933; George Henry and Eleanor Corrin; *m* 1957, Sheila Ann Carpenter; three *s* one *d*. *E* King William's Coll., Isle of Man; St Mary's Hosp. Med. Sch., London Univ. (MB 1956; MD 1962). FRCPath 1977. Res. Pathologist, Birmingham Children's Ho 1957–58; Lectr in Pathology, Univ. of Manchester, 1958–64; Reader in Mor Anatomy, St Thomas's Hosp. Med. Sch., London, 1964–79. Hon. Consultant Patholog Brompton Hosp., 1979–. Pres., London Manx Soc., 1999–2000. *Publications:* The Lu 1990; (ed jtly) Clinical Atlas of Respiratory Disorders, 1990; (ed) Pathology of L Tumors, 1997; Pathology of the Lungs, 2000, 2nd edn (jtly) 2006; (ed jtly) Respirat Medicine, 2003. *Address:* 14 Foxgrove Road, Beckenham, Kent BR3 5AT.

CORRIN, His Honour John William, CBE 1995; Chairman, BlackRock (Isle of M Ltd (formerly Merrill Lynch Investment Managers (Isle of Man) Ltd), 1998–2008; *b* 6 1932; *s* of Evan Cain Corrin and Dorothy Mildred Corrin; *m* 1961, Dorothy Patricia, late J. S. Lace; one *d*. *Educ:* Murrays Road Primary Sch., Douglas; King William's C IOM. Admitted to Manx Bar, 1954. Attorney Gen., IOM, 1974–80; Second Deems 1980–88; HM's First Deemster, Clerk of the Rolls, and Dep. Governor, IOM, 1988– Chairman (all IOM): Criminal Injuries Compensation Tribunal, 1980–88; Licens Appeal Court, 1980–88; Prevention of Fraud (Unit Trust) Tribunal, 1980–88; Inco Tax Appeal Comrs, 1988–2007; Tynwald Ceremony Arrangements Cttee, 1988– Chairman: Manx Blind Welfare Soc.; Manx Workshop for the Disabled; Hon. Memb IOM Med. Soc.; IOM Law Soc.; President: IOM Br., Crossroads Care; Lon Dhoo M Voice Choir; IOM Br., SSAFA; IOM Alcohol Adv. Council; Manx Housing Tr Chm., Douglas Buxton Music Trust; Trustee, Manx Methodist Church; Patron: Smil for the Disabled; Cruse Bereavement Care (IOM). Freeman, Borough of Douglas, 19 Paul Harris Fellow, Rotary Internat., 2007. *Recreations:* music, gardening, bridge. *Addr* Carla Beck, 28 Devonshire Road, Douglas, Isle of Man IM2 3RB. *T:* (01624) 62180

CORRY; *see* Lowry-Corry, family name of Earl of Belmore.

CORRY, Viscount; John Armar Galbraith Lowry-Corry; *b* 2 Nov. 1985; *s* and of Earl of Belmore, *qv*. *Address:* The Garden House, Castle Coole, Enniskillen, N Irel BT74 6JY.

CORRY, Sir James (Michael), 5th Bt *cr* 1885, of Dunraven, co. Antrim; Manager, L Operations, BP Nederland VOF, Netherlands, 1992–2001; *b* 3 Oct. 1946; *e s* of William James Corry, 4th Bt and of Diana Pamela Mary Corry (*née* Lapsley); *S* fath 2000; *m* 1973, Sheridan Lorraine, *d* of A. P. Ashbourne; three *s*. *Educ:* Downside S Joined Shell-Mex and BP Ltd, 1966; British Petroleum Co. Ltd, 1976; BP Nederland 1992. *Recreations:* scuba diving, British Scouts. *Heir:* *s* William James Alexander Corry, Dec. 1981. *Address:* Chackeridge Cottage, Ashbrittle, Wellington, Somerset TA21 0LJ. (01823) 672993; *e-mail:* james.corry@btopenworld.com.

CORSAR, Col Charles Herbert Kenneth, LVO 1989; OBE 1981; TD 1960; retir Vice Lord-Lieutenant, Lothian Region (District of Midlothian), 1993–97; *b* 13 May 19 *s* of Kenneth Charles Corsar and Winifred Paton (*née* Herdman); *m* 1953, M Drummond Buchanan Smith (*see* Hon. Dame Mary Corsar); two *s* two *d* (and one *d* dec *Educ:* Merchiston Castle Sch.; King's Coll., Cambridge (MA). Farmer, 1953– Commnd Royal Scots TA, 1948; comd 8/9 Royal Scots, 1964–67; Edinburgh a Heriot-Watt Univs OTC, 1967–72; TA Col, 1972–75; Hon. ADC to the Que 1977–81; Chm., Lowland TAVRA, 1984–87; Hon. Col., 1/52 Lowland Vols, 1975– Zone Comr, Home Defence, E of Scotland, 1972–74. County Cllr, Midlothian, 1958– Vice-Pres., Boys' Brigade, 1970–91; Chairman: Scottish Standing Conf. of Volunt

Youth Orgns, 1973–78; Earl Haig Fund (Scotland), 1984–90; Mem., Scottish Sports Council, 1972–75; Secretary: Prince's Trust (Lothian & Borders), 1982–93; (for Scotland) Duke of Edinburgh's Award, 1966–87. JP Midlothian, 1964; DL Midlothian, 1975. *Recreation:* gardening. *Address:* Flat 4, 85 South Oswald Road, Edinburgh EH9 2HH. *T:* (0131) 662 0194. *Club:* New (Edinburgh).

CORSAR, Kenneth; Chairman, Lanarkshire NHS Board, since 2006 (non-executive Director, 2003–06); *b* 16 July 1946; *s* of Peter and Ruby Corsar; *m* 1972, Mary Massie; two *s*. *Educ:* Alloa Acad.; St Andrews Univ. (MA Hons 1968); Aberdeen Univ. (DipEd 1970); Aberdeen Coll. of Education (PGCE 1970); Glasgow Univ. (MEd Hons 1976). Teacher of Classics, Dumbarton Acad., 1970–71; Principal Teacher: Kirkintilloch High Sch., 1971–72; Uddingston Grammar Sch., 1972–75; Strathclyde Regional Council: Educn Officer, 1975–86; Sen. Educn Officer, 1986–88; Divl Educn Officer, 1988–93; Depute Dir of Educn, 1993–95; Dir of Educn, Glasgow CC, 1995–2002; Scottish Dir, Nat. Deaf Children's Soc., 2003–06. Advr, Scottish Exec. Educn Dept/COSLA, 2003. Vice-Pres., 1992–93, Pres., 1993–94, Assoc. of Dirs of Educn in Scotland. DUniv Glasgow, 2001. *Publications:* Discovering the Greeks, 1975; Discovering Greek Mythology, 1977; articles in educn press on educn and local govt. *Recreations:* golf, calligraphy, gardening. *Address:* 9 Eaglesfield Crescent, Strathaven, S Lanarks ML10 6HY. *T:* (01357) 520817. *Club:* Strathaven Golf.

CORSAR, Hon. Dame Mary (Drummond), DBE 1993; FRSE; Chairman: TSB Foundation Scotland, 1994–97 (Trustee, 1992–97); Women's Royal Voluntary Service, 1988–93; *b* 8 July 1927; *o d* of Lord Balerno, CBE, TD, DL and Mary Kathleen Smith; *m* 1953, Col Charles Herbert Kenneth Corsar, *qv*; two *s* two *d* (and one *d* decd). *Educ:* Westbourne, Glasgow; St Denis, Edinburgh; Edinburgh Univ. (MA Hons). Dep. Chief Comr, Girl Guides, Scotland, 1972–77; Chm., Scotland WRVS, 1981–88. Member: Vis. Cttee, Glenochil Young Offenders Instn, 1976–94; Parole Bd for Scotland, 1982–89. Hon. Pres., Scottish Women's AAA, 1973–91. Member: Exec. Cttee, Trefoil Centre for Handicapped, 1975–2002; Convocation, Heriot Watt Univ., 1986–96; Royal Anniversary Trust, 1990–93. Gov., Fettes Coll., 1984–99. FRSE 1997. *Recreations:* countryside, hill walking, knitting. *Address:* Flat 4, 85 South Oswald Road, Edinburgh EH9 2HN. *T:* (0131) 662 0194. *Clubs:* New (Edinburgh) (Associate Mem.); Scottish Ladies Climbing.

CORSTON, Baroness *cr* 2005 (Life Peer), of St George in the County and City of Bristol; **Jean Ann Corston;** PC 2003; *b* 5 May 1942; *d* of late Charles Lawrence Parkin and Eileen Ada Parkin; *m* 1st, 1961, Christopher John Davy Corston; one *s* one *d*; 2nd, 1985, Peter Brereton Townsend, *qv*. *Educ:* LSE (LLB 1989). Labour Party posts: Asst Regl Organiser, 1976, Regl Organiser, 1981, South West; Asst National Agent, London, 1985–86. Called to the Bar, Inner Temple, 1991; Bristol chambers. MP (Lab) Bristol East, 1992–2005 (sponsored by TGWU). PPS to Sec. of State for Educn and Employment, 1997–2001. Mem., Select Cttee on Agric., 1992–95, on Home Affairs, 1995–97. Chm., Jt Cttee on Human Rights, 2001–05; Co-Chm., PLP Women's Gp, 1992–97; Chairman: PLP Civil Liberties Gp, 1997–2005; PLP, 2001–05 (Dep. Chm., 1997–98 and 1999–2000; Mem., Parly Cttee, 1997–2005). Chm., Commonwealth Women Parliamentarians, 2000; Mem., Exec. Cttee, CPA, 1998–2005. *Recreations:* gardening, reading, walking. *Address:* House of Lords, SW1A 0PW.

CORTAZZI, Sir (Henry Arthur) Hugh, GCMG 1984 (KCMG 1980; CMG 1969); HM Diplomatic Service, retired; *b* 2 May 1924; *m* 1956, Elizabeth Esther Montagu; one *s* two *d*. *Educ:* Sedbergh Sch.; St Andrews and London Univs. Served in RAF, 1943–47; joined Foreign Office, 1949; Third Sec., Singapore, 1950–51; Third/Second Sec., Tokyo, 1951–54; FO, 1954–58; First Sec., Bonn, 1958–60; First Sec., later Head of Chancery, Tokyo, 1961–65; FO, 1965–66; Counsellor (Commercial), Tokyo, 1966–70; Royal Coll. of Defence Studies, 1971–72; Minister (Commercial), Washington, 1972–75; Dep. Under-Sec. of State, FCO, 1975–80; Ambassador to Japan, 1980–84. Director: Hill Samuel & Co., later Hill Samuel Bank, 1984–91; Foreign and Colonial Pacific Investment Trust, 1984–98; GT Japan Investment Trust plc, 1984–99. Senior Adviser: Mitsukoshi Ltd, 1984–; NEC Corp., Japan, 1992–98; Dai-ichi Kangyo Bank, Japan, 1992–99; Bank of Kyoto, 1992–99; Matsuura Machinery Corp., 1994–2000; Wilde Sapte, solicitors, 1992–99; PIFC, 1993–99. Mem., ESRC, 1984–89. Pres., Asiatic Soc. of Japan, 1982–83; Chm., Japan Soc., of London, 1985–95. Mem., Council and Court, Sussex Univ., 1985–92. Hon. Fellow, Robinson Coll., Cambridge, 1988. Hon. Dr Stirling, 1988; Hon. DLitt East Anglia. Yamagata Banto Prize, Osaka, 1991. Grand Cordon, Order of the Sacred Treasure (Japan), 1995. *Publications:* trans. from Japanese, Genji Keita: The Ogre and other stories of the Japanese Salarymen, 1972; The Guardian God of Golf and other humorous stories, 1972, reprinted as The Lucky One, 1980; (ed) Mary Crawford Fraser, A Diplomat's Wife in Japan: sketches at the turn of the century, 1982; Isles of Gold: antique maps of Japan, 1983; Higashi No Shimaguni, Nishi No Shimaguni (collection of articles and speeches in Japanese), 1984; Dr Willis in Japan, 1985; (ed) Mitford's Japan, 1985; Victorians in Japan: in and around the Treaty Ports, 1987; for Japanese students of English: Thoughts from a Sussex Garden (essays), 1984; Second Thoughts (essays), 1986; Japanese Encounter, 1987; Zoku, Higashi no Shimaguni, Nishi no Shimaguni, 1987; (ed with George Webb) Kipling's Japan, 1988; The Japanese Achievement: a short history of Japan and Japanese culture, 1990; (ed) A British Artist in Meiji Japan, by Sir Alfred East, 1991; (ed) Building Japan 1868–1876, by Richard Henry Brunton, 1991; (ed with Gordon Daniels) Britain and Japan 1859–1991, 1991; Themes and Personalities, 1991; Modern Japan: a concise survey, 1993; (ed with Terry Bennett) Caught in Time: Japan, 1995; Japan and Back and Places Elsewhere, 1998; Collected Writings, 2000; (compiled and ed) Japan Experiences: Fifty Years, One Hundred Views: post-war Japan through British eyes, 2001; (ed) Biographical Portraits of Anglo-Japanese Personalities, vol. IV, 2002, vol. V, 2004, vol. VI, 2007; (ed) British Envoys in Japan 1859–1972, 2004; trans., Crown Prince Naruhito: The Thames and I: a memoir of two years at Oxford, 2005; articles on Japanese themes in English and Japanese pubns. *Recreations:* Japanese studies, the arts including antiques, opera. *Address:* Ballsocks, Vines Cross, Heathfield, E Sussex TN21 9ET. *Club:* Royal Air Force.

CORVEDALE, Viscount; Benedict Alexander Stanley Baldwin; *b* 28 Dec. 1973; *s* and *heir* of 4th Earl Baldwin of Bewdley, *qv*. *Educ:* Newcastle Univ. (BMus 1996).

CORY, Sir (Clinton Charles) Donald, 5th Bt *cr* 1919, of Coryton, Whitchurch, Glamorgan; *b* 13 Sept. 1937; *s* of Sir Clinton James Donald Cory, 4th Bt and Mary, *o d* of Dr Arthur Douglas Hunt; *S* father, 1991. *Educ:* Brighton Coll.; abroad. *Recreations:* collecting Greek and Roman antiquities, student of classical studies. *Heir: kinsman* Douglas Richard Campbell Perkins Cory [*b* 5 May 1940; *m* 1965, Gillian Margaret Sherwood (*d* 2008); one *s* one *d*]. *Address:* 18 Cloisters Road, Letchworth Garden City, Herts SG6 3JS. *T:* (01462) 677206; PO Box 167, Mpemba, Malaŵi, Central Africa.

CORY, Prof. Suzanne, AC 1999; PhD; FRS 1992; FAA; Director, Walter and Eliza Hall Institute of Medical Research, since 1996; Professor of Medical Biology, University of Melbourne, since 1996; *b* 11 March 1942; *d* of Desmond and Joy Cory; *m* 1969, Prof. Jerry Adams; two *d*. *Educ:* Univ. of Melbourne (BSc, MSc); Wolfson Coll., Cambridge (PhD 1968; Hon. Fellow, 2000). Rothmans Fellow, Univ. of Geneva, 1969–71; Walter and Eliza Hall Institute of Medical Research, 1971–: Sen. Principal Res. Fellow, 1988–; Jt Head, Molecular Genetics of Cancer Div., 1988–2005. Internat. Res. Schol., Howard Hughes Med. Inst., 1992–97. FAA 1986. Foreign Mem., NAS, USA, 1997; Foreign Hon. Mem., Amer. Acad. of Arts and Scis, 2001; Assoc. Foreign Mem., French Acad. Sci., 2002; Academician, Pontifical Acad. of Scis, 2004; Assoc. Mem., EMBO, 2007. Hon. DSc: Sydney, 2000; Oxford, 2004. Lemberg Medal, Australian Soc. Biochem. and Molecular Biol., 1995; Burnet Medal, Australian Acad. Sci., 1997; (jtly) Australia Prize, 1998; (jtly) Charles S. Mott Prize, General Motors Cancer Res. Foundn, 1998; Women in Science Award, L'Oréal-UNESCO, 2001; Royal Medal, Royal Soc., 2002. *Publications:* numerous scientific papers and reviews. *Recreations:* camping, hiking, swimming, wilderness photography, ski-ing. *Address:* Walter and Eliza Hall Institute of Medical Research, 1G Royal Parade, Parkville, Vic 3050, Australia. *T:* (3) 93452551.

CORY-WRIGHT, Sir Richard (Michael), 4th Bt *cr* 1903; *b* 17 Jan. 1944; *s* of Capt. A. J. J. Cory-Wright (killed in action, 1944), and Susan Esterel (*d* 1993; she *m* 2nd, 1949, Lt-Col J. E. Gurney, DSO, MC), *d* of Robert Elwes; *S* grandfather, 1969; *m* 1st, 1976, Veronica Bolton (marr. diss. 1994); three *s*; 2nd, 1998, Helga Wright, *e d* of George Godfrey. *Educ:* Eton; Birmingham Univ. *Heir: s* Roland Anthony Cory-Wright, *b* 11 March 1979.

COSFORD, Paul Anthony, FFPHM; Regional Director of Public Health, East of England, Department of Health, since 2006; Medical Director, East of England Strategic Health Authority, since 2006; *b* 20 May 1963; *s* of Brian and Judith Cosford; *m* 2006, Dr Gillian Leng; two step *d*, and one *s* one *d* (and one *s* decd) from a previous marr. *Educ:* Exmouth Ch Primary Sch.; Exeter Sch.; St Mary's Hosp. Med. Sch., Univ. of London (BSc Hons 1984; MB BS (Hons in Pathol.) 1987); St George's Hosp. Med. Sch., Univ. of London (MSc Public Health 1994). MRCPsych 1991; MFPHM 1995, FFPHM 2001; Cert. of Completion of Specialist Trng 1996. Lectr and Hon. Registrar in Psychiatry, St Mary's Hosp. Med. Sch., 1990–92; Consultant in Public Health: Herts, 1996–97; Beds, 1997–2000; Dir of Public Health, Northants HA, 2000–02; Dir, Health Strategy and Public Health, Leics, Northants and Rutland Strategic HA, 2002–06. Hon. Sen. Lectr, Univ. of Leicester, 2005–; Hon. Sen. Fellow, Univ. of Cambridge, 2007–. *Publications:* contribs on health protection, screening and public health to learned jls. *Recreations:* amateur dramatics, golf, gardening, walking. *Address:* 3 Park Palings Walk, Haynes, Beds MK45 3PY; *e-mail:* paulcosford@doctors.org.uk.

COSGRAVE, Liam, SC; *b* April 1920; *s* of late William T. Cosgrave; *m* 1952, Vera Osborne; two *s* one *d*. *Educ:* Synge Street Christian Brothers; Castlenock College, Dublin; King's Inns. Served in Army during Emergency. Barrister-at-Law, 1943; Senior Counsel, 1958. Member, Dail Eireann, 1943–81; Chairman Public Accounts Committee, 1945; Parliamentary Secretary to Taoiseach and Minister for Industry and Commerce, 1948–51; Minister for External Affairs, 1954–57; Leader, Fine Gael Party, 1965–77; Taoiseach (Head of Govt of Ireland), 1973–77; Minister for Defence, 1976. Leader first delegation from Ireland to the UN Assembly, 1956. Hon. LLD: Duquesne Univ., Pittsburg, Pa, and St John's Univ., Brooklyn, 1956; de Paul Univ., Chicago, 1958; NUI, 1974; Dublin Univ., 1974. Knight Grand Cross of Pius IX, 1956. *Address:* Beechpark, Templeogue, Co. Dublin, Ireland.

COSGROVE, Rt Hon. Lady; Hazel Josephine Cosgrove, CBE 2004; PC 2003; a Senator of the College of Justice in Scotland, 1996–2006; *b* 12 Jan. 1946; *d* of late Moses Aron Aronson and Julia Tobias; *m* 1967, John Allan Cosgrove, dental surgeon; one *s* one *d*. *Educ:* Glasgow High Sch. for Girls; Univ. of Glasgow (LLB). Advocate at the Scottish Bar. Admitted to Fac. of Advocates, 1968; QC (Scot.) 1991; Standing Junior Counsel to Dept of Trade, 1977–79; Sheriff of Glasgow and Strathkelvin, 1979–83; Sheriff of Lothian and Borders at Edinburgh, 1983–96. Temporary Judge, High Court and Court of Session, Scotland, 1992–96. Mem., Parole Bd for Scotland, 1988–91; Chairman: Mental Welfare Commn for Scotland, 1991–96; Expert Panel on Sex Offending, Scotland, 1997–2001; Dep. Chm., Boundary Commn for Scotland, 1997–2006. Hon. Fellow, Harris Manchester Coll., Oxford, 2001. Hon. LLD: Napier, 1997; Glasgow, 2002; Strathclyde, 2002; St Andrews, 2003; DUniv Stirling, 2004. *Recreations:* foreign travel, opera, swimming, walking, reading, being a grandmother. *Address: e-mail:* hazelcosgrove@tiscali.co.uk.

COSGROVE, Brian Joseph; Joint Managing Director, Cosgrove Hall Films, 1995–2002; *b* 6 April 1934; *s* of Denis Cosgrove and Martha Cosgrove (*née* Hesketh); *m* 1963, Angela Helen Dyson; two *d*. *Educ:* Manchester Coll. of Art. Nat. Service, Army, 1952–54 (Malayan campaign). TV Graphic Designer, 1967–72; TV Programme Dir, 1972–76; Founder (with Mark Hall), Cosgrove Hall Productions, to produce animated films, 1976–95 (BAFTA Award, 1982, 1983, 1985, 1986, 1987, 2000, 2004; Prix Jeunesse, Munich Film Fest., 1982; Internat. Emmy, 1984, 1991; Prix Danube, Bratislava Film Fest., 1990; 2 Observer Children's Film Awards, 1990; RTS Award, 1999, 2002). Mem., MENSA. *Recreations:* writing, painting, sculpture, gardening. *Address:* Cosgrove Hall Films Ltd, 8 Albany Road, Chorlton-cum-Hardy, Manchester M21 0AW. *T:* (0161) 881 9211.

COSGROVE, Hazel Josephine; *see* Cosgrove, Rt Hon. Lady.

COSSHAM, Christopher Hugh, CB 1989; Senior Assistant Director of Public Prosecutions (Northern Ireland), 1973–89; *b* 12 April 1929; *s* of Lorimer and Gwendolin Cossham; *m* 1958, Joanna Howard Smith; one *s* one *d*. *Educ:* Monkton Combe Sch.; Bristol Univ.; BA Open Univ. Called to Bar, Gray's Inn, 1958. Board of Trade, 1958–62; Director of Public Prosecutions Dept, 1962–73. Dep. Metropolitan Stipendiary Magistrate, 1978–86. Mem., Wkg Party on handling of complaints against police, 1974. *Recreations:* cycling, listening to music, writing humorous verse. *Address:* Valhalla, 1 The Grange, High Street, Portishead, Bristol BS20 6QL. *T:* (01275) 845237. *Clubs:* Civil Service, Northern Law.

COSSONS, Sir Neil, Kt 1994; OBE 1982; Director, Science Museum, 1986–2000; Chairman, English Heritage, 2000–07; *b* 15 Jan. 1939; *s* of Arthur Cossons and Evelyn (*née* Bettle); *m* 1965, Veronica Edwards; two *s* one *d*. *Educ:* Henry Mellish Grammar Sch., Nottingham; Univ. of Liverpool (MA). FSA 1968; FMA 1970. Curator of Technology, Bristol City Museum, 1964; Dep. Dir, City of Liverpool Museums, 1969; Dir, Ironbridge Gorge Museum Trust, 1971; Dir, Nat. Maritime Mus., 1983–86. Comr, Historic Buildings and Monuments Commn for England (English Heritage), 1989–95, and 1999–2000 (Mem., Ancient Monuments Adv. Cttee, 1984–98); Chm., RCHME, 2000–03. Member: Curatorium Internat. Committee for the Conservation of the Industrial Heritage, 1973–78; BBC General Adv. Council, 1987–90; NEDO Tourism and Leisure Industries Sector Gp (formerly Leisure Industries EDC), 1987–90; Council, RCA, 1989– (Pro-Provost and Chm. of Council, 2007–); Design Council, 1990–94; Comité Scientifique, Conservatoire Nat. des Arts et Métiers, 1991–2000. President: Assoc. for Industrial Archaeology, 1977–80; Assoc. of Independent Museums, 1983– (Chm., 1978–83); Museums Assoc., 1981–82; ASE, 1996; RGS-IBG, 2003–06; Member, Council: Newcomen Soc. for Study of Hist. of Engrg and Technol., 1992–2006 (Mem.,

1963–; Pres., 2001–03); FMI, 1993–98. Mem., British Waterways Bd, 1995–2001. Trustee, Civic Trust, 1987–93. Gov., Imperial Coll. of Sci., Technology and Medicine, 1989–93. Collier Prof. in the Public Understanding of Sci., Univ. of Bristol, 2001–02. Hon. Prof., Univ. of Birmingham, 1994–. FRGS 1997; Hon. Fellow: RCA, 1987; BAAS, 2007; Hon. FRIBA 2002; Hon. FCIWEM 2002; Comp IEE, 1991; CCMI (CIMgt 1996); Hon. Mem., SCI, 2002; Hon. CRAeS 1996. Hon. DSocSc Birmingham, 1979; DUniv: Open, 1984; Sheffield Hallam, 1995; York, 1998; Hon. DLitt: Liverpool, 1989; Bradford, 1991; Nottingham Trent, 1994; UWE, 1995; Bath, 1997; Greenwich, 2004; Hon. DSc: Leicester, 1995; Nottingham, 2000; Hon. DArts De Montfort, 1997. Norton Medlicott Medal, Historical Assoc., 1991; President's Medal, Royal Acad. of Engrg, 1993; Dickinson Meml Medal, Newcomen Soc., 2001; Maitland Medal, IStructE, 2002. Series Editor, England's Landscape, 2006. *Publications:* (with R. A. Buchanan) Industrial Archaeology of the Bristol Region, 1968; (with K. Hudson) Industrial Archaeologists' Guide, 1969, 2nd edn 1971; Industrial Archaeology, 1975, 3rd edn 1993; (ed) Transactions of the First International Congress on the Conservation of Industrial Monuments, 1975; (ed) Rees's Manufacturing Industry, 1975; (with H. Sowden) Ironbridge—Landscape of Industry, 1977; (with B. S. Trinder) The Iron Bridge—Symbol of the Industrial Revolution, 1979, 2nd edn (Japanese) 1989, (English) 2002; (ed) Management of Change in Museums, 1985; (ed) Making of the Modern World, 1992; (ed) Perspectives on Industrial Archaeology, 2000; numerous papers, articles and reviews. *Recreations:* travel, design, industrial archaeology. *Address:* The Old Rectory, Rushbury, Shropshire SY6 7EB. *T:* (01694) 771603; *e-mail:* nc@cossons.org.uk. *Club:* Athenæum.

COSTA, António Maria, PhD; Executive Director, United Nations Office on Drugs and Crime, and Director-General, United Nations Office, Vienna, since 2002; *b* 16 June 1941; *s* of Francesco Costa and Maria (*née* Contratto); *m* 1971, Patricia Wallace; two *s* one *d*. *Educ:* Turin Univ. (degree in political sci. 1964); Acad. of Scis, Moscow (Math. Econs 1967); Univ. of Calif at Berkeley (MA Econs 1969; PhD Econs 1971). Sen. Economic Advr, UN, NY, 1971–83; Dep. Sec. Gen. (Special Counsellor), OECD, 1983–87; Dir Gen. for Econs and Finance, Special Advr to Pres., and Mem., Monetary Cttee, EU, Brussels, 1987–92; Dir Gen. for Strategic Planning, Ferrero Gp, 1992–93; Sec. Gen., EBRD, 1994–2002. Member: Wkg Party for Co-ordination of Macroeconomic Policies of G10 Countries, OECD; Bd of Dirs, EIB; EU Rapporteur to EP. Vis. Prof. of Econs, Moscow Univ. and Acad. of Scis, Moscow, 1963–64; Adjunct Professor of Economics: Univ. of Calif at Berkeley, 1968–70; CU NY, 1970–76; New York Univ., 1976–87; Vis. Prof., Free Univ., Brussels, 1990–94. *Address:* United Nations Office on Drugs and Crime, PO Box 500, 1400 Vienna, Austria.

COSTA, Kenneth Johann; Chairman, Lazard International, and Deputy Chairman, Lazard & Co., since 2007; *b* 31 Oct. 1949; *s* of late Joseph Costa and of Martha Costa; *m* 1982, Fiona Morgan-Williams; two *s* two *d*. *Educ:* Univ. of Witwatersrand (BA, LLB); Queens' Coll., Cambridge (LLM, Cert. in Theology). Joined S. G. Warburg, 1976, later SBC Warburg, then Warburg Dillon Read, subseq. UBS Warburg, then UBS Investment Bank: Dep. Chm., 1993; Chm., Investment Banking Bd, Hd of Global Mergers and Acquisitions, 1995; Vice-Chm., 1996–2007; Chm., Investment Banking for Europe, ME and Africa, 2004–07. Vice Chm., Redevelt Adv. Bd and Chm., Tick Tock Club, Gt Ormond Street Hosp.; Trustee, Nelson Mandela Children's Trust UK. Chm., Alpha Internat.; Church Warden, Holy Trinity, Brompton. *Publication:* God at Work, 2007. *Recreations:* country activities, conservation, music, theology. *Address:* Lazard International, 50 Stratton Street, W1J 8LL.

COSTA-LOBO, António; Ambassador of Portugal to the Court of St James's, 1995–97; *b* 22 May 1932; *s* of Gumersindo da Costa Lobo and Maria Magdalena Teixeira Leal da Costa Lobo; *m* 1980, Maria Catarina de Locher Machado. *Educ:* Univ. of Coimbra, Portugal (Law degree). Joined Ministry of Foreign Affairs, Portugal, 1956: served Havana, 1961–63; The Hague, 1964–66; Consul-Gen., San Francisco, 1966–70; Perm. Mission to UN, NY, 1973–77; Council of Europe, 1980–82; Ambassador to China, 1982–85; Perm. Mission, Geneva, 1985–90; Ambassador to Russia, 1990–93; Sec. Gen., Ministry of Foreign Affairs, 1993–95. Visiting Professor: Univ. Católica Portuguese, 1978–80 and 2001–; Univ. Técnica de Lisboa, 1998–2002; Lectr, Univ. Nova de Lisboa, 2003–. Grã-Cruz da Ordem do Infante Dom Henrique (Portugal), 1985; Grã-Cruz da Ordem Militar de Cristo (Portugal), 1997. *Publication:* As Operações de Paz das Nações Unidas, 1969. *Recreations:* reading, bridge, tennis. *Address:* Av. D. Nuno Álvares Pereira 41, 2765-261 Estoril, Portugal. *T:* and *Fax:* (21) 4680508; *e-mail:* acostalobo@netcabo.pt. *Club:* Grémio Literário (Lisbon).

COSTAIN, Janice Elizabeth; *see* Hall, J. E.

COSTAIN, Peter John, FCA; Deputy Chairman, Costain Group Plc, 1995–97 (Group Chief Executive, 1980–95); Director: Pearl Group, 1989–2005; London Life Ltd, 1994–2005; Hendersons (formerly AMP UK, then HHG) plc, 1994–2005; *b* 2 April 1938; *s* of Sir Albert Costain; *m* 1963, Victoria M. Pope; three *s*. *Educ:* Charterhouse. Peat Marwick Mitchell & Co., 1956–63; Richard Costain Ltd, 1963–65; Costain Australia Ltd, 1965–92: Board Member, 1967; Managing Director, 1971; Chief Executive, 1973. Dir, Wessex Water Services Ltd, 1999–. Mem., London Adv. Bd, Westpac Banking Corp., 1981–86. Mem. Bd, CITB, 1989–93. Chm., Tenterden Day Care Centre for the Disabled and Elderly. FAIB. Prime Warden, Basketmakers' Co., 1998–99. *Recreations:* sailing, ski-ing, golf. *Clubs:* Royal Thames Yacht; Athenæum (Melbourne); Rye Golf, Royal St George's Golf.

COSTANZI, Edwin J. B.; *see* Borg Costanzi.

COSTAS, John Peter; Head, Dillon Reed Capital Management LLC, 2005–07; *b* 27 Jan. 1957; *s* of Peter and Louise Costas; *m* 1981, Barbara Slinn. *Educ:* Univ. of Delaware (BA Pol Sci.); Tuck Sch. of Business, Dartmouth (MBA). Credit Suisse First Boston: Fixed Income Associate, 1981–96; Man. Dir, and Co-Head, Global Fixed Income, 1996–97; Sen. Man. Dir, and Co-Head, Global Fixed Income, Union Bank of Switzerland, 1997–98; UBS Warburg: Man. Dir, and Global Head, Fixed Income, Interest Rates, and Fixed Income and Treasury Products, 1998–99; Pres. and Chief Operating Officer, 1999–2001; CEO and Mem., Gp Exec. Bd, UBS AG, 2001–02; CEO, 2001–05, and Chm., 2002, UBS Investment Bank. *Address:* 677 Washington Boulevard, Stamford, CT 06901, USA. *T:* (203) 7193000, *Fax:* (203) 7195413. *Clubs:* Stanwich Golf (Greenwich, Conn); Lake George Sailing (Lake George, NY).

COSTELLO, Declan; President, High Court of the Republic of Ireland, 1995–98; *b* 1 Aug. 1926; *s* of John A. Costello and Ida (*née* O'Malley); *m* 1953, Joan Fitzsimms; three *s* two *d*. *Educ:* Xavier Sch., Dublin; University Coll., Dublin. King's Inns, Dublin; Called to the Bar, 1948; Inner Bar, 1965. TD (FG): Dublin NW, 1951–69; Dublin SW, 1973–77; Attorney-Gen., 1973–77; Judge of the High Court, 1977–95. Mem., Consultative Assembly, Council of Europe, 1957–63. Chairman: Nat. Youth Policy Cttee, Ireland, 1983; Cttee on Fund-raising for Charitable Purposes, Ireland, 1989. *Recreations:* tennis, reading, film-going. *Address:* 8 Eglinton Park, Dublin 4, Republic of Ireland. *T:* (1) 2697963. *Clubs:* St Stephen's Green (Dublin); Fitzwilliam Lawn Tennis (Dublin).

COSTELLO, Elvis; *see* McManus, D. P. A.

COSTELLO, John Francis, MD; FRCP, FRCPI; Consultant Physician: Cromwell Hospital, SW5, since 1983; London Clinic, since 2005; Board Member, Medicsight PLC, since 2003 (Medical Director, 2002–06); Chairman, Capital Hospitals Ltd, since 2006; *b* 22 Sept. 1944; *s* of late William and Sarah Costello; *m* 1972, Dr Christine Ellen McGregor White (marr. diss.); three *s*; *m* 1996, Susanna Clarke; two *s*. *Educ:* Belvedere Coll., Dublin; University Coll., Dublin (MB BCh, BAO Hons 1968; MD 1987). MRCP 1972, FRCP 1982; MRCPI 1995, FRCPI 1996. Hospital appts, Mater Hosp., Dublin, St Stephen's, and Royal Northern; RPMS, 1970–72; Registrar, Brompton Hosp., 1972–73; Lectr, Univ. of Edinburgh, Edinburgh Royal Infirmary, 1973–75; Asst Prof. of Medicine, and attending physician, Univ. of California, San Francisco, 1975–77; King's College Hospital: Consultant Physician, 1977–2003, now Hon. Consultant Physician; Chm. of Consultants, 1989–91; Med. Clinical Dir, Acute Services, 1989–93; Dir, Respiratory Medicine, King's Coll. Sch. of Medicine and Dentistry, 1982–98; Med. Dir, King's Healthcare NHS Trust, 1991–94; Dir of Medicine, King's Healthcare, subseq. KCH, NHS Trust, 1997–2003. Vis. Fellow, KCL, 2003–. Examr in Medicine, Conjoint Bd, 1979–83; Examr, MRCPI 2004–; Med. Vice Chm., SE Thames/S London Regl Cttee for Distinction Awards 1997–2002. Founder Pres., Respiratory Sect., RSocMed, 1991–93; Mem. Council, British Thoracic Soc., 1996. *Publications:* (ed jtly) Beta Agonists in the Treatment of Asthma, 1992; (ed) Methylxanthines and Phosphodiesterase Inhibitors, 1994; (jtly) A Colour Atlas of Lung Infections, 1996; (ed) Sympathomimetic Enantiomers in the Treatment of Asthma, 1997; (ed) Horizons in Medicine, 2002; papers, reviews and chapters on lung disease, esp. asthma, and early detection of lung cancer, bowel cancer and coronary heart disease. *Recreations:* opera, golf. *Address:* 12 Melville Avenue, Wimbledon SW20 0NS. *T:* (020) 8879 1309; *e-mail:* jfcostello@btinternet.com. *Clubs:* Reform; Roya[l] Wimbledon Golf, Portmarnock Golf (Dublin).

COSTELLO, Hon. Peter Howard; MP (L) for Higgins, Victoria, 1990–2007; Treasurer of Australia, 1996–2007; *b* 14 Aug. 1957; *s* of Russell and Anne Costello; *m* 1982, Tanya Pamela Coleman; one *s* two *d*. *Educ:* Carey Baptist Grammar Sch.; Monash Univ. (LLB Hons, BA). Solicitor, 1981–84; Barrister, 1984–90. Shadow Minister for Corporate Law Reform and Consumer Affairs, 1990–92; Shadow Attorney Gen. and Shadow Minister for Justice, 1992–93; Shadow Minister for Finance, 1993–94; Shadow Treasurer, 1994–96; Dep. Leader of Opposition, 1994–96; Dep. Leader, Liberal Party, 1994–2007. *Publication* (with P. Coleman) The Costello Memoirs, 2008. *Recreations:* swimming, football, reading. *Clubs:* Australian (Melbourne); Melbourne Cricket; Essendon Football.

COSTELOE, Prof. Michael Peter, PhD; FRHistS; Professor of Hispanic and Latin American Studies, University of Bristol, 1981–98, now Emeritus; *b* 12 March 1939; *s* of late John Myles Costeloe and of Etheleen Winifred Costeloe, Bishop Auckland; *m* 1962 Eleanor, *d* of late William and Margaret Bonney; one *d*. *Educ:* King James I Grammar Sch. Bishop Auckland; Univ. of Durham (BA 1961); Univ. of Newcastle (DipEd 1962; PhD 1965). FRHistS 1976. University of Bristol: Asst Lectr and Lectr in Latin American Studies, 1965–76; Reader, 1976–81; Dean of Arts, 1993–96. Vis. Prof., Univ. of Texas 1967. Corresp. Fellow, Acad. Mexicana de la Historia, 1995. *Publications:* Church Wealth in Mexico, 1967; (ed and trans.) Alienation of Church Wealth in Mexico, by J. Bazant 1971; (with C. Steele) Independent Mexico, 1973; La primera república federal de Mexico, 1975; Mexico State Papers, 1976; Response to Revolution: Imperial Spain and the Spanish American Revolutions, 1986; The Central Republic in Mexico 1835–1846 1993; Bonds and Bondholders: British investors and Mexico's foreign debt 1824–1888 2003. *Recreations:* Anthony Trollope, golf. *Address:* Department of Hispanic Studies University of Bristol, 15 Woodland Road, Bristol BS8 1TE. *T:* (0117) 928 7496. *Club* Henbury Golf.

COTILL, John Atrill T.; *see* Templeton-Cotill.

COTRAN, His Honour Eugene, LLD; a Circuit Judge, 1992–2007; *b* Jerusalem Palestine, 6 Aug. 1938; *s* of Michael Cotran and Hassiba (*née* Khoury); *m* 1963, Christian Avierino; three *s* one *d*. *Educ:* Victoria Coll., Alexandria, Egypt; Univ. of Leeds (LLB LLM 1958); Trinity Hall, Univ. of Cambridge (Dip. Internat. Law 1959); LLD London 1971. FCIArb. Called to the Bar, Lincoln's Inn, 1959. Res. Officer in African Law, SOAS Univ. of London, 1960–63, Lectr, 1963–77; practised at the Bar, 1963–92; Law Com[m] Kenya, 1967–68; High Court Judge, Kenya, 1977–82; a Recorder, 1989–92. Vis. Prof. o[f] Law and Chm., Centre for Islamic and ME Law, SOAS, 1987–. Internat. and Chartere[d] Arbitrator, Internat. Court of Arbitration, Paris and London, 1985–92; Legal Mem Immigration Appeal Tribunal, 1997–2003. Vice Pres., Med. Aid for Palestinians, 1996– Mem. Bd, Palestinian Ind. Commn for Citizens Rights, 1994–. Gen. Editor, Yearbook o[f] Islamic and Middle Eastern Law, 1994–; Jt Editor, CIMEL Book Series, 1994– *Publications:* Restatement of African Law, Kenya: Vol. I, Marriage and Divorce, Vol. I[I] Succession, 1968; Casebook on Kenya Customary Law, 1987; Butterworth's Immigratio[n] Law Service, 1991; edited jointly: The Role of the Judiciary in the Protection of Huma[n] Rights, 1997; Democracy, the Rule of Law and Islam, 1999; The Palestinian Exodu[s] 1948–1998, 1999; The Rule of Law in the Middle East and the Islamic World: huma[n] rights and the judicial process, 2000; articles in internat. law jls and African law jl[s] *Recreations:* horse-racing, swimming, bridge. *Address:* 32 Gloucester Road, Acton, W[3] 8PD. *T:* (020) 8992 0432, *Fax:* (020) 8992 7228.

COTRUBAS, Ileana, (Mme Manfred Ramin); opera singer, retired 1990; *b* Rumani[a] *d* of Vasile and Maria Cotrubas; *m* 1972, Manfred Ramin. *Educ:* Conservatorul Cipria[n] Porumbescu, Bucharest. Opera and concert engagements all over Europe, N America an[d] Japan. Formerly permanent guest at Royal Opera House, Covent Garden; Membe[r] Vienna State Opera (Hon. Mem., 1991); also frequently sang in Scala, Milan, Munich Berlin, Paris, Chicago, NY Metropolitan Opera. Main operatic roles: Susanna, Pamin[a] Gilda, Traviata, Manon, Tatyana, Mimi, Melisande, Amina, Elisabetta, Nedd[a] Marguerite. Has made numerous recordings. Hon. Citizen, Bucharest, 199[…] Kammersängerin, Austria, 1981; Grand Officer: Sant Iago da Espada (Portugal), 199[…] Steaua României (Romania), 2000. *Publication:* Opernwahrheiten, 1998.

COTTAM, Harold; Founding Partner, Investor Relations Development LLP, 2002–0[…] *b* 12 Oct. 1938; *s* of Rev. Canon Frank and Elizabeth Cottam; *m* 1962, Lyn Minton; tw[o] *d*. *Educ:* Bedford School. FCA. Deloitte & Co., Tanganyika and Peru, 1960–64; Smi[th] Kline UK, 1964–66; Simon Engineering Group, Spain, 1966–68; Ernst & Whinne[y] subseq. Ernst & Young, 1968–92; UK Man. Partner, 1987–92; Chairman: Ernst & Youn[g] Case Services (Internat.), 1992–93; Ernst & Young Pan-European Consulting G[p] 1992–93; Haden MacLellan Hldgs, 1992–97; Anglo United (Coalite Product[s] Charrington and Falkland Is Gp), 1993–96; Rebus Gp, 1996–99; Britannic plc, subse[q] Britannic Gp plc, 1996–2004. Dir, Allied Colloids Gp, 1992–97. *Recreations:* piano, oper[a] tennis. *Address:* 8a Burton Mews, SW1W 9EP.

COTTAM, Maj.-Gen. Nicholas Jeremy, CB 2007; OBE 1990; Reserve Forces Stu[d]y Team Leader, since 2008; *b* 17 Feb. 1951; *s* of late Brig. H. W. Donald Cottam, OBE an[d] Diana Cottam; *m* 1982, Susan Habberfield-Bateman; one *s* one *d*. *Educ:* Univ. of Durha[m]

(BA Hons). Commnd Royal Green Jackets, 1973: CO, 2nd RGJ, 1990–93 (despatches 1993); Comd, 8th Inf. Bde, 1995–96; rcds 1997; Director: Intelligence, MoD, 1998–2000; Personal Services (Army), MoD, 2000–02; GOC 5th Div., 2003–05; Mil. Sec., 2005–08. Col Comdt, 2nd RGJ, 2002–07. *Recreation:* mountaineering. *Address:* c/o Regimental Headquarters The Rifles, Peninsula Barracks, Winchester, Hants SO23 8TS. *Club:* Alpine.

COTTELL, Michael Norman Tizard, OBE 1988; FREng; FICE, FIHT; Chairman and Executive Director, Aspen Consultancy Group, 1996–2001; President, Institution of Civil Engineers, 1992–93; *b* 25 July 1931; *s* of late Norman James Cottell and Eileen Clare Cottell (*née* Tizard); *m* 1957, Joan Florence Dolton; two *s*. *Educ:* Peter Symonds Sch., Winchester; University Coll., Southampton. CEng, FREng (FEng 1990); FIHT 1954; MICE 1958, FICE 1976; MASCE 1990. Trainee Civil Engr, Hants CC, 1949–51; Nat. Service, RE, Malaya and Suez, 1951–53, 1956; Engineering Assistant: Glos CC, 1954–57; Northants CC, 1957–58; Resident Engr, Oxford Western Bypass, 1958–61; Project Engr, M4 Motorway, Glos, 1961–67; Asst County Surveyor, Suffolk CC, 1967–73; Dep. County Surveyor, E Sussex CC, 1973–76; County Surveyor: Northants CC, 1976–84; Kent CC, 1984–91. Exec. Consultant, Travers Morgan, 1991–95. Trustee: Rees Jeffries Road Fund, 1991–; ICE Pensions Funds, 1995–. Lt-Col, RE & Logistics Staff Corps (TA), 1992–. MCMI 1971. *Recreations:* golf, swimming, walking, theatre, jazz, travel, viewing historic buildings, as a spectator keen on most sports. *Address:* Salcey Lawn, Harrow Court, Stockbury, Kent ME9 7UQ. *Clubs:* Athenæum, Royal Automobile.

COTTENHAM, 9th Earl of, *cr* 1850; **Mark John Henry Pepys;** Bt 1784 and 1801; Baron Cottenham 1836; Viscount Crowhurst 1850; *b* 11 Oct. 1983; *s* of 8th Earl of Cottenham; *S* father, 2000. *Educ:* Eton. *Heir: b* Hon. Sam Richard Pepys, *b* 26 April 1986.

COTTER, family name of **Baron Cotter**.

COTTER, Baron *cr* 2006 (Life Peer), of Congresbury in the County of Somerset; **Brian Joseph Michael Cotter;** campaigner on fair trade and overseas development issues; *b* 24 Aug. 1936; *s* of Michael Joseph Cotter and Mary Cotter; *m* 1963, Eyleen Patricia Wade; two *s* one *d*. *Educ:* Downside Sch., Somerset. Sales Manager, then Man. Dir, Plasticable Ltd, 1989–2003. MP (Lib Dem) Weston-super-Mare, 1997–2005; contested (Lib Dem) same seat, 2005. Lib Dem spokesman on small businesses, 1997–2005. Nat. Patron, SURF (charity for Rwandan widows), 1998–. *Recreations:* reading, gardening, films. *Address:* Belmont House, Brinsea Road, Congresbury, Som BS49 5JF. *T:* (01934) 832755; House of Lords, SW1A 0PW. *Club:* National Liberal.

COTTER, Barry Paul; QC 2006; a Recorder, since 2002; *b* 30 July 1963; *s* of Austin and Angela Cotter; *m* 1996, Catherine Maskell; one *s* two *d*. *Educ:* St Theresa's Primary Sch., St Helens; West Park High Sch., St Helens; University Coll. London (LLB 1984). Called to the Bar, Lincoln's Inn, 1985; Dep. Hd, Old Sq. Chambers, 2003–. Mem. Cttee, Personal Injury Bar Assoc., 1995–99 and 2001–03. *Publications:* Cotter: Defective and Unsafe Products: Law and Practice, 1996; (Gen. Ed.) Munkman on Employer's Liability, 14th edn 2006. *Recreations:* family life, being in Holford, walking, Rugby. *Address:* Old Square Chambers, 10–11 Bedford Row, WC1R 4BU. *T:* (020) 7269 0300, *Fax:* (020) 7269 5210; *e-mail:* cotterqc@oldsquare.co.uk.

COTTER, Sir Patrick Laurence Delaval, 7th Bt *cr* 1763, of Rockforest, Cork; *b* 21 Nov. 1941; *s* of Laurence Stopford Llewelyn Cotter; *S* uncle, 2001; *m* 1967, Janet, *d* of George Potter, Barnstaple; one *s* two *d*. *Educ:* Blundell's; RAC Cirencester. *Heir: s* Julius Laurence George Cotter, *b* 5 Jan. 1968.

COTTER, Suzanne Maree; Deputy Director and Senior Curator, Modern Art Oxford, since 2008; *b* Melbourne, Australia, 20 April 1961; *d* of James and Elaine Cotter; *m* 1987, Bruce Manson. *Educ:* Star of the Sea High Sch., Southport, Qld; Queensland Inst. of Technol., Brisbane (Dip. Applied Sci. 1981); Univ. of Melbourne; École du Louvre, Paris (Dip. du Premier Cycle 1994); Courtauld Inst. of Art (MA 1995); City Univ. (Post-grad. Dip. Cultural Leadership 2007). Asst to Australian Cultural Attaché, Paris, 1991–94; Exhibn Organiser, Serpentine Gall., London, 1996–98; Curator, Whitechapel Gall., London, 1998; Exhibns Curator, Hayward Gall., London, 1998–2002; Sen. Curator, Modern Art Oxford, 2002–07. Ext. Examr, MA in Contemp. Curator, RCA, 2007–. Trustee: Paris Calling charity, 2005–; Peer, London, 2005–. Judge, Turner Prize, 2008. FRSA 2005. Chevalier, Ordre des Arts et des Lettres (France), 2005. *Publications:* (ed) Vox Populi, by Fiona Tan, 2006; exhibn catalogues. *Recreations:* tennis, ski-ing, swimming, reading, theatre, films, art. *Address:* Modern Art Oxford, 30 Pembroke Street, Oxford OX1 1BP. *T:* (01865) 813822, *Fax:* (01865) 722573; *e-mail:* suzanne.cotter@modernartoxford.org.uk.

COTTERELL, Geoffrey; author; *b* 24 Nov. 1919; *yr s* of late Graham Cotterell and Millicent (*née* Crews). *Educ:* Bishops Stortford College. Served War of 1939–45, Royal Artillery, 1940–46. *Publications:* Then a Soldier, 1944; This is the Way, 1947; Randle in Springtime, 1949; Strait and Narrow, 1950; Westward the Sun, 1952 (repr. 1973); The Strange Enchantment, 1956 (repr. 1973); Tea at Shadow Creek, 1958; Tiara Tahiti, 1960 (filmed 1962, screenplay with Ivan Foxwell); Go, said the bird, 1966; Bowers of Innocence, 1970; Amsterdam, the life of a city, 1972. *Recreation:* golf. *Address:* 2 Fulbourne House, Blackwater Road, Eastbourne, Sussex BN20 7DN. *Clubs:* Royal Automobile; Cooden Beach Golf.

COTTERELL, Sir John (Henry Geers), 6th Bt *cr* 1805; Vice Lord-Lieutenant, Herefordshire, since 1998; Chairman: Radio Wyvern, 1980–97; Herefordshire Community Health NHS Trust, 1991–97; *b* 8 May 1935; *s* of Sir Richard Charles Geers Cotterell, 5th Bt, CBE, and Lady Lettice Cotterell (*d* 1973), *d* of 7th Earl Beauchamp; *S* father, 1978; *m* 1959, Vanda Alexandra Clare (MBE 1997) (*d* 2005), *d* of Major Philip Alexander Clement Bridgewater; three *s* one *d*. *Educ:* Eton; RMA Sandhurst. Officer, Royal Horse Guards, 1955–61. Vice-Chm. Hereford and Worcs CC, 1973–77, Chm., 1977–81. Pres., Nat. Fedn of Young Farmers Clubs, 1986–91 (Dep. Pres., 1979–86); Mem., Jockey Club, 1990–. Chairman: Hereford Mappa Mundi Trust, 1990–; Rural Voice, 1991–92. *Recreations:* cricket, shooting. *Heir: s* Henry Richard Geers Cotterell [*b* 22 Aug. 1961; *m* 1st, 1986, Carolyn (*d* 1999), *er d* of John Beckwith-Smith, Maybanks Manor, Rudgwick, Sussex; two *s* one *d*; 2nd, 2002, Katherine Bromley; one *s*]. *Address:* Downshill House, Bishopstone, Herefordshire HR4 7JT. *T:* (01981) 590232. *Club:* Turf.

COTTERILL, Kenneth William, CMG 1976; Chairman, Commercial and Political Risk Consultants Ltd, 1986–98 (Deputy Chairman, 1981–86); *b* 5 June 1921; *s* of William and Ada May Cotterill; *m* 1948, Janet Hilda Cox; one *d*. *Educ:* Sutton County Sch.; London School of Economics, BSc (Econ). Served War in Royal Navy, 1941–46. After the war, joined ECGD; Principal, 1956; Asst Sec., 1966; Under Sec., 1970; Dep. Head of Dept, 1976–81. Dir, Tarmac Internat., 1981–86; Consultant: NEI International, 1981–87; Barclays Bank, 1981–87. *Recreations:* reading, walking, gardening. *Address:* 15 Minster Drive, Croydon CR0 5UP. *T:* (020) 8681 6700.

COTTERRELL, Prof. Roger Brian Melvyn, LLD; FBA 2005; Anniversary Professor of Legal Theory, Queen Mary, University of London, since 2005; *b* 30 Nov. 1946; *s* of Walter Leslie Cotterrell and Hilda Margaret Cotterrell (*née* Randle); *m* 1969, Ann Zillah Poyner; one *s* one *d*. *Educ:* King Edward VI Camp Hill Sch., Birmingham; University Coll. London (LLB 1968; LLM 1969); Birkbeck Coll., Univ. of London (MScSoc 1977); LLD London 1988. Lectr in Law, Univ. of Leicester, 1969–74; Queen Mary College, then Queen Mary and Westfield College, subseq. Queen Mary, University of London: Lectr in Law, 1974–78; Sen. Lectr in Law, 1978–85; Reader in Legal Theory, 1985–90; Prof. of Legal Theory, 1990–2005; Actg Hd, 1989–90, Hd, 1990–91, Dept of Law; Dean, Faculty of Laws, 1993–96. Vis. Prof. and Jay H. Brown Centennial Faculty Fellow in Law, Univ. of Texas, Austin, 1989; George Lurcy Lectr, Amherst Coll., Mass, 1989; Visiting Professor: Univ. of Lund, 1996; Katholiek Univ. Brussel and Facultés Universitaires St Louis, Brussels, 1996, 1997; Internat. Inst. for the Sociol. of Law, Onati, Spain, 2003, 2004. Mem., Cttee of Hds of Univ. Law Schs, 1993–96. Mem., Law Panel, RAE, 1999–2001, 2005–08. Trustee, 1996–99, Chm., Articles Prize Cttee, 1999–2000, Law and Soc. Assoc. Mem. Ct, Univ. of Leicester, 2000–03. *Publications:* The Sociology of Law: an introduction, 1984 (trans. Chinese, 1989, Spanish, 1991, Korean, 1992), 2nd edn 1992 (trans. Lithuanian, 1997); (ed jtly) Law, Democracy and Social Justice, 1988; The Politics of Jurisprudence: a critical introduction to legal philosophy, 1989, 2nd edn 2003; (ed) Law and Society, 1994; (ed) Process and Substance: Butterworth lectures on comparative law, 1994; Law's Community: legal theory in sociological perspective, 1995; Emile Durkheim: law in a moral domain, 1999; (ed) Sociological Perspectives on Law, 2 vols, 2001; (with Coleridge Goode) Bass Lines: a life in jazz, 2002; Law, Culture and Society: legal ideas in the mirror of social theory, 2006; (ed) Law in Social Theory, 2006; Living Law: studies in legal and social theory, 2008; contribs to symposia and jls on law, social sci. and phil. *Recreations:* listening to and writing about music, exploring cities, European cinema. *Address:* Law School, Queen Mary, University of London, Mile End Road, E1 4NS. *T:* (020) 7882 5142, *Fax:* (020) 8981 8733; *e-mail:* r.b.m.cotterrell@qmul.ac.uk.

COTTESLOE, 5th Baron (UK) *cr* 1874; **Comdr John Tapling Fremantle,** RN (retired); JP; DL; Bt 1821; Baron of Austrian Empire 1816; Lord-Lieutenant of Buckinghamshire, 1984–97; *b* 22 Jan. 1927; *s* of 4th Baron Cottesloe, GBE and his 1st wife, Lady Elizabeth Harris (*d* 1983), *o d* of 5th Earl of Malmesbury; *S* father, 1994; *m* 1958, Elizabeth Ann, *e d* of late Lt-Col H. S. Barker, DSO; one *s* two *d*. *Educ:* Summer Fields, Hastings; Eton College. Joined RN, 1944; CO HMS Palliser, 1959–61; retired at own request, 1966. Governor, Stowe School, 1983–89. Chm., Radcliffe Trust, 1997–2006 (Trustee, 1983–). Vice President: British Assoc. for Shooting and Conservation, 1975–; Hospital Saving Assoc., 1979–2001; Bucks County Agricl Assoc., 1988–; Bucks Guide Assoc., 1996–; Bucks Fedn of Young Farmers' Clubs, 1997–2000 (Trustee, 1985–96); Dep. Pres., RASE, 1995–96; President: Bucks Br., CLA, 1983–97; HMS Concord Assoc., 1984–; Bucks Assoc. for the Blind, 1997– (Trustee, 1984–96); Bucks Farming and Wildlife Adv. Gp, 1997–2000; Bucks County Rifle Assoc.; Chm., Oxon Bucks Div., Royal Forestry Soc., 1981–83. Councillor, Winslow RDC, 1971–74; Hon. Treas., Aylesbury Vale Assoc. of Local Councils, 1974–84. Patron: RN Assoc. Aylesbury (No 1) Br.; Ferris Foundn. High Sheriff, 1969–70, JP 1984, DL 1978–84, 1997, Bucks. KStJ 1984. DUniv Buckingham, 1993. *Recreations:* shooting, crosswords, steam railways, Sherlock Holmes. *Heir: s* Hon. Thomas Francis Henry Fremantle, *b* 17 March 1966. *Address:* Athawes Farm House, 15 Nearton End, Swanbourne, Milton Keynes, Bucks MK17 0SL. *T:* (home) (01296) 720263, *T:* and *Fax:* (office) (01296) 720256. *Club:* Travellers.

See also Rt Hon. G. I. Duncan Smith.

COTTHAM, (George) William; Chairman, CentreWest London Buses Ltd, 1995–97; *b* 11 July 1944; *s* of George William and Elizabeth Cottham; *m* 1967, Joan Thomas; two *d*. *Educ:* Univ. of London; Polytechnic of Liverpool; Liverpool Coll. of Commerce. BSc 1st Cl. Hons, LLB 2nd Cl. Hons. FCILT. Various posts, Liverpool City Transport, 1960–74; District Transport Manager, St Helens, 1974–77; Transport General Manager, Newport, 1977–80; Gen. Manager, Cleveland Transit, 1980–83; Dir Gen., W Yorks PTE, 1983–86; Chairman and Managing Director: Yorkshire Rider, 1986–94; Rider Hldgs, 1988–94; Rider York, 1990–94. *Recreations:* family, home, garden, music, photography. *Address:* Bismarckia, 1438 Palm Grove Villas, Four Seasons Resort Estates, Nevis, West Indies; Vila Fonte, Algarve, Portugal; Naples Lakes, Naples, FL 34112, USA.

COTTINGHAM, Barrie, FCA; Chairman: SIG plc, 1993–2004; Cattles plc, 1995–2006; *b* 5 Oct. 1933; *s* of John and Eleanor Cottingham; *m* 1957, Kathleen Morton; one *s* (and one *d* decd). *Educ:* Carfield Sch. ATII. Coopers & Lybrand: joined, 1957; partner, 1964–95; Exec. Partner, i/c Regl Practice, 1986–93; Mem. UK Bd, 1974–93. Dep. Chm., Dew Pitchmastic plc, 1997–2005; non-exec. Dir, VP plc, 1996–. Pres., Sheffield and District, Soc. of Chartered Accountants, 1964. *Recreations:* squash, golf, watching Rugby and soccer, theatre, opera. *Address:* Waterstones, 2 Beckside, Cawthorne, Barnsley S75 4EP. *T:* (01226) 791395, *Fax:* (01226) 791506.

COTTON; *see* Stapleton-Cotton, family name of Viscount Combermere.

COTTON, Diana Rosemary, (Mrs R. B. Allan); QC 1983; a Recorder, since 1982; *b* 30 Nov. 1941; *d* of Arthur Frank Edward and Muriel Cotton; *m* 1966, Richard Bellerby Allan; two *s* one *d*. *Educ:* Berkhamsted School for Girls; Lady Margaret Hall, Oxford (MA). Joined Middle Temple, 1961; called to Bar, 1964; Bencher, 1990; Member, Midland Circuit; a Dep. High Ct Judge, 1993–. Member: Criminal Injuries Compensation Bd, 1989–2000; Criminal Injuries Compensation Appeal Panel, 1996–; Pres., Mental Health Ind. Rev. Tribunal for restricted patients, 1997–; Asst Boundary Comr, 2000–05. *Recreation:* her family and other animals. *Address:* Devereux Chambers, Devereux Court, Temple, WC2R 3JH. *T:* (020) 7353 7534. *Club:* Western (Glasgow).

COTTON, Jane Catherine; Human Resources Director, Oxfam, since 1999; *b* 10 Jan. 1959; *d* of Tony and Jean Alderson; *m* 1980, Stephen Paul Cotton. *Educ:* Girton Coll., Cambridge (MA). Department of Transport: graduate trainee posts, 1979–83; Aviation Policy, 1983–88; Personnel, 1989–92; Railways Policy/Finances, 1992–93; Hd of Resources, Charity Commn, 1993–96; Sec. to Board, Dept of Transport, 1996–97; Personnel Dir, DETR, 1997–99. *Recreations:* gardening, walking, football (spectator), theatre. *Address:* Oxfam, Oxfam House, John Smith Drive, Cowley, Oxford OX4 2JY.

COTTON, His Honour John Anthony; a Circuit Judge, 1973–93; *b* 6 March 1926; *s* of Frederick Thomas Hooley Cotton and Catherine Mary Cotton; *m* 1960, Johanna Aritia van Lookeren Campagne; three *s* two *d*. *Educ:* Stonyhurst Coll.; Lincoln Coll., Oxford. Called to the Bar, Middle Temple, 1949; Dep. Chm., W Riding of Yorks QS, 1967–71; Recorder of Halifax, 1971; a Recorder and Hon. Recorder of Halifax, 1972–73. Mem., Parole Bd, 1995–2001. *Recreation:* golf. *Address:* Myrtle Garth, Rossett Beck Close, Harrogate HG2 9NU.

COTTON, Richard Selkirk; Senior Partner, Cluttons LLP, since 2003; Director, Cluttons Private Finance Ltd; *b* 29 March 1947; *s* of Albert George Cotton and Vera May Cotton. *Educ:* Coll. of Estate Mgt (BSc (Estate Mgt) London); Wye Coll., London Univ. (Dip. Farm Business Admin). Partner, Cluttons, 1976. Member: British-Saudi Jt Trade Bd, 2005–; Oman Business Council, 2006–. Chm., UAE Br., 1980–83, Mem., Brooke Rev.

Cttee, 2004, RICS. Mem., Chartered Surveyors' Co., 1997– (Master, 2006–07). *Recreations:* tennis, walking, bridge, travel, theatre. *Address:* Cluttons, Portman House, 2 Portman Street, W1H 6DU; *e-mail:* richard.cotton@cluttons.com; 21C Sunderland Terrace, W2 5PA. *T:* (020) 7727 0313, *Fax:* (020) 7647 7076.

COTTRELL, Sir Alan (Howard), Kt 1971; FRS 1955; FREng; Master of Jesus College, Cambridge, 1974–86 (Hon. Fellow 1986); Vice-Chancellor, University of Cambridge, 1977–79; *b* 17 July 1919; *s* of Albert and Elizabeth Cottrell; *m* 1944, Jean Elizabeth Harber (*d* 1999); one *s. Educ:* Moseley Grammar Sch.; University of Birmingham. BSc 1939; PhD 1942; ScD(Cantab) 1976. Lectr in Metallurgy, University of Birmingham, 1943–49; Prof. of Physical Metallurgy, University of Birmingham, 1949–55; Deputy Head of Metallurgy Division, Atomic Energy Research Establishment, Harwell, Berks, 1955–58; Goldsmiths' Prof. of Metallurgy, Cambridge Univ., 1958–65; Fellow of Christ's Coll., Cambridge, 1958–70, Hon. Fellow, 1970; Dep. Chief Scientific Adviser (Studies), Min. of Defence, 1965–67, Chief Adviser, 1967; Dep. Chief Scientific Advr to HM Govt, 1968–71, Chief Scientific Advr, 1971–74. Part-time Mem., UKAEA, 1962–65, 1983–87; Member: Adv. Council on Scientific Policy, 1963–64; Central Adv. Council for Science and Technology, 1967–; Exec. Cttee, British Council, 1974–87; Adv. Council, Science Policy Foundn, 1976–; Security Commn, 1981–92. Dir, Fisons plc, 1979–90. A Vice-Pres., Royal Society, 1964, 1976, 1977. Foreign Hon. Mem., American Academy of Arts and Sciences, 1960; Foreign Associate: Nat. Acad. of Sciences, USA, 1972; Nat. Acad. of Engrg, USA, 1976; Mem., Academia Europaea, 1991–; Hon. Member: Amer. Soc. for Metals, 1972 (Fellow, 1974); Metals Soc., 1977 (Hon. FIM 1989, Hon. FIMMM); Japan Inst. of Metals, 1981. FIC 1991; FREng (FEng 1979); Fellow, Royal Swedish Acad. of Scis; Hon. Fellow, Internat. Congress on Fracture, 1985–. Hon. DSc: Columbia Univ., 1965; Newcastle Univ., 1967; Liverpool Univ., 1969; Manchester, 1970; Warwick, 1971; Sussex, 1972; Bath, 1973; Strathclyde, 1975; Cranfield, 1975; Aston, 1975; Oxford, 1979; Birmingham, 1983; DUniv Essex, 1982; Hon. DEng Tech. Univ. of Nova Scotia, 1984; Hon. LLD Cantab, 1996. Rosenhain Medallist of the Inst. of Metals; Hughes Medal, 1961, Rumford Medal, 1974, Copley Medal, 1996, Royal Society; Inst. of Metals (Platinum) Medal, 1965; Réaumur Medal, Société Française de Métallurgie, 1964; James Alfred Ewing Medal, ICE, 1967; Holweck Medal, Société Française de Physique, 1969; Albert Sauveur Achievement Award, Amer. Soc. for Metals, 1969; James Douglas Gold Medal, Amer. Inst. of Mining, Metallurgy and Petroleum Engrs, 1974; Harvey Science Prize, Technion Israel Inst., 1974; Acta Metallurgica Gold Medal, 1976; Guthrie Medal and Prize, Inst. of Physics, 1977; Gold Medal, Amer. Soc. for Metals, 1980; Brinell Medal, Royal Swedish Acad. of Engrg Sciences, 1980; Kelvin Medal, ICE, 1986; Hollomon Award, Acta Metallurgica, 1991; Von Hippel Award, Materials Res. Soc., 1996. *Publications:* Theoretical Structural Metallurgy, 1948, 2nd edn 1955; Dislocations and Plastic Flow in Crystals, 1953; The Mechanical Properties of Matter, 1964; Theory of Crystal Dislocations, 1964; An Introduction to Metallurgy, 1967; Portrait of Nature, 1975; Environmental Economics, 1978; How Safe is Nuclear Energy?, 1981; Introduction to the Modern Theory of Metals, 1988; Chemical Bonding in Transition Metal Carbides, 1995; Concepts in the Electron Theory of Alloys, 1998; scientific papers to various learned journals. *Recreations:* music, reading. *Address:* 40 Maids Causeway, Cambridge CB5 8DD. *T:* (01223) 363806.

COTTRELL, Peter John Waraker, AO 1987; OBE 1978; Director, SAHF Enterprises, since 2004; *b* 25 May 1928; *s* of Knowles Waraker Cottrell and Elmira Grenfell Cottrell; *m* 1952, Barbara Jean Wheeler; two *s* two *d. Educ:* Sydney Univ. (BEng, MEng; Univ. Medal (Mech. Eng) 1951); Birmingham Univ. (Postgrad. Dip. in Mgt). Cadet, Qld Irrigation Commn, 1945–46; cadet, then engr, Australian Dept of Munitions, 1947–60; Email Ltd: Manager, 1960–74; Man. Dir, 1974–92; Chm., 1993–98. Chairman: Export Finance & Insurance Corp., 1983–86; Pacifica Gp Ltd, 1989–95; Scania Australia Pty Ltd, 1991–2003; Adelaide Steamship Co. Ltd, 1992–99; Boral Ltd, 1994–2000; Adsteam Marine Ltd, 1997–2001; Dep. Chm., Australian Telecommunications Commn, 1982–87; Dir, Nat. Australia Bank, 1985–98. Vice-Pres., Business Council of Australia, 1991–92. Hon. FIEAust 1994. Hon. DBus Charles Sturt Univ., 1996. Sir James Kirby Medal, IProdE, 1986; Sir Charles McGrath Award, Aust. Marketing Inst., 1989. *Recreations:* golf, family activities. *Address:* 5/125 Merrivale Lane, Turramurra, NSW 2074, Australia. *T:* (2) 99839836. *Clubs:* Royal Sydney Yacht Squadron; Pymble Golf (Sydney).

COTTRELL, Richard John; President, Euroconsult Ltd, since 2002; *b* 11 July 1943; *s* of John Cottrell and Winifred (*née* Barter); *m* 1st, 1965, Dinah Louise (*née* David) (marr. diss. 1986); two *d*; 2nd, 1987, Tracy Katherine (*née* Wade) (marr. diss. 1996); one *d*; 3rd, 1997, Liliana (*née* Velitchkova) (marr. diss. 2001); 4th, 2001, Diana (*née* Kiebdoj); two *d. Educ:* Court Fields Sch., Wellington, Somerset. Journalist: Wellington Weekly News, 1958; South Devon Jl, 1960; Topic (internat. news weekly), 1962; Evening Argus, Brighton, 1963; Lincolnshire Standard, 1964; Evening Post, Bristol, 1965; TWW, subseq. HTV, 1967–79. Chairman: RCA Ltd, 1989–94; Rail Central Europe, 1994–2002. Contested (C) Bristol, European Parly elecn, 1989. MEP (C) Bristol, 1979–89; Sec., backbench cttee, European Dem. Gp, 1979; Member: Transport Cttee, 1979–83; External Econ. Relns Cttee, 1979–82; Information Cttee, 1981–84; ACP-EEC Convention, 1981–84; Agriculture Cttee, 1982–86; Rules Cttee, 1982–89; Environment Cttee, 1983–89; Budget Cttee, 1983–86; Energy Cttee, 1986–88; deleg. to China, 1987. *Publications:* Energy, the Burning Question for Europe (jtly), 1981; (ed and contrib.) Transport for Europe, 1982; Blood on their Hands: the killing of Ann Chapman, 1987; The Sacred Cow, 1987; contribs to Encounter, Contemporary Review. *Recreations:* travel, reading, transport studies, appreciation of real ale, astronomy, ornithology.

COTTRELL, Rt Rev. Stephen Geoffrey; *see* Reading, Area Bishop of.

COTTS, Sir Richard Crichton Mitchell, 4th Bt *cr* 1921, of Coldharbour Wood, Rogate, Sussex; *b* 26 July 1946; *er s* of Sir Robert Crichton Mitchell Cotts, 3rd Bt and Barbara Mary Winifrede (*d* 1982), *o d* of Captain H. J. A. Throckmorton, RN; *S* father, 1995, but his name does not appear on the Official Roll of the Baronetage. *Educ:* Oratory Sch. *Heir: b* Hamish William Anthony Mitchell Cotts [*b* 15 Sept. 1951; *m* 1995, Merlyn Mattiuzzo; three *s* three *d*].

COUCHER, Iain Michael; Chief Executive, Network Rail, since 2007; *b* 22 Aug. 1961; *s* of Brian and Daphne Coucher; *m* 1993, Tanya Nightingale; one *s* one *d. Educ:* Ashville Coll., Harrogate; Imperial Coll., London (BSc Eng Hons Aeronautical Engrg); Henley Mgt Coll. (MBA). Defence project design, Hunting Engrg, and Marconi, 1982–85; project manager and dir, then Head of Transport, EDS, then SD-Scicon, 1985–97; Chief Executive: TranSys Consortium, 1997–99; Tube Lines Gp, 1999–2001; Network Rail: Man. Dir, Jan.–Sept. 2002; Dep. Chief Exec., 2002–07. Dir, Rly Safety and Standards Bd, 2003–. *Recreations:* cycling, birdwatching, films. *Address:* Network Rail, 40 Melton Street, NW1 2EE. *T:* (020) 7557 8000, *Fax:* (020) 7557 9120.

COUCHMAN, James Randall; *b* 11 Feb. 1942; *s* of Stanley Randall Couchman and Alison Margaret Couchman; *m* 1967, Barbara Jean (*née* Heilbrun); one *s* one *d. Educ:* Cranleigh School; King's College, Newcastle upon Tyne; Univ. of Durham. Oil industry, 1964–70; Public House Manager, family company, 1970–74; Gen. Manager, family licensed trade co., 1974–80, Director, 1980–95. Member (C): Bexley LBC, 1974– (Chm., Social Services, 1975–78, 1980–82); Oxford CC, 2005– (Cabinet Mem. for Adu Social Services, 2006–). Chm., Bexley HA, 1981–83. Member: Assoc. of Metropolit Authorities Social Services Cttee, 1975–80; Central Council for Educn and Training Social Workers, 1976–80; Governor, Nat. Inst. for Social Workers, 1976–80. MP (C Gillingham, 1983–97; contested (C) same seat, 1997. PPS to Minister of State for Soc Security, 1984–86, to Minister of Health, 1986–88, to Chancellor of Duchy of Lancast 1988–89, to Sec. of State for Social Security, 1989–90, to Lord Pres. of the Council an Leader of the House, 1995–97. Member: Social Services Select Cttee, 1983–85; Sele Cttee on Health, 1990–92; Public Accounts Cttee, 1992–95; Select Cttee on N 1995–97. Fellow, Industry and Parlt Trust, 1987. Mem., Vintners' Co. *Recreations:* trav reading, listening to music, politics. *Address:* Dovecote House, Filkins Road, Langfor Lechlade, Glos GL7 3LW. *T:* (01367) 860289.

COUCHMAN, Martin, OBE 2005; Deputy Chief Executive, British Hospitali Association, since 1993; *b* 28 Sept. 1947; *s* of late Frederick Alfred James Couchman an Pamela Mary Couchman (*née* Argent); *m* 1983, Carolyn Mary Constance Roberts; thr *s* one *d. Educ:* Sutton Valence Sch.; Exeter Coll., Oxford (BA Jurisprudence). Buildin Industry, 1970–77; National Economic Development Office, 1977–92: Industrial Adv 1977–84; Hd of Administration, 1984–87; on secondment as UK Dir of European Ye of the Environment, 1987–88; Sec., NEDC, 1988–92. Chm., Social Affairs, Europe Confedn of Nat. Assocs of Hotels, Restaurants, Cafés and Similar Estabts, 2001– (Me Exec. Cttee, 1997–2000); Chm., CBI Sectoral Employment Issues Cttee, 2000–. Mer Green Alliance, 1988–. FRSA 1988. *Recreations:* Anglo-Saxon history, armch archaeology, amateur dramatics. *Address:* British Hospitality Association, Queens Hous 55–56 Lincoln's Inn Fields, WC2A 3BH; The Old School, Halstead, Sevenoaks, Ke TN14 7HF. *Club:* St Julians (Sevenoaks).

COUGHLIN, Michael Charles; Chief Executive, Reading Borough Council, sin 2008; *b* London, 13 May 1959; *s* of Dennis and Jean Louise Dorothy Coughlin; *m* 198 Christine Ann Hance; two *s* one *d. Educ:* Thomas Bennett Sch.; Portsmouth Poly. (E Hons Social Admin); Loughborough Univ. (Dip. ILAM); Croydon Coll. (Dip. M Studies, Dip. CI Mktg). Recreation Officer, Crawley BC, 1981–84; Leisure Manage Bexley London Bor., 1984–87; Hd of Leisure and Community Services, Elmbridge B 1987–97; Dir, Leisure and Cultural Services, 1997–2000, Planning and Envmt, 2000–0 Royal Bor. Windsor and Maidenhead; Chief Exec., Crawley BC, 2002–08. *Recreation* music - playing guitar and bass, songwriting, performing, singing, squash - team a league, ballroom and latin dancing, family, friends and holidays, cooking. *Address:* Readin Borough Council, Civic Centre, Reading RG1 7TD. *T:* (0118) 939 0067, 07809 58428 *e-mail:* michael.coughlin@reading.gov.uk.

COUGHLIN, Vincent William; QC 2003; *b* 6 May 1957; *s* of Cornelius and Maure Coughlin; *m* 1988, Elizabeth Anne Ray; one *s* two *d. Educ:* Christ's Hospital, Horshar Queen Mary Coll., London (LLB Hons). Called to the Bar, Middle Temple, 198 practice, SE Circuit, specialising in criminal law and white collar fraud. *Recreations:* ja guitar, sailing, cycling. *Address:* Furnival Chambers, 32 Furnival Street, EC4A 1JQ. (020) 7405 3232, *Fax:* (020) 7405 3322; *e-mail:* vcoughlin@furnivallaw.co.uk. Clu Travellers; Blackwater Sailing.

COULL, Prof. Alexander, PhD; DSc; FRSE; FICE, FIStructE; Regius Professor of Civ Engineering, University of Glasgow, 1977–92; *b* 20 June 1931; *s* of William Coull an Jane Ritchie (*née* Reid); *m* 1962, Frances Bruce Moir; one *s* two *d. Educ:* Peterhead Acac Univ. of Aberdeen (BScEng, PhD; DSc 1983). FRSE 1971; FICE 1972, FIStructE 197 Res. Asst, MIT, USA, 1955; Struct. Engr, English Electric Co. Ltd, 1955–57; Lectr Engrg, Univ. of Aberdeen, 1957–62; Lectr in Civil Engrg, Univ. of Southamptc 1962–66; Prof. of Struct. Engrg, Univ. of Strathclyde, 1966–76. Chm., Clyde Estua Amenity Council, 1981–86. *Publications:* Tall Buildings, 1967; Fundamentals of Structur Theory, 1972; (with B. Stafford Smith) Tall Building Structures: Planning Analysis an Design, 1991; author or co-author of 130 res. papers in scientific jls. *Recreations:* golf, h walking, ski-ing. *Address:* 4 Monaltrie Way, Ballater, Aberdeenshire AB35 5PS. (01339) 755766.

COULL, Ian David, FRICS; Chief Executive, Segro (formerly Slough Estates) plc, sin 2003; *b* 7 June 1950; *s* of John and Davina Coull; *m* 1971, Linda Shepherd; one *s* two *Educ:* Perth Acad.; Coll. of Estate Management. FRICS 1984. Dir, J. Sainsbury pl 1988–2002. Mem., London Regl Bd, Royal and Sun Alliance, 2001–; non-exec. D House of Fraser, 2003–06. Co-Chair, London Sustainable Develt Commn, 2002–0 Member: Sustainable Construction Task Gp, 2003–04; Code for Sustainable Bldgs Se Steering Gp, 2004–. Pres., British Property Fedn, 2005–06. Chm., South Bank Employe Gp, 1994–2003. *Recreations:* Rugby, golf, family. *Address:* Segro plc, 234 Bath Roa Slough SL1 4EE. *T:* (01753) 537171, *Fax:* (01753) 820585. *Clubs:* Temple Golf; Marlo Rugby.

COULL, Maj.-Gen. John Taylor, CB 1992; FRCS; FRCSE; Medico-Legal Advise Army Medical Directorate, Ministry of Defence, 1992–97; *b* 4 March 1934; *s* of late Joh Sandeman Coull and Ethel Marjory (*née* Taylor); *m* 1958, Mildred Macfarlane; three *Educ:* Robert Gordon's College; Aberdeen Univ. Med. Sch. MB ChB. House app Aberdeen Royal Infirmary, 1958–60; Commissioned RAMC, 1960; Surgeon: Colchest Mil. Hosp., 1960–63; Queen Alexandra Mil. Hosp., 1963; Sen. Registrar, Edinburgh Ea Gen. Hosp., 1963–65; Royal Herbert Hosp., 1965–67; Sen. Registrar, Birmingha Accident Hosp., 1967; Consultant Surgeon, BMH Singapore, 1967–70; Lectr, Dept Orthopaedics, Univ. of Edinburgh, 1970–71; Consultant Orthopaedic Surgeon, BAOI 1971–77; Consultant Adviser in Orthop. Surgery and Sen. Consultant, Queen Elizabe Mil. Hosp., 1977–86; Consulting Surgeon, HQ BAOR, 1986–88; Dir of Army Surger 1988–92. Hon. Col 202 (Midland) Field Hosp. RAMC (V), 1992–97; Col Comd RAMC, 1994–99. Mitchiner Meml Lectr, RAMC, 2001. QHS 1988–92. Mitchine Medal, RCS, 1980. OStJ. GSM N Ireland, 1976. *Publications:* chapters in: Field Pock Surgery, 1981; R. Smith's The Hand, 1985; Trauma, 1989; articles in learned j *Recreations:* home maintenance, carpentry, gardening, travel. *Address:* Sheigra, 25 Braem Road, Ballater AB35 5RL. *Club:* Royal Society of Medicine.

COULSFIELD, Rt Hon. Lord; John Taylor Cameron; PC 2000; a Senator of th College of Justice in Scotland, 1987–2002; *b* 24 April 1934; *s* of late John Reid Cameron MA, formerly Director of Education, Dundee; *m* 1961, Bridget Deirdre Sloan; no *c. Edu* Fettes Coll.; Corpus Christi Coll., Oxford; Edinburgh Univ. BA (Oxon), LL (Edinburgh). Admitted to Faculty of Advocates, 1960. Lecturer in Public Law, Edinburg Univ., 1960–64. QC (Scot.) 1973; Keeper of the Advocates' Library, 1977–87; Advocate-Depute, 1977–79. Judge, Courts of Appeal of Jersey and Guernsey, 1986–87; Judge, Employment Appeal Tribunal, 1992–96; Mem., Scottish Court in the Netherland 2000–01; Judge of Appeal, Botswana, 2005–. Chm., Medical Appeal Tribunals, 1985–8 Editor, Scottish Law and Practice Qly, 1995–2003. Chm., Esmée Fairbairn Found Inquiry, Alternatives to Prison, 2003–04. Chairman: Jt Standing Cttee on Legal Educn i Scotland, 1998–2003; Scottish Council for Internat. Arbitration, 2003–. Trustee, Na

Liby of Scotland, 2000–. Hon. Mem., Soc. of Legal Scholars, 2006. *Publications:* Report Disclosures, Scots Criminal Law, 2007; (ed jtly) Gloag and Henderson, The Law of Scotland, 12th edn, 2007; articles in legal jls.

COULSHED, Brian Thomas; Headmaster, Parmiter's School, Hertfordshire, since 1993; *b* St Helens, Lancs, 11 March 1950; *s* of Thomas Cyril and Mary Ann Coulshed; *m* 1982, Gillian Margaret; two *s*. *Educ:* West Park Grammar Sch., St Helens; Univ. of Manchester (BA Hons, PGCE). Asst teacher, then Hd of Year, Longdean Sch., Hemel Hempstead, 1972–79; Hd of Dept, then Hd of Year, Hemel Hempstead Sch., 1979–86; Dep. Headmaster, Goffs Sch., 1986–92. Vis. Fellow, St Catharine's Coll., Cambridge, 2000. Chm., SW Herts Heads' Assoc., 1999–. Pres., Herts Schs FA, 2004–. Headteacher of the Year, 2007. *Publications:* The History of the Parmiter's Estates Foundation, 1997; The History of the Parmiter's Foundation, 2000, 2nd edn 2008. *Recreations:* cricket (playing mem., Leverstock Green CC, 1973–), football, Rugby League (lifelong supporter of Liverpool FC and St Helens Rugby League FC). *Address:* Parmiter's School, High Elms Lane, Garston, Herts WD25 0UU. *T:* (01923) 671424, *Fax:* (01923) 894195; *e-mail:* head@parmiters.herts.sch.uk. *Club:* Leverstock Green Cricket (Pres., 2003–).

COULSON, Mrs Ann Margaret; Chairman, Leamington Hastings Consolidated Charity, since 1998; *b* 11 March 1935; *d* of Sidney Herbert Wood and Ada (*née* Mills); *m* 1958, Peter James Coulson; two *s* one *d*. *Educ:* The Grammar Sch., Chippenham, Wilts; UCL (BScEcon); Univ. of Manchester (DSA); Wolverhampton Technical Teachers' Coll. (CertEd). Hosp. Admin, 1956–62; Lectr in Econs and Management, Bromsgrove Coll. of Further Educn, 1968–76; Asst Dir, North Worcestershire Coll., 1976–80; Service Planning and Develt Co-ordinator, 1980–83, Regl Planning Administrator, 1983–88, Dir of Planning, 1988–91, W Midlands RHA; Gen. Manager, Age Concern, Solihull, 1991–94. City of Birmingham Dist Council, 1973–79; special interest in Social Services. Mem., IBA, 1976–81. Trustee, Age Concern, Warwicks, 1996–2007. *Recreations:* sailing, cooking, music, theatre. *Address:* Rowans, Leamington Hastings, near Rugby, Warwicks CV23 8DY. *T:* (01926) 633264.

COULSON, Hon. Sir Peter (David William), Kt 2008; **Hon. Mr Justice Coulson;** a Judge of the High Court of Justice, Queen's Bench Division, since 2008; *b* 31 March 1958; *s* of David Coulson and Pamela Coulson (*née* Shorter); *m* 1985, Veronica Lachkovic; one *s* two *d*. *Educ:* Lord Wandsworth Coll.; Univ. of Keele (BA Hons 1980). ACIArb 1990. Called to the Bar, Gray's Inn, 1982 (Sir Malcolm Hilbery Award, 1982; Bencher, 2006); in practice, 1984–2004; QC 2001; Recorder, 2002–04; Circuit Judge, 2004–07. Trustee, Orchard Vale Trust, 1999–. Contributor, Lloyd's Law Reports: Professional Negligence, 1999–2000. *Publications:* (jtly) Professional Negligence and Liability, 2000; The Technology and Construction Court, 2006; Construction Adjudication, 2007. *Recreations:* British art 1750–1950, comedy, music, cricket, Watford FC. *Address:* Royal Courts of Justice, Strand, WC2A 2LL. *Club:* Travellers.

COULTASS, (George Thomas) Clive; historian; Keeper of Audio-Visual Records, Imperial War Museum, 1983–91; *b* 5 July 1931; *m* 1962, Norma Morris (*d* 2004). *Educ:* Tadcaster Grammar Sch.; Univ. of Sheffield (BA Hons). Teacher in various London schools, 1955–62; Lectr/Sen. Lectr in History, James Graham Coll., Leeds, 1962–69; Imperial War Museum: Keeper of Film Programming, 1969–70; Keeper, Dept of Film, 1970–83. Vice-Pres., Internat. Assoc. for Audio-Visual Media in Hist. Res. and Educn, 1978–85. Organiser: various film historical confs, 1973–90; exhibn on British film and World War II, 1982. *Publications:* Images for Battle, 1989; sections in: The Historian and Film, 1976; Britain and the Cinema in the Second World War, 1988; articles in various historical jls. *Recreations:* travel, music, including opera, reading, cinema. *Address:* 39 Fairfield Grove, SE7 8UA.

COULTER, Rev. Robert James; Member (UU) Antrim North, Northern Ireland Assembly, since 1998; *b* 23 Oct. 1929; *m* 1956, Elizabeth Holmes; one *s* one *d*. *Educ:* Trinity Coll., Dublin (BA, MA, BD); Univ. of Ulster (MA Educn). Ordained, 1963, Minister, 1963–76, Presbyterian Church in Ireland; Lectr in Further and Higher Educn, 1976–93. Mem. (UU), Ballymena BC, 1985–2001; Mayor of Ballymena, 1993–96. *Recreation:* vintage vehicles. *Address:* 18 Springmount Road, Clough, Ballymena, Co. Antrim BT44 9QQ. *T:* (028) 2568 5694.

COULTON, Very Rev. Nicholas Guy; Residentiary Canon and Sub-Dean, Christ Church, Oxford, 2003–08; House for Duty Priest, North Leigh, Oxford, since 2008; *b* 14 June 1940; *s* of Nicholas Guy Coulton and Audrey Florence Furneaux Coulton (*née* Luscombe); *m* 1978, Edith Mary Gainford; one *s* two *d*. *Educ:* Blundell's School, Tiverton; Cuddesdon Coll., Oxford; BD London (ext.) 1972; MA Oxon 2007. Admitted Solicitor, 1962; Asst Solicitor, Burges, Salmon & Co., Bristol, 1962–65. Ordination training, 1965–67; Curate of Pershore Abbey with Birlingham, Wick and Pinvin, 1967–71; Domestic Chaplain to Bishop of St Albans, 1971–75; Vicar of St Paul's, Bedford, 1975–90; part-time Industrial Chaplain, 1976–89; Provost, subseq. Dean, St Nicholas' Cathedral, Newcastle upon Tyne, 1990–2003, now Dean Emeritus. Proctor in Convocation, 1985–90; Hon. Canon of St Alban's Cathedral, 1989–90. Member: Gen. Synod of C of E, 1998–2003; Legal Adv. Commn of C of E, 2001–. Chm., NE CCJ, 1991–2002; Mem., NE Assembly, 2002–03. Dir, Ecclesiastical Insurance Gp, 1997–2005. Governor: Newcastle upon Tyne Church High Sch., 1990–2003; Dame Allan's Schs, 1990–2003; Ripon Coll., Cuddesdon, 2002–. OStJ 2002. *Publications:* Twelve Years of Prayer, 1989; (ed) The Bible, The Church and Homosexuality, 2005. *Recreations:* gardening, reading, listening to music, historical exploration. *Address:* 123 Merewood Avenue, Oxford OX3 8EQ.

COUNSELL, Her Honour Hazel Rosemary; *see* Fallon, Her Honour H. R.

COUNT, Dr Brian Morrison; Chairman, Progressive Energy; *b* 18 Feb. 1951; *s* of Douglas John Count and Ethel Sarah Count; *m* 1975, Jane Elizabeth Hudson; three *s*. *Educ:* King's College, Cambridge (MA Maths); Exeter Univ. (PhD Physics). Central Electricity Generating Board: Research Dept, 1974–84; Planning Dept, 1984–90; National Power: Project Develt Dir, 1990–95; Dir of Ops, 1995–96; Mem. Bd, 1996–2000; Man. Dir, UK, 1999–2000; Innogy Holdings: Chief Operating Officer, 2000–01; Chief Exec., 2001–03; CEO, RWE Trading, 2003–05. Non-executive Director: Eskom, 2002–; Ceres Power, 2007–. *Recreations:* golf, Rugby, entertaining. *Address:* Oakwood House, Blindmans Gate, Woolton Hill, Newbury, Berks RG20 9XD.

COUPER, Prof. Alastair Dougal; Research Professor, Seafarers International Research Centre for Safety and Occupational Health, University of Wales Cardiff, 1997–98 (Director, 1995–97); Emeritus Professor, University of Cardiff, since 1999; *b* 4 June 1931; *s* of Daniel Alexander Couper and Davina Couper (*née* Rilley); *m* 1958, Norma Milton; two *s* two *d*. *Educ:* Robert Gordon's School of Navigation (Master Mariner); Univ. of Aberdeen (MA, DipEd); Australian National Univ. (PhD). FNI 1979. Cadet and Navigating Officer, Merchant Navy, 1947–57; student, Univ. of Aberdeen, 1958–62, postgraduate teaching course, 1962–63; Research Schol., Sch. of Pacific Studies, ANU, Canberra, 1963–66; Lectr, Univ. of Durham, 1967–70; Prof. of Maritime Studies, UWIST, then UWCC, 1970–97; Prof., World Maritime Univ. (UN), Malmö, Sweden, 1987–89 (on secondment). UN Consultant, 1972–98; Chm., Maritime Bd, CNAA, 1978–85; Assessor, Chartered Inst. of Transport, 1976–85; Founder Mem., Council, British Maritime League, 1982–85; Mem. Exec. Bd, Law of the Sea Inst., USA, 1989–95; Mem., British Commn, Internat. Commn for Maritime History, 1996–99. Thomas Gray Meml Lectr, RSA, 2003. Pres., Neptune Assoc. of Maritime Res. Insts, 1997–98. Trustee, Nat. Maritime Mus., 1992–2000. Editor (and Founder), Journal of Maritime Policy and Management, 1973–84. Hon. DSc Plymouth, 1995. *Publications:* Geography of Sea Transport, 1971; The Law of the Sea, 1978; (ed) Times Atlas of the Oceans, 1983; contrib. Pacific, in World Atlas of Agriculture, 1969; Pacific in Transition (ed Brookfield), 1973; New Cargo Handling Techniques: implications for port employment and skills, 1986; (ed) Development and Social Change in the Pacific, 1988; (ed) The Shipping Revolution, 1992; Voyages of Abuse: Seafarers, Human Rights and International Shipping, 1999; (contrib.) Seafarers' Rights, 2005; several UN Reports, UNCTAD, ILO, IMO; articles in jls; conf. papers. *Recreations:* hill walking, sailing, archaeology, Pacific history. *Address:* 112 Ely Road, Llandaff, Cardiff CF5 2DA. *T:* (029) 2056 5401.

COUPER, Heather Anita, CBE 2007; CPhys, FInstP; FRAS; science broadcaster and author, since 1983; Director, Pioneer TV Productions, 1988–99; *b* 2 June 1949; *o d* of late George Couper Elder Couper and Anita Couper (*née* Taylor). *Educ:* St Mary's Grammar Sch., Northwood, Middx; Univ. of Leicester (BSc Hons Astronomy and Physics); Univ. of Oxford. FRAS 1970; CPhys 1999; FInstP 1999. Management trainee, Peter Robinson Ltd, 1967–69; Res. Asst, Cambridge Observatories, 1969–70; Lectr, Greenwich Planetarium, Old Royal Observ., 1977–83. Gresham Prof. of Astronomy, 1993–96. Mem., Millennium Commn, 1994–2006. President: Brit. Astron. Assoc., 1984–86; Jun. Astron. Soc., 1987–89. Presenter on television: Heavens Above, 1981; Spacewatch, 1983; The Planets, 1985; The Stars, 1988; The Neptune Encounter, 1989; A Close Encounter of the Second Kind, 1992; Stephen Hawking: a profile, 2002; producer/narrator: ET—Please Phone Earth, 1992; Space Shuttle Discovery, 1993; Electric Skies, 1994; Arthur C. Clarke: the Visionary, 1995; On Jupiter, 1996; Black Holes, 1997; narrator/presenter: Rendezvous in Space, and Avalanche, 1995; Raging Planet, 1997; The Sci-Fi Files, Killer Earth, and Stormforce, 1998; producer, Universe, 1999; presenter/producer, Space Shuttle: human time bomb?, 2003; presenter on radio: Science Now, 1983; Cosmic Pursuits, 1985; Seeing Stars, 1991–2001; ET on Trial, 1993; Starwatch, 1996; Sun Science, 1999; The Essential Guide to the 21st Century, 2000; Red Planet (series), 2003; Worlds Beyond (series), 2005; Arthur C. Clark: the Science Behind the Fiction, 2005; A Brief Guide to Infinity, 2006; Britain's Space Race, 2007; Cosmic Quest, 2008; also appearances and interviews on wide variety of television and radio progs. Astronomy columnist: The Independent; BBC Focus Mag. Hon. DLitt Loughborough, 1991; Hon. DSc: Hertfordshire, 1994; Leicester, 1997. *Publications:* Exploring Space, 1980; (jtly) Heavens Above, 1981; Journey into Space, 1984; (jtly) Starfinder, 1984; (jtly) The Halley's Comet Pop-Up Book, 1985; (jtly) The Universe: a 3-dimensional study, 1985; Space Scientist series, 1985–87: Comets and Meteors; The Planets; The Stars; jointly: The Sun; The Moon; Galaxies and Quasars; Satellites and Spaceprobes; Telescopes and Observatories; *with Nigel Henbest:* Space Frontiers, 1978; The Restless Universe, 1982; Physics, 1983; Astronomy, 1983; The Planets, 1985; The Stars, 1988; The Space Atlas, 1992; Guide to the Galaxy, 1994; How the Universe Works, 1994; Black Holes, 1996; Big Bang, 1997; Is Anybody Out There?, 1998; To the Ends of the Universe, 1998; Space Encyclopedia, 1999; Universe, 1999; Mars: the inside story of the red planet, 2001; Extreme Universe, 2001; Philip's Stargazing, annually 2004–08; Out of this World, 2007; Universe, 2007; The History of Astronomy, 2007; numerous articles in nat. newspapers and magazines. *Recreations:* travel, the English countryside, classical music; wine, food and winemaking. *Address:* David Higham Associates, 5–8 Lower John Street, Golden Square, W1R 4HA. *Club:* Groucho.

COUPER, Sir James George, 7th Bt *cr* 1841; *b* 27 Oct. 1977; *o s* of Sir Nicholas Couper, 6th Bt and of 1st wife, Kirsten Henrietta, *d* of Major George Burrell MacKean; *S* father 2002. *Heir: cousin* Jonathan Every Couper, *b* 26 Feb. 1931.

COUPLAND, George, PhD; FRS 2007; Director, Max Planck Institute for Plant Breeding Research, Cologne, since 2001; *b* 20 Dec. 1959; *s* of Walter Archibald Coupland and Margaret Coupland; *m* 1991, Jane Parker; one *s* one *d*. *Educ:* Univ. of Glasgow (BSc 1st Cl. Hons Microbiol. 1981); Univ. of Edinburgh (PhD 1984). Postdoctoral experience, Inst. for Genetics, Univ. of Cologne and Max Planck Inst. for Plant Breeding Res., Cologne, 1985–88; res. gp leader, Plant Breeding Inst., Cambridge and Cambridge Lab., John Innes Centre, Norwich, 1987–2001. Hon. Lectr, UEA, 1993–2001; Hon. Prof., Univ. of Cologne, 2003–. Cttee, Genetical Soc. of UK, 1997–2001; Cttee, UK RAE, 2007–08. Mem., EMBO, 2001; Associate Mem., Class of Scis, Royal Acad. of Belgium, 2006. *Publications:* articles in learned jls incl. Nature, Science, Cell. *Recreations:* ornithology, travel. *Address:* Max Planck Institute for Plant Breeding Research, Plant Developmental Biology, Carl von Linné Weg 10, 50829 Köln, Germany. *T:* (221) 5062205, *Fax:* (221) 5062207; *e-mail:* coupland@mpiz-koeln.mpg.de.

COURAGE, Maj.-Gen. Walter James, CB 1994; MBE 1979; Director, The Risk Advisory Group plc (formerly Ltd), since 1997; *b* 25 Sept. 1940; *s* of late Walter Henry Phipps and of Nancy Mary Courage (*née* Reeves, who *m* 3rd, John Frederick Gardner), and step *s* of late Lt-Col Nigel Anthony Courage, MC; *m* 1964, Lavinia Patricia, *d* of late John Emerson Crawhall Wood; one *s* one *d*. *Educ:* Abingdon Sch.; RMA, Sandhurst. Commnd 5th Royal Inniskilling Dragoon Guards, 1961; served BAOR, Libya and Canada, 1961–81; commanded Regt, 1982–84; Div. Col Staff Coll., 1985; Comdr 4th Armoured Bde, 1985–88; Chief of Staff, UN Force in Cyprus, 1988–90; Chief Joint Services Liaison Officer, BAOR, Bonn, 1990–94; Chief, Ext. Affairs Div., Germany, 1994–95; Dir-Gen., TA, 1995–96. Member: Bd, British American Business Inc., 2001–; Adv. Bd, Moore, Clayton & Co., 2002–; Dir, Janusian Security Risk Mgt, 2002–; Consultant: AMEC Project Investments Ltd, 1997–2004; DLA, 2000–04. Trustee, Shotover Estate, 2005–. FCMI. *Recreations:* shooting, cricket, ski-ing, polo, fine art. *Address:* Brigmerston Farm House, Brigmerston, Salisbury, Wilts SP4 8HX. *Clubs:* Cavalry and Guards, MCC; I Zingari.

COURCY; *see* de Courcy, family name of Baron Kingsale.

COURT, Hon. Richard Fairfax, AC 2003; Premier of Western Australia, Treasurer and Minister for Public Sector Management and for Federal Affairs, 1993–2001; *b* 27 Sept. 1947; *s* of Hon. Sir Charles Walter Michael Court, AK, KCMG, OBE; *m* 1989, Joanne, *d* of B. Moffat; one *d*, and one *s* one *d* by previous marriage. *Educ:* Univ. of Western Australia (BCom). Man. Dir, Court Marine Pty, 1974–82. MLA (L) Nedlands, WA, 1982–2001; Shadow Minister for Small Business, 1986; Dep. Leader, Parly Lib. Party, 1987–90; Shadow Minister for: Resources, Develt, Mines, Fuel and Energy, NW and Goldfields, 1990–91; Resource and Industrial Develt, Mines and Aboriginal Affairs, 1991–92; Public Sector Management, also Leader of the Opposition and Shadow Treas., 1992–93; Minister for: Tourism, 1994–95; Youth, 1996–97.

COURT, Robert Vernon; HM Diplomatic Service; Vice-President, Government Affairs International, GlaxoSmithKline, since 2005 (on secondment); *b* 28 Jan. 1958; *s* of Derrick and Catherine Court; *m* 1983, Rebecca Ophelia Sholl; three *s* one *d*. *Educ:* Churchill Coll., Cambridge (MA). Entered FCO, 1981; Bangkok, 1983–86; First Sec., FCO, 1986–88; Private Sec. to Minister of State, 1988–90; First Secretary: UK Delegn to NATO, 1990–93; UK Perm. Repn to EU, 1993–96; PA to Chm. and CEO, 1997–99, Gp Co-ordinator for Sustainable Develt, 2000–01, Rio Tinto plc; Dep. High Comr, Canberra, 2001–05. *Recreations:* sub-aqua diving, swimming, travel. *Address:* c/o GlaxoSmithKline, 980 Great West Road, Brentford, Middx TW8 9GS. *Club:* Royal Automobile.

COURTAULD, Rev. (Augustine) Christopher (Caradoc); Vicar of St Paul's, Knightsbridge, 1978–99; *b* 12 Sept. 1934; *s* of late Augustine Courtauld and of Lady Butler of Saffron Walden; *m* 1978, Dr Elizabeth Ann Molland, MD, FRCPath, *d* of late Rev. Preb. John W. G. Molland; two *d*. *Educ:* Eton; Trinity College, Cambridge (BA 1958, MA 1961); Westcott House, Cambridge. Deacon 1960, priest 1961, Manchester; Curate of Oldham, 1960–63; Chaplain: Trinity College, Cambridge, 1963–68; The London Hospital, 1968–78. Area Dean, Westminster (St Margaret), 1992–97. *Recreation:* sailing. *Address:* Broke House, The Drift, Levington, Ipswich, Suffolk IP10 0LF.

COURTAULD, George; Vice Lord-Lieutenant of Essex, since 2003; landowner and farmer; *b* 2 May 1938; *s* of George Courtauld and Claudine Suzanne (*née* Booth); *m* 1962, Dominie Jennifer Faith Mirren Riley-Smith; two *s* two *d*. *Educ:* Gordonstoun Coll.; Pembroke Coll., Cambridge (BA 1961). Commnd Grenadier Guards, 1957. With textile manufacturer, Courtaulds Ltd, 1962–83. Queen's Messenger, 1985–2000. Chairman: Haven Gateway Partnership, 2002–08 (Pres., 2008–); NE Essex Strategic LSC, 2004; Harwich Regeneration Gp, 2005–; Essex Br., Prince's Trust, 2005–08; Essex Envmt Trust, 2005–. President: Friends of Essex Churches, 2002–; Chelmsford and Mid Essex Samaritans, 2003–; Halstead Allotment Holders and Leisure Gardeners Assoc., 2006–. Master Patron, Public Catalogue Foundn, Essex, 2006–. Member: Halstead RDC, 1967–74; Braintree DC, 1974–85. Freeman, City of London, 1959; Liveryman: Weavers' Co., 1961–; Goldsmiths' Co., 1970–. High Sheriff, 2001–02, DL 2002, Essex. *Publications:* An Axe, A Spade and Ten Acres, 1983; Odd Noises from the Barn, 1985; The Travels of a Fat Bulldog, 1995; The Fat Bulldog Roams Again, 1998; The Last Travels of a Fat Bulldog, 2000. *Recreations:* travel, plant collecting, forestry. *Address:* Knight's Barn, Colne Engaine, Earls Colne, Essex CO6 2JG. *Clubs:* White's, Special Forces; Essex.

COURTENAY, family name of **Earl of Devon**.

COURTENAY, Lord; Charles Peregrine Courtenay; *b* 14 Aug. 1975; *o s* of Earl of Devon, *qv*; *m* 2004, Allison Joy Langer; one *d*. *Educ:* St John's Coll., Cambridge (BA Hons History of Art, 1997; MA 2001; Rugby half-Blue 1996). Called to the Bar, Inner Temple, 1999; admitted to California Bar, 2004. Associate, Latham & Watkins LLP, Los Angeles, 2005–. London Scottish 1st XV Rugby, 1998–2003; Santa Monica 1st XV Rugby, 2003–05. Mem., Grocers' Co. *Clubs:* St Moritz Tobogganing; Butterflies Cricket.

COURTENAY, Ralph Andrew, RIBA; FCSD; Managing Director, 1992–2007, Senior Vice President, 1998–2007, HOK Europe; *b* 21 Feb. 1943; *s* of Reginald William James Courtenay and Joyce Louisa Courtenay; *m* 1969, Brenda Ruth Caudle; two *d*. *Educ:* Abbey Sch., London; NE London Poly. (Dist. in Thesis). RIBA 1972; FCSD 1984. Austin-Smith, London, 1978–89: Partner, 1980–89; Man. Partner, 1984–89; own practice, Ralph Courtenay Associates, 1989–92; joined HOK, London, 1992, Man. Dir, 1995–2007; Dir, HOK Worldwide, 1996–2007; Chm., HOK European Architects Network, 2000–07. Mem., Soc. of Architectural Illustrators, 1982. *Publications:* contrib. articles to Building Design, Architects Jl and Architectural Rev. *Recreations:* marathon running, golf, tennis, ski-ing, painting, music, opera. *Address:* 1 The Orchards, Mill Road, Winchelsea, E Sussex TN36 4HJ. *Clubs:* Royal Automobile, Arts; Hemstead Forest Golf, Sissinghurst Tennis.

COURTENAY, Sir Thomas Daniel, (Sir Tom), Kt 2001; actor; *b* 25 Feb. 1937; *s* of late Thomas Henry Courtenay and Annie Eliza Quest; *m* 1st, 1973, Cheryl Kennedy (marr. diss. 1982); 2nd, 1988, Isabel Crossley. *Educ:* Kingston High Sch., Hull; University Coll., London (Fellow 1994). RADA, 1958–60; started acting professionally, 1960; Old Vic, 1960–61: Konstantin Treplieff, Poins, Feste and Puck; Billy Liar, Cambridge Theatre, June 1961–Feb. 1962 and on tour; Andorra, National Theatre (guest), 1964; The Cherry Orchard, and Macbeth, Chichester, 1966; joined 69 Theatre Co., Manchester, 1966: Charley's Aunt, 1966; Romeo, Playboy of the Western World, 1967; Hamlet (Edinburgh Festival), 1968; She Stoops to Conquer, (transferred to Garrick), 1969; Peer Gynt, 1970; Charley's Aunt, Apollo, 1971; Time and Time Again, Comedy, 1972 (Variety Club of GB Stage Actor Award, 1972); The Norman Conquests, Globe, 1974; The Fool, Royal Court, 1975; Prince of Homburg, The Rivals, Manchester (opening prods of The Royal Exchange), 1976; Otherwise Engaged, NY, 1977; Clouds, Duke of York's, 1978; Crime and Punishment, Manchester, 1978; The Dresser, Manchester and Queen's, 1980 (Drama Critics Award and New Standard Award for best actor, 1980), NY 1981; The Misanthrope, Manchester and Round House, 1981; Andy Capp, Manchester and Aldwych, 1982; Jumpers, Manchester, 1984; Rookery Nook, Shaftesbury, 1986; The Hypochondriac, Lyric, Hammersmith, 1987; Dealing with Clair, Richmond, 1988; The Miser, Manchester, 1991; Moscow Stations (one-man show), Traverse Theatre, Edinburgh, 1993, 1994, Garrick, 1994 (Evening Standard and Critics Circle Award), NY, 1995; Poison Pen, Manchester, 1993; Uncle Vanya, NY, 1995, Manchester, 2001; Art, Wyndham's, 1996; King Lear, Manchester, 1999; Pretending to be Me (one-man show), W Yorks Playhouse, 2002, Comedy, 2003; The Home Place, Gate, Dublin, transf. Comedy, 2005. Began acting in films, 1962. *Films:* The Loneliness of the Long Distance Runner, Private Potter, 1962; Billy Liar, 1963; King and Country, 1964 (Volpi Cup, 1964); Operation Crossbow, King Rat, Dr Zhivago, 1965; The Night of the Generals, The Day the Fish Came Out, 1967; A Dandy in Aspic, 1968; Otley, 1969; One Day in the Life of Ivan Denisovitch, 1970; Catch Me a Spy, 1971; The Dresser, 1983 (Golden Globe Award); The Last Butterfly, 1990; Let Him Have It, 1991; The Boy from Mercury, 1996; Whatever Happened to Harold Smith?, 1999; Last Orders, 2002; Nicholas Nickleby, 2003; The Golden Compass, 2007; *television* includes: Redemption, 1991; Old Curiosity Shop (film), 1995; A Rather English Marriage, 1998; The Flood, 2007. Best Actor Award, Prague Festival, 1968; TV Drama Award (for Oswald in Ghosts), 1968. *Publication:* Dear Tom: letters from home (memoirs), 2000. *Recreations:* listening to music (mainly classical, romantic and jazz); watching sport (and occasionally taking part in it, in a light-hearted manner), the countryside, playing the flute. *Address:* Putney. *Club:* Garrick.

COURTNEY, Prof. Edward, MA; Gildersleeve Professor of Classics, University of Virginia, 1993–2002, now Emeritus; *b* 22 March 1932; *s* of George and Kathleen Courtney; *m* 1962, Brenda Virginia Meek; two *s*. *Educ:* Royal Belfast Academical Instn; Trinity Coll., Dublin (BA); BA (by incorporation) 1955, MA 1957, Oxford. University studentship, Dublin, 1954–55; Research Lectr, Christ Church, Oxford, 1955–59; Lectr in Classics, 1959, Reader in Classics, 1970, Prof. of Latin, 1977, King's Coll., London; Prof. of Classics, 1982–93, Leonard Ely Prof. of Humanistic Studies, 1986–93, Stanford Univ. *Publications:* (ed) Valerius Flaccus, Argonautica (Leipzig), 1970; (ed jtly) Juvenal, Satires 1, 3, 10, 1977; (ed jtly) Ovid, Fasti (Leipzig), 1978, 4th edn 1997; A Commentary on the Satires of Juvenal, 1980; (ed) Juvenal, The Satires, a text, 1984; (ed) Statius, Silvae, 1990; The Poems of Petronius, 1991; The Fragmentary Roman Poets, 1993, 2nd edn 2003; Musa Lapidaria: a selection of Latin verse inscriptions, 1995; Archaic Latin Prose, 1999; A Companion to Petronius, 2002; many articles and reviews. *Recreation:* chess (schoolboy champion of Ireland, 1950). *Address:* 1500 West Pines Drive, Charlottesville, VA 22901, USA.

COURTNEY, Roger Graham, CPhys, FInstP; CEng, FCIBSE; consultant, construction research and innovation; Professorial Fellow in Construction Innovation, University of Manchester (formerly University of Manchester Institute of Science and Technology), since 2001; *b* 11 July 1946; *s* of late Ronald Samuel Courtney and Marjorie Dixon Courtney; *m* 1973, Rosemary Madeleine Westlake; four *d*. *Educ:* Roan School for Boys, SE3; Trinity Coll., Cambridge (MA); Univ. of Bristol (MSc); Brunel Univ. (MTech(OR)). CPhys 1991, FInstP 1991; MCIOB 1993; FCIBSE 1993; CEng 1994. Building Research Station, later Building Research Establishment, 1969–77: res. on bldg and urban services and energy conservation; Sci. Officer, 1969–72; Sen. Sci. Officer, 1972–75; PSO, 1975–81; Inner Cities Directorate, DoE, 1977–78; Sci. and Technology Secretariat, Cabinet Office, 1978–84 (Sec. to ACARD and IT Adv. Panel); SPSO, 1981–83; DCSO, 1983–86; Technical Dir, Energy Efficiency Office, Dept of Energy, 1984–86; Dep. Dir, 1986–88, Dir, 1988–90, Chief Exec., 1990–97, BRE, DoE; Dep. Chm., BRE Ltd, 1997–99. Vis. Prof., Sch. of Construction Project Mgt, The Bartlett (formerly Bartlett Sch. of Grad. Studies), UCL, 2005–. *Publications:* papers in sci. and professional jls. *Address:* 89 Parkside Drive, Watford WD17 3AY. *T:* (01923) 446767.

COURTNEY, William Reid; Regional Chairman of Industrial Tribunals, Scotland, 1991–93; *b* 22 Nov. 1927; *s* of Samuel Courtney and Louisa Reid or Courtney; *m* 1951, Jean Ursula Page; one *s* two *d*. *Educ:* Allan Glens Sch., Glasgow; Glasgow Univ. (LLB). Solicitor, Supreme Courts. Failed professional cricketer, fell back on Law; Edinburgh solicitor, 1952–77; Chm., Industrial Tribunals, Scotland, 1978–91. *Recreations:* sea, hills. *Address:* 30 Millig Street, Helensburgh, Dunbartonshire G84 9PN. *T:* (01436) 676900. *Clubs:* Royal Northern & Clyde Yacht, Clyde Corinthian Yacht, Clyde Cruising, Old Gaffers.

COURTOWN, 9th Earl of, *cr* 1762; **James Patrick Montagu Burgoyne Winthrop Stopford;** Baron Courtown (Ire.), 1758; Viscount Stopford, 1762; Baron Saltersford (GB), 1796; *b* 19 March 1954; *s* of 8th Earl of Courtown, OBE, TD, DL, and Patricia, 3rd *d* of Harry S. Winthrop, Auckland, NZ; *S* father, 1975; *m* 1985, Elisabeth, *yr d* of I. R. Dunnett, Broad Campden, Glos; one *s* two *d*. *Educ:* Eton College; Berkshire Coll. of Agriculture; RAC, Cirencester. A Lord in Waiting (Govt Whip), 1995–97; an Opposition Whip, 1997–2000; elected Mem., H of L, 1999. *Heir:* s Viscount Stopford, *qv*. *Address:* House of Lords, SW1A 0PW.

See also Lady E. C. Godsal.

COUSE, Philip Edward, FCA; Partner, Coopers & Lybrand, 1966–91; *b* 24 March 1936; *s* of Oliver and Marion Couse; *m* 1st (marr. diss. 1973); two *s* one *d*; 2nd, Carol Ann Johannessen Pruitt; one step *d*. *Educ:* Uppingham Sch.; Hackley Sch., USA. Qualified as Chartered Accountant, 1961. Birmingham Chartered Accountants' Students Society: Sec., 1958–59; Chm., 1967–69; Pres., 1977–78; Birmingham and West Midlands Soc. of Chartered Accountants: Mem. Cttee, 1974–92, Pres., 1982–83; Institute of Chartered Accountants: Mem. Council, 1978–92; Chm. of various cttees; Pres., 1989–90; Chartered Accountants' Dining Club: Mem. Cttee, 1981–92; Treas., 1985–89; Pres., 1989–91. Director: Birmingham Heartlands and Solihull Hosp. NHS Trust, 1991–2000; William King Ltd, 1993–99. Part-time Comr, Friendly Socs Commn, 1992–97. Dir, Hillstone Sch. Trust, Malvern, 1971–86; Chairman: Edgbaston C of E Coll. for Girls, 1982–88; Birmingham Rep. Theatre Foundn, 1991–96; Dir, Birmingham Rep. Th., 1991–96; Chm., Birmingham Dio. Bd of Finance, 1992–2000, and Mem. of various cttees; Mem. C of E Pensions Bd, 1998–99. Mem., Council of Management, Ironbridge Heritage Foundn, 1991–2005 (Treas., 1991–2003); Trustee, Birmingham Eye Foundn, 1981–9[illegible] (Treas., 1981–91). Liveryman, Co. of Chartered Accountants in England and Wales 1977– (Mem., Court, 1987–90). *Recreations:* music, horse racing, woodwork, theatre going. *Address:* 23 Frederick Road, Edgbaston, Birmingham B15 1JN; 715 Greenwood Manor Circle, West Melbourne, FL 32904, USA. *Club:* Royal Automobile.

COUSINS, Air Chief Marshal Sir David, KCB 1996 (CB 1991); AFC 1980; Controller RAF Benevolent Fund, 1998–2006; *b* 20 Jan. 1942; *s* of late Peter and Irene Cousins; *m* 1st, 1966, Mary Edith McMurray (marr. diss. 2003); two *s* one *d*; 2nd, 2006, Maggie Broadbent. *Educ:* St Edward's Sch., Malta; Prince Rupert's Sch., Wilhelmshaven; RAF College; Open Univ. (BA 1992). 92 Sqn (Lightnings), 1965–68; ADC to CAS, 1968–70; 15 Sqn (Buccaneers), 1970–73; Air Plans, HQ RAF Germany, 1973; RAF Staff Coll. 1974; Staff Officer to ACAS (OR), 1975–77; OC 16 Sqn (Buccaneers), 1977–80; Central Trials and Tactics Orgn, 1980; PSO to CAS, 1981–83; OC RAF Laarbruch, 1983–85; RCDS 1986; Dir, Air Offensive, MoD, 1987–89; Dir Gen. Aircraft 2, MoD (PE) 1989–91; AOC and Comdt, RAF Coll., Cranwell, 1992–94; AOC No 38 Gp, and SASO Strike Comd, 1994–95; Air Mem. for Personnel, and AOC-in-C, Personnel and Trng Comd, 1995–98. ADC to the Queen, 1984–85. *Recreations:* dinghy sailing, golf, horology. *Club:* Royal Air Force.

COUSINS, James Mackay; MP (Lab) Newcastle upon Tyne Central, since 1987; *b* 2[illegible] Feb. 1944; *m*; two *s*, and one step *s* one step *d*. *Educ:* New Coll., Oxford (Schol.); London School of Economics. Contract Researcher, and Lectr in job markets, Commn on Industrial Relns and Depts of Employment and the Environment. Member: Wallsend Borough Council, 1969–73; Tyne and Wear County Council, 1973–86 (Dep. Leader 1981–86). Mem., Treasury Select Cttee, 1997–. Member: CND; Amicus. *Address:* (office) 42, 7–15 Pink Lane, Newcastle upon Tyne NE1 5DW; House of Commons, SW1A 0AA; *e-mail:* cousinsj@parliament.uk.

COUSINS, Jeremy Vincent; QC 1999; a Recorder, since 2000; *b* 25 Feb. 1955; *s* of Eri[illegible] Cousins and Joyce Cousins; *m* 1993, Jane Owens; two *s* one *d*. *Educ:* Oxford Sch.; Warwick Univ. Called to the Bar, Middle Temple, 1977; in practice at the Bar, 1977–; an Asst Recorder, 1996–2000. Chm., Commercial Gp, St Philip's Chambers, 2003–. Chm. Midland Chancery and Commercial Bar Assoc., 2002–. Mem. PCC, St Anne's, Moseley 1998–. *Recreations:* wine, travelling in France and Italy. *Address:* St Philip's Chambers, 5 Temple Row, Birmingham B2 5LS. *T:* (0121) 246 7000; Selborne Chambers, 10 Essex Street, WC2R 3AA. *T:* (020) 7420 9500.

COUSINS, John Peter; Chairman, Crown Asset Management Ltd, Hong Kong, since 1994; *b* 31 Oct. 1931; *s* of Rt Hon. Frank Cousins, PC; *m* 1976, Pauline Cousins (*née* Hubbard); three *d*. *Educ:* Doncaster Central Sch. Motor engineering apprentice, 1947–52; RAF Engineering, 1952–55; BOAC cabin crew and clerical work, 1955–63; Full Time Official, TGWU, 1963–75, Nat. Sec., 1966–75; Dir of Manpower and Industrial Relations, NEDO, 1975–79; Dir of Personnel, Plessey Telecommunications and Offic

Systems Ltd, 1979–81; Dir of Personnel and Industrial Relns, John Brown PLC, 1981–83; Gen. Sec., Clearing Bank Union, 1983–86; Head of Personnel, Scottish Daily Record & Sunday Mail (1986) Ltd, 1987; Personnel Dir, Maxwell Pergamon Publishing Corp., 1988–89; Sen. Consultant, Contract 2000, 1989–90; Man. Dir, Cousins Financial Services Ltd (Gibraltar), 1990–. Mem., Transport and Local Govt Cttees, TUC; UK Deleg., ILO; International Transport Workers Federation: Member: Aviation Sect.; Local Govt Cttee; Chemical Cttee; Civil Aviation Cttee; Mem. Industrial Training Bds. Member: Countryside Commn, 1972–84; New Towns Commn, 1975–79; Sandford Cttee to review National Parks in England and Wales, 1972–73; Council, RSPB, 1982; Bd of Trustees, Royal Botanic Gardens, Kew, 1983–88. Chm., British Council of Productivity Assocs, 1977–82. Travelling Fellow, Kingston Reg. Management Centre, 1977. FCMI. *Recreations:* music, golf. *Address:* Apt 1265 Marcopolo Hotel, 3 Salisbury Road, Tsim Sha Tsui, Kowloon, Hong Kong.

COUSINS, Philip, CB 1982; Deputy Comptroller and Auditor General, National Audit Office (formerly Secretary, Exchequer and Audit Department), 1979–84; *b* 28 Feb. 1923; *s* of Herbert and Ella Cousins; *m* 1948, Ruby Laura Morris; two *d. Educ:* Royal Liberty School, Romford. Served in Royal Air Force, 1943–47. Joined Treasury, 1949; Under Secretary, 1974–79. *Address:* 102 Philbeach Gardens, SW5 9ET. *T:* (020) 7373 6164.

COUSINS, Richard John; Chief Executive, Compass Group PLC, since 2006; *b* 29 March 1959; *s* of Philip Cousins and late Marian Cousins; *m* 1982, Caroline Thorpe; two *s. Educ:* Sheffield Univ. (BSc Maths and Stats); Lancaster Univ. (MA Operational Res.). OR Dept, Cadbury Schweppes plc, 1981–84; BTR (Newey and Eyre) Corporate Planning, 1984–90; with BPB plc, 1990–2005: Corporate Planning, 1990–92; Gp Financial Controller, 1992–95; Gen. Manager, Packaging, 1995–96; Man. Dir, Abertay, 1996–98; Pres., BPB Westroc (Canada), 1998–2000; Chief Exec., 2000–05. Non-executive Director: P&O plc, 2005–06; HBOS plc, 2007–. *Recreations:* cricket, walking, photography, history. *Address:* Compass Group PLC, Compass House, Guildford Street, Chertsey, Surrey KT16 9BQ.

COUSSINS, Baroness *cr* 2007 (Life Peer), of Whitehall Park in the London Borough of Islington; **Jean Elizabeth Coussins;** independent consultant on corporate responsibility, since 2006; *b* 26 Oct. 1950; *d* of Walter Leonard Coussins and Jessica Coussins (*née* Hughes); *m* 1976, Roger Hamilton (marr. diss. 1985); one *s* one *d*; one *d. Educ:* Godolphin and Latymer Girls' Sch.; Newnham Coll., Cambridge (BA (Medieval and Modern Langs) 1973; MA 1976). Sec., UN Youth and Student Assoc., 1973–75; Women's Rights Officer, NCCL, 1975–80; Dep. Dir, Child Poverty Action Gp, 1980–83; Sen. Educn Officer, ILEA, 1983–88; Dir, Social Policy Div., 1988–94, Equality Assurance Div., 1994–96, CRE; Chief Exec., Portman Gp, 1996–2006. Non-exec. Dir and Council Mem., ASA, 2003–. Founder Mem. and Chm., Maternity Alliance, 1980–81. Member: Crime Prevention Panel, Foresight Prog., DTI, 2000–03; Scottish Ministerial Adv. Cttee on Alcohol Problems, 2001–06; Adv. Gp on alcohol harm reduction, PM's Strategy Unit, 2003–04; Expert Taskforce on Consumers and Markets, DoH, 2004. Indep. Mem. Adv. Council, BBFC, 2002–05; Comr, Better Regulation Commn, 2004–07. Trustee: Inst. for Citizenship, 1994–99; Drinkaware Trust, 2001–06; Alcohol Educn and Res. Council, 2004–07. Parent Gov., Ashmount Sch., 1980s; Associate Fellow and Mem. Governing Body, Newnham Coll., Cambridge, 2002–05; Mem., Bd Govs, Channing Sch., 2007–. FRSA. *Publications:* Taking Liberties, 1978; (jtly) Shattering Illusions: West Indians in British politics, 1986; (contrib.) Policing Black People, 1990; pamphlets and booklets on equality and maternity rights. *Recreations:* family, travel, food, swimming, football, crosswords. *Address:* House of Lords, SW1A 0PW. *T:* (020) 7219 5353; *e-mail:* coussinsj@parliament.uk. *Club:* Fulham Football.

COUTTS; *see* Money-Coutts.

COUTTS, Anne Jane, MEd; Headteacher, Headington School, since 2003; *b* Watford, 9 April 1956; *d* of Alistair and Mysie Sutherland; *m* 1978, Ian Alexander Coutts; two *d. Educ:* King's High Sch., Warwick; Aspley Grammar Sch.; Univ. of Warwick (BSc, PGCE, MEd). Res. Asst, Nuffield Inst. for Med. Res. and Oxford Inst. of Virol., 1978–80; Teacher of Chemistry: Coventry LEA, 1981–83; Hereford and Worcester LEA, 1983–86; Hd of Gen. Studies, Trent Coll., 1986–88; Dep. Hd, then Actg Hd, Edgbaston Coll. of Educn, 1988–92; Head: Eothen Sch., Caterham, 1992–95; Sutton High Sch., 1995–2003. Mem., QCA Adv. Gp for Res. in Assessment and Qualifications Cttee, HMC Council, 2007–. *Recreations:* photography, singing, saxophone, cooking, reading. *Address:* Headington School, Headington Road, Oxford OX3 7TD. *T:* (01865) 759100; *e-mail:* enquiries@headington.org.uk.

COUTTS, Gordon; *see* Coutts, T. G.

COUTTS, Herbert, MBE 2008; FSAScot; FMA; Director of Culture and Leisure (formerly of Culture and Arts), City of Edinburgh Council, 2001–06; *b* 9 March 1944; *s* of late Herbert and Agnes Coutts, Dundee; *m* 1970, Angela Elizabeth Mason Smith; one *s* three *d. Educ:* Morgan Acad., Dundee. FSAScot 1965; AMA 1970, FMA 1976. Asst Keeper of Antiquities and Bygones, Dundee City Museums, 1965–68, Keeper, 1968–71; Supt, Edinburgh City Museums, 1971–73; City Curator, City of Edinburgh Museums and Art Galls, 1973–96; City of Edinburgh Council: Hd of Museums and Galls, 1996–97; Hd of Heritage and Arts, 1997–99; Dir of Recreation, 1999–2001. Vice Pres., Museums Assts Gp, 1967–70; Member: Bd, Scottish Museums Council, 1971–74, and 1986–88; Govt Cttee on Future of Scotland's Nat. Museums and Galleries, 1979–80 (report publd 1981); Bd, Museums Trng Inst., 1995–2000; Bd, Cultural Heritage NTO, 2000–04; Bd of Trustees, Nat. Galleries of Scotland, 2007–. Member, Council: Museums Assoc., 1977–78, 1987–88; Soc. of Antiquaries of Scotland, 1981–82; Museums Advr, COSLA Arts and Recreation Cttee, 1985–90, 1995–99. Member: Paxton House Trust, 1988–2002, 2006–; E Lothian Community Develt Trust, 1989–; Scottish Catholic Heritage Commn, 2006–; Bd, Order of Malta Dial-a-Journey Ltd, 2007–; Dunbar Community Council, 2007–. External Examr, St Andrews Univ., 1993–97. Building Projects: City of Edinburgh Art Centre (opened 1980); Museum of Childhood Extension (opened 1986); People's Story Museum (opened 1989); City of Edinburgh Art Centre Extension (opened 1992); Scott Monument Restoration (completed 1999); Usher Hall Renovation (completed 2000). Exhibitions at City of Edinburgh Art Centre: The Emperor's Warriors, 1985; Gold of the Pharaohs, 1988; Gold of Peru, 1990; Golden Warriors of the Ukrainian Steppes, 1993; Star Trek—The Exhibition, 1995; Quest for a Pirate, 1996; Gateway to the Silk Road, 1996. Contested (Lab) Angus South, 1970. Founding Fellow, Inst. of Contemp. Scotland, 1999. SBStJ 1977. Baron Bailie of Dolphinstoun, 2007–. *Publications:* Ancient Monuments of Tayside, 1970; Tayside Before History, 1971; Aince a Bailie, Aye a Bailie, 1974; Edinburgh: an illustrated history, 1975; Huntly House, 1980; Lady Stair's House, 1980; (ed) Gold of the Pharaohs, 1988; (ed) Dinosaurs Alive, 1990; (ed) Gold of Peru, 1990; (ed) Golden Warriors of the Ukrainian Steppes, 1993; (ed) Gateway to the Silk Road, 1996; (ed) Quest for a Pirate, 1996; (ed) Faster, Higher, Stronger, 1997; exhibn catalogues; contrib. Museums Jl and archaeol jls. *Recreations:* relaxing with family, gardening, going to the opera, writing, reading, walking. *Address:* Kirkhill House, Queen's Road, Dunbar, East Lothian EH42 1LN. *T:* (01368) 863113.

COUTTS, Ian Dewar, CBE 1982; in practice as chartered accountant, 1950–95; Member, Forestry Commission, 1984–93; Director, Eastern Electricity plc, 1990–95 (Member, Eastern Electricity Board, 1982–90); *b* 15 May 1927; *s* of David Dewar Coutts and Dorothy Helen Coutts; *m* 1st, 1950, Sheila Margaret Cargill (marr. diss. 1983); one *s* two *d*; 2nd 1983, Hilary Ballard; one *s* one *d. Educ:* Ipswich Sch.; Culford Sch.; UEA (BA History, 2000). Chartered Accountant, 1949. Served 1st Essex Regt, 1946–48. Norfolk County Councillor, 1970–89; Leader, Norfolk CC, 1973–79. Chm., ACC Finance Cttee, 1977–83; Mem., Consultative Council on Local Govt Finance, 1977–83. Mem., Local Govt Audit Commn, 1983–90. Chm., S Norfolk Conservative Assoc., 1970–73; Parly Cand., Norwich S, 1979. Mem., Council, Univ. of East Anglia, 1974–86. *Recreation:* sailing.

COUTTS, Russell, DCNZM 2000; CBE 1995 (MBE 1985); yachtsman; *b* 1 March 1962; *s* of late Allan and of Beverley Coutts; *m* 1999, Jennifer Little; two *s* one *d. Educ:* Auckland Univ. (BEng). Gold Medal, Finn Cl., Olympic Games, LA, 1984; World Champion, Match Racing, 1992, 1993 and 1996; ranked No 1, Match Racing Circuit, 1994; winner, Brut Sailing series, 1996; Helmsman: Admiral's Cup winner, Pinta, 1993; America's Cup winners, Black Magic, San Diego, 1995 and Team NZ, Auckland, 2000; World Title, S Australia, 2001; 1st Swedish Match Cup, Marstrand, 2001; winner, World Title, Farr 40, Alinghi, 2001; Skipper and Exec. Dir, America's Cup winner, Alinghi Team, Switzerland, 2003. Yachtsman of the Year, NZ, 1984; Sperry World Sailor of the Year, 1995; Trophée Fabergé, Match Racing, 1996. *Publications:* The Course to Victory, 1996; America's Cup 2000, 1999; Challenge 2000: the race to win the America's Cup, 1999. *Recreation:* golf. *Address: e-mail:* media@russellcoutts.net. *Clubs:* Société Nautique de Genève; New York Yacht; Royal New Zealand Yacht; North Shore Golf, Titirangi Golf (Auckland).

COUTTS, T(homas) Gordon; QC (Scotland) 1973; *b* 5 July 1933; *s* of Thomas Coutts and Evelyn Gordon Coutts; *m* 1959, Winifred Katherine Scott, PhD; one *s* one *d. Educ:* Aberdeen Grammar Sch.; Aberdeen Univ. (MA, LLB). Admitted Faculty of Advocates, 1959; Standing Junior Counsel to Dept Agric. (Scot.), 1965–73; called to the Bar, Lincoln's Inn, 1995. Temporary Judge, Court of Session, Scotland, 1991–2004; Vice Pres. (Scot.), VAT and Duties Tribunals, 1996–2008. Part-time Chairman: Industrial Tribunals, 1972–2003; Medical Appeal Tribunal, 1984–2006; VAT Tribunal, 1990–96; Financial Services and Markets Tribunal, 2001–; Pension Regulator Appeal Tribunal, 2005–08. Mem., Panel of Arbitrators, 1995. FCIArb 1994. *Recreations:* travel, stamp collecting. *Address:* 6 Heriot Row, Edinburgh EH3 6HU. *Club:* New (Edinburgh).

COUTTS, William Walter B.; *see* Burdett-Coutts.

COUTURE, Most Rev. Maurice; Archbishop of Québec, (RC), and Primate of Canada, 1990–2002; *b* 3 Nov. 1926. Perpetual vows with Vincentian Fathers, 1948; ordained priest, 1951; Patros de la Baie, Plessisville, Port Alfred and Bagotville, 1952–55; in charge of Minor Seminary of his Congregation, 1955–65; founder and Rector, Inter-Congregational Seminary, Cap-Rouge, 1965–70; Provincial Superior, 1970–76, Superior General of Congregation, 1976–82; Titular Bishop of Talattula and Auxiliary Bishop of Québec, 1982–88; Bishop of Baie-Comeau, 1988–90. *Address:* c/o Office of the Archbishop of Québec, 1073 Boulevard René Levesque Ouest, Québec, QC G1S 4R5, Canada.

COUZENS, Brian William; classical recording producer; Chairman, Chandos Records Ltd, since 2004; Managing Director, Chandos Music, since 1961; *b* 17 Jan. 1933; *s* of William and Vera Couzens; *m* 1st, 1956, Ilse Elizabeth Hauguth (*d* 2005); three *s* one *d*; 2nd, 2006, Deborah Frogel. Self educated. Musician, 1948–51; Nat. Service, 1951–53; composer and arranger for BBC and publishers, 1954–59; orchestration for films incl. Where Eagles Dare, Magnificent Men in their Flying Machines, 633 Squadron, and 34 films working for Ron Goodwin, John Williams, Dimitri Tiomkin, and others, 1959–69; formed Chandos Music Ltd, 1961; independent sound engr and record producer of classical music, 1969–78; formed Chandos Records Ltd, 1979. Hon Dr, Anglia Ruskin, 2007. Numerous internat. awards incl. Grammy, and Gramophone. *Recreations:* photography, video, nature and wildlife. *Address:* Chandos Records Ltd, Chandos House, Commerce Park, Commerce Way, Colchester CO2 8HX. *T:* (01206) 225200.

COUZENS, Air Vice-Marshal David Cyril, CEng, FIMechE, FRAeS; Senior Directing Staff (Air), Royal College of Defence Studies, 2003–04; *b* 15 Oct. 1949; *s* of Cyril Couzens and Joyce Couzens (*née* Walker); *m* 1977, Deborah Cawse; one *s* one *d. Educ:* Ecclesbourne Sch.; Churchill Coll., Cambridge (MA); Open Univ. Business Sch. (MBA); Loughborough Univ. (Postgrad. Dip). CEng 1979; FIMechE 1991; FRAeS 1995. Joined Royal Air Force, 1968: initial and professional trng, 1968–72; practical aircraft/weapon system appts, 1972–88; personnel mgt, 1988–89; Gp Captain 1990; Superintendent of Armament, 1990–91; Dep. Dir Support Policy (Op. Requirements) (RAF), MoD Policy, 1991–94; rcds 1994; Air Cdre 1995; Air Cdre, CIS, HQ Strike Comd, 1995–97; Dir, Logistic Inf. Strategy (RAF), MoD, 1997–98; AO, Logistic Inf. Strategy and Industrial Interface Study, MoD, 1998–99; Air Vice-Marshal 1999; Dir Gen., Defence Logistics (Communications and Inf. Systems), 1999–2001, Defence Logistics Capability, 2001–02, MoD; COS to Surgeon Gen., MoD, 2002–03. Mem. Council and Chm., Professional Standards Bd, RAeS, 2006–. President: RAF Rugby League, 1999–2004; Combined Services Rugby League, 2002–04. FCMI 2002. *Recreations:* hill-walking, gardening, music. *Club:* Royal Air Force (Chm., 2003–04).

COVENEY, Prof. James; Professor of French, University of Bath, 1969–85, now Professor Emeritus; *b* 4 April 1920; *s* of James and Mary Coveney; *m* 1955, Patricia Yvonne Townsend; two *s. Educ:* St Ignatius Coll., London; Univ. of Reading (BA 1st Cl. Hons French, 1950); Univ. of Strasbourg (Dr Univ. 1953). Served War of 1939–45: Welch Regt; Royal West Kent Regt; RAF (Flt-Lt (Pilot)). French Govt Res. Scholar, 1950–51, Lectr, 1951–53, Univ. of Strasbourg; Lectr in Medieval French, Univ. of Hull, 1953–58; Asst Dir, Civil Service Commn, 1958–59; UN Secretariat, New York, 1959–61; NATO Secretariat, 1961–64; University of Bath: Head of Mod. Langs Gp, 1964–68; Jt Dir, Centre for European Industrial Studies, 1969–75; Head of Sch. of Mod. Langs, 1969–77 and 1980–83. Visiting Professor: Ecole Nat. d'Administration, Paris, 1974–85; Univ. of Buckingham, 1974–86 (Mem., Acad. Adv. Council, 1974–83); Bethlehem Univ., 1985. Consultant: Univ. of Macau, 1988; Internat. Communications Inc., Tokyo, 1991–94. Lang. Trng Advr, McKinsey & Co., 1967–73. Member: British-French Cultural Commn, 1973–79; Bd of Govs, British Inst. in Paris, 1975–79; European League for Econ. Co-operation, 1997. Trustee, Friends of Birzeit Univ., 1991–2004. Corresp. Mem., Académie des Sciences, Agriculture, Arts et Belles-Lettres, Aix-en-Provence, 1975; Confrère de Saint-Etienne, Alsace, 1998. Officier, Ordre des Palmes Académiques (France), 2007 (Chevalier, 1978); Officier, Ordre National du Mérite (France), 1986. *Publications:* La Légende de l'Empereur Constant, 1955; (with S. Moore) Glossary of French and English Management Terms, 1972; (with J. Grosjean) Le français pour l'ingénieur, 1974; (with S. Kempa) Guide to French Institutions, 1978; (with S.

Moore) French Business Management Dictionary, 1993. *Address:* 2 Campions Court, Graemesdyke Road, Berkhamsted, Herts HP4 3PD. *T:* (01442) 865657. *Club:* Travellers.

COVENEY, Michael William; theatre critic and author; *b* 24 July 1948; *s* of William Coveney and Violet Amy Coveney (*née* Perry); *m* 1977, Susan Monica Hyman; one *s*. *Educ:* St Ignatius College, London; Worcester College, Oxford. Editor, Plays and Players, 1975–78; theatre critic: Financial Times, 1981–89; The Observer, 1990–97; Daily Mail, 1997–2004. *Publications:* The Citz, 1990; Maggie Smith, 1992; The Aisle is Full of Noises, 1994; (with Robert Stephens) Knight Errant: memoirs of a vagabond actor, 1995; The World According to Mike Leigh, 1996; Cats on a Chandelier: the Andrew Lloyd Webber story, 1999. *Recreations:* music, running, travel. *Address:* 11 Shirlock Road, NW3 2HR.

COVENTRY, family name of **Earl of Coventry**.

COVENTRY, 13th Earl of, *cr* 1697; **George William Coventry;** Viscount Deerhurst 1697; *b* 5 Oct. 1939; *s* of Comdr Cecil Dick Bluett Coventry, DSC, RD, RNR; *S* kinsman, 2004; *m* 1965, Gillian Frances, *d* of F. W. R. Randall; one *d*. *Educ:* Prince of Wales Sch., Nairobi. *Heir: nephew* David Duncan Sherwood Coventry, *b* 5 March 1973.

COVENTRY, Bishop of, since 2008; **Rt Rev. Christopher John Cocksworth,** PhD; *b* 12 Jan. 1959; *s* of Stanley John Cocksworth and Auriol Gwyneth Cocksworth; *m* 1979, Charlotte Mary Pytches; five *s*. *Educ:* Manchester Univ. (BA (1st cl. Hons) Theol., 1980; PhD 1989); Didsbury Sch. of Educn, Manchester Poly. (PGCE 1981); St John's Theol Coll., Nottingham. Teacher and House Tutor, King Edward's Sch., Witley, Surrey, 1981–84; doctoral res. student, 1986–88. Ordained deacon, 1988, priest, 1989; Asst Curate, Christ Church, Epsom, 1988–92; Chaplain, RHBNC, Univ. of London, 1992–97; Dir, STETS, 1997–2001; Principal, Ridley Hall, Cambridge, 2001–08. Hon. Canon, Guildford Cathedral, 2000–01, now Canon Emeritus. Mem., C of E Liturgical Commn, 1996–2006. *Publications:* Evangelical Eucharistic Thought in the Church of England, 1993; (with Paul Roberts) Renewing Daily Prayer, 1993; (with Alan Wilkinson) An Anglican Companion, 1996, 2nd edn 2001; Holy, Holy, Holy: worshipping the Trinitarian God, 1997; Prayer and the Departed, 1997; (with Jeremy Fletcher) The Spirit and Liturgy, 1998; (with Rosalind Brown) Being a Priest Today, 2002, 2nd edn 2006; Wisdom: the Spirit's gift, 2003; Holding Together: Gospel, Church and Spirit, 2008; various articles in bks and learned jls. *Recreations:* hill-walking, cycling, swimming, film watching. *Address:* Bishop's House, 23 Davenport Road, Coventry CV5 6PW. *T:* (024) 7667 2244.

COVENTRY, Dean of; *see* Irvine, Very Rev. J. D.

COVENTRY, Archdeacon of; *see* Watson, Ven. I. L. S.

COVEY, Donna May; Chief Executive, Refugee Council, since 2007; *b* 20 June 1961; *d* of Mrs Cynthia Covey. *Educ:* Univ. of Warwick (BSc). Nat. Officer, GMB, 1988–98; Dir, Assoc. of CHCs for England and Wales, 1998–2001; Chief Exec., Nat. Asthma Campaign, subseq. Asthma UK, 2001–07. Chm., London Food Commn, 1986–87; Vice Chm., Wandsworth CHC, 1987–88. Member: Gen. Council, TUC, 1988–98; Nat. Women's Cttee, Labour Party, 1992–98. *Publications:* contributed to: Waiting for Change, 1986; Visions of Primary Care, 1999; NHS Frontline: visions for 2010, 2000; A Practical Guide to Primary Care Groups and Trusts, 2001. *Recreations:* rambling, murder mysteries, Tate Gall. *Address:* Refugee Council, 240–250 Ferndale Road, SW9 8BB.

COVILLE, Air Marshal Sir Christopher (Charles Cotton), KCB 2000 (CB 1995); Defence Advisor, BT Defence, since 2003; Managing Director, C4 Defence and Aerospace, since 2003; Chairman, Westland Helicopters, since 2005; Senior Defence Advisor, Rockwell Collins (UK), since 2007; *b* 2 June 1945; *s* of Henry and Anna Coville; *m* 1967, Irene Johnson; one *s* two *d*. *Educ:* De La Salle Grammar Sch., Liverpool; RAF Coll., Cranwell. BA Open. Lightning Pilot and Instructor, 1969–73; Phantom Pilot and Instructor, 1973–78; Central Tactics and Trials Orgn, 1978–80; Personal Staff Officer to UK Mil. Rep., Brussels, 1981–83; OC Ops Wing, RAF Stanley, 1983; OC 111 Fighter Sqn, 1983–85; Gp Capt. Air, HQ 11 Fighter Group, 1985–86; OC RAF Coningsby, 1986–88; RCDS 1989; Air Cdre Flying Training, HQ RAF Support Command, 1990–92; AO Trng and AOC Trng Gp, 1992–94; Chief Exec., Trng Gp Defence Agency, Apr.–Sept. 1994; ACDS, Op. Requirements (Air), 1994–98; Dep. C-in-C, AFCENT, 1998–2000; Dep. C-in-C, AFNORTH, 2000–01; Air Mem. for Personnel, and C-in-C, PTC, 2001–03. President: RAF Microlight Assoc., 1992–2000; RAF Football Assoc., 1996–2002; Vice-Pres., RAFA, 2001–. FCIPD (FITD 1993); FRAeS 1994. *Recreations:* mountaineering, shooting. *Club:* Royal Air Force.

COVINGTON, Nicholas; Director, Office of Manpower Economics, 1986–89; *b* 9 June 1929; *s* of late Cyril Tim Covington and Margaret Joan (*née* Bray); *m* 1st, 1953, Pat Sillitoe; one *s* two *d*; 2nd, 1983, Kathy Hegarty. *Educ:* Cranleigh Sch.; Oriel Coll., Oxford. RAF, 1947–49; TA Commn, 1952. Metal Box Co. Ltd, South Africa, 1952–57; Gen. Manager and Dir, Garnier & Co. Ltd, 1957–66; entered Min. of Labour, 1966; Asst Sec., 1971; Industrial Relns Div., Dept of Employment, 1976–86. *Address:* Dovecote House, Lower Slaughter, near Cheltenham, Glos GL54 2HY.

COWAN, Annella Marie; Sheriff of Grampian, Highland and Islands at Aberdeen, since 1997; *b* 14 Nov. 1953; *m* 1979, James Temple Cowan (marr. diss. 1995). *Educ:* Elgin Acad.; Edinburgh Univ. (LLB 1976; MSc 1984). Admitted Solicitor, 1978; Procurator Fiscal Depute, 1978–86; seconded to Scottish Law Commn, 1984–86; admitted Faculty of Advocates, 1987; Temp. Sheriff, 1991; Sheriff of Tayside, Central and Fife at Stirling, 1993–97. *Recreation:* equestrianism. *Address:* Sheriff's Chambers, Sheriff Court, Aberdeen AB10 1WP. *T:* (01224) 657200.

COWAN, Prof. Charles Donald, (Jeremy), CBE 1988; MA Cantab, PhD London; FRAS; Chairman, External System, University of London, 1993–97; *b* London, 18 Nov. 1923; *s* of W. C. Cowan and Minnie Ethel (*née* Farrow); *m* 1st, 1945, Mary Evelyn (marr. diss. 1960), *d* of Otto Vetter, Perth, WA; two *d*; 2nd, 1962, Daphne Eleanor (*d* 2004), *d* of Walter Rishworth Whittam, Rangoon. *Educ:* Kilburn Grammar Sch.; Peterhouse, Cambridge. Served Royal Navy, 1941–45. Lecturer in History, Raffles Coll., Singapore, 1947–48, and University of Malaya, 1948–50; School of Oriental and African Studies, University of London: Lectr in the History of South-East Asia, 1950–60; Prof., 1961–80, Prof. of Oriental History, 1980–89; Dir, 1976–89; London University: Pro-Vice-Chancellor, 1985–86; Dep. Vice-Chancellor, 1988–90; Chm. of Convocation, 1990–94. Visiting Prof. of Southeast Asian Hist., Cornell Univ., 1960–61. Chm., Cttee for SE Asian Studies, British Acad., 1990–97. Governor: James Allen's Girls School, 1977–89; Alleyn's Sch., 1980–98; Dulwich Coll., 1980–98; Richmond Coll., 1988–92. Trustee, Dulwich Estate, 1985–98. Hon. DSc, London. *Publications:* Nineteenth Century Malaya, 1961; (ed) The Economic Development of South-East Asia, 1964; (ed) The Economic Development of China and Japan, 1964; (with P. L. Burns) Sir Frank Swettenham's Malayan Journals, 1975; (with O. L. Wolters) Southeast Asian History and Historiography, 1976. *Address:* 34 Great Brownings, College Road, SE21 7HP.

COWAN, Brig. Colin Hunter, CBE 1984; Chief Executive, Cumbernaul Development Corporation, 1970–85; *b* 16 Oct. 1920; *s* of late Lt-Col S. Hunter Cowa DSO and Mrs Jean Hunter Cowan; *m* 1st, 1949, Elizabeth Williamson, MD (*d* 1985); on *s* one *d* (and one *s* decd); 2nd, 1988, Mrs Jen Burnett, *widow* of A. H. Burnett. *Edu* Wellington Coll.; RMA Woolwich; Trinity Coll., Cambridge (MA). MICE. Com Engineer Regt, 1960–63; Defence Adviser, UK Mission to the UN, 1964–66; Brigadi Engineer Plans, MoD (Army), 1968–70. DL Dunbartonshire, 1973–88. *Recreations:* musi photography. *Address:* Flat 11, Varrich House, 7 Church Hill, Edinburgh EH10 4BG. *T* (0131) 447 9768. *Club:* New (Edinburgh).

COWAN, Dr George Osborne, OBE 1986; FRCP, FRCPE; Medical Director, Joi Committee on Higher Medical Training, Royal Colleges of Physicians of UK, 2001–0 *b* 5 Sept. 1939; *s* of late John Jardine Cowan and Marion Ramsay Cowan (*née* Corrie); 1981, Beatrice Mary Hill, MA, MPhil, MLitt, *d* of late Leonard Charles Hill, OBE, DS FRGS and Joyce (*née* Snelus). *Educ:* Merchiston Castle Sch., Edinburgh; Univ. of S Andrews (MB ChB 1963); Open Univ. (Dip. Music, 2004; BA 1st Cl. Hons Humaniti with Music, 2007). MRCPE 1967, FRCPE 1978; DTM&H 1968; MRCP 1967, FRC 1983. Commissioned RAMC, 1962; served Australia, Hong Kong, Malaysia, Singapor Nepal, The Gambia, Germany and NI; Consultant Physician in Army Hosps, 1973–9 Prof. of Mil. Medicine, RAMC, 1987–92; Dir of Army Medicine, 1992–93; Comdt an Post-Grad. Dean, Royal Army Med. Coll., 1993–96; QHP 1992–96; retired in rank Maj.-Gen., 1996. Dean of Postgrad. Medicine, Univ. of London (N Thames) (former N Thames (E) Region), 1996–2001. Cohen Lectr, Univ. of Liverpool, 1991. Pres RSTM&H, 1995–97 (Vice-Pres., 1993–95). Hon. FRCPI 2003; FRCPGlas *aeg* 200 Mitchiner Medal, RCS, 1992. OStJ 1994. *Publications:* (ed) Atlas of Medic Helminthology and Protozoology, 3rd edn, 1991; (with B. J. Heap) Clinical Tropic Medicine, 1993; (with N. R. H. Burgess) Atlas of Medical Entomology, 1993. *Recreation* golf, music, medical history. *Clubs:* Army and Navy; Royal & Ancient Golf (St Andrews).

COWAN, James Robertson, CBE 1983 (OBE 1974); CEng, FIMinE; Chairman, NC Coal Products, 1985–88; *b* 12 Sept. 1919; *s* of John and Jean Cowan; *m* 1945, Harri Good Forrest; two *d*. *Educ:* Dalziel High Sch., Motherwell; Glasgow Univ. (BSc 1st C Hons). CEng, FIMinE 1971. National Coal Board: Dir, Scottish Area, 1970–80; B Mem., 1977–85; Mem. for Industrial Relns, 1980–85; Dep. Chm., 1982–85. Chm Scottish Brick Corp., 1980–88 (Dir, 1974–88); Dep. Chm., British Investment Trust (Di 1978–). Vis. Prof., Strathclyde Univ., 1978. CCMI. *Recreation:* golf. *Address:* 11 Th Paddock, Gullane, Scotland EH31 2BW. *T:* (01620) 843398. *Club:* Caledonian.

COWAN, Jeremy; *see* Cowan, C. D.

COWAN, Lionel David, (Nick Cowan); personnel management consultant; *b* 18 De 1929; *m* 1953, Pamela Ida, *e d* of Hubert and Winifred Williams, Totton, Hants; one *s* tw *d*. *Educ:* Surbiton County Grammar Sch.; King's Coll., London (BA Hons Spanish, 1995 Univ. of Salamanca (Dip. in Hispanic Studies, 1994). CCIPD (CIPM 1979; AMIPM 1965). Served Royal Navy, 1945–61: Fleet Air Arm Aircrew (Lieut), 1953; Sen. Inst RAN, 1958–60. Training Officer, Shoe and Allied Trades Res. Assoc., 1961–62; Perki Engines Gp, 1962–72; Dir of Personnel, Philips Electronic and Associated Industrie 1972–78; Gp Personnel Dir, Unigate Ltd, 1978–79; Dir and Sec., Fedn of Londo Clearing Bank Employers, 1980–87; Personnel Dir, TSB England & Wales, 1987–8 Chm., W Lambeth HA, 1982–86; Member: Employment Appeal Tribunal, 1976–200 Editorial Panel, Industrial Relns Law Reports, 1977–; Civil Service Arbitration Tribuna 1979–; Central Arbitration Cttee, 1984–2000; Equal Opportunities Commn, 1988–9 NEDO Enquiry, Industrial Relns Trng for Managers, 1976, Supply and Demand f Skilled Manpower, 1977. Vice-Pres. (Employee Relations), IPM, 1977–79. Directo Oxford Univ. Business Summer Sch., 1980. *Publications:* Personnel Management an Banking, 1984; The Clearing Banks and the Trade Unions, 1984. *Recreations:* thin Spanish, music and opera, bridge. *Address:* 15 Somerville Road, Cobham, Surrey KT 2QT. *T:* (01372) 843441.

COWAN, Robert Charles; writer and broadcaster; *b* 14 April 1948; *s* of Maurice Berna Cowan and Vera Cowan; *m* 1971, Georgina Gilmour; two *d*. *Educ:* Fern Bank Prima Sch.; Leas House Sch.; Pitman's Coll. Asst, Lewis Cranston Public Relns, 196 Advertising Dept, Pergamon Press, 1966–68; Asst Librarian, BBC Record Liby an Concerts Mgt, 1968–69; Advertising Manager, 1970–78, Archivist, 1978–89, Boosey Hawkes Music Publishers Ltd. Ed., Music Diary, 1982–89; contrib. 1985–, Ed., 1989–9 CD Rev. mag.; Ed., Classics mag., 1991–93; contrib., 1993–, Contributing Ed., 1999 Gramophone; writer, The Independent, 1993–; radio: co-presenter, Classic Verdic 1992–95; presenter: Our Musical Yesterdays, 1993; Off the Record, 1996; CD Choic 1998–2000; CD Masters, 2001–07; The Cowan Collection, 2003–07; Rob Cowa Breakfast, 2007–. Grammy Award, 1995. *Publication:* The Guinness Classical 1000, 199 *Recreations:* walking, listening, reading, collecting, travelling, writing (for fun), spendir time with my family. *Address:* 2 Merry Hill Mount, Bushey, Herts WD23 1DJ.

COWAN, Gen. Sir Samuel, KCB 1997; CBE 1988 (OBE 1983); Chief of Defenc Logistics, Ministry of Defence, 1998–2002; Aide-de-camp to the Queen, 2000–02; *b* Oct. 1941; *s* of late Samuel Cowan and Rachel Cowan; *m* 1971, Anne Gretton; one *s* or *d*. *Educ:* Lisburn Technical Coll.; Open Univ. (BA 1980). Commissioned Royal Signal 1963; CO 2 Armd Div. HQ and Signal Regt, 1980–82; Comdr Communications an Comdr 1 Signal Brigade, 1 (BR) Corps, 1985–87; Director of Public Relations (Army 1987–88; Comdt, RMCS, 1989–91; ACDS OR (Land), 1991–94; Inspector Ge Training, MoD, 1995–96; QMG, MoD, 1996–98. Col Comdt, Brigade of Gurkha 1994–2003; Master of Signals, 2003–08. Pres., Gurkha Bde Assoc., 2004–; Dep. Gra Pres., Royal Commonwealth Ex-Services League, 2003–. Hon. FCIPS 2000; Ho FCILT (Hon. FILT 2000). Hon. DSc Cranfield, 1999. *Recreations:* sport, trekking Nepal. *Address:* c/o RHQ Royal Signals, Blandford Camp, Dorset DT11 8RH. (01258) 482082. *Club:* Army and Navy.

COWANS, David; Chief Executive, Places for People Group, since 1999; *b* 3 May 195 *s* of Harry and Margaret Cowans; *m* 1997, Julie Brewerton; one *s* two *d*. *Educ:* Cuthbert's Grammar Sch., Newcastle upon Tyne; New Coll., Durham (Dip. Housin Studies); Birmingham Univ. (MBA). Neighbourhood Officer, Walsall MBC, 1979–8 Area Manager, Sheffield CC, 1982–86; Asst Dir of Housing, Leicester CC, 1986–88; Ge Manager, 1988–94, Dir of Housing, 1994–97, Birmingham CC; Gp Chief Exec., British Housing Gp, 1997–99. Mem. Exec. Council, Nat. Housing Fedn, 1998–200 *Recreations:* cinema, music, my children, social history, gardening. *Address:* Galtres Hous 11 Rawcliffe Lane, Clifton, York YO30 6NP. *T:* (01904) 650150; *e-mail:* david.cowans(placesforpeople.co.uk.

COWARD, David John, CMG 1965; OBE 1962; Registrar General, Kenya, 1955–82; 21 March 1917; *s* of late Robert J. Coward, Exmouth, Devon; *m* 1954, Joan, *d* of la Reginald Frank, Doncaster; three *d*. *Educ:* Exmouth Grammar Sch. and Law Society's Sc of Law. FCIS 1961; ACIArb 1984. Admitted a solicitor, 1938. Joined RN as a rating outbreak of war, 1939; commissioned, 1941; demobilized as Lieut-Comdr (S) RNVR

1947. ADC to Governor of Trinidad, 1947. Joined Colonial Legal Service, 1948, Asst Registrar Gen., Kenya; Dep. Registrar Gen., 1952; Registrar Gen., Official Receiver and Public Trustee, 1955–82. Acted as Permanent Sec. for Justice and Constitutional Affairs, 1963–64. Served in Kenya Police Reserve, 1949–63, latterly as Senior Superintendent i/c Nairobi Area. Chm., Working Party on future of Company Secretarial Profession in Kenya; Mem. Accountants' Registration Bd, 1978–82; Trustee, Nat. Museums of Kenya, 1979–82. Pres., Storrington Br., Royal British Legion, 2002– (Chm., 1993–97). Liveryman, 1985 and Hon. Archivist, 1995–2002, Chartered Secretaries' and Administrators' Co. Silver Medal, Internat. Olympic Cttee, 1981. *Recreations:* golf, genealogy. *Address:* North Perretts, Spinney Lane, West Chiltington, W Sussex RH20 2NX. *T:* (01903) 742521. *Clubs:* Naval; Nairobi and Limuru Country (Kenya).

COWARD, Maj. Gen. Gary Robert, CB 2008; OBE 1996; Chief of Staff (Joint Welfare Development), since 2008; *b* 26 Aug. 1955; *s* of Robert Vacey and Marion Avril Coward; *m* 1978, Chrissie Hamerton; one *s*. *Educ:* Duke of York's Royal Mil. Sch.; RMA Sandhurst. Served RA, 1974–82; transf. to AAC, 1983; OC 656 Sqdn, 1991–93; UN mil. spokesman (UNPROFOR), 1994–95; CO 1 Regt, 1996–98; Sec., Chiefs of Staff Cttee, MoD, 1998–2000; Dep. Comdr, Jt Helicopter Comd, 2000–03; Dir, Equipt Capability (Air and Littoral Manoeuvre), MoD, 2003–05; Comdr, Jt Helicopter Command, 2005–08. CGIA 1988. *Address:* Permanent Joint Headquarters, Northwood, Middx HA6 3HP. *T:* (01923) 838043.

COWARD, Vice Adm. Sir John (Francis), KCB 1990; DSO 1982; Lieutenant Governor and Commander-in-Chief of Guernsey, Channel Islands, 1994–2000; *b* 11 Oct. 1937; *s* of Reginald John Coward and Isabelle (*née* Foreman); *m* 1963, Diana (*née* Taylor); two *s*. *Educ:* Downside; RNC, Dartmouth. Served submarines, 1959–76, i/c HMS Oracle and HMS Valiant; Naval Asst to First Sea Lord, 1978–80; i/c HMS Brilliant, 1980–82; S Atlantic, 1982; Dir, Naval Operational Requirements, 1984; Flag Officer: Sea Trng, 1987–88; Flotilla One, 1988–89; Submarines, and Comdr Submarines Eastern Atlantic, 1989–91; Comdt, RCDS, 1992–94. Rear Adm. 1987; Vice Adm. 1989; retd 1994. Mem. Bd, N. M. Rothschild (CI) Ltd, 2000–07; Chm., Luxury Brands Gp, 2001–02. Underwriting Mem. of Lloyd's, 1978–. Mem., Council, RNLI, 1998–; Younger Brother, Trinity Hse. *Recreations:* sailing, gardening, cricket, golf. *Address:* South Wilcove House, Torpoint, Cornwall PL11 2PE. *T:* (01752) 814331. *Clubs:* Royal Navy of 1919, Royal Navy of 1765 and 1785, Sloane; Royal Yacht Squadron.

COWARD, (John) Stephen; QC 1984; barrister-at-law; a Recorder of the Crown Court, 1980–2003; *b* 15 Nov. 1937; *s* of Frank and Kathleen Coward; *m* 1967, Ann Lesley Pye; four *d*. *Educ:* King James Grammar Sch., Almondbury, Huddersfield; University Coll. London (LLB). Lecturer in Law and Constitutional History, University Coll. London and Police Staff Coll., 1962–64; called to the Bar, Inner Temple, 1964, Bencher, 2002; in practice on Midland and Oxford Circuit, 1964–2007. *Recreation:* trying to grow calceolarias and a decent row of peas. *Address:* The Grange, Scaldwell, Northampton NN6 9JP. *T:* (01604) 880255. *Club:* Scaldwell (Scaldwell, Northants).

COWARD, Nicholas; Chief Executive, British Horseracing Authority, since 2007; *b* 13 Feb. 1966; *s* of John and Jane Coward; *m* Vivien Lyle; one *s* one *d*. *Educ:* Shrewsbury Sch.; Bristol Univ. (LLB 1989); Guildford Coll. of Law. Solicitor, Freshfields, 1990–96; Football Association: Co. Solicitor, 1996–98; Dir, Legal and Corporate Affairs, 1998–2004; Actg Chief Exec., 1998–2000 and 2002–03; Advr to Bd, FA Premier League, 2004–07; Dep. Chm., A. S. Biss & Co., 2004–07; Chief Executive: British Horseracing Bd, 2007; Horseracing Regulatory Authy, 2007. Treas., CCPR, 2004–07. *Recreations:* sports: horseracing, golf, football, music, food, drinking coffee. *Address:* British Horseracing Authority, 151 Shaftesbury Avenue, WC2H 8AL. *T:* (020) 7152 0015, *Fax:* (020) 7152 0002; *e-mail:* ncoward@britishhorseracing.com. *Clubs:* Union, MCC.

COWARD, Dame Pamela (Sarah), DBE 2003; education consultant, since 2004; Headteacher, Middleton Technology School, 1991–2004; *b* 18 Jan. 1944; *d* of late Henry and Faith Coward; *m* 1994, Alan Lowe; one step *s* one step *d*, and one *s* from a previous marriage. *Educ:* City of Leeds Trng Coll. (Teachers' Cert. 1969); Open Univ. (BA 1979; Advanced Dip. in Mgt 1988); Manchester Univ. (Advanced Dip. in Guidance in Educn 1981). Special Needs Co-ordinator, Heywood Community Sch., 1984–88. Council Mem., Specialist Schools' Trust, 1998–2004. FRSA 1993. *Recreations:* theatre, playing with two grandchildren, caravanning.

COWARD, Richard Edgar; retired; Director for Library Planning, OCLC Inc., 1980–81; *b* 19 April 1927; *s* of Edgar Frank Coward and Jean (*née* McIntyre); *m* 1949, Audrey Scott Lintern; one *s* two *d*. *Educ:* Richmond Grammar Sch., Surrey. FCLIP. Dir Gen., Bibliographic Servs Div., British Library, 1975–79. Member: Adv. Cttee on BBC Archives, 1976–79; Library Adv. Council (England), 1976–. *Address:* Allfarthings, West Street, Mayfield, E Sussex TN20 6DT.

COWARD, Stephen; *see* Coward, J. S.

COWBURN, Norman; Chairman, Britannia Building Society, 1987–90 (Managing Director, 1970–84; Deputy Chairman, 1986–87); *b* 5 Jan. 1920; *s* of Harold and Edith Cowburn; *m* 1945, Edna Margaret Heatley; two *s* one *d*. *Educ:* Queen Elizabeth's Grammar Sch., Blackburn. FCIS, FCIB. Burnley Building Soc., 1936. Served War, 1940–46. Burnley Building Soc., 1946; Leek and Westbourne Building Soc., 1954 (re-named Britannia Building Soc., Dec. 1975). *Recreations:* golf, gardening. *Address:* Greywoods, Birchall, Leek, Staffs. *T:* (01538) 383214.

COWDEROY, Brenda; General Secretary, Girls' Friendly Society, 1978–85; *b* 27 June 1925; *o c* of Frederick and Evelyn Cowderoy (*née* Land). *Educ:* Surbiton High Sch.; St Hugh's Coll., Oxford (MA). Called to Bar, Gray's Inn, 1949. John Lewis Partnership: Asst Legal Adviser, 1954–56; Head of Legal Dept, 1956–70; Nat. Gen. Sec., YWCA, 1971–77. *Address:* 26 Rossetti Road, Birchington, Kent CT7 9ER. *Club:* Royal Commonwealth Society.

COWDRAY, 4th Viscount *cr* 1917; **Michael Orlando Weetman Pearson;** Bt 1894; Baron 1910; *b* 17 June 1944; *s* of 3rd Viscount Cowdray and of his 1st wife, Lady Anne Pamela Bridgeman, *d* of 5th Earl of Bradford; *S* father, 1995; one *s* by Barbara Page; *m* 1st, 1977, Ellen (marr. diss. 1984), *d* of Hermann Erhardt; 2nd, 1987, Marina Rose, *d* of late John H. Cordle and of Mrs H. J. Ross Skinner; two *s* three *d*. *Educ:* Gordonstoun. *Recreation:* historic motor racing. *Heir:* *s* Hon. Peregrine John Dickinson Pearson, *b* 27 Oct. 1994. *Address:* Cowdray Park, Midhurst, West Sussex GU29 0AY. *Club:* White's.

COWDREY, Rev. (Herbert Edward) John, FBA 1991; Emeritus Fellow, St Edmund Hall, Oxford, since 1994 (Senior Research Fellow in Modern History, 1987–94); *b* 29 Nov. 1926; *s* of Herbert and Winifred Cowdrey; *m* 1959, Judith Watson Davis (*d* 2004); one *s* two *d*. *Educ:* Queen Mary's Sch., Basingstoke; Trinity Coll., Oxford (BA Modern Hist. and Theology, 1951; MA); St Stephen's House, Oxford (Hon. Fellow, 2005); DD Oxon 2000. Nat. service, RN, 1945–47. Deacon, 1952; priest, 1953; Tutor and Chaplain, St Stephen's House, Oxford, 1952–56; Fellow and Tutor in Modern History, St Edmund Hall, Oxford, 1956–87. Leverhulme Emeritus Fellow, 1996–98. *Publications:* The Cluniacs and the Gregorian Reform, 1970; The Epistolae vagantes of Pope Gregory VII, 1972; Two Studies in Cluniac History, 1978; The Age of Abbot Desiderius, 1983; Popes, Monks and Crusaders, 1984; Pope Gregory VII, 1998; The Crusades and Latin Monasticism, 1999; Popes and Church Reform in the 11th Century, 2000; The Register of Pope Gregory VII, 2002; Lanfranc: scholar, monk and archbishop, 2003; articles and reviews in learned jls. *Recreation:* listening to music. *Address:* 19 Church Lane, Old Marston, Oxford OX3 0NZ. *T:* (01865) 794486.

COWE, Andrew Inglis; Chief Executive, North Lanarkshire Council, 1995–2000; *b* 1943; *s* of Andrew and Alice Cowe; *m* 1964, Mary Geraldine McAleer; three *s* four *d*. *Educ:* Glasgow Sch. of Art (DipTP). MRTPI 1974, FRTPI 1986–2004. Monklands District Council: Dir, Planning and Develt, 1974–84; Depute Chief Exec. (Computer Services and Strategic Issues), 1984–87; Renfrew District Council: Dir of Planning and Develt, 1987–89; Man. Dir, 1989–95. FCMI (FBIM 1990).

COWELL, Peter Reginald; His Honour Judge Cowell; a Circuit Judge, since 1996; *b* 9 March 1942; *s* of Reginald Ernest Cowell and Philippa Eleanor Frances Anne Cowell (*née* Prettejohn); *m* 1975, Penelope Jane Bowring; two *s* one *d*. *Educ:* Bedford Sch.; Gonville and Caius Coll., Cambridge. Called to the Bar, Middle Temple, 1964, Bencher, 1997, Autumn Reader, 2008; Asst Recorder, 1985–92; Recorder, 1992–96. Mem. Senate, Inns of Court, 1975–78. *Recreations:* acting (Mem., Old Stagers), sculling, genealogy. *Address:* Central London Civil Justice Centre, 26 Park Crescent, W1N 4HT. *Club:* Garrick.

COWELL, Prof. Raymond, CBE 2004; Vice-Chancellor, Nottingham Trent University, 1992–2003 (Director and Chief Executive, Trent Polytechnic, Nottingham, then Nottingham Polytechnic, 1987–92); *b* 3 Sept. 1937; *s* of Cecil Cowell and Susan Cowell (*née* Green); *m* 1963, Sheila (*née* Bolton); one *s* one *d*. *Educ:* St Aidan's Grammar Sch., Sunderland; Bristol Univ. (BA, PhD); Cambridge Univ. (PGCE). Head of English, Nottingham Coll. of Educn, 1970–73; Dean of Humanities 1974–81, Dep. Rector 1981–87, Sunderland Polytechnic. Member: CNAA, 1974–77 and 1981–85; Unit for Develt of Adult and Continuing Educn, 1986–90; British Council Cttee for Internat. Co-op. in Higher Educn, 1990–2000; Bd, Greater Nottingham TEC, 1990–93; Directing Gp, Prog. on Instnl Management in Higher Educn, OECD, 1990–97; Council, NCVQ, 1991–97; Bd, Higher Educn Business Enterprise, 1993–95; Policy Liaison Gp, Open Learning Foundn, 1993–95; Adv. Panel, Nat. Reading Initiative, DNH, 1996–97; E Midlands Business Leadership Team, BITC, 2001–03. Chairman: Staff and Educnl Develt Assoc., 1993–99; CVCP working gp on vocational higher educn, 1993–96; Management Bd and Members Adv. Gp, Univs and Colls Staff Develt Agency (formerly Univs Staff Develt Unit), 1993–95; E Midlands Arts Bd Ltd, 1995–2001 (Mem., Arts Council of England, 1996–98). Board Member: Nottingham City Challenge, 1991–93; Opera North, 2000–; Nottingham Bldg Soc., 2003– (Vice-Chm., 2004–); Mem., Bd of Govs, Djanogly City Acad., 2005–; Chair, Bd, Viva Chamber Orch., 2005–. FRSA 1996. DL Notts, 1996. Midlander of the Year, Carlton TV, 2002. *Publications:* Twelve Modern Dramatists, 1967; W. B. Yeats, 1969; (ed) Richard II, 1969; Critics on Yeats, 1971; Critics on Wordsworth, 1973; The Critical Enterprise, 1975; articles and reviews on higher education. *Recreations:* books, music, theatre.

COWEN, Brian; Member (FF) of the Dáil (TD) for Laois-Offaly, since June 1984; Taoiseach (Prime Minister of Ireland), since 2008; President, Fianna Fáil, since 2008; *b* 10 Jan. 1960; *m* 1990, Mary Molloy; two *d*. *Educ:* Cistercian Coll., Roscrea; University Coll., Dublin. Solicitor. Minister: for Labour, 1991–92; for Transport, Energy and Communications, 1992–94; for Health and Children, 1997–2000; for Foreign Affairs, 2000–04; for Finance, 2004–08; Tánaiste (Dep. Prime Minister), 2007–08. *Recreation:* all sports. *Address:* Office of the Taoiseach, Government Buildings, Upper Merrion Street, Dublin 2, Republic of Ireland.

COWEN, Rt Hon. Sir Zelman, AK 1977; GCMG 1977 (CMG 1968); GCVO 1980; Kt 1976; PC 1981; QC; Provost of Oriel College, Oxford, 1982–90; Pro-Vice-Chancellor, University of Oxford, 1988–90; Director, John Fairfax Holdings Ltd, 1992–96 (Chairman, 1992–94); *b* 7 Oct. 1919; *s* of late Bernard and of Sara Cowen; *m* 1945, Anna Wittner; three *s* one *d*. *Educ:* Scotch Coll., Melbourne; Univ. of Melbourne; New and Oriel Colls, Oxford. BA 1939, LLB 1941, LLM 1942, Melbourne; BCL, MA 1947, DCL 1968, Oxford. Lieut, RANVR, 1941–45. Called to Bar, Gray's Inn, 1947; Hon. Bencher, 1978; called to Vic (Aust.) Bar, 1951, Queensland Bar, 1971; QC 1972. Victorian Rhodes Schol., 1941; Vinerian Schol., Oxford Univ., 1947. Fellow and Tutor, Oriel Coll., Oxford, 1947–50, Hon. Fellow 1977; Prof. of Public Law and Dean of Faculty of Law, Univ. of Melbourne, 1951–66; Dominion Liaison Officer to Colonial Office (UK), 1951–66; Prof. Emer., Univ. of Melbourne, 1967; Vice-Chancellor and Professor, Univ. of New England, Armidale, NSW, 1967–70; Vice-Chancellor, Qld Univ., 1970–77; Governor-General of Australia, 1977–82. Visiting Professor: Univ. of Chicago, 1949; Harvard Law Sch. and Fletcher Sch. of Law and Diplomacy, 1953–54 and 1963–64; Univ. of Utah, 1954; Univ. of Illinois, 1957–58; Washington Univ., St Louis, 1959; Tagore Law Prof., Univ. of Calcutta, 1975; Menzies Schol. in Res., Univ. of Va, 1983; Lee Kuan Yew Dist. Vis. Fellow, Singapore, 1986; Dist. Vis. Prof., Victoria Univ. of Technol., 1994–. Broadcaster on radio and TV on nat. and internat. affairs; Mem. and Chm., Victorian State Adv. Cttee of Australian Broadcasting Commn (at various times during 1950's and 1960's); Mem., Chief Justice's Law Reform Cttee, 1951–66; President: Asthma Foundn of Victoria, 1963–66; Adult Educn Assoc. of Australia, 1968–70; Aust. Inst. of Urban Studies, 1973–77; Mem., Law Reform Commn, Australia, 1976–77; Chairman: Aust. Vice-Chancellors' Cttee, 1977; Aust. Studies Centre Cttee, London, 1982–90; Nat Council, Australian Opera, 1983–95; Press Council, 1983–88; Trustees, Visnews Ltd, 1986–91; Victoria League for Commonwealth Friendship, 1987–89; Australian Nat. Acad. of Music, 1995–2000. Mem., Club of Rome, 1974–77. National President: Order of Australia Assoc. Ltd, 1992–95; Australia-Britain Soc., 1993–95. Academic Governor, Bd of Governors, Hebrew Univ. of Jerusalem, 1969–77, 1982–; Mem., Academic Bd of Govrs, Tel Aviv Univ., 1983–; Weizmann Inst., 1988–. Trustee: Van Leer Inst. of Jerusalem, 1985– (Chm. Trustees, 1988–95); Winston Churchill Meml Trust, 1987–89; Sir Robert Menzies Meml Trust, 1987–; Dir, Sir Robert Menzies Meml Foundn Ltd, 1990–97. For. Hon. Mem., Amer. Acad. of Arts and Scis, 1965. Fellow, Australian Nat. Acad. of Music, 2000; Hon. FASSA 1977; Hon. FACE 1978; Hon. FRAIA 1978; Hon. FTS 1979; Hon. FRACP 1979; Hon. FAHA 1980; Hon. FASA 1980; Hon. FRACMA 1981; Hon. FRACOG 1981; Hon. FCA 1981; Hon. FACRM 1982; Hon. Fellow: New Coll. Oxford 1978; University House, ANU, 1978; ANZAAS 1983; TCD, 1985; St John's Coll., Univ. of Qld, 1985; Australian Council of Educnl Admin, 1991. Hon. Law Prof., Griffith Univ., Qld, 1992. Hon. LLD: Hong Kong, 1967; Queensland, 1972; Melbourne, 1973; Western Australia, 1981; Turin, 1981; ANU, 1985; Tasmania, 1990; Victoria Univ. of Technol., 1998; Deakin, 2003; Monash, 2004; Hon. DLitt: New England, 1979; Sydney, 1980; James Cook Univ. of N Qld, 1982; Oxford, 1983; Hon. DHL: Hebrew Union Coll., Cincinnati, 1980; Redlands Univ., Calif., 1986; DUniv: Newcastle, 1980; Griffith, 1981; Sunshine Coast, 1999; Hon. DPhil: Hebrew

Univ. of Jerusalem, 1982; Tel Aviv, 1985. KStJ (A) 1977. Kt Grand Cross, Order of Merit (Italy), 1990. *Publications:* (ed jtly) Dicey's Conflict of Laws, 1949; Australia and the United States: Some Legal Comparisons, 1954; (with P. B. Carter) Essays on the Law of Evidence, 1956; American-Australian Private International Law, 1957; Federal Jurisdiction in Australia, 1959, 3rd edn 2002; (with D. M. da Costa) Matrimonial Causes Jurisdiction, 1961; Sir John Latham and other papers, 1965; British Commonwealth of Nations in a Changing World, 1964; Isaac Isaacs, 1967, 2nd edn 1993; The Private Man, 1969; Individual Liberty and the Law, 1977; The Virginia Lectures, 1984; Reflections on Medicine, Biotechnology, and the Law, 1986; A Touch of Healing, 1986; The Memoirs of Sir Zelman Cowen: a public life, 2006; articles and chapters in legal works in UK, US, Canada, Germany, Australia. *Recreations:* swimming, music, performing and visual arts. *Address:* Commonwealth Offices, 4 Treasury Place, East Melbourne, Vic 3002, Australia. *Clubs:* Oxford and Cambridge; Queensland (Brisbane); Pioneer (Sydney).

COWEY, Prof. Alan, PhD; FMedSci; FRS 1988; Professor of Physiological Psychology, University of Oxford, 1981–2002, now Emeritus; Fellow of Lincoln College, Oxford, 1981–2002, now Supernumerary Fellow; MRC Research Professor, 1997–2002; *b* 28 April 1935; *s* of Harry and Mary Cowey; *m* 1959, Patricia Leckonby; three *d*. *Educ:* Bede Grammar Sch., Sunderland; Emmanuel Coll., Cambridge (MA, PhD). Rockefeller Foundn Fellow, Center for Brain Research, Univ. of Rochester, New York, 1961–62; Univ. Demonstrator in Experimental Psychology, Cambridge, 1962–67; Fellow and Coll. Tutor, Emmanuel Coll., Cambridge, 1964–67; Vis. Sen. Fulbright Fellow, Psychology Dept, Harvard Univ., 1967; Sen. Res. Officer, Inst. of Experimental Psychology, Univ. of Oxford, 1967–68; Nuffield Sen. Res. Fellow, Lincoln Coll., Oxford, 1968–81; Henry Head Res. Fellow of Royal Society, 1968–73; Reader in Physiolog. Psychology, Oxford Univ., 1973–81; Dir, Oxford Res. Centre in Brain and Behaviour, 1991–96. Member: MRC Neurosciences Grants Cttee, 1974–77 (Chm., 1979–81); MRC Neurosciences Board, 1979–83 (Chm., 1981–83); Mem. Council, MRC, 1981–85. President: European Brain and Behaviour Soc., 1986–88; Experimental Psychology Soc., 1990–92; Assoc. for Scientific Study of Consciousness, 2008–. Founder FMedSci 1998. Hon. DSc Durham, 2000. Spearman Medal, British Psychological Soc., 1967. *Publications:* numerous articles in psychological and physiological jls. *Recreations:* gardening, swimming, reading. *Address:* Department of Experimental Psychology, South Parks Road, Oxford OX1 3UD. *T:* (01865) 271352.

COWIE, Hon. Lord; William Lorn Kerr Cowie; a Senator of the College of Justice in Scotland, 1977–94; a Judge of the Court of Appeal, Botswana, 1995–98; *b* 1 June 1926; *s* of late Charles Rennie Cowie, MBE and Norah Slimmon Kerr; *m* 1958, Camilla Henrietta Grizel Hoyle; twin *s* two *d*. *Educ:* Fettes Coll.; Clare Coll., Cambridge; Glasgow Univ. Sub-Lieut RNVR, 1944–47; Cambridge, 1947–49; Glasgow Univ., 1949–51; Mem., Faculty of Advocates, 1952; QC (Scotland) 1967. *Address:* 20 Blacket Place, Edinburgh EH9 1RL. *T:* (0131) 667 8238. *Club:* New (Edinburgh).

COWIE, Ian McGregor; Personal Finance Editor, Daily Telegraph, since 1989; *b* 15 Sept. 1958; *s* of Joseph Cowie and Mary (*née* Proctor); *m* 1987, Susan Carole Fleming; one *s*. *Educ:* William Ellis Sch.; Univ. of York (BA Hons); City Univ. (Postgrad. Dip.). City Reporter, Daily Telegraph, 1986–89. Personal Finance Journalist of the Year: Golden Pen Awards, 1996; Assoc. of British Insurers Awards, 1996, 1997, 1998; Wincott Award, 2007. *Publications:* Daily Telegraph Guides series on savings and investments, 1996–; contrib. Spectator. *Recreation:* sailing close to the wind. *Address:* Daily Telegraph, 111 Buckingham Palace Road, SW1W 0DT. *T:* (020) 7931 2731. *Club:* Royal Ocean Racing.

COWIE, Dr Lennox Lauchlan, FRS 2004; Astronomer, University of Hawaii, since 1997; *b* 18 Oct. 1950. *Educ:* Edinburgh Univ. (BSc 1st cl.); Harvard Univ. (PhD 1976). Res. Astronomer, with rank of Associate Prof., Princeton Univ., 1979–81; Associate Prof. of Physics, MIT, 1981–84; Chief, Acad. Affairs Br., Space Telescope Sci. Inst., and Prof., Johns Hopkins Univ., 1984–86; Associate Dir, Inst. for Astronomy, Univ. of Hawaii, 1986–97. *Publications:* numerous papers in refereed learned jls. *Address:* Institute for Astronomy, University of Hawaii, 2680 Woodlawn Drive, Honolulu, HI 96822, USA.

COWIE, Sir Thomas, (Sir Tom), Kt 1992; OBE 1982; Life President, T. Cowie Ltd, subseq. T. Cowie PLC, now Arriva, motor vehicle distribution and finance, since 1993 (Chairman, 1948–93); *b* 9 Sept. 1922; *s* of late Thomas Stephenson Knowles Cowie and Florence Cowie; *m* 1st, 1948, Lillas Roberts Hunnam (marr. diss.; she *d* 1994); one *s* four *d*; 2nd, 1975, Diana Carole Wentworth Kenyon; three *d*, and one step *s* one step *d*. *Educ:* Bede Grammar School, Sunderland. *Relevant publications:* The Tom Cowie Story, by Phil Martin, 1988; Sir Tom Cowie: a true entrepreneur, by Denise Robertson, 2004. *Recreations:* game shooting, walking, music. *Address:* Broadwood Hall, Lanchester, Co. Durham DH7 0TD. *T:* (01207) 520464.

COWIE, William Lorn Kerr; *see* Cowie, Hon. Lord.

COWLEY, 7th Earl *cr* 1857; **Garret Graham Wellesley;** Baron Cowley, 1828; Viscount Dangan, 1857; Senior Investment Partner, Thos R. Miller & Son (Bermuda), Isle of Man, 1990–2000; *b* 30 July 1934; 3rd *s* of 4th Earl Cowley (*d* 1962) and of Mary (Elsie May), Countess Cowley; *S* nephew, 1975; *m* Paige Deming, Reno, Nevada; one *s* five *d*, and one *s* one *d* of former marriage. *Educ:* Univ. of S California (BSc Finance 1957); Harvard Univ. (MBA 1962). Investment Research Analyst: Wells Fargo Bank, San Francisco, 1962–64; Dodge & Cox, San Francisco, 1964–66; Asst Head, Investment Research Dept, Wells Fargo Bank, 1966–67; Vice-Pres., Investment Counsel, Thorndike, Doran, Paine & Lewis, Los Angeles, 1967–69; Sen. Vice-Pres., Exec. Cttee Mem., Securities, Real Estate and Company Acquisition Advisor, Shareholders Capital Corp., Los Angeles, 1969–74; Vice-Pres., and Sen. Investment Manager, Trust Dept, Bank of America, San Francisco, 1974–78; Gp Vice-Pres. and Dir, Internat Investment Management Service, Bank of America NT & SA, 1980–85; Director: Bank of America Internat., London, 1978–85; BankAmerica Trust Co. (Hong Kong), 1980–85; Bank of America Banking & Trust Co. (Gibraltar), 1981–85; Bank of America Trust Co. (Jersey), 1982–85; Bank of America Banking & Trust Co. (Nassau), 1982–85; Bank of America Banking & Trust Co. (Cayman), 1982–85; indep. financial advr and co. dir, 1985–90; Director: Duncan Lawrie (IOM) Ltd, 1993–2001; Scottish Provident Internat. Ltd, 1998–; L-R Global Fund (New York), 2003–; Kazimir Russia Growth Fund (Moscow), 2005–; Mem., Gen. Cttee of Trustees, Lloyds Register Gp, 2006–. Served US Army Counter Intelligence Corps, primarily in France, 1957–60. Member: Assoc. of Conservative Peers, 1981–; Party Arts and Heritage Gp, 1981–99, Defence Gp, 1982–99, and Anglo-Amer. Gp, 1987–99, H of L. *Heir: s* Viscount Dangan, *qv*. *Clubs:* Brooks's; Pilgrims, Philippics; Harvard (San Francisco).

COWLEY, Prof. Alan Herbert, FRS 1988; FRSC; Robert A. Welch Professor of Chemistry, University of Texas at Austin, since 1991; *b* 29 Jan. 1934; *s* of late Herbert Cowley and Dora Cowley; *m* 1975, Deborah Elaine Cole; two *s* three *d*. *Educ:* Univ. of Manchester (BSc, MSc; Dalton Chem. Schol., 1956–58; PhD 1958). Technical Officer, ICI, 1960–61; University of Texas at Austin: Asst Prof. of Chemistry, 1962–67; Associate Prof., 1967–70; Prof., 1970–84; George W. Watt Centennial Prof., 1984–88; Richard J. V. Johnson Regents Prof. of Chemistry, 1989–91; Sir Edward Frankland Prof. of Inorganic Chem., Imperial Coll., London, 1988–89. Deutsche Akademische Austauschdienst Fellow, 1973; Guggenheim Fellow, 1976–77; von Humboldt Sen. Fellow, 1996; Lectures: Jeremy I. Musher Meml, Hebrew Univ., Jerusalem, 1979; Mobay, Univ. of New Hampshire, 1985; Karcher, Univ. of Oklahoma, 1985; Reilly, Univ. of Notre Dame, 1987; Fischel, Vanderbilt Univ., 1991; Baxter, Northern Illinois Univ., 1992; Etter Meml, Univ. of Minnesota, 1995; Vis. Prof., Univ. of Western Ont., 1987; Gauss Prof., Göttinger Acad. of Scis, 2005. Member: Chem. Soc., subseq. RSC, 1961 (Award for Main-Gp Element Chem., 1980; Centenary Medal and Lectureship, 1986); Amer. Chem. Soc., 1962 (Southwest Regl Award, 1986); Corresp. Member: Mexican Acad. of Scis, 2004; Göttingen Acad. of Scis, 2007; Eur. Acad. of Scis and Arts, 2007. Stiefvater Meml Award and Lectureship, Univ. of Nebraska, 1987; Chemical Pioneer Award, Amer. Inst. of Chemists, 1994; C. N. R. Rao Award, Chem. Res. Soc. of India, 2007. Mem. Bd of Trustees, Gordon Res. Confs, 1989–98 (Chm., 1994–95). Member, Editorial Board: Inorganic Chemistry, 1979–83; Chemical Reviews, 1984–88; Polyhedron, 1984–2000; Jl of Amer. Chem. Soc., 1986–91; Jl of Organometallic Chemistry, 1987–2008; Organometallics, 1988–91; Dalton Trans., 1997–2000; Mem. Bd, Inorganic Syntheses, 1983– (Ed.-in-Chief, vol. 31). FRSC 2004. Dr *hc* Bordeaux I, 2003. *Publications:* over 500 pubns in learned jls. *Recreations:* squash, sailing, music. *Address:* Department of Chemistry and Biochemistry, University of Texas at Austin, 1 University Station A5300, Austin, TX 78712, USA. *Clubs:* Athenæum; Headliners (Austin).

COWLEY, Kenneth Edward, AO 1988; Chief Executive, 1980–97, and Executive Chairman, 1996–97, News Ltd (Chairman, 1992–96); Chairman, Independent Newspapers Ltd (NZ), 2001–04 (Director, since 1990); *b* 17 Nov. 1934; *s* of Edward Clegg Cowley and Patricia Bertha (*née* Curran); *m* 1958, Maureen Yvonne Manahan; one *s* one *d*. Sen. Exec., The Australian, 1964–97; Director: News Ltd, 1976–97; Internat. Bd, News Corp., 1980–; Chairman: PMP Communications (formerly Pacific Magazines and Printing) Ltd, 1991–2001; Ansett Transport Industries, then Ansett Australia Hldgs, 1992–98 (Dir, 1997–2000); R. M. Williams Holdings Ltd, 1994–; Ansett Internat., 1997–2000; Tasman Pacific Airways (traded as Ansett NZ, then Qantas NZ), 1997–2000. Director: Qld Press Ltd, 1987–97; Commonwealth Bank of Australia, 1997–2001; Tower Estate plc, 1998–. Councillor, Royal Agricl Soc. of NSW, 1979–. Life Gov., Art Gall. of NSW, 1997 (Trustee, 1986–97); Chm., Australian Stockman's Hall of Fame & Outback Heritage Centre, 1976–. Hon. DBus NSW, 2008. *Address:* The News Corporation Ltd, 2 Holt Street, Surry Hills, NSW 2010, Australia. *T:* (2) 2883209. *Club:* Union (Sydney).

COWLEY, Prof. Roger Arthur, FRS 1978; FRSE; FRSC; Dr Lee's Professor of Experimental Philosophy, and Fellow of Wadham College, University of Oxford, 1988–2007; *b* 24 Feb. 1939; *s* of Cecil A. Cowley and Mildred S. Cowley; *m* 1964, Sheila J. Wells; one *s* one *d*. *Educ:* Brentwood Sch., Essex; Cambridge Univ. (MA, PhD). FRSE 1972; FRSC 2001. Fellow, Trinity Hall, Cambridge, 1962–64; Research Officer, Atomic Energy of Canada Ltd, 1964–70; Prof. of Physics, Edinburgh Univ., 1970–88; Chm. of Physics, Univ. of Oxford, 1993–96, 1999–2002. Max Born Medal, Inst. of Physics and German Physical Soc., 1973; Holweck Medal and Prize, Inst. of Physics and French Physical Soc., 1990; W. Hälg Medal and Prize, Eur. Neutron Scattering Soc., 2003; Faraday Medal and Prize, Inst. of Physics, 2008. *Publications:* Structural Phase Transitions, 1981; over 350 articles. *Address:* Oxford Physics, Clarendon Laboratory, Parks Road, Oxford OX1 3PU. *T:* (01865) 272224; Tredinnock, Harcourt Hill, Oxford OX2 9AS. *T:* (01865) 247570.

COWLEY, Prof. Stanley William Herbert, PhD; CPhys; FRAS; FBIS; Professor of Solar-Planetary (formerly Space Plasma) Physics, and Head, Radio and Space Plasma Physics Group, Department of Physics and Astronomy, University of Leicester, since 1996; *b* 11 April 1947; *s* of late Herbert William Leslie Cowley and Annie Jenny Cowley (*née* Clark); *m* 1970, Lynn Doreen Moore; two *s* one *d*. *Educ:* Imperial Coll., Univ. of London (BSc, ARCS, PhD, DIC). FBIS 1975; MInstP 1975; FRAS 1986; CPhys 1989. Imperial College, University of London: SERC Advanced Fellow, 1977–82; Lectr, 1982–85; Reader, 1985–88; Prof. of Physics, 1988–95; Head, Space and Atmospheric Physics Gp, Blackett Lab., 1990–95; PPARC Sen. Fellow, 2001–04; Royal Soc. Leverhulme Trust Sen. Res. Fellow, 2006–07. Mem., PPARC, 1994–96. Fellow, Amer. Geophysical Union, 1995. Chapman Medal, 1991, Gold Medal, 2006, RAS; Bartels Medal, Eur. Geoscis Union, 2006. *Publications:* contrib. numerous papers in solar system plasma physics in learned jls. *Recreation:* walking the dog. *Address:* Department of Physics and Astronomy, University of Leicester, University Road, Leicester LE1 7RH. *T:* (0116) 223 1331, (0116) 252 3563.

COWLING, Gareth; *see* Cowling, T. G.

COWLING, (James) Roy; HM Diplomatic Service, retired; Consul-General, Barcelona, 1996–99; *b* 9 Feb. 1940; *m* 1st, 1962, Monique Lassimonillas; 2nd, 1983, Janet Bel Barnshaw. Second Sec., Karachi, 1964; FCO, 1968; First Sec., Buenos Aires, 1972, Copenhagen, 1975; FCO, 1977; on loan to ODA, 1980; First Sec., Nairobi, 1983; First Sec., subseq. Counsellor, FCO, 1987; High Comr, Lesotho, 1992–96. *Address:* c/o Foreign and Commonwealth Office, SW1A 2AH.

COWLING, Peter John; Director, Falmouth Quay Consultants, since 2003; *b* 11 Nov 1944; *s* of Harold Cowling and Irene (*née* Phillips); *m* 1979, Sara Fox; two *d*. *Educ* Bletchley Grammar Sch.; Britannia Royal Naval Coll. Joined RN 1963; commanded HMS Naiad, 1979; HMS York and 3rd Destroyer Sqdn, 1988; Sen. Naval Officer, Middle East, 1991; Dir, Naval Ops, MoD, 1992; retired 1994. Dir, RSA, 1994–96; Head o Corporate Relns, Proshare, 1997–98; Dir, Nat. Maritime Mus. Cornwall, 1998–2003 Chm., Cornwall SSAFA, 2006–. Younger Brother, Trinity House, 1981– (Pilgrim 1996–). Queen's Gold Medal, 1967. *Recreations:* sailing, gardening. *Address:* Parc Vean Mylor Churchtown, Cornwall TR11 5UD.

COWLING, Roy; *see* Cowling, J. R.

COWLING, (Thomas) Gareth; His Honour Judge Cowling; a Circuit Judge, sinc 2004; *b* 12 Nov. 1944; *s* of late Clifford Cowling and Beryl Elizabeth Cowling (*né* Thomas); *m* 1970, Jill Ann Stephens; one *s* one *d*. *Educ:* Eastbourne Coll.; College of Law Articled to Clifford Cowling, of Clifford Cowling & Co., Hampshire, 1964; admitte Solicitor of Supreme Court, 1969; Solicitor, Solicitor's Dept, New Scotland Yard 1969–72; called to Bar, Middle Temple, 1972; private practice at Bar, London an Winchester, Western Circuit, 1972–88; Metropolitan Stipendiary Magistrate, 1988–89 Stipendiary Magistrate, subseq. Dist Judge (Magistrates' Courts), Hampshire, 1989–2004 a Recorder, 1998–2004. Mem., Parole Bd, 2007. *Recreations:* eating and drinking wit family and friends, trying to play golf. *Address:* The Courts of Justice, Winston Churchi Avenue, Portsmouth, Hants PO1 2EB.

COWPER-COLES, Sir Sherard (Louis), KCMG 2004 (CMG 1997); LVO 1991; HM Diplomatic Service; Ambassador to Afghanistan, since 2007; *b* 8 Jan. 1955; *s* of Sherar Hamilton Cowper-Coles and Dorothy (*née* Short); *m* 1982, Bridget Mary Elliott; four one *d.* *Educ:* Freston Lodge Sch.; New Beacon Sch.; Tonbridge Sch.; Hertford Coll., Oxford (MA; Hon. Fellow, 2002). Joined HM Diplomatic Service, 1977: Third, later Second, Sec., Cairo, 1980–83; First Sec., Planning Staff, FCO, 1983–85; Private Sec. to Perm. Under-Sec. of State, 1985–87; First Sec., Washington, 1987–91; Asst, Security Policy Dept, FCO, 1991–93; Res. Associate, IISS, 1993–94; Head, Hong Kong Dept, FCO, 1994–97; Counsellor (Political) Paris, 1997–99; Prin. Private Sec. to Sec. of State for For. and Commonwealth Affairs, 1999–2001; Ambassador to: Israel, 2001–03; Saudi Arabia, 2003–07. Liveryman, Skinners' Co., 1988. *Publication:* contrib. Survival (IISS jl). *Address:* c/o Foreign and Commonwealth Office, King Charles Street, SW1A 2AH. *Club:* Brooks's.

COWTAN, Maj.-Gen. Frank Willoughby John, CBE 1970 (MBE 1947); MC 1942 and Bar, 1945; *b* 10 Feb. 1920; *s* of late Air Vice-Marshal F. C. Cowtan, CB, CBE, KHS and late Mrs N. A. Cowtan (*née* Kennedy); *m* 1949, Rose Isabel Cope; one *s* one *d.* *Educ:* Wellington Coll.; RMA Woolwich. 2nd Lieut Royal Engineers, 1939; served War of 1939–45, BEF, N Africa, Italy, NW Europe (Captain); Palestine, Kenya, Middle East, 1945–50 (Major); psc 1951; Middle East, UK, BAOR, 1952–58; Liaison Officer to US Corps of Engrs, USA, 1958–60 (Bt Lt-Col); CO 131 Parachute Engr Regt, 1960–62; CO Victory Coll., RMA Sandhurst, 1962–65 (Lt-Col); Comd 11 Engr Bde, BAOR, 1965–67 (Brig.); ndc (Canada) 1967–68; Dir of Quartering (Army), 1968–70; Maj.-Gen. 1969; Dep. QMG, 1970–71; Comdt, RMCS, 1971–75, retired. Hon. Col, 131 Indep. Commando Sqn, RE, 1975–80; Col Comdt RE, 1977–82. Dep. Dir, CLA Game Fair, 1978–86. *Recreations:* travel, languages, crosswords, support of field sports. *Address:* Rectory Cottage, Coleshill, Swindon, SN6 7PR.

COX, family name of **Baroness Cox**.

COX, Baroness *cr* 1982 (Life Peer), of Queensbury in Greater London; **Caroline Anne Cox;** a Deputy Speaker, House of Lords, since 1986; Co-Director, Education Research Trust, since 1980; Chief Executive, Humanitarian Aid Relief Trust UK, since 2004; *b* 6 July 1937; *d* of Robert John McNeill Love, MS, FRCS and Dorothy Ida Borland; *m* 1959, Dr Murray Cox, FRCPsych (*d* 1997); two *s* one *d.* *Educ:* Channing School; London Univ. (BSc (Sociology, 1st Cl. Hons) 1967, MSc (Economics) 1969). FRCN 1985. SRN, London Hosp., 1958; Staff Nurse, Edgware Gen. Hosp., 1960; Research Associate, Univ. of Newcastle upon Tyne, 1967–68; Department of Sociology, Polytechnic of North London: Lecturer, Senior Lectr, Principal Lectr, 1969–74; Head of Department, 1974–77; Dir, Nursing Educn Res. Unit, Chelsea Coll., London Univ., 1977–84. Dir, Centre for Policy Studies, 1983–85. A Baroness in Waiting, April–Aug. 1985. Chancellor: Bournemouth Univ., 1992–2001; Liverpool Hope Univ., 2006–. Vice President: RCN, 1990–; Liverpool Sch. of Tropical Medicine, 2006–. Special Rep., FCO Freedom of Religion Panel, 2004–. Chm., Exec. Bd, Internat. Islamic Christian Orgn for Reconciliation and Reconstruction. Hon. Prof. and Trustee, Siberian Med. Univ., Tomsk, Russia; Pres., Tushinskaya Children's Hosp. Trust; Patron, Medical Aid for Poland Fund. Fellow, Goodenough Coll., 2005. Hon. FRCS 1996. Hon. PhD Polish Univ. in London, 1988; Hon. LLD CNAA; DUniv: Surrey; UCE, 1998; Hon. DH Utah; Hon. Dr Yerevan; Hon. DSS QUB, 1996; Hon. DSc: City, 1999; Wolverhampton, 1999. Internat. Mother Teresa Award, All India Christian Council, 2005; Mkhitar Gosh Medal, Republic of Armenia, 2005; 25th Anniv. Medal, Polish Solidarity Movt, 2005. Commander's Cross, Order of Merit (Poland), 1990. *Publications:* (ed jtly) A Sociology of Medical Practice, 1975; (jtly) Rape of Reason: The Corruption of the Polytechnic of North London, 1975; (jtly) The Right to Learn, 1982; Sociology: A Guide for Nurses, Midwives and Health Visitors, 1983; (jtly) The Insolence of Office, 1989; (jtly) Choosing a State School: how to find the best education for your child, 1989; Trajectories of Despair: misdiagnosis and maltreatment of Soviet orphans, 1991; (with John Eibner) Ethnic Cleansing in Progress: war in Nagorno Karabakh, 1993; (jtly) Made to Care: the case for residential and village communities for people with a mental handicap, 1995; (contrib.) Remorse and Reparation, ed Murray Cox, 1998; (jtly) The West, Islam and Islamism, 2003, 2nd edn 2006; (with Catherine Butcher) Cox's Book of Modern Saints and Martyrs, 2006; (with John Marks) This Immoral Trade: slavery in the 21st century, 2006. *Recreations:* campanology, tennis, hill walking. *Address:* House of Lords, SW1A 0PW. *T:* (office) (020) 8204 7336, *Fax:* (020) 8204 5661. *Club:* Royal Over-Seas League.

COX, Sir Alan (George), Kt 1994; CBE 1988; FCA; FCMA; Chief Executive, ASW Holdings PLC, 1981–96; *b* 23 Aug. 1936; *s* of late George Henry Cox and Florence Ivy Cox; *m* 1994, Rosamund Shelley. *Educ:* Oldbury Grammar Sch. FCA 1959; ACMA 1961. Chm. and Chief Exec., GKN Rolled and Bright Steel Ltd, 1978–80; Corporate Management Dir, GKN, PLC, 1980–81; Director: Morgan Crucible Co. plc, 1995–2004; Meggitt plc, 1996–. Chairman: Wales Millennium Centre Ltd, 1996–2001; The Public Ltd (formerly Jubilee/c/Plex Arts), 2001–04. Member: Bd, Cardiff Bay Develt Corp., 1987–2000; School Teachers Review Body, 1991–95; Financial Reporting Council, 1996–99. Chm., Mountview Acad. of Theatre Arts Ltd, 2004–. *Recreations:* cookery, opera, walking. *Address:* PO Box 27, Chepstow, Monmouthshire NP16 6EY. *Club:* Cardiff and County.

COX, Alistair Richard; Chief Executive, Xansa plc, since 2002; *b* 25 Feb. 1961; *s* of Gerald and Jean Cox; *m* 1988, Merete Oftedahl; two *s.* *Educ:* Univ. of Salford (BSc Hons Aeronautical Engrg, Dip. Engrg); Stanford Grad. Sch. of Business (MBA). Aeronautical Engr, British Aerospace UK, 1978–83; Engr and Manager, Schlumberger Wireline Services, Norway and USA, 1983–90; Consultant and Manager, McKinsey & Co., 1990–94; Gp Strategy Dir, 1994–98, Regl Pres. Asia, 1998–2002, Blue Circle Industries, subseq. Lafarge. *Recreations:* scuba diving, mountaineering, sailing, wake boarding, motorsports. *Address:* Xansa plc, 420 Thames Valley Park Drive, Thames Valley Park, Reading, Berks RG6 1PU. *T:* (08702) 416181, *Fax:* (08702) 426282.

COX, Alister Stransom, MA; Headmaster, Royal Grammar School, Newcastle upon Tyne, 1972–94; *b* 21 May 1934; *s* of Rev. Roland L. Cox and F. Ruth Cox; *m* 1960, Janet (*née* Williams); one *s* two *d.* *Educ:* Kingswood School, Bath; New College, Oxford (Scholar). Hon. Mods (1st Class); Lit. Hum. BA 1957, MA 1961. Sixth Form Master, Clifton Coll., 1957–63; Head of Classics, Wellington Coll., 1963–69; Dep. Head, Arnold Sch., Blackpool, 1969–72. Vis. Lectr in Greek, Bristol Univ., 1968. Founder Mem., Sinfonia Chorus, Northern Sinfonia of England, 1973–94 (Mem., Management Cttee, 1980–85). FRSA 1982. *Publications:* Lucretius on Matter and Man, 1967; Didactic Poetry, in Greek and Latin Literature (ed Higginbotham), 1969; articles in Greece and Rome, Times Educnl Supp. and educnl jls. *Recreations:* music, especially singing; French life and politics; touring lecturer Alliance Française. *Address:* 3 Lower Gale, Ambleside, Cumbria LA22 0BD. *T:* (015394) 32634; 36 rue Jeanne d'Arc, Montsoreau 49730, France.

COX, Anthony Robert, PhD, CEng; adviser on science and technology, since 1998; *b* 30 Nov. 1938; *s* of Robert George Cox and Gladys Cox; *m* 1963, Constance Jean Hammond; one *s* two *d.* *Educ:* Brockley County School; Imperial College, London. BScEng (Metallurgy). ARSM, MIMMM. RARDE, 1960–69; Exchange Scientist, US Naval Research Lab., Washington, 1969–71; Dep. Materials Supt, RARDE, 1971–75; Asst Dir, Armour and Materials, Military Vehicle Engineering Estab., 1975–80; MoD Central Staffs Defence Science, 1980–83; Counsellor, Science and Technol., Washington, 1983–87; Superintendent, Radiation Sci. and Acoustics, NPL, 1988–92; Counsellor, Sci. and Technol., Tokyo, 1993–98. Dir, Asia Pacific Technology Network, 1999–2003. Business Mentor, Prince's Trust, 2001–. *Publications:* papers on refractory metals, structure and strengthening mechanism on high strength steel, fractography, explosive effects, archaeological artefacts corrosion, composites, space, robotics, science policy, metrology. *Recreations:* sailing, foreign travel, gardening, industrial archaeology, University of the Third Age.

COX, Archibald, Jr; Chairman: Sextant Group Inc., since 1993; Precision Magnetics Singapore, since 2007; *b* 13 July 1940; *s* of late Prof. Archibald Cox and Frances Bruen (*née* Perkins); *m* 1977, Jean Inge; two *s* one *d*; *m* 2005, Judy Gordon. *Educ:* Harvard Coll. (ABEcon 1962); Harvard Business Sch. (MBA 1964). Associate 1964–70, Vice Pres. 1971–72, Man. Dir, 1973–88, Morgan Stanley & Co. Incorp.; Man. Dir and Head of London Office, Morgan Stanley Internat., 1977–88; Pres. and Chief Exec. Officer, First Boston Corp., 1990–93. Director: Diamar Interactive Corp., 1995–2000; Hutchinson Technol. Inc., 1996–; Harris Chemical Gp, 1997–98; Builders Information Gp, 2004–; Micell Technologies Inc., 2007–. Member: Securities and Investments Board, 1986–88; Bd, Securities Industry Assoc., 1990–93. *Recreations:* cycling, hiking, sailing. *Clubs:* Links (New York); New York Yacht (New York); Bucks Harbor Yacht (Brooksville, Maine).

COX, Barry; *see* Cox, C. B.

COX, Barry Geoffrey; Chairman: Digital UK (SwitchCo), since 2005; Digital Radio Working Group, 2008; Deputy Chairman, Channel Four, 1999–2006; *b* 25 May 1942; *s* of Leonard William Cox and Daisy Miriam; *m* 1st, 1963, Pamela Ann Doran (marr. diss. 1977); two *s* two *d*; 2nd, 1984, Kathryn Diane Kay (marr. diss. 1994); 3rd, 2001, Fiona Pamela Hillary. *Educ:* Tiffin Sch., Kingston-upon-Thames; Magdalen Coll., Oxford (BA Hons). Reporter: The Scotsman, 1965–67; Sunday Telegraph, 1967–70; Producer and Dir, Granada TV, 1970–74; London Weekend Television: Editor, then Controller, 1974–87; Dir, Corporate Affairs, 1987–94; Dir, ITV Assoc., 1995–98; Chm., Digital TV Stakeholders' Gp, 2002–05. News Internat. Vis. Prof. of Broadcast Media, Oxford Univ., 2003. Treas., Inst. of Educn, London Univ., 2000–. Chm., Oval House Theatre, 2001–07. Life Mem., BAFTA. *Publications:* Civil Liberties in Britain, 1975; The Fall of Scotland Yard, 1977; Free For All?, 2004. *Address:* Mapledene TV Productions Ltd, 3 Old Barrack Yard, SW1X 7NP; *e-mail:* Barry.cox3@btopenworld.com.

COX, Brian Denis, CBE 2003; actor, director, teacher and writer; *b* 1 June 1946; *s* of Charles Mcardle Campbell Cox and Mary Ann Gillerline (*née* Mccann); *m* 1st, 1968, Caroline Burt (marr. diss. 1987); one *s* one *d*; 2nd 2001, Nicole Elisabeth Ansari; two *s.* *Educ:* LAMDA. *Stage appearances:* début, Dundee Rep., 1961; Royal Lyceum, Edinburgh, 1965–66; Birmingham Rep., 1966–68; As You Like It, Birmingham and Vaudeville (London début), 1967; title rôle, Peer Gynt, Birmingham, 1967; When We Dead Awaken, Edinburgh Fest., 1968; In Celebration, Royal Court, 1969; The Wild Duck, Edinburgh Festival, 1969; The Big Romance, Royal Court, 1970; Don't Start Without Me, Garrick, 1971; Mirandolina, Brighton, 1971; Getting On, Queen's, 1971; The Creditors, Open Space, 1972; Hedda Gabler, Royal Court, 1972; Playhouse, Nottingham: Love's Labour's Lost, title rôle, Brand, What The Butler Saw, The Three Musketeers, 1972; Cromwell, Royal Court, 1973; Royal Exchange, Manchester: Arms and the Man, 1974; The Cocktail Party, 1975; Pilgrims Progress, Prospect Th., 1975; Emigres, Nat. Theatre Co., Young Vic, 1976; Olivier Theatre: Tamburlaine The Great, 1976; Julius Caesar, 1977; The Changeling, Riverside Studios, 1978; National Theatre: title rôle, Herod, The Putney Debates, 1978; On Top, Royal Court, 1979; Macbeth, Cambridge Th. and tour of India, 1980; Summer Party, Crucible, 1980; Have You Anything to Declare?, Manchester then Round House, 1981; title rôle, Danton's Death, Nat. Theatre Co., Olivier, 1982; Strange Interlude, Duke of York, 1984 (Drama Mag. Best Actor Award, 1985), Nederlander, NY, 1985; Rat in the Skull, Royal Court, 1984 (Drama Mag. and Olivier Best Actor Awards, 1985) and NY, 1985; Fashion, The Danton Affair, Misalliance, Penny for a Song, 1986, The Taming of the Shrew, Titus Andronicus (title rôle), 1987, The Three Sisters, 1989, RSC, and Titus Andronicus on tour, Madrid, Paris, Copenhagen, 1988 (Olivier Award, Best Actor in a Revival, and Drama Mag. Best Actor Award for RSC 1988 season); Frankie and Johnny in the Clare-de-Lune, Comedy, 1989; Richard III, and title rôle, King Lear, National and world tour, 1990–91; The Master Builder, Edinburgh, 1993, Riverside, 1994; St Nicholas, Bush, 1997, NY, 1998 (Lucille Lortel Award, 1998); Skylight, LA, 1997; Dublin Carol, Old Vic, and Royal Court, 2000; Uncle Varrick, Edinburgh Royal Lyceum, 2004; Rock 'n' Roll, Royal Court, 2006; *films:* Nicholas and Alexandra, 1971; In Celebration, 1975; Manhunter, Shoot for the Sun, 1986; Hidden Agenda, 1990; Braveheart, The Cutter, 1994; Rob Roy, 1995; Chain Reaction, The Glimmer Man, Long Kiss Goodnight, 1996; Desperate Measures, Food for Ravens, Poodle Spring, 1997; The Boxer, The Corruptor, Mad About Mamba, The Minus Man, Rushmore, 1998; The Biographer, 2000; Saltwater, Strictly Sinatra, The Affair of the Necklace, 2001; Morality Play, The Rookie, Adaptation, The Bourne Identity, L.I.E., Super Troopers, 2002; 25th Hour, X-Men 2, The Ring, 2003; Troy, The Reckoning, The Bourne Supremacy, 2004; Red-eye, Woman in Winter, The Ringer, 2005; Match Point, Burns, Fourth Wall, Running with Scissors, Shamrock Boy, 2006; The Flying Scotsman, Zodiac, Terra, The Waterhorse: legend of the deep, 2007; Red, The Escapist, Agent Crush, Shoot on Sight, 2008; *TV appearances:* Churchill's People: The Wallace, 1972; The Master of Ballantrae, 1975; Henry II, in The Devil's Crown, 1978; Thérèse Raquin, 1979; Dalhousie's Luck, Bothwell, 1980; Bach, 1981; Pope John Paul II, 1984; Florence Nightingale, 1985; Beryl Markham: a shadow in the sun, 1988; Secret Weapon, Acting in Tragedy (BBC Masterclass), 1990; The Lost Language of Cranes, The Cloning of Joanna May, The Big Battalions, 1992; The Negotiator, 1994; Witness for Hitler, Blow Your Mind See A Play, 1995; Nuremberg (best supporting actor, Emmy Award), 2001; Frasier, 2002; The Strange Case of Sherlock Holmes and Arthur Conan Doyle, Blue/Orange, 2005; Deadwood, 2006; The Outsiders, The Secret of the Nutcracker, 2007; *radio:* James McLevy, 2001–03; *directed:* Edinburgh Festival: The Man with a Flower in his Mouth, The Stronger, 1973; Orange Tree, Richmond: I Love My Love, 1982; Mrs Warren's Profession, 1989; The Crucible, Moscow Art Theatre, London and Edinburgh, 1988–89; The Philanderer, Hampstead Th. Club, 1991 (world première of complete version); Richard III, Regent's Park Open Air Th., 1995. Hon. LLD Dundee, 1994; Hon. DLitt Queen Margaret, 2007; Hon. Dr Napier, 2008. Internat. Theatre Inst. Award, 1990. *Publications:* Salem to Moscow: an actor's Odyssey, 1991; The Lear Diaries, 1992. *Recreations:* keeping fit, tango. *Address:* c/o Conway van Gelder Grant Ltd, 18–21 Jermyn Street, SW1Y 6HP. *T:* (020) 7287 0077. *Clubs:* Savile, Garrick.

COX, Brian (Robert) Escott; QC 1974; a Recorder of the Crown Court, 1972–98; *b* 30 Sept. 1932; *yr s* of late George Robert Escott Cox, solicitor, and Doris Cox; *m* 1st, 1956; one *s* two *d*; 2nd, 1969, Noelle Gilormini; one *s* one *d.* *Educ:* Rugby Sch.; Oriel Coll., Oxford (BA Jurisprudence). Called to the Bar, Lincoln's Inn, 1954, Bencher, 1985; Midland and Oxford Circuit; a Dep. High Court Judge, 1980–98. *Recreations:* listening to and playing jazz. *Address:* 36 Bedford Row, WC1R 4JH. *T:* (020) 7421 8000.

COX, (Charles) Geoffrey; QC 2003; MP (C) Devon West and Torridge, since 2005; *b* 30 April 1960; *s* of Michael and Diane Cox; *m* 1985, Jeanie (*née* McDonald); two *s* one *d*. *Educ:* Downing Coll., Cambridge (BA). Called to the Bar, Middle Temple, 1982; in practice, specialising in criminal law, human rights, constitutional, commercial and defamation law; Hd of Chambers, Thomas More Chambers, 2003–. Contested (C) Devon W and Torridge, 2001. *Recreations:* walking, swimming, theatre, literature, political history, enjoying rural life. *Address:* Thomas More Chambers, 7 Lincoln's Inn Fields, WC2A 3BP. *T:* (020) 7404 7000, *Fax:* (020) 7831 4606; *e-mail:* clerks@thomasmore.co.uk; House of Commons, SW1A 0AA.

COX, Prof. (Christopher) Barry, PhD, DSc; Professor, Division of Life Sciences, and Assistant Principal, King's College London, 1989–96; *b* 29 July 1931; *s* of Herbert Ernest Cox and May Cox; *m* 1st, 1961, Sheila (*née* Morgan) (*d* 1996); two *s* one *d*; 2nd, 1998, Marie-Hélène (*née* Forges). *Educ:* St Paul's Sch., Kensington (Sen. Foundn Scholar); Balliol Coll., Oxford (MA); St John's Coll., Cambridge (PhD); DSc London. Asst Lectr in Zoology, King's Coll. London, 1956–59; Harkness Fellow of Commonwealth Fund, at Mus. of Comparative Zoology, Harvard, 1959–60; King's College London: Lectr in Zoology, 1959–66; Sen. Lectr, 1966–69; Reader, 1970–76; Prof., 1976–96; Head: Dept of Zoology, 1982–85; Dept of Biology, 1985–88; Fulbright Schol., Stanford Univ., Calif, 1988–89. Mem. Council, Palaeontological Assoc., 1967–69, 1974 (Vice-Pres., 1969–81). Editor: Palaeontology, 1975–79; Proc. of Leatherhead & Dist Local Hist. Soc., 2005–. Palaeontological collecting expedns to Central Africa, 1963; Argentina, 1967; N Brazil, 1972; Qld, Aust., 1978. *Publications:* Prehistoric Animals, 1969; (with P. D. Moore) Biogeography—an ecological and evolutionary approach, 1973, 7th edn 2005; (jtly) The Prehistoric World, 1975; (jtly) Illustrated Encyclopedia of Dinosaurs and Prehistoric Animals, 1988; (jtly) Atlas of The Living World, 1989; research papers on vertebrate palaeontology and historical biogeography, in Phil. Trans. Royal Soc., Proc. Zool. Soc., Nature, Bull. Brit. Mus. (Nat. Hist.), Jl Biogeog., etc. *Recreations:* theatre, old Surrey buildings (Chm., Domestic Bldgs Res. Gp, 2000–05; Sec., Surrey Dendrochronology Project, 2002–).

COX, Prof. Sir David (Roxbee), Kt 1985; PhD; FRS 1973; Warden of Nuffield College, Oxford, 1988–94, Hon. Fellow, 1994; *b* 15 July 1924; *s* of S. R. Cox, Handsworth, Birmingham; *m* 1948, Joyce (*née* Drummond), Keighley, Yorks; three *s* one *d*. *Educ:* Handsworth Grammar Sch., Birmingham; St John's Coll., Cambridge (MA). PhD Leeds, 1949. Posts at Royal Aircraft Establishment, 1944–46; Wool Industries Research Assoc., 1946–50; Statistical Laboratory, Cambridge, 1950–55; Visiting Prof., University of N Carolina, 1955–56; Reader in Statistics, 1956–60, Professor of Statistics, 1961–66, Birkbeck Coll. (Fellow, 2001); Prof. of Statistics, 1966–88 and Head of Dept of Maths, 1970–74, Imperial Coll. of Sci. and Technology. SERC Sen. Res. Fellow, 1983–88. President: Bernoulli Soc., 1979–81; Royal Statistical Soc., 1980–82; Pres., ISI, 1995–97. Foreign Member: Royal Danish Acad. of Scis and Letters, 1983; Indian Acad. of Scis, 1997; For. Hon. Mem., Amer. Acad. of Arts and Sciences, 1974; For. Associate, Nat. Acad. of Scis, USA, 1988. FIC 1994. Hon. FIA 1991; Hon. FBA 1997. Hon. DSc: Reading, 1982; Bradford, 1982; Helsinki, 1986; Heriot-Watt, 1987; Limburg's Univ. Centrum, 1988; Queen's Univ., Kingston, Ont, 1989; Waterloo, 1991; Neuchâtel, 1992; Padua, 1994; Minnesota, 1994; Toronto, 1994; Abertay Dundee, 1995; Tech. Univ. of Crete, 1996; Athens Univ. of Economics, 1998; Bordeaux II, 1999; Harvard, 1999; Elche, 1999; Rio de Janeiro, 2000; Leeds, 2005; Southampton, 2006; Gothenburg, 2007. Weldon Meml Prize, Univ. of Oxford, 1984; Kettering Medal, General Motors Cancer Foundn, 1990; (jtly) Max Planck Forschungspreis, 1993. Editor of Biometrika, 1966–91. *Publications:* Statistical Methods in the Textile Industry, 1949 (jt author); Planning of Experiments, 1958; (jtly) Queues, 1961; Renewal Theory, 1962; (jtly) Theory of Stochastic Processes, 1965; (jtly) Statistical Analysis of Series of Events, 1966; Analysis of Binary Data, 1970, 2nd edn 1989; (jtly) Theoretical Statistics, 1974; (jtly) Problems and Solutions in Theoretical Statistics, 1978; (jtly) Point Processes, 1980; (jtly) Applied Statistics, 1981; (jtly) Analysis of Survival Data, 1984; (jtly) Asymptotic Methods, 1989; (jtly) Inference and Asymptotics, 1994; (jtly) Multivariate Dependencies, 1996; (jtly) Theory of Design of Experiments, 2000; (jtly) Components of Variance, 2002; Selected Papers, two vols, 2005; Principles of Statistical Inference, 2006; papers in Jl of Royal Statistical Society, Biometrika, etc. *Address:* Nuffield College, Oxford OX1 1NF.

COX, Dame Elizabeth (Louise); *see* Neville, Dame E. L.

COX, Geoffrey; *see* Cox, C. G.

COX, Sir George (Edwin), Kt 2005; Board Member, NYSE-Euronext, since 2007; Chairman, Design Council, 2004–07; *b* 28 May 1940; *s* of George Herbert Cox and Beatrice Mary Cox; *m* 1st, 1963, Gillian Mary Mannings (marr. diss. 1996); two *s*; 2nd, 1996, Lorna Janet Peach; two *d*. *Educ:* Quintin Sch.; Queen Mary Coll., Univ. of London (BScAeEng). Engineer, BAC, 1962–64; Molins Machine Co.: Systems Designer, 1964–67; Manufacturing Manager, 1967–69; Management Consultant, Urwick Orr & Partners, 1969–73; UK Dir, Diebold Gp, 1973–77; Man. Dir, Butler Cox, 1977–92; Chm., 1992–94, Chief Exec., 1993–94, P-E International; Chief Exec., 1995–96, Chm., 1996–99, Unisys Ltd; Man. Dir, Unisys Inf. Services, Europe, 1996–99; Dir Gen., Inst. of Dirs, 1999–2004. Non-exec. Dir, 2000–07, Sen. Ind. Dir, 2003–07, Bradford & Bingley plc; Member: Bd, Shorts, 2000–; Supervisory Bd, Euronext, 2002–07. Cox Review of Creativity in Business, for HM Treasury, reported 2005. Chm., Merlin (Med. Emergency Relief Internat.), 2001–07. Mem. Bd, LIFFE, 1995–2002. Mem. Bd of Inland Revenue, 1996–99. Vis. Prof., Royal Holloway, Univ. of London, 1995–. Pres., Management Consultancies Assoc., 1991. Pres., Royal Coll. of Speech and Lang. Therapists, 2008–. Mem. Adv. Bd, Warwick Business Sch., 2001– (Chm., 2006–). Trustee, VSO, 2004–07. Mem., Information Technologists Co., 1992–; Master, Guild of Mgt Consultants, 1997–98. CCMI; CRAeS. Hon. Fellow, Queen Mary, Univ. of London, 2007. Hon FIED. DUniv Middlesex, 2002; Hon. DBA Wolverhampton, 2004; Hon. DDes De Montfort, 2007; Hon. DCL Northumbria, 2007; Hon. DSc, Huddersfield, 2008. *Publications:* contribs to various jls. *Recreations:* theatre, rowing (Chief Coach, Univ. of London Boat Club, 1976–78, Chm. of Selectors, GB Men's Rowing, 1978–80), gliding, history of aviation. *Address:* c/o NYSE-Euronext, Cannon Bridge House, 1 Cousin Lane, EC4R 3XX. *Club:* Leander.

COX, Gilbert Kirkwood, MBE; JP; Lord-Lieutenant of Lanarkshire, since 2000; *b* 24 Aug. 1935; *s* of William and Mary Bryce Cox; *m* 1959, Marjory Moir Ross Taylor; two *s* one *d*. *Educ:* Airdrie Acad.; Glasgow Royal Tech. Coll. NCB, 1953–63; David A. McPhail & Sons Ltd, 1963–71; Gen. Manager, Scotland, Associated Perforators & Weavers Ltd, 1971–97. Dir, Airdrie Savings Bank, 1985– (Chm., 1995–97). Chm. Bd of Mgt, Coatbridge Coll., 1996–2000. Hon. Sheriff, Lanarks, 2002–. *Recreations:* golf, photography. *Address:* Bedford House, Commonhead Street, Airdrie, N Lanarkshire ML6 6NS. *T:* (01236) 763331.

COX, Graham Loudon; QC (Scot.) 1993; Sheriff Principal of South Strathclyde, Dumfries and Galloway, 1993–2000; *b* 22 Dec. 1933; *s* of Rev. Thomas Loudon Cox and Leonainie Violet Rose (*née* Watson); *m* 1st, 1959, June Mary Constance Gunner (marr. diss. 1975); three *d*; 2nd, 1977, Jean Nelson. *Educ:* Hamilton Acad.; Grove Acad.; Univ. of Edinburgh (MA 1954; LLB 1956). Commnd RASC, 1957; transferred to Directorate Army Legal Services, 1958–61 (Temp. Major). Called to Scottish Bar, 1962; Advocate Depute, 1967; Sheriff, Tayside Central and Fife, at Dundee, 1968–93. Mem., Scottish Criminal Justice Forum, 1996–2000; Chm., Scottish Adoption Policy Review Gp, 2001–05. Hon. Vice Pres., Scottish Assoc. for Study of Delinquency, 1996–2002; Pres., Sheriffs' Assoc., 1992–93; Mem. Council, Commonwealth Magistrates and Judges Assoc., 1991–94, 1997–2000. Comr, Northern Lighthouse Bd, 1993–2000 (Vice-Chm., 1997–2000). *Recreations:* golf, gardening, travelling. *Address:* Crail House, Crail, Fife KY10 3SJ. *T:* (01333) 450270; *e-mail:* coxcrail@aol.com. *Clubs:* Army and Navy; Royal & Ancient Golf (St Andrews).

COX, John; freelance director of plays, opera, revue and musicals in Britain and abroad; *b* 12 March 1935; *s* of Leonard John Cox and Ethel M. (*née* McGill). *Educ:* Queen Elizabeth's Hosp., Bristol; St Edmund Hall, Oxford (MA; Hon. Fellow, 1991). Vis. Fellow, European Humanities Res. Centre, Oxford, 1995. Freelance dir, 1959–; Dir of Prodn, Glyndebourne Festival Opera, 1971–81; Gen. Adminr, 1981–85, Artistic Dir, 1985–86, Scottish Opera; Prodn Dir, Royal Opera House, Covent Gdn, 1988–94. Productions include: *Glyndebourne:* Richard Strauss cycle, Rake's Progress, The Magic Flute, La Cenerentola; *ENO:* Così fan tutte, Patience; *Scottish Opera:* L'Egisto, Manon Lescaut, Marriage of Figaro, Lulu, Don Giovanni; *Royal Opera:* Manon, Die Fledermaus, Guillaume Tell, Capriccio, Die Meistersinger, Il Viaggio a Reims, Die Frau ohne Schatten, Tosca, Eugene Onegin; *Garsington Opera:* Così fan tutte, Nozze di Figaro, Philosopher's Stone; *Australian Opera:* Barber of Seville, Albert Herring, Patience, Masked Ball, Capriccio (Olympic Arts Fest.), Arabella; *Santa Fe Opera:* L'Egisto, La Calisto, Marriage of Figaro, Arabella; *Monte Carlo Opera:* Rake's Progress, Hamlet, Eugene Onegin, Picture of Dorian Gray (world première), Vanessa, Così fan tutte, Otello; *Salzburg Opera:* Il Re Pastore, Ariadne auf Naxos, Rake's Progress, Der Freischutz, La Traviata; *Madrid:* Eugene Onegin, La Cenerentola, Rake's Progress, Capriccio; *Drottningholm:* Zemire et Azor, Tom Jones; *San Francisco:* Arabella, Magic Flute, Rake's Progress, Capriccio, Don Carlos, Ariadne auf Naxos, Così fan tutte; *Metropolitan, NY:* Barber of Seville, Magic Flute, Capriccio, Werther; *La Scala, Milan:* Rake's Progress, Magic Flute; *Amsterdam:* Der Rosenkavalier, Tannhäuser, Intermezzo; *Chicago Lyric Opera:* Thaïs, Capriccio, Ariadne auf Naxos; *Copenhagen:* Hamlet, Falstaff; also opera in Brussels, Stockholm, Cologne, Frankfurt, Munich, Florence, Spoleto, Turin, Parma, Nice, Strasbourg, Toulouse, Lisbon, Vienna, Leeds, Dallas, San Diego, Los Angeles, Washington, Houston, Wexford, Melbourne, Vancouver, etc. *Address:* 7 West Grove, SE10 8QT. *T:* (020) 8692 2450.

COX, John Colin Leslie, CBE 1994; Chief Executive, Pensions, Protection and Investment Accreditation Board, 2000; Chairman, London Europe Gateway Ltd, since 1996; *b* 23 Oct. 1933; *s* of late Dr Leslie Reginald Cox, OBE, FRS, and Hilda Cecilia Cox; *m* 1983, Avril Joyce Butt; one *s* one *d*. *Educ:* University College Sch., London; Queens' Coll., Cambridge (BA). National Service, 2nd Lieut, 2nd 10th Princess Mary's Own Gurkha Rifles, 1956–58 (GSM Malaya 1958). Joined Shell Group, 1958: Executive positions in Shell Ghana, 1962–65, and in Shell Gp in London, 1966–77; Shell Chemicals UK: Personnel Dir, 1978–81; Dir, Business Devlt, and chm. of subsid. cos, 1981–86; Dir Gen., CIA, 1987–95; Chief Exec., London First Centre, 1995–96. Member: Armed Forces Pay Review Body, 1993–99; Steering Bd, Lab. of the Govt Chemist, 1992–96; Adv. Cttee, European Movement, 1994–; Bd, UK CEED, 1996 (Chm., 1999); Bd, PHLS, 1997; Standards Bd, Edexcel Foundn, 1997–; Envmt Cttee, Knightsbridge Assoc., 1997–; Vice Chm., Defence and Security Forum, 1996–. Mem. (C), Westminster CC, 1998 (Vice Chm., PFI Cttee, 1998, Planning and Licensing Cttee, 2000). Chm., Governing Body, Westminster Adult Educn Service, 1998; Gov., City of Westminster Coll., 2000. Mem., Caux Round Table, 1991–. FRSA 1989. *Recreations:* sailing, antiques, country pursuits, photography. *Address:* London Europe Gateway Ltd, 138 Brompton Road, SW3 1HY. *T:* (020) 7581 9510. *Clubs:* Army and Navy, Hurlingham; Leander (Henley on Thames); Royal Solent Yacht (IoW).

COX, Ven. John Stuart; Archdeacon of Sudbury, 1995–2006, now Archdeacon Emeritus; *b* 13 Sept. 1940; *s* of Arthur F. W. Cox and Clarice M. Cox; *m* Mary Diane Williams; one *s* one *d*. *Educ:* Fitzwilliam House, Cambridge (MA); Linacre Coll., and Wycliffe Hall, Oxford (BA); Birmingham Univ. (DPS). Ordained deacon, 1968, priest 1969; Assistant Curate: St Mary's, Prescot, 1968–71; St George, Newtown, Birmingham 1971–73; Rector, St George, Newtown, Birmingham, 1973–78; Selection Sec., ACCM 1978–83 (Sen. Selection Sec., 1979–83); Canon Residentiary, Southwark Cathedral 1983–91; Diocesan Dir of Ordinands and Dir of Post-Ordination Training, Southwark 1983–91; Vicar, Holy Trinity Church in the Ecumenical Parish of Roehampton 1991–95; Diocesan Dir of Educn, St Edmundsbury and Ipswich, 2006–. *Publications* (contrib.) Religion and Medicine, Vol. 1, 1970; (contrib.) Say One for Me, 1992; A Risk Worth Taking, 2007. *Recreations:* music, reading, theatre, golf, wine-making. *Address:* 2 Bullen Close, Bury St Edmunds, Suffolk IP33 3JP. *T:* and *Fax:* (01284) 766796.

COX, Jonathan Mark, PhD; Headmaster, Royal Grammar School, Guildford, since 2007 *b* 25 Feb. 1966; *s* of Darrell and Nita Cox; *m* 1993, Rosemary Bruce; one *s* two *d*. *Educ* Charlton Prep. Sch.; St Mary's Coll., Southampton; Univ. of Southampton (BSc Hon Physiol. with Pharmacol. 1987; PhD Biochem. 1992); Royal Coll. of Music. Whitgift School: Biology Teacher, 1992–98; Hd of Sixth Form, 1998–2001; Second Master 2001–06. *Recreations:* performing classical music and close-up magic, playing Junior Monopoly with my children, listening to opera, visiting auctions, drinking my father-in law's fine wine. *Address:* c/o The Royal Grammar School, High Street, Guildford, Surrey GU1 3BB. *T:* (01483) 880608, *Fax:* (01483) 306127; *e-mail:* j.cox@rgs-guildford.co.uk *Clubs:* East India, MCC.

COX, Jonson; Group Chief Executive, Anglian Water Group plc, since 2004; *b* 11 Oct 1956; *s* of Peter Cox and Bobbie Cox (*née* Sutton); partner, Barbara Kennedy Wight; one *s* two *d*. *Educ:* King Edward VI Sch., Totnes; Clare Coll., Cambridge (BA Hons Econs). Various posts with companies of Royal Dutch/Shell Gp, 1979–92; Chm. and Man. Dir Yorkshire Envmtl, 1993–96; Managing Director: and Mem. Bd, Kelda Gp plc 1994–2000; Yorkshire Water, 1996–2000; Chief Operating Officer, Railtrack plc 2000–01; Chief Exec., Valpak Ltd, 2002–04. Non-exec. Dir, Wincanton plc, 2005–. *Recreation:* outdoor activities. *Address:* Anglian Water Group plc, Anglian House, Ambury Road, Huntingdon, Cambs PE29 3NZ.

COX, Josephine; writer; *b* 15 July 1940; *d* of Bernard and Mary Jane Brindle; *m* Kenneth George Cox; two *s*. Formerly: clerk, Milton Keynes Devel t Council; secretarial and teaching posts, incl. Lectr in Sociol. and History, Bletchley Coll., Milton Keynes; Partner family landscaping co. *Publications:* as Josephine Cox: Her Father's Sins, 1986; Let Loose the Tigers, 1988; Take This Woman, 1989; Angels Cry Sometimes, 1990; Whistledown Woman, 1990; Outcast, 1991; Alley Urchin, 1991; Don't Cry Alone, 1992; Vagabond; Jessica's Girl, 1993; Nobody's Darling, 1993; More Than Riches, 1994; Born to Serve 1994; Little Badness, 1995; Living a Lie, 1995; A Time For Us, 1996; The Devil Yo

Know, 1996; Miss You Forever, 1997; Cradle of Thorns, 1997; Love Me or Leave Me, 1998; Tomorrow the World, 1998; Gilded Cage, 1999; Somewhere, Someday, 1999; Rainbow Days, 2000; Looking Back, 2000; Let It Shine, 2001; The Woman Who Left, 2001; Jinnie, 2002; Bad Boy Jack, 2002; The Beachcomber, 2003; Lovers and Liars, 2004; Live the Dream, 2004; The Journey, 2005; Journey's End, 2006; The Loner, 2007; as Jane Brindle: Scarlet, 1991; No Mercy, 1992; The Tallow Image, 1994; No Heaven, No Hell, 1995; The Seeker, 1997; Hiding Game, 1998. *Address:* c/o Anthony Sheil, Aitken Alexander Associates, 18–21 Cavaye Place, SW10 9PT.

COX, Hon. Dame Laura (Mary), DBE 2002; **Hon. Mrs Justice Cox;** a Judge of the High Court of Justice, Queen's Bench Division, since 2002; *b* 8 Nov. 1951; *d* of John Arthur Bryant and Mary Eileen Bryant (*née* Clarke); *m* 1970, David Cox; three *s*. *Educ:* Queen Mary Coll., Univ. of London (LLB 1973; LLM 1975). Called to the Bar, Inner Temple, 1975, Bencher, 1999; in practice at the Bar, 1976–2002; QC 1994; Head of Chambers, 1996–2002. A Recorder, 1995–2002; a part-time Judge, Employment Appeal Tribunal, 2000–02. Chairman: Equal Opportunities Cttee, Bar Council, 2000–02; Equal Treatment Adv. Cttee, Judicial Studies Bd, 2003–; Mem., Justice, 1997–. British Mem., ILO Cttee of Experts, 1998–. Chm. Bd, Interights, 2002–05. Pres., Assoc. of Women Barristers, 2005–. Hon. Life Pres., Univ. of Essex Law Soc. Hon. Fellow, Queen Mary, Univ. of London, 2005. *Recreations:* music, theatre, cinema, watching football, cooking, novels, walking, arguing with sons! *Address:* Royal Courts of Justice, Strand, WC2A 2LL.

COX, Nigel John; HM Diplomatic Service, retired; Senior Adviser, East Asia, International Power plc, since 2007; Member, Advisory Panel, PricewaterhouseCoopers LLP, since 2007; *b* 23 April 1954; *s* of late Basil Cox, DFC and of Anne (*née* Webber); *m* 1992, Olivia Jane, *d* of Lt-Col Sir Julian Paget, *qv*. *Educ:* The High Sch., Dublin; Trinity Coll., Dublin (BA, LLB); Ecole Nat. d'Administration, Paris. FCO 1975; Chinese lang trng, Cambridge and Hong Kong, 1976–78; Second Sec., Peking, 1978–81; Second, later First, Sec., FCO, 1981–84; Asst Political Advr, Hong Kong, 1984; First Sec., Paris, 1985–90; Assistant Head: Western European Dept, FCO, 1990–91; Hong Kong Dept, FCO, 1991–92; Counsellor, Peking, 1992–96; Hd of SE Asian Dept, FCO, 1996–99; Minister, Peking, 2000–02; FCO, 2002–03; Dir, Asia-Pacific, FCO, 2003–05; Sen. Advr to Chief Exec., P&O Gp, 2005–06 (on secondment). *Recreations:* sinological claptrap, irony. *Address:* c/o Suite 222, 4 Montpelier Street, SW7 1EE. *Club:* Travellers.

COX, Oliver Jasper, CBE 1982; RIBA; Principal, Oliver Cox, Consultant Architect (Partner, Jean & Oliver Cox, 1989); *b* 20 April 1920; *s* of William Edward and Elsie Gertrude Cox; *m* 1953, Jean (*d* 2007); one *s* two *d*. *Educ:* Mill Hill Sch.; Architectural Association School of Architecture (AADip Hons). DistTP. Architects Dept, Herts CC, New Schools Division, 1948–49; Architects Dept, LCC Housing Division, 1950–59; Dep. Chief Architect, and Leader, Research and Development Gp, Min. of Housing and Local Govt, 1960–64; Partner, Shankland/Cox Partnership, 1965–85. *Publications:* Upgrading and Renewing the Historic City of Port Royal, Jamaica, 1985; (jtly) Lauderdale Revealed, 1993; The Naval Hospitals of Port Royal, Jamaica, 1996; Oracabessa: the town, the people and the waterfront development, 1997; (jtly) Lauderdale Reborn, 2003. *Recreations:* painting, drawing and screen printing. *Address:* 22 Grove Terrace, NW5 1PL. *T:* (020) 7485 6929.
See also P. W. Cox.

COX, Patricia Ann, CB 1989; Under Secretary, Scottish Home and Health Department, 1985–88, retired; *b* 25 May 1931; *d* of Sir (Ernest) Gordon Cox, KBE, TD, FRS. *Educ:* Leeds Girls' High Sch.; Newnham Coll., Cambridge (MA). Asst Principal, Dept of Health for Scotland, 1953; Principal: SHHD, 1959–62; HM Treasury, 1962–65; SHHD, 1965–67; Asst Sec., 1967–76, Under Sec., 1976–85, Scottish Educn Dept. *Publication:* Sandal Ash (novel for children), 1950. *Recreations:* archaeology, needlework, botanical painting. *Address:* 2 Gloucester Place, Edinburgh EH3 6EF. *T:* (0131) 225 6370.

COX, Patricia Anne, (Mrs Roger Cox); *see* Edwards, P. A.

COX, Patrick; President, International European Movement; Member (ELDR), Munster, 1989–2004, and President, 2002–04, European Parliament; *b* 29 Nov. 1952; *m* 1974, Kathleen Tighe; two *s* four *d*. *Educ:* Trinity Coll., Dublin (BA Mod. Econs 1974). Lecturer in Economics: Inst. of Public Admin, Dublin, 1974–76; Nat. Inst. for Higher Educn, Limerick, 1976–82; TV current affairs reporter and presenter, Today Tonight, Dublin, 1982–86. TD (Progressive Democrats), Cork S Central, 1992–94; Leader, Liberal Gp, European Parlt, 1998–2002. Gen. Sec., Progressive Democrat Party, 1985–89. Hon. Life Mem., Irish Inst. of Trng and Develt, 2002. Hon. Fellow, Irish Auctioneers and Valuers Instn, 2002. Freeman, Limerick City, 2002. Hon. LLD NUI, 2002; Hon. DHL American Coll., Dublin/Lynn Univ., Florida, 2002. President's Medal, Univ. of Limerick, 2002; European Movt/Aer Rianta European of Year Award, 2002; Charlemagne Prize, 2004.

COX, Paul William; freelance artist and illustrator, since 1982; *b* 31 July 1957; *s* of Oliver Jasper Cox, *qv*; *m* 1987, Julia Claire Nichol; one *s* one *d*. *Educ:* Port Regis and Stanbridge Earls School; Camberwell Sch. of Art and Crafts (BA Hons); Royal Coll. of Art (MA). Contributor to: The Times, Daily Telegraph, Independent, Express, Spectator, Punch, Sunday Times, Observer, Guardian, New Yorker, Vanity Fair, Town and Country, Wall St Journal, Traditional Home, Chatelaine, Business Week, House Beautiful; founder contributor to Blueprint, 1984; designed: PO stamps for 600th Lord Mayor's Show, 1989; mural for Eleanor Davies Colley Lect. Th., RCS, 2004; sets for 50th anniv. prodn of Salad Days, 2005; 15 paintings for St Charles Hosp., 2007; exhibns of watercolour drawings: Workshop Gallery, 1984; Illustrators' Gallery, 1985; Chris Beetles Gallery, 1989, 1993, 2001, 2006; Molesworth Gall., Dublin, 2001; Durrell Wildlife Conservation Trusts, 2006; historical Illustrations for Drama and Debate exhibn, Hampton Ct Palace, 2004. Vis Lectr in Illustration, Camberwell Sch. of Art and Crafts, 1982–90. *Publications:* illustrated books: Experiences of an Irish RM, 1984; The Common Years, 1984; A Varied Life, 1984; The Outing, 1985; The Character of Cricket, 1986; Romantic Gardens, 1988; Evacuee, 1988; Rebuilding the Globe, 1989; Dear Boy, 1989; Leave it to Psmith, 1989; Three Men in a Boat, 1989; The Cricket Match, 1991; Honourable Estates, 1992; The Darling Buds of May, 1992; The Russian Tea Room, 1993; The Wind in the Willows, 1993; Rumpole, 1994; Look out London, 1995; Jeeves & Wooster, 1996; The Plumbs of P. G. Wodehouse, 1997; Three Men on the Bummel, 1998; Tinkerbill, 1999; Jeeves & Wooster II, 2000; Best After-Dinner Stories, 2003; The Giver, 2003; The Train To Glasgow, 2003; The Best of Blandings, 2004; The Folio Book of Comic Short Stories, 2005; My Family and Other Animals, 2006; The Elevator Man, 2008; Absolute Corkers, 2008. *Address:* Twytten House, Wilmington, E Sussex BN26 5SN. *T:* (01323) 871264, *Fax:* (01323) 871265. *Clubs:* Chelsea Arts; Bembridge Sailing.

COX, Pauline Victoria, MA; Head Teacher, The Tiffin Girls' School, since 1994; *b* 9 Oct. 1948; *d* of Harold and Lily Greenwood; *m* 1970, Stephen James Cox, *qv*; one *s* one *d*. *Educ:* High Storrs Girls' Grammar Sch., Sheffield; Birmingham Univ. (BA Hons Geography 1970); Inst. of Education, London Univ. (PGCE 1973); W London Inst. of HE (RSA Dip. TEFL 1981); MA London 1983. Asst Editor, Polish News Bulletin of British and American Embassies, Warsaw, 1971–72; Teacher, subseq. also Head of Geography, Wandsworth Boys' Sch., 1973–75; Teacher of Geography, Lady Eleanor Holles Sch., Hampton, 1976–77; Lectr in ESL, Univ. of Legon, Accra, Ghana, 1978–80; Teacher of Geography: Tiffin Girls' Sch., 1981–83; Teddington Sch., 1983–84; Head of Geography, Waldegrave Sch. for Girls, Twickenham, 1984–87; Dep. Head, Cranford Community Sch., Hounslow, 1987–94. Mem. Council, London South LSC, 2001–04. Judge, Teaching Awards, 2005–06. Trustee: Smallpeice Trust, 2007; Arkwright Scholarships Trust, 2007. FRGS 1988. *Recreations:* reading crime fiction, listening to the Archers, watching sport. *Address:* The Tiffin Girls' School, Richmond Road, Kingston upon Thames KT2 5PL. *T:* (020) 8546 0773.

COX, Peter Arthur, BSc Eng; FREng, FICE; FCGI; FIC; consulting engineer; *b* 30 Oct. 1922; *m* 1944, Rosemary; one *s* two *d*. *Educ:* Westcliff High Sch., Essex; City and Guilds Coll., Imperial Coll., London (FIC 1991). Commissioned, Royal Engineers, 1942 (despatches). Lewis & Duvivier, 1947; Rendel Palmer & Tritton, 1952; Peter Lind & Co. Ltd, 1954; Sir Bruce White Wolfe Barry & Partners, 1955; Rendel Palmer & Tritton Ltd, Consulting Engineers, 1956, Partner, 1966, Sen. Partner, 1978–85, Chm., 1985–88. Chm., Ceemaid Ltd, 1984–85. Member: Dover Harbour Bd, 1983–89; Nat. Maritime Inst. Ltd, 1983–85; British Maritime Technology Ltd, 1986–93. Institution of Civil Engineers: Pres., 1980–81; Mem., Infrastructure Policy (formerly Planning) Gp, 1981–92 (Chm. 1981–84); Chm., Legal Affairs Cttee, 1988–92; Member: Smeatonian Soc. of Civil Engrs, 1980–; British Acad. of Experts, 1991–96. Mem., Commonwealth Scholarship Commn, 1982–88. Pres., Old Centralians, 1989–90. Governor, Westminster Coll., Wandsworth, 1990–92. *Publications:* papers to Instn of Civil Engrs on Leith Harbour and Belfast Dry Dock; many papers to conferences. *Recreations:* walking, gardening. *Address:* 22 Manor Court, Swan Road, Pewsey, SW9 5DW. *Club:* East India.

COX, Peter Frederick; Head of Information & Archives (formerly of Libraries), BBC, 1993–98; *b* 1 Dec. 1945; *s* of George William and Edna May Cox; *m* 1968, Gillian Mary Stevens; two *d*. *Educ:* Bedford Sch.; University Coll. London (BA); Univ. of Herts (MSc 1999). MCLIP (ALA 1968; MIInfSc). Chartered Librarian, 1968; Sen. Asst County Librarian, Herts, 1979–88; City of Westminster: City Librarian, 1989–92; Asst Dir (Leisure and Libraries), 1992–93. Member: Library and Information Services Council for England and Wales, 1992–95; Cttee on Public Library Objectives, 1992; Adv. Cttee, Nat. Sound Archive, 1996–98. FRSA 1991. JP Stevenage, 1980–88. *Publications:* professional articles and symposia papers. *Recreations:* sailing, painting. *Address:* 14 Ellis Grove, Norton Fitzwarren, Taunton, Somerset TA2 6SY. *T:* (01823) 284780.

COX, Peter Geoffrey; Editor, Daily Record, 2000–03; *b* 4 March 1950; *s* of William and Mary Cox; *m* 1991, Kay McWilliams; two *s* two *d*. *Educ:* Ilford Co. High Sch.; Nottingham Univ. Asst Ed., The Sun, 1983–94; Dep. Ed., New York Post, 1994–95; Exec. Ed., Daily Mirror, 1995–98; Dep. Ed., Daily Record, 1998–99; Ed., Sunday Mail, 1999–2000. *Recreations:* cooking, travel.

COX, Philip Gotsall; Chief Executive Officer, International Power plc, since 2003; *b* 22 Sept. 1951; *m* 1976, Brenda Sadler; one *s* one *d*. *Educ:* Queens' Coll., Cambridge (BA 1973). Gp Controller, 1989–98, Chief Financial Officer, 1998–99, Siebe plc; Sen. Vice-Pres., Ops, Invensys plc, 1999–2000; Chief Financial Officer, International Power plc, 2000–03. *Recreations:* golf, football. *Address:* International Power plc, Senator House, 85 Queen Victoria Street, EC4 4DP. *T:* (020) 7320 8640, *Fax:* (020) 7320 8650; *e-mail:* philip.cox@ipplc.com.

COX, Philip (Joseph), DSC 1943; QC 1967; Honorary Recorder of Northampton, since 1972; *b* 28 Sept. 1922; *s* of Joseph Parriss Cox, Rugby; *m* 1951, Margaret Jocelyn Cox, *d* of R. C. H. Cox, Purley, Surrey; one *s* one *d*. *Educ:* Rugby Sch.; Queens' Coll., Cambridge. Lance-Corp., LDV and HG, 1940–42; RNVR, 1942–46 (Lieut): Radar Officer, Gp B3, N Atlantic Convoy Close Escort Gp, 1943–44; Application Officer for S and X band Radar, Admiralty Signal Establishment, 1944–45; orgn of Radar Section, Royal Hellenic Navy, 1945–46. Called to Bar, Gray's Inn, 1949; Bencher, 1972 (Vice-Treas., 1990; Treas., 1991); practised at Bar, Birmingham, 1949–67, London, 1967–91. Deputy Chairman: Northants QS, 1963–71; Warwicks QS, 1966–71; a Recorder, 1972–94; Leader, Midland and Oxford Circuit, 1975–79; a Dep. High Court Judge, 1977–92. Member: County Court Rules Cttee, 1962–68; Senate, Inns of Court and Bar, 1974–80. Legal Assessor to Disciplinary Cttee, RCVS, 1969–2000; Chm., Cttee of Enquiry into London Smallpox Outbreak, 1973; Chairman: Code of Practice Appeal Bd, Prescription Medicines Code of Practice Authy, 1993–2000; Code of Practice Cttee, Assoc. of British Pharmaceut. Industries, 1978–92; Code of Practice Cttee, Internat. Fedn of Pharmaceut. Manufacturers Assocs, 1985–2000; Gen. Optical Council, 1985–88; Code of Practice Cttee, Nat. Office of Animal Health, 1987–92; WHO Internat. Gp of Experts on Ethical Criteria for Drug Promotion, 1987. Pres., Mental Health Review Tribunals, 1984–95. Chm., Birmingham Forward Br., RBL, 2003–05. Pres., Edgbaston Liberal Assoc., 1974–86. *Recreations:* sailing, golf, gardening, reading, woodwork. *Address:* 9 Sir Harry's Road, Edgbaston, Birmingham B15 2UY. *T:* (0121) 440 0278. *Clubs:* Naval; Royal Cruising, Bar Yacht.

COX, Raymond Edwin; QC 2002; *b* 6 May 1959; s of Edwin David Cox and Catherine (*née* Mook Lan, now Deverill-West); *m* 1990, Alexandra Clare Howell; two *s* two *d*. *Educ:* Mansfield Coll., Oxford (BA Hons Jurisprudence (1st cl.); Eldon Schol.). Called to the Bar, Gray's Inn (Arden Schol.), 1982, Bencher, 2008. Consultant Editor, Civil Procedure Reports, 2005–. *Publications:* (ed jtly) Commercial Court Procedure, 2000; (ed jtly) Law of Bank Payments, 3rd edn, 2004; Private International Law of Reinsurance and Insurance, 2006. *Recreations:* music, ski-ing. *Address:* Fountain Court Chambers, Temple, EC4Y 9DH. *T:* (020) 7583 3335, *Fax:* (020) 7353 0329; *e-mail:* rc@fountaincourt.co.uk.

COX, Richard Charles, MBE 1961; HM Diplomatic Service, retired; *b* 27 May 1920; *s* of Charles Victor Cox and Marjorie Eleanor Cox (*née* Fox); *m* 1941, Constance (*née* Goddard); one *s*. *Educ:* Gravesend Grammar Sch.; BA Open Univ., 1985. Served War of 1939–45, RAF; released with rank of Sqdn Leader, 1946. Entered Colonial Office, 1937; Dominions Office, 1946; High Commn, Colombo, 1949–52; Second Sec., Calcutta, 1953–54; CRO, 1954–56; First Sec., Bombay, 1956–59; CRO, 1960–63; First Sec., Valletta, 1964–68; FCO, 1968–72; NI Office, 1972–74; Dep. Sec. Gen., Cento, 1975–77. *Recreations:* swimming, gardening, watching Rugby football. *Address:* 31 Lotfield Street, Orwell, near Royston, Herts SG8 5QT. *T:* (01223) 207969.

COX, Richard T.; *see* Temple Cox.

COX, Dr Roger; Director, Centre for Radiation, Chemical and Environmental Hazards, Health Protection Agency, since 2005; *b* 26 May 1947; *s* of Thomas and Leonora Cox; *m* 1971, Susan Whisstock; one *s* one *d*. *Educ:* Univ. of Reading (BSc Hons Microbiol. 1968; PhD Microbial Genetics 1973). With MRC, 1971–90; Hd of Dept, and Div. Hd, 1990–2003, Dir, 2003–05, NRPB. Hon. Prof., Brunel Univ., 1999–. Delegate to UN Scientific Cttee on Effects of Atomic Radiation, 2001–. Member: Internat. Commn on Radiological Protection, 1996– (Vice Chm., 2003–); Biol Effects of Ionizing Radiation VII Cttee, NAS, 1999–2005. FMedSci 2006. (Jtly) Weiss Medal, ARR, 1992. *Publications:*

(jtly) Health Risks from Exposure to Low Levels of Ionizing Radiation, 2005; numerous contribs to radiation sci. and cell/molecular biol. jls and reports. *Recreations:* family life, boats, fishing, cinema. *Address:* Health Protection Agency Centre for Radiation, Chemical and Environmental Hazards, Chilton, Didcot, Oxon OX11 0RQ. *T:* (01235) 822618, *Fax:* (01235) 822620; *e-mail:* roger.cox@hpa.org.uk.

COX, His Honour Roger Charles; a Circuit Judge, 1988–2004; *b* 18 April 1941; *s* of late Reginald William Cox and Hilda Cox; *m* 1970, Patricia Anne Edwards, *qv. Educ:* Cheltenham Grammar Sch.; Birmingham Univ. (LLB, LLM). Called to the Bar, Gray's Inn, 1965. Asst Lectr, Faculty of Law, Bristol Univ., 1964–66; Lord Justice Holker Sen. Schol., Gray's Inn, 1966; a Recorder, 1986. *Publication:* (contrib.) Guidelines for the Assessment of Damages in Personal Injury Cases. *Recreations:* travel, music, theatre, reading, Freemasonry.

COX, Roy Arthur, CBE 1987; JDipMA; FCA, FCMA, FCBSI; Chief General Manager, 1970–85, Director, 1976–89, Alliance and Leicester (formerly Alliance) Building Society; *b* 30 Nov. 1925; *s* of J. W. Arthur Cox; *m* 1st, 1951, Joy (*née* Dunsford); one *s* one *d*; 2nd, 1980, Audrey (*née* Brayham); 3rd, 2007, Audrey (*née* Smith). *Educ:* Isleworth Grammar Sch. FCA 1953; FCMA 1957; FCBSI (FBS 1971). War Service, 1944–47. Wells & Partners, Chartered Accountants, 1942–49; Colombo Commercial Co. Ltd, 1950–61; Urwick, Orr & Partners, Management Consultants, 1961–65; Alliance Building Society: Sec., 1965; Gen. Man., 1967. Dir, Southern Bd, Legal & General Assce Soc. Ltd, 1972–86. Building Societies Association: Chm., S Eastern Assoc., 1972–74; Mem. Council, 1973–87; Chm., Gen. Purposes and Public Relations Cttee, 1975–77; Dep. Chm., Council, 1983–85; Chm., Council, 1985–87; Vice-Pres., 1987–. Mem., Royal Commn on Distribution of Income and Wealth, 1974–78; Dir, SE Electricity Bd, 1983–90; Dep. Chm., Seeboard plc, 1990–96; Chairman: PO Staff Superannuation Scheme, 1986–95; PO Pension Scheme, 1987–95; Siebe Pension Trustee Ltd, 1992–2000; Dir, Hermes Pensions Management Ltd, 1995–98. CCMI (CBIM 1980). *Recreations:* golf, snooker, bridge.

COX, Sarah Elizabeth; Director, Change, Cabinet Office, since 2007; *b* 19 May 1967; *d* of Dr Joseph Cox and Dr Barbara Cox (*née* Smith). *Educ:* Arnold Sch., Blackpool; Univ. of Birmingham (BCom Hons 1988). APMI 1991. Commercial Union Assce Co., later CGU and Aviva, 1991–2001: operational mgt, 1991–95; Prog. Dir, 1995–98; IT Service Centre Manager, 1996–98; Sen. Consultant, 1998–2000; Business Develt Manager, Norwich Union Internat., Aviva plc, 2000–01; Partner, Business Change and Delivery, Barclays Solutions, Barclays plc, 2001–04; Dir, Business Change and Delivery, ODPM, 2004–06; a Dir, Capability Rev. Team, Prime Minister's Delivery Unit, Cabinet Office, 2006–07. *Recreations:* golf, season ticket holder at Chelsea FC. *Address:* Change Team, Cabinet Office, Kirkland House, 22–26 Whitehall, SW1A 2WH. *T:* 07917 263864; *e-mail:* sarah.cox@cabinet-office.x.gsi.gov.uk. *Club:* Woodcote Park Golf.

COX, Sebert Leslie, OBE 1994; Partner, Kingston Reid Consulting, since 2001; Chairman: NNTLIFTCo Ltd, since 2004; Key Real Estate Ltd, since 2004; *b* 27 Dec. 1950; *s* of late Maunsell Newton Cox and Anna Louise Cox (*née* Reid); *m* 1974, Christine Lesley Hall; two *d. Educ:* Univ. of Lancaster (MSc). Granada Gp Ltd, 1967–70; Ford Motor Co. Ltd, 1970–72; Easton House Trust, 1972–73; Springboard Trust, 1973–76; Northumbria Probation Service, 1976–90; Develt Advr, Home Office, 1990–2001; Chm., Thames Gateway Ltd Partnership, 2003–05. Chairman: N British Housing Assoc., subseq. Places for People Gp, 1997–2004; Co. Durham Probation Bd, 2007–. Mem., Inst. of Dirs, 1996. *Recreations:* cooking and entertaining, gardening, walking, visiting historic buildings. *Address:* Spurtop House, Whitehall Lane, Iveston, Co. Durham DH8 7TA. *Club:* Royal Commonwealth Society.

COX, Stephen James, CVO 1997; Executive Secretary, Royal Society, since 1997; *b* 5 Dec. 1946; *s* of late Harold James West Cox and of Norah Cox (*née* Wilkinson); *m* 1970, Pauline Victoria Greenwood (*see* P. V. Cox); one *s* one *d. Educ:* Queen Elizabeth Grammar Sch., Blackburn; Atlantic Coll.; Birmingham Univ. (BA Hons Geography 1969); Leeds Univ. (Postgrad. Dip. ESL 1970); Sussex Univ. (MA Educn 1977). VSO, Bolivia, 1965–66. British Council: Warsaw, 1970; Western Europe Dept, London, 1974; Accra, 1977; Staff Training Dept, 1981; Chm., British Council Whitley Council, Trade Union Side, 1981–84; Educn Attaché, Washington DC, 1984–85; Asst Sec., Royal Society, 1985–91; Dir Gen., Commonwealth Inst., 1991–97; Chief Exec., Westminster Foundn for Democracy, 1995–97. Member: Jt Commonwealth Socs Council, 1992–97; Court, RCA, 1993–99; Council, Parly and Scientific Cttee, 1997– (Vice-Pres., 2004–08); Council, BAAS, 1997–. Trustee: Council for Assisting Refugee Academics, 1997–; Internat. Polar Foundn, 2006–. Chm., Duke of Edinburgh Awards Forum, 2003–07. Mem. Bd of Govs, 2002–, and Chair, Audit Cttee, 2004–08, Kingston Univ. FRGS (Member: Sci. and Public Affairs Cttee, 1994–96; Educn Cttee, 1996–98; Expedn and Field Work Cttee, 1998–2004). Hon. Mem., ESU, 1994–. Mem., 1994–, Chm., 2002–06, Editl Bd, Commonwealth Round Table. Hon. DSc Lancaster, 2003. *Recreations:* cricket, travel, visiting galleries, architecture. *Address:* Royal Society, 6 Carlton House Terrace, SW1Y 5AG. *T:* (020) 7839 5561, *Fax:* (020) 7930 2170. *Clubs:* Royal Over-Seas League, Geographical; Middlesex County Cricket.

COX, Prof. Susan Jean; Professor of Safety and Risk Management and Dean, Lancaster University Management School, Lancaster University, since 2001; *b* 17 Oct. 1947; *d* of late Derric and Jean Minshall; *m* 1969, Thomas Rodford Cox, CBE; two *d. Educ:* Univ. of Nottingham (BSc (Chemistry and Psychol.) 1969; MPhil (Psychol.) 1988). Loughborough University: Director: Centre for Extension Studies, 1993–94; Centre for Hazard and Risk Mgt, 1994–97; Loughborough Business Sch., 1997–2001. Chm., Assoc. of Business Schs, 2002–04; Mem., Res. Priorities Bd, ESRC, 2003–07; Dir, Inspire Learning, 2003–06. *Publications:* (with Robin Tait) Reliability, Safety and Risk Management: an integrated approach, 1991, 2nd edn 1998; (with Tom Cox) Safety, Systems and People, 1996. *Recreations:* gardening, theatre, walking, football (Stoke City supporter), reading, travel. *Address:* Walnut Lodge, Rose Grove, Keyworth, Notts NG12 5HE. *T:* (0115) 937 5947, *Fax:* (office) (01524) 594720; *e-mail:* s.cox@lancaster.ac.uk.

COX, Thomas Michael; *b* London, 19 Jan. 1930. *Educ:* state schools; London Sch. of Economics. Electrical worker. Former Mem., Fulham Borough Council; contested (Lab) GLC elections, 1967; contested (Lab) Stroud, 1966. MP (Lab): Wandsworth Central, 1970–74; Wandsworth Tooting, 1974–83; Tooting, 1983–2005. An Asst Govt Whip, 1974–77; a Lord Comr of the Treasury, 1977–79. Member: ETU; Co-operative Party.

COX, Prof. Timothy Martin, MD; FRCP, FMedSci; Professor of Medicine, since 1989 and Fellow of Sidney Sussex College, since 1990, University of Cambridge; *b* 10 May 1948; *s* of late William Neville Cox and Joan Desirèe Cox (*née* Ward); *m* 1975, Susan Ruth Mason; three *s* one *d. Educ:* Oundle Sch.; London Hosp. Med. Coll., Univ. of London (Price Entrance Scholar; James Anderson Prize; MB 1971, MSc 1978, MD 1979); MA Cantab 1990, MD Cantab 1991. FRCP 1984. Junior posts, Med. Unit, Royal London Hosp., 1971; Dept of Morbid Anatomy, Bernard Baron Inst., Hammersmith and United Oxford Hosps, 1972–77; Royal Postgraduate Medical School, London University: MRC Training Fellow, Cell Biology Unit, 1977–79; Wellcome Sen. Clinical Fellow and Se Lectr, Dept of Medicine, 1979–87; Sen. Lectr, Depts of Haematology and Medicin 1987–89. Hon. Consultant Physician, Addenbrooke's Hosp., 1989–. Vis. Scientist, De of Biology, MIT, 1983–84. Lectures: A. J. MacFazean, Univ. of Hong Kong, 199 Schorstein Meml, London Hosp. Med Coll., 1994; Bradshaw, RCP, 1996; Flyn RCPath, 2001. External examiner in Medicine: Univ. of Hong Kong, 1990; Univ. London, 1993–97; RCSI, 1995–97; Chinese Univ. of HK, 2001; Univ. of Oxford, 2001 Member: MRC Grants Cttee, 1990–94; MRC Clin. Trng Career Develt Panel, 2000–0 Mem., Vet. Panel, Wellcome Trust, 1996–98. Trustee, Croucher Foundn, HK, 2001 Mem., Assoc. of Physicians of GB and Ire., 1984– (Mem., Exec. Cttee, 1995–97 Cambridge Philosophical Society: Mem. Council, 1994–; Vice Pres., 1999–2002, 2005 Pres., 2002–03; Sen. Vice Pres., 2003–05. Fellow and Mem. Council, Galton Inst., 2007 Founder FMedSci 1998. FRSA 2000. Syndic, CUP, 1998–; Member, Editorial Boar Qly Jl of Medicine; Reviews in Molecular Medicine. *Publications:* Oxford Textbook Medicine, (contrib.) 3rd edn, 1995, (ed jtly) 5th edn, 2009; (ed jtly) Molecular Biology Medicine, 1997 (trans. Spanish, 1998, Serbo-Croat, 2000); contribs to sci. and med. jls inborn errors metabolism, incl. Cell, New England Jl of Med., Lancet, Jl of Cli Investigation, Jl Biol. Chem., Nature Reviews Genetics. *Recreations:* natural history, pian making cider. *Address:* Department of Medicine, University of Cambridge School Clinical Medicine, Hills Road, Cambridge CB2 2QQ. *T:* (01223) 336864.

COX, Vivienne; Executive Vice President, and Chief Executive Officer, Alternati Energy, BP plc, since 2008; *b* 29 May 1959; *d* of Ewart Arthur Cox and Doreen Oli Cox (*née* Merchant); *m* 2007, Eric Vischer; two *d. Educ:* St Catherine's Coll., Oxford (B 1981, MA); INSEAD (MBA 1989). Joined BP, 1981; Chief Exec., Air BP, 1997–9 Group Vice President: Refining and Mkting, 1999–2001; Integrated Supply and Tradin 2001–05; Exec. Vice Pres., Gas Power and Renewables, 2005–08. Non-exec. Dir, R Tinto, 2005–. Mem., Internat. Council, INSEAD. Patron, St Francis Hospice, 2006 *Recreations:* sailing, swimming, gardening. *Address:* BP plc, 1 St James's Square, SW1 4PD.

COX, Hon. William John Ellis, AC 1999; RFD 1985; ED 1968; Governor, Tasmani 2004–08; *b* 1 April 1936; *s* of Hon. William Ellis Cox, CBE, MC, and Alice Mary Co *m* 1970, Jocelyn Fay Wallace; two *s* one *d. Educ:* Xavier Coll., Melbourne; Univ. Tasmania (BA, LLB). Called to the Bar, Tasmania, 1960; Partner, Dobson, Mitchell Allport, 1961–76; Magistrate, Hobart, 1976–77; Crown Advocate, Tasmania, 1977–8 QC 1978; Judge, Supreme Court of Tasmania, 1982–95; Chief Justice, Tasmani 1995–2004; Lieut Gov., Tasmania, 1996–2004. Dep. Pres., Defence Force Disciplin Appeal Tribunal, 1988–95. Pres., Bar Assoc. of Tasmania, 1973–75. Lt Col, Arm Reserve; CO, 6 Field Regt, RAA, 1972–75; Hon. Col Comdt, RAA (Tas), 1993–97. Di Winston Churchill Meml Trust, 1988– (Nat. Chm., 2000–04). Pres., St John Ambulanc Australia (Tas), 2002–04. Hon. LLD Tasmania, 2005. KStJ 2002. *Recreations:* bus walking, gardening. *Address:* 214 Davey Street, Hobart, Tas 7004, Australia. *Clu* Tasmanian.

COX, William Trevor; *see* Trevor, William.

COXWELL-ROGERS, Col Richard Annesley; Vice Lord-Lieutenant Gloucestershire, 1993–2007; *b* 26 April 1932; *s* of Maj.-Gen. Norman Annesley Coxwel Rogers, CB, CBE, DSO and Diana Coxwell-Rogers (*née* Coston); *m* 1st, 1965, Marth Felicity Hurrell (*d* 1998); two *s*; 2nd, 2003, Louisa, *widow* of David Wagg. *Educ:* Et Coll.; RMA Sandhurst. Commissioned 15th/19th Hussars, 1952; served Germany, U Malaya, Cyprus; Comd 15th/19th Hussars, 1973–75; Col, 15th/19th Hussars, 1988–9 Area Appeals Organiser, CRC, 1982–93. DL Glos 1990; High Sheriff of Glos, 199 *Recreations:* country sports. *Address:* Hookash, Foxcote, Andoversford, Cheltenham, Gl GL54 4LP. *T:* (01242) 821410. *Club:* Cavalry and Guards.

COYLE, Prof. Andrew Gerard, CMG 2003; PhD; Professor of Prison Studies, sin 2003, and Director, International Centre for Prison Studies, 1997–2005, King's Colleg University of London; *b* 17 June 1944; *s* of Andrew Coyle and late Kathleen Coyle (*n* Ward); *m* 1st, Joyce Hamilton (marr. diss.); one *s* three *d*; 2nd, Vivien Stern (*see* Barone Stern). *Educ:* Real Colegio Escocés, Valladolid; Open Univ. (BA); Univ. of Edinburg (PhD 1986). Scottish Prison Service and HM Prison Service, 1973–97: Assista Governor: Edinburgh Prison, 1973–76; Polmont Borstal, 1976–78; Dep. Gov., Sho Prison, 1978–81; Head of Ops, Scottish Prison Service HQ, 1981–86; Governo Greenock Prison, 1986–88; Peterhead Prison, 1988–90; Shotts Prison, 1990–91; Brixto Prison, 1991–97. Man. Ed., Punishment & Society, 1997–. Winston Churchill Travellin Fellow, 1984; Hon. Prof., Min. of Justice Acad. of Law and Mgt, Russia, 2000–. Expe consultant on prison matters: to Office of UN High Comr for Human Rights, 1992–; Council of Europe, 1992–. Expert Mem., Eur. Cttee for Prevention of Torture missio to Iceland, 1998, 2004, Russia, 1998, 1999, Turkey, 2000, Armenia, 2002. Expert advis on prison issues to: Prison Admin of Kazakhstan, 1997–99; Min. of Justice, Chile, 199 NZ Dept of Corrections, 1999; Min. of Justice, Venezuela, 2000; Govt of Mauritiu 2001; Palestinian Authy, 2002; Govts of The Bahamas, 2002, the Dominican Republi 2003, Argentina, 2005, Uruguay, 2005, Algeria, 2006, Cayman Islands, 2006; has visite advised on or lectured in prison systems in numerous countries. Chm., Scottish Pris Governors' Cttee, 1986–89. Associate Mem., Centre for Law and Society, Univ. Edinburgh, 1988. Mem., Centre for Theol. and Public Issues, Univ. of Edinburgh, 1993 Chm., Inst. for Study and Treatment of Delinquency, 1993–97. Chm., Scottish Assoc. f Study of Delinquency, 1989–91; Mem., Prison Health Care Res. Ethics Ctte 1999–2002. Vice Pres., Nat. Assoc. of Prison Visitors, 1999–. Mem., Penal Refor Internat., 1990–. Patron, Unlock, Assoc. of Former Prisoners, 1997–. Trustee: Prisone Abroad, 1999–2007; Unit for Arts and Offenders, 2000–05; Royal London Aid So 2002–05. Bd Mem., Eisenhower Foundn, Washington, 2004–. FKC 2004. Med Russian Penitentiary Service, 2001; Min. of Justice, Russian Fedn, 2002. *Publication* Inside: rethinking Scotland's prisons, 1991; The Prisons We Deserve, 1994; Managi Prisons in a Time of Change, 2002; Human Rights Approach to Prison Manageme handbook for prison staff, 2002; (ed) Capitalist Punishment: prison privatisation a human rights, 2003; Humanity in Prison, 2003; Understanding Prisons, 2005; contribut to: Problems of Long-Term Imprisonment, 1987; Relational Justice, 1994; Couples Care in Custody, 1997; Sentenced to Die?: the problem of TB in prisons in Easte Europe and Central Asia, 1999; Punishment and the Prison: Indian and internatio perspectives, 1999; Imprisonment Today and Tomorrow, 2001; Incident Command: ta from the hot seat, 2002; Handbook of Public Policy in Britain, France and German 2004; Capital Punishment: strategies for abolition, 2004; (contrib. with V. Stern) Heal Care: responding to diversity, 2003; contrib. numerous articles to learned jls on hum rights, prisons, prison mgt and alternatives to prison. *Address:* International Centre f Prison Studies, King's College London, Strand, WC2R 2LS. *T:* (020) 7848 1922, *Fa* (020) 7848 1901; *e-mail:* icps@kcl.ac.uk.

COYLE, Dr Diane; Director, Enlightenment Economics, since 2001; Trustee, BB Trust, since 2007; *b* 12 Feb. 1961; *d* of Joseph and Kathleen Coyle; *m* 1990, Rory Cellar

Jones; two *s. Educ:* Brasenose Coll., Oxford (BA Hons PPE 1981); Harvard Univ. (PhD Econs 1985). Sen. Econ. Asst, HM Treasury, 1985–86; Sen. Economist, DRI Europe, 1986–89; Eur. Ed. and features writer, Investors' Chronicle, 1989–93; Econs Ed., The Independent, 1993–2001. Mem., Competition Commn, 2001–. *Publications:* The Weightless World, 1996 (US edn 1997); Governing the World Economy, 2000; Paradoxes of Prosperity, 2001; Sex, Drugs and Economics, 2002; New Wealth for Old Nations, 2005; The Soulful Science, 2007; contrib. chapters in books and articles to jls. *Recreations:* classical ballet, reading. *Address:* BBC Trust, Room 211, 35 Marylebone High Street, W1U 4AA. *T:* (020) 7208 9666; *e-mail:* diane@enlightenmenteconomics.com. *Club:* Commonwealth.

COYLE, Eurfron Gwynne, (Mrs Michael Coyle); *see* Jones, E. G.

COYNE, James Elliott; Canadian banker and financial consultant; *b* Winnipeg, 17 July 1910; *s* of James Bowes Coyne and Edna Margaret Coyne (*née* Elliott); *m* 1957, Meribeth Stobie; one *s* one *d. Educ:* University of Manitoba (BA); University of Oxford (BCL). RCAF (Flying Officer), 1942–44. Admitted to the Bar, Manitoba, 1934; solicitor and barrister in Manitoba, 1934–38; Financial Attaché, Canadian Embassy, Washington, DC, 1941; Mem. War-time Prices and Trade Board, Ottawa, 1942 (Dep.-Chm.). Bank of Canada, Ottawa: Asst to the Governors, 1944–49; Deputy-Governor, 1950–54; Governor, 1955–61. *Address:* PO Box 864 Station Main, Winnipeg, MB R3C 2P7, Canada.

COYNE, Prof. John; Vice-Chancellor, University of Derby, since 2004; *b* Barnsley, 27 Sept. 1951; *m* Julie; two *d. Educ:* Univ. of Nottingham (BA). University of Nottingham, 1985–90: Lectr, then Sen. Lectr, Dept of Industrial Econs, subseq. Dept of Industrial Econs, Accountancy and Insurance; Warden of Cripps Hall; Co-Dir, Centre for Mgt Buy-out Res.; De Montfort University: Prof. of Business, 1990–2000 (Bass Prof., 1990–93); Hd, Leicester Sch. of Business, 1990–97; Dean, Faculty of Business and Law, 1997–2000; Pro-Vice-Chancellor, 2000–04. *Address:* Office of the Vice-Chancellor, University of Derby, Kedleston Road, Derby DE22 1GB.

COZENS, Andrew Geoffrey, CBE 2005; Strategic Adviser, Children, Adults and Health Services, Improvement and Development Agency, since 2006; *b* 3 June 1955; *s* of late Geoffrey Cozens and Iris Cozens (*née* Hammett). *Educ:* Peter Symonds Sch., Winchester; Magdalene Coll., Cambridge (BA 1977); Green Coll., Oxford (MSc, CQSW 1981). Social Worker, N Yorks CC, 1981–84; Develt Officer, N Yorks Forum for Vol. Orgns, 1984–88; North Yorkshire County Council: Principal Officer, 1988–90; Asst Dir, 1990–94; Sen. Asst Dir, 1994–96; Dir of Social Services, Glos CC, 1996–2000; Dir of Social Services, then of Social Care and Health, and Dep. Chief Exec., Leicester CC, 2000–06. Pres., Assoc. of Dirs of Social Services, 2003–04. Publishing Editor: Platform Mag., 1972–77; Green Horse Pubns, 1974–77; Avalon Editions, 1978–82. Hon. Fellow, Cheltenham and Gloucester Coll. of Higher Educn, 1998. *Recreations:* hill walking, the arts, reading, watching sport. *Address:* Improvement and Development Agency, Layden House, 76–86 Turnmill Street, EC1M 5LG.

COZENS, Robert William, CBE 1989; QPM 1981; Director, Police Requirements for Science and Technology, Home Office, 1985–88, retired; *b* 10 Nov. 1927; *s* of Sydney Robert and Rose Elizabeth Cozens; *m* 1952, Jean Dorothy Banfield; one *s* one *d. Educ:* Stoke C of E Sch., Guildford. Constable to Chief Superintendent, Surrey Constabulary, 1954–72; Asst Dir, Command Courses, Police Staff Coll., Bramshill, 1972–74; Asst Chief Constable, S Yorks Police, 1974–78; seconded to Federal Judicial Police in Mexico for advisory duties, 1975; Dep. Chief Constable, Lincs Police, 1978–81; Chief Constable, W Mercia Constabulary (Hereford, Worcester and Shropshire), 1981–85. *Recreations:* tennis, swimming, making friends.

CRABB, Stephen; MP (C) Preseli Pembrokeshire, since 2005; *b* 20 Jan. 1973; *m* 1996, Béatrice Alice Claude Odile Monnier; one *s* one *d. Educ:* Bristol Univ. (BSc Hons 1995); London Business Sch. (MBA 2004). Res. Asst to Andrew Rowe, MP, 1995–96; Parly Officer, Nat. Council for Voluntary Youth Services, 1996–98; Policy and Campaigns Manager, LCCI, 1998–2002; mktg consultant, 2003–05. *Recreations:* Rugby, cooking, spending time with family. *Address:* House of Commons, SW1A 0AA. *T:* (020) 7219 3000; *e-mail:* crabbs@parliament.uk. *Clubs:* Balfour, Haverfordwest Co. Assoc. Football (Haverfordwest).

CRABB, Tony William; media consultant, since 1992; *b* 27 June 1933; *s* of William Harold Crabb and Ellen Emily Crabb; *m* 1957, Brenda Margaret (*née* Sullman); one *s* one *d. Educ:* Chiswick Grammar School; London School of Economics (BScEcon); Intelligence Corps Russian Interpreters Course, 1952–54. BBC, 1957–88; seconded as news adviser to Govt of Libya, 1968–69; Managing Editor: BBC TV News, 1979–82; BBC Breakfast Time, 1982–84; Controller, Corporate News Services, BBC, 1984–87; Special Asst, News and Current Affairs, BBC, 1987–88; Dep. Dir of Broadcasting, Radio TV Hong Kong, 1988–92. Gen. Manager, CCT Productions Ltd, 1995–97. Mem. (Lib Dem) Spelthorne BC, 1999–2003. FRTS (Mem. Council, 2002–06). *Address:* 38 The Avenue, Sunbury-on-Thames, Middx TW16 5ES; *e-mail:* tony.crabb@tiscali.co.uk.

CRABBIE, Christopher Donald, CMG 1995; HM Diplomatic Service, retired; UK Permanent Representative to OECD, Paris, (with rank of Ambassador), 1999–2003; *b* 17 Jan. 1946; *s* of late William George Crabbie and of Jane (*née* Coe). *Educ:* Rugby Sch.; Newcastle Univ.; Liverpool Univ.; Corpus Christi Coll., Oxford. Second Sec., FCO, 1973–75; First Secretary: Nairobi, 1975–79; Washington, 1979–83; FCO, 1983–85; Counsellor and Hd of European Communities Div., HM Treasury, 1985–87; Counsellor, FCO, 1987–90; Dep. UK Perm. Rep., OECD, Paris, 1990; Counsellor, British Embassy, Paris, 1990–94; Ambassador, Algeria, 1994–95; Ambassador to Romania, 1996–99. *Recreations:* ski-ing, flying, sailing, gardening. *Club:* New (Edinburgh).

CRABTREE, Maj.-Gen. Derek Thomas, CB 1983; *b* 21 Jan. 1930; *s* of late William Edward Crabtree and Winifred Hilda Burton; *m* 1960, Daphne Christine Mason; one *s* one *d. Educ:* St Brendan's Coll., Bristol. Commissioned, 1953; Regimental Service: 13th/18th Royal Hussars (QMO), 1953–56; Royal Berkshire Regt, 1956–59; Technical Staff Course, RMCS, 1960–62; sc Camberley, 1964; BM 11 Inf. Bde, BAOR, 1965–67; CO 1st Bn Duke of Edinburgh's Royal Regt, UK and Berlin, 1970–72; Col GS, MGO Secretariat, MoD, 1974–76; Dep. Comdr and Chief of Staff Headquarters British Forces Hong Kong, 1976–79; Dep. Comdt RMCS, 1979–80; Dir Gen. of Weapons (Army), MoD, 1980–84. Sen. Mil. Advr, Short Bros, 1984–86; Gen. Manager, Regular Forces Employment Assoc., 1987–94. Col, Duke of Edinburgh's Royal Regt, 1982–87, 1988–89. *Recreations:* golf, computing, gardening, beekeeping. *Address:* 53 High Street, Shrivenham, Swindon SN6 8AW. *Club:* Army and Navy.

CRABTREE, Peter Dixon, OBE 1997; a District Judge (Magistrates' Courts), since 2005; *b* 2 March 1956; *s* of Kenneth and Elizabeth Crabtree; *m* 1981, Ann Davina Cooper; three *d. Educ:* Liverpool Coll.; Manchester Poly.; Univ. of Bristol (BA Hons); Inns of Court Sch. of Law. ACIS. Royal Navy, 1979–2005: served HMSs Fearless, Minerva, Ark

Royal, Invincible; Captain. Called to the Bar, Gray's Inn, 1985. *Recreations:* walking, climbing, reading, family. *Address:* c/o Manor Barn, Prinsted, W Sussex PO10 8HR.

CRACKNELL, David John; Founder and Director, Big Tent Communications, since 2008; *b* 5 June 1968; *s* of David Lewis and Norma Rose Cracknell; *m* 1998, Rachel Laurent; one *s* two *d. Educ:* Southampton Univ. (LLB); Pembroke Coll., Oxford (BCL). Reporter, Coventry Evening Telegraph, 1993–95; Lobby Corresp., Press Assoc., 1995–98; Political Ed., Sunday Business, 1998–99; Dep. Political Ed., Sunday Telegraph, 1999–2001; Political Ed., Sunday Times, 2001–08; Chm., FD-LLM, 2008.

CRACKNELL, James Edward, OBE 2005 (MBE 2001); oarsman; *b* 5 May 1972; *s* of John David and Jennifer Ann Cracknell; *m* 2002, Beverley Anne Turner; one *s. Educ:* Kingston Grammar Sch.; Reading Univ. (BSc Geog.); Inst. of Educn, London Univ. (PGCE); Brunel Univ. (MSc). Gold Medal, Jun. World Championships, 1990; Mem., British rowing team, 1991–2006; winner: World Championships: Gold Medal, coxless fours, 1997, 1998 and 1999; (with Matthew Pinsent) Gold Medal, coxed pairs, 2001; Gold Medal, coxless pairs, 2001 and 2002; Gold Medal, coxless fours, Olympic Games, Sydney, 2000 and Athens, 2004. Journalist and columnist, Daily Telegraph, 1998–; broadcaster, ITV, 2005–. *Publication:* (with Ben Fogle) The Crossing: conquering the Atlantic in the world's toughest rowing race, 2006. *Recreations:* motorbikes, surfboards. *Address:* c/o MTC Ltd, 20 York Street, W1V 6PU. *T:* (020) 7935 8000; *Fax:* (020) 7935 8066; *e-mail:* jonathan@mtc-uk.com. *Club:* Leander (Captain, 2000–05) (Henley-on-Thames).

CRACKNELL, Malcolm Thomas; His Honour Judge Cracknell; a Circuit Judge, since 1989; *b* 12 Dec. 1943; *s* of late Percy Thomas Cracknell and Doris Louise Cracknell; *m* 1st, 1968, Ann Carrington (*née* Gooding) (marr. diss. 1980); one *s* one *d;* 2nd, 1988, Felicity Anne Davies; two *s* one *d. Educ:* Royal Liberty Sch., Romford; Hull Univ. (LLB); King's Coll., London (LLM). Called to Bar, Middle Temple, 1969. Lectr in Law, Univ. of Hull, 1968–74; Barrister, NE Circuit, 1970–89; a Recorder, 1988; Designated Family Judge, Hull Combined Court Centre, 1994–2007. *Recreations:* golf, gardening, cricket, reading. *Address:* Hull Combined Court Centre, Lowgate, Hull HU1 2EZ.

CRACKNELL, (William) Martin; Chief Executive, Glenrothes Development Corporation, 1976–93; *b* 24 June 1929; *s* of John Sidney Cracknell and Sybil Marian (*née* Wood); *m* 1962, Gillian Goatcher; two *s* two *d. Educ:* St Edward's School, Oxford; RMA Sandhurst. Regular Army Officer, Royal Green Jackets, 1949–69; British Printing Industries Fedn, 1969–76. Mem. Exec., Scottish Council (Develt and Industry), 1984–90; Chm., Scottish Cttee, German Chamber of Industry and Commerce in UK, 1987–92. Director: Glenrothes Enterprise Trust, 1983–89; New Enterprise Develt, 1987–90. FRSA 1993. Cross of Order of Merit (Germany), 1992. *Address:* West End Cottage, Freuchie, Fife KY15 7EZ. *T:* (01337) 857849. *Club:* Royal Green Jackets.

CRACROFT-ELEY, Bridget Katharine, CVO 2008; Lord-Lieutenant of Lincolnshire, 1995–2008; *b* 29 Oct. 1933; *d* of Weston Cracroft-Amcotts and Rhona (*née* Clifton-Brown); *m* 1959, Robert Peel Charles Cracroft-Eley (*d* 1996); one *s* one *d. Educ:* Lincoln Girls' High Sch.; Crofton Grange Sch., Buntingford, Herts. Voluntary and charity work, including: WRVS, 1974–94; Lincs Old Churches Trust, 1980–; Girl Guides, 1984–; RNIB Looking Glass Appeal, 1990–91. Parish Councillor, Hackthorn and Cold Hanworth, 1980–. Governor: Hackthorn C of E Primary Sch., 1988–2006; King's Sch., Grantham, 1995–. High Sheriff, Lincs, 1989–90. Hon. Col, Lincs ACF, 2001–06. DStJ 1996. Hon. LLD: De Montfort, 1999; Lincoln, 2003. *Recreations:* upholstery, gardening, the arts. *Address:* The Little House, Hackthorn, Lincoln LN2 3PQ. *T:* (01673) 860212.

CRADDOCK, Timothy James; HM Diplomatic Service; UK Permanent Delegate to UNESCO, with personal rank of Ambassador, since 2003; *b* 27 June 1956; *s* of James Vincent Craddock and Kathleen Mary Craddock (*née* Twigg). *Educ:* King Edward's Sch., Birmingham; Gonville and Caius Coll., Cambridge (Exhibnr; MA); School of Oriental and African Studies, London Univ. Entered FCO, 1979; Third Sec. and Vice-Consul, Chad, 1979–80; Vice-Consul, Istanbul, 1981–82; Second Sec., Ankara, 1982–85; Hd of Section, South America Dept, FCO, 1985–87; Sec., FCO Bd of Mgt, 1988–90; First Sec., Paris, 1990–94; Dep. Hd, Aid Policy and Resources Dept, FCO, 1995–97; Ambassador to Estonia, 1997–2000; Hd, Africa Gt Lakes and Horn Dept, DFID (on secondment), 2000–03. *Recreations:* hill walking, opera, London, gardening in France. *Address:* UK Delegation to UNESCO (Paris), King Charles Street, SW1A 2AH; 52 rue du Bourg Voisin, 21140 Semur-en-Auxois, France. *Club:* Royal Commonwealth Society.

CRADDOCK, (William) Aleck, LVO 1981; Director, Harrods Ltd, 1964–88 (Managing Director, 1980–84, Chairman, 1981–86, Deputy Chairman, 1987–88); Director, Cartier Ltd, 1986–97; *b* Nov. 1924; *m* 1947, Olive May Brown; one *s* one *d. Educ:* City of London School. Joined Druce and Craddock, Craddock and Tomkins Ltd (family firm), Meat and Provision Merchants, Marylebone, London, 1946; joined Harrods Ltd as Asst to Food Manager, 1954; Member of the Board, 1964; Director and General Manager, 1970; Asst Managing Director, 1975; a Director of House of Fraser, 1980–91. Vice Chm., Drapers' Cottage Homes, 1987–94 (Pres., Appeal, 1985–86); Pres., Twenty Club, 1988. Liveryman, Worshipful Company of Cooks, 1972 (Mem., Court of Assts, 1993–96). Cavaliere Ufficiale (Fourth Cl.), Order Al Merito Della Repubblica Italiana, 1980. *Recreation:* watercolour painting. *Address:* 17 Tretawn Park, Mill Hill, NW7 4PS. *Club:* Guards' Polo (Life Mem.).

CRADOCK, Rt Hon. Sir Percy, GCMG 1983 (KCMG 1980; CMG 1968); PC 1993; the Prime Minister's Foreign Policy Adviser, 1984–92; *b* 26 Oct. 1923; *m* 1953, Birthe Marie Dyrlund. *Educ:* St John's Coll., Cambridge (MA, LLM; Hon. Fellow, 1982). Pres., Cambridge Union, 1950. Called to the Bar, Middle Temple, 1953. Served Foreign Office, 1954–57; First Sec., Kuala Lumpur, 1957–61; Hong Kong, 1961, Peking, 1962; Foreign Office, 1963–66; Counsellor and Head of Chancery, Peking, 1966–68; Chargé d'Affaires, Peking, 1968–69; Head of Planning Staff, FCO, 1969–71; Under-Sec., Cabinet Office, 1971–75; Ambassador to German Democratic Republic, 1976–78; Leader, UK Delegn to Comprehensive Test Ban Discussions at Geneva, 1977–78; Ambassador to People's Republic of China, 1978–83; Leader of UK team in negotiations over Hong Kong, 1983; Dep. Under Sec. of State, FCO, supervising Hong Kong negotiations, 1984; Chm., Jt Intelligence Cttee, 1985–92. *Publications:* Experiences of China, 1994; In Pursuit of British Interests, 1997; Know Your Enemy, 2002. *Club:* Reform.

CRAFT, Sir Alan (William), Kt 2004; MD; FRCP, FRCP(E), FRCPCH, FMedSci, FFPH, FRCR, FRCA; Director, Northern Institute for Cancer Research, University of Newcastle upon Tyne, since 2007; *b* 6 July 1946; *s* of William and Yvonne Craft; *m* 1st, 1968, Dorothy Noble (decd); one *s;* 2nd, 1992, Anne Nicholson. *Educ:* Rutherford Grammar Sch., Newcastle upon Tyne; Univ. of Newcastle upon Tyne (MB, BS; MD). FRCP 1982; FRCPCH 1997; FFPH (FFPHM 2001); FRCP(E) 2003; FRCP(I) 2003; FAAP 2003; FIAP 2003; FAMM 2003; FACP 2005; FRCR 2006; FRCA 2006. House Officer, Royal Victoria Infirmary, Newcastle upon Tyne, 1969–70; Sen. House Officer, then Registrar and Sen. Registrar, Newcastle Hosps, 1970–77; MRC Trng Fellow, Royal Marsden Hosp., 1976–77; Consultant Paediatrician: N Tyneside Hosp., 1977–86; Royal

Victoria Infirmary, 1977–; Prof. of Paediatric Oncology, 1991–93, Sir James Spence Prof. of Child Health, 1993–2007, Univ. of Newcastle upon Tyne. Chm., European Osteosarcoma Intergroup, 1994–97; Sec. Gen., 1993–99, Pres., 2002–05, Internat. Paediatric Oncology Soc.; President: RCPCH, 2003–06 (Vice-Pres., 1998–2002); Assoc. for Care of Terminally Ill Children, 2001–. Chm., Academy of Med. Royal Colls, 2004–06. FMedSci 2003. *Publications:* papers on childhood cancer and other childhood disorders in BMJ, Lancet, Archives of Disease in Childhood, etc. *Recreations:* marathon running, orienteering, crosswords. *Address:* 1 The Villas, Embleton, Northumberland NE66 3XG. *T:* (01665) 576619. *Club:* Athenæum.

CRAFT, Prof. Ian Logan, FRCS; FRCOG; Director, London Gynaecology and Fertility Centre, since 1990; *b* 11 July 1937; *s* of Reginald Thomas Craft and Lois Mary (*née* Logan); *m* 1959, Jacqueline Rivers Symmons; two *s*. *Educ:* Owens Sch., London; Westminster Med. Sch., Univ. of London (MB, BS). FRCS 1966; MRCOG 1970, FRCOG 1986. Sen. Registrar, Westminster Hosp. Teaching Gp (Westminster Hosp. and Kingston Hosp.), 1970–72; Sen. Lectr and Consultant, Inst. of Obstetrics and Gynaecology, Queen Charlotte's Hosp., London, 1972–76; Prof. of Obstetrics and Gynaecology, Royal Free Hosp., London, 1976–82; Dir of Gynaecology, Cromwell Hosp., 1982–85; Dir of Fertility and Obstetric Studies, Humana Hosp. Wellington, 1985–90. Vis Prof., UCL. *Publications:* contrib. BMJ, Lancet and other medical jls. *Recreations:* art, music, ornithology, sports of most types. *Address:* London Gynaecology and Fertility Centre, Cozens House, 112A Harley Street, W1G 7JH. *T:* (020) 7224 0707; *e-mail:* prof@lfc.org.uk.

CRAFT, Prof. Maurice, PhD, DLitt; Emeritus Professor of Education, University of Nottingham; *b* 4 May 1932; *er s* of Jack and Polly Craft, London; *m* 1957, Alma, *y d* of Elio and Dinah Sampson, Dublin; two *d*. *Educ:* LCC Elem. Sch. and Colfe's Grammar Sch., SE13; LSE, Univ. of London (BSc Econ); Sch. of Education, Trinity Coll., Univ. of Dublin (HDipEd); Inst. of Education, Univ. of London (AcadDipEd); Dept of Sociology, Univ. of Liverpool (PhD 1972); Univ. of Nottingham (DLitt 1990). 2/Lt RAOC (Nat. Service), 1953–55. Asst Master, Catford Secondary Sch., SE6, 1956–60; Princ. Lectr and Head of Dept of Sociology, Edge Hill Coll. of Education, Ormskirk, Lancs, 1960–67; Sen. Lectr in Education, i/c Advanced Courses, Univ. of Exeter, 1967–73; Sub-Dean, Faculty of Educn, 1969–73; Prof. of Education, and Chairman, Centre for the Study of Urban Education, La Trobe Univ., Melbourne, 1973–75; Goldsmiths' Prof. of Education, Inst. of Educn, Univ. of London, and Head of Dept of Advanced Studies in Education, Goldsmiths' Coll., 1976–80; University of Nottingham: Prof. of Educn, and Hd, Div. of Advanced Studies, 1980–89; Dean, Faculty of Educn, 1981–83; Chm., Sch. of Educn, 1983–85, 1988–89; Pro-Vice-Chancellor, 1983–87; Foundn Dean of Humanities and Social Science, Hong Kong Univ. of Science and Technol., 1989–92; Foundn Prof. of Educn, Open Univ. of Hong Kong, 1992–94; Res. Prof. in Educn, Univ. of Greenwich, 1994–97; Vis Prof. of Educn, Goldsmiths' Coll., Univ. of London, 1997–2002. Adviser: Devon CC, 1970–72; Aust. Federal Poverty Commn, 1974–75; ACU, 1976, 1979; CNAA, 1978–89; Centre for Advice and Inf. on Educn Disadvantage (Chm., Teacher Educn Working Gp, 1979–80); Schools Council, 1979; CRE (Chm., Teacher Educn Adv. Gp, 1980–84); H of C Home Affairs Cttee, 1981; Swann Cttee, 1982–84; Leverhulme Trust, 1982–; Macquarie Univ., Aust., 1982; Council for Educn and Trng in Youth and Community Work (Chm., In-service Wkg Gp, 1983); UNESCO, 1985; QUB, 1986; Univ. of Kuwait, 1988; Peshawar Univ., Pakistan, 1988; Hong Kong Council for Academic Accreditation, 1991; Hong Kong Educn Commn, 1991; Lagos Univ., Nigeria, 1991; City Polytechnic of Hong Kong, 1992; Hong Kong Baptist Univ., 1994; Griffith Univ., Aust., 1996; Hong Kong Govt Res. Grants Council, 1996–; Commonwealth of Learning, Vancouver, 1996; ESRC, 1997; Hong Kong Inst. of Educn, 1997; Southampton Univ., 1999; Chester UC, 2000; Surrey Univ., 2000–04; Lewisham PCT, 2003–. Mem., UK Delegn to EEC Colloquium on Ethnic Min. Educn, Brussels, 1979, 1982; UK delegate to: Council of Europe Seminars on Intercultural Trng of Teachers, Lisbon, 1981, Rome, 1982, Strasbourg, 1983; UNESCO Colloquium on Educnl Disadvantage, Thessalonika, 1984. Member: Council of Validating Univs, 1982–89 (Vice-Chm., 1987–89); E Midlands Reg. Consultative Gp on Teacher Educn, 1980–84 (Chm., 1980–84); Exec. Cttee, Univs Council for Educn of Teachers, 1984–88 (Chm., Standing Cttee on Validation, 1984–87); Cttee on Validation, CVCP, 1986–88; Hong Kong Govt Bd of Inquiry in Educn, 1992; Hong Kong Govt Adv. Cttee on Teacher Educn and Qualifications, 1993; Exec. Cttee, Soc. for Educnl Studies, 1996–2002 (Chm., Res. sub-cttee, 1999–2002); Froebel Council, 2000– (Chm., Res. Cttee, 2004–06). Chm., Blackheath Cator Estate Res. Assoc., 2003–06. Non-exec. Dir, Greenwich PCT Bd, 2007–. Member, Editorial Board: Sociology of Educn Abstracts, 1965–; Jl of Multilingual and Multicultural Develt, 1979–96; Multicultural Educn Abstracts, 1981–; Internat. Studies in Sociology of Educn, 1991–; British Jl of Educnl Studies, 1996–2002. FRSA 1989. *Publications:* (ed jtly) Linking Home and School, 1967 (3rd edn, 1980); (ed jtly) Guidance and Counselling in British Schools, 1969 (2nd edn, 1974); (ed) Family, Class and Education: a Reader, 1970; Urban Education—a Dublin case study, 1974; School Welfare Provision in Australia, 1977; (ed) Teaching in a Multicultural Society: the Task for Teacher Education, 1981; (jtly) Training Teachers of Ethnic Minority Community Languages, 1983; (ed jtly) Change in Teacher Education, 1984; (ed) Education and Cultural Pluralism, 1984; The Democratisation of Education, 1985; Teacher Education in a Multicultural Society, 1986; (ed jtly) Ethnic Relations and Schooling, 1995; (ed) Teacher Education in Plural Societies, 1996; contrib. to numerous books and to the following jls: Educnl Research, Internat. Review of Educn, Internat. Jl of Educnl Develt, Educnl Review, Social and Econ. Admin., Cambridge Jl of Educn, Educn for Teaching, British Jl of In-Service Educn, Internat. Social Work, Aust. Jl of Social Work, Aust. Educnl Researcher, THES, Higher Educn Jl, New Society, Education, Administration, New Era, Studies. *Recreations:* music, walking. *T:* (020) 8852 7611; *e-mail:* almacraft@hotmail.com. *Club:* Royal Over-Seas League.

CRAFTS, Prof. Nicholas Francis Robert, FBA 1992; Professor of Economic History, University of Warwick, since 2006; *b* 9 March 1949; *s* of Alfred Hedley Crafts and Flora Geraldine Mary Crafts; *m* 1969, Barbara Daynes; one *s* two *d*. *Educ:* Brunts Grammar Sch., Mansfield; Trinity Coll., Cambridge (BA Econs 1st cl., 1970). Lectr in Econ. Hist., Exeter Univ., 1971–72; Lectr in Econs, Warwick Univ., 1972–77; Fellow in Econs, University Coll., Oxford, 1977–86; Professor of Economic History: Leeds Univ., 1987–88; Univ. of Warwick, 1988–95 (Hon. Prof., 1995–2006); LSE, 1995–2005. Vis. Asst Prof. of Econs, Univ. of Calif., Berkeley, 1974–76; Vis. Prof. of Econs, Stanford Univ., 1982–83. *Publications:* British Economic Growth during the Industrial Revolution, 1985; contrib. to Economic Jl, Jl of Economic Hist., Economic Policy, Population Studies, etc. *Recreations:* betting on horses, drinking beer. *Address:* Department of Economics, University of Warwick, Coventry CV4 7AL. *T:* (024) 7652 3468; *e-mail:* n.crafts@warwick.ac.uk.

CRAGG, Rt Rev. (Albert) Kenneth, DPhil; *b* 8 March 1913; *yr s* of Albert and Emily Cragg; *m* 1940, Theodora Melita (*d* 1989), *yr d* of John Wesley Arnold; three *s* (one *d* decd). *Educ:* Blackpool Grammar Sch.; Jesus Coll., Oxford (Hon. Fellow, 1999); Tyndale Hall, Bristol. BA Oxon 2nd Cl. Hons Mod. Hist., 1934; MA Oxon 1938; DPhil 1950. Ellerton Theol. Essay Prize, Oxford, 1937; Green Moral Philos. Prize, Oxford, 1947. Deacon, 1936; Priest, 1937; Curate, Higher Tranmere Parish Church, Birkenhead,

1936–39; Chaplain, All Saints', Beirut, Lebanon, 1939–47; Warden, St Justin's House, Beirut, 1942–47; Asst Prof. of Philos., Amer. University of Beirut, 1942–47; Rector of Longworth, Berks, 1947–51; Sheriff's Chap., Berks, 1948; Prof. of Arabic and Islamics, Hartford Seminary, Conn, USA, 1951–56; Rockefeller Travelling Schol., 1954; Res. Canon, St George's Collegiate Church, Jerusalem, 1956–61; Fellow, St Augustine's Coll., Canterbury, 1959–60, Sub-Warden, 1960–61, Warden, 1961–67; Examng Chaplain to Archbishop of Canterbury, 1961–67; Hon. Canon of Canterbury, 1961–80; Asst Bishop to Archbishop in Jerusalem, 1970–74; Reader in Religious Studies, Sussex Univ., and Asst Bishop, dio. of Chichester, 1973–78; Vicar of Helme, W Yorks, and Asst Bishop, dio. Wakefield, 1978–81; Asst Bishop, dio. Oxford, 1982–. Select Preacher: Cambridge, 1961; Dublin, 1962; Oxford, 1974. Proctor in Convocation, Canterbury, 1965–68; Visiting Prof., Union Theological Seminary, New York, 1965–66; Lectr, Faculty of Divinity, Cambridge, 1966; Jordan Lectr, Sch. of Oriental and African Studies, University of London, 1967; Vis. Prof., University of Ibadan, Nigeria, 1968; Bye-Fellow, Gonville and Caius Coll., Cambridge, 1968–74; Vis. Prof., Virginia Theol Seminary, 1984, 1985. Hon. DD: Leeds, 1993; Toronto, 2001; DD Lambeth, 2002. Editor, The Muslim World Quarterly, 1952–60. *Publications:* The Call of the Minaret, 1956, 2nd edn 1986; Sandals at the Mosque, 1959; The Dome and the Rock, 1964; Counsels in Contemporary Islam, 1965; Christianity in World Perspective, 1968; The Privilege of Man, 1968; The House of Islam, 1969; Alive to God, 1970; The Event of the Qur'ān, 1971; The Mind of the Qur'ān, 1973; The Wisdom of the Sufis, 1976; The Christian and Other Religion, 1977; Islam from Within, 1979; This Year in Jerusalem, 1982; Muhammad and the Christian, 1983; The Pen and the Faith, 1985; Jesus and the Muslim, 1985; The Christ and the Faiths, 1986; Readings in the Qur'ān, 1988; What Decided Christianity, 1989; The Arab Christian, 1991; Troubled by Truth, 1992; To Meet and to Greet, 1992; Faith and Life Negotiate (autobiog.), 1994; The Lively Credentials of God, 1996; Defending (the) Faith, 1997; Palestine: the prize and price of Zion, 1997; With God in Human Trust, 1999; The Weight in the Word, 1999; The Education of Christian Faith, 2000; Islam Among the Spires, 2000; Muhammad in the Qur'ān, 2002; Am I Not Your Lord?, 2002; Faiths in their Pronouns, 2003; The Christian Jesus, 2003; The Tragic in Islam, 2004; A Certain Sympathy of Scriptures: Biblical and Quranic, 2004; Semitism: the whence and whither, 2005; Faith at Suicide, 2005; God's Wrong is Most of All, 2006; The Qur'an and the West, 2006; The Order of the Wounded Hands, 2007; A Christian/Muslim Inter-Text Now, 2007; Mosque Sermons, 2008; translated: City of Wrong, 1959; The Theology of Unity, 1965; A Passage to France, 1976; The Hallowed Valley, 1977; contributor: Journal of World History, 1957; Religion in the Middle East, 1969. *Address:* 3 Goring Lodge, White House Road, Oxford OX1 4QE.

CRAGG, Prof. Anthony Douglas, CBE 2002; RA 1994; sculptor; *b* 9 April 1949; *m* 1990, Tatjana (*née* Verhasselt); one *s* one *d*, and two *s* by former *m*. *Educ:* Wimbledon Sch. of Art (BA); Royal Coll. of Art (MA). Prof., l'Ecole des Beaux Arts de Metz, 1976; teacher, 1978–88, Prof., 1988–2001, Co-Dir, 1989–2001, Kunstakademie, Düsseldorf; Prof., Univ. der Künste, Berlin, 2001–06. *One-man exhibitions include:* Lisson Gall., 1979, 1980, 1985, 1991, 1992, 1997, 1998, 2001; Whitechapel Art Gall., 1981, 1997; Kanrasha Gall., Tokyo, 1982, 1984, 1989, 1990; Konrad Fischer, Düsseldorf, 1982, 1986, 1989, 1990; Marian Goodman, NY, 1982, 1983, 1986, 1987, 1989; Palais des Beaux-Arts, Brussels, 1985; Brooklyn Mus. of Art, NY, 1986; Venice Biennale, 1986, 1988, 1997; Hayward Gall., 1987; Tate Gall., Liverpool, 1988, 2000; Tate Gall., 1989; Stedelijk Van Abbemus., Eindhoven, 1989, 1991; Corcoran Gall. of Art, Washington, 1991; Wiener Secession, 1991; IVAM, Valencia, 1992; Goodwood Sculpture Park, 2005; *group exhibitions:* Documenta 7, Documenta 8, 1987, Kassel; Mus. van Hedendaagse Kunst, Ghent, 1980; Bienal de São Paulo, 1983; Tate Gall., 1983, 1985; Sydney Biennale, 1984, 1990; Hayward Gall., 1985, 1990; and many others throughout Europe, US, Japan and Australia. Turner Prize, 1988; Shakespeare Prize, 2001; Praemium Imperiale for Sculpture, Japan Art Assoc., 2007. Chevalier des Arts et des Lettres (France), 1992. *Address:* Lise Meitner Strasse 33, 42119 Wuppertal, Germany.

CRAGG, Anthony John, CMG 2000; JP; Senior Associate Research Fellow, Centre for Defence Studies, King's College London, since 2003; Associate Fellow, Royal United Services Institute, since 2003; *b* 16 May 1943; *s* of late Leslie Cragg and Gwendolen Cragg (*née* Pevler); *m* 1971, Jeanette Ann Rix; two *d*. *Educ:* Hastings Grammar School; Lincoln College, Oxford (Open Schol.; BA). Ministry of Defence, 1966–2003: Asst Private Sec to Sec. of State for Defence, 1974; UK Delegn to NATO, 1977; Asst Sec., 1979; Chief Officer, Sovereign Base Areas, Cyprus, 1983–85; RCDS 1988; Asst Under Sec. of State, 1990; Dir Gen. of Mgt Audit, MoD, 1991–93; Chm., Defence Organisation Planning Team, 1991–92; Asst Sec. Gen. for Defence Planning and Policy, then Ops, NATO, 1993–99; Asst Under-Sec. of State, MoD, 1999–2003. Visiting Lecturer: NATO Defence Coll., 2003–; Geneva Centre for Security Policy, 2005–. Chm., MoD Grievance Appeal Panel, 2004–. Lay Mem., Asylum and Immigration Tribunal (formerly Immigration Appeal Tribunal), 2003–. JP London, 2005. *Publications:* articles on internat. security issues in press and specialised jls. *Recreations:* the performing arts, swimming, walking, reading. *Address:* c/o Royal United Services Institute, Whitehall, SW1A 2ET.

CRAGG, Rt Rev. Kenneth; see Cragg, Rt Rev. A. K.

CRAGG, Dr Martin Robert; Chief Executive and Secretary, Institution of Highways and Transportation, 1990–2001; *b* 8 June 1941; *s* of Robert Brooks Cragg and Hilda Cragg (*née* Bateman); *m* 1966, Pamela Watts; one *s* two *d*. *Educ:* Dixie Grammar Sch., Market Bosworth; Sheffield Univ. (BSc Hons Chem.; PhD Fuel Technol. 1966); London Business Sch. (Sloan Fellow). Industrial Advr, NEDO, 1979–88; Dir, then Dir-Gen. and Chief Exec., Business Equipt and Information Technol. Assoc., 1988–89, then Sen. Exec., Electronic and Business Equipt Assoc., 1989–90. *Recreations:* golf, fly fishing, ski-ing. *Address:* 10 Woodside Road, New Malden, Surrey KT3 3AH. *T:* (020) 8942 8008.

CRAGGS, Prof. James Wilkinson, BSc, PhD; Professor of Engineering Mathematics, University of Southampton, 1967–81; *b* 3 Feb. 1920; *s* of Thomas Gibson Craggs and Margaret (*née* Wilkinson); *m* 1946, Mary Baker; two *s* one *d*. *Educ:* Bede Collegiate Sch., Sunderland; University of Manchester (BSc 1941, PhD 1948); PhD Cambridge, 1953. Junior Lectr, Royal Military Coll. of Science, 1941–45; Asst Lectr, University of Manchester, 1947–49; Lecturer, Queen's Coll., Dundee, 1951–52; King's Coll., Newcastle upon Tyne: Lectr, 1952–56; Senior Lecturer, 1956–60; Reader in Mathematics, 1960–61; Prof. of Mathematics, University of Leeds, 1961–63; Prof. of Applied Mathematics, Melbourne Univ., 1963–67. *Publications:* contrib. learned journals regarding the mechanics of solids and fluids. *Recreation:* Methodist lay preacher. *Address:* 23 Redhill, Bassett, Southampton SO16 7BR.

CRAGGS, Madeleine Jennifer; Chief Executive and Registrar, General Osteopathic Council, 1997–2007; *b* 28 Dec. 1945; *d* of René Beaumont-Craggs and Muriel (*née* Robinson). *Educ:* Couvent des Ursulines, Brussels; Alexandra Grammar Sch., Singapore; WRAC Coll., Camberley. MCMI. Commnd WRAC, 1965; served in UK and Germany incl. staff appts, MoD and HQ BAOR; Maj., 1970; WRAC Advr, 16th Signal Regt, 1973–75; Battery Comdr, Royal Sch. Artillery, 1975–77; SO2(A), HQ York Dist,

1977–79; Chief Instructor, WRAC Trng Centre, 1979–81; Detachment Comdr, Manning and Records Office, Chester, 1981–82; SO2 (Manpower & Planning), WRAC Directorate, MoD, 1982–84; Develt Dir, St Bartholomew's Hosp. Med. Coll., 1984–90; Sec., ICRF, 1991–97. *Recreations:* good wine, good food, good company. *Address:* 7 Felstead Gardens, Felstead Wharf, Ferry Street, E14 3BS.

CRAIG, family name of **Viscount Craigavon** and of **Baron Craig of Radley**.

CRAIG OF RADLEY, Baron *cr* 1991 (Life Peer), of Helhoughton in the County of Norfolk; **Marshal of the Royal Air Force David Brownrigg Craig,** GCB 1984 (KCB 1981; CB 1978); OBE 1967; Chief of the Defence Staff, 1988–91; *b* 17 Sept. 1929; *s* of Major Francis Brownrigg Craig and Mrs Olive Craig; *m* 1955, Elisabeth June Derenburg; one *s* one *d. Educ:* Radley Coll.; Lincoln Coll., Oxford (MA; Hon. Fellow 1984). FRAeS 1986. Commnd in RAF, 1951; OC RAF Cranwell, 1968–70; ADC to the Queen, 1969–71; Dir, Plans and Ops, HQ Far East Comd, 1970–71; OC RAF Akrotiri, 1972–73; ACAS (Ops), MoD, 1975–78; AOC No 1 Group, RAF Strike Command, 1978–80; Vice-Chief of Air Staff, 1980–82; AOC-in-C, RAF Strike Command and C-in-C, UK Air Forces, 1982–85; CAS, 1985–88. Air ADC to the Queen, 1985–88. Dir, M. L. Holdings plc, 1991–92. Mem., H of L Select Cttee for Sci. and Technology, 1993–99; Convenor, Cross Bench Peers, 1999–2004. Chm. Council, King Edward VII's Hosp. (Sister Agnes) (formerly King Edward VII's Hosp. for Officers), 1998–2004. Dep. Chm. Council, RAF Benevolent Fund, 1996–. Pres., Not Forgotten Assoc., 1996–. Hon. DSc Cranfield, 1988. *Recreations:* fishing, shooting, golf. *Address:* House of Lords, SW1A 0PW. *Club:* Royal Air Force (Pres., 2002–).

CRAIG, Rev. Canon Alan Stuart; Chaplain to the Bishop of Newcastle and Diocesan Director of Ordinands, 1999–2002; Chaplain to the Queen, 1995–2008; *b* 7 Feb. 1938; *s* of Dr John Gray Craig and Grace Craig (*née* Kay); *m* 1962, Marjorie (*née* Bell); one *s* two *d. Educ:* Uppingham Sch.; Leeds Univ. (BA (Hons)); Cranmer Hall, Durham Univ. (DipTh). Ordained deacon, Lichfield, 1961, priest, 1962; Assistant Curate: St Giles, Newcastle under Lyme, 1961–65; St Mary's, Scarborough, 1965–67; Vicar, Werrington, Stoke-on-Trent, 1967–72; Asst Chaplain, Manchester Prison, 1972–73; Chaplain: Hindley Borstal, 1973–78; Acklington Prison, 1978–84; Vicar, Longhirst and Hebron, Newcastle, 1984–90; Rector of Morpeth, 1990–99; Rural Dean of Morpeth, 1984–95. Hon. Canon, Newcastle Cathedral, 1990–2002. Chm., Newcastle Diocesan Pastoral Cttee, 1994–99. *Recreations:* music, theatre, fell-walking, visual arts. *Address:* 5 Springfield Meadow, Alnwick, Northumberland NE66 2NY. *T:* (01665) 602806; *e-mail:* as.m.craig@talktalk.net.

CRAIG, Sir (Albert) James (Macqueen), GCMG 1984 (KCMG 1981; CMG 1975); HM Diplomatic Service, retired; President, Middle East Association, since 1993 (Director General, 1985–93); *b* 13 July 1924; *s* of James Craig and Florence Morris; *m* 1st, 1952, Margaret Hutchinson (*d* 2001); three *s* one *d*; 2nd, 2002, Bernadette Hartley Lane. *Educ:* Liverpool Institute High Sch.; Queen's Coll., Oxford (Exhibr), 1942; 1st cl. Hon. Mods Classics, 1943 (Hon. Schol.); Hon. Fellow, 2007. Army, 1943–44; 1st cl. Oriental Studies (Arabic and Persian), 1947; Sen. Demy, Magdalen Coll., 1947–48; student, Cairo Univ., 1950–51. Lectr in Arabic, Durham Univ., 1948–55; seconded to FO, 1955 as Principal Instructor at Middle East Centre for Arab Studies, Lebanon; joined Foreign Service substantively, 1956; served: FO, 1958–61; HM Political Agent, Trucial States, 1961–64; 1st Sec., Beirut, 1964–67; Counsellor and Head of Chancery, Jedda, 1967–70; Supernumerary Fellow, St Antony's Coll., Oxford, 1970–71; Head of Near East and N Africa Dept, FCO, 1971–75; Dep. High Comr, Kuala Lumpur, 1975–76; Ambassador to: Syria, 1976–79; Saudi Arabia, 1979–84. Vis. Prof. in Arabic, and Lectr, Pembroke Coll., Univ. of Oxford, 1985–91. Director: Saudi-British Bank, 1985–94; Hong Kong Egyptian Bank, 1987–94; Special Adviser, Hong Kong Bank Gp, 1985–92; Chm., Roxby Engineering Internat., 1988–99. Pres., British Soc. for ME Studies, 1987–94; Vice-Chm., Middle East Internat., 1990–2005. Vice-Chm., Saudi-British Soc., 1986–2003; Chm., Anglo-Arab Assoc., 2000–03. Sen. Associate Mem., St Antony's Coll., Oxford, 1989 (Hon. Fellow, 2008). Hon. Fellow, Middle East Centre, Durham Univ., 1987–. OStJ 1985; Mem. Council, Order of St John, 1985–90. *Publications:* Shemlan: a history of the Middle East Centre for Arab Studies, 1998; (ed) The Arabists of Shemlan, vol. 1, 2006; various articles on the Arab world. *Address:* c/o 33 Bury Street, SW1Y 6AX. *T:* (020) 7839 2137. *Club:* Travellers.

CRAIG, Surgeon Rear-Admiral Alexander; Member, Criminal Injuries Compensation Appeal Panel, 1997–2007; *b* 22 Nov. 1943; *s* of Rev. Dr Albert Craig and Agnes Nicol (*née* Wards); *m* 1968, Kate Margaret Elliott; one *s* two *d. Educ:* George Watson's Boys' Coll., Edinburgh; Edinburgh Univ. (MB ChB 1967). Royal Infirmary, Edinburgh, 1968; Regimental MO, 45 Commando, RM, 1969–72; Jt Services Families Clinic, Malta, 1972–74; OC Med. Sqn, CDO LOG Regt, 1974–78; MoD, 1978–80, NDC 1981; UK Support Unit, Naples, 1981–83; CSO to Surgeon Cdre (NMT), 1983–86; PMO, HMS Sultan, 1986–87; CSO to SRA (OMS), 1987–89; MO i/c, Inst. of Naval Medicine, 1989–90; Dir, Med. Organisation, MoD, 1990–93; Surg. Rear-Adm. Support Med. Services, 1993–94; Med. Dir Gen. (Naval), 1994–97. QHP, 1992–97. *Recreation:* travel. *Address:* Lime Tree House, Bargrennan, Newton Stewart DG8 6RN.

CRAIG, Anne Gwendoline, (Wendy); actress; *b* 20 June 1934; *d* of late George Dixon Craig and Anne Lindsay; *m* 1955, John Alexander, Jack, Bentley (*d* 1994); two *s. Educ:* Durham High Sch. for Girls; Darlington High Sch.; Yarm Grammar Sch.; Central Sch. of Speech and Drama. *Theatre includes:* Ipswich Rep. Theatre, 1953; Royal Court season, 1957; The Wrong Side of the Park, 1960; The Ginger Man, Royal Court, 1964; Ride a Cock Horse, Piccadilly, 1965; I Love You Mrs Patterson; Finishing Touches; Peter Pan; Beyond Reasonable Doubt, Queen's, 1987; Easy Virtue, Chichester Fest., 1999; The Rivals, RSC, 2000; The Circle, Queen's, 2002; The Importance of Being Earnest, nat. tour, 2003; *television includes:* Not in Front of the Children, 1967–70; And Mother Makes Three, 1971–74; And Mother Makes Five, 1974–76; Butterflies, 1978–82; Nanny, 1981–83; Brighton Belles, 1993; The Forsyte Saga, Midsomer Murders, 2002; The Royal, 2002–06; *films include:* The Servant, The Mind Benders, 1963; The Nanny, 1965; Just Like a Woman, 1966; I'll Never Forget Whatsisname, 1967; Joseph Andrews, 1977. Awards incl. BAFTA award for best actress, 1968; BBC Personality of the Year, 1969. Hon. MA Teesside 1994. *Publications:* Happy Endings, 1972; The Busy Mums Cook Book, 1983; The Busy Mums Baking Book, 1986; Show Me the Way, 2006. *Recreations:* music, walking, reading, gardening.

CRAIG, Cairns; *see* Craig, R. C.

CRAIG, Christopher John Sinclair, CB 1991; DSC 1982; RN retired; *b* 18 May 1941; *s* of Richard Michael Craig and Barbara Mary Craig; *m* 1973, Daphne Joan Underwood; two *s. Educ:* Portchester Sch., Bournemouth. Joined RN, 1959; qualified as anti-submarine helicopter pilot, 1963; HMS Eagle, 1964–66; HMS Dido, 1967–69; in command: HMS Monkton, 1970–72; naval air sqdns, 705, 1973–74, and 826, 1975; HMS London, 1976–77; Asst Sec. to Chiefs of Staff, 1978–80; in command: HMS Alacrity, 1980–82 (incl. Falklands War); HMS Avenger and Fourth Frigate Sqdn, 1985–86; RNAS Portland/HMS Osprey, 1986–87; HMS Drake, 1987–89; Comdr, RN Task Gp afloat, Gulf War, 1990–91; COS to FONA, 1991–93; retd 1994. US Bronze Star, 1991. *Publication:* Call for Fire: sea combat in the Falklands and the Gulf War, 1995. *Recreations:* watercolour painting, classical music, reading. *Address:* Greencroft, East Grimstead, near Salisbury, Wilts SP5 3SA.

CRAIG, Daniel Wroughton; actor; *b* Chester, 2 March 1968; *s* of Timothy and Carol Olivia Craig; *m* 1992, Fiona Loudon (marr. diss. 1994); one *d. Educ:* Guildhall Sch. of Music and Drama. *Theatre* includes: Angels in America, A Number, RNT; Hurly Burly, Old Vic; *films* include: The Power of One, 1992; Obsession, 1997; Love and Rage, Elizabeth, Love is the Devil, 1998; The Trench, 1999; I Dreamed of Africa, Some Voices, Hotel Splendide, 2000; Lara Croft: Tomb Raider, 2001; Road to Perdition, Ten Minutes Older: The Cello, Occasional, Strong, 2002; The Mother, Sylvia, 2003; Enduring Love, Layer Cake, 2004; The Jacket, Sorstalanság, Munich, 2005; Casino Royale, 2006; The Golden Compass, Infamous, 2007; Flashbacks of a Fool, Quantum of Solace, 2008; *television* includes: Our Friends in the North, 1996; Sword of Honour, 2001; Copenhagen, 2002; Archangel, 2005. *Address:* c/o Independent Talent Group Ltd, Oxford House, 76 Oxford Street, W1S 1BS.

CRAIG, (David) Jonathan; Member (DemU) Lagan Valley, Northern Ireland Assembly, since 2007; *b* 2 Feb. 1965; *s* of David and Deborah Craig; *m* 1991, S. G. Yvonne; one *s* one *d. Educ:* Univ. of Ulster (HND with Dist. Mech. Engrg). Tool design engr, Shorts Bombardier, 1987–2007. Mem. (DemU) Lisburn CC, 2001– (Mayor, 2005–06). *Recreations:* following motorbike racing, building computers, home DIY. *Address:* (office) 29 Castle Street, Lisburn, Co. Antrim BT27 4DH. *T:* (028) 9266 8378; *e-mail:* jonathan.craig@lisburn.gov.uk.

CRAIG, Prof. David Parker, AO 1985; FRS 1968; FAA 1969; FRSC; University Fellow and Emeritus Professor, Australian National University, since 1985; *b* 23 Dec. 1919; *s* of Andrew Hunter Craig, Manchester and Sydney, and Mary Jane (*née* Parker); *m* 1948, Veronica, *d* of Cyril Bryden-Brown, Market Harborough and Sydney; three *s* one *d. Educ:* Sydney Church of England Grammar Sch.; University of Sydney; University Coll., London. MSc (Sydney) 1941, PhD (London) 1950, DSc (London) 1956. Commonwealth Science Scholar, 1940. War Service: Capt., Australian Imperial Force, 1941–44. Lectr in Chemistry, University of Sydney, 1944–46; Turner and Newall Research Fellow, 1946–49, and Lectr in Chemistry, University Coll., London, 1949–52; Prof. of Physical Chemistry, Univ. of Sydney, 1952–56; Prof. of Chemistry, University Coll., London, 1956–67; Prof. of Chemistry, 1967–85, Dean, Research Sch. of Chemistry, 1970–73 and 1977–81, ANU. Vis. Prof., UCL, 1968–90; Firth Vis. Prof., Univ. of Sheffield, 1973; Vis. Prof., University Coll., Cardiff, 1975–89. Part-time Mem., CSIRO Exec., 1980–85. Chm., Adv. Cttee, Aust. Nat. Botanic Gdns, 1986–89. Pres., Australian Acad. of Sci., 1990–94. Fellow of University Coll., London, 1964–. Hon. FRSC 1987. Hon. Dr Chem Bologna, 1985; Hon. DSc Sydney, 1985. *Publications:* books and original papers on chemistry in scientific periodicals. *Address:* 216 Dryandra Street, O'Connor, ACT 2602, Australia. *Club:* Athenæum.

CRAIG, Douglas, OBE 1965; freelance opera producer, adjudicator and lecturer; *b* 26 May 1916; *m* 1955, Dorothy Dixon; two *d. Educ:* Latymer Upper Sch.; St Catharine's Coll., Cambridge (MA). FRCM, FRSA. Winchester Prize, Cambridge, 1938. Intell. Corps, 1940–46, Major 1944. Baritone, Sadler's Wells Opera and elsewhere, 1946–; Artistic Dir, Opera for All, 1949–65; Stage Dir, Glyndebourne, 1952–55; Asst Gen. Man., Glyndebourne, 1955–59; Producer, Royal Coll. of Music, 1958–; Freelance Opera Producer, 1959–; Dep. Dir, London Opera Centre, 1965–66; Administrator, Welsh Nat. Opera, 1966–70; Dir, Sadler's Wells Theatre, 1970–78; Dir, Opera and Drama Sch., RCM, 1976–80. Master Teacher in Residence, Adelaide Coll. of the Arts, 1981; taught in Adelaide, Canberra, Melbourne, Sydney and Hong Kong, 1984 (specialist tour award from British Council); prodns for S Australia Coll. of Advanced Educn and for NSW State Conservatorium of Music, master classes and lectures, Australia, 1985; Nat. Adjudicator, Australian Singing Competition, 1985. President: Council of Friends of Sadler's Wells, 1982–95; Sussex Opera and Ballet Soc., 1997–. Mem. Exec. and Editor, Music Jl of ISM, 1979–84. *Publication:* (ed) Delius: Koanga (opera), 1975. *Recreation:* travel. *Address:* 43 Park Road, Radlett, Herts WD7 8EG. *T:* (01923) 857240. *Club:* Garrick.

CRAIG, Prof. Edward John, FBA 1993; Knightbridge Professor of Philosophy, University of Cambridge, 1998–2005; Fellow, Churchill College, Cambridge, since 1966; *b* 26 March 1942; *s* of Charles William Craig and Annie (*née* Taylor); *m* 1st, 1973, Isabel Nina Barnard (marr. diss. 1986); two *d*; 2nd, 1987, Gillian Helen Elizabeth Edwards. *Educ:* Charterhouse; Trinity Coll., Cambridge (MA 1966; PhD 1970). Cricket for Cambridge Univ. and Lancs CCC, 1961–63; Cambridge University: Asst Lectr and Univ. Lectr in Philosophy, 1966–92; Reader in Modern Philosophy, 1992–98. Visiting University appointments: Melbourne, 1974; Hamburg, 1977–78; Heidelberg, 1981; Indian Inst. of Advanced Studies, 1996. General Editor: Routledge Encyclopedia of Philosophy, 1991–; Routledge Encyclopedia of Philosophy Online, 2000–; Editor, Ratio, 1988–92. *Publications:* David Hume: eine Einführung in seine Philosophie, 1979; The Mind of God and the Works of Man, 1987; Knowledge and the State of Nature, 1990; Pragmatische Untersuchungen zum Wissensbegriff, 1993; Hume on Religion, 1997; Philosophy: a very short introduction, 2002. *Recreations:* music, golf. *Address:* Churchill College, Cambridge CB3 0DS. *T:* (01223) 336000.

CRAIG, George Charles Graham; Senior Director, Social Affairs (formerly Social Policy and Land Affairs), Welsh Assembly Government, 1999–2003; *b* 8 May 1946; s of late George Craig and of E. S. Craig (*née* Milne); *m* 1968, (Ethne) Marian, *er d* of late H. H. A. Gallagher and of E. F. Gallagher; two *s* one *d. Educ:* Brockley County Grammar Sch.; Nottingham Univ. (BA). Asst Principal, Min. of Transport, 1967; Welsh Office: Private Sec. to Minister of State, 1970–72; Principal, 1972; Private Sec. to Sec. of State for Wales, 1978–80; Asst Sec., 1980; Under Sec., 1986; Dep. Sec., 1999. *Address:* c/o Harries and Wilson, 69 High Street, Swanage, Dorset BH19 2LY.

CRAIG, Gloria Linda; a Director General, Ministry of Defence, since 1999; *b* 23 Nov. 1948; *née* Kristler; adopted *d* of late George Edward Franklin and of Victoria Franklin; *m* 1987, Gordon Montgomery Craig (marr. diss. 2001). *Educ:* St Martin-in-the-Fields High Sch. for Girls; Lady Margaret Hall, Oxford (MA). GB-USSR Assoc., 1970–71; joined MoD, 1971; Private Sec. to Parly Under Sec. of State (Navy), 1975–76; Planning Staff, FCO, 1979–81; Asst Sec., 1984; RCDS 1988; Dep. Dir, Cabinet Office, 1989–92, 1995–99. Non-exec. Mem. Bd, Family Housing Assoc., 1999–2004. *Publications:* papers and lectures on defence and public service issues, white papers and best practice guides. *Recreations:* antiques, music, travel, animals, gardening.

CRAIG, Sir James; *see* Craig, Sir A. J. M.

CRAIG, Dr (James) Oscar (Max Clark), FRCS, FRCP, FRCSI, FRCR; Consultant Radiologist since 1963, and Hon. Senior Clinical Lecturer, since 1987, St Mary's Hospital, London; President, Royal College of Radiologists, 1989–92; *b* 7 May 1927; *s* of James

Oscar Max Clark Craig and Olivia Craig; *m* 1950, Louise Burleigh; four *d. Educ:* Royal College of Surgeons in Ireland. LRCP&SI 1950; FRCSI 1956; DMRD 1959; FRCR (FFR 1962); FRCS 1982; MRCP 1989, FRCP 1993; FRCGP 1991. Asst GP, 1950–51; Ho. Surg., St Helier Hosp., Carshalton, 1951–52; Gen. practice, Sutton, 1952–54. Surg. RAF, 1954–56. Sen. Ho. Officer, Surgery, Hammersmith Hosp., 1956–57; Registrar and Sen. Registrar, Dept of Radiology, St Mary's Hosp., London, 1957–63; Lectr in Radiology, London Univ., 1963–87; Dir of Clinical Studies, 1969–75, Dir of Post Grad. Studies, 1979–81, St Mary's Hosp. Med. Sch. Visiting Professor: UBC, Canada, 1977; Univ. of Queensland, 1984; Concord Hosp., Sydney, 1988. Pres., Harveian Soc. of London, 2002. Fellow, Med Soc. of London, 2001. Hon. Mem., Radiological Soc. of N America, 1993; Hon. FFR RCSI 1985; Hon. Fellow, Hong Kong Coll. of Radiologists, 1995. *Publications:* A Life in Medicine (autobiog.), 2000; Medical Memoirs (autobiog.), 2006; Doctors at War, 2007; numerous papers and chapters in books on clinical radiology, phlebography, lymphangiography, gastro-intestinal radiology, medico-legal medicine and the develt of digital radiology. *Recreation:* country-walking. *Address:* The White House, 18 Sandy Lane, Cheam, Surrey SM2 7NR. *T:* (020) 8642 2696. *Clubs:* Royal Society of Medicine, MCC.

CRAIG, John Egwin, CBE 1998 (OBE 1990); Director, since 2005 and Deputy Chairman, since 2007, New Star Asset Management plc; *b* 16 Aug. 1932; *s* of late Thomas Joseph Alexander Craig, CIE, and Mabel Frances (*née* Quinnell); *m* 1959, Patricia Costa Lopes; three *s. Educ:* Charterhouse. FCA 1961–2000. Cooper Bros (later Coopers & Lybrands), 1958–61; Council of Stock Exchange, 1961–64; N. M. Rothschild & Sons, 1964–91, Dir, 1970–91; Man. Dir, N. M. Rothschild, 1981–89; Chm., Jupiter European Investment Trust, 1990–2000; Dir, New Star Investment Trust, 2001–05 (Chm., 2005). Chairman: Powerscreen Internat. plc, 1989–99; Belfast Internat. Airport Hldgs, 1994–96; Director: Standard Chartered, 1989–94; Jupiter Tyndall Gp, then Jupiter Internat. Gp, 1991–2000 (Vice Chm., 1991–94). Govt Dir, Internat. Fund for Ireland, 1989–96. Member: Exec. Cttee, BBA, 1981–89 (Chm., 1987–89); Deposit Protection Bd, 1986–89. Mem. Council, LPO, 1983–87. Trustee, Restoration of Appearance and Function Trust, 2000–07. FRSA 1988. *Address:* Saxonbury House, Frant, Tunbridge Wells, Kent TN3 9HJ. *Club:* Brooks's.

CRAIG, John Frazer, CB 1994; Director, Economic Affairs (formerly Head of Economic and Industrial Affairs), Welsh Office, 1990–97; *b* 8 Nov. 1943; *s* of late John Frazer Craig and Margaret Jane Gibson Craig; *m* 1st, 1963, Ann Bardo (marr. diss. 1972); two *s* one *d*; 2nd, 1973, Janet Elizabeth. *Educ:* Robert Richardson Grammar Sch., Sunderland. Customs and Excise, 1961–69; Nat. Bd for Prices and Incomes, 1969–70; Welsh Office, 1970–97: Private Sec. to Perm. Sec., 1972–74; Private Sec. to Sec. of State for Wales, 1980–82; Asst Sec., 1982–85, Under Sec. (Dir), 1985–87, Industry Dept; Under Sec. (Principal Finance Officer), Welsh Office, 1987–90; Dep. Sec., 1990–97.

CRAIG, Jonathan; *see* Craig, D. J.

CRAIG, Rev. Maxwell Davidson; General Secretary, Action of Churches Together in Scotland, 1990–98; Chaplain to the Queen in Scotland, 1986–2001, now an Extra Chaplain; *b* 25 Dec. 1931; *s* of Dr William Craig and Alice M. Craig (*née* Semple); *m* 1957, Janet Margaret Macgregor; one *s* three *d. Educ:* Oriel Coll., Oxford (MA (Hons) Lit.Hum.); Edinburgh Univ. (BD); Princeton Theol Seminary, NJ (ThM). 2nd Lieut, 1st Bn Argyll and Sutherland Highlanders, 1954–56. Asst Principal, Ministry of Labour, 1957–61. Ordained minister, Grahamston Parish Church, Falkirk, 1966; Minister: Wellington Church, Glasgow, 1973–89; St Columba's Parish Church, Aberdeen, 1989–90; St Andrew's Ch, Jerusalem, 1999–2000. Convener of the Church and Nation Cttee, Church of Scotland, 1984–88. Chairman: Falkirk Children's Panel, 1970–72; Hillhead Housing Assoc., 1977–89; Scottish Churches Housing Agency, subseq. Action, 2000–06. *Publications:* Stella: the story of Stella J. Reekie, 1984; For God's Sake Unity, 1998. *Recreations:* hill-walking, choral singing. *Address:* 3 Queens Road, Stirling FK8 2QY. *T:* (01786) 472319.

CRAIG, Norman; Assistant Under-Secretary of State, Ministry of Defence, 1972–79; *b* 15 May 1920; *s* of George Craig, OBE; *m* 1st, 1946, Judith Margaret Newling (marr. diss. 1957); one *s*; 2nd, 1960, Jane Hudson; two *s* one *d. Educ:* Penarth County Sch.; Cardiff Univ. Army Service, Royal Sussex Regt, 1940–47. Board of Trade, 1948; Min. of Supply (later Aviation), 1953; Private Sec. to Minister, 1959–60; Min. of Technology, 1964; Sec. to Cttee of Inquiry into Aircraft Industry, 1964–65; course at IDC, 1968; MoD, 1971. Lord Chancellor's Department: official, 1979–85; consultant, 1986–87; lay observer, 1990. *Publication:* The Broken Plume, 1982. *Address:* 51 Hayes Lane, Beckenham, Kent BR3 6RE. *T:* (020) 8650 7916.

CRAIG, Oscar; *see* Craig, J. O. M. C.

CRAIG, Pamela Tudor; *see* Wedgwood, Pamela, Lady.

CRAIG, Prof. Paul Philip, FBA 1998; Professor of English Law, since 1998 (Professor of Law, 1996–98), and Fellow of St John's College, since 1998, University of Oxford; *b* 27 Sept. 1951; *s* of Maurice and Beatrice Craig; *m* 1991, Dr Anita Cooper; one *s. Educ:* Worcester Coll., Oxford (MA, BCL). University of Oxford: Fellow, Worcester Coll., 1976–98, now Emeritus; Reader in Law, 1990–96. Vis. Prof. in Univs of Virginia, Cornell, Connecticut, York (Osgoode Hall) Canada, Indiana, Queensland. Hon. QC 2000. *Publications:* Administrative Law, 1983, 6th edn 2008; Public Law and Democracy in the United Kingdom and the United States of America, 1990; Text, Cases and Materials on Community Law, 1995, 4th edn 2007; Law Making in the European Union, 1998; The Evolution of EU Law, 1999; EU Administrative Law, 2006; articles in jls. *Recreations:* riding, ski-ing, theatre, acting, ballet. *Address:* St John's College, Oxford OX1 3JP. *T:* (01865) 277340.

CRAIG, Prof. R. Cairns, PhD; FBA 2005; FRSE; Glucksman Professor of Irish and Scottish Studies and Director, Research Institute of Irish and Scottish Studies, since 2005, and Director of AHRC Centre for Irish and Scottish Studies, since 2006, University of Aberdeen; *b* 16 Feb. 1949. Lectr, Dept. of English, Univ. of Aberdeen; Department of English Literature, University of Edinburgh: Lectr; Sen. Lectr; Reader; Prof. of Scottish and Modern Literature; Hd of Dept, 1997–2003; Dir, Centre for History of Ideas in Scotland. Hon. Prof. and Chm., Academic Bd, AHRC Centre for Irish and Scottish Studies, Univ. of Aberdeen, 2001–06. FRSE 2003. *Publications:* Yeats, Eliot, Pound and the Politics of Poetry: richest to the richest, 1982; Out of History: narrative paradigms in Scottish and English Culture, 1996; The Modern Scottish Novel: narrative and the national imagination, 1999; Iain Banks's Complicity: a reader's guide, 2002. *Address:* Research Institute of Irish and Scottish Studies, Humanity Manse, 19 College Bounds, Aberdeen AB24 3UG.

CRAIG, Maj.-Gen. (Robert) Peter, MD; FRCS, FCEM; Chairman, Queen Mary's Roehampton Trust, since 2002; Medical Member, Pensions Appeals Tribunals, since 1997 (Medical Chairman, 2000–01); *b* 24 June 1940; *s* of late Dr Robert Theodore Gilpin

Craig, TD, MB BS, MRCGP and Jessie Craig (*née* McKinstry); *m* 1971, Jean Toft, MA; one *s* two *d. Educ:* George Watson's Boys' Coll.; Durham Univ. Med. Sch. (MB BS 1964); MD Newcastle upon Tyne 1987; FRCS 1972; FCEM (FFAEM 1994). Commissioned RA (TA) 1958; RAMC 1963; Royal Victoria Infirmary, Newcastle, 1964–65; RMO 1/2 Gurkha Rifles, 1966–68; Queen Alexandra Mil. Hosp.; Birmingham Accident Hosp.; Dept of Surgery, Univ. of Newcastle upon Tyne; BMH Rinteln; Guy's Hosp., 1974–78; Consultant Surgeon: BMH Hong Kong, 1979–81; Queen Elizabeth Mil. Hosp., 1981–86; Sen. Lectr in Mil. Surgery, Royal Army Med. Coll., 1981–86; BMH Rinteln, 1986–89, CO, 1987–89; Comd Med., 4th Armoured Div., 1989–90; Comd Surgeon, HQ BAOR, 1990–92; Dir of Army Surgery, 1992–93; Comdr Medical, UKLF, 1993–94; Consultant in A & E Medicine, Wansbeck Gen. Hosp., 1994–96. Med. Mem., The Appeals Service, 1998–2008. QHS 1992–94. Liveryman, Soc. of Apothecaries, 2003–. Montefiore Meml Medal, 1979; Leishman Meml Medal, 1987. OStJ 1993. GSM Oman 1973, NI 1979. *Publications:* contribs to surgical jls. *Recreations:* golf, bridge, military history. *Address:* 162 New Kent Road, SE1 4YS. *T:* (020) 7701 6553; *e-mail:* rpetercraig@yahoo.co.uk. *Clubs:* Athenæum, Royal Society of Medicine; Northumberland Golf; Wildernesse (Sevenoaks).

CRAIG, Stuart (Norman), OBE 2003; RDI 2004; film production designer; *b* 14 April 1942; *s* of Norman and Kate Craig; *m* 1965, Patricia Stangroom; two *d. Educ:* Royal Coll. of Art. *Films:* The Elephant Man, 1980 (BAFTA Award); Gandhi, 1982 (Acad. Award); Greystoke, 1984; Cal, 1984; The Mission, 1986; Cry Freedom, 1987; Dangerous Liaisons, 1988 (Acad. Award); Memphis Belle, 1990; Chaplin, 1992; The Secret Garden, 1993; Shadowlands, 1993; Mary Reilly, 1996; The English Patient, 1996 (Acad. Award); In Love and War, 1996; The Avengers, 1998; Notting Hill, 1999; The Legend of Bagger Vance, 2000; Harry Potter I–V, 2001–07. *Address:* c/o Steve Kenis & Co., Royalty House, 72–74 Dean Street, W1D 3SG. *T:* (020) 7434 9055.

CRAIG, Wendy; *see* Craig, A. G.

CRAIG, Rt Hon. William; PC (N Ire.) 1963; solicitor and company director; *b* 2 Dec. 1924; *s* of late John Craig and Mary Kathleen Craig (*née* Lamont); *m* 1960, Doris Hilgendorff; two *s. Educ:* Dungannon Royal Sch.; Larne Grammar Sch.; Queen's Univ., Belfast. Served War of 1939–45, Royal Air Force, 1943–46. Qualified as solicitor, 1952. MP (U) Larne Div. of Antrim, NI Parliament, 1960–73; Mem. (Vanguard Unionist Progressive), N Antrim, NI Assembly, 1973–75; Mem. (UUC), E Belfast, NI Constitutional Convention, 1975–76; MP (UU) Belfast East, Feb. 1974–1979. Chief Whip, Parliament of Northern Ireland, 1962–63; Minister of Home Affairs, 1963–64, and 1966–68; Minister of Health and Local Government, 1964; Minister of Development, 1965–66. Founder: Ulster Vanguard, 1972 (Leader, 1972–77); Vanguard Unionist Party, 1973 (Leader, 1973–77). Member: Council of Europe, 1976–79; WEU, 1976–79. *Recreations:* travel, motoring, shooting.

CRAIG-COOPER, Sir (Frederick Howard) Michael, Kt 1991; CBE 1982; TD 1968 (3 bars); Director: Craig-Lloyd, since 1968; National Bank of Kuwait (International) plc, since 1993; Vice Lord-Lieutenant of Greater London, since 2005; *b* 28 Jan. 1936; *s* of late Frederick William Valentine Craig-Cooper and of Elizabeth Oliver-Thompson Craig-Cooper (*née* Macdonald) (she *m* 1978, Col J. H. Carroll-Leahy, MC (decd)); *m* 1968, Elizabeth Snagge, MVO; one *s. Educ:* Horris Hill; Stowe; College of Law. Solicitor, 1961. National Service, RA, 1954–56; TA, 1956–88; Comdr, Naval Gunfire Liaison Unit, 29 Commando Regt, RA, 1972–75; Mem., Greater London TAVRA (Chm., Employers Support Cttee, 1987–90). Jaques & Co., 1956–61; Allen & Overy, 1962–64; Inco, 1964–85; Director: Paul Ray Internat., 1984–92 (merged with Carre Orban & Partners, 1989); Tichborne Enterprises Ltd, 1993–; non-executive Director: Ely Place Holdings Ltd, 1994–; Craigmyle & Co. Ltd, 1995–; Westminster Forum (formerly WIB Publications) Ltd, 1996–. Royal Borough of Kensington & Chelsea: Councillor, 1968–74; Chief Whip, 1971–74; Chm. Finance Cttee, 1972–74; Alderman, 1974–78; Mem. Investment Cttee, 1973–. Contested (C) Houghton-le-Spring, 1966, 1970; Chm., Cons Nat. Property Adv. Cttee, 1986–93 (Mem., 1993–); Pres., Kensington and Chelsea (formerly Chelsea), Cons. Assoc., 1983–2005 (Chm., 1974–77). Trustee: Copper Develt Trust Fund, 1974–85; Order of Malta Homes Trust, 1980–2003; Orders of St John Trust, 1988–2003. Mem. Council, Mining Assoc., 1977–82; Chm. Disciplinary Appeal Cttee, CIMA, 1994–2005. Comr, Royal Hosp. Chelsea, 1998–2005. Pres., Boys' Brigade (London Dist), 2002–05. Freeman, City of London, 1964; Liveryman, Drapers' Co., 1970– (Mem. Court of Assistants, 1987–; Master, 1997–98). DL Greater London, 1986. Rep. DL Kensington & Chelsea, 1987–2006. FCIArb 1992. KStJ 1990 (Chm., Council for London, 1990–94; Mem., Chapter-Gen., 1993–99). Comdr, SMO Malta, 2001. *Publications:* (with Philippe De Backer) Management Audit: how to create an effective management team, 1993; (jtly) Maw on Corporate Governance, 1994; (jtly) Maximum Leadership, 1995, revd edn as Maximum Leadership 2000, 1997. *Recreation:* admiring wife's gardening. *Clubs:* Beefsteak, Pratt's, White's.

CRAIG-McFEELY, Comdt Elizabeth Sarah Ann, (Mrs C. C. H. Dunlop), CE 1982; DL; Director, Women's Royal Naval Service, 1979–82; *b* 28 April 1927; *d* of late Lt-Col Cecil Michael Craig McFeely, DSO, OBE, MC, and Nancy Sarah (*née* Mann, later Roberts); *m* 1995, Rear-Adm. C. C. H. Dunlop, *qv. Educ:* St Rose's Convent, Stroud, Glos; Anstey College of Physical Educn, Birmingham. DipPhysEducn London. Taught PE at St Angela's Ursuline Convent Sch., 1948–52; joined WRNS, 1952; Third Officer 1953; served in various Royal Naval, Royal Marines and Royal Naval Reserve Establts 1952–67; in charge, WRNS, Far Eastern Fleet, 1967–69; various appts, MoD (Navy) 1969–74; HMS Centurion, 1974–76; Supt WRNS, 1977. Naval member, NAAFI Bd c Management, 1977–79; Hon. ADC to the Queen, 1979–82; retired 1982. DL Ken 1996–2005. *Recreations:* gardening and country pursuits. *Address:* 1 The Gatehouse Elliscombe Park, Holton, Wincanton, Somerset BA9 8EA. *T:* (01963) 31534.

CRAIG-MARTIN, Prof. Michael, CBE 2001; RA 2006; artist; *b* 28 Aug. 1941; *s* of Pat and Rhona Craig-Martin; *m* 1963, Janice Lucia Hashey (separated); one *d. Educ:* Prior Sch., Washington; Yale Univ. Artist in Residence, King's Coll., Cambridge, 1970–72 Sen. Lectr, 1973–79, Prin. Lectr, 1979–85, Millard Prof. of Fine Art, 1994–2000 Goldsmiths' Coll., London (Hon. Fellow, 2001). Trustee, Tate Gall., 1989–99. *Exhibition* include: Hayward Gall., 1972; Tate Gall., 1972; IX Biennale des Jeunes Artistes, Paris 1975; Sydney Biennale, 1976, 1990; Whitechapel Art Gall., 1995; MOMA, NY, 1999 *one-man exhibitions:* Whitechapel Art Gall., 1989 (retrospective); MOMA, NY, 199 Centre Pompidou, Paris, 1994; Hannover Kunstverein, 1998; São Paulo Bienal, 1998 Stuttgart Kunstverein, 1999; Peter Blum, NY, 1999; Waddington Galls, 2000, 2002 IVAM, Valencia, Spain, 2000.

CRAIGAVON, 3rd Viscount *cr* 1927, of Stormont, Co. Down; **Janric Fraser Craig;** B 1918; *b* 9 June 1944; *s* of 2nd Viscount Craigavon; *S* father, 1974. *Educ:* Eton; Londo Univ. (BA, BSc). FCA. Elected Mem., H of L, 1999. *Heir:* none.

CRAIGEN, Desmond Seaward; Director: Prudential Corporation plc, 1982–8 Pioneer Concrete (Holdings) Ltd, 1982–89; *b* 31 July 1916; *s* of late John Craigen and An Amelia Craigen (*née* Brebner); *m* 1961, Elena Ines (*née* Oldham Florez) (*d* 1995); one *s* or *d. Educ:* Holloway Sch.; King's Coll., London (BA Hons). Prudential Assurance Co. Ltd, 1934–81; India, 1950–57; attached O&M Div., Treasury, 1957–58; Dep. General Manager, 1968–69; General Manager, 1969–78; Chief General Manager, 1979–81; Chm., Vanbrugh Life Assurance Co. Ltd, 1982–87. Served War of 1939–45: 53rd Reconnaissance Regt RAC (Major; despatches). *Recreations:* music, reading. *Address:* Tregolls Manor, Tregolls Road, Truro TR1 1XQ.

CRAIGEN, James Mark; Director and Secretary, Scottish Federation of Housing Associations, 1988–90; freelance writer; *b* 2 Aug. 1938; *e s* of James Craigen, MA and Isabel Craigen; *m* 1971, Sheena Millar. *Educ:* Shawlands Academy, Glasgow; Strathclyde University; MLitt Heriot-Watt 1974. Compositor, 1954–61. Industrial Relations Asst, Scottish Gas Bd, 1963–64; Head of Organisation and Social Services at Scottish TUC, 1964–68; Asst Sec., and Industrial Liaison Officer, Scottish Business Educn Council, 1968–74. Glasgow City Councillor, 1965–68, Magistrate, 1966–68. Member: Scottish Ambulance Service Bd, 1966–71; Race Relations Bd, Scottish Conciliation Cttee, 1967–70; Police Adv. Bd for Scotland, 1970–74; ITC Viewer Consultative Council for Scotland, 1990–93; S Scotland Electricity Consumers' Cttee, 1994–97. Contested Ayr constituency, 1970. MP (Lab and Co-op) Glasgow Maryhill, Feb. 1974–1987 (retired on grounds of experience, not age); PPS to Rt Hon. William Ross, MBE, MP, Sec. of State for Scotland, 1974–76; Opposition Spokesman on Scottish Affairs, 1983–85. Member: Select Cttee on Employment, 1979–83 (Chm., 1982–83); Select Cttee on Scottish Affairs, 1987; Chairman: Co-op. Party Parly Group, 1978–79; Scottish Group, Labour MPs, 1978–79; PLP Employment Gp, 1981–83. Member: UK Delegn to Council of Europe Assembly, 1976–80; Extra Parly Panel, Private Legislation Procedure (Scotland) Act 1936, 1996–2005. Trustee, Industry and Parliament Trust, 1983–88 (Fellow, 1978–79). Mem., Bd of Trustees, Nat. Museums of Scotland, 1985–91. Hon. Vice-Pres., Building Societies Assoc., 1985–88. Hon. Lectr, Strathclyde Univ., 1980–85; Fellow, Inst. of Advanced Studies in Humanities, Edinburgh Univ., 1990–91. JP: Glasgow, 1966; Edinburgh, 1975–2007. CCMI. *Publications:* (contrib.) Forward! Labour Politics in Scotland 1888–1988, 1989; contribs to Co-operative News. *Address:* 38 Downie Grove, Edinburgh EH12 7AX.

CRAIGIE, Cathie; Member (Lab) Cumbernauld and Kilsyth, Scottish Parliament, since 1999; *b* Stirling, 14 April 1954; *d* of George Mitchell and Marion (*née* Mandelkau); *m* 1978, Arthur Craigie; one *s* one *d*. *Educ:* Kilsyth Acad. Mem., Ext. Audit Team for Chartered Accountants, 1970–80. Parly Asst to MP, 1992–97. Member (Lab): Cumbernauld and Kilsyth DC, 1984–96: Council Leader, 1994–96; Chm., Planning, Housing, Policy & Resources and Equal Opportunities Cttees, 1984–96; N Lanarks Council, 1995–99: Vice-Chm., Housing, 1995–98; Chairman: Envmtl Services, 1998–99; Kilsyth Local Area Cttee, 1998–99; Cumbernauld Housing Partnership, 1997–98. Scottish Parliament: Member: Audit Cttee, 1999–2000; Social Inclusion, Housing and Voluntary Sector Cttee, 1999–2000; Social Justice Cttee, 2001. Labour Party: Mem., 1974–; Constituency Party Sec., 1992–99; Mem., Nat. Policy Forum, 1998–. *Recreations:* cycling, reading, family holidays. *Address:* Scottish Parliament, Edinburgh EH99 1SP.

CRAIGMYLE, 4th Baron *cr* 1929, of Craigmyle, co. Aberdeen; **Thomas Columba Shaw;** *b* 19 Oct. 1960; *s* of 3rd Baron Craigmyle and of Anthea Esther Christine (*née* Rich); *S* father, 1998; *m* 1987, (Katherine) Alice (*née* Floyd); four *s*. *Heir: e s* Alexander Francis Shaw, *b* 1 July 1988.

CRAIK, Prof. Fergus Ian Muirden, PhD; FRS 2008; FRSC; psychologist; University Professor, University of Toronto, 1997–2000, now Emeritus; Senior Scientist, Rotman Research Institute, Baycrest Centre, Toronto, since 1989; *b* Edinburgh, 17 April 1935; *s* of late George Craik and of Frances Craik; *m* 1961, Anne, *d* of Jack and Rita Catherall; one *s* one *d*. *Educ:* George Watson's Boys' Coll., Edinburgh; Univ. of Edinburgh (BSc 1960); Univ. of Liverpool (PhD 1965). Lectr in Psychol., Birkbeck Coll., Univ. of London, 1965–71; University of Toronto: Associate Prof. of Psychol., 1971–75; Prof. of Psychol., 1975–97; Chm. of Psychol., 1985–90; Glassman Prof. of Neuropsychol., 1996–2000. Fellow, Center for Advanced Study in Behavioral Scis, Stanford Univ., 1982–83; Killam Res. Fellow, 1982–84; Guggenheim Fellow, 1982–83. Ed., Jl of Verbal Learning and Verbal Behavior, 1980–84. Mem., Soc. of Experimental Psychols; Fellow: Canadian Psychol. Assoc. (Hon. Pres., 1997–98); Amer. Psychol. Assoc. FRSC 1985. Hon. Dr Bordeaux 2, 2006. Dist. Scientific Contribution Award, Canadian Psychol. Assoc., 1987; William James Fellow Award, Amer. Psychol. Soc., 1993; Hebb Award, Canadian Soc. for Brain, Behaviour and Cognitive Sci., 1998; Killam Prize, 2000. *Publications:* (ed jtly) Levels of Processing in Human Memory, 1979; Aging and Cognitive Processes, 1982; Varieties of Memory and Consciousness, 1989; The Handbook of Aging and Cognition, 1992, 2008; The Oxford Handbook of Memory, 2000; Lifespan Cognition: mechanisms of change, 2006. *Recreations:* reading, walking, music, tennis. *Address:* Rotman Research Institute of Baycrest, 3560 Bathurst Street, Toronto, ON M6A 2E1, Canada.

See also R. G. Craik.

CRAIK, Roger George; QC (Scot.) 1981; Sheriff of Lothian and Borders, 1984–2005; *b* 22 Nov. 1940; *s* of late George and of Frances Craik; *m* 1964, Helen Sinclair Sutherland; one *s* one *d*. *Educ:* Lockerbie Academy; Breadalbane Academy, Aberfeldy; George Watson's Boys' Coll.; Edinburgh Univ. (MA 1960, LLB 1962). Qualified as solicitor, 1962; worked for Orr Dignam & Co., Solicitors, Pakistan, 1963–65; called to Scottish Bar, 1966. Standing junior counsel to Min. of Defence (Army), 1974–80; Advocate Depute, 1980–83. Temp. Court of Session Judge, 2004–. Mem., Sheriff Court Rules Council, 1990–95. *Publications:* The Advocates' Library 1689–1989, 1989; James Boswell: The Scottish Perspective, 1994; Parliament House Portraits: the art collection of the Faculty of Advocates, 2000. *Recreations:* Scottish antiquities, modern jazz. *Address:* 9 York Road, Trinity, Edinburgh EH5 3EJ.

CRAM, Stephen, MBE 1986; middle distance runner; athletics presenter and commentator; Chairman, English Institute of Sport, since 2002; *b* 14 Oct. 1960; *s* of William Frank Cram and Maria Helene (*née* Korte); *m* 1983, Karen Anne Waters (marr. diss.); one *s* one *d*. *Educ:* Jarrow Grammar Sch.; Newcastle Poly. (BA). Commonwealth Games: Gold Medal for 1500m, 1982, 1986; Gold Medal for 800m, 1986; European Championships: Gold Medal for 1500m, 1982, 1986; Bronze Medal for 800m, 1986; Gold Medal for 1500m, World Championships, 1983; Silver Medal for 1500m, Olympic Games, 1984; Member, British Olympic Squad, 1980, 1984, 1988; former world record for mile, 1500m and 2000m, 1985. Regular contributor, BBC Radio 5 Live, 1995–; athletics presenter and commentator, BBC TV, 1999–; motivational speaker and sports consultant. Chm. and Trustee, Northumberland Sport. Chm. and Dir, Comrades of Children Overseas, 1998–. Patron, Macmillan Cancer Relief. Hon. Fellow Sunderland Univ., 1986. DUniv: Staffordshire, 2001; Sheffield Hallam, 2001. BBC Sports Personality of the Year, 1983. *Recreations:* golf, football, snooker. *Address:* Suite 2/4, 14 Blandford Square, Newcastle upon Tyne NE1 4HZ. *T:* (0191) 230 1124, *Fax:* (0191) 261 8535; *e-mail:* cramka100@hotmail.com. *Clubs:* Jarrow and Hebburn Athletic; Sunderland Association Football (Pres. London and Southern England Br., Supporters' Assoc.).

CRAMOND, Ronald Duncan, CBE 1987; Secretary and Founding Trustee, Intellectual Access Trust, since 1995; *b* 22 March 1927; *s* of Adam and Margaret Cramond; *m* 1st, 1954, Constance MacGregor (*d* 1985); one *s* one *d*; 2nd, 1999, Ann Rayner. *Educ:* George Heriot's Sch.; Edinburgh Univ. (MA). Sen. Medallist History 1949. FSAScot 1978. Commnd Royal Scots, 1950. Entered War Office, 1951; Private Sec. to Parly Under-Sec. of State, Scottish Office, 1956; Principal, Dept of Health for Scotland, 1957; Mactaggart Fellow (Applied Econs), Glasgow Univ., 1962; Haldane Medallist in Public Admin, 1964; Asst Sec., Scottish Develt Dept, 1966, Under Sec., 1973; Under Sec., Dept of Agric. and Fisheries for Scotland, 1977; Dep. Chm., Highlands and Islands Develt Bd, 1983–88. Chairman: Strathclyde Greenbelt Co., then Scottish Greenbelt Foundn, 1992–2000 (Mem., 1992–2005); Greenbelt Foundn, 1999–2002. Dir, Cairngorm Chairlift Co., 1988–90. Chairman: Scottish Museums Council, 1990–93; LandTrust, 1997–98; Member: Scottish Museums Adv. Bd, 1984–85; Scottish Tourist Board, 1985–88; CCS, 1988–92; Trustee: Nat. Museums of Scotland, 1985–96; Scottish Civic Trust, 1988–95; Scottish Fisheries Mus., 2001–04; Vice-Pres., Architectural Heritage Soc. of Scotland, 1988–93. *Publication:* Housing Policy in Scotland, 1966. *Recreation:* showing visitors round the Museum of Scotland.

CRAMP, Leslie Thomas; Deputy Inspector General and Senior Official Receiver, Insolvency Service, since 1998; *b* 25 Oct. 1949; *s* of Noel Clifford Cramp and Doris Nellie Irene Cramp; *m* 1974, Linda Ann Lipscomb; one *s* one *d*. *Educ:* Maidstone Grammar Sch. Local govt post, 1968–70; Insolvency Service, Department of Trade and Industry, 1970–: Companies Winding-up, London, 1970–82; Principal Examr, Policy Unit, 1982–88; Official Receiver, High Court, London, 1988–96; Manager, Anglia Reg., 1996–98. *Recreations:* music, football, reading, gardening. *Address:* Insolvency Service, 21 Bloomsbury Street, WC1B 3QW. *T:* (020) 7291 6728.

CRAMP, Prof. Rosemary Jean, CBE 1987; FBA 2006; Professor of Archaeology, University of Durham, 1971–90, now Emeritus; *b* 6 May 1929; *er d* of Robert Kingston and Vera Cramp, Cranoe Grange, Leics. *Educ:* Market Harborough Grammar Sch.; St Anne's Coll., Oxford (MA, BLitt). Lectr, St Anne's Coll., Oxford, 1950–55; Lectr, Durham Univ., 1955, Sen. Lectr, 1966. Vis. Fellow, All Souls Coll., Oxford, 1992. Commissioner: Royal Commn on Ancient and Historical Monuments of Scotland, 1975–99; Historic Bldgs and Monuments Commn, 1984–89 (Mem., Adv. Cttee (Archaeology), 1984–89). Trustee, BM, 1978–98. Member: Adv. Bd for Redundant Churches, 1984–98; Validation Panel, Museums' Trng Inst., 1993–97; Reviewing Cttee on Export of Works of Art, 1994–2003. Chm., Archaeology Data Service, 1996–2001. President: Council for British Archaeology, 1989–92 (Hon. Vice-Pres., 1992–); Cumberland and Westmorland Antiquarian and Archaeol Soc., 1984–87; Soc. for Church Archaeology, 1996–2001; Soc. of Antiquaries of London, 2001–04 (Hon. Vice-Pres., 2004–); Vice-Pres., Royal Archaeol Inst., 1992–97; Hon. Vice Pres., Soc. for Medieval Archaeol., 2004–. Gen. Editor, Corpus of Anglo-Saxon Stone Sculpture, 1974–. Hon. DSc: Durham, 1995; Bradford, 2002; Hon. DLitt: NUI, 2003; Leicester, 2004. *Publications:* Corpus of Anglo-Saxon Stone Sculpture, vol. I, Durham and Northumberland, 1984, vol. 2, (with R. N. Bailey) Cumberland and Westmorland, 1986, vol. 7, South West England, 2006; Wearmouth and Jarrow Monastic Sites, vol. 1, 2005, vol. 2, 2006; contribs in the field of early monasticism, early medieval sculpture and glass, and northern archaeology. *Address:* 5 Leazes Place, Durham DH1 1RE.

CRAMPIN, Peter; QC 1993; a Recorder, since 1995; *b* 7 July 1946; *s* of John Hames Crampin and Gwendoline Edith (*née* Richardson); *m* 1975, Frida Yvonne Schoemann; one *s*. *Educ:* St Albans Sch.; University Coll., Oxford (Open Exhibnr; MA). Admitted Solicitor, 1973; called to the Bar, Middle Temple, 1976; in practice at Chancery Bar, 1978–; an Asst Recorder, 1990–95; 2nd Jun. Counsel to Attorney General in Charity Matters, 1988–93. *Address:* Radcliffe Chambers, 11 New Square, Lincoln's Inn, WC2A 3QB. *T:* (020) 7831 0081.

CRAMPTON, Prof. Julian Moray, PhD; CBiol, FIBiol; Vice-Chancellor, and Professor of Molecular Biology, University of Brighton, since 2005; *b* 1 Nov. 1952; *s* of late Sqdn Ldr Roy A. V. Crampton and of Jean D. Crampton (*née* Macnair); partner, Dr Teresa F. Knapp. *Educ:* Univ. of Sussex (BSc Biol. 1975); Univ. of Warwick (PhD 1978). CBiol, MIBiol 1997, FIBiol 2004. MRC Postdoctoral Res. Fellow, St Mary's Hosp. Med. Sch., 1978–83; Liverpool School of Tropical Medicine, University of Liverpool: Hd, Wolfson Unit of Molecular Genetics, 1983–96; Wellcome Trust Sen. Res. Fellow, 1986–96; Hd, Div. of Molecular Biol. and Immunol., 1994–96; University of Liverpool: Prof. of Molecular Biol., 1991–2005; Hd, Sch. of Biol Scis, 1996–2000; Pro-Vice-Chancellor, 2000–04; Vis. Prof. 2005–. Chairman: Higher Educn SE, 2006–; Hastings and Bexhill Renaissance Ltd, 2006–; Mem., SE England Sci. Engrg and Technol. Adv. Council, 2006–. Trustee and Gov., Friends of Royal Pavilion, Art Gall. and Mus., 2006–; Trustee, Brighton Dome and Fest. Ltd, 2007–. Ed., Insect Molecular Biol., 1989–99 (Mem., Editl Bd, 1999–). FRSTM&H 1984; FRES 1989 (Hon. FRES 2002). FRSA 2001. *Publications:* (ed jtly) Insect Molecular Science, 1992; (ed jtly) The Molecular Biology of Insect Disease Vector, 1996; numerous contribs to learned jls. *Recreations:* photography, hill-walking, music. *Address:* University of Brighton, Mithras House, Lewes Road, Brighton BN2 4AT. *T:* (01273) 642001.

CRAMPTON, Peter Duncan; *b* 10 June 1932; *s* of Edmund Crampton and Louisa Crampton (*née* Thurman); *m* 1955, Margaret Eva McMillan; two *s*. *Educ:* Blackpool Grammar School; Nottingham Univ. (BA Hons Geography); Birmingham Univ. (MA African Studies); Hull Univ. (Dip. W European Studies); London Univ. (PGCE). Casual work, mainly as farm worker, 1954–55; Statistician, Plessey Co., 1955–56; Geography Teacher, Coventry, 1957–61; Educn Officer, Uganda, 1961–64; Lectr i/c Geography, Technical Coll., Birmingham, 1964–70; Lectr in Geography, Hull Coll. of Educn, then Humberside Coll. of HE, 1970–85; part-time work as lectr, writer, parly assistant, 1985–89. Chairman: European Nuclear Disarmament Campaign, 1984–86; Internat. Cttee, CND, 1988–90. MEP (Lab) Humberside, 1989–99. European Parliament: First Vice-Pres., Political Affairs Cttee, 1989–94, For. Affairs Cttee, 1989–94; Member: Regl Policy Cttee, 1994–99; Fishing Cttee, 1994–99; Vice Pres., Delegn to Mongolia and Central Asia, 1994–96. *Publications:* (contrib.) Voices for One World, 1988; articles in jls on population geography in Africa, electoral behaviour and nuclear disarmament. *Recreations:* travel, hill-walking, music. *Address:* 135 Westbourne Avenue, Hull HU5 3HU. *T:* (01482) 494796.

CRAMPTON, Prof. Richard John, PhD; Professor of East European History, University of Oxford, 1996–2006; Fellow of St Edmund Hall, Oxford, 1990–2006, now Emeritus; *b* 23 Nov. 1940; *s* of John Donald Crampton and Norah Crampton (*née* Haden); *m* 1965, Celia Harriss; two *s*. *Educ:* Univ. of Dublin (MA); MA Oxon; SSEES, Univ. of London (PhD). University of Kent at Canterbury: Lectr, 1967–78; Sen. Lectr, 1978–88; Prof. of East European History, 1988–90; Lectr in History, Univ. of Oxford, 1990–96. Fellow, Woodrow Wilson Internat. Center for Scholars, Washington, 1998–99. Dr *hc* Sofia, 2000. *Publications:* The Hollow Détente, 1981; Bulgaria 1878–1918: a history, 1984; Short History of Modern Bulgaria, 1987; Eastern Europe in the Twentieth Century, 1994;

(with Ben Crampton) Atlas of Eastern Europe in the 20th Century, 1996; Concise History of Bulgaria, 1997; The Balkans since the Second World War, 2002; (contrib.) Oxford History of Modern Europe, 2007. *Recreations:* cooking, bird-watching, trying to avoid pop music and mobile phones. *Address:* St Edmund Hall, Oxford OX1 4AR. *T:* (01865) 279000.

CRAMPTON SMITH, Alex; *see* Smith, A. C.

CRAN, James Douglas; *b* 28 Jan. 1944; *s* of James Cran and Jane McDonald Cran, Aberdeenshire; *m* 1973, Penelope Barbara Wilson; one *d. Educ:* Ruthrieston Sch., Aberdeen; Aberdeen Coll. of Commerce; King's Coll., Univ. of Aberdeen (MA Hons). Researcher, Cons. Res. Dept, 1970–71; Sec., 1971–73, Chief. Exec., 1973–79, Nat. Assoc. of Pension Funds; Northern Dir, 1979–84, West Midlands Dir, 1984–87, CBI. Councillor (C), London Borough of Sutton, 1974–79 (Chm., Health and Housing Cttee). MP (C) Beverley, 1987–97, Beverley and Holderness, 1997–2005. PPS to Sec. of State for NI, 1995–96; an Opposition Whip, 1997–2001 (Pairing Whip, 1998–2000); Opposition Asst Chief Whip, 2001. Member: Select Cttee on Trade and Industry, 1987–92, on NI, 1994–95, on Administration, 1997–98, on Selection, 1998–2001, on Defence, 2001–05; Chairmen's Panel, 2001–05; Vice Chairman: Cons. Backbench NI Cttee, 1992–95; All-Party Anglo-Mongolian Gp, 1993–94; Order of St John All-Party Gp, 1994–95; Secretary: Cons. Backbench Cttee on Constitutional Affairs, 1989–91, on European Affairs, 1989–91; All-Party Anglo-Malta Gp, 1992–94; Co-Founder, Parly Gp on Occupational Pensions, 1992. Mem., Council of Europe and WEU, 2001–02. Mem., NI Grand Cttee, 1996–2001. Fellow: Armed Forces Parly Scheme, attached to RM, 1992; Parlt and Industry Trust, 1994. Parly consultant, Lincoln Nat. (UK) plc, 1994–98. Treas., European Res. Gp, 1994–97; Mem., 92 Gp Steering Cttee, 2001–04. Vice-Pres., Beverley Combined Div., St John Ambulance. Council Mem., Pension Trustees Forum, 1992–95. Member of Court: Univ. of Birmingham, 1984–87; Univ. of Hull, 1987–2005. Dux Medallion, City of Aberdeen, 1959; Daily Mirror Nat. Speaking Trophy, 1969. OStJ. *Recreations:* travelling, reading biographies, autobiographies and military history. *Address:* The Mill House, Ashkirk, Selkirkshire TD7 4NY.

CRAN, Mark Dyson Gordon; QC 1988; a Recorder, since 2000; *b* 18 May 1948; *s* of William Broadbent Gordon Cran and Diana Rosemary Cran (*née* Mallinson); *m* 1983, Prudence Elizabeth Binning (marr. diss.). *Educ:* Gordonstoun; Millfield; Bristol Univ. (LLB). Called to the Bar, Gray's Inn, 1973. *Recreations:* country sports, long walks, convivial disputation, wine and food, performing arts. *Address:* Brick Court Chambers, 7–8 Essex Street, WC2R 3LD. *T:* (020) 7379 3550. *Clubs:* Brooks's, MCC.

CRANBORNE, Viscount; Robert Edward William Gascoyne-Cecil; *b* 18 Dec. 1970; *s* and *heir* of Marquess of Salisbury, *qv*; one *d* by Camilla Mary Davidson.

CRANBROOK, 5th Earl of, *cr* 1892; **Gathorne Gathorne-Hardy;** DL; Viscount Cranbrook, 1878; Baron Medway, 1892; Chairman: Institute for European Environmental Policy, 1990–2005; International Trust for Zoological Nomenclature, 2001–08; *b* 20 June 1933; *er s* of 4th Earl of Cranbrook, CBE, and of the Dowager Countess of Cranbrook (Fidelity, OBE 1972, *o d* of late Hugh E. Seebohm); *S* father, 1978; *m* 1967, Caroline (OBE 2006), *o d* of Col Ralph G. E. Jarvis, Doddington Hall, Lincoln; two *s* one *d. Educ:* Eton; Corpus Christi Coll., Cambridge (MA); University of Birmingham (PhD). Asst, Sarawak Museum, 1956–58; Fellow, Yayasan Siswa Lokantara (Indonesia), 1960–61; Asst Lectr, subseq. Lectr then Sen. Lectr in Zoology, Univ. of Malaya, 1961–70. Editor of Ibis, 1973–80. Mem., H of L Select Cttee on EC, then EU, three terms, 1979–99 (Mem., Envmt Sub-Cttee, 1979–85, 1987–90 (Chm., 1980–83, 1987–90), Chm., Envmt, Public Health and Consumer Protection Sub-Cttee, 1998–99). Bd Mem., Anglian Water Authy, 1987–89; non-exec. Dir, Anglian Water, 1989–98. Chairman: English Nature, 1990–98; ENTRUST, Envmtl Trusts Scheme Regulatory Body, 1996–2002; Member: Royal Commn on Environmental Pollution, 1981–92; NERC, 1982–88; Foundn for Eur. Envmtl Policy, 1987–98 (Chm., 1990–98); UK Round Table on Sustainable Develt, 1994–98; Broads Authy, 1988–99; Harwich Haven Authy, 1989–97 (Vice Chm., 1995–97); NCC, 1990–91; Suffolk Coastal DC, 1974–83; Pres., Suffolk Wildlife Trust (formerly Suffolk Trust for Nature Conservation), 1979–; Chm. Adv. Cttee, NERC Centre for Ecology and Hydrology, 1998–2005; Pres., Haven Gateway Partnership, 2001–. Trustee, BM (Natural History), 1982–86. Skinner and Freeman of the City of London. DL Suffolk, 1984. FZS; FRGS; FIBiol; MBOU. Hon. FCIWEM; Hon. FIWM; Hon. FLS 2006. Hon. DSc: Aberdeen, 1989; Cranfield, 1996. Founder's Medal, RGS, 1995. OStJ. Hon. Johan Bintang Sarawak, 1997; Hon. Panglima Negara Bintang Sarawak, 2005. *Publications:* Mammals of Borneo, 1965, 2nd edn 1977; Mammals of Malaya, 1969, 2nd edn 1978; (with D. R. Wells) Birds of the Malay Peninsula, 1976; Riches of the Wild: mammals of South East Asia, 1987, 2nd edn 1991; (ed) Key Environments: Malaysia, 1988; (with D. S. Edwards) Belalong: a tropical rain forest, 1994; Wonders of Nature in South-East Asia, 1997; (trans.) The Ballad of Jerjezang, 2001; (with C. K. Lim) Swiftlets of Borneo: builders of edible nests, 2002. *Heir: s* Lord Medway, *qv. Fax:* (home) (01728) 663339.

CRANE, Nicholas Peter; writer and broadcaster, since 1979; *b* 9 May 1954; *s* of Harold and Naomi Crane; *m* 1991, Annabel Huxley; one *s* two *d. Educ:* St Cedd's Primary Sch., Chelmsford; Ketteringham Hall Prep. Sch.; Town Close House Prep. Sch., Norwich; Wymondham Coll.; Cambridgeshire Coll. of Arts & Technol., Cambridge (BA Hons Geog., Univ. of London). Cyclists Touring Club, 1976–78. Presenter: documentaries, BBC Radio 4: Journey to the Centre of the Earth, 1987; Forbidden Journey, 1989; From Ancient Sparta to the Gates of Hell, 1990; television: Blazing Pedals, 1990; The Pyrenees (for Wilderness Walks series), 1998; Map Man, Series 1, 2004, Series 2, 2005; Coast, Series 1, Christmas Special, 2005, Series 2, 2006, Series 3, 2007; Great British Journeys, 2007; producer, High Trails to Istanbul, 1995. Pres., Globetrotters Club, 1990–93; Mem. Mgt Cttee, Soc. of Authors, 2000–03; Mem. RSL. FRGS (Chm., Indep. Travellers' Seminar, 1989–90; Mem. Council, 2004–07). Editl Adv. Gp, Geographical magazine, 1999–. Come to Britain Trophy, BTA, 1977; Mungo Park Medal, RSGS, 1993; journalism award, British Guild of Travel Writers, 1996. *Publications:* (jtly) The CTC Route Guide to Cycling in Britain & Ireland, 1980; Cycling in Europe, 1984; (with Richard Crane) Bicycles up Kilimanjaro, 1985; (with Richard Crane) Journey to the Centre of the Earth, 1987; The Great Bicycle Adventure, 1987; Nick Crane's Action Sports, 1989; Atlas Biker, 1990; Clear Waters Rising: a mountain walk across Europe, 1996 (Thomas Cook/Daily Telegraph Travel Book Award, 1997); Two Degrees West: a walk along England's Meridian, 1999; Mercator: the man who mapped the planet, 2002; Great British Journeys, 2007. *Recreations:* walking, sailing. *Address:* c/o A. P. Watt Ltd, 20 John Street, WC1N 2DR. *Club:* Travellers (Hon. Mem.).

CRANE, Hon. Sir Peter (Francis), Kt 2000; a Judge of the High Court of Justice, Queen's Bench Division, 2000–07; *b* 14 Jan. 1940; *s* of late Prof. Francis Roger Crane and Jean Berenice Crane (*née* Hadfield); *m* 1967, Elizabeth Mary Pittman; four *d. Educ:* Nottingham High Sch.; Highgate Sch.; Gonville and Caius Coll., Cambridge (MA, LLM); Tulane Univ., New Orleans (LLM). Called to the Bar, Gray's Inn, 1964 (Barstow Scholar, 1963); in practice on Midland and Oxford Circuit, 1965–87; Recorder, 1982–87; a Circuit Judge, 1987–2000; Resident Judge, Peterborough Crown and County Court, 1992–2000. Mem., Senate of Inns of Court and the Bar, 1983–86 (Member: Professional Conduct Cttee, 1984–86; Bar Cttee, 1985–86). Mem., Judicial Studies Bd, 1993–96, 2001–06 (Chm., Criminal Cttee, 2001–06). Mem., Sentencing Guidelines Council, 2004–06. Chairman: Kettering Constituency Liberal Assoc., 1981–84; Pytchley Parish Council, 1985–86. *Publication:* (co-ed) Phipson on Evidence, 14th edn 1990, 15th edn 2000. *Recreations:* walking, gardening, reading, wine. *Address:* Royal Courts of Justice, Strand, WC2A 2LL.

CRANE, Sir Peter (Robert), Kt 2004; PhD; FRS 1998; John and Marion Sullivan Professor, Department of Geophysical Sciences, University of Chicago, since 2006; *b* 18 July 1954; *s* of Walter Robert Crane and Dorothy Mary Crane; *m* 1986, Elinor Margaret Hamer; one *s* one *d. Educ:* Univ. of Reading (BSc 1975; PhD 1981). Lectr, Dept of Botany, Univ. of Reading, 1978–81; Post-doctoral Res. Schol., Indiana Univ., 1981–82; Field Museum, Chicago: Curator, Dept of Geology, 1982–92; Vice Pres., Acad. Affairs, 1992–99; Dir, 1995–99; Dir, Royal Botanic Gardens, Kew, 1999–2006. Visiting Professor: Univ. of Reading, 1999–2006; Royal Holloway, Univ. of London, 2000–06; ICSTM, 2003–06. President: Paleontol Soc., 1998–2000; Palaeontol Assoc., 2004–06. Foreign Associate, Nat Acad. of Scis, USA, 2001; Foreign Member: Royal Swedish Acad. of Scis, 2002; Acad. Leopoldina, 2004. *Publications:* (ed jtly) The Origins of Angiosperms and their Biological Consequences, 1987; (ed jtly) The Evolution, Systematics and Fossil History of the Hamamelidae, vols 1 and 2, 1989; (jtly) The Origin and Diversification of Land Plants, 1997. *Address:* Department of Geophysical Sciences, University of Chicago, 5734 S Ellis Avenue, Chicago, IL 60637, USA.

CRANFIELD, Rev. Prof. Charles Ernest Burland, FBA 1982; Emeritus Professor of Theology, University of Durham, since 1980; *b* 13 Sept. 1915; *s* of Charles Ernest Cranfield and Beatrice Mary Cranfield (*née* Tubbs); *m* 1953, Ruth Elizabeth Gertrude, *d* of Rev. T. Bole; two *d. Educ:* Mill Hill Sch.; Jesus Coll., Cambridge; Wesley House, Cambridge. MA Cantab. Research in Basel, cut short before it properly began by outbreak of war. Probationer in Methodist Church, 1939; ordained 1941; Minister, Shoeburyness; Chaplain to the Forces, 1942–46; from end of hostilities worked with German prisoners-of-war and was first staff chaplain to POW Directorate, War Office; Minister, Cleethorpes, 1946–50; admitted to Presbyterian Church of England (now United Reformed Church) as a minister, 1954. Lecturer in Theology, Durham Univ., 1950–62; Sen. Lectr, 1962–66; Reader, 1966–78; Prof. of Theology (personal), 1978–80. Joint general editor, new series of International Critical Commentary, 1966–2005. Hon. DD Aberdeen, 1980. Burkitt Medal for Biblical Studies, 1989. *Publications:* The First Epistle of Peter, 1950, 4th imp. 1958; The Gospel according to Saint Mark, 1959, supplemented and somewhat revised over the years, 13th imp. 2000; I and II Peter and Jude, 1960; A Ransom for Many, 1963; The Service of God, 1965; A Commentary on Romans 12–13, 1965; A Critical and Exegetical Commentary on the Epistle to the Romans, vol. 1 1975, 14th imp. 2007, vol. 2 1979, 10th imp. 2006; Romans: a shorter commentary, 1985, 6th imp. 2001; If God Be For Us: a collection of sermons, 1985; The Bible and Christian Life: a collection of essays, 1985; The Apostles' Creed: a faith to live by, 1993, 3rd imp. 2004; On Romans and Other New Testament Essays, 1998; contribs to composite works and to various theological periodicals. *Address:* 30 Albert Street, Western Hill, Durham City DH1 4RL. *T:* (0191) 384 3096.

CRANLEY, Viscount; Rupert Charles William Bullard Onslow; *b* 16 June 1967; *s* and *heir* of 7th Earl of Onslow, *qv*; *m* 1999, Leigh, *d* of late E. Jones-Fenleigh, one *d. Educ:* Eton; Western Kentucky Univ., USA. *Recreations:* photography, riding, shooting. *Address:* Temple Court, Clandon Park, Guildford, Surrey GU4 7RQ.

CRANSTON, David Alan, CBE 1993; Director General, National Association of Pension Funds, 2000–01; *b* 20 Oct. 1945; *s* of Stanley Cranston and Mary Cranston (*née* Fitzherbert); *m* 1968, Pippa Ann Reynolds; three *d. Educ:* Strathallan Sch., Perthshire; RMA, Sandhurst. Commnd RA, 1966; Army Staff Course, 1979–80; transf. to AAC, 1981; COS HQ, British Forces, Belize, 1983; DS, RMCS Shrivenham, 1984–86; Comd, 4th Regt, AAC, 1986–88; COS, 2nd Inf. Div., 1988–90; Higher Comd and Staff Course, 1990; Comd, British Army Aviation, Germany, 1990–92; Dep. Head of Mission, EC Monitor Mission to former Yugoslavia, 1992; rcds, 1993; Dep. Comdr, Multinational Airmobile Div., 1994–95. Head of Mem. Relns, PIA, 1995–97; Head of Gp Compliance, Royal Bank of Scotland, 1997–2000. Chm., British Biathlon Union, 1996–. *Recreations:* gardening, reading, tennis, ski-ing. *Club:* Army and Navy.

CRANSTON, Hon. Sir Ross (Frederick), Kt 2007; FBA 2007; **Hon. Mr Justice Cranston;** a Judge of the High Court of Justice, Queen's Bench Division, since 2007; *b* 23 July 1948; *s* of late Frederick Hugh Cranston and of Edna Elizabeth Cranston (*née* Davies); *m* 1st, 1976, Prof. Jane Stapleton (marr. diss. 1985); 2nd, 1988, Anna Whyatt (marr. diss. 1998); one *d*; *m* 2007, Hazel Phillips. *Educ:* Univ. of Queensland (BA 1970; LLB 1971); Harvard Law Sch. (LLM 1973); Oxford (DPhil 1976; DCL 1998). Called to the Bar, Gray's Inn, 1976, Bencher, 1998; Asst Recorder, 1991–97; Recorder, 1997–2007; QC 1998. Lectr, Univ. of Warwick, 1975–77; Res. Fellow, 1978–81, Sen Lectr, then Reader, 1981–86, Assoc. Dean, 1984–86, Faculty of Law, ANU Canberra; W G. Hart Sen. Fellow, QMC, 1983–84; Queen Mary and Westfield College, London University: Sir John Lubbock Prof. of Banking Law, 1986–92; Dean, Faculty of Laws 1988–91; Dir, Centre for Commercial Law Studies, 1989–92; London School of Economics and Political Science: Cassel Prof. of Commercial Law, 1993–97; Vis. Prof. 1997–2005, 2007–; Centennial Prof. of Law, 2005–07. Acad. Consultant, Woolf Inquiry into Access to Justice, 1994–96; Consultant to various international bodies including World Bank, IMF, UN Conf. on Trade and Develt, Commonwealth Secretariat 1988–96. Contested (Lab) Richmond, Yorks, 1992. MP (Lab) Dudley North, 1997–2005 Solicitor-Gen., 1998–2001. Chairman: All-Party Parly Gp on Alcohol Misuse, 2002–05 All-Party Parly Gp for the Bar, 2002–05. Judiciary Assessment Mission, Turkey, 2005 Justice and Home Affairs Peer Rev. Mission, Bulgaria, 2006, Croatia, 2007, Eur. Commn Vice Pres., 1991–92, Pres., 1992–93, SPTL. Dep. Chm., 1993–96, Chm., 1996–97, Bd of Trustees, Public Concern at Work. Trustee: Build It Internat., 2006–; NOFAS-UK 2006–. Chair, Soc. of Labour Lawyers, 2003–06; Pres., Internat. Acad. of Commercial and Consumer Law, 2004–06. Mem., American Law Inst., 1999. FCIArb 2006. *Publications:* Consumers and the Law, 1978, 3rd edn, as Cranston's Consumers and the Law, 2000 Regulating Business, 1979; Legal Foundations of the Welfare State, 1985; Law Government and Public Policy, 1987; (ed) Banks, Liability and Risk, 1990, 2nd edn 1995 (ed) The Single Market and the Law of Banking, 1991, 2nd edn 1995; (ed with R. M Goode) Contemporary Issues in International Commercial Law, 1993; (ed) European Banking Law, 1993, 2nd edn 1999; (ed) Legal Ethics and Professional Responsibility 1995; (ed with A. Zuckerman) Reform of the Administration of Civil Justice, 1995; (ed) Making Commercial Law, 1997; Principles of Banking Law, 1997, 2nd edn 2002; How Law Works, 2006. *Address:* Royal Courts of Justice, Strand, WC2A 2LL.

CRANWORTH, 3rd Baron *cr* 1899; **Philip Bertram Gurdon;** Lieutenant, Royal Wiltshire Yeomanry; *b* 24 May 1940; *s* of Hon. Robin Gurdon (killed in action, 1942 and Hon. Yoskyl Pearson (she *m* 2nd, 1944, as his 2nd wife, Lieut-Col. Alistair Gibb, and 3rd, 1962, as his 2nd wife, 1st Baron McCorquodale of Newton, PC, KCVO; she *d* 1979), *d* of 2nd Viscount Cowdray; *S* grandfather, 1964; *m* 1968, Frances Henrietta Montagu Douglas Scott (*d* 2000), *d* of late Lord William Scott and Lady William Scott; two *s* one *d*; *m* 2006, Cameron Vail Noble. *Educ:* Eton; Magdalene Coll., Cambridge. *Heir: s* Hon. Sacha William Robin Gurdon, [*b* 12 Aug. 1970; *m* 2001, Susannah, *d* of Martin Bates]. *Address:* Grundisburgh Hall, Woodbridge, Suffolk IP13 6TW.

See also Marquess of Huntly.

CRASTON, Rev. Canon (Richard) Colin; Vicar, then Rector, St Paul with Emmanuel, Bolton, 1977–93, retired; Hon. Canon, Manchester Cathedral, 1968–95, Canon Emeritus, since 1995; Chaplain to the Queen, 1985–92; *b* 31 Dec. 1922; *s* of Albert Edward Craston and Ethel Craston; *m* 1st, 1948, Ruth Taggart (*d* 1992); one *s* one *d*; 2nd, 1993, Rev. Brenda H. Fullalove. *Educ:* Preston Grammar Sch.; Univ. of Bristol (BA Hons); Univ. of London (BD Hons); Tyndale Hall, Bristol. Served War, RN, 1941–46. Ordained 1951; Curate, St Nicholas, Durham, 1951–54; Vicar, St Paul, Bolton, 1954–76; Priest i/c, 1964–66, Vicar, 1966–76, Emmanuel, Bolton; Area Dean of Bolton, 1972–92. Chm., House of Clergy, Dio. of Manchester, 1982–94; Member: Gen. Synod, 1970–95 (Mem., Standing Cttee, 1975–95; Chm., Business Sub-Cttee, 1991–95); ACC, 1981–96 (Mem., Standing Cttee, 1981–96; Vice-Chm., 1986–90; Chm., 1990–96); Crown Appts Commn, 1982–92. DD Lambeth, 1992. *Publications:* Biblical Headship and the Ordination of Women, 1986; (ed) Open to the Spirit—Essays on Renewal, 1987; (contrib.) Authority in the Anglican Communion, 1987; (jtly) Anglicanism and the Universal Church, 1990; (ed) By Word and Deed, 1992; Debtor to Grace, 1998; The Silence of Eternity, 2003; Evangelical and Evolving: following the gospel in a changing world, 2006; contrib. Anvil. *Address:* 12 Lever Park Avenue, Horwich, Bolton BL6 7LE. *T:* (01204) 699972; *e-mail:* colbren@craston.fsnet.co.uk. *Club:* Union Jack.

CRATHORNE, 2nd Baron *cr* 1959; **(Charles) James Dugdale;** JP; Bt 1945; Lord-Lieutenant of North Yorkshire, since 1999; consultant and lecturer in Fine Art; *b* 12 Sept. 1939; *s* of 1st Baron Crathorne, PC, TD, and Nancy, OBE (*d* 1969), *d* of Sir Charles Tennant, 1st Bt; *S* father, 1977; *m* 1970, Sylvia Mary, *yr d* of Brig. Arthur Herbert Montgomery, OBE, TD; one *s* two *d*. *Educ:* Eton College; Trinity Coll., Cambridge. MA Cantab (Fine Arts). Impressionist and Modern Painting Dept, Sotheby & Co., 1963–66; Assistant to the President, Parke-Bernet, New York, 1966–69; James Dugdale & Associates, London, Independent Fine Art Consultancy Service, 1969–77; James Crathorne & Associates, 1977–; Director: Woodhouse Securities, 1989–99; Cliveden Ltd, 1999–2002; Hand Picked Hotels Ltd, 2001–02. Member: Yorks Regl Cttee, NT, 1978–84 and 1988–94; Council, RSA, 1982–88; Exec. Cttee, Georgian Gp, 1985– (Chm., 1990–99); Cons. Adv. Gp on Arts and Heritage, 1988–98; Chm., Jt Cttee, Nat. Amenity Socs, 1996–99 (Dep. Chm., 1993–96); President: Cleveland Assoc., NT, 1982–96; Yarm Civic Soc., 1987–; Hambledon Dist, CPRE, 1988–; Cleveland Family History Soc., 1988–; Cleveland Sea Cadets, 1988–; Cleveland and N Yorks Br., 1997–2003, Cleveland and S Durham Br., 2003–, Magistrates' Assoc.; Cleveland Search and Rescue Team, 1998–; Yorks and Humberside RFCA, 2005– (Vice Pres., 1999–2005); Vice President: Cleveland Wildlife Trust, 1990–; Public Monuments and Sculpture Assoc., 1997–; N Yorks County Scouts, 1998–; N of England RFCA, 2001–; Patron, Cleveland Community Foundn, 1990–. Member: Works of Art Sub-Cttee, H of L, 1983–2001 (Chm., 2004–07); Editorial Bd, House Magazine, 1983–; Hon. Secretary: All-Party Parly Arts and Heritage Gp, 1981–; All-Party Photography Gp, 1997–; elected Mem., H of L, 1999. Trustee: Captain Cook Trust, 1978– (Chm., 1993–); Georgian Theatre Royal, Richmond, Yorks, 1970–; Nat. Heritage Meml Fund, 1992–95; Patron, Attingham Trust for Study of the British Country House, 1991–; Hon. Patron, Friends of Yorks Sculpture Park, 1992–. Church Warden, All Saints, Crathorne, 1977–. Annual lecture tours to America, 1970–90; lecture series, Metropolitan Mus., NY, 1981; Australian Bicentennial Lecture Tour, 1988. Member Court: Univ. of Leeds, 1985–97; Univ. of York, 1999–; Univ. of Hull, 1999–; Gov., Queen Margaret's Sch. York Ltd, 1986–99. FRSA 1972. DL Cleveland, 1983, N Yorks, 1996; JP N Yorks, 1999. KStJ 1999. Golden Jubilee Medal, 2002. *Exhibitions:* Photographs: Middlesbrough Art Gall., 1980; Georgian Th. Royal, Richmond, N Yorks, 2005; All Party Photography Gp annual exhibn, Westminster and touring, 1992–. *Publications:* Edouard Vuillard, 1967; (co-author) Tennant's Stalk, 1973; (co-author) A Present from Crathorne, 1989; Cliveden: the place and the people, 1995; The Royal Crescent Book of Bath, 1998; (co-photographer) Parliament in Pictures, 1999; contribs to Apollo and The Connoisseur. *Recreations:* photography, travel, collecting, country pursuits, jazz. *Heir: s* Hon. Thomas Arthur John Dugdale, *b* 30 Sept. 1977. *Address:* Crathorne House, Yarm, N Yorks TS15 0AT. *T:* (01642) 700431, *Fax:* (01642) 700632; House of Lords, SW1A 0PW. *T:* (020) 7219 5224, *Fax:* (020) 7219 2772; *e-mail:* crathornej@parliament.uk, james@jcrathorne.fsnet.co.uk. *Clubs:* Brooks's, Pratt's.

CRAUFURD, Sir Robert (James), 9th Bt *cr* 1781; *b* 18 March 1937; *s* of Sir James Gregan Craufurd, 8th Bt and Ruth Marjorie (*d* 1998), *d* of Frederic Corder; *S* father, 1970; *m* 1st, 1964, Catherine Penelope (marr. diss.), *yr d* of late Captain Horatio Westmacott, Torquay; three *d*; 2nd, 1987, Georgina Anne, *d* of late John D. Russell, Lymington. *Educ:* Harrow; University College, Oxford. Elected Member of the London Stock Exchange, 1969. *Address:* East Grove, Grove Road, Lymington, Hants SO41 3RF.

CRAUSBY, David Anthony; MP (Lab) Bolton North East, since 1997; *b* 17 June 1946; *s* of Thomas Crausby and Kathleen Lavin; *m* 1965, Enid Anne Noon; two *s*. *Educ:* Derby Grammar Sch., Bury. Apprentice centre lathe turner, 1962, skilled turner, 1967; Works Convenor, AEEU (formerly AEU), 1978–97. Mem (Lab) Bury MDC, 1979–92. Contested (Lab): Bury N, 1987; Bolton NE, 1992. *Recreations:* football, walking, cinema. *Address:* 580 Blackburn Road, Bolton BL1 7AL. *T:* (01204) 303340.

CRAVEN, family name of **Earl of Craven**.

CRAVEN, 9th Earl of, *cr* 1801; **Benjamin Robert Joseph Craven;** Baron Craven, 1665; Viscount Uffington, 1801; *b* 13 June 1989; *s* of 8th Earl and of Teresa Maria Bernadette Craven; *S* father, 1990. *Heir: cousin* Rupert José Evelyn Craven, Lt-Comdr RN [*b* 22 March 1926; *m* 1st, 1955, Margaret Campbell (*d* 1985), *d* of Alexander Smith, MBE; 2nd, 2000, Susan Lilian Margaret Eaton].

CRAVEN, Archdeacon of; *see* Slater, Ven. P. J.

CRAVEN, Janet; *see* Morrison, J.

CRAVEN, Sir John (Anthony), Kt 1996; Member, Board of Managing Directors, Deutsche Bank AG, Frankfurt, 1990–96; Chairman, Morgan Grenfell, later Deutsche Morgan Grenfell, Group PLC, 1989–97 (Chief Executive, 1987–89); *b* 23 Oct. 1940; *s* of William Herbert Craven and Hilda Lucy Craven; *m* 1st, 1961, Gillian Margaret (*née* Murray); one *s* one *d*; 2nd, 1970, Jane Frances (*née* Stiles-Allen); three *s*; 3rd, 2005, Ning Chang. *Educ:* Michaelhouse, S Africa; Jesus Coll., Cambridge (BA Hons Law); Queen's Univ., Kingston, Ont. Clarkson Gordon & Co., Toronto, Chartered Accountants, 1961–64; Wood Gundy, Investment Bankers, 1964–67; S. G. Warburg & Co., 1967–73, Dir 1969–73; Gp Chief Exec., White Weld & Co. Ltd, 1973–78; Vice Chm., S. G. Warburg & Co., 1979; Founder and Chm., Phoenix Securities Ltd, 1981–89; Dir, Mercury Securities Ltd, 1979. Non-executive Chairman: Tootal Group PLC, 1985–91; Lonmin plc (formerly Lonrho), 1997–; GEMS Funds, HK, 1998–; Fleming Family & Partners, 2003–07 (non-exec. Dir, 2000–); Patagonia Gold plc, 2004–; Director: Rothmans Internat. NV, 1993–95; Rothmans Internat. BV, 1995–99; non-executive Director: Reuters plc, 1997–2004; Robert Fleming Hldgs Ltd, 1999–2000; Ducati Motor Hldgs SpA, 1999–2000. Mem., Conseil d'Administration, Société Générale de Surveillance, Switzerland, 1989–98; Dir, SIB, 1990–93. Member: Ontario Inst. of Chartered Accts; Canadian Inst. of Chartered Accountants. *Recreations:* hunting, shooting, ski-ing. *Address:* Lonmin plc, 4 Grosvenor Place, SW1X 7YL. *Clubs:* Links (New York).

CRAVEN, Prof. John Anthony George; Vice-Chancellor, University of Portsmouth, since 1997; *b* 17 June 1949; *s* of late George Marriott Craven and Dorothy Maude Craven (*née* Walford); *m* 1974, Laura Elizabeth Loftis; one *s* one *d*. *Educ:* Pinner GS; King's Coll., Cambridge (BA 1970; MA 1974). Kennedy Meml Schol., MIT, 1970–71; University of Kent at Canterbury: Lectr in Econs, 1971–76; Sen. Lectr, 1976–80; Reader, 1980–86; Prof., 1986–96; Dean of Faculty, Social Scis, 1987–91; Pro Vice-Chancellor, 1991–93; Dep. Vice-Chancellor, 1993–96. Vis. Associate Prof., Univ. of Guelph, 1982–83. Chm., University Alliance, 2006–; Mem. Bd, UUK, 2006–. Mem., Archbishops' Council, 2006–. Chair, St Martin's Trust for the Homeless, 1987–96. Governor: South Kent Coll., 1991–96; Highbury Coll., 1997–2003; St Luke's Sch., Portsmouth, 2002–. Dir, New Th. Royal, Portsmouth, 1999–. Hon. DSc Univ. Teknologi, Malaysia. *Publications:* The Distribution of the Product, 1979; Introduction to Economics, 1984, 2nd edn 1990; Social Choice, 1992; articles in learned jls. *Recreations:* gardening, choral singing, house restoration. *Address:* (home) Fyning Cross, Rogate, Petersfield GU31 5EF. *T:* (01730) 821392; (office) University House, Portsmouth PO1 2UP. *T:* (023) 9284 3190; *e-mail:* john.craven@port.ac.uk.

CRAVEN, Sir Philip (Lee), Kt 2005; MBE 1991; President, International Paralympic Committee, since 2001; *b* 4 July 1950; *s* of Herbert and Hilda Craven; *m* 1974, Jocelyne Halgand; one *s* one *d*. *Educ:* Manchester Univ. (BA Hons (Geog.) 1972). Hd of Secretariat, British Coal Corp., 1986–91; Pres., 1989–2002, CEO, 1994–98, Internat. Wheelchair Basketball Fedn; Performance Dir, GB Men's Wheelchair Basketball Team, 1998–2001. Played wheelchair basketball for GB, 1969–93: Team Captain, 1982–88; Gold Medal, Commonwealth Games, 1970; European Championships: Bronze Medal, 1970; Gold Medal, 1971, 1973, 1974; Silver Medal, 1993; 4th Place, Paralympic Games, 1974; Bronze Medal, World Championship, 1975; Silver Medal, Internat. Stoke Mandeville Games, 1986; Gold Medal, European Champions Cup, 1994; Nat. Table Tennis Champion, 1977. Chm., GB Wheelchair Basketball Assoc., 1977–80, 1984–87 and 1989–94. International Olympic Committee: Mem., 2003–; Member: Sport and Envmt Commn, 2002–05; 2008 Beijing Co-ordination Commn, 2002–; Culture and Olympic Educn Commn, 2005–. Foundn Bd Mem., World Anti-Doping Agency, 2002–. Hon. DSc Manchester Metropolitan, 2006; Hon. LLD Nottingham, 2007. Medaille d'argent de la Jeunesse et des Sports (France), 1973; Grande Ufficiale, Order of Merit (Italy), 2006; Chevalier, Ordre Ducal de la Croix de Bourgogne (France), 2007. *Recreations:* playing wheelchair basketball, gardening, culture of wine. *Address:* International Paralympic Committee, Adenauerallee 212–214, 53113 Bonn, Germany. *T:* (228) 2097200, *Fax:* (228) 2097209; *e-mail:* info@paralympic.org.

CRAWFORD, 29th Earl of, *cr* 1398, **AND BALCARRES,** 12th Earl of, *cr* 1651; **Robert Alexander Lindsay,** KT 1996; GCVO 2002; PC 1972; Lord Lindsay of Crawford, before 1143; Lord Lindsay of Balcarres, 1633; Lord Balniel, 1651; Baron Wigan (UK), 1826; Baron Balniel (Life Peer), 1974; Premier Earl of Scotland; Head of House of Lindsay; Lord Chamberlain to the Queen Mother, 1992–2002; *b* 5 March 1927; *er s* of 28th Earl of Crawford and 11th of Balcarres, KT, GBE, and Mary (*d* 1994), 3rd *d* of late Lord Richard Cavendish, PC, CB, CMG; *S* father, 1975; *m* 1949, Ruth Beatrice, *d* of Leo Meyer-Bechtler, Zürich; two *s* two *d*. *Educ:* Eton; Trinity College, Cambridge. Served with Grenadier Guards, 1945–49. MP (C) Hertford, 1955–74, Welwyn and Hatfield, Feb.–Sept. 1974; Parliamentary Private Secretary: to Financial Secretary of Treasury, 1955–57; to Minister of Housing and Local Government, 1957–60; Opposition front-bench spokesman on health and social security, 1967–70; Minister of State for Defence, 1970–72; Minister of State for Foreign and Commonwealth Affairs, 1972–74. First Crown Estate Comr, 1980–85. Chairman: Lombard North Central Bank, 1976–80; Abela Hldgs (UK), 1983–95; Director: Nat. Westminster Bank, 1975–88; Scottish American Investment Co., 1978–88; a Vice-Chm., Sun Alliance & London Insurance Gp, 1975–91. President, Rural District Councils Assoc., 1959–65; Chairman: National Association for Mental Health, 1963–70; Historic Buildings Council for Scotland, 1976–83; Royal Commn on Ancient and Historical Monuments of Scotland, 1985–95; Bd of Trustees, Nat. Library of Scotland, 1990–2000. DL Fife, 1976–2003. *Heir: s* Lord Balniel, *qv*. *Address:* House of Lords, SW1A 0PW.

CRAWFORD, Alistair Stephen; Chief Executive, Psion, 2003–06; *b* 4 Jan. 1953; *s* of late Daniel Clark Crawford and Joan Crawford; *m* 1981, Susan Potter; two *d*. *Educ:* Oriel Coll., Oxford (MA Jurisprudence). Pres. and CEO, Computer Sciences Corp. (UK), 1989–94; Sen. Vice Pres., Oracle Corp., 1995–2000; Chief Operating Officer, CMG plc, 2001; CEO, Logica CMG plc, 2002–03. *Club:* Reform.

CRAWFORD, Prof. Andrew Charles, FRS 1990; Professor of Neurophysiology, Cambridge University, since 1992; Fellow of Trinity College, Cambridge, since 1974; *b* 12 Jan. 1949; *s* of Charles and Vera Crawford; *m* 1974, Catherine Jones; one *s* one *d*. *Educ:* King Edward VI Camp Hill Sch., Birmingham; Downing Coll., Cambridge (BA 1970); Emmanuel Coll., Cambridge (MA, PhD 1974). Cambridge University: Research Fellow, Emmanuel Coll., 1972; Univ. Demonstrator, 1974; Lectr, 1977; Reader in Sensory Physiology, 1987. *Publications:* contribs on physiology of hearing, in learned jls. *Address:* Physiological Laboratory, Downing Street, Cambridge CB2 3EG. *T:* (01223) 333879.

CRAWFORD, Bruce; *see* Crawford, R. H. B.

CRAWFORD, Charles Graham, CMG 1998; HM Diplomatic Service, retired; consultant/mediator; *b* 22 May 1954; *s* of Graham Wellington James Crawford and Edith Ellen Crawford; *m* 1990, Helen Margaret Walsh; two *s* one *d*. *Educ:* St John's Coll., Oxford (BA Hons Jurisprudence 1976); Lincoln's Inn (part II Bar exams 1977); Fletcher Sch. of Law and Diplomacy, Boston, USA (MA 1979). Entered FCO, 1979; Second, later First Sec., Belgrade, 1981–84; FCO (air services then speechwriter), 1984–87; First Sec., Pretoria/Cape Town, 1987–91; FCO, 1991–93; Political Counsellor, Moscow, 1993–96; Ambassador to Bosnia and Herzegovina, 1996–98; Weatherhead Center for Internat. Affairs, Harvard Univ., 1998–99; Dep. Political Dir, FCO, 1999–2000; Dir, SE Europe, FCO, 2000; Ambassador to Federal Republic of Yugoslavia, subseq. Serbia and Montenegro, 2001–03; Ambassador to Poland, 2003–07. Qualified Mediator, 2007. *Recreations:* chess, music, blogoir. *Address:* *e-mail:* charlescrawf@gmail.com; *web:* www.charlescrawford.biz.

CRAWFORD, Sir Frederick (William), Kt 1986; DL; FREng; Chairman, Criminal Cases Review Commission, 1996–2003; Vice-Chancellor, Aston University, 1980–96; *b* 28 July 1931; *s* of William and Victoria Maud Crawford; *m* 1963, Béatrice M. J. Hutter, LèsL, MA, PhD, Paris; one *d* (one *s* decd). *Educ:* George Dixon Grammar Sch., Birmingham; Univ. of London (BSc Eng (1st cl. hons) 1952; MSc 1958; DSc 1975); Univ. of Liverpool (DipEd 1956; PhD 1955; DEng 1965); Open Univ. (DipStat 2006; BA Maths (1st cl. hons) 2007). Pres., Guild of Undergraduates, 1955–56, Mem. Court, 1955–62 and 1981–, Univ. of Liverpool; Treas., NUS, 1957–59; Winner, NUS-Observer Fifth Nat. Student Debating Tourn., 1958, followed by ESU debating tour of USA. FInstP 1964; FAPS 1965; FIET (FIEE 1965); FIEEE 1972; FIMA 1978; FREng (FEng 1985). Research Trainee, J. Lucas Ltd, 1948–52; Scientist, NCB Mining Res. Estabt, 1956–57; Sen. Lectr in Elec. Engrg, CAT Birmingham, 1958–59; Stanford University, California, 1959–82: Res. Associate, W. W. Hansen Labs of Physics, 1959–64; Institute for Plasma Research: Prof. (Research), 1964–67; Associate Prof., 1967–69; Prof., 1969–82; Consulting Prof., 1983–84; Chm., 1974–80; Dir, Centre for Interdisciplinary Res., 1973–77. Vis. Scientist, French Atomic Energy Commn, and Cons. to Comp. Française Thomson-Houston, 1961–62; Visiting Professor: Japan, 1969; Univ. of Paris, 1971; Australia, 1972; Mathematical Inst., Oxford Univ., 1977–78; Vis. Fellow, St Catherine's Coll., Oxford, 1977–78, 1996–97. Union Radio-Scientifique Internationale: Mem., US Nat. Cttee, 1975–81, UK Nat. Cttee, 1980–84; Commn H (Waves in Plasmas): US Chm., 1975–78; Internat. Chm., 1978–81; UK Rep., 1982–84; Chm. Internat. Sci. Cttee, Internat. Conf. on Phenomena in Ionised Gases, 1979–81; Universities Space Research Association: Member: Council, 1973–81 (Chm. 1977–78); Bd of Trustees, 1975–81 (Chm. 1976–77). Dir, Sigma Xi, 1976–78; Mem. Council, Amer. Assoc. of Univ. Profs, 1980–82; Vice-Chm., CVCP, 1993–95; Dir, HEQC, 1994–96; Vice-Pres., Parly and Scientific Cttee, 1992–95 (Vice-Chm., 1989–92). Member: Council, IEE, 1985–88, 1989–92 and 1993–96; Smeatonian Soc. of Civil Engrs, 1995. Director: Birmingham Technology Ltd, 1982–96; West Midlands Technology Transfer Centre, 1985–93; Legal & General Gp plc, 1988–97; Rexam (formerly Bowater) plc, 1989–97; PowerGen plc, 1990–2002. Member: US-UK Educnl Commn, 1981–84; British-North American Cttee, 1987–; Franco-British Council, 1987–98; Vice-President: Birmingham Civic Soc., 1990– (Chm., 1983–88). Founder Mem., Lunar Soc., Birmingham, 1991. Freeman, City of London, 1986; Master: Co. of Engineers, 1996; Co. of Information Technologists, 2000. High Sheriff, W Midlands, 1995, DL W Midlands, 1995. Hon. Bencher, Inner Temple, 1996. CCMI (CBIM 1986; Special Award for Univ. Mgt, 1992). Hon. FCIL (Hon. FIL 1987). Hon. DSc Buckingham, 1996. *Publications:* numerous papers on plasma physics and higher educn. *Address:* 47 Charlbury Road, Oxford OX2 6UX. *T:* (01865) 554 707. *Club:* Athenæum.

CRAWFORD, Geoffrey Douglas, CVO 2000 (LVO 1995); Director of Corporate Affairs, Australian Broadcasting Corporation, 2002–05; *b* 29 Sept. 1950; *s* of late Rev. Canon Douglas Crawford and of Edna Crawford; *m* 1st, 1980 (marr. diss.); one *s* two *d*; 2nd, 1998, Catherine Banks. *Educ:* King's Sch., Parramatta, NSW; Univ. of Sydney (BA Hons). Entered Australian Dept of Foreign Affairs, 1974: Third Sec., Port Moresby, 1974–75; Vice-Consul, Lae, 1975–76; lang. trng, Cairo, 1978–80; Second Sec., Jeddah, 1980–82; First Sec., Baghdad, 1983–84; seconded as Asst Press Sec. to the Queen, 1988–93; transferred to Civil List, 1991; Dep. Press Sec., 1993–97, Press Sec. to the Queen, 1997–2000; Consultant, Edelman Public Relations Worldwide (Sydney), 2001–02. *Recreations:* swimming, classical music, reading. *Address:* 13 Wandevan Place, Mittagong, NSW 2575, Australia.

CRAWFORD, Iain; Director, Veterinary Field Service, Ministry of Agriculture, Fisheries and Food, 1988–98; *b* 8 April 1938; *s* of James and Agnes Crawford, Baillieston, Glasgow; *m* 1962, Janette Mary Allan; two *s* one *d*. *Educ:* Coatbridge High Sch., Lanarks; Glasgow Univ. (BVMS). MRCVS 1961. Entered private vet. practice, 1961; joined MAFF as a Vet. Officer, 1968; Dep. Regl Vet. Officer, Bristol, 1981; Vet. Head of Sect. (Regl Vet. Officer), 1983; Asst Chief Vet. Officer, 1986. *Recreations:* sailing, walking.

CRAWFORD, Maj.-Gen. (Ian) Patrick, GM 1964; FFCM, FFOM; Commandant and Postgraduate Dean, Royal Army Medical College, Millbank, 1989–93; *b* 11 Oct. 1933; *s* of Donald Patrick and Florence Ireland Crawford; *m* 1956, Juliet Treharne James; two *s* one *d*. *Educ:* Chatham House, Ramsgate; St Thomas' Hosp., London. MRCS, LRCP; FFCM 1982; FFOM 1987; DPH, DIH, DTM&H. House Surgeon, Casualty and Orthopaedics and House Physician, Royal Sussex County Hosp., 1959–60; Nat. Service, RAMC, 1960–63; on active service, Borneo, 1962–64; commnd 1963; Regimental MO, 20 Regt RA and 1st/7th Gurkha Rifles, Malaya and Borneo, 1963–68; Staff Officer: Army Health Home Counties Dist, 1968; HQ Singapore Dist, 1968–70; Instructor, Sch. of Army Health, 1970–71; MoD, 1971–72; Exchange Officer, Australia, 1972–75; MoD, 1975–78; HQ 1 BR Corps, 1978–81; Parkes Prof. of Preventive Medicine, Royal Army Med. Coll., 1981–84; Defence Med. Services Directorate, 1984–86; Comdr, Saudi Arabian Nat. Guard Med. Team, 1986–88; Defence Med. Services Directorate, 1988–89. QHP 1991–93. Specialist in Preventive Medicine, Singapore, Australia, PNG, BAOR, Saudi Arabia and UK; Consultant Advr, Saudi Arabia Nat. Guard, Jeddah, 1986–88. Chm. Court of Govs, 1997–, and Mem. Bd, 1994–, LSHTM. Mem. Council, Shipwrecked Fishermen and Mariners' Royal Benevolent Soc., 1994–; Trustee, Florence Nightingale Mus., 1993–. Hon. Lectr, Dept of Occupational Med., Queensland Univ., 1973–75. FRSocMed 1981. OStJ 1992. *Publications:* papers and pubns on military preventive medicine. *Recreations:* golf, computing, travel, bridge. *Address:* Mill Cottage, Mill Lane, Cocking, near Midhurst, W Sussex GU29 0HJ. *T:* (01730) 817982.

CRAWFORD, Prof. James Richard, DPhil, LLD; FBA 2000; barrister; Whewell Professor of International Law, University of Cambridge, and Fellow of Jesus College, Cambridge, since 1992; *b* 14 Nov. 1948; *s* of James Allen and Josephine Margaret Crawford; *m* 1st, 1971, Marisa Luigina (marr. diss. 1991); two *d*; 2nd, 1992, Patricia Hyndman (marr. diss. 1998); two *d*; 3rd, 1998, Joanna Gomula; one *s*. *Educ:* Adelaide Univ. (LLB Hons; BA 1971); Oxford Univ. (DPhil 1977); LLD Cantab 2004. Called to the Bar, High Court of Australia, 1979; SC, NSW, 1997. University of Adelaide: Lectr, 1974; Sen. Lectr, 1977; Reader, 1982; Prof. of Law, 1983; Challis Prof. of Internat. Law, 1986–92, Dean, Faculty of Law, 1990–92, Univ. of Sydney. Chm., Faculty Bd of Law, Univ. of Cambridge, 2003–06. Comr, Australian Law Reform Commn, 1982–90; Mem., UN Internat. Law Commn, 1992–2001. *Publications:* The Creation of States in International Law, 1979, 2nd edn 2006; Australian Courts of Law, 1982, 4th edn 2003; (ed) The Rights of Peoples, 1988; The International Law Commission's Articles on State Responsibility, 2002; International Law as an Open System, 2002. *Recreations:* cricket, reading. *Address:* Lauterpacht Centre for International Law, 5 Cranmer Road, Cambridge CB3 9LW; *e-mail:* JRC1000@cam.ac.uk.

CRAWFORD, (Jeremy) Patrick (Stewart); Chief Executive, Export Credits Guarantee Department, since 2004; *b* 16 Sept. 1952; *s* of Sir (Robert) Stewart Crawford, GCMG, CVO and Mary Katharine (*née* Corbett); *m* 1980, Charlotte Elisabeth Cecily Burnaby-Atkins; one *s* three *d*. *Educ:* Worcester Coll., Oxford (BA Juris.). Called to the Bar, Middle Temple, 1975; Morgan Grenfell & Co. Ltd, then Deutsche Morgan Grenfell, subseq. Deutsche Bank AG, 1976–2002: Man. Dir and Global Hd, Project and Export Finance, 1998–2001; Global Hd, Project Finance, 2001–02; Man. Dir, Emerging Africa Advisers, fund manager of Emerging Africa Infrastructure Fund, 2002–04. *Address:* Export Credits Guarantee Department, PO Box 2200, 2 Exchange Tower, Harbour Exchange Square, E14 9GS. *T:* (020) 7512 7000, *Fax:* (020) 7512 7649.

CRAWFORD, John Michael; Director of Education (formerly Chief Education Officer), Birmingham, 1977–88; *b* 6 Dec. 1938; *s* of James and Emily Crawford; *m* 1962, Geraldine Kay Weaver; two *d*. *Educ:* Ipswich Sch.; University Coll., London (BA); Fitzwilliam House, Cambridge. Asst Master, Merchant Taylor's, Crosby, 1961–63; Admin. Asst, E Suffolk CC, 1963–66; Sen. Admin. Asst, Lancs CC, 1966–68; Asst Educn Officer, W Riding CC, 1968–73; Dep. Educn Officer, Birmingham, 1973–77. *Address:* July Green, Snuff Mill Walk, Bewdley, Worcs DY12 2HG. *T:* (01299) 400174.

CRAWFORD, Lesley Jane; *see* Anderson, L. J.

CRAWFORD, Lionel Vivian, FRS 1988; Principal Scientist, Imperial Cancer Research Fund Tumour Virus Group, Department of Pathology, Cambridge University, 1988–95; *b* 30 April 1932; *s* of John Mitchell Crawford and Fanny May Crawford (*née* Barnett); *m* 1957, Elizabeth Minnie (*née* Green); one *d*. *Educ:* Rendcomb College, Cirencester; Emmanuel College, Cambridge (BA, MA, PhD). Virus Lab., Berkeley, Calif., 1958–59; Calif. Inst. of Technology, 1959–60; Inst. of Virology, Glasgow, 1960–68; Molecular Virology Lab., Imperial Cancer Res. Fund, 1968–88. Mem., EMBO. FRSE 1970. *Publications:* numerous scientific articles. *Recreation:* wood-turning.

CRAWFORD, Michael, OBE 1987; actor, since 1955; *b* 19 Jan. 1942. *Educ:* St Michael's Coll., Bexley; Oakfield Sch., Dulwich. In orig. prodn of Britten's Noyes Fludde and of Let's Make an Opera; *stage appearances include:* Come Blow Your Horn, Prince of Wales, 1961; Travelling Light, 1965; The Anniversary, 1966; No Sex Please, We're British, Strand, 1971; Billy, Drury Lane, 1974; Same Time, Next Year, Prince of Wales, 1976; Flowers for Algernon, Queen's, 1979; Barnum, Palladium, 1981, 1983, Victoria Palace, 1985–86 (Olivier Award; Show Business Personality of the Year, Variety Club of GB); The Phantom of the Opera, Her Majesty's, 1986 (Olivier Award, Best Actor in a Musical), NY, 1988 (Tony Award, Best Actor in a Musical), Los Angeles, 1989; The Music of Andrew Lloyd Webber (concert tour), USA, Australia and UK, 1991–92; EFX, Las Vegas, 1995–96; Dance of the Vampires, NY, 2002–03; The Woman in White, Palace, 2004. *Films include:* Soap Box Derby; Blow Your Own Trumpet; Two Left Feet; The War Lover; Two Living, One Dead; The Knack, 1964 (Variety Club Award for Most Promising Newcomer); A Funny Thing Happened on the Way to the Forum, 1965; The Jokers, How I Won the War, 1966; Hello Dolly, 1968; The Games, 1969; Hello and Goodbye, 1970; Alice in Wonderland, 1972; The Condorman, 1980. Numerous radio broadcasts and TV appearances; *TV series include:* Some Mothers Do 'Ave 'Em; Chalk and Cheese. *Publication:* Parcel Arrived Safely: Tied with String (autobiog.), 1999. *Address:* c/o Knight Ayton Management, 114 St Martin's Lane, WC2N 4BE. *T:* (020) 7836 5333, *Fax:* (020) 7836 8333.

CRAWFORD, Prof. Michael Hewson, FBA 1980; Professor of Ancient History, University College London, since 1986; *b* 7 Dec. 1939; *s* of late Brian Hewson Crawford and Margarethe Bettina (*née* Nagel). *Educ:* St Paul's School; Oriel College, Oxford (BA, MA). Scholar, British School at Rome, 1962–64; Jane Eliza Procter Visiting Fellow, Princeton Univ., 1964–65; Cambridge University: Research Fellow, 1964–69, Fellow, 1969–86, Christ's Coll.; Lectr, 1969–86. Visiting Professor: Univ. of Pavia, 1983, 1992; Ecole Normale Supérieure, Paris, 1984; Univ. of Padua, 1986; Sorbonne, Paris, 1989; San Marino, 1989; Milan, 1990; L'Aquila, 1990; Ecole des Hautes Etudes, Paris, 1997; Ecole des Hautes Etudes en Sciences Sociales, Paris, 1999; Toronto, 2007; Joseph Crabtree Orator, UCL, 2000. Joint Director: Excavations of Fregellae, 1980–86; Valpolcevera Project, 1987–93; Velleia Project, 1994–95; San Martino Project, 1996–. Chm., JACT, 1992–95 (Chm., Ancient History Cttee, 1978–84); Vice-Pres., Roman Soc., 1981–. Membro Straniero, Istituto Lombardo, 1990; MAE 1995; Mem., Reial Acadèmia de Bones Lletres, 1998; Corresp. Member: Accademia Petrarca, 2004; Académie des Inscriptions et Belles Lettres, 2006. Editor: Papers of the British Sch. at Rome, 1975–79; Jl of Roman Studies, 1980–84. Officier, Ordre des Palmes Académiques (France), 2001. *Publications:* Roman Republican Coin Hoards, 1969; Roman Republican Coinage, 1974; The Roman Republic, 1978; La Moneta in Grecia e a Roma, 1981; (with D. Whitehead) Archaic and Classical Greece, 1982; Sources for Ancient History, 1983; Coinage and Money under the Roman Republic, 1985; (with M. Beard) Rome in the Late Republic, 1985; L'impero romano e la struttura economica e sociale delle province, 1986; (with A. M. Burnett) The Coinage of the Roman World in the Late Republic, 1987; (with C. Ligota and J. B. Trapp) Medals and Coins from Budé to Mommsen, 1990; (ed) Antonio Agustín between Renaissance and Counter-reform, 1993; (ed) Roman Statutes, 1995; contribs to Annales, Economic History Rev., Jl of Roman Studies, etc. *Address:* Department of History, University College, Gower Street, WC1E 6BT.

CRAWFORD, Michael James, CMG 2008; HM Diplomatic Service; Counsellor, Foreign and Commonwealth Office, since 2001; *b* London, 3 Feb. 1954; *s* of Sir (Robert) Stewart Crawford, GCMG, CVO and Mary Katharine Crawford (*née* Corbett); *m* 1984, Georgia Anne Moylan; two *s* one *d* (of whom one *s* one *d* are twins). *Educ:* University Coll., Oxford (BA Juris. 1975); St Antony's Coll., Oxford (MPhil Mid. Eastern Studies 1980). Called to the Bar, Inner Temple, 1981; joined FCO, 2001; Second, then First Sec., Cairo, 1983–84; First Secretary: Sana'a, 1985–86; Riyadh, 1986–90; FCO, 1990–92; Warsaw, 1992–95; FCO, 1995–99; Counsellor, Islamabad, 1999–2001. *Recreations:* travel, reading and writing on Middle East and Islam, second-hand bookshops. *Address:* Foreign and Commonwealth Office, King Charles Street, SW1A 2AH.

See also J. P. S. Crawford.

CRAWFORD, Maj.-Gen. Patrick; *see* Crawford, I. P.

CRAWFORD, Patrick; *see* Crawford, J. P. S.

CRAWFORD, His Honour Peter John; QC 1976; a Senior Circuit Judge, 1992–2002 (a Circuit Judge, 1988–92); *b* 23 June 1930; *s* of William Gordon Robertson and Doris Victoria Robertson (*née* Mann, subseq. Crawford); *m* 1st, 1955, Jocelyn Lavender (marr. diss.; she *d* 2004); two *s* two *d*; 2nd, 1979, Ann Allen Travis. *Educ:* Berkhamsted Sch.; Brasenose Coll., Oxford (MA). Called to Bar, Lincoln's Inn, 1953; Bencher, 1984; a Recorder, 1974–88; Resident Judge, Oxford Crown Court, 1991–92; Recorder of Birmingham, 1992–2001; Additional Judge, Court of Appeal (Criminal Div.), 1995–2002; Hon. Recorder of Oxford, 2001–02. Pres., Trent Region, Mental Health Review Tribunal, 1986–2002; Vice Chm., Appeal Cttee, ICA, 1987–88; Member: Council of Justice, 1986–88; Parole Bd, 1992–96. Chm., Disciplinary Ct, Univ. of Oxford, 2004–. Associate, Kathryn Redway Associates, 2004–. Mem., Paddington Borough Council, 1962–65; Chm., W London Family Service Unit, 1972–79; Mem., Family Service Units Nat. Council, 1975–81. Hon. Pres., English Nat. Sect., Internat. Assoc. of Penal Law,

1998–2002. *Recreation:* gardening. *Address:* 13 King's Bench Walk, Temple, EC4Y 7EN. *Club:* Royal Over-Seas League.

CRAWFORD, Prof. Robert, DPhil; FRSE, FEA; Professor of Modern Scottish Literature, School of English, University of St Andrews, since 1995; *b* 23 Feb. 1959; *s* of Robert Alexander Nelson Crawford and Elizabeth Menzies Crawford; *m* 1988, Alice Wales; one *s* one *d. Educ:* Hutchesons' Grammar Sch., Glasgow; Univ. of Glasgow (MA Hons 1981); Balliol Coll., Oxford (DPhil 1985). Elizabeth Wordsworth Jun. Res. Fellow, St Hugh's Coll., Oxford, 1984–87; British Acad. Postdoctoral Res. Fellow, Univ. of Glasgow, 1987–89; University of St Andrews: Lectr in Modern Scottish Lit., 1989–95; Hd, Sch. of English, 2002–05. Ed., Verse mag., 1984–95; Poetry Ed., Polygon, 1991–99. FRSE 1999; FEA 1999. *Publications:* The Savage and the City in the Works of T. S. Eliot, 1987; A Scottish Assembly, 1990; (with W. N. Herbert) Sharawaggi, 1990; (ed) Other Tongues, 1990; (ed jtly) About Edwin Morgan, 1990; The Arts of Alasdair Gray, 1991; Talkies, 1992; Devolving English Literature, 1992, 2nd edn 2000; (ed jtly) Reading Douglas Dunn, 1992; Identifying Poets, 1993; (ed jtly) Liz Lochhead's Voices, 1993; (ed jtly) Talking Verse, 1995; Literature in Twentieth-Century Scotland, 1995; Masculinity, 1996; (ed) Robert Burns and Cultural Authority, 1997; (ed) The Scottish Invention of English Literature, 1998; (ed jtly) The Penguin Book of Poetry from Britain and Ireland since 1945, 1998; Spirit Machines, 1999; (ed jtly) The New Penguin Book of Scottish Verse, 2000; (ed jtly) Scottish Religious Poetry, 2000; The Modern Poet, 2001; The Tip of My Tongue, 2003; (ed) Heaven-Taught Fergusson, 2003; Selected Poems, 2005; (ed) The Book of St Andrews, 2005; (ed) Apollos of the North, 2006; (ed) Contemporary Poetry and Contemporary Science, 2006; Scotland's Books: the Penguin history of Scottish literature, 2007; Full Volume, 2008; The Bard, Robert Burns, a Biography, 2009; (ed jtly) Best Laid Schemes, 2009; (ed) Poems, Chiefly in the Scottish Dialect, 2009. *Recreations:* walking, Scottish nationalism, internationalism, Anglophilia. *Address:* School of English, University of St Andrews, St Andrews, Fife KY16 9AL. *T:* (01334) 462666, *Fax:* (01334) 462655.

CRAWFORD, Robert Gammie, CBE 1990; Chairman, Highlands and Islands Airports Ltd, 1986–93; *b* 20 March 1924; *s* of William and Janet Beveridge Crawford; *m* 1947, Rita Veiss (*d* 2004); one *d. Educ:* Robert Gordon's Coll., Aberdeen. Solicitor of the Supreme Court, England. Navigator, RAF, 1942–47. Practised as Solicitor, 1950–73, Partner, Ince and Co. (Internat. Shipping Lawyers); Director: UK Freight Demurrage and Defence Assoc. Ltd, 1976– (Chm., 1987–90); UK Mutual Steamship Assurance Assoc. Ltd, 1980–94 (Chm., 1983–90); Sturge Aviation Syndicates Management Ltd, 1994–96; L. R. Integrity Management Ltd, 1994–96; Ockham Sturge Aviation Agency, 1996–97; Chairman: Silver Line Ltd, 1974–83; Silver Line Pension Fund, 1983–; UK Mutual War Risk Assoc. Ltd, 1982– (Dir, 1980–); Independent Claims Services Ltd, 1995–99. Mem., Lloyd's, 1975–95; Mem. Bd, 1982–94, Gen. Cttee, 1982–, Lloyd's Register of Shipping; Trustee, Lloyd's Register Superannuation Fund, 1982–2006. Member: Bd, CAA, 1984–93; Bd, PLA, 1985–92 (Vice Chm., 1986–92). Freeman: City of London, 1988; Co. of Watermen and Lightermen, 1985. *Recreations:* shooting, reading, conversation. *Address:* 9 London House, Avenue Road, NW8 7PX. *T:* and *Fax:* (020) 7483 2754; *e-mail:* r.g.crawford@btinternet.com. *Club:* Royal Northern and University (Aberdeen).

CRAWFORD, (Robert Hardie) Bruce; JP; Member (SNP) Stirling, Scottish Parliament, since 2007 (Scotland Mid and Fife, 1999–2007); Minister for Parliamentary Business, since 2007; *b* 16 Feb. 1955; *s* of Robert and Wilma Crawford; *m* 1980, Jacqueline Hamilton Scott; three *s. Educ:* Kinross High Sch.; Perth High Sch. Personnel Officer, then Equal Opportunities Officer, later Develt Advr, Scottish Office, 1974–99. Member (SNP): Perth and Kinross DC, 1988–96; Perth and Kinross Council, 1995–99 (Leader, 1995–99). Scottish Parliament: Opposition Chief Whip, 1999; Opposition frontbench spokesman on transport and the envmt, 2000–01, on envmt and energy, 2001–03, on Parliament, 2003–07. Business Convenor, SNP, 2005–. Member Board: Scottish Enterprise Tayside, 1996–99; Perthshire Tourist Bd, 1996–99; Perth Coll., 1996–99. Chairman: Perth and Kinross Recreational Facilities Ltd, 1996–99; Kinross-shire Partnership Ltd, 1998–99. JP Perth, Kinross, 1993. *Recreations:* politics, golf, football. *Address:* Scottish Parliament, Edinburgh EH99 1SP. *T:* (0131) 348 5686.

CRAWFORD, Prof. Robert James, (Roy), FREng; Vice-Chancellor, University of Waikato, since 2005; *b* 6 April 1949; *s* of Robert James Crawford and Teresa Harriet Crawford; *m* 1974, Isobel Catherine Allen; two *s* one *d. Educ:* Queen's Univ., Belfast (BSc 1st cl. Hons Mech. Engrg 1970; PhD 1973; DSc 1987). FIMMM (FIM 1985); FIMechE 1986; FREng 1997; FIPENZ 2006. Queen's University, Belfast: Asst Lectr in Engrg, 1972–74; Lectr, 1974–82; Sen. Lectr, 1982–84; Reader, 1984–89; Prof. of Engrg Materials, 1989–2005; Dir, Sch. of Mechanical and Process Engrg, 1989–97; Dir, Polymer Processing Res. Centre, 1996–2005; Pro-Vice-Chancellor, 2001–05. Director: Rotosystems Ltd, 1991–2005; Hughes & McLeod Ltd, 1993–. *Publications:* Plastics Engineering, 1981, 3rd edn 1998; Mechanics of Engineering Materials, 1987, 2nd edn 1996; Rotational Moulding of Plastics, 1992, 2nd edn 1996; (with J. L. Throne) Rotational Molding Technology, 2002; (with M. P. Kearns) Practical Guide to Rotational Moulding, 2003. *Recreations:* reading, golf. *Address:* Vice-Chancellor's Office, University of Waikato, Private Bag 3105, Hamilton, New Zealand.

CRAWFORD, Dr Robert McKay, CBE 2004; Executive Director, Business Development and Commercialisation, Glasgow Caledonian University, since 2006; *b* 14 June 1951; *s* of Robert and Catherine Crawford; *m* 1975, Linda Acheson; one *s* one *d. Educ:* Strathclyde Univ. (BA Hons Politics); Harvard Univ. (John F. Kennedy Schol.); Glasgow Univ. (PhD Govt 1982). Leverhulme Fellow, Fraser of Allander Inst., Strathclyde Univ., 1983–85; Develt Exec., 1985–87, Manager of US Desk, 1987–89, SDA; Dir, N America, 1989–91, Dir, 1991–94, Locate in Scotland; Man. Dir, Scottish Enterprise Ops, 1994–96; Sen. Specialist in Investment, World Bank, 1996–98; Partner, Ernst & Young, 1998–2000; Chief Exec., Scottish Enterprise, 2000–04; Hd of Strategy and Special Projects, Wood Gp, 2004–05; Chief Exec., Mersey Partnership, 2005–06. FRSA 1995. *Recreations:* running, reading, modern history, economics, biography. *Address:* Glasgow Caledonian University, Cowcaddens Road, Glasgow G4 0BA.

CRAWFORD, Sir Robert (William Kenneth), Kt 2007; CBE 2002; Director-General, Imperial War Museum, 1995–2008 (Deputy Director-General, 1982–95); *b* 3 July 1945; *s* of late Hugh Merrall Crawford, FCA, and Mary Crawford (*née* Percival); *m* 1975, Vivienne Sylvia Polakowski; one *d* one *s. Educ:* Culford Sch.; Pembroke Coll., Oxford (Cleoburey Schol.; BA). Joined Imperial War Museum as Research Asst, 1968: Head of Research and Information Office, 1971–89; Keeper, Dept of Photographs, 1975–83; Asst Director, 1979–82. Chairman: UK Nat. Inventory of War Memorials, 1995–; Nat. Mus. Dirs' Conf., 2000–06; Member: British Nat. Cttee for History of Second World War, 1995–2008; Bd, Museum Documentation Assoc., 1998–2006; Nat. Historic Ships Cttee, 2000–06. Trustee: Imperial War Mus. Trust, 1982–2008; Sir Winston Churchill Archives Trust, 1995–2006; Florence Nightingale Mus. Trust, 1999–; Royal Logistic Corps Mus. Trust, 2000–; Fleet Air Arm Mus., 2000–; Horniman Mus. and Public Park Trust, 2001–; Greenwich Foundn for Old Royal Naval Coll., 2007–; Chatham Historic Dockyard Trust, 2008–. Freeman, City of London, 1998; Liveryman, Glovers' Co., 1998–. *Address:* 55 Marlborough Crescent, Riverhead, Sevenoaks, Kent TN13 2HL. *Club:* Special Forces.

CRAWFORD, His Honour William Hamilton Raymund, QC 1980; a Circuit Judge, 1986–2001; *b* 10 Nov. 1936; *s* of late Col Mervyn Crawford, DSO, DL, JP, and Martha Hamilton Crawford; *m* 1965, Marilyn Jean Colville; one *s* two *d. Educ:* West Downs, Winchester; Winchester Coll.; Emmanuel Coll., Cambridge (BA). Commnd 2nd Lt, Royal Scots Greys, 1955–57. Called to the Bar, Inner Temple, 1964; Dep. Chm., Agricultural Land Tribunal, 1978; a Recorder, 1979–86. *Recreations:* hill farming, fishing, shooting (shot for GB in Kolapore Match, and for Scotland in Elcho and Twenty Matches on several occasions; mem., Scottish Rifle Team, Commonwealth Games, Jamaica, 1966). *Club:* Northern Counties (Newcastle).

See also Viscount Dupplin.

CRAWLEY, family name of **Baroness Crawley**.

CRAWLEY, Baroness *cr* 1998 (Life Peer), of Edgbaston in the co. of West Midlands; **Christine Mary Crawley;** a Baroness in Waiting (Government Whip), 2002–08; *b* 9 Jan. 1950; *m*; three *c* (incl. twins). *Educ:* Notre Dame Catholic Secondary Girls' School, Plymouth; Digby Stuart Training College, Roehampton. Formerly teacher; S Oxfordshire District Council; contested (Lab) Staffordshire SE, gen. election, 1983. MEP (Lab) Birmingham E, 1984–99; Dep. Leader, Eur. PLP, 1994–99. Govt spokesman, H of L, on foreign affairs, defence, transport and equal opportunities. Chm., European Parlt Women's Rights Cttee, 1989–94. Chm., Women's Nat. Commn, 1999–2002. Dir, Northfield Regeneration Forum; Chm., W Midlands Regl Cultural Consortium, 1999–. Patron: Orgn for Sickle Cell Anaemia Relief; Women's Returners Network. FRSA. *Address:* House of Lords, SW1A 0PW.

CRAWLEY, David Jonathan; Director, Scottish Executive European Union Office, Brussels, 2005–06; *b* 6 May 1951; *s* of Frederick John Crawley and Olive Elizabeth Crawley (*née* Bunce); *m* 1983, Anne Anderson; one *s* two *d. Educ:* Chichester High Sch.; Christ Church, Oxford (BA Modern Hist. 1972; MA 1973). Scottish Office, 1972–81; Dept of Energy, 1981–84; Asst Sec., Scottish Educn Dept, 1984–87; Principal Private Sec. to Sec. of State for Scotland, 1987–89; Counsellor, UK Representation to EU, Brussels, 1990–94; Asst Dir, Finance, and Hd, Private Finance Unit, 1994–97, Hd, Powers and Functions, Constitution Gp, 1997–98, Scottish Office; Hd of Schs Gp, Scottish Office, then Scottish Exec., Educn Dept, 1998–99; Hd of Agriculture, Rural Affairs, then Envmt and Rural Affairs, Dept, Scottish Exec., 1999–2002; Hd of Dept, Scotland Office, 2002–05. Chm., Audit Cttee, Wales Office, 2005–. Member: Bd, Scottish Natural Heritage, 2006–; Jt Nature Conservation Cttee, 2007–; Dir, Central Scotland Forest Trust, 2007– (Chm., 2008–). Treas., St Fillan's Episcopal Ch, 1998–99. Comr, Queen Victoria Sch., Dunblane, 2006–. *Recreations:* gardening, music.

CRAWLEY, Most Rev. David Perry; Archbishop of Kootenay and Metropolitan of British Columbia and Yukon, 1994–2004; *b* 26 July 1937; *s* of Rev. Canon George Antony Crawley, LTh and Lucy Lillian Crawley (*née* Ball); *m* 1st, 1959, Frances Mary Louise Wilmot; two *d*; 2nd, 1986, Joan Alice Bubbs; one *d* (and one *d* decd). *Educ:* Univ. of Manitoba (BA 1958); St John's Coll., Winnipeg (LTh 1961; DD 1990); Univ. of Kent at Canterbury (MA 1967). Ordained Deacon 1961, Priest 1962. Incumbent, St Thomas', Sherwood Park, Edmonton, 1961–66; Canon Missioner, All Saints Cathedral, Edmonton, 1967–70; Rector, St Matthew's, Winnipeg, 1971–77; Archdeacon of Winnipeg, 1974–77; Archdeacon of Rupert's Land, 1977–81; Lectr, St John's College, Winnipeg, 1981–82; Rector, St Michael and All Angels, Regina, 1982–85; Rector, St Paul's, Vancouver, 1985–90; Bishop of Kootenay, 1990–2004. *Recreations:* ski-ing, hiking. *Address:* c/o Diocese of Kootenay, 1876 Richter Street, Kelowna, BC V1Y 2M9, Canada.

CRAWLEY, Frederick William, CBE 1998; FCIB; FRAeS; Chairman: Alliance & Leicester Building Society, 1991–94 (Director, since 1988; Deputy Chairman, 1990–91); Girobank PLC, 1992–94 (Director, since 1990; Deputy Chairman, 1990–92); *b* 10 June 1926; *s* of William Clement Crawley and Elsie Florence Crawley; *m* 1951, Ruth Eva Jungman (*d* 2003); two *d.* Joined Lloyds Bank, 1942; Chief Accountant, 1969–72; Asst Chief Gen. Man., 1977–78; Dep. Chief Gen. Man., 1978–82; Chief Exec., Lloyds Bank, Calif, 1982–83; Dep. Chief Gen. Man., 1983–84, Chief Gen. Man., 1984–85, Dep. Chief Exec., 1985–87, Lloyds Bank plc. Chairman: Black Horse Agencies Ltd, 1985–88; Betta Stores, 1990–92; Legal & General Recovery Investment Trust, 1994–98; Director: Black Horse Life Assce Co., 1977–82; Lloyds Bank Unit Trust Managers, 1977–82; Lloyds Leasing, 1977–82; Lloyds Development Capital, 1981–82; Lloyds Bank International, 1982–83; Internat. Commodities Clearing House Hldgs, 1984–87; Lloyds Bank, 1984–88; Lloyds Bank Export Finance, 1985–87; Lloyds Bowmaker Finance, 1985–87; FS Assurance, 1988–90; Barratt Developments, 1988–96; Lloyds Development Capital, 1988–92; Legal & General Bank Ltd, 1997–2001; Aeroclub Ltd, 1987–2004; Chm., The Property Jungle Ltd, 2000. RAF Benevolent Fund: Hon. Treas., 1988–2004, and Dep. Chm., 1988–2004, RAF Benevolent Fund Enterprises (formerly Internat. Air Tattoo); Dir, Air Shows Europe (formerly Battle of Britain Appeal,) 1988–2004; Chm., RAF Charitable Trust Enterprises, 2005–; Trustee, RAF Charitable Trust, 2005–. Develt Trustee, Mus. of Army Flying, 1993–2001. Fellow, St Andrews Strategic Management Ltd, 1995–96. FCIB (FIB 1971); FRAeS 2006 (ARAeS 1984). Freeman, City of London, 2006; Freeman, 1992, Liveryman, 2006, GAPAN. *Recreations:* aviation, shooting, photography. *Address:* 4 The Hexagon, Fitzroy Park, N6 6HR. *T:* (020) 8341 2279. *Club:* Royal Air Force.

CRAWLEY, John Maurice, CB 1992; Under Secretary, Inland Revenue, 1979–93; *b* 27 Sept. 1933; *s* of late Charles William and Kathleen Elizabeth Crawley; *m* 1978, Jane Meadows Rendel; three *s. Educ:* Rugby Sch.; New Coll., Oxford (MA). Assistant Principal, Inland Revenue, 1959; Principal, 1963; Asst Secretary, 1969; Under Sec., 1979; seconded to Cabinet Office (Central Policy Review Staff), 1973–76 and 1979–81. *Recreations:* music, walking, book-binding.

CRAWLEY, Prof. Michael John, PhD; FRS 2002; Professor of Plant Ecology, Imperial College, London University, since 1994; *b* 9 March 1949; *s* of John and Isabel Crawley; *m* 1971, Greer Anne Williams. *Educ:* Dukes Grammar Sch., Alnwick; Edinburgh Univ. (BSc Hons 1st Cl. 1970); Imperial Coll., London (DIC, PhD 1973). Lectr, Univ. of Bradford, 1973–79; Lectr, 1979–89, Reader, 1989–94, Imperial Coll., London. *Publications:* Herbivory, 1983; Plant Ecology, 1986; Colonization, Succession and Stability, 1987; Natural Enemies, 1992; GLIM for Ecologists, 1993; Statistical Computing, 2002; The Flora of Berkshire, 2005; The R Book, 2007; papers on plant-herbivore interactions and biological invasions. *Recreations:* BSBI plant recorder for Berkshire, mountains, croquet, Newcastle United. *Address:* Department of Biological Sciences, Silwood Park, Ascot, Berks SL5 7PY. *T:* (020) 7594 2216, *Fax:* (020) 7594 2339; *e-mail:* m.crawley@imperial.ac.uk.

CRAWLEY-BOEVEY, Sir Thomas (Michael Blake), 8th Bt *cr* 1784; *b* 29 Sept. 1928; *er s* of Sir Launcelot Valentine Hyde Crawley-Boevey, 7th Bt, and Elizabeth Goodeth (*d*

1976), *d* of Herbert d'Auvergne Innes, late Indian Police; *S* father, 1968; *m* 1st, 1957, Laura Coelingh (*d* 1979); two *s*; 2nd, 2003, Judith Tillotson. *Educ:* Wellington Coll.; St John's Coll., Cambridge (BA 1952, MA 1956). 2nd Lieut, Durham Light Infantry, 1948. With Shipping Agents, 1952–61; with Consumers' Association, 1961–82; Editor: Money Which?, 1968–76; Which?, 1976–82; Editor-in-Chief, Which? magazines, 1980–82. Master, Girdlers' Co., 1992–93. *Heir: er s* Thomas Hyde Crawley-Boevey [*b* 26 June 1958; *m* 1992, Lynette Claire Gilbert; two *s*]. *Address:* 47 Belvoir Road, Cambridge CB4 1JH. *T:* (01223) 368698.

CRAWSHAW, 5th Baron *cr* 1892, of Crawshaw, co. Lancaster and of Whatton, co. Leics; **David Gerald Brooks;** Bt 1891; *b* 14 Sept. 1934; *s* of 3rd Baron Crawshaw and Sheila (*d* 1964), *o d* of Lt-Col P. R. Clifton, CMG, DSO; *S* brother, 1997; *m* 1970, Belinda Mary, *d* of George Burgess; four *d*. *Educ:* Eton; RAC, Cirencester. *Heir: b* Hon. John Patrick Brooks [*b* 17 March 1938; *m* 1967, Rosemary Vans Agnew, *o d* of C. Vans Agnew Frank; one *s* one *d*].

CRAWSHAW, Steven John; Group Chief Executive, Bradford & Bingley plc, 2004–08; *b* 15 April 1961; *s* of John Crawshaw and Serena Gillean Crawshaw; *m* 1991, Brigid Rushmore; two *s*. *Educ:* Eastbourne Coll.; Univ. of Leicester (LLB); Cranfield Univ. (MBA). Articled clerk and Asst Solicitor, Hewitson Becke & Shaw, 1984–88; Partner, Froggatt & Co., 1988–89; Manager, Legal Dept, 1990–95, Strategic Planner, 1995–96, Hd of Strategy, 1996–97, Cheltenham & Gloucester plc; PA to Gp Dir, Customer Finance, Lloyds TSB plc, 1997–98; Bradford & Bingley plc, 1999–2008, Gp Strategy, HR and IT Dir, 2002–04. *Recreations:* family, hill walking, cooking.

CRAWSHAY, Elisabeth Mary Boyd, (Lady Crawshay), CBE 1986; DL; Chairman, Local Government Boundary Commission, Wales, 1981–94; Deputy Chief Commissioner, St John's Ambulance Brigade, Wales, 1979–84; *b* 2 July 1927; *d* of Lt-Col Guy Franklin Reynolds, late 9th Lancers, and Katherine Isobel (*née* Macdonell); *m* 1950, Col Sir William (Robert) Crawshay, DSO, ERD, TD. *Educ:* Convent of Sacred Heart, Roehampton; St Anne's Coll., Oxford (MA). Mem., Mental Health Act Commn, 1983–88. DL Gwent 1978; JP Abergavenny, 1972–96 (Chm., Juvenile Bench, 1980–95; Mem., Borstal Board of Visitors, 1975–84). DJStJ 1970. *Address:* Ty Carreg, Govilon, Abergavenny, Mon NP7 9PT. *T:* (01873) 832220.

CRAXTON, Christine Elizabeth; *see* Gamble, C. E.

CRAXTON, John Leith, RA 1993; artist; *b* 3 Oct. 1922; *s* of late Harold Craxton, OBE, LRAM and Essie Craxton. *Educ:* various private schs incl. Betteshanger, Kent; Westminster and Central Schs of Art; Goldsmiths' Coll. (with Lucian Freud). First solo exhibn, Leicester Galls, 1944; with Lucian Freud, worked in Scilly Is, then Greece, 1945–47, and held joint exhibn, London Gall., 1947; designed sets and costumes for Daphnis and Chloë, Royal Ballet, 1951, Apollo, 1966; Cotteral Meml Tapestry for Stirling Univ., 1971–74. Principal solo exhibitions include: St George's Gall., London, 1945; Galerie Gasser, Zürich, 1946; British Council, Athens, 1946, 1949, 1985; Mayor Gall., London, 1950; Leicester Galls, London, 1951, 1954, 1956, 1961, 1966; Crane Gall., Manchester, 1955; Whitechapel Art Gall., 1967; Hamet Gall., London, 1971; Christopher Hull Gall., London, 1982, 1985, 1987, 1993; Chrysostomos Gall., Hania, 1985; Pallant House Gall., Chichester, 1998. Work in public collections includes: Tate Gall.; V&A; BM; Gall. of Modern Art, Edinburgh; Nat. Mus. of Wales; Arts Council; British Council; Govt Picture Collection; Nat. Gall., Melbourne; Metropolitan Mus., NY; work in many private collections. HM Consular Correspondent, Hania, Crete, 1992–. *Relevant publication:* Illustrated Monograph 1941–1948, by Geoffrey Grigson, 1948. *Recreations:* music, museums, motorbikes, archaeology, seafood, cooking. *Address:* Moschon 1, Hania, Crete, Greece; c/o Royal Academy of Arts, Burlington House, Piccadilly W1V 0DJ.

CRAXTON, (Katharine) Jane; *see* Carmichael, K. J.

CRAY, Rt Rev. Graham Alan; *see* Maidstone, Bishop Suffragan of.

CREAGH, Mary Helen; MP (Lab) Wakefield, since 2005; *b* 2 Dec. 1967; *d* of Thomas and Elizabeth Creagh; *m* 2001, Adrian Pulham; one *s*. *Educ:* Pembroke Coll., Oxford (BA Jt Hons Modern Langs (French and Italian)); London Sch. of Econs (MSc Eur. Studies). Press Officer: Youth Forum of EU, 1991–95; London Enterprise Agency, 1995–97; Lectr in Entrepreneurship, Cranfield Sch. of Mgt, 1997–2005. Mem. (Lab) Islington BC, 1998–2005 (Leader, Labour Gp, 2000–04). Trustee, Rathbone Trng, 1997–2004. *Recreations:* cycling, yoga, friends and family, pop music. *Address:* House of Commons, SW1A 0AA. *T:* (020) 7219 6984; *e-mail:* mary@marycreagh.co.uk. *Club:* Red Shed (Wakefield).

CREAN, Anthony Joseph Daniel; QC 2006; *b* 9 June 1962; *s* of Michael and Patricia Crean; *m* 2003, Angela Roberts; one *s* two *d*. *Educ:* Univ. of Essex (BA); Univ. of Manchester (MPhil). Called to the Bar, Gray's Inn, 1987; in practice as barrister, 1987–, specialising in planning law. FRGS 2003. *Recreations:* hanging out with Alice, Laura and Francis, scuba-diving, poetry, ski-ing, swimming, chess. *Address:* No5 Chambers, Fountain Court, Steelhouse Lane, Birmingham B4 6DR; *e-mail:* ajc@no5.com.

CREAN, Hon. Francis Daniel, (Hon. Frank); *b* Hamilton, Vic, 28 Feb. 1916; *s* of J. Crean; *m* 1946, Mary Isobel (AM 2006), *d* of late A. E. Findlay; three *s*. *Educ:* Hamilton High Sch.; Melbourne High Sch.; Melbourne Univ. BA Hons; BCom. DPA; FCPA. Income Tax Assessor, 1934–45. MLA: for Albert Park, Vic, 1945–47; for Prahran, 1949–51; MHR for Melbourne Ports, 1951–77; Mem. Exec., Federal Parly Labour Party, 1956–72, Dep. Leader, 1975–76; Mem., Jt Parly Cttee on Public Accounts, 1952–55; Treasurer, Commonwealth of Australia, 1972–74; Minister for Overseas Trade, 1974–75, also Deputy Prime Minister, 1975. Chm., Council of Adult Educn, 1947–74. Pres., Vict. Br., Aust. Inst. Internat. Affairs, 1983–86; Chairman: Vict. Br., Freedom from Hunger Campaign, 1979; South-Central Migrant Resource Centre, 1980–. *Publication:* (with W. J. Byrt) Government and Politics in Australia, 1972, 2nd edn 1982. *Address:* 31/27 Queens Road, Melbourne, Vic 3004, Australia.

See also Hon. S. F. Crean.

CREAN, Hon. Simon (Findlay); MP (ALP) for Hotham, Vic, since 1990; Minister for Trade, Australia, since 2007; *b* 26 Feb. 1949; *s* of Hon. Francis Daniel Crean, *qv* and Mary Isobel Crean, AM; *m* 1973, Carole (*née* Lamb); two *d*. *Educ:* Middle Park Central, Melbourne; Melbourne High Sch.; Monash Univ. (BEc, LLB). Trade Union Official, Federated Storemen and Packers Union of Australia, 1970–85; Pres., ACTU, 1985–90. Federal Minister for: Science and Technology, 1990; Primary Industries and Energy, 1991–93; Employment, Educn and Training, 1993–96; Dep. Leader of the Opposition, 1998–2001; Leader of the Opposition, 2001–03; Shadow Treasurer, 1998–2001, 2003–04; Shadow Trade Minister, 2004–07. Patron, North Melbourne FC. *Recreations:* bushwalking, tennis. *Address:* Parliament House, Canberra, ACT 2600, Australia. *T:* (2) 62774022, *Fax:* (2) 62778495; *e-mail:* s.crean.mp@aph.gov.au. *Club:* North Melbourne Football.

CREDITON, Bishop Suffragan of, since 2004; **Rt Rev. Robert John Scott Even** *b* 29 May 1947; *s* of Reginald Evens and Sheila (*née* Scott); *m* 1972, Sue Hayes; one *s* o *d*. *Educ:* Maidstone Grammar Sch.; Trinity Coll., Bristol (DipTh); ACIB. Na Westminster Bank, 1964–74; ordained deacon, 1977, priest, 1978; Assistant Curate: Simon's, Southsea, 1977–79; St Mary's, Portchester, 1979–83; Vicar, St John's, Loc Heath, 1983–96; RD of Fareham, 1993–96; Archdeacon of Bath, 1996–2004. *Recreation* caravanning in France, gardening, walking with Sue. *Address:* 32 The Avenue, Tiverto EX16 4HW. *T:* (01884) 250002, *Fax:* (01884) 257454; *e-mail:* bishop.of.crediton exeter.anglican.org.

CREECH, Hon. Wyatt (Beetham), CNZM 2003; Director, Open Country Chee Company Ltd; Chairman, Kaimai Cheese Company Ltd; Deputy Prime Minister of Ne Zealand, 1998–99; *b* Oceanside, Calif, 13 Oct. 1946; arrived in NZ 1947; *s* of Jesse Wya Creech and Ellanora Sophia (*née* Beetham); *m* 1981, Diane Marie Rose; three *s*. *Edu* Hadlow Prep. Sch., Masterton; Wanganui Collegiate Sch.; Massey Univ. (Dip. Shee Farming); Victoria Univ. (BA Pol Sci. and Internat. Politics). Farmer, Wairarap 1974–79; horticulturalist (vineyard developer), 1979–88; Accountant, Masterto 1983–87. MP (Nat.) Wairarapa, NZ, 1988–2002; Minister: of Revenue, of Customs, i Public Trust Office and responsible for Govt Superannuation Fund, 1990–91; for Se Citizens, and Associate Minister of Finance and of Social Welfare, 1991–93; for Sta Owned Enterprises, 1993; of Employment, 1993–96; of Revenue and Dep. Minister Finance, 1993–96; Leader of the House, 1996–98; Minister of Educn, 1996–99; Minist of Courts and of Ministerial Services, 1997–98. Dep. Leader, Nat. Party, 1997–200 Indep. Dir, Blue Chip NZ, 2004–06. Mem., Parly Service Commn. *Recreations:* win tasting, gardening, outdoor pursuits. *Address:* 43 Kandy Crescent, Khandallah, Wellingto New Zealand.

CREED, Prof. Francis Hunter, MD; FRCP, FRCPsych, FMedSci; Professor Psychological Medicine, University of Manchester, since 1997; *b* 22 Feb. 1947; *s* of la Albert Lowry Creed and Joyce Marian Creed; *m* 1972, Ruth Alison Kaye; two *s* two *Educ:* Kingswood Sch., Bath; Downing Coll., Cambridge (Pilley Schol.; MB BChir 197 MA; MD 1985); St Thomas' Hosp. Med. Sch., London. FRCP 1991; FRCPsych 199 Registrar, Maudsley Hosp., 1974–76; Sen. Registrar, Maudsley and London Hosp 1976–78; Mental Health Leverhulme Res. Fellow, 1978–80; Sen. Lectr, Univ. Manchester and Consultant Psychiatrist, Manchester Royal Infirmary, 1980–92; Prof. Community Psychiatry, 1992–97, Res. Dean, Faculty of Medicine, Dentistry, Nursin and Pharmacy, 1997–2001, Univ. of Manchester; Hon. Consultant Psychiatris Manchester Royal Infirmary, subseq. Central Manchester Healthcare Trust, then Centr Manchester and Manchester Children's Univ. Hosps NHS Trust, 1981–. Churchi Travelling Fellow, 1993. FRSocMed 1980; FMedSci 2000. *Publications:* Medicine an Psychiatry, 1981; Psychiatry in Medical Practice, 1989, 2nd edn 1994; over 200 articles i learned jls on psychological aspects of medicine and Community Psychiatry. *Recreation* hill walking, swimming, travelling. *Address:* Department of Psychiatry, Mancheste University, Rawnsley Building, Manchester Royal Infirmary, Oxford Road, Mancheste M13 9WL. *T:* (0161) 276 5331.

CREED, Martin; artist; *b* 21 Oct. 1968; *s* of John Creed and Gisela Grosscurth. *Educ:* Slad Sch. of Fine Art, London (BA Hons Fine Art 1990). Exhibitions include: Martin Cree Works (organised by Southampton City Art Gall.), Leeds City Art Gall., Bluecoat Gall Liverpool, Camden Arts Centre, London, 2000; Art Now: Martin Creed, Tate Britain London, 2000. Turner Prize, 2001. *Publication:* the whole world + the work = the whol world, 1996. *Address:* 80 O'Donnell Court, Brunswick Centre, WC1N 1NX. *T:* (020 7837 4097, *Fax:* (020) 7833 8407; *e-mail:* mail@martincreed.com.

CREEDON, Michael Francis; Chief Constable, Derbyshire Constabulary, since 2007; London, 14 June 1958; *s* of Raymond and Elizabeth Creedon; *m* 1994, Sally Deans; tw *s* one *d*. *Educ:* City of Leicester Boys' Sch.; Univ. of Manchester (BA Hons Hist. an Econs); Univ. of Leicester (MA Criminol.). Leicestershire Constabulary, 1980–2003 served as detective in every rank; Basic Comd Unit Comdr, S Area, 2001–03; Derbyshir Constabulary: Asst Chief Constable (Ops), 2003–06; Dep. Chief Constable for ACPO Nat. Co-ordinator for Serious and Organised Crime, 2006–07. Holder, ACPO portfoli for asset recovery and policy lead for kidnap or extortion, 2005–. *Recreations* Middlesbrough Football Club, family, cookery (oriental especially), painting an decorating, running. *Address:* Derbyshire Constabulary HQ, Butterley Hall, Ripon Derbys DE5 3RS.

CREEDON, Roger, CBE 2005; Chief Executive, Electoral Commission, 2000–04; *b* 3 Dec. 1946; *s* of late Patrick Michael Creedon and Norah Creedon (*née* Rice); *m* 1969 Shirley Ann Clay; two *s*. Joined Home Office, 1964; Police Directorate, 1969–77; Ass Sec., Cttee on Obscenity and Film Censorship, 1977–80; Forensic Sci. Service, 1980–83 Gaming Bd, 1983–87; Home Office Finance Directorate, 1987–90; Police Sci. and Technology Gp, 1990–93; Dir, Nat. Criminal Intelligence Service, 1993–96; Corporat Resources and Constitutional Directorates, Home Office 1996–2000. Election Observe for Commonwealth Secretariat, 2005. Lay Member: Information Tribunal, 2006–; GMC Fitness to Practise Panel, 2006–; Rules and Ethics Cttee, SRA, 2007–; Standards Cttee Bar Standards Bd, 2008–. Mem., Kentish Opera Council, 2005–. *Recreations:* backstage opera, walking, reading. *Address: e-mail:* rcreedon@ntlworld.com.

CREELMAN, Graham Murray, OBE 2006; Managing Director, Anglia Television, 1996–2006; Director, Regional Programming, ITV, 2003–06; *b* 20 May 1947; *s* of late Robert Kelly Creelman and of Jean Murray Creelman; *m* 1st, 1969, Eleanor McCulloch McAuslan (marr. diss. 1984); two *d*; 2nd, 1984, Sarah Katharine Bruce-Lockhart (marr. diss. 1996); two *d*; 3rd, 1997, Francesca Vivica Parsons; one step *s* one step *d*. *Educ.* Greenock Acad.; Univ. of Sussex (BA Hons). Journalist, Scotsman, 1969–70; journalist and producer, BBC Scotland, 1970–78; producer and dir documentaries, Anglia TV, 1978–89; Exec. Dir, Survival Anglia Ltd, 1989–94; Dir of Programmes, Anglia TV, 1994–96; Chm., Anglia Multimedia, 1999–2001. Founder, Creelman Associates LTP, 2006. Dir, Eastern Arts Bd, 1995–2002; Chairman: Eastern Screen Commn, 1997–2002; East of England Cultural Consortium, 1999–; Screen East, 2001–06; Council Mem., Arts Council England, East, 2002–. Mem., E of England Regl Assembly, 2001–. Bd Associate, Govt Office for E of England, 2006–. Trustee/Dir, Wildscreen Trustees, 1993–2001; Director: New Writing Partnership, 2004–; Norwich Heritage Economic and Regeneration Trust, 2004–; Chm., Norwich Partnership, 2006–. Dep. Chm., United Wildlife, 1997–2001. Gov., Norwich Sch. of Art and Design, 2004– (Vice-Chm., 2006; Chm., 2007–). *Publications:* contribs to New Statesman, The Listener. *Recreations:* walking in Scotland, fishing, Schubert, the books of John Buchan. *Address:* 22 Christchurch Road, Norwich NR2 2AE.

CREESE, Nigel Arthur Holloway, AM 1988; Executive Officer, Association of Heads of Independent Schools of Australia, 1989–95 (Chairman, 1985–87); *b* 4 June 1927; *s* of late H. R. Creese; *m* 1951, Valdai (*née* Walters); two *s* two *d*. *Educ:* Blundell's Sch.; Brasenose Coll., Oxford. Assistant Master: Bromsgrove Sch., 1952–55; Rugby Sch., 1955–63; Headmaster: Christ's Coll., Christchurch, NZ, 1963–70; Melbourne Grammar

Sch., 1970–87. *Address:* 75 Charles Street, Kew, Vic 3101, Australia. *Clubs:* East India and Public Schools; Melbourne (Melbourne).

CREIGHTON, Alan Joseph, CEng, FRINA; RCNC; Chief Underwater Systems Executive, Ministry of Defence, 1989–91, retired; *b* 21 Nov. 1936; *s* of Joseph Kenneth and Iris Mary Creighton; *m* 1959, Judith Bayford; two *d. Educ:* Gillingham County Grammar School; Royal Naval College, Greenwich. Joined Admiralty, 1953; Cadetship to Royal Corps of Naval Constructors, 1957; pass out, RNC Greenwich, 1961; RCDS 1980; secondment to industry, 1981; resumed MoD (PE) career, 1984; Dir Gen., Surface Ships, 1986–89. *Recreations:* music, dinghy sailing, cabinet making. *Address:* Rose Cottage, West Littleton, Marshfield SN14 8JE. *T:* (01225) 891021.

CREIGHTON, Robert Mandell; Chief Executive, Ealing Primary Care Trust, since 2002; *b* 18 Feb. 1950; *s* of Hugh Creighton and Christian Creighton (*née* Barclay); *m* 1st, 1977, Sok-Chzeng Ong (marr. diss. 1983); 2nd, 1985, Rosanne Jelley; two *d. Educ:* Marlborough Coll.; King's Coll., Cambridge (MA Hist.); King's Coll. London (PGCE). Teacher, King's Coll. Sch., Wimbledon, 1974–78; Internat. Sec., United World Colls, 1978–88; Department of Health: Principal, 1988–91; Asst Sec., 1991–95; Principal Private Sec. to Sec. of State for Health, 1992–94; Chief Exec., Great Ormond Street Hosp. for Children NHS Trust, 1995–2000. *Recreations:* tennis, squash, opera, painting. *Address:* Ealing Primary Care Trust, 1 Armstrong Way, Southall, Middx UB2 4SA. *T:* (020) 8893 0102. *Club:* Wimbledon Tennis and Squash.

CREMONA, Hon. John Joseph; Judge, 1965–92, Vice-President, 1986–92, European Court of Human Rights; Judge, 1985–92, Vice-President, 1987–92, European Tribunal in matters of State immunity; Emeritus Professor, University of Malta, since 1965; Chief Justice of Malta and President of the Constitutional Court, Court of Appeal and Court of Criminal Appeal, 1971–81; *b* 6 Jan. 1918; *s* of late Dr Antonio Cremona, KM, MD and Anne (*née* Camilleri); *m* 1949, Marchioness Beatrice Barbaro of St George (*d* 2001); one *s* two *d. Educ:* Malta Univ. (BA 1936, LLD *cum laude* 1942); Rome Univ. (DLitt 1939); London Univ. (BA 1st Cl. Hons 1946, PhD in Laws 1951). DrJur Trieste, 1972. Crown Counsel, 1947; Lectr in Constitutional Law, Malta Univ., 1947–65, Prof. of Criminal Law, 1959–65; Attorney-Gen., 1957–64; Vice-Pres., Constitutional Court and Court of Appeal, 1965–71; sometime Actg Governor General and Actg Pres., Republic of Malta. Chm., UN Cttee on Elimination of Racial Discrimination (CERD), 1986–88 (Mem., 1984–88). Chairman: Human Rights Section, World Assoc. of Lawyers; Planning Council, Foundn for Internat. Studies, Malta Univ.; Malta Human Rights Assoc.; Vice-Pres., Internat. Inst. of Studies, Documentation and Info. for the Protection of Envt, Italy; Member: Cttee of Experts on Human Rights and Cttee of Experts on State Immunity, Council of Europe, Strasbourg; Inst Internat. de Droits de l'Homme, Strasbourg; Scientific Council, Revue des Droits de l'Homme, Paris; Scientific Council, Centro Internazionale per la Protezione dei Diritti dell' Uomo, Pesaro, Italy; Scientific Council, Faculty of Law, Université de Saint Esprit, Lebanon; Editorial Adv. Board: Checklist of Human Rights Documents, NY; Rivista Internazionale dei diritti dell'Uomo, Milan; delegate and rapporteur, internat. confs. FRHistS; Fellow *ex titulo*, Internat. Acad. of Legal Medicine and Social Medicine; Hon. Fellow, LSE; Hon. Mem., Real Acad. de Jurisprudencia y Legislacion, Madrid. KStJ 1984 (Chm., St John Council, Malta, 1983–). KSG 1972. Kt, 1966, Commendatore al Merito Melitense, 2004, Sovereign Military Order of Malta; Companion, Order of Merit (Malta), 1994. Kt Comdr, 1968, Grand Officier, 1989, Kt Grand Cross, 1995, Order of Merit (Italy); Kt Comdr, 1971, Grand Cross of Merit, 1981, Constantinian Order of St George; Chevalier de la Légion d'Honneur (France), 1990. *Publications:* The Treatment of Young Offenders in Malta, 1956; The Malta Constitution of 1835, 1959; The Doctrine of Entrapment in Theft, 1959; The Legal Consequences of a Conviction, 1962; The Constitutional Development of Malta, 1963; From the Declaration of Rights to Independence, 1965; Human Rights Documentation in Malta, 1966; Selected Papers 1946–1989, 1990, vol. II, 1990–2000, 2002; The Maltese Constitution and Constitutional History, 1994; Malta and Britain: the early constitutions, 1996; six poetry books; articles in French, German, Italian, Portuguese and American law jls. *Recreation:* gardening. *Address:* Villa Barbaro, Zejtun Road, Tarxien, Malta. *T:* 21826414.

CRESSON, Edith; Commandeur du Mérite Agricole, 1983; Chevalier de la Légion d'Honneur; Grand Croix de l'Ordre National du Mérite, 1991; Member, European Commission, 1995–99; *b* 27 Jan. 1934; *née* Campion; *m* Jacques Cresson (*d* 2001); two *d. Educ:* Diplômée de l'Ecole des Hautes Etudes Commerciales; Dr en démographie (doctoral thesis: the life of women in a rural district of Guéméné-Penfao, Loire-Atlantique). Mem., Convention des Institutions Républicaines (responsible for agricl problems), 1966; Dir of Studies, Bureau des Etudes Economiques privés (dealing especially with industrial investment); National Secretary, Parti Socialiste (in charge of youth organisation), 1974; Mem. Directing Cttee, Parti Socialiste; contested (for Parti Socialiste) Châtellerault, 1975; Mem., Eur. Parlt, 1979–81 (Mem., Cttee on Agriculture); elected Deputy, Vienne, 1981, 1986, 1988; Minister: of Agriculture, France, 1981–83; of For. Trade and Tourism, 1983–84; for Industrial Redeployment and Foreign Trade, 1984–86; for European Affairs, 1988–90; Pres.-Dir Gen., Schneider Industries Services Internat., 1990–91; Prime Minister of France, 1991–92; Pres. Dir Gen., Services Industries Strategies Internat. et Envmt, 1993–94. Consultant, Agence pour le Développement de l'Innovation et de la Technologie, 2008–. President: Inst d'Etudes Européennes de Paris 8, 2000–; Fondation des Ecoles de la Deuxième Chance, 2002–; Commission Scientifique de la Fondation France Israël, 2007–. Pres., Assoc. Démocratique des Français à l'Etranger, 1986–91. Member, Conseil Général of Vienne, 1978–98; Mayor of Châtellerault, Vienne, 1983–97 (Dep. Mayor, 1997). Dr *hc* Weizmann Inst., Israel, 1999; DUniv Open, 1999. *Publications:* Avec le soleil, 1976; Innover ou subir, 1998.

CRESSWELL, Rev. Amos Samuel; Chairman, Plymouth and Exeter District of the Methodist Church, 1976–91; President of the Methodist Conference, 1983–84; *b* Walsall Wood, 21 April 1926; *s* of Amos and Jane Cresswell; *m* 1956, Evelyn Rosemary Marchbanks; two *s* one *d. Educ:* Queen Mary's Grammar School, Walsall; University College, Durham Univ.; Wesley House, and Fitzwilliam Coll., Cambridge; Theological Seminary, Bethel bei Bielefeld, Westphalia. BA (Dunelm), Classics, 1947; BA (Cantab), Theology, 1952, MA (Cantab) 1956. Teacher of English and Latin, High School for Boys, Colchester, 1947–49; Methodist Minister, Clitheroe Circuit, 1949–50; Asst Tutor in New Testament, Richmond Coll., London, 1953–56; Minister in Darlaston (Slater St), 1956–61; Tutor in New Testament, Cliff Coll., Derbyshire, 1961–66; Minister in Bramhall Circuit (Cheadle Hulme), 1966–73; Superintendent Minister, Welwyn Garden City, 1973–76. Pres., Devonshire Assoc., 1985–86. Editor, Advance (religious weekly, formerly Joyful News), 1961–63; (with Evelyn Cresswell), Founder, Vigo Press, 1991. *Publications:* The Story of Cliff (a history of Cliff College), 1965, 2nd edn 1983; The Story They Told (a short study of the Passion Narratives in the Gospels), 1966, 2nd edn 1992; Life, Power and Hope—a study of the Holy Spirit, 1972; Lord! I've had enough! (a collection of sermons), 1991; I've Told You Twice (sermons), 1995; (with Maxwell Tow) Dr Franz Hildebrandt: Mr Valiant-for-Truth (biog.), 2000; (ed jtly) Methodist Hymns, Old and New, 2001; Whispers of Love (poems), 2004. *Recreations:* compulsive watching of sport (especially West Bromwich Albion), collecting Roman Imperial coins, reading about American Civil War, listening to music and to Shakespeare, family and friends, research into German church struggle of 1930s and 1940s. *Address:* 2 Sage Park Road, Braunton, North Devon EX33 1HH. *T:* (01271) 813835.

CRESSWELL, Jeremy Michael, CVO 1996; HM Diplomatic Service; High Commissioner to Jamaica and the Commonwealth of the Bahamas, since 2005; *b* 1 Oct. 1949; *s* of late John Cresswell and of Jean Cresswell; *m* 1974, Petra Forwick (marr. diss. 2006); two *c. Educ:* Eton Coll. Choir Sch.; Sir William Borlase's Sch., Marlow; Exeter Coll., Oxford (BA Hons); Johannes-Gutenberg Univ., Mainz, Germany. Entered FCO, 1972: Brussels, 1973–77; Kuala Lumpur, 1977–78; FCO, 1978–82 (Private Sec. to Minister of State, 1980–82); Dep. Pol Advr, BMG, Berlin, 1982–86; Dep. Head, News Dept, 1986–88, Asst Head, S America Dept, 1988–90, FCO; Counsellor (Political), UK Delegn to NATO, 1990–94; Dep. Head of Mission, Prague, 1995–98; Sen. Directing Staff, RCDS, 1998; Hd of EU Dept (Bilateral), FCO, 1999–2001; Minister and Dep. Hd of Mission, Berlin, 2001–05. *Recreations:* tennis, music. *Address:* c/o Foreign and Commonwealth Office, King Charles Street, SW1A 2AH.

CRESSWELL, John Harold; Chief Operating Officer, ITV plc, 2005–06 and since 2007 (Interim Chief Executive Officer, 2006–07; Finance Director, 2006); *b* 2 May 1961; *m* 1987, Sarah Johnston; one *s* two *d. Educ:* Peter Symonds Sch., Winchester; Univ. of Keele (BA Hons Econs and Pols 1983). Practice Dept, KPMG, 1983–87; Gp Financial Accountant, latterly Financial Controller, TVS, 1987–92; United Broadcasting and Entertainment Ltd: Financial Dir, Meridian Broadcasting, 1992–95; Financial Dir, 1996–98; Chief Op. Officer, 1998–2000; Granada Content: Dir of Ops, 2000–01; Chief Op. Officer, 2001–05. *Recreations:* tennis, sport, family. *Address:* ITV plc, 200 Gray's Inn Road, WC1X 8HF; *e-mail:* john.cresswell@itv.com.

CRESSWELL, Michael John, PhD; Director General, Assessment and Qualifications Alliance, since 2003; *b* 11 Dec. 1950; *s* of Sidney Walter Cresswell and Marjorie Mary Cresswell; *m* 1980, Lowena Orchard; one *s* one *d. Educ:* Chelsea Coll., London (BSc 1972; PGCE 1973); Inst. of Educn, London (PhD 1997). Various res. posts, NFER, 1973–80; Res. Officer, then Hd of Res., Associated Examining Bd, 1980–2000; Assessment and Qualifications Alliance: Hd of Res., 2000–02; Dir of Exams, 2002–03. Vis. Prof. of Educn, Inst. of Educn, London, 2000–. *Publications:* (with D. Vincent) Reading Tests in the Classroom, 1976; (with J. Gubb) The Second International Mathematics Study in England and Wales, 1987; (with F. Good) Grading the GCSE, 1988; Research Studies in Public Examining, 2000; over 50 other articles and papers in learned jls and other pubns. *Recreations:* birding, philosophy, theatre, 60s music, non-violent computer games, intermittent t'ai chi. *Address:* Assessment and Qualifications Alliance, Stag Hill House, Guildford, Surrey GU2 7XJ. *T:* (01483) 477706; *e-mail:* mcresswell@aqa.org.uk.

CRESSWELL, Prof. Peter, PhD; FRS 2000; Professor of Immunobiology, and Investigator at Howard Hughes Medical Institute, Yale University, since 1991; *b* 6 March 1945; *s* of Maurice and Mary Cresswell; *m* 1969, Ann K. Cooney; two *s. Educ:* Univ. of Newcastle upon Tyne (BSc, MSc); Guy's Hosp. Med. Sch., Univ. of London (PhD 1971). Post-doctoral Fellow, Harvard Univ., 1971–73; Duke University: Asst Prof., 1973–78; Associate Prof., 1978–85; Prof., 1985–91. *Address:* Section of Immunobiology, Howard Hughes Medical Institute, Yale University School of Medicine, PO Box 208011, New Haven, CT 06520–8011, USA. *T:* (203) 7855176.

CRESSWELL, Hon. Sir Peter (John), Kt 1991; DL; a Judge of the High Court of Justice, Queen's Bench Division, 1991–2008; *b* 24 April 1944; *s* of late Jack Joseph Cresswell and Madeleine Cresswell; *m* 1972, Caroline Ward (*d* 2003); one *s* (and one *s* decd). *Educ:* St John's Sch., Leatherhead; Queens' Coll., Cambridge (MA, LLM). Called to the Bar, Gray's Inn, 1966 (Malcolm Hilbery Award), Bencher, 1989; QC 1983; a Recorder, 1986–91; Nominated Commercial List Judge, 1991 (Judge in Charge, 1993–94). Mem., Senate of Inns of Court and Bar, 1981–84, 1985–86; Chm., Common Law and Commercial Bar Assoc., 1985–87; Mem., 1987–88, Vice Chm., 1989, Chm., 1990, Gen. Council of the Bar. Mem., Civil Justice Council, 1999–2003. Trustee and Mem. Bd, Cystic Fibrosis Trust, 2002–. Hon. Mem., Canadian Bar Assoc., 1990. DL Hants, 2008. *Publication:* Encyclopaedia of Banking Law, 1982, and subseq. service issues. *Recreations:* fly-fishing, river management, the Outer Hebrides. *Club:* Flyfishers' (Pres., 2003–05).

CRETNEY, Stephen Michael, DCL; FBA 1985; Fellow of All Souls College, Oxford, 1993–2001, now Emeritus; *b* 25 Feb. 1936; *yr s* of late Fred and Winifred M. V. Cretney; *m* 1973, Rev. Antonia Lois Vanrenen, *o d* of late Lt-Comdr A. G. G. Vanrenen, RN; two *s. Educ:* Cheadle Hulme Sch.; Magdalen Coll., Oxford; DCL Oxon 1985. Nat. Service, 1954–56. Solicitor. Partner, Macfarlanes, London, 1964; Lecturer: Kenya Sch. of Law, Nairobi, 1966; Southampton Univ., 1968; Fellow and Tutor, Exeter Coll., Oxford, 1969–78; a Gen. Comr of Income Tax, 1970–78; a Law Comr, 1978–83; Prof. of Law, 1984–93, and Dean, Faculty of Law, 1984–88, Univ. of Bristol. Pt-time Chm. of Social Security and other Appeal Tribunals, 1985–96. Member: Departmental Cttee on Prison Disciplinary System, 1984–85; Family and Civil Cttee, Judicial Studies Bd, 1985–90; Lord Chancellor's Adv. Cttee on Legal Educn, 1987–88; President's Ancillary Relief Adv. Gp, 2000–03. Chm., Cttee of Heads of Univ. Law Schs, 1986–88. Bencher (Academic), Inner Temple, 2006. Hon. QC 1992; Hon. LLD Bristol, 2007. *Publications:* Theobald on Wills, (ed jtly) 13th edn 1970; Principles of Family Law, 1974, 7th edn (ed jtly) 2002; Family Law (Teach Yourself series), 1982; Enduring Powers of Attorney, 1986, 4th edn (ed jtly) 1996; Elements of Family Law, 1987, 4th edn 2000; (jtly) Simple Quarrels, 1994; (jtly) Divorce—the New Law, 1996; Law, Law Reform and the Family, 1998; (ed) Family Law at the Millennium, 2000; Family Law in the 20th Century: a history, 2003; Same Sex Relationships: from 'odious crime' to 'gay marriage', 2006; *contributed to:* English Private Law, 2000, 2nd edn 2007; Halsbury's Laws of England, 4th edn; Oxford DNB, 2004; articles and notes in legal jls. *Address:* 8 Elm Farm Close, Wantage, Oxon OX12 9FD. *T:* (01235) 763217; *e-mail:* Smcretney@aol.com; *Club:* Oxford and Cambridge.

CREW, Sir Edward (Michael), Kt 2001; QPM 1991; DL; Chief Constable, West Midlands Police, 1996–2002; *b* 13 Jan. 1946; *s* of Joseph Edwin Crew and Cecilia May Crew (*née* Davis); *m* 1967, Gillian Glover; one *s* one *d. Educ:* Haberdashers' Aske's Hatcham Sch. for Boys; Police Staff Coll. Joined Metropolitan Police from Cadet Corps, 1965; Inspector, 1970; Mem., investigation team into breach of security at Buckingham Palace, 1982; Chief Supt, comdg SE London Traffic Div., 1982–84; Asst Chief Constable, 1984–89, Dep. Chief Constable, 1989–93, Kent County Constabulary; rcds, 1988; Chief Constable, Northants, 1993–96. DL West Midlands, 1999. CCMI 2001. Hon. LLD Birmingham, 2001. OStJ 1989. *Recreations:* good food, walking, gardening, travel.

CREWE, Albert Victor, PhD; Professor, Department of Physics and the Enrico Fermi Institute, 1963–96, now Emeritus (Assistant Professor, 1956–59; Associate Professor, 1959–63; William E. Wrather Distinguished Service Professor, 1977–97), Dean of Physical Sciences Division, 1971–81, University of Chicago; *b* 18 Feb. 1927; US citizen, 1961; *m* 1949, Doreen Patricia Blunsdon; one *s* three *d. Educ:* Univ. of Liverpool (BS,

PhD). Asst Lectr, 1950–52, Lectr, 1952–55, Univ. of Liverpool; Div. Dir, Particle Accelerator Division, Argonne National Laboratory, 1958–61; Dir, Argonne National Laboratory, 1961–67. Mem. Bd of Dirs, R. R. Donnelley & Sons, Co., 1974–93; Pres., Orchid One Corp., 1987–90. Member: Nat. Acad. of Sciences; Amer. Acad. of Arts and Sciences. Artist Mem., Palette and Chisel Acad., Chicago. Hon. FRMS 1984. Named Outstanding New Citizen by Citizenship Council of Chicago, 1962; received Immigrant's Service League's Annual Award for Outstanding Achievement in the Field of Science, 1962; Illinois Sesquicentennial Award, 1968; Industrial Research Award, 1970; Distinguished Service Award, Electron Microscope Soc. of America, 1976; Albert A. Michelson Award, Franklin Inst., 1977; Ernst Abbe Award, NY Microscope Soc., 1979; Duddell Medal, Inst. of Physics, 1980. *Publications:* Research USA (with J. J. Katz), 1964; contribs to: Proc. Royal Soc.; Proc. Phys. Soc.; Physical Review; Science; Physics Today; Jl of Applied Physics; Reviews of Scientific Instruments; Optik; Ultramicroscopy, etc. *Address:* 8 Summit Drive, Dune Acres, IN 46304, USA. *T:* (219) 7875018. *Clubs:* Quadrangle, Wayfarers' (Chicago).

CREWE, Sir Ivor (Martin), Kt 2006; DL; Master, University College, Oxford, since 2008; *b* 15 Dec. 1945; *s* of Francis and Lilly Crewe; *m* 1968, Jill Barbara (*née* Gadian); two *s* one *d. Educ:* Manchester Grammar Sch.; Exeter Coll., Oxford (MA; Hon. Fellow, 1998); London School of Economics (MScEcon). Assistant Lecturer, Univ. of Lancaster, 1967–69; Junior Research Fellow, Nuffield Coll., Oxford, 1969–71; Lectr, Dept of Govt, Univ. of Essex, 1971–74; Dir SSRC Data Archive, 1974–82; University of Essex: Prof. of Govt, 1982–2007; Pro-Vice-Chancellor (Academic), 1992–95; Vice-Chancellor, 1995–2007; Res. Prof., 2007–08. Member: Exec. Cttee and UK Council, UUK, 2000–07 (Chm., England and NI Bd, 2001–03; Pres., 2003–05); Bd, Univ. and Colls Employers Assoc., 2001–07; Bd, Leadership Foundn, 2003–; Governing Body, SOAS, 2007–; Trustee, Higher Educn Policy Inst., 2007–. Dir, USS Ltd, 2006–07. Co-Dir, Feb. 1974, Oct. 1974, 1979 British Election Studies; elections analyst for: BBC TV, 1982–89; The Times, 1990–92; BBC World TV, 1997, 2001, 2005. High Steward, Colchester, 2003–08. Editor, 1977–82, Co-editor, 1984–92, British Journal of Political Science. DL Essex, 2002. Hon. DLitt Salford, 1999. *Publications:* (with A. H. Halsey) Social Survey of the Civil Service (HMSO), 1969; ed, British Political Sociology Yearbook, vol. 1 1974, vol. 2 1975; (with Bo Sarlvik) Decade of Dealignment, 1983; (with Anthony Fox) British Parliamentary Constituencies, 1984; (ed jtly) Electoral Change in Western Democracies, 1985; (ed jtly) Political Communications: the general election campaign of 1983, 1986, of 1987, 1989, of 1992, 1995, of 1997, 1998; (with Anthony Fox and Neil Day) The British Electorate 1963–87, 1991, 2nd edn as The British Electorate 1963–92, 1992; (with Anthony King) SDP: the birth, life and death of the Social Democratic Party, 1995; (jtly) The New British Politics, 1998, 3rd edn 2004; articles in various academic jls on public opinion, parties and elections in Britain. *Recreations:* music, walking, friends, family. *Address:* University College, Oxford OX1 4BH.

CREWE, Susan Anne; Editor, House and Garden, since 1994; *b* 31 Aug. 1949; *d* of late Richard Cavendish and Pamela Cavendish; *m* 1st, 1970, Quentin Crewe (marr. diss.; he *d* 1998); one *s* one *d*; 2nd, 1984, C. N. J. Ryan, *qv* (marr. diss.). *Educ:* St Mary's Sch., Wantage; Cheshire Coll. of Agriculture. Harpers & Queen magazine, 1986–92: shopping editor, 1987; consultant editor, 1990; social editor, 1991–92; subseq. freelance writer, broadcaster, journalist; contribs to The Times, Daily Telegraph, Daily Mail, Evening Standard and Literary Review. *Recreations:* gardening, sea-swimming, music. *Address:* Ladysyke House, Haverthwaite, Ulverston, Cumbria LA12 8PQ. *Club:* Academy.

See also Baron Cavendish of Furness.

CRIBB, Joseph Edmond; Keeper of Coins and Medals, British Museum, since 2003; *b* 30 Oct. 1947; *s* of Peter William Cribb and Rewa Annie Cribb (*née* Bloor); *m* 1971, Margaret Morrison Moore; two *s* two *d. Educ:* Queen Mary Coll., London (BA Hons Latin). British Museum: Curator of Asian coins, Dept of Coins and Medals, 1970–; Curator, HSBC Money Gall., 1997. Hon. Sec., 1983–94, Pres., 2004–Oct. 2009, RNS. Hirayama Inst. of Silk Road Studies (Kamakura) Award, 1997; Silver Medal, RNS, 1999. *Publications:* Money, from Cowrie Shells to Credit Cards, 1986; Money Fun Book, 1986; Money in the Bank, 1987; The Coin Atlas, 1990, 2nd edn 2003; Eyewitness Guide: Money, 1990, 2nd edn 1999; Collected Papers of Nicholas Lowick, vol. I, 1990, vol. II, 1991; Crossroads of Asia, 1992; A Catalogue of Sycee in the British Museum, Chinese Silver Currency Ingots *c.*1750–1933, 1992; Studies in Silk Road Coins and Culture, 1997; Magic Coins of Java, Bali and the Malay Peninsula, 1999; The Order of Industrial Heroism - Eric Gill's Medal for the Daily Herald, 2000; The Chand Collection - Ancient Indian Coins, 2003; The Indian Coinage Tradition, 2005; After Alexander: Central Asia before Islam, 2007; Eric Gill and Ditchling: the workshop tradition, 2007. *Recreations:* history of the Guild of St Joseph and St Dominic, Ditchling, reading Japanese fiction in translation, commuting. *Address:* Department of Coins and Medals, British Museum, WC1B 3DG; *e-mail:* jcribb@thebritishmuseum.ac.uk.

See also P. J. W. Cribb.

CRIBB, Air Cdre Peter Henry, CBE 1957; DSO 1942, and Bar, 1944; DFC 1941; JP; *b* 28 Sept. 1918; *s* of late Charles B. Cribb and Mrs Ethel Cribb; *m* 1949, Vivienne Janet, *yr d* of late Col S. T. J. Perry, MC, TD, DL, Oxton, Birkenhead, Ches; three *s. Educ:* Bradford Grammar Sch.; Prince Henry's Sch., Otley. Flt Cadet, RAF Coll., 1936–38; Flying duties in Bomber Comd, 1938–45 (Comd No. 582 Sqdn, RAF Little Staughton); Comdg RAF Salbani, RAF Peshawar, India and Staff No. 1 Indian Gp, 1945–47; OC 203 Sqdn, 1947, and HQ Staff, 1950, Coastal Comd; RAF Staff Coll., Bracknell, 1951; Asst Dir Tech. Intell., Air Min., 1951–53; Gp Capt. Plans and Policy, HQ Bomber Comd, 1953–57; 2nd TAF, Germany (OC Oldenburg, Ahlhorn and Gutersloh), 1957–60; Air Min., Dep. Dir Air Staff Briefing, 1959–61, Dir, 1961–62; SASO, Air Forces, Middle East, 1962–63; IDC, 1964; Deputy to Asst Chief of Defence Staff (Joint Warfare), MoD 1965–66; retired, 1966. Administrative Manager, Goldsworthy Mining Ltd, 1966–68. Associate Fellow, Australian Inst. of Management, 1969; Past State Pres., Ryder-Cheshire Foundn of WA, Inc.; Patron, Pathfinder Assoc. of WA. Foundn Chm. Council, Univ. of Third Age (Univ. of Western Australia) Inc., 1986–88. Patron (RAF), UK Combined Services Fedn, WA, 1990–. JP Western Australia, 1968. *Recreations:* mainly cerebral. *Address:* Unit 183, RAAFA Estate, 19 Hughie Edwards Drive, Merriwa, WA 6030, Australia.

CRIBB, Phillip James William, PhD; botanist; Deputy Keeper of Herbarium, 1989–2006, Hon. Research Fellow, since 2006, Royal Botanic Gardens, Kew; *b* 12 March 1946; *s* of Peter William Cribb and Rewa Annie, (Nancy), Cribb (*née* Bloor); *m* 1984, Marianne Gafafer. *Educ:* Christ's Coll., Cambridge (BA 1968); Univ. of Birmingham (PhD 1972). Joined Royal Botanic Gardens, Kew, as Higher Scientific Officer, 1974. Hon. Research Associate: Harvard Univ., 1979–90; Royal Holloway and Bedford New Coll., Univ. of London, 2006–. Trustee: Gilbert White & Oates Mus., Selborne, 1993–2006; Jany Renz Foundn, Univ. of Basel, 2003–. Veitch Meml Medal, RHS, 2006; Linnean Medal for Botany, 2007. *Publications:* The Genus Paphiopedilum, 1987; The Genus Cypripedium, 1997; (jtly) Slipper Orchids of Vietnam, 2003; (with M. Tibbs) A Very Victorian Passion, 2004. *Recreations:* natural history, travel. *Address:* The Herbarium, Royal Botanic Gardens, Kew, Richmond, Surrey TW9 3AE. *T:* (020) 8332 5245, *Fax:* (020) 8332 5278; *e-mail:* p.cribb@rbgkew.org.uk.

See also J. E. Cribb.

CRICH, Michael Arthur, FCMA; Director of Resources, English Heritage, 2002–07; *b* 9 Jan. 1957; *s* of Arthur Crich and Elizabeth Crich; *m* 1980, Gillian Anne Chamberlain; three *s* one *d. Educ:* Slough Grammar Sch.; Univ. of Hull; Emile Woolf Coll.; Warwick Business Sch., Univ. of Warwick (MBA 2002). FCMA 1991. Financial Controller, Wendy Restaurants (UK) Ltd, 1981–84; Sketchley Dry Cleaning: Finance Manager, 1984–86; Financial Controller, 1986–87; Financial Dir, 1987–91; London Borough of Brent: Gen. Manager, Contract Services, 1992–93; Dir, Brent Business Support, 1993–96; Exec. Dir, Finance and Corporate Services, London Borough of Lambeth, 1996–2001. *Publication:* (contrib.) Local Government Governance, 2001. *Recreations:* food and wine, live music, motor racing.

CRICHTON, family name of **Earl of Erne**.

CRICHTON, Viscount; John Henry Michael Ninian Crichton; Director, John Crichton Property, since 2008; *b* 19 June 1971; *s* and *heir* of Earl of Erne, *qv. Educ:* Sunningdale Prep. Sch.; Shiplake Coll.; L'Institut de Touraine, Tours. Douglas & Gordon Ltd, 1992–98; Associate Dir, Lane Fox Residential Ltd, 2000–07. *Recreations:* theatre, amateur dramatics, shooting, ski-ing. *Address:* Flat 1, 42 Redcliffe Road, SW10 9NJ; West Wing, Crom Castle, Newtownbutler, Co. Fermanagh, N Ireland. *Club:* Brooks's.

CRICHTON, Maj.-Gen. Edward Maitland-Makgill-, OBE 1948 (MBE 1945); GOC 51st Highland Division, 1966–68, retired; *b* 23 Nov. 1916; *s* of late Lt-Col D. E. Maitland-Makgill-Crichton, Queen's Own Cameron Highlanders and Phyllis (*née* Cuthbert); *m* 1951, Sheila Margaret Hibbins (*d* 2004), Bexhill-on-Sea; two *s* (and one *s* decd). *Educ:* Bedford Sch.; RMC Sandhurst. 2nd Lieut Queen's Own Cameron Highlanders, 1937; Adjt 5th Bn Cameron Highlanders, 1939; served with 5th Cameron Highlanders and 51 (Highland) Div., N Africa, Sicily, Normandy, NW Europe, 1940–45; GSO 1, HQ British Commonwealth Occupation Force, Japan, 1946–47; Mobilisation Br., WO 1948–50; 1st Bn Cameron Highlanders, Tripoli and Canal Zone, 1950–52; Jt Services Staff Coll., 1953 GSO 1, 3rd Inf. Div. (UK Strategic Reserve), Canal Zone, Egypt, UK and Suez, 1953–57 with 1st Bn Cameron Highlanders, Aden, 1957; comd 1st Liverpool Scottish, 1958–61 Comdr 152 (Highland) Inf. Bde, 1962–64; Dep. Dir Army Staff Duties, MoD, 1965–66 *Recreations:* shooting, golf, gardening, fishing. *Address:* c/o Coldon, Port of Menteith Stirling FK8 3RD. *T:* (0131) 447 5662.

CRICHTON, (John) Michael, MD; author; film director; *b* Chicago, 23 Oct. 1942 *Educ:* Harvard Univ. (AB *summa cum laude* 1964); Harvard Med. Sch. (MD 1969). Henry Russell Shaw Travelling Fellow, 1964–65; Vis. Lectr in Anthropology, Univ. o Cambridge, 1965; Post-doctoral Fellow, Salk Inst. for Biol Scis, La Jolla, Calif, 1969–70 Vis. Writer, MIT, 1988. *Television:* creator and Co-Exec. Producer, ER, 1994–; *films* writer/director: Westworld, 1973; Coma, 1977; The Great Train Robbery, 1978; Looker 1981; Runaway, 1984; director: Pursuit, 1972; Physical Evidence, 1989; writer: Rising Sun, 1993; Jurassic Park, 1993; producer: Disclosure, 1995; Twister, 1996; Sphere, 1998 Member: Authors' Guild; Writers' Guild Amer.; Dirs' Guild Amer.; Producers' Guild PEN Amer. *Publications: novels:* The Andromeda Strain, 1969; The Terminal Man, 1972 The Great Train Robbery, 1975; Eaters of the Dead, 1976; Congo, 1980; Sphere, 1987 Jurassic Park, 1990; Rising Sun, 1992; Disclosure, 1993; The Lost World, 1995; Airframe 1996; Timeline, 1999; Prey, 2002; State of Fear, 2004; Next, 2006; (as John Lange): Odd On, 1966; Scratch One, 1967; Easy Go, 1968; The Venom Business, 1969; Zero Cool 1969; Grave Descend, 1970; Drug of Choice, 1970; Binary, 1972; (as Jeffery Hudson) A Case of Need, 1968; (as Michael Douglas) (with D. Crichton) Dealing, 1971; *non-fiction* Five Patients, 1970; Jasper Johns, 1977; Electronic Life, 1983; Travels (autobiog.), 1988 *screenplays:* Westworld, 1975; (with A.-M. Martin) Twister, 1996. *Address:* 2118 Wilshire Boulevard #433, Santa Monica, CA 90403, USA; c/o Jenkins Financial Services, 433 N Camden Drive #770, Beverly Hills, CA 90210, USA.

CRICHTON, Nicholas; a District Judge (Magistrates' Courts) (formerly Metropolitan Stipendiary Magistrate), since 1987; a Recorder, since 1995; *b* 23 Oct. 1943; *s* of late Charles Ainslie Crichton and Vera Pearl McCallum; *m* 1973, Ann Valerie (*née* Jackson) two *s. Educ:* Haileybury & ISC; Queen's Univ., Belfast (LLB, 2nd Cl. Hons) Schoolmaster, Pembroke House Sch., Gilgil, Kenya, 1963; cowhand, Montana, USA 1966; articled to late T. J. Burrows, Currey & Co., SW1, 1968–70; Assistant Solicitor Currey & Co., 1970–71; Nicholls Christie & Crocker, 1972–74; Partner, Nicholls Christie & Crocker, 1974–86. An Asst Recorder, 1991–95. Mem., Family Justice Council, 2004–. *Recreations:* cricket (playing, coaching and watching), golf, watching rugby, gardening, walking, reading, bird watching, photography. *Address:* c/o Inner London Family Proceedings Court, 59–65 Wells Street, W1A 3AE.

CRICHTON-BROWN, Sir Robert, KCMG 1980; Kt 1972; CBE 1970; TD; Executive Chairman, Rothmans International plc, 1985–88; *b* Melbourne, 23 Aug. 1919; *s* of late L Crichton-Brown, Sydney; *m* 1941, Norah Isabelle, *d* of late A. E. Turnbull; one *s* one *d*. *Educ:* Sydney Grammar Sch. Served War, 1939–45, BEF; Major, Royal Artillery and Gen Staff, France, Iceland, India, Burma (despatches twice). Chairman: Lumley Corp. Ltd (formerly Edward Lumley Ltd), 1974–89 (Man. Dir, 1952–82); Lumley Life Ltd, 1961–8 (Dir, 1961–89); Lumley Gen. Insce Ltd, 1974–88 (Dir, 1952–88); NEI Pacific Ltd 1961–85; Rothmans of Pall Mall (Australia) Ltd, 1981–85 (Dir, 1971–85 and 1987–88) Commercial Banking Co. of Sydney Ltd, 1976–82 (Dir, 1970–82); Commercial & General Acceptance Ltd, 1977–82; Westham Dredging Co. Pty Ltd, 1975–85; Vice Chairman: Nat. Australia Bank Ltd, 1982–85; Custom Credit Corp., 1982–85; Director Daily Mail and General Trust Ltd (UK), 1979–95; Edward Lumley Hldgs, 1989–2003 Fed. Pres., Inst. of Dirs in Aust., 1967–80 (Chm., NSW Branch, 1965–80; Councillor 1980–89; Hon. Life Mem.). Mem. Federal Exec. and Federal Hon. Treas., Liberal Part of Australia, 1973–85. Pres., Med. Foundn, Sydney Univ., 1962–87; Dir, Royal Princ Alfred Hosp., 1970–84; Hon. Life Governor, Aust. Postgraduate Fedn in Medicine Member: Cttee, RACP, 1973–85; Adv. Bd, Girl Guides Assoc. of Australia, 1973–85 Adv. Bd, Salvation Army, 1973–85; Internat. Forum and Panel, Duke of Edinburgh's Award, 1979–84 (Nat. Co-ordinator, Duke of Edinburgh's Award Scheme in Aust 1979–84); Council, Imperial Soc. of Knights Bachelor, 1983–97 (Vice-Chm., Pacific Reg.); Nat. Councillor, Scout Assoc. of Aust., 1980–85; Mem. Council, Maritime Trust (formerly Cutty Sark Maritime Trust), 1987–99; Gov., Cutty Sark Soc., 1987–89 Underwriting Mem. of Lloyd's, 1946–97. Hon. Fellow, Sydney Univ., 1987. Mem Australia's winning Admiral's Cup Team (Balandra), UK, 1967; winner, Sydney-Hobart Yacht Race (Pacha), 1970. *Clubs:* White's, Royal Cruising; Royal Yacht Squadron Australian, Union (Sydney); Cruising Yacht Club of Australia, Royal Sydney Yacht Squadron, Royal Prince Alfred Yacht.

CRICHTON-STUART, family name of **Marquess of Bute**.

CRICK, Sir Bernard, Kt 2002; BSc (Econ.), PhD (London); writer; Emeritus Professor, University of London; *b* 16 Dec. 1929; *s* of Harry Edgar and Florence Clara Crick. *Educ:* Whitgift Sch.; University Coll., London. Research student, LSE, 1950–52; Teaching Fellow, Harvard, 1952–54; Asst Prof., McGill, 1954–55; Vis. Fellow, Berkeley, 1955–56; Asst Lectr, later Lectr, later Sen. Lectr, LSE, 1957–65; Prof. of Political Theory and Institutions, Sheffield Univ., 1965–71; Prof. of Politics, Birkbeck Coll., Univ of London, 1971–84. Vis. Prof., Univ. of Glasgow, 2006–07. Joint Editor, Political Quarterly, 1966–80; Chm., Political Qly Publishing Co., 1980–93; Literary Ed., Political Qly, 1993–2000. Joint Sec., Study of Parlt Gp, 1964–68; Jt Chm., British S African Conf., 1991–95. Chairman: Cttee on Teaching Citizenship in English Schs, 1997–98; Living in the UK (adv. gp), 2003–04; Adv. Bd for Naturalisation and Integration, 2004–05. Adviser on Citizenship to: DfEE, 1998–2001; Home Office, 2002–04. Hon. President: Politics Assoc., 1970–76; Assoc. for Citizenship Teaching, 2001–; Vice Pres., Political Studies Assoc., 1995–; Hon. Mem., Hansard Soc., 1993 (Mem. Council, 1962–93). Vis. Fellow, Woodrow Wilson Centre, 1995–96; Hon. Fellow in Politics, Univ. of Edinburgh, 1986–. Hon. Fellow: Birkbeck Coll., 1999; UCL, 2001. Senate of Australia Lectr, 2008. Hon. DSc QUB, 1986; Hon. DLitt: Sheffield, 1990; E London Poly., 1990; Kingston, 1996; Glasgow, 2006. *Publications:* The American Science of Politics, 1958; In Defence of Politics, 1962, 5th edn 2000 (trans. German, Japanese, Spanish, Italian); The Reform of Parliament, 1964, 2nd edn 1968; (ed) Essays on Reform, 1967; (ed with W. A. Robson) Protest and Discontent, 1970; (ed) Machiavelli: The Discourses, 1971; Political Theory and Practice, 1972; (ed with W. A. Robson) Taxation Policy, 1973; Basic Forms of Government, 1973; Crime, Rape and Gin, 1975; (ed with Alex Porter) Political Education and Political Literacy, 1978; George Orwell: a Life, 1980, 3rd edn 1992; (ed) Unemployment, 1981; (ed) Clarendon edn, Orwell's Nineteen Eighty-Four, 1984; (ed with Audrey Coppard) Orwell Observed, 1984; Socialism, 1987; Essays on Politics and Literature, 1989; Political Thoughts and Polemics, 1990; (ed) National Identities, 1991; (with David Millar) To Make the Parliament of Scotland a Model for Democracy, 1995; Essays on Citizenship, 2000; Crossing Borders, 2001; (ed) Citizens: towards a citizenship culture, 2001; Democracy, 2002. *Recreations:* polemicising, talking, theatre, city-walking. *Address:* 8A Bellevue Terrace, Edinburgh EH7 4DT. *T:* (0131) 557 2517. *Club:* Savile.

CRICK, Michael Lawrence; broadcaster and writer; Political Editor, BBC Newsnight, since 2007; *b* 21 May 1958; *s* of John Fairhurst Crick and Patricia Margaret Crick (*née* Wright); *m* 1985, Beatrice Margaret Sarah Hounsell (marr. diss.); one *d*; partner, Lucy Katharine Anna Hetherington; one *d*. *Educ:* Manchester Grammar Sch. (Foundn Schol.); New Coll., Oxford (BA 1st Cl. Hons PPE 1979). Pres., Oxford Union, 1979. Trainee journalist, ITN, 1980–82; Channel 4 News: producer, 1982–84; reporter, 1984–88; Washington Corresp., 1988–90; reporter, Panorama, 1990–92, Newsnight, 1992–2007, BBC. Chm., Young Fabian Gp, 1980–81. Organiser, Shareholders United, 1988–99 (Vice-Chm., 1999–2001). Mem., Manchester United Fans' Forum, 2000–02. *Publications:* (Founder Ed.) Oxford Handbook, 1978; (Founder Ed.) Oxbridge Careers Handbook, 1979; Militant, 1984; Scargill and the Miners, 1985; (with D. Smith) Manchester United: the betrayal of a legend, 1989; Jeffrey Archer: stranger than fiction, 1995; The Complete Manchester United Trivia Factbook, 1996; Michael Heseltine: a biography, 1997; The Boss: the many sides of Alex Ferguson, 2002; In Search of Michael Howard, 2005. *Recreations:* following Manchester United, swimming, hill-walking, collecting political and football books and memorabilia. *Address:* 1 Sumburgh Road, SW12 8AJ. *T:* (020) 7223 5847, 07762 601173, *Fax:* (020) 7924 4556; *e-mail:* CrickML@aol.com. BBC TV Centre, W12 7RJ. *T:* (020) 8624 9820.

CRICK, R(onald) Pitts, FRCS, FRCOphth; Ophthalmic Surgeon, King's College Hospital, 1950–1982 (Hon. Consultant, 1982–87); Recognised Teacher in the Faculty of Medicine, University of London, 1960–87; Lecturer in Opthalmology, King's College Hospital Medical School, 1950–1982, Emeritus Lecturer, 1982–87; *b* 5 Feb. 1917; *yr s* of Owen J. Pitts Crick and Margaret Daw, Minehead, Som; *m* 1941, Jocelyn Mary Grenfell Robins, *yr d* of Leonard A. C. Robins and Geraldine Grenfell, Hendon; four *s* one *d*. *Educ:* Latymer Upper Sch., London; King's Coll. and (Science Schol.) King's Coll. Hosp. Med. Sch., Univ. of London. MRCS, LRCP 1939; DOMS 1946; FRCS 1950; FRCOphth 1988 (Hon. FRCOphth 2008). Surgeon, MN, 1939–40; Surg. Lieut, RNVR, 1940–46. Ophthalmic Registrar, King's Coll. Hosp., 1946–48; Surgical First Asst, Royal Eye Hosp., 1947–50; Ophth. Surg., Epsom County Hosp., 1948–49; Ophth. Registrar, Belgrave Hosp. for Children, 1948–50; Ophth. Surg., Sevenoaks Hosp., 1948–50; Sen. Ophthalmic Surg., Royal Eye Hosp., 1950–69; Ophthalmic Surg., Belgrave Hosp. for Children, 1950–66. Vis. Res. Fellow, Univ. of Sussex, 1976–98. Chm., Ophthalmic Post-Grad. Trng, SE Thames RHA, 1972–82. Examr to RCS for Diploma in Ophthalmology, 1961–68. Hon. Ophth. Surg., Royal London Soc. for the Blind, 1954–57. FRSocMed, Vice-Pres. Ophthalmological Section, 1964, and Mem. Council Ophthalmolog. Section, 1953–54 and 1956–58. Member: Oxford Ophthalmolog. Congress; Southern Ophthalmolog. Soc. (Vice-Pres., 1969; Pres., 1970); Founder and Chm., Internat. Glaucoma Assoc., 1974–2000 (Pres., 2000–05); Charter Member: Internat. Glaucoma Congress, USA, 1977; Internat. Assoc. of Ocular Surgeons, 1981. Alim Meml Lectr, Ophthalmolog. Soc. of Bangladesh, Dhaka, 1991. Sir Stewart Duke-Elder Glaucoma Award, Internat. Glaucoma Congress, 1985; Lederle Medal for Ophthalmology, Amer. Soc. of Contemp. Ophthalmol., 1985. *Publications:* All About Glaucoma, 1981; A Textbook of Clinical Ophthalmology, 1986, 3rd edn (with Peng T. Khaw) 2003; Cardiovascular Affections, Arteriosclerosis and Hypertension (Section in Systemic Ophthalmology, ed A. Sorsby), 1950 and 1958; Computerised Monitoring of Glaucoma (Section in Glaucoma, ed J. G. Bellows), 1979; Diagnosis of Primary Open Angle Glaucoma (in Glaucoma, ed J. E. Cairns), 1986; medical and ophthalmic contribs to Brit. Jl Ophthalmology, BMJ, Lancet, Eye, Ophthalmic and Physiol Optics, etc. *Recreations:* motoring, sailing, economics. *Address:* International Glaucoma Association, Woodcote House, 15 Highpoint Business Village, Henwood, Ashford, Kent TN24 8DH. *T:* (01233) 648160, *Fax:* (01233) 648179; *e-mail:* info@iga.org.uk; 10 Golden Gates, Sandbanks, Poole, Dorset BH13 7QN. *T:* (01202) 707560, *Fax:* (01202) 701560. *Clubs:* Royal Automobile; Royal Motor Yacht.

CRICKHOWELL, Baron *cr* 1987 (Life Peer), of Pont Esgob in the Black Mountains and County of Powys; **Roger Nicholas Edwards;** PC 1979; Chairman, ITNET Plc, 1995–2004; *b* 25 Feb. 1934; *s* of late (H. C.) Ralph Edwards, CBE, FSA, and Marjorie Ingham Brooke; *m* 1963, Ankaret Healing; one *s* two *d*. *Educ:* Westminster Sch.; Trinity Coll., Cambridge, 1954–57; read History: BA 1957, MA 1968. Member of Lloyds, 1965–2002. Dir, 1987–97, Chm., 1997–2002, HTV Ltd; Dir, Associated British Ports Hldgs, 1988–99; Vice-Chm., Anglesey Mining, 1988–2000. MP (C) Pembroke, 1970–87. Opposition spokesman on Welsh affairs, 1975–79; Sec. of State for Wales, 1979–87. Chm., NRA, 1989–96 (Chm., Adv. Cttee, 1988–89). Pres., Univ. of Wales, Cardiff (formerly Univ. of Wales Coll. of Cardiff), 1988–98 (Hon. Fellow, UC, Cardiff, 1985). Dir, WNO, 1988–92. President: Contemporary Art Society for Wales, 1988–93; SE Wales Arts Assoc., 1988–94; Mem., Cttee, AA, 1988–98. Hon. LLD Glamorgan, 2001. *Publications:* Opera House Lottery, 1997; Westminster, Wales and Water, 1999; articles and reviews in The Connoisseur and other jls. *Recreations:* fishing, gardening, collecting watercolours and drawings. *Address:* Pont Esgob Mill, Fforest Coal Pit, near Abergavenny, Monmouthshire NP7 7LS; 4 Henning Street, SW11 3DR. *Club:* Brooks's.

CRICKMAY, Anthony John; photographer, since 1961; *b* 20 May 1937; *s* of Jack and Peggy Crickmay. *Educ:* Belmont Sch., Dorking. Photographer, specialising in theatre, portraits, fashion, reportage; work has appeared in many publications throughout the world; has photographed personalities and stars incl. the Queen, the Queen Mother, the Prime Minister and family, etc. *Publications:* The Principles of Classical Dance, 1979; Lynn Seymour, 1980; Dancers, 1982. *Recreations:* swimming, tennis, but most of all, photography. *Address:* c/o Camera Press, 21 Queen Elizabeth Street, SE1 2PD. *T:* (020) 7378 1300.

CRIDLAND, John Robert, CBE 2006; Deputy Director-General, Confederation of British Industry, since 2000; *b* 3 Feb. 1961; *s* of Walter and Doreen Cridland; *m* 1987, Denise Yates; one *s* one *d*. *Educ:* Christ's Coll., Cambridge (MA). Confederation of British Industry, 1982–: Director: Envmtl Affairs, 1991–95; Human Resources Policy, 1995–2000. Member: Low Pay Commn, 1997–2007; LSC, 2007–; Councillor, ACAS, 1998–2007. *Recreations:* history, cinema, castles. *Address:* Confederation of British Industry, Centre Point, 103 New Oxford Street, WC1A 1DU. *T:* (020) 7395 8005, *Fax:* (020) 7836 0645; *e-mail:* john.cridland@cbi.org.uk.

CRIGMAN, David Ian; QC 1989; *b* 16 Aug. 1945; *s* of late Jack Crigman and of Sylvia Crigman; *m* 1980, Judith Ann Penny; one *s*. *Educ:* King Edward's Sch., Birmingham; Univ. of Leeds (LLB Hons). Called to the Bar, Gray's Inn, 1969; a Recorder, 1985. *Publications:* What's Truth Got To Do With It? (novel), 2006; The Molecule Man (novel), 2008. *Recreations:* tennis, ski-ing, writing, travel. *Address:* St Philips Chambers, 55 Temple Row, Birmingham B2 5LS. *T:* (0121) 246 7000.

CRINE, Simon John Geoffrey; Director, Corporate Affairs, Digital UK, since 2006; *b* Weston-Super-Mare, 30 Nov. 1955; *s* of Geoffrey V. Crine and Ruby E. Crine; *m* Alison Blom-Cooper; one *s* one *d*. *Educ:* Weston-Super-Mare Grammar Sch.; Univ. of York (BA Hons Hist.). Various political and public policy appts, 1979–84; Dir, Nat. Campaign for the Arts, 1985–90; Gen. Sec., Fabian Soc., 1990–96; Dir, Public Affairs, APCO UK, 1997–2004; Dir, England and Industry, Ofcom, 2004–06. Mem., Policy Adv. Bd, Social Market Foundn, 2000–. Harkness Fellow, Washington, DC, 1993–94. *Publications:* various Fabian, WEA and Low Pay Unit reports; occasional journalism. *Recreations:* reading the papers, watching the kids play cricket, tennis or ride horses, playing occasional golf or tennis myself, seeing friends, theatre, history. *Address:* Digital UK, The Met Building, 22 Percy Street, W1T 2BU. *T:* 07711 066378; *e-mail:* simon.crine@digitaluk.co.uk.

CRIPPS, family name of **Baron Parmoor**.

CRISHAM, Catherine Ann; lawyer, Treasury Solicitor's Department, 2003–07; *b* 29 April 1950; *d* of Air Vice-Marshal W. J. Crisham, CB, CBE and late Maureen Teresa Crisham (*née* Bergin). *Educ:* St Anne's Coll., Oxford (BA); Exeter Univ. (LLM). Lecturer in European Community Law: Leiden Univ., 1977–80; London Univ., 1980–82; called to the Bar, Gray's Inn, 1981; private practice, 1982–84; lawyer, MAFF, 1984–88 and 1991–94; Legal Sec., European Court of Justice, 1988–90; Hd, Legal Directorate, MAFF, subseq. DEFRA, 1994–2003. *Recreations:* theatre, cinema, walking.

CRISP, family name of **Baron Crisp**.

CRISP, Baron *cr* 2006 (Life Peer), of Eaglescliffe in the County of Durham; **Edmund Nigel Ramsay Crisp,** KCB 2003; *b* 14 Jan. 1952; *s* of Edmund Theodore Crisp and late Dorothy Sheppard Crisp (*née* Ramsay); *m* 1976, Siân Elaine Jenkins; one *s* one *d*. *Educ:* Uppingham Sch.; St John's Coll., Cambridge (BA Hons 1973; MA 1976). Dep. Dir, Halewood Community Council, 1973; Production Manager, Trebor, 1978; Dir, Cambs Community Council, 1981; Unit Gen. Manager, E Berks HA, 1986; Chief Executive: Heatherwood and Wexham Park Hosps, 1988; Oxford Radcliffe Hosp. NHS Trust, 1993–97; Regl Dir, S Thames, 1977–98, London, 1999–2000, NHS Exec., DoH; Permanent Sec. and Chief Exec., DoH and NHS, 2000–06. CCMI 2002; Companion, Inst. of Healthcare Mgt, 2003. Hon. FRCP, 2004. Hon. DSc City, 2001. *Recreation:* the countryside. *Address:* House of Lords, SW1A 0PW. *Clubs:* Reform; Tutts Clump Tennis.

CRISP, Clement Andrew, OBE 2005; contributor, since 1956, and Dance Critic, since 1970, Financial Times; *b* 21 Sept. 1931; *s* of Charles Evelyn Gifford Crisp and Bertha Dorothy (*née* Dean). *Educ:* Oxted Sch.; Bordeaux Univ.; Keble Coll., Oxford Univ. (BA). Critic and dance writer to various jls, 1956–; Ballet Critic, The Spectator, 1966–70. Lectr, Librarian and Archivist to Royal Acad. of Dancing, 1963–85, Archivist, 1985–2001. Associate Prof., Univ. of Notre Dame (London Faculty), 1987–. Queen Elizabeth II Coronation Award, Royal Acad. of Dancing, 1992; Vaslav Nijinsky Medal, Poland, 1995. Knight, Order of Dannebrog (Denmark), 1992. *Publications include:* (with Peter Brinson) Ballet for All, 1971, rev. edn 1980; with Mary Clarke: Ballet: an illustrated history, 1973, rev. edn 1992; Making a Ballet, 1974; Ballet in Art, 1976; Design for Ballet, 1978; Introducing Ballet, 1978; Ballet-goer's Guide, 1981; History of Dance, 1981; How to Enjoy Ballet, 1983, 2nd edn 1987; Dancer, 1984; Ballerina, 1987; London Contemporary Dance, 1989. *Recreations:* avoiding noise, gardening, despair about dancing. *Address:* 82 Marsham Court, Marsham Street, SW1P 4LA.

CRISP, Sir John Charles, 5th Bt *cr* 1913, of Bungay, Suffolk; *b* 10 Dec. 1955; *s* of Sir (John) Peter Crisp, 4th Bt and Judith Mary Crisp (*née* Gillett); *S* father, 2005; *m* 1992, Mary Jo, *e d* of Dr and Mrs D. MacAuley; one *s*. *Heir: s* George Peter Daniel Crisp, *b* 17 Sept. 1993.

CRISP, June Frances; *see* de Moller, J. F.

CRISPIN, Prof. Sheila Margaret, PhD; FRCVS; Visiting Professorial Fellow, University of Bristol, since 2004; *b* 21 Jan. 1944; *d* of William George Crispin and Winifred Margaret Crispin. *Educ:* Ulverston Grammar Sch.; University Coll. of N Wales (Bangor) (ARC Vet. Trng Schol.; BSc Hons Zool. 1967); Girton Coll., Cambridge (MA, VetMB 1972); Univ. of Edinburgh (PhD 1984). DVA 1976; DVOphthal 1985; DipECVO 1993; FRCVS 1999. In private practice, Cumbria, 1972; Clin. Schol., then Univ. House Surgeon, Univ. of Cambridge, 1972–75; Bye-Fellow and Dir of Studies in Vet. Medicine, Girton Coll., Cambridge, 1974–75; Lectr, Univ. of Edinburgh, 1975–83; University of Bristol: Lectr, 1983–91; Sen. Lectr, 1991–2000; Reader, 2000–02; Prof. of Comparative Ophthalmol., 2002–04; Res. Fellow, 2003–04. Share-Jones Lectr, RCVS, 1991. Bull Fellow, Univ. of Guelph, Canada, 2000. Co-Chm., Quinquennial Sci. Audit, DEFRA Lab. Sci. Agencies, 2005–07; Mem., Sci. Adv. Council, DEFRA, 2006–. Chief Panellist, BVA/Kennel Club/Internat. Sheep Dog Soc. Eye Scheme, 1992–96, 1998–99 and 2008–. Member: Vet. Services Adv. Cttee, BVA, 1995–98; Sci. Adv. Cttee, Animal Health Trust, 1998–; Council, RCVS, 2003– (Chm. of various cttees; Pres., 2006–07). Chm., British Assoc. for Vet. Ophthalmol., 1983–86. Trustee, Wildlife Information Network. Associate MRCOphth 1990. Simon Award, British Small Animal Vet. Assoc., 1989. *Publications:* (ed and contrib. with S. M. Petersen-Jones) Manual of Small Animal

Ophthalmology, 1993, 2nd edn 2002; (ed jtly and contrib.) A Colour Atlas and Text of Equine Ophthalmology, 1995, 2nd edn 2004; (ed and contrib. with K. C. Barnett) Feline Ophthalmology: an atlas and text, 1998; Notes on Veterinary Ophthalmology, 2005; contribs mainly in the field of comparative ophthalmology. *Recreations:* mountaineering, sailing, classical music, environmental stewardship, moral philosophy. *Address:* Cold Harbour Farm, Underbarrow, Kendal, Cumbria LA8 8HD. *T:* and *Fax:* (01539) 568637; *e-mail:* s.m.crispin@bris.ac.uk, s.crispin@rcvs.org.uk. *Clubs:* Farmers', Kennel; Pinnacle.

CRITCHETT, Sir Charles George Montague, 4th Bt *cr* 1908, of Harley Street, St Marylebone; engineer, W. S. Atkins, since 1998; *b* 2 April 1965; *s* of Sir Ian George Lorraine Critchett, 3rd Bt and of Jocelyn Daphne Margret Critchett (*née* Hall); *S* father, 2004; *m* 2004, Joanna Jane Sugden, *d* of late Dr H. J. S. Sugden and of Mrs Pamela Morrow; two *s. Educ:* Harrow; Univ. of Bristol (BEng 1st Cl. Aeronautical Engrg); Wolfson Coll., Cambridge (PGCE Design, Mfr and Mgt). Aerodynamicist and Project Mgr, British Aerospace, 1990–97. *Heir: s* Ralph Henry Anderson Critchett, *b* 22 Jan. 2006. *Address:* 13 Alexandra Park, Redland, Bristol BS6 6QB.

CRITCHLEY, Philip, CB 1990; consultant, Martin Jack & Co., 1991–2005; *b* 31 Jan. 1931; *s* of Henry Stephen and Edith Adela Critchley; *m* 1962, Stella Ann Barnes; two *s* one *d. Educ:* Manchester Grammar Sch.; Balliol Coll., Oxford (MA, 2nd Classical Mods and Greats). National Service, Intelligence Corps, 1953–55. Joined Min. of Housing and Local Govt, later Dept of Environment, 1955: Principal, 1960; Asst Sec., 1969; Under Sec., 1980; Dir of Waste Disposal, 1983; Dir of Contracts, Highways Administration and Maintenance, 1985–90; Dir of Network Mgt and Maintenance, 1990–91, Dept of Transport. Volunteer, Ulverston Br., MIND, 1996–. Advr, S Cumbria Mental Health User and Carer Forum, 2004–. FRSA 1990. *Recreations:* philosophy, writing poetry. *Address:* Infield House, Kendall Ground, Lowick, Ulverston, Cumbria LA12 8ER. *T:* (01229) 885254. *Clubs:* Blackheath Harriers; Oxford Union Society.

CRITCHLEY, Tom; international business adviser, since 1990; *b* 17 Aug. 1928; *s* of late Leonard and Jessie Critchley; *m* 1951, Margaret Bland; one *s. Educ:* Sheffield Coll. of Commerce and Technology (Freshgate Trust Award, 1958). Davy-Ashmore Group, 1951–66; Cammell Laird and Upper Clyde Groups, 1966–69; J. C. B. Group, 1969–70; EMI Group, 1970–80; Head, Investment Casting Mission to Canada; UN Adviser to Tanzanian Govt; Adviser to UN High Commn for Refugees; Chm., MATC Ltd; Senior Partner, internat. consultancy practice, 1980–85; Under Sec., DHSS, subseq. Dept of Health, and NHS Management Bd Mem., 1986–90; Head, healthcare missions to Japan, Philippines, Indonesia, USSR and Poland, 1989–90; UK Chm., Anglo-Soviet Health-care Gp, 1989–91; Managing Director: Bio-Flo Ltd, 1991–95; Eurosep, Poland, 1992–95. Chairman: UK Trade Assoc., 1990–92; European Timeshare Fedn, 1991–92; Mem. Board, Nat. Inst. of Govt Purchasing, USA, 1977–78; Sen. UK Deleg., Internat. Fedn of Purchasing & Materials Management, 1980–85; Dir, Internat. Management Inst., Paris, 1980–88; Faculty Mem., Management Centre Europe, Brussels, 1980–85; Mem., Business in the Community, 1989–92. Institute of Purchasing & Supply, now Chartered Inst. of Purchasing and Supply: Mem., 1959–; FCIPS (Fellow, 1967); Chm. Council, 1974–75; Pres., 1977–78; Chm., Ext. Affairs, 1978–82; Mem., Internat. Council, 1979–82. Pres., Internat. Cttee of Friendship for Internat. Students, Imperial Coll., London, 1996–97. Millennium Adviser: The Children's Soc., 1996–98; Friends of the Elderly, 1998–2000; Business Develt Advr, SE Regl Arts Centre, 2000–02. Chm., Huntleigh Foundn, 1997–2003; Capital Appeal Co-ordinator, Harlington Hospice, 2003–05. Vice-Patron, British Assoc. for Services to Elderly, 2006–. *Recreations:* competitive sports, live theatre, North American history. *Address:* 3 Lincoln Close, Stoke Mandeville, Bucks HP22 5YS. *T:* (01296) 612511, *Fax:* (01296) 614203.

CRITCHLOW, Christopher Allan; His Honour Judge Critchlow; a Circuit Judge, since 2000; *b* 8 July 1951; *s* of late Charles Brandon Critchlow and of Eileen Margerie (*née* Bowers); *m* 1974, Wendy Anne Lucey; one *s* two *d. Educ:* Royal Grammar Sch., Lancaster; Exeter Univ. (LLB). FCIArb 1994. Called to the Bar, Inner Temple, 1973, Bencher, 2003; Mem., Western Circuit; Asst Recorder, 1987–91; a Recorder, 1991–2000. Gov., RGS Guildford, 2004–. *Recreations:* golf, bridge, listening to music, reading history. *Address:* Guildford Crown Court, Bedford Road, Guildford, Surrey GU1 4ST. *Club:* Reform.

CROALL, Simon Martin; QC 2008; *b* Bramhall, Cheshire, 12 Feb. 1963; *s* of Alan and Jean Croall; *m* 1989, Susan Cook (separated 2007); one *s* one *d. Educ:* Stockport Grammar Sch.; Emmanuel Coll., Cambridge (BA Law 1985). Called to the Bar, Middle Temple, 1986; in practice as barrister, 1986–. Mem., Professional Conduct and Complaints Cttee, Bar Council of England and Wales, 2001–04. Gov., Stanley Infant Sch., 1997–2001. *Publication:* (contrib.) Butterworth's Commercial Court & Arbitration Pleadings, 2005. *Recreations:* athletics (including coaching), travel, Wii Sports, time with my children. *Address:* Quadrant Chambers, 10 Fleet Street, EC4Y 1AU. *T:* (020) 7583 4444, *Fax:* (020) 7583 4455; *e-mail:* simon.croall@quadrantchambers.com. *Club:* Kingston Athletics and Polytechnic Harriers Athletic.

CROCKARD, Prof. (Hugh) Alan, DSc; FRCS, FRCP; FDS RCS; National Director for Modernising Medical Careers, Department of Health, 2004–07; Professor of Surgical Neurology, Institute of Neurology, University College London, 2001–06, now Professor Emeritus; Consultant Neurosurgeon, National Hospital for Neurology and Neurosurgery, 1978–2006, now Hon. Consultant; *b* 24 Jan. 1943; *s* of Hugh and Mary Crockard; *m* 1977, Dr Caroline Orr; two *s. Educ:* Royal Belfast Academical Instn; Queen's Univ., Belfast (MB BCh, BAO 1966; DSc 2000). FRCSEd 1970; FRCS 1971; FDS RCS 2001; FRCP 2003. Wellcome Surgical Fellow, 1973; Hunterian Prof., RCS, 1974; Fogarty Internat. Fellow, 1974, Asst Prof., 1975, Univ. of Chicago; Sen. Lectr, QUB, 1975–78. Dir, Raven Dept of Educn, RCS, 1998–2003. Vis. Prof. of Surgical Neurology, Univ. of WA, 2000. Co-Founder, Hill Surgical Workshops, 1990. President: British Cervical Spine Soc., 1997–99 (Co-Founder, 1986); Eur. Cervical Spine Res. Soc., 1999–2001; Member: British Soc. of Neurological Surgeons; Amer. Acad. of Neurological Surgeons. Sinclair Medal for Surgery, QUB, 1966; Olivecrona Lectr, Karolinska Inst., Stockholm, 1995; Harrington Medal, Scoliosis Res. Soc., USA, 1995; Arnott Demonstr., RCS, 1995. *Publications:* (jtly) Trauma Care, 1981; (jtly) Neurosurgery: scientific basis of clinical practice, 1985, 3rd edn 2000; more than 300 papers. *Recreations:* music, travel, sailing, ski-ing, photography. *Address:* Victor Horsley Department of Neurosurgery, National Hospital for Neurology and Neurosurgery, Queen Square, WC1N 3BG. *Clubs:* Athenæum; Royal Ocean Racing.

CROCKER, John Fraser; His Honour Judge Crocker; a Circuit Judge, since 1995; *b* 27 May 1943; *o s* of late Noel John Fraser Crocker and Marjorie Jean Crocker (*née* Heaton); *m* 1969, Janet Butteriss; one *s* twin *d. Educ:* The Leys, Cambridge; Christ's Coll., Cambridge (MA). Admitted Solicitor, 1969; called to the Bar, Inner Temple, 1973; a Recorder, 1991–95. Resident Judge: Isleworth Crown Court, 1999–2003; Guildford Crown Court, 2004–08. *Recreations:* reading thrillers, avoiding gardening. *Address:* Kingston Crown Court, 6–8 Penrhyn Road, Kingston-upon-Thames KT1 2BB.

CROCKETT, Sir Andrew (Duncan), Kt 2003; President, JP Morgan Chase International, since 2003; *b* 23 March 1943; *s* of late Dr Andrew Stuart Crockett and of Sheilah Crockett (*née* Stewart); *m* 1966, Marjorie Frances Hlavacek; two *s* one *d. Educ:* Queens' College, Cambridge (MA Econ.); Yale Univ. (MA). Bank of England, 1966–72; International Monetary Fund, 1972–89; Exec. Dir, Bank of England, 1989–93; Gen. Manager, BIS, 1994–2003. *Publications:* Money: theory, policy, institutions, 1973; International Money: issues and analysis, 1977; contribs to professional jls. *Recreations:* reading, golf, tennis. *Address:* JP Morgan Chase, 272 Park Avenue (15th Floor), New York, NY 10017, USA.

CROFT, family name of **Baron Croft.**

CROFT, 3rd Baron *cr* 1940, of Bournemouth, co. Southampton; **Bernard William Henry Page Croft;** Bt 1924; publisher; *b* 28 Aug. 1949; *s* of 2nd Baron Croft and Lady Antoinette Conyngham (*d* 1959), *o d* of 6th Marquess Conyngham; *S* father, 1997; *m* 1993, Elizabeth Mary Richardson, *o d* of late James Richardson, Co. Tyrone. *Educ:* Stowe; UCW, Cardiff (BScEcon). *Recreations:* shooting, fishing, ski-ing. *Address:* Croft Castle, Leominster, Herefordshire HR6 9PW; 5 Comeragh Mews, Comeragh Road, W14 9HW. *Clubs:* Naval and Military, Hurlingham.

CROFT, Charles Beresford, FRCS, FRCSE; Consultant Surgeon, Royal National Throat, Nose and Ear Hospital, and Royal Free Hospital, 1979–2004, now Emeritus; *b* 14 Jan. 1943; *s* of Arthur James Croft and Margaret Bays Croft (later Conyers); *m* 1968, Hilary Louise Whitaker; one *d. Educ:* Worksop Coll., Notts; Leeds Univ. Med. Sch. (MB BCh Hons 1965). FRCS 1970; FRCSE 1972; Dip. Amer. Bd Otolaryngology, 1979. House Surg., then Physician, Leeds Gen. Infirmary, 1966–68; Demonstrator in Anatomy, Leeds Med. Sch., 1968–69; Surgical Registrar, 1969–73, Sen. Registrar, Otolaryngology, 1971–73, Leeds Gen. Infirmary; Fellow in Head and Neck Surgery, Albert Einstein Med. Sch., NY, 1973–76; Associate Prof. in Otolaryngology, Albert Einstein Med. Sch. and Montefiore Hosp., NY, 1976–79. Civil Consultant Laryngologist, RAF, 1984–2004. FRSocMed. Arnott Demonstrator and Medal, RCS, 1988. *Publications:* chapters and papers on mgt of head and neck tumours, surgery of sleep breathing disorders and sleep apnoea in textbooks on tumour mgt and otolaryngology. *Recreations:* golf, fly fishing, bridge. *Address:* Westward Barn, Woodcock Hill, Rickmansworth, Herts WD3 1PX. *T:* (01923) 897187. *Clubs:* MCC; Moor Park Golf.

CROFT, His Honour David Legh; QC 1982; a Circuit Judge, 1987–2004; *b* 14 Aug. 1937; *s* of late Alan Croft and Doreen Mary Berry (*née* Mitchell); *m* 1963, Susan Mary (*née* Bagnall); two *s. Educ:* Haileybury and ISC; Nottingham Univ. (LLB). Called to the Bar, Middle Temple, 1960; called to the Hong Kong Bar, 1984; a Recorder, 1985–87. *Recreation:* resting. *Club:* The Castle (Rochester).

CROFT, David Michael Bruce; Director, since 1998, Managing Director, since 2002, Yorkshire Television Ltd; *b* 2 April 1955; *s* of late Eric David Croft and of Catherine Margaret Croft (*née* Kelly); *m* 2001, Angela Jane Murray; one *s. Educ:* Epsom Coll.; Magdalen Coll., Oxford (MA Hons Modern Hist.). Ocean Transport & Trading; NFC; Thames TV; Channel Four TV; Director: Tyne Tees TV, 1998–; Granada TV, 1998–; Meridian Broadcasting, 2001–; Border TV, 2001–; Anglia TV, 2001–; Central Independent TV, 2004–; HTV Gp, 2004–; Westcountry TV, 2004–. *Recreations:* golf, horse-racing, travel. *Address:* Yorkshire Television Ltd, Television Centre, Leeds LS3 1JS. *T:* (office) (0113) 243 8283, *Fax:* (0113) 242 3867; Flat 51, 3 Concordia Street, Leeds LS1 4ES; *e-mail:* david.croft@itv.com. *Club:* Royal Liverpool Golf.

CROFT, Frederick Lister; Deputy Legal Adviser, Department for Communities and Local Government (formerly Office of the Deputy Prime Minister), since 2004; *b* 13 April 1951; *s* of Frederick Croft and Eirian Croft (*née* Spickett); *m* 1975, Elizabeth May Cohen; two *s* one *d. Educ:* Highgate Sch.; Jesus Coll., Oxford (MA). Called to the Bar, Middle Temple, 1975; Treasury Solicitor's Department: Litigation Div., 1977–84; Dept of Energy Div., 1984–86; HM Treasury Div., 1986–87, 1989–91; DES Div., 1987–89; Dep. Head of Litigation, 1991–97; Under Sec., 1997; Legal Adviser: DfEE, 1997–98; BBC, 1998–2000; Divl Manager, Legal Gp, DETR, subseq. DTLR, 2000–02, ODPM and Dept of Transport, 2002–04. *Recreations:* reading, theatre, running. *Address:* (office) Eland House, Bressenden Place, SW1E 5DU. *Club:* Thames Hare and Hounds.

CROFT, Giles Laurance; Artistic Director, Nottingham Playhouse, since 1999; *b* 20 June 1957; *s* of John Rothschild Croft and Myrtle Maud Croft (*née* Geal); partner, Rachel Webb. *Educ:* Monckton Combe Sch. Artistic Director: Bath Young People's Th. Co., 1978–80; Gate Th., London, 1985–89; Literary Manager, Nat. Th., 1989–95; Artistic Dir, Palace Th., Watford, 1995–99. Director of plays including: Hinkemann, 1983; Naomi, 1987; Kind Hearts and Coronets (also adapted), 1997; Polygraph, 2001; Rat Pack Confidential, 2002; The Man Who, 2003; The White Album, 2006. Chair, Th. Writing Panel, Arts Council, 2000–03; Vice Pres., Eur. Th. Convention, 2003–. FRSA 1993. *Recreations:* reading, music, walking the pooch. *Address:* Nottingham Playhouse, Wellington Circus, Nottingham NG1 5AF. *T:* (0115) 947 4361; *e-mail:* gilesc@nottinghamplayhouse.co.uk. *Club:* Blacks.

CROFT, (Ivor) John, CBE 1982; painter; Head of Home Office Research and Planning Unit, 1981–83 (Head, Home Office Research Unit, 1972–81); *b* 6 Jan. 1923; *s* of Oswald Croft and Doris (*née* Phillips). *Educ:* Westminster Sch.; Christ Church, Oxford (Hinchcliffe Scholar in Mod. Hist.; MA); Inst. of Education, Univ. of London (MA); LSE. Temp. jun. admin. officer, FO, 1942–45; asst teacher, LCC, 1949–51; Inspector, Home Office Children's Dept, 1952–66; Sen. Research Officer, Home Office Research Unit 1966–72. Member: Criminological Scientific Council, Council of Europe, 1978–83 Chm., 1981–83; Conservative Study Gp on Crime, 1983–87; Kensington Crime Prevention Panel, 1984–87; Tribunal under I of M Interception of Communications Act 1989–94. Mem., Crime Policy Gp, Centre for Policy Studies, 2001–04. Governor, ILEA Secondary Schs, 1959–68. Mem. Exec. Cttee, English Assoc., 1966–77 (Hon. Treas 1972–75); Chairman: Pembridge Assoc., 1985–87; Peel Heritage Trust, 1991–93 (Mem Cttee, 1989–93); Circus Area Residents' Assoc., 1997–99 (Mem. Cttee, 1996–99) Commn on Community Safety, Bath and NE Somerset Council, 1996–97; Working Gp on Evening Economy, Bath, 2004–05. Group shows, 1958, 1963, 1967, 1968, 1969 1973, 1992, 1993, 2002; one-man shows, 1970, 1971, 2007. *Publications:* booklets pamphlets and articles, and various studies of crime, criminological research and the administration of justice. *Address:* 15 Circus Mews, Bath BA1 2PW. *Club:* Reform.

CROFT, Sir Owen (Glendower), 14th Bt *cr* 1671; grazier; *b* 26 April 1932; *s* of Sir Bernard Hugh Denman Croft, 13th Bt, and of Helen Margaret (*née* Weaver); *S* father 1984; *m* 1959, Sally Patricia, *d* of Dr T. M. Mansfield, Brisbane; one *s* two *d. Educ:* Armidale School, NSW. Mem., State Council of Advice to Rural Lands Protection Bd of NSW, 1983–96; Member: NSW Feral Animal Control Council, 1983–96; NSW Footrot Strategic Plan Steering Cttee, 1986–96; NSW Non-Indigenous Species Adv Cttee; Armidale Rural Lands Protection Bd, 1978–2001; NSW National Parks and Wildlife Service: Chm., Armidale Dist Adv. Cttee, 1988–2000; Chm., Northern

Tablelands Region Adv. Cttee, 2000–04. *Recreations:* tennis; National Trust activities. *Heir: s* Thomas Jasper Croft [*b* 3 Nov. 1962; *m* 1989, Catherine Fiona, *d* of Graham William White; two *d*]. *Address:* Salisbury Court, Uralla, NSW 2358, Australia. *T:* (2) 67784624.

CROFT, Roy Henry Francis, CB 1983; Member, Competition (formerly Monopolies and Mergers) Commission, 1995–2001; *b* 4 March 1936; *s* of late William Henry Croft and Dorothy Croft; *m* 1961, Patricia Ainley; one *s* two *d*. *Educ:* Isleworth Grammar Sch.; Christ's Coll., Cambridge (MA). BoT, 1959; Treasury, 1961–62; DEA, 1964–67; Private Sec. to Pres. Bd of Trade, 1968–70; Cabinet Office, 1970–72; Civil Aviation Div., Dept of Trade, 1973–76; Finance and Economic Appraisal Div., DoI, 1976–79; Posts and Telecommunications Div., DoI, 1979–80; Dep. Sec. DTI, 1980–85; Exec. Dir and Chief Operating Officer, SIB, 1985–93. Dir (non-exec.), Morgan Stanley Bank Internat. Ltd, 1999–2005.

CROFT, Rev. Dr Steven John Lindsey; Archbishops' Missioner, and Team Leader, Fresh Expressions, since 2004; *b* 29 May 1957; *s* of James and Marian Croft; *m* 1978, Ann Christine Baker; two *s* two *d*. *Educ:* Worcester Coll., Oxford (BA Hons 1980, MA 1983); St John's Coll., Durham (PhD 1984). Ordained deacon, 1983, priest, 1984; Curate, St Andrew's, Enfield, 1983–87; Vicar, St George's, Ovenden, Halifax, 1987–96; Mission Consultant, Dio. Wakefield, 1993–96; Priest-in-charge, St Augustine, Halifax, 1994–96; Warden, Cranmer Hall, St John's Coll., Durham, 1996–2004. *Publications:* The Identity of the Individual in the Psalms, 1987; Growing New Christians, 1993; Making New Disciples, 1994; (jtly) Emmaus, The Way of Faith, vols 1–6, 1996, vols 7–8, 1998; Man to Man: friendship and faith, 1999; Ministry in Three Dimensions: ordination and leadership in the local church, 1999; (jtly) Travelling Well, 2000; The Lord is Risen, 2001; Missionary Journeys, Missionary Church, 2001; Transforming Communities: re-imagining the Church for the 21st century, 2002; (jtly) Learning for Ministry: making the most of study and training, 2005; Moving On in a Mission-Shaped Church, 2005; The Advent Calendar, 2006; (ed) The Future of the Parish System, 2006; (ed) Mission-shaped Questions, 2008. *Recreations:* walking, cycling, films. *Address:* 15 Fyfield Road, Oxford OX2 6QE. *T:* (01865) 311838; *e-mail:* steven.croft@freshexpressions.org.uk.

CROFT, Sir Thomas (Stephen Hutton), 6th Bt *cr* 1818, of Cowling Hall, Yorkshire; Principal, Thomas Croft, Architects, since 1988; *b* 12 June 1959; *o s* of Major Sir John Croft, 5th Bt and Lucy Elizabeth, *d* of late Major William Dallas Loney Jupp, OBE; *S* father, 1990; *m* 2001, Maxine Julia, *d* of Antonio Benato and Mrs Jean Sichel; one *d*. *Educ:* King's Sch., Canterbury; University Coll., London (BSc); Royal Coll. of Art, London (MA). Architect, Richard Meier & Partners, Architects, New York, 1985–86; Project Architect, Rick Mather, Architects, London, 1986–88. Completed buildings include Royal Yacht Squadron Pavilion, Cowes, 2000. *Address:* (office) 9 Ivebury Court, 325 Latimer Road, W10 6RA. *T:* (020) 8962 0066, *Fax:* (020) 8962 0088; *e-mail:* email@thomascroft.com.

CROFT, Trevor Anthony; Reporter, Scottish Government Directorate for Planning and Environmental Appeals (formerly Scottish Executive Inquiry Reporters Unit), since 2002; *b* 9 June 1948; *s* of late Kenneth Edward Croft and Gladys (*née* Bartle); *m* 1980, Janet Frances Halley; two *d*. *Educ:* Belle Vue Boys' GS, Bradford; Hull Univ. (BSc 1969); Sheffield Univ. (DipTRP 1971). MRTPI 1974. Sen. Asst Planning Officer, Min. of Develt, NI, 1971–72; Asst Planning Officer, Countryside Commn for Scotland, 1972–75; Physical Planning Officer, Office of the President, Malaŵi, 1976–78; Parks Planning Officer, Dept of Nat. Parks and Wildlife, Malaŵi, 1978–82; National Trust for Scotland: Planning Officer, 1982–84; Head of Policy Res., 1984–88; Regl Dir, 1988–95; Dep. Dir and Dir of Countryside, 1995–97; Dir, 1997–2001; Consultant, 2001–03. Mem., Regl Adv. Cttee, S Scotland, Forestry Commn, 1987–90. Member Council: RSGS, 1998–2001, 2003–05 (Mem., Finance Cttee, 2003–08; Chm., Dunferline Br., 1993–96); Europa Nostra, 1999–2001. Chm., British Equestrian Vaulting Ltd, 2002–03; Mem. Bd, BEF, 2002–03. Chm. Awards Panel, Kinross Civic Trust, 2005–. Associate, RSGS, 1995; FRSA 1997. *Recreations:* sailing, travel, motorcycling, restoring Srs 1 Land Rover. *Address:* Glenside, Tillyrie, Kinross KY13 0RW. *T:* (01577) 864105. *Club:* Royal Scots (Edinburgh).

CROFTON, family name of **Baron Crofton.**

CROFTON, 8th Baron *cr* 1797 (Ire.); **Edward Harry Piers Crofton;** Bt 1758; *b* 23 Jan. 1988; *er* twin *s* of 7th Baron Crofton and of Gillian Crofton (*née* Bass); *S* father, 2007. *Educ:* Sandroyd Sch.; Stowe Sch. *Recreations:* travel, popular music, outdoor sports. *Heir: yr* twin *b* Hon. Charles Marcus George Crofton, *b* 23 Jan. 1988. *Address: e-mail:* hcrofton@gmail.com.

CROFTON, (Sir) Hugh Dennis, (8th Bt *cr* 1801, of Mohill); *S* nephew, 1987, but does not use the title and his name does not appear on the Official Roll of the Baronetage. *Heir: b* Major Edward Morgan Crofton.

CROFTON, Sir John (Wenman), Kt 1977; retired; Professor of Respiratory Diseases and Tuberculosis, University of Edinburgh, 1952–77; *b* 27 March 1912; *s* of Dr W. M. Crofton; *m* 1945, Eileen Chris Mercer, MBE 1984; two *s* three *d*. *Educ:* Tonbridge; Sidney Sussex Coll., Cambridge (BA 1933; MB BChir 1937; MD 1947); St Thomas's Hosp. FRCP 1951; FRCPE 1957. War of 1939–45, RAMC; France, Middle East, Germany. Lecturer in Medicine, Postgraduate Medical Sch. of London, 1947–51, Senior Lecturer, 1951; Part-time Tuberculosis Unit, Medical Research Council, Brompton Hosp., 1947–50; Dean of Faculty of Medicine, 1963–66, and Vice-Principal, 1969–70, Univ. of Edinburgh. Vice-Pres., 1972–73, Pres., 1973–76, RCPE. Hon. Mem., Acads of Medicine of Argentina, Catalonia and Singapore. Hon. FRCPI 1975; Hon. FRACP 1976; Hon. FACP 1976; Hon. FFCM 1978; Hon. FRCPE 1987; Hon. FRSE 1997; Hon. FRSocMed 2003. Dr *hc* Bordeaux, 1997; Hon. DSc London, 2001. Weber-Parkes Prize, RCP, 1966; City of Edinburgh Medal for Sci. and Soc., 1995; Galen Medal, Soc. of Apothecaries, 2001; Union Medal, Internat. Union against Tuberculosis and Lung Disease, 2005; Edwin Chadwick Medal, LSHTM, 2008. *Publications:* (jtly) Respiratory Diseases, 1969, 3rd edn 1981; (jtly) Clinical Tuberculosis, 1992, 3rd edn 2008; Housing and Health in Scotland, 1993; (co-ed) Tobacco and Health, 1996; (jtly) Tobacco or Health: a global threat, 2001; contributor to BMJ, Lancet, Thorax, etc. *Recreations:* reading science and history, mountains. *Address:* 13 Spylaw Bank Road, Edinburgh EH13 0JW. *T:* (0131) 441 3730.

CROFTON, Sir Julian (Malby), 7th Bt *cr* 1838, of Longford House, Sligo; *b* 26 Nov. 1958; *s* of Sir Melville Crofton, 6th Bt, MBE and of Mary Brigid Crofton (*née* Riddle), OBE; *S* father, 2003, but his name does not appear on the Official Roll of the Baronetage; *m* 1989, Hilary, *d* of T. J. Twort; two *s* one *d*. *Heir: s* William Robert Malby Crofton, *b* 5 Jan. 1996. *Address:* Broomfield House, Broomfield Park, Ascot, Berks SL5 0JT.

CROFTS, Roger Stanley, CBE 1999; FRSE; independent environment and management adviser; Chief Executive, Scottish Natural Heritage, 1991–2002; *b* 17 Jan. 1944; *s* of Stanley Crofts and Violet May Crofts (*née* Dawson); *m* 1996, Lindsay Manson; one *s* one *d* by previous marriage. *Educ:* Hinckley Grammar Sch.; Liverpool Univ. (BA); Leicester Univ. (PGCE); Aberdeen Univ. (MLitt). Res. Asst to Prof. K. Walton, Aberdeen Univ., 1966–72; British Geomorphological Res. Gp, UCL, 1972–74; Central Res. Unit, Scottish Office, 1974–84; Scottish Office: Head of Highlands and Tourism, 1984–88; Head of Rural Affairs, 1988–91. Visiting Professor: of Geography, 1992–95, of Envmtl Mgt, 1997–2004, Royal Holloway, Univ. of London; of Geoscience, Univ. of Edinburgh, 2004–; Hon. Prof. of Geography, Univ. of Aberdeen, 1997–. Chairman: UK Cttee, IUCN, 1999–2002; Europe Cttee, IUCN World Commn on Protected Areas, 2001–; National Trust for Scotland: Member: Council, 1992–2004; Exec. Cttee, 2003–04; Bd, 2004–; Convener, Conservation Cttee, 2004–. Member: Council, Scottish Wildlife Trust, 1992–97; RSGS, 1994–2000; Scottish Assoc. for Marine Science, 1995–2005; Board Member and Trustee: Plantlife Internat., 2001– (Chm., 2007–); Scottish Agricl Coll., 2002–; Chm., Sibthorp Trust, 2003–. Hon. Pres., Scottish Assoc. of Geography Teachers, 1994–95 (Patron, 2002–). FRSA 1997; FRSE 2001; FRSGS 2001; FRGS 2002. Hon DSc St Andrews, 2004. *Publications:* (with A. McKirdy) Scotland: the creation of its natural landscape, 1999; (ed) Scotland's Environment: the future, 2000; (ed) Conserving Nature: Scotland and the wider world, 2005; (with A. McKirdy and J. Gordon) Land of Mountain and Flood: the geology and landforms of Scotland, 2007; contribs to books on marginal regions, geomorph. mapping, second homes, field studies, conservation, envmtl policy; numerous articles. *Recreations:* designing gardens, choral singing, flower photography, cooking, hill walking. *Address:* 6 Old Church Lane, Duddington Village, Edinburgh EH15 3PX. *T:* (0131) 661 7858.

CROHAM, Baron *cr* 1978 (Life Peer), of the London Borough of Croydon; **Douglas Albert Vivian Allen,** GCB 1973 (KCB 1967; CB 1963); Chairman, Guinness Peat Group, 1983–87; Head of the Home Civil Service and Permanent Secretary, Civil Service Department, 1974–77; *b* 15 Dec. 1917; *s* of late Albert Allen; *m* 1941, Sybil Eileen Allegro (*d* 1994), *d* of late John Marco Allegro; two *s* one *d*. *Educ:* Wallington County Grammar Sch.; London School of Economics. BSc (Econ.) First Class Hons, 1938. Entered Board of Trade, 1939; Royal Artillery, 1940–45; Cabinet Office, 1947; Treasury, 1948–58; Under-Secretary, Ministry of Health, 1958–60; Under-Secretary, Treasury, 1960–62, Third Secretary, 1962–64; Dept of Economic Affairs: Dep. Under-Sec. of State, 1964–66; Second Permanent Under-Sec. of State, May–Oct. 1966; Permanent Under-Sec. of State, 1966–68; Permanent Sec., HM Treasury, 1968–74. Director: Pilkington plc (formerly Pilkington Bros), 1978–92; Guinness Mahon & Co., 1989–92; Dep. Chm., 1978–82, Chm., 1982–85, BNOC; Chm., Trinity Insurance, 1988–92. An Industrial Adviser to the Governor, Bank of England, 1978–83. President: Inst. for Fiscal Studies, 1979–92; British Inst. of Energy Economies, 1985–94. A Trustee, Anglo-German Foundn, 1977– (Chm., 1982–97). CCMI; FRSA 1975. Hon. Fellow, LSE, 1969; Hon. DSc (Social Sciences) Southampton, 1977. *Recreations:* bridge, woodwork. *Address:* 9 Manor Way, South Croydon, Surrey CR2 7BT. *T:* (020) 8688 0496. *Club:* Reform.

CROLL, Prof. James George Arthur, FREng; Professor of Civil Engineering, University College London, since 2003; *b* 16 Oct. 1943; *s* of late Keith Waghorn Croll and Jean Croll; *m* 1966, Elisabeth Joan (*née* Spracket) (marr. diss. 1997; she *d* 2007); one *s* one *d*. *Educ:* Palmerston North Boys' High Sch., NZ; Univ. of Canterbury, NZ (BE 1st cl. Hons, PhD). FIStructE, FICE, FIMA; CEng 1970, FREng (FEng 1990); CMath. Asst Engineer, Min. of Works, NZ, 1962–67; University College London: Res. Fellow, 1967–70; Lectr, 1970–81; Reader in Structural Engrg, 1981–85; Prof. of Structural Engrg, 1985–92; Chadwick Prof. of Civil Engrg, and Hd, Dept of Civil and Envmtl Engrg, 1992–2003. Vis. Fellow, Princeton, 1979; Visiting Professor: Fed. Univ. of Rio de Janeiro, 1973, 1981, 1984; Univ. of Hong Kong, 1985, 2000. FRSA. *Publications:* Elements of Structural Stability, 1972; Force Systems and Equilibrium, 1974. *Recreations:* singing, piano, painting, drawing, sailing, ski-ing, travel. *Address:* 8 Chester Place, Regent's Park, NW1 4NB. *T:* (020) 7486 4310. *Club:* Natural Science (UCL).

CROLL, (Mary) Louise, CBE 1995; HM Diplomatic Service, retired; Ambassador to Costa Rica, 1992–95; *b* 10 Sept. 1935. Joined FO, subseq. FCO, 1953; Bahrain, 1957; Addis Ababa, 1959; UK Mission, NY, 1961; FO, 1964; S America floater, 1967; Bilbao, 1969; Lusaka, 1972; First Sec., Madrid, 1979, FCO, 1984; Consul, Florence, 1988.

CROMARTIE, 5th Earl of, *cr* 1861; **John Ruaridh Grant Mackenzie,** MIExpE; Viscount Tarbat, Baron Castlehaven, Baron MacLeod, 1861; Chief of the Clan Mackenzie; explosives engineer; *b* 12 June 1948; *s* of 4th Earl of Cromartie, MC, TD and Olga (*d* 1996), *d* of late Stuart Laurance; *S* father, 1989; *m* 1973, Helen, *d* of John Murray; (one *s* decd); *m* 1985, Janet Clare, *d* of Christopher J. Harley; two *s*. *Educ:* Rannoch School, Perthshire; Strathclyde University. Pres., Mountaineering Council of Scotland, 2003– (Mem. Council, 1995–); Trustee, John Muir Trust, 2001–. *Publications:* Selected Climbs in Skye, 1982; articles in Classic Rock Climbs and Cold Climbs. *Recreations:* mountaineering, art, astronomy, geology. *Heir: s* Viscount Tarbat, *qv*. *Address:* Castle Leod, Strathpeffer, Ross-shire IV14 9AA. *Clubs:* Army and Navy; Scottish Mountaineering.

CROME, Prof. Ilana Belle, MD; FRCPsych; Professor of Addiction Psychiatry, and Academic Director of Psychiatry, University of Keele, since 2002; Consultant Addiction Psychiatrist, North Staffordshire Combined Healthcare Trust, Stoke-on-Trent, since 2002; *b* 2 Feb. 1951; *d* of late Solomon Glass and Yette Glass (*née* Golombick); *m* 1989, Prof. Peter Crome, *qv*; one *s*. *Educ:* Redhill Sch., Johannesburg; Lauriston Sch., Melbourne; Damelin Coll., Johannesburg; Univ. of Witwatersrand; New Hall, Cambridge (BA 1972, MA 1974); Univ. of Birmingham (MB ChB 1975; MD 1996). FRCPsych 1997. Sen. Lectr, Inst. of Psychiatry and Hon. Consultant, Maudsley and Bethlem Royal Hosp. and KCH, 1989–93; Sen. Lectr and Consultant Psychiatrist, St Bartholomew's Hosp. Med. Coll. and Barts NHS Trust, 1994; Consultant in Gen. Hosp. Liaison Psychiatry, City Gen. Hosp., Stoke-on-Trent, 1994–97; Prof. of Addiction Studies, 1997–98, Prof. and Hd, Dept of Psychiatry, 1998–2002, Univ. of Wolverhampton; Consultant Addiction Psychiatrist, Wolverhampton Healthcare Trust, 1997–2002. Member: Soc. for the Study of Addiction, 1994–; Scientific Cttee on Tobacco and Health, DoH, 2001–; Alcohol Educn and Res. Council, 2001–; Adv. Council on Misuse of Drugs, 2002–. Chair, Faculty of Substance Misuse, RCPsych, 1998–2002. Pres., Drug and Alcohol Section, Assoc. of European Psychiatrists, 2006–08 (Pres.-elect, 2004–06); Hon. Sec., Profs of Psychiatry Club, 2003–. Internat. Ed., American Jl of Addictions, 2002–; Ed., Drugs Educn, Prevention & Policy, 2002–. *Publications:* International Handbook of Addiction Behaviour, 1991; Young People and Substance Misuse, 2004; Psychological Disorders in Obstetrics and Gynaecology, 2006; contrib. papers to Addiction, Drug & Alcohol Dependence, Anaesthesia, Psychiatric Bull., Alcohol & Alcoholism, Acta Psychiatrica Scandinavica, British Jl Psychiatry, Psychol Medicine, Neuropharmacol., Lancet, Psychoneuroendocrinol. Reviews in Gerontology. *Recreations:* painting and paintings, plays and playing, pots and pottering, but not pot! *Address:* Academic Suite, Harplands Hospital, Hilton Road, Harpfields, Stoke-on-Trent, Staffs ST4 6TH. *T:* (01782) 441658, *Fax:* (01782) 441650; *e-mail:* ilana.crome@btinternet.com, pca03@keele.ac.uk.

CROME, Prof. Peter, MD; PhD; FRCPE, FRCP, FRCPGlas; FFPM; Professor of Geriatric Medicine, since 1994, and Head of Postgraduate Medicine, since 2001, Keele University; *b* 4 Feb. 1947; *s* of Leonard Crome, MC, FRCPE, FRCPath and Helena Crome (*née* Huttner); *m* 1989, Ilana Belle Glass (*see* I. B. Crome); one *s*, and one *s* one *d* from a former marr. *Educ:* Dulwich Coll.; King's Coll. London; King's Coll. Hosp. Med. Sch. (MB BS 1970; MD 1980; PhD 1995). LRCP 1970, MRCP 1974, FRCP 1990; MRCS 1970; DObstRCOG 1973; FRCPE 1988; FFPM 1992; FRCPGlas 1995. Consultant Geriatrician, Orpington Hosp., 1981–91; Sen. Lectr, King's Coll. Sch. of Medicine and Dentistry, 1991–94; Dep. Hd, 2001–05, Head, 2005, Med. Sch., Keele Univ. Hon. Consultant: Guy's and St Thomas' Hosp., 1988–2003; King's Healthcare NHS Trust, 1991–94. Dir, Shropshire and Staffs Strategic HA, 2003–06. President: Section of Geriatrics and Gerontol., RSocMed, 2001–03; British Geriatrics Soc., 2006–08 (Pres.-elect, 2004–06); Mem. Council, RCP, 2006–; Sec.-Gen., Clinical Sect., Internat. Assoc. of Gerontol. and Geriatrics, 2007–. *Publications:* (with G. A. Ford) Drugs and the Older Population, 2001; (jtly) Pain in Older People, 2006; contrib. papers on geriatric medicine, stroke and clinical pharmacol. *Recreations:* travel, food, especially cheese. *Address:* Wyke House, 62 Sutherland Drive, Westlands, Newcastle-under-Lyme, Staffs ST5 3NZ. *T:* (01782) 633168; *e-mail:* p.crome@keele.ac.uk. *Club:* Royal Society of Medicine.

CROMER, 4th Earl of, *cr* 1901; **Evelyn Rowland Esmond Baring;** Baron Cromer, 1892; Viscount Cromer, 1899; Viscount Errington, 1901; Chief Executive, Cromer Associates Ltd, since 1994; *b* 3 June 1946; *e s* of 3rd Earl of Cromer, KG, GCMG, MBE, PC and of Hon. Esmé Harmsworth, CVO, *d* of 2nd Viscount Rothermere; *S* father, 1991; *m* 1971, Plern Isarangkun Na Ayudhya (marr. diss. 1993); 2nd, 1993, Shelly Hu Cheng-Yu, *e d* of Hu Guoquin, Shanghai; one *s* one *d*. *Educ:* Eton. Managing Director: Inchcape (China) Ltd, 1979–94; Inchcape Vietnam Ltd, 1987–94; Inchcape Special Markets Ltd, 1990–94; Dir, Inchcape Pacific Ltd, 1985–94. Chairman: Lloyd George Standard Chartered China Fund Ltd (Hong Kong), 1994–2006; Jardine Fleming China Region Fund Inc. (USA), 1994–; Korea Asia Fund Ltd, 1996–2000; Philippine Discovery Investment Co. Ltd, 1997–2006; Cambridge Asia Fund Ltd, 2001–08; China IPO Gp Ltd; Director: Cluff Oil China Ltd (Hong Kong), 1990–99; China & Eastern Investments Ltd, 1991–96; Schroder AsiaPacific Fund Ltd, 1995–; Western Provident Assoc., 2004–; Pacific Basin Shipping Ltd, 2004–08; Japan High Yield Property Fund Ltd, 2005–. Dir, Somerset TEC, 1999–2001; Chm., Business Link Somerset, 1999–. Mem. St John's Council (Hong Kong), 1980–85. *Publication:* The Son from the West, 2007. *Recreations:* mountain climbing, deep sea diving. *Heir: s* Viscount Errington, *qv*. *Address:* 6 Sloane Terrace Mansions, SW1X 9DG. *Clubs:* White's, Oriental; Hong Kong (Hong Kong).

CROMPTON, Sir Dan, Kt 2003; CBE 1996; QPM 1990; HM Inspector of Constabulary, North of England, 1995–2002; *b* 15 Feb. 1941; *s* of Arthur and Elizabeth Crompton; *m* 1962, Olive Ramsden; one *s*. *Educ:* Didsbury Technical Sch., Manchester. Manchester City Police, 1960–68; Manchester and Salford Police, 1968–74; Greater Manchester Police, 1974–87; Nottinghamshire Constabulary, 1987–95 (Chief Constable, 1990–95). *Recreations:* reading, popular classics, gardening, cricket, Rugby. *Address:* 1 Half Acre Lane, Rochdale, Lancs OL11 4BY.

CROMPTON, Prof. Gareth, FRCP, FFPH; Professor of Public Health Medicine, University of Wales College of Medicine, 1989–97, now Emeritus; Hon. Fellow, University of Wales Institute, Cardiff, since 1997; *b* 9 Jan. 1937; *s* of late Edward and Annie Jane Crompton, Drefach-Felindre, Carmarthenshire; *m* 1965; one *d*. *Educ:* Llandysul Grammar Sch.; Welsh Nat. Sch. of Medicine. MB, BCh Wales, 1960; DObstRCOG 1962; DPH Wales, 1964; FFPH (FFCM 1976); FRCP 1986 (MRCP 1980). County Med. Officer, County Welfare Officer and Principal Sch. Med. Officer, Anglesey CC, 1966–73; Area Med. Officer, Gwynedd Health Authority, 1974–77; CMO, Welsh Office, 1978–89; Chief Admin. MO and Dir of Public Health Medicine, S Glam HA, 1989–96. Specialty Advr, Health Service Comr for England and Wales, 1974–77; Advr in Wales, Faculty of Community Medicine, 1974–77. Chm., Anglesey Disablement Adv. Cttee, 1969–77; Sec., Fluoridation Study Gp, Soc. of Med. Officers of Health, 1969–73; Mem., Welsh Hosp. Bd, 1970–74. Member: GMC, 1981–83 and 1987–89; Bd, PHLS, 1990–97; Exec. Bd, FPHM, 1990–95. Med. Fellow, Council of Europe, 1971. QHP 1984–87. Hon. MD Wales, 1999. Alwyn Smith Prize Medal, Faculty of Public Health, RCP, 2000. *Publications:* papers on the effects of fluoridated water supplies on dental caries, and the epidemiology and management of chronic sickness and disablement. *Recreations:* bowls, watching Rugby football and cricket, reading contemporary Welsh verse. *Address:* 19 Kenilworth House, Castle Court, Westgate Street, Cardiff CF10 1DJ. *T:* (029) 2034 3192.

CROMPTON, Kenneth Charles; Chief Executive, General Sir John Monash Foundation, since 2002; *b* 19 July 1948; *s* of late Charles Frederic Crompton and of Margaret Joan Crompton; *m* 1971, Elizabeth Anne Meek; one *s* two *d*. *Educ:* Melbourne Univ. (LLB). Solicitor, Morris Komesaroff, Aarons & Co., 1971–75; Seton Williams & Smyth, 1975–79; Gen. Manager, Legal and Technical Services, Victorian Chamber of Manufactures, 1979–87; Dir, Industrial Relations, 1987–88, Chief Exec. (Vic.), 1988–92, Aust. Chamber of Manufactures; Agent-Gen. for Victoria in London, 1993–96. Dir, Corporate Counsel Pty Ltd. *Recreations:* wind surfing, tennis, photography, walking. *Address:* 104 Scenic Crescent, Eltham, Vic 3095, Australia. *Clubs:* Athenæum (Melbourne); Melbourne Cricket.

CROMWELL, 7th Baron *cr* 1375 (called out of abeyance, 1923); **Godfrey John Bewicke-Copley;** *b* 4 March 1960; *s* of 6th Baron Cromwell and of Vivian, *y d* of late Hugh de Lisle Penfold, Isle of Man; *S* father, 1982; *m* 1990, Elizabeth, *d* of John Hawksley; three *s* (incl. twins) one *d*. *Heir: s* Hon. David Godfrey Bewicke-Copley, *b* 21 Sept. 1997.

CRONIN, Vincent Archibald Patrick; author; *b* 24 May 1924; *s* of late Archibald Joseph Cronin, MD, MRCP, DPH and of Agnes Mary Gibson, MB, ChB; *m* 1949, Chantal, *d* of Comte Jean de Rolland; two *s* three *d*. *Educ:* Ampleforth; Harvard; Trinity Coll., Oxford. Rifle Bde, 1943–45. *Publications:* The Golden Honeycomb, 1954; The Wise Man from the West, 1955; The Last Migration, 1957; A Pearl to India, 1959; The Letter after Z, 1960; Louis XIV, 1964; Four Women in Pursuit of an Ideal, 1965; The Florentine Renaissance, 1967; The Flowering of the Renaissance, 1970; Napoleon, 1971; Louis and Antoinette, 1974; trans., Giscard d'Estaing, Towards a New Democracy, 1977; Catherine, Empress of all the Russias, 1978; The View from Planet Earth, 1981; Paris on the Eve, 1989; Paris: City of Light 1919–1939, 1995. *Address:* Manoir de Brion, Dragey 50530, France.

CROOK, family name of **Baron Crook.**

CROOK, 3rd Baron *cr* 1947, of Carshalton, Surrey; **Robert Douglas Edwin Crook;** *b* 19 May 1955; *S* father, 2001; *m* 1981, Suzanne Jane Robinson, BA, LLB; two *s*. *Educ:* Sir William Borlase's Sch., Marlow; Newcastle Univ. (BSc); MBA. *Heir: s* Hon. Matthew Robert Crook, *b* 28 May 1990.

CROOK, (Alan) Peter, MA; Headmaster, Purcell School, since 2007; *b* 1954; *s* of Donald Hartley Crook and Constance Crook (*née* Llewellyn); *m* 1981, Elaine Joyce Scragg; two *s*. *Educ:* Rydal Sch.; Charterhouse; Royal Acad. Music (BMus Hons; ARCO, ARAM); Univ. of London Inst. of Educn (PGCE); Univ. of Durham (MA). Asst Dir of Music, 1979–83, Dir of Music, 1983–85, Loretto Sch.; Dir of Music, 1985–2003, Co-ordinator of Performing Arts, 2003–07, Rugby Sch. Conductor: Loretto Choral Soc., 1983–85; Rugby Philharmonic Choir and Orch., 1985–2007. FRSA 2007. *Publications:* hymn tunes and arrangements in various hymnals. *Recreations:* family, fiction, fly fishing, over-seas travel. *Address:* Office of the Headmaster, Purcell School, Aldenham Road, Bushey, Herts WD23 2TS. *T:* (01923) 331100, *Fax:* (01923) 331166; *e-mail:* crookp@googlemail.com. *Club:* Royal Over-Seas League.

CROOK, Colin, FREng; special advisor to business, academia, governments and non-governmental organisations on advanced thinking for complex problems; Senior Technology Officer (formerly Chairman, Corporate Technology Committee), Citicorp, 1990–97; *b* 1 June 1942; *s* of Richard and Ruth Crook; *m* 1965, Dorothy Jean Taylor; two *d*. *Educ:* Harris Coll., Preston; Liverpool Polytechnic (ACT Hons; Dip. Elec. Engrg). CEng 1977, FREng (FEng 1981); MIET (MIEE 1976); MIERE 1976; MIEEE 1976; MACM 1977. Electronics Engr, Canadian Marconi, 1962–64; Computer Designer, The Plessey Co., 1964–68; Systems Engr, Eli Lilly Co., 1968–69; sen. appts, Motorola Semiconductor Div., Switzerland and USA, 1969–79; sen. appts, The Rank Organisation, 1979–83, including: Man. Dir, RPI, 1979–81; Man. Dir, Zynar, CEO Nestar Systems, USA, 1981–83; Mem. of Bd, British Telecom, and Man. Dir, BT Enterprises, 1983–84; Sen. Vice Pres., Data General Corp., 1984–89. Sen. Fellow, SEI Inst., Wharton Sch., 1997. Mem., various NAS adv. cttees, USA; advr to various global cos; Member: Bd, Onsett Internat., Boston, 1998–; Adv. Bd, Rein Capital, NJ, 1999–; Advr, IDAnalytics, San Diego, 1999–. Mem. Editl Bd, Emergence Jl, NY. *Publications:* The Power of Impossible Thinking, 2004; articles and learned papers on electronics and computers. *Recreations:* photography, walking, reading, wine, sailing. *Address:* Penberen House, Seifton, Shropshire SY7 9BY.

CROOK, Frances Rachel; Director, Howard League for Penal Reform, since 1986; *b* 18 Dec. 1952; *d* of Sheila Sibson-Turnbull and Maurice Crook; one *d*. *Educ:* Camden School; Liverpool University (BA Hons History). Historical Researcher, Liverpool, 1977–78; Teacher, 1978–79; Campaign Co-ordinator, Amnesty International, 1980–85. Councillor (Lab) Barnet, 1982–90. Mem. Court, Greenwich Univ., 1996–2002 (Chm., Staffing and Gen. Cttee, 1997–2002). Mem., Sch. Food Trust, 2005–08. Chm., Old Barn Youth and Community Centre, Finchley, 1996–97. Freeman, City of London, 1997. Perrie Award, Perrie Lectures Cttee, 2005. *Recreation:* demonstrations. *Address:* The Howard League, 1 Ardleigh Road, N1 4HS. *T:* (020) 7249 7373.

CROOK, Maj.-Gen. James Cooper, MD, FRCPath; late RAMC, retired 1981; Civilian Medical Practitioner, Army Blood Supply Depot, Aldershot, 1982–88; *b* 19 March 1923; *s* of late Francis William Crook and late Mary Catherine Perry, *d* of late Sir Edwin Cooper Perry, GCVO, MD, Superintendent of Guy's Hospital and Vice-Chancellor of London Univ.; *m* 1950, Ruth, *d* of late W. A. Bellamy of Santa Cruz, Tenerife; one *s* two *d*. *Educ:* Worksop Coll.; Guy's Hosp. Med. Sch., Univ. of London. MB BS 1946, MD 1953; DTM&H 1952; FRCPath 1968. Guy's and Pembury Hosps, 1946; Commnd RAMC 1946; served Egypt and N Africa, 1946–49; Pathologist, Queen Alexandra's Mil. Hosp., 1950; David Bruce Laboratories, 1953; med. liaison officer to MRC Radiobiology Unit, AERE, Harwell, 1954; Asst Dir of Pathology, Middle East, 1957; Cons. in Pathology, 1958; RAMC Specialist, Chem. Defence Estab., Porton, 1960; Asst Dir of Pathology, Eastern Comd, 1963; ADGMS, 1966; Comd Cons. in Pathology, BAOR, 1969; Prof. of Pathology, Royal Army Med. Coll., 1974; Dir of Army Pathology and Consulting Pathologist to the Army, 1976–81; Hon. Physician to HM The Queen, 1978–81. Hon Col, 380 Blood Supply Unit RAMC, TAVR, 1982–86. *Publications:* articles in Jl of Clinical Path., Nature, Med. Sci. and the Law, Jl of RAMC, British Jl of Radiology. *Recreations:* gardening, beekeeping. *Address:* Egloshayle, Fore Street, Kingsand, Torpoint, Cornwall PL10 1NB. *T:* (01752) 823666.

CROOK, Rt Rev. John Michael; Bishop of Moray, Ross and Caithness, 1999–2006; *b* 11 June 1940; *s* of late John Hadley Crook and Ada Crook; *m* 1965, Judith Christine Barber; one *s* three *d*. *Educ:* William Hulme's GS, Manchester; St David's Coll., Lampeter (BA 1962); Coll. of the Resurrection, Mirfield. Ordained deacon, 1964, priest, 1965. Curate: Horninglow, 1964–66; Bloxwich, 1966–70; Rector: St Michael, Inverness, 1970–78; St John, Inverness, 1974–78; Aberfoyle, and Callander, and Doune, 1978–87; Bridge of Allan, 1987–99; Canon, St Ninian's Cathedral, Perth, 1985–99. Diocesan Synod Clerk, St Andrews, 1997–99. *Recreation:* bird-watching.

CROOK, Prof. Joseph Mordaunt, CBE 2003; DPhil; FBA 1988; FSA; Professor of Architectural History, University of London at Royal Holloway and Bedford New College (formerly at Bedford College), 1981–99, now Emeritus; *b* 27 Feb. 1937; *e s* of late Austin Mordaunt Crook and late Irene Woolfenden; *m* 1st, 1964, Margaret, *o d* of late James Mulholland; 2nd, 1975, Susan, *o d* of late F. H. Mayor. *Educ:* Wimbledon Coll.; Brasenose Coll., Oxford (BA (1st cl. Mod. Hist.) 1958; DPhil 1961, MA 1962). FSA 1972. Research Fellow: Inst. of Historical Res., 1961–62; Bedford Coll., London, 1962–63; Warburg Inst., London, 1970–71; Asst Lectr, Univ. of Leicester, 1963–65; Lectr, Bedford Coll., London, 1965–75, Reader in Architectural Hist., 1975–81; Dir, Victorian Studies Centre, RHBNC, 1990–99. Slade Prof. of Fine Art, Oxford Univ., 1979–80; Vis. Fellow, Brasenose Coll., Oxford, 1979–80; Humanities Res. Centre, ANU, Canberra, 1985; Waynflete Lectr and Vis. Fellow, Magdalen Coll., Oxford, 1984–85; Vis. Fellow, Gonville and Caius Coll., Cambridge, 1986; Humanities Fellow, Princeton Univ., 1990; Supernumerary Fellow, Brasenose Coll., Oxford, 2002–. Public Orator, Univ. of London, 1988–90. Member: Exec. Cttee, Soc. Architect. Historians of Gt Britain, 1964–77 (Pres. 1980–84); RIBA Drawings Cttee, 1969–75; Exec. Cttee, Georgian Gp, 1970–77; Exec. Cttee, Victorian Soc., 1970–77, Council, 1978–88; Historic Buildings Council for England, 1974–80; Council, Soc. of Antiquaries, 1980–82; Adv. Council, Paul Mellon Centre for Studies in British Art, 1985–90; Gen. Cttee, Incorp. Church Building Soc., 1987–99; Council, British Acad., 1989–92; Adv. Bd for Redundant Churches, 1991–99; Westminster Abbey Architectural Adv. Panel, 1993–99 and Fabric Commn, 2000– (Vice Chm., 2002–). Freeman, 1979, Liveryman, 1984, Worshipful Co. of Goldsmiths. Hon. DLit London, 2004. Editor, Architectural History, 1967–75. *Publications:* The Greek Revival, 1968; Victorian Architecture: A Visual Anthology, 1971; The British Museum, 1972, 2nd edn 1973; The Greek Revival: Neo-Classical Attitudes in British Architecture 1760–1870, 1972, 2nd edn 1995; The Reform Club, 1973; (jtly) The History of the King's Works, Vol. VI, 1782–1851, 1973 (Hitchcock Medallion, 1974), Vol. V, 1660–1782, 1976; William Burges and the High Victorian Dream, 1981; (jtly) Axel Haig and The Victorian Vision of the Middle Ages, 1984; The Dilemma of Style: architectural ideas from the picturesque to the post-modern, 1987, 2nd edn 1989; John Carter and the Mind of the Gothic Revival, 1995; The Rise of the Nouveaux Riches: style and status in Victorian and Edwardian architecture, 1999, 2nd edn 2000; London's Arcadia: John Nash and the Planning of Regent's Park, 2001; The Architect's Secret: Victorian critics and the imag of gravity, 2003; Brasenose: the biography of an Oxford college, 2008; *edited:* Eastlake, A History of the Gothic Revival, 1970, rev. edn, 1978; Emmet, Six Essays, 1972; Kerr, The Gentleman's House, 1972; The Strange Genius of William Burges, 1981; Clark, The Gothic Revival, 1995; Bedford College: memories of 150 years, 2001; *contrib. to:* Concerning Architecture, 1967; The Country Seat, 1970; The Age of Neo-Classicism, 1972; The Building of Early America, 1976; Seven Victorian Architects, 1976; The Ruskin Polygon, 1982; In Search of Modern Architecture, 1983; Rediscovering Hellenism, 1989; The University of London and the World of Learning 1836–1986, 1990; Brooks's: a social history, 1991; London: World City 1800–1840, 1992; Scottish Country Houses, 1995; The Question of Style in Philosophy and the Arts, 1995; Armchair Athenians, 2001; The Impact of the Railway on Society in Britain, 2003; numerous articles in Architect. History, Architect. Review, Country Life, History Today, Jl Royal Soc. Arts, RIBA Jl, Antiquaries Jl, TLS, Architect Design, etc. *Recreation:* strolling. *Address:* 55 Gloucester Avenue, NW1 7BA. *T:* (020) 7485 8280; West Wing, Maristow, near Roborough, Devon PL6 7BZ. *T:* (01752) 696648. *Clubs:* Athenæum, Brooks's.

CROOK, Kenneth Roy, CMG 1978; HM Diplomatic Service, retired; Ambassador to Afghanistan, 1976–79; *b* 30 July 1920; *s* of Alexander Crook, Prescot, Lancs, and Margaret Kay Crook; *m* 1943, Freda Joan Vidler; two *d.* *Educ:* Prescot Grammar Sch., Lancs; Skerry's Coll., Liverpool. Appointed to: Board of Trade, 1937; Min. of War Transport, 1939. Royal Navy, 1941–46. Board of Trade, 1946–49; Commonwealth Relations Office, 1949; Second Sec., Canberra, 1951–54; First Sec., Madras, 1956–59; Deputy High Commissioner: Peshawar, W Pakistan, 1962–64; Dacca, E Pakistan, 1964–67; Counsellor, FCO, 1967; Head of Information Research Dept, FCO, 1969–71; Governor, Cayman Is, 1971–74; Canadian Nat. Defence Coll., 1974–75; Head of Science and Technology Dept, FCO, 1975–76. *Recreations:* walking, gardening, music appreciation. *Address:* 16 Burntwood Road, Sevenoaks, Kent TN13 1PT. *T:* (01732) 452774.

CROOK, Peter; *see* Crook, A. P.

CROOK, Zeinab Mohammed-Khair; *see* Badawi, Z. M. K.

CROOKALL, Ian; Chief Executive, Buckinghamshire County Council, 1995–2001; *b* 28 Dec. 1944; *s* of F. Harold Crookall and M. Ida Crookall (*née* Stubbs); *m* 1974, Georgina; one *s.* *Educ:* Arnold Sch., Blackpool; University Coll. London (LLB Hons). Admitted Solicitor, 1969; Asst Solicitor, N Yorks CC, 1974–82; Asst Clerk, Norfolk CC, 1982–85; Dep. County Solicitor, Dorset CC, 1985–89; Buckinghamshire County Council: County Secretary and Solicitor, 1989–95. *Recreations:* tennis, swimming, walking, theatre. *Address:* Flemings House, Old School, High Street, Wendover HP22 6DU. *T:* (01296) 696410.

CROOKE, Alastair Warren, CMG 2004; Founder, Conflicts Forum, since 2004; *b* 30 June 1949; *s* of Frederick Montague Warren and Shona Ann Crooke (*née* Thomson); *m* 1976, Carole Cecilia (*née* Flaxman); three *s* one *d.* *Educ:* Aiglon Coll., Switzerland; St Andrews Univ. (MA Hons Pol Economy and Philos.). Contrib. to mediation, mgt and resolution of conflict in Ireland, Namibia, Afghanistan, Cambodia and Colombia; co-ordinated hostage negotiations in four overseas locations; Security Adviser: to EU Special Rep. for ME peace process, 1997–2003; to EU High Rep., Javier Solana, 1999–2003; Mem., US Senator George Mitchell's Fact Finding Cttee into causes of Palestinian Intifada, 2000–01; facilitated Israeli/Palestinian ceasefires, 2002, 2003; mediated negotiations that led to ending of siege of Church of Nativity, Bethlehem, 2002; instrumental in negotiations that led to ceasefire declared by Hamas and Islamic Jihad, 2003; initiated bringing together Islamist movts with European and US non-official participants, 2005–06. Has made TV documentaries and broadcasts. *Publications:* various articles in jls and newspapers on ME and Islamic affairs. *Recreations:* scuba diving instructing, climbing, ski-ing, study of 18th century art, architecture and furniture. *Address:* *e-mail:* Alastair@conflictsforum.com.

CROOKENDEN, Simon Robert; QC 1996; a Recorder, since 1998; *b* 27 Sept. 1946; *s* of late Spencer Crookenden and Jean Phyllis (formerly Carter, *née* Dewing); *m* 1983, Sarah Anne Georgina Margaret Pragnell; one *s* two *d.* *Educ:* Winchester Coll.; Corpus Christi Coll., Cambridge (MA Mech. Scis). Management trainee, Westland Aircraft, 1968–69; various posts, incl. Brand Manager, Unilever, 1969–72; Brand Manager, Express Dairies, 1972–74; called to the Bar, Gray's Inn, 1975, Bencher, 2003; in practice as barrister, 1975–; Asst Recorder, 1994–98. *Recreations:* ski-ing, rowing, sailing. *Address:* Essex Court Chambers, 24 Lincoln's Inn Fields, WC2A 3EG. *T:* (020) 7813 8000.

CROOKHAM, Ian; Chief Executive, Kingston upon Hull City Council, 1995–2002; *b* 7 Oct. 1952; *s* of George Edward Crookham and Jean Crookham; *m* 1977, Shirley Ann Green; four *s.* *Educ:* St Margaret's Sch., Liverpool (BA Hons). CPFA 1979. Graduate trainee, Liverpool CC, 1974–77; various finance posts, Gtr Manchester Council, 1977–86; Chief Accountant, Trafford MBC, 1986–88; Asst Dir of Finance, 1988, Sen. Asst Dir of Finance, 1988–94, Humberside CC; Dir of Finance, Hull CC, 1994–95. Clerk to: Hull and Goole Port HA, 1995–2002; Humber Bridge Bd, 1996–2002; Humberside Police Authy, 1997–2002. Co. Sec., Hull City Vision, 1995–2002. Audit Cttee, Univ. of Hull Council, 2003–. Chm. Governors, South Cave Sch., 1993. *Recreations:* aviation, military history, reading.

CROOKS, Air Marshal David Manson, CB 1985; OBE 1969; FRAeS; Chief of Defence Staff, New Zealand Armed Forces, 1986–87, retired; aviation and defence industry consultant, 1988–99; *b* 8 Dec. 1931; *s* of James and Gladys Meta Crooks; *m* 1954, Barbara Naismith McDougall; four *d.* *Educ:* Rangiora, NZ. Joined RNZAF, 1951; Head, NZ Defence Liaison Staff, Singapore, 1967–70; Commanding Officer: RNZAF Base: Ohakea, 1971–72; Wigram, 1973–74; RCDS, UK, 1974–75; AOC RNZAF Ops Gp, 1978–80; DCAS, 1980–83; CAS, RNZAF, 1983–86. *Recreations:* gardening, reading, vintage motoring, sailing. *Address:* 13 Burrows Avenue, Karori, Wellington 6012, New Zealand. *T:* (4) 4764588. *Club:* Wellington (Wellington, NZ).

CROOKS, Emily Jane; *see* Bell, E. J.

CROPPER, James Anthony, FCA; Chairman, James Cropper PLC, since 1971; Lord-Lieutenant of Cumbria, since 1994 (Vice Lord-Lieutenant, 1991–94); *b* 22 Dec. 1938; *s* of Anthony Charles Cropper and Philippa Mary Gloria (*née* Clutterbuck); *m* 1967, Susan Rosemary, *y d* of Col F. J. N. Davis; one *s* one *d* (and one *s* decd). *Educ:* Eton; Magdalene Coll., Cambridge (BA). FCA 1966. James Cropper, 1966–, Dir, 1967–; Dir, East Lancashire Paper Group, 1982–84. Member: Lancs River Authority, 1968–74; NW Water Authority, 1973–80, 1983–89; Dir, NW Water Group, 1989–90. Dir, Cumbria Rural Enterprise Agency, 1986–; Mem., NW Business Leadership Team, 1991–98. Pres., British Paper and Bd Fedn, 1988–90. Chm., Frieda Scott Charitable Trust, 1981–94; Trustee, Lakeland Arts Trust (formerly Abbot Hall Art Gall. and Mus.), 1992– (Chm. Govs, 1983–88). Member (Indep.): S Westmorland RDC, 1967–74; S Lakeland DC, 1974–77. High Sheriff of Westmorland, 1971; DL Cumbria, 1985. KStJ 1997. *Recreations:* shooting, ski-ing, golf. *Address:* Tolson Hall, Kendal, Cumbria LA9 5SE. *T:* (01539) 722011. *Club:* Brooks's.

CROPPER, Peter John, CBE 1988; Special Adviser: to Chief Secretary to the Treasury, 1979–82; to Chancellor of the Exchequer, 1984–88; *b* 18 June 1927; *s* of late Walter Cecil Cropper and Kathleen Cropper; *m* 1965, Rosemary Winning; one *s.* *Educ:* Hitchin Grammar Sch.; Gonville and Caius Coll., Cambridge (MA). Served Royal Artillery, 1945–48. Conservative Research Dept, 1951–53, 1975–79, Dir, 1982–84. *Address:* 77 Hadlow Road, Tonbridge, Kent TN9 1QB. *Club:* Reform.

CROSBIE, Annette, OBE 1998; actress; *b* 12 Feb. 1934; *m* Michael Griffiths; one *s* one *d.* *Educ:* Bristol Old Vic Theatre Sch. *Stage* includes: Citizens' Theatre, Glasgow: A View from the Bridge; The Crucible; The Cherry Orchard; Bristol Old Vic: Romeo and Juliet; The Tempest; A Taste of Honey; Comedy Theatre: Tinker; A Singular Man; The Winslow Boy, New, 1970; Mr Bolfry, Aldwych; The Changeling, Royal Court; The Family Dance, Criterion, 1976; The Trojan War Will Not Take Place, NT, 1983; Curtains, Whitehall, 1988; I Thought I Heard a Rustling, Theatre Royal Stratford, 1991; A Delicate Balance, Haymarket, 1997; The Night Season, NT, 2004; *television* includes: *series and serials:* The Six Wives of Henry VIII, 1970 (BAFTA Award for best actress); Edward VII, 1975 (BAFTA Award for best actress); Lillie, 1978; Paradise Postponed, 1986; Take Me Home, 1989; Summer's Lease, 1989; One Foot in the Grave, 1989–2000; Dr Finlay (Scottish TV Award for best actress), 1993; An Unsuitable Job for a Woman, 1997; *plays:* The Seagull; Waste, 1977; Richard III; Beyond the Pale, 1989; radio plays and serials; *films* include: The Slipper and the Rose (Eve. News British Film Award for best actress), 1975; Ordeal by Innocence; The Pope Must Die, 1990; Calendar Girls, 2003. Founding Mem., Greyhounds UK, 1998; Pres., League Against Cruel Sports, 2002–. Hon. DVMS Glasgow, 2000. *Address:* c/o Independent Talent Group Ltd, Oxford House, 76 Oxford Street, W1D 1BS.

CROSBIE, Hon. John Carnell; PC (Canada) 1979; OC 1998; QC; Counsel, Cox and Palmer (formerly Patterson Palmer Hunt Murphy, then Patterson Palmer), Atlantic Canada lawyers, 1994–2008; Lieutenant Governor of Newfoundland and Labrador, since 2008; *b* 30 Jan. 1931; *s* of Chesley Arthur Crosbie and Jessie Carnell; *m* 1952, Jane Furneaux; two *s* one *d.* *Educ:* Bishop Field Coll., St John's, Nfld; St Andrew's Coll., Aurora, Ont.; Queen's Univ., Kingston, Ont. (Pol Sc. and Econs); Dalhousie Univ., Halifax, NS (Law); LSE, London, Eng. Joined Newfoundland Law Soc. and Newfoundland Bar; entered law practice, St John's, 1957; Mem. City Council, St John's, 1965; Dep. Mayor, 1966; Minister of Municipal Affairs and Housing, Province of Newfoundland, (Lib. Admin), July 1966; MHA, Prov. of Newfoundland, Sept. 1966; Minister of Health, 1967; resigned from Govt, 1968; re-elected Member for St John's West (Progressive Conservative), Provincial election, 1971; Minister of Finance, Pres. of Treasury Bd and Minister of Econ. Develt, 1972–74; Minister of Fisheries, Min. for Intergovtl Affairs and Govt House Leader, 1974–75; Minister of Mines and Energy and Minister for Intergovtl Affairs, 1975–76; resigned from Newfoundland Govt, Sept. 1976; elected to House of Commons, Oct. 1976; MP (PC) St John's West, Newfoundland, 1976–93; Chm. of Progressive Conservative Caucus Cttee on Energy, 1977; PC parly critic for Industry, Trade and Commerce, 1977–79; Minister of Finance, 1979–80; Party Finance Critic, 1980; Party External Affairs Critic, 1981–83; Minister of Justice and Attorney General, 1984–86; Minister of Transport, 1986–88; Minister for International Trade, 1988–91; Minister for Fisheries and Oceans and for Atlantic Canada Opportunities Agency, 1991–93. Dir, Atlantic Inst. of Market Studies, 1996–2008. Hon. Consul of Mexico in Newfoundland and Labrador, 1996–2008. Chancellor, Meml Univ. of Newfoundland, 1994–2008. *Publication:* No Holds Barred (memoirs), 1997. *Address:* Government House, Military Road, PO Box 5517, St John's, NL A1C 5W4, Canada.

CROSBY, Sir James (Robert), Kt 2006; Senior Independent Director: ITV plc (formerly Granada plc), since 2002; Compass Group plc, since 2007; *b* 14 March 1956; *m*; four *d.* *Educ:* Lancaster Royal Grammar Sch.; Brasenose Coll., Oxford (BA Maths). FFA 1980. With Scottish Amicable, 1977–94: posts incl. Investment Dir, 1983, and Hd of Marketing and Finance; Man. Dir, Halifax Life, Halifax Bldg Soc., 1994–96; Dir, Financial Services and Insurance, 1996–99, Chief Exec., 1999–2001, Halifax plc; Gp Chief Exec., HBOS plc, 2001–06. Member: Eur. Adv. Bd, Bridgepoint Capital, 2006–; Finance Cttee of the Delegacy, OUP, 2006–. Dep. Chm., FSA, 2007– (non-exec. Dir, 2004–). Chairman: Public Private Forum on Identity Mgt, 2006–08 (report, Opportunities and Challenges in Identity Assurance, 2008); Private Investment Commn, North Way, 2008–; Wkg Gp, Housing Finance Rev., HM Treasury, 2008–. Trustee, CRUK, 2008–.

CROSFIELD, Rev. Canon (George) Philip (Chorley), OBE 1990; Provost of St Mary's Cathedral, Edinburgh, 1970–90, retired, Hon. Canon, 1991; *b* 9 Sept. 1924; *s* of James Chorley Crosfield and Marjorie Louise Crosfield; *m* 1956, Susan Mary Jullion (*née* Martin); one *s* two *d.* *Educ:* George Watson's Coll., Edinburgh; Selwyn Coll., Cambridge (BA 1950; MA 1955). Royal Artillery, 1942–46 (Captain). Priest, 1952; Asst Curate: St David's, Pilton, Edinburgh, 1951–53; St Andrew's, St Andrews, 1953–55; Rector, St Cuthbert's, Hawick, 1955–60; Chaplain, Gordonstoun School, 1960–68; Canon and Vice Provost, St Mary's Cathedral, Edinburgh, 1968–70. *Recreations:* walking, reading. *Address:* 21 Biggar Road, Silverburn, Penicuik EH26 9LQ. *T:* (01968) 676607.

CROSLAND, Neisha, (Mrs S. Perche), RDI 2006; wallpaper and fabric designer with own business, since 1994; *b* 11 Jan. 1960; *d* of C. R. H. Crosland and Felicity Crosland (*née* d'Abreu); *m* 2002, Stephane Perche; two *s.* *Educ:* Camberwell Sch. of Arts and Crafts (BA 1st Cl. Hons Textile Design); Royal Coll. of Art (MA Printed Textiles). Freelance designer and teaching appointments: Glasgow Sch. of Art, 1989–90; Winchester Sch. of Art, 1991–92; Northbrooke Coll., 1992; freelance designer: designed: Romagna collection for Osborne & Little, 1988; Carnaval collection of wallpaper and fabrics for Harlequin Wall Coverings Ltd, 1990–94; contrib. First Eleven Portfolio, textile agency, 1991; launched: Neisha Crosland Scarves, 1994; Neisha at Debenhams, 1998; Ginka Ready to Wear and own Neisha Crosland Wallpaper Collection, 1999; home decorative and stationery collection and opened first retail outlet, London, 2000–01; licensed collection of scarves and fashion accessories for Hank Yu, Japan, 2002; first collection of home furnishing fabrics, and opened flagship store, 2003; re-designed uniform, scarves and ties for Reed Employment, 2007. Ext. Examr, RCA, 2007. Mem. Panel, RSA Design Bursary Award, 2006–. *Recreations:* food, wine, films, arts, music. *Address:* Unit 40, Battersea Business Centre, 99 Lavender Hill, SW11 5QL. *T:* (020) 7978 4389, *Fax:* (020) 7924 2873; *e-mail:* info@neishacrosland.com. *Club:* Chelsea Arts.

CROSLAND, Susan Barnes; writer; *b* Baltimore, Maryland; *y d* of Susan Owens and Mark Skinner Watson; *m* 1st, Patrick Skene Catling (marr. diss.); two *d*; 2nd, Rt Hon. (Charles) Anthony (Raven) Crosland, PC, MP (*d* 1977). Journalism: Sunday Express, 1960–64; freelance, 1964–; profile-writer and columnist, Sunday Times and various jls. Trustee, Nat. Portrait Gallery, 1978–92. *Publications:* Behind the Image, 1974; Tony Crosland, 1982; Looking Out, Looking In, 1987; Great Sexual Scandals, 2002; *novels:* Ruling Passions, 1989; Dangerous Games, 1991; The Magnates, 1994; The Prime Minister's Wife, 2001. *Recreation:* freedom. *Address:* 16 Stanford Court, 45 Cornwall Gardens, SW7 4AB. *Club:* Academy.

CROSS, Alistair Robert Sinclair B.; *see* Bassett Cross.

CROSS, Anne; *see* McGaughrin, A.

CROSS, Prof. Anthony Glenn, FBA 1989; Professor of Slavonic Studies, 1985–2004, now Emeritus, and Fellow of Fitzwilliam College, 1986–2004, Cambridge University; *b* 21 Oct. 1936; *s* of Walter Sidney Cross and Ada Cross; *m* 1960, Margaret (*née* Elson); two *d. Educ:* High Pavement Sch., Nottingham; Trinity Hall, Cambridge (BA 1960, MA 1964, PhD 1966); Harvard Univ. (AM 1961); LittD East Anglia 1981; LittD Cambridge 1997. Frank Knox Fellow, Harvard Univ., 1960–61; Univ. of East Anglia: Lectr in Russian, 1964–69; Sen. Lectr in Russian, 1969–72; Reader, 1972–81; Roberts Prof. of Russian, Univ. of Leeds, 1981–85. Vis. Fellow: Univ. of Illinois, 1969–70; All Souls Coll., Oxford, 1977–78. Pres., British Univs Assoc. of Slavists, 1982–84; Chm., British Academic Cttee for Liaison with Soviet Archives, 1983–95. Mem., Russian Acad. of Humanities, 1996. Reviews Editor, Jl of European Studies, 1971–; Editor, Study Group on Eighteenth-Century Russia Newsletter, 1973–. Nove Prize, 1997; Antsiferov Prize, St Petersburg, 1998; Dashkova medal, Moscow, 2003. *Publications:* N. M. Karamzin, 1971; Russia Under Western Eyes 1517–1825, 1971; (ed) Russian Literature in the Age of Catherine the Great, 1976; Anglo-Russian Relations in the Eighteenth Century, 1977; (ed) Great Britain and Russia in the Eighteenth Century, 1979; By the Banks of the Thames, 1980; (ed) Russia and the West in the Eighteenth Century, 1981; The Tale of the Russian Daughter and her Suffocated Lover, 1982; (ed jtly) Eighteenth Century Russian Literature, Culture and Thought: a bibliography, 1984; The Russian Theme in English Literature, 1985; (ed jtly) Russia and the World of the Eighteenth Century, 1988; (ed) An English Lady at the Court of Catherine the Great, 1989; Anglophilia on the Throne: the British and the Russians in the age of Catherine II, 1992; (ed) Engraved in the Memory: James Walker, engraver to Catherine the Great and his Russian anecdotes, 1993; Anglo-Russica: aspects of Anglo-Russian cultural relations in the eighteenth and early nineteenth centuries, 1993; (ed jtly) Literature, Lives and Legality in Catherine's Russia, 1994; By the Banks of the Neva: chapters from the lives of the British in eighteenth-century Russia, 1996; (ed) Russia in the Reign of Peter the Great: old and new perspectives, 1998; (ed jtly) Britain and Russia in the Age of Peter the Great: historical documents, 1998; Peter the Great through British Eyes: perceptions and representations of the tsar since 1698, 2000; Catherine the Great and the British, 2001; (ed) St Petersburg 1703–1825: a collection of essays, 2003; (ed) Anglo-Russian Cultural Encounters and Collisions in the Nineteenth and Early Twentieth Centuries, 2005; (ed) Days from the Regions of Eighteenth-Century Russian Rulers, 2007; St Petersburg and the British: the city through the eyes of British visitors and residents, 2008. *Recreations:* book collecting, cricket watching. *Address:* Fitzwilliam College, Storey's Way, Cambridge CB2 0DG. *T:* (01223) 332000; *e-mail:* agc28@cam.ac.uk.

CROSS, Anthony Maurice; QC 2006; a Recorder of the Crown Court, since 2002; *b* 16 June 1958; *s* of Maurice and Mia Cross; *m* 1982, Joanne Corrin; one *s* two *d. Educ:* St Mary's Marist Coll., Blackburn; Univ. of Manchester (LLB Hons). Called to the Bar, Middle Temple, 1982; in practice as a barrister, Manchester. *Recreations:* travel, fashion, theatre, film, football (Burnley FC), cricket (Clitheroe CC). *Address:* Lincoln House, 1 Brazennose Street, Manchester M2 5EL. *T:* (0161) 832 5701, *Fax:* (0161) 832 0839; *e-mail:* anthony.cross@lincolnhse.co.uk. *Clubs:* Burnley Football; Clitheroe Cricket, Clitheroe Tennis.

CROSS, Dr Dolores Evelyn; President, Chicago State University, 1990–98; *b* 29 Aug. 1938; *d* of late Ozie Johnson Tucker and Charles Tucker; *m* 1956, Thomas Edwin Cross (marr. diss.); one *s* one *d. Educ:* Seton Hall Univ. (BS 1963); Hofstra Univ. (MS 1968); Univ. of Michigan (PhD 1971). Teaching posts, NY and Michigan, 1961–71; Asst Prof. in Educn, Northwestern Univ., 1971–74; Associate Prof. in Educn, Claremont Graduate Sch., 1974–78; Vice-Chancellor for student affairs and special programs, City Univ., NY, and Prof. in Educn, Brooklyn Coll., 1978–81; Pres., NY State Higher Educn Services Corp., 1981–88; Associate Provost and Associate Vice-Pres. for Academic Affairs, Univ. of Minnesota, 1988–90; Pres., Morris Brown Coll., Atlanta, 1999–2002. Hon. LLD: Marymount Manhattan, 1984; Skidmore Coll., 1988. NAACP Muriel Silverberg Award, NY, 1987; John Jay Award, NYC Commn of Indep. Colls and Univs, 1989. *Publications:* Influence of Individual Difference on Theories of Instruction, 1974; Teaching in a Multi-Cultural Society, 1977; Breaking Through the Wall: a marathoner's story (autobiog.), 1999. *Recreations:* jogging, marathon running. *Address:* c/o Chicago State University, 95th Street at King Drive Avenue, Chicago, IL 60628, USA. *T:* (312) 9952400.

CROSS, Prof. George Alan Martin, FRS 1984; André and Bella Meyer Professor of Molecular Parasitology, since 1982, and Dean of Graduate and Postgraduate Studies, 1995–99, Rockefeller University, New York; *b* 27 Sept. 1942; *s* of George Bernard and Beatrice Mary Cross; *m*; one *s. Educ:* Cheadle Hulme Sch.; Downing Coll., Univ. of Cambridge (BA, PhD). ICI Postdoctoral Fellow, Biochemistry, Cambridge, 1967–69; Research Fellow, Fitzwilliam Coll., Cambridge, 1967–70; Scientist, MRC Biochemical Parasitology Unit, Molteno Inst., Cambridge, 1969–77; Head, Dept of Immunochemistry, Wellcome Research Laboratories, 1977–82. Fleming Lectr, Soc. for General Microbiology, 1978; Leeuwenhoek Lectr, Royal Soc., 1998. Chalmers Medal, Royal Soc. for Tropical Medicine and Hygiene, 1983; (jtly) Paul Ehrlich and Ludwig Darmstaedter Prize, 1984. *Publications:* in journals of parasitology, biochemistry, microbiology and molecular biology. *Recreations:* sailing, tennis, building projects, observing people. *Address:* Rockefeller University, 1230 York Avenue, New York, NY 10065, USA. *T:* (212) 3277571; *e-mail:* george.cross@rockefeller.edu.

CROSS, Gillian Clare, DPhil; author; *b* 1945; *d* of James Eric Arnold and Joan Emma (*née* Manton); *m* 1967, Martin Francis Cross; two *s* two *d. Educ:* North London Collegiate Sch. for Girls; Somerville Coll., Oxford (MA); Univ. of Sussex (DPhil). Mem., Adv. Council on Libraries, 1995–2000. Mem., Soc. of Authors. Mem., Octavian Droobers. Freeman, Guild of Educators, 2007–. *Publications:* The Runaway, 1979; The Iron Way, 1979; Revolt at Ratcliffe's Rags, 1980; Save Our School, 1981; A Whisper of Lace, 1981; The Dark Behind the Curtain, 1982; The Demon Headmaster, 1982; Born of the Sun, 1983; The Mintyglo Kid, 1983; On the Edge, 1984; The Prime Minister's Brain, 1985; Chartbreak, 1986 (USA as Chartbreaker, 1987); Swimathon, 1986; Roscoe's Leap, 1987; A Map of Nowhere, 1988; Rescuing Gloria, 1989; Wolf, 1990 (Carnegie Medal, LA, 1990); The Monster from Underground, 1990; Twin and Super-Twin, 1990; Gobbo The Great, 1991; Rent-A-Genius, 1991; The Great Elephant Chase, 1992 (Smarties Book Prize and Whitbread Children's Novel Award, 1992); Beware Olga!, 1993; Furry Maccaloo, 1993; The Tree House, 1993; Hunky Parker is Watching You, 1994; What will Emily Do?, 1994; New World, 1994; The Crazy Shoe Shuffle, 1995; Posh Watson, 1995; The Roman Beanfeast, 1996; Pictures in the Dark, 1996; The Demon Headmaster Strikes Again, 1996; The Demon Headmaster Takes Over, 1997; The Goose Girl, 1998; Tightrope, 1999; Down with the Dirty Danes, 2000; The Treasure in the Mud, 2001; Calling a Dead Man, 2001, US edn as Phoning a Dead Man, 2002; Beware of the Demon Headmaster, 2002; Facing the Demon Headmaster, 2002; The Dark Ground, 2004; The Black Room, 2005; The Nightmare Game, 2006; Brother Aelred's Feet, 2007. *Recreations:* playing the piano, orienteering. *Address:* c/o Oxford Children's Books, Oxford University Press, Great Clarendon Street, Oxford OX2 6DP.

CROSS, James Edward Michael; QC 2006; *b* 18 March 1962; *s* of Michael Cross and Mary (*née* Wright); *m* 1994, Victoria Lambert; two *s. Educ:* Shrewsbury Sch.; Magdalen Coll., Oxford (MA Juris; Academical Clerk). Called to the Bar, Gray's Inn, 1985; in practice specialising in construction and engrg law, professional negligence and liability, insurance and product liability. Member: Monitoring of Pupillage Review Panel, Bar Council, 1999–2002; Cttee, London Common Law and Commercial Bar Assoc., 2002–; Chm., Pupillage Cttee, 4 Pump Ct, 2003–06. Lectr in Law, Magdalen Coll., Oxford, 1985–88. *Recreations:* singing (Mem., Vasari Singers, since 1992, Chm., 2004–07), hill walking, gardening. *Address:* 4 Pump Court, Temple, EC4Y 7AN. *Club:* Roehampton.

CROSS, James Richard, (Jasper), CMG 1971; Under-Secretary, Principal Establishment Officer, Department of Energy, 1978–80; *b* 29 Sept. 1921; *s* of J. P. Cross and Dinah Cross (*née* Hodgins); *m* 1945, Barbara Dagg; one *d. Educ:* King's Hosp., Dublin; Trinity Coll., Dublin. Scholar, First Cl. Moderatorship Economics and Polit. Science. RE (Lieut). Asst Principal, Bd of Trade, 1947; Private Sec. to Parly Sec., 1947–49; Principal, 1950; Trade Commissioner: New Delhi, 1953–56; Halifax, 1957–60; Winnipeg, 1960–62; Asst Sec., 1962; Sen. Trade Comr, Kuala Lumpur, 1962–66; Bd of Trade, 1966–67; Under Sec., 1968; Sen. British Trade Comr, Montreal, 1968–70 (kidnapped by terrorists and held for 59 days, Oct.–Dec. 1970); Under-Sec., Export Planning and Develt Div., DTI, 1971–73; Coal Div., DTI, later Dept of Energy, 1973–78. *Recreations:* theatre, bridge. *Address:* 4 Crouchfield Close, Crooked Lane, Seaford, East Sussex BN25 1QE.

CROSS, Linda Mary, MBE 2004; HM Diplomatic Service; Ambassador to Ecuador, since 2008; *b* Dundee, 15 March 1956; *d* of W. Gordon Guild and late Elizabeth Mary Guild; *m* 1989, Michael Cross. *Educ:* Leeds Metropolitan Univ. (BA Hons 1st Cl. Hospitality and Business Mgt). Entered FCO, 1978; Rabat, 1978–81; Prague, 1981–83; Quito, 1983–85; Paris, 1985–88; FCO, 1988–91; Third Sec., Chancery, and Vice-Consul, Vienna, 1992–94; Third Sec., UK Mission to UN, NY, 1995–97; Dep. Hd of Mission, Azerbaijan, 1998–2001; Consul Gen., Yekaterinburg, 2001–05; FCO, 2005–08. *Recreations:* music, reading, swimming, learning languages. *Address:* BFPO 5550, HA4 6EP. *T:* (Ecuador) 2221901, ext. 2204, ext. 8801; *e-mail:* linda.cross@fco.gov.uk; c/o Foreign and Commonwealth Office, King Charles Street, SW1A 2AH.

CROSS, Dame Margaret Natalie; *see* Smith, Dame Maggie.

CROSS, Dr Nigel; consultant in international development; Country Director, Sudan, Netherlands Development Organisation, since 2008; *b* 9 March 1953; *s* of Sir Barry Albert Cross, CBE, FRS and of Audrey Lilian Cross; *m* 1980, Dr Caroline Dakers; two *d. Educ:* Univ. of Sussex (BA English 1974); University Coll. London (PhD 1980). Archivist Royal Literary Fund, 1975–80; Leverhulme Res. Fellow, 1980–81; tutor-counsellor and tutor, third world studies, Open Univ., 1981–87; Sec., British Cttee, SOS Sahel-Internat. 1983–85; Director: SOS Sahel UK, 1985–95; Panos Inst., 1995–99; Dir, 1999–2003 Consultant, 2003–04, Internat. Inst. for Envmt and Develt; Professorial Res. Fellow, Dept of Develt Studies, SOAS, Univ. of London, 2005–08. Board Member: FARM Africa 1989–94; Inst. for Develt Policy and Mgt, Univ. of Manchester, 1992–95; Agency for Co-op. and Res. in Develt (ACORD Africa), 1996–2002 (Chm., 1998–2000); Inst. for Global Envmtl Strategies, Japan, 1999–2003. Ext. collaborator, ILO, Geneva, 1984–86; Member NGO Consultative Gp, IFAD, Rome, 1991–96 (Co-Chm., 1991–92); Adv. Bd, Grid Arendal, Norway, 2000–02. *Publications:* The Common Writer, 1985; (with N. Ardill) Undocumented Lives, 1987; The Sahel: the people's right to development, 1990; (with R. Barker) At The Desert's Edge: oral histories from the Sahel, 1991; (contributing ed.) Listening for a Change, 1993; (ed) Evidence for Hope: the search for sustainable development, 2003; contribs on literature and develt to various newspapers and specialist jls. *Address: e-mail:* nigelcross@ncross.plus.com.

CROSS, Peter H.; *see* Hulme Cross.

CROSS, Stefan Tylney; Senior Partner, Stefan Cross Solicitors, since 2002; *b* Chiswick 5 Oct. 1960; *s* of Brian Cross and Jacqueline Ann Pilling; *m* 1986, Dr Alison Mary Steele two *s* two *d. Educ:* Univ. of Southampton (LLB 1982); Univ. of Leicester (LLM 1990) Admitted solicitor, 1985; trainee solicitor, GA Mooring Aldridge and Brownlee, 1983–86 Partner: Brian Thompson and Partners, 1986–90; Thompsons Solicitors, 1990–2002 Part-time Chm., Employment Tribunal, subseq. Employment Judge, 2005–08. Mem (Lab) Newcastle CC, 1990–98. *Recreations:* Newcastle United Football Club, trashy crim novels, indie rock music, travel, politics. *Address:* 23 Montagu Avenue, Newcastle upo Tyne NE3 4HY. *T:* (0191) 285 6110; *e-mail:* Stc@stefancross.co.uk.

CROSS, Maj.-Gen. Timothy, CBE 2000; FCILT; Director, CROSSTC Ltd, sinc 2006; General Officer Commanding Theatre Troops, 2004–06; *b* 19 April 1951; *s* o Sidney George and Patricia Mary Cross; *m* 1972, Christine Mary Pelly; two *s* one *d. Edu* Welbeck; RMA, Sandhurst; RMCS Shrivenham (BSc Hons, MSc); ato. NI, 1978; Adjt Ordnance Bn, 1979–80; UN, Cyprus, 1981; Army Staff Coll., 1982–83 (psc); Britis Liaison Bureaux, Paris, 1984–85; Co. Comdr, 1 Ordnance Bn, 1986–87; Directing Staf Army Staff Coll., 1988–90; CO, 1 Ordnance Bn, 1990–92; deployed to Kuwait/Irac 1990–91; Comdr, Logistic Support 3 (UK) Div., 1992–96; deployed to Balkans (IFOR 1995–96; HCSC, 1995; Dir, Materiel Support (Army), 1996–97; Comdr, 101 Logisti Bde, 1998–2000; deployed to Balkans/Kosovo, 1998 (SFOR), 2000 (KFOR); rcds 200 Dir Gen., Defence Supply Chain (formerly Defence Logistic Support), 2000–03; deploye to Kuwait/Iraq as UK Deputy in ORHA/CPA, 2003. Col Comdt RLC, 2003–; Ho Col 168 Pioneer Regt, RLC (V), 2007–. Army Advr, Defence Cttee, H of C, 2007– Defence Advisor: Fujitsu, 2007–; Harmonic, 2007–. Has lectured in UK and abroa Visiting Professor: Nottingham Univ., 2007–; Cranfield Univ., 2007–. Director: Centr for Internat. Humanitarian Co-operation, 2004–; Theos, 2007–; Trustee, Leadershi Trust Foundn, 2003–. FCILT 2002. Lay Reader, C of E. Trustee: British and Foreig Bible Soc., 2007–; Accts Mil. Ministries Internat., 2007–. *Publications:* contribs to book and jls. *Recreations:* golf, walking, reading, writing.

CROSSE, Gordon; composer; *b* 1 Dec. 1937; *s* of Percy and Marie Crosse; *m* 196 Elizabeth Bunch. *Educ:* Cheadle Hulme Sch.; St Edmund Hall, Oxford; Accad. di Cecilia, Rome. Music Fellow, Essex Univ., 1969–74; Composer in residence, King Coll., Cambridge, 1974–76; Vis. Lectr, Univ. of Calif at Santa Barbara, 1977–78. Ho RAM, 1980. *Operas:* Purgatory, 1966; The Grace of Todd, 1967; The Story of Vasc 1970; Potter Thompson, 1973; *ballets:* Playground, 1979; Wildboy, 1981; *oth compositions:* Concerto da Camera, 1962; Meet My Folks, 1963; "Symphonies", 196 Second Violin Concerto, 1970; Memories of Morning: Night, 1972; Ariadne, 197 Symphony 2, 1975; Wildboy (clarinet concerto), Play Ground, 1977; Dreamsongs, 197 Cello Concerto, 1979; String Quartet, 1980; Trio for clarinet, cello and piano, 198 Dreamcanon (chorus), 1981; Trio for piano, violin and cello, 1986; Trumpet Concert 1986; much other orchestral, vocal and chamber music. *Address:* Brant's Cottag Blackheath, Wenhaston, Halesworth, Suffolk IP19 9EX.

CROSSETT, Robert Nelson, (Tom), DPhil; Chairman: National Flood Forun 2004–06 (Director, 2003–06); Thames Flood Forum, 2005–08; *b* 27 May 1938; *s*

Robert Crossett and Mary Nelson; *m* 1966, Susan Marjorie Legg; two *s*. *Educ:* British School, Hamburg; Campbell College, Belfast; Queen's Univ., Belfast (BSc, BAgr); Lincoln College, Oxford (DPhil); Univ. of East Anglia. Group Leader Environmental Studies, Aust. Atomic Energy Commn, 1966; Sen. Sci. Officer, ARC Letcombe Lab., 1969; Develt Officer (Crops), Scottish Agricl Develt Council, 1972; PSO, Dept of Agric. and Fisheries for Scotland, 1975; Ministry of Agriculture, Fisheries and Food: Sci. Liaison Officer (Horticulture and Soils), 1978; Head, Food Sci. Div., 1984; Chief Scientist (Fisheries and Food), 1985–89; Head of Envmtl Policy, 1989–90, Envmt Dir, 1990–91, National Power; Sec. Gen., Nat. Soc. for Clean Air and Envmtl Protection, 1992–96; Dir-Gen., Internat. Union of Air Pollution Prevention Assocs, 1996–98. Chairman: Southern Regional Envmtl Protection Adv. Cttee, EA, 1996–2002; SE Water Resources Forum, 2005–. Consultant, SE Inst. of Public Health, 1998–2000. Member: NERC, 1985–89; AFRC, 1985–89; UK Delgn, Tripartite Meetings on Food and Drugs, 1985–88; Cttee on Med. Aspects of Food Policy, 1985–89; Adv. Gp to Sec. of State for Envmt on Eco-Management and Audit, 1994–96; UK Round Table on Sustainable Develt, 1995–97. Vis. Fellow, Sci. Policy Res. Unit, Univ. of Sussex, 1997–2000; Sen. Vis. Fellow, Sch. of Health and Life Scis, KCL, 2000–05. *Publications:* papers in plant physiology, marine biology, food science and envmtl management. *Recreations:* walking, gardening, orienteering, boats.

CROSSICK, Prof. Geoffrey Joel, PhD; Warden, Goldsmiths (formerly Goldsmiths College), University of London, since 2005; *b* 13 June 1946; *s* of Louis Crossick and Rebecca Naomi (*née* Backen); *m* 1973, Rita Geraldine Vaudrey; two *s*. *Educ:* Haberdashers' Aske's Sch., Elstree; Gonville and Caius Coll., Cambridge (BA Hist. 1967); Birkbeck Coll., London (PhD Hist. 1976). Res. Fellow in Hist., Emmanuel Coll., Cambridge, 1970–73; Lectr in Social Hist., Univ. of Hull, 1973–78; University of Essex: Lectr in Hist., 1979–83; Sen. Lectr, 1983–86; Reader, 1986–91; Prof. of Hist., 1991–2002; Dean: Comparative Studies, 1992–95; Grad. Sch., 1996–97; Pro-Vice-Chancellor, 1997–2002; Chief Exec., AHRB, 2002–05. Vis. Prof., Univ. of Lyon 2, 1990–91. Member: Business and Community Strategy Cttee, HEFCE, 2005–; Bd, UUK, 2006–. Member: British Library Adv. Council, 2004–; Council, Royal Coll. Music, 2005–; London Cultural Consortium, 2006–; Bd, UCEA, 2007–; Governing Body, Courtauld Inst., 2007–. Hon. Fellow, Emmanuel Coll., Cambridge, 2004. *Publications:* (ed) The Lower Middle Class in Britain, 1976; An Artisan Elite in Victorian Society, 1978; (ed jtly) Shopkeepers and Master Artisans in 19th Century Europe, 1984; (ed jtly) The Power of the Past: essays for Eric Hobsbawm, 1984; (with H. G. Haupt) The Petite Bourgeoisie in Europe 1780–1914, 1995; (ed) The Artisan and the European Town, 1997; (ed jtly) Cathedrals of Consumption: the European department store 1850–1939, 1998; contrib. articles to learned jls. *Recreations:* Tottenham Hotspur, travel, music. *Address:* Goldsmiths, University of London, New Cross, SE14 6NW. *T:* (020) 7919 7900; *e-mail:* warden@gold.ac.uk.

CROSSLAND, Anthony, FRCO; Organist and Master of the Choristers, Wells Cathedral, 1971–96; *b* 4 Aug. 1931; *s* of Ernest Thomas and Frances Elizabeth Crossland; *m* 1960, Barbara Helen Pullar-Strecker; one *s* two *d*. *Educ:* Christ Church, Oxford. MA, BMus (Oxon), FRCO (CHM), ARCM. Asst Organist: Christ Church Cathedral, Oxford, 1957–61; Wells Cathedral, 1961–71. Conductor: Wells Cathedral Oratorio Soc., 1966–96; Wells Sinfonietta, 1985–96; Organs Advr to dio. of Bath and Wells, 1971–96. Pres., Cathedral Organists' Assoc., 1983–85. DMus Lambeth, 1994. *Recreations:* reading, photography, cooking. *Address:* Barton End, 10b Newtown, Bradford-on-Avon, Wilts BA15 1NE. *T:* (01225) 864496.

CROSSLAND, Sir Bernard, Kt 1990; CBE 1980; MSc (London); PhD (Bristol); DSc (Nottingham); FRS 1979; FREng; FIAE; MRIA; Emeritus Professor, The Queen's University, Belfast, since 1984 (Professor and Head of Department of Mechanical and Industrial Engineering, 1959–82, Research Professor, 1982–84; Dean, 1964–67; Pro-Vice-Chancellor, 1978–82); *b* 20 Oct. 1923; *s* of R. F. Crossland and K. M. Rudduck; *m* 1946, Audrey Elliott Birks; two *d*. *Educ:* Simon Langton's, Canterbury. Apprentice, Rolls Royce Ltd, 1940–44; Nottingham Univ., 1941–43; Technical Asst, Rolls Royce, 1943–45; Asst Lectr, Lectr and then Senior Lectr in Mechanical Engineering, Univ. of Bristol, 1946–59. Member: AFRC, 1981–87; Engrg Council, 1983–88; Chairman: Bd for Engineers' Registration, 1983–86; Youth Careers Guidance Cttee, NI, 1975–79, 1979–81; NI Manpower Council, 1981–86; Adv. Bd for Postgrad. Awards, NI Dept of Educn, 1982–95; Member: NI Training Council, 1964–76, 1977–81; NI Economic Council, 1981–85; NI Industrial Develt Bd, 1982–87. Dir, Gilbert Associates (Europe) Ltd, 1991–94. Assessor, King's Cross Fire Investigation, 1988; Chm., Public Hearing into Bilsthorpe Colliery Accident, 1994; Expert Witness for HSE in prosecution arising from Port of Ramsgate walkway disaster, 1997. Mem. Council and a Vice-Pres., Royal Soc., 1984–86; Mem. Council, Fellowship of Engrg, 1985–88; Pres., Section 6, British Assoc., 1987; Institution of Mechanical Engineers: Chm., Engineering Sciences Div., 1980–84; Vice-Pres., 1983–84; Dep. Pres., 1984–86; Pres., 1986–87; Past Pres., 1987–91; Leonardo da Vinci Lectr, 1970; George Stephenson Lectr, 1989; Thomas Lowe Gray Lectr, 1999; George Stephenson and Thomas Hawksley Medals; Hon. Fellow, 1997; James Watt Internat. Medal, 1999. Lectures: Richard Weck, Welding Inst., 1992; Seamus Timoney, NUI, 1993; McLaughlin, Instn of Engrs of Ireland, 1998. Trustee, Mackie Foundn, 1983–94. Freeman, City of London, 1987; Liveryman, Worshipful Co. of Engrs, 1988. FREng (FEng 1979); Founder FIAE 1998. Hon. MASME 1987; Hon. FWeldI 1990 (Pres., 1995–98); Hon. FIEI 1993; Hon. FIStructE 2001. Hon. Fellow, Univ. of Luton, 1994. Hon. DSc: NUI, 1984; Dublin, 1985; Edinburgh, 1987; QUB 1988; Aston, 1988; Cranfield Inst. of Technology, 1989; Hon. DEng: Bristol, 1992; Limerick, 1993; Liverpool, 1993. Kelvin Medal, ICE, 1992; Cunningham Medal, RIA, 2001; Lifetime Achievement Award, Instn of Engrs of Ireland, 2007. *Publications:* An Introduction to the Mechanics of Machines, 1964; Explosive Welding and its Application, 1982; The Lives of Great Engineers of Ulster, vol. 1, 2003; The Anatomy of an Engineer - an autobiography, 2006; various papers on fatigue of metals and effect of very high fluid pressures on properties of materials; strength of thick-walled vessels, explosive welding, friction welding, design and history of engineering, engineering disasters. *Recreation:* hobbling. *Address:* The Queen's University, Belfast BT7 1NN. *T:* (028) 9038 0860; 16 Malone Court, Belfast BT9 6PA. *T:* (028) 9066 7495. *Club:* Athenæum.

CROSSLEY, family name of **Baron Somerleyton**.

CROSSLEY, Prof. Gary; Principal, Central School of Speech and Drama, 2000–07; *b* 11 Jan. 1946; *s* of John and Patricia Crossley; *m* 1981, Yvonne Stapleton-Henthorne; one *d*. *Educ:* Portsmouth Coll. of Art (BA Hons); Hornsey Sch. of Art (PG Dip.). Hd of Dept, E Ham Coll., 1979–85; Vice Principal, W Surrey Coll. of Art and Design, 1985–89; Dep. Dir, Surrey Inst. of Art and Design, 1989–98; Founding Chm., Consortium of Arts and Design Instns in Southern England, 1998–2000. Mem. Bd, 2000–05, Exec. Council, 2005–07, Standing Conf. of Principals. Mem., Univ. Choice TV Adv. Bd, 2004–. *Recreations:* theatre, film, flyfishing. *Address:* The Chestnuts, Bishops Sutton, Hants SO24 0AN. *T:* (01962) 732469. *Club:* Savile.

CROSSLEY, Geoffrey Allan, CMG 1974; HM Diplomatic Service, retired; Director, External Relations, Continuing Education, European Institute of Business Administration, INSEAD, Fontainebleau, 1980–84; *b* 11 Nov. 1920; *s* of Thomas Crossley and Winifred Mary Crossley (*née* Ellis); *m* 1945, Aline Louise Farcy; two *s* one *d*. *Educ:* Penistone; abroad; Gonville and Caius Coll., Cambridge (Scholar). Served War of 1939–45: Min. of Supply, 1941; Foreign Office, 1942; in Algeria and France. Foreign (later Diplomatic) Service, 1945–80: Second Sec., Paris, 1945–48; FO, 1948–49; Alternate UK Deleg. on UN Balkans Commn, Greece, 1949–52; Dep. Regional Inf. Officer with Commissioner-Gen. for SE Asia, Singapore, 1952–55; FO, 1955–57; Consulate-Gen., Frankfurt, for Saar Transition from France to Germany, 1957–59; Political Office, NE Command, Cyprus (later in charge), 1959–61; Head of Chancery, Berne, 1961–65; on secondment to Min. of Overseas Development, as Head of W and N African Dept, 1965–67; Dep. High Comr, Lusaka, 1967–69; Counsellor, Oslo, 1969–73; Ambassador to Colombia, 1973–77; Envoy to the Holy See, 1978–80. Founder Mem., Cambridge Soc. Mem., French Inst. of Internat. Relations. *Recreations:* various. *Address:* La Houlette, Le Pin, 24520 Saint Germain et Mons, Dordogne, France.

CROSSLEY, Paul Christopher Richard, CBE 1993; concert pianist; Artistic Director, London Sinfonietta, 1988–94; *b* 17 May 1944; *s* of late Frank Crossley and Myra Crossley (*née* Barrowcliffe). *Educ:* Silcoates Sch., Wakefield; Mansfield Coll., Oxford (BA, MA; Hon. Fellow, 1992). International concert pianist; recitals and concerts with all major orchestras; numerous recordings and films for TV. *Recreations:* Mah-Jongg, reading. *Address:* c/o Connaught Artists Management Ltd, 2 Molasses Row, Plantation Wharf, SW11 3UX. *T:* (020) 7738 0017.

CROSSLEY, Maj.-Gen. Ralph John, CB 1987; CBE 1981; *b* 11 Oct. 1933; *s* of Edward Crossley and Eva Mary Crossley (*née* Farnworth); *m* 1957, Marion Hilary Crossley (*née* Bacon); one *s* one *d*. *Educ:* Quainton Sch., Harrow; Felsted School. Commnd 1952 (Nat. Service); Air Observation Post Pilots course, 1953; Regimental Duty: Canal Zone, 1954–56; BAOR, 1956–59; Instructor in Gunnery, Larkhill, 1959–63; Technical Staff Course, 1963–65; Regtl Duty, BAOR, 1965–67, 1969–71; Weapons Staff, UK, 1967–69; Gen. Staff, UK, 1971–72; Instructor, RMCS, 1972–74; CO, 94 Locating Regt, 1974–77; Project Manager, 155 Systems, 1977–81; Dep. Comdt, RMCS, 1981–84; Dir Gen. of Weapons (Army), 1984–86; retired 1986. Defence Advr, Avon Rubber, 1987–91. Chairman: Salisbury HA, 1990–93; Salisbury Healthcare NHS Trust, 1993–97. *Recreations:* golf, walking, gardening, grandchildren.

CROSSLEY, Sir Sloan (Nicholas), 6th Bt *cr* 1909, of Glenfield, Dunham Massey, Chester; Managing Director, Pull Scar Estates (Pty) Ltd, White River, South Africa; *b* 20 March 1958; *s* of late Wing Comdr Michael Nicholson Crossley, RAF, DSO, OBE, DFC and Sylvia Constance Crossley; *S* cousin, 2003; *m* 1999, Jane Elizabeth, *d* of late Henry Cecil Twycross and Katherine Elizabeth Twycross. *Educ:* St Albans Coll., Pretoria; Kingston Polytech., London; Central Sch. of Art and Design, London (BSc Hons Industrial Design (Eng)). *Address:* Pull Scar Estate, PO Box 121, White River, 1240 Mpumalanga, South Africa.

CROSSLEY-HOLLAND, Kevin John William, FRSL; author; *b* 7 Feb. 1941; *s* of late Prof. Peter Charles Crossley-Holland and Joan Mary Crossley-Holland (*née* Cowper), MBE; *m* 1st, 1963, Caroline Fendall, *er d* of Prof. L. M. Thompson; two *s*; 2nd, 1972, Ruth, *er d* of John Marris; 3rd, 1982, Gillian Paula, *er d* of Peter Cook; two *d*; 4th, 1999, Linda Marie, *d* of Abner Jones. *Educ:* Bryanston Sch.; St Edmund Hall, Oxford (MA Hons; Hon. Fellow, 2001). FRSL 1998. Editor, Macmillan & Co., 1962–69; Gregory Fellow in Poetry, Univ. of Leeds, 1969–71; Talks Producer, BBC, 1972; Editl Dir, Victor Gollancz, 1972–77; Lectr in English: Tufts-in-London Program, 1967–78; Regensburg Univ., 1978–80; Arts Council Fellow in Writing, Winchester Sch. of Art, 1983 and 1984; Vis. Prof. of English and Fulbright Scholar, St Olaf Coll., Minnesota, 1987–90; Prof. and Endowed Chair in Humanities and Fine Arts, Univ. of St Thomas, Minnesota, 1991–95; Vis. Lectr for British Council in Germany, Iceland, India, Malawi, Yugoslavia, Slovakia. Editl Consultant, Boydell & Brewer, 1983–90. Chm., Literature Panel, Eastern Arts Assoc., 1986–89; Trustee, Wingfield Coll., 1989–99 (Chm., Friends, 1989–91). Dir, American Composers Forum, 1993–97. Chm., Poetry-next-the-Sea, 1999–2006. Patron: Thomas Lovell Beddoes Soc., 1999–; Soc. for Storytelling, 2002–. Contribs to radio (incl. drama), TV (incl. educl series), and musical works. *Publications:* *poetry:* The Rain-Giver, 1972; The Dream-House, 1976; Time's Oriel, 1983; Waterslain, 1986; The Painting-Room, 1988; New and Selected Poems, 1991; The Language of Yes, 1996; Poems from East Anglia, 1997; Selected Poems, 2001; (with Norman Ackroyd) Moored Man, 2006; *for children:* Havelok the Dane, 1964; King Horn, 1965; The Green Children, 1966 (Arts Council Award); The Callow Pit Coffer, 1968; (with Jill Paton Walsh) Wordhoard, 1969; Storm and Other Old English Riddles, 1970; The Pedlar of Swaffham, 1971; The Sea Stranger, 1973; The Fire-Brother, 1974; Green Blades Rising, 1975; The Earth-Father, 1976; The Wildman, 1976; The Dead Moon, 1982; Beowulf, 1982; (with Gwyn Thomas) The Mabinogion, 1984; Axe-Age, Wolf-Age, 1985; Storm, 1985 (Carnegie Medal); (with Susanne Lugert) The Fox and the Cat, 1985; British Folk Tales, 1987, reissued as The Magic Lands, 2001; Wulf, 1988; (with Gwyn Thomas) The Quest for Olwen, 1988; Piper and Pooka, 1988; Small Tooth Dog, 1988; Boo!, 1988; Dathera Dad, 1989; (with Ian Penney) Under the Sun and Over the Moon, 1989; Sleeping Nanna, 1989; Sea Tongue, 1991; Tales from Europe, 1991; Long Tom and The Dead Hand, 1992; (with Gwyn Thomas) Taliesin, 1992; The Labours of Herakles, 1993; Norse Myths, 1993; The Green Children, 1994; The Dark Horseman, 1995; The Old Stories, 1997; Short!, 1998; The King Who Was and Will Be, 1998; Enchantment, 2000; The Seeing Stone, 2000 (Guardian Children's Fiction Prize; Tir na n-Og Award); At the Crossing-Places, 2001; (with Meilo So) The Ugly Duckling, 2001; Viking!, 2002; King of the Middle March, 2003; (with Peter Malone) How Many Miles to Bethlehem?, 2004; King Arthur's World, 2004; Outsiders, 2005; Gatty's Tale, 2006; Thor and the Master of Magic, 2007; Waterslain Angels, 2008; *play:* (with Ivan Cutting) The Wuffings, 1999; *travel:* Pieces of Land, 1972; *mythology:* The Norse Myths, 1980; *history:* (with Andrew Rafferty) The Stones Remain, 1989; *translations from Old English:* (with Bruce Mitchell) The Battle of Maldon, 1965; (with Bruce Mitchell) Beowulf, 1968; The Exeter Book Riddles, 1978; The Illustrated Beowulf, 1987; The Anglo-Saxon Elegies, 1988; *edited:* Running to Paradise, 1967; Winter's Tales for Children 3, 1967; Winter's Tales 14, 1968; (with Patricia Beer) New Poetry 2, 1976; The Faber Book of Northern Legends, 1977; The Faber Book of Northern Folk-Tales, 1980; The Anglo-Saxon World, 1982; The Riddle Book, 1982; Folk-Tales of the British Isles, 1985; The Oxford Book of Travel Verse, 1986; Northern Lights, 1987; Medieval Lovers, 1988; Medieval Gardens, 1990; Peter Grimes by George Crabbe, 1990; The Young Oxford Book of Folk-Tales, 1998; (with Lawrence Sail) The New Exeter Book of Riddles, 1999; (with Lawrence Sail) Light Unlocked: Christmas card poems, 2005; *operas:* (with Nicola LeFanu): The Green Children, 1990; The Wildman, 1995; (with Rupert Bawden) The Sailor's Tale, 2002. *Recreations:* walks, wine, opera, the company of friends, appreciating East Anglia. *Address:* Chalk Hill, Burnham Market, Norfolk PE31 8JR. *Club:* Garrick.

CROSSMAN, Moira Katherine Brigid; *see* Whyte, M. K. B.

CROUCH, Prof. Colin John, DPhil; FBA 2005; Chair, Institute of Governance and Public Management and Professor of Governance and Public Management, Warwick Business School, University of Warwick, since 2005; *b* 1 March 1944; *s* of Charles and Doris Crouch; *m* 1970, Joan Ann Freedman; two *s*. *Educ:* Latymer Upper Sch.; London School of Economics (BASoc; Pres., Students Union, 1968; Hobhouse Prize, 1969); Nuffield Coll., Oxford (MA, DPhil). Lecturer in Sociology: LSE, 1969–70; Univ. of Bath, 1972–73; Lectr, 1973–79, Sen. Lectr 1979–80, Reader 1980–85, in Sociology, LSE; University of Oxford: Fellow and Tutor in Politics, Trinity Coll., Oxford, 1985–98; Prof. of Sociol., 1996–98; Curator, Bodleian Liby, 1991–95; Jun. Proctor, 1990–91; Deleg., OUP, 1992–98; European University Institute, Florence: Prof. of Comparative Social Instns, 1995–2004; Chm., Dept of Social and Political Scis, 2001–04. External Scientific Mem., Max-Planck Institut für Gesellschaftsforschung, Cologne, 1997–. Mem., Exec. Cttee, Fabian Soc., 1969–78 (Chm., 1976); Dir, Andrew Shonfield Soc., 1989–95. Member: Standing Cttee, Court of Govs, LSE, 1980–84; Scientific Adv. Bd, Univ. of Vienna, 2007–. Fellow, Sunningdale Inst., 2005–. Chm. Editl Bd, The Political Qly, 1999– (Joint Editor, 1985–95). *Publications:* The Student Revolt, 1970; (ed jtly) Stress and Contradiction in Modern Capitalism, 1975; (ed) British Political Sociology Year Book, vol. III, 1977; Class Conflict and the Industrial Relations Crisis, 1977; (ed jtly) The Resurgence of Class Conflict in Western Europe since 1968, 2 vols, 1978; (ed) State and Economy in Contemporary Capitalism, 1979; The Politics of Industrial Relations, 1979, 2nd edn 1982; Trade Unions: the logic of collective action, 1982; (ed jtly) International Yearbook of Organizational Democracy, vol. I, 1983; (ed jtly) The New Centralism: Britain out of step in Europe?, 1989; (ed jtly) European Industrial Relations: the challenge of flexibility, 1990; (ed jtly) Corporatism and Accountability: organised interests in British public life, 1990; (ed jtly) The Politics of 1992: beyond the single European market, 1990; (ed jtly) Towards Greater Europe?, 1992; Industrial Relations and European State Traditions, 1993 (Political Studies Assoc. Book Prize, 1993); (ed jtly) Ethics and Markets: co-operation and competition in capitalist economies, 1993; (ed jtly) Reinventing Collective Action: the global and the local, 1995; (ed jtly) Organized Industrial Relations in Europe: what future?, 1995; (ed jtly) Les capitalismes en Europe, 1996; (ed jtly) Political Economy of Modern Capitalism, 1997; (jtly) Are Skills the Answer?, 1999; Social Change in Western Europe, 1999; (ed jtly) After the Euro, 2000; (ed jtly) Citizenship, Markets and the State, 2001; (ed) Coping with Post-Democracy, 2001; (jtly) Local Production Systems in Europe: rise or demise?, 2001; Commercialisation or Citizenship, 2003; Postdemocrazia, 2003, trans. English as Postdemocracy, 2004; (jtly) Changing Governance of Local Economies: responses of European local production systems, 2004; Capitalist Diversity and Change, 2005; numerous articles on industrial relns, politics, economic sociology and social structure in Britain and Western Europe. *Recreations:* playing violin, music, gardening, watching and refereeing football matches. *Address:* Warwick Business School, University of Warwick, Coventry CV4 7AL. *T:* (024) 7652 4505.

CROUCH, Sybil Edith; Director, Taliesin Arts Centre, Swansea University (formerly University College of Swansea, then University of Wales, Swansea), since 1990; *b* 9 Aug. 1953; *d* of David George and Lilian Crouch. *Educ:* Birkenhead High Sch. for Girls; Swansea Coll. of Art. Specialist Art Teacher. Dep. Dir, W Wales Assoc. for the Arts, 1979–90. Chm., Arts Council of Wales, 1999–2003. FRSA 1999. *Recreation:* the company of friends. *Address:* Taliesin Arts Centre, Swansea University, Singleton Park, Swansea SA2 8PZ.

CROW, Jonathan Rupert; QC 2006; Attorney General to the Prince of Wales, since 2006; *b* 25 June 1958; *s* of Michael Frederick Crow and Edith Mae Crow; *m* 1998, Claudia Jane Turner; two *s* one *d*. *Educ:* St Paul's Sch.; Magdalen Coll., Oxford (BA Modern Hist.). Called to the Bar, Lincoln's Inn, 1981; Treasury Counsel (Chancery), 1994–98; First Treasury Counsel (Chancery), 1998–2006; Dep. High Court Judge, 2001–. *Address:* 4 Stone Buildings, Lincoln's Inn, WC2A 3XT. *T:* (020) 7242 5524, *Fax:* (020) 7831 7907; *e-mail:* clerks@4stonebuildings.com. *Club:* Athenæum.

CROW, Robert; General Secretary, National Union of Rail, Maritime and Transport Workers, since 2002; *b* 13 June 1961; *s* of George William Crow and Lillian (*née* Hutton); partner, Nicola Hoarau; one *s* two *d*. *Educ:* Hainault High Sch. Joined London Underground as railway worker, 1977. Mem. Nat. Exec., 1994–, Asst Gen. Sec., 1997–2002, RMT. *Recreations:* football, boxing, darts. *Address:* National Union of Rail, Maritime and Transport Workers, 39 Chalton Street, NW1 1YD. *Club:* Millwall Football.

CROW, Prof. Timothy John, PhD; FRCP, FRCPsych, FMedSci; Scientific Director, SANE Prince of Wales Centre for Research into Schizophrenia and Depression, University Department of Psychiatry, Warneford Hospital, Oxford, since 1995; Titular Professor of Psychiatry, University of Oxford, since 1998; *b* 7 June 1938; *s* of late Percy Arthur Crow and of Barbara Bonner Davies; *m* 1966, Julie Carol Carter; one *s* one *d*. *Educ:* Shrewsbury Sch.; London Hosp. Med. Coll. MB BS, PhD, DPM. Maudsley Hosp., 1966; University of Aberdeen: Lectr in Physiology, 1966–70; Lectr in Mental Health, 1970–72; Sen. Lectr in Psychiatry, Univ. of Manchester, 1972–73; Head, Div. of Psychiatry, Clinical Res. Centre, Northwick Park Hosp., 1974–94. Part-time Mem., Sci. Staff, Div. Neurophysiology and Neuropharmacology, Nat. Inst. for Med. Res., 1974–83; Dep. Dir, Clinical Res. Centre, 1984–89. Member: MRC Neuroscis Projects Grants Cttee, 1978–80; Neuroscis Bd, 1986–90; Chm., Biol. Psych. Gp, RCPsych, 1983–88 (Sec., 1980–83). Andrew W. Woods Vis. Prof., Univ. of Iowa, 1980; Lectures: St George's Hosp., 1980; St Louis, 1981; Univ. of Minnesota, 1981; Univ. of Ohio, 1986; RSocMed, 1988; Roche, RCPsych, Dublin, 1988; Stockholm, 1988; Maudsley, RCPsych, 1989; APA Internat. Scholars, 1990; Univ. of Oregon, 1991. Founder FMedSci 1998. A. P. Noyes Award, 1988; US Nat. Alliance Lieber Award, 1989; Res. Prize, World Fedn of Socs of Biol Psychiatry, 1991; Alexander Gralnick Award, Amer. Psych. Foundn, 2000; Kurt Schneider Award, 2006. *Publications:* (ed) Disorders of Neurohumoral Transmission, 1982; (ed) Recurrent and Chronic Psychoses, 1987; (ed) The Speciation of Modern Homo Sapiens, 2002; papers on brain reward mechanisms, learning, evolution of language, speciation of Homo Sapiens, and schizophrenia in sci. and med. jls. *Recreations:* sciolistic archaeology, anthropology. *Address:* 16 Northwick Circle, Kenton, Middx HA3 0EJ. *T:* (020) 8907 6124. *Club:* Royal Society of Medicine.

CROWCROFT, Prof. Jonathan Andrew, PhD; FREng, FIET, FBCS; Marconi Professor of Communications Systems, University of Cambridge, since 2001; *b* 23 Nov. 1957; *s* of late Dr Andrew Crowcroft and of Prof. Kyla Crowcroft (*née* Greenbaum); *m* 1988, Noreen McKeever; two *s* one *d*. *Educ:* Trinity Coll., Cambridge (BA 1979); University Coll. London (PhD 1997). FREng 1999; FIET (FIEE 1999); FBCS 2000. Sen. Lectr, 1996–97, Prof. of Networked Systems, 1997–2001, UCL. FIEEE 2003 (SMIEE 1992); FACM 2004 (MACM 1988). *Publications:* WWW: beneath the surf, 1994; Open Distributed Systems, 1997; Internet Multimedia, 2000; Linux Internet Protocols, 2001. *Recreation:* classical guitar. *Address:* The Computer Laboratory, Gates Building, J. J. Thomson Avenue, Cambridge CB3 0FD. *T:* (01223) 763633, *Fax:* (01223) 334678; *e-mail:* jon.crowcroft@cl.cam.ac.uk.

CROWDEN, James Gee Pascoe, CVO 2003; JP; FRICS, FCIArb; Senior Partne Grounds & Co., 1974–88; Lord-Lieutenant and Custos Rotulorum of Cambridgeshir 1992–2002; *b* 14 Nov. 1927; *yr s* of late Lt-Col R. J. C. Crowden, MC, and Nina Ma (*née* Gee), Peterborough; *m* 1st, 1955, Kathleen Mary (*d* 1989), *widow* of Captain F. Grounds and *d* of late Mr and Mrs J. W. Loughlin, Upwell; (one *s* decd), and one step 2nd, 2001, Margaret, *widow* of J. R. Crowden and *d* of late Rev. Wilfred Cole, Oundl four step *d*. *Educ:* Bedford Sch.; Pembroke Coll., Cambridge (MA; Hon. Fellow, 1993 Chartered surveyor; FRICS 1959; FCIArb 1977. Commissioned Royal Lincs Regt, 194 Rowed in Oxford and Cambridge Boat Race, 1951 and 1952 (Pres., 1952); Captai Great Britain VIII, European Championships, Macon, 1951 (Gold Medallists); also rowe in European Championships, Milan, 1950 (Bronze Medallists) and Helsinki Olympic 1952; coached 20 Cambridge crews, 1953–75; Steward, Henley Royal Regatta, 1959 (Mem., Cttee of Management, 1964–92); Mem. Council, Amateur Rowing Assoc 1957–77; Hon. Mem. of Court and Freeman, Co. of Watermen and Lightermen of th River Thames (Master, 1991–92). Vice-Pres., British Olympic Assoc., 1988–; Chairma Cambridgeshire Olympic Appeals, 1984, 1988, 1992, 1996 and 2000; Appeal Exec. Ctte Peterborough Cathedral, 1979–80; Member: Ely Diocesan Pastoral Cttee, 1969–89; E Cathedral Fabric Cttee, 1986–90. Chm., Order of St Etheldreda, 1992–2002. Form Pres., Agricl Valuers' Assocs for Herts, Beds and Bucks, Lincs, Norfolk, Cambs, an Wisbech. Dep. Pres., E of England Agricl Soc., 2001; President: Cambs Fedn of Your Farmers, 1971–73; Cambs Scouts, 1992–2002; Cambs TAVR and Cadet Ctte 1992–2002; E Anglia TAVRA, 1996–2000 (Vice-Pres., 1992–96 and 2000–02); Ho Col, Cambs ACF, 1996–2002. Patron: Cambs RBL, 1992–2006; Cambs Red Cros 1992–2002; Duke of Edinburgh's Award County Cttee, 1992–2002; Cambs St Joh Ambulance, 1993–2002; Cambs Regt Old Comrades' Assoc., 1998–. Governor: Marc Grammar Sch., 1960–70 (Chm., 1967–70); King's Sch., Peterborough, 1980–90; Hugh's Sch., Woodhall Spa, 1981–92. Church Warden, All Saints', Walsoken, 1964–7 and 1983–84. Pres., Old Bedfordians' Club, 1996–98. JP Wisbech, 1969; DL 1971, Vic Lord-Lieut, 1985–92, Cambridgeshire; High Sheriff, Cambridgeshire and Isle of El 1970. Freeman: Town of Wisbech, 2001; Tri-Base (Alconbury, Molesworth an Upwood), USAF, 2001; City of Peterborough, 2007. FRSA 1990. KStJ 1992. *Recreatio* rowing, shooting. *Address:* 19 North Brink, Wisbech, Cambridgeshire PE13 1JR. (01945) 583320. *Clubs:* East India, Devonshire, Sports and Public Schools, Sette of Od Volumes; Hawks', University Pitt, Cambridge County (Cambridge); Leander (Henley on-Thames).

CROWDER, Ven. Norman Harry; Archdeacon of Portsmouth, 1985–93, no Archdeacon Emeritus; *b* 20 Oct. 1926; *s* of Laurence Smethurst Crowder and Franc Annie (*née* Hicks); *m* 1971, Pauleen Florence Alison (*née* Styles); one *s*. *Educ:* Nottingha High School; St John's Coll., Cambridge (MA); Westcott House, Cambridge. Na Service, Flying Officer, RAF Educn Branch, 1948–50. Curate, St Mary's, Radcliffe-on Trent, 1952–55; Residential Chaplain to Bishop of Portsmouth, 1955–59; Asst Chaplai Canford School, 1959–64, Chaplain 1964–72; Vicar, St John's, Oakfield, Ryde, IoW 1972–75; Dir of Religious Educn, Portsmouth Dio., and Res. Canon of Portsmout Cathedral, 1975–85. *Recreations:* water colours of J. M. W. Turner, poetry of T. S. Elio conservation of elephants. *Address:* 37 Rectory Road, Salisbury SP2 7SD. *T:* (0172 320052. *Club:* MCC.

CROWDY, Maj.-Gen. Joseph Porter, CB 1984; Commandant and Postgraduate Dea Royal Army Medical College, 1981–84, retired; Hon. Consultant on nutrition to Arm 1985–88; *b* 19 Nov. 1923; *s* of late Lt-Col Charles R. Crowdy and Kate Crowdy (*n* Porter); *m* 1948, Beryl Elisabeth Sapsford (*d* 1997); four *d*. *Educ:* Gresham's Sch Edinburgh Univ. MB, ChB 1947, DTM&H 1956, DPH 1957, DIH 1957; FFPH (FFC 1974); MFOM 1981; FRIPH (FRIPHH 1982). House Surgeon, Norfolk and Norwic Hosp., 1947–48; joined RAMC, 1949; North Africa, 1952–55; Singapore, 1960–6 Head of Applied Physiology, Army Personnel Res. Estabt, 1963–73; Prof. of Arm Health, Royal Army Med. Coll., 1973–76; SMO, Land Forces Cyprus, 1976–78; Di Army Preventive Medicine, 1978–81. Col Comdt, RAMC, 1985–88. QHP 1981–8 Editor, RAMC Jl, 1978–83. *Publications:* articles in medical jls, on smoking and healt nutrition, physical fitness and obesity. *Recreations:* antique furniture restoration, fami genealogy, embroidery. *Address:* Pepperdon Mine, Lustleigh, Newton Abbot, Devo TQ13 9SN. *T:* and *Fax:* (01647) 277419; *e-mail:* crowdy@btinternet.com.

CROWE, Sir Brian (Lee), KCMG 2002 (CMG 1985); Director General for External an Defence Affairs, Council of the European Union, 1994–2002; *b* 5 Jan. 1938; *s* of Er Crowe and Virginia Crowe; *m* 1969, Virginia Willis; two *s*. *Educ:* Sherborne; Magdale Coll., Oxford (1st Cl. Hons PPE). Joined FO, 1961; served: Moscow, 1962–64; Londo 1965–67; Aden, 1967; Washington, 1968–73; Bonn, 1973–76; Counsellor and Hd Policy Planning Staff, FCO, 1976–78; Hd of Chancery, UK Perm. Representation t EEC, Brussels, 1979–81; Counsellor and Hd of EEC Dept (External), FCO, 1982–8 Minister, Commercial, Washington, 1985–89; Ambassador to Austria, 1989–92; De Under-Sec. of State (Dir Gen.) for Econ. Affairs, FCO, 1992–94. Mem. Counci Chatham House, 2003– (Dep. Chm., 2005–). *Recreations:* winter sports, tennis, ridin swimming. *Address:* 55 Ashley Gardens, Ambrosden Avenue, SW1P 1QF; *e-mai* brian_lee_crowe@hotmail.com.

CROWE, Frank Richard; Sheriff, and Director, Judicial Studies in Scotland, since 200 *b* 15 March 1952; *s* of James Crowe and Helen Mary Harle or Crowe; *m* 1975, Aliso Margaret Purdom or Crowe (separated 1997); two *d*; partner, Margaret Elizabeth Scot QC (Scot.); one *s*. *Educ:* Valley and West Primary Schs, Kirkcaldy; Kirkcaldy High Sch Royal High Sch., Edinburgh; Dundee Univ. (LLB). Admitted solicitor, 1975, NP 199 Solicitor Advocate, 1995; law apprentice, N of Scotland Hydro-Electric Bd, 1973–7 Procurator Fiscal Depute: Dundee, 1975–78; Glasgow, 1978–81; Sen. Legal Asst, Crow Office, 1981–83; Sen. Depute Procurator Fiscal, Edinburgh, 1983–87; Crown Offic Sen. Depute i/c Fraud Unit, 1987–88; Asst Solicitor i/c High Court Unit, 1988–9 Procurator Fiscal, Kirkcaldy, 1991–96; Regl Procurator Fiscal, Hamilton, 1996–9 Deputy Crown Agent, Crown Office, 1999–2001; Sheriff of Tayside Central and Fife, Dundee, 2001–04. Mem., Stephen Lawrence Steering Gp, Scottish Exec., 1999–200 Chm., Adv. Gp to Zone Trng for New Futures, Dundee, 2002–04; consultant to Crimin Justice Oversight Comr, NI, 2003–07. Mem. Council, Law Soc. of Scotland, 1996–9 Mem. and Vice Chm., Lothian Victim Support Scheme, 1983–89. Chm. Bd, Stockbrig Primary Sch., 2006–. *Publication:* (jtly) Criminal Procedure, 1989, 2nd edn, as part of Sta Memorial Encyclopaedia of the Laws of Scotland, 2002. *Recreations:* golf, music, walkin racing, analysis. *Address:* Judicial Studies Committee, Bearford House, 39 Hanover Stree Edinburgh EH2 2PJ. *T:* (0131) 220 9320, *Fax:* (0131) 220 9321; *e-mail:* sheriff.frcrowe@ scotcourts.gov.uk. *Club:* Murrayfield Golf (Edinburgh).

CROWE, His Honour Gerald Patrick; QC 1973; a Circuit Judge, 1980–95; *b* 3 Apr 1930; *y s* of Patrick Crowe and Ethel Maud Crowe (*née* Tooth); *m* 1st, 1954, Catherin Mary (*d* 2000), *d* of Joseph and Rose Murphy, Newry, N Ireland; 2nd, 2004, Mar Therese Murphy. *Educ:* St Francis Xavier's Coll.; Liverpool Univ. (LLB). Called to Ba Gray's Inn, 1952; practised Northern Circuit. A Recorder of the Crown Court, 1976–8

Mem., Lord Chancellor's Adv. Cttee on Legal Aid, 1984–91. *Recreations:* golf, fishing. *Address:* The Spinney, Long Hey Road, Caldy, Cheshire L48 1LY. *T:* (0151) 625 8848.

CROWE, Dr Michael John, DM; FRCP, FRCPsych; Consultant Psychiatrist, Bethlem Royal and Maudsley Hospital, London, 1978–2002; *b* 16 Oct. 1937; *s* of Robert James Crowe and Olive (*née* Kingston-Jones); *m* 1968, Diane Jordan; one *s* one *d.* *Educ:* St Paul's Sch., London; Exeter Coll., Oxford (MA, BM 1963); London Hosp. Med. Coll. MPhil London, 1970; DM Oxon, 1977. MRCP 1967; MRCPsych 1973; FRCPsych 1984; FRCP 1992. House Officer: London Hosp., 1964; Chelmsford and Essex Hosp., 1964; Senior House Officer: Addenbrooke's Hosp., 1965–66; London Hosp., 1966–67; Maudsley Hospital: Registrar, 1967–69; Sen. Registrar, Res. Worker and Lectr, 1970–74; Sen. Lectr, Inst. of Psychiatry, 1974–77 (Course Leader, Couple Therapy Dip. Course, 1989–2002). Vis. Fellow, Univ. of Vermont, USA, 1969. Lectr on behavioural and couple therapy, USA, Trinidad, Denmark, Italy, etc. Founder Mem., Inst. of Family Therapy, London, 1976–. Chm., Assoc. of Sexual and Marital Therapists, 1986–88. Gaskell Gold Medal, RCPsych, 1972. *Publications:* (with J. Ridley) Therapy with Couples, 1990, 2nd edn 2000; Overcoming Relationship Problems, 2005; papers in med. and psychol. jls on behaviour therapy, couple therapy and sexual dysfunctions. *Recreations:* music (performing and listening), poetry, literature, languages, walking. *Address:* 66 Palace View, Shirley, Croydon CR0 8QN. *T:* (020) 8777 4823; 21 Wimpole Street, W1G 8GG. *T:* (020) 7637 0146.

CROWE, Rev. Philip Anthony; Tutor in Ethics, St Asaph Ministry Training Scheme, since 1999 (Director, 1996–2001); *b* 16 Aug. 1936; *s* of late Frederick Francis Crowe and of Hilda Crowe; *m* 1963, Freda Maureen Gill; two *s* one *d.* *Educ:* Repton School; Selwyn Coll., Cambridge; Ridley Hall, Cambridge. National service, RA, 1955–57. Tutor in NT Greek and Mission, Oak Hill, 1962–67; Curate at Christchurch, Cockfosters, 1962–65; Editor, Church of England Newspaper, 1967–70; Sec., Bursary Scheme for Overseas Students, 1967–70; Senior Staff Member, St Martin-in-the Bull Ring, Birmingham, 1970–76; Rector of Breadsall, Derby, 1977–88; Derby Diocesan Missioner, 1977–83; Tutor in Ethics, St John's Coll., Nottingham, 1986–88; Principal, Salisbury and Wells Theol Coll., 1988–94; Rector, Overton, Penley and Erbistock, 1995–97; Hon. Canon, Salisbury Cathedral, 1991–95. Mem., Gen. Synod, C of E, 1992–95. *Publications:* (contrib.) Mission in the Modern World, Church and Sacraments, 1977; Pastoral Reorganisation, 1978; Christian Baptism, 1980; The Use and Abuse of Alcohol, 1980; A Whisper will be Heard, 1994; Strange Design, 1999. *Recreations:* gardening, music, squash, walking, caravanning. *Address:* Alderlea, Babbinswood, Whittington SY11 4PQ. *T:* and *Fax:* (01691) 671698.

CROWLEY, Graham Neil; Professor of Painting, and Head, Department of Painting, Royal College of Art, 1998–2006; *b* 3 May 1950; *s* of Victor Matthew Crowley and Violet Mary Crowley (*née* Lee); *m* 1978, Sally Ann Townshend; two *s.* *Educ:* St Martin's Sch. of Art (DipAD); Royal Coll. of Art (MA). Vis. Lectr, Painting, Royal Coll. of Art, 1978–85; Artist-in-Residence, Oxford Univ. and Fellow, St Edmund Hall, Oxford, 1982–83; Vis. Lectr, Goldsmiths' Coll., London, 1984–86; Sen. Fellow in Painting, S Glamorgan Inst. of Higher Educn, Cardiff, 1986–89; Artist-in-Residence: Riverscape Project, Cleveland, 1991–92; Dulwich Picture Gall., London, 1994–95; Hd of Fine Art, C&G, 1996–98. *One-man exhibitions* include: In Living Memory, Orchard Gall., Derry, and touring, 1987; Millfield Gall., Som, 1993; The Last Decade, Lamont Gall., London, 1995; A Drift, RCA, 1999; Familiar Ground, Beaux Arts, London, 2001; Are you serious?, Wolsey Art Gall., Ipswich, 2002; Graham Crowley, Beaux Arts, 2003, 2005; W Cork Arts Centre, Skibbereen, 2008; *group exhibitions* include: Arnolfini Gall., Bristol, 1977; Open Attitudes, MOMA, Oxford, 1979; South Bank Show, Hayward Gall. and Paris Biennale, 1982; Venice Biennale, 1984; Artists Against Apartheid, RFH, 1985; Edward Totah Gall., London, 1986, 1987; New British Painting, Queens Mus., NY, 1990; Royal Acad. Summer Exhibn, 1990, 1991, 1992; British Liby, 1994; Flowers E Gall., London, annually 1994–98, 2001, 2002; Summer Shows, 2000–02, Art 2001, Art 2002, Beaux Arts; The Discerning Eye, Mall Galls, London, 2000, 2001; British Art Fair, Beaux Arts, RCA, 2001, Commonwealth Inst., 2002; *work in public collections* includes: Imperial War Mus.; V&A Mus.; Contemporary Arts Soc.; Kettles Yard, Cambridge; Castle Mus., Nottingham; Mus. of Auckland, NZ. *Publication:* (with S. Hood) De Sade for Beginners, 1995. *Recreations:* motorcycling, rowing, gardening. *Address:* Rineen, Skibbereen, Co. Cork, Ireland. *T:* (28) 36421.

CROWLEY, Jane Elizabeth Rosser; QC 1998; a Recorder, since 1995; *b* 5 Aug. 1953; *d* of Robert Jenkyn Rosser and Marion Rosser (*née* Davies); *m* 1986, (Jonathan) Mark Crowley; one *s* one *d.* *Educ:* Howell's Sch., Llandaff, Cardiff; King's Coll. London (LLB 1975). Called to the Bar, Gray's Inn, 1976 ; Bencher, 2004; in practice at the Bar, 1976–. Dep. High Ct Judge, Family Div., 1999–. Legal Mem., Mental Health Tribunal Restricted Order Panel, 2000–. *Recreations:* family, music, Pembrokeshire coast, Glamorgan County Cricket Club, good friends, good wine. *Address:* 30 Park Place, Cardiff CF1 3BA. *T:* (029) 2039 8421; 1 Garden Court, Temple, EC4Y 9BJ. *T:* (020) 7797 7900.

CROWLEY, Rt Rev. John; Bishop of Middlesbrough, (RC), 1993–2007; *b* Newbury, 23 June 1941. Ordained priest, 1965; Holy Trinity Parish, Brook Green, W6, 1965–68; Catholic Missionary Soc., 1968–74; Private Sec. to Cardinal Hume, 1974–82; Vicar Gen. for Westminster dio., 1982–86; Auxiliary Bishop of Westminster (Bishop in Central London), and Titular Bishop of Tala, 1986–92. Chairman, Catholic Fund for Overseas Development, 1988–2000. Rep. of Bishops' Conf. of England and Wales to Conf. of European Bishops within EU, 2001. *Address:* c/o Curial Office, 50a The Avenue, Linthorpe, Middlesbrough TS5 6QT.

CROWLEY, John Desmond; QC 1982; a Recorder of the Crown Court, since 1980; *b* 25 June 1938; *s* of late John Joseph Crowley and Anne Marie (*née* Fallon); *m* 1977, Sarah Maria, *er d* of Christopher Gage Jacobs and late Joan Zara (*née* Atkinson); two *d.* *Educ:* St Edmund's College, Ware; Christ's College, Cambridge (BA 1961, LLB 1962). National Service, 2/Lieut 6th Royal Tank Regt, 1957–58. Called to the Bar, Inner Temple, 1962, Bencher, 1989. Member: Criminal Injuries Compensation Bd, 1985–2000; Criminal Injuries Compensation Appeal Panel, 2000–02. Chm., Appeal Cttee, ICAEW, 2000–. *Recreations:* music, the turf, wine. *Address:* Crown Office Chambers, 2 Crown Office Row, Temple, EC4Y 7HJ. *T:* (020) 7797 8100.

CROWLEY, Robert, RDI 1997; set designer for theatre, opera, ballet and film; *b* Cork, 1952. *Educ:* Crawford Municipal Sch. of Fine Art; Bristol Old Vic Theatre Sch. *Sets designed* include: *theatre:* Royal Shakespeare Company: Love's Labour's Lost, 1984; As You Like It, 1985; Les Liaisons Dangereuses, 1986, transf. Ambassadors, NY, LA, Tokyo; Macbeth, A Penny for a Song, Principia Scriptoriae, 1986; The Plantagenets, 1988; Othello, 1989; Hamlet, 1992; National Theatre, later Royal National Theatre: Ghetto (Laurence Olivier Award for Designer of the Year, 1990), Hedda Gabler, Ma Rainey's Black Bottom, 1989; White Chameleon, Murmuring Judges, 1991; Carousel, 1992, transf. Shaftesbury, 1993, NY (Tony Award, 1994); The Coast of Utopia, 2002, NY (Tony Award, 2007); Mourning Becomes Electra, 2003; The History Boys, 2004; Bristol Old Vic: Timon of Athens; A View from the Bridge; Destiny; Women All Over, King's, Edinburgh, 1985; Two Way Mirror, Young Vic, 1989; The Three Sisters, Gate, Dublin, 1990; The Cure at Troy, Guildhall, Derry, then Lyric, Belfast, 1990 (also Jt Dir); Saint Oscar, Field Day Theatre Co., Derry (Dir); Madame de Sade, Tokyo; No Man's Land, Almeida, 1992; When She Danced, Globe; Cunning Little Vixen, Châtelet, Paris; The Judas Kiss, Playhouse, then NY, 1998; The Capeman, NY, 1998; Twelfth Night, NY, 1998; Into the Woods, Donmar Warehouse, 1998; The Seagull, NY, 2001; Sweet Smell of Success, NY, 2002; Mary Poppins, Prince Edward, 2004 (Best Designer, Evening Standard Theatre Awards, 2005; Tony Award, 2007); Moon for the Misbegotten, Old Vic, 2006, transf. NY, 2007; *opera:* Don Giovanni, Kent Opera; The Magic Flute, ENO, 1988, 1997; Aida, NY (Tony Award), 2001; Royal Opera: costumes, The King Goes Forth to France, 1987; The Knot Garden, 1988; La Traviata; Don Carlo, 2008; *ballet:* Anastasia, Pavane, Royal Ballet; Naked, Sadler's Wells, 2005; *films:* Othello; Tales of Hollywood; The Crucible, 1997. *Address:* c/o Simpson Fox Associates Ltd, 52 Shaftesbury Avenue, W1D 6LP.

CROWLEY-MILLING, Michael Crowley, CMG 1982; CEng, FIET; consultant on computer control systems; *b* 7 May 1917; *s* of Thomas William Crowley-Milling and Gillian May (*née* Chinnery); *m* 1958, Gee Dickson (*d* 2005). *Educ:* Radley Coll.; St John's Coll., Cambridge (MA 1943). CEng, FIET (FIEE 1956). R&D on radar systems, Metropolitan-Vickers Electrical Co. Ltd, Manchester, 1938–46; design and develt of electron linear accelerators for physics, medical and irradiation purposes, 1946–63; contrib. to construction of electron synchrotron, Daresbury Nuclear Physics Lab., Warrington, 1963–71; CERN, Geneva: resp. for control system for Super Proton Synchrotron (SPS), 1971–75; SPS Div. Leader, 1977–78; Dir, Accelerator Prog., 1979–80; Consultant, 1982–83; Consultant to: SLAC, Stanford Univ., Calif., 1984–85; Los Alamos Nat. Lab., New Mexico, 1986–94; SSC Lab., Dallas, 1991–93; Dir, Crowley Consultants, 1984–. Crompton Premium, IEE, 1959; Glazebrook Medal, Inst. of Physics, 1980. Captain LMBC, 1938. Patents for improvements in radar systems and particle accelerators, 1940–60. *Publications:* (ed) Accelerator Control Systems, 1986; (ed) Accelerator and Large Experimental Control Systems, 1990, 1994; John Bertram Adams, Engineer Extraordinary, 1993; articles and chapters in books on particle accelerators and computer control systems. *Recreations:* vintage cars, sailing. *Address:* 5 West Court, Hollins Hall, Harrogate HG3 2WY. *Clubs:* Vintage Sports Car, Royal Yacht.

CROWN, Dr June Madge, CBE 1998; FRCP, FFPH; President, Faculty of Public Health Medicine, Royal College of Physicians, 1995–98; *b* 5 June 1938; *d* of late Edward Downes and Madge Edith Downes; *m* 1964, Sidney Crown; two *s* one *d.* *Educ:* Pate's Grammar Sch. for Girls, Cheltenham; Newnham Coll., Cambridge (MA); Middlesex Hosp. Med. Sch. (MB, BChir); London Sch. of Hygiene and Tropical Medicine (MSc). FFPH (FFPHM 1986); FRCP 1991. Area MO, Brent and Harrow AHA, 1980–82; Dir of Public Health, Bloomsbury HA, 1982–91. Dir, SE Inst. of Public Health, UMDS, 1991–99. Chairman: DoH Adv. Gp on Nurse Prescribing, 1988–89; DoH Rev. of Prescribing, 1996–98; Member: Standing Med. Adv. Cttee, DoH, 1984–88 and 1995–98; Clinical Standards Adv. Gp, DoH, 1995–99. Advr to WHO, 1984–; Consultant on Health Sector Mgt Develt to Czech Republic and Slovakia, 1992–93; Advr to NZ Govt and Health Bds on Health Care Reforms, 1992; Chm., UK Inquiry into Mental Health and Well-Being in Later Life, 2005–07. President: Sect. of Epidemiology and Public Health, RSocMed, 1994–96; Medical Action for Global Security (MEDACT), 1993–. Chm., 1998–2002, Vice Pres., 2002–, Age Concern, England; Vice-Pres., Chartered Inst. of Envmtl Health, 2001. Chm., Queen's Nursing Inst., 2002–03 (Mem. Council, 1982–); Member: Bd of Govs, Royal Nat. Orthopaedic Hosp., 1976–82 (Vice-Chm., 1980–82); Inst. of Orthopaedics, Univ. of London, 1978–88 (Chm., 1982–88); Bd of Mgt and Court of Govs, LSHTM, 1983–94; Dep. Chm., Bd of Govs, Univ. of Brighton, 2002– (Mem., 2000–02). Trustee, Help the Aged, 2004–. Chm., Fitzrovia Youth in Action, 2000–. Associate, Newnham Coll., Cambridge, 1992– (Associate Fellow, 1997–99; Chm., Associates, 1998–2000). Hon. Fellow: Soc. of Chiropodists, 1986; Australasian Faculty of Public Health Medicine, 1996; Faculty of Public Health Med., RCPI, 1997; RCPE, 1998; Hon. FDSRCS 2005. *Publications:* Health for All: revised targets, 1993; (with J. Connelly) Homelessness and Ill Health, 1995; Epidemiologically Based Needs Assessment: child and adolescent mental health, 1995. *Recreations:* family, opera, fine art, theatre, travel, jogging. *Address:* 118 Whitfield Street, W1T 5EG. *T:* (020) 7387 6787.

CROWNE, Stephen Thomas; Chief Executive, British Educational Communications and Technology Agency, since 2006; *b* 9 Aug. 1957; *s* of Charles and Beatrice Crowne; *m* 1979, Elizabeth; three *s.* *Educ:* Queens' Coll., Cambridge (BA (Hist.) 1978). Principal Private Sec. to Sec. of State for Educn, 1989–91; Hd, 16–19 Policy, DFEE, 1991–94; Chief Exec., Further Educn Develt Agency, 1994–98; Department for Education and Skills: Hd, Special Educnl Needs Div., 1998–2000; Dep. Dir, then Actg Dir, Standards and Effectiveness Unit, 2001–02; Dir, Sch. Resources, 2002–06. Dir, Partnership for Schs, 2004–06. *Address:* (office) Millburn Hill Road, Science Park, Coventry CV4 7JJ. *T:* (024) 7641 6994; *e-mail:* stephen.crowne@becta.org.uk.

CROWSON, Richard Borman, CMG 1986; HM Diplomatic Service, retired; Chairman, Uweso UK Trust, 1996–2007; *s* of late Clarence Borman Crowson and Cecilia May Crowson; *m* 1st, 1960, Sylvia Cavalier (marr. diss. 1974); one *s* one *d*; 2nd, 1983, Judith Elaine Turner; one step *s.* *Educ:* Downing Coll., Cambridge (MA). FCIS. HMOCS, Uganda, 1955–62; Foreign Office, 1962–63; First Sec. (Commercial), Tokyo, 1963–68; Dep. High Commissioner, Barbados, 1968–70; FCO, 1970–75; Counsellor (Commercial and Aid), Jakarta, 1975–77; Counsellor for Hong Kong Affairs, Washington, 1977–82; Counsellor and Head of Chancery, Berne, 1983–85; High Comr in Mauritius, 1985–89, and Ambassador (non-resident) to Federal Islamic Republic of the Comoros, 1986–89. *Recreations:* music, drama, travel. *Address:* 67 Crofton Road, Orpington, Kent BR6 8HU. *T:* (01689) 891320. *Club:* Royal Commonwealth Society.

CROWTHER, (David) Bruce; Fairtrade Towns Co-ordinator for Fairtrade Foundation, since 2003; *b* 19 Oct. 1959; *s* of late John and Florence Crowther; *m* 1992, (Nancy) Jane Bamber; two *s* one *d.* *Educ:* Queen's Park High Sch., Chester; Liverpool Univ. Vet. Coll. (BVSc 1985). Dep. Vet. Officer, Min. of Agric., Dungannon, NI, 1985; Vet. Surgeon, 1986–2003; Vet. Surgeon (pt-time), 2003–. Started campaigning for Oxfam, 1984; founded Garstang Oxfam Gp, 1992 (Chm., 1992–2002); led campaign to make Garstang the world's first Fairtrade Town, 2000; instigated twinning of Garstang with New Koforidua (a cocoa farming community) in Ghana, 2002. Assoc. Mem., Oxfam, 2001–06. Mem., Calder Bridge Meeting of Religious Soc. of Friends. Hon. Citizen and Sub-Chief (Nana Kwado Osafo I) of New Koforidua, 2004. Beacon Fellow for Creative Giving, 2004. *Recreations:* persuading people to buy, sell or use Fairtrade products, attempting to play the Djembe drum, failing to learn Spanish, watching Manchester United FC live or on TV. *Address:* c/o Fairtrade Foundation, Room 204, 16 Baldwin Gardens, EC1N 7RJ. *T:* (home) (01995) 602637; *e-mail:* bruce@crowther1450.fsnet.co.uk.

CROWTHER, Prof. Derek, PhD; FRCP, FRCR; Professor and Director, Cancer Research Campaign Department of Medical Oncology, Christie Hospital and Manchester University, 1974–97, now Professor Emeritus; *b* 1 July 1937; *s* of Robinson Westgarth

Crowther and Gladys Hannah Crowther; *m* 1959, Margaret Frances Dickinson; two *d* (one *s* decd). *Educ:* City of London Sch.; Clare Coll., Cambridge (Foundn Scholar; MB, BChir, MA 1963); Baylor Univ., Texas (Fulbright Scholar, 1959–60); Royal Postgraduate Medical Sch., London (PhD 1968); Royal Marsden Hosp. MSc Manchester, 1977. FRCP 1976; FRCR 1993. Sen. Registrar and Dep. Dir of Med. Oncology, St Bartholomew's Hosp., 1972–74. CMO, Friends Provident, 1995–2006. Chairman: Leukaemia Res. Fund, Clinical Trials Adv. Panel, 2000–06; London Cancer Res. Mapping Working Gp, 2000–01; Co-Chm., CRUK (formerly CRC) Central Instl Review Bd, 2001–04; Mem., Statutory Gene Therapy Adv. Cttee, 1994–97. Pres., Assoc. of Cancer Physicians, 1999–2007. Mem. Council, Manchester Lit. & Phil. Soc., 2002–. Hon. MRSocMed. Prizes in medicine, paediatrics, and pathology, incl. Gold Medal in Obstetrics and Gynaecology, St Bartholomew's Hosp.; Glyn Evans Gold Medal, RCR, 1980; Award of Distinction, CRC, 1997; Lifetime Achievement in Cancer award, Cancer BACUP, 1999. *Publications:* edited: Manual of Cancer Chemotherapy, 1978 (trans. several langs); Interferons, 1991; more than 300 publications in the field of anti-cancer therapy. *Recreations:* gardening, travel, cosmology, oriental and modern art.

CROWTHER, John Anthony; Chief Executive, 1997–2006, Consultant, 2006–07, Lawn Tennis Association; *b* 16 Oct. 1951; *s* of Charles Alec Crowther and Joan Sylvia (*née* Boddam-Whetham); *m* 1975, Lorraine Ann Chadwick; three *s*. *Educ:* Malvern Coll.; Imperial Coll., London (BSc Eng). ACGI. British Aerospace PLC, 1970–77; Delta Neu Ltd, 1977–78; Panavia Aircraft GmbH, 1978–79; British Aerospace PLC, 1979–90; Vickers Defence Systems: Commercial Dir, 1990–92; Man. Dir, 1992–94; Chief Exec., 1994–96. Confederation of British Industry: Chm., Contracts Panel, 1990–92; Regl Council Mem., Yorks & Humberside, 1994–96. Chm., Leeds Career Guidance, 1995–96. Dir, 2002–03, Chm., Major Spectator Sports Div., 2001–03 (Dep. Chm., 1999–2001), Treas., 2007–, CCPR. Non-executive Director: Sports Leaders UK, 2002–; N Yorks Sport, 2007–; Yorks Culture, 2007–. Mem., Major Match Gp, ECB, 2006–. MInstD 1997. *Recreations:* piano, running, tennis, gardening.

CROWTHER, (Joseph) Stanley; *b* 30 May 1925; *s* of Cyril Joseph Crowther and Florence Mildred (*née* Beckett); *m* 1948, Margaret Royston; two *s*. *Educ:* Rotherham Grammar Sch.; Rotherham Coll. of Technology. Royal Signals, 1943–47. Journalist: Rotherham Advertiser, 1941–43 and 1947–50; Yorkshire Evening Post, 1950–51; freelance, 1951–. Mem., Rotherham Borough Council, 1958–59, 1961–76; Mayor of Rotherham, 1971–72, 1975–76; Chm., Yorkshire and Humberside Develt Assoc., 1972–76. MP (Lab) Rotherham, June 1976–1992. Vice-Pres., Town and Country Planning Assoc., 1990–2000. *Publication:* One Thing After Another (memoirs), 2005. *Recreations:* walking, singing, listening to jazz.

CROWTHER, Dr Richard Anthony, FRS 1993; Member of Scientific Staff, 1969–2007, Visiting Scientist, since 2007, Medical Research Council Laboratory of Molecular Biology, Cambridge; Fellow of Peterhouse, Cambridge, since 1981; *b* 26 July 1942; *s* of Albert Crowther and Joyce Edith Crowther (*née* Anthony); *m* 1964, Susan Elizabeth Hope; two *s*. *Educ:* Manchester Grammar Sch.; Jesus Coll., Cambridge (BA); PhD Cantab. Res. Fellow, Edinburgh Univ., 1968. FMedSci 2007. *Publications:* research papers and reviews in sci. jls. *Recreations:* walking, bird watching. *Address:* MRC Laboratory of Molecular Biology, Hills Road, Cambridge CB2 0QH. *T:* (01223) 402410.

CROWTHER, Stanley; *see* Crowther, J. S.

CROWTHER, Thomas Rowland; QC 1981; **His Honour Judge Crowther;** a Circuit Judge since 1985; a Senior Circuit Judge, since 2001; *b* 11 Sept. 1937; *s* of late Kenneth Vincent Crowther, MB, BCh, and Winifred Anita Crowther, MPS; *m* 1969, Gillian Jane (*née* Prince); one *s* one *d*. *Educ:* Newport High Sch.: Keble Coll., Oxford (MA). President, Oxford Univ. Liberal Club, 1957; Editor, Oxford Guardian, 1957. Called to the Bar, Inner Temple, 1961, Bencher, 2005; Junior and Wine Steward, Wales and Chester Circuit, 1974. A Recorder, 1980–85. Hon. Recorder, Bristol, 2001. Contested (L) General Elections: Oswestry, 1964 and 1966; Hereford, 1970. Founder Mem., Gwent Area Broadcasting, 1981. *Recreations:* garden, trout fishing. *Address:* Lansor, Llandegfedd, Caerleon NP18 1LS. *T:* (01633) 450224.

CROWTHER, William Ronald Hilton; QC 1980; a Recorder, 1984–96; *b* 7 May 1941; *s* of Ronald Crowther and Ann Bourne Crowther; *m* 1964, Valerie Meredith (*née* Richards); one *s*. *Educ:* Oundle Sch.; Univ. of Oxford (BA Jurisprudence). Called to the Bar, Inner Temple, 1963, Bencher, 1985–96. *Recreations:* bird-watching and all aspects of natural history.

CROXALL, Prof. John Patrick, CBE 2004; PhD; FRS 2005; Chair, BirdLife International Global Seabird Programme, since 2006; *b* 19 Jan. 1946; *s* of Harold Eli Croxall and Marjorie (*née* Jones); partner, Alison Jane Stattersfield. *Educ:* King Edward's Sch., Birmingham; Queen's Coll., Oxford (Open Schol.; BA 1st Cl. Hons Zool. 1968; MA 1987); Univ. of Auckland, NZ (Commonwealth Schol.; PhD 1971). Dir, Oiled Seabird Res. Unit and Sen. Res. Associate in Zool., Univ. of Newcastle upon Tyne, 1972–75; British Antarctic Survey: Hd, Birds and Mammals Section, 1976–85; SPSO, 1985; Hd, Higher Predator Section, 1986–2001; DCSO, 1992; Hd of Conservation Biology, 2001–06. Hon. Professor: Univ. of Birmingham, 1998–; Univ. of Durham, 1998–. Mem., Royal Soc. Interdisciplinary Cttee on Antarctic Res., 1997–2001 and 2005–. Scientific Committee for Antarctic Research: Member, Group of Specialists: on Seals, 1984–90; on Southern Ocean Ecol., 1986–96; Mem., Wkg Gp on Biol., 1986–2000; Mem., 1978–, Sec., 1980–85, Chm., 1986–94, Bird Biol Sub Cttee. Chm., Seabird Gp, 1984–87; Mem., 1990–, Mem. Perm. Exec., 1998–, Internat. Ornithol Cttee; British Ornithologists' Union: Mem. Council, 1974–78; Vice-Pres., 1987–91; Pres., 1995–99; Royal Society for the Protection of Birds: Mem. Council, 1989–2003 (Chm., 1998–2003); Chm., Conservation Cttee, 1993–98; Falklands Conservation: Trustee, 1987–; Chm., 1993–98. Scientific Medal, 1984, Marsh Award for Conservation, 2002, Zool Soc. of London; Polar Medal, 1992, clasp, 2004; President's Medal, British Ecol Soc., 1995; Robert Cushman and Murphy Prize and Medal, Internat. Waterbird Soc., 1997; Godman-Salvin Medal, BOU, 2004; Lifetime Achievement Award, Pacific Seabird Gp, 2008. *Publications:* (ed jtly) Status and Conservation of the World's Seabirds, 1984; (ed) Seabirds: feeding ecology and role in marine ecosystems, 1987; (ed with R. L. Gentry) Status, Biology and Ecology of Fur Seals, 1987; Seabird Status and Conservation: a supplement, 1991; contrib. numerous scientific papers and reports. *Recreations:* birdwatching, conservation, pteridology, French wines and countryside. *Address:* BirdLife International, Wellbrook Court, Girton Road, Cambridge CB3 0NA. *T:* (01223) 277318, *Fax:* (01223) 277200; *e-mail:* john.croxall@birdlife.org.

CROXFORD, Ian Lionel; QC 1993; *b* 23 July 1953; *s* of Peter Patrick Croxford, BEM, and Mary Helen Croxford (*née* Richardson); *m* 1976, Sandra McCord; one *s* one *d*. *Educ:* Westcliff High Sch. for Boys; Univ. of Leicester (LLB 1st Cl. Hons). Called to the Bar, Gray's Inn, 1976 (Bacon Schol.), Bencher, 2001; Lincoln's Inn, *ad eundem*, 1977. Gov., Westcliff High Sch. for Boys, 1990– (Chm. Govs, 1995–). *Recreation:* watching sport. *Address:* Wilberforce Chambers, 8 New Square, Lincoln's Inn, WC2A 3QP. *T:* (020) 7306 0102.

CROXON, Raymond Patrick Austen; QC 1983; *b* 31 July 1928; *s* of late Randolph Croxon, bandmaster, Salvation Army, and Rose Harvey, Home League Sec., Salvation Army; *m* 1952, Monica Howard (marr. diss. 1992); two *s* two *d*; *m* 2001, Hara Marinou. *Educ:* Strand College; King's College London. LLB. Served in RAMC, 1946–49. Called to the Bar, Gray's Inn, 1960; Hd of Regency Chambers, 1995–2003. *Recreations:* travel, walking, swimming, reading, music, theatre, modern Greek language. *Club:* Savage.

CROYDON, Area Bishop of, since 2003; **Rt Rev. Nicholas Baines;** *b* 13 Nov. 1957; *s* of Frank Baines and Beryl Amy Baines; *m* 1980, Linda Margaret Higgins; two *s* one *d*. *Educ:* Holt Comprehensive Sch., Liverpool; Univ. of Bradford (BA (Hons) Mod. Langs); Trinity Coll., Bristol (BA (Hons) Theol Studies). Linguist specialist, GCHQ, Cheltenham, 1980–84; ordained deacon, 1987, priest, 1988; Asst Curate, St Thomas, Kendal, 1987–91; Asst Priest, Holy Trinity with St John, Leicester, 1991–92; Vicar, St Mary and St John, Rothley, Leicester, 1992–2000; Archdeacon of Lambeth, 2000–03. English Co-Chair, Meissen Commn. Mem., Gen. Synod of C of E, 1995–2005. Regular broadcaster, BBC Radio. *Publications:* Hungry for Hope, 1991; Speedbumps and Potholes, 2003; Jesus and People Like Us, 2004; Marking Time: 47 reflections on Mark's Gospel for Lent, Holy Week and Easter, 2005; Hungry for Hope?, 2007; Finding Faith, 2008. *Recreations:* music, reading, sport, travelling. *Address:* St Matthew's House, 100 George Street, Croydon, Surrey CR0 1PJ. *T:* (office) (020) 8256 9630, *Fax:* (020) 8256 9631, *T:* (home) (020) 8686 1822, *Fax:* (020) 8649 7658; *e-mail:* bishop.nick@southwark.anglican.org.

CROYDON, Archdeacon of; *see* Davies, Ven. V. A.

CROYDON, Rear-Adm. John Edward Kenneth; JP; DL; CEng, FIET; *b* 25 Feb. 1929; *s* of late Kenneth P. Croydon and Elizabeth V. Croydon; *m* 1953, Brenda Joyce Buss, MA; one *s* two *d*. *Educ:* King Edward's Sch., Birmingham; Selwyn Coll., Cambridge (MA). BA London; CEng, FIET (FIEE 1975); jssc 1969. RN Special Entry Cadet (L) 1947; HMS Verulam and HMS Undine, 1954–55; Royal Naval Coll., Dartmouth 1959–61; HMS Devonshire, 1961–64; HMS London, 1970–72; MoD, 1972–74; Captain Weapon Trials, 1974–77; Dir, Underwater Weapon Projects (Naval), 1978–80; Dir Gen Weapons (Naval), 1981–83; Dep. Controller, Warships Equipment, MoD (Navy) 1983–84, retd. Rear Cdre (Dinghies), Royal Naval Sailing Assoc., 1980. Gov., Milton Abbey Sch., 1985–2002. Chm. Bd of Visitors, HMP Weare, 1997–2000. County Com. for Scouts, Dorset, 1986–93. JP Weymouth, 1985; DL Dorset, 1993. *Recreations:* sailing music, restacking the dishwasher. *Address:* Hillside, Plaisters Lane, Sutton Poyntz Weymouth, Dorset DT3 6LQ. *Clubs:* Royal Naval Sailing Association; Weymouth Sailing.

CROZIER, Adam Alexander; Chief Executive, Royal Mail Group plc, since 2003; *b* 26 Jan. 1964; *s* of Robert and Elinor Crozier; *m* 1994, Annette Edwards; two *d*. *Educ:* Heriot-Watt Univ. (BA Business Orgn). Pedigree Petfoods, Mars (UK) Ltd, 1984–86; Daily Telegraph, 1986–88; Saatchi & Saatchi, 1988–99: Dir, 1990; Media Dir, 1992; Vice Chm. 1994; Chief Exec., 1995; Chief Exec., FA, 2000–02. *Recreations:* football, golf, my children. *Address:* Royal Mail Group plc, 148 Old Street, EC1V 9HQ.

CROZIER, Brian Rossiter; writer and consultant on international affairs; Distinguishe Visiting Fellow, Hoover Institution on War, Revolution and Peace, Stanford University California, 1996–2002; contributor, National Review, New York, since 1982; *b* 4 Aug 1918; *s* of R. H. Crozier and Elsa (*née* McGillivray); *m* 1st, 1940, Mary Lillian Samuel (1993); one *s* three *d*; 2nd, 1999, Jacqueline Marie Mitchell. *Educ:* Lycée, Montpellie Peterborough Coll., Harrow; Trinity Coll. of Music, London. Music and art critic London, 1936–39; reporter-sub-editor, Stoke-on-Trent, Stockport, London, 1940–4 aeronautical inspection, 1941–43; sub-editor: Reuters, 1943–44; News Chronicl 1944–48; and writer, Sydney Morning Herald, 1948–51; corresp., Reuters-AAI 1951–52; features editor, Straits Times, 1952–53; leader writer, corresp. and edito Foreign Report, Economist, 1954–64; commentator, BBC English, French and Spanis overseas services, 1954–66; Chm., Forum World Features, 1965–74; Columnist: Na Review, NY, 1978–95; Now!, 1979–81; The Times, 1982–83; Freedom Today (former The Free Nation), 1982–89. Co-founder, Inst. for the Study of Conflict, 1970 (Di 1970–79). Adjunct Scholar, Heritage Foundn, Washington, 1984–95. *Publications:* Th Rebels, 1960; The Morning After, 1963; Neo-Colonialism, 1964; South-East Asia i Turmoil, 1965 (3rd edn 1968); The Struggle for the Third World, 1966; Franco, 1967 The Masters of Power, 1969; The Future of Communist Power (in USA: Since Stalin 1970; De Gaulle, vol. 1 1973, vol. 2 1974; A Theory of Conflict, 1974; The Man Wh Lost China (Chiang Kai-shek), 1976; Strategy of Survival, 1978; The Minimum State 1979; Franco: crepúsculo de un hombre (Spanish orig.), 1980; The Price of Peace, 198 new edn 1983; (jtly) Socialism Explained, 1984; (jtly) This War Called Peace, 1984; (John Rossiter) The Andropov Deception (novel), 1984 (pubd under own name, NY 1986); Socialism: dream and reality, 1987; (ed) The Grenada Documents, 1987; Th Gorbachev Phenomenon, 1990; Communism: why prolong its death-throes?, 1990; Fre Agent, 1993; The KGB Lawsuits, 1995; (jtly) Le Phénix rouge, 1995; The Rise and Fa of the Soviet Empire, 1999; The Other Brian Croziers, 2003; Political Victory: the elusiv prize of military wars, 2005; contrib. to jls in various countries. *Recreations:* piano, film *Address:* 18 Wickliffe Avenue, N3 3EJ. *T:* (020) 8346 8124. *Club:* Royal Automobile.

CRUDDAS, Jon, PhD; MP (Lab) Dagenham, since 2001; *b* 7 April 1962; *s* of John an Pat Cruddas; *m* 1993, Anna Mary Healy; one *s*. *Educ:* Oaklands RC Comprehensive Sch Waterlooville; Warwick Univ. (BSc, MA; PhD 1991). Labour Party: Policy Office 1989–94; Chief Asst to Gen. Sec., 1994–97; Dep. Political Sec., Prime Minister's Offic 1997–2001. Mem., White Hart Angling Soc., 2000–. Mem., Dagenham Royal Nav Assoc., 2000–. *Recreations:* golf, angling. *Address:* House of Commons, SW1A 0AA. *Clu* Dagenham Working Mens'.

CRUICKSHANK, Alistair Ronald; Trustee, since 2001, and Chair, since 200 EcoLocal (formerly Centre for Environmental Initiatives); *b* 2 Oct. 1944; *s* of late Franc John Cruickshank and Kate Cameron Cruickshank (*née* Brittain); *m* 1967, Sandra Ma Noble; three *d*. *Educ:* Aberdeen Grammar School; Aberdeen University (MA). Joine MAFF as Assistant Principal, 1966; Principal, 1970; Asst Secretary, 1978; Under Se (Animal Health), 1986; Principal Finance Officer, 1989–94; Under Sec. (Agricl Inputs 1995–96. Chairman: Surrey Organic Gardening Gp, 1997–; Sutton Future Networ subseq. Sutton Envmt Network, 2000–; Carshalton Lavender, 2004–; Dir, EcoLoc Services Ltd, 2003–; Mem., Standards Bd, Soil Assoc., 2008–. Vice Pres., London, CPR 2004–06. *Recreations:* gardening, looking at old buildings, various church activities. *Clu* Royal Over-Seas League.

CRUICKSHANK, David Charles, CA, CPFA; independent management consultant; Christchurch, NZ, 22 April 1954; *s* of Clarence Albert Shepperd and Eunice Carolir Cruickshank (formerly Shepperd, *née* Wilson); *m* 1974, Linda Friel; one *d*. *Educ:* Quee Charlotte Coll., Picton, NZ; Victoria Univ. of Wellington (BCA 1979). Audit Dir, Auc

NZ, 1977–98; Chief Financial Officer, Wellington CC, 1998–2002; Dir of Finance, Islington LBC, 2002–05. Mem., Inst. of Chartered Accountants of NZ, 1980– (Chm., Public Sector Cttee, 1997–2002); CPFA 2003. *Publications:* contrib. auditing and accounting articles to Accountants Jl. *Recreations:* cycling, family, golf, mountain biking. *Clubs:* Wellington; Manor Park Golf.

CRUICKSHANK, Sir Donald Gordon, (Sir Don), Kt 2006; Director, Qualcomm Inc., since 2005; *b* 17 Sept. 1942; *s* of Donald Campbell Cruickshank and Margaret Buchan Cruickshank (*née* Morrison); *m* 1964, Elizabeth Buchan Taylor; one *s* one *d*. *Educ:* Univ. of Aberdeen (MA); Inst. of Chartered Accountants of Scotland (CA); Manchester Business School (MBA). McKinsey & Co., 1972–77; Times Newspapers, 1977–80; Pearson, 1980–84; Man. Dir, Virgin Group, 1984–89; Chief Exec., NHS in Scotland, 1989–93; Dir Gen., Oftel, 1993–98; Chairman: Scottish Media Gp, subseq. SMG plc, 1999–2004; London Stock Exchange, 2000–03; Formscape Gp Ltd, 2003–06; Taylor & Francis plc, 2004–05; Clinovia Gp Ltd, 2004–06. Non-exec. Dir, Christian Salvesen, 1994–95. Chairman: Wandsworth HA, 1986–89; Action 2000, 1997–2000; UK Banking Review, 1998–2000. Mem. Court, Univ. of Aberdeen, 2005–. Hon. LLD Aberdeen, 2001. *Recreations:* education, sport, golf, opera.

CRUICKSHANK, Prof. Garth Stuart, PhD; FRCS, FRCSE; Professor of Neurosurgery, University of Birmingham and Queen Elizabeth Hospital, since 1997; *b* 24 Jan. 1951; *s* of Lt Col Alfred, (Jimmy), Cruickshank and Peggy Lillian Cruickshank (*née* Rushton); *m* 1979, Ros Fitzgerald; two *s* two *d*. *Educ:* Wellington Coll., Berks; Univ. of London (BSc Hons 1974); Royal Free Hosp. (PhD 1979; MB BS 1984). FRCS 1989; FRCSE 1989; FRCS (Surgical Neurol.) 1993. Institute of Neurological Sciences, Glasgow: Registrar, 1989–93; Sen. Lectr in Neurosurgery, 1993–97. Member: NCRI Brain Tumour Gp, 1998–; DVLA Adv. Panel, 2001–. *Publications:* publications in the area of brain tumour res., gene therapy and imaging. *Recreation:* sailing. *Address:* Queen Elizabeth Hospital, Edgbaston, Birmingham B15 2TH. *T:* (0121) 697 8225, *Fax:* (0121) 697 8248; *e-mail:* g.s.cruickshank@bham.ac.uk.

CRUICKSHANK, Flight-Lieut John Alexander, VC 1944; ED 1947; late RAF; with Grindlay's Bank Ltd, London, 1952–76; retired; Administrator, Northern Division, North West Securities Ltd, 1977–85; *b* 20 May 1920; *s* of James C. Cruickshank, Aberdeen, and Alice Bow, Macduff, Banffshire; *m* 1955, Marion R. Beverley (*d* 1985), Toronto, Canada. *Educ:* Aberdeen Grammar Sch.; Daniel Stewart's Coll., Edinburgh. Entered Commercial Bank of Scotland, 1938; returned to banking, 1946. Mem. of Territorial Army and called for service, Aug. 1939, in RA; transferred to RAF 1941 and commissioned in 1942; all RAF service was with Coastal Command. ADC to Lord High Commissioner to the Gen. Assembly of the Church of Scotland, 1946–48. *Clubs:* Naval and Military; Royal Northern and University (Aberdeen); Royal Scots (Edinburgh); Merchants of Edinburgh Golf.

CRUICKSHANK, Sheena Carlin; JP; Lord-Lieutenant of Clackmannanshire, since 2001; *b* 26 March 1936; *d* of David Irons Brown and Janet Cameron Carlin Brown; *m* 1957, Alistair Booth Cruickshank; two *s* one *d*. *Educ:* High Sch. of Stirling. Hon. Sheriff, Alloa Sheriff Court, 1996. JP Clackmannan, 1989. *Recreations:* quilting, travel. *Address:* c/o Lieutenancy Office, Caesar and Howie, Solicitors, 27 Mar Street, Alloa, Clackmannanshire FK10 1HX.

CRUISE MAPOTHER, Thomas, IV, (Tom Cruise); actor and producer; *b* 3 July 1962; *s* of late Thomas Cruise Mapother, III and of Mary Lee Cruise Mapother (*née* Pfeiffer); *m* 1st, 1987, Mimi Rogers (marr. diss. 1990); 2nd, 1990, Nicole Mary Kidman, *qv* (marr. diss. 2001); one adopted *s* one adopted *d*; 3rd, 2006, Katie Holmes; one *d*. *Educ:* Glen Ridge High Sch., NJ. *Films:* actor: Endless Love, Taps, 1981; Losin' It, The Outsiders, Risky Business, All the Right Moves, 1983; Legend, 1985; Top Gun, The Color of Money, 1986; Rain Man, 1988; Cocktail, Born on the Fourth of July, 1989; Days of Thunder, 1990; Far and Away, A Few Good Men, 1992; The Firm, 1993; Interview with the Vampire, 1994; Jerry Maguire, 1996; Eyes Wide Shut, 1999; Magnolia, 2000; Vanilla Sky, Minority Report, 2002; Collateral, 2004; War of the Worlds, 2005; actor and producer: Mission Impossible, 1996; Mission Impossible 2, 2000; The Last Samurai, 2003; Mission Impossible 3, 2006; Lions for Lambs, 2007; producer: Without Limits, 1998; The Others, 2001; co-producer: Ask the Dust, 2006. *Address:* c/o CAA, 2000 Avenue of the Stars, Los Angeles, CA 90067, USA.

CRUM, Douglas Vernon E.; *see* Erskine Crum.

CRUMP, Bernard John, FRCP, FFPH; Chief Executive Officer, NHS Institute for Innovation and Improvement, since 2005; *b* 10 Nov. 1956; *s* of Vincent and Bridget Crump; *m* 1990, Izabela Kuncewicz; one *s* one *d*. *Educ:* Burton Grammar Sch.; Univ. of Birmingham (MB ChB). FFPH 1999; FRCP 2005. Engaged in clin. medicine, res. and public health trng, W Midlands and London, 1980–91; Director of Public Health: South Birmingham HA, 1991–95; Leicestershire HA, 1995–2002; CEO, Shropshire and Staffs Strategic HA, 2002–05. Vis. Prof., Public Health and Epidemiology, Univ. of Leicester, 2000–. MInstD. *Publications:* (with M. Drummond) Evaluating Clinical Evidence: a handbook for managers, 1993; articles in health and social care jls. *Recreations:* ski-ing, golf. *Address:* NHS Institute for Innovation and Improvement, University of Warwick Campus, Coventry CV4 7AL. *T:* (024) 7647 5852; *e-mail:* bernard.crump@institute.nhs.uk. *Club:* Leicestershire Golf (Leicester).

CRUMP, Douglas Woodward; Regional Employment Judge (formerly Regional Chairman, Employment Tribunals), Birmingham, since 2007; *b* W Bromwich, 26 May 1944; *s* of W. R. A. Crump and E. M. Crump; *m* 1971, Jennifer Ann Snape; two *d*. Solicitor in private practice, 1968–93; Chm., Employment Tribunals, 1993–2007. *Recreations:* music, fly fishing. *Address:* Employment Tribunals, Phoenix House, 1–3 Newhall Street, Birmingham B3 3NH. *T:* (0121) 236 6051.

CRUMPLER, Peter George; Director of Communications, Archbishops' Council of Church of England, since 2004; *b* 27 Aug. 1956; *m* 1977, Linda Charmaine Smith; one *s* two *d*. *Educ:* Chiswick Sch.; Harlow Coll., Essex (CAM Foundn Dip. in PR 1983). Journalist, Acton Gazette Series, 1975–77; Press Officer, London Bor. of Hillingdon, 1977–79; Press Officer, London Bor. of Hounslow, 1979–81; communications posts with N Thames Gas, 1981–89; PR Manager, British Gas Eastern, 1989–91; Internat. Public Affairs Manager, British Gas, 1991–97; Head: Ext. Affairs, Internat., BG plc, 1997–2000; Communications, BG Gp plc, 2000–01; Communications Officer, Dio. of St Albans, 2001–04. Lay Reader, Dio. of St Albans, 2008–. MIPR 1984, FCIPR (FIPR 2002). *Publications:* Making Friends with the Media, 1989; Keep in Touch!, 1993. *Recreations:* family, films, studying, Brentford FC. *Address:* Church House, Great Smith Street, SW1P 3NZ. *T:* (020) 7898 1462, *Fax:* (020) 7222 6672; *e-mail:* peter.crumpler@c-of-e.org.uk.

CRUMPTON, Michael Joseph, CBE 1992; PhD; FRS 1979; Director of Research (Laboratories), Imperial Cancer Research Fund Laboratories, London, 1991–93, retired (Deputy Director of Research, 1979–91); *b* 7 June 1929; *s* of Charles E. and Edith Crumpton; *m* 1960, Janet Elizabeth Dean; one *s* two *d*. *Educ:* Poole Grammar Sch., Poole; University Coll., Southampton; Lister Inst. of Preventive Medicine, London. BSc, PhD, London. National Service, RAMC, 1953–55. Member, scientific staff, Microbiological Research Estabt, Porton, Wilts, 1955–60; Visiting Scientist Fellowship, Nat. Insts of Health, Bethesda, Maryland, USA, 1959–60; Research Fellow, Dept of Immunology, St Mary's Hosp. Med. Sch., London, 1960–66; Mem., scientific staff, Nat. Inst. for Med. Research, Mill Hill, 1966–79, Head of Biochemistry Div., 1976–79. Visiting Fellow, John Curtin Sch. of Med. Research, ANU, Canberra, 1973–74. Non-exec. Dir, Imperial Cancer Research Technology Ltd, 1989–99 (Chief Operating Officer, 1993–94). Member: WHO Steering Cttee for Encapsulated Bacteria, 1984–91 (Chm., 1988–91); Cell Board, MRC, 1979–83; Scientific Adv. Cttee, Lister Inst., 1986–91; Sloan Cttee, General Motors Res. Foundn, 1986–88 (Chm., 1988); MRC AIDS Directed Prog. Steering Cttee, 1987–91; Scientific Cttee, Swiss Inst. for Experimental Cancer Res., 1989–96; DTI/SERC Biotech. Jt Adv. Bd, 1989–93. Member Council: Royal Instn, 1986–90 (Mem., Davy Faraday Lab. Cttee, 1985–90, Chm. of Cttee, 1988–90); MRC, 1986–90; Royal Soc., 1990–92; Mem. Sci. Council, Celltech Ltd, 1980–90; Chairman: Sci. Adv. Bd, Biomed. Res. Centre, Univ. of British Columbia, Vancouver, 1987–91; DoH/HSE Adv. Cttee on Dangerous Pathogens, 1991–98; Mem. Sci. Adv. Bd, Ciba Foundn, 1990–94. Chm., InferMed Ltd, 1998–2000; non-executive Director: Amersham Internat., 1990–97; Amersham Pharmacia Biotech Ltd, 1997–2001; Amersham Pharmacia Biotech Inc., 2001–02. Mem. Council, Inst. of Cancer Res., 1994–2001; Member, Governing Body: Imperial Coll. of Sci., Technol. and Medicine, 1994–98; BPMF, 1987–95; Gov., Strangeways Res. Lab., 1993–2000. Mem., EMBO, 1982; MAE, 1996; Hon. Mem., Amer. Assoc. of Immunologists, 1995. Trustee: EMF Biol Res. Trust, 1995–2007 (Chm., Sci. Adv. Cttee, 1995–2005); Breakthrough Breast Cancer, 1997–2004. Fellow, Inst. of Cancer Res., 2001. Bernal Lectr, Royal Soc., 2004. Founder FMedSci 1998. Hon. FRCPath 2000. Mem. Editorial Board: Biochemical Jl, 1966–73 (Dep. Chm., 1969–72); Eur. Jl of Immunology, 1972–86; Immunochemistry, 1975–79; Immunogenetics, 1979–85; Biochemistry Internat., 1980–86; Molecular Biol. and Medicine, 1983–86; Human Immunology, 1985–96; Regional Editor, Molecular Immunology, 1982–86. Biochem. Soc. Vis. Lectr, Australia, 1983. Sen. Treas., Royal Soc. Club, 1988–89. *Publications:* contribs to learned scientific jls. *Recreations:* gardening, reading. *Address:* 33 Homefield Road, Radlett, Herts WD7 8PX. *T:* (01923) 854675.

CRUSH, His Honour Harvey Michael; a Circuit Judge, 1995–2001; *b* 12 April 1939; *s* of late George Stanley Crush, Chislehurst, and Alison Isabel Crush; *m* 1st, 1965, Diana Bassett (marr. diss. 1982); one *s* one *d*; 2nd, 1982, Maggie, *d* of Nicholas Dixson. *Educ:* Chigwell Sch. Admitted solicitor, 1963; Partner, Norton Rose, 1968–91; Asst Recorder, 1987–92; Recorder, 1992–95; Higher Courts Advocate, 1994; Dep. Circuit Judge, 2001–04; called to the Bar, 2001. Dir, TOSG Trust Fund Ltd, 1970–95. Mem., Supreme Court Rule Cttee, 1984–88. Mem., Law Soc., 1963–; Vice-Pres., City of London Law Soc., 1989–91. Hon. Solicitor, British Assoc. Aviation Consultants, 1990–95 (Mem. Council, 1991–95, 2001–; Chm., 2002–04). FRAeS 2004 (MRAeS 1980). Hon. Life Member: Solicitors' Assoc. of Higher Ct Advocates (formerly Solicitors' Higher Courts Advocacy Assoc.); London Solicitors' Litigation Assoc. Liveryman: Co. of Solicitors, 1982 (Mem. Court, 1987–; Master, 1994–95); Co. of Farriers, 1984 (Mem. Court, 1997–2003); GAPAN, 2000 (Freeman, 1991). Hon. Life Mem., Sevenoaks & Dist Motor Club (Chm., 1968–71). *Recreations:* flying light aircraft, travel, Spain, walking. *Address:* Quadrant Chambers, 10 Fleet Street, EC4Y 1AU.

CRUTCHLOW, John Adrian; Director of Finance, Metropolitan Police, 1986–96, retired; *b* 30 March 1946; *s* of James William Crutchlow and Elsie Nellie Crutchlow (*née* King); *m* 1971, Valerie Elizabeth Farage. *Educ:* Finchley County Grammar Sch.; HNC (with dist.) in Business Studies; BA Open; postgraduate Dip. Management Studies. Paymaster General's Office, 1962–65; Metropolitan Police Civil Staff, 1965–96; Principal, 1974–81; Dep. Dir of Finance, 1981–84; Dep. Estabt Officer, 1984–86; Asst Sec., 1986–92; Asst Under-Sec. of State, 1992–96; Dep. to Receiver, Metropolitan Police Dist, 1994–96. President: New Scotland Yard Civil Staff Assoc., 1994–96; Metropolitan Police Former (formerly Metropolitan Police Retired) Civil Staff Assoc., 1996–. FCMI (FBIM 1992); FInstAM 1995. *Recreations:* reading, gardening, golf, renovating old houses. *Address:* Friars' Grange, Rushden, Herts SG9 0TF.

CRUTE, Prof. Ian Richard, PhD; Director, Rothamsted Research (formerly Institute of Arable Crops Research), since 1999; *b* 3 June 1949; *s* of Walter and Rose Crute; *m* 1973, J. Elizabeth Harden; two *d*. *Educ:* Univ. of Newcastle upon Tyne (BSc Hons Botany 1970; PhD 1973). Research Leader, Nat. Vegetable Res. Station, Wellesbourne, Warwick, 1973–86; Horticulture Research International: Head, Crop and Envmt Protection Dept, E Malling, Kent, 1987–93; Head, Plant Pathology Dept, 1993–95, Dir, 1995–99, Wellesbourne. Fulbright Fellow, Univ. of Wisconsin, 1986; Vis. Prof. in Plant Pathol., Faculty of Biol Scis, Univ. of Oxford, 1997–. *Publications:* numerous papers on plant pathol. and genetics in scientific jls. *Recreations:* gardening, golf, walking, theatre. *Address:* Rothamsted Research, Harpenden, Herts AL5 2JQ. *T:* (01582) 763133.

CRUTHERS, Sir James (Winter), Kt 1980; AO 2008; company director; Vice-Chairman and Executive Vice-President, News America Publishing Inc., 1984–90 (Director, since 1983); Vice-Chairman, News America Holdings Inc., 1984–90 (Director, since 1984); *b* 20 Dec. 1924; *s* of James William and Kate Cruthers; *m* 1950, Alwyn Sheila Della; one *s* one *d*. *Educ:* Claremont Central State Sch.; Perth Technical College. Started as junior in Perth Daily News, 1939; war service, AIF and RAAF (Pilot), 1942; Journalist, Perth Daily News, 1946; Editor, Weekly Publications, West Australian Newspapers Ltd, 1953; TVW Enterprises Ltd: General Manager, 1958; Managing Director, 1969; Dep. Chm., 1974; Chm., 1976–81; Chm., Australian Film Commn, 1982–83. Director: News Corp. Ltd, 1981–92; Satellite Television plc, 1984–90 (Chm., 1985–88). Western Australian Citizen Of The Year, Industry and Commerce, 1980. *Recreations:* golf, jogging. *Address:* 122/7 Dean Street, Claremont, WA 6010, Australia. *Clubs:* Weld, Lake Karrinyup Country (Perth).

CRUTTWELL, Geraldine, (Mrs Hugh Cruttwell); *see* McEwan, G.

CRUTZEN, Prof. Dr Paul; Director, Atmospheric Chemistry Division, Max-Planck Institute for Chemistry, Germany, 1980–2000; *b* Amsterdam, 3 Dec. 1933; *m* 1958, Terttu Crutzen (*née* Soininen); two *d*. *Educ:* Stockholm Univ. (PhD 1968; DSc 1973). Member: Royal Swedish Acad. of Scis; Royal Swedish Acad. of Engrg Scis; Academia Europaea. Foreign Mem., Royal Soc., 2006. (Jtly) Nobel Prize for Chemistry, 1995. *Address:* c/o Max-Planck Institute for Chemistry, PO Box 3060, 55020 Mainz, Germany.

CRWYS-WILLIAMS, Air Vice-Marshal David Owen, CB 1990; Managing Director, Services Sound and Vision Corporation (SSVC), 1994–2005 (Deputy Managing Director, 1993–94); *b* 24 Dec. 1940; *s* of Gareth Crwys-Williams and Frances Ellen Crwys-Williams (*née* Strange); *m* 1st, 1964, Jennifer Jean (*née* Pearce) (marr. diss. 1971); one *s* one *d*; 2nd, 1973, Irene Thompson (Suzie) (*née* Whan); one *s* two *d*. *Educ:* Oakham Sch.; RAF Coll., Cranwell. Commnd as pilot, RAF, 1961; served No 30 Sqn, Kenya, 1962–64, No 47 Sqn, Abingdon, 1964–66; ADC to C-in-C RAF Trng Comd, 1966–68; OC 46 Sqn, 1969; RAF Masirah, 1972; Army Staff Coll., 1973; Personal Staff Officer to C-in-C NEAF,

1974–75; OC No 230 Sqn, 1976–77; Air Sec. Dept, MoD, 1977–78; Dep. Dir Air Plans, MoD, 1979–82; OC RAF Shawbury, 1983–84; RCDS 1985; Dir of Air Support and Dir of Air Staff Duties, MoD, 1986–88; Comdr, British Forces Falkland Is, 1988–89; Dir Gen., RAF Personal Services, MoD, 1989–92. Gp Captain 1979; Air Cdre 1985; Air Vice-Marshal 1988. Executive Chairman: SSVC Services Ltd, 1994–99; Columbia Communications Europe, 1994–98; VISUA Ltd, 1996–99; Man. Dir, Teleport London Internat., 1994–98; Director: Forces Events Ltd, 1999–; Amersham Business Centre, 2001–. Council Mem., Cinema and Television Benevolent Fund, 1994–2005. Chm., New Island South Conservation Trust, 1995–. Trustee: British Forces Foundn, 1999–; RAF Mus., 2002–; Hearing Dogs for Deaf People, 2006–. Gov., Amersham and Wycombe Coll., 1997– (Vice-Chm., 1998–2000; Chm., 2000–03). Freeman, City of London, 2002; Liveryman, GAPAN, 2003–. MInstD; FICPD (FIPM 1991); FCMI (FIMgt 1993). *Recreations:* furniture restoration, walking, building, fishing. *Address:* c/o Barclays Bank, PO Box 354, Abingdon, Oxon OX14 1FL. *Club:* Royal Air Force.

CRYAN, Donald Michael; His Honour Judge Cryan; a Circuit Judge, since 1996; *b* 18 Jan. 1948; *s* of late Thomas Joseph Cryan and Helen McBeath Cryan (*née* Munro); *m* 1973, Pamela; two *s*. *Educ:* Salvatorian Coll.; UCL (LLB (Hons)). Called to the Bar, Inner Temple, 1970 (Bencher, 1992; Master of the House, 1993–98; Master of Marshals, 2002–); a Recorder, 1993–96; SE Circuit. Designated Family Judge, Medway, 2001–04, Kent, 2004–08. Chm., Working Party on Delay in Family Proceedings Courts, LCD, 2002; Member: Lord Chancellor's Children Act Judicial Case Mgt Adv. Cttee, 2002–04; Unified Admin Judicial Cttee, 2003–05; various cttees/sub-cttees, Judicial Studies Bd, 2003– (Vice Chm., 2005, Chm., 2005–07, Magisterial and Family sub-cttee); Working Party on Authorisation of Magistrates, DCA, 2004–05; Judicial Mem., Courts Bd for Kent, 2005–08; Chm., Family Justice Council for Kent, 2005–08. Freeman, City of London, 1978; Liveryman, Co. of Fruiterers, 1978 (Master, 1999–2000). Member, Committee: Marshall Hall Trust, 1991–2005; Centre for Child and Family Law Reform, City Univ., 1999–. *Recreation:* walking. *Address:* 4 Paper Buildings, Temple, EC4Y 7EX. *T:* (020) 7583 0816. *Club:* Royal Automobile.

CRYER, (Constance) Ann; JP; MP (Lab) Keighley, since 1997; *b* 14 Dec. 1939; *d* of Allen Place and Margaret Ann Place; *m* 1st, 1963, George Robert, (Bob), Cryer, MP (*d* 1994); one *s* one *d*; 2nd, 2003, Rev. John Hammersley (*d* 2004); one step *s* one step *d*. *Educ:* St John's Primary Sch.; Spring Bank Secondary Mod. Sch., Darwen; Bolton Tech. Coll.; Keighley Tech. Coll. Clerk, ICI, 1955–60; telephonist, GPO, 1960–64; researcher, Social Hist. Dept, Essex Univ., 1969; PA to Bob Cryer, MP and MEP, 1974–94. Member: Home Affairs Select Cttee, 2004–; Parly Cttee, PLP, 2005–; Vice Chair, PLP, 2008–. Mem. (Lab), Darwen BC, 1962–65. Mem., Cathedral Council, 1999–, Hon. Lay Canon, 2005–, Bradford Cathedral. JP Bradford, 1996. *Publication:* (contrib.) Boldness be My Friend: remembering Bob Cryer, 1997. *Recreations:* gardening, cinema, theatre, time with my 6 grandchildren and 3 step grandchildren. *Address:* House of Commons, SW1A 0AA; (constituency office) Bob Cryer House, 35 Devonshire Street, Keighley, W Yorks BD21 2BH; 32 Kendall Avenue, Shipley, W Yorks BD18 4DY. *T:* (01274) 584701.

See also J. R. Cryer.

CRYER, John Robert; National Political Officer, T&G section of Unite - the union (formerly Transport and General Workers Union), since 2006; *b* 11 April 1964; *s* of late (George) Robert Cryer, MP and of Ann Cryer, *qv*; *m* 1994, Narinder Bains, *d* of Shiv Singh Bains and Bakhshish Bains; two *s* one *d*. *Educ:* Oakbank Sch., Keighley; Hatfield Poly. (BA). Underwriter, 1986–88; Journalist, Morning Star, 1989–92; Editor, Labour Briefing, 1992–93; Journalist: GPMU Jl, 1992–93; Tribune, 1993–96; Lloyd's of London Pubns, 1996–97; Pol Officer, ASLEF, 2005–06. MP (Lab) Hornchurch, 1997–2005; contested (Lab) same seat, 2005. Chm., Labour Against the Superstate. Trustee, Thames Chase Community Forest. Mem., Editl Bd, Tribune. *Publication:* (jtly) Boldness be My Friend: remembering Bob Cryer, 1997. *Recreations:* most sports, reading, cinema, old cars. *Address:* 62 Springfield Gardens, Upminster, Essex RM14 3ER.

CRYNE, Christine; Senior Director, Consumer Direct, Office of Fair Trading, since 2006; *b* 5 March 1955; *d* of William George and Irene Ethel Austin; *m* 1978, John Michael Cryne. *Educ:* Univ. of Reading (BSc Hons Chem. Physics with Maths). Researcher, Unilever Res., 1977–82; Product Develt Exec., Schweppes, 1982–85; commercial and new product develt roles, RHM Foods, 1985–90; Gp Product Manager, Sharwoods, 1990–92; Marketing Manager, IPC Mags, 1992–94; Hd, Corporate, Trading and Develt, 1994–97, Mktg Dir, 1997–2001, Help the Aged; Exec. Dir, Muscular Dystrophy Campaign, 2001–04; Chief Exec., CIM, 2005–06. A Dir, CAMRA, 1987–98; Mem., British Guild of Beer Writers. MInstD 2000. *Recreations:* swimming, Real Ale, cooking. *Address:* Consumer Direct, Office of Fair Trading, Fleetbank House, Salisbury Square, EC4Y 8JX. *T:* (020) 7211 8931; *e-mail:* christinecryne@oft.gsi.gov.uk.

CRYSTAL, Prof. David, OBE 1995; FBA 2000; author, lecturer, broadcaster on language and linguistics, and reference books editor; Hon. Professorial Fellow, Bangor University (formerly University College of North Wales, then University of Wales, Bangor), since 1985; *b* 6 July 1941; *s* of late Samuel Cyril Crystal, OBE and Mary Agnes Morris; *m* 1st, 1964, Molly Irene Stack (*d* 1976); one *s* two *d* (and one *s* decd); 2nd, 1976, Hilary Frances Norman; one *s*. *Educ:* St Mary's Coll., Liverpool; University Coll. London (BA 1962); London Univ. (PhD 1966). Res. Asst, UCL, 1962–63; Asst Lectr, UCNW, 1963–65; University of Reading: Lectr, 1965–69; Reader, 1969–75; Prof., 1975–85. Vis. Prof., Bowling Green State Univ., 1969. Dir, Ucheldre Centre, Holyhead, 1991–. Member Board: British Council, 1996–2001; ESU, 2001–06. Chm., 2001–06, Hd, R&D, 2006–, Crystal Reference Systems. Sec., Linguistics Assoc. of GB, 1965–70; Chm., Nat. Literacy Assoc., 1995–2003 (Patron, 2004–); Vice-President: Inst. of Linguistics, 1998–; Soc. for Eds and Proofreaders, 2004–; Pres., Johnson Soc., 2005–06. Hon. Vice-Pres., Royal Coll. of Speech and Lang. Therapists, 1995– (Mem., Academic Bd, Coll. of Speech Therapists, 1972–79); FRCSLT (FCST 1983). Hon. President: Nat. Assoc. of Professionals concerned with Lang. Impaired Children, 1985–2002; Internat. Assoc. of Forensic Phonetics, 1991–94; Soc. of Indexers, 1992–95; Patron: Internat. Assoc. of Teachers of English as a Foreign Lang., 1995–; Assoc. for Language Learning, 2006–. Sam Wanamaker Fellow, Shakespeare's Globe, 2003; Hon. Fellow, Wolfson Coll., Cambridge, 2005. Editor: Language Res. in Progress, 1966–70; Jl of Child Language, 1973–85; The Language Library, 1978–2008; Applied Language Studies, 1980–84; Child Language Teaching and Therapy, 1985–96; Linguistics Abstracts, 1985–96; Blackwells Applied Language Studies, 1986–95; Consultant Editor, English Today, 1985–94; Adv. Editor, Penguin Linguistics, 1968–75; Associate Editor, Jl of Linguistics, 1970–73; Co-Editor, Studies in Language Disability, 1974–2006. Regular BBC broadcasts on English language and linguistics. FRSA 1983. Hon. DSc Queen Margaret UC, Edinburgh, 1997; Hon. DLitt Cambridge, 2005; DUniv Open, 2007. *Publications:* Systems of prosodic and paralinguistic features in English (with R. Quirk), 1964; Linguistics, language and religion, 1965; (ed jtly) Proceedings, Modern approaches to language teaching at university level, 1967; What is linguistics?, 1968, 5th edn 1985; Prosodic systems and intonation in English, 1969; (with D. Davy) Investigating English style, 1969; (ed with W. Bolton) The English language, vol. 2, 1969; Linguistics, 1971, 2nd edn 1985; Basic linguistics, 1973; Language acquisition, 1973; The English tone of voice, 1975; (with D. Davy) Advance conversational English, 1975; (with J. Bevington) Skylarks, 1975; (jtly) The grammatic analysis of language disability, 1976, 2nd edn 1989; Child language, learning an linguistics, 1976, 2nd edn 1987; Working with LARSP, 1979; Introduction to languag pathology, 1980, 4th edn (with R. Varley) 1998; A first dictionary of linguistics ar phonetics, 1980, 6th edn 2008; (ed) Eric Partridge: in his own words, 1980; Clinic linguistics, 1981; Directions in applied linguistics, 1981; Profiling linguistic disabilit 1982, 2nd edn 1992; (ed) Linguistic controversies, 1982; Who cares about English usage 1984, 2nd edn 2000; Language handicap in children, 1984; Linguistic encounters wi language handicap, 1984; Listen to your child, 1986; (ed with W. Bolton) The Englis language, 1987; Cambridge Encyclopedia of Language, 1987, 3rd edn 2008; Rediscov grammar, 1988, 3rd edn 2004; The English Language, 1988, 2nd edn 2002; Pilgrimag 1988; (with J. C. Davies) Convent, 1989; (ed) Cambridge Encyclopedia, 1990, 4th ed 2000; Language A to Z, 1991; Making Sense of English Usage, 1991; Ninetie Knowledge, 1992; Introducing Linguistics, 1992; An Encyclopedic Dictionary Language and Languages, 1992, 2nd edn, as The Penguin Dictionary of Language, 199 (ed) Cambridge Concise Encyclopedia, 1992, 2nd edn 1995; (ed) Cambridge Paperbac Encyclopedia, 1993, 3rd edn 1999; (ed) Cambridge Factfinder, 1993, 4th edn 2000; (e Cambridge Biographical Encyclopedia, 1994, 2nd edn 1998; Cambridge Encyclopedia the English Language, 1995, 2nd edn 2003; Discover Grammar, 1996; (ed) Joh Bradburne, Songs of the Vagabond, 1996; Cambridge Biographical Dictionary, 199 English as a Global Language, 1997, 2nd edn 2003; Language Play, 1998; (with H. Crysta Words on Words, 2000 (Wheatley Medal, LA, 2001); Language Death, 2000; (with H Crystal) John Bradburne's Mutemwa, 2000; Happenings, 2000; Language and th Internet, 2001, 2nd edn 2006; (with Ben Crystal) Shakespeare's Words, 2002; (ed) Th New Penguin Encyclopedia, 2002, 3rd edn, as The Penguin Encyclopedia, 2006; (ed) Th New Penguin Factfinder, 2003, 3rd edn, as The Penguin Factfinder, 2007; (ed) Th Concise Penguin Encyclopedia, 2003, 3rd edn 2007; The Stories of English, 2004; Makin Sense of Grammar, 2004; The Language Revolution, 2004; A Glossary of Netspeak an Textspeak, 2004; John Bradburne's Book of Days, 2004; Pronouncing Shakespeare, 200 (with Ben Crystal) The Shakespeare Miscellany, 2005; Johnson's Dictionary: a anthology, 2005; Words, Words, Words, 2006; How Language Works, 2006; The Fig for English, 2006; As They Say in Zanzibar, 2006; By Hook or by Crook, 2007; (ed) Joh Bradburne's Birds, Bees and Beasts, 2007; The Ucheldre Story, 2007; Think on m Words: exploring Shakespeare's language, 2008; Txtng: the Gr8 Db8, 2008; (with J. I Foster) Databank series: Heat, Light, Sound, Roads, Railways, Canals, Manors, Castle Money, Monasteries, Parliament, Newspapers, 1979; The Romans, The Greeks, Th Ancient Egyptians, 1981; Air, Food, Volcanoes, 1982; Deserts, Dinosaurs and Electricit 1983; Motorcycles, Computers, Horses and Ponies, Normans, Vikings, Anglo-Saxon Celts, 1984; The Stone Age, Fishing, 1985; (with J. L. Foster) Datasearch series: Air an Breathing, Heating and Cooling, Light and Seeing, Sound and Hearing, 199 contributions to: The Library of Modern Knowledge, 1978; A Dictionary of Moder Thought, 1978, 2nd edn 1987; Reader's Digest Great Illustrated Dictionary, 198 Reader's Digest Book of Facts, 1985; A Comprehensive Grammar of the Englis Language, 1985; International Encyclopedia of Linguistics, 1992; William Shakespear the Complete Works (ed Wells and Taylor), 2005; and to numerous volumes on languag style, prosody, communication, religion, handicap, teaching and reading; symposia an proceedings of learned socs; articles and reviews in jls on linguistics, English languag speech pathology and education. *Recreations:* cinema, music, bibliophily, development the arts. *Address:* Akaroa, Gors Avenue, Holyhead, Anglesey LL65 1PB. *T:* (0140 762764, *Fax:* (01407) 769728; *e-mail:* david.crystal1@googlemail.com.

CRYSTAL, Michael; QC 1984; a Deputy High Court Judge, since 1995; Senior Visitin Fellow, Centre for Commercial Law Studies, Queen Mary (formerly Queen Ma College, then Queen Mary and Westfield College), University of London, since 199 (Hon. Senior Visiting Fellow, 1987–96); *b* 5 March 1948; *s* of late Dr Samuel Cyr Crystal, OBE, and Rachel Ettel Crystal; *m* 1972, Susan Felicia Sniderman; one *s* one *Educ:* Leeds Grammar Sch.; Queen Mary Coll., Univ. of London (LLB Hons; Hon Fellow, QMW, 1996); Magdalen Coll., Oxford (BCL). Called to the Bar, Middle Templ 1970, Bencher, 1993; called to the Bar *ad eundem*, Gray's Inn, 1989; Lecturer in Law Pembroke Coll., Oxford, 1971–76. Vis. Prof., Dept of Laws, UCL, 2002–. DTI Inspect into County NatWest Ltd and County NatWest Securities Ltd, 1988–89, and int National Westminster Bank plc, 1992. Member: Insolvency Rules Adv. Cttee, 1993–9 Financial Law Panel, 1996–2002; FA Premier League Panel, 2004–; Internat. Insolvenc Inst., 2005–. Mem., Adv. Council, Centre for Commercial Law Studies, QMU (formerly QMC, then QMW), 1996–. Gov., 1988–2006, Hon. Gov., 2007–, RSC Trustee, British Friends of Haifa Univ., 2007–. Fellow: Royal Instn, 2004; Amer. Coll. Bankruptcy, 2006–. Hon. Fellow, Soc. for Advanced Legal Studies, 1997. *Publication* various legal text books. *Recreations:* travel, music, theatre. *Clubs:* Royal Automobil MCC.

CUBBON, Sir Brian (Crossland), GCB 1984 (KCB 1977; CB 1974); Permanent Und Secretary of State, Home Office, 1979–88; Charter Commissioner, Press Complain Commission, since 2004; *b* 9 April 1928; *m* 1956, Elizabeth Lorin Richardson; three *s* on *d*. *Educ:* Bury Grammar Sch.; Trinity Coll., Cambridge. Entered Home Office, 195 Cabinet Office, 1961–63, 1971–75; Private Sec. to Home Sec., 1968–69; Permaner Under-Sec. of State, Northern Ireland Office, 1976–79. Mem., Press Complain Commn, 1995–2002. Vice-Pres., Hakluyt Foundn, 1995–2002. *Address:* Brook Far House, Capel, Tonbridge, Kent TN12 6TT. *T:* (01892) 832534. *Clubs:* Oxford an Cambridge, Beefsteak.

CUBIE, Andrew, CBE 2001; FRSE; consultant to Fyfe Ireland LLP, since 2003 (Senic Partner, 1994–2003); *b* 24 Aug. 1946; *s* of late Dr Alexander Cubie and Elsie B. C. Cubi (*née* Thorburn); *m* 1968, Dr Heather Ann Muir; one *s* two *d*. *Educ:* Dollar Acad Edinburgh Univ. (LLB Hons). WS. Admitted solicitor, 1969; Partner, Fyfe Ireland & Co WS, 1974. Solicitor; Partner, Fyfe Ireland & Co., WS, 1971–87; Partner and Chm., Bir Semple Fyfe Ireland, WS, 1987–94. Chairman: CBI Scotland, 1995–97; Regl Chairme of CBI, 1996–97; Scotland's Health at Work, 1996–2005; Independent Cttee of Inquir into Student Finance, 1999–2000; Quality Scotland Foundn, 1999–; Scottish Credit an Qualification Framework, 2001–; British Council, Scotland, 2002–; Centre for Health Working Lives, 2005–. Member: Consultative Steering Gp, Scottish Parliament, 1997–9 McIntosh Commn in respect of Scottish Local Govt, 1998–99. Fulbright Comr, 2005– Chm., Cttee of Univ. Chairmen, 2007–. Vice Chm., Northern Lighthouse Bd, 2007– Vice-Pres., RNLI, 2000– (Chm., Scottish Council, 1997–); Chm., UK Cttee, VSC 2006– (Vice-Pres., 2001–04, Chm., 2004–05, BESO); Trustee, Common Purpos 2003–. Chairman: Governing Council, George Watson's Coll., 1994–99; Court, Napie Univ., 2001–. FRSE 2001. FRCPSGlas 2006. Hon. DBA Queen Margaret UC Edinburgh, 2000; Hon. LLD: Glasgow, 2001; Glasgow Caledonian, 2001; DUni Edinburgh, 2001. *Recreations:* reading, conversation, sailing. *Address:* The Garden Flat, 1 Moray Place, Edinburgh EH3 6DT. *T:* (0131) 226 3717, *Fax:* (0131) 225 2303; *e-mai*

andrew@cubie-edinburgh.com. *Clubs:* New (Edinburgh); Royal Highland Yacht.
See also G. Cubie.

CUBIE, Andrew MacInnes; Sheriff of Tayside, Central and Fife at Stirling, since 2004; *b* 12 Feb. 1963; *s* of John Pattison Cubie and Mary Moira Keir Cubie; *m* 1987, Joan Crockett; two *s* one *d. Educ:* Univ. of Glasgow (LLB 1st Cl. Hons; DLP). Admitted solicitor, 1986; Partner, Maxwell MacLaurin (Solicitors), Glasgow, until 2003. Temp. Sheriff, 1997–99; Floating Sheriff, 2003–04. Lectr (pt-time), Centre for Professional Legal Studies, Univ. of Strathclyde, 1993–2003. *Publications:* (contrib. ed.) Butterworth's Family Law Service; contrib. articles to Scots Law Time, Green's Family Law Bulletin and Jl Law Soc. of Scotland. *Recreations:* family, music, sports, travel. *Address:* Sheriff Court House, Viewfield Place, Stirling FK8 1NH. *T:* (01786) 462191.

CUBIE, George, CB 2003; Clerk of Committees, House of Commons, 2001–05; *b* 30 Aug. 1943; *s* of late Dr Alexander Cubie and Elsie B. C. Cubie (*née* Thorburn); *m* 1966, Kathleen S. Mullan; one *s. Educ:* Dollar Acad.; Edinburgh Univ. (MA Hons). Clerk in H of C, 1966; Clerk of Financial Cttees, H of C, 1987–89; Sec. to Public Accounts Commn, 1987–89; Clerk of Select Cttees, H of C, 1989–91; Clerk of the Overseas Office, 1991–95; Principal Clerk, Table Office, 1995–97; Clerk Asst, H of C, 1998–2001. *Publications:* (contrib.) Erskine May's Parliamentary Practice, 22nd edn, 1997; (contrib.) Halsbury's Laws of England, 5th edn. *Recreation:* walking.
See also A. Cubie.

CUBITT, family name of **Baron Ashcombe**.

CUBITT, Sir Hugh (Guy), Kt 1983; CBE 1977; FRICS; JP; DL; Chairman, Peabody Trust, 1998–2003 (Governor, 1991–2003); Director, PSIT PLC (formerly Property Security Investment Trust PLC), 1962–97; *b* 2 July 1928; *s* of late Col Hon. (Charles) Guy Cubitt, CBE, DSO, TD, and Rosamond Mary Edith, *d* of Sir Montagu Cholmeley, 4th Bt; *m* 1958, Linda Ishbel, *d* of late Hon. Angus Campbell, CBE; one *s* two *d. Educ:* RNC Dartmouth and Greenwich. Lieut RN, 1949; served in Korea, 1949–51; Flag Lieut to Adm., BJSM Washington, 1952 and to C-in-C Nore, 1953; retd 1953. Qual. Chartered Auctioneer and Estate Agent, 1958; Chartered Surveyor (FRICS) 1970. Partner: Rogers Chapman & Thomas, 1958–67; Cubitt & West, 1962–79. Regl Dir, 1970–77, Dir, 1977–90, Mem., UK Adv. Bd, 1990–91, National Westminster Bank; Chairman: Lombard North Central PLC, 1980–91; The Housing Corp., 1980–90; Rea Brothers Group PLC, 1996–98. Comr, and Chm., London Adv. Cttee, English Heritage, 1988–94. Mem. Westminster City Council, 1963–78; Leader of Council, 1972–76; Alderman, 1974–78; Lord Mayor and Dep. High Steward of Westminster, 1977–78. Pres., London Chamber of Commerce, 1988–91. Chairman: Anchor Trust (formerly Anchor Gp of Housing Assocs), 1991–98; Housing Assocs' Charitable Trust, 1991–97; Chairman of Governors: West Heath Sch., 1978–91; Cranleigh Sch., 1981–95; Dir and Mem. Governing Body, RAM, 1978–98. Hon. Steward, Westminster Abbey, 1978–2002 (Chief Steward, 1997–2002). Mem., Bd of Green Cloth Verge of Palaces, 1980–98. FRSA; Hon. FRAM 1985. JP Surrey, 1964; Chairman: Dorking PSD, 1991–93; SE Surrey PSD, 1993–95. High Sheriff of Surrey, 1983–84; DL Greater London, 1978. *Recreations:* travel, photography, painting. *Address:* Chapel House, Westhumble, Dorking, Surrey RH5 6AY. *T:* (01306) 882994. *Club:* Boodle's.

CUBITT, Maj. Gen. William George, CBE 2005 (OBE 2000); General Officer Commanding, London District, and Major General Commanding Household Division, since 2007; *b* 19 Feb. 1959; *m* 1990, Lucy Jane Brooking (*née* Pym); two *s* one *d. Educ:* Beechwood Park, Herts; Stowe Sch., Bucks; Univ. of Edinburgh (BSc Hons Agric.). Served: Coldstream Guards, 1977–98; Irish Guards, 1998–. Class IV, Order of St Olav (Norway), 1988. *Address:* Headquarters, Household Division and London District, Horse Guards, Whitehall, SW1A 2AX.

CUCKNEY, Baron *cr* 1995 (Life Peer), of Millbank in the City of Westminster; **John Graham Cuckney,** Kt 1978; *b* 12 July 1925; *s* of late Air Vice-Marshal E. J. Cuckney, CB, CBE, DSC and Bar, and Lilian (*née* Williams); *m* 2nd, 1960, Muriel (*d* 2004), *d* of late Walter Scott Boyd; 3rd, 2007, (Priscilla) Jane Newell (*née* Watts), OBE. *Educ:* Shrewsbury; St Andrews Univ. (MA). War Service, Royal Northumberland Fusiliers, King's African Rifles, followed by attachment to War Office (Civil Asst, Gen. Staff), until 1957; subseq. appts with various industrial and financial cos including: Chairman: Brooke Bond Gp, 1981–84 (Dir, 1979–84); Thomas Cook Gp, 1978–87; John Brown, 1983–86 (Dir, 1981–86; Dep. Chm., 1982–83); Westland Gp, 1985–89; Royal Insce Hldgs plc, 1985–94 (Dir, 1979–89; Dep. Chm., 1983–85); Investors in Industry Gp, subseq. 3i Gp, 1987–92 (Dir, 1986–92); Orion Publishing Gp Ltd, 1994–97; Dep. Chm., TI Gp, 1985–90; Vice Chm., Glaxo, 1993–95 (Dir, 1990–95); Director: Lazard Brothers, 1964–70 and 1988–90; Midland Bank, 1978–88; Brixton Estate, 1985–96. Public appointments include: Chm., Mersey Docks and Harbour Board, 1970–72; Chief Executive (Second Perm. Sec.), Property Services Agency, DoE, 1972–74; Chm., International Military Services Ltd (an MoD company), 1974–85; Sen. Crown Agent and Chm. of Crown Agents, for Oversea Governments and Administrations, 1974–78. Advr to Sec. of State for Social Security on Maxwell pensions affair, and Founder Chm., Maxwell Pensioners' Trust, 1992–95. Independent Mem., Railway Policy Review Cttee, 1966–67; special Mem., Hops Marketing Bd, 1971–72; Chairman: EDC for Building, 1976–80; Port of London Authority, 1977–79; Internat. Maritime Bureau, Internat. Chamber of Commerce, 1981–85; NEDC Working Party on European Public Purchasing, 1990–92; Member: Docklands Joint Cttee, 1977–79; Council, British Exec. Service Overseas, 1981–84; Council, Foundn for Science and Technology, 1987–90; Dir, SBAC, 1986–89. Vice Pres., Liverpool Sch. of Tropical Med., 1985–93. Governor, Centre for Internat. Briefing, Farnham Castle, 1974–84; Chm., Understanding Industry Trust, 1988–91; Controller, ROH Develt Land Trust, 1993–96; Trustee, RAF Mus., 1987–99. Freeman, City of London, 1977. Elder Brother of Trinity House, 1980. Hon. DSc Bath, 1991; Hon. LLD St Andrews, 1993. *Address:* House of Lords, SW1A 0PW. *T:* (020) 7219 3000. *Club:* Athenæum.

CUDMORE, Harold; yachtsman/businessman; *b* 21 April 1944; *s* of late Harold Cudmore, LLD and Sheila Coleman; *m* 1993, Lauren E. Dagge; two *d.* Skipper, White Crusader, British challenger, America's Cup, 1986; Manager and sailor, British Admiral's Cup winning team, 1989; Adviser and Coach, America 3, America's Cup winning team, 1992. Winner of many world championships, internat. match-racing regattas and major events. *Recreations:* other sports, walking, travelling, socialising. *Address:* 4 Queen's Road, Cowes, Isle of Wight PO31 8BQ. *T:* (01983) 280466; *e-mail:* haroldcudmore@aol.com. *Clubs:* Royal Thames Yacht, Royal Ocean Racing; Royal Cork Yacht, Island Sailing, Royal Corinthian Yacht, Irish Cruising, Fort Worth Boat.

CUENOD, Hugues; Swiss tenor, retired; *b* 26 June 1902; *s* of Frank Cuenod and Gabrielle de Meuron. *Educ:* Swiss schools and colleges; Conservatoire Basel; Vienna; with Mme Singer-Burian. First concert, Paris, 1928; gave many performances of classical and light music, incl. musical comedy, in Europe and USA; numerous concerts with Clara Haskil and Nadia Boulanger; taught at Conservatoire de Genève, 1940–46; after returning to Paris, concentrated on sacred and classical music; sang in all major opera houses, incl. Glyndebourne (début 1954) and NY Metropolitan (début 1987); latterly specialised in French songs; many master classes; still teaches vocal interpretation of French songs. 33 recordings, of Couperin, Fauré, Debussy, Schubert, Bach, etc, many now re-issued on CD; Grand Prix du Disque, 1980, for Socrate, by Erik Satie. Hon. Citizen of Boston, 1972. Händel and Haydn Soc. Medal, Boston, 1972; Fidelio Medal, Geneva, 1987. Commandeur de l'Ordre des Arts et des Lettres (France), 1976. *Relevant publications:* Hugues Cuenod: un diable de musicien, by Jerôme Spycket, 1978; Hugues Cuenod d'une voix légère: entretiens avec François Hudry, 1995. *Address:* 21 Place du Marché, 1800 Vevey, Switzerland; Château de Lully sur Morges, Vaud, Switzerland.

CUEVAS-CANCINO, Francisco, Hon. GCVO 1985; Founder and Professor, Instituto de Educación Superior Simón Bolívar, Xalapa, Veracruz, since 1997; Mexican Ambassador Emeritus; *b* 7 May 1921; *s* of José Luis Cuevas and Sofia Cancino; *m* 1946, Ana Hilditch; two *s* one *d*; *m* Cristina Flores de Cuevas. *Educ:* Free School of Law, Mexico (lawyer, 1943); McGill Univ., Montreal (MCL 1946). Entered Mexican Foreign Service, as Vice-Consul, 1946, reaching rank of Ambassador by own merit; Permanent Representative to UN, 1965–70; Mexican Rep. to UNESCO, 1971–75, and Mem. Exec. Council during first four years; Perm. Rep. to UN, 1978–79; Ambassador: to Brazil, 1979–80; to Belgium, 1980–83; to UK and to Republic of Ireland, 1983–85; to Austria, 1986–90; Perm. Mexican Rep. to UNIDO and IAEA, 1986. Chm., Group of 77, Vienna, 1988. Order of the Liberator, 1970, Order Andrés Bello, 1971, (Venezuela); Medal of Mexican For. Service (25 years), 1972; Order Cruzeiro do Sul (Brazil), 1980; Great Cross of Order of the Crown (Belgium), 1983. *Publications:* La nullité des actes juridiques, 1947; La doctrina de Suárez en el derecho natural (award, Madrid), 1952; Roosevelt y la buena vecindad, 1955; Del Congreso de Panamá a la Conferencia de Caracas, 1955, re-ed 1979; Tratado sobre la organización internacional, 1962; (ed) Porvenir de México by Luis G. Cuevas, 1961; (ed) Pacto de Familia (vol. forms part of Hist. Archives of Mexican Diplomatic Service, 2nd series), 1963; (ed) Foro Internacional, 1961–62; Cuentos de la Síndone, 1995; Las máscaras americanas del heroísmo, 1997; Homenaje a Agatha Christie, 2000; El asesinato del Gran Mariscal de Ayacucho, 2001; Las Memorias de Hugo Grocio, 2004; Grotius' *De Iure Belli* (modern version in Spanish), 2005; Manual de Derecho Internacional Privado Mexicano, 2007; contrib. to book of essays in homage to Hans Morgenthau, 1978; several works and articles on Bolivarian theatre, and on Simón Bolívar (The Liberator), incl.: Visión Surrealista del Libertador, (Bogotá) 1980; Homenaje a Bolívar en el Sesquicentenario de su Muerte, (Bogotá) 1980. *Address:* Instituto de Educación Superior Simón Bolivar, Revolución 279, Xalapa Centro, 91000 Veracruz, Mexico.

CUI, Prof. Zhanfeng, PhD; CEng; Donald Pollock Professor of Chemical Engineering, and Fellow of Hertford College, Oxford University, since 2000; *b* 16 Nov. 1962; *s* of Chun-Ting Cui and Su-e Li; *m* 1985, Dr Jing Yu; one *s* one *d. Educ:* Inner Mongolia Poly. Univ., China (BSc 1982); Dalian Univ. of Technol., China (MSc 1984; PhD 1987); MA Oxon 1994. CEng 1997. Res. Fellow, Univ. of Strathclyde, 1988–91; Lectr in Chemical Engrg, Edinburgh Univ., 1991–94; Oxford University: Lectr in Engrg Sci., 1994–99; Reader, 1999–2000; Fellow, Keble Coll., 1994–2000. Visiting Professor: Georgia Inst. of Technol., Atlanta, 1999; Univ. of Minnesota, 2004; (also Chang Jiang Scholar) Dalian Univ. of Technol., China, 2005. *Publications:* contrib. numerous res. articles to professional jls, as sole or jt author. *Recreations:* bridge, basketball. *Address:* Department of Engineering Science, Oxford University, Parks Road, Oxford OX1 3PJ. *T:* (01865) 273118.

CULHAM, Michael John, CB 1992; Assistant Under Secretary of State (Civilian Management (Administrators)), Ministry of Defence, 1987–92, retired; *b* 24 June 1933; *s* of Cecil and Constance Culham; *m* 1963, Christine Mary Daish; one *s* two *d. Educ:* Reading Sch.; Lincoln Coll., Oxford (MA); Open Univ. (Dip. French, 1997). National Service, Queen's Own Royal West Kent Regt, RAEC, 1952–54. Exec. Officer, WO, 1957–61; Asst Principal, Air Min., 1962; Private Sec. to Under-Sec. of State for Air, 1962–64; Principal, MoD, 1964–72; Jt Services Staff Coll., 1969; 1st Sec. (Defence), UK Delegn to NATO, Brussels, 1972–74; Asst Sec., MoD, 1974–82; Asst Under-Sec. of State (Adjt-Gen.), MoD, 1982–87. Member: Royal Patriotic Fund Corp., 1983–87; Adv. Council, RMCS, Shrivenham, 1983–87. Commissioner: Duke of York's Royal Mil. Sch., 1982–87; Queen Victoria Sch., 1982–87; Welbeck Coll., 1985–87; Royal Hosp. Chelsea, 1985–88. Chm., Defence Sports and Recreation (formerly MoD Recreation) Assoc., 1985–92; Vice President: CS RFU, 1992–; Farnham Town Boys' FC, 1987– (Chm., 1983–85). Trustee, Nat. Army Mus., 1985–88. *Recreations:* music, sailing, walking, watching cricket. *Address:* 39 Waverley Lane, Farnham, Surrey GU9 8BH. *Clubs:* Civil Service; Surrey County Cricket; Hampshire County Cricket.

CULHANE, Prof. (John) Leonard, FRS 1985; Professor of Physics, 1981–2005, now Emeritus, Director, Mullard Space Science Laboratory, 1983–2003, and Head of Department of Space and Climate Physics, 1993–2003, University College London; *b* 14 Oct. 1937; *s* of late John Thomas Culhane and Mary Agnes Culhane; *m* 1961, Mary Brigid, *d* of James Smith; two *s. Educ:* Clongowes Wood College, Co. Kildare; University College Dublin (BSc Phys 1959; MSc Phys 1960); UCL (PhD Phys 1966). FRAS 1970; FInstP 1991. Physics Department, University College London: Res. Asst, 1963; Lectr, 1967; Reader, 1976; Prof., 1981. Sen. Scientist, Lockheed Palo Alto Res. Lab., 1969–70; Vis. Prof., Inst. of Space and Astronautical Sci., Tokyo, 1997. Chairman: SERC/BNSC Space Sci. Prog. Bd, 1989–92 (Vice-Pres., and UK Deleg., ESA Sci. Prog. Cttee, 1990–94); Royal Soc. Space Res. Cttee, 1990–93; COSPAR Commn E, 1994–2002; Eur. Space Sci. Cttee, ESF, 1997–2002; Member: Council, RAS, 1975–78; Space Sci. Adv. Cttee, ESA, 1985–89 (Chm., Astrophysics Working Group, 1985–89); SERC/BNSC Earth Obs. Prog. Bd, 1986–88; SERC Astron. Plan. Sci. Bd, 1989–92; Adv. Panel, ESA Space Sci. Dept, 1995–2000; PPARC, 1996–2000; Sci. Oversight Cttee, Internat. Space Sci. Inst., Bern, 2004–. Mem. Council, Surrey Univ., 1985–90. MAE 2001; Member: IAU; Amer. Astronomical Soc.; Amer. Geophys. Union; Internat. Acad. of Astronautics; For. Mem., Norwegian Acad. of Scis and Letters, 1966. Fellow, UCL, 2008. Hon. DSc Wroclaw, 1993. Silver Award and Pardoe Space Prize, RAeS, 2005; Gold Medal in Astronomy, Royal Astronomical Soc., 2007. *Publications:* X-ray Astronomy (with P. W. Sanford), 1981; over 320 papers on solar physics, X-ray astronomy, X-ray instrumentation and plasma spectroscopy. *Recreations:* music, racing cars. *Address:* 24 Warnham Road, Horsham, West Sussex RH12 2QU. *T:* (lab.) (01483) 274100; *e-mail:* jlc@mssl.ucl.ac.uk.

CULHANE, Simon Hugh Desmond; Chief Executive, Securities & Investment Institute (formerly Securities Institute), since 2004; *b* 15 Feb. 1960; *m* 1985, Sarah; three *s* one *d. Educ:* St Paul's Sch.; Univ. of Surrey (BSc Hons Econs and Stats). ACIB 1984; FSI 2005. Lloyds TSB Bank, 1981–95; Dep. Dir, Prime Minister's Efficiency Unit, Cabinet Office, 1995–98; Dir, Chairman's Office, Deutsche Bank AG, London, 1998–2002; Foundn Trust Project Dir, UCLH, 2003–04. Non-exec. Dir, Efficiency Project Prog. Bd, Office of Govt Commerce, 2004–07. MInstD 2004; Mem., Guild of Internat. Bankers, 2006–. *Recreations:* sailing, youth cricket, following AFC Wimbledon. *Address:* Securities

& Investment Institute, 8 Eastcheap, EC3M 1AE. *T:* (020) 7645 0600, *Fax:* (020) 7626 3068; *e-mail:* simon.culhane@sii.org.uk. *Club:* Cornhill.

CULL-CANDY, Prof. Stuart Graham, PhD; FMedSci; FRS 2002; Gaddum Professor of Pharmacology and Professor of Neuroscience, University College London, since 2006; *b* 2 Nov. 1946; *s* of Stanley William Cull-Candy and Margaret Cull-Candy; *m* Dr Barbara Paterson Fulton; one *d*. *Educ:* Royal Holloway Coll., Univ. of London (BSc Hons Biology 1969); UCL (MSc Physiology and Biophysics 1971); Univ. of Glasgow (PhD Synaptic Physiology 1974). FBPharmacolS 2005. Royal Society European Exchange Prog. Fellow, Inst. of Pharmacology, Univ. of Lund, Sweden, 1974–75; University College London: Beit Meml Res. Fellow, and MRC Associate Res. Staff, Dept of Biophysics, 1975–82; Wellcome Trust Reader in Pharmacology, Dept of Pharmacology, 1982–90; Prof. of Pharmacology, 1990–2003, Prof. of Neuroscience, 2003–06, UCL. Internat. Res. Scholar, Howard Hughes Medical Inst., 1993–98. Mem., Neurosci. Cttee, MRC, 1987–91; Founder Mem., Wellcome Trust Internat. Interest Gp, 1991–97; Expert Advr, Scientific Bd, INSERM, France, 2007. Member: Royal Soc. Univ. Res. Fellowships Grants Cttee, 2003–, Res. Grants Bd, 2005–; Panel, Leverhulme Trust Sen. Res. Fellowships, 2006–. Mem., Faculty of 1000, 2006–. External Editl Advr in Neuroscience, Nature, 1993–97; Editor: Jl of Physiology, 1987–95; European Jl of Neuroscience, 1988–; Neuron, 1994–98; Reviewing Editor, Jl of Neuroscience, 2000–; Guest Ed., Current Opinions in Neurobiology, 2007. FMedSci 2004. G. L. Brown Prize, Physiological Soc., 1996; Wolfson Award, Royal Soc., 2003. *Publications:* various book chapters; numerous articles on fast synaptic transmission and glutamate receptors in the brain and peripheral nervous system in scientific jls Nature, Neuron, Jl of Neuroscience, Jl of Physiology and Nature Neuroscience. *Recreations:* natural history, local history, antiquarian books relating to medicine and natural history, the Arts and Crafts movement. *Address:* Department of Pharmacology, University College London, Gower Street, WC1E 6BT. *T:* (020) 7679 3766, *Fax:* (020) 7679 7298; *e-mail:* s.cull-candy@ucl.ac.uk.

CULLEN, family name of **Baron Cullen of Whitekirk**.

CULLEN OF ASHBOURNE, 3rd Baron *cr* 1920, of Roehampton, co. Surrey; **Edmund Willoughby Marsham Cokayne;** *b* 18 May 1916; 2nd *s* of 1st Baron Cullen of Ashbourne, KBE and Grace Margaret (*née* Marsham); *S* brother, 2000; *m* 1943, Janet Muirhead Manson (*née* Watson) (*d* 2006); one adopted *d*. *Educ:* Eton; Royal Sch. of Mines. PEng. Served War, Pilot (Flt-Lt) RAF, 1940–46. Jun. Engr, Sons of Gwalia Mine and Zinc Corp., Australia, 1937–40; Chief Engineer: Central Patricia Gold Mine, Ont, Canada, 1946–51; Algoma Ore Properties, Ont, 1951–65; Chief Engr, Mine Supt then Mine Mgr, Craigmont Mines, BC, 1965–76; Mine Mgr then Gen. Mgr, Lakeshore Mine, Casa Grande, Arizona, USA, 1976–84. *Publications:* technical papers. *Recreations:* music, gardening, volunteering. *Heir:* *b* John O'Brien Marsham Cokayne [*b* 11 Oct. 1920; *m* 1948, Anne Frances Clayton (*d* 1971); one *s*]. *Address:* 15–1901 Maxwell Avenue, Merritt, BC V1K 1L9, Canada. *T:* (250) 3789462.

CULLEN OF WHITEKIRK, Baron *cr* 2003 (Life Peer), of Whitekirk in East Lothian; **William Douglas Cullen,** KT 2007; PC 1997; Lord Justice-General of Scotland and Lord President of the Court of Session, 2001–05; *b* 18 Nov. 1935; *s* of late Sheriff K. D. Cullen and Mrs G. M. Cullen; *m* 1961, Rosamond Mary Downer (MBE 2007); two *s* two *d*. *Educ:* Dundee High Sch.; St Andrews Univ. (MA); Edinburgh Univ. (LLB). FRSE 1993. Called to the Scottish Bar, 1960. Standing Jun. Counsel to HM Customs and Excise, 1970–73; QC (Scot.) 1973; Advocate-depute, 1978–81; a Senator of the Coll. of Justice in Scotland, 1986–2005; Lord Justice-Clerk and Pres. of the Second Div. of the Court of Session, 1997–2001. Chairman: Medical Appeal Tribunal, 1977–86; Inquiry into the Piper Alpha disaster, 1988–90; Review of Business of the Outer House of the Court of Session, 1995; Tribunal of Inquiry into the shootings at Dunblane Primary Sch., 1996; Ladbroke Grove Rail Inquiry, 1999–2001. Chm., Bd of Dirs, The Signet Accreditation Ltd, 2007–. Member: Scottish Valuation Adv. Council, 1980–86; Royal Commn on Ancient and Historical Monuments of Scotland, 1987–97. President: SACRO, 2000–; Saltire Soc., 2005–. Chairman: Council, Cockburn Assoc. (Edinburgh Civic Trust), 1984–86; Govs, St Margaret's Sch., Edinburgh, 1994–2001; Mem. Court, Napier Univ., 1996–2005. Hon. Bencher: Inner Temple, 2001; Inn of Court of NI, 2002. Hon. FREng (Hon. FEng 1995); Hon. FRCSEd 2006. Hon. LLD: Aberdeen, 1992; St Andrews, 1997; Dundee, Edinburgh, Glasgow Caledonian, 2000; DUniv Heriot-Watt, 1995. *Publications:* The Faculty Digest Supplement 1951–60, 1965; non-legal booklets on buildings in Edinburgh. *Recreations:* gardening, natural history. *Address:* House of Lords, SW1A 0PW. *Clubs:* Caledonian; New (Edinburgh).

CULLEN, Prof. Alexander Lamb, OBE 1960; DSc(Eng); FRS 1977; FREng, FIET, FIEEE, FInstP, FCGI; Emeritus Professor, University of London; Hon. Research Fellow, Department of Electronic and Electrical Engineering, University College London, since 1984 (SERC Senior Research Fellow, 1980–84); *b* 30 April 1920; *s* of Richard and Jessie Cullen, Lincoln; *m* 1940, Margaret, *er d* of late Andrew Lamb, OBE; two *s* one *d*. *Educ:* Lincoln Sch.; City and Guilds Coll., London. Staff of Radio Dept, RAE Farnborough, working on development of radar, 1940–46; Lectr in Electrical Engineering, University Coll., London, 1946–55 (title of Reader conferred 1955); Prof. of Electrical Engineering, University of Sheffield, 1955–67; Pender Prof. of Electrical Engineering, University College London, 1967–80. Hon. Prof., Northwestern Polytechnical Univ., Xian, China, 1981. Mem., IBA, 1982–89. Institution of Electrical Engineers: Kelvin premium, 1952; Ambrose Fleming premium, 1956 (with J. C. Parr), 1975 (with Dr J. R. Forrest), 1988 (with S. P. Yeo); Duddell premium, 1957 (with Dr H. A. French); Faraday Medal, 1984; Electronics Letters premium, 1985; Maxwell premium, 1996 (jtly). Microwave Career Award, IEEE, 1989. Chm., Brit. Nat. Cttee, URSI, 1981–85; Vice-Pres., Internat. URSI, 1981–87, Pres., 1987–90; Mem. Council, Royal Soc., 1984–86. Clifford Paterson Lecture, Royal Soc., 1984; Clerk Maxwell Lecture, IERE, 1986. FREng (FEng 1977). Hon. FIERE 1987; Hon. Fellow, UCL, 1993. Hon. DSc: Chinese Univ. of Hong Kong, 1981; Kent, 1986. Hon. DEng Sheffield, 1985. Royal Medal, Royal Soc., 1984. *Publications:* Microwave Measurements (jointly with Prof. H. M. Barlow), 1950; a number of papers on electromagnetic waves and microwave measurement techniques in IEE proceedings and elsewhere. *Recreations:* music and reading. *Address:* 3 Felden Drive, Felden, Hemel Hempstead, Herts HP3 0BD.

CULLEN, Sir (Edward) John, Kt 1991; PhD; FREng; Chairman, Health and Safety Commission, 1983–93; *b* 19 Oct. 1926; *s* of William Henry Pearson Cullen and Ellen Emma Cullen; *m* 1954, Betty Davall Hopkins (*d* 2006); two *s* two *d*. *Educ:* Cambridge Univ. (MA 1952, PhD 1956); Univ. of Texas (MS 1953). UKAEA, 1956–58; ICI, 1958–67; Rohm and Haas Co., 1967–83: Eur. Dir for Engrg and Regulatory Affairs, 1981–83; Dep. Chm., Rohm and Haas (UK) Ltd, 1981–83. Chm., British Nat. Cttee for Internat. Engrg Affairs, 1990–96; President: Pipeline Industries Guild, 1996–98; FEANI, 1996–99 (Vice-Pres., 1995–96); British Safety Industries Fedn, 1997–; Mem., Engrg Council, 1990–96. FREng (FEng 1987; Mem. Council, 1991–94); Pres., IChemE, 1988–89. Mem., 1995–99, Chm., 1999–2002, McRobert Award Cttee. MInstD 1978; FRSA 1988. Liveryman, Engineers' Co., 1989–. Hon. DSc Exeter, 1993. *Publications:* articles on gas absorption, in Trans Faraday Soc., Trans IChemE, Chem. Engrg Science; numerous articles on health and safety. *Recreations:* reading (detective stories), photography, swimming, gardening. *Address:* 34 Duchess of Bedford House, W8 7QW. *T:* (020) 7937 0709. *Club:* Athenæum.

CULLEN, Felicity Ann; QC 2008; *b* Talgarth, 5 March 1962; *d* of John Milton and Mary Christine London; *m* 1986, Christopher Cullen; two *s*. *Educ:* Holy Trinity Convent, Kidderminster; St David's Ursuline Convent, Brecon; Brecon High Sch.; Univ. of Birmingham (LLB 1983); Queens' Coll., Cambridge (LLM 1984). Called to the Bar, Lincoln's Inn, 1985; in practice as barrister, specialising in revenue law; Mem., Gray's Inn Tax Chambers, 1986–. *Recreations:* arts, entertaining, architecture and design, adventure travel, go-karting, power boating. *Address:* Gray's Inn Tax Chambers, Gray's Inn, WC1R 5JA. *T:* (020) 7242 2642.

CULLEN, Hon. Michael (John), PhD; MP (Lab) New Zealand, since 1981; Treasurer, Minister of Finance and Leader of the House, since 1999, Deputy Prime Minister, since 2002, Attorney General, since 2005, New Zealand; *b* London, 5 Feb. 1945; adopted NZ citizenship, 1975; *s* of John Joseph Thomas Cullen and Ivy May Cullen; *m* 1st, 1967, Rowena Joy Knight (marr. diss. 1987); two *d*; 2nd, 1989, Lowson Anne Collins. *Educ:* Christ's Coll., Christchurch; Canterbury Univ. (BA 1965; MA Hist. 1967); Edinburgh Univ. (PhD Social and Economic Hist.). Asst Lectr, Univ. of Canterbury; Tutor, Univ. of Stirling; Sen. Lectr, Univ. of Otago. MP (Lab) St Kilda, 1981–96, Dunedin S, 1996–2002, List MP (Lab), 2002–. Sen. Govt Whip, 1984–87; Minister: of Social Welfare, 1987–90; of Revenue, 1999–2005; for Tertiary Education, 2005–; Associate Minister of Finance, 1987–90; Associate Minister of Health, 1988–90; of Labour, 1989–90; opposition spokesperson on social welfare, war pensions and Accident Compensation Corp., 1990–91, on finance, 1991. Dep. Leader, NZ Labour Party, 1996. Vis. Fellow, ANU. *Publications:* The Statistical Movement in Early Victorian Britain, 1974; Lawfully Occupied, 1979; articles in jls. *Recreations:* music, reading, golf, house renovation. *Address:* Parliament Buildings, Wellington, New Zealand.

CULLEN, Paul Benedict; QC (Scot.) 1995; Solicitor General for Scotland, 1995–97; *b* 11 March 1957; *s* of James Finbarr Cullen and Ann Evaline Black or Cullen; *m* 1983, Joyce Nicol; two *s* one *d*. *Educ:* St Augustine's High Sch., Edinburgh; Edinburgh Univ. (LLB Hons). Admitted to Faculty of Advocates, 1982 (Clerk of Faculty, 1986–90); Standing Jun. Counsel to DoE in Scotland, 1988–91; Advocate Depute, 1992–95. Chairman: Police Appeals Tribunal, 2003–; Chm., Appeal Cttee, ICAS, 2005–. Scottish Cons. spokesman on home and legal affairs, 1997–98; Chm. Disciplinary Panel, Scottish Cons. Party, 2000–. Cons. rep. on Scottish Office consultative steering gp on Scottish Parlt, 1998–99. Chm. Gilmerton Limestone Emergency inquiry, 2001–02. Vice Pres., Edinburgh S Cons. & Unionist Assoc., 1997–. Contested (C) Eastwood, 1997. *Recreations:* tennis, bridge. *Address:* Advocates Library, Edinburgh EH1 1RF. *T:* (0131) 226 5071. *Club:* New (Edinburgh).

CULLEN, Terence Lindsay Graham; QC 1978; *b* 29 Oct. 1930; *s* of late Eric Graham Cullen and Jean Morrison Hunter (*née* Bennett); *m* 1958, Muriel Elisabeth Rolfe; three *s*. *Educ:* RNC, Dartmouth. RN, 1948–55; Prestige Group Ltd, 1955–61. Called to the Bar Lincoln's Inn, 1961 (Bencher, 1986); Singapore, 1978; Malaysia, 1980; Hong Kong, 1986 Bermuda, 1990; retired, 1998. *Recreation:* the Turf. *Address:* Flat 510, Bunyan Court Barbican, EC2Y 8DH.

CULLEY, Ronald; Chief Executive, Strathclyde Partnership for Transport, since 2006; 2 Feb. 1950; *s* of Ronald Frank Culley and Mary McTavish Culley (*née* McLeod); *m* 1st 1973, Margaret Ferguson (marr. diss. 1985); two *s*; 2nd, 1994, Jean Pollock; two *s*. *Educ* Craigbank Comprehensive Sch.; Jordanhill Coll. of Educn (Dip. YCS); Moray House Coll. of Educn (CQSW, CSW); Univ. of Strathclyde (MSc). Various social work and social policy posts, Strathclyde Regl Council, 1975–87; Chief Executive: Govan Initiative Ltd, 1987–2000; Scottish Enterprise Glasgow, 2000–06. Mem. Bd, Police Adv. Bd fo Scotland, 1999–2005. Member Board: Scottish Urban Regeneration Foundn, 1992–2006 Quality Scotland, 1999–2000; Glasgow Alliance, 2000–06; Prince's Trust Glasgow 2002–06; Glasgow Economic Forum, 2002–; Wise Gp, 2003–; Glasgow Communit Planning Partnership, 2004–; Clyde Valley Community Planning Partnership, 2004– Glasgow Sci. Centre, 2004–06. Mem., British Transport Police Authy, 2008–. Conteste (SLP) Scotland W, Scottish Parly elecns, 1999. Gov., Scottish Police Trng Coll 1999–2004. Friend of Govan Initiative, 2000–; Sec., Govan Hons Soc., 1999–. Hon Mem., Harmony Row Youth Club, 2000–. *Publications:* (with J. McManus) Merka Forces, 1994; The New Guards, 1999. *Recreations:* family and friends, music, Associatio football (particularly Manchester United), fair weather golf, gardening, socialising, readin biographies, Scottish, American and Irish politics, irreverence, laughing out louc convivial temulence. *Address:* (office) Consort House, 12 West George Street, Glasgov G2 1HN. *T:* (0141) 333 3100; *e-mail:* ron.culley@spt.co.uk. *Club:* Ross Prior (Gartacharn).

CULLIMORE, Charles Augustine Kaye, CMG 1993; HM Diplomatic Service, retirec Chairman, British African Business Association, since 2001; *b* 2 Oct. 1933; *s* of Rev Canon Charles Cullimore and Constance Alicia Kaye Cullimore (*née* Grimshaw); *m* 195 Val Elizabeth Margot (*née* Willemsen); one *s* one *d*. *Educ:* Portora Royal Sch., Enniskiller Trinity Coll., Oxford (MA). N Ireland Short Service Commn, 1955–57. HMOCS Tanganyika, 1958–61; ICI Ltd, 1961–71; joined HM Diplomatic Service, 1971; FCC 1971–73; Bonn, 1973–77; FCO, 1977–79; Counsellor, New Delhi, 1979–82; Dep. Hig Comr, Canberra, 1982–86; FCO, 1986–89; High Comr, Uganda, 1989–93. Chief Exec Southern Africa Business Assoc., 1995–2001. Dir, Transparency Internat. (UK), 1996–9 Council Member: Royal African Soc., 2000–; Overseas Service Pensioners' Assoc., 2004– Member: The Pilgrims, 1993–; RIIA, 1996–; RSAA, 2002 –. *Publication:* contrib. Jl c Mod. African Studies. *Recreations:* theatre, walking, travel. *Address:* Deacon Hous Bidborough, Kent TN3 0UP. *Clubs:* Royal Commonwealth Society, Royal Over-Se League.

CULLIMORE, Colin Stuart, CBE 1978; DL; Chairman, Lincoln Cathedral Counc 2000–07 (Member, Transitional Council, 1998–2000); *b* 13 July 1931; *s* of Reginal Victor Cullimore and May Maria Cullimore; *m* 1952, Kathleen Anyta Lamming; one *Educ:* Westminster Sch.; Grenoble Univ.; National Coll. of Food Technol. Commn Royal Scots Fusiliers, 1951; seconded Parachute Regt; transf. when perm. officer cad formed; Major 1956; 10th Bn Parachute Regt TA, 1960. Gen. Man., Payne & Sc (Butchers) Ltd, 1960; Asst Gen. Man., J. H. Dewhurst Ltd, 1965, Gen. Man. 1969, Ma Dir, 1976–90; Dir of External Affairs, Vestey Gp, 1990–92; Dir, Airborne Initiativ Holdings Ltd, 1991–93; Chm., NAAFI, 1993–96 (non-exec. Dir, 1984–96); Directo Longhurst Housing Assoc., 1996–2001; Longhurst Gp, 2000–02 (Chm., Audit Ctte 2000–02). Trustee, Western United Gp Pension Scheme, 1986–. Chairman: Reta Consortium Food Cttee, 1973–74; Multiple Shops Fedn, 1977–78; Vice-Chairma Multiple Food Retailers Assoc., 1972–74; Retail Consortium, 1982–88 (Vice-Pres 1990–92); Pres., British Retailers Assoc., 1984–89 (Vice Pres., 1978–84); Dep. Chn Meat Promotion Exec., 1975–78; Vice Pres., Bd of Admin, CECD (European Retailers

1986–88 (Mem., 1981–85); Gov., Coll. for Distributive Trades, 1976–79 (Vice Chm.), 1984–88. Member: EDC for Distrib. Trades, 1972–80; Council and Management Cttee, Inst. of Meat (Vice-Chm., 1981–83); Cttee of Commerce and Distribn, EEC, 1984–93; Council, Industry & Parlt Trust, 1987–93. Chm. Council, Westminster Sch. Soc., 1999–2007 (Mem., 1990–2008). Vice Pres., Royal Smithfield Club, 1991– (Mem. Council, 1993–95). Gov., Court of London Inst., 1984–87 and 1989–90; Exec. Trustee, Airborne Assault Normandy Trust, 1983–2004; Chm., Reserve Forces Ulysses Trust, 1992–96; Member: Regtl Council, Parachute Regt, 1991–97; Lincoln Diocese Trust and Bd of Finances, 1993–2001 (Chm. Resources Cttee, 1994–96). FInstD 1979; CCMI (CBIM 1984); FRSA 1987. Liveryman, Butchers' Co. (Mem. Court, 1992–2007; Warden, 1998–2003; Providitor, 2002–03; Master, 2004–05). DL Lincs, 1998. Gold Medal: Inst. of Meat, 1956; Butchers' Co., 1956. OStJ 1988. *Address:* 20 Minster Yard, Lincoln LN2 1PY. *T:* (01522) 569581, *Fax:* (01522) 524205; *e-mail:* colincullimore@yahoo.co.uk. *Club:* Farmers'.

CULLINAN, Edward Horder, CBE 1987; RA 1991 (ARA 1989); Chairman, Edward Cullinan Architects Ltd, since 1989 (Founder, 1965, and Senior Partner, 1965–89, Edward Cullinan Architects); *b* 17 July 1931; *s* of Dr Edward Cullinan and Joy (*née* Horder); *m* 1961, Rosalind Yeates; one *s* two *d. Educ:* Ampleforth Coll.; Cambridge Univ. (Anderson and Webb Schol., 1951; BA); Univ. of California at Berkeley (George VI Meml Fellow, 1956). AADip; RIBA. With Denys Lasdun, 1958–65. Bannister Fletcher Prof., UCL, 1978–79; Graham Willis Prof., Univ. of Sheffield, 1985–87; George Simpson Prof., Univ. of Edinburgh, 1987–90. Mem., Royal Fine Art Commn, 1996–99. Designed and built: Horder House, Hampshire, 1959–60; Minster Lovell Mill, 1969–72; Parish Ch. of St Mary, Barnes, 1978–84; Lambeth Community Care Centre, 1979–84; RMC Internat. HQ, 1985–90; Fountains Abbey visitor centre and landscape, 1987–92; Archeolink Visitor Centre, Oyne, Aberdeenshire, 1994–97; Faculty of Divinity, 1995–2000, Centre for Mathematical Scis, 1996–2002, Cambridge Univ.; Univ. of East London, 1997–99; Downland Gridshell, Weald and Downland Open Air Mus., 1997–2002; Greenwich Millennium Sch. and Health Centre, 1998–2001; Singapore Mgt Univ., 2000–; Masterplans: Univ. of N Carolina, 1996; Bristol Harbourside, 2000–; St Austell Town Centre, 2002–; all have received awards and been published internationally. FRSA 1984; Hon. FRIAS 1995. Royal Gold Medal, RIBA, 2008. *Publications:* Edward Cullinan, Architects, 1984; (with K. Powell) Edward Cullinan, Architects, 1995; contribs to many architectural jls. *Recreations:* horticulture, travel, building, history, geography. *Address:* 1 Baldwin Terrace, N1 7RU. *T:* (020) 7704 1975.

CULLINGFORD, Eric Coome Maynard, CMG 1963; *b* 15 March 1910; *s* of Francis James and Lilian Mabel Cullingford; *m* 1938, Friedel Fuchs (*d* 2003); two *s* one *d. Educ:* City of London Sch.; St Catharine's Coll., Cambridge (Exhibitioner). Entered Ministry of Labour as Third Class Officer, 1932; Principal, 1942. Served with Manpower Div. of CCG, 1946–50. Asst Sec., Min. of Labour, 1954. Labour Attaché, Bonn, 1961–65, 1968–72. Regional Controller, Eastern and Southern Region, Dept of Employment and Productivity, 1966–68; retired 1973. *Publications:* Trade Unions in West Germany, 1976; Pirates of Shearwater Island, 1983. *Address:* The Chace Rest Home, Chase Road, Upper Welland, Worcs WR14 4JY.

CULLIS, Prof. Anthony George, DPhil, DSc; FRS 2004; Professor of Semiconductor Nanocharacterisation (formerly of Electronic and Electrical Engineering), University of Sheffield, since 1995; *b* 16 Jan. 1946; *s* of late George Thomas Cullis and Doris Mary Cullis; *m* 1979, Ruth Edith Allen; one *s* one *d. Educ:* Royal Grammar Sch., Worcester; Wadham Coll., Oxford (MA, DPhil, DSc). Mem. Tech. Staff, Bell Labs, Murray Hill, USA, 1972–75; posts to SPSO (Individual Merit), DERA/QinetiQ, Malvern, 1975–95. Chairman: Electron Microscopy and Analysis Gp, Inst. of Physics, 1980–82; Wkg Party on Transient Annealing, DoI, 1981–84; SERC MSEC Instrumentation Panel, 1988–93; Mem., Functional Materials Coll., EPSRC, 1997–. Pres., Scientific Council, TASC Italian Nat. Lab., Trieste, 2001–03. Ed., Procs vols for Microscopy of Semiconducting Materials internat. conf. series, 1979–; Co-ordinating Ed., Materials Sci. and Engrg Reports, 1994–. Holliday Award, IMMM, 1984. *Publications:* numerous refereed scientific papers in learned jls and other media. *Recreations:* philately, armchair archaeology, motoring. *Address:* Department of Electronic and Electrical Engineering, University of Sheffield, Mappin Street, Sheffield S1 3JD. *T:* (0114) 222 5407, *Fax:* (0114) 272 6391; *e-mail:* a.g.cullis@sheffield.ac.uk.

CULLIS, Prof. Charles Fowler; Professor of Physical Chemistry, City University, 1967–84, now Emeritus (Head, Chemistry Department, 1973–84; Pro-Vice-Chancellor, 1980–84; Saddlers' Research Professor, 1984–87; Leverhulme Emeritus Research Fellow, 1987–89); *b* 31 Aug. 1922; 2nd *s* of late Prof. C. G. Cullis, Prof. of Mining Geology, Univ. of London, and Mrs W. J. Cullis (*née* Fowler); *m* 1958, Marjorie Elizabeth, *er d* of late Sir Austin and Lady Anderson; two *s* two *d. Educ:* Stowe Sch. (Open Schol.); Trinity Coll., Oxford. BA 1944, BSc 1st Cl. Hons Chem. 1945, DPhil 1948, MA 1948, DSc 1960; FRSC (FRIC 1958); FRSA. ICI Research Fellow in Chem., Oxford, 1947–50; Lectr in Phys. Chem., Imperial Coll., London, 1950–59; Sen. Lectr in Chem. Engrg and Chem. Tech., Imperial Coll., 1959–64; Reader in Combustion Chemistry, Univ. of London, 1964–66. Vis. Prof., College of Chem., Univ. of California, Berkeley, 1966; Vis. Scientist, CSIRO, Sydney, 1970. Mem. Council, Chem. Soc., 1969–72, 1975–78; Hon. Sec., Brit. Sect. of Combustion Inst., 1969–74; Mem., Rockets Sub-cttee, 1968–73, and of Combustion Sub-cttee, 1969–72, Aeronautical Research Council; Member: Navy Dept Fuels and Lubricants Adv. Cttee (Fire and Explosion Hazards Working Gp), 1967–83; Safety in Mines Research Adv. Bd, 1973–88 (Chm., 1980–88); Chem. Cttee, Defence Sci. Adv. Council, 1979–82; Chem. Bd, 1982–87, Phys. Sci. Cttee, 1987–89, CNAA. Scientific Editor, Internat. Union of Pure and Applied Chem., 1976–78. Non-exec. Dir, City Technology Ltd, 1977–91. Mem., Mid Sussex DC, 1986–95. Mem. Council, Sussex Univ., 1993–95; Governor, City of London Polytechnic, 1982–84. Trustee, Sino-British Fellowship Trust, 1992–2002. Freeman, City of London, 1983; Liveryman, Bakers' Co., 1983. Joseph Priestley Award, 1974, Combustion Chem. Medal and Award, 1978, Chem. Soc. *Publications:* The Combustion of Organic Polymers (jtly with M. M. Hirschler), 1981; numerous sci. papers in Proc. Royal Soc., Trans Faraday Soc., Jl Chem. Soc., etc, mainly concerned with chemistry of combustion reactions. *Recreations:* music, travel. *Address:* Quinces, Courtmead Road, Cuckfield, W Sussex RH17 5LP. *T:* (01444) 453513. *Club:* Athenæum.

CULLOTY, James Hugh; jockey, retired 2005; *b* 18 Dec. 1973; *s* of Donal and Maureen Culloty; *m* 2004, Susannah Samworth; one *s* one *d. Educ:* St Brendan's Coll., Killarney. Stable jockey to Miss Henrietta Knight, 1996–2005; winner: Grand National, on Bindaree, 2002; Cheltenham Gold Cup, on Best Mate, 2002, 2003, 2004; Irish Grand National, on Timbera, 2003. *Recreations:* golf, farming. *Address:* Mount Corbitt, Churchtown, Mallow, Co. Cork, Ireland. *T:* (22) 49776.

CULME-SEYMOUR, Sir Michael Patrick; *see* Seymour.

CULPIN, Sir Robert (Paul), Kt 2001; Managing Director, Budget and Public Finances, HM Treasury, 1998–2003. *Educ:* Christ's Coll., Cambridge (BA 1968); Harvard Univ.; California Univ. HM Treasury, 1965–2003; Press Sec. and Hd of Information, 1984–87; Under-Sec., Fiscal Policy Div., 1987–93; Dep. Sec., Public Finance, 1993–94; Second Permanent Sec., 1994; Dir, Public Expenditure, then Public Spending, 1994–98. *Address:* c/o HM Treasury, 1 Horse Guards Road, SW1A 2HQ.

CULSHAW, John Douglas; Assistant Chief Scientific Adviser (Capabilities), Ministry of Defence, 1985–87; *b* 22 Oct. 1927; *s* of Alfred Henry Douglas Culshaw and Dorothy Yeats Culshaw (*née* Hogarth); *m* 1951, Hazel Speirs Alexander (*d* 1998); one *s* one *d. Educ:* Washington Alderman Smith Grammar Sch., Co. Durham; University Coll., Nottingham. BSc London 1949; MSc Nottingham 1950. Joined Weapons Dept, Royal Aircraft Estabt, Min. of Supply, Farnborough, 1950; OC (Scientific) 6 Joint Services Trials Unit RAF (UK), 1956; OC (Sci.) 16 JSTU RA Weapons Research Estabt, Salisbury, S Australia, 1961; Co-ordinating Research and Development Authority Technical Project Officer, RAE, 1964; Supt Mine Warfare Br., Royal Armament R&D Estabt, MoD, Sevenoaks, 1967; Director, Scientific Adv. Br., Home Office, 1970; Dept of Chief Scientific Adviser (Army), 1972; Head of Mathematics and Assessment Dept, RARDE, MoD, Sevenoaks, 1974; Head of Defence Science II, MoD, 1975; RCDS 1976; Dep. Dir, Scientific and Technical Intelligence, 1977; Dir, Defence Operational Analysis Estabt and Asst Chief Scientific Advr (Studies), MoD, 1979–84. *Recreation:* historical research. *Club:* Civil Service.

CULSHAW, Robert Nicholas, MVO 1979; Deputy Director, British Antarctic Survey, since 2006; HM Diplomatic Service, retired; *b* 22 Dec. 1952; *s* of late Ivan Culshaw and of Edith Marjorie Jose Barnard; *m* 1977, Elaine Ritchie Clegg; one *s. Educ:* University Coll. Sch., Hampstead; King's Coll., Cambridge (BA 1st Cl. Hons Classics 1974; Major Univ. Scholarship for Classics, 1974; MA 1977). FCO, 1974–75; MECAS, Lebanon and Jordan, 1975–77; 3rd Sec., Muscat, 1977–79; 2nd Sec., Khartoum, 1979–80; 1st Sec., Rome, 1980–84; FCO, 1984–88; Head of Chancery, 1988–90, Dep. Hd of Mission and Consul-Gen., 1991–93, Athens; FCO Spokesman and Hd of News Dept, 1993–95; Minister-Counsellor (Trade and Transport), Washington, 1995–99; Consul Gen., Chicago, 1999–2003; Dir, Americas and Overseas Territories, FCO, 2003–05. Churchill Fellow, Westminster Coll., Fulton, 2001. Mem. Bd, Friends of Leonard Cheshire, 1998–2005; Trustee, Lady Ryder of Warsaw Foundn, 2007–. Mem., Cambridge Univ. Music Soc., 2005–. MCIL (MIL 2004); FRSA 1995; FRGS 2007. *Recreations:* ski-ing, singing, poetry, languages, nostalgia. *Address:* Piney Lodge, 66 Cow Lane, Fulbourn, Cambridge CB21 5HB.

CULVER, John Howard, LVO 2000; HM Diplomatic Service, retired; *b* 17 July 1947; *s* of late Frank and Peggy Culver; *m* 1973, Margaret Ann Davis; two *s* one *d.* Entered FO, 1968; Moscow, 1974–76; La Paz, 1977–80; FCO, 1980–83; Rome, 1983–87; Head of Chancery, Dhaka, 1987–90; FCO, 1990–92; Ambassador to Nicaragua, 1992–97; Consul-General, Naples, 1997–99; Rome, 2000; Ambassador to Iceland, 2001–04; Hd of Resources, Europe Directorate-Gen., FCO, 2004–05; Chargé d'Affaires *ai*, Holy See, 2005. *Address:* *e-mail:* john@theculvers.com.

CULYER, Prof. Anthony John, CBE 1999; Professor of Economics, University of York, since 1979, on leave of absence, 2003–06 (Director of Health Development, 1997–2001); Chief Scientist, Institute for Work and Health, Toronto, 2003–06; Professor of Health Policy and System Design, University of Toronto, since 2007; *b* 1 July 1942; *s* of late Thomas Reginald Culyer and Betty Ely (*née* Headland); *m* 1966, Sieglinde Birgit; one *s* one *d. Educ:* King's Sch., Worcester; Exeter Univ. (BA Hons); Univ. of California at Los Angeles. Tutor and Asst Lectr, Exeter Univ., 1965–69; York University: Lectr, Sen. Lectr and Reader, 1969–79; Dep. Dir, Inst. of Social and Economic Research, 1971–82; Hd, Dept of Econs and Related Studies, 1986–2001; Pro-Vice-Chancellor, 1991–94; Dep. Vice-Chancellor, 1994–97. University of Toronto: Status-only Prof., 1989–2001 and Adjunct Prof., 2003–07. Sen. Research Associate, Ontario Economic Council, 1976, Vis. Professorial Lectr, Queen's Univ., Kingston, 1976; William Evans Vis. Professor, Otago Univ., 1979; Vis. Fellow, Australian National Univ., 1979; Visiting Professor: Trent Univ., 1985–86; Inst. für Med. Informatik und Systemforschung, Munich, 1990–91; Toronto Univ., 1991; Central Inst. of Technology, NZ, 1996. Lectures: Woodward, Univ. of BC, 1986; Perey, McMaster Univ., and Champlain, Trent Univ., Canada, 1990; Francis Fraser, BPMF, 1994; Sinclair, Queen's Univ., Kingston, 2005. Member: Standing Cttee, Conf. of Heads of Univ. Depts of Econs, 1988–2001; Coll. Cttee, King's Fund Coll., London, 1989–92; Res. Adv. Cttee, 1990–2002, Sci. Adv. Cttee, 2002–03 (Sen. Scientist, 2006–07), Inst. for Work and Health, Toronto; Adv. Cttee for Centre for Health and Society, UCL, 1992–99; Rev. Adv. Cttee on London SHAs, 1992–93; Adv. Cttee, Canadian Inst. for Advanced Res., 1992–2002; Future Health Care Options Wkg Pty, IHSM, 1992–93; British Council Health Adv. Cttee, 1995–97; Academic Adv. Council, Univ. of Buckingham, 1996–2004; Chm., Res. Adv. Council, Workers' Safety and Insurance Bd, Ontario, 2006–08; Vice Chm., Nat. Inst. for Clinical Excellence, 1999–2003. Royal School of Church Music: Chm., York Dist, 1984–95, NE Yorks Area, 1995–2003; Mem. Adv. Bd, 2002–; Mem. Council, and Trustee, 2003–. Mem., 1982–90, non-exec. Mem., 1990–92, Northallerton HA; Dep. Chm., N Yorks HA, 1995–99 (non-exec. Mem., 1994–99); Member: Yorks RHA R&D Cttee, 1992–94; Northern and Yorks Regl R&D Adv. Cttee, 1995–; Central R&D Cttee, NHS, 1991–2001; NHS Standing Gp on Health Technol., 1992–97; R&D Cttee of High Security Psychiatric Hosps Commissioning Bd, 1995–99; Chair: Methodology Panel, NHS Standing Gp on Health Technol., 1993–97; NHS Task Force on Supporting R&D in NHS, 1994; Advr to NHS Dir of R&D, 1997–99; Chm., R&D Cttee, NICE, 2007–. Chm., Office of Health Econs, 2001– (Chm., Editl Bd, 1997–); Mem., Economics Adv. Panel, Home Office, 2005–; Special Advr, Canada Health Council, 2005–; Sen. Economic Advr, Cancer Care Ontario, 2006–07. Trustee, Canadian Health Services Res. Foundn, 2000–03. Pres., Econs Section, BAAS, 1994. Founder FMedSci 1998. Co-Editor, Jl of Health Econs, 1982–; Member, Editorial Board: Econ. Rev., 1983–; Med. Law Internat., 1992–; BMJ, 1995–2000; Mem. Managing Cttee, Jl of Med. Ethics, 1994–2001. Hon. DEc Stockholm Sch. of Econs, 1999. *Publications:* The Economics of Social Policy, 1973; (ed with M. H. Cooper) Health Economics, 1973; (ed) Economic Policies and Social Goals, 1974; Need and the National Health Service, 1976; (with J. Wiseman and A. Walker) Annotated Bibliography of Health Economics, 1977; (ed with V. Halberstadt) Human Resources and Public Finance, 1977; Measuring Health: Lessons for Ontario, 1978; (ed with K. G. Wright) Economic Aspects of Health Services, 1978; The Political Economy of Social Policy, 1980; (ed) Health Indicators, 1983; (ed with B. Horisberger) Economic and Medical Evaluation of Health Care Technologies, 1983; Economics, 1985; (ed with G. Terny) Public Finance and Social Policy, 1985; (ed with B. Jonsson) Public and Private Health Services: complementarities and conflicts, 1986; (jtly) The International Bibliography of Health Economics: a comprehensive annotated guide to English language sources since 1914, 1986; Canadian Health Care Expenditures: myth and reality, past and future, 1988; (ed) Standards for the Socio-economic Evaluation of Health Care Products and Services, 1990; (ed jtly) Competition in Health Care: reforming the NHS, 1990; (ed) The Economics of Health, 1991; (ed jtly) Some Recent Developments in Health Economics, 1992; (ed jtly) Swedish Health Care: the best in the world?, 1993; (ed jtly) Reforming Health Care Systems: experiments with the NHS, 1996; (ed jtly)

Being Reasonable about the Economics of Health: selected essays by Alan Williams, 1997; (ed jtly) Handbook of Health Economics, 2001; The Dictionary of Health Economics, 2005; articles in Oxford Econ. Papers, Economica, Scottish Jl of Political Economy, Public Finance, Jl of Public Economics, Kyklos, Qly Jl of Economics, Jl Royal Statistical Soc., Jl of Health Economics, Health Econs, BMJ, Jl Med Ethics, and others. *Recreation:* church music (Organist and Choir Director, St Catherine's, Barmby Moor, 1971–2003). *Address:* Department of Economics and Related Studies, University of York, York YO10 5DD.

CUMANI, Luca Matteo; racehorse trainer; *b* 7 April 1949; *s* of Sergio Cumani and Elena Cardini Cumani; *m* 1979, Sara Doon Plunket; one *s* one *d. Educ:* Milan. Riding career: 85 winners in Italy, France and UK; champion amateur, Italy, 1972; won Moët and Chandon on Meissen, 1972; Prix Paul Noël de la Houtre on Harland, 1970, 1972, 1973; Asst to Sergio Cumani and to H. R. A. Cecil, 1974–75; first held licence, 1976; numerous major races won, incl. St Leger (Commanche Run), 1984; Derby and Irish Sweeps Derby, 1988 (Kahyasi); Breeders Cup Mile, 1994 (Barathea); Derby, 1998 (High Rise); Coral Eclipse Stakes, Sandown, 2003 (Falbrav); Juddmonte Internat. Stakes, 2003 (Falbrav); Queen Elizabeth II Stakes, Ascot, 2003 (Falbrav); Prix du Moulin, Longchamp, 2005 (Starcraft); Japan Cup, 2005 (Alkaased). *Address:* Bedford House Stables, Bury Road, Newmarket, Suffolk CB8 7BX. *T:* (01638) 665432.

CUMBERLEGE, family name of **Baroness Cumberlege**.

CUMBERLEGE, Baroness *cr* 1990 (Life Peer), of Newick in the County of East Sussex; **Julia Frances Cumberlege,** CBE 1985; FRCP, FRCGP; Founder and Director, Cumberlege Connections Ltd, since 2001; Director, Assuring Better Practice (UK) Ltd, 2004–07; Associate, Quo Health, 2001–05; *b* 27 Jan. 1943; *d* of late Dr L. U. Camm and M. G. G. Camm; *m* 1961, Patrick Francis Howard Cumberlege; three *s. Educ:* Convent of the Sacred Heart, Tunbridge Wells. FRCP 2007; FRCGP 2007. Mem., East Sussex AHA, 1977–81; Chairman: Brighton HA, 1981–88; SW Thames RHA, 1988–92; Mem. Council, NAHA, 1982–88 (Vice-Chm., 1984–87; Chm., 1987–88). Member (C): Lewes DC, 1966–79 (Leader, 1977–78); East Sussex CC, 1974–85 (Chm., Social Services Cttee, 1979–82). Chairman: Review of Community Nursing for England, 1985 (report, Neighbourhood Nursing—a focus for care, 1986); Expert Maternity Gp, 1993 (report, Changing Childbirth, 1993). Member: Social Security Adv. Cttee, 1980–82; DHSS Expert Adv. Gp on AIDS, 1987–89; Council, UK Central Council for Nursing, Midwifery and Health Visiting, 1989–92; NHS Policy Bd, 1989–97. Parly Under-Sec. of State, DoH, 1992–97; Co-Chm., Associate Parly Health Gp, 2001–; Jt Chm., All Party Parly Osteoporosis Gp, 2000–; Jt Vice-Chm., All Party Parly Gp on Maternity, 2000–. Exec. Dir, MJM Healthcare Solutions, 1997–2001; Dir, Huntsworth plc, 2001–03. Chairman: AMRC, 2007–; Adv. Bd, Humana Europe. Lay Mem., 1977–83, Mem. Appts Commn, 1984–90, Press Council. Vice President: RCN, 1989–; Royal Coll. of Midwives, 2001–; Pres., Age Concern, E Sussex, 1995–; Mem. Council, ICRF, subseq. Cancer Res. UK, 1998–2007; Trustee: Princess Royal Trust for Carers, 1992–93; Life Education Centres, 1997–99; Patron: Nat. Childbirth Trust; Assoc. for Nurse Prescribing. Sen. Associate, King's Fund. Member Council: Brighton Poly., 1987–89; Univ. of Sussex, 2001–; Chm. Trustees, Chailey Heritage Sch., 1997– (Governor, 1982–88); Chm. Council, St George's, Univ. of London (formerly St George's Hosp. Med. Sch.), 2000–; Trustee, Leeds Castle Foundn, 2005–. Governor: Chailey Comprehensive Sch., 1972–86; Ringmer Comprehensive Sch., 1979–85; Newick Primary Sch., 1977–85. Founder: Newick Playgp; Newick Youth Club. FRSA 1989. DL 1986, Vice Lord-Lieut, 1992, E Sussex; JP East Sussex, 1973–85. DUniv: Surrey, 1990; Brighton, 1994. *Recreations:* bicycling, other people's gardens. *Address:* Snells Cottage, The Green, Newick, Lewes, East Sussex BN8 4LA. *T:* (01825) 722154, *Fax:* (01825) 723873. *Club:* Royal Society of Medicine.

CUMING, Frederick George Rees, RA 1974 (ARA 1969); ARCA 1954; NDD 1948; NEAC 1960; painter; *b* 16 Feb. 1930; *m* 1962, Audrey Lee Cuming; one *s* one *d. Educ:* University School, Bexley Heath; Sidcup Art School; Royal College of Art; travelling schol., Italy. Exhibns in Redfern, Walker, New Grafton, Thackeray, Fieldborne Galleries; Group shows at NEAC, RA, Schools' Exhibn, John Moores London Group; One Man exhibns at Thackeray Gall., galls in Chichester, Lewes, Eastbourne, Guildford, Durham, Chester, Folkstone, Canterbury, New York; featured artist, RA Summer Exhibn, 2001; works in collections: DoE; Treasury; Chantrey Bequest; RA; Kendal Mus.; Scunthorpe Mus.; Bradford; Carlisle; Nat. Mus. of Wales; Brighton and Hove Mus.; Maidstone Mus.; Towner Gall., Eastbourne; Monte Carlo Mus.; St John's Coll., Oxford; Worcester Coll., Oxford; Faringdon Trust, Oxon; ITV collection; Southend Mus.; Preston Mus.; Nat. Trust collection; Baring's Bank; Lloyd's; Guinness collection; W. H. Smith; Nat. Portrait Gall.; City private collections; works in galls in America, Argentina, Canada, Chile, France, Germany, Greece, Holland, Hong Kong and S Africa. Hon. ROI 1992; Hon. RBA. Hon. DLitt Kent, 2004. Grand Prix, Art Contemporaine, Monte Carlo. *Publication:* Figure in a Landscape, 2002. *Address:* The Gables, Wittersham Road, Iden, near Rye, E Sussex TN31 7UY. *T:* (01797) 280322.

CUMMING, Alexander James; Chief Executive (formerly Project Director), IMMPACT (Initiative for Maternal Mortality Project), since 2004; *b* 7 March 1947; *s* of Alexander George Cumming and Jean Campbell (*née* McWilliam); *m* 1973, Margaret Ada Callan; one *s* two *d. Educ:* Fordyce Acad., Banffshire; Robert Gordon's Coll., Aberdeen; Univ. of Aberdeen (MA). Mem., CIMA; IPFA. Volunteer teacher, VSO, India, 1968–70; Trainee Accountant, Wiggins Teape, Papermakers, 1970–72; Company Sec., Glen Gordon Ltd, Aberdeen, 1972–74; Chief Accountant, BOC Offshore, 1974–75; Accountant, then Dir of Finance, Grampian Health Bd., 1975–93; Actg Dir of Finance, Mgt Exec., Scottish Health Service, 1994; Chief Exec., Acute Services Div., NHS Grampian (formerly Aberdeen Royal Hosps, later Grampian Univ. Hosps NHS Trust), 1994–2004. Chm., Langstane Housing Assoc., 1997–2002 (Hon. Treas., 1984–97). *Recreations:* music, literature, history, the outdoors. *Address:* (office) IMMPACT, Medical School, University of Aberdeen, Foresterhill, Aberdeen AB25 2ZY.

CUMMING, Sir Alexander Penrose G.; *see* Gordon Cumming.

CUMMING, Maj.-Gen. Andrew Alexander John Rennie, CBE 1993; Controller, Soldiers, Sailors, Airmen and Families Association—Forces Help, since 2004; *b* 12 March 1948; *s* of Donald Alexander Cumming and Evelyn Julia (*née* Rennie); *m* 1979, Gilly Thompson; three *d. Educ:* Hawtreys Prep. Sch.; Bradfield Coll.; Army Staff Coll. In command 17th/21st Lancers, 1988–90; hcsc 1992; Commander: 20 Armd Bde, 1992; 11 Armd Bde/British Forces, Croatia and Bosnia-Herzegovina, 1992–93; ACOS Ops, HQ LAND, 1993–95; Chief Jt Ops Centre, Intervention Force (IFOR), 1995–96; Comdr, Initial Trng Gp, 1996–99; Comdr, Land Warfare Centre, 1999–2002; UK Co-ordinator, Kosovo Protection Corps, 2002–04. Col, Queen's Royal Lancers, 2006–. Dir, Wincanton Race Course, 2004–. *Recreations:* field sports, racing, walking, sailing, ski-ing, reading. *Address: e-mail:* aajrc@tiscali.co.uk. *Club:* Cavalry and Guards.

CUMMING, Valerie Lynn, FMA; writer and lecturer; Deputy Director, Museum of London, 1988–97; *b* 11 Oct. 1946; *d* of late John Gunson Carter and Edna Ruth Carter (*née* Willis); *m* 1972, John Lawrence Cumming. *Educ:* Abbey Sch., Reading; Univ. of Leicester (BA); Courtauld Inst. of Art (Courtauld Cert. in History of Dress). Admin. trainee, Univ. of Surrey, 1968–69; Asst, Chertsey Mus., 1971–73; Res. Asst, 1973–75, Sen. Asst Keeper, 1975–78, Mus. of London; Curator, Court Dress Collection, Kensington Palace, 1978–81; Asst Dir, Mus. of London, 1981–88. Trustee: Olive Matthews Collection, Chertsey Mus., Surrey, 1983– (Chm., 2003–); Costume Soc., 2001–04 (Chm., 2004–). Curatorial advr, Chartered Insurance Inst., 1991–98. Vis. Lectr, 1997 and 2007, External Examnr, 2003–06, Courtauld Inst. of Art. *Publications:* Exploring Costume History 1500–1900, 1981; Gloves, 1982; A Visual History of Costume: the Seventeenth Century, 1984; (with Aileen Ribeiro) The Visual History of Costume, 1989; Royal Dress, 1989; The Visual History of Accessories, 1998; Understanding Fashion History, 2004; contributed to: Tradescant's Rarities, 1983; The Late King's Goods, 1989; London—World City 1800–1840, 1992; The Oxford Companion to the Body, 2001; The Oxford Encyclopedia of Theatre and Performance, 2003; City Merchants and the Arts 1670–1720, 2004. *Recreations:* gardening, watching cricket. *Address:* 7 Frere Street, SW11 2JA. *T:* (020) 7223 1380.

CUMMINGS, Brian; QC 2008; a Recorder, since 2005; *b* Belfast, 10 April 1965; *s* of late Wilbur Cummings and of Shirley Cummings (*née* Drum). *Educ:* Trinity Coll., Cambridge (BA 1987). Called to the Bar, Lincoln's Inn, 1988; in practice at the Bar, Liverpool, 1989–. *Recreations:* cycling, hill-walking/mountaineering, cricket, foreign travel, the Falkland Islands, foreign languages, reading. *Address:* Exchange Chambers, Pearl Assurance House, Derby Square, Liverpool L2 9XX. *T:* (0151) 236 7747, *Fax:* (0151) 236 3433; *e-mail:* cummingsqc@exchangechambers.co.uk.

CUMMINGS, John Scott; MP (Lab) Easington, since 1987; *b* 6 July 1943; *s* of late George Scott Cummings and Mary (*née* Cain); unmarried. *Educ:* Murton Council Infants, Jun. and Sen. Schs; Easington Technical Coll. Colliery apprentice electrician, 1958–63, colliery electrician, 1963–87, Murton Colliery. Vice-Chm., Coalfields Community Campaign, 1985–87; Member: Northumbrian Water Authority, 1977–83; Aycliffe and Peterlee Develt Corp., 1980–87; Easington RDC, 1970–73; Easington DC, 1973–87 (Chm., 1975–76; Leader, 1979–87). Member: Envmt, Transport and Regions Select Cttee, 1997–2001; ODPM Select Cttee, 2002–; Speaker's Panel of Chairmen, 2000–; Chm., All-Party Czech and Slovak Gp, 1997–; Vice-Chm., All-Party Aluminium Gp, 1999. Mem., Council of Europe, 1992–97. Hon. Parliamentary Adviser: Nat. Assoc. of Councillors; Nat. Assoc. of Licenced House Managers. *Recreations:* Jack Russell terriers, walking, travel. *Address:* (home) 18 Grasmere Terrace, Murton, Seaham, Co. Durham SR7 9NU. *T:* (0191) 526 1142; (constituency) Seaton Holme, Hall Walks, Easington Village, Peterlee, Co. Durham SR8 3BS. *T:* (0191) 527 3773, *Fax:* (0191) 527 9640; House of Commons, SW1A 0AA. *T:* (020) 7219 5122. *Clubs:* Murton Victoria, Democratic, Ex-Servicesman's (Murton); Peterlee Labour; Thornley Catholic.

CUMMINGS, Prof. Keith Richard; Professor of Glass Studies, School of Art and Design, University of Wolverhampton, since 1991; *b* 15 July 1940; *s* of Henry Gordon Cummings and Kathleen Cummings; *m* 1963, Pamela Anne Cornall; two *s. Educ:* Univ. of Durham (BA Hons Fine Art). Sen. Lectr in Glass, Stourbridge Coll. of Art, 1967–85; Tutor, Sch. of Ceramics and Glass, RCA, 1986–89; Principal Lectr, Sch. of Art and Design, Univ. of Wolverhampton, 1989–94. Work exhibited in nat. and internat. collections, incl. V&A, Mus. of Decorative Art, Paris. *Publications:* Techniques of Glassforming, 1980; Techniques of Kiln-Formed Glass, 1997, 3rd edn 2007; A History of Glassforming, 2002. *Recreations:* reading, gardening, table-tennis. *Address:* School of Art and Design, University of Wolverhampton, Molineux Street, Wolverhampton WV1 1SB; *e-mail:* K.R.Cummings@wlv.ac.uk.

CUMMINGS, Laurence Alexander, FRCO; harpsichordist and conductor; Head, Historical Performance, Royal Academy of Music, since 1997; Musical Director: London Handel Society, since 2002; Tilford Bach Society, since 2002; *b* 25 May 1968; *s* of Geoffrey Victor and Maureen Cummings. *Educ:* Christ Church, Oxford (MA); Royal Coll. of Music (ARCM). FRCO 1985. Freelance harpsichordist, 1989–. Conductor: Hallé Orch., 2004; ENO (Semele, 2004); Glyndebourne Fest. Opera (Giulio Cesare, 2005). Co-director: London Handel Fest., 1999–2002; Tilford Bach Fest., 1999–2002. Trustee, Handel House Mus., London, 2002–. Has made recordings. Hon. ARAM 2001. *Recreations:* travelling, reading, walking. *Address:* 81 Chetwynd Road, NW5 1DA. *T:* and *Fax:* (020) 7267 2760; *e-mail:* laurence@chetwynd.clara.co.uk.

CUMMINGS, Peter Joseph; Chief Executive, Corporate, HBOS plc, since 2006 (Director, since 2005); *b* Dumbarton, 19 July 1955; *m* 1978, Margaret Mary Docherty. *Educ:* St Patrick's High Sch., Dumbarton; Glasgow Coll. of Technol.; Univ. of Strathclyde (MBA). Joined Bank of Scotland, 1973; worked in branches in W of Scotland; Chief Manager, Glasgow Chief Office, 1982–85; Advances Manager, Corporate Div., 1985–90; Hd, Corporate Recovery, 1990–93; Regl Manager, N of England, 1993–95; Dir, Corporate Banking, Bank of Scotland, subseq. HBOS plc, 1995–2005; Dep. Chief Exec., Corporate, HBOS plc, 2005–06. Mem., Adv. Cttee, Edinburgh Univ. Business Sch., 2008–. Dir, Maggie's Cancer Care Centres, 2005–. FCIBS 2000. *Recreations:* scuba-diving, swimming, football, music. *Address:* HBOS plc, The Mound, Edinburgh EH1 1YZ. *T:* (0131) 243 7033, *Fax:* (0131) 243 5566; *e-mail:* peter_cummings@bankofscotland.co.uk. *Clubs:* Mark's, George.

CUMMINS, Gus, RA 1992; artist; *b* 28 Jan. 1943; *s* of Harold George Cummins and Honor Cecilia (*née* Bird); *m* 1968, Angela Braven; two *s* one *d. Educ:* Sutton and Wimbledon Schs of Art; RCA (NDD, MA). Part-time teacher at nine art schs and colls, 1969–; currently at RA schs. Exhibns, mainly in UK, also Norway, Holland, UAE and USA, 1980–; 7 solo exhibns, 1991–. Henry Moore Prize, London Gp, 1982; Spirit of London 2nd Prize, 1983; Daler-Rowney Prize, RA, 1987; Hunting Gp 1st Prize, Mall Gall., 1990, RCA, 1999; House & Garden Prize and Blackstone Award, RA Summer Show, 1992; RWS Prize, 2001; Jack Goldhill Sculpture Award, RA, 2005. *Recreations:* music, poetry, literature, swimming, cycling, pubs, snooker. *Address:* Harpsichord House, Cobourg Place, Hastings, Sussex TN34 3HY. *T:* (01424) 426429.

CUMMINS, Sir Michael (John Austin), Kt 2003; Serjeant at Arms, House of Commons, 2000–04; *b* 26 Nov. 1939; *s* of Harold Leslie Cummins and Florence Gladys Cummins (*née* Austin); *m* 1st, 1964, Mary Isobel Farman (marr. diss. 1995); two *s*; 2nd, 1995, Catherine Ellen Lamb; one step *d. Educ:* Queen Mary Sch.; RMA Sandhurst; psc. Commnd 3rd Carabiniers (POW DG), 1959; Royal Scots Dragoon Guards, 1971–81. Serjeant at Arms Dept, H of C, 1981–2004; Dep. Serjeant at Arms, 1995–99. Trustee Selwood Foundn, 1986–. *Publication:* (with Sir Peter Thorne) Serjeant for the Commons 1994, 2nd edn 1999. *Recreations:* equitation, gardening, tennis, tapestry. *Address:* 140A Ashley Gardens, Westminster SW1P 1HN. *Club:* Cavalry and Guards.

CUMPSTY, Prof. Nicholas Alexander, PhD, FREng; Professor of Mechanical Engineering, Imperial College, London, since 2005; *b* 13 Jan. 1943; *s* of Norman and Edith Cumpsty; *m* 1st, 1966, Annette Tischler (*d* 1982); one *s* one *d*; 2nd, 1983, Mary Cecily Hamer (*née* Turner); two step *d. Educ:* Haberdashers' Aske's Sch., Hampstead

Imperial Coll., London (BScEng 1964); Trinity Coll. and Peterhouse, Cambridge (PhD 1967; MA 1968). Post Office Student Apprentice, 1960–64; Peterhouse Research Fellow, 1966–69; Rolls-Royce, 1969–71; Cambridge University: Sen. Asst in Research, Lectr, then Reader, Dept of Engineering, 1972–89; Prof. of Aerothermal Technology, 1989–99; Fellow of Peterhouse, 1972–99, now Emeritus; Chief Technologist, Rolls-Royce plc, 2000–05. Hunsaker Vis. Prof., Dept of Aeronautics and Astronautics, MIT, 1991–92. Mem., Royal Commn on Envmtl Pollution, 2005–. Mem., Defence Scientific Adv. Council, 2005–. FREng (FEng 1995). *Publications:* Compressor Aerodynamics, 1989; Jet Propulsion, 1997; numerous papers on aerodynamics, esp. relating to jet engines. *Recreations:* reading, music, walking. *Address:* Imperial College, London, SW7 2AZ. *T:* (020) 7594 7032; *e-mail:* n.cumpsty@imperial.ac.uk.

CUNDY, Rt Rev. Ian Patrick Martyn; *see* Peterborough, Bishop of.

CUNINGHAME, Sir John Christopher Foggo M.; *see* Montgomery Cuninghame.

CUNINGHAME, Sir Robert Henry F.; *see* Fairlie-Cuninghame.

CUNLIFFE, family name of **Baron Cunliffe.**

CUNLIFFE, 3rd Baron *cr* 1914, of Headley; **Roger Cunliffe,** RIBA; MCMI; micro-landowner; *b* 12 Jan. 1932; *s* of 2nd Baron and Joan Catherine Lubbock (*d* 1980); *S* father, 1963; *m* 1957, Clemency Ann Hoare; two *s* one *d. Educ:* Eton; Trinity Coll., Cambridge (MA); Architectural Association (AA Dipl.); Open Univ. With various architectural firms in UK and USA, 1957–65; Associate, Robert Matthew, Johnson-Marshall & Partners, 1966–69; Dir, Architectural Assoc., 1969–71; Partner, SCP, 1973–78; own practice as architectural, planning and management consultant, 1977–2002; Dir, Exhibition Consultants Ltd, 1981–2004. Member: Urban Motorways Cttee, 1969–72; Council, British Consultants Bureau, 1986–90. Member: Council, Lancing Coll., 1967–85; Delegacy, Goldsmiths' Coll., 1972–78; Bd, Coll. of Estate Management, 1992–2006. Chm., Suffolk Craft Soc., 1994–97. Mem. Ct, Goldsmiths' Co., 1986– (Prime Warden, 1997). *Publications:* (with Leonard Manasseh) Office Buildings, 1962; (with Santa Raymond) Tomorrow's Office, 1996; contrib. various professional jls. *Recreations:* making pots and pottering, baking bread and loafing. *Heir: s* Hon. Henry Cunliffe [*b* 9 March 1962; *m* 2004, Mary Therese, *e d* of Richard Barrett, Minnesota]. *Address:* The Broadhurst, Brandeston, Woodbridge, Suffolk IP13 7AG.

CUNLIFFE, Sir Barrington Windsor, (Sir Barry), Kt 2006; CBE 1994; FBA 1979; FSA; Professor of European Archaeology, Oxford University, and Fellow of Keble College, 1972–2007; *b* 10 Dec. 1939. *Educ:* Portsmouth; St John's Coll., Cambridge (MA, PhD, LittD). Lecturer, Univ. of Bristol, 1963–66; Prof. of Archæology, Univ. of Southampton, 1966–72. O'Donnell Lectr in Celtic Studies, Oxford Univ., 1983–84. Member: Ancient Monuments Bd for England, 1976–84; Historic Bldgs and Monuments Commn for England, 1987–92 (Mem., Ancient Monuments Adv. Cttee, 1984–); Comr, English Heritage, 2006–. President: Council for British Archaeology, 1976–79; Soc. of Antiquaries, 1991–95 (Vice-Pres., 1982–86). Gov., Mus. of London, 1995–99; Trustee, British Mus., 2000–. Hon. DLitt Sussex, 1983; Hon. DSc Bath, 1984; DUniv. Open, 1995. *Publications:* Fishbourne, a Roman Palace and its Garden, 1971; Roman Bath Discovered, 1971, rev. edn 1984; The Cradle of England, 1972; The Making of the English, 1973; The Regni, 1973; Iron Age Communities in Britain, 1974, 4th edn 2005; Rome and the Barbarians, 1975; Hengistbury Head, 1978; Rome and her Empire, 1978; The Celtic World, 1979; Danebury: the anatomy of an Iron Age hillfort, 1984; The City of Bath, 1986; Greeks, Romans and Barbarians, 1988; Wessex before AD 1000, 1991; (ed) The Oxford Illustrated Prehistory of Europe, 1994; Iron Age Britain, 1995; The Ancient Celts, 1997; Facing the Ocean: the Atlantic and its peoples, 2001 (Wolfson History Prize, 2002); The Extraordinary Voyage of Pytheas the Greek, 2001; The Celts: a very short introduction, 2003; (ed) England's Landscape: the west, 2006; Europe Between the Oceans: 9000 BC to AD 1000, 2008; contribs to several major excavation reports and articles to Soc. of Antiquaries, and in other learned jls. *Recreation:* mild self-indulgence. *Address:* Institute of Archaeology, 36 Beaumont Street, Oxford OX1 2PG.

CUNLIFFE, Ven. Christopher John, DPhil; Archdeacon of Derby, since 2006; *b* 25 Sept. 1955; *s* of Joseph and Margaret Cunliffe; *m* 1979, Helen Margaret Ketley (*see* Ven. H. M. Cunliffe); two *s. Educ:* Charterhouse; Christ Church, Oxford (MA, DPhil 1981); Trinity Coll., Cambridge (MA 1986); Westcott House, Cambridge. ARHistS 1993. Ordained deacon, 1983, priest, 1984; Asst Curate, Chesterfield, 1983–85; Chaplain and Jun. Res. Fellow, Lincoln Coll., Oxford, 1985–89; Chaplain, City Univ. and Guildhall Sch. of Music and Drama, 1989–91; Selection Sec. and Vocations Officer, Adv. Bd of Ministry, 1991–96; Bp of London's Advr for Ordained Ministry, 1997–2003; Chaplain to Bp of Bradwell, 2004–06; Canon Residentiary, Derby Cathedral, 2006–08. Clerk, All Saints Educnl Trust, 2004. *Publication:* (ed) Joseph Butler's Moral and Religious Thought, 1992. *Recreations:* walking, reading, listening to music, watching sport. *Address:* Derby Church House, Full Street, Derby DE1 3DR. *T:* (01332) 388676, *Fax:* (01332) 292969; *e-mail:* archderby@derby.anglican.org.

CUNLIFFE, Sir David Ellis, 9th Bt *cr* 1759; business development manager; *b* 29 Oct. 1957; *s* of Sir Cyril Henley Cunliffe, 8th Bt and of Eileen Lady Cunliffe, *d* of Frederick William and Nora Anne Parkins; *S* father, 1969; *m* 1983, Linda Carol, *d* of John Sidney and Ella Mary Batchelor; three *d. Educ:* St Albans Grammar School. *Heir: b* Andrew Mark Cunliffe [*b* 17 April 1959; *m* 1980, Janice Elizabeth, *d* of Ronald William Kyle; one *s* three *d*].

CUNLIFFE, Ven. Helen Margaret; Archdeacon of St Albans, 2003–07; *b* 1954; *m* 1979, Ven. Christopher John Cunliffe, *qv*; two *s. Educ:* Homelands Sch., Derby; St Hilda's Coll., Oxford (BA 1977, MA 1978); Westcott House, Cambridge. Ordained deaconess, 1983, deacon, 1987, priest, 1994; Curate, St Mary and All Saints, Chesterfield, 1983–85; Dss, 1986–87, Parish Deacon, 1987–89, St Mary the Virgin with St Cross and St Peter, Oxford; Chaplain, Nuffield Coll., Oxford, 1986–89; Team Deacon, 1989–94, Team Vicar, 1994–96, Clapham Team Ministry; Residentiary Canon, Southwark Cathedral, 1996–2002; Diocesan Advr for Women in Ministry, Southwark, 1996–2002. Chaplain, Welcare, 1996–2002. *Recreations:* walking, gardening, watching football. *Address:* 1 Thatch Close, Derby DE22 1EA.

CUNLIFFE, Jonathan Stephen, CB 2001; Head of International Economic Affairs, Europe and G8 Sherpa, Prime Minister's Office, since 2007; *b* 2 June 1953; *s* of Ralph and Cynthia Cunliffe; *m* 1984, Naomi Brandler; two *d. Educ:* St Marylebone GS, London; Manchester Univ. (BA Eng. 1975; MA 1976). Lectr in English and Drama, Univ of Western Ontario, 1976–79; res. student, 1979–80; joined Civil Service, 1980; DoE, 1980–85; Department of Transport: Principal, 1985; Pvte Sec. to Sec. of State, 1985–88; Transport Industry Finance, 1988–90; HM Treasury: Asst Sec., Pay Gp, 1990–93; Internat. Financial Instns, and UK Alternate Dir, EBRD (on secondment), 1993–95; Debt and Reserves Mgt, 1995–97; Dep. Dir, Macroeconomic Policy and Prospects, 1997–98; Dep. Dir, then Dir, Internat. Finance, later Macroeconomic Policy and Internat. Finance, 1998–2001; Managing Director: Financial Regulation and Industry, 2001–02; Macroecon. Policy and Internat. Finance, 2002–05; Perm. Sec., Macroecon. Policy and Internat. Finance, subseq. Internat. and Finance, 2005–07. UK Alternate Mem., EU Monetary Cttee, 1996–98; UK Mem., EU Economic and Financial Cttee and G7 Treaty, 2002–. *Recreations:* tennis, cooking, walking. *Address:* 10 Downing Street, SW1A 2AA.

CUNLIFFE, Lawrence Francis; *b* 25 March 1929; *m* 1950, Winifred (marr. diss. 1985), *d* of William Haslem; three *s* two *d. Educ:* St Edmund's RC Sch., Worsley, Manchester. Engr, NCB, 1949–79. Member, Farnworth Borough Council, 1960–74, Bolton MDC, 1974–79. Contested (Lab) Rochdale, Oct. 1972 and Feb. 1974. MP (Lab) Leigh, 1979–2001. An Opposition Whip, 1985–87. JP 1967–79.

CUNLIFFE, Peter Whalley, CBE 1980; Chairman: Pharmaceuticals Division, Imperial Chemical Industries PLC, 1976–87; British Pharma Group, 1987–90; *b* 29 Oct. 1926; *s* of Fred Cunliffe and Lillie Whalley; *m* 1951, Alice Thérèse Emma Brunel; one *d. Educ:* Queen Elizabeth's Grammar Sch., Blackburn; Trinity Hall, Cambridge (Scholar; BA 1st Class Hons, 1948). Joined ICI Ltd, Pharmaceuticals Div., 1950; Services Dir, 1968; Overseas Dir, 1970; Dep. Chm., 1971. Pres., Assoc. of British Pharmaceutical Industry, 1981–83; Member: Council, Internat. Fedn of Pharmaceutical Manufrs Assoc., 1979–87 (Vice Pres., 1982–84, Pres. 1984–86); Exec. Cttee, European Fedn of Pharmaceutical Industries Assocs, 1982–85. *Address:* 11 St Edmund's Terrace, NW8 7QP.

CUNLIFFE, Stella Vivian, MBE 1993; consultant statistician; *b* 12 Jan. 1917; *d* of Percy Cunliffe and Edith Blanche Wellwood Cunliffe. *Educ:* privately, then Parsons Mead, Ashtead; London School of Economics (BScEcon). Danish Bacon Co., 1939–44; Voluntary Relief Work in Europe, 1945–47; Arthur Guinness Son and Co. Ltd, 1947–70; Head of Research Unit, Home Office, 1970–72; Dir of Statistics, Home Office, 1972–77. Statistical Adviser to Cttee of Enquiry into Engineering Profession, 1978–80. Pres., Royal Statistical Soc., 1975–77. *Recreations:* work with youth organisations; gardening; prison after-care. *Address:* 69 Harriotts Lane, Ashtead, Surrey KT21 2QE. *T:* (01372) 272343.

CUNLIFFE-LISTER, family name of **Baroness Masham of Ilton** and **Earl of Swinton.**

CUNLIFFE-OWEN, Sir Hugo Dudley, 3rd Bt *cr* 1920, of Bray; *b* 16 May 1966; *s* of Sir Dudley Herbert Cunliffe-Owen, 2nd Bt, and of Jean, *o d* of late Surg.-Comdr A. N. Forsyth, RN; *S* father, 1983. *Heir:* none.

CUNNAH, Michael Graeme; Director, Aston Villa Football Club, since 2007; *b* 26 Feb. 1958; *s* of Alan and Irene Cunnah; *m* 1984, Julie Kendrew; one *s* one *d. Educ:* Univ. of Aston in Birmingham (BSc Managerial and Admin. Studies). FCMA 1997. Guinness Plc, 1987–96: Financial Controller, Guinness GB, 1987–91; Dir, Corporate Finance, GBW, 1991–92; Finance Dir, Africa/Americas Region, 1992–93; Vice Pres., Finance, Desnoes & Geddes Ltd, Jamaica, 1993–95; Hd, Internal Audit, 1996; Corporate Finance Dir, Coca-Cola Schweppes, 1996–98; Finance Dir, FA, 1998–2002; CEO, Wembley Stadium, 2002–06. Fellow, Aston Univ. Business Sch. *Recreations:* football, music, cricket, golf, reading. *Address:* Aston Villa Football Club, Villa Park, Birmingham B6 6HE; *e-mail:* michaelcunnah@hotmail.com.

CUNNINGHAM, family name of **Baron Cunningham of Felling.**

CUNNINGHAM OF FELLING, Baron *cr* 2005 (Life Peer), of Felling, in the county of Tyne and Wear; **John Anderson, (Jack), Cunningham;** PC 1993; DL; PhD; *b* 4 Aug. 1939; *s* of Andrew Cunningham; *m* 1964, Maureen; one *s* two *d. Educ:* Jarrow Grammar Sch.; Bede Coll., Durham Univ. Hons Chemistry, 1962; PhD Chemistry, 1966. Formerly: Research Fellow in Chemistry, Durham Univ.; School Teacher; Trades Union Officer. MP (Lab) Whitehaven, Cumbria, 1970–83, Copeland, 1983–2005. PPS to Rt Hon. James Callaghan, 1972–76; Parly Under-Sec. of State, Dept of Energy, 1976–79; opposition spokesman on industry, 1979–83; Mem., Shadow Cabinet, 1983–95 and 1996–97; spokesman on the environment, 1983–89; Shadow Leader, H of C, 1989–92; opposition front bench spokesman on foreign and Commonwealth affairs, 1992–94; on trade and industry, 1994–95; on national heritage, 1995–97; Minister of Agriculture, Fisheries and Food, 1997–98; Minister for the Cabinet Office and Chancellor of the Duchy of Lancaster, 1998–99. DL Cumbria, 1991. *Recreations:* fell walking, fly-fishing, gardening, classical and folk music, reading, listening to other people's opinions. *Address:* House of Lords, SW1A 0PW.

CUNNINGHAM, Alexander Alan; Executive Vice President, General Motors, 1984–86, retired; *b* Bulgaria, 7 Jan. 1926; naturalised citizen, US; *m* 1976, Mary Helen; one *s* three *d* of former marr. *Educ:* General Motors Inst., Michigan. BSc (Industrial Engrg) 1951. Served War of 1939–45, navigation electronics radar specialist, RAF. General Motors: Jun. Process Engr, Frigidaire Div., 1951; Asst to Frigidaire Man., NY, Gen. Motors Overseas Ops, 1952; Prodn Planning Technician for Adam Opel AG, Germany, 1953; Exec. Asst to Man. Dir, GM Ltd, London, 1956; Master Mechanic, Gen. Motors do Brasil, 1957, Works Man. 1958; Works Man., Gen. Motors Argentina SA, 1962; Man. Dir, Gen. Motors do Brasil, 1963; Man., Adam Opel's Bochum plant, 1964; Asst Gen. Manufrg Man., Adam Opel AG, 1966, Gen. Manufrg Man. 1969; Man. Dir, Adam Opel AG, 1970; Gen. Dir, European Organisations, Gen. Motors Overseas Corp., 1974–76; Vice Pres., Group Exec. Overseas, 1978; Group Exec., Body Assembly, 1980. Exec. Vice-Pres., N American Cars, 1982. Trustee, Detroit SO, 1983. *Address:* 70–671 Oroville Circle, Rancho Mirage, CA 92270–3414, USA. *T:* (760) 3288621. *Clubs:* Thunderbird Country, Mission Hills Country (Rancho Mirage); Center (Orange County).

CUNNINGHAM, Carey Louise; *see* Bennet, C. L.

CUNNINGHAM, George; *b* June 1931; *s* of Harry Jackson Cunningham and Christina Cunningham, Dunfermline; *m* 1957, Mavis Walton; one *s* one *d. Educ:* Univ. of Manchester (BA 1952); Univ. of London (BSc(Econ) ext. 1969). Nat. Service in Royal Artillery (2nd Lieut), 1954–56; Commonwealth Relations Office, 1956–63; 2nd Sec., British High Commn, Ottawa, 1958–60; Commonwealth Officer of Labour Party, 1963–66; Min. of Overseas Development, 1966–69; Chief Exec., Library Assoc., 1984–92. MP South West Islington, 1970–74, Islington South and Finsbury, 1974–83 (Lab, 1970–81, Ind, 1981–82, SDP, 1982–83). Opposition front bench spokesman (Lab) on home affairs, 1979–81. Contested: (Lab) Henley, 1966; (SDP) Islington South and Finsbury, 1983, 1987. Mem., Parlt of European Community, 1978–79. Pres., Study of Parlt Gp, 2000–03. Chm., Gen. Council for Massage Therapy, 2002–04; Treas., Trigeminal Neuralgia Assoc., 2008–. Mem. Council, Hansard Soc., 1984–2003. Trustee, Children's Aid Direct, 1994–2002. Hon. FCLIP (Hon. FLA 1992). *Publications:* (Fabian pamphlet) Rhodesia, the Last Chance, 1966; (ed) Britain and the World in the Seventies, 1970; The Management of Aid Agencies, 1974; Careers in Politics, 1984. *Address:* 28 Manor Gardens, Hampton, Middlesex TW12 2TU. *T:* (020) 8979 6221.

CUNNINGHAM, Lt-Gen. Sir Hugh (Patrick), KBE 1975 (OBE 1966); *b* 4 Nov. 1921; *s* of late Sir Charles Banks Cunningham, CSI; *m* 1st, 1955, Jill (*d* 1992), *d* of J. S. Jeffrey,

East Knoyle; two *s* two *d*; 2nd, 1995, Zoë Simpson (*née* Andrew), Constantia, Cape Town, S Africa. *Educ:* Charterhouse. 2nd Lieut, RE, 1942; served War of 1939–45, India, New Guinea, Burma; Greece, 1950–51; Egypt, 1951–53; Instructor, Sch. of Infantry, 1955–57, RMA Sandhurst, 1957–60; Cameroons, 1960–61; CRE 3 Div., Cyprus and Aden, 1963–66; comd 11 Engr Bde, BAOR, 1967–69; comd Mons OCS, 1969–70; Nat. Defence Coll., Canada, 1970–71; GOC SW District, 1971–74; ACGS (OR), 1974–75; DCDS (OR), 1976–78, retired. Lieutenant of Tower of London, 1983–86. Col, Queen's Gurkha Engineers (formerly Gurkha Engrs), 1976–81; Col Comdt, RE, 1976–81; Col, Bristol Univ. OTC, 1977–87. Director: Fairey Holdings Ltd, 1978–86; Fairey Engineering, 1981–86; MEL, 1982–89; TREND Communications Ltd, 1984–86, 1990–93; Chairman: LL Consultants Ltd, 1984–89; TREND Group, 1986–90. Pres., Old Carthusian Soc., 1982–87. Master, Glass Sellers' Co., 1981. Chm. of Governors, Port Regis School, 1982–94; Gov., Suttons Hosp. in Charterhouse, 1984–96. *Recreations:* bird-watching, opera, golf. *Address:* Granary Mill House, Fontmell Magna, Shaftesbury, Dorset SP7 0NY. *T:* (01747) 812025. *Club:* Army and Navy.

CUNNINGHAM, James Dolan; MP (Lab) Coventry South, since 1997 (Coventry South East, 1992–97); *b* Coatbridge, 4 Feb. 1941; *s* of Adam and Elizabeth Cunningham; *m* 1985, Marion Douglas; one *s* one *d* and one step *s* one step *d*. *Educ:* St Columbia High Sch., Coatbridge. Trade Union Diplomas in Industrial Law and Social Sciences. Engineer, 1964–88. Mem. (Lab) Coventry CC, 1972–92 (Leader, 1988–92; formerly Dep. Leader, Chief Whip, Chm. and Vice Chm. of Cttees). Chm., W Midlands Jt Cttee of Local Authority, 1990–92; Sec., AMA, 1991–92. PPS to Solicitor Gen., 2005–07, to Minister of State, DWP, 2007–. Chm., HM Treasury Back Bench Cttee, 1997–. Chm., W Midland Gp of MPs, 2005–. Mem., MSF. *Address:* House of Commons, SW1A 0AA.

CUNNINGHAM, Prof. John, CVO 2008; DM, FRCP; Professor of Nephrology, University College London, and Consultant Nephrologist, Royal Free Hospital and University College London Hospitals, since 2003; Physician to the Queen and Head of HM Medical Household, since 2005 (Physician to the Royal Household, 1993–2005); Physician, King Edward VII's Hospital Sister Agnes (formerly King Edward VII's Hospital for Officers), since 1993; *b* 27 June 1949; *s* of late Daniel John Chapman Cunningham and of Judith (*née* Hill); *m* 1st, 1970, Deborah Alison Yeates (marr. diss. 1996); three *s*; 2nd, 2001, Caroline Ann Hughes Hewitt; one *d*. *Educ:* Magdalen Coll. Sch., Oxford; Trinity Hall, Cambridge (BA 1970); St John's Coll., Oxford (BM, BCh 1973; DM 1988). FRCP 1988. Junior appointments, 1973–77: Radcliffe Infirmary, Oxford; Whittington Hosp., London; Brompton Hosp., London; Central Middx Hosp., London; Lectr in Medicine, London Hosp. Med. Coll., 1977–80; Res. Fellow, Washington Univ. Sch. of Medicine, St Louis, USA, 1980–82; Consultant Physician, London, subseq. Royal London, Hosp., 1982–2003; Sub-Dean for Med. Student Admissions, London Hosp. Med. Coll., 1990–97; Prof. of Renal and Metabolic Medicine, Queen Mary, Univ. of London, 2001–03. Special Trustee, Royal London Hosp., 1985–. Jan Brod Meml Lecture, Prague, 1993, and other invited lectures. *Publications:* contrib. chapters in books, reviews and numerous articles in scientific jls. *Recreations:* music, sport, walking. *Address:* 31A King Henry's Road, NW3 3QR. *T:* (020) 7722 3883. *Club:* MCC.

CUNNINGHAM, Rt Rev. John; *see* Galloway, Bishop of, (RC).

CUNNINGHAM, Mark James; QC 2001; *b* 6 June 1956; *s* of late James Arthur Cunningham and Carole Kathleen Cunningham; *m* 1980 (marr. diss. 1995); two *s* two *d*. *Educ:* Stonyhurst Coll.; Magdalen Coll., Oxford (BA Hons Modern Hist.); Poly. of Central London (Dip. Law). Called to the Bar: Inner Temple, 1980; E Caribbean, 2005; Junior Counsel to the Crown: Chancery, 1991–99; A Panel, 1999–2001; DTI Inspector, 1998–99. *Recreations:* cricket, tennis, horses, food, travel. *Address:* Maitland Chambers, 7 Stone Buildings, Lincoln's Inn, WC2A 3SZ. *T:* (020) 7406 1200, *Fax:* (020) 7406 1300; *e-mail:* mcunningham@maitlandchambers.com. *Clubs:* Pegasus, Drayton Parslow Cricket, Stewkley Tennis.

CUNNINGHAM, Merce; Artistic Director, Merce Cunningham Dance Company, since 1953; *b* 16 April 1919; *s* of Clifford D. Cunningham. *Educ:* Cornish Coll., Seattle, Washington. Martha Graham Dance Co., 1939–45; 1st solo concert, NY, 1944; choreographed: The Seasons, for Ballet Society (later NY City Ballet), 1947; Un Jour ou deux, for Ballet of Paris Opéra, 1973; more than 200 works for own company; other works revived for NY City Ballet, American Ballet Theatre, Rambert Dance Co. (formerly Ballet Rambert), Théâtre du Silence, France, Ohio Ballet, Boston Ballet, Pacific Northwest Ballet, Zürich Ballet, Netherlands Ballet, Ballet de Lyon. Hon. Mem., Amer. Acad. and Inst. of Arts and Letters, 1984. DLitt Univ. of Illinois, 1972; Hon. DHL Minnesota, 2004. Samuel H. Scripps American Dance Festival Award for lifetime contribs to dance, 1982; Award of Honor for Arts and Culture, NY, 1983; MacArthur Award, 1985; Kennedy Center Honors, 1985; Laurence Olivier Award, 1985; Meadows Award for excellence in the arts, Meadows Sch. of Arts, Southern Methodist Univ., Dallas, 1987; Nat. Medal of Arts, USA, 1990; Digital Dance Premier Award, 1990; Golden Lion, Venice Biennale, 1995; Premio Internazionale, Gino Tani, 1999; Dorothy and Lillian Gish Prize, 2000; Nijinsky Special Prize, Monaco, 2000; Praemium Imperiale, Tokyo, 2005. Comdr, Order of Arts and Letters, France, 1982; Officier de la Légion d'Honneur, 2004 (Chevalier, 1989). *Publications:* Changes: notes on choreography (ed Frances Starr), 1968; Le Danseur et la danse: entretiens avec Jacqueline Lesschaeve, 1980, English edn The Dancer and the Dance, 1985; Other Animals: drawings and journals, 2002; articles in 7 Arts, trans/formation, TriQuarterly. *Address:* 55 Bethune Street, New York, NY 10014, USA. *T:* (212) 2558240.

CUNNINGHAM, Phyllis Margaret, CBE 1997; Chief Executive, Royal Marsden NHS Trust, 1994–98 (Chief Executive, Royal Marsden Hospital Special Health Authority, 1980–94); *b* 15 Sept. 1937; *d* of late Andrew Cunningham and of Minnie Cunningham (*née* Rees). *Educ:* Chorlton Central Sch., Manchester; Loreburn Coll., Manchester (Dip. in Business Studies, 1956). Trainee Adminr, Withington Hosp., Manchester, 1956–59; PA/Res. Asst to Med. Dir, Geigy Pharmaceutical Co., 1959–62; Unit Adminr, Roosevelt Hosp., NY, 1962–64; Planning Officer, Royal Free Hosp., London, 1964–74; Dep. House Gov./Sec. to Board, Royal Marsden Hosp., 1974–80. Mem., Ministerial Adv. Bd, Med. Devices Agency, 2001–03. Trustee and Mem. Council, St Christopher's Hospice, Sydenham, 1999–; Trustee: Headley Court Trust, 2001–; Lady Capel's Charity, 2003–; Trustee/Chm., Abbeyfield Richmond, Thames and Dist Soc. Ltd, 2002–04; Trustee/Bd Mem., Abbeyfield UK, 2004–07. Governor: Christ's Sch., Richmond, 1996–99; Queen's Sch., Richmond, 2002–. FRSA 1992. *Recreations:* current affairs, travel, theatre, music, gardening. *Address:* 12 Augustus Close, Brentford Dock, Brentford, Middx TW8 8QE. *T:* (020) 8847 1067.

CUNNINGHAM, Roseanna; Member (SNP) Perth, Scottish Parliament, since 1999; *b* 27 July 1951; *d* of Hugh and Catherine Cunningham. *Educ:* Univ. of Western Australia (BA Hons Politics 1975); Edinburgh Univ. (LLB 1982); Aberdeen Univ. (Dip. Legal Practice 1983). SNP Research Asst, 1977–79; Solicitor, 1983–90; admitted Faculty of Advocates, 1990; in practice, 1990–95. MP (SNP) Perth and Kinross, May 1995–1997, Perth, 1997–2001. Scottish Parliament: Convener: Health and Community Care Cttee, 2004–07; Rural Affairs and Envmt Cttee, 2007–. Dep. Leader, SNP, 2000–04. *Recreations:* hill walking, music, reading, stirring up trouble. *Address:* Scottish Parliament, Edinburgh EH99 1SP.

CUNNINGHAM, Thomas Anthony, (Tony); MP (Lab) Workington, since 2001; a Lord Commissioner of HM Treasury (Government Whip), since 2008; *b* 16 Sept. 1952; *s* of late Daniel Cunningham and of Bessie Cunningham; *m* 1985, Anne Gilmore; one *s* one *d*, and one step *s* one step *d*. *Educ:* Workington GS; Liverpool Univ. (BA Hons). Mem., Allerdale DC, then BC, 1987–94 (Leader, 1992–94); Mayor of Workington, 1990–91. MEP (Lab) Cumbria and Lancs N, 1994–99; contested (Lab) NW Reg., 1999. An Asst Govt Whip, 2005–08. *Address:* 17 Carlton Road, Workington, Cumbria CA14 4BX. *T:* (01900) 605799; c/o House of Commons, SW1A 0AA.

CUNNINGHAM, Prof. Valentine David, DPhil; Professor of English Language and Literature, University of Oxford, since 1996; Fellow and Tutor in English, Corpus Christi College, Oxford, since 1972; *b* 28 Oct. 1944; *s* of Rev. Valentine Cunningham and Alma Lilian Cunningham (*née* Alexander); *m* 1966, Carol Ann Shaw; two *s*. *Educ:* Lawrence Sheriff Sch., Rugby; Keble Coll., Oxford (BA); St John's Coll., Oxford (MA, DPhil 1972). University of Oxford: Jun. Res. Fellow, St John's Coll., 1969–72; Dean, 1980–91, Sen. Tutor, 1991–94, Corpus Christi Coll.; Special Lectr, English Faculty, 1996–97. Visiting Professor: Univ. of Massachusetts, 1979–80; Konstanz Univ., 1980, 1983, 1989–90, 1992–93; Scholar-in-Residence, Univ. of Western Australia, 1985; Ständigergastprof., Konstanz Univ., 1994–2001. *Publications:* Everywhere Spoken Against: dissent in the Victorian novel, 1975, 2nd edn 1977; (ed) The Penguin Book of Spanish Civil War Verse, 1979; (ed) Spanish Front: writers on the Civil War, 1986; British Writers of the Thirties, 1988; (ed) Cinco Escritores Britannicos/Five British Writers (bilingual text), 1990; In the Reading Gaol: postmodernity, texts and history, 1994; (ed) Adam Bede, 1996; (ed) The Victorians: an anthology of poetry and poetics, 2000; Reading After Theory, 2001. *Recreations:* playing piano and trumpet (Leader, Dark Blues Jazz Band), listening to jazz, haunting bookshops, going to the cinema, reading bad novels, going to church. *Address:* 26 Frenchay Road, Oxford OX2 6TG. *T:* (01865) 556128; *e-mail:* valentine.cunningham@ccc.ox.ac.uk. *Club:* Ronnie Scott's.

CUNNINGHAM-JARDINE, Ronald Charles, CVO 2007; Lord-Lieutenant, Dumfries and Galloway Region, districts of Nithsdale, Annandale and Eskdale, 1991–2006 (Vice Lord-Lieutenant, 1988–91); *b* 19 Sept. 1931; *s* of Charles Frederick Cunningham and Dorothy Agnes Jessie Jardine; *m* 1959, Constance Mary Teresa Inglis; one *s* one *d*. *Educ:* Ludgrove; Eton College; RMA Sandhurst. Royal Scots Greys, 1950–58; Edinburgh Agricultural College, 1959–60; farming, 1960–95. *Recreations:* all country sports. *Address:* Fourmerkland, Lockerbie, Dumfriesshire DG11 1EH. *T:* (01387) 810226. *Clubs:* White's; Muthaiga (Kenya).

CUNO, James, PhD; President and Director, Art Institute of Chicago, since 2004; *b* St Louis, Mo, 4 April 1951. *Educ:* Willamette Univ. (BA Hist 1973); Univ. of Oregon (MA Hist. of Art 1978); Harvard Univ. (AM Fine Arts 1980; PhD Fine Arts 1985). Asst Curator of Prints, Fogg Art Mus., Harvard Univ., 1980–83; Asst Prof., Dept of Art, Vassar Coll. 1983–86; Adjunct Asst Prof., Dept of Art Hist., and Dir, Grunwald Center for Graphic Arts, UCLA, 1986–89; Adjunct Prof. of Art Hist., and Dir, Hood Mus. of Art, Dartmouth Coll., 1989–91; Prof. of Hist. of Art, Harvard Univ., and Elizabeth and John Moors Cabot Dir, Harvard Univ. Art Mus., 1991–2002; Dir and Märit Rausing Prof., Courtauld Inst of Art, 2003–04. Mem., Nat. Cttee for Hist. of Art, 1998–. Association of Art Museum Directors: Mem., 1990–; Trustee, 1999–; Treas., 1999–2000; Vice-Pres., 2000–01; Pres. 2001–02. Trustee: Mus. of Fine Arts, Boston, 1991–2000; Wadsworth Atheneum Mus. of Art, Hartford, 2000–. Fellow, Amer. Acad. Arts and Scis, 2001. *Publications:* (ed and contrib.) Foirades/Fizzles: echo and allusion in the art of Jasper Johns, 1987; (ed and contrib.) Politics and Polemics: French caricature and the Revolution 1789–1799, 1988; Who Owns Antiquity?: museums and the battle over our ancient heritage, 2008; contrib. numerous articles, reviews and papers to learned jls. *Address:* Art Institute of Chicago, 111 South Michigan Avenue, Chicago, IL 60603, USA.

CUNY, Jean-Pierre; President-Director General: Bigot Mécanique, since 2002; Sopram since 2003; *b* 8 April 1940; *s* of Robert Cuny and Marie Louise Marchal; *m* 1968, Anne-Marie Fousse; two *d*. *Educ:* Ecole Centrale de Paris (Ingénieur); Massachusetts Inst. of Technol. (MSc). Ingénieur, Serete, 1965–68; Director: Firmin Didot, 1968–73; DAFSA 1973–76; Project Manager, CGA, 1976–78; joined Placoplatre, France, 1978: Prodn Dir 1978–82; Commercial Dir, 1982–86; Pres. Dir Gen., BPB France, 1986–92; Dir 1988–99, Chief Exec., 1994–99, BPB plc; Chm., St Eloi Finance, 2000–05. Chevalier de la Légion d'Honneur, 1994. *Recreations:* ski-ing, photography.

CUNYNGHAME, Sir Andrew (David Francis), 12th Bt *cr* 1702; FCA; *b* 25 Dec. 1942; *s* of Sir (Henry) David St Leger Brooke Selwyn Cunynghame, 11th Bt, and of Hon Pamela Margaret Stanley (*d* 1991), *d* of 5th Lord Stanley of Alderley; *S* father, 1978; *m* 1st, 1972, Harriet Ann, *d* of late C. T. Dupont, Montreal; two *d*; 2nd, 1989, Isabella King, of late Edward Everett Watts, Jr and of Isabella Hardy Watts. *Educ:* Eton. *Heir:* *b* John Philip Henry Michael Selwyn Cunynghame [*b* 9 Sept. 1944; *m* 1981, Marjatta, *d* of Martti Markus; one *s* one *d*]. *Address:* 12 Vicarage Gardens, W8 4AH. *Club:* Brooks's.

CUOMO, Mario Matthew; lawyer; Democrat; Partner, Willkie Farr & Gallagher LLP since 1995; *b* 15 June 1932; *s* of late Andrea and Immaculata Cuomo; *m* 1954, Matilda M. Raffa; two *s* three *d*. *Educ:* St John's Coll., NY (Latin Amer. Studies, English, Philosophy BA 1953); St John's Univ. (LLB 1956). Admitted to NY Bar, 1956, US Supreme Court 1960; Asst to Judge A. P. Burke, NY State Court of Appeals, 1956–58; joined Corner, Weisbrod, Froeb & Charles (later Corner, Finn, Cuomo & Charles), 1958, Partner 1963–75; Prof., St John's Univ. Law Sch., 1963–73; Sec. of State for NY, 1975–78 (Chm NY Urban & Rural Affairs, Adv. Council on Disabled; 1st NY Ombudsman); Lt Governor, NY, 1979–82; Governor, NY State, 1983–95. *Publications:* The Forest Hills Controversy: a report and comment, 1972; Forest Hills Diary: the crisis of low income housing, 1974; Diaries of Mario M. Cuomo: the campaign for Governor, 1984; (ed jtly) Lincoln on Democracy, 1990; More than Words: the speeches of Mario Cuomo, 1993; New York Idea: an experiment in democracy, 1994; Reason to Believe, 1995; (for children) The Blue Spruce, 1999; Why Lincoln Matters: today more than ever, 2004; articles in legal jls.

CUPITT, Rev. Don; Fellow of Emmanuel College, 1965–96, now Life Fellow (Dean 1966–91) and University Lecturer in Divinity, 1973–96, Cambridge; *b* 22 May 1934; *s* of late Robert and Norah Cupitt; *m* 1963, Susan Marianne (*née* Day); one *s* two *d*. *Educ:* Charterhouse; Trinity Hall, Cambridge; Westcott House, Cambridge. Curate, St Philip's Church, Salford, 1959–62; Vice-Principal, Westcott House, Cambridge, 1962–65. Writer and presenter, BBC TV series: The Big Question, 1973; Who Was Jesus?, 1976; The Sea of Faith, 1984. Hon. DLitt Bristol, 1985. *Publications:* Christ and the Hiddenness of God, 1971; Crisis of Moral Authority, 1972; The Leap of Reason, 1976; The Worlds of Science and Religion, 1976; (with Peter Armstrong) Who Was Jesus?, 1977; Jesus and the Gospel of God, 1979; The Nature of Man, 1979; The Debate about Christ, 1979; Exploration in Theology, 1979; Taking Leave of God, 1980; The World to Come, 1982; The Sea of Faith, 1984; Only Human, 1985; Life Lines, 1986; The Long-Legged Fly, 1987; The New Christian Ethics, 1988; Radicals and the Future of the Church, 1989; Creation Out of Nothing, 1990; What is a Story?, 1991; Rethinking Religion, 1992; The Time Being, 1992; After All, 1994; The Last Philosophy, 1995; Solar Ethics, 1995; After God, 1997; Mysticism After Modernity, 1998; The Religion of Being, 1998; The Revelation of Being, 1998; The New Religion of Life in Everyday Speech, 1999; The Meaning of It All in Everyday Speech, 1999; Kingdom Come in Everyday Speech, 2000; Philosophy's Own Religion, 2000; Reforming Christianity, 2001; Emptiness and Brightness, 2002; Is Nothing Sacred?, 2002; Life, Life, 2003; The Way to Happiness, 2005; The Great Questions of Life, 2006; Radical Theology, 2006; The Old Creed and the New, 2006; Impossible Loves, 2007; Above Us Only Sky, 2008. *Address:* Emmanuel College, Cambridge CB2 3AP. *T:* (01223) 334200.

CURA, José; singer, composer and conductor; *b* Rosario, Argentina, 5 Dec. 1962; *m* 1985, Silvia Ibarra; two *s* one *d*. *Educ:* Nat. Univ. of Rosario; Sch. of Arts, Teatro Colon, Buenos Aires. Débuts: Father, in Pollicino, Verona, 1992; Stiffelio (title rôle), Royal Opera, Covent Garden, 1995; La Gioconda, La Scala, Milan, 1997; other rôles include: Cavaradossi, in Tosca; Samson, in Samson et Dalila; Don José, in Carmen; Rhadames, in Aida; Otello; Don Carlo; Alfredo, in La Traviata; Manrico, in Il Trovatore; Calaf, in Turandot; Dick Johnson, in La Fanciulla del West. Principal Guest Conductor, Sinfonia Varsovia, 2001–04. Founder and Pres., Cuibar Productions, 2001–. Recordings include: all tenor arias from Puccini's operas; Annelo, Argentine songs; Verismo Arias; Samson et Dalila. *Address:* International José Cura Connexion, 3 Grove Court, Church End, Arlesey, Beds SG15 6UZ.

CURDS, Prof. Colin Robert, DSc, PhD; Keeper of Zoology, 1991–97, Research Associate, since 1997, Natural History Museum; *b* 16 Sept. 1937; *s* of Robert Redvers Curds and Daisy Violet Curds (*née* Howsam); *m* 1961, Pauline (Polly) Armitage; one *s* one *d*. *Educ:* East Ham Grammar Sch.; Univ. of London (BSc 1960; PhD 1963; DSc 1978). FIBiol 1979, CBiol 1982. Jun. Res. Fellow, Water Pollution Res. Lab., 1963–65; Min. of Technology, 1965–71; British Museum (Natural History), 1971–: Dep. Keeper of Zoology, 1976–89; Acting Keeper of Zoology, 1989–91. Visiting Lecturer: Chelsea Coll., 1965–73; Aston Univ., 1967–75; Surrey Univ., 1971–85; Vis. Prof., Mexico Univ., 1989–. Former mem., biol. and microbiol. cttees, 1972–; Member: Publications Policy Cttee, Inst. Biol., 1979–85; Council of Management, Project Urquhart, 1991–. Hon. Mem., Soc. of Protozoology, 1999–. Gov., Powell-Cotton Mus., 1992–97. *Publications:* (ed jtly) Ecological Aspects of Used-water Treatment Processes, vol. 1, 1979, vols 2 and 3, 1983; British and other freshwater ciliated protozoa, Pt 1, 1982, Pt 2 (jtly), 1983; Protozoa in the Water Industry, 1992; contribs to professional jls. *Recreations:* family life, furniture design, cabinet-making, France, cats, snorkelling, genealogy. *Address:* Department of Zoology, Natural History Museum, Cromwell Road, SW7 5BD. *T:* (020) 7942 5149; *e-mail:* curds@wanadoo.fr.

CURL, Philip; His Honour Judge Curl; a Circuit Judge, since 1996; *b* 31 Oct. 1947; *s* of Dr Oliver Curl and Joan Curl; *m* 1983, Nicola Ruth Gurney; two *d*. *Educ:* Radley Coll.; Southampton Univ. (LLB). Called to the Bar, Gray's Inn, 1970; Asst Recorder, 1991–95; Recorder, 1995–96; Designated Family Judge, Norwich, 1998–2007. Legal Mem., Mental Health Review Tribunal (Restricted Patients Panel), 2002–. Mem. Council, Norwich Cathedral, 2002–. Local Steward: Gt Yarmouth and Fakenham Racecourses, 2004–; Newmarket Racecourse, 2007–. *Recreations:* playing and watching sport, art, travel. *Address:* c/o Norwich Combined Courts, Bishopgate, Norwich, Norfolk NR3 1UR. *Clubs:* Boodle's, MCC; Norfolk (Norwich).

CURL, Prof. Robert Floyd, PhD; Kenneth S. Pitzer-Schlumberger Professor of Natural Sciences and University Professor, Rice University, Houston, 2003–05, now Emeritus; *b* 23 Aug. 1933; *s* of Robert Floyd Curl and Lessie Waldeen Curl; *m* 1955, Jonel Whipple; two *s*. *Educ:* Rice Inst. (BA 1954); Univ. of Calif, Berkeley (PhD 1957). Res. Fellow, Harvard, 1957–58; Rice Institute, then Rice University: Asst Prof., 1958–63; Associate Prof., 1963–67; Prof. of Chemistry, 1967–96; Chm., Chemistry Dept, 1992–96; Harry C. and Olga K. Wiess Prof. of Natural Scis, 1996–2003; Master, Lovett Coll., 1968–72. Dr (*hc*): Buenos Aires, 1997; Littoral, 2003. (Jtly) Clayton Prize, IMechE, 1958; (jtly) APS Prize for New Materials, 1992; (jtly) Nobel Prize for Chemistry, 1996; (jtly) Texas Distinguished Scientist, Texas Acad. of Sci., 1997; (jtly) Achievement in Carbon Science, Amer. Carbon Soc., 1997; Order of the Golden Plate, Amer. Acad. of Achievement, 1997. *Publications:* numerous contribs to scientific jls. *Recreations:* contract bridge, squash. *Address:* Chemistry Department, Rice University, Houston, TX 77005, USA. *T:* (713) 3484816; 1824 Bolsover, Houston, TX 77005, USA.

CURLE, James Leonard; Member and Managing Director, Civil Aviation Authority, 1984–87; *b* 14 Nov. 1925; *s* of Leonard and Mary Curle; *m* 1952, Gloria Madaleine Roch; one *s* one *d*. *Educ:* St Joseph's Academy, Blackheath; SE London Technical College; Borough Polytechnic. CEng, MIET. Royal Signals, 1944–49; joined Telecommunications Div., MTCA, 1957; Dir Telecommunications, ATS, 1976–79; Dir Gen. Telecommunications, NATS, 1979–84. *Address:* 6 Nightingale Lane, Bickley, Kent BR1 2QH. *T:* (020) 8460 8023.

CURLEY, Carlo James; international concert organist; *b* 24 Aug. 1952; *s* of James Dennis Curley and Gladys Maynard Curley. *Educ:* N Carolina Sch. of Arts; privately with Virgil Fox, Robert Elmore and Sir George Thalben Ball. Organist/choirmaster, Druid Hills Baptist Ch, Atlanta, Ga, 1968–71; Artist-in-Residence, Fountain St Ch, Grand Rapids, Mich, 1970–71; Summer Organist-in-Residence, Alexandra Palace, London, 1977–78; numerous community and civic concerts, N America, 1979–88; played first solo classic organ recital at the White House, by invitation of the Pres., 1989; various Royal Comd performances; has performed world-wide, both solo and orchestral, 1989–; numerous radio, TV and media appearances world-wide, 1989–; has made numerous recordings. Hon. Fellow, Guild of Musicians and Singers, 1996. *Publication:* In the Pipeline (autobiog.), 1997. *Recreations:* reading, walking, swimming, fine food and wines. *Address:* c/o PVA Management Ltd, Hallow Park, Worcester WR2 6PG. *T:* (01905) 640663, *Fax:* (01905) 641842; *e-mail:* maggie@pva.co.uk.

CURNOCK COOK, Jeremy Laurence; Chairman, Bioscience Managers Ltd, since 2001; consultant, biotechnology industry, since 2000; *b* 3 Sept. 1949; *s* of Colin Curnock Cook and Doris (*née* Wolsey); *m* 1st, 1975, Elizabeth Joanna Badgett (marr. diss. 1981); 2nd, 1987, Mary Elizabeth Thomasson (marr. diss. 1998); one *s* two *d*; 3rd, 2007, Sara Jane Stickland. *Educ:* Lycée Français de Londres; Westminster Sch.; Trinity Coll., Dublin (MA Natural Scis). Res. Scientist, Inst. Cancer Res., London, 1972–73; Managing Director: Badgett-Cook Biochems Ltd, London, 1973–75; Internat. Biochems Ltd, Dublin, London, 1975–87; Rothschild Asset Mgt (Biosci. Unit), 1987–2000. Chairman: Targeted Genetics Inc., 1998–; atugen GmbH, 2002–; Inflazyme Pharmaceuticals Inc., 2006–; Man. Dir, Intersuisse Bioscis Managers, 2005–; Dir, BMI Canada, 2004–; non-executive Director: Cantab Pharmaceuticals plc, 1990–2001; Biocompatibles Internat. plc, 1992–; Vernalis, 1995–2001; Angiotech Pharmaceuticals Inc., 1995–2001; Amrad Corp., 1995–2002; Sirna Therapeutics Inc., 2003–06; Q chip, 2004–06; Silence Therapeutics (formerly S. R. Pharma) plc, 2005–; Gastrotech Pharma, 2005–06; Osteologix Inc., 2006–; Aegera Therapeutics Inc., 2008–; Topigen Pharmaceuticals Inc., 2008–. Mem., Biosci. Futures Forum, 2005–. Mem., Soc. for Gen. Microbiol., 1971–. FInstD 1988; FRSA 1994. *Recreations:* keeping fit, music, ski-ing. *Address:* 2 Balfern Grove, Chiswick, W4 2JX. *Club:* Kildare Street and University (Dublin).

CURNOW, Rt Rev. Andrew William; *see* Bendigo, Bishop of.

CURNOW, (Elizabeth) Ann (Marguerite); QC 1985; a Recorder of the Crown Court, 1980–2000; *b* 5 June 1935; *d* of Cecil Curnow and Doris Curnow (*née* Behr); *m* 1981, (William) Neil Denison, *qv*. *Educ:* St Hilda's Sch., Whitby, Yorks; King's Coll., London (LLB). Called to the Bar, Gray's Inn, 1957, Bencher, 1985. Treasury Counsel, Middx Crown Court, 1972–77; Central Criminal Court: Jun. Treasury Counsel, 1977–81; Sen. Prosecuting Counsel to the Crown, 1981–85. Member: Parole Bd, 1992–94; Criminal Injuries Compensation Bd, 1996–2002; Mental Health Rev. Tribunal, 2000–04. Chm., Victim Support, Lambeth, 1987–2003. *Recreations:* Burmese cats, listening to music, tapestry, gardens. *Address:* 6 King's Bench Walk, Temple, EC4Y 7DR. *T:* (020) 7583 0410, *Fax:* (020) 7353 8791.

CURR, Surgeon Rear Adm. Ralph Donaldson, FRCGP; Medical Director General (Naval), Ministry of Defence, 2002–03; *b* 25 Sept. 1943; *s* of George and Florence Curr; *m* 1972, Susan Brereton; two *s* three *d*. *Educ:* Dulwich Coll.; King's Coll. Hosp. (MB BS; AKC). LRCP, MRCS 1969; DRCOG 1975; FRCGP 1992. Joined RN 1969; HMS Mohawk, 1969; HMS Cleopatra, 1971; Malta, 1972–74; GP, NHS and RNR, HMS Vivid, 1975–76; Clyde Submarine Base, 1976–79; Gibraltar, 1979–81; PMO, HMS Raleigh, 1981–84; HK, 1984–86; HMS Intrepid, 1986–88; Dean of Naval Medicine, 1988–90; PMO, HMS Drake, 1990–95; Dir of Naval Personnel, MoD, 1995–97; COS to Med. Dir Gen. (Naval), MoD, 1997–2000; Dir, Med. Ops, CINCFLEET, 2000–02. QHP 2000–03. Civilian Med. Practitioner, HMS Raleigh, 2004–. Chm., Kosovo Mammography Project; Sec., Tamar Faculty, RCGP. Director: Lord Caradon Trust, 2007–; UK Nat. Defence Assoc. Member: Scotch Malt Whisky Soc., 2001–; Britannia Assoc., 2004–; St Austell Bay Rotary Club, 2006–; Chm., St Austell Sea Cadets, 2006–. OStJ 2001. *Recreations:* walking, church. *Address:* Sea Garth, Pentewan Hill, Pentewan, St Austell, Cornwall PL26 6DD. *T:* (01726) 843106; *e-mail:* rdcurr@hotmail.com. *Club:* Naval.

CURRAN, Edmund Russell, OBE 2006; Editor-in-Chief, Independent News and Media (Northern Ireland), since 2005; *b* 29 Sept. 1944; *s* of William John Curran and Elizabeth (*née* Russell); *m* 1st, 1968, Romaine Carmichael (marr. diss. 1991); two *s* two *d*; 2nd, 1994, Pauline Hall. *Educ:* Royal Sch., Dungannon; Queen's Univ., Belfast (BSc, DipEd). Dep. Editor, Belfast Telegraph, 1974–88; Editor, Sunday Life (NI), 1988–92; Actg Editor, Wales on Sunday, 1991; Editor, Belfast Telegraph, 1993–2005. Mem., Press Complaints Commn, 2002–06. Pres., Soc. of Editors, 2001. Newspaper Focus UK Regl Newspaper Editor of Year, 1991. *Recreations:* golf, reading newspapers. *Address:* Independent News and Media (Northern Ireland), 124/144 Royal Avenue, Belfast BT1 1EB. *T:* (028) 9026 4400. *Clubs:* Belvoir Park Golf (Belfast); Royal County Down Golf (Newcastle).

CURRAN, Frances; Member (Scot. Socialist) Scotland West, Scottish Parliament, 2003–07; *b* 21 May 1961. *Educ:* St Brendan's Sch., Linwood; St Andrew's Secondary Sch., Carntyne, Glasgow. Mem., NEC, Labour Party, 1984–86; worked for campaigns incl. red wedge, anti-poll tax, youth against racism in Europe; involved in launching Scottish Socialist Alliance, 1995, Scottish Socialist Party, 1998. Contested (Scot. Socialist) Glasgow E, July 2008. *Recreations:* reading, bingo, caravanning, socialising.

CURRAN, John Terence; His Honour Judge Curran; a Circuit Judge, since 1996; Resident Judge, Merthyr Tydfil Combined Court Centre, since 1998; *b* 3 Oct. 1941; *s* of Eugene Curran, OBE and Joan Curran; *m* 1971, Elizabeth Ann Bowcott; one *s* one *d*. *Educ:* Ratcliffe; Jesus Coll., Cambridge (MA). Hallinans, solicitors, Cardiff: articled clerk, 1963–68; admitted solicitor, 1968; Partner, 1968–83; called to the Bar, Gray's Inn, 1983; Asst Recorder, 1989–93; Actg Stipendiary Magistrate, 1989; Provincial Stipendiary Magistrate (Mid-Glam), 1990–96; a Recorder, 1993–96. *Recreations:* walking, gardening, history, supporting Cardiff RFC, looking for my spectacles. *Address:* Law Courts, Glebeland Place, Merthyr Tydfil CF47 8BH. *Club:* Cardiff Athletic.

CURRAN, Kevin Barry; General Secretary, GMB, 2003–05; *b* 20 Aug. 1954; *s* of John and Maureen Curran; *m* 1977, June Bartholomew; one *s* one *d*. GMB (formerly General, Municipal, Boilermakers and Allied Trades Union): joined 1975; Health and Safety Officer, London Region, 1988; Regl Organiser, 1990, Regl Industrial Organiser, 1996, Southern Region; Regl Sec., Northern Region, 1997. *Recreations:* football, running, blacksmithing, woodlands, reading, allotment gardening, keeping fit, keeping the foes of working people on their toes. *Club:* Crystal Palace Football.

CURRAN, Maj. Gen. Liam Diarmuid, CB 2001; independent consultant, 2001–06; Engineer Adviser to Defence Procurement Agency and President of the Ordnance Board, 1998–2001; *b* 31 March 1946; *s* of late William James Curran and Genevieve Curran (*née* Lavery); *m* 1971, Evelyn Mary Elizabeth Strang; two *d*. *Educ:* Presentation Coll., Reading; Welbeck Coll.; Royal Military Acad., Sandhurst; Fitzwilliam Coll., Cambridge (MA 1970). CEng 1980; FIET (FIEE 1990). CO, 7 Armd Workshop, REME and Comdr, Fallingbostel Station, 1986–89; Equipt Support Manager on staff of QMG, 1989–91; Project Manager for Light Armd Vehicles, 1991–93; Equipt Support Dir on staff of QMG, 1993–96; Vice-Pres., Ordnance Bd, 1996–98. Col Comdt, REME, 2000–05. *Recreations:* walking, gardening, National Trust. *Address:* c/o Lloyds TSB, 38 Market Place, East Dereham, Norfolk NR19 2AT.

CURRAN, Margaret Patricia; Member (Lab) Glasgow Baillieston, Scottish Parliament, since 1999; *b* 24 Nov. 1958; *d* of James Curran and Rose McConnellogue; *m*; two *s*. *Educ:* Glasgow Univ. (MA Hons Hist. and Econ. Hist.); Cert. Community Educn. Welfare rights officer, 1982–83; community worker, 1983–87, sen. community worker, 1987–89, Strathclyde Regl Council; Lectr, Dept of Community Educn, Univ. of Strathclyde, 1989–99. Scottish Executive: Dep. Minister for Social Justice, 2001–02; Minister: for Social Justice, 2002–03; for Communities, 2003–04; for Parly Business, 2004–07. Contested (Lab) Glasgow East, July 2008. *Recreations:* reading, cinema, being with children. *Address:* Scottish Parliament, Edinburgh EH99 1SP.

CURRAN, Patrick David; QC 1995; **His Honour Judge Patrick Curran;** a Circuit Judge, since 2007; *s* of late David Curran and Noreen Curran; *m* 1976; two *s* two *d*. *Educ:* Ratcliffe; Queen's Coll., Oxford (MA). Called to the Bar, Gray's Inn, 1972, Bencher, 2005; Asst Recorder, 1988–92; Recorder, 1992–2007; admitted to Bar of Ireland, 1993. Asst Comr, Parly Boundary Commn for Wales, 1994–2007. Legal Mem., Mental Health Review Tribunal for Wales, 1995–2008. Legal Assessor, GMC, 2002–07. Governor, Westminster Cathedral Choir Sch., 2000–. FRSocMed 2007. Editor, 1992–2004,

Consultant Editor, 2004–, Personal Injuries and Quantum Reports. *Publications:* Personal Injury Pleadings, 1994, 4th edn 2008; (contrib.) Criminal Law and Forensic Psychiatry, 1995; (ed and contrib.) Personal Injury Handbook, 1997; (contrib.) Clinical Litigation, 2003; contrib. Criminal Law Rev., Personal Injuries and Quantum Reports. *Address:* Cardiff Crown Court, The Law Courts, Cathays Park, Cardiff CF10 3PG.

See also Dame D. J. Hine.

CURRAN, Prof. Paul James, PhD, DSc; CGeog, FRGS; Vice-Chancellor, and Professor of Physical Geography, Bournemouth University, since 2005; *b* 17 May 1955; *s* of late James Patrick Curran and of Betty Doreen (*née* Bott); *m* 1978, Helen Patricia Palin; one *d. Educ:* Longslade Upper Sch., Birstall, Leics; Univ. of Sheffield (BSc Hons Geog. 1976); Univ. of Bristol (PhD 1979, DSc 1991); Univ. of Southampton (MBA Dist. 1998). FRGS 1979; CGeog 2002. Lectr, Univ. of Reading, 1979–81; Lectr, then Sen. Lectr, Univ. of Sheffield, 1981–89; Sen. Res. Associate, NASA Ames Res. Center, Calif, 1988–89; Prof. of Physical Geog., UC of Swansea, 1990–93; University of Southampton: Prof. of Physical Geog., 1993–2005; Hd, Dept of Geog., 1995–99; Dean of Sci., 2000–03; Hd, Winchester Sch. of Art, 2003–04; Dep. Vice Chancellor, 2004–05; Vis. Prof., 2005–. Vis. Res. Fellow, Univ. of NSW, 1986. Member: NERC, 2006– (Mem., Terrestrial Life Scis Cttee, 1989–92); Bd, QAA, 2006–. Member: Sci. Adv. Gp, ESA, 1990–; Earth Observation Prog. Bd, BNSC, 1995–98; Sci. Adv. Cttee, ISPRS, 1999–; Wkg Party on Terrestrial Carbon Sinks, Royal Soc., 2000–01; Geog. Panel, 2001 RAE, HEFCE; Employability, Business and Industry Policy Cttee, 2005–, Research Policy Cttee, 2006–, UUK; Chairman: Wkg Gp on Global Ecosystem Monitoring, ISPRS, 1992–2000; High Level Academic Workforce Steering Gp, HEFCE, 2007–. FRSPS 1995; FCIM 1999. Otto van Gruber Medal, ISPRS, 1988; Cuthbert Peek Award (1883), RGS, 1998; Gold Medal, Remote Sensing Soc., 2000; Patron's Medal, RGS, 2007. *Publications:* Principles of Remote Sensing, 1985; (jtly) Remote Sensing of Soils and Vegetation in the USSR, 1990; (ed) Environmental Remote Sensing from Regional to Global Scales, 1994; Remote Sensing in Biosphere Studies, 1994; Remote Sensing in Action, 1995; Scaling-up from Cell to Landscape, 1997; contrib. chapters in books and articles to conf. proc. and learned jls. *Recreations:* running, travel, family life, art, sea. *Address:* Office of the Vice-Chancellor, Bournemouth University, Poole, Dorset BH12 5BB. *T:* (01202) 965070, *Fax:* (01202) 965069; *e-mail:* vice-chancellor@bournemouth.ac.uk. *Club:* Geographical.

CURRAN, Terence Dominic; HM Diplomatic Service, retired; Consul-General, Toronto, and Director-General of Trade and Investment in Canada, 1996–2000; *b* 14 June 1940; *m* 1969, Penelope Anne Ford; two *s* one *d*. Joined HM Diplomatic Service, 1966; DSAO, 1966–68; Peking, 1968–69; Consul, Dakar, 1970–73; Asst Trade Comr, then Consul (Commercial), Edmonton, 1973–78; FCO, 1978–80; First Sec., Pretoria, 1980–84; FCO, 1984–87; Counsellor (Commercial and Economic), Singapore, 1987–90; Head of Training, FCO, 1990–93; Dep. High Comr, Bombay, 1993–96. *Address:* Rother House, Nyewood, Petersfield, Hants GU31 5HY.

CURRAN, Dr Thomas, FRS 2005; Professor of Anatomy and Neurobiology, University of Tennessee, since 1995; Member and Chairman, Department of Developmental Neurobiology, St Jude Children's Research Hospital, Memphis, Tennessee, since 1995; *b* 14 Feb. 1956; *s* of Thomas and Jane Curran; *m*; one *s*. *Educ:* Univ. of Edinburgh (BS 1978); ICRF Labs and University Coll. London (PhD 1982). Postdoctoral Fellow, Salk Inst., San Diego, Calif, 1982–84; Sen. Scientist, Hoffman-La Roche, Inc., NJ, 1984–85; Asst Mem., 1985–86, Associate Mem., 1986–88, Full Mem., 1988–95, Associate Dir, 1991–95, Roche Inst., Molecular Biol., NJ. Adjunct Prof., Columbia Univ., NY, 1989–95. Mem., Bd of Scientific Advrs, Nat. Cancer Inst., Washington, 2000–05. Pres., Amer. Assoc. for Cancer Res., Philadelphia, 2002. Passano Foundn Young Scientist Award, Baltimore, 1992; Javitz Neurosci. Investigator Award, Nat. Inst. of Neurol Disorder and Stroke, NIH, 2001; Peter M. Steck Meml Award and Lecture, Houston, Texas, 2002; LIMA Internat. Award for Excellence in Pediatric Brain Tumour Res., PBT Foundn, NY, 2004. *Publications:* (ed) The Oncogene Handbook, 1988; Origins of Human Cancer, 1991; contrib. numerous articles to scientific jls and books. *Address:* 6284 Whitmar Place North, Memphis, TN 38120, USA. *T:* (901) 6819937, *Fax:* (901) 4952270; *e-mail:* tom.curran@stjude.org.

CURRIE, family name of **Baron Currie of Marylebone**.

CURRIE OF MARYLEBONE, Baron *cr* 1996 (Life Peer), of Marylebone in the City of Westminster; **David Anthony Currie;** Chairman, Office of Communications, 2002–April 2009; *b* 9 Dec. 1946; *s* of Kennedy Moir Currie and Marjorie Currie (*née* Thompson); *m* 1st, 1975, Shaziye Gazioglu Currie (marr. diss. 1992); two *s*; 2nd, 1995, Angela Mary Piers Dumas. *Educ:* Battersea Grammar Sch.; Univ. of Manchester (BSc 1st cl. Maths); Univ. of Birmingham (MSocSci Econs); PhD Econs London. Economist: Hoare Govett, 1971–72; Economic Models, 1972; Lectr, Reader and Prof. of Economics, Queen Mary College, Univ. of London, 1972–88; London Business School: Prof. of Econs, 1988–2000; Res. Dean, 1989–92; Gov., 1989–95; Dep. Principal, 1992–95; Dep. Dean for External Relations, 1999–2000; Dir, Centre for Econ. Forecasting, 1988–95; Dean, City Univ. Business Sch., subseq. Cass Business Sch., City of London, 2001–07. Res. Fellow, Centre for Economic Policy Research, 1983–. Houblon-Norman Res. Fellow, Bank of England, 1985–86; Vis. Scholar, IMF, 1987. Member: ABRC, 1992–93; Retail Price Index Adv. Cttee, 1992–93; Treasury's Panel of Independent Forecasters, 1992–95; Gas and Electricity Mkts Authy, 2000–02; Bd, Dubai FSA, 2004–. Dir and Chm. Exec. Cttee, 1994–97, Charter 88; Director: Internat. Schs of Business Mgt, 1992–95; Joseph Rowntree Reform Trust (Investments) Ltd, 1989–2002; Joseph Rowntree Reform Trust (Properties) Ltd, 1991–2002; Abbey National plc, 2001–02; non-exec. Dir, BDO Stoy Hayward, 2008–. Chm., Coredeal MTS, 2002–. Mem., Bd, LPO, 2007–. Trustee, Joseph Rowntree Reform Trust, 1991–2002. Hon. Fellow, QMW, 1997. Hon. DLitt Glasgow, 1998. *Publications:* Advances in Monetary Economics, 1985; (with Charles Goodhart and David Llewellyn) The Operation and Regulation of Financial Markets, 1986; (with David Vines) Macroeconomic Interactions Between North and South, 1988; (with Paul Levine) Rules, Reputation and Macroeconomic Policy Co-ordination, 1993; (with David Vines) North-South Linkages and International Macroeconomic Policy, 1995; The Pros and Cons of EMU, 1997; Will the Euro Work?: the ins and outs of EMU, 1998; articles in jls. *Recreations:* music, literature, swimming. *Address:* (until April 2009) Ofcom, Riverside House, 2a Southwark Bridge Road, SE1 9HA; House of Lords, SW1A 0PW.

CURRIE, Maj. Gen. Archibald Peter Neil, CB 2001; Lieutenant Governor, Royal Hospital, Chelsea, since 2005; Director: Blue Force Group Ltd, since 2003; *b* Dar es Salaam, 30 June 1948; *s* of Donald and Ysobel Currie; *m* 1974, Angela Margaret Howell; two *s*. *Educ:* Sao Hill Sch., Tanzania; Monkton Combe Sch.; RMA, Sandhurst; Nottingham Univ. (BA Hons Hist. 1973). 2nd Regt, RA, 1970–75; 22 Regt, RA, 1975–79; RMCS, Shrivenham, 1980; psc, 1981; Operational Requirements, MoD, 1982–83; Batt. Comdr, 22 Regt, RA, 1984–86; Army Staff Duties, MoD, 1986–87; CO, 12 Regt, RA, 1987–90; Instr, Staff Coll., Camberley, 1990–91; Col, Mil. Ops 1, MoD, 1991–93; HCSC, 1993; Comdr Artillery, HQ ARRC, 1994; Dep. Comdr, Multinat. Div. Central (Airmobile), 1995; DPS (Army), MoD, 1996–98; Mil. Advr to High Rep. in Bosnia Herzegovina, 1998–99; COS to Adjt Gen., 1999–2001; Dep. Adjt Gen., MoD, 2001–02. Has served in NI and Falkland Is. Advr to Sunday Mirror, 2003–05. Non-exec. Dir, Close Brothers Mil. Services, 2004–06. Member: Bd, Services Sound and Vision Corp., 2003–; Council, Forces Pension Soc., 2003–; Mgt Cttee, Combat Stress, 2006– (Chm., 2007–). *Recreations:* ski-ing, tennis, opera, walking.

CURRIE, Austin; *see* Currie, J. A.

CURRIE, Brian Murdoch; President, Institute of Chartered Accountants in England and Wales, 1996–97 (Vice-President, 1994–95; Deputy President, 1995–96); *b* 20 Dec. 1934; *s* of William Murdoch Currie and Dorothy (*née* Holloway); *m* 1961, Patricia Maria, *d* of Capt. Frederick Eaton-Farr; three *s* one *d*. *Educ:* Blundell's Sch. (Scholar); Oriel Coll., Oxford (Open Scholar; MA). ACA 1963, FCA 1973; MIMC 1968, FIMC 1990. Commnd RTR, 1957–59; Arthur Andersen Chartered Accountants, 1959–90: Partner, 1970–90; Dep. Man. Partner, 1975; Man. Partner, London, 1977–82; Chm., Partnership Council, 1983–85. Dist Auditor, 1982–87. Dept of Trade Inspector, Fourth City and other cos, 1978; Mem., Foster Cttee of Inquiry into Road Haulage Licensing, 1977. Member: Management Bd, HMSO, 1972–74; Restrictive Practices Court, 1979–2004; Takeover Panel, 1989–97; Lay Mem., GDC, 1994–99; Dep. Chm., Financial Reporting Council, 1996–98. Institute of Chartered Accountants in England and Wales: Mem. Council, 1988–99; Chm., Practice Regulation, 1993; Chm., Chartered Accountants Jt Ethics Cttee, 1994–95; Mem., IFAC Compliance Cttee, 2000–02. Trustee, Oriel Coll. Develt Trust, 1980–94. Chm., Peter Blundell Soc., 1997–2002; Member, Committee: Exmoor Soc., 1993–2002 (Founder's Award, 2002); Glass Assoc., 1998–2003; Founder Mem., Pluralists, 1992–. Gov., Blundell's Sch., 2000–02. Jt Ed., Glass Cone, 1999–2005. *Publications:* A Principle-based Framework for Professional Independence, 1992; official public reports; papers and articles in professional and technical pubns. *Recreations:* natural history, Exmoor, church (lay assisting). *Address:* Westbrook House, Bampton, Tiverton, Devon EX16 9HU. *T:* (01398) 331418. *Club:* Athenæum.

CURRIE, Dr Christopher Richard John, FRHistS, FSA; Senior Research Fellow, Institute of Historical Research, since 2002; Gazette and Deputy Web Editor, Church Times, since 2002; *b* 3 March 1948; *s* of George Samson Currie, MC and Norah Currie (*née* Kennedy); *m* 1981, Katherine Ruth Gommon; one *s* one *d*. *Educ:* Winchester; Balliol Coll., Oxford (MA 1976, DPhil 1976). FRHistS 1979; FSA 1984. Victoria County History: Asst Editor, Staffs, 1972–78; Dep. Editor, 1978–94; Gen. Editor, 1994–2000; Consultant Editor, 2000–02. Mem. Council, RHistS, 1996–2000. Pres., Vernacular Architecture Gp, 2007–; Hon. Editor, Vernacular Architecture, 1980–82. *Publications:* (ed with C. P. Lewis) English County Histories: a guide, 1994; articles in Victoria County Hist. and learned jls. *Recreation:* sleep. *Address:* 14 Keston Road, N17 6PN. *T:* (020) 8801 2185.

CURRIE, Sir Donald Scott, 7th Bt *cr* 1847; Chief of Maintenance, National Park Service, Department of the Interior, 1976; *b* 16 Jan. 1930; *s* of George Donald Currie (*d* 1980) (*g g s* of 1st Bt) and Janet K. (*d* 1990), *d* of late James Scott; *S* cousin, 1987, but his name does not appear on the Official Roll of the Baronetage; *m* 1st, 1948, Charlotte (marr. diss. 1951), *d* of Charles Johnstone; twin *d* (and one *s* decd); 2nd, 1952, Barbara Lee (*d* 1993), *d* of A. P. Garnier; one *s* two *d*; 3rd, 1994, Barbara Lou Lebsack, *d* of Joshua Fenn. Rancher and farmer, 1949–75. *Clubs:* American Legion (Colorado, USA); National Rifle Association (USA); North American Hunting.

CURRIE, Edwina, (Edwina Currie Jones); *b* 13 Oct. 1946; *m* 1st, 1972, Raymond F. Currie, BA, FCA (marr. diss. 2001); two *d*; 2nd, 2001, John Benjamin Paul Jones, former Det. Supt, Met. Police; four step *s*. *Educ:* Liverpool Inst. for Girls; St Anne's Coll., Oxford (scholar; MA 1972); London Sch. of Econs and Pol Science (MSc 1972). Teaching and lecturing posts in econs, econ. history and business studies, 1972–81. Birmingham City Council: Mem., 1975–86; Chm., Social Services Cttee, 1979–80; Chm., Housing Cttee 1982–83. Chm., Central Birmingham HA, 1981–83. MP (C) Derbyshire South, 1983–97; contested (C) same seat, 1997. PPS to Sec. of State for Educn and Science, 1985–86; Parly Under-Sec. of State (Health), DHSS, later Dept of Health, 1986–88. Member: European Movement, 1992– (Vice Chm., 1995–98); Cons. Gp for Europe, 1992– (Chm., 1995–97). Contested (C) Bedfordshire and Milton Keynes, Eur. Parly elecns, 1994. Regular contributor to nat. newspapers and magazines; presenter: Sunday Supplement, TV, 1993; Espresso, TV, 1997; various radio progs, incl. Late Night Currie, 1998–2003, BBC Radio Five Live. Trustee: VOICE (UK) (Chm., 1994–97); The Patients Assoc., 2006–; Patron Redhill Women's Aid, 2005–; MRSA Action UK, 2007–. Dir, Future of Europe Trust (Jt Chm., 1994–97). Speaker of the Year, Assoc. of Speakers' Clubs, 1990; Campaigner of the Year, Spectator Awards, 1994. *Publications:* Financing our Cities (Bow Group pamphlet), 1976; Life Lines, 1989; What Women Want, 1990; (jtly) Three-Line Quips 1992; Edwina Currie Diaries 1987–92, 2002; *novels:* A Parliamentary Affair, 1994; A Woman's Place, 1996; She's Leaving Home, 1997; The Ambassador, 1999; Chasing Men 2000; This Honourable House, 2001. *Recreations:* earning a living, theatre, family, reading other people's books. *Address:* c/o Little, Brown, Brettenham House, Lancaster Place WC2E 7EN. *T:* (020) 7911 8000.

CURRIE, Dr Graham Alan, MD; FRCP, FRCPath; Research Director, Marie Curie 1982–2002; *b* 17 Aug. 1939; *s* of Alan Currie and Dorothy Currie; *m* 1964, Dr Angela Wright; one *s* three *d*. *Educ:* Charing Cross Hosp. Med. Sch. (MB BS; Univ. of London Prize Medal, 1963; MD 1974). FRCPath 1982; FRCP 1984. Jun. appts, Charing Cross Hosp., 1963–69; staff mem., Chester Beatty Res. Inst., 1969–74; Sen. Lectr, Ludwig Inst for Cancer Res., 1974–82; Hon. Consultant Physician, Royal Marsden Hosp., 1974–82 Saltwell Res. Scholar, RCP, 1966; Wellcome Res. Fellow, Charing Cross Hosp., 1968 Founding Ed., Oncogene, 1987. *Publications:* Cancer and the Immune Response, 1974 2nd edn 1980; numerous papers and reviews in learned jls. *Recreations:* art, music, gardens sleep. *Address:* Hunters, Forest Lodge, Epsom Road, Ashtead, Surrey KT21 1JX. *T* (01372) 278707.

CURRIE, Heriot Whitson; QC (Scot.) 1992; *b* 23 June 1952; *s* of Heriot Clunas Currie and Evelyn Whitson; *m* 1st, 1975, Susan Carolyn Hodge (marr. diss. 2001); three *d*; 2nd 2003, Paula Maria Christian. *Educ:* Edinburgh Academy; Wadham Coll., Oxford (MA) Edinburgh Univ. (LLB). Admitted to Faculty of Advocates, 1979; practice as Advocate 1979–; called to the Bar, Gray's Inn, 1991; Mem., Monckton Chambers, 2005– *Recreations:* chamber music, cinema, golf, foreign languages. *Address:* 2 Doune Terrace Edinburgh EH3 6DY; 1 & 2 Raymond Buildings, Gray's Inn, WC1R 5NR. *Club:* New (Edinburgh).

CURRIE, James McGill; Director-General (Environment and Nuclear Safety), European Commission, 1997–2001; *b* 17 Nov. 1941; *s* of late David Currie and of Mary (*née* Smith) *m* 1968, Evelyn Barbara MacIntyre; one *s* one *d*. *Educ:* St Joseph's High Sch., Kilmarnock Blairs Coll., Aberdeen; Royal Scots Coll., Valladolid; Univ. of Glasgow (MA). Asst Principal, Scottish Home and Health Dept, 1968–72; Principal, Scottish Educn Dept 1972–75; Secretary, Management Gp, Scottish Office, 1975–77; Scottish Developmen

Dept: Principal, 1977–79; Asst Sec., 1979–81; Asst Sec., Scottish Economic Planning Dept, 1981–82; Counsellor, UK Perm. Representation to EEC, 1982–87; Dir of Regional Policy, EEC, 1987–89; Chef de Cabinet to Leon Brittan, EEC, 1989–92; Dep. Head, EC Delegn to USA, 1993–96; Dir-Gen. (Customs and Indirect Taxation), EC, 1996–97. Vis. Prof. of Law, Georgetown Law Center, Washington, 1997–. Non-executive Director: Royal Bank of Scotland, 2001–; Total UK, 2004–; Vimetco NV, 2007–; Met Office, 2007–. FRSA 2007. Hon. DLitt Glasgow, 2001. *Recreations:* tennis, golf, guitar, good food. *Address:* Flat 7, 54 Queen's Gate Terrace, SW7 5PJ. *Club:* New (Edinburgh).

CURRIE, (Joseph) Austin; retired politician and author; Minister of State, Departments of Health, Education and Justice, Irish Parliament, 1994–97; only person to have been elected to both Irish Parliaments and to have served as a Minister in both; *b* 11 Oct. 1939; *s* of John Currie and Mary (*née* O'Donnell); *m* 1968, Anne Ita Lynch; two *s* three *d*. *Educ:* Edendork Sch.; St Patrick's Academy, Dungannon; Queen's Univ., Belfast (BA). MP (Nat) Tyrone, Parlt of N Ireland, 1964–72; Founder Mem., SDLP, 1970; Mem. (SDLP), Fermanagh and S Tyrone, NI Assembly, 1973–75, NI Constitutional Convention, 1975–76, NI Assembly, 1982–86; Minister of Housing, Planning and Local Govt, 1974. Contested (FG) Presidency of Ireland, 1990. Irish Parliament: TD (FG), Dublin W, Dail Eireann, 1989–2002. Mem., Anglo-Irish Parly tier; frontbench spokesperson: on communications, 1991–93; on equality and law reform, 1993–94; spokesperson on energy, 1997–2001; dep. spokesperson on foreign affairs, 2001–02. Mem., Forum for Peace and Reconciliation, 1995–. Advr to Eur. Commn, 1984–87. *Publication:* All Hell Will Break Loose (autobiog.), 2004. *Recreations:* Gaelic football, golf, snooker, reading. *Address:* Tullydraw, Derrymullen, Robertstown, Naas, Co. Kildare, Ireland.

CURRIE JONES, Edwina; *see* Currie, E.

CURRIMBHOY, Sir Mohamed; *see* Ebrahim, Sir M. C.

CURRY, Rt Hon. David (Maurice); PC 1996; MP (C) Skipton and Ripon, since 1987; *b* 13 June 1944; *s* of Thomas Harold Curry and Florence Joan (*née* Tyerman); *m* 1971, Anne Helene Maud Roullet; one *s* two *d*. *Educ:* Ripon Grammar Sch.; Corpus Christi Coll., Oxford (MA Hons); Kennedy Sch. of Govt, Harvard (Kennedy Scholar, 1966–67). Reporter, Newcastle Jl, 1967–70; Financial Times: Trade Editor, Internat. Cos Editor, Brussels Corresp., Paris Corresp., and European News Editor, 1970–79. Sec., Anglo-American Press Assoc. of Paris, 1978; Founder, Paris Conservative Assoc., 1977. MEP (C) Essex NE, 1979–89; Chm., Agriculture Cttee, 1982–84; Vice-Chm., Budgets Cttee, 1984–85; spokesman on budgetary matters for European Democratic Gp, 1985–89; Gen. Rapporteur for EEC's 1987 budget. Parly Sec., 1989–92, Minister of State, 1992–93, MAFF; Minister of State, DoE, 1993–97; Shadow Sec. of State for Local and Devolved Govt Affairs, 2003–04. Chairman, Select Committee: on agriculture, 1999–2001; on envmt, food and rural affairs, 2001–03; Member: Public Accounts Cttee, 2004–; Cttee on Standards & Privileges, 2007–. Chm., Dairy UK, 2005–. *Publications:* The Food War: the EEC, the US and the battle for world food markets, 1982; (ed) The Conservative Tradition in Europe, 1998; Lobbying Government, 1999. *Recreations:* digging, windsurfing. *Address:* Newland End, Arkesden, Essex CB11 4HF. *T:* (01799) 550368.

CURRY, Sir Donald (Thomas Younger), Kt 2001; CBE 1997; farmer; Chairman: Meat and Livestock Commission, 1993–2001; NFU Mutual Insurance Society, since 2003 (non-executive Director, since 1997; Vice-Chairman, 2000–03); *b* 4 April 1944; *s* of Robert Thomas Younger Curry and Barbara Ramsey Curry; *m* 1966, Rhoda Mary Murdie; two *s* one *d*. *Educ:* Northumberland Coll. of Agric. Estabd farming business, 1971; farms 450 acres in Northumberland (C&G Farm Mgt and Orgn). Comr, MLC, 1986– (Dep. Chm., 1992–93); Crown Estate Comr, 2000–07. Chm., Commn on the Future of Farming and Food, 2001–02. Founder/Chairman: N Country Primestock (livestock mktg co-op.), 1990–2002; At Home in the Community (provides residential homes for people with a learning disability), 1992–; Farm Assured British Beef and Lamb, 1992–94; *Recreations:* church responsibilities, photography, travel, gardening. *Address:* Middle Farm, Barrasford, Hexham, Northumberland NE48 4DA. *Club:* Farmers'.

CURRY, Dr Gordon Barrett; Reader, Department of Geographical and Earth Sciences (formerly Department of Geology and Applied Geology, then Division of Earth Sciences), University of Glasgow, since 1992 (Royal Society University Research Fellow, 1984–92); *b* 27 June 1954; *s* of Robert and Violet Curry; *m* 1983, Gillian. *Educ:* Masonic Sch., Dublin; Trinity Coll., Dublin (BA Mod.); Imperial Coll. London (PhD, DIC). FGS. University of Glasgow: Research Asst to Sir Alwyn Williams, 1980–84; Dep. Dir, Human Identification Centre, 1995–98; Project Manager, Taxonomy Prog., 1996–99. Treas., Systematics Assoc., 1996–. President's Award, Geol Soc., 1985; Clough Award, Edinburgh Geol Soc., 1985–86; Wollaston Fund, Geol Soc., 1989. *Publications:* (jtly) British Brachiopods, 1979; (ed) Allochthonous Terranes, 1991; (jtly) Molecules through Time: fossil molecules and biochemical systematics, 1991; Biology of Living Brachiopods, 1992; (ed) Biodiversity Databases, 2007; numerous contribs to learned jls. *Recreations:* music, swimming, cricket, golf, travel. *Address:* Department of Geographical and Earth Sciences, Gregory Building, University of Glasgow, Lilybank Gardens, Glasgow G12 8QQ. *T:* (0141) 330 5444; *e-mail:* Gordon.Curry@ges.gla.ac.uk.

CURRY, John Arthur Hugh, CBE 1997; Chairman, All England Lawn Tennis Ground plc, since 1990; *b* 7 June 1938; *s* of Alfred Robert and Mercia Beatrice Curry; *m* 1962, Anne Rosemary Lewis; three *s* one *d*. *Educ:* King's College School, Wimbledon; St Edmund Hall, Oxford (MA); Harvard Univ. Graduate College (MBA). FCA. Arthur Andersen, 1962–64; Man. Dir, Unitech, 1966–86 (non-exec. Dir, 1986–96); Chm., ACAL, 1986–2005. Non-executive Director: Dixons, 1993–2001; Foreign & Colonial Smaller Cos PLC, 1996–2004 (Chm., 2002–04); Terence Chapman Group plc, 1999–2003; Chm., Invicta Leisure Gp, 1999–2002. *Publication:* Partners for Profit, 1966. *Recreations:* tennis, Rugby. *Address:* Stokewood Park House, Sheardley Lane, Droxford, Hants SO32 3QY. *Clubs:* Farmers', Inst. of Dirs; All England Lawn Tennis and Croquet (Chm., 1989–99, Mem. Cttee, 1979–99); International Lawn Tennis of GB.

CURRY, (Thomas) Peter (Ellison); QC 1966, 1973; *s* of Maj. F. R. P. Curry; *m* 1950, Pamela Joyce, *d* of late Group Capt. A. J. Holmes, AFC, JP; two *s* two *d*. *Educ:* Tonbridge; Oriel Coll., Oxford (BA 1948; MA 1951). Served War of 1939–45; enlisted 1939; commnd, 1941; 17th Indian Div., India and Burma, 1941–45. War Office, 1946. Called to Bar, Middle Temple, 1953, Bencher, 1979. QC 1966. Solicitor, 1968; partner in Freshfields, Solicitors, 1968–70; returned to Bar; re-appointed QC 1973. Pres., Aircraft and Shipbuilding Industries Arbitration Tribunal, 1978–80. Chm., Chancery Bar Assoc., 1980–85; Dep. Chm., Barristers' Benevolent Assoc., 1989–91 (Hon. Treas., 1964–71, 1984–89). Rep. Army and Sussex at Squash Racquets (described as fastest mover in squash, 1947); triple blue, squash, cross country and athletics, Oxford (twice cross country winner; unbeaten, cross country, 1946–48); World Student Games (5000 m), 1947; British Steeplechase champion 1948, Olympic Games, 1948. Served on AAA Cttee of Inquiry, 1967. Holder of French certificate as capitaine-mécanicien for mechanically propelled boats. *Publications:* (ed jtly) Palmer's Company Law, 1959; (ed jtly) Crew on Meetings, 1966, 1975. *Recreations:* gardening, the Turf. *Address:* Hurlands, Dunsfold, Surrey GU8 4NT. *T:* (01483) 200356.

CURTEIS, Ian Bayley; dramatist; *b* 1 May 1935; *m* 1st, 1964, Mrs (Dorothy) Joan Macdonald; two *s*; 2nd, 1985, Joanna Trollope, *qv* (marr. diss. 2001); two step *d*; 3rd, 2001, Lady Deirdre Freda Mary Hare, *e d* of 5th Earl of Listowel, GCMG, PC and *widow* of 7th Baron Grantley, MC; two step *s*. *Educ:* Iver Council Sch.; Slough Grammar Sch.; Slough Trading Estate; London Univ. Director and actor in theatres all over Great Britain, and BBC-tv script reader, 1956–63; BBC and ATV staff director (drama), directing plays by John Betjeman, John Hopkins, William Trevor and others, 1963–67. Pres., Writers' Guild of GB, 1998–2001 (Mem. Exec. Council and Chm. various cttees, 1979–2001). Founder and Trustee, Joanna Trollope Charitable Trust, 1995–2003. *Television plays:* Beethoven, Sir Alexander Fleming (BBC's entry at 1973 Prague Fest.), Mr Rolls and Mr Royce, Long Voyage out of War (trilogy), The Folly, The Haunting, Second Time Round, A Distinct Chill, The Portland Millions, Philby, Burgess and Maclean (British entry 1978 Monte Carlo Fest., BAFTA nomination), Hess, The Atom Spies, Churchill and the Generals (BAFTA nomination; Grand Prize, Best Programme of 1980, NY Internat. Film and TV Fest.), Suez 1956 (BAFTA nomination), Miss Morison's Ghosts (British entry 1982 Monte Carlo Fest.), The Mitford Girls, BB and Joe (trilogy), Lost Empires (adapted from J. B. Priestley), The Trials of Lady Sackville, Eureka (1st Euroserial simultaneously shown in UK, West Germany, Austria, Switzerland, Italy and France), The Nightmare Years, The Zimmerman Telegram, The Choir (dramatisation of Joanna Trollope novel), The Falklands Play; also originated and wrote numerous popular television drama series; *film screenplays:* Andre Malraux's La Condition humaine, 1982; Graham Greene's The Man Within, 1983; Tom Paine (for Sir Richard Attenborough), 1983; *play:* A Personal Affair, Globe, 1982; The Bargain, Bath and nat. tour, 2007; *radio plays:* Eroica, 2000; Love, 2001; The Falklands Play, 2002; After the Break, 2002; More Love, 2003; Yet More Love, 2004; Miss Morison's Ghosts, 2004. *Publications: plays:* Long Voyage out of War (trilogy), 1971; Churchill and the Generals, 1979; Suez 1956, 1980; The Falklands Play, 1987; numerous articles and speeches on the ethics and politics of broadcasting. *Recreations:* history of art, history of architecture, country pursuits. *Address:* Markenfield Hall, Ripon, N Yorks HG4 3AD. *T:* (01765) 603411; 2 Warwick Square, SW1V 2AA. *T:* (020) 7821 8606. *Clubs:* Beefsteak, Garrick.

See also T. A. Curteis.

CURTEIS, Tobit Armstrong, FIIC; wall painting conservator and specialist in environmental deterioration, Tobit Curteis Associates, since 1996; *b* 2 March 1966; *s* of Ian Bayley Curteis, *qv* and Dorothy Joan Curteis; *m* 1996, Victoria Ellen Kaye; one *s* one *d*. *Educ:* King's Sch., Canterbury; Univ. of Warwick (BA Hons Hist. of Art 1988); Courtauld Inst. of Art, Univ. of London (Dip. Conservation of Wall Paintings 1991). FIIC 2003. Research and treatment projects include: Winchester Cathedral, 1995; Hill Hall (English Heritage), 1995–2005; Chartwell (NT), 1998–2005; Fitzwilliam Mus., Cambridge, 1999–2001; Peterborough Cathedral, 1999–2005; Cormac's Chapel, Cashel, Ireland, 2001–; St John's Coll., Cambridge, 2002; Golden Temple, Amritsar, 2003; Worcester Cathedral, 2003–06; Hampton Court Palace, 2004–06; Chinese Palace, St Petersburg, Russia (World Monument Fund), 2004–; Blickling Hall, Norfolk (NT), 2005; Lincoln Cathedral, 2006. Consultant to English Heritage on conservation of wall paintings, 2002–; Wall Paintings Advr to NT, 2005–. *Publications:* contrib. numerous articles and published lectures to conf. proc. and professional jls. *Recreations:* paragliding, hill walking, cooking. *Address:* Tobit Curteis Associates, 36 Abbey Road, Cambridge CB5 8HQ. *T:* (01223) 501958, *Fax:* (01223) 304190; *e-mail:* tc@tcassociates.co.uk.

CURTIS, Prof. Adam Sebastian Genevieve, PhD; Professor of Cell Biology, University of Glasgow, 1967–2004, now Emeritus; *b* 3 Jan. 1934; *s* of Herbert Lewis Curtis and Nora Patricia Curtis (*née* Stevens); *m* 1958, Ann Park; two *d*. *Educ:* Aldenham Sch.; King's Coll., Cambridge (BA 1955; MA); Univ. of Edinburgh (PhD 1957). University College London: Hon. Research Asst, 1957–62; Lectr in Zool., 1962–67; University of Glasgow: Head, Molecular and Cellular Biol. Planning Unit, 1991–94; Head, Molecular and Cellular Biol. Div., 1994–95; Jt Dir, Centre for Cell Engrg, 1996–2004. Pres., Tissue & Cell Engrg Soc., 2001–03. Editor in Chief, Exptl Biology Online, 1996–99; Ed., IEEE Trans in Nanobioscience, 2002–. Cuvier Medal, Zool Soc. of France, 1972. *Publications:* The Cell Surface, 1967; (with J. M. Lackie) Measuring Cell Adhesion, 1991; numerous articles in scientific jls; also articles on scuba diving. *Recreations:* scuba diving, underwater photography, gardening. *Address:* 2 Kirklee Circus, Glasgow G12 0TW. *T:* (0141) 339 2152. *Club:* Lansdowne.

CURTIS, Sir Barry (John), Kt 1992; Mayor of Manukau, New Zealand, 1983–2007; *b* 27 Feb. 1939; *s* of John Dixon Cory Curtis and Vera Gladys Curtis (*née* Johnson); *m* 1961, Miriam Ann Brooke (marr. diss. 1991); three *d*. *Educ:* Otahuhu College; Univ. of Auckland (Dip. TP). MRICS, MNZIS, MNZPI, MPMI. Town Planner, Chartered and Registered Surveyor. Manukau City Councillor, 1968–83; Member: Auckland Regl Authy, 1971–84 (Chm., Regl Planning Cttee, 1977–83); Prime Minister's Safer Communities Council, 1990–; Chairman: Hillary Commn Task Force on Recreation, 1988; Jean Batten Meml Trust, 1989; Manukau Healthy City Cttee, 1989–93; Manukau Safer Community Council, 1990–93; Auckland Mayors' Forum, 1990–96, 2004–05; Electoral Coll., Infrastructure Auckland, 1998–2004; Auckland Regl Econ. Devel Strategy Establishment Gp, 2002–04; Nat. Taskforce for Community Violence Reduction Leaders Gp, 2005–07; Dep. Chm., Auckland Regl Growth Strategy Forum, 1996–2007. Past Pres., NZ Sister Cities Cttee. A Dir, XIVth Commonwealth Games Ltd, 1989–92 (Mem. Exec. Bd, 1989–90). Patron, Auckland Hockey Assoc. Valedictory Award, NZ Pacific Business Council, 2007. Seiuli (High Chief Matai title) conferred by HE Malietoa Tanumafili II, Western Samoa, 1993; Kaumatua conferred by Tuhoe and Te Arawa tribes, Aotearoa, 2007; Hon. Residence, Cook Islands, 2005. *Recreations:* jogging, surfing, gardening, follower of Rugby, hockey, cricket, tennis, yachting. *Address:* 3/116 Clovelly Road, Bucklands Beach, City of Manukau, Auckland Region, New Zealand. *T:* (9) 5348153, *Fax:* (9) 5349153. *Clubs:* Pakuranga Combined Bowling (Foundn Chm.), Pakuranga Men's Bowling (Foundn Pres.).

CURTIS, Bronwen Mary, CBE 2008; Chairman, Northampton General Hospital NHS Trust, 1998–2007; a Civil Service Commissioner, 2001–07; *b* 17 May 1955; *d* of Hywel Arwyn Hughes and Doris Winifred Hughes (*née* Billingham); *m* 1990, Alan Curtis (marr. diss. 2002); one *s* (one *d* decd). *Educ:* Sheffield Poly. (HND Business Studies (Dist.)); University Coll., Cardiff (Postgrad. Dip. Personnel Mgt). Avon Cosmetics: Dir, UK Manufg, 1988–90; Vice President: Manufg, 1990–92; Planning and Develt, 1993–95; HR, 1995–2001. Chm., Two Shires Ambulance Trust, 1995–98. Home Sec.'s Rep., Northants Police Authy Selection Panel, 1997–2003; Indep. Mem., Sen. Salaries Rev. Bd, DCMS, 2005–; Mem., Prison Service Pay Rev. Body. Non-executive Director: Nat. Archives; Northants Healthcare Trust. Mem., Forum UK, 1990–. Midlands Businesswoman of Year, Winged Fellowship Trust, 1990. *Recreations:* playing and watching sport, learning from others, solving complex problems and making life easier for others.

CURTIS, Bronwyn Nanette, OBE 2008; Partner and Chief Economist, Arch Financial Products LLP, since 2006; Chairman, Society of Business Economists, since 2006; *b* Bendigo, Australia; *d* of Edward J. and Loris M. Schlotterlein; *m* Paul G. Curtis; one *s* one *d*. *Educ:* La Trobe Univ., Australia (BEc Hons); London Sch. of Econs (MSc Econ.). Sen. Manager, Mars Confectionary, 1977–82; Chief Economist, Gill and Duffus plc, 1982–84; Res. Dir, Landell Mills Commodities Studies, 1984–87; Global Hd, Currency and Fixed Income Strategy, Deutsche Bank, 1987–97; Chief Economist, Nomura Internat., 1997–99; Managing Ed. and Hd, Eur. Broadcasting, Bloomberg LP, 1999–2006. Consultant: UN, 1984–87; World Bank, 1984–87. Vis. Prof., Cass Business Sch., 1997–2005. Non-exec. Dir, OFT, 2007–. Member: ESRC, 1998–2003; Bd of Mgt, NIESR, 2005–. Gov., LSE, 2002–. *Publication:* Cocoa, A Trader's Guide, 1987. *Recreations:* yacht racing and cruising, ballet. *Address:* Society of Business Economists, Dean House, Vernham Dean, Andover, Hants SP11 0JZ. *T:* (01264) 737552; *e-mail:* admin@sbe.co.uk. *Clubs:* Royal Thames Yacht, Royal Southern Yacht.

CURTIS, Prof. Charles David, OBE 2001; Head of Research and Development Strategy, Radioactive Waste Management Directorate, Nuclear Decommissioning Authority, since 2007 (Head of Research and Development Strategy, UK Nirex Ltd, 2004–07); *b* 11 Nov. 1939; *s* of Charles Frederick Curtis and Kate Margaret Curtis (*née* Jackson); *m* 1963, Dr Diana Joy Saxty; two *d*. *Educ:* Imperial College London; Univ. of Sheffield (BSc, PhD). University of Sheffield: Lectr, Sen. Lectr, Reader, 1965–83; Personal Chair in Geochem., 1983–88; University of Manchester: Professor of Geochemistry, 1988–2004, now Emeritus; Hd, Dept of Geology, 1989–92; Res. Dean, Faculty of Science and Engrg, 1994–2000. Vis. Prof., Dept of Geology and Geophys., UCLA, 1970–71; Res. Associate, British Petroleum Res. Centre, 1987–88; Hon. Res. Fellow, Natural Hist. Mus., 1999–. Member: Council, NERC, 1990–93; Radioactive Waste Mgt Adv. Cttee, 1994–2004 (Chm., 1999–2004); Radioactivity Res. and Envmtl Monitoring Cttee, 1995–2004; Bd Assurance Cttee, UKAEA, 2002–. Pres., Geological Soc., 1992–94. Murchison Medal, Geological Soc., 1987. *Publications:* numerous articles in learned jls. *Recreations:* mountaineering, gardening, photography. *Address:* Nuclear Decommissioning Authority, Curie Avenue, Harwell, Didcot, Oxon OX11 0RH. *T:* (01235) 825415.

CURTIS, Colin Hinton Thomson, CVO 1970; ISO 1970; retired; Chairman, Metropolitan Public Abattoir Board, 1971–81; Member, Queensland Meat Industry Authority, 1972–78; *b* 25 June 1920; *s* of A. Curtis, Brisbane; *m* 1943, Anne Catherline Drevesen; one *s*. *Educ:* Brisbane Grammar School. RANR Overseas Service, 1940–45. Sec. and Investigation Officer to Chm., Sugar Cane Prices Board, 1948–49; Asst Sec. to Central Sugar Cane Prices Board, 1949; Sec. to Premier of Queensland, 1950–64; Mem., Qld Trade Missions to SE Asia, 1963 and 1964; Asst Under-Sec., Premier's Dept, 1961–64; Assoc. Dir and Dir of Industrial Development, 1964–66; Under-Sec., Premier's Dept and Clerk of Exec. Council, 1966–70; State Dir, Royal Visit, 1970; Agent-General for Queensland in London, 1970–71. *Recreations:* yachting, swimming. *Address:* 57 Daru Avenue, Runaway Bay, Gold Coast, Qld 4216, Australia. *Club:* RSL Memorial (Queensland).

CURTIS, Daniel Nicholas Mansfield; a District Judge (Magistrates' Courts), since 2005; *b* 15 May 1963; *s* of late Cyril Frank Paul Curtis and of Joyce Mary Curtis (*née* Bailey); two *s*. *Educ:* Boston Spa Comp. Sch.; King's Coll., London (LLB Hons). Partner, Tates, solicitors, 1992–2005; a Dep. District Judge, 2003–05. *Recreations:* motorcycling, travel, running (almost as slowly as District Judge Browne), coaching amateur Rugby (youth). *Address:* Grimsby Magistrates' Court, Victoria Street, Grimsby, Lincs DN31 1PE. *T:* (01472) 320444, *Fax:* (01472) 320440; *e-mail:* districtjudge.curtis@judiciary.gsi.gov.uk. *Club:* Roundhegians (Leeds).

CURTIS, Prof. David Roderick, AC 1992; FRACP 1987; FRS 1974; FAA 1965; Emeritus Professor, Australian National University, since 1993; *b* 3 June 1927; *s* of E. D. and E. V. Curtis; *m* 1951, Lauri Sewell; one *s* one *d*. *Educ:* Univ. of Melbourne; Australian National Univ. MB, BS Melbourne 1950, PhD ANU 1957. John Curtin School of Medical Research, Australian National University: Department of Physiology: Research Scholar, 1954–56; Research Fellow, 1956–57; Fellow, 1957–59; Sen. Fellow, 1959–62; Professorial Fellow, 1962–66; Prof. of Pharmacology, 1966–68; Prof. of Neuropharmacology, 1968–73; Prof. and Foundn Head, Dept of Pharmacology, 1973–88; Chm., Div. of Physiol Sciences, 1988–89; Howard Florey Prof. of Med. Res., and Dir of the Sch., 1989–92; University Fellow, 1993–95. President: Aust. Acad. of Sci., 1986–90 (Burnet Medal, 1983); Australian Physiol and Pharmacol Soc., 1992–95; Chairman: Res. Adv. Bd, Nat. Multiple Sclerosis Soc., Australia, 1978–83, 1993–96; Inaugural Australia Prize Cttee, 1989–90. Centenary Medal, 2003. *Publications:* (with F. J. Fenner) The John Curtin School of Medical Research: the first fifty years, 2001; papers in fields of neurophysiology, neuropharmacology in Jl Physiology, Jl Neurophysiol., Brain Research, Exper. Brain Research. *Recreations:* woodwork, wombling. *Address:* 7 Patey Street, Campbell, Canberra, ACT 2612, Australia. *T:* and *Fax:* (2) 62485664.

CURTIS, Frank; *see* Curtis, R. F.

CURTIS, James William Ockford; QC 1993; a Recorder, since 1991; *b* 2 Sept. 1946; *s* of late Eric William Curtis, MC, TD and Margaret Joan Curtis (*née* Blunt); *m* 1985, Genevra Fiona Penelope Victoria Caws, QC (*d* 1997); one *d*. *Educ:* Bedford Sch.; Worcester Coll., Oxford (MA Jurisp). Called to the Bar, Inner Temple, 1970. *Recreations:* farming, field sports, ski-ing, classics. *Address:* 6 King's Bench Walk, Temple, EC4Y 7DR. *T:* (020) 7583 0410. *Clubs:* Reform, Flyfishers'.

CURTIS, Most Rev. John Barry; Archbishop of Calgary, 1994–99; Metropolitan of Rupert's Land, 1994–99; *b* 19 June 1933; *s* of Harold Boyd Curtis and Eva B. Curtis (*née* Saunders); *m* 1959, Patricia Emily (*née* Simpson); two *s* two *d*. *Educ:* Trinity Coll., Univ. of Toronto (BA 1955, LTh 1958); Theological Coll., Chichester, Sussex. Deacon 1958, priest 1959; Asst Curate, Holy Trinity, Pembroke, Ont, 1958–61; Rector: Parish of March, Kanata, Ont, 1961–65; St Stephen's Church, Buckingham, Que, 1965–69; Church School Consultant, Diocese of Ottawa, 1969; Rector, All Saints (Westboro), Ottawa, 1969–78; Director of Programme, Diocese of Ottawa, 1978–80; Rector, Christ Church, Elbow Park, Calgary, Alta, 1980–83; Bishop of Calgary, 1983–99. Member, Governing Board: Canadian Council of Churches, 1994– (Pres., 1999–); Habitat for Humanity Canada, 1994–. Hon. DD Trinity Coll., Toronto, 1985. Habitat for Humanity, Canada. *Recreations:* reading, hiking, ski-ing, cycling. *Address:* 12 Varanger Place NW, Calgary, AB T3A 0E9, Canada. *T:* (403) 2865127. *Club:* Ranchmen's (Calgary, Alta).

CURTIS, John Edward, OBE 2006; PhD; FBA 2003; FSA; Keeper, Department of Middle East (formerly Department of Western Asiatic Antiquities, then of Ancient Near East), British Museum, since 1989; *b* 23 June 1946; *yr s* of late Arthur Norman Curtis and of Laura Letitia Ladd (*née* Thomas); *m* 1977, Vesta Sarkhosh; one *s* one *d*. *Educ:* Collyer's Grammar Sch., Horsham; Univ. of Bristol (BA); Inst. of Archaeology, Univ. of London (Postgrad. Diploma in Western Asiatic Archaeology; PhD 1979). FSA 1984. Fellow, British Sch. of Archaeology in Iraq, 1969–71; Res. Asst, Dept of Western Asiatic Antiquities, British Museum, 1971–74, Asst Keeper, 1974–89. Chm., British Assoc. for Near Eastern Archaeol., 1996–2001; Hon. Sec. and Trustee, Ancient Persia Fund, 1987–; Member, Governing Council: British Sch. of Archaeol. in Iraq, 1980–2001, 2002–; British Inst. of Persian Studies, 1991–2001, 2002–05. Iran Heritage Foundn Award, 2005. *Publications:* (ed) Fifty Years of Mesopotamian Discovery, 1982; Nush-i Jan III: the Small Finds, 1984; (ed) Bronzeworking Centres of Western Asia *c* 1000–539 BC, 1988; Excavations at Qasrij Cliff and Khirbet Qasrij, 1989; Ancient Persia, 1989, 2nd edn 2000; (ed) Early Mesopotamia and Iran: Contact and Conflict 3500–1600 BC, 1993; (ed with J. E. Reade) Art and Empire: treasures from Assyria in the British Museum, 1995; (ed) Later Mesopotamia and Iran: tribes and empires 1600–539 BC, 1995; (ed) Mesopotamia and Iran in the Persian period: conquest and imperialism 539–331 BC, 1997; (with A. R. Green) Excavations at Khirbet Khatuniyeh, 1997; (ed) Mesopotamia and Iran in the Parthian and Sasanian periods: rejection and revival *c* 238 BC–AD 642, 2000; (with M. Kruszyński) Ancient Caucasian and Related Material in the British Museum, 2002; (ed with N. Tallis) Forgotten Empire: the world of Ancient Persia, 2005; articles in learned jls. *Address:* 4 Hillfield Road, NW6 1QE. *T:* (020) 7435 6153; 1 Francis Cottage, Sandy Hill Road, Saundersfoot, Dyfed SA69 9HW.

CURTIS, John Henry, CB 1981; FTSE; Chairman, Nortel Australia Pty Ltd, 1989–92, retired; *b* 20 March 1920; *s* of K. H. and E. M. Curtis; *m* 1943, Patricia Foote (*d* 1989); one *s* one *d*. *Educ:* Ipswich Grammar Sch.; Queensland Univ. (BE Hons 1950, BSc 1951, BA 1957). FIEAust 1981; FAIM 1970; FTSE (FTS 1979). Dir of Posts and Telegraphs, Qld, 1971–73; Dep. Dir Gen., Postmaster-Gen.'s Dept, 1973–75; Man. Dir, Australian Telecommunications Commn, 1975–81; Chairman: D. Richardson & Sons, later Richardson Pacific, 1982–90; A. W. A. Nortel, 1986–89. Comr, Overseas Telecommunications Commn (Australia), 1974–87. Pres., Victorian Div., Aust. Inst. of Management, 1979–81; Dir, Cttee for Econ. Develt of Aust., 1981–93 (Hon. Life Mem., 1993). Mem., Bd of Management, Defence Aerospace, 1984–86. Gov., Internat. Council for Computer Communication, 1982–94. Hon. Life Mem., IREE, 1982. Centenary Medal, 2004. *Address:* 101 Kadumba Street, Yeronga, Qld 4104, Australia. *T:* (7) 38922743.

CURTIS, Michael Alexander; QC 2008; *b* Birmingham, 4 July 1959; *s* of Frank and Ann Curtis; *m* 2007, Kate Purkiss; one *s* two *d*. *Educ:* King Henry VIII Sch., Coventry; Brasenose Coll., Oxford (MA); King's Coll. London (MSc). Called to the Bar, Middle Temple, 1982; in practice as barrister, specialising in construction, commercial and public law, 1982–. *Publication:* (ed) Emden's Construction Law. *Recreation:* watching football. *Address:* Crown Office Chambers, 2 Crown Office Row, Temple, EC4Y 7HJ. *T:* (020) 7797 8100, *Fax:* (020) 7797 8101; *e-mail:* curtis@crownofficechambers.com. *Club:* Arsenal Football.

CURTIS, Michael John; Director of Finance, Islington Council, since 2006; *b* 2 Aug. 1961; *s* of John and Sylvia Curtis; *m* 1992, Julie Thompson; two *s*. *Educ:* Portsmouth Poly. (BA Hons 1982); Miami Univ., Ohio (MA 1984); St Antony's Coll., Oxford. CPFA 1989. Trainee Accountant, 1986–89, Finance Manager, 1989–90, Kent CC; Projects Consultant, Berks CC, 1990–93; Manager, CSL Managed Services, 1993–95; Head of Financial Services, 1996–98, Dir of Finance, 1998–2001, Broxbourne BC; Asst Dir, Adult Care Services, Herts CC, 2001–06. Bd Mem., Broxbourne Housing Assoc., 2005– (Chm., Audit Cttee). Trustee and Treas., One World Action, 2006–. *Recreations:* travel, walking, reading, cricket, football. *Address:* Islington Council, 222 Upper Street, N1 1XR. *T:* (020) 7527 2294; *e-mail:* mike.curtis@islington.gov.uk.

CURTIS, Monica Anne; Head, Chelmsford County High School for Girls, 1997–2006; *b* 26 May 1946; *d* of H. L. Seale; *m* 1968, Timothy Chaytor Curtis (*d* 1986), former Dep. Dir, Lancashire Poly.; two *s*. *Educ:* Manchester Univ. (BA English and History of Art 1968). Teacher: Urmston Grammar Sch. for Girls, 1968–70; various schs in Newcastle upon Tyne, 1970–80; Lancaster Girls' Grammar Sch., 1980–89; Kesteven and Grantham Girls' Sch., 1989–97. *Address:* The Chestnuts, Braintree Road, Felsted, Dunmow, Essex CM6 3DR.

CURTIS, Hon. Sir Richard Herbert, Kt 1992; a Judge of the High Court of Justice, Queen's Bench Division, 1992–2005; Presiding Judge, Wales and Chester Circuit, 1994–97. *Educ:* Oxford Univ. (MA). Called to Bar, Inner Temple, 1958, Bencher, 1985; QC 1977; a Recorder, 1974–89; Recorder of Birmingham, 1989–92; Hon. Recorder, City of Hereford, 1981–1992; Sen. Circuit Judge, Oxford and Midland Circuit, 1989–92. *Address:* c/o Royal Courts of Justice, Strand, WC2A 2LL.

CURTIS, Richard Whalley Anthony, CBE 2000 (MBE 1995); freelance writer; *b* 8 Nov. 1956; *s* of late Anthony J. Curtis and of Glynness S. Curtis; three *s* one *d* by Emma Vallencey Freud, *d* of Sir Clement Freud, *qv*. *Educ:* Papplewick Sch.; Harrow Sch.; Christ Church, Oxford (BA). Freelance writer: *television:* Not the Nine O'clock News (four series), 1979–83; Blackadder (four series), 1984–89; Mr Bean, 1989–95; Bernard and the Genie, 1993; The Vicar of Dibley, 1994–2000; The Girl in the Café, 2005; *films:* The Tall Guy, 1988; Four Weddings and a Funeral, 1994; Bean, 1997; Notting Hill, 1999; (jtly) Bridget Jones's Diary, 2001; (also dir) Love Actually, 2003; (jtly) Bridget Jones: The Edge of Reason, 2004; producer, Comic Relief, 1985–2003. Campaigner, Make Poverty History and Live 8, 2005. *Recreations:* too much TV, too many films, too much pop music. *Address:* c/o United Agents, 12–26 Lexington Street, W1F 0LE.

CURTIS, Prof. (Robert) Frank, CBE 1985; PhD, DSc; Chairman, Norfolk Mental Health Care NHS Trust, 1994–98; Professor, University of East Anglia, 1977–88, Hon Professor, 1988–2001; *b* 8 Oct. 1926; *s* of late William John Curtis, Somerset, and Ethel Irene Curtis, Bath; *m* 1954, Sheila Rose, *y d* of Bruce Rose, Huddersfield; two *s* one *d*. *Educ:* City of Bath Sch.; Univ. of Bristol (BSc 1949, PhD 1952, DSc 1972). FRIC 1966; FIFST 1977. Johns Hopkins University: W. H. Grafflin Fellow, 1952; Instr in Chemistry, 1953; Technical Officer, ICI Ltd, Manchester, 1954–56; Res. Fellow, Univ. of Wl 1956–57; Lectr in Chem., University Coll., Swansea, 1957–62, Sen. Lectr, 1962–69; Reader, Univ. of Wales, 1969–70; Head, Chem. Div., 1970–77, Dir, 1977–85, ARC Food Res. Inst.; Dir, AFRC Inst. of Food Res., Reading, 1985–88. Chm., Food Adv Cttee, MAFF, 1983–88 (Chm., Food Standards Cttee, 1979–83); Mem. Management Bd AFRC, 1987–88. Mem., Norwich HA, 1989–94 (Vice-Chm., 1993–94); Mem. Council RVC, 1991–2000. Hon. ScD UEA, 1988. *Publications:* res. papers on chemistry and food science in jls of learned socs. *Address:* Manor Barn, Colton, Norwich NR9 5BZ. *T:* (01603) 880379.

CURTIS, Stephen Russell; Managing Director, Professional Services Division, Jordan Ltd, since 1997; *b* 27 Feb. 1948; *s* of Barry Russell and Joyce Muriel (*née* Smith); *m* 1972 Gillian Mary Pitkin; three *s* one *d*. *Educ:* Forest Sch., E17; Exeter Univ. (BA Econs and Stats). Asst Statistician, Business Stats Office, 1970–72; DTI, 1972–78, Statistician, Export Stats, 1975–78; Statistician, 1978–83, Chief Statistician, 1983–85, Business Stats Office; Registrar of Companies, 1985–90, and Chief Exec., 1988–90, Companies House; Chief Exec., DVLA, 1990–95. *Recreations:* travel, photography, walking. *Club:* Civil Service.

CURTIS, Sir William (Peter), 7th Bt *cr* 1802; *b* 9 April 1935; *s* of Sir Peter Curtis, 6th Bt, and Joan Margaret, *d* of late Reginald Nicholson; *S* father, 1976. *Educ:* Winchester College; Trinity College, Oxford (MA); Royal Agricultural College, Cirencester. *Heir: cousin* Major Edward Philip Curtis, 16th/5th The Queen's Royal Lancers (retd) [*b* 25 June 1940; *m* 1978, Catherine, *d* of H. J. Armstrong, Christchurch, NZ; two *s* two *d*. *Educ:* Bradfield; RMA Sandhurst]. *Address:* Oak Lodge, Bank Street, Bishop's Waltham, Hants SO3 1AN.

CURTIS-RALEIGH, Dr Jean Margaret Macdonald; Consultant Psychiatrist, Queen Mary's University Hospital, Roehampton, 1979–98; *b* 12 July 1933; *d* of late Dr Harry Hubert Steadman and Janet Gilchrist Steadman (*née* Macdonald); *m* 1964, His Honour Judge Nigel Hugh Curtis-Raleigh (*d* 1986); five *s*. *Educ:* Convent of the Sacred Heart, Epsom, Surrey; Sutton High Sch. for Girls; Guy's Hospital Med. Sch. (MB BS); FRCPsych; DPM. Psychiatric trng, Maudsley and Bethlem Royal Hosps, 1963–66. Med. Mem., Mental Health Review Tribunal, 1994–2006. Mem., Broadcasting Standards Council, 1988–95. *Recreations:* opera, gardening, walking.
See also J. H. Steadman.

CURTIS-THOMAS, Claire; MP (Lab) Crosby, since 1997; *b* 30 April 1958; *d* of late Joyce Curtis; *m* Michael Lewis; one *s* two *d*. *Educ:* Mynyddbach Comp. Sch. for Girls, Swansea; UC Cardiff (BSc); Aston Univ. (MBA). CEng; FIMechE 1995; FIET (FIEE 2000). Shell Chemicals, 1990–92; Hd, Strategic Planning, 1992–93, Hd R&D Lab., 1993–95, Birmingham CC; Dean, Faculty of Business and Engrg, Univ. of Wales Coll. Newport (formerly Gwent Coll. of Higher Educn), 1996–97. Member: Home Affairs Select Cttee, 2003–05; Sci. and Technology Select Cttee, 1997–2002. Senator, Engrg Council, 1996–2002; Mem., Engrg Technol. Bd, 2002–. Pres., Instn of Engrg Designers, 2003– (Hon. FIED). Pres., SETup (Promotion of Science Engrg and Technol.), 1997–2005; Trustee: Severn Bridges Trust; IMechE, 2005–. FICES 2000; FCGI 2001. Hon. PhD Staffordshire Univ., 1999. *Address:* House of Commons, SW1A 0AA.

CURTISS, Air Marshal Sir John (Bagot), KCB 1981 (CB 1979); KBE 1982; FRAeS; Chairman, Oakhaven Hospice Trust, 2001–04; *b* 6 Dec. 1924; *s* of Major E. F. B. Curtiss, RFC; *m* 1946, Peggy Drughorn Bowie; three *s* one *d*. *Educ:* Radley Coll.; Wanganui Collegiate Sch., NZ; Worcester Coll., Oxford. Served War: Oxford Univ. Air Sqdn, 1942–43; Bomber Comd, 578 and 158 sqdns, 1944–45; Transport Comd, 51 and 59 sqdn, 1945–49; Training Comd, 1950–53; Fighter Comd, 29 and 5 sqdns, 1953–64; Dir, RAF Staff Coll., 1967–69; Stn Comdr RAF Bruggen, RAFG, 1970–72; Gp Capt. Ops, HQ Strike Comd, 1972–74; SASO, HQ 11 Gp, 1974–75; Dir-Gen. Organisation, RAF, 1975–77; Comdt, RAF Staff Coll., 1977–80; Air Comdr, Falklands Operations, 1982; AOC No 18 Gp, 1980–83, retd. Dir and Chief Exec., SBAC, 1984–89; Sec., Defence Inds Council, 1985–89. Mem. Exec. Cttee, Air League, 1982–93; President: Aircrew Assoc., 1987–93; Berlin Airlift Assoc., 1998–; RAF Oxford and Cambridge Soc., 1998–2005, now Pres. Emeritus; Milford-on-Sea Br., RBL, 2002–. Chm., Pathfinders Disaster Relief, 1995–2000; Chief Exec., Assoc. of Pathfinders, 1996–2000. Trustee, Buskaid, 1995–2004 (Chm., 1999–2004). Chm., Governors, Canford Sch., 1990–95. FRAeS 1984. *Recreations:* family, fishing, sailing, reading, bicycling. *Address:* Normandy House, Barnes Lane, Milford-on-Sea, Hants SO41 0RQ. *Clubs:* MCC, Pilgrims; Colonels (Pres. and Founder Mem.); Keyhaven Yacht.

CURWEN, Sir Christopher (Keith), KCMG 1986 (CMG 1982); HM Diplomatic Service, retired; *b* 9 April 1929; *s* of late Rev. R. M. Curwen and Mrs M. E. Curwen; *m* 1st, 1956, Noom Tai (marr. diss. 1977; she *d* 2002); one *s* two *d*; 2nd, 1977, Helen Anne Stirling; one *s* one *d*. *Educ:* Sherborne Sch.; Sidney Sussex Coll., Cambridge (BA). Served HM Forces, 4th Queen's Own Hussars, 1948–49 (despatches). Joined FO, 1952; Bangkok, 1954; Vientiane, 1956; FO, 1958; Bangkok, 1961; Kuala Lumpur, 1963; FO, 1965; Washington, 1968; FCO, 1971; Geneva, 1977; FCO, 1980–88; Dep. Sec., Cabinet Office, 1989–91. Mem., Security Commn, 1991–98. Chm., Century Benevolent Fund, 1993–99; Trustee, Bath Preservation Trust, 1992–2004. *Recreations:* books, gardening, motoring.

CURWEN, Peter Stewart; Director, Europe, HM Treasury, since 2008; *b* 25 Oct. 1963; *s* of Brian Stewart Curwen and late Pamela Westgarth Curwen (*née* Jones); *m* 1996, Helene Radcliffe; one *s* one *d*. *Educ:* King Edward VI Grammar Sch. for Boys, Aston; Manchester Univ. (BA Econ Hons); Warwick Univ. (MA Econs). Economist, MSC, 1985–87; HM Treasury: Macroeconomist, 1987–90; World economy forecaster, Econ. Advr, 1991–94; EU co-ordination and strategy, 1994–96; Dep. Hd, Communications, 1996–97; Head: Communications, 1997–99; EU and Internat. Tax Team, 1999–2002; on secondment to FCO, as Counsellor, Econs, Finance and Tax, UK Perm. Repn to EU, 2002–06; Dir, Budget and Tax Policy, 2006–08. *Recreations:* golf, tennis, ski-ing, campanology. *Address:* HM Treasury, 1 Horse Guards Road, SW1A 2HQ. *T:* (020) 7270 4470; *e-mail:* peter.curwen@hm-treasury.gov.uk. *Club:* Sandy Lodge Golf (Northwood, Middx).

CURZON; *see* Roper-Curzon, family name of Baron Teynham.

CURZON, family name of **Earl Howe** and **Viscount Scarsdale**.

CURZON, Viscount; Thomas Edward Penn Curzon; *b* 22 Oct. 1994; *s* and *heir* of Earl Howe, *qv*.

CUSCHIERI, Prof. Sir Alfred, Kt 1998; MD; FRCS, FRCSE; FRSE; Professor of Surgery, Scuola Superiore S'Anna di Studi Universitari, since 2003; Director, Minimal Access Therapy Unit for Scotland, since 1992; *b* 30 Sept. 1938; *s* of Saviour and Angela Cuschieri; *m* 1966, Marguerite Holley; three *d*. *Educ:* Univ. of Malta (MD 1961); Univ. of Liverpool (ChM 1968). FRCSE 1965; FRCS 1967; FRSE 1998. University of Liverpool: Sen. Lectr in Surgery, 1970–74; Reader, 1974–76; Prof., and Hd of Dept of Surgery, Univ. of Dundee, 1976–2003. Mem. Council, RCSE, 1980–; President: Internat. Hepatobiliary Pancreatic Assoc., 1992–93; European Assoc. Endoscopic Surgeons, 1995–97. Founder FMedSci 1998. Hon. FRCSGlas 1996; Hon. FRCSI 1996. Hon. MD Liverpool, 1997; Hon. DSc: Abertay, 2002; St Andrews, 2007; Hon. LLD Dundee, 2007. Gold Medal, Scandinavian Soc. Gastroenterology, 1990; Society Prize for pioneering work in minimal access surgery, Internat. Soc. of Surgery, 1993. *Publications:* Essential Surgical Practice, 1986, 4th edn 2001; contrib. to learned jls incl. Brit. Jl Surgery, Surgical Endoscopy, Lancet, Annals of Surgery, Archives of Surgery. *Recreations:* music, fly-fishing, carving. *Address:* Denbrae Mill, Strathkinness Low Road, St Andrews, Fife KY16 9TY. *T:* (01334) 475046. *Club:* Athenæum.

CUSENS, Prof. Anthony Ralph, OBE 1989; PhD; FRSE; FREng; FICE, FIStructE; Professor of Civil Engineering, University of Leeds, 1979–92, now Emeritus (Dean, Faculty of Engineering, 1989–91); *b* 24 Sept. 1927; *s* of James Henry Cusens and May Edith (*née* Thomas); *m* 1953, Pauline Shirin German; three *d*. *Educ:* St John's Coll., Southsea; University Coll. London (BSc Eng; PhD 1955). FICE 1966; FIStructE 1972; FAmSCE 1972; FREng (FEng 1988). FRSE 1974. Res. Engr, British Cast Concrete Fedn, 1952–54; Sen. Lectr, RMCS, Shrivenham, 1954–56; Sen. Lectr, Univ. of Khartoum, Sudan, 1956–60; Prof. of Structl Engrg, Asian Inst. of Technol., Bangkok, 1960–65; Prof. of Civil Engineering: Univ. of St Andrews, 1965–67; Univ. of Dundee, 1967–78. Visitor, Transport and Road Res. Lab., 1982–88; President: Concrete Soc., 1983–84; IStructE, 1991–92; Chairman: Jt Bd of Moderators of ICE, IStructE and CIBSE, 1986–89; UK Certifying Authy for Reinforcing Steels, 1994–2001. Mem., Bramham cum Oglethorpe Parish Council, 2001–07. Hon. DSc Aston, 1993. *Publications:* (jtly) Bridge Deck Analysis, 1975; Finite Strip Method in Bridge Engineering, 1978; res. papers on concrete technol. and structures. *Recreations:* golf, gardening, family history. *Address:* Old Hall Cottage, Bramham, West Yorks LS23 6QR. *Clubs:* East India; Pannal Golf (Harrogate).

CUSHING, Penny; District Judge, Principal Registry, Family Division, since 1994; *b* 10 April 1950; *d* of George Norman Cushing and Doris Cushing. *Educ:* Birkenhead High Sch. (GPDST); University Coll., London (LLB Hons 1971). Admitted solicitor, 1974; Solicitor: London Bor. of Harrow, 1974–75; Camden Community Law Centre, 1975–80; Trng Officer, Law Centres Fedn, 1980–83; Partner, Cushing & Kelly, subseq. Clinton Davis Cushing & Kelly, solicitors, 1983–90. Mem., Mental Health Act Commn, 1991–94. *Recreations:* theatre, reading, gardening, walking, allotmenteering. *Address:* Principal Registry, Family Division, First Avenue House, 42–49 High Holborn, WC1V 6NP.

CUSHING, Philip Edward; Chairman: Paragon Print and Packaging Ltd, since 2002; DCI Biologicals Inc., since 2002; Director, Ikon Office Solutions, since 1998; *b* 9 Sept. 1950; *s* of Cyril Edward Willis Cushing and Marguerite Ellen Cushing (*née* Whaite); *m* 1st, 1972, Margareta Barbro Westin (marr. diss.); one *s* one *d*; 2nd, 2000, Ruth Christine Clarke. *Educ:* Highgate Sch.; Christ's Coll., Cambridge (BA 1st Cl. Hons Econs). Marketing Manager, Norprint Ltd, 1972–78; Man. Dir, Modulex Systems, 1978–84; Norton Opax plc: Marketing Dir, 1984–86; Chief Exec., Internat. Ops, 1986–89; Inchcape plc: Chief Exec., Inchcape Berhad, 1990–92; Dir, Services, 1992–95; Gp Man. Dir, 1995–96; Gp Chief Exec., 1996–99; Chief Exec., Vitec, 2000–01. Chm., Strix Investments Ltd, 2007–08. *Recreations:* golf, reading, bridge, cricket, travel, music.

CUSHING, Sir Selwyn (John), KNZM 1999; CMG 1994; FCA; Chairman, New Zealand Rural Property Trust Management Ltd; Chairman and Chief Executive, Brierley Investments Ltd, 1999–2001; *b* 1 Sept. 1936; *s* of Cyril John Cushing and Henrietta Marjory Belle Cushing; *m* 1964, Kaye Dorothy Anderson; two *s*. *Educ:* Hastings High Sch.; Univ. of NZ. FCA 1957; ACIS 1958; CMA 1959. Partner, Esam Cushing & Co., sharebrokers, Hastings, 1960–86; Exec. Dir, Brierley Investments Ltd, 1986–93; Chairman: Carter Holt Harvey Ltd, 1991–93; Electricity Corp. of NZ, 1993–99; Dir, Air New Zealand (Dep. Chm., 1988–98; Chm., 1998–2001). Chm., NZ Symphony Orch. Ltd, 1996–2002. *Recreations:* cricket, music. *Address:* 1 Beatson Road, Hastings, New Zealand. *T:* (6) 8786160. *Clubs:* Wellington; Auckland; Dunedin.

CUSINE, Douglas James; Sheriff of Grampian, Highland and Islands at Aberdeen, since 2001 (at Peterhead, 2000–01); *b* 2 Sept. 1946; *s* of James Fechnie Cusine and Catherine Cusine (*née* McLean); *m* 1973, Marilyn Calvert Ramsay; one *s* one *d*. *Educ:* Hutcheson's Boys' Grammar Sch.; Univ. of Glasgow (LLB (Hons)). Admitted Solicitor, 1971; in private practice, 1971–74; Lectr in Private Law, Univ. of Glasgow, 1974–76; University of Aberdeen: Lectr in Private Law, 1976–82; Sen. Lectr in Conveyancing and Professional Practice of Law, 1982–90; Prof. (personal), 1990–92; Hugh McLennan Prof. of Conveyancing, 1990–2000. Temp. Sheriff, 1998–1999; Hon. Sheriff: Aberdeen; Stonehaven. Member: Council, Law Soc. of Scotland, 1988–2000; Lord President's Adv. Council on Messengers-at-Arms and Sheriff Officers, 1989–2000; Legal Practice Course Bd, Law Soc. (England and Wales), 1993–97; Adv. Cttee on Feudal System, 1997–2000, Adv. Cttee on Real Burdens, 1998–2000, Scottish Law Commn; UK Mem., CCBE, 1997–2000; Rep., Internat. Union of Latin Notaries, 1989–1997. Examiner, Messengers-at-Arms and Sheriff Officers, 1989–92; Examiner in Conveyancing, Faculty of Advocates, 1992–. Mem., AID subcttee, RCOG, 1976–79. Mem., 1978, Fellow, 1981, Eugenics Soc. Review Ed., Jl Law Soc. of Scotland, 1988–98. *Publications:* (ed jtly) The Impact of Marine Pollution: law and practice, 1980; (ed jtly) Scottish Cases and Materials in Commercial Law, 1987, 2nd edn 2002; (ed) A Scots Conveyancing Miscellany: essays in honour of Professor Halliday, 1988; New Reproductive Techniques: a legal perspective, 1988; (jtly) The Law and Practice of Diligence, 1990; (ed jtly) Reproductive Medicine and the Law, 1990; (ed) The Conveyancing Opinions of Professor Halliday, 1992; Standard Securities, 1991, 2nd edn (jtly) 2002; (jtly) Missives, 1993, 2nd edn 1999; (jtly) The Requirements of Writing, 1995; (ed) Green's Practice Styles, vol. 1, 1996; (ed jtly) McDonald's Conveyancing Manual, 6th edn 1997; (jtly) Servitudes and Rights of Way, 1998; articles in legal journals. *Recreations:* golf, swimming, walking, bird watching. *Address:* Sheriff Court House, Castle Street, Aberdeen AB10 1WP. *T:* (01224) 657200.

CUSK, Rachel Emma; novelist and writer; *b* Saskatchewan, 8 Feb. 1967; *d* of Peter Cusk and Carolyn Cusk (*née* Woods); *m* Adrian Clarke; two *d*, and one step *d*. *Educ:* St Mary's Convent, Cambridge; New Coll., Oxford (BA). *Publications:* novels: Saving Agnes, 1992 (Whitbread First Novel Award, 1993); The Temporary, 1995; The Country Life (Somerset Maugham Award), 1997; The Lucky Ones, 2003; In the Fold, 2005; Arlington Park, 2006; A Life's Work: on becoming a mother (autobiog.), 2001; numerous articles and short stories; contrib. The Times, The Guardian, Daily Telegraph, Evening Standard, etc. *Address:* c/o The Wylie Agency, 17 Bedford Square, WC1B 3JA. *T:* (020) 7908 5900.

CUST, family name of **Baron Brownlow**.

CUSTIS, Patrick James, CBE 1981; FCA, FCMA, FCIS; director of companies; *b* 19 March 1921; *er s* of late Alfred and Amy Custis; *m* 1954, Rita, *yr d* of late Percy and Annie Rayner; one *s*. *Educ:* The High Sch., Dublin. JDipMA. FCA 1951; FCMA 1950; FCIS 1945. Served articles with Josolyne Miles & Co., Chartered Accountants, Cheapside, London, 1946–51; Asst to Gen. Man., Rio Tinto Co. Ltd, London, 1952–54; Gp Chief Accountant and Dir of subsid. cos, Glynwed Ltd, W Midlands, 1955–67; Guest Keen & Nettlefolds Ltd, W Midlands, 1967–81 (Dir of Finance, 1974–81); various sen. appts prior to 1974. Mem., Midlands and N Wales Reg. Bd (formerly Birmingham and W Midlands Reg. Bd), Lloyds Bank plc, 1979–91; Director: New Court Property Fund Managers Ltd, 1978–91; Associated Heat Services plc, 1981–90; Leigh Interests PLC, 1982–96 (Dep. Chm., 1990–93; Chm., 1993–96); Wolseley plc, 1982–90; Birmingham Technology Ltd, 1983–93; Wyko Group PLC, 1985–94; Benford Concrete Machinery plc, 1985–86; Chm., MCD Gp plc, 1983–86. Member: Monopolies and Mergers Commn, 1981–82; HM Prisons Bd, Home Office, 1980–85. Chm., Midlands Indust. Gp of Finance Dirs, 1977–80. Trustee, Bi-Centenary Appeal, Birmingham Gen. Hosp., 1978–89. Co-opted Mem. Council, Inst. of Chartered Accountants in England and Wales, 1979–85; Liveryman, Worshipful Co. of Chartered Accountants in England and Wales; Pres., Wolverhampton Soc. of Chartered Accountants, 1985–86. FRSA 1987. *Address:* 18 Richmond Village, Stroud Road, Painswick, Glos GL6 6UH.
See also R. A. Custis.

CUSTIS, Ronald Alfred; Director General, Energy Industries Council, 1981–92; *b* 28 Feb. 1931; *yr s* of late Alfred and Amy Custis, Dublin; *m* 1st, 1957, Enid Rowe (*d* 1984); one *s* one *d*; 2nd, 1986, Valerie Mackett (*née* Holbrook). *Educ:* The High Sch., Dublin.

Joined HM Treasury, 1947; DES, 1964; Min. of Technology, 1964–70: Private Sec. to Permanent Under Sec., 1964–66; Principal, 1967; Sec. to Cttee of Inquiry into the Brain Drain, 1967–68; Min. of Aviation Supply, later MoD (Procurement Exec.), 1970–74: Private Sec. to Sec. of State for Defence, 1971–73; Asst Sec., 1973; Dept of Energy, 1974–81: Private Sec. to successive Secs of State for Energy, 1974–75; Under Sec., 1978; Dir Gen., Offshore Supplies Office, 1980–81. *Recreations:* reading, walking public footpaths, listening to music, gardening. *Address:* 1 The Coaches, Fields Road, Chedworth, Glos GL54 4NQ. *T:* (01285) 720479.

See also P. J. Custis.

CUTHBERT, Prof. Alan William, ScD; FRS 1982; Sheild Professor of Pharmacology, 1979–99, and Deputy Vice-Chancellor, 1995–99, University of Cambridge; Master of Fitzwilliam College, Cambridge, 1990–99 (Hon. Fellow, 1999); *b* 7 May 1932; *s* of late Thomas William Cuthbert and Florence Mary (*née* Griffin); *m* 1957, Harriet Jane Webster; two *s*. *Educ:* Leicester Coll. of Technol.; St Andrews Univ. (BSc); London Univ. (BPharm, PhD); MA, ScD Cantab. Instructor Lieut, RN, 1956–59. Res. Fellow, then Asst Lectr, Dept of Pharmacology, Sch. of Pharmacy, Univ. of London, 1959–63; Demonstrator in Pharmacol., 1963–66, Lectr, 1966–73, and Reader, 1973–79, Dept of Pharmacol., Univ. of Cambridge; Fellow of Jesus Coll., Cambridge, 1968–90 (Hon. Fellow, 1991). Chm. Editorial Bd, British Jl of Pharmacology, 1974–82. For. Sec., British Pharmacol Soc., 1997–2000 (Hon. Mem., 2000; Hon. Fellow, 2004); Pres., Fedn of European Pharmacol Socs, 2002–04. Member: AFRC, 1988–90; Council, Royal Soc., 1986–88; Council, Zool Soc. of London, 1988–91. Gov., De Montfort Univ., 1998–2005. Mem., Academie Royale de Médicine de Belgique, 1996–; MAE, 1996; Founder FMedSci 1998. Fellow, Sch. of Pharmacy, Univ. of London, 1996. Hon. Fellow, Gonville and Caius Coll., Cambridge, 2008. Hon. DSc: De Montfort, 1993; Aston, 1995; Hon. LLD Dundee, 1995. Pereira Medal in Materia Medica, Pharmaceutical Soc. of GB, 1953; Sir James Irvine Medal in Chemistry, St Andrews Univ., 1955; Wellcome Gold Medal, 2005. *Publications:* scientific papers in pharmacol and physiol jls. *Recreations:* travel, painting, growing orchids. *Address:* Department of Medicine, University of Cambridge, Addenbrooke's Hospital, Hills Road, Cambridge CB2 2QQ; 7 Longstanton Road, Oakington, Cambridge CB24 3BB. *T:* (01223) 233676.

CUTHBERT, Ceri Jayne; *see* Jones, C. J.

CUTHBERT, Sir Ian Holm; *see* Holm, Sir Ian.

CUTHBERT, Jeffrey Hambley; Member (Lab) Caerphilly, National Assembly for Wales, since 2003; *b* 4 June 1948; *s* of William and Jennie Cuthbert; *m* 1985, Catherine (marr. diss.); one *s* four *d*. *Educ:* University Coll., Cardiff (BSc Hons; Pres., Students' Union, 1974–75). Mining surveyor, Saudi Arabia, 1978–81, Libya, 1981–82, NCB. Sen. Consultant, Welsh Jt Educn Cttee; Principal (pt-time), Aberbargoed Adult Educn Centre. *Recreations:* reading, politics and trade union studies, walking, travel. *Address:* National Assembly for Wales, Cardiff Bay, Cardiff CF99 1NA; *e-mail:* Jeff.Cuthbert@wales.gov.uk.

CUTHBERT, Stephen Colin, CBE 2005; FCA; Chairman, Iain Rennie Hospice at Home, since 2006; Chief Executive, Port of London Authority, 1999–2004; *b* 27 Oct. 1942; *s* of Colin Samuel Cuthbert and Helen Mary Cuthbert (*née* Scott); *m* 1st, 1969, Jane Elizabeth Bluett (marr. diss. 1984); two *s* one *d*; 2nd, 1987, Susan Melanie Shepherd; one step *s* two step *d*. *Educ:* Trinity Sch. of John Whitgift; Bristol Univ. (BScEng). FCA 1968. Voluntary Service, UNRWA, Jordan, 1964–65; Price Waterhouse, London, 1965–76; Finance Dir, 1976–79, Chief Exec., 1980–93, Brent International plc; Dir Gen., Chartered Inst. of Marketing, 1994–99. Chm., UK Major Ports Gp, 2002–04. Dir, London Chamber of Commerce and Industry, 2000–02. Mem. Council, 1989–99, Chm. Southern Reg., 1992–93, CBI. Freeman: City of London, 1998; Co. of Watermen and Lightermen, 2000; Liveryman: Co. of Marketors, 1998–2006; Co. of Shipwrights, 2003–. *Recreations:* opera, sailing, family pursuits. *Address:* 61 Burkes Road, Beaconsfield, Bucks HP9 1PW.

CUTHBERTSON, Ian Jardine; Senior Partner, Corporate Recovery, Dundas & Wilson, since 1997; *b* 8 May 1951; *s* of James and Catherine Cuthbertson; *m* 1974, Sally Jane Whittick; one *s* two *d*. *Educ:* Jordanhill Coll. Sch.; Univ. of Glasgow (LLB). Admitted solicitor, 1974; NP 1975; licensed as Insolvency Practitioner, 1986; Partner: Boyds, 1978–79; and Jt Founder, Dorman Jeffrey, 1979; Dundas & Wilson, 1997– (following merger with Dorman Jeffrey). FInstD 1988; FIPA 1990; Fellow, Assoc. of Business Recovery Professionals, 1990; Fellow, Inst. of Contemp. Scotland, 2003. *Recreations:* sport (Rugby, football), reading, art. *Address:* Dundas & Wilson, 191 West George Street, Glasgow G2 2LD. *T:* (0141) 222 2200, *Fax:* (0141) 222 2201; *e-mail:* ian.cuthbertson@dundas-wilson.com.

CUTLER, Keith Charles; His Honour Judge Cutler; a Circuit Judge, since 1996; Resident Judge, Salisbury, since 2003; Hon. Recorder of Salisbury, since 2007; *b* 14 Aug. 1950; *s* of Henry Walter Cutler and Evelyn Constance Cutler; *m* 1975, Judith Mary Haddy; one *s* one *d*. *Educ:* Bristol Univ. (LLB Hons). Called to the Bar, Lincoln's Inn, 1972 (Bencher, 2005); Asst Recorder, 1989; Recorder, 1993–96. Dep. Chancellor, dio. of Portsmouth, 2003–; Wilts Magistrates Liaison Judge, 2006–. Judicial Member: Parole Bd, 2001–04; Wilts Courts Bd, 2004–07; Chm., Salisbury and Dist, Mediation, 2001–. Hon. Sec., Council of HM Circuit Judges, 2005– (Asst Sec., 2003–04). *Recreations:* church music, Italian travel, maps. *Address:* The Crown and County Court, Salisbury SP1 2PN. *T:* (01722) 325444.

CUTLER, Robin; *see* Cutler, T. R.

CUTLER, Timothy Robert, (Robin), CBE 1995; Director-General and Deputy Chairman, Forestry Commission, 1990–95; *b* 24 July 1934; *s* of Frank Raymond Cutler and Jeannie Evelyn Cutler (*née* Badenoch); *m* 1958, Ishbel Primrose; one *s* one *d*. *Educ:* Banff Academy; Aberdeen Univ. (BSc Forestry 1956). National Service, Royal Engineers, 1956–58. Colonial Forest Service, Kenya, 1958–64; New Zealand Forest Service: joined 1964; Dir of Forest Management, 1978; Dep. Dir-Gen., 1986; Chief Exec., Min. of Forestry, 1988–90. Hon. DSc Aberdeen, 1992. *Recreations:* tennis, golf, gardening, stamps. *Address:* 14 Swanston Road, Fairmilehead, Edinburgh EH10 7BB.

CUTT, Rev. Canon Samuel Robert; Canon Residentiary, 1979–93, and Treasurer, 1985–93, Wells Cathedral (Chancellor, 1979–85); *b* 28 Nov. 1925; *er s* of Robert Bush Cutt and Lilian Elizabeth Cutt (*née* Saint); *m* 1972, Margaret Eva (*d* 1975), *yr d* of Norman and Eva McIntyre. *Educ:* Skegness Grammar Sch.; Selwyn Coll., Cambridge; Cuddesdon Coll., Oxford. BA Cantab 1950, MA 1954. Deacon 1953, Priest 1954. Asst Curate, St Aidan, West Hartlepool, 1953–56; Tutor for King's Coll. London at St Boniface Coll., Warminster, 1956–59; Sub-Warden for KCL at St Boniface Coll., 1959–65; Lectr and Tutor of Chichester Theol Coll., 1965–71; Priest Vicar of Chichester Cath., 1966–71; Minor Canon, 1971–79, and Succentor, 1974–79, St Paul's Cathedral, and Warden, Coll. of Minor Canons, 1974–79; part-time Lectr, Theological Dept, KCL, 1973–79; Priest in Ordinary to the Queen, 1975–79; Dio. Dir of Ordinands, Bath and Wells, 1979–86; Examining Chaplain to Bishop of Bath and Wells, 1980–93; Warden, Community of St Denys, Warminster, 1987–91. OStJ 1981. *Recreations:* walking, music, biographical studies, heraldry, cooking.

CUTTELL, Very Rev. Dr Jeffrey Charles; Dean of Derby, since 2008; *b* 1959, Giltbrook, Notts; *s* of late Vernon Howard Cuttell and of Joan Cuttell (*née* Brown); *m* 1981, Dr Elizabeth Jane Beton; one *s* one *d*. *Educ:* Broadoak Comp. Sch., Weston-Super-Mare; Birmingham Univ. (BSc 1980; PhD 1983); Trinity Theol Coll., Bristol (DipHE 1986); Sheffield Univ. (MA 1991). Res. Student, AERE Harwell, Oxon, 1980–83; ordained deacon, 1987, priest, 1988; Asst Curate, 1987–91, Vicar, 1991–95, Normanton; producer and presenter, BBC Religious Progs, 1995–99; Rector, Astbury with Smallwood, 1999–2008. Associate Lectr, Cardiff Univ., 2001–06; Tutor, St Michael's Theol Coll., Cardiff, 2001–06. Chaplain, 4th Bn Parachute Regt Res., 1997–2006. *Recreations:* frightening myself, people watching, late night reading, wasting time with my family, walking a large dog. *Address:* Derby Cathedral Centre, 18–19 Iron Gate, Derby DE1 3GP. *T:* (01332) 341201, *Fax:* (01332) 203991; *e-mail:* dean@derbycathedral.org.

CUTTER, Prof. Elizabeth Graham, PhD, DSc; FRSE; FLS; George Harrison Professor of Botany, University of Manchester, 1979–89, now Emeritus; *b* 9 Aug. 1929; *d* of Roy Carnegie Cutter and Alexandra (*née* Graham). *Educ:* Rothesay House Sch., Edinburgh; Univ. of St Andrews (BSc, DSc); Univ. of Manchester (PhD). Asst Lecturer in Botany, 1955–57, Lectr in Botany, 1957–64, Univ. of Manchester; Associate Professor of Botany, 1964–68, Professor of Botany, 1968–72, Univ. of California, Davis; Sen. Lectr in Cryptogamic Botany, 1972–74, Reader in Cryptogamic Botany, 1974–79, Univ. of Manchester. *Publications:* Trends in Plant Morphogenesis (principal editor), 1966; Plant Anatomy: Experiment and Interpretation, pt 1, Cells and Tissues, 1969, 2nd edn 1978; pt 2, Organs, 1971. *Recreations:* photography, fishing. *Address:* Barnyard Butts, Bakers Road, Gattonside, Melrose, Roxburghshire TD6 9NA. *T:* (01896) 822139.

CUTTS, Adrian; Executive Director of Resources, Lancashire County Council, 2006–Oct. 2009; *b* Wingerworth, Derbys, 16 Oct. 1949; *s* of Geoffrey Wilson Cutts and Noel Deidre Cutts; *m* 1979, Lynda Keegan; three *d*. *Educ:* Wade Deacon Grammar Sch., Widnes; Liverpool Coll. of Commerce. CIPFA 1973. Audit Clerk, Widnes BC, 1968; various posts from Audit Asst to Principal Accountant, St Helens CBC, subseq. MBC, 1971–84; Lancashire County Council: Principal Accountant (Educn), 1984–89; Chief Accountant, 1989–2001; Dir of Finance, 2001–06; Treas. to Lancs Fire Authy, 2001–05. *Recreations:* keen fell walker, playing contract bridge at Preston Bridge Club, reading, foreign travel (preferably to mountain regions). *Address:* 6 Forest Way, Fulwood, Preston PR2 8PR. *T:* (01772) 774206, *Fax:* (01772) 264705; *e-mail:* cuttsfamily@blueyonder.co.uk, adrian.cutts@fin.lancscc.gov.uk.

CUTTS, Johannah; QC 2008; a Recorder, since 2002; *b* Taplow, 13 Jan. 1964; *d* of Anthony and Jacqueline Cutts. *Educ:* Sch. of St Helen and St Katherine, Abingdon; Chelmer Inst. of Higher Educn (LLB Hons). Called to the Bar, Inner Temple, 1986; in practice as barrister, specialising in criminal law, particularly in cases involving vulnerable witnesses, 1986–. *Publication:* (contrib.) Rook and Ward on Sexual Offences, 2003. *Recreations:* walking my dogs in Somerset, travelling with my niece, relaxing and eating with friends. *Address:* 9–12 Bell Yard, WC2A 2JR. *T:* (020) 7400 1800, *Fax:* (020) 7404 1405; *e-mail:* jcutts@9-12bellyard.com.

CYPRUS AND THE GULF, Bishop of, since 2007; **Rt Rev. Michael Augustine Owen Lewis;** *b* 8 June 1953; *m* 1979, Julia Donneky (*née* Lennox); two *s* one *d*. *Educ:* Merton Coll., Oxford (BA 1975; MA 1979); Cuddesdon Coll. (BA Oxon 1977). Ordained deacon, 1978, priest, 1979; Curate, Salfords, 1978–80; Chaplain, Thames Poly., 1980–84; Vicar, Welling, 1984–91; Team Rector, Worcester SE Team Ministry, 1991–99; Rural Dean, Worcester E, 1993–99; Canon, Worcester Cathedral, 1998–99; Bishop of Middleton, 1999–2007. Chm., Manchester Diocesan Bd of Educn, 2000–07; Warden of Readers and Lay Assts, dio. of Manchester, 2001–07. *Address:* St Paul's Cathedral, PO Box 22075, Nicosia 1517, Cyprus. *T:* (22) 671220, *Fax:* (22) 674553; *e-mail:* bishop@spidernet.com.cy.

CZAKÓ, Borbála; Ambassador of Hungary to the Court of St James's, since 2007; Budapest, 22 Nov. 1953; *d* of Jozsef Serfozo and Ilona Bock; two *d*. *Educ:* Budapest Tech. Coll. (BA 1975); Univ. of Econs, Budapest (MA 1987); Tulane Univ., New Orleans (MBA 1991). Sen. Manager, Ernst & Young Hungary, 1989–91; Chief of Mission, Hungary, Internat. Finance Corp., 1991–2002; Ernst & Young Hungary: Hd, Corporate Finance, 2002–03; Country Man. Partner and Dep. Man. Partner, Central Europe and South, 2003–06. Pres., Hungarian Business Leaders Forum, 2003–. Mem., Bd of Dirs, Central European Univ., 2003–06. Pro-Europe Award, 2005. *Recreations:* reading, theatre, gardening, cooking. *Address:* Embassy of Hungary, 35 Eaton Place, SW1X 8BY. *T:* (020) 7201 3446, *Fax:* (020) 7823 1348; *e-mail:* Ambassador.LON@kum.hu.

CZERNIN, family name of **Baroness Howard de Walden**.

D

DABER, Timothy Mark; a District Judge (Magistrates' Courts), since 2007; *b* Manchester, 24 Feb. 1958; *s* of Dr Keith Daber and Patricia Daber; *m* 2005, Karen Sonja Vanterpool; one *d*. *Educ:* William Hulme's Grammar Sch., Manchester; Sch. of Oriental and African Studies, Univ. of London (LLB Hons). Called to the Bar, Gray's Inn, 1981; Clerk to Cambs Justices, 2000–07; Dep. Dist Judge (Magistrates' Courts), 2000–07. *Recreations:* golf, ski-ing, travel, food and wine. *Address:* City of Westminster Magistrates' Court, 70 Horseferry Road, SW1P 2AX.

DACOMBE, William John Armstrong; Chairman, Postern Ltd, 1996–2002; *b* 21 Sept. 1934; *s* of late John Christian Dacombe and of Eileen Elizabeth Dacombe; *m* 1962, Margaretta Joanna (*née* Barrington); two *d*. *Educ:* Felsted School; Corpus Christi College, Oxford (MA). Kleinwort Benson, 1961–65; N. M. Rothschild & Sons, 1965–73 (Dir, 1970–73); Dir, 1973–84, Asst Chief Exec., 1979–82, Williams & Glyn's Bank; Group Exec. Dir, Royal Bank of Scotland Group, 1982–84; Chief Exec. Dir, Rea Brothers Group, 1984–88. Chairman: Brown Shipley Holdings, 1991–; Albert E. Sharp Hldgs, 1997–98. Mem., Export Guarantees Adv. Council, 1982–86 (Dep. Chm., 1985–86). *Recreations:* art, historic buildings, reading. *Address:* Mullion Cottage, Well Lane, SW14 7AJ. *T:* (020) 8876 4336. *Clubs:* Brooks's, City of London.

DACRE, Baroness (27th in line), *cr* 1321; **Rachel Leila Douglas-Home;** *b* 24 Oct. 1929; *er* surv. *d* of 4th Viscount Hampden, CMG (*d* 1965) (whose Barony of Dacre was called out of abeyance in her favour, 1970) and Leila Emily (*d* 1996), *o d* of late Lt-Col Frank Evelyn Seely; *m* 1951, Hon. William Douglas-Home (*d* 1992), author and playwright; one *s* three *d*. *Heir: s* Hon. James Thomas Archibald Douglas-Home [*b* 16 May 1952; *m* 1979, Christine (*née* Stephenson) (*d* 2008); one *d*].

DACRE, Prof. Jane Elizabeth, MD; FRCP, FRCPGlas; Professor of Medical Education, Vice Dean, since 2005, and Director, Division of Medical Education, since 2008, University College London; *b* 11 Nov. 1955; *d* of late Peter Verrill and Christine Verrill; *m* 1979, Nigel Dacre, *qv*; one *s* two *d*. *Educ:* Univ. Coll. Hosp. Med. Sch. (BSc 1977; MB BS 1980; MD 1992). MRCP 1983, FRCP 1994; FRCPGlas 1999. Sen. Lectr in Clin. Skills and Consultant Physician and Rheumatologist, St Bartholomew's Med. Coll., 1980–95. Academic Vice-Pres., RCP, 2006–08. FHEA 2007. *Publications:* (with M. Nicol) Clinical Skills: the learning matrix for students of medicine and nursing, 1996; (with P. Kopelman) Handbook of Clinical Skills, 2002; articles on med. educn, assessment, fitness to practice and women in medicine. *Recreations:* family life and all things French. *Address:* Division of Medical Education, Royal Free and University College Medical School, Holborn Union Building, Highgate Hill, N19 5LW. *T:* (020) 7288 5209; *e-mail:* j.dacre@medsch.ucl.ac.uk.

DACRE, Nigel; Managing Director, Ten Alps Digital, since 2007; *b* 3 Sept. 1956; *s* of late Peter and of Joan Dacre; *m* 1979, Jane Verrill (*see* Prof. Jane Elizabeth Dacre); one *s* two *d*. *Educ:* St John's Coll., Oxford (MA, PPE). BBC News Trainee, 1978; Regl Journalist, BBC Bristol, 1980; ITN, 1982–2002: ITN Scriptwriter, 1982; Programme Editor, Super Channel News, 1986; Editor, World News, 1987; Editor, News at One, 1989; Head of Programme Output and Exec. Producer, News at Ten, 1992; Dep. Editor, News Programmes, 1993–95; Editor, ITN News on ITV, subseq. ITV News, 1995–2002; Dean, Sch. of Media, London Coll. of Printing, 2003; Chief Exec., Educn Digital Mgt Ltd (Teachers' TV), 2003–06.

See also P. M. Dacre.

DACRE, Paul Michael; Editor in Chief, Associated Newspapers, since 1998; Editor, Daily Mail, since 1992; *b* 14 Nov. 1948; *s* of Joan and late Peter Dacre; *m* 1973, Kathleen Thomson; two *s*. *Educ:* University College Sch.; Leeds Univ. (Hons English). Reporter, feature writer, Associate Features Editor, Daily Express, 1970–76; Washington and NY corresp., Daily Express, 1976–79; Daily Mail: NY Bureau Chief, 1980; News Editor, 1981–85; Asst Editor (News and Foreign), 1986; Exec. Editor (Features), 1987; Associate Editor, 1989–91; Editor, Evening Standard, 1991–92. Director: Associated Newspaper Holdings, 1991–; Daily Mail & General Trust plc, 1998–; Teletext Hldgs Ltd, 2000–02. Member: Press Complaints Commn, 1998–; Press Bd of Finance, 2004–. Ambassador for Alzheimer's Soc., 2007– Cudlipp Lect., London Coll. of Communication, 2007. FRSA 2007. *Address:* Daily Mail, Northcliffe House, 2 Derry Street, W8 5TT. *T:* (020) 7938 6000. *Club:* Garrick.

See also N. Dacre.

DADSON, Prof. Trevor John, PhD; FBA 2008; Professor of Hispanic Studies, since 2004, and Vice-Principal, since 2006, Queen Mary, University of London; *b* 7 Oct. 1947; *s* of Leonard John Dadson and Chrissie Vera (*née* Black); *m* 1975, Maria Angeles Gimeno; two *s*. *Educ:* Borden Grammar Sch., Sittingbourne; Univ. of Leeds (BA Hons); Univ. of Durham (PGCE); Emmanuel Coll., Cambridge (PhD 1974). Queen's University, Belfast: Lectr, 1978–86; Reader, 1986–88; Prof., 1988–90; University of Birmingham: Prof. of Hispanic Studies, 1990–2004; Head, Sch. of Modern Langs, 1993–97; Dir, Centre for European Langs and Culture, 2001–02. *Publications:* The Genoese in Spain, 1983; Avisos a un Cortesano, 1985; (ed) G. Bocángel, La Lira de las Musas, 1985; (ed) D. Silva y Mendoza, Antología Poética, 1985; (ed) A. Barros, Filosofía Cortesana, 1987; Una Familia Hispano-Genovesa, 1991; Libros, lectores y lecturas: bibliotecas particulares españolas del Siglo de Oro, 1998; (gen. ed) Actas del XII Congreso de la AIH, 1998; (ed) Ludisimo e intertextualidad en la lírica española moderna, 1998; (ed) Voces subversivas: poesía bajo el Régimen, 2000; (ed) G. Bocángel, Obra Completa, 2001; (ed) La poesía española del siglo XX y la tradición literaria, 2003; Estudios sobre poesía contemporánea, 2005; Los moriscos de Villarrubia de los Ojos, siglos XV–XVIII, 2007; numerous articles. *Recreations:* ski-ing, walking, tennis, reading.

DAFFERN, Paul George; Chief Financial Officer, Greenstone Group Ltd, since 2008; *b* 5 May 1953; *s* of late George Thomas Daffern and Kathleen Esther Daffern; *m* 1984, Hilary Margaret Jenkins; one *s* one *d*. *Educ:* Foxford School, Coventry. Unbrako Ltd, 1969–73; Massey-Ferguson UK, 1973–75; Chrysler UK, 1975–77; Lucas Service UK, 1978–79; National Freight Co., 1980–88; Autoglass, 1988–91; Exec. Dir, Finance, AEA Technology, 1991–95; Chief Financial Officer, X/Open Co. Ltd, 1995–97; Finance Dir, Autoglass Ltd, 1998–2000; Dir, IMS, 2000–02; Gp Finance Dir, PD Ports, Logistics and Shipping Gp, then PD Ports Gp Ltd, subseq. PD Ports plc, 2002–06; Finance Dir, Infinis Ltd, 2006–07. *Recreations:* golf, ski-ing.

DAFIS, Cynog Glyndwr; Member (Plaid Cymru) Mid and West Wales, National Assembly for Wales, 1999–2003; *b* 1 April 1938; *s* of Annie and George Davies; *m* 1963, Llinos Iorwerth Jones; two *s* one *d*. *Educ:* Aberaeron County Secondary Sch.; Neath Boys' Grammar Sch.; UCW Aberystwyth (BA Hons English, MEd). Teacher of English: Coll. of Further Educn, Pontardawe, 1960–62; Newcastle Emlyn Secondary Modern Sch., 1962–80; Aberaeron Comprehensive Sch., 1980–84; Dyffryn Teifi Comprehensive Sch., Llandysul, 1984–91; Research Officer, Dept of Adult Continuing Educn, UC Swansea, 1991–92. Contested (Plaid Cymru) Ceredigion and Pembroke North, 1983 and 1987. MP (Plaid Cymru) Ceredigion and Pembroke N, 1992–97, Ceredigion, 1997–Jan. 2000. Member: Select Cttee, Welsh Affairs, 1995–97; Envmtl Audit Cttee, 1997–2000. National Assembly for Wales: Chair: Post-16 Educn and Culture Cttee, 1999–2000; Educn and Lifelong Learning Cttee, 2000–02. Dir of Policy, Plaid Cymru, 1997–2003. *Publications:* Mab y Pregethwr (autobiog.), 2005; pamphlets and booklet (in Welsh) on bilingualism and Welsh politics. *Recreations:* walking, jogging, reading, listening to music. *Address:* Cedrwydd, Llandre, Bow Street, Ceredigion SY24 5AB. *T:* (01970) 828262.

DAHL, Mildred; *see* Gordon, M.

DAHRENDORF, Baron *cr* 1993 (Life Peer), of Clare Market in the City of Westminster; **Ralf Dahrendorf,** KBE 1982; PhD, DrPhil; FBA 1977; Warden of St Antony's College, Oxford, 1987–97; *b* Hamburg, 1 May 1929; adopted British nationality, 1988; *s* of Gustav Dahrendorf and Lina Dahrendorf (*née* Witt). *Educ:* several schools, including Heinrich-Hertz Oberschule, Hamburg; studies in philosophy and classical philology, Hamburg, 1947–52; DrPhil 1952; postgrad. studies at London Sch. of Economics, 1952–54; Leverhulme Research Schol., 1953–54; PhD 1956. Habilitation, and University Lecturer, Saarbrücken, 1957; Fellow at Center for Advanced Study in the Behavioral Sciences, Palo Alto, USA, 1957–58; Prof. of Sociology, Hamburg, 1958–60; Vis. Prof. Columbia Univ., 1960; Prof. of Sociology, Tübingen, 1960–66; Vice-Chm., Founding Cttee of Univ. of Konstanz, 1964–66; Prof. of Sociology, Konstanz, 1966–69; Parly Sec. of State, Foreign Office, W Germany, 1969–70; Mem., EEC, Brussels, 1970–74; Dir, 1974–84, Governor, 1986–, LSE; Prof. of Social Sci., Konstanz Univ., 1984–87. Chm., Delegated Powers Select Cttee, H of L, 2002–06. Member: Hansard Soc. Commn on Electoral Reform, 1975–76; Royal Commn on Legal Services, 1976–79; Cttee to Review Functioning of Financial Instns, 1977–80. Trustee, Ford Foundn, 1976–88. Chm. Bd, Friedrich Naumann Stiftung, 1982–88; non-executive Director: Glaxo Holdings PLC, 1984–92; Bankges. Berlin (UK) plc, 1996–2001. Vis. Prof. at several Europ. and N American univs. Reith Lecturer, 1974; Jephcott Lectr, RSocMed, 1983. Hon. Fellow: LSE; Imperial Coll. Hon. MRIA 1974; Fellow, St Antony's Coll., Oxford, 1976. Foreign Hon. Member: Amer. Acad. of Arts and Sciences, 1975–; Nat. Acad. of Sciences, USA, 1977; Amer. Philosophical Soc., 1977; FRSA 1977; Hon. FRCS 1982. 26 hon. degrees from univs in 12 countries. Journal Fund Award for Learned Publication, 1966; Agnelli Prize, Giovanni Agnelli Foundation, 1992; Heuss Prize, Theodor-Heuss Stiftung, 1997. Grand Croix de l'Ordre du Mérite du Sénégal, 1971; Grosses Bundesverdienstkreuz mit Stern und Schulterband (Federal Republic of Germany), 1974; Grand Croix de l'Ordre du Mérite du Luxembourg, 1974; Grosses goldenes Ehrenzeichen am Bande für Verdienste um die Republik Österreich (Austria), 1975; Grand Croix de l'Ordre de Léopold II (Belgium), 1975; Comdr's Cross, Order of Civil Merit (Spain), 1990. *Publications include:* Marx in Perspective, 1953; Industrie- und Betriebssoziologie, 1956; Soziale Klassen und Klassenkonflikt, 1957 (Class and Class Conflict, 1959); Homo Sociologicus, 1959; Die angewandte Aufklärung, 1963; Gesellschaft und Demokratie in Deutschland, 1965 (Society and Democracy in Germany, 1966); Pfade aus Utopia, 1967 (Uscire dall'Utopia, 1971); Essays in the Theory of Society, 1968; Konflikt und Freiheit, 1972; Plädoyer für die Europäische Union, 1973; The New Liberty, 1975; Life Chances, 1979; On Britain, 1982; Die Chancen der Krise, 1983; Reisen nach innen und aussen, 1984; Law and Order, 1985; The Modern Social Conflict, 1988; Reflections on the Revolution in Europe, 1990; LSE: a history of the London School of Economics and Political Science 1895–1995, 1995; After 1989, 1997; Liberal und unabhängig: Gerd Bucerius und seine Zeit, 2000; Universities after Communism, 2000; Über Grenzen, 2002; Auf der Suche nach einer neuen Ordnung, 2003; Der Wiederbeginn der Geschichte, 2004; Versuchungen der Unfreiheit, 2006. *Address:* House of Lords, SW1A 0PW. *Clubs:* PEN, Reform, Garrick.

DAIN, Sir David (John Michael), KCVO 1997; CMG 1991; HM Diplomatic Service, retired; High Commissioner to Pakistan, 1997–2000; *b* 30 Oct. 1940; *s* of late John Gordon Dain and Joan (*née* Connop); *m* 1969, Susan Kathleen Moss; one *s* four *d*. *Educ:* Merchant Taylors' Sch.; St John's Coll., Oxford (MA Lit.Hum.). Entered HM Diplomatic Service, 1963; Third, later Second Sec., Tehran and Kabul, 1964–68; seconded to Cabinet Office, 1969–72; First Sec., Bonn, 1972–75; FCO, 1975–78; Head of Chancery, Athens, 1978–81; Counsellor and Dep. High Comr, Nicosia, 1981–85; Head of Western European Dept, FCO, 1985–89; on attachment to CSSB, 1989–90; High Comr, Cyprus, 1990–94; Asst Under-Sec. of State, then Dir, S Asian and SE Asian Depts, FCO, 1994–97. Chm., Anglo-Hellenic League, 2007–. FCIL (FIL 1986). Royal Order of Merit, Norway, 1988. *Recreations:* tennis, bridge, flying, golf, walking, natural history. *Address:* Manor

Cottage, Frant, Tunbridge Wells, Kent TN3 9DR. *Clubs:* Oxford and Cambridge; Oxford Union Society.

DAINTITH, Prof. Terence Charles; Professor of Law: University of London, 1988–2004, now Professor Emeritus; University of Western Australia, since 2002; *b* 8 May 1942; *s* of Edward Terence and Irene May Daintith; *m* 1965, Christine Anne Bulport; one *s* one *d.* *Educ:* Wimbledon Coll.; St Edmund Hall, Oxford (BA Jurisp., MA); Univ. of Nancy (Leverhulme European Schol.). Called to the Bar, Lincoln's Inn, 1966; Bencher, 2000. Associate in Law, Univ. of California, Berkeley, 1963–64; Lectr in Constitutional and Admin. Law, Univ. of Edinburgh, 1964–72; University of Dundee: Prof. and Head of Dept of Public Law, 1972–83 ; Dir, Centre for Petroleum and Mineral Law Studies, 1977–83; Prof. of Law, European Univ. Inst., Florence, 1981–87; Dir, Inst. of Advanced Legal Studies, Univ. of London, 1988–95; Dean, Univ. of London Sch. of Advanced Study, 1994–2001. Vis. Fellow, Sch. of Law, Univ. of Melbourne, 2004–. MAE 1989 (Chm., Law Cttee, 1993–96; Chm., Social Scis Section, 1996–98). Editor, Jl Energy and Natural Resources Law, 1983–92. Hon. LLD De Montfort, 2001. *Publications:* The Economic Law of the United Kingdom, 1974; (with G. Willoughby) United Kingdom Oil and Gas Law, 1977, 3rd edn (with A. D. G. Hill) 2000; (with L. Hancher) European Energy Strategy: the legal framework, 1986; (with S. Williams) The Legal Integration of Energy Markets, 1987; Law as an Instrument of Economic Policy, 1988; (with G. R. Baldwin) Harmonisation and Hazard, 1992; Implementing EC Law in the United Kingdom, 1995; (with A. C. Page) The Executive in the Constitution, 1999; Discretion in the Administration of Offshore Oil and Gas, 2006; contribs to UK and foreign law jls. *Recreations:* cycling, carpentry. *Address:* Institute of Advanced Legal Studies, 17 Russell Square, WC1B 5DR. *Club:* Athenæum.

DAINTON, Prof. John Bourke, DPhil; FRS 2002; CPhys, FInstP; Sir James Chadwick Professor of Physics, University of Liverpool, since 2002; Director, Cockcroft Institute of Accelerator Science and Technology, since 2005; *b* 10 Sept. 1947; *s* of Lord Dainton, FRS and of Barbara Hazlitt Dainton (*née* Wright); partner, Josephine Zilberkweit. *Educ:* Merton Coll., Oxford (BA Hons 1969; MA, DPhil 1973). CPhys, FInstP, 1982. Lectr in Physics, Merton Coll., Oxford, 1972–73; Res. Associate, SRC Daresbury Lab., 1973–77; Lectr in Physics, Univ. of Glasgow, 1978–85; University of Liverpool: Lectr in Physics, 1986–88; Sen. Lectr in Physics, 1988–91; Reader in Physics, 1991–94; SERC Sen. Fellow, 1992–97; Prof. of Physics, 1994–2002. Vis. Scientist, DESY, Hamburg, 1980–82, 1997–99; Fellow, Alexander von Humboldt Stiftung, Germany, 2003. Chm., Super Proton Synchrotron and PS Cttee, CERN, 2003–. Freeman, City of London, 1982; Liveryman, Goldsmiths' Co., 1982–. FRSA 2003. Max Born Medal, Inst. of Physics and German Physical Soc., 1999. *Publications:* more than 250 articles in Zeitschrift für Physik C, Nuclear Physics B, Physics Letters B, Jl of Physics G, Nuclear Instruments and Methods, conf. proceedings, SERC and PPARC reports and scientific adv. panels. *Recreations:* music, travelling, taking time to think. *Address:* Cockcroft Institute of Accelerator Science and Technology, Daresbury Science and Innovation Campus, Warrington WA4 4AD. *T:* (01925) 603820; *e-mail:* J.B.Dainton@cockcroft.ac.uk.

DAINTY, Prof. (John) Christopher, PhD; Professor of Applied Physics (formerly Science Foundation Ireland Professor of Experimental Physics), National University of Ireland, Galway, since 2002; Pilkington Professor of Applied Optics, Imperial College, University of London, since 1984 (on leave of absence); *b* 22 Jan. 1947; *s* of Jack Dainty and Mary Elizabeth (*née* Elbeck); *m* 1978, Janice Hancock; one *s* one *d.* *Educ:* George Heriot's, Edinburgh; City of Norwich Sch.; Polytechnic of Central London (Diploma); Imperial Coll. of Science and Technol. (MSc; PhD 1972). Lectr, Queen Elizabeth Coll., Univ. of London, 1974–78; Associate Prof., Inst. of Optics, Univ. of Rochester, NY, USA, 1978–83. Sen. Res. Fellow, SERC, 1987–92; PPARC Sen. Res. Fellow, Imperial Coll., Univ. of London, 2001–02. President: Internat. Commn for Optics, 1990–93; European Optical Soc., 2002–04. Internat. Commn of Optics Prize, 1984; Thomas Young Medal and Prize, Inst. of Physics, 1993; Mees Medal and Prize, Optical Soc. of America, 2003. *Publications:* (with R. Shaw) Image Science, 1974; (ed) Laser Speckle and Related Phenomena, 1975, 2nd edn 1984; (ed with M. Nieto-Vesperinas) Scattering in Volumes and Surfaces, 1989; scientific papers. *Address:* Department of Physics, National University of Ireland, Galway, Ireland. *T:* (91) 492826.

DAKIN, Dorothy Danvers, OBE 1982; JP; Assistant Chaplain, HM Prison and Remand Centre, Pucklechurch, 1984–87; *b* 22 Oct. 1919; *d* of Edwin Lionel Dakin, chartered civil engr and Mary Danvers Dakin (*née* Walker), artist. *Educ:* Sherborne Sch. for Girls; Newnham Coll., Cambridge. MA Geography. 2nd Officer WRNS (Educn), 1943–50; Housemistress, Wycombe Abbey Sch., 1950–60; Headmistress, The Red Maids' School, Bristol, 1961–81; Chm., ISIS Assoc., 1982–84. President: West of England Br., Assoc. of Headmistresses, 1969–71; Assoc. of Headmistresses of Girls' Boarding Schs, 1971–73; Girls' Schs Assoc. (Independent), 1973–75; Chm. Council, ISIS, 1975–81. Licensed Reader, C of E, 1982–86. FRSA 1988. JP Bristol, 1974. *Recreations:* fencing, painting, embroidery. *Address:* 41 Park Grove, Henleaze, Bristol BS9 4LF.

DALAI LAMA; *see* Tenzin Gyatso.

DALAL, Maneck Ardeshir Sohrab, OBE 1997; Director: Tata Ltd, SW1, since 1977 (Managing Director, 1977–88; Vice-Chairman, 1989–94); Tata Industries, Bombay, since 1979; *b* 24 Dec. 1918; *s* of Ardeshir Dalal, OBE and Amy Dalal; *m* 1947, Kathleen Gertrude Richardson; three *d.* *Educ:* Trinity Hall, Cambridge (MA). Cambridge Univ. Captain, tennis and squash rackets. Called to the Bar, Middle Temple, 1945. Manager: Air-India New Delhi, 1946–48; Air-India London, 1948–53; Regional Traffic Manager, 1953–59; Regional Director, 1959–77; Minister for Tourism and Civil Aviation, High Commn for India, 1973–77. President: Indian Chamber of Commerce in Great Britain, 1959–62; Indian Management Assoc. of UK, 1960–63; UK Pres., World Conf. on Religions and Peace, UK and Ireland Gp, 1985–; Vice-Pres., Friends of Vellore, 1979–; Chairman: Foreign Airlines Assoc. of UK, 1965–67; Indian YMCA, London, 1972–98; Bharatiya Vidhya Bhavan, London (Indian Cultural Inst. of Gt Britain), 1975–; Northbrook Soc., 1990– (Mem. Cttee, 1975–); Indian Women's Educn Assoc., 1985–95 (Mem. Cttee, 1975–95); Vice-Chm., Fest. of India in GB, 1980–81; Member: Sub-Cttee on Transport, Industrial Trng Bd of GB, 1975–77; Assembly, British Council of Churches, 1984–87; Internat. Bd, United World Colls, 1985–; Bd Govs, Nat. Inst. for Social Work, 1986–96; Chm. Central Council, Royal Over-Seas League, 1986–89 (Dep. Chm. Central Council, 1982–86; Mem., 1974–; Vice-Pres., 1989–). Patron: Internat. Centre for Child Studies, 1984–; Satyajit Ray Foundn, 1995–; Indian Professionals Assoc., UK, 1996–; Child in Need Internat. (UK), 2001–. FCILT (FCIT 1975); FCMI; FRSA 1997. *Recreations:* reading, walking. *Address:* Tall Trees, Marlborough Road, Hampton, Middx TW12 3RX. *T:* (020) 8979 2065. *Clubs:* Hurlingham, Royal Over-Seas League, MCC; Hawks (Cambridge).

DALBY, David; *see* Dalby, T. D. P.

DALBY, Ven. (John) Mark (Meredith); Chaplain, The Beauchamp Community, Newland, 2000–07; Archdeacon of Rochdale, 1991–2000, now Emeritus; *b* 3 Jan. 1938; *s* of William and Sheila Mary Dalby (*née* Arkell). *Educ:* King George V Sch., Southpor Exeter Coll., Oxford, (MA 1965); Ripon Hall, Oxford; Univ. of Nottingham (Ph 1977). Ordained deacon 1963, priest 1964; Curate: Hambleden, Bucks, 1963–68; Fawle Fingest, Medmenham and Turville, Bucks, 1965–68; Vicar of St Peter, Spring Hi Birmingham, 1968–75; Rural Dean of Birmingham City, 1973–75; Sec., Cttee for The Educn, and Selection Sec., ACCM, 1975–80; Hon. Curate of All Hallows, Tottenhan 1975–80; Vicar of St Mark, Worsley, 1980–84; Team Rector of Worsley, 1984–91; Rur Dean of Eccles, 1987–91. Examining Chaplain to the Bp of Manchester, 1980–200 Member: Gen. Synod of C of E, 1985–95; Liturgical Commn, 1986–95. *Publication* Open Communion in the Church of England, 1959; The Gospel and the Priest, 197 Tottenham Church and Parish, 1979; The Cocker Connection, 1989; Open Baptism 1989; Anglican Missals and their Canons, 1998; Infant Communion: the New Testamer to the Reformation, 2003. *Recreations:* travel, family history, philately, freemasonry liturgy. *Address:* St Christopher's, Beauchamp Community, Newland, Malvern Worcestershire WR13 5AX. *T:* (01684) 899198.

DALBY, Dr (Terry) David (Pereira); Reader in West African Languages, School o Oriental and African Studies, University of London, 1967–83, now Emeritus; Directo Linguasphere Observatory (Observatoire linguistique), since 1987; *b* 7 Jan. 1933; *s* o Ernest Edwin Dalby and Rose Cecilia Dalby; one *s* four *d.* *Educ:* Cardiff High Sch.; Quee Mary Coll., London (BA 1954, PhD 1961; Hon. Life Mem., Queen Mary Coll. Unio Soc., 1954). Served to Lieut, Intell. Corps, 1954–56. United Africa Co. Ltd, London an W Africa, 1957–60; Lectr in Mod. Languages, University Coll. of Sierra Leone, 1961–6 Lectr in W African Langs, SOAS, Univ. of London, 1962–67; Hon. Res. Fellow, Adra y Gymraeg, Univ. of Wales, Cardiff, 1996–2005. Hanns Wolff Vis. Prof., Indiana Univ 1969. Chm., Centre for Afr. Studies, Univ. of London, 1971–74; Dir, Internat. Africa Inst., 1974–80; Chairman: Internat. Conf. on Manding Studies, 1972, and Drought i Africa Conf., 1973; UK Standing Cttee on Univ. Studies of Africa, 1978–82 (Dep. Chm 1975–78). Vice-Pres., Unesco Meeting on Cultural Specificity in Africa, Accra, 198 Member: Governing Body, SOAS, 1969–70; Council, African Studies Assoc. of UK 1970–73; Cttee of Management, British Inst. in Paris, 1975–82; Conseil Internat. d Recherche et d'Etude en Linguistique Fondamentale et Appliquée, 1980–86 (Présiden 1984); Centre Internat. de Recherche sur le Bilinguisme, Laval Univ., Que, 1981–8 Eur. Council on African Studies, 1985–87; Centre Internat. des Industries de la Langu Univ. Paris X, 1993–95; Comité Français des Etudes Africaines, 1993–94; BSI Cttee TS 1, 2001–06; ISO Cttee TC37, 2002–05. Hon. Mem., SOAS, 1983. Editor, Africa Language Review, 1962–72; Co-editor, Africa, 1976–80. Endowed Rhoswen Enfys li awards, Nat. Eisteddfod Wales, 2002–. *Publications:* Lexicon of the Mediaeval Germa Hunt, 1965; Black through White: patterns of communication in Africa and the Ne World, 1970; (ed) Language and History in Africa, 1970; (ed jtly) Drought in Africa, 1 vol. 1973, 2nd vol. 1978; Language Map of Africa and the adjacent islands, 1977; Clavie international de Niamey, 1984; (jtly) Les langues et l'espace du français, 1985; Afrique e la lettre, 1986; (jtly) Thesaurus of African Languages, 1987; Linguasphere Register of th World's Languages and Speech Communities, 2 vols, 2000; articles in linguistic and othe jls. *Recreations:* walking, campaigning for children's rights. *Address:* *e-mail:* dalby(linguasphere.info.

DALDRY, Stephen David, CBE 2004; Director, Stephen Daldry Pictures, since 199 Associate Director, Royal Court Theatre, since 1999; *b* 2 May 1961; *s* of late Patric Daldry and of Cherry (*née* Thompson); *m* 2001, Lucy Sexton; one *d.* *Educ:* Huish G Taunton; Univ. of Sheffield (BA). Trained with Il Circo di Nando Orfei, Italy; Artist Dir, Metro Theatre, 1984–86; Associate Artist, Crucible Theatre, Sheffield, 1986–8 Artistic Director: Gate Theatre, Notting Hill, 1989–92; English Stage Co., Royal Cou Theatre, 1992–99. Major productions include: Damned for Despair, Gate, 1991; A Inspector Calls, RNT, 1992, Aldwych, 1994, Garrick, 1995, NY, 1995, Playhouse, 200 Machinal, RNT, 1993; Royal Court: The Kitchen, 1995; Via Dolorosa, 1998, NY, 199 filmed 1999; Far Away, 2000, transf. Albery, 2001; A Number, 2002; Billy Elliot - th Musical, Victoria Palace, 2005. *Films:* Eight (short), 1998; Billy Elliot, 2000; The Hour 2003. *Address:* c/o Working Title Films, 140 Wardour Street, W1F 8ZT.

DALE, Barry Gordon, FCA; Chairman, Burlington Inns plc, since 2000; Directo Marketfund Ltd, since 1995; *b* 31 July 1938; *s* of Francis and Catherine Dale; *m* 196 Margaret (*née* Fairbrother); one *s* one *d.* *Educ:* Queen Elizabeth Grammar Sch., Blackbur Coopers Lybrand, Montreal, 1960–62; Pilkington Brothers Glass, St Helens, 1962–6 ICI, 1965–85: Mond Div., Cheshire, 1966–68; Head Office, 1968–72; Dep. Chief Acc Mond Div., 1972–78; Finance Dir, ICI Latin America (Wilmington, USA), 1978–8 Chief Acct, Organics Div., Manchester, 1980–84; Bd Mem. for Finance, LRT, 1985–8 Gp Finance Dir, 1988–92, Gp Chief Exec., 1993–95, Littlewoods Orgn. Director: Ellis Everard, 1978–81; Magadi Soda Co. (Kenya), 1980–82; Triplex Lloyd, 1994–98; Londo Buses Ltd, 1985–88; London Underground Ltd, 1985–88; LRT Bus Engineering Lt 1985–88; Greenalls, then De Vere, Gp, 1992–2000; Chairman: London Transport Truste Co., 1985–88; London Transport Pension Fund Trustees, 1985–88; Datanetwork 1987–88; Creightons, 1997–99. Associate, Corporate Development Internat., 2003– *Recreations:* golf, fell walking, other sports. *Address:* Tanglewood, Spinney Lane, Knutsfor WA16 0NQ. *Clubs:* Tatton (Knutsford); Knutsford Golf.

DALE, Maj.-Gen. Ian Conway, CBE 2007; CEng; Director General Land Equipmen Defence Equipment and Support, since 2008; *b* Leicester, 8 Sept. 1957; *s* of Eric Dale an Gwendolen Dale (*née* Mann); *m* 1983, Karen Moore; two *d.* *Educ:* Gateway Gramma Sch., Leicester; Army Apprentices Coll., Arborfield; RMA, Sandhurst; Royal Mil. Col of Sci., Shrivenham (BSc Eng Hons 1983; MSc 1988). CEng 1987; MIET 1986. Troo Comd, 14/20 King's Hussars, Germany and Canada, 1979; 2IC Light Aid Detachmer REME, 14/20 King's Hussars, Germany, 1980; Trng Officer, 20 Electronics Worksho REME, Germany, 1984; OC, 32 Regt RA Workshop REME, Germany, 1985–86; Adj Logistic Bn, Falkland Is, 1987; psc† 1989; Gen. Staff, Directorate of CIS (Army), MoD 1990–91; Co. Comd, 20 Electronics Workshop REME, Germany, 1992–93; Gen. Sta HQ ARRC, Germany and Denmark, 1994–95; CO, 6 Bn REME, UK and Bosni 1996–97; COS Inspector REME, UK, 1998; Comdr Equipment Support, German 1999–2000, DCS, Germany and Oman, 2001, 1 (UK) Armoured Div.; hcsc 200 Commander: 101 Logistic Bde, UK, 2002–03; UK Jt Force Logistics Component, Kuwa and Iraq, 2003; Deputy Chief of Staff: ARRC, Germany, 2004–05; Internat. Securit Assistance Force, Afghanistan, 2006–07; rcds 2007. President: Army Rugby Leagu REME Winter Sports. *Recreations:* mountain sports, ski-ing, deer management. *Addres* RHQ REME, Box H075, HQ DEME(A), Hazebrouck Barracks, Arborfield, Berks RG 9NJ. *T:* (0118) 976 2480.

DALE, Jim, MBE 2003; actor, director, singer, composer, lyricist; *b* 15 Aug. 1935; *m*; thre *s* one *d.* *Educ:* Kettering Grammar School. Music Hall comedian, 1951; singing compèring, directing, 1951–61; *films,* 1965–, include: Lock Up Your Daughters, Th Winter's Tale, The Biggest Dog in the World, National Health, Adolf Hitler—My Pa in his Downfall, Joseph Andrews, Pete's Dragon, Hot Lead Cold Feet, Bloodshy, Th Spaceman and King Arthur, Scandalous, Carry On films: Carry On Cabby, Carry O

Cleo, Carry On Jack, Carry On Cowboy, Carry On Screaming, Carry On Spying, Carry On Constable, Carry On Doctor, Carry On Again Doctor, Carry On Don't Lose Your Head, Carry On Follow that Camel, Carry On Columbus. *Stage:* joined Frank Dunlop's Pop Theatre for Edinburgh Festival, 1967–68; National Theatre, 1969–71: main roles in National Health, Love's Labour's Lost, Merchant of Venice, Good-natured Man, Captain of Kopenick, The Architect and the Emperor of Assyria; also appeared at Young Vic in Taming of the Shrew, Scapino (title rôle and wrote music); title rôle in musical The Card, 1973; Compère of Sunday Night at the London Palladium, 1973–74; Scapino (title rôle), Broadway, 1974–75 (Drama Critics' and Outer Circle Awards for best actor; Tony award nomination for best actor); Privates on Parade, Long Wharf Theatre, New Haven, Conn, 1979; Barnum (title rôle), Broadway, 1980 (Tony award for best actor in a musical, Drama Desk Award); A Day in the Death of Joe Egg, NY, 1985 (Tony nomination for best actor; Outer Circle Award for best actor); Me and My Girl, NY, 1987–88; Privates on Parade, NY, 1989; Oliver!, London Palladium, 1995; The Music Man, Travels With My Aunt, NY (Drama Desk Award, Outer Circle Award and Critics Award, 1995); Comedians, NY, 2003; A Christmas Carol, NY, 2003–04; Address Unknown, NY, 2004; The Threepenny Opera, NY, 2006; Busker Alley, NY, 2006; The Oak Tree, NY, 2007; Don Juan in Hell, Williamstown, 2007. *Television* includes: host of Ringling Brothers Barnum and Bailey Circus (TV special), 1985; Adventures of Huckleberry Finn, 1985; Pushing Daisies, 2007–08. Composed film music for: The Winter's Tale, Shalako, Twinky, Georgy Girl (nominated for Academy Award), Joseph Andrews. Audio recordings incl. Harry Potter series (Grammy Award, best children's audio recording: 2001, for Harry Potter and the Goblet of Fire; 2008, for Harry Potter and the Deathly Hallows), A Christmas Carol, 2004; Peter and the Wolf, The Shoe Bird, 2008. *Address:* c/o Sharon Bierut, CED, 257 Park Avenue South, New York, NY 10010, USA; c/o Janet Glass, Eric Glass Ltd, 25 Ladbroke Crescent, W11 1PS.

DALE, Peter David; Head of More4, Channel 4, since 2005; *b* 25 July 1955; *s* of David Howard Dale and Betty Marguerite Dale (*née* Rosser); *m* 1988, Victoria Francesca Pennington; one *s* two *d*. *Educ:* King Henry VIII Grammar Sch., Coventry; Liverpool Univ. (BA Hons English Lit. and Lang.). BBC Television: research asst trainee, 1980–82; Dir and Producer, 1982–98; Channel 4: Commissioning Ed., Documentaries, 1998–2000; Head of Documentaries, 2000–05. Dir, Sheffield Internat. Documentary Fest., 2002–04. Mem. Exec. Cttee, Guardian Edinburgh TV Fest., 2002–05. Trustee, Grierson Trust, 2007–. Journalism Prize, Anglo-German Foundn, 1992; Best Documentary Award, 1994, Best Documentary Series, 1996, RTS; Producer of Year Award, Broadcast Mag., 1997; Grierson Award for Best British Documentary, BFI, 1997. *Recreations:* family, sailing. *Address:* Channel 4, 124 Horseferry Road, SW1P 2TX. *T:* (020) 7306 8727.

DALE, Robert Alan; business consultant, retired; Director, Business Development, Lucas Industries plc, 1992–93; *b* 31 Oct. 1938; *s* of Horace and Alice Dale; *m* 1963, Sheila Mary Dursley; one *s* one *d*. *Educ:* West Bromwich Grammar Sch.; Birmingham Univ. (BA Hons). Joined Lucas Industries as graduate apprentice, 1960; first management appt, 1965; first Bd appt, 1971; Dir, Lucas CAV, 1972–77; Dir and Gen. Man., Lucas Batteries, 1978–81; joined Exec. Cttee of Lucas (Joseph Lucas Ltd), 1980; Managing Director: Lucas World Service, 1981–85; Lucas Electrical, 1985–87; Lucas Automotive, 1987–92; Dir, Lucas Industries, 1987–93. Vice-Pres., SMMT, 1989–92. *Recreations:* sport, photography, travel.

DALES, Sir Richard (Nigel), KCVO 2001; CMG 1993; HM Diplomatic Service, retired; Ambassador to Norway, 1998–2002; *b* 26 Aug. 1942; *s* of late Kenneth Richard Frank Dales and Olwen Mary (*née* Preedy); *m* 1966, Elizabeth Margaret Martin; one *s* one *d*. *Educ:* Chigwell Sch.; St Catharine's Coll., Cambridge (BA 1964). Entered FO, 1964; Third Sec., Yaoundé, Cameroon, 1965–67; FCO, 1968–70; Second Sec., later First Sec., Copenhagen, 1970–73; FCO, 1973; Asst Private Sec. to Foreign and Commonwealth Sec., 1974–77; First Sec., Head of Chancery and Consul, Sofia, Bulgaria, 1977–81; FCO, 1981; Counsellor and Head of Chancery, Copenhagen, 1982–86; Dep. High Comr, Harare, 1986–89; Head of Southern Africa, later Central and Southern Africa, Dept, FCO, 1989–91; Resident Chm. (FCO), CSSB, 1991–92; High Comr, Zimbabwe, 1992–95; Asst Under-Sec. of State, later Dir, Africa and Commonwealth, FCO, 1995–98. Chm., Anglo-Norse Soc., 2003–; Trustee, Internat. Alert, 2005– (Chm., 2006–). Mem. Bd, Norfolk and Norwich Fest., 2003–06. Mem. Council, UEA, 2004–. *Recreations:* music, walking. *Club:* Oxford and Cambridge.

DALEY, Judith Mary Philomena; Her Honour Judge Daley; a Circuit Judge, since 1994; *b* 12 Aug. 1948; *d* of James Patrick Daley and Mary Elizabeth Daley (*née* Rawcliffe), BA. *Educ:* Seafield Convent Grammar Sch., Crosby; King's Coll. London (LLB Hons). Called to the Bar, Gray's Inn, 1970; Asst Recorder, 1984; Recorder, 1989–94 (Northern Circuit). *Recreations:* opera, music, theatre, travel, gardening. *Address:* Liverpool Civil and Family Courts, 35 Vernon Street, Liverpool L2 2BX. *Club:* Athenæum (Liverpool).

DALGARNO, Prof. Alexander, PhD; FRS 1972; Phillips Professor of Astronomy, since 1977, Chairman of Department of Astronomy, 1971–76, Associate Director of Centre for Astrophysics, 1973–80, Harvard University; Member of Smithsonian Astrophysical Observatory, since 1967; *b* 5 Jan. 1928; *s* of William Dalgarno; *m* 1st, 1957, Barbara Kane (marr. diss. 1972); two *s* two *d*; 2nd, 1972, Emily Izsák (marr. diss. 1987). *Educ:* Southgate Grammar Sch.; University Coll., London (Fellow 1976). BSc Maths, 1st Cl. Hons London, 1947; PhD Theoretical Physics London, 1951; AM Harvard, 1967. The Queen's University of Belfast: Lectr in Applied Maths, 1952; Reader in Maths, 1956; Dir of Computing Lab., 1960; Prof. of Quantum Mechanics, 1961; Prof. of Mathematical Physics, 1966–67; Prof. of Astronomy, Harvard Univ., 1967–; Acting Dir, Harvard Coll. Observatory, 1971–73. Chief Scientist, Geophysics Corp. of America, 1962–63. Vikram A. Sarabhai Prof., Physical Res. Lab., Ahmedabad, 2002; Oort Prof., Leiden Univ., 2003; Charles M. and Martha Hitchcock Prof., Univ. of Calif, Berkeley, 2003. Spiers Meml Lectr and Medal, Faraday Div., RSC, 1992. Editor, Astrophysical Journal Letters, 1973–2002. Fellow: Amer. Acad. of Arts and Sciences, 1968; Amer. Geophysical Union, 1972; Amer. Physical Soc., 1980; FInstP 2000; Member: Internat. Acad. Astronautics, 1972; US Nat. Acad. of Scis, 2001. MRIA 1989. FUMIST 1992. Hon. DSc: QUB, 1980; York, Canada, 2000. Prize of Internat. Acad. of Quantum Molecular Sci., 1969; Hodgkins Medal, Smithsonian Instn, 1977; Davisson-Germer Prize, Amer. Physical Soc., 1980; Gold Medal, Royal Astronomical Soc., 1986; Meggers Prize, Optical Soc. of America, 1986; Fleming Medal, Amer. Geophys. Union, 1995; Hughes Medal, Royal Soc., 2002. *Publications:* numerous papers in scientific journals. *Recreations:* squash, books. *Address:* c/o Harvard-Smithsonian Center for Astrophysics, 60 Garden Street, Cambridge, MA 02138, USA.

DALGETY, Hon. Ramsay Robertson; QC (Scot.) 1986; Judge of the Supreme Court, 1991–95, and sometime Acting Chief Justice, Tonga; *b* 2 July 1945; *s* of James Robertson Dalgety and Georgia Dalgety (*née* Whyte); *m* 1971, Mary Margaret Bernard; one *s* one *d*. *Educ:* High School of Dundee; Univ. of St Andrews (LLB Hons). Advocate, 1972; Temp. Sheriff, 1987–91. Dep. Traffic Comr for Scotland, 1988–93. Councillor, City of Edinburgh, 1974–80. Director/Chairman: Archer Transport Ltd and Archer Transport (London) Ltd, 1982–85; Venture Shipping Ltd, 1983–85. Director: Scottish Opera Ltd, 1980–90; Scottish Opera Theatre Trust Ltd, 1987–90; Chm., Opera Singers Pension Fund, 1990–92 (Dep. Chm., 1989–90; Trustee, 1983–92); Dep. Chm., Edinburgh Hibernian Shareholders Assoc., 1990–92. Sec. Gen., Tonga Chamber of Commerce, 1998–2001. Chm., Tonga Electric Power Bd, 2003–. Vice-Pres. and Treas., Tonga Internat. Gamefishing Assoc., 1994–98; Pres., Tonga Archery Fedn, 1998–; Dep. Chef de Mission, Kingdom of Tonga team, Olympic Games, Athens, 2004. *Recreations:* boating, opera, travel, cricket, football, archery. *Address:* PO Box 869, Nuku'alofa, Kingdom of Tonga, South Pacific. *T:* (office) 8723400, (home) 8723348, *Fax:* 23632. *Club:* Royal Nuku'alofa (Tonga) (Mem. Cttee, 2003–).

DALHOUSIE, 17th Earl of, *cr* 1633; **James Hubert Ramsay;** Baron Ramsay 1618; Lord Ramsay 1633; Baron Ramsay (UK) 1875; Vice Lord-Lieutenant, Angus, since 2002; Director, Jamestown Investments Ltd, since 1987; *b* 17 Jan. 1948; *er s* of 16th Earl of Dalhousie, KT, GCVO, GBE, MC; *S* father, 1999; *m* 1973, Marilyn, *yr d* of Major Sir David Butter, *qv*; one *s* two *d*. *Educ:* Ampleforth. 2nd Bn Coldstream Guards, commnd 1968–71, RARO 1971. Director: Hambros Bank Ltd, 1981–82; (exec.) Enskilda Securities, 1982–87; Capel-Cure Myers Capital Management Ltd, 1988–91; Dunedin Smaller Cos Investment Trust, 1993– (Chm., 1998–); Scottish Woodlands Ltd, 1993–2005 (Chm., 1998–2005). Chm., (Scotland) Mental Health Foundn, 2000–02. Lt, Royal Co. of Archers (The Queen's Body Guard for Scotland), 2007–. Vice Chm., Game Conservancy Trust, 1994–; Pres., British Deer Soc., 1987–. DL Angus, 1993. OStJ 2001. *Heir:* *s* Lord Ramsay, *qv*. *Address:* Brechin Castle, Brechin, Angus DD9 6SH. *Clubs:* White's, Pratt's, Caledonian (Pres., 1990–), Turf.

DALKEITH, Earl of; Walter John Francis Montagu Douglas Scott; *b* 2 Aug. 1984; *s* and *heir* of Duke of Buccleuch, *qv* and of Duchess of Buccleuch, *qv*. A Page of Honour to HM The Queen, 1996–99.

DALLAGLIO, Lawrence Bruno Nero, OBE 2008 (MBE 2004); professional Rugby Union player, 1995–2008; *b* 10 Aug. 1972; *s* of Vincenzo and Eileen Dallaglio; *m* 2006, Alice Corbett; one *s* two *d*. *Educ:* Ampleforth Coll.; Kingston Univ. Debut, Wasps Rugby Union team, 1992, Capt., 1995–2008; Mem., British Lions touring teams, 1997, 2001, 2005; England team: debut, 1995; 85 caps, 1995–2007; Capt., 1998–99 and 2004; Mem., World Cup winning team, Australia, 2003. *Publications:* Diary of a Season, 1997; Know the Modern Game, 1999; It's in the Blood: my life (autobiog.), 2007. *Recreations:* golf, Chelsea supporter. *Address:* c/o Richard Relton, Green Room Sports, 4th Floor, 31 Windmill Street, W1T 2JN. *T:* (020) 7009 6000.

DALLAS, James; Chairman, Denton Wilde Sapte (formerly Denton Hall), since 1996; *b* 21 April 1955; *m* 1979, Annabel Hope; one *s* two *d*. *Educ:* Eton; St Edmund Hall, Oxford (MA Jurisprudence). Trainee and asst solicitor, 1976–81; Sen. Legal Advr, Internat. Energy Develt Corp., 1981–84; Solicitor, 1984–, Partner, 1985–, Denton Hall, subseq. Denton Wilde Sapte. Non-exec. Dir, AMEC plc, 1999–. Member: Corporate Develt Bd, Multiple Sclerosis Soc.; ARK. Trustee, Thames River Restoration Trust. *Recreations:* fishing, birdwatching, cricket. *Address:* Denton Wilde Sapte, 1 Fleet Place, EC4M 7WS.

DALLAT, John James; Member (SDLP) Londonderry East, Northern Ireland Assembly, since 1998; *b* 24 March 1947; *s* of Daniel and Ellen Dallat; *m* 1975, Anne Philomena Long; two *s* one *d*. *Educ:* Coleraine Coll. of Further Educn (qual. teacher, commercial subjects, 1968); North West Inst., Derry (Business Studies Teacher's Dip., 1975); Univ. of Ulster (Dip. in Advanced Studies in Educn, 1979); UC, Galway (Dip. in Rural Studies, 1997). Teacher: Technical Coll., Carndonagh, 1968–74; St Paul's Coll., Kilrea, 1975–98. Mem. (SDLP) Coleraine BC, 1977–98; Mayor of Coleraine, 2001–02. Contested (SDLP) Londonderry East, 2001. Dep. Speaker, NI Assembly, 2007–. Chm., District Policing Partnership, 2007–08. *Recreations:* attending meetings!, walking, reading. *Address:* Northern Ireland Assembly, Stormont Castle, Belfast BT4 3XX. *T:* (028) 2554 0798, *Fax:* (028) 2554 1798.

DALLISTON, Very Rev. Christopher Charles; Dean of Newcastle, since 2003; *b* 2 April 1956; *s* of Gerald and Rosemary Dalliston; *m* 1989, Michelle Aleysha Caron; two *s* two *d*. *Educ:* Diss Grammar Sch.; Peterhouse, Cambridge (MA 1980); St Stephen's House, Oxford (BA 1984). Ford Motor Co., 1978–81. Ordained deacon, 1984, priest, 1985; Curate, Halstead, 1984–87; Domestic Chaplain to Bp of Chelmsford, 1987–91; Vicar, St Edmund, Forest Gate, 1991–95; St Botolph, Boston, 1995–2003. *Recreations:* choral music, folksong, theatre, Norwich City FC, walking. *Address:* The Cathedral Vicarage, 26 Mitchell Avenue, Jesmond, Newcastle upon Tyne NE2 3LA; *e-mail:* DeanNewcastle@aol.com.

DALMENY, Lord; Harry Ronald Neil Primrose; DL; Director, Sotheby's, since 2001; Chairman, Sotheby's Olympia, since 2003; *b* 20 Nov. 1967; *s* and *heir* of 7th Earl of Rosebery, *qv*; *m* 1994, Caroline, *e d* of Ronald Daglish and Mrs William Wyatt-Lowe; one *s* four *d* (incl. triplets). *Educ:* Dragon Sch., Oxford; Eton Coll.; Trinity Coll., Cambridge (BA Hons). Mem., Royal Co. of Archers, The Queen's Body Guard for Scotland, 2002–. DL Midlothian, 2006. *Heir:* *s* Hon. Caspian Albert Harry Primrose, *b* 8 Sept. 2005. *Address:* Dalmeny House, South Queensferry, West Lothian EH30 9TQ. *T:* (0131) 331 1784. *Clubs:* Turf; University Pitt (Cambridge); Midlothian (Edinburgh); St Moritz Tobogganing.

DALRYMPLE, family name of **Earl of Stair**.

DALRYMPLE, Sir Hew (Fleetwood) Hamilton-, 10th Bt *cr* 1697; GCVO 2001 (KCVO 1985; CVO 1974); JP; late Major, Grenadier Guards; Lord-Lieutenant of East Lothian, 1987–2001 (Vice-Lieutenant, 1973–87); *b* 9 April 1926; *er s* of Sir Hew (Clifford) Hamilton-Dalrymple, 9th Bt, JP; *S* father, 1959; *m* 1954, Lady Anne-Louise Mary Keppel, *d* of 9th Earl of Albemarle, MC, and of (Diana Cicely), Diana, Countess of Albemarle, *qv*; four *s*. *Educ:* Ampleforth. Commnd, Grenadier Guards, 1944; Staff Coll., Camberley, 1957; DAAG HQ 3rd Div., 1958–60; Regimental Adjt, Grenadier Guards, 1960–62; retd 1962. Adjt, 1964–85, Pres. of Council, 1988–96, and Captain General and Gold Stick, 1996–2004, Queen's Body Guard for Scotland (Royal Company of Archers). Vice-Chm., Scottish & Newcastle Breweries, 1983–86 (Dir, 1967–86); Chm., Scottish American Investment Co., 1985–91 (Dir, 1967–93). DL 1964, JP 1987, East Lothian. *Heir:* *e s* Hew Richard Hamilton-Dalrymple [*b* 3 Sept. 1955; *m* 1987, Jane Elizabeth, *yr d* of Lt-Col John Morris; one *s* three *d*. *Educ:* Ampleforth; Corpus Christi Coll., Oxford (MA); Clare Hall, Cambridge (MPhil); Birkbeck Coll., London (MSc). ODI Fellow, Swaziland, 1982–84]. *Address:* Leuchie, North Berwick, East Lothian EH39 5NT. *T:* (01620) 892903. *Club:* Cavalry and Guards.

See also W. B. H. Dalrymple.

DALRYMPLE, William Benedict Hamilton; writer; Director, Jaipur Literature Festival, since 2005; *b* 20 March 1965; *s* of Sir Hew (Fleetwood) Hamilton-Dalrymple, *qv*; *m* 1991, Olivia Fraser; two *s* one *d*. *Educ:* Ampleforth Coll.; Trinity Coll., Cambridge (Exhibr; Sen. Hist. Schol., MA Hons 1992). Television series: Stones of the Raj, 1997;

Indian Journeys, 2000 (Grierson Award, Best Documentary Series, 2001); Sufi Soul, 2005; radio series: Three Miles an Hour, 2002; The Long Search, 2002 (Sandford St Martin Prize for Religious Broadcasting), 2003. FRSL 1993; FRGS 1993; FRAS 1998. Hon. DLitt: St Andrews, 2006; Lucknow, 2007; Aberdeen, 2008. Mungo Park Medal, RSGS, 2002; Sir Percy Sykes Meml Medal, RSAA, 2005; Col James Todd Award, Mewar Foundn, 2008. *Publications:* In Xanadu, 1989 (Yorks Post Best First Work Award, Scottish Arts Council Spring Book Award, 1990); City of Djinns, 1993 (Thomas Cook Travel Book Award, Sunday Times Young British Writer of Year Award, 1994); From the Holy Mountain (Scottish Arts Council Autumn Book Award), 1997; The Age of Kali (collected journalism), 1998 (Prix d'Astrolabe, 2005); White Mughals, 2002 (Wolfson Hist. Prize, 2003; Scottish Book of the Year Prize, 2003); The Last Mughal, 2006 (Duff Cooper Memorial Prize, 2007); contribs to jls incl. TLS, Granta, New Yorker, NY Review of Books, Guardian. *Address:* 1 & 2 Pages' Yard, Church Street, Old Chiswick, W4 2PA. *T:* (020) 8742 3233, *Fax:* (020) 8742 3123; *e-mail:* wdalrymple1@aol.com.

DALRYMPLE-HAMILTON of Bargany, Captain North Edward Frederick, CVO 1961; MBE 1953; DSC 1943; JP; Royal Navy; *b* 17 Feb. 1922; *s* of Admiral Sir Frederick Dalrymple-Hamilton of Bargany, KCB; *m* 1st, 1949, Hon. Mary Colville (*d* 1981), *d* of 1st Baron Clydesmuir, PC, GCIE, TD; two *s*; 2nd, 1983, Antoinette, *widow* of Major Rowland Beech, MC. *Educ:* Eton. Entered Royal Navy, 1940; Comdr 1954; Captain 1960. Comdg Officer HMS Scarborough, 1958; Executive Officer, HM Yacht Britannia, 1959; Captain (F) 17th Frigate Squadron, 1963; Dir of Naval Signals, 1965; Dir, Weapons Equipment Surface, 1967; retd, 1970. Lieut, Royal Company of Archers, Queen's Body Guard for Scotland. DL 1973, JP 1980, Ayrshire. *Address:* 3 New Court, Sutton Manor, Sutton Scotney, Winchester SO21 3JX. *T:* (01962) 761862. *Clubs:* Pratt's, MCC.

DALRYMPLE HAMILTON, (North) John (Frederick), OBE 1992; TD 1989; farmer, since 1982; Vice Lord-Lieutenant, Ayrshire and Arran, since 1998; *b* 7 May 1950; *s* of Capt. North Edward Frederick Dalrymple-Hamilton, *qv*, and late Hon. Mary Colville; *m* 1980, Sally Anne How; two *s* one *d*. *Educ:* Eton Coll.; Aberdeen Univ. (MA Hons 1972); E of Scotland Coll. of Agriculture (Cert. Agric. 1983). Sales Manager, Scottish & Newcastle Breweries, 1973–82; Bargany estate, 1983–. Commnd TA, 1970; CO, QOY, 1989–92; Dep. Comdr (Col), 52 Bde, 1993–94. Chm., Lowlands RFCA, 2003–07. DL Ayrshire and Arran, 1995–98. *Address:* Lovestone House, Bargany, Girvan, Ayrshire KA26 9RF. *T:* (01465) 871227. *Club:* New (Edinburgh).

DALRYMPLE-HAY, Sir John (Hugh), 7th Bt *cr* 1798, of Park Place, Wigtownshire; *b* 16 Dec. 1929; 2nd *s* of Lt-Col Brian George Rowland Dalrymple-Hay (*d* 1943) and Beatrice (*d* 1935), *d* of A. W. Inglis; *S* brother 2005; *m* 1962, Jennifer, *d* of Brig. Robert Johnston, OBE; one *s*. *Educ:* Blundell's Sch., Tiverton; RMA Sandhurst. Commnd RSF, 1950; served with KOSB, Korea (despatches, 1952) and Malaya; retired in rank of Captain, 1957. Industrial Relations Manager, Shell Co. (Fedn of Malaya) Ltd, 1960–62; various appointments with: Distillers Co. (CO_2) Ltd; Messer Gresheim. *Recreations:* sailing, ski-ing, golf (mainly golf now). *Heir:* *s* Malcolm John Robert Dalrymple-Hay, FRCS [*b* 1 April 1966; *m* 1998, Vanessa Long; three *d*].

DALRYMPLE-WHITE, Sir Jan Hew, 3rd Bt *cr* 1926, of High Mark, Wigtownshire; *b* 26 Nov. 1950; *o s* of Sir Henry Arthur Dalrymple-White, 2nd Bt and Mary (*née* Thomas); *S* father, 2006, but his name does not appear on the Official Roll of the Baronetage; *m* 1st, 1979, Elizabeth Wallis (marr. diss); 2nd, 1984, Angela Stevenson (marr. diss.); one *s*; 3rd, 1990, Elizabeth Smith. *Educ:* Stowe.

DALTON, Alfred Hyam, CB 1976; Deputy Chairman, Board of Inland Revenue, 1973–82 (Commissioner of Inland Revenue, 1970–82); *b* 29 March 1922; *m* 1946, Elizabeth Stalker (*d* 1992); three *d*; *m* 1995, Sylvia Winifred West (*née* Boyce). *Educ:* Merchant Taylors' Sch., Northwood; Aberdeen Univ. Served War, REME, 1942–45 (despatches). Entered Inland Revenue, 1947; Asst Sec., 1958; Sec. to Board, 1969. *Address:* 22 Clifton Avenue, Eaglescliffe TS16 9BA. *T:* (01642) 648850.

DALTON, Duncan Edward S.; *see* Shipley Dalton.

DALTON, Vice-Adm. Sir Geoffrey (Thomas James Oliver), KCB 1986; Secretary-General of Mencap, 1987–90; *b* 14 April 1931; *s* of late Jack Rowland Thomas Dalton and Margaret Kathleen Dalton; *m* 1957, Jane Hamilton (*née* Baynes); four *s*. *Educ:* Parkfield, Sussex; Reigate Grammar Sch.; RNC Dartmouth. Midshipman 1950; served in HM Ships Illustrious, Loch Alvie, Cockade, Virago, Flag Lieut to C-in-C The Nore, and HMS Maryton (in comd), 1950–61; served HMS Murray, RN Staff Course and HMS Dido, 1961–66; served HMS Relentless (in Comd), RN Sch. of PT, HMS Nubian (in Comd), Staff of Flag Officers Second in Comd Far East Fleet and Second Flotilla, 1966–72; Asst Dir of Naval Plans, 1972–74; RCDS, 1975; Captain RN Presentation Team, 1976–77; in Comd HMS Jupiter, 1977–79 and HMS Dryad, 1979–81; Asst Chief of Naval Staff (Policy), 1981–84; Dep. SACLANT, 1984–87. Commander, 1966; Captain, 1972; Rear-Adm. 1981; Vice-Adm. 1984. President: RBL, 1993–97; Regular Forces Employment Assoc., 1999–2002; Chm., Ex-Services Fellowship Centres, 1991–2006. Hon. Col 71st (Yeomanry) Signal Regt (Volunteers), 1998–2001. Gov., QMW, 1992–2002. Mem. Ct of Assts, Drapers' Co., 1989– (Master, 1996). FCMI (FBIM 1987). *Recreations:* tennis, ski-ing, fishing, gardening, motor cycling, walking. *Address:* Farm Cottage, Catherington, Waterlooville, Hants PO8 0TD.

DALTON, Graham Edward, CEng, FICE; Chief Executive, Highways Agency, since 2008; *b* 24 Sept. 1960; *s* of John and Jocelyn Dalton; *m* 1985, Fiona Jane Iles; three *d*. *Educ:* Gillots Sch., Henley-on-Thames; Imperial Coll., London (BSc 1st Cl. Civil Engrg 1983); Henley Mgt Coll. (MBA 2000). CEng 1989; FICE 2003. Mgt trainee, BR, 1979–88; civil engr, L. G. Mouchel & Partners, 1988–95; Project Manager, Bovis Construction, 1995–2001; Project Dir, Strategic Rail Authy, 2001–05; Dir, Rail Projects, DfT, 2005–08. Mem. Council, ICE, 2004–07. *Recreations:* sailing, walking. *Address:* Highways Agency, 5th Floor, 123 Buckingham Palace Road, SW1W 9HA. *T:* (020) 7153 4700; *e-mail:* Graham.dalton@highways.gsi.gov.uk. *Club:* Dell Quay Sailing (Chichester).

DALTON, Ian Mark Marshall; Chief Executive, North East Strategic Health Authority, since 2007; *b* Welwyn Garden City, 14 Jan. 1964; *s* of Douglas Vivian Marshall Dalton and Helgard Dalton (*née* Herzog); *m* 1992, Juliet Kearsley; one *s* one *d*. *Educ:* Verulam Sch., St Albans; Univ. of York (BA Hons Econs; MA Learning Disabilities Services); Univ. of Durham (MBA). Residential Care Officer, N Yorks CC, 1985–86; Project, 1986–88, Dist Officer, 1988–90, RSMHCA; Develt Manager, Community Mental Health, Durham CC, 1990–91; Policy Officer, Community Care, then Hd of Primary and Community Care, Northern and Yorks (formerly Northern) RHA, 1991–95; Hd, Primary and Community Care, 1995–96, Purchaser Perf. Develt, 1996–97, Northern & Yorks Regl Office, NHS Exec.; Dir, Planning and Develt, Hartlepool and E Durham NHS Trust, 1997–99; Dir, Acute Services, Planning and Develt, N Tees and Hartlepool NHS Trust, 1999–2000; Department of Health: Regl Dir of Perf. Mgt (Northern and Yorks), 2000–02; Dir of Perf. (N), 2002–03; Chief Executive: N Cheshire Hosps NHS Trust, 2003–05; N Tees and Hartlepool NHS Trust, 2005–07. Hon. Col, B (250) Med. Sqdn (V), 5 Gen. Med. Support Regt, RAMC, 2007–. *Recreations:* family, fell walking, reading. *Address:* North East Strategic Health Authority, Riverside House, Goldcrest Way, Newcastle upon Tyne NE15 8NY. *T:* (0191) 210 6410, *Fax:* (0191) 210 6411; *e-mail:* ian.dalton@northeast.nhs.uk.

DALTON, Irwin, CBE 1986; Executive Vice-Chairman, 1985–88, and Chief Executive (Operations), 1986–88, National Bus Company; *b* 25 July 1932; *s* of Harry Farr Dalton and Bessie Dalton; *m* 1954, Marie Davies; two *d*. *Educ:* Cockburn High Sch., Leeds. FCA 1973; FCIT 1978. Accountancy profession, 1947–62; Asst Company Sec., 1962–67, Company Sec., 1968–70, West Riding Automobile, Wakefield; Company Sec., Crosville Motor Services, 1971–74; Dir and Gen. Manager, Ribble Motor Services, 1974–76; National Bus Company: Regional Dir, 1977–81; Mem. for Personnel Services, 1981–83; Exec. Bd Mem., 1983–84. Dir, Leyland Bus Gp, 1987–88. A Vice-Pres., Bus and Coach Council, 1983–87, Pres., 1987–88. *Recreations:* golf, other sporting activities. *Address:* 7 Aultmore Court, Kingswood Road, Tunbridge Wells, Kent TN2 4UF. *T:* (01892) 533459. *Club:* Tunbridge Wells Golf.

DALTON, Maurice Leonard, LVO 1986 (MVO 1981); OBE 1996; HM Diplomatic Service, retired; protocol consultant, since 2000; *b* 18 May 1944; *s* of late Albert William Dalton and Mildred Eliza (*née* Wraight); *m* 1982, Cathy Lee Parker. Joined FO, 1965; Enugu and Lagos, 1967–68; FCO, 1968–70; Attaché, Ankara, 1970–72; Third Secretary: E Berlin, 1973–74; Abu Dhabi, 1974–76; Second Sec., FCO, 1977–79; Second, later First Sec., Oslo, 1979–83; First Secretary: Kuala Lumpur, 1983–86; Peking, 1986; FCO, 1987–92; Asst Head of Protocol Dept, FCO, and HM Asst Marshal of Diplomatic Corps, 1992–96; Counsellor and Head of Conference Dept, FCO, 1996–98; Head of Protocol Dept, FCO, 1998–99; HM First Asst Marshal of Diplomatic Corps, 1998–2000; Protocol Consultant, FCO, 2001–05. Mem. Cttee, Kent and Sussex Br., Benenden Healthcare Soc., 2005– (Sec., 2008–). Royal Norwegian Order: of St Olav, 1981; of Merit, 1994. *Recreations:* genealogy, cross-country ski-ing. *Address:* Brookside, Hope's Grove Lane, Smallhythe Road, Tenterden, Kent TN30 7LT.

DALTON, Sir Richard (John), KCMG 2005 (CMG 1996); HM Diplomatic Service, retired; Director General, Libyan British Business Council, since 2006; *b* 10 Oct. 1948; *s* of Maj.-Gen. John Cecil D'Arcy Dalton, CB, CBE and Pamela Frances (*née* Segrave); *m* 1972, Elisabeth Mary Keays; two *s* two *d* (and one *s* decd). *Educ:* Winchester Coll.; Magdalene Coll., Cambridge (BA). Joined HM Diplomatic Service, 1970: FCO, 1971; MECAS, 1971–73; 3rd Sec., Amman, 1973–75; 2nd, later 1st, Sec., Mission to UN, NY, 1975–79; FCO, 1979–83; Dep. Head of Mission, Muscat, 1983–87; Dep. Head, Southern African Dept, FCO, 1987–88; Head, Tropical Foods Div. and Ext. Relns and Trade Div., MAFF, 1988–91; Vis. Fellow, RIIA, 1991–92; Head, CSCE Unit, FCO, 1992–93; Consul Gen., Jerusalem, 1993–97; Dir (Personnel), FCO, 1998–99; Ambassador to: Libya, 1999–2002; Iran, 2003–06. *Publication:* Peace in the Gulf: a long term view, 1992. *Recreation:* land and woodland management. *Address:* Hauxwell Hall, Leyburn, N Yorks DL8 5LR.

DALTON, Air Marshal Stephen Gary George, CB 2006; FRAeS; Deputy Commander-in-Chief Personnel and Air Member for Personnel, Headquarters Air Command, since 2007; *b* 23 April 1954. *Educ:* Univ. of Bath (BSc). Royal Air Force: exercises in Europe, USA and Canada; psc; qwi 1983; RAF Bradwell, 1990; Comdr, RAF Coltishall and Jaguar Force, 1997–99; Dir, Eurofighter Prog. Assurance Gp, MoD, 2000; hcsc, 2002; Dir Air Ops, MoD, 2002–03; Capability Manager (Information Superiority), 2003–04; Controller Aircraft, 2004–07; Dir Gen. Typhoon, 2006–07. FCMI. *Address:* Headquarters Air Command, RAF High Wycombe, Bucks HP14 4UE.

DALTON, William Robert Patrick, FCIB, FICB; Chief Executive, HSBC (formerly Midland) Bank plc, 1998–2004; *b* 8 Dec. 1943; *s* of Albert and Emily Dalton; *m* 1993, Starr Underhill; one *s* one *d*. *Educ:* Univ. of British Columbia (BComm 1971). FICB 1971; FCIB 1998. Joined Bank of Montreal, 1961; Wardley Canada Ltd, later HSBC Bank, Canada, 1980, Pres. and CEO, 1992–97; Director: HSBC Holdings, 1998–2004; HSBC Private Banking Hldgs (Suisse) SA, 2001–04; Crédit Commercial de France SA, 2000–04; Aegis Insce Services Inc. (formerly Aegis Ltd), 2004–. Non-executive Director: Mastercard Internat., 1998–2004; HSBC Finance Inc. (formerly Household Internat. Inc.), 2003–; First Choice Holidays plc, 2004–07; Swiss Re GB, 2005–; Talisman Energy Inc., 2005–; TUI Travel plc, 2007–. Vice-President: CIB, 2001–; BBA, 2003–. Chm., Young Enterprise UK, 1998–2004; Trustee: Crimestoppers Trust, 2000–04; Duke of Edinburgh's Commonwealth Study Confs (UK Fund), 2002–. Hon. Dr UCE, 2001.

DALTREY, Roger Harry, CBE 2005; singer; *b* Hammersmith, 1 March 1944; *s* of Harry and Irene Daltrey; *m* 1971, Heather Taylor; two *s* two *d*; one *s* by a previous marriage. *Educ:* Acton Co. Grammar Sch. Lead singer, The Detours, later The Who, 1964–84; solo singer, 1984–. Albums with The Who: My Generation, 1965; A Quick One, 1966; Happy Jack, 1967; The Who Sell Out, 1967; Magic Bus, 1968; Tommy, 1969; Who's Next, 1971; Meaty Beefy Big And Bouncy, 1971; Quadrophenia, 1973; The Who By Numbers, 1975; The Story of the Who, 1976; Who Are You, 1978; Face Dances, 1981; Hooligans, 1982; It's Hard, 1982; Once Upon A Time, 1983; Two's Missing, 1987; Endless Wire, 2006; solo albums: Daltrey, 1973; Ride A Rock Horse, 1975; One of the Boys, 1977; Parting Should Be Painless, 1984; Under a Raging Moon, 1985; Can't Wait to See the Movie, 1987; Rocks in the Head, 1992. Actor in films including: Tommy, 1974; Lisztomania, 1975; The Legacy, 1978; McVicar (also prod.), 1980; Mack the Knife, 1990; Buddy's Song (also prod.), 1991. *Address:* c/o Trinifold Management Ltd, 12 Oval Road, NW1 7DH.

DALY, His Eminence Cardinal Cahal Brendan; Roman Catholic Archbishop Emeritus of Armagh and Primate Emeritus of All Ireland; *b* 1 Oct. 1917. *Educ:* St Malachy's Coll., Belfast; Queen's Univ., Belfast (BA Hons, Classics, MA); St Patrick's Coll., Maynooth (LTh 1942, DTh 1944; DD); Institut Catholique, Paris (LPh 1953); DHL Sacred Heart Univ., Conn, USA. Ordained priest, 1941. Classics Master, St Malachy's Coll., Belfast, 1945–46; Lecturer in Scholastic Philosophy, 1946–63; Reader, 1963–67, Queen's Univ., Belfast; consecrated Bishop, 1967; Bishop of Ardagh and Clonmacnois, 1967–82; Bishop of Down and Connor, 1982–90; Archbishop of Armagh and Primate of All Ireland, 1990–96. Cardinal, 1991. Hon. DD: QUB; Exeter; Hon. DLitt TCD; Hon. LLD: NUI; Notre Dame, Indiana; St John's, NY; Sacred Heart, Fairfield, Conn. *Publications:* Morals, Law and Life, 1962; Natural Law Morality Today, 1965; Violence in Ireland and Christian Conscience, 1973; Theologians and the Magisterium, 1977; Peace the Work of Justice, 1979; The Price of Peace, 1991; Tertullian: the Puritan and his influence, 1993; Morals and Law, 1993; Northern Ireland—Peace—Now is the Time, 1994; Love begins at Home, 1995; Moral Philosophy in Britain from Bradley to Wittgenstein, 1996; Steps on my Pilgrim Journey, 1998; The Minding of Planet Earth, 2000; chapters in: Prospect for Metaphysics, 1961; Intellect and Hope, 1968; New Essays in Religious Language, 1969; Understanding the Eucharist, 1969. *Address:* Ard Mhacha, 23 Rosetta Avenue, Belfast BT7 3HG.

DALY, Hon. Francis Lenton; Judge of District Courts, Queensland, Australia, 1989–99; Judge of Planning and Environment Court, Queensland, 1994–99; *b* 23 June 1938; *s* of late Sydney Richard Daly and Lilian May Daly (*née* Lindholm); *m* 1964, Joyce Brenda (*née* Nicholls). *Educ:* Forest School; London School of Economics (LLB). Called to Bar, Gray's Inn, 1961 (Lord Justice Holker Exhibn). English Bar, 1961–66; Legal Secretary, Lord Chancellor's Office, 1966; Bermudian Bar, 1966–72; Asst Judge Advocate General to the Forces, UK, 1972–78; Principal Magistrate, Malaita, Solomon Islands, 1978; Attorney General, 1979, Chief Justice, 1980–84, Solomon Islands; Chief Justice, Nauru, 1983; admitted, Qld Bar, 1984. *Publications:* contribs to International and Comparative Law Qly, Commonwealth Judicial Jl. *Recreations:* yachting, rowing, reading. *Address:* 22 Booth Street, Balmain, NSW 2041, Australia.

See also O. L. Aikin.

DALY, James, CVO 1994; HM Diplomatic Service, retired; re-employed, Foreign and Commonwealth Office, since 2001; *b* 8 Sept. 1940; *s* of late Maurice Daly and Christina Daly; *m* 1970, Dorothy Lillian Powell; two *s*. *Educ:* St Thomas More, Chelsea; University College London (BSc Hons Econ). Served RM, 1958–67. Joined Foreign Office, 1968: Third Secretary: Accra, 1971–73; Moscow, 1973–76; Second Sec., Karachi, 1976–78; First Secretary: FCO, 1978–79; Sofia, 1979–86; Consul-Gen., Paris, 1986–92; Counsellor and Consul-Gen., Moscow, 1992–95; High Commissioner: Vanuatu, 1995–97; Mauritius, 1997–2000. Mem., Special Immigration Appeals Commn, 2002–. Exec. Mem., St Francis Leprosy Guild, 2003–. *Recreations:* reading, music, walking. *Address:* 10 Cardinal Mansions, Carlisle Place, SW1P 1EY. *Club:* Naval and Military.

DALY, Rev. Mgr John Anthony, QHC 2004; VG; Principal Roman Catholic Chaplain, Royal Air Force, 2004–07; *b* 23 Sept. 1952; *s* of Richard and Mary Daly. *Educ:* St Anne's RC Primary Sch., Stretford; St Mary's Secondary Sch., Stretford; Ushaw Coll., Durham. Ordained, 1977; Priest: St Osmund's, Breightmet, Bolton, 1977–83; St Mary's, Radcliffe, Bury, 1983–84; joined RAF, 1985; Gp Captain, 2004. Vicar General, 2004. *Recreations:* supporting Manchester United, squash, golf, folk music. *Address:* c/o Chaplaincy Centre, RAF Halton, Aylesbury HP22 5PG; *e-mail:* john.daly22@btinternet.com.

DALY, Lawrence; General Secretary, National Union of Mineworkers, 1968–84, retired; *b* 20 Oct. 1924; *s* of James Daly and late Janet Taylor; *m* 1948, Renée M. Baxter; four *s* one *d*. *Educ:* primary and secondary schools. Glencraig Colliery (underground), 1939; Workmen's Safety Inspector, there, 1954–64. Part-time NUM lodge official, Glencraig, 1946; Chm., Scottish NUM Youth Committee, 1949; elected to Scottish Area NUM Exec. Cttee, 1962; Gen. Sec., Scottish NUM, 1964; National Exec., NUM, 1965. Mem., TUC General Council, 1971–81. TUC Gold Badge, 1981. *Publications:* (pamphlets): A Young Miner Sees Russia, 1946; The Miners and the Nation, 1968. *Recreations:* literature, politics, folk-song.

DALY, Margaret Elizabeth; *b* 26 Jan. 1938; *d* of Robert and Elizabeth Bell; *m* 1964, Kenneth Anthony Edward Daly; one *d*. *Educ:* Methodist Coll., Belfast. Departmental Head, Phoenix Assurance Co., 1956–60; Trade Union Official, Guild of Insurance Officials, later Union of Insurance Staffs, and subseq. merged with ASTMS, 1960–71; Consultant, Cons. Party, 1976–79; Nat. Dir of Cons. Trade Unionists, 1979–84. MEP (C) Somerset and Dorset W, 1984–94; contested (C) Somerset and N Devon, Eur. Parly elecns, 1994; Mem., Develt Cttee, Eur. Parlt, 1984–94 (Vice Chm., 1987–89; Cons. spokesman, 1989–94); Vice-Pres., Jt EEC/African Caribbean Pacific Lomé Assembly, 1988–94. Contested (C), Weston-super-Mare, 1997. Mem. Bd, Traidcraft PLC, 1995–98. Mem. Bd, South West in Europe, 2000–01; European Movement: Mem. Mgt Bd, 1999–2006; Vice-Pres., Somerset Br., 2002– (Chair, 1999–2001); Pres., Devon Br., 2005–. *Recreations:* swimming, music, travel. *Address:* The Old School House, Aisholt, Bridgwater, Somerset TA5 1AR.

DALY, Michael Francis, CMG 1989; HM Diplomatic Service, retired; *b* 7 April 1931; *s* of late William Thomas Daly and Hilda Frances Daly; *m* 1st, 1963, Sally Malcolm Angwin (*d* 1966); one *d*; 2nd, 1971, Juliet Mary Siragusa (*née* Arning); one step *d*. *Educ:* Downside; Gonville and Caius Coll., Cambridge (Scholar; MA). Mil. Service, 1952–54: 2nd Lieut, Intell. Corps. E. D. Sassoon Banking Co., London, 1954; Transreef Industrial & Investment Co., Johannesburg, 1955–66; General Electric Co., London, 1966; HM Diplomatic Service: 1st Sec., FCO, 1967; 1st Sec. (Commercial), Rio de Janeiro, 1969; 1st Sec. (Inf.) and Head of Chancery, Dublin, 1973; Asst, Cultural Relations Dept, FCO, 1976; Counsellor, Consul-Gen. and Head of Chancery, Brasilia, 1977–78; Ambassador to Ivory Coast, Upper Volta and Niger, 1978–83; Head of West African Dept, FCO, and Ambassador (non-resident) to Chad, 1983–86; Ambassador: to Costa Rica and (non-resident) to Nicaragua, 1986–89; to Bolivia, 1989–91. Sec., Margaret Mee Fellowship Programme, 1993–. Kew Medal, 2002. *Recreations:* sailing, theatre, golf. *Address:* 45 Priory Road, Kew, Surrey TW9 3DQ. *T:* (020) 8940 1272. *Club:* Canning.

DALY, Michael Vincent; Director, Corporate Services Transformation Programme, Department for Children, Schools and Families (formerly Efficiency and Reform Unit, Department for Education and Skills), since 2006; *b* 23 July 1958; *s* of Michael Joseph Daly and Mary Anne Daly. *Educ:* St Philip's Grammar Sch., Edgbaston; Brimingham Univ. (DMS 1989). HEO (D), HSE, 1989; Second Sec. for Social Affairs, UK Repn to EC, 1990; Private Sec. to Parly Under Sec. of State, Dept of Employment, 1990–93; UK Rep. on Social Affairs to Council of Europe, Strasbourg, 1993–95; Divl Manager, DFEE, 1999–2001; Project Dir, No 10 Forward Strategy Unit, 2001–02; Hd, Learning Acad., 2002–04, Dir of Change, 2004–06, DFES. *Recreations:* curate's egg golf, film, early science fiction novels. *Address:* *e-mail:* mike.daly@dcsf.gsi.gov.uk.

DALYELL, Kathleen Mary Agnes, OBE 2005; DL; National Trust for Scotland Administrator at The Binns, since 1972; Chairman, Royal Commission on Ancient and Historical Monuments of Scotland, 2000–05; *b* 17 Nov. 1937; *o d* of Rt Hon. Lord Wheatley and Agnes (Nancy) Lady Wheatley (*née* Nichol); *m* 1963, Tam Dalyell, *qv*; one *s* one *d*. *Educ:* Convent of the Sacred Heart, Aberdeen; Edinburgh Univ. (MA Hons History 1960); Craiglochart Teacher Trng Coll., Edinburgh. Teacher of History: St Augustine's Secondary Sch., Glasgow, 1961–62; James Gillespie's High Sch. for Girls, Edinburgh, 1962–63. Member: Historic Buildings Council for Scotland, 1975–87; Lady Provost of Edinburgh's Delegn to China, 1987; Nat. Cttee of Architectural Heritage Soc. for Scotland, 1983–89 (Vice-Chm., 1986–89); Ancient Monuments Bd for Scotland, 1989–99; Royal Fine Art Commn for Scotland, 1992–2001. Chm., Bo'ness Heritage Trust, 1988–93; Director: Heritage Educn Trust, 1987–2005; Weslo Housing Assoc., 1994–2003; Trustee: Paxton Trust, 1988–92; Carmont Settlement Trust, 1997–; Hopetown Preservation Trust, 2005–; Mus. of Scotland Charitable Trust, 2005–. DL W Lothian, 2001. Mem. Ct, Stirling Univ., 2003–. Hon. Dr Edinburgh, 2006. *Publication:* House of The Binns, 1973. *Recreations:* reading, travel, chess, hill walking. *Address:* The Binns, Blackness, Linlithgow, Scotland EH49 7NA. *T:* (01506) 834255.

DALYELL, Tam, FRSE; *b* 9 Aug. 1932; *s* of late Gordon and Eleanor Dalyell; *m* 1963, Kathleen Mary Agnes Wheatley (*see* K. M. A. Dalyell); one *s* one *d*. *Educ:* Eton; King's Coll., Cambridge; Moray House Teachers' Training Coll., Edinburgh. Trooper, Royal Scots Greys, 1950–52; Teacher, Bo'ness High Sch., 1956–60. Dep.-Dir of Studies on British India ship-school, Dunera, 1961–62. Contested (Lab) Roxburgh, Selkirk, and Peebles, 1959. MP (Lab) West Lothian, 1962–83, Linlithgow, 1983–2005. Member Public Accounts Cttee, House of Commons, 1962–66; Secretary, Labour Party Standing Conference on the Sciences, 1962–64; PPS to Rt Hon. Richard Crossman, Minister of Housing, Leader of H of C, Sec. of State for the Social Services, 1964–70; Opposition spokesman on science, 1980–82; Chairman: PLP Education Cttee, 1964–65; PLP Sports Group, 1964–74; PLP Foreign Affairs Gp, 1974–75; Vice-Chairman: PLP Defence and Foreign Affairs Gps, 1972–74; Scottish Labour Group of MPs, 1973–75; Parly Lab. Party, 1974–76; Sub-Cttee on Public Accounts; Mem., Labour Party NEC, 1986–87. Member: European Parlt, 1975–79; European Parlt Budget Cttee, 1976–79; European Parlt Energy Cttee, 1979; Member: House of Commons Select Cttee on Science and Technology, 1967–69; Liaison Cttee between Cabinet and Parly Labour Party, 1974–76; Chm., All-Pty Latin-America Gp, 1997–2005. Father, H of C, 2001–05. Leader, IPU Delegation: to Brazil, 1976; to Peru, 1999; to Bolivia, 2000; to Libya, 2001. Chm., *ad hoc* Cttee against war in Iraq, 1998. Trustee, History of Parlt Trust, 1999–2005; Mem., Council, National Trust for Scotland. Rector, Edinburgh Univ., 2003–06. Mem., Trade Delegn to China, Nov. 1971, Hon. Pres., 2005–08, Scottish Council for Develt and Industry. Political columnist, New Scientist, 1967–2005. FRSE 2003. Hon. DSc Edinburgh, 1994; Hon. DLitt City Univ., 1998; Hon. Dr: St Andrews, 2001; Northumbria, 2005; Napier, 2005; Stirling, 2006; DUniv Open, 2006. *Publications:* The Case of Ship-Schools, 1960; Ship-School Dunera, 1963; Devolution: the end of Britain?, 1977; One Man's Falklands, 1982; A Science Policy for Britain, 1983; Thatcher's Torpedo, 1983; Misrule, 1987; Dick Crossman: a portrait, 1989. *Recreations:* tennis, swimming. *Address:* The Binns, Linlithgow, Scotland EH49 7NA. *T:* (01506) 834255.

DALZELL PAYNE, Henry Salusbury Legh, (Harry), CBE 1973 (OBE 1970; MBE 1961); Director/Trustee, Mutual Funds Complex, USA, since 1993; *b* 9 Aug. 1929; *m* 1963, Serena Helen (marr. diss. 1980), *d* of Col Clifford White Gourlay, MC, TD; two *d*. *Educ:* Cheltenham; RMA Sandhurst; Staff Coll.; RCDS. Commissioned, 7th Hussars, 1949; served Queen's Own Hussars, 1957–66; seconded to Sultan of Muscat's Armed Forces, 1959–60; commanded: 3rd Carabiniers, 1967–69; 6th Armoured Bde, 1974–75; 3rd Armoured Div., 1979–80; resigned in rank of Maj.-Gen., 1981. Dir, Nat. Securities and Res. Corp., USA, 1983–93. *Recreations:* travel, the turf, fine wines. *Clubs:* Cavalry and Guards, Turf, White's.

DALZIEL, Geoffrey Albert; British Commissioner, Leader of Salvation Army activities in Great Britain, 1974–80; *b* 10 Dec. 1912; *s* of Alexander William and Olive Mary Dalziel; *m* 1937, Ruth Edith Fairbank; two *s* one *d*. *Educ:* Harrow Elementary Sch. Commissioned Salvation Army Officer, 1934; Corps Officer in Gt Britain, to 1946; on Internat. Trng Coll. Staff, 1946–51; Divisional Youth Sec., 1951–59; Trng Coll. Principal, Melbourne, Aust., 1959–64; Chief Side Officer, Internat. Trng Coll., London, 1964–66; Chief Secretary: Sydney, Aust., 1966–68; Toronto, Canada, 1968–70; Territorial Comdr, Kenya, Uganda and Tanzania, E Africa, 1970–74. *Recreations:* walking, gardening, reading.

DALZIEL, Ian Martin; *b* 21 June 1947; *s* of late John Calvin Dalziel and of Elizabeth Roy Dalziel, *e d* of Rev. Ian Bain, FRSE and Mrs Christian Stuart Fisher Bain, Gairloch; *m* 1972, Nadia Maria Iacovazzi; four *s*. *Educ:* Daniel Stewart's Coll., Edinburgh; St John's Coll., Cambridge; Université Libre de Bruxelles (Weiner Anspach Foundation Scholarship, 1970). Mullens & Co., 1970–72; Manufacturers Hanover Ltd, 1972–83. Mem., Richmond upon Thames Council, 1978–79. Mem. (C) Lothian, European Parlt, 1979–84. Chairman: Continental Assets Trust plc, 1989–98; Invesco Smaller Continental Cos Trust plc, 1998–2005; Director: Adam & Co. plc, 1983–92; Lepercq-Amcur Fund NV, 1989–; Gen. Man., Devin SA, 1992–2008; Consultant, Primwest Hldg NV, 1992–2008. Mem., Queen's Body Guard for Scotland (Royal Company of Archers). *Recreations:* golf, shooting, tennis, ski-ing. *Address:* 45 route des Eaux-Belles, 1243 Presinge/Geneva, Switzerland. *T:* (22) 7591935; *e-mail:* imd4@mac.com. *Clubs:* Brooks's; New (Edinburgh); Hawks (Cambridge); Yeamans Hall Golf (Charleston, S Carolina); Royal and Ancient Golf (St Andrews); Hon. Company of Edinburgh Golfers; Sunningdale Golf; Royal St George's Golf (Sandwich); Racquet and Tennis (New York).

DALZIEL, Malcolm Stuart, CBE 1984; international funding consultant, 1991–2003; *b* 18 Sept. 1936; *s* of late Robert Henderson Dalziel and Susan Aileen (*née* Robertson); *m* 1961, Elizabeth Anne Harvey; one *s* two *d*. *Educ:* Banbury Grammar Sch.; St Catherine's Coll., Oxford (BA 1960, MA 1965). National Service, 2nd Lieut Northamptonshire Regt, 1955–57. The British Council, 1960–87: student, SOAS, 1960; Asst Educn Officer, Lahore, Pakistan, 1961–63; Regional Dir, Penang, Malaya, 1963–67; Regional Rep., Lahore, 1967–70; Rep., Sudan, 1970–74; Dir, Management Services Dept, and Dep. Controller, Estabs Div., 1975–79; Rep., Egypt, and Counsellor (Cultural), British Embassy, Cairo, 1979–83; Controller, Higher Educn Div., British Council and Sec., IUPC, 1983–87; Associate Consultant, 1988–96, Dir, 1990–96, Consultants in Economic Regeneration in Europe Services; Associate Consultant, Eur. Econ. Develt Services, 1996–2001. Affiliate, Internat., Develt Centre, Queen Elizabeth House, Oxford Univ., 1988–. Dep. Chm., Council for Educn in the Commonwealth, 1990–2000 (Mem. Exec. Cttee, 1986–2003); Mem. Court, Univ. of Essex, 1986–88. Mem., Methodology Soc., 2004–. Vice-Pres., 1990–2007, Sen. Mem., 2007–, Northants CCC. *Recreations:* theatre, ballet, walking, Rugby. *Address:* 62 Victoria Road, Oxford OX2 7QD. *T:* (01865) 558969. *Club:* Oxford and Cambridge.

DALZIEL, Maureen, MD; FFPH; Director, MD: health consultancy Ltd, since 2004; Secretary, Contract Skill Ltd, 2002–05; *b* 7 April 1952; *d* of late Peter and of Eileen Farrell; *m* 1974, Ian Dalziel. *Educ:* Notre Dame High Sch., Glasgow; Univ. of Glasgow (MB ChB); MD London 2004. MFCM 1985, FFPH (FFPHM 1990). Jun. hosp. posts, Glasgow and Lanarkshire Hosps, 1976–79; GP, E Kilbride, 1979–81; Registrar, then Sen. Registrar in Public Health Medicine: SW Herts HA, 1981–83; Brent HA, 1983–85; Consultant in Public Health Medicine, 1985–89, Associate Dir, 1989, NW Thames RHA; Chief Executive: SW Herts DHA, 1990–93 (Dir, Public Health, 1989–90); Hillingdon Health Agency, 1993–95; Regl Dir of Public Health and Med. Dir, N Thames Regl HA, then N Thames Regl Office, NHS Exec., DoH, 1995–99; Dir, Nat. Co-ordinating Centre for NHS Service Delivery and Orgn, LSHTM, 1999–2001; Med. Dir, NHS Litigation Authy, 1999–2000; Chief Exec., HFEA, 2001–02. Lectr in Public Health Medicine, 1981–85, Sen. Lectr, 1989–90, Hon. Sen. Lectr, 1999–, LSHTM. Mem., European Steering Gp, Mégapoles, 1997–2001; Chm., Sub-network on Social Disadvantage, Mégapoles, 1997–2001. Member Board: Housing 21, 1995–2002; Intensive Care Nat. Audit and Res. Centre, 1997–; Refugee Housing Assoc., 2005–07; Metropolitan Support Trust, 2007– (Trustee, 2007–); Trustee, British Pregnancy Adv. Service, 2007–. *Publications:* numerous articles in learned jls and papers presented at nat. confs. *Recreations:* ski-ing, reading novels and biographies, golf (par 3), watching old films. *Address:* *e-mail:* dalziel@btinternet.com.

DAMAZER, Mark David; Controller, BBC Radio 4 and BBC7, since 2004; *b* 15 April 1955; *s* of Stanislaw and Suzanne Damazer; *m* 1981, Rosemary Jane Morgan; one *s* one *d*. *Educ:* Gonville & Caius Coll., Cambridge (BA History); Harvard Univ. Harkness Fellow,

1977–79; American Political Sci. Fellow, 1978–79. Trainee, ITN, 1979–81; Producer: BBC World Service, 1981–83; TV-AM, 1983–84; BBC: Six O'Clock News, 1984–86; Output Editor, Newsnight, 1986–88; Dep. Editor, 1988–89, Editor, 1989–94, Nine O'Clock News; Editor, TV News, 1994–96; Head: Current Affairs, 1996–98; Political Progs, 1998–2000; Asst Chief Exec. (Dir of Journalism), BBC News, 2000–01; Dep. Dir of News, BBC, 2001–04. Dep. Chm., Internat. Press Inst., 2005–. *Publications:* articles in Economist and various newspapers. *Recreations:* opera, Tottenham Hotspur, gardening, coarse tennis, Italian painting.

DAMER; *see* Dawson-Damer, family name of Earl of Portarlington.

DANCE, Brian David, MA; Headmaster, St Dunstan's College, Catford, 1973–93; *b* 22 Nov. 1929; *s* of late L. H. Dance and Mrs M. G. Swain (*née* Shrivelle); *m* 1955, Chloe Elizabeth, *o d* of late J. F. A. Baker, CB, FEng; two *s* two *d*. *Educ:* Kingston Grammar Sch.; Wadham Coll., Oxford. BA 1952, MA 1956. Asst Master, Kingston Grammar Sch., 1953–59; Sen. History Master: Faversham Grammar Sch., 1959–62; Westminster City Sch., 1962–65; Headmaster: Cirencester Grammar Sch., 1965–66; Luton Sixth Form Coll., 1966–73. Member: Cambridge Local Examination Syndicate, 1968–73; Headmasters' Assoc. Council, 1968–76 (Exec. Cttee, 1972–76, Hon. Legal Sec. 1975–76); Chm., London Area, SHA, 1984–85. Chm., Lewisham Environment Trust, 1987–88. Gov., Bromley High Sch., 1985–2005 (Chm., 2002–05). Hon. Assoc. for Life, GDST, 2005. Vice-Pres., Rugby Fives Assoc., 1993–. *Publications:* articles in: Times Educnl Supp.; Headmasters' Assoc. 'Review'. *Recreations:* watching most ball games (especially cricket and Rugby football), music, philately, theatre. *Address:* 59 Albyfield, Bickley, Bromley, Kent BR1 2HY. *T:* (020) 8467 9458.

DANCE, Charles Walter, OBE 2006; actor; *b* 10 Oct. 1946; *s* of late Walter Dance and Eleanor Dance (*née* Perks); *m* 1970, Joanna Haythorn; one *s* one *d*. *Educ:* Widey Tech. Sch.; Plymouth Sch. of Art; Leicester Poly. Rep. theatre at Nottingham, Leeds, Greenwich and Chichester Fest.; joined RSC, 1975; appeared in Henry IV, Hamlet, Richard III, Perkin Warbeck, As You Like It, The Changeling, Henry VI, title rôles in Henry V and Coriolanus; other *theatre* includes: Irma La Douce, 1978; The Heiress, 1980; Turning Over, 1982; Good, Donmar Warehouse, 1999; Long Day's Journey Into Night, Lyric, 2000; Shadowlands, Wyndham, 2007; *television:* Edward VII, 1973; The Fatal Spring, 1978; Little Eyolf, 1980; Frost in May, Nancy Astor, 1981; Saigon, the Last Day, The Jewel in the Crown, 1982; Rainy Day Women, The Secret Servant, 1984; Thunder Rock, The McGuffin, 1985; Out on a Limb, 1986; Out of the Shadows, First Born, 1988; Goldeneye, The Phantom of the Opera, 1989; Undertow, 1993; In the Presence of Mine Enemies, 1995; Rebecca, 1996; Randall & Hopkirk Deceased, Bloodlines, 1999; Justice in Wonderland, 2000; Nicholas Nickleby, 2001; Trial and Retribution, Henry VIII, Looking for Victoria, 2003; To the Ends of the Earth, Don Bosco, Last Rights, 2004; Bleak House, 2005; Fallen Angel, 2007; Consenting Adults, 2007; *films:* For Your Eyes Only, 1979; Plenty, 1984; The Golden Child, Good Morning Babylon, 1985; White Mischief, Hidden City, 1986; Pascali's Island, Kalkstein, 1989; China Moon, 1990; Alien 3, 1991; Century, Last Action Hero, Exquisite Tenderness, 1992; Kabloonak (Best Actor, Paris Film Fest., 1994), Shortcut to Paradise, 1993; Michael Collins, Space Truckers, 1995; The Blood Oranges, Don't Go Breaking My Heart, What Rats Won't Do, 1997; Hilary and Jackie, 1998; Jurij, 1999; Dark Blue World, Gosford Park, Ali G Indahouse, 2002; Swimming Pool, 2003; Black and White, (writer and dir) Ladies in Lavender, 2004; Remake, Funny Farm, 2005; Starter for Ten, 2006. *Recreations:* tennis, swimming. *Address:* c/o Independent Talent Group Ltd, Oxford House, 76 Oxford Street, W1D 1BS. *T:* (020) 7636 6565. *Club:* Groucho.

DANCER, Eric, CBE 1991; JP; Lord-Lieutenant of Devon, since 1998; Managing Director, Dartington Crystal Ltd, 1986–2000; *b* 17 April 1940; *s* of Joseph Cyril Dancer and Mabel Dancer; *m* 1980, Carole Anne Moxon. *Educ:* King Edward VII Sch., Sheffield; Sheffield Poly. Buyer: Moorwood-Vulcan Ltd, 1959–63; Balfour-Darwins Ltd, 1963–67; Purchasing Officer, Brightside Foundry and Engineering Co. Ltd, 1965–67; Dep. Chief Buyer, Metro-Cammell Ltd, 1967–68; Chief Buyer, Chrysler Parts Div., 1968–69; Supplies Manager, Jensen Motors Ltd, 1969–72; Dir, Anglo Nordic Hldgs plc, 1972–80; Man. Dir, Dartington Hall Corp., 1980–87; Chm., English Country Crystal, 1983–87. Trustee, Dartington Hall Trust, 1984–87. Member: SW Regl IDB, 1984–91; Council, CBI, 1997–2000; Chairman: Devon Cttee, Rural Develt Commn, 1981–86; Devon and Cornwall TEC, 1989–93; Gp of 10, 1990–92; West Country Develt Corp., 1993–99; Nat. Assessor, TEC, 1993–98. Gov., Univ. of Plymouth, 1992–96. CCMI (CIMgt 1987); FCIPS 1990 (President's Prize, 1964); FInstD 1981 (Dip. 1989); FRSA 1984 (Mem. Council, 1994–98). Freeman, City of London, 1992; Liveryman, Co. of Glass Sellers, 1992–. DL Devon, 1998; JP Devon, 1998 (Chm., Adv. Cttee of Magistrates). Hon. Captain RNR, 2001. DUniv Sheffield Hallam, 1999. KStJ 1998. *Recreations:* motor boats, reading, music, private flying and gliding 1956–90. *Address:* The Roundhouse, Moreleigh, Totnes, Devon TQ9 7JN. *T:* (01548) 821465. *Clubs:* Army and Navy; Royal Dart Yacht (Dartmouth).

DANCEY, Roger Michael, MA; Chief Master, King Edward's School, Birmingham, and Educational Adviser, King Edward VI Foundation, 1998–2005; *b* 24 Nov. 1945; *s* of Michael and Rosalind Dancey; *m* 1988, Elizabeth Jane Shadbolt; one step *s* one step *d*. *Educ:* Lancing Coll.; Exeter Univ. (MA). Careers Master, Whitgift Sch., 1972–76; Head of Sixth Form, Greenshaw High Sch., 1976–81; Sen. Master, Royal Grammar Sch., Worcester, 1982–86; Headmaster: King Edward VI Camp Hill Sch. for Boys, 1986–95; City of London Sch., 1995–98. Mem. Council, 1999–2005, Dep. Pro Chancellor, 2005–, Birmingham Univ. Vice Chm., Warwick Ind. Schools Foundn, 2007–. *Recreations:* cricket, golf, theatre, cinema. *Address:* 110 Gough Road, Edgbaston, Birmingham B15 2JQ. *Club:* Edgbaston Golf.

d'ANCONA, John Edward William, CB 1994; consultant; Chairman, Maris International Ltd, 2001–04 (Chief Executive, 2000–03); *b* 28 May 1935; *o s* of late Adolph and Margaret d'Ancona; *m* 1958, Mary Helen, *o d* of late Sqdn-Ldr R. T. Hunter and Mrs Hunter; three *s*. *Educ:* St Edward's Coll., Malta; St Cuthbert's Grammar Sch., Newcastle upon Tyne. BA (Hons) Mod. History, DipEd (Durham). Teacher, 1959–61; Civil Service, 1961–94: Asst Principal, Dept of Educn and Science, 1961; Private Sec. to Minister of State, DES, 1964–65; Principal: DES, 1965–67; Min. of Technology and DTI, 1967–74; Asst Sec., 1974, Under Sec., 1981, DoE; Dir Gen., Offshore Supplies Office, Dept of Energy, then DTI, 1981–94. Chm., UK Maritime Forum, 2000–. Pres., Soc. for Underwater Technol., 1997–99. *Recreations:* cricket, philately, wine-bibbing. *Address:* 33 Culverley Road, Catford, SE6 2LD.
    See also M. R. R. d'Ancona.

d'ANCONA, Matthew Robert Ralph; Editor, The Spectator, since 2006; *b* 27 Jan. 1968; *e s* of John Edward William d'Ancona, *qv*; *m* 2002, Sarah Schaefer (separated); two *s*. *Educ:* St Dunstan's Coll.; Magdalen Coll., Oxford (Demy; H. W. C. Davis Prize in Hist. 1987; BA 1st Cl. Hons Hist. 1989). Fellow, All Souls Coll., Oxford, 1989–96; The Times, 1991–95 (Asst Ed., 1994–95); Sunday Telegraph: Dep. Ed. (Comment), 1996–98; Dep. Ed., 1998–2006; Contributing Ed. and Political Columnist, GQ magazine, 2006–.

Member: Bd of Dirs, Centre for Policy Studies, 1998–2006; Adv. Council, Demos, 1998–2006; Millennium Commn, 2001–06; Policy Adv. Bd, Social Market Foundn, 2002–06; Puttnam Commn on Parliament in the Public Eye, 2004–05. Mem., British Exec., IPI, 1998–2006. Philip Geddes Meml Lectr, St Edmund Hall, Oxford, 2006. FRSA 2004. Charles Douglas-Home Meml Trust Prize, 1995; Political Journalist of the Year: British Press Awards, 2004; Political Studies Assoc. Awards, 2006; Ed. of the Year, Current Affairs Magazines, BSME, 2007. *Publications:* (with C. P. Thiede) The Jesus Papyrus, 1996; The Ties That Bind Us, 1996; (with C. P. Thiede) The Quest for the True Cross, 2000; Going East (novel), 2003; Tabatha's Code (novel), 2006; Confessions of a Hawkish Hack, 2006; Nothing to Fear (novel), 2008. *Recreation:* cinema. *Address:* The Spectator, 22 Old Queen Street, SW1H 9HP. *T:* (020) 7961 0200. *Clubs:* Garrick, Home House, Ivy.

DANCY, Prof. John Christopher, MA; Professor of Education, University of Exeter, 1978–84, now Emeritus; *b* 13 Nov. 1920; *e s* of late Dr J. H. Dancy and Dr N. Dancy; *m* 1944, Angela Bryant; two *s* one *d*. *Educ:* Winchester (Scholar); New Coll., Oxford (Scholar, MA). 1st Class, Classical Hon. Mods, 1940; Craven Scholar, 1946; Gaisford Greek Prose Prize, 1947; Hertford Scholar, 1947; Arnold Historical Essay Prize, 1949. Served in Rifle Brigade, 1941–46; Capt. GSO(3)I, 30 Corps, 1945; Major, GSO(2)I, 1 Airborne Corps, 1945–46. Lecturer in Classics, Wadham Coll., 1946–48; Asst Master, Winchester Coll., 1948–53; Headmaster of Lancing Coll., 1953–61; Master, Marlborough Coll., 1961–72; Principal, St Luke's Coll. of Educn, Exeter, 1972–78. Dir, St Luke's Coll. Foundn, 1978–86. Member, Public Schools' Commission, 1966–68. Chm., Higher Educn Foundn, 1981–86. Chm., British Accreditation Council for Independent Further and Higher Educn, 1984–93. *Publications:* Commentary on 1 Maccabees, 1954; The Public Schools and the Future, 1963; Commentary on Shorter Books of Apocrypha, 1972; Walter Oakeshott: a diversity of gifts, 1995; The Divine Drama: the Old Testament as literature, 2001. *Address:* Wharf House, Mousehole, Penzance, Cornwall TR19 6RX. *T:* (01736) 731137.

DANDEKER, Prof. Christopher, PhD; Professor of Military Sociology, since 1997, and Chairman, War Studies Group, since 2001, King's College London; *b* 12 July 1950; *s* of Arjun Dandeker and Yvonne Margerat (*née* Bogaert); partner, A. F. Alexander-Williams. *Educ:* Worthing High Sch. for Boys; Univ. of Leicester (BSc (Sociol.) 1971; PhD 1978). Lecturer in Applied Social Studies, Hallam Univ., 1973–74; in Sociol., Univ. of Leicester, 1974–90; King's College London: Sen. Lectr in War Studies, 1990–97; Co-Dir, King's Centre for Military Health Res., 2004–; Head, Sch. of Social Sci. and Public Policy, 2005–. *Publications:* The Structure of Social Theory (jtly), 1984; Surveillance, Power and Modernity, 1990; (with B. Boene) Les Armées en Europe, 1998; Nationalism and Violence, 1998; Facing Uncertainty: Sweden in international perspective, 2000; contribs to jls inc. Armed Forces and Society, Political Quarterly, British Jl of Sociol., Sociol Rev., The Lancet. *Recreations:* wine, food, walking, travel, classical music, being near the sea! *Address:* Department of War Studies, King's College London, Strand, WC2R 2LS. *T:* (020) 7848 2673, *Fax:* (020) 7848 2026; *e-mail:* christophe.dandeker@kcl.ac.uk, christopherdndkr@aol.com. *Club:* Travellers.

DANDO, Stephen Gordon; Group Human Resources Director, Reuters, since 2006; *b* 13 Feb. 1962; *s* of Douglas and Anne Dando; *m* 1985, Catherine Macquarrie Fraser; one *s* one *d*. *Educ:* Univ. of Strathclyde (BA Hons 1984); Univ. of Edinburgh (MBA 1990). Mgt Develt Dir, United Distillers, 1995–97; Gp Mgt Develt Dir, Diageo plc, 1997–99; Human Resources Director: (Europe), United Distillers & Vintners, 1999–2000; Guinness Ltd, 2000–01; Dir, Human Resources and Internal Communications, BBC, subseq. BBC People, 2001–06. ChFCIPD 2004; FRSA. *Recreations:* young family, keeping fit, current affairs. *Address:* Reuters, The Reuters Building, 30 South Colonnade, Canary Wharf, E14 5EP. *T:* (020) 7542 6426, *Fax:* (020) 7542 9854; *e-mail:* stephen.dando@reuters.com. *Club:* Roehampton.

DANDY, David James, MD; FRCS; Consultant Orthopaedic Surgeon: Addenbrooke's Hospital, Cambridge, 1975–2003; Newmarket General Hospital, 1975–2002; *b* 30 May 1940; *s* of late James Dandy, Great Shelford, Cambs, and Margaret Dandy (*née* Coe); *m* 1966, (Stephanie) Jane Essex; one *s* one *d*. *Educ:* Forest Sch.; Emmanuel Coll., Cambridge (Windsor Student, 1965; BA 1961, MA 1963; BChir 1964; MB 1965; MD 1990; MChir 1994); London Hosp. Med. Coll. (Robert Milne Prize for Surgery, 1995). LRCP, MRCS 1964, FRCS 1969. Surg. Registrar, St Andrew's Hosp., Bow, 1966–67; Surg., then Orthopaedic Registrar, London Hosp., 1967–69; Orthopaedic Registrar: Royal Nat. Orthopaedic Hosp., 1969–71; St Bartholomew's Hosp., 1971; Princess Alexandra Hosp., Harlow, 1971–72; Norfolk and Norwich Hosp., 1972–73; Sen. Registrar: St Bartholomew's Hosp., 1973–75; Hosp. for Sick Children, Gt Ormond St, 1974; Sen. Fellow, Toronto Gen. Hosp., 1973–74; Associate Lectr, Univ. of Cambridge, 1975–2007; Civilian Advr in Knee Surgery, RN and RAF, 1980–2006. Lectures: Mackenzie Crooks, RAF Hosp., Ely, 1980; Munsif Meml Orator, Bombay, 1987; Sir Ernest Finch Meml, Sheffield, 1990; William Gissane, Inst. of Accident Surgery, 1998; Bradshaw, 2004, Vicary, 2005, RCS. Director: Internat. Soc. of the Knee, 1989–93; European Soc. for Sports Traumatology, Knee Surgery, Sports Medicine and Arthroscopy, 1992–96; President: Internat. Arthroscopy Assoc., 1989–91; British Orthopaedic Sports Trauma Assoc., 1993–95; British Orthopaedic Assoc., 1998–99 (Robert Jones Prize and Assoc. Medal, 1991; Naughton Dunn Lectr, 1991; Mem. Council, 1992–95); Combined Services Orthopaedic Soc., 2001–04; Mem. Council, RCS, 1994–2006 (James Berry Prize, 1985; Hunterian Prof., 1994; Treas., 2003–06; Vice-Pres., 2005–06). Chm., Granta Decorative and Fine Arts Soc., 2007–. Hon. FRCSE 1998; Hon. FFGDP(UK) 2007. *Publications:* Arthroscopy of the Knee, 1973; Arthroscopic Surgery of the Knee, 1981, rev. edn 1987; Arthroscopy of the Knee: a diagnostic atlas, 1984; Essentials of Orthopaedics and Trauma, 1989, rev. edn 2003; articles on surgery of the knee and arthroscopic surgery. *Recreations:* travel, ablative horticulture. *Address:* The Old Vicarage, Great Wilbraham, Cambridge CB21 5JF. *Club:* East India.

DANESH, Prof. John Navid, DPhil; Professor of Epidemiology and Medicine, and Head, Department of Public Health and Primary Care, University of Cambridge, since 2001; *b* 21 April 1968; *s* of Dr Ali Danesh and Dr Mahtaban Danesh (*née* Safapour); *m* 2005, Nathalie Jacoby. *Educ:* Univ. of Otago Med. Sch., NZ (MB ChB Dist. 1992); London Sch. of Hygiene and Trop. Medicine (MSc Epidemiol. Dist. 1995); DPhil Epidemiol. Oxon 2000. MRCP (Dist.) 2005. House Officer, Royal Melbourne Hosp., 1993; Rhodes Schol., New Coll. and Balliol Coll., Oxford, 1994–97; Jun. Res. Fellow, Merton Coll., Oxford, 1997–99; Clin. Res. Fellow, Univ. of Oxford, 1999–2001. *Publications:* (jtly) Reason and Revelation, 2002; Search for Values, 2004; (jtly) The Baha'i Faith in Words and Images, 2008; contrib. articles to scientific jls on epidemiology of chronic diseases, particularly molecular risk factors in heart disease. *Recreations:* food, conversation. *Address:* Department of Public Health and Primary Care, University of Cambridge, Institute of Public Health, Cambridge CB1 8RN. *T:* (01223) 741302, *Fax:* (01223) 741339; *e-mail:* john.danesh@phpc.cam.ac.uk.

DANGAN, Viscount; Garret Graham Wellesley, (Jr); Chief Executive: ODL Securities Ltd, since 2003; ODL Group Ltd, since 2003; *b* 30 March 1965; *s* and *heir* of 7th Earl Cowley, *qv*; *m* 1990, Claire Lorraine, *d* of P. W. Brighton, Stow Bridge, Norfolk; two *s* one *d*. *Educ:* Franklin Coll., Switzerland (Associate of Arts degree). Traded Options, Hoare Govett, 1985–88; Manager, Ing (London) Derivatives Ltd, 1991–94; CEO, IFX Ltd, 1995–2003; Gp Chief Exec., Zetters plc, then IFX Gp plc, 2000–03; Sen. Vice Pres., Index Futures Gp, 1995–2002. Non-exec. Chm., Prestige Asset Management Ltd, 2007–. Non-exec. Chm., Children's Miracle Network UK, 2007–; non-exec. Dir, Redwings Horse Sanctuary, 2002–. *Heir:* *s* Hon. Henry Arthur Peter Wellesley, *b* 3 Dec. 1991. *Address:* Ashbourne Manor, High Street, Widford, Herts SG12 8SZ; ODL Securities Ltd, 8th Floor, The Northern & Shell Building, 10 Lower Thames Street, EC3R 6AD.

DANIEL, Brother; *see* Matthews, Brother D. F.

DANIEL, Gareth John; Chief Executive, London Borough of Brent, since 1998; *b* 30 March 1954; *s* of late Evan John Daniel and of Eileen Marie Daniel; partner, Margaret Wilson; three *s*. *Educ:* St Edward's Coll., Liverpool; Jesus Coll., Oxford (BA Hons); South Bank Poly. (DASS, CQSW). Pres., Oxford Univ. Students' Union, 1974–75. Social worker, London Borough of Ealing, 1976–83; London Borough of Brent, 1986–98: Principal Develt Officer; Divl Manager, Strategy; Head, Central Policy Unit; Dir, Partnership and Res. Member (Lab): Ealing LBC (Chm., Planning and Econ. Develt, 1986–90); Ealing North, GLC, 1981–86. Contested (Lab): Worcs S, 1979; Ealing, Acton, 1983. *Recreations:* family, hill-walking, foreign travel. *Address:* Brent Town Hall, Forty Lane, Wembley, Middx HA9 9HD. *T:* (020) 8937 1007.

DANIEL, His Honour (Gruffydd) Huw Morgan; a Circuit Judge, 1986–2006; Lord-Lieutenant of Gwynedd since 2006; *b* 16 April 1939; *s* of Prof. John Edward Daniel, MA, and Catherine Megan Daniel (*née* Parry Hughes); *m* 1968, Phyllis Margaret (*née* Bermingham); one *d*. *Educ:* Ampleforth; University College of Wales (LLB); Inns of Court School of Law. Commissioned 2nd Lieut First Bn Royal Welch Fusiliers, 1959; Captain 6/7 Bn Royal Welch Fusiliers (TA), 1965; served MELF, Cyprus. Called to the Bar, Gray's Inn, 1967; Wales and Chester Circuit (Circuit Junior, 1975); Recorder, 1980–86; Asst Liaison Judge, 1983–87, Liaison Judge, 1988–2006, Gwynedd; Liaison Judge for N Wales, 1998–2006; Dep. Sen. Judge, 1995–2002, Sen. Judge, 2002–06, Sovereign Base Area, Cyprus. Asst Parly Boundary Comr for Wales, 1981–82, 1985–86; Pres., Mental Health Appeals Tribunal, 2002–. Chm., N Wales Judicial Forum, 2005–06. President: Caerns Br., SSAFA, 1995–; St John's Ambulance in Gwynedd, 2006–; Custos rotulorum of Gwynedd, 2006–; Gwynedd Magistrates' Assoc., 2006–. Hon. Col, 6th Cadet Bn, Royal Welch Fusiliers, 1997–2003. DL Gwynedd, 1993. CStJ 2006. *Recreations:* gardening, shooting, fishing, sailing. *Address:* (residence) Rhiwgoch, Pont y Pandy, Bangor, Gwynedd LL57 3AX. *Clubs:* Reform; Bristol Channel Yacht.

DANIEL, Hamish St Clair, CMG 2008; OBE 2004 (MBE 1992); HM Diplomatic Service, retired; Deputy High Commissioner, Karachi and UK Director of Trade and Investment, Pakistan, 2004–08; *b* 22 Aug. 1953; *s* of James Anderson Daniel and Charlotte Daniel; *m* 2002, Heather Ann Bull; one *s* one *d* from previous marriage. *Educ:* Lerwick Central Public Sch., Scotland. Joined FCO, 1973: Algiers, 1975–77; Prague, 1977; Lisbon, 1978–80; Islamabad, 1980–82; FCO, 1982–85; San Francisco, 1985–88; Second Secretary: Khartoum, 1989–92; FCO, 1992–94; Dep. Hd of Mission, Sana'a, 1994–96; Pol and Econ. Sec., Jakarta, 1997–2001; British Rep., Dili, 2001–02; Ambassador to E Timor, 2002–03. *Recreations:* sailing, golf, walking.

DANIEL, Huw Morgan; *see* Daniel, G. H. M.

DANIEL, Jack; *see* Daniel, R. J.

DANIEL, Joan; *see* Rodgers, J.

DANIEL, John, MA; Headmaster, Royal Grammar School, Guildford, 1977–92; *b* 7 March 1932; *s* of John Daniel and Mary (*née* Young); *m* 1st, 1956, Heather Joy Retey (marr. diss. 2001); two *d*; 2nd, 2001, Beatrice Miller McTighe. *Educ:* Truro Sch.; New Coll., Oxford (Hons Modern Langs 1955). Thomas Hedley & Son, 1955–57; Linton Lodge Hotel, Oxford, 1957–59; Hartford Motors, Oxford, 1959–62; Royal Grammar Sch., Worcester, 1963–65; Malvern Coll., 1965–72; Royal Grammar School, Guildford: Dep. Headmaster, 1972–75; Acting Headmaster, 1975–77. Chm. of Govs, Tormead Sch., Guildford, 1981–97. Asst Dir, Gap Activity Projects Ltd, 1994–2002. Chm., Guildford Symphony Orch., 1995–2002. *Recreations:* watching Rugby football, playing the piano and double bass. *Address:* 2 Oak Tree View, Heath End, Farnham, Surrey GU9 9AG.

DANIEL, Sir John (Sagar), Kt 1994; DSc; President and Chief Executive Officer, Commonwealth of Learning, since 2004; *b* 31 May 1942; *s* of John Edward Daniel and Winifred (*née* Sagar); *m* 1966, Kristin Anne Swanson; one *s* two *d*. *Educ:* Christ's Hosp.; St Edmund Hall, Oxford (BA Metallurgy, MA; Hon. Fellow, 1990); Univ. of Paris (DSc Metallurgy); Thorneloe Univ., Ont (Associate 1992); Concordia Univ., Quebec (MA Educnl Technol. 1995). Asst Prof., then Associate Prof., Ecole Polytechnique, Montreal, 1969–73; Dir, Etudes Télé-Univ., Univ. of Quebec, 1973–77; Vice Pres., Learning Services, Athabasca Univ., Alberta, 1979–80; Vice-Rector, Academic Affairs, Concordia Univ., Montreal, 1980–84; Pres., Laurentian Univ., Sudbury, Ont, 1984–90; Vice-Chancellor, Open Univ., 1990–2001 (Hon. Fellow, 2002); Pres., US Open Univ., 1998–2001; Asst Dir-Gen. for Educn, UNESCO, 2001–04. Chairman: UNESCO-CEPES Adv. Council, 1990–92; Adv. Council for Develt of RN Personnel, 1996–2001; Member: HEQC, 1992–94; Council of Foundn, Internat. Baccalaureate, 1992–99; Council for Industry and Higher Educn, 1994–2001; British N American Cttee, 1995–2001, 2006–; Council, CBI, 1996–98; Steering Cttee, Defence Trng Rev., 1999–2001. Member: Bd of Govs, Commonwealth of Learning, 1988–90; Council, Univ. of Buckingham, 1994–; Council, Open Univ. of Hong Kong, 1996–; Bd, Univ. for Industry, 1999–2001 (Mem. Transition Bd, 1998–99); Canadian Council on Learning, 2005–; Trustee, Carnegie Foundn for Advancement of Teaching, 1993–2001. Mem., Adv. Bd, Xerox, Canada, 1998–99; Dir, Blackwells Publishing, 1998–2001. Hon. Chair, Canadian Soc. for Trng and Develt, 2006–. Licensed Reader: Montreal, 1980–84, Algoma, 1984–90, Anglican Ch of Canada; St Albans, 1990–2001, Europe, 2003–, C of E. Forum Fellow, World Econ. Forum, 1998. Hon. Fellow, Commonwealth of Learning, 2002. CCMI (CIMgt 1997; Pres., Milton Keynes Br., 1998–2001). Hon. FCP 1997. Hon. DLitt: Deakin, Aust., 1985; Athabasca, Canada, 1998; Indira Gandhi Nat. Open Univ., India, 2003; Thompson Rivers, Canada, 2005; Netaji Subhas Open Univ., India, 2005; Kota Open Univ., India, 2007; Hon. DHumLitt: Thomas Edison State Coll., USA, 1997; Richmond Coll., London, 1997; Hon. DSc: Royal Mil. Coll., St Jean, Canada, 1988; Open Univ., Sri Lanka, 1994; Paris VI, 2001; Univ. of Education, Winneba, Ghana, 2006; Hon. DEd: CNAA, 1992; Sukhothai Thammathirat Open Univ., Thailand, 1999; Hon. LLD: Univ. of Waterloo, Canada, 1993; Wales, 2002; Laurentian, Canada, 2006; DUniv: Humberside, 1996; Aberta, Portugal, 1996; Anadolu, Turkey, 1998; Québec, Derby, and New Bulgarian, 2000; Open Univ., Hong Kong, 2001; Stirling, 2002. Individual Excellence Award, Commonwealth of Learning, 1995; Morris T. Keeton Award, Council for Adult and Experiential Learning, USA, 1999. Officier, Ordre des Palmes Académiques (France), 1991 (Chevalier, 1987); Golden Jubilee Medal, Canada, 2002. *Publications:* Learning at a Distance: a world perspective, 1982; Mega-universities and Knowledge Media, 1996; numerous articles to professional pubns. *Address:* Commonwealth of Learning, Suite 1200, 1055 West Hastings, Vancouver, BC V6E 2E9, Canada.

DANIEL, Nicholas; oboe soloist; conductor; *b* 9 Jan. 1962; *s* of late Jeremy Daniel and Margaret Louise Daniel; *m* 1986, Joy Farrall, clarinettist; two *s*. *Educ:* Salisbury Cathedral Sch.; Purcell Sch.; Royal Acad. of Music. ARAM 1986, FRAM 1987; FGSM 1996. Prof., GSMD, 1986–97; Oboe Prof., Indiana Univ., 1997–99; Prince Consort Lectr, RCM, 1999–2002; Prof., Trossingen Musikhochschule, 2004–. Artistic Director: Osnabrück Chamber Music Fest., 2001–04; Leicester Internat. Music Fest., 2004–; Barbirolli-Isle of Man Internat. Oboe Fest. and Competition, 2005–; Associate Artistic Dir, Britten Sinfonia, 2002–. Dedicatee and first performer of many new works; more than 30 recordings and many broadcasts. Internat. appearances in USA, Japan, Europe, Australasia. Competition prize winner: BBC Young Musician of Year, 1980; Munich, 1983; Graz, 1984; Duino, Italy, 1986. Member: Assoc. for Improvement of Maternity Services; Assoc. of Radical Midwives; Good Practice; JABS; The Informed Parent. *Recreations:* childbirth studies (home birth), music, literature, Star Trek, travel, cinema. *Address:* *e-mail:* nicholas@engage.plus.com.

DANIEL, Paul Wilson, CBE 2000; conductor; Principal Conductor and Artistic Advisor, West Australian Symphony Orchestra, since 2009 (Principal Conductor designate, 2007–08); *b* 5 July 1958; *s* of Alfred Daniel and Margaret Daniel (*née* Poole); *m* 1988, Joan Rodgers, *qv*; two *d*. *Educ:* King Henry VIII Sch., Coventry; King's Coll., Cambridge; Guildhall Sch. of Music and Drama. Music Dir, Opera Factory, London, 1987–90; Artistic Dir, Opera North, 1990–97; Principal Conductor, English Northern Philharmonia, 1990–97; Music Dir, ENO, 1997–2005. Has worked with ENO, Royal Opera House, Bayerische Staatsoper, Munich, La Monnaie, Brussels, Geneva Opera and Teatro Real Madrid; has conducted many orchestras incl. Philharmonia, LSO, LPO, RPO, BBC SO, London Sinfonietta, CBSO, Scottish Chamber Orch., and ABC orchestras, Australia; has also conducted in Germany, Holland, France and USA. Co-presenter, Harry Enfield's Guide to Opera, TV series, 1993. Has made numerous recordings. *Address:* c/o Ingpen & Williams, 7 St George's Court, 131 Putney Bridge Road, SW15 2PA. *T:* (020) 8874 3222.

DANIEL, (Reginald) Jack, OBE 1958; FREng, CEng, FRINA, FIMarEST; RCNC; *b* 27 Feb. 1920; *o s* of Reginald Daniel and Florence Emily (*née* Woods); *m* 1st, Joyce Earnshaw (marr. diss.); two *s*; 2nd, 1977, Elizabeth, *o d* of George Mitchell, Long Ashton, Som. *Educ:* Royal Naval Engrg Coll., Keyham; Royal Naval Coll., Greenwich. Grad., 1942; subseq. engaged in submarine design. Served War of 1939–45; Staff of C-in-C's Far East Fleet and Pacific Fleet, 1943–45. Atomic Bomb Tests, Bikini, 1946; Admty, Whitehall, 1947–49; Admty, Bath, Aircraft Carrier Design, 1949–52; Guided Missile Cruiser design, 1952–56; Nuclear and Polaris Submarine design, 1956–65; idc, 1966; Materials, R&D, 1967–68; Head of Forward Design, 1968–70; Director, Submarine Design and Production, 1970–74; Dir-Gen. Ships and Head of RCNC, MoD, 1974–79; British Shipbuilders: Bd Mem., 1979; Man. Dir, for Warshipbuilding, 1980–83; Dir (Training, Educn, Safety), 1981–85; Dir of Technology (Warships), British Shipbuilders, 1983–84; Dir, British Shipbuilders Australia Pty, 1983–86. Dep. Chm., Internationale Schiff Studien GmbH Hamburg, 1984–88; Man. Dir, Warship Design Services Ltd, 1984–87; VSEL Canadian Project Dir, 1987–91; Director: VSEL Australia Pty, 1986–91; VSEL Defence Systems Canada Inc., 1987–91; Chm., VSEL-CAP, 1987–91. Vice Pres., RINA, 1982. Parsons Meml Lect., 1976. Liveryman, Worshipful Co. of Shipwrights, 1980. Hon. Res. Fellow, UCL, 1974. FREng (Founder Fellow, Fellowship of Engineering, 1976). *Publications:* The End of an Era, 2003; Hawkridge series: Murder in the Park, 2006; Murder in Providence, 2006; It Couldn't Happen in Dorset, 2006; The Qatar Affair, 2006; Diamonds in Dorset, 2006; Bedsits in Bath, 2006; Problem in Portland, 2006; Nuclear. No! How?, 2006; Submarines and Swindlers, 2006; Requiem for a Sapper, 2006; Politics and Property, 2006; The Body in the Churchyard, 2006; Chain of Circumstances, 2007; Murder in the Theatre, 2007; The Irish Affair, 2007; The Spetisbury Mystery, 2007; Death Isn't Particular, 2007; Family Affairs, 2007; Nemesis, 2007; Satan's Disciples, 2007; papers on warship design, technology and production. *Recreations:* gardening, motoring, music. *Address:* Meadowland, Cleveland Walk, Bath BA2 6JU.

DANIEL, William Wentworth, CBE 1997; independent social scientist; Director, Policy Studies Institute, 1986–93; *b* 19 Nov. 1938; *s* of late George Taylor Daniel and Margaret Elizabeth Daniel; *m* 1st, 1961, Lynda Mary Coles Garrett (marr. diss.); one *s* two *d*; 2nd, 1990, Eileen Mary Reid (*née* Loudfoot) (*d* 1996). *Educ:* Shebbear Coll., Devon; Victoria Univ. of Manchester (BA Hons); Univ. of Manchester Inst. of Science and Technology (MSc Tech). Directing Staff, Ashorne Hill Management Coll., 1963–65; Sen. Res. Officer, Research Services Ltd, 1965–67; Senior Research Fellow: Bath Univ., 1967–69; PSI (formerly PEP), 1969–81; Dep. Dir, PSI, 1981–86. Member: ESRC, 1992–96; Eur. Foundn for Improvement of Living and Wkg Conditions, Dublin, 1992–96. Dir, Holsworthy Biogas Ltd, 1999. Mem. Bd of Govs, Plymouth Univ., 2001. *Publications:* Racial Discrimination in England, 1968; Whatever Happened to the Workers in Woolwich?, 1972; The Right to Manage?, 1972; A National Survey of the Unemployed, 1974; Sandwich Courses in Higher Education, 1975; Pay Determination in Manufacturing Industry, 1976; Where Are They Now?: a follow-up survey of the unemployed, 1977; The Impact of Employment Protection Laws, 1978; Maternity Rights: the experience of women, 1980; Maternity Rights: the experience of employers, 1981; Workplace Industrial Relations in Britain, 1983; Workplace Industrial Relations and Technical Change, 1987; The Unemployed Flow, 1989; (with Terence Hogarth) Britain's New Industrial Gypsies, 1989. *Recreations:* golf, lawn tennis. *Address:* Bryn-Mor, 7 Maer Down Road, Bude, Cornwall EX23 8NG. *T:* (01288) 356678; Flat 2, 64 Queensway, W2 3RL. *Clubs:* National Liberal; Bude & N Cornwall Golf; David Lloyd Slazenger Racquet (Heston).

DANIELL, Prof. David John, PhD; Professor of English, University College London, 1992–94, now Emeritus Professor; *b* 17 Feb. 1929; *s* of late Rev. Eric Herbert Daniell, MA, and Betty (*née* Heap); *m* 1956, Dorothy Mary Wells; two *s*. *Educ:* Queen Elizabeth GS, Darlington; St Catherine's Coll., Oxford (BA English Lang. and Lit., MA; BA Theol.; Hon. Fellow, 2000); Univ. of Tübingen; UCL (PhD 1972). Radar fitter, RAF, 1947–49. Sixth Form Master, Apsley GS, 1958–69; Lectr, 1969–86, Sen. Lectr, 1986–92, English Dept, UCL. Vis. Prof., KCL, 1995; Vis. Fellow, Magdalen Coll., Oxford, 1996 (Hon. Mem., Sen. Common Room, 1996); Leverhulme Emeritus Fellow, 1997–99; Mayers Fellow, Henry E. Huntington Liby, Calif, 1998; Special Lectr, Magdalen Coll., Oxford, 1999; Oxford Univ. Sermon, 2000. Lectures: Beatrice Warde Meml, 1994; Lambeth Tyndale, 1994; A. G. Dickens, Univ. of Cambridge, 1994; Hertford Tyndale, 1994; Hilda Hulme Meml, 1994; Waynflete, Univ. of Oxford, 1996; Staley, Michigan, 1998; St Paul's Cathedral, 2003; Shakespeare Inst., Illinois, 2005. Asst Ed., The Year's Work in English Studies, 1976–84; Gen. Ed., John Buchan series, OUP World's Classics, 1993–2003; Founder and Ed., Reformation, 1995–97. Mem., Acad. Adv. Cttee, Internat. Shakespeare Globe Centre, 1981–91; Founder and organiser, biennial Oxford Internat. Tyndale Confs,

1994–; Founder and Chm., Tyndale Soc., 1995–. Curator, Let There Be Light Exhibn, British Liby, 1994–97 (London, Calif, NY and Washington). Frequent broadcaster, incl. Tyndale's New Testament, Radio 3, 1993. Lectures widely in UK, Europe and USA. Hon. Fellow, Hertford Coll., Oxford, 1998. *Publications:* The Interpreter's House, 1975; Coriolanus in Europe, 1980; The Best Short Stories of John Buchan, vol. 1, 1980, vol. 2, 1982; The Critics Debate: The Tempest, 1989; (ed) Tyndale's 1534 New Testament, 1989; (ed) Tyndale's Old Testament, 1992; William Tyndale: a biography, 1994; The Arden Shakespeare: Julius Caesar, 1998; (ed) Tyndale, the Obedience of a Christian Man, 2000; The Bible in English, 2003; William Tyndale, Selected Writings, 2003; contrib. Oxford DNB; numerous contribs to learned jls incl. Shakespeare Survey, TLS, The Year's Work in English Studies, MLR, Jl of Ecclesiastical Hist., Jl of Amer. Studies, Jl of Theol Studies, Reformation. *Recreations:* music, reading, hill-walking in Scotland. *Address:* 17 Crossfell Road, Leverstock Green, Hemel Hempstead, Herts HP3 8RF. *T:* (01442) 254766. *Club:* Authors'.

DANIELS, David; countertenor; *b* S Carolina, 12 March 1966. *Educ:* Cincinnati Conservatoire; Univ. of Michigan. Singing début, 1992; début with Metropolitan Opera, as Sesto in Giulio Cesare, 1999; *rôles* include: Rinaldo, Nerone in L'Incoronazione di Poppea, Didymus in Theodora, Hamor in Jeptha, Arsamenes in Xerxes, Oberon in A Midsummer Night's Dream; title rôles in Tamerlano, Giulio Cesare, Orfeo ed Euridice, Orlando; has performed with San Francisco SO, St Louis SO, New World SO, Philharmonia Baroque, San Francisco Opera, Florida Grand Opera, Bavarian State Opera, Glimmerglass Opera Fest., Brooklyn Acad. of Music, Royal Opera, Covent Gdn, Glyndebourne Fest., Salzburg Fest.,, Bayerische Staatsoper, NY City Opera, Canadian Opera Co., Lyric Opera of Chicago, Netherlands Opera, and Paris Opera; extensive recital and concert repertoire performed in US and Europe, incl. Promenade Concerts. Has made numerous recordings. Richard Tucker Award, 1997; Vocalist of Year Award, Musical America, 1999. *Recreations:* theatre, sports, especially baseball. *Address:* c/o Askonas Holt Ltd, Lincoln House, 300 High Holborn WC1V 7JH. *T:* (020) 7400 1700.

DANIELS, Eric; *see* Daniels, J. E.

DANIELS, George, MBE 1982; FSA, FBHI; author, watchmaker; horological consultant to Sotheby's, since 1970; *b* 19 Aug. 1926; *s* of George Daniels and Beatrice (*née* Cadou); *m* 1964, Juliet Anne (*née* Marryat); one *d*. *Educ:* elementary. 2nd Bn E Yorks Regt, 1944–47. Started professional horology, 1947; restoration of historical watches, 1956–; hand watch making to own designs, 1969–; invented co-Axial escapement, 1975, developed and patented, 1980, industrialised by Swiss makers, 1997; designed IOM Millennium postage stamps, commemorating English chronometer inventors, 1999. Horological lectures, both antiquarian and modern technical, to RSA, Royal Instn, Antiquarian Horol Soc., Harvard Univ., Cambridge Phil Soc., British Horol Inst., Amer. Watchmakers' Inst., Swedish Watchmakers' Inst., RAS, RCA. President: British Horological Inst., 1980 (Fellow, 1951); British Clock and Watchmakers' Benevolent Soc., 1980; Chm. and Founder, BHI Educn Trust, 1998. One man exhibition, Goldsmiths' Hall, 1992. Worshipful Co. of Clockmakers: Liveryman, 1968; Warden, 1977; Master, 1980; Tompion Gold Medal, 1981; Asst Hon. Surveyor, 1972–81; Founding Chm., Horological Industries Cttee, 1985–. Freeman, Goldsmiths' Co., 1979; FSA 1976. Hon. DSc City, 1994. Arts, Sciences and Learning Award, City Corporation, London, 1974; Victor Kullberg Medal, Stockholm Watch Guild, 1977; Gold Medal, British Horol Inst., 1981; Gold Badge and Hon. Fellow, Amer. Watchmakers Inst., 1985; Hon. FCGI 1986; City and Guilds Gold Medal for Craftsmanship, 1991; Gaïa Award, Mus. Internat. d'Horlogerie, 2002. *Publications:* Watches (jtly), 1965, 3rd edn 1978 (trans. German, 1982); English and American Watches, 1967; The Art of Breguet, 1975, 3rd edn 1985 (trans. French, 1985, Italian, 1990); (jtly) Clocks and Watches of the Worshipful Company of Clockmakers, 1975; Sir David Salomons Collection, 1978; Watchmaking, 1981, 2nd edn 1985 (trans. French, 1993); The Practical Watch Escapement, 1995, 2nd edn 1997; All in Good Time: reflections of a watchmaker (autobiog.), 2000, rev. edn 2001. *Recreations:* vintage cars, fast motorcycles, opera. *Address:* 34 New Bond Street, W1A 2AA.

DANIELS, Harold Albert; *b* 8 June 1915; *s* of Albert Pollikett Daniels and Eleanor Sarah Maud Daniels (*née* Flahey); *m* 1946, Frances Victoria Jerdan; one *s* decd. *Educ:* Mercers' Sch.; Christ's Coll., Cambridge. BA 1937; Wren Prize 1938; MA 1940. Asst Principal, Post Office, 1938; Admiralty, 1942; Post Office, 1945; Principal, 1946; Asst Sec., 1950; Under-Sec., 1961; Min. of Posts and Telecommunications, 1969; Asst Under Sec. of State, Home Office, 1974–76. *Address:* Lyle Court Cottage, Bradbourne Road, Sevenoaks, Kent TN13 3PZ. *T:* (01732) 454039.

DANIELS, (John) Eric; Chief Executive, Lloyds TSB Group plc, since 2003; *b* Montana, USA, 1951; *m*; one *s*. *Educ:* Cornell Univ. (BA 1973); Massachusetts Inst. of Technol. (MSc 1975). Joined Citibank, USA, 1975; Regl Hd, Citigroup Consumer Bank Europe, 1996; Chief Operating Officer, Citigroup Consumer Bank, 1998; Chm. and CEO, Travelers Life & Annuity, 1998–2000; Chm. and CEO, Zona Financiera, 2000–01; Exec. Dir, UK Retail Banking, Lloyds TSB Gp plc, 2001–03. Non-exec. Dir, BT, 2008–. *Address:* Lloyds TSB Group plc, 25 Gresham Street, EC2V 7HN.

DANKWORTH, Lady; *see* Laine, Dame C. D.

DANKWORTH, Sir John (Philip William), Kt 2006; CBE 1974; FRAM 1973; musician; *b* 20 Sept. 1927; British; *m* 1958, Clementine Dinah Laine, (Cleo) (*see* Dame C. D. Laine); one *s* one *d*. *Educ:* Monoux Grammar Sch. Studied Royal Academy of Music, 1944–46. ARAM 1969. Closely involved with post-war development of British jazz, 1947–60; formed large jazz orchestra, 1953; with Cleo Laine founded Stables Theatre, Wavendon, 1969. Pops Music Dir, LSO, 1985–90; Principal Guest Pops Conductor, San Francisco Orch., 1987–89. *Compositions* for combined jazz and symphonic musicians including: Improvisations (with Matyas Seiber), 1959; Escapade (commissioned by Northern Sinfonia Orch.), 1967; Tom Sawyer's Saturday, for narrator and orchestra (commissioned by Farnham Festival), 1967; String Quartet, 1971; Piano Concerto (commissioned by Westminster Festival), 1972; Grace Abounding (for RPO), 1980; The Diamond and the Goose (for City of Birmingham Choir and Orch.), 1981; Reconciliation (commnd for Silver Jubilee of Coventry Cathedral), 1987; Woolwich Clarinet Concerto (for Emma Johnson), 1995; Mariposas (for Peter Fisher), for violin and piano, 1996, rescored for violin and string orch., 2001; Double Vision (for BBC Big Band, world première, BBC Proms), 1997; Objective 2000 (for combined orchs of Harpur Trust Schs), 2000; many important *film scores*, 1964–, including: Saturday Night and Sunday Morning, Darling, The Servant, Morgan, Accident, Gangster No 1; other works include: Palabras, 1970; dialogue and songs for Colette, Comedy, 1980. Numerous record albums, incl. Echoes of Harlem, Misty, Symphonic Fusions. Variety Club of GB Show Business Personality Award (with Cleo Laine), 1977. Hon. Fellow, Leeds Coll. of Music, 1999. Hon. MA Open Univ., 1975; Hon. DMus: Berklee Sch. of Music, 1982; York, 1993. Distinguished Artists Award, Internat. Soc. for the Performance Arts, 1999; (with Cleo Laine) Bob Harrington Lifetime Achievement Award, Back Stage, 2001; Lifetime Achievement Award, BBC Radio Jazz Awards, 2002. *Publications:* Sax from the Start, 1996; Jazz in Revolution (autobiog.), 1998. *Recreations:* driving, household maintenance. *Address:* The Old Rectory, Wavendon, Milton Keynes MK17 8LT. *Fax:* (01908) 584414.

DANN, Mrs Jill; *b* 10 Sept. 1929; *d* of Harold Norman Cartwright and Marjorie Alice Thornton; *m* 1952, Anthony John Dann (*d* 2000); two *s* two *d* (and one *s* decd). *Educ:* Solihull High Sch. for Girls, Malvern Hall; Birmingham Univ. (LLB); St Hilda's Coll., Oxford (BCL). Called to the Bar, Inner Temple, 1952. Mayoress of Chippenham, 1964–65. Church Commissioner, 1968–93; Member: General Synod of Church of England, 1965–95 (Mem., Standing Cttee, 1971–90; Vice-Chm. House of Laity, 1985–90); Crown Appointments Commn, 1977–87; Chairman: House of Laity, Bristol Diocesan Synod, 1982–88; C of E Evangelical Council, 1985–89; Trustee, Church Urban Fund, 1987–95. Vice Chm., Trinity Coll., Bristol, 1990–2006; Pres. of Fellows, Cheltenham and Gloucester Coll. of Higher Educn, subseq. Univ. of Gloucestershire, 1988–2003. Director: Wiltshire Radio, 1981–88; ARK 2 TV Ltd, 1995–97. Pres., Inner Wheel, 1978–79. *Recreations:* reading, enjoying being a grandmother. *Address:* The Cottage, 21 St Mary Street, Chippenham, Wilts SN15 3JW. *T:* (01249) 464740.

DANN, Most Rev. Robert William; *b* 28 Sept. 1914; *s* of James and Ruth Dann; *m* 1949, Yvonne (*née* Newnham); one *s* two *d*. *Educ:* Trinity Coll., Univ. of Melbourne. BA Hons Melbourne 1946. Deacon, 1945; Priest, 1946. Dir of Youth and Religious Education, Dio. Melbourne, 1946; Incumbent: St Matthew's, Cheltenham, 1951; St George's, Malvern, 1956; St John's, Footscray, 1961; Archdeacon of Essendon, 1961; Dir of Evangelism and Extension, Dio. Melbourne, 1963; Bishop Coadjutor, Dio. Melbourne, 1969–77; Archbishop of Melbourne and Metropolitan of Province of Victoria, 1977–83. *Address:* 101 Cameron Close, 155 Warrigal Road, Burood, Vic 3125, Australia.

DANNATT, Gen. Sir (Francis) Richard, KCB 2004; CBE 1996; MC 1973; Chief of the General Staff, since 2006; Aide-de-Camp General to the Queen, since 2006; *b* 23 Dec 1950; *s* of late Anthony Richard Dannatt and of Mary Juliet Dannatt (*née* Chilvers); *m* 1977, Philippa Margaret Gurney; three *s* one *d*. *Educ:* Felsted Jun. Sch.; St Lawrence Coll. RMA, Sandhurst; Univ. of Durham (BA Hons Econ. Hist. 1976). Commnd Green Howards, 1971; Army Comd and Staff Coll., Camberley, 1982; COS, 20th Armd Bde, 1983–84; MA to Minister of State for Armed Forces, 1986–89; CO, 1 Green Howards, 1989–91; Col Higher Comd and Staff Course, Staff Coll., Camberley, 1992–94; Comdr, 4th Armd Bde, 1994–96; Dir, Defence Progs, MoD, 1996–98; GOC 3rd UK Div., 1999–2000; Dep. Comdr Ops, HQ SFOR, 2000–01; ACGS, 2001–02; Comdr, Allied RRC, 2003–05; C-in-C Land Comd, 2005–06. Col, Green Howards, 1994–2003; Dep Col Comdt, AGC (RMP), 1999–2005; Col Comdt, King's Div., 2001–05. Vice Pres. Officers Christian Union, 1998–; President: Soldiers' and Airmen's Scripture Readers Assoc., 1999–; Army Rifle Assoc., 2000–; Trustee, Windsor Leadership Trust, 2005–. Patron, Hope and Homes for Children, 2006–. *Recreations:* cricket, tennis, fishing shooting. *Address:* Regimental Headquarters, The Green Howards, Holy Trinity Church, Richmond, N Yorks DL10 4QN. *T:* (01748) 822133. *Club:* Army and Navy.

DANNATT, Prof. (James) Trevor, MA; RA 1983 (ARA 1977); FRIBA; Partner Dannatt, Johnson Architects (formerly Trevor Dannatt & Partners), 1975–2003 Consultant, since 2003; Professor of Architecture: Manchester University, 1975–86 Royal Academy, 1988–2005; *b* 15 Jan. 1920; *s* of George Herbert and Jane Ellen Dannatt *m* 1st, 1953, Joan Howell Davies (marr. diss. 1991); one *s* one *d*; 2nd, 1994, Dr Ann Crawshaw (*née* Critchley). *Educ:* Colfes Sch.; Sch. of Architecture, Regent Street Polytechnic (Dip. Arch.). Professional experience in office of Jane B. Drew and E Maxwell Fry, 1943–48; Architects Dept, LCC (Royal Festival Hall Gp), 1948–52 commenced private practice, 1952. Vis. Prof., Washington Univ., St Louis, 1976 and 1987. Assessor for national and international architectural competitions. Member Cathedrals Adv. Commn, 1986–91; Historic Bldgs Adv. Cttee, English Heritage, 1988–9 (Mem., Post War Listing Adv. Cttee, 1986–2003); Fabric Cttees of Cathedrals: Lichfield 1985–97; Portsmouth, 1990–96; St Paul's, 1991–2006. Founder Mem., and Chm., South Bank Gp, 1993–. Pres., 20th Century Soc., 2003–. Trustee, DOCOMOMO (Document of the Modern Movement), 1991–. Editor, Architects' Year Book, 1945–62. Exhibn of paintings and architecture, Whitworth Art Gall., 2006. Architectural work includes private houses, housing, school buildings; university buildings (residences, Leicester, Hull Trinity Hall Combination Room, Cambridge; Vaughan Coll. and Jewry Wall Mus. Leicester; develt plan and extensive works for Univ. of Greenwich, formerly Thames Polytechnic, inc. studies for occupation of several buildings of RNC at Greenwich, incl conversion and refurbishment of Queen Anne Quarters and Dreadnought Seamen' Hosp., 1999, Queen Mary's Quarters, 2000 and King William's Quarters, 2001); work for Univ. of Westminster; welfare buildings and schools for London boroughs conservation and restoration, interiors for private, corporate and public clients; Architect for British Embassy and Diplomatic Staff housing, Riyadh, 1985; Consultant Architects Royal Botanic Gardens, Kew, 1989–2005; Victoria Gate visitor reception and facilitie building; various restorations and new buildings; houses for Morden Coll., Blackheath 2004. Won internat. competition for Conference complex in Riyadh, Saudi Arabia completed 1974. Hon. FAIA 1988. Hon. DDes Greenwich, 2002. *Publications:* Modern Architecture in Britain, 1959; Trevor Dannatt: Buildings and Interiors 1951–72, 1972 (Editorial Adviser, and foreword) Buildings and Ideas 1933–83 from the Studio of Leslie Martin, 1983; (with P. Carolin) Sir Leslie Martin: architecture, education, research, 1996 Maritime Greenwich Campus, 2002; contribs to Architectural Rev., Architects' Jl, and various foreign journals. *Recreations:* the arts, including architecture. *Address:* (office) 52 Borough High Street, SE1 1XN. *T:* (020) 7357 7100; *e-mail:* dja@djarchitects.co.uk *Clubs:* Travellers, Arts.

DANNATT, Gen. Sir Richard; *see* Dannatt, Sir F. R.

DANNATT, Trevor; *see* Dannatt, J. T.

d'ANSEMBOURG, Count Jan Mark Vladimir Anton de Marchant et; *see* de Marchant et d'Ansembourg.

DANSON, Hon. Barnett Jerome; PC (Canada) 1974; OC 1996; author; company director; *b* 8 Feb. 1921; *s* of Joseph B. Danson and Saidie W. Danson, Toronto; *m* 1943 Isobel, *d* of Robert John Bull, London, England; four *s*. *Educ:* Toronto public and high schs. Served War: enlisted Queen's Own Rifles as Rifleman, 1939; commnd, 1943 wounded in France, 1944; retd 1945, Lieut. Manager, Jos. B. Danson & Sons Ltd Toronto, 1945–50; Sales Man., Maple Leaf Plastics Ltd, 1950–53; Principal (Pres.) Danson Corp. Ltd, Scarborough, 1953–74; Chairman: CSPG Consultants, 1980–84; de Havilland Aircraft of Canada Ltd, 1981–84; Canadian Consul General, Boston, Mass 1984–86. Active in Liberal Party, 1946–: MP (L) for York North, 1968–79; Parly Sec. to Prime Minister Trudeau, 1970–72; Minister of State for Urban Affairs, 1974–76; Minister of Nat. Defence, Canada, 1976–79; former Mem., Standing Cttee on Finance, Trade and Econ. Affairs and Ext. Affairs and National Defence. Chm., GSW Thermoplastics Co Dir, Algoma Central Railway Ltd. Dir Emeritus, Canadian Council of Native Business Director: Atlantic Council of Canada; Canadian Inst. of Strategic Studies; Canadian Centre for Global Security; Canadian Exec. Services Orgn, Toronto; Royal Conservatory of Music, Canada; Scholarship Foundn, F. J. L. Woodcock/Sir Arthur Pearson Assoc. of War Blinded; Mem. Council, Canadian Nat. Inst. for Blind. Chm. Bd, No Price Too High Foundn; former Pres. and first Chm. Bd, Soc. of Plastics Industry Inc. Dir, Canadian Council of Christians and Jews. Hon. Dir, Empire Club, Canada. Chm., Adv. Cttee, Canadian War Mus., 1998–. Trustee, Canadian Mus. of Civilisation, 1998–. Former Hon. Lt-Col, Queen's Own Rifles of Canada. Dr of Laws (*hc*) Royal Military Coll. of Canada, 1993; Hon. LLD York Univ., Toronto, 2006. Award for Excellence in the cause of parly democracy, Churchill Soc., 1995; Vimy Award, Conf. of Defence Assocs, 2000. Officer, Order of Merit (France), 1994; Chevalier, Legion of Honour (France), 2007. *Publication:* Not Bad for a Sergeant (memoirs), 2002. *Recreations:* fishing, reading, music. *Address:* 1132 Bay Street, Apt 1501, Toronto, ON M5S 2Z4, Canada.

DANTZIC, Roy Matthew, CA; Chairman, Interior Services Group plc, since 2004; *b* 4 July 1944; *s* of David and Renee Dantzic; *m* 1969, Diane Clapham; one *s* one *d*. *Educ:* Brighton Coll., Sussex. CA 1968. Coopers & Lybrand, 1962–69; Kleinwort, Benson Ltd, 1970–72; Drayton Corporation Ltd, 1972–74; Samuel Montagu & Co. Ltd, 1974–80 (Exec. Dir, 1975); Mem. for Finance, BNOC, subseq. Finance Dir, Britoil plc, 1980–84; Dir, Pallas SA, 1984–85; Dir, Wood Mackenzie & Co., 1985–89; Finance Dir, Stanhope Properties, 1989–95; Dir, Merrill Lynch Internat., 1995–96; Man. Dir, British Gas Properties, then BG Property Hldgs, subseq. SecondSite Property Hldgs, 1996–2003 (non-exec. Dir, 2003–04). Chairman: Premier Portfolio Ltd, 1985–92; Associated British Cinemas Ltd, 1998–2000; Development Securities plc, 2003–07; Dep. Chm., Spazio Investment NV, 2007–; non-executive Director: Moor Park (1958) Ltd, 1980–90; Saxon Oil plc, 1984–85; Total Oil Holdings, 1995–96; Airplanes Ltd, 1996–; Blenheim Bishop Ltd, 2003–07. pt-time Mem., CEGB, 1984–87; Pt-time Dir, BNFL, 1987–91. Mem., Council of Mgt, Architectural Heritage Fund, 2001–. Trustee, Portman Estate, 2005–. Governor, Brighton Coll., 1990–98. *Recreations:* cinema, theatre, playing golf, watching cricket. *Clubs:* MCC; Moor Park Golf.

DARBY, John Oliver Robertson; Chairman, Arthur Young, Chartered Accountants, 1974–87; *b* 5 Jan. 1930; *s* of Ralph Darby and Margaret Darby (*née* Robertson); *m* 1955, Valerie Leyland Cole; three *s*. *Educ:* Charterhouse. FCA 1953. Pilot Officer, RAF, 1953–55; Arthur Young, Chartered Accts, 1955–87, Partner, 1959–87. Chairman: Nat. Home Loans Hldgs PLC, 1985–92; Property Lending Trust, later Property Lending Bank, PLC, 1987–92; Ultramar, 1988–91; BREL Gp, later ABB Transportation (Hldgs) Ltd, 1989–94; Director: British Rail Engineering Ltd, 1986–89; Lightgraphix Ltd, 1996–. *Recreations:* racing, golf. *Address:* The Tithe Barn, Headley, Bordon, Hants GU35 8PW. *Clubs:* Garrick, Royal Thames Yacht; Royal & Ancient Golf (St Andrews); Liphook Golf.

DARBY, Dr Michael Douglas, FRES; Coleoptera recorder for Wiltshire, since 1995; Editor, Recording Wiltshire's Biodiversity, since 1996; *b* 2 Sept. 1944; *s* of Arthur Douglas Darby and Ilene Doris Darby (*née* Eatwell); *m* 1977, Elisabeth Susan Done; two *s*. *Educ:* Rugby School; Reading Univ. (PhD). FRES 1977; FRGS 1984; AMA 1990. Asst to Barbara Jones, 1963; Victoria and Albert Museum: Textiles Dept, 1964–72; Prints and Drawings Dept, 1973–76; Exhibitions Officer, 1977–83; Dep. Dir, 1983–87; Hd of Publications, Exhibitions and Design, 1988–89; Surveyor Gen., Carroll Art Collection, 1990–94. Member: Crafts Council, 1984–88; IoW Adv. Cttee, English Heritage, 1986–; Council, Royal Entomol Soc., 1988–90; Council, National Trust, 1989–93; Council, Wilts Archaeol and Natural Hist. Soc., 1996–2001. FRSA 1989. Natural Hist. Ed., Wiltshire Studies, 2000–. *Publications:* Marble Halls, 1973; Early Railway Prints, 1974, 2nd edn 1979; British Art in the Victoria and Albert Museum, 1983; John Pollard Seddon, 1983; The Islamic Perspective, 1983; articles in art, architectural and entomological periodicals. *Recreations:* beetles, books. *Address:* The Old Malthouse, Sutton Mandeville, near Salisbury, Wilts SP3 5ND. *T:* (01722) 714295.

DARBYSHIRE, Jane Helen, (Mrs Jane Darbyshire-Walker), OBE 1994; Consultant, Jane Darbyshire and David Kendall Ltd (Director, 1995–2000); *b* 5 June 1948; *d* of Gordon Desmond Wroe and Patricia Keough; *m* 1st, 1973, David Darbyshire (marr. diss. 1987); one *d*; 2nd, 1993, Michael Walker. *Educ:* Univ. of Newcastle upon Tyne (BA Hons, BArch Hons). RIBA. Architect: Ryder and Yates, Newcastle upon Tyne, 1972–75; Barnett Winskell, 1975–79; Partner: Jane and David Darbyshire, 1979–87; Jane Darbyshire Associates, 1987–95. Ext. Examr, Newcastle upon Tyne Univ., 1993–95. Mem., RIBA Nat. Council, 1998–2001; Board Member: Tyne and Wear Develt Corp., 1992–98; NE Regl Cultural Consortium, 1999–2001. *Recreations:* classical music, horse riding, art. *Address:* Jane Darbyshire and David Kendall Ltd, Millmount, Ponteland Road, Newcastle upon Tyne NE5 3AL.

DARBYSHIRE, Prof. Janet Howard, (Mrs G. M. Scott), OBE 1996; FRCP, FFPH, FMedSci; Director, MRC Clinical Trials Unit, since 1998; Professor of Epidemiology, University College London, since 1997; Co-Director, UK Clinical Research Network, since 2005; *b* 16 Nov. 1947; *d* of Philip and Jean Darbyshire; *m* 1976, Dr Geoffrey M. Scott, FRCP, FRCPath. *Educ:* Manchester Univ. (MB ChB 1970); London Sch. of Hygiene and Tropical Medicine (MSc 1990). MRCP 1973, FRCP 1988; FFPH 2001; FMedSci 2005. Mem., Scientific Staff, MRC, 1974–. Hon. Professor: Dept of Pharmacol. and Therapeutics, Univ. of Liverpool, 1994–; LSHTM, 1999–; Univ. of Leeds, 2007–. Hon. Consultant Physician: Royal Brompton Hosp., 1982–; Camden PCT, 1997–. *Publications:* contribs on clinical trials and epidemiol studies in tuberculosis, HIV infection and other diseases. *Recreations:* music, horse-riding, walking, reading, cooking, flying. *Address:* MRC Clinical Trials Unit, 222 Euston Road, NW1 2DA. *T:* (020) 7670 4752, *Fax:* (020) 7670 4815; *e-mail:* JHD@ctu.mrc.ac.uk.

DARCY DE KNAYTH, 19th Baron *cr* 1332; **Caspar David Ingrams;** consultant engineer, since 2005; *b* 5 Jan. 1962; *s* of late Rupert George Ingrams and Baroness Darcy de Knayth (18th in line); *S* mother, 2008; *m* 1996, Catherine Ann Baker; three *s*. *Educ:* Eton Coll.; Reading Univ. (BSc (Hons) Mech. Engrg). Ops Mgr, Howden Wade, 1987–98; Engrg Mgr, Airscrew Ltd, 1998–2004. *Recreations:* walking, opera, family. *Heir:* *s* Hon. Thomas Rupert Ingrams, *b* 23 Oct. 1999. *Address:* Morns Field, Crawley, Winchester SO21 2PL. *T:* (01962) 776050. *Club:* Brooks's.

DARELL, Brig. Sir Jeffrey (Lionel), 8th Bt *cr* 1795; MC 1945; *b* 2 Oct. 1919; *s* of late Lt-Col Guy Marsland Darell, MC (3rd *s* of 5th Bt); *S* cousin, 1959; *m* 1953, Bridget Mary, *e d* of Maj.-Gen. Sir Allan Adair, 6th Bt, GCVO, CB, DSO, MC; one *s* two *d*. *Educ:* Eton; RMC, Sandhurst. Commissioned Coldstream Guards, July 1939; served War of 1939–45: Coats Mission, 1940–41 (to guard Royal Family in case of invasion); ADC to GOC-in-C, Southern Comd, 1942; Bde Major, Guards Bde, 1953–55; Officer Comdg 1st Bn Coldstream Guards, 1957–59; GSO1, PS12, War Office, 1959; College Comdr RMA Sandhurst, 1961–64; Comdg Coldstream Guards, 1964–65; Comdr, 56 Inf. Brigade (TA), 1965–67; Vice-Pres., Regular Commns Bd, 1968–70; Comdt, Mons OCS, 1970–72; MoD, 1972–74; retd 1974. ADC to HM the Queen, 1973–74. Trustee and Mem., London Law Trust, 1981–99. High Sheriff, Norfolk, 1985. *Recreations:* normal. *Heir:* *s* Guy Jeffrey Adair Darell [*b* 8 June 1961; *m* 1988, Justine Samantha, *d* of Mr Justice T. Reynolds, Quambi Place, Sydney, Australia; one *s* two *d*]. *Address:* Denton Lodge, Harleston, Norfolk IP20 0AD. *T:* (01986) 788206. *Clubs:* Army and Navy, MCC.

DARESBURY, 4th Baron *cr* 1927, of Walton, co. Chester; **Peter Gilbert Greenall;** DL; Bt 1876; Chairman: Nasstar plc, since 2005; The De Vere (formerly Greenalls) Group plc, 2000–06 (Director, 1982–2006); *b* 18 July 1953; *e s* of 3rd Baron Daresbury and of his 1st wife, Margaret Ada, *y d* of C. J. Crawford; *S* father, 1996; *m* 1982, Clare Alison, *d* of late Christopher Weatherby; four *s*. *Educ:* Eton; Magdalene Coll., Cambridge (MA); London Business Sch. (Sloan Fellowship). Man. Dir, 1992–97, Chief Exec., 1997–2000, Greenalls Gp; Chairman: Aintree Racecourse Co. Ltd, 1988–; Highland Gold Mining Ltd, 2002–04; Kazakh Gold, 2005–07; non-executive Director: Evraz, 2005–06; Jockey Club Racecourses, 2007–; Mallett plc, 2007–. DL Cheshire, 1993. *Heir:* *s* Hon. Thomas Edward Greenall, *b* 6 Nov. 1984. *Address:* Hall Lane Farm, Daresbury, Warrington, Cheshire WA4 4AF. *T:* (home) (01925) 740212, (office) (01925) 740427, *Fax:* (01925) 740884; *e-mail:* peter.daresbury@daresburyltd.co.uk. *Clubs:* Jockey, MCC; Royal & Ancient Golf (St Andrews).

DARKE, Christopher; Head, Regional Services (England), British Medical Association, since 2002; *b* 5 Aug. 1949; *s* of late Derek Herbert Darke and Helen Navina Darke (*née* Davies); *m* 1st, 1976, Marian Dyson (marr. diss. 1982); one *s* one *d*; 2nd, 1992, Lorraine Julie Hinchliffe; two *d*. *Educ:* Handsworth Secondary Sch., Birmingham. Engrg apprentice, GEC, 1967–70; Engrg Draughtsman, Lucas Industries, 1970–77; TU Officer, AUEW-TASS, 1977–82; Nat. Officer, AUEW-TASS, later MSF, 1982–92; Gen. Sec., BALPA, 1992–2002. Mem., Competition (formerly Monopolies and Mergers) Commn, 1998–2005. *Recreations:* flying, travel, reading, gardening. *Address:* (office) BMA House, Tavistock Square, WC1H 9JP.

DARKE, Geoffrey James, RIBA; Principal, Geoffrey Darke Associates, Architects and Planners, since 1987; *b* 1 Sept. 1929; *s* of late Harry James Darke and Edith Anne (*née* Rose); *m* 1959, Jean Yvonne Rose, BA, ARCM; one *s* two *d*. *Educ:* Prince Henry's Grammar Sch., Evesham, Worcs; Birmingham School of Architecture (DipArch); ARIBA 1956. National Service, Malaya, commnd RE, 1954–56. Asst Architect, Stevenage Development Corp., 1952–58; private practice, 1958–61; Partner, Darbourne and Darke, Architects and Landscape Planners, 1961–87. Work has included many large commissions, particularly public buildings. Success in national and internat. competitions, in Stuttgart, 1977, Hanover, 1979 and 1980, and in Bolzano, Italy, 1980; numerous medals and awards for architectural work; co-recipient of Fritz Schumacher Award, Hamburg, 1978, for services to architecture and town planning. Mem. Council, RIBA, 1977–83; Chm., RIBA Competitions Cttee, 1979–84; has served on many professional committees; Mem., Access Cttee for England, 1992–98. Mem., Aldeburgh Foundn, 1979–98. FRSA 1981. *Recreation:* music. *Address:* 2 Murray Court, 80 Banbury Road, Oxford OX2 6LQ.

DARKE, Marjorie Sheila; writer, since 1962; *b* 25 Jan. 1929; *d* of Christopher Darke and Sarah Ann (*née* Palin); *m* 1952; two *s* one *d*. *Educ:* Worcester Grammar Sch. for Girls; Leicester Coll. of Art and Technol.; Central Sch. of Art, London. Worked in textile studio of John Lewis Partnership, 1950–54. *Publications:* Ride the Iron Horse, 1973; The Star Trap, 1974; A Question of Courage, 1975; The First of Midnight, 1977; A Long Way to Go, 1978; Comeback, 1981; Tom Post's Private Eye, 1982; Messages and Other Shivery Tales, 1984; A Rose from Blighty, 1990; *for young children:* Mike's Bike, 1974; What Can I Do, 1975; Kipper's Turn, 1976; The Big Brass Band, 1976; My Uncle Charlie, 1977; Carnival Day, 1979; Kipper Skips, 1979; Imp, 1985; The Rainbow Sandwich, 1989; Night Windows, 1990; Emma's Monster, 1992; Just Bear and Friends, 1996. *Recreations:* reading, music, sewing, country walks. *Address:* c/o Rogers, Coleridge & White Ltd, Literary Agency, 20 Powis Mews, W11 1JN. *Clubs:* Society of Authors; International PEN.

DARLEY, Gillian Mary, FSA; architectural writer and biographer; *b* 28 Nov. 1947; *d* of Lt Col Robert Darley, MC and Caroline (*née* Swanston Ward); *m* 1986, Michael Horowitz, QC; one *d* (one *s* decd). *Educ:* Courtauld Inst. of Art, London Univ. (BA Hons 1969); Birkbeck Coll., London (MSc Politics and Admin 1986). Journalist and broadcaster; contributor to daily and Sunday newspapers, magazines and professional press, 1975–; Architectural correspondent, Observer, 1991–93. Joint Partner, Edifice, architectural photographic liby, 1987–. Dir, Landscape Foundn, 1994–98. Trustee, SPAB (Chm., 1997–2000); Member: Lottery Architecture Adv. Cttee, Arts Council England (formerly Arts Council of England), 1996–2005; Council, NT, 2008. FRSA 1995; FSA 2007. *Publications:* Villages of Vision, 1975, 2nd edn 2007; The National Trust Book of the Farm, 1981; Built in Britain, 1984; (with P. Lewis) Dictionary of Ornament, 1986; Octavia Hill: a life, 1990; (with A. Saint) The Chronicles of London, 1994; John Soane: an accidental romantic, 1999; Factory, 2003; John Evelyn: living for ingenuity, 2006. *Recreations:* gardening in a small space, Jack Russell, deserts.

DARLEY, Kevin Paul; freelance flat race jockey; *b* 5 Aug. 1960; *s* of Clifford Darley and Dorothy Thelma Darley (*née* Newby); *m* 1983, Debby Ford; two *d*. *Educ:* Colton Hills Comprehensive Sch., Wolverhampton. Apprentice Jockey to Reg Hollinshead, 1976–78 (Champion apprentice, 1978, with 70 winners); has ridden over 2,400 winners, incl. 71 Group winners (24 in Gp 1) in Britain and Europe, and 158 in one season, 2001; winner: French Derby, 1995, on Celtic Swing; St Leger, 2002, on Bollin Eric; English and Irish 1,000 Guineas, on Attraction, 2004; Champion Jockey, 2000. Jt Pres., Jockeys' Assoc. of GB, 2003–. *Recreations:* shooting, golf, hunting, ski-ing. *Address:* Ascot House, Lower Dunsforth, York YO26 9RZ. *T:* (01423) 323611.

DARLING; *see* Stormonth Darling.

DARLING, family name of **Baron Darling**.

DARLING, 3rd Baron *cr* 1924; **Robert Julian Henry Darling;** chartered surveyor in private practice, since 1990; *b* 29 April 1944; *s* of 2nd Baron Darling and Bridget Rosemary Whishaw Darling (*née* Dickson); *S* father, 2003; *m* 1970, Janet Rachel (*née* Mallinson); two *s* one *d*. *Educ:* Wellington Coll.; RAC Cirencester. FRICS. Nuffield Scholar, Australia and NZ, 1984. Partner, Smith-Woolley, Chartered Surveyors, 1970–89. Vice-Chairman: Norfolk Mental Healthcare NHS Trust, 1993–97; Nat. Assoc. of Prison Visitors, 2000. Chairman: Gt Yarmouth and Waveney, Mind, 2001–; Land Use and Access Panel, NT, 2007–. *Recreations:* fishing, gardening. *Heir:* *s* Hon. (Robert) James (Cyprian) Darling, *b* 6 March 1972. *Address:* The White House, Intwood, Norwich NR4 6TQ. *T:* (01603) 250450, *Fax:* (01603) 250520; *e-mail:* jdarling@paston.co.uk. *Club:* Norfolk.

DARLING, Rt Hon. Alistair (Maclean); PC 1997; MP (Lab) Edinburgh South West, since 2005 (Edinburgh Central, 1987–2005); Chancellor of the Exchequer, since 2007; advocate; *b* 28 Nov. 1953; *m* 1986, Margaret McQueen Vaughan; one *s* one *d*. *Educ:* Aberdeen Univ. Admitted to Faculty of Advocates, 1984. Member: Lothian Regl Council, 1982–87; Lothian and Borders Police Bd, 1982–86. Shadow Chief Sec. to HM Treasury, 1996–97; Chief Sec. to HM Treasury, 1997–98; Secretary of State: for Social Security, 1998–2001; for Work and Pensions, 2001–02; for Transport, 2002–06; for Scotland, 2003–06; for Trade and Industry, 2006–07. Gov., Napier Coll., Edinburgh, 1982–87. *Address:* House of Commons, SW1A 0AA.

DARLING, Sir Clifford, GCVO 1994; Kt 1977; Governor-General, Bahamas, 1992–94; *b* Acklins Island, 6 Feb. 1922; *s* of Charles and Aremelia Darling; *m* Igrid Smith. *Educ:* Acklins Public Sch.; several public schs in Nassau. Became taxi-driver (Gen. Sec. Bahamas Taxicab Union for 8 yrs, Pres. for 10 yrs). An early Mem., Progressive Liberal Party; MHA for Englerston; Senator, 1964–67; Dep. Speaker, House of Assembly, 1967–69; Minister of State, Oct. 1969; Minister of Labour and Welfare, Dec. 1971; Minister of Labour and Nat. Insurance, 1974–77; Speaker, House of Assembly, 1977–92. Past Chm., Tourist Advisory Bd; instrumental in introd. of a comprehensive Nat. Insce Scheme in the Bahamas, Oct. 1974. Member: Masonic Lodge; Elks Lodge; Acklins, Crooked Is and Long Cays Assoc. *Publication:* A Bahamian Life Story (autobiog.), vol. 1, 1922–1958, 2002. *Address:* PO Box N-1050, Nassau, Bahamas.

DARLING, Rt Rev. Edward Flewett; Bishop of Limerick and Killaloe, 1985–2000; *b* 24 July 1933; *s* of late Ven. Vivian W. Darling and Honor F. G. Darling; *m* 1958, E. E. Patricia Mann; three *s* two *d*. *Educ:* Cork Grammar School; Midleton Coll., Co Cork; St John's School, Leatherhead, Surrey; Trinity Coll., Dublin (MA). Curate: St Luke's, Belfast, 1956–59; St John's, Orangefield, Belfast, 1959–62; Incumbent, St Gall's, Carnalea, Co. Down, 1962–72; Chaplain, Bangor Hosp., Co. Down, 1963–72; Rector, St John's, Malone, Belfast, 1972–85; Chaplain, Ulster Independent Clinic, Belfast, 1981–85. Hon. FGCM 2006. *Publications:* Choosing the Hymns, 1984; (ed) Irish Church Praise, 1990; Sing to the Word, 2000; (ed) Church Hymnal, 5th edn 2000; (jtly) Companion to Church Hymnal, 2005; Understanding Hymns, 2007. *Recreations:* music, gardening. *Address:* 15 Beechwood Park, Moira, Craigavon, Co. Armagh BT67 0LL. *T:* (028) 9261 2982.

DARLING, Paul Antony; QC 1999; *b* 15 March 1960; *s* of William Martindale Darling, *qv*, and Ann Edith Darling; *m* 1st, 1983 (marr. diss.); 2nd, 1994 (marr. diss.). *Educ:* Tonstall Sch., Sunderland; Winchester Coll. (Schol.); St Edmund Hall, Oxford (BA Jurisp. 1981; BCL 1982). Treas., Oxford Union, 1980. Called to the Bar, Middle Temple, 1983, Bencher, 2004; in practice, 1985–. Chairman: Technol. and Construction Bar Assoc., 2003–07; Access to the Bar Cttee, Bar Council, 2007–; Mem., Gen. Council of the Bar, 2007–. Dir, J. M. & W. Darling Ltd (pharmaceutical chemists), 1978–. Non-exec. Dir, Horserace Totalisator Bd, 2006–. Ed., Construction Industry Law Letter, 1990–94; Mem., editl team, Keating on Building Contracts, 5th edn 1991 to 8th edn 2006. Trustee, Free Repn Unit, 2004–. *Recreations:* horse racing, Newcastle United. *Address:* Keating Chambers, 15 Essex Street, WC2R 3AA. *T:* (020) 7544 2600; *e-mail:* pdarling@keatingchambers.com. *Clubs:* Royal Ascot Racing (Mem. Cttee, 2004–06); South Shields and Westoe (South Shields).

DARLING, Susan; writer; *b* 1942; *d* of Eric Francis Justice Darling and Monica Darling. *Educ:* Nonsuch County Grammar Sch. for Girls, Cheam; King's Coll., London (BA Hons). Joined BoT as Asst Principal, 1963; transf. to FCO, 1965; Nairobi, 1967–69; Second, later First Sec., Econ. and Social Affairs, UK Mission to UN, 1969–73; FCO, 1973–74; resigned, 1974; reinstated, 1975; FCO, 1975–78; Dep. High Comr and Head of Chancery, Suva, 1981–84; FCO, 1984–87; Consul-Gen., Perth, WA, 1987–88; resigned FCO, 1988; Dept of Chief Minister, NT, Australia, 1989–90; Quaker Service Australia, 1991–93; Aboriginal and Torres Strait Islander Commn, 1994–96; Law Soc. of England and Wales, 2000–02. *Recreations:* travel, draught horses. *Address:* Mayor House Farm Cottages, Farley Heath, Surrey GU5 9EW.

DARLING, William Martindale, CBE 1988 (OBE 1972); DL; FRPharmS; Managing Director, J. M. & W. Darling Ltd, since 1957; Chairman, Gateshead and South Tyneside (formerly South Tyneside, then South of Tyne) Health Authority, 1974–2002; *b* 7 May 1934; *s* of William Darling, MPS and Muriel Darling; *m* 1958, Ann Edith Allen; two *s*. *Educ:* Mortimer Road Primary Sch.; Newcastle Royal Grammar Sch.; Sunderland Polytechnic Sch. of Pharmacy. MPS 1956. Member: Medicines Commn, 1971–79; Health Educn Council, 1972–80; Pharmacy Bd, CNAA, 1972–78; Cttee on Safety of Medicines, 1979–86; Cttee on Review of Medicines, 1987–90; Health Service Supply Council, 1975–84 (Chm. and Vice-Chm.); Mem., Ministerial Adv. Bd, 2000–, Chm., Audit Cttee, 2005–, NHS Purchasing and Supply Agency; Lay Mem., GMC, 1995–99; Chairman: Standing Pharmaceutical Adv. Cttee, 1974–2001; Nat. Pharmaceutical Supplies Gp, 1984–; Head, UK Pharm. Delegn to EU, 1972–2003; Pres., Pharm. Gp, EU, 1985–86, 2002; Mem., Comité Consultatif pour formation des pharmaciens, 1988–2003. Chairman: Standards Cttee, S Tyneside MBC, 2000–; Nat. Jt Registry Steering Cttee, 2002–; Counter Fraud and Security Mgt Special HA, 2003–06. Pharmaceutical, later Royal Pharmaceutical, Society of Great Britain: Mem. Council, 1962–2001; Vice-Pres., 1969–71; Pres., 1971–73; Treas., 1992–95; Chm., Code of Ethics and Health Wkg Pty, 1970–2001. Mem., Council, NAHA, 1974–90 (Chm., 1980–82; Hon. Treasurer, 1988–89); first Chm., Nat. Assoc. of Health Authorities and Trusts, 1990–93; Pres., Internat. Hosp. Fedn, 1997–2000 (Mem., Exec., 1994–2000). Gov., Univ. of Sunderland (formerly Sunderland Poly.), 1989– (Chm., 1994–2003; Hon. Fellow, 1990). Hon. Life Mem., South Shields and Westoe Club, 1990. DL Tyne and Wear, 2000. Pharm. Soc. Gold Medal, 1985. *Recreations:* horse racing, sunbathing, eating good food, growing prize flowers and vegetables. *Address:* Hartside, 6 Whitburn Road, Cleadon, near Sunderland SR6 7QL. *T:* (0191) 536 2089.
See also P. A. Darling.

DARLINGTON, Joyce B.; *see* Blow Darlington.

DARLINGTON, Stephen Mark, FRCO; Organist and Official Student in Music, Christ Church, Oxford, since 1985; *b* 21 Sept. 1952; *s* of John Oliver Darlington and Bernice Constance Elizabeth (*née* Murphy); *m* 1975, Moira Ellen (*née* Hill); three *d*. *Educ:* King's Sch., Worcester; Christ Church, Oxford (Organ Schol.; MA). Asst Organist, Canterbury Cathedral, 1974–78; Master of the Music, St Albans Abbey, 1978–85. Artistic Dir, Internat. Organ Fest., 1979–85. Pres., RCO, 1998–2000. DMus Lambeth, 2001. *Publication:* (ed jtly) Composing Music for Worship, 2003. *Recreations:* travel, walking, punting, Italian food. *Address:* Christ Church, Oxford OX1 1DP. *T:* (01865) 276195.

DARLOW, Paul Manning; His Honour Judge Darlow; a Circuit Judge, since 1997; *b* 7 Feb. 1951; *s* of late Brig. Eric William Townsend Darlow, OBE and of Elsie Joan Darlow, JP (*née* Ring); *m* 1985, Barbara Joan Speirs; one *d*. *Educ:* Audley House Prep. Sch., St Edward's Sch., Oxford; Mount Hermon Sch., Massachusetts; King's Coll., London (LLB). Called to the Bar, Middle Temple, 1973; in practice as barrister, London, 1974–78, Bristol, 1978–97; Asst Recorder, 1991–94; a Recorder, 1994–97. *Recreations:* sailing, tennis, bridge, walking, ski-ing. *Address:* Plymouth Combined Court Centre, 10 Armada Way, Plymouth, Devon PL1 2ER.

DARNBROUGH, Monica Anne, CBE 2003; PhD; Head of Bioscience Unit, Department of Trade and Industry, 1998–2005; independent consultant; *b* 14 Aug. 1951; *d* of Cecil Charles Webb and Marjorie Edyth (*née* Perring); *m* 1974, Geoffrey Darnbrough (marr. diss.). *Educ:* Univ. of Nottingham (BSc Jt Hons (Physiol. and Psychol.) 1972; PhD (Develtl Biol.) 1979). Police Scientific Devlt Br., Home Office, 1975–79; Department of Industry: Res. and Technol. and Space Div., 1979–80; Rayner study of res. estabts, 1980; Office of Chief Engr and Scientist, 1980–81; Office of Govt Chief Scientific Advr, Cabinet Office, 1981–83; Sec. to ACARD, 1981–83; IT Div., 1984–88, Personnel Div 1989–93, DTI; Counsellor for Sci. and Technol., FCO, Paris, 1994–98. Membe Council, BBSRC, 2002–04; Commonwealth Scholarship Commn, 2006–. Founde Mem., and Mem. Bd, Newton's Apple Science Think Tank, 2006–. Mem., PCC 2001–05, Church Warden, 2005–, St Bartholomew the Great. *Publication:* (contrib. Handbook of Medicinal Chemistry, 2006. *Recreations:* choral singing, photography looking at mountains, walking, travel, French garden. *Address: e-mail:* madarnbro@ukonline.co.uk.

DARNLEY, 11th Earl of, *cr* 1725; **Adam Ivo Stuart Bligh;** Baron Clifton of Leighto Bromswold, 1608; Baron Clifton of Rathmore, 1721; Viscount Darnley, 1723; *b* 8 Nov 1941; *s* of 9th Earl of Darnley and of Rosemary, *d* of late Edmund Basil Potter; *S* half brother, 1980; *m* 1965, Susan Elaine, JP, DL, *y d* of late Sir Donald Anderson; one *s* on *d*. *Educ:* Harrow; Christ Church, Oxford. Dir, City of Birmingham Touring Opera 1990–2000. Chm., Herefordshire Historic Churches Trust, 2003–. Governor: Cobhar Hall Sch., 1981–; Hereford Cathedral Sch., 2003– (Chm., 2006–). *Heir:* *s* Lord Clifton *qv*. *Address:* Netherwood Manor, Tenbury Wells, Worcs WR15 8RT. *Clubs:* Brooks's MCC.

DARRINGTON, Sir Michael (John), Kt 2004; FCA; Group Managing Directo Greggs plc, 1984–2008 (non-executive Director, since 2008); *b* 8 March 1942; *s* of Georg and Kathleen Darrington; *m* 1965, Paula Setterington; one *s* two *d*. *Educ:* Lancing Coll. Harvard Business Sch. (PMD 1974). FCA 1965. Josolyne Miles and Co., 1960–66; Unite Biscuits, 1966–83: posts incl. Gp Export Acct; Commercial Dir, Foods Div.; Man. Di Sayers Confectioners Ltd, 1978–83. Prince of Wales Regl Ambassador, NE, BITC, 2003– Regl Councillor, NE, CBI, 1990–. *Recreations:* sailing, golf, reading, pyrotechnics. *Club* Northern Counties (Newcastle upon Tyne).

DARROCH, Alasdair Malcolm; His Honour Judge Darroch; a Circuit Judge, sinc 2000; *b* 18 Feb. 1947; *s* of Ronald George Darroch and Diana Graburn Darroch; *m* 1972 Elizabeth Lesley Humphrey; one *s*. *Educ:* Harrow Sch.; Trinity Coll., Cambridge. Article Mills & Reeve, Solicitors, Norwich, 1969; admitted as solicitor, 1971; Partner, Mills & Reeve, 1974–2000; a Recorder, 1996–2000. Pres., Norfolk and Norwich Incorporate Law Soc., 1996–97. *Publications:* contrib. articles to legal press. *Recreations:* gardening European travel, real ale. *Address:* The Crown Court, Bishopgate, Norwich NR3 1UR.

DARROCH, Sir (Nigel) Kim, KCMG 2008 (CMG 1998); HM Diplomatic Service; UK Permanent Representative (with personal rank of Ambassador) to the European Union Brussels, since 2007; *b* 30 April 1954; *s* of Alastair Macphee Darroch and Enid Darroc (*née* Thompson); *m* 1978, Vanessa Claire Jackson; one *s* one *d*. *Educ:* Abingdon Sch Durham Univ. (BSc Zool 1975). Joined FCO, 1976; First Secretary: Tokyo, 1980–84 FCO, 1985–86; Private Sec. to Minister of State, FCO, 1987–89; First Sec., Rome 1989–92; Dep. Head, European Integration Dept, FCO, 1993–95; Head, Eastern Adriati Dept, FCO, 1995–97; Counsellor (External Affairs), UK Perm. Rep. to EU, Brussel 1997–98; Foreign and Commonwealth Office: Head, News Dept, 1998–2000; Dir, EU Comd, 2000–03; Dir Gen., EU Directorate, 2003–04; EU Advr to the PM and Hd European Secretariat, 2004–07. *Recreations:* squash, ski-ing, sailing, cinema. *Address:* c/ Foreign and Commonwealth Office, SW1A 2AH.

DART, Dr Edward Charles, CBE 1997; Chairman, Plant Bioscience Ltd (formerly Joh Innes Centre Innovations), since 1999 (non-executive Director, 1997–99); *b* 8 Marc 1941; *s* of late Arthur and Alice Dart; *m* 1964, Jean Ellen Long; one *s* two *d*. *Educ:* Univ of Manchester Inst. of Science and Technol. (BSc 1962; PhD 1965); Univ. of Calif, LA Univ. of Calif, Berkeley. Imperial Chemical Industries: Sen. Res. Scientist, Petrochemica and Polymer Lab. (and Lectr in Org. Chem., Univ. of Liverpool), 1968–71; Sen. Res Scientist, Corporate Lab., 1971–73; Jt Gp Head, Bioscience Gp, 1973–75; Gp Head Bioscience, 1975–78; Jt Lab. Manager, Corporate Lab. Policy Gp, 1981–83; Head Corporate Bioscience and Colloids Lab., 1983–85; Associate Res. Dir, Plant Protectio Div., 1985–86; Res. Dir, ZENECA (formerly ICI) Seeds, 1986–97; Chief Executiv Officer: Norwich Res. Park, 1997–98; AdProTech plc, 1997–99. Chm., Novact Biosystems Ltd, 2004–05; Board Member: Poalis AS, 2004–05; Rainbow Seed Fund 2004–. Science and Engineering Research Council: Mem., Biotechnol. Directorate 1981–84, Chm., 1984–89; Member: Molecular Biology Sub Cttee, 1980–82; Science Bd 1985–88. Member: BBSRC, 1994–98 (Chm., Technol. Interaction Bd, 1994–97; Mem. Appointments Cttee, 1998–; Mem., Strategy Bd, 2005–08); BBSRC/Science Mus Consensus Conf. Steering Cttee, 1994. Chairman: Biotechnol. Jt Adv. Bd, 1992–94 Agric., Horticulture and Forestry Foresight Panel, 1997–99; Member: Adv. Cttee o Genetic Manipulation, 1984–96; DTI/MAFF Agro Food Quality Link Cttee, 1991–98 John Innes Council, 1986–94; MAFF/AFRC Arable Crops Sectoral Gp, 1991–93; Agric and Envmt Biotechnology Commn, 2000–05; Exec. Advr, Kansai Res. Inst., 2008– (Mem., Internat. Adv. Cttee, 2001–07). Pres., Berks and Oxfordshire Assoc. for Scienc Educn, 1989–92. *Publications:* review articles in scientific books; papers in chemical an bioscience jls. *Recreations:* travel, books, music, golf, gardening.

DART, Geoffrey Stanley; Director of Corporate Law and Governance, Department fo Business, Enterprise and Regulatory Reform (formerly Department of Trade an Industry), since 2005; *b* 2 Oct. 1952; *s* of Wilfred Stanley Dart and Irene Jean Dart; *m* 1974, Rosemary Penelope Hinton; one *s* one *d*. *Educ:* Torquay Boys' Grammar Sch.; S Peter's Coll., Oxford (BA and MA Mod. Hist.). Researcher, Electricity Council 1974–77; Department of Energy: Energy Policy, Offshore Supplies, Oil Policy, Gas, Ass Private Sec. to Sec. of State, to 1984; Cabinet Secretariat, 1984–85; Principal Private Sec to Sec. of State for Energy, 1985–87; Asst Sec., Electricity Div., 1987–89; Offshore Safety Div., 1989–91; Estabt and Finance Div., 1991–92; Department of Trade and Industry Competitiveness Div., 1992–94; Under Sec., 1994–; Dir, Deregulation Unit, 1994; Hd Regl Develt Div., 1995–96; Shell UK (on secondment), 1996; Dir, Insurance, 1997–98 Dir, Oil and Gas, 1998–2002; Dir, Strategy, 2003–05. Director: Laing Engineering 1991–96; European Investment Bank, 1994–96. Gov., Gwyn Jones Sch., 1996–. FRSA 2001. *Recreations:* gardening, reading, music, films. *Address:* Department for Business Enterprise and Regulatory Reform, 1 Victoria Street, SW1H 0ET. *T:* (020) 7215 0414.

DARTMOUTH, 10th Earl of, *cr* 1711; **William Legge;** Baron Dartmouth 1682 Viscount Lewisham 1711; Chartered Accountant; *b* 23 Sept. 1949; *e s* of 9th Earl o Dartmouth and of Raine, Countess Spencer, *qv*; *S* father, 1997. *Educ:* Eton; Chris Church, Oxford; Harvard Business Sch. Secretary, Oxford Union Soc., 1969. Contested (C): Leigh, Lancs, Feb. 1974; Stockport South, Oct. 1974; contested (C) Yorkshire an the Humber Region, Eur. Parly elecns, 1999. Mem., UKIP. Founder, Kirklees Cable *Recreation:* tennis. *Heir:* *b* Hon. Rupert Legge [*b* 1 Jan. 1951; *m* 1984, Victoria, *d* of L. E B. Ottley; one *s* one *d*]. *Address:* Blakelea House, Marsden, near Huddersfield, W Yorks HD7 5AU. *Clubs:* Buck's; Travellers (Paris).

DARTON, Prof. Richard Charles, PhD; FREng, FIChemE; Professor of Engineering Science, since 2000, and Head, Department of Engineering Science, since 2004, University of Oxford; Fellow, Keble College, Oxford, since 1992 (by special election,

1992–2001); *b* 1 July 1948; *s* of Allan John Darton and Beryl Clare Darton (*née* Davies); *m* 1974, Diana Mildred Warrell; two *s* one *d*. *Educ:* King's Sch., Rochester; Univ. of Birmingham (BSc 1970); Downing Coll., Cambridge (PhD 1973). FIChemE 1987. ICI Post-doctoral Res. Fellow, Univ. of Cambridge, 1973–75; various appts, Shell Internat. Petroleum, Netherlands, 1975–91; on secondment to Univ. of Oxford, from Shell UK, 1991–99; Reader in Chem. Engrg, Univ. of Oxford, and Sen. Res. Fellow and Tutor, Keble Coll., Oxford, 2001–. Pres., IChemE, 2008–May 2009 (Council Medal, 2005; Dep. Pres., 2007–08). FREng 2000. *Publication:* (ed jtly) Chemical Engineering: visions of the world, 2003. *Recreations:* Scottish country dancing, reading history. *Address:* Department of Engineering Science, University of Oxford, Parks Road, Oxford OX1 3PJ. *T:* (01865) 273002, *Fax:* (01865) 283310; *e-mail:* richard.darton@eng.ox.ac.uk.

DARVILL, Keith Ernest; Partner, Kenneth Elliott & Rowe, Solicitors, since 1999; *b* 28 May 1948; *s* of Ernest Arthur James Darvill and Ellen May (*née* Clarke); *m* 1971, Julia Betina de Saran; two *s* one *d*. *Educ:* Coll. of Law, Chester. Admitted solicitor, 1981. Port of London Authority: clerical posts, 1967–73; Asst Solicitor, 1973–84; Partner, Duthie Hart and Duthie, Solicitors, 1984–93; sole practitioner, 1993–97. MP (Lab) Upminster, 1997–2001; contested (Lab) same seat, 2001 and 2005. Mem. (Lab), Havering LBC, 2002–. Chairman: Havering Fabian Soc.; Front Line Community Assoc.; Trustee: Upminster Windmill Preservation Soc.; Site Action (Havering). Chm. Govs, Havering Sixth Form Coll., 2002–; Governor: Gaynes Sch., Upminster; Kingswood Sch., Harold Hill. *Recreations:* tennis, gardening. *Address:* Kenneth Elliott & Rowe, 88 South Street, Romford RM1 1SX. *Club:* Cranston Park Lawn Tennis (Upminster).

DARWALL SMITH, Simon Crompton; His Honour Judge Simon Darwall Smith; a Circuit Judge, since 1992; *b* 13 April 1946; *s* of late Randle Darwall Smith and Barbara Darwall Smith (*née* Crompton); *m* 1968, Susan Patricia Moss (*see* S. P. Darwall Smith); two *d*. *Educ:* Charterhouse. Called to the Bar, Gray's Inn, 1968; in practice on Western Circuit, 1968–92; a Recorder, 1986–92. *Recreations:* opera, travel, ballet, theatre, concerts. *Address:* The Law Courts, Small Street, Bristol BS1 2HL. *Club:* Army and Navy.

DARWALL SMITH, Susan Patricia; Her Honour Judge Darwall Smith; DL; a Circuit Judge, since 1992; *b* 27 Oct. 1946; *d* of late George Kenneth Moss, JP and of Jean Margaret Moss (*née* Johnston); *m* 1968, Simon Crompton Darwall Smith, *qv*; two *d*. *Educ:* Howell's Sch., Denbigh. Called to the Bar, Gray's Inn, 1968; in practice on Western Circuit, 1968–92; a Recorder, 1986–92. Gov., Red Maids' Sch., Bristol, 1990–. DL Bristol, 2004. *Recreations:* travel, opera, ballet, theatre, gardening. *Address:* The Law Courts, Small Street, Bristol BS1 2HL. *Club:* Army and Navy.

DARWEN, 3rd Baron *cr* 1946, of Heys-in-Bowland; **Roger Michael Davies;** *b* 28 June 1938; *s* of 2nd Baron Darwen and of Kathleen Dora, *d* of George Sharples Walker; *S* father, 1988; *m* 1961, Gillian Irene, *d* of Eric G. Hardy, Bristol; two *s* three *d*. *Educ:* Bootham School, York. *Heir: s* Hon. Paul Davies, *b* 20 Feb. 1962. *Address:* Labourer's Rest, Green Street, Pleshey, Chelmsford CM3 1HT.

DARWENT, Rt Rev. Frederick Charles; JP; Bishop of Aberdeen and Orkney, 1978–92; *b* Liverpool, 20 April 1927; *y s* of Samuel Darwent and Edith Emily Darwent (*née* Malcolm); *m* 1st, 1949, Edna Lilian (*d* 1981), *o c* of David Waugh and Lily Elizabeth Waugh (*née* McIndoe); twin *d*; 2nd, 1983, Roma Evelyn, *er d* of John Michie and Evelyn Michie (*née* Stephen). *Educ:* Warbreck Sch., Liverpool; Ormskirk Grammar Sch., Lancs; Wells Theological Coll., Somerset. Followed a banking career, 1943–61; War service in Far East with Royal Inniskilling Fusiliers, 1945–48. Deacon 1963; priest 1964, Diocese of Liverpool; Curate of Pemberton, Wigan, 1963–65 (in charge of St Francis, Kitt Green, 1964–65); Rector of: Strichen, 1965–71; New Pitsligo, 1965–78; Fraserburgh, 1971–78; Canon of St Andrew's Cathedral, Aberdeen, 1971; Dean of Aberdeen and Orkney, 1973–78. JP Aberdeen City, 1988. Hon. LTh St Mark's Inst. of Theology, 1974. *Recreations:* amateur stage (acting and production), music (especially jazz), calligraphy. *Address:* 107 Osborne Place, Aberdeen AB25 2DD. *T:* (01224) 646497. *Clubs:* Rotary International; Club of Deir (Aberdeens).

DARWIN, Kenneth; retired civil servant; *b* 24 Sept. 1921; *s* of late Robert Lawrence and Elizabeth Darwin (*née* Swain), Ripon, Yorks; unmarried. *Educ:* Elementary Sch.; Ripon Grammar Sch.; University Coll., Durham; Oflag VIIB (1943–45). BA 1947, MA 1948. Served 2nd Bn Lancs Fus., N Africa, (Captain) POW, 1942–46; TA Captain (Intelligence Corps), 1949–54. Asst Keeper, Public Record Office (NI), 1948; Dep. Keeper of Records of N Ireland, 1955–70; Vis. Lectr in Archives, UC Dublin, 1967–71; Fellow Commoner, Churchill Coll., Cambridge, 1970; Asst Sec., Min. of Commerce (NI), 1970–74; Sen. Asst Sec., Dept of Finance (NI) and Dept of Civil Service (NI), 1974–77; Dep. Sec., Dept of Finance (NI), 1977–81. Dir, Fountain Publishing, Belfast, 1995–. Member: Irish MSS Commn, Dublin, 1955–70; Adv. Bd for New History of Ireland, Royal Irish Acad., 1968–; Trustee: Ulster Historical Foundn, 1956–87; Ulster Museum, 1982–88 (Vice-Chm., 1984–86); Lyric Th., Belfast, 1966–69. Mem., Bangor Drama Club. Ed., Familia: Ulster Genealogical Rev., 1985–93. *Publications:* (ed jtly) Passion and Prejudice: Nationalist-Unionist conflict in Ulster in the 1930s and the founding of the Irish Association, 1993; articles on archives, history and genealogy, in jls and Nat. Trust guides. *Recreations:* travel, piano playing, walking, gardening. *Address:* 18 Seymour Road, Bangor, Co. Down BT19 1BL. *T:* (028) 9146 0718. *Clubs:* Royal Commonwealth Society; Royal British Legion (Bangor, Co. Down).

DARZI, family name of **Baron Darzi of Denham**.

DARZI OF DENHAM, Baron *cr* 2007 (Life Peer), of Gerrards Cross in the county of Buckinghamshire; **Ara Warkes Darzi,** KBE 2002; MD; FRCS, FRCSI, FACS, FRCPSGlas, FMedSci; Paul Hamlyn Professor of Surgery, Imperial College London, since 2005; Consultant Surgeon: St Mary's Hospital, Paddington, since 1994; Royal Marsden Hospital, since 2005; Parliamentary Under-Secretary of State, Department of Health, since 2007; *b* 7 May 1960; adopted British citizenship, 2002; *m* 1991, Wendy Hutchinson; one *s* one *d*. *Educ:* RCSI (MB BCh, BAO 1984); TCD (MD 1992). LRCPI 1984; LRCSI 1984, FRCSI 1992; FRCS 1995; FACS 1998; FRCPSGlas 2003; FMedSci 2003. Consultant Surgeon/Sen. Lectr, Central Middx Hosp., 1993–94; Prof. of Surgery, 1995–, Hd, Div. of Surgery, Anaesthetics and Intensive Care, 2004–07, Imperial Coll., London. FCGI 2004. Hon. FREng 2006; Hon. FRCSE 2005. *Publications:* Laparoscopic Inguinal Hernia Repair, 1994; Laparoscopic Colorectal Surgery, 1995; Clinical Surgery, 1996, 2nd edn 2003; Atlas of Operative Laparoscopy, 1997; over 400 articles in learned jls. *Address:* Imperial College London, St Mary's Hospital Campus, 10th Floor, QEQM Building, Praed Street, W2 1NY. *T:* (020) 7886 1310, *Fax:* (020) 7886 6950; *e-mail:* a.darzi@imperial.ac.uk. *Clubs:* Athenæum, Mosimann's.

DASGUPTA, Partha; Chief Executive Officer, Pension Protection Fund, 2006–June 2009 (Director of Investment and Finance, 2005–06); *b* 23 Jan. 1969; *s* of Purnendu Dasgupta and Chandana Dasgupta; *m* 2000, Uttara Moorthy. *Educ:* Links Primary Sch., Edinburgh; Leith Acad.; Heriot-Watt Univ. (BSc 1st Cl. Maths 1990). Valuation Analyst, Prudential, 1991–94; Barclays Global Investors: Associate, 1994–98; Principal, 1998–2003; Man. Dir, 2003–05. *Recreations:* reading, yoga, hill walking in Scotland. *Address:* c/o Pension Protection Fund, Knollys House, 17 Addiscombe Road, Croydon CR0 6SR.

DASGUPTA, Sir Partha (Sarathi), Kt 2002; PhD; FRS 2004; FBA 1989; Frank Ramsey Professor of Economics, Cambridge University, since 1994 (Professor of Economics, 1985–94), and Fellow of St John's College, Cambridge, since 1985; *b* 17 Nov. 1942; *s* of late Prof. Amiya Dasgupta and Shanti Dasgupta, Santiniketan, India; *m* 1968, Carol Margaret, *d* of Prof. James Meade, CB, FBA; one *s* two *d*. *Educ:* Univ. of Delhi (BSc Hons 1962); Univ. of Cambridge (BA 1965, PhD 1968; Stevenson Prize, 1967). Res. Fellow, Trinity Hall, Cambridge, 1968–71, Supernumerary Fellow, 1971–74; Lectr, 1971–75, Reader, 1975–78, Prof. of Econs, 1978–84, LSE (Hon. Fellow, 1994); Prof. of Econs and Philosophy, Stanford Univ., 1989–92. Sen. Res. Fellow, Inst. for Policy Reform, 1992–94. Visiting Professor: Stanford Univ., 1974–75 and 1983–84; Delhi Univ., 1978; Harvard Univ., 1987; Princeton Univ., 1988. Res. Advr, WIDER (UN Univ., 1989–94); Univ. Fellow, Resources for the Future, Washington, 1998–. Mem., Expert Panel on Environmtl Health, WHO, 1975–85. Chm., Beijer Internat. Inst. of Ecological Econs, Stockholm, 1991–97; Member: Science Cttee, Santa Fe Inst., 1992–96; External Adv. Council, World Bank Inst., 1999–; Millennium Ecosystem Assessment Panel, 2000–05; External Adv. Bd, Earth Inst., Columbia Univ., 2002–. President: European Econ. Assoc., 1999; REconS, 1998–2001; Sect. F, BAAS, 2006; Pres.-elect, European Assoc. of Environmental and Resource Economists. For. Hon. Mem., Amer. Acad. of Arts and Scis, 1991; For. Mem., Royal Swedish Acad. of Scis, 1991; Hon. Mem., Amer. Econ. Assoc., 1997; Mem., Pontifical Acad. of Social Scis, 1998; For. Associate, US Nat. Acad. of Scis, 2001; For. Mem., Amer. Phil Soc., 2005. Fellow: Econometric Soc., 1975; Third World Acad. of Sci., 2002. Dr *hc* Wageningen, 2000; Catholic Univ. of Louvain, 2007. Jt winner, Volvo Envmt Prize, 2002; John Kenneth Galbraith Award, Amer. Agricl Econs Assoc., 2007. *Publications:* (with S. Marglin and A. K. Sen) Guidelines for Project Evaluation, 1972; (with G. Heal) Economic Theory and Exhaustible Resources, 1979; The Control of Resources, 1982; (with K. Binmore) Economic Organizations as Games, 1986; (with K. Binmore) The Economics of Bargaining, 1987; (with P. Stoneman) Economic Policy and Technological Performance, 1987; An Inquiry into Well-Being and Destitution, 1993; (with K. G. Mäler) The Environment and Emerging Development Issues, vols 1 and 2, 1997; (with I. Serageldin) Social Capital: a multifaceted perspective, 1999; Human Well-Being and the Natural Environment, 2001; Economics: a very short introduction, 2007; articles on develt planning, optimum population, taxation and trade, welfare and justice, nat. resources, game theory, indust. org. and technical progress, poverty and unemployment, in Econ. Jl, Econometrica, Rev. of Econ. Stud., etc. *Address:* 1 Dean Drive, Holbrook Road, Cambridge CB1 7SW. *T:* (01223) 212179. *Club:* MCC.

DASH, Penelope Jane; Health Care Expert, McKinsey & Co., since 2002; *b* 27 Jan. 1963; *d* of Hugo and Margaret Dash; *m* 1998, Guy Palmer; three *s*. *Educ:* Robinson Coll., Cambridge (BA Hons 1984); Middlesex Hosp. Med. Sch., London Univ. (MB BS 1987); LSHTM (MSc 1992); Stanford Univ. (MBA 1994). MRCP 1990. Jun. hosp. posts, UCH and Middlesex Hosps, 1987–88; Barnet Gen. Hosp., 1988; Northwich P Hosp., 1988–90; Registrar in Public Health Medicine, NW Thames RHA, 1990–92; Mgt Consultant, Boston Consulting Gp, 1994–99; Hd of Strategy and Planning, DoH, 2000–01.

DASHWOOD, Prof. (Arthur) Alan, CBE 2004; Professor of European Law, University of Cambridge, since 1995; Fellow, Sidney Sussex College, Cambridge, since 1995 (Vice-Master, 1997–2000); *b* 18 Oct. 1941; *s* of late Alan Stanley Dashwood and of Dorothy Mary Dashwood (*née* Childe); *m* 1971, Julie Rosalind Pashley. *Educ:* Michaelhouse, Natal, SA; Rhodes Univ., Grahamstown, SA (BA Hons 1962); Oriel Coll., Oxford (MA). Called to the Bar, Inner Temple, 1969, Bencher, 2001. Asst Lectr, Dept of Civil Law, Univ. of Glasgow, 1966–67; Lecturer: Dept of Law, UCW, Aberystwyth, 1968–73; Centre of European Governmental Studies, Univ. of Edinburgh, 1973–75; Reader, Univ. of Sussex, 1975–78; Legal Sec. to Advocate General, Court of Justice of ECs, 1978–80; Prof. of Law, Univ. of Leicester, 1980–87; Dir, Legal Service, Council of EU, 1987–94. Editor: European Law Rev., 1975–91; Common Market Law Rev., 1995–. *Publications:* The Substantive Law of the EEC, 1980, 5th edn (with D. Wyatt) as Wyatt and Dashwood's European Community Law, 2006; contrib. to legal jls. *Recreation:* salmon and trout fishing. *Address:* Sidney Sussex College, Cambridge CB2 3HU. *T:* (01223) 338874; Henderson Chambers, 2 Harcourt Buildings, Temple, EC4Y 9DB. *T:* (020) 7583 9020. *Club:* Athenæum; Porcupines.

DASHWOOD, Sir Edward (John Francis), 12th Bt *cr* 1707, of West Wycombe, Buckinghamshire; Premier Baronet of Great Britain; *b* 25 Sept. 1964; *o s* of Sir Francis Dashwood, 11th Bt and Victoria Ann Elizabeth Gwynne (*née* de Rutzen); *S* father, 2000; *m* 1989, Lucinda Nell (*née* Miesegaes); two *s* one *d*. *Educ:* Eton; Reading Univ. (BSc Estate Mgt). MRICS. Land Agent. *Recreations:* shooting, fishing, tennis, bridge. *Heir: s* George Francis Dashwood, *b* 17 June 1992. *Address:* West Wycombe Park, High Wycombe, Bucks HP14 3AJ. *T:* (01494) 524411/2. *Clubs:* White's, Pitt, Daniel's; Shikar; Eton Ramblers.

DASHWOOD, Sir Richard (James), 9th Bt *cr* 1684, of Kirtlington Park; TD 1987; Senior Director, EFG Harris Allday (formerly Partner, Harris Allday Lea & Brooks, then Harris Allday), stockbrokers; *b* 14 Feb. 1950; *s* of Sir Henry George Massy Dashwood, 8th Bt, and Susan Mary (*d* 1985), *er d* of late Major V. R. Montgomerie-Charrington, Hunsdon House, Herts; *S* father, 1972; *m* 1984, Kathryn Ann (marr. diss. 1993), *er d* of Frank Mahon, Eastbury, Berks; one *s*. *Educ:* Maidwell Hall Preparatory Sch.; Eton College. Commissioned 14th/20th King's Hussars, 1969, later King's Royal Hussars; T&AVR, 1973– (Major 1992). *Heir: s* Frederick George Mahon Dashwood, *b* 29 Jan. 1988. *Address:* Ledwell Cottage, Sandford St Martin, Oxfordshire OX7 7AN. *T:* (01608) 683267.

DATTA, Dr Naomi, FRS 1985; Professor Emeritus, London University; *b* 17 Sept. 1922; *d* of Alexander and Ellen Henrietta Goddard; *m* 1943, S. P. Datta; two *d* one *s*. *Educ:* St Mary's Sch., Wantage; University Coll. London; W London Hosp. Med Sch. MB BS (external); MD London. Junior medical posts, 1946–47; Bacteriologist in PHLS, 1947–57; Lectr, later Prof. of Microbiol Genetics, RPMS, London Univ., 1957–84; retired 1984. *Publications:* papers on the genetics and epidemiology of antibiotic resistance in bacteria. *Recreations:* gardening, cooking, travelling. *Address:* 9 Duke's Avenue, W4 2AA. *T:* (020) 8995 7562.

DAUBENY DE MOLEYNS, family name of **Baron Ventry**.

DAUNCEY, Brig. Michael Donald Keen, DSO 1945; DL; *b* 11 May 1920; *o s* of late Thomas Gough Dauncey and Alice Dauncey (*née* Keen); *m* 1945, Marjorie Kathleen, *d* of H. W. Neep, FCA; one *s* two *d*. *Educ:* King Edward's School, Birmingham; Inter. Exam., Inst. of Chartered Accountants. Commissioned, 22nd (Cheshire) Regt, 1941; seconded to Glider Pilot Regt, 1943; Arnhem, 1944 (wounded three times; taken prisoner, later escaped); MA to GOC-in-C, Greece, 1946–47; seconded to Para. Regt, 1948–49; Staff Coll., 1950; Instructor, RMA, 1957–58; CO, 1st Bn 22nd (Cheshire) Regt, 1963–66,

BAOR and UN peace keeping force, Cyprus; DS plans, JSSC, 1966–68; Comdt, Jungle Warfare Sch., 1968–69; Comdt, Support Weapons Wing, Sch. of Infantry, 1969–72; Defence and Military Attaché, Madrid, 1973–75; retired 1976. Col, 22nd (Cheshire) Regt, 1978–85; Hon. Col, 1st Cadet Bn, Glos Regt (ACF), 1981–90. President: Glider Pilot Regtl Assoc., 1994–98; Double Hills Arnhem Commemoration-1978, 1999–; Vice Pres., Arnhem 1944 Veterans' Club, 2007–; Leader, Airborne Pilgrimage to Arnhem, 2000, 2008. DL Glos 1983. *Recreations:* travelling, tennis; also under-gardener. *Address:* Uley Lodge Coach House, Uley, Dursley, Glos GL11 5SN. *T:* (01453) 860216. *Club:* Army and Navy.

DAUNT, Patrick Eldon; Head of Bureau for Action in favour of Disabled People, EEC, 1982–87, retired; international consultant on education and disability; *b* 19 Feb. 1925; *s* of Dr Francis Eldon Daunt and Winifred Doggett Daunt (*née* Wells); *m* 1958, Jean Patricia, *d* of Lt-Col Percy Wentworth Hargreaves and of Joan (*née* Holford); three *s* one *d*. *Educ:* Rugby Sch.; Wadham Coll., Oxford (BA, 1st Cl. Hons Lit. Hum., 1949, MA 1954). Housemaster, Christ's Hosp., 1959; Headmaster, Thomas Bennett Comprehensive Sch., Crawley, 1965. Chm., Campaign for Comprehensive Educn, 1971–73; Principal Administrator, EEC, 1974–82. Vis. Fellow, London Inst. of Educn, 1988–94. Chm., ASBAH, 1990–95. UNESCO consultant, special educn in Romania, 1992–97; ILO consultant, 1998–99. Ravenswood Foundn Internat. Award, 1992. *Publications:* Comprehensive Values, 1975; Meeting Disability, a European Response, 1991; (ed) Teacher Education for Special Needs in Europe, 1995. *Recreations:* books, botany. *Address:* 4 Bourn Bridge Road, Little Abington, Cambridge CB21 6BJ. *T:* (01223) 891485. *Club:* Oxford and Cambridge.

DAUNT, Sir Timothy Lewis Achilles, KCMG 1989 (CMG 1982); HM Diplomatic Service, retired; Lieutenant-Governor of the Isle of Man, 1995–2000; *b* 11 Oct. 1935; *s* of L. H. G. Daunt and Margery (*née* Lewis Jones); *m* 1962, Patricia Susan Knight; one *s* two *d*. *Educ:* Sherborne; St Catharine's Coll., Cambridge. 8th KRI Hussars, 1954–56. Entered Foreign Office, 1959; Ankara, 1960; FO, 1964; Nicosia, 1967; Private Sec. to Permanent Under-Sec. of State, FCO, 1970; Bank of England, 1972; UK Mission, NY, 1973; Counsellor, OECD, Paris, 1975; Head of South European Dept, FCO, 1978–81; Associate at Centre d'études et de recherches internationales, Paris, 1982; Minister and Dep. UK Perm. Rep. to NATO, Brussels, 1982–85; Asst Under-Sec. of State (Defence), FCO, 1985–86; Ambassador to Turkey, 1986–92; Dep. Under-Sec. of State (Defence), FCO, 1992–95. Chm., British Inst. of Archaeol., Ankara, 1995–2006. Chairman: Anglo-Turkish Soc., 2001–; Ottoman Fund Ltd, 2005–. *Address:* 20 Ripplevale Grove, N1 1HU.

DAUNTON, Prof. Martin James, PhD, LittD; FBA 1997; Professor of Economic History, University of Cambridge, since 1997; Master of Trinity Hall, Cambridge, since 2004; *b* 7 Feb. 1949; *s* of Ronald James Daunton and Dorothy May Daunton (*née* Bellett); *m* 1984, Claire Hilda Gabriel Gobbi. *Educ:* Barry Grammar Sch.; Univ. of Nottingham (BA 1970); Univ. of Kent (PhD 1974); LittD Cambridge, 2005. Lectr in Economic History, Univ. of Durham, 1973–79; University College London: Lectr in Economic History, 1979–85; Reader, 1985–89; Prof. of Modern History, 1989–92; Astor Prof. of British History, 1992–97; Fellow, Churchill Coll., Cambridge, 1997–2004; Chm., Faculty of History, 2001–03; Sch. of Humanities and Soc. Scis, 2003–05, Cambridge Univ. Vis. Fellow, ANU, 1985, 1994; Vis. Prof., Nihon Univ., Tokyo, 2000. Trustee: Nat. Maritime Mus., 2002–; Barings Archive, 2007–; Syndic, Fitzwilliam Mus., 2006–. Pres., RHistS, 2004–08 (Hon. Treas., 1986–91; Vice-Pres., 1996–2000; Convener, Studies in History, 1994–2000). Chair, Inst. of Historical Res., 1994–98; Mem. Adv. Bd, Inst. of Advanced Studies, Univ. of Durham, 2006–. Consultant Ed., Oxford DNB, 1993–98; Member: Editorial Board: Historical Jl, 2000–; English Historical Rev., 2001–. Hon. DLitt UCL, 2006. *Publications:* Coal Metropolis: Cardiff 1870–1914, 1977; House and Home in the Victorian City, 1983; Royal Mail: the Post Office since 1840, 1985; A Property Owning Democracy?, 1987; Progress and Poverty: an economic and social history of Britain 1700–1850, 1995; Cambridge Urban History of Britain, 2000; Trusting Leviathan: the politics of taxation in Britain 1799–1914, 2001; Just Taxes: the politics of taxation in Britain 1914–79, 2002; Organisation of Knowledge in Victorian Britain, 2005; Wealth and Welfare: an economic and social history of Britain 1851–1951, 2007; State and Market in Victorian Britain, 2008; articles in learned jls. *Recreations:* collecting modern ceramics, opera, architectural tourism. *Address:* Master's Lodge, Trinity Hall, Trinity Lane, Cambridge CB2 1TJ. *T:* (01223) 332540; *e-mail:* mjd42@cam.ac.uk. *Clubs:* Reform, Oxford and Cambridge.

DAUSSET, Prof. Jean Baptiste Gabriel Joachim; Grand Croix de la Légion d'Honneur; Professeur de Médecine Expérimentale au Collège de France, 1977–87; *b* 19 Oct. 1916; *s* of Henri Dausset and Elizabeth Brullard; *m* 1962, Rose Mayoral; one *s* one *d*. *Educ:* Lycée Michelet, Paris; Faculty of Medicine, University of Paris. Associate Professor, 1958–68, Professor of Immunohaematology, 1968–77, University of Paris. Institut Nationale de la Santé et de la Recherche Médicale: Director of Research Unit on Immunogenetics of Human Transplantation, 1968–84; Centre National de la Recherche Scientifique: Co-Director, Oncology and Immunohaematology Laboratory, 1968–84. Gairdner Foundn Prize, 1977; Koch Foundn Prize, 1978; Wolf Foundn Prize, 1978; Nobel Prize for Physiology or Medicine, 1980. *Publications:* Immuno-hématologie biologique et clinique, 1956; (with F. T. Rapaport) Human Transplantation, 1968; (with G. Snell and S. Nathanson) Histocompatibility, 1976; (with M. Fougereau) Immunology 1980, 1980; (with M. Pla) HLA, 1985; Clin d'oeil à la vie (autobiog.), 1998. *Recreation:* plastic art. *Address:* 44 rue des Ecoles, 75005 Paris, France.

DAVAN WETTON, Hilary John; Conductor-in-residence, Wellington College, since 2007; conductor; *b* 23 Dec. 1943; *s* of late Eric Davan Wetton, CBE and (Kathleen) Valerie Davan Wetton (*née* Edwards); *m* 1st, 1964, Elizabeth Jane Tayler; three *d*; 2nd, 1989, Alison Mary Moncrieff Kelly; one *s* one *d*; 3rd, 2003, Dr Antonia Louise Vincent; one *d*. *Educ:* Westminster Sch.; Royal Coll. of Music (ARCM); Brasenose Coll., Oxford (BA, MA, DipEd). Director of Music: St Alban's Sch., 1965–67; Cranleigh Sch., 1967–74; Stantonbury Music Centre, 1974–78; St Paul's Girls' Sch., 1978–93; Tonbridge Sch., 1993–2006. Conductor: Guildford Choral Soc., 1968–; Milton Keynes City Orch., 1974–; Holst Singers, 1978–91; City of London Choir, 1989–; Wren Orch., 1990–; Scottish Schools Orch., 1984–95; Edinburgh Youth Orch., 1994–97; guest conducting and recording with Philharmonia, LPO, Royal Phil. Orch., BBC Concert Orch., Ulster Orch., orchestras in Bulgaria, Iceland, USA, Australia. Presenter, Classic FM Masterclass. Member: RSA; Pepys Soc. Hon. MA Open, 1984; Hon. DMus De Montfort, 1994. Diapason d'Or for Holst recording, 1994. *Publications:* contrib. musical jls and Guardian. *Recreation:* tennis. *Address:* Carrsleigh, Church Road, Southborough, Kent TN4 0RT. *Club:* Garrick.

See also P. H. D. Wetton.

DAVENPORT; see Bromley-Davenport.

DAVENPORT, (Arthur) Nigel; President, British Actors' Equity Association, 1986–92; *b* 23 May 1928; *s* of Arthur Henry Davenport and Katherine Lucy (*née* Meiklejohn); *m* 1st, 1951, Helena White (*d* 1978); one *s* one *d*; 2nd, 1972, Maria Aitken, *qv* (marr. diss.); one

s. *Educ:* Cheltenham Coll.; Trinity Coll., Oxford (MA). Entered acting profession, 1951; for first ten years worked almost exclusively in theatre; original mem. English Stage Co. at Royal Court Th., 1956; A Taste of Honey, on Broadway, 1960; television and films, 1961–; Murder is Easy, Duke of York's, 1993; Our Betters, Chichester, 1997; toured England: King Lear (title rôle), 1986; The Old Country, 1989; Sleuth, 1990; The Constant Wife, 1994–95; Brideshead Revisited, 1995; On That Day, 1996; *films:* Look Back in Anger, 1958; Peeping Tom, 1960; In the Cool of the Day, 1963; The Third Secret, 1964; A High Wind in Jamaica, Life at the Top, Sands of the Kalahari, Where the Spies Are, 1965; A Man for All Seasons, 1966; Play Dirty, Sebastian/Mr Sebastian, The Strange Affair, 1968; Royal Hunt of the Sun, Sinful Davey, The Virgin Soldiers, 1969; The Last Valley, The Mind of Mr Soames, No Blade of Grass, 1970; Mary, Queen of Scots, Villain, 1971; Living Free, 1972; Charlie One-Eye, 1973; La Regenta, Phase IV, 1974; The Island of Dr Moreau, Stand Up Virgin Soldiers, 1977; The Omega Connection, Zulu Dawn, 1979; Chariots of Fire, Den Tuchtigen gehört Die Welt, Nighthawks, 1981; Strata, 1982; Greystoke, 1984; Caravaggio, 1986; Without a Clue, 1988; The Cutter, 1992; Hotel Shanghai, 1995; La Revuelta de El Coyote, 1997; David Copperfield, 1999; *television:* South Riding; George III in The Prince Regent; Howard's Way, 1987–88, 1990; Trainer, 1991; The Treasure Seekers, The Opium Wars, 1996; Longitude, 1999. Mem. Council, British Actors' Equity, 1976 (Vice-Pres., 1978–82, 1985–86). *Recreations:* gardening, horse racing.

See also H. B. Davenport.

DAVENPORT, Major (retd) David John Cecil, CBE 1989; DL; Member, Rural Development Commission, 1982–90 (Deputy Chairman, April–Oct. 1988); *b* 28 Oct. 1934; *s* of late Major John Lewes Davenport, DL, JP, and Louise Aline Davenport; *m* 1st, 1959, Jennifer Burness (marr. diss. 1969); two *d*; 2nd, 1971, Lindy Jane Baker; one *s*. *Educ:* Eton College; Royal Military Academy, Sandhurst. Commnd into Grenadier Guards, 1954, retired 1967. RAC, Cirencester, 1968–69. Chairman, Leominster District Council, 1975–76. Chm., CoSIRA, 1982–88. Chm., Regional Adv. Cttee of the Forestry Commn (SW), 1974–87; Pres., Royal Forestry Soc., 1991–93. DL 1974, High Sheriff, 1989–90, Hereford and Worcester. *Address:* Mansel Lacy House, Hereford HR4 7HQ. *T:* (01981) 590224. *Clubs:* Boodle's, MCC.

DAVENPORT, Hugo Benedick; editorial consultant, freelance writer and broadcaster, since 2001; *b* 6 June 1953; *s* of Arthur Nigel Davenport, *qv*; *m* 1988, Sarah Mollison; one *s* one *d*. *Educ:* Westminster Sch.; Univ. of Sussex (BA 1st Cl. Hons). With Visnews Ltd, 1976–77; trainee journalist, Liverpool Daily Post & Echo, 1977–80; reporter/diarist, Observer, 1981–84; feature writer, Mail on Sunday, 1985–87; news feature writer, then film critic, Daily Telegraph, 1987–96; contributor, BBC World Service, 1992–96; editor: FT New Media Markets, 1997–2000; Broadband Media, 2000–01; Sen. Consultant, Caseworks Ltd, 2005–. FRSA 2003. Envmtl Reporting Award, Population Inst., Washington, 1988. *Publication:* Days that Shook the World, 2003. *Recreations:* walking, reading, music, painting. *Address:* 6 Ann's Close, Kinnerton Street, SW1X 8EG; *e-mail:* hugo.davenport@tiscali.co.uk.

DAVENPORT, Maurice Hopwood, FCIB; Director, First National Finance Corporation plc, 1985–95; *b* 19 March 1925; *s* of Richard and Elizabeth Davenport; *m* 1954, Sheila Timms; one *s* two *d*. *Educ:* Rivington and Blackrod Grammar Sch. FIB 1982. Served RN, 1943–46. Joined Williams Deacon's Bank, 1940; Sec., 1960; Asst Gen. Man., 1969; Dir, 1978–85, Man. Dir, 1982–85, Williams & Glyn's Bank; Dir, Royal Bank of Scotland Gp and Royal Bank of Scotland, 1982–85. *Recreations:* walking, gardening, reading. *Address:* Pines, Dormans Park, East Grinstead, West Sussex RH19 2LX. *T:* (01342) 870439.

DAVENPORT, Michael Hayward, MBE 1994; HM Diplomatic Service; Director for Russia, Central Asia and South Caucasus, Foreign and Commonwealth Office, since 2007; *b* 25 Sept. 1961; *s* of Montague Davenport and late Olive Margaret Davenport (*née* Brabner); *m* 1992, Lavinia Sophia Braun; one *s* two *d*. *Educ:* Gonville and Caius Coll., Cambridge (BA 1983, MA 1985); Coll. of Law, London. Lectr, Graz Univ., Austria, 1983–84; with Macfarlanes, Solicitors, 1986–88; admitted solicitor, 1988; joined FCO, 1988: est. British Know-How Fund for Poland, Warsaw, 1990–93; Hd, Peacekeeping Section, FCO, 1993–95; First Sec. (Political), Moscow, 1996–99; Dir of Trade Promotion and Consul-Gen., Warsaw, 2000–03; Dep. Hd of Mission, Cairo, 2004–07. *Recreations:* tennis, German literature, cooking. *Address:* c/o Foreign and Commonwealth Office, King Charles Street, SW1A 2AH.

DAVENPORT, Nigel; see Davenport, A. N.

DAVENPORT, Sara Jane; Founder, and Trustee, Breast Cancer Haven (formerly Haven Trust), since 1997; *b* 11 March 1962; *d* of David Davenport and Jennifer Davenport (*née* Burness, now Zulidis Duridis); *m* 1988, Adrian Kyriazi (marr. diss. 2002); two *d*. *Educ:* N Foreland Lodge; Fitzwilliam Coll., Cambridge (BA 1983). Publicity Dept, Hodder & Stoughton, 1983–84; Manager, Cadogan Gall., 1985–87; Sara Davenport Gall., Walton St, London, 1987–97; founded Haven Trust (breast cancer charity), 1997; opened London Haven, 2000, Hereford Haven, 2004. Trng and work as kinesiologist, 2002–. *Recreations:* travel, friends, providing a taxi service to my children! *Address:* 58 Chelsea Park Gardens, SW3 6AE. *T:* (020) 7352 4032; *e-mail:* saradavenport@hotmail.com.

DAVENPORT-HANDLEY, Sir David (John), Kt 1980; OBE 1962; JP; DL; Chairman, Clipsham Quarry Co., since 1947; *b* 2 Sept. 1919; *s* of John Davenport-Handley, JP; *m* 1943, Leslie Mary Goldsmith; one *d* (one *s* decd). *Educ:* RNC Dartmouth RN retd 1947. Chm., Rutland and Stamford Conservative Assoc., 1952–65; Treasurer, East Midlands Area Conservative Assoc., 1965–71, Chm. 1971–77; Vice-Chm., Nat. Union of Conservative & Unionist Assocs, 1977–79, Chm., 1979–80. Member: Consumers' Cttees for GB and for England and Wales, 1956–65; Parole Bd, 1981–84. Chm., Rutland Historic Churches Preservation Trust, 1987–2005. President: E Midlands Area Cons. Assoc., 1987–94; Nat. Union of Cons. and Unionist Assocs, 1990–91. Governor, Swinton Conservative Coll., 1973–77; Chairman: Board of Visitors, Ashwell Prison, 1955–73; Governors, Casterton Community Coll., 1960–78; Trustee, Oakham Sch., 1970–86. JP 1948, High Sheriff 1954, DL 1962, Vice-Lieutenant 1972, Rutland. Chm., Rutland Petty Sessional Div., 1957–84; DL Leicestershire 1974. *Recreations:* gardening, music. *Address:* Clipsham Hall, Oakham, Rutland, Leics LE15 7SE. *T:* (01780) 410204.

DAVENTRY, 4th Viscount *cr* 1943; **James Edward FitzRoy Newdegate;** Director R. K. Harrison Insurance Brokers Ltd; *b* 27 July 1960; *s* of 3rd Viscount Daventry and Hon. Rosemary, *e d* of 1st Baron Norrie, GCMG, GCVO, CB, DSO, MC; *S* father, 2000; *m* 1994, Georgia, *yr d* of John Stuart Lodge; one *s* two *d*. *Educ:* Milton Abbey; RAC Cirencester (MRAC). Gov., The Lady Katherine Leveson Charity. Patron, Mary Ann Evans Hospice. *Recreations:* shooting, fishing, racing, golf, farming, occasional gardening. *Heir:* *s* Hon. Humphrey John FitzRoy Newdegate, *b* 23 Nov. 1995. *Address:* Arbury, Nuneaton, Warwickshire CV10 7PT. *Clubs:* White's, Turf, MCC.

DAVEY, Alan; Chief Executive, Arts Council England, since 2008; *b* 12 Nov. 1960; *s* of William Patrick Davey and Alwyn Davey (*née* Dorrington); partner, Patrick Feeny, *qv. Educ:* Univ. of Birmingham (BA Hons (English Lang. and Lit.) 1982); Merton Coll., Oxford (MLitt (English) 1985); Birkbeck Coll., London (MA Hist. 1998). Admin. Trainee, DHSS, 1985; Sec. to Inquiry into Child Abuse in Cleveland, 1987; Private Sec. to Minister of State for Health, 1988–90; Hd, AIDS Treatment and Care, DoH, 1990–92; Hd, Nat. Lottery Bill Team, DNH, 1992–93; Principal Private Sec. to Sec. of State for Nat. Heritage, 1993–94; Hd, European Business, Medicines Control Agency, 1995–97; Sec., Royal Commn on Long Term Care, 1997–99; Fulbright/Helen Hamlyn Scholar, 1999; Hd, Arts Div., 2001–03; Dir of Arts and Culture, subseq. of Culture, 2003–08, DCMS. *Recreations:* music, football, medieval Scandinavian literature, ancient history, cultural theory, Apple Macintosh computers. *Address:* Arts Council England, 14 Great Peter Street, SW1P 3NQ. *T:* (020) 7973 5191; *e-mail:* alan.davey@artscouncil.org.uk. *Club:* Two Brydges.

DAVEY, Hon. Sir David Herbert P.; *see* Penry-Davey.

DAVEY, Edward Jonathan; MP (Lib Dem) Kingston and Surbiton, since 1997; *b* 25 Dec. 1965; *s* of late John George Davey and Nina Joan (*née* Stanbrook); *m* 2005, Emily Jane Gasson; one *s. Educ:* Nottingham High Sch.; Jesus Coll., Oxford (BA 1st Cl. Hons PPE); Birkbeck Coll., London (MSc Econs). Sen. Econs Advr to Lib Dem MPs, 1989–93; Mgt Consultant, Omega Partners, 1993–97. Lib Dem spokesman: on econ. affairs, 1997–2001; for London, 2000–01; on Treasury affairs, 2001–02; on ODPM affairs, 2002–05; for education and skills, 2005–06; for trade and industry, 2006; on foreign affairs, 2007–; Chm., Lib Dem Campaigns and Communications, 2006–; Chief of Staff to Lib Dem Leader, 2006–07. Mem., Treasury Select Cttee, 1999–2001. FRSA 2001. Hon. Testimonial, RHS, and Cert. of Commendation from Chief Constable of Brit. Transport Police (for rescuing a woman who had fallen on the track at Clapham Junction), 1995. *Recreations:* walking, music. *Address:* House of Commons, SW1A 0AA. *T:* (020) 7219 3512; *e-mail:* daveye@parliament.uk. *Clubs:* National Liberal; Surbiton (Surbiton).

DAVEY, Eric; Chairman, Sea Fish Industry Authority, 1996–2002 (Deputy Chairman, 1990–96); *b* 16 Jan. 1933; *s* of William James Davey and Doris Evelynne Davey; *m* 1955, Janet Nicholson; two *d. Educ:* Woodbridge Sch.; Ilminster Sch. With Bank of England, 1953–88, Agent, Newcastle Br., 1980–88; Newcastle Building Society: Dir, 1988–2001; Dep. Chm., 1992–98; Chm., 1998–2001; Pres., 2001–04. *Recreations:* foreign travel, motoring, reading, theatre.

DAVEY, Francis, MA; Headmaster of Merchant Taylors' School, 1974–82; *b* 23 March 1932; *er s* of Wilfred Henry Davey, BSc and Olive (*née* Geeson); *m* 1st, 1960, Margaret Filby Lake, MA Oxon, AMA (marr. diss. 2004), *o d* of Harold Lake, DMus Oxon, FRCO; one *s* one *d;* 2nd, 2005, Patricia Quaife, *er d* of late Alfred Grover Quaife. *Educ:* Plymouth Coll.; New Coll., Oxford (Hon. Exhibr); Corpus Christi Coll., Cambridge (Schoolmaster Fellow Commoner). 1st cl. Class. Hon. Mods 1953, 2nd cl. Lit. Hum. 1955, BA 1955, MA 1958. RAF, 1950–51; Classical Upper Sixth Form Master, Dulwich Coll., 1955–60; Head of Classics Dept, Warwick Sch., 1960–66; Headmaster, Dr Morgan's Grammar Sch., Bridgwater, 1966–73. *Publications:* (with R. Pascoe) The Camino Portugués, 1997; William Wey, 2000; (with P. Quaife) The Camino Inglés, 2000; articles in Enciclopedia dello Spettacolo, Classical Review, Jl of Royal Instn of Cornwall, Devon and Cornwall Notes and Queries. *Recreations:* Rugby, swimming, gardening, travel. *Address:* 1 North Street, Topsham, Exeter, Devon EX3 0AP. *T:* and *Fax:* (01392) 873251. *Clubs:* East India, Devonshire, Sports and Public Schools; Union (Oxford).

DAVEY, Grenville; artist; Visiting Professor, University of the Arts, London (formerly London Institute), since 1997; *b* 28 April 1961; *s* of Clifford Henry and Lillian Joyce Davey. *Educ:* Goldsmiths' Coll., London. Exhibitions: Lisson Gall., London, 1987; Stichting De Appel Foundn, Amsterdam, 1990; Kunsthalle, Berne, 1991; Kunstverein für die Rheinlande und Westfalen, Dusseldorf, 1992; Le Crypte Jules-Noriac, Limoges, 1993; Württembergisher, Kunstverein, Stuttgart, 1994; Henry Moore Foundn, Dean Clough Foundn, 1994; Mus. of Modern Art, Vienna, Kunstverein, Hanover, 1996; Odense, Denmark, and Yorks Sculpture Park, 1999; Peggy Guggenheim, Venice, 2002; LSHTM, 2004; Tate Modern, 2005; William Morris Gall., London, 2006; No 1 Canada Square, London, 2007. Turner Prize, 1992. *Recreation:* work.

DAVEY, Jon Colin; Chairman, Media Matrix Partnership, 1996–2003; *b* 16 June 1938; *s* of late Frederick John Davey and Dorothy Mary Davey; *m* 1962, Ann Patricia Streames; two *s* one *d. Educ:* Raynes Park Grammar Sch. Joined Home Office, 1957; served in Civil Defence, Immigration, Criminal Policy, Prison and Criminal Justice Depts; Asst Sec., Broadcasting Dept, 1981–85; Dir-Gen., Cable Authy, 1985–90; Dir of Cable and Satellite, ITC, 1991–96; Dir, Communications Equity Associates Internat., 1996–98. Asst Sec. Franks Cttee on Sect. 2 of Official Secrets Act, 1971–72; Secretary: Williams Cttee on Obscenity and Film Censorship, 1977–79; Hunt Inquiry into Cable Expansion and Broadcasting Policy, 1982. Vice-Chm., Media Policy Cttee, Council of Europe, 1983–84; Member: British Screen Adv. Council, 1990–96; Adv. Panel on Public Appointments, DCMS, 1999–2007. Ed., Insight, 1997–2008. Hon. Fellow, Soc. of Cable Television Engrs, 1994. Silver Medal, RTS, 1999. *Recreations:* lawnmaking, Bach, English countryside. *Address:* 71 Hare Lane, Claygate, Esher, Surrey KT10 0QX. *T:* (01372) 810106; *e-mail:* joncdavey@ntlworld.com.

DAVEY, Julian; mountaineer and mountain leader, since 1998; *b* 24 July 1946; *s* of Frederick Victor Davey and Dorothy Davey (*née* Stokes); *m* 1971, Prof. Katherine O'Donovan (marr. diss. 2004); one *d; m* 2007, Dr Kate Keohane. *Educ:* Kingston Grammar Sch.; Selwyn Coll., Cambridge; Inst. of Education, London Univ. (MA 1973). British Council: Ethiopia, 1969–72; E Africa Dept, 1973–75; Mgt Accountant, 1975–78; Malaysia, 1978–81; Dep. Controller, Finance, 1981–85; Dir, Hong Kong, 1985–90; Regl Dir, Asia-Pacific, 1992–94; Internat. Advr, Anglia Polytechnic Univ., 1994–97. Chm., Hesket Newmarket Brewery, 2000–. *Recreations:* climbing, ski-mountaineering, caving, performing arts, landscape gardening. *Address:* Potts Gill, Caldbeck, Cumbria CA7 8LB. *T:* (016974) 78773. *Clubs:* Royal Commonwealth Society, Alpine; Eagle Ski; Eden Valley Mountaineering; Hong Kong (Hong Kong).

DAVEY, Marcus John; Artistic Director and Chief Executive Officer, The Roundhouse, since 1999; *b* Malvern, 5 July 1967; *s* of Robin and Ruth Davey; *m* 1997, Tatty Theo; two *s. Educ:* Dartington Coll. of Arts (BA Hons). Administrator, Dartington Internat. Summer Sch., 1989–95; Dir, Dartington Arts Centre, 1992–95; Artistic Dir, Norfolk and Norwich Fest., 1995–99. Chairman: Hackney Youth Orchestras Trust, 1991–97; PRS Foundn, 1999–2006; Mem. Adv. Bd, Clore Leadership Foundn, 2004–. FRSA. *Recreations:* cooking, music, walking. *Address:* The Roundhouse, Chalk Farm Road, NW1 8EH. *T:* (020) 7424 9991, *Fax:* (020) 7424 9992; *e-mail:* marcus.davey@roundhouse.org.uk. *Clubs:* Savile, Soho House, Groucho.

DAVEY, Peter Gordon, CBE 1986; Partner, Crossfell Consultants, since 1998; *b* 6 Aug. 1935; *s* of late Lt-Col Frank Davey, Royal Signals and H. Jean Davey (*née* Robley); *m*

1961; two *s* two *d. Educ:* Winchester Coll.; Gonville and Caius Coll., Cambridge (Mech. Scis Tripos, pt 2 Electrical; MA 1961). MIET; MBCS 1967. Engineer: GEC Applied Electronics Labs, Stanmore, 1958–61; Lawrence Radiation Lab., Berkeley, Calif, 1961–64; Guest Researcher, Heidelberg Univ., 1964–65; Oxford University: Project Engr, Nuclear Physics Lab., 1966–79; Co-ordinator, Indust. Robotics Research Prog., SERC, 1979–84; Head of Inter-active Computing Facility, Rutherford Lab., SRC, 1978–80; of Robot Welding Project, Engrg Sci. Lab., 1979–84; Sen. Res. Fellow, St Cross Coll., 1981–89. Tech. Dir, Electro Pneumatic Equipment Ltd, Letchworth, 1968–87; Man. Dir, Meta Machines Ltd, 1984–87 (Dir, 1984–91); Man. Dir, Oxford Intelligent Machines Ltd, 1990–98; Dep. Chm., Oxim Ltd, 1999–2000. Ed., Open University Press Industrial Robotics Series, 1982–92. Hon. Prof., UCW, Aberystwyth, 1988–93. Hon. DSc Hull, 1987. *Publications:* (with W. F. Clocksin) A Tutorial Introduction to Industrial Robotics: artificial intelligence skills, 1982; (contrib.) Robot Vision, 1982; contribs to learned jls on robotics and image analysis systems. *Recreations:* buildings restoration, squash, sailing. *Address:* Trewennack, Raginnis, Penzance, Cornwall TR19 6NJ.

DAVEY, Peter John, OBE 1998; architectural writer and critic; Editor, The Architectural Review, 1981–2005; *b* 28 Feb. 1940; *s* of John Davey and Mary (*née* Roberts); *m* 1968, Carolyn Pulford; two *s. Educ:* Oundle Sch.; Edinburgh University (BArch). RIBA. News and Features Editor, 1974, Man. Editor, 1978, Architects' Journal; Managing Editor, Architectural Review, 1980. Mem. Council, RIBA, 1990–93 (Vice Pres. and Hon. Librarian, 1991–93). Editl Dir, EMAP Construct, 1995–2005. Member Jury, including: RIBA Royal Gold Medal, 1990–95, 2007, 2008; Carlsberg Architecture Prize, 1992, 1995, 1998; Brunel Prize, 1996; Constitutional Court Competition, S Africa, 1997–98; Hellenic Inst. of Arch. Nat. Prize, 2000; competition for Oil Ministry HQ bldg, Tehran, Iran, 2002; Jury Chairman: Prague Castle Pheasantry (pleasure grounds) Competition, 1997; Emerging Architecture Awards, 1999–2007; Commonwealth Assoc. of Architects Student Comp., Wellington, NZ, 2000, Bloemfontein, S Africa, 2003, Dhaka, Bangladesh, 2007; Internat. Architectl Photography Comp., Stuttgart, 2005. FRSA. Pierre Vago Award, Internat. Cttee of Architectl Critics, 2005; Médaille d'argent de l'Analyse Architecturale, Acad. d'Architecture, Paris, 2005; Jean Tschumi Prize for architectl criticism, Internat. Union of Architects, 2005. Kt 1st Cl., Order of White Rose (Finland), 1991. *Publications:* Architects' Journal Legal Handbook (ed), 1973; Arts and Crafts Architecture, 1980, 2nd edn 1995; Heikkinen & Komonen, 1997; Peter Zumthor, 1998; numerous articles in architectural jls and books. *Recreations:* pursuit of edible fungi, fishing, cooking, classical music, travelling in Italy. *Address:* 44 Hungerford Road, N7 9LP. *Club:* Athenæum.

DAVEY, Dr Ronald William, LVO 2001; Physician to the Queen, 1986–2001; *b* 25 Oct. 1943; *s* of Frederick George Davey and Cissy Beatrice Davey (*née* Lawday); *m* 1966; one *s* one *d. Educ:* Trinity School of John Whitgift; King's College London; King's College Hosp. (MB BS; FFHom; AKC); MD Imperial Coll., London, 1997. Gen. med. practice, 1970–77; private homoeopathic medical practice, 1978–2001; research into: electro-stimulation and drug addiction, 1978–79; pain relief in spinally injured, 1983–94; antibiotic properties of propolis, 1984–94. Hon. Med. Res. Dir, Blackie Foundn Trust, 1980–98; Hon. Res. Fellow, Nat. Heart and Lung Inst., Univ. of London, 1990 (Blackie Res. Fellow, 1988–90); Vis. Schol., Green Coll., Oxford, 1998. Former Consultant to Res. Council for Complementary Medicine (Vice-Chm., 1986–87). Freeman, City of London, 1997; Liveryman, Barbers' Co., 2001– (Freeman, 1997); Liveryman, Apothecaries' Soc., 2005–. *Publications:* medical papers. *Recreations:* Scottish reeling, opera, reading, writing. *Address:* 1 Upper Wimpole Street, W1G 6LA.

DAVEY, Valerie; *b* 16 April 1940; *m* 1966, Graham Davey; twin *d* one *s. Educ:* Birmingham Univ. (MA); London Univ. Inst. of Educn (PGCE). Teacher: Wolverhampton; Tanzania; FE Coll. Mem. (Lab) Avon CC, 1981–96. MP (Lab) Bristol West, 1997–2005; contested (Lab) same seat, 2005. Mem., Educn and Employment Select Cttee, 1997–2005. Exec. Chair, Council for Educn in the Commonwealth, 2005–. Mem., Amnesty International. *Recreations:* gardens, cooking esp. marmalade.

DAVEY, Prof. William, CBE 1978; PhD; FRSC; President, Portsmouth Polytechnic, 1969–82; Honorary Professor, University of Westminster (formerly Polytechnic of Central London), since 1979; *b* Chesterfield, Derbyshire, 15 June 1917; *m* 1941, Eunice Battye; two *s. Educ:* University Coll., Nottingham; Technical Coll., Huddersfield. BSc, PhD (London, external). Chemist: ICI Scottish Dyes, 1940; Boots, 1941; Shell, 1942–44. Lectr and Sen. Lectr in Organic Chemistry, Acton Techn. Coll., 1944–53; Head of Dept of Chemistry and Biology, The Polytechnic, Regent Street, London, W1, 1953–59; Principal, Coll. of Technology, Portsmouth, 1960–69. FRSA, FRSC, CCMI. DUniv Portsmouth, 1993. *Publications:* Industrial Chemistry, 1961; numerous original papers in: Jl Chem. Soc., Inst. Petroleum, Jl Applied Chem. *Recreations:* motoring, foreign travel. *Address:* 67 Ferndale, Waterlooville, Portsmouth PO7 7PH. *T:* (023) 9226 3014.

DAVEY SMITH, Prof. George, MD, DSc; Professor of Clinical Epidemiology, University of Bristol, since 1994; *b* 9 May 1959; *s* of George Davey Smith and Irmgaard Davey Smith (*née* Beckmann). *Educ:* Stockton Heath Primary Sch.; Lymm Grammar Sch.; Queen's Coll., Oxford (BA 1981; DSc 2000); Jesus Coll., Cambridge (MB BChir 1984; MD 1991); London Sch. of Hygiene and Tropical Medicine (MSc 1988). Clinical Res. Fellow (Hon. Clinical Med. Officer), Welsh Heart Prog., Cardiff, 1985–86; Wellcome Res. Fellow in Clinical Epidemiol., Dept of Community Medicine, UCL and Middlesex Sch. of Medicine, 1986–89; Lectr in Epidemiol., LSHTM, 1989–92; Sen. Lectr in Public Health and Epidemiol., and Hon. Sen. Registrar, 1992–93, Consultant in Public Health Medicine, 1993–94, Univ. of Glasgow. Hon. Prof., Dept of Public Health, Univ. of Glasgow, 1996–. Vis. Prof., Dept of Epidemiol. and Popn Health, LSHTM, 1999–. FMedSci 2006. *Publications:* (ed jtly) The Sociology of Health Inequalities, 1998; (jtly) The Widening Gap: health inequalities and policy in Britain, 1999; (ed jtly) Inequalities in Health: the evidence presented to the independent inquiry into inequalities in health, 1999; (ed jtly) Systematic Reviews in Health Care: meta-analysis in context, 2nd edn, 2001; (ed jtly) Poverty, Inequality and Health in Britain, 1800–2000: a reader, 2001; Health Inequalities: lifecourse approaches, 2003; (with M. Shaw) Cultures of Health, Cultures of Illness, 2004; (jtly) The Handbook of Inequality and Socioeconomic Position: concepts and measures, 2007; over 600 articles in jls. *Recreations:* poor squash, bad tennis and abysmal badminton. *Address:* Department of Social Medicine, University of Bristol, Canynge Hall, Whiteladies Road, Bristol BS8 2PR. *T:* (0117) 928 7329.

DAVID, family name of **Baroness David.**

DAVID, Baroness *cr* 1978 (Life Peer), of Romsey in the City of Cambridge; **Nora Ratcliff David;** JP; *b* 23 Sept. 1913; *d* of George Blockley Blakesley, JP, and Annie Edith Blakesley; *m* 1935, Richard William David, CBE (*d* 1993); two *s* two *d. Educ:* Ashby-de-la-Zouch Girls' Grammar School; St Felix, Southwold; Newnham Coll., Cambridge (MA; Hon. Fellow 1986). Mem. Bd, Peterborough Develt Corp., 1976–78. A Baroness-in-Waiting (Government Whip), 1978–79; Opposition Whip, 1979–82; Dep. Chief Opposition Whip, 1982–87; opposition spokesman on education, 1987–97. Member:

Cambridge City Council, 1964–67, 1968–74; Cambs County Council, 1974–78. Fellow, Anglia Ruskin Univ (formerly Anglia Poly. Higher Educn Coll.), 1989. JP Cambridge City, 1965. *Recreations:* theatre, travel. *Address:* 50 Highsett, Cambridge CB2 1NZ. *T:* (01223) 350376; Cove, New Polzeath, Cornwall PL27 6UF. *T:* (01208) 863310; House of Lords, SW1A 0PW. *T:* (020) 7219 3159.

DAVID, Prof. Anthony Sion, MD; FRCP, FRCPGlas, FRCPsych, FMedSci; Professor of Cognitive Neuropsychiatry, King's College London, since 1996; *b* 27 Sept. 1958. *Educ:* Univ. of Glasgow (MB ChB 1980; MD 1993); MSc Cognitive Neuropsychol. London 1990. FRCP 1994; FRCPGlas 1994; FRCPsych 1998; FMedSci 2002. Registrar: in Neurol., Southern Gen. Hosp., Glasgow, 1982–84; in Psychiatry, Maudsley Hosp., London, 1984–87; Institute of Psychiatry, University of London: Lectr, 1987–90; Sen. Lectr, 1990–94; Reader, 1994–96. *Publications:* (ed with X. Amador) Insight and Psychosis, 1998, 2nd edn 2004; (with T. Kircher) Self in Neuroscience and Psychiatry, 2003; contrib. scientific articles on schizophrenia and neuropsychol. *Recreations:* football, jazz piano. *Address:* Institute of Psychiatry, King's College London, PO Box 68, De Crespigny Park, SE5 8AF. *T:* (020) 7848 0138; *e-mail:* a.david@iop.kcl.ac.uk.

DAVID, Sir (Jean) Marc, Kt 1986; CBE 1982; QC (Mauritius) 1969; Barrister, in private practice 1964–2005, and consultant, 2005; Hon. Professor of Law, University of Mauritius, since 1990; *b* 22 Sept. 1925; *s* of late Joseph Claudius David and Marie Lucresia David (*née* Henrisson); *m* 1948, Mary Doreen Mahoney; three *s* three *d*. *Educ:* Royal Coll., Port Louis; Royal Coll., Curepipe, Mauritius (Laureate (classical side) of English Scholarship, 1945); LSE (LLB Hons). Called to the Bar, Middle Temple, 1949. Barrister in private practice, 1950–54; Dist Magistrate, then Crown Law Officer (Crown Counsel, Sen. Crown Counsel and Actg AAG), 1954–64. Chm., Mauritius Bar Assoc., 1968, 1979, 2000. Chairman: various arbitration tribunals, commns of enquiry and cttees apptd by govt, 1958–; Electoral Supervisory and Boundaries Commns, 1973–82 (Mem., 1968–73); Mem., Panel of Conciliators and Arbitrators, Internat. Centre for Settlement of Investment Disputes, 1969–. Visitor, Univ. of Mauritius, 1980–81. *Recreations:* reading, listening to music, horse racing. *Address:* Le Flamboyant, Bonne Terre, Vacoas, Mauritius. *T:* 6961667. *Club:* Turf, Racing (Mauritius).

DAVID, Prof. Paul Allan, PhD; FBA 1995; Senior Research Fellow, All Souls College, 1994–2003, now Fellow Emeritus, and Professor of Economics and Economic History, 1998–2003, now Professor Emeritus, University of Oxford; Senior Fellow, Oxford Internet Institute, since 2002; Professor of Economics, 1969–2005, now Emeritus, and Senior Fellow, Stanford Insitute for Economic Policy Research, since 1990, Stanford University, California; *b* 24 May 1935; *s* of Henry David and Evelyn (*née* Levinson); *m* 1st, 1958, Janet Williamson (marr. diss. 1982); one *s* one *d*; 2nd, 1982, Sheila Ryan Johansson; one step *s* one step *d*. *Educ:* High Sch. of Music and Art, NYC; Harvard Coll. (AB *summa cum laude* 1956); Pembroke Coll., Cambridge (Fulbright Schol.); Harvard Univ. (PhD 1973); MA Oxon. Stanford University, California: Asst Prof. of Econs, 1961–66; Associate Prof., 1966–69; William Robertson Coe Prof. of American Econ. Hist., 1978–94. Vis. Fellow, All Souls Coll., Oxford, 1967–68 and 1992–93; Vis. Prof. of Econs, Harvard Univ., 1972–73; Pitt Prof. of American Hist. and Institutions, Univ. of Cambridge, 1977–78; Vis. Res. Prof. in Econs of Sci. and Technol., Rijksuniversiteit Limburg, 1993–; Marshall Lectr, Univ. of Cambridge, 1992. Guggenheim Fellow, 1975–76; Fellow, Center for Advanced Study in the Behavioral Scis, 1978–79. Director: Cie Saint-Gobain, 2002–; Science Commons, 2005–. Pres.-Elect and Pres., Econ. Hist. Assoc., 1987–89. Mem. Council, REconS, 1996–2002. Fellow: Internat. Econometrics Soc., 1975; Amer. Acad. Arts and Scis, 1979; Amer. Philos. Soc., 2003. Phi Beta Kappa, Harvard, 1956. Hon. Dr Inf. and Commns Scis, Torino, 2003. *Publications:* (ed) Households and Nations in Economic Growth, 1974; Technical Choice, Innovation and Economic Growth, 1975, 2nd edn 2003; Reckoning with Slavery, 1976; The Economic Future in Historical Perspective, 2003; Behind the Diffusion Curve, 2008; From the Economics of QWERTY to the Millennium Bug, 2008; Networks, Standards and Markets, 2008; numerous articles and contribs to books. *Recreations:* photography, Chinese cooking, tennis, walking. *Address:* All Souls College, Oxford OX1 4AL. *Fax:* (01865) 279299; *e-mail:* pdavid@herald.ox.ac.uk; (Sept.–March) Department of Economics, Stanford University, Stanford, CA 94305–6072, USA. *Fax:* (650) 7255702; *e-mail:* pad@stanford.edu.

DAVID, Robert Allan; Head of International and Tourism Division, Department of Employment, 1989–91; *b* 27 April 1937; *s* of George David and Mabel Edith David; *m* 1961, Brenda Marshall; three *d*. *Educ:* Cathays High Sch., Cardiff. BoT, 1955–71; Dept of Employment, 1971–91. Mem. (Ind.), Tandridge DC, 2003–. *Recreations:* badminton, tennis, gardening. *Address:* The Briars, Ninehams Road, Tatsfield, Westerham, Kent TN16 2AN. *T:* (01959) 577357.

DAVID, His Honour Sir Robert Daniel George, (Sir Robin), Kt 1995; QC 1968; DL; a Circuit Judge (formerly Chairman, Cheshire Quarter Sessions), 1968–97; *b* 30 April 1922; *s* of late Alexander Charles Robert David and late Edrica Doris Pole David (*née* Evans); *m* 1st, 1944, Edith Mary Marsh (*d* 1999); two *d*; 2nd, 2000, Zena (*née* Cooke). *Educ:* Christ Coll., Brecon; Ellesmere Coll., Salop. War Service, 1943–47, Captain, Royal Artillery. Called to Bar, Gray's Inn, 1949; joined Wales and Chester Circuit, 1949. Dep. Chairman, Cheshire QS, 1961; Dep. Chairman, Agricultural Land Tribunal (Wales), 1965–68; Commissioner of Assize, 1970; Dep. Presiding Judge, Judicial Trng, 1970–74; Mem., Parole Bd for England and Wales, 1971–74. DL Cheshire 1972. *Publication:* The Magistrate in the Crown Court, 1982. *Address:* Fieldgate, Willington Lane, Kelsall, Tarporley CW6 0PR. *T:* (01829) 751453.

DAVID, Timothy James; HM Diplomatic Service, retired; High Commissioner, Zambia, 2002–05; *b* 3 June 1947; *s* of late Herman Francis David and Mavis Jeanne David (*née* Evans); *m* 1996, Rosemary (*née* Kunzel); one *s* one *d*. *Educ:* Stonyhurst Coll.; New Coll., Oxford (BA Hons 1969; MA Hons 1978); Univ. of Rhodesia (Grad. Cert. in Educn 1972); Univ. of London. Volunteer Teacher, Southern Rhodesia, 1965–66; Headmaster, St Peter's Community Secondary Sch., Salisbury (now Harare, Zimbabwe), 1970–71; British Council, 1973; Educn Dir, Help the Aged, 1974; FCO by open competition, 1974; 2nd, later 1st, Sec., Dar es Salaam, and, non-resident, Antananarivo, 1977–80; Commonwealth Co-ordination Dept, 1980–82; Sec. to UK Delegn to Commonwealth Heads of Govt Meeting, Melbourne, 1981; UKMIS to UN, NY, 1982; Central and Southern Africa Dept, ODA, 1983–84; UKMIS to UN, Geneva, 1985–88; Head of Internat. and Planning Section and Dep. Head, Aid Policy Dept, ODA/FCO, 1988–89; Counsellor and Head, Narcotics Control and Aids Dept, FCO, 1989–91; Ambassador to Fiji and High Comr to Nauru and Tuvalu, 1992–95, and to Kiribati, 1994–95; Counsellor, Middle East Dept, FCO, 1995; Dep. High Comr, Harare, 1996–98; High Comr, Belize, 1998–2001; Dean, Diplomatic Corps in Belize, 2001. UK Dir, Tuvalu Trust Fund, 1992–95. Member: Council, Univ. of S Pacific, 1993–95; Rhodes Scholarship Selection Cttee, Zambia, 2002–05; Chm., Marlborough Brandt Gp, 2007–. Mem., Royal African Soc., 2004–08. Patron, SCF (Fiji), 1993–95. Chm., Bd of Trustees, AbleChildAfrica. Governor: Oaksey Village Primary Sch., 2006–; Emmaus (Gloucester), 2007–; Trustee, Oaksey Playing Field Trust, 2006–. Hon. Citizen, Gunjur, The Gambia. *Recreations:* friends, reading, music, tennis, squash, walking. *Address:* The Old House, The Stre Oaksey, near Malmesbury, Wilts SN16 9TD. *Club:* All England Lawn Tennis a Croquet.

DAVID, Prof. Timothy Joseph, PhD, MD; FRCP, FRCPCH; Professor of Ch Health and Paediatrics, University of Manchester, and Hon. Consultant Paediatricia Booth Hall Children's Hospital, Manchester, since 1991; two *s*. *Educ:* Clifton Co Bristol; Univ. of Bristol (MB ChB 1970; PhD 1975; MD 1981); DCH 1976 (RC MRCP 1976, FRCP 1986; FRCPCH 1997. Posts in Bristol, Taunton and Plymou 1970–78; Tutor/Lectr in Child Health, 1978–81, Sen. Lectr, Dept of Child Heal 1981–91, Univ. of Manchester. *Publications:* (jtly) Applied Paediatric Nursing, 1982; (e Cystic Fibrosis in Children, 1986; (ed) Recent Advances in Paediatrics, vol. 9, 1991–v 23, 2006; (ed) Role of the Cystic Fibrosis Nurse Specialist, 1992; Food and Food Additi Intolerance in Childhood, 1993; Symptoms of Disease in Childhood, 1995 (Dutch ed 1999); (jtly) Eczema in Children, 1995; (ed) Major Controversies in Infant Nutritic 1996; (jtly) Problem-based Learning in Medicine, 1999; author or editor of over 3 scientific and med. pubns, inc. conf. procs. *Recreations:* baseball, cricket, cricket umpirii classical music, opera. *Address:* Booth Hall Children's Hospital, Charlestown Ro Blackley, Manchester M9 7AA. *T:* (0161) 795 7000, *Fax:* (0161) 904 9320.

DAVID, Wayne; MP (Lab) Caerphilly, since 2001; Parliamentary Under-Secretary State, Wales Office, since 2008; *b* 1 July 1957; *s* of late D. Haydn David and of Edna David; *m* 1991, Catherine Thomas (marr. diss. 2007). *Educ:* Cynffig Comprehensive Sc University Coll., Cardiff (BA Hons History; PGCE); University Coll., Swansea. Histo teacher, Brynteg Comprehensive Sch., Bridgend, 1983–85; Mid Glam Tutor Organis S Wales Dist, WEA, 1985–89. Policy Advr, Wales Youth Agency, 1999–2001. MEP (La S Wales, 1989–94, S Wales Central, 1994–99. Treas., 1989–91, Leader, 1994–9 European Parly Labour Party (formerly British Labour Gp); 1st Vice-Pres., Regl Poli and Planning Cttee, Eur. Parlt, 1992–94; Sec., Tribune Gp of MEPs, 1992–94. Men Labour Party NEC, 1994–98. PPS to Minister of State for Armed Forces, 2005–06; an A Govt Whip, 2007–08. Mem., European Scrutiny Select Cttee, 2001–07; Chm., All Pa Parly Gp on EU, 2006–07. Sec., DWP Gp, 2002–07, Wales Gp, 2003–07, PLP; Se Labour Movt for Europe, 2003–07. Bd Mem., European Movt, 2002–07; Pres., Wa Council, European Movt, 2006–. Pres., Council for Wales of Voluntary Youth Servic 2001–; Vice-Pres., City of Cardiff Br., UNA, 1989–; Mem., Cefn Cribwr Commun Council, 1985–91. President: Aber Valley Male Voice Choir, 2001–; Caerphilly Lo Hist. Soc., 2006–. Fellow, Univ. of Wales Coll. of Cardiff, 1995. *Publications:* (contri Oxford Companion to the Literature of Wales, 1986; Remaining True: a biography Ness Edwards, 2006; three pamphlets; contrib. Llafur—Jl of Welsh Labour Histo *Recreations:* music, reading. *Address:* c/o House of Commons, SW1A 0AA. *T:* (020) 72 8152.

DAVID-WEILL, Michel Alexandre; Chairman, Lazard Frères & Co., LLC, New Yo 1977–2005; Partner, Lazard Frères et Cie, Paris, 1965–2005; *b* 23 Nov. 1932; *s* of Bert Haardt and Pierre David-Weill; *m* 1956, Hélène Lehideux; four *d*. *Educ:* Institut Sciences Politiques, Paris; Lycée Français de New York. Brown Brothers Harrim 1954–55; Lehman Brothers, NY, 1955–56; Lazard Frères & Co., NY, 1956–, Partn 1961, Sen. Partner, 1977; Lazard Brothers & Co., London, Dir, 1965–; Chm., Laza Partners, 1984–. Dir, French Amer. Foundn, NY; Member Council: Musée de la Légi d'Honneur, Paris, 1975; Cité Internat. des Arts, Paris, 1976; Mem., Acad. des Beaux-Ar 1983; Pres., Conseil Artistique de la Réunion des Musées Nationaux, Paris. Gov., N Hosp. Officier, Legion of Honour (France), 1990. *Address:* c/o Lazard Frères & Co., Rockefeller Plaza, New York, NY 10020, USA. *T:* (212) 6326000. *Clubs:* Knickerbock Brook (NY); Creek (Locust Valley).

DAVIDSON, family name of **Viscount Davidson**.

DAVIDSON, 2nd Viscount *cr* 1937, of Little Gaddesden; **John Andrew Davidso** Captain of the Yeomen of the Guard (Deputy Government Chief Whip), 1986–91; *b* Dec. 1928; *er s* of 1st Viscount Davidson, GCVO, CH, CB, PC, and Frances Joa Viscountess Davidson (Baroness Northchurch), DBE (*d* 1985), *y d* of 1st Baron Dickinso KBE, PC; *S* father, 1970; *m* 1st, 1956, Margaret Birgitta Norton (marr. diss. 1974); thr *d* (including twin *d*) (and one *d* decd); 2nd, 1975, Mrs Pamela Dobb (*née* Vergette) 2006). *Educ:* Westminster School; Pembroke College, Cambridge (BA). Served in T Black Watch and 5th Bn KAR, 1947–49. Pres., CU Footlights Club, 1951. A Lord Waiting (Govt Whip), 1985–86. Director: Strutt & Parker (Farms) Ltd, 1960–75; Lo Rayleigh's Farms Inc., 1960–75; Member of Council: CLA, 1965–75; RASE, 197 Chm., Management Committee, Royal Eastern Counties Hospital, 1966–72; Mem., E Anglia Economic Planning Council, 1971–75. *Recreation:* music. *Heir:* *b* Hon. Malco William Mackenzie Davidson [*b* 28 Aug. 1934; *m* 1970, Mrs Evelyn Ann Carew Perfe *yr d* of William Blackmore Storey; one *s* one *d*]. *Address:* 19 Lochmore House, Cun Street, SW1W 9JX.

See also Baron Rayleigh.

DAVIDSON OF GLEN CLOVA, Baron *cr* 2006 (Life Peer), of Glen Clova in Ang **Neil Forbes Davidson;** QC (Scot.) 1993; Advocate General for Scotland, since 2006 13 Sept. 1950; *s* of John and Flora Davidson; *m* 1980, Regina Anne Sprissler, Philadelph *Educ:* Univs of Stirling (BA), Bradford (MSc), Edinburgh (LLB, LLM). Admitted Facul of Advocates, 1979; called to the Bar, Inner Temple, 1990; Standing Jun. Counsel Registrar Gen., 1982, to Depts of Health and Social Security, 1988; Solicitor Gen. Scot., 2000–01. Dir, City Disputes Panel, 1993–2000. ICJ missions to Egypt, 1997, 199 Reviewer, Davidson Review on UK Implementation of EU Legislation, 2005–(*Publications:* (jtly) Judicial Review in Scotland, 1986; (contrib.) ADR in Scotland, 199 *Address:* House of Lords, SW1A 0PW.

DAVIDSON, Hon. Lord; Charles Kemp Davidson, FRSE 1985; a Senator of t College of Justice in Scotland, 1983–96; Chairman, Scottish Law Commission, 1988–9 *b* Edinburgh, 13 April 1929; *s* of Rev. Donald Davidson, DD, Edinburgh; *m* 1960, Ma (OBE 1994), *d* of Charles Mactaggart, Campbeltown, Argyll; one *s* two *d*. *Educ:* Fet Coll., Edinburgh; Brasenose Coll., Oxford; Edinburgh Univ. Admitted to Faculty Advocates, 1956; QC (Scot.) 1969; Vice-Dean, 1977–79; Dean, 1979–83; Keep Advocates' Library, 1972–76. Procurator to Gen. Assembly of Church of Scotlar 1972–83. Dep. Chm., Boundary Commn for Scotland, 1985–96. *Address:* 22 Dub Street, Edinburgh EH1 3PP. *T:* (0131) 556 2168.

DAVIDSON, Arthur; QC 1978; *b* 7 Nov. 1928. *Educ:* Liverpool Coll.; King George Sch., Southport; Trinity Coll., Cambridge. Served in Merchant Navy. Barrister, Midd Temple, 1953. Trinity Coll., Cambridge, 1959–62; Editor of the Granta. Legal Direct Associated Newspapers Hldgs, 1987–90; Mirror Gp, 1991–93. MP (Lab) Accringto 1966–83; PPS to Solicitor-General, 1968–70; Chm., Home Affairs Gp, Parly Labo Party, 1971–74; Parly Sec., Law Officers' Dept, 1974–79; Opposition spokesman Defence (Army), 1980–81, on legal affairs, 1981–83, Shadow Attorney-General, 1982–8 Member: Home Affairs Select Cttee, 1980–83; Armed Forces Bill Select Cttee, 1981–8

Contested (Lab): Blackpool S, 1955; Preston N, 1959; Hyndburn, 1983. Member: Council, Consumers' Association, 1970–74; Exec. Cttee, Soc. of Labour Lawyers, 1981; Nat. Exec., Fabian Soc.; Council, Nat. Youth Jazz Orchestra; Chm., House of Commons Jazz Club, 1973–83. *Recreations:* lawn tennis, ski-ing, theatre, listening to good jazz and playing bad jazz; formerly Member Cambridge Univ. athletics team. *Address:* Cloisters, 1st Floor, 1 Pump Court, Temple, EC4Y 7AA. *Clubs:* James Street Men's Working (Oswaldtwistle); Free Gardeners (Rishton); King Street, Marlborough Working Men's (Accrington).

DAVIDSON, Basil Risbridger, MC 1945; author and historian; *b* 9 Nov. 1914; *s* of Thomas and Jessie Davidson; *m* 1943, Marion Ruth Young; three *s.* Served War of 1939–45 (despatches twice, MC, US Bronze Star, Jugoslav Zasluge za Narod); British Army, 1940–45 (Balkans, N Africa, Italy); Temp. Lt-Col demobilised as Hon. Major. Editorial staff of The Economist, 1938–39; The Star (diplomatic correspondent, 1939); The Times (Paris correspondent, 1945–47; chief foreign leader-writer, 1947–49); New Statesman (special correspondent, 1950–54); Daily Herald (special correspondent, 1954–57); Daily Mirror (leader-writer, 1959–62). Vis. Prof., Univ. of Ghana, 1964; Vis. Prof., 1965, Regents' Lectr, 1971, Univ. of California; Montagu Burton Vis. Prof. of Internat. Relations, Edinburgh Univ., 1972; Sen. Simon Res. Fellow, Univ. of Manchester, 1975–76; Hon. Res. Fellow, Univ. of Birmingham, 1978–; Agnelli Vis. Prof., Univ. of Turin, 1990. A Vice-Pres., Anti-Apartheid Movement, 1969–85. Author/presenter, Africa (8-part TV documentary series), 1984. Associate Mem., Acad. des Scis d'Outre-Mer, Paris, 1973. Freeman of City of Genoa, 1945. Hon. Fellow, SOAS, London Univ., 1998. DLitt *hc*: Ibadan, 1975; Dar es Salaam, 1985; Edinburgh, 1981; Western Cape, S Africa, 1997; Bristol, 1999; DUniv Open, 1980. Haile Selassie African Research Award, 1970. Medalha Amílcar Cabral (Republic of Guinea-Bissau), 1976; Grand Officer, Order of Prince Henry the Navigator (Portugal), 2002; First Degree, Order Amílcar Cabral (Republic of Cape Verde), 2003. *Publications: novels:* Highway Forty, 1949; Golden Horn, 1952; The Rapids, 1955; Lindy, 1958; The Andrassy Affair, 1966; *non-fiction:* Partisan Picture, 1946; Germany: From Potsdam to Partition, 1950; Report on Southern Africa, 1952; Daybreak in China, 1953; (ed) The New West Africa, 1953; The African Awakening, 1955; Turkestan Alive, 1957; Old Africa Rediscovered, 1959; Black Mother, 1961, rev. edn 1980; The African Past, 1964; Which Way Africa?, 1964; The Growth of African Civilisation: West Africa AD 1000–1800, 1965; Africa: History of a Continent, 1966; A History of East and Central Africa to the late 19th Century, 1967; Africa in History: Themes and Outlines, 1968; The Liberation of Guiné, 1969; The Africans, An Entry to Cultural History, 1969; Discovering our African Heritage, 1971; In the Eye of the Storm: Angola's People, 1972; Black Star, 1974; Can Africa Survive?, 1975; Discovering Africa's Past, 1978 (Children's Rights Workshop Award, 1978); Africa in Modern History, 1978; Crossroads in Africa, 1980; Special Operations Europe, 1980; The People's Cause, 1980; No Fist is Big Enough, 1981; Modern Africa, 1982, 3rd edn 1994; The Story of Africa, 1984; The Fortunate Isles, 1989; African Civilisation Revisited, 1991; The Black Man's Burden: Africa and the curse of the nation-state, 1992; The Search for Africa (essays), 1994; West Africa before the Colonial Era: a history to 1850, 1998.

DAVIDSON, Charles Kemp; *see* Davidson, Hon. Lord.

DAVIDSON, Charles Peter Morton; a District Judge (Magistrates' Courts) (formerly Metropolitan Stipendiary Magistrate), 1984–2004; a Deputy District Judge (Magistrates' Courts), since 2004; *b* 29 July 1938; *s* of late William Philip Morton Davidson, MD, and Muriel Maud Davidson (*née* Alderson); *m* 1966, Pamela Louise Campbell-Rose. *Educ:* Harrow; Trinity Coll., Dublin (MA, LLB). Called to the Bar, Inner Temple, 1963; employed by Legal and General Assurance Soc., 1963–65; in practice at Bar, 1966–84; a Recorder, 1991–99. Chairman, London Rent Assessment Panel, 1973–84; part-time Immigration Appeals Adjudicator, 1976–84; a Chairman: Inner London Juvenile Courts, 1985–88; Family Court, 1991–2004. Contested (C) North Battersea, 1966. Member: Wandsworth BC, 1964–68; Merton BC, 1968–71. *Recreations:* music, gardening. *Club:* Hurlingham.

DAVIDSON, David; Managing Director: Earlston Ltd, since 1984; Carse Ltd, since 1996; *b* 25 Jan. 1943; *s* of John and Marjory Davidson; *m* 1968, Christine Hunter; three *s* two *d.* *Educ:* Heriot-Watt Univ. (Pharmacy); Manchester Business Sch. (DipBA). MRPharmS. Manager, 1966–69, Proprietor, 1969–74, community pharmacy, Kent; developed gp of community pharmacies in Scotland and Northern England, 1974–93; Dir, Unichem Ltd, 1977–90; Regl Chm., Unichem plc, 1990–93. Associate Dir, Caledonia Consulting, 2007–. Mem. (C) Stirling Council, 1995–99. MSP (C) Scotland NE, 1999–2007. Founder Chm., Assoc. Scottish Community Councils, 1993–95. *Recreations:* country pursuits, pedigree stock breeding, Rugby football, travel. *Address:* North Hilton, Netherley, by Stonehaven, Kincardine, Aberdeenshire AB39 3QL. *T:* (01569) 730449.

DAVIDSON, Dennis Arthur; Chairman, DDA Public Relations Ltd, since 1970; *b* Chester, 11 March 1947; *s* of Arthur Davidson and Elizabeth Joan Morgan; *m* 1991, Janette Graydon Dickson; three *s* one *d.* *Educ:* Helsby Grammar Sch.; Ellesmere Port Grammar Sch. Associated British Picture Corp., 1964–70. Member: BAFTA; Acad. of Motion Picture Arts and Scis, 1980. FCIPR 1995; FRSA 2007; FInstD 2008. *Recreations:* tennis, cinema, food and wine consumption, Rugby Union. *Address:* Barrihurst House, Cranleigh, Surrey GU6 8LQ. *T:* (01483) 279779; *e-mail:* dennis.davidson@ddapr.com. *Clubs:* Hurlingham, Groucho, Soho House.

DAVIDSON, Duncan Henry; Chairman, 1972–2006, Life President, since 2006, Persimmon plc; *b* 29 March 1941; *s* of late Col Colin Keppel Davidson, CIE, OBE, RA (killed in action 1943) and late Lady (Mary) Rachel Davidson (later Lady (Mary) Rachel Pepys, DCVO); *m* 1965, Sarah Wilson; four *d.* *Educ:* Ampleforth Coll. Lieut, Royal Scots Greys, 1959–63; Manager, George Wimpey plc, 1963–65; Founder and Chm., Ryedale Homes Ltd, 1965–72. *Recreation:* country pursuits. *Address:* Lilburn Tower, Alnwick, Northumberland NE66 4PQ. *T:* (01668) 217291. *Clubs:* White's, Turf.

DAVIDSON, Edward Alan; QC 1994; *b* 12 July 1943; *o s* of late Alan T. Davidson and H. Muriel Davidson, Sheffield; *m* 1973, Hilary Jill, *er d* of late Major N. S. Fairman, MBE; two *s.* *Educ:* King's Sch., Canterbury; Gonville and Caius Coll., Cambridge (schol., Tapp Postgrad Schol.; MA, LLB). Called to the Bar, Gray's Inn, 1966 (Atkin and Birkenhead Schol.), Bencher, 2002. Chm., Summer Fields Sch. Trust, 2007– (Gov., 1998–). *Recreations:* tennis, bridge, gardening. *Address:* Thatch End, Furneux Pelham, Buntingford, Herts SG9 0LW.

DAVIDSON, Ian Graham; MP (Lab and Co-op) Glasgow South West, since 2005 (Glasgow, Govan, 1992–97; Glasgow, Pollok, 1997–2005); *b* 8 Sept. 1950; *s* of Graham Davidson and Elizabeth Crowe; *m* 1978, Morag Mackinnon; one *s* one *d.* *Educ:* Jedburgh Grammar Sch.; Galashiels Acad.; Edinburgh Univ. (MA Hons); Jordanhill Coll. (Teacher Cert.). Chm., Nat. Orgn of Labour Students, 1973–74; Pres., Jordanhill Coll. Students' Assoc., 1975–76; PA/Researcher, Janey Buchan, MEP, 1978–85; Community Service Volunteers, 1985–92. Councillor, Strathclyde Region, 1978–92 (Chm., Educn Cttees, 1986–92). Member: Public Accounts Select Cttee, 1997–; Select Cttee on Scottish Affairs, 2005–; Chairman: MSF Parly Gp, 1996–97; Co-op Gp, 1998–99; Bermuda Gp, 1998–; Secretary: New Europe Parly Gp, 2001–; British/German All Party Parly Gp, 1998–2002; British/Japanese All Party Parly Gp, 1998–; Aerospace All Party Parly Gp, 1998–2001; Ship Building and Repair All Party Parly Gp, 2000–; Parly Rugby Union team, 1996–. Secretary: Tribune Gp of MPs, 1997–; Trade Union Gp of Lab MPs, 1998–; Vice Chm., Scotland Lab Gp; Chm., Lab Against the Euro. *Recreations:* running, swimming, family. *Address:* House of Commons, SW1A 0AA.

DAVIDSON, James Duncan Gordon, OBE 1984; MVO 1947; Chief Executive, Royal Highland and Agricultural Society of Scotland, 1970–92; *b* 10 Jan. 1927; *s* of Alastair Gordon Davidson and M. Valentine B. Davidson (*née* Osborne); *m* 1st, 1955, Catherine Ann Jamieson; one *s* two *d*; 2nd, 1973, Janet Stafford; one *s.* *Educ:* RN Coll., Dartmouth; Downing Coll., Cambridge. Active List, RN, 1944–55. Subseq. farming, and political work; contested (L) West Aberdeenshire, 1964; MP (L) West Aberdeenshire, 1966–70. FRAgS; MIEx. *Publications:* Scots and the Sea, 2003; Admiral Lord St Vincent: saint or tyrant?, 2006. *Recreations:* family, walking, music, forestry, naval history. *Address:* Coire Cas, Newtonmore, Inverness-shire PH20 1AR. *T:* (01540) 673322.

DAVIDSON, James Patton, CBE 1980; *b* 23 March 1928; *s* of Richard Davidson and Elizabeth Ferguson Carnichan; *m* 1st, 1953, Jean Stevenson Ferguson Anderson (marr. diss. 1981); two *s*; 2nd, 1981, Esmé Evelyn Ancill. *Educ:* Rutherglen Acad.; Glasgow Univ. (BL). Mil. service, commissioned RASC, 1948–50. Clyde Navigation Trust, 1950; Asst Gen. Manager, 1958. Clyde Port Authority: Gen. Manager, 1966; Managing Dir, 1974; Dep. Chm. and Man. Dir, 1976; Chm., 1980–83. Chairman: Ardrossan Harbour Co. Ltd, 1976–83; Clydeport Stevedoring Services Ltd, 1977–83; Clyde Container Services Ltd, 1968–83; S. & H. McCall Transport (Glasgow) Ltd, 1972–83; Rhu Marina Ltd, 1976–80; Scotway Haulage Ltd, 1976–81; R. & J. Strang Ltd, 1976–81; Nat. Assoc. of Port Employers, 1974–79; British Ports Assoc., 1980–83 (Dep. Chm., 1978–80); Port Employers' & Registered Dock Workers' Pension Fund Trustee Ltd, 1978–83; Pilotage Commn, 1983–91 (Mem., 1979–83); UK Dir, 1976–83 and Mem., Exec. Cttee, 1977–83, Hon. Mem., 1983, Internat. Assoc. of Ports and Harbours. Dir, Iron Trades Insurance Gp, 1981–94; Chm., Foods & Feeds (UK), 1982–83. FCIT, CCMI; FRSA. *Recreations:* golf, bridge, travel, reading.

DAVIDSON, Jane Barbara; *see* Stevenson, J. B.

DAVIDSON, Jane Elizabeth; Member (Lab) Pontypridd, National Assembly for Wales, since 1999; Minister for Environment, Sustainability and Housing, since 2007; *b* 19 March 1957; *d* of Dr Lindsay Alexander Gordon Davidson and Dr Joyce Mary Davidson; *m* 1994, Guy Roger George Stoate; one *d*, and two step *s.* *Educ:* Malvern Girls' Coll.; Birmingham Univ. (BA 2nd Cl. Hons English); UCW, Aberystwyth (PGCE). Teacher, Cardigan and Pontypridd, 1981–83; Develt Officer, YHA, 1983–86; youth and community worker, Dinas Powys Youth Centre, 1986–89; researcher to Rhodri Morgan, MP, 1989–94; Welsh Co-ordinator, Nat. Local Govt Forum Against Poverty, 1994–96; Hd, Social Affairs, Welsh Local Govt Assoc., 1996–99. National Assembly for Wales: Dep. Presiding Officer, 1999–2000; Sec., then Minister, for Educn and Lifelong Learning, subseq. Minister for Educn, Lifelong Learning and Skills, 2000–07; Minister for Sustainability and Rural Develt, 2007. *Publications:* The Anti Poverty Implications of Local Government Reorganisation, 1990; contrib. to social policy jls. *Recreations:* theatre, walking, cycling. *Address:* National Assembly for Wales, Crickhowell House, Cardiff Bay, Cardiff CF99 1NA. *T:* (constituency office) (01443) 406400.

DAVIDSON, Prof. John Frank, FRS 1974; FREng; Shell Professor of Chemical Engineering, University of Cambridge, 1978–93 (Professor of Chemical Engineering, 1975–78); Vice-Master, Trinity College, Cambridge, 1992–96; Adjunct Professor, Monash University, Australia, 1996–99; *b* 7 Feb. 1926; *s* of John and Katie Davidson; *m* 1948, Susanne Hedwig Ostberg; one *s* one *d.* *Educ:* Heaton Grammar Sch., Newcastle upon Tyne; Trinity Coll., Cambridge. MA, PhD, ScD; FIChemE, MIMechE. 1st cl. Mech. Scis Tripos, Cantab, 1946, BA 1947. Engrg work at Rolls Royce, Derby, 1947–50; Cambridge Univ.: Research Fellow, Trinity Coll., 1949; research, 1950–52; Univ. Demonstrator, 1952; Univ. Lectr, 1954; Steward of Trinity Coll., 1957–64; Reader in Chem. Engrg, Univ. of Cambridge, 1964–75. Visiting Professor: Univ. of Delaware, 1960; Univ. of Sydney, 1967. Member: Flixborough Ct of Inquiry, 1974–75; Adv. Cttee on Safety of Nuclear Installations, HSC, 1977–87. Pres., IChemE, 1970–71; Vice Pres. and Mem. Council, Royal Soc., 1988. FREng (Founder FEng, 1976). For. Associate, Nat. Acad. of Engrg, US, 1976; For. Fellow, Indian National Science Acad., 1990; For. Mem., Russian Engrg Acad., 1998. Dr *hc* Institut Nat. Polytech. de Toulouse, 1979; Hon. DSc Aston, 1989. Leverhulme Medal, Royal Soc., 1984; Messel Medal, Soc. of Chemical Industry, 1986; Royal Medal, Royal Soc., 1999. *Publications:* (with D. Harrison): Fluidised Particles, 1963; Fluidization, 1971, 2nd edn (with R. Clift and D. Harrison), 1985; (with D. L. Keairns) Fluidization (Conference Procs), 1978. *Recreations:* hill walking, gardening, upholstery, mending domestic artefacts. *Address:* 5 Luard Close, Cambridge CB2 8PL. *T:* (01223) 246104.

See also I. G. Letwin.

DAVIDSON, John Roderick, OBE 2004; Director of Administration, 1991–2004, Clerk of the Council, 1994–2004, University of London; *b* 29 Jan. 1937; *yr s* of late Alexander Ross Davidson and Jessie Maud (*née* Oakley). *Educ:* Portsmouth Northern Grammar Sch.; Univ. of Manchester (BA). Advr to students, Chelsea Sch. of Art, 1966–68; Asst Sch. Sec., RPMS, 1968–74; Imperial College of Science, Technology and Medicine: Asst Sec., 1974–77; Personnel Sec., 1977–85; Admin. Sec., 1985–89; London University: Clerk of Senate, 1989–94; Member: Exams and Assessment Council, 1991–2000; Bd, British Inst. in Paris, 1993–2004. Director: London E Anglian Gp, 1990–96; Superannuation Arrangements of Univ. of London Trustee Co., 1993–98; London and S Eastern Library Region, 1995–2001; Senate House Services Ltd, 1996–2004; Digital Preservation Coalition Ltd, 2002–04. Chm., Lansdowne (Putney) Ltd, 1999–. Trustee: Univ. of London Convocation Trust, 1997–2004; St Stephen's AIDS Trust, 2003–. Governor: Charterhouse Sch., 1994–2003; More House Sch., 2000– (Chm., 2005–); Wimbledon High Sch., 2001–. *Recreations:* theatre, opera, genealogy. *Address:* 10 Lansdowne, Carlton Drive, SW15 2BY. *T:* (020) 8789 0021. *Club:* Athenæum.

DAVIDSON, Martin Stuart, CMG 2007; Chief Executive, British Council, since 2007; *b* 14 Oct. 1955; *s* of Westland Davidson and Freda (*née* Hill); *m* 1980, Elizabeth Fanner; two *s* one *d.* *Educ:* Royal Grammar Sch., Guildford; St Andrews Univ. (MA). Admin. Officer, Hong Kong Govt, 1979–83; British Council: Peking, 1984–87; Regl Officer, China, 1987–89; Dir, S China, 1989–93; Asst Regl Dir, E and S Europe, 1993–95; Cultural Counsellor and Dir, British Council, Peking, 1995–2000; Dir, E Asia and Americas, 2000–03; Dir, Europe, Americas and Middle East, 2003–05; Dep. Dir-Gen., 2006–07. *Recreations:* hill walking, reading, Rugby. *Address:* c/o British Council, 10 Spring Gardens, SW1A 2BN. *Clubs:* Royal Commonwealth Society; Foreign Correspondents (Hong Kong).

DAVIDSON, Nicholas Ranking; QC 1993; a Deputy High Court Judge, since 2000; *b* 2 March 1951; *s* of late Brian Davidson, CBE and Priscilla Margaret (*née* Chilver); *m* 1978, Gillian Frances Watts; two *d*. *Educ:* Winchester (Schol.); Trinity Coll., Cambridge (Exhibnr; BA; MA). Called to the Bar, Inner Temple, 1974 (Treas.'s Prize, Hughes Parry Prize and Inner Temple Scholarship, 1974); Bencher, 1998. Chm., Professional Negligence Bar Assoc., 1997–99. MCIArb 2004. Governor, St Mary's Sch., Ascot, 1996–2006. *Publications:* (contrib.) Now and Then, 1999; (contrib.) Professional Negligence and Liability, 2000. *Recreations:* bridge, music, ski-ing. *Address:* 4 New Square, Lincoln's Inn, WC2A 3RJ. *T:* (020) 7822 2000.

DAVIDSON, Prof. Peter Robert Keith Andrew, PhD; Professor of Renaissance Studies and Scholar-Keeper of University Renaissance Collections, University of Aberdeen, since 2005; *b* 14 May 1957; *s* of Robert Ritchie Davidson and Daphne Davidson (*née* Sanderson); *m* 1989, Jane Barbara Stevenson, *qv*. *Educ:* Clare Coll., Cambridge (BA 1979; PhD 1986); Univ. of York (MA 1980). FSAScot 1984. Lectr, Univ. of St Andrews, 1989–90; Docent in Lit. and Book Studies, Universitet Leiden, Netherlands, 1990–92; University of Warwick: Lectr in English, 1992–97; Sen. Lectr, 1997–99; Reader, 1999–2000; Chalmers Regius Prof. of English, Aberdeen Univ., 2000–05. *Publications:* (with A. H. van der Weel) Poems of Sir Constantijn Huygens, 1996; The Vocall Forest, 1996; The Poems and Translations of Sir Richard Fanshawe, vol. I, 1998, vol. II, 1999; Poetry and Revolution, 1998; (with Jane Stevenson) Early Modern Women's Verse, 2000; The Idea of North, 2005; (with Anne Sweeney) Collected Poems of St Robert Southwell, SJ, 2007; The Universal Baroque, 2007; (with Jill Bepler) The Triumphs of the Defeated, 2007; The Palace of Oblivion, 2008. *Recreation:* casuistry. *Address:* Art History, King's College, Aberdeen AB24 3FX.

DAVIDSON, Very Rev. Prof. Robert, FRSE; Professor of Old Testament Language and Literature, University of Glasgow, 1972–91; Principal, Trinity College, Glasgow, 1982–91; *b* 30 March 1927; *s* of George Braid Davidson and Gertrude May Ward; *m* 1952, Elizabeth May Robertson; four *s* four *d*. *Educ:* Univ. of St Andrews (MA 1st Cl Hons Classics, 1949; BD, Distinction in Old Testament, 1952). FRSE 1989. Asst Lectr, then Lectr in Biblical Studies, Univ. of Aberdeen, 1953–60; Lectr in Hebrew and Old Testament, Univ. of St Andrews, 1960–66; Lectr in Old Testament Studies, Univ. of Edinburgh, 1966–69, Sen. Lectr, 1969–72. Edward Cadbury Lectr, Birmingham Univ., 1988–89. Moderator, Gen. Assembly, Church of Scotland, 1990–91. Hon. DD: Aberdeen, 1985; Glasgow, 1993. *Publications:* The Bible Speaks, 1959; The Old Testament, 1964; (with A. R. C. Leaney) Biblical Criticism (Vol. 3 of Pelican Guide to Modern Theology), 1970; Genesis 1–11 (Cambridge Bible Commentary), 1973; Genesis 12–50 (Cambridge Bible Commentary), 1979; The Bible in Religious Education, 1979; The Courage to Doubt, 1983; Jeremiah 1–20 (Daily Study Bible), 1983; Jeremiah II, Lamentations (Daily Study Bible), 1986; Ecclesiastes and Song of Songs (Daily Study Bible), 1986; Wisdom and Worship, 1990; A Beginner's Guide to the Old Testament, 1992; Go By the Book, 1996; The Vitality of Worship, 1998; articles in Vetus Testamentum, Annual Swedish Theol Inst., Expository Times, Scottish Jl of Theol., Epworth Review and The Furrow. *Recreations:* music, gardening. *Address:* 30 Dumgoyne Drive, Bearsden, Glasgow G61 3AP. *T:* (0141) 942 1810.

DAVIDSON, Stephen Robert; DL; Headmaster, Bradford Grammar School, since 1996; *b* 20 Oct. 1950; *er s* of Robert Davidson and late Joan Davidson, Tynemouth; *m* 1983, Carol, *d* of Ralston and Dorothy Smith, St Bees; one *s*. *Educ:* Univ. of Manchester Inst. of Sci. and Technol. (BSc Hons Engrg 1972); Univ. of Newcastle (PGCE 1974). Teacher, Lord Wandsworth Coll., 1974–83; Middle Sch. Master, Manchester Grammar Sch., 1983–96. DL W Yorks, 2001. *Recreations:* travel (especially USA), sport, civil aviation. *Address:* Bradford Grammar School, Keighley Road, Bradford BD9 4JP. *T:* (01274) 553702; *e-mail:* hmsec@bradfordgrammar.com.

DAVIE, Alan, CBE 1972; RWA 1991; HRSA 1977; painter, poet, musician, silversmith and jeweller; *b* 28 Sept. 1920. *Educ:* Edinburgh Coll. of Art. DA. Gregory Fellowship, Leeds Univ., 1956–59. Teaching, Central Sch. of Arts and Crafts, London, 1953–56 and 1959–60, and Emily Carr Coll. of Art, Vancouver, 1982. *One-man exhibitions:* Gimpel Fils Galleries in London, Zürich and New York, 1946–; Edinburgh Fest., 1972; Brussels, Paris, Athens and London, 1977; London, Florida, Stuttgart, Zürich, Amsterdam, St Andrews and Edinburgh, 1978; Florida, Edinburgh Fest., Belgium, Sydney and Perth, Australia, 1979; New York, Australia, Colchester and Philadelphia, 1980; London, Frankfurt, NY and Toronto, 1981; Toronto, Edinburgh, Basle, Harrogate, Hong Kong, Paris (Foire Internat. d'Art Contemporain) and Vancouver, 1982; Amsterdam, FIAC Paris, Basel, Madrid, Glasgow and London, 1983; New York, Frankfurt, Cologne, Edinburgh, Windsor, Hertford and Bath, 1984; London (Art Fair, Olympia), Edinburgh and Bonn, 1985; London, Arizona and NY, 1986; Gal. Carre and FIAC, Paris, London, Edinburgh, 1987; Paintings 1956–88, touring Scotland, Helsingborg, 1988; Edinburgh (Scottish Art Gall., and Nat. Gall. of Modern Art), and galleries and museums in Scotland and Sweden, 1989; Madrid, Paris, Helsingford, New York, 1990; Bath, Cracow, Penzance, Copenhagen, 1991; Edinburgh, Vienna, and British Council Travelling Exhibn, 1992; Brighton, Hastings, Ramsgate, Newcastle upon Tyne, Nottingham, Stirling, 1993; Porto, Lisbon, 1994; Brighton, Chichester, 1996; Edinburgh, Brighton, London, Chichester, NY, Inverness, 1997; Pier Arts Centre, Stromness, 1998; Milan, 2001; Tate St Ives, 2003; *retrospective exhibitions:* Sheffield and Lincoln, 1965; Texas, Montreal and Oakland, 1970; Edinburgh, 1972; Germany, 1973; Edinburgh, and Glasgow, 1992; S America, 1993; Barbican, NY and Ireland, 1993; Chicago, 1994; Edinburgh (Scottish Nat. Gall. of Modern Art), 2000; (small paintings) Brighton and Edinburgh Univs, London (Gimpel Fils), Holland, 2001. Work represented in exhibitions: 4th Internat. Art Exhibn, Japan; Pittsburgh Internat.; Documenta II & III, Kassel, Germany; British Painting 1700–1960, Moscow; Salon de Mai, Paris; Peggy Guggenheim Collection; ROSC Dublin; Peter Styvesant Collection; British Painting and Sculpture 1960–1970, Washington; III Bienal de Arte Coltejer, Colombia; Hannover, 1973; British Paintings, 1974; Hayward Gall., 1974; Paris, 1975; Lausanne, 1975; 25 years of British Art, RA, 1977; South America, 1977; Kassell, 1977; Sydney, 1979; Works on paper, Gimpel Fils, 1989; SW Arts Touring Exhibn, 1989; Glasgow and Edinburgh, and Royal W of England Acad., 1992. Works in Public Collections: Tate Gall., Gulbenkian Foundn London, Belfast, Bristol, Durham, Edinburgh, Hull, Leeds, Manchester, Newcastle, Wakefield; Boston, Buffalo, Dallas, Detroit, Yale New Haven, Phoenix, Pittsburgh, Rhode Island, San Francisco, NY (MOMA); Ottawa, Adelaide, Sydney, Auckland, São Paulo, Tel Aviv, Venice, Vienna, Baden-Baden, Bochum, Munich, Amsterdam, Eindhoven, The Hague, Rotterdam, Oslo, Basle, Stockholm, Gothenburg, St Paul de Vence and Paris. Created mural, Tarot Sculpture Gdn, Garavicchio, Tuscany, 1987; commnd to design tapestry, Edinburgh Hosp., 2001. First public recital of music, Gimpel Fils Gall., 1971; music and lecture tour, Sydney, Melbourne, Canberra, 1979. Vis. Prof., Brighton Univ., 1993–. Hon. DLitt: Heriot-Watt, 1994; Hertfordshire, 1995. Prize for Best Foreign Painter, VII Bienal de São Paulo, 1963; Saltire Award, 1977. *Publications:* Magic Reader: eighteen original lithographs, 1992; Alan Davie Drawings, 1997; *relevant publications:* Alan Davie (ed Alan Bowness), 1967; Alan Davie, by D. Hall and M. Tucker, 1992; Alan Davie: the quest for the miraculous (ed Michael Tucker), 1993. *Address:* Gamels Studio, Rush Green, Hertford SG13 7SB.

DAVIE, Sir Michael F.; *see* Ferguson Davie.

DAVIE, Rex; *see* Davie, S. R.

DAVIE, Ronald, PhD; FBPsS; Director, National Children's Bureau, 1982–90; *b* 25 Nov. 1929; *s* of late Thomas Edgar Davie and Gladys (*née* Powell); *m* 1957, Kathleen, *d* of William Wilkinson, Westhoughton, Lancs; one *s* one *d*. *Educ:* King Edward VI Grammar Sch., Aston, Birmingham; Univ. of Reading (BA 1954); Univ. of Manchester (PGCE and Dip. Deaf Educn 1955); Univ. of Birmingham (Dip. Educnl Psych. 1961); Univ. of London (PhD 1970). FBPsS 1973. Teacher, schs for normal and handicapped children, 1955–60; Co. Educnl Psychologist, IoW, 1961–64; Nat. Children's Bureau, London: Sen. Res. Officer, 1964; Dep. Dir, 1968; Dir of Res., 1972; Prof. of Educnl Psychology, Dept of Educn, UC Cardiff, 1974–81. Mem., Special Educnl Needs Tribunal, 1994–2003. Visiting Professor: Oxford Poly., later Oxford Brookes Univ., 1991–97; Cheltenham and Gloucester Coll. of Higher Educn, later Univ. of Gloucestershire, 1997–2006; Visiting Fellow: Inst. of Educn, Univ. of London, 1985–93; Univ. of Newcastle, 1995–2006; Hon. Res. Fellow, UCL, 1991–2006. Co-Dir, Nat. Child Develt Study, 1968–77; Scientific Adviser: Local Authority Social Services Res. Liaison Gp, DHSS, 1975–77; Mental Handicap in Wales Res. Unit, 1977–79; Mental Handicap Res. Liaison Gp, DHSS, 1977–81; Prof. Advr, All Party Parly Gp for Children, 1983–91; Consultant, Whitefield Sch., 1994–98 (Chm., Academic Bd, 1991–94); Hon. Consultant: Play Board, 1984–87; 1981 Educn Act Res. Dissemination Project, 1986–89. President: Links Assoc., 1977–90; Child Develt Soc., 1990–91; Nat. Assoc. for Special Educnl Needs, 1992–94; Vice-Pres., British Assoc. for Early Childhood Educn, 1984–95, Young Minds, 1991–2007; Chairman: Trng and Educn Cttee, Nat. Assoc. Mental Health, 1969–72; Assoc. for Child Psychol. and Psychiatry, 1972–73 (Hon. Sec. 1965–70); Standing Conf. of Professional Assocs in S Wales Concerned with Children, 1974–84; Working Party, Children Appearing Before Juvenile Courts, Children's Reg. Planning Cttee for Wales, 1975–77; Develt Psychol. Section, Brit. Psychol. Soc., 1975–77 (Treas. 1973–75); Wales Standing Conf. for Internat. Year of the Child, 1978–79; Steering Cttee, Child Health and Educn Study, 1979–84; Adv. Bd, Whitefield Library, 1983–98; Task Gp on Special Educnl Needs, 1989, Steering Gp on Severe Learning Difficulties, 1991, Nat. Curriculum Council; Policy Sub-Cttee, Nat. Assoc. for Special Educnl Needs, 1994–97; Bd of Trustees, Eden Valley Hospice, 2000 (Trustee, 1998–2006; Vice Chm., 2001). Member: Council of Management, Nat. Assoc. Mental Health, 1969–77; Working Party, Children at Risk, DHSS, 1970–72; Educn and Employment Cttee, Nat. Deaf Children's Soc., 1972–78; Management Cttee, Craig y Parc Sch., 1974–76; Cttee, Welsh Br., Assoc. for Child Psychol. and Psychiatry, 1975–80; Bd of Assessors, Therapeutic Educn, 1975–82; Council, British Psychol Soc., 1977–80; Experimental Panel on Children in Care, SSRC, 1978–79; NCSE Internat. Conf. Prog. Cttee, 1982–85; Council, Child Accident Prevention Trust, 1982–88; Evaluation Panel, Royal Jubilee Trusts, 1982–94; Steering Cttee on Special Educn Needs Res., DES, 1983–86; Bd of Trustees, Stress Syndrome Foundn, 1983–85; Adv. Bd, Ravenswood Village, 1984–91; Bd of Governors, Elizabeth Garrett Anderson Sch., 1985–88; Council, Caldecott Community, 1985–96; Research Cttee, Froebel Inst., 1987–88; Nat. Curriculum Council, 1988–90; BBC/IBA Central Appeals Adv. Cttee, 1989–93. Chm. Govs, Fellview Sch., 1998–2001. Patron, Action for Special Educnl Needs, 1994–97. Church Warden, St Kentigern's, Caldbeck, 2004–. FRSA 1991. Hon. FRCPCH 1996. Hon. DEd: CNAA, 1991; UWE, 1998; Hon. DLitt Birmingham, 1999. Member Editorial Board: Internat. Jl of Adolescence and Youth 1986–2003; Children and Society, 1987–90. *Publications:* (co-author) 11,000 Seven-Year Olds, 1966; Directory of Voluntary Organisations concerned with Children, 1969; Living with Handicap, 1970; From Birth to Seven, 1972; Child Sexual Abuse: the way forward after Cleveland, 1989; Listening to Children in Education, 1996; The Voice of the Child 1996; chapters in books and papers in sci. and other jls on special educn, psychol., child care health, effects of TV on children, and children's ownership and use of mobile phones. *Recreations:* photography, antiques, good music of all kinds. *Address:* Bridge House, Upton Caldbeck, Cumbria CA7 8EU.

DAVIE, (Stephen) Rex, CB 1993; Member: Council on Tribunals, 1995–2001; Civil Service Appeal Board, 1995–2001; Principal Establishment and Finance Officer (Under Secretary), Cabinet Office, 1989–93; *b* 11 June 1933; *s* of late Sydney and Dorothy Davie *m* 1955, Christine Stockwell; one *s* one *d*. *Educ:* Ilfracombe Grammar Sch. Executive Officer, Inland Revenue, 1951. National Service, RAF, 1952–54. Office of Minister for Science, 1962; NEDO, 1967; CSD, 1970; Asst Sec. 1979; Cabinet Office, 1983; Sen. Sec. Security Commn, 1979–89. Mem. Council, Inst. of Cancer Res., 1993– (Vice Chm. 1995–2003). *Recreations:* reading, travel. *Address:* 2 Linnet Close, Basingstoke, Hant RG22 5PD. *Clubs:* Athenæum, Civil Service.

DAVIE, Timothy Douglas; Director, BBC Audio and Music, since 2008; *b* 25 April 1967; *s* of Douglas John Davie and Alicia Margaret Davie; *m* 1997, Anne Claire Shotbolt three *s*. *Educ:* Selwyn Coll., Cambridge (BA 1989). Brand Manager, Procter and Gamble 1989–93; Vice Pres., Pepsico, 1993–2005; Dir, Marketing, Communications and Audiences, BBC, 2005–08. Dir, Digitaluk (formerly Switchco), 2005–; Chm., Freesat 2007. Mem., Mktg Gp of GB, 2001–. Trustee, Children in Need, 2005–. *Recreations:* my young family, running, reading, ski-ing, dance music, fresh air, strong coffee. *Address:* BBC Media Centre, Wood Lane, W12 7TS. *T:* (020) 8008 2115; *e-mail:* tim.davie@bbc.co.uk. *Club:* Soho House.

DAVIES; *see* Prys-Davies.

DAVIES, family name of **Barons Darwen**, **Davies**, **Davies of Coity** and **Davies of Oldham**.

DAVIES, 3rd Baron *cr* 1932, of Llandinam; **David Davies,** CEng, MICE; Vice Lord Lieutenant of Powys, since 2004; Chairman, Welsh National Opera Company 1975–2000; *b* 2 Oct. 1940; *s* of 2nd Baron and Ruth Eldrydd (*d* 1966), 3rd *d* of Major W M. Dugdale, CB, DSO; *S* father (killed in action), 1944; *m* 1972, Beryl, *d* of W. J. Oliver two *s* two *d*. *Educ:* Eton; King's Coll., Cambridge (MA); MBA. DL Powys, 1997. *Heir:* Hon. David Daniel Davies [*b* 23 Oct. 1975; *m* 2001, Leyla Natasha, *d* of Martin and Elain Pope]. *Address:* Plas Dinam, Llandinam, Powys SY17 5DQ.

DAVIES OF COITY, Baron *cr* 1997 (Life Peer), of Penybont, in the co. of Mid Glamorgan; **David Garfield Davies,** CBE 1996; General Secretary, Union of Shop Distributive and Allied Workers, 1986–97; *b* 24 June 1935; *s* of David John Davies and Lizzie Ann Davies; *m* 1960, Marian (*née* Jones); four *d*. *Educ:* Heolgam Secondary Modern School; Bridgend Tech Coll. (part time). Served RAF, 1956–58. Junior operative electrical apprentice and electrician, British Steel Corp., Port Talbot, 1950–69; Area Organiser, USDAW, Ipswich, 1969–73; Dep. Divl Officer, USDAW, London/Ipswich 1973–78; Nat. Officer, USDAW, Manchester, 1978–85. Mem., TUC Gen. Council 1986–97; Chm., TUC Internat. Cttee, 1992–94; TUC spokesperson on internat. affairs

1994–97. Member: Exec. Bd, ICFTU, 1992–97; Exec. Cttee, ETUC, 1992–97. Mem., Employment Appeal Tribunal, 1991–2006. Governor, Birmingham Coll. of Food, Tourism and Creative Studies, 1995–99. JP 1972–79. Trustee, Royal Sch. for the Deaf and Communication Disorders, Manchester, 2004–07. President: Kidney Res. UK, 2002–; Manchester S Scout Council, 2004–. *Recreations:* swimming, reading, spectator sports (supporter, Stockport County FC); formerly soccer, cricket, Rugby. *Address:* 64 Dairyground Road, Bramhall, Stockport, Cheshire SK7 2QW. *T:* (0161) 439 9548. *Clubs:* Reform, Union Jack; Lancashire CC.

DAVIES OF OLDHAM, Baron *cr* 1997 (Life Peer), of Broxbourne in the co. of Hertfordshire; **Bryan Davies;** PC 2006; Captain of the Yeomen of the Guard (Deputy Chief Whip, House of Lords), since 2003; *b* 9 Nov. 1939; *s* of George William and Beryl Davies; *m* 1963, Monica Rosemary Mildred Shearing; two *s* one *d. Educ:* Redditch High Sch.; University Coll. London (BA Hons History); Inst. of Education (CertEd); London Sch. of Economics (BScEcons). Teacher, Latymer Sch., 1962–65; Lectr, Middlesex Polytechnic at Enfield, 1965–74. Sec., Parly Labour Party, 1979–92. Contested (Lab): Norfolk Central, 1966; Newport W, 1983. MP (Lab): Enfield North, Feb. 1974–1979; Oldham Central and Royton, 1992–97. An Asst Govt Whip, 1978–79; front bench spokesman on Further and Higher Educn, 1993–97. Member: Select Cttee on Public Expenditure, 1975–79; Select Cttee on Overseas Develt, 1975–79; Select Cttee on Nat. Heritage, 1992–93. A Lord in Waiting (Govt Whip), 2000–03. Chm., FEFCE, 1998–2000. Mem., MRC, 1977–79. Pres., RoSPA, 1998–2000. *Recreations:* sport, literature. *Address:* 28 Churchfields, Broxbourne, Herts EN10 7JS. *T:* (01992) 410418.

DAVIES, Adele, (Mrs R. O. Davies); *see* Biss, A.

DAVIES, Alan Roger; actor and comedian; *b* 6 March 1966; *s* of Roy and Shirley Davies; *m* 2007, Katie Maskell. *Educ:* Bancroft's Sch.; Loughton Coll. of Further Educn; Univ. of Kent (BA Hons 1988). Stand-up comedian, 1988–; Live at the Lyric, 1994; Urban Trauma (one-man show), Duchess Th., 1998; *television* series include: Jonathan Creek, 1996–2003; Bob and Rose, 2001; QI, 2003–; The Brief, 2004, 2005; *radio* includes: The Alan Davies Show, Radio 4, 1998; *films* include: Angus, Thongs and Perfect Snogging, 2008. Columnist, The Times, 2003–06. Hon. DLitt Kent, 2003. *Recreations:* Arsenal FC, motor cycling, scuba diving. *Address:* c/o ARG, 4 Great Portland Street, W1W 8PA; *e-mail:* alandavies4@aol.com.

DAVIES, Sir Alan (Seymour), Kt 2000; JP; Headmaster, Copland Community School and Technology Centre Foundation, since 1988; *b* 21 Feb. 1947; *s* of Seymour George Davies and Sarah Louise Davies; *m* 1972, Frances Patricia Williamson; one *s* two *d. Educ:* Inst. of Educn, London Univ. (BEd, CertEd); NE London Poly. (MEd). Teacher, E Barnet Sch., 1972–75; Teacher, 1975–80, Dep. Head, 1980–86, McEntee Sen. High Sch.; Headteacher, Sidney Chaplin Sch., 1986–88. Consultant Headteacher, London Leadership Challenge, 2003. Chm. of Govs, Chalkhill Primary Sch., 2003; Governor: Park Lane Primary Sch., 1998; Mitchell Brook Primary Sch., 1999; Harlesden Primary Sch., 2000. JP Barnet, 1984. *Recreation:* sport. *Address:* 39 Grants Close, Mill Hill, NW7 1DD. *T:* (020) 8349 9731.

DAVIES, Prof. Alwyn George, FRS 1989; Professor of Chemistry, University College London, 1969–91, now Emeritus; *b* 13 May 1926; *s* of John Lewis and Victoria May Davies; *m* 1956, Margaret Drake; one *s* one *d. Educ:* Hamond's Grammar Sch., Swaffham; University College London (BSc, PhD, DSc; Fellow 1991). CChem, FRSC. Lectr, Battersea Polytechnic, 1949; Lectr, 1953, Reader, 1964, UCL. Ingold Lectr, RSC, 1992–93. Medal for Organic Reaction Mechanism, RSC, 1989; Humboldt Prize, Freiburg Univ., 1994. *Publications:* Organic Peroxides, 1959; Organotin Chemistry, 1997, 2nd edn 2004; scientific papers on physical organic chemistry and organometallic chemistry in learned jls. *Address:* Chemistry Department, University College London, 20 Gordon Street, WC1H 0AJ. *T:* (020) 7679 4701; *e-mail:* a.g.davies@ucl.ac.uk.

DAVIES, Andrew; *see* Davies, D. A.

DAVIES, Andrew L.; *see* Lloyd-Davies.

DAVIES, Andrew Robert Tudor; Member (C) South Wales Central, National Assembly for Wales, since 2007; *b* 8 April 1968; *s* of Tudor John Davies and Margaret Elizabeth Rees Davies; *m* 1991, Julia Mary; two *s* two *d. Educ:* Balfour House Sch., St Athan; Wycliffe Coll., Stonehouse. Partner, family farming and agricl business. National Farmers Union: Chm., 2001, Pres., 2002, Glamorgan; Mem., Welsh Council, 2002–07; Mem., Nat. Combinable Crops Bd, 2004–07. Chm., Creative Rural Communities, 2003–04. Various positions in Cons Party. Gov., Llanfair Primary Sch., 2001–07. Chm., Llantrisant Young Farmers' Club, 1988. *Recreations:* work, travel, family. *Address:* Foxwood House, The Garn Farm, St Hilary, Vale of Glamorgan CF71 7DP. *T:* (01446) 773493; *e-mail:* aroberttdavies@aol.com. *Club:* Farmers (Glamorgan).

DAVIES, Andrew Wynford; writer; *b* Rhiwbina, Cardiff, 20 Sept. 1936; *e s* of Wynford and Hilda Davies; *m* 1960, Diana Lennox Huntley; one *s* one *d. Educ:* Whitchurch Grammar Sch., Cardiff; University College London. Teacher: St Clement Danes Grammar Sch., 1958–61; Woodberry Down Comprehensive Sch., 1961–63; Lecturer: Coventry Coll. of Educn, 1963–71; Univ. of Warwick, 1971–87. Hon. Fellow, Univ. of Wales, Cardiff, 1997. Hon. DLitt: Coventry, 1994; Warwick, 2004; UCL, 2006; Hon. DArts De Montfort, 2003; DUniv Open, 2004. Guardian Children's Fiction Award, 1979; Boston Globe Horn Award, 1979; BPG Award, 1980, 1990, 1995, 1997, 2000, 2006; Pye Colour TV Award, best children's writer, 1981; writer's awards: RTS, 1986–87, 2006; BAFTA, 1989, 1993, 1998, 2006 (Fellow 2002); Writers' Guild, 1991, 1992, 1996; Primetime Emmy, 1991. *Television includes:* To Serve Them All My Days, 1979; A Very Peculiar Practice, 1986–87; Mother Love, 1989; House of Cards, 1990; Filipina Dreamers, 1991; The Old Devils, Anglo-Saxon Attitudes, A Very Polish Practice, 1992; Anna Lee, Harnessing Peacocks, To Play the King, 1993; Middlemarch, 1994; Game On, Pride and Prejudice, The Final Cut, 1995; Emma, Moll Flanders, Wilderness, 1996; A Few Short Journeys of the Heart, Bill's New Frock, 1997; Getting Hurt, Vanity Fair, A Rather English Marriage, 1998; Wives and Daughters, 1999; Take a Girl Like You, 2000; Othello, The Way We Live Now, 2001; Tipping the Velvet, Dr Zhivago, Daniel Deronda, 2002; Boudica, 2003; He Knew He Was Right, 2004; Falling, Bleak House, 2005; The Chatterley Affair, The Line of Beauty, 2006; Northanger Abbey, The Diary of a Nobody, Fanny Hill, A Room With A View, 2007; Sense and Sensibility, Affinity, Sleep With Me, Little Dorrit, 2008; *stage plays:* Rose, 1981; Prin, 1990; *film screenplays:* Circle of Friends, 1995; B. Monkey, 1996; Bridget Jones's Diary, The Tailor of Panama, 2001; Bridget Jones: The Edge of Reason, 2004. *Publications: for children:* The Fantastic Feats of Dr Boox, 1972; Conrad's War, 1978; Marmalade and Rufus, 1980; Marmalade Atkins in Space, 1981; Educating Marmalade, 1982; Danger Marmalade at Work, 1983; Marmalade Hits the Big Time, 1984; Alfonso Bonzo, 1987; Marmalade on the Ball, 1995; (with Diana Davies): Poonam's Pets, 1990; Raj in Charge, 1994; *fiction:* A Very Peculiar Practice, 1986; The New Frontier, 1987; Getting Hurt, 1989; Dirty Faxes, 1990; B. Monkey, 1992. *Recreations:* tennis, food, alcohol. *Address:* c/o The Agency, 24 Pottery Lane, W11 4LZ.

DAVIES, Prof. Anna Elbina, (A. Morpurgo Davies), Hon. DBE 2000; FBA 1985; Diebold Professor of Comparative Philology, Oxford University, 2003–04 (Professor of Comparative Philology, 1971–2003), now Emeritus; Fellow of Somerville College, Oxford, 1971–2004, now Emeritus; *b* Milan, 21 June 1937; *d* of Augusto Morpurgo and Maria (*née* Castelnuovo); *m* 1962, J. K. Davies, *qv* (marr. diss. 1978). *Educ:* Liceo-Ginnasio Giulio Cesare, Rome; Univ. of Rome. Dott.lett. Rome, 1959; Libera docente, Rome, 1963; MA Oxford, 1964. Asst in Classical Philology, Univ. of Rome, 1959–61; Junior Research Fellow, Center for Hellenic Studies, Harvard Univ., 1961–62; Univ. Lectr in Classical Philology, Oxford, 1964–71; Fellow of St Hilda's Coll., Oxford, 1966–71, Hon. Fellow, 1972–. Visiting Professor: Univ. of Pennsylvania, 1971; Yale Univ., 1977; Pavia, 2005; Berkeley, 2006, 2007; Collitz Prof. of Ling. Soc. of America, Univ. of South Florida, 1975; Webster Vis. Prof., Stanford Univ., 1988; Sather Prof. of Classics, Univ. of Calif at Berkeley, 2000. Lectures: Semple, Univ. of Cincinnati, 1983; Jackson, Harvard Univ., 1990; Sather, Berkeley, 2000. Pres., Philological Soc., 1976–80, Hon. Vice-Pres., 1980–. Delegate, Oxford University Press, 1992–2004. FSA 1974; Foreign Mem., Amer. Philosophical Soc., 1991; Foreign Hon. Mem., Amer. Acad. of Arts and Sciences, 1986; Corresponding Member: Österreichische Akademie der Wissenschaften, Vienna, 1988; Inst. de France (Acad. des inscriptions et belles-lettres), 1992; Bayerische Akademie der Wissenschaften, 1998; Mem., Academia Europaea, 1989; Hon. Mem., Linguistic Soc. of America, 1993. Hon. DLitt St Andrews, 1981. Premio linceo per la linguistica, Accad. dei Lincei, 1996. *Publications:* (as A. Morpurgo) Mycenaeae Graecitatis Lexicon, 1963; (ed with W. Meid) Studies in Greek, Italic and Indo-European Linguistics, festschrift for L. R. Palmer, 1976; (ed with Y. Duhoux) Linear B: a 1984 survey, 1985; La linguistica dell'Ottocento, 1996; Nineteenth-Century Linguistics, 1998; *festschrift:* Indo-European Perspectives, ed by J. H. W. Penney, 2004; articles and reviews on comparative and classical philology in learned jls. *Address:* Somerville College, Oxford OX2 6HD; 22 Yarnells Hill, Oxford OX2 9BD. *T:* (01865) 247099.

DAVIES, Ven. Anthony; *see* Davies, Ven. V. A.

DAVIES, (Anthony) Roger; a District Judge (Magistrates' Courts) (formerly Metropolitan Stipendiary Magistrate), 1985–2005; Chairman, Family Courts, 1989–2005; a Recorder, 1993–2005; *b* 1 Sept. 1940; *er s* of late R. George Davies and Megan Davies, Penarth, Glam; *m* 1967, Clare, *e d* of Comdr W. A. Walters, RN; twin *s* one *d. Educ:* Bridgend; King's Coll., London. LLB (Hons); AKC. Called to the Bar, Gray's Inn, 1965 (Lord Justice Holker Sen. Schol.). Practised at Bar, London and SE Circuit, 1965–85. *Recreations:* reading (history, biography), music (especially opera), travel, family life. *Club:* Travellers.

DAVIES, Barry George, MBE 2005; broadcaster, BBC Television sport and events; *b* 24 Oct. 1937; *s* of Roy Charles Davies and Dorothy Davies; *m* 1968, Edna (Penny) Pegna; one *s* one *d. Educ:* Cranbrook Sch., Kent; London Univ. (King's Coll. Royal Dental Hosp.). Commnd RASC, 1960. Sub-editor/reporter, The Times, 1963–66; Independent Television, 1966–69; commentator, World Cup 1966, Olympic Games 1968; joined BBC Television, 1969; commentator, Match of the Day, 1969–2004; commentator and presenter covering variety of sports, including: World Cup, 1970–2002; Olympic Games, 1972–; Winter Olympics, 1984–; Commonwealth Games, 1978–; Wimbledon, 1983–; University Boat Race, 1993–2004; commentator, LBC, University Boat Race, 2008–. Commentator: Lord Mayor's Show, 1996–2003; (last) Royal Tournament, 1999; All the Queen's Horses, 2003. Presenter, Maestro Series, 1985–87. *Publication:* Interesting, Very Interesting: the autobiography, 2007. *Recreations:* family, theatre, political biographies, all sports (enthusiasm way ahead of talent). *Address:* Luxton Harris Ltd, 2 Deanery Street, W1K 1AU. *Clubs:* Lord's Taverners; Hawks (Cambridge); Wentworth.

DAVIES, Brian; *see* Davies, E. B.

DAVIES, Prof. Brian Lawrence, PhD, DSc; FREng, FIMechE; Professor of Medical Robotics, Imperial College, London, since 2000; *b* 18 July 1939; *s* of William and Elizabeth Davies; *m* 1975, Marcia Mills; one *d. Educ:* Harrow Grammar Sch.; UCL (MPhil 1970); Imperial Coll., London (PhD 1995; DSc 2001). CEng 1973, FREng 2005; FIMechE 1990. GEC Ltd: indentured apprenticeship, 1955–60; design engr, 1960–63; Res. Asst in Mech. Engrg, 1963–69, Lectr, 1969–83, UCL; Lectr, 1983–89, Sen. Lectr, 1989–93, Reader, 1993–2000, in Mech. Engrg, Imperial Coll., London. Founder and Tech. Dir, Acrobot Co. Ltd, 1999–. Institute of Mechanical Engineering: Mem. Bd, 1990–, Chm., 1998–2001, Med. Engrg Div.; Mem. Council, 1998–2001. Chm., Strategic Acad. Bd, Swiss Nat. Computer Aided Med. Engrg, 2001–. *Publications:* Engineering Drawing and Computer Graphics, 1986; (jtly) Computer-aided Drawing and Design, 1991; Computer Integrated Surgery, 1995; over 200 refereed papers mainly on computer-aided surgery and med. robotics. *Recreations:* painting, walking. *Address:* Department of Mechanical Engineering, Imperial College, London, SW7 2AZ. *T:* (020) 7594 7054, *Fax:* (020) 7584 7239.

DAVIES, Brian Meredith; *see* Davies, J. B. M.

DAVIES, Brigid Catherine Brennan; *see* Gardner, B. C. B.

DAVIES, Bryn, CBE 1987 (MBE 1978); DL; Member, General Council, Wales Trades Union Congress, 1974–91 (Vice-Chairman, 1983–84, Chairman, 1984–85); *b* 22 Jan. 1932; *s* of Gomer and Ann Davies; *m* 1st, 1956, Esme Irene Gould (*d* 1988); two *s*; 2nd, 1991, Katherine Lewis. *Educ:* Cwmlai School, Tonyrefail. Served HM Forces (RAMC), 1949–51; Forestry Commn, 1951–56; South Wales and Hereford Organiser, Nat. Union of Agricultural and Allied Workers, subseq. TGWU (following merger), 1956–91. Chm., Mid Glamorgan AHA, 1978–94; Member: Welsh Council, 1965–81; Development Commn, 1975–81; Nat. Cttee (Wales), Forestry Commn, 1978–86; Nat. Water Council, 1982–85; Council, British Heart Foundn, 1986–. Trustee, Sir Geraint Evans Wales Heart Res. Inst. Patron, Mencap Jubilee Festival. DL Mid Glamorgan, 1992. *Recreations:* cricket, Rugby football. *Address:* 3 Lias Cottages, Porthcawl, Mid Glamorgan CF36 3AD. *T:* (01656) 785851. *Clubs:* Tonyrefail Rugby (Pres., 1985–88); Pyle and Kenfig Golf; Pyle Rugby; Pirates (Porthcawl).

DAVIES, Byron, OBE 2008; CEng, FICE; Chief Executive, Cardiff County Council, since 1996; *b* 23 April 1947; *s* of Cecil and Elizabeth Gwendoline Davies; *m* 1972, Sarah Kay Lott; one *s* one *d. Educ:* Swansea Univ. (BSc Hons); Univ. of Glamorgan (MPhil). CEng 1976; FICE 1992. Work in private sector orgns, 1968–72; with Swansea CC and Devon CC, 1972–77; South Glamorgan County Council, 1977–96: various sen. civil engrg, property develt and gen. mgt posts; Dir, Property Services, 1990–92, Chief Exec., 1992–96. Director: Cardiff-Wales Airport, 1992–; Millennium Stadium plc, 1996–; Cardiff Chamber of Trade and Commerce, 1999–; Cardiff Marketing, 1999–; Cardiff Initiative, 1999–. Clerk to Lieutenancy of S Glam, 1992–; Sec. to Lord Chancellor's Adv. Cttee for S Glam, 1992–. Sec., Soc. of Local Authority Chief Execs and Sen. Managers in Wales, 2004–; Jun. Vice-Pres., SOLACE UK, 2005–; Vice Pres., Union des Dirigeants Territoriaux de l'Europe, 2006–. Ex-Officio Mem., Council and Court, Univ. of Wales, Cardiff, 1992–. FCMI (FIMgt 1992); Pres., Cardiff Inst. of Mgt, 1999–. *Publications:*

contrib. on engrg and mgt to professional jls. *Recreations:* walking, sport, cinema, photography. *Address:* The Cottage, Ystradowen, Cowbridge, CF71 7SZ.

DAVIES, Sir (Charles) Noel, Kt 1996; CEng, FIMechE; Chairman, Ricardo PLC (formerly Ricardo Group plc), 1997–2003; *b* 2 Dec. 1933; *s* of Henry Norman Davies and Vena Mary Bebb; *m* 1958, Sheila Rigby; two *s* one *d*. *Educ:* Ellesmere Coll., Shropshire; Imperial Coll., London (BSc). CEng 1956; FIMechE 1980; FCGI 1980. Dir, Vickers PLC, 1980–84; Chief Executive: 600 Gp, 1984–89; VSEL PLC, 1989–95; Dep. Chm., British Energy PLC, 1995–99; Chairman: Nuclear Electric Ltd, 1995–98; Powell Duffryn PLC, 1996–2000. Mem., Sec. of State's Industrial Develt Adv. Bd, 1987–94. Pres., EEF, 1994–96. *Recreations:* vintage cars, motor-cycles, gardening.

DAVIES, Prof. Christine Tullis Hunter, OBE 2006; PhD; FInstP; FRSE; Professor of Physics, University of Glasgow, since 1999; *b* Clacton, 19 Nov. 1959; *d* of Crawford Stewart and Elizabeth Stewart (*née* Clachan); *m* 1982, John Davies; two *d*. *Educ:* Colchester Co. High Sch. for Girls; Churchill Coll., Cambridge (BA 1981; PhD 1984). FInstP 1988. Postdoctoral res. associate, Cornell Univ., NY, 1984–86; SERC Advanced Fellow, 1987–93; Lectr, 1993–96, Reader, 1996–99, Univ. of Glasgow. Fulbright Schol. and Leverhulme Trust Fellow, Univ. of Calif at Santa Barbara, 1997–98. Mem., Particle Physics Grants Panel (theory), 2006–09, Educn, Trng and Careers Cttee, 2006–09, STFC; Mem., Physics Rev. Panel, Res. Council UK, 2008. Mem. Council, Inst. of Physics, 2007– (Chm., Diversity Cttee, 2007–). FRSE 2001. *Publications:* contrib. jls on theoretical particle physics. *Recreations:* walking, photography. *Address:* Department of Physics and Astronomy, University of Glasgow, Glasgow G12 8QQ. *T:* (0141) 330 4710.

DAVIES, Christopher Graham, (Chris); Member (Lib Dem) North West Region, England, European Parliament, since 1999; *b* 7 July 1954; *s* of Caryl St John Davies and Margaret (*née* McLeod); *m* 1979, Carol Hancox; one *d*. *Educ:* Cheadle Hulme Sch.; Gonville and Caius Coll., Cambridge (BA 1975, MA 1978); Univ. of Kent. Member: Liverpool City Council, 1980–84 (Chm., Housing Cttee, 1982–83); Oldham MBC, 1994–98. Manager: Public Affairs Div., Extel, 1983–85; Northern PR, Liverpool, 1985–87; Dir, Abercromby Consultancy Ltd, 1988–91; marketing and communications consultant, 1991–95; Sen. Consultant, Concept Communications, 1997–99. Contested (Lib Dem) Littleborough and Saddleworth, 1987, 1992. MP (Lib Dem) Littleborough and Saddleworth, July 1995–1997; contested (Lib Dem) Oldham East and Saddleworth, 1997. Leader, British Lib Dem MEPs, 2004–06; Lib Dem spokesman on envmt and climate change (formerly on envmt), 1999–. *Recreation:* fell running. *Address:* 4 Higher Kinders, Greenfield, Oldham OL3 7BH; European Parliament, Rue Wiertz, 1047 Brussels, Belgium. *T:* (2) 2847353.

DAVIES, Prof. Colin; architectural journalist; Professor of Architectural Theory, London Metropolitan University (formerly University of North London), since 2000 (Lecturer, 1992–2000); *b* 24 March 1948; *s* of John and Hazel Davies; *m* 1st, 1973, Diana Lamont (marr. diss.); one *s*; 2nd, 1992, Susan Wallington. *Educ:* King Henry VIII Sch., Coventry; Oxford Polytechnic; Architectural Assoc.; University College London (MSc). AADip, RIBA. Asst Editor, Building Magazine, 1975–77; Associate Partner, Derek Stow and Partners, 1977–81; freelance journalist, 1981–88; Editor, Architects' Jl, 1989–90. Lectr, Bartlett, Canterbury and Brighton Schs of Architecture, 1983–91. *Publications:* High Tech Architecture, 1988; Century Tower, 1992; Hopkins, 1993; Commerzbank, Frankfurt, 1997; Hopkins 2, 2001; The Prefabricated Home, 2005; Key Houses of the Twentieth Century, 2006; contribs to arch. jls. *Recreation:* choral singing. *Address:* 3 The Copse, Fortis Green, N2 9HL.

DAVIES, Colin Godfrey, CEng, FIET; FRAeS; Director (formerly Director General, Projects and Engineering), National Air Traffic Services, 1991–97; *b* 9 Nov. 1934; *s* of Thomas William Godfrey Davies and Kathleen Mabel Davies; *m* 1966, Enid Beryl Packham; two *s*. *Educ:* King's Sch., Bruton; Loughborough Univ. (BSc Hons). FIET (FIEE 1986); FRAeS 1995. RAF Flying Officer (Aircrew), 1952–54. Cable and Wireless, 1955–90: Radio Technician, 1955–59; student, 1960–64; Special Projects Engr, Engr-in-Chief's Dept, 1964–68; Project Manager, 1968–75; Manager Transmission, Omantel, 1975–76; Manager Engrg, Fintel, 1976–77; Chief Engr Long Distance Services, Emirtel, 1978–79; Manager Internat. Services, 1980–82, Gen. Manager, 1983–87, Qatar; Dir of Corporate Technology and of two associated cos, 1987–90; Dep. Dir, Communications, NATS, 1990–91. Sen. Advr, Frequentis, Vienna, 1998–2003. *Recreations:* sport (badminton, sailing, ski-ing), gardening, photography. *Address:* Ibex House, Church Lane, Worplesdon, Guildford, Surrey GU3 3RU. *T:* (01483) 233214.

DAVIES, Cynog Glyndwr; *see* Dafis, C. G.

DAVIES, Cyril James, CBE 1987; DL; Chief Executive, City of Newcastle upon Tyne, 1980–86; *b* 24 Aug. 1923; *s* of James and Frances Davies; *m* 1948, Elizabeth Leggett; two *s* two *d*. *Educ:* Heaton Grammar Sch. CIPFA. Served RN, Fleet Air Arm, 1942–46. Entered City Treasurer's Dept, Newcastle upon Tyne, 1940: Dep. City Treas., 1964; City Treas., 1969; Treas., Tyne and Wear Co., 1973–80. Mem. Court, Univ. of Newcastle upon Tyne, 1999–2005. DL Tyne and Wear, 1989. Hon. DCL Newcastle, 1998. *Recreations:* theatre, walking, music. *Address:* 4 Montagu Court, Gosforth, Newcastle upon Tyne NE3 4JL. *T:* (0191) 285 9685.

DAVIES, Dai; *see* Davies, David Clifford.

DAVIES, Dr David; Director: Elmhirst Trust, 1987–2002; Open College of the Arts, 1989–99 (Administrative Director, 1988–89); *b* 11 Aug. 1939; *s* of late Trefor Alun and Kathleen Elsie Davies; *m* 1968, Joanna Rachel, *d* of late David Brian Peace, MBE; one *s* three *d*. *Educ:* Nottingham High Sch.; Peterhouse, Cambridge. MA, PhD. Res. Scientist, Dept of Geophysics, Cambridge, 1961–69; Leader, Seismic Discrimination Gp, MIT Lincoln Laboratory, 1970–73; Editor of Nature, 1973–79; Dir, Dartington N Devon Trust, 1980–87. Rapporteur, Seismic Study Gp of Stockholm Internat. Peace Res. Inst. (SIPRI), 1968–73; Chm., British Seismic Verification Res. Project, 1987–91. Member: Warnock Cttee on artificial human fertilisation, 1982–84; BMA Working Party on Surrogacy, 1988–89. Chm., Ivanhoe Trust, 1986–2001. Member Council: Internat. Disaster Inst., 1979; Beaford Arts Centre, 1980–87; Voluntary Arts Network, 1992–95; Trustee: Bristol Exploratory, 1983–90; Cooper Art Gall., Barnsley, 1994–2001; Yorks Organiser, Open Coll. of the Arts, 1987–89. Musical Director: Blackheath Opera Workshop, 1977–79; Winterbourne Opera, 2006–; Conductor, Exmoor Chamber Orchestra, 1980–87; Member: Musica Rustica, 2002–; Cross Keys Ensemble, 2006–; Producer, Ebblesway Opera, 2004–. Hon. Lectr, Bretton Hall Coll., 1987–2001. Hon. Fellow: Univ. of Leicester, 1988; Univ. of Leeds, 1989. *Publications:* Seismic Methods for Monitoring Underground Explosions, 1968; numerous scientific papers. *Recreation:* keyboard playing.

DAVIES, (David) Andrew; Member (Lab) Swansea West, National Assembly for Wales, since 1999; Minister for Finance and Public Service Delivery, since 2007; *b* 5 May 1952; *s* of Wallace Morton Davies and Elizabeth Muriel Jane Davies (*née* Baldwin); *m* 1978, Deborah Frost (marr. diss. 1991). *Educ:* UC, Swansea (BSc Econ 1979; PGCE 1981); Gwent Coll. of Higher Educn (Dip. Counselling). Lectr in Adult and Further Educn, Swansea Univ., WEA and Swansea Coll., 1980–84; Regl Official, Wales Labour Party, 1984–91; Head of Employee Develt and Assistance Prog., Ford Motor Co., 1991–96; Lectr, Swansea Coll., 1994–97; Special Projects Officer (Referendum), Wales Labour Party, 1997–98; Associate Dir, Welsh Context, 1998–99. National Assembly for Wales: Chief Whip, Labour Gp, 1999–2000; Business Manager, then Minister for Assembly Business, 1999–2002; Minister: for Econ. Develt, 2002–06; for Transport, 2003–06; for Enterprise, Innovation and Networks, 2006–07; for Social Justice and Public Service Delivery, 2007. *Recreations:* bird watching, cooking, gardening, the arts (especially contemporary dance and film). *Address:* National Assembly for Wales, Cardiff Bay, Cardiff CF99 1NA. *T:* (029) 2089 8249.

DAVIES, David Clifford, (Dai); MP (Ind) Blaenau Gwent, since June 2006; 26 Nov. 1959; *m* Amanda Gearing; one *s*. *Educ:* secondary sch.; served electrical apprenticeship. Steelworker, British Steel, subseq. Corus, Blaenau Gwent, 1976–2002; work with trade unions, 2002–05. Researcher for Peter Law, MP, 2005–06. *Address:* House of Commons, SW1A 0AA.

DAVIES, David Cyril, BA, LLB; Headmaster, Crown Woods School, 1971–84; *b* 7 Oct. 1925; *s* of D. T. E. Davies and Mrs G. V. Davies, JP; *m* 1952, Joan Rogers, BSc; one *s* one *d*. *Educ:* Lewis Sch., Pengam; UCW Aberystwyth. Asst Master, Ebbw Vale Gram. Sch., 1951–55; Head, Lower Sch., Netteswell Bilateral Sch., 1955–58; Sen. Master and Dep. Headmaster, Peckham Manor Sch., 1958–64; Headmaster: Greenway Comprehensive Sch., 1964–67; Woodberry Down Sch., 1967–71. Pres., Inverliever Lodge Trust, 1971–84. *Recreations:* reading, Rugby and roughing it. *Address:* 9 Plaxtol Close, Bromley, Kent BR1 3AU. *T:* (020) 8464 4187.

DAVIES, Sir David (Evan Naunton), Kt 1994; CBE 1986; PhD, DSc; FRS 1984; FREng; Chairman, Hazard Forum, since 2003; President, Royal Academy of Engineering, 1996–2001; *b* 28 Oct. 1935; *s* of David Evan Davies and Sarah (*née* Samuel); *m* 1st, 1962, Enid Patilla (*d* 1990); two *s*; 2nd, 1992, Jennifer E., (Jenna), Rayner. *Educ.* Univ. of Birmingham (MSc 1958; PhD 1960; DSc 1968). FIET (FIEE 1969); FIERE 1975; FREng (FEng 1979). Lectr and Sen. Lectr in Elec. Engrg, Univ. of Birmingham, 1961–67 (also Hon. SPSO, RRE, Malvern, 1966–67); Asst Dir of Elec. Res., BR Bd, Derby, 1967–71; Vis. Industrial Prof. of Elec. Engrg, Loughborough Univ. of Technol., 1969–71; University College London: Prof. of Elec. Engrg, 1971–88; Pender Prof. and Hd of Dept of Electronic and Electrical Engrg, 1985–88; Vice-Provost, 1986–88; Vice-Chancellor, Loughborough Univ. of Technology, 1988–93; Chief Scientific Advr, MoD, 1993–99. Chm., Railway Safety, 2001–03; Safety Advr, Nat. Grid Transco, 2002–08. Non-executive Director: Gaydon Technology (Rover Group), 1986–88; Loughborough Consultants, 1988–93; Inst. Consumer Ergonomics, 1988–93; ERA Technology, 1996–2003; Lattice plc, 2000–02; ERA Foundn, 2002–07. Member: SERC, 1985–89; IT Adv. Bd, DTI, 1988–91; EPSRC, 1994–99; Chm., Defence Scientific Adv. Council 1992–93. Pres., IEE, 1994–95; Vice Pres., Royal Acad. of Engrg, 1995–96. Pro Chancellor, Univ. of Sussex, 1998–2001. Hon. FIChemE 1997; Hon. FIMechE 1998 Hon. FIStructE 2001; Hon. FIEE 2002; Hon. Fellow UCL, 2006. Hon DSc Birmingham, Loughborough, South Bank, 1994; Bradford, 1995; Surrey, 1996; Bath Warwick, 1997; Heriot-Watt, 1999; Wales, 2002; Hon. DEng UMIST 2000. Rank Prize for Optoelectronics, 1984; Callendar Medal, Inst. of Measurement & Control, 1984 Faraday Medal, IEE, 1987; President's Medal, RAEng, 2006. *Publications:* technical paper and articles on radar, antennae and aspects of fibre optics. *Address:* Church Hill House Church Lane, Danehill, Haywards Heath, W Sussex RH17 7EY. *T:* (01825) 790321.

DAVIES, Hon. Sir (David Herbert) Mervyn, Kt 1982; MC 1944; TD 1946; a Judge of the High Court of Justice, Chancery Division, 1982–93; *b* 17 Jan. 1918; *s* of Herber Bowen Davies and Esther Davies, Llangunnor, Carms; *m* 1951, Zita Yollanne Angelique Blanche Antoinette, 2nd *d* of Rev. E. A. Phillips, Bale, Norfolk. *Educ:* Swansea Gram Sch. Solicitor, 1939 (Travers Smith Scholar and Daniel Reardon Prize, Law Soc., 1939) 18th Bn Welch Regt and 2nd London Irish Rifles, Africa, Italy and Austria, 1939–45 Called to Bar, Lincoln's Inn, 1947; Bencher, 1974; QC 1967; a Circuit Judge, 1978–82 Mem., Bar Council, 1972; Mem., Senate of Inns of Court, 1975. *Address:* The White House, Great Snoring, Norfolk NR21 0AH. *T:* (01328) 820575. *Club:* Army and Navy.

DAVIES, (David) Hywel, MA, PhD; FREng; FIET; consultant; Deputy Director General for Science, Research and Development, EEC, Brussels, 1982–86; *b* 28 Marcl 1929; *s* of John and Maggie Davies; *m* 1961, Valerie Elizabeth Nott; one *s* two *d*. *Edu* Cardiff High Sch.; Christ's Coll., Cambridge. Radar Research Estabt, 1956; Head o Airborne Radar Group, RRE, 1970; Head of Weapons Dept, Admty Surface Weapon Estabt, 1972; Asst Chief Scientific Advr (Projects), MoD, 1976–79; Dir, RARDE, MoD 1979–80; Dep. Controller, Res. Programmes, MoD, 1980–82. Man. Dir, Topexpress Ltd 1988–89. FREng (FEng 1988). *Publications:* papers on electronics, radar and remot sensing, in Proc. IEE, etc. *Recreations:* Europe, computing, knots. *Address:* 52 Brittain Lane, Sevenoaks, Kent TN13 2JP. *T:* (01732) 456359.

DAVIES, (David) Ian, MA; Headmaster, Brentwood School, since 2004; *b* 17 May 1959 *s* of Dillwyn and Morfydd Davies; *m* 1989, Sara Stern. *Educ:* St John's Coll., Oxford (MA 1980); Fitzwilliam Coll., Cambridge (PGCE 1981). Hd, Lower Sch., Latymer Upper Sch 1992–98; Headmaster, St Dunstan's Coll., 1998–2004. Boarding Headmaster, Admiralt Bd, 2000–04; Indep. Schs Advr to Duke of Edinburgh's Award Scheme, 2004–. Chm. London Div. (S), HMC, 2002. Liveryman, Co. of Wax Chandlers. *Recreations:* golf, tennis cricket, reading, France. *Address:* Brentwood School, Brentwood, Essex CM15 8AS. *T:* (01277) 243243, *Fax:* (01277) 243299; *e-mail:* headmaster@brentwood.essex.sch.uk *Clubs:* East India; Thorndon Park Golf.

DAVIES, Sir David (John), Kt 1999; Director, European Financial Group, EFG Bank since 2006 (Chairman, EFG Private Bank Ltd, 1999–2006); *b* 1 April 1940; *s* of late Stanle Kenneth Davies, CBE and Stephanie Davies; *m* 1st, 1967, Deborah Frances Loeb (marr diss.); one *s*; 2nd, 1985, Linda Wong Lin-Tye; one *s* two *d*. *Educ:* Winchester Coll Winchester; New Coll., Oxford (MA); Harvard Business Sch. (AMP). Chase Manhatta Bank, 1963–67; Hill Samuel Group, 1967–73: Dir, Hill Samuel Inc., New York 1970–73; Dir, Hill Samuel Ltd, London, 1973; Finance Dir, 1973–83, and Vice-Chm 1977–83, MEPC Ltd; Man. Dir, The Hongkong Land Co. Ltd, 1983–86; Chm., Hon Kong Land Property Co. Ltd, 1983–86; Dir, 1986–88, Chief Exec. and Exec. Vice Chm 1987–88, Hill Samuel Gp; Jt Chm., Hill Samuel & Co., 1987–88. Chm., 1990–98, Chi Exec., 1994–98, Johnson Matthey plc. Chairman: Wire Ropes Ltd, Wicklow, 1979– Mandarin Oriental Hotel Group, 1983–86; Dairy Farm Ltd, 1983–86; Imry Merchan Developers (formerly Imry Internat.), 1987–89; Imry Holdings, 1992–98; MBO Partne Ltd, HK, 1992–2000; Semara (formerly Sketchley) PLC, 1990–2000; Dep. Chm., Charte Consolidated, 1988–89; Director: Jardine Matheson Group, 1983–86; Hong Kon Electric Co., 1983–85; American Barrick Resources Corp., Toronto, 1986–94; Delawar North Cos Inc., Buffalo, NY, 1986–; Singapore Land Ltd, 1986–90; Fitzwilton PLC Dublin, 1987–90; Asia Securities, Hong Kong, 1987–89; Hardwicke Ltd, Dublin, 1987–

TSB Group, 1987–89; First Pacific Co., Hong Kong, 1988–91; Irish Life Assce, 1991–97; The Wharf (Holdings) Ltd, Hong Kong, 1992–99; Wheelock NatWest, 1994–97; Glyndebourne Productions Ltd, 1990–2000; Hilton Gp (formerly Ladbroke Gp) plc, 1997–2001; General Enterprise Mgt Services Ltd, 1998–2001; Gluskin Sheff and Associates, Toronto, 2007–. Chm., Adv. Cttee on Business and the Envmt, 1995–98 (Mem., 1993–98); Dep. Chm., Prince of Wales' Business Leaders Forum, 1997–98 (Dir, 1991–96); Mem., Prince of Wales Business and the Envmt Prog., 1993–99. Member: Council, Ireland Fund of GB, 1988–2002; Bd, Wales Millennium Centre, 2004–; Governing Council, Centre for Study of Financial Innovation, 2004–; Chm., Adv. Council, Global Leadership Foundn, 2004– (Trustee, 2004–); Chm., Global Leadership Foundn, UK, 2008–). Director: Irish Georgian Foundn, 2002–; Everard Read Gall., 2005–. Chairman: Wexford Fest. UK Trust, 1997–; Grange Park Opera, 1998–2005 (Chm., Adv. Council, 2005–); Vice-Pres., Leeds Internat. Piano Comp., 2004–. Chairman: Irish Heritage Trust, 2006–; Develt Bd, Saïd Business Sch., Univ. of Oxford, 2007–; Member: Adv. Cttee for Fund Raising, Ashmolean Mus., 1991–96; New Coll. Develt Fund, 1995– (Chm., 2007–; Mem., New Coll. Endowment Cttee, 1994–2007); Winchester Coll. Develt Council, 2002–; Dep. Chm., Campaign for Oxford, 2008–; Trustee: Anglo-Hong Kong Trust, 1989–2004; Monteverdi Trust, 1991–97; Royal Opera House Trust, 1997–2001 (Mem., Appeal Cttee, 1997–2001); St Catherine Foundn, 2001–; World Monuments Fund in Britain, 2002–07; Cape Town Opera, 2004–. *Recreations:* trees, walking, opera. *Address:* 148 Tai Hang Road, Apartment 4 (4th Floor), Hong Kong. *Clubs:* Beefsteak, Garrick; All England Lawn Tennis; Cardiff and County (Cardiff); Kildare Street and University (Dublin); Hong Kong, China (Hong Kong).

DAVIES, Rt Hon. (David John) Denzil; PC 1978; *b* 9 Oct. 1938; *s* of G. Davies, Conwil Elfed, Carmarthen; *m* 1963, Mary Ann Finlay (marr. diss. 1988), Illinois; one *s* one *d. Educ:* Queen Elizabeth Grammar Sch., Carmarthen; Pembroke Coll., Oxford. Bacon Scholar, Gray's Inn, 1961; BA (1st cl. Law) 1962; Martin Wronker Prize (Law), 1962. Teaching Fellow, Univ. of Chicago, 1963; Lectr in Law, Leeds Univ., 1964; called to Bar, Gray's Inn, 1964. MP (Lab) Llanelli, 1970–2005. Member: Select Cttee on Corporation Tax, 1971; Jt Select Cttee (Commons and Lords) on Delegated Legislation, 1972; Public Accounts Cttee, 1974; PPS to the Secretary of State for Wales, 1974–76; Minister of State, HM Treasury, 1975–79; Opposition spokesman on Treasury matters, 1979–81, on foreign affairs, 1981–82, on defence, 1982–83; chief opposition spokesman: on Welsh affairs, 1983; on defence and disarmament, 1983–88.

DAVIES, Prof. David Roy, OBE 1995; PhD; Professor of Applied Genetics, University of East Anglia, 1968–94, now Professor Emeritus (Dean of School of Biological Sciences, 1985–91); Deputy Director, John Innes Institute, 1978–94; *b* 10 June 1932; *s* of late J. O. Davies and A. E. Davies; *m* 1957, Winifred Frances Davies, JP, BA (*née* Wills); two *s* two *d. Educ:* Llandyssul and Grove Park, Wrexham Grammar Schs; Univ. of Wales. BSc, PhD. UK Atomic Energy Authority, 1956–62 and 1963–68; US Atomic Energy Commn, 1962–63. Editor, Heredity, 1975–82. *Publications:* edited: The Plant Genome, 1980; Temperate Legumes, 1983; Peas: genetics, molecular biology and biotechnology, 1993; papers on radiobiology and plant genetics in scientific jls. *Address:* 57 Church Lane, Eaton, Norwich NR4 6NY. *T:* (01603) 451049.

DAVIES, His Honour David Theodore Alban; a Circuit Judge, 1994–2007; *b* 8 June 1940; *s* of late John Rhys Davies, Archdeacon of Merioneth, and Mabel Aeronwy Davies; *m* 1966, Janet Mary, *er d* of late Frank and Barbara Welburn, Cheadle Hulme, Cheshire; one *s* one *d. Educ:* Rossall School (Scholar); Magdalen College, Oxford (Exhibnr, 2nd cl. Mods 1960, 1st cl. Lit Hum, 1962, BA 1962; Eldon Law Schol., 1963; MA 1967). Called to the Bar, Gray's Inn, 1964 (Entrance Schol., Arden Atkin and Mould Prize, Lord Justice Holker Sen. Schol.). Practised SE Circuit, 1965–83; Registrar, then a Dist Judge, Family Div., High Court, 1983–94; a Recorder, 1989–94; Designated Family Judge, Rhyl County Court, 1994–2007. Chancellor, dio. of Bangor, 1995–. Sec., Family Law Bar Assoc., 1976–80, Treasurer, 1980–83; Member: Senate Law Reform Cttee, 1979–83; Civil and Family Cttee, 1988–93, Main Bd, 1991–93, Judicial Studies Bd. *Publication:* (ed jtly) Jackson's Matrimonial Finance and Taxation, 2nd edn 1975, 5th edn 1992. *Recreations:* reading, walking, history. *Address:* c/o Rhyl County Court, Clwyd Street, Rhyl, Denbighshire LL18 3LA.

DAVIES, David Thomas Charles; MP (C) Monmouth, since 2005; *b* 27 July 1970; *s* of Peter Hugh Charles Davies and Kathleen Diane Davies (*née* Elton); *m* 2003, Aliz Harnisföger; one *s* two *d. Educ:* Clytha Sch., Newport; Bassaleg Sch., Newport. MInstTA; MILog; MIFF. BSC, 1988–89; grape picking, working on roads, rickshaw driver in tourist resort, Australia, 1989–91; Gen. Manager, Tea Importing and Shipping Co. (family business), 1991–99. Mem. (C) Monmouth, Nat. Assembly for Wales, 1999–2007. Contested (C) Bridgend, 1997. *Recreations:* surfing, long distance running, keeping fit. *Address:* (constituency office) The Grange, 16 Maryport Street, Usk, Monmouthshire NP15 1AB; House of Commons, SW1A 0AA. *Clubs:* Oriental; Abergavenny Constitutional; Chepstow Conservative; Monmouth Conservative; Usk Conservative.

DAVIES, Deborah; see Arnott, D.

DAVIES, Rt Hon. Denzil; see Davies, Rt Hon. David J. D.

DAVIES, Dickie; television sports presenter, since 1964; *s* of Owen John Davies and Ellen Davies; *m* 1962, Elisabeth Ann Hastings Mann; twin *s. Educ:* William Ellis Sch., Highgate; Oldershaw Grammar Sch., Wallasey, Cheshire. Purser, Cunard Line, 1953–60; Television Announcer, Southern TV, 1960–63; World of Sport Presenter, 1964–85, Presenter: ITV Sport, 1985–89; Sportsmasters, 1988–92; The World of Golf, 1990; Classic FM, 1995–; Bobby Charlton's Football Scrapbook, Sky Sports TV, 1995–; Dickie Davies's Sporting Heroes, 1998–; World Cup Classics, 1999. *Recreations:* golf, walking our dogs.

DAVIES, Donald, CBE 1978 (OBE 1973); consultant; *b* 13 Feb. 1924; *s* of late Wilfred Lawson Davies and Alwyne Davies; *m* 1948, Mabel (*née* Hellyar); two *d. Educ:* Ebbw Vale Grammar Sch.; UC Cardiff (BSc). CEng, FIMinE. National Coal Board: Colliery Man., 1951–55; Gp Man., 1955–58; Dep. Prodn Man., 1958–60; Prodn Man., 1960–61; Area Gen. Man., 1961–67; Area Dir, 1967–73; Bd Mem., 1973–84; Chairman: Nat. Fuel Distributors, 1973–89; Southern Depot Co., 1973–89; NCB (Ancillaries), 1979–89; Horizon Exploration, 1981–89. *Recreations:* golf, walking. *Address:* Wendy Cottage, Dukes Wood Avenue, Gerrards Cross, Bucks SL9 7LA. *T:* (01753) 885083.

DAVIES, Douglas; see Davies, Percy D.

DAVIES, Rev. Prof. Douglas James, PhD, DLitt; Professor in the Study of Religion, University of Durham, since 2000 (Head, Department of Theology, 2002–05); *b* 11 Feb. 1947; *s* of Llewelyn James Davies and Gladys Evelyn Davies (*née* Morgan). *Educ:* Lewis Sch., Pengam; St John's Coll., Durham (BA 1969); St Peter's Coll., Oxford (MLitt 1972); PhD Nottingham 1980; DLitt Oxon 2004. Ordained deacon 1975; priest 1976; University of Nottingham: Lectr in Theology, 1974–90; Sen. Lectr, 1990–93; Prof. of Religious Studies, 1993–97; Principal, Coll. of St Hild and St Bede, and Prof. of Theol., Univ. of

Durham, 1997–2000. Vis. Res. Fellow, Rothermere American Inst., Oxford Univ., 2006–07; Mayers Fellow, Huntington Library, Calif, 2006–07. Hon. DTheol Uppsala, 1998. *Publications:* Meaning and Salvation in Religious Studies, 1984; Mormon Spirituality, 1987; (jtly) Church and Religion in Rural England, 1991; Frank Byron Jevons: an evolutionary realist, 1991; (jtly) Reusing Old Graves, 1995; (ed) Mormon Identities in Transition, 1996; Death, Ritual and Belief, 1997; The Mormon Culture of Salvation, 2000; Private Passions, 2000; Anthropology and Theology, 2002; Introduction to Mormonism, 2003; A Brief History of Death, 2004; (ed jtly) Encyclopedia of Cremation, 2005; (jtly) Studying Local Churches, 2005; (jtly) Bishops, Wives and Children: spiritual capital across the generations, 2007; The Theology of Death, 2008. *Recreations:* squash, cacti. *Address:* Department of Theology and Religion, Abbey House, Palace Green, Durham DH1 3RS. *Club:* Royal Over-Seas League.

DAVIES, Ednyfed Hudson, BA (Wales); MA (Oxon); barrister; Chairman, Lincs FM plc, since 1991; *b* 4 Dec. 1929; *s* of Rev. E. Curig Davies and Enid Curig (*née* Hughes); *m* 1972, Amanda Barker-Mill, *d* of Peter Barker-Mill and Elsa Barker-Mill; two *d. Educ:* Friars Sch., Bangor; Dynevor Grammar Sch., Swansea; University College of Swansea; Balliol Coll., Oxford. Called to the Bar, Gray's Inn, 1975. Lecturer in Dept of Extra-Mural Studies, University of Wales, Aberystwyth, 1957–61; Lecturer in Political Thought, Welsh Coll. of Advanced Technology, Cardiff, 1961–66. MP: (Lab) Conway, 1966–70; Caerphilly, 1979–83 (Lab, 1979–81, SDP, 1981–83); Mem., H of C Select Cttee on Energy, 1980–83; Sec., H of C All-Party Tourism Cttee, 1979–83. Contested (SDP) Basingstoke, 1983. Part-time TV and radio commentator and interviewer on current affairs, 1962–66; on full-time contract to BBC presenting Welsh-language feature programmes on overseas countries, 1970–76; Chm., Wales Tourist Board, 1976–78. Dep. Chm., Ocean Sound Radio, 1989–94 (Dir, 1986–94); Dir, Southern Radio, 1989–94. Director: New Forest Butterfly Farm, 1984–94; New Forest Industrial Assoc. Ltd, 1989–. Trustee, 1986–, Chm., 1994–, New Forest Ninth Centenary Trust. *Address:* Lincs FM plc, Witham Park, Waterside South, Lincoln LN5 7JN. *Clubs:* Cardiff and County (Cardiff); Royal Welsh Yacht (Caernarfon) (Cdre, 2002–03); Royal Lymington Yacht; Royal Southampton Yacht.

DAVIES, Prof. (Edward) Brian, DPhil; FRS 1995; Professor of Mathematics, King's College London, since 1981; *b* 13 June 1944; *s* of Arthur Granville Davies and Mary Davies (*née* Scudamore); *m* 1968, Jane Christine Phillips; one *s* one *d. Educ:* Jesus Coll., Oxford (BA 1965; MA). Brasenose Coll., Oxford (DPhil Maths 1968). Tutorial Fellow, St John's Coll., Oxford, 1970–81; Univ. Lectr, Oxford Univ., 1973–81; Head, Dept of Maths, KCL, 1990–93; FKC 1996. Pres., London Mathematical Soc., 2007–09. Editor, Qly Jl of Mathematics, 1973–81; Founding Editor, London Mathematical Soc. Student Text Series, 1983–90. *Publications:* Quantum Theory of Open Systems, 1976; One-Parameter Semigroups, 1980; Heat Kernels and Spectral Theory, 1989; Spectral Theory and Differential Operators, 1995; Science in the Looking Glass, 2003. *Recreations:* family, scientific reading. *Address:* Department of Mathematics, King's College, Strand, WC2R 2LS.

DAVIES, (Edward) Hunter; author, journalist; *b* Renfrew, Scotland, 7 Jan. 1936; *s* of late John Hunter Davies and Marion (*née* Brechin); *m* 1960, Margaret Forster, *qv*; one *s* two *d. Educ:* Creighton Sch., Carlisle; Carlisle Grammar Sch.; University Coll., Durham (BA 1957, DipEd 1958; Editor of Palatinate; Hon. Fellow 2007). Reporter: Manchester Evening Chronicle, 1958–59; Sunday Graphic, London, 1959–60; Sunday Times, 1960–84; Atticus, 1965–67; Chief Feature Writer, 1967; Editor, Sunday Times Magazine, 1975–77; Columnist: Punch, 1979–89; Stamp News, 1981–86; London Evening Standard, 1987; The Independent, 1989–93; New Statesman & Society, 1996–; Money section, Sunday Times, 1999–. Presenter, Bookshelf, Radio 4, 1983–86. Mem., British Library Consultative Gp on Newspapers, 1987–89; Dir, Edinburgh Book Festival Bd, 1990–95; Chm., Cumbria Wildlife Trust, 1995–2008. Dep. Pro-Chancellor, Lancaster Univ., 1996–97. *Television:* The Playground (play), 1967; The Living Wall, 1974; George Stephenson, 1975; A Walk in the Lakes, 1979. *Publications: fiction:* Here We Go, Round the Mulberry Bush, 1965 (filmed, 1968); The Rise and Fall of Jake Sullivan, 1970; (ed) I Knew Daisy Smuten, 1970; A Very Loving Couple, 1971; Body Charge, 1972; Flossie Teacake's Fur Coat, 1982; Flossie Teacake—Again!, 1983; Flossie Teacake Strikes Back, 1984; Come on Ossie!, 1985; Ossie Goes Supersonic, 1986; Ossie the Millionaire, 1987; Saturday Night, 1989; S.T.A.R.S (12 books in Penguin series), 1989–90; Snotty Bumstead, 1991; Striker, 1992; Snotty Bumstead and the Rent-a-Mum, 1993; Snotty the Hostage, 1995; Flossie Wins the Lottery, 1996; Flossie Teacake's Holiday, 2000; *non-fiction:* The Other Half, 1966; (ed) The New London Spy, 1966; The Beatles, 1968, 2nd edn 1985, illus. edn 2002; The Glory Game, 1972, 4th edn 2000; A Walk Along the Wall, 1974, 2nd edn 1984; George Stephenson, 1975, 2nd edn 2004; The Creighton Report, 1976; (ed) Sunday Times Book of Jubilee Year, 1977; A Walk Around the Lakes, 1979, 2nd edn 2000; William Wordsworth, 1980, 2nd edn 1997; The British Book of Lists, 1980; The Grades, 1981; Father's Day, 1981 (television series, 1983); Beaver Book of Lists, 1981; A Walk Along the Tracks, 1982, 2nd edn 2002; England!, 1982; (with Frank Herrmann) Great Britain: a celebration, 1982; A Walk Round London Parks, 1983; The Joy of Stamps, 1983; London at its Best, 1984; (also publisher) The Good Guide to the Lakes, 1984, 6th edn 2003; The Grand Tour, 1986; The Good Quiz Book to the Lakes, 1987; Back in the USSR, 1987; Beatrix Potter's Lakeland, 1988; My Life in Football, 1990; In Search of Columbus, 1991; Teller of Tales: in search of Robert Louis Stevenson, 1994; Hunting People: thirty years of interviews with the famous, 1994; Wainwright: the biography, 1995; Living on the Lottery, 1996; Born 1900, 1998; London to Loweswater, 1999; Dwight Yorke, 1999; A Walk Around the West Indies, 2000; Joe Kinnear: still crazy, 2000; The Quarrymen, 2001; The Eddie Stobart Story, 2001; Hurry, Hurry While Stocks Last, 2001; The Best of Lakeland, 2002; Relative Strangers, 2003; Boots, Balls and Haircuts, 2003; The Fan (anthol.), 2003; (jtly) Gazza—My Story, 2004; The Best of Wainwright, 2004; Strong Lad Wanted for Strong Lass, 2004; Mean With Money (anthol.), 2005; (jtly) Being Gazza, 2006; I Love Football, 2006; The Beatles, Football and Me: a memoir, 2006; The Second Half (anthol.), 2006; (jtly) Wayne Rooney, 2006; The Bumper Book of Football, 2007; (jtly) Prezza: my story - pulling no punches, 2008. *Recreations:* walking, Lakeland books, Beatles memorabilia, swimming, football memorabilia. *Address:* 11 Boscastle Road, NW5 1EE; Grasmoor House, Loweswater, Cumbria CA13 0RU.

DAVIES, Edwin, OBE 2000; FCMA; investment advisor; *b* 18 June 1946; *s* of Edwin Davies and Hannah Davies (*née* Kelly); *m* 1989, Susan Chinn Crellin; one *s* one *d. Educ:* Farnworth Grammar Sch.; Durham Univ. (BA 1st Cl. Hons Maths). FCMA 1985; CCMI 2005. Asst Gp Man. Dir, Scapa Gp plc, 1968–84; Chm., Strix Gp Ltd, 1984–2006. Dir, Bolton Wanderers FC Ltd, 1999–. Trustee, V&A Mus., 2006–. *Recreations:* travel, archaeology, soccer. *Address:* Moorecroft, Crossag Road, Ballasalla, Isle of Man IM9 3EF. *T:* (01624) 828730, *Fax:* (01624) 824578; *e-mail:* gilly@fildraw.com.

DAVIES, Emrys Thomas, CMG 1988; HM Diplomatic Service, retired; *b* 8 Oct. 1934; *s* of Evan William Davies and Dinah Davies (*née* Jones); *m* 1960, Angela Audrey, *er d* of late Paul Robert Buchan May, ICS and of Esme May; one *s* two *d. Educ:* Parmiters

Foundation Sch. RAF, 1953–55; commnd RAFVR, 1955. Sch. of Slavonic Studies, Cambridge Univ., 1954; Sch. of Oriental and African Studies, London Univ., 1955–56. Served Peking, 1956–59; FO, 1959–60; Bahrain, 1960–62; FO, 1962–63; Asst Political Adviser to Hong Kong Govt, 1963–68; First Sec., British High Commn, Ottawa, 1968–71; FCO, 1972–76; Commercial Counsellor, Peking, 1976–78 (Chargé, 1976 and 1978); Oxford Univ. Business Summer Sch., 1977; NATO Defense Coll., Rome, 1979; Dep. High Comr, Ottawa, 1979–82; Overseas Inspector, FCO, 1982–84; Dep. UK Perm. Rep. to OECD, and Counsellor (Econ. and Financial) to UK Delegn, Paris, 1984–87; Ambassador to Hanoi, 1987–90; High Comr, Barbados, Grenada, St Lucia, Dominica, Antigua and Barbuda, St Vincent and the Grenadines, and St Kitts and Nevis, 1990–94; Hd, UK Delegn to EC Monitoring Mission to former Yugoslavia, 1995 and 1998–99. Sec. Gen., Tripartite Commn for Restitution of Monetary Gold, Brussels, 1995–98. Appointments Advr to Welsh Office, 1997–2002; Pol Advr, EU Police Mission to Bosnia and Herzegovina, 2003. *Address:* Edinburgh House, 8 Alison Way, Winchester, Hants SO22 5BT. *Club:* Royal Air Force.

DAVIES, Dr Ernest Arthur; JP; management consultant and lecturer, retired 1987; *b* 25 Oct. 1926; *s* of Dan Davies and Ada (*née* Smith), Nuneaton; *m* 1st, 1956, Margaret Stephen Tait Gatt (marr. diss. 1967), *d* of H. Gatt, Gamesley, near Glossop; no *c*; 2nd, 1972, Patricia (marr. diss. 1980), *d* of S. Bates, Radford, Coventry; no *c*. *Educ:* Coventry Jun. Techn. Coll.; Westminster Trng Coll., London; St Salvator's Coll., University of St Andrews; St John's Coll., Cambridge. PhD Cantab 1959; MInstP 1959, CPhys 1986. RAF Aircraft Apprentice, 1942–43 (discharged on med. grounds). Westminster Trng Coll., 1946–48; Teacher, Foxford Sch., Coventry, 1948–50; University of St Andrews, 1950–54 (1st cl. hons Physics, Neil Arnott Prize, Carnegie Schol.); subseq. research in superconductivity, Royal Society Mond Lab., Cambridge; AEI Research Scientist, 1957–63; Lectr in Physics, Faculty of Technology, University of Manchester, 1963–66; Management Selection Consultant, MSL, 1970–81; Lectr in Business Studies, Hammersmith and West London Coll., 1981–87. MP (Lab) Stretford, 1966–70; Parliamentary Private Secretary to: PMG (Mr Edward Short), Nov.–Dec. 1967; Foreign Secretary (Mr George Brown), Jan.–Mar. 1968; Foreign and Commonwealth Sec. (Mr Michael Stewart), 1968–69; Jt Parly Sec., Min. of Technology, 1969–70. Co-Vice-Chm., Parly Labour Party's Defence and Services Group; Mem., Select Cttee on Science and Technology, 1966–67, 1967–68, 1968–69; Parly Deleg. to 24th Gen. Assembly of UN (UK Rep. on 4th Cttee). Councillor: Borough of Stretford, 1961–67; Borough of Southwark, 1974–82. JP Lancs, 1962, Inner London, 1972. *Publications:* contribs to Proc. Royal Society, Jl of Physics and Chem. of Solids. *Recreations:* reading, walking, art and design practice, computer studies. *Address:* 43 Frensham Drive, Nuneaton, Warwickshire CV10 9QH.

DAVIES, Prof. (Eurfil) Rhys, CBE 1990; FRCR, FRCPE; FFR (RCSI); FDSRCS; Professor of Clinical Radiology (formerly Radiodiagnosis), University of Bristol, 1981–93; *b* 18 April 1929; *s* of late Daniel Haydn Davies and Mary Davies; *m* 1962, Zoë Doreen Chamberlain; three *s*. *Educ:* Rhondda Grammar Sch.; Llandovery Coll.; Clare Coll., Cambridge (MB, BChir 1953; MA); St Mary's Hosp., London. FRCR (FFR 1964); FRCPE 1971; FFR (RCSI) 1978; FDSRCS 1989. Served RAMC, 1954–56 (Regtl MO 24 Regt). Sen. Registrar, St Mary's Hosp., 1963–66; Consultant Radiologist, United Bristol Hosps, 1966–81; Clinical Lectr, 1972–81, Hd, Clinical Sch., 1992–93, Univ. of Bristol. Vis. Sen. Lectr, Lagos Univ., 1971; Mayne Vis. Prof., Queensland Univ., 1982. Civilian Cons. Advr to RN, 1989–94. Mem., Bristol and Weston DHA, 1983–86. Member: Admin of Radio Active Substances Adv. Cttee, DHSS, 1978–83; Clin. Standards Adv. Cttee, 1991–93; GMC, 1989–93; Ionising Radiation Adv. Cttee, HSC, 1995–97 (Mem., Working Gp, 1987–95). Royal Coll. of Radiologists: Sen. Examr, 1973–74; Mem., Fellowship Bd, 1974–76; Registrar, 1976–81; Chm., Examining Bd, 1981–84; Warden of the Fellowship, 1984–86; Pres., 1986–89; Chm., Nuclear Medicine Cttee, 1972–78; Knox Lectr, 1990. Pres., Nuclear Medicine Soc., 1974–76 (Sec., 1972–74); Chm., Inter Collegiate Standing Cttee for Nuclear Medicine, 1982–84 (Sec., 1980–82). *Publications:* (contrib.) Textbook of Radiology, ed Sutton, 1969, Associate Editor, 6th edn 1998; (contrib.) Textbook of Urology, ed J. P. Blandy, 1974; (jtly) Radioisotopes in Radiodiagnosis, 1976; (contrib.) Radiological Atlas of Biliary and Pancreatic Disease, 1978; Textbook of Radiology by British Authors, 1984; (ed with W. E. G. Thomas) Nuclear Medicine for Surgeons, 1988; papers in Clin. Radiology, British Jl of Radiology, Lancet. *Recreations:* theatre, cooking, wine, travel. *Address:* 19 Hyland Grove, Bristol BS9 3NR.

DAVIES, (Evan) Huw; QC 2006; *b* 22 Jan. 1962; *s* of John and Joan Davies; *m* 1988, Alison Susan Keen; one *s* one *d*. *Educ:* Carr Lane Primary Sch., Hull; Wolfreton Comprehensive Sch., Hull; Imberhorne Comprehensive Sch., E Grinstead; University Coll., Cardiff (LLB 1st Cl. Hons). Called to the Bar, Gray's Inn, 1985; in practice, specialising in commercial litigation and arbitration. CEDR accredited mediator. *Recreations:* Rugby, ski-ing, mountaineering, cycling, golf (still learning), travel, food. *Address:* Essex Court Chambers, 24 Lincoln's Inn Fields, WC2A 3EG. *T:* (020) 7873 8000; *e-mail:* hdavies@essexcourt.net.

DAVIES, (Evan) Mervyn, CBE 2002; FCIB; Chairman, Standard Chartered plc, since 2006 (Director, since 1997); *b* 21 Nov. 1952; *s* of Richard Aled Davies and Margaret Davies; *m* 1979, Jeanne Marie (*née* Gammie); one *s* one *d*. *Educ:* Rydal Sch., N Wales; Harvard Business Sch. (PMD). FCIB 1990. Man. Dir, UK Banking and Sen. Credit Officer, Citibank, 1983–93; Standard Chartered plc, 1993–; Gp Chief Exec., 2001–06; Dir, Standard Chartered Bank, Hong Kong, 1997–2001. Chairman: Fleming Family and Partners, 2007–; Nordic Windpower Ltd, 2008–; Mem., Corsair Private Equity Bd, 2007–; Dir, FF&P Private Equity Ltd, 2007–. Non-executive Director: Tesco plc, 2003–; Tottenham Hotspur FC, 2004–; Breakingviews Ltd, 2007–. Member: Singapore Business Council; UK-India Forum; Heads Up Finance Gp, UK-China Forum; Asia House Internat. Adv. Council; UK-India Business Council, 2007–; Special Govt Taskforce on China; Dir, Hong Kong Assoc., 2006–; Chairman: Prime Minister's Business Council for Britain, 2007–08; Interim Exec. Cttee, ICFR, 2007–. Former Chairman: British Chamber of Commerce, HK; HK Assoc. of Banks; HK Youth Arts Fest.; Asia Youth Orch.; Generations Appeal, Breakthrough Breast Cancer. Mem., Burlington Project Appeal Cttee, 2007–; Corporate Bd Mem., RA, 2006–; Chm., Major Projects Bd, Roundhouse, 2008–. Chm., Council, Bangor Univ., 2008–. Trustee, Sir Kyffin Williams Trust, 2007–. JP Hong Kong, 2000. *Recreations:* soccer, cricket, golf, Rugby, Welsh art, antiques. *Address:* Standard Chartered plc, 1 Aldermanbury Square, EC2V 7SB. *T:* (020) 7280 7088, *Fax:* (020) 7600 2546; *e-mail:* emd@uk.standardchartered.com. *Clubs:* Mark's; Hong Kong, Shek O (Hong Kong).

DAVIES, Rt Rev. (Francis James) Saunders; Bishop of Bangor, 2000–04; *b* 30 Dec. 1937; *s* of Tom and Clara Davies; *m* 1963, (Marianne) Cynthia Young; one *s* one *d*. *Educ:* UCNW Bangor (BA Hons Welsh and accessory Hebrew 1960; Hon. Fellow, 2002); Selwyn Coll., Cambridge (MA Theol. 1966); St Michael's Coll., Llandaff; Bonn Univ., Germany. Ordained deacon, 1963, priest, 1964; Curate, Holyhead, 1963–67; Minor Canon, Bangor Cathedral and Hon. Staff Mem., SCM, 1967–69; Rector, Llanllyfni, 1969–75; Canon Missioner, Bangor Dio., 1975–78; Vicar, Gorseinon, 1978–86; Rural Dean, Llwchwr, 1983–86; Vicar, Eglwys Dewi Sant, Cardiff, 1986–93; Rector, Criccieth with Treflys and Archdeacon of Meirionnydd, 1993–2000; permission to officiate, dio. of St Davids, 2004–. Tutor: NSM Course, Llandaff Dio., 1987–93; for Continuing Educn, UC Cardiff, 1988–93. Vice-Chm., Cardiff Christian Adult Educn Centre, 1990–93. *Publications:* (ed jtly) Euros Bowen Poet-Priest/Bardd Offeiriad, 1993; Y Daith Anorfod: a commentary on St Luke's Gospel, 1993. *Recreations:* reading, walking, listening to classical music, going to the theatre and the Nat. Eisteddfod of Wales. *Address:* 5 Maes-y-coed, Cardigan SA43 1AP.

DAVIES, Sir Frank (John), Kt 1999; CBE 1993; Chairman, Health and Safety Commission, 1993–99; *b* 24 Sept. 1931; *s* of late Lt-Col F. H. Davies and Veronica Josephine Davies; *m* 1956, Sheila Margaret Bailey; three *s*. *Educ:* Monmouth Sch.; UMIST. BPB Industries plc, 1953–63; RTZ Piller Ltd, 1964–67; Alcan Aluminium (UK) Ltd, 1967–83: Div. Man. Dir, 1971–83; Dir, 1977–83; Dir, Alcan Booth, 1972–82; Gp Chief Exec., Rockware Gp, 1983–93. Chairman: Dartington Crystal, 1989–94; ACI Europe Ltd, 1991–93; Bardon Gp plc, 1994–97; Mediwatch plc, 2003–05; non-executive Director: Ian Proctor M. Masts, 1974–83; Ardagh plc, 1985–2003; BTR Nylex, 1991–94; Saltire (formerly Cannon St Investments), 1993–99; Aggregate Industries plc, 1997–2002; Investor Champions plc, 2000–04; Ardagh Glass Gp, 2003–. Mem., Oxfordshire HA, 1981–90; Chm., Nuffield Orthopaedic Centre NHS Trust, 1990–98. Dep. Chm., Railway Safety, 2001–03; non-exec. Dir, Railway Safety and Standards Board, 2003–08. President: Glass Manufrs Fedn, 1985, 1986; Fédn Européene du Verre d'Emballage, 1987–88; Member: Council, Cttee Permanent Industrie du Verre, Brussels, 1984–86; Council, Aluminium Fedn, 1980–82; Council, CBI, 1985–93; Council, Industry Council for Packaging and the Envmt, 1986–93; Packaging Standards Council, 1992–93; Vice-President: Inst. of Packaging, 1992; Inst. of Occupational Safety & Health, 1995. Trustee, British Occupnl Health Res. Foundn, 1993–99; Chm. of Trustees, Back Care, 1998–2004. Governor: Inst. of Occupl Medicine, 2000–; British Safety Council, 2000–06 (Chm., 2001–). CCMI (CBIM 1986); FRSA 1986. Freeman, City of London, 1986; Liveryman: Basketmakers' Co., 1987; Glass-Sellers' Co., 1990. OStJ 1977 (Mem., Council of St John, Oxfordshire, 1973–2000); Vice-Pres., Oxfordshire St John Ambulance, 1973–2000. *Recreations:* NHS, gardening, theatre, travel. *Address:* Stonewalls, Castle Street, Deddington, Banbury, Oxon OX15 0TE. *Clubs:* Carlton, Royal Automobile.

DAVIES, Col (Frederic) Nicolas (John), LVO 2002; JP; DL; non-executive Director, Guildford and Waverley Primary Care Trust, 2003–06; Secretary for Appointments and Chief Clerk, Duchy of Lancaster, 1992–2002; *b* 11 May 1939; *s* of late Rev. William John Davies and Winifred Mary Davies (*née* Lewis); *m* 1970, Caroline Tweedie; one step *s* one step *d*, and one *s* one *d* by previous *m*. *Educ:* King's Coll., Taunton; RMA Sandhurst. Nat. Service, Queen's Royal Regt, 1957; commnd Royal Regt of Artillery, 1959; served in UK, Cyprus, Hong Kong and Germany; COS, Catterick Garrison, N Yorks, 1982–85; Defence and Military Attaché, Hungary, 1986–91; retd 1992. Independent Member: Standards Cttee, Surrey CC, 2001– (Chm., 2007); Standards Cttee, Waverley BC, 2001– (Chm., 2002). Trustee, Queen's Royal Surrey Regtl Mus., 2003– (Chm., 2006–). Member: St John Council for Surrey, 1995– (Pres., Haslemere Div., 2000); Court, Univ. of Surrey, 1997–. Mem., Ex-Services Mental Welfare Soc. (Combat Stress), 2007–. Gov., Corp. of Sons of the Clergy, 1997– (Mem., Court of Assts, 1999–2005). JP Inner London 1997, SW Surrey 2002; DL Surrey, 1997. Hon. Mem., Order of Vitéz (Hungary), 1994. *Recreations:* walking, gardening, reading. *Club:* Army and Navy.

DAVIES, Gareth, CBE 1992; FCA; Group Chief Executive, 1984–93, Chairman, 1986–98, Glynwed International plc; *b* 13 Feb. 1930; *s* of Lewis and Margaret Ann Davies; *m* 1953, Joan Patricia Prosser; one *s*. *Educ:* King Edward's Grammar School, Aston, Birmingham. Joined Glynwed Group, 1957; Computer Manager, 1964; Financial Dir, 1969; Man. Dir, 1981. Non-executive Director: Midlands Electricity Plc, 1989–96; Midlands Indep. Newspapers plc, 1994–97; Lloyds Chemists plc, 1995–97. *Recreations:* music, gardening. *Address:* 4 Beechgate, Roman Road, Little Aston Park, Sutton Coldfield, West Midlands B74 3AR. *T:* (0121) 353 4780.

DAVIES, Gareth; *see* Davies, W. G.

DAVIES, His Honour Gareth Lewis; a Circuit Judge, 1990–2002; *b* 8 Sept. 1936; *s* o David Edward Davies and Glynwen Davies; *m* 1st, 1962; two *s* two *d*; 2nd, 2001, Emma Messenger. *Educ:* Brecon County Grammar Sch.; Univ. of Wales (LLB). National Service, RAF, 1954–56. Articled 1959, qualified Solicitor, 1962; Partner, Ottaways', Solicitors, St Albans, 1965–90; a Recorder, 1987. *Recreations:* sailing instructor, ski guide, classic cars, cycling. *Address:* Bronllys Castle, Bronllys, Brecon, Powys LD3 0HL. *T:* (01874) 711930.

DAVIES, Gavyn, OBE 1979; Chairman, Fulcrum Asset Management; Principal, Prisma Capital Partners, since 2005; *b* 27 Nov. 1950; *s* of W. J. F. Davies and M. G. Davies; *m* 1989, Susan Jane Nye; two *s* one *d*. *Educ:* St John's Coll., Cambridge (BA); Balliol Coll. Oxford. Economic Advr, Policy Unit, 10 Downing Street, 1974–79; Economist, Phillips and Drew, 1979–81; Chief UK Economist, Simon & Coates, 1981–86; Goldman Sachs Chief UK Economist, 1986–93; Partner, 1988–2001; Hd of Investment Res. (London) 1991–93; Head, later Co-Head, Eur. Investment Res., 1993–99; Chief Internat Economist, 1993–2001; Chm., Investment Res. Dept, 1999–2001; Adv. Dir, 2001. Vis Prof. of Economics, LSE, 1988–98. Principal Econs Commentator, The Independent 1991–99. Mem., HM Treasury's Indep. Forecasting Panel, 1993–97. Chairman: Future Funding of the BBC (govt inquiry), 1999; Bd of Govs, BBC, 2001–04 (Vice-Chm. 2001). Fellow, Univ. of Wales, Aberystwyth, 2002. Hon. DSc (Social Sci.) Southampton 1998; Hon. LLD Nottingham, 2002. *Recreation:* Southampton FC.

DAVIES, George William; Chairman, Per Una clothing for Marks and Spencer plc, since 2001 (Chief Executive, 2004–05); *b* 29 Oct. 1941; *s* of George and Mary Davies; *m* 1st 1964, Anne; three *d*; 2nd, 1985, Liz; two *d*; 3rd, 1992, Fiona; two *s*. *Educ:* Netherton Moss Primary Sch.; Bootle Grammar Sch.; Birmingham Univ. Littlewoods, 1967–72; School Care (own business), 1972–75; Pippa Dee (subsid. of Rosgill Hldgs)—Party Plan/Lingerie 1975–81; J. Hepworth & Son plc (responsible for launch of Next), 1981; Jt Gp Man. Dir J. Hepworth & Son, 1984; Chief Exec., 1985–88, Chm., 1987–88, Next (name changed from J. Hepworth & Son); Managing Director: George Davies Partnership plc 1989–2000; George Clothing, 1995–2000; Pres., Asda Gp, 1995–2000; Chm., S. Porter Ltd, 1995–2007. Sen. Fellow, RCA, 1988. FRSA 1987; Hon. FSDC 2004. Hon. DBA Liverpool Polytechnic, 1989; Hon. DDes: Nottingham Trent, 1996; Middlesex, 2002; De Montfort, 2006; Hon. DLitt Heriot-Watt, 2003; Hon. DCL Northumbria, 2005 Guardian Young Businessman of the Year, 1985; Wood Mackenzie Retailer of the Year 1987; Marketing Personality of the Year, 1988; Lifetime Achievement Award, Drapers Co., 2003; Designer of the Decade, Prima mag., 2004; Forum Award, Textil Wirtschaft mag., 2004. *Publication:* What Next? (autobiog.), 1989. *Recreations:* tennis, golf, cycling *Clubs:* Formby Golf; Liverpool Ramblers; Blackwell Golf.

DAVIES, Geraint Rhys; Member (Plaid Cymru) Rhondda, National Assembly for Wales 1999–2003; *b* 1 Dec. 1948; *s* of John Davies and Sarah Olwen Davies; *m* 1973, Merr

Margaret Williams; three *s* one *d*. *Educ:* Pentre Grammar Sch.; Chelsea Coll., London (BPharm). MRPharmS. Community pharmacist: Boots, Treorci, Rhondda, 1972–75; self-employed, 1975–. Member (Plaid Cymru): Rhondda CBC, 1983–95; Rhondda Cynon Taff CBC, 1995. Contested (Plaid Cymru) Rhondda, Nat. Assembly for Wales, 2003. *Recreations:* playing tennis, listening to music, reading.

DAVIES, Geraint Richard; Chair, Flood Risk Management Wales, since 2005; *b* 3 May 1960; *s* of David Thomas Morgan Davies and Betty Ferrer Davies; *m* 1991, Dr Vanessa Catherine Fry; three *d*. *Educ:* Llanishen Comp. Sch., Cardiff; Jesus Coll., Oxford (JCR Pres.; BA Hons PPE, MA). Joined Brooke Bond Oxo as sales and mkting trainee, 1982; subseq. Gp Product Manager, Unilever; Marketing Manager, Colgate Palmolive Ltd; Founder, and Director: Pure Crete, 1989–; Pure Aviation, 1996–; Dir, Equity Creative Ltd, 1989–2001. Mem., Croydon BC, 1986–97 (Chm. of Housing, 1994–96; Leader of Council, 1996–97); Chm., London Boroughs Housing Cttee, 1994–96. Contested (Lab): Croydon S, 1987; Croydon Central, 1992. MP (Lab) Croydon Central, 1997–2005; contested (Lab) same seat, 2005. Team PPS, Dept of Constitutional Affairs, 2003–05. Mem., Public Accounts Select Cttee, 1997–2003. Sec., Parly Gp on Domestic Violence, 2003–05; Parly Ambassador, NSPCC, 2003–05. Chair: Lab. Finance and Industry Gp, 1998–2003 (Mem. Exec., 1994–; Vice Pres., 2003–); Deptl Cttee, Envmt, Transport and Regions, 1997–2003. Published parliamentary bills: Physical Punishment of Children (Prohibition) Bill, 2003; Regulation of Child Care Providers Bill, 2003; Regulation of Hormone Disrupting Chemicals Bill, 2004; School Meals and Nutrition Bill, 2005. *Recreation:* spending time with the family.

DAVIES, Geraint Talfan; Chairman, Institute of Welsh Affairs, since 1992; *b* 30 Dec. 1943; *s* of late Aneirin Talfan Davies, OBE and Mary Anne (*née* Evans); *m* 1967, Elizabeth Shân Vaughan (*née* Yorath); three *s*. *Educ:* Cardiff High Sch.; Jesus Coll., Oxford (MA). Western Mail, Cardiff, 1966–71; The Journal, Newcastle upon Tyne, 1971–73; The Times, 1973; Asst Editor, Western Mail, Cardiff, 1974–78; HTV Wales: Head, News and Current Affairs, 1978–82; Asst Controller of Progs, 1982–87; Dir of Progs, Tyne Tees TV, 1987–90; Controller, BBC Wales, 1990–2000. Non-executive Director: Glas Cymru Cyf, 2000–; Wales Millennium Centre, 2000–03, 2006–; Mem., BT Wales Adv. Forum, 2001–. Chairman: Newydd Housing Assoc., 1975–78; Cardiff Bay Arts Trust, 1997–2003; Wales Internat. Film Festival, 1998–2001; Arts Council of Wales, 2003–06. Mem., Prince of Wales' Cttee, 1993–95; Trustee: Tenovus Cancer Appeal, 1984–87; British Bone Marrow Donor Appeal, 1987–95; Media Standards Trust, 2006–. Member: Management Cttee, Northern Sinfonia, 1989–90; Radio Authy, 2001–; UK Cttee, Europ. Cultural Foundn, 2005–; Chm., WNO, 2000–03, 2006–. Governor: Welsh Coll. of Music and Drama, 1993–97; UWIC, 2000–06. *Recreations:* theatre, music, architecture. *Address:* 15 The Parade, Whitchurch, Cardiff CF14 2EF. *T:* (029) 2062 6571; *e-mail:* geraint.talfan@btopenworld.com.

DAVIES, Dr Gillian; DL; barrister; Chairman, Technical Board of Appeal, European Patent Office, Munich, 1997–2005; *b* 5 April 1940; *d* of late Ninian Rhys Davies and Gweneth Elizabeth Davies (*née* Griffith). *Educ:* Cheltenham Ladies' Coll.; Grenoble Univ.; Univ. of Wales, Aberystwyth (PhD 1997). Called to the Bar, Lincoln's Inn, 1961; in practice at the Bar, 1961–63, and 2005–. Legal Assistant: De La Rue Co., 1963–65; United Internat. Bureaux for Protection of Intellectual Property, Geneva, 1965–70; Legal Advr, 1970–73, Asst Dir Gen., 1973–80, Associate Dir Gen. and Chief Legal Advr, 1980–91, IFPI. Res. Fellow, Max Planck Inst. for Foreign and Internat. Patent, Copyright, and Competition Law, Munich, 1990; Hon. Prof., Univ. of Wales, Aberystwyth, 1994–; Vis. Prof., QMIPRI, Univ. of London, 2007–. Mem., Wkg Gp on the Rôle of the State vis-à-vis the Cultural Industries, Council of Europe, 1980–86; Legal Mem., Bds of Appeal, 1991, Mem., Enlarged Bd of Appeal, 1996, European Patent Office. DL Gwynedd, 2001. Liveryman, Welsh Livery Guild, 2007. *Publications:* Piracy of Phonograms, 1981, 2nd edn 1986; Private Copying of Sound and Audiovisual Recordings, 1984; (jtly) Challenges to Copyright and Related Rights in the European Community, 1983; (jtly) Music and Video Private Copying, 1993; Copyright and the Public Interest, 1994, 2nd edn 2002; Copinger and Skone James on Copyright, suppl. (jtly) 1994, 14th edn (ed jtly) 1999, 15th edn (ed jtly) 2005, suppls (jtly) 2006, 2007; many articles in intellectual property law jls. *Recreations:* golf, tennis, art, travel. *Address:* Hogarth Chambers, 5 New Square, Lincoln's Inn, WC2A 3RJ; Trefaes, Abersoch, Gwynedd LL53 7AD. *T:* (01758) 712426. *Clubs:* Royal Anglo-Belgian, Hurlingham.

DAVIES, Rt Rev. Glenn Naunton, PhD; Assistant Bishop, Diocese of Sydney, and Bishop of North Sydney, since 2002; *b* 26 Sept. 1950; *s* of Rodger Naunton Davies and Dorothy Joan Davies; *m* 1979, Dianne Frances Carlisle; two *d*. *Educ:* Univ. of Sydney (BSc 1972); Westminster Theol Seminary, Philadelphia (MDiv, ThM 1979); Moore Theol Coll. (DipA 1981); Sheffield Univ. (PhD 1988). Ordained deacon, priest, 1981; Asst Minister, St Stephen's, Willoughby, 1981–82; Lectr, Moore Theol Coll., 1983–95; Rector, St Luke's, Miranda, 1995–2001. Canon Theologian, dio. Ballarat, 2000–. Centenary Medal, Australia, 2003. *Publications:* Job, 1989; Faith and Obedience: studies in Romans 1–4, 1990. *Address:* PO Box Q190, QVB Post Office, NSW 1230, Australia.

DAVIES, Glyn; *see* Davies, R. H. G.

DAVIES, Glyn; Member (C) Mid & West Wales, National Assembly for Wales, 1999–2007; *b* 16 Feb. 1944; *m* 1969, Bobbie; three *s* one *d*. *Educ:* Caereinion High Sch.; UCW, Aberystwyth. Mem. (C) Montgomeryshire DC, 1985–88 (Chm.). Chm., Develt Bd for Rural Wales, 1989–94. *Recreations:* countryside, sport. *Address:* Cil Farm, Berriew, Welshpool, Montgomeryshire, Mid Wales SY21 8AZ. *T:* (01686) 640698.

DAVIES, Prof. Glyn Arthur Owen, FRAeS; FCGI; Professor of Aeronautical Structures, 1985–99, and Senior Research Fellow in Aerostructures, since 1999, Imperial College of Science, Technology and Medicine, London (Head of Department of Aeronautics, 1982–89; Pro-Rector (Resources), 1997–99); *b* 11 Feb. 1933; *s* of Arthur and Florence Davies; *m* 1959, Helen Rosemary (*née* Boot); two *d*. *Educ:* Liverpool Inst., Univ. of Liverpool (BEng); Cranfield Inst. of Technology (DCAe); PhD Sydney, 1966. Res. Asst, MIT, 1956; Advanced Project Engr, Brit. Aerospace, 1957–59; Lectr, Sen. Lectr, Dept of Aeronautics, Univ. of Sydney, 1959–66; Lectr, Sen. Lectr, Dept of Aeronautics, Imperial Coll. of Sci. and Technol., 1966–72. Consultant to: ARC, 1975–81; MoD, 1980–; Nat. Agency for Finite Element Methods and Standards, 1983–95; SERC, 1986–90 (Supercomputing, 1991–93); The Computer Bd, 1989–91; ABRC (Supercomputing), 1991–94; UFC (IT), 1991–93; DTI (Aviation), 1991–2005; RAeS, 1994–; EPSRC, 1994–2005; OST (Foresight) Defence & Aerospace, 1994–2002. FRAeS 1987; FCGI 2000. *Publications:* Virtual Work in Structural Analysis, 1982; Mathematical Methods in Engineering, 1984; Finite Element Primer, 1986; Background to Benchmarks, 1993; Finite Element Modelling of Composite Materials and Structures, 2002; The Standard Handbook for Aeronautical and Astronautical Engineers, 2003. *Recreations:* photography, archaeology, painting, theatre, music, allotment. *Address:* Hedsor School House, Bourne End, Bucks SL8 5JJ.

DAVIES, Sir Graeme (John), Kt 1996; FREng; FRSE; Vice-Chancellor, University of London, since 2003; *b* 7 April 1937; *s* of Harry John Davies and Gladys Edna Davies (*née* Pratt); *m* 1959, Florence Isabelle Martin; one *s* one *d*. *Educ:* Mount Albert Grammar School, Auckland, NZ; Univ. of Auckland (BE, PhD); St Catharine's College, Cambridge (MA, ScD). FREng (FEng 1988). Junior Lectr, Univ. of Auckland, 1960–62; University of Cambridge: TI Research Fellow, 1962–64; Univ. Demonstrator in Metallurgy, 1964–66; Lectr, 1966–76; Fellow of St Catharine's Coll., 1967–77 (Hon. Fellow 1989); Prof. of Metallurgy, Univ. of Sheffield, 1978–86; Vice Chancellor, Univ. of Liverpool, 1986–91; Chief Executive: UFC, 1991–93; PCFC, 1992–93; HEFCE, 1992–95; Principal and Vice-Chancellor, Univ. of Glasgow, 1995–2003. Visiting Professor: Brazil, 1976–77; Israel, 1978; Argentina, 1980; China, 1981; Hon. Professor: Zhejiang Univ., China, 1985; Yantai Univ., China, 1996. Chm., Univs Superannuation Scheme, 1996–2006. Mem., ACOST, 1991–93. Member: Merseyside Enterprise Forum, 1986–90; London Economic Panel, 2004–; Chairman: Scottish Educn and Trng, 1996–2001; Observatory on Borderless Higher Educn, 2001–; Higher Educn Policy Inst., 2006–. Guardian, Sheffield Assay Office, 1983–86; Chairman: CCLRC, 2001–07; Glasgow Sci. Centre, 2002–06, 2007–; Member Council: Inst. Metals, 1981–86; Sheffield Metallurgical and Engineering Assoc., 1977–86 (Pres., 1984–85); ACU, 1987–91, 1998–2002; UUK (formerly CVCP), 1996–; Pres., Council of Military Educn Cttees, 2006–. Trustee: Bluecoat Soc. of Arts, 1986–91; Museums and Galls on Merseyside, 1987–92; Iona Trust, 1995–2003; Carnegie Trust for the Univs of Scotland, 1995–2003; Scottish Science Trust, 1996–2003. Governor: Shrewsbury Sch., 1989–95; Glasgow Sch. of Art, 2004–. FRSA 1989; FRSE 1996; CCMI (CBIM 1991). Freeman, City of London, 1987; Liveryman, Co. of Ironmongers, 1989 (Mem., Court, 1992–; Master, 2005–06); Freeman and Burgess Holder, City of Glasgow, 1996. DL Merseyside, 1989–92. Hon. FTCL 1995; FRCPSGlas 1999; Hon. FCIPS 2003; Hon. FIPENZ 2007. Hon. LLD: Liverpool, 1991; Strathclyde, 2000; Edinburgh, 2003; Hon. DSc: Nottingham, 1995; Ulster, 2004; Hon. DMet Sheffield, 1995; Hon. DEng: Manchester Metropolitan, 1996; Auckland, 2002; DUniv: Glasgow, 2004; Paisley, 2004; London South Bank, 2006. Rosenhain Medal, Inst. of Metals, 1982. *Publications:* Solidification and Casting, 1973; Texture and Properties of Materials, 1976; Solidificação e Fundicao das Metais e Suas Ligas, 1978; Hot Working and Forming Processes, 1980; Superplasticity, 1981; Essential Metallurgy for Engineers, 1985; papers to learned jls. *Recreations:* cricket, birdwatching, golf, The Times crossword. *Address:* University of London, Senate House, Malet Street, WC1E 7HU. *Club:* Athenæum.

DAVIES, Prof. Graham Arthur, PhD, DSc; FREng; Professor and Head of Chemical Engineering Department, University of Manchester Institute of Science and Technology, 1989–2001; *b* 2 July 1938; *s* of Evan Henry Davies and Esther Davies; *m* 1963, Christine; one *s* one *d*. *Educ:* Wolverhampton Grammar Sch.; Univ. of Birmingham (BSc 1st Cl. Hons; PhD 1963; DSc 1987). FREng (FEng 1995). R&D Div., Procter & Gamble Ltd, 1961–65; Lectr, 1965–69, Sen. Lectr, 1969–74, Reader, 1974–89, Chemical Engrg Dept, UMIST. *Publications:* Recent Advances in Liquid-Liquid Extraction, 1971; Hydrometallurgy, 1985; Science and Practice of Liquid Liquid Extraction, 1993. *Recreations:* golf, music. *Address:* c/o University of Manchester, Oxford Road, Manchester M13 9PL.

DAVIES, Prof. Graham Ivor, PhD, DD; FBA 2003; Professor of Old Testament Studies, University of Cambridge, since 2001, Fellow, Fitzwilliam College, Cambridge, since 1983; *b* 26 Sept. 1944; *s* of late Ivor Samuel Davies and of Pauline Beryl Davies (*née* Serjeant); *m* 1971, Nicola Rina Galeski; three *s* one *d*. *Educ:* King's Coll. Sch., Wimbledon; Merton Coll., Oxford (Postmaster in Classics; BA 1st cl. hons Lit. Hum. 1967; 1st cl. hons Theol. 1969; MA 1970; DD 1998); Peterhouse, Cambridge (PhD 1975). FSA 1987. Asst Lectr, then Lectr, in Theol., Univ. of Nottingham, 1971–78; University of Cambridge: Lectr in Divinity, 1979–93; Reader in OT Studies, 1993–2001; Chm., Faculty Bd of Divinity, 1995–97. Director of Studies in Theology: Pembroke Coll., 1979–87; Peterhouse, 1979–88; Fitzwilliam Coll., 1983–2008; Director: Hebrew Inscriptions Project, 1987–2003; Cambridge Centre, Semantics of Ancient Hebrew Database, 1995– (Sec., ESF Network Co-ordinating Cttee, 1991–95). Mem., Exec. Cttee, Palestine Exploration Fund, 1981–2001; Sec., Fifteenth Congress, Internat. Orgn for Study of OT, Cambridge, 1995. Chm., Theol. and Religious Studies Section, British Acad., 2006–July 2009. Macbride Sermon, Oxford, 1986. Editor: Cities of the Biblical World series, 1981–96; Palestine Exploration Qly, 1990–2000; Internat. Critical Commentary (OT), 2004–; Editl Bd, Zeitschrift für die Alttestamentliche Wisenschaft, 2007–. *Publications:* The Way of the Wilderness, 1979; Megiddo (Cities of the Biblical World), 1986; Ancient Hebrew Inscriptions: corpus and concordance, vol. 1, 1991, vol. 2, 2004; Hosea (New Century Bible Commentary), 1992; Hosea (Old Testament Guide), 1993; (with A. N. S. Lane) John Calvin's The Bondage and Liberation of the Will, 1996; contrib. Vetus Testamentum, Palestine Exploration Qly, Jl of Semitic Studies and other learned jls and collections of essays. *Recreations:* steam trains, Rugby football, hill-walking, gardening, religious poetry. *Address:* Faculty of Divinity, University of Cambridge, West Road, Cambridge CB3 9BS. *T:* (01223) 763002, *Fax:* (01223) 763003; *e-mail:* gid10@cam.ac.uk.

DAVIES, Prof. Graham James, PhD, DSc; CEng, FREng, FIET, FInstP, FIMMM; Sir James Timmins Chance Professor of Engineering and Head, School of Engineering, University of Birmingham, since 2001; *b* 2 July 1946; *s* of William Thomas and Amy Davies; *m* 1975, Frances Vivienne Martin; two *s*. *Educ:* UCW Aberystwyth (BSc; PhD 1971; DSc 1986). MRSC 1969; CEng, FIET (FIEE 1998); FInstP 1990; FIMMM 2002. Res. Officer, KCL, 1971–72; Post Office Research: Jun. Res. Fellow, 1972–75; Hd of Gp, 1975–84; British Telecom Research Laboratories: Head: Advanced Materials and Devices Section, 1984–90; Competitor Analysis Section, 1990–93; Director: Corporate Res., 1993–98; Technol. Acquisition, 1998–2001. Chm., Foresight Materials Panel, DTI, 2000–04. Director: Inst. of Physics Publishing, 2001–03; Birmingham R&D, 2001–; Diamond Light Source, 2003–. Mem. Council, CCLRC, 2003–07. FREng 1999. Liveryman, Co. of Engrs, 2003. *Publications:* (with R. H. Williams) Semiconductor Growth, Surfaces and Interfaces, 1994; (jtly) Chemical Beam Epitaxy and Related Techniques, 1997; numerous papers in learned jls. *Recreations:* walking, music, golf, reading. *Address:* School of Engineering, University of Birmingham, Edgbaston, Birmingham B15 2TT. *T:* (0121) 414 4155, *Fax:* (0121) 414 4269; *e-mail:* G.J.Davies@bham.ac.uk.

DAVIES, Prof. Graham Michael; JP; Professor of Psychology, University of Leicester, 1989–2006, now Emeritus; Hon. Professor, Universities of Birmingham and Coventry, since 2007; *b* 19 Feb. 1943; *s* of Harold Cecil Davies and Mona Florence Daisy Wisbey; *m* 1st, 1966, Heather Jane Neale; one *s* one *d*; 2nd, 1987, Noelle Robertson; two *d*. *Educ:* Bodmin Grammar Sch.; Univ. of Hull (BA, PhD, DSc). CPsychol, FBPsS. Lectr in Psychology, 1967–77, Sen. Lectr, 1977–87, Univ. of Aberdeen; Prof. of Psychology, NE London Poly., 1987–89. Chm., Soc. for Applied Res. in Memory and Cognition, 1998–99; Pres., Eur. Assoc. for Psychology and Law, 2003–06. Founding Editor, Applied Cognitive Psychology, 1987. JP Melton, Belvoir and Rutland, 2000. *Publications:* edited jointly: Perceiving and Remembering Faces, 1981; Identification Evidence: a psychological evaluation, 1982; Memory in Context, 1988; Memory in Everyday life, 1993; Psychology, Law and Criminal Justice: international developments in research and practice, 1995; Recovered Memories: seeking the middle ground, 2001; Children's Testimony: a handbook of psychological research and forensic practice, 2002; Practical Psychology for Forensic Investigations and Prosecutions, 2006; Forensic Psychology, 2008; reports for the Home Office: An evaluation of the live link for child witnesses, 1991; (jtly) Videotaping of Children's Evidence: an evaluation, 1995. *Recreations:* reading, walking. *Address:* School of Psychology, Wellcome Building, University of Leicester, Lancaster Road, Leicester LE1 9HN. *T:* (0116) 229 7176.

DAVIES, Grahame Brian; Chairman, London Internet Exchange, since 1999; *b* 6 May 1961; *s* of Brian and Joyce Davies; *m* 1990, Karen Uridge; two *s*. *Educ:* Haberdashers' Aske's Boys' Sch., Elstree. Computer operator, Unilever Computer Services Ltd, 1979–81; computer programmer, Impetus Computer Services, 1981–83; Dir, Demon Systems Ltd, 1983–95; Founder, Demon Internet, 1992; Gp Man. Dir, Easynet Gp plc, 1995–2001; Dir, Internet Watch Foundn, 1997–2002; Dir, Great Scores, digital sheet music, 2005–, and other internet start-ups. *Recreations:* playing the piano, sport. *Address:* e-mail: grahame@tptb.co.uk.

DAVIES, (Gwilym) E(dnyfed) Hudson; *see* Davies, Ednyfed H.

DAVIES, Howard; *see* Davies, S. H.

DAVIES, (Sir) Howard (John), Kt 2000; Director, London School of Economics, since 2003; *b* 12 Feb. 1951; *s* of late Leslie Powell Davies and of Marjorie Davies; *m* 1984, Prudence Mary Keely; two *s*. *Educ:* Manchester Grammar Sch.; Memorial Univ., Newfoundland; Merton Coll., Oxford (MA History and Mod. Langs); Stanford Graduate Sch. of Business, USA (MS Management Science). Foreign Office, 1973–74; Private Sec. to HM Ambassador, Paris, 1974–76; HM Treasury, 1976–82; McKinsey & Co. Inc., 1982–87 (Special Adviser to Chancellor of the Exchequer, 1985–86); Controller, Audit Commn, 1987–92; Dir Gen., CBI, 1992–95; Dep. Gov., 1995–97, Dir, 1998–2003, Bank of England; Chm., FSA, 1997–2003. Director: GKN plc, 1990–95; Morgan Stanley Inc., 2004–; Paternoster Ltd, 2006–; Mem., NatWest Internat. Adv. Bd, 1992–95. Director: BOTB, 1992–95; BITC, 1992–95. Trustee, Tate Gall., 2002–. Pres., Age Concern England, 1994–98. Governor: De Montfort Univ. (formerly Leicester Polytechnic), 1988–95; Royal Acad. of Music, 2005–. Chm. Judges, Man Booker Prize for Fiction, 2007. *Publications:* The Chancellors' Tales, 2006; Global Financial Regulation: the essential guide, 2008. *Recreations:* cricket, children. *Address:* London School of Economics, Houghton Street, WC2A 2AE. *Clubs:* Barnes Common Cricket; Manchester City Supporters.

DAVIES, Rt Rev. Howell Haydn; Bishop of Karamoja, Uganda, 1981–87; Vicar of St Jude's Parish, Wolverhampton, 1987–93, now retired; *b* 18 Sept. 1927; *s* of Ivor Thomas Davies and Sarah Gladys Davies (*née* Thomas); *m* 1958, Jean Wylam (*née* King); three *s* three *d*. *Educ:* Birmingham; DipArch (Birm.) 1954; ARIBA 1955. Corporal Clerk (Gen. Duties) RAF, Mediterranean and Middle East, 1945–48. Assistant Architect, 1952–56. Deacon 1959, priest 1960; Curate, St Peter's Parish, Hereford, 1959–61; Missionary of Bible Churchmen's Missionary Soc., Kenya, 1961–79, Uganda, 1981–87; Archdeacon of Maseno North, 1971–74; Provost of Nairobi, 1974–79; Vicar of Woking, 1979–81. Buildings designed and completed in Kenya: Church Trng Centre, Kapsabet; Teachers' Coll. Chapel, Mosoriot; St Andrew's Parish Centre, Kapenguria; Cathedral Church of the Good Shepherd, Nakuru; three-storey admin block, bookshop and staff housing for Maseno N Dio., Kakamega; various church and mission staff housing in Kenya and Uganda. *Recreations:* walking, reading, d-i-y, building design. *Address:* 2 Cherry Tree Close, Cherry Tree Road, Sheffield S11 9AF.

DAVIES, Hugh Llewelyn, CMG 1994; HM Diplomatic Service, retired; Senior Partner, Orient Asian Partners, since 2005; *b* 8 Nov. 1941; *s* of late Vincent Davies (formerly ICS), OBE, and Rose (*née* Temple); *m* 1968, Virginia Ann Lucius; one *d* one *s*. *Educ:* Rugby School; Churchill College, Cambridge (Hons History degree). HM Diplomatic Service, 1965–99: Chinese Language Studies, Hong Kong, 1966–68; Second Sec., Office of British Chargé d'Affaires, Peking, 1969–71; Far Eastern Dept, FCO, 1971–74; First Sec. (Econ.), Bonn, 1974–77; Head of Chancery, Singapore, 1977–79; Asst Head, Far Eastern Dept, FCO, 1979–82; on secondment, Barclays Bank International, 1982–83; Commercial Counsellor, Peking, 1984–87; Dep. British Permanent Rep., OECD, Paris, 1987–90; Hd, Far Eastern Dept, FCO, 1990–93; Sen. British Trade Comr, Hong Kong, June–Sept. 1993; British Sen. Rep., (Ambassador), Sino-British Jt Liaison Gp, Hong Kong, 1993–97; Special Enquiry on China Trade and Special Co-ordinator, China, Taiwan and Hong Kong, FCO, 1997–98; Exec. Dir, Prudential Corp. Asia, 1999–2005; Sen. Advr, China, Old Mutual, 2005–06. Chm., China Assoc., 2002–; Mem. Bd, China Britain Trade Council, 1999–; Vice Chm., GB China Centre, 2003–. *Recreations:* watersports, sketching, tennis, gardens, walking. *Address:* Church Farm, Cucklington, Wincanton, Somerset BA9 9PT.

See also Sir J. M. Davies.

DAVIES, Hunter; *see* Davies, E. H.

DAVIES, Huw; QC 2001; a Recorder, since 1998; *b* 25 Oct. 1955; *s* of Walter Stephen Davies and May Davies. *Educ:* UCW, Aberystwyth (LLB); Sidney Sussex Coll., Cambridge (MPhil). Called to the Bar, Gray's Inn, 1978; Asst Recorder, 1994–98; Standing Counsel to HM Customs and Excise, Wales and Chester Circuit, 1996–2001. *Recreation:* flying. *Address:* 30 Park Place, Cardiff CF10 3BS. *T:* (029) 2039 8421. *Clubs:* Carlton; Tiger.

DAVIES, Huw; *see* Davies, E. H.

DAVIES, Huw Humphreys; Chief Executive, Channel Television, 2000–06; *b* 4 Aug. 1940; *s* of William Davies and Harriet Jane Davies (*née* Humphreys); *m* 1966, Elizabeth Shân Harries; two *d*. *Educ:* Llangynog Primary School; Llandovery College; Pembroke College, Oxford. MA (Lit.Hum) 1964. Director/Producer: Television Wales and West, 1964; HTV, 1968; HTV Cymru/Wales: Asst Controller of Programmes, 1978; Controller of Programmes, 1979–81; Dir of Programmes, 1981–87; Chief Exec., 1987–91; Gp Dir of Television, HTV, 1989–94; Pres., HTV Internat., 1994–96; Chm., Square Circle Prodns Ltd, 1996–2002; Director: Winchester Entertainment (formerly Winchester Multimedia), 1996–2003 (Chm., 2003–04); Content Film, 2004–. Produced and directed many programmes and series in English and Welsh; latterly numerous plays and drama-documentaries. Chm., Regional Controllers, ITV, 1987–88. Mem., Gorsedd of Bards. *Recreations:* reading, swimming. *Address:* 41 Victoria Road, Penarth, S Glamorgan CF64 3HY.

DAVIES, Hywel; *see* Davies, D. H.

DAVIES, Lt-Col Hywel William; Chairman, Peatland Goup, since 2000; Managing Director, Peatland Smokehouse Ltd, since 2002; *b* 28 June 1945; *s* of late William Lewis Davies, JP and Barbara Beatrice Eleanor Davies, JP, MFH, Pantyderi, Boncath, Pembs; *m* 1969, Patricia, *d* of late Lt-Col E. B. Thornhill, MC; one *s* one *d*. *Educ:* Harrow; Magdalene Coll., Cambridge (MA). Commnd RHG (The Blues, later Blues & Royals), 1965; Staff Coll., 1977; Operational Requirements, MoD, 1978–80; Defence Intelligence, MoD, 1982–84; CO, Blues & Royals, 1985–87; with Pilkington Optronics, 1988–89; Chief Executive: RHASS, 1991–98; BHS, 1998–2000. Director: G. D. Golding & Son Ltd, 1988–; Challenger Consultancy Ltd, 1987–91; Ingliston Hotels Ltd, 1997–98; Scottish Farming and Educnl Trust, 1991–98; Scottish Agricl & Rural Develt Centre Ltd, 1992–98; The Countryside Movt, 1995–97; Ingliston Develt Trust, 1996–98; British Horse Soc. Trading Co. Ltd, 1998–2000. Mem., Countryside Cttee, Countryside Alliance, 1997–99. Chairman: Assoc. of Show and Agricl Orgns, 1998–99 (Hon. Life Mem., 2000); Draught Horse Trng Cttee, 1998–2000; Royal Internat. Horse Show, 1998–2000. Mem. (C) S Ayrshire Council, 2003– (Convenor, Rural Affairs Cttee and HR Cttee, 2005). Chairman: Central Region, 1998, Ayr and Arran, 2004–, Assoc. of Order of St John; W Lowland Cadet Force League, 2001–; Vice Pres., Ayrshire and Arran Red Cross, 2002–04. ARAgS 1996. OStJ 1997. *Recreations:* equestrian pursuits (Mem., Coaching Club; represented UK at Four-in-Hand Carriage Driving, 1984–87), shooting, fishing, gardening. *Address:* Peatland, Gatehead, Ayrshire KA2 9AN. *T:* (01563) 851020. *Club:* Farmers'.

DAVIES, Ian; HM Diplomatic Service; Foreign Office Response Centre, Foreign and Commonwealth Office, since 2005; *b* 1 Aug. 1956; *s* of late John Davies and of Freda Mary Davies; *m* 1979, Purificación Bautista Hervias; two *d*. *Educ:* Queen Mary Coll., London (BSc Econs 1983); Birkbeck Coll., London (MSc Econs 1985). Joined FCO, 1976; Moscow, 1978–80; Protocol Dept, FCO, 1983–85; Paris, 1985–88; Moscow, 1988–90; Far Eastern Dept, FCO, 1990–93; Dep. Head of Mission, Bolivia, 1993–96; Consul Gen., Marseille, 1997–2001; Dep. Head of Mission, Peru, 2002–05. *Recreations:* walking, classical music, cinema, theatre. *Address:* c/o Foreign and Commonwealth Office, King Charles Street, SW1A 2AH.

DAVIES, Ian; *see* Davies, D. I.

DAVIES, (Ifor) Huw I.; *see* Irranca-Davies.

DAVIES, Isobel Mary M.; *see* Macdonald-Davies.

DAVIES, Prof. (Ivor) Norman (Richard), CMG 2001; PhD; FBA 1997; historian; Senior Research Associate, Oxford University, since 1997; Fellow, St Antony's College, Oxford, since 2007; Supernumerary Fellow, Wolfson College, Oxford, 1998–2005; Professor of Polish History, School of Slavonic and East European Studies, University of London, 1985–96, now Emeritus; *b* Bolton, 8 June 1939; *s* of Richard Davies and Elizabeth Bolton; *m* 1st, 1966, Maria Zielińska; one *s*; 2nd, 1984, Maria Korzeniewicz; one *s*. *Educ:* Bolton Sch.; Grenoble Univ.; Magdalen Coll., Oxford (MA); Sussex Univ. (MA); Jagiellonian Univ., Cracow (PhD). Asst Master, St Paul's Sch., London, 1963–65; Alistair Horne Res. Fellow, St Antony's Coll., Oxford, 1969–71; Lectr, 1971–84, Reader, 1984–85, SSEES, London Univ. Visiting Professor: Columbia Univ., 1974; McGill Univ., 1977–78; Hokkaido Univ., 1982–83; Stanford Univ., 1985–86; Harvard Univ., 1991; Univ. of Adelaide, 1998; ANU, Canberra, 1999; Clare Hall, Cambridge, 2006–07; Vis. Fellow, Clare Hall, Cambridge, 2006–07. FRHistS 1974. Dr *hc*: Marie Curie-Skłodowska Univ., Lublin, 1993; Univ. of Gdańsk, 2000; Jagiellonian Univ., 2003; Sussex, 2006; Warsaw, 2007. Hon. Citizen: Cracow, 1999; Lublin, 2000; Wrocław, 2002. Kt Cross, Order of Polonia Restituta (Poland), 1984; Commander Cross, 1992, Grand Cross, 1998, Order of Merit (Poland). *Publications:* White Eagle, Red Star: the Polish-Soviet war of 1919–20, 1972; Poland Past and Present: a bibliography of works in English on Polish history, 1976; God's Playground: a history of Poland, 2 vols, 1981; Heart of Europe: a short history of Poland, 1984; (ed with A. Polonsky) The Jews in Eastern Poland and the Soviet Union 1939–45, 1991; Europe: a history, 1996; The Isles: a history, 1999; (with Roger Moorhouse) Microcosm: portrait of a central European city, 2002; Rising '44: the battle for Warsaw, 2003; Europe East & West, 2006; Europe at War 1939–1945: no simple victory, 2006. *Recreation:* not writing. *Address:* St Antony's College, Oxford OX2 6JF.

DAVIES, Jacqueline, (Mrs P. N. R. Clark); Her Honour Judge Jacqueline Davies; a Circuit Judge, since 1993; *b* 21 May 1948; one *d*; *m* 1997, Paul Nicholas Rowntree Clark, *qv*. *Educ:* Manchester High Sch. for Girls; Univ. of Leeds (LLB Hons). Called to the Bar, Middle Temple, 1975, Bencher, 2004; a Recorder, 1991–93. *Address:* Doncaster Crown Court, College Road, Doncaster DN1 3HS.

DAVIES, (James) Brian Meredith, MD, DPH, FFPH; Director of Social Services, City of Liverpool, 1971–81; *b* 27 Jan. 1920; *s* of late Dr G. Meredith Davies and Caroline Meredith Davies; *m* 1944, Charlotte (*née* Pillar); three *s*. *Educ:* Bedford Sch.; Medical Sch. St Mary's Hosp., London Univ. MB, BS (London) 1943, MD (London) 1948; DPH 1948; FFPH (MFCM 1972, FFCM 1974). Various hosp. appts. Served War, RAMC, Captain 1944–47. Asst MOH, Lancashire CC, 1948–50; Dep. MOH, City of Oxford, 1950–53; Clin. Asst (infectious Diseases), United Oxford Hosps, 1950–53; Dep. MOH, 1953–69; Dir of Personal Health and Social Services, 1969–71, City of Liverpool; pt-time Lectr in Public Health, 1953–71, and Hon. Lectr in Preventive Paediatrics, 1964–85, Liverpool Univ. Chm., Liverpool div., BMA, 1958–59; Council of Europe Fellowship, to study Elderly: in Finland, Sweden, Norway and Denmark, 1964 (report awarded special prize); Mem. Public Health Laboratory Service Bd, 1966–71. Teaching Gp of Soc. of Community Med. (Sec. of Gp, 1958–72, Pres. Gp, 1972–73). Member: Personal Social Services Council, 1978–80; Mental Health Review Tribunal, Mersey Area, 1982–; Governor, Occupational Therapy Coll., Huyton, Liverpool, 1969–85; Dir of MERIT (Merseyside Industrial Therapy Services Ltd), 1970–75; Mem. Council, Queen's Inst. of District Nursing, 1971–78; Assoc. of Dirs of Social Services: Chm., NW Br., 1971–73; Mem. Exec. Council, 1973–78; Pres. 1976–77; Mem. Exec. Cttee of Central Council for the Disabled, 1972–76; Adviser to Social Services Cttee of Assoc. of Metropolitan Authorities, 1974–81; Member: RCP Cttee on Rheumatism and Rehabilitation, 1974–83; DES Cttee of Enquiry into Special Educn for Disabled Children, 1975–78; Exec. Cttee, Liverpool Personal Services Soc., 1973–81; Adv. Panel Inf. Service, Disabled Living Foundn, 1979–81; UK Steering Cttee, Internat. Year for the Disabled, 1979–80; J Cttee on Mobility of Blind and Partially Sighted People, 1980–81; Exec. Cttee, N Regional Assoc. for the Blind, 1980–81. Vice Pres., MIND Appeal, 1978–79. Christopher Kershaw Meml Lectr, London, 1984. Pres., Merseyside Ski Club, 1970–77. Mem. Council, Prospect Hall Coll., 1973–77; Chm., Bd of Governors, William Rathbone Staff Coll., Liverpool, 1961–75. Duncan Medal, 1998 (for services to public health in Liverpool, 1953–71). *Publications:* Community Health and Social Services, 1965, 6th edn as Public Health, Preventive Medicine and Social Services, 1995; Community Health, Preventive Medicine and Social Services, 1966, 6th edn 1993; (contrib.) Going Home (a Guide for helping the patient on leaving hospital), 1981; The Disabled Child and Adult, 1982; (contrib.) Rehabilitation: a practical guide to the management of physical disability in adults, 1988; numerous papers on Public Health, Physically and Mentally Handicapped and various social services, in scientific and other jls. *Recreations:* ski-ing, golf, fishing gardening, music. *Address:* Tree Tops, Church Road, Thornton Hough, Wirral, Merseyside CH63 1JN. *T:* (0151) 336 3435. *Club:* Bromborough Golf.

DAVIES, Janet; Member (Plaid Cymru) South West Wales, National Assembly for Wales, 1999–2007; *b* 29 May 1938; *d* of late David Rees and Jean Wardlaw Rees; *m* 1965, Basil Peter Ridley Davies (*d* 2000); one *s* one *d*. *Educ:* Howell's Sch., Llandaff; Trinity Coll., Carmarthen (BA); Open Univ. (BA Hons Social Scis). Mem. (Plaid Cymru) Taff Ely BC, 1983–96 (Leader, 1991–96); Mayor, Taff Ely, 1995–96. National Assembly for Wales: Plaid Cymru spokesperson on local govt, 1993–99, on housing, 1999–2002, for envmt, planning and transport, 2002, for transport, 2003–07; Plaid Cymru Chief Whip, 2003–07; Chm., Audit Cttee, 2003–07. Dir of Elections, Plaid Cymru, 1996–2001.

DAVIES, Janet Mary H.; *see* Hewlett-Davies.

DAVIES, Jill Adrian; *see* Kraye, J. A.

DAVIES, Jocelyn Ann; Member (Plaid Cymru) SE Wales, National Assembly for Wales, since 1999; *b* 18 June 1959; *d* of Edward and Marjorie Davies; one *s* two *d* by Michael Davies. *Educ:* Harris Manchester Coll., Oxford. Work in local govt, Islwyn BC and Newport BC, 1976–80. Mem. (Plaid Cymru) Islwyn BC, 1987–91. Dep. Minister for Housing, Nat. Assembly for Wales, 2007–. *Recreations:* walking, people watching. *Address:* National Assembly for Wales, Cardiff Bay, Cardiff CF99 1NA. *T:* (constituency) (01633) 220022, *Fax:* (01633) 220603.

DAVIES, Prof. John Brian, FREng; Professor of Electrical Engineering, University College London, 1985–97, now Emeritus Professor; *b* 2 May 1932; *s* of John Kendrick Davies and Agnes Ada Davies; *m* 1956, Shirley June (*née* Abrahart); one *s* two *d*. *Educ:* Jesus Coll., Cambridge (MA); Univ. of London (MSc, PhD, DSc Eng). Research Engineer, Mullard Res. Labs, Redhill, 1955–63; Lectr, Dept of Electrical Engineering, Univ. of Sheffield, 1963; Sen. Lectr 1967, Reader 1970–85, Dean of Engrg, 1989–91, University College London. Vis. Scientist, Nat. Bureau of Standards, Boulder, Colo, 1971–72; Visitor, Univ. of Oxford, 1983; Vis. Prof., Univ. of Colorado, 1988–89. FREng (FEng 1988). *Publications:* Electromagnetic Theory, vol. 2, 1972; (contrib.) Numerical Techniques for Microwave and Millimeter Wave Passive Structures, 1989. *Recreations:* fell walking, music.

DAVIES, Rt Rev. John David Edward; *see* Swansea and Brecon, Bishop of.

DAVIES, Rt Rev. John Dudley; Hon. Assistant Bishop, diocese of Lichfield, 1995–2005; Bishop Suffragan, then Area Bishop, of Shrewsbury, 1987–94; *b* 12 Aug. 1927; *s* of Charles Edward Steedman Davies and Minnie Paton Davies; *m* 1956, Shirley Dorothy Gough; one *s* two *d*. *Educ:* Trinity Coll., Cambridge (BA 1951, MA 1963); Lincoln Theol Coll. Deacon 1953, priest 1954, dio. Ripon; Curate: Halton, Leeds, 1953–56; Yeoville, Johannesburg, 1957; Priest-in-Charge, Evander, dio. Johannesburg, 1957–61; Rector and Dir of Missions, Empangeni, dio. Zululand and Swaziland, 1961–63; Anglican Chaplain, Univ. of Witwatersrand and Johannesburg Coll. of Educn, 1963–70; Chm., Div. of Christian Educn, S African Council of Churches, 1964–70; Mem. Exec., Univ. Christian Movement of Southern Africa, 1966–69; Sec. for Chaplaincies of Higher Educn, C of E Bd of Educn, 1970–74; Vicar of Keele and Chaplain, Univ. of Keele, 1974–76; Principal, Coll. of Ascension, Selly Oak, 1976–81; Preb. of Sandiacre, Lichfield Cathedral, 1976–87; Diocesan Missioner, St Asaph, 1982–87; Canon Res. and Hellins Lectr, St Asaph, 1982–85; Vicar/Rector, Llanrhaeadr-ym-Mochnant, Llanarmon-Mynydd-Mawr, Pennant, Hirnant and Llangynog, 1985–87. *Publications:* Free to Be, 1970; Beginning Now, 1971; Good News in Galatians, 1975; Creed and Conflict, 1979; The Faith Abroad, 1983; (with John J. Vincent) Mark at Work, 1986; World on Loan, 1992; The Crisis of the Cross, 1997; Be Born in us Today, 1999; God at Work, 2001; Only Say the Word, 2002; A Song for Every Morning, 2008; contribs to jls. *Address:* Nyddfa, By Pass Road, Gobowen, Oswestry SY11 3NG. *T:* (01691) 653434.

DAVIES, John Duncan, OBE 1984; DSc, PhD; Director, Polytechnic of Wales, 1978–92, then University of Glamorgan, Jan.–Oct. 1992, now Emeritus Professor; *b* 19 March 1929; *s* of Ioan and Gertrude Davies; *m* 1949, Barbara, *d* of Ivor and Alice Morgan; three *d*. *Educ:* Pontardawe School; Treforest School of Mines. BSc, MSc, PhD, DSc, Univ. of London. Junior Engineer, Consulting Engineers, 1949; Site Engineer, Cleveland Bridge Co., 1950–54; Royal Engineers, 1952–53; Design Engineer, Local Authority, 1955–56; Asst Lectr, Manchester Univ., 1957–58; University College, Swansea: Lecturer, 1959; Senior Lecturer, 1965; Reader, 1968; Professor of Civil Engineering, 1971–76; Dean, 1974–76; Principal, West Glamorgan Inst. of Higher Education, 1976–77. Member: Open University Delegacy, 1978–83; OU Cttee, 1987–90; Manpower Services Cttee (Wales), 1980–83; Wales Adv. Bd for Public Sector Higher Educn, 1982–83, 1986–89; Council, CNAA, 1985–93; Chm., Coleg Powys Corp., 1994–98. Hon. Fellow, Univ. of Wales, 1996. Hon. DTech Glamorgan, 1995. *Publications:* contribs to Structural Mechanics.

DAVIES, John Hamilton, OBE 2005; Chairman, Civil Service Appeal Board, since 1999; *b* 24 Nov. 1943; *s* of Albert Victor Davies and Betty Davies; *m* 1971, Helen Ruth Thomas; three *s*. *Educ:* Lewis Sch., Pengam, S Wales; Selwyn Coll., Cambridge (MA). ACIB 1970, FCIB 1991; FCIPD (FIPD 1991). With Barclays Bank, 1966–98: Local Dir, Chelmsford Reg., 1983–86; Hd, Career Planning, Gp Personnel, 1986–90; Dep. Dir, Gp Personnel, 1991–95; Dir, Personnel, Barclays UK Banking Services, 1995–98. Non-exec. Dir, ILX Gp (formerly Intellexis plc), 2001–06. Vis. Fellow, Cranfield Univ. Sch. of Mgt, 1998–2002. Board Member: Employers' Forum on Disability, 1991–96; BESO, 1991–98; Member: CBI Employment Policy Cttee, 1996–98; Armed Forces Pay Review Body, 1999–2005; Prison Service Pay Review Body, 2007–. Treas. and Mem., Exec. Bd, CIB, 1998–99. Gov., Felsted Sch., 1990–95 and 1998– (Chm., 2007–). Trustee, Farleigh Hospice, Chelmsford, 2000–. Freeman, City of London, 2002; Liveryman, Curriers' Co., 2002–. *Recreations:* walking, Church of England, music, travel. *Address:* Denbies, Bardfield Saling, Essex CM7 5EG. *T:* (01371) 850735. *Clubs:* Oxford and Cambridge; Essex.

DAVIES, Rev. Canon John Howard; Director of Theological and Religious Studies, University of Southampton, 1981–94; *b* 19 Feb. 1929; *s* of Jabez Howard and Sarah Violet Davies; *m* 1956, Ina Mary (*d* 1985), *d* of Stanley William and Olive Mary Bubb; two *s* (and two *s* decd). *Educ:* Southall Grammar Sch.; St John's Coll., Cambridge (MA); Westcott House, Cambridge; Univ. of Nottingham (BD); FRCO 1952. Ordained deacon, 1955, priest 1956. Succentor of Derby Cathedral, 1955; Chaplain of Westcott House, 1958; Lectr in Theology, Univ. of Southampton, 1963, Sen. Lectr 1974. Canon Theologian of Winchester, 1981–91. *Publication:* A Letter to Hebrews, 1967. *Recreations:* music, architecture, the countryside. *Address:* 13 Glen Eyre Road, Southampton SO16 3GA. *T:* (023) 8067 9359.

DAVIES, John Irfon, CBE 1998 (MBE (mil.) 1963); Under Secretary, Welsh Office, 1985–90, retired; Chairman, Health Promotion Authority for Wales, 1992–99; *b* 8 June 1930; *s* of late Thomas M. Davies and Mary M. Davies (*née* Harris); *m* 1950, Jean Marion Anderson (*d* 2000); one *d*. *Educ:* Stanley School; Croydon Polytechnic. Joined RAF, 1948, commissioned 1950, Specialist Navigator 1957; psc 1963; MoD, 1964–66; Chief Navigation Instructor, Cranwell, 1967; OC Flying, Muharraq, 1967–69; awc 1970; MoD, 1970–72; Cabinet Office, 1972–74; retd from RAF, 1974; Principal, Welsh Office, 1974, Asst Sec., 1978. Mem., GMC, 1990–99. *Recreations:* golf, piano, fishing, books. *Address:* 7 Danybryn Close, Radyr, Cardiff CF15 8DJ. *Clubs:* Royal Air Force; Cardiff and County; Radyr Golf.

DAVIES, Prof. John Kenyon, MA, DPhil; FSA; FBA 1985; Rathbone Professor of Ancient History and Classical Archaeology, University of Liverpool, 1977–2003; *b* 19 Sept. 1937; *s* of Harold Edward Davies and Clarice Theresa (*née* Woodburn); *m* 1st, 1962, Anna Elbina Morpurgo (*see* Anna Elbina Davies) (marr. diss. 1978); 2nd, 1978, Nicola Jane, *d* of Dr and Mrs R. M. S. Perrin; one *s* one *d*. *Educ:* Manchester Grammar Sch.; Wadham Coll., Oxford (BA 1959; MA 1962; DPhil 1966). FSA 1986. Harmsworth Sen. Scholar, Merton Coll., Oxford, 1960–61 and 1962–63; Jun. Fellow, Center for Hellenic Studies, Washington, DC, 1961–62; Dyson Jun. Res. Fellow, Balliol Coll., Oxford, 1963–65; Lectr in Ancient History, Univ. of St Andrews, 1965–68; Fellow and Tutor in Ancient History, Oriel Coll., Oxford, 1968–77; Pro-Vice-Chancellor, Univ. of Liverpool, 1986–90. Leverhulme Res. Prof., 1995–2000. Vis. Lectr, Univ. of Pennsylvania, 1971; Sen. Fellow, Istituto di Studi Avanzati, Univ. di Bologna, 2006. Chairman: St Patrick's Isle (IOM) Archaeological Trust Ltd, 1982–86; NW Archaeol Trust, 1982–91. Editor: Jl of Hellenic Studies, 1972–77; Archaeol Reports, 1972–74. *Publications:* Athenian Propertied Families 600–300 BC, 1971; Democracy and Classical Greece, 1978, 2nd edn 1993 (Spanish trans. 1981, German and Italian trans. 1983, Polish trans. 2003, Russian trans. 2004); Wealth and the Power of Wealth in Classical Athens, 1981; (ed with L. Foxhall) The Trojan War: its historicity and context, 1984; (ed jtly) Hellenistic Economies, 2001; (ed jtly) Making, Moving, and Managing, 2005; articles and reviews in learned jls. *Recreation:* choral singing. *Address:* 20 North Road, Grassendale Park, Liverpool L19 0LR. *T:* (0151) 427 2126.

DAVIES, Sir (John) Michael, KCB 2002; Clerk of the Parliaments, House of Lords, 1997–2003; *b* 2 Aug. 1940; *s* of late Vincent Ellis Davies, OBE and Rose Trench (*née* Temple); *m* 1971, Amanda Mary Atkinson; two *s* one *d*. *Educ:* The King's Sch., Canterbury; Peterhouse, Cambridge. Joined Parliament Office, House of Lords, 1964; seconded to Civil Service Dept as Private Sec. to Leader of House of Lords and Govt Chief Whip, 1971–74; Establishment Officer and Sec. to Chm. of Cttees, 1974–83; Principal Clerk, Overseas and European Office, 1983–85; Principal Clerk, Private Bill and Overseas Offices and Examiner of Petitions for Private Bills, 1985–88; Reading Clerk, 1988–90, and Clerk of Public Bills, 1988–94; Clerk Asst, 1991–97, and Principal Finance Officer, 1994–97. Secretary: Soc. of Clerks-at-the-Table in Commonwealth Parlts, and Jt Editor, The Table, 1967–83; Statute Law Cttee, 1974–83. Pres., Assoc. of Secs-General of Parlts, 1997–2000. Chm., BACSA, 2008–. *Address:* 26 Northchurch Terrace, N1 4EG.

See also H. L. Davies.

DAVIES, (John) Quentin; MP Grantham and Stamford, since 1997 (Stamford and Spalding, 1987–97) (C, 1997–2007, Lab, since 2007); Parliamentary Under-Secretary of State, Ministry of Defence, since 2008; *b* 29 May 1944; *e s* of late Dr Michael Ivor Davies and Thelma Davies (*née* Butler), Oxford; *m* 1983, Chantal, *e d* of late Lt-Col R. L. C. Tamplin, 17/21 Lancers, Military Kt of Windsor, and Claudine Tamplin (*née* Pleis); two *s*. *Educ:* Dragon Sch.; Leighton Park (exhibnr); Gonville and Caius Coll., Cambridge (Open Scholar; BA Hist. Tripos 1st cl. Hons 1966; MA); Harvard Univ. (Frank Know Fellow, 1966–67). HM Diplomatic Service, 1967; 3rd Sec., FCO, 1967–69; 2nd Sec., Moscow, 1969–72; 1st Sec., FCO, 1973–74. Morgan Grenfell & Co.: Manager, later Asst Dir, 1974–78; Rep. in France, later Dir-Gen. and Pres., Morgan Grenfell France SA, 1978–81; Director (main bd), and Hd of Eur. Corporate Finance, 1981–87; Consultant, 1987–93. Director: Dewe Rogerson International, 1987–95; SGE, later Vinci SA, 1999–2001, 2003–; Vinci UK (formerly Norwest Holst), 2001–. Adviser: NatWest Securities, then NatWest Markets, 1993–99; Royal Bank of Scotland, 1999–2003. Mem. Council, Lloyds of London, 2004–07. Parly Advr, Chartered Inst. of Taxation, 1993–. Contested (C) Birmingham, Ladywood, Aug. 1977. Parliamentary Private Secretary: to Minister of State for Educn, 1988–90; to Minister of State, Home Office, 1990–91; Opposition spokesman on social security and pensions, 1998–99; Shadow Paymaster-Gen., 1999–2000; Opposition spokesman on defence, 2000–01; Shadow NI Sec., 2001–03. Member: Treasury Select Cttee, 1992–98; Cttee on Standards and Privileges, 1995–98; Eur. Standing Cttee, 1991–97; Eur. Legislation Cttee, 1997–98; Internat. Devclt Cttee, 2003–07; Jt Chm., 1997–2005, Chm., 2005–, British-German Parly Gp; Vice Chairman: Anglo-French Parly Gp, 1997–; British-Netherlands Parly Gp, 1999–; British-Italian Parly Gp, 2005–; Chm., Conservative Gp for Europe, 2006–07. Chm., City in Europe Cttee, 1975. Freeman, City of London; Liveryman, Goldsmiths' Co. Trustee and Mem. Council, Centre for Econ. Policy Res., 1996–. Freedom of Information Award, 1996; Guardian Backbencher of the Year Award, 1996; Spectator Parliamentarian of the Year Award, 1997. *Publication:* Britain and Europe: a Conservative view, 1996. *Recreations:* reading, walking, riding, ski-ing, travel, playing bad tennis, looking at art and architecture. *Address:* House of Commons, SW1A 0AA. *Clubs:* Brooks's, Beefsteak, Travellers.

DAVIES, John Richard; QC 2003; *b* 18 Sept. 1958; *s* of late Geoffrey William and Jean Dawson Davies; partner, Barbara Kelly; one *d*. *Educ:* Eastbourne Coll.; Downing Coll., Cambridge (BA 1980, MA 1984). Called to the Bar, 1981; in practice as commercial, company and employment barrister, 1981–. *Recreations:* Burgundy (both red and white), Bordeaux, golf and almost all matters sporting. *Address:* Littleton Chambers, 3 King's Bench Walk North, Temple, EC4Y 7HR. *T:* (020) 7797 8600, *Fax:* (020) 7797 8699.

DAVIES, Rt Rev. John Stewart; Bishop of St Asaph, 1999–2008; *b* 28 Feb. 1943; *s* of John Edward Davies and Dorothy Stewart Davies (*née* Jones); *m* 1965, Joan Patricia Lovatt; two *s*. *Educ:* St John's Sch., Leatherhead; UCNW, Bangor (BA Hebrew); Westcott House, Cambridge; Queens' Coll., Cambridge (MLitt 1974). Journalism, 1960–68; ordained deacon, 1974, priest, 1975; Curate, Hawarden, 1974–78; Vicar: Rhosymedre, 1978–87; Mold, 1987–92; Archdeacon of St Asaph, 1991–99. *Recreations:* hill walking, cycling.

DAVIES, John Thomas, FCIB; Director, 1990–98, a Deputy Chairman, 1995–98, Lloyds Bank plc; a Deputy Chairman, Lloyds TSB Group plc, 1995–98; *b* 9 Feb. 1933; *s* of Joseph Robert and Dorothy Mary Davies; *m* 1957, Margaret Ann Johnson; two *s* three *d*. *Educ:* King Edward's Grammar Sch., Camp Hill, Birmingham. FCIB. Joined Lloyds Bank, 1949; served RAF, 1951–53; Lloyds Bank: Manager of branches, 1963–78; Gen. Management, 1978–89; Dir, Internat. Banking Div., 1989–91; Asst Chief Exec., 1991–92; Dep. Chief Exec., 1992–94. Director: Nat. Bank of NZ, 1989–90 and 1995–98; Cheltenham & Gloucester Building Society, 1995–98; Dir, 1995–98, Chm., 1997–98, Lloyds Abbey Life, later Lloyds TSB Financial Hldgs plc. Chm. Bd, OBO Property (formerly Office of the Banking Ombudsman), 1995–2004. *Recreations:* opera, gardening, walking, reading. *Address:* c/o Lloyds TSB Group plc, 25 Gresham Street, EC2V 7HN.

DAVIES, Jonathan, MBE 1995; writer and commentator on Rugby Union and League football; *b* 24 Oct. 1962; *s* of late Len and of Diana Davies; *m* 1984, Karen Hopkins (*d* 1997); one *s* two *d*; *m* 2002, Helen Jones. *Educ:* Gwendraeth Grammar Sch. Rugby Union footballer to 1989; played for Neath and Llanelli; 28 Wales caps, 4 as Captain; transferred to Rugby League, 1989; with Widnes, 1989–93, Warrington, 1993–95; returned to Rugby Union, 1995; with Cardiff, 1995–97, retired. Player of the Year Award, 1991, 1994; Stones Bitter Man of Steel, 1994. *Publication:* Jonathan (autobiog.), 1989. *Recreations:* golf, football. *Address:* c/o Cardiff RUFC, Cardiff Arms Park, Cardiff CF1 1JL.

DAVIES, Prof. Julian Edmund, PhD; FRS 1994; FRSC 1996; Professor and Head of Department of Microbiology and Immunology, University of British Columbia, 1992–97, now Professor Emeritus; *b* 9 Jan. 1932; *s* of Norman Alfred Davies and Lilian Constance (*née* Clarke); *m* 1957, Dorothy Jean Olney; two *s* one *d*. *Educ:* Univ. of Nottingham (BSc Hons Chem., Maths and Phys.; PhD 1956). Lectr in Chem., Univ. of Manchester, 1959–62; Associate in Bacteriol., Harvard Univ., 1962–67; University of Wisconsin: Associate Prof. of Biochem., 1967–70; Prof., 1970–80; Biogen: Res. Dir, 1980–83; Pres., 1983–85; Prof., Inst. Pasteur, Paris, 1986–91; Dir, West-East Center, Univ. of BC, 1993–96; Chief Scientific Officer, and Vice-Pres. of Res., TerraGen Diversity Inc., 1996–2000; Exec. Vice-Pres. for Technology Develt, Cubist Pharmaceuticals, Vancouver, 2000–04; Dir, Life Scis Inst., Univ. of British Columbia, 2005–06. President: Amer. Soc. for Microbiol., 1999–2000; Internat. Union Microbiol. Soc., 2002–05. Hoechst-Roussel Award, Amer. Soc. for Microbiol., 1986; Thom Award, Soc. for Industrial Microbiol., 1993; Scheele Prize, Swedish Acad. of Pharmaceutical Scis, 1997; Bristol Myers Squibb Award, 1999. *Publications:* Elementary Biochemistry, 1980; Milestones in Biotechnology, 1992. *Recreations:* cycling, ski-ing, tennis, wine. *Address:* 4428 West 6th Avenue, Vancouver, BC V6R 1Z3, Canada. *T:* (604) 2228235.

DAVIES, Karl; *see* Davies, R. K.

DAVIES, Dame Kay (Elizabeth), DBE 2008 (CBE 1995); DPhil; FMedSci; FRS 2003; Dr Lee's Professor of Anatomy, and Fellow of Hertford College, Oxford University, since 1998; Hon. Director, MRC Functional Genetics Unit, since 1999; Co-Director, Oxford Centre for Gene Function, since 2001; *b* 1 April 1951; *d* of Harry Partridge and Florence Partridge (*née* Farmer); *m* 1973, Stephen Graham Davies (marr. diss. 2000); one *s*. *Educ:* Stourbridge Girl's High Sch.; Somerville Coll., Oxford (BA, MA; DPhil; Hon. Fellow, 1995). MRCPath 1990, FRCPath 1997. Guy Newton Jun. Res. Fellow, Wolfson Coll., Oxford, 1976–78; Royal Soc. European Post-doctoral Fellow, Service de Biochimie, Centre d'Etudes, Gif-sur-Yvette, France, 1978–80; St Mary's Hospital Medical School: Cystic Fibrosis Res. Fellow, 1980–82; MRC Sen. Res. Fellow, 1982–84; Nuffield Department of Clinical Medicine, John Radcliffe Hospital, Oxford: MRC Sen. Res. Fellow, 1984–86; MRC Ext. Staff, 1986–92; Univ. Res. Lectr, 1990; MRC Ext. Staff, Inst. of Molecular Medicine, Oxford, 1989–95; Fellow of Green Coll., Oxford, 1990–95; MRC Res. Dir, MRC Clin. Scis Centre, Hammersmith Hosp., 1992–94; Prof. of Genetics, and Fellow, Keble Coll., Oxford Univ., 1995–98. Mem., MRC, 2002–08. Editor (with S. Tilghman), Genome Analysis Reviews, 1990–. Bristol-Myers Prof., USA, 1986; 7th Annual Colleen Giblin Dist. Lectr, Columbia Univ., 1992; Dist. Lectr, Mayo Clinic, USA, 1994. Founder FMedSci 1998. Hon. FRCP 1994. Hon. DSc Victoria, Canada, 1990; DUniv Open, 1999. Wellcome Trust Award, 1996; SCI Medal, 1999. *Publications:* (with A. P. Read) Molecular Analysis of Inherited Diseases, 1988, rev. edn 1992; (ed) Human Genetics Diseases: a practical approach, 1988, rev. edn 1993; (ed) Genome Analysis: a practical approach, 1988; (ed) The Fragile X Syndrome, 1989; (ed) Application of Molecular Genetics to the Diagnosis of Inherited Diseases, 1989; numerous reviews and 250 peer-reviewed pubns. *Recreations:* sport, music, gardening. *Address:* Department of Physiology, Anatomy and Genetics, University of Oxford, South Parks Road, Oxford OX1 3QX.

DAVIES, Keith Laurence M.; *see* Maitland Davies.

DAVIES, Sir Lancelot Richard B.; *see* Bell Davies.

DAVIES, Laura Jane, CBE 2000 (MBE 1988); professional golfer; *b* 5 Oct. 1963; *d* of David Thomas Davies and Rita Ann Davies (*née* Foskett). *Educ:* Fullbrook County Secondary Sch. Mem., Curtis Cup team, 1984; professional début, 1985; Mem., Solheim Cup team, 1990, 1992, 1994, 1996, 1998, 2000, 2003; Winner: Belgian Ladies' Open, 1985; Ladies' British Open, 1986; US Ladies' Open, 1987; Italian Open, 1987, 1988, 1996; Ford Classic, Woburn, 1988; Biarritz Ladies' Open, 1988; Itoki Classic, Japan, 1988; European Open, 1992; Thailand Ladies' Open, 1993, 1994; English Open, 1993, 1995; Australian Ladies' Masters, 1993, 1994, 2003; LPGA Championship, 1994, 1996; Irish Open, 1994, 1995; Scottish Open, 1994; French Masters, 1995; Danish Open, 1997; Championship of Europe, 1999; Norwegian Masters, 2002, 2006. Mem., Golf Foundn. *Publication:* Carefree Golf, 1991. *Address:* c/o Ladies European Tour Ltd, The Tytherington Club, Dorchester Way, Tytherington, Macclesfield SK10 2JP.

DAVIES, Leighton; *see* Davies, R. L.

DAVIES, Lewis Mervyn, CMG 1966; CBE 1984 (OBE 1962); HM Overseas Civil Service, retired; *b* 5 Dec. 1922; *s* of late Rev. Canon L. C. Davies; *m* 1st, 1950, Ione Podger (*d* 1973); one *s*; 2nd, 1975, Mona A. Birley; two step *s*. *Educ:* St Edward's Sch., Oxford. Served with Fleet Air Arm, 1941–46: Lieut A, RNVR. Administrative Officer, Gold Coast, 1948; Western Pacific: Senior Asst Secretary, 1956–62; Financial Secretary, 1962–65; Chief Secretary, 1965–70; Deputy Governor, Bahamas, 1970–73; Secretary for Security, 1973–82, Secretary (Gen. Duties), 1983–85, Hong Kong. Commandeur de l'Ordre National du Mérite, 1966. *Address:* Carrer Cals Julians 16, 07141 Sa Cabaneta-Marratxi, Mallorca, Spain. *T:* and *Fax:* (971) 602519. *Club:* Oriental.

DAVIES, Linda Hillary; Her Honour Judge Linda Davies; a Circuit Judge, since 1992; *b* 31 May 1945; *d* of Lt-Col Robert Blowers and Doris Rhoda (*née* Hillary); *m* 1966, Michael Llewelyn Lifton Davies; two *d*. *Educ:* Folkestone Grammar Sch. for Girls; King's Coll., London (LLB Hons). Called to the Bar, Gray's Inn, 1969; Barrister, 1972–92, a Recorder, 1990–92, Western Circuit. Part-time Chm., Industrial Tribunals, 1986–92.

DAVIES, Dr Lindsey Margaret, CBE 2004; FFPH; National Director of Pandemic Influenza Preparedness, Department of Health, since 2006; *b* 21 May 1953; *d* of Dr Frank Newby and Margaret Newby; *m* 1974, Peter Davies (marr. diss. 1994); two *s*. *Educ:* Univ. of Nottingham (BM, BS). MHSM 1987; FFPH (FFPHM 1991). Community paediatrics, 1976–82; trainee in public health medicine, 1982–85; Director of Public Health: Southern Derbys HA, 1985–89; Nottingham HA, 1989–92; Hd, Public Health Div., NHS Exec., DoH, 1992–94; Dir of Public Health, Trent RHA, 1994–96; Dir of Public Health and Med. Dir, Trent Regl Office, NHS Exec., DoH, 1996–2002; Regl Dir of Public Health, E Midlands, DoH, 2002–06. Special Prof., Nottingham Univ. Med. Sch., 2001–. British Medical Association: Mem. Council, 1989–92; Chm., Cttee for Public Health Medicine and Community Health, 1990–92. *Publications:* contribs to learned jls. *Recreations:* family life, enjoying modern architecture. *Address:* Department of Health, Richmond House, 79 Whitehall, SW1A 2NS. *T:* (020) 7210 5753.

DAVIES, Ven. Lorys Martin; Archdeacon of Bolton, 1992–2001, now Emeritus; *b* 14 June 1936; *s* of Evan Tudor Davies and Eigen Morfydd Davies; *m* 1960, Barbara Ethel (*née* Walkley); two *s*. *Educ:* Whitland Grammar Sch.; St David's Coll., Lampeter, Univ. of Wales (BA Hons); Philips Hist. Schol.; Organ Exhibnr. Wells Theol Coll. ALCM 1952. Ordained: deacon, 1959; priest, 1960; Curate, St Mary's, Tenby, 1959–61; Asst Chaplain, Brentwood Sch., 1962–66; Chaplain and Head of Dept, Solihull Sch., 1966–68; Vicar, St Mary's, Moseley, 1968–81; Residentiary Canon, Birmingham Cathedral, 1981–92; Diocesan Dir of Ordinands, Birmingham, 1982–90; Advr to Bishop of Manchester on Hosp. Chaplaincies, 1992–2001, Warden of Readers, 1994–2000, dio. of Manchester. Chm., House of Clergy, Birmingham Diocesan Synod, 1990–91; Proctor in Convocation, 1998–2001. Member: Nat. Stewardship Cttee, 2000–05; Hosp. Chaplaincies Council, 2000–05 (Vice-Chm., 2003–05). Reviewer: Community Health Improvement, 2001–04; Healthcare Commn, 2004–07. JP Birmingham, 1978–92. *Recreations:* sport, theatre, music, reading. *Address:* Heolcerrig, 28 Penshurst Road, Bromsgrove, Worcestershire B60 2SN.

DAVIES, Rt Rev. Mark; *see* Middleton, Bishop Suffragan of.

DAVIES, Mark Edward Trehearne; Chairman, FF&P Asset Management Ltd, since 2003; Director: Fleming Family & Partners Ltd, since 2003; FF&P Capital Management Ltd, since 2004; *b* 20 May 1948; *s* of Denis Norman Davies and Patricia Helen (*née* Trehearne); *m* 1987, Antonia Catharine Chittenden; two *s* two *d*. *Educ:* Stowe. Chief Exec., Gerrard Gp plc, 1995–2001 (Dir, 1986–2001); Chairman: Townhouse Hotel Investments Ltd, 1994–2006; Thornhill Nominees (formerly Thornhill Hldgs) Ltd, 2001–; Director: Thornhill Investment Mgt Ltd, 2001–; Thornhill Hldgs (formerly Thornhill Acquisitions) Ltd, 2001–; Thornhill Unit Trust Managers Ltd, 2001–; Ascot Authority (Hldgs) Ltd, 2002–; Caledonia Investments plc, 2002–; FCM Seed LLP, 2006–. Director: Rank Foundn Ltd, 1991–; Admington Hall Farms Ltd, 1995–; Racing Welfare, 2001–; Racing Welfare (Enterprises) Ltd, 2006–. *Publication:* (jtly) Trading in Commodities, 1974. *Recreations:* hunting, racing. *Address:* 26 Chester Street, SW1X 7BL; Fleming Family & Partners Ltd, 15 Suffolk Street, SW1Y 4HG. *Club:* White's.

DAVIES, Hon. Sir Mervyn; *see* Davies, Hon. Sir D. H. M.

DAVIES, Mervyn; *see* Davies, E. M.

DAVIES, Sir Michael; *see* Davies, Sir J. M.

DAVIES, Michael Jeremy Pugh, CBE 2000; RIBA; FICPD; Founder Director, Rogers Stirk Harbour & Partners (formerly Richard Rogers Partnership), Architects, since 1977; *b* 23 Jan. 1942; *er s* of late Leonard Gwerfyl Davies and of Nancy Hannah Davies; *m* 1977, Elizabeth Renee Yvonne Escalmel; one *s* one *d*. *Educ:* Highgate Sch.; Architectural Assoc. (AA Dip.); UCLA (Charles Scott Fellow; MArch Urban Design). Dir, Airstructures Design, 1966–68; Partner, Chrysalis USA, 1969–72; Project architect, Piano and Rogers, 1972–77; Partner, Chrysalis Architects (London), 1978–83. Richard Rogers Partnership projects incl. Project Director: Millennium Dome, London, 1996–2000; Terminal 5, Heathrow Airport, 2000–. Has lectured at univs, confs and schools of architecture worldwide. FRGS; FICPD 1998; FRSA; FRAS. *Publications:* contrib. articles and papers to professional jls. *Recreations:* astronomy, sailing. *Address:* Rogers Stirk Harbour & Partners, Thames Wharf, Rainville Road, W6 9HA. *T:* (020) 7385 1235.

DAVIES, Prof. Nicholas Barry, DPhil; FRS 1994; Professor of Behavioural Ecology, University of Cambridge, since 1995, and Fellow of Pembroke College, Cambridge, since 1979; *b* 23 May 1952; *s* of Anthony Barry Davies and Joyce Margaret Davies; *m* 1979, Jan Parr; two *d*. *Educ:* Merchant Taylors' Sch., Crosby; Pembroke Coll., Cambridge (BA 1973, MA 1977); Edward Grey Inst., Oxford Univ. (DPhil 1976). Demonstrator, Dept of Zoology (Edward Grey Inst. of Field Ornithology), Oxford Univ., 1976–79, and Jun. Res. Fellow, Wolfson Coll., Oxford, 1977–79; Demonstrator and Lectr in Zoology, 1979–92, Reader in Behavioural Ecology, 1992–95, Univ. of Cambridge. Pres., Internat. Soc. for Behavioural Ecology, 2000–02. Scientific Medal, Zool Soc., 1987; Cambridge Foundn Teaching Prize, 1995; William Bate Hardy Prize, Cambridge Phil Soc., 1995; Medal, Assoc. Study Animal Behaviour, 1996; Frink Medal, Zool Soc. of London, 2001; Elliott Coues Award, Amer. Ornithologists' Union, 2005. *Publications:* (ed with J. R. Krebs) Behavioural Ecology, 1978, 4th edn 1997; (with J. R. Krebs) An Introduction to Behavioural Ecology, 1981, 3rd edn 1993; Dunnock Behaviour and Social Evolution, 1992; Cuckoos, Cowbirds and other Cheats, 2000; contribs to learned jls. *Recreations:* bird watching, cricket. *Address:* Department of Zoology, Downing Street, Cambridge CB2 3EJ. *T:* (01223) 336600.

DAVIES, Nicola Velfor; QC 1992; a Recorder, since 1998; a Deputy High Court Judge, since 2003; *b* 13 March 1953. *Educ:* Bridgend Girls' Grammar School; Birmingham Univ. (LLB). Called to the Bar, Gray's Inn, 1976, Bencher, 2001. *Address:* 3 Serjeants Inn, EC4Y 1BQ. *T:* (020) 7353 5537.

DAVIES, Col Nicolas; *see* Davies, Col F. N. J.

DAVIES, Sir Noel; *see* Davies, Sir C. N.

DAVIES, Rev. Noel Anthony, OBE 2003; PhD; Minister, Swansea and Clydach Ecumenical Pastorate, since 2000; Associate Lecturer, Cardiff University (formerly University of Wales, Cardiff), since 2000; *b* 26 Dec. 1942; *s* of late Rev. Ronald Anthony Davies and of Anne Davies; *m* 1968, Patricia Barter. *Educ:* UCNW, Bangor (BSc Chem and Biochem.); Mansfield College, Oxford (BA Theol.); PhD Wales 1998. Ordained 1968; Minister, Bryn Seion Welsh Congregational Church, Glanaman, 1968–77; General Secretary: Council of Churches for Wales and Commn of Covenanted Churches in Wales, 1977–90; Cytûn: Churches Together in Wales, 1990–98. Pres., Union of Welsh Independents (Congregational), 1998–99 (Chm. Council, 1990–93); Moderator Churches' Commn on Mission, CCBI, 1991–95. Pres., Welsh Nat. Centre for Ecumenical Studies, Trinity Coll., Carmarthen, 2001–. *Publications:* Wales: language nation, faith and witness, 1996; (ed jtly) Wales: a moral society?, 1996; Un er mwyn y byd (A History of Welsh Ecumenism), 1998; God in the Centre, 1999; Religion and Ethics 2003; articles in ecumenical jls and Welsh language items. *Recreations:* classical music and hi-fi, gardening, West Highland White terriers, oriental cookery. *Address:* 16 Maple Crescent, Uplands, Swansea SA2 0QD.

DAVIES, (Norah) Olwen, MA; Headmistress, St Swithun's School, Winchester 1973–86; *b* 21 March 1926; *d* of late Rev. and Mrs E. A. Davies. *Educ:* Tregaron County Sch.; Walthamstow Hall, Sevenoaks; Edinburgh Univ. (MA). DipEd Oxon. Staff of Girls Remand Home, Essex, 1948–50; Russell Hill Sch., Purley, 1950–53; Woodford House NZ, 1953–57 (Dep. Headmistress); Westonbirt Sch., 1957–65; Headmistress, St Mary's Hall, Brighton, 1965–73. Pres., Girls' Schools Association, 1981–82. *Address:* 28 Arle Gardens, Alresford, Hants SO24 9BA.

DAVIES, Norman; *see* Davies, I. N. R.

DAVIES, Col Norman Thomas, OBE 1996 (MBE (mil.) 1970); Registrar, General Dental Council, 1981–96; *b* 2 May 1933; *s* of late Edward Ernest Davies and Elsie Davies (*née* Scott); *m* 1961, Penelope Mary, *e d* of late Peter Graeme Agnew, MBE and (Mary

Diana Agnew; one *s* one *d*. *Educ:* Holywell; RMA, Sandhurst; Open Univ. (BA 1979). Commnd RA, 1954; Regtl and Staff Appts, Malaya, Germany and UK, 1954–64; ptsc 1966; psc 1967; Mil. Asst to C of S Northern Army Gp, 1968–69; Commanded C Bty RHA and 2IC 3RHA, 1970–72; GSOI (DS), Staff Coll., Camberley, and Canadian Land Forces Comd and Staff Coll., 1972–74; Commanded 4 Field Regt, RA, 1975–77; Mil. Dir of Studies, RMCS, Shrivenham, 1977–80. Mem., EEC Adv. Cttee on the Training of Dental Practitioners, 1983–96. Vice Pres., British Dental Hygienists Assoc., 1996–99. Hon. Mem., BDA, 1990; Hon. FDSRCS 1997. JP Hants, 1984–2003. *Recreations:* Rugby football (Treas., RARFC, 1984–2000), the renaissance of Welsh Rugby football, fly fishing, gardening, wine, keeping four grandchildren happy. *Address:* 6 Weatherby Gardens, Hartley Wintney, Hook, Hants RG27 8PA. *T:* (01252) 843303.

DAVIES, Olwen; *see* Davies, N. O.

DAVIES, Owen Handel; QC 1999; a Recorder, since 2000; *b* 22 Sept. 1949; *s* of Trevor Davies and Mary Davies (*née* Jacobs); *m* 1971, Dr Caroline Jane Smith; one *s* one *d*. *Educ:* Hazelwick Sch.; Magdalene Coll., Cambridge (MA). Called to the Bar, Inner Temple, 1973, Bencher, 2001; in practice at the Bar, 1974–; Jt Head of Chambers, 1980–. Chm., Admin. Law Bar Assoc., 2002–05; Mem., Bar Council, 1998–2002. *Publications:* numerous contribs on humanitarian laws of conflict, extradition, information technol. and legal practice. *Recreations:* silversmithing, stained glass windows, narrowboating. *Address:* Garden Court Chambers, 57–60 Lincoln's Inn Fields, WC2A 3LS. *T:* (020) 7993 7721; *e-mail:* owend@gclaw.co.uk. *Club:* India.

DAVIES, Patrick Taylor, CMG 1978; OBE 1967; HM Overseas Civil Service, retired; *b* 10 Aug. 1927; *s* of Andrew Taylor Davies and Olive Kathleen Mary Davies; *m* 1959, Marjorie Eileen (*née* Wilkinson); two *d*. *Educ:* Shrewsbury Sch.; St John's Coll., Cambridge (MA); Trinity Coll., Oxford. Lieut, RA, Nigeria, 1945–48. Colonial Admin. Service, Nigeria, 1952; Permanent Sec., Kano State, 1970; Chief Inspector, Area Courts, Kano State, 1972–79. *Address:* 1 Millfield Drive, Market Drayton, Shropshire TF9 1HS. *T:* (01630) 653408.

DAVIES, Paul; General Manager, St John's, Smith Square, since 1985; *b* 28 Dec. 1955; *s* of Thomas Rees Davies and Eirlys Davies. *Educ:* Gowerton Boys' Grammar Sch.; University Coll. London (BA Hons English). Asst, Camden Fest. and Shaw Theatre, 1978–79; Wigmore Hall: Concert Asst, 1979–84; Dep. Manager, 1984–85. *Recreations:* music, opera, theatre, reading. *Address:* St John's, Smith Square, SW1P 3HA.

DAVIES, Dr Paul Charles, CB 2006; JP; CEng, FRSC; Chief Scientist, and Director, Corporate Science and Analytical Services Directorate, Health and Safety Executive, 1999–2006; *b* 25 April 1948; *s* of Philip Davies and Edith Mary Davies (*née* Johnson); *m* 1970, Sheila Tatham; one *s* one *d*. *Educ:* James Watt Tech. High Sch., Smethwick; Leicester Poly. (BSc 1st Cl. Hons Applied Chem.); Univ. of Leicester (PhD 1974). FRSC 1990; CEng 1996. With Unilever, 1968–69; Health and Safety Executive, 1975–2006: Factory Inspector, 1975–83; Major Hazards Assessment Unit, 1983–86; Hazardous Installations Policy Unit, 1986–89; Area Dir, London, 1989–93; Hd, Occupational Health Br., 1993–96; Mem. Bd, and Hd, Chemical and Hazardous Installations Div., 1996–99; Dir, Hazardous Installations Directorate, 1999–2002. Mem., Internat. Adv. Cttee on Health & Safety, Govt of Singapore, 2006–. Dir, Crosby Housing Assoc., 2005–. JP Ormskirk, 2004. *Publications:* contrib. papers on risk management. *Recreations:* walking, music, gardening, Aston Villa FC. *Address:* 18 Barrow Nook Lane, Bickerstaffe, Lancs L39 0ET.

DAVIES, Prof. Paul Charles William, AM 2007; PhD; College Professor and Director, Beyond: Center for Fundamental Concepts in Science, Arizona State University, since 2006; *b* London, 22 April 1946; *s* of Hugh Augustus Robert Davies and Pearl Vera Davies; *m* 2003, Pauline. *Educ:* University Coll. London (BSc 1st Cl. 1967; PhD 1970). Res. Fellow, Inst. of Theoretical Astronomy, Univ. of Cambridge, 1970–72; Lectr in Maths, KCL, 1972–80; Prof. of Theoretical Physics, Univ. of Newcastle upon Tyne, 1980–90; Prof. of Mathematical Physics, 1990–93, Prof. of Natural Philos., 1993–97, Univ. of Adelaide; Prof. of Natural Philos., Macquarie Univ., Sydney, 2001–06. Vis. Prof., Imperial Coll., London, 1998–2003; Adjunct Prof., Univ. of Queensland, 1998–. Hon. DSc Macquarie, 2006. *Publications:* The Physics of Time Asymmetry, 1974; Space and Time in the Modern Universe, 1977; The Runaway Universe, 1978; The Forces of Nature, 1979, 2nd edn 1986; Other Worlds, 1980; The Search for Gravity Waves, 1980; The Edge of Infinity, 1981; The Accidental Universe, 1982; (with N. D. Birrell) Quantum Fields in Curved Space, 1982; God and the New Physics, 1983; Superforce, 1983; Quantum Mechanics, 1984, 2nd edn (with D. Betts) 1994; (with J. R. Brown) The Ghost in the Atom, 1986; Fireball, 1987; The Cosmic Blueprint, 1987, rev. edn 2004; (with J. R. Brown) Superstrings: a theory of everything?, 1988; (ed) The New Physics, 1989; (with J. Gribbin) The Matter Myth, 1991; The Mind of God, 1992; The Last Three Minutes, 1994; About Time: Einstein's unfinished revolution, 1995; Are We Alone?: the philosophical basis of the search for extraterrestrial life, 1995; (with Phillip Adams) The Big Questions, 1996; One Universe or Many Universes?, 1998; (with Phillip Adams) More Big Questions, 1998; The Fifth Miracle: the search for the origin of life, 1998, rev. edn as The Origin of Life, 2003; How to Build a Time Machine, 2001; (ed jtly) Science and Ultimate Reality, 2004; The Goldilocks Enigma: why is the universe just right for life?, 2006 (US title, Cosmic Jackpot, 2007); (ed with Philip Clayton) The Re-Emergence of Emergence, 2006; (ed jtly) Instruments, Methods and Missions for Astrobiology, 2007. *Recreation:* keeping fit. *Address:* PO Box 3215, Tempe, Arizona 85280–3215, USA. *T:* (480) 3021066; *e-mail:* deepthought@asu.edu. *Club:* Victory Services.

DAVIES, Prof. Paul Lyndon, FBA 2000; Cassel Professor of Commercial Law, London School of Economics and Political Science, since 1998; *b* 24 Sept. 1944; *s* of John Clifford Davies and Kathleen Gertrude Davies (*née* Webber); *m* 1973, Saphié Ashtiany; two *d*. *Educ:* Cardiff High Sch.; Balliol Coll., Oxford (BA, MA); London Sch. of Econs and Pol Sci. (LLM); Yale Univ. (LLM). Lectr, Univ. of Warwick, 1969–73; University of Oxford: CUF Lectr, 1973–91; Reader in Law of Enterprise, 1991–96, Prof., 1996–98; Chm. Bd, Faculty of Law, 1992–95; Balliol College: Fellow and Tutor in Law, 1973–98, Emeritus Fellow, 1998; Estates Bursar, 1983–86. Mem., Steering Gp, Co. Law Rev., 1999–2001. Dep. Chm., Central Arbitration Cttee, 2001–. Vice-Pres., Industrial Law Soc., 2001. Hon. QC 2006; Hon. Bencher, Gray's Inn, 2007. *Publications:* (with K. W. Wedderburn) Employment Grievances and Disputes Procedures in Britain, 1969; Takeovers and Mergers, 1976; (with M. R. Freedland) Labour Law: text and materials, 1979, 2nd edn 1984; (with M. R. Freedland) Labour Legislation and Public Policy, 1993; (ed) Gower's Principles of Modern Company Law, 6th edn 1997, 7th edn 2003; Introduction to Company Law, 2002; (ed) Palmer's Company Law, 23rd edn 1982 to 25th edn 1992; (jtly) Anatomy of Corporate Law, 2004; (with M. R. Freedland) Towards a Flexible Labour Market, 2007. *Recreation:* walking.

DAVIES, Paul Windsor; Member (C) Preseli Pembrokeshire, National Assembly for Wales, since 2007; *b* 2 Jan. 1969; *s* of Timothy Iorwerth Davies and Mair Elizabeth Davies; *m* 2006, Julie Wheeler. *Educ:* Tregroes Primary Sch.; Llandysul Grammar Sch.; Newcastle Emlyn Comp. Sch. Lloyds Bank, subseq. Lloyds TSB, 1987–2007, Business Manager, Haverfordwest, 1994–2007. *Recreations:* reading, visiting historical attractions, Rugby. *Address:* National Assembly for Wales, Cardiff Bay, Cardiff CF99 1NA. *T:* (029) 2089 8725; *e-mail:* Paul.Davies2@wales.gov.uk.

DAVIES, Pauline Elizabeth, MEd; Headmistress, Wycombe Abbey School, 1998–2008; *b* 8 April 1950; *d* of Gordon White and Petrula White (*née* Theohari); *m* 1970, Alan Henry Davies; two *s*. *Educ:* Univ. of Manchester (BSc Jt Hons 1971; PGCE 1972; MEd 1978). Teacher of Biology, 1972–77, Head of Dept, 1974–77, Urmston Girls' Grammar Sch.; various posts, incl. Dep. Head and Head of Middle Sch., King Edward VI Grammar Sch. for Boys, Chelmsford, 1979–90; Headmistress, Croydon High Sch., 1990–98. Pres., GSA, 2003. *Recreations:* reading, theatre, music, travel. *Club:* Lansdowne.

DAVIES, (Percy) Douglas, CB 1981; *b* 17 Sept. 1921; *m* 1947, Renée Margaret Billings (*d* 2001); one *s* one *d*. *Educ:* Liverpool Collegiate School; Open Univ. (BA 1989). Clerical Officer, Ministry of Transport, 1938; served Royal Armoured Corps, 1941–46; Chief Executive Officer, Min. of Transport, 1963; Asst Secretary, 1966; Principal Establishment Officer, Under Secretary, Property Services Agency, Dept of the Environment, 1972–81. Chm., Council of Management, London Hostels Assoc., 1983–2000. *Recreations:* gardening, making things work. *Address:* 3 Court Avenue, Old Coulsdon, Surrey CR5 1HG. *T:* (01737) 553391.

DAVIES, Peter Douglas Royston, CMG 1994; HM Diplomatic Service, retired; international business consultant, Lewis Companies Inc., and MEC International; *b* 29 Nov. 1936; *e s* of Douglas and Edna Davies; *m* 1967, Elizabeth Mary Lovett Williams; one *s* two *d*. *Educ:* Brockenhurst County High Sch.; LSE (BSc(Econ)). Joined HM Diplomatic Service, 1964; FO, 1964–66; Second Sec., Nicosia, 1966–67; FO, 1967–68; First Sec., Budapest, 1968–71; FCO, 1971–74; Consul (Commercial), Rio de Janeiro, 1974–78; Counsellor (Commercial): The Hague, 1978–82; Kuala Lumpur, 1982–83; Dep. High Comr, Kuala Lumpur, 1983–85; RCDS 1986; Head of Arms Control and Disarmament Dept, FCO, 1987–91; Consul-Gen., Toronto, and Dir-Gen. of Trade and Investment in Canada, 1991–96. Pres., Peter Davies Associates, 1997–2000. *Recreations:* golf, ski-ing, biography, travel. *Address:* South Wing, The Manor, Moreton Pinkney, Northants NN11 3SJ.

DAVIES, Sir Peter Maxwell; *see* Maxwell Davies.

DAVIES, Rear-Adm. Peter Roland, CB 2005; CBE 1996 (MBE 1984); Principal and Chief Executive, City Literary Institute, since 2004; *b* 2 April 1950; *s* of Roland and Winifred Davies; *m* 1974, Dianne Whittaker; one *s* one *d*. *Educ:* Thornleigh Grammar Sch., Bolton; King's Coll. London (BSc Elec. Engrg 1971); RMCS Schrivenham (MSc Guided Weapons Systems 1977). Naval service, 1973–89: Weapon Engineer Officer: HMS Opportune, 1973–75; HMS Narwhal, 1975–77; Submarine Harpoon Project, 1978–80; Weapon Engineer Officer: 3rd Submarine Sqn, 1980–82; HMS Courageous, 1982–84; 2nd Submarine Sqn, 1984–87; Submarine Senser's Commns Office Flag Officer Submarine Staff, 1987–89; Ministry of Defence: Future Projects, 1991–92; Res. Requirements, 1992–93; Project Manager: Sonar, 1993–95, Tomahawk, 1995–97, Procurement Exec.; Asst Dir, (Command, Control, Computers, Commns, Intel) Directorate of Communication & Inf. Systems (Navy), 1997–98; CO, HMS Collingwood, 1998–2001; FO Trng and Recruiting and Chief Exec., Naval Recruiting and Trng Agency, 2001–04. *Recreations:* music, sailing, swimming. *Address:* City Literary Institute, Keeley Street, Covent Garden, WC2B 4BA. *Clubs:* Royal Naval Sailing Assoc.; Royal Naval Swimming Assoc.

DAVIES, Maj.-Gen. Peter Ronald, CB 1992; Director General, World Society for the Protection of Animals (WSPA), since 2002; *b* 10 May 1938; *e s* of Lt-Col Charles Henry Davies and Joy Davies (*née* Moore); *m* 1960, (Rosemary) Julia, *er d* of late David Felice of Douglas, IoM; one *s* one *d*. *Educ:* Llandovery College; Welbeck College; RMA Sandhurst; student: RMCS 1969; Staff Coll., 1970; RCDS, 1985. Commissioned Royal Corps of Signals, 1958; service in BAOR, Berlin, Borneo, Cyprus and UK, 1958–68; OC Artillery Bde Sig. Sqn, 1971–72; Bde Maj., 20 Armd Bde, 1973–75; Directing Staff, Staff Coll., Camberley, 1975–76; CO 1 Armd Div. Signal Regt, 1976–79; Col GS SD, HQ UKLF, 1979–82; Brigade Comdr, 12 Armd Brigade, 1982–84; Dep. Comdt and Dir of Studies, Staff College, Camberley, 1985–86; Comdr Communications, BAOR, 1987–90; GOC Wales, 1990–91. Dir-Gen., RSPCA, 1991–2002. Mem., Internat. Strategic Planning and Adv. Bd, Andrew Corp., USA, 1991–92. Director: WSPA Internat., 1992–2002 (Vice Pres., 1998–2000; Pres., 2000–02); Eurogroup for Animal Welfare, 1992–2002; Chairman: Freedom Food Ltd, 1994–2002; Animals in War Meml Fund, 1996–; Trustee: Flora for Fauna Soc., 2000–; Wildlife Inf. Network, 2002–04. Colonel, King's Regt, 1986–94; Chm., Regtl Council and King's and Manchester Regts' Assoc., 1986–94; Col Comdt, RCS, 1990–96; Life Pres., Jullunder Bde Assoc., 1990. Member, Executive Committee: Lord Roberts Workshops and Forces Help Soc., 1994–96; Addaction (Drug and Alcohol Abuse), 1997–2000. Gov., Welbeck Coll., 1980–81; Trustee, Llandovery Coll., 1992–2003. CCMI (CIMgt 1994); FIPD 1991; FRSA 2002. Queen Victoria Silver Medal, RSPCA, 2003; Angell Humanitarian Award, Mass Soc. for Prevention Cruelty to Animals, USA, 2003; Assisi Medal, NZ Companion Animals, 2007. *Recreations:* music, wine, Welsh nostalgia. *Address:* World Society for the Protection of Animals, 89 Albert Embankment, SE1 7TP. *T:* (020) 7587 5000, *Fax:* (020) 7793 0208; *e-mail:* peterdavies@wspa-international.org. *Clubs:* Buck's, Army and Navy, Kennel; Fadeaways.
See also T. D. H. Davies.

DAVIES, Peter Wilton; DL; Member, Executive Board, South West Strategic Health Authority (NHS South West), since 2006; *b* 7 March 1945; *s* of late John Finden Davies and Mary (*née* Harrison); *m* 1971, Ann Mary Dawn Jones; two *d*. *Educ:* Blundell's Sch.; Southampton Inst. FCIPD (FIPD 1979). Grad. trainee, Devon CC, 1964–67; Personnel Officer, Berkshire CC, 1967–69; Sen. Personnel Officer, Camden LBC, 1969–70; Industrial Relns Officer, Hampshire CC, 1970–74; Dep. County Personnel Officer, 1974–81, Dir of Personnel, 1981–99, Chief Exec., 1999–2002, Cornwall CC. Chairman: Central Cornwall PCT, 2002–06; Royal Cornwall Hosps NHS Trust, 2007–08. Mem., Lord Chancellor's Adv. Cttee for Cornwall on JPs, 1998–. Chm., Common Purpose Cornwall, 2001–06; Mem. Devon and Cornwall Regl Cttee, NT, 2002–. FCMI (FIMgt 1988); FRSA 1994. DL Cornwall, 2002. *Recreations:* bee-keeping, walking, shooting, the arts. *Address:* Trehane Mill, Tresillian, Truro, Cornwall TR2 4AS. *T:* (01872) 520427.

DAVIES, Philip Andrew; MP (C) Shipley, since 2005; *b* 5 Jan. 1972; *s* of Peter Davies and Marilyn (*née* Johnson, now Lifsey); *m* 1994, Debbie Hemsley; two *s*. *Educ:* Univ. of Huddersfield (BA Hons Histl and Pol Studies). Asda: various positions, 1993–2000; Customer Service Project Manager, 2000–04; Mktg Manager, 2004–05. Contested (C) Colne Valley, 2001. Member: Culture, Media and Sport Select Cttee, 2006–; Modernisation Select Cttee, 2007–. Mem. Exec. Cttee, 1922 Cttee, 2006–. *Recreation:* horse racing. *Address:* House of Commons, SW1A 0AA; *e-mail:* daviesp@parliament.uk.

DAVIES, Philip John, CB 2001; Parliamentary Counsel, since 1994; *b* 19 Sept. 1954; *s* of late Glynn Davies and of Mary (*née* Adams); *m* 1981, Jacqueline Sara Boutcher; one *d*. *Educ:* St Julian's High Sch., Newport, S Wales; Hertford Coll., Oxford (MA, BCL). Called to the Bar, Middle Temple, 1981; Lectr in Law, Univ. of Manchester, 1977–82; Asst and Sen. Asst Parly Counsel, 1982–90; Dep. Parly Counsel, 1990–94 (seconded to Law Commn, 1992–94). *Publications:* articles and notes in Law Qly Rev., Modern Law Rev. and other legal jls. *Recreations:* family, Welsh terriers, the garden. *Address:* Pinecroft, The Downs, Givons Grove, Leatherhead, Surrey KT22 8JY. *T:* (01372) 373915; Office of the Parliamentary Counsel, 36 Whitehall, SW1A 2AY. *T:* (020) 7210 6630, *Fax:* (020) 7210 6638; *e-mail:* philip.j.davies@cabinet-office.x.gsi.gov.uk.

DAVIES, Maj.-Gen. Philip Middleton, OBE 1975; *b* 27 Oct. 1932; *s* of late Hugh Davies and Miriam Allen (*née* Tickler); *m* 1956, Mona Wallace; two *d*. *Educ:* Charterhouse; RMA, Sandhurst. Commnd Royal Scots, 1953; served Korea, Canal Zone, Cyprus, Suez, Berlin, Libya 1st Bn Royal Scots, 1953–63; Staff Coll., 1963; National Defence Coll., 1971; commanded 1st Bn Royal Scots, Norway, Cyprus, N Ireland (despatches), 1973–76; DS, Staff Coll., 1976–77; comd 19 Bde/7 Fd Force, 1977–79; RCDS, 1980; Comd Land Forces, Cyprus, 1981–83; GOC NW Dist, 1983–86; retired. *Recreations:* fishing, gardening.

DAVIES, Quentin; *see* Davies, J. Q.

DAVIES, Rhodri; *see* Davies, W. R.

DAVIES, Rhys; *see* Davies, E. R.

DAVIES, His Honour Sir Rhys (Everson), Kt 2000; QC 1981; a Senior Circuit Judge, 1990–2003; retired; *b* 13 Jan. 1941; *s* of late Evan Davies and Nancy Caroline Davies; *m* 1963, Katharine Anne Yeates; one *s* one *d*. *Educ:* Cowbridge Grammar School; Neath Grammar School; Victoria University of Manchester. LLB (Hons). Called to the Bar, Gray's Inn, 1964, Bencher, 1993. Northern Circuit, 1964–90; a Recorder, 1980–90; Hon. Recorder of Manchester, 1990–2003. Mem., Sentencing Adv. Panel, 2000–05. Pres., Manchester and District Medico-Legal Soc., 2002–04 (Patron, 2004–). Ind. Monitor, Criminal Records Bureau, 2004–. Mem. Court and Council, Victoria Univ. of Manchester, 1993–2004 (Dep. Chm. Council, 2000–04); Visitor, Univ. of Manchester, 2004–. *Recreations:* music, conversation.

DAVIES, Prof. Richard Bees, PhD; Vice-Chancellor, Swansea University (formerly University of Wales, Swansea), since 2003; *m*; three *c*. *Educ:* Milford Haven Grammar Sch.; Sidney Sussex Coll., Cambridge (BA 1968); Univ. of Birmingham (MSc); Univ. of Bristol (PhD). Lectr, then Sen. Lectr, Dept of Town Planning, UWIST, subseq. UWCC; Univ. of Lancaster, 1989–2003: Prof. and Dir, Centre for Applied Statistics; Dean, Faculty of Engrg, Computing and Math. Scis; Pro-Vice-Chancellor. *Address:* Swansea University, Singleton Park, Swansea SA2 8PP.

DAVIES, Richard John; Management Board Director and Head, Department for Public Services and Performance, Welsh Assembly Government, since 2006; *b* 12 Aug. 1949; *s* of Sydney John Davies and Valerie Reynolds Davies; *m* 1971, Margaret Mary Goddard; one *s* one *d*. *Educ:* King's Coll., Taunton; Univ. of Liverpool (BA Hons 1971; MA 1976). Teaching Asst, Dept of Political Theory and Instns, Liverpool Univ., 1972–73; entered Civil Service, 1973; MoD, FCO, MPO, etc, 1973–84; Welsh Office: Asst Sec., 1985; Head of Division: Health Mgt, Systems and Personnel, 1985–87; Health and Social Services Policy, 1987–89; Housing, 1989–94; School Performance, 1994–97; Gp Dir, Educn Dept, Welsh Office, subseq. Dept for Trng and Educn, Nat. Assembly for Wales, 1997–2006. Vis. Prof., Univ. of Glamorgan, 2006–. Nuffield-Leverhulme Fellow, 1990. *Recreations:* family, walking, swimming, music. *Address:* Public Services and Performance Department, Welsh Assembly Government, Cathays Park, Cardiff CF1 3NQ. *T:* (029) 2082 3207.

DAVIES, Richard Llewellyn; QC 1994; *b* 7 April 1948; *s* of Richard Henry Davies and Margaret Davies; *m* 1979, Elizabeth Ann Johnston; one *s* one *d*. *Educ:* St Julian's High Sch., Newport, Gwent; Univ. of Liverpool (LLB Hons). Called to the Bar, Inner Temple, 1973, Bencher, 2002. *Recreations:* music, wine, reading, cycling. *Address:* 39 Essex Street, WC2R 3AT.

DAVIES, (Robert Harold) Glyn; HM Diplomatic Service, retired; Ambassador to Panama, 1999–2002; *b* 23 March 1942; *s* of late Robert Leach Davies and Edith Greenwood Davies (*née* Burgoyne); *m* 1968, Maria Del Carmen Diaz; one *s*. *Educ:* Hulme Grammar Sch., Oldham; St John's Coll., Cambridge. Joined FO, 1963; Havana, 1964; FO, 1964; Third, later Second Sec., Mexico, 1968; FCO, 1972; Consul (Commercial), Zagreb, 1980; First Sec., on loan to Cabinet Office, 1983; First Sec., Consul and Head of Chancery, Luanda, 1986; FCO, 1989; High Commissioner to Namibia, 1996–98. *Address:* c/o Foreign and Commonwealth Office, SW1A 2AH.

DAVIES, Dr Robert James; Lecturer in Computing, North West Kent College, since 2003; Managing Director, Masters-in-Science (formerly Partner, Masters-in-Science.com), since 2004; *b* 24 Feb. 1943; *s* of late Rev. Canon Dilwyn Morgan Davies and Kate Davies (*née* Maltby); *m* 1st, 1969 (marr. diss. 1980); two *s*; 2nd, 1981, Karen, *d* of Dennis Henley. *Educ:* St Catharine's Coll., Cambridge (BA 1964); St Thomas's Hosp. Med. Sch. (BChir 1967; MB BS, MA 1968); Univ. of Cambridge (MD 1977); Univ. of Greenwich (MSc Computing and Info. Systems (Distinction) 2003; PGCE 2003). FRCP 1982. Res. Fellow, Brompton Hosp., 1971–73; Lectr in Medicine, St Thomas's Hosp., 1973–76; MRC Res. Fellow, Univ. of Tulane, New Orleans, 1976–77; St Bartholomew's Hospital: Consultant Physician, 1977–82; Dir, Asthma & Allergy Res. Dept, 1981–99; Reader in Respiratory Medicine, 1982–90; Dir, General and Emergency Medicine, 1994–96; Prof. of Respiratory Medicine, St Bartholomew's and Royal London Sch. of Medicine and Dentistry, QMW, London Univ., 1991–99; Cons. Physician, 1994–99, Dir of R&D, 1995–97, Royal Hosps NHS Trust. British Allergy Foundn: Founder and Chm., 1991–97; Pres., 1997–2002; Dir of Tech. and Educn, Allergy UK, 2000–02; Scientific Dir, Allergy Res. Ltd, 2000–02. Ed., Respiratory Medicine, 1988–95. Pres., Brit. Soc. for Allergy and Clin. Immunology, 1987–90; 2nd Vice Pres., Internat. Assoc. of Allergology and Clin. Immunology, 1997–99 (Treas., 1985–94); Chm., World Allergy Forum, 1996–99; Mem., Collegium Internationale Allergologicum, 1998–2000. Hon. Mem., Argentinian Assoc. of Allergy and Immunology, 1997. Fellow, Amer. Acad. Allergy, Asthma and Immunology, 1984. Medal, Faculty of Medicine, Univ. of Montpellier, 1981. *Publications:* Allergy The Facts, 1989; (ed) Formoterol: clinical profile of a new long acting inhaled B2-Agonist, 1990; Hay Fever and Other Allergies, 1995; contrib. Allergy. *Recreations:* hill-walking, mountain and moorland ponies. *Address:* 96 Vanbrugh Park, Blackheath, SE3 7AL.

DAVIES, Robert John; Chairman, Biffa plc, since 2006; Chief Executive, Arriva plc, 1999–2006; *b* 12 Oct. 1948; *s* of William Davies and Janet Davies (*née* Robinson); *m* 1971, Eileen Susan Littlefield; one *s*. *Educ:* Univ. of Edinburgh (LLB Law and Econs). FCMA 1976. With Ford Motor Co., in UK, USA and latterly as Finance Dir, Ford Spain, 1970–85; Coopers & Lybrand, 1985–87; Finance Director: Waterford Wedgwood plc, 1987–91; Ferranti Internat. plc, 1991–93; Finance Dir, 1994–97, Chief Exec., 1997–98, E Midlands Electricity plc. Non-executive Director: T & S Stores plc, 1998–2003; Geest plc, 1998–2004; Barratt Developments plc, 2004–; British Energy, 2006–. Chm., NE Regl Council, CBI, 2007–. Chm. Bd Govs, Sunderland Univ., 2003–. *Recreations:* golf, vintage cars.

DAVIES, (Robert) Karl; Head, Governance and Accountability Wales, BBC Trust, since 2007; *b* 26 July 1963; *s* of R. Keith Davies and Dilys Catherine Davies (*née* Hughes). *Educ:* Ysgol Glan Clywd, St Asaph; University Coll. of Wales, Aberystwyth (BA). Editor, Tafod Y Ddraig, 1983–84; Chm., Welsh Lang. Soc., 1984–85; Res. Dir, Plaid Cymru, 1985–89; BBC Wales: Producer, Radio, 1989–90; Parly Editor, 1990–93; Chief Exec., Plaid Cymru, 1993–2002; Dir for Wales, NAHT, 2002–03; Sec., BBC Wales, 2003–06. Mem. Council, UCW, Aberystwyth, 1988–91. Fellow, British American Proj., 1996–. *Publication:* Beth am Gynnau Tân?, 1985. *Recreations:* travel, cinema, gossip, Italy. *Address:* Room E5108, BBC Broadcasting House, Llandaff, Cardiff CF5 2YQ. *T:* (029) 2032 2004, *Fax:* (029) 2032 2280; *e-mail:* karl.davies-cf@bbc.co.uk.

DAVIES, (Robert) Leighton; QC 1994; a Recorder, since 1994; *b* 7 Sept. 1949; *s* of Robert Brinley Davies and Elizabeth Nesta Davies (*née* Jones); *m* 1979, Linda Fox; two *s* one *d*. *Educ:* Rhondda Co. Grammar Sch., Porth, Rhondda; Corpus Christi Coll., Oxford (MA, BCL; boxing blue, 1971–72); Inns of Court Sch. of Law. Called to the Bar, Gray's Inn, 1975, Bencher, 2002; practising on Wales and Chester Circuit, 1975–; Asst Recorder, 1990–94. *Recreations:* fly-fishing, gardening, military history. *Address:* Farrar's Building, Temple, EC4Y 7BD. *T:* (020) 7583 9241; Bryn Corun, Glyncoli Road, Treorchy, Rhondda CF42 6SB. *T:* (01443) 774559. *Club:* Vincent's (Oxford).

DAVIES, (Robert) Russell; freelance writer and broadcaster, since 1970; *b* 5 April 1946; *s* of late John Gwilym Davies and of Gladys Davies (*née* Davies); *m* 1972, Judith Anne Slater (separated); one *s*. *Educ:* Manchester Grammar Sch.; St John's Coll., Cambridge (Scholar; BA Mod. Langs). Comedy actor and TV presenter, 1970–71; literary reviewer and caricaturist, 1972–; football reporter, 1973–76, film critic, 1973–78, Observer; TV critic, Sunday Times, 1979–83; Dep. Editor and acting Editor, Punch, 1988; sports columnist, Sunday Telegraph, 1989–94. Presenter and feature-maker, 1979–: radio includes: When Housewives had the Choice; Turns of the Century; Word of Mouth (Premio Ondas, 1997); Jazz Century; television includes: What the Papers Say (also Annual Awards, 1989–97); jazz weeks and weekends; Saturday Review. *Publications:* Vicky (with Liz Ottaway), 1987; Ronald Searle, 1990; (ed) The Kenneth Williams Diaries, 1993; (ed) The Kenneth Williams Letters, 1994. *Recreations:* playing trombone, tuba and piano, comic art, cartooning, American cookery, following baseball. *Address:* c/o United Agents, 12–26 Lexington Street, W1F 0LE.

DAVIES, Prof. Rodney Deane, CBE 1995; DSc, PhD; FRS 1992; CPhys, FInstP; FRAS; Professor of Radio Astronomy, University of Manchester, 1976–97, now Professor Emeritus; Director, Nuffield Radio Astronomy Laboratories, Jodrell Bank, 1988–97; *b* 8 Jan. 1930; *s* of Holbin James Davies and Rena Irene (*née* March), Mallala, S Australia; *m* 1953, Valda Beth Treasure; one *s* two *d* (and one *s* decd). *Educ:* Adelaide High Sch.; Univ. of Adelaide (BSc Hons, MSc); Univ. of Manchester (PhD, DSc). Research Officer, Radiophysics Div., CSIRO, Sydney, 1951–53; Univ. of Manchester: Asst Lectr, 1953–56; Lectr, 1956–67; Reader, 1967–76. Visiting Astronomer, Radiophysics Div., CSIRO, Australia, 1963. Member: Internat. Astronomical Union, 1958; Org. Cttee and Working Gps of various Commns; Bd and various panels and cttees of Astronomy Space and Radio Bd and Science Bd of Science Research Council; British Nat. Cttee for Astronomy, 1974–77. Royal Astronomical Society: Mem. Council, 1972–75 and 1978–89; Sec., 1978–86; Vice-Pres., 1973–75 and 1986–87; Pres., 1987–89. *Publications:* Radio Studies of the Universe (with H. P. Palmer), 1959; Radio Astronomy Today (with H. P. Palmer and M. I. Large), 1963; The Crab Nebula (co-ed with F. G. Smith), 1971; numerous contribs to Monthly Notices of RAS and internat. jls on the galactic and extragalactic magnetic fields, structure and dynamics of the Galaxy and nearby external galaxies, use of radio spectral lines, the early Universe and studies of the Cosmic Microwave Background. *Recreations:* gardening, fell-walking. *Address:* University of Manchester, Jodrell Bank Observatory, Macclesfield, Cheshire SK11 9DL. *T:* (01477) 571321.

DAVIES, Roger; *see* Davies, A. R.

DAVIES, Prof. Roger Llewelyn, PhD; FRAS; Philip Wetton Professor of Astrophysics, since 2002, Chairman of Physics, since 2005, Oxford University; Student, since 2002, Dr Lee's Reader in Physics, since 2006, Christ Church, Oxford; *b* 13 Jan. 1954; *s* of Albert Edward Davies and Gwendoline Mary Davies; *m* 1982, Ioana Christina Westwater; one *s* one *d*. *Educ:* John Leggott Grammar Sch., Scunthorpe; University Coll. London (BSc Physics 1975); Inst. of Astronomy and Churchill Coll., Cambridge (PhD 1979). FRAS 1979. Lindemann Fellow, Lick Observatory, Calif, 1979–80; Res. Fellow, Christ's Coll., Cambridge, 1979–82; Staff Mem., US Nat. Optical Astronomy Observatories, Tucson, Arizona, 1982–88; Scientist, UK Gemini Project, 1988–96; Lectr in Physics, Oxford Univ. and Fellow, St Peter's Coll., Oxford, 1992–94; Prof. of Astronomy, Dept of Physics, Univ. of Durham, 1994–2002; Hd, Sub-Dept of Astrophysics, Oxford Univ., 2004–05. PPARC Senior Res. Fellow, 2001–04 (Mem. Council, PPARC, 1999–2001, 2006–07). Vis. Prof., Beihang Univ., Beijing, 2006. Chairman: Anglo-Australian Telescope Bd, 1997–99 (Mem., 1996–99); Eur. Space Telescope Co-ordinating Facility Users Cttee, 2001–03; Gemini Telescopes Bd, 2002–03 (Mem., 2001–04; Chm., UK Gemini Telescopes Steering Cttee, 1996–99); Extremely Large Telescope Standing Review Cttee, ESO, 2006–. Mem., VISTA Telescope Bd, 1999–2001; Vice-Pres., Commn 28, Galaxies, IAU, 2006–08. Member: IAU, 1980; AAS, 1980; Council, RAS, 2005–08 (Vice-Pres., 2006–08). Dr *hc* Univ. Claude Bernard Lyon 1, 2006. Daiwa-Adrian Prize, Daiwa Anglo Japanese Foundn, 2001. *Publications:* contrib. papers to Astrophysical Jl, Monthly Notices of RAS, Astronomical Jl and conf. procs. *Recreations:* hiking, swimming, photography, films, listening to music. *Address:* Denys Wilkinson Building, Keble Road, Oxford OX1 3RH. *T:* (01865) 272253.

DAVIES, Roger Oliver; *b* 4 Jan. 1945; *s* of Griffith William Davies and Dorothy Anne Davies; *m* 1973, Adele Biss, *qv*; one *s*. *Educ:* Reading Sch.; Devonport High Sch.; London School of Economics (BScEcon). Marketing Dir, 1972, Man. Dir, 1977, Thomson Holidays; Man. Dir, 1982, Chm., 1984–90, Thomson Travel Gp; Chairman: Going Places, 1994–97; Sunway Travel, 1997–2000; Travel Chest.com, 2000; Dir, Airtours PLC, 1994–2000. Mem., Monopolies and Mergers Commn, 1989–98. Governor, LSE 1995–. Commandeur de la République (Tunisia), 1987. *Recreations:* walking, ski-ing reading. *Address:* 7 Elsworthy Road, NW3 3DS.

DAVIES, Rt Hon. Ronald; PC 1997; Member (Ind), Caerphilly County Borough Council, since 2008; *b* 6 Aug. 1946; *s* of late Ronald Davies; *m* 1981, Christina Elizabeth Rees (marr. diss. 2000); one *d*; *m* 2002, Lynne Hughes; one *d*. *Educ:* Bassaleg Grammar Sch.; Portsmouth Polytechnic; University Coll. of Wales, Cardiff. Schoolteacher 1968–70; WEA Tutor/Organiser, 1970–74; Further Educn Adviser, Mid-Glamorgan LEA, 1974–83. Councillor, Rhymney Valley DC (formerly Bedwas and Machen UDC)

1969–84 (Vice-Chm.). MP (Lab) Caerphilly, 1983–2001. Opposition Whip, 1985–87; Opposition spokesman on agriculture and rural affairs, 1987–92, front bench spokesman on Wales, 1992–97; Sec. of State for Wales, May 1997–Oct. 1998. National Assembly for Wales: Mem. (Lab) Caerphilly, 1999–2003; Mem., Econ. Develt Cttee, 1999–2003 (Chm., 1999). Dir, Valleys Race Equality Council, 2003–. Highest Order, Gorsedd of the Bards, 1998. *Publication:* paper on devolution. *Address:* Wernddu House, Wernddu, Caerphilly CF83 3DA.

DAVIES, Rt Rev. Ross Owen; *see* Murray, Bishop of The.

DAVIES, Rt Rev. Roy Thomas; Bishop of Llandaff, 1985–99; *b* 31 Jan. 1934; *s* of Hubert and Dilys Davies; unmarried. *Educ:* St David's Coll., Lampeter (BA); Jesus Coll., Oxford (BLitt); St Stephen's House, Oxford. Asst Curate, St Paul's, Llanelli, 1959–64; Vicar of Llanafan, 1964–67; Chaplain to Anglican Students, University Coll. of Wales, Aberystwyth, 1967–73; Sec., Provincial Council for Mission and Unity of Church in Wales, 1973–79; Vicar of St David's, Carmarthen, 1979–83; Vicar of Llanegwad, 1983–85; Archdeacon of Carmarthen, 1982–85; Clerical Sec., Governing Body of Church in Wales, 1983–85. ChStJ 1986–2000. *Recreations:* walking, reading. *Address:* 25 Awel Tywi, Llangunnor, Carmarthen SA31 2NL.

DAVIES, Russell; *see* Davies, Robert R.

DAVIES, Ryland; opera singer; tenor; *b* 9 Feb. 1943; *s* of Gethin and Joan Davies; *m* 1st, 1966, Anne Elizabeth Howells, *qv* (marr. diss. 1981); 2nd, 1983, Deborah Rees; one *d*. *Educ:* Royal Manchester College of Music (Fellow, 1971) (studied with Frederic R. Cox, OBE). Voice teacher, RNCM, 1987–94; teaches privately and gives masterclasses at home and abroad. Début as Almaviva in The Barber of Seville, WNO, 1964; Glyndebourne Fest. Chorus, 1964–66; has since sung with Royal Opera, Sadler's Wells Opera, WNO, Scottish Opera, at Glyndebourne, and in Brussels, Chicago, NY, San Francisco, Houston, Paris, Salzburg, Buenos Aires, Hong Kong, Berlin, Hamburg and Stuttgart; solo rôles include: Belmonte in Il Seraglio; Fenton, and Dr Caius, in Falstaff; Ferrando in Così Fan Tutte; Flamand in Capriccio; Tamino in The Magic Flute; Essex in Britten's Gloriana; Hylas in The Trojans; Don Ottavio in Don Giovanni; Cassio in Otello; Ernesto in Don Pasquale; Lysander in A Midsummer Night's Dream; title rôle in Werther; Prince in L'Amour des Trois Oranges; Nemorino in L'Elisir d'amore; Don Basilio in Le Nozze di Figaro; Rector in Peter Grimes; Triquet in Eugene Onegin; Alfredo in La Traviata, Pelléas in Pelléas et Melisande; Eneas in Esclarmonde; Jack in The Midsummer Marriage; Chaplin in Dialogues des Carmelites; Remendado in Carmen; Sellem in The Rake's Progress; Albazar in The Turk in Italy; Gaudenzio in Leoncavallo's La Bohème; Hauk Šendorf in The Makropulos Case; Francis Flute in A Midsummer Night's Dream. Many concerts at home with all major British orchestras, and abroad with such orchestras as: Boston Symphony, Cleveland Symphony, Chicago Symphony, Philadelphia, San Francisco, Los Angeles, Bavarian Radio and Vienna Symphony. Principal oratorio rôles include: Bach, B minor Mass; Beethoven: Mass in C; Berlioz, narrator in L'Enfance du Christ; Elgar, St John, in The Kingdom; Handel: Acis, in Acis and Galatea; title rôle, Judas Maccabaeus; Messiah; Jonathan, in Saul; Haydn: Nelson Mass; The Seasons; Mendelssohn: Obadiah, in Elijah; Hymn of Praise; Rossini, Messe Solennelle; Schubert, Lazarus; Tippett, Child of Our Time. Has sung in all major religious works including: Missa Solemnis, Verdi's Requiem, Dream of Gerontius, St Matthew Passion, The Creation. Many recordings incl. Il Seraglio, The Trojans, Saul, Così Fan Tutte, Thérèse, Monteverdi Madrigals, Idomeneo, Haydn's The Seasons, Messiah, L'Oracolo (Leone), Judas Maccabaeus, Il Matrimonio Segreto (Cimarosa), L'Amore dei Tre Re (Montemezzi), La Navarraise (Massenet), Lucia di Lammermoor (Donizetti). FRWCMD (FWCMD 1996). John Christie Award, 1965. *Recreations:* antiques, art, cinema, sport. *Address:* c/o Hazard Chase Ltd, 25 City Road, Cambridge CB1 1DP.

DAVIES, Prof. Sally Claire; Director General (formerly Director) of Research and Development, Department of Health, since 2004 (Deputy Director, 1997–2004); Consultant Haematologist, Central Middlesex Hospital, since 1985; *b* 24 Nov. 1949; *d* of John Gordon Davies and Emily Mary Davies (*née* Tordoff); *m* 1st, 1974, R. F. W. Skilbeck (marr. diss. 1982); 2nd, 1982, P. R. A. Vulliamy (*d* 1982); 3rd, 1989, W. H. Ouwehand; two *d*. *Educ:* Manchester Univ. (MB ChB); London Univ. (MSc). FRCP 1992; FRCPath 1997; FRCPCH 1997; FFPH (FFPHM 1999). House Phys. and Surg., and SHO, Manchester, 1972–74; clin. assistant in cardiology, Clínica la Concepción, Fundación Jimenez Díaz, Madrid, 1974–77; SHO in Paediatrics, Middlesex Hosp., 1978–79; Lectr, 1979–83, MRC Fellow in Recombinant DNA Technology, 1983–85, Middlesex Hosp. Med. Sch. Wkg Gp on Haemoglobinopathies, European Haematology Assoc., 1999–. FMedSci 2002. Ed. for haemoglobinopathies, Internat. Cochrane Collaboration. Hon. MD Southampton, 2007. *Publications:* contribs to med. jls, mainly relating to sickle cell disease and the haemoglobinopathies. *Recreations:* travel, opera, music, cooking, art, architecture. *Address:* Department of Health, 79 Whitehall, SW1A 2NS.

DAVIES, Sam; *see* Davies, Stanley M.

DAVIES, Rt Rev. Saunders; *see* Davies, Rt Rev. F. J. S.

DAVIES, Sîan; Chief Executive, Henley Centre HeadlightVision (formerly Henley Centre); *b* Long Eaton, 1 Aug. 1966; *d* of Alyn and Margaret Davies; *m* Chad Wollen; one *d*. *Educ:* Hertford Coll., Oxford (BA PPE). Mercer Mgt Consulting, 1988–96; with Henley Centre, subseq. Henley Centre HeadlightVision, 1996–. Mem., Mktg Soc. *Recreations:* contemporary art, photography. *Address:* Henley Centre HeadlightVision, 6 More London Place, Tooley Street, SE1 2QY. *T:* (020) 7955 1830; *e-mail:* sian.davies@hchlv.com.

DAVIES, Simon James; Firmwide Managing Partner, Linklaters, since 2008; *b* London, 29 May 1967; *s* of T. D. Davies and late M. J. Davies; *m* 2007, Minori Mano; one *d*. *Educ:* Emmanuel Coll., Cambridge (BA Law 1989). Admitted Solicitor, 1992; Linklaters: Solicitor, 1992–99; Partner, 1999–2003; Man. Partner, Asia, 2003–07. *Recreations:* theatre, Rugby, running. *Address:* Linklaters, One Silk Street, EC2Y 8HQ. *T:* (020) 7456 3354, *Fax:* (020) 7456 2222; *e-mail:* simon.davies@linklaters.com.

DAVIES, Simon Philip; Headmaster, Eastbourne College, since 2005; *b* 27 July 1964; *s* of late Ven. Philip Bertram Davies and of Jane Davies (*née* Richardson); *m* 1991, Robina Pelham Burn; two *s* one *d*. *Educ:* Radley Coll.; Lady Margaret Hall, Oxford (MA); Inst. of Educn, Univ. of London (PGCE 1994). Grad. trainee, Chase Manhattan Bank, 1986–87; Futures and Options Broker, James Capel, London and Goodbody James Capel, Dublin, 1987–92; Form Teacher, Hereward House Prep. Sch., 1992–93; Hd of Biol. and Sen. Housemaster, Abingdon Sch., 1994–2002; Vice Master and Usher, Bedford Sch., 2002–05. *Recreations:* walking, fly fishing. *Address:* Headmaster's House, Eastbourne College, Eastbourne, E Sussex BN21 4JX. *T:* (01323) 452320, *Fax:* (01323) 452327; *e-mail:* spdavies@eastbourne-college.co.uk. *Club:* East India.

DAVIES, Siobhan; *see* Davies, Susan.

DAVIES, Stanley Mason, (Sam), CMG 1971; Director, ACM (formerly Alliance) International Health Care Fund (formerly Trust), 1986–2002 (Consultant, 1984–86); *b* 7 Feb. 1919; *s* of late Charles Davies, MBE and Constance Evelyn Davies; *m* 1943, Diana Joan (*née* Lowe); three *d*. *Educ:* Bootle Grammar School. War Service, UK and W Europe, 1939–46; Royal Army Dental Corps, 1939–41 (Sgt); Corps of Royal Engineers, 1941–46 (Staff Captain). Clerical Officer, Min. of Labour, 1936; Exec. Officer, Inland Revenue, 1938; Higher Exec. Officer, Min. of Pensions, 1946–53; Min. of Health, 1953–68; Asst Sec., DHSS, 1968–75; Under Sec., Industries and Exports Div., DHSS, 1975–76. Consultant: Monsanto Health Care, 1977–85; Sterling Winthrop Drug, 1977–86. FSAScot. Croix de Guerre (France), 1944. *Recreations:* reading, archæology, philately. *Address:* 31 Leverstock Green Road, Hemel Hempstead, Herts HP2 4HH. *T:* (01442) 217142.

DAVIES, (Stephen) Howard; Associate Director, National Theatre, since 1989; *b* 26 April 1945; *s* of late Thomas Emrys Davies and (Eileen) Hilda Davies; *m* Susan Wall (marr. diss.); two *d*. *Educ:* Christ's Hosp.; Univ. of Durham; Univ. of Bristol. Associate Dir, Bristol Old Vic, 1971–73; Associate Dir, RSC, 1976–86; freelance dir, 1974–76; Founder, The Warehouse, RSC, 1977, Co. Dir, 1977–82. *Productions* include: Royal Shakespeare Company: Troilus and Cressida; Bandits, Bingo, 1977; The Jail Diary of Albie Sachs, 1979; Much Ado About Nothing, 1980; Piaf; Henry VIII, 1983; Les Liaisons Dangereuses, 1986; Royal National Theatre: The Shaughraun; Cat on a Hot Tin Roof, 1988; The Secret Rapture; Hedda Gabler, 1989; The Crucible, 1990; A Long Day's Journey into Night; Mary Stuart, 1996; Chips with Everything, 1997; Flight, 1998; Battle Royal, 1999; All My Sons, 2000 (Best Dir, Laurence Olivier Awards, 2001); The Talking Cure, 2003; Mourning Becomes Electra, 2003; Cyrano de Bergerac, 2004; The House of Bernarda Alba, 2005; The Life of Galileo, 2006; Philistines, 2007; Present Laughter, 2007; Never So Good, Her Naked Skin, 2008; Almeida: Who's Afraid of Virginia Woolf?, 1996; The Iceman Cometh, 1998 (Best Dir, Evening Standard Awards, Lawrence Olivier Awards); Conversations After a Burial, 2000; Period of Adjustment, 2006; Albery: Vassa, 1999; Private Lives, 2001; The Breath of Life, Haymarket, 2002; A Moon for the Misbegotten, Old Vic, 2006, transf. NY, 2007. Director: film, The Secret Rapture, 1993; television: Tales from Hollywood, 1992; Armadillo, 2001; Copenhagen, 2002; Blue/Orange, 2005. *Address:* c/o National Theatre, South Bank, SE1 9PX.

DAVIES, Stephen Rees; QC 2000; *b* 2 May 1960; *s* of John Stephen Davies and Auriol (*née* Huber, now Barriball); partner, Romola Anne Pocock; one *s* one *d*. *Educ:* Stanwell Comprehensive Sch.; Cowbridge Comprehensive Sch.; London Sch. of Economics (LLB 1981); Trinity Hall, Cambridge (LLB 1982). Called to the Bar, Gray's Inn, 1983, Bencher 2006; in practice at the Bar, 1983–. Trustee: CLIC, subseq. CLIC Sargent, 2003–06; Jessie May Trust, 2006–. Mem., Woodside Saturday Club (for children with special needs), Bristol. *Recreations:* music, poetry, Welsh Rugby. *Address:* 5–8 Broad Street, Bristol BS1 3HW; *e-mail:* stephen.davies@guildhallchambers.co.uk.

DAVIES, Stephen Richard; His Honour Judge Stephen Davies; a Circuit Judge, since 2007; a Specialist Circuit Judge, Technology and Construction Court, since 2007; *b* 7 Feb. 1963; *s* of Robert Alun Davies and Merle June Davies; *m* 1996, April Anne Marland; two *d*. *Educ:* Baines Sch., Poulton-Le-Fylde, Lancs; Downing Coll., Cambridge (BA Law 1984). Called to the Bar, Middle Temple, 1985; a Recorder of the Crown Court, 2002–07; Recorder, Technol. and Construction Court, 2006–07. *Address:* Manchester Civil Justice Centre, 1 Bridge Street West, Manchester M3 3FX.

DAVIES, Susan, (Siobhan), CBE 2002 (MBE 1995); freelance choreographer; Director, Siobhan Davies Dance Company, since 1988; *b* 18 Sept. 1950; *d* of Grahame Henry Wyatt Davies and Tempé Mary Davies (*née* Wallich); lives with David John Buckland; one *s* one *d*. *Educ:* several schools, ending with Queensgate School for Girls; Hammersmith College of Art and Building. With London Contemporary Dance Theatre, 1967–87: first choreography, 1972; Associate Choreographer, 1971; Associate Dir, 1983. Formed Siobhan Davies and Dancers, 1980; Jt Dir, with Ian Spink and Richard Alston, Second Stride, 1981–86; Associate Choreographer, Rambert Dance Co., 1988–93. Choreographed works include: White Man Sleeps, 1988; Art of Touch, 1995; Eighty-Eight, 1998; 13 Different Keys, 1999; Wild Air, 1999; Of Oil and Water, 2000; Plants and Ghosts, 2002; Bird Song, 2004; In Plain Clothes, 2006; Two Quartets, 2007. Hon. FTCL 1996. DUniv: Surrey, 1999; Leicester, 2003. Arts Award, Fulbright Commn, 1987, to travel and study in America; Digital Dance Award, 1988, 1989, 1990, 1992; Laurence Olivier Award for Outstanding Achievement in Dance, 1993, 1996; Prudential Award for Dance, Evening Standard Dance Award, 1996; Time Out Award, 1997; South Bank Show Award for Dance, Prudential Creative Britons Award, 2000. *Address:* Siobhan Davies Studios, 85 St George's Road, SE1 6ER.

DAVIES, Susan Elizabeth, (Mrs John Davies), OBE 1988; Founder and Director, Photographers' Gallery, 1971–91; freelance consultant; *b* 14 April 1933; *d* of Stanworth Wills Adey and Joan Mary Margaret Adey (*née* Charlesworth); *m* 1954, John Ross Twiston Davies (*d* 2004); two *d* (and one *d* decd). *Educ:* Nightingale Bamford Sch., NY; Eothen Sch., Caterham. Municipal Journal, 1952–54; local and voluntary work, 1960–67; Artists Placement Group, 1967–68; ICA, 1968–71. Curator, Istanbul Photo-Biennial, 1995–96. Mem. (Ind) S Bucks DC, 1995–99; Parish Councillor, Burnham, Bucks, 1995–2003. Hon. FRPS (President's Medal, 1982). Photokina Award, 1986; National Artist Karel Plicka Medal, Czechoslovakia, 1989. *Recreations:* jazz live and recorded, reading, gardening. *Address:* 57 Sandilands Road, Fulham, SW6 2BD. *Club:* Chelsea Arts.

DAVIES, Dr Susan Jane; Lecturer in Palaeography, Aberystwyth University (formerly University of Wales, Aberystwyth), since 1979; *b* 4 April 1941; *d* of Iorwerth Howells and Megan Howells; *m* 1966, Brian Harold Davies; one *s* one *d*. *Educ:* Queen Elizabeth Grammar Sch. for Girls, Carmarthen; University Coll. of Wales, Aberystwyth (BA Hist., Dip. in Palaeography and Archive Admin, PhD). Trustee, Nat. Mus. Wales (formerly Mem., Council and Court of Govs, Nat. Museums and Galls of Wales), 1994–2007 (Vice-Pres., 2002–07); Mem., Royal Commn on Historical Manuscripts, 1995–2003. *Address:* Department of History and Welsh History, Aberystwyth University, Aberystwyth SY23 3DY.

DAVIES, Prof. Trevor David, PhD; FRMetS; Professor of Environmental Sciences, since 1993, and Pro Vice-Chancellor, Research, since 2004, University of East Anglia; *b* 29 March 1946; *s* of David Vincent Davies and Alice Beatrice Davies (*née* Savage); *m* 1970, Sandra Patricia Rowles (marr. diss. 2007); one *s* one *d*. *Educ:* Saltley Grammar Sch., Birmingham; Univ. of Sheffield (BSc 1967, PhD 1970). FRMetS 1974. Res. Asst, Univ. of New England, Australia, 1967; University of East Anglia: Lectr in Meteorol., 1970–88; Reader in Atmospheric Scis, 1988–93; Dir, Climatic Res. Unit, 1993–98; Dean, Sch. of Envmtl Scis, 1998–2004. Mem., NERC, 2001–. *Publications:* contrib. numerous scientific papers to specialist jls. *Recreations:* many things. *Address:* Vice-Chancellor's Office, University of East Anglia, Norwich NR4 7TJ. *T:* (01603) 592836; *e-mail:* t.d.davies@uea.ac.uk.

DAVIES, Tristan David Henry; Executive Editor, Sunday Times, since 2008; *b* 26 Oct. 1961; *s* of Maj.-Gen. Peter Ronald Davies, *qv*; *m* 2006, Shane, *d* of Maj.-Gen. Andrew Linton Watson, *qv*; two *s* one *d* from a former marriage. *Educ:* Douai; Bristol Univ. (English and Hist. (failed)). Editor: Covent Gdn Courier, 1983–86; Piazza Mag., 1986–87; joined The Independent, 1987: Listings Ed., 1988–90; Arts and Weekend Ed., 1990–93; Dep. Features Ed., 1993–96; Asst Ed., Mail on Sunday, Night and Day Mag., 1996–98; Exec. Ed., The Independent, 1998–2001; Ed., Independent on Sunday, 2001–07. *Recreations:* football, singing. *Address:* The Sunday Times, 1 Pennington Street, E98 1ST. *Club:* Groucho.

DAVIES, Ven. (Vincent) Anthony; Archdeacon of Croydon, since 1994; *b* 15 Sept. 1946; *s* of Vincent Davies and Maud Mary Cecilia Davies (*née* Hackett); unmarried. *Educ:* Brasted Place Theol Coll.; St Michael and All Angels Theol Coll., Llandaff. Curate: St James, Owton Manor, dio. Durham, 1973–76; St Faith, Wandsworth, dio. Southwark, 1976–78; Parish Priest: St Faith, Wandsworth, 1978–81; St John, Walworth, 1981–94; RD of Southwark and Newington, 1988–93. FRSA. *Recreations:* walking, swimming, country pubs, all things Italian. *Address:* 246 Pampisford Road, South Croydon, Surrey CR2 6DD. *T:* (020) 8688 2943; (office) St Matthew's House, 100 George Street, Croydon CR0 1PE. *T:* (020) 8256 9630. *Club:* National Liberal.

DAVIES, Vivian; *see* Davies, W. V.

DAVIES, Walter, OBE 1966; Secretary-General and Chief Executive of The British Chamber of Commerce for Italy 1961–86, retired; *b* 7 Dec. 1920; *s* of late William Davies and late Frances Poole; *m* 1947, Alda, *d* of Tiso Lucchetta, Padua; two *d*. *Educ:* St Margaret's Higher Grade Sch., Liverpool; Liverpool Coll. of Commerce. Served War: RA, 1940–41; Scots Guards, 1942–47. Commendatore dell'Ordine al Merito della Repubblica Italiana, 1967. *Recreations:* good food, good company, fishing, motoring. *Address:* Via G. Dezza 27, 20144 Milan, Italy. *T:* (2) 4694391.

DAVIES, Prof. Wendy Elizabeth, OBE 2008; FSA; FRHistS; FBA 1992; Professor of History, 1985–2007, now Emerita, and Pro-Provost, 1995–2007, University College London; *b* 28 Aug. 1942; *d* of Douglas Charles Davies and Lucy (*née* Evans). *Educ:* University Coll. London (BA, PhD). Temporary Lectr 1970, Res. Fellow 1971, Lectr 1972, Univ. of Birmingham; University College London: Lectr 1977; Reader 1981; Hd, Dept of Hist., 1987–92; Dean of Arts, 1991–94; Dean of Social and Historical Scis, 1994–95; Fellow, 1997. Member: Ancient Monuments Bd for Wales, 1993–2003; Humanities Res. Bd, 1996–98. Vice-Pres., British Acad., 2003–05. UK Team Mem., Bologna Experts (formerly Promoters), 2004–. Gov., Mus. of London, 1995–2001. *Publications:* An Early Welsh Microcosm, 1978; The Llandaff Charters, 1979; Wales in the Early Middle Ages, 1982; (ed with P. Fouracre) Settlement of Disputes in Early Medieval Europe, 1986; Small Worlds: the village community in early medieval Brittany, 1988; Patterns of Power, 1990; (with G. Astill) The East Brittany Survey, Field Work and Field Data, 1994; (ed with P. Fouracre) Property and Power, 1995; (with G. Astill) A Breton Landscape, 1997; Inscriptions of Early Medieval Brittany, 2000; (ed) From the Vikings to the Normans, 2003; (ed jtly) People and Space, 2006; Acts of Giving: individual, community and church in tenth-century Christian Spain, 2007; papers in Eng. Historical Rev., Past and Present, Francia, Bull. of Bd of Celtic Studies, Etudes Celtiques, Hist. and Anthropology, Oxford Jl of Archaeology, etc. *Recreations:* walking, gardening, friends, early music.

DAVIES, Dame Wendy (Patricia), DBE 2001; Head Teacher, Selly Park Technology College (formerly Selly Park School), 1986–2003; *b* 19 Dec. 1942; *d* of Cecil and Mary Trotter; *m* 1967, Mansel John Davies; one *s* (one *d* decd). *Educ:* Portsmouth High Sch., GPDST; UCNW (BSc Hons); DipEd Oxford Univ. Teacher, Birmingham LEA, 1966; Dep. Hd, 1969–74, Hd, 1974–80, Dept of Maths; Dep. Head Teacher, 1980–86. Associate Dir, Specialist Schs Trust, 2005–; Trustee, e-Learning Foundn. *Recreations:* maths, travelling, reading, ICT. *Address:* 82 Lugtrout Lane, Solihull, W Midlands B91 2SN. *T:* (0121) 624 2693. *Club:* Selly Park Technol. Coll. Saturday.

DAVIES, (William) Gareth; Head, Australia and New Zealand, International Business Wales, since 2006; *b* 29 Sept. 1955; *s* of late David Elvet Davies and Sarah Davies; *m* 1979, Helen (marr. diss. 2003); two *d*. *Educ:* UWIST, Cardiff (BSc). Oxford Univ. Manager, Burnley Bldg Soc. (Nat. and Provincial Bldg Soc.), 1979–87; Asst Dir, CBI, Wales, 1987–89; Hd of Sport, BBC Wales, 1989–94; Chief Exec., Cardiff Rugby Club, 1994–99; Commissioning Ed., Sports and Events (formerly Sports Advr), S4C, 1999–2006; Dir for Welsh Affairs, Royal Mail Gp, 2003–06. Chm., Sports Council for Wales, 1999–2003. Rugby journalist: Independent on Sunday, 1999; Sunday Times, 2002–06. Hon. Fellow, Cardiff Univ., 1995. *Publication:* Standing Off, 1985. *Recreations:* golf, wine (Burgundy and Bordeaux). *Address:* International Business Wales, Level 31, Phillip Street, Sydney, NSW 2000, Australia. *Club:* Royal Porthcawl Golf.

DAVIES, William Llewellyn M.; *see* Monro Davies.

DAVIES, (William) Rhodri; QC 1999; a Recorder, since 2004; *b* 29 Jan. 1957; *s* of His Honour (Lewis) John Davies, QC; *m* 1984, Vicky Platt; three *d*. *Educ:* Winchester Coll.; Downing Coll., Cambridge (BA Hons Law). Called to the Bar, Middle Temple, 1979; practising barrister, 1980–. *Recreations:* running, sailing, swimming. *Address:* 1 Essex Court, Temple, EC4Y 9AR. *T:* (020) 7583 2000. *Club:* Thames Hare and Hounds.

DAVIES, Rev. Dr William Rhys; Principal of Cliff College, Sheffield, 1983–94; Moderator of the Free Church Federal Council, 1991–92; *b* Blackpool, 31 May 1932; *m* 1955, Barbara; one *s* one *d*. *Educ:* Junior, Central Selective and Grammar schools, Blackpool; Hartley Victoria Methodist Coll., Manchester; Univ. of Manchester. BD London 1955; MA 1959, PhD 1965, Manchester. Junior Rating and Valuation Officer (Clerical), Blackpool Corp., 1950–51. Methodist Circuit Minister: Middleton, Manchester, 1955–60; Fleetwood, 1960–65; Stockton-on-Tees, 1965–66; Sen. Lectr in Religious Studies, Padgate Coll. of Higher Education, and Methodist Minister without pastoral charge on Warrington Circuit, 1966–79; Superintendent Minister, Bradford Methodist Mission, 1979–83. Nat. Advr, Aglow Internat. (GB), 1983–. Pres., Methodist Conf., 1987–88. Methodist Committees: Chairman: Cttee for Relations with People of Other Faiths, 1988–98; Ministerial Candidates Appeals Cttee, 1994–2004. Member: Cliff Coll. Gen. Cttee, 1974–77 and 1981–94; Faith and Order Cttee, 1975–82; Doctrinal Cttee, 1979–82; Divl Bd for Social Responsibility, 1982–85; Home Mission Bd, 1983–94. Mem. Council, Garden Tomb (Jerusalem) Assoc., 1992–95. Patron: Pen-y-Rhondda Trust, 2003–; Philippi Trust, 2007–. Co-Editor, Dunamis (renewal magazine for Methodists), 1972–94. *Publications:* (with Ross Peart) The Charismatic Movement and Methodism, 1973; Spirit Baptism and Spiritual Gifts in Early Methodism, (USA) 1974; Gathered into One (Archbishop of Canterbury's Lent Book), 1975; (with Ross Peart) What about the Charismatic Movement?, 1980; (contrib.) A Dictionary of Christian Spirituality, 1983; Rocking the Boat, 1986; Spirit without Measure, 1996; (contrib.) An Encyclopedia: Jesus in history, thought and culture, 2003; contribs to jls. *Recreations:* reading, sport (soccer). *Address:* 25 Grange Avenue, Thornton Cleveleys, Lancs FY5 4PA. *T:* (01253) 864678.

DAVIES, (William) Vivian, FSA 1980; Keeper, Ancient Egypt and Sudan (formerly Egyptian Antiquities), British Museum, since 1988; *b* 14 Oct. 1947; *s* of late Walter Percival Davies and Gwenllian Davies (*née* Evans); *m* 1970, Janet Olwen May Foat (marr. diss. 1994); one *s* one *d*; *m* 1996, Renée Frances Friedman. *Educ:* Llanelli Grammar Sch.; Jesus Coll., Oxford (BA, MA). Randall-MacIver Student in Archaeology, Queen's Coll., Oxford, 1973–74; Asst Keeper, 1974–81, Dep. Keeper, 1981–88, Dept of Egyptian Antiquities, BM. Vis. Prof. of Egyptology, Univ. of Heidelberg, 1984–85. Hon. Librarian, 1975–85, Gen. Ed. of Pubns, 1990–99, Egypt Exploration Soc.; Chm., Sudan Archaeol Res. Soc., 1991–; Member: Governing Council, British Inst. in Eastern Africa, 1989–2005; German Archaeol Inst., 1992–. Reviews Editor, Jl of Egyptian Archaeology, 1975–85. *Publications:* A Royal Statue Reattributed, 1981; (with T. G. H. James) Egyptian Sculpture, 1983; The statuette of Queen Tetisheri: a reconsideration, 1984; (with A. el-Khouli, A. B. Lloyd, A. J. Spencer) Saqqara Tombs, I: The Mastabas of Mereri and Wernu, 1984; (ed with J. Assmann and G. Burkard) Problems and Priorities in Egyptian Archaeology, 1987; Egyptian Hieroglyphs, 1987; Catalogue of Egyptian Antiquities in the British Museum, VII: Tools and Weapons—1: Axes, 1987; (ed) Egypt and Africa: Nubia from prehistory to Islam, 1991; (ed with R. Walker) Biological Anthropology and the Study of Ancient Egypt, 1993; (ed with J. Putnam) Time Machine: Ancient Egypt and contemporary art, 1994; (ed with L. Schofield) Egypt, the Aegean and the Levant: interconnections in the second millennium BC, 1995; (with R. Friedman) Egypt, 1998; (ed) Studies in Egyptian Antiquities: a tribute to T. G. H. James, 1999; (ed) Colour and Painting in Ancient Egypt, 2001; (ed with D. Welsby) Uncovering Ancient Sudan: a decade of discovery by the Sudan Archaeological Research Society, 2002; contribs to: Egypt's Golden Age: the art of living in the New Kingdom, 1982; Excavating in Egypt: The Egypt Exploration Society 1882–1982, 1982; Tanis: l'or des pharaons, 1987; Africa: the art of a continent, 1996; Sudan: ancient treasures, 2004; Hatshepsut, from Queen to Pharaoh, 2005; reviews and articles in learned jls. *Address:* Department of Ancient Egypt and Sudan, British Museum, WC1B 3DG. *T:* (020) 7323 8306.

DAVIGNON, Viscount Etienne; Minister of State and Ambassador of HM the King of the Belgians; Chairman: Foundation P. H. Spaak, since 1983; Royal Institute for International Relations, since 1987; Vice-Chairman, Suez-Tractebel, since 2003; *b* Budapest, 4 Oct. 1932; *m* 1959, Françoise de Cumont; one *s* two *d*. *Educ:* University of Louvain (LLD). Diplomat; Head of Office of Minister for Foreign Affairs, Belgium, 1963; Political Director, Ministry for Foreign Affairs, Belgium, 1969; Chm., Gov. Board, Internat. Energy Agency, 1974. Mem., 1977–84 (with responsibility for internal mkt, customs, union and industl affairs), and Vice-Pres., 1981–84 (with responsibility for industry, energy and research policies), EEC. Chairman: CMB (Belgium), 2002–; Recticel (Belgium), 2004–; Vice-Chairman: Fortis, 1989–2004; ACCOR, 2000– (Dir, 1990–2000); Société Gén. de Belgique, 2001–03 (Chm., 1989–2001); Director: Umicore 1989–92 and 2000–05 (Chm., 1992–2000); Suez, 1989–; Gilead (USA), 1990–. *Recreations:* tennis, golf. *Address:* 12 Avenue des Fleurs, 1150 Brussels, Belgium.

DAVIS; *see* Clinton-Davis.

DAVIS; *see* Hart-Davis.

DAVIS, Prof. Adrian Charles, OBE 2007; PhD; Professor of Hearing and Communication, and Director, MRC Hearing and Communication Group, University of Manchester, since 2004; *b* 21 March 1950; *s* of Albert H. W. Davis and G. H., (Trudy) Davis; *m* 1978, Kathryn Southworth; two *s* one *d*. *Educ:* Douai Sch.; University Coll London (Dip. Theol. 1970; PhD Psychol. 1984); Univ. of Exeter (BSc Mathematical Stat and Psychol. 1973); Stirling Univ. (MSc Mathematical Psychol. 1974). Lectr in Community Medicine, St Thomas's Hosp. Med. Sch., 1977–78; SRC Res. Fellow (Psychol.), Lancaster Poly., 1978; Sen. Scientific Epidemiologist, MRC Inst. of Hearing Res., 1978–2004. Special Prof., Dept of Surgery, Univ. of Nottingham, 1996–; Hon Consultant Clinical Scientist, Queens Med. Centre, Nottingham, 1996–; Hon Consultant, Central Manchester and Manchester Children's Univ. NHS Trust, 2005–. Director: NHS Newborn Hearing Screening Prog., 2001–; NHS Clinical Audiology Res Network, 2005–; DoH Advr, Audiology, 2005–; DoH Clinical/Scientific Audiology Champion for Physiol Measurement Strategy Gp, 2005–. Medal, Swedish Med. Assoc. 1992; Amer. Auditory Soc. Award, 1998; Thomas Simm Littler Prize, British Soc. of Audiology, 1999. *Publications:* Hearing in Adults, 1995; over 100 books, conf. papers and over 100 articles in scientific jls. *Recreations:* badminton, running. *Address:* MRC Hearing and Communication Group, 3rd Floor, Block A, Ellen Wilkinson Building, University of Manchester, Oxford Road, Manchester M13 9PL; *e-mail:* adrian.davis@manchester.ac.uk.

DAVIS, Alan Henry; strategy consultant; Director of Neighbourhood Renewal Strategy Department for Communities and Local Government (formerly Office of the Deputy Prime Minister), 2004–07; *b* 1 May 1948; *s* of Arthur Wallace Davis and Phyllis Marjorie Davis (*née* Grudgings); *m* 1972, Angela Joy Wells (marr. diss. 2003); two *s* one *d*. *Educ:* Wyggeston Boys' Sch., Leicester; University Coll., Oxford (MA Chem. 1973). Joined DoE, 1973; on secondment to GLC, 1979–80; Private Sec. to successive Secs of State 1983–85; Asst Sec., 1986; Head of Divs in Local Govt, Housing, Global Atmosphere Principal Private Sec. to Sec. of State, 1994–97; Under-Sec., 1997; Director: Water and Land, DETR, 1997–2001; Integrated and Local Transport, DfT (formerly DETR, then DTLR), 2001–04. *Recreations:* gardening, walking, watching sport. *Address:* 269 Gladbeck Way, Enfield EN2 7HR. *T:* (020) 8362 1181.

DAVIS, Ven. Alan Norman; Archdeacon of West Cumberland, 1996–2004; *b* 27 July 1938; *s* of Arthur William and Bertha Eileen Davis; *m* 1966, Françoise Marguerite Blondet; one *s* two *d*. *Educ:* King Edward's Sch., Birmingham; Durham Univ.; Lichfield Theol Coll.; Open Univ. (BA). Ordained deacon, 1965, priest, 1966; Asst Curate, St Luke's Birmingham, 1965–68; Priest-in-charge, 1968–73, Vicar, 1973–75, St Paul Wordsworth Avenue, Sheffield; Vicar, St James and St Christopher, Shiregreen, Sheffield 1975–80; Team Rector, Maltby, Sheffield, 1980–89; Archbishop's Officer for Urban Priority Areas, 1990–92; Priest-in-charge, St Cuthbert, Carlisle, and Diocesan Communications Officer, 1992–96; Area Dean, Sparkenhoe W, Dio. Leicester, 2007–. *Recreation:* French holidays. *Address:* 71 North Street, Atherstone, Warwicks CV9 1JW. *T:* (01827) 718210.

DAVIS, Alan Roger M.; *see* Maryon Davis.

DAVIS, Andrew; Founder and Executive Chairman, von Essen group of companies, since 1997; Executive Chairman, Premier Aviation Services Ltd, since 2007; *b* 22 Feb. 1964; *s* of Brendon G. F. Davis and Catharine Agnes Davis (*née* Smyth); one *s*. Farmer; property devélt and investment; art consulting. *Address:* von Essen Hotels Ltd, Ston Easton Park Ston Easton, Bath BA3 4DF; *e-mail:* chairman@vonessenhotels.co.uk.

DAVIS, Sir Andrew (Frank), Kt 1999; CBE 1992; conductor; Musical Director, Chicago Lyric Opera, since 2000; *b* 2 Feb. 1944; *m* 1989, Gianna Rolandi; one *s*. *Educ:* Watford Grammar Sch.; King's Coll., Cambridge (MA, BMus); Accademia di S Cecilia, Rome. Assistant Conductor, BBC Scottish Symphony Orchestra, 1970–72; Asst Conductor, New Philharmonia Orchestra, 1973–77; Artistic Dir and Chief Conductor, Toronto Symphony, 1975–88, now Conductor Laureate; Musical Dir, Glyndebourne Fest. Opera, 1988–2000; Chief Conductor, BBC SO, 1989–2000, now Conductor Laureate. Principal Guest Conductor: Royal Liverpool Philharmonic Orchestra, 1974–77; Royal Stockholm Philharmonic, 1995–2000. Has conducted major US orchestras: New York, Boston, Chicago, Cleveland, Philadelphia and LA. Particularly noted for interpretations of Strauss operas; conducts at: La Scala, Milan; Metropolitan Opera, NY; Chicago Lyric; San Francisco; Glyndebourne; Royal Opera House, Covent Gdn; Bayreuth Fest. Toronto Symphony Orchestra tours: US Centres, China, Japan, 1978; Europe, 1983, 1986, incl. London, Helsinki, Bonn, Paris and Edinburgh Fest.; BBC SO tours: Far East, 1990; Europe, 1992 and 1996; Japan, 1993; N America, 1995 and 1998; Korea and Japan, 1997; Salzburg Fest., 1997; other tours include: Australia, 2002; LSO, 2002, 2004. Many commercial recordings include: complete Dvorak Symphonies, Philharmonia Orch.; Mendelssohn Symphonies, Bavarian Radio Symphony; Borodin Cycle, Holst's The Planets and Handel's Messiah, Toronto Symphony; Tippett's The Mask of Time, BBC SO and Chorus (Record of the Year, Gramophone Awards, 1987); The British Line (British Orchestral Series), BBC SO; world première of Elgar/Payne Symphony No 3. *Recreation:* the study of mediaeval stained glass. *Address:* c/o Columbia Artists Management Inc., 1790 Broadway, New York, NY 10019–1412, USA.

DAVIS, Ann-Louise; *see* Kinmonth, A.-L.

DAVIS, Anthony Ronald William James; media consultant, since 1990; *b* 26 July 1931; *e s* of Donald William Davis, Barnes and Mary Josephine Davis (*née* Nolan-Byrne), Templeogue Mill, Co. Dublin; *m* 1960, Yolande Mary June, *o d* of Patrick Leonard, retd civil engr; one *s* two *d* (and one *d* decd). *Educ:* Hamlet of Ratcliffe and Oratory; Regent Street Polytechnic. Joint Services School for Linguists on Russian course as National Serviceman (Army), 1953–55; Architectural Asst, Housing Dept, Middx County Architect's Dept, 1956–58; Sub-Editor, The Builder, 1959; Editor: Official Architecture and Planning, 1964–70; Building, 1970–74; Director, Building, 1972–77; Editor-in-Chief, New World Publishers Ltd, 1978–83; Editl Dir, New World Publishers Ltd, Middle East Construction and Saudi Arabian Construction, 1983–86; Editor, World Property, 1986–90. Member Board: Architecture and Planning Publications Ltd, 1966; Building (Publishers) Ltd, 1972. Mem. Council, Modular Soc., 1970–71. JP Berkshire, 1973–81. *Publications:* contribs to various, architectural and technical. *Recreations:* collecting porcelain, music and dreaming. *Address:* Farm Cottage, Grantham Road, Old Somerby, Grantham, Lincs NG33 4AB. *T:* (01476) 569778.

DAVIS, (Arthur) John, RD 1967; FCIB; Vice-Chairman, Lloyds Bank, 1984–91 (Chief General Manager, 1978–84); *b* 28 July 1924; *s* of Alan Wilfrid Davis and Emily Davis; *m* 1950, Jean Elizabeth Edna Hobbs (*d* 2004); one *s* one *d* (and one *d* decd). *Educ:* grammar schs. FCIB (FIB 1969). Served War, RN, 1942–46. Entered Lloyds Bank, 1941; Jt Gen. Manager, 1973; Asst Chief Gen. Man., 1973; Dep. Chief Gen. Man., 1976. Pres., Chartered Inst. of Bankers, 1985–87. *Recreations:* gardening, music, country pursuits. *Address:* The Granary, Stocks Road, Aldbury, Tring, Herts HP23 5RX. *T:* (01442) 851321.

DAVIS, Barbara Ann; *see* Cassani, B. A.

DAVIS, Dr Brian Elliott, CBE 2000; Chief Executive, Nationwide Building Society, 1994–2001; *b* 22 Sept. 1944; *s* of William and Bessie Davis; *m* 1972, Elizabeth Rose; one *s* two *d*. *Educ:* St John's Coll., Southsea; Sussex Univ. (BSc); Sheffield Univ. (PhD). FCIB 2000. With Esso Petroleum Co., 1969–86; joined Nationwide Building Soc., 1986; Gen. Manager (Technology), 1987; Resource Dir, 1989; Ops Dir, 1992. Chm., BSA, 1996–98. *Recreations:* tennis, golf, amateur dramatics, computing.

DAVIS, Maj.-Gen. Brian William, CB 1985; CBE 1980 (OBE 1974); Head of Public Affairs, Royal Ordnance plc, 1987–94 (Director, Product Support Group, 1985–87); *b* 28 Aug. 1930; *s* of late Edward William Davis, MBE, and Louise Jane Davis (*née* Webber); *m* 1954, Margaret Isobel Jenkins; one *s* one *d*. *Educ:* Weston-super-Mare Grammar Sch.; Mons OCS, Aldershot. Commissioned Royal Artillery, 1949; Regtl Duty, 1949–56 and 1960–61, UK/BAOR; Instr-in-Gunnery, 1956–59; Staff Coll. Camberley, 1962; DAA and QMG HQ 7 Armd Bde BAOR, 1963–66; GSO2 SD UN Force, Cyprus, 1966; Regtl Duty, 1967–69; Lt-Col 1969, Directing Staff, Staff Coll. Camberley, 1969–71; CO 32 Lt Regt RA BAOR/England/N Ireland, 1971–74; Col AQ Ops HQ BAOR, 1975; Brig. 1975; CRA 3 Div., 1976–77; RCDS 1978; Chief of Staff N Ireland, 1979–80; Chief of Comdrs-in-Chief Mission to Soviet Forces in Germany, 1981–82; Maj. Gen., 1982; C of S, Logistic Exec. (Army), 1982–83; DGLP (A) (formerly VQMG), MoD, 1983–85, retired. Col Comdt RA, 1987–93. Mem., HAC, 1987–95. *Recreations:* Rugby (President, RARFC, 1975–78; Dep. Pres., Army Rugby Union, 1984–89), cricket, fishing, ornithology. *Clubs:* Special Forces, MCC; Army Rugby Union; Fadeaways; Piscatorial Society (Pres., 2003–07).

DAVIS, Carl, Hon. CBE 2005; composer; *b* 28 Oct. 1936; *s* of Isadore and Sara Davis; *m* 1971, Jean Boht; two *d*. *Educ:* New England Conservatory of Music; Bard Coll. (BA). Associate Conductor, London Philharmonic Orchestra, 1987–88; Principal Conductor, Bournemouth Pops, 1984–87; Principal Guest Conductor, Munich SO, 1990–93; Artistic Dir, Liverpool Philharmonic Summer Pops, 1993–2000; *major TV credits:* The Snow Goose, 1971; World at War (Emmy Award), 1972; The Naked Civil Servant, 1975; Marie Curie, 1977; Our Mutual Friend, 1978; Prince Regent, The Old Curiosity Shop, 1979; Hollywood, Oppenheimer, The Sailor's Return, Fair Stood the Wind for France, 1980; The Commanding Sea, Private Schulz, 1981; The Last Night of the Poms, Home Sweet Home, La Ronde, 1982; The Unknown Chaplin, The Tale of Beatrix Potter, The Far Pavilions, 1983; The Day the Universe Changed, 1985; Hotel du Lac, 1986; The Accountant (BAFTA Award), The Pied Piper, 1989; Flight Terminal, Secret Life of Ian Fleming, 1990; The Black Velvet Gown, Buried Mirror, Yellow Wallpaper, The Last of the Romantics, Ashenden, Separate But Equal, 1991; The Royal Collection, A Very Polish Practice, A Sense of History, Fame in the 20th Century, 1992; A Year in Provence, Genghis Cohen, Thatcher: the Downing Street Years, 1993; Red Eagle, Hope in the Year 2, 1994; Pride and Prejudice, 1995; A Dance to the Music of Time, 1997; Cold War, Good Night Mr Tom, Seesaw, Coming Home, 1998; The Great Gatsby, 2000; Christopher Columbus, 2002; Promoted by Glory, 2003; *radio:* presenter, Carl Davis Classics, R2, 1997–2000; *scores:* for RSC and National Theatre; *musicals:* The Projector, 1971; Pilgrim, 1975; Cranford, 1976; Alice in Wonderland, 1978; The Wind in the Willows, 1985; Kip's War, 1987; *opera:* Peace, 1978; *TV operas:* The Arrangement, 1967; Orpheus in the Underground, 1976; *West End:* Forty Years On, 1969; Habeas Corpus, 1973; *films:* The French Lieutenant's Woman (BAFTA Original Film Score Award), 1981; Champions, 1984; King David, 1985; Girl in a Swing, Scandal, The Rainbow, 1988; Frankenstein Unbound, Fragments of Isabella, 1989; Crucifer of Blood, Raft of the Medusa, 1991; The Voyage, 1992; The Trial, 1993; Widows Peak, 1994; Topsy-Turvy, 1999; Book of Eve, 2002; *silent films:* Napoleon, 1980, newly adapted, 2000; The Crowd, 1981; Flesh and the Devil, Show People, How to Make Movies, 1982; Broken Blossoms, The Wind, The Musketeers of Pig Alley, An Unseen Enemy, 1983; Thief of Bagdad, 1984; The Big Parade, Greed, 1985; The General, Ben Hur, 1987; Mysterious Lady, Intolerance, City Lights (re-creation of Chaplin score), 1988; Safety Last, Kid Brother, 1989; The Immigrant, 1991; IT, The Four Horsemen of the Apocalypse, 1992; Wings; The Gold Rush (re-creation of Chaplin score), 1993; The Wedding March, 1998; Old Heidelberg, 1999; The Iron Mask, 1999; The Adventurer, 2000; The Rink, Behind the Screen (Chaplain short films), 2003; *ballets:* Dances of Love and Death, 1981; Fire and Ice (ice ballet for Torvill and Dean), 1986; The Portrait of Dorian Gray (for SWRB), 1987; A Simple Man (based on L. S. Lowry, for Northern Ballet Theatre), 1987; Liaisons Amoureuses, 1988; Lipizzaner (Northern Ballet Theatre), 1988; A Christmas Carol (Northern Ballet Theatre), 1992; Savoy Suite (English Nat. Ballet), 1993; Alice in Wonderland (English Nat. Ballet), 1995; Aladdin (Scottish Ballet), 2000; Cyrano (Birmingham Royal Ballet), 2007; *orchestral compositions:* Lines on London (symphony), 1984 (commnd by Capital Radio); Clarinet Concerto, 1984; Fantasy for flute, 1985 (commnd by Acad. of St Martin's-in-the-Fields); Glenlivet Firework Music, 1987; Beginners Please!, 1987; (with Paul McCartney) Paul McCartney's Liverpool Oratorio, 1991; On the Beach at Night Alone, 1999. Has made numerous recordings. Mem. BAFTA, 1979–. First winner, BAFTA Award for Original TV Music, 1981; BAFTA Lifetime Achievement Award for Contribution to Film and TV, 2003. Chevalier de L'Ordre des Arts et des Lettres, 1983. *Publications:* sheet music of television themes. *Recreations:* reading, gardening, playing chamber music, cooking. *Address:* c/o Paul Wing, Selbourne, 3 Deermead, Little Kings Hill, Great Missenden, Bucks HP16 OEY. *T:* (01494) 890511, *Fax:* (01494) 890522; *e-mail:* admin@winfordm.co.uk.

DAVIS, Christine Agnes Murison, CBE 1997; Chairman, Scottish Legal Aid Board, 1991–98 (Member, 1986–89, 1990–91); *b* 5 March 1944; *d* of William Russell Aitken and Betsy Mary Murison or Aitken; *m* 1968, Robin John Davis; twin *d*. *Educ:* Perth Acad.; Ayr Acad.; St Andrews Univ. (MA Hons Modern History 1966); Aberdeen Univ. (DipEd 1967). Teacher of History and Modern Studies: Cumbernauld High Sch., 1967–68; High Sch. of Stirling, 1968–69; HM Instn, Cornton Vale, 1979–87. Member: Dunblane Town Council (non-political), 1972–75; (ex-officio) Perth and Kinross Jt County Council, 1972–75. Mem., 1974–77, Vice Chm., 1978–79, Chm., 1980–90, Electricity Consultative Council for N of Scotland Dist; Member: N Scotland Hydro Electric Bd, 1980–90; Legal Aid Central Cttee, 1980–87; Scottish Econ. Council, 1987–95; Scottish Cttee, Council on Tribunals, 1989–95; Rail Users' Consultative Cttee for Scotland, subseq. Rail Passengers' Cttee Scotland, 1997–2005; Vice Chm., IT82 Scottish Cttee, 1981–83; Chm., Scottish Agricl Wages Bd, 1995–2004 (Mem., 1991–95); Ind. Advr on Public Appts, 1998–2002. Trustee: Nat. Energy Foundn, 1991–2002; Energy Action Scotland, 1991–2002, 2003– (Convener, 2004–); Joseph Rowntree Charitable Trust, 1996–. Co-opted Mem. Court, Univ. of St Andrews, 2004– (Gen. Council Assessor, 2000–03). Is a Quaker; a Pres., CCBI, 1990–92. *Recreations:* gardening, walking, sewing. *Address:* 24 Newton Crescent, Dunblane, Perthshire FK15 0DZ. *T:* (01786) 823226, *Fax:* (01786) 825633; *e-mail:* christine.amd@btinternet.com. *Club:* Penn.

DAVIS, Sir Colin (Rex), CH 2001; Kt 1980; CBE 1965; Principal Conductor, 1995–2007, President, since 2007, London Symphony Orchestra; *b* 25 Sept. 1927; *s* of Reginald George and Lillian Davis; *m* 1949, April Cantelo (marr. diss. 1964); one *s* one *d*; *m* 1964, Ashraf Naini; three *s* two *d*. *Educ:* Christ's Hospital; Royal College of Music. Orchestral Conductor, Freelance wilderness, 1949–57; Asst Conductor, BBC Scottish Orchestra, 1957–59. Conductor, Sadler's Wells, 1959, Principal Conductor, 1960–65, Musical Director, 1961–65; Chief Conductor, BBC Symphony Orchestra, 1967–71, Chief Guest Conductor, 1971–75; Musical Dir, Royal Opera House, Covent Garden, 1971–86; Chief Conductor, Bavarian Radio Symphony Orch., 1983–92; Principal Guest Conductor: Boston SO, 1972–84; LSO, 1975–95; NY Philharmonic, 1998–2003; Hon. Conductor, Dresden Staatskapelle, 1990. Conducted at: Metropolitan Opera House, New York, 1969, 1970, 1972; Bayreuth Fest., 1977; Vienna State Opera, 1986; Bavarian State Opera, 1994. Hon. DMus: RAM 2002; Keele, 2002; Dr *hc* La Sorbonne, 2006. Freedom, City of London, 1992; Hon. Freedom, Co. of Musicians, 2005. Sibelius Medal, Finland Sibelius Soc., 1977; Grosse Schallplattenpreis, 1978; Gold Medal, Royal Philharmonic Soc., 1995; Distinguished Musician Award, ISM, 1996; Sibelius Birthplace Medal, 1998. Commendatore of Republic of Italy, 1976; Commander's Cross, Order of Merit (FRG), 1987; Commandeur, l'Ordre des Arts et des Lettres (France), 1990; Commander, Order of Lion (Finland), 1992; Order of Merit (Bavaria), 1993; Officier, Légion d'Honneur (France), 1999 (Chevalier, 1982); Order of Maximilian (Bavaria), 2000. *Recreations:* reading, cooking, gardening, knitting. *Address:* c/o Alison Glaister, 39 Huntingdon Street, N1 1BP. *Club:* Athenæum.

DAVIS, Prof. (Conrad) Glyn, AC 2002; PhD; Vice-Chancellor and President, University of Melbourne, since 2005. *Educ:* Univ. of NSW (BA 1st Cl. Hons Pol Sci. 1981); ANU (PhD 1985). FIPAA 1995; FASSA 2003. Lectr in Politics and Public Policy, Griffith Univ., 1985; Harkness Fellow, Univ. of Calif, Berkeley, Brookings Instn, Washington and John F. Kennedy Sch. of Govt, Harvard, 1987–88; Griffith University: Aust. Res. Council QE II Res. Fellow, 1992–95, 1996–98; Prof., 1998; Vice-Chancellor and Pres., 2002–05; on secondment to Queensland Government: as Comr for Public Sector Equity, Qld Public Sector Mgt Commn, 1990–93; as Dir Gen., Office of the Cabinet, 1995–96; as Dir Gen., Qld Dept of the Premier and Cabinet, 1998–2002. Chm., Aust. and NZ Sch. of Govt, Univ. of Melbourne, 2002–06. Director: South Bank Corp., 1998–2001; Qld Theatre Co., 2002–05; Melbourne Theatre Co., 2005–. DUniv Griffith, 2006. *Publications:* Breaking Up the ABC, 1988; A Government of Routines, 1995; (with P. Bridgman) The Australian Policy Handbook, 1998, 4th edn (with P. Bridgman and C. Althaus) 2007; (ed with M. Keating) The Future of Australian Governance: policy choices, 2000; (ed with P. Weller) Are You Being Served?: state, citizens and governance, 2001. *Address:* Vice-Chancellor's Office, University of Melbourne, Vic 3010, Australia.

DAVIS, Sir Crispin Henry Lamert, Kt 2004; Chief Executive Officer, Reed Elsevier, since 1999; *b* 19 March 1949; *s* of late Walter Patrick Carless Davis and Jane (*née* Lamert); *m* 1970, Anne Richardson; three *d*. *Educ:* Charterhouse; Oriel Coll., Oxford (MA Mod. Hist.). Joined Procter & Gamble, 1970: Man. Dir, Procter & Gamble Germany, 1981–84; Vice-Pres., Food Div., Procter & Gamble USA, 1984–90; European Man. Dir, 1990–92, Gp Man. Dir, 1992–94, United Distillers; CEO, Aegis plc, 1994–99. Non-exec. Dir, GlaxoSmithKline plc, 2003–. Trustee, Nat. Trust, 2005–. *Recreations:* sport: tennis, squash, golf, ski-ing; gardening, art, antique furniture. *Address:* Hills End, Titlarks Hill, Sunningdale, Berks SL5 0JD. *T:* (01344) 291233. *Clubs:* Royal Automobile, MCC.
See also I. E. L. Davis, *Hon. Sir* N. A. L. Davis.

DAVIS, Rt Hon. David (Michael); PC 1997; MP (C) Haltemprice and Howden, 1997–June 2008 and since July 2008 (Boothferry, 1987–97); *b* 23 Dec. 1948; *s* of Ronald and Elizabeth Davis; *m* 1973, Doreen Margery Cook; one *s* two *d*. *Educ:* Warwick Univ. (BSc); London Business Sch. (MSc); Harvard (AMP). Joined Tate & Lyle, 1974: Strategic

Planning Dir, 1984–87; Dir, 1987–89. PPS to Parly Under-Sec. of State, DTI, 1989–90; an Asst Govt Whip, 1990–93; Parly Sec., Office of Public Service and Science, Cabinet Office, 1993–94; Minister of State, FCO, 1994–97; Chm., Cons. Party, 2001–02; Shadow Sec. of State, ODPM, 2002–03; Shadow Home Sec., 2003–08. Chm., H of C Public Accounts Cttee, 1997–2001. Resigned seat June 2008 to contest by-election on civil liberties issue; re-elected July 2008. Mem., Financial Policy Cttee, CBI, 1977–79; Exec. Mem., Industrial Soc., 1985–87. Chm., Fedn of Cons. Students, 1973–74. *Recreations:* writing, flying, mountaineering. *Address:* House of Commons, SW1A 0AA.

DAVIS, Dennis Tyrone, CBE 2004 (OBE 1996); QFSM 1991; CEng, FIFireE; independent fire adviser, since 2004; HM Chief Inspector of Fire Services for Scotland, 1999–2004; *b* 10 Feb. 1947; *s* of Dennis and Winifred Davis; *m* 1968, Maureen; two *s*. *Educ:* Queen Mary's Grammar Sch., Walsall; MPhil Univ. of Central Lancs 2005. Joined Fire Bde, 1965; Walsall, 1965–71; Cheshire, 1971–99, Chief Fire Officer, 1986–99. Chm., Fire Confs and Exhibitions Ltd, 1990–2005 (Dir, 1990–). Chm., Fedn of British Fire Orgns, 2006– (Vice Chm., 2004–06). FIFireE 1981 (Chm., 1988–2006; Life Fellow, 1999); CEng 1998; MEI (MInstE 1998); CCMI (CIMgt 1995). OStJ 1996. *Recreation:* old cars. *Address:* 11 Private Walk, Chester CH3 5XB.

DAVIS, Derek Alan, CEng; Director, World Energy Council Commission, 1990–93; *b* 5 Oct. 1929; *s* of Irene Davis (*née* Longstaff) and Sydney George Davis; *m* 1954, Ann Margery Willett; three *s*. *Educ:* private schools; Battersea Polytechnic; London University. BScEng (First Hons) 1950; MIMechE; CBIM. De Havilland Engine Co. Ltd: post-graduate apprentice, 1950–52; develt engineer, Gas Turbine Div., 1952–53, Rocket Div., 1953–56; Central Electricity Generating Board: Research Labs, 1956–60; Manager, Mech. and Civil Engineering, 1960–65; Group Head Fuel, 1965, System Econ. Engineer, 1970, System Planning Engineer, 1973–75, Planning Dept; Dir, Resource Planning, later Dir Production, NE Region, 1975–81; Dir Corporate Strategy Dept, 1981–84; Mem., 1984–90. Member: SERC, 1989–94; Meteorology Cttee, MoD, 1986–99; ACORD, Dept of Energy, 1990–92. *Publications:* articles in tech. and engineering jls. *Recreations:* playing, now watching, sport; gardening, DIY, reading.

DAVIS, Derek Richard; Chairman, British Geological Survey, since 2005 (Board Member, since 2004); *b* 3 May 1945; *s* of late Stanley Lewis Davis, OBE and Rita Beatrice Rachel Davis (*née* Rosenheim), MBE; *m* 1987, Diana Levinson; one *s* one *d*. *Educ:* Clifton Coll., Bristol; Balliol Coll., Oxford (BA 1967). Asst Principal, BoT, 1967; Pvte Sec. to Perm. Sec., DTI, 1971–72; Principal, 1972; Asst Sec., Dept of Energy, 1977; Secretary: Energy Commn, 1977–79; NEDC Energy Task Force, 1981; seconded to NCB, 1982–83; Under Sec., Gas Div., 1985–87, Oil and Gas Div., 1987–93, Dept of Energy, subseq. DTI; Dir Gen., BNSC, 1993–99; Dir, Chemicals, Biotechnology, Consumer Goods and Posts, 1999–2002, Nuclear and Coal Liabilities, 2002–04, DTI. Member: BBSRC, 2000–02. Trustee, Nat. Space Sci. Centre, 1998–99. *Address:* 6 Roman Road, Bedford Park, W4 1NA. *T:* (020) 8747 3931.

DAVIS, Evan Harold; Presenter, Today programme, Radio 4, since 2008; *b* 8 April 1962; *s* of Quintin Visser Davis and Hazel Noreen Davis. *Educ:* Ashcombe Sch., Dorking; St John's Coll., Oxford (PPE Hons 1984); Kennedy Sch. of Government, Harvard Univ. (MPA 1988). Res. Officer, Inst. for Fiscal Studies, 1984–86; Res. Fellow, London Business Sch., 1988–92; Res. Co-ordinator, Inst. for Fiscal Studies, 1992–93; Econs Correspondent, 1993–2001, Econs Ed., 2001–08, BBC. *Publications:* Public Spending, 1998; (jtly) Penguin Dictionary of Economics, 4th edn 1987 to 7th edn 2003; (jtly) New Penguin Dictionary of Business, 2003. *Address:* Room G630, BBC Television Centre, Wood Lane, W12 7RJ. *T:* (020) 8624 9843; *e-mail:* evan.davis@bbc.co.uk.

DAVIS, Gareth; Chief Executive Officer, Imperial Tobacco Group plc, since 1996; *b* 13 May 1950; *m* 1973, Andrea Allan; one *d* (and one *d* decd). *Educ:* Beal Grammar Sch., Ilford; Univ. of Sheffield (BA Hons Econ.). Mgt trainee, Imperial Tobacco, 1972; W. D. & H. O. Wills: Prodn Manager, Newcastle, 1973–79; Prodn Control Manager, Bristol, 1979–83; Factory Manager, Players, Nottingham, 1983–89; Mfg Dir, Imperial, 1987–95, and Man. Dir, Imperial Internat., 1988–95. *Recreations:* most sports, especially cricket, golf, soccer. *Address:* (office) PO Box 244, Southville, Bristol BS99 7UJ. *T:* (0117) 963 6636.

DAVIS, Prof. Glyn; *see* Davis, C. G.

DAVIS, Rear-Adm. Graham Noel, CB 1993; software development consultant, since 1993; *b* 24 Dec. 1937; *s* of Edward Davis and Ruth (*née* Bullen); *m* 1964, Mary Jenkins; one *s* one *d*. *Educ:* Eltham Coll.; London Univ. (BSc Hons Physics). Joined RN 1963: Comdr, 1973; Capt., 1981; Dean, RNC, Greenwich, 1981–83; rcds 1983; Dir, various depts, MoD, 1984–90; Rear-Adm., 1991; Dir-Gen., Fleet Support for Ops and Plans, 1991–93. Chm., Sussex Ouse Restoration Soc., 2000–03. *Recreations:* cooking, pottery, exploring UK and European canals by boat. *Address: e-mail:* davis5@which.net.

DAVIS, Gray; *see* Davis, J. G.

DAVIS, Rt Hon. Helen Elizabeth; *see* Clark, Rt Hon. H. E.

DAVIS, Ian Edward Lamert; Worldwide Managing Director, McKinsey & Company Inc., since 2003; *b* 10 March 1951; *s* of late Walter Patrick Carless Davis and Jane Davis (*née* Lamert); *m* 1st, 1977, Sally J. Fuller; one *s* one *d*; 2nd, 1994, Penny A. Thring. *Educ:* Charterhouse; Balliol Coll., Oxford (MA). Bowater, 1972–79; McKinsey & Company: Associate, 1979–85; Principal, 1985–90; Dir, 1990–; Man. Dir, UK, 1996–2003. *Recreations:* the Alps, watching cricket, golf, biographies. *Clubs:* Hurlingham, Queen's; Berkshire Golf.

See also Sir C. H. L. Davis, Hon. Sir N. A. L. Davis.

DAVIS, Ian Paul, CEng; Operations Director, National House-Building Council, since 2006; *b* 26 Dec. 1954; *s* of George Davis and Margaret Davis (*née* Proctor); *m* 1978, Jane Fidell; two *d*. *Educ:* Grove Sch., Newark; Univ. of Liverpool (BEng 1976); Open Univ. (MBA 1999). CEng, MICE 1982. Site Engr, Head Wrightson Process Engrg, 1976–78; Design Engr, Simpson Coulson & Partners, 1978–80; Project Engr, Davy International, 1980–83; Regl Engr, 1983–90, Dir of Standards, 1990–94, Dep. Chief Exec., 1994–97, NHBC; Dir Gen., Fedn of Master Builders, 1997–2006. Chm., Soha Housing (formerly S Oxfordshire Housing Assoc.), 2000–03 (Dir, 1996–2005). *Address:* National House-Building Council, Buildmark House, Chiltern Avenue, Amersham HP6 5AP.

DAVIS, Ivan, OBE 2005; Member (UU) Lagan Valley, Northern Ireland Assembly, 1998–2003; *b* 16 April 1937; *s* of late James and Susan Davis; *m* 1960, Hannah Elizabeth (Betty), Murphy; three *s* one *d*. *Educ:* Lisburn Public Elementary Sch. Lisburn Borough Council: Mem., 1973–2002; Chairman: Police Liaison Cttee, 1977–81; Recreation and Allied Services, 1977–79, 1993–95; Housing Liaison Cttee, 1984–2002; Planning Cttee, 1987–89; Leisure Services Cttee, 1997–99; Capital Develt Cttee, 1997–99; Member: Health Cttee, 1994–96; Strategic Policy Cttee, 1997–99; Dep. Mayor of Lisburn, 1989–91, Mayor, 1991–93. Member: NI Assembly, 1982–86; NI Forum (Dep. Chm.), 1996–98. Northern Ireland Assembly: Dep. Whip, 1998–2002; Chief Whip, 2002; Member: Culture, Arts and Leisure Cttee; Business Cttee, 1998–2002; Cttee on Procedures, 2001–02. Member: UUP, 1987– (Mem. Exec. Cttee, 1993–99, 2000–); UU Council, 1993– (Mem., Exec. Cttee, 1993–99). Member: Lisburn Sports Adv. Council, 1989–; SE Educn and Liby Bd, 1993–95; Lisburn CAB, 1997–; Cttee, Lisburn Partnership of Peace and Reconciliation, 1997–. Pres., Kirkpatrick Charity Cttee, 1988–; Vice President: Lisburn Amateur Boxing Club, 1985–; Lisburn Swimming Club, 1989–. *Address:* 29 Roseville Park, Lisburn BT27 4XT. *T:* (028) 9267 8164. *Club:* Lambeg Golf (Pres., 1998–2000).

DAVIS, James Gresham, CBE 1988; FCILT; FICS; Chairman: International Maritime Industries Forum, since 1981; Global Ocean Carriers Ltd, since 1996 (Director, since 1988); British Committee, ClassNK, since 2003; *b* 20 July 1928; *s* of Col Robert Davis, OBE, JP and Josephine Davis (*née* Edwards); *m* 1973, Adriana Johanna Verhoef, Utrecht, Holland; three *d*. *Educ:* Bradfield Coll.; Clare Coll., Cambridge (MA). FCILT (FCIT 1969, FILT); FIEx; FInstLM (FISM 1989); FNI. Served RN, 1946–49. P&OSN Co., 1952–72: Calcutta, 1953; Kobe, Japan, 1954–56; Hong Kong, 1956–57; Director: P&O Lines, 1967–72; Kleinwort Benson Ltd, 1973–88; DFDS Ltd, 1975–97 (Chm., 1984–95; Advr, 1995–97); Pearl Cruises of Scandinavia Inc., 1982–86; Rodskog Shipbrokers (Hong Kong) Ltd, 1983–88; Associated British Ports Holdings plc, 1983–97; Transport Develt Gp plc, 1984–91; TIP Europe Plc, 1987–93 (Chm., 1990–93); Sedgwick Energy & Marine Ltd, 1988–99; Sedgwick Gp Develt Ltd, 1991–99; Hempel Paints Ltd, 1992–2000; Tsavliris Salvage (International) Ltd, 1994–2000; 2M Invest AS (Copenhagen), 1996–2000; Catenas Ltd, 2000–02; Foresight Ltd, 2002–; Shipserve Ltd, 2002–; Chairman: Bromley Shipping, 1989–94; Trinitas Services Ltd, 1993–2006; Marine Risk Mgt Services, 1995–99; Liberia Maritime Adv. Bd, 1998–2001; Wigham Richardson Shipbrokers Ltd, 2003–; Caterham Leasing Ltd, 2003–06; Dep. Chm., Hanjin Eurobulk Ltd, 2003–07; Member Advisory Board: J. Lauritzen A/S, Copenhagen, 1981–85; DFDS A/S, Copenhagen, 1981–85; Adviser, Tjaerborg (UK) Ltd, 1985–87. Mem. (part-time), British Transport Docks Bd, 1981–83; Chm., SITPRO, 1987–98; Dir, British Internat. Freight Assoc., 1989–; Chm., Danish-UK Chamber of Commerce, 1992–2001 (Pres., 2001–). Chairman: Friends of the World Maritime Univ., 1985–; Marine Soc., 1987–93 (Vice-Pres., 1993); Anglian Bd, BR, 1988–92; Trinitas Management Services Ltd (Trinity House), 1999–2006; Mem. Council, Missions to Seamen, subseq. Mission to Seafarers, 1981–. President: World Ship Soc., 1969, 1971, 1984–86, 2003–; CIT, 1981–82; Inst. of Freight Forwarders, 1984–86; National Waterways Transport Assoc., 1986–91; Inst. of Supervisory Management, 1989–92; Inst. of Chartered Shipbrokers, 1990–92 (Vice-Pres., 1988–90); Inst. of Export, 1995–2001 (Vice Pres., 1991–95); Harwich Lifeboat, RNLI, 1984–; Vice-President: British Maritime League, 1984–88; British Maritime Charitable Foundn, 1992–; Member: Baltic Exchange, 1973–; Greenwich Forum, 1982–; Internat and UK Cttees, Bureau Veritas, 1989–; Gen. Cttee, Lloyds Register, 1998–. Trustee, Nat Maritime Mus., 1993–98. Lectures: Grout, CIT, 1975; Wakeford Meml, Southampton Univ., 1993; Thomas Gray Meml, RSA, 1990. FRSA 1986. Hon. FNI 1985; Hon. FIFF 1986. Freeman, City of London, 1972; Liveryman and Mem., Court of Assts, Shipwrights Co.; Master, World Traders' Co., 1996–97; Associate Mem., Master Mariners' Co., 1998 Younger Brother, Trinity House, 1989. Seatrade Personality of the Year, Seatrade Orgn 2002. Knight Commander, Order of Dannebrog (Denmark), 1996. *Publication:* You and Your Ships (autobiog.), 2007. *Recreations:* golf, family, ships. *Address:* 115 Woodsford Square, W14 8DT. *T:* (020) 7602 0675; Summer Lawn, Dovercourt, Essex CO12 4EF *T:* (01255) 502981. *Clubs:* Brooks's, Hurlingham, Golfers; Fanlingerers (Hong Kong) Harwich & Dovercourt Golf, Royal Calcutta Golf; Holland Park Lawn Tennis.

DAVIS, John; *see* Davis, A. J.

DAVIS, Prof. John Allen, MD, FRCP, FRCPCH; Professor of Paediatrics, and Fellow of Peterhouse, University of Cambridge, 1979–88, now Professor Emeritus and Fellow Emeritus; *b* 6 Aug. 1923; *s* of Major H. E. Davis, MC, and Mrs M. W. Davis; *m* 1st, 1957 Madeleine Elizabeth Vinicombe Ashlin (author with D. Wallbridge of Boundary and Space: introduction to the work of D. W. Winnicott, 1981) (*d* 1991); three *s* two *d*; 2nd 2005, Prof. Ann-Louise Kinmonth, *qv*. *Educ:* Blundells Sch., Tiverton (Scholar); St Mary's Hosp. Med. Sch. (Scholar; MB, BS 1946; London Univ. Gold Medal); MSc Manchester 1967; MA Cantab 1979, MD 1988. FRCP 1967. Army Service, BAOR, 1947–49. House Physician: St Mary's Hosp., 1947; Gt Ormond St Hosp. for Sick Children, 1950 Registrar/Sen. Registrar, St Mary's Paediatric Unit and Home Care Scheme, 1951–57 Sen. Asst Resident, Children's Med. Centre, Boston, Mass, and Harvard Teaching Fellow 1953; Nuffield Res. Fellowship, Oxford, 1958–59; Sen. Lectr, Inst. of Child Health, and Reader, Hammersmith Hosp., 1960–67; Prof. of Paediatrics and Child Health, Victoria Univ. of Manchester, 1967–79. Second Vice Pres., RCP, 1986; Member: Assoc. of Physicians; Société française de pédiatrie; Hon. Member: BPA (former Chm., Academic Bd); Hungarian Acad. Paediatrics; Neonatal Soc.; Pres., Eur. Soc. for Pediatric Research 1984–85; Patron: Arts for Health, 1989–; Squiggle Foundn, 1993–. Greenwood Lectr Univ. of Exeter, 1981; Teale Lectr, RCP, 1990. Hon. FRSocMed 2006. Dawson Williams Prize, BMA, 1986; James Spence Medal, BPA, 1991; Hunterian Medal Hunterian Soc., 1995. *Publications:* Scientific Foundations of Paediatrics (ed and contrib.) 1974 (2nd edn 1981); Place of Birth, 1978; (ed jtly) Parent-Baby Attachment in Premature Infants, 1984; Mortalia and Other Things (verse), 2003; papers in various medical and scientific jls. *Recreations:* collecting and painting watercolours, gardening, reading, music *Address:* Four Mile House, 1 Cambridge Road, Great Shelford, Cambridge CB2 5JE.

DAVIS, Brig. John Anthony; Chairman, Commonwealth Society for the Deaf (Sound Seekers), 2006–June 2009 (Chief Executive, 1994–2003; Director, 2003–06; Trustee since 2003); *b* 2 Dec. 1936; *s* of late Horace Albert Davis and Jean Isobel Davis (*née* Marshall); *m* 1960, Deirdre Telford; two *d*. *Educ:* Hurstpierpoint Coll.; RMA, Sandhurst FCIS 1979. Commnd York and Lancaster Regt, 1958; served BAOR, Cyprus, Swaziland Aden, Kenya; Green Howards, 1968, tranf. RAPC, 1970; HQ 1 Armd Div., 1966–68 DAA&QMG, HQ Dhekelia Area, 1972–74; Staff Paymaster, HQ 2 Armd Div., 1978–80 Chief Instructor, RAPC Trng Centre, 1980–83; Comd Finance HQ 1 (BR) Corps 1983–86; Regtl Paymaster, Regtl Pay Office, Glasgow, 1986–88; Dep. Paymaster-in-Chief, 1988–89; Comd Finance HQ BAOR, 1989–92. Dep. Controller, SSAFA 1992–94. *Recreations:* photography, travel. *Address:* Pear Tree Cottage, 31 Basingbourne Road, Fleet, Hants GU52 6TG.

DAVIS, Sir John (Gilbert), 3rd Bt *cr* 1946; *b* 17 Aug. 1936; *s* of Sir Gilbert Davis, 2nd Bt, and of Kathleen, *d* of Sidney Deacon Ford; *S* father, 1973; *m* 1960, Elizabeth Margaret *d* of Robert Smith Turnbull; one *s* two *d*. *Educ:* Oundle School; Britannia RNC Dartmouth. RN, 1955–56. Joined Spicers Ltd, 1956; emigrated to Montreal, Canada 1957; joined Inter City Papers and progressed through the company until becoming Pres 1967; transf. to parent co., Abitibi-Price Inc., 1976 and held several exec. positions before retiring as Exec. Vice-Pres., 1989; co-developer, Greenfield de-inked pulp business Château Thierry, France. *Recreations:* golf, tennis, music, reading. *Heir:* *s* Richard Charles Davis, *b* 11 April 1970. *Address:* 3900 Yonge Street, Apt 603, Toronto, ON M4N 3N6 Canada. *T:* (416) 2224916. *Clubs:* Donalda, Rosedale Golf (Toronto).

DAVIS, John Horsley Russell, PhD; FBA 1988; Warden of All Souls College, Oxford, 1995–2008; *b* 9 Sept. 1938; *s* of William Russell Davis and Jean (*née* Horsley); *m* 1981, Dymphna Gerarda Hermans; three *s*. *Educ:* University Coll., Oxford (BA); Univ. of London (PhD). University of Kent, 1966–90: progressively, Lectr, Sen. Lectr, Reader, Social Anthropology; Prof., 1982–90; Prof. of Social Anthropology, and Fellow of All Souls College, Univ. of Oxford, 1990–95. Chm., European Assoc. of Social Anthropologists, 1993–94; Pres., Royal Anthropological Inst., 1997–2001. *Publications:* Land and Family in Pisticci, 1973; People of the Mediterranean, 1977; Libyan Politics: tribe and revolution, 1987; Exchange, 1992. *Recreations:* gardens, music. *Address:* All Souls College, Oxford OX1 4AL.

DAVIS, Joseph Graham, (Gray), Jr; Counsel, Loeb & Loeb LLP, Los Angeles, since 2004; Governor of California, 1999–2003; *b* New York City, 26 Dec. 1942; *s* of Joseph G. and Doris Davis; *m* 1983, Sharon Ryer. *Educ:* Stanford Univ. (BA Hist. *cum laude*); Columbia Univ. Law Sch. (JD). Served US Army, 1967–69 (Bronze Star for Meritorious Service, Vietnam War). Chief of Staff to Gov. of Calif., Edmund G. Brown Jr, 1975–81; Mem. for Los Angeles, Calif. State Assembly, 1983–87; Controller, State of Calif., 1987–95; Lt Gov., Calif., 1995–99. Mem., Calif. State Bar, 1969–. *Recreations:* golf, reading.

DAVIS, Dame Karlene (Cecile), DBE 2001; General Secretary, Royal College of Midwives, 1997–2008; *b* 10 Oct. 1946; *d* of late Herman Leiba and of Inez Leiba; *m* 1975, Victor Davis; one *s*. *Educ:* Titchfield Secondary Sch., Port Antonio, Jamaica; BEd Hons South Bank Poly. 1986; MA Inst. of Educn, London Univ. 1989. RN 1970; RM 1974; MTD 1980. SRN, 1967–70; SCM, 1973–74; Midwife Clinician, 1974–80; Midwife Tutor, Pembury Hosp., 1980–84; Sen. Midwife Teacher, Mayday Hosp., Croydon, 1984–87; Dir, Midwifery Educn, Olive Hayden Sch. of Midwifery, Guy's, St Thomas' and Lewisham Hosps, 1987–91; Regl Nurse, Midwifery Practice and Educn, SE Thames RHA, 1991–94; Dep. Gen. Sec., Royal Coll. of Midwives, 1994–97. Mem., Modernisation Bd overseeing implementation of NHS plan, 2000–04. Dir, WHO Collaborating Centre for Midwifery, 1997–. Pres., Internat. Confedn of Midwives, 2005–08. FRSocMed 1998; FFPH 2003. Hon. DSc: Brighton, 2001; Kingston, 2002; Greenwich, 2002; Nottingham, 2004; City, 2004; Wolverhampton, 2004. *Recreations:* theatre, reading, travel. *Address:* c/o Royal College of Midwives, 15 Mansfield Street, W1G 9NH. *T:* (020) 7312 3443.

DAVIS, Kenneth Joseph; Director of Children and Young People Services, London Borough of Bromley, 2006; *b* 19 March 1948; *s* of late Kenneth Sydney Joseph Davis and of Dorothy May Davis (now Addison); *m* 1970, Susan Mary Thompson; one *s*. *Educ:* Mark Hall Sch., Harlow; City of Portsmouth Coll. of Education (BEd Hons); Wolverhampton Poly. (DMS 1978); Inst. of Education, London Univ. (MA 1981). Computer operator, London & Manchester Assce Co., 1966–67; Asst Teacher, Brune Pk Comp. Sch., Gosport, 1971–73; Head of Physics, Darlaston Comp. Sch., Walsall, 1973–78; Professional Asst, E Sussex CC, 1978–80; Kent County Council: Asst Educn Officer, 1980–83; Divl Educn Officer, 1983–86; Area Educn Officer, 1986–89; Area Dir of Educn Services, 1989–96; Dir of Educn, 1996–2004, of Educn and Libraries, 2004–06, Bromley LBC. FCMI. *Recreations:* sailing, ski-ing. *Address:* 18 Admiralty Mews, The Strand, Walmer, Kent CT14 7AZ. *Club:* Downs Sailing.

DAVIS, Dom Leo Richard M.; *see* Maidlow Davis.

DAVIS, Leonard Andrew, (Leon), AO 2004; Chairman, Westpac Banking Corporation, 2000–07; *b* 3 April 1939; *s* of Leonard Harold Davis and Gladys Davis; *m* 1963, Annette Brakenridge; two *d*. *Educ:* S Australian Inst. of Technol. (Dip. in Primary Metallurgy). Man. Dir, Pacific Coal, 1984–89; Gp Exec., CRA Ltd, 1989–91; Mining Dir, RTZ Corp., 1991–94; Man. Dir and Chief Exec., CRA Ltd, 1994–95; Chief Operating Officer, RTZ-CRA, 1996; Chief Exec., 1997–2000, Dep. Chm., 2000–05, Rio Tinto. Dir, Codan Ltd, 2000–04. Bd Mem., Walter and Eliza Hall Inst. of Med. Res., 2001– (Pres., 2003–). Hon. DSc: Curtin Univ., 1998; Qld Univ., 2004; DUniv S Australia, 2005. Centenary Medal, Australia, 2003. *Address:* Box 627 PO, East Melbourne, Vic 3002, Australia. *Clubs:* Melbourne; Brisbane.

DAVIS, Madeline; *see* Gibson, M.

DAVIS, Prof. Mark Herbert Ainsworth; Professor of Mathematics, Imperial College London, since 2000; *b* 1 May 1945; *s* of Christopher A. Davis and Frances E. Davis (*née* Marsden); *m* 1988, Jessica I. C. Smith. *Educ:* Oundle Sch.; Clare College, Cambridge (BA 1966, MA 1970, ScD 1983); Univ. of California (PhD 1971). FSS 1985; FIMS 1994. Research Asst, Electronics Res. Lab., Univ. of California, Berkeley, 1969–71; Lectr, 1971–79, Reader, 1979–84, Prof. of System Theory, 1984–95, Imperial College, London; Hd of Res. and Product Develt, Tokyo-Mitsubishi Internat., 1995–99. Visiting appointments: Polish Acad. of Sciences, 1973; Harvard, 1974; MIT, 1978; Washington Univ., St Louis, 1979; ETH Zurich, 1984; Oslo Univ., 1991; Technical Univ., Vienna, 2000. Hon. FIA 2001. Editor, Stochastics and Stochastics Reports, 1978–95; Founding Co-Editor, Mathematical Finance, 1990–93. *Publications:* Linear Estimation and Stochastic Control, 1977, Russian edn 1984; (with R. B. Vinter) Stochastic Modelling and Control, 1985; Markov Models and Optimization, 1993; (with A. Etheridge) Louis Bachelier's Theory of Speculation: the origins of modern finance, 2006; jl articles on stochastic analysis, control theory, maths of finance. *Recreation:* classical music (violin and viola). *Address:* 11 Chartfield Avenue, SW15 6DT. *T:* (020) 8789 7677; Department of Mathematics, Imperial College London, SW7 2AZ. *T:* (020) 7594 8486.

DAVIS, Dr Michael; Hon. Director General, European Commission, Brussels, since 1989; *b* 9 June 1923; *s* of William James Davis and Rosaline Sarah (*née* May); *m* 1951, Helena Hobbs Campbell, *e d* of Roland and Catherine Campbell, Toronto. *Educ:* Exeter Univ. (BSc); Bristol Univ. (PhD). CEng, FIMMM; CPhys, FInstP. Radar Officer, Flagship, 4th Cruiser Sqdn, British Pacific Fleet, Lieut (Sp. Br.) RNVR, 1943–46 (despatches). Res. Fellow, Canadian Atomic Energy Project, Toronto Univ., 1949–51; Sen. Sci. Officer, Services Electronics Res. Lab., 1951–55; UKAEA: Commercial Dir and Techn. Adviser, 1956–73; Dir of Nuclear Energy, Other Primary Sources and Electricity, EC, 1973–81; Dir for Energy Saving, Alternative Sources of Energy, Electricity and Heat, EC, 1981–88. Chm., OECD Cttee on World Uranium Resources, 1965–73; Dir, NATO Advanced Study Inst., 1971; advised NZ Govt on Atomic Energy, 1967. Mem., Ecumenical Commn, Westminster Dio., 1966–73. McLaughlin Meml Lectr, Instn of Engineers of Ireland, 1977. *Publications:* (ed jtly) Uranium Prospecting Handbook, 1972; papers in various sci. jls. *Recreations:* sculpture, writing. *Club:* Oxford and Cambridge.

DAVIS, Brig. Sir Miles Garth H.; *see* Hunt-Davis.

DAVIS, Hon. Sir Nigel (Anthony Lamert), Kt 2001; **Hon. Mr Justice Davis;** a Judge of the High Court, Queen's Bench Division, since 2001; a Presiding Judge for Wales (formerly Wales and Chester Circuit), since 2005; *b* 10 March 1951; *s* of late Walter Patrick Carless Davis and Jane (*née* Lamert); *m* 1st, 1977, Sheila Ann Gillies Nickel (marr. diss. 1992); three *d*; 2nd, 2001, Emma Douglas. *Educ:* Charterhouse; University Coll., Oxford (BA 1973; MA 1983). Called to the Bar, Lincoln's Inn, 1975 (Hardwicke Schol., Kennedy Schol.; Bencher, 2000). Jun. Counsel to Crown (Chancery), 1985–92; QC 1992; an Asst Recorder, 1995–98; a Recorder, 1998–2001. Counsel to inquiry of Bd of Banking Supervision into collapse of Baring's Bank, 1995. *Address:* Royal Courts of Justice, Strand, WC2A 2LL. *Clubs:* MCC; Vincent's (Oxford).

See also Sir C. H. L. Davis, I. E. L. Davis.

DAVIS, Peter Anthony; Director General, National Lottery, 1993–98; *b* 10 Oct. 1941; *s* of late Stanley H. S. Davis and Betty H. Davis (*née* Back); *m* 1971, Vanessa C. E. Beale; two *s*. *Educ:* Winchester Coll.; Lincoln Coll., Oxford (MA Law). CA 1967. With Price Waterhouse, 1963–80, Gen. Audit Partner, 1974–80; Exec. Dep. Chm., Harris Queensway PLC, 1980–87; Sturge Holdings PLC: Gp Finance Dir, 1988–93; Dep. Chm., 1991–93; Abbey National PLC: non-exec. Dir, 1982–94; Dep. Chm., 1988–94; Chm., Audit Cttee, 1988–93, and Scottish Adv. Bd, 1989–92. Non-executive Director: Horne Bros, 1984–87; Symphony Gp, 1984–87; Avis Europe, 1987–89; Provident Financial, 1994–2000; Proned Holdings, 1992–94; Equitable Life Assurance Soc., 1995–2001; Boosey & Hawkes, 1998–2003; non-exec. Chm., Ascent Gp, 2001–. Institute of Chartered Accountants in England and Wales: Council Mem., 1989–95; Chm., Bd for Chartered Accountants in Business, 1991–94; Mem., Senate, 1989–99. MInstD 1993. *Recreations:* fishing, tennis, football, theatre. *Address:* 29 Arthur Road, SW19 7DN. *Club:* Hurlingham.

DAVIS, Sir Peter (John), Kt 1997; Chairman, Marie Curie Cancer Care, since 2006; *b* 23 Dec. 1941; *s* of John Stephen Davis and Adriaantje de Baat; *m* 1968, Susan Hillman; two *s* one *d*. *Educ:* Shrewsbury Sch.; Grad. Inst. of Marketing (Drexler Travelling Schol., 1961). Management trainee and sales, Ditchburn Orgn, 1959–65; marketing and sales posts, General Foods Ltd, Banbury, 1965–72; Fitch Lovell Ltd, 1973–76: Marketing Dir, Key Markets; Man. Dir, Key Markets and David Greig; J. Sainsbury, 1976–86: Marketing Dir, 1977; Asst Man. Dir, 1979; Dep. Chief Exec., 1986, Chief Exec., 1986–92, Chm., 1990–94, Reed Internat.; Chief Exec., 1993, Chm., 1993–94, Reed Elsevier; Gp Chief Exec., Prudential Corp., 1995–2000; Chief Exec., 2000–04, Chm., 2004, J. Sainsbury plc. Director: Boots Co. PLC, 1991–2000; UBS AG, 2001–07; Mem., Adv. Bd, Permira Advisers Ltd, 2005–. Chairman: Basic Skills Agency (formerly Adult Literacy and Basic Skills Unit), 1989–97; Nat. Adv. Council for Educn and Training Targets, 1993–97; BITC, 1997–2002 (Dep. Chm., 1991–97); Welfare to Work New Deal Task Force, 1997–2000. Vice Pres., Chartered Inst. of Marketing, 1991–. Dir, Royal Opera House, 1999–2005 (Trustee, 1994–2005); Trustee, V&A Mus., 1994–97. Vice Pres. and Mem. Council, Bangor Univ. Governor: Duncombe Sch., Hertford, 1976–2005; Queenswood Sch., 1993–95. FRSA. Hon. LLD Exon, 2000. *Recreations:* sailing, reading, opera, wine. *Clubs:* Garrick, Royal Automobile; Trearddur Bay Sailing (Cdre, 1982–84).

See also C. V. Gipps.

DAVIS, Philip Michael; transport specialist and consumer/community representative; Board Member, Commission for Integrated Transport, since 2007; *b* 15 May 1954; *o s* of late Ronald Davis and of Joan Davis; *m* 1977, Susan Jean Wolton; one *s* two *d*. *Educ:* Holly Lodge High Sch.; Southampton Univ. (BA Jt Hons Mod. Hist./Politics); Warwick Univ. (Master Ind. Relns). Full-time Officer, GMB, 1979–2000. Member (Lab): Wrekin DC, 1979–97 (Chm., Planning and Envmt Cttee, 1991–97); Telford and Wrekin Council, 1997–2006 (Leader, 2000–04). Chairman: W Midlands Constitnl Convention, 1999–; W Midlands Regl Assembly, 2001–03; Sen. Vice-Chm., W Midlands LGA, 2003–05 (Vice-Chm., 2000–01); Mem., LGA Regeneration Bd, 2004–06. Chairman: W Midlands Low Pay Unit, 1989–2000; W Midlands Regl Mus Council, 1995–2000; Midlands Rail Passengers' Cttee, 1999–2005; Campaign for English Regions, 2003–; Founder Chair, TravelWatch Midlands West, 2005–; Mem., Nat. Rail Passengers' Council, 1999– (Mem., Passenger Focus Bd, 2005–); Public Mem., Network Rail, 2002–06; Network Dir, Regl Action W Midlands, 2006–07. Comr, English Heritage, 1999–2002. Pres., Eurotowns, 2001–04. Founder Chm., UK World Heritage Forum, 1995–2005 (Hon. Pres., 2005–07); Trustee, Ironbridge Mus. Trust, 1982– (Mem. Bd, 1982–2005). Contested (Lab): Ludlow, 1983; W Midlands, EP, 1999. *Address:* 208 Islington Gates, Fleet Street, Birmingham B3 1JH.

DAVIS, Richard Cuthbert Tolly M., (Dom Leo Richard M.); *see* Maidlow Davis.

DAVIS, (Richard) Simon; His Honour Judge Simon Davis; a Circuit Judge, since 2004; *b* 29 July 1956; *s* of Peter Richard Davis and Evelyn Davis; *m* 1980, Caroline Jane Neal; two *s* one *d*. *Educ:* Wellington Sch., Somerset; Univ. of Leicester (LLB Hons). Called to the Bar, Inner Temple, 1978, Bencher, 2007; a Recorder, 1998–2004. *Recreations:* sport, theatre, travel. *Address:* Inner London Crown Court, Sessions House, Newington Causeway, SE1 6AZ. *T:* (020) 7234 3100. *Club:* Lansdowne.

DAVIS, Air Vice-Marshal Robert Leslie, CB 1984; RAF, retired 1983; *b* 22 March 1930; *s* of Sidney and Florence Davis; *m* 1956, Diana, *d* of Edward William Bryant; one *s* one *d*. *Educ:* Wolsingham Grammar Sch., Co. Durham; Bede Sch. Collegiate, Sunderland, Co. Durham; RAF Coll., Cranwell. Commnd, 1952; served fighter units, exchange posting, USAF, Staff Coll., OR and Ops appts, MoD, DS Staff Coll., 1953–69; comd No 19 Sqdn, 1970–72; Dep. Dir Ops Air Defence, MoD, 1972–75; comd RAF Leuchars, 1975–77; Comdr RAF Staff, and Air Attaché, British Defence Staff, Washington, DC, 1977–80; Comdr, British Forces Cyprus, and Administrator, Sovereign Base Areas, Cyprus, 1980–83, retired. Man. Dir, Bodenseewerk Geratetechnik/British Aerospace GmbH, 1983–86, retd. Chm. Durham Br., SSAFA Forces Help, 1993–2002. *Recreations:* golf, antiques, music. *Address:* High Garth Farm, Witton-le-Wear, Bishop Auckland, Co. Durham DL14 0BL.

DAVIS, Prof. Roger John, PhD; FRS 2002; Professor of Molecular Medicine and H. Arthur Smith Professor of Cancer Research, University of Massachusetts Medical School; Investigator, Howard Hughes Medical Institute. *Educ:* Queens' Coll., Cambridge (BA 1979; PhD 1983). Damon Runyon-Walter Winchell Cancer Fund Fellow, Dept of Biochem. and Molecular Biol., Univ. of Massachusetts Med. Sch. *Address:* Program in Molecular Medicine, University of Massachusetts Medical School, 373 Plantation Street, Suite 309, Worcester, MA 01605, USA.

DAVIS, Simon; *see* Davis, R. S.

DAVIS, Prof. Stanley Stewart, CChem, FRSC; Lord Trent Professor of Pharmacy, Nottingham University, 1975–2003, now Emeritus Professor; *b* 17 Dec. 1942; *s* of William Stanley and Joan Davis; *m* 1984, Lisbeth Illum; three *s*. *Educ:* Warwick Sch.; London Univ. (BPharm, PhD, DSc). FRPharmS. Lecturer, London Univ., 1976–80; Sen. Lectr, Aston Univ., 1970–75. Fulbright Scholar, Univ. of Kansas, 1978–79; various periods as visiting scientist to pharmaceutical industry. Founder: Danbiosyst (UK) Ltd; Pharmaceutical Profiles Ltd. Mem., Medicines Commn, 1994–97. *Publications:* (co-ed) Radionuclide Imaging in Drug Research, 1982; (co-ed) Microspheres and Drug Therapy, 1984; (co-ed) Site Specific Drug Delivery, 1986; (co-ed) Polymers in Controlled Drug

Delivery, 1988; (co-ed) Drug Delivery to the Gastrointestinal Tract, 1989; (co-ed) Pharmaceutical Application of Cell and Tissue Culture to Drug Transport, 1991; ed jtly over 700 research pubns in various scientific jls. *Recreations:* tennis, ski-ing, painting. *Address:* 19 Cavendish Crescent North, The Park, Nottingham NG7 1BA. *T:* (0115) 948 1866; University of Nottingham, University Park, Nottingham NG7 2RD. *T:* (0115) 951 5121.

DAVIS, Steve, OBE 2000 (MBE 1988); snooker player; *b* 22 Aug. 1957; *s* of Harry George Davis and Jean Catherine Davis; *m* 1990, Judy Greig; two *s. Educ:* Alexander McLeod Primary School and Abbey Wood School, London. Became professional snooker player, 1978; has won numerous championships in UK and abroad; major titles include: UK Professional Champion, 1980, 1981, 1984, 1985, 1986, 1987; Masters Champion, 1981, 1982, 1988, 1997; International Champion, 1981, 1983, 1984, 1987, 1988, 1989; World Professional Champion, 1981, 1983, 1984, 1987, 1988, 1989. BBC Sports Personality of the Year, 1988. Mem. Bd, World Professional Billiards and Snooker Assoc., 1993–. *Publications:* Steve Davis, World Champion, 1981; Frame and Fortune, 1982; Successful Snooker, 1982; How to be Really Interesting, 1988. *Recreations:* chess, keep fit, listening to records (jazz/soul), Tom Sharpe books. *Address:* Mascalls, Mascalls Lane, Brentwood, Essex CM14 5LJ. *T:* (01277) 359900. *Club:* Matchroom (Romford).

DAVIS, Susan; *see* Gubbay, S.

DAVIS, Rt Hon. Terence Anthony Gordon, (Terry); PC 1999; Secretary General, Council of Europe, since 2004; *b* 5 Jan. 1938; *s* of Gordon Davis and Gladys (*née* Avery), Stourbridge, West Midlands; *m* 1963, Anne, *d* of F. B. Cooper, Newton-le-Willows, Lancs; one *s* one *d. Educ:* King Edward VI Grammar Sch., Stourbridge, Worcestershire; University Coll. London (LLB; Fellow 2007); Univ. of Michigan, USA (MBA). Company Executive, 1962–71. Motor Industry Manager, 1974–79. Joined Labour Party, 1965; contested (Lab): Bromsgrove, 1970, Feb. and Oct. 1974; Birmingham, Stechford, March 1977. MP (Lab): Bromsgrove, May 1971–Feb. 1974; Birmingham, Stechford, 1979–83; Birmingham, Hodge Hill, 1983–2004. Opposition Whip, 1979–80; opposition spokesman: on the health service and social services, 1980–83; on Treasury and economic affairs, 1983–86; on industry, 1986–87. Member: Public Accounts Cttee, 1987–94; Adv. Council on Public Records, 1989–94. Chm., Birmingham Lab. MPs, 1992–97. Leader: British delegn to WEU Assembly, 1997–2002 (Mem., 1992–2004; Leader, Lab. delegn, 1995–97; Pres., Socialist Gp, 1996–99; Vice Pres. Assembly, 1997–2001); British delegn to Council of Europe Assembly, 1997–2002 (Mem., 1992–2004; Leader, Labour delegn, 1995–97; Chairman: Econ. Affairs and Develt Cttee, 1995–98; Pol Affairs Cttee, 2000–02; Vice Pres. Assembly, 1997–2002; Pres., Socialist Gp, 2002–04); British Delegn to OSCE Assembly, 2002–04 (Mem., 1997–2004). Mem., MSF. Member, Yeovil Rural District Council, 1967–68. *Address:* Council of Europe, Avenue de l'Europe, 67075 Strasbourg, France.

DAVIS, Trevor Fraser C.; *see* Campbell Davis.

DAVIS, William; author, publisher, and columnist; Chairman, Headway Publishing, 1999–2004; *b* 6 March 1933; *m* 1967, Sylvette Jouclas. *Educ:* City of London Coll. On staff of Financial Times, 1954–59; Editor, Investor's Guide, 1959–60; City Editor, Evening Standard, 1960–65 (with one year's break as City Editor, Sunday Express); Financial Editor, The Guardian, 1965–68; Editor, Punch, 1968–77; Editor-in-Chief: High Life, 1973–97; Financial Weekly, 1977–80. Presenter: Money Programme, BBC TV, 1967–69; World at One, BBC Radio, 1972–79. Chairman: Headway Publications, 1977–90; BTA, 1990–93; English Tourist Bd, 1990–93; Allied Leisure, 1993–94; Premier Magazines, 1992–99; Director: Fleet Publishing International, Morgan-Grampian, and Fleet Holdings, 1977–80; Thomas Cook, 1988–98; British Invisibles, 1990–93. Editor and Publr, Private Patient, 2000–02. Mem., Develt Council, Royal Nat. Theatre, 1990–92. Knight, Order of Merit of Italian Republic. *Publications:* Three Years Hard Labour: the road to devaluation, 1968; Merger Mania, 1970; Money Talks, 1972; Have Expenses, Will Travel, 1975; It's No Sin to be Rich, 1976; (ed) The Best of Everything, 1980; Money in the 1980s, 1981; The Rich: a study of the species, 1982; Fantasy: a practical guide to escapism, 1984; The Corporate Infighter's Handbook, 1984; (ed) The World's Best Business Hotels, 1985; The Supersalesman's Handbook, 1986; The Innovators, 1987; Children of the Rich, 1989; The Lucky Generation: a positive view of the 21st century, 1995; Great Myths of Business, 1997; Business Life: Wit and Wisdom, a treasury of international quotations, 1998; The Alien: an autobiography, 2003; How to be British, 2005; The Rich: a new study of the species, 2006. *Recreations:* travel, tennis, lunch. *T:* (020) 7730 1373. *Club:* Garrick.

DAVIS, William Easthope; QC 1998; **His Honour Judge William Davis;** a Circuit Judge, since 2008; *b* 20 June 1954; *s* of Prof. Ralph Davis, FBA and Dorothy Davis (*née* Easthope); *m* 1990, Susan Virginia Smith; one *s* one *d. Educ:* Wyggeston Boys' Sch., Leicester; Queen Mary Coll., London (LLB 1974). Called to the Bar, Inner Temple, 1975, Bencher, 2007; Recorder, 1995–2008. Asst Treas., Midland and Oxford Circuit, 1992–99. *Recreations:* Rosie and Ralph, writing and performing in sketches, wine. *Address:* Birmingham Crown Court, Queen Elizabeth II Law Courts, 1 Newton Street, Birmingham B4 7NA.

DAVIS, Hon. William Grenville; PC (Can.) 1982; CC (Canada) 1986; QC (Can.); barrister and solicitor; Counsel to Torys LLP, Toronto; Member of the Provincial Parliament, Ontario, 1959–85; Premier of Ontario, Canada, and President of the Council, Ontario, 1971–85; Leader, Progressive Conservative Party, 1971–85; *b* Brampton, Ont., 30 July 1929; *s* of Albert Grenville Davis and Vera M. Davis (*née* Hewetson); *m* 1st, 1953, Helen MacPhee (*d* 1962), *d* of Neil MacPhee, Windsor, Ontario; 2nd, 1963, Kathleen Louise, *d* of Dr R. P. Mackay, California; two *s* three *d. Educ:* Brampton High Sch.; University Coll., Univ. of Toronto (BA); Osgoode Hall Law Sch. (grad. 1955). Called to Bar of Ontario, 1955; practised gen. law, Brampton, 1955–59. Elected Mem. (C) Provincial Parlt (MPP) for Peel Riding, 1959, 1963, Peel North Riding, 1967, 1971, Brampton Riding, 1975, 1977, 1981. Minister of Educn, 1962–71; also Minister of Univ. Affairs, 1964–71; Special Envoy on Acid Rain, apptd by Prime Minister of Canada, 1985–86. Director: First American Title Insurance Co.; Magellan Aerospace Corp.; BPO Properties Ltd; First American Financial Corp.; Home Capital Gp Inc. A Freemason. Chevalier, Légion d'Honneur. Holds hon. doctorates in Law from eight Ontario Univs: Waterloo Lutheran, W Ontario, Toronto, McMaster, Queen's, Windsor; Hon. Graduate: Albert Einstein Coll. of Med.; Yeshiva Univ. of NY; NUI; Ottawa; Tel Aviv. Amer. Transit Assoc. Man of the Year, 1973. *Publications:* Education in Ontario, 1965; The Government of Ontario and the Universities of the Province (Frank Gerstein Lectures, York Univ.), 1966; Building an Educated Society 1816–1966, 1966; Education for New Times, 1967. *Address:* 61 Main Street South, Brampton, ON L6Y 1M9, Canada; Torys LLP, Suite 3000, TD/Waterhouse Tower, PO Box 270, Toronto-Dominion Centre, Toronto, ON M5K IN2, Canada. *Clubs:* Kiwanis, Shriners, Masons, Albany (Ont.).

DAVIS, William Herbert, BSc; CEng, FIMechE; former executive with BL and Land Rover Ltd, retired 1983; *b* 27 July 1919; *s* of William and Dora Davis; *m* 1945, Barbara Mary Joan (*née* Sommerfield); one *d. Educ:* Waverley Grammar Sch.; Univ. of Aston in Birmingham (BSc). Army Service, France, Belgium, Egypt, Libya, Iraq, Cyprus and Italy, 1939–46. Austin Motor Co.: Engr Apprentice, 1935–39; Mech. Engr and Section Leader, Works Engrs, 1946–51; Supt Engr, 1951; Asst Production Manager, 1954; Production Manager, 1956; Dir and Gen. Works Manager, 1958. British Motor Corp. Ltd: Dir of Production, 1960; Dep. Managing Dir (Manufacture and Supply), 1961; Dep. Managing Dir, British Leyland (Austin-Morris Ltd), 1968; Chairman and Chief Executive, Triumph Motor Co. Ltd, 1969; Managing Dir, Rover Triumph BLUK Ltd, 1972; Dir (Manufacture), British Leyland Motor Corporation, 1973; Dir, Military Contracts and Govt Affairs, Leyland Cars, 1976–81; Consultant, BL and Land Rover Ltd, 1981–83; Dir, Land Rover Santana (Spain), 1976–83. Member: Engrg ITB, 1976–81; CBI Regl Council, 1978–83. Gov., Solihull Coll. of Technol., 1978–87. FIIM, SME(USA). Silver Jubilee Medal, 1977. *Recreations:* motoring, photography; interests in amateur boxing. *Address:* The Courtyard House, Marley, South Brent, Devon TQ10 9JX.

DAVIS-GOFF, Sir Robert William; *see* Goff.

DAVIS-WHITE, Malcolm; QC 2003; *b* 18 Sept. 1960; *m* 1989, Sarah O'Hara; two *s* one *d. Educ:* Hertford Coll., Oxford (BCL; MA). Called to the Bar, Middle Temple, 1984; JC to the Crown (A Panel), 1994. *Publications:* (with Adrian Walters) Directors' Disqualification and Bankruptcy Restrictions: law and practice, 1999, 2nd edn 2004; (contrib.) Atkin's Court Forms, vol. 9 Companies General, 1999, 2004, vol. 9 (2)-(4) Companies (Insolvency), 2000, 2006; (contrib.) Annotated Companies Acts, 2007. *Recreations:* walking, gardening, sailing, opera. *Address:* 4 Stone Buildings, Lincoln's Inn, WC2A 3XT. *T:* (020) 7242 5524, *Fax:* (020) 7831 7907; *e-mail:* clerks@4stonebuildings.com.

DAVISON, Prof. Alan, PhD; FRS 2000; Professor of Inorganic Chemistry, Massachusetts Institute of Technology, 1974–2005, now Emeritus; *b* 24 March 1936. *Educ:* UC, Swansea; Imperial Coll. (DIC). Lectr in Chemistry, Harvard Univ., 1962–64; Asst Prof., 1964–67, Associate Prof., 1967–74, MIT. Alfred P. Sloan Foundn Fellow, 1967–69. *Publications:* articles in learned jls. *Address:* Department of Chemistry, Massachusetts Institute of Technology, 77 Massachusetts Avenue, Cambridge, MA 02139–4307, USA.

DAVISON, Alan John, EdD; Headteacher, Dame Alice Owen's School, since 2005; *b* 9 April 1956; *s* of Sydney and Margaret Davison; *m* 2002, Kholoud Porter; one *s* one *d*, and two step *s. Educ:* Durham Inst. of Educn (Cert Ed 1977); Univ. of Leicester (MBA 1994; EdD 1998). Headteacher: Notley High Sch., 1993–97; Mill Hill County High Sch., 1997–2003; Strategic Dir, London Leadership Strategy, London Challenge, 2003–05; Lectr (pt-time), Univ. of Leicester, 1999–2002. Advisor to Department for Education and Skills: Educn Action Zones, 1999; Teacher Threshold, 2000–02; Transforming Sch Workforce Pathfinder Proj., 2002–04. *Publication:* (contrib.) Raising Boys' Achievement in Schools, 1998. *Recreations:* ski-ing, theatre, cinema, travel. *Address:* Dame Alice Owen's School, Dugdale Hill Lane, Potters Bar, Herts EN6 2DU; *e-mail:* head@damealiceowens.herts.sch.uk.

DAVISON, Air Vice Marshal Christopher, MBE 1978; Director, RAF Sports Board, since 2001; *b* 26 Sept. 1947; *s* of Dixon and Kathleen Lillian Davison; *m* 1971, Rosemary Stamper; one *s* one *d. Educ:* Tynemouth Grammar Technical Sch.; Borough Road Coll. London. Joined RAF Phys. Educn Br., 1970; RAF Halton, Inst. of Aviation Medicine Farnborough and RAF Hereford, 1970–76; Comd, RAF Outdoor Activity Centre Scotland, 1976–78; Sqn Leader, 1978; HQ Strike Comd, 1979–80; Chief Instr, RAF Sch of Physical Trng, RAF Cosford, 1981–82; RAF Staff Coll., Bracknell, 1983; PSO to Controller Aircraft, MoD, 1984–85; Wing Comdr, 1985; OC Admin Wing, RAF Wattisham, 1985–87; Dep. Comdr, Support Gp, HQ AFCENT, 1987–89; Gp Capt. 1989; Admin Trng, HQ Support Comd, 1989–91; OC RAF Swinderby, 1991–93; Head of Physical Educn Specialisation, RAF, 1994; Air Cdre, 1994; AOA and AOC Directly Administered Units, RAF HQ PTC, 1994–96 and 2000–01; Dir Personnel (Airmen) and Controller Reserve Forces, RAF, 1997–99; retd 2001. *Recreations:* golf, ski-ing, Rugby. *Address:* c/o National Westminster Bank plc, 225 High Street, Lincoln LN2 1AZ. *Club:* Royal Air Force.

DAVISON, Ian Frederic Hay, CBE 2003; Chairman, Ruffer LLP, since 2002; Managing Partner, Arthur Andersen & Co., 1966–82; Deputy Chairman and Chief Executive, Lloyd's of London, 1983–86; *b* 30 June 1931; *s* of late Eric Hay Davison, FCA, and Ine Davison; *m* 1955, Maureen Patricia Blacker; one *s* two *d. Educ:* Dulwich Coll.; LSE (BScEcon; Hon. Fellow, 2004); Univ. of Mich. ACA 1956, FCA 1966. Chairman: Crédit Lyonnais Capital Markets, 1988–91; Storehouse plc, 1990–96; NMB Group plc, 1992–2000; McDonnell Information Systems, later Northgate plc, 1993–99; Director: Midland Bank, 1986–88; Newspaper Publishing, 1986–94 (Chm., 1993–94); Chloride plc, 1988–98; Cadbury-Schweppes plc, 1990–2000; CIBA plc, 1991–96. Mem. Council, ICA, 1975–99; Chm., Accounting Standards Cttee, 1982–84. Mem., NEDC for Bld Industry, 1971–77; Member: Price Commn, 1977–79; Audit Commn, 1983–85. Chairman: EDC for Food and Drink Manufg Industry, 1981–83; Securities Review Cttee, Hong Kong, 1987–88. Dept of Trade Inspector, London Capital Securities, 1975–77; Inspector, Grays Building Soc., 1978–79. Chm., Regulatory Council, Dubai FSA, 2002–04. Trustee: V&A Museum, 1984–93 (Chm., V&A Enterprises Ltd, 1993–2002); Holburne Mus., Bath, 2005–; Dir, Royal Opera House, 1984–86; Chairman: Monteverdi Trust, 1979–84; Sadler's Wells Foundation, 1995–2003. Pres., Nat. Council for One Parent Families, 1991–2004; Chairman: SANE, 2000–02; Railway Heritage Cttee, 2000–04. Council Mem., Nat. Trust, 1992–94. Governor, LSE, 1982–2007; Pro-Provost and Chm. Council, RCA, 1996–2007. Chairman: Wells Cathedral Trust, 1997–; Council, Exeter Cathedral, 2002–. Councillor and Alderman, London Bor. of Greenwich, 1961–73. Hon. DSc Aston, 1985; Hon. LLD Bath, 1998. *Publication:* A View of the Room: Lloyd's change and disclosure, 1987. *Recreations:* opera, theatre, music, gardening under supervision, bell-ringing. *Address:* 13 Catharine Place, Bath BA1 2PR. *Clubs:* Athenæum, Beefsteak, MCC; Bath and County.

DAVISON, (John) Stanley, OBE 1981; Secretary General, World Federation of Scientific Workers, 1987–2001; *b* 26 Sept. 1922; *s* of George Davison and Rosie Davison (*née* Segger); *m* 1959, Margaret Smith; two *s* one *d. Educ:* Timothy Hackworth Sch., Shildon, Co. Durham; Shildon Senior Boys' Sch.; St Helens Tech. Coll. RAF, 1941–46; Civil Servant (Technical), 1946–52; Regional Organiser, 1953–60, Dep. Gen. Sec., 1960–68, Assoc. of Scientific Workers; Dep. Gen. Sec., ASTMS, 1968–87. Member, Engineering Council, 1986–94; Heavy Electrical NEDO, 1976–87; Exec. Council, CSEU, 1981–88; Exec. Council, Internat. Metalworkers' Fedn, 1986–87; All Party Energy Cttee, 1982–88; Chm., Trade Union Side, GEC NJC, 1965–87; Governor, Aston CAT, 1955–60; Mem. Council, Brunel Univ., 1989–2000. MUniv Brunel, 200[illegible] *Recreations:* science policy, amateur dramatics, bridge, caravanning. *Address:* 1 Hazel Close, Shefford, Beds SG17 5YE. *Clubs:* Players' Theatre; Addington Theatre Group (Hon. Mem.); Caravan.

DAVISON, Peter; *see* Moffett, P.

DAVISON, Rt Hon. Sir Ronald (Keith), GBE 1978; CMG 1975; PC 1978; Chief Justice of New Zealand, 1978–89; *b* 16 Nov. 1920; *s* of Joseph James Davison and Florence May Davison; *m* 1948, Jacqueline May Carr; one *s* one *d* (and one *s* decd). *Educ:* Auckland Univ. (LLB). Admitted as barrister and solicitor, 1948; QC (NZ) 1963. Chairman: Environmental Council, 1969–74; Legal Aid Bd, 1969–78; Member: Council, Auckland Dist Law Soc., 1960–65 (Pres., 1965–66); Council, NZ Law Soc., 1963–66; Auckland Electric Power Bd (13 yrs); Aircrew Indust. Tribunal, 1970–78. Chm., Montana Wines Ltd, 1971–78; Dir, NZ Insurance Co. Ltd, 1975–78. *Recreations:* golf, fishing, bowls. *Address:* 1 Lichfield Road, Parnell, Auckland, New Zealand. *T:* (9) 3020493. *Clubs:* Wellington; Northern (Auckland, NZ).

DAVISON, Stanley; *see* Davison, J. S.

DAVISON, Timothy Paul; Chief Executive, NHS Lanarkshire, since 2005; *b* 4 June 1961; *s* of late John Paul Davison and of Patricia Davison; *m* 1984, Hilary Williamson Gillick (separated 2001); one *s*. *Educ:* Univ. of Stirling (BA Hons Hist.); Univ. of Glasgow (MBA, MPH); DipHSM. NHS nat. mgt trainee, 1983–84; Gen. Services Manager, Stirling Royal Infirmary, 1984–86; Asst Unit Administrator, Royal Edinburgh Hosp., 1986–87; Patient Services Manager, Lothian Mental Health Unit, 1987–88; Hosp. Administrator, Glasgow Royal Infirmary, 1988–90; Sector Gen. Manager, Gartnavel Royal Hosp., 1990–91; Unit Gen. Manager, Gtr Glasgow Community and Mental Health Unit (formerly Gtr Glasgow Mental Health Unit), 1991–94; Chief Executive: Gtr Glasgow Community and Mental Health Services NHS Trust, 1994–99; Gtr Glasgow Primary Care NHS Trust, 1999–2002; NHS Gtr Glasgow, N Glasgow Univ. Hosps NHS Trust, subseq. N Glasgow Univ. Hosps Div., 2002–05. Non-exec. Dir, Clinical Standards Bd for Scotland, 1999–2002. Mem. Ct, UWS, 2007–. *Recreations:* tennis, military and political history, motor-cycling. *Address:* NHS Lanarkshire, 14 Beckford Street, Hamilton, S Lanarkshire ML3 0TA.

d'AVRAY, Prof. David Levesley, DPhil; FBA 2005; Professor of History, University College London, since 1996; *b* 3 Feb. 1952; *s* of Hector Anthony d'Avray and Audrey Sabina d'Avray (*née* Atkinson); *m* 1985, Julia Caroline Walworth. *Educ:* St John's Coll., Cambridge (BA 1973, MA 1977); DPhil Oxon 1977. Lectr, 1977–93, Reader, 1993–96, UCL. *Publications:* The Preaching of the Friars, 1985; Death and the Prince, 1994; Medieval Marriage Sermons, 2001; Medieval Marriage, 2005. *Recreations:* alpine walking, domestic discussion of television. *Address:* Department of History, University College London, Gower Street, WC1E 6BJ; *e-mail:* ucradav@ucl.ac.uk.

DAVSON, Sir George Trenchard Simon, 4th Bt *cr* 1927, of Berbice, British Guiana; *b* 5 June 1964; *s* of Sir Christopher Davson, 3rd Bt and of Evelyn Mary Davson (née Wardrop); *S* father, 2004; *m* 1985, Joanna (marr. diss. 1996), *e d* of Rev. Dr James Bentley; one *s* one *d*. *Heir:* *s* James Davson, *b* 23 Dec. 1990.

DAVY, Margaret Ruth; *see* Bowron, M. R.

DAW, Roger Keith; Director, Policy, Crown Prosecution Service, since 2007; *b* 10 March 1959; *s* of Owen William Albert Daw and late Mavis Hilda Daw (*née* Elson); partner, Courtney David Spence. *Educ:* Tiffin Sch., Kingston-upon-Thames; Birmingham Univ. (LLB). Called to the Bar, Middle Temple, 1982. Chief Crown Prosecutor, Hants and IoW, 1999–2003; Speaker's Sec., H of C, 2003–04; Prog. Dir, Police Reform, CPS, 2005–07. *Recreations:* genealogy, theatre. *Address:* Crown Prosecution Service Headquarters, 50 Ludgate Hill, EC4M 7EX.

DAWANINCURA, Sir John (Norbert), Kt 1999; OBE 1992; Secretary General, Papua New Guinea Sports Federation, since 1994 (Vice President, 1983); *b* 25 May 1945; *s* of Stephen Joe Frank Dawanincura and Giro Paulo; *m* Lenah; one *s* two *d*. *Educ:* Chevalier Coll., NSW. Dist Valuer, W Highlands Province, Valuer Gen.'s Office; Manager, E Highlands Province, Bureau of Mgt Services; Graemme Dunnage Real Estate, 1977–78; Partner, Property Mgt and Maintenance, 1979–85. Rugby Football Union Player, Papua New Guinea team, 1965–70; Gen. Team Manager, PNG Contingents, 1981–86; Chief of PNG Delegation: Olympic Games, 1984–; Commonwealth Games, 1982–97, 1999–; S Pacific Games, 1983–98 (Chm. of Sports, Organising Cttee, Port Moresby, 1991); Mini S Pacific Games, 1981–; Mem., 1984–97, Vice Pres., 1993–97, 2001–04, Oceania Nat. Olympic Cttee (Chm., Develt Commn, 1993–97); Alternate Mem., PNG Sports Commn, 1992–; Schol. Mem., Mgt Cttee, Oceania Olympic Trng Coll., 1993–97; Mem. Mgt Cttee, Australia S Pacific 2000 Prog., 1995–97; Mem., Assoc. of Nat. Olympic Cttees, 1993–97; Deleg., 1981–86, Bd Mem., 1987–91, Pres. and Chm., 1995–99, S Pacific Games Council; Mem., Nat. Coaching Council, 1988–. Sir Buri Kidu Heart Inst., 1996–. *Recreations:* golf, circuit training, fishing. *Address:* PO Box 467, Boroko, NCD, Papua New Guinea. *T:* 3251411, 3251449. *Clubs:* Carbine, Golf, Yacht (Papua New Guinea).

DAWBARN, Sir Simon (Yelverton), KCVO 1980; CMG 1976; HM Diplomatic Service, retired; *b* 16 Sept. 1923; *s* of Frederic Dawbarn and Maud Louise Mansell; *m* 1948, Shelby Montgomery Parker; one *s* two *d*. *Educ:* Oundle Sch.; Corpus Christi Coll., Cambridge. Served in HM Forces (Reconnaissance Corps), 1942–45. Reckitt & Colman (Overseas), 1948–49. Joined Foreign Service, 1949. Foreign Office, 1949–53; Brussels, 1953; Prague, 1955; Tehran, 1957; seconded to HM Treasury, 1959; Foreign Office, 1961; Algiers, 1965; Athens, 1968; FCO, 1971–75. Head of W African Dept and concurrently non-resident Ambassador to Chad, 1973–75; Consul-General, Montreal, 1975–78; Ambassador to Morocco, 1978–82. *Address:* 44 Canonbury Park North, N1 2JT. *T:* (020) 7226 0659.

DAWE, Howard Carlton; Chairman, Bellway plc, since 1999; *b* 7 April 1944; *s* of Sydney Carlton Dawe and Dorothy Dawe (*née* Cooke); *m* 1968, Kathryn Jennifer Adcock; one *s* two *d*. *Educ:* Newlands Sch., Newcastle; Durham Cathedral Choir Sch.; Newcastle Royal Grammar Sch.; various tech. colls. MCIOB 1969. Joined Bellway, 1961; Man. Dir, 1984–99. *Recreations:* country pursuits, photography, environmental travel (particularly rainforests and Africa). *Address:* Fenham Grange, Fenham le Moor, Belford, Northumberland NE70 7PN.

DAWE, Roger James, CB 1988; OBE 1970; educational consultant, KPMG, since 2001; *b* 26 Feb. 1941; *s* of late Harry James and Edith Mary Dawe; *m* 1965, Ruth Day Jolliffe; one *s* one *d*. *Educ:* Hardyes Sch., Dorchester; Fitzwilliam House, Cambridge (MA; Hon. Fellow, Fitzwilliam Coll., 1996). Entered Min. of Labour, 1962; Dept of Economic Affairs, 1964–65; Private Sec. to Prime Minister, 1966–70; Principal, Dept of Employment, 1970; Private Sec. to Secretary of State for Employment, 1972–74; Asst Sec., Dept of Employment, 1974–81; Under Sec., MSC, 1981; Chief Exec., Trng Div., MSC, 1982–84; Dep. Sec., Dept of Employment, 1985–87; Dir Gen., MSC, then Training Commn, subseq. Training Agency, 1988–90; Dir Gen., Training, Enterprise and Educn Directorate, Dept of Employment, 1990–92; Dep. Sec., Further and Higher Educn, DFE, 1992–95; Dir Gen. for Further and Higher Educn and Youth Trng, DFEE, 1995–2000. Chm., Strategy and Resources Cttee, Methodist Church, 2000–06. Dep. Chm., Council, Open Univ., 2003– (Mem., 2001–). FRSA. Hon. DEduc UWE, 2000. *Recreations:* tennis, Plymouth Argyle supporter, music, theatre, cinema.

DAWES, Prof. Edwin Alfred, CBiol, FIBiol; CChem, FRSC; Reckitt Professor of Biochemistry, University of Hull, 1963–90, now Emeritus; *b* 6 July 1925; *s* of late Harold Dawes and Maude Dawes (*née* Barker); *m* 1950, Amy Rogerson; two *s*. *Educ:* Goole Grammar Sch.; Univ. of Leeds. (BSc, PhD, DSc). Asst Lectr, later Lectr, in Biochemistry, Univ. of Leeds, 1947–50; Lectr, later Sen. Lectr, Univ. of Glasgow, 1951–63; Hull University: Head of Biochemistry Dept, 1963–86; Dean of Science, 1968–70; Pro-Vice-Chancellor, 1977–80; Dir, Biomed. Res. Unit, 1981–92. Visiting Lecturer: Meml Univ., Newfoundland, Dalhousie Univ., 1959; Univ. of Brazil, 1960, 1972; Univ. of S California, 1962; Univ. of Rabat, 1967; Univ. of Göttingen, 1972; Osmania Univ., Hyderabad, 1986; Univ. of Massachusetts, Amherst, 1989; Univ. of Padua, 1991; Lectures: Biochemical Soc., Australia and NZ, 1975; Amer. Medical Alumni, Univ. of St Andrews, 1980–81; Biodegradable Plastics Soc., Japan, 1991. Editor, Biochemical Jl, 1958–65; Editor-in-Chief, Jl of Gen. Microbiol., 1976–81; Man. Editor, Fedn of European Microbiol Socs, and Editor-in-Chief, FEMS Microbiology Letters, 1982–90. Vice Chm., 1987–, Chm., Scientific Adv. Cttee, 1978–2006, Yorks Cancer Res. Campaign; Member: Scientific Adv. Cttee, Whyte-Watson-Turner Cancer Res. Trust, 1984–91; Adv. Gp for Cancer Res., Sheffield Univ., 1991–96. President: Hull Lit. Philosophical Soc., 1976–77; British Ring of Internat. Brotherhood of Magicians, 1972–73; Hon. President: Scottish Conjurers' Assoc., 1973–; Scottish Assoc. Magical Socs, 1996–; Hon. Vice-Pres., Magic Circle (Official Historian, 1987–; Mem., 1959–; Maskelyne Trophy, 1998; David Devant Internat. Award, 2002); Chm., Centre for the Magic Arts Ltd, 2005–. Chm., Philip Larkin Soc., 1995–. Governor, Pocklington Sch., 1965–74; Member, Court: Leeds Univ., 1974–2002; Bradford Univ., 1985–2002. Mem., Hall of Fame and H. A. Smith Literary Award, Soc. Amer. Magicians, 1984, 1997; Literary Fellowship and Hon. Life Mem., Acad. Magical Arts, USA, 1985; Hon. Mem. Bd, Houdini Historical Center, Wisconsin, 1990–. Consultant, The Mysteries of Magic, Learning Channel, 1998. Hon DSc Hull, 1992. Maskelyne Literary Award, 1988; Literary Award, Milbourne Christopher Foundn, USA, 1999. *Publications:* Quantitative Problems in Biochemistry, 1956, 6th edn 1980; (jtly) Biochemistry of Bacterial Growth, 1968, 3rd edn 1982; The Great Illusionists, 1979; Isaac Fawkes: fame and fable, 1979; The Biochemist in a Microbial Wonderland, 1982; Vonetta, 1982; The Barrister in the Circle, 1983; (ed) Environmental Regulation of Microbial Metabolism, 1985; (ed) Enterobacterial Surface Antigens, 1985; Microbial Energetics, 1985; (jtly) The Book of Magic, 1986, re-issued as Making Magic, 1992; The Wizard Exposed, 1987; (ed) Continuous Culture in Biotechnology and Environment Conservation, 1988; (contrib.) Philip Larkin: the man and his work, 1989; Henri Robin: expositor of science and magic, 1990; (ed) Molecular Biology of Membrane-Bound Complexes in Photosynthetic Bacteria, 1990; (ed) Novel Biodegradable Microbial Polymers, 1990; The Magic of Britain, 1994; Charles Bertram: the court conjurer, 1997; Stodare: the Enigma variations, 1998; (ed jtly) The Annals of Conjuring, 2001; Stanley Collins: conjuror and iconoclast, 2002; Harry Leat, 2003; The Great Lyle, 2005; (ed jtly and contrib.) Circle Without End, 2005; (jtly) David Nixon: entertainer with the magic touch, 2008; numerous papers in scientific jls. *Recreations:* conjuring, book-collecting. *Address:* Dane Hill, 393 Beverley Road, Anlaby, E Yorkshire HU10 7BQ. *T:* (01482) 657998, *Fax:* (01482) 655941.

DAWES, Melanie Henrietta; Acting Director General, Business Tax, HM Revenue and Customs, since 2007; *b* 9 March 1966; *d* of Nigel G. K. Dawes and Rosalie J. Dawes (*née* Wood); *m* 1992, Benedict Brogan; one *d*. *Educ:* Malvern Girls' Coll.; New Coll., Oxford (BA Hons); Birkbeck Coll., London (MSc Econ.). Econ. Asst, Dept of Transport, 1989–91; joined HM Treasury, 1991: Econ. Advr, then Team Leader, Econ. and Monetary Union, 1996–98; Head: Work Incentives and Poverty Analysis, 1998–2001; Educn and Culture, 2001–02; Dir (Europe), 2002–06; Dir, Large Business Service, HMRC, 2006–07. Chair, Alcohol Recovery Project, 2003–05. *Address:* HM Revenue and Customs, 100 Parliament Street, SW1A 2BQ.

DAWES, Rt Rev. Peter Spencer; Bishop of Derby, 1988–95; *b* 5 Feb. 1928; *s* of Jason Spencer Dawes and Janet Dawes; *m* 1954, Ethel Marrin; two *s* two *d*. *Educ:* Bickley Hall School; Aldenham School; Hatfield Coll., Durham (BA); Tyndale Hall, Bristol. Assistant Curate: St Andrew's, Whitehall Park, 1954–57; St Ebbe's, Oxford, 1957–60; Tutor, Clifton Theological Coll., 1960–65; Vicar, Good Shepherd, Romford, 1965–80; Archdeacon of West Ham, 1980–88. Examining Chaplain to Bishop of Chelmsford, 1970–88. Member, General Synod, 1970–95. *Address:* 45 Arundell, Ely, Cambs CB6 1BQ. *T:* (01353) 661241.

DAWES, Prof. William Nicholas, PhD; FREng, FRAeS; Francis Mond Professor of Aeronautical Engineering, Cambridge University, since 1996; Fellow of Churchill College, Cambridge, since 1984; *b* 5 Sept. 1955; *s* of Kenneth Frederick Dawes and Doris Jacyntha Hulm; *m* 1980, Luigia Cuomo; two *d*. *Educ:* Churchill Coll., Cambridge (BA, MA, PhD). CEng; FRAeS 1997; FREng 2000. Res. Officer, CEGB, 1980–84; Sen. Res. Asst, 1984–86, Lectr, 1986–96, Engrg Dept, Cambridge Univ. Mem., Amer. Inst. Aeronautics and Astronautics, 1990. *Publications:* articles in professional jls. *Recreations:* Italy, good food and good wine. *Address:* Church Farm, 7 Church Lane, Little Eversden CB23 1HQ. *T:* (01223) 263318.

DAWICK, Viscount; Alexander Douglas Derrick Haig; farmer; *b* 30 June 1961; *s* and *heir* of 2nd Earl Haig, *qv*; *m* 2003, Jane Hartree Risk, *widow* of Michael Risk and *d* of late Donald Grassick Crieff. *Educ:* Stowe School; Royal Agricl Coll., Cirencester. *Address:* Findas Farm, Chance Inn, Cupar, Fife KY15 5PQ. *Club:* New (Edinburgh).

DAWID, Prof. (Alexander) Philip, ScD; Professor of Statistics, University of Cambridge, since 2007; Fellow, Darwin College, Cambridge, since 2007; *b* 1 Feb. 1946; *s* of Israel Dawid and Rita Dawid; *m* 1974, Fatemeh Elahe Madjd; one *s* one *d*. *Educ:* Trinity Hall and Darwin Coll., Cambridge (BA 1966; Dip. Math. Statistics 1967; ScD 1982). CStat 1993. Lectr, UCL, 1969–78; Prof. of Statistics, City Univ., 1978–81; University College London: Reader, 1981–82; Prof. of Statistics, 1982–2007; Hon. Prof., 2007–. Editor: Jl of Royal Stat. Soc. Series B, 1992; Biometrika, 1992–96; Bayesian Analysis, 2005–. *Publications:* (ed jtly) Bayesian Statistics 4, 1992, 5, 1996, 6, 1999, 7, 2003, 8, 2007; (jtly) Probabilistic Networks and Expert Systems, 1999. *Recreation:* music. *Address:* Darwin College, Silver Street, Cambridge CB3 9EU; *e-mail:* apd25@cam.ac.uk.

DAWKINS, Prof. (Clinton) Richard, FRS 2001; Charles Simonyi Professor of the Public Understanding of Science, University of Oxford, 1995–2008; Fellow, New College, Oxford, since 1970; *b* 26 March 1941; *s* of Clinton John Dawkins and Jean Mary Vyvyan (*née* Ladner); *m*; one *d*. *Educ:* Oundle Sch.; Balliol Coll., Oxford (MA, DPhil, DSc; Hon. Fellow 2004). Asst Prof. of Zoology, Univ. of California, Berkeley, 1967–69; Oxford University: Lectr, 1970–89; Reader in Zoology, 1989–95. Gifford Lectr, Glasgow Univ., 1988; Sidgwick Meml Lectr, Newnham Coll., Cambridge, 1988; Kovler Vis. Fellow, Univ. of Chicago, 1990; Nelson Lectr, Univ. of California, Davis, 1990; Royal Instn Christmas Lects for Young People, 1991. Presenter, BBC TV Horizon progs, 1985,

1986. Editor: Animal Behaviour, 1974–78; Oxford Surveys in Evolutionary Biology, 1983–86. FRSL 1997. Hon. Fellow, Regent's Coll., London, 1988. Hon. DLitt: St Andrews, 1995; ANU, 1996; Hon. DSc: Westminster, 1997; Hull, 2001; DUniv Open, 2003. Silver Medal, Zool Soc., 1989; Michael Faraday Award, Royal Soc., 1990; Nakayama Prize, Nakayama Foundn for Human Scis, 1994; Internat. Cosmos Prize, 1997; Kistler Prize, Foundn for the Future, 2001; Shakespeare Prize, 2005; Lewis Thomas Prize, Rockefeller Univ., NY, 2007; Deschner Prize, Johan-Wolfgang Goethe Univ., Frankfurt, 2007. *Publications:* The Selfish Gene, 1976, 2nd edn 1989; The Extended Phenotype, 1982; The Blind Watchmaker, 1986 (RSL Prize 1987; LA Times Lit. Prize 1987); River Out of Eden, 1995; Climbing Mount Improbable, 1996; Unweaving the Rainbow: science, delusion and the appetite for wonder, 1998; A Devil's Chaplain and Other Selected Essays, 2003; The Ancestor's Tale, 2004; The God Delusion, 2006 (Book of Year, Galaxy Book Awards, 2007). *Recreation:* the Apple Macintosh. *Address:* New College, Holywell Street, Oxford OX1 3BN.

DAWKINS, Douglas Alfred; Associate Director, Bank of England, 1985–87; *b* 17 Sept. 1927; *s* of Arthur Dawkins and Edith Annie Dawkins; *m* 1953, Diana Pauline (*née* Ormes); one *s* one *d*. *Educ:* Edmonton County Secondary Sch.; University Coll. London (Rosa Morison Scholar; BA Hons). Entered Bank of England, 1950; Bank for Internat. Settlements, 1953–54; Adviser to Governors, Bank of Libya, 1964–65; Asst Chief of Overseas Dept, 1970; First Dep. Chief of Exchange Control, 1972; Chief of Exchange Control, 1979; Asst Dir, 1980. *Address:* c/o Bank of England, Threadneedle Street, EC2R 8AH.
   See also M. Dawkins.

DAWKINS, Hon. John Sydney, AO 2000; economist, consultant, company director; Chairman: John Dawkins & Co., since 1994; M & C Saatchi (Australia), since 1996; Retail Energy Market Company, since 2002; *b* 2 March 1947; *s* of Dr A. L. Dawkins and M. Dawkins (*née* Lee Steere); *m* 1987, Maggie Maruff; one *d*, one step *s*, and one *s* one *d* by previous marr. *Educ:* Roseworthy Agricl Coll., SA (RDA); Univ. of WA (BEc). MHR, Tangney, 1974–75; Press Officer, WA Trades and Labor Council, 1976–77; MP (ALP) Fremantle, WA, 1977–94; Shadow Minister for Educn, 1980–83; Minister: for Finance and assisting Prime Minister for Public Service Matters, 1983–84; for Trade and assisting Prime Minister for Youth Affairs, 1984–87; for Employment, Educn and Trng, 1987–91; Treasurer of Australia, 1991–93. Special investment rep., 1994–95; Director: Sealcorp Hldgs, 1994–2004; Govt Relations Australia, 2000–; Genetic Technologies, 2004–; Elders Rural Bank, 2006– (Chm., 1998–2006); Chairman: Med. Corp. of Australasia, 1997–2000; Law Central, 2000–06. Chairman: Botanic Gardens of Adelaide, 2003–05; Inst. of Trade, 2005–. Bd Mem., Fred Hollows Foundn, 1995–2004. Hon. Dr: Univ. of S Australia, 1996; Queensland Univ. of Technol., 1997. Centenary Medal, Australia, 2003. *Address:* 36 Howard Street, Collinswood, SA 5081, Australia.

DAWKINS, Mark; Managing Partner, Simmons & Simmons, since 2005; *b* 2 May 1960; *s* of Douglas Alfred Dawkins, *qv; m* 2002, Kim (*née* Taylor); two *s* two *d*. *Educ:* Exeter Univ. (LLB). Admitted solicitor, 1985; Simmons & Simmons: Partner, 1990; Hd of Litigation, 1997–2000; Hd, Financial Mkts, 2000–05. *Recreations:* family, tennis, squash, Southern African history, photography. *Address:* c/o Simmons & Simmons, CityPoint, One Ropemaker Street, EC2Y 9SS. *T:* (020) 7628 2020; *e-mail:* mark.dawkins@simmons-simmons.com.

DAWKINS, Richard; see Dawkins, C. R.

DAWKINS, Simon John Robert, MA; Headmaster, Merchant Taylors' School, Crosby, 1986–2005; *b* 9 July 1945; *s* of Col William John Dawkins, TD and Mary Doreen Dawkins (*née* King); *m* 1968, Janet Mary Stevens; one *s* one *d*. *Educ:* Solihull Sch.; Univ. of Nottingham (BA); Queens' Coll., Cambridge (PGCE); Birkbeck Coll. London (MA distn). Head of Economics: Eltham Coll., 1968–71; Dulwich Coll., 1971–86 (Housemaster, 1979–86). Headmasters' Conference: Chm. NW Div., 1996 (Sec., 1995); Member: Memship Cttee, 1996–99; Academic Policy Cttee, 2000–04. *Recreations:* physical exercise, tennis, golf, reading. *Address:* Brackenwood, St George's Road, Hightown, Liverpool L38 3RT. *T:* (0151) 929 3546. *Clubs:* Hightown (Lancs); Formby Golf, St Enodoc Golf.

DAWNAY, family name of **Viscount Downe.**

DAWNAY, (Charles) James (Payan); Chairman, CCLA Investment Management Ltd, since 2004; *b* 7 Nov. 1946; *s* of late Capt. Oliver Dawnay, CVO and of Lady Margaret Dawnay (*née* Boyle, now Lady Margaret Stirling-Aird); *m* 1978, Sarah Stogdon; one *s* three *d*. *Educ:* Trinity Hall, Cambridge (BA 1968). Investment Manager, M & G Gp Ltd, 1969–78; Export Sales Dir, Alginate Industries Ltd, 1979–81; Man. Dir, Vannick Products Ltd, 1981–83; S G Warburg & Co. Ltd, 1983–87 (Dir, 1984–87); Dir, Mercury Asset Mgt Gp plc, 1987–92; Chm., Mercury Fund Managers Ltd, 1987–92; Business Develt Dir, 1992–99, Dep. Chm., 1999–2000, Martin Currie Ltd; Chairman: China Heartland Fund Ltd, 1997–2006; Northern Aim VCT plc, 2000–; Gurr Johns Ltd, 2000–06; Investec High Income Trust plc, 2001–; Resources Investment Trust plc, 2001–; New Opportunities Investment Trust plc, 2002–06; Director: Govett Strategic Trust plc, 2000–03; Taiwan Opportunities Trust Ltd, 2001–. Mem. Bd of Trustees, Nat. Galls of Scotland, 2003–. Mem., Finance Cttee, NT, 1991–2005; Mem. Finance Cttee, 1993–2005, Dir NTS Enterprises, 2001–05 and Chm. Commercial Develt Cttee, 2001–05, Nat. Trust for Scotland, 1993–2005. Chairman: Biggar Mus. Trust, 1993–; Penicuik House Preservation Trust, 2001–. *Recreations:* collecting, conservation, country sports. *Address:* Symington House, by Biggar, Lanarkshire ML12 6LW. *T:* (01899) 308211, *Fax:* (01899) 308727; *e-mail:* jdawnay@yahoo.co.uk. *Clubs:* Brooks's, Pratt's; New (Edinburgh); Biggar.

DAWNAY, Lady Jane Meriel; Member of Board, Historic Buildings Council for Scotland, 1996–99; *b* 8 Feb. 1953; *yr d* of 5th Duke of Westminster, TD and Hon. Viola Maud Lyttelton (*d* 1987); *m* 1st, 1977, Duke of Roxburghe, *qv* (marr. diss. 1990); two *s* one *d*; 2nd, 1996, Edward William Dawnay. *Educ:* Collegiate Sch., Enniskillen; Sherborne Hill; Switzerland; Bedgebury Park; Paris. Vice Pres., Arthritis & Rheumatism Council for Res., 1998– (Regl Chm., 1983–98); Macmillan Cancer Relief (formerly Cancer Relief Macmillan Fund): Vice Pres., Scotland, 1994– (Dir and Bd Mem., 1990–94); Chm., Scotland and NI, 1989–94. Mem. Bd, Ancient Monuments Scotland, 1993–96; Member: Adv. Cttee, Royal Parks, 1994–99; Royal Highland & Agricultural Soc. of Scotland, 1998 (Pres., 1998–). Trustee, Atlantic Salmon Trust Scotland, 1995–. Director: Beltane Partners Ltd, 1994–98; Radio Borders, 1992–98. Mem., Racehorse Owners' Assoc. Vice Pres., NW Norfolk Cons. Assoc. (Pres., 1999–2002). Pres., W Norfolk, King's Lynn and Wisbech Br., NSPCC, 2007–. Patron, British Lymphology Soc., 1998–; Life Patron, George Thomas Soc.; Vice Patron, Norfolk Community Foundn, 2006–. MInstD 1997. Freeman, City of Chester, 1997. Queen Elizabeth the Queen Mother's Award for Envmt, Scotland, 1996. *Recreations:* fishing, gardening, reading, horses. *Address:* Hillington Hall, Hillington, King's Lynn, Norfolk PE31 6BW; 48 Eaton Square, SW1W 9BD.
   See also Marquis of Bowmont and Cessford.

DAWOOD, Nessim Joseph; Arabist and Middle East Consultant; Chairman, The Arabic Advertising and Publishing Co. (Aradco) Ltd, London, since 2000 (Managing Director, 1958–2000); *b* Baghdad, 27 Aug. 1927; 4th *s* of late Yousef Dawood, merchant, and Muzli (*née* Tweg); *m* 1949, Juliet, 2nd *d* of late M. and N. Abraham, Baghdad and New York; three *s*. *Educ:* The American Sch. and Shamash Sch., Baghdad; Iraq State Scholar in England, UC Exeter, 1945–49; Univ. of London, BA (Hons). FCIL (FIL 1959). Dir, Bradbury Wilkinson (Graphics) Ltd, 1975–86. Has written and spoken radio and film commentaries. *Publications:* The Muqaddimah of Ibn Khaldun, 1967 (US, 1969); Penguin Classics: The Thousand and One Nights, 1954; The Koran, 1956, 59th edn 2007, parallel Arabic/English edn, 1990; Aladdin and Other Tales, 1957; Tales from The Thousand and One Nights, 1973, 38th edn 2008; Arabian Nights (illus. children's edn), 1978; Puffin Classics: Aladdin & Other Tales, 1989; Sindbad the Sailor & other Tales, 1989; contribs to specialised and technical English-Arabic dictionaries; translated numerous technical publications into Arabic; occasional book reviews. *Recreation:* going to the theatre. *Address:* (office) Aradco House, 132 Cleveland Street, W1T 6AB. *T:* (020) 7692 7700. *Club:* Hurlingham.

DAWS, Dr Christine; Director of Finance, Welsh Assembly Government, since 2006; *b* Rugby, 3 Feb. 1955; *d* of Harold and Daphne Sellar; *m* 1993, Robert Daws (*d* 2001). *Educ:* Durham Univ. (BA Hons Econs); Loughborough Univ. (MSc Recreation Mgt); Texas A&M Univ. (PhD Agricl Econs 1982). Dir of Finance, Bucks HA, 1995–99; Dep. Dir of Finance, DoH, 1999–2003; Dir of Finance, NHS Wales Dept, 2003–06. Non-exec. Dir, Shared Services Audit Cttee, DWP, 2007–. *Recreations:* gardening, golf. *Address:* Welsh Assembly Government, Cathays Park, Cardiff CF10 3NQ.

DAWSON, (Archibald) Keith; educational consultant, since 1996; Headmaster, Haberdashers' Aske's School, Elstree, 1987–96; *b* 12 Jan. 1937; *s* of Wilfred Joseph and Alice Marjorie Dawson; *m* 1961, Marjorie Blakeson; two *d*. *Educ:* Nunthorpe Grammar School for Boys, York; The Queen's College, Oxford. MA, Dip Ed distinction. Ilford County High School for Boys, 1961–63; Haberdashers' Aske's Sch., 1963–71 (Head of History, 1965–71); Headmaster, John Mason Sch., Abingdon, 1971–79; Principal, Scarborough Sixth Form Coll., 1979–84; Principal, King James's College of Henley, 1984–87. Liveryman, Haberdashers' Co., 1996–. *Publications:* Society and Industry in 19th Century England (with Peter Wall), 1968; The Industrial Revolution, 1971. *Recreations:* theatre, 'cello, cricket, hill walking. *Address:* Puffins, 77 Chapel Street, Sidbury, Sidmouth EX10 0RQ.

DAWSON, Celia Anne, (Mrs D. Charlton); a District Judge (Magistrates' Courts), since 2004; *b* 25 Sept. 1959; *d* of David and Jean Dawson; *m* 1983, Dr David Charlton; one *s* two *d*. *Educ:* Essex Univ. (BA Hons (Lit.) 1981); Coll. of Law. Admitted solicitor, 1983; Partner, Thompson Smith and Puxon, Solicitors, Colchester, 1987–91; Sen. Legal Advr Essex Magistrates' Courts, 1991–98; Partner, Birkett Long, Solicitors, Colchester 1998–2004; Dep. Dist Judge, Sussex, 2001–04. Mem. Bd, and Chm., Mgt Cttee, Colne Housing Soc., 1999–2004. Trustee, Children's Legal Centre, Univ. of Essex, 2007–. *Recreations:* obsessive sailing, unsuccessful garden taming, making a mess in the kitchen. *Address:* Stratford Magistrates' Court, 389 High Street, Stratford, E15 4SB. *T:* (020) 8522 5000. *Clubs:* Brightlingsea Sailing, Colne Yacht.

DAWSON, Hon. Sir Daryl (Michael), AC 1988; KBE 1982; CB 1980; Justice of the High Court of Australia, 1982–97; Non permanent Member, Hong Kong Court of Final Appeal, 1997–2003; Professorial Fellow, University of Melbourne, since 1998; *b* 12 Dec. 1933; *s* of Claude Charles Dawson and Elizabeth May Dawson; *m* 1971, Mary Louise Thomas. *Educ:* Canberra High Sch.; Ormond Coll., Univ. of Melbourne (LLB Hons) LLM Yale. Sterling Fellow, Yale Univ., 1955–56. QC 1971; Solicitor-General for Victoria, 1974–82. Mem. Council, Univ. of Melbourne, 1976–86; Chm. Council Ormond Coll., Univ. of Melbourne, 1991–92. Adjunct Prof. of Law, Monash Univ. 1997–2006. Chairman: Australian Motor Sport Appeal Court, 1986–88 (Mem., 1970–86) Longford Royal Commn, 1998–99; Trade Practices Act Review Cttee, 2002–03. Chm. Menzies Foundn, 1998–; Gov., Ian Potter Foundn, 1998–. Hon. LLD Monash, 2006 *Recreation:* gardening. *Address:* PO Box 147, East Melbourne, Vic 3002, Australia. *Clubs:* Melbourne, Savage, RACV, Beefsteaks (Melbourne).

DAWSON, Dee; see Dawson, J. D.

DAWSON, (Edward) John; Assistant Chief Executive, 1989–90, and Director, 1989–91 Lloyds Bank; *b* 14 Oct. 1935; *s* of late Edward Dawson and Kathleen Dawson (*née* Naughton); *m* 1st, 1963, Ann Prudence (*née* Hicks) (marr. diss. 1997); one *s* one *d* (and one *s* decd); 2nd, 1998, Jill Solveig (*née* Linton). *Educ:* St Joseph's Coll., Blackpool; London Graduate Sch. of Business Studies (Sloan Fellow, 1969–70); Manchester Coll. Univ. of Oxford (BA Hons PPE 1994; MA 1998). FCIB. Entered Lloyds Bank, 1952 served RAF, 1954–56; General Manager, Lloyds Bank and Exec. Dir, Lloyds Bank International, 1982–84; Asst Chief Gen. Manager, 1985, Dir, UK Retail Banking 1985–88, Lloyds Bank; Chairman: Lloyds Bowmaker Finance, 1988–90 (Dir, 1985–90) Black Horse Agencies, 1988–89 (Dir, 1985–89). Chm., Walsingham Community Home Ltd, 1991–96. *Recreations:* life in South Africa during Northern winter, golf, cricket tennis, choral singing, hiking, climbing, T'ai chi ch'uan. *Address:* c/o Lloyds TSB Westminster House, 4 Dean Stanley Street, SW1P 3HU. *Clubs:* MCC; Wareham Golf.

DAWSON, Hilton; see Dawson, T. H.

DAWSON, Sir (Hugh) Michael (Trevor), 4th Bt *cr* 1920, of Edgewarebury; *b* 28 March 1956; *s* of Sir (Hugh Halliday) Trevor Dawson, 3rd Bt; *S* father, 1983. *Heir: b* Nicholas Antony Trevor Dawson, *b* 17 Aug. 1957.

DAWSON, Ian David; Assistant Under-Secretary of State (Policy), Ministry of Defence 1991–93; *b* 24 Nov. 1934; *s* of Harry Newton Dawson and Margaret (*née* Aspinall); *m* 1955, Barbara (*née* Mather); two *s* one *d*. *Educ:* Hutton Grammar Sch.; Fitzwilliam House Cambridge (MA). Directorate of Military Survey, 1958–71; Principal, MoD, 1971 Private Sec. to CAS, 1975–77; Asst Sec., Naval Staff, 1977–80; Sec., AWRE, 1980–83 RCDS, 1984; Dir, Defence and Security Agency, WEU, Paris, 1986–88; Asst Under-Sec of State (Resources), MoD, 1988–90; Fellow, Center for Internat. Affairs, Harvard 1990–91. *Recreations:* music, mountaineering, travel. *Address:* 7 Claremont Falls, Killigarth Polperro, Cornwall PL13 2HT.

DAWSON, James Grant Forbes, CEng, FICE; Strategic Development Director, BS Consultants, since 2002; Chairman, Vilnius Consult, since 2002; Associate, First Class Partnerships, since 2003; *b* 5 Sept. 1940; *s* of William Maxwell Hume Dawson and Caroline Margaret Storey Dawson; *m* 2nd, 1993, Joan Margaret Davison. *Educ:* Edinburgh Univ. (BSc). FIPENZ (FNZIE); Eur Ing. GIBB Ltd: Chief Engr, 1975–78; Associate 1978–80; Head of Transport, 1980–82; Partner, 1982; Director, 1989; Chm., 1995–2000 Chm. Emeritus, Jacobs GIBB Ltd, 2001–. Consultant: RSM Robson Rhodes, 2002–0. MVA, 2005–06. Member: DTI Cttee for S Africa Trade, 1998–2001; E Europe Trade Council, 1999–2001; Mem., ME and African Gp, 2001–03, Chm., Ports and Logistics Gp

British Trade Investments. Chm., ACE, 1999–2000. Liveryman, Engineers' Co., 2001–. *Recreations:* golf, gardening. *Address:* Woodpeckers, Pangbourne Hill, Pangbourne, Berks RG8 8JS. *Club:* East India.

DAWSON, Joan Denise, (Dee); Medical Director, Rhodes Farm Clinic, since 1991; *b* 17 Jan. 1947; *d* of Horace and Joan Webb; *m* 1st, 1969, Stephen Dawson (marr diss.); 2nd, 1979, Ian Dear (marr. diss.); one *s* four *d*; 3rd, 2002, Eberhard von Wick. *Educ:* Chelsea Coll., London Univ. (BSc); London Business Sch.; Royal Free Hosp. Sch. of Medicine (MB BS 1989). Voluntary Teacher, VSO, Madagascar, 1969–71; Mkt Res. Manager, Parker Ltd, 1974–75; Man. Dir, Dee Dawson Fashion Ltd, 1977–84; House Physician, 1989–90, House Surgeon, 1990–91, North Middx Hosp.; set up Rhodes Farm Clinic, first residential unit, incl. full-time school, dedicated solely to treatment of anorexic children, 1991. *Publications:* A Quick Guide to Eating Disorders, 1995; Anorexia and Bulimia - a parents' guide, 2001. *Recreations:* tennis, water ski-ing. *Address:* The Old House, Totteridge Green, N20 8PA.

DAWSON, John; *see* Dawson, E. J.

DAWSON, Prof. John Alan, FRSE; Professor of Marketing, University of Edinburgh, since 1990; Professor of Retail Studies, University of Stirling, since 2005; *b* 19 Aug. 1944; *s* of Alan and Gladys Dawson; *m* 1967, Jocelyn M. P. Barker (marr. diss. 2007); one *s* one *d*. *Educ:* University College London (BSc, MPhil); University of Nottingham (PhD). Lectr, Univ. of Nottingham, 1967–71; Lectr, 1971, Sen. Lectr, 1974, Reader, 1981–83, Univ. of Wales, Lampeter; Fraser of Allander Prof. of Distributive Studies, and Dir, Inst. for Retail Studies, Univ. of Stirling, 1983–90. Vis. Lectr, Univ. of Western Australia, 1973; Vis. Res. Fellow, ANU, 1978; Vis. Prof., 2000–, Dist. Prof., 2003–, Univ. of Mktg and Distbn Sci., Kobe; Visiting Professor: Florida State Univ., 1982; Chuo Univ., 1986; Univ. of S Africa, 1999; Sch. for Higher Mgt and Business Strategy, Barcelona, 2000–; Bocconni Univ., Milan, 2000; Saitama Univ., 2002. Chm., Nat. Museums of Scotland Retailing Co., 1992–2003. Member: Distributive Trades EDC, 1984–87; Board, Cumbernauld Develt Corp., 1987–96. Hon. Sec., Inst. of British Geographers, 1985–88. FRSE 2003. *Publications:* Evaluating the Human Environment, 1973; Man and His World, 1975; Computing for Geographers, 1976; Small Scale Retailing in UK, 1979; Marketing Environment, 1979; Retail Geography, 1980; Commercial Distribution in Europe, 1982; Teach Yourself Geography, 1983; Shopping Centre Development, 1983; Computer Programming for Geographers, 1985; Shopping Centres Policies and Prospects, 1985; Evolution of European Retailing, 1989; Competition and Markets, 1991; Retail Environments in Developing Countries, 1991; Distribution Statistics, 1992; Internationalisation of Retailing in Asia, 2003; International Retailing Plans and Strategies in Asia, 2005; Strategic Issues in International Retailing, 2006; The Retail Reader, 2008; articles in geographical, management and marketing jls. *Recreations:* sport, travel. *Address:* School of Management, University of Edinburgh, Edinburgh EH8 9JY. *T:* (0131) 650 3830.

DAWSON, John Anthony Lawrence, FICE, FIHT; Chairman and Managing Director, European Road Assessment Association, since 2005; Chairman, International Road Assessment Programme, since 2005; *b* 6 Feb. 1950; *m* 1980, Frances Anne Elizabeth Whelan; two *d*. *Educ:* Mill Hill Sch.; Southampton Univ. British Rail Engineering Scholar, 1968–72; Depts of Envt and Transport, 1972–81; Overseas Transport Consultant, 1981–85; Dir (Transport), London Regl Office, Dept of Transport, 1985–88; Chief Road Engineer, Scottish Develt Dept, 1988; Dir of Roads and Chief Road Engr, Scottish Office, 1989–95; Automobile Association: Policy Dir, 1995–2004; Internat. Dir, 2003–04; Mem. Cttee, 1996–99; Man. Dir, AA Foundn for Road Safety Research, 1995–2004; Dir, AA Motoring Trust, 2003–04; Man. Exec., Road Safety Foundn, 2005–. Mem. Bd, Ertico, 1995–97, 1999–2002. Trustee, Air Ambulance Assoc., 1999–2002; Sec., FIA Foundn for Automobile and Soc., 2001–. *Recreations:* touring, music. *Address:* EuroRAP AISBL, Worting House, Basingstoke, Hants RG23 8PX. *T:* (01256) 345598.

DAWSON, John Kelvin; Agent-General for Queensland in London, and Commissioner, Europe, since 2001; *b* Melbourne, 15 Sept. 1943; *s* of John Inglis Dawson and Marie Victoria Dawson; one *s* one *d*. *Educ:* Ivanhoe Grammar Sch.; Univ. of Melbourne (BA). National Australia Bank Ltd: Gen. Manager, Strategic Develt, 1991–93; Man. Dir, UK and Europe, 1993–95; Gp Gen. Manager, Asian and Internat. Banking, 1995; CEO, Bank of Queensland Ltd, 1996–2001. Director: Clydesdale Bank, 1993–95; Nat. Irish Bank, 1993–95; Northern Bank, Belfast, 1993–95; Yorkshire Bank, 1993–95; Bank of Hawaii Internat., 1999–2001. Chm., Exec. Cttee, Aust. Bankers' Assoc., 1992–93. Dir, British-Aust. Soc., 2001–. Freeman, City of London, 2004. *Recreations:* all sports, wine, reading. *Address:* Queensland Government Office Europe, 392 Strand, WC2R 0LZ. *Clubs:* East India; Australian, Melbourne Cricket (Melbourne); Brisbane, Tattersalls (Qld); Hong Kong Foreign Correspondents.

DAWSON, Keith; *see* Dawson, A. K.

DAWSON, Sir Michael; *see* Dawson, Sir H. M. T.

DAWSON, Ven. Peter; Archdeacon of Norfolk, 1977–93, now Emeritus; *b* 31 March 1929; *s* of late Leonard Smith and Cicely Alice Dawson; *m* 1955, Kathleen Mary Sansome; one *s* three *d*. *Educ:* Manchester Grammar School; Keble Coll., Oxford (MA); Ridley Hall, Cambridge. Nat. service, Army, 1947–49; University, 1949–52; Theological College, 1952–54. Asst Curate, St Lawrence, Morden, Dio. Southwark, 1954–59; Vicar of Barston, Warwicks, Dio. Birmingham, 1959–63; Rector of St Clement, Higher Openshaw, Dio. Manchester, 1963–68; Rector of Morden, Dio. Southwark, 1968–77, and Rural Dean of Merton, 1975–77. *Recreations:* gardening, politics, the rural community, historical studies. *Address:* The Coach House, Harmony Hill, Milnthorpe LA7 7QA. *T:* (015395) 62020.

DAWSON, Rev. Peter, OBE 1986; education consultant, since 1985; employment law consultant, since 2002; *b* 19 May 1933; *s* of Richard Dawson and Henrietta Kate Dawson (*née* Trueman); *m* 1957, Shirley Margaret Pentland Johnson; two *d*. *Educ:* Beckenham Technical Sch.; Beckenham Grammar Sch.; London School of Economics (BScEcon); Westminster Coll. (Postgrad. CertEd). Schoolmaster Fellow Commoner, Keble Coll., Oxford, 1969, and Corpus Christi Coll., Cambridge, 1979. Asst Master, Roan Grammar School for Boys, London, 1957–62; Head of Upper School, Sedgehill Sch., London, 1962–67; Second Master, Gateacre Comprehensive Sch., Liverpool, 1967–70; Headmaster, Eltham Green Sch., London, 1970–80; Gen. Sec., Professional Assoc. of Teachers, 1980–92; OFSTED Registered Inspector of Schs, 1993–2000. Methodist Minister, ordained 1985; Asst Minister, Queen's Hall Methodist Mission, Derby, 1984–87; Minister, Spondon Methodist Ch., Derby, 1989–90; Free Church Minister, Church on Oakwood, Derby, 1990–94; Minister, Mayfield Rd Methodist Church, Derby, 1994–98. Member: Burnham Cttee, 1981–87; Council of Managerial and Professional Staffs, 1989–92 (Pres.); Econ. and Social Cttee, EC, 1990–94; Employment Appeal Tribunal, 1992–2004. Chm., East Midlands RSA, 2004–06. *Publications:* Making a Comprehensive Work, 1981; Teachers and Teaching, 1984; Why Preach?, 2000; A Short History of the Employment Appeal Tribunal, 2002, rev. and updated edn 2004. *Recreations:* reading, theatre, cinema, grandparenthood. *Address:* 30 Elm Street, Borrowash, Derby DE72 3HP. *T:* (01332) 672669.

DAWSON, Prof. Peter, PhD; FRCP, FRCR, FInstP; Professor of Radiology and Consultant Radiologist, since 1999, Chairman and Clinical Director of Radiology, since 2002, University College London Hospitals; *b* 17 May 1945; *s* of Frederick and May Dawson; *m* 1968, Hilary Sturley; one *s* one *d*. *Educ:* Firth Park Sch., Sheffield; King's Coll. London (BSc 1st Cl. Hons 1966; PhD 1970); Westminster Med. Sch. (MB BS 1978). FRCR 1984; FRCP 1994; FInstP 2005. Sen. Lectr and Reader in Radiology, 1985–96, Prof. of Med. Imaging, 1996–99, RPMS. Pres., BIR, 1994–95; Royal College of Radiologists: Roentgen Prof. 2002; Registrar, 2002–. Mem., Internat. Commn on Radiation Units and Measurements, 1999–; Special Asst to IAEA, 2003–. Bd Mem., Internat. Soc. of Radiology, 2002–; Mem. Res. Cttee, European Assoc. of Radiology, 2005–. Barclay Prize, 1984, Barclay Medal, 1998, BIR; (jtly) Finzi Prize, RSM, 1991, 1993. *Publications:* Contrast Media in Practice, 1993; Functional CT, 1997; A Textbook of Contrast Media, 1999; Protocols for Multi-slice Computed Tomography, 2006; some 250 papers on physics and medical imaging in learned jls. *Recreations:* music, mathematics, wine, scuba diving. *Address:* Beechers, Green Lane, Chesham Bois, Bucks HP6 5LQ. *T:* (01494) 728222; *e-mail:* phda728222@aol.com. *Club:* Royal Society of Medicine.

DAWSON, Peter; Secretary, Royal and Ancient Golf Club of St Andrews, since 1999; *b* 28 May 1948; *s* of George Dawson and Violet Dawson (*née* Smith); *m* 1969, Juliet Ann Bartlett; one *s* one *d*. *Educ:* Westcliff High Sch.; Corpus Christi Coll., Cambridge (MA). Managing Director: Grove Cranes, 1977–83; Blackwood Hodge (UK), 1983–89; Grove Europe, 1989–93; Thos Storey, 1994–97. *Address:* Royal and Ancient Golf Club of St Andrews, Fife KY16 9JD. *T:* (01334) 460000. *Clubs:* Northumberland Golf; Royal Worlington and Newmarket Golf; Golf House (Elie).

DAWSON, Rex Malcolm Chaplin, FRS 1981; PhD, DSc; Deputy Director and Head of Biochemistry Department, Institute of Animal Physiology, Babraham, Cambridge, 1969–84, retired (Deputy Chief Scientific Officer, 1969–84); *b* 3 June 1924; *s* of late James Dawson and Ethel Mary Dawson (*née* Chaplin); *m* 1946, Emily Elizabeth Hodder; one *s* one *d*. *Educ:* Hinckley Grammar Sch.; University Coll., London (BSc 1946, DSc 1960); Univ. of Wales (PhD 1951). MRC Fellowship followed by Beit Meml Fellowship, Neuropsychiatric Res. Centre, Whitchurch Hosp., Cardiff, 1947–52; Betty Brookes Fellow, Dept of Biochemistry, Univ. of Oxford, 1952–55. Vis. Res. Fellow, Harvard Univ., 1959; Vis. Prof., Northwestern Univ., Chicago, 1974. International Lipid Prize, Amer. Oil Chemists' Assoc., 1981. *Publications:* Metabolism and Physiological Significance of Lipids, 1964; Data for Biochemical Research, 1959, 3rd edn 1986; Form and Function of Phospholipids, 1973; numerous papers on structure, turnover and role of phospholipids in cell membranes in various scientific jls. *Recreations:* mercantile marine history, sailing, gardening. *Address:* Kirn House, Holt Road, Langham, Norfolk NR25 7BX. *T:* (01328) 830396.

DAWSON, Dame Sandra (June Noble), DBE 2004; KPMG Professor of Management Studies, since 1995, and Master of Sidney Sussex College, 1999–Aug. 2009, University of Cambridge (Director, Judge Business School (formerly Judge Institute of Management Studies), 1995–2006); *b* 4 June 1946; *d* of Wilfred Denyer and Joy (*née* Noble); *m* 1969, Henry R. C. Dawson; one *s* two *d*. *Educ:* Dr Challoner's Grammar Sch., Amersham; Univ. of Keele (BA 1st Cl. Hons Hist. and Sociol. 1968). Research Officer, Govt Social Survey, 1968–69; Imperial College of Science, Technology and Medicine: Res. Officer, Lectr, then Sen. Lectr, Industrial Sociol. Unit, Dept of Social and Econ. Studies, 1969–90; Prof. of Organisational Behaviour, Mgt Sch., 1990–95; Fellow, Jesus Coll. Cambridge, 1995–99. Non-exec. Dir, Riverside HA, 1990–92; Chm., Riverside Mental Health Trust, 1992–95. Member: Res. Strategy Bd, Offshore Safety Div., HSE, 1991–95; Strategic Review Gp, PHLS, 1994; Sen. Salaries Review Body, 1997–2003; Futures and Innovation Bd, DTI, 1998–2002; Res. Priorities Bd, ESRC, 2000–03; Task Force on Accounting for People, 2003; Fire and Rescue Service Ministerial Adv. Gp, 2004–. Chm., Exec. Steering Cttee, ESRC Advanced Inst. of Mgt, 2007–. Non-executive Director: Cambridge Econometrics, 1996–; Fleming Claverhouse Investment Trust, 1996–2003; PHLS, 1997–99; Soc. for Advancement of Mgt Studies, 1999–2003; Barclays plc, 2003–; Oxfam, 2006–. Mem. Adv. Bd, Alchemy Partners, 2000–04. Member: UK-India Roundtable, 2006–; Adv. Bd, UK India Business Council, 2007–. Trustee, RANDEurope (UK), 2001–04. Companion, Assoc. of Business Schs. Internat. Women's Forum Hall of Fame, 2007. *Publications:* Analysing Organisations, 1986, 3rd edn 1996; Safety at Work: the limits of self regulation, 1988; Managing in the NHS, 1995; (ed) Future Health Organisations and Systems, 2005; (ed) Policy Futures for UK Health, 2005; contribs to mgt learned jls. *Recreations:* music, walking, family. *Address:* Judge Business School, Trumpington Street, Cambridge CB2 1AG. *T:* (01223) 339700.

DAWSON, Stephen Eric; a District Judge (Magistrates' Courts) (formerly Metropolitan Stipendiary Magistrate), since 1994; a Recorder, since 2000; *b* 16 Feb. 1952; *s* of late Leslie Eric Dawson and of Margaret Kathleen Dawson; *m* 1977, Sandra Mary Bate; two *d*. *Educ:* St Joseph's Acad., Blackheath; Coll. of Law. Admitted Solicitor, 1977. Articled and subseq. Partner, Victor Lissack, solicitors, 1978–82; Partner, Reynolds Dawson, 1982–94; an Asst Recorder, 1998–2000. Treas. and Mem. Council, British Acad. of Forensic Scis, 1985–2005; Treas. and Mem. Cttee, London Criminal Courts Solicitors' Assoc., 1987–94; Member: Criminal Law Cttee, Law Soc., 1993–2000; Inner London Magistrates' Courts Cttee, 1997–2000; Gtr London Magistrates' Cts Authy, 2000–02. *Publication:* Profitable Legal Aid, 1991. *Recreations:* occasional gardening, gentle jogging. *Address:* c/o The Chief Magistrate's Office, Westminster City Magistrates' Court, 70 Horseferry Road, SW1P 2AX.

DAWSON, (Thomas) Hilton; Chairman, National Academy for Parenting Practitioners, since 2007; Development Consultant, Serco Education and Children's Services; *b* 30 Sept. 1953; *s* of late Harry Dawson and of Sally Dawson; *m* 1973, Susan, *d* of Ellis and Alice Williams; two *d*. *Educ:* Warwick Univ. (BA Hons Philos. and Pols 1975); Lancaster Univ. (Dip. in Social Work 1982). Brickworks labourer, 1975; clerk, 1976; kibbutz volunteer, 1976; community worker, 1977; social worker, 1979; Lancs Social Services, 1982–97; youth justice worker, 1983; social work manager, 1989. Mem. (Lab) Lancaster CC, 1987–97. MP (Lab) Lancaster and Wyre, 1997–2005. Chief Exec., Shaftesbury Homes and Arethusa, subseq. Shaftesbury Young People, 2005–08. *Recreations:* family, the arts, walking, keeping fit. *Address:* 36 Morwick Road, Warkworth, Northumberland NE65 0TD. *T:* (01665) 711817.

DAWSON-DAMER, family name of **Earl of Portarlington**.

DAWTRY, Sir Alan, Kt 1974; CBE 1968 (MBE (mil.) 1945); TD 1948; Chief Executive (formerly Town Clerk), Westminster City Council, 1956–77; Chairman: Sperry Rand Ltd, 1977–86; Sperry Rand (Ireland) Ltd, 1977–86; President, London Rent Assessment Panel, 1979–86; *b* 8 April 1915; *s* of Melancthon and Kate Nicholas Dawtry, Sheffield; *m* 1997, Sally Ann, *d* of Mr and Mrs D. P. Chalklin. *Educ:* King Edward VII Sch., Sheffield; Sheffield Univ. (LLB). Served War of 1939–45: commissioned RA; campaigns France, N

Africa, Italy (MBE, despatches twice); released with rank of Lt-Col. Admitted Solicitor, 1938; Asst Solicitor, Sheffield, 1938–48; Deputy Town Clerk, Bolton, 1948–52; Deputy Town Clerk, Leicester, 1952–54; Town Clerk, Wolverhampton, 1954–56; Hon. Sec., London Boroughs Assoc., 1965–78. Member: Metrication Bd, 1969–74; Clean Air Council, 1960–75; Council of Management, Architectural Heritage Fund, 1977–89; CBI Council, 1982–86. Pres., Soc. of Local Authority Chief Execs, 1975–76. Vice-Chm., Dolphin Square Trust, 1985–99. FCMI (FBIM 1975); FRSA 1978. Hon. LLD Sheffield, 2007. Foreign Orders: The Star (Afghanistan); Golden Honour (Austria); Leopold II (Belgium); Rio Branco (Brazil); Merit (Chile); Legion of Honour (France); Merit (W Germany); the Phœnix (Greece); Merit (Italy); Homayoun (Iran); The Rising Sun (Japan); the Star (Jordan); African Redemption (Liberia); Oaken Crown (Luxembourg); Loyalty (Malaysia); the Right Hand (Nepal); Orange-Nassau (Netherlands); the Two Niles (Sudan); the Crown (Thailand); Zaire (Zaire). *Address:* 901 Grenville House, Dolphin Square, SW1V 3LR. *T:* (020) 7798 8100.

DAY, Prof. Alan Charles Lynn; Professor of Economics, London School of Economics, University of London, 1964–83, now Professor Emeritus; *b* 25 Oct. 1924; *s* of late Henry Charles Day, MBE, and Ruth Day; *m* 1962, Diana Hope Bocking (*d* 1980); no *c*; *m* 1982, Dr Shirley E. Jones. *Educ:* Chesterfield Grammar Sch.; Queens' Coll., Cambridge. Asst Lecturer, then Lecturer, LSE, 1949–54; Economic Adviser, HM Treas., 1954–56; Reader in Economics, London Univ., 1956–64. Ed., National Inst. Econ. Review, 1960–62; Econ. Correspondent, The Observer, intermittently, 1957–81. Economic Adviser on Civil Aviation, BoT, later Dept of Trade and Industry, 1968–72; Economic Adviser, Civil Aviation Authority, 1972–78. Member: Council, Consumers' Assoc., 1963–82; Board, British Airports Authority, 1965–68; SE Region Econ. Planning Council, 1966–69; Home Office Cttee on the London Taxicab Trade, 1967–70; Layfield Cttee on Local Govt Finance, 1974–76; Air Transport Users' Cttee, CAA, 1978–79; Home Office Adv. Panel on Satellite Broadcasting Standards, 1982. British Acad. Leverhulme Vis. Prof., Graduate Inst. for International Studies, Geneva, 1971. Governor, LSE, 1971–76, 1977–79, Pro-Director, 1979–83; Hon. Fellow, 1988. *Publications:* The Future of Sterling, 1954; Outline of Monetary Economics, 1956; The Economics of Money, 1959; (with S. T. Beza) Wealth and Income, 1960. *Address:* Chart Place, Chart Sutton, Maidstone, Kent ME17 3RE. *T:* (01622) 842236; 13 Gower Mews Mansions, WC1E 6HP. *T:* (020) 7631 3928.

DAY, Andrew Christopher King, CBE 2003; Deputy Bailiff, 1999–2002, Lieutenant Bailiff, 2002–05, Guernsey; *b* 30 Oct. 1941; *m* José Guillemette; one *s* two *d*. *Educ:* Gresham's Sch., Holt; Magdalen Coll., Oxford (BA 1964); Inst. of Educn, London Univ. (Cert. Ed. 1965). Teacher, Kenya, 1965–69; called to the Bar, Gray's Inn, 1970; Advocate, Royal Court of Guernsey, 1971; in private practice, 1971–82; QC (Guernsey) 1989; Solicitor General, HM Comptroller, 1982–92, Attorney General, HM Procureur and Receiver General, 1992–99, Guernsey. *Address:* Sans Souci, Les Dunes, Vazon, Castel, Guernsey GY5 7LQ.

DAY, Bernard Maurice, CB 1987; Chairman, The Riverside (East Molesey) Management Co., 1996–99, 2004–05 (Director, 1999–2004); *b* 7 May 1928; *s* of M. J. Day and Mrs M. H. Day; *m* 1956, Ruth Elizabeth Stansfield; two *s* one *d*. *Educ:* Bancroft's Sch.; London School of Economics (BScEcon). Army service, commnd RA, 1946–48. British Electric Traction Fedn, 1950–51; Asst Principal, Air Ministry, 1951; Private Sec. to Air Mem. for Supply and Organisation, 1954–56; Principal, 1956; Cabinet Secretariat, 1959–61; Asst Sec., 1965; Sec., Meteorological Office, 1965–69; Estabt Officer, Cabinet Office, 1969–72; Head of Air Staff Secretariat, MoD, 1972–74; Asst Under Sec. of State, MoD, 1974; Civilian Staff Management, 1974–76; Operational Requirements, 1976–80; Programmes and Budget, 1980–82; Supply and Orgn, Air, 1982–84; Resident Chm., CSSB, 1984–85; Asst Under-Sec. of State (Fleet Support), MoD, 1985–88. Panel Chm., CSSB, 1988–96. Chairman: MoD Branch, First Div. Assoc., 1983–84; MoD Liaison Cttee with CS Benevolent Fund, 1975–84. Pres., Fellowship Club, Weybridge, 2008. *Recreations:* local church, arts and environment. *Address:* 26 The Riverside, Graburn Way, East Molesey, Surrey KT8 9BF. *T:* (020) 8941 4520. *Club:* Royal Commonwealth Society.

DAY, Prof. Christopher, DPhil; Professor, School of Education, University of Nottingham, since 1993; *b* 3 May 1943; *s* of Walter Day and Patricia Jane Day; *m* 1984, Alison Jane Stewart; two *s*. *Educ:* St Luke's Coll., Exeter (Cert Ed 1964); Univ. of Sussex (MA 1976; DPhil 1979); Univ. of Nottingham (DLitt 2008). LRAM 1966. School teacher, 1964–68; Lectr, 1968–71; LEA Advr, London Borough of Barking and Dagenham, 1972–76; Associate Prof., Univ. of Calgary, Alberta, 1979–81; Lectr, Sen. Lectr and Reader, Univ. of Nottingham, 1981–93. Editor, Developing Teachers and Schools series, 1991–94; Founding Editor, Teachers and Teaching, 1995–; Co-Editor: Jl of In-Service Teacher Educn, 1975–2002; Educational Action Res. Jl, 1993–. FRSA 1972. Hon. PhD Linköping, Sweden, 1993. *Publications:* Developing Teachers: the challenges of lifelong learning, 1999; A Passion for Teaching, 2004; *jointly:* Managing Primary Schools, 1985; Appraisal and Professional Development in Primary Schools, 1987; Reconceptualising School-Based Curriculum Development, 1990; Managing Primary Schools in the 1990s, 1990; Leadership and Curriculum in Primary Schools, 1993; Developing Leadership in Primary Schools, 1998; Leading Schools in Times of Change, 2001; Effective Leadership for School Improvement, 2003; Teachers Matter: connecting work, lives and effectiveness, 2007; *edited jointly:* Staff Development in Secondary Schools, 1986; Partnership in Educational Management, 1988; Insights into Teachers' Thinking and Practice, 1990; Managing the Professional Development of Teachers, 1991; Research on Teacher Thinking, 1993; Childen and Youth at Risk and Urban Education, 1997; Teachers and Teaching: international perspectives on school reform and teacher education, 1997; The Life and Work of Teachers in Changing Times: international perspectives, 1999; Developing Teachers and Teaching Practice, 2002; Theory and Practice in Action Research, 2002; (and contrib.) International Handbook of the Continuing Professional Development of Teachers, 2004; Successful Principal Leadership in Times of Change: an international perspective, 2007. *Recreations:* walking, tennis, reading. *Address:* School of Education, University of Nottingham, Jubilee Campus, Wollaton Road, Nottingham NG8 1BB. *T:* (0115) 951 4423.

DAY, Rev. David Vivian; Principal, St John's College, University of Durham, 1993–99; non-stipendiary Curate, St Nicholas, Durham, since 1999; *b* 11 Aug. 1936; *s* of Frederick Vivian Day and Enid Blodwen (*née* Evans); *m* 1959, Lorna Rosemary Taylor; two *s* one *d*. *Educ:* The Grammar Sch., Tottenham; QMC, Univ. of London (BA Classics); Univ. of Nottingham (MEd, MTheol). Classics Master, Southgate County Sch., 1958–64; Head of Religious Education: Southgate Sch., 1964–66; Bilborough Sch., 1966–73; Sen. Lectr in Theol., Bishop Lonsdale Coll., Derby, 1973–79; Sen. Lectr in Educn, Univ. of Durham, 1979–97. Ordained deacon, 1999, priest, 2000. *Publications:* This Jesus, 1980, 2nd edn 1981; Jeremiah: speaking for God in a time of crisis, 1987; Teenage Beliefs, 1991; (ed jtly) The Contours of Christian Education, 1992; Beyond the Here and Now, 1996; A Preaching Workbook, 1998, 4th edn 2004; Pearl beyond Price, 2002; Christ Our Life, 2003; (ed jtly) A Reader on Preaching, 2005; Embodying the Word, 2005. *Recreations:* keeping fit, watching Rugby and soccer. *Address:* 35 Orchard Drive, The Sands, Durham DH1 1LA. *T:* (0191) 386 6909.

DAY, Sir Derek (Malcolm), KCMG 1984 (CMG 1973); HM Diplomatic Service, retired; High Commissioner to Canada, 1984–87; *b* 29 Nov. 1927; *s* of late Mr and Mrs Alan W. Day; *m* 1955, Sheila Nott; three *s* one *d*. *Educ:* Hurstpierpoint Coll.; St Catharine's Coll., Cambridge. Royal Artillery, 1946–48. Entered HM Foreign Service, Sept. 1951; Third Sec., British Embassy, Tel Aviv, 1953–56; Private Sec. to HM Ambassador, Rome, 1956–59; Second, then First Sec., FO, 1959–62; First Sec., British Embassy, Washington, 1962–66; First Sec., FO, 1966–67; Asst Private Sec. to Sec. of State for Foreign Affairs, 1967–68; Head of Personnel Operations Dept, FCO, 1969–72; Counsellor, British High Commn, Nicosia, 1972–75; Ambassador to Ethiopia, 1975–78; Asst Under-Sec. of State, 1979, Dep. Under-Sec. of State, 1980, and Chief Clerk, 1982–84, FCO. Dir, Monenco Ltd (Canada), 1988–92; Chm., Crystal Palace Sports and Leisure Ltd, 1992–97. Mem., Commonwealth War Graves Commn, 1987–92; Vice-Chm. of Council, British Red Cross, 1988–94. Chm. Governors, Hurstpierpoint Coll., 1987–97; Gov., Bethany Sch., 1987–2000. GB Hockey XI, Olympic Games, 1952. *Address:* Pedlars End, The Plain, Goudhurst, Kent TN17 1AD. *Clubs:* Royal Commonwealth Society; Hawks.

See also W. M. Day.

DAY, Douglas Henry; QC 1989; a Recorder, since 1987; *b* 11 Oct. 1943; *s* of James Henry Day and Nancy Day; *m* 1970, Elizabeth Margaret (*née* Jarman); two *s* one *d*. *Educ:* Bec Sch.; Selwyn Coll., Cambridge (MA). Called to the Bar, Lincoln's Inn, 1967, Bencher, 1996. Asst Parly Boundary Comr, 1994–. Treas., Gen. Council of the Bar, 1999–2001. *Address:* Farrar's Building, Temple, EC4Y 7BD. *T:* (020) 7583 9241. *Clubs:* Garrick; Bec Old Boys Rugby.

DAY, Sir Graham; *see* Day, Sir J. G.

DAY, (Henrietta Miriam) Ottoline; *see* Leyser, H. M. O.

DAY, John Leigh, MD; FRCP; Professor of Internal Medicine, Catholic University of Mozambique, since 2002; *b* 30 Nov. 1939; *s* of Peter Leigh Day and Jean Metcalfe Bailey; *m* 1972, Anne Pamela Northcote; two *s* one *d*. *Educ:* King's Coll., London (MD 1973). FRCP 1979. Medical Registrar: Ipswich and E Suffolk Hosp., 1966; KCH, 1967; Lectr in Medicine, KCL; Consultant Physician, 1972, now Emeritus, Clinical Dir of Medicine, 1998–2002, Ipswich Hosp. Advr on Educn, WHO, 1990–95. Chm., Educn Adv. Cttee, Diabetes UK, 1985–92; Pres., Diabetes Educn Study Gp, European Assoc. of Diabetes, 1985–92. Hon. DSc UEA, 2000. *Publications:* Learning Diabetes Type 1, and Type 2 Diabetic, 1986, 3rd edn 2001; res. articles in Diabetes Educn and Care, Diabetes Medicine, Patient Educn and Counselling, BMJ. *Recreations:* golf, canal boating. *Address:* Playford Grange, Great Bealings, Woodbridge, Ipswich IP13 6PH. *T:* (01473) 735444; *e-mail:* days_bealings@hotmail.com. *Club:* Woodbridge Golf.

DAY, Air Chief Marshal Sir John (Romney), KCB 1999; OBE 1985; FRAeS; Senior Military Adviser, BAE Systems, since 2003; *b* 15 July 1947; *er s* of John George Day and Daphne Myrtle Day (*née* Kelly); *m* 1969, Jane Richards; two *s*. *Educ:* King's Sch., Canterbury; Imperial Coll., Univ. of London (BSc Aer. Eng.). FRAeS 2002. No 72 Sqn, 1970–73; Flying Instructor, RAF Linton-on-Ouse, 1973–76; OC Oxford Univ. Air Sqn, 1976–79; RAF Staff Coll., 1981; PSO to Air Mem. for Personnel, 1982–83; OC No 72 Sqn, 1983–85; OC RAF Odiham, 1987–89; RCDS, 1990; Dir, Air Force Plans and Progs, MoD, 1991–94; AOC No 1 Gp, 1994–97; DCDS (Commitments), MoD, 1997–2000; AMP and C-in-C, RAF PTC, 2000–01; C-in-C Strike Comd, 2001–03; Air ADC to the Queen, 2001–03. FCGI 2002. *Address:* c/o Lloyds TSB, Ashford, Kent TN24 8SS. *Club:* Royal Air Force.

See also N. J. Day.

DAY, Jonathan Stephen, CBE 1999; Director General, Operational Policy, Ministry of Defence, since 2007; *b* 23 April 1954; *s* of late Peter Alan John Day and of Josephine Day; *m* 1980, Sandra Ayres; one *d*. *Educ:* Marling Sch., Stroud; Univ. of Nottingham (LLB Hons 1976). Ministry of Defence: admin trainee, 1979; early posts included Naval, out-of-area and policy studies secretariats, and Asst Private Sec. to Armed Forces Minister; seconded: to FCO in UK Delegn to NATO, Brussels, 1988–92; to NATO as Hd, Force Planning, 1992–95; Dep. Comd Sec., Land Comd, 1995–97; Dir, Defence Policy, 1997–99; sabbatical, Harvard Univ., 1999–2000; seconded: to Cabinet Office as Chief, Jt Intelligence Cttee Assessments Staff, 2000–01; to NATO as Dir, Sec. Gen.'s Private Office, 2001–03; Comd Sec., Fleet Comd, 2004–06. *Publication:* Gloucester and Newbury 1643, Turning Point of the Civil War, 2007. *Recreations:* history, reading, theatre and cinema, cricket, walking, unsuitably juvenile loud music. *Address:* c/o Ministry of Defence, SW1A 2EU.

DAY, Sir (Judson) Graham, Kt 1989; Chairman, PowerGen, 1990–93 (Director, 1990–93); *b* 3 May 1933; *s* of Frank Charles Day and Edythe Grace (*née* Baker); *m* 1958, Leda Ann (*née* Creighton); one *s* two *d*. *Educ:* Queen Elizabeth High Sch., Halifax, NS; Dalhousie Univ., Halifax, NS (LLB). Private practice of Law, Windsor, Nova Scotia, 1956–64; Canadian Pacific Ltd, Montreal and Toronto, 1964–71; Chief Exec., Cammell Laird Shipbuilders Ltd, Birkenhead, Eng., 1971–75; Dep. Chm., Organising Cttee for British Shipbuilders and Dep. Chm. and Chief Exec. designate, British Shipbuilders, 1975–76; Prof. of Business Admin and Dir, Canadian Marine Transportation Centre, Dalhousie Univ., NS, 1977–81; Vice-Pres., Shipyards & Marine Devélt, Dome Petroleum Ltd, 1981–83; Chm. and Chief Exec., British Shipbuilders, 1983–86; Chief Exec., 1986–88, Chm., 1986–91, BL, subseq. The Rover Gp Hldgs. Chm., Cadbury Schweppes, 1989–93 (Dir, 1988–93); Deputy Chairman: MAI plc, 1989–93 (Dir, 1988–93); Ugland Internat. Hldgs plc, 1997–; Director: The Laird Gp plc, 1985; British Aerospace, 1986–92 (Chairman, 1991–92); Extendicare (formerly Crownx) Inc. (Canada), 1989–; Bank of Nova Scotia (Canada), 1989–2004; NOVA Corp. of Alberta, 1990–; EMI Gp, 1991; Empire Co. Ltd, 1991–; Sobeys Inc., 1998–. Counsel, Stewart McKelvey (formerly Stewart McKelvey Stirling Scales), 1991–. Pres., ISBA, 1991–93. Member: Nova Scotia Barristers' Soc.; Law Soc. of Upper Canada; Canadian Bar Assoc. Freeman, City of London. ARINA. Hon. Fellow, Univ. of Wales Coll. of Cardiff, 1990. Hon. doctorates: Dalhousie; City; CNAA; Cranfield; Aston; Warwick; Humberside; South Bank. *Recreation:* reading. *Address:* 18 Avon Street, PO Box 423, Hantsport, NS B0P 1P0, Canada.

DAY, Lance Reginald; Keeper, Science Museum Library, 1976–87; *b* 2 Nov. 1927; *s* of late Reginald and Eileen Day; *m* 1959, Mary Ann Sheahan; one *s* two *d*. *Educ:* Sherrardswood Sch., Welwyn Garden City; Alleyne's Grammar Sch., Stevenage; Northern Polytechnic (BSc London); University Coll., London (MSc Hist. and Philos. of Sci.). Res. Asst, Science Museum Library, 1951–64, Asst Keeper 1964–70; Asst Keeper, Science Museum, Dept of Chemistry, 1970–74; Keeper, Science Museum, Dept of Communications and Electrical Engrg, 1974–76. Sec., Nat. Railway Museum Cttee, 1973–75; Newcomen Society: Hon. Sec., 1973–82; Mem., 1996; Ed., Trans of

Newcomen Soc. (Chm., Editl Bd, 1990–2000). *Publications:* Broad Gauge, 1985; (contrib.) Encyclopaedia of the History of Technology, 1990; (ed jtly and contrib.) Biographical Dictionary of the History of Technology, 1996; reviews and articles. *Recreation:* music. *Address:* 12 Rhinefield Close, Brockenhurst, Hants SO42 7SU. *T:* (01590) 622079.

DAY, Lucienne, OBE 2004; RDI 1962; in freelance practice, since 1948; Consultant, with Robin Day, to John Lewis Partnership, 1962–87; *b* 1917; *d* of Felix Conradi and Dulcie Lilian Duncan-Smith; *m* 1942, Robin Day, *qv*; one *d*. *Educ:* Convent Notre Dame de Sion, Worthing; Croydon School of Art; Royal Coll. of Art. ARCA 1940; FSIAD 1955. Teacher, Beckenham Sch. of Art, 1942–47; began designing full-time, dress fabrics and later furnishing fabrics, carpets, wallpapers, table-linen, 1947 for Edinburgh Weavers, Heal's Fabrics, Cavendish Textiles, Tomkinsons, Wilton Royal, Thos Somerset etc, and firms in Scandinavia, USA and Germany; also china decoration for Rosenthal China, Selb, Bavaria, 1956–68; work for Barbican Art Centre, 1979; currently designing and making silk wall-hangings (silk mosaics). Retrospective exhibitions: Whitworth Art Gall., Manchester, and RCA, 1993; Aberdeen, 1994; Barbican, 2001; Mackintosh Gall., Glasgow, 2003. Work in permanent collections: V&A; Whitworth Art Gall. Museum; Trondheim Museum, Norway; Cranbrook Museum, Michigan, USA; Art Inst. of Chicago; Röhsska Mus., Gothenberg, Sweden; Musée des Arts Décoratifs, Montreal. Member: Rosenthal Studio-line Jury, 1960–68; Cttee, Duke of Edinburgh's Prize for Elegant Design, 1960–63; Council, RCA, 1962–67; RSA Design Bursaries Juries; Cttee, Sir Misha Black Awards, 1980–2007. Master, Faculty of Royal Designers for Industry, 1987–89. Hon. FRIBA 1997. Sen. Fellow, RCA, 1999. Hon. DDes: Southampton, 1995; Buckingham, 2003. First Award, Amer. Inst. of Decorators, 1950; Gold Medal, 9th Triennale di Milano, 1951; Gran Premio, 10th Triennale di Milano, 1954; Design Council Awards, 1957, 1960, 1968; Silver Medal, Weavers' Co., 2005. *Relevant publication:* Robin and Lucienne Day: pioneers of contemporary design, by Lesley Jackson, 2001. *Recreation:* gardening. *Address:* 21 West Street, Chichester, W Sussex PO19 1QW. *T:* (01243) 781429.

DAY, Sir Michael (John), Kt 1992; OBE 1981; Chairman, Commission for Racial Equality, 1988–93; *b* 4 Sept. 1933; *s* of Albert Day and Ellen Florence (*née* Itter); *m* 1960, June Marjorie, *d* of late Dr John William and Edith Mackay; one *s* one *d*. *Educ:* University College Sch., Hampstead; Selwyn Coll., Cambridge (MA); London School of Economics (Cert. Social Work and Social Admin). Probation Officer, Surrey, 1960–64; Sen. Probation Officer, W Sussex, 1964–67; Asst Prin. Probation Officer, 1967–68, Chief Probation Officer, 1968–76, Surrey; Chief Probation Officer, W Midlands, 1976–88. Chm., Chief Probation Officers' Conf., 1974–77; First Chm., Assoc. Chief Officers of Probation, 1982–84. Member: Probation Adv. and Trng Bd, Home Office, 1970–73; Adv. Council for Probation and Aftercare, 1973–78. Member Council: Howard League for Penal Reform, 1966–73; Volunteer Centre, 1977–81; Grubb Inst., 1980–93. Dir, Shropshire and Mid Wales Hospice, 1998–2003. *Publications:* contribs to professional jls and others. *Recreations:* books, music, woodturning, gardening, the countryside. *Address:* 30 Broad Street, Ludlow, Shropshire SY8 1NJ.

DAY, Michael Patrick; Chief Executive, Historic Royal Palaces, since 2003; *b* 20 Feb. 1953; *s* of Harry and Anne Day; *m* 1998, Anne Murch; one *s* one *d*. *Educ:* Nottingham High Sch.; Univ. of Leeds (BA Hons (English) 1974). Graduate trainee, Mus. Asst, then Asst Keeper of Social Hist., Norfolk Mus Service, 1974–83; Curator of Social Hist., Ironbridge Gorge Mus. Trust, 1983–86; Dir, Jersey Heritage Trust, 1987–2003. Mem. Faculty, Mus. Leadership Prog., UEA, 1994–; Co-Dir, Nordic Mus. Leadership Prog., Copenhagen, 2001–. FMA 1994; FRSA 1995; FCMI (FIMgt 1999); CCMI 2007. *Recreations:* family and friends, ski-ing, sailing, Aston Villa FC, real tennis, music, cinema. *Address:* Historic Royal Palaces, Apt 39, Hampton Court Palace, Surrey KT8 9AU. *T:* (020) 8781 9751; *e-mail:* michael.day@hrp.org.uk. *Clubs:* Ski Club of Great Britain; Royal Tennis Court; St Catherine's Sailing (St Martin, Jersey).

DAY, Prof. Nicholas Edward, CBE 2001; PhD; FRS 2004; FRCPath, FMedSci; MRC Research Professor in Epidemiology, 1999–2004, and Fellow of Hughes Hall, since 1992, University of Cambridge; *b* 24 Sept. 1939; *s* of late John King Day, TD and Mary Elizabeth (*née* Stinton); *m* 1961, Jocelyn Deanne Broughton; one *s* one *d*. *Educ:* Magdalen Coll., Oxford (BA Maths); Aberdeen Univ. (PhD Med. Stats). FRCPath 1997. Res. Fellow, Aberdeen Univ., 1962–66; Fellow, ANU, 1966–69; Statistician, 1969–78, Head, Unit of Biostats and Field Studies, 1979–86, Internat. Agency for Res. on Cancer, Lyon; Cancer Expert, Nat. Cancer Inst., USA, 1978–79; Dir, 1986–89, Hon. Dir, 1989–99, MRC Biostats Unit; Prof. of Public Health, Cambridge Univ., 1989–99; Fellow, Churchill Coll., Cambridge, 1986–92. Founder FMedSci 1998. *Publications:* Statistical Methods in Cancer Research, vol. 1 1980, vol. 2 1988; Screening for Cancer of the Uterine Cervix, 1986; Screening for Breast Cancer, 1988; over 300 articles in scientific jls. *Recreations:* sea fishing, fruit growing. *Address:* La Cordonnerie, La Bellieuse, St Martin's, Guernsey GY4 6RP. *T:* (01481) 238740.

DAY, Air Vice Marshal Nigel James, CBE 2000; FRAeS; Senior Defence Adviser, MBDA Missile Systems, since 2004; *b* 13 Feb. 1949; *s* of John George Day and Daphne Myrtle Day (*née* Kelly); *m* 1971, Gillian Cronk; one *s* one *d*. *Educ:* King's Sch., Canterbury; Imperial Coll., Univ. of London (BSc). No 45 Sqn, 1974; No 17 Sqn, 1975–76; No 31 Sqn, 1976–78; No 725 Sqn, Royal Danish Air Force, 1979–81; Flight Comdr, No 226 (Jaguar) OCU, 1982–83; RAF Staff Coll., 1984; Operational Requirements Staff, MoD, 1985–87; OC No 617 (DamBusters) Sqn, 1987–90; Air Offensive Staff, MoD, 1990–93; OC RAF Lossiemouth, 1993–95; rcds, 1996; OC Brit. Forces, Gulf Region, 1997; Dir, Air Ops, Strike Command, 1997–99; Dep. UK Mil. Rep. to NATO, 1999–2001; Capability Manager (Strike), MoD, 2001–04. FRAeS 2004. *Publications:* contrib. to RUSI jl. *Recreations:* dog walking, sailing, painting. *Club:* Royal Air Force.

See also Air Chief Marshal Sir J. R. Day.

DAY, Prof. Peter, DPhil; FRS 1986; Fullerian Professor of Chemistry, Royal Institution, since 1994; Royal Institution Professorial Research Fellow, University College London, since 1995 (Honorary Fellow, 2003); *b* 20 Aug. 1938; *s* of Edgar Day and Ethel Hilda Day (*née* Russell); *m* 1964, Frances Mary Elizabeth Anderson; one *s* one *d*. *Educ:* Maidstone Grammar School; Wadham College, Oxford (BA 1961; MA, DPhil 1965; Hon. Fellow, 1991). Cyanamid European Research Institute, Geneva, 1962; Jun. Res. Fellow, 1963–65, Official Fellow, 1965–91, Hon. Fellow, 1994, St John's College, Oxford; Departmental Demonstrator, 1965–67, Lectr in Inorganic Chemistry, 1967–89, *ad hominem* Prof. of Solid State Chemistry, 1989–91, Oxford Univ. Dir, Inst. Laue-Langevin, Grenoble, 1988–91 (on secondment); Royal Institution: Dir, 1991–98; Resident Prof. of Chemistry, 1991–94; Dir, Davy Faraday Res. Lab., 1991–98. Prof. Associé, Univ. de Paris-Sud, 1975; Guest Prof., Univ. of Copenhagen, 1978; Iberdrola Prof., Univ. of Valencia, 2001. Vis. Fellow, ANU, 1980; Senior Research Fellow, SRC, 1977–82. Lectures: Du Pont, Indiana Univ., 1988; Royal Soc. Blackett Meml, 1994; Bakerian, 1999; ACL, Chinese Univ. Hong Kong, 1997; Birch, ANU, 1997; Humphry Davy, 2002. Science and Engineering Research Council: Member: Neutron Beam Res. Cttee, 1983–88; Chemistry Cttee, 1985–88; Molecular Electronics Cttee, 1987–88; Nat. Cttee on Superconductivity, 1987–88; Materials Commn, 1988–90; COPUS, 1991–98. Member: Sci. and Engrg Cttee, British Council, 1991–98; Phys. and Engrg Sci. Cttee, ESF, 1994–2000; Medicines Commn, 1998–2005; Council Member: Inst. for Molecular Scis, Okazaki, Japan, 1991–95; Parly and Scientific Cttee, 1992–98. Royal Society of Chemistry: Vice-Pres., Dalton Div., 1986–88; Corday-Morgan Medal, 1971; Solid State Chem. Award, 1986; Daiwa Adrian Prize, Daiwa Foundn, 1998. Gov., Birkbeck Coll., London, 1993–2001. Mem., Academia Europaea, 1992 (Mem. Council, 2000–; Treas., 2000–; Trustee, 2002–). Hon. Foreign Mem., Indian Soc. of Materials Res., 1994. Hon. Fellow, Indian Acad. of Sci., 1995. Hon. DSc: Newcastle, 1994; Kent, 1999. *Publications:* Physical Methods in Advanced Inorganic Chemistry (ed with H. A. O. Hill), 1968; Electronic States of Inorganic Compounds, 1974; Emission and Scattering Techniques, 1980; Electronic Structure and Magnetism of Inorganic Compounds, vols 1–7, 1972–82; (ed with A. K. Cheetham) Solid State Chemistry, vol. 1 1987, vol. 2 1992; The Philosopher's Tree, 1999; Nature Not Mocked, 2006; Molecules into Materials, 2007; papers in Jl Chem. Soc.; Inorg. Chem. *Recreation:* cultivating gardens (horticultural and Voltairean). *Address:* 21 Albemarle Street, W1S 4BS. *T:* (020) 7679 2979.

DAY, Peter Rodney, PhD; Founding Director, Biotechnology Center for Agriculture and the Environment (formerly Center for Agricultural Molecular Biology), Rutgers University, New Jersey, 1987–2001; *b* 27 Dec. 1928; *s* of Roland Percy Day and Florence Kate (*née* Dixon); *m* 1950, Lois Elizabeth Rhodes; two *s* one *d*. *Educ:* Birkbeck Coll., Univ. of London (BSc, PhD). John Innes Institute, 1946–63; Associate Prof. of Botany, Ohio State Univ., 1963–64; Chief, Dept of Genetics, Connecticut Agricl Experiment Station, 1964–79; Dir, Plant Breeding Inst., Cambridge, 1979–87. Sec., Internat. Genetics Fedn, 1984–93. Special Prof. of Botany, Nottingham Univ., 1982–88. Commonwealth Fund Fellow, 1954; John Simon Guggenheim Meml Fellow, 1973. *Publications:* Fungal Genetics (with J. R. S. Fincham), 1963, 4th edn 1979; Genetics of Host-Parasite Interaction, 1974; (with H. H. Prell) Plant-Fungal Pathogen Interaction, 2001; contrib. Genetical Research, Genetics, Heredity, Nature, Proc. Nat. Acad. Sci., Phytopathology, etc. *Recreation:* Scottish country dancing. *Address:* Biotechnology Center for Agriculture and the Environment, Rutgers, State University of New Jersey, NJ 08901–8520, USA. *T:* (732) 9328165; *e-mail:* peterday@optonline.net.

DAY, Robin, OBE 1983; RDI 1959; FCSD (FSIAD 1948); design consultant and freelance designer; *b* 25 May 1915; *s* of Arthur Day and Mary Shersby; *m* 1942, Lucienne Conradi (*see* Lucienne Day); one *d*. *Educ:* Royal Coll. of Art (ARCA). National scholarship to RCA, 1935–39; teacher and lectr for several yrs; Design Consultant: Hille International, 1948–; John Lewis Partnership, 1962–87. Commissions include: seating for many major concert halls, theatres, stadia, etc.; interior design of Super VC10 and other aircraft. Mem., juries for many national and internat. indust. design competitions. Sen. Fellow, RCA, 1991; Hon. FRIBA; Hon. Fellow, Kent Inst. of Art & Design, 1998. Hon. DDes Buckingham Chilterns UC, 2003. Many awards for design work, including: 6 Design Centre awards; Gold Medal, Triennale di Milano, 1951, and Silver Medal, 1954; Designs Medal, SIAD, 1957. *Relevant publication:* Robin and Lucienne Day: pioneers of contemporary design, by Lesley Jackson, 2001. *Recreations:* mountaineering, ski touring, hill-walking. *Address:* 21 West Street, Chichester, W Sussex PO19 1QW. *T:* (01243) 781429. *Clubs:* Alpine, Alpine Ski.

DAY, Rosemary; non-executive Director, Northern Ireland Department of Regional Development, since 2007; *b* 20 Sept. 1942; *d* of Albert Rich and Alice Rich (*née* Wren); *m* (marr. diss.). *Educ:* Bedford Coll., Univ. of London (BA Hons 1964). ATII 1978. Asst Dir Gen., GLC, 1964–83; Admin. Dir, London Transport, 1983–88; Ops Dir, Allied Dunbar, 1988–94; Chm., London Ambulance Service, 1995–99. Non-executive Director: Nationwide Building Soc., 1984–88; Milk Mktg Bd, 1993–95; London Transport, 1994–99; Govt Offices Mgt Bd, 1996–98; NATS, 1997–2001; UKAEA, 1999–2006; Picker Inst. Europe, 2002–05. Member: Legal Aid Adv. Bd, 1992–94; Member, Sen. Salaries Review Body, 1994–2000. Chm., Joyful Company of Singers, 1988–2001. Trustee: Railway Children, 1999–; Chiswick House and Grounds Trust, 2005–. CCMI (CBIM 1984); FRSA. *Recreations:* the arts, gardening, books. *Address:* 63a Barrowgate Road, W4 4QT.

DAY, Sir Simon (James), Kt 1997; farmer; *b* 22 Jan. 1935; *s* of late John Adam Day and Kathleen Day (*née* Hebditch); *m* 1959, Hilary Maureen Greenslade Gomm; two *s* (and one *s* decd). *Educ:* S Devon Tech. Coll.; Emmanuel Coll., Cambridge (MA Hist.). Nat. Service, RN, 1954–56. Devon County Council: Councillor, Modbury Div., 1964–74, Modbury and Salcombe Div., 1974–2005, Thurlestone, Salcombe and Allington Div., 2005–; Whip, 1981–89; Dep. Leader, 1989, Leader, 1991–93; Opposition Leader, 1993–99; Chm., 2001–02. Non-exec. Dir, SW Water, 1989–98; Regl Dir, Portman Building Soc., 1989–91; Director: Plymouth Sound Radio, 1966–80; Plymouth Develt Corp., 1993–96; Exeter Internat. Airport, 1997–2006; Chm., West of England Newspapers Gp, 1981–86. Mem., Exec. Council, ACC, 1981–85, 1990–96 (Chm., Police Cttee, 1991–93; Dep. Leader, 1992; Vice Chm., 1993–95; Cons. Leader, 1993–95); Chm., Devon and Cornwall Police Authy, 1990–93; Member: Police Adv. Bd, Home Office, 1989–93; Police Negotiating Bd, 1989–93; Chairman: Devon Sea Fisheries Cttee, 1986–95; Assoc. of Sea Fisheries Cttees, England and Wales, 1993–96 (Vice-Chm., 1991–93); Mem., Govt Salmon Adv. Cttee, 1987–90; Chm., Devon and Cornwall Develt Bureau, 1989–91; Vice Chairman: Nat. Parks Cttee for England and Wales, 1981–83; Local Govt Finance Cttee, 1983–85; Member: Consultative Council, Local Govt Finance, 1983–85 and 1993; Standing Conf. of Local and Regl Authies, Council of Europe, 1990–97; Cttee of Regions, EU, 1994–97, 1998–2001, 2002–05, 2006– (Vice-Chm., UK Delegn, 2006–); Chm., Cons. Nat. Local Govt Adv. Cttee, 1994–95; Cons. Leader and Vice Chm., SW Regl Assembly, 2004–; Mem. Bd (formerly Dir), Europ. and Internat. Unit, LGA (formerly Local Govt Internat. Bureau), 2004–07. President: S Devon Herd Book Soc., 1986; Devon County Agricl Assoc., 1996–97; Devon Co. Show, 2006–07. Chm. Govs, Bicton Coll. of Agric., 1983–2000. Trustee, West Country Rivers Trust, 1997–. Mem. Court, Exeter Univ., 1964–. Pres., Devon County LTA, 2002–. Contested (C): Carmarthen, 1966, by-election 1966; N Cornwall, 1970. High Sheriff, Devon, 1999–2000. Hereditary Freeman, City of Norwich. *Recreations:* shooting, sailing, fishing. *Address:* Keaton House, near Ivybridge, Devon PL21 0LB. *T:* (01752) 691212. *Clubs:* Buck's, Royal Thames Yacht; Royal Yacht Squadron; Hawks (Cambridge) (Hon. Mem., 1995).

DAY, Stephen Charles; Chief Executive, Norfolk and Norwich University Hospital NHS Trust, 2003–04; *b* 17 Feb. 1954; *s* of Peter Charles Day and June Lillian Day; *m* 1975 (marr. diss.); one *s* one *d*; *m* 2000, Dr V. A. Chishty. *Educ:* Queen Elizabeth's GS for Boys, Barnet. CPFA 1978. Various NHS posts, 1972–84; Dep. Treas., Canterbury and Thanet HA, 1984–86; Dep. Regl Treas., South Western RHA, 1986–89; Dir of Finance and Computing, Southmead HA, 1989–92; Dir of Finance, Southmead Health Services NHS Trust, 1992–93; Regl Dir of Finance, W Midlands RHA, 1993–96; Regl Dir, W Midlands, NHS Exec., DoH, 1996–2002; Chief Exec., Broadland PCT, 2002. *Recreations:* classical music, gardening.

DAY, Stephen Nicholas; a District Judge (Magistrates' Courts) (formerly Stipendiary Magistrate), Middlesex, since 1991; *b* 17 Aug. 1947; *s* of late Robert Weatherston Day and Margaret Diana (*née* McKenzie); *m* 1973, Shama (*née* Tak); one *s* one *d*. *Educ:* St Mary's Coll., Southampton; King Edward VI Sch., Southampton; Brasenose Coll., Oxford (MA). Called to the Bar, Middle Temple, 1972. Sen. Court Clerk, Nottingham, 1973–77; Justices Clerk, Abingdon, Didcot and Wantage, 1977–91. Member: Gtr London Magistrates' Courts Authy, 2002–05; Sentencing Adv. Panel, Sentencing Guidelines Council, 2006–. *Address:* c/o Feltham Magistrates' Court, Hanworth Road, Feltham, Middlesex TW13 5AF. *T:* (020) 8917 3400. *Club:* Oxford and Cambridge.

DAY, Stephen Peter, CMG 1989; HM Diplomatic Service, retired; consultant, Middle East affairs; *b* 19 Jan. 1938; *s* of Frank William and Mary Elizabeth Day; *m* 1965, Angela Doreen (*née* Waudby); one *s* two *d*. *Educ:* Bancroft's School; Corpus Christi Coll., Cambridge. MA. Entered HMOCS as Political Officer, Western Aden Protectorate, 1961, transf. to FO, 1965; Senior Political Officer, South Arabian Federation, 1964–67; FO, 1967–70; First Sec., Office of C-in-C, Far East, Singapore, 1970–71; First Sec. (Press), UK Mission to UN, NY, 1971–75; FCO, 1976–77; Counsellor, Beirut, 1977–78; Consul-Gen., Edmonton, 1979–81; Ambassador to Qatar, 1981–84; Head of ME Dept, FCO, 1984–87; attached to Household of the Prince of Wales, 1986; Ambassador to Tunisia, 1987–92; Sen. British Trade Comr, Hong Kong, 1992–93; Dir, Council for Advancement of Arab-British Understanding, 1993–94. Dir, Claremont Associates, 1995–. Mem., Exec. Cttee, Soc. for Arabian Studies, 1995–2000. Chairman: British-Tunisian Soc., 1993–; Palestine Exploration Fund, 1995–2000; British-Yemeni Soc., 1998–99; MBI Trust, SOAS, 2000–03; MBI Foundn, 2002–07. Governor, Qatar Academy, 1996–2002. Comdr, Order of the Republic (Tunisia), 2002. *Publication:* At Home in Carthage, 1991. *Recreations:* walking, family. *Address:* 15 St James's Place, SW1A 1NP. *T:* 07971 806677. *Clubs:* Oriental; Hong Kong.

DAY, Stephen Richard; public affairs consultant; *b* 30 Oct. 1948; *s* of late Francis and of Anne Day; one *s* by former marriage. *Educ:* Otley Secondary Modern Sch.; Park Lane Coll., Leeds; Leeds Polytechnic. MIEx 1972. Sales Clerk, William Sinclair & Sons, stationary manufrs, Otley, W Yorks, 1965–70, Asst Sales Manager (working in Home and Export Depts), 1970–77; Sales Representative: Larkfield Printing Co. Ltd (part of Hunting Group), Brighouse, W Yorks, 1977–80; A. H. Leach & Co. (part of Hunting Gp), photographic processing lab., Brighouse, 1980–84; Sales Executive: PPL Chromacopy, photographic labs, Leeds and Manchester, 1984–86; Chromogene, photographic lab., Leeds, 1986–87. Vice-President: Stockport Chamber of Commerce, 1987–2001; Stockport and Dist Heart Foundn, 1985–. Chm., Yorks Area Cons. Political Centre, 1983–86; Vice-Chm., NW Leeds Constituency, 1983–86. Town Councillor, Otley, 1975–76 and 1979–83; City Councillor, Leeds, 1975–80. Contested (C): Bradford West, 1983; Cheadle, 2001; Prospective Parly Cand. (C) Cheadle, 2002. MP (C) Cheadle, 1987–2001. An Opposition Whip, 1997–2001. Member: Select Cttee on Social Security, 1990–97; Select Cttee on Envmt, Transport and Regions, 1997; Co-Chm., Parly Adv. Council for Transport Safety, 1989–97; Vice-Chm., All-Party Non-Profit-Making Clubs Gp, 1995–2001; Co-Chm., All-Party West Coast Main Line Gp, 1993–2001. Sponsor, Private Member's Bill to introduce compulsory wearing of rear car seat belts by children, 1988. Vice-Chm., CPA (UK), 1996–97; Nat. Chm., Assoc. of Cons. Clubs, 1997– (Vice-Chm., 1995–97). Pres., Council of Registered Club Assocs, 2002–. Mem., Bramhall and Woodford Rotary Club; Pres., Cheadle Hulme Br., RBL, 2001–. *Publications:* pamphlets on Otley and on rate reform. *Recreations:* movies, music, history (particularly Roman). *Club:* Cheadle Hulme Conservative (Cheadle Hulme).

DAY, William, PhD; CPhys; Director, Silsoe Research Institute, BBSRC, 1999–2006; Visiting Professor, Cranfield University at Silsoe, since 2003; *b* 11 June 1949; *s* of late Arthur Thomas Day and Barbara Nan Day; *m* 1973, Virginia Lesley Elisabeth Playford; two *s* one *d*. *Educ:* Norwich Sch.; Gonville and Caius Coll., Cambridge (MA Natural Scis (Physics)); PhD Physics Cantab 1974. CPhys 1980. Higher Scientific Officer, SSO, then PSO, Physics Dept, Rothamsted Exptl Stn, 1974–81 Head: Envmtl Physiol. Gp, Long Ashton Res. Stn, 1982–83; Physiology and Envmtl Physics Dept, Rothamsted Exptl Stn, 1983–88; Process Engrg Div., Silsoe Res. Inst., 1988–99. Special Prof. of Agricl Engrg, Univ. of Nottingham, 1993–2002. Ed.-in-Chief, Biosystems Engineering, 2007–. *Publications:* contribs relating to interaction between biological systems and envmt in numerous jls, include. Jl Agricl Sci., Agricl and Forest Meteorol. and Phytopathol. *Recreations:* bird watching, choral singing, running.

DAY, William Michael; Senior Associate, University of Cambridge Programme for Industry, since 2003; Special Adviser, United Nations Development Programme, since 2004; *b* 26 June 1956; *s* of Sir Derek (Malcolm) Day, *qv*; *m* 1986, Kate Gardener; one *s* two *d*. *Educ:* Univ. of Exeter (BA). Save the Children Fund: Uganda, 1983; Ethiopia, 1983–84; Sudan, 1984–86; BBC World Service for Africa, 1986–87; Oxfam, Ethiopia, 1987–88; Grants Dir for Africa, Charity Projects/Comic Relief, 1988–94; Dir, Opportunity Trust, 1994–96; Chief Exec., CARE International UK, 1996–2004. Non-exec. Dir, S Kent Hosps NHS Trust, 1994–96. Public Appts Ind. Assessor, DCMS, 1999–; Mem. Council, ODI, 2000–; Chm., Water and Sanitation for the Urban Poor, 2006–. Member: BBC Central Appeals Cttee, 1992–2003 (Chm., 1997–2003); Grants Council, Charities Aid Foundn, 1990–94; Globalisation and Global Poverty Commn, 2006–; Trustee: BBC Children in Need, 1998–2008 (Chm., 2006–08); Disasters Emergency Cttee, 1998–2004. *Address:* Pilgrims, Hastingleigh, Ashford, Kent TN25 5HP. *T:* (01233) 750196; *e-mail:* william.day@phonecoop.coop.

DAY-LEWIS, Daniel; actor; *s* of late Cecil Day-Lewis, CBE, CLit and Jill Angela Henriette Balcon; *m* 1996, Rebecca, *d* of Arthur Miller, playwright; two *s*. *Educ:* Bedales; Bristol Old Vic Theatre Sch. *Stage:* The Recruiting Officer, Troilus and Cressida, Funny Peculiar, Old King Cole, A Midsummer Night's Dream, Class Enemy, Edward II, Oh! What a Lovely War, Look Back in Anger, Dracula, Another Country, Romeo and Juliet, The Futurists, Hamlet; *films:* Gandhi, 1981; The Saga of HMS Bounty, 1983; My Beautiful Laundrette, 1985; A Room With a View, 1985; Nanou, 1985; The Unbearable Lightness of Being, 1986; Stars and Bars, 1987; My Left Foot, 1988 (Oscar best actor and numerous other awards); Ever Smile New Jersey, 1988; Last of the Mohicans, 1991 (Variety Club best actor); Age of Innocence, 1992; In the Name of the Father, 1993; The Crucible, 1997; The Boxer, 1998; Gangs of New York, 2002; The Ballad of Jack and Rose, 2006; There Will Be Blood, 2008 (Oscar and BAFTA for best actor); principal roles in TV. *Address:* c/o Julian Belfrage Associates, Adam House, 14 New Burlington Street, W1S 3BQ.

DAY-LEWIS, Séan; journalist and author; *b* 3 Aug. 1931; *s* of late Cecil Day-Lewis, CBE, CLit and Mary Day-Lewis; *m* 1960, Anna Mott; one *s* one *d*. *Educ:* Allhallows Sch., Rousdon, Devon. National Service, RAF, 1949–51. Bridport News, 1952–53; Southern Times, Weymouth, 1953–54; Herts Advertiser, St Albans, 1954–56; Express and Star, Wolverhampton, 1956–60; The Daily Telegraph, 1960–86 (first nat. newspaper Arts Reporter, 1965–70; TV and Radio Editor, 1970–86); TV Editor, London Daily News, 1987; TV Critic, Country Life, 1989–2003. Arts Editor, Socialist Commentary, 1966–71; Founder-Chm., 1975, Chm., 1990–92, BPG; Vice Pres., Bulleid Soc., 1970; Member, BAFTA, 1976. *Publications:* Bulleid: last giant of steam, 1964; C. Day-Lewis: an English literary life, 1980; (ed) One Day in the Life of Television, 1989; TV Heaven: a review of British television from the 1930s to the 1990s, 1992; Talk of Drama: views of the television dramatist now and then, 1998. *Recreations:* music (J. S. Bach preferred), tennis, walking, giving in to temptation. *Address:* Restorick Row, Rosemary Lane, Colyton, Devon EX24 6LW. *T:* (01297) 553039.

DAYAN, Edouard; General Director, International Bureau, Universal Postal Union, since 2005. La Poste, France: Hd, Air Transport Bureau, 1984–86; Manager, Dept of Internat. Mail Mgt and Internat. Accounting, then Internat. Partnership Strategy Dept, 1986–92; European Commission: expert, 1992–93; Dep. Dir, 1993–97, Dir, 1998–2005, Eur. and Internat. Affairs. Chm., Eur. Social Dialogue Cttee for postal sector, 1994–; former Mem., Mgt Bd, PostEurop; Universal Postal Union: Chm., Tech. Co-operation Action Gp; Chm., Bd of Trustees, Quality Service Fund. Chevalier: Ordre national du Mérite (France); Légion d'Honneur (France). *Address:* Universal Postal Union, Weltpoststrasse 4, 3000 Bern 15, Switzerland.

DAYKIN, Christopher David, CB 1993; FIA; Government Actuary, 1989–2007; *b* 18 July 1948; *s* of John Francis Daykin and Mona Daykin; *m* 1977, Kathryn Ruth (*née* Tingey); two *s* one *d*. *Educ:* Merchant Taylors' Sch., Northwood; Pembroke Coll., Cambridge (BA 1970, MA 1973). FIA 1973. Government Actuary's Department, 1970; VSO, Brunei, 1971; Govt Actuary's Dept, 1972–78; Principal (Health and Social Services), HM Treasury, 1978–80; Govt Actuary's Dept, 1980–2007, Principal Actuary, 1982–84, Directing Actuary (Social Security), 1985–89. Mem., Council, Inst. of Actuaries, 1985–99 (Hon. Sec., 1988–90; Vice Pres., 1993–94; Pres., 1994–96); Chm., Internat. Forum of Actuarial Assocs, 1996–97; Chairman: Perm. Cttee for Statistical, Actuarial and Financial Studies, ISSA, 1992–2007; Educn Cttee, Groupe Consultatif Actuariel Européen, 1992–2007. Mem. Pensions Observatory, EC Commn, 1992–96. Chm., CS Insce Soc. Visiting Professor: City Univ., 1997–; Shanghai Univ. of Finance and Econs, 1998–. Treasurer, Emmanuel Church, Northwood, 1982–87 and 1998–2008; Chm., VSO Harrow and Hillingdon, 1976–91. Hon. DSc City, 1995. *Publications:* Practical Risk Theory, 1993; articles and papers on pensions, demography, consumer credit, social security and insurance. *Recreations:* travel, photography, languages. *Address:* c/o Institute of Actuaries, Staple Inn Hall, High Holborn, WC1V 7QJ.

DEACON, Keith Vivian; international tax and management consultant, 1996–2004; Under Secretary, 1988–95, and Director of Quality Development, 1993–95, Inland Revenue; *b* 19 Nov. 1935; *s* of Vivian and Louisa Deacon; *m* 1960, Brenda Chater; one *s* one *d*. *Educ:* Sutton County Grammar School; Bristol Univ. (BA Hons English Lang. and Litt.). Entered Inland Revenue as Inspector of Taxes, 1962; Regional Controller, 1985; Dir, Technical Div. I until Head Office reorganisation, 1988; Dir, Insce and Specialist Div., 1988–91; Dir of Operations, 1991–93. Part time work for Civil Service Selection Board: Observer, 1969–72; Chairman, 1985–87. FRSA 1992. *Recreations:* living for part of the year in France, keeping up with four grandchildren, photography, music, reading, architecture.

DEACON, Richard, CBE 1999; RA 1998; sculptor; *b* Bangor, 15 Aug. 1949; *s* of late Gp Capt. Edward William Deacon, RAF (retd) and Dr Joan Bullivant Winstanley; *m* 1977, Jacqueline Poncelet (marr. diss. 2000); one *s* one *d*. *Educ:* Somerset Coll. of Art; St Martin's Sch. of Art; RCA; Chelsea Sch. of Art. *Solo exhibitions* include: Orchard Gall., Londonderry, 1983; Lisson Gall., 1983, 1985, 1987, 1992, 1995, 1999, 2002; Riverside Studios, Chapter Arts Centre, Cardiff, and Fruitmarket Gall., Edinburgh, 1984; Tate Gall., 1985; Marian Goodman Gall., NY, 1986, 1988, 1990, 1992, 1997; Whitechapel Art Gall., Musée Nat. d'Art Moderne, Paris, 1989; Kunstnernes Hus, Oslo, and Mala Galerija, Slovenia, 1990; Kunstverein Hanover, 1993; LA Louver, 1995, 2001; tour of South America, 1996–97; Musée de Rochechouart, 1997; Tate Gall., Liverpool, 1999; Dundee Contemp. Arts, 2001; PSI Center for Art and Urban Resources, NY, 2001; Museum Ludwig, Cologne, 2003; Atelier Brancusi, CNAC, Paris, 2003; Tate St Ives, 2005; Museo Artium, Vitoria-Gasteiz, Spain, 2005; Sara Hilden Art Mus., Tampere, Finland, 2005–06; Arp Mus., Remagen, Germany, 2006; Ikon Gall., Birmingham, 2007; Wales at the Venice Biennale, 2007; represented in collections in: Tate Gall.; Mus. of Modern Art, NY; Art Gall. of NSW, Sydney; Musée Beaubourg, Paris; Bonnefanten Mus., Maastricht. Vis. Prof., Chelsea Sch. of Art, 1992–; Prof., Ecole Nat. Superieure des Beaux-Arts, Paris, 1998–. Member: Grants to Artists Sub Cttee, 1986–92, Visual Arts Adv. Gp, 1990–93, British Council; Architecture Adv. Gp, Arts Council of England, 1996–2000; Trustee, Tate Gall., 1991–96; Vice Chm. Trustees, Baltic Flour Mills Centre for Contemporary Art, 1999–2004. Turner Prize, 1987; Robert Jakobsen Prize, Mus. Wurth, Germany, 1995. Chevalier des Arts et des Lettres (France), 1997. *Publications:* Stuff Box Object, 1972, 1984; For Those Who Have Ears #2, 1985; Atlas: Gondwanaland & Laurasia, 1990; In Praise of Television, 1997; About the Size of It, 2005. *Address:* c/o Lisson Gallery, 67 Lisson Street, NW1 5DA.

DEACON, Prof. Susan Catherine; Professor of Social Change, Queen Margaret University, since 2007; speaker, adviser and consultant on public policy, strategy and change; *b* 2 Feb. 1964; *d* of James Deacon and Barbara Deacon (*née* Timmins); partner, John Boothman; one *s* one *d*. *Educ:* Edinburgh Univ. (MA Hons 1987; MBA 1992). Local Govt officer, 1987–94; Open Univ. Tutor (part-time), 1992–94; sen. mgt consultant, 1994; Dir of MBA Programmes, Edinburgh Business Sch., Heriot-Watt Univ., 1994–98; business consultant, 1998–99. Mem. (Lab) Edinburgh E and Musselburgh, Scottish Parlt, 1999–2007; Minister for Health and Community Care, 1999–2001. *Address:* Queen Margaret University, Edinburgh EH21 6UU. *T:* (0131) 474 0000; *e-mail:* sdeacon@qmu.ac.uk.

DEAKIN, Prof. (John Francis) William, PhD; FRCPsych; Professor of Psychiatry, Manchester University, since 1990; *b* 5 July 1949; *s* of John Deakin and Kathleen Brown; *m* 1973, Hildur Jakobsdottir; three *d*. *Educ:* Eltham Coll., Kent; Leeds Univ. (BSc 1st Cl. Physiol. 1970; MB Hons, ChB dist. and prize 1973); PhD London 1982. MRCPsych 1984, FRCPsych 1990. MRC Trng Fellow, NIMR, Mill Hill, and Clin. Res. Centre, Harrow, 1974–83; Sen. Lectr, Manchester Univ., 1983–90. FMedSci 2000. *Publications:* contrib. numerous articles to learned jls on neuroscientific basis of mental illness, especially the rôle of serotonin in neuroses. *Recreations:* listening to jazz, playing the game of Go, speculation of all kinds. *Address:* 3 Chesham Place, Bowdon, Cheshire WA14 2JL. *T:* (0161) 941 6385.

DEAKIN, Michael; writer, documentary and film maker; Director, Gryphon Productions Ltd, 1985–2005; *b* 21 Feb. 1939; *s* of Sir William Deakin, DSO, and Margaret Hodson (*née* Beatson-Bell). *Educ:* Bryanston; Univ. d'Aix-Marseille; Emmanuel Coll., Cambridge (MA Hons). Founding Partner, Editions Alecto, Fine Art Publishers, 1960–64; Producer, BBC Radio Current Affairs Dept, 1964–68; Producer, then Editor, Yorkshire Television Documentary Unit, 1968–81; Sen. Vice-Pres., Paramount/Revcom, 1987–93. Documentary film productions include: Out of the Shadow into the Sun—The Eiger; Struggle for China; The Children on the Hill; Whicker's World—Way Out West; The

Japanese Experience; The Good, the Bad and the Indifferent; Johnny Go Home (British Academy Award, 1976); David Frost's Global Village; The Frost Interview—The Shah; Rampton—The Secret Hospital; Painting With Light (co-prodn with BBC); other films: Act of Betrayal, 1987; Not a Penny More, Not a Penny Less, 1990 (TV mini series); Secret Weapon, 1990; The Supergun, 1994; Good King Wenceslas, 1994; The Human Bomb, 1996; The Place of Lions, 1997; Varian's War, 2001; also many others. Founding Mem., TV-am Breakfast Television Consortium, 1980; Consultant, TV-am, 1984–87 (Dir of Programmes, 1982–84; Bd Mem., 1984–85). *Publications*: Restif de la Bretonne—Les Nuits de Paris (critical edn and trans. with Nicholas Deakin), 1968; Gaetano Donizetti—a biography, 1968; (for children) Tom Grattan's War, 1970, 2nd edn 1971; The Children on the Hill, 1972, 9th edn 1982; (with John Willis) Johnny Go Home, 1976; (with Antony Thomas) The Arab Experience, 1975, 2nd edn 1976; Flame in the Desert, 1976; (with David Frost) I Could Have Kicked Myself, 1982, 2nd US edn 1983; (with David Frost) Who Wants to be a Millionaire, 1983; (with David Frost) If You'll Believe That You'll Believe Anything…, 1986. *Recreations*: travel, music, books, pictures, motorcycling. *Address*: 6 Glenhurst Avenue, NW5 1PS; La Marsaulaie, Saint Mathurin 49250, France. *Club*: Hat.
See also N. D. Deakin.

DEAKIN, Prof. Nicholas Dampier, CBE 1997; Professor of Social Policy and Administration, University of Birmingham, 1980–98, now Emeritus Professor (Dean, Faculty of Commerce and Social Science, 1986–89; Foundation Fellow, 2006); Visiting Professor: London School of Economics, 1998–2004; Warwick Business School, 1998–2001; *b* 5 June 1936; *s* of Sir (Frederick) William Deakin, DSO and Margaret Ogilvy Hodson; *m* 1st, 1961, Rose Albinia Donaldson (marr. diss. 1988), *d* of Baron Donaldson of Kingsbridge, OBE and Frances Donaldson; one *s* two *d*; 2nd, 1988, Lucy Moira, *d* of Jack and Moira Gaster. *Educ*: Westminster Sch.; Christ Church Coll., Oxford (BA (1st cl. Hons) 1959, MA 1963); DPhil Sussex 1972. Asst Principal, Home Office, 1959–63, Private Sec. to Minister of State, 1962–63; Asst Dir, Nuffield Foundn Survey of Race Relations in Britain, 1963–68; Res. Fellow, subseq. Lectr, Univ. of Sussex, 1968–72; Head of Social Studies, subseq. Head of Central Policy Unit, GLC, 1972–80. Scientific Advr, DHSS, later Dept of Health, 1986–91. Chm., Indep. Commn on Future of Voluntary Sector in England, 1995–96. Vice-Chm., Social Affairs Cttee, ESRC, 1984–86. Chair, Social Policy Assoc., 1989–92; Member: Exec. Cttee, NCVO, 1988–90; Council, RIPA, 1984–88; Governing Council, Family Policy Studies Centre, 1987–2001. Trustee: Nationwide Foundn, 1999–2005; Baring Foundn, 2005–. Chair, Birmingham City Pride, 1998–2001. FRSA 1996. *Publications*: (ed and trans.) Memoirs of the Comte de Gramont, 1965; Colour and the British Electorate 1964, 1965; Colour, Citizenship and British Society, 1969; (with Clare Ungerson) Leaving London, 1977; (jtly) Government and Urban Poverty, 1983; (ed) Policy Change in Government, 1986; The Politics of Welfare, 1987, 2nd edn 1994; (ed jtly) Consuming Public Services, 1990; (jtly) The Enterprise Culture and the Inner Cities, 1992; (ed jtly) The Costs of Welfare, 1993; (jtly) Public Welfare Services and Social Exclusion, 1995; (jtly) Contracting for Change, 1997; (with Richard Parry) The Treasury and Social Policy, 2000; In Search of Civil Society, 2001; (ed jtly) Welfare and the State, 2003; (contrib.) Angleterre ou Albion, entre fascination et répulsion, ed by G. Millat, 2006; contribs to other vols and learned jls. *Recreations*: reading fiction, music. *Address*: Chedington, Lynmouth Road, N2 9LR.
See also M. Deakin.

DEAKIN, Prof. Simon Francis, PhD; FBA 2005; Professor of Law, University of Cambridge, since 2006; Fellow, Peterhouse, Cambridge, since 1990; *b* 26 March 1961; *s* of Anthony Francis and Elizabeth Mary Deakin; *m* 1989, Elaine Skidmore; one *s*. *Educ*: Netherthorpe Grammar Sch., Staveley; Peterhouse, Cambridge (BA 1983, MA 1985, PhD 1990). Res. Fellow, Peterhouse, Cambridge, 1985–88; Lectr in Law, QMC, 1987–90; Cambridge University: Asst Lectr, Lectr, then Reader in Law, 1990–2001; Asst Dir, Centre for Business Res., 1994–; Robert Monks Prof. of Corporate Governance, Judge Inst. of Mgt, subseq. Judge Business Sch., 2001–06. Bigelow Fellow, Univ. of Chicago Law Sch., 1986–87; Visiting Fellow: Univ. of Nantes, 1993, 1995; Univ. of Melbourne, 1996; European Univ. Inst., Florence, 2004; Doshisha Univ., Kyoto, 2004–; Vis. Prof., Columbia Univ., 2003. Mem. Exec. Cttee, Inst. of Employment Rights, 1990–2002. Mem., Ind. Commn of Inquiry into Drug Testing at Work, 2003–05. *Publications*: (with B. S. Markesinis) Tort Law, 3rd edn 1994, 4th edn 1999, 5th edn 2003, 6th edn (with A. Johnston) 2007; (with G. S. Morris) Labour Law, 1995, 3rd edn 2001; (ed with J. Michie) Contracts, Co-operation and Competition, 1997; (ed with A. Hughes) Enterprise and Community, 1997; (with F. Wilkinson) The Law of the Labour Market: industrialization, employment and legal evolution, 2005; Tanner Lectures: Corporate Governance and Human Development, 2008; contribs to jls in law, econs, corporate governance and industrial relns. *Recreation*: fell walking. *Address*: Peterhouse, Cambridge CB2 1RD. *T*: (01223) 338200, *Fax*: (01223) 337578; *e-mail*: s.deakin@cbr.cam.ac.uk.

DEAKIN, William; see Deakin, J. F. W.

DEAKINS, Eric Petro; international public affairs consultant; *b* 7 Oct. 1932; *er s* of late Edward Deakins and Gladys Deakins; *m* 1990, Sandra Weaver; one *s* two *d*. *Educ*: Tottenham Grammar Sch.; London Sch. of Economics. BA (Hons) in History, 1953. Executive with FMC (Meat) Ltd, 1956; General Manager, Pigs Div., FMC (Meat) Ltd, 1969. Contested (Lab): Finchley, 1959; Chigwell, 1966; Walthamstow W, 1967. MP (Lab): Walthamstow W, 1970–74; Walthamstow, 1974–87. Parly Under-Sec. of State, Dept of Trade, 1974–76, DHSS, 1976–79. *Publications*: A Faith to Fight For, 1964; You and your MP, 1987; What Future for Labour?, 1988. *Recreations*: writing, cinema, squash, football. *Address*: 36 Murray Mews, NW1 9RJ.

DEAL, Hon. Timothy Edward; Senior Vice President, United States Council for International Business, Washington, since 1996; *b* 17 Sept. 1940; *s* of Edward Deal and Loretta (*née* Fuemuller); *m* 1964, Jill Brady; two *s*. *Educ*: Univ. of California at Berkeley (AB Pol Sci.). First Lieut, US Army, 1963–65. Joined Foreign Service, US Dept of State, 1965; served Tegucigalpa, Honduras, Warsaw, Poland, and Washington, 1965–76; Sen. Staff Mem., Nat. Security Council, 1976–79 and 1980–81; Special Asst to Asst Sec. of State for European Affairs, 1979–80; Counsellor for Econ. Affairs, London, 1981–85; Dep. US Rep., OECD, Paris, 1985–88; Dir, Office of Eastern European Affairs, Washington, 1988–89; Special Asst to President and Sen. Dir for Internat. Econ. Affairs, Nat. Security Council, 1989–92; Minister and Dep. Chief of Mission, US Embassy, London, 1992–96. Presidential Awards for: Meritorious Service, 1991; Distinguished Service, 1993. *Recreations*: theatre, cinema, horse racing. *Address*: 5721 MacArthur Boulevard NW, Washington, DC 20016, USA.

DEALTRY, Prof. (Thomas) Richard; Managing Director, Intellectual Partnerships Consultancy Ltd, since 1999; Programmes Director: BAA plc, since 1997; University of Surrey Management Learning Partnership, since 1997; *b* 24 Nov. 1936; *s* of George Raymond Dealtry and Edith (*née* Gardner); *m* 1962, Pauline (*née* Sedgwick) (marr. diss. 1982); one *s* one *d*. *Educ*: Cranfield Inst. of Advanced Technol.; MBA. CEng, MIMechE; MInstM; FIMCB. National Service Commn, 1959–61: Temp. Captain 1960. Divl Exec.,

Tube Investments Ltd, 1967–71; Sen. Exec., Guest, Keen & Nettlefold Gp Corporate Staff, 1971–74; Dir, Simpson-Lawrence Ltd, and Man. Dir, BUKO BV, Holland, 1974–77; Under Sec./Industrial Adviser, Scottish Econ. Planning Dept, 1977–78; Director, Gulf Regional Planning, Gulf Org. for Industrial Consulting, 1978–82; Man. Dir, RBA Management Services Ltd, London and Kuwait, 1982–85; Regl Dir, Diverco Ltd, 1985–; Prof. of Strategic Mgt, Internat. Mgt Centres, Buckingham, 1989–97. *Recreations*: golf, squash. *Address*: 43 Hunstanton Avenue, Harborne, Birmingham B17 8SX.

DEAN OF HARPTREE, Baron *cr* 1993 (Life Peer), of Wedmore in the County of Somerset; **Arthur Paul Dean,** Kt 1985; PC 1991; company director; *b* 14 Sept. 1924; *s* of Arthur Percival Dean and Jessie Margaret Dean (*née* Gaunt); *m* 1st, 1957, Doris Ellen Webb (*d* 1979); 2nd, 1980, Peggy Parker (*d* 2002). *Educ*: Ellesmere Coll., Shropshire; Exeter Coll., Oxford (MA, BLitt). Former President Oxford Univ. Conservative Assoc. and Oxford Carlton Club. Served War of 1939–45, Capt. Welsh Guards; ADC to Comdr 1 Corps BAOR. Farmer, 1950–56. Resident Tutor, Swinton Conservative Coll., 1957; Conservative Research Dept, 1957–64, Assistant Director from 1962. MP (C) Somerset North, 1964–83, Woodspring, Avon, 1983–92. A Front Bench Spokesman on Health and Social Security, 1969–70; Parly Under-Sec. of State, DHSS, 1970–74; Dep. Chm. of Ways and Means and Dep. Speaker, 1982–92. Member: Exec. Cttee, CPA, UK Branch, 1975–92; House of Commons Services Select Cttee, 1979–82; House of Commons Chairman's Panel, 1979–82; Chm., Conservative Health and Social Security Cttee, 1979–82. A Dep. Speaker, H of L, 1995–. Mem., Exec. Cttee, Assoc. of Conservative Peers, 1995–. Formerly, Member Governing Body of Church in Wales. *Publications*: contributions to political pamphlets. *Recreation*: fishing. *Address*: Archer's Wyck, Knightcott, Banwell, Weston-super-Mare, Avon BS24 6HS. *Club*: Oxford and Cambridge.

DEAN OF THORNTON-LE-FYLDE, Baroness *cr* 1993 (Life Peer), of Eccles in the Metropolitan County of Greater Manchester; **Brenda Dean;** PC 1998; Chairman, Housing Corporation, 1997–2003; *b* 29 April 1943; *d* of Hugh Dean and Lillian Dean; *m* 1988, Keith Desmond McDowall, *qv*. *Educ*: St Andrews Junior Sch., Eccles; Stretford High Sch. for Girls. Admin. Sec., SOGAT, 1959–72; SOGAT Manchester Branch: Asst Sec., 1972–76; Sec., 1976–83; Mem., Nat. Exec. Council, 1977–83; Pres., 1983–85, Gen.-Sec., 1985–91, SOGAT '82; Dep. Gen. Sec., Graphical, Paper and Media Union, 1991–92; Chm., ICSTIS, 1993–99 (Mem., 1991–93). Non-executive Director: Inveresk plc, 1993–97; Chamberlain Phipps Gp plc, 1994–96; Takare plc, 1995–98; Assured British Meat, 1997–2001; George Wimpey plc, 2003–07; Dawsons plc, 2004–; Taylor Wimpey plc, 2007–. Co-Chm., Women's Nat. Commn, 1985–87; Dep. Chm., UCL Hosps NHS Trust, 1993–98; Chairman: Armed Forces Pay Review Body, 1999–2004 (Mem., 1993–94); Covent Gdn Mkt Authy, 2005– (Mem., 2004–05); Member: Printing and Publishing Trng Bd, 1974–82; Supplementary Benefits Commn, 1976–80; Price Commn, 1977–79; Occupational Pensions Bd, 1983–87; Gen. Adv. Council, BBC, 1984–88; TUC Gen. Council, 1985–92; NEDC, 1989–92; Employment Appeal Tribunal, 1991–93; Broadcasting Complaints Commn, 1993–94; Press Complaints Commn, 1993–98; Nat. Cttee of Inquiry into Future of Higher Educn, 1996–97; Royal Commn on H of L reform, 1999; H of L Appts Commn, 2000–; Bd, Gen. Ins. Standards Council, 1999–2005; Sen. Salaries Review Body, 1999–2004. Mem. Council, ABSA, 1990–95. Member: Council, City Univ., 1991–96; Bar Council of Legal Educn, 1992–95; Council, Open Univ., 1996–98; Court of Governors, LSE, 1996–98; Gov., Ditchley Foundn, 1992–. Pres., Coll. of Occupational Therapy, 1995–2004. Mem. Adv. Bd of Mgt, PYBT, 1999–2002 (Trustee, 1996–99); Trustee, Prince's Foundn, 1999–. FRSA 1992. Hon. Fellow, Lancs Poly., 1991. Hon. MA: Salford, 1986; South Bank, 1995; Hon. DCL City, 1993; Hon. LLD: North London, 1996; Exeter, 1999; Hon. LLB De Montfort, 1998. *Recreations*: sailing, reading, relaxing, thinking! *Address*: House of Lords, SW1P 0PW. *Clubs*: Reform; Royal Cornwall Yacht.

DEAN, Caroline, OBE 2004; DPhil; FRS 2004; Associate Research Director, John Innes Centre, since 1999; *b* 2 April 1957; *d* of late D. H. Dean and of Alice Joy Dean; *m* 1991, Jonathan Dallas George Jones, *qv*; one *s* one *d*. *Educ*: Univ. of York (BA Hons (Biol.); DPhil (Biol.) 1982). Res. Scientist, Advanced Genetic Sciences, Oakland, Calif, 1983–88; Project Leader, John Innes Centre, Norwich, 1988–99. Hon. Chair, UEA, 2000–. Medal, Genetics Soc., 2007. *Publications*: numerous articles in learned jls, incl. Science, Cell, Plant Cell, Plant Jl, EMBO Jl, Nature, Nature Genetics. *Recreation*: sailing. *Address*: John Innes Centre, Colney Lane, Norwich NR4 7UH. *T*: (01603) 450526, *Fax*: (01603) 450022; *e-mail*: caroline.dean@bbsrc.ac.uk.

DEAN, (Catherine) Margaret; HM Lord Lieutenant of Fife, since 1999; *b* 16 Nov. 1939; *d* of Thomas Day McNeil Scrimgeour and Catherine Forbes Scrimgeour (*née* Sunderland); *m* 1962, Brian Dean; three *d*. *Educ*: George Watson's Ladies' Coll., Edinburgh; Univ. of Edinburgh (MA). *Address*: (home) Viewforth, 121 Rose Street, Dunfermline, Fife KY12 0QT. *T*: (01383) 722488, *Fax*: (01383) 738027; (office) Clerk to the Lieutenancy, Fife House, North Street, Glenrothes, Fife KY7 5LT. *T*: 08451 555555, ext. 442301, *Fax*: (01592) 414200; *e-mail*: linda.bissett@fife.gov.uk.

DEAN, (Cecil) Roy; HM Diplomatic Service, retired; writer and composer; *b* 18 Feb. 1927; *s* of Arthur Dean and Flora Dean (*née* Clare); *m* 1954, Heather Sturtridge; three *s*. *Educ*: Watford Grammar Sch.; London Coll. of Printing and Graphic Arts (diploma); Coll. for Distributive Trades (MCIPR). Sec., Watford Boys' Club, 1943–45. Served RAF, 1945–48, SEAC; Central Office of Information, 1948–58; Second, Later First Sec., Colombo, 1958–62; Vancouver, 1962–64; Lagos, 1964–68; FCO, 1968–71; Consul, Houston, 1971, Acting Consul-Gen., 1972–73; FCO, 1973–76; Dir, Arms Control and Disarmament Res. Unit, 1976–83; Dep. High Comr, Accra, 1983–86, Acting High Comr, 1984 and 1986. Mem., UN Sec.-General's expert group on disarmament instns, 1980–81; UK Rep., UNESCO Conf. on Disarmament Educn, 1980. Contested (Lab) Bromley LBC, 1990 and 1994. Trustee, Urbanaid, 1987–96. Mem., RSL. Editor: Insight, 1964–68; Arms Control and Disarmament, 1979–83; author and presenter, The Poetry of Popular Song (BBC Radio Four series), 1989–91. Vice-Pres., Bromley Arts Council; Press Officer: Bromley Music Soc.; Biggin Hill Br., RAFA. *Compositions*: A Century of Song, 1996; A Shropshire Lass, 2000; Three Moons: a lyric suite, 2003; Hymn to the Laureate, 2004; Ceremonial March: Betjemania, 2005; A Somerset Lad, 2005. *Publications*: Peace and Disarmament, 1982; chapter in Ethics and Nuclear Deterrence, 1982; Mainly in Fun, 1998, enlarged edn 2002; A Simple Songbook, 2002; Great British Lyric Writers 1890–1950, 2006; Victor in the Battle of Britain, 2006; Translations from Eight French Poets, 2007; numerous research papers; contribs to learned jls. *Recreations*: crosswords (Times national champion, 1970 and 1979, world record for fastest solution, 1970), humour, light verse, setting puzzles. *Address*: 14 Blyth Road, Bromley, Kent BR1 3RX. *T*: (020) 8402 0743.

DEAN, Christopher Colin, OBE 2000 (MBE 1981); professional ice skater; *b* 27 July 1958; *s* of Colin Gordon Dean and Mavis (*née* Pearson) and step *s* of Mary Betty (*née* Chambers); *m* 1st, 1991, Isabelle Duchesnay (marr. diss. 1993); 2nd, 1994, Jill Trenary;

two *s*. *Educ:* Calverton Manor Sch., Nottingham; Sir John Sherbrooke Sch., Nottingham; Col Frank Seely Sch., Nottingham. Police constable, 1974–80. Ice dancer, with Jayne Torvill, *qv*: British Champions, 1978, 1979, 1980, 1981, 1982, 1983, 1994; European Champions, 1981, 1982, 1984, 1994; World Champions, 1981, 1982, 1983, 1984; World Professional Champions, 1984, 1985, 1990, 1995 and 1996; Olympic Champions, 1984; Olympic Bronze Medallists, 1994. Choreographer, Encounters, English Nat. Ballet, 1996; trainer, choreographer and performer: Stars on Ice, USA, 1998–99, 1999–2000; Dancing on Ice, ITV, 2006, 2007 and 2008. Hon. MA Nottingham Trent, 1993. With Jayne Torvill: BBC Sportsview Personality of the Year, 1983–84; Figure Skating Hall of Fame, 1989. *Publication:* (with Jayne Torvill) Facing the Music, 1995. *Recreations:* motor racing, films, dance. *Address:* PO Box 32, Heathfield, E Sussex TN21 0BW. *T:* (01435) 867825. *Club:* Groucho.

DEAN, Janet Elizabeth Ann; MP (Lab) Burton, since 1997; *b* 28 Jan. 1949; *d* of late Harry Gibson and Mary Gibson (*née* Walley); *m* 1968, Alan Dean (*d* 1994); two *d*. *Educ:* Winsford Verdin County Grammar Sch., Cheshire. Clerk: Barclays Bank, 1965–69; Bass Charrington, 1969–70. Member (Lab): Staffordshire County Council, 1981–97; E Staffordshire BC, 1991–97; Uttoxeter Town Council, 1995–97. *Recreations:* dressmaking, reading.

DEAN, His Honour Joseph (Jolyon); a Circuit Judge, South Eastern Circuit, 1975–87; *b* 26 April 1921; *s* of late Basil Dean, CBE; *m* 1962, Hon. Jenefer Mills, *yr d* of late 5th Baron Hillingdon, MC, TD; one *s* two *d*. *Educ:* Elstree Sch.; Harrow Sch.; Merton Coll., Oxford (MA Classics and Law). 51st (Highland) Div., RA, 1942–45. Called to the Bar, Middle Temple, 1947; Bencher 1972. Member (C): Westminster City Council, 1961–65; Ashford BC, 1991–95. Chm., E Ashford Rural Trust, 1988–91. *Publication:* Hatred, Ridicule or Contempt, 1953 (paperback edns 1955 and 1964). *Address:* The Hall, West Brabourne, Ashford, Kent TN25 5LZ.
See also Winton Dean.

DEAN, Margaret; *see* Dean, C. M.

DEAN, Michael; QC 1981; **His Honour Judge Dean;** a Circuit Judge, since 1991; *b* 2 Feb. 1938; *s* of late Henry Ross Dean and Dorothea Alicia Dean; *m* 1st, 1967, Diane Ruth Griffiths; 2nd, 1992, Jane Isabel Glaister; one *s*. *Educ:* Altrincham Co. Grammar Sch.; Univ. of Nottingham (LLB 1st Cl. Hons 1959). Lectr in Law, Univ. of Manchester, 1959–62; called to the Bar, Gray's Inn, 1962 (Arden Scholar and Holker Sen. Scholarship, 1962); Northern Circuit, Manchester, 1962–65; Lectr in Law, LSE, 1965–67; practice at the Bar, London, 1968–91; an Asst Recorder, 1986–89; a Recorder, 1989–91. *Publications:* articles in various legal periodicals. *Recreations:* conversation, music, theatre, sailing, family life.

DEAN, Nicholas Arthur; QC 2003; a Recorder, since 2001; *b* 11 July 1960; *s* of John and Alwyne Dean; *m* 1987, Nicola Anne Kay Carslaw; one *s* one *d*. *Educ:* Wyggeston Boys' Sch.; Univ. of Leeds (LLB Hons). Called to the Bar, Lincoln's Inn, 1982; in practice specialising in crime, clinical negligence and commercial competition law. *Recreations:* cycling, reading, keeping chickens, listening to the Archers. *Address:* Ilam House, 221 Forest Road, Woodhouse, Leics LE12 8TZ. *T:* (01509) 891105; *e-mail:* Nicholas.Dean@btinternet.com.

DEAN, Dr Paul, CB 1981; Director, National Physical Laboratory, 1977–90 (Deputy Director, 1974–76); *b* 23 Jan. 1933; *s* of late Sydney and Rachel Dean; *m* 1961, Sheila Valerie Gamse; one *s* one *d*. *Educ:* Hackney Downs Grammar Sch.; Queen Mary Coll., Univ. of London (Fellow, 1984). BSc (1st cl. Hons Physics), PhD; CPhys; FInstP, FIMA, CMath. National Physical Laboratory: Sen. Sci. Officer, Math. Div., 1957; Principal Sci. Officer, 1963; Sen. Principal Sci. Officer (Individual Merit), 1967; Head of Central Computer Unit, 1967; Supt, Div. of Quantum Metrology, 1969; Under-Sec., DoI (Head of Space and Air Res. and R&D Contractors Divs), 1976–77; initiated testing lab. accreditation in UK, leading to NAMAS, 1985. Part-time Head, Res. Estabts Management Div., DoI, 1979–82; Exec. Dep. Chm., Council of Res. Estabts, 1979–82. Mem., Internat. Cttee of Weights and Measures, 1985–90; Pres., Comité Consultatif pour les Etalons de Mesure des Rayonnements Ionisants, 1987–90; Founder Pres., British Measurement and Testing Assoc., 1990–95; First Chm., EUROMET, 1988–90. *Publications:* papers and articles in learned, professional and popular jls. *Recreations:* mathematics, computing, astronomy, chess, music, bridge. *Address:* Dorset.

DEAN, Peter Henry, CBE 1993; Chairman, Gambling Commission, 2005–07 (Chairman, Gaming Board for Great Britain, 1998–2005); *b* 24 July 1939; *s* of late Alan Walduck Dean and Gertrude (*née* Bürger); *m* 1965, Linda Louise Keating; one *d*. *Educ:* Rugby Sch.; London Univ. (LLB). Admitted Solicitor, 1962. Joined Rio Tinto-Zinc Corp., 1966; Sec., 1972–74; Dir, 1974–85; freelance business consultant, 1985–96. Director: Associated British Ports Holdings, 1982–2001 (Mem., British Transport Docks Bd, 1980–82); Liberty Life Assce Co., 1986–95; Seeboard, 1993–96. Chm., G. H. Dean & Co., 2001– (Dir, 1999–). Dep. Chm., Monopolies and Mergers Commn, 1990–97 (Mem., 1982–97); Investment Ombudsman, 1996–2001. Chm., Council of Management, Highgate Counselling Centre, 1991–2002 (Mem., 1985–2002); Chairman: English Baroque Choir, 1985–89, 1999–2000; City Chamber Choir, 2003–07. *Recreations:* choral singing, ski-ing. *Address:* 52 Lanchester Road, Highgate, N6 4TA. *T:* (020) 8883 5417, *Fax:* (020) 8365 2398; *e-mail:* phdean@blueyonder.co.uk.

DEAN, Prof. Roger Thornton, DSc, DLitt, PhD; FAHA; Research Professor of Sonic Communication, Auditory Laboratories of Macarthur Auditory Research Centre Sydney, University of Western Sydney, since 2007; *b* UK, 6 Sept. 1948; *s* of Cyril Thornton Dean and Kathleen Ida Dean (*née* Harrington); *m* 1973, Dr Hazel Anne Smith. *Educ:* Corpus Christi Coll., Cambridge (BA 1970; PhD 1974); Brunel Univ. (DSc 1984, DLitt 2002). FIBiol 1988. Post-Doctoral Fellow, Dept of Exptl Pathol., UCH Med. Sch., 1973–76; MRC Scientist, Div. of Cell Pathol., Clinical Res. Centre, London, 1976–79; Brunel University: Hd, Cell Biol. Res. Gp, and Reader in Applied Biol., 1979–84; Hd, Cell Biol. Res. Gp, and Prof. of Cell Biol., 1984–88; Hon. Prof., Faculty of Medicine, Sydney Univ., 1988–2002; Foundn Exec. Dir, Heart Res. Inst. Ltd, Sydney, Australia, 1988–2002; University of Canberra: Vice-Chancellor and Pres., and Prof., 2002–07; Founder, Sonic Communications Res. Gp, 2004. Founder and Artistic Dir, LYSIS and austraLYSIS, internat. sound and intermedia creative and perf. gp, 1975–. FAICD 2003; FAHA 2004. Musical and multimedia compositions, many included in compact disc pubns as creator and performer. Centenary Medal, Australia, 2003. *Publications:* include: (with Dr M. Davies) Protein Oxidation (monograph), 1997; Hyperimprovisation, 2003; contrib. learned jls in cell biol., music and humanities res. *Recreations:* film, visual arts. *Address:* MARCS Auditory Laboratories, University of Western Sydney, Locked Bag 1797, Penrith South Distribution Centre, NSW 1797, Australia. *T:* (2) 97726695; *e-mail:* roger.dean@uws.edu.au.

DEAN, Roy; *see* Dean, C. R.

DEAN, Winton (Basil), FBA 1975; author and musical scholar; *b* Birkenhead, 18 March 1916; *e s* of late Basil Dean, CBE, and Esther, *d* of A. H. Van Gruisen; *m* 1939, Hon. Thalia Mary Shaw (*d* 2000), 2nd *d* of 2nd Baron Craigmyle; one *s* one adopted *d* (and two *d* decd). *Educ:* Harrow; King's Coll., Cambridge (MA). Translated libretto of Weber's opera Abu Hassan (Arts Theatre, Cambridge) 1938. Served War of 1939–45: in Admiralty (Naval Intelligence Div.), 1944–45. Member: Music Panel, Arts Council, 1957–60, Cttee of Handel Opera Society (London), 1955–60; Council, Royal Musical Assoc., 1965–98 (Vice-Pres., 1970–98; Hon. Mem., 1998–). Ernest Bloch Prof. of Music, 1965–66, Regent's Lectr, 1977, Univ. of California (Berkeley); Matthew Vassar Lectr, Vassar Coll., Poughkeepsie, NY, 1979. Member: Management Cttee, Halle Handel Soc., 1979– (Vice-Pres., 1991–99; Hon. Mem., 1999); Kuratorium, Göttingen Handel Fest., 1981–97 (Hon. Mem., 1997–); Corresp. Mem., Amer. Musicological Soc., 1989–. Ed, with Sarah Fuller, Handel's opera Julius Caesar (Barber Inst. of Fine Arts, Birmingham), performed 1977. Hon. RAM 1971. Hon. MusD Cambridge, 1996. City of Halle Handel Prize, 1995. *Publications:* The Frogs of Aristophanes (trans. of choruses to music by Walter Leigh), 1937; Bizet (Master Musicians), 1948 (3rd rev. edn, 1975); Carmen, 1949; Introduction to the Music of Bizet, 1950; Franck, 1950; Hambledon *v* Feathercombe, the Story of a Village Cricket Match, 1951; Handel's Dramatic Oratorios and Masques, 1959; Shakespeare and Opera (Shakespeare in Music), 1964; Georges Bizet, His Life and Work, 1965; Handel and the Opera Seria, 1969, Japanese rev. edn 2005; Beethoven and Opera (in The Beethoven Companion), 1971; ed, Handel, Three Ornamented Arias, 1976; (ed) E. J. Dent, The Rise of Romantic Opera, 1976; The New Grove Handel, 1982; (with J. M. Knapp) Handel's Operas 1704–1726, 1987 (Yorkshire Post Lit. Prize, 1988), 2nd edn 1995; Essays on Opera, 1990; (ed jtly) Handel, Julius Caesar, 1999; Handel's Operas 1726–1741, 2006; contributed to Grove's Dictionary of Music and Musicians (5th and 6th edns), New Oxford History of Music and to musical periodicals and learned journals. *Recreations:* cricket, shooting, salmon fishing, naval history. *Address:* Hambledon Hurst, Godalming, Surrey GU8 4HF. *T:* (01428) 682644.
See also J. J. Dean.

DEANE, family name of **Baron Muskerry**.

DEANE, Derek, OBE 2000; choreographer; Artistic Director, English National Ballet, 1993–2001; *b* 18 June 1953; *s* of William Gordon Shepherd and Margaret Shepherd; adopted Deane as stage name. *Educ:* Royal Ballet School. With Royal Ballet Co., 1972–89; Asst Dir, Rome Opera, 1990–92. *Recreations:* theatre, all performing arts, travelling, tennis.

DEANE, Prof. Phyllis Mary, FBA 1980; Professor of Economic History, University of Cambridge, 1981–83; Fellow of Newnham College, 1961–83, Hon. Fellow, 1983; *b* 13 Oct. 1918; *d* of John Edward Deane and Elizabeth Jane Brooks; single. *Educ:* Chatham County Sch.; Hutcheson's Girls' Grammar Sch., Glasgow; Univ. of Glasgow (MA Hons Econ. Science 1940); MA Cantab. Carnegie Research Scholar, 1940–41; Research Officer, Nat. Inst. of Econ. and Social Research, 1941–45; Colonial Research Officer, 1946–48; Research Officer: HM Colonial Office, 1948–49; Cambridge University: Dept of Applied Econs, 1950–61; Lectr, Faculty of Econs and Politics, 1961–71; Reader in Economic History, 1971–81. Vis. Prof., Univ. of Pittsburgh, 1969. Editor, Economic Jl, 1968–75. Pres., Royal Economic Soc., 1980–82. Hon. DLitt Glasgow, 1989. *Publications:* (with Julian Huxley) The Future of the Colonies, 1945; The Measurement of Colonial National Incomes, 1948; Colonial Social Accounting, 1953; (with W. A. Cole) British Economic Growth 1688–1959, 1962; The First Industrial Revolution, 1965; The Evolution of Economic Ideas, 1978; The State and the Economic System, 1989; The Life and Times of Neville Keynes, 2001; papers and reviews in econ. jls. *Address:* Flat 11 Gretton Court, 3–5 High Street, Girton, Cambridge CB3 0QN.

DEANE, Robert Edward; HM Diplomatic Service; Counsellor, Rome, since 2007; *b* 28 Sept. 1962; *s* of Edward Stuart Deane and Jennifer Mary Deane; *m* 1993, Corinna Osmann; one *s* two *d*. *Educ:* London Sch. of Economics (BSc 1984); Univ. of Southampton (MSc 1985). HM Treasury, 1985–94; Bonn, 1994–99; First Sec., FCO, 1999–2005; Dep. Hd of Mission, Abu Dhabi, 2005–07. *Recreations:* photography, diving, travel, sailing. *Address:* c/o Foreign and Commonwealth Office, SW1A 2AH.

DEANE, Hon. Sir William (Patrick), AC 1988; KBE 1982; Governor General of the Commonwealth of Australia, 1996–2001; *b* 4 Jan. 1931; *s* of C. A. Deane, MC and Lillian Hussey; *m* 1965, Helen, *d* of Dr Gerald and Kathleen Russell; one *s* one *d*. *Educ:* St Christopher's Convent, Canberra; St Joseph's College, Sydney; Univ. of Sydney (BA LLB); Trinity Coll., Dublin; Dip. Internat. Law, The Hague. Called to the Bar of NSW 1957. Teaching Fellow in Equity, Univ. of Sydney, 1956–61 (Actg Lectr in Public Internat. Law, 1956–57); QC 1966; Judge, Supreme Court of NSW, 1977; Judge, Fed Court of Australia, 1977–82; Pres., Trade Practices Tribunal, 1977–82; Justice of the High Court of Australia, 1982–95. Hon. LLD: Sydney, NSW, Griffith, Notre Dame, TCD UTS, Melbourne, Queensland; DUniv: Southern Cross, Aust. Cath., Western Sydney Qld Univ. of Technol.; Hon. Dr Sac. Theol. Melbourne Coll. of Divinity. KStJ 1996 *Address:* PO Box 4168, Manuka, ACT 2603, Australia.

DEANE-DRUMMOND, Maj.-Gen. Anthony John, CB 1970; DSO 1960; MC 1942 and Bar, 1945; *b* 23 June 1917; *s* of late Col J. D. Deane-Drummond, DSO and Bar, OBE MC; *m* 1944, Mary Evangeline Boyd (*d* 2002); four *d*. *Educ:* Marlborough Coll.; RMA Woolwich. Commissioned Royal Signals, 1937. War Service in Europe and N Africa POW, Italy, 1941 (escaped, 1942); Staff Coll., 1945; Bde Major, 3rd Parachute Bde 1946–47; Instructor, Sandhurst, 1949–51 and Staff Coll., 1952–55; CO, 22 Special Air Service Regt, 1957–60; Bde Comdr, 44 Parachute Bde, 1961–63; Asst Comdt, RMA Sandhurst, 1963–66; GOC 3rd Division, 1966–68; ACDS (Operations), 1968–70, retired 1971. Col Comdt, Royal Corps of Signals, 1966–71. Director: Paper and Paper Products Industry Trng Bd, 1971–79; Wood Burning Centre, 1980–83. British Gliding Champion 1957; Pilot, British Gliding Team, 1958, 1960, 1963, 1965. *Publications:* Return Ticket 1951; Riot Control, 1975; Arrows of Fortune (autobiog.), 1991; (contrib.) The Imperial War Museum Book of Modern Warfare, 2002. *Recreations:* carpentry and carving, antique furniture restoration, shooting. *Address:* c/o Royal Bank of Scotland, PO Box 412, 62–63 Threadneedle Street, EC2R 8LA.

DEANFIELD, Prof. John Eric, FRCP; British Heart Foundation Vandervell Professor of Cardiology, University College London (Professor of Cardiology, 1996); Consultant Cardiologist, since 1984, and Academic Head, Cardiothoracic Unit, Great Ormond Street Hospital; *b* 28 April 1952; *s* of Sigmund and Tina Deanfield; *m* 1983, Melanie Fulford; one *s* one *d*. *Educ:* Churchill Coll., Cambridge (BA 1972); Middlesex Hosp. Med. Sch. (MB BChir 1975). FRCP 1993. MRC Trng Fellow, RPMS, 1980–83; Sen. Registrar in Cardiol., Gt Ormond St Hosp., 1983–84. FACC; FESC. *Publications:* numerous peer reviewed contribs to med. jls. *Recreations:* fencing (represented GB in Fencing at Olympics 1972, 1976, 1980), wine tasting, antique collecting (English porcelain lectr). *Address:* Cardiothoracic Unit, Great Ormond Street Hospital, WC1N 3JH. *T:* (020) 7404 5094 *Fax:* (020) 7813 8263; *e-mail:* J.deanfield@ich.ucl.ac.uk.

DEAR, family name of **Baron Dear**.

DEAR, Baron *cr* 2006 (Life Peer), of Willersey in the County of Gloucestershire; **Geoffrey James Dear,** Kt 1997; QPM 1982; Vice Lord-Lieutenant, Worcestershire, 1998–2001; HM Inspector of Constabulary, 1990–97; *b* 20 Sept. 1937; *er s* of Cecil William Dear and Violet Mildred (*née* Mackney); *m* 1st, 1958, Judith Ann Stocker (*d* 1996); one *s* two *d*; 2nd, 1998, Alison Jean Martin Jones. *Educ:* Fletton Grammar Sch., Hunts; University Coll., London (LLB). Joined Peterborough Combined Police after cadet service, 1956; Mid-Anglia (now Cambridgeshire) Constab., 1965; Bramshill Scholarship, UCL, 1965–68 (Fellow, 1990); Asst Chief Constable (Ops), Notts (City and County), 1972–80; seconded as Dir of Comd Training, Bramshill, 1975–77; Metropolitan Police: Dep. Asst Comr, 1980–81; Asst Comr, 1981–85 (Personnel and Trng, 1981–84; Ops, 1984–85); Chief Constable, W Midlands Police, 1985–90. Member: Govt Adv. Cttee on Alcoholism, 1975–78; Glidewell Rev. into CPS, 1997–98; Council, RUSI, 1982–89 (Mem. Cttee, 1976–94). Lecture tour of Eastern USA univs, 1978; visited Memphis, Tenn, USA to advise on reorganisation of Police Dept, 1979. Non-executive Chairman: Image Metrics plc, 2001–03; Skyguard Technologies Ltd, 2001–; Omniperception plc, 2005–; Key Forensic Services Ltd, 2005–; Forensic DNA Services Ltd, 2006–; Adv. Bd, Pegasus Bridge Fund Mgt Ltd, 2006–; non-executive Director: Reliance Security Services Ltd, 1997–2005; Reliance Custodial Services, subseq. Reliance Secure Task Management Ltd, 1999–2005. Chm., Action against Business Crime, 2004–. Vice Chm., London and SE Reg., Sports Council, 1984–85. Vice President: Warwickshire CCC, 1985–; W Midlands and Hereford & Worcester Grenadier Guards Assocs, 1992–. Hon. Fellow, Birmingham City Univ. (formerly Univ. of Central England in Birmingham), 1991. FRSA 1990. DL W Midlands, 1985, Hereford and Worcester, 1995. CStJ 1996. Queen's Commendation for Bravery, 1979. *Publications:* (contrib.) The Police and the Community, 1975; articles in Police Jl and other pubns. *Recreations:* field sports, Rugby football (Pres., Met. Police RFC, 1983–85), fell-walking, literature, gardening, music, fine arts. *Address:* The Old Rectory, Willersey, Broadway, Worcs WR12 7PN; House of Lords, SW1A 0PW. *Clubs:* East India, Special Forces.

DEAR, Jeremy; General Secretary, National Union of Journalists, since 2002; *b* 6 Dec. 1966; *s* of John and Jan Dear; *m* 1999, Paula Jolly. *Educ:* Coventry Polytech. (BA Hons Mod. Studies); UC Cardiff (Postgrad. Dip. Journalism). Journalist, freelance, and on staff of Essex Chronicle Series, and The Big Issue, 1989–94; Ed., Big Issue in the Midlands, 1994–97; Nat. Organiser, Newspapers, NUJ, 1997–2001. *Address:* National Union of Journalists, Headland House, 308 Grays Inn Road, WC1X 8DP. *T:* (020) 7278 7916, *Fax:* (020) 7837 8143; *e-mail:* jeremyd@nuj.org.uk.

DEARING, family name of **Baron Dearing**.

DEARING, Baron *cr* 1998 (Life Peer), of Kingston upon Hull in the co. of the East Riding of Yorkshire; **Ronald Ernest Dearing,** Kt 1984; CB 1979; *b* 27 July 1930; *s* of late E. H. A. Dearing and of M. T. Dearing (*née* Hoyle); *m* 1954, Margaret Patricia Riley; two *d*. *Educ:* Doncaster Grammar Sch.; Hull Univ. (BScEcon); London Business Sch. (Sloan Fellow). Min. of Labour and Nat. Service, 1946–49; Min. of Power, 1949–62; HM Treasury, 1962–64; Min. of Power, Min. of Technology, DTI, 1965–72; Regional Dir, N Region, DTI, 1972–74, and Under-Sec., DTI later Dept of Industry, 1972–76; Dep. Sec. on nationalised industry matters, Dept of Industry, 1976–80; Dep. Chm., 1980–81, Chm., 1981–87, Post Office Corp.; Chairman: Co. Durham Develt Co., 1987–90; Northern Develt Co., 1990–94; Camelot Gp, 1993–95. Director (non-executive): Whitbread Co. plc, 1987–90; Prudential plc, 1987–91; IMI plc, 1988–95; British Coal, 1988–91; Erisson Ltd, 1988–93; English Estates, 1988–90; SDX Business Systems, 1996–99. Chairman: NICG, 1983–84; Accounting Standards Review Cttee, CCAB, 1987–88; Financial Reporting Council, 1990–93. Mem. Council, Industrial Soc., 1985–99. CCMI (CBIM 1981; Mem. Council, 1985–88; Vice-Chm., 1986; Gold Medal, 1994). Chairman: CNAA, 1987–88; PCFC, 1988–93; UFC, 1991–93; HEFCE, 1992–93; SCAA, 1993–96; Nat. Cttee of Inquiry into Higher Educn, 1996–97; Cttee of Inquiry into Church Schs, 2000–01; Report on Languages in Schs, 2007. McKechnie Lectr, Liverpool Univ., 1995. Mem. Governing Council, London Business Sch., 1985–89, Fellow, 1988; Member: Council, Durham Univ., 1988–91; Governing Body, Univ. of Melbourne, 1997–2000; Chm., London Educn Business Partnership, 1989–92; Chm. Trustees, Higher Educn Policy Inst., 2002–04. Pres., Council of Church Colls Assoc., 2000–03. Chm., Northern Sinfonia Appeals Cttee, 1993–94. Pres., Inst. of Direct Mkting, 1994–97. Chancellor, Nottingham Univ., 1993–2001. Patron: Sascha Lasserson Meml Trust, 1995; Music in Allendale, 1995; Univ. for Industry, 2000– (Chm., 1999–2000); Guildford Community Family Trust, 2001–; Trident Trust, 2005–. Trustee, TRAC, 1995–97. Freeman, City of London, 1982. Hon. FREng (Hon. FEng 1992); Hon. FTCL 1993; Hon. Fellow, Inst. of Educn, 1995. Hon. Fellow, Sunderland Poly., 1991. Hon. DSc Hull, 1986; Hon. DTech: CNAA, 1991; Staffordshire, 1995; Hon. DCL: Durham, 1992; Northumbria, 1993; Hon. LLD Nottingham, 1993; Dr *hc* Humberside, 1993; DUniv Open, 1995; Hon. DLitt: Brighton, 1998; Exeter, 1998; Melbourne, 2000; Gloucestershire, 2002. *Recreations:* car boot sales, DIY, gardening. *Address:* House of Lords, SW1A 2PW.

DEARLOVE, Sir Richard (Billing), KCMG 2001; OBE 1984; Master of Pembroke College, Cambridge, since 2004; Deputy Vice-Chancellor, University of Cambridge, since 2005; *b* 23 Jan. 1945; *m* 1968, Rosalind McKenzie; two *s* one *d*. *Educ:* Monkton Combe Sch.; Kent Sch., Conn, USA; Queens' Coll., Cambridge (MA; Hon. Fellow, 2004). Entered FO, 1966; Nairobi, 1968–71; Prague, 1973–76; FCO, 1976–80; First Secretary: Paris, 1980–84; FCO, 1984–87; Counsellor: UKMIS Geneva, 1987–91; Washington, 1991–93; Secret Intelligence Service: Dir, Personnel and Admin, 1993–94; Dir, Ops, 1994–99; Asst Chief, 1998–99; Chief, 1999–2004. Chm., Ascot Underwriting Ltd, 2006–. Vis. Lectr, Fletcher Sch., Tufts Univ., Boston, USA, 2005–. Advr, Monitor Gp, 2005–; Mem. Adv. Bd, AIG, 2005–. Chm. Trustees, Cambridge Union Soc., 2007; Trustee, Kent Sch., Conn, USA, 2001–. Gov., ESU, 2008. Hon. LLD Exeter, 2007. *Address:* The Master's Lodge, Pembroke College, Cambridge CB2 1RF.

DEARNALEY, Dr Geoffrey, FRS 1993; President, Cambritec Consulting, since 1999; Vice-President, Materials and Structures Division, Southwest Research Institute, 1994–99; *b* 22 June 1930; *s* of Eric and Dora Dearnaley; *m* 1957, Jean Rosalind Beer; two *s*. *Educ:* Univ. of Cambridge (MA 1955; PhD 1956). Research Fellow, Pembroke Coll., Cambridge, 1955–58; joined AERE, Harwell, Nuclear Physics Division, 1958: Individual Merit Promotion, 1975; Chief Scientist, Surface Technologies, 1991–93; joined Southwest Res. Inst., Texas, 1993, Inst. Scientist, 1993–94. Vis. Prof. in Physics, Sussex Univ., 1972–. *Publications:* Semiconductor Counters for Nuclear Radiations, 1963; Ion Implantation, 1973; numerous articles on interaction of energetic ion beams with materials. *Recreations:* travel, walking, the life and work of William Blake. *Address:* Southwest Research Institute, 6220 Culebra Road, PO Drawer 28510, San Antonio, TX 78228–0510, USA. *T:* (210) 5225579.

DEARY, Prof. Ian John, PhD; FRCPE; FRCPsych; FBA 2003; FRSE; FMedSci; Professor of Differential Psychology, University of Edinburgh, since 1995; *b* 17 May 1954; *s* of Hugh McCulloch Deary and Isobelle Ferguson Deary; *m* 1978, Ann Marie Barclay; one *s* two *d*. *Educ:* Hamilton Acad.; Univ. of Edinburgh (BSc; MB ChB; PhD 1992). MRCPsych 1991, FRCPsych 2008; FRCPE 1996; FRSE 2003. Med. House Officer, 1983–84, Surgical House Officer, 1984, Royal Infirmary of Edinburgh; Sen. House Officer, Psychiatry, Bethlem Royal and Maudsley Hosps, 1984–85; Lectr, 1985–90, Sen. Lectr, 1990–92, Reader, 1992–95, in Psychology, Univ. of Edinburgh; Registrar, Psychiatry, Royal Edinburgh Hosp., 1989–90. FMedSci 2007. *Publications:* (with G. Matthews) Personality Traits, 1998, 2nd edn 2003; Looking Down on Human Intelligence: from psychometrics to the brain, 2000; Intelligence: a very short introduction, 2001; over 300 articles in learned jls on human mental abilities, personality, psychometrics and med. aspects of psychology. *Recreations:* cycling, lyric writing, saxophone, Motherwell FC, English Romantic composers, late Victorian English novelists. *Address:* Department of Psychology, University of Edinburgh, 7 George Square, Edinburgh EH8 9JZ. *T:* (0131) 650 3452, *Fax:* (0131) 651 1771; *e-mail:* I.Deary@ed.ac.uk.

DEATHRIDGE, Prof. John William, DPhil; FRCO; King Edward Professor of Music, King's College London, since 1996; *b* 21 Oct. 1944; *s* of Leslie and Iris Deathridge; *m* 1985, Victoria L. Cooper; one *d*. *Educ:* King Edward's Sch., Birmingham; Lincoln Coll., Oxford (MA; DPhil 1974). FRCO 1967. Organist and Choirmaster, St Wolfgang, Munich, 1971–81; Ed., Richard Wagner-Gesamtausgabe, Munich, 1981–83; University of Cambridge: Fellow, and Dir, Studies in Music, King's Coll., 1983–96; Lectr in Music, 1983–95; Reader in Music, 1995–96. Pres., Royal Musical Assoc., 2005– (Vice-Pres., 2002–05). Corresp. Mem., Amer. Musicological Soc., 2002. *Publications:* Wagner's Rienzi: a reappraisal based on a study of the sketches and drafts, 1977; (with C. Dahlhaus) The New Grove Wagner, 1984; (jtly) Verzeichnis der musikalischen Werke Richard Wagners und ihrer Quellen, 1986; (ed) Family Letters of Richard Wagner, 1991; (ed jtly) Wagner Handbook, 1992; Wagner Beyond Good and Evil, 2008; edited with K. Döge: Richard Wagner: Lohengrin, 3 vols, 1996–2000; Dokumente und Texte zu "Lohengrin", 2003; contribs to Musical Times, 19th Century Music, Cambridge Opera Jl, Jl Royal Musical Assoc., Opera Quarterly. *Recreations:* keep fit, films, pond care. *Address:* 12 Cook Close, Cambridge CB4 1PH; Music Department, King's College London, Strand, WC2R 2LS; *e-mail:* john.deathridge@kcl.ac.uk.

DEAVE, John James; former barrister-at-law; *b* 1 April 1928; *s* of Charles John Deave and Gertrude Debrit Deave; *m* 1958, Gillian Mary, *d* of Adm. Sir Manley Power, KCB, CBE, DSO; one *s* one *d*. *Educ:* Charterhouse; Pembroke Coll., Oxford (MA). Served RA, 2nd Lieut, 1946–48; Pembroke Coll., 1948–51; called to the Bar, Gray's Inn, 1952; in practice at Nottingham, 1957–98; a Recorder, 1980–98. *Recreations:* history, gardening. *Address:* Greensmith Cottage, Stathern, Melton Mowbray, Leics LE14 4HE. *T:* (01949) 860340. *Club:* Nottinghamshire United Services.

DEAYTON, (Gordon) Angus; writer and presenter; *b* 6 Jan. 1956; *s* of Roger Davall Deayton and Susan Agnes Deayton (*née* Weir). *Educ:* Caterham Sch.; New Coll., Oxford (BA Modern Langs (French and German)). Dir, Oxford Revue, 1979. Writer and performer: *radio:* Radio Active, 1980–87 (Mem., Hee Bee Gee Bees pop parody band); *stage:* Rowan Atkinson's Stage Show, 1986–90; *television:* Alexei Sayle's Stuff, 1987–90; KYTV, 1990–93; One Foot in the Grave, 1990–2000; Have I Got News For You?, 1990–2002; TV Hell, 1992; End of the Year Show, 1995–2000; Before They Were Famous, 1997–2004; Not Another Awards Show, 1999; Not Another Game Show, News Bulletin, Eurovision, 2002; University Challenge (for Comic Relief), 2002, 2004; Nighty Night, 2003; Absolute Power, 2004–; Hell's Kitchen, 2004–07; Bognor or Bust, 2004; Heartless, New Year's Honours List, Marigold, Stick to What You Know, 2005; Help Yourself, Only Fools On Horses, 2006; Would I Lie to You?, 2007–08; Comedy Sketchbook, 2008; *documentaries:* In Search of Happiness, 1995; The Lying Game, 1997; The Temptation Game, 1998; The History of Alternative Comedy, 1999; Posh 'n Becks: the Reign in Spain, 2003. *Publications:* Radio Active Times, 1986; The Uncyclopaedia of Rock, 1987; Have I Got News For You?, 1994; In Search of Happiness, 1995; Have I Got 1997 For You?, 1997. *Recreations:* soccer, tennis, ski-ing. *Address:* c/o Independent Talent Group Ltd, Oxford House, 76 Oxford Street, W1D 1BS. *Clubs:* Garrick, Groucho, Soho House, Home House.

de BASTO, Gerald Arthur; Judge of the High Court of Hong Kong, 1982–89; *b* London, 31 Dec. 1924; *s* of Bernard de Basto and Lucie Marie, *d* of Raoul Melchior Pattard, Paris; *m* 1961, Diana, *d* of Dr Frederick Osborne Busby Wilkinson; two *s*. *Educ:* Riverview Coll., Sydney, Australia; Univ. of Sydney (LLB). Called to the Bar: Supreme Court of New South Wales and High Court of Australia, 1952; Lincoln's Inn, 1955; admitted to the Hong Kong Bar, 1957; Chairman, Hong Kong Bar, 1968–70, 1973; QC 1968; Judge of the District Court of Hong Kong, 1973–82; Pres., Deportation Tribunal, 1986–89. *Recreations:* antiques, travel, reading. *Address:* 3 Roderick Way, Constantia, 7806, South Africa. *T:* (21) 7942778. *Clubs:* Boodle's; Hong Kong, Hong Kong Jockey (Hong Kong).

de BELLAIGUE, Sir Geoffrey, GCVO 1996 (KCVO 1986; CVO 1976; LVO 1968); FSA; FBA 1992; Director of the Royal Collection, 1988–96; Surveyor of the Queen's Works of Art, 1972–96, now Surveyor Emeritus; *b* 12 March 1931; *s* of late Vicomte Pierre de Bellaigue and Marie-Antoinette Ladd; *m* 1971, Sheila, (LVO 2000), 2nd *d* of late Rt Rev. J. K. Russell; two *d*. *Educ:* Wellington Coll.; Trinity Coll., Cambridge (BA 1954, MA 1959); Ecole du Louvre. With J. Henry Schroeder & Co., 1954–59; with the National Trust, Waddesdon Manor, 1960–63 (Keeper of the Collection, 1962–63); Dep. Surveyor, the Queen's Work's of Art, 1963–72. Mem., Exec. Cttee, NACF, 1977–2005. Trustee, Wallace Collection, 1998–2006. Hon. Pres., French Porcelain Soc., 1985–99. Officier de l'Ordre des Arts et des Lettres (France), 1987; Officier, Légion d'Honneur, 1999. *Publications:* The James A. de Rothschild Collection at Waddesdon Manor: furniture, clocks and gilt bronzes, 1974; (jtly) Buckingham Palace, 1986; Sèvres Porcelain in the Collection of HM the Queen, Vol. I, 1986; (with S. Eriksen) Sèvres Porcelain, 1987; articles in art historical jls and exhibn catalogues, principally for The Queen's Gallery. *Address:* 85 Tantallon Road, SW12 8DQ.

DE BENEDETTI, Carlo; Cavaliere del Lavoro, Italy, 1983; Chairman: Compagnie Industriali Riunite, since 1995 (Vice-Chairman and Chief Executive, 1976–95); Compagnia Finanziaria De Benedetti, since 1995 (Chief Executive, 1991–95); Cerus, since 1986; Sogefi, 1981–2005, now Hon. Chairman; *b* 14 Nov. 1934; *m*; three *s*. *Educ:* Turin Polytechnic (degree in electrotech. engrg). Chm./Chief Exec., Gilardini, 1972–76; Chief Exec., Fiat, 1976; Olivetti SpA: Chief Exec., 1978–96; Chm., 1983–96; Hon. Chm., 1996–99. Director: Pirelli SpA; Valeo; l'Espresso SpA; Mem., European Adv. Cttee, NY Stock Exchange, 1985–2005. Dir, Center for Strategic and Internat. Studies, Washington, 1978; Mem. Bd of Trustees, Solomon R. Guggenheim Foundn, NY, 1984; Vice Chm., Eur. Roundtable of Industrialists, Brussels, 1999–2004. Foreign Mem., Royal Swedish Acad. of Engrg Scis, Stockholm, 1987. *Publications:* lectures and articles in business jls. *Address:* CIR SpA, Via Ciovassino 1, 20121 Milano, Italy. *T:* (2) 722701.

DEBENHAM, Sir Thomas Adam, 4th Bt *cr* 1931, of Bladen, co. Dorset; *b* 28 Feb. 1971; *s* of George Andrew Debenham and of Penelope Jane (*née* Carter); *S* grandfather, 2001; *m* 1998, Melanie Bargh. *Heir: uncle* William Michael Debenham [*b* 30 June 1940; *m* 1974, Gunnel Birgitta Holmgren; two *s*].

DEBENHAM TAYLOR, John, CMG 1967; OBE 1959; TD 1967; HM Diplomatic Service, retired; *b* 25 April 1920; *s* of John Francis Taylor and Harriett Beatrice (*née* Williams); *m* 1966, Gillian May James; one *d*. *Educ:* Aldenham School. Eastern Counties Farmers Assoc. Ltd, Ipswich and Great Yarmouth, 1936–39. Commd in RA (TA), Feb. 1939; served War of 1939–46 in Finland, Middle East, UK and SE Asia (despatches, 1946). Foreign Office, 1946; Control Commn for Germany, 1947–49; 2nd Sec., Bangkok, 1950; Actg Consul, Songkhla, 1951–52; Vice-Consul, Hanoi, 1952–53; FO, 1953–54; 1st Sec., Bangkok, 1954–56; FO, 1956–58; Singapore, 1958–59; FO, 1960–64; Counsellor, 1964; Counsellor: Kuala Lumpur, 1964–66; FCO (formerly FO), 1966–69; Washington, 1969–72; Paris, 1972–73; FCO, 1973–77. *Recreations:* walking, reading, history. *Address:* The East Wing, Gunton Hall, Norfolk NR11 7HJ. *T:* (01263) 768301. *Club:* Naval and Military.

de BERNIÈRE-SMART, Louis Henry Piers; author, as Louis de Bernières; *b* 8 Dec. 1954; *s* of Major Reginald Piers Alexander de Bernière-Smart, *qv*. *Educ:* Grenham House; Bradfield Coll.; Manchester Univ. (BA Hons Philosophy 1977); Leicester Poly. (PGCE 1981); Inst. of Educn, London Univ. (MA 1985). Landscape gardener, 1972–73; teacher and rancher, Colombia, 1974; philosophy tutor, 1977–79; car mechanic, 1980; English teacher, 1981–84; bookshop asst, 1985–86; supply teacher, 1986–93. FTCL 1999. *Publications:* The War of Don Emmanuel's Nether Parts, 1990; Señor Vivo and the Coca Lord, 1991; The Troublesome Offspring of Cardinal Guzman, 1992; Captain Corelli's Mandolin, 1994 (filmed, 2001); Red Dog, 2001; Sunday Morning at the Centre of the World, 2001; Birds Without Wings, 2004; A Partisan's Daughter, 2008. *Recreations:* music, literature, golf, fishing, carpentry, gardening, cats. *Address:* c/o Lavinia Trevor Agency, 29 Addison Place, W11 4RJ. *T:* (020) 7603 5254.

de BERNIÈRE-SMART, Major Reginald Piers Alexander; Director, The Shaftesbury Homes and Arethusa, 1988–89, retired (General Secretary, 1971–88); general duties, Chichester Division, SSAFA/FHS, 1995–2000 (caseworker, 1990–94); *b* 3 March 1924; *s* of Kenneth de Bernière-Smart and Audrey (*née* Brown); *m* 1951, Jean Ashton Smithells; one *s* two *d*. *Educ:* Bowden House, Seaford; Bradfield Coll. Commnd The Queen's Bays (2nd Dragoon Guards), 1943; Italian Campaign, 1944–45 (despatches); Staff, RAC OCTU and Mons OCS, 1948–49; GSO 3 7th Armd Bde, 1951; Adjt, The Queen's Bays, 1952–54; Adjt, RAC Centre, Bovington, 1956–58; retired from 1st The Queen's Dragoon Guards, 1959. Exec. Sec., British Diabetic Assoc., 1960–65; joined Shaftesbury Homes and Arethusa exec. staff, 1966. Dir, Wad (West Wittering) Management Co., 1992–94. Chm., Management Cttee, Bradfield Club, Peckham, 1990–92 (Mem. Council, 1992–2000). Member: IAM, 1959–; NCVCCO, 1971–89. West Wittering PCC, 1991–97; Foundn Gov., W Wittering Parochial C of E Sch., 1997–2000 (Chm. of Govs, 1998–2000). Hon. Fellow, Cancer Res. UK, 2003. *Publication:* (as Piers Alexander) Golden Apples (poetry), 2006. *Recreations:* open air activities, photography, steam and model railways, theatre, poetry, militaria. *Address:* 9 The Wad, West Wittering, Chichester, W Sussex PO20 8AH. *T:* (01243) 511072. *Clubs:* Cavalry and Guards, Victoria League for Commonwealth Friendship.

See also L. H. P. de Bernière-Smart.

de BERNIÈRES, Louis; *see* de Bernière-Smart, L. H. P.

de BLANK, Justin Robert; Chairman, The Justin de Blank Co. Ltd, since 2002 (Vice-Chairman, 1996–2002); *b* 25 Feb. 1927; *s* of William de Blank and Agnes Frances de Blank (*née* Crossley); *m* 1st, 1972, Mary Jacqueline Christina du Bois Godet (Molly); 2nd, 1977, Melanie Alexandra Margaret Irwin; three *d*. *Educ:* Grenham House School, Birchington-on-Sea; Marlborough College; Corpus Christi College, Cambridge (BA); Royal Acad. Sch. of Architecture. Unilever, 1953–58; J. Walter Thompson, London and Paris, 1958–66; Conran Design Group, 1967; formed own company, 1968; Chm. and Man. Dir, Justin de Blank Provisions Ltd, 1968–93; Chm., de Blank Restaurants, 1986–95; Pres., Justin de Blank Foods Ltd, 1993–95. Director: Kitchen Range Foods Ltd, 1976–96; Millers Damsels Ltd, 1989–96; The Original Porter's Provisions Co. Ltd, 1993–96; Chm., Chantdene, 1999–2002. *Recreations:* gardening, golf, food and wine. *Club:* Royal West Norfolk Golf.

de BLOCQ van KUFFELER, John Philip; Chairman, Provident Financial plc, since 1997; *b* 9 Jan. 1949; *s* of late Captain Frans de Blocq van Kuffeler and Stella de Blocq van Kuffeler (*née* Hall); *m* 1971, Lesley Callander; two *s* one *d*. *Educ:* Atlantic Coll.; Clare Coll., Cambridge (MA). FCA 1975. Peat Marwick & Mitchell, 1970–77; Grindlays Bank: Manager, 1977–80; Head of Corporate Finance, 1980–82; Brown Shipley & Co.: Head: Corporate Finance, 1983–88; Investment Banking, UK and USA, 1986–88; Gp Chief Exec., 1988–91; Chief Exec., Provident Financial plc, 1991–97. Council Mem., CBI, 1997–99. Exec. Chm., Huveaux plc, 2001–; non-exec. Chm., Eidos plc, 2002–05; non-exec. Dir, Medical Defence Union, 2001–04. Mem. Council, Prince's Trust, 2001–. *Recreations:* field sports, opera. *Address:* Provident Financial plc, Colonnade, Sunbridge Road, Bradford BD1 2LQ. *T:* (01274) 731111. *Club:* City of London.

de BONO, Dr Edward Francis Charles Publius; Lecturer in Medicine, Department of Medicine, University of Cambridge, 1976–83; Director of The Cognitive Research Trust, Cambridge, since 1971; Secretary-General, Supranational Independent Thinking Organisation (SITO), since 1983; *b* 19 May 1933; *s* of late Prof. Joseph de Bono, CBE and of Josephine de Bono (*née* O'Byrne); *m* 1971, Josephine, *d* of Maj. Francis Hall-White, MBE; two *s*. *Educ:* St Edward's Coll., Malta; Royal Univ. of Malta; Christ Church, Oxford (Rhodes Scholar). BSc, MD Malta; DPhil Oxon; PhD Cantab. Research Asst, Dept of Regius Prof. of Medicine, Univ. of Oxford, 1958–60; Jun. Lectr in Med., Oxford, 1960–61; Asst Dir of Res., Dept of Investigative Medicine, Cambridge Univ., 1963–76. Research Associate: also Hon. Registrar, St Thomas' Hosp. Med. Sch., Univ. of London; Harvard Med. Sch., and Hon. Consultant, Boston City Hosp., 1965–66. Hon. Prof. of Thinking, Univ. of Pretoria, 2003; Da Vinci Prof. of Thinking, Univ. of Advancing Technol., Arizona, 2005–; Prof. of Constructive Thinking, Dublin City Univ., 2005–. Chm. Council, Young Enterprise Europe, 1998–. Established World Centre for New Thinking, Malta, 2004. TV series: The Greatest Thinkers, 1981; de Bono's Thinking Course, 1982. Hon. LLD Dundee, 2005; Hon. DDes RMIT, 2003. Planet DE73 named edebono after him, 1997. Carl Sloans Award, Internat. Assoc. Mgt Consulting Firms, 2006. *Publications:* The Use of Lateral Thinking, 1967; The Five-Day Course in Thinking, 1968; The Mechanism of Mind, 1969; Lateral Thinking: a textbook of creativity, 1970; The Dog Exercising Machine, 1970; Technology Today, 1971; Practical Thinking, 1971; Lateral Thinking for Management, 1971; Beyond Yes and No, 1972; Children Solve Problems, 1972; Eureka!: an illustrated history of inventions from the wheel to the computer, 1974; Teaching Thinking, 1976; The Greatest Thinkers, 1976; Wordpower, 1977; The Happiness Purpose, 1977; The Case of the Disappearing Elephant, 1977; Opportunities: a handbook of business opportunity search, 1978; Future Positive, 1979; Atlas of Management Thinking, 1981; de Bono's Thinking Course, 1982; Tactics: the art and science of success, 1984; Conflicts: a better way to resolve them, 1985; Six Thinking Hats, 1985; Masterthinker's Handbook, 1985; Letters to Thinkers, 1987; I am Right, You are Wrong, 1990; Positive Revolution for Brazil, 1990; Handbook for a Positive Revolution, 1990; Six Action Shoes, 1992; Sur/Petition, 1992; Serious Creativity, 1992; Teach Your Child to Think, 1992; Water Logic, 1993; Parallel Thinking, 1994; Teach Yourself to Think, 1995; Mind Pack, 1995; Edward de Bono's Textbook of Wisdom, 1996; How To Be More Interesting, 1997; Simplicity, 1998; New Thinking for the New Millennium, 1999; Why I want to be King of Australia, 1999; The de Bono Code Book, 2000; Why So Stupid: how the human race has never really learned to think, 2003; How to have a Beautiful Mind, 2004; Six Value Medals, 2005; H+, 2006; How to have Creative Ideas, 2007; Free or Unfree?: are Americans really free?, 2007; contribs to Nature, Lancet, Clinical Science, Amer. Jl of Physiology, etc. *Recreations:* travel, toys, thinking. *Address:* L2 Albany, Piccadilly, W1V 9RR. *Club:* Athenæum.

de BOTTON, Alain; author, since 1993; *b* 20 Dec. 1969; *s* of late Gilbert de Botton and of Jacqueline (*née* Burgauer); *m* 2003, Charlotte Neser; two *s*. *Educ:* Gonville and Caius Coll., Cambridge (BA Hist. 1st Cl. Hons). *Publications:* Essays in Love, 1993; The Romantic Movement, 1994; Kiss and Tell, 1995; How Proust Can Change Your Life, 1997; The Consolations of Philosophy, 2000; The Art of Travel, 2002; Status Anxiety, 2004; The Architecture of Happiness, 2006. *Recreations:* French Cinema 1960–1970, nature, art. *Address:* c/o Caroline Dawnay, United Agents, 12–26 Lexington Street, W1F 0LE.

de BOTTON, Hon. Janet Frances Wolfson, CBE 2006; Trustee, Wolfson Foundation, since 1987; *b* 31 March 1952; *d* of Baron Wolfson, *qv* and Ruth, Lady Wolfson; *m* 1st, 1972, Michael Philip Green, *qv* (marr. diss. 1989); two *d*; 2nd, 1990, Gilbert de Botton (*d* 2000). *Educ:* St Paul's Girls' Sch. Dir. Christie's International, 1994–98. Trustee, Tate Gall., 1992–2002. Chm. Council, Tate Modern, 1999–2002. *Address:* c/o Tate Gallery, Millbank, SW1P 4RG. *T:* (020) 7887 8000.

DEBRÉ, Jean Louis; President, Constitutional Council, France, since 2007; *b* Toulouse, 30 Sept. 1944; *s* of late Michel Jean-Pierre Debré; *m* 1971, Anne-Marie Engel; two *s* one *d*. *Educ:* Lycée Janson-de-Sailly; Institut d'Etudes Politiques, Paris; Faculté de Droit, Paris (DenD); Ecole Nationale de la Magistrature. Asst, Faculté de Droit, Paris, 1972–75. Technical Counsellor, then Chargé de Mission, office of Jacques Chirac, as Minister of Agric., 1973–74, Minister of the Interior, 1974, and Prime Minister, 1974–76; Dep. Public Prosecutor, High Court of Evry, 1976–78; Magistrate, Central Admin, Ministry of Justice, 1978; Chef de Cabinet to Minister of the Budget, 1978; Examng Magistrate, High Court of Paris, 1979. Dep. (RPR) for Eure, Nat. Assembly, 1986–95 and 1997–2007. Minister of the Interior, France, 1995–97; Pres., Nat. Assembly, 2002–07; Vice-Pres. 1990–95, Pres., 1997–2007, RPR Gp in Nat. Assembly. Councillor: Evreux, 1989–95; Paris, 1995–97; Conseiller Général, Canton de Nonancourt, 1992–; Mayor of Evreux, 2001–07. *Publications:* Les Idées constitutionnelles du Général de Gaulle, 1974; La Constitution de la Ve République, 1974; Le Pouvoir politique, 1977; Le Gaullisme, 1978; La Justice au XIXe, 1981; Les Républiques des Avocats, 1984; Le Curieux, 1986; En mon for intérieur, 1997; Pièges, 1998; Le Gaullisme n'est pas une nostalgie, 1999; Qu'est ce que l'Assemblée Nationale?, 2006; Quand les brochets font courir les carpes, 2008; Les oubliés de la République, 2008. *Recreations:* horse-riding, tennis. *Address:* Conseil Constitutionnel, 2 rue de Montpensier, 75001 Paris, France.

de BROKE; *see* Willoughby de Broke.

de BRÚN, Bairbre; Member (SF) Northern Ireland, European Parliament, since 2004. *Educ:* University Coll., Dublin (BA Hons 1974); Queen's Univ., Belfast (PGCE 1980). Teacher, specialised in Irish Medium Educn, 1991–97. Mem. (SF) W Belfast, NI Assembly, 1998–2004; Minister of Health, Social Services and Public Safety, NI, 1999–2002. *Recreations:* hill-walking, theatre, cinema. *Address:* Sinn Féin Offices, 51–55 Falls Road, Belfast BT12 4PD. *T:* (028) 9052 1675.

DEBY, John Bedford; QC 1980; a Recorder of the Crown Court, 1977–95; *b* 19 Dec. 1931; *s* of Reginald Bedford Deby and Irene (*née* Slater). *Educ:* Winchester Coll.; Trinity Coll., Cambridge (MA). Called to the Bar, Inner Temple, 1954, Bencher, 1986. *Address:* 11 Britannia Road, Fulham, SW6 2HJ. *T:* (020) 7736 4976. *Club:* Athenæum.

de CARDI, Beatrice Eileen, OBE 1973; FBA 2002; archaeologist; *b* 5 June 1914; *d* of Edwin Count de Cardi and Christine Berbette Wurfflein. *Educ:* St Paul's Girls' Sch.; University Coll. London (BA; Fellow, 1995). Secretary (later Asst), London Museum, 1936–44; Personal Asst to Representative of Allied Supplies Exec. of War Cabinet in China, 1944–45; Asst UK Trade Comr: Delhi, 1946; Karachi, 1947; Lahore, 1948–49. Asst Sec. (title changed to Sec.), Council for British Archæology, 1949–73. Archæological research: in Kalat, Pakistan Baluchistan, 1948; in Afghanistan, 1949; directed excavations in Kalat, 1957; at Bampur, Persian Baluchistan, 1966; survey in Ras al-Khaimah (then Trucial States), 1968; Middle East lecture tour for British Council, 1970; survey with RGS's Musandam Expedn (Northern Oman), 1971–72; directed archæological research projects: in Qatar, 1973–74; in Central Oman, 1974–76, 1978; survey in Ras al-Khaimah, 1977, 1982, 1992. Winston Churchill Meml Trust Fellowship for work in Oman, 1973. Hon. Vis. Prof., UCL, 1998–. FSA 1950 (Vice-Pres., 1976–80; Dir, 1980–83). Al-Qasimi Medal (UAE), 1989 (for services to Ras al-Khaimah); Burton Meml Medal, RAS, 1993; Soc. of Antiquaries Medal, 2003. *Publications:* Excavations at Bampur, a third millennium settlement in Persian Baluchistan, 1966 (Vol. 51, Pt 3, Anthropological Papers of the American Museum of Natural History), 1970; Archaeological Surveys in Baluchistan 1948 and 1957 (Inst. of Archaeology, Occasional Paper No 8), 1983; contribs to Antiquity, Iran, Pakistan Archæology, East and West, Jl of Oman Studies, Oriens Antiquus, Proc. Seminar for Arabian Studies. *Recreations:* archæological fieldwork, travel, cooking. *Address:* 1 Douro Place, Victoria Road, W8 5PH. *T:* (020) 7937 9740.

de CARMOY, Hervé Pierre; Comte de Carmoy; Managing Director, Rhône Group LLC, New York, 1999–2003; *b* 4 Jan. 1937; *s* of Guy de Carmoy and Marie de Gourcuff; *m* Roseline de Rohan Chabot; two *c*. *Educ:* Institut d'Etudes Politiques, Paris; Cornell Univ. Gen. Man., Western Europe, Chase Manhattan Bank, 1963–78; Chm., Exec. Bd, Midland Bank, Paris, 1978–79; Gen. Man., Europe, Midland Bank, London, 1979–84; Chief Exec., Internat. Midland Bank, London, 1984–86; Dir and Chief Exec., Global Banking Sector, Midland Bank, 1986–88; Chief Exec. Officer, Société Générale de Belgique, 1988–91; Chairman and Chief Executive: Union Minière, 1989–91; Banque Industrielle et Mobilière Privée, 1992–98. Chairman: Cimenteries Belges Réunies, 1989–; Gechem, 1989–; Parvalind Gérance, 1991–; Almatis, 2003–07; Supervisory Bd, Etam, 2008–; Vice Chm., Générale de Banque, 1989–. Prof. of Internat. Strategy, Institut d'Etudes Politiques, Paris, 1996–2002. Chm., France, 1989–2004, Vice-Chm., Europe, 2004–, Trilateral Commn. Commandeur de la Légion d'Honneur (Côte d'Ivoire), 1978; Chevalier de l'Ordre du Mérite (France), 1987; Chevalier de la Légion d'Honneur (France), 1992. *Publications:* Third World Debt, 1987; Stratégie Bancaire: le refus de la dérive, 1988; La Banque du XXIe Siècle, 1996; L'entreprise, l'individu, l'Etat: conduire l changement, 1999; Euramérique, 2007. *Recreations:* tennis, music. *Address:* 10 rue Guynemer, 75006 Paris, France.

de CHARETTE, Hervé; Deputy (UDF) for Maine-et-Loire, 1988–93, and since 1997; Deputy President, Union pour la Démocratie Française, since 1999; *b* 30 July 1938; *s* of Hélion de Charette; *m* 1980, Michelle Delor; one *d*, and one *s* three *d* by former marriage. *Educ:* Institut des Etudes Politiques; HEC; Ecole Nationale de l'Administration. Conseil d'Etat: Mem., 1966–; Auditor, 1966–73; Dep. Sec. Gen., 1969–73; Maître des Requêtes, 1973–; tech. advr to Minister of Social Affairs, 1973–74; Cabinet Director for: Sec. of State for Immigration, 1974–76; Minister of Employment, 1976–78; Chargé de Mission for Minister of Commerce, 1978–81; Conseil d'Etat, 1982–86; Asst to Prime Minister and Minister of Public Service, Planning and Social Econs, 1986–88; Minister of Housing, 1988–95; Minister for Foreign Affairs, 1995–97. Vice-Pres., UDF, 1989; Delegate-Gen., 1995–97, Pres., 1997–, PPDF. Vice-Pres., Pays-de-Loire Regl Council, 1992–; Mayor, St Florent-le-Vieil, 1989–. Pres., St Florent-le-Vieil Music and Dance Fest., 1989–. *Publications:* Whirlwind over the Republic, 1995; Lyautey, 1997. *Address:* 250 boulevard Saint Germain, 75007 Paris, France.

de CHASSIRON, Charles Richard Lucien, CVO 2000; HM Diplomatic Service, retired; Chairman, Spencer House, since 2006; Diplomatic Consultant, Royal Garden Hotel, London, since 2006; *b* 27 April 1948; *s* of Hugo and Deane de Chassiron; *m* 1974, Britt-Marie Medhammar; one *s* one *d*. *Educ:* Jesus Coll., Univ. of Cambridge (BA Hons 1969, MA 1973); Univ. of Harvard (MPA 1971). Joined Diplomatic Service, 1971; service in: Stockholm, 1972–75; Maputo, 1975–78; Mem., UK Delegn at Lancaster House Conf. on Rhodesia, 1979; FCO, 1980–82; service in Brasilia, 1982–85; Asst Hd, later Hd, S America Dept, FCO, 1985–89; Counsellor (Comm./Econ.), Rome, 1989–94; Ambassador to Estonia, 1994–97; Dir-Gen. for British Trade Develt in Italy, and Consul-Gen., Milan, 1997–2001; Vice-Marshal, Diplomatic Corps, and Hd, Protocol Div., FCO, 2002–06. Chm., British-Italian Soc., 2006–. *Recreations:* art history, walking, Italian culture. *Address:* 47 College Road, Epsom, Surrey KT17 4HQ.

de CHASTELAIN, Gen. (Alfred) John (Gardyne Drummond), OC 1993; CMM 1984; CH 1999; Chairman, Independent International Commission on Decommissioning, Northern Ireland, since 1997; *b* Bucharest, 30 July 1937; *s* of late Alfred George Gardyne de Chastelain, DSO, OBE, and Marion Elizabeth de Chastelain (*née* Walsh); *m* 1961, MaryAnn Laverty; one *s* one *d*. *Educ:* Fettes Coll., Edinburgh; Mount Royal Coll., Calgary, Alberta; Royal Mil. Coll. of Canada (BA Hons Hist. 1960); Army Staff Coll., Camberley. Commnd 2nd Lieut, 2nd Bn, PPCLI, 1960; Capt. 1962; Maj. 1967; Lt-Col 1970; CO, 2nd Bn, PPCLI 1970–72; Col 1974; Commander: Canadian Forces Base, Montreal, 1974–76; Canadian Contingent, UN Forces, Cyprus, 1976–77; Brig. Gen. 1977; Comdt, RMC of Canada, 1977–80; Comdr, 4th Canadian Mechanized Bde Gp, Germany, 1980–82; Maj.-Gen. 1983; Dep. Comdr, Mobile Comd, Quebec, 1983–86; Lt-Gen. 1986; Asst Dep. Minister (Personnel), NDHQ, 1986–88; Vice Chief, Defence Staff, 1988–89; Gen. 1989; Chief of Defence Staff, 1989–92; Ambassador for Canada to USA, 1993; Chief of Defence Staff, 1994–95; Mem., Internat. Body on Decommissioning of Arms in NI, 1995–96; Chm., Business Cttee and Co. Chm., Strand Two Talks, NI Peace Process, 1996–98. Col of Regt, PPCLI, 2000–03. Hon. Fellow, LMH, Oxford, 2006. Hon. DScMil RMC, Canada, 1996; Hon. LLD: Royal Roads, Canada, 2001; Carleton, Ontario, 2006; Queen's, Kingston, 2007; Hon. DPhil (Educn) Nipissing, Ontario, 2006. CStJ 1991. CD (Canada), 1968; Medal of Merit and Honour (Greece), 1992; Comdr, Legion of Merit (USA), 1995. *Publications:* (contrib.) Canada on the Threshold of the 21st Century, 1992; contrib. to Canadian Defence Qly. *Recreations:* painting, fishing, bagpipes. *Address:* 170 Acacia Avenue, Ottawa, ON K1M 0R3, Canada. *T:* (613) 7447300.

DECIE, Elizabeth Anne Scott P.; *see* Prescott-Decie.

DECIES, 7th Baron *cr* 1812 (Ire.); **Marcus Hugh Tristram de la Poer Beresford;** *b* 5 Aug. 1948; *o s* of 6th Baron Decies and of his 2nd wife, Diana, *d* of Wing Comdr George Turner-Cain and *widow* of Major David Galsworthy; *S* father, 1992; *m* 1st, 1970, Sarah Jane Gunnell (marr. diss. 1974); 2nd, 1981, Edel Jeannette, *d* of late Vincent Hendron; two *s* two *d*. *Educ:* St Columba's Coll.; Dublin Univ. (MLitt). FCIArb. *Heir: s* Hon. Robert Marcus Duncan de la Poer Beresford, *b* 14 July 1988.

DE CLERCQ, Willy; Member (L) European Parliament, 1979–81, and 1989–2004; Minister of State, Belgium, since 1985; *b* 8 July 1927; *s* of Frans De Clercq; *m* 1953, Fernande Fazzi; two *s* one *d*. *Educ:* Ghent Univ. (Dr in Law 1950); Univ. of Syracuse, USA (MA SocSci 1951). Called to Belgian Bar, 1951; Municipal Councillor, Ghent, 1952–79; Dep. Sec.-Gen., Belgian Liberal Party, 1957; MP Ghent-Eeklo, 1958–85; Dep. State Sec., Min. of Budget, 1960; Leader, Parly Gp of Belgian Liberal Party, 1965; Dep. Prime Minister, 1966–68; created Flemish Liberal Party (PVV) (Chm., 1972–73 and 1977–81); Dep. Prime Minister, 1973; Minister of Finance, 1974–77 (Chm., Interim Cttee, IMF; Mem., Bd of Governors, EIB; Governor, World Bank); Dep. Prime Minister and Minister of Finance and Foreign Trade, 1981–85; Mem., Commn of European Communities, 1985–88. European Parliament: Chairman: External Econ. Relations Cttee, 1989–97; Cttee on Legal Affairs and Citizens' Rights, 1997–2004. Pres., European Liberal Democrat and Reform Party (formerly Fedn of Europ. Liberal Democratic and Reform Parties), 1981–85 and 1991–95 (Hon. Pres., 1995). President: Eur. Movt, Belgium, 1992 (Hon. Pres.); Eur. Federalist Movt, Belgium, 1992 (Hon. Pres.). Comdr, Order of Leopold; Grand Cross, Order of Leopold II; holds numerous foreign decorations. *Address:* Cyriel Buyssestraat 12, 9000 Ghent, Belgium. *T:* (9) 2211813.

de CLIFFORD, 27th Baron *cr* 1299; **John Edward Southwell Russell;** *b* 8 June 1928; *s* of 26th Baron de Clifford, OBE, TD, and Dorothy Evelyn (*d* 1987), *d* of late Ferdinand Richard Holmes Meyrick, MD; *S* father, 1982; *m* 1959, Bridget Jennifer, *yr d* of Duncan Robertson, Llangollen, Denbighshire. *Educ:* Eton; RAC Cirencester. *Heir: b* Hon. William Southwell Russell [*b* 26 Feb. 1930; *m* 1961, Jean Brodie, *d* of Neil Brodie Henderson; one *s* two *d*]. *Address:* Riggledown, Pennymoor, Tiverton, Devon EX16 8LR. *Club:* Naval and Military.

de COSSART, Linda, FRCS; Consultant Vascular and General Surgeon, Countess of Chester Hospital, since 1988; *b* Swansea, 9 Nov. 1947; *d* of Leonard and Elizabeth Jones; *m* 1979, Michael de Cossart (*d* 1989). *Educ:* Univ. of Liverpool Med. Sch. (MB ChB 1972; ChM 1983). FRCS 1977. Mersey Deanery: Associate Postgrad. Dean, 1993–2006; Prog. Dir, Gen. Surgery, 1993–2004. Jt Vice Pres., RCS, 2008– (Mem. Council, 1999–). Hon. Sec., Vascular Soc. of GB and Ire., 1994–98. Member: Liverpool Medical Instn, 1977–; Travelling Surgical Soc., 1995–. *Publications:* Cultivating a Thinking Surgeon, 2005; Developing the Wise Doctor, 2007; articles in vascular and general surgery jls. *Recreations:* cooking, poetry, writing. *Address:* The Lodge, Cranham Corner, Cranham, Glos GL4 8HB. *T:* 07778 215801; *e-mail:* decossart@btinternet.com. *Clubs:* Lister; Needles.

de COURCY, family name of **Baron Kingsale**.

de COURCY-IRELAND, Patrick Gault, CVO 1980; HM Diplomatic Service, retired; Director of Marketing, Alireza Group of Companies, since 1987; Director, Rezayat Europe Ltd, since 1988; *b* 19 Aug. 1933; *e s* of late Lawrence Kilmaine de Courcy-Ireland and Elizabeth Pentland Gault; *m* 1957, Margaret Gallop; one *s* three *d*. *Educ:* St Paul's Sch.; Jesus Coll., Cambridge (MA). HM Forces (2nd Lieut), 1952–54. Joined Foreign Service, 1957; Student, ME Centre for Arab Studies, 1957–59; Third, later Second Sec., Baghdad, 1959–62; Private Sec. to HM Ambassador, Washington, 1963; Consul (Commercial), New York, 1963–67; UN (Polit.) Dept, 1967–69; Asst Head of Amer. Dept, 1969–71; First Sec. and Hd of Chancery, Kuwait, 1971–73; Asst Hd of SW Pacific Dept, 1973–76; Hd of Trng Dept and Dir, Diplomatic Serv. Language Centre, FCO, 1976–80; Consul-Gen., Casablanca, 1980–84; Consul-Gen., Jerusalem, 1984–87. Chm., British Sch. of Archaeology in Jerusalem, 1990–99; Member: Exec. Cttee, Palestine Exploration Fund, 1991–95; Council, Soc. for Moroccan Studies, 1992–99; Sec., MECAS Assoc., 2002–. Director: Napier Court Freehold Ltd, 2003–; Napier Court Management Ltd, 2005–. MEI (MInstPet 1992). Great Comdr, Order of KHS, 1985. *Recreations:* book collecting, opera. *Address:* 49 Napier Court, Ranelagh Gardens, SW6 3UU. *T:* (020) 7736 0622.

DeCRANE, Alfred Charles, Jr; Chairman of the Board, 1987–96, and Chief Executive Officer, 1993–96, Texaco Inc.; *b* 11 June 1931; *s* of Alfred Charles DeCrane and Verona (Marquard) DeCrane; *m* 1954, Joan Hoffman; one *s* five *d*. *Educ:* Notre Dame Univ. (BA); Georgetown Univ. (LLB). Texaco Inc.: Attorney, Houston and NY, 1959–65; Asst to Vice-Chm., 1965–67; Asst to Chm., 1967–68; Gen. Manager, 1968–70, Vice-Pres., 1970–76, Producing Dept, E Hemisphere; Sen. Vice-Pres., General Counsel, 1976–78; Board Dir, 1977–96; Exec. Vice-Pres., 1978–83; Pres., 1983. *Address:* Two Greenwich Plaza, PO Box 1247, Greenwich, CT 06836, USA.

de DENEY, Sir Geoffrey Ivor, KCVO 1992 (CVO 1986); Clerk of the Privy Council, 1984–92; Chief Executive, Royal College of Anaesthetists, 1993–97; *b* 8 Oct. 1931; *s* of late Thomas Douglas and Violet Ivy de Deney; *m* 1959, Diana Elizabeth Winrow; two *s*. *Educ:* William Ellis Sch.; St Edmund Hall, Oxford (MA, BCL); Univ. of Michigan. Home Office: joined, 1956; Asst Principal, 1956–61 (Private Sec. to Parly Under Sec. of State, 1959–61); Principal, 1961–69; Sec. to Graham Hall Cttee on maintenance limits in magistrates' courts; Sec. to Brodrick Cttee on Death Certification and Coroners; Private Sec. to Sec. of State, 1968; Asst Sec., 1969–78; seconded to Cabinet Office, 1975; Asst Under Sec. of State, 1978–84; Community Programmes and Equal Opportunities Dept, 1978–80; General Dept (and Registrar of the Baronetage), 1980–84. Trustee, Gordon House Assoc., 1990– (Chm., 2002–). Hon. FRCA 1997. *Recreations:* books, walking. *Address:* 17 Ladbroke Terrace, W11 3PG.

DEDMAN, Peter George; His Honour Judge Peter Dedman; a Circuit Judge, since 2000; *b* 22 May 1940; *s* of late George Stephen Henry Dedman and Jessie Maud Dedman (*née* Hanson); *m* 1965, Patricia Mary Gordon, JP, RGN, RHV; one *d*. *Educ:* Tottenham Grammar Sch. Magistrates' Courts Service, Brentford, Tottenham and Newham; Principal Asst to Clerk to the Justices, Newham, 1965–69; called to the Bar, Gray's Inn, 1968 (amongst first to qualify following removal of embargo on Justices' Clerks and their assts from reading for the Bar); in practice at the Bar, specialising in personal injury litigation; a Recorder, 1992–2000; South Eastern Circuit. *Recreations:* music – playing the piano and trombone, theatre, film, attending concerts. *Address:* Chelmsford Crown Court, New Street, Chelmsford, Essex CM1 1EL. *T:* (01245) 603000.

de DUVE, Prof. Christian René Marie Joseph, Grand Cross Order of Leopold II 1975; Professor of Biochemistry, Catholic University of Louvain, 1951–85, now Emeritus; Founding Member, and President 1974–91, International Institute of Cellular and Molecular Pathology, Brussels; Andrew W. Mellon Professor at Rockefeller University, New York, 1962–88, now Emeritus; *b* England, 2 Oct. 1917; *s* of Alphonse de Duve and Madeleine Pungs; *m* 1943, Janine Herman; two *s* two *d*. *Educ:* Jesuit Coll., Antwerp; Catholic Univ. of Louvain; Med. Nobel Inst., Stockholm; Washington Univ., St Louis. MD 1941, MSc 1946, Agrégé de l'Enseignement Supérieur 1945, Louvain. Lectr, Med. Faculty, Catholic Univ. of Louvain, 1947–51. Vis. Prof. at various univs. Mem. editorial and other bds and cttees; mem. or hon. mem. various learned socs, incl. For. Assoc. Nat. Acad. of Scis (US) 1975, and For. Mem of Royal Soc., 1988. Holds hon. degrees. Awards incl. Nobel Prize in Physiol. or Med., 1974. *Publications:* A Guided Tour of the Living Cell, 1985; Blueprint for a Cell, 1991; Vital Dust, 1995; numerous scientific. *Recreations:* tennis, ski-ing, bridge. *Address:* Le Pré St Jean, 239 rue de Weert, 1390 Nethen (Grez-Doiceau), Belgium. *T:* (10) 866628; 80 Central Park West, New York, NY 10023, USA. *T:* (212) 7248048; Christian de Duve Institute of Cellular Pathology, Avenue Hippocrate 75, 1200 Brussels, Belgium; Rockefeller University, 1230 York Avenue, New York, NY 10021, USA.

DEE, Janie, (Mrs R. S. M. Wickham); actress; *b* 20 June 1962; *d* of John Henry Leonard Lewis and Ruth Winifred Lewis (*née* Miller); adopted stage name Janie Dee; *m* 1995, Rupert Stewart Makepeace Wickham; one *s* one *d*. *Educ:* Arts Educational Schs, London. *Theatre* includes: Carousel, RNT, 1992 (Best Supporting Performance in a Musical, Olivier awards, 1993); Comic Potential, Lyric, 1999, transf. NY, 2000 (Best Actress, Evening Standard, Critics' Circle, Olivier awards, 2000; Obie award, and Best Newcomer, Theater World Award, 2001); My One and Only, Chichester Fest. Th., 2001, transf. Piccadilly, 2002; Three Sisters, Chichester Fest. Th., 2001; Paradise Moscow, Opera North, UK tour, 2001; Women of Troy, NT, 2001; Divas at the Donmar, Donmar Warehouse, 2002; Much Ado About Nothing, Peter Hall Co., Bath, 2003; Mack and Mabel, Criterion, 2006; Old Times, UK tour, 2007; Shadowlands, Wyndham's, 2007; *television* includes: Death in Holy Orders, 2003; The Murder Room, 2004; Celebration. Dir, Royal Theatrical Fund, 2002–. Trustee, Arts Educnl Schs, 2001–. *Recreations:* sailing, ballet.

DEECH, family name of **Baroness Deech**.

DEECH, Baroness *cr* 2005 (Life Peer), of Cumnor in the County of Oxfordshire; **Ruth Lynn Deech,** DBE 2002; Independent Adjudicator for Higher Education, 2004–08; *b* 29 April 1943; *d* of Josef Fraenkel and Dora (*née* Rosenfeld); *m* 1967, Dr John Stewart Deech; one *d*. *Educ:* Christ's Hosp., Hertford; St Anne's Coll., Oxford (BA 1st Cl. 1965; MA 1969; Hon. Fellow, 2004); Brandeis Univ., USA (MA 1966). Called to the Bar, Inner Temple, 1967, Hon. Bencher, 1996. Legal Asst, Law Commn, 1966–67; Asst Prof., Faculty of Law, Univ. of Windsor, Canada, 1968–70; Oxford University: Fellow and Tutor in Law, 1970–91, Vice-Principal, 1988–91, Principal, 1991–2004, St Anne's Coll.; CUF Lectr in Law, 1971–91; Sen. Proctor, 1985–86; Mem., Hebdomadal Council, 1986–2000; Chm., Jt Undergrad. Admissions Cttee, 1993–97, Admissions Exec., 2000–03; Pro-Vice-Chancellor, 2001–04. Chm., HFEA, 1994–2002. Member: Cttee of Inquiry into Equal Opportunities on Bar Vocational Course, 1993–94; Human Genetics Commn, 2000–02. A Governor, BBC, 2002–06. Non-exec. Dir, Oxon HA, 1993–94. Mem., Exec. Council, Internat. Soc. on Family Law, 1988–. Visiting Professor: Osgoode Hall Law Sch., York Univ., Canada, 1978; Univ. of Florida, 2004; Santa Clara Univ., 2006. Governor: Carmel Coll., 1980–90; Oxford Centre for Hebrew and Jewish Studies, 1994–2000; UCS, 1997–2002. Rhodes Trustee, 1997–2006; Mandela Rhodes Foundn

Trustee, 2003–06. Gov., United Jewish Israel Appeal, 1997–99. Freeman, City of London, 2003; Hon. Freeman, Drapers' Co., 2003. FRSocMed 2001. Hon. Fellow, Soc. for Advanced Legal Studies, 1997. Hon. LLD: Strathclyde, 2003; Richmond American Internat. Univ. in London, 2006. *Publications:* From IVF to Immortality, 2007; articles on family law and property law. *Recreations:* after-dinner speaking, music, entertaining. *Address:* House of Lords, SW1A 0PW; *e-mail:* deechr@parliament.uk.

DEEDES, Hon. Jeremy (Wyndham); non-executive Chairman, Pelham Public Relations, since 2007; *b* 24 Nov. 1943; *s* of Baron Deedes, KBE, MC, PC; *m* 1973, Anna Gray, *d* of late Maj. Elwin Gray; two *s*. *Educ:* Eton Coll. Reporter: Kent and Sussex Courier, 1963–66; Daily Sketch, 1966–69; Londoner's Diary, Evening Standard, 1969–76; Dep. Editor, Daily Express, 1976–79; Managing Editor: Evening Standard, 1979–85; Today, 1985–86; Editorial Dir, Daily Telegraph and Sunday Telegraph, 1986–96; Man. Dir, 1996–2003, Dep. Chm. and Chief Exec., 2004–05, Telegraph Gp Ltd; Chm., The Sportsman, 2005–06. Chm., Trafford Park Printers, 1998–2000; Dep. Chm., West Ferry Printers, 1998–2005; Director: Millbourne Productions (Watermill Theatre), 1985–; Horserace Totalisator Bd, 1992–98; Warwick Racecourse, 2005– (Chm., 2002–05). Chm., Nat. Publishers Assoc., 1998–99. *Recreations:* racing, cricket, golf, cabinet making. *Address:* Hamilton House, Compton, Newbury, Berks RG20 6QJ. *T:* (01635) 578695. *Clubs:* Boodle's; Sunningdale Golf, Huntercombe Golf; Royal Cape (Cape Town).

DEEKS, Rev. David Gerald; General Secretary of the Methodist Church, 2003–08; *b* 5 July 1942; *s* of Horace J. Deeks and Irene Deeks; *m* 1967, Jennifer Wakefield; one *s* two *d*. *Educ:* Downing Coll., Cambridge (MA); Wesley House, Cambridge. Asst Tutor, Richmond Coll., Surrey, 1966–70; Ecumenical Lectr, Lincoln Theol Coll., 1970–74; Minister, Maidstone Circuit, 1974–80; Tutor, Wesley House, Cambridge, 1980–88; Minister, Bristol (Clifton and Redland) Circuit, and Methodist Chaplain, Univ. of Bristol, 1988–92; Gen. Sec., Div. of Social Responsibility, 1992–96, Co-ordinating Sec., Church and Society, 1996–2003, Methodist Church. *Publications:* Calling, God?, 1976; Pastoral Theology: an inquiry, 1987. *Recreations:* walking, art, music. *Address:* 1 Shields Avenue, Bristol BS7 0RR; *e-mail:* david.deeks@gmail.com.

DEELEY, Michael; film producer; *b* 6 Aug. 1932; *s* of John Hamilton-Deeley and Anne Deeley; *m* 1955, Teresa Harrison; one *s* two *d*; *m* 1970, Ruth Stone-Spencer. *Educ:* Stowe. Entered film industry as film editor, 1952; Distributor, MCA TV, 1958–60; independent producer, 1961–63; Gen. Man., Woodfall Films, 1964–67; indep. prod., 1967–72; Man. Director: British Lion Films Ltd, 1973–76; EMI Films Ltd, 1976–77; Pres., EMI Films Inc., 1977–79; Chief Exec. Officer, Consolidated Television Inc., 1984–90. Dep. Chm., British Screen Adv. Council, 1985–. Member: Prime Minister's Film Industry Working Party, 1975–76; Film Industry Interim Action Cttee, 1977–84. *Films* include: Robbery; The Italian Job; The Knack; Murphy's War; Conduct Unbecoming; The Man who fell to Earth; The Deer Hunter (Academy Award, Best Picture Producer, 1978); Convoy; Blade Runner; many TV films and series. *Address:* 36 Elizabeth Court, SW10 0DA; 1010 Fairway Road, Santa Barbara, CA 93108, USA. *Clubs:* Garrick; Santa Barbara Polo and Racquet.

DEEM, Prof. Rosemary, PhD; Professor of Education, since 2001, and Research Director, Faculty of Social Sciences and Law, since 2007, University of Bristol; *b* 18 Jan. 1949; *d* of Leslie Thomas George Deem and Peggy Deem (*née* Stoyle); *m* 1985, Kevin Joseph Brehony. *Educ:* Univ. of Leicester (BA Hons Social Scis (Sociol.) 1970; MPhil Sociol. 1973); Open Univ. (PhD Sociol. of Leisure 1990). Lectr in Sociol., N Staffs Poly., 1975–79; Lectr in Sociol. of Educn, 1980–87, Sen Lectr in Educn, 1987–91, Open Univ.; Prof. of Educnl Res., 1991–2000, Dean of Social Scis, 1994–97, Univ. of Lancaster; Founding Dir, Univ. of Lancaster Grad. Sch., 1998–2000. Jt Man. Ed., Sociol. Rev., 2001–. Dir, UK Subject Centre for Educn (ESCalate), Learning and Teaching Support Network, 2001–04. Chairman: British Sociol Assoc., 1986–87 and 1994–96; Publications Cttee, SRHE, 2004–; Develt Cttee, SRHE, 2007–. AcSS 2006. *Publications:* Women and Schooling, 1978; (ed) Schooling for Women's Work, 1980; (ed) Co-education Reconsidered, 1984; All Work and No Play, 1986; Work, Unemployment and Leisure, 1988; (with K. J. Brehony and S. J. Heath) Active Citizenship and the Governing of Schools, 1995; (with S. Hillyard and M. Reed) Knowledge, Higher Education and the New Managerialism: the changing management of UK universities, 2007; contrib. numerous articles and chapters in social sci. jls and academic books. *Recreations:* walking, cycling (Mem., Cyclists Touring Club), photography, camping and caravanning (Mem., Camping and Caravanning Club), reading. *Address:* Graduate School of Education, Helen Wodehouse Building, University of Bristol, 35 Berkeley Square, Bristol BS8 1JA. *T:* (0117) 928 7013, *Fax:* (0117) 925 1537; *e-mail:* R.Deem@bristol.ac.uk.

DEENY, Hon. Sir Donnell (Justin Patrick), Kt 2004; DL; **Hon. Mr Justice Deeny;** a Judge of the High Court of Justice, Northern Ireland, since 2004; *b* 25 April 1950; *y s* of late Dr Donnell McLarnon Deeny, JP and Annie (*née* McGinley); *m* 1st, 1975, S. M. Duff (marr. diss.); two *d*; 2nd, 1998, Alison Jane, *y d* of late Ian Scott and of Tressan Scott; one *s* two *d*. *Educ:* Clongowes Wood Coll.; TCD (Auditor, The Hist.; MA); QUB. Called to the Bar: NI, 1974 (Bencher, 2001); Ireland, 1986; Middle Temple, 1987 (Bencher, 2006); one of Attorney Gen.'s Counsel, NI, 1985–2003; QC (NI) 1989; SC (Ireland) 1996. Mem., UK Spoliation Adv. Panel, 2001–. Dir, Hearth Social Housing, 1999–2003. Mem. (APNI), Belfast CC, 1981–85. Mem., 1991–93, Chm., 1993–98, Arts Council of NI; Vice Chm., 1984–88, Chm., 1988–93, Opera NI. Trustee, Ulster Mus., 1983–85; Chm., Ireland Chair of Poetry Trust, 1997–; Dir, Tyrone Guthrie Centre, 2001–06; Pres., Ulster Architectural Heritage Soc., 2006–. High Sheriff 1983, DL 2003, Belfast; JP Co. Down, 1988. *Publication:* (ed) To the Millennium: a strategy for the arts in Northern Ireland, 1995. *Recreations:* books, the arts, ski-ing. *Address:* Royal Courts of Justice, Chichester Street, Belfast BT1 3JF.

See also M. F. A. Cook, M. E. McL. Deeny.

DEENY, Michael Eunan McLarnon, FCA; Chairman, Association of Lloyd's Members, since 1998 (Director, since 1995); *b* 12 Nov. 1944; *s* of late Dr Donnell McLarnon Deeny and Annie Deeny (*née* McGinley); *m* 1975, Dr Margaret Irene Vereker, *d* of late Dr Richard Vereker and of Judy Vereker; one *s* two *d*. *Educ:* Clongowes Wood Coll., Ireland; Magdalen Coll., Oxford (MA). FCA 1974. Articled Clerk, Chalmers Impey, 1966–70; Chief Accountant, Peter Kennedy Ltd, 1970–71; Manager (Murray Head, Horslips, Noosha Fox, Barry McGuigan, etc), 1971–91; Concert Promoter (U2, Bruce Springsteen, Nirvana, The Eagles, Aerosmith, Luciano Pavarotti, etc), 1984–. Chairman: Gooda Walker Action Gp, 1993–2008; Litigating Names' Cttee, 1994–. Dir, GW Run-Off, 1995–97; Dep. Chm., Equitas Trust, 1996–; Dir, Equitas Ltd, 1996–. Mem. Council, Lloyd's 1996–97. *Recreation:* taking risks and living to tell the tale. *Address:* c/o Association of Lloyd's Members, 100 Fenchurch Street, EC3M 5LG.

See also M. F. A. Cook, Hon. Sir D. J. P. Deeny.

DEER, Prof. William Alexander, MSc Manchester, PhD Cantab; FRS 1962; FGS; Emeritus Professor of Mineralogy and Petrology, Cambridge University; Hon. Fellow of Trinity Hall, Cambridge, 1978; *b* 26 Oct. 1910; *s* of William Deer; *m* 1939, Margaret Marjorie (*d* 1971), *d* of William Kidd; two *s* one *d*; *m* 1973, Rita Tagg. *Educ:* Manchester Central High Sch.; Manchester Univ.; St John's Coll., Cambridge. Graduate Research Scholar, 1932, Beyer Fellow, 1933, Manchester Univ.; Strathcona Studentship, St John's Coll., Cambridge, 1934; Petrologist on British East Greenland Expedition, 1935–36; 1851 Exhibition Senior Studentship, 1938; Fellow, St John's Coll., Cambridge, 1939; served War of 1939–45, RE, 1940–45. Murchison Fund Geological Soc. of London, 1945 (Murchison Medal, 1974); Junior Bursar, St John's Coll., 1946; Leader NE Baffin Land Expedition, 1948; Bruce Medal, Royal Society of Edinburgh, 1948; Tutor, St John's Coll., 1949; Prof. of Geology, Manchester Univ., 1950–61; Fellow of St John's Coll., Cambridge, 1961–66, Hon. Fellow, 1969; Prof. of Mineralogy and Petrology, 1961–78, Vice-Chancellor, 1971–73, Cambridge Univ.; Master of Trinity Hall, Cambridge, 1966–75. Percival Lecturer, Univ. of Manchester, 1953; Joint Leader East Greenland Geological Expedition, 1953; Leader British East Greenland Expedition, 1966. Trustee, British Museum (Natural History), 1967–75. President: Mineralogical Soc., 1967–70; Geological Soc., 1970–72; Member: NERC, 1968–71; Marshall Aid Commemoration Commn, 1973–79. Hon. DSc Aberdeen, 1983. *Publications:* (jtly) Rock-forming Minerals, 5 vols, 1962–63, 2nd edn 1978– (vol. IIA 1978, vol. IA 1982, vol. IB 1986, vol. IIB 1997, Introduction 1992); Introduction to Rock-forming Minerals, 1966, 2nd edn 1992; papers in Petrology and Mineralogy. *Address:* 12 Barrington House, Southacre Drive, Cambridge CB2 2TY.

de FERRANTI, Sebastian (Basil Joseph) Ziani; DL; Chairman, Ferranti plc, 1963–82 (Managing Director, 1958–75; Director 1954); Director, GEC plc, 1982–97; *b* 5 Oct. 1927; *er s* of Sir Vincent de Ferranti, MC, and late Dorothy H. C. Wilson; *m* 1st, 1953, Mona Helen, *d* of T. E. Cunningham; one *s* two *d*; 2nd, 1983, Naomi Angela Rae, DL (*d* 2001). *Educ:* Ampleforth. 4th/7th Dragoon Guards, 1947–49; Cheshire Yeo. Brown Boveri, Switzerland, and Alsthom, France, 1949–50. Director: British Airways Helicopters, 1982–84; Nat. Nuclear Corp., 1984–88. President: Electrical Research Assoc., 1968–69; BEAMA, 1969–70; Centre for Educn in Science, Educn and Technology, Manchester and region, 1972–82. Chm., Internat. Electrical Assoc., 1970–72. Member: Nat. Defence Industries Council, 1969–77; Council, IEE, 1970–73. Trustee, Tate Gallery, 1971–78; Chm., Civic Trust for the North-West, 1978–83; Comr, Royal Commn for Exhibn of 1851, 1984–97. Pres., Hallé Concerts Soc., 1997– (Chm., 1988–96). Mem. Bd of Govs, RNCM, 1988–2000 (Hon. RNCM 1997). Chm. assessors, architect for Manchester City Art Gall extn, 1995–. FRSA 1972 (Vice-Pres., 1980–84). Lectures: Granada, Guildhall, 1966; Royal Instn, 1969; Louis Blériot, Paris, 1970; Faraday, 1970–71. High Sheriff of Cheshire, 1988–89; DL Cheshire, 1995. Hon. Fellow, UMIST. Hon. DSc: Salford Univ., 1967; Cranfield Inst. of Technology, 1973; Hon. LLD Manchester, 1998. *Address:* Henbury Hall, Macclesfield, Cheshire SK11 9PJ. *Clubs:* Cavalry and Guards, Pratt's.

DEFFEE, Leslie Ann; *see* Morphy, L. A.

de FONBLANQUE, John Robert, CMG 1993; HM Diplomatic Service, retired; Director, Office of High Commissioner on National Minorities, Organisation for Security and Co-operation in Europe, 2004–07; *b* 20 Dec. 1943; *s* of late Maj.-Gen. E. B. de Fonblanque, CB, CBE, DSO and of Elizabeth de Fonblanque; *m* 1984, Margaret Prest; one *s*. *Educ:* Ampleforth; King's College, Cambridge (MA); London School of Economics (MSc). FCO, 1968; Second Sec., Jakarta, 1969; Second, later First Sec., UK Representation to European Community, Brussels, 1972; Principal, HM Treasury, 1977; FCO, 1980; Asst Sec., Cabinet Office, 1983; Head of Chancery, New Delhi, 1986; Counsellor (Pol and Instnl), UK Repn to EC, Brussels, 1988; Vis. Fellow, RIIA, 1993; Asst Under-Sec. of State, Internat. Orgns, then Dir, Global Issues, FCO, 1994–98; Dir (Europe), FCO, 1998–99; Hd, UK Delegn to OSCE, Vienna (with rank of Ambassador) 1999–2003. Mem., PPARC, 1994–98. *Recreation:* mountain walking.

de FRANCIA, Prof. Peter Laurent; Professor, School of Painting, Royal College of Art, London, 1972–86; *b* 25 Jan. 1921; *s* of Fernand de Francia and Alice Groom. *Educ:* Academy of Brussels; Slade Sch., Univ. of London. Canadian Exhibition Commn, Ottawa, 1949–50; American Museum, Central Park West, NY, 1950–51; Talks Producer, BBC, Television, 1951–52; Teacher, St Martin's Sch., London, 1953–68; Tutor, Royal College of Art, 1963–69; Principal, Dept of Fine Art, Goldsmiths Coll., 1969–72. Work represented in public collections: Tate Gall.; Nat. Portrait Gall.; V&A Mus.; Mus. of Modern Art, NY; Arts Council of GB; British Mus.; Ashmolean Mus., Oxford; Graves Art Gall., Sheffield; Mus. of Modern Art, Prague; Scottish Nat. Gall. of Modern Art, Edinburgh; Imperial War Mus.; Ulster Mus., Belfast; Pallant House, Chichester; British Council, New Delhi; Wimbledon Sch. of Art, London. *Publications:* (trans. with Anna Bostock) Le Corbusier, The Modulor and The Modulor 2, 1954; Léger: the great parade, 1969; Fernand Léger, 1983; "Untitled", 1990; Fables, 2002. *Address:* 44 Surrey Square, SE17 2JX. *T:* (020) 7703 8361.

DE FREYNE, 7th Baron *cr* 1851; Feudal Baron of Coolavin; **Francis Arthur John French;** Knight of Malta; *b* 3 Sept. 1927; *s* of 6th Baron and Victoria (*d* 1974), *d* of Sir J. Arnott, 2nd Bt; *S* father 1935; *m* 1st, 1954 (marr. diss. 1978); two *s* one *d*; 2nd, 1978, Sheelin Deirdre, *widow* of William Walker Stevenson and *y d* of late Lt-Col H. K. O'Kelly, DSO. *Educ:* Ladycross, Glenstal. *Heir: s* Hon. Fulke Charles Arthur John French [*b* 21 April 1957; *m* 1986, Julia Mary, *o d* of Dr James H. Wellard; two *s*]. *Address:* The Old School, Sutton Courtenay, Oxon OX14 4AW.

DEFRIEZ, Alistair Norman Campbell, FCA; consultant; Managing Director, UBS Investment Bank (formerly Warburg Dillon Read, then UBS Warburg), 1999–2007; *b* 2 Nov. 1951; *s* of Norman William Defriez and late Helen Catherine Defriez (*née* Maclean); *m* 1978, Linda Mavis Phillips, BSc, PGCE, ACA; two *s* one *d*. *Educ:* Dulwich Coll.; University Coll., Oxford (Open Gladstone Schol., MA). FCA 1981. With Coopers & Lybrand, 1973–78; joined S. G. Warburg & Co. Ltd, 1978, Dir, 1987; Dir-Gen., Panel on Takeovers and Mergers, 1996–99 (on secondment) (Mem., 2008–). *Recreations:* golf, Rugby, music, reading. *Clubs:* Bankers', London Scottish; Royal Wimbledon Golf; St George's Hill Golf; Rye Golf.

DE FRUTOS, Javier; Artistic Director, Phoenix Dance Theatre, since 2006; *b* Caracas, 15 May 1963; *s* of Esteban De Frutos and Angela Fernandez. *Educ:* Caracas Sch. of Contemporary Dance; Merce Cunningham Sch., NY; London Sch. of Contemporary Dance. Dancer, Laura Dean Dancers and Musicians, NY, 1988–92; Choreographer in Residence, Movement Res., NYC, 1993; Founder and Artistic Dir, Javier De Frutos Dance Co., 1994–2000. Fellow, Arts Council of England, 2000–02. *Choreographed:* for De Frutos Dance Co.: D, 1990; The Montana Affair, J, Trilogy + Country, Consecration, 1991; Almost Montana, Meeting, Hemisphere, Jota Dolce, 1993; Simone and the Jacaranda Tree, Dialogue Between Hemispheres, Frasquita, The Palace Does Not Forgive, Gota a Gota, 1994; Sweetie J, Meeting J, 1995; Carnal Glory, Out of J, Transatlantic, 1996; Grass, Weed, The Golden Impossibility, 1997; The Hypochondriac Bird, 1998; Mazatlan, 1999; Affliction of Loneliness, 2000; for Phoenix Dance Theatre: Nopalitos, 2006; Los Picadores, Paseillo, Blue Roses, 2007; Cattle Call, 2008; for Ricochet Dance Co.: E Muoio Disperato, 1995 (Bagnolet Prix d'Auteur, France, 1996); All visitors bring happiness, some by coming, some by going, 1995 (S Bank Award, 1997); for Rambert Dance Co.: The Celebrated Soubrette, 2000 (re-staged for Royal NZ Ballet, 2004); Elsa Canesta, 2003; for Royal NZ Ballet: Milagros, 2003; Banderillero, 2006; The Misty Frontier for Royal Ballet, 2001; *theatre*: Carousel, Chichester Fest., 2006; Cabaret, Lyric, 2006 (Olivier Award for Best Th. Choreographer, 2007). Paul Hamlyn Foundn Award, 1995; Critics' Circle Nat. Dance Award for Best Choreog. (Contemp.), 2005. *Address*: Phoenix Dance Theatre, Yorkshire Dance, 3 St Peter's Buildings, St Peter's Square, Leeds LS9 8AH. *T*: (0113) 242 3486, *Fax*: (0113) 244 4736; *e-mail*: jdf@phoenixdancetheatre.co.uk, javierdefru@hotmail.com.

de GARR ROBINSON, Anthony John; QC 2006; *b* 4 July 1963; *s* of Peter de Garr Robinson and Audrey Robinson; *m* 1997, Miranda Wilson; one *s* one *d*. *Educ*: Brighton Coll.; University Coll., Oxford; Grad. Sch. of Arts and Scis, Harvard Univ.; Inns of Court Sch. of Law. Called to the Bar, Lincoln's Inn, 1987; in practice as barrister specialising in commercial and chancery law. Chancery Bar Association: Mem., Cttee; Chm., Internat. Relns Cttee. *Recreation*: Halo 2. *Address*: One Essex Court, Middle Temple, EC4Y 9AR. *T*: (020) 7583 2000.

de GIER, Johannes Antonie, (Hans); President, Executive Board, Julius Baer Group, and Group Chief Executive Officer, Julius Baer Holding Ltd, since 2005; *b* 24 Dec. 1944; *s* of W. G. de Gier and A. M. de Gier (*née* van Heijningen); *m* 1969, Anne-Marie Wintermans; one *s* one *d*. *Educ*: Amsterdam Univ. (LLM). Legal counsel, ABN, 1970–73; Divl Man., Capital Markets, 1975–78, Dep. Gen. Man., Internat. Finance, 1978–79, AMRO; Dir, Corporate Finance, Orion Bank, 1979–80; Swiss Bank Corporation: Exec. Dir, Corporate Finance, 1980–87; Man. Dir and Chief Exec. Officer, 1987–96; Mem., Exec. Bd, and Hd, Global Corporate Finance, 1991–96; Mem., Gp Exec. Cttee, 1996; Chm. and Chief Exec., SBC Warburg, then Warburg Dillon Read, 1996–99; UBS AG: Mem., Gp Exec. Bd, 1998–99; Advr, 1999–2001; Vice Chm., 2001–03; Chm., SBC Wealth Mgt, 2003–05. Vice-Chm., Banco di Lugano, 2003–06; Ehinger & Armand von Ernst, 2003–06 (latterly Chm.); Ferrier Lullin & Cie SA, 2003–06 (latterly Vice-Chm.); Member: Supervisory Bd, SHV Hldgs; Bd, Groupe Lhoist. Vice-Chm., Centre for Econ. Policy Res., 2000–02. Trustee, Fitzwilliam Mus., 2000–. *Recreations*: wildlife, music, art. *Club*: Turf.

de GREY, family name of **Baron Walsingham.**

de GREY, Flavia, (Lady de Grey), (Flavia Irwin), RA 1996; RWEA; painter; *b* 15 Dec. 1916; *d* of Clinton and Everilda Irwin; *m* 1942, Sir Roger de Grey, KCVO, PPRA (*d* 1995); two *s* one *d*. *Educ*: Hawnes Sch., Ampthill; Chelsea Sch. of Art. Teacher, 1960–97: Bexley Girls' Sch.; Sheppey Comprehensive Sch.; Medway Coll. of Art; City and Guilds of London Art Sch. (Head of Decorative Arts). Exhibitions include: London Gp, 1938; Andsell Gall. (solo); Shad Thames, 1994; Curwen and Phoenix Galls, 1996; Friends' Room, RA (solo), 2001. Pictures in various public and private collections, incl. Carlisle City Art Gall. and Walker Art Gall. *Recreations*: swimming, walking. *Address*: Camer Street, Meopham, Kent DA13 0XR.

   See also S. T. de Grey.

de GREY, Spencer Thomas, CBE 1997; RIBA; Design Partner, since 1991, and Deputy Chairman, since 2005, Foster + Partners; *b* 7 June 1944; *s* of Sir Roger de Grey, KCVO, PPRA, and of Flavia de Grey, *qv*; *m* 1977, Hon. (Amanda) Lucy, *d* of Baron Annan, OBE; one *s* one *d*. *Educ*: Eton Coll.; Churchill Coll., Cambridge (BA 1966; MA 1970; DipArch 1969). ARCUK 1969; RIBA 1993. Architect, Merton LBC, 1969–73; joined Foster Associates, later Foster & Partners, 1973–: estabd Hong Kong office, 1979; Dir, 1981– (responsible for Third London Airport, Stansted, 1991, and Sackler Galls, Royal Acad., 1991); *projects* include: Lycée Albert Camus, Fréjus, 1995; Law Faculty, Univ. of Cambridge, 1995; EDF Regl operational centre, Bordeaux, 1996; Commerzbank HQ, Frankfurt, 1997; World Squares for All, London, 1997–2003; HM Treasury, Whitehall, 1997–2004; Sir Alexander Fleming Med. Bldg, Imperial Coll., London, 1998; Great Court, BM, 2000; Nat. Botanical Gdns for Wales, 1999; Dresden Stn, 1999–2002; Mus. of Fine Art, Boston, USA, 1999–; Opera House, Dallas, USA, 2001–; eight City Academies, 2002–; Avery Fisher Hall, Lincoln Center, NY, 2003–; Tanaka Business Sch., Imperial Coll., London, 2004; Smithsonian Instn, 2004–07; Sage Music Centre, Gateshead, 2005; Parliament Square, 2005–. Architectural Advr, Royal Botanical Gardens, Kew, 2003– (Trustee, 1995–2003); Gov., Bldg Centre Trust, 1998– (Chm., 2005–). FRSA 2006. *Recreations*: music, theatre, travel. *Address*: (office) Riverside Three, 22 Hester Road, SW11 4AN. *T*: (020) 7738 0455, *Fax*: (020) 7738 1107.

DE GROOT, Prof. Gerard Jan, PhD; Professor of History, University of St Andrews, since 2000; *b* 22 June 1955; *s* of Jan De Groot and Johanna Hendrika De Groot (*née* Jansen); *m* 1991, Sharon Lynn Roe; one *s* one *d*. *Educ*: Whitman Coll., USA (BA 1977); Edinburgh Univ. (PhD 1983). Beach lifeguard, San Diego, Calif, 1973–77; insce adjuster, Portland, Oregon, 1977–80; lollipop man, Edinburgh, 1980–81; pt-time Tutor, WEA and Edinburgh Univ., 1983–85; Lectr, Univ. of St Andrews, 1985–2000. Freelance journalist, 1988–. RUSI Westminster Medal for Mil. Lit., 2001. *Publications*: Douglas Haig 1861–1928, 1988; Liberal Crusader, 1993; Blighty, 1996; Military Miscellany, 1997; Student Protest, 1998; A Noble Cause, 1999; A Soldier and a Woman, 2000; The First World War, 2001; The Bomb: a life, 2004; Dark Side of the Moon, 2006. *Recreations*: cooking, carpentry, following baseball on the internet. *Address*: 11 Walker Place, St Andrews, Fife KY16 9NY. *T*: (01334) 473107; *e-mail*: gjdg@st-andrews.ac.uk.

de GROOT, Lucy Manuela; Executive Director, Improvement and Development Agency, since 2003; *b* 7 June 1951. *Educ*: St Anne's Coll., Oxford (BA 1973); LSE. Prin. Employment Officer, Hackney BC, 1985–87; Employment Policy Advr, ALA, 1987–89; Hd of Policy, Lewisham BC, 1989–93; Hd of Policy, 1993–94, Chief Exec., 1995–2000, Bristol CC; Dir of Public Services, HM Treasury, 2000–03. Vis. Prof., UWE, 2002–. Trustee: Common Purpose UK, 2000–; Campaign for Learning, 2002–; Coram (formerly Coram Family) (Gov., 2004). FRSA. *Address*: Improvement and Development Agency, Layden House, 76–86 Turnmill Street, EC1M 5LG; (home) 8 Southcote Road, N19 5BJ.

de GRUBEN, Baron Thierry; Ambassador of Belgium to the Court of St James's, 2002–06, now Hon. Ambassador; *b* 17 Nov. 1941; *s* of Baron Guy de Gruben and Baroness Guy de Gruben (*née* Monique Dierckx de Casterlé); *m* 1980, Françoise Francq; one *s*. *Educ*: Namur; Univ. of Leuven (law degree). Joined diplomatic service, 1969; diplomatic trainee, NATO, Brussels, 1969–70; Press Service, Min. of Foreign Affairs, Brussels, 1970–71; Attaché, then Sec., Moscow, 1971–76; Sec., then First Sec., London, 1976–80; Consul General, Bombay, 1980–82; Private Office, Minister of External Relns, Brussels, 1982–85; Ambassador: Warsaw, 1985–90; Moscow, 1990–95; Dep. Pol Dir, Brussels, and Special Envoy for E Slavonia, Croatia, 1995–97; Ambassador and Perm. Rep. of Belgium to NATO, Brussels, 1997–2002. Commandeur, Ordre de Léopold (Belgium), 1996; Grand Officier: Ordre de Léopold II (Belgium), 2000; Ordre de la Couronne (Belgium), 2003. *Address*: 4 rue Descartes, 75005 Paris, France; *e-mail*: dgrubf@hotmail.com.

de GRUCHY, Nigel Ronald Anthony; General Secretary, National Association of Schoolmasters Union of Women Teachers, 1990–2002; *b* 28 Jan. 1943; *s* of Robert Philip de Gruchy and Dorothy Louise de Gruchy (*née* Cullinane); *m* 1970, Judith Ann Berglund, USA; one *s*. *Educ*: De La Salle Coll., Jersey; Univ. of Reading (BA Hons (Econs and Philosophy) 1965); PGCE London Univ. 1969; Cert. Pratique de Langue Française, Paris Univ., 1968; Cert. de Française Parlé et du Diplôme de Langue Française, L'Alliance Française, 1968. TEFL, Berlitz Schs, Santander, 1965–66; Versailles, 1966–67; student of French/Tutor in English, Paris, 1967–68; Head of Econs Dept, St Joseph's Acad., ILEA, 1968–78; Asst Sec., 1978–82, Dep. Gen. Sec., 1982–89, NAS UWT. Sec., London Assoc., 1975–78, Mem., Nat. Exec., 1975–78, NAS UWT. Member: Gen. Council, TUC, 1989–2003 (Pres., 2002–03); Exec., The Educn Internat., 1993–2004; Accountancy Foundn, 2000–04. *Publications*: contribs to Career Teacher. *Recreations*: golf, cricket, football, literature, music, opera, France, Spain. *Address*: 26 Glentrammon Road, Green Street Green, Orpington, Kent BR6 6DE.

de HAAN, Kevin Charles; QC 2000; a Recorder, since 2002; *b* 30 Oct. 1952; *s* of Michael James de Haan and Barbara Ada de Haan; *m* 1983, Katy Monica Foster. *Educ*: Davenant Foundn Grammar Sch.; Queen Mary Coll., Univ. of London (LLB); Vrije Univ., Brussels (LLM Internat. and Comparative Law). Called to the Bar, Inner Temple, 1976, Bencher, 1997. *Publications*: Food Safety Law and Practice, 1994; Pollution in the United Kingdom, 1994; (contrib.) Smith & Monckom, The Law of Betting, Gaming and Lotteries, 2nd edn 2000. *Recreations*: ski-ing, flying light aircraft, mountain bicycling, cooking. *Address*: Francis Taylor Building, Inner Temple, EC4Y 7BY. *Club*: Ski of GB.

de HAAS, Margaret Ruth, (Mrs I. S. Goldrein); QC 1998; Her Honour Judge de Haas; a Circuit Judge, since 2004; *b* 21 May 1954; *d* of Josef and Lilo de Haas; *m* 1980, Iain Saville Goldrein, *qv*; one *s* one *d*. *Educ*: Townsend Sch., Zimbabwe; Bristol Univ. (LLB Hons 1976). Called to the Bar, Middle Temple, 1977; in practice at the Bar, 1977–2004; a Recorder, 1999–2004. Mem., Criminal Injuries Compensation Bd, 1999–. *Publications*: (jtly) Butterworths Personal Injury Litigation Service, 1988–; (jtly) Property Distribution on Divorce, 1989; (jtly) Domestic Injunctions, 1997; (jtly) Medical Negligence: cost effective case management, 1997; (jtly) Structured Settlements, 1997. *Recreations*: family, swimming, reading, theatre. *Address*: c/o Liverpool Family and Civil Courts, 35 Vernon Street, Liverpool L2 2BX.

DEHAENE, Jean-Luc; Member (PPE-DE), European Parliament, since 2004; *b* Montpellier, 7 Aug. 1940; *s* of late Albert Dehaene and of Andrée Verstraete; *m* 1965, Celie Verbeke; four *c*. *Educ*: Univ. of Namur; Univ. of Kul. Comr, Flemish Assoc. of Catholic Scouts, 1963–67; Christian Social Party (CVP): Nat. Vice Pres., CVP Youth, 1967–71; Mem., Nat. Cttee; Councillor: for Public Works, 1972–73; for Public Health, 1973–74; then Leader of Cabinet for Econ. Affairs, 1974–77; Leader of Cabinet for Flemish Affairs, 1977–78; Pres., CVP, Bruxelles-Hal-Vivorde, 1977–81; Leader of Cabinet, 1979–81; Leader of Cabinet for Instnl Reforms, 1981; co-opted Senator, 1982–87; Deputy, 1987–99; Minister of Social Affairs and Instnl Reforms, 1981–88; Dep. Prime Minister and Minister of Communications and Instnl Reforms, 1988–92; Prime Minister of Belgium, 1992–99. A Vice-Chm., Eur. Convention, 2002–03. Mayor of Vilvoorde, 2001–07. *Address*: Berkendallaan 52, 1800 Vilvoorde, Belgium.

de HALPERT, Rear-Adm. Jeremy Michael, CB 2001; Deputy Master, Trinity House, since 2002; *b* 9 July 1947; *s* of late Lt Comdr Michael Frances de Halpert and of Eleanor Anne Love de Halpert; *m* 1972, Jane Fattorini, *d* of late Joseph Fattorini; two *s* one *d*. *Educ*: Canford Sch., Wimborne. Joined Royal Navy, 1966. BRNC, Dartmouth; served HM Ships Aurora, Chilcompton, London, Phoebe, Lowestoft, 1967–75; CO, HMS Sheraton, 1975–76; Specialised Principal Warfare Officer (Navigation): HMS Dryad and HMS Mercury, 1977–78; HMS Ajax and HMS Ariadne, 1978–80; HMS Bristol and Falklands Campaign, 1982–84; Comdr, 1984; CO, HMS Apollo, 1985–86; jsdc 1987; Directorate of Naval Staff Duties, MoD, 1987–89; USN War Coll., Newport, RI, 1989–90; Capt., 1990; CO, HMS Campbeltown, 1990–92; CoS, Flag Officer Surface Flotilla, 1992–94; Dep. UK Mil. Rep., SHAPE, 1994–96; Cdre, 1996; Dir, Overseas Mil. Activity, MoD, 1996–98; Rear-Adm., 1998; Naval Sec., and Chief Exec., Naval Manning Agency, 1998–2002. Dir, Standard (London) P & I Club, 2002–. Gov., Canford Sch., 2002–. Younger Brother, 1993, Elder Brother, 2001, Trinity House. Trustee, Marine Soc. & Sea Cadets (formerly Marine Soc.), 2002–. HM Lieut, City of London, 2006. Liveryman, Shipwrights' Co., 2003–. Mem., Tennis & Racquets Assoc. MRIN 1980, FRIN 2002. Commandeur de Bordeaux à Londres, 2005. *Recreations*: Royal tennis, ski-ing, squash, cricket, military history. *Address*: Corporation of Trinity House, Trinity House, Tower Hill, EC3N 4DH. *Clubs*: Boodle's, Royal Navy of 1765 and 1785, MCC.

de HAMEL, Christopher Francis Rivers, DPhil, PhD; FSA; FRHistS; Donnelley Librarian, and Fellow, Corpus Christi College, Cambridge, since 2000; *b* 20 Nov. 1950; *s* of Dr Francis Alexander de Hamel and Joan Littledale de Hamel (*née* Pollock); *m* 1st, 1978 (marr. diss. 1989); two *s*; 2nd, 1993, Mette Tang Simpson (*née* Svendsen) (*see* M. T. de Hamel). *Educ*: Otago Univ., NZ (BA Hons); Oxford Univ. (DPhil); PhD Cambridge 2005. FSA 1981; FRHistS 1986. Sotheby's: cataloguer of medieval manuscripts, 1975; Asst Dir, 1977; Dir, Western and Oriental, later Western, Manuscripts, 1982–2000. Vis. Fellow, All Souls Coll., Oxford, 1999–2000; Sandars Reader in Bibliography, Univ. of Cambridge, 2003–04. Chm., Assoc. for Manuscripts and Archives in Res. Collections, 2000–. Hon. LittD St John's, Minn, 1994; Hon. DLitt Otago, 2002. *Publications* include: Glossed Books of the Bible and the Origins of the Paris Booktrade, 1984; A History of Illuminated Manuscripts, 1986, 2nd edn 1994; (with M. Manion and V. Vines) Medieval and Renaissance Manuscripts in New Zealand Collections, 1989; Syon Abbey, The Library of the Bridgettine Nuns and their Peregrinations after the Reformation, 1991; Scribes and Illuminators, 1992; The British Library Guide to Manuscript Illumination, 2001; The Book: a history of the Bible, 2001; The Rothschilds and their Collections of Illuminated Manuscripts, 2004. *Address*: Corpus Christi College, Trumpington Street, Cambridge CB2 1RH. *Clubs*: Roxburghe; Grolier (New York); Association Internationale de Bibliophilie (Paris).

de HAMEL, Mette Tang, FIIC; art conservator; *b* Copenhagen, 15 May 1945; *d* of late Axel Tang Svendsen and Grethe Svendsen (*née* Selchau); *m* 1st, 1965, David Melville Bromby Simpson (marr. diss.); two *s*; 2nd, 1993, Dr Christopher Francis Rivers de Hamel, *qv*. *Educ*: Newcastle upon Tyne Poly. (BA Hons History of Art 1979; Dip. in Conservation 1982). Conservator, Bowes Mus., 1979–80; Lectr, Newcastle upon Tyne Poly., 1982–86; Dir, Textile Conservation Centre, Hampton Court Palace, 1986–88; Sen. Conservator, Sotheby's, 1988–99. *Recreations*: painting, gardening. *Address*: 40 Lansdowne Gardens, SW8 2EF. *Club*: Sloane.

de HAVILLAND, Olivia Mary; actress; *b* Tokyo, Japan, 1 July 1916; *d* of Walter Augustus de Havilland and Lilian Augusta (*née* Ruse) (parents British subjects); *m* 1st, 1946, Marcus Aurelius Goodrich (marr. diss., 1953); one *s*; 2nd, 1955, Pierre Paul Galante (marr. diss. 1979); one *d*. *Educ*: in California; won scholarship to Mills Coll., but career prevented acceptance. Played Hermia in Max Reinhardt's stage production of Midsummer Night's Dream, 1934. *Legitimate theatre* (USA): Juliet in Romeo and Juliet, 1951; Candida, 1951 and 1952; A Gift of Time, 1962. Began film career 1935, Midsummer Night's Dream. Nominated for Academy Award, 1939, 1941, 1946, 1948, 1949; Acad. Award, 1946, 1949; New York Critics' Award, 1948, 1949; San Francisco Critics' Award, 1948, 1949; Venice Fest. Award, 1999. Hollywood Foreign Press Assoc. Golden Globe Award, 1949, 1986; Women's National Press Club Award for 1950; French Winged Victory Award, 1950; Belgian Prix Femina, 1957; British Films and Filming Award, 1967; Filmex Tribute, 1978; Amer. Acad. of Achievement Award, 1978. *Important films:* The Adventures of Robin Hood, 1938; Gone With the Wind, 1939; Hold Back the Dawn, 1941; Princess O'Rourke, 1943; To Each His Own, 1946; The Dark Mirror, 1946; The Snake Pit, 1948; The Heiress, 1949; My Cousin Rachel, 1952; Not as a Stranger, 1955; The Ambassador's Daughter, 1956; Proud Rebel, 1957; The Light in the Piazza, 1961; Lady in a Cage, 1963; Hush ... Hush, Sweet Charlotte, 1965; Airport '77, 1976. *Television includes:* Noon Wine, 1966; The Screaming Woman, 1971; Roots, The Next Generations, 1979; 3 ABC Cable-TV Cultural Documentaries, 1981; Murder is Easy, 1982; Charles & Diana, a Royal Romance, 1982; North and South, Book II, 1986; Anastasia, 1986; The Woman He Loved, 1988. US Lecture tours, 1971, 1972, 1973, 1974, 1975, 1976, 1978, 1979, 1980. Pres. of Jury, Cannes Film Festival, 1965. Took part in narration of France's BiCentennial Gift to US, Son et Lumière, A Salute to George Washington, Mount Vernon, 19 May 1976; read excerpts from Thomas Jefferson at BiCentennial Service, American Cathedral in Paris, 4 July 1976. Hon. DHL Amer. Univ. of Paris, 1994; Hon. Dr Letters Univ. of Hertfordshire, 1998. Amer. Legion Humanitarian Medal, 1967; Freedoms Foundn Exemplar American Award, 1981. *Publications:* Every Frenchman Has One, 1962; (contrib.) Mother and Child, 1975. *Address:* BP 156–16, 75764 Paris, Cedex 16, France.

DEHENNIN, Baron Herman; Hon. Grand Marshal of Belgian Royal Court; Hon. Belgian Ambassador; *b* 20 July 1929; created Baron, 1990; *s* of Alexander Dehennin and Flora Brehmen; *m* 1954, Margareta-Maria Donvil; two *s*. *Educ:* Catholic Univ. of Leuven. Dr in Law 1951. Lieut, Royal Belgian Artillery, 1951–53; entered Belgian Diplomatic Service, 1954; served The Hague, New Delhi, Madrid, the Congo; Ambassador to Rwanda, 1966–70; Economic Minister, Washington, 1970–74; Dir-Gen., Foreign Econ. Relations, Brussels, 1974–77; Ambassador to Japan, 1978–81; Grand Marshal, Belgian Royal Court, 1981–85; Ambassador: to USA, 1985–91; to UK, 1991–94. Pres., Special Olympics, Belgium, 1995–. Chm., Club Chateau Ste Anne, Brussels, 1997–. Grand Cross, Order of Leopold, 1985; Grand Cross, Order of the Crown, 1983; foreign Orders: Comoros, France, Greece, Japan, Luxembourg, Mexico, Netherlands, Portugal, Rwanda, Sweden, Zaire. *Recreations:* hiking, tennis, fishing, hunting, reading (history, philosophy). *Clubs:* Travellers, Royal Anglo-Belgian; University Foundation, Cercle Gaulois, Cercle Royal Africain (Brussels); Royal Golf of Belgium.

DEHMELT, Prof. Hans Georg; Professor of Physics, University of Washington, Seattle, 1961–2002; *b* 9 Sept. 1922; *s* of Georg Karl Dehmelt and Asta Ella Dehmelt (*née* Klemmt); US Citizen, 1961; *m* 1st; one *s*; 2nd, 1989, Diana Elaine Dundore. *Educ:* Graues Kloster, Berlin; Technische Hochschule, Breslau; Univ. of Göttingen (Dr rer. nat. 1950). Res. Fellow, Inst. Kopfermann, Göttingen, 1950–52; Res. Associate, Duke Univ., USA, 1952–55; Vis. Asst Prof., 1955, Associate Prof., 1957, Univ. of Washington. Consultant, Varian Associates, Palo Alto, Calif, 1956–70. Member: Amer. Acad. of Arts and Scis; Nat. Acad. of Scis; Fellow, Amer. Phys Soc.; FAAAS. Numerous awards and hon. degrees; Nobel Prize for Physics (jtly), 1989; Nat. Medal of Science, US, 1995. Leader of group which first saw with own eyes individual atom at rest in free space, 1979, reported 1980; isolated individual electron/positron at rest in empty space, 1973, 1981, and precisely measured its magnetism and size, 1976–87. *Publications:* papers on electron and atomic physics, charged atoms, proposed cosmonium world-atom hypothesis of big bang.

DEHN, Conrad Francis; QC 1968; Barrister; a Recorder of the Crown Court, 1974–98; a Deputy High Court Judge, 1988–96; *b* London, 24 Nov. 1926; *o s* of late C. G. Dehn, Solicitor and Cynthia Dehn (*née* Fuller) painter, as Francyn; *m* 1st, 1954, Sheila (*née* Magan) (marr. diss.); two *s* one *d*; 2nd, 1978, Marilyn, *d* of late Peter and Constance Collyer. *Educ:* Charterhouse (Sen. Exhibr); Christ Church, Oxford (Holford Schol.). Served RA, 1945–48, Best Cadet Mons Basic OCTU, 1946, 2nd Lieut 1947. 1st cl. hons PPE Oxon. 1950, MA 1952; Holt Schol., Gray's Inn, 1951; Pres., Inns of Court Students Union, 1951–52. WEA Tutor, 1951–55. Called to Bar, Gray's Inn, 1952; Bencher, 1977; Chm., Management Cttee, 1987; Vice-Treas., 1995; Treas., 1996. Head, Fountain Court Chambers, 1984–89. Chairman: Bar Council Working Party on Liability for Defective Products, 1975–77; Planning Cttee, Senate of Inns of Court and Bar, 1980–83; London Univ. Disciplinary Appeals Cttee, 1986–90; Adv. Cttee, Gen. Comrs of Income Tax, Gray's Inn, 1994–2003. Dir, Bar Mutual Indemnity Fund Ltd, 1988–. Mem., Foster Cttee of Inquiry into Operators' Licensing, Dept of Transport, 1978. Member: Council of Legal Educn, 1981–86; London Legal Aid Cttee, 1965–92 (Vice-Chm., 1987–92); Hon. Advr, S London Psychotherapy Centre, 1982–2001; Hon. Legal Adviser: Age Concern London, 1987–2002 (Vice-Pres., 2001–02); Southwark Action for Voluntary Orgns, 2003–08. Pres., Camberwell Soc., 1996–2007. Member: Governing Body, United Westminster Schs, 1953–57; Adv. Bd, Inst. of Law, City Univ., 2002–; Gov., Inns of Court Sch. of Law, 1996–2002. Appeared in film, The History Boys, 2007. Hon. Liberty, Camberwell, 2006. *Publications:* (contrib.) Ideas, 1954; (contrib.) Reform of Civil Procedure, 1996; (ed) Commercial Court Practice, 1999, 2nd edn 2000. *Recreations:* theatre, living in France. *Address:* Fountain Court, Temple, EC4Y 9DH. *T:* (020) 7583 3335. *Club:* Reform.

De HOCHEPIED LARPENT, Lt Col Andrew Lionel Dudley, OBE 1992; Chief Executive, Somerset Care Group, since 2001; *b* 10 Feb. 1951; *s* of Douglas De Hochepied Larpent and Patience (*née* Johnson); *m* 1974, Anne Marion Knights; two *s* one *d*. *Educ:* Bradfield Coll.; RMA Sandhurst; Reading Univ. (BSc Hons Estate Mgt 1976). Royal Regt of Fusiliers, 1969–94, CO, 3rd Bn, 1990–92; Dir, Rehau Ltd, 1994–96; construction industry consultant, 1996–97; CEO, Cancer and Leukaemia in Childhood, 1997–2001. Chairman: Care Focus Somerset, 2005–07; Nat. Care Forum, 2006–; Mem. Bd, Internat. Assoc. of Homes and Services for the Ageing, 2006–. *Recreations:* country pursuits, ski-ing.

de HOGHTON, Sir (Richard) Bernard (Cuthbert), 14th Bt *cr* 1611; KM; DL; *b* 26 Jan. 1945; 3rd *s* of Sir Cuthbert de Hoghton, 12th Bt, and of Philomena, *d* of late Herbert Simmons; *S* half-brother, 1978; *m* 1974, Rosanna Stella Virginia (*née* Buratti); one *s* one *d*. *Educ:* Ampleforth College, York; McGill Univ., Montreal (BA Hons); Birmingham Univ. (MA); PhD (USA). Turner & Newall Ltd, 1967–70; international fund management, Vickers Da Costa & Co. Ltd, 1970–77; international institutional brokerage, de Zoete & Bevan & Co., 1977–86 (Partner, 1984–86); Dir, BZW Ltd (Europe), 1986–89; Asst Dir, Brown Shipley, 1989–94; Associate Dir, Teather & Greenwood, 1994–98; Dir, Tutton & Saunders Ltd, 1998–99. Pres., Royal Lancs Agricl Soc., 1995; Nat. Vice-Pres., Internat. Tree Foundn, 1983–. Patron: ACU (NW), 1980–; Internat. Spinal Res. Trust, 1984–. Historic house and estate management, 1978–. DL Lancs, 1988. Constantinian Order of S George (Naples), 1984; Kt SMO, Malta, 1980. *Recreations:* tennis, shooting, travelling, local historical research. *Heir: s* Thomas James Daniel Adam de Hoghton, *b* 11 April 1980. *Address:* Hoghton Tower, Hoghton, Preston, Lancs PR5 0SH.

de HOOP SCHEFFER, Jakob Gijsbert, (Jaap); Secretary-General, NATO, since 2004; *b* 3 April 1948; *m* Jeannine van Oorschot; two *d*. *Educ:* Leiden Univ. (law degree 1974). Joined Foreign Service, Netherlands, 1976; Accra, 1976–78; Perm. Delegn, NATO, Brussels, 1978–80; i/c pvte office, Minister of Foreign Affairs, Netherlands, 1980–86. MP (Christian Democratic Alliance), Netherlands, 1986–2003; Minister of Foreign Affairs, 2002–03. Dep. Leader 1995–97, Leader, 1997–2001, Christian Democratic Alliance. *Address:* NATO, Boulevard Leopold III, 1110 Brussels, Belgium.

DEIGHTON, Paul Clive; Chief Executive, London Organising Committee, 2012 Olympic Games, since 2006; *b* 18 Jan. 1956; *s* of Walter Francis and Mabel Alice Deighton; *m* 1985, Alison Zoe Klebanoff; two *s*. *Educ:* Trinity Coll., Cambridge (BA 1978). Goldman Sachs International, 1983–2006: Investment Banking Div., 1983–93; Head of Controllers Dept, NY, 1993–96; Partner and Man. Dir, 1996–2000; Chief Operating Officer, Europe, 2000–06. *Address:* London Organising Committee, 2012 Olympic Games, 23rd Floor, 1 Churchill Place, Canary Wharf, E14 5LN. *T:* (020) 3201 2085.

DEIN, David; Vice Chairman, Arsenal Football Club, 1984–2007; *b* 7 Sept. 1943; *s* of Isidore and Sybil Dein; *m* 1972, Barbara Einhorn; two *s* one *d*. *Educ:* Orange Hill Grammar Sch., Edgware. Proprietor, sugar and commodity trading business, 1961–88; Dir, 1983–2007, full-time exec. role, 1988–2007, Arsenal FC. Chm., Stage One (formerly Theatre Investment Fund), 2001–. *Recreations:* theatre, films, tennis.

DEISENHOFER, Prof. Johann, PhD; Regental Professor and Professor in Biochemistry, University of Texas Southwestern Medical Center at Dallas, since 1988; Investigator, Howard Hughes Medical Institute, since 1988; *b* 30 Sept. 1943; *s* of Johann and Thekla Deisenhofer; *m* 1989, Kirsten Fischer-Lindahl, PhD. *Educ:* Technische Universität München (Physics Diploma 1971; PhD 1974). Max-Planck-Institut für Biochemie: graduate student, 1971–74; Postdoctoral Fellow, 1974–76; Staff Scientist, 1976–88. (Jtly) Biological Physics Prize, Amer. Physical Soc., 1986; (jtly) Otto Bayer Preis, 1988; (jtly) Nobel Prize in Chemistry, 1988. *Publications:* contribs to Acta Crystallographica, Biochemistry, Jl of Molecular Biology, Nature, Science, etc. *Recreations:* ski-ing, swimming, classical music. *Address:* University of Texas Southwestern Medical Center, Howard Hughes Medical Institute, 6001 Forest Park Road, Dallas, TX 75390–9050, USA. *T:* (214) 6455941.

DEJARDIN, Ian Alan Charles; Director, Dulwich Picture Gallery, since 2005; *b* 26 Aug. 1955; *s* of Alan A. Dejardin and Pamela B. Dejardin (*née* Wilcock); civil partnership 2007, Eric Pearson. *Educ:* Daniel Stewart's Coll., Edinburgh; Univ. of Edinburgh (MA 1st Cl. Hons Hist. of Art 1977); Univ. of Manchester (Dip. Art Gall. and Mus. Studies 1987). Curatorial Asst, Royal Acad. of Arts, 1988–90; English Heritage: Curator of Paintings, London Historic Houses, 1990–94; Sen. Curator of Collections, 1994–96, Hd, Historic Team, 1996–97, Historic Properties, London Reg.; Curator, Dulwich Picture Gall., 1998–2005. *Publications:* exhibition catalogues: Paintings from the Chantrey Bequest, 1989; Henry Moore at Dulwich Picture Gallery, 2004; Desideratum: a cycle of work 1998–2004 by Nicholas Charles Williams, 2004. *Recreations:* piano, ice skating. *Address:* Dulwich Picture Gallery, Gallery Road, SE21 7AD. *T:* (020) 8299 8702, *Fax:* (020) 8299 8700.

de JERSEY, Hon. Paul, AC 2000; Chief Justice of Queensland, since 1998; a Judge of the Supreme Court, Queensland, since 1985; *b* 21 Sept. 1948; *s* of Ronald Claude and Moya Clarice de Jersey; *m* 1971, Kaye Brown; one *s* two *d*. *Educ:* C of E Grammar Sch., Brisbane; Univ. of Qld (BA, LLB Hons). Admitted to Qld Bar, 1971; QC (Qld) 1981. Chm., Qld Law Reform Commn, 1996–98; Pres., Industrial Court of Qld, 1996–98. Chm. Judicial Section, Law Assoc. for Asia and Pacific, 2006–. Chancellor, Anglican Dio. Brisbane, 1991–. Chm., Qld Cancer Fund, 1994–2001; Pres., Australian Cancer Soc., 1998–2001. Visitor, Univ. of South Pacific, 2006–. Hon. LLD Qld, 2000. *Recreations:* reading, music. *Address:* Chief Justice's Chambers, Supreme Court, George Street, Brisbane, Qld 4000, Australia. *T:* (7) 32474279. *Clubs:* Queensland, United Service (Brisbane).

de JONGH, Nicholas Raymond; Theatre Critic, Evening Standard, since 1991; *b* London; *s* of Louis de Jongh and late Vivian (*née* Creditor). *Educ:* Hall Sch., Hampstead; St Paul's Sch.; University Coll. London (BA Hons, MPhil 1983). Secker & Warburg, 1967; Scriptwriter, BBC External Services, 1968; The Guardian: Reporter, 1968; Theatre Reviewer, 1969; Dep. Theatre Critic, 1970–91; Arts Reporter, 1973–78; Arts Corresp., 1978–90; Theatre Critic, Mail on Sunday, 1983. Chm., Drama Section, Critics' Circle, 1984–86. Writer of play, Plague Over England, Finborough Th., 2008. *Publications:* (ed) Bedside Guardian, 1989, 1990; Not in Front of the Audience, 1992; (contrib.) Approaching the Millennium: essays on Angels in America, 2000; Politics, Prudery and Perversions (Theatre Book Prize, Soc. of Theatre Res.), 2000; (contrib.) British Theatre of the 1990s, 2007. *Recreations:* fantasising, riding hobby-horses. *Address:* Evening Standard, Northcliffe House, 2 Derry Street, W8 5EE. *Club:* Groucho.

DEJOUANY, Guy Georges André; Commandeur, Légion d'Honneur; Hon. Chairman, Vivendi (Chairman and Managing Director, Compagnie Générale des Eaux, 1976–96); *b* 15 Dec. 1920; *s* of André Dejouany and Jeanne (*née* Imbard); *m* (wife decd); two *s* one *d*; *m* 1996, Renée Marnet. *Educ:* Ecole Polytechnique, Paris; Ponts et Chaussées, Paris. Civil Engineer: Metz, 1945–49; Paris, 1949–50; joined Compagnie Générale des Eaux, 1950; Manager, 1961–65; Dep. Man. Dir, 1965–72; Man. Dir, 1972–73; Dir, 1973–, co. name now Vivendi. Chm. and Man. Dir, Cie des Eaux et de l'Ozone, 1970–96; Man. Dir, Soc. Monégasque des Eaux, 1970–96. *Address:* (office) 52 rue d'Anjou, 75008 Paris, France; 2 rue de Franqueville, 75116 Paris, France.

de KLERK, Frederik Willem; Leader of the Opposition, National Assembly of South Africa, 1996–97; *b* 18 March 1936; *s* of J. de Klerk; *m* 1st, 1959, Marike Willemse (marr. diss. 1998; she *d* 2001); two *s* one *d*; 2nd, 1998, Elita Georgiadis. *Educ:* Monument High School, Krugersdorp; Potchefstroom Univ. Law practice, 1961–72; MP (Nat. Party) Vereeniging, 1972–89; Information Officer, Transvaal, Nat. Party, 1975; Minister: of Posts and Telecommunications and Social Welfare and Pensions, 1978; of Posts and Telecommunications and of Sport and Recreation, 1978–79; of Mines, Energy and Environmental Planning, 1979–80; of Mineral and Energy Affairs, 1980–82; of Internal Affairs, 1982–85; of Nat. Educn and Planning, 1984–89; Leader, Nat. Party, 1989–97 (Transvaal Leader, 1982–89); Chm., Council of Ministers, 1985–89; State President, 1989–94, Dep. President, 1994–96, S Africa. Hon. LLD: Potchefstroom Univ., 1990; Bar Ilan Univ., Tel Aviv; Hon. DPhil: Stellenbosch Univ., 1990; Nat. Chengchi Univ., Taipei, Taiwan. Nobel Peace Prize (with N. R. Mandela), 1993. *Publication:* The Last Trek: a new beginning, 1999. *Address:* PO Box 15785, Panorama, 7506, Cape Province, South Africa.

de KRETSER, Prof. David Morritz, AC 2006 (AO 2000); MD; FRACP, FAA, FTSE; Governor of Victoria, Australia, since 2006; *b* Colombo, Sri Lanka, 27 April 1939; *s* of Percival Shirley de Kretser and Iris Aileen de Kretser; *m* 1962, Janice Margaret Warren four *s. Educ:* Camberwell Grammar Sch.; Univ. of Melbourne (MS BS 1962); Monash Univ. (MD 1969). FRACP 1976; FAA 1996; FTSE 2001. Lectr, 1966–68, Sen. Lectr, 1968, Dept of Anatomy, Monash Univ.; Sen. Fellow in Endocrinol., Dept of Medicine, Univ. of Washington, and USPHS Postdoctoral Fellow, 1969–71; Monash University: Sen. Lectr, Depts of Medicine and Anatomy, 1971–75; Reader in Anatomy, 1976–78; Prof. of Anatomy, 1978–2006; Hd, Dept of Anatomy, 1978–91; Dir, Centre for Reproductive Biol., 1989–91; Dir, Inst. of Reproduction and Develt, subseq. Monash Inst. of Med. Res., 1991–2005; Associate Dean, Biotechnol. Develt, 2002–06; Prince Henry's Hospital: Asst Endocrinologist, 1971–85; Physician, 1973–74; Sen. Res. Fellow, 1974–78, Associate Dir, 1977–78, Med. Res. Centre; Consultant, Reproductive Medicine Clinic, Inst. of Med. Res., 1976–2006. Centenary Medal, Aust., 2003. *Publications:* The Pituitary and Testis: clinical and experimental studies, 1983; papers on reproductive biology and male infertility. *Recreations:* squash, fishing, tennis. *Address:* Government House, Melbourne, Vic 3004, Australia. *Club:* Athenæum (Melbourne).

de LA BARRE de NANTEUIL, Luc; Commandeur de l'Ordre National du Mérite; Officier de la Légion d'Honneur; Ambassadeur de France; Chairman, Les Echos Group, 1991–2003; *b* 21 Sept. 1925; *m* 1st, Philippa MacDonald; one *s*; 2nd, 1973, Hedwige Frerejean de Chavagneux; one *s* one *d. Educ:* school in Poitiers; BA, LLB Lyon and Paris; Dip. d'Etudes Supérieures (Econ); Graduate, Ecole Nat. d'Admin, 1949. French Ministry of Foreign Affairs: Economic Affairs Dept, 1950–51; Secrétariat Général, 1951–52; Pacts Service, 1952–53; Econ. Affairs Dept, 1954–59; First Sec., London, 1959–64; Asst Dir, Afr. and ME Affairs Dept, 1964–70; Hd of Econ. Co-operation Service, Directorate of Econ. Affairs, 1970–76; Ambassador to the Netherlands, 1976–77; French Permanent Representative: to EEC, Brussels, 1977–82 and 1985–86; to Security Council and to UN, New York, 1981–84; Diplomatic Adviser, 1986; Ambassador to UK, 1986–91. *Publication:* David (Jacques Louis), 1985.

De la BÈRE, Sir Cameron, 2nd Bt *cr* 1953; jeweller, Geneva; *b* 12 Feb. 1933; *s* of Sir Rupert De la Bère, 1st Bt, KCVO, and Marguerite (*d* 1969), *e d* of late Sir John Humphery; *S* father, 1978; *m* 1964, Clairemonde (*d* 2004), *o d* of late Casimir Kaufmann, Geneva; one *d. Educ:* Tonbridge, and on the Continent. Translator's cert. in Russian. British Army Intelligence Corps, 1951–53. Company director of Continental Express Ltd (subsid. of Hay's Wharf), 1958–64. Engaged in promotion of luxury retail jewellery stores, Switzerland and France, 1965–. Liveryman, Skinners' Co. *Recreations:* riding, swimming, history. *Heir: b* Adrian De la Bère, *b* 17 Sept. 1939. *Address:* 1 Avenue Theodore Flournoy, 1207 Geneva, Switzerland. *T:* (22) 7860015. *Clubs:* Hurlingham, Société Litéraire (Geneva).

de la BILLIÈRE, Gen. Sir Peter (Edgar de la Cour), KCB 1988; KBE 1991 (CBE 1983); DSO 1976; MC 1959 and Bar 1966; DL; Chairman, Meadowland Meats Ltd, 1994–2002; *b* 29 April 1934; *s* of Surgeon Lieut Comdr Claude Dennis Delacour de Labillière (killed in action, HMS Fiji, 1941) and of Frances Christine Wright Lawley; *m* 1965, Bridget Constance Muriel Goode; one *s* two *d. Educ:* Harrow School; Staff College. Joined KSLI 1952; commissioned DLI; served Japan, Korea, Malaya (despatches 1958), Jordan, Borneo, Egypt, Aden, Gulf States, Sudan, Oman, Falkland Is; CO 22 SAS Regt, 1972–74; GSO1 (DS) Staff Coll., 1974–77; Comd British Army Training Team, Sudan, 1977–78; Dir SAS and Comd, SAS Group, 1978–82; RCDS 1983; Comd, British Forces Falkland Is and Mil. Comr, 1984–85; GOC Wales, 1985–87; GOC SE Dist, and Perm. Peace Time Comdr, Jt Forces Operations Staff, 1987–90; Comdr British Forces, ME, 1990–91; ME Advr to MOD, 1991–92, retd. Col Comdt, Light Div., 1986–89. Chm., ME Div., Robert Fleming Hldgs, 1998–99 (non-exec. Dir, 1992–98). Mem. Council, RUSI, 1975–77. Chm., FARM Africa, 1998–2001 (Mem. Bd, 1992–2001; Vice-Chm., 1995–98). Chm., Jt Services Hang Gliding, 1986–89; Cdre, Army Sailing Assoc., 1989–91. President: SAS Assoc., 1991–96; ACF, 1992–99. Vice-Pres., UK Falkland Is Assoc., 1993–. Comr, Duke of York's Mil. Sch., 1988–90. Presenter, TV series, Clash of the Generals, 2004. Trustee, Imperial War Mus., 1992–99; President: Imperial War Mus. Friends, 2001–08; Harrow Sch. Assoc., 2001–05. Patron: Jt Educnl Trust, 1998–; Farm Africa, 2001–; Gallantry Medallists' League, 2005–; St Dunstan's for blind servicemen, 2007–. Freeman, City of London, 1991; Hon. Freeman, Fishmongers' Co., 1991. Stowaway Mem., Southampton Master Mariners Assoc., 1992. DL Hereford and Worcester, 1993. Hon. DSc Cranfield Inst. of Technol., 1992; Hon. DCL Durham, 1993. Order of Bahrain, 1st Cl., 1991; Chief Comdr, Legion of Merit (USA), 1992; Meritorious Service Cross, (Canada), 1992; Order of Abdul Aziz, 2nd Cl. (Saudi Arabia), 1992; Kuwait Decoration, 1st Cl., 1992; Qatar Sash of Merit, 1992. *Publications:* Storm Command: a personal story, 1992; (autobiog.) Looking for Trouble, 1994; Supreme Courage: 150 years of the Victoria Cross, 2004. *Recreations:* family, squash, down market apiculture, tennis, farming, sailing. *Clubs:* Farmers', Naval and Military (Trustee, 1999–2003).

DELACOUR, Jean-Paul; Officer of Legion of Honour; Knight of National Order of Merit; Inspector General of Finance; Hon. Vice-Chairman, Société Générale, Paris (Chief Operating Officer, 1986–95; Vice-Chairman, 1992); *b* 7 Nov. 1930; *s* of Henri Delacour and Denise Brochet; *m* 1958, Claude Laurence; four *s* one *d. Educ:* Inst. of Political Studies, Paris (Dipl.); ENA (Nat. Sch. of Administration). Inspector of Finance, 1955–61; Dep. Dir, Crédit National, 1961–68; Dir, 1969, Dep. Gen. Manager, 1974, Bd Mem. and Man. Dir, 1986, Société Générale; Chm. and Chief Exec. Officer, Soc. Gén. Alsacienne de Banque, 1978–82; Chm., Sogebail, 1985–2000; senior functions in internat. banking and financial insts. Chm., Bd of Catholic Inst. Paris, 1984–2005. *Address:* Société Générale, 29 boulevard Haussmann, 75009 Paris, France. *T:* 42142336.

DELACOURT-SMITH OF ALTERYN, Baroness *cr* 1974 (Life Peer), of Alteryn, Gwent; **Margaret Delacourt-Smith;** *b* 1916; *d* of Frederick James Hando; *m* 1st, 1939, Charles Smith (subsequently Lord Delacourt-Smith, PC) (*d* 1972); one *s* two *d*; 2nd, 1978, Professor Charles Blackton. *Educ:* Newport High School for Girls; St Anne's College, Oxford (MA).

de LACY, Richard Michael; QC 2000; *b* 4 Dec. 1954; *e s* of Michael de Lacy, MN, and Barbara de Lacy (*née* Greene), Hobart, Tasmania; *m* 1980, Sybil del Strother (marr. diss. 2003); one *s* two *d. Educ:* Hymers Coll., Kingston upon Hull; Clare Coll., Cambridge (BA 1975; MA 1979). Called to the Bar, Middle Temple, 1976 (Harmsworth Schol.), Bencher, 2001; in practice at the Bar, 1976–, specialising in commercial law, 1986–. Member: Practice Regulation Review Cttee, ICAEW, 1998–2004; Panel, Accountancy and Actuarial Discipline (formerly Accounting Investigation and Discipline) Bd, 2004–. Jt Hon. Treas., Barristers' Benevolent Assoc., 1989–99; Chm., Endeavour Trng, 2005–. FCIArb 1991 (Chartered Arbitrator 2000); accredited Mediator, CEDR, 1998. *Recreations:* music, history. *Address:* 3 Stone Buildings, Lincoln's Inn, WC2A 3XL. *T:* (020) 7242 4937. *Club:* Travellers'.

DELAHUNTY, Johanne Erica; QC 2006; barrister; *b* 15 Sept. 1963; *d* of Pauline Delahunty; *m* 1990, Jonathan Light; one *s* two *d. Educ:* Copthall Comp. Sch., Mill Hill; St Anne's Coll., Oxford (BA Law Juris. 1983, MA). Called to the Bar, Middle Temple, 1986; in practice, 1986–, specialist child abuse and family law practitioner; accredited specialist in family law and child protection. Member: Family Law Bar Assoc.; Assoc. of Lawyers for Children; Assoc. of Women Barristers. Member: Amnesty; ChildRIGHT; NSPCC; Barnardo's; Save the Children; Help the Aged; Soc. of Decorative Arts. *Publications:* contribs to specialist child care and family law publications. *Recreations:* married to my partner of 26 years with 3 children and 2 dogs to occupy a life outside the Bar, skilled at finding time to read Vogue, to indulge in a passion for modern British jewellery and retail therapy, guilt pangs alleviated by fine wine and good friends. *Address:* Garden Court Chambers, 57–60 Lincoln's Inn Fields, WC2A 3LS. *T:* (020) 7993 7600, *Fax:* (020) 7993 7700; *e-mail:* jod@gclaw.co.uk.

de la LANNE-MIRRLEES, Robin Ian Evelyn Stuart; *see* Mirrlees.

de la MADRID HURTADO, Miguel; President of Mexico, 1982–88; Director General, Fondo de Cultura Económica, 1990–2000; *b* 12 Dec. 1934; *m* 1959, Paloma Cordero de la Madrid; four *s* one *d. Educ:* Nat. Autonomous Univ., Mexico (Law degree with hon. mention for thesis; with master); Harvard Univ. (MPA). Legal Dept, Nat. Bank of Foreign Trade, 1953–57; Asst Gen. Man., Bank of Mexico, 1960–64; Asst Dir Gen., Credit Mexican, Min. of Treasury, 1965–70; Dir of Finance, Pemex, 1970–72; Gen. Dir, Credit, 1972–75, Under Sec., 1975–79, Min. of Treasury; Minister, Nat. Planning and Budget, Govt of Mexico, 1979–81. Pres., Nat. Assoc. of Lawyers, 1989–. Pres., Mexican Inst. of Culture, 1989–. Mem., InterAction Council, 1989–. *Publications:* economic and legal essays. *Address:* (office) Parras #46, Barrio Sta Catarina, Deleg. Coyoacán, 04010, México DF. *T:* (525) 6584459.

de la MARTINEZ, Odaline, (Odaline de la Caridad Martinez), FRAM; Cuban conductor and composer; *b* 31 Oct. 1949; *d* of Julian J. Martinez and Odaline M. Martinez. *Educ:* schs and univ. in USA; Royal Acad. of Music, London; Surrey Univ. Jt Founder and Artistic Dir, Lontano (chamber ensemble), 1976–; first woman to conduct an entire Promenade Concert programme, Royal Albert Hall, 1984; Dir, European Women's Orchestra, 1990–; Principal Guest Cond., Camerata of the Americas, 1998–. Founder, 1992, and Man. Dir, Lorelt recording co. Founder Mem., Women in Music, 1985. *Compositions include:* First String Quartet; *opera:* Sister Aimée: an American Legend, 1984. *Publications:* Mendelssohn's Sister, 1999; Latin American Music, 1999. *Address:* c/o Lontano Trust Ltd, 35A Copeland Road, E17 9DB.

DELAMERE, 5th Baron *cr* 1821; **Hugh George Cholmondeley;** *b* 18 Jan. 1934; *s* of 4th Baron Delamere, and Phyllis Anne (*d* 1978), *e d* of late Lord George Scott, OBE; *S* father, 1979; *m* 1964, Mrs Ann Willoughby Tinne, *o d* of late Sir Patrick Renison, GCMG and Lady Renison, Mayfield, Sussex; one *s. Educ:* Eton; Magdalene Coll., Cambridge. MA Agric. *Heir: s* Hon. Thomas Patrick Gilbert Cholmondeley [*b* 19 June 1968; *m* 1998, Dr Sally Brewerton, *d* of Prof. and Mrs Derrick Brewerton; two *s*]. *Address:* Soysambu, Elmenteita, Kenya.

de la MORENA, Felipe, Hon. CBE 2001; Ambassador of Spain; Chairman, British Hispanic Foundation, Madrid, since 1993; *b* 22 Oct. 1927; *s* of Felipe de la Morena and Luisa Calvet; *m* 1958, María Teresa Casado Bach; two *s* two *d. Educ:* Univ. Complutense de Madrid; Univs of Grenoble and Oxford; Diplomatic Sch., Madrid. Entered diplomatic service 1957; served Beirut, Berne, Washington and Min. of Foreign Affairs, Madrid; Dir, Technical Office, later Dir-Gen., Territorial Planning, Min. of Develt Planning, 1974–76; Minister Counsellor, Lisbon, 1976; Ambassador to People's Republic of China, 1978; Dir-Gen., Foreign Policy for Latin America, 1982; Ambassador to Syria and Cyprus (residence Damascus), 1983; Ambassador to Tunisia, 1987, to UK, 1990–93. Orders: Alfonso X el Sabio, 1965; Mérito Civil, 1973; Isabel la Católica, 1970; Carlos III, 1980; Gran Cruz del Mérito Naval, 1992; SM Orden Constantiniana de San Jorge, 1993; holds foreign decorations. *Recreation:* golf. *Address:* Fundación Hispano-Británica, Avda. Pío XII 92, 28036 Madrid, Spain. *Clubs:* Travellers; Puerta de Hierro, Real Automóvil de España, Gran Peña (Madrid).

DELANEY, Francis James Joseph, (Frank); writer and broadcaster, since 1972; *b* 24 Oct. 1942; 5th *s* of Edward Delaney and Elizabeth Josephine O'Sullivan; *m* 1st, 1966, Eilish (*née* Kelliher) (marr. diss. 1978); three *s*; 2nd, 1988, Susan Jane Collier (marr. diss. 1997); 3rd, 2002, Diane Meier. *Educ:* Abbey Schools, Tipperary, Ireland; Rosse Coll., Dublin. Bank of Ireland, 1961–72; journalism, 1972–: includes: broadcasting news with RTE, Dublin; current affairs with BBC Northern Ireland, BBC Radio Four, London, and BBC Television. Chm., NBL, 1984–86. *Publications:* James Joyce's Odyssey, 1981; Betjeman Country, 1983; The Celts, 1986; A Walk in the Dark Ages, 1988; A Walk to the Western Isles, 1993; Simple Courage, 2006; *fiction:* My Dark Rosaleen, 1989; The Sins of the Mothers, 1992; Telling the Pictures, 1993; A Stranger in their Midst, 1995; The Amethysts, 1997; Desire and Pursuit, 1998; Pearl, 1999; At Ruby's, 2001; The Bell Walk, 2003; Ireland: a novel, 2004; Tipperary: a novel, 2007; (as Francis Bryan) Jim Hawkins and the Curse of Treasure Island, 2001; sundry criticisms and introductions. *Recreations:* reading, conversation, walking. *Address: e-mail:* frankdelaney@frankdelaney.com. *Clubs:* Athenæum, Chelsea Arts.

DELANEY, Ven. Peter Anthony, MBE 2001; Archdeacon of London, since 1999; *b* 20 June 1939; *s* of Anthony Mario Delaney and Ena Margaret Delaney. *Educ:* King's Coll., London (AKC); St Boniface Coll., Warminster. Ordained deacon, 1966, priest, 1967; Curate, St Marylebone Parish Church, 1966–70; Chaplain, London University Church of Christ the King, 1970–74; Canon Residentiary and Precentor, Southwark Cathedral, 1974–77; Vicar, All Hallows by the Tower, 1977–2004; Guild Vicar, St Katharine Cree, 1997–2002; Rector, St Stephen Walbrook, 2005–. Hon. Canon, St Paul's Cathedral, Nicosia, Dio. Cyprus and the Gulf, 1984–; Prebendary, St Paul's Cathedral, London, 1995–99. Dir, City Churches Develt Gp, 1997–2000. Gov., St Dunstan's Coll., Catford, 1977–2000; Master: Co. of World Traders of City of London, 1994–95; Gardeners' Co., 1999–2000. Kt Comdr, SMO of Knights Templars. *Publications:* The Artist and his Exploration into God, 1981; (contrib.) The Canon Law of the Church of England, 1975. *Recreations:* painting, theatre, gardening. *Address:* Archdeacon's Office, The Old Deanery, Dean's Court, EC4V 5AA. *T:* (020) 7236 7891, *Fax:* (020) 7248 7455; *e-mail:* archdeacon.london@london.anglican.org.

DELANEY, Shelagh; playwright; *b* Salford, Lancs, 25 Nov. 1939; one *d. Educ:* Broughton Secondary Sch. *Plays:* A Taste of Honey, Theatre Royal, Stratford, 1958 and 1959, Wyndhams, 1959, New York, 1960 and 1961, off-Broadway revival, trans. to Broadway, 1981 (Charles Henry Foyle New Play Award, Arts Council Bursary, New York Drama Critics' Award); The Lion in Love, Royal Court 1960, New York 1962. *Films:* A Taste of Honey, 1961 (British Film Academy Award, Robert Flaherty Award); The White Bus, 1966; Charlie Bubbles, 1968 (Writers Guild Award for best original film writing); Dance with a Stranger, 1985 (Prix Film Jeunesse-Etranger, Cannes, 1985). *TV plays:* St Martin's Summer, LWT, 1974; Find Me First, BBC TV, 1979; *TV series:* The House that Jack Built, BBC TV, 1977 (stage adaptation, NY, 1979). *Radio plays:* So Does the Nightingale, BBC, 1980; Don't Worry About Matilda, 1983; Tell Me a Film, 2003; Country Life, 2004. FRSL 1985. *Publications:* A Taste of Honey, 1959 (London and New York); The Lion in Love, 1961 (London and New York); Sweetly Sings the Donkey, 1963 (New

York), 1964 (London). *Address:* c/o Sayle Literary Agency, 1 Petersfield, Cambridge CB1 1BB.

DÉLANO ORTÚZAR, Juan Carlos; Director, Universidad Adolfo Ibañez, 1998–2004; *b* Santiago, 14 June 1941; *m* Maria Paz Valenzuela; three *s* one *d*. *Educ:* St George's Coll., Catholic Univ., Chile; OCD, Belgium. Private enterprise: Distribuidora Audicol SA, Commercial Magara Ltd; Pres., Trading Assoc. of Chile, Dir, Chamber of Commerce of Santiago, 1979–83; Pres., Chilean Nat. Chamber of Commerce and Advr to Confedn of Trade and Industry, 1983–85; Minister of Economy, Promotion and Reconstruction, 1985–87; Ambassador to UK, 1987–90. Chief Exec. Officer, Equs SA, 1990–; Dir, Icare, 1990–. *Address:* Americo Vespucio Norte 1776, Dept 31, Vitacura, Santiago, Chile; *e-mail:* juancdelano@yahoo.com. *Club:* Polo.

de LAROSIÈRE de CHAMPFEU, Jacques (Martin Henri Marie), Hon. KBE 1998; Commander, Legion of Honour, 1996; Chevalier, National Order of Merit, 1970; Inspector General of Finance, since 1981; Adviser, BNP Paribas, since 1998; *b* 12 Nov. 1929; *s* of Robert de Larosière and Hugayte de Champfeu; *m* 1960, France du Bos; one *s* one *d*. *Educ:* Institut d'Etudes Politiques, Paris (L ès L, licencié en droit); Nat. Sch. of Administration, Paris. Inspecteur des Finances, 1958; appointments at: Inspectorate-General of Finance, 1961; External Finance Office, 1963; Treasury 1965; Asst Dir, Treasury, 1967; Dep. Dir then Head of Dept, Min. of Economics and Finance, 1971; Principal Private Sec. to Minister of Economics and Finance, 1974; Dir, Treasury, 1974–78; Man. Dir, IMF, 1978–87; Gov., Bank of France, 1987–93; Pres., EBRD, 1993–98. Director: Renault, 1971–74; Banque Nat. de Paris, 1973–78; Air France and French Railways, 1974–78; Société nat. industrielle aérospatiale, 1976–78; Power Corp., 1998–2001; Alstom, 1998–2000; France Telecom, 1998–; Trustee, Reuters, 1999–2004. Director appointed by Treasury, General Council, Bank of France, 1974–78; Auditor: Crédit national, 1974–78; Comptoir des entrepreneurs, 1973–75; Crédit foncier de France, 1975–78. Vice Pres., Caisse nat. des télécommunications, 1974–78; Pres., Observatoire de l'Epargne Européenne, 1999–; Co-Chm., Eurofi, 2000–. Member: Internat. Adv. Bd, AIG, 2002–; Adv. Bd, China Develt Bank, 2005–; Chm. Adv. Bd, Mid Europa Fund, 2006–. Chairman: OECD Econ. and Develt Review Cttee, 1967–71; Deputies Gp of Ten, 1976–78; Cttee of Gp of Ten, 1990–93; Co-Chm., Cttee on Crisis Mgt and Crisis Resolution in Emerging Markets, Inst. of Internat. Finance, 2003–. Dir, Stichting NYSE Euronext (Dutch Foundn); Trustee, NYSE Gp Trust I (US Trust), 2007–. Prés., Assoc. Internat. Cardinal Henri de Lubac. Mem., Acad. of Moral and Pol Scis, 1993; Hon. Mem., Société des Cincinnati de France, 1992. Grand Cordon: Order of Sacred Treasure (Japan), 1993; Order of the Brilliant Star (Taipei), 1998; Grand Cross, Order of Merit: Argentina, 1992; Italy, 1993; Stana Platina (Bulgaria), 1993; Order of Aztec Eagle (Mexico), 1994; Cross, Order of Merit (Germany), 1996; Comdr, Order of Merit (Poland), 1997; Order of Friendship (Russia), 1997; Order of Merit (Hungary), 1998; Comdr, Order of Southern Cross (Brazil), 1999; Order of Cross of Terra Mariana (Estonia), 2001. *Address:* BNP Paribas, 3 rue d'Antin, 75002 Paris, France.

de la RÚA, Fernando; President of Argentina, 1999–2001; *b* 15 Sept. 1937; *m* Inés Pertiné; three *c*. *Educ:* Liceo Militar General Paz, Córdoba Univ. (Dr of Laws). Mem., Unión Cívica Radical. Advr, Min. of the Interior, Argentina, 1963–66; Senator (UCR) for Buenos Aires, 1973–76 and 1989; Nat. Senator (UCR), 1983–89, 1992–99; Nat. Deputy (UCR), 1991; (Pres., UCR Gp); Mayor, City Buenos Aires, 1996. *Publication:* Operación Política: la causa del senado, 2006.

de la RUE, Sir Andrew (George Ilay), 4th Bt *cr* 1898, of Cadogan Square; company director; farmer; *b* 3 Feb. 1946; *s* of Sir Eric Vincent de la Rue, 3rd Bt and Cecilia (*d* 1963), *d* of late Maj. Walter Waring and Lady Clementine Waring, *d* of 10th Marquess of Tweedale; *S* father, 1989; *m* 1984, Tessa Ann, *er d* of David Dobson; two *s*. *Educ:* Millfield. With Lloyd's (Insurance), 1966; Dir, Private Company, 1976–. *Recreations:* shooting, coursing, tennis. *Heir: s* Edward Walter de la Rue, *b* 25 Nov. 1986. *Address:* Stragglethorpe Grange, Brant Broughton, Lincolnshire LN5 0RA. *T:* (01636) 626505.

de la TOUR, Frances; actress; *b* 30 July 1944; *d* of Charles de la Tour and Moyra (*née* Fessas); one *s* one *d*. *Educ:* Lycée français de Londres; Drama Centre, London. Royal Shakespeare Company, 1965–71: rôles include Audrey in As You Like It, 1967; Hoyden in The Relapse, 1969; Helena in A Midsummer Night's Dream (Peter Brooks's production), 1971 (also USA tour); Belinda in The Man of Mode, 1971; Violet in Small Craft Warnings, Comedy, 1973 (Best Supporting Actress, Plays and Players Award); Ruth Jones in The Banana Box, Apollo, 1973; Isabella in The White Devil, Old Vic, 1976; appearances at Hampstead Theatre, and Half Moon Theatre incl. title rôle in Hamlet, 1979; Stephanie in Duet for One, Bush Theatre and Duke of York's, 1980 (Best New Play, and Best Perf. by Actress, Drama Awards, Best Perf. by Actress in New Play, SWET Award, Best Actress, New Standard Award); Jean in Skirmishes, Hampstead, 1982 (also television, 1982); Sonya in Uncle Vanya, Haymarket, 1982; Josie in A Moon for the Misbegotten, Riverside, 1983 (SWET Best Actress award); title rôle in St Joan, NT, 1984; Dance of Death, Riverside, 1985; Sonya and Masha in Chekhov's Women, Lyric, 1985; Brighton Beach Memoirs, NT, 1986; Lillian, Lyric, 1986, Fortune, 1987; Façades, Lyric, Hammersmith, 1988; Regan in King Lear, Old Vic, 1989; Arkadina, Ranyevskaya and Olga Knipper in Chekhov's Women, Moscow Art Theatre, 1990; Miss Belzer in When She Danced, Globe, 1991 (Olivier Award); Witch in The Pope and the Witch, Comedy, 1992; Yoko Sitsuki in Greasepaint, Lyric, Hammersmith, 1993; Leonie in Les Parents Terribles, RNT, 1994; Three Tall Women, Wyndham's, 1994; Elinor in Blinded by the Sun, RNT, 1996; the woman in The Play about the Baby, Almeida, 1998; Raisa in The Forest, RNT, 1999; Cleopatra in Antony and Cleopatra, RSC, 1999; Jane in Fallen Angels, Apollo, 2000 (Variety Club Best Actress award); The Good Hope, 2001, Pinter Sketches, 2002, NT; Alice in Dance of Death, Lyric, 2003; Mrs Lintott in The History Boys, NT, 2004, NY, 2006 (Tony Award); Bertha in Boeing-Boeing, Comedy, 2007. *Films* include: Rising Damp, 1979 (Best Actress, New Standard British Film Award, 1980); The Cherry Orchard, 1998; Love Actually, 2002; Harry Potter and the Goblet of Fire, 2005; The History Boys, 2006; The Nutcracker, 2008. *Television* includes: Play for Today (twice), 1973–75; Rising Damp (series), 1974, 1976; Flickers, 1980; Duet for One, 1985; Cold Lazarus, 1995; Tom Jones, 1997; The Egg, 2002; Death on the Nile, 2003; Waking the Dead, 2004; Sensitive Skin, 2005. *Address:* c/o Claire Maroussas, Independent Talent Group Ltd, Oxford House, 76 Oxford Street, W1D 1BS. *T:* (020) 7636 6565.

DE LA WARR, 11th Earl *cr* 1761; **William Herbrand Sackville;** DL; Baron De La Warr, 1299 and 1572; Viscount Cantelupe 1761; Baron Buckhurst 1864; Director, Shore Capital Stockbrokers Ltd, since 2004; farmer; *b* 10 April 1948; *s* of 10th Earl De La Warr and of Anne Rachel, *d* of Geoffrey Devas, MC; *S* father, 1988; *m* 1978, Anne, Countess of Hopetoun, *e d* of Arthur Leveson; two *s* and two step *s*. *Educ:* Eton. Stockbroker, Credit Lyonnais Securities (formerly Laing & Cruickshank), 1980–2004. DL E Sussex, 2006. *Heir: s* Lord Buckhurst, *qv*. *Address:* Buckhurst Park, Withyham, Sussex TN7 4BL; 14 Bourne Street, SW1W 8JU. *Clubs:* White's, Turf.

See also Hon. T. G. Sackville.

DELAY, Thomas Auguste Read, CEng; Chief Executive, Carbon Trust, since 2001; *b* London, 15 April 1959; *s* of Francis and Jill Delay; *m* 1991, Valerie; two *s*. *Educ:* Univ. of Southampton (BSc Mech. Engrg 1981); INSEAD, Fontainbleau (MBA 1988). CEng, MIMechE 1985. Engrg/Ops Manager, Shell Djibouti, 1982–85; Project Engr, Shell UK, 1985–87; Sales/Mktg Manager, Shell Lubricants, 1988–90; Planning Manager, Shell UK, 1990–92; Gen. Manager, Pizo Shell, Gabon, 1992–96; Mgt Consultant, McKinsey & Co., 1996–98; Principal, A. T. Kearney, 1999–2001. *Recreations:* looking for powder snow, Surrey walks in my 1977 Fiat Spyder, cooking pasta, playing a reasonable game of tennis. *Address:* c/o The Carbon Trust, 8th Floor, 3 Clement's Inn, WC2A 2AZ. *T:* (020) 7170 7000; *e-mail:* tom.delay@carbontrust.co.uk.

DELBRIDGE, Richard; Director: Tate & Lyle PLC, since 2000; Fortis Group, since 2004; JP Morgan Cazenove Holdings, since 2005; *b* 21 May 1942; *s* of late Tom Delbridge and Vera Kate Delbridge (*née* Lancashire); *m* 1966, Diana Genevra Rose Bowers-Broadbent; one *s* two *d*. *Educ:* Copleston Sch., Ipswich; LSE (BSc Econ); Univ. of California at Berkeley (MBA). FCA. Arthur Andersen & Co., subseq. Andersen Consulting, 1963–66 and 1968–76, Partner 1974–76; Morgan Guaranty Trust Co., NY: Vice-Pres., 1976–79; Sen. Vice-Pres. and Comptroller of Morgan Guaranty Trust Co. and J. P. Morgan Inc., 1979–85; Sen. Vice-Pres. and Asst Gen. Manager, 1985–87, Man. Dir and Gen. Manager, 1987–89, London offices, J. P. Morgan Inc.; Dir, Group Finance, Midland Bank, 1990–92; Gp Finance Dir, HSBC Hldgs, 1993–95; Dir and Chief Financial Officer, NatWest Gp, 1996–2000. Director: Innogy plc, 2000–02; Egg plc, 2000–03; Cazenove Gp, 2002–05; Balfour Beatty plc, 2002–05; Gallaher Gp Plc, 2002–07. Member: Bd, Securities Assoc., 1988–89; UK Council, INSEAD, 1993–99; Financial Reporting Review Panel, 1998–2007. Dir, City Arts Trust, 1998–2001. Trustee, Wordsworth Trust, 2000–07. Mem. Council and Treas., Open Univ., 2001–. CCMI; FRSA. *Recreations:* hill walking, books.

DELIGHT, Ven. John David; Archdeacon of Stoke, 1982–90, Archdeacon Emeritus 1990; *b* 24 Aug. 1925; *s* of Rev. Sidney John Delight and Elizabeth Ethel (*née* Tuckett); *m* 1952, Eileen Elsie Braden; four *s* two *d*. *Educ:* Christ's Hospital, Horsham; Liverpool Univ.; Oak Hill Theol Coll.; Open Univ. RNVR (Fleet Air Arm), 1942–46. Curate, Tooting Graveney, 1952–55; Wallington, 1955–58; Travelling Sec., Inter-Varsity Fellowship, 1958–61; Vicar, St Christopher's, Leicester, 1961–69; Chaplain, Leicester Prison, 1965–67; Rector of Aldridge, 1969–82; RD, Walsall, 1981–82; Prebendary of Lichfield Cathedral, 1980–82; volunteer associate of Crosslinks (formerly BCMS) and CMS, to develop theol educn by extension in dio. of Machakos, Kenya, 1990–94; retired 1994 and licensed to officiate, dio. of Chester. Hon. Canon, All Souls Cathedral, Machakos. *Publication:* (contrib.) Families, Facts and Frictions, 1976. *Recreations:* travel, music, gardening, reading.

DE L'ISLE, 2nd Viscount *cr* 1956; **Philip John Algernon Sidney,** MBE 1977; Baron De L'Isle and Dudley 1835; Bt 1806; Bt 1818; Vice Lord-Lieutenant of Kent, since 2002; *b* 21 April 1945; *s* of 1st Viscount De L'Isle, VC, KG, GCMG, GCVO, PC and Hon. Jacqueline Vereker (*d* 1962), *o d* of Field-Marshal 6th Viscount Gort, VC, GCB, CBE, DSO, MVO, MC; *S* father, 1991; *m* 1980, Isobel Tresyllian, *y d* of Sir Edmund Compton, GCB, KBE; one *s* one *d*. *Educ:* Tabley House; Mons OCS; RMA Sandhurst. Commd Grenadier Guards, 1966. Served BAOR, UKLF, NI, Belize and Sudan at Regtl Duty; GSO3 Ops/SD HQ 3 Inf. Bde, 1974–76; retired 1979. Landowner, 1979–. Member: H of L Adv. Panel on Works of Art, 1994–97; Lord Chancellor's Adv. Council on Nat. Records and Archives, 2004–. Chm., Kent County Cttee, CLA, 1983–85. Chm., Canterbury Cathedral Trust Fund, 2007–. Hon. Colonel: 5th (V) Bn, Princess of Wales' Royal Regt, 1992–99; Kent ACF, 2006–. Freeman, City of London; Liveryman, Goldsmiths' Co. DL Kent, 1996. *Heir: s* Hon. Philip William Edmund Sidney, *b* 2 April 1985. *Address:* Penshurst Place, Penshurst, Tonbridge, Kent TN11 8DG. *T:* (01892) 870307, *Fax:* (01892) 870866; *e-mail:* delisle@penshurstplace.com. *Clubs:* White's, Pratt's.

de LISLE, Timothy John March Phillipps; journalist, since 1979; *b* 25 June 1962; *s* of late Everard March Phillipps de Lisle and of Hon. Mary Rose de Lisle (*née* Peake); *m* 1991, Amanda Barford; one *s* one *d*. *Educ:* Sunningdale; Eton; Worcester Coll., Oxford (BA Hons). Freelance journalist, 1979–86, revs and features for LAM, Smash Hits, Harpers & Queen and The Observer; Founder, Undergraduate Tutors, 1982–86; The Daily Telegraph: diary reporter, 1986–87; chief rock critic, 1986–89; news reporter, 1987; feature writer, 1987–89; arts editor, The Times, 1989; Weekend editor, The Daily Telegraph, 1989–90; Independent on Sunday: cricket correspondent, 1990–91; arts editor, 1991–95; freelance, 1995–: features: Independent on Sunday and Daily Telegraph, 1995–98; The Guardian G2, 2004–; cricket column: Independent, 1995–96; 1999–2003; Evening Standard, 1997–98; The Times, 2004–06; rock column, Mail on Sunday, 1999–; Wisden, 1996–2003: Editor: Wisden Cricket Monthly, 1996–2000 (Editor of the Year, Special Interest Mags, British Soc. of Mag. Editors, 1999); Wisden Online, 1999–2002; Wisden Cricketers' Almanack, 2003; Intelligent Life, 2008– (Dep. Ed., 2007–08); founder and consultant editor, Wisden Asia Cricket mag., 2001–05; columnist, Cricinfo.com, 2006–08. *Publications:* (ed) Lives of the Great Songs, 1994, rev. edn 1995; Young Wisden, 2007. *Recreations:* swimming, photography, reading His Dark Materials aloud. *Address:* c/o Mail on Sunday, 2 Derry Street, W8 5TS; *e-mail:* tim.delisle@gmail.com. *Clubs:* Eton Ramblers; Cricket Writers'.

DELL, Prof. Anne, PhD; FRS 2002; Professor of Carbohydrate Biochemistry, Imperial College London, since 1991; *b* 11 Sept. 1950; *d* of Edgar Dell and Elneth Dell; one *d*. *Educ:* Univ. of Western Australia (BSc); King's Coll., Cambridge (PhD). Imperial College: Lectr, 1979–86; Reader, 1986–91; Hd, Dept of Biochemistry, 1999–2001. Mem., BBSRC, 2007– (Professorial Fellow, 2002–07). *Recreations:* theatre, gardening, reading. *Address:* Division of Molecular Biosciences, Imperial College London, SW7 2AZ. *T:* (020) 7594 5219, *Fax:* (020) 7225 0458; *e-mail:* a.dell@imperial.ac.uk.

DELL, David Michael, CB 1986; Deputy Secretary, Department of Trade and Industry, 1983–91; *b* 30 April 1931; *s* of late Montague Roger Dell and Aimée Gabrielle Dell; partner, 1971, Eliseo Cabrejos (*d* 1995), Lima, Peru. *Educ:* Rugby Sch.; Balliol Coll., Oxford (MA). 2nd Lieut Royal Signals, Egypt and Cyprus, 1954–55. Admiralty, 195[illegible]; MoD, 1960; Min. of Technol., 1965; DTI, 1970; DoI, 1974, Under Sec., 1976; Regl Dir, Yorks and Humberside, DTI, 1976–78; Dir, EIB, 1984–87; Chief Exec., BOTB, 1987–91. Dir, Nesbit Evans Gp, 1991–93. Mem., British-Peruvian Trade & Investment Gp, 1997–2001. Chm., Christ Church Bentinck Sch., 1979–92. Sec., London Numismatic Club, 1995–97; Mem. Council, Oxford Soc., 1995–2001; Dep. Chm., Anglo-Peruvian Soc., 2005–07. *Clubs:* Oriental, Royal Automobile, St Stephen's.

DELL, Michael S.; Chairman, since 1984, Chief Executive Officer, 1984–2004 and since 2007, Dell Inc. (formerly PCs Ltd, then Dell Computer Corporation); *b* Houston, Texas, 23 Feb. 1965; *s* of Alexander and Lorraine Dell; *m* 1989, Susan Lieberman; four *c* (incl. twins). *Educ:* Univ. of Texas. Founder, PCs Ltd, 1984; co. renamed Dell Computer Corp., 1987. Member: Computer Systems Policy Proj.; The Business Council; Member Board, US Chamber of Commerce; World Econ. Forum. *Publication:* Direct From Dell: strategi that revolutionized an industry, 1999. *Address:* Dell Inc., 1 Dell Way, Round Rock, TX 78682, USA.

DELL, Dame Miriam (Patricia), ONZ 1993; DBE 1980 (CBE 1975); JP (NZ); Hon. President, International Council of Women, 1986–88 (President, 1979–86; Vice-President, 1976–79); *b* 14 June 1924; *d* of Gerald Wilfred Matthews and Ruby Miriam Crawford; *m* 1946, Richard Kenneth Dell; four *d.* *Educ:* Epsom Girls Grammar Sch.; Univ. of Auckland (BA); Auckland Teachers' Coll. (Teachers' Cert. (Secondary Sch.)). Teaching, 1945–47, 1957–58 and 1961–71. Nat. Pres., Nat. Council of Women, 1970–74 (Vice-Pres., 1967–70); Chm., Cttee on Women, NZ, 1974–81; Chm., Envmt and Conservation Orgns of NZ, 1989–94; Chm., 1993 Suffrage Centennial Year Trust, 1991–94; Chair, Landmarks Project - Celebrating Women Trust, 1999–. Member: Nat. Develt Council, 1969–74; Cttee of Inquiry into Equal Pay, 1971–72; Nat. Commn for UNESCO, 1974–83; Social Security Appeal Authority, 1974–99; Anglican Provincial Commn on Ordination of Women, 1974; Project Develt Bd, Mus. of NZ, 1988–92; Dep. Chm., Wellington Conservation Bd, 1990–98; Nat. Convener, Internat. Women's Year, 1975; Co-ordinator, Internat. Council of Women Develt Prog., 1988–91; Sec., Inter-Church Council on Public Affairs, 1986–89 (Chm., 1982–86); Convener, Public Affairs Unit, Anglican Church of NZ, 1988–92. JP NZ 1975. Jubilee Medal, 1977; NZ Commemoration Medal, 1990; NZ Suffrage Centennial Medal, 1993. *Publications:* Role of Women in National Development, 1970; numerous articles in popular and house magazines, on role and status of women. *Recreations:* gardening, reading, handcrafts, beachcombing. *Address:* 62 Venice Street, Martinborough 5711, New Zealand. *T:* (6) 3068836.

DELLAL, Jack; Chairman, Allied Commercial Holdings Ltd; *b* 2 Oct. 1923; *s* of Sulman and Charlotte Dellal; *m* 1st, 1952, Zehava Helmer (marr. diss. 1975); one *s* five *d* (and one *d* decd); 2nd, 1997, Ruanne Louw; one *s* one *d.* *Educ:* Heaton Moor Coll., Manchester. Chm., Dalton, Barton & Co. Ltd, 1962–72; Dep. Chm., Keyser Ullman Ltd, 1972–74; Chm., Highland Electronics Group Ltd, 1971–76; Director: Anglo African Finance PLC, 1983–; General Tire & Rubber (SA) Ltd, 1983–87; Williams, Hunt South Africa Ltd, 1983–87. Vice-Pres., Anglo-Polish Conservative Society, 1970–. Officer, Order of Polonia Restituta, 1970. Freeman Citizen of Glasgow, 1971. *Recreations:* lawn tennis, squash, music, art. *Clubs:* Royal Thames Yacht, Queen's, Hurlingham.

DELLER, Jeremy; artist; *b* London, 1966. *Educ:* Dulwich Coll.; Courtauld Inst. of Art (BA Art Hist. 1988); Sussex Univ. (MA Art Hist. 1992). Curator, producer and dir of projects, incl. orchestrated events, films and pubns. *Works include:* Acid Brass (collaboration with Williams Fairey Brass Band), 1997; (with A. Kane) Folk Archive, 2000; The Battle of Orgreave (filmed re-enactment), 2001; Social Parade (video), Five Memorials, This is US (CD), 2003; Memory Bucket (mixed-media installation), 2003 (Turner Prize, 2004); group exhibn, New British Art 2000: Intelligence, Tate Britain, 2000. Mem. Bd, Artangel, 2005–. Trustee, Tate Gall., 2007– (Mem., Collection Cttee); Mem. Council, Tate Liverpool. *Address:* c/o Tate Britain, Millbank, SW1P 4RG.

DELLOW, Sir John (Albert), Kt 1990; CBE 1985 (OBE 1979); DL; Deputy Commissioner, Metropolitan Police, 1987–91; *b* 5 June 1931; *s* of Albert Reginald and Lily Dellow; *m* 1952, Heather Josephine Rowe; one *s* one *d.* *Educ:* William Ellis Sch., Highgate; Royal Grammar Sch., High Wycombe. Joined City of London Police, 1951; seconded Manchester City Police, 1966; Superintendent, Kent County Constabulary, 1966, Chief Supt, 1968; jssc 1969; Asst Chief Constable, Kent Co. Constabulary, 1969; Metropolitan Police: Deputy Assistant Commissioner: Traffic Planning, 1973; Personnel, 1975; No 2 Area, 1978; 'A' Dept Operations, 1979; Inspectorate, 1980; Assistant Commissioner: 'B' Dept, 1982; Crime, 1984; Asst Comr (Specialist Ops), 1985–87. Pres., ACPO, 1989–90 (Vice-Pres., 1988–89). Former Chairman: Metropolitan Police History Soc.; Metropolitan Police Climbing, Canoe, Rowing and Heavy Boat Sections; Cdre, Metropolitan Police Sailing Club. Member Council: London Dist, Order of St John of Jerusalem, 1988–96; RUSI, 1991–95. DL Greater London, 1991. *Publications:* contrib. RUSI Defence Studies series and other jls. *Recreations:* walking, history, listening to wireless, water colour painting.

DELORS, Jacques Lucien Jean; President, Council for Employment, Income and Social Cohesion, since 2000; President, Commission of the European Economic Community, 1985–95; *b* Paris, 20 July 1925; *s* of Louis Delors and Jeanne (*née* Rigal); *m* 1948, Marie Lephaille; one *d* (one *s* decd). *Educ:* Paris Univ.; Dip., Centre for Higher Studies of Banking. Joined Banque de France, 1945; in office of Chief of Securities Dept, 1950–62, and in Sect. for the Plan and Investments, Conseil Economique et Social, 1959–61; Chief of Social Affairs, Gen. Commissariat of Plan Monnet, 1962–68; Gen. Sec. for Perm. Trng and Social Promotion, 1968; Gen. Sec., Interministerial Cttee for Professional Educn, 1969–73; Mem., Gen. Council, Banque de France, 1973–79, and Dir, on leave of absence, 1973. Special Advr on Social and Cultural Affairs to Prime Minister, 1969–72. Socialist Party Spokesman on internat. econ. matters, 1976–81; Minister of the Economy and Finance, 1981–83; Minister of Economy, Finance and Budget, 1983–84. Mem., European Parlt, 1979–81 (Pres., Econ. and Financial Cttee, 1979–81). Mayor of Clichy, 1983–84. Pres., Internat. Commn on Educn for the Twenty First Century, UNESCO, 1993–96. Associate Prof., Univ. of Paris-Dauphine, 1973–79. Dir, Work and Society Res. Centre, 1975–79; President: Bd of Admin, College of Europe, Bruges, 1996–2000; Notre Europe, 1996–2004. Founder, Club Echange et Projets, 1974–79. Hon. doctorates from 24 univs. Awards and honours from 15 countries. *Publications:* Les indicateurs sociaux, 1971; Changer, 1975; (jtly) En sortir ou pas, 1985; La France par L'Europe, 1988 (Our Europe: the community and national development, 1992); Le Nouveau Concert Européen, 1992; L'unité d'un homme, 1994; Combats pour l'Europe, 1996; Mémoires, 2004; L'Europe tragique et magnifique, 2006; essays, articles and UN reports on French Plan. *Address:* Conseil de l'emploi, des revenus et de la cohésion sociale, 113 rue de Grenelle, 75007 Paris, France; *e-mail:* jacques.delors@cerc.gouv.fr.

DELPY, Prof. David Thomas, DSc; FMedSci; FRS 1999; FREng; ; Chief Executive, Engineering and Physical Sciences Research Council, since 2007; *b* 11 Aug. 1948; *s* of R. M. Delpy and M. H. Delpy; *m* 1972, Margaret E. Kimber; two *s.* *Educ:* Heaton Grammar Sch., Newcastle upon Tyne; Brunel Univ. (BSc 1st Cl. Hons Applied Phys); UCL (DSc Med. Phys London). Technical Mgt Services, Darchem Ltd, Darlington, 1970–71; Non-clinical Lectr, UCL Med. Sch., 1971–76; University College Hospital, London: Sen. Physicist, 1976–82; Principal Physicist, 1982–86; University College London: Sen. Lectr, 1986–91; Hd, Dept of Med. Phys and Bioengrg, 1992–99; Hamamatsu Prof. of Med. Photonics, 1991–2007; Vice Provost, 1999–2007. Mem., BBSRC, 2004–07. FMedSci 2000; FREng 2002. *Publications:* numerous scientific papers. *Recreations:* work, classical music, gardening. *Address:* Engineering and Physical Sciences Research Council, Polaris House, North Star Avenue, Swindon SN2 1ET.

DELVIN, Lord; title borne by eldest son of Earl of Westmeath, *qv*; not at present used.

DELVIN, Dr David George; television and radio broadcaster, writer and doctor; Director, The Medical Information Service, since 1995; *b* 28 Jan. 1939; *s* of William Delvin, Ayrshire and Elizabeth Falvey, Kerry; *m* 1st, Kathleen Sears, SRN, SCM; two *s* one *d*; 2nd, Christine Webber. *Educ:* St Dunstan's Coll.; King's Coll., Univ. of London; King's Coll. Hosp. (MB, BS 1962; psychol medicine, forensic medicine and public health prizes, 1962). LRCP, MRCS 1962; MRCGP 1974; DObstRCOG 1965; DCH 1966; DipVen, Soc. of Apothecaries, 1977; FPA Cert. 1972; FPA Instructing Cert. 1974. Dir, Hosp. Medicine Film Unit, 1968–69. Vice-Chm., 1982–87, Chm., 2007–, Med. Journalists' Assoc.; General Medical Council: Elected Mem., 1979–94; Member: Health Cttee 1980–86; Professional Conduct Cttee, 1987–94; Standards & Ethics Cttee, 1992–94. Member: Educn Cttee, Back Pain Assoc., 1983–87; Faculty of Family Planning, RCOG, 1993–. Medical Consultant: FPA, 1981–90; Nat. Assoc. of Family Planning Doctors, 1990–93; Medical Advisor to: various BBC and ITV progs, 1974–; NetDoctor website, 1999–. Med. Editor, General Practitioner, 1972–90; Sen. Editor, The Lancet, 1996–98; Chm., Editorial Boards of Medeconomics, Monthly Index of Med. Specialities, and MIMS Magazine, 1988–91; Mem. Editorial Adv. Bd, British Jl of Family Planning, 1994–2002; Dr Jekyll Columnist in World Medicine, 1973–82; Columnist, BMA News Review, 1992–98; Med. Columnist, Glasgow Herald, 1995–97. Fellow, Faculty of Reproductive Health Care, RCOG, 2005. Cert. of Special Merit, Med. Journalists' Assoc., 1974 and (jtly) 1975. American Medical Writers' Assoc. Best Book Award, 1976; Consumer Columnist of the Year Award, 1986. Médaille de la Ville de Paris (échelon argent), 1983. *Publications:* The Good Sex Guide, 1994, and other books, articles, TV and radio scripts, short stories, humorous pieces, medical films and videos; papers on hypertension and contraception in BMJ etc. *Recreations:* athletics, opera, orienteering, scuba-diving, hang-gliding (retired hurt). *Address:* c/o Coutts, 2 Harley Street, W1A 1EE. *Club:* Royal Society of Medicine.

DEMACK, (James) David; a Special Commissioner of Income Tax, since 2000; Vice-President for England and Wales, VAT and Duties Tribunals, since 2001; *b* 1 March 1942; *s* of James and Edith Annie Demack; *m* 1969, Ruth Cicely Hosker. *Educ:* Balshaw's Grammar Sch., Leyland, Lancs; Manchester Univ.; Manchester Poly.; Salford Poly. CTA (FTII 1982). Admitted solicitor, 1965; solicitor, private practice, 1965–93. Mem., 1986–92, pt-time Chm., 1990–93, full-time Chm., 1993–2001, VAT Tribunals, subseq. VAT and Duties Tribunals. Mem. UK Panel, Adv. Commn under EU Arbitration Convention, EU Jt Transfer Pricing Forum, 2002–. Trustee, Cuerden Valley Park Trust, 1998–. *Recreations:* rehabilitation of disabled wild birds of prey, walking, golf, classical music, railways. *Address:* Combined Tax Tribunals, 9th Floor, West Point, 501 Chester Road, Old Trafford, Manchester M16 9HU. *T:* (0161) 868 6600, *Fax:* (0161) 876 4479; *e-mail:* David.Demack@judiciary.gsi.gov.uk. *Clubs:* Royal Over-Seas League; Leyland Golf.

de MARCHANT et d'ANSEMBOURG, Count Jan Mark Vladimir Anton; Ambassador of the Netherlands to the Court of St James's, 2003–06; *b* 9 Oct. 1941; *s* of Count François de Marchant et d'Ansembourg and Fernandine, Countess de Bombelles; *m* 1979, Countess Nicole de Marchant et d'Ansembourg-Rougé; (one *s* decd). *Educ:* Leyden Univ. (MA Law). Lieut, military service, 1961–63; diplomatic postings, Damascus, NY, The Hague, 1970–82; Counsellor, Paris, 1982; Dep. Hd of Delegation, CSCE Meeting, Vienna, 1986; Dir, UN Dept, Min. of Foreign Affairs, 1989; Dep. Permanent Rep., Permanent Mission to NY, 1990–94; Dir European Dept, Min. of Foreign Affairs, 1994–96; Ambassador at large, 1996; Dep. Political Dir, 1997; Ambassador to Spain, 1998–2003. Officer, Order of Orange Nassau (Netherlands), 1994; Commander: Cross of St Olav (Norway), 1996; Ordre du Mérite (France), 1997; Grand Cross, Isabella la Católica (Spain), 2001. *Address:* 9 rue Colbert, 7800 Versailles, France. *Club:* Haagsche (The Hague).

de MARCO, Prof. Guido, KUOM 1999; LLD; President of Malta, 1999–2004; Lecturer and Professor of Criminal Law, University of Malta, since 1967; *b* 22 July 1931; *s* of Emanuele de Marco and Giovanna (*née* Raniolo); *m* 1956, Violet Saliba; one *s* two *d.* *Educ:* St Joseph High Sch.; St Aloysius Coll.; Royal Univ. of Malta (BA Philosophy, Econs and Italian 1952; LLD 1955). Warrant of Advocate, Superior Courts of Malta, 1956; Crown Counsel, 1964–66. MP (Nat.) Malta, 1966–99; Dep. Prime Minister and Minister of Interior and Justice, 1987–90; Dep. Prime Minister and Minister of Foreign Affairs, 1990–96; Shadow Minister and Opposition Spokesman on Foreign Affairs, 1996–98; Dep. Prime Minister and Minister of Foreign Affairs, 1998–99. Nationalist Party: Sec. Gen., 1972–77; Dep. Leader, 1977–99. Rep. of Maltese Parlt, Council of Europe, 1967–87 and 1996–98 (Chm., Monitoring Cttee, 1997–98); Pres., UN Gen. Assembly (45th Session), 1990. Hon. LLD Seconda Università degli Studi di Napoli, 1999. *Publications:* A Presidency with a Purpose: United Nations General Assembly 45th Session, 1991; Malta's Foreign Policy in the Nineties: its evolution and progression, 1996; (with M. Bartolo) A Second Generation United Nations: for peace in freedom in the 21st century, 1997; Momentum, 2001; Momentum II, 2004. *Recreations:* reading, travelling. *Address:* L'Orangerie, Mile End Street, Hamrun, Malta.

DEMARCO, Prof. Richard, CBE 2007 (OBE 1985); RSW; Professor of European Cultural Studies, Kingston University, 1993–2000, now Professor Emeritus; *b* 9 July 1930; *s* of Carmine Demarco and Elizabeth (*née* Fusco); *m* 1957, Anne Muckle. *Educ:* Holy Cross Academy, Edinburgh; Edinburgh College of Art. National Service, KOSB and RAEC, 1954–56. Art Master, Duns Scotus Academy, Edinburgh, 1956–67; Co-Founder, Traverse Theatre Club; Vice-Chm. and Director, Traverse Art Gall., 1963–67; Dir, Richard Demarco Gall., Melville Crescent, Edinburgh, 1966–92, appointed by co-founders John Martin, Andrew Elliott and James Walker; introduced contemporary visual arts into official Edinburgh Festival programme with Edinburgh Open 100 Exhibn, 1967; introduced work of 330 internat. artists to UK, mainly through Edinburgh Fest. exhibns, from Canada, 1968, W Germany, 1970, Romania, 1971, Poland, 1972 and 1979, France, 1973, Austria, 1973, Yugoslavia, 1975, Aust. and NZ, 1984, Netherlands, 1990; incl. Joseph Beuys, 1970, Gunther Uecker, 1991, and Tadeusz Kantor's Cricot Theatre, with prodns of The Water Hen, 1972, Lovelies and Dowdies, 1973, The Dead Class, 1976. Has presented, 1969–, annual programmes of theatre, music and dance prodns, incl. the Freehold Company's Antigone, 1970; Dublin Project Company's On Baille Strand, 1977; Mladen Materio's Obala Theatre from Sarajevo, 1988 and 1989; Teatro Settimo from Turin, and Grupa Chwilowa from Lublin, 1991; Yvette Bozsik Theatre from Budapest, 1993; prod Macbeth for Edinburgh Fest., on Inchcolm Is, 1988 and 1989. Director: Sean Connery's Scottish Internat. Educn Trust, 1972–74; Edinburgh Arts annual summer sch. and expedns, 1972–92; Artistic Advr, Eur. Youth Parlt, 1992–. Has directed annual exhibn prog. with Special Unit, HM Prison, Barlinnie, with partic. reference to sculpture of James Boyle, 1974–80; directed Edinburgh Fest. Internat. Confs, Towards the Housing of Art in the 21st Century, 1983, Art and the Human Environment, 1984 (also at Dublin Fest.). Was subject of film, Walkabout Edinburgh, dir. by Edward McConnell, 1970; acted in feature films: Long Shot, 1978; That Sinking Feeling, 1980; subject of TV film, The Demarco Dimension, 1987. Has broadcast regularly on television and radio, 1966–; has lectured in over 150 univs, art colls, schools, art galls; as water-colour painter and printmaker is represented in over 1600 public and private collections, incl. Nat. Gall. of Modern Art of Scotland, V&A Museum, Scottish Arts Council. Trustee: Kingston Demarco European Art Foundn, 1993–; Green Cross (UK), 1999–; Vice-Pres., Kingston

Th. Trust, 2001–. Contributing Editor, Studio International, 1982–. SSA 1964; RWSScot 1966. Mem., AICA, 1992; FRSA 1998. Hon. FRIAS 1991; HRSA 2001; Hon. Fellow, Inst. of Contemp. Scotland, 2002. Hon. DFA Atlanta Coll. of Art, 1993. Gold Order of Merit, Polish People's Republic, 1976; Order of the Cavaliere della Repubblica d'Italia, 1987; Chevalier de l'Ordre des Arts et des Lettres, France, 1991. *Publications:* The Artist as Explorer, 1978; The Road to Meikle Seggie, 1978; A Life in Pictures, 1994. *Recreations:* exploring: the small and secret spaces in townscape; cathedrals, abbeys, parish churches; coastlines and islands and The Road to Meikle Seggie. *Address:* 23A Lennox Street, Edinburgh EH4 1PY. *T:* (0131) 343 2124. *Club:* Scottish Arts (Hon. Mem.) (Edinburgh).

de MAULEY, 7th Baron *cr* 1838; **Rupert Charles Ponsonby,** TD 1988; *b* 30 June 1957; *s* of Hon. Thomas Maurice Ponsonby, TD and of Maxine Henrietta Ponsonby (*née* Thellusson); *S* uncle, 2002; *m* 2002, Hon. Lucinda Katherine Fanshawe Royle, *d* of Baron Fanshawe of Richmond, KCMG. *Educ:* Eton. FCA 1990 (ACA 1980). Director: Samuel Montagu & Co. Ltd, 1990–93; Standard Chartered Merchant Bank Asia Ltd, Singapore, 1994–99 (Man. Dir, 1996–99); FixIT Worldwide Ltd, 1999–2006. CO, The Royal Wessex Yeomanry (TA), 2003–04 (commnd, 1976). Elected Mem., H of L, March 2005; Opposition Whip and Opposition BERR (formerly DTI) spokesman, 2005–; Opposition spokesman, Cabinet Office, 2006–. *Heir: b* Hon. (Ashley) George Ponsonby [*b* 17 Nov. 1959; *m* 2006, Mrs Camilla Gordon Lennox (*née* Pilkington)]. *Club:* Cavalry and Guards.

DEMBRI, Mohamed-Salah; Ambassador of Algeria to the Court of St James's, and also to Ireland, since 2005; *b* 30 Jan. 1938; *s* of Hardjem Dembri and Zelikha Dembri (*née* Bendaoud); *m* 1960, Monique Paule Alleaume; one *s* one *d. Educ:* Sorbonne Univ. (BA; Higher Educn Dip.). Secretary General: Min. of Higher Educn and Scientific Res., 1973–79; Min. of Foreign Affairs, 1979–82; Ambassador to Canada, 1982–84; Sec. Gen., Min. of Labour and Social Affairs, 1988–89; Official Rep. (Special Advr) to Hd of Govt on political and diplomatic issues, 1989–91; Ambassador to Hellenic Republic, 1991–93; Minister of Foreign Affairs, 1993–96; Ambassador to UN, Geneva, 1996–2004 and (non-resident), to Holy See, 1997–2004. Jubilee Medal (Bulgaria), 1979; Kt, Nat. Order of Chad, 1994; Gt Cross, Order of St Gregory the Gt (Vatican), 1999; Grand Officer, Nat. Order of Mono (Togo), 2002. *Publications:* contribs to Algerian Arts and Human Scis Rev., Algerian Notebooks of Comparative Lit., and publications of Algerian Inst. of Global Strategy and UN; papers on Euro-Mediterranean relations and on St Augustine. *Recreations:* reading, cinema, theatre, sight-seeing, tourism. *Address:* Embassy of the People's Democratic Republic of Algeria, 54 Holland Park, W11 3RS. *T:* (020) 7221 7800, *Fax:* (020) 7221 0448, (020) 7792 5513; *e-mail:* msdembri@algerianembassy.org.uk.

DEMERITTE, Richard Clifford; Managing Partner, MGI Richard C. Demeritte & Co., Chartered Accountants, since 1997; Auditor-General, Commonwealth of the Bahamas, 1980–84 and 1988–96; *b* 27 Feb. 1939; *s* of R. H. Demeritte and late Miriam Demeritte (*née* Whitfield); *m* 1966, Ruth Smith; one *s* two *d. Educ:* Bahamas Sch. of Commerce; Metropolitan Coll., London; Century Univ., USA. Treasury Department, Bahamas: Asst Accountant, 1967; Accountant, 1969–71; Asst Treasurer, Jan.–Dec. 1972; Dep. Treasurer, 1973–79; High Comr, London, 1984–88; Amb. to EEC, 1986–88, and to Belgium, France, FRG, 1987–88. Exec. Partner, Caribo Partners, 1996–. Mem., Midsnell Gp Internat. (Mem. Nominating Cttee, N America, 1999–); Pres., Universal Financial and Business Consultants, 1996–. Fellow: Inst. of Admin. Accountants, London, 1969; Corp. of Accountants and Auditors, Bahamas, 1971 (Pres., 1973–84; Hon. Fellow, 1983); Assoc. of Internat. Accountants, 1976 (Pres./Chm. Council, 1985); FCGA 1996 (Certified Gen. Accountant, 1982); Mem., Bahamas Inst. of Chartered Accountants, 1991; Certified Fraud Examr, 2001. President: Certified Gen. Accts Assoc., Bahamas, 1996–; Certified Gen. Accts Assoc., Caribbean, 1996–; Mem., Nat. Assoc. of Fraud Investigators, 2001–. FCMI (FBIM 1985); FRSA 1988. Hon. Life Pres.: YMCA (Grand Bahama); Toastmasters Internat. (Grand Bahama). *Recreations:* chess, golf, billiards, weightlifting. *Address:* (office) PO Box CB 11001, Nassau, Bahamas; (home) Rurick, Cable Beach, PO Box CB 11001, Nassau, Bahamas.

DEMEURE de LESPAUL, Edouard Henri; Officer, Order of Leopold II; General Manager, Marketing, Petrofina SA, 1993; *b* 6 Jan. 1928; *s* of Charles Demeure de Lespaul and Adrienne Demeure de Lespaul (*née* Escoyez); *m* 1953, Myriam van Cutsem; two *d. Educ:* Univ. of Louvain (Mining Engineering); ENSP 1952 (Petroleum Engineering). Petrofina: Exploration and Production Dept, Brussels, 1952–53; Manager, Drilling Activities, Congo, 1955–56; Man. Dir, Egypt, 1956–61; Manager, Exploration and Production, Brussels, 1961–63; Chm. and Man. Dir, Finaneste NV, Belgium, 1963–89; Man. Dir and Chief Exec., Petrofina UK, later Fina plc, 1989–92. Military Medal, war voluntary. *Recreations:* swimming, history reading, mountain walking.

De MEYER, Prof. Arnoud Cyriel Leo, PhD; Director, Judge Business School, University of Cambridge, since 2006; *b* 12 April 1954; *s* of Eugeen De Meyer and Emma (*née* De Winter). *Educ:* Univ. of Ghent (MSc Electrical Engrg; PhD Mgt 1983). Institut Européen d'Administration des Affaires (INSEAD): Prof. of Technol. Mgt, 1983–2006; Associate Dean for Exec. Educn, 1992–99; Dir Gen., Euro-Asia Centre, 1995–99; Akzo Nobel Fellow in Strategic Mgt, 1997–2006; Dean, Campus in Asia, 1999–2002; Dep. Dean, then Dean of Admin and Ext. Relns, 2001–06. Pt-time Prof., De Vlerick Leuven Gent Mgt Sch., Univ. of Ghent, 1988–2004. Vis. Prof., Grad. Sch. of Business Admin, Waseda Univ., Tokyo, 1999–2000. Board Member: Option Internat., NV, 1997–; Dassault Systemes, 2005–. *Publications:* (jtly) Benchmarking for Global Manufacturing, 1992; Creating Product Value: a strategic manufacturing perspective, 1992; (jtly) The Bright Stuff, 2001; Belgique On Line: 30 propositions pour la e-Belgique de demain, 2002; (jtly) Global Future, The Next Challenge for Asian Business, 2005; (with S. Garg) Inspire to Innovate, Management of Innovation in Asia, 2005; (jtly) Managing the Unknown: a new approach to managing high uncertainty and risk in projects, 2006; (jtly) The Information Society in an Enlarged Europe, 2006; contrib. articles to jls incl. R&D Mgt, IEEE Trans on Engrg Mgt, Sloan Mgt Rev., Strategic Mgt Jl. *Address:* Judge Business School, Trumpington Street, Cambridge CB2 1AG.

DEMIDENKO, Nikolai Anatolyevich; concert pianist; *b* 1 July 1955; *s* of Anatoli Antonovich Demidenko and Olga Mikhailovna Demidenko; granted British citizenship, 1995; *m* 1994, Julia B. Dovgiallo; one *s* by a previous marriage. *Educ:* Gnessin Music Sch., Moscow; Moscow State Conservatoire. Professional début, 1975; British début, 1985; NY début, 2001. Teacher: Moscow State Conservatoire, 1979–84; Yehudi Menuhin Sch. of Music, 1990–95; Vis. Prof., Univ. of Surrey. 2nd prize, Montreal Piano Competition, 1976; 3rd prize, Moscow Tchaikovsky Competition, 1978. Has made numerous recordings. Gramophone Award, 1992; Classic CD Award, 1995. *Recreations:* photography, computing. *Address:* Georgina Ivor Associates, 28 Old Devonshire Road, SW12 9RB.

de MILLE, Peter Noël; His Honour Judge de Mille; a Circuit Judge, since 1992 (Midland and Oxford Circuit, 1992–2002; South Eastern Circuit, since 2002); *b* 19 Nov. 1944; *s* of late Noël James de Mille and Ailsa Christine de Mille (*née* Ogilvie); *m* 1977, Angela Mary Cooper; one *d. Educ:* Fettes Coll.; Trinity Coll., Dublin (BA, LLB). Called to the Bar, Inner Temple, 1968; a Recorder, 1987–92. *Recreations:* sailing, music, theatre. *Address:* Judges Chambers, Crown and County Court, Crown Buildings, Rivergate, Peterborough PE1 1EJ. *Club:* Aldeburgh Yacht.

de MOLEYNS; *see* Daubeny de Moleyns, family name of Baron Ventry.

de MOLLER, June Frances; Managing Director, Carlton Communications plc, 1993–99; *b* 25 June 1947; *m* 1st, 1967 (marr. diss. 1980); 2nd, 1996, John Robert Giles Crisp. *Educ:* Roedean; Hastings Coll.; Sorbonne Univ., Paris. Exec. Dir, Carlton Communications, 1983–99. Non-executive Director: Anglian Water plc, 1992–2000; Riverside Mental Health NHS Trust, 1992–96; Lynx Gp plc, 1999–2002; Cookson Gp plc, 1999–2004; British Telecommunications plc, 1999–2002; J. Sainsbury plc, 1999–2005; Archant (formerly Eastern Counties Newspapers Gp) Ltd, 1999–; London Merchant Securities plc, subseq. Derwent London plc, 2002–; Temple Bar Investment Trust plc, 2006–. Mem., Listed Cos Adv. Cttee, Stock Exchange, 1998–99. Mem., Adv. Bd, Judge Inst. for Management Studies, Cambridge, 1996–2004. Member Council: Aldeburgh Productions 2000–; UEA, 2002–. Mem. Cttee, Home of Rest for Horses, 1999–2005. *Recreations* reading, tennis, breeding Red Poll cows.

de MONTEBELLO, (Guy) Philippe (Lannes); Director, since 1978, and Chief Executive Officer, since 1999, Metropolitan Museum of Art; *b* 16 May 1936; *s* of Roger Lannes de Montebello and Germaine (*née* Croisset); *m* 1961, Edith Bradford Myles; two *s* one *d. Educ:* Harvard Coll. (BA *magna cum laude*); New York Univ., Inst. of Fine Arts (MA). Curatorial Asst, European Paintings, Metropolitan Mus. of Art, 1963; Asst Curator Associate Curator, MMA, until 1969; Director, Museum of Fine Arts, Houston, Texas 1969–74; Vice-Director: for Curatorial Affairs, MMA, Jan.–June 1974; for Curatorial and Educnl Affairs, 1974–77; Actg Dir, MMA, 1977–78. Gallatin Fellow, New York Univ. 1981; Hon. LLD: Lafayette Coll., East Pa, 1979; Bard Coll., Annandale-on-Hudson, NY 1981; Dartmouth Coll., 2004; Hon. DFA Iona Coll., New Rochelle, NY, 1982; Hon DArts: Harvard, 2006; New York, 2007. Alumni Achievement Award, New York Univ. 1978; Nat. Medal of Arts (USA), 2003; Amigos del Museo del Prado Prize, 2004. Officier Ordre Nat. de la Légion d'Honneur (France), 2005. *Publication:* Peter Paul Rubens, 1968 *Club:* Knickerbocker (New York).

DEMPSEY, Andrew; *see* Dempsey, J. A.

DEMPSEY, Dr Anthony Michael; Headmaster, Tiffin School, 1988–2004; *b* 12 June 1944; *s* of Michael and Bertha Laura Dempsey; *m* 1970, Sandra Lynn Atkins; one *s. Educ* Tiffin Sch.; Bristol Univ. (BSc, PhD). Chemistry Teacher, King's College Sch., 1969–73 Heathland School, Hounslow: Head of Sci., 1973–75; Head, Maths and Sci. Faculty 1975–79; Feltham Community School: Dep. Head, 1979–82; Sen. Dep. Head, 1982–88 *Publications:* Visual Chemistry, 1983; Science Master Pack, 1985; contrib. to Nuffield Chemistry books; papers in carbohydrate res. *Recreations:* walking, travel, sport, church industrial archaeology. *Address:* 63 Gilpin Crescent, Twickenham TW2 7BP. *T:* (020 8898 2860.

DEMPSEY, (James) Andrew; independent exhibition curator and organiser, since 1996 *b* 17 Nov. 1942; *s* of James Dempsey, Glasgow; *m* 1st, 1966, Grace (marr. diss. 1998), *d* of Dr Ian MacPhail, Dumbarton; one *s* one *d*; 2nd, 2006, Catherine, *d* of Chester Lampert Bethesda, Md. *Educ:* Ampleforth Coll.; Glasgow Univ. Whistler Research Asst, Fine Art Dept, Univ. of Glasgow, 1963–65; exhibn work for art dept of Arts Council, 1966–71 Keeper, Dept of Public Relations, V&A, 1971–75; Asst Dir of Exhibitions, Arts Council of GB, 1975–87; Asst Dir, 1987–94, Associate Curator, 1994–96, Hayward Gall., S Bank Centre. *T:* (020) 7241 2065.

DEMPSEY, Michael Bernard, RDI 1994; FCSD; Founder, Studio Dempsey, 2008; *b* 2 July 1944; *s* of John Patrick Dempsey and Britannia May (*née* Thompson); *m* 1st, 1967 Sonja Green (marr. diss. 1988); two *s* one *d*; 2nd, 1989, Charlotte Antonia Richardson three *d. Educ:* St Vincent RC Primary Sch., Dagenham; Bishop Ward RC Secondar Mod. Sch., Dagenham. Asst designer, Cheveron Studio, 1963–64; in-house designer Bryan Colmer Artist Agent, 1964–65; freelance designer, 1965–66; Designer, Cato Peter O'Brien, 1966–68; Art Director: William Heinemann Publishers, 1968–74; William Collins Publishers, 1974–79; Founder Partner, Carroll & Dempsey Ltd, 1979–85; Partner 1985–2007, Chm. and Creative Dir, 1993–2007, Carroll, Dempsey Thirkell Ltd, late CDT Design Ltd. Consultant Art Dir to Royal Mail for 1999 Millennium stamps 1997–99, designer: Mind and Matter stamps, 2000; Definitive stamps, Sounds of Britai stamps, 2006; identity and communications consultant, DCMS, 1997–99; Art Dir an Mem., Editl Bd, RSA Jl, 1997–2002; feature writer: Design Week, 2001–; Blueprin 2006–. Pres., British Design and Art Dirs Assoc., 1997–98. Master of Faculty, RDI 2005–07. Member: AGI, 1998–2000; BAFTA, 2003–. *Publications:* Bubbles: earl advertising art from A. & F. Pears, 1978; The Magical Paintings of Justin Todd, 1978; Pip Dreams: early advertising art from the Imperial Tobacco Company, 1982. *Recreation* living. *Address:* The Hayloft, Church Lane, Osmington, Dorset DT3 6EZ. *T:* (01305 832520. *Club:* Groucho.

DEMPSTER, John William Scott, CB 1994; Director, United Kingdom Major Por Group Ltd, 1999–2007; *b* 10 May 1938; *m* 1965, Ailsa Newman (marr. diss. 1972). *Edu* Plymouth Coll.; Oriel Coll., Oxford (MA(PPE)). HM Inspector of Taxes, Inlan Revenue, 1961–65; Ministry of Transport: Asst Principal, 1965–67; Principal, 1967–7 Asst Sec., Property Services Agency, 1973–76; Principal Private Sec. to Sec. of State fo the Environment, 1976–77; Asst Sec., Dept of Transport, 1977–80; Principal Estabt an Finance Officer, Lord Chancellor's Dept, 1980–84; Department of Transport: Head o Marine Directorate, 1984–89; Principal Establishment Officer, 1989–90; Princip Establishment and Finance Officer, 1990–91; Dir Gen. of Highways, 1991–94; Dep. Sec Aviation and Shipping, 1994–96; Dir, Bahamas Maritime Authy, 1996–99. Hon. Sec Parly Maritime Gp, 2008–. *Recreations:* mountaineering, sailing, bridge, Munro collectin *Address:* 7 Willow Bridge Road, N1 2LB. *T:* (020) 7226 7553. *Clubs:* Fell and Rock; Swi Alpine (Pres., Association of British Members, 2006–).

DEMPSTER, Prof. Michael Alan Howarth, PhD; Professor of Management, Judg Institute of Management, 1996–2005, now Emeritus, and Director, Centre for Financi Research, since 1997, University of Cambridge (Director of Research, 1997–200 Director, PhD Programme, 1997–2002); Fellow, Hughes Hall, Cambridge, since 2002; 10 April 1938; *s* of Cedric William Dempster and Honor Fitz Simmons Dempster (*n* Gowan); *m* 1st, 1963, Ann Laura Lazier (marr. diss. 1980); one *d*; 2nd, 1981, Eler Anatolievna Medova; one *d. Educ:* Univ. of Toronto (BA 1961); Carnegie-Mellon Uni (MS 1963; PhD 1965); Oxford Univ. (MA 1967); Cambridge Univ. (MA 2005). IB Res. Fellow, Math. Inst., Oxford, 1965–66; Jun. Res. Fellow, Nuffield Coll., Oxfor 1966; Fellow, Tutor and Univ. Lectr in Maths, 1967–81, Lectr in Maths, 1982–87, Balli Coll., Oxford; R. A. Jodrey Res. Prof. of Mgt and Inf. Scis, Sch. of Business Admin, an Prof. of Maths, Stats and Computing Science, Dalhousie Univ., 1981–93; Prof. of Math 1990–95, and Dir, Inst. for Studies in Finance, 1993–95, Univ. of Essex. Fellow, Cent for Advanced Study in Behavioral Scis, Stanford, 1974–75; Sen. Res. Scholar, Interna Inst. for Applied Systems Analysis, Laxenberg, Austria, 1979–81; Vis. Prof., Univ.

Rome, La Sapienza, 1988–89; Vis. Fellow, Princeton Univ., 1995. Chm., Oxford Systems Associates Ltd, 1974–79; Man. Dir, Cambridge Systems Associates Ltd, 1996–. Cons. to numerous cos and govts, 1965–. Mem., Res. Adv. Bd, Canadian Inst. for Advanced Res., 1986–2002. FIMA 1974. Hon. FIA 2000. Ed., Quantitative Finance, 2000–. *Publications:* (jtly) Introduction to Optimization Methods, 1974; (ed) Stochastic Programming, 1980; (ed jtly) Analysis and Optimization of Stochastic Systems, 1980; (ed jtly) Large-Scale Linear Programming, 1981; (ed jtly) Deterministic and Stochastic Scheduling, 1982; (ed jtly) Mathematical Models in Economics, 1994; (ed jtly) Mathematics of Derivative Securities, 1997; (ed) Risk Management: value at risk and beyond, 2002; (ed jtly) Quantitative Fund Management; *translations* from Russian: (jtly) Stochastic Models of Control and Economic Dynamics, 1987; (jtly) Sequential Control and Incomplete Information, 1990. *Recreations:* reading, gardening, tennis, sailing, ski-ing. *Address:* 1 Earl Street, Cambridge CB1 1JR; Judge Business School, University of Cambridge, Trumpington Street, Cambridge CB2 1AG.

DENARO, Maj.-Gen. Arthur George, CBE 1996 (OBE 1991); DL; Extra Equerry to the Prince of Wales, since 2000; Adviser to Court of Crown Prince of Bahrain, 2003–07; *b* 23 March 1948; *s* of late Brig. George Tancred Denaro, CBE, DSO and of Francesca Violet Denaro (*née* Garnett); *m* 1980, Margaret Roney Acworth, *widow* of Major Michael Kealy, DSO; one *s* one *d*, and one step *s* two step *d*. *Educ:* Downside Sch.; RMA Sandhurst. Commissioned Queen's Royal Irish Hussars, 1968; Staff Coll., 1979–80; CO QRIH, 1989–91; Comdr 33 (later 20) Armd Bde, 1992–94; RCDS 1994; COS HQ UNPROFOR, former Yugoslavia, 1994–95; COS HQ British Forces, Cyprus, 1995–96; Chief, Combat Support, HQ ARRC, 1996–97; Comdt, RMA Sandhurst, 1997–2000; GOC 5th Div., 2000–03. Middle East Adviser: to Sec. of State for Defence, 1997–2002; to JCB, 2003–; Special Adviser: Strategic Real Estate Advrs, 2007–; Inspirational Develt Gp, 2007–. Col, Queen's Royal Hussars (Queen's Own and Royal Irish), 2004–; Hon. Colonel: Royal Glos Hussars, 2003–; Royal Wessex Yeomanry, 2003–. Pres., Combined Irish Regts Assoc., 2003–. Chairman: Prince's Trust Team Prog., 2000–; Army Benevolent Fund (Hereford), 2003–. President: Army Rugby Union, 2001–03; Army Polo Assoc., 2002–. DL Herefordshire, 2008. *Recreations:* fieldsports, polo, ski-ing. *Club:* Cavalry and Guards.

de NAVARRO, Michael Antony; QC 1990; a Recorder, since 1990; *b* 1 May 1944; *s* of A. J. M. (Toty) de Navarro and Dorothy M. de Navarro; *m* 1975, Jill Margaret Walker; one *s* two *d*. *Educ:* Downside School; Trinity College, Cambridge (BA Hons). Called to the Bar, Inner Temple, 1968, Bencher, 2000; pupil of Hon. Mr Justice Cazalet and Hon. Mr Justice Turner; Mem., Western Circuit. Chm., Personal Injuries Bar Assoc., 1997–99. Trustee, Longborough Fest. Opera. *Recreations:* opera, cricket, gardening, cooking. *Address:* 2 Temple Gardens, Temple, EC4Y 9AY. *T:* (020) 7822 1200.

DENBIGH, 12th Earl of, *cr* 1622, **AND DESMOND,** 11th Earl of, *cr* 1622; **Alexander Stephen Rudolph Feilding;** Baron Feilding 1620; Viscount Feilding 1620; Viscount Callan 1622; Baron St Liz 1663; *b* 4 Nov. 1970; *o s* of 11th Earl of Denbigh and of Caroline Judith Vivienne, *o d* of Lt-Col Geoffrey Cooke; *S* father, 1995; *m* 1996, Suzanne Jane, *d* of Gregory R. Allen; one *s* one *d*. *Heir: s* Viscount Feilding, *qv*. *Address:* Newnham Paddox, Monks Kirby, Rugby CV23 0RX; 34 Keildon Road, Battersea, SW11 1XH.

DENCH, Dame Judith Olivia, (Dame Judi Dench), CH 2005; DBE 1988 (OBE 1970); actress (theatre, films and television); *b* 9 Dec. 1934; *d* of Reginald Arthur Dench and Eleanora Olave Dench (*née* Jones); *m* 1971, Michael Leonard Williams, actor (*d* 2001); one *d*. *Educ:* The Mount Sch., York; Central Sch. of Speech and Drama. *Theatre:* Old Vic seasons, 1957–61: parts incl.: Ophelia in Hamlet; Katherine in Henry V; Cecily in The Importance of Being Earnest; Juliet in Romeo and Juliet; also 1957–61: two Edinburgh Festivals; Paris-Belgium-Yugoslavia tour; America-Canada tour; Venice (all with Old Vic Co.). Subseq. appearances incl.: Royal Shakespeare Co., 1961–62: Anya in The Cherry Orchard; Titania in A Midsummer Night's Dream; Dorcas Bellboys in A Penny for a Song; Isabella in Measure for Measure; Nottingham Playhouse tour of W Africa, 1963; Oxford Playhouse, 1964–65: Irina in The Three Sisters; Doll Common in The Alchemist; Nottingham Playhouse, 1965: Saint Joan; The Astrakhan Coat (world première); Amanda in Private Lives; Variety London Critics' Best Actress of the Year Award for perf. as Lika in The Promise, Fortune, 1967; Sally Bowles in Cabaret, Palace, 1968; Associate Mem., RSC, 1969–; London Assurance, Aldwych, 1970, and New, 1972; Major Barbara, Aldwych, 1970; Bianca in Women Beware Women, Viola in Twelfth Night, doubling Hermione and Perdita in The Winter's Tale, Portia in The Merchant of Venice, the Duchess in The Duchess of Malfi, Beatrice in Much Ado About Nothing, Lady Macbeth in Macbeth, Adriana in The Comedy of Errors, Regan in King Lear, Imogen in Cymbeline; The Wolf, Oxford and London, 1973; The Good Companions, Her Majesty's, 1974; The Gay Lord Quex, Albery, 1975; Too True to be Good, Aldwych, 1975, Globe, 1976; Pillars of the Community, The Comedy of Errors, Aldwych, 1977; The Way of the World, 1978; Juno and the Paycock, Aldwych, 1980 (Best Actress award, SWET, Evening Standard, Variety Club, and Plays and Players); The Importance of Being Earnest, A Kind of Alaska, Nat. Theatre, 1982; Pack of Lies, Lyric, 1983 (SWET award); Mother Courage, Barbican, 1984; Waste, Barbican and Lyric, 1985; Mr and Mrs Nobody, Garrick, 1986; Antony and Cleopatra (Best Actress award, SWET, Evening Standard), Entertaining Strangers, Nat. Theatre, 1987; Hamlet, Royal Nat. Theatre, and Dubrovnik Theatre Fest., 1989; The Cherry Orchard, Aldwych, 1989; The Plough and the Stars, Young Vic, 1991; The Sea, Nat. Theatre, 1991; Coriolanus, Chichester, 1992; The Gift of the Gorgon, Barbican, 1992, transf. Wyndham's, 1993; The Seagull, RNT, 1994; Absolute Hell, RNT, 1995 (Best Actress, Olivier award, 1996); A Little Night Music, RNT, 1995 (Best Actress in a Musical, Olivier award, 1996); Amy's View, RNT, 1997, transf. Aldwych (Critics' Circle Drama Award), 1998, NY (Tony Award), 1999; Filumena, Piccadilly, 1998; The Royal Family, 2001, The Breath of Life, 2002, Theatre Royal, Haymarket; All's Well That Ends Well, RSC Stratford, transf. Gielgud, 2004; Hay Fever, Th. Royal, Haymarket, 2006; Merry Wives - The Musical, RSC Stratford, 2006; Director, for Renaissance Theatre Co.: Much Ado About Nothing, 1988; Look Back in Anger, 1989; Director: The Boys from Syracuse, Regent's Park, 1991; Romeo and Juliet, Regent's Park, 1993. Recital tour of W Africa, 1969; RSC tours: Japan and Australia, 1970; Japan, 1972. *Films:* He Who Rides a Tiger; A Study in Terror; Four in the Morning (Brit. Film Acad. Award for Most Promising Newcomer, 1965); A Midsummer Night's Dream, 1968; The Third Secret; Dead Cert; Saigon: Year of the Cat; Wetherby, 1984; A Room with a View, 1985 (Best Supporting Actress, BAFTA award, 1987); 84 Charing Cross Road, 1986; A Handful of Dust (Best Supporting Actress, BAFTA award), 1988; Henry V, 1990; Goldeneye, 1995; Mrs Brown (Best Actress awards: BAFTA Scotland, 1997; Golden Globe, London Film Critics, BAFTA, and Screen Actors' Guild, NY, 1998), Tomorrow Never Dies, 1997; Shakespeare in Love (Oscar and BAFTA Award for Best Supporting Actress), Tea with Mussolini, The World is Not Enough, 1999; Chocolat, 2001; Iris (Best Actress, BAFTA award), The Shipping News, The Importance of Being Earnest, Die Another Day, 2002; Ladies in Lavender, The Chronicles of Riddick, 2004; Pride and Prejudice, Mrs Henderson Presents, 2005; Casino Royale, 2006; Notes on a Scandal, 2007. *Television* appearances include, 1957–: Talking to a Stranger (Best Actress of Year award, Guild of Television Dirs, 1967); Major Barbara; Hilda Lessways; Langrishe, Go Down; Macbeth; Comedy of Errors; On Giant's Shoulders; A Village Wooing; Love in a Cold Climate; Saigon; A Fine Romance (BAFTA Award, 1985); The Cherry Orchard; Going Gently; Mr and Mrs Edgehill (Best Actress, Amer. Cable Award, 1988); The Browning Version; Make or Break; Ghosts; Behaving Badly; Absolute Hell; Can You Hear Me Thinking?; As Time Goes By (8 series); Last of the Blonde Bombshells, 2000 (Best Actress, BAFTA TV Award, 2001); Cranford, 2007. Mem. Bd, Royal Nat. Theatre, 1988–. Awards incl. British and foreign, for theatre, films and TV, incl. BAFTA award for best television actress, 1981, Rothermere Award for Lifetime Achievement, 1997, and Critics' Circle Award for Outstanding Achievement, 1998; William Shakespeare Award, Washington, DC, 2004; Evening Standard Lifetime Achievement Award, 2004. Fellow BAFTA, 2001. Hon. DLitt: Warwick, 1978; Birmingham, 1989; Loughborough, 1991; London, 1994; Oxford, 2000; DUniv: York, 1983; Open, 1992; RSAMD, 1995; Surrey, 1996. *Publication:* Scenes from My Life, 2005. *Recreations:* sewing, drawing, catching up with letters.

DENEGRI, Simon; Chief Executive, Association of Medical Research Charities, since 2006; *b* 17 March 1967; *s* of Donald and Ann Denegri; *m* 2006, Nicola Margaret Bain; three *s* from former marr. *Educ:* Dean Row Jun. Sch., Handforth; New Beacon Sch., Sevenoaks; Judd Grammar Sch., Tonbridge; Univ. of Hull (BA Hons Politics and Legislative Studies). Hd, Public Affairs, Alzheimer's Soc., 1992–97; Corporate and Financial Media Relns Manager, Procter and Gamble, USA, 1997–2000; Dir, Communications, Sainsbury Centre for Mental Health, 2001–03; Asst Chief Exec., Alzheimer's Soc., 2003; Dir, Corporate Communications, RCP, 2003–06. MCIPR 2003. FRSA 2006. *Recreations:* playing guitar, going to the cinema, live music, writing poetry, exploring London, modern political history. *Address:* c/o Association of Medical Research Charities, 61 Gray's Inn Road, WC1X 8TL. *T:* (020) 7269 8820, *Fax:* (020) 7269 8821; *e-mail:* s.denegri@amrc.org.uk.

DENEUVE, Catherine; French film actress; *b* 22 Oct. 1943; *d* of Maurice Dorléac and Renée (*née* Deneuve); one *s* by Roger Vadim (*d* 2000); *m* 1967, David Bailey, *qv* (marr. diss.); one *d* by Marcello Mastroianni (*d* 1996). *Educ:* Lycée La Fontaine, Paris. Pres.-Dir Gen., Films de la Citrouille, 1971–79. Chm. Jury, Cannes Film Fest., 1994. *Films include:* Les petits chats, 1959; Les portes claquent, 1960; Le vice et la vertu, 1962; Les parapluies de Cherbourg, 1963; La Constanza della Ragione, 1964; Repulsion, 1964; Liebes Karusell, 1965; Belle de jour, 1967; Folies d'avril, 1969; Un flic, 1972; Le sauvage, 1975; Âmes perdues, 1976; Hustle, 1976; A nous deux, 1978; Le dernier métro, 1980 (César for best actress, 1981); Le choc, 1982; The Hunger, 1982; Le bon plaisir, 1984; Let's Hope It's A Girl, 1987; Drôle d'Endroit pour une Rencontre (Strange Place to Meet), 1989; Indochine, 1992; Ma Saison préférée, 1994; The Convent, 1995; Les voleurs, 1996; Genealogie d'un Crime, 1997; Place Vendôme, 1998; Pola X, Time Regained, Dancer in the Dark, East-West, 2000; The Musketeer, 8 Women, 2002; Les temps qui changent, 2005; Rois et Reine, 2005; Persepolis, 2008. *Publication:* A l'ombre de moi-même, 2004 (Close Up and Personal, 2005). *Address:* c/o Artmédia, 20 avenue Rapp, 75007 Paris, France.

DENHAM, 2nd Baron *cr* 1937, of Weston Underwood; **Bertram Stanley Mitford Bowyer,** KBE 1991; PC 1981; Bt 1660, of Denham; Bt 1933, of Weston Underwood; Captain of the Gentlemen at Arms (Government Chief Whip in the House of Lords), 1979–91; an Extra Lord-in-Waiting to the Queen, since 1998; *b* 3 Oct. 1927; *s* of 1st Baron and Hon. Daphne Freeman-Mitford (*d* 1996), 4th *d* of 1st Baron Redesdale; *S* father, 1948; *m* 1956, Jean, *o d* of Kenneth McCorquodale, Fambridge Hall, White Notley, Essex; three *s* one *d*. *Educ:* Eton; King's Coll., Cambridge. Mem. Westminster CC, 1959–61. A Lord-in-Waiting to the Queen, 1961–64 and 1970–71; Opposition Jun. Whip, 1964–70; Captain of the Yeomen of the Guard, 1971–74; Opposition Dep. Chief Whip, 1974–78; Opposition Chief Whip, 1978–79; elected Mem., H of L, 1999–. Countryside Comr, 1993–99. Dep. Pres., British Field Sports Soc., 1992–98. *Publications:* The Man who Lost his Shadow, 1979; Two Thyrdes, 1983; Foxhunt, 1988; Black Rod, 1997. *Recreations:* field sports. *Heir: s* Hon. Richard Grenville George Bowyer [*b* 8 Feb. 1959; *m* 1st, 1988, Eleanor (marr. diss. 1993), *o d* of A. Sharpe; 2nd, 1996, Dagmar, *o d* of Karel and Jaroslava Božek, Břeslaw, Czech Republic]. *Address:* The Laundry Cottage, Weston Underwood, Olney, Bucks MK46 5JZ. *T:* (020) 7219 6056. *Clubs:* Pratt's, Garrick.

DENHAM, Ernest William; Deputy Keeper of Public Records, Public Record Office, 1978–82; *b* 16 Sept. 1922; *s* of William and Beatrice Denham; *m* 1957, Penelope Agatha Gregory; one *s* one *d*. *Educ:* City of London Sch.; Merton Coll., Oxford (Postmaster). MA 1948. Naval Intell., UK and SEAC, 1942–45. Asst Sec., Plant Protection Ltd, 1947–49; Asst Keeper 1949, Principal Asst Keeper 1967, Records Admin. Officer 1973, Public Record Office; Lectr in Palaeography and Diplomatic, UCL, 1957–73. *Recreation:* armchair criticism. *Address:* 4 The Ridge, 89 Green Lane, Northwood, Middx HA6 1AE. *T:* (01923) 827382.

See also J. M. G. Denham.

DENHAM, (John Martin) Giles, CBE 2004; Director of Policy, Health and Safety Executive, since 2005; *b* 13 Feb. 1959; *s* of Ernest William Denham, *qv* and Penelope Agatha Denham; *m* 1986, Heather Gillian Yarker; three *d*. *Educ:* Merchant Taylors' Sch., Northwood; Christ Church, Oxford (MA 1981). Various Civil Service appts, DHSS, HM Treasury and DoH, 1981–90; Gen. Manager, Eastman Dental Hosp., 1990–95; Branch Head, Dentistry, Community Pharmacy, Optometry and Community Care, 1995–2001, Hd of Policy, Children, Older People and Social Care, 2001–03, DoH; Dir, Civil Affairs, Coalition Provl Authy, Iraq, 2004. Trustee: Marie Curie Cancer Care, 1991–2000; Kepplewray Trust, 2001–. *Address:* Health and Safety Executive, Rose Court, 2 Southwark Bridge, SE1 9HS. *T:* (020) 7717 6203. *Clubs:* Athenæum; Eastcote Lawn Tennis.

DENHAM, Rt Hon. John (Yorke); PC 2000; MP (Lab) Southampton, Itchen, since 1992; Secretary of State for Innovation, Universities and Skills, since 2007; *b* 15 July 1953; *s* of Albert Edward Denham and Beryl Frances Ada Denham; *m* 1979, Ruth Eleanore Dixon (marr. diss.); one *s* one *d*; partner, Susan Jane Littlemore; one *s*. *Educ:* Woodroffe Comprehensive Sch., Lyme Regis; Univ. of Southampton (BSc Hons Chemistry; Pres., Students' Union, 1976–77). Advr, Energy Advice Service, Durham, 1977; Transport Campaigner, Friends of the Earth, 1977–79; Head, Youth Affairs, British Youth Council, 1979–82; Publications Sec., Clause IV Publications, 1982–84; Campaigns Officer, War on Want, 1984–88; Consultant to develt NGOs, 1988–92. Member (Lab): Hants CC, 1981–89; Southampton CC, 1989–93 (Chm., Housing Cttee, 1990–92). Contested (Lab) Southampton, Itchen, 1983, 1987. Parly Under-Sec. of State, DSS, 1997–98; Minister of State: DSS, 1998; Dept of Health, 1998–2001; Home Office, 2001–03. Chm., Select Cttee on Home Affairs, 2003–07. *Address:* House of Commons, SW1A 0AA.

DENHAM, Pamela Anne, CB 1997; DL; PhD; management consultant, since 1998; Regional Director, Government Office for the North East, 1994–98; *b* 1 May 1943; *d* of late Matthew Gray Dobson and Jane (*née* Carter); *m* 1965, Paul Denham (marr. diss. 1980); partner, Brian Murray (*d* 1993). *Educ:* Central Newcastle High Sch.; King's Coll., Univ.

of London (BSc 1964; PhD 1969). Asst Principal, Ministry of Technol., 1967–72; Department of Trade and Industry: Principal, 1972–79; Asst Sec., 1979–85; Under Sec., 1985–89; Under Sec., Cabinet Office (Office of Minister for CS), 1989–90; Regl Dir, DTI NE, 1990–94. Non-executive Director: Mono Pumps and Saunders Valve, 1982–85; Newcastle Primary Care Trust, 2001–. Member: Governing Body, Sunderland Univ., 1993, 1998–2007; Local Governing Body, Central Newcastle High Sch., 1992–2006 (Chair, 2001–06); Trustee, Univ. of Sunderland Develt Trust, 1999–. Chair, Project North East, 1998–; Mem. Bd, Community Foundn serving Tyne & Wear and Northumberland, 2001–07. Trustee: Age Concern, Newcastle, 2000–; Age Concern England, 2002–05. FRSA. DL Tyne and Wear, 2000. Hon. LLD Sunderland, 1994. *Publications:* papers in scientific jls. *Recreations:* travel, reading, walking, cooking. *Address:* 43 Lindisfarne Close, Jesmond, Newcastle upon Tyne NE2 2HT. *T:* (0191) 212 0390.

DENHAM, Lt-Col Sir Seymour Vivian G.; *see* Gilbart-Denham.

DENHAM, Susan Gageby; Hon. Mrs Justice Denham; Judge, Supreme Court of Ireland, since 1992; *b* 22 Aug. 1945; *d* of late Douglas Gageby and Dorothy Mary Gageby (*née* Lester); *m* 1970, Brian Denham; three *s* one *d* (and one *s* decd). *Educ:* Trinity Coll. Dublin (BA (Mod.), LLB); Columbia Univ., NY (LLM). Called to the Irish Bar, 1971 (Bencher, King's Inns, 1991); in practice on Midland Circuit, 1971–87; SC, called to Inner Bar, 1987; Judge of High Court, 1991–92. Chair: Working Gp on Courts Commn, 1995–98; Courts Service Bd, 1999–; Cttee on Court Practice and Procedure, 2000–; Wkg Gp on a Court of Appeal, 2007–. Hon. Sec., Cttee on Judicial Conduct and Ethics, 1999–2002. Pro-Chancellor, Dublin Univ., 1996–. Hon. Bencher, Middle Temple, 2005. Hon. LLD QUB, 2002. *Recreations:* gardens, horses, reading. *Address:* The Supreme Court, Four Courts, Dublin, Ireland. *T:* (1) 8886533.

DENHOLM, Allan; *see* Denholm, J. A.

DENHOLM, Sir Ian; *see* Denholm, Sir J. F.

DENHOLM, (James) Allan, CBE 1992; Chairman, East Kilbride Development Corporation, 1983–94 (Member, 1979–94); Director, William Grant & Sons Ltd, 1975–96 (Secretary, 1966–96); President, Institute of Chartered Accountants of Scotland, 1992–93; *b* 27 Sept. 1936; *s* of James Denholm and Florence Lily Keith (*née* Kennedy); *m* 1964, Elizabeth Avril McLachlan, CA; one *s* one *d*. *Educ:* Hutchesons' Boys' Sch., Glasgow. CA. Apprentice with McFarlane Hutton & Patrick, 1954–60; Chief Accountant, A. & W. Smith & Co. Ltd, 1960–66. Councillor, Eastwood DC, 1962–64. Mem., Council, Inst. of Chartered Accountants, Scotland, 1978–83 (Sen. Vice-Pres., 1991–92). Chm., Glasgow Jun. Chamber of Commerce, 1972–73. Director: Scottish Cremation Soc. Ltd, 1980–; Scottish Mutual Assurance PLC, 1987–2003 (Dep. Chm., 1992–2003); Abbey National PLC, 1992–97; Deputy Chairman: Abbey National Life PLC, 1997–2003; Scottish Provident Instn PLC, 2001–03 (Mem., Adv. Cttee, 2001–06). Visitor, Incorporation of Maltmen, Glasgow, 1980–81. Trustee: Scottish Cot Death Trust, 1985–96; Neurosciences Foundn, Glasgow, 2003–; Dir, Assoc. for the Relief of Incurables in Glasgow and W of Scotland, 1999–. Mem., W of Scotland Adv. Bd, Salvation Army, 1996–. Elder, New Kilpatrick Parish Church, Bearsden, 1971–. Preses, Weavers' Soc., Anderston, 1994–95; President: 49 Wine & Spirit Club of Scotland, 1983–84; Assoc. of Deacons of the Fourteen Incorporated Trades, Glasgow, 1994–95; Deacon Convener, The Trades House, Glasgow, 1998–99; Deacon, Soc. of Deacons and Free Preseses, Glasgow, 1999–2000. Patron, Royal Incorp. of Hutchesons' Hosp., 1998–. FSAScot 1987. FRSA 1992. *Recreations:* golf, shooting. *Address:* Greencroft, 19 Colquhoun Drive, Bearsden, Glasgow G61 4NQ. *T:* and *Fax:* (0141) 942 1773. *Club:* Western (Glasgow) (Chm., 2004–05).

DENHOLM, Sir John Ferguson, (Sir Ian), Kt 1989; CBE 1974; JP; DL; Chairman, J. & J. Denholm Ltd, 1974–98; *b* 8 May 1927; *s* of Sir William Lang Denholm, TD; *m* 1952, Elizabeth Murray Stephen; two *s* two *d*. *Educ:* St Mary's Sch., Melrose; Loretto Sch., Musselburgh. Joined J. & J. Denholm Ltd, 1944. Chm., Murray Investment Trusts, 1985–93; Dep. Chm., P&O, 1980–85 (Dir, 1974–85); Director: Fleming Mercantile Investment Trust, 1985–94; Murray Trusts, 1973–93; Murray Johnstone, 1985–93; Member: London Bd, Bank of Scotland, 1988–91; West of Scotland Bd, Bank of Scotland, 1991–95. Member: Nat. Ports Council, 1974–77; Scottish Transport Gp, 1975–82. President: Chamber of Shipping of the UK, 1973–74; Gen. Council of British Shipping, 1988–89; British Internat. Freight Assoc., 1990–91; Baltic and Internat. Maritime Council, 1991–93. Hon. Norwegian Consul in Glasgow, 1975–97. DL 1980, JP 1984, Renfrewshire. *Recreation:* fishing. *Clubs:* Western (Glasgow); Royal Thames Yacht, Royal Northern and Clyde Yacht.

DE NIRO, Robert; actor and producer; *b* NYC, 17 Aug. 1943; *s* of late Robert De Niro and of Virginia Admiral; *m* 1st, 1976, Diahnne Abbott (marr. diss. 1988); one *s*, and one adopted *d*; 2nd, 1997, Grace Hightower (marr. diss. 1999; remarried 2004); one *s*; twin *s* by Toukie Smith. *Educ:* Rhodes Sch., NY; High Sch. of Music and Art, NY. Co-founder and Pres., Tribeca Prodns, 1989–. Co-creator, We Will Rock You (musical), 2002. *Films include:* The Wedding Party, 1969; Jennifer on my Mind, Bloody Mama, Born to Win, The Gang That Couldn't Shoot Straight, 1971; Bang the Drum Slowly, Mean Streets, 1973; The Godfather Part II, 1974 (Acad. Award for best supporting actor, 1975); The Last Tycoon, Taxi Driver, 1976; 1900, New York, New York, 1977; The Deer Hunter, 1978; Raging Bull (Acad. Award for best actor), 1980; True Confessions, 1981; The King of Comedy, 1983; Once Upon a Time in America, Falling in Love, 1984; Brazil, 1985; The Mission, 1986; Angel Heart, The Untouchables, 1987; Midnight Run, Letters Home from Vietnam, 1988; Jacknife, We're No Angels (also prod.), 1989; Stanley and Iris, Goodfellas, Awakenings, Fear No Evil, 1990; Guilty by Suspicion, Backdraft, Cape Fear, 1991; Mad Dog and Glory, Night and the City, Mistress (also co-prod.), 1992; This Boy's Life, A Bronx Tale (also dir and co-prod.), 1993; Mary Shelley's Frankenstein, 1994; Casino, Heat, 1995; The Fan, Sleepers, Marvin's Room (also prod.), 1996; Cop Land, Jackie Brown, Wag the Dog (also prod.), 1997; Great Expectations, Ronin, 1998; Analyse This, 1999; Flawless (also prod.), Meet the Parents (also prod.), 2000; The Adventures of Rocky and Bulwinkle (also prod.), Men of Honour, 15 Minutes (also prod.), The Score, 2001; Showtime, City By the Sea, 2002; Analyse That, Godsend, 2003; Meet the Fockers (also prod.), Hide and Seek, 2005; The Good Shepherd (also dir), Stardust, 2007; What Just Happened?, 2008; *producer:* Thunderheart, 1992; Entropy, 1999; Conjugating Niki, 2000; Prison Song, About a Boy, 2001; Stage Beauty, 2004. *Address:* c/o CAA, 2000 Avenue of the Stars, Los Angeles, CA 90067, USA; Tribeca Productions, 375 Greenwich Street, New York, NY 10013, USA.

DENISON, family name of **Baron Londesborough**.

DENISON, Ann, (Mrs W. N. Denison); *see* Curnow, E. A. M.

DENISON, Dulcie Winifred Catherine, (Dulcie Gray), CBE 1983; actress, playwright, authoress; *b* 20 Nov. 1915; *d* of late Arnold Savage Bailey, CBE, and of Kate Edith (*née* Clulow Gray); *m* 1939, Michael Denison, CBE (*d* 1998). *Educ:* England and Malaya. In Repertory in Aberdeen, 1st part Sorrel in Hay Fever, 1939; Repertory in Edinburgh, Glasgow and Harrogate, 1940; BBC Serial, Front Line Family, 1941; Shakespeare, Regents Park; Alexandra in The Little Foxes, Piccadilly; Midsummer Night's Dream, Westminster, 1942; Brighton Rock, Garrick; Landslide, Westminster, 1943; Lady from Edinburgh, Playhouse, 1945; Dear Ruth, St James's; Wind is 90, Apollo, 1946; on tour in Fools Rush In, 1946; Rain on the Just, Aldwych, 1948; Queen Elizabeth Slept Here, Strand, 1949; The Four-poster, Ambassadors, 1950 (tour of S Africa, 1954–55); See You Later (Revue), Watergate, 1951; Dragon's Mouth, Winter Garden, 1952; Sweet Peril, St James's, 1952; We Must Kill Toni, Westminster; The Diary of a Nobody, Arts, 1954; Alice Through the Looking Glass, Chelsea Palace, 1955, Ashcroft Theatre, Croydon, 1972; appeared in own play, Love Affair, Lyric Hammersmith, 1956; South Sea Bubble, Cape Town, 1956; Tea and Sympathy, Melbourne and Sydney, 1956; South Sea Bubble, Johannesburg, 1957; Double Cross, Duchess, 1958; Let Them Eat Cake, Cambridge, 1959; Candida, Piccadilly and Wyndham's, 1960; Heartbreak House, Wyndham's, 1961; A Marriage Has Been Arranged, and A Village Wooing (Hong Kong); Shakespeare Recital (Berlin Festival); Royal Gambit for opening of Ashcroft Theatre, Croydon, 1962; Where Angels Fear to Tread, Arts and St Martin's, 1963; An Ideal Husband, Strand, 1965; On Approval, St Martin's, 1966; Happy Family, St Martin's, 1967; Number 10, Strand, 1967; Out of the Question, St Martin's, 1968; Three, Fortune, 1970; The Wild Duck, Criterion, 1970; Clandestine Marriage (tour), 1971; Ghosts, York; Hay Fever (tour), 1972; Dragon Variation (tour), 1973; At the End of the Day, Savoy, 1973; The Sack Race, Ambassadors, 1974; The Pay Off, Comedy, 1974, Westminster, 1975; Time and the Conways (tour), 1976; Ladies in Retirement (tour), 1976; Façade, QEH, 1976; The Cabinet Minister (tour), 1977; A Murder is Announced, Vaudeville, 1977; Bedroom Farce, Prince of Wales, 1979; The Cherry Orchard, Exeter, 1980; Lloyd George Knew my Father (tour), 1980; The Kingfisher, Windsor, 1980, Worthing and on tour, 1981; Relatively Speaking (Dinner Theatre Tour, Near and Far East), 1981; A Coat of Varnish, Haymarket, 1982; Cavell, Chichester Fest., 1982; School for Scandal, Haymarket, transf. to Duke of York's, and British Council 50th Anniversary European Tour, 1983; There Goes the Bride (Dinner Theatre tour, Near and Far East), 1985; The Living Room, Royalty, 1987; The Chalk Garden, Windsor and tour, 1989; The Best of Friends (tour) 1990, 1991; The Importance of Being Earnest (tour), 1991; Tartuffe, Playhouse, 1991–92; Bedroom Farce (tour), 1992; An Ideal Husband, Globe, 1992, tour, 1993, Haymarket and NY, 1996, Haymarket, transf. Gielgud, 1997; Pygmalion, and The Schoolmistress, Chichester Fest., 1994; Two of a Kind (tour), 1995; The Importance of Being Earnest, Leatherhead, 1995; The Ladykillers (tour), 1999; Les Liaisons Dangereuses (tour), 2000; The Lady Vanishes (tour), 2000; Three Sisters (tour), 2002. *Films include:* They were Sisters, 1944; Wanted for Murder, 1945; A Man about the House, 1946; Mine Own Executioner, 1947; My Brother Jonathan, 1947; The Glass Mountain, 1948; The Franchise Affair, 1951; Angels One Five, 1952; There was a Young Lady, 1953; A Man Could Get Killed, 1965; The Black Crow, 1994. Has appeared in television plays and radio serials; *television series:* Howard's Way, 1985–90. Fellow, Linnean Soc., 1984. FRSA. Queen's Silver Jubilee Medal, 1977. *Publications: play:* Love Affair; *books:* Murder on the Stairs; Murder in Melbourne; Baby Face; Epitaph for a Dead Actor; Murder on a Saturday; Murder in Mind; The Devil Wore Scarlet; No Quarter for a Star; The Murder of Love; Died in the Red; The Actor and His World (with Michael Denison); Murder on Honeymoon; For Richer, For Richer; Deadly Lampshade; Understudy to Murder; Dead Give Away; Ride on a Tiger; Stage-Door Fright; Death in Denims; Butterflies on my Mind (TES Senior Information Book Prize, 1978); Dark Calypso; The Glanville Women; Anna Starr; Mirror Image; Looking Forward, Looking Back (autobiog.); J. B. Priestley (biog.). *Recreations:* swimming, butterflies. *Address:* Shardeloes, Amersham, Bucks HP7 0RL; c/o Burnett Granger Crowther, 3 Clifford Street, W1S 2LF. *T:* (020) 7437 8008.

DENISON, His Honour (William) Neil; QC 1980; a Circuit Judge, 1985–2001; Common Serjeant in the City of London, 1993–2001; *b* 10 March 1929; *s* of William George Denison and Jean Brodie; *m*; three *s*; *m* 1981, Elizabeth Ann Marguerite Curnow, *qv*. *Educ:* Queen Mary's Sch., Walsall; Univ. of Birmingham (LLB); Hertford Coll., Univ. of Oxford (BCL). Called to the Bar, Lincoln's Inn, 1952, Bencher, 1993. A Recorder of the Crown Court, 1979–85. Liveryman, Wax Chandlers' Co., 1988 (Master, 2001–02). *Recreations:* walking, reading rubbish. *Club:* Garrick.

DENISON-PENDER, family name of **Baron Pender**.

DENISON-SMITH, Lt-Gen. Sir Anthony (Arthur), KBE 1995 (MBE 1973); DL; Lieutenant, HM Tower of London, 1998–2001; *b* 24 Jan. 1942; *s* of late George Denison-Smith and Dorothy Gwendolin Phillips; *m* 1966, Julia Henrietta Scott; three *s*. *Educ:* Harrow; RMA, Sandhurst. Commissioned Grenadier Guards, 1962; Staff Coll., 1974; Brigade Major, 7th Armoured Brigade, 1977–79; Directing Staff, Staff Coll., 1979–81; CO 2nd Bn Grenadier Guards, 1981–83; Chief of Staff, 4th Armoured Div., 1983–85; Comdr, 22nd Armoured Brigade, 1985–87; Chief of Staff, 1 (BR) Corps, 1987–89; Dir Gen. Trng and Doctrine (Army), 1990–91; Comdr, 4th Armoured Div., 1991–93; Comdr, 1st (UK) Armoured Div., 1993–94; GOC Southern Dist, 1994–95; GOC 4th Div., 1995–96. Col, Princess of Wales's Royal Regt (Queen's and Royal Hampshires), 1992–99. Chm., ACFA, 1996–2001; Pres., Essex Br., Grenadier Guards Assoc., 1998–. Hon. Col, Essex ACF, 2002–07. Consultant, Rave Technologies Ltd (formerly Karnataka Gp Ltd), 1996–. DL Essex, 2001. Comdr (1st cl.), Order of the Dannebrog (Denmark), 1996. *Recreations:* family, friends, Hawkwoods. *Address:* Hawkwoods, Gosfield, Halstead, Essex CO9 1SB. *Clubs:* MCC; Essex.

DENMAN, family name of **Baron Denman**.

DENMAN, 5th Baron *cr* 1834; **Charles Spencer Denman,** CBE 1976; MC 1942; TD; Bt 1945; Senior Advisor: Close Brothers; Merchant Bridge; *b* 7 July 1916; *e s* of Hon. Sir Richard Douglas Denman, 1st Bt; *S* father, 1957 and to barony of cousin, 1971; *m* 1943, Sheila Anne (*d* 1987), *d* of late Lt-Col Algernon Bingham Anstruther Stewart, DSO, Seaforth Highlanders, of Ornockenoch, Gatehouse of Fleet; three *s* one *d*. *Educ:* Shrewsbury. Served War of 1939–45 with Duke of Cornwall's Light Infantry (TA), India, Middle East, Western Desert and Dodecanese Islands; Major, 1943. Contested (C) Leeds Central, 1945. Director: Close Brothers Group Plc; British Water & Wastewater Ltd; Albaraka Internat. Bank Ltd; Arab-British Centre Ltd; New Zealand Holdings (UK) Ltd; formerly Chairman: Marine and General Mutual Life Assurance Soc.; Tennant Guaranty Ltd; Gold Fields Mahd adh Dhahab Ltd; Arundell House Plc; formerly Director: C. Tennant Sons & Co. Ltd; Consolidated Gold Fields Plc; British Bank of the Middle East; Saudi British Bank; British Arabian Corp.; Fletcher Challenge Corp.; MGM Life Assurance Soc. Member: Cttee for ME Trade, 1963 (Chm., 1971–75); Advisory Council of Export Credits Guarantee Department, 1963–68; British National Export Council, 1965; Cttee on Invisible Exports, 1965–67; British Invisible Exports Council; Guild of World Traders in London; Res. Inst. for Study of Conflict and Terrorism; UK/Saudi Jt Cultural Cttee; Lord Kitchener Nat. Meml Fund. President: RSAA, 1984–; NZ-UK Chamber of Commerce and Industry; Vice President: ME Assoc.; Saudi-British Soc.; Chm., Arab British Chamber Charitable Foundn; formerly Chm., Governors of

Windlesham House Sch. *Heir:* *s* Hon. Richard Thomas Stewart Denman [*b* 4 Oct. 1946; *m* 1984, (Lesley) Jane, *d* of John Stevens; one *s* three *d*]. *Club:* Brooks's.

DENMAN, Sylvia Elaine, CBE 1994; Member, Housing Corporation, 1996–2002; Member, 1992–2000, Chairman, 1996–2000, Camden and Islington (formerly Bloomsbury and Islington) Health Authority; *b* Barbados; *d* of late Alexander Yarde and Euleen Yarde (*née* Alleyne), Barbados; *m* Hugh Frederick Denman (marr. diss.); one *d*. *Educ:* Queen's College, Barbados; LSE (LLM); called to the Bar, Lincoln's Inn, 1962. Lectr then Sen. Lectr, Oxford Polytechnic, 1965–76; Sen. Lectr and Tutor, Norman Manley Law Sch., Univ. of West Indies, Jamaica, 1977–82; Fulbright Fellow, New York Univ. Sch. of Law, 1982–83; Prin. Equal Opportunities Officer, ILEA, 1983–86; Pro Asst Dir, Polytechnic of South Bank, 1986–89; Dep. Dir of Educn, ILEA, 1989–90. Sole Ind. Chair, Ind. Internal Inquiry, CPS, 2000–02. Member: Oxford Cttee for Racial Integration, 1965–76; Oxford, Bucks and Berks Conciliation Cttee, Race Relations Bd, 1965–70; London Rent Assessment Panel, 1968–76 and 1984–2002; Race Relations Bd, 1970–76; Equal Opportunities Commission, 1975–76; Lord Chancellor's Adv. Cttee on Legal Aid, 1975–76; Criminal Justice Consultative Council, 1991–97; Council, NACRO, 1994–99; SSAC, 1998–2001. Trustee: Runnymede Trust, 1985–91; Windsor Fellowship, 1994–98; CAF, 1997–2001. Governor: Haverstock Sch., 1989–94; Oxford Brookes Univ., 1996–2000. *Recreations:* music, theatre, wandering about in the Caribbean.

DENNAY, Charles William, CEng; Consultant, Quantel Ltd, 1993–2001; *b* 13 May 1935; *s* of Charles Dennay and Elsie May Smith; *m* 1955, Shirley Patricia Johnston; one *s*. *Educ:* Humberston Foundation Sch.; Borough Polytechnic. DiPEE, MIERE. Scientific Asst (Govt), 1953; Technician, BBC, 1956; Transmitter Engineer, 1958; Asst Lectr/Lectr, 1961; Head of Ops Transmitters, 1973; Head of Engrg Transmitter Ops, 1976; Asst Chief Engineer, Transmitters, 1978; Chief Engineer, External Broadcasting, 1979; Controller, Ops and Engineering Radio, 1984; Asst Dir of Engineering, 1985; Dir of Engineering, 1987; Man. Dir, Resources Engrg and Services, 1993, retd. Director: Brighton Fest. Soc. Ltd, 1996–2000; Brighton Dome & Museum Develt Co. Ltd, 1999–2005. Mem., Steering Bd, Radio Communication Agency, 1996–2003. Vis. Prof., Internat. Acad. of Broadcasting, Montreux, 1994–98. President: IEEIE, 1994–98 (Vice-Pres., 1990–94); IIE, 2001–03. FRTS 1997 (a Vice-Pres., 1989–94); FIIE 1998, Hon. FIIE 2003. FRSA 1993. Hon. FIET; Hon. FBKS 1990. *Recreations:* photography, music, civil aviation. *Address:* Montmore Cottage, 1 Orchard Dean, Alresford, Hants SO24 9DE. *T:* (01962) 735103.

DENNE, Christopher James Alured, CMG 1991; HM Diplomatic Service, 1967–78 and 1983–98; *b* 20 Aug. 1945; *s* of late Lt Comdr John Richard Alured Denne, DSC, RN and Alison Patricia Denne; *m* 1968, Sarah Longman; two *s* one *d*. *Educ:* Wellington Coll.; Southampton Univ. (BSc Soc. Sci. 1967). Entered Diplomatic Service, 1967; New Delhi, 1969–72; Second Sec., FCO, 1972–74; First Sec. (Information), Lagos, 1974–77; FCO, 1977; resigned, 1978; BBC External Services, 1979–80; reinstated FCO, 1983; First Sec. and Dep. Permanent Rep., UK Mission to UN, Vienna, 1985–89; Head of Consular Dept, FCO, 1989–92; Dep. Hd of Mission, Athens, 1993–97. Chm., Tamar Br., European Movt, 2007–. *Address:* Churchtown Farm, Sydenham Damerel, Tavistock, Devon PL19 8PU.

DENNEN, Ven. Lyle; Archdeacon of Hackney, and Vicar, St Andrew, Holborn, since 1999; *b* 8 Jan. 1942; *s* of Ernest and Rose Dennen; *m* 1977, Xenia Howard-Johnston, *d* of Rear Adm. C. D. Howard-Johnston, CB, DSO, DSC, and Lady Alexandra Haig (who *m* 1954, Hugh Trevor-Roper (later Lord Dacre of Glanton)); two *s*. *Educ:* Trinity Coll., Cambridge (BA 1970, MA 1975); Harvard Law Sch. (DJur); Harvard Univ. (PhD); Cuddesdon Coll., Oxford. Ordained deacon, 1972, priest, 1973; Curate, St Anne, S Lambeth, Southwark, 1972–75; Curate in charge, St Matthias, Richmond, 1975–78; Vicar, St John the Divine, Kennington, 1978–99; RD of Brixton, 1988–99. Hon. Canon, Southwark Cathedral, 1999. Chairman of Governors: St John the Divine Primary Sch., 1978–99; Charles Edward Brooke Secondary Sch., 1978–99; Chm., Lambeth WelCare, 1978–99. Chairman: London Cttee, Southwark & London Diocesan Housing Assoc., 1999–; Alexander Stafford Trust, 1999–; Trustee: St Gabriel's Coll. Trust, 1978–99; Bromfield Educnl Charity, 1999–; Lady Elizabeth Hatton Charity, 1999–; Lady Nevill Charity, 1999–; St Andrew Holborn Ch Foundn, 1999–; St Andrew Holborn Parish Estates Charity, 1999–; St Andrew Holborn Charity, 2002–. *Recreation:* sailing. *Address:* 5 St Andrew Street, EC4A 3AB. *T:* (020) 7353 3544, *Fax:* (020) 7583 2750; *e-mail:* archdeacon.hackney@london.anglican.org. *Clubs:* Athenæum; Harlequins Supporters.

DENNER, Dr (William) Howard (Butler); freelance photographer, especially of pop, blues and jazz musicians, since 1996; *b* 14 May 1944; *s* of late William Ormonde Ralph Denner and Violet Evelyn Arscott; *m* 1966, Gwenda Williams; two *d*. *Educ:* Cyfarthfa Castle Grammar School, Merthyr Tydfil; UCW Cardiff (BSc, PhD Biochem.). Research Associate: Miami Univ., 1968; Cardiff Univ., 1969; Ministry of Agriculture, Fisheries and Food, 1972–96: Secretary: Food Additives and Contaminants Cttee, 1974–84; Cttee on Toxicity of Chemicals in Food, Consumer Products and the Environment, 1978–84; Mem., Jt FAO/WHO Expert Cttee on Food Additives, 1978–85; Head of Food Composition and Information Unit, 1984; Chm., Codex Cttee on Fats and Oils, 1987–92; Assessor, Adv. Cttees on Novel Foods and Processes and on Genetic Modification, 1985–92; Head of Food Sci. Div. II, 1989; Chief Scientist (Food), 1992–96. Lectr and Judge, E Anglia Fedn of Photographic Alliance of GB, 1978–88; Judge, Essex Internat. Salon of Photography, 1987–88. One-man exhibn of photographs, Half Moon Gallery, 1974; individual photographs in internat. exhibns, newspapers, jls and books. AFIAP 1972. *Publications:* papers on food safety in learned jls. *Recreations:* photography, golf. *Address:* 33 Waldegrave Gardens, Upminster, Essex RM14 1UT. *T:* (01708) 223742; *e-mail:* h.denner@ntlworld.com.

DENNEY, Stuart Henry MacDonald; QC 2008; *b* Welwyn, Herts, 15 June 1959; *s* of late Robert Waterson Denney and of Jane Denney (*née* Kemp); *m* 1988, Anna Louise Bancroft; one *s*. *Educ:* Gonville & Caius Coll., Cambridge (BA 1980). Called to the Bar, Inner Temple, 1982; in practice as a barrister, specialising in criminal and regulatory law. *Recreation:* Rugby Union. *Address:* Deans Court Chambers, 24 St John Street, Manchester M3 4DF. *T:* (0161) 214 6000, *Fax:* (0161) 214 6001; *e-mail:* clerks@deanscourt.co.uk. *Club:* London Scottish Football.

DENNINGTON, Dudley, FREng; FICE; FIStructE; Partner, 1972–92, Senior Partner, 1989–92, Bullen and Partners; *b* 21 April 1927; *s* of John Dennington and Beryl Dennington (*née* Hagon); *m* 1951, Margaret Patricia Stewart; two *d*. *Educ:* Clifton Coll., Bristol; Imperial Coll., London Univ. (BSc). National Service, 2nd Lieut, RE, 1947–49; Sandford Fawcett and Partners, Consulting Engineers, 1949–51; D. & C. Wm Press, Contractors, 1951–52; AMICE 1953; Manager, Design Office, George Wimpey & Co., 1952–65; GLC 1965–72: Asst Chief Engineer, Construction, 1965–67; Chief Engineer, Construction, 1967–70; Traffic Comr and Dir of Development, 1970–72. Mem., Bd for Engineers' Registration, Engrg Council, 1983–85. Pres., British Sect., Conseil Nat. des Ingénieurs et des Scientifiques de France, 1992. Vis. Prof., King's Coll., London Univ., 1978–81. Chm., Blythe Sappers, 1997. FICE 1966 (Mem. Council, 1975–78 and 1981–84; Vice-Pres., 1990–92); FCGI 1984; FREng (FEng 1985). *Recreations:* mathematics, painting. *Address:* 25 Corkran Road, Surbiton, Surrey KT6 6PL.

DENNIS, Maj.-Gen. Alastair Wesley, CB 1985; OBE 1973; *b* 30 Aug. 1931; *s* of late Ralph Dennis and of Helen (*née* Henderson); *m* 1st, 1957, Susan Lindy Elgar (*d* 1998); one *s* two *d*; 2nd, 2000, Caroline Brenda Dowdall. *Educ:* Malvern Coll.; RMA, Sandhurst. Commanded 16th/5th The Queen's Royal Lancers, 1971–74; Col GS, Cabinet Office, 1974–75; Comd 20 Armoured Bde, 1976–77; Dep. Comdt, Staff Coll., 1978–80; Director of Defence Policy (B), MoD, Whitehall, 1980–82; Dir, Military Assistance Overseas, MoD, 1982–85. Sec., Imperial Cancer Res. Fund, 1985–91; Chm., Assoc. of Med. Res. Charities, 1987–91. Mem., Malvern Coll. Council, 1988–92. Col, 16th/5th The Queen's Royal Lancers, 1990–93, The Queen's Royal Lancers, 1993–95. *Recreations:* fishing, golf, gardening. *Address:* St Maur, Long Street, Sherborne, Dorset DT9 3BS.

DENNIS, Geoffrey Adrian; Chief Executive, CARE International UK, since 2004; *b* 15 Aug. 1951; *s* of Clive Gardner Dennis and Audrey Joan Dennis; *m* 1998, Joanna Mary Snook; one *s*. *Educ:* Enfield Coll. (BA Hons); Univ. of Sussex (MA 1976). Main Bd Dir, Ewbank Preece Consultants, 1979–90; Man. Dir, Travers Morgan Consultants (Environmental), 1990–92; Internat. Dir, British Red Cross, and Hd of Delegn, Dem. People's Rep. of Korea, Internat. Fedn of the Red Cross, 1992–98; Hd of Regl Delegn, S Asia, Internat. Fedn of the Red Cross, 1998–2000; CEO, Friends of the Elderly, 2000–04. Chm., Rocking Horse Appeal (volunteer), 2004–. Badge of Honour, British Red Cross, 1998. *Recreations:* hockey (Sussex County 1st Eleven, Brighton Hockey Club), squash, travel. *Address:* Cuckfield, Sussex.

DENNIS, Rt Rev. John; Bishop of St Edmundsbury and Ipswich, 1986–96; an Hon. Assistant Bishop, Diocese of Winchester, since 2000; *b* 19 June 1931; *s* of late Hubert Ronald and Evelyn Dennis; *m* 1956, Dorothy Mary (*née* Hinnels); two *s*. *Educ:* Rutlish School, Merton; St Catharine's Coll., Cambridge (BA 1954; MA 1959); Cuddesdon Coll., Oxford (1954–56). RAF, 1950–51. Curate, St Bartholomew's, Armley, Leeds, 1956–60; Curate of Kettering, 1960–62; Vicar of the Isle of Dogs, 1962–71; Vicar of John Keble, Mill Hill, 1971–79; Area Dean of West Barnet, 1973–79; Prebendary of St Paul's Cathedral, 1977–79; Bishop Suffragan of Knaresborough, 1979–86; Diocesan Dir of Ordinands, Dio. Ripon, 1980–86; Asst Bp, Ely, 1996–99. Episcopal Guardian of Anglican Focolarini, 1981–96; Chaplain to Franciscan Third Order, 1988–94. Co-Chairman: English ARC, 1988–92; Anglican-Oriental Orthodox Dialogue, 1989–95. *Recreations:* walking, toy making, wood working. *Address:* 7 Conifer Close, Winchester, Hants SO22 6SH.

See also J. D. Dennis.

DENNIS, John David; HM Diplomatic Service; Additional Director, Asia, Foreign and Commonwealth Office, since 2007; *b* 6 Aug. 1959; *s* of Rt Rev. John Dennis, *qv*; *m* 1989, Jillian Kemp; two *s*. *Educ:* Haberdashers' Aske's Sch., Elstree; St Catharine's Coll., Cambridge (BA Hons 1981). Entered FCO, 1981; Hong Kong, 1983–85; Peking, 1985–87; Hd, Political Section, Kuala Lumpur, 1992–96; on secondment to Standard Chartered Bank, 1997–98; Dir, Automotive, DTI, 1998–2001; Dir, Trade and Investment Promotion, New Delhi, 2001–03; Minister, Consul-Gen. and Dep. Head of Mission, Beijing, 2003–06. *Recreations:* my children, reading, creative writing. *Address:* Foreign and Commonwealth Office, King Charles Street, SW1A 2AH; *e-mail:* dennisjj14@hotmail.com.

DENNIS, Mark Jonathan; QC 2006; Senior Treasury Counsel, Central Criminal Court, 1998–2006; a Recorder, since 2000; *b* 15 March 1955; *s* of Edward John Dennis and Patricia Edna Dennis; *m* 1985, Christabel Birbeck; one *s* one *d*. *Educ:* Battersea Grammar Sch.; Peterhouse, Cambridge (MA Law). Called to the Bar, Middle Temple, 1977; Jun. Treasury Counsel, Central Criminal Court, 1993–98. *Address:* (chambers) 6 King's Bench Walk, Temple, EC4Y 7DR. *T:* (020) 7583 0410.

DENNIS, Ronald, CBE 2000; Chairman and Chief Executive, McLaren Group, since 2000; *b* 1 June 1947; *s* of late Norman Stanley Dennis and of Evelyn (*née* Reader); *m* 1985, Lisa Ann Shelton; one *s* two *d*. *Educ:* Guildford Technical Coll. (vehicle technology course). Apprentice, Thomson & Taylor; Owner/Manager, Project Four Team, 1976–80 (winners: Procar Championship, 1979; Formula 3 Championship, 1979–80); merged with McLaren Team, 1980; McLaren Formula 1 Racing Team (winners: Constructors' Championship 1984, 1985, 1988, 1989, 1990, 1991, 1998; 9 Drivers' Championships). Co-Chm., Tommy's Campaign. Hon. DTech De Montfort, 1996; Hon. DSc City, 1997; DUniv Surrey, 2000. *Recreations:* golf, snow and water ski-ing, diving, shooting. *Address:* McLaren Group, McLaren Technology Centre, Chertsey Road, Woking, Surrey GU21 4YH. *T:* (01483) 261002, *Fax:* (01483) 261261. *Club:* British Racing Drivers'.

DENNISTON, Rev. Robin Alastair, PhD; Oxford Publisher and Senior Deputy Secretary to the Delegates, Oxford University Press, 1984–88 (Academic and General Publisher, 1980–84); Priest-in-charge of Great with Little Tew and Over Worton with Nether Worton, 1995–2002; *b* 25 Dec. 1926; *s* of late Alexander Guthrie Denniston, CMG, CBE, head of Govt code and cipher school, and late Dorothy Mary Gilliat; *m* 1st, 1950, Anne Alice Kyffin Evans (*d* 1985), *y d* of late Dr Geoffrey Evans, MD, FRCP, consulting Physician at St Bartholomew's Hosp., and late Hon. E. M. K. Evans; one *s* two *d*; 2nd, 1987, Dr Rosa Susan Penelope Beddington, FRS (*d* 2001). *Educ:* Westminster Sch. (King's Schol.; Captain of School, 1945); Christ Church, Oxford (Classical Schol.; 2nd cl. Hons Lit. Hum.); MSc Edinburgh 1992; PhD London 1997. National Service: commnd into Airborne Artillery, 1948. Editor at Collins, 1950–59; Man. Dir, Faith Press, 1959–60; Editor, Prism, 1959–61; Promotion Man., Hodder & Stoughton Ltd, 1960–64, Editorial Dir, 1966, Man. Dir, 1968–72; Dir, Matthew Hodder Ltd (and subsid. cos), 1968–72; Dep. Chm., George Weidenfeld & Nicolson (and subsid. cos), 1973–75; non-exec. Chm., A. R. Mowbray & Co., 1974–88; Dir, Thomson Publications Ltd, 1975–77; also Chm. of Michael Joseph Ltd, Thomas Nelson & Sons (and subsid. cos), George Rainbird Ltd, 1975–77 and Sphere Books, 1975–76; Academic Publisher, OUP, 1978; non-exec. Dir, W. W. Norton, 1989–. Student of Christ Church, 1978–88. Ordained Deacon, 1978, Priest, 1979; Hon. Curate: Clifton-on-Teme, 1978; New with South Hinksey, 1985; Non-Stipendiary Minister: Great with Little Tew, 1987–90 and 1995–2001; West Fife Team Ministry, 1990–93. A Church Comr, 1989–90. *Publications:* The Young Musicians, 1956; Partly Living, 1967; (ed) Part Time Priests?, 1960; (co-ed) Anatomy of Scotland, 1992; Churchill's Secret War, 1997; Trevor Huddleston: a life, 1999; Thirty Secret Years: A. G. Denniston's work in signals in intelligence 1914–44, 2007; contrib. Oxford DNB. *Recreations:* reading, walking, music. *Address:* 25 Pyndar Court, Newland, Malvern, Worcs WR13 5AX.

DENNY, Sir Anthony Coningham de Waltham, 8th Bt *cr* 1782, of Tralee Castle, Co. Kerry, Ireland; designer; Consultant, Verity and Beverley, Architects and Designers (offices in Tetbury, Lisbon and New York), since 2002 (Partner, 1959–2001); *b* 22 April 1925; *s* of Rev. Sir Henry Lyttleton Lyster Denny, 7th Bt, and Joan Lucy Dorothy, *er d* of Major William A. C. Denny, OBE; *S* father, 1953; *m* 1949, Anne Catherine, *e d* of S. Beverley, FRIBA; two *s* one adopted *d*. *Educ:* Clayesmore Sch. Served War of 1939–45:

Middle East, RAF (Aircrew), 1943–47. Anglo-French Art Centre, 1947–50; Mural Painter and Theatrical Designer, 1950–54. Trustee: Waltham Abbey; Emery Walker Trust. Hereditary Freeman of City of Cork. FRSA; MCSD. *Recreations:* architecture, painting. *Heir: s* Piers Anthony de Waltham Denny [*b* 14 March 1954; *m* 1987, Ella Jane, *o d* of Peter P. Huhne; two *d*]. *Address:* Almonry Cottage, Muchelney, Langport, Somerset TA10 0DG. *T:* (01458) 252621. *Club:* Chelsea Arts.

See also B. L. Denny.

DENNY, Barry Lyttelton, LVO 1979; HM Diplomatic Service, retired; *b* 6 June 1928; *s* of Rev. Sir Henry Lyttelton Lyster Denny, 7th Bt, and Joan Lucy Dorothy, *er d* of Major William A. C. Denny, OBE; *m* 1st, 1951 (marr. diss. 1968); one *s* one *d*; 2nd, 1969, Anne Rosemary Jordon, *o d* of late Col James F. White, MC; one *d*. *Educ:* Clayesmore Sch.; RMA, Sandhurst. Indian Army Cadet, 1946–47; commnd RA, 1949; retd from HM Forces as Captain (Temp. Major), 1960. Joined Foreign Office, 1962; First Sec., Nicosia, 1964; FO, later FCO, 1966; Kaduna, 1969; FCO, 1972; Vientiane, 1973; FCO, 1975; Kuwait, 1977; Counsellor, Oslo, 1980; seconded to MoD, 1984–89. Comdr, Order of St Olav (Norway), 1981. *Recreations:* collecting, my family.

See also Sir A. C. de W. Denny.

DENNY, Sir Charles Alistair Maurice, 4th Bt *cr* 1913, of Dumbarton, co. Dunbarton; Associate Director, HSBC Bank plc, since 2004; *b* 7 Oct. 1950; *e s* of Sir Alistair Maurice Archibald Denny, 3rd Bt and of Elizabeth Hunt, *y d* of Major Sir Guy Lloyd, 1st Bt, DSO; *S* father, 1995; *m* 1981, Belinda (marr. diss. 2002), *yr d* of J. P. McDonald; one *s* one *d*. *Educ:* Wellington Coll.; Edinburgh Univ. *Heir: s* Patrick Charles Alistair Denny, *b* 2 Jan. 1985. *Address:* The Ridge, 2 Oakfield, Hawkhurst, Kent TN18 4JR.

DENNY, John Ingram, CMG 1997; RIBA; Managing Director, Property Consulting Ltd, 2001–05; *b* 28 May 1941; *s* of Thomas Ingram Denny, Macclesfield and Claire Dorothy Denny (*née* Lewis); *m* 1967, Carol Ann Frances, *d* of Walter James Hughes, St Leonards, Bournemouth; one *s* two *d*. *Educ:* Normain Coll., Chester; Northern Poly. (Dip. Arch. (Hons)); Univ. of Reading (MSc). RIBA 1967. Partner, 1970–90, Sen. Partner, 1990–95, Man. Dir, 1995–2001, Cecil Denny Highton, architects and project managers; Jt Man. Dir, HOK Internat., 1995–2001; Sen. Vice Pres., Hellmuth, Obata + Kassabaum Inc., 1995–2001. Involved in architecture, conservation and mgt; Consultant to FCO, Home Office, MoD, Parly Works Office, Royal Household, HM Treasury, Cabinet Office, PACE and Natural Hist. Mus. *Recreations:* golf, photography.

DENNY, Rev. Norwyn Ephraim; retired Methodist minister; President of the Methodist Conference, 1982–83; *b* 23 Oct. 1924; *s* of Percy Edward James Denny and Dorothy Ann Denny (*née* Stringer); *m* 1950, Ellen Amelia Shaw; three *d*. *Educ:* City of Norwich School; Wesley College, Bristol. BD (Hons), London Univ. Ordained Methodist Minister, 1951; Methodist Minister in Jamaica, 1950–54; Minister in Peterborough, 1955–61; Member of Notting Hill Group (Ecumenical) Ministry, 1961–75; Chm., Liverpool Dist Methodist Church, 1975–86; Supt, Lowestoft and E Suffolk Methodist Circuit, 1986–91. Mem., Fellowship of Reconciliation. *Publications:* (with D. Mason and G. Ainger) News from Notting Hill, 1967; Caring, 1976; Worship, 1995; Words on the Way, 2005. *Recreations:* gardening, astronomy, association football, World Development movement. *Address:* 5 Red Hill, Lodge Park, Redditch, Worcs B98 7JE. *T:* (01527) 522426.

DENNY, Ronald Maurice; Director, The Catalogue Co. Ltd (Malta), 1991–2004; *b* 11 Jan. 1927; *s* of Maurice Denny and Ada (*née* Bradley); *m* 1st, 1952, Dorothy Hamilton (*d* 2003); one *s* two *d*; 2nd, 2005, Audrey Halls. *Educ:* Gosport County Sch. CEng, FIET. BBC Engineering, 1943; served Royal Navy, 1946–49; BBC Engr (TV), 1949–55; ATV Ltd, 1955, Gen. Man., ATV, 1967; Rediffusion Ltd, 1970; Chief Exec., 1979–85, Chm., 1985–89, Rediffusion PLC; Director: (non-exec.) Thames Television, 1981–89; BET, 1983–89; Electrocomponents, 1984–95. Mem. of Trust, Philharmonia Orch., 1983–93. Hon. Mem., RCM, 1984–. FRSA 1985. *Recreation:* music. *Address:* 7 The Holt, Bishop's Cleeve, Cheltenham GL52 8NQ. *T:* (01242) 677151. *Club:* Arts.

DENNY, William Eric, CBE 1984; QC 1975; a Recorder of the Crown Court, 1974–93; *b* 2 Nov. 1927; *s* of William John Denny and Elsie Denny; *m* 1960, Daphne Rose Southern-Reddin; one *s* two *d*. *Educ:* Ormskirk Grammar Sch.; Liverpool Univ. (Pres., Guild of Undergraduates, 1952–53; LLB). Served RAF, 1946–48. Called to the Bar, Gray's Inn, 1953, Bencher, 1985. Lectured at LSE, 1953–58. Chm., Home Secretary's Adv. Bd on Restricted Patients, 1980–85 (Mem., 1979). *Recreations:* music, sailing, gardening.

DENNYS, Nicholas Charles Jonathan; QC 1991; a Recorder, since 2000; *b* 14 July 1951; *m* 1977, Frances Winifred Markham (marr. diss. 2001); four *d*. *Educ:* Eton; Brasenose Coll., Oxford (BA 1973). Admitted Middle Temple, 1973; called to the Bar, 1975, Bencher, 2001; Asst Recorder, 1996–2000. Chm. Trustees, China Oxford Scholarship Fund. *Recreations:* windsurfing, golf, music. *Address:* 26 Ansdell Terrace, W8 5BY.

DENT, Helen Anne; Chief Executive, Family Welfare Association, since 1996; *b* 29 June 1951; *d* of Frederick and Muriel Dent. *Educ:* Lancaster Univ. (BEd 1977); South Bank Poly. (MSc 1987). London Bor. of Enfield, 1981–86; Cambs CC, 1986–90; NCH, 1990–96. Mem., ESRC, 2003–07. Non-exec. Dir, Gt Ormond St Hosp. for Children NHS Trust, 1998–. *Recreations:* music: choral and opera, theatre, cinema, reading, gardening. *Address:* Family Welfare Association, 501–505 Kingsland Road, E8 4AU; *e-mail:* helen.dent@fwa.org.uk.

DENTON, Dame Catherine Margaret Mary; *see* Scott, Dame M.

DENTON, Charles; Head of Drama, BBC Television, 1993–96; *b* 20 Dec. 1937; *s* of Alan Charles Denton and Mary Frances Royle; *m* 1961, Eleanor Mary Player; one *s* two *d*. *Educ:* Reading Sch.; Bristol Univ. BA History (Hons). Deckhand, 1960; advertising trainee, 1961–63; BBC TV, 1963–68; freelance television producer with Granada, ATV and Yorkshire TV, 1969–72; Dir, Tempest Films Ltd, 1969–71; Man. Dir, Black Lion Films, 1979–81; ATV: Head of Documentaries, 1974–77; Controller of Programmes, 1977–81; Dir of Progs, Central Indep. TV, 1981–84; Dir, Central Indep. Television plc, 1981–87; Chief Exec., Zenith Prodns, 1984–93; Chairman: Zenith North Ltd, 1988–93; Action Time Ltd, 1988–93; Producers Alliance for Cinema and TV, 1991–93; Cornwall Film, 2001–03. Mem., Arts Council of England, 1996–98. Governor, BFI, 1992–99; Mem. Bd, Film Council, 1999–2002; Chm., Nat. Film Trustee Co., 2001–08. FRSA 1988; FRTS 1988. *Recreations:* walking, music.

DENTON, Prof. Derek Ashworth, (Dick), AC 2005; FRACP, FRCP; FRS 1999; Founding Director, Howard Florey Institute of Experimental Physiology and Medicine, Melbourne, 1971–89, Emeritus Director and Consultant Scientist, since 1990; *b* 27 May 1924; *s* of Arthur A. and Catherine Denton; *m* 1953, Catherine Margaret Mary Scott (*see* Dame Margaret Scott); two *s*. *Educ:* Launceston Grammar Sch.; Univ. of Melbourne (MB BS). FAA 1979; FRACP 1986; FRCP 1988. Haley Res. Fellow, Walter & Eliza Hall Inst., Melbourne, 1948; Med. Res. Fellow, then Sen. Med. Res. Fellow, 1948–62, Principal Res. Fellow, 1962–70, NH&MRC. Adjunct Scientist, SW Foundn for Biomed. Res., San Antonio, Texas, 1991–; Pres., Howard Florey Biomed. Foundn, Melbourne, 1997–. Dir, David Syme Ltd, 1984–93. First Vice-Pres., Internat. Union of Physiol. Sci., 1983–89 (Chm., Nominating Cttee, and Cttee on Commns, 1986–93). Mem. Jury, Albert and Mary Lasker Foundn Awards in Med. Sci., 1979–90. For. Med. Mem., Royal Swedish Acad. of Sci., 1974; Mem., Amer. Acad. Arts & Sci., 1986; Foreign Associate: NAS, 1995; French Acad. of Scis, 2000. *Publications:* The Hunger for Salt, 1982; The Pinnacle of Life, 1994 (trans. French, 1997, Japanese, 1998); Les emotions primordiales et l'éveil de la conscience, 2005 (The Primordial Emotions: the dawning of consciousness, 2006). *Recreations:* wine, tennis, fly-fishing. *Address:* Department of Physiology, University of Melbourne, Parkville, Vic 3052, Australia; 816 Orrong Road, Toorak, Vic 3142, Australia. *Club:* Melbourne (Melbourne).

DENTON, Jane, CBE 2007; Director, Multiple Births Foundation, since 1999; *b* 30 June 1953; *d* of Ronald and Joan Gulliver; *m* 1987, Nigel Denton. *Educ:* Nottingham Bluecoat Sch.; St Bartholomew's Hosp., London (RGN 1974); Mill Rd Maternity Hosp., Cambridge (RM 1976). Staff Nurse, St Bartholomew's Hosp., 1974–76; Midwife, Mill Road Maternity Hosp., 1977–78; Nursing Director: Hallam Med. Centre, 1978–91; Multiple Births Foundn, 1991–99. Mem., HFEA, 1992–2004 (Dep. Chm., 1997–2000). FRCN 2006. *Publications:* (ed jtly) Infertility: nursing and caring, 1995; contrib. articles on multiple births. *Recreations:* music, walking. *Address:* Multiple Births Foundation, Queen Charlotte's and Chelsea Hospital, W12 0HS. *T:* (020) 8383 3519.

DENTON, Prof. John Douglas, PhD; FRS 2000; FREng; Professor of Turbomachinery Aerodynamics, Cambridge University, 1991–2005; Fellow of Trinity Hall, Cambridge, 1977–2005, now Emeritus (Vice-Master, 2002–05); *b* 1 Dec. 1939; *s* of Donald and Mary Denton; *m* 1966, Maureen Hunt; three *d*. *Educ:* Trinity Hall, Cambridge (BA, PhD); Univ. of British Columbia (MASc). MIMechE, CEng, FREng (FEng 1993). Lectr, Univ. of East Africa, 1967–69; Res. Officer, later Section Head, CEGB, 1969–77; Lectr, Dept of Engrg, Cambridge, 1977–91. *Recreations:* travel, mountain walking, bee keeping.

DENTON, John Grant, AM 2005; OBE 1977; General Secretary, General Synod of Anglican Church of Australia, 1969–94 (part time until 1977); *b* 16 July 1929; *s* of Ernest Bengrey Denton and Gladys Leonard Stevenson; *m* 1956, Shirley Joan Wise; two *s* two *d*. *Educ:* Camberwell C of E Grammar School, Melbourne. Personnel and Industrial Relations Dept, Mobil Oil (Aust.), 1950–54; Administrative Sec., Dio. of Central Tanganyika, as CMS missionary, 1954–64; Dir of Information, Dio. of Sydney, 1964–69; Registrar, Dio. of Sydney, 1969–77 (part time). Mem., ACC, 1976–84 (Chm., 1980–84); Chm., Aust. Churches' Cttee for Seventh Assembly of WCC, Canberra, 1991. Mem., Central Coast Regl Council, dio. of Newcastle, 1997–2005. Chm., Sydney Bethel Union Trust, 1986–2002. *Recreation:* model railway. *Address:* 14A Torres Street, Killarney Vale, NSW 2261, Australia.

DENTON, Dame Margaret; *see* Scott, Dame M.

DENTON, Prof. Richard Michael, PhD, DSc; FMedSci; FRS 1998; Professor of Biochemistry, University of Bristol, since 1987; *b* 16 Oct. 1941; *s* of Arthur Benjamin Denton and Eileen Mary Denton (*née* Evans); *m* 1965, Janet Mary Jones; one *s* two *d*. *Educ:* Wycliffe Coll.; Christ's Coll., Cambridge (MA, PhD 1967); Univ. of Bristol (DSc 1976). University of Bristol: Lectr in Biochemistry, 1967–78; Reader in Biochemistry, 1978–87; Hd, Dept of Biochemistry, 1995–2000; Chm., Med. Scis, 2000–04; Founder Dean, Med. and Vet. Scis, 2003–04. MRC Sen. Res. Leave Fellow, 1984–88. Mem., MRC, 1999–2004. Founder FMedSci 1998. *Publications:* more than 240 res. papers, mainly on molecular basis of effects of insulin on metabolism, and role of calcium ions in mitochondria, in internat. res. jls. *Recreations:* family, walking, keeping fit, cooking. *Address:* Department of Biochemistry, University of Bristol School of Medical Sciences, University Walk, Bristol BS8 1TD. *T:* (0117) 331 2184.

DENTON-THOMPSON, Aubrey Gordon, OBE 1958; MC 1942; *b* 6 June 1920; *s* of late M. A. B. Denton-Thompson; *m* 1944, Ruth Cecily Isaac (*d* 1959); two *s* (one *d* decd); *m* 1961, Barbara Mary Wells. *Educ:* Malvern Coll. Served in RA 1940–44; seconded to Basutoland Administration, 1944; apptd to HM Colonial Service, 1945; transferred to Tanganyika as Asst District Officer, 1947; seconded to Colonial Office, 1948–50, District Officer; seconded to Secretariat, Dar es Salaam, as Asst Sec., 1950; Colonial Sec., Falkland Islands, 1955–60; Dep. Permanent Sec., Ministry of Agriculture, Tanganyika, 1960–62; retired from Tanganyika Civil Service, 1963. Man. Dir, Tanganyika Sisal Marketing Assoc. Ltd, 1966–68 (Sec. 1963); Sen. Agricl Advr, UNDP, 1968–78, and FAO Country Rep.: Korea, 1970–73, Indonesia, 1973–76, Turkey, 1976–78; Sen. Advr to Director General, FAO, Rome, July–Dec. 1978; retd Jan. 1979. Chm., New Forest Conservative Assoc., 1985–88 (Dep. Chm., 1983–85). *Address:* Octave Cottage, 43 Ramley Road, Pennington, Lymington, Hants SO41 8GZ. *T:* (01590) 676626.

DENYER, Roderick Lawrence; QC 1990; **His Honour Judge Denyer;** a Circuit Judge, since 2002; *b* 1 March 1948; *s* of Oliver James Denyer and Olive Mabel Jones; *m* 1st, 1973, Pauline (*née* Vann) (marr. diss.); two *d*; 2nd, Yoko Ujile; two step *d*. *Educ:* Grove Park Grammar School for Boys, Wrexham; London School of Economics (LLM). Called to the Bar, Inner Temple, 1970, Bencher, 1996; Lectr in Law, Bristol Univ., 1971–73; in practice at Bar, 1973–2002; a Recorder, 1990–2002. Vis. Fellow, UWE, 1994–. Mem., Bar Council, 1992–95. *Publications:* Children and Personal Injury Litigation, 1993, 2nd edn 2002; contrib. legal jls. *Recreations:* cricket, 19th century history, theatre, restaurants. *Address:* Cardiff Crown Court, Law Courts, Cathays Park, Cardiff CF1 3PE.

DENZA, Mrs Eileen, CMG 1984; Visiting Professor, University College London, since 1997 (Senior Research Fellow, 1996–97); Second Counsel to Chairman of Committees and Counsel to European Communities Committee, House of Lords, 1987–95; *b* 23 July 1937; *d* of Alexander L. Young and Mrs Young; *m* 1966, John Denza; two *s* one *d*. *Educ:* Aberdeen Univ. (MA); Somerville Coll., Oxford (MA); Harvard Univ. (LLM). Called to the Bar, Lincoln's Inn, 1963. Asst Lectr in Law, Bristol Univ., 1961–63; Asst Legal Adviser, FCO (formerly FO), 1963–74; Legal Counsellor, FCO, 1974–80; Counsellor (Legal Adviser), Office of UK Perm. Rep. to European Communities, 1980–83; Legal Counsellor, FCO, 1983–86. Pupillage and practice at the Bar, 1986–87. Member: EC Law Section of Adv. Bd, British Inst. of Internat. and Comparative Law, 1988–; Adv. Bd, Inst. of European Public Law, 1992–96; Justice Expert Panel on Human Rights in the EU, 1997–2002. FRSA 1995. *Publications:* Diplomatic Law, 1976, 3rd edn 2008; The Intergovernmental Pillars of the European Union, 2002; contribs to: Satow's Guide to Diplomatic Practice, 5th edn; Essays in Air Law; Lee's Consular Law and Practice, 2nd edn; Institutional Dynamics of European Integration; The European Union and World Trade Law; Evans' International Law; EU Law for the 21st Century; The Harvard Research in Internat. Law; articles in British Yearbook of Internat. Law, Revue du Marché Commun, International and Comparative Law Quarterly, Statute Law Review, Common Market Law Review, European Foreign Affairs Review.

de OSUNA, Sheelagh Marilyn; Ambassador of Trinidad and Tobago to Venezuela and (non-resident) to Peru, Ecuador, Colombia and Bolivia, 2002–06; *b* 25 March 1948; *d* of Henry Wells Macnaughton-Jones and Cynthia Maud Macnaughton-Jones; *m* 1971, Alfredo Osuna (marr. diss. 1980); one *d*. *Educ:* Univ. of Sussex (BA Hons Internat. Relns); Universidad Javeriana, Bogotá (Dip. in Spanish); Internat. Law Inst., Georgetown Univ., Washington (Dip. in Loan Negotiation and Renegotiation). Entered Foreign Service of Trinidad and Tobago, 1970: Second Sec., Perm. Mission to UN, Geneva, 1970–72; First Sec., Caracas, 1972–77; Foreign Service Officer III, Political Bureau, Min. of Foreign Affairs, 1977–79; Econ. Counsellor, Washington, 1979–88; Dir, Internat. Econ. Relns Div., Min. of Foreign Affairs, 1988–92; Dep. High Comr, London, 1992–95; Ambassador for Trade, Min. of Trade and Industry, Port-of-Spain, 1995–96; High Comr, London and Ambassador (non-res.) to Germany, Norway, Sweden and Denmark, 1996–2000; Perm. Sec., Min. of Foreign Affairs and Hd of Foreign Service, 2001. *Recreations:* swimming, scuba diving, theatre and opera, foreign travel, cooking. *Clubs:* Royal Over-Seas League; Country, Union (Port-of-Spain, Trinidad).

DEPARDIEU, Gérard; actor; *b* 27 Dec. 1948; *m* 1970, Elisabeth Guignot (marr. diss. 1996); one *s* one *d*. *Educ:* Ecole d'art dramatique de Jean Laurent Cochet. Pres., Cannes Film Fest. Jury, 1992. Fellow BFI, 1989. Chevalier, Ordre Nat. du Mérite (France), 1985; Chevalier, Légion d'Honneur (France), 1996. *Stage:* Les Garçons de la Bande, Th. Edouard VII, 1968; Une fille dans ma soupe, 1970, Galapagos, 1971, Th. de la Madeleine; Saved, Th. Nat. de Chaillot, 1972; Home, 1972, Isme, Isaac, 1973, La Chevauchée sur le Lac de Constance, 1974, Espace Pierre Cardin; Les Gens deraisonnables sont en voie de disparition, Nanterre, 1977; Tartuffe, Strasbourg, 1983; Lily Passion (musical), Zénith, 1986. *Films:* Le Tueur, 1971; L'affaire Dominici, Un peu de soleil dans l'eau froide, Au rendez-vous de la mort joyeuse, La Scoumoune, Deux hommes dans la ville, Le viager, 1972; Rude journée pour la reine, Stavisky, Les Gaspards, Les Valseuses, 1973; Vincent, François, Paul et les autres, Pas si méchant que ça, 1974; 1900, La dernière femme, Sept morts sur ordonnance, Maîtresse, 1975; Barocco, René la Canne, Baxter, Vera Baxter, 1976; Dites-lui que je l'aime, Le Camion, La nuit tous les chats sont gris, Préparez vos mouchoirs, Rêve de singe, 1977; Le Sucre, Les chiens, Le Grand embouteillage, 1978; Buffet froid, Rosy la bourrasque, Loulou, Mon oncle d'Amérique, 1979; Le dernier métro (Caesar best actor award, 1980), Inspecteur la Bavure, Je vous aime, 1980; Le Choix des armes, La Femme d'à côté, La Chèvre, Le Retour de Martin Guerre, Danton, 1981; Le Grand frère, La Lune dans le caniveau, 1982; Les Compères, Fort Saganne, 1983; Tartuffe (also dir), Rive droite, rive gauche, Police, 1984; Une femme ou deux, Tenue de soirée, Jean de Florette, 1985; Les Fugitifs, Sous le soleil de Satan, 1986; Camille Claudel, 1987; Drôle d'endroit pour une rencontre, Deux, Trop belle pour toi, I Want to go Home, 1988; Cyrano de Bergerac, 1989 (Best Actor, Cannes, 1990; Caesar and de Donatello best actor awards, 1991); Green Card (Golden Globe award, 1991), Uranus, Merci la vie, 1990; Mon Père ce héros, 1492: Colombus, Tous les matins du monde, 1991; Hélas pour moi, Germinal, 1992; Une pure formalité, Le Colonel Chabert, 1993; La Machine, Elisa, Les Cents et une nuits, Les anges gardiens, 1994; Unhook the Stars, 1995; Hamlet, 1997; The Man in the Iron Mask, 1998; Asterix et Obelix contre César, Un pont entre deux rives (dir), 1999; 102 Dalmatians, 2000; Astérix et Obelix: Mission Cléopatre, The Closet, 2002; Bon voyage, Nathalie, 2004; Les temps qui changent, 2005; Last Holiday, 36 Quai des Orfèvres, 2006; La Môme, La vie en rose, The Singer, 2007; Astérix aux Jeux Olympiques, Babylon A. D., 2008; has also appeared on TV. *Publication:* Lettres volées, 1988. *Address:* c/o Artmédia, 20 avenue Rapp, 75007 Paris, France.

de PAULA, (Frederic) Clive, CBE 1970; TD 1950 and Clasp 1951; FCA, JDipMA; Chairman, Dennys Sanders & Greene Ltd, 1987–2008; *b* 17 Nov. 1916; 2nd *s* of late F. R. M. de Paula, CBE, FCA, and Agnes Smithson de Paula (*née* Clark) (American Medal of Freedom, 1947). *Educ:* Rugby Sch.; Spain and France. ACA 1940, FCA 1951; JDipMA 1966. Articled to de Paula, Turner, Lake & Co., chartered accountants, London, 1934–39. 2nd Lieut, TA, 1939; Liaison Officer, Free French Forces in London and French Equatorial Africa, 1940; Specially employed Middle East and E Africa, 1941; SOE Madagascar, 1942; comd special forces unit with 11th E African Div., Ceylon and Burma, 1943; Finance Div., Control Commn, Germany, 1945; demobilised as Major, 1946; Captain 21st Special Air Service Regt (Artists) TA, 1947–56. Joined Robson, Morrow & Co., management consultants, 1946; Partner, 1951; seconded to DEA then to Min. of Technology as an Industrial Adviser, 1967; Co-ordinator of Industrial Advisers to Govt, 1969; returned as Sen. Partner, Robson, Morrow & Co., 1970–71; Man. Dir, Agricultural Mortgage Corp. Ltd, 1971–81; Dir, 1972–83, Dep. Chm., 1978–80, Chm., 1980–83, Tecalemit plc; non-exec. Dir, Green's Economiser Group plc, 1972–83; Dep. Chm., C. & J. Clark Ltd, 1985–86. Mem., EDC for Agric., 1972–81. Member: ICAEW, 1940–; Inst. of Cost & Works Accountants, 1947–72; British Computer Soc., 1964–74 (Mem. Council, 1965–68); Management Consultants Assoc., 1964–72 (Mem. Council, 1970–71); BIM, 1970–84 (Mem. Council, 1971–76; CIMgt 1970). Gen. Comr of Income Tax, Winslow Div., Bucks, 1965–82. Vice Pres., Schoolmistresses and Governesses Benevolent Instn, 1982–2003 (Hon. Treas., 1947–81); Chm., Internat. Wine and Food Soc., 1980–83 (Silver Medal, 1996). *Publications:* first published paper in world to forecast coming impact of electronic computers on accountancy, 1952; Accounts for Management, 1954; (ed) P. Tovey, Balance Sheets: how to read and understand them, 4th edn, 1954; (ed) F. R. M. de Paula, The Principles of Auditing, 12th edn 1957 (trans. Sinhalese, 1967), (with F. A. Attwood) 15th edn as Auditing: Principles and Practice, 1976, (with F. A. Attwood and N. D. Stein) 17th edn as de Paula's Auditing, 1986; Management Accounting in Practice, 1959 (trans. Japanese, 1960); (ed with A. G Russell) A. C. Smith, Internal Control and Audit, 2nd edn, 1968; (with A. W. Willsmore) The Techniques of Business Control, 1973; (with F. A. Attwood) Auditing Standards, 1978. *Address:* c/o National Westminster Bank, 60 High Street, Esher, Surrey KT10 9QY.

de PENCIER, Theo; Chief Executive, Freight Transport Association, since 2007; *b* Carlisle, 16 Feb. 1952; *s* of Edwin and Maria de Pencier; *m* 1976, Fiona Margaret Lyall; one *s* two *d*. *Educ:* Taunton Sch., Som; Univ. of Newcastle upon Tyne (BA Hons Econ 1974). Grad. trainee, Tube Investments Ltd, 1970–74; Mktg Exec., H. J. Heinz Ltd, 1974–79; Senior Manager: Grand Metropolitan plc, 1980–85; NFC plc, 1985–95; Managing Director: Danzas Ltd, 1995–99; Bibby Line Gp, 1999–2007. MInstD 2006. FCILT 2001. Liveryman, Co. of Carmen. *Recreations:* travel, Rugby, theatre. *Address:* Freight Transport Association Ltd, Hermes House, St John's Road, Tunbridge Wells, Kent TN4 9UZ. *T:* (01892) 526171, *Fax:* (01892) 552371; *e-mail:* tdepencier@fta.co.uk.

de PEYER, David Charles; Director General, Cancer Research Campaign, 1984–96; *b* 25 April 1934; *s* of late Charles de Peyer, CMG and Flora (*née* Collins); *m* 1959, Ann Harbord. *Educ:* Rendcomb Coll., Cirencester; Magdalen Coll., Oxford (BA PPE). Asst Principal, Min. of Health, 1960; Sec., Royal Commn on NHS, 1976–79; Under Sec., DHSS, 1979–84. Vice-Chm., Suffolk HA, 1996–98. Mem., Criminal Injuries Compensation Appeals Panel, 1997–2006. Trustee: Disabled Living Foundn, 1988–2004; Res. into Ageing, 1996–2001. *Address:* 21 Southwood Park, N6 5SG.

de PEYER, Gervase; solo clarinettist; conductor; Founder and Conductor, Melos Sinfonia of Washington, 1992; Director, London Symphony Wind Ensemble; solo clarinettist, Chamber Music Society of Lincoln Center, New York, since 1969; Co-founder and Artistic Director, Innisfree Music Festival, Pa, USA; *b* London, 11 April 1926; *m* 1980, Katia Perret Aubry; one *s* two *d* by a previous marriage. *Educ:* King Alfred's, London; Bedales; Royal College of Music. Served HM Forces, 1945 and 1946. Founder Mem., Melos Ensemble of London, 1950–72; Principal Clarinet, London Symphony Orchestra, 1955–72; formerly: Associate Conductor, Haydn Orch. of London; Resident Conductor, Victoria Internat. Fest., BC, Canada. ARCM; FRCM 1992; Hon. ARAM. Gold Medallist, Worshipful Co. of Musicians, 1948; Charles Gros Grand Prix du Disque, 1961, 1962; Plaque of Honour for recording, Acad. of Arts and Sciences of America, 1962. Most recorded solo clarinettist in world. *Recreations:* travel, cooking, kite-flying, sport, theatre. *Address:* 42 Tower Bridge Wharf, 86 St Katherine's Way, E1W 1UR. *T:* and *Fax:* (020) 7265 1110; *e-mail:* gervase@depeyer.freeserve.co.uk; *web:* www.GervasedePeyer.net; La Source, Chemin de La Hournère, 4770 Casteljaloux, France. *T:* (5) 53833154.

DEPLEDGE, Prof. Michael Harold, PhD, DSc; Professor of Environment and Human Health, Peninsula Medical School, since 2007; *b* 8 Jan. 1954; *s* of Clifford and Edna Depledge; *m* 1977, Juliana Eileen Dearden; two *s*. *Educ:* Leeds Modern Grammar Sch.; Westfield Coll., Univ. of London (BSc 1st Cl. Hons Biol Scis 1975; PhD 1982; DSc 1996). Res. Fellow, Brompton Hosp., London, 1979; Clinical Scientist, Royal Marsden Hosp., Sutton, 1979–82; Lectr in Physiol., Med. Sch., Univ. of Hong Kong, 1983–87; Prof. of Ecotoxicol., Odense Univ., Denmark, 1987–94; Prof. of Ecotoxicol. and Dir, Plymouth Envmtl Res. Centre, Univ. of Plymouth, 1994–2002; Hd of Sci., 2002–05, Chief Scientific Advr, 2005–06, Envmt Agency. Keeley Vis. Fellow, Wadham Coll., Oxford, 2006. Member: NERC, 2003–06; Natural England, 2006–; Royal Commn on Envmtl Pollution, 2006–; Vice-Chm., Sci. Adv. Cttee, DG Research, EC, 2006–. Advr to various UN bodies, 1990–. *Publications:* contrib. numerous peer-reviewed scientific papers, book chapters and abstracts to internat. scientific literature and learned jls, incl. Lancet, Thorax, Envmtl Sci. and Technol., Envmtl Health Perspectives, Marine Biol., Aquatic Toxicol. *Recreations:* travel, guitar, football, sailing, reading. *Address:* Peninsula Medical School, John Bull Building, Research Way, Plymouth PL6 8BU. *T:* (01752) 437402; *e-mail:* michael.depledge@pms.ac.uk.

DEPP, John Christopher, (Johnny); actor; *b* 9 June 1963; *s* of John Christopher Depp and Betty Sue Depp (*née* Palmer); *m* 1983, Lori Anne Allison (marr. diss. 1985); partner, Vanessa Chantal Paradis; one *s* one *d*. *Television series:* 21 Jump Street, 1987–90; United States of Poetry, 1995. *Films include:* A Nightmare on Elm Street, 1984; Private Resort, 1985; Platoon, 1986; Cry Baby, Edward Scissorhands, 1990; Freddy's Dead: The Final Nightmare, 1991; Benny and Joon, What's Eating Gilbert Grape, Arizona Dream, 1993; Ed Wood, Don Juan DeMarco, 1994; Dead Man, Nick of Time, 1995; The Brave (also writer and dir), Donnie Brasco, 1997; Fear and Loathing in Las Vegas, 1998; The Astronaut's Wife, The Ninth Gate, Sleepy Hollow, 1999; The Man Who Cried, Before Night Falls, Chocolat, 2000; Blow, From Hell, 2001; Pirates of the Caribbean: The Curse of the Black Pearl, Once Upon a Time in Mexico, 2003; Secret Window, Finding Neverland, The Libertine, 2004; Charlie and the Chocolate Factory, 2005; Pirates of the Caribbean: Dead Man's Chest, 2006; Pirates of the Caribbean: At World's End, 2007; Sweeney Todd: The Demon Barber of Fleet Street, 2008. *Address:* 9100 Wilshire Boulevard, Suite 725, East Beverly Hills, CA 90212, USA.

de PURY, Christopher Mark; Partner, Berwin Leighton Paisner LLP, since 2008; *b* London, 11 Feb. 1968; *s* of Andrew and Lois de Pury; *m* 2000, Carolyn Sara Rice-Oxley; two *s* one *d*. *Educ:* Christ Church, Oxford (MA Hons Juris.). Admitted solicitor, 1992; Solicitor, Herbert Smith LLP, Partner, 1998–2008. *Recreations:* theatre, drama, the arts, family. *Address:* *e-mail:* chris.de.pury@blplaw.com.

de QUINCEY, Paul Morrison; Director and Cultural Counsellor, France, British Council, since 2004; *b* 23 June 1954; *s* of Ronald Anthony and Margaret Claire de Quincey; *m* 1976, Theresa Elizabeth Patricia Casabayo; one *s* one *d*. *Educ:* Univ. of Leeds (BA Hons English 1975; PGCE English/Drama 1976; MA Linguistics 1979). Teacher: of English, Ubiaja, Nigeria, 1976–78; of English and Drama, Wakefield, 1979–81; British Council, 1981–: Asst Rep., S Korea, 1981–84; Consultant, ELSD, London, 1984–87; Deputy Director: Algeria, 1987–91; Czechoslovakia, 1991–93; Director: Venezuela, 1993–98; Americas, 1998–2000; UK, 2000–02; Grant Funded Services, 2002–04. *Recreations:* fishing, shooting, the arts. *Address:* 5 Avenue F. D. Roosevelt, 75008 Paris, France. *T:* (6) 82574433; *e-mail:* paul.dequincey@britishcouncil.fr; 167 Kennington Road, SE11 6SF.

DE RAMSEY, 4th Baron *cr* 1887, of Ramsey Abbey, Huntingdon; **John Ailwyn Fellowes;** DL; Chairman, Environment Agency, 1995–2000; *b* 27 Feb. 1942; *s* of 3rd Baron De Ramsey, KBE and Lilah Helen Suzanne (*d* 1987), *d* of Frank Labouchere; *S* father, 1993; *m* 1st, 1973, Phyllida Mary Forsyth; one *s*; 2nd, 1984, Alison Mary Birkmyre; one *s* two *d*. *Educ:* Winchester Coll.; Writtle Inst. of Agriculture. Dir, Cambridge Water Co., 1974–94 (Chm., 1983–89). Crown Estate Comr, 1994–2002. President: CLA, 1991–93; Assoc. of Drainage Authorities, 1993–94 and 2004–. FRAgS 1993 (Pres., 2001–02). DL Cambs, 1993. Hon. DSc Cranfield, 1997. *Recreations:* golf, fishing, fine arts. *Heir:* *s* Freddie John Fellowes, *b* 31 May 1978. *Address:* Abbots Ripton Hall, Huntingdon PE28 2PQ. *T:* (01487) 773555. *Club:* Boodle's.

DERBY, 19th Earl of, *cr* 1485; **Edward Richard William Stanley;** DL; Bt 1627; Baron Stanley 1832; Baron Stanley of Preston 1886; Chairman, FF&P Trustee Co. Ltd, since 2004; *b* 10 Oct. 1962; *er s* of Hon. Hugh Henry Montagu Stanley (*d* 1971), *g s* of 17th Earl, and of Mary Rose Stanley (*née* Birch); *S* uncle, 1994; *m* 1995, Hon. Caroline Emma Neville, *d* of 10th Baron Braybrooke, *qv*; two *s* one *d*. *Educ:* Ludgrove; Eton Coll.; RAC Cirencester. Commnd Grenadier Guards, 1982, resigned 1985. Merchant banker with Robert Fleming Hldgs Ltd, 1987–2001. Director: Fleming Private Fund Management Ltd, 1991–96; Fleming Private Asset Management Ltd, 1992–2000; The Haydock Park Racecourse Co. Ltd, 1994–; Robert Fleming & Co. Ltd, 1996–98; Robert Fleming Internat. Ltd, 1998–2001; Fleming Family & Partners, 2001–. Trustee, Nat. Mus Liverpool (formerly Nat. Mus and Galls on Merseyside), 1995–2006 (Mem., Finance Cttee, 2006–). President: Liverpool Chamber of Commerce and Industry, 1995–; Knowsley Chamber of Commerce and Industry, 1995–; Sefton Chamber of Commerce and Industry, 1998; Liverpool Council of Social Service, 1996–. Aintree Trustee, 1995–. President: Royal Liverpool Philharmonic Soc., 1995–; Rugby Football League Assoc., 1997–; Vice Pres., PGA, 2001–. Mem. Council, Univ. of Liverpool, 1998–2004. DL Merseyside, 1999. *Publication:* Ouija Board: a mare in a million, 2007. *Recreations:* shooting, ski-ing, food and wine. *Heir:* *s* Lord Stanley, *qv*. *Address:* Knowsley, Prescot, Merseyside L34 4AF. *T:* (0151) 489 6148, *Fax:* (0151) 482 1988; *e-mail:* private.office@knowsley.com. *Clubs:* White's, Jockey Club Rooms.

DERBY, Bishop of, since 2005; **Rt Rev. Dr Alastair Llewellyn John Redfern;** *b* 1 Sept. 1948; *s* of Victor Redfern and Audrey Joan Redfern; *m* 1st, 1974, Jane Valerie Straw (*d* 2004); two *d*, 2nd, 2006, Caroline Elizabeth Boddington, *qv*. *Educ:* Christ Church, Oxford (MA Modern Hist.); Trinity Coll., Cambridge (MA Theol.); Westcott House, Cambridge; PhD Theol. Bristol. Curate, Wolverhampton, 1976–79; Lectr in Church

History, 1979–87, Vice Principal, 1985–87, Ripon Coll., Cuddesdon; Dir, Oxford Inst. for Church and Society, 1979–83; Curate, All Saints, Cuddesdon, 1983–87; Canon Theologian, Bristol Cathedral, 1987–97; Bishop Suffragan of Grantham, 1997–2005. Dean of Stamford, 1997–2005; Canon and Preb., Lincoln Cathedral, 2000–05. *Publications:* Ministry and Priesthood, 1999; Being Anglican, 2000. *Recreations:* reading, walking. *Address:* The Bishop's House, 6 King Street, Duffield, Derby DE56 4EU. *T:* (office) (01332) 840132, *Fax:* (01332) 840397; *e-mail:* bishop@bishopofderby.org.

DERBY, Dean of; *see* Cuttell, Very Rev. Dr J. C.

DERBY, Archdeacon of; *see* Cunliffe, Ven. C. J.

DERBYSHIRE, Sir Andrew (George), Kt 1986; FRIBA; Chairman, Robert Matthew, Johnson-Marshall & Partners & RMJM Ltd, 1983–89; President, RMJM Group, 1989–98; *b* 7 Oct. 1923; *s* of late Samuel Reginald Derbyshire and late Helen Louise Puleston Derbyshire (*née* Clarke); *m* Lily Rhodes (*née* Binns), *widow* of late Norman Rhodes; three *s* one *d*. *Educ:* Chesterfield Grammar Sch.; Queens' Coll., Cambridge; Architectural Assoc. MA (Cantab), AA Dip. (Hons). Admty Signals Estabt and Bldg Research Station, 1943–46. Farmer & Dark, 1951–53 (Marchwood and Belvedere power stations); West Riding County Architect's Dept, 1953–55 (bldgs for educn and social welfare). Asst City Architect, Sheffield, 1955–61; responsible for central area redevelt. Mem. Research Team, RIBA Survey of Architects' Offices, 1960–62. Since 1961, as Mem. RM, J-M & Partners, later RMJM Ltd, responsible for: develt of Univ. of York, 1961–98, Central Lancs New Town, NE Lancs Impact Study, Univ. of Cambridge, West Cambridge Develt and New Cavendish Laboratory, Preston Market and Guildhall, London Docklands Study, Hillingdon Civic Centre, Cabtrack and Minitram feasibility studies, Suez Master Plan Study; Castle Peak Power Stations, and Harbour Reclamation and Urban Growth Study, Hong Kong. Consultant on envmtl impact issues, listing of post-war bldgs and res. on feedback for construction industry, 1998–. Member: RIBA Council, 1950–72, 1975–81 (Senior Vice-Pres., 1980); NJCC, 1961–65; Bldg Industry Communications Res. Cttee, 1964–66 (Chm. Steering Cttee); DoE Planning and Transport Res. Adv. Council, 1971–76; Commn on Energy and the Environment, 1978–81. Pt-time Mem., CEGB, 1973–84; Board Member: Property Services Agency, 1975–79; London Docklands Develt Corp., 1984–88 (Chm., Planning Cttee, 1984–88); Construction Industry Sector Group, NEDC, 1988–92; Mem., Construction Industry Council, 1990–94. Hoffman Wood Prof. of Architecture, Univ. of Leeds, 1978–80; External Prof., Dept of Civil Engineering, Univ. of Leeds, 1981–85; Gresham Prof. of Rhetoric, Gresham Coll., 1990–92; Hon. Fellow, Inst. of Advanced Architectural Studies, Univ. of York, 1994; Hon. FIStructE 1992. FRSA 1981 (Chm., Art for Architecture Project, 1994–98). DUniv York, 1972. *Publications:* The Architect and his Office, 1962; on professional consultancy, town planning, public transport, and energy conservation in construction; incl. papers on architecture, science and conservation of 20th century buildings, 1998–. *Recreations:* his family, the garden. *Address:* 4 Sunnyfield, Hatfield, Herts AL9 5DX. *T:* (01707) 265903.

DERHAM, Catherine Beatrice Margaret, (Katie), (Mrs J. Vincent); newscaster, ITV News, since 1999, and ITV Evening News, since 2001; presenter, ITV lunchtime news, since 2005; *b* 18 June 1970; *d* of John and Margaret Derham; *m* 1999, John Vincent; two *d*. *Educ:* Cheadle Hulme Sch.; Magdalene Coll., Cambridge (BA Econ). Joined BBC, 1993: researcher, Money Box, Radio 4, 1993–94; Producer, Radio Business Progs, 1994–95; Presenter, Money Check, Radio 5 Live, 1995–96; Consumer Affairs Corresp., TV business progs, 1996–97; reporter, Film '96, '97; Media and Arts Corresp., 1998–2001, Media and Arts Editor, 2001–03, ITN; presenter, London Tonight, ITV, 2004–. Presenter: Classical Brit Awards, annually, 2001–04; Classic FM, 2002–; LBC, 2003. *Recreations:* reading, travel, music - listening and playing, film, sailing. *Address:* ITN, 200 Gray's Inn Road, WC1X 8XZ. *T:* (020) 7833 3000.

DERHAM, Patrick Sibley Jan, MA; Head Master, Rugby School, since 2001; *b* 23 Aug. 1959; *s* of John Joseph Sibley Derham and Helena Petronella Trimby (*née* Verhagen); *m* 1982, Alison Jane Sheardown; one *s* one *d*. *Educ:* Training Ship Arethusa; Pangbourne Coll. (Hd of Sch.); Pembroke Coll., Cambridge (Foundn Schol., 1st Cl. Hons Hist. 1982, MA 1985). Assistant Master: Cheam, 1982–84; Radley Coll., 1984–96 (Hd of Hist. and Tutor, 1990–96); Headmaster, Solihull Sch., 1996–2001. Trustee: Solihull Community Foundn, 1998–2001; IntoUniversity, 2006–. *Publications:* The Irish Question 1868–1886: a collection of documents, 1988; contrib. articles and reviews. *Recreations:* quizzes, collecting Tom Merry political cartoons, reading contemporary fiction, running, family. *Address:* Rugby School, Rugby, Warwickshire CV22 5EH. *T:* (01788) 556216. *Club:* East India.

DERHAM, Sir Peter (John), AC 2001; Kt 1980; FAIM; FPIA; FInstD; Chairman: Circadian Technologies Ltd (formerly Circadian Pharmaceuticals Ltd), 1984–2006; See Australia (formerly Partnership Australia Domestic Ltd), 1999–2005; Red Hill Wines plc, 2001–05; *b* 21 Aug. 1925; *s* of John and Mary Derham; *m* 1950, Averil C. Wigan; two *s* one *d*. *Educ:* Melbourne Church of England Grammar School; Univ. of Melbourne (BSc 1958); Harvard Univ. (Advanced Management Programme, 1965). Served RAAF and RAN, 1944–46. Joined Moulded Products (Australasia) Ltd (later Nylex Corp.), 1943; Dir, 1953–82, Sales Dir, 1960, Gen. Manager, 1967, Man. Dir, 1972–80. Chairman: Internat. Pacific Corp. Ltd, later Rothschild Australia Ltd, 1981–85; Australia New Zealand Foundn, 1978–83; Australian Canned Fruits Corp., 1981–89; Robert Bryce & Co. Ltd, 1982–91; Davy McKee Pacific Pty, 1984–90; Leasing Corp. Ltd, 1987–93; Multistack, 1993–99; Greenchip Develt Capital Ltd, 1993–99; Greenchip Investments Ltd, 1997–99; Vos Industries Ltd, 1997–2001; Bays and Peninsulas, 1999–2000; Deputy Chairman: Prime Computer of Australia Ltd, 1986–92; Australian Mutual Provident Society State Board of Advice, 1990–91 (Dir, Victoria Br. Bd, 1974–90); Director: Lucas Industries Aust., 1981–84; Station 3XY Pty, 1980–87; Radio 3XY Pty, 1980–87; Perpetual Trustees Victoria Ltd, 1992–93; Perpetual Trustees Australia Ltd, 1993–97; Advance Australia Foundn, 1983–96; Jt Chm., Advance Australia America Cup Challenge Ltd, 1981–83; Councillor Enterprise Australia, 1975–82 (Dep. Chm., 1975–78). Chairman: Nat. Training Council, 1971–80; Adv. Bd, CSIRO, 1981–86; Australian Tourist Commn, 1981–85; Member: Manufg Industries Adv. Council, 1971–74; Victorian Econ. Develt Corp., 1981–82. Federal Pres., Inst. of Directors in Australia, 1980–82 (Mem., 1975–89, Chm., 1975–82, Victorian Council; Life Mem., 1986); Councillor: Yooralla Soc. of Victoria, 1972–79 (Chm. Workshops Cttee, 1972–81); Aust. Industries Develt Assoc., 1975–80; State Councillor, Industrial Design Council, 1967–73, Federal Councillor, 1970–73; Mem. Council, Inst. of Public Affairs, 1971–; Life Mem., Plastics Inst. of Australia Inc. (Victorian Pres., 1964–66; Nat. Pres., 1971–72); Mem. Board of Advisors, Inst. of Cultural Affairs, 1971–81. Victorian State Treas., Liberal Party of Australia, 1981–83. Member: Rotary Club of Melbourne (Mem., Bd of Dirs, 1974–75, 1975–76); Victorian State Cttee, Child Accident Prevention Foundn of Australia; Appeal Cttee, Royal Victorian Eye and Ear Hosp.; Bd of Management, Alfred Hosp., 1980–93 (Pres., 1990–92), Amalgamated Alfred, Caulfield and Royal Southern Meml Hosp., 1987–93; Alfred Foundn Bd, 1993–; St John Ambulance, 1988– (Chm., State Council, 1991–96; Pres., Victoria, 1996–99); Chm., Caulfield Hosp. Cttee, 1984–87 (Dir, 1981–87; Vice Pres., 1989). President: Alcohol and Drug Foundn (formerly Victorian Foundn on Alcoholism and Drug Dependence), 1986–91 (Appeal Chm., 1981–86); Victorian Soc. for Prevention of Child Abuse and Neglect, 1987–96; Dep Chm., Australian Assoc. for Support of Educn, 1983–87; Mem., Melbourne C of E Grammar Sch. Council, 1974–75, 1977–80; Pres., Old Melburnians, 1974–75; Governor, Ian Clunies Ross Meml Foundn, 1981–99; Chairman: Trade & Industry Cttee, Victoria's 150th Anniv. Celebration; Police Toy Fund for Underprivileged Children; Pres., Somers Area, Boy Scout Assoc. of Australia, 1985–90; Vict. Trustee, Australian Koala Foundn Inc., 1986–92; Trustee, H & L Hecht Trust, 1990–; Life Governor, Assoc. for the Blind. Rotary Paul Harris Fellowship, 1997. CStJ 1995. *Recreations:* golf, sailing, tennis, gardening, viticulture. *Address:* 2a Ashley Grove, Malvern, Vic 3144, Australia. *T:* (3) 98220770; *e-mail:* pjderham@bigpond.com. *Clubs:* Australian, Melbourne (Melbourne); Royal Melbourne Golf, Flinders Golf.

de RIVAZ, Vincent; Chief Executive, EDF Energy plc, since 2003; *b* Paris, 4 Oct. 1953; *s* of François de Rivaz and Isabelle de Rivaz (*née* de Buttet); *m* 1980, Anne de Valence de Minardière; three *s*. *Educ:* Ecole Nat. Superieur d'hydraulique, Grenoble. Hydraulic engineer; Electricité de France: joined External Engrg Centre, 1977; Manager, Faraday Div., 1985–91; Man. Dir, Hydropower Dept, 1991–94; Dep. Hd, Internat. Develt, i/c New Projects Develt, 1995–98; Corporate Finance and Treasury Dir, 1999–2001; Chief Exec., London Electricity, 2002–03; Mem., Exec. Cttee, EDF Gp, 2004–. Melchett Medal, Energy Inst., 2006. *Recreations:* photography, cycling. *Address:* EDF Energy plc, 40 Grosvenor Place, SW1X 7EN. *T:* (020) 7752 2101, *Fax:* (020) 7752 2104; *e-mail:* vincent.de-rivaz@edfenergy.com.

DERMODY, Paul Bernard, OBE 2004; Director, 1997–2003, Chief Executive, 2000–03, De Vere Group plc (formerly Greenalls Group plc); *b* 1 Oct. 1945; *s* of Bernard and Jessie Dermody; *m* 1967, Margaret Eileen Horsfield; one *s* one *d*. *Educ:* De La Salle Coll., Salford; Salford Tech. Coll. ACMA 1971. Mgt accounting trainee, 1963–68, Asst Accountant, 1968–72, Groves & Whitnall; Mgt Accountant, Greenalls Brewery, 1972–77; Financial Controller, Greenalls Retail Div., 1977–84; Finance Dir and Dep. Man. Dir, 1984–89, Dep. Chm., 1989–95, De Vere Hotels; Chief Exec., Premier House & Village Leisure Hotels, 1995–97; Man. Dir, Greenalls Hotels & Leisure Ltd, 1997–2000. Non-executive Director: Majestic Wine, 2004–; Aga Foodservice Gp plc, 2004–. Chm., Nat. Football Mus., 2005–. School Governor. FIH (FHCIMA 1997); FBAHA 1985; FRSA 2000; CCMI. *Recreations:* singing, swimming, reading. *Address:* 6 Roe Green, Worsley, Manchester M28 2RF.

DERNIE, Prof. David James, RIBA; Head, Manchester School of Architecture, since 2005; Professor of Architecture, Manchester Metropolitan University, since 2005; Principal, David Dernie Architects, since 2000; *b* 16 Dec. 1962; *s* of B. S. Broughton and M. J. Dernie; *m* 1997, Anna Reali; one *s*. *Educ:* Lancaster Royal Grammar Sch.; Fitzwilliam Coll., Cambridge (BA 1985; DipArch 1988). RIBA 1990. Rome Scholar, British Sch. at Rome, 1991–93; Lectr in Architecture, Univ. of Cambridge, and Fellow, Fitzwilliam Coll., Cambridge, 1998–2005; Reader in Architecture, Univ. of Nottingham, 2005. Vis. Prof. of Architecture, Univ. of Lincoln, 2003–. *Publications:* Victor Horta, 1995; Villa D'Este at Tivoli, 1996; New Stone Architecture, 2003; Material Imagination, 2005; Exhibition Design, 2006. *Recreations:* painting, music, travel. *Address:* 86 Oxford Road, Cambridge CB4 3PL. *T:* 07866 602574; *e-mail:* david@dd-a.co.uk.

de ROS, 28th Baron *cr* 1264 (Premier Barony of England); **Peter Trevor Maxwell;** *b* 23 Dec. 1958; *s* of Comdr John David Maxwell, RN, and late Georgiana Angela Maxwell, 27th Baroness de Ros; *S* mother, 1983; *m* 1987, Siân Ross; one *s* one *d*. *Educ:* Headfort School, Kells, Co. Meath; Stowe School, Bucks; Down High School, Co. Down. Upholstered furniture maker. *Recreations:* gardening, travel and sailing. *Heir: s* Hon. Finbar James Maxwell, *b* 14 Nov. 1988.

de ROTHSCHILD; *see* Rothschild.

DERRETT, Prof. (John) Duncan (Martin), MA, PhD, DCL, LLD, DD; Professor of Oriental Laws in the University of London, 1965–82, now Emeritus; *b* 30 Aug. 1922; *s* of John West Derrett and Fay Frances Ethel Kate (*née* Martin); *m* 1950, Margaret Esmé Griffiths; four *s* one *d*. *Educ:* Emanuel Sch., London; Jesus Coll., Oxford; Sch. of Oriental and Afr. Studies, London; Inns of Court School of Law. MA 1947, DCL 1966 (Oxon); PhD 1949, LLD 1971, DD 1983 (London). Called to the Bar, Gray's Inn, 1953. Lectr in Hindu Law, SOAS, 1949; Reader in Oriental Laws, 1956, Prof. of Oriental Laws, 1965, Univ. of London; Tagore Prof. of Law, Univ. of Calcutta, 1953 (lectures delivered, 1955); Vis. Professor: Univ. of Chicago, 1963; Univ. of Michigan, 1970; Wilde Lectr in Natural and Compar. Religion, Univ. of Oxford, 1978–81; Japan Soc. Prom. Sci. Fellow and Vis. Prof., Oriental Inst., Univ. of Tokyo, 1982. Fellow, Indian Law Inst., Delhi, 1988. Mem., Editorial Bd, Zeitschrift für vergleichende Rechtswissenschaft, 1954–85, subseq. of Kannada Studies, Bharata Manisha, Kerala Law Times. Mem., Stud. Novi Test. Soc., 1971–2001. Barcelona Prize in Comparative Law, 1954; N. C. Sen-Gupta Gold Medal, Asiatic Soc. (Calcutta), 1977. *Publications:* The Hoysalas, 1957; Hindu Law Past and Present, 1957; Introduction to Modern Hindu Law, 1963; Religion, Law and the State in India, 1968, repr. 1999; Critique of Modern Hindu Law, 1970; Law in the New Testament, 1970, repr. 2005; Jesus's Audience, 1973; Dharmaśāstra and Juridical Literature, 1973; History of Indian Law (Dharmaśāstra), 1973; Henry Swinburne (?1551–1624) Civil Lawyer of York, 1973; trans. R. Lingat, Classical Law of India, 1973, repr. 1998; Bhāruci's Commentary on the Manusmrti, 1975; Essays in Classical and Modern Hindu Law, vols I-IV, 1976–79; Studies in the New Testament, vols I-VI, 1977–96; The Death of a Marriage Law, 1978; Beiträge zu Indischem Rechtsdenken, 1979; The Anastasis: the Resurrection of Jesus as an Historical Event, 1982; A Textbook for Novices: Jayarakshita's Perspicuous Commentary on the 'Compendium of Conduct', 1983; The Making of Mark, 1985; New Resolutions of Old Conundrums: a fresh insight into Luke's Gospel, 1986; The Ascetic Discourse: an explanation of the Sermon on the Mount, 1989; The Victim: the Johannine passion narrative reexamined, 1993; The Sermon on the Mount, 1994; Prophecy in the Cotswolds 1804–1947, 1994; Studies in Hindu Law, 1994; Two Masters: the Buddha and Jesus, 1995; Some Telltale Words in the New Testament, 1997; Law and Morality, 1998; The Bible and the Buddhists, 2000; *edited:* Studies in the Laws of Succession in Nigeria, 1965; Introduction to Legal Systems, 1968; (with W. D. O'Flaherty) The Concept of Duty in South Asia, 1978; A Second Blockley Miscellany, 1994; collab. with Yale Edn, Works of St Thomas More, Société Jean Bodin, Brussels, Max Planck Inst., Hamburg, Fritz Thyssen Stiftung, Cologne, Institut für Soziologie, Heidelberg, Aufstieg und Niedergang der Römischen Welt, Tübingen, and Sekai Kyusei Kyo, Atami; *Festschriften:* Indology and Law, 1982; Novum Testamentum, 24, 1982, fasc. 3 and foll. *Address:* Half Way House, High Street, Blockley, Moreton-in-Marsh, Glos GL56 9EX. *T:* (01386) 700828.

DERRICK, Peter; Chamberlain, City of London Corporation (formerly Corporation of London), 1999–2007; *b* 2 April 1948; *s* of John Moorhead Derrick and Lucy (*née* Norman); *m* 1972, Joyce Bainbridge; two *d*. *Educ:* Univ. of Lancaster (BA Hons Politics

1974). CPFA 1971. Gateshead CBC, 1965–71; Principal Accountant, Carlisle CC, 1974–77; Chief Tech. Asst, Knowsley MBC, 1977–79; Principal Accountant, Lothian Regl Council, 1979–81; Under Sec. (Finance), ADC, 1981–85; Director of Finance: London Bor. of Hounslow, 1985–88; London Bor. of Camden, 1988–91; Chief Exec., London Bor. of Hammersmith and Fulham, 1991–93; Dir, Finance and Corporate Services, Surrey CC, 1993–98. Actg Prin., GSMD, 2003–04. Chm., London Financial Adv. Cttee, CIPFA, 2000–06; Chm., Officer Adv. Gp, Local Govt Pension Scheme, Local Govt Employers Orgn, 1997–2006; Mem., Employer Task Force on Pensions, DWP, 2003–04. Council Mem., Nat. Assoc. of Pension Funds, 1997–2002; Pres., Soc. of London Treasurers, 2003–04. Order of the Dannebrog (Denmark), 2000. *Recreations:* football, golf, squash, film, opera. *Address:* 352 Wimbledon Central, Wimbledon, SW19 4BJ. *Clubs:* Wimbledon Racquets and Fitness; Wimbledon Park Golf; Sunderland AFC Supporters.

DERRY, Bishop of, (RC), since 1994; **Most Rev. Séamus Hegarty;** *b* 26 Jan. 1940; *s* of James Hegarty and Mary O'Donnell. *Educ:* Kilcar National School; St Eunan's Coll., Letterkenny; St Patrick's Coll., Maynooth; University Coll., Dublin. Priest, 1966; post-grad. studies, University Coll., Dublin, 1966–67; Dean of Studies 1967–71, President 1971–82, Holy Cross College, Falcarragh; Bishop of Raphoe, 1982–94. *Publication:* contribs to works on school administration and student assessment. *Recreations:* bridge, angling. *Address:* St Eugene's Cathedral, Derry BT48 9AP. *T:* (028) 7126 2302, *Fax:* (028) 7137 1960; *e-mail:* office@derrydiocese.org.

DERRY AND RAPHOE, Bishop of, since 2002; **Rt Rev. Kenneth Raymond Good;** *b* 1 Nov. 1952; *s* of (William Thomas) Raymond Good and Jean Beryl (*née* Hewson); *m* 1977, Mary Knox; two *s* one *d*. *Educ:* Dublin Univ. (BA 1974); Nottingham Univ. (BA Theol., 1976); NUI (HDipEd 1981, MEd 1984). Ordained deacon, 1977, priest, 1978; Curate, Willowfield Parish, Belfast, 1977–79; Chaplain and Hd of Religious Educn, Ashton Comprehensive Sch., Cork, 1979–84; Rector: Dunganstown Union, dio. Glendalough, 1984–90; Shankill Parish, Lurgan, 1990–2002; Archdeacon of Dromore, 1997–2002. *Publication:* A Heart for the Unchurched, 1996. *Recreations:* golf, swimming, opera. *Address:* The See House, 112 Culmore Road, Londonderry, Northern Ireland BT48 8JF; *e-mail:* bishop@derry.anglican.org.

DERVAIRD, Hon. Lord; John Murray; Dickson Minto Professor of Company Law, Edinburgh University, 1990–99, now Professor Emeritus; a Senator of the College of Justice in Scotland, 1988–89; *b* 8 July 1935; *o s* of J. H. Murray, farmer, Stranraer; *m* 1960, Bridget Jane, *d* of Sir William Godfrey, 7th Bt, and of Lady Godfrey; three *s*. *Educ:* Stranraer schs; Edinburgh Academy; Corpus Christi Coll., Oxford (BA 1st cl. Lit. Hum., 1959); Edinburgh Univ. (LLB 1962). FCIArb 1991. Advocate, 1962; QC (Scot.) 1974. Dean, Faculty of Law, Edinburgh Univ., 1994–96. Mem., Scottish Law Commn, 1979–88. Chairman: Scottish Lawyers' European Gp, 1975–78; Scottish Council of Law Reporting, 1978–88; Scottish Cttee on Law of Arbitration, 1986–96; Scottish Council for Internat. Arbitration, 1989–2003; Panel of Professional Adjudicators, 2004–; Member: City Disputes Panel, 1994–; Panel of Arbitrators, Internat. Centre for Investment Disputes, 1998–2004; Adv. Bd, Internat. Arbitration Inst., Paris, 2000–; Academic Council, SICA-FICA, 2002–; Vice-Pres., Centre of Conciliation and Arbitration for Advanced Techniques, Paris, 2000–. Vice-President: Agricultural Law Assoc., 1985–91 (Chm., 1979–85); Comité Européen de Droit Rural, 1989–91, 1995–96. Hon. Pres., Advocates' Business Law Group, 1988–. Dir and Chm., BT Scottish Ensemble, 1988–2000. Corresp. Mem., ICC Cttee on Business Law, Paris, 1994–. Trustee, David Hume Inst., 1994–2007. Grand Chaplain, Von Poser Soc. of Scotland, 1995; Knight, Order of Von Poser, 1996. *Publications:* contributed to: Festschrift für Dr Pikalo, 1979; Mélanges offert à Jean Megret, 1985; Stair Encyclopedia of Scots Law, 1987, 1992, 1998, 2001; Scottish Legal Tradition, 1991; Corporate Law—the European Dimension, 1991; European Company Law, 1992; International Handbook on Commercial Arbitration, 1995; Essays in Honour of Lord Mackenzie-Stuart of Dean, 1996; Science and Law, 2000; articles in legal and ornithological jls. *Recreations:* farming, gardening, birdwatching, music, curling, field sports. *Address:* Auchenmalg House, Auchenmalg, Glenluce, Wigtownshire DG8 0JS. *T:* (01581) 500205, *Fax:* (01581) 500324; Wood of Dervaird Farm, Glenluce DG8 9JT. *T:* (01581) 300222; *e-mail:* murraydervaird@talk21.com. *Clubs:* New, Puffins (Edinburgh); Aberlady Curlers.

DERWENT, 5th Baron *cr* 1881; **Robin Evelyn Leo Vanden-Bempde-Johnstone,** LVO 1957; Bt 1795; DL; Deputy Chairman, Hutchison Whampoa (Europe) Ltd, 1998–2007 (Managing Director, 1985–97); *b* 30 Oct. 1930; *s* of 4th Baron Derwent, CBE and Marie-Louise (*d* 1985), *d* of Albert Picard, Paris; *S* father, 1986; *m* 1957, Sybille, *d* of late Vicomte de Simard de Pitray and Madame Jeanine Hennessy; one *s* three *d*. *Educ:* Winchester College; Clare Coll., Cambridge (Scholar, MA 1953). 2nd Lieut 1949, 60th Rifles; Lieut 1950, Queen Victoria's Rifles (TA). HM Diplomatic Service, 1954–69; served FO, Paris, Mexico City, Washington. Director, NM Rothschild & Sons, Merchant Bankers, 1969–85. Director: F&C (Pacific) Investment Trust Ltd, 1989–2001; Scarborough Building Soc., 1991–2001. Chm., London & Provincial Antique Dealers' Assoc., 1989–95. Mem., N York Moors Nat. Park Authy, 1997–99. Chm., Scarborough Mus Trust, 2004–. DL N Yorks, 1991. Chevalier de la Légion d'Honneur (France), 1957; Officier de l'Ordre National du Mérite (France), 1978. *Recreations:* shooting, fishing. *Heir:* *s* Hon. Francis Patrick Harcourt Vanden-Bempde-Johnstone [*b* 23 Sept. 1965; *m* 1990, Cressida, *o d* of Christopher John Bourke, *qv*]. *Address:* Hackness Hall, Hackness, Scarborough YO13 0BL; Flat 6, Sovereign Court, 29 Wrights Lane, W8 5SH. *Club:* Boodle's.

DERWENT, Henry Clifford Sydney, CB 2006; President and Chief Executive Officer, International Emissions Trading Association, since 2008; *b* 19 Nov. 1951; *s* of late Clifford Sydney Derwent and Joan Kathleen (*née* Craft); *m* 1988, Rosemary Patricia Jesse Meaker; three *d*. *Educ:* Berkhamsted Sch.; Worcester Coll., Oxford. Department of the Environment, 1974–86: planning policy; PSA; London housing; commercial property; Rayner scrutiny; seconded to Midland Bank; inner cities; Department of Transport, subseq. DETR, now DEFRA, 1986–2008: private office; local finance; vehicle licensing; central finance; highways; Under Sec., then Dir, Nat. Roads Policy, 1992–97; (on secondment) Corporate Finance Div., SBC Warburg, later UBS Warburg, 1997–99; Dir, Envmt: Risks and Atmosphere, subseq. Climate, Energy and Envmtl Risk, then Internat. Climate Change Air and Analysis, 1999–2008. *Recreations:* flute, trombone, tenor sax, riding, watercolours. *Address:* International Emissions Trading Association, Avenue Merle d'Aubigné, Geneva 1207, Switzerland.

DERX, Donald John, CB 1975; non-executive Director, Glaxo Holdings, later Glaxo Wellcome plc, 1991–97; *b* 25 June 1928; *s* of John Derx and Violet Ivy Stroud; *m* 1956, Luisa Donzelli; two *s* two *d*. *Educ:* Tiffin Boys' Sch., Kingston-on-Thames; St Edmund Hall, Oxford (BA). Asst Principal, BoT, 1951; seconded to Cabinet Office, 1954–55; Principal, Colonial Office, 1957; Asst Sec., Industrial Policy Gp, DEA, 1965; Dir, Treasury Centre for Admin. Studies, 1968; Head of London Centre, Civil Service Coll., 1970; Under Sec., 1971–72, Dep. Sec., 1972–84, Dept of Employment; Dir, Policy Studies Inst., 1985–86; with Glaxo Holdings plc, 1986–90.

DERYCKE, Erik; a Judge, Court of Arbitration, Belgium, since 2001; *b* Waregem, Flanders, 28 Oct. 1949. *Educ:* State Univ. of Ghent (degree in Law 1972). Lawyer, 1972–2001. Flemish Socialist Party: Mem. Council, W Flanders, 1975–84; Mem., Public Commn for Social Assistance, Waregem, 1976–88; Municipal Councillor, Waregem, 1988–2001; Mem., Exec. Cttee; National Parliament: MP (Flemish Socialist) Kortrijk, 1984–2001; Dep. Minister, Sci. Policy, 1990–92, and Minister of Develt Co-operation, 1991–92; Dep. Minister of Develt Co-operation, 1992–95; Minister of Foreign Affairs and Develt Co-operation, March–June 1995; Minister of Foreign Affairs, 1995–99; Belgian Rep. at Council of Europe and WEU, 1988–89 and 1999–2001. *Address:* Court of Arbitration, 7 Place Royale, 1000 Brussels, Belgium.

DESAI, family name of **Baron Desai**.

DESAI, Baron *cr* 1991 (Life Peer), of St Clement Danes in the City of Westminster; **Meghnad Jagdishchandra Desai,** PhD; Professor of Economics, 1983–2003, now Emeritus, and Director, Centre for the Study of Global Governance, 1992–2003, London School of Economics and Political Science; *b* 10 July 1940; *s* of late Jagdishchandra and of Mandakini Desai; *m* 1st, 1970, Gail Graham Wilson (marr. diss. 2004); one *s* two *d*; 2nd, 2004, Kishwar Ahluwalia. *Educ:* Univ. of Bombay (BA Hons, MA); Univ. of Pennsylvania (PhD 1964). Associate Specialist, Dept of Agricultural Econs, Univ. of Calif, Berkeley, 1963–65; London School of Economics: Lectr, 1965–77, Sen. Lectr, 1977–80, Reader, 1980–83, Dept. of Econs; Head, Develt Studies Inst., 1990–95. Pres., Assoc. of Univ. Teachers in Econs, 1987–90; Mem. Council, REconS, 1988. Life Pres., Islington South and Finsbury Constituency Labour Pty, 1993– (Chm., 1986–92). Hon. DSc Kingston, 1992; Hon. DSc (Econ) E London, 1994; DUniv Middlesex, 1993; Hon. DPhil London Guildhall, 1996; Hon. LLD Monash, 2005. *Publications:* Marxian Economic Theory, 1974; Applied Econometrics, 1976; Marxian Economics, 1979; Testing Monetarism, 1981; (Asst Editor to Prof. Dharma Kumar) The Cambridge Economic History of India 1757–1970, 1983; (ed jtly) Agrarian Power and Agricultural Productivity in South Asia, 1984; (ed) Lenin on Economics, 1987; Macroeconomics and Monetary Theory: selected essays, vol. 1, 1995; Poverty, Famine and Economic Development: selected essays, vol. 2, 1995; (ed jtly) Global Governance, 1995; (ed) On Inequality, 1995; Marx's Revenge, 2002; Nehru's Hero: Dilip Kumar in the life of India, 2004; Development and Nationhood, 2005; contrib. Econometrica, Econ. Jl, Rev. of Econ. Studies, Economica, Econ. Hist. Rev. *Address:* House of Lords, SW1A 0PW.

DESAI, Anita, FRSL; novelist; *b* 24 June 1937; *d* of Toni Nimé and D. N. Mazumbar; *m* 1958, Ashvin Desai; two *s* two *d*. *Educ:* Queen Mary's Sch., Delhi; Miranda House, Univ. of Delhi (BA Hons). FRSL 1963. First story published 1946; novelist and book reviewer (freelance), 1963–. Helen Cam Vis. Fellow, 1986–87, Hon. Fellow, 1988, Girton Coll., Univ. of Cambridge; Elizabeth Drew Prof., Smith Coll., USA, 1987–88; Purington Prof. of English, Mount Holyoke Coll., USA, 1988–92; Prof. of Writing, MIT, 1993–; Ashby Fellow, 1989, Hon. Fellow, 1991, Clare Hall, Univ. of Cambridge. Hon. Mem., Amer. Acad. of Arts and Letters, 1993. Neil Gunn Prize for Internat. Writers, Scotland, 1993; Alberto Moravia Prize for Internat. Writers, Italy, 1999. Padma Sri, 1990. *Publications:* Cry, The Peacock, 1963; Voices in the City, 1965; Bye-Bye Blackbird, 1971; Where Shall We Go This Summer?, 1973; Fire on the Mountain, 1978 (Winifred Holtby Award, RSL, 1978); Games at Twilight, 1979; Clear Light of Day, 1980; The Village by the Sea, 1983 (Guardian Prize for Children's Fiction, 1983; filmed, 1992); In Custody, 1984 (screenplay, filmed 1994); Baumgartner's Bombay, 1988 (Hadassah Prize, Hadassah Magazine, NY, 1989); Journey to Ithaca, 1995; Fasting, Feasting, 1999; Diamond Dust and Other Stories, 2000; The Zigzag Way, 2004. *Address:* c/o Rogers, Coleridge & White Ltd, 20 Powis Mews, W11 1JN.

de SAUMAREZ, 7th Baron *cr* 1831; **Eric Douglas Saumarez;** Bt 1801; farmer; *b* 13 Aug. 1956; *s* of 6th Baron de Saumarez and Joan Beryl, (Julia) (*d* 2004), *d* of late Douglas Raymond Charlton; *S* father, 1991; *m* 1st, 1982, Christine Elizabeth (marr. diss. 1990), *yr d* of B. N. Halliday; two *d*; 2nd, 1991, Susan M. Hearn. *Educ:* Milton Abbey; Nottingham Univ.; RAC, Cirencester. *Recreations:* flying, shooting, ski-ing, fishing. *Heir:* *twin b* Hon. Victor Thomas Saumarez, *b* 13 Aug. 1956. *Address:* Les Beaucamps de Bas, Castel, Guernsey GY5 7PE.

de SAVARY, Peter John; international entrepreneur; *b* 11 July 1944; *m* 1986, (Lucille) Lana Paton; three *d* (and two *d* by a former marriage). *Educ:* Charterhouse. Activities in the energy, property, finance, maritime and leisure fields. Chm., Victory Syndicate, Admiral's Cup, 1981 and 1983 British Challenge for America's Cup. Founder of Clubs: Carnegie (Chm., 1994–2003); Carnegie Abbey; Cherokee Plantation; Abaco; London Outpost; St James's, NY, Antigua, London, Paris, LA. Contested (Referendum) Falmouth and Camborne, 1997. Tourism Personality of the Year, English Tourist Bd, 1988. *Recreations:* sailing, riding, carriage driving. *Clubs:* St James's, Royal Automobile, Royal Thames Yacht; Royal Burnham Yacht, Royal Torbay Yacht, Royal Corinthian Yacht, Royal Cornwall Yacht; New York Yacht.

de SILGUY, Count Yves-Thibault Christian Marie; Chairman, VINCI, since 2006; *b* Rennes, 22 July 1948; *s* of Raymond de Silguy and Claude de Pompery; *m* 1976, Jacqueline de Montillet de Grenaud (decd); one *s* one *d*. *Educ:* Collège Saint-Martin; Univ. of Rennes (Law and Econ Scis); Sch. of Public Service, Institut d'Etudes Politiques, Paris (Dip.); Ecole Nationale d'Administration. Sec. for Foreign Affairs to Dir for Econ. and Financial Affairs, 1976–80; Advr, then Dep. Staff Dir for Vice-Pres. Ortoli, Comr for Econ. and Monetary Affairs, 1981–84; Advr i/c Econ. Affairs, French Embassy in Washington, 1985–86; Tech. Advr to Prime Minister i/c European Affairs and Internat. Econ. and Financial Affairs, 1986–88; Manager, Internat. Business Div. and Gp Internat. Business Dir, Usinor Sacilor, 1988–93; Sec. Gen., Interministerial Cttee for European Econ. Co-operation and Advr for European Affairs to Prime Minister, 1993–95; Mem., European Commn, i/c economic, monetary and financial affairs, 1995–99. Bd Mem., 2000–02, Sen. Exec. Vice-Pres., 2002–06, SUEZ. Gen. Deleg. of French Steel Fedn, 1990–93; Chm. Bd, Professional Center for Steel Stats, 1990–93; Chm., Finance Cttee, Eurofer, 1990–93. Commandeur, Ordre des Arts et des Lettres (France) (Officier, 1994); Officier: du Mérite Agricole (France), 1995; Ordre Nat. du Mérite (France), 2000; Légion d'Honneur (France). *Recreations:* tennis, yachting, hunting. *Address:* VINCI, 1 cours Ferdinand de Lesseps, 92851 Rueil-Malmaison Cedex, France. *Clubs:* Polo, Cercle de l'Union Interallié (Paris).

de SILVA, Sir Desmond (George Lorenz), Kt 2007; QC 1984; international lawyer; Chief Prosecutor, International Criminal Court, Sierra Leone, 2005–06; *b* 13 Dec. 1939; *s* of late Edmund Frederick Lorenz de Silva, MBE, and Esme Gregg de Silva; *m* 1987, HRH Princess Katarina of Yugoslavia, *d* of HRH late Prince Tomislav of Yugoslavia and of HRH Princess Margarita of Baden; one *d*. *Educ:* Dulwich College Prep Sch.; Trinity College, Ceylon. Served with 3rd Carabiniers (3rd Dragoon Guards). Called to the Bar: Middle Temple, 1964; Sierra Leone, 1968; The Gambia, 1981; Gibraltar, 1992; a Dep.

Circuit Judge, 1976–80; Dep. Prosecutor, Internat. War Crimes Court for Sierra Leone, 2002–05. UNDP Envoy to Belgrade, 2004. Vice-Chm., Westminster Community Relations Council, 1980–82; Councilman, City of London, 1980–95; Main Session Chm., First Internat. Conf. on Human Value, 1981. Member: Home Affairs Standing Cttee, Bow Gp, 1982; Editl Adv. Bd, Crossbow, 1984; Crime and Juvenile Delinquency Study Gp, Centre for Policy Studies, 1983–87. Sen. Associate Mem., St Antony's Coll., Oxford, 2005–. Member: Governing Council, Manorial Soc. of GB, 1982–; Nat. Cttee for 900th anniv. of Domesday; Internat. Assoc. of Prosecutors; Imperial Soc. of Kts Bachelor, 2007–. Mem., Racehorse Owners Assoc. Patron: Meml Gates Trust, 1999–; PRESET, 2000–. Liveryman, Gunmakers' Co. Vice-Pres., St John Ambulance London (Prince of Wales's) Dist, 1984–; Mem., St John Council for London, 1986–; KStJ 1994. *Publication:* (ed) English Law and Ethnic Minority Customs, 1986. *Recreations:* politics, shooting, travel. *Address:* Marlands House, Itchingfield, Horsham, W Sussex RH13 0NN; 2 Paper Buildings, Temple, EC4Y 7ET; Taprobane Island, off Weligama, Sri Lanka. *Clubs:* Brooks's, Naval and Military, Carlton; Orient (Colombo).

de SILVA, Harendra (Aneurin Domingo); QC 1995; a Recorder, since 1991; *b* 29 Sept. 1945; *s* of Annesley de Silva and Maharani of Porbandar; *m* 1972, Indira Raj; one *s* one *d*. *Educ:* Doon Sch., Dehra Dun, India; Millfield Sch.; Queens' Coll., Cambridge (MA, LLM). Called to the Bar, Middle Temple, 1970, Bencher, 2003. *Recreations:* golf, bridge. *Address:* 2 Paper Buildings, Temple, EC4Y 7ET. *T:* (020) 7556 5500. *Clubs:* Oxford and Cambridge, Roehampton; Ooty (Ootacamund, S India).

DESLANDES, Ian Anthony; Chief Executive, Construction Confederation, 1997–99; *b* 17 July 1941; *s* of Albert Deslandes and Christine Veronica Deslandes (*née* Hale); *m* 1965, Mary Catherine Bowler; two *s*. *Educ:* Stonyhurst Coll.; St Catherine's Coll., Oxford. Conservative Res. Dept., 1965–70; PA to Conservative Party Chm., 1970–72; Dir, Housebuilders' Fedn, 1973–78; Dir, Manpower Services, 1978–86, Dep. Dir Gen., 1985–92, Dir Gen., 1992–97, Building Employers' Confedn. CBI: Chm., Trade Assoc. Council, 1999; Mem., Council and President's Cttee, 1999. *Recreations:* reading, jazz, gardening, walking. *Address:* Greystones, Downhouse Lane, Higher Eype, Bridport, Dorset DT6 6AH. *T:* (01308) 424498.

DESLONGCHAMPS, Prof. Pierre, OC 1989; OQ 1997; PhD; FRS 1983; FRSC 1974; FCIC; Professor of Organic Chemistry, Université de Sherbrooke, Canada, 1972–2006, now Emeritus; *b* 8 May 1938; *s* of Rodolphe Deslongchamps and Madeleine Magnan; *m* 1st, 1960, Micheline Renaud (marr. diss. 1975); two *c*; 2nd, 1976, Shirley E. Thomas (marr. diss. 1983); 3rd, 1987, Marie-Marthe Leroux. *Educ:* Univ. de Montréal (BSc Chem., 1959); Univ. of New Brunswick (PhD Chem., 1964). FCIC 1980; FAAAS 1988. Post-doctoral Student with Dr R.B. Woodward, Harvard Univ., USA, 1965; Asst Prof., Univ. de Montréal, 1966; Asst Prof. 1967, Associate Prof. 1968, Univ. de Sherbrooke. A.P. Sloan Fellow, 1970–72; E. W. R. Steacie Fellow, 1971–74. Member: Amer. Chem. Soc.; Ordre des Chemistes du Québec; Assoc. Canadienne-Française pour l'Avancement des Sciences; Fellow, World Innovation Foundn (UK), 2002; For. Asst Mem., Acad. des Scis de Paris, 1995. Dr *hc:* Univ. Pierre et Marie Curie, Paris, 1983; Bishop's Univ., Univ. de Montréal, and Univ. Laval, 1984; New Brunswick Univ., 1985; Univ. of Moncton, 1995. Scientific Prize of Québec, 1971; E. W. R. Steacie Prize (Nat. Scis), NRCC, 1974; Médaille Vincent, ACFAS, 1975; Merck, Sharp and Dohme Lectures Award, CIC, 1976; Canada Council Izaak Walton Killam Meml Scholarship, 1976–77; John Simon Guggenheim Meml Foundn Fellow, 1979; Médaille Pariseau, ACFAS, 1979; Marie-Victorin Médaille, Province of Que., 1987; Alfred Bader Award in Organic Chemistry, Canadian Soc. of Chemistry, 1991; Canada Gold Medal for Science and Engrng, NSERCC, 1993; Lemieux Award, Canadian Soc. for Chemistry, 1994. Holder of 19 patents. *Publications:* Stereoelectronic Effects in Organic Chemistry, 1983; over 230 contribs on organic chemistry in Tetrahedron, Jl Amer. Chem. Soc., Canadian Jl of Chem., Pure Applied Chem., Synth. Commun., Nouv. Jl Chim., Heterocycles, Jl Molecular Struct., Interface, Aldrichimica Acta, and Bull. Soc. Chim., France. *Recreations:* fishing, reading. *Address:* Department of Chemistry, Institut de pharmacologie, Université de Sherbrooke, Sherbrooke, QC J1H 5N4, Canada. *T:* (819) 5645300, *Fax:* (819) 8206823; *e-mail:* pierre.deslongchamps@usherbrooke.ca; 161 de Vimy, Sherbrooke, QC J1J 3M6, Canada. *T:* (819) 5638788.

DESMOND, Denis Fitzgerald, CBE 1989; Lord-Lieutenant of Co. Londonderry, since 2000; Chairman, Desmond & Sons Ltd, 1970–95; *b* 11 May 1943; *s* of late Major James Fitzgerald Desmond, DL, JP and Harriet Ivy Desmond (*née* Evans); *m* 1965, Anick Marie Françoise Marguerite Faussemagne; one *d*. *Educ:* Trinity Coll., Glenalmond. 2nd Lieut, then Lieut RCT (TA), 1964–69. ADC to Governor of NI, 1967–69. Dir, Ulster Bank, 1990–97. Chm., Altnagelvin Hosps Health Trust, 1996–2004. Dir, Ulster Orchestra Soc. Ltd, 2008. Mem. Council, Prince's Trust, NI, 2008. High Sheriff 1973, DL 1992–2000, Co. Londonderry. Hon. DSc: QUB, 1987; Ulster, 1991. *Address:* Bellarena, Limavady, Co. Londonderry BT49 0HZ. *Club:* Queen's.

DESMOND, Michael John; International Adviser, Hunan Broadcasting Company, since 2006; *b* 10 March 1959; *s* of Frank and Eileen Desmond; *m* 1984, Christine; one *s* two *d*. *Educ:* Leeds Univ. Gp Sales Manager, Anglia TV, 1982–86; Sales Controller, HTV, London, 1986–88; Sales Controller, 1988–92, Sales Dir, 1992–94, Granada; Chief Executive Officer: Laser, 1994–98; Granada Media Sales, 1998; Granada Broadcasting and Enterprises; Jt Man. Dir, ITV, 2002–04; Chief Exec., ITV Broadcast, 2004–05. *Recreations:* golf, tennis, watching most sports. *Address:* 5 Copse Hill SW20 0NB. *Club:* Solus.

DESMOND, Richard Clive; Chairman, Northern & Shell Network, since 1974; Proprietor, Express Newspapers, since 2000; *b* 8 Dec. 1951; *s* of Cyril and Millie Desmond; *m* 1983, Janet Robertson; one *s*. *Educ:* Christ's Coll., Finchley. Musician, 1967; Advertisement Exec., Thomson Gp, 1967–68; Group Advertisement Manager, Beat Pubns Ltd, 1968–74; launched International Musician, 1974 (separate editions in US, Europe, Australia and Japan); publr of numerous magazines in areas incl. leisure, music, hi tech, fitness, cooking, envmt, business, automative, and men's and women's lifestyle; De Monde Advertising Ltd, 1976–89; OK! magazine, 1993–; Fantasy Channel, 1995–; OK! TV, 1999–; launched: Daily Star Sunday, 2002; New! mag., and Star mag., 2003. Pres., Norwood, 2006–. *Recreations:* music, fitness. *Address:* Northern & Shell Building, Number 10 Lower Thames Street, EC3R 6EN. *T:* 0871 4341010.

de SOUZA, Christopher Edward; freelance composer; broadcaster; Artistic Director, Southern Sinfonia, since 1998; *b* 6 June 1943; *s* of Denis Walter de Souza and Dorothy Edna (*née* Woodman); *m* 1971, Robyn Ann Williams (marr. diss. 1981); partner, Elinor Anne Kelly; two *s*. *Educ:* Prior Park Coll., Bath; Univ. of Bristol (BA Music 1966); Old Vic Theatre Sch. Head of Music, St Bernadette's RC Comp. Sch., Bristol, 1966–70; Producer, Sadlers Wells/ENO, 1971–75; Arts Producer, BBC Radio London, 1975–79; Producer, BBC Radio 3, 1980–95. Founder Dir, Liszt Fest. of London, 1977; (with J. Piper) music organiser, HM Silver Jubilee Fireworks, 1977. Director: UK stage premières: Don Sanche (Liszt), 1977; The Mother of Us All (Virgil Thompson), 1979; The Duenna (Prokofiev), 1980; Palestrina (Pfitzner), 1981; William Tell (Gretry), 1984; USA première: Don Sanche (Liszt), 1986. *Compositions include:* music for TV, incl. Maharajahs, 1987; orch., chamber and choral works including The Ides of March, 1993; (with Adrian Morris) Children of the Light (musical), 2001; Missa Douensis, 2003. *Publications:* A Child's Guide to Looking at Music, 1979; (ed jtly) Liszt: Don Sanche, 1985; Kingfisher Book of Music, 1996; contrib. to The Listener, Music and Musicians, Musical Times, Radio Times, Strad, The Times, British Music Year Book. *Recreations:* reading, travel, swimming, drawing. *Address:* Westbrook Farm Cottage, Boxford, Berks RG20 8DL. *Club:* Royal Over-Seas League.

DESPONTIN, Dr Brenda; Principal, British School of Brussels, since 2008; *b* 22 Oct. 1950; *d* of Telford and Nancy Betty Griffiths; *m* 1975, Robert Despontin; one *s*. *Educ:* University Coll., Cardiff (BA Hons Psychol.; MA English; PhD English - Children's Lit 1996); Univ. of Bath (PGCE (Dist.)); Univ. of Hull (MBA). Teacher, British Sch. of Brussels, 1973–77; residential social worker, 1977–78; teacher: Willlows Sch., Cardiff 1978–85; New Coll., Cardiff, 1985–92; Principal, Girls' Div., King's Sch., Macclesfield 1992–97; Headmistress, Haberdashers' Monmouth Sch. for Girls, 1997–2008. Pres., GSA 2006. MCMI (MBIM 1995). Teachers' Award for Sch. Leadership in Wales, 2003. *Publications:* (contrib. and ed jtly) Leading Schools in the 21st Century, 3 vols, 2008; contrib. The Times, Daily Telegraph, FT, Independent, TES. *Recreations:* writing, reading, people-watching, following Fox's advice to 'walk cheerfully'. *Address:* British School of Brussels, Leuvensesteenweg 19, 3080 Tervuren, Belgium.

DESPRÉS, Robert, OC 1978; GOQ 2003; President, DRM Holdings Inc., since 1987; Chairman, Cominar Real Estate Investment Trust, since 2006 (Director, since 1998); *b* 2[illegible] Sept. 1924; *s* of Adrien Després and Augustine Marmen; *m* 1949; two *s* two *d*. *Educ:* Académie de Québec (BA 1943); Laval Univ. (MCom 1947); (postgrad. studies) Western Univ. Comptroller, Québec Power Co., 1947–63; Reg. Manager, Administration & Trust Co., 1963–65; Dep. Minister, Québec Dept of Revenue, 1965–69; Pres. and Gen. Man. Québec Health Insurance Bd, 1969–73; Pres., Université du Québec, 1973–78; Pres. and Chief Exec. Officer, National Cablevision Ltd, 1978–80, and Netcom Inc., 1978–89; Chm. of the Bd, Atomic Energy of Canada Ltd, 1978–86. Chm., Domosys Corp. Director: Sidbec Corp.; HRS Holdings Ltd; Infectio Diagnostic Inc.; GeneOhm Scis Inc. Obzerv Technologies Inc. (Chm.). Director: Nat. Optics Inst.; Canadian Certified General Accountants' Res. Foundn; Council for Canadian Unity; la Soc. du Musée du Séminaire de Québec; Inst de cardiologie de Québec. *Publications:* contrib. Commerce and Soc. of Management Accountants Revue. *Recreations:* golf, reading. *Clubs:* Rideau; Cercle Universitaire; Lorette Golf.

de SWIET, Eleanor Jane, MA; Headteacher, The Henrietta Barnett School, 1989–99; retired; *b* 18 Aug. 1942; *d* of Richard and Joan Hawkins; *m* 1964, Prof. Michael de Swiet; two *s* one *d*. *Educ:* Girton Coll., Cambridge (MA Classics); Inst. of Education (PGCE). Teacher of Classics: Francis Holland Sch., 1965–67; St Paul's Girls' Sch., 1967–70; Queen's Coll., London, 1975–84; City of London Sch., 1984–89. President: JACT 1995–97; Assoc. of Maintained Girls' Schs, 1997–98. Mem. Council, Cheltenham Ladies' Coll., 1999–2008. Trustee: Open Door, 2000–; Toynbee Hall, 2001–. *Recreations:* walking, reading, Yorkshire, travelling. *Address:* 60 Hornsey Lane, N6 5LU. *T:* (020) 727[illegible] 3195; *e-mail:* jdeswiet@blueyonder.co.uk.

DETMER, Prof. Don Eugene, MD; President and Chief Executive Officer, American Medical Informatics Association, since 2004; Professor of Medical Education, University of Virginia, since 1999; *b* 3 Feb. 1939; *s* of Lawrence D. Detmer and Esther B. Detmer (*née* McCormick); *m* 1961, Mary Helen McFerson; two *d*. *Educ:* Univ. of Kansas (MD 1965); MA Cantab 2002. Asst Prof., 1973–77, Associate Prof., 1977–80, Prof., 1980–84, of Surgery and Preventive Medicine, Univ. of Wisconsin-Madison; Vice Pres. for Health Sci., and Prof. of Surgery and Med. Informatics, Univ. of Utah, 1984–88; University of Virginia: Vice Pres. for Health Sci., and Prof. of Surgery and Business Admin, 1988–92; Co-Dir, Virginia Health Policy Center, 1992–99; Vice Pres. and Provost for Health Sci. and Prof. of Health Policy and Surgery, 1993–96; Louis Nerancy Prof. of Health Sci. Policy, Univ. Prof. and Sen. Vice Pres., 1996–99; Prof. Emeritus, 1999; Dennis Gillings Prof. of Health Mgt, Cambridge Univ., 1999–2003; Fellow, Clare Hall, Cambridge 2000–; Sen. Associate, Judge Inst. of Mgt, subseq. Judge Business Sch., Univ. of Cambridge, 2004–. *Publications:* (ed jtly and contrib.) The Computer-Based Patient Record: an essential technology for health care, 1991, rev. edn 1997; articles in jls and contribs to books. *Recreations:* fly-fishing, reading biographies, wilderness canoeing, handcrafts. *Address:* Branch Point Farm, 5245 Brown's Gap Turnpike, Crozet, VA 22932, USA. *Club:* Cosmos (Washington DC).

de TRAFFORD, Sir Dermot Humphrey, 6th Bt *cr* 1841; VRD 1963; Director 1977–90, Chairman, 1982–90, Low & Bonar plc (Deputy Chairman, 1980–82); Chairman: GHP Group Ltd, 1965–77 (Managing Director, 1961); Calor Gas Holding 1974–88; *b* 19 Jan. 1925; *s* of Sir Rudolph de Trafford, 5th Bt, OBE and June Lady Audley (*née* Chaplin), MBE (*d* 1977); *S* father, 1983; *m* 1st, 1946, Patricia Mary Beeley (marr. diss. 1973); three *s* five *d* (and one *d* decd); 2nd, 1973, Mrs Xandra Caradini Walter (*d* 2002). *Educ:* Harrow Sch.; Christ Church, Oxford (MA). Trained as Management Consultant, Orr & Boss and Partners Ltd, 1949–52; Director: Monks Investment Trust; Imperial Continental Gas Assoc., 1963–87 (Dep. Chm., 1972–87); Petrofina SA, 1971–87. Chm. Council, Inst. of Dirs, 1990–93. *Recreations:* theatre, travel. *Heir:* *s* John Humphrey de Trafford [*b* 12 Sept. 1950; *m* 1975, Anne, *d* of J. Faure de Pebeyre; one *s* one *d*]. *Address:* 1 Roper's Orchard, Danvers Street, SW3 5AX. *Clubs:* White's, Royal Ocean Racing; Island Sailing.

DETTORI, Lanfranco, (Frankie), Hon. MBE 2000; flat race jockey; *b* Italy, 15 Dec. 1970; *s* of Gianfranco Dettori and Maria Dettori (*née* Nieman); *m* 1997, Catherine, *d* of W. R. Allen, *qv*; two *s* three *d*. Winner: World Young Jockey Championship, Japan, 1992, 1993; Ascot Gold Cup, on Drum Taps, 1992, 1993, on Papineau, 2004; French Derby, German Derby; Nonthorpe; Sussex Stakes; Fillies Mile; Irish Derby, on Balanchine, 1994; Oaks, on Balanchine, 1994, on Moonshell, 1995, on Kazzia, 2002; Queen Elizabeth II, on Lammtarra, 1995; St Leger, on Classic Cliché, 1995, on Shantou, 1996, on Scorpion, 2005, on Sixties Icon, 2006; Prix de l'Arc de Triomphe, on Lammtarra, 1995, on Sakhee, 2001, on Marienbard, 2002; Two Thousand Guineas, on Mark of Esteem, 1996, on Island Sands, 1999; One Thousand Guineas, on Cape Verdi, 1998; on Kazzia, 2002; French Two Thousand Guineas, on Bachir, 2000, on Noverre, 2001, on Shamardal, 2005; Irish Champion Stakes, and Breeders' Cup Turf, NY, on Fantastic Light, 2001; Irish Oaks, on Vintage Tipple, 2003; Prix de l'Abbaye, Longchamp, on Var, 2004; Epsom Derby, on Authorized, 2007; all seven winners, Ascot, 28 Sept. 1996. Champion Jockey, 1994, 1995, 2004. Jt Proprietor, Frankie's Italian Bar and Grill, 2004–. *Publications:* A Year in the Life of Frankie Dettori, 1996; (with Jonathan Powell) Frankie: the autobiography of Frankie Dettori, 2004. *Address:* c/o Peter Burrell, 5 Jubilee Place, SW3 3TD. *T:* (020) 7352 8899.

DEUCHAR, Rev. Canon Andrew Gilchrist; Rector of St Peter and All Saints (formerly St Peter with St James), Nottingham, 2000–08; Priest-in-charge, St Mary the Virgin, Nottingham, 2004–08; a Chaplain to the Queen, 2004–08; *b* 3 June 1955; *s* of late David and of (Lucretia) Marian Deuchar; *m* 1977, Francesca Fowler; three *s* two *d*. *Educ:* Royal Hospital Sch., Ipswich; Southampton Univ. (BTh); Salisbury and Wells Theol Coll. HM

Diplomatic Service, 1974–81; ordained deacon, 1984, priest, 1985; Asst Curate, Alnwick, Northumberland, 1984–88; Team Vicar, S Wye Team Ministry, Hereford, 1988–90; Social Responsibility Advr, Canterbury and Rochester dios, 1990–94; Archbp of Canterbury's Sec. for Anglican Communion Affairs, 1994–2000. Hon. Canon, Canterbury Cathedral, 1995–2000. Chaplain to High Sheriff of Notts, 2007–. Mem. Bd of Trustees, USPG, 2003–06. Patron, Bishop Mubarak Scholarship Fund, 2004–. *Publications:* (contrib.) Anglicanism: a global communion, 1998; (contrib.) An Introduction to the Anglican Communion, 1998; (ed) A Last Embrace: essays in honour of Nadir Dinshaw, 2003. *Recreations:* music, travel, walking, football, the Isle of Skye. *Club:* Nikaean.

See also P. L. Deuchar.

DEUCHAR, Patrick Lindsay; *b* 27 March 1949; *s* of late David and of Marian Deuchar; *m* Gwyneth Miles (marr. diss.); one *s* one *d*; *m* 1997, Liz Robertson; one *d*. *Educ:* Christ's Hospital; Lackham Coll. of Agriculture. Farming, 1967–72; IPC Business Press, 1972–74; PR Manager, RASE, 1974–77; PR Manager, Earls Court and Olympia, 1977–80; European Dir, World Championship Tennis, 1981–89; Chief Exec., Royal Albert Hall, 1989–98; Chm., London Centre Mgt Co., 1998–99; Chief Exec., Rugby Hospitality for Rugby World Cup, 1998–99; Events Consultant: Somerset House Trust Ltd, 1998–99; 7th Regt Armory Conservancy, NY, 1998–99. Director: London First, 1996–99; TS2K (Trng and Skills 2000) (formerly Trafalgar Square 2000), 1996– (Dep. Chm.); Covent Gdn Fest., 1998–2001; (non-exec.) Cavendish Consultancy, 2000–. Chm., Sparks Charity, 1992–96; Member: Nat. Fundraising Cttee, Muscular Dystrophy Group, 1989–92; Nat. Music Day Cttee, 1993–97; London Visitor Council, 1994–97; Royal Concert Cttee, 1994–97; Mem. Council, 1995–, Chm. Develt Cttee, 2000–, RCM. Trustee: Albert Meml Trust, 1994–99; Cardiff Bay Opera House, 1994–96. Barker, Variety Club of GB, 1992; Mem., Inst. of Dirs. FRSA 1992. *Recreations:* music, theatre, art, cooking, wines, family life. *Address:* Flat 1, 27 Sloane Gardens, SW1W 8EB.

See also Rev. Canon A. G. Deuchar.

DEUCHAR, Dr Stephen John; Director, Tate Britain, since 1998; *b* 11 March 1957; *s* of late Rev. John Deuchar and of Nancy Dorothea Deuchar (*née* Jenkyns); *m* 1982, Dr Katie Scott; one *s* three *d*. *Educ:* Dulwich Coll. (Schol.); Univ. of Southampton (BA 1st Cl. Hons Hist.); Westfield Coll., London (PhD Hist. of Art 1986). National Maritime Museum: Curator of Paintings, 1985–87; Curator, Armada exhibn, 1987–88; Corporate Planning Manager, 1988–89; organizer of various exhibns and display projects, 1990–95; Dir, Neptune Court Project, 1995–97. Andrew W. Mellon Fellow in British Art, Yale Univ., 1981–82. Member: Council, Southampton Univ., 2004–; Adv. Cttee, Govt Art Collection, 2006–. Trustee, Metropole Arts Centre Trust, 2005–. *Publications:* Noble Exercise: the sporting ideal in 18th century British art, 1982; Paintings, Politics and Porter: Samuel Whitbread and British art, 1984; (jtly) Concise Catalogue of Oil Paintings in the National Maritime Museum, 1988; Sporting Art in 18th Century England: a social and political history, 1988; (jtly) Nelson: an illustrated history, 1995; contrib. articles on British art. *Recreation:* kart racing. *Address:* Tate, Millbank, SW1P 4RG. *T:* (020) 7887 8048.

DEUKMEJIAN, George; lawyer; Partner, Sidley & Austin, 1991–2000; Republican; *b* 6 June 1928; *s* of C. George Deukmejian and Alice (*née* Gairdan); *m* 1957, Gloria M. Saatjian; one *s* two *d*. *Educ:* Watervliet Sch., NY; Siena College (BA 1949); St John's Univ., NY (JD 1952). Admitted to NY State Bar, 1952, Californian Bar, 1956, US Supreme Court Bar, 1970. US Army, 1953–55. Law practice, Calif., 1955; Partner, Riedman, Dalessi, Deukmejian & Woods; Mem., Calif. Assembly, 1963–67; Mem., Calif. Senate (minority leader), 1967–79; Attorney Gen., Calif., 1979–83; Governor, California, 1983–91. *Address:* 5366 E Broadway, Long Beach, CA 90803–3549, USA.

DEUTCH, John Mark, PhD; Institute Professor, Department of Chemistry, Massachusetts Institute of Technology, since 1990; Director of Central Intelligence, USA, 1995–96; *b* 27 July 1938; *s* of Michael Joseph Deutch and Rachel Felicia Deutch (*née* Fischer); *m* Pat Lyon; three *s* by previous marriage. *Educ:* Amherst Coll. (BA 1961); MIT (BChemEng 1961; PhD PhysChem 1965). Sec. of Defence Office, 1961; Nat. Bureau of Standards, 1966; Asst Prof., Princeton, 1967–70; Prof., Chemistry Dept, MIT, 1971– (Mem. Faculty, 1976–; Dean of Science, 1982–85; Provost, 1985–90); Dept of Energy, 1977–80; Department of Defence: Under-Sec., 1993–94, Dep. Sec., 1994–95. Member: Army Sci. Adv. Panel, 1975–78; President's Commn on Strategic Forces, 1983; White House Sci. Council, 1985–89; President's Foreign Intell. Adv. Bd, 1990–93. Mem., Amer. Acad. of Arts and Scis. Hon. DSc Amherst, 1978; Hon. DPhil: Lowell, 1986; Northeastern, 1995. *Publications:* numerous research articles. *Recreations:* tennis, squash, reading. *Address:* Department of Chemistry, Room 6–215, Massachusetts Institute of Technology, Cambridge, MA 02139, USA.

DEUTSCH, Anthony Frederick; Sheriff of Glasgow and Strathkelvin, since 2005; *b* 9 June 1952; *s* of Robert and Elizabeth Deutsch; *m* 1977, Barbara MacDonald; two *s* one *d*. *Educ:* Univ. of Edinburgh (MA, LLB). Admitted solicitor, 1978; Partner, Macdonalds Solicitors, Glasgow, 1980–2005. *Recreations:* reading (mostly history), walking (mostly Isle of Arran), cooking, wine. *Address:* Sheriff Court House, 1 Carlton Place, Glasgow G5 9DA; *e-mail:* sheriffadeutsch@scotcourts.gov.uk.

DEUTSCH, Prof. David Elieser, DPhil; FRS 2008; Visiting Professor, Centre for Quantum Computation, Clarendon Laboratory, University of Oxford, since 1999; *b* Haifa, 18 May 1953; *s* of Oskar Deutsch and Tikva Deutsch. *Educ:* William Ellis Sch., London; Clare Coll., Cambridge (BA Natural Scis, Math. Tripos Pt III 1974); Wolfson Coll., Oxford (DPhil Theoretical Physics). *Publication:* The Fabric of Reality, 1997. *Address:* Centre for Quantum Computation, Clarendon Laboratory, Parks Road, Oxford OX1 3PU; *e-mail:* david.deutsch@qubit.org.

DEUTSCH, James Chobot, PhD; Director, Africa Programme, Wildlife Conservation Society, since 2002; *b* 28 Nov. 1963; *s* of Harold Kauffman Deutsch and late Barbara Hope Deutsch (*née* Chobot). *Educ:* St George's Sch., Newport, RI; Harvard Coll. (AB 1987); King's Coll., Cambridge (MPhil 1988, PhD 1992). Temp. Lectr, UEA, 1992–93; Res. Fellow, Churchill Coll., Cambridge, 1993–95; Lectr, Imperial Coll., London, 1995–97. Dir, AIDS Treatment Project, 1996–2000; Chief Exec., Crusaid, 1997–2002. Chm., Aidspan, 2002–; Member: Exec. Cttee, British HIV Assoc., 1999–2001; Council, Crusaid, 2002–. *Publications:* contrib. articles to Nature, Proc. Royal Soc., Evolution, HIV Medicine, Animal Behaviour, Conservation Biol., African Jl Ecol., and other jls. *Address:* International Conservation, Wildlife Conservation Society, 2300 Southern Boulevard, Bronx, NY 10460, USA. *T:* (646) 2291724.

DEVA, Niranjan Joseph Aditya, (Nirj); DL; Member (C) South East Region, England, European Parliament, since 1999; Director-General, Policy Research Centre for Business, since 1997; *b* Colombo, 11 May 1948; *s* of late Thakur Dr Kingsley de Silva Deva Aditya and of Zita Virginia Deva; *m* Indra Lavinia, *d* of Romy Govindia; one step *s*. *Educ:* St Joseph's Coll., Colombo; Loughborough Univ. of Technol. (BTech Hons Aero. Eng.). Company dir and adviser; Dep. Chm., Symphony Environmental Plastics Ltd; Director: Orient Garments (Sri Lanka) Ltd; Ceylon and Foreign Trades (Sri Lanka) Ltd; Distilleries

Co. of Sri Lanka Ltd, 2006–; Aitken Spence Ltd, Sri Lanka, 2006–. Pol. Officer, 1979, Chm., 1981, Bow Gp. Organiser, Conf. on Overseas Develt and Brandt Report, 1979. Member: Governing Council, Royal Commonwealth Soc., 1979–83; Nat. Consumer Council, 1982–88; Dept of Employment Adv. Cttee, 1988–91; Chairman: DTI/NCC Cttee on De-regulation of European Air Transport, 1985–86; One Nation Forum Political Cttee, 1986–91. Pres., Bow Group Trade and Industry Cttee, 1996. Contested (C) Hammersmith, 1987; MP (C) Brentford and Isleworth, 1992–97; contested (C) same seat, 1997. PPS to Minister of State, Scottish Office, 1996–97. Mem., Select Cttee on Parly Admin (Ombudsman), 1992–96, on Educn, 1995–96; Vice-Chm., Cons. back bench Aviation Cttee, 1994–97 (Jt Sec., 1992); Member: Asylum Bill Cttee, 1992; Deregulation Bill Cttee, 1994–97; Caravans Rating Bill Cttee, 1996–97; Asylum and Immigration Bill Cttee, 1996–97; European Standing Cttee B, 1992–97; All-Party Manufacturing Gp, 1993–97; Hon. Sec., All-Party Uganda Gp, 1994–97. European Parliament: spokesman, overseas develt and co-operation, 1999–; Member: Envmt Cttee, 1999–; EU-ACP Delegn, 1999–; Delegn to ASEAN countries, 2002–; Delegn to South Asian Assoc. for Regl Cooperation, 2004– (Vice Chm., 2007–); Foreign Affairs Cttee, 2004–June 2009; Rapporteur: WTO and Develt Issues of World Trade, 2000–; Aid to Uprooted People in Asia and Latin America, 2000–; Chairman: Indonesia Gp, 2000–; Afghan Gp, 2000–; EU-India Chamber of Commerce, 2005–; EU-China Friendship Gp, 2006–; Wkg Gp 'A', Develt Cttee, 2006–; Vice Pres., India Gp, 2001–; EPP-ED Coordinator, Develt Commn, 2004–; Co-Chairman: Wkg Gp on Colombia, 2004–; Delgn to UN World Summit and Gen. Assembly, 2005; Tsunami Co-ordinator, 2005–; budget draftsman, Develt Budget, 2006. Hon. Advr to Prime Minister of Sri Lanka, 2002–. Editor, Crossbow, 1983–85. Presenter, Deva's Hour, Sunrise Radio, 1995, 1998–99. FRSA 1997. DL Greater London, 1986. Hon. Ambassador-at-Large for Sri Lanka, 2003–. Wishwa Kirthi Sri Lanka Ahbimani, 2005. Knight of Merit with Star, Sacred Military Constantian Order of St George. *Publications:* Wealth of Nations Part II: Adam Smith revisited, 1998; various pamphlets and memoranda for Bow Group, 1980–85. *Recreations:* riding, reading, tennis. *Address:* Policy Research Centre for Business, 169 Kennington Road, SE11 6SF. *T:* (office) (01784) 432070, (mobile) 07976 734722; European Parliament, 43–60 rue Wiertz, 1047 Brussels, Belgium; *T:* (22) 847245; *e-mail:* office@nirjdeva.com; *web:* www.nirjdeva.com. *Clubs:* Carlton; Hounslow Conservative.

DEVANE, Ciarán Gearóid; Chief Executive, Macmillan Cancer Support, since 2007; *b* 25 Oct. 1962; *s* of Micheal and Eibhlín Devane; *m* 1998, Katy Ashburner (*d* 2003). *Educ:* University Coll., Dublin (BEng); George Washington Univ. (Masters Internat. Policy and Practice). Process Engr, ICI, 1984–93; Mgt Consultant, Gemini Consulting, 1993–2003; Chm., Pavilion Housing Gp, 2004–05; Mem. Bd, First Wessex Housing Gp, 2006–. *Recreations:* hill walking, theatre. *Address:* c/o Macmillan Cancer Support, 89 Albert Embankment, SE1 7UQ. *Club:* Royal Automobile.

DEVANEY, John Francis, CEng, FIET, FIMechE; Chairman: telent (formerly Marconi) plc, since 2002; National Air Traffic Services, since 2005; *b* 25 June 1946; *s* of late George Devaney and Alice Ann Devaney; two *s* one *d*. *Educ:* St Mary's Coll., Blackburn; Sheffield Univ. (BEng). FIMechE. Perkins Engines, 1968–89: manufacturing positions, Peterborough, 1968–76; Project Manager, Ohio, 1976–77; Director posts, UK, 1977–82; President, 1983–88; Group Vice-Pres., European Components Group, Peterborough, 1988 and Enterprises Group, Toronto, 1988–89; Chm. and Chief Exec. Officer and Group Vice-Pres., Kelsey-Hayes Corp., Michigan, 1989–92; Man. Dir, 1992, Chief Exec., 1993, Exec. Chm., 1995–98, Eastern Electricity plc, later Eastern Gp plc; Chm., NFC, subseq. Exel, plc, 2000–02 (Dir, 1996–2002). Non-executive Director: HSBC (formerly Midland Bank), 1994–; British Steel, 1998–. President: Electricity Assoc., 1994–95; Inst. for Customer Services, 1998–. *Recreations:* ski-ing, golf, tennis, sailing. *Address:* telent plc, 6th Floor, Tower 3, Harbour Exchange Square, E14 9GE. *Club:* Reform.

DEVANY, Rev. Mgr Thomas James, QHC 2000; VG; Principal Roman Catholic Chaplain, Royal Air Force, 1999–2004; *b* 5 July 1943; *s* of Joseph and Mary Devany. *Educ:* St Bede's, Manchester; Upholland Coll. Ordained priest, 1969; joined RAF 1982; has served in Germany, N Ireland and on UK mainland. VG 1999. *Recreations:* golf, opera.

DEVAUX, John Edward; His Honour Judge Devaux; a Circuit Judge, since 1993; *b* 1947; *s* of Henry Edward Devaux and Anne Elizabeth Devaux; *m* 1979, Fiona O'Conor; two *d*. *Educ:* Beaumont Coll.; Bristol Univ. (LLB). Called to the Bar, Lincoln's Inn, 1970; a Recorder, 1989–93; Resident Judge, Ipswich, 1998–2007. Hon. Recorder of Ipswich, 2000. *Address:* Ipswich Crown Court, The Courthouse, 1 Russell Road, Ipswich, Suffolk IP1 2AG. *T:* (01473) 228585.

DEVENPORT, Rt Rev. Eric Nash; Hon. Assistant Bishop: in the diocese of Europe, since 1992; Diocese of Norwich, since 2000; *b* 3 May 1926; *s* of Joseph and Emma Devenport; *m* 1954, Jean Margaret Richardson; two *d*. *Educ:* Kelham Theological Coll. BA (Open Univ.). Curate, St Mark, Leicester, 1951–54; St Matthew, Barrow-in-Furness, 1954–56; Succentor, Leicester Cathedral, 1956–59; Vicar of Shepshed, 1959–64; Oadby, 1964–73; Proctor in Convocation, 1964–80; Hon. Canon of Leicester Cathedral, 1973–80; Leader of Mission, Diocese of Leicester, 1973–80; Bishop Suffragan of Dunwich, 1980–92, retd; Archdeacon of Italy and Chaplain of St Mark's, Florence, 1992–97. Chairman: Diocesan Communication Officers Cttee, 1986–92; C of E Hospital Chaplaincies Council, 1986–91; Jt Hosp. Chaplaincies Cttee, 1988–91; E Anglian Ministerial Trng Course, 1990–92. Chaplain, Worshipful Company of Framework Knitters, 1964–80; Area Chaplain, Actors' Church Union, 1980–92. Chm., Local Radio Adv. Council for Radio Suffolk, 1990–92. *Publication:* Preaching at the Parish Communion: ASB Gospels-Sundays: Year One, Vol. 2, 1989. *Recreation:* theatre. *Address:* 6 Damocles Court, Pottergate, Norwich NR2 1HN. *T:* (01603) 664121.

de VERE, Anthony Charles Mayle, CMG 1986; HM Diplomatic Service, retired; Foreign and Commonwealth Office, 1986–93; *b* 23 Jan. 1930; *m* 1st, 1959, Geraldine Gertrude Bolton (*d* 1980); 2nd, 1986, Rosemary Edith Austin. *Educ:* St John's College, Cambridge. Served Army, Malaya, 1950–52; joined Colonial Service (later HMOCS), 1953, Provincial Admin, Tanganyika; Kibondo, 1953–56; in charge Kondoa-Irangi Develt Scheme, 1957–59; Res. Magistrate, Singida, 1959; Dist Comr, Tunduru, 1960–61, Kigoma, 1961–62; Head of local govt, Western Region, 1962–63, retired 1963; joined FO, later FCO, 1963; First Sec., Lusaka, 1967–70, NY, 1972–74; Counsellor, Washington, 1982–86. *Recreations:* riding, most things rural, sculpture, music, books. *Address:* Haddiscoe Hall, Norfolk NR14 6PE.

de VERE WHITE, Hon. Mrs; see Glendinning, Hon. Victoria.

DEVEREAU, (George) Michael, CB 1997; Head of Government Information Service, 1990–97; Chief Executive (formerly Director General), Central Office of Information, 1989–96; *b* 10 Nov. 1937; *s* of George Alfred Devereau and Elspeth Mary Duff Devereau; *m* 1961, Sarah Poupart; four *s*. *Educ:* King William's Coll., Isle of Man; University Coll. London. Asst Ed., Architects' Jl, 1962; Information Officer, MPBW, BRE and DoE, 1967–75; Chief Information Officer: Price Commn, 1975; DoE, 1978; Dept of Transport,

1982; Gp Dir, 1985, Dep. Dir Gen., 1987, COI. Trustee, Manx Nat. Heritage, 2007–. *Publication:* Architects Working Details, 1964. *Recreations:* house restoration, travel. *Address:* Magher Breck, Quaker Road, Maughold, Isle of Man IM7 1EF.

DEVERELL, Gen. Sir John Freegard, (Sir Jack), KCB 1999; OBE 1986; Commander-in-Chief, Allied Forces North, 2001–04; *b* 27 April 1945; *s* of Harold James Frank Deverell and Joan Beatrice Deverell (*née* Carter); *m* 1973, Jane Ellen Solomon; one *s* one *d*. *Educ:* King Edward's Sch., Bath; RMA Sandhurst. Commnd Somerset and Cornwall LI, 1965; RN Staff Coll., Greenwich, 1977; Comd 3rd Bn LI, 1984–86; Mil. Dir of Studies, RMCS, Shrivenham, 1988; Higher Command and Staff Course, Camberley, 1988; Comdr 1st Infantry Bde (UK Mobile Force), 1988–90; NDC, India, 1991; Dir, Army Recruiting, 1992–93; Dir Gen., Army Manning and Recruiting, 1993–95; Comdt, RMA Sandhurst, 1995–97; Dep. C-in-C, HQ Land Comd and Inspr Gen. TA, 1997–98 and 1999–2001; Dep. Comdr (Ops), HQ SFOR, Bosnia, 1998–99. Chm., Nat. Army Museum, 2004–. Pres., ACFA, 2004–. FICPD; FRSA. *Recreations:* golf, cricket, horses. *Clubs:* Army and Navy, Mounted Infantry.

DEVERELL, Richard George; Controller, BBC Children's, since 2006 (Chief Operating Officer, 2005–06); *b* 4 Dec. 1965; *s* of Geoff and Pauline Deverell; *m* 1993, Sarah Ann Inigo-Jones; one *s* two *d*. *Educ:* St Mary's Coll., Southampton; Magdalene Coll., Cambridge (BA Nat. Scis 1987). Associate Consultant, LEK Partnership, 1990–92; joined BBC, 1992; Sen. Advr, Policy and Planning, 1992–96; Head: Strategy and Mktg, BBC News, 1996–2000; BBC News Interactive, 2000–05. Trustee, Royal Botanic Gdns, Kew, 2003–. *Recreations:* cooking, triathlon. *Address:* c/o BBC Television Centre, Wood Lane, W12 7RJ. *T:* (020) 8576 1280, *Fax:* (020) 8576 9949; *e-mail:* Richard.deverell@bbc.co.uk.

DEVEREUX, family name of **Viscount Hereford**.

DEVEREUX, Alan Robert, CBE 1980; DL; Founder Director, Quality Scotland Foundation, since 1991; Director, Scottish Mutual Assurance Society, since 1975; *b* 18 April 1933; *s* of Donald Charles and Doris Devereux; *m* 1st, 1959, Gloria Alma Hair (*d* 1985); one *s*; 2nd, 1987, Elizabeth Tormey Docherty. *Educ:* Colchester School; Clacton County High School; Mid-Essex Technical Coll. CEng, MIET, CIMgt. Marconi's Wireless Telegraph Co., 1950–56; Halex Div. of British Xylonite Co., 1956–58; Spa Div., Sanitas Trust, 1958–65; Gen. Man., Dobar Engineering, 1965–67; Norcros Ltd, 1967–69; Gp Man. Dir 1969–78, Dep. Chm. 1978–80, Scotcros Ltd; Dir-Gen., Scotcros Europe SA, 1976–79. Director: Walter Alexander PLC, 1980–90; Hambros Scotland Ltd, 1984–; Abbey National Life, 1999–2003; Scottish Advisor, Hambros Bank, 1984–90. Dep. Chm. 1975–77, Chm. 1977–79, CBI Scotland; CBI: Council Mem., 1972–; Mem. President's Adv. Cttee, 1979; UK Regional Chm., 1979; Mem., F and GP Cttee, 1982–84. Chairman: Small Industries Council for Rural Areas of Scotland, 1975–77; Scottish Tourist Bd, 1980–90; Scottish Ambulance Service NHS Trust, 1994–97; Member: Scottish Development Agency, 1977–82; BTA, 1980–90. Chairman: Mission Aviation Fellowship, 2004–; Police Dependants' Trust, Scotland. Scottish Free Enterprise Award, 1978. DL Renfrewshire, 1985. *Recreations:* clock restoration, walking, Christian charities. *Address:* South Fell, 24 Kirkhouse Road, Blanefield, Stirlingshire G63 9BX. *T:* (01360) 770464. *Club:* East India, Devonshire, Sports and Public Schools.

DEVEREUX, Robert Harold Ferrars; Chairman: New Forests Company Holding Ltd, since 2007; Business Clubs Ltd, since 2007; *b* Woking, 11 April 1955; *s* of Robert Humphrey Bouchier Devereux and Barbara Devereux (*née* Heywood); *m* 1983, Vanessa, *d* of Edward James Branson, *qv*; three *s* one *d*. *Educ:* Marlborough Coll.; Downing Coll., Cambridge (BA Hons 1978). Founding shareholder, 1979–96, Chm., Communications and Entertainment Gp, 1989–2006, Virgin Gp. Mem., DCMS Creative Industries Task Force. Trustee and Chm., Portobello Trust, 1993–2003; Chm., Trustees, Save the Rhino Internat., 1997–2006; Gov., South Bank Centre, 1997–. *Recreations:* contemporary art, walking. *Address:* 5 Ladbroke Terrace, W11 3PG. *T:* 07768 270416; *e-mail:* robert.hfd@virgin.net. *Clubs:* Soho House, One Alfred Place.

See also Sir R. C. N. Branson.

DEVEREUX, Robert John; Permanent Secretary, Department for Transport, since 2007; *b* 15 Jan. 1957; *s* of Roy Devereux and Mary Margaret Devereux; *m* 1980, Margaret Alexandra Johnson; two *d*. *Educ:* St John's Coll., Oxford (MA Maths); Edinburgh Univ. (MSc Stats). ODA, 1979–83; HM Treasury, 1984–94 (Hd, Defence Expenditure, 1992–94); Guinness Brewing Worldwide, 1995–96 (on secondment); Department for Social Security: Hd, Family Policy, 1996–98; Director: Fraud Strategy, 1998–2000; Working Age Strategy, 2000–01; Dir, Planning and Performance, DWP, 2001–02; Dir Gen., Roads, Regl and Local Transport, subseq. Road Transport, Aviation and Shipping, DfT, 2003–07. *Recreations:* painting, singing. *Address:* Department for Transport, Great Minster House, 76 Marsham Street, SW1P 4DR. *T:* (020) 7944 3017; *e-mail:* robert.devereux@dft.gsi.gov.uk.

de VESCI, 7th Viscount *cr* 1766; **Thomas Eustace Vesey;** Bt 1698; Baron Knapton, 1750; Managing Director, Horticultural Coir Ltd; *b* 8 Oct. 1955; *s* of 6th Viscount de Vesci and Susan Anne (*d* 1986), *d* of late Ronald (Owen Lloyd) Armstrong-Jones, MBE, QC, DL, and of the Countess of Rosse; *S* father, 1983; *m* 1987, Sita-Maria, *o c* of late Brian de Breffny; two *s* one *d*. *Educ:* Eton; St Benet's Hall, Oxford. *Address:* 14 Rumbold Road, SW6 2JA.

See also Earl of Snowdon.

DEVESI, Sir Baddeley, GCMG 1980; GCVO 1982; Deputy Prime Minister and Minister for Transport, Works, Communication and Aviation, Solomon Islands, 1996–2000; *b* 16 Oct. 1941; *s* of late Mostyn Tagabasoe Norua and Laisa Otu; *m* 1969, June Marie Barley; six *s* three *d* (and one *d* decd). *Educ:* St Stephen's Sch., Auckland, NZ; Ardmore Teachers' Coll., Auckland, NZ; Univ. of Western Aust.; Univ. of S Pacific. MLC and Mem. Exec. Council, 1967–69. Headmaster, St Nicholas Sch., Honiara, 1968; Educn Officer and Lectr, Solomon Is Teachers' Coll., 1970–71; Sen. Asst Sec., Solomon Is, 1972; Dist. Officer, 1973; District Comr, District Magistrate and Clerk to Malaita Council, 1974–75; Permanent Sec., Ministry of Transport and Communications, 1976; Governor-Gen. of the Solomon Islands, 1978–88; Minister for Home Affairs and Dep. Prime Minister, 1989; Minister for For. Affairs and Trade Relations and Dep. Prime Minister, 1990–92; Minister for Health and Med. Services and Dep. Prime Minister, 1993; Leader of the Opposition, 1994. Dep. Chm., Solomon Islands Broadcasting Corp., 1976; Chm., AcP, 1990–91. Chancellor, Univ. of S Pacific, 1980–83. Captain, Solomon Islands team, 2nd South Pacific Games, 1966. Comr, Boy Scouts Assoc., 1968; Chief Scout, 1980–88. Hon. DU Univ. of the South Pacific, 1981. KStJ 1984. *Recreations:* reading, snooker, golf. *Address:* PO Box 227, Honiara, Solomon Islands.

DE VILLE, Sir Harold Godfrey, (Sir Oscar), Kt 1990; CBE 1979; PhD; Chairman, Meyer International plc, 1987–91 (Deputy Chairman, 1985–87; Director, 1984–91); *b* Derbyshire, 11 April 1925; *s* of Harold De Ville and Anne De Ville (*née* Godfrey); *m* 1947, Pamela Fay Ellis; one *s*. *Educ:* Burton-on-Trent Grammar Sch.; Trinity Coll., Cambridge (MA); PhD London 1995. Served RNVR, 1943–46. Ford Motor Co. Ltd, 1949–65; BICC, 1965–84: Dir, 1971–84; Exec. Dep. Chm., 1978–84. Director: Balfour Beatty Ltd, 1971–78; Phillips Cables Ltd, Canada, 1982–84; Metal Manufacturers Ltd, Australia, 1983–84; Scottish Cables Ltd, S Africa, 1983–84. Mem., BRB, 1985–91. Chairman: Iron and Steel EDC, 1984–86; Govt Review of vocational qualifications, 1985–86; NCVQ, 1986–90; Nat. Jt Council for Engrg Construction Industry, 1985–87. Member: Commn on Industrial Relations, 1971–74; Central Arbitration Cttee, 1976–77; Council: ACAS, 1976–91; BIM, 1982–86; Confederation of British Industry, 1977–85 (Chm., Working Party on Employee Participation, 1975–78). Mem. Council, Reading Univ., 1985–91. *Recreation:* genealogy.

de VILLEPIN, Dominique Marie François René Galouzeau; Prime Minister of France, 2005–07; *b* Rabat, Morocco, 14 Nov. 1953; *s* of Xavier Galouzeau de Villepin and Yvonne (*née* Hétier); *m* 1985, Marie-Laure Le Guay; one *s* two *d*. *Educ:* Ecole Nat. d'Admin; Paris Inst. of Pol Scis (BA Arts and Law). Ministry of Foreign Affairs, France: Sec. of Foreign Affairs, Dept for African Affairs, 1980–81; Hd of Mission, Dept for African Affairs and Analysis and Forecasting Centre, 1981–84; First Sec., 1984–87, Press Officer and Spokesperson, 1987–89, Washington; Second Counsellor, 1989–90, First Counsellor, 1990–92, New Delhi; Dep. Hd, African Affairs, Min. of Foreign Affairs, 1992–93; COS to Minister of Foreign Affairs, 1993–95; Sec. Gen. of Presidency of Republic, 1995–2002. Minister of Foreign Affairs, 2002–04; Rep., Convention on Future of Europe, 2002. Minister of the Interior, Internal Security and Local Rights, 2004–05. Chm., Admin Council, Nat. Forests Office, 1996–99. Légion d'Honneur (France). *Publications:* Les Cent Jours ou l'esprit de sacrifice, 2001; Le cri de la gargouille, 2002; Eloge des voleurs de feu, 2003; "Un autre monde": Cahiers de l'Herne, 2003; Le requin et la mouette, 2004; L'homme européen, 2005; *poetry:* Parole d'exil, 1986; Le droit d'aînesse, 1988; Sécession, 1996; Elégies barbares, 1996. *Address:* c/o Office of the Prime Minister, 57 rue de Varenne, 75007 Paris, France.

de VILLIERS, 4th Baron cr 1910; **Alexander Charles de Villiers;** *b* 29 Dec. 1940; *o s* of 3rd Baron de Villiers and Edna Alexis Lovett (*née* MacKinnon); *S* father, 2001; *m* 1966 (marr. diss.); *m* 1987, Christina Jacobsen.

de VILLIERS, Dawid Jacobus, DPhil; Advisor to the Secretary General of the United Nations World Tourism Organisation, since 2006; Deputy Secretary General, World Tourism Organisation, 1997–2005; *b* 10 July 1940; *m* 1964, Suzaan Mangold; one *s* three *d*. *Educ:* Univ. of Stellenbosch (BA Hons Philosophy; BTh, DPhil); Rand Afrikaans Univ. (MA Phil., 1972). Abe Bailey Scholar, 1963–64; Markotter Scholar, 1964. Part-time Lect in Philosophy, Univ. of Western Cape, 1963–64; Minister of Dutch Reformed Church, Wellington, Cape, 1967–69; Lectr in Philosophy, 1969–72, and Pres. Convocation, 1973–96, Rand Afrikaans Univ.; MP for Johannesburg W, 1972–79, for Piketberg, 1981–94, list MP, 1994–97; Chm., Nat. Party's Foreign Affairs Cttee in Parlt; Ambassador of S Africa to London, 1979–80; Minister: of Trade and Industry (formerly Industries, Commerce and Tourism), SA, 1980–86; of Budget and Welfare, 1986–88; for Admin and Privatisation, 1988–90; for Public Enterprises, 1989–91; for Mineral and Energy Affairs, 1990–91; for Economic Co-ordination, 1991–92; for Public Enterprises, 1992–94; for the Envmt and Tourism, 1994–96; Leader, Houses of Parliament, 1989–92. Leader, Nat Party, Cape Province, 1990–96. National Party Delegn Leader, Constitutional Conf. Convention for a Democratic S Africa, 1992. Visited: USA on US Leaders Exchange Prog., 1974; UK as guest of Brit. Govt, 1975; Israel as guest of Israeli Govt, 1977. Represented S Africa in internat. Rugby in S Africa, UK, Ireland, Australia, NZ, France and the Argentine, 1962–70 (Captain, 1965–70). State President's Award for Sport, 196[illegible] and 1970; S African Sportsman of the Year, 1968; Jaycee's Outstanding Young Man of the Year Award, 1971; State President's Decoration for Meritorious Service, Gold, 1988. *Recreations:* sports, reading. *Address:* Koloniesland 8, Stellenbosch, 7600, South Africa.

DEVINE, Hon. (Donald) Grant; founder and President, Grant Devine Managemen Inc., since 1991; President, Grant Devine Farms & Consulting Services Ltd; Premier o Saskatchewan, 1982–91; *b* Regina, 5 July 1944; *m* 1966, (Adeline) Chantal Guillaume two *s* three *d*. *Educ:* Saskatchewan Univ. (BScA 1967); Alberta Univ. (MSc 1969; MBA 1970); Ohio State Univ. (PhD 1976). Farming, 1962–; marketing specialist, Fed. Govt Ottawa, 1970–72; Graduate Assistant, Ohio State Univ., 1972–76; Prof. of Agricl Econs Saskatchewan Univ., 1976–79. Leader, Progressive Cons. Party of Saskatchewan 1979–92; MLA for Estevan, 1982–95; Leader, Official Opposition, Saskatchewan 1991–92; Minister of Agriculture, 1985–91. Advisor: Food Prices Rev. Bd and Provincial Govts; Sask. Consumers' Assoc. Member: Amer. Econ. Assoc.; Amer. Marketing Assoc Amer. Assoc. for Consumer Res.; Canadian Agricl Econs Soc.; Consumers' Assoc. o Canada. *Publications:* contribs to professional jls on retail food pricing and marke performance. *Recreations:* golf, ski-ing, baseball, horses.

DEVINE, Prof. Fiona, PhD; Professor of Sociology, since 2001, and Head of Sociology 2004–07, University of Manchester; *b* 6 June 1962; *d* of Patrick Noel Devine and Marth (*née* Daly); partner, James B. Husband. *Educ:* Univ. of Essex (BA Sociol. and Govt 1983 MA Sociol.; PhD Sociol. 1990). Res. officer, PSI, 1988–89; Lectr in Sociol., Univ. o Liverpool, 1989–94; University of Manchester: Lectr, 1994–97; Sen. Lectr, 1997–99 Reader, 1999–2001. Mem. Council, ESRC, 2003–07 (Chm., Internat. Adv. Cttee 2003–07). *Publications:* Affluent Workers Revisited, 1992; Social Class in America and Britain, 1997; (with S. Heath) Sociological Research Methods in Context, 1999; Clas Practices, 2004. *Recreations:* walking in Spain, bird-watching, classical and world music swimming, badminton. *Address:* Sociology, School of Social Sciences, University o Manchester, Oxford Road, Manchester M13 9PL. *T:* (0161) 275 2508; *e-mai* Fiona.Devine@manchester.ac.uk.

DEVINE, James; MP (Lab) Livingston, since Sept. 2005; *b* 24 May 1953; *s* of James and Rose Devine; *m* 1974, Elizabeth (marr. diss.); one *s* one *d*. *Educ:* St Mary's Acad., W Lothian; Moray House Coll. Sch. of Nursing. Student teacher, 1970–72; student nurse 1972–75; Staff Nurse, Bangour Hosp., 1975–77; Charge Nurse, psychiatric nursing team Blackburn Health Centre, 1977–82; union official, COHSE, then Unison (Head o Health, Scotland), 1982–2005. Hon. Lectr in Industrial Relns, Stirling Univ., 1985–2005 Agent, Rt Hon. Robin Cook, MP, 1982–2005. Mem., Scottish Exec., Labour Party 1983–95; Chm., Scottish Labour Party, 1996–95. *Recreations:* reading, chess, footbal horse racing. *Address:* c/o House of Commons, SW1A 0AA; *e-mail:* devinej@ parliament.uk. *Club:* Loganlea Miners.

DEVINE, Rt Rev. Joseph; *see* Motherwell, Bishop of, (RC).

DEVINE, Prof. Thomas Martin, OBE 2005; PhD, DLitt; FBA 1994; FRSE; FRHistS Sir William Fraser Professor of Scottish History and Palaeography, University o Edinburgh, since 2006; *b* 30 July 1945; *s* of Michael Gerard Devine and Norah Martin; *m* 1971; Catherine Mary Lynas; two *s* three *d*. *Educ:* Strathclyde Univ. (BA; PhD 1972; DLitt 1992). FRHistS 1980; FRSE 1992. University of Strathclyde: Lectr in History, 1969–78 Sen. Lectr in History, 1978–83; Reader in Scottish History, 1983–88; Prof. of Scottish History, 1988–98; Dir, Res. Centre in Scottish History, 1993–98; Dean, Faculty of Ar and Social Studies, 1993–94; Dep. Principal, 1994–97; Aberdeen University: Univ. Res. Prof. in Scottish Hist. and Dir, Res. Inst. of Irish and Scottish Studies, 1998–2003; Dir, AHRB, subseq. AHRC Centre for Irish-Scottish Studies, 2001–06; Glucksman Res. Prof., 2004–06. Adjunct Professor in History: Univ. of Guelph, Canada, 1989–; Univ. of N Carolina, 1997–. Member: Sec. of State for Scotland's Adv. Cttee, 2001–04; Res. Awards Adv. Cttee, Leverhulme Trust, 2002–; Adv. Cttee, ESRC Prog. on Devolution, 2002–06. Chm., Econ. and Social History Soc. of Scotland, 1984–88; Convenor of Council, Scottish Catholic Historical Assoc., 1990–95; Convener, Irish-Scottish Academic Initiative, 1998–2001; UK Rep., Internat. Commn for Hist. of Towns, 2000–06. Mem. Council, British Acad., 1998–2001. Trustee, 1995–2002, Chair, European Ethnol Res. Centre, Nat. Museums of Scotland. Gov., St Andrews Coll. of Educn, 1990–94. Prothero Lectr, RHistS, 2005. Hon. MRIA 2001. Hon. Fellow, Bell Coll., 2005. Hon. DLitt: QUB; Abertay Dundee; DUniv Strathclyde, 2006. Sen. Hume Brown Prize in Scottish Hist., 1976; Saltire Prize, 1992; Henry Duncan Prize, 1994, Royal Medal, 2001, RSE; John Aitkenhead Award and Medal, Inst. of Contemp. Scotland, 2006. *Publications:* The Tobacco Lords, 1975, 2nd edn 1990; (ed) Ireland and Scotland 1600–1850, 1983; (ed) Farm Servants and Labour in Lowland Scotland, 1984; A Scottish Firm in Virginia 1767–77, 1984; (ed) People and Society in Scotland, 1988; The Great Highland Famine, 1988; (ed) Improvement and Enlightenment, 1989; (ed) Conflict and Stability in Scottish Society 1700–1850, 1990; (ed) Irish Immigrants and Scottish Society in 18th and 19th Centuries, 1991; Scottish Emigration and Scottish Society, 1992; The Transformation of Rural Scotland 1660–1815, 1994; Clanship to Crofters' War, 1994; (ed) Scottish Elites, 1994; Glasgow, vol. I, 1995; Exploring The Scottish Past, 1995; (ed) Scotland in the Twentieth Century, 1996; (ed) Eighteenth Century Scotland: new perspectives, 1999; (ed) Celebrating Columba: Irish-Scottish connections 1597–1997, 1999; The Scottish Nation 1700–2000, 1999; (ed) Scotland's Shame?: bigotry and sectarianism in modern Scotland, 2000; (ed) Being Scottish: personal reflections on Scottish identity, 2002; Scotland's Empire 1600–1815, 2003; (ed jtly) The Transformation of Scotland, 2005; Clearance and Improvement: land, power and people in Scotland, 1660–1860, 2006; The Scottish Nation 1700–2007, 2006; (ed) Scotland and the Union, 1707 to 2007, 2008; articles in learned jls. *Recreations:* grandchildren, walking in the Hebrides, foreign travel, music, watching skilful soccer. *Address:* School of History, Classics and Archaeology (Scottish History), University of Edinburgh, 17 Buccleuch Place, Edinburgh EH8 9LN. *T:* (0131) 650 4029; *e-mail:* t.m.devine@ed.ac.uk.

de VIRION, Tadeusz, Cross of Valour, Cross of the Home Army, Warsaw Uprising Cross, 1944; practising lawyer in penal law; Polish Ambassador to the Court of St James's, 1990–93; *b* 28 March 1926; *s* of Jerzy de Virion (killed in Auschwitz, 1941); *m* 1985, Jayanti Hazra; two *d.* *Educ:* Univ. of Warsaw (LLM). Barrister, 1950–, specialising in criminal law; Judge of Tribunal of State, elected by Polish Parlt, 1989, 1990, 1993–. Cross of Knights of Malta, 1980; Golden Insignia of Barrister's Merit, 1988; Comdr's Cross, Order of Polonia Restituta; Grand Officier, Order of Pro Merito Melitensi. *Recreations:* Jayanti, books. *Address:* ul. Zakopiańska 17, 03 934 Warsaw, Poland. *T:* (2) 6178880. *Clubs:* Polish Hearth, Travellers, Special Forces; Polish Business Centre (Warsaw).

DEVITT, Sir James (Hugh Thomas), 3rd Bt *cr* 1916, of Chelsea, Co. London; hotel and leisure consultant; Director, CB Richard Ellis Hotels, since 2003; *b* 18 Sept. 1956; *o s* of Sir Thomas Gordon Devitt, 2nd Bt and of Janet Lilian, *o d* of Col H. S. Ellis, CBE, MC; *S* father, 1995; *m* 1985, Susan Carol (*née* Duffus); two *s* one *d.* *Educ:* Corpus Christi Coll., Cambridge (MA). MRICS. *Recreations:* family, football. *Heir: s* Jack Thomas Michael Devitt, *b* 29 July 1988. *Address:* The Old Rectory, Ford Lane, Alresford, Colchester, Essex CO7 8AX. *T:* (01206) 827315.

DEVLIN, Alexander, OBE 1977; JP; Member, Glenrothes New Town Development Corporation, 1958–78; *b* 22 Dec. 1927; *s* of Thomas Devlin and Jean Gibson; *m* 1949, Annie Scott Gordon. *Educ:* Cowdenbeath St Columba's High Sch.; National Council of Labour Colls (Local Govt and Public Speaking). Member: Fife CC, 1956–74; Fife Regional Council, 1974–78; Chm., Fife Educn Cttee, 1963–78; Vice-Chm., Educn Cttee of Convention of Scottish Local Authorities, 1974–78. Member: Dunning Cttee on Scottish System for Assessment of Pupils after 4 years Secondary Educn, 1974–77; Scottish Sports Council, 1964–74; Manpower Services Commn, 1978–79. Mem. Bd, 1992, Fellow, 1996–, Glenrothes Coll. Pres., Glenrothes & Dist Burns Club, 1995–97. JP Fife, 1963.

DEVLIN, Rt Rev. Mgr Bernard Patrick, CMG 1996; RC Bishop of Gibraltar, 1985–98, now Emeritus; *b* Youghal, Co. Cork, 10 March 1921. *Educ:* Mount Melleray Cistercian Coll.; Holy Cross Seminary, Dublin; Nat. Univ. of Ireland (BA 1942); Pontifical Beda Coll. Ordained, 1945; Curate, Cathedral of St Mary the Crowned, Gibraltar, 1946–60; Parish Priest, St Theresa's Church, Gibraltar, 1961–85; Vicar General, 1976–85. Freeman, City of Gibraltar, 1999. *Recreations:* golf, painting. *Address:* c/o Cathedral of St Mary the Crowned, 215 Main Street, Gibraltar. *T:* 76688.

DEVLIN, (Josephine) Bernadette; *see* McAliskey, J. B.

DEVLIN, His Honour Keith Michael, PhD; a Circuit Judge, 1984–95; a Deputy Circuit Judge, 1995–99; *b* 21 Oct. 1933; *e s* of late Francis Michael Devlin and of Norah Devlin (*née* Gregory); *m* 1958, Pamela Gwendoline Phillips; two *s* one *d.* *Educ:* Price's Sch., Fareham; Eaton Hall OCS; King's Coll., London Univ. (LLB 1960, MPhil 1968); PhD Brunel 1976. Commnd RAOC, 1953. Called to the Bar, Gray's Inn, 1964; Dep. Chief Clerk, Metropolitan Magistrates' Courts Service, 1964–66; various appts as Dep. Metropolitan Stipendiary Magistrate, 1975–79; Asst Recorder, 1980–83; a Recorder, 1983–84; Liaison Judge, Bedfordshire, 1990–93; Resident Judge, Luton Crown Court, 1991–93. Brunel University: Lectr in Law, 1966–71; Reader in Law, 1971–84; Associate Prof. of Law, 1984–96; Professorial Res. Fellow, 1996–; Mem., Court, 1985–88. Fellow, Netherlands Inst. for Advanced Study in the Humanities and Social Sciences, Wassenaar, 1975–76. Chm., Mental Health Review Tribunals, 1991–93, 1995–98. Mem., Consumer Protection Adv. Cttee, 1976–81. MRI (Member: Finance Cttee, 1988–97; Council, 1994–97). Magistrates' Association: Mem., 1974–, Vice-Chm., 1984–89, Legal Cttee; co-opted Mem. Council, 1980–88; a Vice-Pres., Bucks Br., 1993–. Mem. Court, Luton Univ., 1994–98. Mem., Inst. of Cancer Res., 1999– (Mem. Council, 1999–2001; Chm., Ethics Cttee, 2000–03). JP Inner London (Juvenile Court Panel), 1968–84 (Chm., 1973–84). Liveryman, Feltmakers' Co. (Mem., Ct of Assts, 1991–; Master, 1998–99). FRSA 1989. Jt Founder and Editor, Anglo-Amer. Law Rev., 1972–84. *Publications:* Sentencing Offenders in Magistrates' Courts, 1970; (with Eric Stockdale) Sentencing, 1987; articles in legal jls. *Recreations:* watching cricket, fly-fishing, Roman Britain. *Clubs:* Athenæum, MCC; Hampshire County Cricket.

DEVLIN, Stuart Leslie, AO 1988; CMG 1980; goldsmith, silversmith and designer in London since 1965; Goldsmith and Jeweller by appointment to HM the Queen, 1982; *b* 9 Oct. 1931; *m* 1986, Carole Hedley-Saunders. *Educ:* Gordon Inst. of Technology, Geelong; Royal Melbourne Inst. of Technology; Royal Coll. of Art. DesRCA (Silversmith), DesRCA (Industrial Design/Engrg). Art Teacher, Vic. Educn Dept, 1950–58; Royal Coll. of Art, 1958–60; Harkness Fellow, NY, 1960–62; Lectr, Prahran Techn. Coll., Melbourne, 1962; one-man shows of sculpture, NY and Sydney, 1961–64; Inspr Art in Techn. Schs, Vic. Educn Dept, 1964–65; exhibns of silver and gold in numerous cities USA, Australia, Bermuda, Middle East and UK, 1965–. Mem., Royal Mint Adv. Cttee, 1998–2007. Executed many commissions in gold and silver: designed coins for Australia, Singapore, Cayman Is, Gibraltar, IoM, Burundi, Botswana, Ethiopia and Bhutan; designed and made: cutlery for State Visit to Paris, 1972; Duke of Edinburgh trophy for World Driving Championship, 1973; silver to commemorate opening of Sydney Opera House, 1973; Grand National Trophy, 1975, 1976; Australian Bravery Awards, 1975; Regalia for the Order of Australia, 1975–76; Queen's Silver Jubilee Medal, 1977; Centrepiece for RE to commemorate their work in NI, 1984; Bas-relief portrait of Princess of Wales for Wedgwood, 1986; full set of Defence Awards for Australia, 1989; portraits of HM the Queen Mother, HRH the Princess of Wales, HRH the Princess Royal, HRH the Princess Margaret, 1991; British Athletics Fedn Badge and Chain of Office, 1992; 24 Sydney 2000 Olympic coins, 1997; Millennium commemorative dishes for Goldsmiths' Co. and Inf. Technologists' Co., 2000. Developed strategy for use of champagne diamonds in jewellery for Argyle Diamond Mines, 1987. Computer presentations in USA and UK; Inaugural Chm., Engrg Modelling Systems Special Interest Gp, 1993; Vice Chm., Intergraph Graphics Users' Gp UK, 1996. Freeman, City of London, 1966; Liveryman, 1972, Mem. Ct of Assts, 1986–2007, Prime Warden, May 1996–97, Goldsmiths' Co. Hon. DocArts RMIT, 2000. *Recreations:* work, computer graphics. *Address:* Fordwych, Angmering Lane, East Preston, W Sussex BN16 2TA. *T:* (01903) 858939.

DEVLIN, Tim; Founder, Tim Devlin Enterprises, public relations consultancy, 1989; *b* 28 July 1944; 3rd *s* of Rt Hon. Lord Devlin, PC, FBA, and of Madeleine, *yr d* of Sir Bernard Oppenheimer, 1st Bt; *m* 1967, Angela Denise, *d* of late A. J. G. and Mrs Laramy; two *s* two *d.* *Educ:* Winchester Coll.; University Coll., Oxford (Hons degree, History). Feature Writer, Aberdeen Press & Journal, 1966; Reporter, Scotsman, 1967; Educn Reporter, Evening Echo, Watford, 1968–69; Reporter, later News Editor, The Times Educnl Supplement, 1969–71; Reporter, The Times, 1971–73, Educn Corresp., 1973–77; Nat. Dir, ISIS, 1977–84; Public Relations Dir, Inst. of Dirs, 1984–86; Assoc. Dir, Charles Barker Traverse-Healy, 1986–89. *Publications:* (with Mary Warnock) What Must We Teach?, 1977; Good Communications Guide, 1980; Independent Schools—The Facts, 1981; Choosing Your Independent School, 1984; (with Brian Knight) Public Relations and Marketing for Schools, 1990; (with Hywel Williams) Old School Ties, 1992; (with Angela Devlin) Anybody's Nightmare, 1998; Public Relations Manual for Schools, 1998. *Recreations:* writing, art, tennis. *T:* (01205) 290176.

DEVLIN, Timothy Robert; barrister; *b* 13 June 1959; *e s* of late H. Brendan Devlin, CBE, FRCS and of Anne Elizabeth Devlin, MB BCh; *m* 1st, 1986 (marr. diss. 1989); 2nd, 1991, Carol-Anne Aitken (marr. diss. 2002). *Educ:* Dulwich Coll.; LSE; City Univ. Called to the Bar, Lincoln's Inn, 1985 (Hardwick and Thomas More Scholar; Mem., Finance Cttee, 2006). Sen. Expert, Technical Assistance to CIS, EU, 1998–99; Consultant, Stanbrook & Hooper, Brussels, 1999–2000. Dep. Chm., NHS Tribunal, 2001–. Mem., Cons. Research Dept, 1981; former Chm., LSE Conservatives; Chm., Islington North Cons. Assoc., 1986. MP (C) Stockton South, 1987–97; contested (C) same seat, 1997, 2001. PPS to Attorney Gen., 1992–94; PPS to Ministers of Trade and Industry, 1995–97. Mem., Select Cttee on Scottish Affairs, 1995–97; formerly Chm., Parly Panel on Charity Law; Chm., Northern Gp of Cons. MPs, 1992–97. Dep. Chm., Foreign Affairs Forum, 1990–92; Mem., Bar Council, 2007. Member: Islington South Cons. Assoc.; Soc. of Cons. Lawyers; European Bar Assoc.; Friends of the RA. Trustee, NSPCC, 1993–95; Gov., Yarm Sch., 1988–98. *Recreations:* sailing, opera, travel. *Address:* 32 Furnival Street, EC4A 1JQ. *Club:* Royal Cinque Ports Yacht.

DEVON, 18th Earl of, *cr* 1553; **Hugh Rupert Courtenay;** Bt 1644; Vice Lord-Lieutenant of Devon, since 2002; landowner, farmer; *b* 5 May 1942; *o s* of 17th Earl of Devon, and Venetia, former wife of 6th Earl of Cottenham and *d* of Captain J. V. Taylor; *S* father, 1998; *m* 1967, Diana Frances, *er d* of J. G. Watherston, Jedburgh, Roxburghshire; one *s* three *d.* *Educ:* Winchester; Magdalene Coll., Cambridge (BA). MRICS. Captain, Wessex Yeomanry, retd. Chm., Devon Br., CLA, 1987–89. DL Devon, 1991. *Recreations:* riding, hunting, shooting. *Heir: s* Lord Courtenay, *qv.* *Address:* Powderham Castle, near Exeter, Devon EX6 8JQ. *T:* (01626) 890370.

DEVONPORT, 3rd Viscount *cr* 1917, of Wittington, Bucks; **Terence Kearley;** Bt 1908; Baron 1910; architect and landowner; Chairman: Peasmarsh Place (Country Care), since 1984; Millhouse Developments Ltd, since 1989; *b* 29 Aug. 1944; *s* of 2nd Viscount Devonport and Sheila Isabel, *e d* of Lt-Col C. Hope Murray; *S* father, 1973; *m* 1st, 1968, Elizabeth Rosemary (marr. diss. 1979), *d* of late John G. Hopton; two *d*; 2nd, 2000, Dr Meiyi Pu, *d* of Prof. Wan Jun Pu, Beijing; one *d.* *Educ:* Aiglon Coll., Switzerland; Selwyn Coll., Cambridge (BA, DipArch, MA); Newcastle Univ. (MPhil). Architect: Davis Brody, New York City, 1967–68; London Borough of Lambeth, 1971–72; Barnett Winskell, Newcastle-upon-Tyne, 1972–75; landscape architect, Ralph Erskine, Newcastle, 1977–78; in private practice, 1979–84 (RIBA, ALI); Forestry Manager, 1973–; farmer, 1978–. Chairman: Cape Acre Ltd; Devonport Farms Ltd; Devonport Estates; Man. Dir, Tweedswood Enterprises, 1979–, and dir various other cos, 1984–. Member: Lloyds, 1976–90; Internat. Dendrology Soc., 1978– (Council, 1995–); N Adv. Cttee, TGEW, 1978–94; N Adv. Cttee, CLA, 1980–85; Nat. Land Use and Envmt Cttee, TGUK, 1984–87. Pres., Arboricultural Assoc., 1995–2001; Forestry Commn Reference Panel, 1987–94. MInstD. Order of Mark Twain (USA), 1977. *Recreations:* nature, travel and good food; interests: trees, the arts, country sports. *Heir: cousin* Chester Dagley Hugh Kearley [*b* 29 April 1932; *m* 1974, Josefa Mesquida; one *s* one *d*]. *Address:* Ray Demesne, Kirkwhelpington, Newcastle upon Tyne NE19 2RG. *Clubs:* Royal Automobile, Beefsteak, Farmers', MCC; Northern Counties (Newcastle upon Tyne).

DEVONSHIRE, 12th Duke of, *cr* 1694; **Peregrine Andrew Morny Cavendish,** CBE 1997; DL; Baron Cavendish, 1605; Earl of Devonshire, 1618; Marquess of Hartington, 1694; Earl of Burlington, 1831; Baron Cavendish (UK), 1831; Her Majesty's Representative and Chairman, Ascot Racecourse, since 1998; *b* 27 April 1944; *s* of 11th Duke of Devonshire, KG, MC, PC and of Dowager Duchess of Devonshire, *qv*; *S* father, 2004; *m* 1967, Amanda Carmen, *d* of late Comdr E. G. Heywood-Lonsdale, RN, and of Mrs Heywood-Lonsdale; one *s* two *d.* *Educ:* Eton; Exeter Coll., Oxford. Dep. Chm., Sen. Steward, Jockey Club, 1989–94; Chm., British Horseracing Bd, 1993–96. Dep. Chm., Sotheby's Holdings Inc., 1996– (Dir, 1994–). Trustee: Wallace Collection, 2007–; Storm King Art Centre, New York, 2007–; Sheffield Galls and Mus Trust, 2007–. Patron, Sheffield Botanical Gardens, 2007–. DL Derbys, 2008. *Heir: s* Earl of Burlington, *qv.* *Address:* Chatsworth, Bakewell, Derbyshire DE45 1PP.

DEVONSHIRE, Dowager Duchess of; Deborah Vivien Cavendish, DCVO 1999; housewife; Trustee, Royal Collections Trust, 1993–99; *b* 31 March 1920; 6th *d* of 2nd Baron Redesdale and Sydney (*née* Bowles); *m* 1941, Lord Andrew Cavendish (later 11th Duke of Devonshire, KG, MC, PC) (*d* 2004); one *s* two *d.* *Educ:* private. Director: Peacock Hotel (Baslow) Ltd, 1975–; Elm Tree Farm Ltd, 1975–; Chatsworth House

Trust, 1981–2006; Devonshire Arms Hotel (Bolton Abbey) Ltd, 1981–2006; Partner, Chatsworth Partners, 1981–2006; non-executive Director: Tarmac plc, 1984–92; W. & F. C. Bonhams & Sons Ltd, 1988–95. President: Royal Smithfield Show, 1972–74 and 1985; Royal Smithfield Club, 1975 (Vice-Pres., 1974–); RASE, 1995; Vice-Pres., Derbys Br., BRCS; Pres. or Patron, local charitable orgns, Derbys. Hon. Fellow, Sheffield City Poly., 1990. DUniv Middlesex, 1996; Hon. LittD Sheffield, 1998; Hon. Dr Derby, Buxton, 2006. *Publications:* The House: a portrait of Chatsworth, 1982; The Estate: a view from Chatsworth, 1990; Farm Animals, 1991; Treasures of Chatsworth: a private view, 1991; The Garden at Chatsworth, 1999; Counting My Chickens … and Other Home Thoughts, 2001; Chatsworth: the house, 2002; The Duchess of Devonshire's Chatsworth Cookery Book, 2003; Round about Chatsworth, 2005; Memories of Andrew Devonshire, 2007; contribs to Spectator, Daily Telegraph. *Address:* 1 Old Vicarage, Edensor, Bakewell, Derbyshire DE45 1PH. *T:* (01246) 584020, *Fax:* (01246) 584021.

See also Baron Margadale, Lady E. Tennant.

DEVONSHIRE, His Honour Michael Norman, TD 1969; a Circuit Judge, 1991–2000; *b* 23 May 1930; *s* of late Norman George Devonshire and late Edith Devonshire (*née* Skinner); *m* 1962, Jessie Margaret Roberts. *Educ:* King's Sch., Canterbury. Military Service, 2nd Lt, RA, served Korea, 1953–55; 4/5 Bn Queen's Own Royal West Kent Regt TA and 8 Bn Queen's Regt TA, 1955–69; retired in rank of Major, 1969. Admitted Solicitor, 1953; Partner, Doyle Devonshire Co., 1957–79; Master of the Supreme Court, Taxing Office, 1979–91; a Recorder, 1987–91; Dep. Circuit Judge, 2000–01. Chm., SE London Area Adv. Cttee on Magistracy, 1995–99. Pres., London Solicitors' Litigation Assoc., 1974–76; Mem., Law Soc. Family Law and Contentious Remuneration Cttees, 1969–79. Mem., Recreation and Conservation Cttee, Southern Water Authy, 1984–89. Mem., Council, Royal Yachting Assoc., 1978–92 and 1993–96 (Trustee, Seamanship Foundn, 1981–85; Chairman: Gen. Purposes Cttee, 1982–87; Regl Cttee, 1987–92; Internat. Affairs Cttee, 1990–2004; SE Region, 1993–98; Hon. Life Mem., 2000); Chm., Internat. Regs Cttee, ISAF (formerly IYRU), 1994–2004 (Mem., 1986–90; Vice Chm., 1991–94); Mem., Pleasure Navigation Commn, Union Internat. de Motorautique, 1986–2000. FRIN 2004. Outstanding Service Award, Royal Norwegian Boating Fedn, 2004. *Recreations:* sailing, photography. *Club:* Royal Thames Yacht.

de VOS, Niels; Chief Executive Officer, UK Athletics, since 2007; *b* 27 March 1967; *s* of Leendert and Christine de Vos; *m* 1990, Kirsten Macleod; two *s* one *d*. *Educ:* Dorridge Jun. Sch.; King Edward's Sch., Edgbaston; Keble Coll., Oxford (BA Hons Modern Hist.). Hd, Corporate Relns, Barnardo's, 1994–97; Commercial Gen. Manager, Millennium Dome, 1997–99; Commercial Dir, Manchester 2002 Commonwealth Games, 1999–2002; CEO, Sale Sharks Rugby Club, 2002–07. Founder and Trustee, Children's Promise, 1999–. *Recreations:* football, running, films, family holidays, supporting Birmingham City FC. *Address:* c/o UK Athletics, Athletics House, Central Boulevard, Blythe Valley Park, Solihull, W Midlands B90 8JA.

DEVOY, Dame Susan (Elizabeth Anne), DNZM 1998; CBE 1993 (MBE 1986); professional squash rackets player, 1982–92, retired; formerly Chief Executive Officer, then Chairperson, Sport Bay of Plenty; *b* 4 Jan. 1964; *d* of John and Tui Devoy; *m* 1986, John Brandon Oakley; four *s*. *Educ:* McKillop Coll., Rotorua. Ranked no 1 internat. women's squash rackets player, 1984–92; winner: World Championships: Dublin, 1985; Auckland, 1987; Sydney, 1990; Vancouver, 1992; British Open Championships, 1984–90, 1992; 86 other internat. titles. Walked length of NZ in 53 days, raising NZ$500,000 for Muscular Dystrophy, 1988. Chm., Halberg Trust for Crippled Children, 1996–. NZ Sportsperson of Year, Halberg Trust, 1985–87, 1990, 1992. *Publications:* Susan Devoy on Squash, 1988; Out on Top, 1993. *Recreation:* yoga.

DEW, John Anthony; HM Diplomatic Service; Ambassador to Colombia, since 2008; *b* 3 May 1952; *s* of Roderick Dew and Katharina (*née* Kohlmeyer); *m* 1975, Marion, *d* of late Prof. Kenneth Kirkwood; three *d*. *Educ:* Hastings Grammar Sch.; Lincoln Coll., Oxford (Schol.); Ruskin Sch. of Drawing, Oxford. Joined HM Diplomatic Service, 1973; Third Sec., Caracas, 1975–79; FCO, 1979–83; First Sec., UK Delegn to OECD, Paris, 1983–87; Asst Hd, Falkland Is and Resource Mgt Depts, FCO, 1987–92; Counsellor, Dublin, 1992–96; Minister, Madrid, 1996–2000; Hd of Latin America and Caribbean Dept, FCO, 2000–03; on secondment to Lehman Brothers Internat., 2003–04; Ambassador to Cuba, 2004–08. *Recreations:* books, pictures, printmaking. *Address:* c/o Foreign and Commonwealth Office, King Charles Street, SW1A 2AH. *Club:* Gran Pena (Madrid).

DEW, Most Rev. John Atcherley; *see* Wellington (NZ), Archbishop of, (RC).

DEW, Prof. Ronald Beresford; Professor of Management Sciences, University of Manchester Institute of Science and Technology, 1967–80, now Professor Emeritus, University of Manchester; *b* 19 May 1916; *s* of Edwyn Dew-Jones, FCA, and Jean Robertson Dew-Jones, BA, (*née* McInnes); *m* 1940, Sheila Mary Smith, BA; one *s* one *d*. *Educ:* Sedbergh; Manchester Univ. (LLB); Cambridge Univ. (MA). FCA 1947. Barrister-at-Law, Middle Temple, 1965. Lieut, RNVR, 1940–45. Asst Managing Dir, P-E Consulting Gp, 1952–62. Visiting Prof. of Industrial Administration, Manchester Univ., 1960–63; Head of Dept of Management Sciences, Univ. of Manchester Inst. of Science and Technology, 1963–70 and 1974–77; Prof. of Industrial Administration, Manchester Univ., 1963–67. Mem. Council, Internat. Univ. Contact for Management Educn, 1966–71; Dir, Centre for Business Research, 1965–69; Dir, European Assoc. of Management Training Centres, 1966–71; Dep. Chm., Manchester Polytechnic, 1970–72; Co-Chm., Conf. of Univ. Management Schools (CUMS), 1970–73. Member: Council of BIM, 1971–76 (Bd of NW Region, 1966–80); Council of Manchester Business School, 1967–76; Court of Manchester Univ., 1978–80; Trustee, European Foundation for Management Develt, 1975–77. *Recreations:* archaeology, ornithology, travel. *Address:* University of Manchester, School of Management, Sackville Street, Manchester M60 1QD.

de WAAL, Sir Constant Hendrik, (Sir Henry), KCB 1989 (CB 1977); QC 1988; First Parliamentary Counsel, 1987–91; *b* 1 May 1931; *s* of late Hendrik de Waal and Elizabeth von Ephrussi; *m* 1964, Julia Jessel (MBE 2008); two *s*. *Educ:* Tonbridge Sch. (scholar); Pembroke Coll., Cambridge (scholar; Hon. Fellow, 1992). 1st cl. Law Tripos, 1st cl. LLM. Called to the Bar, Lincoln's Inn, 1953, Bencher 1989; Buchanan Prize, Cassel Scholar. Fellow of Pembroke Coll., Cambridge, and Univ. Asst Lectr in Law, 1958–60. Entered Parliamentary Counsel Office, 1960; with Law Commission, 1969–71; Parly Counsel, 1971–81; Second Parly Counsel, 1981–86; Parly Counsel to Law Commn, 1991–96. *Recreation:* remaining (so far as possible) unaware of current events. *Address:* 21 Warwick Square, SW1V 2AB.

See also Rev. V. A. de Waal.

de WAAL, Prof. Edmund Arthur Lowndes; potter and writer; Professor of Ceramics, University of Westminster, since 2004; *b* 10 Sept. 1964; *s* of Rev. Victor Alexander de Waal, *qv*; *m* 1997, Susan Chandler; two *s* one *d*. *Educ:* Trinity Hall, Cambridge (BA 1st cl. Hons (English Lit.) 1986); Sheffield Univ. (Postgrad. Dip. Japanese Lang. 1992). Apprenticeship with Geoffrey Whiting, 1981–83; Cwm Pottery, 1986–88; studios in Sheffield, 1988–92; London, 1993–. Daiwa Anglo-Japanese Foundn Schol., 1991–93; Leverhulme Special Res. Fellow, 1999–2001, Sen. Res. Fellow in Ceramics, 2000–02, Univ. of Westminster. Mem., Arts Adv. Cttee, Nat. Mus. and Gall. of Wales, Cardiff, 2000–. Chm. Trustees, Crafts Study Centre, Surrey Inst. of Art and Design, 2004–. FRSA 1996. *Solo exhibitions* include: Galerie Besson, London, 1997; Garth Clark Gall., NY, 1998; High Cross House, Dartington Hall, 1999; Geffrye Mus., London, 2002; New Art Centre, Roche Court, Salisbury, 2004; Kunstindustrie Mus., Copenhagen, 2004; Kettle's Yard, Cambridge, 2007; Middlesbrough Inst. of Modern Art, 2007; work exhibited in selected gp exhibns, 1996–2003; *work in public collections* includes: Mus. of Arts and Design, NY; Mus. of Fine Arts, Houston; V&A Mus.; Mus. of Western Australia, Perth; Fitzwilliam Mus., Cambridge; York Mus. and Art Gall.; Geffrye Mus., London. *Publications:* Bernard Leach, 1998, 2nd edn 2003; 20th Century Ceramics, 2003. *Recreation:* cooking. *Address:* 97 Grove Park, SE5 8LE. *T:* (020) 8674 1122; *e-mail:* studio@edmunddewaal.com; *web:* www.edmunddewaal.com.

de WAAL, Sir Henry; *see* de Waal, Sir C. H.

de WAAL, Judith Mary; *see* Slater, J. M.

de WAAL, Rev. Victor Alexander; Dean of Canterbury, 1976–86; *b* 2 Feb. 1929; *s* of late Hendrik de Waal and Elizabeth von Ephrussi; *m* 1960, Esther Aline Lowndes Moir, PhD; four *s*. *Educ:* Tonbridge School; Pembroke Coll., Cambridge (MA); Ely Theological College. With Phs van Ommeren (London) Ltd, 1949–50; Asst Curate, St Mary the Virgin, Isleworth, 1952–56; Chaplain, Ely Theological Coll., 1956–59; Chaplain and Succentor, King's Coll., Cambridge, 1959–63; Chaplain, Univ. of Nottingham, 1963–69; Chancellor of Lincoln Cathedral, 1969–76; Chaplain, SSC, Tymawr, 1990–2000. Hon. DD Nottingham, 1983. *Publications:* What is the Church?, 1969; The Politics of Reconciliation: Zimbabwe's first decade, 1990; Holy Wisdom: Father Augustine Baker (1575–1641), 2008; contrib.: Theology and Modern Education, 1965; Stages of Experience, 1965; The Committed Church, 1966; Liturgy Reshaped, 1982; Liturgie et Espace Liturgique, 1987; Vie Ecclesiale—communauté et communautés, 1989; Beyond Death, 1995; La Confession et les Confessions, 1995; Les Artisans de Paix, 1996; Travail et Repos, 2000; Loi et Transgression, 2002. *Address:* 6 St James Close, Bishop Street, N1 8PH. *T:* (020) 7354 2741.

See also Sir C. H. de Waal, E. A. L. de Waal.

DEWAR, family name of **Baron Forteviot**.

DEWAR, Alison Fettes; *see* Richard, A. F.

DEWAR, David Alexander; an Assistant Auditor General, National Audit Office, 1984–94; *b* 28 Oct. 1934; *s* of James and Isabella Dewar; *m* 1959, Rosalind Mary Ellen Greenwood; one *s* one *d*. *Educ:* Leith Academy, Edinburgh. Entered Exchequer and Audit Dept, 1953; Chief Auditor, 1966; Deputy Director of Audit, 1973; Director of Audit, 1977; Dep. Sec. of Dept, 1981. *Recreations:* gardening, golf. *Address:* 2 Coltsfoot Road, Lindford, Bordon, Hants GU35 0YS. *T:* (01420) 479655.

DEWAR, Ian Stewart; JP; Member: South Glamorgan County Council, 1985–93 (Vice Chairman, 1990–91; Finance Chairman, 1992–93); South Wales Valuation Tribunal, 1995–2001; *b* 29 Jan. 1929; *er s* of late William Stewart Dewar and Eileen Dewar (*née* Godfrey); *m* 1968, Nora Stephanie House; one *s* one *d*. *Educ:* Penarth County Sch.; U. Cardiff; Jesus Coll., Oxford (MA). RAF, 1947–49. Asst Archivist, Glamorgan County Council, 1952–53. Entered Min. of Labour, 1953; Asst Private Sec. to Minister, 1956–58; Principal, Min. of Labour and Civil Service Commn, 1958–65; Asst Sec., Min. of Labour; Dept of Employment and Commn on Industrial Relations, 1965–70; Asst Sec., 1970–7; and Under-Sec., 1973–83, Welsh Office. Member, Governing Body: Univ. of Wales, 1985–93; Nat. Mus. of Wales, 1985–93; Chm., Museum Schs Service Cttee, 1989–9; Mayor of Penarth, 1998–99. JP S Glam, 1985. *Address:* 59 Stanwell Road, Penarth, South Glamorgan CF64 3LR. *T:* (029) 2070 3255.

DEWAR, Robert James, CMG 1969; CBE 1964; World Bank, retired 1984; *b* 13 Jan. 1923; *s* of late Dr Robert Scott Dewar, MA, MB, ChB, and Mrs Roubaix Dewar, Dumbreck, Glasgow; *m* 1947, Christina Marianne, *d* of late Olof August Ljungberger, Stockholm, Sweden; two *s* one *d*. *Educ:* High Sch. of Glasgow; Edinburgh Univ. (BSc Forestry); Wadham Coll., Oxford. Asst Conservator of Forests, Colonial Forest Service, Nigeria and Nyasaland, 1944–55; Dep. Chief Conservator of Forests, Nyasaland, 1955–6; Chief Conservator of Forests, Dir of Forestry and Game, Nyasaland (now Malawi), 1961–64; Mem. Nyasaland Legislative Council, 1960. Permanent Secretary, Malawi: Min. of Natural Resources, 1964–67 and 1968–69; Min. of Economic Affairs, 1967–68; retd from Malawi CS, 1969; World Bank: Sen. Agriculturalist, 1969–74; Chief of Agricl Div. Regl Mission for Eastern Africa, 1974–84. Mem. Nat. Development Council, Malawi, 1966–69. Chm. of Trustees, Zimbiala Trust, 2002–. Chm., Friends of Malawi Assoc. 1996–. *Recreations:* gardening, golf, angling. *Address:* Dundurn, 5 Knock Road, Crieff, Perthshire PH7 4AH. *T:* (01764) 654830. *Clubs:* Royal Commonwealth Society, New Cavendish.

See also R. S. Dewar.

DEWAR, Robert Scott, CMG 2006; HM Diplomatic Service; High Commissioner to Nigeria, since 2007; *b* 10 June 1949; *s* of Robert James Dewar, *qv* and Christina Marianne Dewar (*née* Ljungberger); *m* 1979, Jennifer Mary Ward; one *s* one *d*. *Educ:* Loretto; Brasenose Coll., Oxford. VSO, Port Sudan, 1971–72; Scottish Office, 1972–73; FCO, 1973; served Colombo and FCO, to 1981, Asst Sec. Gen. to Lancaster House Conf. on Southern Rhodesia, 1979; Head of Chancery, Luanda, 1981–84; FCO, 1984–88; Dep. Head of Mission, Dakar, 1988–92; Dep. High Comr, Harare, 1992–96; Ambassador to Republic of Madagascar and concurrently (non-res.) to Federal Islamic Republic of the Comoros, 1996–99; FCO, 1999–2000; High Comr to Mozambique, 2000–0; Ambassador to Ethiopia and (non-resident) to Djibouti, and Permanent Rep. to the African Union, 2004–07. *Recreations:* sport, esp. fly fishing. *Address:* c/o Foreign and Commonwealth Office, SW1A 2AH.

DEWAR, Sally Marie; Managing Director, Wholesale and Institutional Markets, Financial Services Authority, since 2008; *b* Farnham, 25 Dec. 1968. *Educ:* Univ. of Manchester Inst. of Sci. and Technol. (BSc 1st Cl. Jt Hons Pure Maths and French). Corporate Finance Manager: KPMG Manchester, 1991–97; BOC, 1997–98; Associate, 1998–99, Manager, 1999–2000, Equity Mkts, UK Listing Authy, London Stock Exchange; Chief Financial Officer, LeisureHunt.com, 2000–01; Hd, Corporate Projects and Actions, UK Listing Authy, FSA, 2001; Hd, Corporate Actions and Projects, London Stock Exchange, 2001–02; Hd, UK Listing Authy, 2002–05, Dir of Mkts, 2005–07, FSA; Mem., Business Develt Cttee, LPO, 2007–. Mem., Bd of Trustees, Disability Challengers, 2007–. *Address:* Financial Services Authority, 25 The North Colonnade, Canary Wharf, E14 5HS. *T:* (020) 7066 1000.

DEWAR-DURIE, Andrew Maule, CBE 1999; DL; Chairman, Seafish Industry Authority, 2002–07 (Deputy Chairman, 2000–02); *b* 13 Nov. 1939; *s* of late Lt Col Raymond Varley Dewar-Durie and Frances St John Dewar-Durie (*née* Maule); *m* 1972, Marguerite Maria Jarmila Kottulinsky; two *s* one *d*. *Educ:* Cheam Sch.; Wellington Coll. Nat. Service, Argyll and Sutherland Highlanders, 1958–68, retd with rank of Captain. Export Rep. to Sen. Export Dir, White Horse Distillers, 1968–83; Internat. Sales Dir, Long John Distillers, 1983–87; Internat. Sales Dir, Man. Dir, then CEO, James Burrough Ltd, 1987–92; Man. Dir, 1992–97, Chm., 1997–99, Allied Distillers. Dir, Britannic Asset Mgt, 2001–04. Vice-Chm., 1996–97, Chm., 1997–99, CBI Scotland. Dir, 2000–08, Vice Chm., 2008–, Edinburgh Mil. Tattoo. DL Dunbartonshire, 1996. *Publication:* The Scottish Sheep Industry: a way forward, 2000. *Recreations:* tennis, ski-ing, rough shooting. *Address:* Finnich Malise, Croftamie, W Stirlingshire G63 0HA. *T:* (01360) 660257, *Fax:* (01360) 660101; *e-mail:* dewardurie@tiscali.co.uk. *Club:* New (Edinburgh).

de WARDENER, Prof. Hugh Edward, CBE 1982 (MBE (mil.) 1946); MD, FRCP; Professor of Medicine, University of London, Charing Cross Hospital, 1960–81, now Emeritus; Honorary Consultant Physician to the Army, 1975–80; *b* 8 Oct. 1915; *s* of Edouard de Wardener and Becky (*née* Pearce); *m* 1st, 1939, Janet Lavinia Bellis Simon (marr. diss. 1947; now decd); one *s*; 2nd, 1947, Diana Rosamund Crawshay (marr. diss. 1954); 3rd, 1954, Jill Mary Foxworthy (marr. diss. 1969); one *d*; 4th, 1969, Josephine Margaret Storey, MBE; two *s*. *Educ:* Malvern Coll. St Thomas's Hosp., 1933–39; RAMC, 1939–45; St Thomas's Hosp., 1945–60, Registrar, Senior Lecturer, Reader. MRCP 1946, MD 1949, FRCP 1958. Hon. MD: Univ. Pierre et Marie Curie, Paris, 1980; Univ. Paul Sabatier, Toulouse, 1996. President: Internat. Soc. of Nephrology, 1969–72; Renal Assoc., 1973–76; Mem. Council, Imp. Cancer Res. Fund, 1981–88. *Publications:* The Kidney: An Outline of Normal and Abnormal Structure and Function, 1958, 5th edn 1986; (with G. A. MacGregor) Salt, Diet and Health, 1998; papers in various scientific journals. *Recreations:* writing, walking. *Address:* 9 Dungarvan Avenue, Putney, SW15 5QU. *T:* (020) 8878 3130.

de WATERVLIET, Jean-Michel V.; *see* Veranneman de Watervliet.

DEWBERRY, David Albert; HM Diplomatic Service, retired; Deputy Head of Mission, the Holy See, Rome, 1996–2001; *b* 27 Sept. 1941; *s* of Albert Dewberry and Grace Dewberry (*née* Tarsey); *m* 1974, Catherine Mary (*née* Stabback); three *s* one *d*. *Educ:* Cray Valley Sch., Foots Cray, Kent. Joined CRO, 1958; Karachi, 1963; Kingston, 1966; Warsaw, 1970; Brussels, 1971; Second Sec. (Aid), Dhaka, 1972; FCO, 1974; Consul: Mexico City, 1977; Buenos Aires, 1980; FCO, 1982; Dep. High Comr, Dar es Salaam, 1987; FCO, 1991–96. *Recreations:* reading, walking. *Address: e-mail:* dadewberry@hotmail.com.

DEWE, Roderick Gorrie; Chairman: Dewe Rogerson Group Ltd, 1969–99; Roddy Dewe Consultants Ltd, 1997–2003; *b* 17 Oct. 1935; *s* of Douglas Percy Dewe and Rosanna Clements Gorrie (*née* Heggie); *m* 1964, Carol Anne Beach Thomas; one *s* one *d*. *Educ:* abroad and University Coll., Oxford (BA Hons). Treasury, Fedn of Rhodesia and Nyasaland Govt, 1957–58; Angel Court Consultants, 1960–68; founded Dewe Rogerson, 1969, Chm., 1969–95. Hon. FCIPR. *Recreations:* golf, flyfishing, travel. *Address:* Old Southill Station House, near Biggleswade, Beds SG18 9LP. *T:* (01462) 811274. *Clubs:* City of London, Beefsteak, Savile.

DEWE MATHEWS, Marina Sarah, (Mrs John Dewe Mathews); *see* Warner, M. S.

de WET, Dr Carel; South African Ambassador to the Court of St James's, 1964–67 and 1972–77; director of companies; farmer; *b* Memel, OFS, S Africa, 25 May 1924; *g s* of Gen. Christian de Wet; *m* 1949, Catharina Elizabeth (Rina) Maas, BA; one *s* three *d*. *Educ:* Vrede High Sch., OFS; Pretoria Univ. (BSc); University of Witwatersrand (MB, BCh). Served at Nat. Hosp., Bloemfontein; subseq. practised medicine at Boksburg, Transvaal, at Winburg, OFS, and, from 1948, at Vanderbijlpark, Transvaal. Mayor of Vanderbijlpark, 1950–53; MP (Nat. Party) for Vanderbijlpark, 1953–64, for Johannesburg West, 1967–72; Mem. various Parly and Nat. Party Cttees, 1953–64; Minister of Mines and Health, Govt of S Africa, 1967–72. *Recreations:* game farming, golf, rugby, cricket, hunting, deep sea fishing. *Address:* PO Box 70292, Bryanston, 2021, South Africa. *T:* (office) 8051948, *Fax:* 8053902; (home) 7066202. *Clubs:* Royal Automobile, East India, Institute of Directors, MCC, Les Ambassadeurs, Eccentric, Wentworth; Here XVII (Cape Town); Constantia (Pretoria); New, Rand Park Golf, Country (Johannesburg); Maccauvlei Country (Vereeniging), Emfuleni Golf (Vanderbijlpark).

DEWEY, Sir Anthony Hugh, 3rd Bt *cr* 1917; JP; *b* 31 July 1921; *s* of late Major Hugh Grahame Dewey, MC (*e s* of 2nd Bt), and Marjorie Florence Isobel (who *m* 2nd, 1940, Sir Robert Bell, KCSI; she *d* 1988), *d* of Lieut-Col Alexander Hugh Dobbs; *S* grandfather, 1948; *m* 1949, Sylvia, *d* of late Dr J. R. MacMahon, Branksome Manor, Bournemouth; two *s* three *d*. JP Somerset, 1961. *Heir: s* Rupert Grahame Dewey [*b* 29 March 1953; *m* 1978, Suzanne Rosemary, *d* of late Andrew Lusk, Perthshire; two *s* one *d*]. *Address:* Rag, Galhampton, Yeovil, Som BA22 7AJ. *T:* (01963) 440213. *Club:* Army and Navy.

DEWEY, Prof. John Frederick, FRS 1985; FGS; Professor of Geology, University of Oxford, 1986–2001, now Emeritus; Fellow, since 1986 and Senior Research Fellow, since 2001, University College, Oxford; Professor of Geology, University of California, Davis, 2001–06, now Distinguished Professor Emeritus; *b* 22 May 1937; *s* of John Edward and Florence Nellie Mary Dewey; *m* 1961, Frances Mary Blackhurst, MA, DSc; one *s* one *d*. *Educ:* Bancroft's School; Queen Mary Coll. and Imperial Coll., Univ. of London (BSc, PhD, DIC); MA 1965, ScD 1988, Cantab; DSc Oxon 1989. CGeol 1990. Lecturer: Univ. of Manchester, 1960–64; Univ. of Cambridge, 1964–70; Prof., State Univ. of New York at Albany, 1970–82; Prof. of Geology, Durham Univ., 1982–86. Vis. Res. Fellow, British Geol Survey, 2001–; Vis. Res. Prof., Imperial Coll., Univ. of London, 2001–. MAE, 1990. Hon. DSc Meml Univ. of Newfoundland, 1996; Hon. LLD NUI, 1998. Numerous honours and awards, UK and overseas, incl. Penrose Medal, Geol Soc. of America, 1992; Arthur Holmes Medal, Europ. Union of Geoscis, 1993; Wollaston Medal, Geol Soc. of London, 1999; Fourmarier Medal, Royal Acad. of Scis, Belgium, 1999. *Publications:* 160 scientific papers; contribs to Geol Soc. of America Bulletin, Geol Soc. London Jl, Jl Geophysical Res. and other learned jls. *Recreations:* ski-ing, cricket, water colour painting, English music 1850–1950, model railways. *Address:* University College, Oxford OX1 4BH.

de WILDE, (Alan) Robin; QC 1993; *b* 12 July 1945; *s* of late Capt. Ronald Cedric de Wilde and of Dorothea Elizabeth Mary (*née* Fenningworth); *m* 1977, Patricia Teresa Bearcroft; three *s*. *Educ:* Dean Close Sch.; RAF Coll., Cranwell; Inns of Court Sch. of Law. Called to the Bar, Inner Temple, 1971, Bencher, 1996; a Recorder, 2000–04. Mem., Bar Council, 1985–90, 1998–99, 2002–04; Chm., Professional Negligence Bar Assoc., 1995–97 (Hon. Vice Pres., 1998–; Chm., Ogden Working Party, 2003–; Gen. Editor, Facts & Figures - Tables for the Calculation of Damages, annually 1996–); Mem. Council, Bodily Injury Claims Mgt Assoc., 2003–. FRSocMed 1997. *Address:* London Chambers, 218 Strand, WC2R 1AT. *T:* (020) 7353 3936.

de WINTER, Carl; Secretary General, Federation of British Artists, 1978–84; *b* 18 June 1934; *s* of Alfred de Winter; *m* 1958, Lyndall Bradshaw; one *s* one *d*. *Educ:* Pangbourne. Purser, Orient Line, 1951–60. Art Exhibitions Bureau: PA to Man. Dir, 1961–66; Director, 1967–84; Royal Soc. of Portrait Painters: Asst Sec., 1962–78; Sec., 1978–84; Royal Soc. of Miniature Painters, Sculptors and Gravers: Asst Sec., 1964–67; Sec., 1968–84; Hon. Mem., 1984; Royal Soc. of Marine Artists: Asst Sec., 1964–70; Sec., 1971–78; Royal Soc. of British Artists: Asst Keeper, 1969–73; Keeper, 1974–84; Royal Inst. of Oil Painters: Sec., 1973–84; Royal Inst. of Painters in Watercolours: Sec., 1979–84; National Soc. of Painters, Sculptors and Printmakers: Sec., 1973–84; New English Art Club: Sec., 1973–84; United Soc. of Artists: Sec., 1975–81.

DE WITT, Prof. Sir Ronald (Wayne), Kt 2002; Chief Executive, HM Courts Service, 2004–07; *b* 31 March 1948; *s* of James Goldwyn De Witt and Una Doreen De Witt (*née* Lane). *Educ:* Sch. of Advanced Nursing, Wellington, NZ (RN; Dip. N 1978); Univ. of Humberside (BA Hons Business Studies, MA Health Mgt 1992; Hon. Fellow 1998). Registered Comprehensive Nurse 1970, NZ 1975, Canada 1970; SRN; Cert. of Burns and Plastic Surgery, 1971; Cert. of Mgt, 1976. Chief Nurse, Auckland Health Bd, 1988–89; Dist Manager, Central Auckland Health Services, 1989–90; Chief Executive: Auckland Hosp., 1990–91; Hull Acute Services, Hull HA, later Royal Hull Hosps NHS Trust, 1991–96; Leeds HA, 1996–99; KCH NHS Trust, 1999–2002; NW London Strategic HA, 2002–04. Chm., English Nat. Bd for Nursing, Midwifery and Health Visiting, 1996–2001. Trustee: Foundn of Nursing Studies, 2005–; Cancer BACUP, subseq. Cancerbackup, 2005–; Gen. Nursing Council, 2005–. Hon. DCL Humberside, 2004. *Publications:* (contrib.) Public Health, 1999; Managing the Business of Health Care, 2001. *Recreations:* travel, reading, walking, books, antiques.

DEWS, Vivienne Margaret, (Mrs Alan Cogbill); Executive Director of Corporate Services, Office of Fair Trading, since 2008; *b* 29 Dec. 1952; *d* of Albert Dews and Eva Margaret Dews (*née* Hayman); *m* 1st, 1972, Stephen Ladner (marr. diss. 1977); 2nd, 1979, Alan Cogbill; one *s* one *d* (and two *d* decd). *Educ:* Northampton High Sch. for Girls; Newnham Coll., Cambridge (BA 1974). Joined Home Office, 1974; Private Sec. to Minister for Police and Prisons, 1980–82; Dep. Dir, Top Mgt Prog., Cabinet Office, 1982–89; Home Office: Head: Immigration Policy, 1989–91; After Entry Casework and Appeals, 1991–93; Consulting Efficiency and Market Testing, 1994–95; Dir, Finance and Services, Immigration and Nationality Directorate, 1995–99; Chief Exec., Police Inf. Technol. Orgn, 1999–2001; Dir, Modernising Corporate Support, Inland Revenue, 2002; Dir, Resources and Planning, HSE, 2002–08. Mem., CIPFA, 2007. *Recreations:* family, home, garden, Italy. *Address:* Office of Fair Trading, Fleetbank House, 2–6 Salisbury Square, EC4Y 8JX.

DEXTER, Colin; *see* Dexter, N. C.

DEXTER, Edward Ralph, CBE 2001; Managing Director, Ted Dexter & Associates, since 1978; *b* 15 May 1935; *m* 1959, Susan Georgina Longfield; one *s* one *d*. *Educ:* Radley College; Jesus College, Cambridge (Captain of cricket and of golf). Served 11th Hussars, 1956–57 (Malaya Campaign Medal 1955). Cricketer, 1958–68; Captain of Sussex, 1960–65; Captain of England, 1962–65; freelance journalist, 1965–88; sports promotion consultant, 1978–. Chm., England (Cricket) Cttee, TCCB, 1989–93. Contested (C) Cardiff, 1965. *Publications:* Ted Dexter's Cricket Book, 1963; Ted Dexter Declares, 1966; (jtly) Test Kill, 1976; Deadly Putter, 1979; From Bradman to Boycott, 1981; My Golf, 1982; Ted Dexter's Little Cricket Book, 1996. *Recreations:* golf, reading. *Address:* 167 Tettenhall Road. Wolverhampton, W Midlands WV6 0BZ. *Clubs:* MCC (Chm., Cricket Cttee, 1998–2003; Pres., 2001–02); Sunningdale Golf, Royal and Ancient Golf.

DEXTER, Michael; *see* Dexter, T. M.

DEXTER, (Norman) Colin, OBE 2000; author of crime novels; *b* 29 Sept. 1930; *s* of Alfred Dexter and Dorothy Dexter (*née* Towns); *m* 1956, Dorothy Cooper; one *s* one *d*. *Educ:* Stamford Sch.; Christ's Coll., Cambridge (MA). Assistant Classics Master: Wyggeston Boys' Sch., Leicester, 1954–57; Loughborough GS, 1957–59; Sen. Classics Master, Corby GS, 1959–66; Sen. Asst Sec., Oxford Delegacy of Local Exams, 1966–88. Member: CWA, 1978; Detection Club, 1980. Freedom, City of Oxford, 2001. Hon. Fellow, St Cross Coll., Oxford, 2005. Hon. MA Leicester, 1996; Hon. DLitt Oxford Brookes, 1998. Cartier Diamond Dagger, CWA, 1998. *Publications:* Last Bus to Woodstock, 1975; Last Seen Wearing, 1976; The Silent World of Nicholas Quinn, 1977; Service of All the Dead (Silver Dagger, CWA), 1979; The Dead of Jericho (Silver Dagger, CWA), 1981; The Riddle of the Third Mile, 1983; The Secret of Annexe 3, 1986; The Wench is Dead (Gold Dagger, CWA), 1989; The Jewel that was Ours, 1991; The Way Through the Woods (Gold Dagger, CWA), 1992; Morse's Greatest Mystery, 1993; The Daughters of Cain, 1994; Death is Now My Neighbour, 1996; The Remorseful Day, 1999. *Recreations:* poetry, crosswords, Wagner. *Address:* 456 Banbury Road, Oxford OX2 7RG.

DEXTER, Dr (Thomas) Michael, FRS 1991; non-executive Director, since 2003, Chairman, 2003–06, Stem Cell Sciences Ltd; *b* 15 May 1945; *s* of Thomas Richard Dexter and Agnes Gertrude Deplege; *m* 1966, Frances Ann Sutton (marr. diss. 1978); one *s* one *d* (twins); one *s* one *d* by Dr Elaine Spooncer. *Educ:* Salford Univ. (BSc 1st class Hons 1970; DSc 1982); Manchester Univ. (PhD 1973). MRCPath 1987, FRCPath 1997; CBiol, FIBiol 1997. Lady Tata Meml Scholar, 1970–73; Paterson Institute for Cancer Research: Res. Scientist, 1973; Prof. of Haematology and Hd of Dept of Exptl Haematol., 1982–98; Dep. Dir, 1994–97; Dir, 1997–98; Dir, Wellcome Trust, 1998–2003. Chairman: Centre for Life, Newcastle upon Tyne, 2003–07; Cockcroft Inst. for Accelerator Science, 2004–. Internat. Scientific Advr, Rothschild Asset Mgt, 2003–. Life Fellow, Cancer Res. Campaign, Manchester, 1978; Personal Chair, Univ. of Manchester, 1985; Gibb Res. Fellow, CRC, 1992–97. Visiting Fellow: Sloan Kettering Inst., NY, 1976–77; Weizmann Inst., Israel, 1980. Lectures: Annual, Leukaemia Res. Fund, 1987; Michael Williams, RSM, 1990; Maximov, Leningrad, 1990; Almoth-Wright, St Mary's, London, 1992; Medawar, RPMS, 1994; Henry Hallett Dale, Nat. Inst. of Biol Standards of Control, 1997; Annual, British Soc. of Haematology, 1998; Inst. Distinguished, Inst. of Cancer Res., 1999; 5th Chamlong-Harinasuta, Bangkok, 1999; Lloyd Roberts, RCP, 2000. Member: MRC, 1993–96 (Chairman: Molecular and Cellular Medicine Bd, 1994–96; Human Genome Mapping Project Co-ordinating Cttee, 1996–98); Scientific Cttee, Leukaemia Res. Fund, 1983–86; Scientific Grants Cttee, CRC, 1987–93; Scientific Adv. Bd, Biomedical Res. Center, BC, 1987–91; Scientific Adv. Bd, Wellcome/CRC Inst., Cambridge, 1992–98; AFRC Grants Cttee, 1992–94; Cttee on Med. Aspects of Radiation in Envmt, 1994–98; Adv. Bd, EMF Trust, 1995–; NW Sci. Council, 2003–. Pres., Internat. Soc. for Exptl Hematology, 1988. Founder FMedSci 1998. Hon. MRCP 1995, Hon. FRCP 1998. Hon. DSc: Salford, 1998; UMIST, 1999; London, 2002; Lancaster, 2006. *Publications:* author of 360 articles in scientific jls; editor of four books. *Recreations:* folk singing, gardening, poetry, dominoes.

DEYERMOND, Prof. Alan David, DLitt; FSA; FBA 1988; Professor of Spanish, Queen Mary and Westfield College, London (formerly Westfield College), 1969–97, now

Research Professor; *b* 24 Feb. 1932; *s* of late Henry Deyermond and Margaret Deyermond (*née* Lawson); *m* 1957, Ann Marie Bracken; one *d*. *Educ:* Quarry Bank High Sch., Liverpool; Victoria Coll., Jersey; Pembroke Coll., Oxford (MA; BLitt 1957; DLitt 1985). FSA 1987. Westfield, subseq. Queen Mary and Westfield, College, London: Asst Lectr, 1955; Lectr, 1958; Reader, 1966; Senior Tutor, 1967–72; Dir, Medieval Hispanic Res. Seminar, 1967–97; Dean, Faculty of Arts, 1972–74, 1981–84; Head of Dept of Spanish, 1983–89; Vice-Principal, 1986–89; Dir of Grad. Studies, Sch. of Modern Langs, 1995–97; Hon. Fellow, 2000. Visiting Professor, Universities of: Wisconsin, 1972; California LA, 1977; Princeton, 1978–81; Victoria, 1983; N Arizona, 1986; Johns Hopkins, 1987; Nacional Autónoma de México, 1992; A Coruña, 1996; California Irvine, 1998–99; Consejo Superior de Investigaciones Científicas, 2002–; Scholar in Residence, Indiana Univ., 1998. Lectures: Sir Henry Thomas, Univ. of Birmingham, 1985; Taylorian, Univ. of Oxford, 1999; Ramsden and Gybbon-Monypenny., Univ. of Manchester, 2003. Chm. Trustees, Kentish's Educnl Foundn, 1992–98. President: London Medieval Soc., 1970–74; Internat. Courtly Literature Soc., 1977–83, Hon. Life Pres., 1983; Asociación Internacional de Hispanistas, 1992–95 (Vice-Pres., 1983–89; Hon. Life Pres., 1995). Corresponding Fellow: Medieval Acad. of America; Real Acad. de Buenas Letras de Barcelona; Mem., Hispanic Soc. of America; Hon. Fellow: Asociación Hispánica de Literatura Medieval; Sociedad de Estudios Medievales y Renacentistas. Hon. LHD Georgetown, 1995; Dr *hc* Valencia, 2005. Premio Internacional Elio Antonio de Nebrija, 1994. Gen. Ed., Papers of Medieval Hispanic Res. Seminar, 1995–. *Publications:* The Petrarchan Sources of La Celestina, 1961, 2nd edn 1975; Epic Poetry and the Clergy, 1969; A Literary History of Spain: The Middle Ages, 1971; Apollonius of Tyre, 1973; Lazarillo de Tormes: a critical guide, 1975; Historia y crítica de la literatura española: Edad Media, 1980, supplement, 1991; El Cantar de Mio Cid y la épica medieval española, 1987; Tradiciones y puntos de vista en la ficción sentimental, 1993; La literatura perdida de la Edad Media castellana: catálogo y estudio, vol. 1, 1995; Point of View in the Ballad, 1996; The Libro de Buen Amor in England, 2004; The Department of Hispanic Studies: a biographical dictionary, 2005; Poesía de cancionero del siglo xv, 2007; (ed) A Century of Medieval Studies, 2007; contribs to Hispanic Res. Jl etc. *Recreations:* psephology, vegetarian cookery. *Address:* 20 Lancaster Road, St Albans, Herts AL1 4ET. *T:* (01727) 855383; *e-mail:* alandeyermond@waitrose.com.

d'EYNCOURT, Sir Mark Gervais T.; *see* Tennyson-d'Eyncourt.

DHAMIJA, Dinesh; Chairman and Chief Executive, ebookers plc, since 1999; *b* 28 March 1950; *s* of Jagan and Devika Dhamija; *m* 1977, Tani Malhotra; two *s*. *Educ:* King's Sch., Canterbury; Fitzwilliam Coll., Cambridge (BA 1974). Founded first travel agency, Dabin Travel Ltd, 1980; estabd Flightbookers, 1983; Royal Nepal Airlines: Gen. Sales Agent, UK and Ireland, 1987–93; Regl Dir, Europe, 1993–96; established: Flightbookers.com, 1996; ebookers, 1999. *Recreations:* golf, tennis. *Address:* (office) ebookers plc, White Ladies, Portnall Drive, Virginia Water, Surrey GU25 4NR. *Clubs:* Royal Automobile, Oxford and Cambridge; Wentworth.

DHANDA, Parmjit Singh; MP (Lab) Gloucester, since 2001; *b* 17 Sept. 1971; *s* of Balbir Singh Dhanda and Mrs Balbir Singh Dhanda; *m* 2003, Rupi Rai. *Educ:* Mellow Lane Comprehensive, Hayes, Middx; Univ. of Nottingham (BEng (Hons) Elec Eng; MSc IT 1995). Labour Party Organiser, W London, 1996–98; Asst Nat. Organiser, Connect, 1998–2001. Mem. (Lab), Hillingdon BC, 1998–2002. Contested (Lab) SE Reg., England, EP elecn, 1999. An Asst Govt Whip, 2005–06; Parly Under-Sec. of State, DES, then Dept for Children, Schools and Families, 2006–07; Parly Under-Sec. of State, DCLG, 2007–08. Member: Fabian Society; Co-operative Society; USDAW. *Recreations:* football, cricket, writing. *Address:* House of Commons, SW1A 0AA.

DHENIN, Air Marshal Sir Geoffrey (Howard), KBE 1975; AFC 1953 and Bar, 1957; GM 1943; MA, MD, DPH; FFCM 1975; FRAeS 1971; Director-General, Medical Services (RAF), 1974–78; *b* 2 April 1918; *s* of Louis Richard Dhenin and Lucy Ellen Dagg; *m* 1st, 1946, Claude Andree Evelyn Rabut (*d* 1996); one *s* two *d* (and one *s* decd); 2nd, 2002, Syvia Howard. *Educ:* Hereford Cathedral Sch.; St John's Coll., Cambridge; Guy's Hosp., London. Joined RAF; various sqdn and other med. appts, Bomber Comd, 2nd TAF, 1943–45 (despatches 1945); pilot trng, 1945–46; various med. officer pilot appts, 1946–58; Staff Coll., Bracknell, 1958–59; comd Princess Mary's RAF Hosp. Akrotiri, Cyprus, 1960–63; comd RAF Hosp. Ely, 1963–66; PMO Air Support Comd, 1966–68; Dir of Health and Research, RAF, 1968–70; Dep. DGMS, RAF, 1970–71; PMO Strike Comd, 1971–73. Fellow, Internat. Acad. of Aerospace Medicine, 1972. CStJ 1974. QHP 1970–78. Adviser to Saudi Arabian Nat. Guard, 1978–79. *Publication:* (ed) Textbook of Aviation Medicine, 1978. *Recreations:* golf, ski-ing, sub-aqua. *Address:* Long Furrow, Abbot's Drive, Virginia Water, Surrey GU25 4SF. *T:* (01932) 563624. *Clubs:* Royal Air Force; Wentworth; Royal Porthcawl Golf.

DHOLAKIA, family name of **Baron Dholakia**.

DHOLAKIA, Baron *cr* 1997 (Life Peer), of Waltham Brooks in the co. of West Sussex; **Navnit Dholakia,** OBE 1994; JP, DL; *b* 4 March 1937; *s* of Permananddas Mulji Dholakia and Shantabai Permananddas Dholakia; *m* 1967, Ann McLuskie; two *d*. *Educ:* Home Sch. and Inst. of Science, Bhavnagar, Gujarat; Brighton Tech. Coll. Medical Lab. Technician, Southlands Hosp., Shoreham-by-Sea, 1960–66; Develt Officer, Nat. Cttee for Commonwealth Immigrants, 1966–68; Sen. Develt Officer, 1968–74, Principal Officer and Sec., 1974–76, Community Relns Commn; Commission for Racial Equality: Principal Fieldwork, Admin. and Liaison Officer, 1976–78; Principal Officer, Management, 1978–81; Head of Admin., Justice Section, 1984–94. Lib Dem spokesman on home affairs, 1997–; an Asst Lib Dem Whip, 1997–99, Dep. Leader of LibDems, 2004–, H of L. Member: Hunt Cttee on Immigration and Youth Service, 1967–69; Bd of Visitors, HM Prison, Lewes, 1978–95; Home Office Inter-Deptl Cttee on Racial Attacks and Harassment, 1987–92; Carlisle Cttee on Parole Systems Review, 1987–88; Sussex Police Authority, 1991–94; Ethnic Minority Adv. Cttee, Judicial Studies Bd, 1992–96; Council, Howard League for Penal Reform, 1992–94 (Mem. Editl Bd, Howard Jl of Criminology, 1993–); Police Complaints Authy, 1994–97. Mem., H of L Appts Commn, 1999–. Pres., NACRO, 2003– (Mem. Council, 1984–; Chm., Race Issues Adv. Cttee, 1989–; Vice-Chm., 1995–98; Chm., 1998–2003); Vice-Chm., Policy Res. Inst. on Ageing and Ethnicity, 1999–. Vice Pres., Mental Health Foundn, 2002– (Trustee, 1997–2002); Trustee: British Empire and Commonwealth Mus., Bristol, 1999–2005; Pallant House Gall., Chichester, 2000–; Police Foundn, 2002–. Gov., Commonwealth Inst., 1998–2005. Chairman: Brighton Young Liberals, 1959–62; Brighton Liberal Assoc., 1962–64; Sec., Race and Community Relns Panel, Liberal Party, 1969–74; Mem., Federal Policy and Federal Exec. Cttee, Liberal Democrats, 1996–97; Pres., Lib Dem Party, 1999–2004. Mem. (L) Brighton CBC, 1961–64. Mem. Council, SCF, 1992– (Chm., Programme Adv. Cttee, 1992–). JP Mid Sussex, 1978; DL West Sussex, 1999. *Publications:* articles on criminal justice. *Recreations:* photography, travel, gardening, cooking exotic dishes. *Address:* House of Lords, SW1A 0PW.

DHRANGADHARA, Maharaja Sriraj of Halvad-, His Highness Jhaladhip Maharana Sriraj Meghrajji III, KCIE 1947; 45th Ruler and Head of Jhalla-Makhvan Clan; *b* 3 March 1923; *s* of HH Ghanashyamsinhji Bava, GCIE, KCSI; *S* father 1942, assumed powers 1943 on termination of political minority; *m* 1943, Princess Brijrajkunvarba of Jodhpur; three *s*. *Educ:* Dhrangadhara Rajmahal Shala (Palace Sch.) which was moved to UK to become Millfield Sch., Som., 1935; Heath Mount Sch.; Haileybury Coll.; St Joseph's Acad., Dehra Dun; Sivaji Military Sch., Poona; later, Christ Church, Oxford, 1952–58 (Mem. High Table and Sen. Common Room); Philosophy course; Ruskin Sch. of Drawing; Associate Vice Pres., Amateur Fencing Assoc. of GB; Postgrad. Diploma in Social Anthropology (with distinction), 1955; research in Hindu sacraments, 1956–58; BLitt (Oxon). FRAS, FRAI; Associate, RHistS. As Darbar-in-Council proclaimed fundamental rights; estab. public adv. body; accepted attachment of Lakhtar, Sayla, Chuda and Muli States and the transfer of British suzerainty over them to the Dhrangadhara Darbar, 1943, and laws enacted: local self-govt, removal of untouchability, compulsory free primary educn, women's property rights, Hindu widows' remarriage, child marriage restraint, labour laws. Mem., Standing Cttee, Chamber of Princes, 1945–47; proposed Confedn of Saurashtra, 1945, and carried it in States-General meeting (as Chm.), 1946; received in private audience by King George VI and witnessed final reading of India Independence Bill, H of C, 1947; reserving sovereignty acceded to India, 1947; instituted Dhrangadhara Coronation Medal, 1942 and Accession to India Medal, 1947; under Covenant ceded admin and army to United State of Saurashtra, 1948; nominated to India's Constituent Assembly, instead became Uparajpramukh, Actg Rajpramukh and C-in-C of State Forces of United State of Saurashtra, 1948–52; First Pres., State Bank of Saurashtra; proclaimed India's constitution for United State of Saurashtra, 1949; resigned to attend Oxford Univ., 1952. Elected Mem. for Jhalavad (Gujarat), Lok Sabha, 1967–70 (introd. Referendum Bill to counter Bill empowering Parlt to abridge fundamental rights; led resistance to Govt's derecognition of all Rulers); Intendant General, Consultation of Rulers of Indian States in Concord for India, 1967. Life Member: Indian Council of World Affairs and Inst. of Const. and Parly Studies, 1967; Indian Parly Gp and CPA, 1967; Linguistic Soc. of India; Internat. Phonetic Assoc. and Simplified Spelling Soc., London; WWF; Wildlife Preservation Soc. of India; Cricket Club of India; India Internat. Centre. Perm. Pres., Srirajman (Educ.) Foundn; Founder President: Śriraj Jhalleśvar Rajkarma Śakti Âsthâ, 1990; Jhâlâmâ Unnati Âsthâ, 1990. Pres., Rajkumar Coll., Rajkot, 1966–2000. Patron, Bhandarkar Oriental Res. Inst. *Heir: s* Maharajkumar Shri Sodhsalji, *b* 22 March 1944. *Address:* Ajitnivas Palace, Dhrangadhara, Jhalavad, Gujarat 363310, India.

DIACK, Lamine; President, International Association of Athletics Federations (formerly International Amateur Athletics Federation), since 1999; *b* 7 June 1933; *s* of Ibrahima Diack and Aissatou Cisse; *m* 1st, 1962, Tondut Fatoumata Bintou; four *s* seven *d* (and one *s* decd); 2nd, 1964, Gaye Ngoné Diaba (*d* 1981); one *s* three *d*; 3rd, 1988, Sy Aissatou (*d* 1994). *Educ:* Dakar Univ. (MA); Ecole Nationale des Impots de Paris (Inspecteur des Impots et Domaines). French long jump Champion, 1958; French Univ. long jump Champion, 1959; holder, French/W African long jump record, 1957–60; Member: Sengalese Volleyball team, 1953–59; Sengalese Football team, 1954–61. Football Coach, Foyer France Senegal, 1964–69; Tech. Dir, nat. football team, Senegal, 1966–69; Gen. Comr for State Sport, 1969–70; State Sec. for Youth and Sport, 1970–73; Pres., Assoc. Sportive et Culturelle Diarafs de Dakar, 1974–78 and 1994–; MP (Socialist Party) Senegal, 1978–93; Dep. Speaker, Nat. Assembly of Senegal, 1988–93; Chm., Nat. Water Co. of Senegal, 1995–2001. Member: Exec. Cttee, Supreme Council for Sport in Africa, 1973–87; Nat. Olympic Cttee of Senegal, 1974– (Pres., 1985–2002); IOC, 1999–; Vice-Pres., 1976–91, Sen. Vice Pres., 1991–99, IAAF. Gen. Sec., 1963–64, Pres., 1974–78, Hon. Pres., 1978–, Senegalese Athletic Fedn; Pres., African Amateur Athletic Confedn, 1973–. Holds numerous decorations and orders, including: Olympic Order, 1994; Order of Merit, IAAF, 1997; Chevalier: Ordre Nat. du Lion (Senegal), 1976; Légion d'Honneur (France), 1984; Comdr, Order of Good Hope (RSA), 1999; Comdr of Distinction (Jamaica), 2002; Grand Cordon of Order of the Rising Sun (Japan), 2007. *Recreations:* reading, family (grandchildren). *Address:* International Association of Athletics Federations, 17 rue Princesse Florestine, BP 359, MC 98007, Monaco. *T:* 93108888, *Fax:* 93159515; *e-mail:* president@iaaf.org. *T:* (Senegal) 338202405, *Fax:* 338202406; *e-mail:* iaaf.dkr.office@orange.sn.

DIAMANTOPOULOU, Anna; MP (PASOK), Greece, since 2004; *b* 1959; *m*; one *c*. *Educ:* Aristotle Univ. of Thessaloniki (Civil Engrg); Panteion Univ. of Athens (Postgrad. Studies in Regl Develt). Civil engr, 1981–85; Lectr, Insts of Higher Technol Educn, 1983–85; Prefect of Kastoria, 1985–86; Sec. Gen. for Adult Educn, 1987–88, for Youth, 1988–89; Man. Dir, regl develt co., 1989–93; Sec. Gen. for Industry, 1994–96; MP for Kozani, 1996–99; Dep. Minister for Develt, Greece, 1996–99; Mem., European Commn, 1999–2004. Mem. Central Cttee, Panhellenic Socialist Movt, 1991–99. *Address:* Hellenic Parliament, Vas. Sophias 2, 100 21 Athens, Greece.

DIAMOND, Prof. Derek Robin; Professor of Geography with special reference to Urban and Regional Planning, London School of Economics and Political Science, 1982–95, now Emeritus Professor; *b* 18 May 1933; *s* of John Diamond (Baron Diamond, PC) and Sadie Diamond; *m* 1957, Esme Grace Passmore; one *s* one *d*. *Educ:* Oxford Univ. (MA); Northwestern Univ., Illinois (MSc). Lecturer: in Geography, 1957–65, in Town and Regional Planning, 1965–68, Glasgow Univ.; Reader in Geography, London School of Economics, 1968–82. Pres., IBG, 1994–95. Hon. MRTPI, 1989. Hon. Fellow LSE, 2006. Hon. Prof. of Human Geography, Inst. of Geography, Beijing, 1990. Editor: Progress in Planning, 1973–2003; Geoforum, 1974–93. *Publications:* Regional Policy Evaluation, 1983; Infrastructure and Industrial Costs in British Industry, 1989; Evaluating the Effectiveness of Land Use Planning, 1992; Metropolitan Governance: its contemporary transition, 1997; Managing the Metropolis in the Global Village, 2002. *Recreation:* philately. *Address:* 9 Ashley Drive, Walton-on-Thames, Surrey KT12 1JL. *T:* (01932) 223280. *Club:* Geographical.

DIAMOND, Prof. Ian David, PhD; FBA 2005; Chief Executive, Economic and Social Research Council, since 2003 (Member, since 2000); *b* 14 March 1954; *s* of Harold and Sylvia Diamond; *m* 1997, Jane Harrison; one *s*, and one step *s* one step *d*. *Educ:* LSE (BSc (Econ.) 1975; MSc 1976); Univ. of St Andrews (PhD 1981). Lectr, Heriot Watt Univ., 1979; University of Southampton: Lectr, 1980–88; Sen. Lectr, 1988–92; Prof. of Social Statistics, 1992–2002; Dep. Vice-Chancellor, 2001–02. AcSS 2000. *Publications:* (with J. Jefferies) Beginning Statistics in the Social Sciences, 2001; over 100 articles in acad. jls, incl. Jl of Royal Statistical Soc., Demography and Popn Studies. *Recreations:* family, swimming, running, football. *Address:* Economic and Social Research Council, Polaris House, North Star Avenue, Swindon SN2 1UE. *T:* (01793) 413004, *Fax:* (01793) 413002; *e-mail:* ian.diamond@esrc.ac.uk. *Club:* Bradford on Avon Swimming.

DIAMOND, (Peter) Michael, OBE 1996; MA, FMA; Director, Birmingham City Museums and Art Gallery, 1980–95; *b* 5 Aug. 1942; *s* of late William Howard and Dorothy Gladys Diamond; *m* 1968, Anne Marie; one *s* one *d*. *Educ:* Bristol Grammar Sch.; Queens' Coll., Cambridge (BA Fine Art 1964, MA 1966). Dip. of Museums Assoc. 1968, FMA 1980. Sheffield City Art Galleries: Art Asst, 1965; Keeper, Mappin Art Gall., 1967; Dep. Dir, 1969; City Arts and Museums Officer, Bradford, 1976. Chairman: Gp of Dirs of

Museums, 1985–89; Public Art Commns Agency, 1987–88. Chm., Avoncroft Mus. of Historic Buildings, 2005–; Member, Executive Committee: Yorks Arts Assoc., 1977–80; Yorks Sculpture Park, 1978–82 (Chm., 1978–82); Pres., Yorks Fedn of Museums, 1978–80; Member: Crafts Council, 1980–84; Council, Museums Assoc., 1987–90; Board, Museums Training Inst., 1990–93; Board, Worcester Porcelain Mus., 2001–; Fabric Adv. Cttee, Lichfield Cathedral, 2001–. Mem. Council, Aston Univ., 1983–92. Hon. DSc Aston, 1993. *Publications:* numerous exhibition catalogues incl. Victorian Paintings, 1968; Art and Industry in Sheffield 1850–75, 1975; Bike Art, 1994; (contrib.) Manual of Curatorship, 1984 and 1992; articles in Museums Jl and Internat. Jl of Arts Mgt. *Address:* 5 Anchorage Road, Sutton Coldfield, W Midlands B74 2PJ.

DIAMOND, Prof. Philip John, PhD; Professor of Radio Astronomy, since 2002, and Head of Astronomy and Astrophysics and Director, Jodrell Bank Centre for Astrophysics, since 2006, University of Manchester; *b* Bude, 18 Feb. 1958; *s* of John Diamond and Denise Diamond; *m* 1985, Jill Hamblett; one *s* one *d.* *Educ:* Leeds Univ. (BSc Hons Physics with Astrophysics 1979); Manchester Univ. (Dip. Advanced Studies in Sci. 1980; PhD Radio Astronomy 1982). Royal Soc. Post-doctoral Res. Fellow, Onsala Space Observatory, Sweden, 1982–84; Staff Scientist, Max-Planck Inst. für Radioastronomie, Bonn, 1984–86; Asst Scientist, Computer Div., NRAO, Charlottesville, 1987–91; National Radio Astronomy Observatory, Socorro, USA: Asst Scientist, 1991–92, Associate Scientist, 1992–93, Scientist, 1994–95, Very Long Baseline Array Operations; Dep. Asst Dir for Very Large Array/Very Long Baseline Array Ops and Computing, 1995–99; Dir, Multi-Element Radio-Linked Interferometer Network and Very Long Baseline Interferometry Nat. Facility, Jodrell Bank Observatory, 1999–2006. Coordinator: RadioNet (EC-funded Integrated Infrastructure Initiative), 2003–; EC 7th Framework Prog. Preparatory Phase Proposal for Square Kilometre Array, 2007–. *Publications:* contrib. numerous papers to jls incl. Nature and Science. *Recreations:* reading, playing squash, worldwide travel, Rugby Union, football.

DIAMOND, Yasmin; Director of Communication, Home Office, since 2007; *b* 27 Oct. 1967; *d* of Barkat Ali and Khurshid Begum; *m* 1999, Mark Diamond; one *s* one *d.* *Educ:* Univ. of Leeds (BA Hons Hist. with Business Mgt); Leeds Business Sch. (Postgrad. DipM). Sen. Communications Manager, NHS Exec., 1995–99; Publicity Comr, BBC Broadcast, 1999–2000; Head: Welfare to Work, DfEE, 2000–01; Strategic Mktg, DfES, 2001–05; Dir of Communications, DEFRA, 2005–07. *Recreations:* spending leisure time with my family and friends, travelling, fashion and design. *Address:* c/o Home Office, 2 Marsham Street, SW1P 4DF. *Club:* Soho House.

DIAS, His Eminence Cardinal Ivan Cornelius, DCnL; Prefect, Congregation for the Evangelisation of Peoples, since 2006; *b* 14 April 1936; *s* of late Carlos Nazario Dias and Maria Martins Dias. *Educ:* Pontifical Ecclesiastical Academy, Rome; DCnL Lateran Univ., Rome, 1964. Ordained priest, Bombay, 1958. Trained for Diplomatic Service, 1961–64; Foreign Service of Holy See, 1964–97; served Vatican Secretariat of State, preparing visit of HH the Pope to Bombay, Internat. Eucharistic Congress, 1964; Sec., Apostolic Nunciatures in Scandinavian countries, Indonesia and Madagascar, 1965–73; Chief of Desk at Vatican Secretariat of State for USSR, Baltic States, Byelorussia, Ukraine, Poland, Bulgaria, China, Vietnam, Laos, Cambodia, S Africa, Namibia, Lesotho, Swaziland, Zimbabwe, Ethiopia, Rwanda, Burundi, Uganda, Zambia, Kenya, Tanzania, 1973–82; Titular Archbishop of Rusubisir and Apostolic Pro-Nuncio to Ghana, Togo and Benin, 1982–87; Apostolic Pro-Nuncio: S Korea, 1987–91; Albania, 1991–97; Archbishop of Bombay, (RC), 1997–2006. Cardinal, 2001. Co-Pres., 10th Ordinary Gen. Assembly, Synod of Bishops, Rome, 2001. Special Papal Envoy to: Albania, 10th anniv. celebrations of Pope John Paul II's visit, 2003; Ghana, Centenary Celebrations of Evangelization in Northern Ghana, 2007. Member: Congregation for Doctrine of the Faith, 2001–; Congregation for Divine Worship and Discipline of the Sacraments, 2001–; Congregation for Catholic Educn, 2001–; Pontifical Council for Laity, 2001–; Pontifical Council for Culture, 2001–; Pontifical Commn for Cultural Heritage of Church, 2001–; Pontifical Council for Interreligious Dialogue, 2005–. *Address:* Palazzo di Propaganda Fide, Piazza di Spagna 48, 00187 Rome, Italy.

DIAS, Julia Amanda, (Mrs S. J. Orford); QC 2008; barrister; *b* Cambridge, 31 Jan. 1959; *d* of Reginald Walter Michael Dias and Norah Hunter Dias (*née* Crabb); *m* 1983, Stuart John Orford; one *s* one *d.* *Educ:* Perse Sch. for Girls, Cambridge; Trinity Hall, Cambridge (BA 1981). MCIArb. Called to the Bar, Inner Temple, 1982. FRSA. *Recreations:* classical music, tennis, reading. *Address:* 7 King's Bench Walk, Temple, EC4Y 7DS. *T:* (020) 7910 8300, *Fax:* (020) 7910 8400; *e-mail:* jdias@7kbw.co.uk.

DIBBEN, Michael Alan Charles; HM Diplomatic Service, retired; High Commissioner, Fiji, also accredited to Tuvalu, Kiribati and Nauru, 1997–2000; *b* 19 Sept. 1943; *s* of Lt-Col Alan Frank Dibben and late Eileen Beatrice Dibben (*née* Donoghue). *Educ:* Dulwich College. With Ottoman Bank, London, 1961–64; CRO 1964; Min. of Overseas Develt, 1965; Protocol Dept, FCO, 1966; served Montreal, Nassau, Stuttgart, Port of Spain, Douala; First Sec., 1981; Nuclear Energy Dept, FCO, 1981–83; Munich and Hamburg, 1983–87; Inf. Dept, FCO, 1987–90; Ambassador to Paraguay, 1991–95; Head of Contracts, Travel and Related Services Gp, FCO, 1995–96. Mem., Horners' Co. *Recreations:* reading, walking, golf, classical music.

DIBBLE, Roy Edwin, CEng, FBCS; HM Diplomatic Service, retired; Chief Executive Services, Foreign and Commonwealth Office, 2000–01; *b* 16 Dec. 1940; *s* of Edwin Dibble and Gwendoline Vera Dibble (*née* Nicholls); *m* 1967, Valerie Jean Denham Smith. *Educ:* Maidstone Tech. High Sch. DipEE; MIET. Central Computer Telecommunications Agency: Head of Div., HM Treasury, 1985–91, Cabinet Office, 1991–94; Dir, OPS, Cabinet Office, 1994–96; Dir, Gen. Services, FCO, 1996–2000. *Recreation:* sailing.

DICE, Brian Charles, OBE 1997; Chief Executive, British Waterways Board, 1986–96; *b* 2 Sept. 1936; *s* of late Frederic Charles Dice; *m* 1965, Gwendoline Tazeena Harrison; two *d.* *Educ:* Clare College, Cambridge; Middle Temple. Cadbury Schweppes, 1960–86, Director, 1979; Managing Director, Schweppes, 1983. *Address:* Stratton Wood, Beaconsfield, Bucks HP9 1HS.

DICK, Sir Iain Charles M.; *see* Mackay-Dick.

DICK, James Brownlee, CB 1977; MA, BSc, FInstP, FCIBS, FIOB; retired consultant; *b* 19 July 1919; *s* of James Brownlee Dick and Matilda Forrest; *m* 1944, Audrey Moira Shinn (*d* 2007); two *s.* *Educ:* Wishaw High Sch.; Glasgow Univ. Royal Naval Scientific Service, 1940. Building Research Station, later Building Research Establishment: Physics Div., 1947; Head of User Requirements Div., 1960; Head of Production Div., 1963; Asst Dir, 1964; Dep. Dir, 1969; Dir, 1969–79. Pres., Internat. Council for Building Res., 1974–77. *Publications:* papers in professional and scientific journals. *Address:* 10 Stanier Rise, Berkhamsted, Herts HP4 1SD. *T:* (01442) 862580.

DICK-LAUDER, Sir Piers Robert; *see* Lauder.

DICKENS, Frank; *see* Huline-Dickens, F. W.

DICKENS, James McCulloch York, OBE 1991; Chief Personnel Officer, Agricultural and Food Research Council, 1983–91; *b* 4 April 1931; *e s* of A. Y. Dickens and I. Dickens (*née* McCulloch); *m* 1st, 1955, M. J. Grieve (marr. diss. 1965); 2nd, 1969, Mrs Carolyn Casey. *Educ:* Shawlands Academy, Glasgow; Newbattle Abbey Coll., Dalkeith, Midlothian; Ruskin Coll. and St Catherine's Coll., Oxford. Administrative Asst, National Coal Board, 1956–58; Industrial Relations Officer, National Coal Board, 1958–65; Management Consultant, 1965–66; MP (Lab) West Lewisham, 1966–70; Asst Dir of Manpower, Nat. Freight Corp., 1970–76; National Water Council: Asst Dir (Ind. Rel.), Manpower Services Div., 1976–80; Dir of Manpower, 1980–82; Dir of Manpower and Trng, 1982–83. Mem. (Lab), Westminster CC, 1962–65. Chm., Governing Body, Anerley Primary Sch., 2001–03. *Recreations:* music, theatre, the countryside. *Address:* 64 Woodbastwick Road, Sydenham, SE26 5LH.

DICKENSON, Prof. Anthony Henry, PhD; Professor of Neuropharmacology, University College London, since 1995; *b* 5 Oct. 1952; *s* of Henry and Kathleen Dickenson; *m* 1975, Joanna Schepp; two *d.* *Educ:* St Mary's Coll., Southampton; Univ. of Reading (BSc 1974); PhD London 1977. MRC French Exchange Fellow, 1978–79; Scientific Staff, MRC, 1979–83; University College London: Lectr, 1983–90; Sen. Lectr, 1990–92; Reader, 1992–95. Mem. Council, Internat. Assoc. for Study of Pain, 1996–2002. Vis. Prof., Univ. of Calif, 1986; RSocMed Vis. Prof., USA, 1995; Medal and Lecture in Neuroscience, Univ. of Pavia, Italy, 1993. FMedSci 2007. *Publications:* (with M. M. Dale and D. G. Haylett) Companion to Pharmacology, 1993, 2nd edn 1995; (with J.-M. Besson) Pharmacology of Pain, 1997; contrib. chapters in books; numerous contribs to learned jls. *Recreations:* drum and bass, friends, family, travel, tennis. *Address:* Department of Pharmacology, University College, Gower Street, WC1E 6BT. *T:* (020) 7679 3742.

DICKENSON, Sir Aubrey Fiennes T.; *see* Trotman-Dickenson.

DICKENSON, Joseph Frank, PhD, CEng, FIMechE; Director, North Staffordshire Polytechnic, 1969–86, retired; *b* 26 Nov. 1924; *s* of late Frank Brand Dickenson and late Maud Dickenson (*née* Beharrell); *m* 1948, Sheila May Kingston; two *s* one *d.* *Educ:* College of Technology, Hull. BSc (1st Cl. Hons) Engrg, PhD (both London). Engrg apprenticeship and Jun. Engr's posts, 1939–52; Lectr and Sen. Lectr, Hull Coll. of Technology, 1952–59; Head of Dept of Mechanical Engrg and later Vice-Principal, Lanchester Coll. of Technology, 1960–64; Principal, Leeds Coll. of Technology, 1964–69. *Recreations:* motor cars, computers. *Address:* 6 Burlington Court, Burlington Place, Eastbourne BN21 4AU. *T:* (01323) 725039.

DICKIE, Brian James; General Director, Chicago Opera Theater, since 1999; *b* 23 July 1941; *s* of late Robert Kelso Dickie, OBE and Harriet Elizabeth (*née* Riddell); *m* 1st, 1968, Victoria Teresa Sheldon (*née* Price); two *s* one *d*; 2nd, 1989, Nancy Gustafson; 3rd, 2002, Elinor Rhys Williams; one *d.* *Educ:* Haileybury; Trinity Coll., Dublin. Admin. Asst, Glyndebourne Opera, 1962–66; Administrator, Glyndebourne Touring Opera, 1967–81; Glyndebourne Festival Opera: Opera Manager, 1970–81; Gen. Administrator, 1981–89. Artistic Dir, Wexford Fest., 1967–73; Artistic Advr, Théâtre Musical de Paris, 1981–87; Gen. Dir, Canadian Opera Co., 1989–93; Artistic Counsellor, Opéra de Nice, 1994–97; Gen. Dir, EU Opera, 1997–99. Member: Bd, Opera America, 1991–93, 2005–; Bd, Chicago Coll. of the Performing Arts, 2003–; Music Vis. Cttee, Univ. of Chicago, 2006–. Chm., London Choral Soc., 1978–85; Vice-Chm., TNC, 1980–85 (Chm., TNC Opera Cttee, 1976–85); Vice-Pres., Theatrical Management Assoc., 1983–85. *Address:* Chicago Opera Theater, 70 East Lake Street, Suite 815, Chicago, IL 60601, USA. *T:* (312) 7048420, *Fax:* (312) 7048421. *Club:* Garrick.

DICKIE, John; Director of Strategy and Policy, London First, since 2008; *b* 31 Aug. 1965; *s* of John Dickie and Gladys Dickie (*née* O'Neil); *m* 1991, Susan Grunstein; one *s* one *d.* *Educ:* Morecambe High Sch.; Worcester Coll., Oxford (BA Mod. Hist.); London Business Sch. (MBA). Grad. trainee, Swiss Bank Corp. Internat., 1987–89; Prima Europe, 1989–98 (Man. Dir, 1997–98); GPC International: Man. Dir, GPC London, 1998–99; Hd, Internat. Regulatory Practice, 1999–2000; Dir, Regulatory Affairs, European Competitive Telecommunications Assoc., 2000–03; Hd, Political and Parly Affairs, 2003–06, Corporate Affairs, 2006–08, BBC. Mem., Camden LBC, 1994–2003 (Dep. Leader, 2000–03). *Recreations:* film, opera, reading, gym. *Address:* c/o London First, 1 Hobhouse Court, Suffolk Street, SW1Y 4HH. *T:* (020) 7665 1500; *e-mail:* jdickie@London-first.co.uk; 49 Burghley Road, NW5 1UH. *Club:* Reform.

DICKINS, Mark Frederick Hakon S.; *see* Scrase-Dickins.

DICKINS, Robert, CBE 2002; Chairman, Instant Karma Ltd, 1999–2007; *b* 24 July 1950; *s* of late Percy Charles Dickins and Sylvia Marjorie Dickins; *m* 2000, Cherry Ann Gillespie. *Educ:* Ilford Co. High Sch. for Boys; Loughborough Univ. (BSc Politics, Sociol. and Russian 1971). Man. Dir, Warner Bros Music Ltd, 1974–79; Sen. Vice Pres., Warner Brothers Music Corp., 1979–83; Chairman: Warner Music Gp UK, 1983–98; Dharma Music Ltd, 1999–. Vis. Prof., Univ. of the Arts, London, 2005–. Chm., British Phonographic Industry, 1986–88 and 1997–2002. Chm., Nat. Mus. of Childhood, Bethnal Green, 2002–07; Trustee: BRIT Trust, 1997–; Nat. Foundn for Youth Music, 1999–2006; V&A Mus., 2000–07; Watts Gall., 2004–. FRSA 2007. Hon. DLitt Loughborough, 2002. *Recreations:* art, film, photography, music, design. *Address:* Church Gate Hall, Church Gate, SW6 3LD. *T:* (020) 7384 0933, *Fax:* (020) 7384 0934; *e-mail:* rob@instantkarma.co.uk. *Club:* Groucho.

DICKINSON, family name of **Baron Dickinson.**

DICKINSON, 2nd Baron *cr* 1930, of Painswick; **Richard Clavering Hyett Dickinson;** *b* 2 March 1926; *s* of late Hon. Richard Sebastian Willoughby Dickinson, DSO (*o s* of 1st Baron) and May Southey, *d* of late Charles Lovemore, Melsetter, Cape Province, S Africa; *S* grandfather, 1943; *m* 1st, 1957, Margaret Ann (marr. diss. 1980), *e d* of late Brig. G. R. McMeekan, CB, DSO, OBE; two *s*; 2nd, 1980, Rita Doreen Moir. *Heir:* *s* Hon. Martin Hyett Dickinson, *b* 30 Jan. 1961. *Address:* The Stables, Gloucester Road, Painswick, Glos GL6 6TH. *T:* (01452) 813646.

See also Very Rev. H. G. Dickinson, Hon. P. M. de B. Dickinson.

DICKINSON, Anne; *see* Dickinson, V. A.

DICKINSON, Prof. Anthony, DPhil; FRS 2003; Professor of Comparative Psychology, University of Cambridge, since 1999; Fellow of Hughes Hall, Cambridge, since 1999; *b* 17 Feb. 1944; *m* 1977, Susan Caroline Melhuish; one *s* two *d.* *Educ:* Univ. of Manchester (BSc 1967); Univ. of Sussex (DPhil 1971); MA Cantab 2001. Postdoctoral Res. Fellow, Sussex Univ., 1971–77; Cambridge University: Demonstrator, 1977–78, Lectr, 1978–94, Dept of Exptl Psychol.; Reader in Comparative Psychol., 1994–99. *Address:* Department of Experimental Psychology, University of Cambridge, Downing Street, Cambridge CB2 3EB.

DICKINSON, Brian Henry Baron; Under Secretary, Animal Health Group, Ministry of Agriculture, Fisheries and Food, 1996–2000; *b* 2 May 1940; *s* of Alan and Ethel Dickinson; *m* 1971, Sheila Minto Lloyd (*d* 2006). *Educ:* Leighton Park School, Reading; Balliol College, Oxford (BA). Ministry of Agriculture, Fisheries and Food, 1964; Dept of Prices and Consumer Protection, 1975; MAFF, 1978; Under Sec., 1984; Principal Finance Officer, 1986; Under Sec. (Food Safety), 1989. FRSA 1995. *Recreations:* bird-watching, bridge, island living.

DICKINSON, Prof. (Christopher) John, DM, FRCP; ARCO; Professor of Medicine and Chairman, Department of Medicine, St Bartholomew's Hospital Medical College, 1975–92, now Professor Emeritus; *b* 1 Feb. 1927; *s* of Reginald Ernest Dickinson and Margaret Dickinson (*née* Petty); *m* 1953, Elizabeth Patricia Farrell; two *s* two *d*. *Educ:* Berkhamsted School; Oxford University (MA, MSc, DM); University College Hospital Medical College. FRCP 1968. Junior med. posts, UCH, 1953–54; RAMC (Junior Med. Specialist), 1955–56; Registrar and Research Fellow, Middlesex Hosp., 1957–60; Rockefeller Travelling Fellow, Cleveland Clinic, USA, 1960–61; Lectr, then Sen. Lectr and Consultant, UCH and Med. Sch., 1961–75. R. Samuel McLoughlin Vis. Prof., McMaster Univ., Canada, 1970; King Edward Fund Vis. Fellow, NZ, 1972. Examr in Medicine, UC Dublin and Univs of Oxford, Cambridge, London, Sheffield, Leeds, Southampton, Hong Kong, Singapore, Kuwait. Sec., European Soc. for Clinical Investigation, 1969–72; Censor, 1978–80, Senior Censor and Vice-Pres., 1982–83, Croonian Lectr, 1986, RCP; Pres., Sect. of Medicine, RSM, 1975–76. Chairman: Med. Research Soc., 1983–87; Assoc. of Professors of Medicine, 1983–87; Vice Chm. Council, BHF, 1995–2000; Mem., MRC, 1986–90. Medical Adviser: Jules Thorn Charitable Trust, 1994–98; St Thomas'/Guy's Hosps' Special Trustees, 1996–98; Trustee: St Bartholomew's Hosp. Foundn for Res., 1983–; BHF, 1995–2000; Chronic Disease Res. Foundn, 1996– (Chm., 1996–). ARCO 1987. FRSA 1995. *Publications:* Electrophysiological Technique, 1950; Clinical Pathology Data, 1951, 2nd edn 1957; (jtly) Clinical Physiology, 1959, 5th edn 1984; Neurogenic Hypertension, 1965; A Computer Model of Human Respiration, 1977; (jtly) Software for Educational Computing, 1980; Neurogenic Hypertension, 1991; 21 Medical Mysteries, 2000; Motorcycling in Towns and Cities, 2002; Medical Mysteries: the testament of a clinical scientist, 2005; papers on hypertension, respiratory physiology, and general medicine. *Recreations:* theatre, opera, playing the organ, squash. *Address:* Wolfson Institute of Preventive Medicine, Charterhouse Square, EC1M 6BQ. *T:* (020) 7882 6219; Griffin Cottage, 57 Belsize Lane, NW3 5AU. *T:* (020) 7431 1845. *Club:* Garrick.

DICKINSON, David Roscoe; Partner, since 1988, Senior Partner, since 2006, Simmons & Simmons (Managing Partner, 1999–2005); *b* 13 Dec. 1950; *s* of John Roscoe Dickinson and Barbara Fleetwood Dickinson (*née* Thomas); *m* 1975, Linda Susan Voneshen; two *s* one *d*. Admitted solicitor: England and Wales, 1974; Hong Kong, 1998; Dir, Legal Services, UBS (Securities) Ltd, 1984–88. *Recreations:* family, garden, collecting. *Address:* c/o Simmons & Simmons, CityPoint, One Ropemaker Street, EC2Y 9SS. *T:* (020) 7628 2020, *Fax:* (020) 7628 2070; *e-mail:* david.dickinson@simmons-simmons.com.

DICKINSON, Gregory David Mark; QC 2002; a Recorder, since 2000; *b* 26 Aug. 1959; *s* of David and Ethel Dickinson; *m* 1989, Frances Judith Betts. *Educ:* Poole Grammar Sch.; Univ. of Leicester (LLB Hons 1980). Called to the Bar, Gray's Inn, 1981; in practice, specialising in criminal law; Asst Recorder, 1998–2000. Midland Circuit Rep., Bar Council, 2004–08. *Recreations:* gardening, walking, travelling, watching old movies with my wife. *Address:* 1 High Pavement, Nottingham NG1 1HF. *T:* (0115) 9418218, *Fax:* (0115) 9418240; *e-mail:* gdqc@1highpavement.co.uk.

DICKINSON, Sir Harold (Herbert), Kt 1975; *b* 27 Feb. 1917; *s* of late William James Dickinson and Barwon Venus Clarke; *m* 1946, Elsie May Smith; two *d*. *Educ:* Singleton Public Sch.; Tamworth High Sch.; Univ. of Sydney (LLB, 1st Cl. Hons). Barrister-at-Law. Served War, 2nd AIF HQ 22 Inf. Bde, 1940–45 (despatches); Japanese POW (Sgt). Dept of Lands, NSW, 1933–40; NSW Public Service Bd, 1946–60: Sec. and Sen. Inspector, 1949–60; Chief Exec. Officer, Prince Henry Hosp., 1960–63; NSW Public Service Bd: Mem., 1963–70; Dep. Chm., 1970–71; Chm., 1971–79. Formerly: Chm., AFT Property Co.; Director: Development Finance Corp.; Australian Fixed Trusts Ltd. Hon. Mem., NSW Univs Bd, 1967–71; Hon. Dir, Prince Henry, Prince of Wales, Eastern Suburbs Teaching Hosps, 1965–75, Chm. of Dirs, 1975–82; Governor, NSW Coll. of Law, 1972–77. *Publications:* contribs to administration jls. *Recreation:* sailing. *Address:* 15/8–10 Diaram Street, Hunters Hill, NSW 2110, Australia. *Club:* Probus (Sydney).

DICKINSON, Prof. Harry Thomas, DLitt; FRHistS; FHA; FRSE; Richard Lodge Professor of British History, University of Edinburgh, 1980–2006, now Emeritus; *b* 9 March 1939; *s* of Joseph Dickinson and Elizabeth Stearman Dickinson (*née* Warriner); *m* 1961, Jennifer Elizabeth Galtry; one *s* one *d*. *Educ:* Gateshead Grammar Sch.; Durham Univ. (BA 1960, DipEd 1961, MA 1963); Newcastle Univ. (PhD 1968); DLitt Edinburgh 1986. FRSE 1998. History Master, Washington Grammar Sch., 1961–64; Earl Grey Fellow, Newcastle Univ., 1964–66; Edinburgh University: Asst Lectr, Lectr and Reader, 1966–80; Associate Dean of Arts (Postgrad. Studies), 1992–95; Convener (Senatus, Postgrad. Studies), 1998–2001. Fulbright Award, 1973; Huntington Library Fellowship, 1973; Folger Shakespeare Library Sen. Fellowship, 1973; Winston Churchill Meml Trust Travelling Fellowship, 1980; Leverhulme Award, 1986–87; William Andrews Clark Library Fellow, 1987. Vis. Prof., Nanjing Univ., 1980, 1983, 1994, Concurrent Prof. of Hist., 1987–; Douglas Southall Freeman Prof., Univ. of Richmond, Va, 1997; Vis. Prof., Beijing Univ., 2004. Anstey Meml Lectr, Kent Univ., 1989; Vis. Lectr to USA, Japan, Taiwan, Canada, France, Czech Republic, Italy, Poland, Norway, Sweden, Estonia and Germany; Dean, Scottish Universities Summer School, 1979–85. Acad. Sponsor, Scotland's Cultural Heritage, 1984–91; Mem., Marshall Aid Commemoration Commn, 1986–98; Specialist Advr, CNAA, 1987–93 (Mem., Cttee on Humanities, 1990–93); Auditor, Quality Assurance Gp, Higher Educn Quality Council, 1992–2001; Mem., Hist. Panel, UFC RAE, 1992; Team Assessor (Hist.), Teaching Quality Assessment, SHEFC, 1995–96; Hist. Benchmarking Panel, 1998–99, Academic Reviewer, 1999–2001, QAA; Chm., Hist. Panel, AHRC (formerly AHRB), 2002–06 (Mem., 1999–2002); Mem., Lord Chancellor's Adv. Council on Nat. Records and Archives, 2002–. Vice-Pres., RHistS, 1991–95 and 2003– (Mem., Council, 1986–90); Historical Association: Mem. Council, 1982–; Vice-Pres., 1995–96, 2005–07; Dep. Pres., 1996–98; Pres., 2002–05; Chm. of Publications, 1991–95; FHA 2007. FHEA 2007. Editor, History, 1993–2000; Mem. Editl Bds, Nineteenth Century Short Title Catalogue and Nineteenth Century Microfiche Series. *Publications:* (ed) The Correspondence of Sir James Clavering, 1967; Bolingbroke, 1970; Walpole and the Whig Supremacy, 1973; (ed) Politics and Literature in the Eighteenth Century, 1974; Liberty and Property, 1977; (ed) The Political Works of Thomas Spence, 1982; British Radicalism and the French Revolution 1789–1815, 1985; Caricatures and the Constitution 1760–1832, 1986; (ed) Britain and the French Revolution 1789–1815, 1989; The Politics of the People in Eighteenth Century Britain, 1995; (ed) Britain and the American Revolution, 1998; (ed jtly) The Challenge to Westminster, 2000; (ed) A Companion to Eighteenth-Century Britain, 2002; (ed) Constitutional Documents of the United Kingdom 1776–1849, 2005; (ed) British Pamphlets on the American Revolution, 8 vols, 2007–08; pamphlets, essays, articles and reviews. *Recreations:* films, watching sports. *Address:* 44 Viewforth Terrace, Edinburgh EH10 4LJ. *T:* (0131) 229 1379.

DICKINSON, Very Rev. Hugh Geoffrey; Dean of Salisbury, 1986–96, now Emeritus; *b* 17 Nov. 1929; *s* of late Hon. Richard Sebastian Willoughby Dickinson, DSO (*o s* of 1st Baron Dickinson) and of May Southey, *d* of late Charles Lovemore; *m* 1963, Jean Marjorie Storey; one *s* one *d*. *Educ:* Westminster School (KS); Trinity Coll., Oxford (MA, DipTh); Cuddesdon Theol Coll. Deacon 1956, priest 1957; Curate of Melksham, Wilts, 1956–58; Chaplain: Trinity Coll., Cambridge, 1958–63; Winchester College, 1963–67; Bishop's Adviser for Adult Education, Diocese of Coventry, 1969–77; Vicar of St Michael's, St Albans, 1977–86. *Recreations:* woodturning, fishing, gardening. *Address:* 5 St Peter's Road, Cirencester, Glos GL7 1RE. *T:* (01285) 657710.

See also Hon. P. M. de B. Dickinson.

DICKINSON, Prof. Hugh Gordon; Sherardian Professor of Botany, Oxford, 1991–Sept. 2009, then Emeritus Professor; Fellow of Magdalen College, Oxford, since 1991; *b* 5 Aug. 1944; *s* of Reginald Gordon Dickinson and Jean Hartley Dickinson; *m* 1980, Alana Gillian Fairbrother; one *s* one *d*. *Educ:* St Lawrence Coll., Ramsgate; Univ. of Birmingham (BSc, PhD, DSc). Postdoctoral Fellow, UCL, 1969–72; University of Reading: Lectr, 1972–79; Reader, 1979–85; Prof. of Plant Cell Genetics, 1985–91. Trustee, Royal Botanic Gardens, Kew, 1996–2001; Council Mem., John Innes Centre, 1999–. *Publications:* (ed with C. W. Evans) Controlling Events in Meiosis, 1984; (ed with P. Goodhew) Proceedings of IXth European Congress for Electron Microscopy, 1988; (ed jtly) Post-Translational Modification in Plants, 1992; contribs to internat. sci. jls and magazines. *Recreations:* owning and restoring Lancia cars of the '50s and '60s, rock music 1955–75, Mozart operas. *Address:* Magdalen College, Oxford OX1 4AU.

DICKINSON, John; *see* Dickinson, C. J.

DICKINSON, Mark; *see* Dickinson, S. M. and Dickinson, W. M. L.

DICKINSON, Matthew John, (Matt); Chief Sports Correspondent, The Times, since 2007; *b* 16 Nov. 1968; *s* of Jimmy Gordon and Celia Dickinson; *m* 2000, Helen Willis; two *s*. *Educ:* Perse Sch., Cambridge; Robinson Coll., Cambridge (MA); NCTJ Postgrad Dip in Journalism, Cardiff. Staff News Reporter, Cambridge Evening News, 1992–94; Sports Reporter: Daily Express, 1994–97; The Times, 1997–: Football Correspondent, 2000–02; Chief Football Correspondent, 2002–07. Young Sports Writer of the Year, Sports Council, 1992; Sports Journalist of the Year, British Press Awards, 2000; Specialist Correspondent of the Year, British Sports Journalism Awards, 2002, 2005. *Publication:* (assisted with) David Beckham: My World, 2000. *Recreations:* playing football, golf, film, travel. *Address:* c/o The Times, 1 Pennington Street, E98 1XY. *Clubs:* Roehampton; Cambridge University Lightweight Rowing.

DICKINSON, Patric Laurence, LVO 2006; Richmond Herald of Arms, since 1989; Earl Marshal's Secretary, since 1996; Secretary, Order of the Garter, since 2004; *b* 24 Nov. 1950; *s* of late John Laurence Dickinson and April Katherine, *d* of Robert Forgan, MC, MD, sometime MP. *Educ:* Marling Sch.; Exeter Coll., Oxford (Stapeldon Schol.; MA). Pres., Oxford Union Soc., 1972. Called to the Bar, Middle Temple, 1979. Res. Asst, College of Arms, 1968–78; Rouge Dragon Pursuivant, 1978–89. Hon. Treasurer: English Genealogical Congress, 1975–91; Bar Theatrical Soc., 1978–; Treas., Coll. of Arms, 1995–. Hon. Sec. and Registrar, British Record Soc., 1979–; Vice-Pres., Assoc. of Genealogists and Researchers in Archives (formerly Assoc. of Genealogists and Record Agents), 1988–; President: Soc. of Genealogists, 2005– (Vice-Pres., 1997–2005); Bristol and Glos Archaeol Soc., 1998–99. Vice-Pres., Anthony Powell Soc., 2008– (Chm., 2003–07). FSG 2000. *Recreation:* catching trains. *Address:* College of Arms, Queen Victoria Street, EC4V 4BT. *T:* (020) 7236 9612; 13 Old Square, Lincoln's Inn, WC2A 3UA. *Club:* Brooks's.

DICKINSON, Prof. Peter, DMus; composer, writer, pianist; Head of Music, Institute of United States Studies, University of London, 1997–2004; Professor of Music, Goldsmiths College, London University, 1991–97, now Emeritus; *b* 15 Nov. 1934; *s* of late Frank Dickinson, FBOA (Hons), FAAO, DOS, FRSH, contact lens specialist, and Muriel Porter; *m* 1964, Bridget Jane Tomkinson, *d* of late Lt-Comdr E. P. Tomkinson, DSO, RN; two *s*. *Educ:* The Leys Sch.; Queens' Coll., Cambridge (organ schol., Stewart of Rannoch schol.; MA); Juilliard Sch. of Music, New York (Rotary Foundn Fellow). DMus London 1992; LRAM, ARCM; FRCO. Teaching and freelance work in New York, 1958–61, London and Birmingham, 1962–74; first Prof. of Music, Keele Univ., 1974–84, subseq. Prof. Emeritus; founded Centre for American Music, Keele. Broadcasts and records as pianist (mostly with sister Meriel Dickinson, mezzo soprano, 1966–94). Member, Board: Trinity Coll. of Music, 1984–98; Inst. of US Studies, London Univ., 1994–2000. Trustee: Berners Trust, 1988–; Bernarr Rainbow Trust, 1996–. Contributor, Gramophone mag., 1989–. Hon. FTCL 1992. Hon. DMus Keele, 1999. *Publications: compositions include: orchestral:* Monologue for Strings, 1959; Five Diversions, 1969; Transformations, 1970; Organ Concerto, 1971; Piano Concerto, 1984; Violin Concerto, 1986; Jigsaws, 1988; Merseyside Echoes, 1988; *chamber:* String Quartet No 1, 1958; Juilliard Dances, 1959; Fanfares and Elegies, 1967; Translations, 1971; String Quartet No 2, 1975; American Trio, 1985; London Rags, 1986; Sonatas for piano and tape playback, 1987; Auden Studies, 1988; Swansongs, 1992; works for solo organ, piano, clavichord, recorder, flute, violin, guitar and baryton; *vocal:* Four Auden Songs, 1956; A Dylan Thomas Cycle, 1959; Elegy, 1966; Five Poems of Alan Porter, 1968; Extravaganzas, 1969; An E. E. Cummings Cycle, 1970; Winter Afternoons (Emily Dickinson), 1970; Three Comic Songs (Auden), 1972; Surrealist Landscape (Lord Berners), 1973; Lust (St Augustine), 1974; A Memory of David Munrow, 1977; Reminiscences (Byron), 1979; The Unicorns (John Heath-Stubbs), 1982; Stevie's Tunes (Stevie Smith), 1984; Larkin's Jazz (Philip Larkin), 1989; Summoned by Mother (Betjeman), 1991; *choral:* Martin of Tours (Thomas Blackburn), 1966; The Dry Heart (Alan Porter), 1967; Outcry, 1969; Late Afternoon in November, 1975; A Mass of the Apocalypse, 1984; Tiananmen 1989, 1990; *ballet:* Vitalitas, 1959; *musical drama:* The Judas Tree (Thomas Blackburn), 1965; various church music; (ed) Twenty British Composers, 1975; (ed) Songs and Piano Music by Lord Berners, 1982, 2nd edn 2000; The Music of Lennox Berkeley, 1989, 2nd edn 2003; Marigold: the music of Billy Mayerl, 1999; (ed) Copland Connotations, 2002; (ed) Collected Works for Solo Piano by Lennox Berkeley, 2003; (ed) CageTalk: dialogues with and about John Cage, 2006; Lord Berners: composer, writer, painter, 2008; contrib. to The New Grove, and various books and periodicals. *Recreation:* rare books. *Address:* c/o Novello & Co., 14–15 Berners Street, W1T 3LJ. *Club:* Garrick.

DICKINSON, Hon. Peter Malcolm de Brissac, FRSL; author; *b* 16 Dec. 1927; *s* of late Hon. Richard Sebastian Willoughby Dickinson and of May Southey (Nancy) Lovemore; *m* 1st, 1953, Mary Rose Barnard (*d* 1988); two *d* two *s*; 2nd, 1992, Robin McKinley. *Educ:* Eton; King's Coll., Cambridge (BA). Asst Editor, Punch, 1952–69. Chm., Management Cttee, Soc. of Authors, 1978–80. FRSL 1999. *Publications: children books:* The Weathermonger, 1968; Heartsease, 1969; The Devil's Children, 1970 (trilog republished 1975 as The Changes); Emma Tupper's Diary, 1970; The Dancing Bear, 1972; The Gift, 1973; The Iron Lion, 1973; Chance, Luck and Destiny, 1975; The Blue Hawk, 1976 (Guardian Award); Annerton Pit, 1977; Hepzibah, 1978; Tulku, 1979 (Whitbread Prize; Carnegie Medal); The Flight of Dragons, 1979; City of Gold, 1980 (Carnegie Medal); The Seventh Raven, 1981; Healer, 1983; Giant Cold, 1984; (ed) Hundreds and Hundreds, 1984; A Box of Nothing, 1985; Mole Hole, 1987; Merlin Dreams, 1988; Eva, 1988; AK, 1990 (Whitbread Children's Award); A Bone from a Dry Sea, 1992; Time and the Clockmice etcetera, 1993; Shadow of a Hero, 1994; Chuck and Danielle, 1996; The Kin, 1998; Touch and Go, 1999; The Lion Tamer's Daughter, 1999; The Ropemaker, 2001; (with Robin McKinley) Elementals: Water, 2002; The Tears of the Salamander, 2003; The Gift Boat, 2004; Angel Isle, 2006; *TV series*, Mandog (Mandog, by Lois Lamplugh, 1972, is based on the Changes series); *novels:* Skin Deep, 1968; A Pride of Heroes, 1969; The Seals, 1970; Sleep and His Brother, 1971; The Lizard in the Cup, 1972; The Green Gene, 1973; The Poison Oracle, 1974; The Lively Dead, 1975; King and Joker, 1976; Walking Dead, 1977; One Foot in the Grave, 1979; A Summer in the Twenties, 1981; The Last House-party, 1982; Hindsight, 1983; Death of a Unicorn, 1984; Tefuga, 1986; Perfect Gallows, 1988; Skeleton-in-Waiting, 1989; Play Dead, 1991; The Yellow Room Conspiracy, 1994; Some Deaths Before Dying, 2000; *poetry:* The Weir, 2008. *Recreation:* manual labour. *Address:* 1 Arlebury Park Mews, Alresford, Hants SO24 9ER.

See also Baron Dickinson, Very Rev. H. G. Dickinson.

DICKINSON, Robert Henry, CBE 1998; DL; Senior Partner, Dickinson Dees, 1987–97; Chairman, Northern Rock PLC (formerly Northern Rock Building Society), 1992–99; *b* 12 May 1934; *s* of Robert Joicey Dickinson and Alice Penelope Dickinson (*née* Barnett); *m* 1963, Kyra Irina Boissevain; one *s* two *d*. *Educ:* Harrow; Christ Church, Oxford (MA). Admitted solicitor (Hons), 1960; Partner, Dickinson Dees, 1963–97. Chairman: Northern Investors PLC, 1984–2005; Grainger Trust PLC, 1992–2007; Director: Reg Vardy PLC, 1988–2002; Yorkshire Tyne Tees TV PLC, 1992–97. Chm., Univ. of Newcastle upon Tyne Develt Trust, 2000–05. DL Northumberland, 1992. *Recreations:* shooting, fishing. *Address:* Styford Hall, Stocksfield, Northumberland NE43 7TX. *T:* (01434) 682467, *Fax:* (01434) 634634. *Clubs:* Boodle's, Pratt's, Beefsteak; Northern Counties (Newcastle).

DICKINSON, Sally Jane; Secretary, Magistrates' Association, since 1994; *b* 12 Sept. 1955; *d* of Colin James Rayner Godden and Margaret Godden (*née* Cowin); *m* 1987, James Anthony Dickinson. *Educ:* Chatham Grammar Sch. for Girls; Bristol Univ. (BA Theol); Bristol Poly. (BA Law). Clerical Officer, Inland Revenue Collection, 1978–81; Exec. Officer, Law Soc. (Legal Aid), 1981–85; Regl Dir, Apex Charitable Trust, 1985–92; Cttee Sec., Magistrates' Assoc., 1992–93. *Recreations:* walking, sleeping, dogs. *Address:* 55 Noah's Ark, Kemsing, Kent TN15 6PA.

DICKINSON, Simon Clervaux; Chairman: Simon C. Dickinson Ltd, Agents and Dealers in Fine Art, since 1993; Dickinson Roundell Inc., since 1993; *b* 26 Oct. 1948; *s* of Peter Dickinson and Anne Dickinson (*née* Chayter); *m* 1983, Hon. Jessica, *d* of 2nd Baron Mancroft, KBE, TD; one *s* two *d*. *Educ:* Aysgarth Sch.; Harrow (art schol.; Mem., First cricket and football XIs). Christie's: joined 1968; Dir, 1974–93; Sen. Picture Dir, 1990–93. *Recreations:* gardening, shooting, fishing, golf, tennis. *Address:* Simon C. Dickinson Ltd, 58 Jermyn Street, SW1Y 6LX. *T:* (020) 7493 0340, *Fax:* (020) 7493 0796; *e-mail:* simon@simondickinson.com. *Clubs:* White's, Boodle's.

DICKINSON, (Stephen) Mark; Editorial Director, Trinity Mirror Midlands, since 2005; *b* 20 Jan. 1951; *s* of Stanley Park Dickinson and Beatrice Joan Dickinson; *m* 1981, Pauline Patricia Mills; two *s* two *d*. *Educ:* Dame Alice Owen's Sch.; Univ. of Manchester (BA 2nd Cl. Hons Psychol). Publicity asst, Macmillan Jls, 1975–76; sub-editor, Daily Telegraph, Manchester, 1976–87; author, 1988–89; Chief Sub Editor: Tonight, Chester, 1990–91; Aberdeen Evening Express, 1991–92; Asst Ed., The Journal, Newcastle, 1992–93; Dep. Ed. in Chief, Chronicle Newspapers, Chester, 1993–96; Editor: The Journal, Newcastle, 1996–2000; Liverpool Echo, 2000–05; Ed.-in-Chief, Trinity Mirror NW and N Wales, 2002–05. *Publications:* The Manchester Book, 1984; To Break a Union, 1986; Goodbye Piccadilly: the history of abolition of Greater Manchester Council, 1990. *Recreations:* reading, gardening, football, Rugby, sailing, entertaining, my family. *Address:* c/o Birmingham Evening Mail, Weaman Street, Birmingham B4 6AV.

DICKINSON, (Vivienne) Anne, (Mrs Basil Phillips); Chairman, Forexia UK, 1997–98; Director, Leedex Public Relations, 1993–96; *b* 27 Sept. 1931; *d* of F. Oswald Edward Dickinson and M. Ida Ismay Dickinson; *m* 1st, 1951, John Kerr Large (marr. diss.); one *s* decd; 2nd, 1979, David Hermas Phillips (*d* 1989); 3rd, 1993, Basil B. Phillips, OBE. *Educ:* Nottingham Girls' High School. Account Executive, W. S. Crawford, 1960–64; Promotions Editor: Good Housekeeping, 1964–65; Harpers Bazaar, 1965–67; Dir in charge of Promotions, Nat. Magazine Co., 1967–68; Dir, Benson PR (later Kingsway), 1968–69; Chm. and Chief Exec., Kingsway Public Relations Ltd (later Kingsway Rowland), 1969–89; Chairman: The Rowland Co., 1989–90; Graduate Appointments Ltd, 1993–94; Dir, Birkdale Group plc, 1991–96. Chm., PR Consultants' Assoc., 1989 (Chm., Professional Practices Cttee, 1989). Chm., Family Welfare Assoc., 1990–94. Member: Rye Town Council, 1995–99; Bd, Rye Health & Care Ltd, 1996–2004 (Vice Pres., 2004–). FCIPR (FIPR 1985); CCMI (CBIM 1986). PR Professional of the Year, PR Week, 1988–89. *Recreations:* friends, food, dogs. *Address:* St Mary's House, 62 Church Square, Rye TN31 7HF. *Club:* Sloane.

DICKINSON, (Woodman) Mark (Lowes), OBE 2000; HM Diplomatic Service; Head of Office, Pristina, Kosovo, 2002–06; *b* 16 Jan. 1955; *s* of Woodman Gilbert Dickinson and Dorothy Priscilla Dickinson (*née* Cashmore); *m* 1st, 1986, Francesca Infanti (marr. diss. 1995); 2nd, 1995, Christina Houlder (*née* Bass); one *s*. *Educ:* Christ's Hosp.; Sidney Sussex Coll., Cambridge (MA). Joined HM Diplomatic Service, 1976; Second Sec., Ankara, 1979–82; FCO, 1982–87; First Sec., Dublin, 1987–90; FCO, 1990–94; Bank of England, 1994–97; Ambassador to Macedonia, 1997–2001. Actg Chief Exec., Westminster Foundn for Democracy, 1992. *Address:* c/o Foreign and Commonwealth Office, King Charles Street, SW1A 2AH.

DICKS, Prof. Anthony Richard; QC (Hong Kong) 1994; Professor of Chinese Law, 1995–2002, now Emeritus, and Professorial Research Associate, since 2003, School of Oriental and African Studies, University of London; *b* 6 Jan. 1936; *s* of Henry Victor Dicks and Pretoria Maud Dicks (*née* Jeffery); *m* 1969, Victoria Frances Mayne. *Educ:* Westminster Sch.; Trinity Coll., Cambridge (Open and Westminster Exhibnr; BA Hist. and Law, LLB 1st Cl., MA). Called to the Bar, Inner Temple, 1961; admitted Hong Kong Bar, 1965, Brunei Bar, 1971. Nat. Service, 2nd Lieut, 3rd King's Own Hussars, 1954–56. Teaching Fellow, Univ. of Chicago Law Sch., 1960–61; Res. Fellow, Brit. Inst. Internat. and Comparative Law and Inst. Current World Affairs, London, Hong Kong and Japan, 1962–68; Fellow, Trinity Hall, and Univ. Asst Lectr in Law, Cambridge, 1968–70; Lectr in Oriental Laws, SOAS, 1970–74; in practice as barrister and arbitrator, Hong Kong, 1974–94. Vis. Prof., SOAS, 1987–94. Mem., various acad., professional and public cttees in Hong Kong, 1974–94. Advr, Foreign Compensation Commn on China Claims, 1987–88; Arbitrator in Internat. Chamber of Commerce, London Court of Internat. Arbitration, Hong Kong Internat. Arbitration Centre and China Internat. Econ. and Trade Arbitration Commn and other arbitrations. *Publications:* articles in China Qly and other jls. *Address:* School of Oriental and African Studies, Thornhaugh Street, Russell Square, WC1H 0XG. *Clubs:* Athenæum; Hong Kong (Hong Kong).

DICKS, Terence Patrick, (Terry); *b* 17 March 1937; *s* of Frank and Winifred Dicks; *m*; one *s* two *d*; *m* 1985, Janet Cross; one *d*. *Educ:* London Sch. of Econs and Pol Science (BScEcon); Oxford Univ. (DipEcon). Clerk: Imperial Tobacco Co. Ltd, 1952–59; Min. of Labour, 1959–66; Admin. Officer, GLC, 1971–86. Contested (C) Bristol South, 1979. MP (C) Hayes and Harlington, 1983–97. Mem., Select Cttee on Transport, 1986–92. Member: Council of Europe, 1993–97; WEU, 1993–97. Mem. (C), Surrey CC, 1999–.

DICKSON, Arthur Richard Franklin, CBE 1974; QC (Belize), 1979; Commissioner for Law Revision, Belize, 1978; *b* 13 Jan. 1913; *m* 1949, Joanna Maria Margaretha van Baardwyk (*d* 1998); four *s*. *Educ:* Rusea's Secondary Sch. and Cornwall Coll., Jamaica. Called to the Bar, Lincoln's Inn, 1938. Judicial Service. HM Overseas Judiciary: Jamaica, 1941; Magistrate, Turks and Caicos Islands, 1944–47; Asst to Attorney-Gen., and Legal Draftsman, Barbados, 1947–49; Magistrate, British Guiana, 1949–52; Nigeria, 1952–62: Magistrate, 1952–54; Chief Magistrate, 1954–56; Chief Registrar, High Court, Lagos, 1956–58; Judge of the High Court, Lagos, 1958–62; retired. Temp. appointment, Solicitors Dept, GPO London, 1962–63; served Northern Rhodesia (latterly Zambia), 1964–67; Judge of the High Court, Uganda, 1967–71; Deputy Chm., Middlesex QS, July–Aug., 1971; Chief Justice, Belize, 1973–74; Judge of the Supreme Court, Anguilla (part-time), 1972–76; part-time Chm., Industrial Tribunals, England and Wales, 1972–85. *Publications:* Revised Ordinances (1909–1941) Turks and Caicos Islands, 1944; (ed) Revised Laws of Belize, 1980. *Recreations:* gardening, walking, swimming. *Address:* 14 Meadow Lane, Lindfield, Haywards Heath, West Sussex RH16 2RJ. *T:* (01444) 484450.

DICKSON, Brice; *see* Dickson, S. B.

DICKSON, David John Scott; Director, Science and Development Network (SciDev.Net), since 2001; *b* 30 Aug. 1947; *s* of David and Rachel Mary Dickson; *m* 1973, Prudence Mary (marr. diss. 1999); one *s* one *d*. *Educ:* Westminster Sch.; Trinity Coll., Cambridge. Medical News, 1968–70; Sec., Brit. Soc. for Social Responsibility in Science, 1970–72; science corresp., 1973–75, features editor, 1975–77, THES; Washington corresp., Nature, 1977–82; European corresp., Science, 1982–89; news editor, 1989–90, Editor, 1990–92, New Scientist; News Editor, Nature, 1993–2001. Lectures organiser, ICA, 1976–77. Recorder, Gen. Section, BAAS, 2001–. Visiting Research Fellow: Univ. of Linköping, Sweden, 1981; Open Univ., 1989; Hon. Res. Fellow, UCL, 2002. Award for Meritorious Achievement, Council of Sci. Editors, 2006; (jtly) Assoc. of British Sci. Writers Award, 2006. *Publications:* Alternative Technology, 1974; The New Politics of Science, 1984; Het verval van de Geest (The Death of the Spirit), 1990; contribs to various jls on science, technology and society. *Recreations:* music, photography, painting. *Address:* SciDev.Net, 97–99 Dean Street, W1D 3TE.

DICKSON, George, CBE 1991 (OBE 1974); HM Diplomatic Service, retired; Consul General, Amsterdam, 1987–91; *b* 23 May 1931; *s* of late George James Stark Dickson and of Isobel (*née* Brown). *Educ:* Aberdeen Acad. DSIR, 1952; CRO, 1952–54; Karachi, 1954–56; Penang, 1957–59; Nicosia, 1960–62; Kampala, 1962–66; FCO, 1966–68; Manila, 1968–71; Jakarta, 1971–75; Stuttgart, 1975–76; Beirut, 1976–79; Baghdad, 1979–81; Asst Dir, Internat. Affairs, Commonwealth Secretariat, 1981–85; Dep. High Comr, Kingston, Jamaica, 1985–87. *Address:* Milton of Braichlie, by Ballater, Aberdeenshire AB35 5SQ. *T:* (01339) 755708.

DICKSON, Prof. Gordon Ross; Professor of Agriculture, University of Newcastle upon Tyne, 1973–97; Chairman, North England Regional Advisory Committee, Forestry Commission, 1987–97; *b* 12 Feb. 1932; *s* of T. W. Dickson, Tynemouth; *m* 1st, 1956, Dorothy Stobbs (*d* 1989); two *s* one *d*; 2nd, 1991, Violet Adams. *Educ:* Tynemouth High Sch.; Durham Univ. BSc (Agric) 1st cl. hons 1953, PhD (Agric) 1958, Dunelm. Tutorial Research Student, Univ. Sch. of Agric., King's Coll., Newcastle upon Tyne, 1953–56; Asst Farm Dir, Council of King's Coll., Nafferton, Stocksfield-on-Tyne, 1956–58; Farms Director for the Duke of Norfolk, 1958–71; Principal, Royal Agric. Coll., Cirencester, 1971–73. Chm., Agricl Wages Bd for England and Wales, 1981–84; Dep. Chm., Home-Grown Cereals Authy, 1982–94. FRAgS; FIAgrM 1992. *Address:* The West Wing, Bolam Hall, Morpeth, Northumberland NE61 3UA.

DICKSON, Jennifer (Joan), (Mrs R. A. Sweetman), CM 1995; RA 1976 (ARA 1970); RE 1965; graphic artist, photographer and painter; *b* 17 Sept. 1936; 2nd *d* of late John Liston Dickson and Margaret Joan Turner, S Africa; *m* 1962, Ronald Andrew Sweetman; one *s*. *Educ:* Goldsmith's College Sch. of Art, Univ. of London; Atelier 17, Paris. Taught at Eastbourne Sch. of Art, 1959–62 (French Govt Schol., to work in Paris under S. W. Hayter). Directed and developed Printmaking Dept, Brighton Coll. of Art, 1962–68; developed and directed Graphics Atelier, Saidye Bronfman Centre, Montreal, 1970–72. Exhibn, L'Ultimo Silenzio, Palazzo Te, Mantua, Italy, 1993. Has held appointments of Vis. Artist at following Universities: Ball State Univ., Muncie, Indiana, 1967; Univ. of the West Indies, Kingston, Jamaica, 1968; Univ. of Wisconsin, Madison, 1972; Ohio State Univ., 1973; Western Illinois Univ., 1973; Haystack Mountain Sch. of Crafts, Maine, 1973; Vis. Artist, Queen's Univ., Kingston, Ont., 1977; part-time Instructor of Drawing, 1980–81, 1983, Sessional Instructor, 1980–85, Ottawa Univ.; Vis. Prof., 1987, Hon. LLD 1988, Univ. of Alberta. Founder Mem., Brit. Printmakers' Council. Prix des Jeunes Artistes (Gravure), Biennale de Paris, 1963; Major Prize, World Print Competition, San Francisco, 1974; Norwegian Print Biennale Prize, 1981. *Publications:* suites of original prints and photographs: Genesis, 1965; Alchemic Images, 1966; Aids to Meditation, 1967; Eclipse, 1968; Song of Songs, 1969; Out of Time, 1970; Fragments, 1971; Sweet Death and Other Pleasures, 1972; Homage to Don Juan, 1975; Body Perceptions, 1975; The Secret Garden, 1976; Openings, 1977; Three Mirrors to Narcissus, 1978; Il Paradiso Terrestre, 1980; Il Tempo Classico, 1981; Grecian Odes, 1983; Aphrodite Anadyomene, 1984; The Gardens of Paradise, part 1, 1984, part 2, 1985; Reflected Palaces, 1985; The Gilded Cage, 1986; Water Gardens, 1987; The Hospital for Wounded Angels, 1987; The Gardens of Desire, 1988; Pavane to Spring, 1989; Sonnet to Persephone, 1990; The Gardener's Journal, 1990; Cadence and Echo: the song of the garden, 1991; The Spirit of the Garden, 1992; The Haunted Heart, 1993; Sanctuaries and Paradeisos, 1994; Old and New Worlds, 1995; Quietude and Grace, 1996; Water Song, 1997; Sanctuary: a landscape of the mind, 2000; Nature and Artifice, 2003; Time is the Thief of Time, 2006. *Address:* 20 Osborne Street, Ottawa, ON K1S 4Z9, Canada. *T:* (613) 7302083, *Fax:* (613) 7301818.

DICKSON, Martin Charles Gregor; Deputy Editor, Financial Times, since 2005; *b* London, 21 Aug. 1948; *s* of George and Stella Dickson; *m* 1973, Hilary Wilce; one *s* two *d*. *Educ:* Haileybury; Trinity Hall, Cambridge (BA Hist. 1970); Univ. of London (BSc Econ. ext.). VSO, Thailand, 1966–67; journalist, Reuters, UK, S Africa and Turkey, 1970–76; Financial Times: journalist, 1976–; Africa Ed., 1978–79; Energy Corresp.,

1980–82; NY Bureau Chief, 1990–94; Financial Ed., 1994–2000; Lombard Columnist, 2001–05. *Recreations:* singing, running, travel, wine, galleries, gardening. *Address:* Financial Times, 1 Southwark Bridge, SE1 9HL; *e-mail:* martin.dickson@ft.com.

DICKSON, Michael George Tufnell, CBE 2005; FREng; Founding Partner, since 1976, and Chairman, 1996–2005, Buro Happold; *b* 22 Sept. 1944; *s* of late George Frederick Thomas Benson Dickson and Rosamond Mary (*née* Tufnell); *m* 1980, Euphemia Anne Galletly; two *d*. *Educ:* Trinity Coll., Cambridge (BA Mech. Scis Tripos); Cornell Univ., NY (MS Structural Engrg and Town Planning). CEng 1975; FREng 1999; FIStructE 1997; FICE 2000. Engineer, Ove Arup, 1968–76. Visiting Professor: of Engrg Design, Univ. of Bath, 1996–; Innsbruck, 2000. Mem., Lord Justice Taylor's Tech. Cttee on Safety of Sports Grounds, 1987; Chairman: Construction Industry Council, 2000–02; Construction Res. and Innovation Strategy Panel, 2002–04. Pres., IStructE, 2005–06 (Chm., Towards Sustainable Devel: construction without depletion, 1999; Vice Pres., 2002–05). Trustee and Bd Mem., Theatre Royal, Bath, 1986–. Mem., AA; FRSA 1992. Hon. FRIBA 2001. Hon. DEng Bath, 2007. *Publication:* (ed with Michael Barnes) Widespan Roof Structures, 2000. *Recreations:* reading, walking, tennis, cricket, engineering design. *Address:* Netherfield, Cleveland Walk, Bath BA2 6JW. *T:* (01225) 464370, (office) (01225) 320626; *e-mail:* michael.dickson@burohappold.com. *Clubs:* Athenæum, MCC.

DICKSON, Niall Forbes Ross; Chief Executive, The King's Fund, since 2004; *b* 5 Nov. 1953; *s* of late Sheriff Ian Anderson Dickson, WS and Margaret Forbes Ross or Dickson; *m* 1979, Elizabeth Selina Taggart, *d* of late James Mercer Taggart, Lisburn, Co. Antrim; one *s* two *d*. *Educ:* Glasgow Acad.; Edinburgh Acad.; Edinburgh Univ. (MA Hons; DipEd); Moray House Coll. of Educn (Cert Ed). Teacher, Broughton High Sch., Edinburgh, 1976–78; Publicity Officer, Nat. Corp. for Care of Old People, 1978; Press Officer, 1978–79, Hd of Publishing, 1979–81, Age Concern England; Editor: Therapy Weekly, 1981–83; Nursing Times, 1983–88; BBC News: Health Corresp., 1988–90; Chief Social Affairs Corresp., 1990–95; Social Affairs Editor, 1995–2004. Chairman: Direct Payments Steering Gp, DoH, 2004–06; Individual Budgets Reform Gp, 2006–. Member: NHS Modernisation Bd, 2004–05; Nat. Leadership Network, DoH, 2005–; CMO's Review of Med. Regulation and Related Matters, 2005–; Wkg Party on Med. Professionalism, RCP, 2005–06; Health Honours Cttee, 2005–. Mem. Council, Which?, 2006–. Mem. Ct of Govs, LSHTM, 2005–. Hon. Fellow: Univ. of Cardiff, 2006; Inst. of Educn, Univ. of London, 2007. Charles Fletcher Med. Broadcaster of Year, BMA, 1997. *Publications:* contribs to newspapers, jls and specialist pubns on health and social issues. *Recreations:* golf, tennis, history, current affairs. *Address:* The King's Fund, 11–13 Cavendish Square, W1G 0AN. *T:* (020) 7307 2487. *Clubs:* Reform; Golf House (Elie), Hever Castle Golf.

See also R. H. Dickson.

DICKSON, Prof. Peter George Muir, DPhil, DLitt; FBA 1988; Professor of Early Modern History, University of Oxford, 1989–96; Fellow, St Catherine's College, Oxford, since 1960; *b* 26 April 1929; *s* of William Muir Dickson, and Regina Dowdall-Nicolls; *m* 1964, Ariane Faye; one *d*. *Educ:* St Paul's Sch.; Worcester Coll., Oxford (Schol.; BA (1st Cl. Hons), MA, DPhil); DLitt Oxon 1992. FRHistS. Research Fellow, Nuffield Coll., Oxford, 1954–56; Tutor, St Catherine's Soc., Oxford, 1956–60; Vice-Master, St Catherine's Coll., 1975–77; Reader in Modern Hist., Oxford Univ., 1978–89. *Publications:* The Sun Insurance Office 1710–1960, 1960; The Financial Revolution in England 1688–1756, 1967, rev. edn 1993; Finance and Government under Maria Theresia 1740–1780, 2 vols, 1987. *Recreations:* tennis, cinema, art. *Address:* Field House, Iffley, Oxford OX4 4EG. *T:* (01865) 779599.

DICKSON, Prof. Robert Andrew, DSc; FRCS, FRCSE; Professor and Head of Department of Orthopaedic Surgery, University of Leeds, 1981; Consultant Surgeon, St James's University Hospital, Leeds, and Leeds General Infirmary, 1981; *b* 13 April 1943; *s* of Robert Campbell Miller Dickson and late Maude Evelyn Dickson; *m* 1980, Ingrid Irene Sandberg; one *s*. *Educ:* Edinburgh Academy; Edinburgh Univ. (MB, ChB 1967, ChM 1973); MA 1979, DSc 1992, Oxon. FRCSE 1972; Moynihan Medal (Assoc. of Surgeons of GB and Ire.), 1977; FRCS *ad eund*. 1982. Lecturer, Nuffield Dept of Orthopaedic Surgery, Univ. of Oxford, 1972–75; Fellow in Spinal Surgery, Univ. of Louisville, Kentucky, 1975–76; Reader, Nuffield Dept of Orthopaedic Surgery, Univ. of Oxford, 1976–81. Chm., Professional Conduct Cttee, GMC, 2003–. Arris and Gale Lectr, and Hunterian Prof., RCS. Fellow, Brit. Orthopaedic Assoc. (Chm., Res. and Scholarship Cttee, 1999–); Member: Brit. Soc. for Surgery of the Hand; Brit. Orthopaedic Research Soc.; Brit. Scoliosis Soc. Treas., Council of Mgt, Jl of Bone and Jt Surgery, 2002–. *Publications:* Surgery of the Rheumatoid Hand, 1979; Musculo-skeletal disease, 1984; Management of spinal deformities, 1984; Management of spinal deformities, 1988; papers on scoliosis and spinal surgery. *Recreations:* squash, music. *Address:* 14A Park Avenue, Leeds LS8 2JH.

DICKSON, Robert Hamish, WS; Sheriff of South Strathclyde, Dumfries and Galloway, at Airdrie, since 1988; *b* 19 Oct. 1945; *s* of late Sheriff Ian Anderson Dickson, WS, and Mrs Margaret Forbes Ross or Dickson; *m* 1976, Janet Laird (*d* 2004), *d* of late Alexander Campbell, Port of Menteith; one *s*. *Educ:* Glasgow Acad.; Drumtochty Castle; Glenalmond; Glasgow Univ. (LLB). WS 1969. Solicitor: Edinburgh, 1969–71; Glasgow, 1971–86 (Partner, Brown Mair Mackintosh, 1973–86); Sheriff of South Strathclyde, Dumfries and Galloway, at Hamilton, 1986–88 (floating). Pres., Sheriffs' Assoc., 2006–. Pres., Scottish Medico Legal Soc., 2004–08. *Publications:* (jtly) Powers & Harris' Medical Negligence, 2nd edn 1994, 4th edn 2007; Medical and Dental Negligence, 1997; articles in medical legal jls. *Recreations:* golf, music, reading. *Address:* Airdrie Sheriff Court, Airdrie ML6 6EE. *T:* (01236) 751121. *Clubs:* Royal and Ancient Golf, Elie Golf House (Capt., 1997–99).

See also N. F. R. Dickson.

DICKSON, Robert Maurice French C.; *see* Chatterton Dickson.

DICKSON, Prof. (Sidney) Brice; Professor of International and Comparative Law, Queen's University, Belfast, since 2005; *b* 5 Dec. 1953; *s* of Sidney Dickson and Mary Dickson (*née* Murray); *m* 1993, Patricia Mary Josephine Mallon; one step *d* (one step *s* decd). *Educ:* Wadham Coll., Oxford (BA, BCL); Univ. of Ulster (MPhil). Called to the Bar, NI, 1976; Lectr in Law, Univ. of Leicester, 1977–79; Lectr, 1979–89, Sen. Lectr, 1989–91, QUB; Prof. of Law, Univ. of Ulster, 1991–99; Chief Comr, NI Human Rights Commn, 1999–2005. Leverhulme Eur. Student, 1976–77; Salzburg Fellow, 1985; Churchill Fellow, 1994; Leverhulme Res. Fellow, 1999. *Publications:* The Legal System of Northern Ireland, 1984, 5th edn 2005; Introduction to French Law, 1994; (ed) Human Rights and the European Convention, 1997; (ed) Civil Liberties in Northern Ireland: the CAJ handbook, 1990, 4th edn 2003; (ed with P. Carmichael) The House of Lords: its parliamentary and judicial roles, 1999; (ed) Judicial Activism in Common Law Supreme Courts, 2007. *Recreations:* modern fiction, travel, philately. *Address:* 33 Maryville Park, Belfast BT9 6LP.

DICKSON, Susan Jane; HM Diplomatic Service; Legal Counsellor, Foreign and Commonwealth Office, since 2003; *b* 30 July 1964; *d* of John Morton Dickson and Marlene Linek Dickson (*née* Allan). *Educ:* Mearns Castle High Sch.; Univ. of Strathclyde (LLB Hons 1986; DipLP 1988); Europa Inst., Univ. of Amsterdam (Dip. in European Law 1987). Admitted solicitor (Scotland), 1989; Asst, then Sen. Asst, Legal Advr, FCO, 1990–97; First Sec. (Legal), UK Mission to UN, NY, 1997–2000; First Sec. (Legal Advr British Overseas Territories), British High Commn, Bridgetown, 2000–03. *Recreations:* yoga, tennis, reading, interior design, Caribbean beaches. *Address:* Legal Advisers, Foreign and Commonwealth Office, King Charles Street, SW1A 2AH. *T:* (020) 7008 3000, *Fax:* (020) 7008 2280; *e-mail:* susan.dickson@fco.gov.uk.

DICKSON WRIGHT, Clarissa Teresa; cook; TV presenter and countryside campaigner; *b* 24 June 1947; *d* of Arthur Dickson Wright and Molly Bath. *Educ:* Sacred Heart Convent, Hove; University Coll. London (LLB). Called to the Bar, Gray's Inn, 1968; barrister; pheasant plucker; Proprietor, The Cooks' Bookshop, Edinburgh. Lord Rector, Aberdeen Univ., 1999–2005. Mem., Gen. Council, NT, 2002–03. Pres., Farmers' Markets Assoc., Scotland; Patron, Farmers' Markets Assoc., England. Co-Pres., Union Country Sports Workers. Presenter, TV series: with Jennifer Paterson, Two Fat Ladies, 1996–99; with Sir John Scott, Clarissa and the Countryman, 2000–03. Member: Butchers' Co., 2000; Yorks Guild of Butchers, 2007. *Publications:* The Haggis: a history, 1996; Heiland Foodie, 1997; Spilling the Beans (autobiog.), 2007; (with Jennifer Paterson): Two Fat Ladies, 1996; Two Fat Ladies Ride Again, 1997; Two Fat Ladies Full Throttle, 1998; Two Fat Ladies Obsessions, 1999; (with Sir John Scott): Clarissa and the Countryman, 2000; Clarissa and the Countryman Sally Forth, 2001; A Sunday Roast, 2002; The Game Cookbook, 2004; A Greener Life, 2005; Spilling the Beans, 2007. *Recreations:* hunting, shooting, fishing, food, Rugby, men.

DIEHL, John Bertram Stuart; QC 1987; **His Honour Judge Diehl;** a Circuit Judge, since 1990; Hon. Recorder of Swansea, since 2001; *b* 18 April 1944; *s* of late E. H. S. Diehl and C. P. Diehl; *m* 1967, Patricia L. Charman; two *s*. *Educ:* Bishop Gore Grammar Sch., Swansea; University Coll. of Wales, Aberystwyth (LLB 1965). Called to the Bar, Lincoln's Inn, 1968, Additional Bencher, 2007. Asst Lectr and Lectr in Law, Univ. of Sheffield, 1965–69; barrister, in practice on Wales and Chester Circuit, 1969–90; Asst Recorder, 1980–84; Recorder, 1984–90. *Address:* c/o Crown Court, St Helen's Road, Swansea SA1 4PF. *T:* (01792) 637000.

DIEPPE, Prof. Paul Adrian, MD; FRCP; MRC Senior Clinical Scientist, MRC Epidemiology Resource Centre, and Hon. Professor of Musculoskeletal Sciences, University of Oxford, since 2007; *b* 20 May 1946; *s* of Richard Willan Dieppe and Muriel Grace Dieppe (*née* Gascoigne); *m* 1970, Elizabeth Anne Stadward; two *d*. *Educ:* Caterham Sch.; St Bartholomew's Hosp. Med. Coll. (BSc 1967; MB BS 1970; MD 1985). FRCP 1985. General medical trng posts in London and Southend, 1970–74; Rheumatology Registrar, Guy's Hosp., London, 1974–75; Res. Fellow and Sen. Registrar in Medicine and Rheumatology, St Bartholomew's Hosp., London, 1975–78; University of Bristol: Consultant Sen. Lectr, 1978–87; ARC Prof. of Rheumatology, 1987–97; Res. Dir, Clinical Medicine and Dentistry, 1993–95; Dean, Faculty of Medicine, 1995–97; Hon. Prof. of Health Services Res., 1997–2007; Dir, MRC Health Services Res. Collaboration, 1997–2007; Hon. Consultant Rheumatologist: to Bristol and Bath hosps, 1978–2007; United Bristol Healthcare NHS Trust, 1992–2007; N Avon Hosp. Trust, 1997–2007. *Publications:* Crystals and Joint Disease, 1983; Rheumatological Medicine, 1985; Atlas of Clinical Rheumatology, 1986; Arthritis: BMA Family Doctor Guide, 1988; Rheumatology, 1993, 2nd edn 1997; contrib. chapters in books and numerous papers in jls. *Recreations:* sailing, running, Real tennis, reading, writing, resting.

DIESKAU, Dietrich F.; *see* Fischer-Dieskau.

DIFFLEY, Dr John Francis Xavier, FRS 2005; Principal Scientist, Cancer Research UK, London Research Institute, since 2002; *b* 4 March 1958; *s* of John and Joan Diffley. *Educ:* New York Univ. (BA 1978; PhD 1985). Postdoctoral Fellow, Cold Spring Harbor Lab., 1984–90; Imperial Cancer Research Fund, Clare Hall Laboratories: res. scientist, 1990–95; Sen. Scientist, 1995–99; Principal Scientist, 1999–2002. *Recreations:* playing the guitar, cycling. *Address:* Cancer Research UK, London Research Institute, Clare Hall Laboratories, South Mimms EN6 3LD.

DIGBY, family name of **Baron Digby**.

DIGBY, 12th Baron (Ire.) *cr* 1620, and 5th Baron (GB) *cr* 1765; **Edward Henry Kenelm Digby,** KCVO 1999; JP; DL; Lord-Lieutenant, Dorset, 1984–99 (Vice Lord-Lieutenant, 1965–84); Captain, late Coldstream Guards; *b* 24 July 1924; *o s* of 11th and 4th Baron Digby, KG, DSO, MC, and Hon. Pamela Bruce, OBE (*d* 1978), *y d* of 2nd Baron Aberdare; *S* father, 1964; *m* 1952, Dione Marian Sherbrooke (*see* Lady Digby); two *s* one *d*. *Educ:* Eton; Trinity Coll., Oxford; RMC. Served War of 1939–45. Capt. Coldstream Guards, 1947; Malaya, 1948–50; ADC to C-in-C: FARELF, 1950–51; BAOR, 1951–52. Director: Brooklyns Westbrick Ltd, 1970–83; Beazer plc, 1983–91; Kier Internat., 1986–91; Gifford-Hill Inc., 1986–91; PACCAR (UK) Ltd, 1990–97. Dep. Chm., SW Economic Planning Council, 1972–77. Mem. Council, Royal Agricultural Soc. of England, 1954; Chm., Royal Agricultural Soc. of Commonwealth, 1966–77, Hon. Fellow 1977. Pres., 1976, Vice Pres., 1977, Royal Bath and West Soc. Dorchester Rural District Councillor, 1962–68; Dorset County Councillor, 1966–81 (Vice Chm. CC, 1977–81). President: Wessex Br., Inst. of Dirs, 1980–97; Council, St John, Dorset, 1984–99; Patron, Dorset Br., British Red Cross Soc. Hon. Col, 4th Bn, Devonshire and Dorset Regt, 1992–96. DL 1957, JP 1959, Dorset. KStJ 1985. *Recreations:* ski-ing, shooting, tennis. *Heir:* *s* Hon. Henry Noel Kenelm Digby, ACA [*b* 6 Jan. 1954; *m* 1st, 1980, Susan (marr. diss. 2001), *er d* of Peter Watts; one *s* one *d*; 2nd, 2002, Sophie, *d* of Robin Malim; one *s* two *d* (of whom one *s* one *d* are twins)]. *Address:* Minterne, Dorchester, Dorset DT2 7AU. *T:* (01300) 341425. *Clubs:* Pratt's, Farmers'.

DIGBY, Lady; Dione Marian Digby, DBE 1991; DL; Founder Chairman and Hon. Secretary, Summer Music Society of Dorset, 1964–2005, Artistic Director, since 2005; *b* 23 Feb. 1934; *d* of Rear-Adm. Robert St Vincent Sherbrooke, VC, CB, DSO, and of Rosemary Neville Sherbrooke (*née* Buckley), Oxton, Notts; *m* 1952, Baron Digby, *qv*; two *s* one *d*. *Educ:* Talindert State Sch., Victoria, Australia; Southover Manor Sch., Lewes, Sussex. Chairman: Dorset Assoc. of Youth Clubs, 1966–73; Dorset Community Council, 1977–79; Standing Conf. of Rural Community Councils and Councils of Voluntary Service SW Region, 1977–79. Councillor (Ind.) W Dorset DC, 1976–86; Mem. Dorset Small Industries Cttee, CoSIRA, 1977 (Chm. 1982–85); Mem., Wessex Water Authority, 1983–89; National Rivers Authority: Mem., 1989–96; Chm., Wessex Regl Adv. Bd, 1989–93; Co-Chm., S Western Adv. Bd, 1993–95; Chm., Southern Regl Adv. Bd, 1995–96. Dir, SW Regl Bd, then Western Adv. Bd, Nat. Westminster Bank, 1986–92. Member: BBC/IBA Central Appeals Adv. Cttee, 1975–80; Ethical Trust Adv. Bd, Scottish Widows Investment Partnership (formerly Abbey Life Investment Services), 1996–2003; Cttee of Reference, Credit Suisse Fellowship Trust, 1997–. Governor: Dorset Coll. of Agriculture, 1978–83; Sherborne Sch., 1986–2000; Chm. Adv. Bd, Jt Univ.

Centre at Yeovil Coll., Bournemouth and Exeter Univs; Mem. Council, Exeter Univ., 1981–96; Chancellor, Bournemouth Univ., 2007– (Pro-Chancellor, 2001–06). Mem. Bath Festival Soc. Council of Management, 1971–81 (Chm. of the Society, 1976–81); Chm. Bath Fest. Friends Trust, 1982–87; Foundation Trustee, RAM, 1985–2000; Trustee, Tallis Scholars Trust, 1984–2004. Member: SW Arts Management Cttee, 1981–86; Arts Council of GB, 1982–86 (Chm., Trng Cttee; Vice-Chm., Dance Panel; Mem., Music Panel); South Bank Bd, 1985–88 (Gov., 1988–90); Bd of Mgt, Bournemouth Orchs, 1989–2000 (Mem. Bd of Mgt, Western Orchestral Soc., 1989–91); Chm., S and W Concerts Bd, 1989–2001; President: Dorset Opera, 1975–; Dorset Youth Assoc., 1994–2004. Mem., Council of Management, The Joseph Weld and Trimar (formerly Dorset Respite) Hospice Trust, 1990– (Pres., 1993–2007). DL Dorset, 1983. Hon. DArts Bournemouth, 1997. *Recreations:* music and the arts, ski-ing, sailing; interest in local government, politics, history, people. *Address:* The West Wing, Minterne House, Dorchester, Dorset DT2 7AX. *T:* (01300) 341425.

DIGGLE, Prof. James, LittD; FBA 1985; Professor of Greek and Latin, University of Cambridge, since 1995; Fellow of Queens' College, since 1966; *b* 29 March 1944; *m* 1973, Sedwell Mary Chapman; three *s*. *Educ:* Rochdale Grammar School; St John's College, Cambridge (Major Scholar; Classical Tripos Pt I, first cl., 1964, Pt II, first cl. with dist., 1965; Pitt Scholar, Browne Scholar, Hallam Prize, Members' Latin Essay Prize, 1963; Montagu Butler Prize, Browne Medals for Greek Elegy and Latin Epigram, 1964; Porson Prize, Chancellor's Classical Medal, Craven Student, Allen Scholar, 1965; BA 1965; MA 1969; PhD 1969; LittD 1985). Queens' College, Cambridge: Research Fellow, 1966–67; Official Fellow, 1967–; Sen. Fellow, 2007–; Director of Studies in Classics, 1967–; Librarian, 1969–77; Praelector, 1971–73, 1978–; Cambridge University: Asst Lectr in Classics, 1970–75; Lectr, 1975–89; Reader in Greek and Latin, 1989–95; Chm., Faculty Bd of Classics, 1989–90; Orator, 1982–93. Jt Editor, Cambridge Classical Texts and Commentaries, 1977–. Corresponding Mem., Acad. of Athens, 2001. *Publications:* The Phaethon of Euripides, 1970; (jtly) Flavii Cresconii Corippi Iohannidos, Libri VIII, 1970; (ed jtly) The Classical Papers of A. E. Housman, 1972; (ed jtly) Dionysiaca: nine studies in Greek poetry, presented to Sir Denys Page, 1978; Studies on the Text of Euripides, 1981; Euripidis Fabulae (Oxford Classical Texts), vol. ii 1981, vol. i 1984, vol. iii 1994; (ed jtly) Studies in Latin Literature and its Tradition, in honour of C. O. Brink, 1989; The textual tradition of Euripides' Orestes, 1991; (ed jtly) F. R. D. Goodyear, Papers on Latin Literature, 1992; Euripidea: collected essays, 1994; Cambridge Orations 1982–1993: a selection, 1994; Tragicorum Graecorum Fragmenta Selecta, 1998; Theophrastus: Characters, 2004; (with R. Bittlestone and J. Underhill) Odysseus Unbound: the search for Homer's Ithaca, 2005. *Recreation:* family life. *Address:* Queens' College, Cambridge CB3 9ET. *T:* (01223) 335527; *e-mail:* jd10000@cam.ac.uk.

DIGGLE, Judith Margaret, (Mrs P. J. Diggle); *see* Brown, J. M.

DIGGORY, Dr Colin; Headmaster, Alleyn's School, since 2002; *b* 22 July 1954; *s* of late John Harold Diggory and Olga (*née* Midcalf); *m* 1976, Susan Janet Robinson; one *s* two *d*. *Educ:* Sir William Turner's Sch., Redcar; Univ. of Durham (BSc 1st cl. Hons Maths, PGCE); Open Univ. (MA 1999; EdD 2005 (Sir John Daniel Award, 2005)). CMath, FIMA 1994. Assistant Master: Manchester Grammar Sch., 1976–83; St Paul's Sch., Barnes, 1983–87; Head of Maths, Merchant Taylors' Sch., 1987–90; Second Master, 1990–91, Headmaster, 1991–2002, Latymer Upper Sch. Chief Examr, A Level Maths, Univ. of London, 1989–91. Chm., London Div., 1999, Jun. Schs Sub-Cttee, 1999–2001, HMC. Trustee: Dulwich Picture Gall., 2005–; Soc. of Schoolmasters and Schoolmistresses, 2004–. Gov., Highgate Sch., 2003–. FRSA 1994. *Recreations:* walking, theatre. *Address:* Alleyn's School, Dulwich, SE22 8SU. *Clubs:* East India, Devonshire, Sports and Public Schools.

DIGHT, Marc David; His Honour Judge Dight; a Senior Circuit Judge, since 2007; *b* 27 Feb. 1961; *s* of Harvey Dight and Gillian Dight (*née* Strauss). *Educ:* Bancroft's Sch.; Univ. of Bristol (LLB Hons 1983). Called to the Bar, Inner Temple, 1984; admitted Lincoln's Inn *ad eundem*, 1986; Recorder, 2002–07. Dep. Adjudicator, HM Land Registry, 2004–. Trustee, Counsel and Care for the Elderly, 2003– (former Hon. Treas.; Chm., Fundraising Cttee). *Recreations:* Swedish horticulture, Thai cuisine. *Address:* Central London Civil Justice Centre, 26 Park Crescent, W1B 1HT.

DIGNAN, Maj.-Gen. (Albert) Patrick, CB 1978; MBE 1952; FRCS, FRCSI; Director of Army Surgery and Consulting Surgeon to the Army, 1973–78; Hon. Consultant Surgeon, Royal Hospital, Chelsea, 1973–78; Hon. Consultant in Radiotherapy and Oncology, Westminster Hospital, 1974–78; *b* 25 July 1920; *s* of Joseph Dignan; *m* 1952, Eileen Helena White (*d* 2001); two *s* one *d*. *Educ:* Trinity Coll., Dublin (Med. Schol.). MB, BCh, BAO, BA 1943, MA, MD 1968, FRCSI 1947, FRCS 1976. Prof. of Physiol. Prize, TCD. Posts in Dublin, Belfast and Wigan; subseq. NS Sen. Specialist in Surgery, Major RAMC Malaya; Sen. Registrar in Surgery, Bristol Royal Infirmary and Wanstead Hosp.; Sen. Specialist in Surgery, BAOR Mil. Hosps and Consultant Surg., Brit. Mil. Hosps Singapore and Tidworth, 1953–68; Brig., and Consulting Surg., Farelf, 1969–70; Consultant Surg., Mil. Hosp. Tidworth, 1971–72; Consultant Surgeon, Queen Alexandra Mil. Hosp. Millbank, 1972–73; Consultant in Accident and Emergency, Ealing Dist, DHSS, 1978–79. Pres., Army Med. Bds, 1980–90. Fellow, Association of Surgeons of GB and Ireland; FRSocMed. Mem., Acad. of Medicine, Singapore, 1969–71. QHS, 1974–78. *Publications:* A Doctor's Experiences of Life (autobiog.), 1994; papers in Brit. Jl Surgery, BMJ, Jl of RAMC, Postgrad. Med. Jl, Univ. Singapore Med. Soc. Med. Gazette. *Recreations:* gardening, golf.

DILHORNE, 2nd Viscount *cr* 1964, of Green's Norton; **John Mervyn Manningham-Buller;** Bt 1866; Baron 1962; Barrister-at-Law; *b* 28 Feb. 1932; *s* of 1st Viscount Dilhorne, PC, and Lady Mary Lilian Lindsay, 4th *d* of 27th Earl of Crawford, KT, PC; *S* father, 1980; *m* 1st, 1955, Gillian Evelyn (marr. diss. 1973), *d* of Colonel George Stockwell; two *s* one *d*; 2nd, 1981, Prof. Susannah Jane Eykyn, MB BS, FRCS, FRCP, FRCPath. *Educ:* Eton; RMA Sandhurst. Called to the Bar, Inner Temple, 1979. Formerly Lieut, Coldstream Guards. Managing Director, Stewart Smith (LP&M) Ltd, 1970–74. Mem., Wilts County Council, 1967–70. Chm., VAT Tribunal, 1988–95; Member, Joint Parliamentary Committee: on Statutory Instruments, 1981–88; on Consolidation Bills, 1994–99; Mem., EC Select Cttee (Law and Instns), 1989–92. FTII (Mem. Council, 1967–74). *Heir: s* Hon. James Edward Manningham-Buller, formerly Captain Welsh Guards [*b* 20 Aug. 1956; *m* 1985, Nicola Marion, *e d* of Sven Mackie; one *s* one *d*. *Educ:* Harrow; Sandhurst]. *Address:* 382 Imperial Court, 225 Kennington Lane, SE11 5QN. *T:* (020) 7820 1660, *Fax:* (020) 7820 1418; The Dower House, Minterne Parva, Dorchester, Dorset DT2 7AP. *T:* (01300) 341392. *Clubs:* Pratt's, Buck's, Beefsteak; Swinley Forest Golf.

See also Baroness Manningham-Buller.

DILKE, Rev. Sir Charles (John Wentworth), 6th Bt *cr* 1862, of Sloane Street; FRAS; priest of the London Oratory, since 1966; *b* 21 Feb. 1937; *er s* of Sir John Dilke, 5th Bt and of Sheila (*née* Seeds, now Knapp); *S* father, 1998. *Educ:* Ashdown House, Sussex; Winchester Coll.; King's Coll., Cambridge (BA). Joined the London Oratory, 1961; ordained priest, 1966; elected Provost (Superior), 1981–87. FRAS 2004. *Recreations:* painting, study of architecture, astronomy. *Heir: b* Dr Timothy Fisher Wentworth Dilke [*b* 1 Aug. 1938; *m* 1965, Caroline Sophia Dilke; one *s* one *d*]. *Address:* The Oratory, SW7 2RP. *T:* (020) 7808 0900. *Club:* Athenæum.

DILKE, Mary Stella F.; *see* Fetherston-Dilke.

DILKS, Prof. David Neville, FRHistS; FRSL; Vice-Chancellor, University of Hull, 1991–99; *b* Coventry, 17 March 1938; *s* of Neville Ernest Dilks and Phyllis Dilks; *m* 1963, Jill Medlicott; one *s*. *Educ:* Royal Grammar Sch., Worcester; Hertford Coll., Oxford (BA Modern Hist., Class II, 1959); St Antony's Coll., Oxford (Curzon Prizeman, 1960). Research Assistant to: Rt Hon. Sir Anthony Eden (later Earl of Avon), 1960–62; Marshal of the RAF Lord Tedder, 1963–65; Rt Hon. Harold Macmillan, 1964–67; Asst Lectr, then Lectr, in International History, LSE, 1962–70; University of Leeds: Prof. of Internat. History, 1970–91; Chm., Sch. of History, 1974–79; Dean, Faculty of Arts, 1975–77. Vis. Fellow, All Souls' Coll., Oxford, 1973. Consultant, Sec.-Gen. of the Commonwealth, 1967–75; Chm., Commonwealth Youth Exchange Council, 1968–73. Member: Adv. Council on Public Records, 1977–85; Central Council, 1982–85, Library Cttee, 1982–91, Royal Commonwealth Soc.; British Nat. Cttee for History of Second World War, 1983–2006 (Pres., Internat. Cttee, 1992–2000); UFC, 1989–91; Adv. Council, Politeia, 1995–. Trustee: Edward Boyle Meml Trust, 1982–96 (Hon. Sec., 1981–82); Imperial War Museum, 1983–90; Lennox-Boyd Meml Trust, 1984–91; Nathaniel Trust, 1986–90. Pres., Worcester Old Elizabethans' Assoc., 1986–87. FRSL 1986; FCGI 1999. Liveryman, Goldsmiths' Co., 1984– (Freeman, 1979). Wrote and presented BBC TV series, The Loneliest Job, 1977; interviewer in BBC TV series, The Twentieth Century Remembered, 1982; historical consultant, TV films, The Gathering Storm, 2002, Winston Churchill at War, 2008. Hon. Dr of History, Russian Acad. of Scis, 1996. Médaille de Vermeil, Acad. Française, 1994. Emery Reves Award, Churchill Center, USA, 2006. *Publications:* Curzon in India, Vol. I, 1969, Vol. II, 1970; (ed) The Diaries of Sir Alexander Cadogan, 1971; (contrib.) The Conservatives (ed Lord Butler of Saffron Walden), 1977; (ed and contrib.) Retreat from Power, vol. 1, 1906–1939, Vol. 2, After 1939, 1981; (ed and contrib.) Britain and Canada (Commonwealth Foundn Paper), 1980; (ed and contrib.) The Missing Dimension: governments and intelligence communities in the twentieth century, 1984; Neville Chamberlain, Vol. I: Pioneering and Reform 1869–1929, 1984; (ed jtly and contrib.) Grossbritannien und der deutsche Widerstand, 1994; (ed jtly) Barbarossa: the axis and the allies, 1994; The Great Dominion: Winston Churchill in Canada 1900–1954, 2005; reviews and articles in English Historical Rev., Survey, History, Scandinavian Jl of History, etc. *Recreations:* ornithology, painting, railways, Bentley cars. *Address:* Wits End, Long Causeway, Leeds LS16 8EX. *T:* (0113) 267 3466. *Clubs:* Brooks's, Special Forces.

DILKS, John Morris Whitworth; Managing Director, Peribase Ltd, since 1999; Chairman, Britannia Movers International plc, since 2004; *b* 10 Feb. 1950; *s* of John Amos Whitworth Dilks and Margaret (*née* Thraves); *m*; one *s* one *d*. *Educ:* Oakham Sch.; Sheffield Univ. (BA Hons). ACMA; CIGEM. Audit Manager, British Gas E Midlands, 1980–85; Asst Dir of Finance, British Gas, 1985–86; Regl Dir of Finance, British Gas NE, 1986–91; Regl Chm., British Gas Eastern, 1991–93; Dir, Transco, 1994–98. *Recreations:* sailing, walking, gardening. *Address:* Rosemount, Stockwell Lane, Woodmancote, Cheltenham, Glos GL52 9QG.

DILLAMORE, Ian Leslie, PhD, DSc; FREng; FIMMM; Chairman and Chief Executive, Doncasters plc, 1996–2000; *b* 22 Nov. 1938; *s* of Arthur Leslie Dillamore and Louise Mary Dillamore; *m* 1962, Maureen Birch; two *s*. *Educ:* Birmingham Univ. (BSc, MSc, PhD, DSc). ICI Research Fellow, Birmingham Univ., 1962–63, Lectr in Physical Metallurgy, 1963–69; Head of Phys. Metallurgy, BISRA, 1969–72; Head of Metals Technology Unit, British Steel Corp., 1972–76; Head of Metallurgy Dept, Aston Univ., 1976–81, Dean of Engineering, 1980–81; Director of Research and Development, INCO Europe, 1981–82; Dir of Technology, 1982–87, Gp Man. Dir, 1987–96, INCO Engineered Products Ltd. Hon. Professor of Metallurgy, Birmingham Univ., 1981–. Mem. Council: Metals Soc., 1980–84; Instn of Metallurgists, 1981–84; Vice-Pres., Inst. of Metals, 1985–88; Mem. SRC Metallurgy Cttee, 1972–75, Materials Cttee, 1977–82; Chm., Processing Sub-Cttee, SRC, later SERC, 1979–82; Mem., DTI Non Ferrous Metals Exec. Cttee, 1982–85; Pres. Birmingham Metallurgical Assoc., 1980–81. FREng (FEng 1985). Hon. DEng Birmingham, 1999. Sir Robert Hadfield Medal and Prize, Metals Soc., 1976; Platinum Medal, Inst. of Materials, 1999. *Publications:* numerous contribs to metallurgical and engrg jls. *Recreation:* industrial archaeology. *Address:* 4 Heather Court Gardens, Sutton Coldfield, W Midlands B74 2ST. *T:* (0121) 308 1363.

DILLON, family name of **Viscount Dillon**.

DILLON, 22nd Viscount *cr* 1622, of Castello Gallen, Co. Mayo, Ireland; **Henry Benedict Charles Dillon;** Count in France, 1711; *b* 6 Jan. 1973; *s* of 21st Viscount Dillon and of Mary Jane, *d* of late John Young, Castle Hill House, Birtle, Lancs; *S* father, 1982. *Heir: uncle* Hon. Richard Arthur Louis Dillon [*b* 23 Oct. 1948; *m* 1975, Hon. Priscilla Frances Hazlerigg, *d* of 2nd Baron Hazlerigg, MC, TD; one *s* one *d*].

DILLON, Andrew Patrick, CBE 2003; Chief Executive, National Institute for Health and Clinical Excellence (formerly for Clinical Excellence), since 1999; *b* 9 May 1954; *s* of Patrick Joseph Dillon and Kathleen Mary Dillon; *m* 1991, Alison Goodbrand; two *d*. *Educ:* St Ambrose Coll., Hale Barns, Cheshire; North Cheshire Coll. of Further Educn; Univ. of Manchester (BSc Hons Geog.). Dip. IHSM 1978. Asst Sector Adminr, Bolton Royal Infirmary, 1978–81; Unit Adminr, Queen Elizabeth Hosp. for Children, London, 1981–83; Dep., then Actg Unit Adminr, Royal London Hosp., 1983–86; Unit Gen. Manager, Royal Free Hosp., 1986–91; Chief Exec., St George's Gp, then St George's Healthcare NHS Trust, 1991–99. Non-exec. Dir, Health Technology Assessment Internat., 2003–05. Mem. Council, NHS Trust Fedn, 1995–97. FRSA 1998. *Recreation:* family. *Address:* National Institute for Health and Clinical Excellence, Midcity Place, 71 High Holborn, WC1V 6NA. *T:* (020) 7045 2043.

DILLON, His Honour Thomas Michael; QC 1973; a Circuit Judge, 1985–2000; *b* 29 Nov. 1927; *yr s* of Thomas Bernard Joseph Dillon, Birmingham, and Ada Gladys Dillon (*née* Noyes); *m* 1956, Wendy Elizabeth Marshall Hurrell; two *s* one *d*. *Educ:* King Edward's Sch., Aston, Birmingham; Birmingham Univ. (LLB); Lincoln Coll., Oxford (BCL). Called to Bar, Middle Temple, 1952, Master of the Bench 1981. 2nd Lieut, RASC, 1953–54. In practice as barrister, 1954–85; a Recorder, 1972–85; Part-time Chm. of Industrial Tribunals, 1968–74. *Recreations:* reading, listening to music.

DILLWYN-VENABLES-LLEWELYN, Sir John Michael; *see* Venables-Llewelyn.

DILNOT, Andrew William, CBE 2000; Principal, St Hugh's College, Oxford, since 2002; Pro-Vice-Chancellor, University of Oxford, since 2005; *b* 19 June 1960; *s* of Anthony William John Dilnot and Patricia Josephine Dilnot; *m* 1984, Catherine Elizabeth Morrish; two *d*. *Educ:* Olchfa Comprehensive Sch.; St John's Coll., Oxford (BA Hons

PPE; Hon. Fellow, 2002). Institute for Fiscal Studies: Res. Asst, 1981–83; Res. Officer, 1983–84; Sen. Res. Officer, 1984–86; Prog. Dir, 1986–90; Dep. Dir, 1990–91; Dir, 1991–2002. Lectr (part-time) in Econs, Exeter Coll., Oxford, 1988–89. Vis. Fellow, ANU, 1986; Downing Meml Fellow, Melbourne Univ., 1989. Presenter: Analysis, Radio 4, 1994–; More or Less, Radio 4, 2001–. Member: Social Security Adv. Cttee, 1992–2002; Retirement Income Inquiry, 1994–95; Foresight Panel on Aging Population, 1999–2001; Evidence Based Policy Panel, HM Treasury, 2001–03; Balance of Funding Inquiry, ODPM, 2002–04; Bd, NCC, 2003–; OST Rev. of Use of Science in ODPM, 2005–06. Member: Council, REconS, 1993–98; Acad. Social Scis, 1999–. Mem. Council, Westfield Coll., then QMW, Univ. of London, 1987–95. Mem. Bd, World Vision UK, 1991–97. Trustee: Relate, Oxon, 1999–2004; Our Right to Read, 2004–06. Patron, Oxford Youth Works, 2007–. Hon. FIA 2001. Hon. Fellow: Queen Mary, Univ. of London, 2004; Swansea Inst. of HE, 2004. Hon. DSc City, 2002. *Publications:* The Reform of Social Security, 1984; The Economics of Social Security, 1989; Pensions Policy in the UK: an economic analysis, 1994; The Tiger That Isn't: seeing through a world of numbers, 2007; contrib. articles on taxation, public spending and economics of public policy. *Address:* St Hugh's College, Oxford OX2 6LE. *T:* (01865) 274900.

DILNOT, Mary, (Mrs Thomas Ruffle), OBE 1982; Director, IPC Women's Magazines Group, 1976–81; Editor, Woman's Weekly, 1971–81; *b* 23 Jan. 1921; 2nd *d* of George Dilnot, author, and Ethel Dilnot; *m* 1974, Thomas Ruffle. *Educ:* St Mary's Coll., Hampton. Joined Woman's Weekly, 1939. *Recreations:* home interests, reading, travel. *Address:* 28 Manor Road South, Hinchley Wood, Esher, Surrey KT10 0QL.

DILWORTH, Prof. Jonathan Robin, DPhil, DSc; FRSC; Professor of Chemistry, University of Oxford, since 1998; Fellow of St Anne's College, Oxford, since 1997; *b* 20 Aug. 1944; *s* of Robert Arnold Dilworth and Jean Marion Dilworth; *m* 1971, Nicola Jane Still; two *d*. *Educ:* Jesus Coll., Oxford (BA 1967, MA 1972); Univ. of Sussex (DPhil 1970; DSc 1983). FRSC 1984. AFRC Unit of Nitrogen Fixation, 1967–85; Prof. of Chemistry, Univ. of Essex, 1985–97. *Publications:* some 280 papers and review articles in internat. chemistry jls. *Recreations:* tennis, badminton, golf. *Address:* The Croft, Newland Close, Eynsham, Oxon OX29 4LE. *T:* (01865) 884102.

DIMAS, Stavros; Member, European Commission, since 2004; *b* 30 April 1941. *Educ:* Univ. of Athens; NY Univ. (LLM). Sullivan & Cromwell, law firm, NY, 1969–70; lawyer, Internat. Finance Corp., World Bank, 1970–75; Dep. Gov., Hellenic Industrial Develt Bank, 1975–77. MP (New Democracy), Greece, 1977–2004; Dep. Minister of Econ. Co-ordination, 1977–80; Minister: of Trade, 1980–81; of Agriculture, 1989–90; of Industry, Energy and Technol., 1990–91. Sec. Gen., Party of New Democracy, 1995–2000. *Address:* European Commission, Rue de la Loi 200, 1049 Brussels, Belgium.

DIMBLEBY, David; broadcaster; Chairman, Dimbleby & Sons Ltd, 1986–2001 (Managing Director, 1966–86); *b* 28 Oct. 1938; *e s* of (Frederick) Richard and Dilys Dimbleby; *m* 1st, 1967, Josceline Rose Gaskell (*see* J. R. Dimbleby) (marr. diss. 2000); one *s* two *d*; 2nd, 2000, Belinda Giles; one *s*. *Educ:* Glengorse Sch.; Charterhouse; Christ Church, Oxford (MA); Univs of Paris and Perugia. News Reporter, BBC Bristol, 1960–61; Presenter and Interviewer on network programmes on: religion (Quest), science for children (What's New?), politics (In My Opinion), Top of the Form, etc, 1961–63; Reporter, BBC2 (Enquiry), and Dir films, incl.: Ku-Klux-Klan, The Forgotten Million, Cyprus: Thin Blue Line, 1964–65; Special Correspondent CBS News, New York; documentary film (Texas-England) and film reports for '60 minutes', 1966–68; Reporter, BBC1 (Panorama), 1967–69; Presenter, BBC1 (24 Hours), 1969–72; Yesterday's Men, 1971; Chm., The Dimbleby Talk-In, 1971–74; films for Reporter at Large, 1973; Presenter: BBC 1 (Panorama), 1974–77, 1980–82, 1989–94; (People and Power), 1982–83; (This Week, Next Week), 1984–86; Chm., BBC Question Time, 1994–; Election Campaign Report, 1974; BBC Election and Results programmes, 1979, 1983, 1987, 1992, 1997, 2001, 2005; film series: The White Tribe of Africa, 1979 (Royal TV Soc. Supreme Documentary Award); An Ocean Apart, 1988; The Struggle for South Africa, 1990 (Emmy Award, 1991; Golden Nymph Award, 1991); David Dimbleby's India, 1997; live commentary, funerals of Diana, Princess of Wales, 1997 and of HRH the Queen Mother, 2002; Mandela: The Living Legend, 2003; A Picture of Britain, 2005; How We Built Britain, 2007. Richard Dimbleby Award, BAFTA, 1998. *Publications:* An Ocean Apart (with David Reynolds), 1988; A Picture of Britain, 2005; How We Built Britain, 2007. *Address:* c/o Coutts & Co., 440 Strand, WC2R 0QS. *T:* (office) (020) 8755 5809.

See also J. Dimbleby.

DIMBLEBY, Jonathan; freelance broadcaster, journalist and author; *b* 31 July 1944; *s* of Richard and Dilys Dimbleby; *m* 1st, 1968, Bel Mooney, *qv* (marr. diss. 2006); one *s* one *d*; 2nd, 2007, Jessica Ray; one *d*. *Educ:* University Coll. London (BA Hons Philosophy). TV and Radio Reporter, BBC Bristol, 1969–70; BBC Radio, World at One, 1970–71; for Thames TV: This Week, 1972–78, 1986–88; TV Eye, 1979; Jonathan Dimbleby in South America, 1979; documentary series, Witness (Editor), 1986–88; for Yorkshire TV: series, Jonathan Dimbleby in Evidence: The Police, 1980; The Bomb, 1980; The Eagle and the Bear, 1981; The Cold War Game, 1982; The American Dream, 1984; Four Years On—The Bomb, 1984; First Tuesday (Associate Editor/Presenter), 1982–86; for TV-am: Jonathan Dimbleby on Sunday (Presenter/Editor), 1985–86; for BBC TV: On the Record, 1988–93; Election Call, 1992; documentary series, The Last Governor (presenter/producer), 1997; series, Russia: A Journey with Jonathan Dimbleby, 2008; for Central TV: Charles: the private man, the public role (documentary), 1994; for LWT: Jonathan Dimbleby, 1995–2005; for ITV: chief presenter, Gen. Election coverage, 1997, 2001, 2005; An Ethiopian Journey (writer/producer/dir), 1998; A Kosovo Journey (writer/presenter), 2000; Heseltine—A Life in the Political Jungle (writer/presenter), 2000; for Teachers TV: The Big Debate (series), 2006–; Presenter, BBC Radio 4: Any Questions?, 1987–; Any Answers, 1989–; The Candidate, 1998. Pres., Soil Assoc., 1997–; Vice-Pres., CPRE, 1997– (Pres., 1992–97); President: VSO, 1999–; RSPB, 2001–03; Bath Fests Trust, 2003–06 (Chm., 1996–2003); Trustee: Richard Dimbleby Cancer Fund, 1966–; Forum for the Future, 1995–2005. SFTA Richard Dimbleby Award, for most outstanding contribution to factual TV, 1974. *Publications:* Richard Dimbleby, 1975; The Palestinians, 1979; The Prince of Wales: a biography, 1994; The Last Governor, 1997; Russia: a journey to the heart of a land and its people, 2008. *Recreations:* music, sailing, tennis. *Address:* c/o David Higham Associates Ltd, 5 Lower John Street, W1R 4HA.

DIMBLEBY, Josceline Rose; cookery and travel writer; *b* 1 Feb. 1943; *d* of late Thomas Josceline Gaskell and Barbara Montagu-Pollock; *m* 1967, David Dimbleby, *qv* (marr. diss. 2000); one *s* two *d*. *Educ:* Cranborne Chase Sch., Dorset; Guildhall School of Music. Contributor, Daily Mail, 1976–78; cookery writer for Sainsbury's, 1978–; Cookery Editor, Sunday Telegraph, 1982–97. André Simon Award, 1979. *Publications:* A Taste of Dreams, 1976, 3rd edn 1984; Party Pieces, 1977; Josceline Dimbleby's Book of Puddings, Desserts and Savouries, 1979, 2nd edn 1983; Favourite Food, 1983, 2nd edn 1984; Josceline Dimbleby's Complete Cookbook, 1997; Josceline Dimbleby's Cooking Course, 1999; Josceline Dimbleby's Almost Vegetarian Cookbook, 1999; A Profound Secret: May Gaskell, her daughter Amy, and Edward Burne-Jones, 2004, US edn as May and Amy 2005; (for Sainsbury's): Cooking for Christmas, 1978; Family Meat and Fish Cookery 1979; Cooking with Herbs and Spices, 1979; Curries and Oriental Cookery, 1980; Salad for all Seasons, 1981; Marvellous Meals with Mince, 1982; Festive Food, 1982; Swee Dreams, 1983; First Impressions, 1984; The Josceline Dimbleby Collection, 1984; Mai Attractions, 1985; A Traveller's Tastes, 1986; The Josceline Dimbleby Christmas Book 1987; The Josceline Dimbleby Book of Entertaining, 1988; The Essential Joscelin Dimbleby, 1989; The Cook's Companion, 1991; The Almost Vegetarian Cookbook 1994; The Christmas Book, 1994. *Recreations:* singing, travel, photography. *Address:* c/o Lucas Alexander Whitley, 14 Vernon Street, W14 0RJ.

DIMMOCK, Peter, CVO 1968; OBE 1961; Chairman, Zenith Entertainment (formerly Television Enterprise and Asset Management) plc, 1991–2000; *e s* of late Frederick Dimmock, OBE, and Paula Dimmock (*née* Hudd); *m* 1st, 1960, Mary Freya, (Polly) (1987), *e d* of late Hon. Mr Justice Elwes, OBE, TD; three *d*; 2nd, 1990, Christabe Rosamund, *e d* of Sir John Bagge, 6th Bt, ED, DL and *widow* of James Hinton Scott. *Educ* Dulwich Coll.; France. TA; RAF pilot, instr, and Air Ministry Staff Officer, 1939–45 After demobilisation became Press Association correspondent; joined BBC as Televisio Outside Broadcasts Producer and commentator, 1946; produced both studio and outsid broadcasts, ranging from documentaries to sporting, theatrical and public events; ha produced or commentated on more than 500 television relays, including Olympic Game 1948, Boat Race 1949, first international television relay, from Calais, 1950, King Georg VI's Funeral, Windsor, 1952. Produced and directed television outside broadcast of th Coronation Service from Westminster Abbey, 1953; first TV State Opening of Parliament 1958; first TV Grand National, 1960; TV for Princess Margaret's Wedding, 1960. Create BBC Sportsview Unit and introduced new television programme Sportsview, 1954 regular presenter of this live weekly network programme, 1954–64; Gen. Manager an Head of Outside Broadcasts, BBC TV, 1954–72; responsible for Liaison between BB and Royal Family, 1963–77; Gen. Manager, BBC Enterprises, 1972–77; Vice-Pres., AB Worldwide Sales and Marketing TV Sports, 1978–86; Vice-Pres. and Consultant, AB Video Enterprises Div., Capital Cities/ABC Inc., NY, 1984–91; Dir, Entertainment an Sports Cable Network, 1984–90. Chm. Sports Cttee and Adviser, European Broadcastin Union, 1959–72. Mem., Greater London and SE Sports Council, 1972–77; Chm., Sport Develt Panel, 1976–77. FRTS 1978 (Hall of Fame, 1996). Freeman, City of London 1977. *Publications:* Sportsview Annuals, 1954–65; Sports in View, 1964; (contrib.) Th BBC Book of Royal Memories, 1990. *Recreations:* flying, winter sports, golf. *Address:* c/ Coutts & Co., 440 Strand, WC2R 0QS. *Clubs:* Garrick, Boodle's; Berkshire Golf; S Enedoc Golf; New York Athletic.

DIMMOCK, Rear-Adm. Roger Charles, CB 1988; Chairman, Archer Mullins Ltd 1989–2004; *b* 27 May 1935; *s* of late Frank Dimmock and Ivy Dimmock (*née* Archer); *m* 1958, Lesley Patricia Reid; two *d* (and one *d* decd). *Educ:* Price's School. Entered Roya Navy, 1953; pilot's wings FAA, 1954, USN, 1955; qualified Flying Instructor, 1959 Master Mariner Foreign Going Cert. of Service, 1979. Served RN Air Sqdns and HM Ships Bulwark, Albion, Ark Royal, Eagle, Hermes, Anzio, Messina, Murray, Berwic (i/c), Naiad (i/c), to 1978; CSO to FO Carriers and Amphibious Ships, 1978–80; Com RNAS Culdrose, 1980–82; Comd HMS Hermes, 1982–83; Dir, Naval Air Warfare MoD, 1983–84; Naval Sec., 1985–87; FONAC, 1987–88. Dir, Charnauds (formerl Manufg and Marketing Services) Ltd, 1993–98. Mem. Cttee of Management, RNL 1987– (Pres., Denmead and Hambledon Br., 1981–). Chm. Trustees, Fleet Air Arm Museum, 1987–88. President: RN Hockey Assoc., 1985–89; CS Hockey Assoc. 1987–93; Vice Pres., Hockey Assoc., 1997–. Mem., Royal Aero Club, 1988–. *Recreations* hockey (player and umpire), cricket, squash, golf, family, home and garden, RNL *Address:* Beverley House, Beverley Grove, Farlington, Portsmouth PO6 1BP. *T:* (023 9261 7224. *Club:* Royal Navy of 1765 and 1785.

DIMOND, Paul Stephen, CMG 2005; HM Diplomatic Service, retired; Outplacemen Adviser, Foreign and Commonwealth Office, since 2006; Deputy Chairman, JAK Simpson Group plc and JAKS Ltd, since 2007; *b* 30 Dec. 1944; *yr s* of late Cyril Jame Dimond and of Dorothy Mabel Louisa Hobbs (*née* Knight); *m* 1965, Carolyn Susan Davis Mees, *er d* of late Dennis Charles Mees and of Eileen Lilian (*née* Barratt); two *s*. *Educ:* S Olave's and St Saviour's Grammar Sch. for Boys, Bermondsey. FCIM 1989; FCIL (FI 1988). British Bakeries Ltd, 1962–63; FO, 1963–65; Diplomatic Service Admin, 1965–66 Japanese lang. student, Tokyo, 1966–68; Vice-Consul (Commercial), 1968–70, Consu (Commercial), 1970–72, Osaka; Second Sec. (Commercial), Tokyo, 1972–73; seconde to Dept of Trade as assistant to Special Advr on Japanese Mkt, BOTB, 1973–75; FCO 1975–76; First Secretary: (Economic), Stockholm, 1977–80; FCO, 1980–81 (Commercial), Tokyo, 1981–86; FCO, 1986–88; seconded to Smiths Industries plc a Strategic Marketing Advr, Smiths Industries Med. Systems, 1988–89; Commercia Counsellor, Tokyo, 1989–93; Dep. Hd of Mission, The Hague, 1994–97; Consul-Gen. Los Angeles, 1997–2001; Ambassador to the Philippines, 2002–04. Director: Intralink Ltd 2005–; Baillie Gifford Japan Trust plc, 2006–; Westminster Gardens Ltd, 2006– (Chm. 2007–). Fund Develt Officer, British Neurological Res. Trust, 2005–; Sen. Advr, Thin London, 2005–; Global Advr, Oakbridge Internat. Bd, 2006–; Sen. Consultant, ME Internat., 2006–. Sec., First Anglo-Mongolian Round Table, Ulaan Baatar, 1987; Chm. FriendsPhilippines, 2006–. Member: BAFTA, 2002–; Council, Japan Soc., 2005– London Reg. Cttee, RSA, 2005–; Central Council, ROSL, 2006–. Governor: Britis Sch. in the Netherlands, 1994–97; British Film Office, LA, 1998–2000. FRSA 1980 *Recreations:* the arts, vintage Batsfords, walking. *Address:* 100 Westminster Gardens Marsham Street, SW1P 4JG. *Clubs:* Travellers, Royal Over-Seas League.

di MONTEZEMOLO, Luca Cordero; Chairman: Ferrari SpA, since 1991 (Chie Executive Officer, 1991–2006); Fiat SpA, since 2004; *b* Bologna, 1947. *Educ:* Univ. o Rome (Law degree); Columbia Univ., NY (Internat. Commercial Law). Worked wit Chiomenti law firm, Rome; with Bergreen & Bergreen, NY, until 1973; Asst to Enz Ferrari and Team Manager, Maranello racing team, 1973–77 (won 2 Formula 1 worl drivers' championships, 1975 and 1977); Sen. Vice Pres., Ext. Relns, Fiat Gp, 1977–81 Chief Executive Officer: ITEDI SpA (holding co. for Fiat Gp publishing activities) 1981–83; Cinzano Internat. SpA, 1984–86; Dir, Organizing Cttee, 1990 Italian Worl Cup Football Championship, 1986–90; CEO, RCS Video and Mem. Bd of Dirs, TF 1990–91; Chm. and CEO, Maserati SpA, 1997–2005; Chm., Confindustria, 2004–08 Member Board: PPR; Tod's; Merloni Elettrodomestici; Le Monde. Former Presiden Industrialists of Modena; FIEG (Italian Newspaper Publishers Assoc.); President: Bologn Internat. Trade Fair; Libera Università Internazionale degli Studi Sociali; Vice Pres UNICE. Hon. Dr Mech. Engrg Modena. Cavaliere del Lavoro (Italy); Legion d'Honneu (France), 2005. *Address:* Via Nizza 250, 10126 Turin, Italy. *T:* (011) 006111.

DINEEN, Peter Brodrick K.; *see* Kerr-Dineen.

DINES, Rev. Griff; *see* Dines, Rev. P. J. G.

DINES, Peter Munn, CBE 1991; Secretary, School Examinations and Assessmen Council, 1988–91; *b* 29 Aug. 1929; *e s* of Victor Edward Dines and Muriel Eleanor Dine (*née* Turner); *m* 1952, Kathleen Elisabeth Jones; two *s* one *d*. *Educ:* Palmer's Sch., Grays, Essex; Imperial Coll. London (ARCS; BSc 1st cl. 1949); Inst. of Education, London (PGCE 1950); Bristol Univ. (MEd 1968). RAF, 1950–53. Teaching maths, 1953–69; Headmaster, Cramlington High Sch., 1969–76; Jt Sec., Schools Council, 1976–78; Headmaster, Sir John Leman High Sch., Beccles, 1978–80; Examinations Officer, Schools Council, 1980–83; Dep. Chief Exec., 1983–87, Chief Exec., 1988, Secondary Examinations Council. Educn Consultant, British Council, Swaziland, 1993 and Pakistan, 1994. Mem., Schools Broadcasting Council, later Educn Broadcasting Council, 1982–91; occasional broadcaster on radio and TV. *Recreations:* sailing, esp. on W coast of Scotland; walking. *Address:* Applegarth, Middleton, Pickering, N Yorks YO18 8NU.

See also Rev. P. J. G. Dines.

DINES, Rev. (Philip Joseph) Griff, PhD; Business Manager and Associate, Macdonald Associates Consultancy, since 2005; Partner, McDougall Dines LLP, since 2005; *b* 22 June 1959; *s* of Peter Munn Dines, *qv* and Kathleen Elisabeth Dines; *m* 1987, Dr Margaret Owen (marr. diss. 2006); two *d*. *Educ:* Royal Grammar Sch., Newcastle upon Tyne; University Coll. London (BScEng 1980); Clare Coll., Cambridge (PhD 1984); Westcott House, Cambridge; MA (Theol) Manchester 1993. Ordained deacon, 1986, priest, 1987; Curate: St Mary, Northolt, 1986–89; St Paul, Withington, 1989–91; Vicar, St Martin, Wythenshawe, 1991–98, and Priest-in-charge, St Francis, Newall Green, 1995–98; Provost and Rector, St Mary's Cathedral, Glasgow, 1998–2005. Founder Mem., Unicorn Grocery Co-op., Manchester, 1996. Mem., Iona Community, 1999–. *Recreations:* travelling hopefully, exploring the boundaries, art of navigation, sailing. *Address:* 42 Luss Road, Govan, Glasgow G51 3YD; *e-mail:* griff@dines.org.

DINEVOR; *see* Dynevor.

DINGEMANS, James Michael; QC 2002; barrister; a Recorder, since 2002; *b* 25 July 1964; *s* of Rear-Adm. Peter George Valentin Dingemans, *qv*; *m* 1991, Janet Griffiths; one *s* two *d*. *Educ:* Mansfield Coll., Oxford (Rugby Union blue, 1985; BA Jurisprudence 1986). Called to the Bar, Inner Temple, 1987. Leading Counsel to Hutton Inquiry, 2003. Mem., Exec. Cttee, Commonwealth Lawyers' Assoc., 2002–; Vice-Chm., Internat. Relns Cttee, Bar Council, 2006–. Judicial Mem., Adv. Panel, Rugby Football League, 2005–. *Recreations:* Rugby, sailing, cricket. *Address:* 3 Hare Court, Temple, EC4Y 7BJ. *T:* (020) 7415 7800, *Fax:* (020) 7415 7811; *e-mail:* clerks@3harecourt.com. *Clubs:* Broadhalfpenny Brigands Cricket; Bar Yacht.

DINGEMANS, Rear-Adm. Peter George Valentin, CB 1990; DSO 1982; Director, Sussex Innovation Centre Management Ltd, since 2004; Governor, Queen Victoria Hospital Foundation Trust, since 2005; *b* 31 July 1935; *s* of late Dr George Albert and Marjorie Dingemans; *m* 1961, Faith Vivien Bristow; three *s*. *Educ:* Brighton College. Entered RN 1953; served HM Ships Vanguard, Superb, Ark Royal, 1953–57; qualified Torpedo Anti Submarine specialist, 1961; Comd, HMS Maxton, 1967; RAF Staff Course, 1968; Directorate of Naval Plans, 1971–73; Comd, HMS Berwick, HMS Lowestoft, 1973–74; Staff Asst, Chief of Defence Staff, 1974–76; Captain, Fishery Protection, 1977–78; rcds, 1979; Comd HMS Intrepid, 1980–83 (incl. service South Atlantic, 1982); Commodore, Amphibious Warfare, 1983–85; Flag Officer Gibraltar, 1985–87; COS to C-in-C Fleet, 1987–90, retd. Director: Administration, Argosy Asset Management PLC, 1990–91; Ivory and Sime, 1991–92; Hd, Benefits Payroll and Insurances, Slaughter and May, 1992–2001; Strategic Advr, St Dunstan's, 2001–05. President: Royal Naval Assoc., Horsham, 1994–; British Legion, Cowfold, 1994–; Assoc. of Old Brightonians, 1995–97. Mem. Council, Sussex Univ., 1999–2005; Mem. Bd, Brighton Coll., 2001–06 (Mem. Council, 1998–2001). Trustee, Brighton Coll. Scholarship Trust Fund, 1999–. FCMI (FBIM 1990). Freeman, City of London, 1984; Liveryman, Coach Makers and Coach Harness Makers Co., 1984. *Recreations:* family and friends, tennis. *Address:* c/o Lloyds TSB, Steyning, Sussex BN44 3ZA. *Club:* Royal Naval of 1765 and 1785 (Trustee, 1995–, Chm. Trustees, 1996–2006).

See also J. M. Dingemans.

DINGLE, John Thomas, PhD, DSc; President, Hughes Hall, Cambridge, 1993–98 (Hon. Fellow, 1998); *b* 27 Oct. 1927; *s* of Thomas Henry and Violet Nora Dingle; *m* 1953, Dorothy Vernon Parsons; two *s*. *Educ:* King Edward Sch., Bath; London Univ. (BSc, DSc); Clare Coll., Cambridge (PhD). Royal National Hosp. for Rheumatic Diseases, Bath, 1951–59; Research Fellowship, Strangeways Research Laboratory, Cambridge, 1959–61; MRC External Staff, 1961–79; Strangeways Research Laboratory: Head of Tissue Physiology Dept, 1966; Dep. Dir, 1970–79; Dir, 1979–93; Fellow, Corpus Christi Coll., Cambridge, 1968–93 (Life Fellow, 1998); Bursar of Leckhampton, 1972–80, Warden, 1980–86. Co-Dir, Rheumatism Res. Unit, Addenbrooke's Hosp., 1997–2001. Visiting Professor: of Biochemistry, Royal Free Hosp. Med. Sch., 1975–78; of Rheumatology, New York Univ., 1977. Chm., British Connective Tissue Soc., 1980–87. Chm. Editorial Bd, Biochemical Jl, 1975–82. Pres., Cambridge Univ. RFC, 1990–2002 (Treas., 1982–90). Heberden Orator and Medalist, 1978; American Orthopaedic Assoc. Steindler Award, 1980. *Publications:* communications to learned jls. *Recreations:* Rugby football (playing member, Bath, Bristol, Somerset RFCs, 1943–57), sailing. *Address:* Hughes Hall, Cambridge CB1 2EW; Corpus Christi College, Cambridge CB2 1RH; Middle Watch, Mount Boone Hill, Dartmouth, Devon TQ6 9NZ. *Club:* Hawks (Cambridge).

See also T. T. Dingle.

DINGLE, Prof. Robert Balson, PhD; FRSE; Professor of Theoretical Physics, University of St Andrews, 1960–87, now Emeritus; *b* 26 March 1926; *s* of late Edward Douglas Dingle and Nora Gertrude Balson; *m* 1958, Helen Glenronnie Munro; two *d*. *Educ:* Bournemouth Secondary Sch.; Cambridge University. PhD 1951. Fellow of St John's Coll., Cambridge, 1948–52; Theoretician to Royal Society Mond Lab., 1949–52; Chief Asst in Theoretical Physics, Technical Univ. of Delft, Holland, 1952–53; Fellow, Nat. Research Council, Ottawa, 1953–54; Reader in Theoretical Physics, Univ. of WA, 1954–60. *Publications:* Asymptotic Expansions: their derivation and interpretation, 1973; contribs to learned journals. *Recreations:* music, local history, gastronomy. *Address:* 6 Lawhead Road East, St Andrews, Fife, Scotland KY16 9ND. *T:* (01334) 474287.

DINGLE, Timothy Thomas; Headmaster, Royal Grammar School, High Wycombe, 1999–2006; *b* 9 June 1959; *s* of Dr John Thomas Dingle, *qv*. *Educ:* Perse Sch., Cambridge; UEA (BSc 1980; PGCE 1981); Univ. of Westminster (MBA 1998). Mill Hill School: Head of Biology Dept, 1985–90; Housemaster, 1990–95; Dep. Head, 1995–99. Member: Cttee, Nat. Grammar Schs Assoc., 1999–2006; Conservative Party Task Force on Grammar Schs, 2000–06. Nat. Selector (Rugby), 1998; Member: Middlesex RFU, 1985–2001; London and SE RFU, 1990; Cttee, England Schs RFU, 2002 (Chm., 16 Gp, 2003). Governor: Highcrest Community Sch., 2001; Davenies Prep. Sch., 2001. Winston Churchill Fellow, 2002. MInstD. *Publications:* Cartilage Disc Degeneration, 1981; European Dimension in Schools, 1994. *Recreations:* Rugby, cricket, painting, sailing, travel, poetry. *Clubs:* MCC; Cambridge University RUF.

DINGWALL, Baron; *see* Lucas of Crudwell and Dingwall.

DINHAM, Martin John, CBE 1997; Director General, International, Department for International Development, since 2008; *b* 9 July 1950; *s* of late John A. Dinham and Gwenyth Dinham; *m* 1980, Jannie Sanderson; one *s* one *d*. *Educ:* Haberdashers' Aske's Sch., Elstree; Christ's Coll., Cambridge (BA Mod. Langs 1971). Joined ODM, later ODA, as exec. officer, 1974; Asst Private Sec. to successive Ministers for Overseas Develt, 1978–79; Desk Officer for Zambia and Malawi, ODA, 1979–81; on secondment to World Bank, Washington, as Asst to UK Exec. Dir, 1981–83; Hd, Personnel Br., ODA, 1983–85; Private Sec. to successive Ministers for Overseas Develt, 1985–87; Hd, SE Asia Develt Div., ODA, Bangkok, 1988–92; on secondment to Hong Kong Govt as Advr to Governor, 1992–97; Department for International Development: Hd of Personnel and Principal Estabt Officer, 1997–2000; Dir, Asia and the Pacific, then Asia, 2000–04; Dir, Europe, Middle E and Americas, subseq. Europe, Middle E, Americas, Central and E Asia, 2005–07; Dir, UN, Conflict and Humanitarian Div., 2007. *Recreations:* tennis, cinema, planning holidays, rock concerts for the over 50s. *Address:* Department for International Development, 1 Palace Street, SW1E 5HE. *T:* (020) 7023 0674.

DINKIN, Anthony David; QC 1991; barrister; a Recorder of the Crown Court, since 1989; *b* 2 Aug. 1944; *s* of late Hyman Dinkin and Mary (*née* Hine); *m* 1968, Derina Tanya (*née* Green), MBE. *Educ:* Henry Thornton Grammar Sch., Clapham; Coll. of Estate Management, London (BSc (Est. Man.)). Called to the Bar, Lincoln's Inn, 1968, Bencher, 2003. Legal Mem., Lands Tribunal, 1998–; Mem., Mental Health Review Tribunal, 2000–. Examr in Law, Reading Univ., 1985–93; Ext. Examr, City Univ., 2003–. Pres., Estate Mgt Club, 1998–99. *Recreations:* gardening, theatre, music, travel. *Address:* 2–3 Gray's Inn Square, WC1R 5JH. *T:* (020) 7242 4986.

DINWIDDY, Bruce Harry, CMG 2003; HM Diplomatic Service, retired; Governor, Cayman Islands, 2002–05; *b* 1 Feb. 1946; *s* of late Thomas Lutwyche Dinwiddy and Ruth Dinwiddy (*née* Abbott); *m* 1974, Emma Victoria Llewellyn; one *s* one *d*. *Educ:* Winchester Coll.; New Coll., Oxford (MA). Economist, Govt of Swaziland (ODI Nuffield Fellow), 1967–70; Res. Officer, ODI, 1970–73; HM Diplomatic Service, 1973; First Sec., UK Deleg. to MBFR talks, Vienna, 1975–77; FCO, 1977–81; Head of Chancery, Cairo, 1981–83; FCO, 1983–86; Asst Sec., Cabinet Office, 1986–88; Counsellor, Bonn, 1989–91; Dep. High Comr, Ottawa, 1992–95; Head of African Dept (Southern), FCO, 1995–98; Comr (non-resident), British Indian Ocean Territory, 1996–98; High Comr, Tanzania, 1998–2001; on secondment to Standard Chartered Bank, 2001–02. Mem. Council, and Chm., Wider Caribbean Wkg Gp, UK Overseas Territories Conservation Forum, 2006–; Consultant, UK Trade and Investment, 2007–. *Publication:* Promoting African Enterprise, 1974. *Recreations:* golf (captained Oxford *v* Cambridge, 1967), swimming, music. *Address:* 8 Connaught Avenue, East Sheen, SW14 7RH. *Clubs:* Vincent's (Oxford); Aldeburgh Golf, Royal Wimbledon Golf.

DIOUF, Jacques, PhD; Director-General, United Nations Food and Agriculture Organization, since 1994; *b* 1 Aug. 1938; *m* 1963, Aïssatou Seye; one *s* four *d*. *Educ:* Ecole nationale d'agriculture, Grignon-Paris (BSc Agric.); Ecole nationale d'application d'agronomie tropicale, Nogent-Paris, (MSc Trop. Agronomy); Panthéon-Sorbonne, Paris (PhD Agricl Econs). Dir, European Office and Agricl Prog. of Mkting Bd, Dakar/Paris, 1963–64; Executive Secretary: African Groundnut Council, Lagos, 1965–71; W Africa Rice Develt Assoc., Liberia, 1971–77; Sec. of State for Sci. and Technol., Senegal, 1978–83; MP Senegambian Confedn, 1983–84: Chm. and Elected Sec., Foreign Relns Cttee, 1983–84; Chm., Friendship Parly Gp, Senegal-UK, 1983–84; Advr to Pres. and Regl Dir, Internat. Develt Res. Centre, Ottawa, 1984–85; Central Bank for W African States, Dakar: Sec.-Gen., 1985–90; Special Advr to Governor, 1990–91; Ambassador, Senegal Perm. Mission to UN, 1991–93. Comdr Legion of Honour (France), 1998; Grand Comdr, Order of Star of Africa (Liberia), 1977. Comdr, Order of Agricl Merit (Canada), 1995; Grand Cross, Order of Merit in Agric., Fisheries and Food (Spain), 1996; Grand Cross, Order of May for Merit (Argentina), 1998; Order of Solidarity (Cuba), 1998. *Publications:* contrib. to learned jls. *Address:* United Nations Food and Agriculture Organization, Viale delle Terme di Caracalla, 00153 Rome, Italy.

DI PALMA, Vera June, (Mrs Ernest Jones), OBE 1986; FCCA, FTII; Chairman, Mobile Training Ltd, 1978–2003; *b* 14 July 1931; *d* of late William Di Palma and Violet Di Palma; *m* 1972, Ernest Jones (*d* 1995). *Educ:* Haverstock Central Sch., London. Accountant in public practice, 1947–64; Taxation Accountant, Dunlop Co., 1964–67; Sen. Lectr in Taxation, City of London Polytechnic, 1967–71; taxation consultant, 1971–80. Pres., Assoc. of Certified Accountants, 1980–81 (Dep. Pres., 1979–80); Public Works Loan Comr, 1978–2002 (Dep. Chm., 1997–2002); Dep. Chm., Air Travel Trust Cttee, 1986–2000; Mem., VAT Tribunals, 1977–2000; non-exec. Mem., S Warwicks HA, 1991–93. *Publications:* Capital Gains Tax, 1972, 5th edn 1981; Your Fringe Benefits, 1978. *Recreations:* dog-walking, bridge, tennis, dancing, gardening. *Address:* Hogsbottom, North Aston Road, Middle Aston, Oxon OX25 5RH. *T:* (01869) 349242.

DI ROLLO, Simon Ronald; QC (Scot.) 2002; *b* 28 Oct. 1961; *s* of late Rino Di Rollo and of Theresa Di Rollo (*née* de Marco); *m* 1990, Alison Margaret Lafferty; one *s* one *d*. *Educ:* Holy Cross Acad., Edinburgh; Scotus Acad., Edinburgh; Univ. of Edinburgh (LLB Hons 1983; DLP 1984). Admitted: solicitor, 1986; to Faculty of Advocates, 1987; Advocate Depute, 1997. Lectr (pt-time) in Civil Procedure, Univ. of Edinburgh, 1999–. Mem., Sheriff Court Rules Council, 2002–. *Recreations:* Italian, walking, food and drink. *Address:* Advocates' Library, Parliament House, Edinburgh EH1 1RF; *e-mail:* sdirollo@advocates.org.uk; 2 West Savile Road, Edinburgh EH16 5NG. *Club:* Scottish Arts (Edinburgh).

DISKI, Jenny, FRSL; writer, since 1984; *b* 8 July 1947; *d* of James Simmonds (*né* Israel Zimmerman) and Rene Simmonds (*née* Rachel Rayner); *m* 1976, Roger Diski (*né* Roger Marks) (marr. diss. 1993); partner, Ian Patterson. *Educ:* St Christopher's Sch., Letchworth (expelled); King Alfred's Sch., London; Wandsworth Tech. Coll. (Cert. Proficiency for 16mm projection); UCL (BSc Anthropol. unfinished). Teacher: Freightliners Free Sch., 1972–73; Haggerston Comprehensive Sch., 1973–77; Islington 6th Form Centre, 1980–84. FRSL 1999. *Publications:* Nothing Natural, 1986; Rainforest, 1987; Like Mother, 1989; Then Again, 1990; Happily Ever After, 1991; Monkey's Uncle, 1994; The Vanishing Princess, 1995; The Dream Mistress, 1996; Skating to Antarctica, 1997; Don't, 1998; Only Human, 2000; Stranger on a Train, 2002; A View From the Bed, 2003; After These Things, 2004; On Trying to Keep Still, 2006; Apology for the Woman Writing, 2008. *Recreations:* online poker, taking baths, middle-distance staring. *Address:* c/o Derek Johns, A. P. Watt, 20 John Street, WC1N 2DR. *T:* (020) 7405 6774; *e-mail:* djohns@apwatt.co.uk; *web:* www.jennydiski.co.uk.

DISLEY, John Ivor, CBE 1979; Co-founder, and Director, London Marathon Ltd, since 1980; Chairman, London Marathon Trust, since 2006; *b* Gwynedd, 20 Nov. 1928; *s* of Harold Disley and Marie Hughes; *m* 1957, Sylvia Cheeseman; two *d*. *Educ:* Oswestry High Sch.; Loughborough Coll. (Hon. DCL). Schoolmaster, Isleworth, 1951; Chief Instructor, CCPR Nat. Mountaineering Centre, 1955; Gen. Inspector of Educn, Surrey, 1958–71. Director: Ski Plan, 1971–75; Reebok, 1985–95. Member: Adv. Sports Council, 1964–71; Mountain Leadership Trng Bd, 1965–; Canal Adv. Bd, 1965–66; Internat. Orienteering

Fedn, 1972–78; Countryside Commn, 1974–77; Water Space Adv. Council, 1976–81; Royal Commn on Gambling, 1976–78. Vice-Chm., Sports Council, 1974–82; Chairman: Nat. Jogging Assoc., 1978–80; The Olympians, 1996–2002; Pres., Snowdonia Soc., 2003–. Mem., British athletics team, 1950–59; Brit. record holder steeplechase, 1950–56; Welsh mile record holder, 1952–57; bronze medal, Olympics, Helsinki, 1952; Sportsman of the Year, 1955; Athlete of the Year, 1955. *Publications:* Tackle Climbing, 1959; Young Athletes Companion, 1961; Orienteering, 1966; Expedition Guide for Duke of Edinburgh's Award Scheme, 1965; Your Way with Map and Compass, 1971. *Recreations:* orienteering, mountain activities. *Address:* Hampton House, Upper Sunbury Road, Hampton, Middx TW12 2DW. *T:* (020) 8979 1707. *Clubs:* Alpine, Climbers'; Southern Navigators; London Athletic.

See also S. J. Cleobury.

DISMORE, Andrew; MP (Lab) Hendon, since 1997; *b* 2 Sept. 1954; *s* of late Ian and of Brenda Dismore. *Educ:* Warwick Univ. (LLB 1972); LSE, London Univ. (LLM 1976). Educn Asst, GMWU, 1976–78; Partner: Robin Thompson & Partners, Solicitors, 1978–95; Russell Jones & Walker, Solicitors, 1995–2003, consultant, 2003–. Mem. (Lab), Westminster CC, 1982–97 (Leader, Labour Gp, 1990–97). Chm., Jt Cttee on Human Rights, H of C, 2005–; Mem., Standards and Privileges Cttee. *Recreations:* gardening, travel, Greece, Greek culture. *Address:* House of Commons, SW1A 0AA. *T:* (020) 7219 3000.

DISS, Eileen, (Mrs Raymond Everett), RDI 1978; freelance designer for theatre, film and television, since 1959; *b* 13 May 1931; *d* of Thomas and Winifred Diss; *m* 1953, Raymond Everett; two *s* one *d. Educ:* Ilford County High Sch. for Girls; Central Sch. of Art and Design. FRSA. BBC Television design, 1952–59. *Television* series and plays: Maigret, 1962–63; The Tea Party, 1964; Up the Junction, 1965; Somerset Maugham, 1969; Uncle Vanya, 1970; The Duchess of Malfi, and Candide, 1972; The Importance of Being Earnest, and Pygmalion, 1973; Caesar and Cleopatra, 1974; Moll Flanders, 1975; Ghosts, and The Winslow Boy, 1976; You Never Can Tell, 1977; The Rear Column, Hedda Gabler, 1980; The Potting Shed, 1981; Porterhouse Blue, 1987; Behaving Badly, 1989; Jeeves & Wooster, 1989, 1990, and 1992; Best of Friends, 1991; Head Over Heels, 1993; Love on a Branch Line, 1993; A Dance to the Music of Time, 1997; television opera: The Merry Widow, 1968; Tales of Hoffmann, 1969; Die Fledermaus, 1971; Falstaff, 1972; The Yeomen of the Guard, 1974; television films: Cider with Rosie, 1971; Robinson Crusoe, 1974; Longitude, 1999; Dead Gorgeous, 2002. *Theatre:* Exiles, 1969; Butley, 1971; The Caretaker, 1972 and 1991; Otherwise Engaged, 1975; The Apple-cart, 1977; The Rear Column, The Homecoming, 1978; The Hothouse, 1980; Translations, Quartermaine's Terms, Incident at Tulse Hill, 1981; Rocket to the Moon, 1982; The Communication Cord, 1983; The Common Pursuit, 1984; Other Places, The Seagull, Sweet Bird of Youth, 1985; Circe and Bravo, 1986; The Deep Blue Sea, 1988; Veterans Day, The Mikado, Steel Magnolias, 1989; Burn This, 1990; The Philanthropist, 1991; Private Lives, A Month in the Country, 1992; Oleanna, 1993; Pinter Fest., Dublin, 1994; Cell Mates, 1995; Taking Sides, The Hothouse, 1995; Twelve Angry Men, 1996; Ashes to Ashes, 1996; Life Support, 1997; A Letter of Resignation, 1997; The Heiress, 1997; Arcadia, 1999; The Late Middle Classes, 1999; The Room, and Celebration, 2000; Port Authority, and The Homecoming, 2001; The Dwarfs, 2002; The Old Masters, 2004; Endgame, 2006; National Theatre: Blithe Spirit, 1976; The Philanderer, 1978; Close of Play, When We Are Married, 1979; Watch on the Rhine, 1980; The Caretaker, 1980; Measure for Measure, 1981; The Trojan War Will Not Take Place, 1983; Landscape, 1994; No Man's Land, 2001. *Films:* Joseph Losey's A Doll's House, 1972; Sweet William, 1978; Harold Pinter's Betrayal, 1982; Secret Places, 1984; 84 Charing Cross Road, 1986; A Handful of Dust, 1988; August, 1994. Television Design Award, 1962, 1965, 1974, 1992 and 2000, Lifetime Achievement Award, 2006, BAFTA; RTS Lifetime Achievement award, 2002. *Recreations:* music, cinema. *Address:* 4 Gloucester Walk, W8 4HZ. *T:* (020) 7937 8794.

DITLHABI OLIPHANT, Tuelonyana Rosemary; High Commissioner of Botswana to Zambia, also accredited to Tanzania, Uganda, Kenya and Democratic Republic of the Congo, since 2005; *b* 13 Sept. 1954; *d* of late Matlhape Ditlhabi and of Tsetsele Ditlhabi; *m* 1986, Clement S. Oliphant; one *s. Educ:* Univ. of Botswana (BA Admin 1977); Pennsylvania State Univ. (MPA 1981). Joined Public Service, Botswana, 1977: Asst, Sen. and Principal Admin Officer, Min. of Mineral Resources and Water Affairs, 1977–85; transferred to Dept of Foreign Affairs, 1985: Counsellor: Washington, 1985–88; NY, 1988–90; High Comr, Namibia and Ambassador, Angola, 1990–96; Doyenne of Diplomatic Corps and African Gp, 1992–96; High Comr, UK, 1996–98; Dep. Perm. Sec., 1998–99, Perm. Sec. for Pol Affairs, 1999–2005. *Recreations:* music, reading, swimming, squash. *Address:* Botswana High Commission, PO Box 31910, Lusaka, Zambia; *e-mail:* toliphant@gov.bw.

DITTNER, Patricia Ann; *see* Troop, P. A.

DIVALL, Prof. Colin Michael, PhD; Professor of Railway Studies, University of York, and Head, Institute of Railway Studies and Transport History, National Railway Museum and University of York, since 1995; *b* 8 Nov. 1957; *s* of late (Ernest) Gordon Divall and of Gwen(doline) Florence Divall; partner, Karen Hunt. *Educ:* Univ. of Bristol (BSc Physics and Phil. 1979); Victoria Univ. of Manchester (MSc Structure and Orgn of Sci. and Technol. 1980; PhD 1985). Ops mgt, BR, 1984–85; Res. Associate, Centre for Hist. of Sci., Technol. and Medicine, Univ. of Manchester, 1986–88; Sen. Lectr in Social Studies of Technol., Manchester Metropolitan Univ., 1989–94. *Publications:* (with S. F. Johnston) Scaling Up: the Institution of Chemical Engineers and the rise of a new profession, 2000; (with A. Scott) Making Histories in Transport Museums, 2001; (ed with W. Bond) Suburbanizing the Masses: public transport and urban development in historical perspective, 2003. *Recreations:* observing the feline world, listening to jazz, failing to build Wimborne Station at 1/76th scale. *Address:* National Railway Museum, Leeman Road, York YO26 4XJ. *T:* (01904) 686229; Department of History, University of York, Heslington, York YO10 5DD. *T:* (01904) 432990; *e-mail:* cd11@york.ac.uk.

DIX, Geoffrey Herbert, OBE 1979; Secretary-General, The Institute of Bankers, 1971–82; *b* 1 March 1922; *o s* of late Herbert Walter and Winifred Ada Dix; *m* 1945, Margaret Sybil Outhwaite, MA (Cantab) (*d* 1981); one *s. Educ:* Watford Grammar Sch.; Gonville and Caius Coll., Cambridge. MA (Mod. langs). Served War, 1942–45: commissioned into Royal Devon Yeomanry; later served with HQ 1st Airborne Corps. Inst. of Export, 1946–51; with Inst. of Bankers, 1951–82: Asst Sec., 1956; Under-Sec. 1962; Dep. Sec. 1968. Mem., Jt Cttee for National Awards in Business Studies, 1960–76. *Recreations:* Mozart, theatre. *Address:* 2 Kirklands, Old Costessey, Norwich NR8 5BW. *T:* (01603) 745181. *Club:* Caterham Players.

DIX, Prof. Gerald Bennett, RIBA; Lever Professor of Civic Design, University of Liverpool, 1975–88; Professor Emeritus and Hon. Senior Fellow, Liverpool University, since 1988; Hon. Senior Research Fellow, Chinese Research Academy of Environmental Sciences, since 1989; *b* 12 Jan. 1926; *s* of late Cyril Dix and Mabel Winifred (*née* Bennett); *m* 1st, 1956 (marr. diss.); two *s*; 2nd, 1963, Lois Nichols; one *d. Educ:* Altrincham Grammar Sch.; Univ. of Manchester (BA (Hons Arch.), DipTP (dist.)); Harvard Univ. (MLA). Studio Asst, 1950–51, Asst Lectr in Town and Country Planning, 1951–53, Manchester Univ.; Asst Architect, 1954; Chief Architect-Planner, Addis Ababa, and chief asst to Sir Patrick Abercrombie, 1954–56; Planning Officer, Singapore, 1957–59; Acting Planning Adviser, 1959; Sen. Research Fellow, Univ. of Science and Technol., Ghana, 1959–63; UN Planning Mission to Ghana, 1962; Planner, later Sen. Planner, BRS/ODM, 1963–65 (adv. missions to W Indies, W Africa, Aden, Bechuanaland, Swaziland, Cyprus); Nottingham University: Lectr, 1966–68; Sen. Lectr, 1968–70; Prof. of Planning, and Dir, Inst. of Planning Studies, 1970–75; Liverpool University: Chm., Fac. of Social and Environmental Studies, 1983–84; Pro Vice-Chancellor, 1984–87. Dir, Cyprus Planning Project, 1967–71; adv. visits on planning educn, to Uganda 1971, Nigeria 1972, Sudan 1975, Mexico 1978, Egypt 1980; UK Mem., Adv. Panel on planning Canal towns, Egypt, 1974, and Western Desert, 1975; Jt Dir, Alexandria Comprehensive Master Plan Project, 1980–86. Member: Professional Literature Cttee, RIBA, 1966–80, 1981–88 (Chm. 1975–80); Library Management Cttee, 1969–72, 1975–80; Historic Areas Adv. Cttee, English Heritage, 1986–88. Vice-Pres., World Soc. for Ekistics, 1975–79, Pres., 1987–90. Editorial adviser, Ekistics (journal), 1972–; Chm., Bd of Management, Town Planning Rev., 1976–88; (Founder) Editor, Third World Planning Rev., 1978–90. FRTPI (resigned 2001); FRSA. Hon. DEng Dong-A Univ., Korea, 1995. *Publications:* ed, C. A. Doxiadis, Ecology and Ekistics, 1977, Boulder, Colo, 1978, Brisbane, 1978; numerous planning reports to govts in various parts of world; articles and reviews in Town Planning Rev., Third World Planning Rev., Ekistics, RIBA Jl, Arch. Rev. *Recreations:* photography, listening to music, travel, cooking. *Address:* 49 Gaveston Gardens, Deddington, Banbury, Oxon OX15 0NX. *T:* (01869) 336215. *Club:* Athenæum.

DIX, (Walter) Malcolm (Hutton); Secretary, Sport Newcastle, since 2000; *b* 10 May 1942; *s* of Charles Walter Dix and Rita May Dix; *m* 1964, Mary Johanne Nilsen; one *s* four *d. Educ:* Ascham House Sch., Gosforth; St Bees Sch., Cumbria; Coll. of Commerce, Newcastle upon Tyne (Business Studies). Drawing office, Walter Dix & Co., Newcastle, 1958–62; tech. sales rep., William Dickinson, Newcastle, 1962–68; Sales Manager, British Rototherm Ltd, London and S Wales, 1968–71; Chm. and Jt Man. Dir, Walter Dix & Co., Newcastle, 1971–97. Chairman: Newcastle Sports Council, 1977–92; Tyne & Wear Sports Council, 1980–86. Executive Member: NE Fedn of Sport and Recreation, 2000–; NE Sport, 2000–. Sec., Newcastle Sports Develt Trust, 2000–. Chm., Beamish Develt Trust, 1995–99; Dir, Friends of Beamish Mus., 1999–. Chm., Tyne Th. and Opera Hse Preservation Trust, 2002–. Trustee: McCrory Foundn, 2005–; Newcastle Eagles Community Foundn, 2005–. Chm., NE Br., St Beghian Soc., 1992– (Pres., 2006–08). Mem. Council for Northumbria, OStJ, 2004–. Consultant, Special Events Cttee, Variety Club of GB, 2000–. Chairman: Newcastle Supporters Assoc., 1978–82; Newcastle Gosforth Rugby Club, 1989–92 (Sen. Vice-Pres., 1992–95). Outstanding Contribution to Sport award, Newcastle upon Tyne Sports Council, 1992. *Recreations:* walking, reading and writing, music, all types (managed pop groups in the 1960s), driving, practically all sport. *Address:* 41 Ingram Drive, Chapel Park, Newcastle upon Tyne NE5 1TG. *T:* (0191) 267 6342; *e-mail:* Dixysport5@aol.com. *Clubs:* Newcastle United Football (Hon. Life Vice-Pres., 1992); Newcastle Falcons Rugby; Jesmond Lawn Tennis.

DIXEY, John, OBE 1976; Development Co-ordinator, Evening Standard Company, 1987–91; *b* 29 March 1926; *s* of John Dixey and Muriel Doris Dixey; *m* 1948, Pauline Seaden; one *s* one *d. Educ:* Battersea Grammar Sch. Served Royal Marines and Royal Fusiliers, 1944–47. Press Telegraphist, Yorkshire Post and Glasgow Herald, 1948–59; Asst to Gen. Sec., Nat. Union of Press Telegraphists, 1959; Labour Officer, Newspaper Soc., 1959–63; Labour Adviser, Thomson Organisation Ltd, 1963–64; Asst Gen. Manager, Liverpool Daily Post & Echo, 1964–67; Executive Dir, Times Newspapers, 1967–74; Special Adviser to Man. Dir, Thomson Org., 1974; Dir, Newspaper Publishers Assoc. Ltd, 1975–76; Employment Affairs Advr, IPA, 1977–79; Sec., Assoc. of Midland Advertising Agencies, 1977–79; Production Dir and Bd Mem., The Guardian, 1979–84; Asst Man. Dir, Mirror Gp Newspapers, 1985; Newspaper Consultant, 1986. Chm., Advertising Assoc. Trade Union Liaison Group, 1975–84; Mem., TUC New Daily Newspaper Advisory Group, 1982–83. Ward-Perkins Vis. Fellow, Pembroke Coll., Oxford, 1978. Mem., Printing and Publishing Industry Trng Bd, 1975–76; Governor, London Coll. of Printing, 1975–76. *Recreations:* cooking, photography. *Address:* 1 Hornor Close, Norwich NR2 2LY. *T:* (01603) 505656.

DIXIT, Prof. Avinash Kamalakar; John J. F. Sherrerd '52 Professor of Economics, Princeton University, USA, since 1989 (Professor of Economics, 1981–89); *b* 8 June 1944; *s* of Kamalakar Ramchandra Dixit and Kusum Dixit (*née* Phadke). *Educ:* Bombay Univ. (BSc); Cambridge Univ. (BA, MA); Massachusetts Inst. of Technology (PhD). Acting Asst Professor, Univ. of California, Berkeley, 1968–69; Lord Thomson of Fleet Fellow and Tutor in Economics, Balliol Coll., Oxford, 1970–74; Professor of Economics, Univ. of Warwick, 1974–80. Guggenheim Fellowship, 1991–92. Pres., Amer. Economic Assoc., 2008 (Vice-Pres., 2002). Fellow: Econometric Society, 1977 (Pres., 2001); Amer. Acad. of Arts and Scis, 1992; US Nat. Acad. of Scis, 2005. Corresp. FBA 2005. Co-Editor, Bell Journal of Economics, 1981–83. *Publications:* Optimization in Economic Theory, 1976; The Theory of Equilibrium Growth, 1976; (with Victor Norman) Theory of International Trade, 1980; (with Barry Nalebuff) Thinking Strategically, 1991; (with Robert S. Pindyck) Investment Under Uncertainty, 1994; The Making of Economic Policy: a transaction-cost politics perspective, 1996; (with Susan Skeath) Games of Strategy, 1999; Lawlessness and Economics, 2004; several articles in professional jls. *Recreations:* listening to music (pre-Schubert only), watching cricket (when possible). *Address:* Department of Economics, Princeton University, Princeton, NJ 08544–1021, USA. *T:* (609) 2584013; *e-mail:* dixitak@princeton.edu.

DIXON; *see* Graham-Dixon.

DIXON, family name of **Barons Dixon** and **Glentoran**.

DIXON, Baron *cr* 1997 (Life Peer), of Jarrow in the co. of Tyne and Wear; **Donald Dixon;** PC 1996; DL; *b* 6 March 1929; *s* of late Christopher Albert Dixon and Jane Dixon; *m* Doreen Morad; one *s* one *d. Educ:* Ellison Street Elementary School, Jarrow. Shipyard Worker, 1947–74; Branch Sec., GMWU, 1974–79. Councillor, South Tyneside MDC, 1963–81. MP (Lab) Jarrow, 1979–97. An Opposition Whip, 1984–96, Dep. Chief Opposition Whip, 1987–96. Mem. Select Cttee on H of C Services; Chm., PLP Shipbuilding Gp. Freeman of: Jarrow, 1972; S Tyneside, 1998. DL Tyne and Wear, 1997. *Recreations:* football, reading. *Address:* 1 Hillcrest, Jarrow NE32 4DP. *T:* (0191) 897635. *Clubs:* Jarrow Labour, Ex Servicemen's (Jarrow); Hastings (Hebburn).

DIXON, Prof. Adrian Kendal, MD; FRCP, FRCR, FRCS, FMedSci; Professor of Radiology, University of Cambridge, since 1994; Master of Peterhouse, Cambridge, since 2008 (Fellow, since 1986); *b* 5 Feb. 1948; *s* of Kendal Cartwright Dixon and Anne Sybil (*née* Darley); *m* 1979, Anne Hazel Lucas; two *s* one *d. Educ:* Uppingham; King's Coll., Cambridge; St Bartholomew's Hosp. Med. Coll., London; MDCantab 1988. FRCR 1978; FRCP 1991; FRCS 2003. Medical posts in: St Bartholomew's Hosp., 1972–79; Gen. Hosp., Nottingham, 1973–75; Hosp. for Sick Children, Gt Ormond St, 1978; Lectr,

Dept of Radiology, Univ. of Cambridge, 1979–94; Hon. Cons. Radiologist, Addenbrooke's Hosp., Cambridge, 1979–. Visiting Professor: Md and Washington, 1988; Dublin, 1991; Univ. of Otago, NZ, 1992; Stanford, 2002; Edmonton, 2007. Arnott Demonstrator, RCS, 1995; Skinner Lectr, RCR, 1996. Warden, RCR, 2002–06. FMedSci 1998. Hon. Fellow, Faculty of Radiology, RCSI, 1999 (Houghton Medal, 1999); Hon. FRANZCR 2001; Hon. Member: Swedish Soc. of Radiology, 2001; Hungarian Soc. of Radiologists, 2002; Soc. Française de Radiologie, 2003. Editor: Clinical Radiology, 1998–2002; European Radiology, 2007–. *Publications:* Body CT, 1983; CT and MRI, Radiological Anatomy, 1991; Human Cross Sectional Anatomy, 1991, 2nd edn as Human Sectional Anatomy, 1999; (jtly) Diagnostic Radiology, 4th edn, 2002, 5th edn, 2007; papers on computed tomography, magnetic resonance imaging and radiological strategies. *Recreations:* family, golf. *Address:* Peterhouse, Cambridge CB2 1RD. *T:* (01223) 336890.

DIXON, Barry, CBE 2007; QFSM 1999; DL; County Fire Officer and Chief Executive, Greater Manchester County Fire Service, since 2002; *b* 5 Jan. 1951; *s* of Thomas Henry and Ruby Harriet Dixon; *m* 1976, Jill Ormrod; one *s* one *d*. *Educ:* Stand Grammar Sch. Joined Manchester City Fire Bde as jun. fireman, 1967; Gtr Manchester Fire Service, 1974; progressed through ranks; posts in Rochdale, Oldham and Bury; Asst Co. Fire Officer (Ops), 1995–2000; Dep. Co. Fire Officer, 2000–02. DL Gtr Manchester, 2008. *Recreations:* clay pigeon shooting, fishing, countryside in general. *Address:* Greater Manchester County Fire Service, Headquarters, 146 Bolton Road, Swinton, Manchester M27 8US. *T:* (0161) 736 5866, *Fax:* (0161) 743 1777; *e-mail:* postmaster@greatermanchesterfire.gov.uk.

DIXON, Dr Bernard, OBE 2000; science writer and consultant; *b* Darlington, 17 July 1938; *s* of late Ronald Dixon and Grace Peirson; *m* 1963, Margaret Helena Charlton (marr. diss. 1988); two *s* one *d*; partner, Kath Adams. *Educ:* Queen Elizabeth Grammar Sch., Darlington; King's Coll., Univ. of Durham; Univ. of Newcastle upon Tyne. BSc, PhD. Luccock Res. Fellow, 1961–64, Frank Schon Fellow, 1964–65, Univ. of Newcastle; Asst Editor, 1965–66, Dep. Editor, 1966–68, World Medicine; Editor, New Scientist, 1969–79; European Editor: The Scientist, 1986–89; Bio Technology, 1989–97; Amer. Soc. for Microbiol., 1997–; Member, Editorial Board: Biologist, 1988–2005; World Jl of Microbiology and Biotechnology, 1988–2002; Columnist, Current Biol., Lancet, Infectious Diseases. Chm., Cttee, Assoc. of British Science Writers, 1971–72; Member: Soc. for General Microbiology, 1962–; European Assoc. of Sci. Eds, 1980–; Amer. Assoc. for Advancement of Sci., 1980–; CSS, 1982–91 (Vice-Chm., 1989–91); Soc. for Applied Microbiol. (formerly Applied Bacteriol.), 1989–; Amer. Soc. for Microbiol., 1995–; Council, BAAS, 1977–83 (Pres., Section X, 1979; Vice-Pres., Gen. Section, 1986–96); Bd, Edinburgh Internat. Science Fest., 1990–2003. Convenor, Eur. Fedn of Biotechnol. Task Gp on Public Perceptions of Biotechnol., 1996–. FIBiol 1982; CBiol 1984. Hon. DSc Edinburgh, 1996. Charter Award, Inst. of Biol., 1999; Biochemical Soc. Award, 2002. *Publications:* (ed) Journeys in Belief, 1968; What is Science For?, 1973; Magnificent Microbes, 1976; Invisible Allies, 1976; Beyond the Magic Bullet, 1978; (with G. Holister) Ideas of Science, 1984; Health and the Human Body, 1986; Engineered Organisms in the Environment, 1986; Recombinant DNA: what's it all about, 1987; The Science of Science: changing the way we think, 1989; The Science of Science: changing the way we live, 1989; (ed) From Creation to Chaos: classic writings in science, 1989; (with A. L. W. F. Eddleston) Interferons in the Treatment of Chronic Virus Infections of the Liver, 1989; (with E. Millstone) Our Genetic Future: the science and ethics of genetic technology, 1992; Genetics and the Understanding of Life, 1993; Power Unseen: how microbes rule the world, 1994; Enzymes Make the World Go Round, 1994; *contributor to:* Animal Rights—A Symposium, 1979; The Book of Predictions, 1980; Development of Science Publishing in Europe, 1980; Medicine and Care, 1981; From Biology to Biotechnology, 1982; Encyclopædia Britannica, 15th edn, 1984; Encyclopædia Britannica Yearbook, 1986–2001; Inquiry into Life, 1986; The Domesday Project, 1986; Industrial Biotechnology in Europe: issues for public policy, 1986; Biotechnology Information, 1987; Future Earth, 1989; Harrap's Illustrated Dictionary of Science, 1989; Biotechnology—A Brave New World?, 1989; Soundings from BMJ columnists, 1993; Taking Sides: clashing views on controversial issues in health and society, 1993; Wider Application and Diffusion of Bioremediation Technologies, 1996; Biotechnology for Clean Industrial Products and Processes, 1998; numerous articles in scientific and general press on microbiology, and other scientific topics. *Recreation:* listening to Elgar, Mahler and Scottish traditional music, collecting old books. *Address:* 130 Cornwall Road, Ruislip Manor, Middlesex HA4 6AW. *T:* (01895) 632390, *Fax:* (01895) 678645.

DIXON, Bernard Tunbridge; legal consultant; *b* 14 July 1928; *s* of Archibald Tunbridge Dixon and Dorothy Dixon (*née* Cardinal); *m* 1962, Jessie Netta Watson Hastie; one *s* three *d*. *Educ:* Owen's Sch.; University Coll. London (LLB). Admitted Solicitor, 1952 (Edmund Thomas Child Prize); Partner in Dixon & Co., Solicitors, 1952–59; Legal Asst/Sen. Legal Asst with Treasury Solicitor, 1959–67; Sen. Legal Asst with Land Commission, 1967–70; Sen. Legal Asst with Charity Comrs, 1970–74; Dep. Charity Comr, 1975–81; Charity Comr, 1981–84. *Recreations:* photography, exploring Lancashire. *Address:* c/o Maxwell Hodge, 9C Altway, Old Roan, Aintree, Liverpool L10 3JA.

DIXON, Sir (David) Jeremy, Kt 2000; RIBA; architect in private practice; Principal, Dixon Jones Ltd (formerly Jeremy Dixon·Edward Jones), since 1991; *b* 31 May 1939; *s* of late Joseph Lawrence Dixon and Beryl Margaret Dixon (*née* Braund); *m* 1964, Fenella Mary Anne Clemens (separated 1990); one *s* two *d*; partner, Julia Somerville, *qv*. *Educ:* Merchant Taylors' School; Architectural Assoc. Sch. of Architecture (AA Dip. (Hons)). Principal: Jeremy Dixon, 1975–90 (with Fenella Dixon); Jeremy Dixon BDP, 1983–90. Work includes: international competitions, first prize: Northampton County Offices, 1973; Royal Opera House, 1983; Piazzale Roma, Venice, 1990; other competitions won: Tate Gallery Coffee Shop and Restaurant, 1984; Study Centre, Darwin Coll., Cambridge, 1988; Robert Gordon Univ. Residence, Aberdeen, 1991; Portsmouth Univ. Science Bldg, 1993; Nat. Portrait Gallery extension, 1994; Saïd Business Sch., Oxford, 1996; Magna Carta Building, Salisbury Cathedral, 2001; Panopticon, UCL, 2001; Kings Place Develt, 2002; Exhibition Road Project, 2004; other works: reconstruction of Tatlin Tower, 1971; London housing, St Mark's Road, 1975; Compass Point, Docklands, 1989; Henry Moore Sculpture Inst., Leeds, 1988; Sainsbury's superstore, Plymouth, 1991; Regent Palace Development, 2005. Tutor: Architectural Assoc., 1974–83; RCA, 1979–81. Chm., RIBA Regl Awards Gp, 1991–. Exhibitions: Venice Biennale, 1980, 1991; Paris, 1981; Bordeaux Chateau, Paris, 1988. *Recreations:* walking in English landscape, contemporary sculpture and painting, music. *Address:* (office) 2–3 Hanover Yard, Noel Road, N1 8YA. *T:* (020) 7483 8888; *e-mail:* jeremydixon@dixonjones.co.uk.

DIXON, Prof. Gordon Henry, OC 1993; PhD; FRS 1978; FRSC; Professor of Medical Biochemistry, 1974–94, now Emeritus, and Head of the Department, 1983–88, Faculty of Medicine, University of Calgary; *b* 25 March 1930; *s* of Walter James Dixon and Ruth Nightingale; *m* 1954, Sylvia Weir Gillen; three *s* one *d*. *Educ:* Cambs High Sch. for Boys; Trinity Coll., Cambridge (Open Schol. 1948; BA Hons, MA); Univ. of Toronto (PhD). FRSC 1970. Res. Asst Prof., Dept of Biochem., Univ. of Washington, Seattle, USA, 1954–58; Mem. staff, MRC Unit for res. in cell metabolism, Univ. of Oxford, 1958–59; Univ. of Toronto: Res. Associate, Connaught Med. Res. Lab., 1959–60; Associate Prof., Dept of Biochem., 1960–63; Prof., Dept of Biochem., Univ. of BC, Vancouver, 1963–72; Prof., Biochem. Group, Univ. of Sussex, 1972–74. Vis. Fellow Commoner, Trinity Coll., Cambridge, 1979–80. Mem. Exec., IUBMB (formerly IUB), 1988–94; President: Canadian Biochemical Soc., 1982–83; Pan-American Assoc. of Biochemical Socs, 1987–90 (Vice-Pres., 1984–87; Past Pres., 1990–93). Ayerst Award, Canadian Biochemistry Soc., 1966; Steacie Prize, 1966; Flavelle Medal, RSC, 1980; Izaak Walton Killam Meml Prize, 1991. Golden Jubilee Medal, 2002. *Publications:* over 200 pubns in learned jls, incl. Jl Biol Chem., Proc. Nat. Acad. Sci. (US), Nature, and Biochemistry. *Recreations:* hiking, reading, gardening. *Address:* 4402 Shore Way, Victoria, BC V8N 3T9, Canada.

DIXON, (Henry) Joly, CMG 2004; Chairman, Strategic Advisory Board for Intellectual Property, since 2008; *b* 13 Jan. 1945; *s* of late Gervais Joly Dixon and Kay Dixon; *m* 1976, Mary Minch; three *s* two *d*. *Educ:* Shrewsbury Sch.; York Univ. Lecturer in: Econs and Stats, York Univ., 1970–72; Econs, Exeter Univ., 1972–74; European Commission, 1975–2003: Econ. Advr to Jacques Delors, 1987–92; Dir for Internat. Econ. and Financial Affairs, 1992–99; Dep. Special Rep. i/c econ. reconstruction and develt, UN Mission, Kosovo, on secondment, 1999–2001; Principal Advr, Directorate Gen. for Econ. and Financial Affairs, 2001–02; Special Advr to Pascal Lamy, EC, 2003–05; Statistics Comr, 2006–08; Sen. Advr, Office of Chief Economist, EBRD, 2007–. Associate, GPlus Europe, 2006–. Chairman: Indirect Tax Policy Commn, Bosnia and Herzegovina, 2003–04; Governing Bd, Indirect Tax Policy Authority, Bosnia and Herzegovina, 2004–06; Fiscal Policy Panel, Jersey, 2007–. Guest Scholar, Brookings Instn, Washington, 1980. Liveryman, Cordwainers' Co., 1969–. Fellow, Royal Statistical Soc., 2006. *Recreations:* gardening, photography. *Address:* 47 Clanricarde Gardens, W2 4JN; *e-mail:* jdx@skynet.be.

DIXON, Dr Jennifer, FFPH; Director, Nuffield Trust, since 2008; Member Board: Audit Commission, since 2004; Healthcare Commission, since 2005; *b* 25 April 1960; *m* 2002, John Simon Vorhaus; two *d*. *Educ:* Bristol Univ. (MB ChB); London Sch. of Hygiene and Tropical Medicine (MSc Public Health; PhD 2002). FFPH (FFPHM 1999). Harkness Fellow, Commonwealth Fund of NY, 1990–91; Sen. Registrar in Public Health and Hon. Lectr, LSHTM, 1991–95; Fellow, King's Fund Inst., 1995–98; Policy Advr to Chief Exec., NHS, 1998–2000; Dir of Policy, King's Fund, 2000–08. *Publication:* (with A. H. Harrison) The NHS: facing the future, 2000. *Recreation:* reading Russian literature and history. *Address:* The Nuffield Trust, 59 New Cavendish Street, W1G 7LP.

DIXON, Sir Jeremy; *see* Dixon, Sir D. J.

DIXON, John Watts; His Honour Judge Dixon; a Circuit Judge, since 2004; *b* 27 Sept. 1951; *s* of John David Dixon and Carol Emmie Lucinda Dixon; *m* 1980, Catherine Barbara Borton; one *s* four *d*. *Educ:* Harrow Sch.; Queen's Coll., Oxford (MA Jurisprudence). Called to the Bar, Middle Temple, 1975; in practice as barrister, 1975–2004; Legal Reader, Associated Newspapers, 1981–2004; Asst Recorder, 1998–2000, Recorder, 2000–04. Chm., British-Ukrainian Law Assoc., 2000–. Freeman, City of London, 1977. *Recreations:* joys of family life, gardening, cycling, the stage. *Address:* The Law Courts, Winchester, Hants SO23 9EL. *T:* (01962) 814100.

DIXON, Joly; *see* Dixon, H. J.

DIXON, Jon Edmund, CMG 1975; Under Secretary, Ministry of Agriculture, Fisheries and Food, 1971–85; *b* 19 Nov. 1928; *e s* of Edmund Joseph Claude and Gwendoline Alice Dixon; *m* 1953, Betty Edith Stone; two *s* one *d* (and one *d* decd). *Educ:* St Paul's Sch., West Kensington; Peterhouse, Cambridge (Natural Sciences Tripos Part I and Part II (Physiology); MA). Asst Principal, Min. of Agric. and Fisheries, 1952; Private Sec. to successive Parliamentary Secretaries, 1955–58; Principal, 1958; Asst Sec., 1966; Under-Sec., 1971; Minister in UK Delegn, subseq. Office of Permanent Rep., to EEC, 1972–75. Founder, Music Publisher and Gen. Editor, JOED Music, 1988– (editing and publishing Renaissance polyphonic choral music). Recordings: Choral, Organ and String Music: a selection of works by Jon Dixon, 1970–85, 1986; Missa pro defunctis super Regina coeli à 8, 2001. *Publications:* Calico Pie (suite for vocal sextet), 1988; The Leuven Carols, 1988; The Pobble Who Has No Toes (4 part-songs), 1989; Missa pro defunctis super Regina coeli (for double choir), 1999; editions of Renaissance choral music by Aichinger, Animuccia, Arcadelt, Byrd, Clemens, Croce, Dering, Ferrabosco, Festa, A. Gabrieli, G. Gabrieli, Gombert, Guerrero, Hassler, Josquin, Lassus, de Monte, Morales, Mouton, Mundy, Palestrina, Philips, Hieronymus Praetorius, Schütz, Senfl, Sheppard, Taverner, Tallis, de Silva, Victoria (complete works), Walther, White and Willaert; contribs to Early Music News, Early Music Review, Musical Times. *Recreations:* singing, musical composition, oil painting, building harpsichords, gardening, walking.

DIXON, Sir Jonathan (Mark), 4th Bt *cr* 1919, of Astle, Chelford, Co. Chester; *b* 1 Sept. 1949; *s* of Captain Nigel Dixon, OBE, RN (*d* 1978), and of Margaret Josephine Dixon; *S* uncle, 1990; *m* 1978, Patricia Margaret, *d* of James Baird Smith; two *s* one *d*. *Educ:* Winchester Coll.; University Coll., Oxford (MA). *Recreation:* fishing. *Heir: s* Mark Edward Dixon, *b* 29 June 1982.

DIXON, Kenneth Herbert Morley, CBE 1996; DL; Chairman: Joseph Rowntree Foundation, 2001–04; Rowntree (formerly Rowntree Mackintosh) plc, 1981–89, retired; Vice-Chairman, Legal & General Group, 1986–94 (Director, 1984–94); Deputy Chairman, Bass, 1990–96 (Director, 1988–96); *b* 19 Aug. 1929; *yr s* of Arnold Morley Dixon and Mary Jolly; *m* 1955, Patricia Oldbury Whalley; two *s*. *Educ:* Cathedral Sch., Shanghai; Cranbrook Sch., Sydney, Australia; Manchester Univ. (BA(Econ) 1952); Harvard Business Sch. AMP, 1969. Lieut Royal Signals, 1947–49. Calico Printers Assoc., 1952–56; joined Rowntree & Co. Ltd, 1956; Dir, 1970; Chm., UK Confectionery Div., 1973–78; Dep. Chm., 1978–81. Dir, Yorkshire-Tyne Tees (formerly Yorks) TV Hldgs, 1989–97; Mem., British Railways Bd, 1990–97. Member: Council, Incorporated Soc. of British Advertisers, 1971–79; Council, Cocoa, Chocolate and Confectionery Alliance, 1972–79; Council, Advertising Assoc., 1976–79; BIM Econ. and Social Affairs Cttee, 1980–84; Council, CBI, 1981–90 (Mem., Companies Cttee, 1979–84; Mem., Employment Policy Cttee, 1983–90); Governing Council, Business in the Community, 1983–90; Council, Food from Britain, 1986–89; Exec. Cttee, Food and Drink Fedn, 1986–89 (Mem. Council, 1986–87); Council for Industry and Higher Educn, 1986–97; Council, Nat. Forum for Management Educn & Develt, 1987–96; HEQC (Chm., Quality Audit Steering Council, 1993–97); Chm., Cttee of Univ. Chairmen, 1998–2000. Chm., Food Assoc., 1986. Mem. Exec. Cttee and Council, York Civic Trust, 1996–2004. Trustee, Joseph Rowntree Foundn, 1996–2004 (Dep. Chm., 1998). Treas., York Archaeol Trust, 1993–97. Mem. Council, York Univ., 1983–2001 (Chm., 1990–2001), Pro-Chancellor, 1987–2001; Chm., Vis. Cttee, Open Univ., 1990–92. FRSA; CCMI. Member: Co. of Merchant Adventurers, 1981–; Co. of Merchant Taylors, 1981–. DL N Yorks, 1991. Morrell Fellow, Univ. of York, 2007. DUniv: York, 1993; Open, 1997.

Recreations: reading, music, fell walking. *Address:* Joseph Rowntree Foundation, The Homestead, Water End, York YO30 6WP. *T:* (01904) 615901. *Club:* Reform.

DIXON, Dr Michael; Director, The Natural History Museum, since 2004; *b* 16 March 1956; *s* of Walter Dixon and late Sonia Ivy Dixon (*née* Doidge); *m* 1st, 1988, Richenda Milton-Thompson (marr. diss. 1999); one *s* one *d*; 2nd, 2001, Deborah Mary Reece (*née* McMahon); one *s. Educ:* Tiffin Boys' Sch., Kingston-upon-Thames; Imperial Coll., London (BSc; ARCS); Univ. of York (DPhil 1984). Sponsoring Ed., Pitman Publishing Ltd, 1980–83; Publisher, then Publishing Dir, John Wiley & Sons Ltd, 1983–96; Man. Dir, Thomson Sci. Europe, 1996–98; Gp Man. Dir, Sweet & Maxwell Ltd, 1998–99; Dir Gen., Zool Soc. of London, 2000–04. Chief Scientific Advr to Dept of Culture, Media and Sport, 2006–07. Trustee, Internat. Trust for Zool Nomenclature, 2004– (Chm., 2008–). Mem. Council, Royal Albert Hall, 2004–; Member of Court: Univ. of Reading, 2005–; Imperial Coll., London, 2007–. *Recreations:* natural history, photography, music. *Address:* The Natural History Museum, Cromwell Road, SW7 5BD. *Club:* Royal Society of Medicine.

DIXON, Michael David, OBE 2001; General Practitioner; Chairman, NHS Alliance, since 1998; *b* 12 May 1952; *s* of Anthony Neville Dixon and Hazel Dixon; *m* 1982, Joanna Withers-Lancashire; one *s* two *d. Educ:* Eton Coll.; Exeter Coll., Oxford (MA Hons 1973); Guy's Medical Sch. (MB BS 1979). LRCP 1979; DRCOG, MRCOG 1984; FRCGP 2001. House Surgeon, Royal Devon and Exeter Hosp., 1979; House Physician, Guy's Hosp., 1980; Exeter GP Vocational Trng Scheme, 1980–84; GP, College Surgery, Cullompton, 1984–. Chm. NHS Nat. Life Check Bd, 2007–. Hon. Sen. Fellow, Sch. of Public Policy, Univ. of Birmingham, 2004–; Sen. Associate, King's Fund, 2005–; Hon. Sen. Lectr in Integrated Health, Peninsula Med. Sch., 2005–; Vis. Prof., Univ. of Westminster, 2006–. Trustee, Prince's Foundn for Integrated Health, 2003–. *Publications:* (ed jtly) The Locality Commissioning Handbook, 1998; (ed with Kieran Sweeney) The Human Effect in Medicine, 2000; (ed with Kieran Sweeney) A Practical Guide to Primary Care Groups and Trusts, 2001; contrib. articles in all main med. jls. *Recreations:* fishing, gardening, writing. *Address:* College Surgery Partnership, Culm Valley Integrated Centre for Health, Willand Road, Cullompton, Devon EX15 1FE. *T:* (01884) 831300. *Clubs:* Royal Society of Medicine, National Liberal.

DIXON, Peter John Bellett; Chairman: University College London Hospitals NHS Foundation Trust (formerly NHS Trust), since 2001; Housing Corporation, since 2003; Office of Public Management, since 2007; *b* 18 May 1945; *s* of Hugh and Mildred Dixon; *m* 1967, Judith Ann Duckworth; one *s* one *d* (and one *d* decd). *Educ:* Caterham Sch., Surrey; Corpus Christi Coll., Cambridge (MA); London Business Sch. (MSc). Asst Dir, Edward Bates & Sons Ltd, 1975–77; Managing Director: Metal Pretreatments Ltd, 1977–86; Turner Curzon Ltd, 1979–86; British Pepper & Spice Co. Ltd, 1981–83; Hd, Capital Markets, Den norske Bank, 1986–90; Chairman: Ketlon Ltd, 1991–93; Welpac PLC, 1994–95; Union Discount Ltd, 1997–2001; Manifest Voting Agency Ltd, 1998–2005. Chm., Enfield and Haringey HA, 1998–2001. Lay Mem., Inf. Tribunal, 2003–. Board Member: New Islington and Hackney Housing Assoc., 1976–98 (Chm., 1995–98); Focus Housing Gp, 1996–97; English Churches Housing Gp, 2000–01; London & Quadrant Housing Trust, 2001–03; Mem. Council, NHS Confedn, 1998– (Trustee, 2002–). *Recreations:* sailing, mountains, music, theatre. *Address:* The Smea, Hickling, Norfolk NR12 0YL. *T:* (office) (020) 7380 9634; *e-mail:* peterjbdixon@hotmail.com.

DIXON, Dr Philip Willis, FSA, FRHistS; Reader in Archaeology, University of Nottingham, 1996–2003; *b* 2 Jan. 1945; *s* of Dr C. Willis Dixon and Marjorie Dixon (*née* Harbron); *m* 1st, 1968, Doris Janet Davenport Sisson (marr. diss. 1973); 2nd, 1979, Patricia Borne (*d* 1987); 3rd, 2001, Jan White (*née* Greenwood). *Educ:* Tiffin Sch.; New Coll., Oxford (MA 1971; DPhil 1976). FSA 1977; FRHistS 1995. Lectr, 1972–81, Sen. Lectr, 1981–96, Nottingham Univ. Vis. Prof., Univ. of Aarhus, Denmark, 1997, 2006. Comr, Cathedrals Fabric Commn, 1996–2006. Sec., 1981–95, Pres., 1995–98, Council for British Archaeol. Director of excavations: Crickley Hill, Glos, 1969–96; Greenwich Palace, 1970–71; Richmond Palace, 1972, and other sites. Archaeologist: for Cathedrals of Ely, Lincoln, Southwell and Sheffield; for Selby Abbey. *Publications:* Excavations at Greenwich Palace, 1972; Barbarian Europe, 1976; Crickley Hill: the Defences, 1994, the Hillfort Settlement, 2004; Knights and Castles, 2007; (with Jane Kennedy) Mont Orgueil Castle: a review, 2001; Mont Orgueil Castle, 2002; contrib. numerous articles to learned jls. *Recreation:* visiting places, photographing them and consuming their food and drink. *Address:* Castle End, Dunstanburgh Road, Craster, Alnwick, Northumberland NE66 3TT. *T:* (01665) 576064; 24 Crown Street, Newark, Notts NG24 4UY. *T:* (01636) 659464.

DIXON, Piers; *b* 29 Dec. 1928; *s* of late Sir Pierson Dixon (British Ambassador in New York and Paris) and Lady (Ismene) Dixon; *m* 1st, 1960, Edwina (marr. diss. 1973), *d* of Rt Hon. Lord Duncan-Sandys, CH, PC; two *s*; 2nd, 1976, Janet (marr. diss. 1981), *d* of R. D. Aiyar, FRCS, and *widow* of 5th Earl Cowley; 3rd, 1984, Anne (marr. diss. 1985), *d* of John Cronin; one *s*; 4th, 1994, Ann Mavroleon, *d* of John Davenport. *Educ:* Eton (schol.); Magdalene Coll., Cambridge (exhibnr); Harvard Business Sch. Grenadier Guards, 1948. Merchant banking, London and New York, 1954–64; Sheppards and Chase, stockbrokers, 1964–81. Centre for Policy Studies, 1976–78. Contested (C) Brixton, 1966; MP (C) Truro, 1970–Sept. 1974; Sec., Cons. Backbenchers' Finance Cttee, 1970–71, Vice-Chm., 1972–74; sponsor of Rehabilitation of Offenders Act, 1974. *Publications:* Double Diploma, 1968; Cornish Names, 1973. *Recreations:* tennis, modern history. *Address:* 22 Ponsonby Terrace, SW1P 4QA. *T:* (020) 7828 6226. *Clubs:* Brooks's, Pratt's.

DIXON, Prof. Raymond Alan, DPhil; FRS 1999; Research Group Leader, Nitrogen Fixation Laboratory and Department of Molecular Microbiology, John Innes Centre, since 1995; *b* 1 Dec. 1947; *s* of late Henry George Dixon and Emily Dixon (*née* Emmins); *m* 1st, 1971, Ing-Britt Maj Wennerhag (marr. diss. 1980); one *d*; 2nd, 1985, Greta Margaret Dunne (marr. diss. 1995). *Educ:* Univ. of Reading (BSc 1st cl. Hons Microbiology 1969; Univ. of Sussex (DPhil Microbial Genetics 1972). University of Sussex: Postdoctoral Res. Fellow, 1973–75; Higher Scientific Officer, 1975–76, SSO, 1976–78, PSO, 1978–87, SPSO, 1987–95, Unit of Nitrogen Fixation. Hon. Prof., UEA, 1998–. Mem., EMBO, 1987. Fleming Medal, Soc. for Gen. Microbiology, 1984. *Publications:* numerous articles in learned jls. *Recreations:* music, various outdoor pursuits. *Address:* Department of Molecular Microbiology, John Innes Centre, Norwich NR4 7UH. *T:* (01603) 450747.

DIXON, Prof. Richard Newland, PhD, ScD; FRS 1986; CChem, FRSC; Senior Research Fellow, since 1996, and Alfred Capper Pass Professor of Chemistry, 1990–96, now Emeritus Professor, University of Bristol; *b* 25 Dec. 1930; *s* of late Robert Thomas Dixon and Lilian Dixon; *m* 1954, Alison Mary Birks; one *s* two *d. Educ:* The Judd Sch., Tonbridge; King's Coll., Univ. of London (BSc 1951); St Catharine's Coll., Univ. of Cambridge (PhD 1955; ScD 1976). FRSC 1976. Scientific Officer, UKAEA, 1954–56; Res. Associate, Univ. of Western Ontario, 1956–57; Postdoctoral Fellow, NRCC, Ottawa, 1957–59; ICI Fellow, Univ. of Sheffield, 1959–60, Lectr in Chem., 1960–69;

Bristol University: Prof. and Hd of Dept of Theoretical Chemistry, 1969–90; Dean, Faculty of Science, 1979–82; Pro-Vice-Chancellor, 1989–92. Sorby Res. Fellow, Royal Soc., 1964–69; Vis. Schol., Stanford Univ., 1982–83. Leverhulme Emeritus Fellow, 1996–98. Hallam Lectr, Univ. of Wales, 1988; Harkins Lectr, Univ. of Chicago, 1994. Mem. Council, Faraday Div., RSC, 1985–98, Vice-Pres., 1989–98; Mem., and Chm. sub-cttee, Laser Facility Cttee, 1987–90, and Mem., Physical Chem. Cttee, 1987–90, SERC. Non-exec. Dir, United Bristol Healthcare NHS Trust, 1994–2003 (Vice-Chm., 1995–2003). Trustee, Charitable Trusts for United Bristol Hosps, 2003– (Chm., 2006–). Corday-Morgan Medal, Chemical Soc., 1966; RSC Award for Spectroscopy, 1984; Liversidge Lectr and Medal, RSC, 1993–94; Rumford Medal, Royal Soc., 2004. *Publications:* Spectroscopy and Structure, 1965; Theoretical Chemistry: Vol. 1, 1974, Vol. 2, 1975, Vol. 3, 1978; numerous articles in res. jls of chemistry and physics. *Recreations:* mountain walking, travel, theatre, concerts. *Address:* 22 Westbury Lane, Bristol BS9 2PE. *T:* (0117) 968 1691; School of Chemistry, The University, Bristol BS8 1TS. *T:* (0117) 928 7661; *e-mail:* r.n.dixon@bris.ac.uk.

DIXON, Maj.-Gen. Roy Laurence Cayley, CB 1977; CVO 1991; MC 1944; Chapter Clerk, College of St George, Windsor Castle, 1981–90; *b* 19 Sept. 1924; *s* of Lt-Col Sidney Frank Dixon, MC and Edith Mary (Sheena) (*née* Clark); *m* 1986, Anne Maureen Aspeslåen (marr. diss. 1988). *Educ:* Haileybury; Edinburgh Univ. Commnd Royal Tank Regt, 1944; served in armd units and on staff; psc 1956; Instructor, Staff Coll., 1961–64; comd 5th Royal Tank Regt, 1966–67; Comdr Royal Armd Corps, Germany, 1968–70; Royal Coll. of Defence Studies, 1971; qual. helicopter pilot, 1973; Dir, Army Air Corps, 1974–76; Chief of Staff, Allied Forces Northern Europe, 1977–80. Col Comdt, RTR, 1978–83. Vice-Pres., Salisbury Civic Soc., 1998– (Chm., 1991–97). Freeman, City of London, 1990. *Address:* c/o Lloyds TSB, Cox's & Kings Branch, PO Box 1190, 7 Pall Mall, SW1Y 5NA. *Club:* Army and Navy.

DIXON-LEWIS, Prof. Graham, DPhil; FRS 1995; Professor of Combustion Science, University of Leeds, 1978–87, now Emeritus; *b* Newport, Gwent, 1 July 1922; *s* of Daniel Watson Dixon-Lewis and Eleanor Jane Dixon-Lewis; *m* 1950, Patricia Mary Best; one *s* two *d. Educ:* Newport High Sch.; Jesus Coll., Oxford (MA; DPhil 1948). Research Chemist, Courtaulds, 1946–49; Sen. Scientific Officer, Gas Res. Bd, Beckenham, 1949–53; University of Leeds: Gas Council Sen. Res. Fellow, 1953–70; Reader, 1970–78. Vis. Prof., Applied Physics Lab., Johns Hopkins Univ., 1965; Vis. Scientist, Sandia Nat. Labs, Calif, 1987. Alfred Egerton Gold Medal 1990, Silver Medal 1990, Combustion Inst.; Award for Combustion and Hydrocarbon Oxidation Chemistry, RSC, 1993; Dionizy Smoleński Medal, Thermodynamics and Combustion Cttee, Polish Acad. of Scis, 1995. *Publications:* numerous scientific papers on combustion topics, chemically reacting flows, and molecular transport processes. *Recreations:* walking, gardening. *Address:* 16 West Park Grove, Leeds LS8 2HQ. *T:* (0113) 266 2269.

DIXON-SMITH, family name of **Baron Dixon-Smith.**

DIXON-SMITH, Baron *cr* 1993 (Life Peer), of Bocking in Essex; **Robert William Dixon-Smith;** DL; farmer, since 1958; *b* 30 Sept. 1934; 2nd *s* of Dixon Smith, Braintree, Essex and Winifred Smith (*née* Stratton); Dixon Smith adopted by Deed Poll as surname, 1961; *m* 1960, Georgina Janet, *d* of George Cook, Halstead, Essex and Kathleen Cook; one *s* one *d. Educ:* Oundle; Writtle Coll. Nat. Service, 2nd Lt, King's Dragoon Guards, 1955–57. Member: Essex CC, 1965–93 (Chm., 1986–89); Association of County Councils, 1983–93 (Chm., 1992–93). Member: H of L EC Cttee sub-cttee C (Envmt), 1994–96; H of L Select Cttee on Sci. and Technol., 1994–98. Opposition spokesman, House of Lords: on local govt, 1998–2001, on home affairs, 2001–02, on envmtl affairs, 2003–07, on communities and local govt, 2007–. Member: Local Govt Management Bd, 1991–93; Council, Essex Univ., 1991–94; Chm., Anglia Polytechnic Univ., 1992–93. Governor, Writtle Coll., 1967–94 (Chm., 1973–85; Fellow, 1993). Hon. Dr Anglia Poly. Univ., 1995. Freeman, City of London, 1988; Liveryman, Farmers' Co., 1991. DL Essex, 1986. *Recreations:* shooting, fishing, golf. *Address:* Lyons Hall, Braintree, Essex CM7 6SH. *T:* (01376) 326834.

DIXSON, Maurice Christopher Scott, DPhil; FRAeS; Executive Chairman, Cranfield Aerospace Ltd, since 2003; Chairman, Southside Thermal Sciences Ltd, since 2004; *b* 5 Nov. 1941; *s* of late Herbert George Muns Dixson and Elizabeth Eileen Dixson; *m* 1965, Anne Beverley Morris. *Educ:* Palmers Grammar Sch.; University Coll., Swansea (BA Jt Hons); Carleton Univ., Ottawa (MA); Pembroke Coll., Oxford (DPhil). Commercial Exec., Hawker Siddeley Aviation, 1969–74; Contracts Manager, Export, later Commercial Manager, Export, Mil. Aircraft Div., BAC, 1974–80; British Aerospace: Warton Division: Div. Commercial Manager, 1980–81; Exec. Dir, Contracts, 1981–83; Divl Commercial Dir, 1983–86; Military Aircraft Division: Dir-in-Charge, Saudi Arabian Ops, March–Aug. 1986; Commercial Dir and Dir-in-Charge, Saudi Arabian Ops, 1986–87; Chief Exec., Royal Ordnance PLC, 1987–88; Man. Dir, British Aerospace (Commercial Aircraft), 1988–90; Supervisory Man. Dir, Electronic Metrology and Components Groups, and Main Bd Dir, GEC, 1990–93; Chief Exec., Simon Engineering, then Simon Gp, 1993–2002; Dir, Higgs & Hill, then Swan Hill plc, 1994–2003. Chm., Kington Langley Parish Council, 2008–. *Recreations:* played representative soccer at school and university, supporter of Tottenham Hotspur Football Club, fishing, shooting, sport, fine arts, politics and current affairs. *Address:* The Poundhouse, Middle Common, Kington Langley, Chippenham, Wilts SN15 5NW. *Club:* Royal Automobile.

DJANOGLY, Sir Harry Ari Simon, Kt 1993; CBE 1983; non-executive Director, Carpetright plc, 1993–2005; *b* 1 Aug. 1938. Former Man. Dir and Dep. Chm., Vantona Viyella; Chm., Coats Viyella, subseq. Coats, plc, 1999–2003; Dir, 1987–2003, Dep. Chm., 1999–2003, Singer & Friedlander; former Chm., Nottingham Manufacturing Co. Ltd.

DJANOGLY, Jonathan Simon; MP (C) Huntingdon, since 2001; *b* 3 June 1965; *s* of Sir Harry Djanogly, *qv* and Lady Djanogly; *m* 1991, Rebecca Silk; one *s* one *d. Educ:* University Coll. Sch.; Oxford Poly. (BA Hons); Guildford Law Sch. Admitted solicitor 1990; Partner, S J Berwin LLP, 1998–. Mem. (C) Westminster LBC, 1994–2001 (Chairman: Traffic and Works Cttee, 1995; Planning Applications Cttee, 1995; Contracts Cttee, 1996; Social Services Cttee, 1998; Envmt Cttee, 1999). Contested (C) Oxford East, 1997. Shadow Minister, Constitutional, Legal and Home affairs, 2004–05; Shadow Solicitor Gen., and Shadow Trade and Industry Minister, 2005–. Mem., Trade and Industry Select Cttee, 2001–05. Officer, Westminster N Cons. Assoc., 1993–94. *Recreations:* sports, arts. *Address:* House of Commons, SW1A 0AA. *T:* (020) 7219 2367.

DLHOPOLČEK, František, PhD; Deputy Secretary General and Director of Human Resources, Ministry of Foreign Affairs, Slovakia; *b* 13 Sept. 1953; *s* of Jozef Dlhopolček and Anna Pončková; *m* 1977, Dagmar Izraelova; one *s* one *d. Educ:* Sch. of Econs, Banská Bystrica, Czechoslovakia; Diplomatic Acad., Moscow (PhD History and Politology 1989). Univ. Asst Lectr, Sch. of Econs, Banská Bystrica, 1977–79; joined Federal Ministry of Foreign Affairs, Czechoslovakia, 1979: Diplomatic Officer: Nairobi, 1979–83; African Dept, 1983–84; Office of Minister of Foreign Affairs, 1984–87; Dept of Arab and Africa

Countries, 1989–90; Dir, African Dept, 1990–91; Consul-Gen., Pretoria, 1991–92; Ambassador of Czech and Slovak Fed. Republic (subseq. of Slovak Republic) to RSA, 1992–93; Dir-Gen., Political Affairs, Min. of Foreign Affairs 1993–94; Ambassador to Israel, 1994–98; Political Dir Gen., Min. of Foreign Affairs, 1998–2000; Ambassador to UK, 2000–05. *Address:* c/o Ministry of Foreign Affairs, Hlboká 2, 83336 Bratislava, Slovak Republic.

DOBBIE, Dr Robert Charles, CB 1996; public sector consultant; *b* 16 Jan. 1942; *s* of Scott U. Dobbie and Isobel M. Dobbie (*née* Jamieson); *m* 1964, Elizabeth Barbour (separated); three *s. Educ:* Univ. of Edinburgh (BSc); Univ. of Cambridge (PhD). Res. Fellow, Univ. of Alberta, 1966–67; ICI Res. Fellow, Univ. of Bristol, 1967–68; Lectr in Inorganic Chemistry, Univ. of Newcastle upon Tyne, 1968–76; sabbatical, California State Univ., LA, 1974; Tutor, Open Univ., 1975–85; Principal, DTI, 1976–83; Asst Sec., Dept of Industry, 1983–90; Under Sec., DTI, 1990–97; Dir, Merseyside Task Force, 1990–92 (seconded to DoE); Head, Competitiveness Unit (formerly Industrial Competitiveness Div.), DTI, 1992–97; Regl Dir, Govt Office for NE, 1998–2001. Vis. Prof., Univ. of Newcastle upon Tyne, 2002–04. *Publications:* on inorganic and organometallic chemistry. *Recreations:* theatre, hill walking, malt whisky. *Address:* 1 Oak Hill Park, NW3 7LB.

See also S. J. Dobbie.

DOBBIE, Scott Jamieson, CBE 1998; Senior Advisor, Deutsche Bank AG, London, since 1999; Chairman, Securities and Investment Institute (formerly Securities Institute), since 2000; *b* 24 July 1939; *s* of Scott U. Dobbie and Isobel M. Dobbie (*née* Jamieson); *m* 1962, Brenda M. Condie; two *d. Educ:* Dollar Acad.; Univ. of Edinburgh (BSc). Industrial mktg, Unilever, 1961–66, and ICI, 1966–72; Wood Mackenzie & Co., stockbrokers, 1972–88: Partner, 1975–82; Man. Partner, 1982–88; acquired by NatWest Securities, 1988: Man. Dir, 1988–93; Chm., 1993–98; acquired by Bankers Trust Internat., 1998–99 (Vice-Chm.). Chairman: CRESTCo Ltd, 1996–2001; Standard Life European Private Equity Trust, 2001–; Edinburgh Investment Trust PLC, 2003– (non-exec. Dir, 1998–2002); non-executive Director: Murray VCT4 plc, 2000–03; Premier Oil plc, 2000–08; Scottish Financial Enterprise, 2001–05; FRESCO SICAV, 2001–03. Director: SFA, 1993–2001; Financial Services NTO, 2001–04; Comr, Jersey Financial Services Commn, 1999–; Mem., Regulatory Decisions Cttee, FSA, 2001–05. Ind. Mem., Standards Cttee, Corp. of London, 2001– (Chm., 2007–). *Recreations:* mechanical objects, buildings, books. *Address:* Securities and Investment Institute, 8 Eastcheap, EC3M 1AE. *T:* (020) 7645 0600.

See also R. C. Dobbie.

DOBBIN, David; *see* Dobbin, T. D.

DOBBIN, James; MP (Lab and Co-op) Heywood and Middleton, since 1997; *b* 26 May 1941; *s* of William Dobbin and Catherine McCabe; *m* 1964, Pat Russell; two *s* two *d. Educ:* St Columba's High Sch., Cowdenbeath; St Andrew's High Sch., Kirkcaldy; Napier Coll., Edinburgh. Microbiologist, NHS, 1966–94. Mem., Rochdale MBC, 1983–97 (Leader, 1996–97). Contested (Lab) Bury N, 1992. Mem., Eur. Scrutiny Select Cttee, 1998–. Chm., All-Pty Pro Life Gp, 2002–. *Address:* House of Commons, SW1A 0AA; 43 Stonehill Drive, Rochdale, Lancs OL12 7JN.

DOBBIN, (Timothy) David, CBE 2005; Group Chief Executive, United Dairy Farmers Ltd, since 2000; *b* 1 May 1955; *s* of George and Phoebe Dobbin; *m* 1977, Pauline Gregg; two *s. Educ:* Grosvenor Grammar Sch., Belfast; Queen's Univ., Belfast (BSc 1st cl. Hons Mech Engrg). Cert. of Professional Competence in Nat. Road Haulage Ops. CEng, MIMechE 1983. Manfg Manager, Rothmans Internat., 1977–83; Gen. Manager, Northern Publishing Office, 1983–85; Ops Dir, Cantrell & Cochrane, 1985–89; Regl Dir, Dalgety Agriculture, 1989–95; Gp Develt Dir, Boxmore Internat. plc, 1995–2000. Dir, Medevol, 2002–. Non-executive Director: CBI, 2005–08 (Chm., CBI NI, 2003–05); Strategic Investment Bd, 2005–; Mem. Adv. Bd, BT Ireland, 2007–. Vice Chm. and Dir, Belfast Port Employers Assoc., 1989–94; Pres. and Exec. Mem., NI Grain Trade Assoc., 1989–95; Director: Food and Drink Industry Trng Adv. Council NI, 1992–95; LEDU, 1998–2002; Investment Belfast, 1998–2002; Dairy UK and NI Dairy Council, 2002–; NI Food and Drink Assoc., 2002–; Chairman: NI Quality Centre, 1995–97; NI Agricl Res. Council, 1997–2000; Intertrade Ireland, 2007–; UK Internat. Dairy Fedn, 2007–; Member: NI Water Council, 1986–92; Food from Britain Council, 2003–. Chm., Sentinus, 1995–2003; Trustee, Prince's Trust, 2005– (Chm., Prince's Trust NI, 2005–). Hon. DScEcon QUB, 2005. Hon. Chinese Citizenship, Kunshan City, 1998. Lunn's Award for Excellence, IoD, 2008. *Recreations:* golf, gardening, Rugby (spectator only!), music, Irish art. *Address:* Dale Farm House, 15 Dargan Road, Belfast BT3 9LS. *T:* (028) 9037 2237, *Fax:* (028) 9037 2206; *e-mail:* david.dobbin@utdni.co.uk. *Clubs:* Farmers; Ulster Reform; Knock Golf.

DOBBIN, Rev. Dr Victor, CB 2000; MBE 1980; QHC 1993; Chaplain General to the Forces, 1995–2000; *b* 12 March 1943; *s* of late Vincent Dobbin and Annie Dobbin (*née* Doherty); *m* 1967, Rosemary Gault; one *s* one *d. Educ:* Trinity Coll., Dublin (MA 1967); Queen's Univ., Belfast (MTh 1979; PhD 1984). Asst Minister, Rosemary Presbyterian Ch, Belfast, 1970–72; joined RAChD, 1972; Dep. Warden, RAChD Centre, 1982–86; Sen. Chaplain, 3rd Armd Div., 1986–89; Staff Chaplain, HQ BAOR, 1989–91; Sen. Chaplain, SE Dist, 1991–93; Asst Chaplain Gen., Southern Dist, 1993–94. Mem., Council of Reference, Barnabas Fund, 1998–. Hon. DD Presbyterian Theol Faculty, Ireland, 1995. *Recreations:* golf, walking, cycling, reading. *Address:* Glenview, 20 Cushendall Road, Bonamargy, Ballycastle, Co. Antrim, N Ireland BT54 6QR.

DOBBS, Prof. (Edwin) Roland, PhD, DSc; Hildred Carlile Professor of Physics, University of London, 1973–90, and Head of Department of Physics, Royal Holloway and Bedford New College, 1985–90; Emeritus Professor of Physics, University of London, 1990; *b* 2 Dec. 1924; *s* of late A. Edwin Dobbs, AMIMechE, and Harriet Dobbs (*née* Wright); *m* 1947, Dorothy Helena (*d* 2004), *o d* of late Alderman A. F. T. Jeeves, Stamford, Lincs; two *s* one *d. Educ:* Ilford County High Sch.; Queen Elizabeth's Sch., Barnet; University College London. BSc (1st cl. Physics) 1943, PhD 1949; DSc London 1977; FInstP 1964; FIOA 1977. Radar research, Admiralty, 1943–46; DSIR Res. Student, UCL, 1946–49; Lectr in Physics, QMC, Univ. of London, 1949–58; Fulbright Scholar, Applied Maths, 1958–59, Associate Prof. of Physics, 1959–60, Brown Univ., USA; AEI Fellow, Cavendish Lab., Univ. of Cambridge, 1960–64; Prof. and Head of Dept of Physics, Univ. of Lancaster, 1964–73; Bedford College, London University: Head of Dept of Physics, 1973–85; Vice-Principal, 1981–82; Dean, Faculty of Science, 1980–82; Chm., Bd of Studies in Physics, Univ. of London, 1982–85; Vice-Dean, 1986–88, Dean, 1988–90, Faculty of Science, Univ. of London. Member: Physics Cttee, SRC, 1970–73, SERC, 1983–86; Nuclear Physics Bd, SRC, 1974–77; Paul Instrument Fund Cttee, 1984–2002. Visiting Professor: Brown Univ., 1966; Wayne State Univ., 1969; Univ. of Tokyo, 1977; Univ. of Delhi, 1983; Cornell Univ., 1984; Univ. of Florida, 1989; Univ. of Sussex, 1989–2003. Pres., Inst. of Acoustics, 1976–78; Hon. Sec., Inst. of Physics, 1976–84. Convenor, Standing Conf. of Profs of Physics of GB, 1985–88. Member: Caius Coll. Club; Physical Soc. Club. Hon. Fellow: Indian Cryogenics Council, 1977; Inst. of Acoustics, 2007. Freeman, City of London, 2005. *Publications:* Electricity and Magnetism, 1984 (trans. Chinese 1990); Electromagnetic Waves, 1985 (trans. Chinese 1992); Basic Electromagnetism, 1993; Solid Helium Three, 1994; Helium Three, 2001; research papers on metals and superconductors in Procs of Royal Soc., on solid state physics and acoustics in Jl of Physics, Physical Rev. Letters, Physical Acoustics, and on superfluid helium 3 in Jl Low Temperature Physics, etc. *Recreations:* travel, opera, gardening. *Address:* Merryfield, Best Beech Hill, Wadhurst, E Sussex TN5 6JT. *Club:* Athenæum.

See also M. A. Jeeves.

DOBBS, Hon. Dame Linda (Penelope), DBE 2004; **Hon. Mrs Justice Dobbs;** a Judge of the High Court of Justice, Queen's Bench Division, since 2004; *b* 3 Jan. 1951; *m* (marr. diss.). *Educ:* Univ. of Surrey (BSc 1976); London School of Economics and Political Science (LLM 1977; PhD 1980). Called to the Bar, Gray's Inn, 1981, Bencher, 2002; QC 1998; in practice at the Bar, 1982–2004. Chm., Criminal Bar Assoc., 2003–04. *Publications:* (with M. Lucraft) Road Traffic Law and Practice, 1993, 3rd edn 1995; (Contributing Ed.) Archbold, Road Traffic Bulletin, 1998–; (jtly) Fraud: law practice and procedure, 2004. *Recreations:* reading, music, theatre, travel, food and wine. *Address:* Royal Courts of Justice, Strand, WC2A 2LL.

DOBBS, Mattiwilda; Order of North Star (Sweden), 1954; opera singer (coloratura soprano); *b* Atlanta, Ga, USA, 11 July 1925; *d* of John Wesley and Irene Dobbs; *m* 1957, Bengt Janzon, retired Dir. of Information, Nat. Ministry of Health and Welfare, Sweden; no *c. Educ:* Spelman Coll., USA (BA 1946); Columbia Univ., USA (MA 1948). Studied voice in NY with Lotte Leonard, 1946–50; special coaching Paris with Pierre Bernac, 1950–52. Marian Anderson Schol., 1948; John Hay Whitney Schol., 1950; 1st prize in singing, Internat. Comp., Geneva Conservatory of Music, 1951. Appeared Royal Dutch Opera, Holland Festival, 1952. Recitals, Sweden, Paris, Holland, 1952; appeared in opera at La Scala, Milan, 1953; Concerts, England and Continent, 1953; Glyndebourne Opera, 1953–54, 1956, 1961; Covent Garden Opera, 1953, 1954, 1956, 1958; command performance, Covent Garden, 1954. Annual concert tours: US, 1954–; Australia, New Zealand, 1955, 1959, 1968; Australia, 1972, 1977; Israel, 1957 and 1959; USSR concerts and opera (Bolshoi Theater), 1959; San Francisco Opera, 1955; début Metropolitan Opera, 1956; there annually, 1956–64. Appearances Hamburg State Opera, 1961–63; Royal Swedish Opera, 1957 and there annually, 1957–73; Norwegian and Finnish Operas, 1957–64. Vis. Prof., Univ. of Texas at Austin, 1973–74; Professor: Univ. of Illinois, 1975–76; Univ. of Georgia, 1976–77; Howard Univ., Washington, 1977–91. Hon. Dr of Music: Spelman Coll., Atlanta, 1979; Emory Univ., Atlanta, 1980. *Address:* 1101 South Arlington Ridge Road, Apt 301, Arlington, VA 22202, USA.

DOBBS, Michael John; novelist and broadcaster; *s* of Eric William Dobbs and Eileen Dobbs; *m*; four *s. Educ:* Christ Church, Oxford (MA); Fletcher School of Law and Diplomacy, USA (PhD, MALD, MA). Govt Special Adviser, 1981–87; Chief of Staff, Conservative Party, 1986–87; Dep. Chm., Saatchi & Saatchi, 1983–86, 1988–91; Jt Dep. Chm., Cons. Party, 1994–95. Presenter, Despatch Box, BBC, 1999–2001. *Publications:* House of Cards, 1989 (televised, 1990); Wall Games, 1990; Last Man to Die, 1991; To Play the King, 1992 (televised, 1993); The Touch of Innocents, 1994; The Final Cut, 1995 (televised, 1995); Goodfellowe MP, 1996; The Buddha of Brewer Street, 1998; Whispers of Betrayal, 2000; Winston's War, 2002; Never Surrender, 2003; Churchill's Hour, 2004; Churchill's Triumph, 2005; First Lady, 2006; The Lord's Day, 2007; The Edge of Madness, 2008. *Recreations:* genealogy, singing in the bath. *Address:* c/o Bell-Lomax-Moreton, James House, 1 Babmaes Street, SW1Y 6HF; *web:* www.michaeldobbs.com. *Club:* Royal Automobile.

DOBBS, Roland; *see* Dobbs, E. R.

DOBKIN, Ian James; His Honour Judge Dobkin; a Circuit Judge, since 1995; *b* 8 June 1948; *s* of Morris Dobkin, dental surgeon, Leeds, and Rhoda Dobkin; *m* 1980, Andrea, *d* of Jack and Rose Dante; two *s. Educ:* Leeds Grammar Sch.; Queen's Coll., Oxford (Hastings Exhibnr in Classics; BA Jurisp. 1970; MA 1974). Called to the Bar, Gray's Inn, 1971; barrister, North Eastern Circuit, 1971–95; Asst Recorder, 1986–90; Recorder, 1990–95; Liaison Judge, Leeds Area Magistrates' Courts, 2002–07. Judicial Mem., W Yorks Probation Bd, 2002–. Mem., Adv. Cttee, Centre for Criminal Justice Studies, Univ. of Leeds, 1987–. United Hebrew Congregation, Leeds: Vice-Pres., 1981–84 and 1992–96; Pres., 1984–88, 1996–99 and 2005–06; Hon. Life Vice-Pres., 2003; Vice-Chm., Leeds Hillel Foundn, 1989–. Contested (C) Penistone, July 1978, gen. election, 1979. *Recreations:* crosswords, reading, music. *Address:* Leeds Combined Court Centre, Leeds LS1 3BE. *Clubs:* Moor Allerton Golf (Leeds); Yorkshire County Cricket.

DOBLE, Denis Henry; HM Diplomatic Service, retired; Consul-General, Amsterdam, 1991–96; *b* 2 Oct. 1936; *s* of Percy Claud Doble and Dorothy Grace (*née* Petley); *m* 1975, Patricia Ann Robinson; one *d* one *s. Educ:* Dover Grammar School; New College, Oxford (MA Modern Hist.). RAF, 1955–57. Colonial Office, 1960–64; Asst Private Sec. to Commonwealth and Colonial Sec., 1963–64; HM Diplomatic Service, 1965; First Sec., Brussels, 1966–68, Lagos, 1968–72; S Asian and Defence Depts, FCO, 1972–75; First Sec. (Economic), Islamabad, 1975–78; Head of Chancery, Lima, 1978–82; E African Dept, FCO, 1982–84; Actg Dep. High Comr, Bombay, 1985; Deputy High Commissioner: Calcutta, 1985–87; Kingston, 1987–91. Mem. Council, Anglo-Netherlands Soc., 1996–; Member, Committee: BACSA, 1998–; London Br., Oxford Univ. Soc., 2002–. Mem. Council, USPG: Anglicans in World Mission (formerly USPG), 2000–; Member, Committee: Oxford Mission, 2001–; London Br., Prayer Book Soc., 2002–. Member: Battersea Pk Rotary Club, 1998– (Pres., 2003–04); P. G. Wodehouse Soc., 2006–; Life Mem., RAFA. FRGS 1997; Mem., Royal Soc. for Asian Affairs, 1997–. Trustee, Friends of Georgian Soc. of Jamaica, 2007–. SBStJ 1972. *Recreations:* cricket, tennis, long rail and road journeys, British colonial history, English cathedrals, quizzes. *Address:* 38 Eglantine Road, Wandsworth, SW18 2DD. *Clubs:* Royal Commonwealth Society, MCC (Life Mem.); Lord's Taverners; Petworth House Tennis.

DOBLE, John Frederick, OBE 1981; HM Diplomatic Service, retired; High Commissioner to Swaziland, 1996–99; *b* 30 June 1941; *s* of Comdr Douglas Doble, RN and Marcella (*née* Cowan); *m* 1975, Isabella (marr. diss. 1992), *d* of late Col W. H. Whitbread, TD; one *d. Educ:* Sunningdale; Eton (Scholar); RMA Sandhurst; Hertford College, Oxford. 17th/21st Lancers, 1959–69 (Captain); attached Lord Strathcona's Horse (Royal Canadians), 1967–69; joined HM Diplomatic Service, 1969; Arabian Dept, FCO, 1969–72; Beirut, 1972–73; UK Delegn to NATO, Brussels, 1973–77; Commonwealth Dept, FCO, 1977–78; Maputo, 1978–81; Inf. Dept, FCO, 1981–83; attached Barclays Bank International, 1983–85; Consul General, Edmonton, Canada, 1985–89; Consul General, Johannesburg, 1990–94. *Recreations:* mountaineering, history, manual labour. *Address:* Hole Farm, Hockworthy, Devon TA21 0NQ.

DOBREV, Valentin; Ambassador of Bulgaria to the Court of St James's, 1998–2005; *b* Varna, 21 Nov. 1955. Joined Bulgarian Foreign Service, 1982; Trainee Attaché, Budapest, 1982–83; Third Sec., Legal and Treaty Dept, 1984–90, and Head, Law of the Sea and Implementation of Internat. Treaties Sect., 1987–90, Min. of Foreign Affairs; Second Sec.,

Helsinki, 1990–91; Dep. Foreign Minister, 1991–93; Govt Co-ordinator for Bulgaria's accession to Council of Europe and EU, 1992; Ambassador and Perm. Rep. to UN, Geneva, 1993–96; First Dep. Foreign Minister, 1997; Foreign Policy Sec. to Pres. of Bulgaria, 1997–98.

DOBROSIELSKI, Marian, PhD; Banner of Labour, 1st Class 1975 (2nd Class 1973); Knight Cross of the Order of Polonia Restituta, 1964; Professor of Philosophy, Warsaw University, 1974–88; Ambassador *ad personam*, since 1973; *b* 25 March 1923; *s* of Stanislaw and Stefania Dobrosielski; *m* 1950; one *d*. *Educ:* Univ. of Zürich (PhD); Univ. of Warsaw. Served in Polish Army in France, War of 1939–45. With Min. of Foreign Affairs, 1948–81; Polish Legation, Bern, 1948–50; Head of Section, Min. of Foreign Affairs, 1950–54; Asst Prof., Warsaw Univ. and Polish Acad. of Sciences, 1954–57; Mem. Polish delegn to UN Gen. Assembly, 1952, 1953, 1958, 1966, 1972, 1976. First Sec., Counsellor, Polish Embassy in Washington, 1958–64; Min. of Foreign Affairs: Counsellor to Minister, 1964–69; Acting Dir, Research Office, 1968–69; Polish Ambassador to London, 1969–71; Dir, Polish Inst. of Internat. Affairs, 1971–80; Dep. Minister of Foreign Affairs, 1978–81. Univ. of Warsaw: Associate Prof., 1966; Vice-Dean of Faculty of Philosophy, 1966–68; Dir, Inst. of Philosophy, 1971–73 (Chm. Scientific Council, 1969). Chair of Diplomacy, Private Coll. of Business and Admin, Warsaw, 1999–. Chm., Editorial Bd of Studia Filozoficzne, 1968–69; Sec., Polish Philos. Soc., 1955–57 and 1965–69. Chm., Polish Cttee for European Security and Co-operation, 1973–79 (Vice-Chm., 1971–73); Vice-Chm., Cttee on Peace Research, Polish Acad. of Scis, 1984–91; Chm., Scientific Council, Inst. of Peace Res. and Security Policy, Univ. of Hamburg, 1987–97. Hon. Vice-Pres., Scottish-Polish Cultural Assoc., Glasgow, 1969–71; Chm., Polish delegn to: 2nd stage Conf. on Security and Co-operation in Europe, 1973–75; CSCE Belgrade Meeting, 1977–78; CSCE Meeting, Madrid, 1980–81. Chm., Polish Nat. Interest Club, 1991–98. Hon. Mem., World Innovation Foundn, 1999. *Publications:* A Basic Epistemological Principle of Logical Positivism, 1947; The Philosophical Pragmatism of C. S. Peirce, 1967; On some contemporary problems: Philosophy, Ideology, Politics, 1970; (trans. and introd) Selection of Aphorisms of G. C. Lichtenberg, Oscar Wilde, Karl Kraus, M. von Ebner-Eschenbach, Mark Twain, C. Norwid, 1970–85; On the Theory and Practice of Peaceful Coexistence, 1976; Belgrad 77, 1978; Chances and Dilemmas, 1980; The Crisis in Poland, 1984; On Politics and Philosophy, 1988; Philosophy of Reason, 1988; Karl R. Popper's Philosophy of History and Politics, 1991; (jtly) Next Europe, 1993; (jtly) Prominent Diplomats of the XX Century, 1996; Rationalism and Irrationalism, 1999; On History, Myths and Facts - Politico-philosophical Essays, 2004; Poland-Germany-Europe, 2007; numerous articles on philosophy and internat. problems in professional jls. *Address:* Kozia Street 9–14, 00–070 Warszawa, Poland.

DOBRY, His Honour George Leon Severyn, CBE 1977; QC 1969; a Circuit Judge, 1980–92; arbitrator, since 1993; *b* 1 Nov. 1918; *m* 1948, Margaret Headley Smith (*d* 1978); two *d*; *m* 1982, Rosemary Anne Alexander, *qv*. *Educ:* Warsaw Univ.; Edinburgh Univ. (MA). ACIArb. Served War of 1939–45: Army, 1939–42 (despatches); Air Force, 1942–46. Called to Bar, Inner Temple, 1946; Bencher 1977. A Recorder of the Crown Court, 1977–80. Legal Sec., Internat. Commn of Jurists, 1955–57. Founder Member, Justice, 1956–, Mem., Council on Law Reporting, 1984–94. Adviser to Sec. of State for Environment and Sec. of State for Wales on Develt Control, 1973–75; Mem., Docklands Jt Cttee, 1974–76; Inspector, Inquiry into M25, 1978–79; Review of Internat. Legal Relns for Lord Chancellor, 2000. Founder, British Centre for English Legal Studies, Warsaw Univ., 1991. Founder, and Chm. Trustees, Lord Slynn of Hadley European Law Foundn, 1997–2004. Trustee, Roy Jenkins Meml Foundn, 2005–. Founder, British-Polish Legal Assoc. Hon. Dr Juris Warsaw, 1994. Comdr, Starred Cross of Merit (Poland), 1999 (Order of Merit, 1993). Gold Medal, Polish Bar, 1999. *Publications:* Woodfall's Law of Landlord and Tenant, 25th edition (one of the Editors), 1952; Blundell and Dobry, Town and Country Planning, 1962; Blundell and Dobry, Planning Appeals and Inquiries, 1962, 5th edn, as Planning, 1996; Review of the Development Control System (Interim Report), 1972 (Final Report), 1975; (ed jtly) Development Gains Tax, 1975; Hill and Redman, Landlord and Tenant (Cons. Editor), 16th edn, 1976; (Gen. Editor) Encyclopedia of Development Law, 1976; articles on town planning and internat. law. *Address:* 105 Whitelands House, Cheltenham Terrace, SW3 4RA. *T:* (020) 7730 7335; Serle Court, 6 New Square, Lincoln's Inn, WC2A 3QS. *e-mail:* george@georgedobry.com. *Clubs:* Garrick, Beefsteak.

DOBRY, Rosemary Anne; *see* Alexander, R. A.

DOBRYNIN, Anatoly Fedorovich; Hero of Socialist Labour; Order of Lenin (five awards); Order of Red Banner of Labour; Secretary, Central Committee, Communist Party of the Soviet Union, 1986–91; Deputy, Supreme Soviet of the USSR, 1986–91; *b* 16 Nov. 1919; *m* Irina Nikolaevna Dobrynina; one *d*. *Educ:* Moscow Inst. of Aviation, 1942; Higher Sch. of Diplomacy, 1946 (doctorate in History). Asst to Dean of Faculty, Moscow Inst. of Aviation, engr-designer, 1942–44; Official, Min. of For. Affairs, 1946–52; Counsellor, Counsellor-Minister, Embassy to USA, 1952–54; Asst to Minister for For. Affairs, 1955–57; Dep. Sec. Gen., UN, 1957–60; Chief, Dept of Amer. Countries, Min. of For. Affairs, 1960–62; Amb. to USA, 1962–86. Mem., CPSU Central Cttee, 1971–91 (Candidate Mem., 1966–71); Chief, Internat. Dept, CPSU Central Cttee, 1986–91. *Publication:* In Confidence: Moscow's Ambassador to six Cold War presidents, 1995.

DOBSON, Prof. Christopher Martin, DPhil; ScD; FRS 1996; FMedSci; John Humphrey Plummer Professor of Chemical and Structural Biology, University of Cambridge, since 2001; Master, St John's College, Cambridge, since 2007 (Fellow, since 2001); *b* 8 Oct. 1949; *s* of Arthur Dobson and Mabel Dobson (*née* Pollard); *m* 1977, Dr Mary Janet Schove (*see* M. J. Dobson); two *s*. *Educ:* Abingdon Sch.; Keble and Merton Colls, Oxford (BSc, MA, DPhil); ScD Cambridge, 2007. Jun. Res. Fellow, Merton Coll., Oxford, 1974–76; IBM Res. Fellow, Linacre Coll., Oxford, 1976–77; Asst Prof. of Chemistry, Harvard Univ., 1977–80; Vis. Scientist, MIT, 1977–80; University of Oxford: Lectr in Chemistry, 1980–95; Reader in Chemistry, 1995–96; Aldrichian Praelector, 1995–2001; Prof. of Chemistry, 1996–2001; Dir, Oxford Centre for Molecular Scis, 1998–2001; Fellow, LMH, 1980–2001, Emeritus Fellow, 2002, Hon. Fellow, 2008; Lectr, Brasenose Coll., Oxford, 1980–2001. Howard Hughes Med. Inst. Internat. Res. Scholar, 1992–97; Royal Soc. Leverhulme Trust Sen. Res. Fellow, 1993–94; Presidential Vis. Prof., Univ. of Calif at San Francisco, 2001–02; Vis. Prof., Univ. of Florence, 2002–; Dist. Vis. Prof., Rutgers Univ., 2007; Sammet Guest Prof., J. W. Goethe Univ., Frankfurt, 2007. Lectures: Nat., Biophysical Soc., USA, 1998; John S. Colter, Univ. of Alberta, 1998; Frederic M. Richards, Yale Univ., 1999; Cynthia Ann Chan Meml, Univ. of Calif, Berkeley, 1999; A. D. Little, MIT, 2001; Sackler, Univ. of Cambridge, 2002; Royal Soc. Bakerian, 2003; Wills, Univ. of London, 2003; Bayer Dist., Univ. of Washington, St Louis, 2003; Anfinsen Meml, Johns Hopkins Univ., 2003; Joseph Black, Glasgow Univ., 2003; Centenary, Strathclyde Univ., 2004; Presidential, Scripps Res. Inst., La Jolla, 2005; Burroughs Wellcome, Univ. of E Carolina, 2005; 50th Anniv., IUBMB, 2005; Sir John Kendrew, Weizmann Inst., 2005; William H. Stein Meml, Rockefeller Univ., 2006; John D. Ferry, Madison Univ., 2006; Linus Pauling, Stanford Univ., 2006; James B. Sumner, Cornell Univ., 2008; Ada Doiry Meml, Illinois Univ., 2008; Weaver, Univ. of Calif, Davis, 2008. Mem., EMBO, 1999. Pres., Protein Soc., 1999–2001. Fellow, Eton Coll., 2001–. FMedSci 2005. Hon. Fellow, Linacre Coll., Oxford, 2008. For. Hon. Mem., American Acad. of Arts and Scis, 2007. Dr *hc* Leuven, 2001; Liege, 2007; Hon. DM: Umea, Sweden, 2005; Florence, 2006. Corday Morgan Medal and Prize, 1983, Interdisciplinary Award, 1999, RSocChem; Dewey and Kelly Award, Univ. of Nebraska, 1997; Bijvoet Medal, Univ. of Utrecht, 2002; Silver Medal, Italian Soc. of Biochemistry, 2002; Stein and Moore Award, Protein Soc., 2003; Davy Medal, Royal Soc., 2005; Hans Neurath Award, Protein Soc., 2006. *Publications:* numerous contribs to learned jls. *Recreations:* family, friends, travel. *Address:* Department of Chemistry, University of Cambridge, Lensfield Road, Cambridge CB2 1EW. *T:* (01223) 763070, *Fax:* (01223) 763418; *e-mail:* cmd44@cam.ac.uk; Master's Lodge, St John's College, Cambridge CB2 1TP.

DOBSON, Vice-Adm. Sir David (Stuart), KBE 1992; Secretary-General, Institute of Investment Management and Research, later Chief Executive, UK Society of Investment Professionals, 1995–2002; *b* 4 Dec. 1938; *s* of Walter and Ethel Dobson; *m* 1962, Joanna Mary Counter; two *s* one *d*. *Educ:* English School, Nicosia, Cyprus; RN College, Dartmouth. Joined RN 1956; qualified Observer, 1961; served HM Ships Ark Royal, Protector, Eagle; BRNC Dartmouth, 1968–70; Flight Comdr, HMS Norfolk, 1970–72; Staff of FO Naval Air Comd, 1972–74; CO HMS Amazon, 1975–76; Naval Sec's Dept, MoD, 1976–78; Naval and Air Attaché, Athens, 1980–82; Senior Naval Officer, Falklands, 1982–83; Captain 5th Destroyer Sqdn (HMS Southampton), 1983–85; Captain of the Fleet, 1985–88; Naval Sec., 1988–90; Chief of Staff to Comdr Allied Naval Forces Southern Europe, 1991–94. Chm. of Trustees, Hands Around the World, charity, 1995–. Vice-Pres., Royal Star and Garter Home, Richmond, 2004– (Gov., 1996–2003; Chm. Govs, 1999–2003). Mem. Council, Union Jack Club, 1996– (Pres., 2001–). *Recreations:* tennis, hill walking, bird watching, choral singing. *Address:* c/o Lloyds TSB, Petersfield, Hants GU32 3HL. *Clubs:* Army and Navy, Royal Navy of 1765 and 1785 (Chm., 1995–98).

DOBSON, Rt Hon. Frank (Gordon); PC 1997; MP (Lab) Holborn and St Pancras, since 1983 (Holborn and St Pancras South, 1979–83); *b* 15 March 1940; *s* of late James William and Irene Shortland Dobson, York; *m* 1967, Janet Mary, *d* of Henry and Edith Alker; three *c*. *Educ:* Dunnington County Primary Sch., York; Archbishop Holgate's Grammar Sch., York; London School of Economics (BScEcon). Administrative jobs with Central Electricity Generating Bd, 1962–70, and Electricity Council, 1970–75; Asst Sec., Commn for Local Administration (local Ombudsman's office), 1975–79. Member, Camden Borough Council, 1971–76 (Leader of Council, 1973–75); Chm., Coram's Fields and Harmsworth Meml Playground, 1977–. Front bench spokesman on educn, 1981–83, on health, 1983–87; Shadow Leader of the Commons and Party Campaign Co-ordinator, 1987–89; opposition front bench spokesman on energy, 1989–92, on employment, 1992–93, on transport, 1993–94, on London, 1993–97, and on the envmt, 1994–97; Sec. of State for Health, 1997–99. Chm., NHS Unlimited, 1981–89. Governor: LSE, 1986–2001; Inst. of Child Health, 1987–92. *Address:* House of Commons, SW1A 0AA; 22 Great Russell Mansions, Great Russell Street, WC1B 3BE. *T:* (020) 7242 5760. *Club:* Covent Garden Community Centre.

DOBSON, Keith; *see* Dobson, W. K.

DOBSON, Dr Mary Janet; author; Director, Wellcome Unit for the History of Medicine and Reader in the History of Medicine, University of Oxford, 1999–2001; Fellow, Green College, Oxford, 1997–2001; *b* 27 Dec. 1954; *d* of late Derek Justin Schove and of Vera Florence Schove; *m* 1977, Christopher Martin Dobson, *qv*; two *s*. *Educ:* Sydenham High Sch. (GPDST); St Hugh's Coll., Oxford (BA 1st Cl. Hons Geog. 1976); Harvard Univ (AM 1980); Nuffield Coll., Oxford (DPhil 1982). Harkness Fellow, Harvard Univ., 1978–80; University of Oxford: E. P. Abraham and Prize Res. Fellow, Nuffield Coll., 1981–84; Deptl Demonstrator, Sch. of Geog., 1983–89; Lectr in Human Geog., Keble Coll., 1985–88; Res. Fellow, Wolfson Coll., 1987–94; Wellcome Fellow in Health Services Res., Dept of Community Medicine and Gen. Practice, 1989–90; Wellcome Unit for History of Medicine: Wellcome Res. Fellow in Historical Epidemiol., 1990–93; Sen. Res. Officer, 1993–98; Actg Dir and Wellcome Trust Unit Fellow, 1998–99. FRSTM&H 1997. Member: Soc. of Authors, 1996–; Historical Novel Soc., 1997–. *Publications:* Contours of Death and Disease in Early Modern England, 1997; Tudor Odours, 1997; Roman Aromas, 1997; Victorian Vapours, 1997; Reeking Royals, 1998; Vile Vikings, 1998; Wartime Whiffs, 1998; Greek Grime, 1998; Mouldy Mummies, 1998; Medieval Muck, 1998; Messy Medicine, 1999; Disease: the extraordinary stories behind history's deadliest killers, 2008. *Address:* Master's Lodge, St John's College, Cambridge CB2 1TP.

DOBSON, Captain Michael F.; *see* Fulford-Dobson.

DOBSON, Michael William Romsey; Chief Executive, Schroders plc, since 2001; *b* 13 May 1952; *s* of Sir Denis (William) Dobson, KCB, OBE, QC; *m* 1998, Frances, *d* of Count Charles de Salis; two *d*. *Educ:* Eton; Trinity Coll., Cambridge. Joined Morgan Grenfell, 1973: Morgan Grenfell NY, 1978–80, Man. Dir, 1984–85; Hd, Investment Div. 1987–88; Dep. Chief Exec., 1988–89; Gp Chief Exec., Morgan Grenfell, then Deutsche Morgan Grenfell, 1989–97; Mem., Bd of Man. Dirs, Deutsche Bank AG, 1996–2000; Chm., Beaumont Capital Mgt, 2001. *Address:* Schroders plc, 31 Gresham Street, EC2V 7QA.

DOBSON, Sir Patrick John H.; *see* Howard-Dobson.

DOBSON, Prof. Richard Barrie, FSA; FRHistS; FBA 1988; Professor of Medieval History, and Fellow of Christ's College, University of Cambridge, 1988–99; Hon Professor of History, University of York, since 1999; *b* 3 Nov. 1931; *s* of Richard Henry Dobson and Mary Victoria Dobson (*née* Kidd); *m* 1959, Narda Leon; one *s* one *d*. *Educ:* Barnard Castle Sch.; Wadham Coll., Oxford (BA 1st cl. Modern Hist.; MA 1958; DPhil 1963; Hon. Fellow, 1989). Senior demy, Magdalen Coll., Oxford, 1957–58; Lectr in Medieval History, Univ. of St Andrews, 1958–64; University of York: Lectr, Sen. Lectr, Reader, Prof. of History, 1964–88; Dep. Vice-Chancellor, 1984–87. British Acad. Fellow, Folger Shakespeare Liby, Washington, 1974; Cornell Vis. Prof., Swarthmore Coll., USA, 1987; Vis. Fellow, Trinity Coll., Toronto, 1994. FRHistS 1972 (Vice-Pres., 1985–89); FSA 1979; President: Surtees Soc., 1987–2002; Jewish Historical Soc. of England, 1990–91; Ecclesiastical History Soc., 1991–92; Chairman: York Archaeol Trust, 1990–96; Friends of the PRO, 1994–98. Trustee, York Glaziers Trust, 2004–. Life Mem., Merchant Taylors' Co., York (Master, 2003–04). Gen. Editor, Yorks Archaeol. Soc., Record Series, 1981–86. *Publications:* The Peasants' Revolt of 1381, 1971, 2nd edn 1983; Durham Priory 1400–1450, 1973; The Jews of Medieval York and the Massacre of March 1190, 1974; (with J. Taylor) Rymes of Robyn Hood, 1977; (ed) York City Chamberlains' Account 1396–1500, 1980; (ed) The Church, Politics and Patronage in the Fifteenth Century, 1984; (contrib.) A History of York Minster, 1977; (contrib.) History of the University of Oxford, Vol. II, 1993; Church and Society in the Medieval North of England, 1996; (e with D. Smith) The Merchant Taylors of York: a history, 2006; articles in learned jls. *Recreations:* hill walking, cinema, chess, modern jazz. *Address:* Centre for Medieval Studies, University of York, The King's Manor, York YO1 2EP. *T:* (01904) 433910.

DOBSON, Roger Swinburne, OBE 1987; FREng, FICE; Managing Director, Hill Farm Orchards Ltd, since 2000; *b* 24 June 1936; *s* of Sir Denis William Dobson, KCB, OBE, QC and Thelma Swinburne; *m* 2nd, Deborah Elizabeth Sancroft Burrough; one *s* one *d. Educ:* Bryanston Sch.; Trinity Coll., Cambridge (MA); Stanford Univ., Calif (DofEng). FICE 1990; FREng 1993. Qualified pilot, RN, 1955. Binnie & Partners, 1959–69; Bechtel Ltd, 1969–90: Gen. Manager, PMB Systems Engrg, 1984–86; Man. Dir, Laing-Bechtel Petroleum Develt, 1986–90; Dir-Gen. and Sec., ICE, 1990–99. Deputy Chairman: Thomas Telford (Holdings) Ltd, 1990–99; Thomas Telford Ltd (formerly Thomas Telford Services Ltd), 1991–99; Director: Yearco Ltd, 1996–98; Quinco: campaign to promote engineering, 1997–2002 (Founding Chm., 1997–98; Trustee, 1997–2002; Hon. Treas., 1998–2002). Chairman: Computer Aided Design Computer Aided Manufacturing Gp, NEDC, 1981–85; Energy Industries Council, 1987–90; Mem., Construction Industry Sector Gp, NEDC, 1988–92. Dir, Pathfinder Fund Internat., 1997–2002. *Publications:* Applications of Digital Computers to Hydraulic Engineering, 1967; contrib. Procs of ICE and IMechE. *Recreations:* sailing, tennis, fishing, gardening. *Address:* Etchilhampton House, Etchilhampton, Devizes, Wilts SN10 3JH. *Club:* Royal Ocean Racing.

See also M. W. R. Dobson.

DOBSON, Ronald James, QFSM 2005; Commissioner for Fire and Emergency Planning, London Fire Brigade, since 2007; *b* Lambeth, 9 March 1959; *s* of Ronald and Patricia Dobson; *m* 1979, Jacqueline Joy Willson; two *s* one *d.* MIFireE 1996. Joined London Fire Bde, 1979; Asst Divl Officer, 1988–92, Divl Officer, 1992–96, Southwark Trng Centre; Divl Comdr, Ops, Eastern Comd, 1996–2000; Asst Comr, 2000–07. Dir, Chief Fire Officers Assoc., 2007–. Pres., London Fire Bde Retd Mems' Assoc., 2008–. *Recreations:* golf, music, walking. *Address:* London Fire Brigade, 169 Union Street, Southwark, SE1 0LL. *T:* (020) 8555 1200, ext. 30000, *Fax:* (020) 7960 3600; *e-mail:* ron.dobson@london-fire.gov.uk. *Club:* Sunridge Park Golf (Bromley).

DOBSON, Sue; freelance travel writer and editor; Travel Editor, Choice, since 2002 (Editor-in-chief, 1994–2002); *b* 31 Jan. 1946; *d* of Arthur and Nellie Henshaw; *m* 1966, Michael Dobson (marr. diss. 1974). *Educ:* convent schs; BA Hons CNAA. From 1964, worked for a collection of women's magazines, including Femina and Fair Lady in S Africa, variously as fashion, cookery, beauty, home and contributing editor, editor at SA Institute of Race Relations and editor of Wedding Day and Successful Slimming in London, with breaks somewhere in between in PR and doing research into the language and learning of children; Editor, Woman and Home, 1982–94. Mem. Bd, Plan Internat., 1993–2004. *Publications:* The Wedding Day Book, 1981, 2nd edn 1989; Travellers Cape Verde, 2008; Travellers Namibia, 2008. *Recreations:* travelling, photography, reading, exploring.

DOBSON, (William) Keith, OBE 1988; Director, Interstate Programmes Ltd, since 2005; *b* 20 Sept. 1945; *s* of Raymond Griffin Dobson and Margaret (*née* Wylie); *m* 1972, Valerie Guest; two *d. Educ:* King Edward's Grammar School, Camp Hill, Birmingham; Univ. of Keele (BA Internat. Relns 1968); Univ. of Essex (DipSoc 1972). With Clarks Ltd, Shoemakers, 1968–71; British Council, 1972–2000: Lagos, 1972–75; London, 1975–77; Ankara, 1977–80; Caracas, 1980–84; Budapest, 1984–87; London, 1987–90; Europe Div., 1990–93; Dir, Germany, 1993–2000; Sec.-Gen., Anglo-German Foundn, 2000–05. Gov., ESU, 2002–. *Recreations:* music, cinema, bridge, woodworking. *Address:* Interstate Programmes Ltd, 1 Grove Mews, W6 7HS; *e-mail:* keithdobson@interstate.org.uk.

DOCHERTY, Dame Jacqueline, DBE 2004; Executive Director of Nursing and Operations, since 1996, Deputy Chief Executive, since 2007, King's College Hospital; *b* 19 Feb. 1950; *d* of William Docherty and Elizabeth Barrie Docherty. *Educ:* Hairmyres Hosp. (RGN; Gold Medallist); Caledonian Univ. (MBA Dist.; DMS Dist.). Sen. Sister, Royal Free Hosp., London, 1973–79; Nursing Officer, Inverclyde Royal Infirmary, Greenock, 1979–80; Sen. Nurse, Royal Infirmary, Glasgow, 1980–90; Dep. Dir of Nursing, St John's Hosp., W Lothian, 1990–92; Nursing Officer, Scottish Office, DoH, 1992–96. Ind. Consultant, Evidence-based Medicine Prog., Mexican Dept of Health, 1997–2000. Visiting Prof., S Bank Univ., 2004–; KCL, 2006–. Trustee: GNC Trust, 2007–; King's Fund, 2007–. *Publications:* (contrib.) A Critical Guide to the UKCC's Code of Conduct, 1999; contribs to DoH (Scotland) clinical pubns, and various articles in professional jls. *Recreations:* country walks, antiques, music, socialising with friends. *Address:* King's College Hospital NHS Trust, Denmark Hill, SE5 9RS. *T:* (020) 3299 3939, *Fax:* (020) 3299 5665; *e-mail:* jacqueline.docherty@kch.nhs.uk.

DOCHERTY, Michael, FCCA, CPFA; Chief Executive, South Lanarkshire Council, 1999–2006; *b* 12 Jan. 1952; *s* of Michael and Susan Docherty; *m* 1972, Linda Thorpe; two *s* one *d. Educ:* St Mungo's Acad., Glasgow. FCCA 1978; CPFA 1986. Accountancy trainee, S of Scotland Electricity Bd, 1970–74; Accounts Asst, Coatbridge Burgh Council, 1974–75; Accountant: Monklands DC, 1975–77; Stirling DC, 1977–79; Sen. Accountant, 1979–80, Principal Accountant, 1980–82, Monklands DC; Principal Accountant, Renfrew DC, 1982–84; Depute Dir of Finance, Motherwell DC, 1984–92; Dir of Finance, 1992–94, Chief Exec., 1994–95, Hamilton DC; Depute Chief Exec. and Exec. Dir, Corporate Resources, 1995–97, Depute Chief Exec. and Exec. Dir, Enterprise Resources, 1997–99, S Lanarkshire Council. *Recreations:* music, reading, running, golf.

DOCHERTY, Paul Francis; Director, Italy, British Council, since 2003; *b* 17 Sept. 1951; *s* of Joseph Docherty and Elizabeth Eileen Docherty (*née* Waters); *m* 1987, Karen Leithead (marr. diss. 2007); three *s. Educ:* Queen Victoria Sch., Dunblane; Univ. of Strathclyde (BA Hons 1977; MLitt 1985). English teacher, Spain, 1977–83; Lectr in English, Moscow State Univ., 1983–84; joined British Council, 1985: Helsinki, 1986–89; English Language Div., 1989–93; Moscow, 1993–96; Corporate Affairs, 1996–97; Sec., 1997–2000; Dir, Czech Republic, and Cultural Counsellor, Prague, 2000–03. Gov., British Inst., Florence, 2003–. FRSA 2008. *Recreations:* listening to opera, playing blues/rock guitar, film and television. *Address:* c/o British Council, 10 Spring Gardens, SW1A 2BN. *T:* (020) 7930 8466.

DOCKER, Rt Rev. Ivor Colin; Bishop Suffragan of Horsham, 1975–91; an Assistant Bishop, diocese of Exeter, since 1991; *b* 3 Dec. 1925; *s* of Colonel Philip Docker, OBE, TD, DL, and Doris Gwendoline Docker (*née* Whitehill); *m* 1950, Thelma Mary, *d* of John William and Gladys Upton; one *s* one *d. Educ:* King Edward's High Sch., Birmingham; Univ. of Birmingham (BA); St Catherine's Coll., Oxford (MA). Curate of Normanton, Yorks, 1949–52; Lecturer of Halifax Parish Church, 1952–54; CMS Area Sec., 1954–59; Vicar of Midhurst, Sussex, 1959–64; RD of Midhurst, 1961–64; Vicar and RD of Seaford, 1964–71; Canon and Prebendary of Colworth in Chichester Cathedral, 1966–81; Vicar and RD of Eastbourne, 1971–75; Proctor in Convocation, 1970–75. Chm., Nat. Council for Social Concern (formerly C of E Nat. Council for Social Aid), 1987–2001 and 2003– (Vice-Chm., 2002–03); Chm., CARA (Caring and Resource for People with HIV/

AIDS), 1995–97 (Patron, 2001–). *Recreations:* photography, travel, reading. *Address:* Braemar, Bradley Road, Bovey Tracey, Newton Abbot, Devon TQ13 9EU. *T:* (01626) 832468.

DOCKRAY, Prof. Graham John, PhD; FRS 2004; FMedSci; Professor of Physiology, since 1982, Deputy Vice-Chancellor, since 2006, University of Liverpool; *b* 19 July 1946; *s* of Ben and Elsie Dockray; *m* 1985, Andrea Varro; one *s* one *d. Educ:* Univ. of Nottingham (BSc 1st cl. Hons (Zool.) 1967; PhD 1971). University of Liverpool: Lectr in Physiol., 1970–78; Sen. Lectr, 1978–80; Reader, 1980–82; Pro-Vice-Chancellor, 2004–06. Fogarty Internat. Fellow, UCLA/Veterans Hosp., LA, 1973–74. FMedSci 1998. Hon. FRCP 2001. *Publications:* Cholecystokinin (CCK) in the Nervous System: current developments in neuropeptide research, 1987; The Neuropeptide Cholecystokinin (CCK), 1989; Gut Peptides: physiology and biochemistry, 1994; numerous papers in peer-reviewed jls. *Recreation:* gardening. *Address:* Physiological Laboratory, School of Biomedical Sciences, University of Liverpool, Crown Street, Liverpool L69 3BX. *T:* (0151) 794 5324, *Fax:* (0151) 794 5315; *e-mail:* g.j.dockray@liverpool.ac.uk.

DOCTOR, Brian Ernest; QC 1999; *b* 8 Dec. 1949; *s* of Hans and Daphne Doctor; *m* 1973, Estelle Ann Lewin; three *s. Educ:* Balliol Coll., Oxford (BCL); Univ. of Witwatersrand (BA, LLB). Solicitor, 1978–80; Advocate, S Africa, 1980–92; SC S Africa 1990; called to the Bar, Lincoln's Inn, 1991; in practice at the Bar, 1992–. *Recreations:* reading, theatre, opera, tennis, cycling. *Address:* Fountain Court Chambers, Temple, EC4Y 9DH. *T:* (020) 7583 3335.

DOCTOROW, Edgar Lawrence; Glucksman Professor of American and English Letters, New York University, since 1987; *b* 6 Jan. 1931; *s* of David R. Doctorow and Rose Doctorow Buck; *m* 1954, Helen Setzer; one *s* two *d. Educ:* Kenyon College (AB 1952); Columbia Univ. (graduate study). Script-reader, Columbia Pictures, NY, 1956–59; sen. editor, New American Library, 1959–64; editor-in-chief, 1964–69, publisher, 1968–69, Dial Press; writer-in-residence, Univ. of California, Irvine, 1969–70; Mem., Faculty, Sarah Lawrence Coll., NY, 1971–78; Creative Writing Fellow, Yale Sch. of Drama, 1974–75; Vis. Sen. Fellow, Council on Humanities, Princeton, 1980–81. Hon. degrees from Brandeis Univ., Kenyon, Hobart and William Smith Colls. Guggenheim Fellowship, 1972; Creative Arts Service Fellow, 1973–74. *Publications:* Welcome to Hard Times, 1960; Big as Life, 1966; The Book of Daniel, 1971; Ragtime, 1975 (Amer. Acad. Award, Nat. Book Critics Circle Award); Drinks Before Dinner, 1979 (play, 1978); Loon Lake, 1980; Lives of the Poets, 1984; World's Fair, 1985 (Nat. Book Award); Billy Bathgate, 1989 (Howells Medal, Amer. Acad.; PEN/Faulkner and Nat. Books Critics Awards; Premio Letterario Internationale, 1991); The Waterworks, 1994; City of God, 2000; Reporting the Universe, 2003; Sweet Laud Stories, 2004; The March, 2006 (PEN/Faulkner and Nat. Book Critics Circle Awards). *Address:* c/o Random House Publishers, 1745 Broadway, New York, NY 10019, USA. *Club:* Century Association (NY).

DODD, John Stanislaus; QC 2006; a Recorder, since 2000; *b* 3 April 1957; *s* of James and Mary Dodd; *m* 1990, Margaret Ann Roberts; two *s. Educ:* St Aloysius' Coll.; Univ. of Leicester (LLB Hons 1978); London Sch. of Economics. Called to the Bar, Gray's Inn, 1979; barrister, specialist in criminal law. Standing Counsel to HM Customs and Excise, subseq. HMRC, 2002–06. Member: Cttee, SE Circuit, 1995–; Bar Council, 1998–2006; Magistrates' Courts Rules Cttee; Sec., Criminal Bar Assoc., 2002–03. *Recreations:* long-distance cycling, squash, playing violin. *Address:* 2 Bedford Row, WC1R 4BU.

DODD, Kenneth Arthur, (Ken Dodd), OBE 1982; comedian, singer and actor; *b* 8 Nov. 1927; *s* of late Arthur and Sarah Dodd; unmarried. *Educ:* Holt High School, Liverpool. Made professional début at Empire Theatre, Nottingham, 1954; created record on London Palladium début, 1965, by starring in his own 42 week season; his record, Tears, topped British charts for six weeks; awarded numerous Gold, Platinum, and Silver Discs (Love Is Like A Violin, Happiness, etc); has starred in numerous pantomimes (holds box office record at Birmingham Hippodrome), summer seasons and Royal Variety Performances, and travels widely with his Happiness Show; starred in own TV and radio series. Shakespearean stage début as Malvolio in Twelfth Night, Playhouse Th., Liverpool, 1971; film début as Yorick in Hamlet, 1997; Mr Mouse in Alice in Wonderland, C4 TV, 1999. Freeman, City of Liverpool, 2001. Hon. Fellow, Liverpool John Moores Univ., 1997. First member, TV Times Hall of Fame, 2002; Living Legend Award, Brit. Comedy Soc., 2003; Lifetime Achievement Award, Brit. Comedy Awards, 1993; voted Greatest Merseysider of All Time by people of Merseyside, 2003. *Relevant publication:* How Tickled I Am: Ken Dodd, by Michael Billington, 1977. *Recreations:* reading, relaxing. *Address:* 76 Thomas Lane, Knotty Ash, Liverpool L14 5NX.

DODD, Philip; Founder, Made in China, consultancy, 2004; *b* Grimethorpe, 25 Oct. 1949; *s* of Ernest and Mavis Dodd; *m* 1976, Kathryn; two *s. Educ:* UC, Swansea (BA Hons); Univ. of Leicester (MA). Lectr in English Literature, Univ. of Leicester, 1976–89; Dep. Editor, New Statesman and Society, 1989–90; Editor, Sight and Sound, BFI, 1990–97; Dir, ICA, 1997–2004. Visiting Professor: KCL, 2000–03; Univ. of the Arts London, 2004–. Consultant, Music and Arts: BBC, 1986–91; Wall to Wall TV, 1991–97. Presenter, Night Waves, BBC Radio 3, 2000–. Chief Internat. Advr, Shanghai eArts Festival, 2007–; Advr, Beijing Internat. Cultural and Creative Industry Expo, 2008. Small Publisher of the Year, PPA, 1993; Sony Radio Award, 1996. *Publications:* (ed jtly) Englishness: politics and culture 1880–1920, 1986; (jtly) Relative Values: what's art worth, 1991; The Battle over Britain, 1995; (ed jtly) Spellbound, Art and Film, 1996.

DODD, Philip Kevin, OBE 1987; a District Judge (Magistrates' Courts) (formerly Stipendiary Magistrate), Cheshire, 1991–2004; *b* 2 April 1938; *s* of Thomas and Mary Dodd; *m* 1962, Kathleen Scott; one *s* one *d. Educ:* St Joseph's Coll., Dumfries; Leeds Univ. (BA, LLB). Admitted Solicitor, 1966. Articled Clerk, Ashton-under-Lyne Magistrates' Court, 1961–63; Dep. Justices' Clerk, 1963–67; Justices' Clerk: Houghton-le-Spring and Seaham, 1967–70; Wolverhampton, 1970–76; Manchester, 1976–91. Council Member: Justices' Clerks' Soc., 1974–89 (Pres., 1985–86); Manchester Law Soc., 1978–91 (Pres., 1987–88). Sec., Standing Conf., Clerks to Magistrates' Courts Cttees, 1974–82 (Chm., 1983–84). *Recreation:* planning holidays.

DODDS, Nigel Alexander, OBE 1997; MP (DemU) Belfast North, since 2001; Member (DemU) Belfast North, Northern Ireland Assembly, since 1998; Minister for Enterprise, Trade and Investment, Northern Ireland, since 2007; barrister; *b* 20 Aug. 1958; *s* of Joseph Alexander and Doreen Elizabeth Dodds; *m* 1985, Diana Jean Harris; two *s* one *d. Educ:* Portora Royal Sch., Enniskillen; St John's Coll., Cambridge (MA); Inst. of Professional Legal Studies, Belfast (Cert. of Professional Legal Studies). Called to the Bar, NI, 1981. Mem., Belfast City Council, 1985– (Chairman: F and GP Cttee, 1985–87; Develt Cttee, 1997–); Lord Mayor of Belfast, 1988–89 and 1991–92; Alderman, Castle Area, 1989–97. Minister for Social Develt, NI, 1999–2000 and 2001–02. Vice Pres., Assoc. of Local Authorities of NI, 1988–89. Mem., NI Forum, 1996–98. Mem., Senate, QUB, 1987–93. *Address:* City Hall, Belfast BT1 5GS; House of Commons, SW1A 0AA.

DODDS, Sir Ralph (Jordan), 2nd Bt *cr* 1964; *b* 25 March 1928; *o s* of Sir (Edward) Charles Dodds, 1st Bt, MVO, FRS, and Constance Elizabeth (*d* 1969), *o d* of late J. T. Jordan, Darlington; *S* father, 1973; *m* 1954, Marion, *er d* of late Sir Daniel Thomas Davies, KCVO; two *d*. *Educ:* Winchester; RMA, Sandhurst. Regular commission, 13/18th Royal Hussars, 1948; served UK and abroad; Malaya, 1953 (despatches); resigned, 1958. Underwriting Member of Lloyd's, 1964–97. *Address:* 49 Sussex Square, W2 2SP. *Clubs:* Cavalry and Guards, Hurlingham.

DODDS, (Robert) Stephen; His Honour Judge Dodds; a Circuit Judge, since 2007; *b* Blackburn, 6 Nov. 1952; *s* of George Dodds and Edith Mary Dodds; *m* 1980, Kathryn Hadley; one *s* one *d*. *Educ:* Queen Elizabeth's Grammar Sch., Blackburn; Leeds Poly. (LLB); Coll. of Law. Called to the Bar, Gray's Inn, 1976; Asst Recorder, 1995–99; Recorder, 1999–2007. Asst Parly Boundary Comr, 2003–07. *Recreations:* watching Blackburn Rovers FC, collecting football programmes, collecting malt whisky, reading, cricket (Lancashire CCC). *Address:* Lancaster Crown Court, 2nd Floor, Mitre House, Church Street, Lancaster LA1 1UZ. *T:* (01524) 68112. *Club:* District and Union (Blackburn).

DODGSHON, Prof. Robert Andrew, PhD; FBA 2002; Gregynog Professor of Human Geography, Institute of Geography and Earth Sciences, University of Wales, Aberystwyth, 2001–07, now Emeritus (Director, 1998–2003); *b* 8 Dec. 1941; *s* of Robert and Dorothy Dodgshon; *m* 1969, Katherine Simmonds; two *d*. *Educ:* Liverpool Univ. (BA 1963, PhD 1969). Asst Keeper, Mus. of English Rural Life, Univ. of Reading, 1966–70; Lectr, 1970–80, Sen. Lectr, 1980–84, Reader, 1984–88, Prof., 1988–2001, UCW Aberystwyth, subseq. Univ. of Wales, Aberystwyth. Council Member: Countryside Council for Wales, 1997–2004; NT, 2001–; Mem., JNCC, 2003–04. Pres., Soc. for Landscape Studies, 1997–. Murchison Award, RGS, 1996; Scottish Geographical Medal, RSGS, 2003. *Publications:* (ed jtly) An Historical Geography of England and Wales, 1978, 2nd edn 1990; The Origin of British Field Systems, 1980; Land and Society in Early Scotland, 1980; The European Past, 1987; From Chiefs to Landlords, 1998; Society in Time and Space, 1998; (ed jtly) An Historical Geography of Europe, 1998; The Age of the Clans, 2002. *Recreations:* travel, landscape, walking, music. *Address:* Institute of Geography and Earth Sciences, Aberystwyth University, Aberystwyth, Ceredigion SY23 3DB. *T:* (01970) 622631, *Fax:* (01970) 622659; *e-mail:* rad@aber.ac.uk.

DODGSON, Clare; Independent Director, Agriculture and Horticulture Development Board, Department for Environment, Food and Rural Affairs, since 2007; *b* 10 Sept. 1962; *d* of William Baxter and Ann Baxter (*née* Mattimoe); *m* 1988, Gerard Dodgson. *Educ:* St Robert of Newminster Sch., Washington; Newcastle Business Sch. (MBA). Dir of Planning and Service Develt, S Tyneside FHSA, 1990–92; Chief Executive: Newcastle FHSA, 1992–93; Sunderland HA, 1993–99; Dir, Jobcentre Services, subseq. Chief Operating Officer, Employment Services Agency, DfEE, 1999–2002; Chief Operating Officer, DWP, Jobcentre Plus, 2002–03; Chief Exec., Legal Services Commn, 2003–06. Non-executive Director: NW London Strategic HA, 2002–06; HMRC Prosecution Office, 2008–. Mem., Healthcare Commn, 2007–. *Recreations:* travel, fast cars, good food and wine. *Address:* c/o Healthcare Commission, Finsbury Tower, 103–105 Bunhill Row, EC1Y 8TG. *T:* (020) 7759 0000.

DODGSON, Paul; His Honour Judge Dodgson; a Circuit Judge, since 2001; *b* 14 Aug. 1951; *s* of late Reginald Dodgson and of Kathleen Dodgson; *m* 1982, Jan Hemingway; one *s* two *d*. *Educ:* Tiffin Sch.; Univ. of Birmingham (LLB Hons). Called to the Bar, Inner Temple, 1975; Asst Recorder, 1992–96; a Recorder, 1996–2001. Mem., Parole Bd of Eng. and Wales, 2003–. Treas., Criminal Bar Assoc., 1992–94. *Recreations:* ski-ing, sailing, golf, socialising. *Club:* Clandon Regis Golf.

DODS, Roanne Watson; Director, Jerwood Charitable Foundation, since 1998; *b* 16 Sept. 1965; *d* of Robin and Jean Dods; *m* 1999, Paul Harkin; one *s*. *Educ:* St Andrews Univ. (MA); Edinburgh Univ. (LLB; DipLP); Laban Centre, London (MA). Solicitor: Loudons WS, 1990–94; Erskine McAskill, 1994–96; Balfour & Manson, 1996–97; Consultant to Lottery Project, Laban Centre, London, 1998. Vice-Chm., Scottish Ballet; Chm., Innovative Craft; Co-Dir, Mission Models Money; Mem. Bd, Sistema Scotland. *Recreations:* windsurfing, triathlon, swimming, contemporary dance, contemporary fiction, dreaming, photography. *Address:* 11 Glencairn Drive, Glasgow G41 4QP. *T:* (0141) 423 7516; Jerwood Charitable Foundation, 171 Union Street, Bankside, SE1 0LN. *e-mail:* roanne.dods@jerwood.org.

DODSON, family name of **Baron Monk Bretton**.

DODSON, Prof. Eleanor Joy, FRS 2003; Research Fellow, University of York, since 1976; *b* 6 Dec. 1936; *d* of Arthur McPherson and Alice Power; *m* 1965, (George) Guy Dodson, *qv*; three *s* one *d*. *Educ:* Univ. of Melbourne (BA Hons). Res. Asst, Lab. of Dorothy Hodgkin, Univ. of Oxford, 1961–76. *Recreations:* family, theatre, opera. *Address:* 101 East Parade, York YO31 7YD. *T:* (01904) 424449; *e-mail:* E.Dodson@ysbl.york.ac.uk.

DODSON, Prof. (George) Guy, PhD; FRS 1994; Professor of Biochemistry, University of York, since 1985; Head, Division of Protein Structure, MRC National Institute for Medical Research, London, since 1993; *b* 13 Jan. 1937; *m* 1965, Eleanor Joy McPherson (*see* E. J. Dodson); three *s* one *d*. *Educ:* New Zealand Univ. (MSc, PhD). Rockefeller res. award, Oxford Univ., 1962; Res. Fellow, Wolfson Coll., Oxford, 1973; Lectr, 1976, Reader, 1983, York Univ. FMedSci 2002; FIASc 2004; Fellow, INSA, 2004. *Publications:* (ed jtly) Structural Studies on Molecules of Biological Interest, 1981; articles in learned jls on protein structure and function, particularly insulin and proteins of medical interest. *Recreations:* music, wife's gardening, cricket. *Address:* Department of Chemistry, University of York, York YO10 5DD. *T:* (01904) 432520, *Fax:* (01904) 410519; MRC National Institute for Medical Research, Mill Hill, NW7 1AA. *T:* (020) 8959 3666, *Fax:* (020) 8906 4477.

DODSON, Joanna; QC 1993; *b* 5 Sept. 1945; *d* of late Jack Herbert Dodson and Joan Muriel (*née* Webb); *m* 1974 (marr. diss. 1981). *Educ:* James Allen's Girls' Sch.; Newnham Coll., Cambridge (entrance exhibnr; BA 1967; MA 1971). Called to the Bar, Middle Temple, 1971, Bencher, 2000. Gov., James Allen's Girls' Sch., 1999–. *Address:* Renaissance Chambers, 5th Floor, Gray's Inn Chambers, Gray's Inn, WC1R 5JA. *T:* (020) 7404 1111.

DODSON, Robert North; *see* North, R.

DODSWORTH, Geoffrey Hugh; JP; FCA; Chairman, Dodsworth & Co. Ltd, since 1988; *b* 7 June 1928; *s* of late Walter J. J. Dodsworth and Doris M. Baxter; *m* 1st, 1949, Isabel Neale (decd); one *d*; 2nd, 1971, Elizabeth Ann Beeston; one *s* one *d*. *Educ:* St Peter's Sch., York. MP (C) Herts SW, Feb. 1974–Oct. 1979, resigned. Mem. York City Council, 1959–65; JP York 1961, later JP Herts. Dir, Grindlays Bank Ltd, 1976–80; Chief Exec., Grindlay Brandts Ltd, 1977–80; Pres. and Chief Exec., Oceanic Finance Corp., 1980–85, Dep. Chm., 1985–86; Chm., Oceanic Financial Services, 1985–86; Director: County Properties Group, 1987–88; First Internat. Leasing Corp., 1990–94. *Recreation:* riding. *Address:* Mill Hill House, Constable Burton, Leyburn, N Yorks DL8 5RQ. *T:* (01677) 450448, *Fax:* (01677) 450335; *e-mail:* dodsworth@jorvikf.demon.co.uk. *Club:* Carlton.

DODSWORTH, Prof. (James) Martin; Professor of English, Royal Holloway (formerly Royal Holloway and Bedford New College), University of London, 1987–2001, now Emeritus; *b* 10 Nov. 1935; *s* of Walter Edward and Kathleen Ida Dodsworth; *m* 1967, Joanna Rybicka; one *s*. *Educ:* St George's Coll., Weybridge; Univ. of Fribourg, Switzerland; Wadham Coll., Oxford (MA). Asst Lectr and Lectr in English, Birkbeck Coll., London, 1961–67; Lectr and Sen. Lectr, Royal Holloway Coll., later Royal Holloway and Bedford New Coll., London, 1967–87. Vis. Lectr, Swarthmore Coll., Pa, 1966. Chairman: English Assoc., 1987–92 (Centenary Hon. Fellow, 2006); Cttee for University English, 1988–90; Mem., Common English Forum, 2001–05. Editor, English, 1976–87; Advr, Agenda, 2004–. *Publications:* (ed) The Survival of Poetry, 1970; Hamlet Closely Observed, 1985; (ed) English Economis'd, 1989; (ed) The Penguin History of Literature, vol. 7: The Twentieth Century, 1994; (with J. B. Bamborough) Commentary to Robert Burton, the Anatomy of Melancholy, vol. 1, 1998, vols 2 and 3, 2000; Assessing Research Assessment in English, 2006; contribs to The Guardian, Essays in Criticism, The Review, etc. *Recreations:* reading, eating and drinking, short walks. *Address:* 59 Temple Street, Brill, Bucks HP18 9SU. *T:* (01844) 237106.

DODSWORTH, Sir John Christopher S.; *see* Smith-Dodsworth.

DODSWORTH, Martin; *see* Dodsworth, J. M.

DODWELL, Christina; writer and explorer; Chairman, Dodwell Trust, since 1996; Senior Attaché, Madagascar Consulate, since 1990; *b* Nigeria, 1 Feb. 1951; *d* of Christopher Bradford Dodwell and Evelyn Dodwell (*née* Beddow); *m* 1991, Stephen Hobbs. *Educ:* Southover Manor, Lewes; Beechlawn Coll., Oxford. Journeys through Africa by horse, 1975–78, and through Papua New Guinea by horse and canoe, 1980–81; presenter, BBC films: River Journey-Waghi, 1984 (BAFTA award); Black Pearls of Polynesia, 1991; African Footsteps—Madagascar, 1996; over 40 documentary progs for BBC Radio 4. FRGS 1982. Mungo Park Medal, RSGS, 1989. *Publications:* Travels with Fortune, 1979; In Papua New Guinea, 1982; An Explorer's Handbook, 1984; A Traveller in China, 1986; A Traveller on Horseback, 1987; Travels with Pegasus, 1989; Beyond Siberia, 1993; Madagascar Travels, 1995. *Address:* c/o Madagascar House, 16 Lanark Mansions, Pennard Road, W12 8DT.

DODWORTH, Air Vice-Marshal Peter, CB 1994; OBE 1982; AFC 1971; DL; FRAeS; Royal Air Force, retired; Military Adviser to Vosper Thornycroft (formerly Bombardier Aerospace Defence Services), 1996–2003; *b* 12 Sept. 1940; *e s* of Eric and Edna Dodworth; *m* 1963, Kay Parry; three *s* (and one twin *s* decd). *Educ:* Southport Grammar Sch.; Leeds Univ. (BSc Physics, 1961). FRAeS 1997. Served: 54 Sqn Hunters, 1963–65; 4 FTS Gnats, 1965–67; Central Flying Sch., 1967–68; Harrier Conversion Team, 1969–72; Air Staff RAF Germany, 1972–76; OC Ops, RAF Wittering, 1976–79; ndc 1980; Air Comdr, Belize, 1980–82; staff, RAF Staff Coll., 1982–83; Stn comdr, RAF Wittering, 1983–85; Command Group Exec., HQ AAFCE, Ramstein, 1985–87; RCDS, 1987; Dir of Personnel, MoD, 1988–91; Defence Attaché and Hd, British Defence Staff (Washington), 1991–94; Sen. DS (A), RCDS, 1995–96. DL Lincs, 2004. Vice Chm., Burma Star Assoc., 2006–. Chm. of Govs., Stamford Endowed Sch., 2005–. *Recreations:* golf, DIY, reading. *Club:* Royal Air Force.

DOE, Rt Rev. Michael David; General Secretary, USPG: Anglicans in World Mission (formerly United Society for the Propagation of the Gospel), since 2004; an Hon. Assistant Bishop, Diocese of Southwark, since 2004; *b* Lymington, Hants, 24 Dec. 1947; *s* of late Albert Henry Doe and of Violet Nellie Doe (*née* Curtis). *Educ:* Brockenhurst Grammar Sch.; Durham Univ. (BA 1969); Ripon Hall Theol Coll., Oxford. Ordained deacon, 1972, priest, 1973; Asst Curate, 1972–76, Hon. Curate, 1976–81, St Peter, St Helier, Morden; Youth Sec., BCC, 1976–81; Priest-Missioner, 1981–88, Vicar, 1988–89, Blackbird Leys LEP, Oxford; RD, Cowley, 1986–89; Social Responsibility Advr, dio. of Portsmouth, and Canon Residentiary, Portsmouth Cathedral, 1989–94; Suffragan Bp of Swindon, 1994–2004. Hon. LLD Bath, 2002. *Publication:* Seeking the Truth in Love, 2000. *Recreations:* the media, English fiction. *Address:* USPG: Anglicans in World Mission, 200 Great Dover Street, SE1 4YB; *e-mail:* michaeld@USPG.org.uk.

DOE, Prof. William Fairbank, FRCP, FRACP, FMedSci; Professor and Head of Medical School, University of Birmingham, 1998–2007, now Professor Emeritus of Medicine (Dean of Medicine, Dentistry and Health Sciences, 1998–2002; Dean of Medicine, 2002–07); *b* 6 May 1941; *s* of Asa Garfield Doe and Hazel Thelma Doe; *m* 1982, Dallas Elizabeth Edith Ariotti; two *s*. *Educ:* Newington Coll., Sydney; Univ. of Sydney (MB BS); Chelsea Coll., Univ. of London (MSc). FRACP 1978; FRCP 1982. MRC Fellow, 1970–71, Lectr, 1973–74, RPMS; Consultant, Hammersmith Hosp., 1973–74; Lilly Internat. Fellow, 1974–75, NIH Fellow, 1975–77, Scripps Clinic and Res. Foundn, Calif; Associate Prof., Univ. of Sydney, and Hon. Physician, Royal N Shore Hosp., 1978–81; Prof. of Medicine and Clin. Scis, 1982–88, Head of Div. of Molecular Medicine, 1988–98, John Curtin Sch. of Med. Res., ANU; Dir of Gastroenterology, Canberra Hosp., 1991–97; Prof. of Medicine, Univ. of Sydney, 1995–98. WHO Cons., Beijing, 1987; Dist. Vis. Fellow, Christ's Coll., Cambridge, 1988–89. Dep. Chm., Council of Hds of Med. Schs, 2002–06. Non-exec. Dir, 1998–2003, Dep. Chm., 2000–03, Birmingham HA; non-exec. Dir, Birmingham and Black Country Strategic HA, 2003–06. Pres., Gastroenterological Soc. of Australia, 1989–91 (Dist. Res. Medal, 1997); Member: NH&MRC Social Psychiatry Adv. Cttee, 1982–92; Council, Nat. Centre for Epidemiology Population Health, 1987–98; Aust. Drug Evaluation Cttee, 1988–95; Council, RACP, 1993–98 (Censor, 1980–87); NH&MRC Res. Strategy Cttee, 1997–98; Workforce Develt Confedn, 2002–06; Wkg Party, Defining and Maintaining Professional Values in Medicine, RCP, 2004–07. Mem. Council, Univ. of Birmingham, 2004–06; Gov., Univ. of Worcester (formerly UC Worcester), 2004–. Mem., Lunar Soc., 1999–. FMedSci 1999. Sen. Editor, Jl Gastroenterology and Hepatology, 1993–2001. *Publications:* numerous scientific papers on molecular cell biology of mucosal inflammation and colon cancer. *Recreations:* opera, reading, wine, tennis. *Address:* Medical School, University of Birmingham, Edgbaston, Birmingham B15 2TT. *T:* (0121) 414 4044; *e-mail:* w.f.doe@bham.ac.uk. *Clubs:* Athenæum; Commonwealth (Canberra).

DOERR, Michael Frank, FIA; Group Chief Executive, Friends Provident Life Office, 1992–97; *b* 25 May 1935; *s* of Frank and May Doerr; *m* 1958, Jill Garrett; one *s* one *d*. *Educ:* Rutlish Sch. FIA 1959. Friends Provident Life Office, 1954–97: Pensions Actuary, 1960–66; Life Manager, 1966–73; Gen. Manager, Marketing, 1973–80; Gen. Manager, Ops, and Dir, 1980–87; Dep. Man. Dir, 1987–92. Director: Endsleigh Insce Services Ltd, 1980–94; Seaboard Life Insce Co. (Canada), 1987–92; Friends Provident Life Assce Co. (Australia), 1990–92; Friends Provident Life Assce Co. (Ireland), 1990–92; Friends Vilas-Fischer Trust Co. (US), 1996–98. Chairman: Preferred Direct Insce, 1992–97; FP Asset Mgt, 1996–97. *Recreations:* golf, tennis, chess, theatre, sailing. *Clubs:* Royal Automobile; Royal Southern Yacht.

DOERRIES, Chantal-Aimée Renée Amelia Annemarie; QC 2008; *b* 26 Aug. 1968; *d* of Dr Reinhard R. Doerries and Elaine L. Doerries (*née* Sulli). *Educ:* Roedean Sch.; Univ. of Pennsylvania; New Hall, Cambridge (BA 1990). Pres., Cambridge Union Soc., 1989. Called to the Bar, Middle Temple, 1992 (Maj. Harmsworth Entrance Exhibn and Diplock Schol.). Vice-Chm., Technol. and Construction Bar Assoc., 2007–. Jt Ed., Building Law Reports, 1999–. Gertrude de Gallaix Achievement Award, Fedn of Amer. Women's Clubs Overseas, 1990. *Address:* 1 Atkin Building, Gray's Inn, WC1R 5AT. *T:* (020) 7404 0102; *e-mail:* clerks@atkinchambers.com.

DOGGART, George Hubert Graham, OBE 1993; Headmaster, King's School, Bruton, 1972–85; *b* 18 July 1925; *e s* of late Alexander Graham Doggart and Grace Carlisle Hannan; *m* 1960, Susan Mary, *d* of R. I. Beattie, Eastbourne; one *s* one *d* (and one *d* decd). *Educ:* Winchester; King's Coll., Cambridge. BA History, 1950; MA 1955. Army, 1943–47 (Sword of Honour, 161 OCTU, Mons, 1944); Coldstream Guards. On staff at Winchester, 1950–72 (exchange at Melbourne C of E Grammar Sch., 1963); Housemaster, 1964–72. HMC Schools rep. on Nat. Cricket Assoc., 1964–75; President: English Schools Cricket Assoc., 1965–2000; Quidnuncs, 1983–88; Cricket Soc., 1983–98; Member: Cricket Council, 1968–71, 1972, 1983–92; MCC Cttee, 1975–78, 1979–81, 1982–92 (Pres., 1981–82; Treas., 1987–92). Captain, Butterflies CC, 1986–97. Chm., Friends of Arundel Castle CC, 1992–2003. *Publications:* (ed) The Heart of Cricket: memoir of H. S. Altham, 1967; (jtly) Lord Be Praised: the story of MCC's bicentenary celebrations, 1988; (jtly) Oxford and Cambridge Cricket, 1989; (ed) Reflections in a Family Mirror, 2002; (contrib.) A Breathless Hush: the MCC anthology of cricket verse, 2004. *Recreations:* literary and sporting (captained Cambridge v Oxford at cricket, Association football, rackets and squash, 1949–50; played in Rugby fives, 1950; played for England v W Indies, two tests, 1950; captained Sussex, 1954). *Address:* 19 Westgate, Chichester, West Sussex PO19 3ET. *Clubs:* MCC; Lord's Taverners; Hawks (Cambridge).

DOGGETT, (Thomas) Stephen; Executive Director, Cottage and Rural Enterprises Ltd, 1990–98 (Director of Development, 1984–90); *b* 7 Jan. 1935; *s* of Arthur Francis Doggett and Mary Elizabeth Doggett (*née* Horder); *m* 1960, Susan Gillian Tyndale; two *s* one *d*. *Educ:* St Faith's, Cambridge; Gresham's Sch., Holt; Queens' Coll., Cambridge (BA Nat. Scis 1958; MA 1963). Nat. Service, Royal Signals, 1953–55. Sketchley PLC, 1958–84; Technical Dir, Sketchley Cleaners, 1978–84. Pres., Assoc. of British Launderers and Cleaners, 1981–83. *Recreations:* ski-ing, golf, vintage and classic cars, family. *Address:* Bay Tree Cottage, 47 Lutterworth Road, Burbage, Hinckley, Leics LE10 2DJ. *T:* (01455) 239410.

DOHA, Aminur Rahman S.; see Shams-ud Doha, A. R.

DOHERTY, Berlie; author, playwright and librettist, since 1982; *b* 6 Nov. 1943; *d* of Walter and Margaret Hollingsworth; *m* 1966, Gerard Doherty (marr. diss. 1996); one *s* two *d*. *Educ:* Upton Hall Convent; Durham Univ. (BA Hons English); Liverpool Univ. (Postgrad. Cert. Social Studies); Sheffield Univ. (Postgrad. Cert Ed). Social worker, Leics Social Services, 1966–67; English teacher, Sheffield, 1979–82; on secondment to BBC Radio Sheffield Schools Progs, 1980–82. Various writing workshops for WEA, Sheffield Univ. and Ardon Foundn, 1978–90. Hon. Dr Derby, 2002. *Publications:* How Green You Are!, 1982; The Making of Fingers Finnigan, 1983; Tilly Mint Tales, 1984; White Peak Farm, 1984; Children of Winter, 1985; Granny Was a Buffer Girl, 1986; Tilly Mint and the Dodo, 1988; Tough Luck, 1988; Paddiwak and Cosy, 1988; Spellhorn, 1989; Dear Nobody, 1991; Requiem, 1991; Snowy, 1993; Walking on Air, 1993; Big Bulgy Fat Black Slugs, 1993; Old Father Christmas, 1993; Street Child, 1993; The Vinegar Jar, 1994; Willa and Old Miss Annie, 1994; The Magical Bicycle, 1995; The Golden Bird, 1995; The Snake-Stone, 1995; Our Field, 1996; Daughter of the Sea, 1996; Running on Ice (collected stories), 1997; Bella's Den, 1997; Tales of Wonder and Magic, 1997; Midnight Man, 1998; The Forsaken Merman, 1998; The Sailing Ship Tree, 1998; The Snow Queen, 1998; Fairy Tales, 2000; The Famous Adventures of Jack, 2000; Zzaap and the Wordmaster, 2000; Holly Starcross, 2001; The Nutcracker, 2002; Blue John, 2003; Coconut Comes to School, 2003; Deep Secret, 2003; Tricky Nelly's Birthday Treat, 2003; The Starburster, 2004; Jinnie Ghost, 2005; Jeannie of White Peak Farm, 2005; The Humming Machine, 2006; Abela: the girl who saw lions, 2007; The Oxford Book of Bible Stories, 2007; The Windspinner, 2008; *plays include:* Sacrifice, 1985; Return to the Ebro, 1986; Morgan's Field, 1995; Heidi, 1996; The Water Babies, 1998; Lorna Doone, 2001; *operas include:* The Magician's Cat, 2004; Wild Cat, 2007. *Recreations:* walking, music (a late learner of piano, folk fiddle and penny whistle), reading, theatre and opera going. *Address:* c/o David Higham Associates Ltd, 5–8 Lower John Street, Golden Square, W1R 4HA.

DOHERTY, (Joseph) Raymond; QC (Scot.) 1997; *b* 30 Jan. 1958; *s* of James Doherty and Mary Doherty (*née* Woods); *m* 1994, Arlene Donaghy; one *s* two *d*. *Educ:* St Mungo's Primary Sch., Alloa; St Joseph's Coll., Dumfries; Univ. of Edinburgh (LLB 1st Cl. Hons 1980); Hertford Coll., Oxford (BCL 1982); Harvard Law Sch. (LLM 1983). Lord Reid Schol., 1983–85; admitted Faculty of Advocates, 1984; Standing Junior Counsel: MoD (Army), Scotland, 1990–91; Scottish Office Industry Dept, 1992–97; Advocate Depute, 1998–2001. Clerk of the Faculty of Advocates, 1990–95. *Publications:* (ed jtly) Armour on Valuation for Rating, 1990–; (contrib.) Stair Memorial Encyclopaedia of the Laws of Scotland. *Address:* Advocates Library, Parliament House, Parliament Square, Edinburgh EH1 1RF. *T:* (0131) 226 5071.

DOHERTY, Michael Eunan; Chairman, Epsom and St Helier NHS Trust, 2002–07; *b* 21 Sept. 1939; *s* of Michael Joseph Doherty and Grace Doherty (*née* Gallagher); *m* 1965, Judy Battams; two *s* two *d*. *Educ:* St Bernard's RC Sch., London. FCA 1977. Partner, Turquands Barton Mayhew, 1960–72; Man. Dir, Anglo-Thai Gp, 1973–82; Chief Exec., Cope Allman Internat. plc, 1982–88; Chairman: Henlys plc, 1985–88, 1991–97; Norcros plc, 1988–97. Chm., King's Healthcare, then King's Coll. Hosp., NHS Trust, 1996–2002; Trustee, KCH Charitable Trust, 1999–2004. Chm. Govs, St John's Sch., Leatherhead, 1997–2006. CCMI (CIMgt 1985). *Recreations:* golf, music, reading, politics. *Address:* Willow Court, 18 The Gables, Oxshott, Surrey KT22 0SD. *T:* (01372) 841558. *Club:* Royal Automobile.

DOHERTY, Pat; MP (SF) Tyrone West, since 2001; Member (SF) Tyrone West, Northern Ireland Assembly, since 1998; *b* Glasgow, 18 July 1945; *m*; two *s* three *d*. Sinn Féin: Dir of Elections, 1984–85; Nat. Organiser, 1985–88; Vice-Pres., 1988–; Leader of delegn to Forum for Peace and Reconciliation, Dublin, 1994–96. Chm., Enterprise, Trade and Investment Cttee, NI Assembly, 1999–2002. Contested (SF) Tyrone West, 1997. *Address:* (office) 12 Bridge Street, Strabane, Co. Tyrone BT82 9AE; Northern Ireland Assembly, Stormont Castle, Belfast BT4 3XX; c/o House of Commons, SW1A 0AA.

DOHERTY, Prof. Peter Charles, AC 1997; FRS 1987; FAA 1983; Laureate Professor, Department of Microbiology and Immunology, University of Melbourne, since 2002; *b* 15 Oct. 1940; *s* of Eric C. and Linda M. Doherty; *m* 1965, Penelope Stephens; two *s*. *Educ:* Univ. of Queensland (BVSc, MVSc); Univ. of Edinburgh (PhD). Veterinary Officer,

Queensland Dept of Primary Industries, 1962–67; Scientific Officer, Moredun Research Inst., Edinburgh, 1967–71; Research Fellow, Dept of Microbiology, John Curtin Sch. of Med. Research, Canberra, 1972–75; Associate Prof., later Prof., Wistar Inst., Philadelphia, 1975–82; Prof. of Experimental Pathology, John Curtin Sch. of Medical Res., ANU, 1982–88; Chm., Dept of Immunology, St Jude Children's Res. Hosp., Memphis, 1988–2002. Bd Mem., Internat. Lab. for Res. on Animal Disease, Nairobi, 1987–92. Mem., US Nat. Acad. of Sci., 1998. Hon. doctorates from 16 univs. Paul Ehrlich Prize and Medal for Immunology, 1983; Gairdner Internat. Award for Med. Research, 1987; Alumnus of Year, Univ. of Queensland, 1993; Lasker Award for Basic Med. Res., 1995; (jtly) Nobel Prize in Physiology or Medicine, 1996. *Publications:* The Beginner's Guide to Winning the Nobel Prize, 2005; A Light History of Hot Air, 2007; papers in scientific jls. *Recreations:* walking, reading. *Address:* Department of Microbiology and Immunology, University of Melbourne, Vic 3010, Australia. *T:* (3) 83447968, *Fax:* (3) 83447990.

DOHERTY, Raymond; see Doherty, J. R.

DOHMANN, Barbara; QC 1987; *b* Berlin; *d* of Paul Dohmann and Dora Dohmann (*née* Thiele). *Educ:* schools in Germany and USA; Univs of Erlangen, Mainz and Paris. Called to the Bar, Gray's Inn, 1971, Bencher, 2007; a Recorder, 1990–2002; a Dep. High Court Judge, 1994–2003. Judge (part-time) of Civil and Commercial Court, Qatar Financial Centre, Doha, 2007–. Mem., Learned Soc. for Internat. Civil Procedure Law, 1991–; Chm., Commercial Bar Assoc., 1999–2001 (Treas., 1997–99; Mem. Cttee, 2001–); Member: Gen. Council of the Bar, 1999–2001; Legal Services Cttee, 2000–01; Bar Eur. Gp, Eur. Circuit, 2000–; Standing Cttee of Internat. Law (North Cttee), 2007–; Special Cttee, London Metal Exchange, 2007–. Member: Bd of Govs, London Inst. Higher Educn Corp., 1993–2000; Chancellor's Forum, Univ. of the Arts, London (formerly London Inst. Higher Educn Corp.), 2000–. *Recreations:* gardening, mountain walking, opera, art. *Address:* Blackstone Chambers, Blackstone House, Temple, EC4Y 9BW. *T:* (020) 7583 1770. *Club:* Athenæum.

DOHNÁNYI, Christoph v.; see von Dohnányi.

DOIG, David William Neal; Clerk of Bills, House of Commons, since 2006; *b* 15 Jan. 1950; *s* of William Doig and Audrey Doig; *m* 1977, Alison Dorothy Farrar; one *s* three *d*. *Educ:* Perse Sch., Cambridge; Jesus Coll., Cambridge (BA Mod. and Mediaeval Langs 1972); City of London Poly. (Dip. Tech. and Specialist Translation 1973). House of Commons: Asst Clerk, 1973–77; Sen. Clerk, 1977–85; Dep. Principal Clerk, 1985–2000; Registrar of Members' Interests, 2000; Principal Clerk of Select Cttees, 2001–06. *Recreations:* gardening, cricket, meccano. *Address:* Quayham, Foots Lane, Burwash Weald, E Sussex TN19 7LE.

DOLAN, Dorothy Elizabeth; see Porter, D. E.

DOLAN, Prof. Raymond Joseph, MD; FRCP, FRCPsych, FMedSci; Kinross Professor of Neuropsychiatry, since 2001, and Director, Wellcome Trust Centre for Neuroimaging, since 2006, University College London; *b* 21 Jan. 1954; *s* of John Dolan and Julia Dolan (*née* Coppenger); *m* 1996, Sheela Kulaveerasingham; three *s*. *Educ:* St Jarlath's Coll., Tuam; University Coll. Galway Medical Sch. (MB BCh BAO Hons 1977; MD 1987). FRCPsych 1995; FRCP 2002. Psychiatry trng, Royal Free and Maudsley Hosps; Sen. Lectr, Royal Free Hosp. Sch. of Medicine, 1987–94; Reader, Inst. of Neurology, 1995–96; Prof., Inst. of Neurology, UCL, 1996–2001. FMedSci 2000. *Publications:* Human Brain Function, 1997, 2nd edn 2004; over 300 papers in jls incl. Nature, Science, Neuron, Jl of Neuroscience, Nature Neuroscience, Brain. *Recreations:* walking, reading, music, fly-fishing, midnight rambling. *Address:* Wellcome Trust Centre for Neuroimaging, 12 Queen Square, WC1N 3BG. *T:* (020) 7833 7456; *e-mail:* r.dolan@fil.ion.ucl.ac.uk. *Clubs:* Groucho; Country Half-Life.

DOLBY, Elizabeth Grace; see Cassidy, E. G.

DOLBY, Ray Milton, Hon. OBE 1986; PhD; engineering company executive; electrical engineer; Founder and Chairman, Dolby Laboratories Inc., San Francisco and London, since 1965; *b* Portland, Ore, 18 Jan. 1933; *s* of Earl Milton Dolby and Esther Eufemia (*née* Strand); *m* 1966, Dagmar Baumert; two *s*. *Educ:* San Jose State Coll.; Washington Univ.; Stanford Univ. (Beach Thompson award, BS Elec. Engrg); Pembroke Coll., Cambridge (Marshall schol., 1957–60, Draper's studentship, 1959–61, NSF Fellow, 1960–61; PhD Physics 1961; Fellow, 1961–63; research in long-wave length x-rays, 1957–63; Hon. Fellow 1983). Electronic technician/jun. engr, Ampex Corp., Redwood City, Calif, 1949–53. Served US Army 1953–54. Engr, 1955–57; Sen. Engr, 1957; UNESCO Advr, Central Sci. Instruments Org., Punjab, 1963–65; Cons., UKAEA, 1962–63. Inventions, research, pubns in video tape rec., x-ray microanalysis, noise reduction and quality improvements in audio and video systems; 50 UK patents. Trustee, Univ. High Sch., San Francisco, 1978–84; Mem., Marshall Scholarships Selection Cttee, 1979–85; Dir, San Francisco Opera; Governor, San Francisco Symphony. Mem., Acad. of Motion Picture Arts and Scis, 2001. Fellow: Audio Engrg Soc. (Silver Medal, 1971; Gold Medal, 1992; Governor, 1972–74, 1979–84; Pres., 1980–81); Brit. Kinematograph, Sound and Television Soc. (Outstanding Technical and Scientific Award, 1995); Soc. Motion Picture, TV Engrs (S. L. Warner award, 1978; Alexander M. Poniatoff Gold Medal, 1982; Progress Medal, 1983; Hon. Mem., 1992); Inst. of Broadcast Sound, 1987; Amer. Acad. of Arts and Scis, 2003; Hon. Fellow, Assoc. of Motion Picture Sound, 1999; Hon. FR.Eng 2004. MIEEE (Ibuka Award, 1997); Tau Beta Pi. Hon. ScD Cambridge, 1997; DUniv York, 1999. Other Awards: Emmy, for contrib. to Ampex video recorder, 1957, and for noise reduction systems on video recorder sound tracks, 1989; Trendsetter, Billboard, 1971; Lyre, Inst. High Fidelity, 1972; Emile Berliner Assoc. Maker of Microphone award, 1972; Top 200 Execs Bi-Centennial, 1976; Sci. and Engrg, 1979, Oscar, 1989, Acad. of Motion Picture Arts and Scis; Man of the Yr, Internat. Tape Assoc., 1987; Pioneer Award, Internat. Teleproduction Soc., 1988; Eduard Rhein Ring, Eduard Rhein Foundn, 1988; Life Achievement Award, Cinema Audio Soc., 1989; Grammy, Nat. Acad. of Recording Arts and Scis, 1995; Medal of Achievement, Amer. Electronics Assoc., 1997; Nat. Medal of Technol., US Dept of Commerce, 1997; inductee, Hall of Fame, Consumer Electronics Assoc., 2000; Internat. Honour for Excellence (John Tucker Award), Internat. Broadcasting Convention, 2000; Lifetime Achievement Award, Acad. of TV Arts and Scis, USA, 2005. *Recreations:* yachting, ski-ing, flying. *Address:* (home) 3340 Jackson Street, San Francisco, CA 94118, USA. *T:* (415) 5636947; (office) 100 Potrero Avenue, San Francisco, CA 94103, USA. *T:* (415) 5580200.

DOLCE, Domenico; Chief Executive Officer, Dolce & Gabbana; *b* 13 Sept. 1958; *s* of Saverio Dolce. Worked in father's clothing factory, Sicily; Asst in design studio, Milan; with Stefano Gabbana opened fashion consulting studio, 1982; Co-founder, Dolce & Gabbana, 1985; first major women's collection, 1986; knitwear, 1987; beachwear, lingerie, 1989; men's collection, 1990; women's fragrance, 1992; D&G line, men's fragrance, 1994; eyewear, 1995; opened boutiques in major cities in Europe, America and Asia. *Publications:* (with Stefano Gabbana): 10 Years Dolce & Gabbana, 1996; Wildness, 1997; Mémoires de la Mode, 1998; Animal, 1998; Calcio, 2004; Music, 2005; 20 Years

Dolce & Gabbana, 2005; (with Eve Claxton and Stefano Gabbana) Hollywood, 2003. *Address:* Dolce & Gabbana, Via Santa Cecilia 7, 20122 Milan, Italy.

DOLE, Bob; *see* Dole, R. J.

DOLE, Robert Joseph, (Bob); Purple Heart; special counsel, Alston & Bird, since 2003; founder, Bob Dole Enterprises Inc.; *b* Russell, Kansas, 22 July 1923; *s* of Doran and Bina Dole; *m* 1975, Elizabeth Hanford; one *d. Educ:* Univ. of Kansas (AB); Washburn Municipal Univ. (LLB). Served US Army, 1943–48; Platoon Ldr, 10th Mountain Div., Italy; wounded and decorated twice for heroic achievement. Captain. Kansas Legislature, 1951–53; Russell County Attorney, Kansas, 1953–61; US House of Reps, 1960–68; US Senator, 1968–96; Republican Leader, 1985–96, Leader, 1995–96, US Senate; Leader, Republican Party, US, 1992–96; Republican Nominee for President, 1996. Special Counsel, Verner, Liipfert, Bernhard, McPherson and Hand, 1999–2003. Chairman: Internat. Commn on Missing Persons, 1997–; Nat. World War II Meml. US Presidential Medal of Freedom, 1997. *Publications:* (ed) Great Political Wit, 1998; (ed) Great Presidential Wit; One Soldier's Story (autobiog.), 2005. *Address:* c/o Alston & Bird LLP, 10th Floor, The Atlantic Building, 950 F Street NW, Washington, DC 20004–1404, USA.

D'OLIVEIRA, Basil Lewis, CBE 2005 (OBE 1969); retired cricketer; *b* 4 Oct. 1931; *s* of Lewis and Moira D'Oliveira; *m* 1960, Naomi Brache; two *s.* Cricketer: played for: Middleton CC, Central Lancs League, 1960–63; Worcs CCC, 1964–80; MCC, 1964–71; England, 1966–72 (44 caps); coach, Worcs CCC, 1980–90. Order of Ikhamanga for excellence in sports (SA), 2003. *Publication:* Time to Declare: an autobiography, 1980; relevant publication: Basil D'Oliveira: cricket and controversy, by Peter Oborne, 2004. *Address:* c/o Worcestershire County Cricket Club, County Ground, New Road, Worcester WR2 4QQ.

DOLLERY, Sir Colin (Terence), Kt 1987; FRCP, FMedSci; Senior Consultant, Research and Development, GlaxoSmithKline (formerly Smithkline Beecham) plc, since 1996; Dean, Royal Postgraduate Medical School, 1991–96, Pro-Vice-Chancellor for Medicine (formerly Medicine and Dentistry), 1992–96, University of London; *b* 14 March 1931; *s* of Cyril Robert and Thelma Mary Dollery; *m* 1958, Diana Myra (*née* Stedman); one *s* one *d. Educ:* Lincoln Sch.; Birmingham Univ. (BSc, MB,ChB); FRCP 1968. House officer: Queen Elizabeth Hosp., Birmingham; Hammersmith Hosp., and Brompton Hosp., 1956–58; Hammersmith Hospital: Med. Registrar, 1958–60; Sen. Registrar and Tutor in Medicine, 1960–62; Consultant Physician, 1962–; Lectr in Medicine, 1962–65, Prof. of Clinical Pharmacology, 1965–87, Prof. of Medicine, 1987–91, Royal Postgrad. Med. Sch. Member: MRC, 1982–84; UGC, subseq. UFC, 1984–91. Founder FMedSci 1998; FIC 2003. Hon. Mem., Assoc. of Amer. Physicians, 1982. Chevalier de l'Ordre National du Mérite (France), 1976. *Publications:* The Retinal Circulation, 1971 (New York); Therapeutic Drugs, 1991, 2nd edn 1998; numerous papers in scientific jls concerned with high blood pressure and drug action. *Recreations:* travel, amateur radio, work. *Address:* 101 Corringham Road, NW11 7DL. *T:* (020) 8458 2616. *Club:* Athenæum.

DOLMAN, Edward James; Chief Executive Officer, Christie's International plc, since 1999; *b* 24 Feb. 1960; *s* of James William Dolman and Jean Dolman; *m* 1987, Clare Callaghan; one *s* one *d. Educ:* Dulwich Coll.; Southampton Univ. (BA Hons History). Joined Christie's, 1984; Dir and Head of Furniture Dept, Christie's S Kensington, 1990–95; Man. Dir, Christie's Amsterdam, 1995–97; Commercial Dir, 1997, Man. Dir, 1998–99, Christie's Europe; Dir, Christie, Manson & Woods Ltd, 1997; Man. Dir, Christie's America, 1999–2000. Mem., Internat. Adv. Bd, British American Business Inc., 2006–. Mem., Council of Trustees, Specialist Schs and Academies Trust, 2006–07. Légion d'Honneur (France), 2007. *Recreations:* art history, Rugby, cricket, sailing. *Address:* Christie's, 8 King Street, St James's, SW1Y 6QT. *T:* (020) 7389 2881. *Clubs:* Royal Automobile, Old Alleynian (Vice Pres., 1998–).

DOLMAN, Rev. Dr William Frederick Gerrit; JP; HM Deputy Coroner, East London, since 2007; HM Assistant Deputy Coroner, South London, since 2008; *b* 14 Nov. 1942; *s* of Dr Gerrit Arnold Dolman and Madeline Joan Dolman. *Educ:* Whitgift Sch., Croydon; KCH Med. Sch., Univ. of London (MB BS 1965); LLB Hons London (ext.) 1987; SE Inst. of Theol Educn (DipTh Univ. of Kent (ext.) 2007). MRCS 1965; LRCP 1965; FFFLM 2005. Principal in Gen. Practice, 1967–74; Asst Dep. Coroner, 1974–86, Dep. Coroner, 1986–93, S London; Medical Referee, Croydon Crematorium, 1986–; Asst Dep. Coroner, 1988–89, Dep. Coroner, 1989–93, Inner W London; Coroner, N London, 1993–2007. Associate Dermatology Specialist, St Helier Hosp., Carshalton, 1992–2000. BBC Radio Doctor, Jimmy Young Show, Radio 2, 1977–2002. FRSocMed 1967 (Mem. Council, Forensic and Legal Medicine Section, 1996–2000); Pres., Croydon Medical Soc., 2002; Med. Sec., Coroners' Soc., 2004–. Examiner, Soc. of Apothecaries, 2002–04 and 2007–. Med. Editor, Modern Medicine, 1976–80; Editor: Coroner sect., Atkin's Court Forms, 2003–08; The Coroner, 2003–. Ordained deacon, 2006, priest, 2007; NSM, Beckley and Peasmarsh, 2006–. JP Croydon, 1975 (Chm. Bench, 2007–08). *Publications:* Can I Speak to the Doctor?, 1981; Doctor on Call, 1987. *Recreations:* classical music, good food, fine wine, real ale, sitting in the garden looking at work that ought to be done. *Address:* Coroner's Court, Barclay Road, Croydon CR9 3NE. *Club:* Authors' (Chm., 2000–04).

DOLPHIN, Prof. David Henry, PhD; FRS 2002; FRS(Can); FRSC, FCIC; QLT/NSERC Industrial Research Professor of Photodynamic Technology, University of British Columbia, since 2005 (Professor of Chemistry, 1979–2005, now Emeritus). *Educ:* Univ. of Nottingham (BSc 1962; PhD 1965; DSc 1982). FRS(Can) 2001; FCIC 1981. Joined Harvard Univ. as Res. Fellow, 1965, subseq. Associate Prof. of Chemistry, until 1974; Associate Prof. of Chemistry, Univ. of BC, 1974. Vice-Pres., Technol. Devélt, Quadra Logic Technologies, Vancouver, 1992. Guggenheim Fellow, 1980; Univ. Killam Prof., 2004. Gold Medal in Health Scis, Sci. Council of BC, 1990; Syntex Award, CIC, 1993; Bell Canada Forum Award, 1993; Izaak Walton Killam Res. Prize, Canada Council, 1996; Prix Galien Award, 2002; Friesen-Rygiel Prize, 2002; Award of Leadership in Canadian Pharmaceutical Scis, Canadian Soc. for Pharmaceutical Scis, 2002; Academic of the Year, Confedn of Univ. Faculty Assocs of BC, 2003; Hero of Chemistry, Amer. Chem. Soc., 2004; Award of Excellence, 2004, Herzberg Award, 2006, NSERC. *Publications:* (jtly) Tabulation of Infrared Spectral Data, 1977; (ed jtly) Biological Aspects of Inorganic Chemistry, 1977; (ed jtly) The Porphyrins, vol. I–VII, 1978–79; (ed jtly) Biomimetic Chemistry, 1980; Murakami and I. Tabushi, 1980; (ed) B12, 2 vols, 1982; (ed jtly) Biological Chemistry of Iron, 1982; (ed jtly) Coenzymes and Cofactors, vol. 1, 1986, vol. 2, 1987, vol. 3, 1989; articles in jls. *Address:* Department of Chemistry, University of British Columbia, 2036 Main Mall, Vancouver, BC V6T 1Z1, Canada.

DOMB, Prof. Cyril, PhD; FRS 1977; Professor of Physics, Bar-Ilan University, 1981–89, now Emeritus; *m* Shirley Galinsky; three *s* three *d. Educ:* Hackney Downs Sch.; Pembroke Coll., Cambridge. Major Open Schol., Pembroke Coll., 1938–41; Radar Research, Admiralty, 1941–46; MA Cambridge, 1945; Nahum Schol., Pembroke Coll., 1946; PhD Cambridge, 1949; ICI Fellowship, Clarendon Laboratory, Oxford, 1949–52; MA Oxon 1952; University Lecturer in Mathematics, Cambridge, 1952–54; Prof. of Theoretical Physics, KCL, 1954–81; FKC 1978. Max Born Prize, Inst. of Physics and German Physical Soc., 1981. *Publications:* (ed) Clerk Maxwell and Modern Science, 1963; (ed) Memories of Kopul Rosen, 1970; Phase Transitions and Critical Phenomena, (ed with M.S. Green) vols 1 and 2, 1972, vol. 3, 1974, vols 5a, 5b, 6, 1976, (ed with J. L. Lebowitz) vols 7 and 8 1983, vol. 9, 1984, vol. 10, 1986, vol. 11, 1987, vol. 12, 1988, vol. 13, 1989, vol. 14 1991, vol. 15, 1992, vol. 16, 1994, vol. 17, 1995, vols 18–20, 2001; (ed with A. Carmell) Challenge, 1976; The Critical Point, 1996; articles in scientific journals. *Recreations:* swimming. *Address:* Department of Physics, Bar-Ilan University, 52900 Ramat-Gan Israel; 32 Cumberland Gardens, NW4 1LD.

DOMINGO, Placido, Hon. KBE 2002; tenor singer, conductor; General Director Washington Opera, since 1996; Los Angeles Opera, since 2000; *b* Madrid, 21 Jan. 1941; *s* of Placido Domingo and Pepita (*née* Embil), professional singers; *m* 1962, Marta Ornelas lyric soprano; two *s* (and one *s* by former marriage). *Educ:* Instituto, Mexico City; Nat Conservatory of Music, Mexico City. Operatic début, Monterrey, as Alfredo in La Traviata, 1961; with opera houses at Dallas, Fort Worth, Israel, to 1965; débuts: NY City Opera, 1965; at NY Metropolitan Opera, as Maurizio in Adriana Lecouvreur, 1968; at La Scala, title role in Ernani, 1969; at Covent Garden, Cavaradossi in Tosca, 1971; has sung record 125 tenor rôles, 1961–2007. Has conducted in Vienna, Barcelona, NY and Frankfurt; début as conductor in UK, Covent Garden, 1983. *Films:* La Traviata, 1983 Carmen, 1984; Otello, 1986; appears on TV, makes recordings, throughout USA and Europe. FRCM; FRNCM. Hon. doctorates include: RNCM, 1982; Philadelphia Coll of Performing Arts, 1982; Complutense, Madrid, 1989; Anáhuac, Mexico, 2001; Hon DMus Oxon, 2003. Medal of City of Madrid; Orden de Isabel la Católica (Spain), 1986 Gran Cruz, Orden del Mérito Civil (Spain), 2002; foreign orders include: Chevalier Legion of Honour (France), 2002 (Officer, 1983); US Medal of Freedom, 2002; Comdr Ordre des Arts et des Lettres (France); Grande Ufficiale, Ordine al Merito della Repubblica Italiana; Grand Cross, Order of Infante Dom Henrique (Portugal); Order of Aztec Eagle (Mexico). *Publication:* My First Forty Years (autobiog.), 1983. *Recreations:* piano, swimming. *Address:* c/o Petra Weiss, PO Box 2018, 68710 Schwetzingen Germany.

DOMINIAN, Dr Jacobus, (Jack), MBE 1994; FRCPEd, FRCPsych; DPM; Hon Consultant, Central Middlesex Hospital, since 1988 (Senior Consultant Psychiatrist 1965–88); *b* 25 Aug. 1929; *s* of late Charles Joseph Dominian and Mary Dominian (*née* Scarlatou); *m* 1955, Edith Mary Smith (*d* 2006); four *d. Educ:* Lycée Leonin, Athens; St Mary's High Sch., Bombay; Stamford Grammar Sch., Lincs; Cambridge Univ.; Oxford Univ. MA, MB BChir (Cantab). Postgraduate work in medicine, various Oxford hosps 1955–58, Maudsley Hosp. (Inst. of Psychiatry), 1958–64; training as psychiatrist at Maudsley Hosp.; Dir, One Plus One: Marriage and Partnership Research, 1971–. Hon DSc Lancaster, 1976. *Publications:* Psychiatry and the Christian, 1961; Christian Marriage 1967; Marital Breakdown, 1968; The Church and the Sexual Revolution, 1971; Cycles of Affirmation, 1975; Depression, 1976; Authority, 1976; (with A. R. Peacocke) From Cosmos to Love, 1976; Proposals for a New Sexual Ethic, 1977; Marriage, Faith and Love 1981; Make or Break, 1984; The Capacity to Love, 1985; Sexual Integrity: the answer to AIDS, 1987; Passionate and Compassionate Love, 1991; (with Edmund Flood) The Everyday God, 1993; Marriage, 1995; One Like Us, 1998; Let's Make Love, 2001; Living Love, 2004; A Guide to Loving, 2005; Being Jack Dominian: reflections on marriage, sex and love, 2007; contribs to Lancet, BMJ, the Tablet, TLS. *Recreations:* enjoyment of the theatre, music, reading and writing. *Address:* Pefka, 19 Clements Road, Chorleywood Herts WD3 5JS. *T:* (01923) 283115.

DOMINIC, Zoë Denise, OBE 2007; FBIPP, FRPS; professional photographer; *b* 4 July 1920; *d* of Lionel J. Levi and Dora Jane Macdonald; name changed to Dominic by Deed Poll, 1960. *Educ:* Francis Holland Sch., Regent's Park. FRPS 1972 (Hood Medal, 1986) FBIPP 1993. Photographer, stage, opera and ballet: English Stage Co. at Royal Court Theatre, 1957–67; National Theatre, 1963–70; Royal Shakespeare Co., 1958; Royal Ballet; Royal Opera Co.; ENO; English Music Theatre; WNO; Stratford, Ontario, 1975 Chm., Avenue Productions, 1987– (Dir, 1986); produced: A Private Treason, Watford 1986; Blithe Spirit, Vaudeville, 1987; Noël and Gertie, Donmar Warehouse 1987 Comedy, 1989; specialist photographer on films: Dr Zhivago, Nijinsky, Reds, Travels With My Aunt, Victor Victoria; exhibns of ballet photographs, Photographers' Gallery 1971, Riverside Studios, 1979. Mem. Council, LAMDA, 1989– (Mem., Finance Cttee (Chm., 1991–94)). Trustee, Theatre Projects Trust, 1970 (Chm., 1983–92). *Publications:* Frederick Ashton, 1971; (jtly) John Cranko and the Stuttgart Ballet, 1973; Theatre at Work (text Jim Hiley), 1981; Full Circle (text Dame Janet Baker), 1982; The Best of Plays and Players 1953–68, 1987. *Recreation:* gardening. *Address:* 3 Lexham Walk, W8 5JD. *T:* (020) 7373 6461.

DOMINICZAK, Prof. Anna Felicja, OBE 2005; MD; FRCPGlas; FMedSci; FRSE British Heart Foundation Professor of Cardiovascular Medicine, University of Glasgow since 1998; *b* 26 Aug. 1954; *d* of Jacob Penson and Joanna Muszkowska; *m* 1976, Marek Dominiczak; one *s. Educ:* Medical Sch., Gdansk, Poland (MD Hons); Univ. of Glasgow (MD); MRCPGlas 1986, FRCPGlas 1995. Jun. House Officer, Glasgow Royal Infirmary 1982; Sen. House Officer and Registrar, Royal Alexandra Hosp., Paisley, 1983–86; MRC Clin. Scientist and Sen. Registrar, Western Infirmary, Glasgow, 1986–89; Res. Fellow and Associate Prof., Univ. of Michigan, Ann Arbor, 1990–91; Clin. Lectr and Hon. Sen Registrar, Univ. of Glasgow, 1992–93; University of Glasgow and Western Infirmary Glasgow: BHF Sen. Res. Fellow, 1993–97; Sen. Lectr, 1993–96; and Reader in Medicine 1996–97; Hon. Consultant Physician and Endocrinologist, 1993–. FMedSci 2001; FRSE 2003. *Publications:* (ed) Genetics of Essential Hypertension, 1999; (ed) Genetics of Hypertension, 2007. *Recreation:* modern literature. *Address:* BHF Glasgow Cardiovascular Research Centre, University of Glasgow, 126 University Place, Glasgow G12 8TA. *T:* (0141) 330 2738, *Fax:* (0141) 330 6997; *e-mail:* ad7e@clinmed.gla.ac.uk.

DOMOKOS, Dr Mátyás; Ambassador, retired; General Director, CD Hungary (formerly Diplomatic Service Directorate, Ministry of Foreign Affairs, Hungary), 1989–95; *b* 2 Oct. 1930; *m* 1956, Irén Beretyán; one *d. Educ:* Karl Marx Univ. of Econs, Budapest Foreign trading enterprises, 1954–57; Commercial Sec., Damascus and Trade Comr Khartoum, 1958–61; various posts in Ministry for Foreign Trade, Hungary, 1961–74 Ambassador to UN, Geneva, 1974–79; Head of Dept of Internat. Organisations, Ministry of Foreign Affairs, 1979–84; Ambassador to UK, 1984–89. *Recreations:* gardening, chess *Address:* 32 Str. Árnyas, 1121 Budapest, Hungary.

DON, Montagu Denis Wyatt, (Monty); writer and broadcaster; *b* 8 July 1955; *s* of late Denis Don and Janet Wyatt; *m* 1983, Sarah; two *s* one *d. Educ:* Magdalene Coll Cambridge (MA Eng. 1979). Jt Founder, Monty Don Ltd (costume jewellery co.) 1981–91; freelance gardening journalist, 1988–; TV broadcaster, 1989–; presenter Gardeners' World, 2002–08. Gardening Editor, The Observer, 1994–2006. *Publications:* The Prickotty Bush, 1990; The Weekend Gardener, 1995; The Sensuous Garden, 1997

Gardening Mad, 1997; Urban Jungle, 1998; Fork to Fork, 1999; The Complete Gardener, 2003; (with Sarah Don) The Jewel Garden, 2004; Gardening from Berryfield, 2005; My Roots, 2005; Growing out of Trouble, 2006; Around the World in 80 Gardens, 2008. *Recreations:* gardening, farming.

DON, Nigel Anderson; Member (SNP) Scotland North East, Scottish Parliament, since 2007; *b* 16 April 1954; *s* of Derek Don and Margaret Don; *m* 1977, Wendy Wrieden; one *s* one *d*. *Educ:* King's College Sch., Wimbledon; Pembroke Coll., Cambridge (BA 1975; MEng 2001); Univ. of London (LLB (ext.) 1982). Chemical engr, Unilever plc, 1976–89; self-employed musician, 1989–2007. Mem. (SNP), Dundee CC, 2003–07. *Recreations:* music, walking. *Address:* Scottish Parliament, Edinburgh EH99 1SP. *T:* (0131) 348 5996, *Fax:* (0131) 348 6998; *e-mail:* nigel.don@scottish.parliament.uk.

DON-WAUCHOPE, Sir Roger (Hamilton), 11th Bt *cr* 1667 (NS), of Newton Don and of Edmonstone; chartered accountant, retired, South Africa; Partner, Deloitte & Touche, 1972–98; *b* 16 Oct. 1938; *s* of Sir Patrick George Don-Wauchope, 10th Bt and Ismay Lilian Ursula (who later *m* George William Shipman), *d* of Sidney Richard Hodges; *S* father, 1989; *m* 1963, Sallee, *yr d* of Lt-Col Harold Mill-Colman, OBE, AMICE, Durban; two *s* one *d*. *Educ:* Hilton Coll., Natal; Univ. of Natal, Durban; Univ. of Natal, Pietermaritzburg (Higher Diploma in Taxation). Gov. and Vice-Chm., Hiltonian Soc., Hilton Coll. Trustee: Tembaletu Educn Trust; Emuseni Centre for the Aged. Mem. Cttee, Senior Golfers' Soc. of KwaZulu-Natal. *Heir: s* Dr Andrew Craig Don-Wauchope [*b* 18 May 1966; *m* 1990, Louise Sylvia, *d* of John Crawford Johnstone-Dougall; one *s* one *d*]. *Address:* Newton, 53 Montrose Drive, Pietermaritzburg 3201, KwaZulu-Natal, South Africa. *T:* (033) 3471107; *e-mail:* Don-Wauchope@interkom.co.za. *Clubs:* Victoria Country (Chm., 1993–95), Fleur-de-Lys (Treas.) (Pietermaritzburg); Durban Country (Durban); Old Hiltonian (Chm., 1992–97; Vice Pres., 1998–); Prince's Grant Golf (Stanger).

DONAGHY, Rita Margaret, CBE 2005 (OBE 1998); FCIPD; Chair, Advisory, Conciliation and Arbitration Service, 2000–07; *b* 9 Oct. 1944; *d* of late William Scott Willis and Margaret Brenda Willis (*née* Howard, later Bryan); *m* 1968, James Columba Donaghy (*d* 1986); *m* 2000, Ted Easen-Thomas. *Educ:* Leamington Coll. for Girls; Durham Univ. (BA 1967). FCIPD 2002. Tech. asst, NUT, 1967–68; Asst Registrar, 1968–84, Perm. Sec., Students' Union, 1984–2000, Inst. of Educn, Univ. of London. Member: Low Pay Commn, 1997–2000; Cttee on Standards in Public Life, 2001–07 (Interim Chm., 2007). Member: Nat. Exec. Council, NALGO/UNISON, 1973–2000; TUC Gen. Council, 1987–2000; President: NALGO, 1989–90; TUC, 2000; Mem. Exec., Eur. TUC, 1992–2000. Non-exec. Dir, KCH NHS Trust, 2005–. Member: Business Adv. Bd, Birmingham Univ., 2006–; Adv. Bd, Modern Records Centre, Warwick Univ., 2007–. DUniv: Open, 2002; Keele, 2004; Hon. DBA Greenwich, 2005. *Recreations:* theatre, gardening, photography, watching cricket, eating out, reading. *Address:* 35 Lyndhurst Grove, SE15 5AN. *Club:* Surrey County Cricket.

DONAHOE, Arthur Richard; QC (Can.) 1982; Secretary-General, Commonwealth Parliamentary Association, 1993–2001; *b* 7 April 1940; *s* of Richard A. Donahoe and Eileen (*née* Boyd); *m* 1972, Carolyn Elizabeth MacCormack. *Educ:* public schools in Halifax, NS; St Mary's Univ. (BComm 1959); Dalhousie Univ. (LLB 1965). Admitted to Bar of Nova Scotia, 1966; Exec. Asst to Leader of Opposition, Senate of Canada, 1967; barrister and solicitor, 1968–81; Lectr in Commercial Law, St Mary's Univ., 1972–75; MLA (PC), Nova Scotia, 1978–92, Speaker, 1981–91. Canadian Regl Rep., CPA Exec. Cttee, 1983–86. *Publications:* contrib. articles to Parliamentarian, Canadian Parly Rev., and Round Table. *Recreations:* golf, reading, bridge. *Address:* Unit 13, 6770 Jubilee Road, Halifax, NS B3H 2H8, Canada. *T:* (902) 4227937. *Clubs:* Ashburn Golf (Pres., 1982–83), Halifax (Halifax, NS).

DONALD, Sir Alan (Ewen), KCMG 1988 (CMG 1979); HM Diplomatic Service, retired; *b* 5 May 1931; 2nd *s* of Robert Thomson Donald and Louise Turner; *m* 1958, Janet Hilary Therese Blood; four *s*. *Educ:* Aberdeen Grammar Sch.; Fettes Coll., Edinburgh; Trinity Hall, Cambridge. BA, LLM. HM Forces, RA (L Battery, 2nd Regt RHA), 1949–50. Joined HM Foreign Service, 1954: Third Sec., Peking, 1955–57; FO, 1958–61: Private Sec. to Parly Under-Sec., FO, 1959–61; Second, later First Sec., UK Delegn to NATO, Paris, 1961–64; First Sec., Peking, 1964–66; Personnel Dept, Diplomatic Service Admin. Office, later FCO, 1967–71; Counsellor (Commercial), Athens, 1971–73; Political Advr to Governor of Hong Kong, 1974–77; Ambassador to: Republics of Zaire, Burundi and Rwanda, 1977–80; People's Republic of the Congo, 1978–80; Asst Under-Sec. of State (Asia and the Pacific), FCO, 1980–84; Ambassador to: Republic of Indonesia, 1984–88; People's Republic of China, 1988–91. Director: China Fund Inc. (NY), 1992–2003; HSBC China Fund Ltd, 1994–2004; J. P. Morgan Fleming Asian Investment Trust Ltd (formerly Fleming Asian Investment Trust), 1997–2001 (Fleming Far Eastern Investment Trust, 1991–97). Pres., China Assoc., 2003–08. Hon. LLD Aberdeen, 1991. *Recreations:* music, military history, water colour sketching. *Address:* Applebys, Chiddingstone Causeway, Kent TN11 8JH.

DONALD, Prof. Athene Margaret, PhD; FRS 1999; Professor of Experimental Physics, since 1998, and Deputy Head, Department of Physics, University of Cambridge; Fellow of Robinson College, Cambridge, since 1981; *b* 15 May 1953; *d* of Walter Griffith and Annette Marian (*née* Tylor); *m* 1976, Matthew J. Donald; one *s* one *d*. *Educ:* Camden Sch. for Girls; Girton Coll., Cambridge (BA, MA; PhD 1977). Postdoctoral researcher, Cornell Univ., 1977–81; University of Cambridge: SERC Res. Fellow, 1981–83; Royal Soc. Univ. Res. Fellow, 1983–85; Lectr, 1985–95; Reader, 1995–98. Mem., Governing Council, Inst. Food Res., 1999–2003. Bakerian Prize Lect., Royal Soc., 2006; Samuel Locker Award in Physics, Birmingham Univ., 1989; Charles Vernon Boys Prize, 1989, Mott Prize, 2005, Inst. of Physics; Rosenhain Medal and Prize, Inst. Materials, 1995; William Hopkins Prize, Cambridge Philosophical Soc., 2003. *Publications:* (with A. H. Windle) Liquid Crystalline Polymers, 1992, 2nd edn (with S. Hanna and A. H. Windle) 2006; (jtly) Starch: structure and function, 1997; Starch: advances in structure and function, 2001; articles on polymer, biopolymer, colloid and food physics in learned jls. *Address:* Cavendish Laboratory, University of Cambridge, J. J. Thomson Avenue, Cambridge CB3 0HE.

DONALD, Brian George; Sheriff of Tayside, Central and Fife at Kirkcaldy, since 1999; *b* 11 July 1944; *s* of George J. Donald and Anna Auchterlonie Donald. *Educ:* Lawside Acad., Dundee; Univ. of St Andrews (LLB 1965). Postgrad. legal trng, Edinburgh, 1965–67; admitted as solicitor, 1967; Asst Solicitor, Ayr, 1967–69; admin, London Univ., 1969; teacher of English, Shenker Inst., Rome, 1970–72; resumed legal practice, with J. & A. Hastie, SSC, Edinburgh, Glasgow and Galashiels, 1972, Partner, 1973–90; Lectr in Civil Advocacy, Law Faculty, Edinburgh Univ., 1981–91; Temp. Sheriff, 1984–99; Consultant, Gillam Mackie, SSC and Fyfe Ireland, WS, 1997–99. Member: Stewart Cttee on Alternatives to Prosecution, 1978–83; (Founder) Scottish Legal Aid Bd, 1986–91. *Recreations:* theatre, music, choral singing, good food and wine, foreign travel, maintaining fluent French and Italian and improving German. *Address:* Sheriff's Chambers, Kirkcaldy Sheriff Court, Kirkcaldy, Fife KY1 1XQ; *e-mail:* sheriff.bgdonald@scotcourts.gov.uk. (home) 20 Howe Street, Edinburgh EH3 6TG. *T:* (0131) 225 8755.

DONALD, George Malcolm, RSA 1992 (ARSA 1975); RSW 1976; SSA 1976; Keeper, Royal Scottish Academy, since 2003; *b* 12 Sept. 1943; *s* of George Donald and Margaret (*née* Tait); *m* 1966 (marr. diss.); one *s* one *d*. *Educ:* Edinburgh Coll. of Art (DA 1966; Post Grad. Dip. 1967); Hornsey Coll. of Art, London Univ. (ATC 1969); Edinburgh Univ. (MEd 1980). ILTM 2002. Edinburgh College of Art: Lectr, Sch. of Drawing and Painting, 1972–96; Tutor and Asst to Vice Principal (Art and Design), 1984–87; Director: Summer Sch., 1991–2004; Centre for Continuing Studies, 1996–2001. Printmaker in Residence, Soulisquoy Print Workshop, Orkney Is, 1988; Visiting Artist: Szechuan Fine Art Inst., China, 1989; Silpakorn Univ., Thailand, 1989; Chulalongkorn Univ., Thailand, 1989; Visiting Professor: Zhejiang Acad. Fine Art, China, 1994–; Univ of Sharja, 2003–; British Council Vis. Prof., Kyoto, 1999, 2002, Korea, 2000; Adjunct Prof., Univ. of Central Florida, 2002–. Solo exhibitions include: Art Dept Gall., Univ. of Central Florida, 1985, 2002, 2003; Dept of Fine Art, Univ. of Georgia, 1987; Open Eye Gall., Edinburgh, 1987, 1990, 1993, 1995, 1998, 2002, 2003, 2005, 2007; Galerija Fakulteta Likovnih Umetnosti, Belgrade, 1987; touring exhibn, UK and France, 1990; Christopher Hull Gall., London, 1992; World Trade Centre, Dubai, 1994; Art Connection, Dubai, 2003, 2007; commissions: portrait, Glasgow Univ., Univ. of Edinburgh and Scottish Arts Council, 1985; window design, New Scottish Nat. Lib., Edinburgh, 1986; portrait: Edinburgh Chamber of Commerce, 1986; St John's Hosp., Livingston, 1994; public collections include: Scottish Arts Council; Edinburgh, Aberdeen and Leeds CCs; Hunterian Mus., Glasgow Univ.; Heriot Watt Univ.; Victoria and Albert Mus.; IBM; BBC; Nat. Library of Scotland; private collections in UK, Europe, Canada and USA, Asia and Australia. Latimer Award 1970, Guthrie Award 1973, Royal Scottish Acad.; Scottish Arts Council Bursary, 1973; Gillies Bequest Travel Award to India, Royal Scottish Acad., 1978, 2003. *Publications:* The New Maths, 1969; An Account of Travels in Turkey, Iran, Afghanistan, Pakistan, India, Kashmir and Nepal, 1969; An Indian Diary, 1980; Aims and Objectives in Teaching Drawing and Painting, 1980; The Day Book, 1987; Anatomia: an artists' book, 2004. *Recreations:* music, travelling. *Address:* c/o Royal Scottish Academy, Edinburgh EH2 2EL.

DONALD, James Graham, FRICS; Consultant, Strutt & Parker, since 2004 (Chairman 1996–2003); *b* 4 April 1944; *s* of William Graham Donald and Jean (Bubbles) Donald; *m* 1976, Jennifer Seaman; one *s* two *d*. *Educ:* Cranleigh Sch.; Coll. of Estate Mgt (BSc Estate Mgt). FRICS 1981. Savills, 1966–72; joined Strutt & Parker, 1972, Partner, 1978–2004. *Recreations:* sport, running around after the children, cycling, travel, reading. *Address:* c/o Strutt & Parker, 13 Hill Street, W1J 5LQ. *T:* (020) 7318 5020. *Clubs:* Boodle's; Wisley; Richmond FC; Old Cranleighans.

DONALD, Air Marshal Sir John (George), KBE 1985 (OBE 1972); Medical Adviser, AMI Middle East Services Ltd, 1989–95; *b* 7 Nov. 1927; *s* of John Shirran Donald and Janet Knox (*née* Napier); *m* 1954, Margaret Jean Walton; one *s* two *d*. *Educ:* Inverurie Acad.; Aberdeen Univ. (MB, ChB 1951); DTM&H Edin 1964; MRCGP 1971, FRCGP 1977; MFCM 1972, FFCM 1985; MFOM 1982 (AFOM 1980); FRCPE 1986. Commnd RAF, 1953; Senior Medical Officer: Colombo, Ceylon, 1954–57; RAF Stafford, 1957–60; RAF Waddington, 1960–63; student, RAF Staff Coll., 1965; SMO, HQ AFCENT, France and Holland, 1966–68; Dep. Dir, Medical Personnel (RAF), 1969–72; OC, The Princess Mary's RAF Hosp., Akrotiri, Cyprus, 1972–76; OC, RAF Hosp., Ely, 1976–78; PMO, RAF Germany, 1978–81; PMO, RAF Strike Comd, 1981–84; Dir-Gen., RAF Med. Services, 1984–85; Dep. Surg. Gen. (Ops), MoD, and Dir Gen., RAF Med. Services, 1985–86; Med. Dir, Security Forces Hosp., 1986–89. QHS, 1983–86. CStJ 1984. *Recreations:* golf, ski-ing, camping, ornithology. *Address:* 8 Oratory Gardens, Canford Cliffs, Poole, Dorset BH13 7HJ. *Club:* Royal Society of Medicine.

DONALD, Rob, CEng, FCILT; Director General, Centro (West Midlands Passenger Transport Executive), 1995–2006; *b* 25 March 1949; *s* of John Donald and Mary Donald (*née* Gardiner); *m* 1st, 1972, Yvonne Dyer (marr. diss.); two *d*; 2nd, 1991, Marilyn Downie. *Educ:* George Heriot's Sch., Edinburgh; Univ. of Edinburgh (BSc Hons); Imperial Coll., Univ. of London (MSc). MICE 1976; CEng 1976; FCILT (FCIT 1996). Graduate Asst, Brian Colquhoun and Partners, Consultants, London, 1971–73; Sen. Asst Officer, SIA Transport Consultants, London, 1973–75; Project Leader, County Surveyor's Dept, Kent CC, 1975–79; Chief Transportation Officer, Jt Transportation Unit, Merseyside CC, 1979–86; Merseytravel: Section Leader, then Manager, 1986–91; Passenger Services Dir, 1991–95. *Recreations:* travelling, computing, hill-walking. *Address:* Norton Lodge, 32 Greyhound Lane, Stourbridge, W Midlands DY8 3AG. *T:* (01384) 838735.

DONALDSON, Dr Alexander Ivan, OBE 2003; Managing Director and International Veterinary Consultant, Bio-Vet Solutions Ltd, since 2003; Visiting Professor, Royal Veterinary College, University of London, since 2008; *b* 1 July 1942; *s* of Basil Ivan Donaldson and Dorothy Cunningham Donaldson; *m* 1966, Margaret Ruth Elizabeth Swan; one *d* one *s*. *Educ:* High Sch., Dublin; Trinity Coll., Univ. of Dublin (BA 1965; MVB 1965; MA 1968; ScD 1983); Ontario Veterinary Coll., Univ. of Guelph (PhD1969). MRCVS 1965. Post-doctoral research, 1969–71, Vet. Res. Officer, 1973–76, Principal Vet. Res. Officer, 1976–89, Animal Virus Res. Inst., subseq. AFRC. Inst. for Animal Health, Pirbright Lab.; Head: World Ref. Lab. for Foot-and-Mouth Disease, 1985–89; Pirbright Lab., Inst. for Animal Health, 1989–2002. Vis. Prof., Ontario Vet. Coll., Univ. of Guelph, 1972–73. Hon. FRCVS 2003. Hon. DVM&S Edinburgh, 2002. Research Medal, RASE, 1988; Gold Medal, World Orgn for Animal Health, 2004. *Publications:* numerous articles on animal virology in learned jls. *Recreations:* reading, jogging, photography. *Address:* 290 London Road, Burpham, Guildford, Surrey GU4 7LB.

DONALDSON, Brian; HM Diplomatic Service, retired; Ambassador to Republic of Madagascar, 2002–05; *b* 6 April 1946; *s* of late William Donaldson and of Elsie Josephine Donaldson; *m* 1969, Elizabeth Claire Sumner; three *s*. Assistant, Establishments Office, Min. of Civil Aviation, 1963–65; joined HM Diplomatic Service, 1965: Mgt Officer, Algiers, 1968–71; Archivist, La Paz, 1971–73; Communications Ops Dept, FCO, 1974–75; Entry Clearance Officer, Lagos, 1975–79; Vice Consul, Luxembourg, 1979–82; Second Sec., Trade Relns and Exports Dept, FCO, 1982–83; Asst Private Sec. to Minister of State, FCO, 1983–85; Second, later First Sec., Port Louis, Mauritius, 1985–89; Dep. Hd of Mission, Yaoundé, Cameroon, 1989–92; First Sec., Dhaka, 1992–96; Personnel Mgt Dept, FCO, 1996–97; Dep. Hd, Information Dept, FCO, 1997–99; High Comr, Republic of Namibia, 1999–2002. Dir Gen., President of Madagascar's Small Grants Scheme, 2005–08. Patron, Madagascar Development Fund, 2008–; Trustee, Equitrade Foundn, 2006–. Council Mem., Assoc. of Business Execs, 2006–. Chm., Grants Cttee, Kitchen Table Charities Trust, 2006–. *Recreations:* family, amateur dramatics, people watching. *Address:* Rose Cottage, High Street, Milverton, Somerset TA4 1LL.

DONALDSON, Prof. (Charles) Ian (Edward), FBA 1993; Foundation Director, 1974–90, Director, since 2004, Humanities Research Centre, Australian National University; *b* 6 May 1935; *s* of Dr William Edward Donaldson and Elizabeth Donaldson (*née* Weigall); *m* 1st, 1962, Tamsin Jane Procter (marr. diss. 1990); one *s* one *d*; 2nd, 1991, Grazia Maria Therese Gunn. *Educ:* Melbourne Grammar Sch.; Melbourne Univ. (BA 1957); Magdalen Coll., Oxford (BA 1960; MA 1964). Sen. Tutor in English, Univ. of Melbourne, 1958; Oxford University: Harmsworth Sen. Scholar, Merton Coll., 1960–62; Fellow and Lectr in English, Wadham Coll., 1962–69; CUF Lectr in English, 1963–69; Prof. of English, ANU Canberra, 1969–91; Regius Prof. of Rhetoric and English Lit., Univ. of Edinburgh, 1991–95; University of Cambridge: Grace I Prof. of English, 1995–2002; Fellow, King's College, 1995–2005; Dir, Centre for Res. in the Arts, Social Scis and Humanities, 2001–03. Vis. appts, Univ. of California Santa Barbara, Gonville and Caius Coll., Cambridge, Cornell Univ., Melbourne Univ. Syndic, CUP, 1997–2001. FAHA 1975; corresp. FBA 1987; FRSE 1993. *Publications:* The World Upside-Down: comedy from Jonson to Fielding, 1970; (ed) Ben Jonson Poems, 1975; The Rapes of Lucretia, 1982; (ed) Jonson and Shakespeare, 1983; (ed) Transformations in Modern European Drama, 1983; (ed with Tamsin Donaldson) Seeing the First Australians, 1985; (ed) Ben Jonson, 1985; (ed jtly) Shaping Lives: reflections on biography, 1992; (ed) Ben Jonson: Selected Poems, 1995; Jonson's Magic Houses, 1997. *Address:* Humanities Research Centre, Australian National University, Canberra, ACT 0200, Australia. *T:* (2) 61250528.

DONALDSON, David Torrance; QC 1984; a Recorder, since 1994; *b* 30 Sept. 1943; *s* of Alexander Walls Donaldson and Margaret Merry Bryce. *Educ:* Glasgow Academy; Gonville and Caius College, Cambridge (Maj. Schol.; MA); University of Freiburg i. Br., West Germany (Dr jur). Fellow, Gonville and Caius College, Cambridge, 1965–69. Called to the Bar, Gray's Inn, 1968, Bencher, 1995. *Address:* Blackstone Chambers, Blackstone House, Temple, EC4Y 9BW. *T:* (020) 7583 1770.

DONALDSON, Graham Hunter Carley; Senior Chief Inspector of Education in Scotland, since 2002; *b* 11 Dec. 1946; *s* of Matthew and Margaret Donaldson; *m* 1972, Dilys Lloyd; two *s* one *d*. *Educ:* High Sch. of Glasgow; Univ. of Glasgow (MA, DipEd, MEd). Teacher, Glasgow, 1970–73; Hd of Dept, Dumbartonshire, 1973–75; Lectr, Jordanhill Coll. of Educn, 1975–83; Inspector of Schs, 1983–90; Chief Inspector, 1990–96; Depute Sen. Chief Inspector, 1996–2002. Nat. Curriculum Evaluator, 1975–83. FRSA 2003. *Publications:* James IV: a Renaissance King, 1975; Industry and Scottish Schools, 1981. *Recreations:* golf, supporting Motherwell FC, reading, particularly history and biographies. *Address:* HM Inspectorate of Education, Denholm House, Almondvale Business Park, Almondvale Way, Livingston EH54 6GA. *T:* (01506) 600366, *Fax:* (01506) 600388; *e-mail:* graham.donaldson@hmie.gsi.gov.uk.

DONALDSON, Hamish; DL; Chairman, Haslemere Festival, since 2003; *b* 13 June 1936; *s* of late James Donaldson and Marie Christine Cormack; *m* 1965, Linda, *d* of late Dr Leslie Challis Bousfield; three *d*. *Educ:* Oundle School; Christ's College, Cambridge (MA). Nat. Service, 2nd Lieut, Seaforth Highlanders, 1955–57. De La Rue Bull, 1960–66; Urwick, Orr & Partners, 1966–73; Hill Samuel & Co., 1973–91; Man. Dir, Hill Samuel Merchant Bank (SA), 1985–86; Chief Exec., Hill Samuel Bank, 1987–91. Chairman: London Bridge Finance, 1993–95; Gresham Telecomputing, 1993–97; Director: TSB Bank, 1988–91; TSB Group, 1990–91; Macquarie Bank, 1989–91; RSH Trading Ltd, 1994–. Chm., Guildford DAC for the Care of Churches and Churchyards, 1992–; Founder Chm., Surrey Churches Preservation Trust, 1997–. Gov., Royal Sch., Haslemere, 1994–. Freeman, City of London, 1988; Liveryman, Information Technologists' Co., 1992–. DL Surrey, 2004. *Publications:* a Guide to the Successful Management of Computer Projects, 1978; Mantrap: avoiding the pitfalls of project management, 2006. *Recreation:* amateur operatics. *Address:* Edgecombe, Hill Road, Haslemere, Surrey GU27 2JN. *T:* (01428) 644473.

DONALDSON, Ian; *see* Donaldson, C. I. E.

DONALDSON, Rt Hon. Jeffrey (Mark); PC 2007; MP Lagan Valley, since 1997 (UU, 1997–2003, DUP, since 2004); Member, Lagan Valley, Northern Ireland Assembly, since 2003 (UU, 2003–04, DUP, since 2004); Junior Minister, Office of the First Minister and Deputy First Minister, Northern Ireland, since 2008; *b* 7 Dec. 1962; *s* of James Alexander Donaldson and Sarah Anne Donaldson; *m* 1987, Eleanor Mary Elizabeth Cousins; two *d*. *Educ:* Castlereagh Coll. (DipEE); Chartered Insurance Inst. (Financial Planning Cert.). Agent to Rt Hon. J. Enoch Powell, MP, 1983–85; Mem., NI Assembly, 1985–86; Partner in financial services/estate agency practice, 1986–97. Mem., NI Forum, 1996–98. Alderman, Lisburn CC, 2005–. Hon. Sec., 1988–2000, Vice-Pres., 2000–03, UU Council. *Recreations:* travelling, walking, reading, war graves and battlefield heritage. *Address:* House of Commons, SW1A 0AA. *T:* (020) 7219 3407; Old Town Hall, 29 Castle Street, Lisburn, Co. Antrim BT27 4ST. *T:* (028) 9266 8001.

DONALDSON, Julia Catherine; writer of books, songs and plays for children; *b* 16 Sept. 1948; *d* of James Shields and Elizabeth Shields (*née* Ede); *m* 1972, Malcolm Donaldson; two *s* (and one *s* decd). *Educ:* Camden Sch. for Girls; Univ. of Bristol (BA Drama and French 1970); Falmer Coll. of Educn (PGCE English 1976). Editl Asst, Michael Joseph, 1971–72; Short-Story Editor, BBC Radio Bristol, 1973–74; Editor, Robert Tyndall, 1974–75; English Teacher, St Mary's Hall, Brighton, 1976–78; freelance contrib. of songs to BBC television progs, 1974–. Writer in Residence, Easterhouse, Glasgow, 1998–2001. Chm., Assoc. of Children's Writers and Illustrators in Scotland, 2001–03. Volunteer, CAB, Glasgow, 1993–97. *Publications:* A Squash and a Squeeze, 1993; The Gruffalo, 1999; Monkey Puzzle, Follow the Swallow, Tales from Acorn Wood: Fox's Socks, Rabbit's Nap, Postman Bear, Hide and Seek Pig, 2000; Room on the Broom, 2001; The Dinosaur's Diary, Night Monkey Day Monkey, 2002; The Smartest Giant in Town, Spinderella, The Head in the Sand, Bombs and Blackberries, The Magic Paintbrush, Conjuror Cow, Princess Mirror-Belle, The Snail and the Whale, Brick-A-Breck, 2003; The Wrong Kind of Bark, Wriggle and Roar, Sharing a Shell, The Giants and the Joneses, The Gruffalo's Child, One Ted Falls out of Bed, Crazy Mayonnaisy Mum, 2004; The Gruffalo Song and other Songs, Princess Mirror-Belle and the Magic Shoes, Chocolate Mousse for Greedy Goose, Rosie's Hat, The Jungle House, The Quick Brown Fox Cub, Charlie Cook's Favourite Book, 2005; Hippo Has a Hat, Princess Mirror-Belle and the Flying Horse, Play Time!, The Princess and the Wizard, (with John Henderson) Fly Pigeon Fly, 2006; Room on the Broom and other Songs, Tyrannosaurus Drip, Tiddler, 2007; One Mole Digging a Hole, Stick Man, 2008; also various educnl pubns incl. Songbirds (series of 48 phonic reading books), part of Oxford Reading Tree, 2006–08. *Recreations:* piano playing, singing, walking, study of flowers and fungi. *Address:* c/o Macmillan Children's Books, 20 New Wharf Road, N1 9RR.

DONALDSON, Sir Liam (Joseph), Kt 2002; MD; FRCP, FRCPE, FRCSE, FFPH, FRCGP; Chief Medical Officer, Department of Health, since 1998; *b* 3 May 1949. *Educ:* Univ. of Bristol (MB, ChB 1972); Univ. of Birmingham (MSc 1976); Univ. of Leicester (MD 1982). FRCSE 1977; FFPH (FFCM 1987; FFPHM 1990); FRCP 1997; FRCGP 1999; FRCPE 1999. House Officer, United Bristol Hosps, 1972–73; Lectr in Anatomy, Univ. of Birmingham, 1973–75; Surgical Registrar, United Birmingham Hosps, 1975–77; Lectr in Anatomy, then Sen. Lectr in Epidemiol., Univ. of Leicester, 1977–86; Regl Med. Officer and Head of Clinical Policy, then Director of Public Health, Northern RHA, 1986–92; Regl Gen. Manager and Dir of Public Health, Northern and Yorks RHA, later Regl Dir and Dir of Public Health, Northern and Yorks NHS Exec., 1994–98. Hon. Prof. of Applied Epidemiol., Univ. of Newcastle upon Tyne, 1989–. Chm., WHO World Alliance for Patient Safety, 2004–. QHP 1996–99. Hon. doctorates from univs of Bristol, Leicester, Cranfield, Huddersfield, Portsmouth, York, Sheffield, Teesside, Birmingham, De Montfort, Nottingham, Hull and East Anglia. Gold Medal, RCSE, 2000. *Publications:* (with R. J. Donaldson) Essential Community Medicine, 1983, rev. edn as Essential Public Health, 2003; (ed with B. R. McAvoy) Health Care for Asians, 1990; (with S. Sheard) The Nation's Doctor, 2005; over 100 papers on various aspects of health services research. *Address:* Department of Health, Richmond House, 79 Whitehall, SW1A 2NS.

DONALDSON, Air Vice-Marshal Michael Phillips, MBE 1973; Chief Executive and Principal, Yorkshire Coast College, 1996–2003; *b* 22 July 1943; *s* of George Millar Donaldson and Mabel Donaldson (*née* Phillips); *m* 1970, Mavis Cornish; one *s* one *d*. *Educ:* Chislehurst and Sidcup Grammar Sch. for Boys. RAF Gen. Duties; Pilot and Weapons Instructor; No 23 Sqn (Lightning), 1965–68; No 226 OCU, 1969; USAF Florida (F106), 1970–73; No 29 Sqn (Phantom), 1974–76; No 228 OCU, 1977; Army Staff Coll., 1978; PSO to Dep. Comdr in Chief AFCENT, Brunssum, 1979–80; MoD, 1980–83; OC 19 Sqn, 1983–85; OC 23 Sqn (Falkland Is), 1985; Dep. PSO to CDS, 1986–87; OC RAF Wattisham, 1987–89; RCDS 1990; SASO, 11 Group, 1990–93; Comdt, RAF Staff Coll., 1993–96. Life Vice-Pres., RAF Squash Rackets Assoc., 1996. MInstD; FRAeS 1997; FRSA 1999. *Recreations:* music, history, squash, tennis, golf. *Club:* Royal Air Force.

DONALDSON, Dame Patricia Anne; *see* Hodgson, Dame P. A.

DONALDSON, Prof. Simon Kirwan, DPhil; FRS 1986; Professor of Pure Mathematics, Imperial College, London University, since 1998; *b* 20 Aug. 1957; *m* 1986, Ana Nora Hurtado; two *s* one *d*. *Educ:* Sevenoaks Sch., Kent; Pembroke Coll., Cambridge (BA 1979; Hon. Fellow, 1992); Worcester Coll., Oxford (DPhil 1983). Jun. Res. Fellow, All Souls Coll., Oxford, 1983–85; Wallis Prof. of Maths, and Fellow, St Anne's Coll., Univ. of Oxford, 1985–98, Hon. Fellow, 1998. Fields Medal, IMU, 1986. *Publications:* (with P. B. Kronheimer) The Geometry of Four-manifolds, 1990; papers in mathematical jls. *Recreation:* sailing. *Address:* Department of Mathematics, Imperial College, 180 Queen's Gate, SW7 2BZ.

DONCASTER, Bishop Suffragan of, since 2000; **Rt Rev. Cyril Guy Ashton;** *b* 6 April 1942; *s* of William Joseph Ashton and Margaret Anne Ashton (*née* Todd); *m* 1965, Muriel Ramshaw; three *s* one *d*. *Educ:* Oak Hill Theol Coll.; Lancaster Univ. (MA 1986). Ordained deacon, 1967, priest, 1968; Curate, St Thomas', Blackpool, 1967–70; Vocations Sec., CPAS, 1970–74; Vicar, St Thomas', Lancaster, 1974–91; Dir of Training, Dio. Blackburn, 1991–2000. Hon. Canon, Blackburn Cathedral, 1991–2000. *Publications:* Church on the Threshold, 1988, 2nd edn 1991; Threshold God, 1992; (with Jack Nicholls) A Faith Worth Sharing?: a Church Worth Joining?, 1995. *Recreations:* motorcycling, swimming, cycling, vintage cars. *Address:* Bishop's House, 3 Farrington Court, Goose Lane, Wickersley, Rotherham S66 1JQ.

DONCASTER, Archdeacon of; *see* Fitzharris, Ven. R. A.

DONE, Frances Winifred, CBE 2003; FCA; Chair, Youth Justice Board, since 2008; *b* 6 May 1950; *d* of Rt Hon. Lord Bishopston, PC and Winifred Mary (*née* Bryant); *m* 1981, James Hancock; two *s*. *Educ:* Manchester Univ. (BA Econ.). FCA 1976. Chm., Finance Cttee, Manchester CC, 1984–88; Treas., 1991–98, Chief Exec. and Treas., 1998–2000, Rochdale MBC; Chief Exec., Manchester 2002 Ltd, XVII Commonwealth Games Org. Cttee, 2000–03; Man. Dir, Local Govt, Housing and Criminal Justice, subseq. Local Govt and Housing, Audit Commn, 2003–06; Interim Dir Gen., RBL, 2007. Trustee, Waterways Trust, 2003–. *Recreations:* canals, walking, family.

DONEGALL, 8th Marquess of, *cr* 1791 (Ire.); **Arthur Patrick Chichester;** Viscount Chichester and Baron Chichester of Belfast, 1625; Earl of Donegall, 1647; Earl of Belfast, 1791; Baron Fisherwick (GB), 1790; Baron Templemore (UK), 1831; Hereditary Lord High Admiral of Lough Neagh; Governor of Carrickfergus Castle; farmer; *b* 9 May 1952; *s* of 7th Marquess of Donegall, LVO and Lady Josceline Gabrielle Legge, *y d* of 7th Earl of Dartmouth, GCVO, TD; *S* father, 2007; *m* 1989, Caroline, *er d* of Major Christopher Philipson; one *s* one *d*. *Educ:* Harrow; Royal Agricl Coll., Cirencester. Coldstream Guards. *Recreations:* hunting, shooting, fishing. *Heir: s* Earl of Belfast, *qv*. *Address:* Dunbrody Park, Arthurstown, Co. Wexford, Eire; Howthill, Jedburgh, Roxburghshire TD8 6QR.

DONERAILE, 10th Viscount *cr* 1785 (Ire.); **Richard Allen St Leger;** Baron Doneraile, 1776; *b* 17 Aug. 1946; *s* of 9th Viscount Doneraile and of Melva, Viscountess Doneraile; *S* father, 1983; *m* 1970, Kathleen Mary Simcox, Churchtown, Mallow, Co. Cork; one *s* one *d*. *Educ:* Orange Coast College, California; Mississippi Univ. Served US Army. Air Traffic Control specialist; antiquarian book appraiser, 1970–73; food marketing analyst, 1974. *Recreations:* outdoor sports, ski-ing, golf, sailing. *Heir: s* Hon. Nathaniel Warham Robert St John St Leger, *b* 13 Sept. 1971. *Club:* Yorba Linda Country (California).

DONLEAVY, James Patrick; author and artist; *b* 23 April 1926; *m* Valerie Heron (marr. diss.); one *s* one *d*; *m* Mary Wilson Price (marr. diss.); one *s* one *d*. *Educ:* schs in USA; Trinity Coll., Dublin. Evening Standard Drama Critics' Award, 1961; Brandeis Univ. Creative Arts Award, 1962; AAAL Grantee, 1975; Worldfest Houston Gold Award, 1992. *Art exhibitions:* Painter's Gall., Dublin, 1950, 1951; Bronxville, NY, 1959; Langton Galls, London, 1975; Caldwell Galls, Belfast, 1987; Anna Mei Chadwick Gall., London, 1989, 1991; Alba Fine Art Gall., London, 1991; The Front Lounge, Dublin, 1995; Walton Gall., London, 2002; Molesworth Gall., Dublin, 2006. *Publications:* The Ginger Man (novel), 1955; Fairy Tales of New York (play), 1960; What They Did In Dublin With The Ginger Man (introd. and play), 1961; A Singular Man (novel), 1963 (play, 1964); Meet My Maker The Mad Molecule (short stories), 1964; The Saddest Summer of Samuel S (novella), 1966 (play, 1967); The Beastly Beatitudes of Balthazar B (novel), 1968 (play, 1981); The Onion Eaters (novel), 1971; The Plays of J. P. Donleavy, 1972; A Fairy Tale of New York (novel), 1973; The Unexpurgated Code: a complete manual of survival and manners, 1975; The Destinies of Darcy Dancer, Gentleman (novel), 1977; Schultz (novel), 1980; Leila (novel), 1983; De Alfonce Tennis: the superlative game of eccentric champions, its history, accoutrements, rules, conduct and regimen (sports manual), 1984; J. P. Donleavy's Ireland, in all her Sins and in some of her Graces, 1986 (Cine Golden Eagle Award, 1993, for television prodn (writer and narrator)); Are You Listening Rabbi Low (novel), 1987; A Singular Country, 1989; That Darcy, That Dancer, That Gentleman (novel), 1990; The History of the Ginger Man (autobiog.), 1994; The Lady Who Liked Clean Rest Rooms (novella), 1996; An Author and His Image: the collected short pieces, 1997; Wrong Information Is Being Given Out at Princeton (novel), 1998; A Letter Marked Personal (novel), 2005; contribs to jls etc, incl. The Observer, The Times (London), New York Times, Washington Post, Daily Telegraph, Daily Mail, Irish Ind., Esquire, Envoy, Punch, Guardian, Saturday Evening Post, Holiday, Atlantic Monthly, Saturday Review, The New Yorker, Queen, Vogue, Penthouse, Playboy, Architectural Digest, Vanity Fair,

Rolling Stone, Liberation (Paris). *Address:* Levington Park, Mullingar, Co. Westmeath, Ireland.

DONN, Mary Cecilia; *see* Spinks, M. C.

DONNACHIE, Prof. Alexander, FInstP; Professor of Physics, 1969–2001, now Emeritus, and Hon. Professor of Physics and Astronomy, since 2001, University of Manchester; *b* 25 May 1936; *s* of John Donnachie and Mary Ramsey Donnachie (*née* Adams); *m* 1960, Dorothy Paterson; two *d. Educ:* Kilmarnock Acad.; Glasgow Univ. (BSc, PhD). DSIR Res. Fellow 1961–63, Lectr 1963–65, UCL; Res. Associate, CERN, Geneva, 1965–67; Sen. Lectr, Univ. of Glasgow, 1967–69; University of Manchester: Hd of Theoretical Physics 1975–85; Dean of Faculty of Science, 1985–87; Chm., Dept of Physics, 1988–94; Dir of Physical Labs, 1989–94; Dean, Faculty of Science and Engrg, 1994–97. Mem., SERC, 1989–94 (Chm., Nuclear Phys Bd, 1989–93); CERN: Chairman: Super Proton Synchrotron Cttee, 1988–90; Super Proton Synchrotron and LEAR Cttee, 1991–93; Member: Res. Bd, 1988–95; Sci. Policy Cttee, 1988–93; Council, 1989–94; Particle, Space and Astronomy Bd, 1993–94; Sec., C11 Commn, IUPAP, 1989–91. *Publications:* Electromagnetic Interactions of Hadrons, vols I and II, 1978; Pomeron Physics and QCD, 2002; Electromagnetic Interactions and Hadronic Structure, 2007; nearly 200 articles in learned jls of Particle Physics. *Recreations:* sailing, walking. *Address:* School of Physics and Astronomy, University of Manchester, Manchester M13 9PL. *T:* (0161) 275 4193.

DONNAI, Prof. Dian, CBE 2005; FRCP, FRCPCH, FRCOG, FMedSci; Professor of Medical Genetics, University of Manchester, since 2001 (Hon. Professor, 1994–2001); Consultant Clinical Geneticist, Regional Genetics Service, St Mary's Hospital, Manchester, since 1980; *b* 15 Feb. 1945; *d* of Arnold Sydney Aughton and May Aughton; *m* 1968, Paul Donnai; one *s* one *d. Educ:* Whitchurch Girls' High Sch., Shropshire; St Mary's Hosp. Med. Sch., London Univ. (MB BS 1968). FRCP 1984; FRCPCH 1997; FRCOG *ad eundem* 1995; FMedSci 2001. Consultant Advr in Genetics to CMO, DoH, 1998–2003. Pres., Med Scis Section, BAAS, 2007. *Publications:* (ed jtly) Congenital Malformation Syndromes, 1996; (ed jtly) Antenatal Diagnosis of Fetal Abnormalities, 1991; (ed jtly) Early Fetal Growth and Development, 1994; (with A. Read) New Clinical Genetics, 2007; numerous articles on genetic disorders and syndromes. *Recreation:* learning French. *Address:* Academic Unit of Medical Genetics and Regional Genetics Service, St Mary's Hospital, Hathersage Road, Manchester M13 0JH. *T:* (0161) 276 6002, *Fax:* (0161) 276 6145; *e-mail:* Dian.Donnai@cmmc.nhs.uk.

DONNE, David Lucas; Director, Marathon Asset Management, since 1989; *b* 17 Aug. 1925; *s* of late Dr Cecil Lucas Donne, Wellington, NZ; *m* 1st, 1957, Jennifer Margaret Duncan (*d* 1975); two *s* one *d;* 2nd, 1978, Clare, *d* of Maj. F. J. Yates. *Educ:* Stowe; Christ Church, Oxford (MA Nat. Science). Called to the Bar, Middle Temple, 1949. Studied Business Admin, Syracuse Univ., 1952–53; Charterhouse Group, 1953–64; William Baird, 1964–67. Chairman: Crest Nicholson, 1973–92; Dalgety, 1977–86 (Dep. Chm., 1975–77); Steetley, 1983–92 (Dep. Chm., 1979–83); ASDA-MFI, 1986–87; Argos, 1990–95; Director: Royal Trust Bank, 1972–93 (Dep. Chm., 1989–93); Sphere Investment Trust, 1982–95 (Chm., 1989–95). Member: Nat. Water Council, 1980–83; Bd, British Coal (formerly NCB), 1984–87; Stock Exchange Listed Cos Adv. Cttee, 1987–91. Trustee, Cancerbackup (formerly CancerBACUP), 1993–; Chm., Calibre Cassette Liby for the Blind, 1997–2004. Fellow, Game Conservancy, 1987. *Recreations:* shooting, opera, sailing. *Address:* 8 Montagu Mews North, W1H 2JU. *Club:* Royal Thames Yacht.

DONNE, Hon. Sir Gaven (John), KBE 1979; Chief Justice: of Nauru, 1985–2000; of Tuvalu, 1986–2001; Member, Kiribati Court of Appeal, 1987–92; *b* 8 May 1914; *s* of Jack Alfred Donne and Mary Elizabeth Donne; *m* 1946, Isabel Fenwick, *d* of John Edwin Hall; two *s* two *d. Educ:* Palmerston North Boys' High Sch.; Hastings High Sch.; Victoria Univ., Wellington; Auckland Univ. (LLB New Zealand). Called to the Bar and admitted solicitor, 1938. Military Service, 2nd NZEF, Middle East and Italy, 1941–45. Stipendiary Magistrate, NZ, 1958–75; Puisne Judge, Supreme Court of Western Samoa, 1970–71; Chief Justice, Western Samoa, 1972–75, Mem. Court of Appeal of Western Samoa, 1975–82; Judge, High Court of Niue, 1973; Chief Justice of the Cook Islands, 1975–82, and of Niue, 1974–82; Queen's Rep. in the Cook Islands, 1982–84. Hon. Counsellor, Internat. Assoc. of Youth Magistrates, 1974–. Member: Takapuna Bor. Council, 1957–58; Auckland Town Planning Authority, 1958; Bd of Governors, Westlake High Sch., 1957–58. Grand Cross 2nd Cl., Order of Merit of Fed. Republic of Germany, 1978. *Recreation:* walking. *Address:* Otaramarae, Rotorua, New Zealand. *Club:* University (Auckland).

DONNE, Jeremy Nigel, RD 1992; QC 2003; a Recorder, since 1998; *b* 22 Jan. 1954; *s* of Tom and Shirley Donne; *m* 1984, Caroline Susan O'Brien-Gore; two *d. Educ:* County Grammar Sch., Merthyr Tydfil; Cyfarthfa High Sch., Merthyr Tydfil; Inns of Court Sch. of Law. Called to the Bar, Middle Temple, 1978; specialises in criminal, regulatory and disciplinary law. Mem., RNSA, 1980–. Chm., Govs, All Saints C of E Sch., Putney, 2006–. *Recreations:* sailing, ski-ing, cycling. *Address:* Queen Elizabeth Building, Temple, EC4Y 9BS. *T:* (020) 7583 5766, *Fax:* (020) 7353 0339; *e-mail:* jdonne@holliswhiteman.co.uk. *Clubs:* Winchester House, Royal Naval Volunteer Reserve Yacht (Cdre, 2007–), Royal Thames Yacht, Bar Yacht.

DONNE, Sir John (Christopher), Kt 1976; Chairman, National Health Service Training Authority, 1983–86; *b* 19 Aug. 1921; *s* of late Leslie Victor Donne, solicitor, Hove, and Mabel Laetitia Richards (*née* Pike); *m* 1945, Mary Stuart (*née* Seaton); three *d. Educ:* Charterhouse. Royal Artillery, 1940–46 (Captain); served Europe and India. Solicitor, 1949; Notary Public; Consultant, Donne Mileham & Haddock, 1985–92; Pres., Sussex Law Soc., 1969–70. Chairman: SE (Metropolitan) Regional Hosp. Bd, 1971–74; SE Thames RHA, 1973–83. Governor, Guy's Hosp., 1971–74, Guy's Hosp. Med. Sch., 1974–82; Dep. Chm., RHA Chairmen, 1976–78 (Chm., 1974–76); Mem., Gen. Council, King Edward's Hosp. Fund for London, 1972–91 (Mem., Management Cttee, 1978–84); a Governing Trustee, Nuffield Provincial Hosp. Trust, 1975–98; Dir, Nuffield Health and Soc. Services Fund, 1976–98. Member: Council, Internat. Hosp. Fedn, 1979–85; Council, Inst. for Med. Ethics (formerly Soc. for Study of Medical Ethics), 1980–86; Court of Univ. of Sussex, 1979–87. FRSA 1985–92; FRSocMed 1985. Mem. Ct of Assts, Hon. Company of Broderers, 1979– (Master, 1983–84). Mem., Editorial Bd, Jl Medical Ethics, 1977–79. *Recreations:* genealogy, gardening, photography, listening to music. *Address:* The Old School House, Acton Burnell, Shrewsbury SY5 7PG. *T:* and *Fax:* (01694) 731647. *Clubs:* Pilgrims, MCC; Butterflies, Sussex Martlets.

DONNELLAN, Declan Michael Martin; Joint Artistic Director, Cheek By Jowl, since 1981; Associate Director, Royal National Theatre, 1989–97; *b* 4 Aug. 1953; *s* of Thomas Patrick John Donnellan and Margaret Josephine Donnellan. *Educ:* Queens' Coll., Cambridge (MA). Called to the Bar, Middle Temple, 1978. Associate Dir, Russian Th. Confedn, 1999–. Productions: Cheek By Jowl: Twelfth Night, 1987; Lady Betty, 1989; As You Like It, 1992, 1995; Measure for Measure, 1994; Duchess of Malfi, 1996; Much Ado About Nothing, 1998; Othello, 2004; The Changeling, 2006; Cymbeline, 2007; Three Sisters, 2007; Royal National Theatre: Fuente Ovejuna, 1989; Peer Gynt, 1990; Angels in America: part 1, Millennium, 1991, part 2, Perestroika, 1993; Sweeney Todd, 1992; The Mandate, 2004; Royal Shakespeare Company: The School for Scandal, 1998; King Lear, 2002; Great Expectations, 2005; Russian Theatre Confederation: Boris Godunov, 2000; Twelfth Night, 2003; Three Sisters, 2005; The Winter's Tale, Maly Drama Theatre, St Petersburg, 1997; Le Cid, Avignon Fest., 1998; The Homebody, and Kabul, NY, 2001; Falstaff, Salzburg Fest., 2001; Romeo and Juliet, Bolshoi Ballet, Moscow, 2003. Several internat. awards incl. Observer Award for Outstanding Achievement. Chevalier, Ordre des Arts et des Lettres (France). *Publication:* The Actor and the Target, 2002 (trans. several languages). *Address:* c/o Cheek By Jowl, Barbican Centre, Silk Street, EC2Y 8DS.

DONNELLY, Alan John; Executive Chairman, Sovereign Strategy, since 2000; Secretary, Co-operative Commission, since 2000; *b* 16 July 1957; *s* of John and Josephine Donnelly; *m* 1979 (marr. diss. 1982); one *s. Educ:* Valley View Primary School and Springfield Comprehensive School, Jarrow; Sunderland Poly. (Hon. Fellow, Sunderland Univ., 1993). GMBATU Northern Region: Health and Safety Officer, 1978–80; Education Officer, 1980–84; Finance and Admin Officer, 1984–87; GMB Central Finance Manager, 1987–89. European Parliament: Member (Lab): Tyne and Wear, 1989–99; NE Reg., England, 1999–Jan. 2000; Pres., Delegn, Relations with USA, 1992–98; Leader, Lab. Party, 1998–2000; a Vice Pres., Socialist Gp. Mem., S Tyneside MBC, 1979–82. B Director, Unity Trust Bank, 1987–89. Kt Comdr, Order of Merit (Germany), 1991. *Recreations:* tennis, swimming, reading.

DONNELLY, Brendan Patrick; Director, Federal Trust, since 2003; Chairman Federal Union, since 2003; *b* 25 Aug. 1950; *s* of Patrick Aloysius Donnelly and late Mary Josephine Donnelly (*née* Barrett). *Educ:* Christ Church, Oxford (BA Classics 1972; MA 1976). Theodor Heuss Travelling Scholar, Munich, 1974–76; FCO, 1976–82; Private Sec. to Sir Henry Plumb, 1983–86; on staff of Lord Cockfield, a Vice-Pres. of CEC, 1986–87; Political Consultant on EC, 1987–90; Special Advr to Leader of Conservatives in EP, 1990–94. MEP (C) Sussex S and Crawley, 1994–99. *Publications:* (jtly) Not in Our Name, 2005; numerous articles on European Union. *Recreations:* watching cricket, modern languages, modern history. *Address:* 61 Leopold Road, N2 8BG. *T:* (020) 8444 0154.

DONNELLY, Sir Brian; *see* Donnelly, Sir J. B.

DONNELLY, Prof. Christl Ann, ScD; Professor of Statistical Epidemiology, Imperial College London, since 2002; *b* 19 June 1967; *d* of Rett F. Donnelly and Lou Ellen Donnelly (*née* Hartke); *m* 2000, Ben Hambly; two *s. Educ:* Oberlin Coll., Ohio (BA 1988); Harvard Univ. (MSc 1990; ScD 1992). Lectr, Univ. of Edinburgh, 1992–95; Hd, Statistics Unit, Wellcome Trust Centre for Epidemiol. of Infectious Disease, Univ. of Oxford, 1995–2000; Lectr, St Catherine's Coll., Oxford, 1998–2000; Reader, Imperial Coll., London, 2000–02. Dep. Chm., Ind. Scientific Gp on Cattle TB, 1998–2007. Mem. Council, Royal Statistical Soc., 2001–05. Associate Ed., Applied Statistics, 2001–04; Mem., Edtl Bd, Internat. Jl of Biostatistics, 2004–. Franco-British Prize, Acad. des Scis, Paris, 2002; Dist. Alum Award, Dept of Biostats, Harvard Univ., 2005. *Publications:* (with N. M. Ferguson) Statistical Aspects of BSE and vCJD: models for epidemics, 2000; many contribs to learned jls, inc. Nature, Science and Lancet. *Recreation:* travel. *Address:* Department of Infectious Disease Epidemiology, Faculty of Medicine, Imperial College London, St Mary's Campus, Norfolk Place, W2 1PG. *T:* (020) 7594 3394, *Fax:* (020) 7262 3180; *e-mail:* c.donnelly@imperial.ac.uk.

DONNELLY, Christopher Nigel, CMG 2004; TD 1982; Senior Fellow, Defence Academy of the United Kingdom, since 2003; Director, Institute of Statecraft and Governance, Oxford, since 2005; *b* 10 Nov. 1946; *s* of Anthony Donnelly and Dorothy Mary Donnelly (*née* Morris); *m* 1971, Jill Norris; one *s* one *d. Educ:* Cardinal Langley Sch., Middleton, Lancs; Manchester Univ. (BA Hons (Russian Studies) 1969). Royal Military Academy Sandhurst: Instructor, 1969–72; Sen. Lectr, 1972–79, Dir, 1979–89, Soviet Studies Res. Centre; Special Advr for Central and E European affairs to Sec. Gen. of NATO, 1989–2003. Adjunct Professor: Carnegie Mellon Univ., 1985–89; Georgia Inst. of Technol., 1989–93. TA Officer (Intelligence Corps), 1970–93. *Publications:* Red Banner, 1988, 2nd edn 1989; War and the Soviet Union, 1990; Gorbachev's Revolution, 1991; Nations, Alliances and Security, 2004. *Recreations:* shooting, fishing. *Address:* Headquarters, Defence Academy of the United Kingdom, Shrivenham, Swindon, Wilts SN6 8LA. *T:* (01793) 788195, *Fax:* (01793) 788287; *e-mail:* cdonnelly.hq@da.mod.uk. *Club:* Army and Navy.

DONNELLY, Jane Caroline; *see* Owen, J. C.

DONNELLY, Sir (Joseph) Brian, KBE 2003; CMG 1998; HM Diplomatic Service, retired; Ambassador (formerly High Commissioner) to Zimbabwe, 2001–04; *b* 24 April 1945; *s* of Joseph Donnelly and Ada Agnes (*née* Bowness); *m* 1st, 1966, Susanne Gibb (marr. diss. 1994); one *d;* 2nd, 1997, Julia Mary Newsome; one step *s* one step *d. Educ:* Workington Grammar Sch.; Queen's Coll., Oxford (Wyndham Scholar, MA); Univ. of Wisconsin (MA). Admin. trainee, GCHQ, 1970; joined HM Diplomatic Service, 1973; 2nd Sec., FCO, 1973; 1st Sec., UK Mission to UN, NY, 1975–79; Head of Chancery, Singapore, 1979–82; Asst Head, Personnel Policy Dept, FCO, 1982–84; Dep. to Chief Scientific Adviser, Cabinet Office, 1984–87; Counsellor and Consul General, Athens, 1988–91; RCDS, 1991; Head of Non-Proliferation Dept, FCO, 1992–95; Minister and Dep. Perm. Rep., UK Delegn to NATO and WEU, Brussels, 1995–97; Ambassador to Yugoslavia, 1997–99; Dir and Special Rep. for SE Europe, FCO, 1999–2000, on secondment to BP Amoco, 2000–01. Special Advr to Sec. of State for Foreign and Commonwealth Affairs, 2005–06. Mem., Commonwealth Scholarships Commn, 2006–; Trustee, Senhouse Museum Trust, 2007–. *Recreations:* MG cars, flying kites, reading, golf. *Address:* *e-mail:* donnewjb@yahoo.co.uk. *Clubs:* Royal Commonwealth Society; MG Owners'; Maryport Golf.

DONNELLY, Martin Eugene, CMG 2002; Senior Partner, Office of Communications, since 2008 (on secondment); *b* 4 June 1958; *s* of Eugene Lawrence Donnelly and Mary Jane Ormsby; *m* 1st, 1985, Carol Jean Heald (*d* 1996); three *d;* 2nd, 1998, Susan Jane Catchpole. *Educ:* Campion Hall, Oxford (MA); Coll. of Europe (Dip. European Studies 1980). Joined HM Treasury, 1980; Private Sec. to Financial Sec., 1982–83; Ecole Nationale d'Admin, Paris, 1983–84; Principal, HM Treasury, 1984–87; Private Sec. to Sec. of State for NI, 1988; Mem., cabinet of Sir Leon Brittan, EC, 1989–92; Asst Sec., Defence Team, HM Treasury, 1993–95; chargé de mission, Direction du Trésor, Finance Min., France, 1995–96; Team Leader, Economic and Monetary Union, HM Treasury, 1996–97; Dep. Hd, European Secretariat, Cabinet Office, 1997–2003; Dep. Dir Gen., Immigration and Nationality Directorate, Home Office, 2003–04; Dir Gen. (Econ.), subseq. (Europe and Globalisation), FCO, 2004–08. *Publications:* articles on G-8, European Commission and cabinet system. *Recreations:* reading, music, walking. *Address:* Office of Communications, Riverside House, 2a Southwark Bridge Road, SE1 9HA.

DONNELLY, Prof. Peter Duncan, MD; FRCP, FRCPE, FFPH; Deputy Chief Medical Officer to the Scottish Government (formerly Scottish Executive), since 2004; *b* 27 Jan. 1963; *s* of Dr James Donnelly and Gwyneth Donnelly; *m* 1988, Joan Dymock; three *s*. *Educ:* Univ. of Edinburgh (MB ChB; MD 1999); Univ. of Stirling (MBA 1989, NHS Mgt Develt Gp scholar); Univ. of Wales Coll. of Medicine (MPH); Harvard Univ. (PMD). FFPH 1997; FRCP 2000; FRCPE 2001. Junior hosp. doctor appts, 1985–88; South Glamorgan Health Authority: Registrar, 1989–90; Sen. Registrar, 1990–92; Consultant in Public Health Medicine, 1992–93; Actg Dir, Planning and Procurement, 1993–94; Dep. Chief Admin MO/Dep. Dir of Public Health Medicine, 1994–96; Dir of Public Health and Exec. Mem. Bd, Morgannwg HA, 1996–2000; Dir, Public Health and Health Policy, Lothian Health Bd, 2000–04. Lectr, 1989–92, Sen. Lectr, 1992–96, Hon. Sen. Lectr, 1996–2000, in Public Health Medicine, UWCM; Hon. Sen. Lectr in Public Health Medicine, Univ. of Wales, Swansea, 1996–2000; Hon. Prof. of Public Health, Univ. of Edinburgh, 2002–. Pres., Assoc. of Dirs of Public Health, 1999–2001; Vice Pres., Faculty of Public Health Medicine, RCP, 2001–04 (Treas., 1999–2001). Hon. DSc Napier, 2003. *Publications:* articles in scientific and professional press on public health and resuscitation. *Recreations:* running, ski-ing, reading, cooking, coaching children's football. *Address:* Scottish Government Health Department, St Andrew's House, Regent Road, Edinburgh EH1 3DG. *T:* (0131) 244 2270, *Fax:* (0131) 244 3477; *e-mail:* peter.donnelly@scotland.gsi.gov.uk.

DONNELLY, Prof. Peter James, DPhil; FRS 2006; Professor of Statistical Science, since 1996, and Director, Wellcome Trust Centre for Human Genetics, since 2007, University of Oxford; Fellow of St Anne's College, Oxford, since 1996; *b* 15 May 1959; *s* of late Augustine Stanislaus Donnelly and of Sheila Bernadette Donnelly (*née* O'Hagan); *m* 1986, Dr Sarah Helen Harper (marr. diss. 2006); one *s* two *d*; one *d* by Kerstin Sallows. *Educ:* St Joseph's Coll., Brisbane; Univ. of Queensland (BSc 1979; Univ. Medal 1980); Balliol Coll., Oxford (Rhodes Schol., DPhil 1983). Vis. Asst Prof., Michigan Univ., 1983–84; Res. Fellow, UC Swansea, 1984–85; Lectr, UCL, 1985–88; Prof. of Math. Stats and Operational Res., QMW, 1988–94; Prof. of Stats and Ecology and Evolution, Chicago Univ., 1994–96. Hon. FIA 1999. Mitchell Prize, Amer. Statistical Soc., 2002; Guy Medal, Silver, Royal Statistical Soc., 2004. *Publications:* (ed jtly) Progress in Population Genetics and Human Evolution, 1997; (ed jtly) Genes, Fossils and Behaviour, 2001; contrib. to learned jls. *Recreations:* sport, music, children. *Address:* Wellcome Trust Centre for Human Genetics, Roosevelt Drive, Oxford OX3 7BN. *T:* (01865) 287725.

DONNISON, David Vernon; Hon. Research Fellow, Glasgow University, since 1991; *b* 19 Jan. 1926; *s* of late Frank Siegfried Vernon Donnison, CBE and Ruth Seruya Singer, MBE, JP; *m* 1st, Jean Kidger; two *s* two *d*; 2nd, 1987, Catherine McIntosh, (Kay), Carmichael, *qv*. *Educ:* Marlborough Coll., Wiltshire; Magdalen Coll., Oxford. Asst Lectr and Lectr, Manchester Univ., 1950–53; Lectr, Toronto Univ., 1953–55; Reader, 1956–61, Prof. of Social Administration, 1961–69, LSE (Hon. Fellow, 1981); Dir, Centre for Environmental Studies, 1969–75; Chm., Supplementary Benefits Commn, 1975–80; Prof. of Town and Regl Planning, Glasgow Univ., 1980–91, now Emeritus. Chm., Public Schs Commn, 1968–70. Hon. doctorates: Bradford, 1973; Hull, 1980; Leeds, Southampton, 1981. *Publications:* The Neglected Child and the Social Services, 1954; Welfare Services in a Canadian Community, 1958; Housing since the Rent Act, 1961; The Government of Housing, 1967; An Approach to Social Policy, 1975; Social Policy and Administration Revisited, 1975; (with Paul Soto) The Good City, 1980; The Politics of Poverty, 1982; (with Clare Ungerson) Housing Policy, 1982; (ed with Alan Middleton) Regenerating the Inner City: Glasgow's Experience, 1987; (ed with D. Maclennan) The Housing Service of the Future, 1991; A Radical Agenda, 1991; Long-term Unemployment in Northern Ireland, 1996; Policies for a Just Society, 1998; Last of the Guardians, 2005. *Address:* 23 Bank Street, Glasgow G12 8JQ. *T:* (0141) 334 5817.

DONNISON, Kay; *see* Carmichael, C. M.

DONOGHUE, Barbara Joan, (Mrs S. Vavalidis); Adviser, Manzanita Capital, since 2007; *b* 16 July 1951; *d* of Hubert Graham Donoghue and Marjorie Larlham Donoghue; *m* 1976, Stefanos Vavalidis; two *s*. *Educ:* McGill Univ., Montreal (BCom 1972; Schol.; Transportation Develt Agency Fellow, 1974; MBA 1974). Canadian Pacific Ltd, 1973–77; Bank of Nova Scotia, 1977–79; Vice Pres., Bankers Trust Co., 1979–93; Man. Dir, NatWest Markets/Hawkpoint Partners, 1994–98; Teaching Fellow, London Business Sch., 2000–04; Dir, Noventus Partners, 2004–06. Non-exec. Dir, Eniro AB, 2003–. Member: ITC, 1999–2003; Competition Commn, 2005–. *Recreation:* learning Greek. *Address:* *e-mail:* barbara.donoghue@btinternet.com. *Club:* Hurlingham.

DONOGHUE, Prof. Denis, MA, PhD, LittD; literary critic; Henry James Professor of Letters, New York University, since 1979; *b* 1 Dec. 1928. *Educ:* University College, Dublin. BA 1949, MA 1952, PhD 1957; MA Cantab 1965. Admin. Office, Dept of Finance, Irish Civil Service, 1951–54. Asst Lectr, Univ. Coll., Dublin, 1954–57; Coll. Lectr, 1957–62; Visiting Schol., Univ. of Pennsylvania, 1962–63; Coll. Lectr, Univ. Coll., Dublin, 1963–64; University Lectr, Cambridge Univ., 1964–65; Fellow, King's Coll., Cambridge, 1964–65; Prof. of Modern English and American Literature, University Coll., Dublin, 1965–79. Mem. Internat. Cttee of Assoc. of University Profs of English. Mem. BBC Commn to monitor the quality of spoken English on BBC Radio, 1979. Reith Lectr, BBC, 1982. *Publications:* The Third Voice, 1959; Connoisseurs of Chaos, 1965; (ed jtly) An Honoured Guest, 1965; The Ordinary Universe, 1968; Emily Dickinson, 1968; Jonathan Swift, 1969; (ed) Swift, 1970; Yeats, 1971; Thieves of Fire, 1974; (ed) W. B. Yeats, Memoirs, 1973; Sovereign Ghost: studies in Imagination, 1978; Ferocious Alphabets, 1981; The Arts without Mystery, 1983; We Irish (selected essays), 1987; Pure Good of Theory, 1992; Walter Pater: lover of strange souls, 1995; The Practice of Reading, 1998; Words Alone: the poet T. S. Eliot, 2001; Adam's Curse, 2001; Speaking of Beauty, 2003; The American Classics: a personal essay, 2005; contribs to reviews and journals. *Address:* New York University, English Department, 19 University Place (5th Floor), New York, NY 10003, USA; Gaybrook, North Avenue, Mount Merrion, Dublin, Ireland.

DONOHOE, Brian Harold; MP (Lab) Ayrshire Central, since 2005 (Cunninghame South, 1992–2005); *b* 10 Sept. 1948; *s* of late George Joseph Donohoe and Catherine Sillars Donohoe (*née* Ashworth); *m* 1973, Christine Pawson; two *s*. *Educ:* Irvine Royal Academy; Kilmarnock Technical Coll. Apprentice fitter-turner, 1965–69; draughtsman, 1969–81; Trade Union Official, NALGO, 1981–92. Member, Select Committee: on transport, 1993–97 and 2002–05; on environment, transport and the regions, 1997–2001; on transport, local govt and the regions, 2001–02; Admin, 2005–. Jt Chm., All Party Parly Gp against Fluoridation, 2005–; Secretary: All Party Parly Gardening and Horticl Gp, 1994–; All Party Parly Scotch Whisky and Spirits Gp (formerly Scotch Whisky Gp), 1996–; Hon. Treas., British-American Parly Gp, 2002–; Chm., PLP Transport Cttee, 2004–. Trustee, Thrive, 2003–. *Recreation:* gardening. *Address:* 5 Greenfield Drive, Irvine KA12 0ED. *T:* (01294) 274419. *Club:* NALGO Staff Social.

DONOHOE, Peter Howard; pianist; *b* 18 June 1953; *s* of Harold Donohoe and Marjorie Donohoe (*née* Travis); *m* 1980, Elaine Margaret Burns; one *d*. *Educ:* Chetham's School of Music, Manchester; Leeds Univ.; Royal Northern Coll. of Music; Paris Conservatoire. BMus; GRNCM, ARCM; Hon. FRNCM 1983. Professional solo pianist, 1974–; London début, 1978; concert tours in Europe, USA, Canada, Australia, Asia, USSR; regular appearances at Royal Festival Hall, Barbican Hall, Queen Elizabeth Hall, Henr Wood Promenade concerts, 1979–; numerous TV and radio broadcasts, UK and overseas; recordings include music by Rachmaninov, Stravinsky, Prokofiev, Britten, Messiaen, Muldowney, Tchaikovsky; British piano concertos. Competition finalist: British Liszt, London, 1976; Liszt-Bartok, Budapest, 1976; Leeds International Piano, 1981; winner Internat. Tchaikovsky competition, Moscow, 1982. Concerto Recording Award Gramophone, 1988; Grand Prix Internat. du Disque Liszt. *Recreations:* jazz, golf, helping young musicians, clock collecting. *Address:* c/o Askonas Holt Ltd, Lincoln House, 30 High Holborn, WC1V 7JH. *T:* (020) 7400 1700.

DONOHOE, Prof. Timothy James, DPhil; Professor of Chemistry, since 2004, an Head of Organic Chemistry, since 2006, University of Oxford; Fellow, Magdale College, Oxford, since 2001; *b* Darwen, Lancs, 28 Jan. 1967; *s* of William Thomas an Christine Ruth Donohoe; *m* 1991, Ann Louise Budge; two *s*. *Educ:* Tarleton High Sch Hutton Grammar Sch.; Univ. of Bath (BSc Hons); Univ. of Oxford (DPhil 1992). Post doctoral researcher, Univ. of Texas at Austin, 1993–94; Lectr in Chem., 1994–200 Reader in Chem., 2000–01, Univ. of Manchester; Lectr, Univ. of Oxford, 2001–04 Corday Morgan Medal, RSC, 2006. *Publications:* Oxidation and Reduction in Organi Synthesis, 2000; contrib. papers to learned jls. *Recreations:* squash, golf. *Address:* Chemistr Research Laboratory, Department of Chemistry, University of Oxford, Mansfield Roac Oxford OX1 3TA.

DONOUGHMORE, 8th Earl of, *cr* 1800; **Richard Michael John Hely-Hutchinson** Baron Donoughmore, 1783; Viscount Hutchinson (UK), 1821; Chairman, Hodde Headline (formerly Headline Book Publishing) PLC, 1986–97; *b* 8 Aug. 1927; *er s* of 7t Earl of Donoughmore and Dorothy Jean (MBE 1947) (*d* 1995), *d* of late J. B. Hotham; father, 1981; *m* 1st, 1951, Sheila (*d* 1999), *o c* of late Frank Frederick Parsons and M Learmond Perkins; four *s*; 2nd, 2001, Margaret, *widow* of Comdr J. M. W. Morgan, RN and *d* of late E. C. Stonehouse. *Educ:* Winchester; New College, Oxford (MA; BM, BCh *Heir:* *s* Viscount Suirdale, *qv*. *Address:* The Manor House, Bampton, Oxon OX18 2LQ.
See also Hon. T. M. Hely Hutchinson.

DONOUGHUE, family name of **Baron Donoughue**.

DONOUGHUE, Baron *cr* 1985 (Life Peer), of Ashton in the County c Northamptonshire; **Bernard Donoughue;** *b* 8 Sept. 1934; *s* of late Thomas Josep Donoughue and of Maud Violet Andrews; *m* 1959, Carol Ruth Goodman (marr. dis 1989); two *s* two *d*. *Educ:* Secondary Modern Sch. and Grammar Sch., Northamptor Lincoln Coll. and Nuffield Coll., Oxford. BA (1st class hons), MA, DPhil (Oxon FRHistS. Henry Fellow, Harvard, USA. Mem., Editorial Staff: The Economist, Sunda Times, Sunday Telegraph. Sen. Res. Officer, PEP, 1960–63; Lectr, Sen. Lectr, Reade LSE, 1963–74; Sen. Policy Advr to the Prime Minister, 1974–79; Development Di Economist Intelligence Unit, 1979–81; Asst Editor, The Times, 1981–82; Partne 1983–86, Head of Res. and Investment Policy, 1984–86, Grieveson, Grant & Co; Di 1986–88, Head of Res., 1986–87, of Internat. Res. and Investment Policy, 1987–8 Kleinwort Grieveson Securities; Exec. Vice-Chm., London and Bishopsgate Interna Investment Holdings, 1988–91. Opposition spokesman on Treasury, 1991–92, on Energ 1991–93, on Nat. Heritage, 1992–97; Parly Under-Sec. of State, MAFF, 1997–99; Mem H of L Select Cttee on Stem Cell Res., 2001–02; Treas., All Party Parly Gp on Integrate Educn in NI; Sec., All Party Racing and Bloodstock Cttee, 2001–; Mem., All Party Scrutiny Cttee on Gambling, 2003–04. Chairman: British Horseracing Bd Comm Inquiry into stable staff, 2003–04; Starting Price Regulatory Bd, 2003–; Future Fundin of Racing Gp, 2005–06; Inquiry into Regulation of British Greyhound Industr 2007–08. Dir, Towcester Racecourse Ltd, 1992–97. Vis. Prof., LSE, 2000–. Membe Sports Council, 1965–71; Commn of Enquiry into Association Football, 1966–68; Ct Governors, LSE, 1968–74, 1982–97; Civil Service Coll. Adv. Council, 1976–79; Adv. B Wissenschaftzentrum, Berlin, 1978–91; Bd, Centre for European Policy Studies, Brussel 1982–87; London Arts Bd, 1991–97. Trustee, Inst. for Policy Res., 1990–. Consultar British Horse Industry Confedn, 1999–. Chm. Exec. Cttee, London Symphony Orch 1978–93 (Patron, 1989–96); Vice-Pres., Newbury Music Fest., 1995–. Associate Mem Nuffield Coll., Oxford, 1982–87; Mem., Sen. Common Room, Lincoln Coll., Oxfor 1985– (Hon. Fellow, 1986); Patron: Inst. of Contemporary British History, 1988 Hansard Soc., 2001–; Vice Pres., Assoc. of Comprehensive Schs, 2000–. Pres., Gamblir Care, 1997; Trustee: Dorneywood Trust, 1997–; Internat. League for Protection Horses, 2002–. FRSA. Hon. Fellow: LSE, 1989; Northampton Univ., 2006. Hon. LL Leicester, 1990. *Publications:* (ed jtly) Oxford Poetry, 1956; Wage Policies in the Publ Sector, 1962; Trade Unions in a Changing Society, 1963; British Politics and th American Revolution, 1964; (with W. T. Rodgers) The People into Parliament, 196 (with G. W. Jones) Herbert Morrison: portrait of a politician, 1973; Prime Minister, 198 The Heat of the Kitchen (memoirs), 2003; Downing Street Diary: with Harold Wilson Number Ten, 2005. *Recreations:* politics, sport, economics, music. *Address:* House Lords, SW1A 0PW. *Club:* Pratt's.

DONOVAN, Prof. Desmond Thomas; Yates-Goldsmid Professor of Geology ar Head of Department of Geology, University College, London, 1966–82; Hon. Curato Wells Museum, Somerset, 1982–85; *b* 16 June 1921; *s* of T. B. Donovan and M. Donovan (*née* Benker); *m* 1959, Shirley Louise Saward (*d* 2007); two *s* one *d*. *Educ:* Epso Coll.; University of Bristol (BSc 1942; PhD 1951; DSc 1960). FGS 1942, CGeol 199 FLS 1960. Asst Lectr in Geology, University of Bristol, 1947–50; Lectr in Geolog Bristol, 1950–62; Prof. of Geology, University of Hull, 1962–66. Geologist on Lau Koch's Danish expeditions to E Greenland, 1947–57. Pres., Palaeontographical So 1979–84. *Publications:* Stratigraphy: An Introduction to Principles, 1966; (ed) Geology Shelf Seas, 1968; papers on fossil cephalopods, Jurassic stratigraphy, Quaternary deposi marine geology. *Recreation:* opera. *Address:* 4 North Grove, Wells, Somerset BA5 2TD. (01749) 677981.

DONOVAN, Ian Edward, FRAeS; FCMA; Director: Cranfield Aerospace Ltd, 200 Aeronautical Trusts Ltd, 2002–07; *b* 2 March 1940; *s* of late John Walter Donovan ar Ethel Molyneux; *m* 1969, Susan Betty Harris; two *s*. *Educ:* Leighton Park, Readin FCMA 1985. Gen. Factory Manager, Lucas CAV, 1969–72; Finance Man., Lucas Girlin 1972–78; Finance Director: Lucas Girling, Koblenz, 1978–81; Lucas Electrical Lt 1982–84; Mem., 1985–88, Gp Dir, Finance and Central Services, 1986–88, CAA; Dir a Gp Controller, 1988–98, Gp Dir, Aerospace, 1998–2000, Smiths Industries Aerospace Defence Ltd; Chm., Chart Co. Ltd, 1998–2000; Pres., Lambda Advanced Analog In 2000. Dir, English Symphony Orch., 2000–02. Mem. Council, SBAC, 1994–97; Ho Treasurer: Air League, 1995–2000 and 2002–05; Homeless Network, 1999–200 Trustee, Air League Educnl Trust, 1995–2000 and 2002–05; Chm. of Trustees, RA Pension and Assce Scheme, 2007–. FRAeS 2001. *Recreations:* fly fishing, sailing, gardenir music, golf. *Address:* Lawn Farm, Church Lane, Tibberton, Droitwich, Worcs WR9 7NW. *Club:* Royal Air Force.

DONOVAN, Judith, CBE 1997; Chairman, DIY Direct Marketing, since 2000; *b* 5 July 1951; *d* of late Ernest and Joyce Nicholson; *m* 1977, John Patrick Donovan. *Educ:* Univ. of Hull (BA Hons English 1973); DipCAM 1979. Mktg Asst, Ford Motor Co., 1973–75; Account Handler, J. Walter Thomson, 1975–77; Advertising Manager, Grattan, 1977–82; Chm., JDA, 1982–2000. Dir, British Direct Marketing Assoc., 1987–91; Chm., Direct Marketing Assoc., 1999–2001 (Dir, 1991–2001); Pres., Bradford Chamber of Commerce, 1999–2001 (Dir, 1988–2003); Director: Bradford City Challenge, 1988–89; Business Link West Yorks, 2001–03; Dep. Chm., Bradford Breakthrough, 1988–90; Chairman: Bradford & Dist TEC, 1989–98; Postwatch, N of England (formerly Northern Region) 2000–08 (Vice Chair, Postwatch Nat. Council, 2007–08). Member: Millennium Commn, 2000–06; Health and Safety Commn, 2000–; UK Bd, Big Lottery Fund, 2007–. Chm., Yorks Tourist Bd, 2005–08. Dir, Northern Ballet Theatre, 1991–. Freeman, City of London, 1999; Liveryman, Co. of Marketors, 1999. Gov., Margaret McMillan Sch., 1985–87. Gov., Legacy Trust, 2007–. FRSA 1996; FCAM 1996; FCIM 1998; FInstD 2000; CCMI (CIMgt 2000); FIDM 2001. Hon. Dr Leeds Metropolitan, 2003. *Recreations:* after dinner speaking, the Western Front, pets. *Address:* DIY Direct Marketing, Biggin Barns, Ringbeck, Kirkby Malzeard, Ripon, N Yorks HG4 3TT. *T:* (01765) 650000, *Fax:* (01765) 650153; *e-mail:* judith@diydirectmarketing.co.uk.

DONOVAN, Katharine Mary; *see* Barker, K. M.

DONOVAN, Stephen Kenneth, PhD, DSc; Researcher (formerly Curator) of Palaeozoic and Mesozoic Macroinvertebrates, Nationaal Natuurhistorisch Museum, Netherlands, since 2001; *b* 3 June 1954; *s* of Alfred Haig Donovan and Beatrice Georgina Donovan (*née* Nichols); *m* 1st, 1997, Catriona Margaret Isobel MacGillivray, PhD (*d* 2003); one *s* one *d*; 2nd, 2005, Fiona Elizabeth Fearnhead. *Educ:* Univ. of Manchester (BSc 1980); Univ. of Liverpool (PhD 1983; DSc 1994). Royal Soc. Res. Fellow, TCD, 1983–84; Higher Scientific Officer, NERC, 1985–86; University of West Indies, Jamaica: Lectr, 1986–89; Sen. Lectr, 1989–92; Reader in Palaeozoology, 1992–96; Prof. of Palaeozoology, 1996–98; Keeper of Palaeontology, Natural Hist. Mus., 1998–2001. Sen. Res. Fellow, Nat. Mus. of Natural History, Smithsonian Instn, Washington, 1994–95; Visiting Professor: Univ. of Portsmouth, 1996–2004; UCL, 2000–01; Univ. of Liverpool, 2001–02; Adjunct Prof., Univ. of New Brunswick, 2000–. Ed., Scripta Geologica, 2002–. FLS 2004. Linnean Medal for Zoology, 2008. *Publications:* (ed) Mass Extinctions: processes and evidence, 1989; (ed) The Processes of Fossilization, 1991; (ed) The Palaeobiology of Trace Fossils, 1994; (ed jtly) Caribbean Geology: an introduction, 1994; (ed jtly) The Adequacy of the Fossil Record, 1998; (ed) The Pliocene Bowden Shell Bed, Southeast Jamaica, 1998; (ed) The Mid-Cainozoic White Limestone Group of Jamaica, 2004; (ed) Palaeontological Papers in Honour of Chris Paul, 2005; (ed) Trace Fossils in the Museum, 2006; (ed) Crustal and Biotic Evolution of the Caribbean Plate, 2008; numerous res. papers and reviews, particularly on palaeontology and Caribbean geology. *Recreations:* reading, writing, walking, cricket, tramway and railway history. *Address:* Nationaal Natuurhistorisch Museum, Postbus 9517, 2300 RA Leiden, Netherlands. *T:* (71) 5687642.

DOOCEY, Elizabeth, (Dee), OBE; Member (Lib Dem), London Assembly, Greater London Authority, since 2004; *m* James Doocey; one *s*. Finance Dir, Lib Dem Party; Financial Advr, Lib Dem Parly Party; Gp Man. Dir, internat. fashion co.; mgt consultant. Mem. (Lib Dem) Richmond-upon-Thames BC, 1986–94. Chm., Econ. Devlt, Culture, Sport and Tourism Cttee, GLA. Mem., Metropolitan Police Authy. *Address:* Greater London Authority, City Hall, Queen's Walk, SE1 2AA.

DOOGE, Prof. James Clement Ignatius; Professor of Civil Engineering, University College, Dublin, 1970–84, now Professor Emeritus; research consultant; Consultant: United Nations specialised agencies; European Commission; President, Royal Irish Academy, 1987–90; *b* 30 July 1922; *s* of Denis Patrick Dooge and Veronica Catherine Carroll; *m* 1946, Veronica O'Doherty; two *s* three *d*. *Educ:* Christian Brothers' Sch., Dun Laoghaire; University Coll., Dublin (BE, BSc 1942, ME 1952); Univ. of Iowa (MSc 1956). FICE; FASCE. Jun. Civil Engr, Irish Office of Public Works, 1943–46; Design Engr, Electricity Supply Bd, Ireland, 1946–58; Prof. of Civil Engrg, UC Cork, 1958–70. Irish Senate: Mem., 1965–77 and 1981–87; Chm., 1973–77; Leader, 1983–87; Minister for Foreign Affairs, Ireland, 1981–82. President: ICEI, 1968–69 (Hon. FICEI; Kettle Premium and Plaque, 1948, 1985; Mullins Medal, 1951, 1962); Internat. Assoc. for Hydrologic Scis, 1975–79; Member: Exec. Bureau, Internat. Union for Geodesy and Geophysics, 1979–87; Gen. Cttee, ICSU, 1980–86, 1988– (Sec. Gen., 1980–82; Pres., 1993–96). Fellow, Amer. Geophysical Union (Horton Award, 1959; Bowie Medal, 1986); Hon. Mem., Eur. Geophysical Soc., 1993 (John Dalton Medal, 1998). Foreign Member: Polish Acad. of Scis, 1985; Russian Acad. of Scis, 1994; Spanish Acad. of Sci., 1998; Royal Acad. of Engrg, 2000. Hon. DrAgrSc Wageningen, 1978; Hon. DrTech. Lund, 1980; Hon. DSc: Birmingham, 1986; Heriot-Watt, 2000; NUI, 2000; Univ. Complutense, Madrid, 2001; Hon. ScD Dublin, 1988; Hon. Dr Technical Univ. of Cracow, 2000. Internat. Prize for Hydrology, 1983; Internat. Prize for Meteorology, 1999; Prince Philip Gold Medal, Royal Acad. of Engrg, 2005. *Address:* Centre for Water Resources Research, University College, Earlsfort Terrace, Dublin 2, Ireland.

DORAN, Frank; MP (Lab) Aberdeen North, since 2005 (Aberdeen Central, 1997–2005); *b* 13 April 1949; *s* of Francis Anthony Doran and Betty Hedges or Doran; *m* 1967, Patricia Ann Govan or Doran (marr. diss.); two *s*. *Educ:* Ainslie Park Secondary Sch.; Leith Acad.; Dundee Univ. (LLB Hons). Admitted Solicitor, 1977. Eur. Parly Cand. (Lab) NE Scotland, 1984. MP (Lab) Aberdeen South, 1987–92; contested (Lab) same seat, 1992. Chm., Admin Select Cttee, H of C, 2005–. Sec., Trade Union Gp of Lab. MPs, 2001–. Asst Editor, Scottish Legal Action Group Bulletin, 1975–78. *Recreations:* cinema, art, sports. *Address:* House of Commons, SW1A 0AA. *Club:* Aberdeen Trades Council.

DORAN, Gregory; Chief Associate Director, Royal Shakespeare Company, since 2005 (Associate Director, 1996–2005); *b* 24 Nov. 1958; *s* of John Doran and Margaret Freeman; civil partnership 2005, Sir Antony Sher, *qv*. *Educ:* Bristol Univ. (BA Hons); Bristol Old Vic Theatre Sch. Joined RSC 1987; *RSC productions include:* The Odyssey, 1992; Henry VIII, 1996; Cyrano de Bergerac, 1997; The Merchant of Venice, The Winter's Tale, 1998; Oroonoko, Timon of Athens, Macbeth, 1999; As You Like It, 2000; King John, Jubilee, 2001; Much Ado About Nothing, The Island Princess, 2002; The Taming of the Shrew, The Tamer Tamed, All's Well That Ends Well, 2003; Othello, Venus and Adonis, 2004; A Midsummer Night's Dream, Sejanus, Canterbury Tales, 2005; Antony and Cleopatra, Merry Wives (musical), 2006; Coriolanus, 2007; Hamlet, Love's Labour's Lost, 2008; *other productions include:* Long Day's Journey into Night, Waiting for Godot, Nottingham Playhouse, 1982–83; Titus Andronicus, Market Th., Johannesburg, and RNT, 1995 (TMA Award for Best Production); Black Comedy, and The Real Inspector Hound, Comedy Th., 1998; York Millennium Mystery Plays, York Minster, 2000; Mahler's Conversion, Aldwych, 2001; The Merchant of Venice, Japan, 2007; The Giant, Hampstead Th., 2007; *film:* Macbeth, 1999. Hon. Dr Huddersfield, 2004. Olivier Award for Outstanding Achievement of the Year, 2003. *Publication:* (with Sir Antony Sher) Woza Shakespeare!, 1996. *Address:* c/o Royal Shakespeare Theatre, Stratford-upon-Avon, Warwicks CV37 6BB.

DORBER, Very Rev. Adrian John; Dean of Lichfield, since 2005; *b* 23 Sept. 1952; *s* of John and Thelma Dorber; *m* 1984, Caroline Perry; three *s* two *d*. *Educ:* St John's Coll., Durham (BA 1974); King's Coll. London (MTh 1991); Westcott House, Cambridge. Ordained deacon, 1979, priest, 1980; Curate, St Michael and St Mary Magdalene, Easthampstead, 1979–85; Priest-in-charge, St Barnabas, Emmer Green, 1985–88; Chaplain, Portsmouth Poly., 1988–92; Lectr, 1991–97, Sen. Chaplain and Public Orator, 1992–97, Portsmouth Univ.; Priest-in-charge, Brancepeth, 1997–2000; Dir, Ministries and Trng, Dio. Durham, 1997–2005. Hon. Chaplain, Portsmouth Cathedral, 1992–97; Hon. Canon, Durham Cathedral, 1997–2005. *Recreations:* gardening, modern fiction, cinema, good food. *Address:* The Deanery, The Close, Lichfield, Staffs WS13 7LD. *T:* (01543) 306250; *e-mail:* adrian.dorber@lichfield-cathedral.org.

DORCHESTER, Area Bishop of, since 2000; **Rt Rev. Colin William Fletcher,** OBE 2000; *b* 17 Nov. 1950; *s* of Alan Philip Fletcher, QC; *m* 1980, Sarah Elizabeth Webster; one *s* two *d*. *Educ:* Marlborough Coll.; Trinity Coll., Oxford (MA 1976). Ordained deacon, 1975, priest, 1976; Asst Curate, St Peter, Shipley, 1975–79; Tutor, Wycliffe Hall, Oxford and Asst Curate, St Andrew, N Oxford, 1979–84; Vicar, Holy Trinity, Margate, 1984–93; Rural Dean of Thanet, 1988–93; Chaplain to the Archbishop of Canterbury, 1993–2000. *Recreations:* ornithology, walking, sport. *Address:* Arran House, Sandy Lane, Yarnton, Oxford OX5 1PB. *T:* (01865) 208218.
See also P. J. Fletcher.

DORE, Prof. Ronald Philip, CBE 1989; FBA 1975; Associate, Centre for Economic Performance, London School of Economics and Political Science (Senior Research Fellow, 1991); *b* 1 Feb. 1925; *s* of Philip Brine Dore and Elsie Constance Dore; *m* 1957, Nancy Macdonald; one *s* one *d*; one *s* with Maria Paisley. *Educ:* Poole Grammar Sch.; SOAS, Univ. of London (BA). Lectr in Japanese Instns, SOAS, London, 1951; Prof. of Asian Studies, Univ. of BC, 1956; Reader, later Prof. of Sociol., LSE, 1961–69 (Hon. Fellow, 1980); Fellow, IDS, Univ. of Sussex, 1969–82; Asst Dir, Technical Change Centre, 1982–86; Dir, Japan-Europe Industry Res. Centre, ICSTM, 1986–91. Vis. Prof. of Sociol., Harvard Univ., 1986–89; Adjunct Prof., MIT, 1989–94. Mem., Academia Europaea, 1989. Hon. Foreign Mem., Amer. Acad. of Arts and Scis, 1978; Hon. Foreign Fellow, Japan Acad., 1986–. Order of the Rising Sun (Third Class), Japan, 1988. *Publications:* City Life in Japan, 1958, 2nd edn 1999; Land Reform in Japan, 1959, 2nd edn 1984; Education in Tokugawa Japan, 1963, 2nd edn 1983; (ed) Aspects of Social Change in Modern Japan, 1967; British Factory, Japanese Factory, 1973, 2nd edn 1990; The Diploma Disease, 1976, 2nd edn 1997; Shinohata: portrait of a Japanese village, 1978, 2nd edn 1992; (ed with Zoe Mars) Community Development, Comparative Case Studies in India, The Republic of Korea, Mexico and Tanzania, 1981; Energy Conservation in Japanese Industry, 1982; Flexible Rigidities: structural adjustment in Japan, 1986; Taking Japan Seriously: a Confucian perspective on leading economic issues, 1987; (ed jtly) Japan and World Depression, Then and Now: essays in memory of E. F. Penrose, 1987; (with Mari Sako) How the Japanese Learn to Work, 1988, rev. edn 1998; (ed jtly) Corporatism and Accountability: organized interests in British public life, 1990; Will the 21st Century be the Age of Individualism?, 1991; (ed with Masahiko Aoki) The Japanese Firm: the source of competitive strength, 1994; Japan, Internationalism and the UN, 1997; Stockmarket Capitalism, Welfare Capitalism: Japan and Germany *vs* the Anglo Saxons, 2000; Social Evolution, Economic Development and Culture, 2001; Collected writing of Ronald Dore, 2002. *Address:* 157 Surrenden Road, Brighton, East Sussex BN1 6ZA. *T:* (01273) 501370.

DOREY, Sir Graham (Martyn), Kt 1993; Bailiff of Guernsey, 1992–99 (Deputy Bailiff, 1982–92); a Judge of the Court of Appeal of Jersey, 1992–99; President, Guernsey Court of Appeal, 1992–99; *b* 15 Dec. 1932; *s* of late Martyn Dorey and Muriel (*née* Pickard); *m* 1st, 1962, Penelope Cecile (*d* 1996), *d* of Maj. E. A. Wheadon, ED; two *s* two *d*; 2nd, 1998, Mrs Cicely Ruth Lummis. *Educ:* Kingswood Sch., Bath; Ecole des Roches, Verneuil; Univs of Bristol and Caen. Admitted Solicitor, 1959; Advocate, Royal Court of Guernsey, 1960; called to the Bar, Gray's Inn, 1992; People's Deputy, States of Guernsey, 1970; Solicitor Gen., 1973, Attorney Gen., 1977, Guernsey. KStJ 1996 (CStJ 1992). *Recreations:* sailing, maritime history, music. *Address:* Les Marchez Farm, La Rue des Reines, St Pierre du Bois, Guernsey GY7 9AE. *T:* (01481) 266186, *Fax:* (01481) 266289. *Clubs:* Royal Ocean Racing; Royal Yacht Squadron.

DOREY, Gregory John, CVO 1997; HM Diplomatic Service; Ambassador to the Republic of Hungary, since 2007; *b* 1 May 1956; *s* of Michael John Dorey and Avril Dorey (*née* Gregory); *m* 1981, Alison Patricia Taylor; two *s* one *d*. *Educ:* Painswick Co. Primary Sch.; Rendcomb Coll., Cirencester; Exeter Coll., Oxford (MA Modern Hist.); Open Univ. (Post Grad. Cert. in Business Admin). Nat. Westminster Bank, 1973–74; Supply and Transport Service, RN, 1977–78; Army Dept, 1978–79, Defence Secretariat, 1979–81, MoD; UK Delegn to NATO, 1982–84; MoD PE, 1984–86; Soviet Dept, FCO, 1986; Asst Hd, CSCE Dept, FCO, 1986–89; First Sec., Budapest, 1989–92; Private Sec., Minister of State, FCO, 1992–94; Asst Hd, ME Dept, FCO, 1994–96; Counsellor, then Dep. Head of Mission, Islamabad, 1996–99; on secondment to HSBC plc, 2000; Dep. Hd of Mission, Hong Kong, 2000–04; Asst Dir (Ops), HR Directorate, FCO, 2005–07. *Recreations:* literature, theatre, cinema, tennis, dragon boat racing, extreme gardening, travel. *Address:* c/o Foreign and Commonwealth Office, King Charles Street, SW1A 2AH.

DORFMAN, Prof. Ariel; Walter Hines Page Professor of Literature and Latin American Studies, Duke University, since 1984; author, poet, playwright and journalist; *b* Buenos Aires, 6 May 1942; *s* of Adolfo Dorfman and Fanny Zelicovich; naturalized Chilean citizen; *m* 1966, Angelica Malinarich; two *s*. *Educ:* Univ. of Chile. Univ. of Chile, Santiago, 1965–73; Sorbonne, Paris VI, 1975–76; Univ. of Amsterdam, 1976–80. Member: Acad. Universelle des Cultures, Paris, 1993–; Amer. Acad. Arts and Scis, 2001–. Hon. LitD Wooster Coll., 1991; Hon. DHL Bradford Coll., 1993. *Publications: fiction:* Hard Rain, 1973; My House is on Fire, 1979; Widows, 1983, 2nd edn 2002; The Last Song of Manuel Sondero, 1986; Mascara, 1988, 2nd edn 2004; Konfidenz, 1995, 2nd edn 2003; The Nanny and the Iceberg, 1999, 2nd edn 2003; Blake's Therapy, 2001; The Rabbit's Rebellion, 2001; (with J. Dorfman) The Burning City, 2003; *poetry:* Missing, 1982; Last Waltz in Santiago and Other Poems of Exile and Disappearance, 1988; In Case of Fire in a Foreign Land, 2002; *plays:* (adaptation, with Tony Kushner) Widows, 1988; Death and the Maiden, 1991; Reader, 1992; (with R. Dorfman) Who's Who, 1997; The Resistance Trilogy, 1998; Speak Truth to Power: voices from beyond the dark, 2000; Manifesto for Another World, 2004; The Other Side, 2004; Purgatorio, 2005; Picasso Lost and Found, 2005; *non-fiction:* (with A. Mattelart) How to Read Donald Duck, 1971; The Empire's Old Clothes, 1983; Some Write to the Future, 1991; Heading South, Looking North: a bilingual journey (memoir), 1998; Exorcising Terror: the incredible unending trial of Gen. Augusto Pinochet, 2002; Desert Memories: journeys through the Chilean

North, 2004; Other Septembers, Many Americas: selected provocations 1980–2004, 2004. *Address:* John Hope Franklin Center, PO Box 90404, Duke University, Durham, NC 27708, USA.

DORFMAN, Lloyd Marshall, CBE 2008; Chairman, Travelex Group, since 2005 (Chairman and Chief Executive, 1977–2005); *b* 25 Aug. 1952; *s* of Harold and Anita Dorfman; *m* 1974, Sarah (*née* Matthews); one *s* two *d*. *Educ:* St Paul's Sch. Non-exec. Dir, M & C Saatchi plc, 2004–; Dep. Chm., Quest Ltd, 2007–. Chm., Roundhouse, 2007–; Dir., Royal Nat. Theatre, 2007–. Trustee, Prince's Trust, 2007– (Dep. Chm., Prince's Trust Develt Bd, 2003–07). Gov., St Paul's Sch., London, 2005–. Hon. Fellow, St Peter's Coll., Oxford, 2003. FRSA 2006. *Recreations:* travel, theatre. *Address:* Travelex plc, 65 Kingsway, WC2B 6TD. *T:* (020) 7400 4000, *Fax:* (020) 7400 4001; *e-mail:* directors@travelex.com.

DORGAN, John Christopher, FRCS; Consultant Orthopaedic Surgeon, Royal Liverpool Children's Hospital, since 1984; *b* 26 Nov. 1948; *s* of William Leonard Dorgan and Mary Ellen Dorgan (*née* Gorringe); *m* 1978, Ann Mary Gargan (*d* 2003); three *d*. *Educ:* Thornleigh Salesian Coll., Bolton; Liverpool Univ. (MB ChB 1973; MChOrth 1979). FRCS 1977. House Officer, Walton Hosp., Liverpool, 1973–74; Sen. House Officer, Royal Southern Hosp., Liverpool, 1974–75; Registrar, Whiston and St Helens Hosps, 1975–77; Research Fellow, Univ. of Liverpool, 1977–78; Registrar, Broadgreen Hosp. and Royal Liverpool Children's Hosp., 1978–80; Lectr, Dept of Orthopaedic Surgery, Univ. of Liverpool, 1981–84; Consultant Orthopaedic Surgeon, Royal Liverpool Univ. Hosp., 1984–96. Pres., British Scoliosis Soc., 2005–06 (Hon. Sec. and Treas., 1999–2002; Mem., Exec. Cttee, 2002–03). *Publications:* articles on orthopaedic and spinal surgery in med. jls. *Recreations:* member of trad jazz band, watching Bolton Wanderers FC. *Address:* 47 Rodney Street, Liverpool L1 9EW. *T:* (0151) 708 0935.

DORIN, Bernard Jean Robert, Hon. GCVO; Officier de la Légion d'Honneur; Officier de l'Ordre National du Mérite; Ambassadeur de France; Conseiller d'Etat, 1993–97, now honorary; *b* 25 Aug. 1929; *s* of Robert Dorin and Jacqueline Dorin (*née* Goumard); *m* 1971, Christine du Bois de Meyrignac; two *s* two *d*. *Educ:* Inst. d'Etudes Politiques, Paris; Ecole Nat. d'Administration. Attaché, French Embassy, Ottawa, 1957–59; Min. of Foreign Affairs, 1959–64; technical adviser: for sci. research, nuclear and space, 1966–67; to Minister of Nat. Educn, 1967–68; to Minister for sci. research, 1968–69; Harvard Univ., 1969–70; Min. of Foreign Affairs, 1970–71; Ambassador in Port-au-Prince, 1972–75; Head of Francophone Affairs Dept, 1975–78; Ambassador in Pretoria, 1978–81; Dir for America, Min. of Foreign Affairs, 1981–84; Ambassador, Brazil, 1984–87, Japan, 1987–90, UK, 1990–93. Hon. Pres., Avenir de la langue française (Pres., 1998); President: Les Amitiés francophones, 1998–; Les Amitiés Acadiennes, 1998–. *Recreation:* collections of naïve paintings. *Address:* 59 rue Michel Ange, 75016 Paris, France.

DORIS, Robert Joseph; Member (SNP) Glasgow, Scottish Parliament, since 2007; *b* 11 May 1973; *s* of Robert Doris and Mary Drummond Doris; partner, Janet Tyson. *Educ:* Univ. of Glasgow (MA Soc. Sci. with Distn 1994); St Andrews Coll. (PGCE (secondary) Hist. and Mod. Studies 1995). Teacher, Hist. and Mod. Studies, 1995–2007. Mem., Local Govt and Communities Cttee, Scottish Parlt, 2007–. *Recreations:* eating out, playing pool (badly), supporting Celtic FC. *Address:* Parliamentary Constituency Office, Baltic Chambers, Wellington Street, Glasgow G2 6HJ; Scottish Parliament, Edinburgh EH99 1SP. *e-mail:* bob.doris.msp@scottish.parliament.uk.

DORKEN, (Anthony) John; Chief Executive, British Tyre Manufacturers' Association, since 2006; Secretary, Tyre Industry Federation, since 2005; *b* 24 April 1944; *s* of late Oscar Roy Dorken, OBE and of Margaret Dorken; *m* 1972, Satanay Mufti; one *s* one *d*. *Educ:* Mill Hill Sch.; King's Coll., Cambridge (BA Classics 1965; MA 1969). VSO, Libya, 1965–66; Asst Principal, BoT, 1967–71; Private Sec. to Parly Under Sec. of State for Industry, 1971–72; Principal, DTI, later Dept of Energy, 1972–77; seconded to Cabinet Office, 1977–79; Asst Sec., Dept of Energy, 1980–86; seconded to Shell UK Exploration and Prodn, 1986–89; Dir of Resource Management, Dept of Energy, 1989–92; Dep. Dir Gen., Office of Gas Supply, 1992–93; Head of Consumer Affairs Div., DTI, 1993–96; Dep. Dir, 1996–97, Dir, 1997–2005, British Rubber Manufacturers' Assoc. Sec. and Treas., Medical Aid and Relief for Children of Chechnya, 2001–. *Publications:* articles on gas regulation in specialist jls. *Recreations:* reading, walking, music, squash, tennis. *Address:* 10 Connaught Gardens, N10 3LB. *T:* (020) 8372 6213. *Club:* Stormont Lawn Tennis and Squash Rackets (Highgate).

DORKING, Bishop Suffragan of, since 1996; **Rt Rev. Ian James Brackley;** *b* 13 Dec. 1947; *s* of Frederick Arthur James Brackley and Ivy Sarah Catherine (*née* Bush); *m* 1971, Penny Saunders; two *s*. *Educ:* Westcliff High Sch.; Keble Coll., Oxford (MA); Cuddesdon Coll., Oxford. Ordained deacon, 1971, priest, 1972; Asst Curate, Lockleaze, Bristol, 1971–74; Asst Chaplain, 1974–76, Chaplain, 1976–80, Bryanston Sch., Dorset; Vicar, East Preston with Kingston, 1980–88; Team Rector, St Wilfrid, Haywards Heath, 1988–96. Rural Dean: Arundel and Bognor, 1982–87; Cuckfield, 1989–95. *Recreations:* golf, cricket, classical music, pipe organs. *Address:* 13 Pilgrims Way, Guildford, Surrey GU4 8AD. *T:* (01483) 570829, *Fax:* (01483) 567268; *e-mail:* bishop.ian@cofeguildford.org.uk.

DORKING, Archdeacon of; *see* Henderson, Ven. J. T.

DORMAN, Sir Philip (Henry Keppel), 4th Bt *cr* 1923, of Nunthorpe, co. York; tax accountant; *b* 19 May 1954; *s* of Richard Dorman (*d* 1976) and of Diana Keppel (*née* Barrett); *S* cousin, 1996; *m* 1982 (marr. diss. 1992); one *d*; *m* 1996 (marr. diss. 2004). *Educ:* Marlborough; Univ. of St Andrews. Life Protector, Dorman Mus., Middlesbrough, 1996–. *Recreation:* golf. *Address:* *e-mail:* pd@philipdorman.co.uk. *Clubs:* MCC; Lewes Golf.

DORMAN, Richard Bostock, CBE 1984; HM Diplomatic Service, retired; High Commissioner to Vanuatu, 1982–85; Chairman, British Friends of Vanuatu, 1990–99 (Co-ordinator, 1986–90); *b* 8 Aug. 1925; *s* of late John Ehrenfried and Madeleine Louise Dorman; *m* 1950, Anna Illingworth; one *s* two *d*. *Educ:* Sedbergh Sch.; St John's Coll., Cambridge. Army Service (Lieut, S Staffs Regt), 1944–48; Asst Principal, War Office, 1951; Principal, 1955; transferred to Commonwealth Relations Office, 1958; First Sec., British High Commission, Nicosia, 1960–64; Dep. High Commissioner, Freetown, 1964–66; SE Asia Dept, FO, 1967–69; Counsellor, Addis Ababa, 1969–73; Commercial Counsellor, Bucharest, 1974–77; Counsellor, Pretoria, 1977–82. Order of Merit (Vanuatu), 1999. *Address:* 67 Beresford Road, Cheam, Surrey SM2 6ER. *T:* (020) 8642 9627. *Club:* Royal Commonwealth Society.

DORMANN, Jürgen; Chairman: Metall Zug AG, since 2008; V-Zug AG; *b* Heidelberg, 12 Jan. 1940. Joined Hoechst AG as mgt trainee, 1963; Fiber Sales Dept, 1965–72; Corporate Staff Dept, 1973–84 (Head of Dept, 1980–84); Dep. Mem., Bd of Mgt, 1984–87; Chief Financial Officer, 1987–94; Chm., 1994–99; Hoechst merged with Rhône-Poulenc to form Aventis, 1999; Chm., Bd of Mgt, 1999–2002, Chm., Supervisory Bd, 2002–04, Aventis; Dir, 1998–2007, Chm., 2001–07, CEO, 2002–04, ABB; Vice-Chm., Sanofi-Aventis, 2004–07; Dir, 2004–, Chm., 2007–08, Adecco. Non-executive Director: IBM, 1999; Allianz AG, 1999; BG Gp, 2005–. *Address:* Metall Zug AG, Industriestrasse 66, 6301 Zug, Switzerland.

DORMENT, Richard, PhD; Art Critic, Daily Telegraph, since 1986; *b* 15 Nov. 1946; *s* of James Dorment and Marguerite Dorment (*née* O'Callaghan); *m* 1st, 1970, Kate S. Ganz (marr. diss. 1981); one *s* one *d*; 2nd, 1985, Harriet Mary Waugh. *Educ:* Georgetown Prep. Sch.; Princeton Univ. (BA 1968); Columbia Univ. (MA 1969, MPhil, PhD 1975). Faculty Fellow, Columbia Univ., 1968–72; Asst Curator, European Painting, Philadelphia Mus. of Art, 1973–76; Curator, Alfred Gilbert: Sculptor and Goldsmith, RA, 1985–86; Art Critic, Country Life, 1986; Co-curator, James McNeill Whistler, Tate Gall., 1994–95. Member: Judging Panel, Turner Prize, 1989; Adv. Cttee, Govt Art Collection, 1996–2005; Reviewing Cttee on the Export of Works of Art, 1996–2002; British Council Visual Arts Adv. Cttee, 1997–2006. Trustee: Watts Gallery, 1996–; Wallace Collection, 2003–. Hawthornden Prize for art criticism in Britain, 1992; Critic of the Year, British Press Awards, 2000. *Publications:* Alfred Gilbert, 1985; British Painting 1750–1900: A Catalogue of the British Paintings in the Philadelphia Museum of Art, 1986; Alfred Gilbert: Sculptor and Goldsmith, 1986; (with Margaret McDonald) James McNeill Whistler, 1994; contributor to exhibition catalogues: Victorian High Renaissance, 1978; Pre-Raphaelite and Other Masters: the Andrew Lloyd Webber Collection, 2003; Manet and the Sea, 2003; reviews for NY Rev. of Books; contrib. to Burlington Magazine, TLS, Literary Rev. *Address:* 10 Clifton Villas, W9 2PH. *T:* (020) 7266 2057. *Club:* Brooks's.

DORMER, family name of **Baron Dormer**.

DORMER, 17th Baron *cr* 1615, of Wenge, co. Buckingham; **Geoffrey Henry Dormer;** Bt 1615; *b* 13 May 1920; *s* of Captain Edward Henry Dormer (*d* 1943) and Hon. Vanessa Margaret Dormer (*d* 1962), *d* of 1st Baron Borwick; *S* cousin, 1995, but does not use the title; *m* 1st, 1947, Janet Readman (marr. diss. 1957); two *d*; 2nd, 1958, Pamela Simpson; two *s*. *Educ:* Eton; Trinity Coll., Cambridge. RNVR Officer, 1939–46; RNR Officer, 1960–70 (Lt-Comdr 1968); RNVR Officer, 1970–81. Farmer until 1958; small-holder gardener. *Recreations:* sailing, gardening. *Heir:* *s* Hon. William Robert Dormer [*b* 8 Nov 1960; *m* 1985, Paula, *d* of Peter Robinson; one *s* one *d*]. *Address:* Dittisham, Devon.

DORMER, Robin James; Parliamentary Counsel, since 2005; on secondment to Law Commission, since 2006; *b* 30 May 1951; *s* of Dudley James Dormer and Jean Mary (*née* Brimacombe). *Educ:* Internat. Sch. of Geneva, Switzerland; University Coll. of Wales Aberystwyth (LLB). Admitted solicitor, 1980; articled clerk and asst solicitor, Messrs Coward Chance, 1976–80; Mem. Staff, Law Commn, 1980–87; Asst Parly Counsel, Office of Parly Counsel, 1987–90; Solicitor's Office, DoH, 1990–99, Grade 5 (Sen. CS), 1992–99; Office of the Parliamentary Counsel, 1999–: Prin. Asst Parly Counsel, 1999–2000; Dep. Parly Counsel, 2000–05. Mem., Legal Services Gp, Terrence Higgins Trust, 1987–99. Co. Sec., Food Chain, 2003–06. *Address:* Law Commission, Steel House, 11 Tothill Street, SW1H 9LJ. *T:* (020) 3334 0200.

DORNAN, Prof. James Connor, MD; FRCOG, FRCPI; Consultant, Royal Maternity Hospital, Belfast, since 1986; Senior Vice President, Royal College of Obstetricians and Gynaecologists, 2004–07; *b* 5 Feb. 1948; *s* of James Dornan and Clare Elizabeth Dornan (*née* Dunn); *m* 1st, 1970, Lorna Jordan (*d* 1998); one *s* two *d*; 2nd, 2002, Samina Mahsud. *Educ:* Bangor Grammar Sch.; Queen's Univ. of Belfast (MB BCh, BAO; MD 1981). MRCOG 1978, FRCOG 1991; FRCPI 2003. Queen's University of Belfast: Sen. Lectr and Consultant, Sch. of Clinical Medicine, 1986–92; Hon. Clinical Lectr, 1993–98; Hon. Sen. Clinical Lectr, 1998–2002; Hon. Reader, 2002–06; Hon. Prof. of Fetal Medicine, 2006–. Hon. Prof. of Health and Life Scis, Univ. of Ulster, 2003–. Mem. Council, RCOG, 1999–2004. Pres., NI Mother and Baby Action, 2006– (Chm., 1996). *Publications:* contrib. chapters to med. textbooks; contrib. numerous papers to learned jls on biophysical assessment of fetal well-being and fetal behaviour; many contribs to med. jls. *Recreations:* tennis, golf, good conversation. *Address:* 8 Clanbrassil Road, Holywood, Cultra, Co. Down, Northern Ireland BT18 0AR. *T:* (028) 9042 5515; *e-mail:* jcdcultra@btinternet.com. *Clubs:* Royal Society of Medicine; Gynaecological Travellers; Royal Belfast Golf; Royal Northern Ireland Yacht.

DORNAN, Prof. Peter John, DSc; FRS 2003; FInstP; Professor of Physics, and Head, High Energy Physics Group, Imperial College London, since 1991; *b* 5 Sept. 1939; *s* of Philip James and Edith Mary Dornan; *m* 1963, Mary Gwendoline Clarke; one *s* one *d*. *Educ:* Lancaster Royal Grammar Sch.; Emmanuel Coll., Cambridge (BA 1961; PhD 1965). FInstP 1992. Res. Associate, Brookhaven Nat. Lab., NY, 1965–68; Lectr, ICSTM, 1968–91. Scientific Associate, CERN, Geneva, 1989–91 and 1997–2000 (Spokesman, Aleph Experiment, 1997–2000). Hon. DSc Lancaster, 2000. *Publications:* contribs to Physics Letters, Physics Reports, Jl European Physics, Nuclear Instruments and Methods. *Recreations:* walking, ski-ing, squash, food, wine, travel. *Address:* Blackett Laboratory, Imperial College London, SW7 2BW. *T:* (020) 7594 7822, *Fax:* (020) 7823 8830; *e-mail:* p.dornan@imperial.ac.uk.

DORR, Noel; Personal Representative of Irish Minister for Foreign Affairs, European Union Intergovernmental Conference, 1996–97 and 2000; *b* Limerick, 1933; *m* 1983, Caitríona Doran. *Educ:* St Nathy's Coll., Ballaghaderreen; University Coll., Galway (BA, BComm, HDipEd); Georgetown Univ., Washington, DC (MA). Entered Dept of Foreign Affairs, 1960; Third Sec., 1960–62; Third Sec., Brussels, 1962–64; First Sec., Washington, 1964–70; First Sec., Dept of For. Affairs, 1970–72; Counsellor (Press and Inf.), Dept of For. Affairs, 1972–74; Asst Sec., Political Div., and Political Dir, 1974–77; Dep. Sec. and Political Dir, 1977–80; Perm. Rep. of Ireland to UN, New York, 1980–83; Rep of Ireland, Security Council, 1981–82; Ambassador of Ireland to UK, 1983–87; Sec., Dept of Foreign Affairs, Ireland, 1987–95. Chm., Inst. for British-Irish Studies. Hon. LLD NUI, 2002. *Address:* c/o Department of Foreign Affairs, 80 St Stephen's Green, Dublin 2, Ireland.

DORRANCE, Dr Richard Christopher; Chief Executive, Council for Awards in Children's Care and Education, since 1994; Partner, since 1996, Company Secretary, since 2000, Brilliant Publications Ltd; *b* 25 Feb. 1948; *s* of Eric and Joan Dorrance; *m* 1996, Priscilla Hannaford; one *s* one *d*. *Educ:* Wolverhampton GS; Aylesbury GS; Univ. of East Anglia (BSc Chem. 1969; PhD 1973); London Univ. (PGCE 1974 ext.). FRSC. Res. into properties of detergents, Unilever and UEA, 1969–72; taught chemistry and geology, Royal GS, High Wycombe (and i/c stage lighting), 1972–80; Head of Science, Monk Walk Sch., Welwyn Garden City, 1980–83; Gen. Advr, Berks CC, 1983–88; Asst Chief Exec., Nat. Curriculum Council, 1989–91; Dep. Chief Exec., Sch. Exams and Assessment Council, 1991–93 (acting Chief Exec., 1991–92); Chief Exec., Early Years NTO, 1998–2005. Mem. UK Cttee, Organisation Mondiale pour l'Education Prescolaire, 1996–99 (Treas., 1998–99). Gov., West Herts Coll., 1997–2001. Advr, Nursery World magazine, 1997–2007. Trustee, Northall Village Hall Mgt Cttee, 2007–. *Publications:* Ey (computer prog.), 1983; GAS 81, 1982; papers in professional jls. *Recreations:* walking, foreign travel, natural history, bowling, gardening, model making, photography. *Address*

The Old School Yard, Leighton Road, Northall, Dunstable, Beds LU6 2HA. *T:* (01525) 221273.

DORRELL, Rt Hon. Stephen James; PC 1994; MP (C) Charnwood, since 1997 (Loughborough, 1979–97); *b* 25 March 1952; *s* of Philip Dorrell; *m* 1980, Penelope Anne Wears, *y d* of Mr and Mrs James Taylor, Windsor; three *s* one *d.* *Educ:* Uppingham; Brasenose Coll., Oxford (BA 1973). Personal asst to Rt Hon. Peter Walker, MBE, MP, Feb. 1974; contested (C) Kingston-upon-Hull East, Oct. 1974. PPS to the Secretary of State for Energy, 1983–87; Asst Govt Whip, 1987–88; a Lord Comr of HM Treasury (Govt Whip), 1988–90; Parly Under-Sec. of State, DoH, 1990–92; Financial Sec. to HM Treasury, 1992–94; Secretary of State: for Nat. Heritage, 1994–95; for Health, 1995–97; Shadow Sec. of State for Educn, 1997–98. *Recreations:* aviation, reading. *Address:* House of Commons, SW1A 0AA.

DORRIAN, Hon. Lady; Leeona June Dorrian; a Senator of the College of Justice in Scotland, since 2005; *b* 16 June 1957; *d* of Thomas and June Dorrian. *Educ:* Cranley Sch.; Univ. of Aberdeen (LLB 1977). Admitted to Faculty of Advocates, 1981; QC (Scot.) 1994; Standing Jun. Counsel, Health and Safety Exec. and Commn, 1987–94; Advocate Depute, 1988–91; Standing Jun. Counsel, Dept of Energy, 1991–94; a Temp. Judge, Court of Session, 2002–05. Mem., English Bar, Inner Temple, 1991–. Mem., CICB, 1998–2002. *Address:* Court of Session, Parliament House, Parliament Square, Edinburgh EH1 1RF. *Clubs:* Royal Automobile; Scottish Arts (Edinburgh); Royal Forth Yacht; Merchants of Edinburgh Golf.

DORRIES, Nadine; MP (C) Mid Bedfordshire, since 2005; *b* 21 May 1957; *d* of George and Sylvia Bargery; *m* 1984, Paul Dorries (marr. diss.); three *d.* *Educ:* Halewood Grange Comprehensive Sch., Liverpool; Warrington Dist Sch. of Nursing. Former nurse and businesswoman. Dir, BUPA. Advr to Oliver Letwin, MP. Contested (C) Hazel Grove, 2001. *Address:* House of Commons, SW1A 0AA; *e-mail:* dorriesn@parliament.uk. *Club:* Carlton.

DORSET, Archdeacon of; *see* Magowan, Ven. A. J.

DORWARD, David Keay; Director of Finance, Dundee City Council, since 1995; *b* 24 May 1954; *s* of David Dorward and Christina Dorward (*née* Keay); *m* 1977, Gail Elizabeth Bruce; three *d.* *Educ:* Kinross High Sch.; Perth High Sch.; Glasgow Coll. of Technology. CPFA 1982. Trainee Accountant, Perth and Kinross Jt CC, 1971–75; Tayside Regional Council: Trainee Accountant, 1975–82; Sen. Accountant, 1982–83; Principal Accountant, 1983–84; Financial Planning Officer, 1984–86; Chief Financial Planning Officer, 1986–93; Depute Dir of Finance, 1993–95. *Recreations:* golf, supporting Dundee United, bowls, going to the theatre. *Address:* 4 Norrie Street, Broughty Ferry, Dundee DD5 2SD. *T:* (01382) 739006. *Clubs:* Dundee United Businessmen's (Dundee); Broughty Bowling; Abertay Golf.

DOSANJH, Hon. Ujjal; PC (Can.) 2004; QC (BC) 1995; MP (L) Vancouver South, Canada, since 2004; *b* India, 9 Sept. 1947; *s* of Giani Pritam Singh Dosanjh and Surjit Kaur Dosanjh; *m* Raminder; three *s.* *Educ:* Simon Fraser Univ. (BA); Univ. of BC (LLB). Called to Canadian Bar, 1977; opened law practice, Dosanjh & Pirani, 1979, subseq. Dosanjh Woolley, now Vertlieb Dosanjh. MLA (NDP) Vancouver-Kensington, 1991–2001; Attorney Gen., BC, 1995–2000; Premier, BC, 2000–01. Leader, NDP, 2000–01. Hon. LLD Guru Nanak Dev Univ., Amritsar, 2001. *Recreations:* jogging, reading. *Address:* 2520 SW Marine Drive, Vancouver, BC V6P 6C2, Canada.

DOSSER, Prof. Douglas George Maurice; Professor of Economics, University of York, 1965–81; retired, 1981; *b* 3 Oct. 1927; *s* of George William Dosser; *m* 1954, Valerie Alwyne Elizabeth, *d* of Leslie Jack Lindsey; three *d.* *Educ:* Latymer Upper School; London School of Economics. Lecturer in Economics, Univ. of Edinburgh, 1958–62; Vis. Prof. of Economics, Univ. of Washington, Seattle, 1960; Vis. Res. Prof. of Economics, Columbia Univ., NY, 1962; Reader in Economics, Univ. of York, 1963–65. *Publications:* Economic Analysis of Tax Harmonisation, 1967; (with S. Han) Taxes in the EEC and Britain, 1968; (with F. Andic) Theory of Economic Integration for Developing Countries, 1971; European Economic Integration and Monetary Unification, 1973; (with K. Hartley) The Collaboration of Nations, 1981; articles in Economic Jl, Economica, Rev. of Economic Studies. *Recreations:* art and antiques.

DOSSETT, David Patrick; Chief Executive: BEAMA (formerly British Electrotechnical and Allied Manufacturers' Association) Ltd, since 2001 (Director General, 1998–2001); BEAMA Installation Ltd; *b* 20 Oct. 1943; *s* of John Dossett and Elizabeth Dossett (*née* Walsh); *m* 1964, Teresa Richards; four *s* two *d.* *Educ:* City Univ., London (BSc (Electrical and Electronic Engrg)). MIET (MIEE 1990). Distribn engr, London Electricity Bd, 1967–71; Tech. Officer, BSI, 1971–77; Hd of Standards, Kala (Iranian oil co.), 1977–84; Sen. Tech. Officer, AMDEA, 1984–91; Dir, EIEMA, 1991–98. Director: ASTA BEAB (formerly Asta) Certification Services, 1991–2007; Electrical Safety Council (formerly NICEIC), 2001– (Vice-Chm., 2005–07, Chm., 2007–March 2009). Chm., Orgalime, 2005–07. Gov., St Bede's Sch., Romford, 1978–88 (Chm., 1984–88). *Recreations:* West Ham United, real ale, 10 grandchildren. *Address:* BEAMA, Westminster Tower, 3 Albert Embankment, SE1 7SL. *T:* (020) 7793 3009, *Fax:* (020) 7793 3003; *e-mail:* dd@beama.org.uk.

DOTRICE, Roy, OBE 2008; actor (stage, films and television); *b* 26 May 1925; *m* 1946, Kay Newman (*d* 2007), actress; three *d.* *Educ:* Dayton and Intermediate Schs, Guernsey, CI. Served War of 1939–45: Air Gunner, RAF, 1940; PoW, 1942–45. Acted in Repertory, 1945–55; formed and directed Guernsey Theatre Co., 1955; Royal Shakespeare Co., 1957–65 (Caliban, Julius Caesar, Hotspur, Firs, Puntila, Edward IV, etc); World War 2½, New Theatre, London, 1966; Brief Lives, Golden Theatre, New York, 1967; Latent Heterosexual and God Bless, Royal Shakespeare Co., Aldwych, 1968; Brief Lives (one-man play), Criterion, 1969 (over 400 perfs, world record for longest-running solo perf.), toured England, Canada, USA, 1973, Mayfair, 1974 (over 150 perfs), Broadway season, and world tour (over 1,700 perfs), 1974, Australian tour, 1975, UK revival, 2008; Peer Gynt, Chichester Festival, 1970; One At Night, Royal Court, 1971; The Hero, Edinburgh, 1970; Mother Adam, Arts, 1971; Tom Brown's Schooldays, Cambridge, 1972; The Hollow Crown, seasons in USA 1973 and 1975, Sweden 1975; Gomes, Queen's, 1973; The Dragon Variation, Duke of York's, 1977; Australian tour with Chichester Festival, 1978; Passion of Dracula, Queen's, 1978; Oliver, Albery, 1979; Mister Lincoln (one-man play on Abraham Lincoln), Washington, NY and TV special, 1980, Fortune, 1981; A Life, NY, 1980–81; Henry V, and Falstaff in Henry IV, American Shakespeare Theatre, Stratford, Conn, 1981; Murder in Mind, Strand, 1982; Winston Churchill (one-man play), USA 1982 (also CBS TV); Kingdoms, NY, 1982; The Genius, Los Angeles, 1984 (Dramalogue Best Perf. Award); Down an Alley, Dallas, 1984; Great Expectations, Old Vic, 1985; Enemy of the People, NY, 1985; Hay Fever, NY and Washington, 1986; The Homecoming, NY, 1991; The Best of Friends, NY, 1993, Hampstead Th., London, 2006; The Woman in Black, USA, 1995, A Moon for the Misbegotten, NY, 2000 (Tony, Critics' Circle, Drama Desk and Jefferson Awards for best actor); The Islander, Theatre Royal, Lincoln, 2002; Carousel, Chichester, 2006; *films include:* Heroes of Telemark, Twist of Sand, Lock up Your Daughters, Buttercup Chain, Tomorrow, One of Those Things, Nicholas and Alexandra, Amadeus, Corsican Brothers, The Eliminators, Camilla, L-Dopa, The Lady Forgets, Lounge People, The Cutting Edge, The Scarlet Letter, Swimming with Sharks, The Beacon, La Femme Musketeer, Go Go Tales, Hellboy II. *Television:* appearances in: Dear Liar, Brief Lives, The Caretaker (Emmy award), Imperial Palace, Misleading Cases, Clochemerle, Dickens of London, Stargazy on Zummerdown, Strange Luck, Babylon 5, Earth 2, Mr and Mrs Smith (series), Murder She Wrote, Picket Fences (series), Children of the Dark, Family Reunion (USA), Tales of the Gold Monkey (USA), The Wizard (USA), A Team (USA), Tales from the Dark-Side (USA), Beauty and the Beast (USA), Going to Extremes (series) (USA), The Good Policeman (USA), Madigan Men (series) (USA), Heartbeat, Doctors, Are You Jim's Wife. TV Actor of the Year Award, 1968; Tony Nomination for A Life, 1981. *Recreations:* fishing, soccer. *Address:* c/o Eric Glass Ltd, 25 Ladbroke Crescent, W11 1PS. *Club:* Garrick.

DOUBLE, Paul Robert Edgar; Remembrancer, since 2003, and Parliamentary Agent, since 2004, City of London; *b* 4 Oct. 1951; *s* of Edgar Harold Double and Iris Joan Double; *m* 1986, Glynis Mycock; one *s* three *d.* *Educ:* Univ. of Bristol (BSc); University Coll. London (LLM). MRSC 1984. Called to the Bar, Middle Temple, 1981; joined Civil Service, 1974; seconded to Univ. of Aston, 1975; Sec., Industry Adv. Cttee, Dept of Employment, and Mem., Legislation Review Unit, 1976–84; joined City Remembrancer's Office, following pupillage in chambers of Hon. Sir Michael Turner, 1985; Asst Remembrancer, 1994–98; Dir, 1998–2003. Dir, Lord Mayor's Show Ltd, 2004–. Vis. Lectr in Law, Univ. of London, 1983–98. Freeman, City of London, 1985. *Recreations:* sailing, ski-ing. *Address:* Guildhall, EC2P 2EJ. *T:* (020) 7332 1200, *Fax:* (020) 7332 1895. *Club:* Guildhall.

DOUBLEDAY, John Vincent; sculptor since 1968; *b* 9 Oct. 1947; *s* of late Gordon V. and Margaret E. V. Doubleday; *m* 1969, Isobel J. C. Durie; two *s* (and one *s* decd). *Educ:* Stowe; Goldsmiths' College School of Art. *Exhibitions include:* Waterhouse Gallery, 1968, 1969, 1970, 1971; Galerie Sothmann, Amsterdam, 1969, 1971, 1979; Richard Demarco Gallery, Edinburgh, 1973; Laing Art Gallery, Newcastle, Bowes Museum, Barnard Castle, 1974; Pandion Gallery, NY, Aldeburgh Festival, 1983; *works include:* Baron Ramsey of Canterbury, 1974; King Olav of Norway, 1975; Prince Philip, Duke of Edinburgh, Earl Mountbatten of Burma, Golda Meir, 1976; Charlie Chaplin (Leicester Square), 1982; Beatles (Liverpool), Dylan Thomas, 1984; Royal Marines Commando Meml, Lympstone, Devon, 1986; Sherlock Holmes (Meiringen), 1991; Dorothy L. Sayers (Witham), J. B. Pflug (Biberach), 1994; Nelson Mandela (Mbabane and London), 1997; Gerald Durrell (Jersey Zoo), Sherlock Holmes (Baker Street Stn, London), 1999; The Dorset Shepherd (Dorchester), 2000; Col Jabara (USAF ACAD., Colorado Springs), 2004; Nelson (Gibraltar), 2005; Battle of Maldon Monument (Blackwater Estuary, Essex), 2006; *works in public collections:* Ashmolean Mus., British Mus., Herbert F. Johnson Mus., USA, Tate Gall., V & A, Nat. Mus. of Wales. *Recreation:* enthusiasm for the unnecessary. *Address:* Goat Lodge, Goat Lodge Road, Great Totham, Maldon, Essex CM9 8BX. *T:* (01621) 891329.

DOUCE, Prof. John Leonard, FREng; FIET; Professor of Electrical Science, Warwick University, 1965–94 (part-time 1989–94), now Emeritus; *b* 15 Aug. 1932; *s* of John William and Florrie Douce; *m* 1959, Jean Shanks; one *s* one *d.* *Educ:* Manchester Grammar Sch.; Manchester Univ. (BSc, MSc, PhD, DSc). Lectr, Sen. Lectr, Reader, Queen's Univ., Belfast, 1958–65. Member: Technology Sub-Cttee, UGC, 1980–89; Engrg Bd, 1987–91, Science Bd, 1989–91, SERC; Contract Assessor, HEFCE, 1993–94. FREng 1991. Sir Harold Hartley Silver Medal, Inst. of Measurement and Control, 1989. *Publications:* Introduction to Mathematics of Servomechanisms, 1963, 2nd edn 1972; papers on control engineering. *Recreations:* bridge, boating, home-brewing. *Address:* 259 Station Road, Balsall Common, Coventry CV7 7EG. *T:* (01676) 532070; *e-mail:* jdouce@iee.org.

DOUEK, Ellis Elliot, FRCS; Consultant Otologist, 1970–99, now Emeritus, and Chairman, Hearing Research Group, 1974–99, Guy's Hospital; author; *b* 25 April 1934; *s* of Cesar Douek and Nelly Sassoon; *m* 1993, Gill Green; two *s* by former marriage. *Educ:* English School, Cairo; Westminster Medical School. MRCS, LRCP 1958; FRCS 1967. House appts, St Helier Hosp., 1959, and Whittington Hosp., 1963; nat. service, RAMC, 1960–62; ENT Registrar, Royal Free Hosp., 1966; Sen. Registrar, King's College Hosp., 1968. Mem., MRC working party on Hearing Research, 1975; MRC Rep. to Europ. Communities on Hearing Res., 1980; UK Rep. to Europ. Communities on Indust. Deafness, 1983; Mem., Scientific Cttee, Inst. de Recherche sur la surdité, Paris, 1989–. Littman Meml Lect., UCL, 2005. Dalby Prize for hearing research, RSM, 1978. *Publications:* Sense of Smell—Its Abnormalities, 1974; Eighth Nerve, in Peripheral Neuropathy, 1975; Olfaction, in Scientific Basis of Otolaryngology, 1976; Cochlear Implant, in Textbook of ENT, 1980; A Middle Eastern Affair (autobiog.), 2004; papers on hearing and smell. *Recreations:* drawing and painting, studying history. *Address:* (home) 14 Heathcroft, Hampstead Way, NW11 7HH. *T:* (020) 8455 6427; Consulting Rooms, Princess Grace Hospital, 42–52 Nottingham Place, W1U 5NY. *e-mail:* elgildouek@aol.com. *Club:* Athenæum.

DOUETIL, Dane Jonathan, CBE 2007; Group Chief Executive Officer, Brit Insurance Holdings PLC, since 2005 (Director, since 1999); Chief Executive, Brit Syndicates Ltd, since 2002; Head, Brit Group Underwriting, since 2002; *b* 28 July 1960; *s* of Dane Peter Douetil and Fleur Caroline Douetil; *m* 1986, Antonia Clare Williamson; three *d.* *Educ:* Birmingham Univ. (BA Hons Commerce 1982). Willis Faber Gp, 1982–89 (Dir, Political and Financial Risk Div., 1988–89); Founding Shareholder and Dir, Special Risk Services Ltd, 1989–94; Consultant, Benfield Gp, 1997; Dir and Chief Exec., Brit Insce Ltd, 1998–. Mem., and Chm., London Mkt Reform Gp, 2006–07. *Recreations:* fishing, shooting, wine. *Address:* Brit Insurance PLC, 55 Bishopsgate, EC2N 3AS. *T:* (020) 7984 8800; *e-mail:* dane.douetil@britinsurance.com. *Club:* Boodle's.

DOUGAL, Andrew James Harrower; Director and Chairman, Audit Committee, Taylor Wimpey plc, since 2007; *b* 2 Sept. 1951; *s* of Andrew James Harrower Dougal and Muriel Mary Dougal (*née* MacDonald); *m* 1978, Margaret Mairi MacDonald; two *s* one *d.* *Educ:* Greenock Acad.; Paisley GS; Glasgow Univ. (BAcc 1972). CA 1975. Articled Clerk, then Asst Manager, Arthur Young Glasgow, 1972–77; Gp Chief Accountant, Scottish & Universal Investments Ltd, 1977–86; Hanson plc, 1986–2002: Finance Comptroller, 1986–89; Finance Dir, ARC Ltd, 1989–92; Man. Dir, ARC Southern, 1992–93; Dep. Finance Dir, 1993–95; Finance Dir, 1995–97; Chief Exec., 1997–2002; Dir, Taylor Woodrow plc, 2002–07 (Chm., Audit Cttee, 2003–07). Non-executive Director: BPB, 2003–05; Celtel Internat. BV, 2004–05; Premier Farnell, 2006–; Creston, 2006–. Mem., Qualification Bd, ICAS, 2000–05. CCMI (CIMgt 1999); FRSA 2005. *Recreations:* family, sports, travel, history. *Address:* Gameswood, Crawley Drive, Camberley, Surrey GU15 2AA; *e-mail:* a.dougal@btinternet.com.

DOUGAL, James Joseph; writer and broadcaster, public affairs consultant and media trainer; Director, Dougal Media, since 2006; *b* 19 March 1945; *s* of Samuel and Christine Dougal; *m* 1970, Deirdre O'Neill; one *s* three *d.* *Educ:* St Mary's Christian Brothers

Grammar Sch., Belfast; St Gabriel's Seminary, Enniskillen. NI Pol and News Ed., RTE, 1977–90; NI Pol Ed., BBC, 1990–97; Hd of NI Repn, 1997–2002, Hd of Repn in UK, 2002–04, EC. Presenter, BBC Radio, 2004–; maker of documentaries for Ulster TV. DUniv QUB, 2003. *Recreations:* walking, driving, going to the gym.

DOUGAL, Malcolm Gordon; HM Diplomatic Service, retired; *b* 20 Jan. 1938; *s* of late Eric Gordon Dougal and Marie (*née* Wildermuth); *m* 1st, 1964, Elke (marr. diss.); one *s*; 2nd, 1995, Brigid Pritchard (*née* Turner) (*d* 2000); two step *s*; 3rd, 2003, Diana Blade (*née* Price); two step *s*. *Educ:* Ampleforth Coll., Yorkshire; The Queen's Coll., Oxford (MA Mod. History). National Service in Korea and Gibraltar with Royal Sussex Regt, 1956–58; Oxford, 1958–61; Contracts Asst, De Havilland Aircraft, Hatfield, 1961–64; Asst to Export Manager, Ticket Equipment Ltd (Plessey), 1964–66; Export Manager, Harris Lebus Ltd, 1967–69; entered HM Diplomatic Service, 1969; Foreign Office, 1969–72; 1st Secretary (Commercial): Paris, 1972–76; Cairo, 1976–79; Foreign Office, 1979–81; Consul Gen., Lille, 1981–85; Dep. High Comr and Head of Chancery, Canberra, 1986–89; RCDS, 1990; Dir, Jt FCO/DTI Directorate of Overseas Trade Services, FCO, 1991–94; Consul Gen., San Francisco, 1994–98. Warden, John Spedan Lewis Trust for the Advancement of the Natural Scis, 1998–2005. *Publication:* (contrib.) The Third Battle of Ypres (Seaford House Papers), 1990. *Recreations:* natural history, history, walking, books, sport, horse racing, wine. *Address:* Eglesfield Cottage, Monk Sherborne, Tadley, Hants RG26 5HH.

DOUGAN, Dr David John; County Arts Officer, Essex County Council, 1989–97; *b* 26 Sept. 1936; *s* of William John Dougan and Blanche May; *m* 1st, 1959, Eileen Ludbrook (marr. diss. 1985); one *s*; 2nd, 1986, Barbara Taylor; one *s* one *d*. *Educ:* Durham Univ. (BA, MA); City Univ. (PhD 1982); BA Open Univ. 2002. Reporter, Tyne Tees Television, 1963; presenter, BBC, 1966; Director, Northern Arts, 1970; Dir, Crafts Council, 1984–88. Chairman: Nat. Youth Dance Trust, 1985–91; Dance East, 1999–2003; Suffolk Univs of the Third Age, 2005–. Special Advr, H of C Educn, Sci. and Arts Cttee, 1981–82; Mem., Calouste Gulbenkian Foundn Enquiry into the Arts in Schs, 1982. *Publications:* History of North East Shipbuilding, 1966; Great Gunmaker, 1968; Shipwrights Trade Union, 1971; The Jarrow March, 1976; To Return a King, 2006. *Recreations:* theatre, music, tennis. *Address:* Grovelands, 1 Grove Road, Bury St Edmunds, Suffolk IP33 3BE. *T:* (01284) 752588.

DOUGHERTY, Air Vice-Marshal Simon Robert Charles, QHP 2002; FFOM; Chief of Staff Health and Director-General Medical Services, Royal Air Force, 2006–08 (Director-General Medical Services (RAF), 2004–06); *b* 26 Feb. 1949; *s* of Patrick Cecil George Dougherty and Valerie June Dougherty (*née* Appleby); *m* 1971, Margaret Snape; two *s* one *d*. *Educ:* Framlingham Coll.; London Hosp. Med. Coll. (MB BS 1971); LSHTM (MSc Occupational Medicine 1986). DObstRCOG 1976; DAvMed (Stewart Meml Prize) 1979; AFOM 1980, MFOM 1984, FFOM 1993. Commnd RAF Med. Br., 1969; MO, RAF Binbrook, 1974–75; UK Deleg & Support Unit HQ AFCENT, 1975–77; Sen. MO, UK Support Unit, HQ AAFCE, 1977–78; DAvMed course, RAF Inst. of Aviation Medicine, 1979; Chief Instructor, RAF Aviation Medicine Trng Centre, 1979–82; Sen. MO, TriNat. Tornado Trng Est., RAF Cottesmore, 1982–85; Deputy Principal Medical Officer: (Occupational Health and Safety) HQ RAF Support Comd, 1986–87; HQ RAF Germany, 1987–91; jsdc, Greenwich, 1991–92; Officer Commanding: RAF Inst. of Health and Med. Trng, 1992–94; Princess Mary's Hosp., RAF Halton, 1994; Dep. Dir, Med. Policy and Plans (RAF), HQ PTC, 1994–96; CO, The Princess Mary's Hosp., RAF Akrotiri and Comd Med. Advr, HQ British Forces Cyprus, 1996–99; Dir Health Services (RAF), HQ PTC, 1999–2001; Dir Med. Personnel, Policy and Plans (RAF), HQ PTC, 2001–02; Dir Med. Policy, Defence Med. Services Dept, MoD, 2002–04. Taylor Prof. of Occupational Medicine, Jt RAF and RCP, 1990–96; Consultant Advr, Occupational Medicine, RAF, 1997–2002. Member: Ct of Govs, LSHTM, 2004–07; Fellowship Cttee, Faculty of Occupational Medicine, 2006–08. Chm. of Trustees, Stewart Meml Trust, 2004–08; Governor: Royal Star and Garter Home, 2004–; Framlingham Coll., 2008–. Mem. SOM, 1980; MRAeS 1982, FRAeS 2000; FRSocMed 1994 (United Services Section Council, 2002–08; Vice Pres., 2004–08); MIHM 1999; FCMI (FIMgt 1999). Freeman, City of London, 2008. Member: Soc. of Apothecaries, 2006–; GAPAN, 2007–. Vice Pres., Soc. of Old Framlinghamians, 2003–. OStJ 1991. *Recreations:* travelling, ski-ing, computers, gardening, watching Rugby. *Club:* Royal Air Force.

DOUGHTY, Sir (Graham) Martin, Kt 2001; Chair, Natural England, since 2006; *b* 11 Oct. 1949; *s* of late Harold Doughty and of Eva Mary (*née* Swift); *m* 1st, 1974, Eleanor Lamont (*d* 1988); two *d*; 2nd, 1996, Gillian Gostick. *Educ:* New Mills Grammar Sch.; Imperial Coll., London (BSc Eng, MSc). Res. Chem. Engr, Booth (Internat.), 1971–72; Lectr, 1973–90, Sen. Lectr, 1990–95, Sheffield Poly., later Sheffield Hallam Univ. Mem. (Lab), Derbys CC, 1981–2005 (Chairman: Highways and Transport, 1983–86; Planning and Countryside, 1986–92; Council Leader, 1992–2001). Chair, English Nature, 2001–06. Board Member: E Midlands Develt Agency, 1998–2001; Countryside Agency, 1999–2005. Mem., Peak Dist Nat. Park Authy, 1987–2005 (Chm., 1993–2002, Vice-Chm., 2002–04); Chm., Assoc. of Nat. Park Authorities, 1997–2001; Mem., Rural Affairs Forum for England, 2002–04. Non-executive Director: Entrust, 1996–2003; Derbys Ambulance Services NHS Trust, 1996–98. Vice-Pres., Arkwright Soc., 2003–. Nat. Forest Ambassador, 2004–; Patron, Inst. of Ecology and Envmtl Mgt, 2002–. DUniv: Sheffield Hallam, 2002; Derby, 2006; Hon. DSc Cranfield, 2005. *Publication:* The Park under the Town, 2001. *Recreations:* hill-walking, gardening, cooking fish well, natural history. *Address:* Natural England, 1 East Parade, Sheffield S1 2ET; *e-mail:* martin.doughty@naturalengland.org.uk. *Club:* Royal Commonwealth Society.

DOUGHTY, Nigel Edward; Joint Founder, and Chief Executive, Doughty Hanson & Co., since 1989; *b* 10 June 1957; *s* of Francis Edward Doughty and Mercia Mary Doughty (*née* Lambert); *m* 1st, 1985, Carol Elizabeth Green (marr. diss. 1997); one *s* one *d*; 2nd, 2004, Lucy Vasquez; two *s*. *Educ:* Magnus Sch., Newark; Cranfield Univ. (MBA 1984). American Express/Shearson Lehman, 1979–83; Standard Chartered Bank, 1984–89 (Anglo-American Banking Schol., 1985). Chairman: Tarkett AG, 1994–98; Geberit AG, 1997–99; Dunlop Standard Aerospace, 1998–2004; Umbro plc, 2000–08; Nottingham Forest FC, 2002–; Tumi Inc., 2005–; Dir, Tag Heuer, SA, 1995–97. Mem., World Econ. Forum, Davos, 1998. Dir, Bridges Community Ventures, 2003–; Trustee, Doughty Hanson Charitable Foundn, 1998–; Founder, Doughty Centre for Corporate Responsibility, 2007. Dist. Alumni Award, Cranfield Sch. of Mgt, 2004. *Recreations:* Nottingham Forest FC, gardening. *Address:* c/o Doughty Hanson & Co., 45 Pall Mall, SW1Y 5JG. *T:* (020) 7663 9300, *Fax:* (020) 7747 9320; *e-mail:* nigel.doughty@doughtyhanson.com. *Club:* Metropolitan (New York).

DOUGHTY, Stuart John, CMG 2005; CEng, FICE; Chief Executive, Costain Group plc, 2001–05; non-executive Chairman, Somero plc, since 2006; Senior non-executive Director, Scott Wilson plc; *b* 13 Sept. 1943; *s* of late Henry John Doughty and of Marie Louise Doughty; *m* Penelope Ann; one *d* (one *s* decd). *Educ:* UC, Cardiff (BSc). CEng; FICE; FIHT. John Laing Construction: grad. trainee, 1965; Regl Manager, 1974–84;

Man. Dir, Civil Engrg Div., 1984–86; Exec. Dir, Tarmac Construction, 1986–91; Chm and Man. Dir, Construction Div., Alfred McAlpine, 1991–94; Dir, Hyder Plc, 1994–97 Chm., Alstec Ltd, Beck & Pollitzer, and Kennedy Construction, 1997–2001. Non-exec Dir, Viborant plc, 1997–2001. Chm., UK Trade Internat. (Sectors), DTI, 1997–. Mem Council, ECGD, 1997–2001. Lt Col, Engr and Logistics Staff Corps, 1998–. Gov., King's Sch., Worcester, 1999–. *Recreations:* classic and historic motor sport and houses. *Address* Bradley Farm House, Kinlet, Bewdley, Worcs DY12 3BU. *T:* (01299) 841327.

DOUGHTY, Susan Kathleen, (Mrs D. Orchard); Director, Corporate Climate Ltd since 2006; *b* 13 April 1948; *d* of Ronald and Olive Powell; *m* 1st, 1974, John Dought (marr. diss.); two *s*; 2nd, 1995, David Orchard; two step *d*. *Educ:* Northumberland Col of Educn (CertEd); holds various business qualifications. Primary sch. teacher, 1969–7 Work Study Analyst, Northern Gas Mgt Services, 1970–73; Work Study Officer, CEB Mgt Services, 1974–75; Orgn and Method Analyst, Wilkinson Match Mgt Service 1976–77; career break (charity work), 1977–83; Indep. Mgt Consultant, 1984–89 1999–2001; Project Manager, Thames Water, 1989–98. MP (Lib Dem) Guildford 2001–05; contested (Lib Dem) same seat, 2005; Prospective Parly Cand. (Lib Dem Guildford, 2007–. Lib Dem spokesman on envmt, 2001–03, front bench spokesman o envmt, 2003–05. Mem., Envmtl Audit Select Cttee, 2001–05. Chm., Thatchan Children's Centre, 1982–84. *Recreations:* gardening, cricket, walking, theatre, opera *Address:* 3 Wharf Cottages, Stonebridge Wharf, Shalford, Surrey GU4 8EH. *Club:* County (Guildford).

DOUGHTY, Sir William (Roland), Kt 1990; Chairman, North West Thames Region Health Authority, 1984–94; Deputy Chairman, Britannia Refined Metals Ltd, later MIM UK Ltd, 1982–94 (Director, 1978–94); *b* 18 July 1925; *s* of Roland Gill Doughty an Gladys Maud Doughty (*née* Peto); *m* 1952, Patricia Lorna Cooke; three *s*. *Educ:* Headstor Sch.; Acton Technical Coll.; Trinity Coll., Dublin (MA); Harvard Business Sch. (AMP Metal Box Co. Ltd, 1953–66; Molins Ltd, 1966–69, Dir, 1967; Cape Industries, 1969–84 Dir, 1972, Man. Dir, 1980–84; Chairman: Surgicare Ltd, 1995–2001; The Nex Challenge Ltd, 1998–2001. Member: SE Economic Planning Council, 1966–79 (Chm Industry and Employment Cttee, 1972–79); CBI Council, 1975–86 (Chm., London Region, 1981–83). Founder and Chm., Assoc. for Conservation of Energy, 1981–8 (Pres., 1985–). Gov., SE Tech. Coll., 1967–69; Trustee, Gt Ormond St Hosp. for Sic Children, 1978–90; Mem., Gen. Council, King Edward VII's Hosp. Fund for Londo 1984– (Mem., Management Cttee, 1987–95); Chairman: King's Fund Centre Ctte 1991–95; Adv. Cttee on Distinction Awards, NHS, 1994–97. Chairman: Cord Bloo Charity, 1998–2004; Headway, The Brain Injury Assoc., 1999–2004; Inventure Trus 2001–03. Life Mem., Sickle Cell Soc. (Patron, 2007–). Chm., Thorpe House Sch. Trus 1995–2005. LHSM 1986. CCMI; FRSA. *Recreations:* cricket, theatre, golf, horse racing *Clubs:* Savile, MCC.

DOUGILL, John Wilson, FREng, FICE, FIStructE, FASCE; Chief Executive an Secretary, Institution of Structural Engineers, 1994–99 (Director of Engineerin 1987–94); *b* 18 Nov. 1934; *s* of William John Dougill and Emily Firmstone Wilson; 1959, Daphne Maude Weeks; one *s* one *d*. *Educ:* Trinity Sch. of John Whitgift, Croydo King's Coll., London; Imperial Coll. of Science and Technology. MScEng, DIC, PhI FREng 1990. Engineer with George Wimpey, 1956–58 and 1960–61; Research Asst Prof. A. L. L. Baker, Imperial Coll., 1961–64; King's College London: Lectr in Civ Engrg, 1964–73; Reader in Engrg Science, 1973–76; Prof. of Engrg Science, 1976–8 Prof. of Concrete Structures and Technology, Imperial Coll., 1981–87. Vis. Re Engineer, Univ. of California, Berkeley, 1967–68; Visiting Professor: Dept of Civil Engr Imperial Coll., 1991–97; Sch. of Engrg, Univ. of Surrey, 2000–06; South China Univ. Technol., 2001–. Chm., SERC Civil Engrg Sub-Cttee, 1982–83; Mem., NEDO Re Strategy Cttee, 1983–85. Sec. Gen., Fedn Internat. de la Precontrainte, 1992–98. Mer Court of Governors, Whitgift Foundn, 1981–2007. FCGI. *Publications:* papers in jls engrg mech., materials and struct. engrg. *Recreations:* coarse gardening, travel, good foo walking. *Address:* Ashcroft, Larch Close, The Glade, Kingswood, Surrey KT20 6JF. (01737) 833283.

DOUGLAS, family name of **Viscount Chilston**, **Earl of Morton**, and **Marquess o Queensberry**.

DOUGLAS AND CLYDESDALE, Marquess of; Alexander Douglas-Hamilton; 31 March 1978; *s* and *heir* of Duke of Hamilton, *qv*.

DOUGLAS, Anthony Gordon, CBE 2008; Chief Executive, Children and Family Cou Advisory and Support Service, since 2004; *b* 4 July 1949; *s* of late Gordon Louis Albe Douglas and Lily Douglas (*née* Graves); *m* 1975, Margaret Olga Jean Friedlander; two *Educ:* St Nicholas Grammar Sch., Northwood; St Peter's Coll., Oxford (Pt I PPE); London Poly. (CQSW 1980); Open Univ. (BSc 1984). Social worker, Hackney Soci Services, 1976–83; various mgt posts in Southwark, Barnet and Newham Council London, 1983–91; Asst Dir of Social Services, Hackney, 1991–96; Havering Council: D Social Services, 1996–98; Exec. Dir, Community Services, 1998–2002; Dir, Social Ca and Health, Suffolk CC, 2002–04. Vis. Fellow, UEA, 2003–. Chair: London Assoc. Dirs of Social Services, 1997–2000; British Assoc. for Adoption and Fostering, 2003 *Publications:* (with T. Philpot) Caring and Coping, 1998; (with A. Weir) Child Protecti and Adult Mental Health: conflicts of interest, 1999; Is Anyone Out There?, 2002; (wit T. Philpot) Adoption: changing families, changing times, 2003. *Recreations:* cricket, oper *Address:* CAFCASS, 8th Floor, South Quay Plaza 3, 189 Marsh Wall, E14 9SH. *T:* (02 7510 7027; *e-mail:* anthony.douglas@cafcass.gov.uk. *Club:* Groucho.

DOUGLAS, Anthony Jude; Director, Gravitas Communications, since 2001; *b* 14 De 1944; *s* of Arthur Sidney Douglas and Margaret Mary Douglas; *m* 1968, Jacqueline Englis two *d*. *Educ:* Cardinal Vaughan Grammar Sch., London; Southampton Univ. (BA Ho English). Head of Client Services, Lintas Advertising, 1967–81; Jt Chm. and Chief Exec DMB&B Advertising, 1981–95; Chief Exec., COI, 1996–98; Chm., FCB Europ 1998–99. Dir, Effective TV, 2003–. *Recreations:* cooking, walking, reading, anthropolog *Address:* 20 Malbrook Road, Putney, SW15 6UE. *T:* (020) 8788 3209.

DOUGLAS, Barry; see Douglas, W. B.

DOUGLAS, Boyd; farmer; Member (U) Limavady Borough Council, since 1997; *b* 1 July 1950; *s* of William Douglas and late May Douglas; *m* 1972, Kathleen Semple; two two *d*. *Educ:* Burnfoot Primary Sch.; Dungiven Secondary Sch.; Strabane Agriculture Co Farmer, 1970–. Mem. (U) E Londonderry, NI Assembly, 1998–2003. *Address:* 27 Drumrane Road, Dungiven, Co. Londonderry BT47 4NL.

DOUGLAS, Colin Antony; Director of NHS Communications, Department of Healt since 2008; *b* 10 Sept. 1963; *s* of Kendric Manasseh Douglas and Adassa Beatrice Dougla *m* 1992, Petrina Hall; two *s*. *Educ:* Tulse Hill Comprehensive Sch., S London; Keble Col Oxford (BA Hons PPE); Oxford Brookes Univ. (MBA). Dip. Mktg, CIM. Dir, Citiga Public Relns, 1994–99; Dir of Communications, Sport England, 1999–2001; Dir

Public Affairs, Transport for London, 2001–02; Director of Communications: Audit Commn, 2002–04; HSE, 2004–08. Non-exec. Dir, London Ambulance Service, 1996–2006. *Publication:* West Indian Women at War: British racism in World War II, 1991. *Recreations:* photography, Afro-Caribbean history, trying to keep up with two growing kids. *Address:* c/o Department of Health, Richmond House, 79 Whitehall, SW1A 2NS.

DOUGLAS, Derek Jack, CBE 2006; CA; Founder, Chairman and Chief Executive Officer, Adam Smith Ltd, since 1988; *b* 17 Oct. 1953. *Educ:* Heriot Watt Univ. (BSc); Aberdeen Univ. CA 1982. Chartered accountant: Coopers & Lybrand, 1978–81; Arthur Young, 1981–83; Gen. Manager, NZ United Corp., 1983–85; Barclays de Zoete Wedd, 1985–88. Chairman: Digital Animations Gp plc, 1996–2001; Kymata Ltd, 1998–99; Acuid Corp. Ltd, 2001–06; Carlton Bingo Plc, 2001–; Dir, Bremner plc, 1990–91. Chm. and Trustee, Maggie Keswick Jencks Cancer Caring Centres Trust, 1996–2003; Dir and Trustee, Macmillan Cancer Support, 2006–. FRSA 2003. Hon. DBA Abertay, 2003. *Publications:* contribs to Jl ICAS. *Recreations:* sailing, golf. *Address:* Adam Smith Ltd, Adam Smith House, Melville Castle Estate, Lasswade, Edinburgh EH18 1AW. *T:* (0131) 654 7000. *Club:* Bruntsfield Links Golfing Society.

DOUGLAS, Henry Russell, FCIJ; journalist; Legal Manager, News Group Newspapers, 1976–89; *b* Bishopbriggs, Lanarkshire, 11 Feb. 1925; 2nd *s* of late Russell Douglas and Jeanie Douglas (*née* Drysdale); *m* 1951, Elizabeth Mary, *d* of late Ralph Nowell, CB; two *s* three *d*. *Educ:* various Scottish and English Grammar Schools; Lincoln Coll., Oxford (MA Hons). Served RNVR, 1943–46 (Sub-Lt, submarines). Merchant Navy, 1946–47; Oxford Univ., 1947–50; Liverpool Daily Post, 1950–69; The Sun, 1969–76. Inst. of Journalists, 1956: Fellow, 1969; Pres., 1972–73; Chm. of Executive, 1973–76; Member: Press Council, 1972–80; Council, Newspaper Press Fund, 1972–76, 1986–2004 (Chm., 1990–91); Founder Mem., Media Society, 1973 (Treas., 1973–86, Vice-Pres., 1987–89); Founder, Soc. of Fleet Street Lawyers, 1989. *Recreations:* chess, painting, history. *Address:* Austen Croft, 31 Austen Road, Guildford, Surrey GU1 3NP. *T:* (01483) 576960. *Club:* Naval.

DOUGLAS, Hilary Kay, CB 2002; Chief Operating Officer, Department for Business, Enterprise and Regulatory Reform (formerly Department of Trade and Industry), since 2006; *b* 27 July 1950; *d* of late James Robert Keith Black and of Joan Margaret Black (*née* Boxall); *m* 1972, Robert Harold Douglas; two *s*. *Educ:* Wimbledon High Sch.; New Hall, Cambridge (BA Hons History 1971). Press Librarian, RIIA, 1971–73; joined DES, 1973: Sec. of State's Private Office, 1975–76; appts in teacher trng, educnl disadvantage and local authy finance, 1977–84; Head: Teacher Supply Div., 1985–87; School Govt Div., 1987–89; freelance consultancy and teaching, Netherlands, 1989–91; Sec., FEFC, 1991–92; set up SCAA, 1992–93; Hd of Personnel, DFE, 1993–94; Dir of Admin, Office for Standards in Educn, 1994–96; Dir, Civil Service Employer Gp, Cabinet Office, 1996–97; Dir, Personnel and Support Services, DfEE, 1997–2000; Man. Dir, Corporate Services and Develt, HM Treasury, 2000–04; Chief Operating Officer, ONS, 2004–06. *Recreations:* travel, European languages, singing. *Address:* Department for Business, Enterprise and Regulatory Reform, 1 Victoria Street, SW1H 0ET.

DOUGLAS, Janet Elizabeth, CMG 2008; HM Diplomatic Service; Head, Africa Department (Southern), Foreign and Commonwealth Office, since 2007; *b* Deal, Kent, 6 Jan. 1960; *d* of Duncan and Mary Douglas. *Educ:* Cheltenham Ladies' Coll.; St Catharine's Coll., Cambridge (BA Hons Archaeol. and Anthropol. 1982). Joined FCO, 1985; Second, later First Sec., Ankara, 1988–92; UN Dept, FCO, 1992–94; on secondment to ODA, 1994–96; First Sec. (EU), Stockholm, 1996–2000; Dep. Hd, Africa Dept (Southern), 2000–02; Head: Personnel Mgt Unit, HR Directorate, 2002–04; Consular Assistance Gp, Consular Directorate, 2004–07. *Recreations:* ski-ing, sailing (fair weather only), visiting art galleries and museums, reading crime fiction. *Address:* c/o Foreign and Commonwealth Office, King Charles Street, SW1A 2AH.

DOUGLAS, Kenneth, CBE 1991; CEng; Managing Director, Austin and Pickersgill Ltd, 1958–69, and 1979–83; Chairman, Kenton Shipping Services, Darlington, 1968–83; *b* 28 Oct. 1920; British; *m* 1942, Doris Lewer; one *s* two *d*. *Educ:* Sunderland Technical Coll. (Dip. Naval Architecture). CEng. Dep. Shipyard Manager, Vickers Armstrong Naval Yard, Newcastle-upon-Tyne, 1946–53; Dir and Gen. Manager, Wm Gray & Co. Ltd, West Hartlepool, 1954–58; Man. Dir, Upper Clyde Shipbuilders Ltd, Chm., Simons Lobnitz Ltd and Chm., UCS Trng Co., 1969–73; Dep. Chm., Govan Shipbuilders, 1971–73; Chm., Douglas (Kilbride) Ltd, 1972–77; Chm. and Man. Dir, Steel Structures Ltd, 1974–76; Shiprepair Marketing Dir, British Shipbuilders, 1978–79; Mem. Bd, PCEF, 1988–91. Mem., Tyne and Wear Residuary Body, DoE, 1985–89. Hon. Fellow, Sunderland Univ., 1993 (Fellow, 1980 and 1992–93, Chm. of Govs, 1982–93, Sunderland Poly., subseq. Univ.). Formerly: FRINA, MBIM, MInstD. *Recreations:* fishing, golf. *Address:* 2 Abbots Lea, Dalton Piercy, Hartlepool, Cleveland TS27 3JS.

DOUGLAS, Kenneth George, ONZ 1999; President, New Zealand Council of Trade Unions, 1987–99; *b* 15 Nov. 1935; *s* of John Atholwood Douglas and Marjorie Alice (*née* Farrow); *m* 1956, Lesley Barbara Winter (marr. diss. 1986); two *s* two *d*; partner, Marilyn Gay Tucker. *Educ:* Wellington Coll. President: Wellington Section, Drivers Union, 1958–79; NZ Drivers Fedn, 1972–79; Treas., Nat. Sect., NZ Fedn of Labour, 1979–87. Mem., Exec. Bd, ICFTU, 1987–99; Pres., ICFTU-Asia Pacific Regl Orgn, 1990–99. Mem., Prime Minister's Enterprise Council, 1990–99. Mem. (Ind.), Porirua CC, 1998–. JP Porirua, 1999. Hon. LLD Victoria Univ. of Wellington, 1999. *Publications:* contrib. articles on industrial relns and Labour movement to jls. *Recreation:* golf. *Address:* 8 View Road, Titahi Bay, Porirua, New Zealand. *T:* (4) 2368857. *Clubs:* Porirua, Titahi Golf (NZ).

DOUGLAS, Lesley; Controller, BBC Radio 2 and 6 Music, since 2004; *b* 7 June 1963; *d* of William and Sarah Douglas; *m* Nick Scripps; one *s* one *d*. *Educ:* Manchester Univ. (BA English). Joined BBC, 1986: prodn asst, res. dept, then David Jacobs Show, 1986–87; Promotions Asst, 1987–88; Producer: Music Dept, 1988–90; Promotions, 1990–93; Ed., Presentation and Planning, Radio 2, 1993–97; Managing Ed., 1997–2000, Hd of Progs, 2000–04, Radio 2. Chm., Steering Cttee, Radio Fest. Fellow, Radio Acad. Woman of Year Award, Music Ind., 2004. *Address:* c/o BBC, Western House, 99 Great Portland Street, W1A 1AA.

DOUGLAS, Michael John; QC 1997; a Recorder, since 2000; *b* 7 Aug. 1952; *s* of late James Murray Douglas, CBE. *Educ:* Westminster Sch.; Balliol Coll., Oxford (BA Hons Jurisprudence). Called to the Bar, Gray's Inn, 1974. *Recreations:* theatre, cinema, eating out, football, travel. *Address:* 4 Pump Court, Temple, EC4Y 7AN. *T:* (020) 7842 5555.

DOUGLAS, Michael Kirk; actor and producer; *b* 25 Sept. 1944; *s* of Kirk Douglas, actor and Diana Douglas; *m* 1977, Diandra Morrell Luker (marr. diss.); one *s*; *m* 2000, Catherine Zeta-Jones; one *s* one *d*. *Educ:* Univ. of Calif at Santa Barbara (BA 1967). *Films include: actor:* Hail Hero, 1969; Napoleon and Samantha, 1972; Star Chamber, 1983; A Chorus Line, 1985; Black Rain, 1990; The War of the Roses, 1990; Shining Through, 1992; Basic Instinct, 1992; Falling Down, 1993; Disclosure, 1994; The American President, 1995; The Game, 1997; Traffic, 2001; Don't Say a Word, 2002; The In-Laws, 2003; You, Me and Dupree, 2006; The Sentinel, 2006; *producer:* One Flew Over the Cuckoo's Nest, 1975; Flatliners, 1990; (jtly) Made in America, 1993; The Rainmaker, 1997; A Song for David, 2000; *actor and producer:* The China Syndrome, 1979; Romancing the Stone, 1984; The Jewel of the Nile, 1985; Fatal Attraction, 1987; Wall Street, 1988 (Academy Award for best actor); A Perfect Murder, 1998; Wonder Boys, 1999; Still Life, 1999; One Night at McCool's, 2001; It Runs in the Family, 2003; The Sentinel, 2006; narrator, One Day in September (documentary), 2000; *television* includes: Streets of San Francisco, 1972–76. UN Messenger of Peace, 1998; UN Ambassador for Nuclear Disarmament, 2000. *Address:* c/o Creative Artists Agency, 2000 Avenue of the Stars, Los Angeles, CA 90067, USA.

DOUGLAS, Neil; Sheriff of North Strathclyde at Paisley, since 1996; *b* 15 Oct. 1945; *s* of Dr Neil Douglas and Doreen Douglas; *m* 1971, Morag Isles; two *d*. *Educ:* Glasgow Acad.; Glasgow Univ. (LLB). Solicitor, 1968; Notary Public, 1972. Trainee solicitor, Brechin Welsh & Risk, Glasgow, 1968–70; Asst Solicitor, Ross Harper & Murphy, Glasgow, 1970–72; Partner, Brechin Robb, Glasgow, 1972–95; Floating Sheriff, All Scotland, 1995–96. *Recreations:* hill-walking, ski-ing, Scottish country dancing. *Address:* Paisley Sheriff Court, St James Street, Paisley PA3 2HW. *T:* (0141) 887 5291.

DOUGLAS, Prof. Neil James, MD, DSc; FRCP, FRCPE; Professor of Respiratory and Sleep Medicine, University of Edinburgh, since 1995; President, Royal College of Physicians of Edinburgh, since 2004 (Dean, 1995–2000; Vice-President, 2000–03); *b* 28 May 1949; *s* of Sir Donald Macleod Douglas, MBE and of (Margaret) Diana Douglas; *m* 1977, Susan McLaren Galloway; one *s* one *d*. *Educ:* Glenalmond Coll.; St Andrews Univ. (Schol.); Univ. of Edinburgh (MB ChB 1973; MD 1983; DSc 2003). FRCPE 1985; FRCP 1998. University of Edinburgh: Lectr in Medicine, 1975–83; Sen. Lectr, 1983–91; Reader in Medicine, 1991–95. MRC Fellow, Univ. of Colorado, 1980–81; Dir, Scottish Nat. Sleep Centre, Royal Infirmary, Edinburgh, 1983–. Hon. Sec., British Thoracic Soc., 1988–90. Ed.-in-Chief, Clinical Science, 1990–92. *Publications:* Clinicians' Guide to Sleep Medicine, 2002; over 300 papers in jls, mainly on breathing during sleep. *Recreations:* hill-walking, fishing, ski-ing, sailing. *Address:* Respiratory Medicine, Royal Infirmary, 51 Little France Crescent, Edinburgh EH16 4SA. *T:* (0131) 242 1836, *Fax:* (0131) 242 1776; *e-mail:* n.j.douglas@ed.ac.uk; Royal College of Physicians, 9 Queen Street, Edinburgh EH2 1JQ. *T:* (0131) 247 3638, *Fax:* (0131) 220 3939; *e-mail:* n.j.douglas@rcpe.ac.uk.

DOUGLAS, Richard Giles; *b* 4 Jan. 1932; *m* 1954, Jean Gray, *d* of Andrew Arnott; two *d*. *Educ:* Co-operative College, Stanford Hall, Loughborough; Univ. of Strathclyde; LSE; Univ. of St Andrews (MA 2003). Engineer (Marine). Tutor organiser in Adult Educn, Co-operative movement, 1957; Sectional Educn Officer, Scotland, 1958–61; Lectr in Economics, Dundee Coll. of Technol., 1964–70. Contested (Lab): South Angus, 1964, Edinburgh West, 1966, Glasgow Pollok, March 1967; (Lab and Co-op) Clackmannan and E Stirlingshire, Oct. 1974; MP (Lab and Co-op) Clackmannan and E Stirlingshire, 1970–Feb. 1974; MP Dunfermline, 1979–83, Dunfermline West, 1983–92 (Lab and Co-op, 1979–90, SNP, 1990–92); contested (SNP) Glasgow, Garscadden, 1992. Contested (SNP) Scotland Mid and Fife, Euro. Parly elecns, 1994. Chm., Scottish Water and Sewerage Customers' Council, 1995–98. *Address:* Braehead House, High Street, Auchtermuchty, Fife KY14 7AR.

DOUGLAS, Richard Philip, CB 2006; Director General Finance and Chief Operating Officer (formerly Director of Finance), Department of Health, since 2001; *b* 20 Nov. 1956; *s* of William Ronald Douglas and Margery Alice Douglas; *m* 1978, Carole Elizabeth Hodgson; two *s* one *d*. *Educ:* Archbishop Holgate's Grammar Sch., York; Hull Univ. (BA Hons). HM Customs and Excise, 1978–80; Exchequer and Audit Dept, later Nat. Audit Office, 1980–96 (Dir, 1994–96); Dep. Dir of Finance, NHS Exec., 1996–99; Dir of Finance, Nat. Savings, 1999–2001. Mem., CIPFA, 1983. *Recreations:* reading, gardening, walking. *Address:* Department of Health, Richmond House, 79 Whitehall, SW1A 2NS.

DOUGLAS, Hon. Sir Roger (Owen), Kt 1991; Director, Brierley Investments Ltd, 1990–99 (Chairman, 1998); *b* 5 Dec. 1937; *s* of Norman and Jennie Douglas; *m* 1961, Glennis June Anderson; one *s* one *d*. *Educ:* Auckland Grammar Sch.; Auckland Univ. (Accountancy Degree). Company Sec. and Acct. MP (Lab) Manurewa, 1969–90; Cabinet Minister, NZ, 1972–75; Minister in Charge of Inland Revenue Dept and Minister in Charge of Friendly Societies, 1984; Minister of Finance, 1984–88; Minister of Immigration and Minister of Police, 1989–90. Finance Minister of the Year, Euromoney Mag., 1985; Freedom Prize, Max Schmidheiny Foundn, 1996; Ludwig Erhard Prize for Economic Journalism, 1997; Friedrich von Hayek Medal, 2001. *Publications:* There's Got to be a Better Way, 1981; papers on NZ economy: An Alternative Budget, 1980; Proposal for Taxation, 1981; Toward Prosperity, 1987; Unfinished Business, 1993; Completing the Circle, 1996. *Recreations:* cricket, Rugby League, reading. *Address:* 411 Redoubt Road, Manukau City 2016, Auckland, New Zealand. *T:* (9) 2639596.

DOUGLAS, Steven Franklyn; Chief Executive, Housing Corporation, since 2007; *b* Hackney, 1964; *s* of Baldwin Douglas and Pamela Douglas (*née* Rodney); three *s*. *Educ:* Sedgehill Comprehensive Sch.; Corpus Christi Coll., Oxford (BA PPE 1985). Sen. Valuation Surveyor, London & Quadrant Housing Trust, 1986–89; Project Manager, Carr Gomm Soc., 1989; Hd of Develt, London & Quadrant Housing Trust, 1989–94; Chief Executive: Spitalfields Housing Assoc., 1994–96; ASRA Housing Assoc., 1996–2001; Housing Corporation: Dir, Investment and Regeneration, 2001–04; Dir (London), 2004–05; Dep. Chief Exec., 2005–06. Member: Public Sector Clients Forum, Office of Govt Commerce, 2005–; Callcutt rev. gp into house bldg delivery, 2006–07; Commn on Integration and Cohesion, 2006–07. Vice Chm., Williams Commn into Design and Quality in Thames Gateway, 2006–07. Chairman: London Housing Fedn Develt Gp, 1994–97; Lewisham Housing Assoc. Liaison Gp, 1994 and 1999; Greenwich Jt Commng Forum, 1994–99; London Develt Conf., 1997–99; Member: Housing Mgt and Maintenance Cttee, Nat. Housing Fedn, 1994–99; Bd, Hexagon Housing Assoc., 1994–99. *Recreations:* football, watching and playing, particularly with my boys, Aaron, Ethan and Freddie, Arsenal, R&B music, Mary J. Blige, dancing. *Address:* Housing Corporation, Maple House, 149 Tottenham Court Road, W1T 7BN.

DOUGLAS, Susan; *see* Douglas Ferguson, S. M.

DOUGLAS, Prof. Thomas Alexander; Professor of Veterinary Biochemistry and Head of Department of Veterinary Biochemistry (Clinical), University of Glasgow, 1977–90; *b* 9 Aug. 1926; *s* of Alexander and Mary Douglas; *m* 1957, Rachel Ishbel McDonald; two *s*. *Educ:* Battlefield Public Sch.; High Sch. of Glasgow; Glasgow Vet. Coll., Univ. of Glasgow (BSc; Animal Health Schol., 1950–54; PhD). MRCVS. General Veterinary Practice: Ulverston, 1948–49; Lanark, 1949–50; University of Glasgow: Faculty of Sci., 1950–54; Asst Lectr, Biochemistry, 1954–57; Lectr 1957–71, Sen. Lectr 1971–77, in Vet. Biochem., Vet. Sch.; Dean of Faculty of Vet. Medicine, 1982–85. Mem. Council, RCVS, 1982–85. Mem., UGC, 1986–89 (Chm., Agriculture and Veterinary Studies Sub-Cttee, 1986–89). *Publications:* sci. articles in vet. and biochem. jls. *Recreations:* golf, hill walking. *Address:* 77 South Mains Road, Milngavie, Glasgow G62 6DE. *T:* (0141) 956 2751.

DOUGLAS, (William) Barry, OBE 2002; concert pianist; *b* 23 April 1960; *m* Deirdre O'Hara; two *s* one *d*. *Educ:* Royal College of Music; private study with Maria Curcio. Gold Medal, Tchaikovsky International Piano Competition, Moscow, 1986; Berlin Philharmonic début, 1987; engagements incl. regular appearances in major European, US and Far East cities; European première, Penderecki piano concerto Resurrection, 2002. Artistic Founder Dir, Camerata Ireland, 1999– (first all-Ireland orch.; concerts in Ireland and abroad; début USA tour, 2001). Prince Consort Prof. of Piano, Royal Coll. of Music, 1998–. Recordings incl. Tchaikovsky Concerto No 1 and Sonata in G, Mussorgsky Pictures at an Exhibition, Brahms Piano Quintet in F minor and Piano Concerto No 1, Liszt Concertos Nos 1 and 2, Beethoven Sonata Op 106, Prokofiev Sonatas 2 and 7, Rachmaninov Concerto No 2, Reger Concerto, Strauss Burleske, Britten Concerto, Debussy Fantaisie. Vis. Fellow, Oriel Coll., Oxford, 1992–93. Hon. DMus QUB, 1986. *Recreations:* driving, reading, food and wine. *Address:* c/o IMG Artists, The Light Box, 111 Power Road, Chiswick, W4 5PY.

DOUGLAS FERGUSON, Niall Campbell; *see* Ferguson.

DOUGLAS FERGUSON, Susan Margaret; Creative Director, PFD, since 2008; *b* 29 Jan. 1957; *d* of Kenneth Frank Douglas and Vivienne Mary Douglas; *m* 1994, Niall Campbell Ferguson (*see* N. C. D. Ferguson); two *s* one *d*. *Educ:* Tiffin Girls' Sch., Kingston; Southampton Univ. (BSc Hons Biochem.). Management consultant, Arthur Andersen & Co., 1978–79; Haymarket Publishing, 1979; reporter, writer, Sunday Express, Johannesburg, 1979–80; Mail on Sunday: medical corresp., 1980–81; Features Editor and Associate Editor, 1981–86; Asst Editor, Daily Mail, 1986–91; Sunday Times: Associate Editor, 1991–94; Dep. Editor, 1995; Editor, Sunday Express, 1996; Consultant Editor, Scotsman, Scotland on Sunday, Edinburgh Evening News, Sunday Business, and Gear magazine (NY), 1997–2001; Exec. Consultant, Sunday Business, 1998–2001; Dir, 1999–2001, Pres., 2001–07, New Business, Condé Nast. *Recreations:* riding, hunting. *Address:* Middle Park Farm, Beckley, Oxon OX3 9SX; *e-mail:* susandouglas@aol.com. *Clubs:* Chelsea Arts, Royal Automobile.

DOUGLAS-HAMILTON, family name of **Duke of Hamilton and Brandon, Earldom of Selkirk** and **Baron Selkirk of Douglas**.

DOUGLAS-HOME, family name of **Earl of Home** and **Baroness Dacre**.

DOUGLAS-HOME, Jessica Violet, (Lady Leach of Fairford); painter; freelance theatre set and costume designer, since 1968; *b* 7 Feb. 1944; *d* of John Gwynne and Patricia (*née* Morrison-Bell); *m* 1st, 1966, Charles Cospatrick Douglas-Home (*d* 1985), Editor, The Times; two *s*; 2nd, 1993, (Charles Guy) Rodney Leach (*see* Baron Leach of Fairford). *Educ:* Cranbourne Chase Sch.; Chelsea Sch. of Art; Slade Sch. of Fine Art. Productions include: When We Are Married, RNT, 1979; Watch on the Rhine, 1980; Anyone for Dennis, Whitehall, 1981; The Mikado, Savoy, 1989. Solo exhibns of paintings and etchings in London, Brussels, Washington and Princeton, USA, 1977–85. Worked with dissidents behind the Iron Curtain, 1983–90. Trustee: Jan Hus Foundn and Jagiellonian Trust, 1983–; Butrint Foundn, 2002–; Founder and Chm., Mihai Eminescu Trust, 1987–. Europa Nostra Cultural Heritage Award, 2007. Officer, National Order for Faithful Service (Romania), 2007. *Publications:* Violet: the life and loves of Violet Gordon Woodhouse, 1996; Once Upon Another Time, 2000; contributed drawings: Book on Dinosaurs, 1975; Love Life, 1979; The English Taste, 1991. *Recreations:* reading, riding. *Address:* Knights Mill, Quenington, Cirencester, Glos GL7 5BN.

DOUGLAS HOME, Mark; Editor, The Herald, 2000–05; *b* 31 Aug. 1951; *s* of late Edward Charles Douglas Home and Nancy Rose Douglas Home; *m* 1976, Colette O'Reilly; one *s* one *d*. *Educ:* Eton Coll.; Univ. of Witwatersrand. Scottish corresp., The Independent, 1986–90; News Ed., 1990–93, Asst Ed., 1993–94, The Scotsman; Deputy Editor: Scotland on Sunday, 1994–98; Sunday Times Scotland, 1998–99; Scotland Editor, Sunday Times, 1999–2000. *Recreation:* gardening.

DOUGLAS MILLER, Robert Alexander Gavin; Director, Edinburgh Worldwide Investment Trust, 1988–2008; *b* 11 Feb. 1937; *s* of late F. G. Douglas Miller and Mora Kennedy; *m* 1963, Judith Madeleine Smith; three *s* one *d*. *Educ:* Harrow; Oxford Univ. (MA). 9th Lancers, 1955–57; Oxford, 1958–61. Treasurer, Queen's Body Guard for Scotland (Royal Company of Archers), 1977–88. Chm., Jenners (Princes St Edinburgh) Ltd, 1975–2005; Director: Kennington Leasing Ltd, 1977–2005; Dunedin Income Growth Trust, 1988–2006. Pres., Edinburgh Chamber of Commerce & Manufactures, 1985–87. Mem., Kyle & Sutherland Fishery Bd, 1980–2007; Member, Council: Assoc. of Scottish Salmon Fishery Bds, 1984–90; Atlantic Salmon Trust, 1989–90; Chm., Game Conservancy (Scotland), 1990–94. Chm., Outreach Trust, 1976–94. Pres., Royal Warrant Holders, 1987–88. *Recreations:* shooting, fishing. *Address:* Bavelaw Castle, Balerno, Midlothian EH14 7JS. *T:* (0131) 449 3972; Forneth Estate, Blairgowrie, Perthshire PH10 6SN. *T:* (01250) 884255. *Club:* New (Edinburgh).

DOUGLAS-PENNANT, family name of **Baron Penrhyn**.

DOUGLAS-SCOTT, Douglas Andrew Montagu; *see* Scott.

DOUGLAS-SCOTT-MONTAGU, family name of **Baron Montagu of Beaulieu**.

DOUGLAS-WILSON, Ian, MD; FRCPE; Editor of the Lancet, 1965–76; *b* 12 May 1912; *o s* of late Dr H. Douglas-Wilson; *m* 1939, Beatrice May, *e d* of late R. P. Bevan; one *s* two *d*. *Educ:* Marlborough Coll.; Edinburgh Univ. MB ChB 1936; MD (commended) Edinburgh 1938; FRCP Edinburgh 1945. Served with RAMC, 1940–45 (temp. Major). House-physician, Royal Infirmary, Edinburgh, 1937; joined the Lancet staff, 1946; Asst Ed., 1952–62; Dep. Ed., 1962–64. Corresp. Mem., Danish Soc. of Int. Med., 1965. Dr (*hc*) Edinburgh, 1974. *Address:* 10 Homan Court, Friern Watch Avenue, N12 9HW. *T:* (020) 8446 9047.

DOULTON, John Hubert Farre; Principal, Elizabeth College, Guernsey, 1988–98; *b* 2 Jan. 1942; *s* of late Alfred John Farre, CBE, TD; *m* 1986, Margaret Anne (*née* Ball); two step *d*. *Educ:* Rugby School; Keble College, Oxford (1st Mods, 2nd Greats). Teacher: Rugby, 1965–66; Radley, 1966–88. *Recreations:* music, walking, boats, foreign travel, carpentry. *Address:* 15 Hungerford Hill, Lambourn, Berks RG17 8NP.

DOUNE, Lord; John Douglas Stuart; *b* 29 Aug. 1966; *s* and *heir* of 20th Earl of Moray, *qv*; *m* 2000, Catherine Jane, *d* of Prof. Wilfred Alan Lawson; two *s*. *Educ:* Loretto School, Musselburgh; University Coll. London (BA Hist. of Art). *Address:* Doune Park, Doune, Perthshire FK16 6HA; Darnaway Castle, Forres, Moray.

DOURO, Marquess of; Arthur Charles Valerian Wellesley, OBE 1999; DL; Chairman, Richemont Holdings UK Ltd (formerly Vendôme Luxury Group Ltd), since 1993; Director: Global Asset Management Worldwide Inc., since 1984; Compagnie Financière Richemont, since 1999; *b* 19 Aug. 1945; *s* and *heir* of 8th Duke of Wellington, *qv*; *m* 1977, Antonia von Preussen (*see* Marchioness of Douro); two *s* three *d*. *Educ:* Eton; Christ Church, Oxford. Deputy Chairman: Thames Valley Broadcasting, 1975–84; Deltec Panamerica SA, 1985–89; Guinness Mahon Hldgs, 1988–91; Director: Antofagasta and Bolivia Railway Co., 1977–80; Eucalyptus Pulp Mills, 1979–88; Transatlantic Hldgs, 1983–95; Continental and Industrial Trust plc, 1987–90; Sanofi-Synthélabo SA, 2002–; Pernod Ricard SA, 2003–; Chairman: Deltec Securities (UK) Ltd, 1985–89; Dunhill Holdings, 1991–93; Sun Life Corp., subseq. Sun Life and Provincial Hldgs plc, 1995–2000; Framlington Gp plc, 1994–2005. Comr, English Heritage, 2003–07. MEP (C): Surrey, 1979–84, Surrey West, 1984–89; contested (C) Islington N, Oct. 1974; Mem., Basingstoke Borough Council, 1978–79. DL Hants, 1999. Chm. Council, KCL 2007–. Kt Comdr, Order of Isabel the Catholic (Spain), 1986; Grand Officer, Order o[f] Merit (Portugal), 1987. *Heir: s* Earl of Mornington, *qv*. *Address:* Apsley House, Piccadilly, W1J 7NT; Stratfield Saye House, Hants RG7 2BZ.

DOURO, Marchioness of; Antonia Elisabeth Brigid Luise Wellesley, OBE 2008; Trustee, since 1976, and President, since 2007, Guinness Trust (Chairman, 1984–2007); *b* 28 April 1955; *d* of late Prince Friedrich of Prussia and Lady Brigid (*née* Guinness; she *m* 2nd, Maj. A. P. Ness); *m* 1977, Marquess of Douro, *qv*; two *s* three *d*. *Educ:* Cobham Hall, Kent; King's Coll., London (BA). Director: Thames Valley Broadcasting, 1984–87; English Nat. Ballet, 1987–90; Scenarist, Frankenstein (ballet), Covent Garden, 1987. Mem. Cttee, London Library, 1981–86; Trustee: Getty Endowment Fund for Nat. Gall. 1985–92; Hermitage Develt Trust, Somerset House, 2000–05; NPG, 2004–. Pres., Roya[l] Hosp. for Neuro-disability, 1991–2001. Patron, Loddon Sch., 1996–. *Address:* Stratfield Saye House, Hants RG7 2BZ; Apsley House, Piccadilly, W1J 7NT.

DOVE, Arthur Allan, CBE 1998; CEng, CStat; Chairman, Council for Registered Ga[s] Installers, 1994–2000; *b* 20 May 1933; *s* of William Joseph Dove and Lucy Frances Dove; *m* 1958, Nancy Iris Powell; two *s* one *d*. *Educ:* Taunton's Sch., Southampton; King's Coll and London Sch. of Econs and Pol. Science, Univ. of London (BSc; AKC 1954). CEng FIGEM (FIGasE 1974); MIS 1962. Asst Statistician, 1958, Marketing Officer, 1961 Southern Gas; Controller of Sales and Marketing, Scottish Gas, 1965; Commercial Sale[s] Manager, Gas Council, 1969; Dep. Chm., South Eastern Gas, 1973; Regl Chm., Britis[h] Gas plc, S Eastern, 1982–87, N Thames, 1988–91; Managing Director: Regions, 1991–92 Regl Services, 1992–93. Chm., Parkside Housing Gp, 1998–2002. *Recreation:* sailing. *Address:* 19 Sunning Avenue, Sunningdale, Berks SL5 9PN.

DOVE, Ian William; QC 2003; a Recorder, since 2003; *b* 31 Dec. 1963; *s* of Jack Richar[d] Dove and Janet Yvonne Dove; *m* 1988, Juliet Caroline Gladston; two *s*. *Educ* Northampton Sch. for Boys; St Catherine's Coll., Oxford (MA); Inns of Court Sch. o[f] Law. Called to the Bar, Inner Temple, 1986; in practice, specialising in planning an[d] environmental law. Immigration Adjudicator (pt-time), 2001–04; Mem., Immigratio[n] Appeal Tribunal, 2004–05; an Immigration Judge, 2005–. *Recreations:* walking, poetry, th[e] visual arts, good food, music, bell ringing. *Address:* No 5 Chambers, Fountain Court Steelhouse Lane, Birmingham B4 6DR. *T:* (0121) 606 0500, *Fax:* (0121) 606 1501; *e-mail* id@no5.com.

DOVE, Jonathan; composer; Music Adviser, Almeida Theatre, since 1990; Nationa[l] Theatre Associate, since 2003; *b* 18 July 1959; *s* of Myles Harrison Dove and Deirdr[e] Cecily Dove. *Educ:* St Joseph's Acad., Blackheath; ILEA Centre for Young Musicians Trinity Coll., Cambridge (MA); Goldsmiths' Coll., London (MMus). Asst Chorus Maste[r] Glyndebourne, 1987–88; Artistic Director, Spitalfields Fest., 2001–06. Composer of score[s] for 30 plays (Almeida, NT, RSC) and of music for film and television. Trustee: Stephe[n] Oliver Trust, 1997–2006; Michael Tippett Foundn, 1999–. Patron: London Fest. o[f] Contemp. Church Music, 2007–; Durham Opera Ensemble, 2007–. *Compositions* include Figures in the Garden, 1991; Seaside Postcards, Tuning In, 1995; The Ringing Isle, 1997 The Magic Flute Dances, 1999; The Passing of the Year, 2000; Stargazer, Out of Time 2001; Moonlight Revels, Koethener Messe, 2002; The Middleham Jewel, The Fa[r] Theatricals of Day, Run to the Edge, The Crocodiamond, 2003; Out of Winter, 2003 Across the Walls, 2004; All the Future Days, 2004; On Spital Fields, Work in Progress Fourteen Site-Visits for Piano and Orch. with Film, 2004; Airport Scenes, 2005; Hojok 2006; It sounded as if the Streets were running, 2007; Minterne, 2007; *operas:* Pig, 1992 L'Augellino Belverde, Siren Song, 1994; Flight, 1998; Tobias and the Angel, 1999; Th[e] Palace in the Sky, 2000; The Hackney Chronicles, L'Altra Euridice, 2001; When Sh[e] Died: Death of a Princess, 2002; La Dama ed il Pulitore di Damasco, Le Porte di Bagdad 2003; Kwasi & Kwame (formerly The Two Hearts of Kwasi Boachi), 2005; Th[e] Enchanted Pig, Man on the Moon, An Old Way to Pay New Debts, 2006; Th[e] Adventures of Pinocchio, 2007. Hon. DMus East London, 2006. *Recreation:* photography *Address:* c/o Peters Edition Ltd, 10-12 Baches Street, N1 6DN. *T:* (020) 7553 4000.

DOVER, Bishop Suffragan of, and Bishop in Canterbury, since 1999; **Rt Rev Stephen Squires Venner;** Bishop for the Falkland Islands, since 2007; *b* 19 June 194[4] *s* of Thomas Edward Venner and Hilda Lester Venner; *m* 1972, Judith Sivewrigh[t] Johnstone; two *s* one *d*. *Educ:* Hardyes Sch., Dorchester; Birmingham Univ. (BA); Linacr[e] Coll., Oxford (MA); London Univ. (PGCE). Curate, St Peter, Streatham, 1968–71; Hon Curate: St Margaret, Streatham Hill, 1971–72; Ascension, Balham, 1972–74; Head of RE St Paul's Girls' Sch., Hammersmith, 1972–74; Vicar, St Peter, Clapham and Bishop Chaplain to Overseas Students, 1974–76; Vicar: St John, Trowbridge, 1976–82; Hol[y] Trinity, Weymouth, 1982–94; RD of Weymouth, 1988–94; Canon and Prebendary o[f] Salisbury Cathedral, 1989–94; Bishop Suffragan of Middleton, 1994–99. Chaplain to Lor[d] Warden of Cinque Ports, 2004–. Pro-Chancellor, Canterbury Christ Church Univ 2005–. Vice Pres., Woodard Corp., 1995–98 (Pres., 1999–2002); Co-Chm., Church o[f] England/Moravian Contact Gp, 1996–99. Mem. Council, Greater Manchester, 1996–9[9] Kent, 2000–, Order of St John. *Recreations:* being a grandfather, playing organ and pian[o] watersports, computing, reading adventure novels. *Address:* Upway, 52 St Martin's Hil[l] Canterbury, Kent CT1 1PR. *T:* (home) (01227) 464537, (office) (01227) 459382, *Fax* (01227) 784987; *e-mail:* bishop@bischcaut.org. *Club:* Farmers'.

DOVER, Den; Member (C) North West Region, England, European Parliament, sinc[e] 1999; *b* 4 April 1938; *s* of Albert and Emmie Dover; *m* 1st, 1959, Anne Marina Wrigh[t] (marr. diss. 1986); one *s* one *d*; 2nd, 1989, Kathleen Edna Fisher. *Educ:* Mancheste[r] Grammar Sch.; Manchester Univ. BSc Hons. CEng, MICE. John Laing & Son Lt[d] 1959–68; National Building Agency: Dep. Chief Executive, 1969–70; Chief Exec 1971–72; Projects Dir, Capital and Counties Property Co. Ltd, 1972–75; Contrac[ts] Manager, Wimpey Laing Iran, 1975–77. Director of Housing Construction, GLC 1977–79. Member, London Borough of Barnet Council, 1968–71. MP (C) Chorley 1979–97; contested (C) same seat, 1997. Mem., Commons Select Cttee on Transpor[t] 1979–87, on Envmt, 1995–97. European Parliament: Budgets Spokesman, 2000–05; Re[gl] Develt Spokesman, 2005–; Chief Whip (C), 2007–08. *Recreations:* cricket, hockey, gol[f] Methodist. *Address:* 30 Countess Way, Euxton, Chorley, Lancs PR7 6PT; 166 Furzehi[ll] Road, Boreham Wood, Herts WD6 2DS. *T:* (020) 8953 5945.

DOVER, Sir Kenneth James, Kt 1977; DLitt; FRSE 1975; FBA 1966; Chancello[r] University of St Andrews, 1981–2005; *b* 11 March 1920; *o s* of P. H. J. Dover, Londo[n] civil servant; *m* 1947, Audrey Ruth Latimer; one *s* one *d*. *Educ:* St Paul's Sch. (Scholar Balliol Coll., Oxford (Domus Scholar); Gaisford Prize, 1939; 1st in Classical Hon. Mods

1940; Ireland Scholar, 1946; Cromer Prize (British Academy), 1946; 1st in Lit. Hum., Derby Scholar, Amy Mary Preston Read Scholar, 1947; Harmsworth Sen. Scholar, Merton Coll., 1947 (Hon. Fellow, 1980); DLitt Oxon 1974. Served War of 1939–45: Army (RA), 1940–45; Western Desert, 1941–43, Italy, 1943–45 (despatches). Fellow and Tutor, Balliol Coll., 1948–55 (Hon. Fellow, 1977); Prof. of Greek, 1955–76, Dean of Fac. of Arts, 1960–63, 1973–75, Univ. of St Andrews; Pres., Corpus Christi Coll., Oxford, 1976–86 (Hon. Fellow, 1986); Prof. of Classics (Winter Quarter), Stanford Univ., 1988–92. Vis. Lectr, Harvard, 1960; Sather Prof. of Classical Literature, Univ. of California, 1967; Prof.-at-large, Cornell Univ., 1984–89. President: Soc. for Promotion of Hellenic Studies, 1971–74; Classical Assoc., 1975; Jt Assoc. of Classical Teachers, 1985. Pres., British Acad., 1978–81. For. Hon. Mem., Amer. Acad. of Arts and Sciences, 1979; For. Mem., Royal Netherlands Acad. of Arts and Sciences, 1979. Hon. LLD: Birmingham, 1979; St Andrews, 1981; Hon. DLitt: Bristol, 1980; London, 1980; St Andrews, 1981; Durham, 1984; Hon. LittD Liverpool, 1983; Hon. DHL Oglethorpe, 1984. Kenyon Medal, British Acad., 1993. *Publications:* Greek Word Order, 1960; Commentaries on Thucydides, Books VI and VII, 1965; (ed) Aristophanes' Clouds, 1968; Lysias and the Corpus Lysiacum, 1968; (with A. W. Gomme and A. Andrewes) Historical Commentary on Thucydides, vol. IV, 1970, vol. V, 1981; (ed) Theocritus, select poems, 1971; Aristophanic Comedy, 1972; Greek Popular Morality in the Time of Plato and Aristotle, 1974; Greek Homosexuality, 1978; (ed) Plato, Symposium, 1980; (ed and co-author) Ancient Greek Literature, 1980; The Greeks, 1980 (contrib., The Greeks, BBC TV series, 1980); Greek and the Greeks, 1987; The Greeks and their Legacy, 1989; (ed) Perceptions of the Ancient Greeks, 1992; (ed) Aristophanes, Frogs, 1993; Marginal Comment (memoirs), 1994; The Evolution of Greek Prose Style, 1997; articles in learned journals; Co-editor, Classical Quarterly, 1962–68. *Recreations:* historical linguistics, gardening. *Address:* 49 Hepburn Gardens, St Andrews, Fife KY16 9LS.

DOW, Andrew Richard George; railway historian and writer; *b* 1 Dec. 1943; *s* of late George Dow and Doris Mary Dow (*née* Soundy); *m* 1973, Stephanie Brenda Murphy; one *s* one *d. Educ:* The Hall, Hampstead; Brighton Coll. Chartered Secretary; ACIS. Commercial Apprentice, Bristol Siddeley Engines, 1962–67; appts in Bristol Siddeley and Rolls-Royce Commercial Depts, Bristol, Coventry and New Jersey, 1967–89; Commercial Exec., 1989; Head of Business (Mil.), 1990; Head, Nat. Railway Mus., 1992–94; Contracts Manager, BR Special Trains Unit, and Commercial Man., BR Infrastructure Services, 1994–95; Dir, 1995–97, and Commercial Dir, 1996–97, Fastline Track Renewals Ltd. Director: Fastline Group Ltd, 1996–97; Fastline Hldgs Ltd, 1996–97; Lynton and Barnstaple Light Railway Co., 1995–2001 (Chm., 2000–01); Locomotive Construction Co., 1997–99; Fastline Photographic Ltd, 2000–05; Tornado Steam Traction Ltd, 2001–04; Fastline Films Ltd, 2005–. Director: York Visitor and Conf. Bureau, 1992–94; FNRM Enterprises Ltd, 1992–94, 1999–2006; A1 Steam Locomotive Trust, 1994–2004; Gresley Soc. Trust Ltd, 1999–. President: Leighton Buzzard Narrow Gauge Rly Soc., 1994–99; Lynton and Barnstaple Rly Assoc., 1994–2002. Pres., Stephenson Locomotive Soc., 2000– (Vice-Pres., 1992–2000); Vice-President: Great Central Rly Soc., 1994–; British Overseas Rly Historical Trust, 1994–; Vice-Chm., Gresley Soc., 1997–; Trustee, Darlington Rly Mus. Trust, 2002–. Fellow, Permanent Way Instn, 1994. Editor and writer, Behind the Scenes (series of archive DVDs). *Publications:* Norfolk and Western Coal Cars, 1998 (US); Telling the Passenger Where to Get Off, 2005; Dow's Dictionary of Railway Quotations, 2006; book reviews, monthly column, and articles in British and American railway jls. *Recreations:* family life, railways, travel, photography, collecting. *Address:* Wyverns, Newton-on-Ouse, York YO30 2BR. *T:* (01347) 848808, *Fax:* (01347) 848169.

DOW, Carol, CMG 2003; Chief Medical Adviser, Foreign and Commonwealth Office, 1998–2003; Consultant in Occupational Health, Guy's and St Thomas' Hospital NHS Trust, London, 1989–2003; *b* 3 April 1951; *d* of John Dickson Dow and Catherine Dow (*née* Robertson). *Educ:* St Bartholomew's Hospital Medical Sch., London Univ. (MB BS 1976; DTM&H 1988); Univ. of Glasgow (Dip. Travel Medicine 1996). MRCP 1981; AFOM 1992. Registrar, St George's Hosp., 1982–86; Malaria Emergency Unit and Air Evacuation Service, African Med. and Res. Foundn, Nairobi, 1983–84; Registrar, Hosp. for Tropical Diseases, London, 1986–88; Med. Registrar, Middlesex Hosp., 1988–89; Principal Med. Advr, FCO, 1989–98. *Publications:* (contrib.) Health Information for Overseas Travel, 1995, 2nd edn 2001; (contrib.) Dawood's Travellers' Health: how to stay healthy abroad, 4th edn 2002. *Recreations:* travel, fishing, hill-walking, medicine. *Address:* Upper Camerory, Ballieward, Grantown-on-Spey, Moray PH26 3PR. *T:* (01479) 872548; *e-mail:* carol@dow3pr.fsnet.co.uk.

DOW, Rear-Adm. Douglas Morrison, CB 1991; DL; Director, National Trust for Scotland, 1992–97; *b* 1 July 1935; *s* of George Torrance Dow and Grace Morrison MacFarlane; *m* 1959, Felicity Margaret Mona Napier, *d* of John Watson Napier and Beatrix Mary Carson; two *s. Educ:* George Heriot's School; BRNC Dartmouth. Joined RN, 1952; served HMS Sheffield, 1957–59; Staff of C-in-C Plymouth, 1959–61; HMS Plymouth, 1961–63; RN Supply Sch., 1963–65; Staff of Comdr FEF, 1965–67; HMS Endurance, 1968–70; BRNC Dartmouth, 1970–72; Asst Dir, Officer Appointments (S), 1972–74; Sec. to Comdr British Navy Staff, Washington, 1974–76; HMS Tiger, 1977–78; NDC Latimer, 1978–79; CSO(A) to Flag Officer Portsmouth, 1979; Sec. to Controller of the Navy, 1981; Captain, HMS Cochrane, 1983; Commodore, HMS Centurion, 1985; RCDS 1988; Dir Gen., Naval Personal Services, 1989–92. Hon. ADC to the Queen, 1986–89. President: South Queensferry Sea Cadets, 1994–; Royal Naval Assoc., Edin., 1996–. Gov., George Heriot's Sch., 1993– (Vice Chm., 1997–). DL Edinburgh, 1996. *Recreations:* Royal Navy Rugby Union (Chairman, 1985–91), fly fishing, shooting, golf, gardening.

DOW, Rt Rev. Geoffrey Graham; *see* Carlisle, Bishop of.

DOW, Harold Peter Bourner; QC 1971; *b* 28 April 1921; *s* of late Col H. P. Dow and P. I. Dow; *m* 1943, Rosemary Merewether (*d* 2002), *d* of late Dr E. R. A. Merewether, CB, CBE, FRCP; two *s* one *d. Educ:* Charterhouse; Trinity Hall, Cambridge (MA). Served RAF (Air Crew), 1941–42. Min. of Supply, 1943–45. Barrister, Middle Temple, 1946. *Publications:* Restatement of Town and Country Planning, 1947; National Assistance, 1948; (with Q. Edwards) Rights of Way, 1951; (ed) Hobsons Local Government, 1951 and 1957 edns. *Recreations:* music, painting. *Address:* Mustow House, Mustow Street, Bury St Edmunds, Suffolk IP33 1XL. *T:* (01284) 725093.

DOW, Simon Charles; Chief Executive, Guinness Trust Group, since 2001; *b* 21 Sept. 1950; *s* of Alan Dow and Rosamund Dow; *m* 1984, Virginia Anne, *d* of late Arthur Charles William Crook; one *s* one *d. Educ:* King's Sch., Chester; United World Coll. of the Atlantic (Internat. Bacc.; RNLI coxswain); SOAS, London Univ. (BA Hons); Brunel Univ. (MA Public Admin). Notting Hill Housing Trust, 1974–78; Dep. Dir, New Islington and Hackney Housing Assoc., 1978–87; Sen. Regulation Manager, Housing Corp., 1985–87 (on secondment); Gp Chief Exec., Samuel Lewis Housing Trust, subseq. Southern Housing Gp, 1987–95; Housing Corporation: Dep. Chief Exec., 1995–97; Chief Ops Officer, 1997–2000; Actg Chief Exec. and Accounting Officer, 2000. Dir,

ARHAG Housing Assoc., 2006–. Chm., London Housing Foundn, 1991–; Dir, Housing Forum, 2000–02 (Chm., Off-site Manufg Gp, 2001–03); Member: Nat. Council, 2002–; Bd of Dirs, 2003–; Nat. Housing Fedn; Dep. Prime Minister's Home Ownership Task Force, 2003; ODPM Ministerial Task Force on Planning Obligations, 2004–06; Ind. Ext. Chm., Audit Cttee, Ind. Police Complaints Commn, 2005–. MInstD 2003. *Recreations:* sailing, cooking, being outdoors. *Address:* Guinness Trust Group, 17 Mendy Street, High Wycombe, Bucks HP11 2NZ. *T:* (01494) 535823, *Fax:* (01494) 459502; *e-mail:* simon.dow@guinness.org.uk.

DOWD, James Patrick; MP (Lab) Lewisham West, since 1992; *b* Germany, 5 March 1951; *s* of late James Patrick Dowd and Elfriede Anna Dowd (*née* Janocha). *Educ:* Dalmain JM&I Sch., London; Sedgehill Comprehensive, London; London Nautical School. Apprentice telephone engineer, GPO, 1967–72; Station Manager, Heron petrol stations, 1972–73; Telecomms Engineer, Plessey Co., later GPT, 1973–92. Group Rep. and Br. Cttee, PO Engrg Union, 1967–72; Sen. Negotiator, ASTMS, then MSF. Lewisham Council: Councillor, 1974–94: Chief Whip; Chm. of Cttees; Dep. Leader; Dep. Mayor, 1987, 1991; Mayor, 1992. Former Mem., Lewisham and Southwark DHA. Contested (Lab): Beckenham, 1983; Lewisham W, 1987. An Opposition Whip, 1993–95; opposition front-bench spokesman on Northern Ireland, 1995–97; a Lord Comr of HM Treasury (Govt Whip), 1997–2001. Mem., Select Cttee on Health, 2001–. Former school governor. *Recreations:* music, reading, theatre, Cornwall, being with friends. *Address:* House of Commons, SW1A 0AA. *T:* (020) 7219 4617. *Club:* Bromley Labour.

DOWDALL, John Michael, CB 2003; Comptroller and Auditor-General for Northern Ireland, since 1994; *b* 6 Sept. 1944; *s* of late Lt-Col W. Dowdall, MBE, and E. Dowdall; *m* 1964, Aylerie (*née* Houston); three *s* one *d. Educ:* King Edward's Sch., Witley, Surrey; Queen's Univ., Belfast (BScEcon). CPFA 2001. Lectr in Economics, Royal Univ. of Malta, 1966–69; Lectr in Political Econ., King's Coll., Univ. of Aberdeen, 1969–72; Economic Advr, Dept of Commerce, N Ireland, 1972–78, Principal, Dept of Commerce, 1978–82; Asst Sec., Dept of Finance and Personnel, N Ireland, 1982–85; Dep. Chief Exec., Industrial Develt Bd, NI, 1986–89; Under Sec., Dept of Finance and Personnel, NI, 1989–94. Vis. Prof., Faculty of Business and Mgt, Univ. of Ulster, 2002–.

DOWDEN, Richard George; Africa analyst and writer; Executive Director, Royal African Society, since 2002; *b* 20 March 1949; *s* of late Peter Dowden and Eleanor Dowden; *m* 1976, Penny Mansfield; two *d. Educ:* St George's Coll., Weybridge, Surrey; London Univ. (BA History). Volunteer Teacher, Uganda, 1971–72; Asst Sec., Justice and Peace Commn, 1973–76; Editor, Catholic Herald, 1976–79; journalist, The Times, 1980–86; Africa Editor, 1986–94, Diplomatic Editor, 1994–95, The Independent; Africa Editor, The Economist, 1995–2001. *Address:* 7 Highbury Grange, N5 2QB.

DOWDESWELL, Prof. Julian Andrew, PhD; Professor of Physical Geography, since 2001, and Director, Scott Polar Research Institute, since 2002, University of Cambridge; Fellow, Jesus College, Cambridge, since 2002; *b* 18 Nov. 1957; *s* of Robert Dowdeswell and Joan Marion Dowdeswell (*née* Longshaw); *m* 1983, Evelyn Kae Lind; one *s* one *d. Educ:* Magdalen Coll. Sch., Oxford; Jesus Coll., Cambridge (BA 1980; schol., 1980; PhD 1985); Univ. of Colorado (MA 1982). Research Associate, Scott Polar Res. Inst., Univ. of Cambridge, 1985; Lectr, Univ. of Wales, Aberystwyth, 1986–89; University of Cambridge: Sen. Asst in Research, 1989–92; Asst Dir of Res., Scott Polar Res. Inst., 1992–94; Dir, Centre for Glaciology, 1994–98, and Dir, Inst. of Geog. and Earth Scis, 1997–98, Univ. of Wales, Aberystwyth; Prof. of Physical Geog. and Dir, Bristol Glaciology Centre, Bristol Univ., 1998–2001. Natural Environment Research Council: Member: Polar Science and Technol. Bd, 1995–97; Earth Scis Res. Grants and Training Awards Cttee, 1996–2000; Polar Scis Expert Gp, 1997–99; Earth Scis Bd, 1997–2000; Peer Review Coll., 2003–06. Hd of Glaciers and Ice Sheets Div., Internat. Commn for Snow and Ice, 1999–. Chm., UK Nat. Cttee on Antarctic Res., 2002–06; UK Alternate Deleg. to Council, Scientific Cttee on Antarctic Res., 2002–06; UK Deleg. to Council, Internat. Arctic Science Cttee, 2002–; UK Mem., Arctic Ocean Sci. Bd, 2006–. Mem. Council, Internat. Glaciol Soc., 1993–96. Gov., Plascrug Sch., Aberystwyth, 1996–98. FRGS 1985. Polar Medal, 1995; Gill Meml Award, 1998, Founder's Medal, 2008, RGS. *Publications:* (ed jtly) Glacimarine Environments: processes and sediments, 1990; (ed jtly) The Arctic and Environmental Change, 1996; (ed jtly) Glacial and Oceanic History of the Polar North Atlantic Margins, 1998; Islands of the Arctic, 2002; (ed jtly) Glacier-influenced sedimentation on high-latitude continental margins, 2002; The Antarctic Paintings of Edward Seago, 2006; papers in learned jls on glaciology, glacier-marine interactions, cryosphere and climate change, and satellite remote sensing of ice. *Recreations:* hill-walking, ski-ing, watching Oxford United FC. *Address:* Jesus College, Cambridge CB5 8BL.

DOWDING, family name of **Baron Dowding.**

DOWDING, 3rd Baron *cr* 1943, of Bentley Priory, Middlesex; **Piers Hugh Tremenheere Dowding;** Professor of English, Okayama Shoka University, Japan, since 1999 (Associate Professor, 1977–99); *b* 18 Feb. 1948; *s* of 2nd Baron Dowding and of his 2nd wife, Alison Margaret, *d* of Dr James Bannerman and *widow* of Major R. W. H. Peebles; *S* father, 1992; *m* Noriko Shiho; two *d. Educ:* Fettes Coll.; Amherst Coll., Mass (BA 1971). LTCL. Life Pres., Dumfries and Galloway Aircrew Assoc., 1996–. *Heir: b* Hon. Mark Denis James Dowding, *b* 11 July 1949.

DOWDING, Nicholas Alan Tatham; QC 1997; *b* 24 Feb. 1956; *s* of Alan Lorimer Dowding and Jennifer Mary Dowding (*née* Hughes); *m*; three *d. Educ:* Radley Coll.; St Catharine's Coll., Cambridge (BA 1978; MA 1982). Called to the Bar, Inner Temple, 1979. Chm., Property Bar Assoc., 2006–; Hon. RICS 2007. *Publications:* (ed jtly) Handbook of Rent Review, 1980–85; (ed jtly) Woodfall on Landlord and Tenant, 1994–; (jtly) Dilapidations: the modern law and practice, 1995, 3rd edn 2004; (ed) Landlord and Tenant Reports, 1998–. *Recreations:* sailing, music, juggling, limericks. *Address:* Falcon Chambers, Falcon Court, EC4Y 1AA. *T:* (020) 7353 2484, *Fax:* (020) 7353 1261; *e-mail:* dowding@falcon-chambers.com.

DOWDING, Hon. Peter M'Callum; SC 2003; barrister; *b* 6 Oct. 1943; *m*; five *c. Educ:* Hale School, Perth; Univ. of Western Australia (LLB 1964). Churchill Fellowship, 1974, UK and Canada. In practice as solicitor and barrister until 1983 and as barrister, 1990–; Partner, Briggs Paul Dowding, 1992–94; Man. Partner, DCH Legal Gp, 1994–96. Dir, Biotech Internat. Ltd, 1998–2001. MLC North Province, WA, 1980–86; MLA (ALP) Maylands, 1986–90; Cabinet Member, 1983–90; Minister for: Mines, Fuel and Energy, 1983; Planning, and Employment and Training, 1983–84; Consumer Affairs, 1983–86; Minister assisting the Minister for Public Sector Management, 1984–88; Minister for Works and Services, Labour, Productivity and Employment, and assisting the Treasurer, 1987–88; Treasurer, and Minister for Productivity, 1988–89; Leader, WA Parly Lab. Party, 1987–90; Premier, WA, 1988–90; Minister, Public Sector Management, and Women's Interests, 1989–90. *Recreations:* sailing, bushwalking, reading. *Address:* PO Box 3344, Adelaide Terrace, Perth, WA 6832, Australia. *T:* (8) 93237790, *Fax:* (8) 93237791;

e-mail: pdowding@peterdowding.com.au. Level 3, 27–29 St George's Terrace, Perth, WA 6000, Australia.

DOWELL, Sir Anthony (James), Kt 1995; CBE 1973; Senior Principal, 1967–2001, Director, 1986–2001, Royal Ballet, Covent Garden (Assistant to Director, 1984–85; Associate Director, 1985–86); *b* 16 Feb. 1943; *s* of late Catherine Ethel and Arthur Henry Dowell; unmarried. *Educ:* Hampshire Sch., St Saviour's Hall, Knightsbridge; Royal Ballet Sch., White Lodge, Richmond, Surrey; Royal Ballet Sch., Barons Court. Joined Opera Ballet, 1960, Royal Ballet, for Russian Tour, 1961; promoted Principal Dancer, 1966. *Principal roles with Royal Ballet include:* La Fête Etrange, 1963; Napoli, 1965; Romeo and Juliet, 1965; Song of the Earth, 1966; Card Game, Giselle, Swan Lake, 1967; The Nutcracker, Cinderella, Monotones, Symphonic Variations, new version of Sleeping Beauty, Enigma Variations, Lilac Garden, 1968; Raymonda Act III, Daphnis and Chloe, La Fille Mal Gardée, 1969; Dances at a Gathering, 1970; La Bayadère, Meditation from Thaïs, Afternoon of a Faun, Anastasia, 1971; Triad, Le Spectre de la Rose, Giselle, 1972; Agon, Firebird, 1973; Manon, 1974; Four Schumann Pieces, Les Sylphides, 1975; Four Seasons, 1975; Scarlet Pastorale, 1976; Rhapsody, 1981; A Month in the Country, The Tempest, Varii Capricci, 1983; Sons of Horus, Frankenstein: the modern Prometheus, 1986; Ondine, 1988. Guest Artist with Amer. Ballet Theater, 1977–79; *performed in:* The Nutcracker; Don Quixote; Other Dances; *created:* The Dream, 1964; Shadow Play, 1967; Pavane, 1973; Manon, 1974; Contredanses; Solor in Makarova's La Bayadère; Fisherman in Le Rossignol (Ashton's choreography), NY Metropolitan Opera, 1981; Winter Dreams, 1991. Narrator in A Wedding Bouquet (first speaking role), Joffrey Ballet, 1977; guest appearances with Nat. Ballet of Canada (The Dream, Four Schumann Pieces), 1979 and 1981; Anthony Dowell Ballet Gala, Palladium, 1980 (for charity); narrated Oedipus Rex, NY Metropolitan Opera, 1981. *Television performances:* La Bayadère (USA); Swan Lake, Cinderella, Sleeping Beauty, A Month in the Country, The Dream, Les Noces (all BBC); Winter Dreams; All the Superlatives (personal profile), Omnibus, BBC. Dance Magazine award, NY, 1972. *Recreations:* painting, paper sculpture, theatrical costume design. *Address:* c/o Royal Opera House, Covent Garden, WC2E 9DD.

DOWELL, Ian Malcolm, MBE 1999; Editor, Birmingham Evening Mail, 1987–2001; *b* 15 Nov. 1940; *s* of late James Mardlin and Lilian Dowell; *m* 1st, 1967, Maureen Kane; two *d*; 2nd, 1980, Pauline Bridget Haughian. *Educ:* Exmouth Grammar Sch., Devon. Reporter, Exmouth and East Devon Journal, 1958; Sub-Editor, Woodrow Wyatt Newspapers, 1960; Editor, Wallingford News, Berks, 1962; Dep. Editor, Birmingham Planet, 1964–66; Birmingham Evening Mail: Sub-Editor, 1966; Dep. Features Editor, 1972; Chief Sub-Editor, 1976; Asst Editor, 1981; Dep. Editor, 1985. Bd Mem., Birmingham Post & Mail Ltd, 1992–2001. Chm., W Midlands Reg. Guild of Editors, 1994; Mem., Code of Practice Cttee, Newspaper and Magazine Publishing in the UK, 1996–2001. Pres., Black Country Olympics Cttee, 1985–94; Mem. Foundn Bd, Solihull Coll., 1994–98. Chm., Birmingham Mail Christmas Tree Fund, 1992–2001; Member: Bd, Birmingham Jazz Festival, 1996–2001; Birmingham Town Hall Adv. Panel, 1999–2001. Fellow, RSPB, 1987. *Recreations:* the countryside, gardening. *Address:* 3 Cutters Wharf, Exmouth Quay, Exmouth, Devon EX8 1XS.

DOWELL, Prof. John Derek, FRS 1986; CPhys, FInstP; Poynting Professor of Physics, University of Birmingham, 1997–2002, now Emeritus; *b* 6 Jan. 1935; *s* of William Ernest Dowell and Elsie Dorothy Dowell (*née* Jarvis); *m* 1959, Patricia Clarkson; one *s* one *d*. *Educ:* Coalville Grammar Sch., Leics; Univ. of Birmingham (BSc, PhD) CPhys, FInstP 1987. Research Fellow, Univ. of Birmingham, 1958–60; Res. Associate, CERN, Geneva, 1960–62; University of Birmingham: Lectr, 1962–70; Sen. Lectr, 1970–75; Reader, 1975–80; Prof. of Elementary Particle Physics, 1980–97. Vis. Scientist, Argonne Nat. Lab., USA, 1968–69. CERN, Geneva: Scientific Associate, 1973–74, 1985–87; Mem., Scientific Policy Cttee, 1982–90, 1993–96; Mem., Res. Bd, 1993–96; Chairman: Large Electron Positron Collider Cttee, 1993–96; ATLAS Collaboration Bd, 1996–97. Mem., Nuclear Physics Bd, 1974–77, 1981–85, Chm., Particle Physics Cttee, 1981–85, SERC; Member: Europ. Cttee for Future Accelerators, 1989–93; BBC Science Consultative Gp, 1992–94; Deutsches Elektronen Synchrotron Extended Scientific Council, 1992–98; PPARC, 1994–97. Mem., Panel for Physics, 2001 RAE, HEFCE. Vice Pres. and Mem. Council, Royal Soc., 1997–98. Lay Chm., Birmingham Children's Hosp. NHS Trust, 2004–. Mem. Court, Univ. of Warwick, 1992–2001. Fellow, APS, 2004. Rutherford Prize and Medal, InstP, 1988. *Publications:* numerous, in Phys. Letters, Nuovo Cimento, Nuclear Phys., Phys. Rev., Proc. Royal Soc., and related literature. *Recreations:* piano, amateur theatre, ski-ing. *Address:* 57 Oxford Road, Moseley, Birmingham B13 9ES; School of Physics and Astronomy, University of Birmingham, Birmingham B15 2TT.

DOWER, Michael Shillito Trevelyan, CBE 1996; Director-General, Countryside Commission, 1992–96; *b* 15 Nov. 1933; *s* of late John Gordon Dower and Pauline Dower; *m* 1960, Agnes Done; three *s*. *Educ:* Leys Sch., Cambridge; St John's Coll., Cambridge (MA); University Coll. London (DipTP). MRTPI, MRICS. Town Planner: LCC, 1957–59; Civic Trust, 1960–65; Amenity and Tourism Planner, UN Develt Prog., Ireland, 1965–67; Dir, Dartington Amenity Res. Trust and Dartington Inst., Devon, 1967–85; Nat. Park Officer, Peak Park Jt Planning Bd, 1985–92. Vis. Prof., Univ. of Glos (formerly Cheltenham and Gloucester Coll. of HE), 1996–. Chm., Public Inquiry into Foot and Mouth Disease in Northumberland, 2002. Member: Sports Council, 1965–72; English Tourist Bd, 1969–76; Founder Chm., Rural Voice, 1980; European Council for Village and Small Town: Pres., 1986–90; Sec.-Gen., 1995–2000; Vice-Pres., 2000–04. Vice-President: YHA, 1996–; BTCV, 1996–; Hon. Councillor, Rural Buildings Preservation Trust, 1996–2000; Patron, Landscape Design Trust, 1997. Trustee, Afghanaid, 2002–03. Hon. FLI 1995. Hon. DSc Plymouth, 1994. *Publications:* Fourth Wave, 1965; Hadrian's Wall, 1976; (jtly) Leisure Provision and People's Needs, 1981; research and consultancy reports. *Recreations:* walking, landscape painting, sculpture, travel. *Address:* 56 Painswick Road, Cheltenham, Glos GL50 2ER. *T:* (01242) 226511.

DOWLEY, Dominic Myles; QC 2002; *b* 25 March 1958; *s* of Laurence Edward Dowley and Audrey Virginia Dowley (*née* Jorgensen); *m* 1985, Emma Sîan Elizabeth (*née* Lewis); five *d*. *Educ:* Ampleforth Coll., Yorks; New Coll., Oxford (MA Hons). Called to the Bar, Gray's Inn, 1983. *Address:* 6 New Square, Lincoln's Inn, WC2A 3QS. *Clubs:* Garrick, MCC; Royal West Norfolk Golf.

DOWLING, Prof. Dame Ann Patricia, (Dame Ann Hynes), DBE 2007 (CBE 2002); PhD, ScD; FRS 2003; FREng; FIMechE; FRAeS; Professor of Mechanical Engineering, University of Cambridge, since 1993; Fellow, Sidney Sussex College, Cambridge, since 1979; *b* 15 July 1952; *d* of Mortimer Joseph Patrick Dowling and Joyce Dowling (*née* Barnes); *m* 1974, Dr Thomas Paul Hynes. *Educ:* Ursuline Convent Sch., Westgate, Kent; Girton Coll., Cambridge (BA 1973; MA 1977; PhD 1978; ScD 2006). CEng, FIMechE 1990; FREng (FEng 1996); FRAeS 1997; Fellow, Inst. Acoustics, 1989. Cambridge University: Res. Fellow, 1977–78, Dir of Studies in Engrg, 1979–90, Sidney Sussex Coll.; Asst Lectr in Engrg, 1979–82; Lectr, 1982–86; Reader in Acoustics, 1986–93; Dep. Hd, Engrg Dept, 1990–93, 1996–99. Jerome C. Hunsaker Vis. Prof., MIT, 1999–2000; Moore Dist. Schol., CIT, 2001–02. Member: AIAA, 1990; Defence and Aerospace Technology Foresight Panel, 1994–97; Defence Sci. Adv. Council, 1998–2001; EPSRC, 2001–06 (Mem., 1998–2002, Chm., 2003–06, Technical Opportunities Panel). Non-exec. Dir DRA, 1995–97; Mem. Scientific Adv. Bd, DERA, 1997–2001. Mem. Council, Royal Acad. of Engrg, 1998–2002 (Vice-Pres., 1999–2002). Trustee: Ford of Britain Trust, 1993–2002; Cambridge European Trust, 1994–; Nat. Mus. of Sci. and Industry, 1999–2008. Gov., Felsted Sch., 1994–99. Foreign Associate: French Acad. of Scis, 2002; US NAE, 2008. A. B. Wood Medal, Inst. of Acoustics, 1990. *Publications:* (with J. E. Ffowcs Williams) Sound and Sources of Sound, 1983; (with D. G. Crighton *et al.*) Modern Methods in Analytical Acoustics, 1992; contribs to scientific and engrg jls, mainly on fluid mechanics, combustion, vibration and acoustics. *Recreations:* opera, walking. *Address:* Engineering Department, Cambridge University, Trumpington Street, Cambridge CB2 1PZ. *T:* (01223) 332739.

DOWLING, Rt Rev. Owen Douglas; Bishop of Canberra and Goulburn, 1983–92; *b* 11 Oct. 1934; *s* of Cecil Gair Mackenzie Dowling and Winifred Hunter; *m* 1st, 1958, Beverly Anne Johnston (*d* 1985); two *s* one *d*; 2nd, 1993, Gloria Helen Goodwin. *Educ:* Melbourne High School; Trinity Coll., Melbourne Univ. (BA, DipEd, ThL). Victoria Education Dept, Secondary Teacher, 1956–60; ordained to ministry of Anglican Church, 1960; Asst Curate, Sunshine/Deer Park, Dio. Melbourne, 1960–62; Vicar of St. Philip's, W Heidelberg, 1962–65; Precentor and Organist, St Saviour's Cathedral, Goulburn, 1965–67; Rector of South Wagga Wagga, 1968–72; Rector of St John's, Canberra, 1972–81; Archdeacon of Canberra, 1974–81; Asst Bishop, Dio. Canberra and Goulburn, 1981–83; Rector: St James's, New Town, Hobart, 1993–96; Christ Church, Longford, Tas, 1996–99. Comr, Australian Heritage Commn, 1993–95. *Recreation:* pipe organ and piano playing. *Address:* 1/12 Key Street, Campbell, ACT 2612, Australia. *Club:* Southern Cross (Canberra).

DOWLING, Prof. Patrick Joseph, CBE 2001; DL; PhD; FRS 1996; FREng; Chairman, British Association for the Advancement of Science, since 2005; Surrey Community Foundation, since 2005; *b* 23 March 1939; *s* of John Dowling and Margaret McKittrick, Dublin; *m* 1966, Grace Carmine Victoria Lobo, *d* of Palladius Lobo and Marcilia Moniz, Zanzibar; one *s* one *d*. *Educ:* Christian Brothers Sch., Dublin; University Coll., Dublin (BE NUI 1960); Imperial Coll. of Science and Technol., London (DIC 1961; PhD 1968; FIC 1997). FRINA 1985; FIStructE 1978; FICE 1979; FREng (FEng 1981); FCGI 1989; FIAE 2000. Demonstr in Civil Engrg, UC Dublin, 1960–61; Post-grad. studies, Imperial Coll., London, 1961–65; Bridge Engr, British Constructional Steelwork Assoc., 1965–68; Imperial Coll., London: Res. Fellow, 1968–74; Reader in Structural Steelwork, 1974–79; British Steel Prof. of Steel Structures, 1979–94; Hd of Civil Engrg Dept, 1985–94; Vice-Chancellor and Chief Exec., Univ. of Surrey, 1994–2005. Partner, Chapman and Dowling, Consulting Engineers, 1981–94. Chm., Eurocode 3 (Steel Structures) Drafting Cttee, 1981–94. Mem. UK Bd, UUK, 2000–05. Mem. Council, RHBNC, 1990–95. Pres., IStructE, 1994–95; Chairman: Steel Construction Inst., 1998–2002; Engrg Council, 2002–03 (Senator, 1996–2002); Mem., Engrg Technology Bd, 2002–. Foreign Member, Nat. Acad. of Engrg, Korea, 1997; Yugoslav Acad. of Engrg, 2003; Corresponding Member: Nat. Acad. of Engrg of Argentina, 2001; Nat. Acad. of Exact, Physical and Natural Scis, Argentina, 2001. Patron, Yvonne Arnaud Th., 2007– (Mem. Bd of Trustees, 2002–). Editor, Jl of Constructional Steel Research, 1980–. DL Surrey, 1999. Hon. Mem. RIA, 2007. Hon. LLD: NUI, 1995; Roehampton, 2005; Hon. DSc: Vilnius Tech. Univ., 1996; Ulster, 1998; Hon. PhD Kuopio, 2005; DUniv Surrey, 2006. Institution of Structural Engineers: Oscar Faber Award, 1971; Henry Adams Medal, 1976; Guthrie Brown Medal, 1979; Oscar Faber Medal, 1985, 1996; Telford Premium, ICE, 1976; Gustave Trasenster Medal, Assoc. des Ingénieurs sortis de l'Univ. de Liège, 1984; Silver Medal, RINA, 1993; Curtin Medal, ICE, 1993; James Alfred Ewing Medal, ICE, 2006. *Publications:* Steel Plated Structures, 1977; Buckling of Shells in Offshore Structures, 1982; Structural Steel Design, 1988; Constructional Steel Design, 1992; technical papers on elastic and inelastic behaviour and design of steel and composite land-based and offshore structures. *Recreations:* travelling, theatre, reading, the enjoyment of good company. *Address:* A4 Trinity Gate, Epsom Road, Guildford, Surrey GU1 3PJ. *Clubs:* Athenæum, Chelsea Arts; Guildford County; National Yacht of Ireland.

DOWLING, Sir Robert, Kt 2002; Headmaster, George Dixon International School, Birmingham, since 1998; *b* 8 Sept. 1940; *s* of Nicholas and Elizabeth Dowling; *m* 1967, Helen Bernadette Ryan; two *s* one *d*. *Educ:* St Mary's Coll., Twickenham (qualified teacher, London Univ.); Cambridge Inst. (Dip Exp. Psychology); Nottingham Univ. (MEd); University Coll. Northampton (Dip SPLD). Headmaster: Collingwood Sch., Birmingham, 1976–90; Selly Oak Special Sch., Birmingham, 1990–96; Uffculme Sch., Birmingham, 1996–98. Sen. Educn Advr, Birmingham LEA, 1988–92. Member, Catenian Assoc.; Birmingham and Edgbaston Debating Soc. *Recreations:* golf, theatre, music, reading, debating. *Address:* 4 Victoria Road, Harborne, Birmingham B17 0AH. *e-mail:* dow@blueyonder.co.uk. *Club:* Edgbaston Golf.

DOWN AND CONNOR, Bishop of, (RC), since 1991; **Most Rev. Patrick Joseph Walsh;** *b* 9 April 1931; *s* of Michael and Nora Walsh. *Educ:* Queen's Univ. Belfast (MA); Christ's Coll., Cambridge (MA); Pontifical Lateran Univ., Rome (STL). Ordained 1956; Teacher, St MacNissi's Coll., Garron Tower, 1958–64; Chaplain, Queen's Univ., Belfast, 1964–70; Pres., St Malachy's Coll., Belfast, 1970–83; Auxiliary Bishop of Down and Connor, 1983–91. *Recreations:* walking, music, theatre. *Address:* 73 Somerton Road, Belfast BT15 4DE. *T:* (028) 9077 6185.

DOWN AND DROMORE, Bishop of, since 1997; **Rt Rev. Harold Creeth Miller;** *b* 23 Feb. 1950; *s* of Harold Miller and Violet (*née* McGinley); *m* 1978, Elizabeth Adelaide Harper; two *s* two *d*. *Educ:* Trinity Coll., Dublin (MA); Nottingham Univ. (BA Hons Theol.); St John's Theol Coll., Nottingham (DPS). Ordained deacon, 1976, priest, 1977; Asst Curate, St Nicholas, Carrickfergus, 1976–79; Dir of Extension Studies and Chaplain, St John's Coll., Nottingham, 1979–84; Chaplain, QUB, 1984–89; Rector of Carrigrohane Union of Parishes, Cork, 1989–97. *Publications:* Anglican Worship Today, 1980; Whose Office? daily prayer for the people of God, 1982; Finding a Personal Rule of Life, 1984, 2nd edn 1987; New Ways in Worship, 1986; Making an Occasion of It, 1994; Outreach in the Local Church, 2000; The Desire of our Soul, 2004; articles in Search. *Recreations:* caravanning, music, travel, phillumeny. *Address:* The See House, 32 Knockdene Park South, Belfast BT5 7AB. *T:* (028) 9023 7602; *e-mail:* bishop@down.anglican.org.

DOWN, Antony Turnbull L.; *see* Langdon-Down.

DOWN, Ven. Philip Roy; Archdeacon of Maidstone, since 2002; *b* 28 March 1953; *s* of Keith Phillip Down and Ivy Olive Down; *m* 1972, Christine Mary Oakley; one *s* three *d*. *Educ:* Royal Melbourne Inst. of Technol. (Dip. Applied Sci. 1976); Melbourne Coll. of Divinity (BTh 1982, MTh 1988); Hull Univ. (MA 1993). Medical scientist: Dept of Pathology, Austin Hosp., Melbourne, 1971–76; Macleod Pathology Services, Melbourne, 1976–78; Siddons Fellow (postgrad. teaching fellowship), Melbourne Coll. of Divinity, 1982; Minister, Brighton Parish, Uniting Ch in Aust., 1983–86; Associate Minister, British Methodist Conf., Scunthorpe Circuit and Westcliffe LEP, and Chaplain (part-time), Scunthorpe Gen. Hosp., 1986–89; ordained deacon and priest, 1989; Curate, 1989–9

Team Vicar, 1991–95, Grimsby; Rector, St Stephen's, Canterbury, 1995–2002; Area Dean of Canterbury, 1999–2002. *Recreations:* opera, poetry, music, natural history, travel, theatre, cinema, dogs, bantam chickens. *Address:* The Old Rectory, The Street, Pluckley, Kent TN27 0QT. *T:* (01233) 840291, *Fax:* (01233) 840759; *e-mail:* pdown@archdeacmaid.org.

DOWN, Rt Rev. William John Denbigh; Assistant Bishop of Leicester and Priest-in-charge, St Mary, Humberstone, 1995–2001; Hon. Assistant Bishop, Diocese of Oxford, since 2001; *b* 15 July 1934; *s* of late William Leonard Frederick Down and Beryl Mary Down (*née* Collett); *m* 1960, Sylvia Mary Aves; two *s* two *d*. *Educ:* Farnham Grammar School; St John's Coll., Cambridge (BA 1957; MA 1961); Ridley Hall, Cambridge. Deacon 1959, priest 1960, Salisbury; Asst Curate, St Paul's Church, Salisbury, 1959–63; Chaplain, Missions to Seamen, 1963–74: South Shields, 1963–65; Hull, 1965–71; Fremantle, WA, 1971–74; Dep. Gen. Secretary, Missions to Seamen, 1975, Gen. Sec. 1976–90; Chaplain, St Michael Paternoster Royal, 1976–90; Hon. Asst Curate, St John's, Stanmore, 1975–90; Bishop of Bermuda, 1990–95. Hon. Canon of Gibraltar, 1985–90, of Kobe, 1987–. Chaplain RANR, 1972–74. Hon. Chaplain, Worshipful Co. of Carmen, 1977–90 (Hon. Chaplain Emeritus, 1990), of Farriers, 1983–90 (Hon. Chaplain Emeritus, 1990), of Innholders, 1983–90. Freeman, City of London, 1981. Hon. FNI 1991. *Publications:* On Course Together, 1989; (contrib.) Chaplaincy, 1999; Down to the Sea (autobiog.), 2004; The Bishop's Bill of Fare, 2005; contrib. to Internat. Christian Maritime Assoc. Bulletin. *Recreations:* sport (keen follower of soccer, cricket, golf), ships and the sea, travel, walking. *Address:* 54 Dark Lane, Witney, Oxon OX28 6LX. *T:* (01993) 706615; *e-mail:* Bishbill@aol.com. *Clubs:* MCC; Chipping Norton Golf.

DOWNE, 12th Viscount *cr* 1680; **Richard Henry Dawnay;** Bt 1642; Baron Dawnay of Danby (UK) 1897; *b* 9 April 1967; *o s* of 11th Viscount Downe and of Alison Diana (*née* Sconce); *S* father, 2002. *Educ:* Eton. *Heir: cousin* Thomas Payan Dawnay, *b* 24 July 1978.

DOWNER, Hon. Alexander John Gosse; MP (L) Mayo, South Australia, since 1984; *b* 9 Sept. 1951; *s* of Hon. Sir Alexander Downer, KBE and of Mary Downer (*née* Gosse); *m* 1978, Nicola Robinson; one *s* three *d*. *Educ:* Geelong GS, Vic; Radley Coll., Oxford; Univ. of Newcastle upon Tyne (BA Hons Pol. and Econs). Economist, Bank of NSW, Sydney, 1975–76; Australian Diplomatic Service, 1976–82: Mission to EEC, Representation to NATO, and Belgium and Luxembourg, 1977–80; Sen. Foreign Affairs Rep., S Australia, 1981; political advr to Prime Minister and Federal Leader of Opposition, 1982–83; Exec. Dir, Australian Chamber of Commerce, 1983–84; Shadow Minister: for Arts, Heritage and Envmt, 1987; for Housing, Small Business and Customs, 1988–89; for Trade and Trade Negotiations, 1990–92; for Defence, 1992–93; Shadow Treas., 1993–94; Leader of Opposition, 1994–95; Shadow Minister for Foreign Affairs, 1995–96; Minister for Foreign Affairs, 1996–2007. *Recreations:* reading, music, tennis, golf. *Address:* Parliament House, Canberra, ACT 2600, Australia. *Club:* Adelaide.

DOWNER, Dame Jocelyn Anita; *see* Barrow, Dame J. A.

DOWNER, Prof. Martin Craig; Hon. Professor, Universities of London and Manchester, since 1996; Director, Oral Health Consultancy Services, since 1996; *b* 9 March 1931; *s* of Dr Reginald Lionel Ernest Downer and Mrs Eileen Maud Downer (*née* Craig); *m* 1961, Anne Catherine (*née* Evans); four *d*. *Educ:* Shrewsbury Sch.; Univ. of Liverpool; Univ. of Manchester (PhD 1974; DDS 1989); Univ. of London. LDSRCS 1958; DDPH RCS 1969. Dental Officer, St Helens Local Authority, 1958–59; gen. dental practice, 1959–64; Dental Officer, Bor. of Haringey, 1964–67; Principal Dental Officer, Royal Bor. of Kensington and Chelsea, 1967–70; Res. Fellow in Dental Health, Univ. of Manchester, 1970–74; Area Dental Officer, Salford HA (also Hon. Lectr, Univ. of Manchester), 1974–79; Chief Dental Officer, SHHD (also Hon. Sen. Lectr, Univs of Edinburgh and Dundee), 1979–83; Chief Dental Officer (Under Sec.), Dept of Health (formerly DHSS), 1983–90; Prof. and Head of Dept, Dental Health Policy, and Hon. Consultant in Dental Public Health, Eastman Dental Inst., London Univ., 1990–96. *Publications:* contribs to books and papers in learned jls in gen. field of dental public health, incl. epidemiology and biostatistics, clin. trials and trial methodology, inf. systems, health services res., and econs of dental care. *Recreations:* music, reading, cookery, natural history, vintage aviation, walking. *Address:* 16A Westbury Park, Westbury Park, Bristol BS6 7JA. *T:* (0117) 974 3703.

DOWNES, Prof. David Malcolm; Professor of Social Administration, London School of Economics, 1987–2003, now Emeritus; *b* 26 Aug. 1938; *s* of Bernice Marion Downes and Herman Leslie Downes; *m* 1961, Susan Onaway Correa-Hunt; one *s* two *d*. *Educ:* King Edward VII Grammar Sch., Sheffield; Keble Coll., Oxford (BA Hons Mod. Hist. 1959); LSE (PhD Criminology 1964). London School of Economics: Asst Lectr, Lectr, Sen. Lectr in Social Admin, 1963–82; Reader, 1982–87; Dir, Mannheim Centre for Criminology and Criminal Justice, 1998–2003; Vice-Chm., Academic Bd, 1996–99. Sen. Res. Fellow, Nuffield Coll., Oxford, 1970–72. Visiting Professor/Academic Visitor: Univ. of California at Berkeley, 1975; Univ. of Toronto, 1977; Free Univ. of Amsterdam, 1981; Univ. of Bologna, 1991. British Mem., Harvard Internat. Seminar, 1966. Member, Council: Centre for Crime and Justice Studies, KCL, 1998–; Liberty, 2003–. Mem., Family Commn, Nat. Family and Parenting Inst., 2004–05. Mem., BFI. Editor, British Jl of Criminology, 1985–90. *Publications:* The Delinquent Solution, 1966, 3rd edn 1973; Gambling, Work and Leisure, 1976; (ed with Paul Rock) Deviant Interpretations, 1979; (with Paul Rock) Understanding Deviance, 1982, 5th edn 2007; Contrasts in Tolerance: postwar penal policy in the Netherlands and England and Wales, 1988; (ed) Crime and the City: essays in memory of John Mays, 1989; (ed) Unravelling Criminal Justice, 1992; (ed jtly) Crime, Social Control and Human Rights: from moral panics to states of denial - essays in honour of Stanley Cohen, 2007. *Recreations:* modern literature, cinema, theatre. *Address:* 25 Rosehill Road, Wandsworth, SW18 2NY. *T:* (020) 8870 3410.

DOWNES, Sir Edward (Thomas), Kt 1991; CBE 1986; Associate Music Director and Principal Conductor, Royal Opera House, Covent Garden, since 1991; *b* 17 June 1924. FRCM. Royal Opera House, Covent Garden, 1952–69; Music Dir, Australian Opera, 1972–76; Prin. Conductor, BBC Northern Symphony Orch., subseq. BBC Philharmonic Orch., 1980–91. *Address:* c/o Royal Opera House, Covent Garden, WC2E 7QA.

DOWNES, Giles Patrick Stretton, CVO 1998; RIBA; Partner, Sidell Gibson Partnership, since 1988; *b* 11 Nov. 1947; *s* of late George Stretton Downes, CBE; *m* 1989, Jessica Jane Harness; one *d*. *Educ:* Wimbledon Coll.; Kingston Coll. of Art (DipArch 1972). ARCUK 1973; RIBA 1989. Foster Associates, 1969–73; Farrell Grimshaw Partnership, 1973–74; joined Sidell Gibson Partnership, 1974: Associate in charge of Housing Projects, 1980; Equity Partner, 1988. *Projects* include: Sheltered Housing Schemes for English Courtyard Assoc., 1978– (Housing Design Awards, 1983 (2), 1987 (3), 1989, 1991, 1993 (2)); Redevelt of Winchester Peninsula Barracks, 1988; Prince of Wales Sch., Dorchester, 1992; Thomas Hardye Sch., Dorchester, 1993; New Design Areas for Fire Restoration of Windsor Castle, 1994 (Bldg of the Year award, Royal Fine Art Commn, for Lantern Lobby, RIBA Award, RICS Conservation Award, 1998; Carpenters Special Award, 1999; Europa Nostra Conservation Award, 2000); 3 Sheldon Square, Paddington (British Council for Offices Award, 2003). Mem., Inst. of Wood Science, 2008. Gov., Building Crafts Coll., 2002–. Liveryman, Carpenters' Co., 2001– (Middle Warden, 2008–Aug. 2009). *Recreations:* sculpture, ceramics, building craft skills, sketching. *Address:* Sidell Gibson Partnership, Holford Mews, Cruikshank Street, WC1X 9HW. *T:* (020) 7284 9005.

See also Dame J. S. Higgins.

DOWNES, Prof. Kerry John, OBE 1994; FSA; Professor of History of Art, University of Reading, 1978–91, now Emeritus; *b* 8 Dec. 1930; *s* of late Ralph William Downes, CBE and Agnes Mary Downes (*née* Rix); *m* 1962, Margaret Walton (*d* 2003). *Educ:* St Benedict's, Ealing; Courtauld Institute of Art. BA, PhD London. Library, Courtauld Inst. of Art, 1954–58; Librarian, Barber Inst. of Fine Arts, Univ. of Birmingham, 1958–66; Lectr in Fine Art, Univ. of Reading, 1966–71, Reader, 1971–78. Vis. Lectr, Yale Univ., 1968; Hon. Vis. Prof., Univ. of York, 1994–. Mem., Royal Commission on Historical Monuments of England, 1981–93; Pres., Soc. of Architectural Historians of GB, 1984–88. Consultant for Trophy Room, St Paul's Cathedral, 1995–97. Hon. DLitt Birmingham, 1995. *Publications:* Hawksmoor, 1959, 2nd edn 1979; English Baroque Architecture, 1966; Hawksmoor, 1969; Christopher Wren, 1971; Whitehall Palace, in Colvin and others, History of the King's Works, V, 1660–1782, 1976; Vanbrugh, 1977; The Georgian Cities of Britain, 1979; Rubens, 1980; The Architecture of Wren, 1982, 2nd edn 1988; Sir John Vanbrugh, a Biography, 1987; Sir Christopher Wren: Design for St Paul's Cathedral, 1988; St Paul's and its Architecture, 1998; Christopher Wren, 2007; contribs to Oxford DNB, Burlington Magazine, Architectural History, Architectural Rev., TLS, Alexander Jl, etc. *Recreations:* drawing, making music, baking, procrastination. *Address:* c/o Department of History of Art, School of Humanities, University of Reading, Whiteknights, PO Box 218, Reading RG6 6AA. *T:* (0118) 378 8890.

DOWNES, Paul Henry; His Honour Judge Downes; a Circuit Judge, since 1995; *b* 23 Nov. 1941; *s* of Eric and Lavinia Downes; *m* 1st; two *s* one *d*; 2nd, 1986, Beverley Jill Rogers; one *s*. *Educ:* Ducie High Sch., Manchester; Coll. of Commerce, UMIST; Coll. of Law, London (Bar degree 1967); Cardiff (LLM Canon Law 2003). Deputy Magistrates' Clerk: Manchester Co. Magistrates' Court, 1960–63; Sheffield City Magistrates' Court, 1963–67; Nottingham City Magistrates' Court, 1967; County Prosecuting Service, Suffolk, 1967–71; in private practice at Norwich Bar, 1971–95; Asst Recorder, 1991–94; Recorder, 1994–95. Vice Chancellor, Dio. St Edmundsbury and Ipswich, 2001–; Chancellor: Dio. of Wakefield, 2007–; Dio. of Norwich, 2007–. Hon. LLD UEA, 2008. *Recreations:* music, singing, chamber choir, instrumental playing, reading, walking, solo baritone singing. *Address:* c/o Norwich Combined Court, Bishopgate, Norwich NR3 1UR.

DOWNEY, Sir Gordon (Stanley), KCB 1984 (CB 1980); Parliamentary Commissioner for Standards, 1995–98; Comptroller and Auditor General, 1981–87; *b* 26 April 1928; *s* of Stanley William and Winifred Downey; *m* 1952, Jacqueline Goldsmith; two *d*. *Educ:* Tiffin's Sch.; London Sch. of Economics (BSc(Econ)). Served RA, 1946–48. Ministry of Works, 1951; entered HM Treasury, 1952; Asst Private Sec. to successive Chancellors of the Exchequer, 1955–57; on loan to Ministry of Health, 1961–62; Asst Sec., 1965, Under-Sec., 1972, Head of Central Unit, 1975; Dep. Sec., 1976–81; on loan as Dep. Head, Central Policy Review Staff, Cabinet Office, 1978–81. Special Advr, Ernst & Young (formerly Ernst & Whinney), 1988–90; Complaints Comr, The Securities Assoc., 1989–90; Chairman: FIMBRA, 1990–93; PIA, 1993. Readers' Rep., The Independent, 1990–95. Chm., Delegacy, King's College Med. and Dental Sch., 1989–91; Mem. Council, KCL, 1989–91; FKC 2002. *Recreations:* reading, visual arts, tennis. *Address:* 137 Whitehall Court, SW1A 2EP. *T:* (020) 7321 0914. *Club:* Athenæum.

DOWNEY, Air Vice-Marshal John Chegwyn Thomas, CB 1975; DFC 1945, AFC; Deputy Controller of Aircraft (C), Ministry of Defence, 1974–75, retired; *b* 26 Nov. 1920; *s* of Thomas Cecil Downey and Mary Evelyn Downey; *m* Diana, (*née* White); one *s* two *d*. *Educ:* Whitgift Sch. Entered RAF 1939; served War of 1939–45 in Coastal Command (DFC 1945 for his part in anti-U-boat ops). Captained Lincoln Aries III on global flight of 29,000 miles, during which London-Khartoum record was broken. RAE Farnborough 1956–58; commanded Bomber Comd Devel t Unit 1959–60; head of NE Defence Secretariat, Cyprus, 1960–62; Comd RAF Farnborough, 1962–64; a Dir, Op. Requirements (RAF) MoD, 1965–67; IDC, 1968; Comdt, RAF Coll. of Air Warfare, Manby, Jan./Oct. 1969; Comdr Southern Maritime Air Region, 1969–71; Senior RAF Mem., RCDS, 1972–74. *Publications:* Management in the Armed Forces: an anatomy of the military profession, 1977; (contrib.) Yearbook of World Affairs, 1983. *Recreations:* sailing, ski-ing. *Address:* c/o Lloyds TSB, 7 Pall Mall, SW1Y 5NA. *Club:* Royal Air Force.

DOWNIE, Caren; Buying Director, Womenswear, ASOS plc, since 2008; *b* Enfield, 24 Dec. 1960; *d* of Roger and Margaret Wheaton; *m* 1988, Charles Downie. *Educ:* London Sch. of Econs (BSc Hons Internat. Trade and Develt). Began career at Warehouse, subseq. progressed via many High St names; Buying Dir, Topshop, 2003–08. Mem. Panel, New Generation, British Fashion Council, 2000–; Ext. Examnr, Univ. of the Arts, London (formerly London Inst.), 2000–. *Publications:* articles in Elle mag. and Daily Telegraph. *Recreations:* shopping the world, collecting expensive shoes. *Address:* c/o ASOS plc, Greater London House, Hampstead Road, NW1 7FB; *e-mail:* carend@asos.com.

DOWNIE, Prof. Robert Silcock, FRSE 1986; Professor of Moral Philosophy, 1969–2002, now Emeritus, Hon. and Professorial Research Fellow, since 2002, Glasgow University; *b* 19 April 1933; *s* of late Robert Mackie Downie and late Margaret Barlas Downie; *m* 1958, Eileen Dorothea Flynn; three *d*. *Educ:* The High Sch. of Glasgow; Glasgow Univ. (MA, first cl. hons, Philosophy and Eng. Lit., 1955); The Queen's Coll., Oxford (Ferguson Schol., 1958; BPhil 1959). Russian linguist, Intelligence Corps, 1955–57; Glasgow University: Lectr in Moral Philosophy, 1959; Sen. Lectr in Moral Philosophy, 1968; Stevenson Lectr in Med. Ethics, 1985–88. Vis. Prof. of Philosophy, Syracuse Univ., NY, USA, 1963–64. FRSA 1997. *Publications:* Government Action and Morality, 1964; (jtly) Respect for Persons, 1969; Roles and Values, 1971; (jtly) Education and Personal Relationships, 1974; (jtly) Values in Social Work, 1976; (jtly) Caring and Curing, 1980; Healthy Respect, 1987; (jtly) Health Promotion: models and values, 1990; (jtly) The Making of a Doctor, 1992; (ed) Francis Hutcheson: selected writings, 1994; (ed) The Healing Arts: an Oxford anthology, 1994; Palliative Care Ethics, 1996; (ed) Medical Ethics, 1996; Clinical Judgement: evidence in practice, 2000; (jtly) The Philosophy of Palliative Care, 2006; Bioethics and the Humanities, 2007; contribs to: Mind, Philosophy, Analysis, Aristotelian Society, Political Studies. *Recreation:* music. *Address:* Department of Moral Philosophy, University of Glasgow G12 8QQ. *T:* (0141) 330 5692.

DOWNING, Anne Elizabeth; *see* Fleming, A. E.

DOWNING, Dr Anthony Leighton, FREng; Consultant, Binnie & Partners, Consulting Engineers, 1986–96 (Partner, 1974–86); *b* 27 March 1926; *s* of Sydney Arthur Downing and Frances Dorothy Downing; *m* 1952, Kathleen Margaret Frost; one *d*. *Educ:* Arnold Sch., Blackpool; Cambridge and London Universities. BA Cantab. 1946; BSc Special Degree 2 (1) Hons. London, 1950; DSc London 1967. Joined Water Pollution

Research Lab., 1946; seconded to Fisheries Research Lab., Lowestoft, 1947–48; granted transfer to Govt Chemist's Lab., 1948; returned to WPRL as Scientific Officer, 1950; subsequently worked mainly in field of biochemical engrg; Dir, Water Pollution Res. Lab., 1966–73. Vis. Prof., Imperial Coll. of Science and Technology, 1978–82. FIChemE 1975; FIWPC 1965 (Pres., 1979); FIBiol 1965; Hon. FIPHE 1965; FIWES 1975; Hon. FCIWEM 1987; FREng (FEng 1991). Freeman, City of London, 1988. Member: Probus Club, Stevenage, 1995– (Chm., 2002); CGA, 2000–. *Publications:* Water on the Brain (memoirs), 2005; 120 papers in scientific and technical journals. *Recreations:* golf, snooker, gardening. *Address:* 2 Tewin Close, Tewin Wood, Welwyn, Herts AL6 0HF. *T:* (01438) 798474. *Club:* Knebworth Golf.

DOWNPATRICK, Lord; Edward Edmund Maximilian George Windsor; *b* 2 Dec. 1988; *s* and *heir* of Earl of St Andrews, *qv*. *Educ:* King's Coll. Sch., Cambridge; Dragon Sch., Oxford; Eton Coll.; Keble Coll., Oxford. Officer Cadet, Oxford Air Sqdn, 2008–. Jun. Capt., Royal W Norfolk Golf Club, 2005–06. *Recreations:* languages, tennis, ski-ing, shooting.

DOWNS, Carolyn Grace; Deputy Permanent Secretary and Director General, Corporate Performance, Ministry of Justice, since 2009; *b* 25 Feb. 1960; *d* of Eric and Mildred Downs; *m* 1988, Prof. Jonathan Michie, *qv*; two *s*. *Educ:* Kingston Univ. (BA Hons French and Politics); UCL (Postgrad. DipLib, MA Liby and Inf. Studies). Asst Dir of Leisure Services, Stevenage BC, 1994–96; Dir of Leisure Services, Calderdale MBC, 1996–99; Corporate Dir, 1999–2003, Chief Exec., 2003–09, Shropshire CC. *Recreations:* tennis, ski-ing, watching Manchester United. *Address:* Ministry of Justice, Selborne House, 54–60 Victoria Street, SW1E 6QW.

DOWNS, Sir Diarmuid, Kt 1985; CBE 1979; FRS 1985; FREng, FIMechE; Managing Director, 1967–84, Chairman, 1976–87, Ricardo Consulting Engineers plc; *b* 23 April 1922; *s* of John Downs and Ellen McMahon; *m* 1951, Mary Carmel Chillman; one *s* three *d*. *Educ:* Gunnersbury Catholic Grammar Sch.; Northampton Poly. (BScEng London Univ., 1942). CEng, FIMechE 1961. Ricardo Consulting Engineers Ltd, 1942–87: Head, Petrol Engine Dept, 1947; Dir, 1957. Mem., Adv. Council for Applied R&D, 1976–80; Member: SERC, 1981–85 (Chm., Engineering Bd); Design Council, 1981–89; Bd of Dirs, Soc. of Automotive Engineers Inc., 1983–86; Bd of British Council, 1987–93; Council, Motor Industry Res. Assoc., 1987–89. President: Assoc. of Indep. Contract Res. Organisations, 1975–77; Fédération Internationale des Sociétés d'Ingénieurs des Techniques de L'Automobile, 1978 (Vice-Pres., 1975); IMechE, 1978–79 (Vice-Pres., 1971–78); Section G, British Assoc. for Advancement of Science, 1984; Royal Commn for Exhibn of 1851, 1985–96. Chm., Technology Activities Cttee, Royal Soc., 1989–95; Mem., Adv. Bd, Parly Office of Science and Technology, 1988–93. Dir, Gabriel Communications (formerly Universe Publications) Ltd, 1986–93. Vis. Fellow, Lincoln Coll. Oxford, 1987–88. Hinton Lecture, Fellowship of Engrg, 1987. Pres., Smeatonian Soc. of Civil Engrs, 2003. Foreign Associate, Nat. Acad. of Engrg, USA, 1987; Hon. Mem., Hungarian Acad. of Scis, 1988. Liveryman, Co. of Engineers, 1984–. Pro Chancellor, Surrey Univ., 1992–94 (Mem. Council, 1983–94, Chm., 1989–92); Mem. Council, City Univ., 1980–82. Hon. Fellow, St Mary's UC, Strawberry Hill, 1995. Hon. DSc: City, 1978; Cranfield Inst. of Technol., 1981; DUniv Surrey, 1995. George Stephenson Research Prize, 1951, Crompton Lanchester Medal, 1951 and Dugald Clerk Prize, 1952, IMechE; James Alfred Ewing Medal, ICE, 1985; Medal, Internat. Fedn of Automobile Engrs' and Technicians' Assocs, 1986. KSG 1993. *Publications:* papers on internal combustion engines in British and internat. engrg jls and conf. proc. *Recreation:* theatre. *Address:* The Downs, 143 New Church Road, Hove, East Sussex BN3 4DB. *T:* (01273) 419357. *Club:* Hove (Hove).

DOWNSHIRE, 9th Marquess of, *cr* 1789 (Ire.); **Arthur Francis Nicholas Wills Hill;** Viscount Hillsborough, Baron Hill, 1717; Earl of Hillsborough, Viscount Kilwarlin, 1751; Baron Harwich (GB), 1756; Earl of Hillsborough, Viscount Fairford (GB), 1772; Hereditary Constable of Hillsborough Fort; company director and landowner; *b* 4 Feb. 1959; *e s* of 8th Marquess of Downshire and Hon. Juliet Mary (*d* 1986), *d* of 7th Baron Forester; *S* father, 2003; *heir-pres.* to Baron Sandys; *m* 1990, Janey, *d* of Gerald Bunting; one *s* three *d*. *Educ:* Eton College; Royal Agricultural Coll., Cirencester; Central London Polytechnic. ACA 1985. Touche Ross & Co., 1981–87; Finance Controller, 1988–89, Finance Dir, 1989–2001, Scheduling Technol. Gp Ltd; Director: Animalcare Group plc (formerly Ritchey Tagg Ltd, then Ritchey plc), 1998–; Farmway Ltd, 2007–; Chm., Identify UK Ltd, 2001–; Man. Dir, Fearing Internat., 2001–; Dir, base2stay (formerly Western Heritable Apartco) Ltd, 2004–. *Recreations:* country pursuits, sport. *Heir: s* Earl of Hillsborough, *qv*.

DOWNSIDE, Abbot of; *see* Bellenger, Rt Rev. Dr D. T. J.

DOWNWARD, Prof. Julian, PhD; FRS 2005; Principal Scientist, since 1996, and Associate Director, since 2005, Cancer Research UK, London Research Institute; *b* 25 Oct. 1960; *s* of Maj.-Gen. Sir Peter Aldcroft Downward, *qv*; *m* 1997, Tanya Basu; two *d*. *Educ:* Eton Coll.; Clare Coll., Cambridge (BA 1982); ICRF/Imperial Coll. London (PhD 1986). Res. Fellow, MIT, 1986–89; Hd, Signal Transduction Lab., CRUK, London Res. Inst. (formerly ICRF Lab.), 1989–. Hon. Professor: Biochem. Dept, UCL, 1997–; Barts and the London, Queen Mary Sch. of Medicine and Dentistry, 2004–. *Publications:* contrib. papers on molecular biol. of cancer to scientific jls. *Recreations:* ski-ing, theatre, scuba diving, music. *Address:* Signal Transduction Laboratory, Cancer Research UK, London Research Institute, 44 Lincoln's Inn Fields, WC2A 3PX. *T:* (020) 7269 3533, *Fax:* (020) 7269 3094; *e-mail:* downward@cancer.org.uk.

DOWNWARD, Maj.-Gen. Sir Peter (Aldcroft), KCVO 1999; CB 1979; DSO 1967; DFC 1952; Governor, Military Knights of Windsor, 1989–2000; *b* 10 April 1924; *s* of late Aldcroft Leonard and Mary Downward; *m* 1st, 1953, Hilda Hinckley Wood (*d* 1976); two *s*; 2nd, 1980, Mrs Mary Boykett Procter (*née* Allwork) (*d* 2008). *Educ:* King William's Coll., Isle of Man. Enlisted 1942; 2nd Lieut, The South Lancashire Regt (Prince of Wales's Volunteers), 1943; served with 13th Bn (Lancs) Parachute Regt, NW Europe, India, Far East, 1944–46, Greece and Palestine, 1947; transf. to Glider Pilot Regt, 1948; Berlin Airlift, 1949, Korea, 1951–53; 1st Bn The South Lancs Regt (PWV) in Egypt and UK, 1953–54; instructor at Light Aircraft Sch., 1955–56; RAF Staff Coll., 1958; War Office, 1959–60; BAOR, 1961–63; Brigade Major 127 Bde, 1964; Comd 4th Bn The East Lancs Regt, 1965–66; Comd 1st Bn The Lancs Regt (PWV), Aden, 1966–67; Allied Forces N Europe, Oslo, 1968–69; instructor, Sch. of Infantry, 1970–71; Comd Berlin Inf. Bde. 1971–74; Comdt, Sch. of Infantry, 1974–76; GOC West Midland District, 1976–78; Lt-Governor and Sec., The Royal Hosp., Chelsea, 1979–84. Col, The Queen's Lancashire Regt, 1978–83; Col Comdt, The King's Division, 1979–83; Hon. Col, Liverpool Univ. OTC, 1980–89. Dir, Oxley Develts Co. Ltd, 1984–89. Chm., Museum of Army Flying, 1984–88; President: British Korean Veterans Assoc., 1986–97; Assoc. of Service Journals (formerly of Service Newspapers), 1986–2003; Trustee, Princess Christian Hosp., Windsor, 1989–94. *Address:* 71 Kings Road, Windsor, Berks SL4 2AD.

See also J. Downward.

DOWSE, John; His Honour Judge Dowse; a Circuit Judge, since 2001; *b* 12 Nov 1946; *s* of Douglas Richard Maurice Dowse and Lilian Maude Dowse (*née* Cade); *m* 2000 Elaine Winstanley (*née* McLean); two step *s* one step *d*, and one *s* two *d* from forme marriage. *Educ:* Univ. of Leeds (LLB Hons 1972); Univ. of Wales, Cardiff (LLM 1996) Called to the Bar, Lincoln's Inn, 1973; Asst Recorder, 1990–94; Recorder, 1994–2001 Magistrates' Court Liaison Judge, N Bank of Humberside, 2002. *Recreations:* cooking eating out, tennis, snooker, chess. *Address:* Hull Combined Court Centre, Lowgate, Hu HU1 2EZ. *T:* (01482) 586161; *e-mail:* judge@tiscali.co.uk.

DOWSON, Prof. Duncan, CBE 1989; FRS 1987; FREng; Professor of Engineerin Fluid Mechanics and Tribology, 1966–93, now Professor Emeritus, Hon. Fellow, sinc 1993, and Research Professor, since 1995, Leeds University; *b* 31 Aug. 1928; *o s* of Wilfri and Hannah Dowson, Kirkbymoorside, York; *m* 1951, Mabel, *d* of Mary Jane and Herbe Strickland; one *s* (and one *s* decd). *Educ:* Lady Lumley's Grammar Sch., Pickering, Yorks Leeds Univ. (BSc Mech Eng. 1950; PhD 1952; DSc 1971) FIMechE; Fellow ASME 197 (Life Fellow); FREng (FEng 1982); Fellow ASLE 1983. Research Engineer, Sir W. G Armstrong Whitworth Aircraft Co., 1953–54; Univ. of Leeds: Lecturer in Mechanica Engineering, 1954; Sen. Lecturer, 1963; Reader, 1965; Dir, Inst. of Tribology, Dept c Mech. Engrg, 1967–87; Pro-Vice-Chancellor, 1983–85; Head of Dept of Mech. Engrg 1987–92; Dean for Internat. Relns, 1987–93. Hon. Professor: Hong Kong Univ., 1992– Bradford Univ., 1996–; External Prof., Loughborough Univ., 2001–; Dist. Res. Prof Univ. of Cardiff, 2004–07. Hinton Lectr, Royal Acad. of Engrg, 1990. Pres., IMechE 1992–93 (Chm., Tribology Group Cttee, 1967–69). Chm., Yorks Region, RSA 1992–97. Mem., EPSRC Peer Rev. Coll., 2003–05. Editor: Pt H (Engrg in Medicine) 1981–90, Pt C, Jl Mech. Engrg Sci., 1990–, IMechE Proceedings; WEAR, 1983–98, nov Emeritus; Engrg Res. Bk Series, 1999–. Foreign Mem., Royal Swedish Acad. of Engr Sciences, 1986. FCGI, 1997. Hon. FIPEM 1998; Hon. Fellow, Soc. of Tribologists an Lubrication Engrs; Hon. FIMechE 2001. Hon. DTech Chalmers Univ. of Technology Göteborg, 1979; Hon. DSc: Institut Nat. des Sciences Appliquées de Lyon, 199 Loughborough, 2005; Dr *hc* Liège, 1996; DEng *hc*: Waterloo, Canada, 2001; Bradforc 2003; Leeds, 2004. Institution of Mechanical Engineers: James Clayton Fund Prize (jtly 1963; Thomas Hawksley Gold Medal, 1966; James Clayton Prize, 1978; Tribology Gol Medal, 1979; James Clayton Meml Lectr, 2000; James Watt Internat. Gold Medal, 200 (jtly) Water Arbitration Prize, 2004; Gold Medal, British Soc. of Rheology, 1969; Na Award, ASLE, 1974; American Society of Mechanical Engineers: Lubrication Div. Be Paper Awards (jt), 1975, 1976, 1999; Melville Medal (jt), 1976; Mayo D. Hersey Awar 1979; Engr Historian Award, 1995; first Robert Henry Thurston Award, 2000; (jtl Tribology Best Paper Award, 1999; Kelvin Medal, ICE, 1998; Sarton Medal, Univ. c Gent, 1998. *Publications:* Elastohydrodynamic Lubrication—the fundamentals of roller an gear lubrication (jtly), 1966, 2nd edn 1977; History of Tribology, 1979, 2nd edn 199 (jtly) An Introduction to the Biomechanics of Joints and Joint Replacement, 1981; (jtl Ball Bearing Lubrication: The Elastohydrodynamics of Elliptical Contacts, 1981; papers o tribology and bio-medical engrg, published by: Royal Society; Instn of Mech. Engineer Amer. Soc. of Mech. Engineers; Amer. Soc. of Lubrication Engineers. *Recreation* genealogy, calligraphy. *Address:* Ryedale, 23 Church Lane, Adel, Leeds LS16 8DQ. *T* (0113) 267 8933.

DOWSON, Sir Philip (Manning), Kt 1980; CBE 1969; MA; PPRA (RA 1986; AR 1979); RIBA, FCSD; a Senior Partner, Ove Arup Partnership, 1969–90, Consultant, sinc 1990; Architectural Founder Partner, Arup Associates, architects and engineers; Presiden Royal Academy of Arts, 1993–99; *b* 16 Aug. 1924; *m* 1950, Sarah Crewdson (MBE 199 one *s* two *d*. *Educ:* Gresham's Sch.; University Coll., Oxford; Clare Coll., Cambridg (Hon. Fellow, 1991); Architectural Association. AA Dip. Lieut, RNVR, 1943–4 Award-winning work includes: university and college buildings in Oxford, Cambridg Birmingham and Leicester; headquarter buildings; buildings for music and the arts; urba and landscape projects. Member: Royal Fine Art Commn, 1971–97; Craft Adv. Ctte 1972–75. Governor, St Martin's Sch. of Art, 1975–82. Trustee: The Thomas Cubitt Trus 1978–98; Royal Botanic Gdns, Kew, 1983–95; Royal Armouries, 1984–89; Nat. Portra Gall., 1993–99; Coram Foundn, 1993–99. Hon. Fellow, Duncan of Jordanstone Coll. Arts, 1985; Hon. FAIA; Hon. FRCA, 1989; Hon. FRIAS. Hon. DArt De Montfor 2000. Royal Gold Medal for Architecture, RIBA, 1981. *Recreation:* sailing. *Clubs:* Garric MCC.

DOYLE, Most Rev. Adrian Leo; *see* Hobart (Australia), Archbishop of, (RC).

DOYLE, Dr Anthony Ian, FBA 1992; Hon. Reader in Bibliography, Durha University, since 1985; *b* 24 Oct. 1925; *s* of Edward Doyle and Norah Keating. *Educ:* Mary's Coll., Great Crosby, Liverpool; Downing Coll., Cambridge (BA 1945; MA 194 PhD 1953). Durham University: Asst Librarian, 1950–59; Keeper of Rare Book 1959–82; Reader in Bibliography, 1972–85. Pres., Assoc. for Manuscripts and Archives Res. Collections, 2000–. Mem., Comité Internat. de Paléographie Latine, 1979. Corres Fellow, Mediaeval Academy of America, 1991. Hon. Fellow, UC, Durham, 2004. Isra Gollancz Prize, British Academy, 1983. *Publications:* Palaeographical introductions facsimiles of the Hengwrt Manuscript, 1979, Vernon Manuscript, 1987, and Ellesme Manuscript, 1995, and of Hoccleve's autograph poems, 2003; articles on medieval MS early printed books and collectors. *Address:* University Library, Palace Green, Durha DH1 3RN. *T:* (0191) 334 2951.

DOYLE, Bernard; *see* Doyle, F. B.

DOYLE, Dr Brian John; Regional Employment Judge (formerly Regional Chairman Employment Tribunals), Manchester and Liverpool, since 2003; *b* 12 Jan. 1955; *s* of Ju Doyle and late Mary Doyle (*née* Clancy); *m* 1986, Antoinette Cecile Chang (marr. dis 2006); one *d*; *m* 2007, Helen Rippon Wile (*née* Glover). *Educ:* St Joseph's Primary Sc Crayford; St Joseph's Acad., Blackheath; Queen Mary Coll., Univ. of London (LLB Ho 1976, LLM 1978); Coll. of Law, London; PhD Salford 1993. Called to the Bar, Inn Temple, 1977; Res. Asst in Law, Poly of N London, 1978–80; Lectr in Law, 1980–8 Sen. Lectr in Law, 1988–95, Univ. of Salford; Prof. of Law, and Dean, Faculty of La Univ. of Liverpool, 1995–2000; Chm., Employment Tribunals, 2000–03. *Publication* New Directions Towards Disabled Workers' Rights, 1994; Disability Discrimination ar Equal Opportunities, 1994; Disability Discrimination: the new law, 1995; Disabili Discrimination Law and Practice, 1996, 6th edn 2008; Employment Tribunals: the ne law, 1998; contrib. articles to Industrial Law Jl, Modern Law Rev. *Recreations:* tenn travel, literature, computing, theatre. *Address:* Employment Tribunals, Alexandra Hous 14–22 The Parsonage, Manchester M3 2JA. *T:* (0161) 833 6100, *Fax:* (0161) 832 0249

DOYLE, David Charles; His Honour Deemster Doyle; HM Second Deemster, Is of Man, since 2003; *b* 26 April 1960; *s* of late David Gordon Doyle and Beatrice Lili Doyle (*née* Cain); *m* 1991, Barbara, *d* of late John Denton and Doreen Holgate; three *Educ:* King William's Coll., I of M; Univ. of Newcastle Upon Tyne (LLB 1981). Call to the Bar, Gray's Inn, 1982; admitted to the Manx Bar, 1984; partner, Dickins Cruickshank & Co., Advocates, 1985–2003. Deputy High Bailiff and Coroner of Inques 2002–03. Isle of Man Law Society: Mem. Council, 1997–2003; Chm., Educn Ctte

1997–2003; Chm., Human Rights Cttee, 2001–03; Vice Pres., 2003. Mem. Council, I of M Chamber of Commerce, 1997–2003; Mem., Corporate Services Review Cttee, 2001–03. Parent Governor, Peel Clothworkers' Sch., 2001. *Publications: contributions to:* Solly's Government and Law in the Isle of Man, 1994; Solly's Isle of Man Partnership Law, 1996; International Tracing of Assets, 1998; Offshore Cases and Materials, 1999; Offshore Financing: security and insolvency, 1998; various articles on legal topics in professional jls. *Recreations:* family, Manx law past, present and future, running, walking, coaching junior football. *Address:* Isle of Man Courts of Justice, Deemsters Walk, Bucks Road, Douglas, Isle of Man IM1 3AR. *T:* 685248, *Fax:* 685236; Ballagyr Farm, Peel, Isle of Man IM5 2AD. *T:* 844020; *e-mail:* daviddoyle@manx.net.

DOYLE, Elaine Mary; *see* Griffiths, E. M.

DOYLE, (Frederick) Bernard; Partner, Gatenby Sanderson, since 2005; *b* 17 July 1940; *s* of James Hopkinson Doyle and Hilda Mary Doyle (*née* Spotsworth); *m* 1963, Ann Weston; two *s* one *d*. *Educ:* St Bede's Coll.; Univ. of Manchester (BSc Hons); Harvard Business Sch., 1965–67 (MBA). CEng 1965; FICE 1980; FIWEM (FIWES 1986). Resident Civil Engineer with British Rail, 1961–65; Management Consultant with Arthur D. Little Inc., 1967–72; Booker McConnell Ltd: Secretary to Executive Cttee, 1973; Director, Engineering Div., 1973–76; Chairman, General Engineering Div., 1976–78; Chm. and Chief Exec., Booker McConnell Engineering, and Director, Booker McConnell, 1978–81; Chief Executive: SDP, 1981–83; Welsh Water Authy, 1983–87; MSL International, then MSL Search and Selection: Dir, Public Sector Ops, 1988–90; Dir, 1994–97; Man. Dir, 1997–99; Man. Dir, Hamptons, 1990–92; Gen. Manager, Bristol & West Building Soc., 1992–94; Dir, MSL Gp, 1996–99; Hd of Public Sector Practice, Hoggett Bowers Exec. Search and Selection, 1999–2000; Dir, KPMG Search and Selection, 2001–05. Chm., Sustainability W Midlands, 2003–07. Vice-Chm., NE Worcester Coll., 1998–2002, 2003–07. CCMI (CBIM 1987); FRSA 1987. *Recreations:* sailing (Times Clipper 2000 Round the World Yacht Race), theatre, reading, walking, bird watching. *Address:* 38A West Road, Bromsgrove, Worcs B60 2NQ. *T:* (01527) 873565.

DOYLE, John Howard, MBE 1995; PPRWS (RWS 1968); landscape painter; President, Royal Watercolour Society, 1996–2000; *b* 15 Feb. 1928; *s* of Eric Howard Doyle and Frances Doyle (*née* Maclean); *m* 1st, 1956, Caroline Knapp-Fisher (marr. diss.); one *s* one *d*; 2nd, 1968, Elizabeth Rickatson-Hatt; one *s* one *d*. *Educ:* Sherborne Sch. Dir, C. F. Doyle Ltd, 1961–96; Chm., Thomas Seager Ltd, 1968–86. Mem., Canterbury DAC, 1975–85 (Advr, 1985–). Founder Mem. and Chm., Romney Marsh Historic Churches Trust, 1980–90 (Pres., 1986–). Exhibitions: Chapter House, Canterbury Cathedral, 1973–76 and 1997; Spink & Sons, 1981–84, 1991, 1997; Catto Gall., 1988; Sanders of Oxford, 1999; Chris Beetles Gall., 2002; exhibitor, RA, 1982–90. Hon. RE 1996; Hon. RI 1996. *Publications:* An Artist's Journey down the Thames, 1993. *Recreations:* golf, gardening. *Address:* Church Farm, Warehorne, Ashford, Kent TN26 2LP. *Clubs:* Garrick; Rye Golf.

DOYLE, Hon. John Jeremy, AC 2002; Chief Justice, Supreme Court of South Australia, since 1995; *b* 4 Jan. 1945; *s* of John Malcolm Doyle and Mary Margaret Doyle; *m* 1969, Marie McLoughlin; two *s* three *d*. *Educ:* St Ignatius' Coll., Norwood; Univ. of Adelaide (LLB); Magdalen Coll., Oxford (BCL). Partner, Kelly & Co., 1970–77; called to the Bar, SA, 1970; Barrister, Hanson Chambers, 1977–86; QC (SA) 1981; Solicitor-General for S Australia, 1986–95. Pro-Chancellor, Flinders Univ. of S Australia, 1988–2001. Chm., Nat. Judicial Coll. of Australia, 2002–07. Hon. LLD Flinders, 2002. *Address:* c/o Chief Justice's Chambers, Supreme Court, 1 Gouger Street, Adelaide, SA 5000, Australia. *T:* (8) 82040390, *Fax:* (8) 82040442.

DOYLE, John Michael; freelance theatre director and writer; *b* 9 Nov. 1952; *s* of John Martin Doyle and Mary Christina Doyle; one *d*; partner, Robert Wilson. *Educ:* RSAMD (DSD); Univ. of Glasgow (CertDS). Jun. Artist-in-Residence, Univ. of Georgia, 1973–74; Dir, Tie-up Th. Co., 1975–78; Dir of Prodns, Eden Court Th., Inverness, 1979–80; Artistic Director: Swan Th., Worcester, 1982–85; Everyman Th., Cheltenham, 1985–89; Everyman Th., Liverpool, 1989–93; Theatre Royal, York, 1993–97; Associate Dir, Watermill Th., Newbury, 1997–2005. Visiting Artist: Univ. of Western Kentucky, 1997, 2000, 2003; Oregon State Univ., 2002. Fellow, Rose Bruford Coll., 2004. FRSA 2001. *Publications:* (with R. Lischner) Shakespeare for Dummies, 1999; contribs to acad. textbooks. *Recreations:* music, tennis, being in Italy. *Address:* 28 Baldslow Road, Hastings, E Sussex TN34 2EZ. *T:* (01424) 426961; *e-mail:* j.m.doyle@btinternet.com.

DOYLE, (Michael) Leo (Haygarth), CB 2004; Director for Policy and Resources, Government Communications Headquarters, 2003–04; non-executive Director, Great Western Ambulance Service NHS Trust, since 2006; *b* 14 March 1944; *s* of late James Harold Doyle and Florence Doyle (*née* Brown); *m* 1967, Barbara Sillence; two *d*. *Educ:* St John's Coll., Cambridge (Maths Tripos; BA 1965, MA 1969). Joined GCHQ, 1965; on secondment to Diplomatic Service, Washington, 1986–89. *Recreations:* bell-ringing, gardening. *Address:* *e-mail:* leo@doylehome.org.uk.

DOYLE, Patrick; composer of film and television scores; *b* 6 April 1953; *s* of Patrick and Sarah Doyle; *m* 1978, Lesley Howard; two *s* two *d*. *Educ:* Royal Scottish Acad. of Music (FRSAM 2004). Composer and musical dir, Renaissance Th. Co., 1987–1992; *compositions* include: The Thistle and the Rose (song cycle for soprano and mixed choir) to commemorate 90th birthday of the Queen Mother, 1990; *TV scores include:* Look Back in Anger; Twelfth Night; *film scores* include: Henry V, 1989 (Ivor Novello Award for Best Film Theme); Shipwrecked, 1990; Dead Again, 1991; Indochine, Into the West, 1992; Much Ado About Nothing, Carlito's Way, 1993; Frankenstein, 1994; A Little Princess (LA Critics Best Film Score), Une Femme Française, Sense and Sensibility, 1995; Mrs Winterbourne, Hamlet, 1996; Donnie Brasco, 1997; (and songs) Great Expectations, 1998; East West, 1999; Love's Labour's Lost, 2000; Bridget Jones's Diary, Gosford Park, 2001; Killing Me Softly, 2002; Calendar Girls, 2003; Nouvelle France, 2004; Man to Man, Jekyll & Hyde, Nanny McPhee, Harry Potter and the Goblet of Fire, 2005; Wah Wah, 2006; As You Like It, Pars Vite et Reviens Tard, Eragon, The Last Legion, Sleuth, 2007; Nim's Island, 2008. *Recreations:* swimming, tennis. *Address:* c/o Air-Edel, 18 Rodmarton Street, W1U 8BJ. *T:* (020) 7486 6466, *Fax:* (020) 7224 0344; *e-mail:* air-edel@air-edel.co.uk. *Club:* Glasgow Arts.

DOYLE, Dr Peter, CBE 1992; FRSE; Chairman, Biotechnology and Biological Sciences Research Council, 1998–2003; *b* 6 Sept. 1938; *s* of late Peter and Joan Penman Doyle; *m* 1962, Anita McCulloch; one *s* one *d*. *Educ:* Univ. of Glasgow (BSc Hons 1st class 1960; PhD 1963). FRSE 1993. Research Chemist, ICI Pharmaceuticals, 1963; Manager, Quality Control Dept, 1973–75; Manager, Chemistry Dept, 1975–77; Research Dir, ICI Plant Protection, 1977–86; Business Dir, ICI Seeds, 1985–86; Dep. Chm. and Technical Dir, ICI Pharmaceuticals, 1986–88; Res. and Technol. Dir, ICI Gp, 1989–93; Dir, Zeneca Gp, 1993–99. Dir, AFRC Rothamsted Experimental Station, 1991–98; non-exec. Dir, Oxford Molecular Group PLC, 1997–2000. Member: ACOST, 1989–93; MRC, 1990–94; Royal Commn on Envmtl Pollution, 1994–98; Central R&D Cttee for NHS, 1995–98; UK Round Table on Sustainable Develt, 1998–. Trustee, Nuffield Foundn, 1998–. Foreign Mem., Royal Swedish Acad. of Engineering Scis, 1990. Liveryman, Salters' Co., 1983 (Master, 2003–04). Hon. DSc: Glasgow, 1992; Nottingham, 1993; Dundee, 1995; Sussex, 1996. *Publications:* contribs to Chemical Communications and Jl Chem. Soc. *Recreation:* golf.

DOYLE, Peter John; QC 2002; *b* 29 Dec. 1951; *s* of Kenneth Charles Doyle and Margaret Doyle (*née* Porter); *m* 1977, Gail Patricia Horspool; one *s* two *d*. *Educ:* Portchester Sch.; Southampton Univ. (LLB Hons). Called to the Bar, Middle Temple, 1975; in practice in criminal law, particularly fraud; appeared in Public Inquiries incl. Stephen Lawrence, Marchioness, Victoria Climbié. Mem., Internat. Soc. for Reform of Criminal Law. *Recreation:* the operas of Gene Tyburn. *Address:* QEB Hollis Whiteman, Third Floor, Queen Elizabeth Building, Temple, EC4Y 9BS. *T:* (020) 7583 5766, *Fax:* (020) 7353 0339; *e-mail:* pd@hwqeb.fsnet.co.uk.

DOYLE, Rt Rev. Peter John Haworth; *see* Northampton, Bishop of, (RC).

DOYLE, Sir Reginald (Derek Henry), Kt 1989; CBE 1980; HM Chief Inspector of Fire Services, 1987–94; *b* 13 June 1929; *s* of John Henry and Elsie Doyle; *m* 1953, June Margretta (*née* Stringer); two *d*. *Educ:* Aston Commercial College. RN 1947–54. Fire Brigades, 1954–84; Chief Fire Officer: Worcester City and County, 1973; Hereford and Worcester County, 1974; Kent County, 1977; Home Office Fire Service Inspector, 1984–87. Warden, Guild of Fire Fighters. OStJ 1990. *Recreations:* shooting, swimming, badminton, horses. *Club:* Rotary (Weald of Kent).

DOYLE, Prof. William, DPhil; FBA 1998; FRHistS; Professor of History, 1986–2008, Senior Research Fellow, since 2008, University of Bristol; *b* 4 March 1942; *s* of Stanley Joseph Doyle and Mary Alice Bielby; *m* 1968, Christine Thomas. *Educ:* Bridlington Sch.; Oriel Coll., Oxford (BA 1964; MA, DPhil 1968). FRHistS 1976. University of York: Asst Lectr, 1967; Lectr, 1969; Sen. Lectr, 1978; Prof. of Modern History, Univ. of Nottingham, 1981–85. Visiting Professor: Univ. of S Carolina, 1969–70; Univ. de Bordeaux III, 1976; Ecole des Hautes Etudes en Sciences Sociales, Paris, 1988; Vis. Fellow, All Souls Coll., Oxford, 1991–92; Hans Kohn Mem., IAS, Princeton, 2004. Dr *hc* Bordeaux, 1987. *Publications:* The Parlement of Bordeaux, 1974; The Old European Order 1660–1800, 1978; Origins of the French Revolution, 1980; The Ancien Régime, 1986; (ed jtly) The Blackwell Dictionary of Historians, 1988; The Oxford History of the French Revolution, 1989; Officers, Nobles and Revolutionaries, 1995; Venality: the sale of offices in eighteenth century France, 1996; (ed jtly) Robespierre, 1999; Jansenism, 1999; La Vénalité, 2000; (ed) Old Regime France, 2001; The French Revolution: a very short introduction, 2001; contribs to Past and Present, Historical Jl, French Historical Studies, Studies on Voltaire, Trans RHistS. *Recreations:* books, decorating, travelling about. *Address:* (home) Linden House, College Road, Lansdown, Bath BA1 5RR. *T:* (01225) 314341. *Clubs:* Athenæum, Oxford and Cambridge.

DOYLE, William Patrick, PhD; President/Proprietor, Middle East-Asia Consultants, since 1997; President, Texaco Middle East/Far East, 1991–96; *b* 15 Feb. 1932; *s* of James W. Doyle and Lillian I. Doyle (*née* Kime); *m* 1957, Judith A. Gosha; two *s* one *d* (and one *s* decd). *Educ:* Seattle Univ. (BS 1955); Oregon State Univ. (PhD 1959). Texaco, USA: Chemist, 1959; Res. Supervisor, 1966; Asst to Vice Pres. of Petrochemicals, 1968; Asst to Sen. Vice Pres. of Supply and Distribn, 1971; Asst Manager, Producing, 1972; Asst Regional Man., Marketing, 1974; Texaco Ltd: Dep. Man. Dir, 1977; Man. Dir, Exploration and Production, 1981; Vice President: Texaco Europe, 1987; Texaco Latin America and Africa, 1989. Pres., UK Offshore Operators Assoc., 1985 (Vice Pres., 1984). Mem. Council, Amer. Geographic Soc., 1994–; Vice Chm., Forum of World Affairs, 1998. CCMI (FBIM 1980); MInstD 1982. *Publications:* contrib. Jl of Amer. Chem. Soc. *Recreations:* tennis, music, theatre. *Address:* PO Box 246, Williamsburg, VA 23187–0246, USA.

D'OYLY, Sir Hadley Gregory, 15th Bt *cr* 1663, of Shottisham, Norfolk; *b* 29 May 1956; *o s* of Sir Nigel D'Oyly, 14th Bt and Dolores, *d* of R. H. Gregory; *S* father, 2000; *m* 1st, 1978, Margaret May Dent (marr. diss. 1982); 2nd, 1991, Annette Frances Elizabeth (*née* White); two *d*. *Educ:* Milton Abbey.

DRABBLE, Jane; *see* Drabble, M. J.

DRABBLE, Dame Margaret, (Dame Margaret Holroyd), DBE 2008 (CBE 1980); author; *b* 5 June 1939; 2nd *d* of His Honour J.F. Drabble, QC and late Kathleen Marie Bloor; *m* 1st, 1960, Clive Walter Swift, *qv* (marr. diss. 1975); two *s* one *d*; 2nd, 1982, Michael (de Courcy Fraser) Holroyd (*see* Sir Michael Holroyd). *Educ:* The Mount Sch., York; Newnham Coll., Cambridge. Lives in London and W Somerset. Chm., Nat. Book League, 1980–82 (Dep. Chm., 1978–80). E. M. Forster Award, 1973, Hon. Mem., 2002, Amer. Acad. of Arts and Letters; Hon. Fellow, Sheffield City Polytechnic, 1989. Hon. DLitt: Sheffield, 1976; Manchester, 1987; Keele, 1988; Bradford, 1988; Hull, 1992; UEA, 1994; York, 1995; Cambridge, 2006. St Louis Literary Award, St Louis Univ. Liby Associates, 2003. *Publications:* A Summer Birdcage, 1963; The Garrick Year, 1964; The Millstone (John Llewellyn Rhys Prize), 1966 (filmed, as A Touch of Love, 1969); Jerusalem the Golden (James Tait Black Meml Prize), 1967; The Waterfall, 1969; The Needle's Eye, 1972; (ed with B. S. Johnson) London Consequences, 1972; The Realms of Gold, 1975; The Ice Age, 1977; The Middle Ground, 1980; The Radiant Way, 1987; A Natural Curiosity, 1989; The Gates of Ivory, 1991; The Witch of Exmoor, 1996; The Peppered Moth, 2001; The Seven Sisters, 2002; The Red Queen, 2004; The Sea Lady, 2006; *non-fiction:* Wordsworth, 1966; Arnold Bennett, a biography, 1974; (ed) The Genius of Thomas Hardy, 1976; (ed jtly) New Stories 1, 1976; For Queen and Country, 1978; A Writer's Britain, 1979; (ed) The Oxford Companion to English Literature, 5th edn, 1985, 6th edn 2000; (ed with Jenny Stringer) The Concise Oxford Companion to English Literature, 1987; Safe as Houses, 1989; Angus Wilson: a biography, 1995. *Recreations:* walking, dreaming. *Address:* c/o Peters, Fraser & Dunlop, Drury House, 34–43 Russell Street, WC2B 5HA.

See also R. J. B. Drabble.

DRABBLE, (Mary) Jane, OBE 2000; Director of Education, BBC, 1994–99; *b* 15 Jan. 1947; *d* of late Walter Drabble and of Molly (*née* Boreham). *Educ:* Bristol Univ. (BA Hons 1968). BBC: Studio Manager, 1968–72; Producer, Radio Current Affairs, 1972–75; Asst Producer, then Producer, TV Current Affairs, 1975–87; Editor, Everyman, 1987–91; Head of Factual Progs, 1993–94, Asst Man. Dir, 1991–94, Network TV. Comr for Judicial Appts, 2001–06; Capability Reviews Team, Cabinet Office, 2006–. Mem., LSC, 2000–06; Vice-Chm., Basic Skills Agency, 2001–04. Chair: Mental Health Media, 2002–06; Nat. Skills Academies Panel, 2005–; Arts Award Partnership Bd, 2005–. Dir, Birmingham Royal Ballet, 2002–; Gov., 2002–, Bd Mem., 2003–, RSC. *Recreations:* music, theatre, walking. *Address:* 2 Greenend Road, W4 1AJ.

DRABBLE, Richard John Bloor; QC 1995; *b* 23 May 1950; *s* of His Honour John Frederick Drabble, QC and late Kathleen Marie Drabble; *m* 1980, Sarah Madeleine Hope

Lewis; two *s* (and one *s* decd). *Educ:* Leighton Park Sch., Reading; Downing Coll., Cambridge (BA Hons). Called to the Bar, Inner Temple, 1975, Bencher, 2002; Junior Counsel to the Crown, Common Law, 1992. Chm., Administrative Law Bar Assoc., 1999–2001. *Publications:* (contrib.) Judicial Review, ed Supperstone and Goudie, 1992, 3rd edn 2006; (ed) Local Authorities and Human Rights, 2004; various articles. *Recreations:* reading, walking. *Address:* Landmark Chambers, 180 Fleet Street, EC4A 2HG. *T:* (020) 7430 1221.

See also Dame A. S. Byatt, Dame M. Drabble.

DRABU, Khurshid Hassan; a Senior Immigration Judge, Asylum and Immigration Tribunal (formerly a Vice President, Immigration Appeal Tribunal), since 2000; *b* Srinagar, Kashmir, 8 March 1946; *o s* of Ghulam Nabi and late Zarifa Nabi Drabu; *m* 1972, Reefat Khurshid Drabu, GP; one *s* three *d*. *Educ:* Univ. of Jammu and Kashmir (BA Hons 1967); Aligarh Muslim Univ., India (LLB 1st Cl., Gold Medal, 1969). Called to the Bar, Inner Temple, 1977; Counsellor, 1977–84, Dep. Dir, 1984–89, UKIAS; Dep. Legal Dir and Hd of Litigation, CRE, 1990–97; Special Adjudicator, Immigration Appeals, 1997–2000. Part-time Legal Mem., Mental Health Rev. Tribunal, 1987–2000. Muslim Council of Britain: Advr on Constitutional Affairs, 1996–; Convenor, Bd of Counsellors, 2006–; Chm., Friends, 2006–. Muslim Advr to MoD, 2002–; Advr, Fest. of Muslim Cultures, 2006–. Founder Trustee, Kashmir Med. Relief Trust UK, 1982–; Chm., Kashmiri Assoc. of GB, 1997–2005; Chm., Art Asia Trust Ltd, 1996–2002. Mem., Editl Bd, Immigration and Nationality, Law and Practice, 1985–89. Hon. Advr, British Muslims Human Rights Centre, 2006–. JP Eastleigh, 1985–98. Lifetime Achievement Award, Global Peace and Unity, 2007; Lifetime Achievement Award, Assoc. of Muslim Lawyers UK, 2007; 'Good Citizenship' Alija Izetbegović Prize, Muslim News Awards for Excellence, 2007. *Publication:* Mandatory Visas, 1991. *Recreations:* cricket, gardening, photography, travel.

DRACE-FRANCIS, Charles David Stephen, CMG 1987; *b* 15 March 1943; *m* 1967, Griselda Hyacinthe Waldegrave; two *s* one *d*. *Educ:* Magdalen Coll., Oxford. HM Diplomatic Service, 1965–2001: Third Sec., FO, 1965; Tehran, 1967; Second, later First Sec., FCO, 1971; Asst Political Advr, Hong Kong, 1974; First Sec., Office of UK Rep. to EEC, Brussels, 1978; FCO, 1980; All Souls Coll., Oxford, 1983; Chargé d'affaires, Kabul, 1984; Counsellor, Lisbon, 1987; Govt Affairs Dir, BAe, 1991 (on secondment); Head, West Indian and Atlantic Dept, FCO, 1994–97; High Comr, PNG, 1997–2000.

DRAINEY, Rt Rev. Terence Patrick; *see* Middlesbrough, Bishop of, (RC).

DRAKE, David Paul, FRCS, FRCPCH; Consultant Paediatric Surgeon, Great Ormond Street Hospital for Children, since 1988 (Medical Director, 2002–05); *b* 9 Feb. 1945; *s* of late Ronald Ingram Drake and of Diana Louisa Drake (*née* Markham); *m* 1976, Linda Ann Callear; two *s*. *Educ:* Clare Coll., Cambridge (MA; MB BChir). FRCS 1974; FRCPCH 1997. Hon. Sen. Lectr, Inst. of Child Health, Univ. of London, 1988–. Hon. Paediatric Surgeon, St Luke's Hosp. for the Clergy, 1989–2004. Mem., Christian Med. Fellowship. *Publications:* contrib. chapter on neonatal surgery to The New Aird's Companion in Surgical Studies, ed K. Burnand and A. Young, 1992, 2nd edn 1998; contrib. papers to surgical and paediatric jls on neonatal surgical and paediatric surgical topics. *Recreations:* swimming, sailing, water-colour painting. *Address:* 14 College Gardens, Dulwich, SE21 7BE. *T:* (020) 8693 3220, *Fax:* (020) 7813 8229; *e-mail:* Draked@gosh.nhs.uk. *Club:* Royal Society of Medicine.

DRAKE, Sir (Frederick) Maurice, Kt 1978; DFC 1944; a Judge of the High Court of Justice, Queen's Bench Division, 1978–95; *b* 15 Feb. 1923; *o s* of late Walter Charles Drake and Elizabeth Drake; *m* 1954, (Alison) May, *d* of late W. D. Waterfall, CB; two *s* three *d*. *Educ:* St George's Sch., Harpenden; Exeter Coll., Oxford. MA Hons 1948. Served War of 1939–45 as Navigator, RAF 96 and 255 Nightfighter Squadrons. Called to Bar, Lincoln's Inn, 1950, QC 1968, Bencher, 1976. Dep. Chm., Beds QS, 1966–71; a Recorder of the Crown Court, 1972–78; Dep. Leader, Midland and Oxford Circuit, 1975–78, Presiding Judge, 1979–83. Standing Senior Counsel to RCP, 1972–78. Nominated Judge for appeals from Pensions Appeal Tribunal, 1985–95. Vice-Chm., Parole Bd, England and Wales, 1985–86 (Mem., 1984–86). Treas., Lincoln's Inn, 1997. Chm. Governors, Aldwickbury Prep. Sch. (Trust), 1969–80; Governor, St George's Sch., Harpenden, 1975–79. Hon. Alderman, St Albans DC, 1976–. *Recreations:* music, opera, gardening. *Address:* The White House, West Common Way, Harpenden, Herts AL5 2LH. *T:* (01582) 712329.

DRAKE, Howard Ronald, OBE 2002; HM Diplomatic Service; Ambassador to Chile, since 2005; *b* 13 Aug. 1956; *s* of Ronald Henry Drake and late Marie Kathleen Drake; *m* 1988, Gillian Summerfield; one *s* one *d*. *Educ:* Churcher's Coll., Petersfield. Joined Foreign and Commonwealth Office, 1975; Vice-Consul (Commercial), Los Angeles, 1981–83; Second Sec. (Political), Santiago, 1985–88; First Sec., FCO, 1988–92; First Sec. and Head of Chancery, Singapore, 1992–95; Dep. Head, Non-Proliferation Dept, FCO, 1995–97; Dir, Invest in Britain Bureau USA, subseq. Invest UK-USA, and Dep. Consul-Gen., NY, 1997–2002; Asst Dir, Human Resources, FCO, 2002–05. *Recreations:* cricket, tennis, golf, squash, ski-ing, music. *Address:* c/o Foreign and Commonwealth Office, King Charles Street, SW1A 2AH.

DRAKE, Jack Thomas Arthur H.; *see* Howard-Drake.

DRAKE, John Gair; Chief Registrar and Chief Accountant, Bank of England, 1983–90; *b* 11 July 1930; *s* of John Nutter Drake and Anne Drake; *m* 1957, Jean Pamela Bishop; one *s* one *d*. *Educ:* University College School; The Queen's College, Oxford. MA. Joined Bank of England, 1953; editor, Quarterly Bulletin, 1971; Asst Chief Cashier, 1973; Management Development Manager, 1974; Dep. Chief, Economic Intell. Dept, 1977; Dep. Chief Cashier and Dep. Chief, Banking Dept, 1980. Governor, South Bank Univ. (formerly Poly.), 1987–96 (Hon. Fellow, 1997). *Address:* 42B Manor Avenue, Caterham, Surrey CR3 6AN. *T:* (01883) 346130. *Clubs:* MCC; Chaldon Cricket; Bletchingly Golf.

DRAKE, Julius Michael; pianist and accompanist; Director, Perth International Chamber Music Festival, Australia, 2001–03; *b* 5 April 1959; *s* of Michael Drake and late Jean Drake (known professionally as Jean Meikle); *m* 1987, Belinda, *d* of Gen. Sir (James) Michael Gow, *qv*; two *d*. *Educ:* Purcell Sch.; Royal Coll. of Music (ARCM). Débuts: Wigmore Hall, with Nicholas Daniel, 1983; Paris, with Sally Burgess, 1990; New York, with Derek Lee Ragin, 1991; Tokyo, with Emma Johnson, 1993; since 1983 has appeared regularly at all major concert halls in Europe and USA, with Victoria de los Angeles, Simon Keenlyside, Sir Thomas Allen, Olaf Bär, Ian Bostridge, Wolfgang Holzmair, Thomas Quasthoff, Angelika Kirchschlager, Dorothea Röschman, Alice Coote, Gerald Finley, Christopher Maltman, etc; has also performed in vocal and instrumental recitals in Amsterdam, Cologne, Salzburg Fest., Edinburgh Fest., Frankfurt, London, NY, Chicago, Paris, San Francisco, Vienna and Zurich; taken masterclasses in Amsterdam, Oxford, Vienna, Brussels, Porto, and Cleveland, Ohio. Devised song recital series: Schumann, S Bank, 1990; Britten, 1995–96, Nineties, 1997–98, Vaughan Williams, 2008–09, Wigmore Hall; Brahms, Concertgebouw Amsterdam, 2002–03; Schumann in the Temple: Julius Drake and Friends, Middle Temple Hall, 2005–06, 2007–08, 2008–09. Broadcasts include: presenting and performing Complete Songs of Gabriel Fauré (radio), 1994; with Ian Bostridge, Schubert's Winterreise (TV film and documentary), 1997. Recordings with world's leading singers incl. Britten Songs, Schumann Myrten op. 25, Howells Complete Songs, Schumann Dichterliebe, French Sonatas, Schubert Lieder (2 vols), Schumann Lieder, The English Songbook, Sibelius Songs, Gurney Songs, Britten Canticles, Ives Songs, Spanish Songs, Barber Songs, Mahler Songs, Schumann Frauenliebe und Leben, Grieg Songs, Schumann Heine Songs. Hon. FRAM. Gramophone Award, 1998; Edison Prize, 2002. *Recreations:* theatre, novels, walking, tennis. *Address:* c/o IMG Artists, The Light Box, 111 Power Road, Chiswick W4 5PY. *T:* (020) 7957 5800, *Fax:* (020) 8742 8758; *e-mail:* Bsegal@imgartists.com.

DRAKE, Madeline Mary; consultant and writer; Chief Executive, Richmond Fellowship, 1995–2001; *b* 5 Oct. 1945; *d* of Ernest and Olive Drake; *m* 1st, 1971, Anthony Gerald Biebuyck (marr. diss.); 2nd, 1983, Prof. Stephen Bernard Torrance; one *s* one *d*. *Educ:* Birmingham Univ. (BA Hons Russian/French; DipSocSc). Home Office researcher, 1972–73; researcher, Centre for Envmtl Studies, 1973–80; Founder and Dir Housing and Social Policy Res., 1980–95. Member, Board: Circle Thirty Three Gp 1976– (Vice-Chm., 1987–94); Shelter, 1987–; Mem. Council, Internat. Year for Shelter for Homeless, 1987. Lectures, broadcasts. FRSA; IPSM. *Publications:* Single and Homeless 1981; Homelessness: a capital problem, 1984; Managing Hostels, 1986; Housing Associations and 1992, 1992; Europe and 1992, 1992; numerous articles on housing Europe and the Soviet Union in nat. and internat. jls. *Recreations:* violin, walking, riding gardening. *Address:* 13 Quernmore Road, N4 4QT.

DRAKE, Sir Maurice; *see* Drake, Sir F. M.

DRAPER, Alan Gregory; Director, Defence Procurement Management Group, Royal Military College of Science, 1988–91; *b* 11 June 1926; *e s* of late William Gregory Draper and Ada Gertrude (*née* Davies); *m* 1st, 1953, Muriel Sylvia Cuss, FRSA (marr. diss.); three *s*; 2nd, 1977, Jacqueline Gubel (*d* 2006); one step *d*. *Educ:* Leeds Grammar Sch.; The Queen's Coll., Oxford (Scholar 1944; MA 1951). RNVR, 1945; Sub-Lt, 1946–47 Admiralty: Asst Principal, 1950; Private Sec. to Civil Lord of the Admiralty, 1953–55 MoD, 1957–60; Head of Polit. Sect., Admiralty 1960–64; First Sec., UK Delegn to NATO, 1964–66; Asst Sec., MoD, 1966; Counsellor, UK Delegn to NATO, 1974–77 Chm., NATO Budget Cttees, 1977–81; Royal Ordnance Factories: Personnel Dir 1982–84; Dir Gen., Personnel, 1984; Dir, Management/Career Develt, Royal Ordnance plc, 1985; Sen. Lectr, Defence Procurement, RMCS, 1986–91. MIPM 1985. *Publication* British Involvement in Major European Collaborative Defence Projects 1957–87, 1990 *Recreations:* reading, music, writing letters. *Address:* 8 rue du Logis, 85200 Bourneau France.

DRAPER, Gerald Carter, OBE 1974; Chairman: G. Draper Consultancy, since 1988 Draper Associates Ltd, 1982–88; *b* 24 Nov. 1926; *s* of Alfred Henderson Draper and Mona Violanta (*née* Johnson); *m* 1951, Winifred Lilian Howe; one *s* three *d*. *Educ:* Univ. of Dublin, Trinity Coll. (MA). FInstM, FCIT. Joined Aer Lingus, 1947; Advertising and PR Manager, 1950; Commercial Man., Central Afr. Airways, 1959; British European Airways: Advertising Man., 1964; Asst Gen. Man. (Market Develt), 1966; Gen. Man. and Dir, Travel Sales Div., 1970; British Airways: Dir, Travel Div., 1973; Marketing Dir 1977; Dir, Commercial Ops, 1978; Mem. Bd, 1978–82; Man. Dir, Intercontinental Services Div., 1982. Chairman: British Air Tours Ltd, 1978–82; Silver Wing Surface Arrangements Ltd, 1971–82; Deputy Chairman: Trust Houses Forte Travel Ltd, 1974–82 ALTA Ltd, 1977–82; Hoverspeed, 1984–87; Member Board: Internat. Aeradio Ltd 1971–82; British Airways Associated Cos Ltd, 1972–82; British Intercontinental Hotels Ltd, 1976–82; Communications Strategy Ltd, 1984–86; AGB Travel Research Internat Ltd, 1984–86; Centre for Airline and Travel Marketing Ltd, 1986–; BR (Southern Region), 1990–92; British Travel Educnl Trust, 1990–2005. Chm., Outdoor Advertising Assoc., 1985–92. Mem., Samuel Pepys Club. Master, Co. of Marketors, 1990; Mem. Guild of Freemen, 1991. FRSA 1979. Chevalier de l'Ordre du Tastevin, 1980 Chambellan de l'Ordre des Coteaux de Champagne, 1982. *Recreations:* shooting, golf *Address:* Old Chestnut, Onslow Road, Burwood Park, Walton-on-Thames, Surrey KT12 5AY. *Clubs:* British Sporting Rifle; National Clay Shooting Centre (Bisley).

DRAPER, Michael William; Under Secretary, Department of Health and Social Security, 1976–78, retired; *b* 26 Sept. 1928; *s* of late John Godfrey Beresford Draper and Aileen Frances Agatha Draper (*née* Masefield); *m* 1952, Theodora Mary Frampton, *o d* of late Henry James Frampton, CSI, CIE; one *s* two *d*. *Educ:* St Edward's Sch., Oxford. FCA Chartered Accountant, 1953; various posts in England, Ireland, Burma, Nigeria, Unilever Ltd, 1953–64; joined Civil Service, 1964; Principal, Min. of Power, 1964; Asst Sec DHSS, 1972–76. Sec., Diocese of Bath and Wells, 1978–88; mem. of staff team, Lamplugh House, Christian Renewal Conf. Centre, 1988–89; working with Anglican Church in Zambia, 1991; associated with Sharing of Ministries Abroad, 1992–2000. *Recreations* mountain walking, church affairs. *Address:* 21 Kent Park Avenue, Kendal, Cumbria LA9 5JT.

DRAPER, Prof. Paul Richard, PhD; Professor of Finance, and Head of School of Business and Economics, University of Exeter, since 2002; *b* 28 Dec. 1946; *s* of James Krishen Draper and Dorothy Jean Draper; *m* 1972, Janet Margaret Grant; one *s* one *d*. *Educ:* Univ. of Exeter (BA Econs 1968); Univ. of Reading (MA Econs 1969); Univ. of Stirling (PhD Finance 1973). Esmée Fairbairn Lectr, Univ. of St Andrews, 1973–75; Lectr Univ. of Edinburgh, 1976–78; University of Strathclyde: Esmée Fairbairn Sen. Lectr 1976–86, Prof., 1986–95; Hd, Dept of Accounting and Finance, 1990–95; Vice Dean Business Sch., 1993–97; University of Edinburgh: Walter Scott and Partners Prof. of Finance, 1997–2001; Hd, Sch. of Business and Econs, 2000–01. Dir, Thomas Hall Estates 2005–. Member: Panel for Accounting and Finance, 2001 and 2008 RAEs; Acad. Bd, Inst of Financial Services, 2005–. *Publications:* The Scottish Financial Sector (jtly), 1988 Investment Trust Industry in the UK, 1989; articles in Jl of Derivatives, Jl of Futures Markets, Jl of Financial Res., Jl of Business Finance and Accounting, European Financial Mgt, Financial Analysts Jl, etc. *Recreations:* travel, urban walking, houses. *Address:* School of Business and Economics, University of Exeter Streatham Court, Rennes Drive, Exeter EX4 4PU. *T:* (01392) 263218, *Fax:* (01392) 263256; *e-mail:* P.R.Draper@ex.ac.uk.

DRAPER, Peter Sydney, CB 1994; Director, City of Cambridge Brewery Company Ltd since 2002; Member, Civil Service Appeal Board, 1996–2002; *b* 18 May 1935; *s* of late Sydney George Draper and Norah Draper; *m* 1959, Elizabeth Ann (*née* French); three *s* *Educ:* Haberdashers' Aske's; Regent Polytechnic Sch. of Management (Dip. in Management Studies). Joined GCHQ, Cheltenham, 1953; Min. of Transport, 1956–70 Principal, 1969; Department of the Environment, 1970–95: Directorate of Estate Management Overseas, PSA, 1970; Asst Sec., 1975; Head of Staff Resources Div 1975–78; Asst Dir, Home Regional Services, 1978–80; RCDS, 1981; Dir, Eastern Reg 1982–84, Under Sec., Dir of Defence Services II, 1985–87, Principal Establishment Officer, 1987–93, Principal Estabt and Finance Officer, 1993–95, PSA. *Recreations* gardening, golf, walking. *Address:* Langdale, 22 Brewery Road, Pampisford, Cambs CB22 3EN. *Club:* Saffron Walden Golf.

DRAPER, Roger James; Chief Executive, Lawn Tennis Association, since 2006; *b* 19 Jan. 1970; *s* of Eric Draper and Marjorie Draper; *m* 1994, Nicola Entract; two *s. Educ:* Bolton Sch.; Winstanley Coll.; Loughborough Univ. (BSc Hons (PE, Sports Sci. and Recreation Mgt)). Dir of Develt, LTA, 1998–2002; Sport England: Chief Operating Officer, 2002–03; Chief Exec., 2003–06. MInstD 1999; Mem., Inst. of Leisure and Amenity Mgt, 2000–. *Recreations:* Rugby League (professional player, GB Students Rugby League, 1988–94), tennis (winner, British Univs Tennis Championship, 1989–92; senior county player; Captain, Lancs and Surrey, 1996–). *Address:* Lawn Tennis Association, National Tennis Centre, 100 Priory Lane, Roehampton, SW15 5JQ. *T:* (020) 8487 7000. *Club:* International Club of GB.

DRAPER, Prof. Ronald Philip, PhD; Regius Chalmers Professor of English, University of Aberdeen, 1986–94, now Professor Emeritus; *b* 3 Oct. 1928; *s* of Albert William and Elsie Draper; *m* 1950, Irene Margaret Aldridge; three *d. Educ:* Univ. of Nottingham (BA, PhD). Educn Officer, RAF, 1953–55. Lectr in English, Univ. of Adelaide, 1955–56; Lectr, Univ. of Leicester, 1957–68, Sen. Lectr, 1968–73; Prof., Univ. of Aberdeen, 1973–86. *Dramatic scripts:* (with P. A. W. Collins) The Canker and the Rose, Mermaid Theatre, 1964; (with Richard Hoggart) D. H. L., A Portrait of D. H. Lawrence, Nottingham Playhouse, 1967 (televised 1980). *Publications:* D. H. Lawrence, 1964, 3rd edn 1984; (ed) D. H. Lawrence, The Critical Heritage, 1970, 3rd edn 1986; (ed) Hardy, The Tragic Novels, 1975, rev. edn 1991; (ed) George Eliot, The Mill on the Floss and Silas Marner, 1977, 3rd edn 1984; (ed) Tragedy, Developments in Criticism, 1980; Lyric Tragedy, 1985; The Winter's Tale, Text and Performance, 1985; (ed) Hardy, Three Pastoral Novels, 1987; (ed) The Literature of Region and Nation, 1989; (with Martin Ray) An Annotated Critical Bibliography of Thomas Hardy, 1989; (ed) The Epic: developments in criticism, 1990; (ed with P. Mallett) A Spacious Vision: essays on Hardy, 1994; An Introduction to Twentieth-Century Poetry in English, 1999; Shakespeare: the comedies, 2000; contrib. Oxford DNB; articles and reviews in Archiv für das Studium der Neueren Sprachen und Literaturen, Critical Qly, Essays in Criticism, Etudes Anglaises, English Studies, Jl of D. H. Lawrence Soc., Lit. of Region and Nation, Longman Critical Essays, MLR, New Lit. Hist., Notes and Queries, Revue des Langues Vivantes, Rev. of English Studies, Shakespeare Qly, Studies in Short Fiction, THES, Thomas Hardy Annual, Thomas Hardy Jl. *Recreations:* reading, listening to music. *Address:* Maynestay, Chipping Campden, Glos GL55 6DJ. *T:* (01386) 840796.

DRAYCOTT, Simon Douglas; QC 2002; a Recorder, since 2000; *b* 29 Sept. 1950; *s* of Douglas and Elizabeth Draycott; three *d. Educ:* Uppingham; Guildhall Sch. of Music and Drama; Coll. of Law. Called to the Bar, Middle Temple, 1977. *Recreation:* sailing. *Address:* 5 St Andrews Hill Chambers, EC4V 5BZ.

DRAYSON, family name of **Baron Drayson**.

DRAYSON, Baron *cr* 2004 (Life Peer), of Kensington in the Royal Borough of Kensington and Chelsea; **Paul Rudd Drayson;** PC 2008; PhD; Minister of State, Department for Innovation, Universities and Skills, since 2008; Founder, Drayson Motor Racing LLP; *b* 5 March 1960; *s* of Michael Rudd Drayson and Ruth Irene Drayson; *m* 1994, Elspeth Jane Bellhouse; three *s* two *d. Educ:* St Dunstan's Coll., London; Aston Univ. (BSc Hons; PhD). Man. Dir, Lambourn Food Co., 1986–91; founder and Dir, Genysys Develt Ltd, 1991–95; co-founder, 1993 and Chief Exec., 1993–2003, PowderJect Pharmaceuticals; Entrepreneur in Residence, Saïd Business Sch., Oxford Univ., 2003–05. Parly Under-Sec. of State, MoD, 2005–07; Minister of State, MoD and BERR, 2007. Chm., BioIndustry Assoc., 2001–02. Chm., Oxford Children's Hosp. Campaign, 2002–05. *Recreations:* sword fencing, motor racing. *Address:* House of Lords, SW1A 0PW. *Club:* Salle d'Armes.

DRAYSON, Robert Quested, DSC 1943; MA; *b* 5 June 1919; *s* of late Frederick Louis Drayson and late Elsie Mabel Drayson; *m* 1943, Rachel, 2nd *d* of Stephen Spencer Jenkyns; one *s* two *d. Educ:* St Lawrence Coll., Ramsgate; Downing Coll., Cambridge, 1938–39, 1946–47 (History Tripos, BA 1947; MA 1950). Served RNVR, 1939–46; Lieut in command HM Motor Torpedo Boats. Asst Master and Housemaster, St Lawrence Coll., 1947–50; Asst Master, Felsted Sch., 1950–55; Headmaster, Reed's Sch., Cobham, 1955–63; Headmaster of Stowe, 1964–79; Resident Lay Chaplain to Bishop of Norwich, 1979–84; Lay Reader, 1979. Member: HMC Cttee, 1973–75 (Chm., Midland Div., 1974–75); Council, McAlpine Educnl Endowments Ltd, 1979–97; Allied Schools Council, 1980–94; Gen. Council, S Amer. Missionary Soc., 1980–96 (Chm. Selection Cttee, 1980–95); Scholarship Cttee, Indep. Schs Travel Assoc., 1982–2003; Martyrs' Meml and C of E Trust, 1983–94. Treas., Swifts Sports Trust, 1988–2004. Chm. of Govs, Riddlesworth Hall, 1980–84; Governor: Parkside, 1958–63; Beachborough, 1965–79; Bilton Grange, 1966–79; Beechwood Park, 1967–79; Monkton Combe, 1976–85; Felixstowe Coll., 1981–84; Vice President: Reed's Sch., 1991–; St Lawrence Coll., 1993– (Gov., 1977–93). Chm., E Sussex Coastal Forces Veterans Assoc., 2000–; Organiser, Sandhurst WRVS Social Car Service, 1988–2008 (Queen's Long Service Medal). FRSA 1968. *Recreations:* formerly hockey (Cambridge Blue, 1946, 1947; Kent XI (Captain), 1947–56; England Final Trial, 1950); now walking, reading. *Address:* Three Gables, Linkhill, Sandhurst, Cranbrook, Kent TN18 5PQ. *T:* (01580) 850447. *Clubs:* Hawks (Cambridge); Acrostics; Rye Golf; Band of Brothers.

See also Dame G. M. Pugh.

DRECHSLER, Paul Joseph; Executive Chairman, Wates Group Ltd, since 2006 (Chief Executive, 2004–06); *b* 16 April 1956; *s* of Frank Stephen Drechsler and Marie Winifred Drechsler (*née* Clancy); *m* 1981, Wendy Isobel Hackett; two *s* one *d. Educ:* Trinity Coll., Dublin (BA); INSEAD (IEP). Chief Executive Officer: ICI Brasil SA, 1992; ICI Acrylics Inc., 1993–96; ICI Polyester, 1996–98; Quest Internat., 1998–2003; Exec. Dir, ICI plc, 1999–2003. Sen. Ind. Dir, Filtrona plc, 2005–. Mem., Adv. Bd, Business Sch., TCD, 2005–. *Recreations:* Blues music, ski-ing, golf, family vacations, music of Eric Clapton. *Address:* Wates Group Ltd, Wates House, Station Approach, Leatherhead, Surrey KT22 7SW. *T:* (01372) 861071, *Fax:* (01372) 861072; *e-mail:* Paul.Drechsler@Wates.co.uk.

DREHER, Derek; Consultant, Northern Ireland Office, since 1997; *b* 12 Jan. 1938; *s* of Frederick Charles Dreher and Mary Emily Dreher (*née* Rutherford); *m* 1961, Patricia Audrey Dowsett; one *s* one *d. Educ:* Roan Grammar Sch., Greenwich. Joined War Office as Exec. Officer, 1956; Nat. Service, RAF, 1956–58 (trained as Russian linguist); with War Office, 1958–64, then MoD; postings include: Cyprus, 1962–65; NI, 1969–71; on secondment to Treasury, 1976–79; Asst Sec., 1980; Asst Under Sec. of State, 1992–97. *Recreations:* all forms of sport, but particularly tennis, theatre, foreign travel, reading, particularly political works. *Address:* Kantara, Church Road, Hartley, Kent DA3 8DL. *Club:* Hartley Country.

DREW, David Elliott; MP (Lab and Co-op) Stroud, since 1997; *b* 13 April 1952; *s* of Ronald Montague Drew and late Maisie Joan Drew; *m* 1990, Anne Baker, *d* of Brian and Sheila Baker; two *s* two *d. Educ:* Kingsfield Sch., Glos; Nottingham Univ. (BA Hons 1974); Birmingham Univ. (PGCE 1976); Bristol Poly., later UWE (MA 1988; MEd 1994). Teacher: Princethorpe Coll., Warwicks, 1976–78; St Michael's Sch., Stevenage, 1978–82; Maidenhill Sch., Glos, 1982–85; Dene Magna Sch., Glos, 1985–86; Sen. Lectr, Bristol Poly., later UWE, 1986–97. Member: Stevenage BC, 1981–82; Stroud DC, 1987–95; Stonehouse Town Council, 1987–; Glos CC, 1993–97. Contested (Lab) Stroud, 1992. *Address:* House of Commons, SW1A 0AA.

DREW, David Ernest, MBE 2006; Character Principal Dancer, Royal Ballet, since 1974; choreographer; Founder, Ballet Scenarios, 2007; *b* London, 12 March 1938; *s* of Thomas Ernest Drew and Phyllis Adelaide (*née* Talbot-Tindale); *m* 1st, 1962, Avril Bergen (marr. diss. 1973); one *s*; 2nd, 1985, June Ritchie; one step *d. Educ:* Bristol Grammar Sch.; Westbury Sch. of Dancing, Bristol; Royal Ballet Upper Sch. Nat. Service, commnd RCS, 1958–60. Joined Royal Ballet at Royal Opera House, Covent Gdn, 1955: Soloist, 1961; Prin. Dancer, 1974; *created rôles* with Royal Ballet include: Bay Middleton, Mayerling; Demetrius, The Dream; Max Merx, Isadora; Celestial, Shadow-Play; Gaoler, Manon; The Master, Rituals; The Captain, Different Drummer; Leading Baboon, Prince of the Pagodas; G. B. Shaw, Grand Tour; Giles, The Crucible; *major rôles* include: Von Rothbart, Swan Lake; Monsieur G. M., Manon; Hilarion and Duke of Courtland, Giselle; Thomas, La Fille Mal Gardée; Catalabutte and King, Sleeping Beauty; Mercutio, Lord Capulet and Tybalt, Romeo and Juliet; Ugly Sister, Cinderella; Ivan and Kostchei, The Firebird; Mrs Pettitoes, Tales of Beatrix Potter; Armand's Father, Marguerite and Armand; Rajah and Brahmin, La Bayadère; *choreographic work* includes: five ballets for Sadler's Wells Royal Ballet: Intrusion, 1969; From Waking Sleep, 1970; St Thomas' Wake, 1971; Sacred Circles, 1972; Sword of Alsace, 1973; *musicals* include: Canterbury Tales, 1968; His Monkey Wife, 1970; *operas* include: Dido and Aeneas; Macbeth; Die Fledermaus; writer of scenario, The Three Musketeers, Northern Ballet Th., 2006; also contribs to theatre and TV. Teacher, Royal Ballet Upper Sch., Pas de Deux at all levels, incl. Grad. Class, 1976–99; assisted in Direction of Choreographic Composition Course, 1986–99. Founder Pres., Ballet Assoc., 1975. Gold Medal, Royal Acad. of Dancing, 1954. *Recreations:* writing, gardening, theatre, art, photography, playing and inventing games. *Address:* c/o Royal Opera House, Covent Garden, WC2 9DD.

DREW, Dorothy Joan; a Vice President, Immigration Appeal Tribunal, 2000–01; *b* 31 March 1938; *d* of late Francis Marshall Gant and Wilhelmina Frederica Gant (*née* Dunster); *m* 1959, Patrick K. Drew; two *s* one *d. Educ:* Sch. of St Helen and St Katharine; Univ. of London (LLB ext.). Called to the Bar, Gray's Inn, 1981; Chm. (pt-time), Social Security Appeal Tribunal, 1986–92; Adjudicator, Immigration Appeal Tribunal, 1989–93 (Special Adjudicator, 1993–2000); Regl Adjudicator, Hatton Cross, 1998–2000; Chm., Child Support Appeal Tribunal, 1993–94. JP Reading, 1975–95. *Recreations:* music, theatre, family and friends, walking in Cornwall.

DREW, John Sydney Neville; Jean Monnet Visiting Professor of European Business and Government, European Business School, London, since 2007; *b* 7 Oct. 1936; *s* of late John William Henry Drew and Kathleen Marjorie (*née* Wright); *m* 1962, Rebecca Margaret Amanda (*née* Usher); two *s* one *d. Educ:* King Edward's Sch., Birmingham; St John's Coll., Oxford (MA); Fletcher School of Law and Diplomacy, Tufts Univ. (AM). Sloan Fellow of London Business Sch., 1971. 2nd Lieut, Somerset LI, 1955–57. HM Diplomatic Service, 1960–73: Third Sec., Paris, 1962; MECAS, 1964; Second Sec., Kuwait, 1965; First Sec., Bucharest, 1968; FCO, 1970; Dir of Marketing and Exec. Programmes, London Business Sch., 1973–79; Dir of Internat. Corporate Affairs, Rank Xerox, 1979–84; Dir of European Affairs, Touche Ross Internat., 1984–86; Head of UK Offices, EEC, 1987–93; Dir, Europa Times, 1993–94; Dep. Chm., ESG, 1993–95; Dir, Change Gp Internat., 1996–2003. Associate Fellow, Templeton Coll., Oxford, 1982–86; Visiting Professor of European Management: Imperial Coll. of Science and Technology, 1987–91; Open Univ., 1993–99. Durham University: Special Advr, Howlands Trust, 1994–95; Dir, Res. Inst. for the Study of Change, subseq. Chm., Durham Res. Inst., later Durham Inst., 1996–2003; Vis. Prof. of European Business, 1995–2004. Chm., DSL Ltd, 1995–97. President: Inst. of Linguists, 1993–99 (Hon. FIL 1993); European Transpersonal Assoc., 1998–2003. Trustee, Thomson Foundn, 1996–2007. Hon. Editor, European Business Jl, 1987–2002. Hon. MBA Univ. of Northumbria, 1991. *Publications:* Doing Business in the European Community, 1979, 3rd edn 1991 (trans. Spanish and Portuguese 1987); Networking in Organisations, 1986; (ed) Readings in International Enterprise, 1995, 2nd edn 1999; (ed) Ways Through the Wall, 2005; articles on European integration and management development. *Recreations:* travel, personal development, golf. *Address:* 49 The Ridgeway, NW11 8QP. *Club:* Oxford and Cambridge.

DREW, Philippa Catherine, CB 2001; Chair, Diplomatic Service Appeal Board, since 2006; *b* 11 May 1946; *d* of Sir Arthur Charles Walter Drew, KCB and Rachel Anna Drew (*née* Lambert). *Educ:* St Paul's Girls' Sch.; St Anne's Coll., Oxford (MA Hons 1968 PPE); Univ. of Pennsylvania (MA Hons 1969 Internat. Relations). Foreign and Commonwealth Office: Central and Southern Africa Dept, 1969; New Delhi, 1970–74; First Sec., S Asia Dept, 1974–75; Home Office: EEC Referendum Count Unit, 1975; Criminal Dept, 1975–78; Police Dept, 1978–81; Gen. Dept, 1981–84; Prison Dept, 1984–85; Field Dir, SCF, Nepal, 1985–87; Head, Probation Service Div., 1987–91; Dir of Custody, HM Prison Service, 1992–95; Dir, Personnel and Office Services, then Corporate Resources, Home Office, 1995–99; Dir for Educn, Trng, Arts and Sport, DCMS, 1999–2002; Dir, Global Issues, FCO, 2002–06. Member: London Probation Bd, 2007–; Bd, Oxford Research Gp, 2007–. *Recreations:* opera, travel, talk. *Address:* 12 Thorney Hedge Road, Chiswick, W4 5SD. *T:* (020) 8747 0836.

See also J. R. Bretherton.

DREWIENKIEWICZ, Maj.-Gen. Karol John, CB 1998; CMG 2000; Consultant, Peace Support Operations, 2001, 2003 and since 2006; *b* 2 Jan. 1946; *s* of late Wojciech Drewienkiewicz and of Barbara Drewienkiewicz; *m* 1970, Christine Elizabeth Bailey; two *s. Educ:* Stamford Sch.; RMA, Sandhurst; Sidney Sussex Coll., Cambridge (BA 1970; MA 1974; Hon. Fellow, 2007). Commnd RE, 1966; Staff Coll., Camberley, 1978 and 1985; CO, 22 Engr Regt, 1985–88; Sec. to UK Chiefs of Staff, MoD, 1988–90; Comdr, RE Trng Bde, 1990–91; RCDS 1992; Dir of Manning, Army, 1993–94; Engr-in-Chief, Army, 1994–95; Dir of Support, HQ Allied Land Forces, Central Europe, 1995–96; COS HQ IFOR/SFOR (Sarajevo), 1996–97; Comdg Gen., SFOR Support Comd (Zagreb), May–Aug. 1997; Dir of Support, HQ Allied Land Forces, Central Europe, Sept.–Dec. 1997; Mil. Advr to High Representative, Sarajevo, 1998; Dep. Hd of Mission, OSCE Kosovo Verification Mission, 1998–99; Sen. Army Mem., RCDS, 1999–2000; retd 2001; Chief, Plans, 2002, Dir and Mil. Advr to High Representative, Sarajevo, 2004–05, Dept for Security Co-operation, OSCE Mission to Bosnia and Herzegovina. Vis. Fellow, Dept of Internat. Studies, Univ. of Cambridge, 2002–03. Trustee: Haig Homes, 2004–; Cleared Ground Demining, 2006–. Pres., Cambridge Univ. Engrs Alumni, 2006–. Pres., American Civil War Round Table UK, 2007–. *Publications:* Training the Territorial Army in 1939 and 1940, 1992; (contrib.) The Battle for France and Flanders Sixty Years On, 2001; Budgets as Arms Control, 2003. *Recreations:* military history, wargaming, gardening. *Address:* c/o Cox's & Kings, 7 Pall Mall, SW1Y 5NA.

DREWITT, (Lionel) Frank; Managing Director, Harrods Ltd, 1984–87; *b* 24 Sept. 1932; *s* of William and Jeanne Drewitt; *m* 1959, Doris Else Heybrok; three *d*. *Educ:* London Univ. (BSc Econ). FCA. National Service, 1951–53. Wells & Partners, later Thornton Baker, 1956–64; Chartered Accountant, 1961; joined Harrods Store group, 1964; positions incl. Asst Internal Auditor, Chief Accountant, Company Sec., Asst Man. Dir. *Recreation:* cottages.

DREWRY, Prof. David John; Vice-Chancellor and Professor, University of Hull, since 1999; *b* 22 Sept. 1947; *s* of late Norman Tidman Drewry and Mary Edwina Drewry (*née* Wray); *m* 1971, Gillian Elizabeth (*née* Holbrook). *Educ:* Havelock School, Grimsby; Queen Mary Coll., Univ. of London (BSc 1st cl. hons 1969; Hon. Fellow, QMW, 1992); Emmanuel College, Cambridge (PhD 1973; Hon. Fellow, 2007). FRGS 1972, CGeog 2002. UK-US Antarctic Expdns, 1969–70 and 1971–72; Sir Henry Strakosh Fellow, 1974; UK-US Antarctic Expdns, 1974–75, 1977–78 (leader), 1978–79 (leader); Sen. Asst in Research, Univ. of Cambridge, 1978–83; leader, UK-Norwegian Svalbard Expdns, 1980, 1983, 1985, 1986; Asst Dir of Research, Univ. of Cambridge, 1983; Director: Scott Polar Res. Inst., Univ. of Cambridge, 1984–87; British Antarctic Survey, 1987–94; Sci. and Technol., NERC, 1994–98; Dir Gen., British Council, 1998. Vis. Fellow, Green Coll., Oxford, 1995; Vis. Prof., QMW, 1996–98; Vis. Scholar, Univ. of Cambridge, 1999; Guest Prof., Xiamen Univ., China, 2006–. Vice-President: Council, RGS, 1990–93 (Mem., 1986–93 and 1995–96); Council, Internat. Glaciological Soc., 1990–96 (Mem., 1980–82); Member: Council of Managers, Nat. Antarctic Programmes, 1988–95 (Chm., 1988–91); Royal Soc. Interdisciplinary Scientific Cttee on Antarctic Res., 1990–98; Internat. Arctic Sci. Cttee, 1994–2002 (Pres., 1997–2002); Exec. Council, ESF, 1996–98 (Mem., Eur. Polar Bd); Trustee, Antarctic Heritage Trust, 1993–; UK alternate deleg., Sci. Cttee on Antarctic Res., 1985–97. Trustee, Nat. History Mus., 2008–. Chm., Yorkshire Univs, 2002–04; Mem., Yorkshire Science, 2005–. Non-executive Director: Hull Urban Regeneration Co., 2003–; The Deep, 2006–. CCMI (Pres., Humberside Br., 2002–04); FRSA 1998. Hon. DSc: Robert Gordon, 1993; Humberside, 1994; Anglia Poly. Univ., 1998. US Antarctic Service Medal, 1979; Cuthbert Peek Award, 1979, Patron's Medal, 1998, RGS; Polar Medal, 1986; Prix de la Belgica Gold Medal, Royal Acad. of Belgium, 1995. *Publications:* Antarctica: glaciological and geophysical folio, 1983; Glacial Geologic Processes, 1986; papers on polar glaciology, geophysics, remote sensing, science policy in learned jls. *Recreations:* music, ski-ing, walking, gastronomy. *Address:* University of Hull, Hull HU6 7RX. *T:* (01482) 465131. *Clubs:* Athenæum, Geographical.

DREYFUS, Prof. Laurence, PhD; FBA 2002; Professor of Music, University of Oxford, since 2006 (Lecturer, 2005–06); Fellow of Magdalen College, Oxford, since 2005; *b* Boston, Mass, 28 July 1952; naturalised British citizen, 2002. *Educ:* studied 'cello with Leonard Rose, Juilliard Sch.; Yeshiva Univ. (BA Pol Sci. 1973); Columbia Univ. (MA 1975, MPhil 1976, PhD 1980, in Musicology); studied viola da gamba with Wieland Kuijken, Royal Conservatory, Brussels, 1979–81 (Premier Prix, 1980; Diplôme supérieur, 1981). Lectr, Univ. of Wisconsin-Madison, 1979; Mellon Fellow in Humanities, Columbia Univ., 1979–81; Asst Prof., Washington Univ. in St Louis, 1981–82; Asst Prof., 1982–88, Associate Prof. of History of Music and Sen. Faculty Fellow, 1988–89, Yale Univ.; Associate Professor of Music: Univ. of Chicago, 1989–90; Stanford Univ., 1990–93; King's College, London: Prof. of Perf. Studies in Music, with the RAM, 1992–96; Thurston Dart Prof. of Perf. Studies in Music, 1996–2005; Hd, Dept of Music, 1995–99. *Appearances* include: Bergen Fest., Norway, 1990; Early Music Network tour of GB, 1990; Utrecht Early Music Fest., 1991; San Francisco SO, 1992; Skálholt Music Fest., Iceland, 1992–95; London Bach Fest., 1993, 1994; Three Choirs Fest., 2006; Edinburgh Fest., 2007. Dir-at-Large, Amer. Musicol Soc., 1989–91 (Otto Kinkeldey Prize, 1997); Vice-Pres., Amer. Bach Soc., 1992–94; Mem. Council, RMA, 1994–98. Hon. RAM 1995. First Prize, Bodky Competition in Early Music, Boston, 1978. Several solo and chamber recordings, incl. Purcell's Complete Fantasies for Viols (Gramophone award for best baroque instrumental recording, 1997) and Orlando Gibbons' Consorts for Viols (Gramophone award, 2004). Jt Gen. Ed., Musical Performance and Reception (formerly Cambridge Musical Texts and Monographs), 1994–. *Publications:* Bach's Continuo Group: players and practices in his vocal works, 1987; Bach and the Patterns of Invention, 1996; (contrib.) The Cambridge Companion to Bach, 1997; papers, and articles in jls. *Address:* Magdalen College, Oxford OX1 4AU. *T:* (01865) 276038; *e-mail:* laurence.dreyfus@magd.ox.ac.uk.

DRIELSMA, Sir Claude Dunbar H.; *see* Hankes-Drielsma.

DRIFE, Prof. James Owen, MD; FRCOG, FRCSE, FRCPE; Professor of Obstetrics and Gynaecology, University of Leeds, since 1990; *b* 8 Sept. 1947; *s* of late Thomas Drife and Rachel Drife (*née* Jones); *m* 1973, Diana Elizabeth, *d* of late Ronald Haxton Girdwood, CBE; one *s* one *d*. *Educ:* Cumnock Acad.; Univ. of Edinburgh (BSc Hons; MB ChB 1971; MD 1982). FRCPE 1998. Hosp. appts, Edinburgh, 1971–79; MRC Res. Fellow in Reproductive Biology, Edinburgh, 1974–76; Lectr in Obst. and Gyn., Univ. of Bristol, 1979–82; Dept of Surgery, Frenchay Hosp., Bristol, 1980–81; Sen. Lectr, Obst. and Gyn., Univ. of Leicester, 1982–90. Non-Exec. Dir, United Leeds Teaching Hosps NHS Trust, 1991–98. Mem., Cases Cttee, Medical Protection Soc., 1985–94; Assessor for England, Enquiries into Maternal Deaths, 1992–; Mem., Midwifery Cttee, UKCC, 1993–99; Mem. Council, RCOG, 1993–2008 (Convenor of Study Gp, 1989–92; Chm., Liby Cttee, 1994–97; Jun. Vice-Pres., 1998–2001); Mem., GMC, 1994–2005; Chairman: Assoc. of Profs of Obstetrics and Gynaecology, 2002–06; Academic Assoc. of Obstetrics and Gynaecology, 2006–07; Pres., N of England Obstetric and Gynaecol Soc., 2007–08. FRSA 1997. Hon. FASPOG, 1988; Hon. Fellow, Amer. Gynecol and Obstetrical Soc., 1998; Hon. FCOG(SA) 2002; Hon. Mem., Jordanian Soc. of Obstetricians and Gynaecologists, 2000. Editor or co-editor, obst. and gyn. jls, 1985–; Co-Editor-in-Chief, Eur. Jl of Obstetrics and Gynaecology, 2003–. *Publications:* Dysfunctional Uterine Bleeding and Menorrhagia, 1989; (jtly) Micturition, 1990; (with J. Studd) HRT and Osteoporosis, 1990; (with D. Donnai) Antenatal Diagnosis of Fetal Abnormalities, 1991; (with A. Calder) Prostaglandins and the Uterus, 1992; (with A. Templeton) Infertility, 1992; (with D. Baird) Contraception, 1993; The Benefits and Risks of Oral Contraceptives, 1994; (with J. J. Walker) Caesarean Section, 2001; (with B. Magowan) Clinical Obstetrics and Gynaecology, 2004; (jtly) Obstetrics and Gynaecology for the MRCOG, 2004; contribs to BMJ. *Recreations:* songwriting (founder Mem., Abracadabarets; perf. at Edinburgh Fringe Fest., 1974, 1979, 1982, 1989, 1997, 2000, 2002, 2007), theatre going, visiting the pub with wife. *Address:* School of Medicine, Clarendon Wing, Belmont Grove, Leeds LS2 9NS. *T:* (0113) 292 3888. *Clubs:* Athenæum, National Liberal, Royal Society of Medicine.

DRING, Richard Paddison; Editor of Official Report (Hansard), House of Commons, 1972–79; *b* 6 Nov. 1913; *s* of late Fred Dring and late Florence Hasleham Dring, East Sheen; *m* 1939, Joan Wilson (*d* 1999); one *s*; *m* 2000, Margaret Foorde (*d* 2007). *Educ:* St Paul's School. Captain, RAOC during the War, serving in Europe and later in India with IA. Herts Advertiser, 1932; Press Association, 1936; Official Report (Hansard), House of Commons, 1940: Asst Editor, 1954; Dep. Editor, 1970. *Recreation:* golf. *Address:* 28 Vicarage Drive, SW14 8RX. *T:* (020) 8878 6604. *Club:* Richmond Golf.

DRINKALL, John Kenneth, CMG 1973; HM Diplomatic Service, retired; High Commissioner to Jamaica, and Ambassador (non-resident) to Haiti, 1976–81; *b* 1 Jan 1922; *m* 1961, Patricia Ellis; two *s* two *d*. *Educ:* Haileybury Coll.; Brasenose Coll., Oxford Indian Army, 1942–45. Entered HM Foreign Service, 1947; 3rd Sec., Nanking, 1948 Vice-Consul, Tamsui, Formosa, 1949–51; Acting Consul, 1951; Foreign Office, 1951–53 1st Sec., Cairo, 1953–56; Foreign Office, 1957–60; 1st Sec., Brasilia, 1960–62; Foreign Office, 1962–65. Appointed Counsellor, 1964; Counsellor: Nicosia, Cyprus, 1965–67 British Embassy, Brussels, 1967–70; FCO, 1970–71; Canadian Nat. Defence Coll. 1971–72; Ambassador to Afghanistan, 1972–76. *Recreations:* lawn tennis, golf, racquets and squash. *Address:* 68 Rivermead Court, Ranelagh Gardens, SW6 3RZ. *Clubs:* Hurlingham All England Lawn Tennis.

DRINKWATER, Surgeon Rear-Adm. John Brian, FRCS; Clinical Medical Officer Community Child Health, Mid Argyll, Kintyre, Islay and Jura, 1989–97; *b* 5 June 1931; of Ellis Drinkwater and Hilda May Drinkwater; *m* 1958, Rosalind Joy Taylor; two *d*; 1986, Carole Anne Coutts; two *d*. *Educ:* Henry Mellish Grammar Sch., Nottingham Sheffield Univ. Med. Sch. (MB, ChB). FRCS 1961. House appts, 1954–55; joined RN 1955: SMO, 6th FS (Cyprus, Suez), 1955–57; RN Hosp., Haslar, 1957; Hammersmith Hosp., 1961; HMS Ganges, 1962; RN Hosps, Malta, Gibraltar, Plymouth, Haslar 1962–67; Gt Ormond St Hosp., 1967; Consultant Surgeon, RN Hosps, 1968–82; Adv in Surgery, 1981–82; Dir of Medical Orgn, 1982–83; MO i/c RN Hosp., Haslar 1983–84; QHS 1983–87; Dep. Med. Dir Gen. (Naval), 1984; Surgeon Rear-Adm (Operational Med. Services), 1985–87; Dir of Support Services, Muscular Dystrophy Gp 1987–88. Member: British Soc. for Digestive Endoscopy, 1972; British Soc. of Gastroenterology, 1980–83. FRSM 1961; Fellow, Assoc. of Surgeons, 1974. OStJ 1983 *Recreations:* music, bridge. *Address:* c/o HSBC, 567 Fulham Road, SW6 1EX.

DRINKWATER, Sir John (Muir), Kt 1988; QC 1972; a Commissioner of Income Tax 1983–2000; *b* 16 March 1925; *s* of late Comdr John Drinkwater, OBE, RN (retd); *m* 1st 1952, Jennifer Marion (*d* 1990), *d* of Edward Fitzwalter Wright, Morley Manor, Derbs one *s* three *d* (and one *d* decd); 2nd, 1998, Deirdre, *d* of Derek Curtis-Bennett, QC and *widow* of James Boscawen. *Educ:* RNC Dartmouth. HM Submarines, 1943–47; Flag Lieu to C-in-C Portsmouth and First Sea Lord, 1947–50; Lt-Comdr 1952; invalided 1953 Called to Bar, Inner Temple, 1957, Bencher, 1979; a Recorder, 1972–90. Mem., Parl Boundary Commn for England, 1977–80. Mem. Bd, British Airports Authy, 1985–87 Dir, BAA plc, 1987–94. Life Mem. Council, SPAB, 1982. Pres., Cotswold Cons. Assoc 1999– (Chm., 1995–99). Governor, St Mary's Hosp., 1960–64. *Recreations:* gardening reading, travel. *Address:* Glebe Court, Fairford, Glos GL7 4JL. *T:* (01285) 712305 Lohitzun, 64120 St Palais, France. *Clubs:* Garrick, Pratt's.

DRISCOLL, Daphne Jane; *see* Todd, D. J.

DRISCOLL, James; Senior Partner, Woodcote Consultancy Services, 1990–96; *b* 24 Apr 1925; *s* of Henry James Driscoll and Honorah Driscoll; *m* 1955, Jeanne Lawrenc Williams, BA, CertEd; one *s* one *d*. *Educ:* Coleg Sant Illtyd, Cardiff; University Coll Cardiff (BA 1st Cl. Hons). Chm., Welsh Young Conservatives, 1948–49; Nat. Dep Chm., Young Conservatives, 1950; Dep. Chm., Univ. Cons. Fedn, 1949–50; Dep. Chm NUS, 1951–53. Vice-Chm., European Youth Campaign, 1951–53. Contested (C Rhondda West, 1950. Asst Lectr, UC Cardiff, 1950–53; Council of Europe Re Fellowship, 1953. Joined British Iron and Steel Fedn, 1953; various econ. and interna posts; Econ. Dir and Dep. Dir-Gen., 1963–67; various posts, British Steel Corporatior 1967–80; Man. Dir, Corporate Strategy, 1971–76, Board Adviser, 1976–80; Di 1976–90, Policy Advr, 1990–96, NICG; Chm. and Man. Dir, Woodcote Consultants Lt 1980–90; Chm., Webb Estate Ltd, 2001–03. Chm., Lifecare NHS Trust, 1990–9 Member: Grand Council, FBI, 1957–65; CBI Council, 1970–93; Observer, NEDC 1977–91; Lay Mem., Investigation Cttee, ICA, 1991–96. Chm., Econ. Studies Ctte Internat. Iron and Steel Inst., 1972–74. Vice-Chm., Croydon Mencap Ltd, 1997–200 Mem., Court of Governors, Cardiff Univ. (formerly UC, Cardiff, then Univ. of Wal Coll. of Cardiff), 1970–2005 (Fellow, 1986). FREconS; FRSA. *Publications:* vario articles and pamphlets on econ. and internat. affairs, esp. steel affairs, European integratio wages policy and financing of world steel investment. *Recreations:* travel, bridge, readin *Address:* Foxley Hatch, 10A Upper Woodcote Village, Purley, Surrey CR8 3HE.

DRISCOLL, Dr James Philip, CEng; independent management consultant; Partne PricewaterhouseCoopers (formerly Coopers & Lybrand, then Coopers & Lybran Deloitte), 1990–99, retired; *b* 29 March 1943; *s* of Reginald Driscoll and Janetta Bridg Driscoll; *m* 1969, Josephine Klapper, BA; two *s* two *d*. *Educ:* St Illtyd's Coll., Cardif Birmingham Univ. (BSc 1964; PhD 1972); Manchester Business Sch. MIChemE 197 MIGEM (MIGasE 1975); MInstF 1975. Taught at St Illtyd's Coll., Cardiff, 1964; res. pos with Joseph Lucas, Solihull, 1968–69; British Steel Corporation: res. posts, 1969–7 commercial posts, 1971–79, incl. Manager, Divl Supplies, 1973; Reg. Manager, BS (Industry), 1979–82; Dir, S Wales Workshops, 1980–82; Industrial Dir, Welsh Offic 1982–85; Associate Dir, 1985–87, Dir, 1987–90, Coopers & Lybrand Associates. Nor exec. Dir of a number of companies. Member: Glas Cymru; Welsh Industrial Develt Ad Bd. *Publications:* various technical papers. *Recreations:* family, sport. *Address:* 6 Co Crescent, Wyndham Park, Peterston-super-Ely, Cardiff CF5 6LS. *T:* (01446) 76037 *Club:* Peterston Football (Cardiff).

DRISCOLL, Lindsay Jane; Consultant, Bates Wells & Braithwaite, since 2008; *b* 17 Ap 1947; *d* of Clement Milligan Woodburn and Evelyn Miriam Woodburn; *m* 1978, Re Canon David Driscoll; two *s*. *Educ:* Queen's Sch., Chester; St Hugh's Coll., Oxford (M Hons Jurisp.). Admitted Solicitor, 1971; Asst Solicitor, Biddle & Co., 1971–73; Asst Publ Trustee of Kenya, 1973–78; Lectr, Kenya Sch. of Law, 1973–78; charity law consultan 1982–87; Consultant, Bowling & Co., 1985; Asst Legal Advr, 1987–90, Legal Adv 1990–95, NCVO; Partner, 1995–2000, Consultant, 2000–03, Sinclair Taylor & Marti Non-exec. Dir, Internat. Center for Not for Profit Law, US, 1996–2003 and 2007 Mem., Exec. Cttee, Charity Law Assoc., 1997–2003; Charity Comr, 2003–08. Truste Newham Community Renewal Prog., 1981–87; Friends of Internat. Centre of Inse Physiology and Ecology Trust, 1997–2005; Assoc. of Church Accountants and Treasure 1998–2000; Womankind Worldwide, 1998–2006; ICNL Charitable Trust, 1998–200 Widows Rights Internat. (formerly Empowering Widows in Develt), 2000–05; Balka Community Initiatives Fund, 2002–06; Historia Theatre Co., 2003–; St Katherine ar Shadwell Trust, 2005–; Darue United, 2006–. Gov., Davenant Foundn Sch., 1990–9 *Publications:* (with Bridget Phelps) The Charities Act 1992: a guide for charities and oth voluntary organisations, 1992, 2nd edn as The Charities Acts 1992 and 1993, 1993, 4 edn 1995; articles on charity law in charity and legal press. *Recreations:* travel, walkin theatre.

DRISCOLL, Michael John; QC 1992; *b* 22 Feb. 1947; *s* of John and Gladys Ma Driscoll; *m* 1970, Heather Edyvean Nichols (marr. diss. 1986); one *s* two *d* (and one decd). *Educ:* Rugby Sch.; St John's Coll., Cambridge (BA, LLB). Asst Lectr, Manchest Univ., 1969–70; called to the Bar, Middle Temple, 1970; Bencher, Lincoln's Inn, 200

Recreation: family. *Address:* Maitland Chambers, 7 Stone Buildings, Lincoln's Inn, WC2A 3SZ.

DRISCOLL, Prof. Michael John; Professor of Economics, since 1989, and Vice-Chancellor, since 1996, Middlesex University (formerly Middlesex Polytechnic); *b* 27 Oct. 1950; *s* of late Michael Driscoll and of Catherine Driscoll; one *s* one *d*. *Educ:* Boteler GS, Warrington; Trent Poly. (BA 1973). Res. Asst, Sheffield Univ., 1973–77; Lectr, Birmingham Univ., 1977–89; Economist, OECD, Paris, 1986–89; Middlesex Polytechnic, later University: Hd of Sch. of Econs, 1989–91; Dean of Business Sch., 1991–95; Pro Vice-Chancellor, 1993–95; Dep. Vice-Chancellor, 1995–96. Visiting Professor: Indian Statistics Inst., 1978; Centre for Econs and Maths Inst., Moscow, 1981; Limoges Univ. (annually), 1981–89; Univ. of the S Pacific, 1984. Chair, Lee Valley Business and Innovation Centre, 1996; Member: Ealing Tertiary Coll. Corp., 1995–96; Weald Coll. Corp., 1996–98; Coll. of NE London Corp., 1997–2005. Member: Council, London Playing Fields Soc., 1998–2000; Steering Cttee, London Higher (formerly London Higher Educn Consortium), 2000–06; N London LSC, 2001–04; Bd, UUK, 2001–; Chairman: Higher Educn Partnership for Sustainability, 2000–04; CMU, 2003–07. Patron, N London Hospice, 2002–. MInstD 1997; CCMI (FIMgt 1995); FRSA 1995. *Publications:* (jtly) Risk and Uncertainty in Economics, 1994; (jtly) The Effects of Monetary Policy on the Real Sector, 1994; numerous articles in academic jls. *Recreations:* following Aston Villa FC, the arts, water sports, walking, mountain biking, food and wine. *Address:* Middlesex University, Trent Park, Bramley Road, N14 4YZ. *T:* (020) 8411 5606, *Fax:* (020) 8411 5465; *e-mail:* m.driscoll@mdx.ac.uk.

DRIVER, Anne; *see* Phillips, A.

DRIVER, Bryan; Vice-Chairman, Rail Access Disputes (formerly Rail Access Disputes Resolution) Committee, since 2002 (Chairman, 1996–2002); *b* 26 Aug. 1932; *s* of Fred and Edith Driver; *m* 1955, Pamela Anne (*née* Nelson); two *d*. *Educ:* Wath-upon-Dearne Grammar School. Joined British Railways (Junior Clerk), 1948; Royal Air Force, 1950–52; management training with BR, 1958–59; posts in London, Doncaster, Newcastle, 1959–69; Divisional Operating Manager, Norwich, 1969–71, Liverpool Street, 1971–72; Divisional Manager, West of England, 1972–75, South Wales, 1975–77; Dep. Gen. Manager, Eastern Region, 1977–82; Man. Dir, 1982–87, Chm., 1985–87, Freightliners Ltd; Bryan Driver Associates, 1987–96; Consultant Advr, 1987–88, Ops Dir, then Dir, Ops and Rolling Stock, 1988–93, Transmanche-Link (Channel Tunnel Contractors). *Recreations:* cricket, Rugby football, golf. *Address:* Riverds Lea, 4 Shilton Garth Close, Earswick, York YO32 9SQ. *T:* (01904) 762848. *Clubs:* Savile, MCC; York Golf.

DRIVER, Charles Jonathan, MPhil; writer and school consultant; Master of Wellington College, 1989–2000; *b* 19 Aug. 1939; *s* of Rev. Kingsley Ernest Driver and Phyllis Edith Mary (*née* Gould); *m* 1967, Ann Elizabeth Hoogewerf; two *s* one *d*. *Educ:* St Andrews Coll., Grahamstown; Univ. of Cape Town (BA Hons, BEd, STD); Trinity Coll., Oxford (MPhil). Pres., National Union of S African Students, 1963–64; Asst Teacher, Sevenoaks Sch., 1964–65 and 1967–68; Housemaster, Internat. Sixth Form Centre, Sevenoaks Sch., 1968–73; Dir of Sixth Form Studies, Matthew Humberstone Sch., 1973–78; Res. Fellow, Univ. of York, 1976; Principal, Island Sch., Hong Kong, 1978–83; Headmaster, Berkhamsted Sch., 1983–89. Hon. Sen. Lectr, Sch. of Lit. and Creative Writing, UEA, 2007–. FRSA. Trustee: Lomans Trust, 1986–; Beit Trust, 1998–; Governor: Benenden Sch., 1987–2005 (Advr, 2006–); Eagle House Prep. Sch., 1989–2000; Milton Abbey Sch., 1998–2005 (Visitor, 2005–); Farlington Sch., 1999–2004 (Chm. Governors, 2000–04); Millfield, 2001–; Frewen Coll., 2002–. Editor, Conference and Common Room, 1993–2000. *Publications: novels:* Elegy for a Revolutionary, 1968; Send War in Our Time, O Lord, 1969; Death of Fathers, 1972; A Messiah of the Last Days, 1974; Shades of Darkness, 2004; *poetry:* I Live Here Now, 1979; (with Jack Cope) Occasional Light, 1979; Hong Kong Portraits, 1986; In the Water-Margins, 1994; Holiday Haiku, 1997; Requiem, 1998; So Far: selected poems 1960–2004, 2005; *biography:* Patrick Duncan, 1980, 2nd edn 2000. *Recreations:* keeping fit, playing the violin, reading, Rugby. *Address:* Apple Yard Cottage, Mill Lane, Mill Corner, Northiam, Rye, E Sussex TN31 6JU; *e-mail:* jontydriver@hotmail.com.

DRIVER, Sir Eric (William), Kt 1979; retired; Chairman: Mersey Regional Health Authority, 1973–82; National Staff Committee, (Works), 1979–82; *b* 19 Jan. 1911; *s* of William Weale Driver and Sarah Ann Driver; *m* 1st, 1938, Winifred Bane; two *d*; 2nd, 1972, Sheila Mary Johnson. *Educ:* Strand Sch., London; King's Coll., London Univ. (BSc). FICE. Civil Engr with ICI Ltd, 1938–73, retd as Chief Civil Engr Mond Div. *Recreations:* walking, gardening, travel, bridge, chess. *Address:* Conker Tree Cottage, South Bank, Great Budworth, Cheshire CW9 6HG. *Club:* Budworth Sailing.

DRIVER, Most Rev. Jeffrey William; *see* Adelaide, Archbishop of.

DRIVER, Prof. Jonathon Stevens, DPhil; FMedSci; FBA 2008; Professor of Cognitive Neuroscience, since 1998, and Director, Institute of Cognitive Neuroscience, since 2004, University College London; *b* 4 July 1962; *s* of Dennis and Jane Driver; *m* 1995, Nilli Lavie; two *s*. *Educ:* Queen's Coll., Oxford (MA Exptl Psychol. 1984; DPhil Exptl Psychol. 1988). Jun. Res. Fellow, Christ Ch, Oxford, 1988–90; Lectr in Exptl Psychol., 1991–96, and Fellow, Gonville and Caius Coll., 1994–96, Univ. of Cambridge; Prof. of Psychol., Birkbeck Coll., London, 1997–98. FMedSci 2005. *Publications:* Control of Cognitive Processes, 2000; Crossmodal Space and Crossmodal Attention, 2004; Mental Processes and the Human Brain, 2008; over 250 papers in learned jls. *Recreations:* the three Fs (family, fishing, football), science, guitar. *Address:* UCL Institute of Cognitive Neuroscience, 17 Queen Square, WC1N 3AR. *Clubs:* Piscatorial Society, Red Spinners Angling Society.

DRIVER, Olga Lindholm; *see* Aikin, O. L.

DRIVER, Paul William; writer and critic; *b* 14 Aug. 1954; *s* of Thomas Driver and Thelma Driver (*née* Tavernor). *Educ:* Salford Grammar Sch.; St Edmund Hall, Oxford (MA Hons English Lit.). Contrib. music reviews, later book and theatre reviews to FT, 1979–95; Music Critic: Daily Telegraph, 1982–83; Boston Globe, 1983–84; Sunday Times, 1984–; contributor to: The Listener, Tempo, Musical Times, TLS, London Rev. of Books, Guardian, NY Times and numerous other pubns; frequent broadcasts on Radio 3, Radio 4, BBC 2, Channel 4, etc; has lectured on music in Britain and USA. Mem. Bd, Contemporary Music Rev., 1981–. Patron, Manchester Musical Heritage Trust, 2000–. *Publications:* (ed) A Diversity of Creatures, by Rudyard Kipling, 1987; (ed jtly) Music and Text, 1989; (ed) Penguin English Verse, 1995; (ed) Penguin Popular Poetry, 6 vols, 1996; Manchester Pieces, 1996; (contrib.) Sing, Ariel, 2003. *Recreations:* walking, swimming, travel. *Address:* 15 Victoria Road, NW6 6SX. *T:* (020) 7624 4501. *Club:* Critics' Circle.

DRIVER, Ven. Penelope May; Archdeacon of Exeter, since 2006; *b* 20 Feb. 1952; *d* of Arthur Anderson Glover and Bessie Glover. *Educ:* All Saints' Coll., London (Teaching Cert.); Northern Ordination Course (DipTh 1983); Manchester Univ. (MEd Adult Educn 1992). Ordained deacon, 1987, priest, 1994; Diocesan Youth Advr, dio. Newcastle, 1986–88; Curate of Cullercoats, Newcastle, 1987–88; Youth Chaplain, Ripon, 1988–96; Diocese of Ripon and Leeds: Asst Dir of Ordinands, 1996–98, Diocesan Dir of Ordinands, 1998–2006; Bishop's Advr in Women's Ministry, 1991–2006; Minor Canon, 1996–2006, Hon. Canon, 1998–2006, Ripon Cathedral. *Recreations:* entertaining, singing, ski-ing, fell walking. *Address:* Emmanuel House, Station Road, Ide, Exeter EX2 9RS. *T:* (01392) 425577; *e-mail:* archdeacon.of.exeter@exeter.anglican.org.

DRIVER, Sheila Elizabeth; a District Judge (Magistrates' Courts) (formerly Stipendiary Magistrate), South Yorkshire, since 1995; *b* 7 Oct. 1950; *d* of Alfred Derek Robinson and Joan Elizabeth Robinson; *m* 1974, John Graham Driver; one *s* two *d*. *Educ:* Bradford Girls' GS; Leeds Univ. (BA Hons Hist.); London School of Economics (MA Internat. Hist.). Admitted Solicitor, 1978; Solicitor: City of Bradford MDC, 1978–79; County Prosecuting Office, W Yorks, 1979–80; in private practice, 1981–95. *Recreations:* amateur dramatics, reading.

DROGHEDA, 12th Earl of, *cr* 1661 (Ireland); **Henry Dermot Ponsonby Moore;** Baron Moore of Mellifont, 1616; Viscount Moore, 1621; Baron Moore of Cobham (UK), 1954; photographer, professional name Derry Moore; *b* 14 Jan. 1937; *o s* of 11th Earl of Drogheda, KG, KBE and of Joan *o d* of late William Henry Carr; *S* father, 1989; *m* 1st, 1968, Eliza Lloyd (marr. diss. 1972), *d* of Stacy Barcroft Lloyd, Jr, and Mrs Paul Mellon; 2nd, 1978, Alexandra, *d* of Sir (John) Nicholas Henderson, *qv*; two *s* one *d*. *Educ:* Eton; Trinity College, Cambridge. *Publications:* (as Derry Moore): (with Brendan Gill) The Dream Come True, Great Houses of Los Angeles, 1980; (with George Plumptre) Royal Gardens, 1981; (with Sybila Jane Flower) Stately Homes of Britain, 1982; (with Henry Mitchell) Washington, Houses of the Capital, 1982; (with Michael Pick) The English Room, 1984; (with Alvilde Lees-Milne) The Englishwoman's House, 1984; (with Alvilde Lees-Milne) The Englishman's Room, 1986; (with the Marchioness of Salisbury) The Gardens of Queen Elizabeth the Queen Mother, 1988; (with Sarah Hollis) The Shell Guide to the Gardens of England and Wales, 1989; Evening Ragas, 1997; (with Clive Aslet) The House of Lords, 1998; Rooms, 2006; Notting Hill, 2007; (with The Dowager Marchioness of Salisbury) A Gardener's Life, 2008. *Heir: s* Viscount Moore, *qv*. *Address:* 40 Ledbury Road, W11 2AB; *e-mail:* moorederry@aol.com. *Club:* Brooks's.

DROMGOOLE, Dominic Charles Fleming; Artistic Director, Shakespeare's Globe Theatre, since 2006; *b* 25 Oct. 1963; *s* of Patrick Shirley Brookes Fleming Dromgoole, *qv*; partner, Sasha Hails; three *d*. *Educ:* Millfield Sch.; St Catharine's Coll., Cambridge (BA (English Lit.) 1985). Artistic Dir, Bush Th., 1990–96; New Plays Dir, Old Vic Th., 1997; Artistic Dir, Oxford Stage Co., 1999–2005. Director: Shadow of a Gunman, Tricycle, 2004; Someone Who'll Watch Over Me, New Ambassadors, 2005. Producer, Saltwater (film), 2000. Essayist, Sunday Times and others, 2001–. *Publications:* The Full Room, 2001; Will and Me: how Shakespeare took over my life, 2006. *Recreations:* walking, drinking. *Address:* 73 Cobbold Road, W12 9LA.

DROMGOOLE, Jolyon; Director (Council Secretariat), Institution of Civil Engineers, 1985–91; Deputy Under-Secretary of State (Army), Ministry of Defence, 1984–85; *b* 27 March 1926; 2nd *s* of late Nicholas and Violet Dromgoole; *m* 1956, Anthea, *e d* of Sir Anthony Bowlby, 2nd Bt; five *d* (incl. triplets). *Educ:* Christ's Hospital; Dulwich Coll.; University Coll., Oxford (matric. 1944; BA 2nd Cl. Hons (History) 1950; MA). Entered HM Forces, 1944; commissioned 14/20 King's Hussars, 1946. Entered Administrative Cl., Civil Service; assigned to War Office, 1950; Private Sec. to Permanent Under-Sec., 1953; Principal, 1955; Private Sec. to Sec. of State, 1964–65; Asst Sec., 1965; Command Sec., HQ FARELF, Singapore, 1968–71; Royal Coll. of Defence Studies, 1972; Under-Sec., Broadcasting Dept, Home Office, 1973–76; Asst Under-Sec. of State, Gen. Staff, 1976–79, Personnel and Logistics, 1979–84, MoD. FRSA 2000. Trustee and Gov., Royal Sch., Hampstead, 1985–99. Mem., Samuel Pepys Club, 1993–; Chm., Samuel Pepys Award Trust, 2002–07. *Recreations:* literature, publisher. *Address:* 13 Gladstone Street, SE1 6EY. *T:* (020) 7928 2162; Montreal House, Barnsley, Glos GL7 5EL. *T:* (01285) 740331. *Club:* Athenæum.

See also P. S. B. F. Dromgoole.

DROMGOOLE, Patrick Shirley Brookes Fleming; Chairman, PDP Ltd, since 1992; *b* 30 Aug. 1930; *s* of late Nicholas and Violet Dromgoole; *m* 1st, 1960, Jennifer Veronica Jill Davis (marr. diss. 1991); two *s* one *d*; 2nd, 1991, June Kell Morrow. *Educ:* Dulwich Coll.; University Coll., Oxford (MA). Actor and various employments in London and Paris, 1947–51; BBC Drama Producer/Dir, 1954–63; freelance theatre, film and television dir (directed first plays in West End of Orton, Wood, Welland, Halliwell and others), 1963–69; directed regularly Armchair Theatre for ABC TV and Thames TV; made number of films for cinema; joined HTV Ltd as Programme Controller, 1969; Asst Man. Dir, 1981; Man. Dir, HTV, 1987; Chief Exec., HTV Gp, 1988–91. Various awards incl. Pye Oscar, RTS, for Thick as Thieves, 1971; Best Play of the Year, for Machinegunner, 1973; Amer. Emmy, for D.P., 1985. FRTS 1978; FRSA 1989. *Recreations:* travel, œnophilia, pre-Raphaelite art, reading. *Address:* Penkill Castle, Girvan, Ayrshire KA26 9TQ. *Clubs:* Savile, Garrick, Groucho.

See also D. C. F. Dromgoole, J. Dromgoole.

DROMORE, Bishop of, (RC), since 1999; **Most Rev. John McAreavey;** *b* Banbridge, Ireland, 2 Feb. 1949. *Educ:* St. Colman's Coll., Newry; Maynooth Coll.; Pontifical Univ., Maynooth; Pontifical Gregorian Univ., Rome. Ordained priest, 1973; Teacher, St Colman's Coll., Newry, 1978–79; Vice Judicial Vicar, 1979–83, Judicial Vicar, 1983–88, Armagh Regl Marriage Tribunal; Prof. of Canon Law, St Patrick's Coll., Maynooth, 1988–99. *Address:* Bishop's House, 44 Armagh Road, Newry, Co. Down BT35 6PN.

DRONKE, Prof. (Ernst) Peter (Michael), FBA 1984; Fellow of Clare Hall, 1964–2001, now Emeritus, and Professor of Medieval Latin Literature, 1989–2001, now Emeritus, University of Cambridge; *b* 30 May 1934; *s* of Senatspräsident A. H. R. Dronke and M. M. Dronke (*née* Kronfeld); *m* 1960, Ursula Miriam (*née* Brown); one *d*. *Educ:* Victoria University, NZ (MA 1st Cl. Hons 1954); Magdalen College, Oxford (BA 1st Cl. Hons 1957; MA 1961); MA Cantab 1961. Research Fellow, Merton Coll., Oxford, 1958–61; Lectr in Medieval Latin, 1961–79, Reader, 1979–89, Univ. of Cambridge. Guest Lectr, Univ. of Munich, 1960; Guest Prof., Centre d'Etudes Médiévales, Poitiers, 1969; Leverhulme Fellow, 1973; Guest Prof., Univ. Autónoma, Barcelona, 1977; Vis. Fellow, Humanities Res. Centre, Canberra, 1978; Vis. Prof. of Medieval Studies, Westfield Coll., 1981–86. Lectures: W. P. Ker, Univ. of Glasgow, 1976; Matthews, Birkbeck Coll., 1983; Jackson, Harvard Univ., 1992; O'Donnell, Univ. of Toronto, 1993; Barlow, UCL, 1995. Corresp. Fellow: Real Academia de Buenas Letras, 1976; Royal Dutch Acad., 1997; Medieval Acad. of America, 1999; Austrian Acad. of Scis, 2001; Fondazione Lorenzo Valla, 2006; Istituto Lombardo Acad. of Scis and Letters, 2007. Hon. Pres., Internat. Courtly Literature Soc., 1974. Co-Editor, Mittellateinisches Jahrbuch, 1977–2002. Premio Internazionale Ascoli Piceno, 1988. *Publications:* Medieval Latin and the Rise of European Love-Lyric, 2 vols, 1965–66; The Medieval Lyric, 1968; Poetic Individuality in the Middle Ages, 1970; Fabula, 1974; Abelard and Heloise in Medieval Testimonies, 1976; (with Ursula Dronke) Barbara et antiquissima carmina, 1977; (ed) Bernardus Silvestris, Cosmographia, 1978; Introduction to Francesco Colonna, Hypnerotomachia, 1981;

Women Writers of the Middle Ages, 1984; The Medieval Poet and his World, 1984; Dante and Medieval Latin Traditions, 1986; Introduction to Rosvita, Dialoghi drammatici, 1986; (ed) A History of Twelfth-Century Western Philosophy, 1988; Hermes and the Sibyls, 1990; Latin and Vernacular Poets of the Middle Ages, 1991; Intellectuals and Poets in Medieval Europe, 1992; Verse with Prose: from Petronius to Dante, 1994; Nine Medieval Latin Plays, 1994; (ed with A. Derolez) Hildegard of Bingen, *Liber divinorum operum*, 1996; Sources of Inspiration, 1997; Dante's Second Love, 1997; Introduction to Alessandro nel medioevo occidentale, 1997; (with Ursula Dronke) Growth of Literature: the sea and the God of the sea, 1998; (ed) Etienne Gilson's Letters to Bruno Nardi, 1998; (ed with Charles Burnett) Hildegard of Bingen: the context of her thought and art, 1998; Imagination in the late Pagan and Early Christian World, 2003; Forms and Imaginings, 2007; The Spell of Calcidius, 2008; essays in learned jls and symposia. *Recreations:* music, film, Brittany. *Address:* 6 Parker Street, Cambridge CB1 1JL.

DROWN, Julia Kate; *b* 23 Aug. 1962; *d* of David Christopher Robert Drown and Audrey Marion Harris; *m* 1999, Bill Child; one *s* one *d* (and one *d* decd). *Educ:* Hampstead Comprehensive Sch.; University Coll., Oxford (BA); Educn and Trng Coll., CIPFA. Unit Accountant, Oxfordshire Unit for People with Learning Difficulties, 1988–90; Dir of Finance, Radcliffe Infirmary, Oxford, 1990–96. Mem. (Lab) Oxfordshire CC, 1989–96. MP (Lab) Swindon South, 1997–2005. Mem., Select Cttee on Health, 1997–99 and 2001–03; Chair, Select Sub-cttee on Maternity Services, 2003; All Party Groups: Chair: on Maternity, 2000–05; on Heavily Indebted Poor Countries (formerly Third World Debt), 2001–05; Co-Chair, on Illegal Camping and Traveller Mgt, 2002–05; Vice Chair, on Further Educn, 1998–99; Hon. Secretary: on Osteoporosis, 1999–2005; on Rwanda, the Great Lakes Region and the Prevention of Genocide, 2001–05. Vice-Chair, Voice, 1998–2004. Mem., CIPFA, 1989–2005. *Recreations:* family, walking, ballet.

DRU DRURY, Martin; *see* Drury.

DRUCKMAN, Paul Bryan, FCA; Chairman, Clear Group, since 2005; *b* 23 Dec. 1954; *s* of Leonard and Phoebe Druckman; *m* 1983, Angela Samuel; one *s* one *d*. *Educ:* King's Coll. Sch., Wimbledon; Warwick Univ. (PGCE 1981). Dip. Envmtl Mgt, British Safety Council, 2002. FCA 1979. Sales Dir, Orchard Business Systems Ltd, 1986–90; Managing Director: Dit Ltd, 1990–99; Aston IT Gp, 1999–2001; Chairman: IT Faculty, 2001–02; SME Forum, 2001–03; Director: Business Link for London Ltd, 2004–06; Access Technol. Gp (formerly Access Accounts), 2004–; Rugged Logic Ltd, 2007–. Pres., ICAEW, 2004–05. Mem., Takeover Panel, 2004–05; Dir, Financial Reporting Council, 2004–07; Chm., CCAB, 2004–05. Chairman: Corporate Responsibility Adv. Gp, ICAEW, 2006–; Sustainability Policy Gp, FEE, 2007–; Prince of Wales's Accounting for Sustainability Forum (formerly Ext. Reporting Wkg Party), 2007–. Freeman, City of London, 2003; Mem., Ct of Assts, Chartered Accountants' Co., 2004–05. *Recreations:* golf, tennis. *Address:* c/o Clear Group, Charlton House, 173 Kingston Road, Surrey KT3 3SS; *e-mail:* paul@druckman.co.uk. *Clubs:* Coombe Hill Golf; Westside Lawn Tennis (Wimbledon).

DRUMLANRIG, Viscount; Sholto Francis Guy Douglas; *b* 1 June 1967; *s* and *heir* of 12th Marquess of Queensberry, *qv*.

DRUMM, Rev. Mgr Walter Gregory; Rector, Pontifical Beda College, Rome, 1987–91; *b* 2 March 1940; *s* of Owen and Kathleen Drumm. *Educ:* St Joseph's Sch. and St Aloysius' Coll., Highgate; Balliol Coll., Oxford (MA). Tutor, The Grange, Warlingham, 1962–66; studied at Beda Coll., 1966–70; ordained, Westminster Dio., 1970; Asst Priest, Wood Green, 1970–73; Chaplain, Oxford Univ., 1973–83; Parish Priest, Our Lady of Victories, Kensington, 1983–87. Prelate of Honour to the Pope, 1988. *Address:* Nazareth House, 162 East End Road, N2 0RU.

DRUMMOND, family name of **Earl of Perth** and **Baron Strange**.

DRUMMOND, Maj.-Gen. Anthony John D.; *see* Deane-Drummond.

DRUMMOND, Caroline Jane, (Mrs Philip Ward); Chief Executive, LEAF (Linking Environment and Farming), since 1991; Director, LEAF Marque, since 2004; *b* Hill Head, Fareham, Hants, 24 June 1963; *d* of Lt Comdr (Geoffrey) Mortimer Heneage Drummond and Sarah Drummond; *m* 1998, Philip Ward; one *d*. *Educ:* Rookesbury Park, Wickham; St Swithun's, Winchester; Seale Hayne Agricultural Coll. (BSc Hons Agric.). Agronomy Lectr, Shuttleworth Agric. Coll., 1989–91. Dir, Oxford Farming Conf., 2003–05 (Chm., 2005). Governor: Inst. of Envmt and Grassland Res., 2005–08; Rothamsted Experimental Station, 2007–; Trustee, CPRE, 2008–. FRAgS 1998. Pioneer to Life of the Nation, 2003. *Publications:* numerous scientific and farming articles, papers and comments. *Recreations:* singing, countryside matters, scientific kitchen experiments and art projects with my daughter. *Address:* LEAF, National Agricultural Centre, Stoneleigh, Warwicks CV8 2LZ. *T:* (024) 7641 3911, *Fax:* (024) 7641 3636; *e-mail:* caroline.drummond@leafuk.org; Butterwell, Horningtops, Liskeard, Cornwall PL14 3QD.

DRUMMOND, Colin Irwin John Hamilton; Executive Director, Pennon Group plc, since 1992; Chief Executive, Viridor Waste Management Ltd, since 2002 (Chief Executive, Viridor Ltd, 1998–2002); *b* 22 Feb. 1951; *s* of Rev. William Balfour Drummond, MA and Annie Rebecca Drummond (*née* Roy); *m* 1975, Georgina Lloyd; two *s*. *Educ:* Wadham Coll., Oxford (BA (double 1st Cl. Hons Classics), MA 1978); Harvard Graduate Sch. of Business Admin (Harkness Fellow; MBA 1977). LTCL 1969 (Colman Prize). Asst Superintendent, Economic Intelligence Dept, Bank of England, 1973–78; Consultant, Boston Consulting Gp, 1978–84; Dir for Corporate Develt, Renold plc, 1984–86; Chief Exec., Yarns Div., Coats Viyella plc, 1986–92. Non-exec. Dir, Vymura plc, 1998–99. Member: Adv. Cttee on Business and the Envmt, 2001–03; Council, SW Reg., CBI, 1997–2003. Dir, Sustainability SW, 2005–. Chairman: Envmtl Sector Adv. Gp, 2005–; Envmtl Knowledge Transfer Network, 2007–. Vis. Sen. Fellow, Earth Scis, Oxford Univ., 2007–. CCMI 2002. Freeman, City of London, 1999; Liveryman, 1999–, Mem., Ct of Assts, and Master, 2007–08, Co. of Water Conservators. Organist and choirmaster, parish church of St John the Baptist, Wellington, Somerset, 1993–2006. *Recreations:* sport, gardening. *Address:* Pennon Group plc, Great Western House, Station Approach, Taunton, Somerset TA1 1QW. *T:* (01823) 721400. *Club:* Oxford and Cambridge.

DRUMMOND, David Classon, FIBiol; Deputy Director, Research and Development Service, Agricultural Development Advisory Service, Ministry of Agriculture, Fisheries and Food, 1987–88, retired; *b* 25 July 1928; *s* of Roger Hamilton Drummond and Marjorie Holt Drummond; *m* 1952, Barbara Anne, *d* of late Prof. Alfred Cobban; three *d*. *Educ:* St Peter's Sch., York; University Coll., London (BSc 1952); Pennsylvania State Univ., USA (Kellogg Fellow; MS 1962). FIBiol 1975. Project Manager, FAO, UN, Karachi, 1971–72; Agricultural Science Service, MAFF: Head of Rodent Res. Dept, and Officer i/c Tolworth Lab., 1974–82; Head of Biol. Div., and Officer i/c Slough Lab., 1982–85; Sen. Agricl Scientist with special responsibilities for R&D, 1985–87. Mem., WHO Expert Adv. Panel on Vector Biology and Control, 1980–97. *Publications:* William C. Hooker's Great American Mouse Trap, 2002; Nineteenth Century Mouse Traps Patented in the USA, 2004; Mouse Traps: a quick scamper through their long history, 2005; McGill Mouse Traps and the Stilson Brothers, 2006; Twentieth Century Mouse Traps Patented in the USA, 1900–1924, 2007; British Mouse Traps and their Markets, 2008; scientific papers and reviews mainly concerned with rodent biology and control and develt of agricl and urban rat control programmes. *Recreations:* travel, gardening, history of mouse traps and rat catching. *Address:* 22 Knoll Road, Dorking, Surrey RH4 3EP.

DRUMMOND, Gillian Vera, OBE 2008; DL; Commissioner, English Heritage, since 2002; *b* 15 Sept. 1939; *d* of Gavin and Vera Clark; *m* 1st, 1958, Graham Turner Laing (marr. diss. 1978; he *d* 2007); three *d* (and one *s* decd); 2nd, 1978, Maldwin Andrew Cyril Drummond, *qv*; one *s*. *Educ:* Roedean Sch.; Poggio Imperiale, Florence. Founder Chm., Hampshire Gardens Trust, 1984–96; Mem., Council of Mgt, Sir Harold Hillier Gardens & Arboretum, 1989–; Chairman: Wessex Region, Historic Houses Assoc., 2000–05; Historic Parks and Gardens Panel, English Heritage, 2001–; Pres., Assoc. of Gardens Trusts, 1995– (Chm., 1992–95). Trustee: Learning Through Landscape Trust, 1991–; Gilbert White's House and Oates Meml Mus., 1992–; Chawton House Library, 1993–; Nat. Maritime Mus., 2005–; Chiswick House and Park Trust, 2006–; Llanthony Secunda Priory Trust, 2007–. Patron: Folly Fellowship, 2001–; Green Space, 2002–. Sen. Judge, Southern Region In Bloom, 1986–2002. County Pres., St John Ambulance Bde, 1990–2003. DL Hants, 1994. Gold Veitch Meml Medal, RHS, 1996. *Recreations:* gardening, sailing, art, architecture. *Address:* Stanswood Farmhouse, Fawley, Southampton SO45 1AB. *T:* (023) 8089 1543; Wester Kames Castle, Port Bannatyne, Isle of Bute PA20 0QW. *T:* (01700) 503983; *e-mail:* gd@cadland.org.uk. *Clubs:* Royal Cruising (Assoc. Mem.); Royal Yacht Squadron (Lady Assoc. Mem.).

See also S. H. Turner Laing.

DRUMMOND, James Robert; Director, South Asia Division, Department for International Development, since 2007; *b* 12 July 1953; *s* of Brian and Isobel Drummond; *m* 1988, Glynis Joan Fell; two *s* one *d*. *Educ:* Trinity Coll., Cambridge (MA Hist. 1979). Head: Develt Sect., British High Commn, New Delhi, 1989–92; Central and Southern Africa Dept, 1992–95, Personnel, 1995–97, ODA; Central Africa, Harare, DFID, 1997–2000; Asst Hd, Defence and Overseas Secretariat, Cabinet Office, 2000–03; Dir, Iraq, 2003–04, UN Conflict and Humanitarian Div., 2005–07, DFID. *Recreations:* village cricket, birds, recent history of Zimbabwe, music of 'Jokes On You'. *Address:* Department for International Development, 1 Palace Street, SW1E 5HE. *Club:* Shamley Green Cricket.

DRUMMOND, Kevin; *see* Drummond, T. A. K.

DRUMMOND, Maldwin Andrew Cyril, OBE 1990; DL; farmer and author; *b* 30 April 1932; *s* of late Maj. Cyril Drummond, JP, DL, and Mildred Joan Quinnell; *m* 1st, 1955, Susan Dorothy Cayley (marr. diss. 1977); two *d*; 2nd, 1978, Gillian Vera Turner Laing (*see* G. V. Drummond); one *s*. *Educ:* Eton Coll.; Royal Agricl Coll., Cirencester; Univ. of Southampton (Cert. in Environmental Sci., 1972). 2nd Lieut, Rifle Bde, 1950–52; Captain, Queen Victoria's, later Queen's, Royal Rifles (TA), retd 1967. Official Verderer of the New Forest, 1999–2002 (Verderer of New Forest, 1961–90); Chairman: Heritage Coast Forum, 1989–95; New Forest Cttee, 1990–98 (Chm., Consultative Panel, 1982–98); Mem., Countryside Commn, 1980–86. Member: Southampton Harbour Bd, 1967; British Transport Docks Bd, Southampton, 1968–74; Southern Water Authority, 1984–87. Chairman: Sail Training Assoc., 1967–72; Maritime Trust, 1979–89; Cutty Sark Soc., 1979–89; Warrior (formerly Ships) Preservation Trust, 1979–91; Pres., Shellfish Assoc. of GB, 1987–2008; Vice-Pres., 1983–, and Chm. Boat Cttee, 1983–92, RNLI; Trustee, World Ship Trust, 1980–91; Chairman: Hampshire Bldgs Preservation Trust, 1986–92; Hampshire and Wight Trust for Maritime Archeology, 2003–. Younger Brother of Trinity House, 1991–. Prime Warden, Fishmongers' Co., 1996–97. Mem., New Forest RDC, 1957–66; Hampshire: County Councillor, 1967–75; JP 1964–98 (Chm., New Forest Bench, 1992–97); DL 1975; High Sheriff, 1980–81. FRGS 1978; FRSA 1987; FSA 2003. Hon. DSc: Bournemouth, 1994; Southampton Inst., 1996. *Publications:* Conflicts in an Estuary, 1973; Tall Ships, 1976; Salt-Water Palaces, 1979; (with Paul Rodhouse) Yachtsman's Naturalist, 1980; (with Philip Allison) The New Forest, 1980; The Riddle, 1985; West Highland Shores, 1990; (ed) Lord Bute, 1996; (with Robin MacInnes) The Book of the Solent, 2001; After You Mr Lear, 2007. *Recreations:* cruising under sail and wondering about the sea. *Address:* Stanswood Farmhouse, Stanswood Road, Fawley, Southampton SO45 1AB. *T:* (office) (023) 8089 2039, (home) (023) 8089 1543; Wester Kames Castle, Port Bannatyne, Isle of Bute PA20 0QW. *T:* (01700) 503983. *Clubs:* White's, Pratt's, Royal Cruising; Royal Yacht Squadron (Cdre, 1991–96) (Cowes); Leander (Henley).

DRUMMOND, Rev. Norman Walker, MA, BD; FRSE; Chairman: Drummond International, since 1999; Lloyds TSB Foundation for Scotland, since 2003; Founder and Chairman, Columba 1400, Community and International Leadership Centre, Isle of Skye, since 1997; Founding Chairman, Inspiring Scotland; *b* 1 April 1952; *s* of late Edwin Payne Drummond and Jean (*née* Walker); *m* 1976, Lady Elizabeth Helen Kennedy, *d* of 7th Marquess of Ailsa, OBE; three *s* two *d*. *Educ:* Merchiston Castle Sch.; Fitzwilliam Coll., Cambridge (MA Law); New Coll., Univ. of Edinburgh (BD). FRSE 2008. Ordained as Minister of the Church of Scotland, and commnd to serve as Chaplain to HM Forces in the Army, 1976; Chaplain: Depot, Parachute Regt and Airborne Forces, 1977–78; 1st Bn The Black Watch (Royal Highland Regt), 1978–82; to the Moderator of the Gen. Assembly of the Church of Scotland, 1980; Fettes Coll., 1982–84; Headmaster, Loretto Sch., 1984–95; Minister of Kilmuir and Stenscholl, Isle of Skye, 1996–98. Chaplain to Gov. of Edinburgh Castle, 1991–93; Chaplain to the Queen in Scotland, 1993–. BBC Nat. Gov., and Chm., Broadcasting Council for Scotland, 1994–99; Mem., Scottish Broadcasting Commn, 2007–08. Chm., BBC Children in Need, 1997–99. Chairman: Musselburgh and Dist Council of Social Service, 1984–94; Community Action Network, Scotland, 2001–03; Founder and non-exec. Chm., The Change Partnership Scotland, 1999–2003. Non-exec. Dir, J. & J. Denholm Ltd, 2002–. Mem., Queen's Bodyguard for Scotland (Royal Co. of Archers), 1990–. Mem. Court, Heriot-Watt Univ., 1986–92; Gov., Gordonstoun Sch., 1995–2000; Chm. Govs, Aiglon Coll., Switzerland, 1999–2005. Former Trustee: Arthur Smith Meml Trust; Foundn for Skin Res. President: Edinburgh Bn, Boys' Bde, 1993–98; Victoria League in Scotland, 1995–98. Cambridge Univ. Rugby Blue, 1971; Captain: Scottish Univs XV, 1974; Army XV and Combined Services XV, 1976–77. *Publications:* The First Twenty-five Years: official history of The Black Watch Kirk Session, 1979; Mother's Hands (collection of short stories for children, parents and teachers), 1992; The Spirit of Success: how to connect your heart to your head in work and life, 2004. *Recreations:* Rugby football, cricket, golf, curling, traditional jazz, Isle of Skye. *Address:* 35 Drummond Place, Edinburgh EH3 6PW. *Clubs:* MCC; New (Edinburgh); Hawks (Cambridge).

DRUMMOND, Roderick Ian; HM Diplomatic Service; Foreign and Commonwealth Office, London, since 2008; *b* 7 Sept. 1962; *s* of Ian Drummond and Sarah (*née* Laird); partner, Yasmin Kamal; one s two *d* by former marriage. *Educ:* Edinburgh Univ. (MA

Hons Hist.). Entered FCO, 1985; lang. trng, SOAS, 1986, Univ. of Jordan, 1987; Second Sec. (Pol/Econ.), Algiers, 1988–92; First Sec., FCO, 1992–96; Dep. Consul-Gen., Johannesburg, 1996–98; UK Rep. to EU, Brussels, 1998–2002; Deputy Head of Mission: Amman, 2002–04; Damascus, 2004–07; Hd of Mission, Doha, 2007–08. *Recreations:* Rugby, cooking, wine, whisky, jazz. *Address:* c/o Foreign and Commonwealth Office, King Charles Street, SW1A 2AH. *Club:* Damascus Rugby.

DRUMMOND, (Thomas Anthony) Kevin; QC (Scot.) 1987; Sheriff of Lothian and Borders at Jedburgh, Selkirk and Duns, since 2000; *b* 3 Nov. 1943; *s* of Thomas Drummond, BSc, and Mary (*née* Hughes); *m* 1966, Margaret Evelyn Broadley; one *d* (and one *d* decd). *Educ:* Blair's Coll., Aberdeen; St Mirin's Acad., Paisley; Edinburgh Univ. (LLB). Estate Duty Office, CS, 1963–70; Solicitor, 1970; admitted Faculty of Advocates, 1974; Advocate-Depute, 1985–90, Home Advocate-Depute, 1996–97, Crown Office, Edinburgh; Sheriff of Glasgow and Stathkelvin, 1997–2000. Member: Criminal Injuries Compensation Bd, 1990–96; Firearms Consultative Cttee, 1990–97; Criminal Injuries Compensation Authy, 1996. Chm., Discipline Tribunal, Inst. of Chartered Accts of Scotland, 1994–. Cartoonist, Scots Law Times, 1981–. *Publications:* legal cartoons under name of TAK: The Law at Work, 1982; The Law at Play, 1983; Great Defences of Our Time, 1995. *Recreations:* shooting, hill-walking, fishing, underwater hang-gliding. *Address:* Pomathorn House, Howgate, Midlothian EH26 8PJ. *T:* (01968) 74046.

DRUMMOND YOUNG, Hon. Lord; James Edward Drummond Young; a Senator of the College of Justice in Scotland, since 2001; Chairman, Scottish Law Commission, since 2007; *b* 17 Feb. 1950; *s* of late Duncan Drummond Young, MBE, DL, Edinburgh, and Annette (*née* Mackay); *m* 1991, Elizabeth Mary, *d* of John Campbell-Kease; one *d*. *Educ:* John Watson's Sch.; Sidney Sussex Coll., Cambridge (BA 1971); Harvard Univ. (Joseph Hodges Choate Meml Fellow, 1971–72; LLM 1972); Edinburgh Univ. (LLB 1974). Admitted to Faculty of Advocates, 1976. Standing Jun. Counsel in Scotland to Bd of Inland Revenue, 1986–88; QC (Scot.) 1988; Advocate-Depute, 1999–2001. *Publications:* (with J. B. St Clair) The Law of Corporate Insolvency in Scotland, 1988, 3rd edn 2004; (contrib.) Stair Memorial Encyclopaedia of Scots Law, 1989. *Recreations:* music, travel.

DRUMMOND YOUNG, James Edward; *see* Drummond Young, Hon. Lord.

DRUON, Maurice Samuel Roger Charles, Hon. KBE 1999 (Hon. CBE 1988); Grand Croix de la Légion d'Honneur; Commandeur des Arts et Lettres; author; Member of the French Academy since 1966 (Permanent Secretary, 1986–2000); Member: French Parliament (Paris), 1978–81; Assembly of Council of Europe, 1978–81; European Parliament, 1979–80; Franco-British Council, since 1972; *b* Paris, 23 April 1918; *s* of René Druon de Reyniac and Léonilla Jenny Samuel-Cros; *m* 1968, Madeleine Marignac. *Educ:* Lycée Michelet and Ecole des Sciences Politiques, Paris. Ecole de Cavalerie de Saumur, aspirant, 1940; joined Free French Forces, London, 1942; Attaché Commissariat à l'Intérieur et Direction de l'Information, 1943; War Correspondent, 1944–45; Lieut de réserve de cavalerie. Journalist, 1946–47; Minister for Cultural Affairs, France, 1973–74. Member: Acad. of Morocco, 1980; Athènes' Acad., 1981; Acad. Bresilienne de Lettres, 1995; Acad. Roumaine, 1996; Acad. Sciences Russie, 2006; Pres., Franco-Italian Assoc., 1985–91. Dr *hc*: York Univ., Ontario, 1987; Boston Univ.; Tirana Univ. Prix de Monaco, 1966. Commandeur du Phénix de Grèce; Grand Officer de l'Ordre de l'Honneur de Grèce; Grand Officier du Mérite de l'Ordre de Malte; Commandeur de l'Ordre de la République de Tunisie; Grand Officier du Lion du Sénégal; Grand Croix du Mérite de la République Italienne; Grand Croix de l'Aigle Aztèque du Mexique; Grand Officier Ouissam Alaouite (Morocco); Commandeur de Saint-Charles de Monaco; Grand Officier, Cruseiro del Sul (Brazil); Grand Officier, Ordre du Cèdre (Lebanon); Comdr, Ordre de Léopold (Belgium); Grand Officier, Ordre de Mai (Argentina); Grand Officier, Etoile (Romania); Commandeur du Mérite Culturel (Monaco); Grand Croix, Ordre du Christ (Portugal), 1994. *Publications:* Lettres d'un Européen, 1944; La Dernière Brigade (The Last Detachment), 1946 (publ. in England 1957); Les Grandes Familles (Prix Goncourt, 1948), La Chute des Corps, Rendez-Vous aux Enfers, 1948–51 (trilogy publ. in England under title The Curtain falls, 1959); La Volupté d'Etre (Film of Memory), 1954 (publ. in England 1955); Les Rois Maudits (The Accursed Kings), 1955–60 (six vols: The Iron King, The Strangled Queen, The Poisoned Crown, The Royal Succession, The She-Wolf of France, The Lily and the Lion, publ. in England 1956–61); Tistou les pouces verts (Tistou of the green fingers), 1957 (publ. in England 1958); Alexandre le Grand (Alexander the God), 1958 (publ. in Eng. 1960); Des Seigneurs de la Plaine- (The Black Prince and other stories), 1962 (publ. in Eng. 1962); Les Mémoires de Zeus I (The Memoirs of Zeus), 1963 (in Eng. 1964); Bernard Buffet, 1964; Paris, de César à Saint Louis (The History of Paris from Caesar to St Louis), 1964 (in Eng. 1969); Le Pouvoir, 1965; Le Bonheur des Uns, 1967; Les Mémoires de Zeus II (The Memoirs of Zeus II), 1967; L'Avenir en désarroi, 1968; Vézelay, colline éternelle, 1968; Nouvelles lettres d'un Européen, 1970; Une Eglise qui se trompe de siècle, 1972; La Parole et le Pouvoir, 1974; Oeuvres complètes, 25 vols, 1973–79; Quand un roi perd la France (Les Rois Maudits 7), 1977; Attention la France!, 1981; Réformer la Démocratie, 1982; Lettre aux Français sur leur langue et leur âme, 1994; Circonstances, 1997; Circonstances politiques, 1998 (Prix Saint Simon, 1998); Circonstances politiques II, 1999; La France aux ordres d'un cadavre, 2000 (Prix Agrippa d'Aubigné); Ordonnances pour un Etat malade, 2002; Le Franc-parler, 2003; L'Aurore vient du fond du ciel (mémoires), vol. 1, 2006; *plays:* Mégarée, 1942; Un Voyageur, 1953; La Contessa, 1962; *song:* Le Chant des Partisans (with Joseph Kessel and Anna Marly), 1943 (London). *Recreations:* riding, travel. *Address:* 81 rue de Lille, 75007 Paris, France; Abbaye de Faise, 33570 Les Artigues de Lussac, Lussac, France. *Clubs:* Savile, Garrick; Travellers (Paris).

DRURY, Very Rev. John Henry; Chaplain and Fellow, All Souls College, Oxford, since 2003; *b* 23 May 1936; *s* of Henry and Barbara Drury; *m* 1972, (Frances) Clare Nineham (*d* 2004), *d* of Rev. Prof. D. E. Nineham, *qv*; two *d*. *Educ:* Bradfield; Trinity Hall, Cambridge (MA (Hist. Pt 1, Cl. 1; Theol. Pt 2, Cl. 2/1); Hon. Fellow, 1997); Westcott House, Cambridge. Curate, St John's Wood Church, 1963; Chaplain of Downing Coll., Cambridge, 1966; Chaplain and Fellow of Exeter Coll., Oxford, 1969 (Hon. Fellow, 1991); Res. Canon of Norwich Cathedral and Examining Chaplain to Bp of Norwich, 1973–79; Vice-Dean of Norwich, 1978; Fleck Resident in Religion, Bryn Mawr Coll., USA, 1978; Lectr in Religious Studies, Sussex Univ., 1979–81; Dean, 1981–91, Fellow, 1982–91, King's College, Cambridge; Dean, Christ Church, Oxford, 1991–2003 (Hon. Student, 2003). Syndic, Fitzwilliam Museum, Cambridge, 1988–91. Examining Chaplain to Bp of Chichester, 1980–82. Mem., Doctrine Commn for C of E, 1978–82. Hussey Lectr, Univ. of Oxford, 1997. Jt Editor, Theology, 1976–86. *Publications:* Angels and Dirt, 1972; Luke, 1973; Tradition and Design in Luke's Gospel, 1976; The Pot and The Knife, 1979; The Parables in the Gospels, 1985; Critics of the Bible 1724–1873, 1989; The Burning Bush, 1990; Painting the Word, 1999; articles and reviews in Jl of Theol. Studies, Theology, Expository Times, TLS. *Recreations:* drawing, carpentry, reading. *Address:* All Souls College, Oxford OX1 4AL.

DRURY, Martin Dru, CBE 2001; FSA; Director-General, National Trust, 1996–2001 (Deputy Director-General, 1992–95); *b* 22 April 1938; *s* of late Walter Neville Dru Drury, TD; *m* 1971, Elizabeth Caroline, *d* of Hon. Sir Maurice Bridgeman, KBE; two *s* one *d*. *Educ:* Rugby. Commissioned, 3rd Hussars, 1957. Insurance Broker at Lloyd's, 1959–65; Mallett & Son (Antiques) Ltd, 1965–73 (Associate Dir, 1970–73); joined National Trust as Historic Buildings Rep., SE, and Furniture Advr, 1973; Historic Buildings Sec., 1981–95. Comr, Royal Hosp. Chelsea, 2002–. Trustee: Landmark Trust, 1988– (Chm., 1992–95, 2001–); Heritage of London Trust, 1996– (Chm., 2007–); Wallace Collection, 2001–; Vice-Chm., Attingham Trust, 1982–. Chm., Stowe Adv. Panel, 2005–. Member: Council, Georgian Group, 1994– (Mem. Exec. Cttee, 1976–94); Fabric Adv. Cttee, St Paul's Cathedral, 1991–; Exec. Cttee, SPAB, 2006–. Mem. Council, UK Overseas Territories Conservation Forum, 2000–05. FSA 1992. Mem., Court of Assts, Goldsmiths' Co., 1994– (Prime Warden, 2005–06). Hon. DArts Greenwich, 2000. Esher Award, for services to SPAB, 2002. *Address:* 3 Victoria Rise, SW4 0PB; 18 The Street, Stedham, West Sussex GU29 0NQ. *Clubs:* Brooks's, Pratt's; Seaview Yacht.

DRURY, Sir Michael; *see* Drury, Sir V. W. M.

DRURY, Raymond Michael; Under Secretary and Executive Director (Personnel), NHS Executive, Department of Health, 1993–95; *b* 28 Sept. 1935; *s* of late James Joseph Drury and Annie Drury (*née* Greenwood); *m* 1959, Joyce Mary (*née* Clare); two *s* two *d*. *Educ:* Manchester Grammar Sch.; University Coll. London (BA Hons Classics (Latin and Greek)). Exec. Officer, Nat. Assistance Bd, 1958–64; HEO and Manager, Legal Aid Assessment Office, N Western Reg., 1964–70; Principal, DHSS, 1970–77; Asst Sec. and Dir (Exports), DHSS, 1977–79; Sec. of State's Rep. on Mgt Sides of Whitley Councils for Health Services (GB) responsible for NHS pay and conditions of service, 1979–88; Hd, Industrial Relns and Negotiations, DoH, 1988–93. *Recreations:* family, gardening, walking, DIY. *Address:* Penlan, Main Street, Clopton, Kettering, Northants NN14 3DZ. *T:* (01832) 720129.

DRURY, Sir (Victor William) Michael, Kt 1989; OBE 1978; FRCP; FRCGP; FRACGP; Professor of General Practice, University of Birmingham, 1980–91, now Emeritus; Vice President, Age Concern England, since 1995 (Chairman, 1992–95); *b* 5 Aug. 1926; *s* of Leslie and Beatrice Drury; *m* 1950, Joan (*née* Williamson); three *s* one *d*. *Educ:* Bromsgrove Sch.; Univ. of Birmingham (MB ChB Hons; Foundn Fellow 2006); MRCS LRCP 1949; FRCGP 1970 (MRCGP 1963); FRCP 1988; FRACGP 1988. Ho. Surg., Birmingham Gen., 1949–50; RSO, Kidderminster, 1950–51; Major, RAMC, 1951–53; Principal in Gen. Practice, Bromsgrove, 1953–91; Nuffield Trav. Fellow, 1965; Clarkson Sen. Clin. Tutor, Univ. of Birmingham, 1973–80. Lectures: James MacKenzie, 1983, Eli Lilley, 1984; Sir David Bruce, 1985; Gale, 1986; Fulton, 1996. Royal College of General Practitioners: Mem. Council, 1971–85 (Vice-Chm., 1980); Chm., Practice Org., 1966–71, Cttee and Res. Div., 1983–85; Pres., 1985–88. Member: Cttee on Safety of Medicines (Adverse Drug Reaction), 1975–79; Prescription Pricing Authy, 1981–86; DHA, 1981–85; Res. Cttee, RHA, 1982–86; GMC, 1984–94; Standing Cttee, Post Grad. Med. Educn, 1988–93. Chairman: Med. and Social Services Cttee, Muscular Dystrophy Gp, 1992–99; UK Centre for Advancement of Interprofessional Educn, 1994–97; Trustee, Nat. Asthma Trng Centre, 1991–2002. Civilian Advr in Gen. Practice to Army, 1984–91. Mem. Ct, Liverpool Univ., 1980–87; Vice-Pres., Bromsgrove Sch., 2004– (Gov. and Trustee, 1990–2003). Mem., Lunar Soc., 1993–. Hon. FRCPCH 1996. *Publications:* Introduction to General Practice, 1974; (ed) Treatment, 1978–; Medical Secretaries Handbook, 6th edn 1992; Treatment and Prognosis, 1990; The New Practice Manager, 1990, 3rd edn 1994; Teaching and Training Techniques for Hospital Doctors, 1998; General Practice and Clinical Negligence, 2000; various chapters in books on Drug Safety, Gen. Practice, etc; res. articles in Lancet, BMJ, Brit. Jl of Surgery, Jl RCGP. *Recreations:* gardening, reading, bridge, talking and listening. *Address:* Magellan House, Bourton Road, Moreton-in-Marsh, Glos GL56 0BD. *T:* (01608) 812325.

DRY, Philip John Seaton; Partner, Biggart Baillie, 1971–2007; President, Law Society of Scotland, 1998–99 (Vice-President, 1997–98); *b* 21 April 1945; *s* of William Good Dry and Georgina Wilson Macpherson or Dry; *m* 1970, Joyce Christine Hall; one *s* one *d*. *Educ:* George Watson's Coll.; Greenock Acad.; Glasgow Univ. (LLB). Apprenticeship, 1966–68, Asst Solicitor, 1968–70, with Biggart Lumsden & Co. Dir, Fyfe Chambers (Glasgow) Ltd, 1990–98. Mem., Disciplinary Appeal Bd, Faculty of Actuaries, 1999–2005. Dir, Westcot Homes plc and Westcot Homes II plc, 1989–2000. Mem., PO Users' Council for Scotland, 1994–98. Director: Scots Law Trust, 1998–99; Scottish Council of Law Reporting, 1998–99. Dir, Glasgow Renfrewshire Soc. *Recreations:* sailing, the garden, opera, swimming, travel. *Address:* 107 Octavia Terrace, Greenock, Renfrewshire PA16 7PY. *Club:* Royal Gourock Yacht.

DRYDEN, Sir John (Stephen Gyles), 8th and 11th Bt *cr* 1795 and 1733; *b* 26 Sept. 1943; *s* of Sir Noel Percy Hugh Dryden, 7th and 10th Bt, and Rosamund Mary (*d* 1994), *e d* of late Stephen Scrope; *S* father, 1970; *m* 1970, Diana Constance, *o d* of late Cyril Tomlinson, Highland Park, Wellington, NZ; one *s* one *d*. *Educ:* Oratory School. *Heir:* *s* John Frederick Simon Dryden, *b* 26 May 1976. *Address:* Spinners, Fairwarp, East Sussex TN22 3BE.

DRYSDALE, Laura, (Mrs John Tipler); consultant to museums and heritage organisations; *b* 28 April 1958; *d* of Andrew and Merida Drysdale; *m* 1989, John Tipler; one *s* one *d*, and one step *s* one step *d*. *Educ:* Charterhouse; St Andrews Univ. (MA 1979); City Univ. (C&G MA 1987). Textile Conservator: Dalmeny House, 1979–81; V&A Mus., 1981–83; Textile Conservation Studio, 1983–86; Conservation Projects, 1986–92; Partner, Drysdale and Halahan, 1992–96; Head of Collections Conservation, English Heritage, 1996–99; Head of Adv. Services, Mus and Galls Commn, 1999–2000; Dir, Sector and Professional Services, Resource: Council for Mus, Archives and Libraries, 2000. FIIC 1996. *Publications:* articles in learned jls, conf. proceedings. *Recreation:* treading grapes. *Address:* 49 The Close, Norwich NR1 4EG.

DRYSDALE, Thomas Henry, WS; solicitor, retired; *b* 23 Nov. 1942; *s* of late Ian Drysdale and Rosalind Marion Drysdale (*née* Gallie); *m* 1967, Caroline, *d* of late Dr Gavin B. Shaw; one *s* two *d*. *Educ:* Cargilfield; Glenalmond; Edinburgh Univ. (LLB). Partner, Shepherd & Wedderburn WS, 1967–99 (Man. Partner, 1988–94); Dep. Keeper of HM Signet, 1991–98; Partner, Olivers WS, 1999–2004, retd. Key Stakeholder Rep., Automated Registration of Title to Land, Registers of Scotland, 2004–07. Dir, Edinburgh Solicitors' Property Centre, 1976–89 (Chm., 1981–88). Legal Chm., Tribunals Service, 2003–. Hon. Consul in Scotland, Republic of Hungary, 2001–. Sec. and Treas., Stair Soc., 1998–. *Recreations:* ski-ing, walking, reading. *Address:* 6 The Glebe, Manse Road, Dirleton, East Lothian EH39 5FB. *Club:* New (Edinburgh).

DRYSDALE WILSON, John Veitch, Eur Ing, CEng, FIMechE, FCIArb; Deputy Secretary, Institution of Mechanical Engineers, 1979–90; *b* 8 April 1929; *s* of Alexander Drysdale Wilson and Winifred Rose (*née* Frazier); *m* 1954, Joan Lily, *e d* of Mr and Mrs John Cooke, Guildford; one *s* one *d*. *Educ:* Solihull School; Guildford Technical Coll. Dennis Bros Ltd, Guildford: Engineer Apprentice, 1946–50; MIRA Research Trainee, 1949–50; Jun. Designer, 1950–51. National Service Officer, REME, 1951–53, Captain on

Staff of CREME, 6th Armd Div. Management Trainee, BET Fedn, 1953–55; Technical Sales Engr, subseq. Head of Mechanical Laboratories, Esso Petroleum Co. Ltd, 1955–66; Chief Engr, R&D, Castrol Ltd, subseq. Burmah Oil Trading Ltd and Edwin Cooper Ltd, 1966–77; Projects and Res. Officer, Instn of Mechanical Engineers, 1977–79. Director: Mechanical Engineering Publications Ltd, 1979–90; Professional Engineers Insurance Bureau Ltd, 1989–90. Freeman, City of London, 1986; Liveryman: Co. of Engineers, 1987; Co. of Arbitrators, 1987. Mem., Casterbridge Probus Club. *Publications:* numerous papers to learned societies in USA and Europe on subjects related to engine lubrication. *Recreations:* travel, genealogy, horology, ink sketching, water colour painting. *Club:* Caravan.

D'SOUZA, family name of **Baroness D'Souza**.

D'SOUZA, Baroness *cr* 2004 (Life Peer), of Wychwood in the County of Oxfordshire; **Frances Gertrude Claire D'Souza,** CMG 1999; DPhil; Director, 2002–04, Consultant, 2004–06, Redress Trust; *b* 18 April 1944; *d* of Robert Anthony Gilbert Russell and Pauline Mary Russell (*née* Parmet); *m* 1st, 1959, Stanislaus D'Souza (marr. diss. 1974); two *d*; 2nd, 1985, Martin Griffiths (marr. diss. 1994); remarried 2003, Stanislaus D'Souza. *Educ:* St Mary's, Princethorpe; UCL (BSc 1970); Lady Margaret Hall, Oxford (DPhil 1976). Ford Foundn Res. Fellow in Comparative Physiology, Nuffield Inst. of Comparative Medicine, 1973–77; pt-time adult educn lectr, Morley Coll. and City Lit., 1973–78; pt-time Lectr on Race and Culture, LSE, 1974–80; Sen. Lectr, Dept of Humanities, Oxford Poly., 1977–80; Founder Dir and Res. Dir, Internat. Relief and Develt Inst., 1977–85; Indep. Res. Cons. for UN, SCF, Ford Foundn, carrying out field work in Africa, Asia, S Europe, Pacific Region, 1985–88; ODA Res. Fellow, 1988–89; Exec. Dir, Article 19, Internat. Centre against Censorship, 1989–98; Fellow, Open Soc. Inst. (Soros Inst.), 1998–99. Mem., RGS expedn to the Karakorums, 1980. Regular broadcasts, 1989–98. Editor, Internat. Jl of Disaster Studies and Practice, 1978–82. *Publications:* (ed) Striking a Balance: hate speech, freedom of expression and non-discrimination, 1992; (jtly) The Right to Know: human rights and access to reproductive health information, 1995; numerous reports, scientific papers, contribs to books and articles in jls, incl. Nature, Scientific American, Third World Qly. *Recreations:* music (opera and string quartets), serious walking.

D'SOUZA, Most Rev. Henry Sebastian; Archbishop of Calcutta, (RC), 1986–2002, now Emeritus; *b* 20 Jan. 1926; *s* of George William and Aurelia Clotilde D'Souza. *Educ:* Papal Atheneum, Kandy (LPH, LD); Urban Univ., Rome (DCL). Ordained priest, 1948; Bishop of Cuttack-Bhubaneswar, 1974–85; Coadjutor Archbishop, Calcutta, 1985–86. Secretary General: Catholic Bishops' Conference of India, 1979–82; Federation of Asian Bishops' Confs, 1983–93. Pres., Conf. of Catholic Bishops of India (Latin Rite), 1988–94, 1998–2002. *Address:* The Presbytery, 9/3 Middleton Row, Kolkata 700071, India.

DUBE, Alfred Uyapo Majaye; Managing Director, Lazare Kaplan Botswana (Pty) Ltd, since 2006; *b* 8 June 1949; *s* of Mbangwa Edison Majaye and Phakela Majaye; *m* 1977, Elvyn Jones; three *s*. *Educ:* Poly. of North London; Univ. of Essex (BA Hons Govt). Librarian, Nat. Liby Service, 1971–74; Foreign Service Officer, Dept of Ext. Affairs, Botswana, 1977–79; First Sec., Botswana Embassy and Mission to EC, Brussels, 1979–80; Counsellor, London, 1980–81; Under-Sec., Min. of Mineral Resources and Water Affairs, 1981–83; Minister Counsellor, Brussels, 1983–87; Under-Sec., Dept of Ext. Affairs, 1987–89; Ambassador to Sweden, all Nordic countries and USSR/Russia, 1989–93; High Comr, UK, 1993–96; Ambassador to People's Republic of China, 1996–2001, and concurrently High Comr to Malaysia and Singapore; Special Envoy on Diamonds, 2001–02; Perm. Rep. to UN, 2002–05; High Comr to Jamaica and Guyana, and Ambassador to Cuba, 2002–05. *Recreations:* reading, jazz, wine, golf. *Address:* Lazare Kaplan Botswana (Pty) Ltd, Private Bag 0034, Gaborone, Botswana.

DUBERLY, (Archibald) Hugh, CBE 1996; Crown Estate Commissioner, since 2002; Lord-Lieutenant for Cambridgeshire, since 2003; *b* 4 April 1942; *s* of Commander Archibald Gray, DSO, RN, and Grey Cunliffe Gray (*née* Duberly); adopted surname Duberly, 1963; *m* 1967, Sarah Elizabeth Robertson; two *s* one *d*. *Educ:* Winchester Coll. Pres., Country Landowners' Assoc., 1993–95; Dir, Agricultural Mortgage Corp. Plc, 1995–2002. Chm., Ely Diocesan Bd of Finance, 1992–. Chairman: Papworth Trust, 1995–; Shuttleworth Trust, 2001–. Chm., Kimbolton Sch., 1992–2000; Gov., Writtle Coll., 1997–. DL 1989, High Sheriff, 1991–92, Cambs. *Address:* Place House, Great Staughton, Huntingdon PE19 5BB. *T:* (01480) 860305. *Club:* Boodle's.

DUBLIN, Archbishop of, and Primate of Ireland, since 2002; **Most Rev. John Robert Winder Neill;** *b* 17 Dec. 1945; *s* of Eberto Mahon Neill and Rhoda Anne Georgina Neill; *m* 1968, Betty Anne (*née* Cox); three *s*. *Educ:* Sandford Park School, Dublin; Trinity Coll., Dublin (Foundation Schol., BA 1st Cl., MA); Jesus Coll., Cambridge (MA, Gardiner Memorial Schol., Univ. of Cambridge); Ridley Hall, Cambridge (GOE). Curate Asst, St Paul's, Glenageary, Dublin, 1969–71; Lectr (Old Testament) in Divinity Hostel, 1970–71; Bishop's Vicar and Dio. Registrar, Kilkenny, 1971–74; Rector of Abbeystrewry, Skibbereen, Co. Cork, 1974–78; Rector of St Bartholomew's, and Leeson Park, Dublin, 1978–84; Lectr (Liturgy) in Theological Coll., 1982–84; Exam. Chaplain to Archbishop of Dublin, 1982–84; Dean of Christ Church Cathedral, Waterford, 1984–86; Archdeacon of Waterford, 1984–86; Bishop: of Tuam, Killala and Achonry, 1986–97; of Cashel and Ossory, 1997–2002; of Dublin and Glendalough, 2002–. Sec., Irish House of Bishops, 1988–95; Mem., Central Cttee, WCC, 1994–2006; Pres., CTBI, 1999–2002. Hon. LLD NUI, 2003. *Publications:* contribs to Theology, New Divinity, Search, Doctrine and Life and Intercom. *Recreations:* photography, travel. *Address:* The See House, 17 Temple Road, Milltown, Dublin 6, Ireland.

DUBLIN, Archbishop of, and Primate of Ireland, (RC), since 2004; **Most Rev. Diarmuid Martin;** *b* Dublin, 8 April 1945. *Educ:* UC Dublin; Dublin Diocesan Seminary; Pontifical Univ. of St Thomas Aquinas (Angelicum), Rome. Ordained priest, 1969; Curate, St Brigid, Cabinteely, 1973–74; respons. for pastoral care of Dublin pilgrims in Rome, 1975; entered service of Holy See, 1976, Pontifical Council for the Family; Under-Sec., 1986, Sec., 1994, Pontifical Council for Justice and Peace; Titular Bp of Glendalough, 1999–2003; Archbishop, 2001, Permanent Observer of Holy See at UN, Geneva, 2001–03; Coadjutor Archbishop of Dublin, 2003–04. *Address:* Archbishop's House, Drumcondra, Dublin 9, Ireland.

DUBLIN, (Christ Church), Dean of; *see* Dunne, Very Rev. D. P. M.

DUBLIN, (St Patrick's), Dean of; *see* MacCarthy, Very Rev. R. B.

du BOULAY; *see* Houssemayne du Boulay.

DUBOWITZ, Prof. Victor, MD, PhD; FRCP, FRCPCH; Professor of Paediatrics, University of London, at the Royal Postgraduate Medical School, 1972–96, now Emeritus; Consultant Paediatrician, Hammersmith Hospital, 1972–96; Director, Muscle Research Centre, Royal Postgraduate Medical School, 1975–96; *b* 6 Aug. 1931; *s* of late Charley and Olga Dubowitz (*née* Schattel); *m* 1960, Dr Lilly Magdalena Suzanne Sebok; four *s*. *Educ:* Beaufort West Central High Sch., S Africa; Univ. of Cape Town (BSc, MB, ChB, 1954; MD 1960). PhD Sheffield, 1965; DCH 1958; FRCP 1972; FRCPCH 1997. Intern, Groote Schuur Hosp., Cape Town, 1955; Sen. House Officer, Queen Mary's Hosp. for Children, Carshalton, 1957–59; Res. Associate in Histochem., Royal Postgrad. Med. Sch., 1958–59; Lectr in Clin. Path., National Hosp. for Nervous Diseases, Queen Square, London, 1960; Lectr in Child Health, 1961–65, Sen. Lectr, 1965–67, and Reader, 1967–72, Univ. of Sheffield; Res. Associate, Inst. for Muscle Diseases, and Asst Paediatrician, Cornell Med. Coll., New York, 1965–66; Dir of Therapeutic Studies, European Neuro Muscular Centre, 1999–2003. Several lectureships and overseas vis. professorships. President: British Paediatric Neurol. Assoc., 1992–94; European Paediatric Neurology Soc., 1994–97; World Muscle Soc., 1995–; Medical Art Soc., 1996–2000. Curator of Art, RCPCH, 1997–. Founding Editor: Neuromuscular Disorders, 1990–; European Jl of Paediatric Neurology, 1996–2003. Hon. FRCPCH 1997. Arvo Ylppö Gold Medal, Finland, 1982; Baron ver Heyden de Lancey Prize, Med. Art Soc., 1980, 1982, 2002; Jean Hunter Prize, RCP, 1987; Gaetano Conte Medal, Italy, 1991; Cornelia de Lange Medal, Netherlands, 1997; Duchenne Erb Prize, German Speaking Muscular Dystrophy Assocs, 1999; James Spence Medal, RCPCH, 2007. Comdr, Order of Constantine the Great, 1980. *Publications:* Developing and Diseased Muscle: a histochemical study, 1968; The Floppy Infant, 1969, 2nd edn 1980; (with M. H. Brooke) Muscle Biopsy: a modern approach, 1973, 3rd edn (with C. Sewry) 2006; (with L. M. S. Dubowitz) Gestational Age of the Newborn: a clinical manual, 1977; Muscle Disorders in Childhood, 1978, 2nd edn 1995; (with L. M. S. Dubowitz) The Neurological Assessment of the Preterm and Full-term Newborn Infant, 1981, 2nd edn 2000; Colour Atlas of Muscle Disorders in Childhood, 1989; (jtly) A Colour Atlas of Brain Lesions in the Newborn, 1990; Ramblings of a Peripatetic Paediatrician, 2005; chapters in books and articles in learned jls on paediatric topics, partic. muscle disorders and newborn neurology. *Recreations:* sculpting, photography. *Address:* 25 Middleton Road, Golders Green, NW11 7NR. *T:* (020) 8455 9352.

DUBS, family name of **Baron Dubs**.

DUBS, Baron *cr* 1994 (Life Peer), of Battersea in the London Borough of Wandsworth; **Alfred Dubs;** Chairman, Broadcasting Standards Commission, 2001–03 (Joint Deputy Chairman, 1997); *b* Prague, Czechoslovakia, Dec. 1932; *m*; one *s* one *d*. *Educ:* LSE. BSc (Econs). Local govt officer. Mem., Westminster CC, 1971–78; Chm., Westminster Community Relns Council, 1972–77; Mem., Kensington, Chelsea and Westminster AHA, 1975–78. Dir, British Refugee Council, 1988–95. Member: TGWU; Co-operative Party. Contested (Lab): Cities of London and Westminster, 1970; Hertfordshire South, Feb. and Oct. 1974; Battersea, 1987 and 1992. MP (Lab): Wandsworth, Battersea S, 1979–83; Battersea, 1983–87. Mem., Home Affairs Select Cttee, 1981–83 (Mem., Race Relations and Immigration Sub-Cttee, 1981–83); opposition front bench spokesman on home affairs, 1983–87. House of Lords: an Opposition Whip, 1994–97; opposition front bench spokesman on energy, 1995–97, on health and safety, 1996–97; Parly Under-Sec. of State, NI Office, 1997–99; Member: Select Cttee on European Communities, 1995–97; Sub-Cttee F, European Select Cttee, 2003–07. Chairman: All Pty Parly Gp on Eur. Enlargement, 2000–, on Integrated Educn in NI, 2000–, on Moldova, 2006–, on Portugal, 2008–; Lab Party in H of L, 2000–06; Mem., Jt Cttee on Human Rights, 2007–. Mem., 1988–94, Dep. Chm., 1995–97, Broadcasting Standards Council; Vice-Chm., ITC, 2000–01; Chm., Road Safety Foundn, 2007–. Chm., Ind. Code Panel, Assoc. of Energy Suppliers, 2004–. *Recreation:* walking in the Lake District. *Address:* c/o House of Lords, SW1P 0PW.

DU CANE, John Peter, OBE 1964; Director, Amax Inc., 1966–91; *b* 16 April 1921; *s* of Charles and Mathilde Du Cane; *m* 1945, Patricia Wallace (*née* Desmond); two *s*. *Educ:* Canford Sch., Wimborne. Pilot, Fleet Air Arm, RN, 1941–46. De Beers Consolidated Mines, 1946–54; Sierra Leone Selection Trust, 1955–63; Director: Consolidated African Selection Trust, 1963–81; Selection Trust Ltd, 1966–81 (Man. Dir, 1975–80; Chm., 1978–81); BP International Ltd, 1981; Chief Exec., BP Minerals Internat. Ltd, 1980–81; Director: Australian Consolidated Minerals Pty, 1981–86 (Dep. Chm., 1983–86); Ultramar Plc, 1983–87; Austamax Resources Ltd, 1984–86 (Dep. Chm., 1984–86). Mem., RNSA. *Recreations:* sailing, fishing, photography. *Club:* Naval and Military.

du CANN, Col Rt Hon. Sir Edward (Dillon Lott), KBE 1985; PC 1964; Chairman, Lonrho Plc, 1984–91 (Director, 1972–92; Joint Deputy Chairman, 1983–84); *b* 28 May 1924; *er s* of late C. G. L. du Cann, Barrister-at-Law, and Janet (*née* Murchie); *m* 1st, 1962, Sallie Innes (marr. diss. 1990; she *d* 2007), *e d* of late James Henry Murchie, Caldy, Cheshire; one *s* two *d*; 2nd, 1990, Jenifer Patricia Evelyn (*d* 1995), *yr d* of late Evelyn Mansfield King, and *widow* of Sir Robert Cooke. *Educ:* Colet Court; Woodbridge Sch.; St John's Coll., Oxford (MA, Law). Served with RNVR, 1943–46 (CO, HMMTB 5010). Vice-Pres., Somerset and Wilts Trustee Savings Bank, 1956–75; Founder, Unicorn Group of Unit Trusts, 1957 (pioneered modern British unit trust industry and equity linked life assurance); Chairman: Barclays Unicorn Ltd and associated cos, 1957–72; Keyser Ullmar Holdings Ltd, 1970–75; Cannon Assurance Ltd, 1972–80. Chm., Association of Unit Trust Managers, 1961. Contested: West Walthamstow Div., 1951; Barrow-in-Furness Div., 1955. MP (C) Taunton Div. of Somerset, Feb. 1956–1987. Economic Sec. to the Treasury, 1962–63; Minister of State, Board of Trade, 1963–64. Mem., Lord Chancellor's Adv. Cttee on Public Records, 1960–62; Joint Hon. Sec.: UN Parly Group, 1961–62; Conservative Parly Finance Group, 1961–62; Mem., Select Cttee on House of Lords Reform, 1962; Founder Chairman: Select Cttee on Public Expenditure, 1971–73; All-Party Maritime Affairs Parly Gp, 1984–87; Mem., Select Cttee on Privilege, 1972–87; Chairman: Select Cttee on Public Accounts, 1974–79; 1922 Cttee, 1972–84; Liaison Cttee of Select Cttee Chairmen, 1974–83; (founder) Select Cttee on Treasury and Civil Service Affairs, 1979–83; (first) Public Accounts Commn, 1984–87; Cons. Party Organisation, 1965–67; Burke Club, 1968–79. President: (founder) Anglo-Polish Cons. Soc., 1972–74; Nat. Union of Conservative and Unionist Assocs, 1981–82; Cons. Parly European Community Reform Gp, 1985–87; Vice-Chm., British American Parly Gp 1978–81. Jt Leader, British-American Parly Gp delegns to USA, 1978, 1980; Leader British Parly Gp delegn to China, IPU, 1982. Dir, James Beattie Ltd, 1965–79. Pres., Inst. of Freight Forwarders Ltd, 1988–89; Vice-Pres., British Insurance Brokers Assoc., 1978; Patron, Assoc. of Insurance Brokers, 1974–77. Visiting Fellow, Univ. of Lancaster Business School, 1970–82. Member: Panel of Judges, Templeton Foundn, 1984; Management Council, GB-Sasakawa Foundn, 1984–91. Patron, Human Ecology Foundn, 1987–2007. Mem. Governing Council, Taunton Sch., 1972–93; Governor, Hatfield Coll., Durham Univ., 1988–92. Vice Pres., Limassol Hospice, 2002–; Pres., Macmillan Cancer Appeal, 1985. Commodore, 1962, Admiral, 1974–87, House of Commons Yacht Club; President, Cyprus Branch: RN Assoc., 2003–; Oxford Univ. Soc. 2005–. Hon. Col, 155 (Wessex) Regt, RCT (Volunteers), 1972–82; Hon. Life Member, Instn of RCT, 1983; Taunton Racecourse, 1991. Sen. Pres., Oxford Univ. Rugby League FC, 2004–. Lecturer, broadcaster. Mem. Court of Assts, Fruiterers' Co. (Master, 1990); elected first Freeman of Taunton Deane Borough, 1977. FRSA 1986. *Publications:* Investing Simplified, 1959; Two Lives: the political and business careers of Edward du

Cann, 1995; Wellington Caricatures, 2000; pamphlets, and articles on financial and international affairs (incl. The Case for a Bill of Rights, How to Bring Government Expenditure within Parliamentary Control, A New Competition Policy, Hoist the Red Ensign). *Recreations:* travel, gardening, sailing. *Address:* Lemona, 8545 Pafos, Cyprus; Flat 7, 42 Great Smith Street, SW1P 3BU. *Clubs:* Carlton (Hon. Mem.); Royal Western Yacht.

DUCAT, Rt Hon. Dawn, (Mrs Thomas Ducat); *see* Primarolo, Rt Hon. D.

duCHARME, Gillian Drusilla Brown; educational consultant, since 2000; Headmistress, Benenden School, 1985–2000; *b* 23 Jan. 1938; *d* of Alfred Henry Brown and Alice Drusilla Grant; *m* 1969, Jean Louis duCharme (marr. diss.). *Educ:* Girton College, Cambridge. BA 1960, MA 1964. British Council, 1964–66; Chm., French Dept and Head of Upper Sch., Park Sch., Brookline, Mass, 1969–77; Registrar, Concord Acad., Concord, Mass, 1977–80; Headmistress, The Town Sch., New York City, 1980–85. Governor: Marlborough House Sch., 1987–; Wellington Coll., Crowthorne, 1996–2006. Member: Council, Friends of Nat. Maritime Mus., 2001– (Chm., 2004–07); Bd, Internat. Rescue Cttee, UK, 2004–. Hon. DEd Greenwich, 2005. *Recreations:* tennis, hill-walking, art, design and architecture, film, birdwatching, travel, books. *Address:* 3 Saint Alfege Passage, Greenwich, SE10 9JS. *T:* (020) 8858 8186; *e-mail:* gillianducharme@hotmail.com.

DUCIE, 7th Earl of, *cr* 1837; **David Leslie Moreton;** Baron Ducie, 1763; Baron Moreton, 1837; *b* 20 Sept. 1951; *e s* of 6th Earl of Ducie and Alison May, *d* of L. A. Bates; *S* father, 1991; *m* 1975, Helen, *er d* of M. L. Duchesne; one *s* one *d*. *Educ:* Cheltenham College; Wye Coll., London Univ. (BSc 1973). *Heir: s* Lord Moreton, *qv*. *Address:* Talbots End Farm, Cromhall, Glos GL12 8AJ.

DUCK, Hywel Ivor, CMG 1998; Hon. Director-General, Council of the European Union, since 1998; Director of Fisheries, Secretariat General, Council of Ministers of European Communities, 1987–98; *b* 12 June 1933; *s* of Dr Ernest Frank Duck and Minnie Isabel Duck (*née* Peake); *m* 1st, 1963, Theodora Mary Fitzgerald Mugnaini (*née* Creighton) (marr. diss. 1975); four step *d*; 2nd, 1980, Dr Barbara Elisabeth Huwe (*d* 1994); one *s* one *d*; 3rd, 2002, Patricia Anne-Louise de Graeve. *Educ:* King's School, Canterbury; Trinity College, Cambridge (MA); Diplôme d'Etudes Supérieures Européennes, Nancy. ARCO 2002. Called to the Bar, Gray's Inn, 1956. Foreign Office, 1956; served Warsaw, FO, Cairo, Khartoum, Damascus; Second later First Sec., Bonn, 1964; DSAO, later FCO, 1968; Consul (Commercial), Zürich and Dep. Dir, British Export Promotion in Switzerland, 1970–73; Head of Div., Secretariat Gen., Council of Ministers, EC, 1973–75; Dir of Ops and Translation, 1975–84; Dir, Directorate-Gen. for Agriculture and Fisheries, 1984–87. *Recreation:* classical music. *Club:* Oxford and Cambridge.

DUCKWORTH, His Honour Brian Roy; DL; a Circuit Judge, 1983–2004; Deputy Senior Judge, Cyprus Sovereign Base Areas Court, since 1998; *b* 26 July 1934; *s* of late Roy and Kathleen Duckworth; *m* 1964, Nancy Carolyn Duckworth, JP, *d* of late Chris and Annie Holden; three *s* one *d*. *Educ:* Sedbergh Sch.; Worcester Coll., Oxford (MA). Called to Bar, Lincoln's Inn, 1958; a Recorder of the Crown Court, 1972–83; Member: Northern Circuit; Bar Council, 1979–82. Councillor, Blackburn RDC, 1960–74 (Chm. 1970–72); Mem., Blackburn HMC, 1966–74. Liaison Judge and Hon. Pres., South Cumbria Magistracy, 1987–92; Liaison Judge, SW Lancs Magistracy, 1993–2004. Member: Lord-Lieut's Magistracy Adv. Cttee, 1993–2004; Lancs Probation Cttee, 1991–2001; Cttee, Council of Circuit Judges, 1995–2004. Chm., Samlesbury Hall Charitable Trust, 1993–. Vice-Pres., 2003–06, Pres., 2006–, Blackburn Br., Prayer Book Soc. Mem. Court, Lancaster Univ., 2003–. Pres., Old Sedberghian Club, 1996–99. DL Lancs 1995. *Recreations:* golf, sailing, gardening, motor sport. *Address:* c/o The Crown Court, Ringway, Preston PR1 2LL. *T:* (01772) 844700. *Club:* Pleasington Golf.

DUCKWORTH, Eric; *see* Duckworth, W. E.

DUCKWORTH, Sir James Edward Dyce, 5th Bt *cr* 1909, of Grosvenor Place, City of Westminster; *b* 20 Dec. 1984; *s* of Sir Edward Richard Dyce Duckworth, 4th Bt and of Patricia, *o d* of Thomas Cahill; *S* father, 2005, but his name does not appear on the Official Roll of the Baronetage. *Heir: uncle* Antony George Dyce Duckworth [*b* 20 Nov. 1946; *m* 1974, Geraldine Broderick; one *s*].

DUCKWORTH, John Alan, (Joe); Chief Executive, London Borough of Newham, since 2008; *b* St Helens, 18 May 1955; *s* of George and Alice Duckworth; *m* 1990, Julie Ratty; two *s* one *d*. *Educ:* Bristol Univ. (BSc Hons Econs); Manchester Univ. (MA Econs). National Research Officer: USDAW, 1980–83; Instn of Professionals, Managers and Specialists, 1983–91; Dir of Personnel, York CC, 1991–95; County Personnel Officer, Surrey CC, 1995–97; Exec. Dir, London Bor. of Hackney, 1997–2000; Dir, Envmt and Leisure, 2000–04, Dep. Chief Exec., 2004–06, Westminster CC; Chief Exec., Isle of Wight Council, 2006–08. *Recreation:* cycling. *Address:* Chief Executive's Office, London Borough of Newham, Building 1000, Dockside Road, E16 2QU. *T:* (020) 8430 3499; *e-mail:* joe.duckworth@newham.gov.uk.

DUCKWORTH, John Clifford, FREng; FIET, FInstP; Managing Director, National Research Development Corporation, 1959–70; *b* 27 Dec. 1916; *s* of late H. Duckworth, Wimbledon, and of Mrs A. H. Duckworth (*née* Woods); *m* 1942, Dorothy Nancy Wills; three *s*. *Educ:* KCS, Wimbledon; Wadham Coll., Oxford (MA). FIET (FIEE 1957); FInstP 1957; Sen. FInstE 1957; FREng (FEng 1976). Radar Research and Development, Telecommunications Research Establishment, Malvern, 1939–46; National Research Council, Chalk River, Ont, 1946–47; Atomic Energy Research Establishment, Harwell, 1947–50; Chief Engineer, Wythenshawe Laboratories, Ferranti Ltd, 1950–54; Nuclear Power Engineer, Brit. Electricity Authority, 1954–58; Central Electricity Authority, 1957–58; Chief Research and Development Officer, Central Electricity Generating Board, 1958–59. Mem. Bd, AEA, 1963–68. Mem., Defence Res. Adv. Council, 1955–65. Chm., IDJ Investment Services Ltd, 1970–82; Chm. or non-exec. dir of various public cos, 1970–83. Pres., Institute of Fuel, 1963–64; Vice-Pres., Parliamentary and Scientific Cttee, 1964–67. Chairman: MacRobert Award Cttee, 1970–76; Science Mus. Adv. Council, 1972–84; Trustee, Science Mus., 1984–90. Vice-Pres., IEE, 1974–77. *Publication:* Weighty Matters, Worthy People, 2007. *Address:* Pengilly, Little-in-Sight, Mawnan Smith, Falmouth TR11 5EY. *Club:* Athenæum.

DUCKWORTH, Prof. Roy, CBE 1987; MD; FRCS, FDSRCS, FRCPath; Emeritus Professor of Oral Medicine, University of London; Dean, The London Hospital Medical College, 1986–94; *b* Bolton, 19 July 1929; *s* of Stanley Duckworth and Hilda Evelyn Moores; *m* 1953, Marjorie Jean Bowness, Flimby; two *s* one *d*. *Educ:* King George V Sch., Southport; Univ. of Liverpool (BDS; MD 1964). FDSRCS 1957; FRCPath 1973; FRCS 1986. Served RAF Dental Br., 1953–55. Nuffield Fellow, RPMS and Guy's Hosp. Dental Sch., 1959–61; The London Hospital Medical College: Sen. Lectr in Oral Medicine, 1961; Reader in Oral Medicine, 1965; Dean of Dental Studies, 1969–75; Prof. and Head, Dept of Oral Medicine, 1968–90. Consultant in Oral Medicine, The London Hosp., 1965–90. Dean, Faculty of Dental Surgery, RCS, 1983–86. Civil Consultant: in Dental Surg., to Army, 1977–90; in Oral Medicine and Oral Path., to RN, 1982–90; Temp. Consultant, WHO, 1973; British Council Visitor, 1977. Vis. Prof. in many countries. President: British Soc. of Periodontology, 1972–73; British Soc. for Oral Medicine, 1986–87; BDA, 1990–91. Chm., Standing Dental Adv. Cttee, Dept of Health, 1988–92 (Mem., 1984–88); Member: Adv. Council on Misuse of Drugs, 1977–85; Medicines Commn, 1980–83; Council, Fédération Dentaire Internationale, 1981–90 (Mem., List of Honour, 1993); GDC, 1984–89. Hon. Fellow, QMW, 1997. Scientific Adviser, British Dental Jl, 1975–82; Editor, Internat. Dental Jl, 1981–90. *Publications:* contrib. professional jls. *Recreation:* sailing.

DUCKWORTH, (Walter) Eric, OBE 1991; PhD; FREng; FIMMM, FInstP; Managing Director, Fulmer Ltd (formerly Fulmer Research Institute), 1969–90; Chairman: Bournville Consultants Ltd, since 1994; Digital Doctor Ltd, since 2006; *b* 2 Aug. 1925; *s* of Albert Duckworth and Rosamund (*née* Biddle); *m* 1949, Emma Evans; one *s*. *Educ:* Cambridge Univ. (MA, PhD). Research Manager, Glacier Metal Co., 1955; Asst Director, BISRA, 1966; Chm., Yarsley Technical Centre, 1973–89; Director: Ricardo Consulting Engineers plc, 1978–85; H. Darnell Ltd, 1982–94; Fleming Technol. Investment Trust plc, 1984–90. Chm., Council of Science and Technology Insts, 1977–78; first Charter Pres., Instn of Metallurgists, 1974–75; Pres., Assoc. of Independent Res. and Technol. Organisations (formerly Assoc. of Indep. Contract Res. Organs), 1978–79, 1988–89; Hon. Treas., Metals Soc., 1981–84; Chm., Professional Affairs Bd, Inst. of Metals, 1985–88. Member: Parly and Scientific Cttee, 1968–94; Res. and Technol. Cttee, 1979–88, and Indust. Policy Cttee, 1983–88, Council, 1988–89, CBI; Nominations Cttee, 1983–88, Standing Cttee on Industry, 1988–94, Engrg Council; Engrg Bd, SERC, 1985–87; Council, Assoc. for Schools' Sci., Engrg and Technol. (formerly Standing Conf. on Schools' Sci. and Technol.), 1994–99. Chm., Christian Nationals Evangelism Commn, 1974–93; Trustee: Comino Foundn, 1981–; FMI, 1995–99 (Mem. Council, 1995–99); Vice-Pres., St Mary's Hosp. Med. Sch., 1976–97; Mem. Court, Brunel Univ., 1978–85, and 1991–. Liveryman: Worshipful Co. of Scientific Instrument Makers; Co. of Engineers; Freeman, City of London. First Edwin Liddiard Meml Lectr, London Metallurgical Soc. of Inst. of Metals, 1982. FREng (FEng 1980). Hon. DTech Brunel, 1976; DUniv Surrey, 1980. Editor, 1978–85, Chm., Editorial Bd, 1985–92, Materials and Design. *Publications:* A Guide to Operational Research, 1962, 3rd edn 1977; Statistical Techniques in Technological Research, 1968; Electroslag Refining, 1969; Manganese in Ferrous Metallurgy, 1976; Contract Research, 1991; *circa* 100 contribs to learned and other jls on many topics. *Recreations:* gardening, photography, changing other people's attitudes. *Address:* Orinda, Church Lane, Stoke Poges, Bucks SL2 4PB. *T:* (01753) 645778.

du CROS, Sir Claude Philip Arthur Mallet, 3rd Bt *cr* 1916; *b* 22 Dec. 1922; *s* of Sir (Harvey) Philip du Cros, 2nd Bt, and of Dita, *d* of late Sir Claude Coventry Mallet, CMG; *S* father, 1975; *m* 1st, 1953, Mrs Christine Nancy Tordoff (marr. diss. 1974; she *d* 1988), *d* of late F. R. Bennett, Spilsby, Lincs; one *s*; 2nd, 1974, Mrs Margaret Roy Cutler (marr. diss. 1982), *d* of late R. J. Frater, Gosforth, Northumberland. *Heir: s* Julian Claude Arthur Mallet du Cros [*b* 23 April 1955; *m* 1984, Patricia, *o d* of Gerald Wyatt, Littlefield School, Liphook; one *s* two *d*].

DUDBRIDGE, Prof. Glen, PhD; FBA 1984; Shaw Professor of Chinese, University of Oxford, 1989–2005; Fellow of University College, Oxford, 1989–2005, now Emeritus; *b* 2 July 1938; *s* of George Victor Dudbridge and Edna Kathleen Dudbridge (*née* Cockle); *m* 1965, Sylvia Lo (Lo Fung-young); one *s* one *d*. *Educ:* Bristol Grammar School; Magdalene College, Cambridge (MA, PhD); New Asia Institute of Advanced Chinese Studies, Hong Kong. MA Oxon. Nat. Service, RAF, 1957–59. Research Fellow, Magdalene College, Cambridge, 1965; Lectr in Modern Chinese, 1965–85 and Fellow, Wolfson Coll., 1966–85 (now Emeritus Fellow), Univ. of Oxford; Prof. of Chinese and Fellow, Magdalene Coll., Univ. of Cambridge, 1985–89. Visiting Professor: Yale Univ., 1972–73; Univ. of California, Berkeley, 1980, 1998. Hon. Mem., Chinese Acad. of Social Scis, 1996. *Publications:* The Hsi-yu chi: a study of antecedents to the sixteenth century Chinese novel, 1970; The Legend of Miao-shan, 1978, 2nd edn 2004 (Chinese edn, 1990); The Tale of Li Wa: study and critical edition of a Chinese story from the ninth century, 1983; Religious experience and lay society in T'ang China, 1995; Lost Books of Medieval China, 2000; Books, Tales and Vernacular Culture: selected papers on China, 2005. *Address:* University College, Oxford OX1 4BH.

DUDDING, Richard Scarbrough; Director for Environment and Economy, Oxfordshire County Council, since 2003; *b* 29 Nov. 1950; *s* of Sir John Scarbrough Dudding and Lady (Enid Grace) Dudding; *m* 1987, Priscilla Diana Russell; two *s*. *Educ:* Cheltenham Coll.; Jesus Coll., Cambridge (MA 1st Cl. Hons History). Joined DoE, 1972; Private Sec. to John Smith, MP, 1976–78; Principal, 1977; Asst Sec., 1984; Sec., Cttee of Inquiry into Conduct of Local Govt Business, 1985–86; Under Sec., 1990; Finance Dir, 1990–93; Director: Pollution Control and Wastes, 1993–96; Personnel and Central Support Services, 1996–97; Dir Gen., Strategy and Corporate Services, DETR, then DTLR, 1997–2002. *Recreations:* gardening, walking, family. *Address:* (office) Speedwell House, Speedwell Street, Oxford OX1 1NE.

DUDDRIDGE, James Philip; MP (C) Rochford and Southend East, since 2005; *b* 26 Aug. 1971; *s* of Philip and Jennifer Duddridge; *m* 2004, Kathryn Brigid Thompson; two *s*. *Educ:* Univ. of Essex (BA Politics). With Barclays Bank, 1993–2002: Sales Dir, Ivory Coast, 1997–98; Sales Manager for unit trust business, UK, 1998–2001; Service Delivery Dir, Botswana, 2001–02; Account Dir, YouGov, 2001–05; Dir, Okavango Ltd, 2002–05. An Opposition Whip, 2008–. *Recreations:* running, cycling, real ale. *Address:* House of Commons, SW1A 0AA. *T:* (020) 7219 4830, *Fax:* (020) 7219 3888; *e-mail:* james@jamesduddridge.com. *Clubs:* Southend United Football, Southampton Football.

DUDLEY, 4th Earl of, *cr* 1860; **William Humble David Ward;** Baron Ward, 1644; Viscount Ednam, 1860; *b* 5 Jan. 1920; *e s* of 3rd Earl of Dudley, MC, TD, and Rosemary Millicent, RRC (*d* 1930), *o d* of 4th Duke of Sutherland; *S* father, 1969; *m* 1st, 1946, Stella (marr. diss., 1961), *d* of M. A. Carcano, KCMG, KBE; one *s* twin *d*; 2nd, 1961, Maureen Swanson; one *s* five *d*. *Educ:* Eton; Christ Church, Oxford. Joined 10th Hussars, 1941, Adjt, 1944–45; ADC to Viceroy of India, 1942–43. Served War of 1939–45 (wounded). *Heir: s* Viscount Ednam, *qv*. *Clubs:* White's, Pratt's.

DUDLEY, 15th Baron *cr* 1439 (called out of abeyance, 1916); **Jim Anthony Hill Wallace;** *b* 9 Nov. 1930; *e s* of Baroness Dudley (14th in line) and Guy Raymond Hill Wallace; *S* mother, 2002; *m* 1962, Nicola Jane, *d* of Lt-Col P. W. E. L. Dunsterville; two *s*. *Educ:* Lancing. *Recreations:* photography, listening to classical music, model engineering, restoring vintage vehicles and old machinery. *Heir: s* Hon. Jeremy William Guilford Wallace, *b* 12 Sept. 1964.

DUDLEY, Suffragan Bishop of; Rt Rev. David Stuart Walker; appointed Area Bishop of Dudley, 2000, Suffragan Bishop, since 2002; *b* 30 May 1957; *s* of late Fred Walker and of Joyce Walker; *m* 1980, Susan Ann (*née* Pearce); one *s* one *d*. *Educ:* King's Coll., Cambridge (MA 1981); Queen's Coll., Birmingham (DipTh 1982). Ordained deacon, 1983, priest, 1984; Curate, Handsworth, Sheffield, 1983–86; Team Vicar, Maltby, 1986–91; Industrial Chaplain, 1986–91; Vicar, Bramley and Ravenfield, 1991–95; Team Rector, Bramley and Ravenfield with Hooton Roberts and Braithwell, 1995–2000. Member: Gen. Synod, 2005–; C of E Pensions Bd, 2006–. Chairman: Housing Justice, 2003–07; Housing Assocs Charitable Trust, 2004–. Member: Council, Nat. Housing Fedn, 1996–2002; Govt Policy Action Team on Housing Mgt, 1998–2001; Lay Adv. Panel, Nat. Police Improvement Agency (formerly Central Police Trng Agency), 2005–. FRSA 2007. *Publications:* (contrib.) Changing Rural Life, 2005; Communion by Extension, 2006; Belonging to Rural Community and Church, 2006; various articles in housing jls. *Recreations:* cricket, hill walking, embroidery, reading. *Address:* Bishop's House, Bishop's Walk, Cradley Heath, W Midlands B64 7RH. *T:* (0121) 550 3407, *Fax:* (0121) 550 7340; *e-mail:* bishop.david@CofE-worcester.org.uk.

DUDLEY, Archdeacon of; *see* Trethewey, Ven. F. M.

DUDLEY, Prof. Hugh Arnold Freeman, CBE 1988; FRCSE, FRCS, FRACS; Professor of Surgery, St Mary's Hospital, London University, 1973–88, now Emeritus; *b* 1 July 1925; *s* of W. L. and Ethel Dudley; *m* 1947, Jean Bruce Lindsay Johnston; one *s* one *d* (and one *s* decd). *Educ:* Heath Grammar Sch., Halifax; Edinburgh and Harvard Univs. MB, ChB Edin. 1947; ChM (Gold Medal and Chiene Medal) Edin. 1958; FRCSE 1951; FRACS 1965; FRCS 1974. Research Fell., Harvard Univ., 1953–54; Lecturer in Surgery, Edinburgh Univ., 1954–58; Sen. Lectr, Aberdeen Univ., 1958–63; Foundation Prof. of Surgery, Monash Univ., Melbourne, 1963–72. President: Surgical Res. Soc. of Australasia, 1968; Biol. Engrg Soc. of GB, 1978–80; Surgical Res. Soc. of GB, 1981. Regl Research Co-ordinator, NW Thames RHA, 1989–92. Chairman, Independent Ethics Committee: Army Personnel Res. Estabt, Farnborough, 1989–94; Chemical and Biological Defence Estabt, Porton Down, 1988–96 (Mem. Council, 1992–94). Chm., Med. Writers Gp, 1980–83, Mem. Cttee, 1984–87, Soc. of Authors. Corresponding Member: Surgical Res. Soc., Australia; Surgical Res. Soc. of SA; Vascular Soc. of SA; Hon. Member: Hellenic Soc. of Experimental Medicine; Aberdeen Medico-Chirurgical Soc.; Hon. Fellow: Amer. Surgical Assoc.; Amer. Assoc. for the Surgery of Trauma; S African Coll. of Surgeons. Chm. Editorial Board of Br. Jl of Surgery and of Br. Jl Surgery Soc. Ltd, 1980–88; Associate Editor, BMJ, 1988–91. *Publications:* Principles of General Surgical Management, 1958; (jtly); Access and Exposure in Abdominal Surgery, 1963; (jtly) Guide for House Surgeons in the Surgical Unit, 5th edn 1974, to 8th edn 1988; (ed) Rob and Smith's Operative Surgery, 3rd edn 1976, 4th edn 1988; Hamilton Bailey's Emergency Surgery, 10th edn 1977, 11th edn 1986; Communication in Medicine and Biology, 1977; (ed) Aid to Clinical Surgery, 2nd edn 1978 to 4th edn 1988; (jtly) Practical Procedures for House Officers, 1988; (jtly) The People's Hospital of North East Scotland, 1992; (ed jtly) Scientific Foundations of Trauma, 1996; papers in med. and sci. jls. *Recreations:* missing pheasants; annoying others; surgical history. *Address:* Glebe Cottage, Glass, Huntly, Aberdeenshire AB54 4XH. *T:* (01466) 700376; *e-mail:* dudleyhughd@aol.com.

DUDLEY, Rev. Martin Raymond, PhD; Rector, Priory Church of St Bartholomew the Great, London, since 1995; *b* 31 May 1953; *s* of Ronald Frank Dudley and Joyce Mary (*née* Gardiner); *m* 1976, Paula Jones; two *s*. *Educ:* King Edward's Sch., Birmingham; RMA Sandhurst; KCL (BD, AKC 1977, MTh 1978); St Michael's Coll., Llandaff; PhD London 1994; Cass Business Sch., City Univ. (MSc 2006). Ordained deacon, 1979, priest, 1980; Curate, Whitchurch, 1979–83; Vicar, Weston, 1983–88; Priest i/c, Ardeley, 1986–88; Vicar, Owlsmoor, 1988–95. Chaplain: Imperial Soc. of Kts Bach., 1995–2005; Butchers' Co., 1995–; Co. of Chartered Secretaries and Administrators, 1995–2000; Hackney Carriage Drivers' Co., 1998–; Master, Farmers' Co., 1999–2000, 2002–03; Co. of Inf. Technologists, 2001–; Master, Fletchers' Co., 2001–02, 2004–April 2009; Tax Advisers' Co., 2002–; Aldermanic Sheriff, City of London, 2003–04; City of London Br., Royal Soc. of St George, 2003–; Public Relations Practitioners' Co., 2003–. Mem., London Dio. Synod, 2003–06 (Mem., Bp's Council, 2003–06). Common Councilman (Aldersgate Ward), Corp. of London, 2002–. Member, Professional Conduct and Complaints Committee: Bar Council, 2000–07; CIArb, 2005–. Member: Hampstead Heath Mgt Cttee, 2003–04; Court, Bridewell Royal Foundn, 2003–; Licensing Cttee, 2004–, Planning & Transportation Cttee, 2005–, Community and Children's Services Cttee, 2006–, City Bridge Trust, 2007–, Standards Cttee, 2007–, City of London Corp. (formerly Corp. of London). Chm., Resource Centre (London) Ltd, 2007–. Governor: City Lit. Inst., 2001–03; City of London Sch. for Girls, 2002–; City of London Acad., Southwark, 2003–; Mus. of London, 2007–. Trustee: Butchers' and Drovers' Charitable Instn, 1996–2004; London Liby, 2003–07; City Parochial Foundn, 2005–. Liveryman, Farriers' Co., 2000; Hon. Freeman: Farmers' Co., 2000; Guild of Public Relns Practitioners, 2005; Pres., Faringdon Ward Club, 2008–April 2009 (Sen. Vice-Pres., 2007–08). FRHistS 1995; FSA 1997; FRSA 2006. SBStJ 1998. *Publications:* The Collect in Anglican Liturgy, 1994; (ed) Like a Two-edged Sword, 1995; A Manual of Ministry to the Sick, 1997; Humanity and Healing, 1998; Ashes to Glory, 1999; A Herald Voice, 2000; Risen, Ascended, Glorified, 2001; Crowning the Year, 2003; with Virginia Rounding: Churchwardens: a survival guide, 2003; The Parish Survival Guide, 2004; Serving the Parish, 2006. *Recreations:* visiting French cathedrals, reading modern fiction. *Address:* St Bartholomew the Great Parish Office, 6 Kinghorn Street, EC1A 7HW. *T:* (020) 7606 5171. *Clubs:* Athenæum, Guildhall.

DUDLEY, Michael John; His Honour Judge Dudley; a Circuit Judge, since 2003; *b* 24 Jan. 1947; *s* of John Kenneth and Ruby Marguerite Dudley; *m* 1968, Barbara; one *s* one *d*. *Educ:* Magdalen Coll. Sch., Brackley; Univ. of Birmingham (LLB); Univ. of Leeds (PGCE). Called to the Bar, Lincoln's Inn, 1972; specialised in crime and general common law; Dep. Stipendiary Magistrate, 1984–90; Asst Recorder, 1993–99, Recorder, 1999–2003. *Recreations:* walking, golf, photography, music, Rugby. *Address:* Wolverhampton Combined Court, Piper's Row, Wolverhampton WV1 3LQ. *Clubs:* Sutton Coldfield Rugby Football; Sutton Coldfield Golf.

DUDLEY, William Stuart, RDI 1989; Associate Designer, Royal National Theatre, since 1981; *b* 4 March 1947; *s* of William Dudley and Dorothy Stacey. *Educ:* Highbury Sch., London; St Martin's School of Art; Slade School of Art. DipAD, BA Fine Art; UCL Postgrad. Dip. Fine Art. First production, Hamlet, Nottingham Playhouse, 1970; subseq. prodns include: The Duchess of Malfi and Man is Man, Royal Court, 1971; *National Theatre,* 1971–: Tyger, 1974; The Good-Natured Man, 1974; The Passion, 1977; Lavender Blue, 1977; The World Turned Upside Down, Has Washington Legs?, 1978; Dispatches, Lost Worlds, Lark Rise to Candleford, Undiscovered Country (SWET award, Designer of the Year, 1980), 1979; Good Soldier Schweyk, 1982; Cinderella, 1983; The Mysteries, Real Inspector Hound/The Critic, 1985 (Laurence Olivier (formerly SWET) Award, Designer of the Year, 1985); Futurists, 1986; Waiting for Godot, 1987; Cat on a Hot Tin Roof, The Shaughraun, and The Changeling, 1988; Bartholemew Fair, 1988; The Crucible, 1990; The Coup, 1991; Pygmalion, 1992; On the Ledge, 1993; Under Milk Wood, 1995; Mary Stuart, 1996; The Homecoming, 1997; The London Cuckolds, 1998; All My Sons, 2000 (Laurence Olivier Awards, Best Set Designer, 2001); The Coast of Utopia, 2002; Honour, 2003; The Permanent Way, Cyrano de Bergerac, 2004; *Royal Court:* Live Like Pigs, 1972; Merry-Go-Round, 1973; Magnificence, 1975; The Fool, 1975; Small Change, 1976; Hamlet, 1980; Kafka's Dick, 1986; Etta Jenks, 1990; I Licked a Slag's Deodorant, 1996; Hitchcock Blonde, 2003, transf. Lyric, 2003; *RSC:* Twelfth Night, 1974; Ivanov, 1976; That Good Between Us, 1977; Richard III, The Party, Today, 1984; Merry Wives of Windsor, 1985, 1992; A Midsummer Night's Dream, Richard II, 1986; Kiss Me Kate, 1987; *West End:* Mutiny, Piccadilly, 1985; Heartbreak House, Haymarket, 1992; A Streetcar Named Desire, Haymarket, 1996; The Breath of Life, Haymarket, 2002; Woman in White, Palace, 2004; *other productions:* The Ship, Glasgow, 1990; The Deep Blue Sea, Almeida, 1993; The Big Picnic, Glasgow, 1994; Some Sunny Day, Hampstead, 1996; The Alchemist, Birmingham, 1996; Titus Andronicus, Shakespeare's Globe, 2006; Betrayal, Donmar Warehouse, 2007; *opera:* WNO: Il barbiere di Siviglia, 1976; Idomeneo, 1991; Metropolitan, NY: Billy Budd, 1978; Glyndebourne: Die Entführung aus dem Serail, 1980; Il barbiere di Siviglia, 1981; Royal Opera: Les Contes d'Hoffman (sets), 1980; Don Giovanni, 1981; The Cunning Little Vixen, 1990, revived 2003; Bayreuth: Der Ring des Nibelungen, 1983; Der Rosenkavalier, 1984; Salzburg Festival: Un ballo in maschera, 1989; *television film:* Persuasion, 1994 (BAFTA and RTS Awards for set design). Designer of the Year, Laurence Olivier Awards, 1980, 1985, 1986, 1993. *Recreation:* playing the concertina. *Address:* 11 Halstow Road, SE10 0LD.

DUDLEY-SMITH, Rt Rev. Timothy, OBE 2003; Bishop Suffragan of Thetford, 1981–92; *b* 26 Dec. 1926; *o s* of Arthur and Phyllis Dudley Smith, Buxton, Derbyshire; *m* 1959, June Arlette MacDonald (*d* 2007); one *s* two *d*. *Educ:* Tonbridge Sch.; Pembroke Coll., and Ridley Hall, Cambridge. BA 1947, MA 1951; Certif. in Educn 1948. Deacon, 1950; priest, 1951; Asst Curate, St Paul, Northumberland Heath, 1950–53; Head of Cambridge Univ. Mission in Bermondsey, 1953–55; Hon. Chaplain to Bp of Rochester, 1953–60; Editor, Crusade, and Editorial Sec. of Evangelical Alliance, 1955–59; Asst Sec. of Church Pastoral-Aid Soc., 1959–65, Sec., 1965–73; Archdeacon of Norwich, 1973–81; Commissary to Archbp of Sydney, 1971–92; Exam. Chap. to Bp of Norwich, 1971–85. President: Evangelical Alliance, 1987–91; C of E Evangelical Council, 1990–93; Vice-Pres., UCCF, 1992–. Chm. of Govs, 1992–96, Patron, 1996–, Monkton Combe Sch. Fellow, Hymn Soc. in the US and Canada, 1997; Hon. Vice-Pres., Hymn Soc. of GB and Ireland, 2003. MLitt Lambeth, 1991. *Publications:* Christian Literature and the Church Bookstall, 1963; What Makes a Man a Christian?, 1966; A Man Named Jesus, 1971; Someone who Beckons, 1978; Lift Every Heart, 1984; A Flame of Love, 1987; Songs of Deliverance, 1988; Praying with the English Hymn Writers, 1989; A Voice of Singing, 1992; John Stott: a comprehensive bibliography, 1995; (compiled) Authentic Christianity, 1995; Great is the Glory, 1997; John Stott: the making of a leader, 1999; John Stott: a global ministry, 2001; (jtly) Beneath a Travelling Star, 2001; A House of Praise, 2003; A Door for the Word, 2006; (jtly) A Calendar of Praise, 2006; (jtly) High Days and Holy Days, 2007; (jtly) The Voice of Faith, 2008; (jtly) Above Every Name, 2009; contributor to hymn books. *Recreations:* reading, verse, DIY, family and friends. *Address:* 9 Ashlands, Ford, Salisbury, Wilts SP4 6DY. *T:* (01722) 326417.

DUDLEY-WILLIAMS, Sir Alastair (Edgcumbe James), 2nd Bt *cr* 1964, of Exeter; Director, Wildcat Consultants, since 1986; *b* 26 Nov. 1943; *s* of Sir Rolf Dudley Dudley-Williams, 1st Bt and Margaret Helen, *er d* of F. E. Robinson, OBE; *S* father, 1987; *m* 1972, Diana Elizabeth Jane, twin *d* of R. H. C. Duncan; three *d*. *Educ:* Pangbourne College. Hughes Tool Co. (Texas), 1962–64; Bay Drilling Corp. (Louisiana), 1964–65; Bristol Siddeley Whittle Tools Ltd, 1965–67; Santa Fe Drilling Co., 1967–72; Inchcape plc, 1972–86. *Recreations:* shooting, fishing. *Heir:* *b* Malcolm Philip Edgcumbe Dudley-Williams [*b* 10 Aug. 1947; *m* 1973, Caroline Anne Colina, twin *d* of R. H. C. Duncan; two *s* one *d*]. *Address:* 34 Trafalgar Court, Farnham, Surrey GU9 7QF.

DUERDEN, Prof. Brian Ion, CBE 2008; MD; FRCPath, FRCPE; Inspector of Microbiology and Infection Control (formerly of Microbiology), Department of Health, since 2004; Professor of Medical Microbiology, Cardiff University (formerly University of Wales College of Medicine), since 1991; *b* 21 June 1948; *s* of Cyril Duerden and Mildred (*née* Ion); *m* 1972, Marjorie Hudson. *Educ:* Nelson Grammar Sch., Nelson, Lancs; Edinburgh Univ. (BSc Hons Med. Sci. Bacteriol. 1970; MB ChB 1972; MD 1979). MRCPath 1978, FRCPath 1990; FRCPE 2005. House Officer, Thoracic Surgery, 1972–73, and Infectious Diseases, 1973, City Hosp., Edinburgh; Lectr in Bacteriol., Univ. of Edinburgh Med. Sch., 1973–76; University of Sheffield Medical School: Lectr in Med. Microbiol., 1976–79; Sen. Lectr, 1979–83; Prof. of Med. Microbiol., 1983–90; Hon. Consultant in Med. Microbiol., Sheffield Children's Hosp., 1979–90; Dir, Cardiff Public Health Lab., and Hd, S Glamorgan Microbiol. Services, 1991–95; Dep. Dir, 1995–2002 and Med. Dir, 1999–2002, Dir, 2002–03, PHLS; Dir, Clinical Quality, HPA, 2003. Ed. in Chief, Jl Med. Microbiol., 1983–2002. *Publications:* (contrib. and vol. ed.) Topley and Wilson's Principles of Bacteriology, Virology and Immunology, 7th edn 1980 to 9th edn 1997; Textbook of Microbial and Parasitic Infection, 1987, 2nd edn 1993; Anaerobes in Human Disease, 1991; contrib. numerous scientific articles to professional jls. *Recreations:* travel, photography, music, cricket. *Address:* Department of Medical Microbiology, Cardiff University, Heath Park, Cardiff CF14 4XN. *T:* (029) 2074 2168, *Fax:* (029) 2074 2169; *e-mail:* brian.duerden@dh.gsi.gov.uk.

DUFF, Andrew Nicholas, OBE 1997; Member (Lib Dem) Eastern England, European Parliament, since 1999; *b* 25 Dec. 1950; *s* of Norman Bruce Duff and Diana (*née* Wilcoxson). *Educ:* Sherborne Sch.; St John's Coll., Cambridge (MA; MLitt 1978); Université Libre de Bruxelles. Res. Officer, Hansard Soc. for Parly Govt, 1974–76; consultant and researcher on EC affairs, 1977–88 (clients incl. BBC, Cambridge Univ., EC, Federal Trust for Educn and Res., PSI); Res. Fellow, Joseph Rowntree Reform Trust, 1989–92; Dir, Federal Trust, 1993–99. Mem. (L), 1982–87, (Lib Dem), 1987–90, Cambridge CC. Contested: (L) Cambridge and N Beds, 1984, (Lib Dem) Cambridgeshire, 1989, 1994, EP elecns; (Lib Dem) Huntingdon, Parly elecns, 1992. Vice Pres., Liberal Democrats, 1994–97. European Parliament: Constitutional Affairs spokesman, Eur. Lib Dem Gp, 1999–; Leader, UK Lib Dems, 2007–; Vice-Pres., delegn to Convention on Future of Europe, 2002–03. *Publications:* include: (ed jtly) Maastricht and Beyond: building the European Union, 1994; Reforming the European Union, 1997; (ed) The Treaty of Amsterdam, 1997; The Struggle for Europe's Constitution, 2005. *Recreation:* music. *Address:* Orwell House, Cowley Road, Cambridge CB4 0PP; *e-mail:* mep@andrewduffmep.org. *Club:* National Liberal.

DUFF, Anthony Michael; communications strategist and executive coach, since 1999; *b* 7 Aug. 1946; *s* of Anthony Duff and Alice Mary Duff (*née* Conway); *m* 1997, Marisol de Lafuente. *Educ:* St Conleth's Coll., Dublin; University Coll., Dublin (BA Hons). LGSM (Drama) 1968; LRAM (Drama) 1970; RSA Dip. TEFLA 1972. Dir, Teacher Trng and Foundn Dir, Café Théatre Anglais, Internat. House, Paris, 1971–74; Vis. Lectr in Drama, Thomond Coll., Co. Limerick, 1975–76; Pedagogic Advr to Longman Italia, 1977–79; International House, London: Dir of Educn, 1979–83; Dir, 1984–89; Dir-Gen., 1990–99. FRSA 1993. *Publications:* English For You, 2 vols, 1979, 1981; (ed) Explorations in Teacher Training, 1989. *Recreations:* music, reading, the theatre, walking, being solitary. *Address:* 39 St Dunstan's Road, W6 8RE.

DUFF, Antony; see Duff, R. A.

DUFF, Sir Gordon (William), Kt 2007; PhD; FRCP, FRCPE, FMedSci, FRSE; Lord Florey Professor of Molecular Medicine, University of Sheffield, since 1991; Chairman: National Biological Standards Board, since 2002; Commission on Human Medicines, since 2005; Scientific Pandemic Influenza Advisory Committee, since 2008; *b* 27 Dec. 1947; *s* of William Munro Duff and Marion Gertrude Duff; *m* 1969, Naida Margaret, *d* of Air Cdre Charles Clarke, OBE and Eileen Clarke; two *d*. *Educ:* Perth Acad.; Hipperholme GS, Yorks; St Peter's Coll., Oxford (BA 1969, MA 1975; BM BCh 1975; Hon. Fellow, 2006); St Thomas's Hosp. Med. Sch., Univ. of London (PhD 1980); Saybrook Coll., Yale Univ. FRCPE 1989; FRCP 1998. House Officer in Medicine, St Thomas's Hosp., London, and in Surgery, Stracathro Hosp., Brechin, 1975–76; Senior House Officer in Medicine: RAF Unit, King Edward VII Hosp., Midhurst, 1976–77; (Clinical Pharmacol.) Hammersmith Hosp. and RPMS, 1977–78; Med. Registrar posts, 1978–80; Yale University School of Medicine: Res. Associate, Internal Medicine (Infectious Diseases) and Pathol. (Immunol.), 1980–83; Associate Investigator, Howard Hughes Inst. of Cellular and Molecular Immunol., 1981–83; Clin. Lectr in Rheumatol., 1984–86, Clin. Sen. Lectr, Dept of Medicine, 1986–90, Univ. of Edinburgh; Hon. Consultant Physician, Lothian Health Bd, 1986–90; University of Sheffield: Res. Dean, Sheffield Med. Sch., 1997–2002; Director: Div. of Molecular and Genetic Medicine, 1997–2000; of Res., Faculty of Medicine, 1999–2002; Div. of Genomic Medicine, 2000–06; Hon. Consultant Physician, Sheffield Teaching Hosps NHS Trust, 1991–. RSocMed Vis. Prof. to USA (Yale, NIH, Pfizer Res.), 1995; Lectures: Honiman-Gillespie, Univ. of Edinburgh, 1991; Harry Bostrom, Swedish Soc. Med., 1996; Faculty, Univ. of Geneva, 2001. Founding Ed., Cytokine, 1988–. Committee on Safety of Medicines: Mem., 1995–2005, Chm. 2003–05; Chairman: Biol Sub-cttee, 1998–2003 (Mem., 1995–2005); vCJD and Blood Products Expert Gp, 1998–2005; vCJD and Vaccines Expert Gp, 2000–05; Tissue Engrg Expert Gp, 2001–05; Mem., Safety and Efficacy Sub-cttee, 1992–95. Chairman: Foresight Internat. Health Gp, DTI (OST), 1998–2000; Gene Therapy Commissioning Gp, DoH, 2004; Member: Health and Life Scis Foresight Panel, DTI, 1997–99; Genomic Medicine Gp, Foresight Healthcare, 1999–2000; Adv. Gp on Genetics Res., DoH, 2003–07. Member: Adv. Bd, MRC, 1997–2005; Health Metrology Panel, EPSRC, 2000. Expert Advr (Biol Medicines), EMEA, 2001–. Clin. Trials Monitor, WHO, 1995–97. Member: R&D Exec., Central Sheffield Univ. Hosp. NHS Trust, 1996–99 (Chm., Res. Mgt Cttee, 1996–98); R&D Strategy Gp, Trent RHA, 2000–04. Mem., Internat. Scientific Adv. Bd, Medical Solutions plc, 1999–2005. Member: Council, Internat. Cytokine Soc., USA, 1992– (Pres., 1997–98); Council, Eur. Cytokine Soc., Paris, 1997–; International Scientific Advisory Board: DeutschesRheumaForschungZentrum, Berlin, 1996–99; Dublin Molecular Medicine Centre, 2000–. Mem., Clin. Interest Gp, Wellcome Trust, 1994–97. Member: Res. Cttee, Arthritis and Rheumatism Council, 1993–97; Scientific Cttee, DEBRA (Fragile Skin Diseases), 1996–99; Scientific Cttee, GDBA, 1996–99. Mem. Council, Univ. of Sheffield, 2000–04. FMedSci 1999; FRSE 2008. Mem., Assoc. of Physicians of GB and Ireland, 1986–. MD (hc) Edinburgh, 2008. (Jtly) Sir Hiram Maxim Award for Res. in Immunol., 1987; Medal, Swedish Soc. Med., 1996. *Publications:* contribs to res. jls in fields of inflammation, immunology and genetics; thirty patents in field of genetic diagnostics for common diseases. *Recreations:* ski-ing, hill-walking, botany, carpentry. *Address:* Royal Hallamshire Hospital, Sheffield S10 2JF. *T:* (0114) 271 2830, *Fax:* (0114) 278 0125; *e-mail:* g.w.duff@sheffield.ac.uk. *Clubs:* Athenæum, Royal Over-Seas League.

DUFF, Graham, CB 1999; barrister; *b* 7 Jan. 1947; *s* of Norman Alexander Duff and Doris Duff; *m* 1987, Jacqueline Tremble; one *s* one *d*. *Educ:* Newcastle Royal Grammar Sch.; Univ. of Durham (BA (Hons) Law); Univ. of Newcastle upon Tyne (Grad. Cert Ed). Called to the Bar, Lincoln's Inn, 1976. Asst Dir of Public Prosecutions, 1986; Br. Crown Prosecutor, Inner London, 1986; Chief Crown Prosecutor, Northumbria and Durham, 1987; a Dir, CPS, 1990–98. Mem., Cartington Parish Council, 2002–. *Recreations:* old Riley motor cars, Northumbrian countryside. *Address:* Trinity Chambers, Custom House, Quayside, Newcastle upon Tyne NE1 3DE. *T:* (0191) 232 1927.

DUFF, Prof. (Robin) Antony, FBA 2004; FRSE; Professor, Department of Philosophy, University of Stirling, since 1990; *b* 9 March 1945; *s* of Rt Hon. Sir (Arthur) Antony Duff, GCMG, CVO, DSO, DSC, PC and of Pauline Marion Duff; partner, Sandra Marshall. *Educ:* St Peter's Sch., Seaford; Sedbergh Sch.; Christ Church, Oxford (BA). Vis. Lectr, Dept of Philos., Univ. of Washington, Seattle, 1968–69; University of Stirling: Lectr, Dept of Philos., 1970–80; Sen. Lectr, 1980–90; Reader, 1990. FRSE 1996. *Publications:* Trials and Punishments, 1986; Intention, Agency and Criminal Liability, 1990; Criminal Attempts, 1996; Punishment, Communication and Community, 2001; Answering for Crime, 2007; The Trial on Trial, 2007. *Address:* Department of Philosophy, University of Stirling, Stirling FK9 4LA; *e-mail:* r.a.duff@stir.ac.uk.

DUFF GORDON, Sir Andrew (Cosmo Lewis), 8th Bt *cr* 1813; *b* 17 Oct. 1933; *o s* of Sir Douglas Duff Gordon, 7th Bt and Gladys Rosemary (*d* 1933), *e d* of late Col Vivien Henry, CB; *S* father, 1964; *m* 1st, 1967, Grania Mary (marr. diss. 1975), *d* of Fitzgerald Villiers-Stuart, Ireland; one *s*; 2nd, 1975, Eveline Virginia, BA, *d* of S. Soames, Newbury; three *s*. *Educ:* Repton. Served with Worcs Regiment and 1st Bn Ches Regt, 1952–54. Mem. of Lloyd's, 1962–91. Jt Hon. Pres., Nomadic Preservation Soc., 2006–. *Publication:* (with R. W. D. Fenn) The Life and Times of Sir George Cornewall Lewis, Bt, 2005. *Recreations:* golf, shooting, ski-ing. *Heir: s* Cosmo Henry Villiers Duff Gordon [*b* 18 June 1968; *m* 2006, Araminta de Clermont; one *s*]. *Address:* Downton House, Walton, Presteigne, Powys LD8 2RD. *T:* (01544) 350223; 27 Cathcart Road, SW10 9JG. *T:* (020) 7351 1170. *Clubs:* Kington Golf; Sunningdale Golf.

DUFFELL, Lt-Gen. Sir Peter Royson, KCB 1992; CBE 1988 (OBE 1981); MC 1966; Manager, Dechert LLP (formerly Titmuss Sainer Dechert), since 2006 (Chief Executive, 1995–2006); *b* 19 June 1939; *s* of late Roy John Duffell, Lenham, Kent, and Ruth Doris (*née* Gustaffson); *m* 1982, Ann Murray, *d* of late Col Basil Bethune Neville Woodd, Rolvenden, Kent; one *s* one *d*. *Educ:* Dulwich Coll. psc, rcds. FRGS 1975; FRAS 1992. Commnd 2nd KEO Gurkha Rifles, 1960; Staff Coll., Camberley, 1971; Bde Major 5 Bde, 1972–74; MA to C-in-C UKLF, 1976–78; Comdt 1st Bn 2nd KEO Gurkha Rifles, 1978–81; Col GS, MoD, 1981–83; Comdr Gurkha Field Force, 1984–85; COS 1 (BR) Corps, 1986–87; RCDS, 1988; Cabinet Office Efficiency Unit, 1989; Comdr, British Forces Hong Kong, and Maj.-Gen. Brigade of Gurkhas, 1989–92; Inspector Gen. Doctrine and Trng, MoD, 1992–95. Col, Royal Gurkha Rifles, 1994–99. Mem., Internat. Adv. Bd, SOAS, 2006–. Trustee, Foyle Foundn, 2006–. Gov., Sandroyd Sch., 1995–. Freeman, City of London, 2001; Liveryman, Paviours' Co., 2001–. *Recreations:* family, drinking wine, taking photographs, playing elephant polo, watching cricket. *Clubs:* Travellers, Pratt's, MCC.

DUFFERIN AND CLANDEBOYE, 11th Baron *cr* 1800 (Ire.); **John Francis Blackwood;** Bt (Ire.) 1763; Bt (UK) 1814; architect; *b* 18 Oct. 1944; *s* of 10th Baron and of Margaret Alice, *d* of Hector Kirkpatrick; *S* father, 1991 (claim to peerage not yet established); *m* 1971, Annette Kay, *d* of Harold Greenhill; one *s* one *d*. *Educ:* Barker Coll., Hornsby; Univ. of NSW (BArch). ARAIA. *Recreations:* organic farming, fishing. *Heir: s* Hon. Francis Senden Blackwood, *b* 6 Jan. 1979. *Address:* PO Box 1815, Orange, NSW 2800, Australia. *T:* (2) 63625399.

DUFFETT, Roger Hugh Edward; Secretary, Royal College of Surgeons of England, 1988–97; *b* 20 Jan. 1936; *s* of Dr Edward Cecil Duffett and Cicely Duffett (*née* Haw); *m* 1959, Angela Julie Olden; one *d* (one *s* decd). *Educ:* Sherborne Sch. (Scholar); Peterhouse, Cambridge (Scholar; MA). Commissioned RA (Nat. Service), 1954–56; British Petroleum Co.: joined 1956; refinery process foreman, 1959–60; research, molecular sieve properties of synthetic zeolites and reactions of frozen free radicals, 1960–64; creation of computerised manpower planning models, 1964–68; creation and operation of computerised linear programming models for integrated oil ops, 1968–71; application of mathematical models to corporate planning, 1971–73; planning, internat. ops for lubricants, 1973–78; negotiation and op., crude oil contracts, 1978–79; consultancy for analysis and resolution of orgnl problems: in shipping, research, engrg, marketing and personnel; for management of secondary schools, Cambs; Unicef (UK); employment of secondees to Enterprise Bds, 1979–87; orgn and systems consultant for BP Oil Internat., for Riding for Disabled, 1987–88. Gov., Basingstoke NHS Foundn Trust, 2006–. Member, Management Committee, Clare Park, 1979–83; Riding for Disabled, 1990–2004 (Trustee, 1999–2004; Hon. Life Vice Pres., 2007); Dir, Quinta Nursing Home, Farnham, 1983–88. Freeman, Barbers' Co., 1998. Hon. FRCS 1997; Hon. DGDP 1998. *Publications:* contribs to learned jls. *Recreations:* golf, servicing golf club website magazine, coarse gardening, creating brain teasers, writing, reading. *Address:* Tavistock Cottage, Bentley, Farnham, Surrey GU10 5JA. *T:* and *Fax:* (01420) 520283; *e-mail:* r.duffett@btinternet.com. *Club:* Liphook Golf.

DUFFIELD, Christopher Paul; Town Clerk and Chief Executive, City of London Corporation (formerly Corporation of London), since 2003; *b* 20 May 1952; *s* of late Jack and Irene Duffield; *m* 1st, 1971 (marr. diss. 1979); one *s*; 2nd, 1987, Tricia Jackson; two *s*. *Educ:* St Albans Sch.; Univ. of Newcastle-upon-Tyne (BA Hons 1973). CPFA 1978. Asst Dir of Finance, GLC, 1983–85; Dep. Dir of Finance, London Bor. of Redbridge, 1985–87; Dep. County Treas., Essex CC, 1988–91; London Borough of Bexley: Dir of Finance, 1991–95; Chief Exec., 1995–2003. Mem., London Regl Risk and Audit Cttee, HM Courts Service, 2006–. Mem., London Regl Resilience Forum, 2004– (Chm., Local Authy Panel, 2008–); Chm., Central London Resilience Forum, 2006–. Dep. Chm., Bexley PCT, 2001–03. *Address:* City of London Corporation, Guildhall, EC2P 2EJ.

DUFFIELD, Linda Joy, CMG 2002; HM Diplomatic Service; Ambassador to the Czech Republic, since 2004; *b* 18 April 1953; *d* of Bryan Charles Duffield and Joyce Eileen Duffield (*née* Barr). *Educ:* St Mary's Sch., Northwood, Middx; Exeter Univ. (BA Hons 1975). DHSS, 1976–85; Ecole Nat. d'Admin, Paris, 1985–86; joined FCO, 1987; First Sec., Moscow, 1989–92; First Sec., later Counsellor, FCO, 1993–95; Dep. High Comr, Ottawa, 1995–99; High Comr, Sri Lanka, 1999–2002; Dir, Wider Europe, FCO, 2002–04. *Recreations:* music, ski-ing. *Address:* c/o Foreign and Commonwealth Office, King Charles Street, SW1A 2AH.

DUFFIELD, Dame Vivien (Louise), DBE 2000 (CBE 1989); *b* 26 March 1946; *d* of Sir Charles Clore and Mrs Francine Clore (*née* Halphen); *m* 1969, John Duffield (marr. diss. 1976); one *s* one *d*. *Educ:* Cours Victor Hugo, Paris; Lycée Français de Londres; Heathfield Sch.; Lady Margaret Hall, Oxford (MA). Member: NSPCC Centenary Appeal Cttee, 1983; NSPCC Financial Develt Cttee, 1985; Vice-Chairman: Great Ormond Street Hosp. Wishing Well Appeal, 1987; Royal Marsden Hosp. Cancer Appeal, 1990; Campaign Chm., Univ. of Oxford, 2007–; Director: Royal Opera House Trust, 1985–2001 (Dep. Chm., 1988–2001); Royal Opera House, 1990–2001 (Chm., Royal Opera House Endowment Fund, 2005–); South Bank Bd, 2002–; Mem., Royal Ballet Bd, 1990–; Gov., Royal Ballet, 2002–; Trustee: Dulwich Coll. Picture Gall., 1993–2002; Jewish Community Centre for London, 2004–. Mem. Bd, Clore Leadership Prog., 2004–. Hon. DLitt Buckingham, 1990; Hon. DPhil Weizmann Inst., 1985; Hon. RCM, 1987. *Recreations:* ski-ing, opera, ballet, shooting. *Address:* c/o Clore Duffield Foundation, 3 Chelsea Manor Studios, Flood Street, SW3 5SR; 39 Quai Wilson, Geneva 1201, Switzerland.

DUFFY, Sir (Albert Edward) Patrick, Kt 1991; PhD; *b* 17 June 1920. *Educ:* London Sch. of Economics (BSc (Econ.), PhD); Columbia Univ., Morningside Heights, New York, USA. Served War of 1939–45, Royal Navy, incl. flying duties with FAA. Lecturer, University of Leeds, 1950–63, 1967–70. Visiting Professor: Drew Univ., Madison, NJ, 1966–70; Amer. Grad. Sch. of Internat. Business, 1982–93; Internat. Business Inst., Wheaton, Ill, 1992–; Associate, Centre of Defence Studies, Univs of Hull and Lancaster, 1997–. Contested (Lab) Tiverton Division of Devon, 1950, 1951, 1955. MP (Lab): Colne Valley Division of Yorks, 1963–66; Sheffield, Attercliffe, 1970–92. PPS to Sec. of State for Defence, 1974–76; Parly Under-Sec. of State for Defence (Navy), MoD, 1976–79; opposition spokesman on defence, 1979–80, 1983–84. Chairman: PLP Economic and Finance Gp, 1965–66, 1974–76; Trade and Industry Sub-Cttee of Select Cttee on Expenditure, 1972–74; PLP Defence Cttee, 1984; Vice-Chairman: PLP Defence Gp, 1979–84; Anglo-Irish Gp, 1979–92. Pres., N Atlantic Assembly, 1988–90 (Mem. 1979–92; Chm., Defence Co-op. sub-cttee, 1983–87); Dep. Chm., Atlantic Council of UK, 1994–97. President: Lower Don Valley Community Devlt Trust, 1997–; The Labour Life Gp, 2001–; Doncaster Mayo Assoc., 2001–. Member: Catholic Club, Doncaster; Irish Soc., Doncaster. Hon. DHL Dominican Univ., Illinois, 1993. *Publications:* contrib. to Economic History Review, Victorian Studies, Manchester School, Annals of Amer. Acad. of Pol. and Soc. Sci., etc. *Recreation:* annual pilgrimages on foot, incl. Walsingham, Croagh Patrick, Co. Mayo and Santiago de Compostela. *Address:* 153 Bennetthorpe, Doncaster, South Yorks DN2 6AH. *Clubs:* Naval; Trades and Labour (Doncaster).

DUFFY, Dame Antonia Susan; see Byatt, Dame A. S.

DUFFY, Carol Ann, CBE 2002 (OBE 1995); FRSL; poet and freelance writer; *b* 23 Dec. 1955; *d* of Frank Duffy and May Black; one *d*. *Educ:* St Joseph's Convent, Stafford; Stafford Girls' High Sch.; Univ. of Liverpool (BA Hons Philosophy 1977). FRSL 1999; FRSA 2001. Hon. DLitt: Hull, 2001; Warwick, 2001. *Awards:* Eric Gregory, 1983; Somerset Maugham, 1987; Dylan Thomas, 1990; Cholmondeley, 1992; Whitbread Poetry, 1993; Forward Poetry, 1993; Lannan, USA, 1995; Signal Poetry, 1997. *Plays:* Take My Husband, 1982; Cavern of Dreams, 1984; Little Women, Big Boys, 1986; Loss (radio), 1986; Grimm Tales, 1994, More Grimm Tales, 1996, Young Vic; Beasts and Beauties, Bristol Old Vic, 2004; Casanova, W Yorks Playhouse, 2007. *Publications:* Standing Female Nude, 1985; Selling Manhattan, 1987, 4th edn 1994; (ed) Home and Away, 1988; The Other Country, 1990; (ed) I Wouldn't Thank You for a Valentine, 1992; Mean Time, 1993 (Whitbread Prize, Forward Prize); Selected Poems, 1994; (ed) Anvil New Poets, 1995; (ed) Stopping for Death, 1996; The Pamphlet, 1998; The World's Wife (poetry), 1999; Meeting Midnight (for children), 1999; Rumpelstiltskin and other Grimm Tales (for children), 1999; (ed) Time's Tidings (poetry), 1999; The Oldest Girl in the World (for children), 2000; (ed) Signal Poetry, 2000; (ed) E. M. Forster, 2001; (ed) Hand in Hand, 2001; Feminine Gospels (poetry), 2002; Underwater Farmyard (for children), 2002;

Queen Munch and Queen Nibble (for children), 2002; (ed) Overheard on a Saltmarsh, 2003; (ed) Out of Fashion: an anthology of poems, 2004; Doris the Giant (for children), 2004; Rapture (poetry), 2005 (T. S. Eliot Prize, 2006); The Hat (poetry), 2007. *Address:* c/o Anvil Press, 69 King George Street, SE10 8PX. *T:* (020) 8858 2946.

DUFFY, Prof. Eamon, PhD, DD; FBA 2004; Professor of the History of Christianity, University of Cambridge, since 2003; Fellow, Magdalene College, Cambridge, since 1979 (President (Senior Fellow and Vice-Master), 2001–06); *b* Dundalk, Eire, 9 Feb. 1947; *s* of Patrick Duffy and Lillian Frances Duffy (*née* Todd); *m* 1968, Jennifer Elizabeth Browning; one *s* two *d. Educ:* Univ. of Hull (BA 1968); Selwyn Coll., Cambridge (PhD 1972); Magdalene Coll., Cambridge (DD 1994). Res. Fellow in Arts, Dept of Hist., Univ. of Durham, 1971–74; Lectr in Ecclesiastical Hist., KCL, 1974–79; Lectr in Divinity, 1979–94, Reader in Church Hist., 1994–2003, Univ. of Cambridge. Mem., Pontifical Historical Commn, 2001–. President: Ecclesiastical Hist. Soc., 2004–05; Catholic Theol Assoc. of GB, 2004–06. Chm. Editl Bd, Calendar of Papal Registers, 1999–. Hon. Fellow, St Mary's Coll., Strawberry Hill, 2003. Hon. DD Hull, 2004. Hawthornden Prize for Lit., 2002. *Publications:* (ed and contrib.) Challoner and His Church: a Catholic bishop in Georgian England, 1981; (ed and contrib. with B. Bradshaw) Humanism, Reform and Reformation: the career of Bishop John Fisher, 1988; The Stripping of the Altars, 1992; (jtly) A History of Magdalene College, Cambridge 1428–1988, 1994; The Creed in the Catechism: the life of God for us, 1996; Saints and Sinners: a history of the Popes, 1997, 2nd edn 2001 (trans. several langs); Catholicism and Its Pasts, 2000; The Voices of Morebath: Reformation and rebellion in an English village, 2001; Faith of Our Fathers: reflections on Catholic tradition, 2004; (ed jtly) The Church of Mary Tudor, 2006; Walking to Emmaus, 2006; Marking the Hours: English people and their prayers 1240–1570, 2006. *Recreations:* early music, landscape painting in watercolour. *Address:* Magdalene College, Cambridge CB3 0AG; *e-mail:* ed10000@cam.ac.uk.

DUFFY, Dr Francis Cuthbert, CBE 1997; PPRIBA; Founder, DEGW plc, 1974; with DEGW North America, 2001–04; *b* 3 Sept. 1940; *s* of late John Austin Duffy and Annie Margaret Duffy (*née* Reed); *m* 1965, Jessica Bear; three *d. Educ:* Architectural Assoc. Sch. (AA Dip Hons); Univ. of California at Berkeley (MArch); Princeton Univ. (MA, PhD). Asst Architect, Nat. Building Agency, 1964–67; Commonwealth Fund Harkness Fellow, Berkeley and Princeton, 1967–70; established London office, JFN Associates (of NY), 1971. Member: Council, RIBA, 1989–97 (Pres., 1993–95); Architects Registration Bd, 1997–2003; Pres., Architects' Council of Europe, 1994. Chairman: Architecture, Design and Workplace Cttee, BBC, 2006–; Stratford City Design Rev. Panel, 2006–. Trustee, Architecture Foundn, 1999–. Visiting Professor: MIT, 2001–04; Reading Univ., 2007–. Editor, AA Jl, 1965–67; founder Editor, Facilities, 1985–90. President's Award for Lifetime Achievement in Workplace Design, British Council of Offices, 2004. *Publications:* Office Landscaping, 1966; (jtly) Planning Office Space, 1976; (jtly) The Changing City, 1989; The Changing Workplace, 1992; (jtly) The Responsible Workplace, 1993; The New Office, 1997; Architectural Knowledge, 1998; (jtly) New Environments for Working, 1998. *Recreations:* walking, talking, reading. *Address:* DEGW plc, The Merchant Centre, 1 New Street Square, EC4A 3BF. *T:* (020) 7239 7777; Threeways, The Street, Walberswick, Suffolk IP18 6TZ. *T:* (01502) 723814. *Clubs:* Athenæum, Reform; Princeton (NY).

DUFFY, Most Rev. Joseph; *see* Clogher, Bishop of, (R.C.).

DUFFY, Joseph Michael; a Judge of the High Court, Hong Kong, 1987–96; *b* 6 Dec. 1936; *s* of John Joseph Duffy and Mary Frances Mullaney; *m* 1962, Patricia Ann Scott; one *s* two *d. Educ:* St Andrews Univ. (MA, LLB). Solicitor, Scotland, 1965, Hong Kong, 1976; Advocate, Scotland, 1981; QC Hong Kong, 1983. Apprentice, then Solicitor, Dundee, 1963–72; Crown Counsel and Sen. Crown Counsel, Hong Kong, 1972–76 and 1978–80 (Solicitor, Hong Kong, 1976–78); Dep. Dir and Dir of Public Prosecutions, Hong Kong, 1980–86; Solicitor-General, Hong Kong, 1986–87. *Recreations:* golf, tennis, travelling, music. *Club:* Panmure Golf.

DUFFY, Maureen Patricia, FRSL 1985; author; *b* 1933; *o c* of Grace Rose Wright. *Educ:* Trowbridge High Sch. for Girls; Sarah Bonnell High Sch. for Girls; King's College, London (BA; FKC 2002). Chairman: Greater London Arts Literature Panel, 1979–81; Authors Lending and Copyright Soc., 1982–94 (Pres. of Honour, 2002–); British Copyright Council, 1989–98 (Vice Chm., 1981–86; Vice-Pres., 1998–2003; Hon. Pres., 2003); Copyright Licensing Agency, 1996–99 (Vice-Chm., 1994–96). Pres., Writers' Guild of GB, 1985–88 (Jt Chm., 1977–78); Co-founder, Writers' Action Group, 1972–79; Pres., European Writers Congress, 2003–05 (Vice-Pres., 1992–2003). Gold Medal for Lit., CISAC, 2002; Benson Silver Medal for Lit., RSL, 2004. *Publications:* That's How It Was, 1962; The Single Eye, 1964; The Microcosm, 1966; The Paradox Players, 1967; Lyrics for the Dog Hour (poetry), 1968; Wounds, 1969; Rites (play), 1969; Love Child, 1971; The Venus Touch, 1971; The Erotic World of Faery, 1972; I want to Go to Moscow, 1973; A Nightingale in Bloomsbury Square (play), 1974; Capital, 1975; Evesong (poetry), 1975; The Passionate Shepherdess, 1977; Housespy, 1978; Memorials of the Quick and the Dead (poetry), 1979; Inherit the Earth, 1980; Gorsaga, 1981 (televised as First Born, 1988); Londoners: an elegy, 1983; Men and Beasts, 1984; Collected Poems 1949–84, 1985; Change (novel), 1987; A Thousand Capricious Chances: Methuen 1889–1989, 1989; Illuminations (novel), 1991; Occam's Razor (novel), 1993; Henry Purcell (biog.), 1994; Restitution (novel), 1998; England: The Making of the Myth, 2001; Alchemy (novel), 2004; Family Values (poetry), 2008; *visual art:* Prop art exhibn (with Brigid Brophy), 1969. *Address:* 18 Fabian Road, SW6 7TZ. *T:* (020) 7385 3598.

DUFFY, Sir Patrick; *see* Duffy, Sir A. E. P.

DUFFY, Peter Clarke, QPM 1979; Director General, Federation Against Copyright Theft, 1985–89, retired; *b* Hamilton, Scotland, 10 May 1927; *s* of Hugh Duffy and Margaret Archibald; *m* 1958, S. M. Joyce (marr. diss.); one *s* two *d. Educ:* Our Lady's High Sch., Motherwell. MInstAM 1983. Served Army, Western Arab Corps, Sudan Defence Force, 1945–48 (War Medal). Joined Metropolitan Police, 1949; Criminal Investigation Dept, 1954; Comdr, New Scotland Yard, 1976–83; Dir, Investigations, Fedn Against Copyright Theft, 1983–85. *Recreations:* golf, living. *Club:* Royal Automobile.

DUFFY, Simon Patrick; Executive Chairman, QXL Ricardo, since 2007; *b* 27 Nov. 1949; *s* of Patrick and Eileen Duffy; *m* 1978, Katherine Haney; two *s. Educ:* Brasenose Coll., Oxford (BA (PPE)); Harvard Business Sch. (MBA; Harkness Fellow). Analyst: N. M. Rothschild & Sons, 1973–76; Shell, 1978–80; Consultant, Bain & Co., 1980–82; Gen. Manager, Planning and Treasury, Consolidated Gold Fields, 1982–86; Dir, Corporate Finance, Guinness, 1986–89; Ops Dir, United Distillers, 1989–92; Group Finance Director: Thorn EMI, 1992–96; EMI Gp, 1996–99 (also Dep. Chm.); Dep. Chm. and CEO, World Online Internat., 1999–2001; CEO, End2End, 2001–02; Chief Financial Officer, Orange SA, 2002–03; CEO, 2003–06, Exec. Vice-Chm., 2006–07, ntl. FRSA 1995. *Recreations:* music, literature, science, politics. *Address:* (office) QXL Ricardo plc, 91 Peterborough Road, SW6 3BU. *T:* (020) 7384 6310, *Fax:* (020) 7384 6321. *Club:* Brooks's.

DUGDALE, family name of **Baron Crathorne**.

DUGDALE, Sir William (Stratford), 2nd Bt *cr* 1936; CBE 1982; MC 1943; DL; Director and Chairman, General Utilities PLC, 1988–99; *b* 29 March 1922; *er s* of Sir William Francis Stratford Dugdale, 1st Bt, and Margaret, 2nd *d* of Sir Robert Gordon Gilmour, 1st Bt, of Liberton and Craigmillar; *S* father, 1965; *m* 1st, 1952, Lady Belinda Pleydell-Bouverie (*d* 1961), 2nd *d* of 6th Earl of Radnor; one *s* three *d*; 2nd, 1967, Cecilia Mary, *e d* of Sir William Malcolm Mount, 2nd Bt; one *s* one *d. Educ:* Eton; Balliol Coll., Oxford. Served War of 1939–45, Grenadier Guards (Captain), Admitted as Solicitor, 1949. Director: Phoenix Assurance Co., 1968–85; Lee Valley Water Co., 1989–90; North Surrey Water Co., 1989–98; Chairman: Severn Trent Water Authority, 1974–83 National Water Council, 1982–83; Birmingham Diocesan Board of Finance, 1979–92 Steward, Jockey Club, 1985–87. Chm., Wolverhampton Racecourse PLC, 1965–91. Governor, Lady Katherine Leveson's Hosp., Temple Balsall, 1956–99. Mem., Warwicks CC, 1964–76; High Steward, Stratford upon Avon, 1977. JP 1951–97, DL 1955, High Sheriff 1971, Warwicks. *Publications:* contrib. DNB. *Heir:* s William Matthew Stratford Dugdale [*b* 22 Feb. 1959; *m* 1990, Paige Sullivan; two *s* two *d*]. *Address:* Blyth Hall, Coleshill, Birmingham B46 2AD. *T:* (01675) 462203; Merevale Hall, Atherstone CV9 2HG. *T:* (01827) 713143; 24 Bryanston Mews West, W1H 7FR. *T:* (020) 7262 2510 *Clubs:* Brooks's, White's, MCC, Jockey (Newmarket).

DUGGAN, (James) Ross; His Honour Judge Duggan; a Circuit Judge, since 2006; Designated Family Judge, Stoke-on-Trent, and a Deputy High Court Judge, since 2007 *b* 14 July 1956; *s* of late Leonard Heaton Duggan and of Dr Mona Leslie Duggan; *m* 1983 Fiona Elspeth Robb Fowlie. *Educ:* Merchant Taylors' Sch., Crosby; Univ. of Liverpool (LLB Hons 1977). Called to the Bar, Middle Temple, 1978; barrister, Northern Circuit (Liverpool), 1979–2006; Circuit Junior, 1981; Asst Recorder, 1993–97; Recorder, 1997–2006. Dir, Local Solutions (formerly Merseyside CVS), 1990–. *Recreations:* cricket, soccer, countryside, theatre. *Address:* Stoke-on-Trent Combined Court, Bethesda Street, Hanley, Stoke-on-Trent ST1 3BP. *T:* (01782) 854000. *Club:* Lancashire County Cricket.

DUGGAN, Patrick Gerald; actor (as **Patrick Malahide**) and writer; *b* 24 March 1945; *s* of John Cuthbert Duggan and Mary Clementine Duggan (*née* Andrews); *m* 1st, 1970, Rosemary Wright (marr. diss. 1990); one *s* one *d*; 2nd, 1993, Jo Ryan. *Educ:* Douai Sch.; Edinburgh Univ. Stage Manager, 1969, Dir of Prodns, 1970–72, Byre Th., St Andrews joined Royal Lyceum Th., Edinburgh, as actor, 1972–76; *plays* include: The Android Circuit, Traverse and ICA, 1978; Judgement (one man show), Liverpool Playhouse, and subseq. at Edinburgh, Dublin and Amsterdam Fests, 1979; The Tempest, 1980, King Lear 1981, Bristol Old Vic; Operation Bad Apple, Royal Court, 1982; Cock-ups, Manchester Royal Exchange, 1983; Bristol Old Vic: The Cherry Orchard, 1987; In The Ruins (one man show), transf. Royal Court, 1989–90; Clandestine Marriage, Uncle Vanya, 1990 Map of the Heart, Globe, 1991; Mutabilitie, RNT, 1998; Hinterland, RNT, 2002; Embers, Duke of York's, 2006; *television* series and serials include: Minder, 1979–87; Charlie, The Pickwick Papers, 1984; The Singing Detective, 1986; The One Game, The Franchise Affair, 1988; Children of the North, 1990; The Secret Agent, 1991; The Blackheath Poisonings, 1992; The Inspector Alleyn Mysteries, 1993–94; Middlemarch 1994; In Search of the Brontës, 2003; Elizabeth I, 2005; Five Days, 2007; *plays:* Miss Julie 1987; A Doll's House, 1991; All the King's Men, 1999; Victoria and Albert, 2001 Goodbye Mr Chips, 2002; Friends and Crocodiles, 2005; *films* include: The Killing Fields, Comfort and Joy, 1984; A Month in the Country, 1987; December Bride, 1990; A Man of No Importance, 1994; Two Deaths, Cutthroat Island, 1995; The Long Kiss Goodnight 1996; US Marshals, 1998; The World is not Enough, 1999; Billy Elliot, Quills, 2000 Captain Corelli's Mandolin, 2001; Sahara, 2005; Brideshead Revisited, 2008. Patron, Byre Theatre Appeal Fund, 1999–; Dir, Bristol Old Vic Trust, 2008–. *Publications:* screenplays as P. G. Duggan: Reasonable Force, 1988; The Writing on the Wall, 1996; Pleas and Directions, 2002. *Recreations:* sailing, walking. *Address:* c/o Independent Talent Group Ltd, Oxford House, 76 Oxford Street, W1D 1BS. *Club:* Royal Fowey Yacht.

DUGGAN, Ross; *see* Duggan, J. R.

DUGGIN, Sir Thomas (Joseph), Kt 2004; HM Diplomatic Service, retired; Vice President, Global Strategies Group (Colombia) Ltd, since 2006; *b* 15 Sept. 1947; *s* of late Joseph Duggin and of Alice Lilian (*née* Mansfield); *m* 1st, 1968 (marr. diss.); two *s*; 2nd 1983 (marr. diss.); 3rd, 1999, Janette Mortimer (*née* David). *Educ:* Thornleigh Salesian Coll. Joined HM Diplomatic Service, 1967; Third Sec., Oslo, 1969–73; Third, later Second Sec. (Commercial), Bucharest, 1973–75; FCO, 1976–79; Second Sec., Bangkok 1979–82; FCO, 1982–85; Head of Chancery and HM Consul, La Paz, 1985–88; Head of Chancery, Mexico City, 1989–91; High Comr, Vanuatu, 1992–95; Hd of Security Dept then Asst Dir for Security, subseq. Hd of Security Comd, then Hd of Security Strategy Unit, FCO, 1995–2001; Ambassador to Colombia, 2001–05. Bd Mem., British and Colombian Chamber of Commerce, 2005–. MSM, Order of Vanuatu, 1992. *Recreations:* walking, tennis, reading, music. *Address:* Crossed Palms, 14 Five Arches, Orton Wistow Peterborough PE2 6FG.

DUGGLEBY, (Charles) Vincent (Anstey), MBE 2005; freelance broadcaster and financial journalist, since 1989; *b* 23 Jan. 1939; *s* of late Bernard Waldby Duggleby and Vivien Duggleby (*née* Hawkins); *m* 1964, Elizabeth Nora Frost; two *d. Educ:* Blundell's Sch.; Worcester Coll., Oxford (BA 1962, MA 2005). FRPSL 1979. Reporter, Bristol Evening Post, 1957–59; Sub-editor, Daily Express, 1960; BBC, 1963–89: sub-editor and sports presenter, 1963–67; Asst Sports Editor, 1967–70; Asst Editor, Current Affairs 1970–80; Financial Editor, 1980–89. Mem., Royal Mint Adv. Cttee, 1987–94. Royal Philatelic Society: Mem. Council, 1979–2002; Hon. Treas., 1988–93; Vice-Pres. 1994–99. Numerous awards, including: Broadcasting Financial Journalist of Year, Harold Wincott Foundn, 1992; Best Personal Finance Broadcaster, ABI, 1997. *Publications:* Highlights from 21 Years of Sports Report, 1969; English Paper Money, 1975, 7th edn 2006; (with Louise Botting) Making the Most of Your Money, 1984, 2nd edn 1985; Days Beyond Recall: a brief history of the Duggleby family, 2005. *Recreations:* philately, genealogy, classic jazz. *Address:* 41 Devonshire Place, W1N 1PE. *T:* (020) 7486 1044.

DUGUID, Andrew Alexander; Integration, Marketing & Planning Executive, Global Aerospace, 2001–04; *b* 22 June 1944; *s* of Wing Comdr (retd) Alexander Gordon Duguid and Dorothy Duguid (*née* Duder); *m* 1967, Janet Hughes; two *s* one *d. Educ:* Whitby Dist High Sch.; Ashbury Coll., Ottawa; Sidcot Sch.; LSE (BSc Econs); Univ. of Lancaster (MA Marketing). Res. Assistant, Brunel Univ., 1967–69; Marketing Executive: Interscan Ltd 1969–72; Ogilvy Benson and Mather, 1972–73; joined DTI as Principal, 1973; Prin. Pvte Sec. to Sec. of State for Industry, 1977–79; Asst Sec., seconded to Prime Minister's Policy Unit, 1979; returned to set up Policy Planning Unit, Dept of Industry, later DTI, 1982 Under Sec., DTI, 1985–86; Lloyd's of London: Head of Regulatory Services, 1986–88 Head of Market Services, 1988–92; Dir, Marketing Services, 1993–94; Dir, Policy and Planning, and Sec. to Council of Lloyd's, 1995–99; Dir, Develt, 1999–2000. Non-executive Director: Kingsway Public Relations, 1982–85; Hammersmith and Fulham NHS PCT, 2005–. Gov., Sir John Cass Foundn, 2005–. *Publication:* (with Elliott Jaques) Case Studies in Export Organisation, 1971. *Recreations:* tennis, ski-ing, walking, canoeing,

Address: 1 Binden Road, W12 9RJ. *T:* (020) 8743 7435. *Clubs:* Reform; Hartswood Lawn Tennis (Pres., 2006–).

DUGUID, Prof. James Paris, CBE 1979; MD, BSc; FRCPath; Professor of Bacteriology, University of Dundee, 1967–84; Consultant, Tayside Health Board, 1963–84; *b* 10 July 1919; *s* of late Maj.-Gen. David Robertson Duguid, CB, and Mary Paris; *m* 1944, Isobel Duff; one *s* three *d*. *Educ:* Edinburgh Academy; Univ. of Edinburgh (MB ChB Hons 1942; BSc 1st Cl. Hons 1943; MD (Gold Medal) 1949); FRCPath 1966. Lectr, Sen. Lectr and Reader, Univ. of Edinburgh, 1944–62; Prof. of Bacteriology, Univ. of St Andrews, 1963–67; Director of Postgrad. Medical Educn, Univ. of Dundee, 1968–71; Dean of Faculty of Medicine, 1971–74; Mem. Univ. Court, 1977–81. Cons. Adviser in Microbiology, Scottish Home and Health Dept, 1967–85; Mem. Adv. Cttee on Medical Research, 1967–71; Member: Eastern Regional and Tayside Health Bds, 1967–77; Adv. Cttee on Laboratory Services, Scottish Health Serv. Council, 1967–74 (Chm., Epidemiology Sub-cttee, 1966–71); Scottish Health Services Planning Council, 1974–77 (Member: Adv. Cttee on New Developments in Health Care, 1976–84; Scientific Services Adv. Gp, 1975–79; Chm., Microbiology and Clin. Immunology Cttees, 1975–77); Jt Cttee on Vaccination and Immunisation, Health Services Councils, 1967–74; GMC, 1975–81; Council for Professions Supp. to Medicine, 1978–86; Independent Adv. Gp on Gruinard Island, 1986–87; Optimum Population Trust, 1993–; Migration Watch UK, 2002–. Hon. Member: Pathol Soc. of GB and Ireland, 1985; Soc. for General Microbiology, 2001. Co-Editor: Jl of Pathology and Bacteriology, 1959–68; Jl of Medical Microbiology, 1968–71. *Publications:* (co-ed) Mackie and McCartney, Medical Microbiology, 11th edn 1969, 12th edn 1973, 13th edn 1978; (ed) Mackie and McCartney, Practical Medical Microbiology, 1989; scientific papers on bacterial fimbriae, adhesins, biotyping and phylogeny, airborne infection, and the action of penicillin. *Recreations:* grandchildren, gardening, presbyterian atheism, population studies. *Address:* Oaklands, Merlewood Road, Inverness IV2 4NL. *T:* (01463) 220118.

DUKAKIS, Michael Stanley; Distinguished Professor of Political Science, Northeastern University, since 1991; Governor, Commonwealth of Massachusetts, 1975–79, and 1983–90; *b* 3 Nov. 1933; *s* of Panos Dukakis and Euterpe Boukis-Dukakis; *m* 1963, Katharine Dickson; one *s* two *d*. *Educ:* Brookline High Sch. (Dip. 1951); Swarthmore Coll., Pa (BA 1955); Harvard Law Sch. (JD 1960). Attorney, Hill & Barlow, Boston, Mass, 1960–74; Lectr and Dir, Intergovtl Studies, John F. Kennedy Sch. of Govt, Harvard Univ., 1979–82. Visiting Professor: Univ. of Hawaii, 1991; UCLA, 1991–. Dir, Amtrack, 1998–2003. Moderator of public television's The Advocates, 1971–73. State Representative, Brookline, Mass, 1963–71; Democratic Candidate for the Presidency of the USA, 1988. *Publications:* (with Rosabeth Moss Kanter) Creating the Future: Massachusetts comeback and its promise for America, 1988; (jtly) The Crisis Strikes, 2001; (jtly) How to get into politics—and why. *Recreations:* walking, playing tennis, gardening. *Address:* 85 Perry Street, Brookline, MA 02446–6935, USA.

DUKE, family name of **Baron Merrivale.**

DUKE, Rt Rev. Michael Geoffrey H.; *see* Hare Duke.

DUKE, Timothy Hugh Stewart; Chester Herald of Arms, since 1995; *b* 12 June 1953; *s* of William Falcon Duke and Mary Cecile Duke (*née* Jackson). *Educ:* Uppingham; Fitzwilliam Coll., Cambridge (MA). Peat, Marwick, Mitchell & Co., 1974–81; Research Asst, Coll. of Arms, 1981–89; Rouge Dragon Pursuivant, 1989–95; Registrar, Coll. of Arms, 2000–07. Hon. Sec., Harleian Soc., 1994–. *Address:* College of Arms, Queen Victoria Street, EC4V 4BT. *T:* (020) 7236 7728. *Club:* Travellers.

DUKES, Alan M.; Director General, Institute of European Affairs, Dublin, since 2002; *b* 22 April 1945; *s* of James and Rita Dukes; *m* 1968, Fionnuala Corcoran; two *d*. *Educ:* Colaiste Mhuire, Dublin; University College Dublin (MA). Chief Economist, Irish Farmers' Assoc., 1967–72; Dir, Irish Farmers' Assoc., Brussels, 1973–76; Personal Advr to Comr of European Communities, 1977–80. TD (FG) Kildare, 1981–2002; Minister for Agriculture, 1981–82; opposition spokesman on agric., March-Dec. 1982; Minister: for Finance, 1982–86; for Justice, 1986–87; for Transport, Energy and Communications, 1996–97; opposition spokesman on envmt and local govt, then on agriculture, marine and natural resources, 1977–2002. Leader, 1987–90, President, 1987–92, Fine Gael Party. Chm., Jt Oireachtas Cttee on Foreign Affairs, 1995–96. Vice-President: Internat. European Movt, 1991–96 (Pres., 1987–91, Chm., 1997–2000, Irish Council); European People's Party, 1987–96; Mem., Council of State, 1988–90. Adjunct Prof. of Public Admin/Management, Univ. of Limerick, 1991–2000. Governor: EIB, 1982–86; IMF. Officier, Légion d'Honneur (France), 2004; Comdr's Cross, OM (Poland), 2004. *Address:* Tully West, Kildare, Co. Kildare, Eire.

DUKES, Justin Paul; Chairman, ECIC Management (formerly European Communications Industries Consortium), since 1990; *s* of late John Alexander Dukes and Agnes Dukes; *m* 1990, Jane Macallister; one *s* one *d*, and two *s* one *d* by a previous marriage. *Educ:* King's Coll., Univ. of Durham. Dir, Financial Times Ltd, 1975–81; Chm., Financial Times (Europe) Ltd, 1978–81; Man. Dir, Channel Four TV Co., 1981–88; Chief-Exec., Galileo Co., 1988–89. Chm., Risk Avert, 2005–; Dir, Herald Investment Trust plc, 1994–2005. Pres., Inst. of Information Scientists, 1982–83; Mem. Council, Foundn for Management Educn, 1979–90. Mem., British Screen Adv. Council, 1986–88. Trustee, Internat. Inst. of Communications, 1986–91. FRTS 1986; FRSA 1986; CCMI (CBIM 1988). Chevalier, Ordre des Arts et des Lettres (France), 1988. *Recreations:* changing institutions, walking.

DUKES, Philip Timothy, FGSM; international viola soloist and conductor; *b* 7 Jan. 1968; *s* of Ronald and Enid Dukes; *m* 2002, Caroline Lefilliatre; two *s*. *Educ:* Wells Cathedral Sch.; Guildhall Sch. of Music and Drama (FGSM 2006). Artist-in-Residence, Queen's Univ., Belfast, 2000–; Prof. of Viola, Royal Acad. of Music, 2003–; Artistic Director: Fest. International de Musique de la Hague, 2005–; Marlborough Coll., 2008–. Hon. ARAM 2007. *Recreations:* cricket, fine wines, food, obsession with Birmingham City Football Club. *Address:* Hamelin, Bath Road, Marlborough, Wilts SN8 1NN. *Club:* Royal Over-Seas League.

DULBECCO, Dr Renato; Senior Clayton Foundation Investigator, since 1979, and President Emeritus, since 1993, The Salk Institute for Biological Studies (President, 1989–93); *b* Italy, 22 Feb. 1914; USA citizen; *s* of late Leonardo Dulbecco and late Maria Virdia; *m* 1963, Maureen R. Muir; one *d*; one *d* (one *s* decd) by previous marriage. *Educ:* Univ. of Turin Medical Sch. (MD). Assistente, Univ. of Turin: Inst. Pathology, 1940–46; Anatomical Inst., 1946–47; Res. Assoc., Indiana Univ., 1947–49; Sen. Res. Fellow, 1949–52, Assoc. Prof., 1952–54, Prof. 1954–63, California Inst. Technology; Vis. Prof., Rockefeller Inst., 1962; Royal Soc. Vis. Prof. at Univ. of Glasgow, 1963–64; Salk Institute: Resident Fellow, 1963–72, Fellow, 1972–77; Distinguished Res. Prof., 1977–82; Imperial Cancer Research Fund: Asst Dir of Res., 1972–74; Dep. Dir of Res., 1974–77; Prof. of Pathology and Medicine, Univ. of Calif San Diego Med. Sch., 1977–81. MNAS; Member: Fedn of Amer. Scientists; Amer. Assoc. for Cancer Research; Cancer

Center, Univ. of Calif at San Diego; Bd of Scientific Counselors, Dept of Cancer Etiology, NCI; Amer. Acad. of Arts and Scis; Internat. Physicians for Prevention of Nuclear War, Inc.; Pres., Amer.-Ital. Foundn for Cancer Res. Trustee: Amer.-Italian Foundn for Cancer Res.; La Jolla Country Day School. Foreign Member: Academia dei Lincei, 1969; Royal Society, 1974; Hon. Member: Accademia Ligure di Scienze e Lettere, 1982; Società Medico-Chirurgica di Modena, 1985; Tissue Culture Assoc., 1988. Has given many lectures to learned instns. Hon. DSc Yale, 1968; Hon. LLD Glasgow, 1970; *hc* Dr Med., Vrije Universiteit Brussel, Brussels, 1978; Hon. DSc Indiana, 1984. (Jtly) Nobel Prize for Physiology or Medicine, 1975; Premio Fregene, Italy, 1988; numerous other prizes and awards. *Publications:* (jtly) Microbiology, 1967; numerous in sci. jls. *Recreation:* music. *Address:* The Salk Institute, PO Box 85800, San Diego, CA 92186–5800, USA.

DULVERTON, 3rd Baron *cr* 1929, of Batsford; **Gilbert Michael Hamilton Wills;** Bt 1897; farmer, forester and industrialist; *b* 2 May 1944; *s* of 2nd Baron and his 1st wife, Judith Betty (*d* 1983), *d* of Lt-Col Hon. Ian Leslie Melville, TD; *S* father, 1992; *m* 1st, 1980, Rosalind van der Velde-Oliver (marr. diss. 1999); one *s* one *d*; 2nd, 2000, Mrs Mary Vicary. *Educ:* Gordonstoun; RAC, Cirencester. Chm., Thwaites Ltd; Director: W Highland Woodlands Ltd; Batsford Estates (1983) Co. Ltd. Trustee, Dulverton Trust. *Heir: s* Hon. Robert Anthony Hamilton Wills, *b* 20 Oct. 1983.

DUMAS, Roland; Officier de la Légion d'Honneur; Croix de Guerre (1939–45); Croix du Combattant Volontaire; Minister of Foreign Affairs, France, 1988–93; *b* Limoges, Haute-Vienne, 23 Aug. 1922; *s* of Georges Dumas and Elisabeth (*née* Lecanuet); *m* 1964, Anne-Marie Lillet; two *s* one *d*. *Educ:* Lycée de Limoges; Faculté de Droit de Paris; Ecole des Sciences Politiques de Paris; Univ. of London; Ecole de langues orientales de Paris. LLL; Diplomas: in Advanced Studies in Laws; in Political Science, Paris, and London School of Economics. Counsel, Court of Appeal, Paris, 1950–; journalist; Sen. Political Dir, Journal Socialiste Limousin; Political Dir of weekly, La Corrèze Républicaine et Socialiste, 1967–; Deputy: UDSR, Haute Vienne, 1956–58; FGDS, Corrèze, 1967–68; Socialiste de la Dordogne, 1981–83, 1986–88; Minister for European Affairs, 1983–84; Govt spokesman, 1984; Minister for External Relations, 1984–86; Pres. Commn for Foreign Affairs, Nat. Assembly, 1986–87. Pres., Conseil Constitutionel, 1995–99. Grand Cross, Order of Isabel (Spain), 1982. *Publications:* J'ai vu vivre la Chine, 1960; Les Avocats, 1970; Le Droit de l'Information et de la Presse, 1981; Plaidoyer pour Roger Gilbert Lecomte, 1985; Le droit de la propriété littéraire et artistique, 1986; Le Peuple Assemblé, 1989; Le Fil et la Pelote (memoirs), 1996; L'Epreuve, 2003; Diplomatie: les nœuds de l'histoire, 2007. *Address:* 19 quai de Bourbon, 75004 Paris, France.

DUMBELL, Dr Keith Rodney; Senior Specialist in Microbiology, Medical School, University of Cape Town, 1982–90, retired; *b* 2 Oct. 1922; *s* of late Stanley Dumbell and Dorothy Ellen (*née* Hewitt); *m* 1st, 1950, Brenda Margaret (*née* Heathcote) (*d* 1971); two *d*; 2nd, 1972, Susan (*née* Herd); two *s*. *Educ:* Wirral Gram. Sch.; University of Liverpool, MB, ChB 1944; MD (Liverpool), 1950; DSc (Med) Cape Town, 2001. FRCPath 1975. Asst Lecturer, Dept of Bacteriology, University of Liverpool, 1945–47; Mem. of Scientific Staff, MRC, 1947–50; Junior Pathologist, RAF, 1950–52; Asst in Pathology and Microbiology, Rockefeller Inst. for Medical Research (Dr Peyton Rous' laboratory), 1952–53; Lecturer in Bacteriology, University of Liverpool, 1952–58; Senior Lecturer, 1958–64; Prof. of Virology, Univ. of London at St Mary's Hosp. Med. Sch., 1964–81. Vis. Prof., Univ. of Florida, 1994. Dir, WHO Collaborative Centre for Poxvirus Res., London, 1969–82; Mem., Global Commn for Certification of Smallpox Eradication, 1977–79. *Publications:* articles in various medical and scientific journals. *Address:* PO Box 1933, Somerset West, Western Cape 7129, South Africa.

DUMBRECK, Nicholas John, FIA; Consulting Actuary, Watson Wyatt Ltd (formerly R. Watson & Sons, later Watson Wyatt Partners, then Watson Wyatt LLP), since 1986; *b* Woking, 12 Nov. 1954; *s* of Alan Edwin Dumbreck and Sibyll Elisabeth Dumbreck; *m* 1978, Lesley Ann Devlin; one *s* two *d*. *Educ:* Royal Grammar Sch., Guildford; Jesus Coll., Cambridge (BA Maths 1976). FIA 1982. Various posts incl. Corporate Actuary, Imperial Life Assce Co. of Canada, 1976–86. Institute of Actuaries: Mem. Council, 1993–98 and 1999–; Hon. Sec., 1996–98; Vice Pres., 2003–05; Pres., 2006–08. Chm., Staple Inn Actuarial Soc., 2002–04. *Recreations:* opera, watching cricket, wine, travel, art. *Address:* Meadow Barn, Priorsfield Road, Godalming, Surrey GU7 2RQ. *T:* (01483) 415258; *e-mail:* nick.dumbreck@btinternet.com.

DUMFRIES, Earl of; John Bryson Crichton-Stuart; *b* 21 Dec. 1989; *s* and *heir* of Marquess of Bute, *qv*.

DUMMETT, (Agnes Margaret) Ann, (Lady Dummett); writer; *b* 4 Sept. 1930; *d* of Arthur William Chesney and late Kitty Mary Chesney; *m* 1951, Michael Anthony Eardley Dummett (*see* Sir Michael Dummett); three *s* two *d* (and one *s* one *d* decd). *Educ:* Guildhouse Sch., Pimlico; Ware Grammar Sch. for Girls; Somerville Coll., Oxford (MA). Pres., Oxford Univ. Liberal Club, 1949. Community Relations Officer, Oxford, 1966–69; teaching in further education, 1969–71; Research Worker: Inst. of Race Relations, 1971–73; Runnymede Trust, 1975, 1977; Jt Council for the Welfare of Immigrants, 1978–84; Dir, Runnymede Trust, 1984–87. Consultant (pt-time) on Eur. policies, CRE, 1990–98. *Publications:* A Portrait of English Racism, 1973; Citizenship and Nationality, 1976; A New Immigration Policy, 1978; (with Ian Martin) British Nationality: a guide to the new law, 1982; (ed) Towards a Just Immigration Policy, 1986; chapters in: Justice First (with Michael Dummett), 1969; Colloque de la Société Française pour le Droit International, 1979; Moral Philosophy, 1979; (with Andrew Nicol) Subjects, Citizens, Aliens and Others, 1990; Free Movement, 1992; Individual Rights and the Law in Britain, 1994; (ed) Racially Motivated Crime, 1997; numerous articles and pamphlets. *Recreations:* walking about cities, theatre going, popular music. *Address:* 54 Park Town, Oxford OX2 6SJ. *T:* (01865) 558698.

DUMMETT, Sir Michael (Anthony Eardley), Kt 1999; FBA; Wykeham Professor of Logic in the University of Oxford, 1979–92, Professor Emeritus 1992; Emeritus Fellow, All Souls College, Oxford, 1979; *b* 27 June 1925; *s* of George Herbert Dummett and Iris Dummett (*née* Eardley-Wilmot); *m* 1951, Ann Chesney (*see* A. M. A. Dummett); three *s* two *d* (and one *s* one *d* decd). *Educ:* Sandroyd Sch.; Winchester Coll. (1st Schol.); Christ Church, Oxford (major hist. schol., 1942; First Class Hons, PPE 1950); DLitt Oxford, 1989. Served in Army, 1943–47: in RA and Intell. Corps (India, 1945, Malaya, 1946–47, Sgt). Asst Lectr in Philosophy, Birmingham Univ., 1950–51; Commonwealth Fund Fellow, Univ. of California, Berkeley, 1955–56; Reader in the Philosophy of Mathematics, Univ. of Oxford, 1962–74; All Souls College, Oxford: Fellow, 1950–79, Senior Research Fellow, 1974–79; Sub-Warden, 1974–76; Fellow, 1979–92, Emer. Fellow, 1992–98, Hon. Fellow, 1998, New Coll., Oxford. Vis. Lectr, Univ. of Ghana, 1958; Vis. Professor: Stanford Univ., several occasions, 1960–66; Univ. of Minnesota, 1968; Princeton Univ., 1970; Rockefeller Univ., 1973; William James Lectr in Philosophy, Harvard Univ., 1976; Alex. von Humboldt-Stiftung Vis. Res. Fellow, Münster Univ., 1981; Gifford Lectr, St Andrews Univ., 1996–97; Dewey Lectr, Columbia Univ., 2002. Founder Mem., Oxford Cttee for Racial Integration, 1965 (Chm., Jan.-May 1966); Member: Exec. Cttee, Campaign Against Racial Discrimination, 1966–67; Legal and Civil Affairs Panel, Nat. Cttee for Commonwealth Immigrants, 1966–68; Chairman: Jt Council for the Welfare of Immigrants, 1970–71 (Vice-Chm., 1967–69, 1973–75); unofficial cttee of enquiry into events in Southall 23 April 1979, 1979–80; shadow board, Barclays Bank, 1981–82. FBA 1968–84, re-elected 1995. For. Hon. Mem., Amer. Acad. of Arts and Scis, 1985. Hon. PhD Nijmegen, 1983; Hon. DLitt: Caen, 1993; Aberdeen, 1993; Athens, 2005; DUniv Stirling, 2002. Lakatos Award in Phil. of Sci., LSE, 1994; Rolf Schock Prize for Logic and Philosophy, Royal Swedish Acad. of Scis, 1995. *Publications:* Frege: philosophy of language, 1973, 2nd edn 1981; The Justification of Deduction, 1973; Elements of Intuitionism, 1977, rev. edn 2000; Truth and other Enigmas, 1978; Immigration: where the debate goes wrong, 1978; Catholicism and the World Order, 1979; The Game of Tarot, 1980; Twelve Tarot Games, 1980; The Interpretation of Frege's Philosophy, 1981; Voting Procedures, 1984; The Visconti-Sforza Tarot Cards, 1986; Ursprünge der analytischen Philosophie, 1988, 2nd edn as Origins of Analytical Philosophy, 1993; Frege and Other Philosophers, 1991; The Logical Basis of Metaphysics, 1991; Frege: Philosophy of Mathematics, 1991; Grammar and Style for Examination Candidates and Others, 1993; The Seas of Language, 1993; Il Mondo e l'Angelo, 1993; I Tarocchi Siciliani, 1995, 2nd edn 2002; (jtly) A Wicked Pack of Cards, 1996; Principles of Electoral Reform, 1997; On Immigration and Refugees, 2001; La Natura e il futuro della filosofia, 2001; (jtly) A History of the Occult Tarot 1870–1970, 2002; Truth and the Past, 2004; (jtly) A History of Games Played with the Tarot Pack, 2004; Thought and Reality, 2006; *contributions to:* Mind and Language, 1975; Truth and Meaning, 1976; Studies on Frege, 1976; Contemporary British Philosophy, 1976; Meaning and Use, 1979; Perception and Identity, 1979; Perspectives on the Philosophy of Wittgenstein, 1981; Approaches to Language, 1983; Frege: tradition and influence, 1984; Reflections on Chomsky, 1989; Meaning and Method, 1990; What is a Philosophical Question?, 2002; contrib. entry on Frege, to Encyclopedia of Philosophy (ed P. Edwards), 1967; (with Ann Dummett) chapter on Rôle of the Government, in Justice First (ed L. Donnelly), 1969; preface to R. C. Zaehner, The City Within the Heart, 1980; articles in: Aristotelian Soc. Proceedings, Philos. Review, Bull. of London Math. Soc., Synthese, Inquiry, Econometrica, Jl of Symbolic Logic, Zeitschrift für mathematische Logik, Dublin Review, New Blackfriars, Clergy Review, Jl of Warburg and Courtauld Insts, Jl of Playing-Card Soc., Artibus et Historiae. *Recreations:* listening to the blues, investigating the history of card games. *Address:* 54 Park Town, Oxford OX2 6SJ. *T:* (01865) 558698.

DUMONT, Dame Ivy (Leona), DCMG 1995; DPA; Governor-General of the Bahamas, 2001–05; *b* 2 Oct. 1930; *d* of Alphonso Tennyson Turnquest and Cecilia Elizabeth Turnquest; *m* 1951, Reginald Deane Dumont; one *s* one *d*. *Educ:* Univ. of Miami (BEd 1970); Nova Univ., USA (DPA 1978). Teacher, later Dep. Dir of Educn, Min. of Educn and Culture, Bahamas, 1945–75; Dep. Permanent Sec., Min. of Works and Utilities, 1975–78; Trng Officer, Personnel Manager then Gp Relations Manager, Natwest Trust Corp. (Bahamas) Ltd, then Coutts & Co., 1978–91; Minister of Health and Envmt, 1992–94; Minister of Education, 1995–2001. Mem. (FNM), Senate, 1992–2001 (Govt Leader, 1992–2001). *Recreations:* dressmaking and design, horticulture (roses), public speaking, family. *Address:* c/o Government House, Government Hill, PO Box N8301, Nassau, Bahamas. *T:* 3221875; PO Box SS-5316, Nassau, Bahamas. *T:* 3234188.

DUMPER, Rt Rev. Anthony Charles; Hon. Assistant Bishop, diocese of Birmingham, since 1993; *b* 4 Oct. 1923; *s* of Charles Frederick and Edith Mildred Dumper; *m* 1948, Sibylle Anna Emilie Hellwig (*d* 2001); two *s* one *d*. *Educ:* Surbiton Grammar School; Christ's Coll., Cambridge (MA); Westcott House, Cambridge. Relief Worker, Germany, 1946–47; ordained, 1947; Curate, East Greenwich, 1947–49; Vicar of South Perak, Malaya, 1949–57; Archdeacon of North Malaya, 1955–64; Vicar of Penang, Malaya, 1957–64; Dean of St Andrew's Cathedral, Singapore, 1964–70; Vicar of St Peter's, Stockton on Tees, and Rural Dean of Stockton, 1970–77; Bishop Suffragan of Dudley, 1977–93. *Publication:* Vortex of the East, 1963. *Recreations:* walking, gardening. *Address:* 117 Berberry Close, Bournville, Birmingham B30 1TB.

DUMVILLE, Prof. David Norman, PhD; FRHistS; FRSAI, FSA, FSAScot; Professor of History, Palaeography and Celtic, since 2005, and Associate Director, Research Institute of Irish and Scottish Studies, since 2006, University of Aberdeen; Fellow, Girton College, Cambridge, since 1978; *b* 5 May 1949; *s* of late Norman Dumville and Eileen Florence Lillie Dumville (*née* Gibbs); *m* 1974, Sally Lois Hannay (*d* 1989); one *s*. *Educ:* Emmanuel Coll., Cambridge (BA Hons, MA); Ludwig-Maximilian Universität, Munich; Univ. of Edinburgh (PhD 1976). FRHistS 1976; FRSAI 1989; FSAScot 1999. Fellow, Univ. of Wales, Swansea, 1975–77; Asst Prof. of English, Univ. of Pennsylvania, 1977–78; O'Donnell Lectr in Celtic Studies, Univ. of Oxford, 1977–78; Lectr in Anglo-Saxon, Norse and Celtic, Univ. of Cambridge, 1977–91; British Acad. Res. Reader in Humanities, 1985–87; Reader in Early Mediaeval History and Culture of British Isles, 1991–95, Prof. of Palaeography and Cultural History, 1995–2004, Univ. of Cambridge. Res. Associate, Sch. of Celtic Studies, Dublin Inst. for Advanced Studies, 1989– (Vis. Prof., 1996–97); Visiting Professor of Mediaeval Studies: UCLA, 1995; Univ. of Calif, Berkeley, 1997. Vice-Pres., Centre International de Recherche et de Documentation sur le Monachisme Celtique, 1986–. Hon. MA Pennsylvania, 1979. *Publications:* (with Kathryn Grabowski) Chronicles and Annals of Mediaeval Ireland & Wales, 1984; (with Michael Lapidge) The Annals of St Neots, 1985; The Historia Brittonum, 1985; (ed jtly) The Anglo-Saxon Chronicle, 1985, 1995, 2007; Histories and Pseudo-Histories of the Insular Middle Ages, 1990; Wessex and England from Alfred to Edgar, 1992; Liturgy and the Ecclesiastical History of Late Anglo-Saxon England, 1992; Britons and Anglo-Saxons in the Early Middle Ages, 1993; English Caroline Script and Monastic History, 1993; Saint Patrick, 1993; The Churches of North Britain in the First Viking-Age, 1997; Three Men in a Boat (inaugural lect.), 1997, 2nd edn 2004; Councils and Synods of the Gaelic Early and Central Middle Ages, 1997; A Palaeographer's Review, vol. 1 1999, vol. 2 2004; Saint David of Wales, 2001; Annales Cambriae, 2002–; The Annals of Iona, 2002; (with Pádraig Ó Néill) Cáin Adomnáin and Canones Adomnani, 2003; The Early Mediaeval Insular Churches and the Preservation of Roman Literature, 2004; Abbreviations used in Insular Script before AD 850, 2004; Brenhinoedd y Saeson, 2005–. *Recreations:* travelling in North America, politics and other arguments. *Address:* Department of Divinity, History and Philosophy, University of Aberdeen, G11 Crombie Annexe, Meston Walk, Old Aberdeen AB24 3FX. *T:* (01224) 272199.

DUN, Peter John; HM Diplomatic Service; Adviser, Directorate-General for External Relations, European Commission, Brussels, since 2002; *b* 6 July 1947; *s* of Herbert Ernest Dun and late Joyce Hannah Dun (*née* Tozer); *m* 1984, Cheng Kiak Pang; two *s*. *Educ:* Bristol Grammar Sch.; Univ. of Birmingham (BA); Univ. of Cologne; Univ. of Freiburg; Univ. of Strasbourg. British High Commn, Kuala Lumpur, 1972–76; FCO, 1976–80; UK Repn to EU, 1980–83; UK Mission to UN, 1983–87; Dep. Hd, Disarmament Dept, FCO, 1987–89; rcds, 1989; British High Commission, Islamabad, 1990–93; Foreign Policy Advr to Ext. Affairs Comr, EC, Brussels, 1993–96; Hd of Information Dept, FCO, 1996–2000; Counsellor, Berlin, 2000–02; Asst to EU Special Rep. for Afghanistan, 2002. Vis. Fellow, Stiftung Wissenschaft und Politik, Berlin, 2000–. *Recreations:* music, travel, maps. *Address:* 170 rue de la Loi, 1049 Brussels, Belgium.

DUNALLEY, 7th Baron *cr* 1800 (Ire.), of Kilboy, Tipperary; **Henry Francis Cornelius Prittie;** Social Worker, Shetland Islands Council, since 2003; *b* 30 May 1948; *s* of 6th Baron Dunalley and of Mary Philippa, *o c* of late Hon. Philip Cary; *S* father, 1992; *m* 1978, Sally Louise, *er d* of Ronald Vere; one *s* three *d*. *Educ:* Gordonstoun Sch.; Trinity Coll., Dublin (BA); Bedford Coll., Univ. of London (CQSW). Probation Officer: Inner London Probation Service, 1977–80; Buckinghamshire Probation Service, 1980–83; Oxfordshire and Bucks Probation Service, 1983–2001; Thames Valley Probation Service, 2001–03. *Heir:* *s* Hon. Joel Henry Prittie, *b* 29 April 1981. *Address:* Ruach, Bridge End, Shetland ZE2 9LE. *T:* (01595) 859447.

DUNANT, Sarah; novelist and broadcaster; *b* 8 Aug. 1950; *d* of David Dunant and Estelle (*née* Joseph); two *d* by Ian Willox. *Educ:* Godolphin and Latymer Girls' Sch.; Newnham Coll., Cambridge (BA Hons 1972). Actress, 1972–73; producer, Radio 4, 1974–76; freelance writer, TV and radio broadcaster and journalist, 1977–; The Late Show, BBC 2, 1989–95. *Publications:* as Peter Dunant, (with Peter Busby): Exterminating Angels, 1983; Intensive Care, 1986; as Sarah Dunant: Snow Storms in a Hot Climate, 1988; Birth Marks, 1991; Fatlands, 1993 (Silver Dagger Award); (ed) The War of the Words, 1994; Under my Skin, 1995; (ed jtly) Age of Anxiety, 1996; Transgressions, 1997; Mapping the Edge, 1999; The Birth of Venus, 2003; In the Company of the Courtesan, 2006. *Recreations:* movies, travel. *Address:* c/o Clare Alexander, Aitken Alexander Associates, 18–21 Cavaye Place, SW10 9PT. *T:* (020) 7373 8672.

DUNBABIN, Dr Jean Hymers; Senior Research Fellow, St Anne's College, Oxford, since 2004 (Fellow and Tutor, 1973–2004); Reader in Medieval History, University of Oxford, 1997–2004; *b* 12 May 1939; *d* of David Mackay and Peggy Mackay (*née* Stewart); *m* 1962, John Dunbabin; two *d*. *Educ:* St Leonard's Sch., St Andrews; St Hilda's Coll., Oxford (MA, DPhil 1965). Jun. Research Fellow, Somerville Coll., Oxford, 1961–63; Vice-Principal, St Anne's Coll., Oxford, 1994–97. Mem., IAS, Princeton, 1989. Ed., English Historical Rev., 2000–03. *Publications:* France in the Making 843–1180, 1985, 2nd edn 2000; A Hound of God: Pierre de la Palud and the Fourteenth Century Church, 1991; Charles I of Anjou: power, kingship and state-making in thirteenth-century Europe, 1998; Captivity and Imprisonment in Medieval Europe 1000–1300, 2002; contributions to: The Cambridge History of Later Medieval Philosophy, 1982; The Cambridge History of Medieval Political Thought, 1988; The New Cambridge Medieval History, vol. III, 1999; contrib. various jls. *Recreations:* walking, travelling. *Address:* St Anne's College, Oxford OX2 6HS. *T:* (01865) 274872.

DUNBAR, Alexander Arbuthnott; *b* 14 March 1929; *yr s* of Sir Edward Dunbar, Bt (*d* 1969); *m* 1965, Elizabeth Susannah, *d* of Rev. Denzil Wright; one *s* one *d*. *Educ:* Wellington Coll., Berks; Pembroke Coll., Cambridge (MA); Edinburgh Sch. of Agriculture, 1980–81. Mil. Service, Lieut QO Cameron Highlanders, 1947–49. Called to the Bar, Inner Temple, 1953. Joined ICI, 1954: Asst Sec., Wilton Works, 1959–63. Joined North Eastern Assoc. for the Arts, 1963, Sec. 1964, Dir 1967; Director: Northern Arts, 1967–69; UK and British Commonwealth Branch, Calouste Gulbenkian Foundn, 1970–71; Scottish Arts Council, 1971–80. Chm., Northern Adv. Cttee, Scottish Wildlife Trust, 1986–93; Member: Arts and Disability Enquiry, Carnegie UK Trust, 1982–85; Museums and Galleries Commn Wkg Party on Museums in Scotland, 1984–86. DL Moray, 1987–2004. *Recreations:* art, theatre, conservation, history, travel. *Address:* Pitgaveny, Elgin, Moray IV30 5PQ.

DUNBAR of Northfield, Sir Archibald (Ranulph), 11th Bt *cr* 1700; *b* 8 Aug. 1927; *er s* of Sir (Archibald) Edward Dunbar, 9th Bt (by some reckonings 10th Bt) and Olivia Douglas Sinclair (*d* 1964), *d* of Maj.-Gen. Sir Edward May, KCB, CMG; *S* father, 1969; *m* 1974, Amelia Millar Sommerville, *d* of Horace Davidson; one *s* two *d*. *Educ:* Wellington Coll.; Pembroke Coll., Cambridge; Imperial Coll. of Tropical Agriculture, Trinidad. Mil Service, 2nd Lt, Cameron (att. Gordon) Highlanders, 1945–48. Entered Colonial Agricultural Service, Uganda, as Agricultural Officer, 1953; retired, 1970. Hon. Sheriff, Sheriff Court District of Moray, 1989–. Kt of Honour and Devotion, SMO Malta, 1989. *Publications:* A History of Bunyoro-Kitara, 1965; Omukama Chwa II Kabarega, 1965; The Annual Crops of Uganda, 1969; various articles in Uganda Jl. *Heir:* *s* Edward Horace Dunbar, Younger of Northfield, *b* 18 March 1977. *Address:* The Old Manse, Duffus, Elgin, Scotland IV30 5QD. *T:* (01343) 830270.
See also A. A. Dunbar.

DUNBAR, Sir David H.; *see* Hope-Dunbar.

DUNBAR, Ian Duncan; Sheriff of Tayside Central and Fife at Dunfermline, since 2005; *b* 31 Oct. 1948; *s* of John Duncan Dunbar and Mary Golden; *m* 1973, Sue Young. *Educ:* Lawside Acad., Dundee; Queen's Coll., Dundee (St Andrews Univ., subseq. Dundee Univ.) (LLB 1969). Apprentice Solicitor, Soutar Reid & Mill, Dundee, 1969–71; Sneddon Campbell & Munro, Perth, later Miller Sneddon, then Miller Hendry, Perth and Dundee: Asst Solicitor, 1971–72; Partner, 1972–98; Chm., 1994–98; Floating Sheriff, 1998–2000; Sheriff of Tayside Central and Fife at Dundee, 2000–05. Pres., Law Soc. of Scotland, 1993–94 (Vice Pres., 1992–93). Trustee, Perth Coll. Develt Trust, 1995–98. *Recreations:* golf, Rugby, cooking, food, wine. *Address:* Craigrownie, Bridge of Earn, Perth PH2 9HA. *Club:* Blairgowrie Golf (Capt., 2005–06).

DUNBAR, Ian Malcolm, CB 1993; Director of Inmate Administration, Prison Service, Home Office, 1990–94; *b* 6 Jan. 1934; *s* of Thomas Dunbar and Rose (*née* Hook); *m* 1966, Sally Ann Hendrickson; two *s* one *d*. *Educ:* Buckhurst Hill County High Sch.; Keele Univ.; Reed Coll., Portland, USA; LSE. Joined Prison Service, 1959; Leyhill Prison, 1960; Prison Service Coll., 1965; Dep. Gov., Long Lartin, 1970; Gov., Usk Borstal and Detention Centre, 1972; Prison Dept 4 Div., Home Office, 1974; Governor: Feltham Borstal, 1978; Wakefield Prison, 1979; Wormwood Scrubs, 1983; seconded to HM Inspectorate of Prisons, 1985; Regl Dir, SW Reg., Prison Service, 1985. NI Sentence Review Comr, 1998– (NI Transitional Life Sentence Review Comr, 2001–02). *Publications:* A Sense of Direction, 1985; (with A. Langdon) Tough Justice: sentencing and penal policies in the 1990s, 1998. *Recreations:* bee-keeping, gardening, photography, walking, reading.

DUNBAR of Mochrum, Colonel Sir James Michael, 14th Bt *cr* 1694 (NS), of Mochrum, Wigtownshire; *b* 17 Jan. 1950; *s* of Sir Jean Ivor Dunbar, 13th Bt and of Rose Jeanne, *d* of Henry William Hertsch; *S* father, 1993; *m* 1st, 1978, Margaret Jacobs (marr. diss. 1989; she *d* 1991); two *s* one *d*; 2nd, 1989, Margaret, *d* of Roger Gordon Talbot; one *d*. Colonel, USAF. *Heir:* *s* Michael Joseph Dunbar, *b* 5 July 1980.

DUNBAR, John Greenwell, OBE 1999; architectural historian; Secretary, Royal Commission on the Ancient and Historical Monuments of Scotland, 1978–90; *b* 1 March 1930; *o s* of John Dunbar and Marie Alton; *m* 1974, Elizabeth Mill Blyth. *Educ:* University College Sch., London; Balliol Coll., Oxford (MA). FSA. Joined staff of Royal Commission on the Ancient and Historical Monuments of Scotland, 1953; Member: Ancient Monuments Board for Scotland, 1978–90; Regl Adv. Cttee, Forestry Commn, 1997–2000. Vice-President: Soc. for Medieval Archaeology, 1981–86; Soc. of Antiquaries of Scotland, 1983–86. Lectures: Lindsay-Fischer, Oslo, 1985; Rhind, Edinburgh, 1998. Hon. FRIAS; Hon. FSA Scot. *Publications:* The Historic Architecture of Scotland, 1966, revd edn 1978; (contrib.) The Cilician Kingdom of Armenia, 1978; (ed with John Imrie) Accounts of the Masters of Works 1616–1649, 1982; Sir William Burrell's Northern Tour 1758, 1997; Scottish Royal Palaces, 1999; (jtly) The Buildings of Scotland: Borders, 2006; numerous articles in archaeological jls, etc. *Address:* Patie's Mill, Carlops, By Penicuik, Midlothian EH26 9NF. *T:* (01968) 660250. *Club:* New (Edinburgh).

DUNBAR of Hempriggs, Sir Richard (Francis), 9th Bt *cr* 1706 (NS); *b* 8 Jan. 1945; *s* of Lady Dunbar of Hempriggs, Btss (8th in line) and Leonard James Blake (*d* 1989); assumed the name of Dunbar, 1965; *S* to mother's Btcy, 1997; *m* 1969, Elizabeth Margaret Jane Lister; two *d. Educ:* Charterhouse. Businessman. *Heir:* (to father's Btcy) *d* Emma Katherine Dunbar of Hempriggs, *b* 9 Nov. 1977.

DUNBAR of Durn, Sir Robert (Drummond Cospatrick), 10th Bt *cr* 1698 (NS); *b* 17 June 1958; *o s* of Sir Drummond Cospatrick Ninian Dunbar, 9th Bt, MC and Sheila Barbara Mary, *d* of John B. de Fonblanque; *S* father, 2000; *m* 1994, Sarah Margaret, *yr d* of Robert Anthony Brooks; one *s* one *d. Educ:* Harrow; Christ Church, Oxford (MA). Associate, Soc. of Investment Professionals. Allen & Overy (Private Client Dept), 1982–86; Merrill Lynch Investment Managers, 1986–2003. *Heir: s* Alexander William Drummond Dunbar, Younger of Durn, *b* 1 March 1995.

DUNBAR, Prof. Robin Ian MacDonald, PhD; FBA 1998; FRAI; Professor of Evolutionary Anthropology, University of Oxford, since 2007; Fellow, Magdalen College, Oxford, since 2007; *b* 28 June 1947; *s* of George MacDonald Dunbar and Betty Lilian (*née* Toon); *m* 1971, Eva Patricia Melvin; two *s* one *d. Educ:* Magdalen Coll. Sch., Brackley; Magdalen Coll., Oxford (BA 1969); Univ. of Bristol (PhD 1974). FRAI 1992. SERC Advanced Res. Fellow, King's Coll., Cambridge, 1977–80; Res. Fellow, Zool. Dept, Univ. of Cambridge, 1980–82; docent, Zool Inst., Univ. of Stockholm, 1983; Res. Fellow, Zool. Dept, Liverpool Univ., 1985–87; University College London: Lectr, Anthropol. Dept, 1987–92; Prof. of Biol Anthropol., 1992–94; Prof. of Evolutionary Psychol., Univ. of Liverpool, 1994–2007. Mem., Animal Procedures Cttee, Home Office, 1997–2004. Member: Assoc. for Study of Animal Behaviour, 1970–; Primate Soc., 1973– (Pres., 1990–92); British Ecol. Soc., 1979–; Galton Inst., 1988– (Galton Lect., 2006); Internat. Behaviour Ecol. Soc., 1995–; Assoc. for Child Psychology and Psychiatry, 1999–2003; Human Behaviour & Evolution Soc., 1999–; BAAS, 2000–; Amer. Psychol Assoc., 2000–. Member: Save British Sci., 1998–; BACSA, 1998–; Chester Caledonian Assoc., 2001–; Council for British Archaeology, 2001–; Ramblers Assoc., 2003–. Osman Hill Medal, Primate Soc. of GB, 1994. Co-editor, Animal Behaviour, 1994–95. *Publications:* Social Dynamics of Galada Baboons, 1975; Reproductive Decisions, 1984; Primate Social Systems, 1988; World of Nature, 1988; The Trouble with Science, 1995; (ed) Human Reproductive Decisions, 1995; Grooming, Gossip and the Evolution of Language, 1996; (ed) The Evolution of Culture, 1999; Primate Conservation Biology, 2000; Cousins, 2000; Human Evolutionary Psychology, 2002; The Human Story, 2004; Evolutionary Psychology, 2005; Handbook of Evolutionary Psychology, 2007. *Recreations:* poetry, Medieval and Renaissance music, hill-walking. *Address:* Institute of Cognitive and Evolutionary Anthropology, School of Anthropology, University of Oxford, Oxford OX2 6PE.

DUNBAR-NASMITH, Sir James (Duncan), Kt 1996; CBE 1976; RIBA; PPRIAS; FRSA, FRSE; Partner, Law & Dunbar-Nasmith, architects, Edinburgh, Forres, 1957–99; Professor Emeritus, Heriot-Watt University, since 1988; *b* 15 March 1927; *y s* of late Adm. Sir Martin Dunbar-Nasmith, VC, KCB, KCMG, DL and Justina Dunbar-Nasmith, CBE, DStJ. *Educ:* Lockers Park; Winchester; Trinity Coll., Cambridge (BA); Edinburgh Coll. of Art (DA; Hon. Fellow 2007). ARIBA 1954. Architekten Kammer Hessen, 1994. Lieut, Scots Guards, 1945–48. Prof. and Hd of Dept. of Architecture, Heriot-Watt Univ. and Edinburgh Coll. of Art, 1978–88. President: Royal Incorporation of Architects in Scotland, 1971–73; Edinburgh Architectural Assoc., 1967–69. Member: Council, RIBA, 1967–73 (a Vice-Pres., 1972–73; Chm., Bd of Educn, 1972–73); Council, ARCUK, 1976–84 (Vice-Chm., Bd of Educn, 1977); Royal Commn on Ancient and Historical Monuments of Scotland, 1972–96; Ancient Monuments Bd for Scotland, 1969–83 (interim Chm., 1972–73); Historic Buildings Council for Scotland, 1966–93; Edinburgh New Town Conservation Cttee/Edinburgh World Heritage Trust, 1972–2004; Council, Europa Nostra, 1986–2004 (Vice-Pres., 1997–2004; Hon. Life Mem., 2005); Dep. Chm., Edinburgh Internat. Festival, 1981–85; Pres., Scottish Civic Trust, 2003– (Chm., 1995–2003); Trustee, Architectural Heritage Fund, 1976–97; Theatres Trust, 1983–95. *Recreations:* music, theatre, ski-ing, sailing. *Address:* Sandbank, Findhorn, Moray IV36 3YY. *T:* (01309) 690445. *Clubs:* Royal Ocean Racing; New (Edinburgh).

DUNBOYNE, 29th Baron by Prescription, 1324, 19th Baron by Patent, *cr* 1541 (Ire.); **John Fitzwalter Butler;** *b* 31 July 1951; *o s* of 28th/18th Baron Dunboyne and Anne Marie, *d* of Sir Victor Mallet, GCMG, CVO; *S* father, 2004; *m* 1975, Diana Caroline, *yr d* of Sir Michael Sanigear Williams, KCMG; one *s* two *d* (and one *d* decd). *Educ:* Winchester; Trinity Coll., Cambridge (BA 1973; MA 1977); London Business Sch. (Sloan Fellow, 1979). Hill Samuel Gp, 1974–75; Stolt Nielsen Inc., 1977–78; Lazard Brothers & Co. Ltd, 1979–80; mgt consultant, 1980–; Dir, Fitzwalter & Co. Ltd, 1985– (projects include: EU consortium for privatisation in Kazakstan, 1994; EU Tacis Enterprise Support Centres for Large and Medium-sized Enterprises in Western Siberia, 1998–99; ISCRA investment support centres to Russia, 2000–02; EU Tacis Assistance to Kabardino-Balkarian Republic, 2004). Transatlantic voyage in small sailing boat, 1975–76. *Recreations:* international relations, sailing, country pursuits, quixotic causes. *Heir: s* Hon. Richard Pierce Theobald Butler, *b* 5 July 1983. *Address:* Argos Hill House, Rotherfield, East Sussex TN6 3QG. *Clubs:* Butler Society (Vice-Pres.), Irish Peers Association; Cruising Association.

DUNCAN, Agnes Lawrie Addie, (Laura); Sheriff of Glasgow and Strathkelvin, 1982–2006; *b* 17 June 1947; *d* of late William Smith, District Clerk, and Mary Marshall Smith McClure; *m* 1990, David Cecil Duncan, farmer, cricket coach, *y s* of late Dr and Mrs H. C. Duncan, Edinburgh; one *s. Educ:* Hamilton Acad.; Glasgow Univ. (LLB 1967). Admitted Solicitor, 1969; called to the Scottish Bar, 1976. Solicitor, private practice, 1969–71; Procurator Fiscal Depute, 1971–75; Standing Junior Counsel to Dept of Employment, 1982. Winner, Scottish Ladies Single handed Dinghy Championship, 1990. *Recreations:* sailing, walking.

DUNCAN, Alan James Carter; MP (C) Rutland and Melton, since 1992; *b* 31 March 1957; 2nd *s* of late Wing Comdr J. G. Duncan, OBE and Anne Duncan (*née* Carter). *Educ:* Merchant Taylors' Sch.; St John's Coll., Oxford. Pres., Oxford Union, 1979. With Shell Internat. Petroleum, 1979–81; Kennedy Schol., Harvard Univ., 1981–82; oil trader, Marc Rich & Co., 1982–88; self-employed oil broker, 1988–92. PPS to Min. of State, DoH, 1993–94, to Chm. of Cons. Party, 1995–97; a Vice Chm. of Cons. Party, 1997–98; Parly Political Sec. to Leader of the Opposition, 1997; Opposition spokesman on health, 1998–99, on trade and industry, 1999–2001, on foreign affairs, 2001–03; Shadow Sec. of State for Constitutional Affairs, 2003–04, for Internat. Develt, 2004–05, for Transport, 2005, for Trade and Industry, 2005–07, for Business, Enterprise and Regulatory Reform, 2007–. Mem., Select Cttee on Social Security, 1993–95. Contested (C) Barnsley W and Penistone, 1987. Vis. Parly Fellow, St Antony's Coll., Oxford, 2002–03. Freeman, City of London, 1980; Liveryman, Merchant Taylors' Co., 1987. *Publications:* An End to Illusions, 1993; (with D. Hobson) Saturn's Children: how the state devours liberty, prosperity and virtue, 1995. *Address:* House of Commons, SW1A 0AA. *Club:* Beefsteak.

DUNCAN, Dr Allan George; environmental consultant, since 2000; *b* 17 Oct. 1940; *s* of Donald Allan Duncan and Annabella Duncan (*née* Thom); *m* 1972, Alison Patricia Reid; two *s* one *d. Educ:* Robert Gordon's Coll., Aberdeen; Aberdeen Univ. (BSc Hons 1963); New Coll., Oxford, (DPhil 1966). CEnv 2006. Research Engineer: California Univ., 1966–67; US Nat. Bureau of Standards, 1967–69; UKAEA, Harwell, 1969–79; Radiochemical Inspectorate, DoE, 1979–87 (Dep. Chief Inspector, 1984–87); HM Inspectorate of Pollution, 1987–96 (Chief Inspector, 1995–96); Hd, Radioactive Substances Regulation, EA, 1996–2000. Member: EC Network of Envmtl Regulators, 1993–2000; Euratom Scientific and Tech. Cttee, 1994–; Envmtl Assessment Panel, UK Accreditation Service, 1994–99. MIEMA; FRSA. *Publications:* various contribs to scientific literature. *Recreations:* sailing, walking, North American history. *Address:* 14 Rawlings Grove, Abingdon, Oxon OX14 1SH. *T:* (01235) 529096.

DUNCAN, Andy; Chief Executive, Channel Four, since 2004; *b* 31 July 1962. *Educ:* Univ. of Manchester Inst. of Sci. and Technol. (BSc). Joined Unilever, 1984; Chm., Business Unit and Mktg Controller for spreads and margarines, 1995–97, Mktg Dir, 1997–99, Van Den Bergh Foods; Eur. Category Dir, Food and Beverages Div., 1999–2001; Dir, Marketing and Communications, subseq. Marketing, Communications and Audiences, BBC, 2001–04. *Address:* Channel Four, 124 Horseferry Road, SW1P 2TX.

DUNCAN, Prof. Archibald Alexander McBeth, FBA 1985; FRSE; Professor of Scottish History and Literature, Glasgow University, 1962–93; *b* 17 Oct. 1926; *s* of Charles George Duncan and Christina Helen McBeth; *m* 1954, Ann Hayes Sawyer, *d* of W. E. H. Sawyer, Oxford; two *s* one *d. Educ:* George Heriot's Sch.; Edinburgh Univ.; Balliol Coll., Oxford. Lecturer in History, Queen's Univ., Belfast, 1951–53; Lecturer in History, Edinburgh Univ., 1953–61; Leverhulme Research Fellow, 1961–62. Glasgow University: Clerk of Senate, 1978–83; Dean of Faculties, 1998–2000. Mem., Royal Commn on the Ancient and Historical Monuments of Scotland, 1969–92. FRSE 1979. DUniv Glasgow, 2001. *Publications:* Scotland: The Making of the Kingdom, 1975; (ed and revised) W. Croft Dickinson's Scotland from the Earliest Times to 1603, 3rd edn 1977; Regesta Regum Scottorum, v, The Acts of Robert I, 1306–29, 1988; (ed, with trans. and notes), John Barbour, The Bruce, 1997; The Kingship of the Scots 842–1292, 2002. *Address:* 17 Campbell Drive, Bearsden, Glasgow G61 4NF.

DUNCAN, Rev. Canon Bruce, MBE 1993; Principal, Sarum College, and Canon and Prebendary of Salisbury Cathedral, 1995–2002, now Canon Emeritus; *b* 28 Jan. 1938; *s* of late Andrew Allan Duncan and of Dora Duncan (*née* Young); *m* 1966, Margaret Holmes Smith; three *d. Educ:* St Albans Sch.; Univ. of Leeds (BA 1960); Cuddesdon Coll., Oxford. Founder/Director: Children's Relief Internat., 1960–62; Northorpe Hall Trust, 1962–65; ordained deacon, 1967, priest, 1968; Curate, St Bartholomew, Armley, Leeds and Curate in charge, St Mary of Bethany, Leeds, 1967–69; Hon. Curate, St Mary the Less, Cambridge, 1969–70; Chaplain, Order of Holy Paraclete, Whitby, 1970–71; Chaplain to HM Ambassadors in Austria, Hungary and Czechoslovakia, based in Vienna, 1971–75; Vicar, Collegiate Church of Holy Cross and the Mother of Him Who Hung Thereon, Crediton, Devon, 1976–82; Rural Dean of Cadbury, 1976–81; Rector, Crediton and Shobrooke, 1982–86; Residentiary Canon, Manchester Cathedral and Fellow, Coll. of Christ in Manchester, 1986–95. Commissary in UK for Bp of N Eastern Caribbean and Aruba, 2006–. Internat. Consultant, Trinity Inst. for Christianity and Culture, 2004–. Lazenby and St Luke's Chaplain, Exeter Univ., 2003–04. Chairman of Trustees: St Luke's Coll. Foundn, 2006–; Families for Children Adoption Agency, 2006–; Hon. Pres., Northorpe Hall Child and Family Trust, 1997–. FRSA 1989. Hon. Fellow, Sarum Coll., 2006. Hon. DD Graduate Theol. Foundn, Indiana, 2002. Cross of St Augustine, 2004. *Publications:* Children at Risk (ed A. H. Denney), 1968; Sich Selbst Verstehen, 1993; Pray Your Way, Your Personality and God, 1993. *Recreations:* travel, walking, Jungian psychology. *Address:* 92 Harnham Road, Salisbury, Wilts SP2 8JW; *e-mail:* churchpath@fsmail.net. *Club:* Athenæum.

DUNCAN, Craig; Adviser to the President, Royal College of Surgeons of England, since 2005; *b* 1 May 1951; *s* of William Sneddon Duncan and of Jessie Clark Sloan Duncan (*née* Mackie); *m* 1st, 1975, Janet Elizabeth Gillespie (marr. diss. 1988); one *s* one *d*; 2nd, 1998, Jane Alison Pavitt. *Educ:* Allan Glen's Sch., Glasgow; Univ. of Strathclyde (BA 1st Cl. Hons Geog.). Administrative Assistant: Univ. of Durham, 1973–76; Univ. of Southampton, 1976–82; Royal College of Surgeons of England, 1982–: Admin. Asst and Asst Sec., 1982–88; Asst Sec., Inst. Basic Med. Scis, 1982–86; Secretary: Hunterian Inst., 1986–88; for Ext. Affairs, 1989–97; Senate of Surgery of GB and Ireland, 1993–97; Coll. Secretary, 1997–2001; Chief Exec., 2001–05. McNeill Love Medal, RCS, 2007. *Recreations:* music, reading, water-colour painting, golf. *Address:* Royal College of Surgeons of England, 35–43 Lincoln's Inn Fields, WC2A 3PN. *T:* (020) 7869 6020. *Club:* South Winchester Golf.

DUNCAN, Rev. Denis Macdonald, MA, BD; *b* 10 Jan. 1920; *s* of late Rev. Reginald Duncan, BD, BLitt and late Clarice Ethel (*née* Hodgkinson); *m* 1942, Henrietta Watson McKenzie (*née* Houston) (*d* 1993); one *s* one *d. Educ:* George Watson's Boys' Coll., Edinburgh; Edinburgh Univ.; New Coll., Edinburgh. Ordained, 1943; Minister of: St Margaret's, Juniper Green, Edinburgh, 1943–49; Trinity Duke Street Parish Church, Glasgow, 1949–57; Founder-editor, Rally, 1956–67; Managing Editor, British Weekly, 1957–70 (Man. Dir, 1967–70); Managing Director: DPS Publicity Services Ltd, 1967–74; Arthur James Ltd (Publishers), 1983–94; broadcaster and scriptwriter, Scottish Television, 1963–68; concert promotion at Edinburgh Festival and elsewhere, 1966–; Concert series "Communication through the Arts" poetry/music anthologies (with Benita Kyle), 1970–80. Dir, Highgate Counselling Centre, 1969–86; Associate Dir and Trng Supervisor, Westminster Pastoral Foundn, 1971–79; Chm., Internat. Cttee of World Assoc. of Pastoral Care and Counselling, 1977–79; Dir, Churches' Council for Health and Healing. 1982–88; Moderator of the Presbytery of England, Church of Scotland, 1984. PhD Somerset Univ., 1989. *Publications:* (ed) Through the Year with William Barclay, 1971; (ed) Through the Year with Cardinal Heenan, 1972; (ed) Daily Celebration, vol. 1, 1972, vol. 2, 1974; Marching Orders, 1973; (ed) Every Day with William Barclay, 1973; (ed) Through the Year with J. B. Phillips, 1974; Marching On, 1974; Here is my Hand, 1977; Creative Silence, 1980; A Day at a Time, 1980; Love, the Word that Heals, 1981; The Way of Love, 1982; Victorious Living, 1982; Health and Healing: a ministry to wholeness, 1988; Be Still and Know …: 100 Daily Telegraph meditations, 1994; Solitude, stillness, serenity …: a further 75 Daily Telegraph meditations, 1997; The Road Taken: autobiographical reflections on communication, 1997; Rainbows Through the Rain: a third collection of 75 Daily Telegraph Meditations, 2000; Meditations through the Year:

367 Daily Telegraph meditations, 2003; (ed) Morning and Evening: William Barclay's meditations, 2003. *Recreation:* cricket. *Address:* 80A Woodland Rise, N10 3UJ. *T:* (020) 8883 1831, *Fax:* (020) 8374 4708.

DUNCAN, Geoffrey Stuart, OBE 1998; General Secretary, General Synod Board of Education and National Society for Promoting Religious Education, 1990–98; *b* 10 April 1938; *s* of Alexander Sidney Duncan and Gertude Ruth (*née* Page); *m* 1962, Shirley Bernice Matilda Vanderput; one *d* (one *s* decd). *Educ:* Hemel Hempstead Grammar Sch.; Univ. of London (BScEcon); Univ. of Exeter (MA). Served RAEC, 1960–64. School and technical coll. teaching, 1964–72; LEA Advr and Officer, 1972–82; Schs Sec. and Dep. Sec., Gen. Synod Bd of Educn and Nat. Soc. for Promoting Religious Educn, 1982–90. Part-time WEA Tutor, 1966–70; part-time Open Univ. Counsellor, 1971–72. Dir, Urban Learning Foundn, 1990–98; Company Sec., Inst. of Consumer Scis, 2000–01. Trustee: St Gabriel's Educnl Trust, 1990–98; St Christopher's Educnl Trust, 1990–98; Winchester Shoei Coll. Foundn, 1990–. Governor, Coll. of St Mark & St John, Plymouth, 1990–2005. MUniv Surrey, 1998. *Publications:* contributor to: Faith for the Future, 1986; Schools for Tomorrow, 1988; various educn jls. *Recreations:* campanology, travel. *Address:* 14 Compton Lodge, Compton Place Road, Eastbourne BN21 1EQ. *T:* (01323) 416746.

DUNCAN, George; Chairman, Laporte plc, 1995–2001 (Director, 1987–95); *b* 9 Nov. 1933; *s* of William Duncan and Catherine Gray Murray; *m* 1965, Frauke Ulrike Schnuhr (marr. diss.); one *d*. *Educ:* Holloway County Grammar Sch.; London Sch. of Economics (BSc(Econ)); Wharton Sch.; Univ. of Pennsylvania (MBA). Mem., Inst. of Chartered Accountants (FCA). Chief Executive, Truman Hanbury Buxton and Co. Ltd, 1967–71; Chief Executive, Watney Mann Ltd, 1971–72; Vice-Chm., Internat. Distillers and Vintners Ltd, 1972; Chm., Lloyds Bowmaker Finance Ltd (formerly Lloyds and Scottish plc), 1976–86; Dir, Lloyds Bank Plc, 1982–87. Chairman: Allied Steel and Wire (Hldgs) Ltd, subseq. ASW Hldgs plc, 1986–2002; Household Mortgage Corp., 1986–94; Humberclyde Finance Gp, 1987–89; Whessoe PLC, 1987–97; Rubicon Group plc, 1992–95; Higgs and Hill plc, subseq. Swan Hill Gp, 1993–2003; Alldays plc, 1999–2001; Hurlingham School Ltd, 2000–; Director: Pauls & Whites, 1974–86; Haden plc, 1974–85 (Dep. Chm., 1984–85); Fitch Lovell plc, 1976–86; City of London Investment Trust (formerly TR City of London Trust PLC), 1977–2000; BET plc, 1981–96; Associated British Ports PLC, 1986–2003 (Dep. Chm., 1998–2003); Newspaper Publishing plc, 1986–93; Crown House PLC, 1987; Dewe Rogerson Gp Ltd, 1987–95; Calor Gp, 1990–97. Chm., CBI Companies Cttee, 1980–83; Mem., CBI President's Cttee, 1980–83. Mem., Eur. Adv. Bd, Wharton Sch., 1995–99. Freeman, City of London, 1971. *Recreations:* opera, golf. *Address:* 16 Belgrave Mews West, SW1X 8HT. *Club:* Brooks's.

DUNCAN, Very Rev. Gregor Duthie, PhD; Dean of the Diocese of Glasgow and Galloway, since 1996; Rector of St Ninian's, Pollokshields, since 1999; *b* 11 Oct. 1950; *s* of Edwin John Duncan and Janet Brown Duncan. *Educ:* Univ. of Glasgow (MA Hons 1972); Clare Coll., Cambridge (PhD 1977); Oriel Coll., Oxford (BA Hons 1983); Ripon Coll., Cuddesdon. Ordained deacon, 1983, priest, 1984; Asst Curate, Oakham with Hambleton and Egleton, and Braunston with Brooke, 1983–86; Chaplain, Edinburgh Theol Coll., 1987–89; Rector of St Columba's, Largs, 1989–99. *Recreations:* collecting gramophone records, cooking. *Address:* St Ninian's Rectory, 32 Glencairn Drive, Pollokshields, Glasgow G41 4PW. *T:* (0141) 423 1247, *Fax:* (0141) 424 3332; *e-mail:* dean@glasgow.anglican.org.

DUNCAN, Jacqueline Ann, FBIDA; Principal of Inchbald Schools of Design and Fine Arts, since 1960; *b* 16 Dec. 1931; *d* of Mrs Donald Whitaker; *m* 1st, 1955, Michael Inchbald, *qv* (marr. diss. 1964); one *s* one *d*; 2nd, 1974, Brig. Peter Trevenen Thwaites (*d* 1991); 3rd, 1994, Col Andrew Tobin Warwick Duncan, LVO, OBE. *Educ:* Convent of the Sacred Heart, Brighton; House of Citizenship, London. FBIDA (FIDDA 1991; FIIDA 1994). Founded: Inchbald Sch. of Design, 1960; Inchbald Sch. of Fine Arts, 1970; Inchbald Sch. of Garden Design, 1972; Inchbald Online, 2008. Member: Monopolies Commn, 1972–75; Whitfield Cttee on Copyright and Design, 1974–76; London Electricity Cons. Council, 1973–76; Westminster City Council (Warwick Ward), 1974–78. Mem., Vis. Cttee, RCA, 1986–90; International Society of Interior Designers: Acting Pres., London Chapter, 1987–90; Chm., 1990–92. Trustee, St Peters' Research Trust, 1987–90. JP South Westminster, 1976–2001. Outstanding Contribution Award, BIDA, 2006. *Publications:* Directory of Interior Designers, 1966; Bedrooms, 1968; Design and Decoration, 1971. *Recreations:* fishing, travel. *Address:* Lime Tree House, Fifehead Magdalen, Gillingham, Dorset SP8 5RT; (office) 32 Eccleston Square, SW1V 1PB.

DUNCAN, Sir James (Blair), Kt 1981; Chairman: Transport Development Group, 1975–92; Boalloy Industries Ltd, 1992–2005; *b* 24 Aug. 1927; *s* of late John Duncan and Emily MacFarlane Duncan; *m* 1974, Dr Betty Psaltis (*d* 2005), San Francisco. *Educ:* Whitehill Sch., Glasgow. Qualified as Scottish Chartered Accountant. Joined Transport Development Group, 1953; Dir, 1960; Chief Exec., 1970–90; retd, 1992. Mem., LTE (part-time), 1979–82. Scottish Council: Mem. 1976–2002, and Chm. 1982–99, London Exec. Cttee; Vice Pres., 1983–99, Pres., 1999–2002. Confedn of British Industry: Mem. Council, 1980–82; Mem. 1979–90, and Chm. 1983–88, London Region Roads and Transportation Cttee; Mem., Transport Policy Cttee, 1983–92. London Chamber of Commerce: Mem. Council, 1982–; Mem., Gen. Purposes Cttee, 1983–90; Dep. Chm., 1984–86; Chm., 1986–88; Chm., Commercial Educn Trust, 1992–98. Pres., IRTE, 1984–87. FCILT (Pres., CIT, 1980–81; Spurrier Meml Lectr, 1972; Award of Merit, 1973; Herbert Crow Medal, 1978); CCMI; FRSA 1977. Liveryman, Co. of Carmen, 1983– (Award of Merit, 1992); Freeman, Co. of Watermen & Lightermen of the River Thames, 1982. *Publications:* papers on transport matters. *Recreations:* travel, reading, walking, swimming, theatre, golf. *Address:* 17 Kingston House South, Ennismore Gardens, SW7 1NF. *T:* (020) 7589 3545. *Clubs:* Hurlingham, Caledonian, Royal Automobile; Wisley Golf.

DUNCAN, Prof. James Playford, DSc Manchester; CEng; FIMechE, FIET; Professor of Mechanical Engineering, University of British Columbia, 1966–84, now Emeritus; Adjunct Professor, University of Victoria, 1985–87; *b* 10 Nov. 1919; *s* of late Hugh Sinclair Duncan and late Nellie Gladys Duncan; *m* 1942, Jean Marie Booth; three *s* one *d*. *Educ:* Scotch Coll., Adelaide; University of Adelaide, S Australia (ME). MInstP. Executive Engineer, Richards Industries Ltd, Keswick, S Australia, 1941–46; Senior Physics Master, Scotch Coll., Adelaide, 1946–47; Lecturer in Mechanical Engineering, University of Adelaide, 1948–49, Senior Lecturer, 1950–51 and 1953–54; Turbine Engineer, Metropolitan Vickers Electrical Co., Trafford Park, Manchester, 1952; Turner and Newall Research Fellow, University of Manchester, 1955; Lecturer in Mechanical Engineering, University of Manchester, 1956; Prof. of Mechanical Engineering, University of Sheffield, 1956–66. *Publications:* Sculptured Surfaces in Engineering and Medicine, 1983; Computer Aided Sculpture, 1989. *Recreations:* sailing, flautist. *Address:* 21771 Ridgeway Crescent, Maple Ridge, BC V2X 3Y6, Canada.

DUNCAN, Ven. John Finch, MBE 1991; Archdeacon of Birmingham, 1985–2001; *b* 9 Sept. 1933; *s* of John and Helen Maud Duncan; *m* 1965, Diana Margaret Dewes (*d* 2001); one *s* two *d*. *Educ:* Queen Elizabeth Grammar School, Wakefield; University Coll., Oxford; Cuddesdon Coll. MA (Oxon). Curate, St John, South Bank, Middlesbrough, 1959–61; Novice, Society of St Francis, 1961–62; Curate, St Peter, Birmingham, 1962–65; Chaplain, Univ. of Birmingham, 1965–76; Vicar of All Saints, Kings Heath, Birmingham, 1976–85. Chairman: Copec Housing Trust, 1970–91; Focus Housing Assoc., 1991–96. *Recreations:* golf, theatre, convivial gatherings. *Address:* 66 Glebe Rise, Kings Sutton, Banbury, Oxon OX17 3PH. *T:* (01295) 812641.

DUNCAN, John Lawrence, QPM 1999; Lord Lieutenant for Ayrshire and Arran, since 2006; *b* 15 Oct. 1942; *s* of John Duncan and Emily Gordon Duncan (*née* Legge); *m* 1st, 1964, Margaret Thomson Clark (*d* 1993); one *s* one *d*; 2nd, 2005, Jess Young; one step *d*. *Educ:* Buckie High Sch. Renfrew and Bute Constabulary, 1959–75 (Cadet, 1959–61); Strathclyde Police, 1975–2001: Head, Complaints and Discipline Br., 1989–92; Divl Comdr, Ayr, 1992–95; Head: of Force Inspectorate, 1995–96; of Force Personnel, 1996; Asst Chief Constable, 1996–99; Dep. Chief Constable, 1999–2001. Chm., Ayr United FC, 2003–04. *Recreations:* football, reading, music, art, church, Rotary. *Address:* Braeside, Stewarton, Kilmarnock KA3 5LL. *T:* (01560) 484050; *e-mail:* johnlduncan@btinternet.com. *Club:* Glasgow Art.

DUNCAN, Prof. John Sidney, DM; FRCP, FMedSci; Professor of Neurology, Institute of Neurology, University College London, since 1998; *b* 12 Dec. 1955; *s* of John Graham Duncan and Elizabeth Mabella Duncan; *m* 1983, Elizabeth Hills; one *s* one *d*. *Educ:* Westminster Sch.; Worcester Coll., Oxford (BM BCh 1979; MA 1980; DM 1988). FRCP 1994. Sen. Lectr in Neurology and Consultant Neurologist, Nat. Hosp. for Neurology and Neurosurgery, 1989–98. Med. Dir, Nat. Soc. for Epilepsy, 1998–. FMedSci 2005. *Publications:* Clinical Epilepsy, 1995; MRI Neuroanatomy, 1996; Functional Imaging of the Epilepsies, 2000; contrib. original papers on treatment of epilepsy and brain imaging applied to epilepsy. *Recreations:* opera, horse riding. *Address:* National Hospital for Neurology and Neurosurgery, Queen Square, WC1N 3BG. *T:* (020) 7391 8905, *Fax:* (020) 7391 8984; *e-mail:* j.duncan@ion.ucl.ac.uk.

DUNCAN, John Stewart, OBE 1993; HM Diplomatic Service; Ambassador for Multilateral Arms Control and Disarmament and UK Permanent Representative to Conference on Disarmament, Geneva, since 2006; *b* 17 April 1958; *s* of Ernest Stewart Duncan and Joyce Fenner Duncan (*née* Austin); *m* 1984, Anne Marie Jacq; one *s* one *d*. *Educ:* Wycliffe Coll.; Univ. de Paris-Sorbonne (dip. langue et civilisation); Keele Univ. (BA Hons); NATO Defence Coll. Entered FCO, 1980; Scandinavia Desk, FCO, 1980–82; Chancery, Paris, 1982–84; Overseas Aid Admin, Khartoum, 1984–88; Head of Section: Defence Sales and Policy, FCO, 1988–89; Non-Proliferation, FCO, 1989–91; Asst Private Sec. to Minister for Overseas Aid and Africa, 1991–92; Chargé d'Affaires, Tirana, 1992–93; Mem., UK Delegn, NATO, 1993–96; Deputy Head: S Atlantic Dependent Territories Dept, FCO, 1996–97; Security Policy Dept, FCO, 1998; UK Pol Advr to SACEUR and Dep. SACEUR, 1998–2001; Dir, Trade and Investment, Paris, 2002–06. *Publication:* Rethinking NATO, 2002. *Recreations:* windsurfing, military history, gardening, jazz. *Address:* c/o Foreign and Commonwealth Office, King Charles Street, SW1A 2AH; UKDIS, 58 Ave Louis Casaï, Case Postale 6 1216 Cointrin, Geneva, Switzerland. *Club:* National Liberal.

DUNCAN, Laura; *see* Duncan, A. L. A.

DUNCAN, Lindsay Vere; actress; *b* 7 Nov. 1950; *m* Hilton McRae, actor; one *s*. *Educ:* Central Sch. of Speech and Drama. *Television:* series: Dead Head, 1985; Traffik, 1989; GBH, 1991; A Year in Provence, 1993; Get Real, 1998; Dirty Tricks, 2000; Rome, 2005; Spooks, 2005–06; serials: The Rector's Wife, 1994; Oliver Twist, 1999; Shooting the Past, 1999; Perfect Strangers, 2001; *theatre:* Les Liaisons Dangereuses, RSC, 1986 (Olivier Award); Hedda Gabler, Hampstead, 1988; Cat on a Hot Tin Roof, NT, 1988 (Evening Standard Award); A Midsummer Night's Dream, RSC; Berenice, NT, 1990; Three Hotels, Tricycle, Kilburn, 1993; The Cryptogram, Ambassadors, 1994; Ashes to Ashes, Royal Court Upstairs, 1996; The Homecoming, RNT, 1997; Celebration, and The Room, Almeida, 2000; Mouth to Mouth, Royal Court (Critics' Circle Award), 2001; Private Lives, Albery, 2001, NY, 2002 (Critics' Circle, Olivier, Tony, NY Drama Desk and Variety Club Awards, 2002); That Face, Royal Court, 2007, transf. Duke of York's, 2008; *films:* Prick Up Your Ears, 1987; Manifesto, 1988; The Reflecting Skin, 1990; City Hall, 1995; A Midsummer Night's Dream, 1996; Mansfield Park, 2000; An Ideal Husband, 2000; Under the Tuscan Sun, 2003; Afterlife, 2004 (Bowmore Scottish Screen Award, Best Actress, Bratislava Film Fest.); Starter for Ten, 2006; (for TV) Longford, 2006. *Address:* c/o Independent Talent Group Ltd, 76 Oxford Street, W1D 1BS.

DUNCAN, Martin David Anson; Joint Artistic Director, Chichester Festival Theatre, 2002–05; *b* 12 July 1948; *s* of Ronald Francis Hamilton Anson Duncan and Margaret Elizabeth (*née* Thurlow). *Educ:* Durston House Sch., Ealing; Westminster Sch.; LAMDA (Stage Mgt). Actor in rep., West End, television and film, 1968–89; composer of musical scores for over 50 theatre prodns; Associate Artist, Crucible Theatre, Sheffield, 1988; Artistic Dir, Nottingham Playhouse, 1994–99. *Theatre productions include:* Rocky Horror Show, Munich and Milan, 1985; School for Clowns, Lilian Baylis Th., 1988; Performance, Pet Shop Boys' tour (Associate Dir), 1991; The Nutcracker, Opera North (Dir and co-writer), 1992; The Comedy of Errors, Berlin, 2001; The Blacks, Johannesburg and Stockholm, 2001; *National Theatre of Brent:* The Greatest Story Ever Told, 1987; The French Revolution, 1989; All the World's a Globe, 1990; Love upon the Throne, 1998; Massive Landmarks of the 20th Century, 1999; The Wonder of Sex, 2001; *Nottingham Playhouse:* The Nose, 1995, The Adventures of Pinocchio, 1995; Happy End, Time and the Room, 1996; Le Bourgeois Gentilhomme, 1998; Endgame, and Krapp's Last Tape, 1999; *Chichester:* The Gondoliers, 2003; Out of this World, Seven Doors, 2004; How to Succeed in Business Without Really Trying, The Government Inspector, 2005; *opera productions:* Opera North: L'heure Espagnole, Gianni Schicchi, 1990; The Thieving Magpie, 1992, 2005; Iolanta, Orpheus in the Underworld, 1992; The Adventures of Pinocchio, 2007; Bavarian State Opera, Munich: Xerxes, 1996; La Clemenza di Tito, 1999; The Rake's Progress, 2002; Die Entführung aus dem Serail, 2003; Albert Herring, Canadian Opera Co., 1991; The Magic Flute, Scottish Opera, 1993; HMS Pinafore, Die Fledermaus, D'Oyly Carte Opera Co., 1994; Ariadne auf Naxos, Scottish Opera, 1997; The Last Supper, Berlin State Opera, 2000; The Love of Three Oranges, Cologne Opera, 2001; The Last Supper, Glyndebourne, 2001; Pagliacci/Cavalleria Rusticana, Royal Albert Hall, 2002; La Traviata, Flanders Opera, 2003.

DUNCAN, Peter; Chief Scout, 2004–09; actor, presenter, theatre director, documentary maker; *b* 3 May 1954; *s* of Alan Gale and Patricia Kaye; *m* 1985, Annie Francis; one *s* three *d*. *Educ:* Hawes Down Sec. Mod. Sch.; Italia Conti Stage Sch.; Open Univ. Actor: NT, 1970–72; theatre, film and television, 1973–80; Presenter: Blue Peter, 1980–84, 1985–86 (Gold Blue Peter Badge); Duncan Dares, 1984–86; Peter Duncan's Family Travels, 2000–06; actor, including: The Card, Regent's Park Th., 1993; Me and My Girl, UK tour, 1995; title rôle in Barnum, UK tour, 1999; theatre and documentary producer, 1987–2005. *Recreations:* organic gardening, singing, football, travel, yoga, green and ethical campaigning, pantomime, journalism. *Address:* 24 Wimbledon Park Road, SW18 1LT; *web:* www.heresoneimadeearlier.com.

DUNCAN, Peter John; Member (C) Dumfries and Galloway Council, since 2007 (Chairman of Resources, since 2007); *b* 10 July 1965; *s* of late Ronald Duncan and Aureen Duncan (*née* Anderson); *m* 1994, Lorna Forbes; one *s* one *d*. *Educ:* Univ. of Birmingham (BCom Hons). Project Manager, Mackays Stores Ltd, 1985–88; Man. Dir, John Duncan & Son, 1988–2000; freelance business consultant, 1998–2000. MP (C) Galloway and Upper Nithsdale, 2001–05; contested (C) Dumfries and Galloway, 2005. Shadow Sec. of State for Scotland, 2003–05. Chm., Scottish Conservative and Unionist Party, 2004–07. *Recreations:* Scottish Rugby, English Test and county cricket. *Address:* 2 St Andrew Street, Castle Douglas, Dumfries and Galloway DG7 1DE.

DUNCAN, Sean Bruce; His Honour Judge Duncan; a Circuit Judge, since 1988; *b* 21 Dec. 1942; *s* of late Joseph Alexander Duncan and Patricia Pauline Duncan; *m* 1974, Dr Diana Bowyer Courtney; three *s* one *d*. *Educ:* Shrewsbury Sch.; St Edmund Hall, Oxford (MA). Called to the Bar, Inner Temple, 1966; Northern Circuit (Hon. Sec., Circuit Cttee, 1985–88); a Recorder, 1984–88. Pres., Council of HM Circuit Judges, 2002 (Hon. Sec., 1996–99). Served with Cheshire Yeomanry (TA), 1963–68. Chairman: Old Swan Boys Club, Liverpool, 1974–79; Liverpool Youth Organisations Cttee, 1977–83; Vice-Chm., Liverpool Council of Voluntary Service, 1982–88. *Recreations:* theatre, sport, music. *Address:* c/o Queen Elizabeth II Law Courts, Derby Square, Liverpool L2 1AX. *Clubs:* Royal Liverpool Golf (Capt., 2003); Liverpool Ramblers AFC (Pres., 2000–02).

DUNCAN, Stanley Frederick St Clair, CMG 1983; HM Diplomatic Service, retired; *b* 13 Nov. 1927; *yr s* of late Stanley Gilbert Scott and Louisa Elizabeth Duncan; *m* 1967, Jennifer Jane Bennett; two *d*. *Educ:* Latymer Upper Sch.; Open Univ. (Dip. European Humanities 1999; BA Hons 2002). FRGS. India Office, 1946; CRO, 1947; Private Sec. to Parly Under-Sec. of State, 1954; Second Sec., Ottawa, 1954–55; Brit. Govt Information Officer, Toronto, 1955–57; Second Sec., Wellington, 1958–60; First Sec., CRO, 1960; seconded to Central African Office, 1962–64; Mem., Brit. Delegn to Victoria Falls Conf. on Dissolution of Fedn of Rhodesia and Nyasaland, 1963; First Sec., Nicosia, 1964–67; FCO, 1967–70; FCO Adviser, Brit. Gp, Inter-Parly Union, 1968–70; Head of Chancery and First Sec., Lisbon, 1970–73; Consul-General and subsequently Chargé d'Affaires in Mozambique, 1973–75; Counsellor (Political), Brasilia, 1976–77; Head of Consular Dept, FCO, 1977–80; Canadian Nat. Defence Coll., 1980–81; Ambassador to Bolivia, 1981–85; High Comr in Malta, 1985–87. Mem., UN Observer Mission to S African elections, 1994. Officer, Military Order of Christ (Portugal), 1973. *Address:* Tucksmead, Longworth, Oxon OX13 5ET.

DUNCAN-JONES, Prof. Katherine Dorothea, FRSL; Fellow, and Tutor in English Literature, Somerville College, Oxford, 1966–2001; Professor of English Literature, University of Oxford, 1998–2001; Senior Research Fellow, Somerville College, and Faculty of English, University of Oxford, since 2001; *b* 13 May 1941; *d* of late Prof. Austin Ernest Duncan-Jones and Elsie Elizabeth Duncan-Jones (*née* Phare); *m* 1971, Andrew N. Wilson, *qv* (marr. diss. 1990); two *d*. *Educ:* King Edward VI High Sch. for Girls, Birmingham; St Hilda's Coll., Oxford (BLitt, MA). Mary Ewart Res. Fellow, Somerville Coll., Oxford, 1963–65; Fellow, New Hall, Cambridge, 1965–66. Hon. Res. Fellow, UCL, 2000–. FRSL 1992; FEA 2000. Ben Jonson Discoveries Prize, 1996. *Publications:* (ed jtly) Miscellaneous Prose of Sir Philip Sidney, 1977; (ed) Sir Philip Sidney, 1989; Sir Philip Sidney: courtier poet (biog.), 1991; (ed) Shakespeare's Sonnets, 1997; Ungentle Shakespeare (biog.), 2001; Shakespeare's Life and Work, 2004; (ed jtly) Shakespeare's Poems, 2007; contrib. numerous articles in Rev. of English Studies, TLS, and other jls. *Recreations:* swimming, theatre-going. *Address:* Somerville College, Oxford OX2 6HD. *T:* (01865) 281267.

See also R. P. Duncan-Jones, Viscount Runciman of Doxford.

DUNCAN-JONES, Richard Phare, PhD; FBA 1992; Fellow, Gonville and Caius College, Cambridge, since 1963; *b* 14 Sept. 1937; *s* of late Austin Ernest Duncan-Jones and Elsie Elizabeth Duncan-Jones; *m* 1986, Julia Elizabeth Poole. *Educ:* King Edward's Sch., Birmingham; King's Coll., Cambridge (MA, PhD). Gonville and Caius College, Cambridge: W. M. Tapp Res. Fellow, 1963–67; Domestic Bursar, 1967–84; Official Fellow, 1967–; College Lectr and Dir of Studies in Classics, 1984–2004. Mem., Inst. for Advanced Study, Princeton, 1971–72. *Publications:* The Economy of the Roman Empire, 1974, 2nd edn 1982; Structure and Scale in the Roman Economy, 1990; Money and Government in the Roman Empire, 1994; articles in learned jls. *Recreations:* wine tasting, walking, continental cinema. *Address:* Gonville and Caius College, Cambridge CB2 1TA. *T:* (01223) 332394.

See also K. D. Duncan-Jones.

DUNCAN SMITH, Rt Hon. (George) Iain; PC 2001; MP (C) Chingford and Woodford Green, since 1997 (Chingford, 1992–97); Leader of the Conservative Party, and Leader of the Opposition, 2001–03; *b* 9 April 1954; *s* of late Group Captain W. G. G. Duncan Smith, DSO (Bar), DFC (2 Bars) and of Pamela Mary Duncan Smith (*née* Summers); *m* 1982, Hon. Elizabeth Wynne Fremantle, *er d* of Baron Cottesloe, *qv*; two *s* two *d*. *Educ:* HMS Conway (Cadet School); RMA Sandhurst; Dunchurch Coll. of Management. Scots Guards, 1975–81; ADC to Gen. Sir John Acland, 1979–81; GEC, 1981–88; Dir, Bellwinch (Property), 1988; Dir, Jane's Inf. Group, 1989–92. Vice-Chm., Fulham Cons. Assoc., 1991; contested (C) Bradford West, 1987. Shadow Secretary of State: for social security, 1997–99, for defence, 1999–2001. Member, Select Committee: on Health, 1994–95; on Nolan, 1995; on Standards and Privileges, 1996–97. Sec., Cons. Backbench Cttee on Foreign and Commonwealth Affairs, 1992–97; Vice Chm., Cons. European Affairs Cttee, 1996–97; Mem., Cons. Party Adv. Council, 2003–. Chm., Centre for Social Justice, 2004–. Trustee: Lygon Alms-house, 1985–91; Whitefield Develt Trust. Freeman, City of London. *Publications:* The Devil's Tune (novel), 2003; Breakdown Britain, 2006; Breakthrough Britain, 2007; various pamphlets on social security, European and defence issues; occasional journalism. *Recreations:* family, painting, fishing, cricket, tennis, shooting, opera, reading. *Address:* House of Commons, SW1A 0AA. *T:* (020) 7219 1210 and 3000.

DUNCANNON, Viscount; Frederick Arthur William Ponsonby; *b* 9 Aug. 1974; *e s* and *heir* of Earl of Bessborough, *qv*; *m* 2005, Emily, *d* of Dr Peter D. Mott, Pittsford, NY; one *s* one *d*. *Educ:* Harrow; UEA. *Heir:* *s* Hon. William Ponsonby, *b* 6 May 2008.

DUNCOMBE, family name of **Baron Feversham**.

DUNCOMBE, Sir Philip (Digby) Pauncefort-, 4th Bt *cr* 1859; DL; one of HM Body Guard, Honourable Corps of Gentlemen-at-Arms, since 1979 (Harbinger, 1993–97); *b* 18 May 1927; *o s* of Sir Everard Pauncefort-Duncombe, 3rd Bt, DSO, and Evelyn Elvira (*d* 1986), *d* of Frederick Anthony Denny; *S* father, 1971; *m* 1951, Rachel Moyra, *d* of Major H. G. Aylmer; one *s* two *d*. *Educ:* Stowe. 2nd Lieut, Grenadier Guards, 1946; served in Palestine, 1947–48; Malaya, 1948–49; Cyprus, 1957–59; Hon. Major, retired 1960, Regular Army Reserve. County Comdt, Buckinghamshire Army Cadet Force, 1967–70. DL Bucks 1971, High Sheriff, 1987–88. CStJ 1992. *Heir:* *s* David Philip Henry Pauncefort-Duncombe [*b* 21 May 1956; *m* 1987, Sarah, *d* of late Reginald Battrum and of Mrs Reginald Battrum; one *s* one *d*]. *Address:* Church Close, Church Lane, Great Brickhill, Bucks MK17 9AE. *T:* (01525) 261205. *Club:* Cavalry and Guards.

DUNCOMBE, Roy, VRD 1957; Chairman, Nationwide Building Society, 1989–91; *b* 7 June 1925; *s* of Joseph William Duncombe and Gladys May Duncombe (*née* Reece); *m* 1946, Joan Thornley Pickering; one *s* two *d*. *Educ:* Hinckley Grammar School. RNR, 1943–68 (Lt-Comdr (A); Pilot, Fleet Air Arm). Financial Dir, Ferry Pickering Gp, 1965–87; Chm., Anglia Building Soc., 1985–87; following merger with Nationwide Bldg Soc., Vice Chm., Nationwide Anglia Bldg Soc., 1987–89; name changed to Nationwide Bldg Soc., 1989. *Recreations:* walking, swimming, photography, ornithology. *Address:* Westways, Market Bosworth, Nuneaton, Warwickshire CV13 0LQ. *T:* (01455) 291728; 3 The Old Grammar School, Chipping Campden, Glos GL55 6HB. *T:* (01386) 841455. *Club:* Naval and Military.

DUNCUMB, Dr Peter, FRS 1977; Director and General Manager, Tube Investments, later TI Group, Research Laboratories, 1979–87; *b* 26 Jan. 1931; *s* of late William Duncumb and of Hilda Grace (*née* Coleman); *m* 1955, Anne Leslie Taylor; two *s* one *d*. *Educ:* Oundle Sch.; Clare Coll., Cambridge (BA 1953, MA 1956, PhD 1957). Commnd GD Br., RAF, qualif. Pilot, 1949–50; No 22RFS Cambridge, RAFVR, 1950–54; DSIR Res. Fellow, Cambridge Univ., 1957–59; Tube Investments, subseq. TI Group, Research Laboratories: Res. Scientist and Gp Leader, 1959–67, Head, Physics Dept, 1967–72; Asst Dir, 1972–79. Hon. Prof., Warwick Univ., 1990–2000. FInstP 1969. Hon. Member: Microbeam Analysis Soc. of America, 1973; European Microbeam Analysis Soc., 1997. C. V. Boys Prize, Inst. of Physics, 1966; Henry Clifton Sorby Award, Internat. Metallographic Soc., 1996. *Publications:* numerous on electron microscopy and analysis in various jls. *Recreations:* photography, orienteering, family genealogy. *Address:* 5A Woollards Lane, Great Shelford, Cambridge CB22 5LZ. *T:* (01223) 843064.

DUNDAS, family name of **Viscount Melville,** and of **Marquess of Zetland**.

DUNDAS, James Frederick Trevor; Chairman: Macmillan Cancer Support (formerly Macmillan Cancer Relief), since 2001 (non-executive Director, since 1996); Jupiter Asset Management, since 2008; *b* 4 Nov. 1950; *s* of Sir Hugh Dundas, CBE, DSO, DFC, and of Hon. Lady Dundas; *m* 1979, Jennifer Daukes; one *s* two *d*. *Educ:* Eton; New Coll., Oxford (BA Hons Jurisp.). Called to the Bar, Inner Temple, 1972; Morgan Grenfell & Co. Ltd, 1972–91: Dir, 1981–91; Head, Corporate and Internat. Banking, 1987–91; Mem., Mgt Cttee, Morgan Grenfell Gp plc, 1989–91; Finance Dir, Hong Kong Airport Authy, 1992–96; Finance Dir, 1997–99, Chief Exec., 1999–2003, MEPC plc. Non-executive Director: J. Sainsbury plc, 2000–07; Standard Chartered PLC, 2004–; Drax Gp plc, 2005–.

DUNDAS-BEKKER, Althea Enid Philippa; DL; owner and administrator, Arniston House, Midlothian; *b* 4 Nov. 1939; *d* of Sir Philip Dundas, 4th Bt and Jean Marion Dundas; *m* 1972, Aedrian Ruprecht Bekker (*d* 1990); two *d*. *Educ:* Inverleny, Callander; Oakfield Sch., Kirkby Lonsdale. Inherited Arniston House, 1970. Mem., Royal Commn on Historical MSS, 1994–2003. DL Midlothian, 1991. *Recreations:* Scottish history and songs, walking dogs. *Address:* Arniston House, Gorebridge, Midlothian EH23 4RY. *T:* (01875) 830238, *Fax:* (01875) 830573; *e-mail:* email@dundasbekker.fsnet.co.uk.

DUNDEE, 12th Earl of, *cr* 1660 (Scotland); **Alexander Henry Scrymgeour;** DL; Viscount Dudhope and Lord Scrymgeour, 1641 (Scotland); Lord Inverkeithing, 1660 (Scotland); Lord Glassary (UK), 1954; Hereditary Royal Standard-Bearer for Scotland; *b* 5 June 1949; *s* of 11th Earl of Dundee, PC, and of Patricia Katherine, *d* of late Col Lord Herbert Montagu Douglas Scott; *S* father, 1983; *m* 1979, Siobhan Mary, *d* of David Llewellyn, Gt Somerford, Wilts; one *s* three *d*. *Educ:* Eton; St Andrews Univ. Contested (C) Hamilton, by-election May 1978. A Lord in Waiting (Govt Whip), 1986–89; elected Mem., H of L, 1999. DL Fife, 2003. *Heir:* *s* Lord Scrymgeour, *qv*. *Address:* Farm Office, Birkhill, Cupar, Fife KY15 4QP. *Clubs:* White's; New (Edinburgh).

DUNDONALD, 15th Earl of, *cr* 1669; **Iain Alexander Douglas Blair Cochrane;** Lord Cochrane of Dundonald, 1647; Lord Cochrane of Paisley and Ochiltree, 1669; Chairman, Duneth Securities and associated companies, since 1986; *b* 17 Feb. 1961; *s* of 14th Earl of Dundonald and Aphra Farquhar (*d* 1972), *d* of late Comdr George Fetherstonhaugh; *S* father, 1986; *m* 1987, Beatrice, *d* of Adolphus Russo; two *s* one *d*. *Educ:* Wellington College; RAC Cirencester. DipREM. Director: Anglo Pacific Gp, 1995–98; Anglo Scientific (formerly Anglo Digital) Ltd, 2000–. Mem. Council, PITCOM, 1994–99. Hon. Consul in Scotland for Chile, 1993–. *Recreations:* rural affairs, sailing, innovation. *Heir:* *s* Lord Cochrane, *qv*. *Address:* Lochnell Castle, Ledaig, Argyll PA37 1QT.

DUNEDIN, Bishop of, since 2005; **Rt Rev. George Howard Douglas Connor;** *b* 27 Feb. 1942; *s* of George Sherwood Connor and Elizabeth Agnes (*née* Gordon); step *s* of John Edward Marshall Ball; *m* 1967, Nonie Saxby; two *s* two *d*. *Educ:* St John's Coll., Auckland; LTh (1st cl. Hons) 1965, LTh (Aotearoa) 1992. Ordained deacon, 1965, priest, 1966; Theol Tutor, Ch of Melanesia, 1967–73; Maori Mission priest, Waiapu dio., 1975–86; Archdeacon of Waiapu, 1981–86, Canon Theologian Emeritus, 1986; Regional Bishop in the Bay of Plenty, 1989–2005. Protector Gen., SSF, 2001–08. *Address:* PO Box 13–170, Green Island, 9052, Dunedin, New Zealand; *e-mail:* bishop@dn.anglican.org.nz.

DUNFORD, Dr John Ernest, OBE 1994; General Secretary, Association of School and College Leaders, since 1998; *b* Burnham-on-Sea, Som, 10 Nov. 1946; *s* of Leslie Donald Dunford and Mary Dunford; *m* 2001, Sue Rust D'Eye; one *s* one *d* and two step *d*. *Educ:* Cheltenham Coll.; Univ. of Nottingham (BSc Jt Hons Maths and Econs; PGCE); Univ. of Durham (MEd 1976; PhD 1992). Pres. of Union, Univ. of Nottingham, 1968–69. Teacher of Maths: Mundella Sch., Nottingham, 1970–72; Hylton Red House Sch., Sunderland, 1972–73; Framwellgate Moor Comp. Sch., Durham, 1973–78 (Sen. Teacher, 1974–78); Dep. Head, Bede Sch., Sunderland, 1979–82; Hd, Durham Johnston Comprehensive Sch., 1982–98. Trustee: Worldwide Volunteering, 1995–; Teach First, 2003–; Board Member: Future Leaders, 2006–; Specialist Schs and Acads Trust, 2007–. *Publications:* Her Majesty's Inspectorate of Schools 1860–1870, 1980; Her Majesty's Inspectorate of Schools since 1944, 1998; (ed) State Schools: New Labour and the Conservative legacy, 1999; School Leadership: national and international perspectives, 2000. *Recreations:* cooking, birdwatching, opera, gardening, golf. *Address:* Cobblestones, Church Street, North Kilworth, Leics LE17 6EZ; *e-mail:* john.dunford@ascl.org.uk. *Club:* Commonwealth.

DUNGARVAN, Viscount; Rory Jonathan Courtenay Boyle; naval architect; *b* 10 Dec. 1978; *o s* and *heir* of Earl of Cork and Orrery, *qv*. *Educ:* Harrow; Newcastle Univ. (BEng). *Recreations:* sailing, ski-ing, design, country sports, dancing reels. *Address:* c/o Lickfold House, Petworth, West Sussex GU28 9EY.

DUNGAVELL, Ian Robert, PhD; FSA; Director, The Victorian Society, since 2000; *b* 4 Sept. 1966; *s* of Robert Charles Dungavell and Barbara Marie Dungavell. *Educ:* ANU (BA Hons Art Hist. 1989); Royal Holloway, London (PhD Architectl Hist. 1999). FSA 2007. Assoc. Lectr, ANU, 1992–93; Lectr, Sotheby's Inst., 1998–2000. Dir, Summer Sch., Victorian Soc., 1998–99. Member: Exec. Cttee, Soc. of Architectl Historians of GB,

1996–99; Places of Worship Forum, English Heritage, 2006–; Conservation Working Gp, Conservation Trust, 2007–. Hon. Sec., Jt Cttee of Nat. Amenity Socs, 2005–. Winston Churchill Travelling Fellow, 2005. *Publications:* (contrib.) Birmingham (Pevsner City Guide), 2005; (ed with D. Crellin) Architecture and Englishness 1880–1914, 2006; (contrib.) Building Conservation Directory, 2007; contrib. Oxford DNB; contribs to Jl of Decorative Arts Soc., Crafts Mag., Ceramics: Art and Perception, Period Ideas. *Recreations:* architecture, swimming, eating. *Address:* The Victorian Society, 1 Priory Gardens, W4 1TT. *T:* (020) 8994 1019, *Fax:* (020) 8747 5899; *e-mail:* ian@dungavell.net.

DUNGER, Dame Jane (Elisabeth); *see* Roberts, Dame J. E.

DUNGEY, Prof. James Wynne, PhD; Professor of Physics, Imperial College, University of London, 1965–84; *b* 30 Jan. 1923; *s* of Ernest Dungey and Alice Dungey; *m* 1950, Christine Scotland (*née* Brown); one *s* one *d*. *Educ:* Bradfield; Magdalene Coll., Cambridge (MA, PhD). Res. Fellow, Univ. of Sydney, 1950–53; Vis. Asst Prof., Penn State Coll., 1953–54; ICI Fellow, Cambridge, 1954–57; Lectr, King's Coll., Newcastle upon Tyne, 1957–59; Sen. Principal Scientific Officer, AWRE, Aldermaston, 1959–63; Res. Fellow, Imperial Coll., London, 1963–65. Fellow, Amer. Geophysical Union, 1973. Hon. Mem., European Geophysical Soc., 1994. Chapman Medal, RAS, 1982; Gold Medal for Geophysics, RAS, 1990; Fleming Medal, Amer. Geophysical Union, 1991. *Publications:* Cosmic Electrodynamics, 1958; papers on related topics. *Address:* 20 Walkers Court, 101 Southdown Road, Harpenden, Herts AL5 1QL.

DUNGLASS, Lord; Michael David Alexander Douglas-Home; *b* 30 Nov. 1987; *s* and *heir* of Earl of Home, *qv*. A Page of Honour to the Queen, 1998–2000. *Address:* The Hirsel, Coldstream, Berwickshire TD12 4LP.

DUNHILL, Rosemary Carole, OBE 2003; FSA; County Archivist, Hampshire Record Office, 1982–2001, retired; *b* 21 June 1944; *d* of Harold John Dunhill and Freda Dunhill (*née* Best); *m* 2007, David Lloyd. *Educ:* Palmer's Girls' Sch., Grays; Cheadle Grammar Sch.; Methodist Coll., Belfast; Somerville Coll., Oxford (BA Modern Hist. 1965, MA). Archivist: Harrowby MSS Trust, 1969–71; Devon Record Office, 1972–76; Northants Record Office, 1976–82; (pt-time) Jesus Coll., Oxford, 2002–07. Member: Royal Commn on Historical MSS, 1999–2003; Lord Chancellor's Adv. Council on Public Records, 1999–2001; Adv. Council on Nat. Records and Archives, 2003–05. Chm., Assoc. of Chief Archivists in Local Govt, 1997–99. FSA 1996. Hon. DLitt King Alfred's Coll., Winchester, 2000. Ellis Prize, Soc. of Archivists, 1996. *Publication:* (with D. Burrows) Music and Theatre in Handel's World: the family papers of James Harris 1735–1780, 2002. *Recreations:* nephews and nieces, archives, fair trade. *Address:* 27 Sunnydown Road, Winchester, Hants SO22 4LD. *T:* (01962) 869007; *e-mail:* rcdunhill@tiscali.co.uk.

DUNION, Kevin Harry, OBE 1999; Scottish Information Commissioner, since 2003; *b* 20 Dec. 1955; *s* of late Harry Dunion and of Mary Leckie Bertolini; *m* 1st, 1978, Christine Elizabeth Hannam (marr. diss. 1997); two *s*; 2nd, 1997, Linda Gray. *Educ:* St Andrews High Sch., Kirkcaldy; St Andrews Univ. (MA Hons); Edinburgh Univ. (MSc Dist.). HM Inspector of Taxes, 1978–80; Administrator, Edinburgh Univ. Students' Assoc., 1980–84; Scottish Campaign Manager, OXFAM, 1984–91; Dir, Friends of the Earth Scotland, 1991–2003; Chm., Friends of the Earth Internat., 1996–99. Mem., Cabinet sub-cttee on Sustainable Scotland, Scottish Exec., 2000–03; Mem. Bd, Scottish Natural Heritage, 2000–03. Editor, Radical Scotland mag., 1981–85. FRSA 1997. *Publications:* Living in the Real World: the international role for Scotland's Parliament, 1995; Troublemakers: the struggle for environmental justice in Scotland, 2003; The Democracy of War, 2007. *Recreation:* living by the seaside. *Address:* The Beach House, 39B John Street, Cellardyke, Anstruther, Fife KY10 3BA. *T:* (01333) 312818.

DUNITZ, Prof. Jack David, FRS 1974; Professor of Chemical Crystallography at the Swiss Federal Institute of Technology (ETH), Zürich, 1957–90; *b* 29 March 1923; *s* of William Dunitz and Mildred (*née* Gossman); *m* 1953, Barbara Steuer; two *d*. *Educ:* Hillhead High Sch., Glasgow; Hutchesons' Grammar Sch., Glasgow; Glasgow Univ. (BSc, PhD). Post-doctoral Fellow, Oxford Univ., 1946–48, 1951–53; California Inst. of Technology, 1948–51, 1953–54; Vis. Scientist, US Nat. Insts of Health, 1954–55; Sen. Res. Fellow, Davy Faraday Res. Lab., Royal Instn, London, 1956–57. Overseas Fellow, Churchill Coll., Cambridge, 1968; Vis. Professor: Iowa State Univ., 1965; Tokyo Univ., 1967; Technion, Haifa, 1970; Hill Vis. Prof., Univ. of Minnesota, 1983; Fairchild Distinguished Scholar, CIT, 1985; Hooker Distinguished Vis. Prof., McMaster Univ., 1987; Alexander Todd Vis. Prof., Cambridge Univ., 1990; Oscar K. Rice Vis. Prof., Univ. of N Carolina, Chapel Hill, 1991; Robert B. Woodward Vis. Prof., Harvard Univ., 1992. Lectures: British Council, 1965; Treat B. Johnson Meml, Yale Univ., 1965; 3M Univ. of Minnesota, 1966; Reilly, Univ. Notre Dame, US, 1971; Kelly, Purdue Univ., 1971; Gerhard Schmidt Meml, Weizmann Inst. of Sci., 1973; George Fisher Baker, Cornell Univ., 1976; Centenary, Chem. Soc., 1977; Appleton, Brown Univ., 1979; H. J. Backer, Gröningen Univ., 1980; Havinga, Leiden Univ., 1980; Karl Folkers, Wisconsin Univ., 1981; A. L. Patterson Meml, Inst. for Cancer Res., Philadelphia, 1983; C. S. Marvel, Illinois Univ., 1987; Birch, Canberra, 1989; Dwyer, Sydney, 1989; Bijvoet, Utrecht Univ., 1989; Bragg, British Crystallographic Assoc., 1999. Foreign Member: Royal Netherlands Acad. of Arts and Sciences, 1979; Amer. Phil Soc., 1997; Member: Leopoldina Acad., 1979; European Acad. of Scis and Arts, 1991; Foreign Associate, US Nat. Acad. of Scis, 1988; Mem., Academia Europaea, 1989; Hon. Member: Swiss Soc. of Crystallography, 1990; Swiss Chem. Soc., 2004; For. Hon. Mem., Amer. Acad. of Arts and Scis, 1997; Fellow AAAS, 1981. Hon. FRSC 2000. Hon. DSc: Technion, Haifa, 1990; Weizmann Inst. of Sci., 1992; Glasgow Univ., 1999. Tishler Award, Harvard Univ., 1985; Paracelsus Prize, Swiss Chem. Soc., 1986; Gregori Aminoff Prize, Swedish Royal Acad., 1990; Martin Buerger Award, Amer. Crystallographic Assoc., 1991; Arthur C. Cope Scholar Award, ACS, 1997. Jt Editor, Perspectives in Structural Chemistry, 1967–71; Mem. Editorial Bd: Helvetica Chimica Acta, 1971–85; Structure and Bonding, 1971–81. *Publications:* X-ray Analysis and the Structure of Organic Molecules, 1979; (with E. Heilbronner) Reflections on Symmetry in Chemistry… and Elsewhere, 1993; papers on various aspects of crystal and molecular structure in Acta Crystallographica, Helvetica Chimica Acta, Jl Chem. Soc., Jl Amer. Chem. Soc., etc. *Recreation:* walking. *Address:* Obere Heslibachstrasse 77, 8700 Küsnacht, Switzerland. *T:* (44) 9101723; (office) Chemistry Department, ETH-Zürich, 8093 Zürich, Switzerland. *T:* (44) 6322892.

DUNKELD, Bishop of, (RC), since 1981; **Rt Rev. Vincent Logan;** *b* 30 June 1941; *s* of Joseph Logan and Elizabeth Flannigan. *Educ:* Blairs College, Aberdeen; St Andrew's Coll., Drygrange, Melrose. Ordained priest, Edinburgh, 1964; Asst Priest, St Margaret's, Davidson's Mains, Edinburgh, 1964–66; Corpus Christi Coll., London, 1966–67 (DipRE); Chaplain, St Joseph's Hospital, Rosewell, Midlothian, 1967–77; Adviser in Religious Education, Archdiocese of St Andrews and Edinburgh, 1967; Parish Priest, St Mary's, Ratho, 1977–81; Episcopal Vicar for Education, Archdiocese of St Andrews and Edinburgh, 1978. *Address:* Bishop's House, 29 Roseangle, Dundee DD1 4LS. *T:* (01382) 224327.

DUNKLEY, Christopher; freelance journalist and broadcaster; *b* 22 Jan. 1944; 2nd *s* o late Robert Dunkley and Joyce Mary Dunkley (*née* Turner); *m* 1967, Carolyn Elizabeth (marr. diss. 2004), *e d* of Col A. P. C. Lyons; one *s* one *d*. *Educ:* Haberdashers' Aske's (expelled). Various jobs, incl. theatre flyman, cook, hospital porter, 1961–63; genera reporter, then cinema and theatre critic, Slough Observer, 1963–65; feature writer and news editor, UK Press Gazette, 1965–68; night news reporter, then mass media correspondent and TV critic, The Times, 1968–73; TV Critic, Financial Times 1973–2002; feature writer, Daily Mail, 2002–03. Frequent radio broadcaster, 1963–; Presenter, Feedback, Radio 4, 1986–98; occasional television presenter/script writer/chairman. Critic of the Year, British Press Awards, 1976, 1986; Broadcast Journalist of the Year, TV-am Awards, 1989; Best Individual Contrib. to Radio, Voice of the Listener and Viewer Awards, 1998. *Publication:* Television Today and Tomorrow: Wall to Wall Dallas? 1985. *Recreations:* motorcycling, collecting almost everything, especially dictionaries, tin toys, Victorian boys' books. *Address:* May Villas, 20 Byfield Road, Isleworth, Middx TW7 7AF.

DUNLEATH, 6th Baron *cr* 1892, of Ballywalter, co. Down; **Brian Henry Mulholland** Bt 1945; *b* 25 Sept. 1950; *o s* of 5th Baron Dunleath and Elizabeth (*d* 1989), twin *d* o Laurence B. Hyde; *S* father, 1997; *m* 1st, 1976, Mary Joan (marr. diss. 2005), *y d* of Major R. J. F. Whistler; two *s* one *d*; 2nd, 2006, Vibeke, *yr d* of late Col Jens Christian Lunn Denmark. *Educ:* Eton. Director: Dunleath Estates Ltd, 1994– (Chm., 1998–) Downpatrick Race Club Ltd, 1999–. *Recreations:* shooting, fishing, gardening. *Heir:* *s* Hon Andrew Henry Mulholland, *b* 15 Dec. 1981. *Address:* (office) The Estate Office Ballywalter Park, Newtownards, Northern Ireland BT22 2PA. *T:* (028) 4275 8264, *Fax* (028) 4275 8818; (home) Ballywalter Park, Newtownards, Northern Ireland BT22 2PP *e-mail:* bd@dunleath-estates.co.uk. *Clubs:* MCC; Kildare Street (Dublin); Royal Ulster Yacht.

DUNLEAVY, Prof. Patrick John, DPhil; AcSS; Professor of Political Science and Public Policy (formerly of Government), London School of Economics and Political Science since 1989; *b* 21 June 1952; *s* of Vincent Dunleavy and Kathleen Mary Dunleavy; *m* 1974 Sheila Dorothea Squire; two *s* one *d*. *Educ:* St Mary's Grammar Sch., Sidcup; Corpus Christi Coll., Oxford (MA 1973); Nuffield Coll., Oxford (DPhil 1978). Research Fellow Nuffield Coll., Oxford, 1976–78; Lectr in Urban Studies, Open Univ., 1978–79; London School of Economics and Political Science: Lectr in Govt, 1979–86; Reader, 1986–89 Mem. Exec., UK Political Studies Assoc., 1980–83, 1993–94 and 1999–2005. Councillor Bucks CC, 1981–85. Mem., Milton Keynes CHC, 1982–90. AcSS 1999. Founding Ed. Politics, 1980–82; Editor: Political Studies, 1999–2005; Political Studies Review 2003–05; mem. editl bd, various jls. *Publications:* Urban Political Analysis, 1980; The Politics of Mass Housing in Britain, 1981; (ed jtly) Developments in British Politics, vol 1, 1983, vol. 2, 1986, vol. 3, 1990, vol. 4, 1993, vol. 5, 1997, vol. 6, 2000; (with C. T Husbands) British Democracy at the Crossroads, 1985; Studying for a Degree, 1987; (with B. O'Leary) Theories of the State, 1987; Democracy, Bureaucracy and Public Choice 1991; (ed with R. A. W. Rhodes) Prime Minister, Cabinet and Core Executive, 1995 (jtly) Making Votes Count, 1997; (with H. Margetts) Government on the Web, 1999; (ed jtly) British Political Science, 2000; (with H. Margetts) Government on the Web 2, 2002 Authoring a PhD, 2002; (with H. Margetts) Difficult Forms, 2003; (jtly) Citizen Redress 2005; (jtly) Digital-Era Governance, 2006; (jtly) Government on the Internet, 2007 articles in learned jls. *Recreations:* family, travel, undermining the (old) constitution *Address:* Department of Government, London School of Economics, Houghton Street WC2A 2AE. *T:* (020) 7955 7178; *e-mail:* p.dunleavy@lse.ac.uk.

DUNLOP; *see* Buchanan-Dunlop.

DUNLOP, Rear-Adm. Colin Charles Harrison, CB 1972; CBE 1963; *b* 4 March 1918 *s* of late Engr Rear-Adm. S. H. Dunlop, CB; *m* 1st, 1941, Moyra Patricia O'Brien Gorge (*d* 1991); two *s* (and one *s* decd); 2nd, 1995, Comdt Elizabeth Craig-McFeely, *qv*. *Educ* Marlborough Coll. Joined RN, 1935; served War of 1939–45 at sea in HM Ships Kent Valiant, Diadem and Orion; subseq. HMS Sheffield, 1957–59; Sec. to 1st Sea Lord 1960–63; comd HMS Pembroke, 1964–66; Programme Evaluation Gp, MoD, 1966–68 Director, Defence Policy (A), MoD, 1968–69; Comdr, British Navy Staff, Washington 1969–71; Chief Naval Supply and Secretariat Officer, 1970–74; Flag Officer, Medway and Port Adm., Chatham, 1971–74, retd 1974. Director General: Cable TV Assoc. 1974–83; Nat. TV Rental Assoc., 1974–83. DL Kent 1976. *Recreations:* cricket, country pursuits. *Address:* 1 The Gatehouse, Elliscombe Park, Holton, Wincanton, Som BA9 8EA *T:* (01963) 31534. *Clubs:* Army and Navy; MCC, I Zingari, Free Foresters, RN Cricket Band of Brothers.

DUNLOP, Elizabeth Sarah Ann, (Mrs C. C. H. Dunlop); *see* Craig-McFeely, E. S. A

DUNLOP, Frank, CBE 1977; theatre director; Director, Edinburgh International Festival 1983–91; *b* 15 Feb. 1927; *s* of Charles Norman Dunlop and Mary Aarons. *Educ:* Kibworth Beauchamp Grammar Sch.; University Coll., London (Fellow, 1979). BA Hons, English Postgrad. Sch. in Shakespeare, at Shakespeare Inst., Stratford-upon-Avon; Old Vic Sch. London. Served with RAF before going to University. Director: (own young theatre co. Piccolo Theatre, Manchester, 1954; Arts Council Midland Theatre Co., 1955; Associate Dir, Bristol Old Vic, 1956; Dir, Théâtre de Poche, Brussels, 1959–60; Founder and Dir Pop Theatre, 1960; Dir, Nottingham Playhouse, 1961–63; New Nottingham Playhouse 1963–64; (dir.) The Enchanted, Bristol Old Vic Co., 1955; (wrote and dir.) Les Frères Jaques, Adelphi, 1960; Director: London Première, The Bishop's Bonfire, Mermaid 1960; Schweyk, Mermaid, 1963; The Taming of the Shrew, Univ. Arts Centre Oklahoma, 1965; Any Wednesday, Apollo, 1965; Too True to be Good, Edinburgh Fest. also Strand and Garrick, 1965; Saturday Night and Sunday Morning, Prince of Wales 1966; The Winter's Tale and The Trojan Women, Edin. and Venice Festivals, also Cambridge Theatre, London, 1966; The Burglar, Vaudeville, 1967; Getting Married Strand, 1967; A Midsummer Night's Dream and The Tricks of Scapin, Edin. Fest. and Saville Theatre, London, 1967; A Sense of Detachment, Royal Court, 1972; Sherlock Holmes, Aldwych, 1974, NY 1974; Habeas Corpus, NY 1975; The New York Idea, The Three Sisters, NY 1977; The Devil's Disciple, LA and NY, 1978; The Play's the Thing Julius Caesar, NY, 1978; The Last of Mrs Cheyney, USA, 1978; Rookery Nook Birmingham and Her Majesty's, 1979; Camelot, USA, 1980, London, 1996; Sherlock Holmes, Norwegian Nat. Th., Oslo, 1980; Lolita, NY, 1981; Oberon (Weber) Edinburgh, Frankfurt, 1986 (filmed); L'Elisir d'Amore, Opéra de Lyon, 1992 (filmed 1996); My Fair Lady, European tour, 1994; Carmen, Royal Albert Hall, 1997; Ecole de Femmes, Belgium, 1998; The Invisible Man, USA, 1998–99; Scapino, Tel Aviv, 1999 Napoleon at St Helena, Waterloo, 2000, Monte Carlo, 2001; Turn of the Screw, Belgium 2001; (adapted and dir.) Address Unknown, NY, 2004; Oscar and the Pink Lady, San Diego, 2007, NY, 2008; *National Theatre:* Assoc. Dir, 1967–71 and Admin. Dir, 1968–73 productions: *Nat. Theatre:* Edward II (Brecht and Marlowe); Home and Beauty Macrune's Guevara; The White Devil; Captain of Kopenick; *Young Vic:* Founder, 1969 Mem. Bd, 1969–92; Dir, 1969–78 and 1980–83; Consultant, 1978–80; productions (author and Dir) Scapino 1970, 1977, NY 1974, LA 1975, Australia 1975, Oslo 1975; The

Taming of the Shrew, 1970, 1977; The Comedy of Errors, 1971; The Maids, Deathwatch, 1972; The Alchemist, 1972; Bible One, 1972; French Without Tears, 1973; Joseph and the Amazing Technicolor Dreamcoat (Roundhouse and Albery Theatre), 1973, NY 1976; Much Ado About Nothing, 1973; Macbeth, 1975; Antony and Cleopatra, 1976; King Lear, 1980; Childe Byron, 1981; Masquerade, 1982; *for Théâtre National de Belgique:* Pantagleize, 1970; Antony and Cleopatra, 1971; Pericles, 1972. Mem., Arts Council Young People's Panel, 1968. Governor, Central School of Arts and Crafts, 1970. Hon. Fellow of Shakespeare Inst. Hon. Dr of Theatre, Philadelphia Coll. of Performing Arts, 1978; DUniv Heriot-Watt, 1989; Dr *hc* Edinburgh, 1990. Chevalier, Order of Arts and Literature (France), 1987. *Recreations:* reading and looking. *Address:* c/o Piccolo Theatre Co., 13 Choumert Square, SE15 4RE; c/o E. Nives, Miracle Management LLP, 1775 Broadway, Suite 417, New York, NY 10019, USA. *T:* (212) 2658787.

DUNLOP, Rev. Canon Ian Geoffrey David, FSA; Canon and Chancellor of Salisbury Cathedral, 1972–92, Canon Emeritus, since 1992; *b* 19 Aug. 1925; *s* of late Walter N. U. Dunlop and Marguerite Irene (*née* Shakerley); *m* 1957, Deirdre Marcia, *d* of late Dr Marcus Jamieson; one *s* one *d*. *Educ:* Winchester Coll.; New Coll., Oxford (MA); Strasbourg Univ. (Diploma); Lincoln Theol Coll. FSA 1965. Served Irish Guards, 1944–46 (Lieut). Curate, Hatfield, 1956–60; Chaplain, Westminster Sch., 1960–62; Vicar of Bures, Suffolk, 1962–72. Member: Gen. Synod, 1975–85; Cathedrals' Adv. Commn, 1981–86. Trustee, Nat. Churches Trust (formerly Historic Churches Preservation Trust), 1969–. *Publications:* Versailles, 1956, 2nd edn 1970; Palaces and Progresses of Elizabeth I, 1962; Châteaux of the Loire, 1969; Companion Guide to the Ile de France, 1979, 2nd edn 1985; Cathedrals Crusade, 1981; Royal Palaces of France, 1985; Thinking It Out, 1986; (contrib.) Oxford Companion to Gardens, 1986; Burgundy, 1990; Marie-Antoinette: a portrait, 1993; Louis XIV, 1999 (Enid McLeod Prize, Franco-British Soc., 2000); Edward VII and the Entente Cordiale, 2004; weekly column in Church Times, 1970–90. *Recreations:* painting, bird watching. *Address:* Gowanbrae, The Glebe, Selkirk TD7 5AB. *T:* (01750) 20706; Hill Cottages, Marsh Lane, Felixstowe, Suffolk IP11 9RP. *T:* (01394) 286118.

DUNLOP, Very Rev. John, CBE 2004; Minister, Presbyterian Church in Ireland, since 1966; *b* 19 Sept. 1939; *s* of Joseph and Annie Dunlop; *m* 1965, Rosemary Willis; one *s* one *d*. *Educ:* QUB (BA); Univ. of Edinburgh (BD). Minister: Fitzroy Avenue Presbyterian Ch, Belfast, 1966–68; United Ch of Jamaica and Grand Cayman, 1968–78; Rosemary Presbyterian Ch, Belfast, 1978–2004; Moderator, Gen. Assembly of Presbyterian Ch in Ireland, 1992–93. Hon. DD: Presbyterian Theol Faculty of Ireland, 1992; TCD, 1993; Hon. LLD: Ulster, 2001; QUB, 2001. *Publication:* A Precarious Belonging: Presbyterians and the conflict in Ireland, 1995. *Address:* 98 Whitehouse Park, Newtownabbey, BT37 9SH.

DUNLOP, John Leeper, OBE 1996; racehorse trainer, since 1965; *b* 10 July 1939; *s* of Dr John Leeper Dunlop, MC, FRCS and Margaret Frances Mary Dunlop; *m* 1965, Susan Jennifer Page; two *s* (and one *s* decd). *Educ:* Marlborough Coll. Royal Ulster Rifles, 1959–61. Leading trainer, 1984; champion trainer, 1995; wins include: Shirley Heights, Derby, 1978; Circus Plume, Oaks, 1984; Salsabil, Oaks, 1990; Erhaab, Derby, 1994; One Thousand Guineas: Quick as Lightning, 1980; Salsabil, 1990; Shadayid, 1991; St Leger: Moon Madness, 1986; Silver Patriarch, 1997; Millenary, 2000. Flat Trainer of the Year, Derby Awards, 1995. *Recreations:* breeding race horses and show horses. *Address:* House on the Hill, Arundel, West Sussex BN18 9LJ. *T:* (01903) 882106. *Club:* Turf.

DUNLOP, Robert Alastair, QC (Scot.) 1990; Sheriff Principal of Tayside Central and Fife, since 2000; *b* 30 June 1951; *s* of Robert Jack Dunlop and Dorothy Shirley Dixon or Dunlop; *m* 1st, 1975, Jane Christian Rankin (marr. diss. 1998); one *s* two *d*; 2nd, 1999, Evelyn Templeton Mackenzie. *Educ:* Trinity Coll., Glenalmond; Univ. of Dundee (LLB). Admitted solicitor, Scotland, 1976; admitted to Faculty of Advocates and called to Scottish Bar, 1978; Advocate Depute, 1985–88; Standing Jun. Counsel, Dept of Transport, 1988–90; part-time Chairman: Pensions Appeal Tribunal, 1991–2000; Employment Tribunals, 1998–2000. Procurator to Gen. Assembly of Ch of Scotland, 1991–2000. Comr, Northern Lighthouses, 2000–. *Recreations:* sailing, golf, music, ski-ing. *Address:* 5 Temple Village, Gorebridge, Midlothian EH3 4SQ. *T:* (01875) 830344. *Clubs:* New (Edinburgh); Royal Northern and Clyde Yacht.

DUNLOP, Sir Thomas, 4th Bt *cr* 1916, of Woodbourne, co. Renfrew; *b* 22 April 1951; *o s* of Sir Thomas Dunlop, 3rd Bt and of Adda Mary Alison Dunlop (*née* Smith); *S* father, 1999; *m* 1984, Eileen, *er d* of A. H. Stevenson; one *s* one *d*. *Educ:* Rugby; Aberdeen Univ. (BScFor). MICFor. *Heir:* *s* Thomas Dunlop, *b* 11 March 1990. *Address:* Bredon Croft, Bredons Norton, Tewkesbury, Glos GL20 7HB.

DUNLOP, William; Sheriff of North Strathclyde, since 1995; *b* 7 March 1944; *s* of William Dunlop and Catherine (*née* McKenzie); *m* 1st, 1968, Katherine Frances Howden (marr. diss. 1976); one *s* one *d*; 2nd, 1979, Janina Marthe Merecki; one *d*. *Educ:* High Sch. of Glasgow; Univ. of Glasgow (LLB 1965). Solicitor in family firm, 1968; called to the Scottish Bar, 1985; in practice at the Bar, 1985–95. Mem. Council, Sheriffs' Assoc., 2001–04. Six Nations Match Comr, Scottish Rugby Union, 2000–. Governor, High Sch. of Glasgow, 1999–. *Recreations:* watching Rugby football, playing bad golf, enjoying good food and wine. *Address:* The Sheriff Court House, Dumbarton G82 1QR. *T:* (01389) 763266. *Club:* Glasgow Golf.

DUNLOP, Prof. William, CBE 2005; PhD; FRCSE, FRCOG; Professor of Obstetrics and Gynaecology, University of Newcastle upon Tyne, 1982–2006; President, Royal College of Obstetricians and Gynaecologists, 2001–04; *b* 18 Aug. 1944; *s* of Alexander Morton Dunlop and Annie Denham Rennie (*née* Ingram); *m* 1968, Sylvia Louise Krauthamer; one *s* one *d*. *Educ:* Kilmarnock Acad.; Glasgow Univ. (MB ChB 1967); Univ. of Newcastle upon Tyne (PhD 1982). FRCSE 1971; MRCOG 1971, FRCOG 1984. Various junior posts in obstetrics and gynaecol., Glasgow Univ., 1969–74; seconded as Lectr, Univ. of Nairobi, 1972–73; on MRC scientific staff, 1974–75, Sen. Lectr, 1975–82, Univ. of Newcastle upon Tyne. Vis. Associate Prof., Medical Univ. of S Carolina, 1980. Royal College of Obstetricians and Gynaecologists: Hon. Sec., 1992–98; Chm., Exam. Cttee, 1990–92; Chm., Specialist Trng Cttee, 1999–2001; Hon. Treasurer: European Bd and Coll. of Obstetrics and Gynaecology, 1999–2005 (Pres., 2005–); UEMS Sect. of Obstetrics and Gynaecology, 2002–05. Chairman: Professional Adv. Panel, NHS Litigation Authority, 2002–04; Jt Consultants Cttee, 2003–; Vice-Chairman: Acad. of Medical Royal Colls, 2002–04; Specialist Trng Authority, 2002–04. Chm., Assoc. of Profs of Obstetrics and Gynaecology, 1999–2002. Chm., Blair-Bell Research Soc., 1989–92. Hon. Member: S African Soc. of Obstetricians and Gynaecologists, 2003; Soc. of Obstetricians and Gynaecologists of Canada, 2003; Soc. of Gynaecol. and Obstetrics of Nigeria, 2003; Hon. Fellow: Acad. of Medicine, Singapore, 2002; FFPRHC 2005; Hon. Fellow *qua* Surgeon RCPSG, 2003; FRCP 2003; Hon. FACOG 2003; Hon. FRCPI 2003; Hon. FCPS (Pak) 2004; Hon. FSLCOG 2004. Dr *hc* Athens, 2006. Editor-in-Chief, Fetal and Maternal Medicine Rev., 1989–99. *Publications:* (ed jtly) High Risk Pregnancy, 1992; Recent Advances in Obstetrics and Gynaecology, 2003. *Recreations:* music, drama, literature. *Address:* Department of Obstetrics and Gynaecology, 3rd Floor, Leech Building, Medical School, University of Newcastle, Newcastle upon Tyne NE2 4HH. *T:* (0191) 232 4218.

DUNLUCE, Viscount; Randal Alexander St John McDonnell; Partner, Sarasin & Partners (formerly Sarasin Chiswell), since 2008 (Director, 2004–08); *b* 2 July 1967; *o s* and heir of Earl of Antrim, *qv*; *m* 2004, Aurora, *d* of David Gunn; one *s* one *d*. *Educ:* Gresham's Sch., Holt; Worcester Coll., Oxford (BA Hons). Fund Manager: NCL Investments Ltd, 1992–97; Sarasin Investment Mgt Ltd, 1998–2004. Director: Game Conservancy Trust, 2003–06; Irish Landmark Trust, 2004–; Glenarm Bldgs Preservation Trust, 2005–; Northern Salmon Co., 2006–; Irish Grouse Conservation Trust, 2006–. *Heir:* *s* Hon. Alexander David Somerled McDonnell, *b* 30 June 2006. *Address:* Glenarm Castle, Glenarm, Ballymena, Co. Antrim BT44 0BD. *Clubs:* Beefsteak, White's.

DUNMORE, 12th Earl of, *cr* 1686 (Scot.); **Malcolm Kenneth Murray;** Viscount of Fincastle, Lord Murray of Blair, Moulin and Tillimet, 1686; Electrical Technical Officer, Air Services Australia, now retired; *b* 17 Sept. 1946; *er s* of 11th Earl of Dunmore and Margaret Joy (*d* 1976), *d* of P. D. Cousins; *S* father, 1995; *m* 1970, Joy Anne, *d* of A. Partridge; one *s* one *d* (both adopted). *Educ:* Launceston Technical High School (Board A Certificate and various tech. qualifs). Patron: Tasmanian Caledonian Council; Launceston Caledonian Soc.; Armorial and Heraldry Soc. of Australasia Inc.; Scottish Australian Heritage Council; Sunnybank Br., RSL; Murray Clan Soc. of NZ; Patron and Member: St Andrew Soc., Tas; Murray Clan Soc. of Vic and Qld. High Comr for Clan Murray in Australia and NZ, 2006–. Past Master, Concord Masonic Lodge, No 10 Tasmanian Constitution. *Recreations:* flying (Tow Master for Soaring Club of Tasmania), astronomy. *Heir:* *b* Hon. Geoffrey Charles Murray [*b* 31 July 1949; *m* 1974, Margaret Irene, *d* of H. Bulloch]. *Address:* PO Box 100E, East Devonport, Tas 7310, Australia. *Club:* Soaring Club of Tasmania.

DUNMORE, Helen, FRSL; poet and novelist; *b* 12 Dec. 1952; *d* of Maurice Dunmore and Betty (*née* Smith); *m* 1980, Francis Charnley; one *s* one *d* and one step *s*. *Educ:* Univ. of York (BA Hons). FRSL 1997. Hon. DLitt: Glamorgan, 1998; Exeter, 2001. *Publications:* *poetry:* The Apple Fall, 1983; The Sea Skater, 1986 (Alice Hunt Bartlett Prize, Poetry Soc., 1987); The Raw Garden, 1988; Short Days, Long Nights: new and selected poems, 1991; Recovering a Body, 1994; Bestiary, 1997; Out of the Blue: new and selected poems, 2001; Glad of These Times, 2007; *fiction:* Zennor in Darkness, 1993 (McKitterick Prize, Soc. of Authors, 1994); Burning Bright, 1994; A Spell of Winter, 1995 (Orange Prize for Fiction, 1996); Talking to the Dead, 1996; Love of Fat Men, 1997; Your Blue-eyed Boy, 1998; With Your Crooked Heart, 1999; Ice Cream, 2000 (short stories); The Siege, 2001; Mourning Ruby, 2003; Rose, 1944 (short stories), 2005; House of Orphans, 2006; Counting the Stars, 2008; *for children:* Going to Egypt, 1994; Secrets (Signal Poetry for Children Award), 1994; In the Money, 1995; Amina's Blanket, 1996; Go Fox, 1996; Fatal Error, 1996; Allie's Apples, 1997; Great-grandma's Dancing Dress, 1998; Clyde's Leopard, 1998; Brother Brother, Sister Sister, 1999; Allie's Rabbit, 1999; Zillah and Me, 2000; The Zillah Rebellion, 2001; Snollygoster, 2001; Ingo, 2005; The Tide Knot, 2006; The Deep, 2007; The Crossing of Ingo, 2008. *Address:* c/o A. P. Watt Ltd, 20 John Street, WC1N 2DR. *T:* (020) 7405 6774; *web:* www.helendunmore.com.

DUNMORE, Stephen Lloyd; Chief Executive, Big Lottery Fund, 2004–08 (Chief Executive: New Opportunities Fund, 1998–2004; Community Fund, 2003–04); *b* 4 Dec. 1948; *s* of Leslie Alfred Dunmore and Josephine Mary Dunmore (*née* Bettles); *m* 1987, Isabel Mary Robertson; one *d*. *Educ:* Kettering Grammar Sch.; King's Coll. London (BA Hons Hist.). Urban Archaeol Officer, Ipswich BC, 1974–76; Department of the Environment: Inspector of Ancient Monuments, 1976–84; Principal, Housing, Construction Industry, Inner Cities, 1984–90; on secondment as Actg Chief Exec., Liverpool HAT, 1990–91; Principal, Citizen's Charter Unit, Cabinet Office, 1991; Regl Controller, Urban and Economic Affairs, Merseyside Task Force, 1991–94; Dir, Regeneration, Transport and Planning, Govt Office for Merseyside, 1994–98. *Recreations:* cricket, books, walking. *Address:* 37 Pages Hill, N10 1EH. *T:* (020) 8883 3905.

DUNN, Baroness *cr* 1990 (Life Peer), of Hong Kong Island in Hong Kong and of Knightsbridge in the Royal Borough of Kensington and Chelsea; **Lydia Selina Dunn,** DBE 1989 (CBE 1983; OBE 1978); Executive Director, John Swire & Sons Ltd, since 1996; *b* 29 Feb. 1940; *d* of Yencheun Yeh Dunn and Chen Yin Chu; *m* 1988, Michael David Thomas, *qv*. *Educ:* St Paul's Convent Sch., Hong Kong; Univ. of Calif, Berkeley. MLC, Hong Kong, 1976–88 (Sen. Mem., 1985–88); MEC, 1982–95 (Sen. Mem., 1988–95). Director: John Swire & Sons (HK) Ltd, 1978–2003; Swire Pacific Ltd, 1981–; Hongkong and Shanghai Banking Corp., subseq. HSBC Hldgs plc, 1981–2008 (Dep. Chm., 1992–2008); Volvo AB, 1991–93 (Mem. Internat. Adv. Bd, 1985–91); Christie's Internat. plc, 1996–98; Christie's Fine Art Ltd, 1998–2000; Marconi (formerly GEC) plc, 1997–2002; Advr to Bd, Cathay Pacific Airways Ltd, 1997–2002 (Dir, 1985–97). Chairman: Hong Kong/Japan Business Co-operation Cttee, 1988–95 (Mem., 1983–88); Hong Kong Trade Develt Council, 1983–91; Mem., Hong Kong/US Econ. Co-op. Cttee, 1984–93. Chm., Lord Wilson Heritage Trust, 1993–95. Hon. LLD: Chinese Univ. of Hong Kong, 1984; Univ. of Hong Kong, 1991; Univ. of British Columbia, 1991; Leeds Univ., 1994; Hon. DSc Univ. of Buckingham, 1995. Prime Minister of Japan's Trade Award, 1987; USA Sec. of Commerce's To Peace and Commerce Award, 1988. *Publication:* In the Kingdom of the Blind, 1983. *Recreation:* art and antiquities. *Address:* John Swire & Sons Ltd, Swire House, 59 Buckingham Gate, SW1E 6AJ.

DUNN, Anderson; Assistant Commissioner, Metropolitan Police, 1994–2001; *b* 6 May 1944; adopted *s* of William Rennie and Wilma Rennie (*née* Turner); *m* 1967, Margaret Docherty; one *s* one *d*. *Educ:* Queen Mary Coll., London (LLB Hons; Hon. Fellow, QMW, 1998). Joined Metropolitan Police, 1963; transf. to Thames Valley Police as Chief Supt, 1987; Asst Chief Constable, Operations, 1988–93; Dep. Chief Constable, Northants, 1993–94. Former Mem. Bd, Northants Probation Service. *Recreations:* walking, reading, most sports.

DUNN, David Hedley; HM Diplomatic Service; High Commissioner to Papua New Guinea, since 2007; *b* 21 Sept. 1968; *s* of Francis Hedley Dunn and Jean Mary Dunn (*née* Osborne). *Educ:* Penrice Comp. Sch.; St Austell Coll. Joined HM Diplomatic Service, 1991; Political Attaché: Oslo, 1992–94; Suva, 1996–97; Third, later Second, Sec., NY, 1997–98; on secondment to UN, 1998–2000; First Sec., Stockholm, 2000–01; Private Sec. to the Minister for Europe, FCO, 2001–03; Dep. High Comr, Freetown, 2004–06. *Recreations:* Cornish Rugby Union, squash, running, euchre. *Address:* c/o Foreign and Commonwealth Office, King Charles Street, SW1 2AH.

DUNN, Prof. Douglas Eaglesham, OBE 2003; FRSL; poet and short-story writer; Professor of English, since 1991, and Director, St Andrews Scottish Studies Institute, since 1992, St Andrews University; *b* 23 Oct. 1942; *s* of William Douglas Dunn and Margaret McGowan; *m* 1st, 1964, Lesley Balfour Wallace (*d* 1981); 2nd, 1985, Lesley Jane Bathgate; one *s* one *d*. *Educ:* Univ. of Hull (BA). Became full-time writer, 1971. St Andrews University: Fellow in Creative Writing, 1989–91; Hd, Sch. of English, 1994–99. Hon. Vis. Prof., Dundee Univ., 1987–89. Mem., Scottish Arts Council, 1992–94. FRSL 1981.

Hon. Fellow, Humberside Coll., 1987. Hon. LLD Dundee, 1987; Hon. DLitt Hull, 1995. Cholmondeley Award, 1989. *Publications:* Terry Street, 1969 (Somerset Maugham Award, 1972); The Happier Life, 1972; (ed) New Poems, 1972–73, 1973; Love or Nothing, 1974 (Geoffrey Faber Meml Prize, 1976); (ed) A Choice of Byron's Verse, 1974; (ed) Two Decades of Irish Writing, 1975 (criticism); (ed) The Poetry of Scotland, 1979; Barbarians, 1979; St Kilda's Parliament, 1981 (Hawthornden Prize, 1982); Europa's Lover, 1982; (ed) A Rumoured City: new poets from Hull, 1982; (ed) To Build a Bridge: celebration of Humberside in verse, 1982; Elegies, 1985 (Whitbread Poetry Prize, 1985; Whitbread Book of the Year Award, 1986); Secret Villages, 1985 (short stories); Selected Poems 1964–1983, 1986; Northlight, 1988 (poetry); New and Selected Poems 1966–1988, 1989; Andromache, 1990; (ed) The Essential Browning, 1990; (ed) Scotland: an anthology, 1991; (ed) Faber Book of 20th Century Scottish Poetry, 1992; Dante's Drum-Kit, 1993; Boyfriends and Girlfriends, 1995 (short stories); Oxford Book of Scottish Short Stories, 1995; The Donkey's Ears, 2000 (poetry); The Year's Afternoon, 2000 (poetry); New Selected Poems, 2003; contrib. to Counterblast pamphlet series, Glasgow Herald, New Yorker, TLS, etc. *Recreations:* playing the clarinet and saxophone, listening to jazz music, philately, gardening. *Address:* School of English, St Andrews University, St Andrews, Fife KY16 9AL.

DUNN, Hubert; *see* Dunn, W. H.

DUNN, Inga Margaret Amy; *see* Grimsey, I. M. A.

DUNN, Prof. James Douglas Grant, PhD, DD; FBA 2006; Lightfoot Professor of Divinity, University of Durham, 1990–2003, now Professor Emeritus; *b* 21 Oct. 1939; *s* of David and Agnes Dunn; *m* 1963, Meta Russell; one *s* two *d*. *Educ:* Hutchesons' Boys' Grammar Sch., Glasgow; Univ. of Glasgow (MA 1961, BD 1964); Clare Coll., Cambridge (PhD 1968; BD 1976; DD 1991). Chaplain to Overseas Students, Edinburgh, 1968–70; Lectr, 1970–79, Reader, 1979–82, Univ. of Nottingham; Prof. of Divinity, 1982–90, Chm., Dept of Theol., 1984–86 and 1996–99, Univ. of Durham. Sir Derman Christopherson Foundn Fellow, 1999–2000. Numerous invited (named) and vis. lectureships. Ed., New Testament Theol. series (16 vols), 1991–2003. Pres., UK New Testament Conf., 1980–82 and 1992–96. Founder and Chm., Assoc. of Univ. Depts of Theol. and Religious Studies, 1985–92. Vice-Pres. Council, St John's Coll., Durham, 1995–2005 (Hon. Life Fellow, 2007). Pres., SNTS, 2002–03. *Publications:* Baptism in the Holy Spirit, 1970 (trans. Spanish 1977); Jesus and the Spirit, 1975 (trans. Spanish 1981); Unity and Diversity in the New Testament, 1977, 3rd edn 2006 (trans. Russian 1997); Christology in the Making, 1980, 2nd rev. edn 1989; The Evidence for Jesus, 1985 (trans. Dutch 1987); The Living Word, 1987; (with J. P. Mackey) New Testament Theology in Dialogue, 1987; Word Biblical Commentary, Vol. 38, Romans, 2 vols, 1988; Jesus, Paul and the Law, 1990; The Partings of the Ways between Christianity and Judaism and their Significance for the Character of Christianity, 1991, 2nd edn 2006; Jesus' Call to Discipleship, 1992 (Japanese edn 1996); Christian Liberty, 1993; A Commentary on the Epistle to the Galatians, 1993 (Japanese edn 1998); (with A. M. Suggate) The Justice of God, 1993; Epistles to the Colossians and to Philemon, 1996; The Acts of the Apostles, 1996; The Theology of Paul the Apostle, 1998 (trans. Italian 1999, Korean edn 2003); Christianity in the Making: Vol. 1: Jesus Remembered, 2003 (trans. Italian 2006); (ed) The Cambridge Companion to St Paul, 2003; (Gen. Ed.) Eerdmans Commentary on the Bible, 2003; A New Perspective on Jesus, 2005; The New Perspective on Paul: collected essays, 2005; (ed with S. McKnight) The Historical Jesus in Recent Research, 2005; contrib. numerous articles to jls, Festschriften, symposia and dictionaries. *Recreations:* choral singing, local preaching, fell walking, writing and reading, sudoku, visiting new places, checking out The Good Pub Guide. *Address:* 4 Fieldhouse Terrace, Durham DH1 4NA. *T:* (0191) 386 4080; *e-mail:* j.d.g.dunn@btopenworld.com.

DUNN, Prof. John Montfort, FBA 1989; Professor of Political Theory, University of Cambridge, 1987–2007, now Emeritus; Fellow of King's College, Cambridge, since 1966; *b* 9 Sept. 1940; *s* of Col. Henry George Montfort Dunn and Catherine Mary Dunn; *m* 1st, 1965, Susan Deborah Fyvel (marr. diss. 1971); 2nd, 1973, Judith Frances Bernal (*see* J. F. Dunn) (marr. diss. 1987); one *s* (and one *s* decd) by Dr Heather Joan Glen; 3rd, 1997, Ruth Ginette Scurr; two *d*. *Educ:* Winchester Coll.; King's Coll., Cambridge (BA 1962). Harkness Fellow, Graduate Sch. of Arts and Sciences, Harvard Univ., 1964–65; Official Fellow in History, Jesus Coll., Cambridge, 1965–66; Dir of Studies in History, King's Coll., Cambridge, 1966–72; Lectr in Pol Science, 1972–77, Reader in Politics, 1977–87, Cambridge Univ. Vis. Lectr, Dept of Pol Science, Univ. of Ghana, 1968–69; Visiting Professor: Dept of Civics and Politics, Univ. of Bombay, 1979–80; Faculty of Law, Tokyo Metropolitan Univ., 1983–84; Chiba Univ., Japan, 2007–; Distinguished Vis. Prof., Murphy Inst. of Pol Economy, Tulane Univ., New Orleans, 1986; Benjamin Evans Lippincott Dist. Prof., Minnesota Univ., 1990; Olmsted Vis. Prof., 1991, Leitner Vis. Prof. in Political Sci. and Internat. Affairs, 2008, Yale Univ. Foreign Hon. Mem., Amer. Acad. of Arts and Scis, 1991. Mem., Bd of Consultants, Kim Dae-Jung Peace Foundn for the Asia-Pacific Region, 1994–. Mem. Council, British Acad., 2004–07. FRSA 1993. Sir Isaiah Berlin Prize, British Political Studies Assoc., 2007. *Publications:* The Political Thought of John Locke, 1969; Modern Revolutions, 1972; Dependence and Opportunity: political change in Ahafo, 1973; (ed) West African States: failure and promise, 1978; Western Political Theory in the Face of the Future, 1979; Political Obligation in its Historical Context, 1980; Locke, 1984, rev. edn as Locke: A Very Short Introduction, 2003; The Politics of Socialism, 1984; Rethinking Modern Political Theory, 1985; (ed) The Economic Limits to Modern Politics, 1989; (ed) Contemporary West African States, 1989; Interpreting Political Responsibility, 1990; (ed) Democracy: the unfinished journey, 1992; Contemporary Crisis of the Nation State?, 1995; The History of Political Theory, 1995; (ed with Ian Harris) Great Political Thinkers, 20 vols, 1997; The Cunning of Unreason: making sense of politics, 2000; Pensare la politica, 2002; Setting the People Free: the story of democracy, 2005. *Address:* The Merchant's House, 31 Station Road, Swavesey, Cambridge CB24 4QJ. *T:* (01954) 231451.

DUNN, Prof. Judith Frances, PhD; FBA 1996; Research Professor, Social, Genetic and Developmental Psychiatry Research Centre, Institute of Psychiatry, King's College London, since 1995; *d* of James Pace and Jean Stewart; *m* 1st, 1961, Martin Gardiner Bernal (marr. diss.); 2nd, 1973, John Montfort Dunn, *qv* (marr. diss. 1987); 3rd, 1987, Robert Plomin. *Educ:* New Hall, Cambridge (BA 1961; MA 1968); King's Coll., Cambridge (PhD 1982). MRC Develt and Integration of Behaviour Unit, and Fellow, King's Coll., Cambridge, 1978–86; Evan Pugh Professor of Human Develt, Pennsylvania State Univ., 1986–95. *Publications:* (jtly) First Year of Life: psychological and medical implications of early experience, 1979; (jtly) Siblings: love, envy and understanding, 1982; Sisters and Brothers, 1984; (ed with R. Plomin) Study of Temperament: changes, continuities and challenges, 1986; Beginnings of Social Understanding, 1988; (jtly) Separate Lives, 1990; (ed jtly) Children's Sibling Relationships, 1992; Young Children's Close Relationships, 1993; (ed jtly) Stepfamilies, 1994; (ed) Connections between Emotion and Understanding in Development, 1995. *Address:* Social, Genetic and Developmental Psychiatry Research Centre, Institute of Psychiatry, King's College London, De Crespigny Park, Denmark Hill, SE5 8AF.

DUNN, Martin; Deputy Publisher/Editor-in-Chief, New York Daily News, since 2003; *b* 26 Jan. 1955. *Educ:* Dudley Grammar Sch., Worcs. Dudley Herald, 1974–77; Birmingham Evening Mail, 1977; Birmingham Post, 1978; Daily Mail, 1978–79; freelance journalist, 1979–83; New York Correspondent, The Sun, 1983–84; The Sun, London, 1984–88; Deputy Editor: News of the World, 1988–89; The Sun, 1989–91; Editor: Today, 1991–93; The Boston Herald, 1993; Editor-in-Chief, The New York Daily News, 1993–96; Editor, Channel One Television, 1996–98; Managing Director: DMG New Media, 1998–2000; DMG Front of Mind Ltd, 2000–03. *Recreations:* squash, running, golf. *Address:* New York Daily News, 450 W 33rd Street, New York, NY 10001–2681, USA. *T:* (212) 210 2100.

DUNN, Most Rev. Patrick James; *see* Auckland (NZ), Bishop of, (RC).

DUNN, Rt Hon. Sir Robin Horace Walford, Kt 1969; MC 1944; PC 1980; a Lord Justice of Appeal, 1980–84; *b* 16 Jan. 1918; *s* of late Brig. K. F. W. Dunn, CBE, and of Ava, *d* of Brig.-Gen. H. F. Kays, CB; *m* 1941, Judith (*d* 1995), *d* of late Sir Gonne Pilcher, MC; one *d* (one *s* and one *d* decd); *m* 1997, Joan, *e d* of Sir Cecil Stafford-King-Harman, 2nd Bt and *widow* of Captain George Dennehy. *Educ:* Wellington; Royal Military Academy, Woolwich (Sword of Honour). First Commissioned, RA, 1938; RHA, 1941; Staff Coll., 1946; retired (hon. Major), 1948. Served War of 1939–45; France and Belgium, 1939–40; Western Desert and Libya, 1941–42; Normandy and NW Europe, 1944–45 (wounded thrice, despatches twice, MC); Hon. Col Comdt, RA, 1980–84, Hon. Col 1984–. Called to Bar (Inner Temple), 1948; Master of the Bench, Inner Temple, 1969. Western Circuit, Junior Counsel to Registrar of Restrictive Trading Agreements, 1959–62; QC 1962; Judge of the High Court of Justice, Family Division (formerly Probate, Divorce and Admiralty Division), 1969–80; Presiding Judge, Western Circuit, 1974–78. Treas., Gen. Council of the Bar, 1967–69 (Mem., 1959–63); Chm. Betting Levy Appeal Tribunal, 1964–69; Dep. Chm., Somerset QS, 1965–71; Mem., Lord Chancellor's Cttee on Legal Educn, 1968–69. *Publication:* Sword and Wig: memoirs of a Lord Justice, 1994. *Recreation:* hunting. *Address:* Lynch Mead, Allerford, Somerset TA24 8HJ. *T:* (01643) 862509. *Club:* Cavalry and Guards.

DUNN, Rosamund Mary; Director, Local Development and Renewal, Department for Communities and Local Government, since 2007; *b* 10 June 1952; *d* of Stelio Democratis and Grace Matchette; *m* 1975, Patrick Dunn (separated 1999); three *d*. *Educ:* Univ. of Hull (BA Hons Philosophy). HM Treasury: Head: Resource Accounting and Budgeting Team, 1995–2000; Devolved Countries and Regions Team, 2000–04; Dir, Strategy and Corporate Planning, London Develt Agency, 2004–06; Dir, Thames Gateway Strategy, DCLG, 2006. *Recreations:* theatre, cinema, socialising, visiting holiday home in France. *Address:* Department for Communities and Local Government, Eland House, Bressenden Place, SW1E 5DU; *e-mail:* ros.dunn@communities.gsi.gov.uk.

DUNN, William Francis N.; *see* Newton Dunn.

DUNN, His Honour (William) Hubert; QC 1982; a Circuit Judge, 1993–2005, a Senior Circuit Judge, 1998–2005; Chief Immigration Adjudicator, 1998–2001; *b* 8 July 1933; *s* of William Patrick Millar Dunn and Isabel (*née* Thompson); *m* 1971, Maria Henriqueta Theresa d'Arouje Perestrello de Moser; one *s* one *d*. *Educ:* Rockport, Co. Down, N Ireland; Winchester Coll.; New Coll., Oxford (Hons degree PPE) (Half-Blue fencing 1954–55). 2nd Lieut, Life Guards, 1956–57; Household Cavalry Reserve of Officers, 1957–64. Cholmondeley Scholar, Lincoln's Inn, 1958, called to Bar, 1958; Bencher, Lincoln's Inn, 1990. A Recorder, 1980–93. Fellow, Soc. for Advanced Legal Studies, 1998. *Recreations:* travel, literature. *Address:* 207 Ashley Gardens, Emery Hill Street, SW1P 1PA. *Club:* Boodle's.

DUNNE, Very Rev. Dermot Patrick Martin; Dean of Christ Church Cathedral, Dublin, since 2008; *b* Portarlington, Co. Laois, 25 March 1959; *s* of late Michael Dunne and of Brigid Dunne (*née* Whelan); *m* Celia Dorothy, *d* of late James and Dorothy Burl. *Educ:* Pontifical Univ., Maynooth (Dip. Phil. 1980; DipTh 1983); Church of Ireland Theol Coll.; Chiron Centre for Integrative Psychotherapy (Cert. Psychotherapy 1995), Dublin City Univ. (BA 2004). Ordained deacon, 1983, priest, 1984, Church of Ireland priest, 1998; various posts in RC Church, 1983–95; Dean's Vicar, Christ Church Cathedral, Dublin, 1999–2001; Rector, Crosspatrick Gp of Parishes, Dio. of Ferns, 2001–08; Precentor, Ferns Cathedral, 2004–08; Archdeacon of Ferns, 2007–08. Warden, Cashel and Ossory Guild of Lay Readers, 2007–. *Address:* 24 Wainsfort Manor Crescent, Terenure, Dublin 6, Ireland. *T:* (office) (1) 6778099, *Fax:* (office) (1) 6798991; *e-mail:* revdunne@eircom.net.

DUNNE, Martin; JP; Lord-Lieutenant of Warwickshire, since 1997; *b* 30 March 1938; *s* of Philip Dunne, MC and Margaret Dunne (*née* Walker); *m* 1964, Alicia Juliet Barclay; three *d*. *Educ:* Eton; Christ Church, Oxford. High Sheriff, 1982–83, JP 1984, DL 1993, Warwicks.

See also Sir T. R. Dunne.

DUNNE, Philip Martin; MP (C) Ludlow, since 2005; *b* 14 Aug. 1958; *m* 1989, Domenica Margaret Anne Fraser; two *s* two *d*. *Educ:* Eton Coll.; Keble Coll., Oxford (BA 1980; MA 2006). S. G. Warburg & Co. Ltd, 1980–88; Dir, Corp. Develt, James Gulliver Associates, 1988–90; Partner, Phoenix Securities, 1991–97; a Man. Dir, Donaldson, Lufkin & Jenrette, 1997–2001; Dir, Business Develt, 2002–05, non-exec. Dir, 2006–, Ruffer LLP. Co-founder, Dir, 1987–97, non-exec. Chm., 1997–2006, Ottakar's plc; non-exec. Chm., Baronsmead VCT 4 plc, 2001–. Partner, Gatley Farms, 1987–. Mem. (C), S Shropshire DC, 2001–07. Member: Work and Pensions Select Cttee, 2005–06; Public Accounts Cttee, 2006–; Treasury Select Cttee, 2007–. Dir, Juvenile Diabetes Res. Foundn, 1999–2005. *Address:* (office) 54 Broad Street, Ludlow, Shropshire SY8 1GP; House of Commons, SW1A 0AA.

DUNNE, Sir Thomas (Raymond), KG 2008; KCVO 1995; JP; Lord-Lieutenant for Herefordshire, 1998–2008, and for Worcestershire, 1998–2001 (Lord-Lieutenant, County of Hereford and Worcester, 1977–98); *b* 24 Oct. 1933; *s* of Philip Dunne, MC, and Margaret Walker; *m* 1957, Henrietta Crawley; two *s* two *d*. *Educ:* Eton; RMA Sandhurst. Served Army, 1951–59: Royal Horse Guards. Herefordshire CC, 1962–68. President: 3 Counties Agric. Soc., 1977; W Midlands TA Assoc., 1988–98; National Vice Pres., Royal British Legion, 1982–89. Mem., West Mercia Police Authy, 1980–99; Dir, West Regional Bd, Central TV, 1981–92. Chm., Lord-Lieutenants' Assoc., 2001–08. Chm., Hereford Cathedral Council, 2001–. Trustee: Dyson Perrins Mus. Trust, 1980–; Worcester Mus. of Porcelain, 1980–2007 (Chm., 1984–2000). Hon. Colonel: 4th Worcester and Sherwood Foresters (formerly 2nd Mercian Volunteers), 1987–93; 5th Bn LI, 1993–98. High Sheriff 1970, DL 1973, Herefordshire; JP Hereford and Worcester, 1977. Hon. Fellow, Univ. of Worcester, 2008. KStJ 1978. *Address:* Trippleton, Leintwardine, Shropshire SY7 0LR.

See also M. Dunne.

DUNNELL, Karen Hope; National Statistician and Chief Executive, Office for National Statistics, since 2005; *b* 16 June 1946; *d* of Richard Henry Williamson and Winifred May

Beeching; *m* 1st, 1969, Keith Malvern Dunnell (marr. diss. 1976); 2nd, 1979, Prof. Michael William Adler, *qv* (marr. diss. 1994); two *d*. *Educ*: Bedford Coll., London (BSc Sociology 1967); MA Oxon, 1987. Res. Officer, Inst. of Community Studies, 1967–71; Lectr, St Thomas's Hosp. Med. Sch., 1971–74; Office of Population Censuses and Surveys, then Office for National Statistics, 1974–: Dep. Dir, 2000–02, Actg Dir, 2001–02, of Social Stats; Exec. Dir of Surveys and Admin. Sources, 2002–05; Registrar Gen. for England and Wales, 2005–08. Vis. Fellow, Nuffield Coll., Oxford, 1987–95; Vis. Prof., LSHTM, 1999–. *Publications*: (with Ann Cartwright) Medicine Takers, Prescribers and Hoarders, 1972; Family Formation 1976, 1979; Nurses Working in the Community, 1982. *Recreations*: yoga, reading modern novels and biography, small house in South of France. *Address*: Office for National Statistics, Government Building, Cardiff Road, Newport, Gwent NP10 8XG. *T*: (01633) 455 333, *Fax*: (01633) 652 500; *e-mail*: karen.dunnell@ons.gov.uk.

DUNNETT, Anthony Gordon, CBE 2004; President, International Health Partners (UK) Ltd, since 2004; *b* 17 June 1953; *s* of Peter Sydney Dunnett and Margaret Eileen (*née* Johnson); *m* 1975, Ruth Elizabeth Barker; one *s* two *d*. *Educ*: St Dunstan's Coll.; McGill Univ. (BComm, DipCS); Exeter Univ. (MA Econs). FCIB 1981. Nat. Westminster Bank, 1975–77; Royal Bank of Canada, Montreal, 1977–80 and 1982–86, Curaçao, 1980–82; Midland Bank: Corporate Banking Dir, 1986–88; Corporate Banking Dir, Samuel Montagu, 1988–89; Corporate Dir, 1990–91; Finance Dir, Corporate and Instnl Banking, 1991–94; Dir, Industrial Develt Unit, DTI, 1994–96; Chief Executive: English Partnerships, 1996–98; SEEDA, 1999–2003. Chm., Two-Five-Four-0 LLP, 2004–07. Member: Steering Bd, Insolvency Service, 1994–96; Urban Task Force, 1998–; Adv. Bd, Relationships Foundn, 2000–; Bd, Berks Learning and Skills Council, 2001–05. Director: Countryside Maritime, 1997–2004; Citylife Ltd, 2001–06; Mem., Bd of Trustees, Internat. Health Partners (UK) Ltd, 2004–. Mem., Mgt Bd, Kingsmead Homes, 1997–99. FRSA 1997; MInstD 1999. *Recreations*: local church, gardening, theatre, opera, sports. *Address*: The Fold, Beech Hill, Wadhurst, E Sussex TN5 6JR. *T*: (01483) 484118, *Fax*: (01483) 484696.

DUNNETT, Denzil Inglis, CMG 1967; OBE 1962; HM Diplomatic Service, retired; *b* 21 Oct. 1917; *s* of late Sir James Dunnett, KCIE and late Annie (*née* Sangster); *m* 1946, Ruth Rawcliffe (*d* 1974); two *s* (one *d* decd). *Educ*: Edinburgh Acad.; Corpus Christi Coll., Oxford. Served with RA, 1939–45. Diplomatic Service: Foreign Office, 1947–48; Sofia, 1948–50; Foreign Office, 1950–53; UK Delegn to OEEC, Paris, 1953–56; Commercial Sec., Buenos Aires, 1956–60; Consul, Elisabethville, 1961–62; Commercial Counsellor, Madrid, 1962–67; seconded to BoT, 1967–70; Counsellor, Mexico City, 1970–73; Ambassador to Senegal, Mauritania, Mali and Guinea, 1973–76, and to Guinea-Bissau, 1975–76; Diplomatic Service Chm., CS Selection Bd, 1976–77. London Rep., Scottish Develt Agency, 1978–82. *Publications*: Bird Poems, 1989; The Weight of Shadows: poems descriptive and religious, 2001; Wounds (poems), 2007. *Recreations*: chess, music. *Address*: 11 Victoria Grove, W8 5RW. *T*: (020) 7584 7523. *Club*: Caledonian.

DUNNETT, Maj. Graham Thomas, TD 1964; JP; Lord-Lieutenant of Caithness, 1995–2004; *b* 8 March 1929; *s* of late Daniel Dunnett and Elizabeth E. Macadie, Wick; *m* 1963, Catherine Elizabeth Sinclair, Westerdale; three *s*. *Educ*: Wick High Sch.; Archbishop Holgate's Grammar Sch., York. 1st Seaforth Highlanders, Malaya, 1948–51; 11th Seaforth Highlanders, Caithness, 1951–71; Major and Company Comdr, 1964. DL 1975, Vice Lord-Lieutenant 1986, JP 1996, Caithness. *Recreations*: gardening, walking, country dancing. *Address*: Cathel Sheiling, Loch Calder, Thurso, Caithness KW14 7YH. *T*: (01847) 871220.

DUNNETT, John Jacob, (Jack); President, Football League, 1981–86 and 1988–89 (Member, Management Committee, 1977–89); *b* 24 June 1922; *m* 1951; two *s* three *d*. *Educ*: Whitgift Middle Sch., Croydon; Downing Coll., Cambridge (BA 1947; LLB 1949; MA 1950; LLM 1989). Served with Cheshire Regt, 1941–46 (Capt.). Admitted Solicitor, 1949. Middlesex CC, 1958–61; Councillor, Enfield Borough Council, 1958–61; Alderman, Enfield Borough Council, 1961–63; Councillor, Greater London Council, 1964–67. MP (Lab) Central Nottingham, 1964–74, Nottingham East, 1974–83; former PPS to: Minister of State, FCO; Minister of Transport. Mem. FA Council, 1977–89, Vice-Pres., 1981–86, 1988–89; Mem., Football Trust, 1982–89; Chm., Notts County FC, 1968–87; Vice-Chm., Portsmouth FC, 1989–90. *Recreation*: watching professional football.

DUNNETT, Stephen Bruce, DSc; Professor, School of Biosciences, Cardiff University, since 2005 (Cardiff Professorial Research Fellow, 2000–05); *b* 28 Jan. 1950; *s* of Peter Sidney Dunnett and Margaret Eileen Dunnett (*née* Johnson); *m* 1984, Dr Sarah-Jane Richards. *Educ*: Eltham Coll.; Churchill Coll., Cambridge (BA Hons 1972; MA 1976; PhD 1981; DSc 1999); Poly. of N London (Dip in Social Work, CQSW 1976); Birkbeck Coll., Univ. of London (BSc Hons 1978). Social worker, London Borough of Southwark, 1972–78; research student, Churchill Coll., Cambridge, 1978–81; Fellow, Clare Coll., Cambridge, 1981–99; Department of Experimental Psychology, University of Cambridge: Wellcome Trust Mental Health Res. Fellow, 1982–83; Demonstrator, 1983–86; Lectr, 1986–95; Reader in Neurobiology, 1995–99; Dir, Scientific Progs, MRC Cambridge Centre for Brain Repair, 1992–99. Vis. Scientist, Univ. of Lund, Sweden, 1981–82. FMedSci 2003. Spearman Medal, BPsS, 1988; Alfred Meyer Medal, British Neuropathol Soc., 1998. *Publications*: (ed with S.-J. Richards) Neural Transplantation: from molecular basis to clinical application, 1990; (ed with A. Björklund): Neural Transplantation: a practical approach, 1992; Functional Neural Transplantation, 1994; Functional Neural Transplantation II, 2000; (with R. A. Barker) Neural Repair, Transplantation and Rehabilitation, 1999; (ed jtly) Neural Transplantation Methods, 2000; (jtly) Brain Damage, Brain Repair, 2001; Dopamine, 2005; over 510 research papers on topics of brain function and neural transplantation. *Recreations*: flying, food and wine, France. *Address*: School of Biosciences, Cardiff University, Box 911, Museum Avenue, Cardiff CF10 3US. *Club*: Royal Society of Medicine.

DUNNILL, Prof. Peter, OBE 1999; DSc, PhD, FREng, FIChemE; Professor of Biochemical Engineering, University College London, since 1984; Chairman, The Advanced Centre for Biochemical Engineering, since 2001 (Director, 1991–2001); *b* 20 May 1938; *s* of Eric and Marjorie Dunnill; *m* 1962, Patricia Mary Lievesley; one *s*. *Educ*: University College London (BSc; DSc 1978; Fellow, 1991). Royal Instn MRC staff, 1963–64; Lectr, 1964–79, Reader, 1979–84, UCL. Member: Internat. Cttee on Econ. and Applied Microbiol., 1974–82; Scientific and Technical Cttee, Central Lab. of Nat. Blood Transfusion Service, 1978–82; Biotechnol. Directorate Management Cttee, SERC, 1982–88, 1993–94; Biotechnol. Adv. Gp to Heads of Res. Councils, 1987–90; Biotechnol. Jt Adv. Bd, 1989–92; BBSRC, 1994–96; Steering Gp, BioSci. Innovation and Growth Team, DTI and DoH, 2002–03. FREng (FEng 1985). Donald Medal, IChemE, 1995; Heatley Medal, Biochem. Soc., 1997. *Publications*: *c* 200 pubns in learned jls. *Recreation*: music. *Address*: The Advanced Centre for Biochemical Engineering, University College London, Torrington Place, WC1E 7JE. *T*: (020) 7679 7031.

DUNNING, Graham; QC 2001; *b* 13 March 1958; *s* of Maj. James E. Dunning and Jane P. Dunning (*née* Hunt); *m* 1986, Claire Abigael Williams; three *s* one *d*. *Educ*: King Edward VI Sch., Southampton; Emmanuel Coll., Cambridge (MA); Harvard Law Sch. (LLM). Called to the Bar, Lincoln's Inn, 1982; joined Essex Court Chambers, 1983; in practice at commercial bar and as internat. arbitrator, 1983–. *Recreations*: travel, ski-ing, golf. *Address*: Essex Court Chambers, 24 Lincoln's Inn Fields, WC2A 3EG. *T*: (020) 7813 8000. *Clubs*: Woking Golf; Rye Golf.

DUNNING, Prof. John Harry, OBE 2008; PhD; Emeritus Professor of International Business, University of Reading, since 1992; State of New Jersey Professor of International Business, Rutgers University, US, 1989–2002; *b* 26 June 1927; *m* 1st, 1948, Ida Teresa Bellamy (marr. diss. 1975); one *s*; 2nd, 1975, Christine Mary Brown. *Educ*: Lower Sch. of John Lyon, Harrow; University Coll. London (BSc (Econ); PhD). Sub-Lieut, RNVR, 1945–48. Research Asst, University Coll. London, 1951–52; Lectr and Sen. Lectr, Univ. of Southampton, 1952–64; University of Reading: Prof. of Economics, 1964–74; Hd of Dept of Economics, 1964–87; Esmée Fairbairn Prof. of Internat. Investment and Business Studies, 1975–87; ICI Res. Prof. of Internat. Business, 1988–92. Visiting Professor: Univ. of Western Ontario, Canada, 1968–69; Univ. of California (Berkeley), 1968, 1987; Boston Univ., USA, 1976; Stockholm Sch. of Economics, 1978; HEC, Univ. of Montreal, Canada, 1980; Walker-Ames Prof., Univ. of Washington, Seattle, 1981; Seth Boyden Distinguished Prof., Rutgers Univ., 1987; Hon. Prof., Univ. of Internat. Business and Econs, Beijing, 1995. Consultant to UN, 1974–; OECD, 1975–; and EC, 1985–. Member: SE Economic Planning Council, 1966–68; Chemicals EDC, 1968–77; UN Study Gp on Multinational Corps, 1973–74. Chm., Economists Advisory Gp Ltd, 1975–2001. Pres., Internat. Trade Assoc., 1994. Fellow, Acad. of Internat. Business (Pres., 1987–88). Hon. Dr: Uppsala, 1975; Universidad Autónoma de Madrid, 1990; Antwerp, 1997; Chinese Culture Univ., Taiwan, 2007; Lund, 2007; Reading, 2008. *Publications*: American Investment in British Manufacturing Industry, 1958, 2nd edn 1998; (with C. J. Thomas) British Industry, 1963; Economic Planning and Town Expansion, 1963; Studies in International Investment, 1970; (ed) The Multinational Enterprise, 1971; (with E. V. Morgan) An Economic Study of the City of London, 1971; (ed) International Investment, 1972; (ed) Economic Analysis and the Multinational Enterprise, 1974; US Industry in Britain, 1976; (with T. Houston) UK Industry Abroad, 1976; International Production and the Multinational Enterprise, 1981; (ed with J. Black) International Capital Movements, 1982; (with J. Stopford) Multinationals: Company Performance and Global Trends, 1983; (with R. D. Pearce) The World's Largest Industrial Companies 1962–83, 1985; (ed) Multinational Enterprises, Economic Structure and International Competitiveness, 1985; Japanese Participation in British Industry, 1986; (with J. Cantwell) World Directory of Statistics on International Direct Investment and Production, 1987; Explaining International Production, 1988; Multinationals, Technology and Competitiveness, 1988; (ed with A. Webster) Structural Change in the World Economy, 1990; Multinational Enterprises and the Global Economy, 1993, new and rev. edn (with S. Lundan) 2008; The Globalization of Business, 1993; (ed with R. Narula) Foreign Direct Investment and Governments, 1996; (ed with K. Hamdani) The New Globalism and Developing Countries, 1997; Alliance Capitalism and Global Business, 1997; (ed) Governments, Globalisation and International Business, 1997; (ed) Globalization, Trade and Foreign Direct Investment, 1998; (ed) Regions, Globalisation and the Knowledge Based Economy, 2000; Global Capitalism at Bay, 2001; Theories and Paradigms of International Business Activity, 2002; Global Capitalism FDI and Competitiveness, 2002; (ed) Making Globalisation Good, 2003; (with R. Narula) Multinationals and Industrial Competitiveness: a new agenda, 2004; (ed with P. Gugler) Foreign Direct Investment, Location and Competitiveness, 2008; Seasons of a Scholar, 2008; numerous articles in learned and professional jls. *Address*: School of Business, University of Reading, Whiteknights Park, Reading, Berks RG6 2AA; *e-mail*: jill.mturner@virgin.net. *Club*: Athenæum.

DUNNING, Joseph, CBE 1977; Chairman, Lothian Health Board, 1983–84; Principal, Napier College of Commerce and Technology, Edinburgh, 1963–81, retired; *b* 9 Oct. 1920; *s* of Joseph and Elizabeth Ellen Dunning; *m* 1st, 1948, Edith Mary Barlow (*d* 1972); one *s* one *d*; 2nd, 1992, Eileen Murdoch, OBE. *Educ*: London University (BSc Hons); Durham University (MEd); Manchester College of Technology (AMCT). Metallurgical Industry and lecturing, 1936–56; Principal, Cleveland Technical College, 1956–63. MA Open Univ.; FEIS. Hon. Fellow, Napier Polytech. of Edinburgh, 1989. Hon. DEd CNAA, 1983. *Recreations*: silversmithing, photography. *Address*: 3 Barnes Green, Great Salkeld, Penrith, Cumbria CA11 9LU. *Club*: New (Edinburgh).

DUNNING, Sir Simon (William Patrick), 3rd Bt *cr* 1930; *b* 14 Dec. 1939; *s* of Sir William Leonard Dunning, 2nd Bt, and Kathleen Lawrie (*d* 1992), *d* of J. P. Cuthbert, MC; *S* father, 1961; *m* 1975, Frances Deirdre Morton, *d* of Major Patrick Lancaster; one *d*. *Educ*: Eton. *Address*: Low Auchengillan, Blanefield, by Glasgow G63 9AU. *T*: (01360) 770323. *Club*: Turf.

DUNNINGTON-JEFFERSON, Sir Mervyn (Stewart), 2nd Bt *cr* 1958; Company Director, since 1968; *b* 5 Aug. 1943; *s* of Sir John Alexander Dunnington-Jefferson, 1st Bt, DSO, and of Frances Isobel, *d* of Col H. A. Cape, DSO; *S* father, 1979; *m* 1971, Caroline Anna, *o d* of J. M. Bayley; one *s* two *d*. *Educ*: Eton College. Joined Charrington & Co. Ltd (Brewers), 1961; left in 1968 to become self-employed. *Recreations*: sport—cricket, ski-ing, golf, etc. *Heir*: *s* John Alexander Dunnington-Jefferson, *b* 23 March 1980. *Address*: 7 Bolingbroke Grove, SW11 6ES. *T*: (020) 8675 3395. *Clubs*: MCC, Queen's, Turf.

DUNRAVEN and MOUNT-EARL, 7th Earl of, *cr* 1822; **Thady Windham Thomas Wyndham-Quin;** Baron Adare, 1800; Viscount Mountearl, 1816; Viscount Adare, 1822; Bt 1871; *b* 27 Oct. 1939; *s* of 6th Earl of Dunraven and Mount-Earl, CB, CBE, MC, and Nancy (*d* 1994), *d* of Thomas B. Yuille, Halifax County, Va; *S* father, 1965; *m* 1969, Geraldine, *d* of Air Commodore Gerard W. McAleer, CBE, MB, BCh, DTM&H, Wokingham; one *d*. *Educ*: Ludgrove; Le Rosey. *Heir*: none. *Address*: Kilgobbin House, Adare, Co. Limerick, Ireland. *Club*: Kildare Street and University (Dublin).

See also Sir F. G. W. Brooke, Bt.

DUNROSSIL, 3rd Viscount *cr* 1959; **Andrew William Reginald Morrison;** Director, Brundage Management Company, San Antonio, Texas, since 1990; *b* 15 Dec. 1953; *e s* of 2nd Viscount Dunrossil, CMG and of Mavis Dawn (*née* Spencer-Payne); *S* father, 2000; *m* 1986, Carla Marie Brundage; one *s* three *d*. *Educ*: Eton (KS); University Coll., Oxford (BA Lit Hum). FCO, 1978–79; Kleinwort Benson Ltd, 1979–89. Chairman: Amer. Financial Services Assoc., 2007–08; Nat. Inst. of Consumer Credit Mgt. Hon. British Consul, San Antonio, Texas, 2004–. Dist. Service Award, Amer. Financial Services Assoc., 2005. *Recreations*: clan history, theology, poetry, sports. *Heir*: *s* Hon. Callum Alasdair Brundage Morrison, *b* 12 July 1994. *Address*: 410 E Rosewood, San Antonio, TX 78212, USA. *T*: (office) (210) 7359393. *Clubs*: San Antonio Country, Giraud, Argyle (San Antonio); Withington Cricket (Glos).

DUNSANY, 20th Baron of, *cr* 1439; **Edward John Carlos Plunkett;** *b* 10 Sept. 1939; *o s* of 19th Baron of Dunsany and Vera Plunkett, *d* of G. de Sà Sottomaior; *S* father, 1999; *m* 1982, Maria Alice Villela de Carvalho; two *s*. *Educ:* Eton; Slade Sch. of Fine Art; Ecole des Beaux Arts, Paris. *Heir: s* Hon. Randal Plunkett, *b* 9 March 1983. *Address:* Dunsany Castle, Co. Meath, Eire.

DUNSMORE, Rev. Barry William; Minister, St Columba's Church of Scotland, Pont Street, London, since 2000; *b* 27 Jan. 1954; *s* of late William Dunsmore and of Mildred Dunsmore (*née* Laing); *m* 1978, Dr Hilda Burns; one *s* one *d*. *Educ:* Hillhead High Sch., Glasgow; Univ. of Glasgow (MA, BD). Post-grad. res., Univ. of Nairobi, 1980–81; ordained and inducted, Erskine Ch, Saltcoats, 1982; inducted: St Columba's Ch, Stirling, 1988; Presbytery Clerk, Presbytery of Stirling, 1994–2000; Vice-Convener, Ch of Scotland Bd of Ministry, 2003–05. *Recreations:* golf, music, travel. *Address:* St Columba's Church of Scotland, Pont Street, SW1X 0BD. *T:* (020) 7584 2321, *Fax:* (020) 7584 5446; *e-mail:* office@stcolumbas.org.uk. *Club:* Caledonian.

DUNSTAN, (Andrew Harold) Bernard, RA 1968 (ARA 1959); painter; *b* 19 Jan. 1920; *s* of late Dr A. E. Dunstan; *m* 1949, Diana Maxwell Armfield, *qv*; two *s* (and one *s* decd). *Educ:* St Paul's; Byam Shaw Sch.; Slade Sch. Has exhibited at RA since 1945. Many one-man exhibitions. Pictures in public collections include Royal Collection, London Museum, Bristol Art Gall., Nat. Gall. of NZ, Arts Council, Nat. Portrait Gall., many in private collections. Member: NEAC; RWA (Pres., 1980–84); Pastel Soc. Chm., Artists' General Benevolent Instn, 1987–91. Trustee, RA, 1989–95. *Publications:* Learning to Paint, 1970; Painting in Progress, 1976; Painting Methods of the Impressionists, 1976; (ed) Ruskin, Elements of Drawing, 1991; The Paintings of Bernard Dunstan, 1993. *Recreation:* music. *Address:* 10 High Park Road, Kew, Richmond, Surrey TW9 4BH. *T:* (020) 8876 6633. *Club:* Arts.

DUNSTAN, Lt-Gen. Sir Donald (Beaumont), AC 1991; KBE 1980 (CBE 1969; MBE 1954); CB 1972; Governor of South Australia, 1982–91; *b* 18 Feb. 1923; *s* of late Oscar Reginald Dunstan and Eileen Dunstan; *m* 1948, Beryl June Dunningham; two *s*. *Educ:* Prince Alfred Coll., South Australia; RMC, Duntroon. Served War of 1939–45: Regimental and Staff appts in SW Pacific Area, 1942–45. Served in Korea, 1954; Instructor: RMC Duntroon, 1955–56, 1963; Staff Coll., Queenscliff, 1958; Staff Coll., Camberley, 1959–60; Dep. Comdr 1 Task Force, Vietnam, 1968–69; Comdr, 10th Task Force, Holsworthy, NSW, 1969; idc 1970; Commander Aust. Force, Vietnam, 1971; Chief of Materiel, 1972–74; GOC Field Force Comd, 1974–77; CGS, 1977–82. KStJ 1982. *Address:* 52 Martin Court, West Lakes, SA 5021, Australia. *Clubs:* Australian (Sydney); Royal Sydney Golf, Royal Adelaide Golf.

DUNSTAN, Ivan, PhD; CChem, FRSC; FCQI; Director-General International, British Standards Institution, 1991–93; *b* 27 Aug. 1930; *s* of Edward Ernest and Sarah Kathleen Dunstan; *m* 1955, Monica Jane (*née* Phillips); two *s* one *d*. *Educ:* Falmouth Grammar Sch.; Bristol Univ. (BSc). Joined Scientific Civil Service, working at Explosives Research and Development Estabt, Waltham Abbey, 1954; became Supt of Gen. Chemistry Div., 1967; Warren Spring Laboratory (DTI) as Dep. Dir (Resources), 1972–74; Dir, Materials Quality Assurance, MoD (PE), 1974–79; Dir, Bldg Res. Estabt, DoE, 1979–83; Standards Dir, 1983–86, Dir-Gen., 1986–91, BSI. Chm., UK Nat. Forum for Quality Policy and Conformity Assessment, 1993–2001. President: RILEM, 1988; European Standards Organ, 1990; European Orgn for Testing and Certification, 1990–92; Inst. of Quality Assurance, 1997–2002 (Vice-Pres., 1986–97); Mem., British Bd of Agrément, 1987. CCMI (CBIM 1986). *Recreations:* golf, opera, gardening. *Address:* 6 High Oaks Road, Welwyn Garden City, Herts AL8 7BH. *T:* (01707) 322272.

DUNSTAN, Tessa Jane; Director, Legal Services A, Department of Trade and Industry, 2001–04; retired; Appeal Officer for community interest companies, since 2006; *b* 18 July 1944; *d* of Alfred Thomas Fripp and Kathleen Jennie (*née* Kimpton); *m* 1973, Richard James Rowley Dunstan; two *s* two *d*. *Educ:* Convent of the Sacred Heart, Woldingham, Surrey; Lady Margaret Hall, Oxford (MA). Called to the Bar, Middle Temple, 1967; Legal Asst, Solicitor's Office, BoT, 1968; Sen. Legal Asst, Solicitor's Office, DTI, 1973–84; Legal Advr, Office of Telecommunications; 1984–87; Solicitor's Office/Legal Department, Department of Trade and Industry, 1987–2004: Investigations Div., 1989–98; Grade 3, Dir Legal Services D, 1998–2001; Legal Project Dir (Co. Law Review), Legal Services, DTI, 2001. *Recreations:* opera, gardening. *Address:* Shalesbrook, Forest Row, Sussex RH18 5LS. *T:* (01342) 823079.

DUNSTONE, Charles; Founder and Chief Executive Officer, The Carphone Warehouse, since 1989; *b* 21 Nov. 1964; *s* of Denis and Anne Dunstone. *Educ:* Uppingham Sch. Sales Manager, Communications Div., NEC, 1985–89. Non-executive Director: Halifax, 2000–01; Hbos, 2001–08; Daily Mail & Gen. Trust. *Recreation:* sailing. *Address:* The Carphone Warehouse, 1 Portal Way, W3 6RS. *Clubs:* Royal Ocean Racing, Royal Thames Yacht.

DUNT, Vice Adm. Sir John (Hugh), KCB 1998; CEng, FIET; Chief of Fleet Support and Member, Admiralty Board, 1997–2000; *b* 14 Aug. 1944; *s* of Harris Hugh Dunt and Margaret Rea Dunt (*née* Morgan); *m* 1972, Alynne Margaret Wood; two *d*. *Educ:* Duke of York Sch., Nairobi; RNEC Manadon (BScEng). Joined RN at BRNC Dartmouth, 1963; served in HM Ships Kent, Ajax, Dundas, Collingwood, Nubian; MoD (PE); Staff, C-in-C Fleet, 1980; Naval Operational Requirements, 1980–82; HMS Invincible, 1982–84; Staff Weapon Engr Officer to FO Sea Training, 1984; Naval Staff Duties, 1985–87; RCDS 1988; Higher Command and Staff Course, Camberley, 1989; Captain, HMS Defiance, 1989–90; Dir, Defence Systems, MoD, 1991–93; Dir, Gen. Fleet Support (Ops and Plans), 1993–95; DCDS (Systems), MoD, 1995–97. Defence Advr, Cap Gemini Ernst & Young, 2001–03. Chm. Trustees, Armed Forces Memorial Trust, 2003–. Gov., Royal Sch., Haslemere, 1992–; Chm. Govs, Royal Star and Garter Home, Richmond, 2003–. *Publications:* articles in naval and professional jls. *Recreations:* sport (cricket, squash), gardening, travel. *Address:* Woodley House, Hill Brow, Liss, Hants GU33 7QG. *Clubs:* MCC; Royal Navy Cricket; Liphook Golf.
See also Vice-Adm. P. A. Dunt.

DUNT, Vice Adm. Peter Arthur, CB 2002; Chief Executive, Defence Estates, 2002–07; *b* 23 June 1947; *s* of Harris Hugh Dunt and Margaret Rae Dunt; *m* 1974, Lesley Gilchrist; two *d*. *Educ:* Duke of York Sch., Nairobi; Merchant Taylors' Sch., Liverpool; BRNC, Dartmouth. Midshipman, HMS Arethusa, 1966; Sub Lieut courses, 1967–69; Captain's Sec., HMS Charybdis, 1969–71; Flag Lieut to Flag Officer, Medway, 1971–74; Dep. Supply Officer, HMS Kent, 1974; Supply Officer, HMS Aurora, 1975–77; Officer's Trng Officer, HMS Pembroke, 1977–79; Asst Sec. to Vice Chief of Naval Staff, 1979–82; Comdr, 1982; Sec. to Flag Officer, 1st Flotilla, 1982–84 (Gp Logistics Officer, HMS Hermes, Falklands Conflict); Supply Officer, BRNC, Dartmouth, 1984–86; Sec. to Dir Gen. Naval Manpower and Trng, 1986–88; Captain, 1988; Dep. Dir Naval Staff Duties, 1988; Sec. to 2nd Sea Lord, 1989–92; Captain, HMS Raleigh, 1992–94; Dir Naval Personnel Corporate Programming, 1994–97; rcds 1997; Rear Adm., 1998; COS to Second Sea Lord and C-in-C Naval Home Command, 1998–2000; Sen. Naval Directing Staff, RCDS and Chief Naval Supply Officer, 2000–02. FCIPD 2000. *Recreations:* cricke golf, squash, walking, gardening, DIY. *Address:* The Lodge, Great Tangley, Guildfor Surrey GU5 0PT. *Club:* Army and Navy.
See also Vice-Adm. Sir J. H. Dunt.

DUNTZE, Sir Daniel Evans, 9th Bt *cr* 1774, of Tiverton, Devon; *b* 11 Aug. 1960; *o s* Sir Daniel Evans Duntze, 8th Bt and of Marietta Duntze (*née* Welsh); *S* father, 1997, bu his name does not appear on the Official Roll of the Baronetage. *Address:* 6811 Universit Drive 2E, St Louis, MO 63130–4658, USA.

DUNWICH, Viscount; Robert Keith Rous; *b* 17 Nov. 1961; *s* and *heir* of Earl Stradbroke, *qv*.

DUNWICH, Bishop Suffragan of, since 1999; **Rt Rev. Clive Young;** *b* 31 May 194 *s* of William Alfred Young and late Dorothy Young; *m* 1971, Susan Elizabeth Tucke *Educ:* King Edward VI Grammar Sch., Chelmsford; St John's Coll., Durham (BA Hons Ridley Hall, Cambridge. Ordained: deacon, 1972; priest, 1973; Assistant Curate: Neasde cum Kingsbury St Catherine, London, 1972–75; St Paul, Hammersmith, 1975–79; Pries in-charge, 1979–82, Vicar, 1982–92, St Paul with St Stephen, Old Ford; Area Dea Tower Hamlets, 1988–92; Archdeacon of Hackney and Vicar of Guild Church of Andrew, Holborn, 1992–99. *Recreations:* music, gardening. *Address:* 28 Westerfield Roa Ipswich, Suffolk IP4 2UJ. *T:* (01473) 222276.

DUNWOODY, Richard; *see* Dunwoody, T. R.

DUNWOODY, Tamsin; Member (Lab) Preseli Pembrokeshire, National Assembly f Wales, 2003–07; *b* 3 Sept. 1958; *d* of late Dr John Elliott Orr Dunwoody, CBE ar Gwyneth Patricia Dunwoody, MP; *m* 1992 (marr. diss. 2006); two *s* three *d*. *Educ:* Uni of Kent (BA); Univ. of South Bank (AHSM 1982). NHS Manager, St Mary Whittington, Royal Northern and Royal Free Hosps, London, 1979–91; Co. Sec., David's Care in the Community, 1992–97; small business advr/commercial tuto 1997–2003. Deputy Minister: for Econ. Develt and Transport, 2005–07; for Envr Planning and the Countryside, 2005–07. Contested (Lab) Preseli Pembrokeshire, Na Assembly for Wales, 2007; (Lab) Crewe and Nantwich, May 2008. Mem., Labour Part 1973–. Mem., RHS, 1993–. *Recreations:* smallholder, embroidery, reading. *T:* (0134 881510; *e-mail:* tamsin.dunwoody@btinternet.com.

DUNWOODY, (Thomas) Richard, MBE 1993; National Hunt jockey, 1982–99; *b* Jan. 1964; *s* of George Rutherford and Gillian Mary Dunwoody; *m* 1988, Carol Ar Abraham (marr. diss. 2000). *Educ:* Rendcomb Coll., Glos. Wins include: Grand Nationa on West Tip, 1986, on Miinnehoma, 1994; Cheltenham Gold Cup, on Charter Part 1988; King George VI Chase, on Desert Orchid, 1989 and 1990, on One Man, 1995 a 1996; Champion Hurdle, on Kribensis, 1990; Breeders' Cup Steeplechase, on Highla Bud, 1989 and 1992; Champion National Hunt Jockey, 1992–93, 1993–94 and 1994–9 1699 National Hunt wins, incl. ten consecutive centuries, 1999. Jt Pres., Jockeys' Asso 1993–99. Completed 680 mile Shackleton South Pole expedn, 2008. *Publications:* (wi Marcus Armytage) Hell for Leather, 1993; (with S. Magee) Duel, 1994; (with Marc Armytage) Hands and Heels, 1997; (with David Walsh) Obsessed: the autobiograph 2000; Horses of My Life, 2005. *Recreations:* sport, travel. *Address:* 129 New Kings Roa Fulham, SW6 4SL.

DUNWORTH, John Vernon, CB 1969; CBE 1955; President, International Committe of Weights and Measures, Sèvres, France, 1975–85 (Vice President, 1968–75); *b* 24 Fe 1917; *o c* of late John Dunworth and Susan Ida (*née* Warburton); *m* 1967, Patricia No Boston; one *d*. *Educ:* Manchester Grammar Sch.; Clare Coll., Cambridge (Denman Bayn Research Studentship, 1937, Robins Prize, 1937); Trinity Coll., Cambridge (Twisd Studentship and Fellowship, MA, PhD 1941). War Service: Ministry of Supply on Ra Development, 1939–44; National Research Council of Canada, on Atomic Ener Development, 1944–45. Univ. Demonstrator in Physics, Cambridge, 1945. Join Atomic Energy Research Establishment, Harwell, 1947; Dir, NPL, 1964–76. Alterna United Kingdom Member on Organising Cttee of UN Atoms for Peace Confs in Genev 1955 and 1958. Fellow Amer. Nuclear Soc. 1960. Chm., British Nuclear Energy So 1964–70; Vice-President, Institute of Physics: Physical Soc., 1966–70. CEng 196 Comdr (with Star), Order of Alfonso X el Sabio, Spain, 1960. *Address:* Apartment 9 Kings Court, Ramsey, Isle of Man IM8 1LP. *T:* (01624) 813003. *Club:* Athenæum.

DUPAS, Gabrielle Teresa S.; *see* Solti-Dupas.

Du PLESSIS, Barend Jacobus; Minister of Finance, Republic of South Africa, 1984–9 MP (National Party) Florida, 1974–92; Leader of National Party of Transvaal, 1989–92 19 Jan. 1940; *s* of late Jan Hendrik Du Plessis and of Martha J. W. Du Plessis (*née* Both *m* 1962, Antoinette (*née* Van Den Berg); three *s* one *d*. *Educ:* Potchefstroom Univ. Christian Higher Educn (BSc); Potchefstroom Teachers' Trng Coll. (THE Mathematics Teacher, Hoër Seunskool Helpmekaar, Johannesburg and Johannesbu Technical Coll., 1962; Engineering Div., Data Processing and Admin. Sec., SAB 1962–68; Systems Engineering and Marketing in Banking and Finance, IBM (S 1968–74. Dep. Minister of Foreign Affairs and Information, 1982; Minister of Educn a Trng, 1983.

Du PLESSIS, Jan Petrus; Chairman: British American Tobacco plc, since 2004; RH 2005–07; *b* 22 Jan. 1954; *m* 1978, Magdalena, (Leni), Nel; two *s* one *d*. *Educ:* Univ. Stellenbosch (BCom Law 1973, LLB 1977). CA 1980 (SA). Internat. Financial Manag Rembrandt Gp Ltd, 1981–87; Group Finance Director: Co. Financière Richemont, S 1988–2004; Rothmans International plc, 1990–96. Non-exec. Dir, Lloyds TSB, 200 *Recreations:* golf, ski-ing, scuba diving, walking. *Address:* British American Tobacco p Globe House, 4 Temple Place, WC2 2PG. *T:* (020) 7845 1000. *Club:* Beaconsfield Go

DUPPLIN, Viscount; Charles William Harley Hay, MA; barrister; Director Mergers and Acquisitions, Hiscox Ltd, since 2000; *b* 20 Dec. 1962; *s* and *heir* of 15th E of Kinnoull, *qv*; *m* 2002, Clare, *d* of His Honour William Hamilton Raymund Crawfo *qv*; three *d* (incl. twins). *Educ:* Summer Fields; Eton; Christ Church, Oxford (Schola City Univ. (Dip. in Law); Inns of Court Sch. of Law. Called to the Bar, Middle Temp 1990. Associate, Credit Suisse First Boston Ltd, 1985–88; Underwriter, Roberts & Hisco then Hiscox Syndicates Ltd, 1990–95; Man. Dir (Europe), Hiscox Insce Co. L 1995–2000. Non-executive Director: Construction & Gen. Guarantee Insce Co., 200 Amorphous Sugar Ltd, 2001–; HIM Capital Ltd, 2007–; non-exec. Chm., Herita Group Ltd, 2001–05. Lieut, Atholl Highlanders, 1993–. Mem., Queen's Bodyguard Scotland (Royal Co. of Archers), 2000–. Pres., London Mems, NT for Scotland, 200 Chm., Royal Caledonian Ball, 1996– (Trustee, 1992–). Mem., Develt Cttee, Christ C Oxford, 2004–. FRPSL 2006 (Mem., 2000). *Publication:* contrib. Jl of Chem. S *Recreations:* cricket, Cresta Run, Real tennis, ski-ing, philately. *Address:* 17 Cumberla Street, SW1V 4LS. *T:* (020) 7976 6973; Pitkindie House, Abernyte, Perthshire PH 9RE. *T:* (01828) 686342. *Clubs:* White's, Turf, MCC; Royal Perth (Perth); Jock (Vienna).

DUPRE, Sir Tumun, Kt 1993; OBE 1988; President, South Wahgi Local Government Council, Papua New Guinea, 1967–88 and 1990 (Councillor, 1988–90); *b* 1923; *s* of Awil Dupre and Dop Amban Ai; *m* 1st, Abamp; 2nd, Kawil; 3rd, Danamp; 4th, Muru; 5th, Wai; thirteen *s* two *d*. *Educ:* no formal schooling. Government interpreter, 1948–63; Luluai (people's representative, apptd by govt), 1956–63. Rep. of Minj Dist, and MEC, W Highlands Province; Minister for Police, Justice, Village Courts, and Peace and Good Order. PNG Independence Medal, 1975; 10th Anniversary Medal, 1985; Provincial Medal, 1988. *Recreation:* village life. *Address:* c/o South Wahgi Local Government Council, Post Office Box, Minj, Papua New Guinea.

DUPREE, Sir (Thomas William James) David, 6th Bt *cr* 1921, of Craneswater, Portsmouth; *b* 5 Feb. 1930; *s* of James Dupree, 5th *s* of 1st Bt and Mary Ethel Gillott (*née* Reid); *S* cousin, 2006. *Heir: cousin* Michael John Dupree [*b* 29 April 1947; *m* 1982, Alexandra Columbia Smollett; one *d*].

Du QUESNAY, Heather Le Mercier, CBE 1996; Chief Executive, English Schools Foundation, Hong Kong, since 2005; *b* 10 Nov. 1947; *d* of Eric William and Agnes Elizabeth Openshaw; *m* 1969, Ian Mark Le Mercier Du Quesnay; two *d*. *Educ:* Univ. of Birmingham (BA, Cert Ed). Teacher, 1972–78, Dep. Head, 1978–83, Bartley Green Girls' Sch., Birmingham; Educn Officer, Cambs CC, 1983–89; Dep. Co. Educn Officer, Essex CC, 1989–90; Dir of Educn, Herts CC, 1991–96; Exec. Dir of Educn, 1996–2000, Interim Chief Exec., 2000, Lambeth BC; Chief Exec., Nat. Coll. for Sch. Leadership, 2000–05. FRSA 1994. Hon. DEd de Montfort, 1997; DUniv UCE, 2002. *Publications:* essays and articles in educ. jls and newspapers. *Recreations:* walking, food, wine, family. *Address:* English Schools Foundation, 43B Stubbs Road, Hong Kong.

DURAND, Sir Edward (Alan Christopher David Percy), 5th Bt *cr* 1892, of Ruckley Grange, Salop; *b* 21 Feb. 1974; *s* of Rev. Sir (Henry Mortimer) Dickon (Marion St George) Durand, 4th Bt and of Stella Evelyn Durand (*née* L'Estrange); *S* father, 1993; *m* 2004, Rachel King; one *d*. *Educ:* St Columba's Coll., Dublin; Milltown Inst., Dublin (Nat. Cert. in Philosophy); Univ. of Ulster at Coleraine (BA Phil.); Nat. Trng Authy dips in herbalism and parapsychology. *Recreation:* mysticism. *Heir: b* David Michael Dickon Percy Durand, *b* 6 June 1978. *Address:* Lisnalurg House, Sligo, Eire.

DURAND, (Julia) Alison; *see* Noble, J. A.

DURANT, Sir Anthony; *see* Durant, Sir R. A. B.

DURANT, Prof. John Robert, PhD; Director, MIT Museum, since 2005; Adjunct Professor, Science, Technology and Society Program, Massachusetts Institute of Technology, since 2005; *b* 8 July 1950; *s* of Kenneth Albert James Durant and Edna Kathleen Durant (*née* Norman); *m* 1st, 1977, Nirmala Naidoo (marr. diss. 1996); two *s* one *d*; 2nd, 2000, Prof. Anne Harrington; one *s*. *Educ:* Queens' College, Cambridge (MA Nat. Scis; PhD Hist. of Sci.). Staff Tutor in Biological Scis, Dept of Extramural Studies, UC Swansea, 1976–82; Staff Tutor in Biol Scis, Dept of External Studies, Univ. of Oxford, 1983–89; Hd, then Dir, Sci. Communication, Sci. Mus., 1989–2000; Chief Exec., At-Bristol, 2000–05. Imperial College London: Vis. Prof. of Hist. and Public Understanding of Sci., 1989–93; Prof., 1993–2002, Vis. Prof., 2002–05, of Public Understanding of Sci.; Vis. Prof., UWE, 2001–05. *Publications:* (ed) Darwinism and Divinity, 1985; (with P. Klopfer and S. Oyama) Aggression: conflict in animals and humans reconsidered, 1988; (ed) Museums and Public Understanding of Science, 1992; (ed) Public Participation in Science, 1995; (ed) Biotechnology in the Public Sphere: a European sourcebook, 1998; articles in professional jls. *Recreations:* family, writing, broadcasting. *Address:* MIT Museum, 265 Massachusetts Avenue N51–201, Cambridge, MA 02139, USA. *T:* (617) 2535653; *e-mail:* jdurant@mit.edu.

DURANT, Louise; *see* Charlton, L.

DURANT, Sir (Robert) Anthony (Bevis), Kt 1991; *b* 9 Jan. 1928; *s* of Captain Robert Michael Durant and Mrs Violet Dorothy Durant (*née* Bevis); *m* 1958, Audrey Stoddart; two *s* one *d*. *Educ:* Dane Court Prep. Sch., Pyrford, Woking; Bryanston Sch., Blandford, Dorset. Royal Navy, 1945–47. Coutts Bank, Strand, 1947–52; Cons. Party Organisation, 1952–67 (Young Cons. Organiser, Yorks; Cons. Agent, Clapham; Nat. Organiser, Young Conservatives). MP (C): Reading N, Feb. 1974–1983; Reading W, 1983–97. PPS to Sec. of State for Transport and to Sec. of State for Employment, 1983–84; Asst Govt Whip, 1984–86; a Lord Comr of HM Treasury, 1986–88; Vice-Chamberlain of HM Household, 1988–90. Member: Select Cttee Parly Comr (Ombudsman), 1973–83, 1990–93; Select Cttee on Members' Interests, 1993–95; Chm., Select Cttee on Channel Tunnel Rail Link Bill, 1995–96; Mem., Exec., 1922 Cttee, 1990–97; Chairman: All Party Gp on Widows and One Parent Families, 1977–85; All Party Gp on Inland Waterways, 1992–97; Cons. Nat. Local Govt Adv. Cttee, 1981–84; Backbench Envmt Cttee, 1991–97; All Party Gp on Film Industry, 1991–97; Vice-Chm., Parly Gp for World Govt, 1979–84. Leader, UK delegn to Council of Europe, 1996–97 (Mem., 1992–96); Chm., British Br., CPA, 1988–90; Mem., Council of Europe, 1981–83, 1990–97 (Ldr, UK Delegn, 1996–97). Dir, Southern Demolition Co. Ltd, 1998–; former Consultant: The Film Production Association of Great Britain Ltd; Delta Electrical Div. of Delta Metal Co. Ltd; Allied Industrial Designers. Dir, British Industrial Scientific Film Assoc., 1967–70; Mem. Bd of Govs, BFI, 1992–98. Chm., Sports Aid Foundn (Southern Region), 1996–. Mem., Inland Waterways Adv. Council, 1975–84; President: Kennet and Avon Canal Trust, 1996–; River Thames Soc., 1996–. Freeman: City of London, 1997; Watermen and Lightermen's Co., 1998–. *Recreations:* boating, golf. *Address:* Hill House, Surley Row, Caversham, Reading RG4 8ND.

DURANTE, Viviana Paola; Guest Artist, Royal Ballet Company; *b* Italy, 8 May 1967. *Educ:* Royal Ballet School. Came to England in 1977; joined Royal Ballet Co., 1984; soloist, 1987; Principal Dancer, 1989; Guest Artist, 1999; first major rôle, Swan Lake, Covent Garden, 1988; rôles include Manon, Ondine, La Bayadère, Giselle, Kitri (in Don Quixote), Aurora, Cinderella, Juliet, Carmen, Coppelia. Principal Dancer, American Ballet Theater, 1999. Evening Standard Ballet Award, 1989; Laurence Olivier Award, 1997.

DURÃO BARROSO, José Manuel; President, European Commission, since 2004; Professor of International Relations, Universidade Lusíada (Head of Department, 1995–99); *b* 23 March 1956; *s* of Luís Barroso and Marie Elisabete Durão; *m* 1980, Maria Margarida Pinto Ribeiro de Sousa Uva Barroso; three *s*. *Educ:* Univ. of Lisbon (LLD Hons 1978); Univ. of Geneva (Master in Pol Sci. 1981); European Univ. Inst., Univ. of Geneva (Dip.). Lecturer: Faculty of Law, Lisbon Univ., 1978–81; Pol Sci. Dept, Geneva Univ., 1981–85. Vis. Scholar, 1985, Vis. Prof., 1996–98, Univ. of Georgetown, Washington. Ed., Revista de Ciência Política. MP (PSD): Lisbon, 1985–87, 1995–2004; Viseu, 1987–95; Secretary of State for: Home Affairs, 1985–87; Foreign Affairs and Co-operation, 1987–92; Minister for Foreign Affairs, Portugal, 1992–95; Prime Minister of Portugal, 2002–04. Chm., Commn for For. Affairs, Portuguese Parlt, 1995–99. Leader, PSD, 1999–2004 (Mem., Nat. Council, 1984–2004; Chm., Dept for Internat. Relns). Leader, Internat. Inst. for Democracy and Electoral Assistance mission to Bosnia Hercegovina, 1996; UN Advr, Project for Peace Process in Africa, Tanzania, 1997. Vice President: EPP, 1999–2002; Center Democrats Intl, 2001–05. Scholarship Fellow: Swiss Confedn; CEC; Volkswagenwerk Foundn; NATO; Swiss Nat. Fund for Scientific Res. *Publications:* (jtly) Governmental System and Party System, 1980; Le Système Politique Portugais face à l'Intégration Européenne, 1983; Política de Cooperacão, 1990; Uma Certa Ideia de Europa, 1999; Uma Ideia para Portugal, 2000; Mudar de Modelo, 2001; Reformar: dois anos de governo, 2004; contrib. to collective works, encyclopaedias and internat. scientific jls. *Address:* European Commission, 200 Rue de la Loi, 1049 Brussels, Belgium.

DURBIN, Prof. James, FBA 2001; Professor of Statistics, University of London (London School of Economics), 1961–88, now Emeritus; *b* 30 June 1923; *m* 1958, Anne Dearnley Outhwaite; two *s* one *d*. *Educ:* Wade Deacon GS, Widnes; St John's Coll., Cambridge. Army Operational Research Group, 1943–45. Boot and Shoe Trade Research Assoc., 1945–47; Dept of Applied Economics, Cambridge, 1948–49; Asst Lectr, then Lecturer in Statistics, London Sch. of Economics, 1950–53; Reader in Statistics, 1953–61. Visiting Professor: Indian Statistical Inst., 1953; Univ. of North Carolina, 1959–60; Stanford Univ., 1960; Univ. of Wisconsin, 1965; Johns Hopkins Univ., 1965–66; Univ. of Washington, 1966; ANU, 1970–71; Univ. of Calif, Berkeley, 1971; Univ. of Cape Town, 1978; UCLA, 1984; Univ. of Calif, Santa Barbara, 1989; Nat. Univ. of Singapore, 1989–90; Univ. of Trento, Italy, 1991; Ohio State Univ., 1993; Moscow Acad. of Scis, 1995; Hon. Prof., UCL, 2007–. Research Fellow: US Bureau of the Census, 1992; Statistics Canada, 1994; Statistics NZ, 1997. Member: Home Office Data Protection Cttee, 1976–78; Dept of Transport Adv. Cttee on Trunk Rd Assessment, 1977–81. Member: ESRC, 1983–86 (Chm., Res. Resources and Methods Cttee, 1982–85); Internat. Statistical Inst., 1955 (Pres., 1983–85; Hon. Mem., 1999); Bd of Dirs, Amer. Statistical Assoc., 1980–82 (Fellow, 1960); Fellow, Inst. of Mathematical Statistics, 1958; Fellow, Econometric Soc., 1967; Royal Statistical Society: Vice Pres., 1969–70 and 1972–73; Pres. 1986–87; Guy Medal in Bronze, 1966, in Silver, 1976, in Gold, 2008. Dr *hc* Tucuman, Argentina, 2001. *Publications:* Distribution Theory for Tests based on the Sample Distribution Function, 1973; (with S. J. Koopman) Time Series Analysis by State Space Methods, 2001; articles in statistical journals, incl. Biometrika, Jl of Royal Statistical Society, etc. *Recreations:* travel, opera, theatre, visiting Suffolk. *Address:* 31 Southway, NW11 6RX. *T:* (020) 8458 3037; *e-mail:* durbinja@aol.com.
See also R. M. Durbin.

DURBIN, Richard Michael, PhD; FRS 2004; Principal Investigator, The Wellcome Trust Sanger Institute (formerly Sanger Centre), Hinxton, Cambridge, since 1992 (Deputy Director, 1997–2006; Joint Head, 1992–94, Head, 1994–2006, Informatics Division); *b* 30 Dec. 1960; *s* of Prof. James Durbin, *qv*; *m* 1996, Dr Julie Ahringer; one *s* one *d*. *Educ:* Highgate Sch.; St John's Coll., Cambridge (BA Maths 1982; PhD Biology 1987). Res. Fellow, King's Coll., Cambridge, 1986–88; Vis. Fellow, Stanford Univ., 1988–90; Staff Scientist, MRC Lab. of Molecular Biology, 1990–96. Member: Human Genome Org., 1994–; Sci. Cttee, UK BioBank, 2003–05. Mem., Internat. Soc. for Computational Biology, 2000–; FSS 2003. Mullard Medal, Royal Soc., 1994; Lord Lloyd of Kilgerran Award, 2004. *Publications:* (jtly) Biology Sequence Analysis, 1998; papers in jls on genomic and computational biology. *Recreation:* walking in wild places. *Address:* The Wellcome Trust Sanger Institute, The Wellcome Trust Genome Campus, Hinxton, Cambs CB10 1SA; *e-mail:* richard.durbin@sanger.ac.uk; 141 Huntingdon Road, Cambridge CB3 0DH.

DURELL, Prof. John Leonard, PhD; CPhys, FInstP; Professor of Nuclear Physics, since 1998, and Head, School of Physics and Astronomy, since 2004, University of Manchester; *b* 26 Oct. 1945; *s* of Leonard Joseph John Durell and Hilda Durell; *m* 1968, Susan Rolfe; two *d*. *Educ:* Beckenham Grammar Sch.; Univ. of Liverpool (BSc Hons; PhD 1970). CPhys, FInstP 1995. Royal Soc. Fellow, Max-Planck Inst., Heidelberg, 1970–71; University of Manchester: Lectr in Physics, 1971–82; Sen. Lectr, 1982–95; Reader in Physics, 1995–98; Hd, Dept of Physics and Astronomy, 2000–02; Dean, Faculty of Sci. and Engrg, 2002–04. Mem. Council, CCLRC, 2002–05. *Publications:* numerous papers in acad. jls. *Recreation:* birdwatching. *Address:* School of Physics and Astronomy, University of Manchester, Manchester M13 9PL. *T:* (0161) 306 9222; *e-mail:* john.durell@manchester.ac.uk.

DURHAM, 7th Earl of, *cr* 1833; **Edward Richard Lambton;** Baron Durham 1828; Viscount Lambton 1833; *b* 19 Oct. 1961; *o s* of Antony Claud Frederick Lambton, (Viscount Lambton), who disclaimed his peerages for life, and Belinda Bridget (*née* Blew-Jones); *S* father, 2006; *m* 1st, 1983, Christabel McEwen (marr. diss. 1995); one *s*; 2nd, 1995, Catherine (marr. diss. 2002), *e d* of D. J. V. Fitz-Gerald, *qv*. *Heir: s* Viscount Lambton, *qv*.

DURHAM, Bishop of, since 2003; **Rt Rev. (Nicholas) Thomas Wright,** DPhil, DD; *b* 1 Dec. 1948; *s* of Nicholas Irwin Wright and Rosemary (*née* Forman); *m* 1971, Margaret Elizabeth Anne Fiske; two *s* two *d*. *Educ:* Sedbergh Sch.; Exeter Coll., Oxford (BA 1st cl. Hons LitHum 1971; MA 1975; DPhil 1981; DD 2000); Wycliffe Hall, Oxford (BA 1st cl. Hons Theology 1973). Ordained deacon, 1975, priest 1976; Jun. Res. Fellow, 1975–78, Jun. Chaplain, 1976–78, Merton Coll., Oxford (Hon. Fellow, 2004); Fellow and Chaplain, Downing Coll., Cambridge, 1978–81 (Hon. Fellow, 2003); Asst Prof. of New Testament Studies, McGill Univ., Montreal, and Hon. Prof., Montreal Dio. Theol Coll., 1981–86; Lectr in Theology, Oxford Univ., and Fellow, Tutor and Chaplain, Worcester Coll., Oxford, 1986–93; Dean of Lichfield, 1994–99; Canon of Westminster, 2000–03. Fellow, Inst. for Christian Studies, Toronto, 1992–; Canon Theologian, Coventry Cathedral, 1992–99. Visiting Professor: Hebrew Univ., Jerusalem, 1989; Harvard Div. Sch., 1999; Gregorian Univ., Rome, 2002; Vis. Res. Fellow, Merton Coll., Oxford, 1999. Member: Doctrine Commn of C of E, 1979–81, 1989–95; Internat. Anglican Doctrinal and Theological Commn, 1991, 2001–; Lambeth Commn, 2004. Presenter, various radio and television series, 1996–: Jesus Then and Now, BBC1, 1996; presenter and writer: Resurrection, Channel 4, 2004; Spring Journey, Radio 3, 2004; Evil, Channel 4, 2005; participant, The Brains Trust, Radio 3, 1999–2002. Hon. DD: Aberdeen, 2001; Wycliffe Coll., Toronto, 2006; Nashotah House, Wisconsin, 2006; Durham, 2007; Hon. DLitt Gordon Coll., Mass, 2003. *Publications:* Small Faith, Great God, 1978; The Work of John Frith, 1983; The Epistles of Paul to the Colossians and to Philemon, 1987; (ed jtly) The Glory of Christ in the New Testament, 1987; (with S. Neill) The Interpretation of the New Testament 1861–1986, 1988; The Climax of the Covenant, 1991; New Tasks for a Renewed Church, 1992; The Crown and the Fire, 1992; The New Testament and the People of God, 1992; Who Was Jesus?, 1992; Following Jesus, 1994; Jesus and the Victory of God, 1996; The Lord and His Prayer, 1996; What Saint Paul Really Said, 1997; For All God's Worth, 1997; Reflecting the Glory, 1998; (with M. Borg) The Meaning of Jesus, 1999; The Myth of the Millennium, 1999; (ed jtly) Romans and the People of God, 1999; Holy Communion for Amateurs, 1999, reissued as The Meal Jesus Gave Us, 2002; The Challenge of Jesus, 2000; Twelve Months of Sundays, Year C, 2000; (with Paul Spicer) Easter Oratorio, 2000; Twelve Months of Sundays, Year A, 2001; Luke for Everyone,

2001; Mark for Everyone, 2001; Paul for Everyone: Galatians and Thessalonians, 2002; Matthew for Everyone, 2002; Paul for Everyone: the prison letters, 2002; John for Everyone, 2002; Twelve Months of Sundays, Year B, 2002; (contrib.) New Interpreters Bible, vol. X, 2002; The Contemporary Quest for Jesus, 2002; The Resurrection of the Son of God, 2003; Paul for Everyone: 1 Corinthians, 2003; Paul for Everyone: 2 Corinthians, 2003; Quiet Moments, 2003; Hebrews for Everyone, 2003; For All the Saints?, 2003; Paul for Everyone: the pastoral letters, 2003; Paul for Everyone: Romans, 2004; (ed jtly) Dictionary for Theological Interpretation of Scripture, 2005; Scripture and the Authority of God, 2005; Paul: fresh perspectives, 2005; The Scriptures, the Cross and the Power of God, 2005; Simply Christian, 2006; Evil and the Justice of God, 2006; (jtly) The Resurrection of Jesus: John Dominic Crossan and N. T. Wright in dialogue, 2006; Judas and the Gospel of Jesus, 2006; The Cross and the Colliery, 2007; Surprised by Hope, 2007; Acts for Everyone, 2008. *Recreations:* music, hill walking, poetry, golf. *Address:* Auckland Castle, Bishop Auckland, Co. Durham DL14 7NR. *T:* (01388) 602576, *Fax:* (01388) 605264; *e-mail:* bishops.office@durham.anglican.org; 14 High Newton Farm, Alnwick, Northumberland NE66 3ED. *T:* (01665) 576140, *Fax:* (01665) 576956.

DURHAM, Dean of; *see* Sadgrove, Very Rev. Michael.

DURHAM, Archdeacon of; *see* Jagger, Ven. I.

DURHAM, John Clive; HM Diplomatic Service, retired; Ambassador to Mongolia, 1997–99; *b* 12 July 1939; *s* of Fred Durham and Eva Lucy (*née* Sykes); *m* 1962, Sandra Kay, (Shan), Beaumont; one *s* one *d*. *Educ:* Castleford Grammar Sch.; Leeds Coll. of Commerce. Min. of Pensions and Nat. Insce, 1955–67; joined HM Diplomatic Service, 1967: FCO, 1967–69; 3rd Sec., Wellington, NZ, 1969–72; Vice-Consul, Mogadishu, 1972–74; seconded to DTI, 1974–77; 2nd, later 1st Sec. (Commercial), Khartoum, 1977–81; Consul (Commercial), Frankfurt, 1981–86; FCO, 1986–93; Consul-Gen., Brisbane, 1993–97. *Recreations:* fell walking, travel, genealogy, steam locomotion. *Address:* 31 Crescent Wood Road, SE26 6SA. *Club:* Royal Over-Seas League.

DURHAM, Kenneth John; Headmaster, University College School, since 1996; *b* 23 Oct. 1953; *s* of John Clifford Durham and Geraldine Mary Durham (*née* Trinder); *m* 1984, Vivienne Mary Johnson. *Educ:* St John's Sch., Leatherhead; Brasenose Coll., Oxford. St Albans Sch., 1975–87, Head of Econs, 1984–87; Head of Econs, 1987–92, Dir of Studies, 1991–96, King's Coll. Sch., Wimbledon. Chautauqua Bell Tower Scholarship to USA, ESU, 1989. *Publication:* The New City, 1992. *Recreations:* reading, theatre, music, film, walking, history of Polar exploration. *Address:* 5 Redington Road, Hampstead, NW3 7QX.

DURHAM HALL, Jonathan David; QC 1995; **His Honour Judge Durham Hall;** a Circuit Judge, since 2003; *b* 2 June 1952; *s* of Peter David Hall and Muriel Ann Hall, Sheffield; *m* 1973, Patricia Helen Bychowski (marr. diss. 1995), *d* of Stefan Bychowski, Whitehaven; one *s* one *d*; *m* 1996, J. Hilary Hart, GRSM, LRAM, *d* of late Edgar Alfred Hart, Hants. *Educ:* King Edward VII Sch., Sheffield; Nottingham Univ. (LLB Hons). Called to the Bar, Gray's Inn, 1975; joined North Eastern Circuit, 1976: Junior, 1982; Cryer, 1990–95; an Asst Recorder, 1991–95; a Recorder, 1995–2003. Head of Chambers, 1993–2003. Part-time Chm., Mental Health Review Tribunal, 2001–. Mem., Bar Council, 1994–95. Legal Assessor, GMC Professional Conduct Cttee, 2002–. *Recreations:* the creation and preservation of woodland, the plays of Shakespeare, all things Portuguese. *Address:* The Law Courts, Exchange Square, Bradford BD1 1JA.

DURIE, Andrew Maule D.; *see* Dewar-Durie.

DURIE, Sir David Robert Campbell, KCMG 2003 (CMG 1995); Chairman, Responsibility in Gambling Trust, 2004–06; *b* 21 Aug. 1944; *s* of late Frederick Robert Edwin Durie and Joan Elizabeth Campbell Durie (*née* Learoyd); *m* 1966, Susan Frances Weller; three *d*. *Educ:* Fettes Coll., Edinburgh; Christ Church, Oxford (MA Physics). Asst Principal, 1966, Pvte Sec. to Perm. Sec., 1970, Min. of Technology; Principal, DTI, 1971; First Sec., UK Delegn to OECD, 1974; Dept of Prices and Consumer Protection, 1977; Asst Sec., 1978; Dept of Trade, 1979; Cabinet Office, 1982; DTI, 1984; Under Sec., 1985–91; Dep. Sec., 1991; Minister and Dep. UK Perm. Rep. to EC/EU, Brussels, 1991–95; Dir Gen. (formerly Dep. Sec.), Enterprise and Regions, DTI, 1995–2000; Gov. and Comdr-in-Chief, Gibraltar, 2000–03. Mem., Lord Chancellor's Adv. Panel on Nat. Records and Archives, 2005–. CCMI (CIMgt 2000). FRSA 1996. KStJ 2000. Kt Comdr, Royal Order of Francis I, 2003. *Recreations:* moderately strenuous outdoor exercise, theatre, admiring my grandchildren. *Address:* 62 Burlington Avenue, Kew Gardens, Richmond, Surrey TW9 4DH.

DURIE, Thomas Peter, OBE 2003 (MBE 1958); GM 1951; Chairman, United Bristol Healthcare NHS Trust, 1991–94; *b* 1 Jan. 1926; *s* of Col Thomas Edwin Durie, DSO, MC, late RA and Madeleine Louise Durie; *m* 1st, 1952, Pamela Mary Bowlby (*d* 1982); one *s* one *d*; 2nd, 1983, Constance Christina Mary Linton. *Educ:* Fettes Coll.; Queen's Univ., Belfast. Commissioned RA 1945, served with RHA and Airborne Forces, India, Palestine, Cyprus, BAOR; Lt Col Directing Staff, Staff Coll., Camberley; retired 1964; Courage Ltd, 1964–86 (Main Bd Dir and Group Asst Man. Dir, 1974); Chm., Bristol & Weston DHA, 1986–90. University of Bristol: Mem. Court and Council, 1982–2001; Chm., Buildings Cttee, 1992–96; Pro-Chancellor, 1994–2004. Master, Soc. of Merchant Venturers, 1988–89. DL Avon, 1992–96, Somerset, 1996–2002. Hon. LLD Bristol, 2002. *Recreations:* gardening, music, ski-ing, tennis. *Address:* 2 Bells Walk, Wrington, Somerset BS40 5PU. *Club:* Army and Navy.

DURKAN, (John) Mark; MP (SDLP) Foyle, since 2005; Member (SDLP) Foyle, Northern Ireland Assembly, since 1998; Leader, Social Democratic and Labour Party, since 2001; *b* 26 June 1960; *s* of Brendan Durkan and Isobel Durkan (*née* Tinney); *m* 1993, Jackie Green; one *d*. *Educ:* St Columb's Coll., Derry; Queen's Univ., Belfast. Asst to John Hume, 1984–98. Mem. (SDLP) Derry CC, 1993–2000. Member: Forum for Peace and Reconciliation, Dublin, 1994–96; NI Forum (Talks Negotiator), 1996–98. Northern Ireland Assembly: Minister for Finance and Personnel, 1999–2001; Dep. First Minister, 2001–02; Chm., Cttee for Enterprise, Trade and Investment, 2007–. Chairperson, SDLP, 1990–95. *Address:* (office) 23 Bishop Street, Derry BT48 6PR. *T:* (028) 7136 0700, *Fax:* (028) 7136 0808.

DURKIN, Claire; Director, Europe and International Trade Policy, Department for Business, Enterprise and Regulatory Reform, since 2008; *b* 18 May 1956; *d* of Richard Durkin and Mollie (*née* Frazer); *m* 1990, Stephen Morgan. *Educ:* Liverpool Univ. (BA 1st cl. Hons); Univ. of Victoria, BC (MA); Wolverhampton Poly. (PGCE). Lectr, Further and Higher Educn, Vauxhall Coll., South Bank Polytech., 1982–88; Department of Employment: Principal, 1988–89; Private Secretary: to Minister for Employment, 1989–90; to Minister for Educn, 1990–91; Asst Dir, Labour Mkt Policies, 1991–95; Asst Dir Deregulation, Central Policy Unit, DTI, 1995–97; Asst Sec., 1997–98, Sec., 1998–2000, Low Pay Commn; Dir, Consumer and Competition Policies, 2000–02, Energy Innovation and Businesses, 2003–05, Energy Markets, 2005–08, DTI, subseq. BERR. *Recreations:* reading, walking the dog. *Address:* Department for Business Enterprise and Regulatory Reform, 1 Victoria Street, SW1H 0ET; *e-mail:* claire.durkin@berr.gov.uk.

DURLACHER, Nicholas John, CBE 1995; Chairman, Elexon Ltd, since 2000; *b* 2 March 1946; *s* of late John Sidney Durlacher, MC and of Alma Gabrielle (*née* Adams); *m* 1971, Mary Caroline Mclaren; one *s*. *Educ:* Stowe; Magdalene Coll., Cambridge (BA Econs). Mem., Stock Exchange, 1970–1986; Partner, Wedd Durlacher, 1972–86; Director: BZW Ltd, 1986–98; BZW Futures, 1986–96; U.F.J. Internat., 2002–04; Chairman: Ennismore Smaller Cos Fund, 1999–; EMX, 2000–07; BSC Co. Ltd, 2000–; Ffastfill, 2000–02. Dir, 1984–96, Chm., 1992–95, LIFFE; Dir, 1987–95, Chm., 1995–2001, SFA; Dir, Investor's Compensation Scheme, 1992–2001; Chm., Balancing and Settlement Code Panel, 2000–. Trustee and Dir, Brain and Spine Foundn, 1994–. *Recreations:* ski-ing, golf, tennis. *Address:* 10 Rutland Street, SW7 1EH. *Clubs:* White's; Hawks.

DURMAN, David John; Editor-in-Chief, IPC Magazines, 1994–99; *b* 10 July 1948; *s* of late John Durman and Joan Durman; *m* 1973, Hilary Pamela Aldrick. *Educ:* Leeds Univ. (BA). Editor, Woman, 1988–94; Dep. Editor, Woman's Own, 1992–94. Chm., BSME 1996. *Recreations:* reading, theatre, life. *Address:* c/o IPC Media, Blue Fin Building, 110 Southwark Street, SE1 0SU.

DURNING, Josephine Marie; independent consultant, since 2005; Co-Director, Europe and World Trade, Department of Trade and Industry, 2003–05; *b* 27 Aug. 1952; *d* of late Cecil and of Isobel M. Durning; *m* 1984, Paul Stephen Capella (*d* 2004); one *s* one *d*. *Educ:* Loreto Coll., St Albans; Univ. of Keele (BA Hons Eng. and Politics 1974). Entered CS as admin trainee, 1974; Private Sec. to Parly Under-Sec. of State, Dept of Employment, 1978–79; Sec. to HSE, 1982–85; Labour Attaché, Paris, 1985–89; Head of Sen. Mgt Support Unit, Dept of Employment, 1990–91; Head of Internat. and Gen. Policy, HSE, 1991–96; with Econ. and Domestic Secretariat, Cabinet Office, 1996–98; Dir, Transdept Gp, OST, 1998–2002, Head, Community Interest Company Team, 2002–03, DTI. FRSA 2000. *Recreation:* reading, riding. *Address:* The Paddox, Debden Road, Saffron Walden, Essex CB11 4AB.

DURR, Kent Diederich Skelton; consultant, and trustee of family trusts, since 2005; *b* 28 March 1941; *s* of Dr John Michael Durr and Diana (*née* Skelton); *m* 1966, Suzanne Wiese; one *s* two *d*. *Educ:* South African Coll. Schs; Cape Town Univ. Dir, family publishing co., 1966–68; Founder and later Man. Dir, Durr Estates, 1968–84. Elected to Provincial Council of Cape, 1974; MP for Maitland, SA, 1977–91; Dep. Minister, Trade and Industry, 1984–86, Finance, 1984–88; Minister of Budget and Public Works in Ministers' Council, 1988–89; Cabinet Minister of Trade and Industry and Tourism, 1989–91; S African Ambassador to UK, 1991–94; High Comr for S Africa in London, 1994–95; Chairman: Fuel-Tech NV, 1995–97; Clean Diesel Technologies, Inc, 1995–97; Commonwealth Investment Guarantee Agency Ltd, 1997–99; MP (African Christian Democratic Party) Western Cape Province, 1999–2005. Mem., SA Nat. Foundn for Conservation of Coastal Birds, 1985 (Award of Honour, 1987). Freeman: City of London, 1995; Vintners' Co., 1995. *Publications:* numerous articles in newspapers and jls on econs, foreign affairs, constitutional affairs, urban renewal, conservation and business. *Recreations:* history, field sports, conservation. *Address:* 7 Bosch Heuvel, Violet Road, Upper Claremont 7708, Cape Town, South Africa. *Club:* Kelvin Grove (Cape Town, SA).

DURRANDS, Prof. Kenneth James, CBE 1992; DGS (Birm), MSc, CEng, FIMechE, FIET; Vice-Chancellor and Rector, University of Huddersfield, 1992–95 (Rector, The Polytechnic, Huddersfield, 1970–92; Professor, 1985); *b* 24 June 1929; *s* of A. I. Durrands, Croxton Kerrial; *m* 1956 (marr. diss. 1971); one *s*; *m* 1983, Jennifer Jones; one *s*. *Educ:* King's Sch., Grantham; Nottingham Technical Coll.; Birmingham Univ. Min. of Supply Engrg Apprentice, ROF, Nottingham, 1947–52; Techn. Engr, UKAEA, Risley, 1954–58; Lecturer in Mechanical and Nuclear Engrg, Univ. of Birmingham, 1958–61; Head of Gen. Engrg Dept, Reactor Engrg Lab., UKAEA, Risley, 1961–67; Technical Dir, Vickers Ltd, Barrow Engrg Works, 1967–70. Vis. Lectr, Manchester Univ., 1962–68. Member: DoI Educn and Training Cttee, 1973–75 (Chm., 1975–80); DoI Garment and Allied Industries Requirements Bd, 1975–79 (Chm. Computer Cttee, 1975–79); BEC Educn Cttee, 1975–79; BEC Business Studies Bd, 1976–79; Inter-Univ. and Polytechnic Council, 1978–81; Yorks Consumers' Cttee, Office of Electricity Regulation, 1990–9; British Council: Higher Educn Cttee, 1981–91; Engrg and Technology Adv. Cttee, 1981–90; Cttee, CICHE, 1985–95; Council for the Accreditation of Teacher Educn, 1991–92; Hon. Sec./Treas., Cttee of Dirs of Polytechnics, 1970–79. Educn Comr, MSC, subseq. Training Commn, 1986–89. Mem. Council, IMechE, 1963–66. Preliminary Judge, Prince of Wales Award for Industrial Innovation and Production, 1982–9; Member, Court: Leeds Univ., 1970–95; Bradford Univ., 1973–95; Mem. Council, Barnsley Coll., 1996–2000; Governor, King's Sch., Grantham, 1999– (Vice-Chm. 2004–). Founder Chm., Assoc. of Lincs Sch. Governing Bodies, 2005–07 (Mem. Exec Cttee, 2005–; Mem., Lincs Schs' Forum, 2007–). *Publications:* technical and policy papers. *Recreations:* gardening, squash rackets. *Address:* Church Cottage, Croxton Kerrial, Grantham, Lincolnshire NG32 1PY. *Club:* Athenæum.

DURRANT, His Honour Anthony Harrisson; a Circuit Judge, 1991–99; *b* 3 Jan. 193; *s* of Frank Baston Durrant and Irene Maud Durrant; *m* 1956, Jacqueline Ostroumoff; one *s* two *d*. *Educ:* Sir Joseph Williamson's Mathematical Sch., Rochester. Admitted Solicitor 1956; Partner, 1960, Sen. Partner, 1976–91, Horwood & James, Aylesbury; a Recorder 1987–91. Dep. Chm., Agricl Land Tribunal, 1987–91. Pres., Berks, Bucks and Oxon Incorp. Law Soc., 1977–78; Chm., Berks, Bucks and Oxon Jt Consultative Cttee of Barristers and Solicitors, 1985–91.

See also A. J. Trace.

DURRANT, Jennifer Ann, RA 1994; painter; began living and working in Umbria 2000; *b* 17 June 1942; *d* of Caleb John Durrant and Winifred May (*née* Wright); *m* 196 William Alistair Herriot Henderson (marr. diss. 1976); *m* 2000, Richard Alban Howard Oxby. *Educ:* Varndean Grammar Sch. for Girls, Brighton; Brighton Coll. of Art; Slade Sch. of Fine Art; University Coll. London (Dip. Fine Art). FRCA 1993. Postgrad. Scholar Slade Sch. of Fine Art, 1965–66. Artist in Residence, Somerville Coll., Oxford, 1979–8 Part-time Lecturer: RCA, 1979–2000; Royal Acad. Schs, 1990–98. External Assessor Reading Univ. MA Fine Art, 1980s; Duncan of Jordanstone Coll. of Art, Univ. of Dundee, 1993–97; Limerick and Cork Colls of Art, 1998–2001; Falmouth Coll. of Art 1998–2002. *Solo exhibitions* include: Arnolfini Gall., Bristol, 1979; Mus. of Modern Art Oxford, 1980; Nicola Jacobs Gall., London, 1982 and 1983; Serpentine Gall., 198 Newlyn Orion Gall., Penzance, 1988; Concourse Gall., Barbican, 1992; Salander O'Reilly Galls, NY, 1993 and 2000; Francis Graham-Dixon Gall., London, 1996; Friends Room, Royal Acad., 1996 and 2005; Art First Contemporary Art, Cork St, 2005; *group exhibitions* include: Hayward Gall., 1976, 1979, 1980 and 1990; Mus. of Fine Art, Boston Mass and Royal Acad., 1977; Salander-O'Reilly Galls, NY, 1981; Tate Gall. and Carnegie Inst., Pittsburgh, 1982; Serpentine Gall., 1983 and 1984; Royal Acad., 1985; Mall Gall

London, 1990–92; also in provincial galls in UK, and in Europe; has exhibited at Royal Acad. Summer Exhibn, 1986, 1987 and annually, 1989–; *works in public collections* including: Arts Council, British Council; Contemporary Art Soc.; Mus. of Fine Arts, Boston, Mass; Tate Gall.; Govt Art Collection; Neue Galerie, Aachen; Trinity Coll., Cambridge; *commissions:* Newham Hosp.; R. P. Scherer 50th Anniv., Swindon, 1987; Thomas Neal, Covent Gdn, 1992; Glaxo UK, Stevenage, 1994. Arts Council Award, 1976; Arts Council Major Award, 1978; Gtr London Arts Assoc. Award, 1980; Athena Art Award, 1988; Artist of the Year, Independent on Sunday, 1996. *Recreations:* classical music, opera, archaeology, museums, painting and sculpture, the natural world. *Address:* La Vigna, Via Bondi 14, 06069 Tuoro-sul-Trasimeno (PG), Italy. *T:* and *Fax:* (075) 829010.

DURRANT, Sir William (Alexander Estridge), 8th Bt *cr* 1784, of Scottow, Norfolk; *b* 26 Nov. 1929; *o s* of Sir William Henry Estridge Durrant, 7th Bt and Georgina Beryl Gwendoline (*d* 1968), *d* of Alexander Purse; *S* father, 1994; *m* 1953, Dorothy, *d* of Ronal Croker, Quirindi, NSW; one *s* one *d*. *Heir: s* David Alexander Durrant [*b* 1 July 1960; *m* 1st, 1989, Maria Lucia Leonard (marr. diss. 2002); three *s*; 2nd, 2006, Mary Josephine]. *Address:* Red Hill, Nundle Road, Nemingha, NSW 2340, Australia.

DURRINGTON, Prof. Paul Nelson, MD; FRCP, FRCPath, FMedSci; Professor of Medicine, University of Manchester, since 1995; Hon. Consultant Physician, Manchester Royal Infirmary, since 1982; *b* 24 July 1947; *s* of Alec Edward Durrington and May Ena Durrington (*née* Nelson); *m* 1969, Patricia Joyce Gibbs; one *s* two *d*. *Educ:* Chislehurst and Sidcup Grammar Sch. for Boys; Univ. of Bristol (BSc Hons Physiol. 1969; MB ChB 1972; MD 1978). MRCP 1975, FRCP 1987; MRCPath 1982, FRCPath 1994. Hse Officer and SHO appts in medicine, paediatrics and surgery, Bristol, 1972–76; Lectr, 1976–82, Sen. Lectr, 1982–92, Reader, 1992–95, in Medicine, Univ. of Manchester. Travelling Fellow, BHF and Amer. Heart Assoc. (Vis. Prof., Div. of Metabolism, Dept of Medicine, UCSD), 1979–80. Dir, R&D, Central Manchester Healthcare NHS Trust, 1997–2001. Med. Dir, Family Heart Assoc., 1995–. Chm., British Hyperlipidaemia Assoc., 1992–95. Mem., Assoc. of Physicians of GB and Ireland, 1992. FMedSci 2001; Fellow, Amer. Heart Assoc. 2001. *Publications:* Hyperlipidaemia, Diagnosis and Treatment, 1989, 2nd edn 1995; Pocketbook of Preventative Cardiology, 1993, 2nd edn 2001; (with A. Sniderman) Hyperlipidaemia, 2000, 2nd edn 2002; contrib. articles on lipid metabolism, diabetes and coronary heart disease to learned jls. *Recreations:* angling (Mem., Prince Albert Angling Soc.), hill-walking, cartology. *Address:* Cardiovascular Research Group, Division of Cardiovascular and Endocrine Sciences, Core Technology Facility (3rd Floor), University of Manchester, 46 Grafton Street, Manchester M13 9NT. *T:* (0161) 275 1200, *Fax:* (0161) 275 1183; *e-mail:* pdurrington@manchester.ac.uk.

DURWARD, (Alan) Scott; Director, 1985–91, and Group Chief Executive, 1989–91, Alliance & Leicester Building Society; Chairman, Girobank Plc, 1990–91; *b* 30 Aug. 1935; *o c* of late Prof. Archibald Durward, MD and Dorothy Durward; *m* 1962, Helen Gourlay; two *s*. *Educ:* Stowe; St John's Coll., Cambridge (MA). Imperial Tobacco Co. Ltd, 1958–65; Rowntree & Co. Ltd, 1965–67; Cheltenham & Gloucester Bldg Soc., 1967–75; Leicester Building Society: Dep. Gen. Man., 1975–77; Gen. Man., 1977–81; Dir and Chief Gen. Man., 1981–85; merger with Alliance Bldg Soc. to form Alliance & Leicester Bldg Soc., 1985; Jt Chief Gen. Manager, 1985–86; Chief Gen. Manager, 1986–89. Chm., Midland Assoc. of Bldg Socs, 1984–85; Member: Council, Bldg Socs Assoc., 1981–85 and 1987–91; Council, Eur. Fedn of Bldg Socs, 1987–91. Director: Gourlay Properties, 1985–99; John Laing plc, 1987–89; Mem. Bd, BR (London Midland), 1990–92. Dir, Leics Ambulance and Paramedic Service NHS Trust, 1993–99. General Comr for Income Tax, 1994–. Chm., Peterborough Diocesan Bd of Finance, 1993–2003. Mem. Council, Loughborough Univ. of Technology, 1984–97 (Treas., 1991–97). JP Leicester, 1999–2004. *Recreations:* tennis, fishing. *Club:* Oxford and Cambridge.

du SAUTOY, Prof. Marcus Peter Francis, DPhil; Professor of Mathematics, University of Oxford, since 2002; Fellow, Wadham College, Oxford, since 2005; *b* 26 Aug. 1965; *s* of Bernard and Jennifer du Sautoy; *m* 1994, Shani Ram; one *s* twin *d* (and one *s* decd). *Educ:* Gillotts Comprehensive Sch., Henley-on-Thames; King James Sixth Form Coll., Henley-on-Thames; Wadham Coll., Oxford (BA Hons Maths 1986); DPhil Oxon 1989. SERC Postdoctoral Res. Fellow, QMW, Univ. of London, 1989–90; Postdoctoral Res. Fellow, All Souls Coll., Oxford, 1990–95; Royal Society University Research Fellow: Univ. of Cambridge, 1995–2001; Univ. of Oxford, 2001–05. Christmas Lectr, Royal Instn, 2006. BBC presenter: Mindgames, 2004–05; Music of the Primes, 2005; The Story of Maths, 2008. Berwick Prize, LMS, 2001. *Publications:* The Music of the Primes, 2003, 6th edn 2007; Finding Moonshine: a mathematician's journey through symmetry, 2008. *Recreations:* No 17 for Recreativo Hackney FC, playing the trumpet, theatre. *Address:* Wadham College, Oxford OX1 3PN; *e-mail:* dusautoy@maths.ox.ac.uk.

DUTHIE, Prof. Sir Herbert Livingston, Kt 1987; MD; FRCS, FRCSEd; Provost of the University of Wales College of Medicine (formerly the Welsh National School of Medicine, University of Wales), 1979–94; *b* 9 Oct. 1929; *s* of Herbert William Duthie and Margaret McFarlane Livingston; *m* 1959, Maureen McCann; three *s* one *d*. *Educ:* Whitehill Sch., Glasgow; Univ. of Glasgow (MB, ChB 1952; MD Hons 1962; ChM Hons 1959). FRCSEd 1956; FRCS 1957. Served RAMC, 1954–56. Sen. House Officer, Registrar, and Lectr in Surgery, Western Infirmary, Glasgow, 1956–59; Rockefeller Travelling Fellow, Mayo Clinic, Rochester, Minn, USA, 1959–60; Lectr in Surg., Univ. of Glasgow, 1960–61; Sen. Lectr in Surg., Univ. of Leeds, 1961–63, Reader, 1964; Prof. of Surg., Univ. of Sheffield, 1964–79 (Dean, Faculty of Medicine, 1976–78). Mem., S Glam HA, 1980–94. Chm., Med. Adv. Cttee, CVCP, 1992–93. President: Surgical Res. Soc., 1978–80; Assoc. of Surgeons of GB and Ireland, 1989–90; Member: GMC, 1976–99 (Treas., 1981–94); Welsh Med. Cttee, 1980–94. Hon. LLD: Sheffield, 1990; Wales, 1995. *Publications:* articles on gastroenterological topics. *Address:* 1 The Malverns, Malvern Place, Cheltenham GL50 2JL. *T:* (01242) 583938. *Club:* Army and Navy.

DUTHIE, Sir Robert Grieve, (Sir Robin), Kt 1987; CBE 1978; CA; Vice Chairman, Advisory Board for Scotland, BP, 1990–2002; *b* 2 Oct. 1928; *s* of George Duthie and Mary (*née* Lyle); *m* 1955, Violetta Noel Maclean; two *s* one *d*. *Educ:* Greenock Academy. Apprentice Chartered Accountant with Thomson Jackson Gourlay & Taylor, CA, 1946–51 (CA 1952); joined Blacks of Greenock, 1952: Man. Dir, 1962; Chairman: Black & Edgington Ltd, 1972–83; Insight Internat. Tours Ltd, 1979–94; Bruntons (Musselburgh), 1984–86; Britoil, 1988–90; Tay Residential Investment Ltd, 1989–96; Neill Clerk Gp plc, 1994–98; Director: British Assets Trust, 1977–98; Royal Bank of Scotland, 1978–99; Investors Capital Trust, 1985–94; Carclo Engineering Gp, 1986–98; British Polythene Industries (formerly Scott & Robertson), 1989–99; Devol Engineering Ltd, 1994–2004. Chm., Greenock Provident Bank, 1974; Dir, Greenock Chamber of Commerce, 1967–68; Tax Liaison Officer for Scotland, CBI, 1976–79. Chm., SDA, 1979–88; Member: Scottish Telecommunications Bd, 1972–77; E Kilbride Develt Corp., 1976–78; Clyde Port Authority, 1971–83 (Chm., 1977–80); Council, Inst. of Chartered Accountants of Scotland, 1973–78; Scottish Econ. Council, 1980–95; Council, Strathclyde Business Sch., 1986–94; Governing Council, Scottish Business in the Community, 1987–95. Chm., Made Up Textiles Assoc. of GB, 1972; Pres., Inverkip Soc., 1966; Mem. of Council, Royal Caledonian Curling Club, 1985–88. Commissioner: Queen Victoria Sch., Dunblane, 1972–89; Scottish Congregational Ministers Pension Fund, 1973–2003; Treasurer, Greenock W URC, 1970–. Fellow, Scottish Vocational Council, 1988. CCMI (CBIM 1976); FRSA 1983. Hon. FRIAS, 1989. Hon. Fellow, Paisley Coll., 1990. Hon. LLD Strathclyde, 1984; Hon. DTech Napier Coll., 1989. *Recreation:* golf. *Address:* Fairhaven, Finnart Street, Greenock PA16 8JA. *T:* (01475) 722642.

DUTTON, Maj.-Gen. Bryan Hawkins, CB 1997; CBE 1990 (OBE 1984; MBE 1978); Director-General, Leonard Cheshire Disability (formerly Leonard Cheshire Foundation), since 1998; *b* 1 March 1943; *s* of late Ralph Dutton and Honor Badcoe (formerly Dutton, *née* Morris); *m* 1972, Angela Margaret Wilson; one *s* one *d*. *Educ:* Lord Weymouth Sch.; RMA Sandhurst. Commissioned, Devonshire and Dorset Regt, 1963; served NI, British Guiana, Libya, Belize, Germany, UK; Instructor, Sch. of Infantry, 1969–71; RMCS and Staff Coll., 1974–75; C-in-C's Mission to Soviet Forces in Germany, 1976–78; Co. Comdr, 1st Devonshire and Dorset, 1978–79 (despatches 1979); Planning Staff, NI Office, 1979–81; Instructor, Staff Coll., 1981–82; MA to Adjutant-Gen., 1982–84; CO 1st Bn Devonshire and Dorset Regt, 1984–87; Ops Staff, UKLF, 1987; Comdr 39 Infantry Brigade, 1987–89; Dir, Public Relations (Army), 1990–92; Dir of Infantry, 1992–94; Comdr British Forces, Hong Kong, 1994–97. Col Comdt, POW Div., 1996–99; Col, Devonshire and Dorset Regt, 1998–2003. Chm., Voluntary Orgns Disability Gp, 2004–. Gov., Hayes Dashwood Foundn, 1999–. FRSA; CCMI. *Recreations:* offshore sailing, fishing, wild-life, Rugby spectator, history, classical music. *Address:* (office) 30 Millbank, SW1P 4QD. *Club:* Army and Navy.

DUTTON, Lt-Gen. James Benjamin, CBE 2003; Deputy Commander International Security and Assistance Force, Afghanistan, since 2008; *b* 21 Feb. 1954; *s* of Edgar and Aileen Dutton; *m* 1978, Elizabeth Waddell; one *s* one *d*. *Educ:* King's Sch., Chester; City Univ., London (BSc Hons (Systems and Mgt)); RCDS. Joined RM, 1972; COS, 3 Commando Bde, 1991–93; Comdr, RM Officers' Trng, 1993; Asst Dir, Jt Warfare, MoD, 1996; CO, 40 Commando, 1996–98; Dir, NATO Policy, MoD, 1998–2000; seconded to Jt Staff, Pentagon, 2001–02; Comdr, 3 Commando Bde, 2002–04; Comdr Multinat. Div. SE and GOC British Forces Iraq, 2005; Comdt Gen., Royal Marines, and Comdr, UK Amphibious Forces, 2004–06; COS (Capability) to C-in-C Fleet, 2006–07; Dep. Chief of Jt Ops (Ops), later COS (Ops), MoD, 2007–08. *Recreations:* sailing, running. *Address:* Permanent Joint Headquarters, Sandy Lane, Northwood, Middlesex HA6 3HP.

DUTTON, Prof. P(eter) Leslie, FRS 1990; Professor of Biochemistry and Biophysics, since 1981 (Chairman, Department of Biochemistry and Biophysics, since 1994), and Director, Johnson Foundation for Molecular Biophysics, since 1991, University of Pennsylvania; *b* 12 March 1941; *s* of Arthur Bramwell Dutton and Mary Dutton; *m* 1965, Dr Julia R. Dwyer; two *s* one *d*. *Educ:* Univ. of Wales (BSc Hons Chem.; PhD Biochem.). PD Fellow, Dept of Biochem. and Soil Science, Univ. of Wales, 1967–68; University of Pennsylvania: PD Fellow, 1968–71, Asst Prof., 1971–76, Johnson Res. Foundn; Associate Prof., Dept of Biochem. and Biophysics, 1976–81; Hon. MA 1976. *Recreations:* painting (several one-man and group shows in Wales and USA), sailing. *Address:* Department of Biochemistry and Biophysics, University of Pennsylvania, Stellar-Chance Building, Suite 1005, 422 Curie Boulevard, Philadelphia, PA 19104–6059, USA. *T:* (215) 8980991, *Fax:* (215) 5732235; 654 West Rose Tree Road, Media, PA 19063, USA. *Clubs:* Mantoloking Yacht (NJ); Corinthian Yacht (Philadelphia).

DUTTON, Roger Thomas; His Honour Judge Dutton; a Circuit Judge, since 1996; *b* 24 March 1952; *s* of Donald Roger Dutton and Doreen May Dutton (*née* Ankers); *m* 1977, Elaine Alison Dixon; one *s* two *d*. *Educ:* Acton Sch., Wrexham; Grove Park Grammar Sch., Wrexham; Univ. of Kent (BA Hons Law 1973); Inns of Court Sch. of Law. Called to the Bar, Middle Temple, 1974; in practice at the Bar, 1974–96; Mem., Wales and Chester Circuit. Asst Recorder, 1988–92; Recorder, 1992–96; Liaison Judge, N Wales Magistrates, 1998–2007, Macclesfield, Crewe and Nantwich Magistrates, 2007–; Disciplinary Investigating Judge, 2007–; Interviewing Judge for Judicial Appts Commn. Circuit Rep., Cttee of Council of HM's Circuit Judges, 2004–05 (Hon. Treas., 2005–). Mem., Tutor Judge Panel, Judicial Studies Bd, 2007–. Former Mem. Bd. Govs, N Wales Inst. of Higher Educn. *Recreations:* golf, walking, travel, gardening, watching cricket, soccer, Rugby Union. *Address:* The Crown Court, The Castle, Chester CH1 2AN. *T:* (01244) 317606. *Clubs:* Lansdowne; Chester City; Wrexham Golf.

DUTTON, Timothy James; QC 1998; a Recorder, since 2000; *b* 25 Feb. 1957; *s* of J. D. Dutton, MA, JP and J. R. Dutton (*née* Parsons); *m* 1987, Sappho Raschid-Dias; one *d*. *Educ:* Repton Sch.; Keble Coll., Oxford (BA Jurisp. 1978). Called to the Bar, Middle Temple, 1979, Bencher, 2003; an Asst Recorder, 1998–2000. Leader, SE Circuit, 2004–06. Advocacy teaching, for Nat. Inst. for Trial Advocacy and the Bar, UK and USA, 1987–. Chm., Inns of Court Advocacy Trng Cttee, 2000–; Bar Council: Vice-Chm., Direct Access Cttee, 2001–03; Chm., Wkg Party into Advocacy Trng, 2002–; Vice-Chm., Educn and Trng Cttee, 2003–; Vice-Chm., 2007; Chm., 2008. Member: Admin. Law Bar Assoc.; Commercial Bar Assoc. *Publications:* contribs to Lloyds List, Financial Times, (on insce law) World Policy Review Guide. *Recreations:* music (French Horn), sailing. *Address:* Fountain Court Chambers, Temple, EC4Y 9DH. *T:* (020) 7583 3335.

DUTTON, Prof. William Harold, PhD; Professor of Internet Studies, University of Oxford, and Director, Oxford Internet Institute, since 2002; Fellow, Balliol College, Oxford, since 2002; *b* 23 Aug. 1947; *s* of Paul V. Dutton and Rosa Lee Dutton; *m* 1981, Diana; two *d*. *Educ:* Univ. of Missouri, Columbia (BA Hons Pol Sci. 1969); State Univ. of NY, Buffalo (MA 1971; PhD Pol Sci. 1974); MA Oxon 2002. Instructor, Dept of Pol Sci., SUNY, Buffalo, 1972–73; Asst Prof., Dept of Pol Sci., Univ. of S Florida, 1973–74; Asst Res. Pol Scientist, Public Policy Res. Orgn, Univ. of Calif, Irvine, 1974–78; Associate Prof., Sch. of Public Admin and Urban Studies, San Diego State Univ., 1978–80; Annenberg School for Communication, University of Southern California: Associate Prof., 1980–82; Associate Prof. (with tenure), 1983–89; Prof., 1990–2002. Vis. Res. Pol Scientist, Univ. of Calif, Irvine, 1979–82; Brunel University: Fulbright Schol. and Vis. Prof., Dept of Human Scis, 1986–87; Nat. Dir, Prog. on Inf. and Communication Technol., ESRC and Vis. Prof., Dept of Human Scis, 1993–95. *Publications:* (jtly) The Management of Information Systems, 1981; (jtly) Computers and Politics: high technology in American local governments, 1982; (with K. L. Kraemer) Modeling as Negotiating: the political dynamics of computer models in the policy process, 1985; (ed jtly) Information and Communication Technologies: visions and realities, 1996; (ed jtly) The Social Shaping of the Information Superhighway: European and American roads to the information society, 1997; Society on the Line: information politics in the digital age, 1999; (ed jtly) Digital Academe, 2002; Social Transformation in the Information Society, 2004; (ed jtly) Transforming Enterprise, 2005; contrib. chapters in books; contrib. articles to professional jls incl. Prometheus, Information, Communication & Society. *Recreations:* jogging, surfing, piano. *Address:* Oxford Internet Institute, University of Oxford, 1 St Giles, Oxford OX1 3JS. *T:* (01865) 287210, *Fax:* (01865) 287211; *e-mail:* william.dutton@oii.ox.ac.uk.

DUVAL, Robin Arthur Philip, CBE 2005; Director, British Board of Film Classification, 1999–2004; *b* 28 April 1941; *s* of Arthur and Jane Duval; *m* 1968, Lorna Eileen Watson; four *d* (one *s* decd). *Educ:* King Edward's Sch., Birmingham; University Coll. London (BA); Univ. of Michigan. Studio manager, BBC, 1964–65; TV producer, J. Walter Thompson, 1965–68; documentary and film producer, COI, 1968–78; Hd, Overseas Prodn, COI, 1978–81; Principal, Home Office, 1981–83; Hd, UK Prodn, COI, 1983–85; Chief Asst, Television, IBA, 1985–90; Dep. Dir, Programmes, ITC, 1991–98. *Recreations:* music, food, Aston Villa.

DUVALL, Leonard, OBE 1998; Member (Lab) Greenwich and Lewisham, London Assembly, Greater London Authority, since 2000; Chairman, Metropolitan Police Authority, since 2004; *b* 26 Sept. 1961; *m* (marr. diss.); two *s*. *Educ:* Hawthorn Sch., London. Mem., Greenwich LBC, 1990–2000 (Leader of Council, 1992–2000). Chairman: London Thames Gateway Partnership, 1997–2000; Local Govt Improvement and Develt Agency, 1998–2000; Dep. Chm., Assoc. of London Govt, 1996–2000; Chm., Commonwealth Local Govt Forum, 2000–05 (Vice-Chm., 1998–2000). Vice-Chm., London Develt Agency, 2000–03; Chm., London Health Commn, 2002–04. Chm., Gtr London Lab. Party, 2002–. Non-exec. Dir, Tilfen Land, 2001–. Trustee, Greenwich Foundn for Old Royal Naval Coll., 1997–2002; non-exec. Dir, Royal Artillery Museums Trust, 1998–. *Address:* Greater London Authority, City Hall, Queen's Walk, SE1 2AA. *T:* (020) 7983 4408/4517.

DUXBURY, Philip Thomas; Chairman, Bradford and Bingley Building Society, 1988–91; *b* 4 Sept. 1928; *s* of Tom Duxbury and Ellen Duxbury (*née* Hargreaves); *m* 1952, Katherine Mary Hagley; three *s*. *Educ:* Bradford Grammar School. Magnet and Southerns plc, 1944–84 (Dir, 1963; Man. Dir, 1975); Dir, Bradford and Bingley Building Soc., 1980–91. *Recreations:* DIY, travel. *Address:* Highfield House, East Morton, Keighley BD20 5SE. *T:* (01274) 564894.

DUXFIELD, Julian; Human Resources Director, Cash Division, Group 4 Securicor, since 2007; *b* 9 Sept. 1962; *s* of John and Wendy Duxfield; partner Lucie Carrington; two *s* one *d*. *Educ:* Corpus Christi Coll., Oxford (BA PPE); London Sch. of Econs (MSc HR Mgt). HR rôles in Unilever, 1988–2000; HR Dir, Carlsberg UK, 2000–03; Dir, Human Resources, DfT, 2003–07. Member: Climbers' Club; Fell and Rock Climbing Club. *Recreation:* mountaineering. *Address:* Group 4 Securicor, Sutton Park House, 15 Carshalton Road, Sutton, Surrey SM1 4LD; *e-mail:* Julian.duxfield@uk.g4s.com.

DWEK, Prof. Raymond Allen, DPhil, DSc; FRS 1998; CChem, FRSC; CBiol, FIBiol; Professor of Glycobiology, and Director of Glycobiology Institute (formerly Unit), University of Oxford, since 1988; Professorial Fellow, Exeter College, Oxford, since 1988 (Fellow, 1974–88); *b* 10 Nov. 1941; *s* of Victor Joe Dwek and Alice Liniado; *m* 1964, Sandra (*née* Livingstone); two *s* two *d*. *Educ:* Carmel Coll.; Manchester Univ. (BSc 1st Cl. Hons Chemistry and Mercer Scholar, 1963; MSc 1964); Lincoln Coll., Oxford (DPhil 1966; Hon. Fellow 2004); Exeter Coll., Oxford (DSc 1985). CChem, FRSC 1993; CBiol, FIBiol 1999. Oxford University: Deptl Demonstrator, 1969–74; Lectr, 1976–88; Associate Hd, 1996–2000, Head, 2000–06, Biochem. Dept; Royal Soc. Locke Res. Fellow, 1974–76; Christ Church: Res. Lectr in Physical Chemistry, 1966–68, in Biochem., 1975–76; Lectr in Inorganic Chem., 1968–75; Lectr in Biochem., Trinity Coll., 1976–84. Vis. Royal Soc. Res. Fellow, Weizmann Inst., Rehovot, Israel, 1969; Kluge Chair of Technol. and Soc., Liby of Congress, Washington, 2007; Visiting Professor: Duke Univ., NC, seconded to Inst. of Exploratory Res., Fort Monmouth, NJ, 1968; Univ. of Trieste, Italy, 1974; Univ. of Lund, Sweden, 1977; Inst. of Enzymology, Budapest, 1980. Boyce Thompson Dist. Lectr in Glycobiology, Cornell Univ., USA, 1997. Dir and Founding Scientist, Oxford GlycoScience (formerly Oxford GlycoSystems) Ltd, 1988–2003; Chm., Oxford University Consulting Ltd, 2000–02; Director: United Therapeutics, 2002–; Isis Innovation, 2003–. Member: Oxford Enzyme Gp, 1971–88; MRC AIDS Antiviral Steering Cttee, 1987–89; Founder Mem., Oxford Oligosaccharide Gp, 1983. Mem., Bd of Scientific Governors, 2003–, and Inst. Prof., Scripps Res. Inst., La Jolla; Special Advr on Biotechnol. to Pres., Ben Gurion Univ. of the Negev, 2001–. Pres., Inst. Biol., 2008–. Hon. FRCP. Foreign Mem., Amer. Philosophical Soc., 2007. Mem., editl bds. Wellcome Trust Award, for research in biochemistry related to medicine, 1994. Hon. Dr Leuven, 1996; Hon. PhD Ben Gurion Univ. of Negev, 2001; Hon. DSc Scripps Res. Inst., USA, 2004; Dr *hc* Cavsa Cluj, Romania, 2006. First Scientific Leadership Award, Hepatitis B Foundn, Philadelphia, 1997; Centennial Award, Delaware Valley Coll., Penn, 1997; Huxley Medal, Inst. Biol., 2007. Comdr, Nat. Order for Merit (Romania), 2000. *Publications:* Nuclear Magnetic Resonance (NMR) in Biochemistry, 1973; (jtly) Physical Chemistry Principles and Problems for Biochemists, 1975, 3rd edn 1983; (jtly) NMR in Biology, 1977; (jtly) Biological Spectroscopy, 1984; articles in books and jls on physical chemistry, biochemistry and medicine; various patents. *Recreations:* family, Patent Law, sport, listening to music. *Address:* Exeter College, Oxford OX1 3DP. *T:* (01865) 275344; Glycobiology Institute, Department of Biochemistry, University of Oxford, South Parks Road, Oxford OX1 3QU.

DWIGHT, Reginald Kenneth; *see* John, Sir E. H.

DWORKIN, Prof. Gerald; Herbert Smith Professor of European Law and Director, Centre of European Law, King's College, University of London, 1993–97, now Professor Emeritus; Director, Intellectual Property Academy, Singapore, 2003–05; *b* 8 July 1933; *s* of Louis and Rose Dworkin; *m* 1960, Celia Sharon Levin; two *s* one *d*. *Educ:* Raines Grammar Sch., London; Univ. of Nottingham (LLB 1954). Admitted solicitor of Supreme Court, 1957; Asst Lectr, Lectr, then Reader, LSE, 1958–67; Prof. of Law, Univ. of Southampton, 1968–86; Herchel Smith Prof. of Intellectual Property Law, QMW, Univ. of London, 1986–92. Visiting Professor: Univ. of Monash, 1965–67, 1980, 1987; Univ. of NSW, 1975; Nat. Univ. of Singapore, 1985, 1991, 1997; Arizona State Univ., 1985. Mem., EC Cttee, Academic Experts on Copyright Law. Member: Council, Intellectual Property Inst. (formerly Common Law Inst. of Intellectual Property); Brit. Literary and Artistic Copyright Soc.; Law Soc. Sub-cttee on Intellectual Property. Chm., British Copyright Council. FRSA 1993. Member of Board: Mod. Law Rev.; European Intellectual Property Law Rev.; Intellectual Property Jl. *Publication:* (with R. Taylor) Guide to Copyright Law, 1989. *Address:* Rosebery, 7A Branksome Wood Road, Bournemouth, Dorset BH2 6BT. *T:* (01202) 555522.

See also P. D. Dworkin.

DWORKIN, Paul David, FSS; an Assistant Director, Central Statistical Office, 1989–91; *b* 7 April 1937; *s* of Louis and Rose Dworkin; *m* 1959, Carole Barbara Burke; two *s*. *Educ:* Hackney Downs Grammar Sch., London; LSE (BScEcon 1958). FSS 1969. E Africa High Commn, Dar es Salaam, Tanganyika, 1959; E African Common Services Org., Nairobi, Kenya, 1961; Asst Statistician, BoT, 1962, Stat. 1965; Chief Statistician: DTI, 1972; Dept of Employment, 1977; Under Secretary: Depts of Trade and Industry, 1977–81; Central Statistical Office, 1982–83; Dir of Stats, Dept of Employment, 1983–89. *Recreation:* bowling. *Club:* Civil Service.

See also G. Dworkin.

DWORKIN, Prof. Ronald Myles, FBA 1979; Bentham Professor of Jurisprudence University College London, since 2004 (Quain Professor of Jurisprudence, 1998–2004); 11 Dec. 1931; *s* of David Dworkin and Madeline Talamo; *m* 1958, Betsy Celia Ross (2000); one *s* one *d*. *Educ:* Harvard Coll.; Oxford Univ.; Harvard Law Sch. Legal Sec. t Judge Learned Hand, 1957–58; Associate, Sullivan & Cromwell, New York, 1958–6; Yale Law School: Associate Prof. of Law, 1962–65; Prof. of Law, 1965–68; Wesley N Hohfeld Prof. of Jurisprudence, 1968–69; Prof. of Jurisprudence, Oxford Univ., 1969–9 now Emeritus; Fellow of UC, Oxford, 1969–98, now Emeritus. Vis. Prof. of Philosophy Princeton Univ., 1974–75; Prof. of Law, 1975–, Sommer Prof. of Law and Philosophy 1984–, NY Univ. Law Sch.; Prof.-at-Large, Cornell Univ., 1976–80; Vis. Prof. o Philosophy and Law, Harvard Univ., 1977, Vis. Prof. of Philosophy, 1979–82. Membe Council, Writers & Scholars Educnl Trust, 1982–; Programme Cttee, Ditchley Found 1982–. Co-Chm., US Democratic Party Abroad, 1972–76. Fellow, Amer. Acad. of Ar and Scis, 1979. Hon. QC 1998; Hon. Fellow, UCL, 2004. Hon. Bencher, Midd Temple, 1999. *Publications:* Taking Rights Seriously, 1977; (ed) The Philosophy of Lav 1977; A Matter of Principle, 1985; Law's Empire, 1986; Philosophical Issues in Seni Dementia, 1987; A Bill of Rights for Britain, 1990; Life's Dominion, 1993; Freedom Law, 1996; Sovereign Virtue, 2000; Justice in Robes, 2005; Is Democracy Possible Here 2006; several articles in legal and philosophical jls. *Address:* 17 Chester Row, SW1W 9J *Club:* Oxford American Democrats (Oxford).

DWYER, Aileen Margaret; *see* Keel, A. M.

DWYER, Glenn N.; *see* Neil-Dwyer.

DWYER, Sir Joseph (Anthony), Kt 2001; FREng; Group Chairman, George Wimpe PLC, 1996–99 (Director, 1988; Group Chief Executive Officer, 1991–98); *b* 20 Jun 1939. CEng, FREng (FEng 1997); FICE, FCIOB. President: CIOB, 1998–99; IC 2000–01. Dir, ETB, 2001–02. Chairman: Liverpool Vision (Urban Regeneration Co. 1999–; Construction for Merseyside Ltd, 2004–. Hon. Fellow, Liverpool John Moor Univ., 2003. Hon. LLD Liverpool, 2002; Hon. DSc Nottingham, 2004. *Address:* Waysid 24B Westcliffe Road, Southport, Merseyside PR8 2BU.

DYCHE, Dame Rachael (Mary), DBE 1997 (CBE 1992); Regional Director, Midland Conservative Party, 1993–98; *b* 29 Nov. 1945; *d* of George Henry Dyche and late Doree Mary Dyche (*née* Rudgard). *Educ:* Burton upon Trent Tech. High Sch. Conservativ Party: Agent: Burton, 1968–72; Harwich, 1972–75; Deputy Central Office Agent: Wale 1975–76; W Midlands, 1976–85; Wessex, 1985–88; Central Office Agent, E Midland 1988–93. Mem., Nat. Soc. Cons. and Unionist Agents, 1968–. Member: PCC, All Sain Lubenham, 2003– (Asst Church Warden, 2004–07; Church Warden, 2007–); Village Ha Cttee, Lubenham, 1999–; Heritage Gp, Ludenham, 2001–. *Recreations:* golf, gardenin music. *Address:* 11 Acorn Close, Lubenham, Market Harborough, Leics LE16 9SP. (01858) 432379.

DYE, Maj.-Gen. Jack Bertie, CBE 1968 (OBE 1965); MC 1945; Vice Lord-Lieutena of Suffolk, 1983–94; Director, Volunteers, Territorials and Cadets, 1971–74; Majo General late Royal Norfolk Regiment; *b* 13 Dec. 1919. Served War of 1939–45 (MC Brigadier, 1966; idc, psc. Commanded South Arabian Army, 1966–68; GOC Easte District, 1969–71. Col Comdt, The Queen's Division, 1970–74; Col, Royal Anglia Regt, 1976–82 (Dep. Col, 1974–76). DL Suffolk, 1979.

DYE, Air Vice-Marshal Peter John, OBE 1992; CEng; Head of Collocate Headquarters, since 2006, and of RAF Transformation, since 2007; *b* 17 Aug. 1953; *s* Roy Mackenzie Dye and Margaret Mary Dye (*née* Chauffourier); *m* 1985, Anne Catheri Waine; two *d*. *Educ:* Sevenoaks Sch.; Imperial Coll., Univ. of London (BSc Eng 1975 RAF Coll., Cranwell. CEng 1898; MRAeS 1989. Commnd RAF, 1972; served U Germany and Canada; Sen. Engrg Officer, No IX Sqdn, 1986–88; OC Engrg and Supp Wing, RAF Coltishall, 1990–91; PSO AOC-in-C, RAF Support Comd, 1991–94 ar AOC-in-C, Logistics Comd, 1994; Dir, Dept of Specialist Ground Trng, 1994–96; rc 1997; AO Wales, 1999–2001; Air Cdre Ground Trng, 2001–05; Dep. C-in-C, Personn and Trng Comd, and COS to Air Mem. for Personnel, 2005–07; Hd, RAF Process ar Orgn Rev., 2006–07. ACGI 1975. Pres., Cross and Cockade, First World War Aviatic Histl Soc. *Publications:* articles and reviews. *Recreations:* aviation history, archaeolog *Address:* c/o Air Command, RAF High Wycombe, Bucks HP14 4UE. *T:* (0149 496644. *Club:* Royal Air Force.

DYER, Alexander Patrick; Chief Executive and Deputy Chairman, BOC Group p 1993–96; Deputy Chairman, Bunzl plc, 1996–2005 (Chairman 1993–96); *b* 30 Aug. 193 *m* 1954, Shirley Shine; one *s* (and one *s* decd). *Educ:* US Military Acad. (BSc Engrg Harvard Business Sch. (MBA). US Army, 1954–57; Esso Corp., 1959–63; Air Produc 1963–89; Gp Vice Pres., Gases, 1978–87; Exec. Vice Pres., Gas and Equipment, 1987–8 Bd Dir, 1988–89; Man. Dir, Gases, BOC Gp, 1989–93. *Recreations:* golf, skeet. *Addre* 1803 Apple Tree Lane, Bethlehem, PA 18105, USA. *Clubs:* University (New York Saucon Valley Country; Gulf Stream Golf, Gulf Stream Bath and Tennis; Weyhill Ske Blooming Grove Hunting and Fishing; Ocean (Florida).

DYER, Charles; playwright and novelist; actor-director (as Raymond Dyer); *b* 7 Ju 1928; *s* of James Sidney Dyer and Florence (*née* Stretton); *m* 1959, Fiona Thomson, actre three *s*. *Educ:* Queen Elizabeth's Sch., Barnet. *Plays:* Clubs Are Sometimes Trumps, 194 Who On Earth!, 1951; Turtle in the Soup, 1953; The Jovial Parasite, 1954; Single Tick Mars, 1955; Time, Murderer, Please, and Poison In Jest, 1956; Wanted—One Body 1958; Prelude to Fury, 1959 (also wrote theme music); Rattle of A Simple Man, 1962 (al in Berlin, Paris, NY, Rome and London), 1981, 2004, USA, 1985, 1990, Netherland 1988, Germany, 1993, Scandinavia, 1993, 1995; Staircase, 1966 (for RSC; also in N Paris (1968, 1982, 1986, 1992), Amsterdam, Berlin, Rome, 1988, 1992, Vienna, Braz 1992, trans-Germany, 1992–95); Mother Adam, Paris, Berlin, 1970, London, 1971, 197 NY, 1974; The Loving Allelujah, 1974; Circling Dancers, 1979; Lovers Dancing, 198 1983; Futility Rites, 1981; as R. Kraselchik: Red Cabbage and Kings, 1960 (also wrc theme music); *screenplays:* Rattle, 1964; Insurance Italian Style, 1967; Staircase, 196 Brother Sun and Sister Moon, 1970. Also directed plays for the stage and television. *Act* in 230 plays and films; London début as Duke in Worm's Eye View, Whitehall, 1948; *fil* include: Cuptie Honeymoon, 1947; Britannia Mews, 1949; Road Sense, 1950; Off T Record, 1952; Pickwick Papers, 1952; Dockland Case, 1953; Strange Case of Blond 1953; Naval Patrol, 1959; Loneliness of the Long Distance Runner, 1962; Mouse On T Moon, 1962; Knack, 1964; Rattle of A Simple Man, 1964; How I Won The War, 196 Staircase, 1968; *television:* Charlie in Staircase, BBC, 1986; *television series:* Hugh and 1964. *Publications:* (as Charles Dyer): plays: Wanted—One Body!, 1961; Time, Murdere Please, 1962; Rattle Of A Simple Man, (Fr.) 1963; Staircase, 1966; Mother Adam, 197 The Loneliness Trilogy, 1972; Hot Godly Wind, 1973; novels: Rattle Of A Simple Ma 1964; Charlie Always Told Harry Almost Everything, 1969 (USA and Europe, 1970); T Rising of our Herbert, 1972; Wilderness of Monkeys (autobiog.), 2005. *Recreation* amateur music and carpentry. *Address:* Old Wob, Austenwood Common, Gerrards Cro Bucks SL9 8SF.

DYER, Prof. Christopher Charles, CBE 2008; PhD; FBA 1995; FSA; Professor of Regional and Local History, University of Leicester, since 2001; *b* 24 Dec. 1944; *s* of Charles James Dyer and Doris Mary Dyer; *m* 1967, Jenifer Ann Dent; one *s* one *d*. *Educ:* Univ. of Birmingham (BA, PhD). Asst Lectr in History, Univ. of Edinburgh, 1967–70; Lectr, Sen. Lectr, then Reader, 1970–90, Prof. of Medieval Social History, 1991–2001, Univ. of Birmingham. Ford Lectr in Medieval Hist., Oxford Univ., 2000–01. President: Soc. for Medieval Archaeology, 1998–2001; Bristol and Glos Archaeol Soc., 2001–02; British Agricl Hist. Soc., 2004–07. Chairman: Victoria County History Cttee, 1997–2004; Dugdale Soc., 2003–; Records of Social and Economic History Cttee, British Acad., 2004–. FSA 1994; AcSS 2006. *Publications:* Lords and Peasants in a Changing Society, 1980; Standards of Living in the later Middle Ages, 1989; Everyday Life in Medieval England, 1994; Making a Living in the Middle Ages 850–1520, 2002; An Age of Transition, 2005. *Address:* Centre for English Local History, University of Leicester, Marc Fitch House, 5 Salisbury Road, Leicester LE1 7QR. *T:* (0116) 252 2762.

DYER, Sir Henry Peter Francis S.; *see* Swinnerton-Dyer.

DYER, James Archibald Thomson, OBE 2003; FRCPsych; Scottish Parliamentary Standards Commissioner, since 2003; Medical Member, Mental Health Tribunal for Scotland, since 2005; *b* 31 Dec. 1946; *s* of Rev. Thomas James Dyer, MA and Mary Watt Dyer; *m* 1969 (marr. diss. 1994); two *s* one *d*; *m* 1994, Suzanne Paula Whitaker; one step *s* two step *d*. *Educ:* Bo'ness Acad.; Robert Gordon's Coll., Aberdeen; Univ. of Aberdeen (MB ChB Hons 1970). FRCPsych 1992. Various trng posts in psychiatry, Royal Edinburgh Hosp., 1972–77; SO, MRC Unit for Epidemiological Studies in Psychiatry, 1977–81; Consultant Psychiatrist, Royal Edinburgh Hosp. and Hon. Sen. Lectr in Psychiatry, Univ. of Edinburgh, 1981–91; Medical Comr, 1991–2003, and Dir, 1993–2003, Mental Welfare Commn for Scotland. FRSA 2000; FFCS 2001. *Publications:* contrib. book chapters; contrib. articles and res. papers on parasuicide and suicide, schizophrenia, mental health services, mental health law and psychological aspects of nuclear war. *Recreations:* reading, photography, Radio 4, swimming. *Address:* Scottish Parliament, Edinburgh EH99 1SP. *T:* (0131) 348 6666; *e-mail:* standards.commissioner@scottish.parliament.uk.

DYER, Lois Edith, OBE 1984; FCSP; international physiotherapy consultant; *b* 18 March 1925; *d* of Richard Morgan Dyer and Emmeline Agnes (*née* Wells). *Educ:* Middlesex Hospital. FCSP 1986. Variety of posts as physiotherapist in Britain, Southern, Central and North Africa, 1948–71; extensive travel world wide, visiting and lecturing at national and internat. conferences. First Physiotherapist Member, NHS Health Adv. Service, 1971; first Advr in Physiotherapy, DHSS, 1976–85. Mem., Camden (formerly Hampstead) CHC, 1996–2001. First non-medical Chm., Chartered Society of Physiotherapy, 1972–75; Founder Mem., Soc. for Res. in Rehabilitation, 1978–; Hon. Life Vice-Pres., S African Soc. of Physiotherapy. Editor-in-Chief, Physiotherapy Practice, 1985–90. CMLJ 2001. *Publications:* Care of the Orthopaedic Patient (jtly), 1977; numerous papers in professional jls. *Recreations:* music, country pursuits, bird watching, bridge, ecology, wildlife, conservation. *Address:* Garden Flat, 6 Belsize Grove, NW3 4UN. *T:* (020) 7722 1794.

DYER, His Honour Mark; a Circuit Judge, 1977–96; a Senior Circuit Judge, 1996–2001; *b* 20 Nov. 1928; *er s* of late Maj.-Gen. G. M. Dyer, CBE, DSO, and Evelyn Mary (*née* List); *m* 1953, Diana, *d* of Sir Percy Lancelot Orde, CIE; two *d*. *Educ:* Ampleforth Coll.; Christ Church, Oxford (MA). 2nd Lieut, Royal Scots Greys, 1948–49; The Westminster Dragoons (2nd CLY) TA, 1950–58, Captain. Called to the Bar: Middle Temple, 1953; Inner Temple, 1972, Bencher, 1998; part-time Lectr in Law, Univ. of Southampton, 1957–67; Dep. Chm., Isle of Wight QS, 1971; a Recorder of the Crown Court, 1972–77; Liaison Judge for Wiltshire, 1981; Hon. Recorder: Devizes, 1988; Bristol, 1996–2001. Mem., Parole Bd, 1992–96, 2002–05. Member: Gen. Council of the Bar, 1965–69; Judicial Studies Bd, 1986–91. Pres., Council of HM Circuit Judges, 1992 (Hon. Sec., 1989–91). FRSA 1994. Hon. LLD UWE, 2001. *Recreation:* enjoying retirement. *Address:* The Court Service, 2nd Floor, Southside Offices, Law Courts, Winchester, Hants SO23 9DL. *Club:* Cavalry and Guards.

DYER, Nigel Ingram John; QC 2006; *b* 21 Sept. 1957; *s* of Derek Ingram Dyer and Elizabeth Dyer; *m* 1986, Victoria Duckham; one *s* one *d*. *Educ:* St Mary's Sch., Nairobi; Oratory Sch.; Durham Univ. (BA Jt Hons Law and Politics). Called to the Bar, Inner Temple, 1982; Mem., Western Circuit. Member: President's Ancillary Relief Adv. Gp, Family Div., 2000–05; Money and Property Cttee, Family Justice Council, 2005–. Fellow, Internat. Acad. Matrimonial Lawyers, 2006. *Publication:* (ed jtly) Rayden and Jackson on Divorce and Family Matters, 18th edn 2005. *Recreations:* gardening, opera, theatre. *Address:* 1 Hare Court, Temple, EC4Y 7BS. *T:* (020) 7797 7070, *Fax:* (020) 7797 7435; *e-mail:* dyer@1hc.com. *Clubs:* Hurlingham, MCC; Rye Tennis.

DYER, Dr Richard George, OBE 2007; Chief Executive, Biosciences Federation, since 2006; *b* 18 July 1943; *s* of late Comdr Charles William Dyer, RN and Dorothy Patricia Victoria Vaughan-Hogan; *m* 1st, 1967, Shirley James Foulsham (marr. diss. 1995); two *s* one *d*; 2nd, 2000, Dr Caroline Edmonds (*née* Porter); one *d*. *Educ:* Churcher's Coll., Petersfield; Univ. of London (BSc 1967); Univ. of Birmingham (MSc 1968); Univ. of Bristol (PhD 1972). Research, Dept of Anatomy, Bristol Med. Sch., 1968–74; ARC Institute of Animal Physiology, subseq. AFRC Institute of Animal Physiology and Genetics Research, then Babraham Institute: Head, Dept of Neuroendocrinology, 1985–90; Head, Cambridge Station, 1989–90; Associate Dir of Inst., 1991–93; Exec. Dir, 1993–94; Dir, 1994–2005. Teacher of Physiol., Jesus Coll., Cambridge, 1977–90; Res. Fellowships, Germany and France; Consultant for WHO, Shanghai, 1983–86. Member: AFRC Animals Res. Bd, 1992–93; AFRC Strategy Bd, 1993; BBSRC Animal Sci. and Psych. Cttee, 1994–96; Cttee, R&D Soc., 1998–2000; European Science Foundation: Member: Life and Envmtl Scis Standing Cttee, 1995–2000; Eur. Medical Res. Councils, 1996–2000; Exec. Bd, 1999–; Chm., Finance and Audit Cttee, 2004–; Vice-Pres., 2004–. Member, Board: Babraham Bioscience Technologies Ltd, 1998– (Chm., 2000–); Univ. of Cambridge Challenge, then Venture, Fund, 1999–2004. Medal, Soc. for Endocrinology, 1986; Medal, Polish Physiol. Soc., 1987. Former Member, Editorial Board: Exptl Brain Res.; Jl of Endocrinology. *Publications:* (ed with R. J. Bicknell) Brain Opioid Systems in Reproduction, 1989; numerous papers on neuroendocrine topics in learned jls. *Recreations:* finding bargains, escaping to mountains and sea, lively dinners. *Address:* Biosciences Federation, PO Box 502, Cambridge CB1 0AL.

DYET, Fergus John C.; *see* Cochrane-Dyet.

DYKE; *see* Hart Dyke.

DYKE, Gregory; Chairman: HIT Entertainment Ltd, since 2005; Brentford Football Club, since 2006; British Film Institute, since 2008; *b* 20 May 1947; *s* of Joseph and Denise Dyke; partner, Sue Howes; one *s* one *d*; one step *s* one step *d*. *Educ:* Hayes Grammar Sch.; York Univ. (BA Politics). Varied career, 1965–83; Editor in Chief, TV-am, 1983–84; Dir of Programmes, TVS, 1984–87; London Weekend Television: Dir of Progs, 1987–91; Dep. Man. Dir, 1989–90; Man. Dir, subseq. Gp Chief Exec., 1990–94; Chm., GMTV, 1993–94; Director: Channel Four Television, 1988–92; BSkyB, 1995; Chm. and Chief Exec., Pearson Television, 1995–99; Exec. Dir, Pearson plc, 1996–99; Chm., Channel 5 Broadcasting, 1997–99; Dir-Gen., BBC, 2000–04. Non-exec. Dir, ITN, 1990–92. Chm., ITV Council, 1992–94. Non-executive Director: Manchester United FC, 1997–99; ProSiebenSat.1 Media AG, 2004–. Chancellor, York Univ., 2004–. Trustee: Science Museum, 1996–2005; English Nat. Stadium Trust, 1997–99. *Publication:* Inside Story (memoirs), 2004. *Recreations:* football, tennis, horse-riding, movies, theatre. *Address:* PO Box 49142, London SW19 5XH.

DYKES, family name of **Baron Dykes**.

DYKES, Baron *cr* 2004 (Life Peer), of Harrow Weald in the London Borough of Harrow; **Hugh John Maxwell Dykes;** *b* 17 May 1939; *s* of Richard Dykes and Doreen Ismay Maxwell Dykes; *m* 1965, Susan Margaret Dykes (*née* Smith) (marr. diss. 2000); two *s* (and one *s* decd). *Educ:* Weston super Mare Grammar Sch.; Pembroke Coll., Cambridge. Partner, Simon & Coates, Stockbrokers, 1968–78; Associate Mem., Quilter, Hilton, Goodison, Stockbrokers, 1978. MSI, 1993. Dir, Dixons Stores Far East Ltd, 1985. Contested (C) Tottenham, 1966. MP (C) Harrow East, 1970–97; contested (C) same seat, 1997; joined LibDem party, 1997; contested (Lib Dem) London Region, Eur. Parly elecns, 1999. PPS: to three Parly Under-Secs of State for Defence, 1970; to Parly Under-Sec. of State in Civil Service Dept attached to Cabinet Office, 1973; Mem., H of C EEC Select Cttee, 1983–97. Mem., European Parlt, Strasbourg, 1974–77; Chairman: Cons. Parly European Cttee, 1979–80 (Vice-Chm., 1974–79); Commons Euro-Gp, 1988–97; Vice-Pres., Cons. Gp for EEC, 1982–86 (Chm., 1978–81). Chm., European Movement, 1990–97 (Jt Hon. Sec., 1982–87). Mem., Lib Dem Team on EU, Foreign Affairs and Defence Policy, 1997–2004; Lib Dem spokesman on EU, H of L, 2005–. Research Sec., Bow Gp, 1965; Chm., Coningsby Club, 1969. Governor: Royal Nat. Orthopaedic Hosp., 1975–82; N London Collegiate Sch., 1982. Order of Merit (Germany), 1993; Médaille pour l'Europe (Luxembourg), 1993; Chevalier: Ordre National du Mérite (France), 1994; Légion d'Honneur (France), 2003. *Publications:* (ed) Westropp's "Invest £100", 1964, and Westropp's "Start Your Own Business", 1965; many articles and pamphlets on political and financial subjects. *Recreations:* music, theatre, swimming, travel, gardening. *Address:* House of Lords, SW1A 0PW. *Clubs:* Garrick, Beefsteak.

DYKES, David Wilmer, MA, PhD; Director, National Museum of Wales, 1986–89; *b* 18 Dec. 1933; *s* of late Captain David Dykes, OBE and Jenny Dykes; *m* 1967, Margaret Anne George; two *d*. *Educ:* Swansea Grammar Sch.; Corpus Christi Coll., Oxford (MA); PhD (Wales). FRNS 1958 (Parkes-Weber Prize, 1954); FRSAI 1963; FRHistS 1965; FSA 1973. Commnd RN and RNR, 1955–62. Civil Servant, Bd of Inland Revenue, 1958–59; administrative appts, Univ. of Bristol and Univ. Coll. of Swansea, 1959–63; Dep. Registrar, Univ. Coll. of Swansea, 1963–69; Registrar, Univ. of Warwick, 1969–72; Sec., Nat. Museum of Wales, 1972–86, Acting Dir, 1985–86. Hon. Lectr in History, University Coll., Cardiff, later Univ. of Wales Coll. of Cardiff, 1975–95. Pres., British Numismatic Soc., 1999–2003 (Mem. Council, 1966–70 and 1997–). Liveryman: Worshipful Co. of Tin Plate Workers, 1985; Welsh Livery Guild, 1993; Freeman, City of London, 1985. KStJ 1993 (CStJ 1991; Chancellor, Priory for Wales, 1991–98; Bailiff of St Davids, 1999–2002). *Publications:* Anglo-Saxon Coins in the National Museum of Wales, 1977; (ed and contrib.) Alan Sorrell: Early Wales Re-created, 1980; Wales in Vanity Fair, 1989; The University College of Swansea: an illustrated history, 1992; The Eighteenth Century Token, 2007; articles and reviews in numismatic, historical and other jls. *Recreations:* numismatics, writing, gardening. *Address:* 3 Peverell Avenue East, Poundbury, Dorchester, Dorset DT1 3RH. *Clubs:* Athenæum; Cardiff and County (Cardiff).

DYKES, Richard Thornton Booth; Chairman, Carrenza Ltd, since 2001; *b* 7 April 1945; *s* of Alan Thornton Dykes and Myra McFie Dykes (*née* Booth); *m* 1970, Janet Rosemary Cundall (marr. diss. 1995); one *s*. *Educ:* Rossall Sch. Articled clerk, Dehn & Lauderdale, solicitors, 1965–67; EO, later HEO, Min. of Labour, 1967–73; Private Sec. to Sec. of State for Employment, 1974–76; Principal, Econ. Policy Div., Dept of Employment, 1976–77; Dir, Industrial Relns, British Shipbuilders, 1977–80; Non-exec. Dir, Austin & Pickersgill Ltd, Sunderland, 1979–80; Principal Private Sec. to Sec. of State for Employment, 1980–82; Department of Employment: Hd, Unemployment Benefit Service, 1982–85; Sec., Sen. Mgt Gp, 1985–86; Hd, Inner Cities Central Unit, 1986; Post Office Counters Ltd: Gen. Manager for Gtr London, 1986–87; Dir of Ops, 1987–92; Man. Dir, 1993–96; Gp Man. Dir, Royal Mail, and Exec. Bd Mem., The Post Office, later Consignia plc, 1996–2001. Non-exec. Dir, Employment Service, 1998–2002. Member: Forensic Sci. Service Adv. Bd, Home Office, 1991–98; EDC, BITC, 1994–2003; Design Council, 1994–2001; Chm., HSC and DTLR Work-related Road Safety Task Gp, 2000–01. *Recreations:* travel, hill-walking. *Address:* The Old Rectory, Upper Slaughter, Glos GL54 2JB.

DYKSTRA, Ronald Gerrit Malcolm; Senior Partner, Addleshaw Sons & Latham, solicitors, 1987–94, retired; *b* 4 March 1934; *s* of Gerrit Abe Dykstra and Margaret Kirk Dykstra (*née* McDonald); *m* 1st, 1960, Jennifer Mary Cramer (marr. diss. 1985); three *s*; 2nd, 1986, Sonia Hoole. *Educ:* Edinburgh Academy. Admitted Solicitor, 1957; Asst Solicitor, 1957, Partner, 1961, Addleshaw Sons & Latham, Manchester. Mem., Wilmslow Green Room Soc. *Recreations:* swimming, cycling, amateur drama, walking, sailing. *Address:* 7 Racecourse Road, Wilmslow, Cheshire SK9 5LF. *T:* (01625) 525856.

DYLAN, Bob; *see* Zimmerman, R. A.

DYMOCK, Vice Adm. Sir Anthony Knox, KBE 2008; CB 2003; UK Military Representative to NATO, 2006–08; *b* 18 July 1949; *s* of Richard Challis Dymock and Irene Mary Dymock (*née* Knox); *m* 1977, Elizabeth Mary Frewer; one *s* one *d*. *Educ:* Brighton, Hove and Sussex Grammar Sch.; Univ. of E Anglia (BA Hons Russian and Philosophy). MNI 1992. BRNC, 1969–70; served: HMS Yarmouth, 1972–74; HMS Brighton, 1974; HMS Antrim, 1981–83 (Falklands War); i/c HMS Plymouth, 1985–88; MoD, Whitehall, 1989–91; HMS London, 1991–92 (Gulf War); i/c HMS Campbeltown, 1992–93; MoD Naval Staff, 1993–96; i/c 2nd Frigate Sqdn, HMS Cornwall, 1996–98; Dep. Comdr, UK Task Gp (HMS Invincible), Gulf and Kosovo, 1998–99; Dep. Comdr, Striking and Support Forces Southern Region, 2000–02; Defence Attaché and Hd of British Defence Staff, Washington, 2002–05. FRSA 2005. Member: RYA; RNSA. *Publications:* contribs to Naval Rev. *Recreations:* sailing, ski-ing.

DYMOKE, Lt-Col John Lindley Marmion, MBE 1960; Vice Lord-Lieutenant of Lincolnshire, 1991–2001; 34th Hereditary Queen's Champion, 1946; *b* 1 Sept. 1926; *s* of late Lionel Marmion Dymoke and Rachel, *d* of Hon. Lennox Lindley; *m* 1953, Susan Cicely Fane; three *s*. *Educ:* Christ's Hosp. Commnd Royal Lincs Regt, 1946; Staff Coll., 1957; Armed Forces Staff Coll., USA, 1964; Coll. Chief Instructor, RMA Sandhurst, 1961–64; Comd 3rd Bn, Royal Anglian Regt, 1966–69; military service included: India, Sumatra, Malaya, Egypt, Jordan, Aden, France, Germany, USA and UK; retired 1972. Farmer and landowner, 1972–. Mem., E Lindsey DC, 1973–99. President: Lincs Br., CLA, 1995–2002 (Chm., 1982–85); Lincs Agricl Soc., 1995. Chm., Horncastle Grammar Sch., 1979–91. Master, Grocers' Co., 1977–78. DL 1976, High Sheriff 1979, Lincs.

Recreation: care of Scrivelsby Estate. *Address:* Scrivelsby Court, near Horncastle, Lincolnshire LN9 6JA. *T:* (01507) 523325.

DYNEVOR, 9th Baron *cr* 1780; **Richard Charles Uryan Rhys;** *b* 19 June 1935; *s* of 8th Baron Dynevor, CBE, MC; *S* father, 1962; *m* 1959, Lucy (marr. diss. 1978), *d* of Sir John Rothenstein, CBE; one *s* three *d*. *Educ:* Eton; Magdalene Coll., Cambridge. *Heir: s* Hon. Hugo Griffith Uryan Rhys, *b* 19 Nov. 1966.

DYSART, Countess of (12th in line) *cr* 1643; **Katherine Grant of Rothiemurchus;** Lady Huntingtower, 1643; *b* 1 June 1918; *yr d* of Owain Greaves and Wenefryde Agatha Greaves (*née* Scott), Countess of Dysart (10th in line); *S* sister, 2003; *m* 1941, Colonel John Peter Grant of Rothiemurchus, MBE (*d* 1987); one *s* one *d*. *Educ:* Oxenfoord Castle, Ford, Midlothian. Wartime ambulance driver, 1939–41. WRVS; Red Cross Rep.; SSAFA Rep. *Heir: s* Lord Huntingtower, *qv*. *Address:* Rothiemurchus, Aviemore PH22 1QR. *T:* (01479) 810357. *Clubs:* Royal Over-Seas League; Royal Overseas (Edinburgh).

DYSON, Prof. Freeman John, FRS 1952; Professor, School of Natural Sciences, Institute for Advanced Study, Princeton, New Jersey, 1953–94, Professor Emeritus since 1994; *b* 15 Dec. 1923; *s* of late Sir George Dyson, KCVO; *m* 1st, 1950, Verena Esther (*née* Huber) (marr. diss. 1958); one *s* one *d*; 2nd, 1958, Imme (*née* Jung); four *d*. *Educ:* Winchester; Cambridge; Cornell University. Operational research for RAF Bomber Command, 1943–45. Fellow of Trinity Coll., Cambridge, 1946–50, Hon. Fellow, 1989; Commonwealth Fund Fellow at Cornell and Princeton, USA, 1947–49; Mem. of Institute for Advanced Study, Princeton, USA, 1949–50; Professor of Physics, Cornell Univ., Ithaca, NY, USA, 1951–53. Mem. of National Academy of Sciences (USA), 1964; For. Associate, Acad. des Scis, Paris, 1989. Gifford Lectr, Aberdeen, 1985; Radcliffe Lectr, Oxford, 1990. Lorentz Medal, Royal Netherlands Acad. of Sciences, 1966; Hughes Medal, Royal Soc., 1968; Max Planck Medal, German Physical Soc., 1969; Templeton Prize, 2000. *Publications:* Disturbing the Universe, 1979; Weapons and Hope, 1984; Origins of Life, 1986; Infinite in All Directions, 1988; From Eros to Gaia, 1991; Imagined Worlds, 1997; The Sun, the Genome and the Internet, 1999; The Scientist as Rebel, 2006; A Many-Colored Glass, 2007; contrib. to The Physical Review, Annals of Mathematics, etc. *Address:* School of Natural Sciences, Institute for Advanced Study, Einstein Drive, Princeton, NJ 08540, USA.

DYSON, Sir James, Kt 2007; CBE 1998; RDI 2005; FREng; FCSD; Founder and Chairman, Dyson Ltd (formerly Prototypes Ltd, then Dyson Research), since 1992; *b* 2 May 1947; *s* of late Alec Dyson and Mary (*née* Bolton); *m* 1967, Deirdre Hindmarsh; two *s* one *d*. *Educ:* Gresham's Sch.; Royal Coll. of Art (MDes). FCSD 1996; FREng 2005. Dir, Rotork Marine, 1970–74 (design and manufacture of Sea Truck high speed landing craft); Man. Dir, Kirk-Dyson, 1974–79 (design and manufacture of Ballbarrow wheelbarrow); developed and designed Dyson Dual Cyclone vacuum cleaner, 1979–93, Contrarotator washing machine, 2000, Dyson Digital Motor, 2004, Airblade Handrier, 2006. Mem., Design Council, 1997–; Chm., Design Mus., 1999–2004. Mem. Council, RCA, 1998– (Ext. Examr, 1993–96). Trustee, Roundhouse Th., London. Estabd James Dyson Foundn (Registered Charity), 2002. Dyson vacuum cleaners on permanent display in museums: Sci. Mus., V&A and Design Mus., London; MOMA, NY; Boymans Mus., Rotterdam; Powerhouse Mus., Sydney; San Francisco Mus. of Modern Art; Mus. of Scotland; Design Mus., Zurich; Mus. für angewandte Kunst, Germany. Hon. FRIBA 2006. Hon. doctorates: Oxford Brookes, 1997; Brunel, 1999; RCA, Bath, 2000; Imperial Coll. London, 2001. Awards incl.: Design and Innovation Award for Ballbarrow, Building Design, 1976; Internat. Design Fair Prize, Japan, 1991; Minerva Award, CSD, 1995; Gerald Frewer Trophy, Inst. Engrg Designers, 1996; Industrial Design Prize of America, 1996; Eversheds Grand Prix Trophy, Design Council, 1996; European Design Prize, EC, 1997; Prince Philip's Designers Prize; European Design Prize, 1997; French Oscar, Livre Mondial des Inventions, 1997; Gold Award, Industrial Design Promotion Orgn, Japan, 1999; Gal. Lafayette Prix Innovation-Design, France, 1999; Mingay Most Innovative Product Award, Australia, 2000; Lord Kilgerran Prize, Royal Soc.; Queen's Award for Innovation, 2003; Giant of Design, USA, 2004; Queen's Award for Export, 2006. *Publications:* Doing a Dyson, 1996; Against the Odds (autobiog.), 1997; History of Great Inventions, 2001. *Recreations:* running, garden design, bassoon, opera, tennis. *Address:* Tetbury Hill, Malmesbury, Wilts SN16 0RP. *T:* (01666) 828282. *Club:* Chelsea Arts.

DYSON, John Alva, MVO 1995; HM Diplomatic Service, retired; Ambassador to Montenegro, 2006–07; *b* 15 April 1949; *s* of Louis and Myrtle Dyson; *m* 1971, Deirdre Anne George; two *s*. *Educ:* Devonport High Sch., Plymouth. Entered HM Diplomatic Service, 1966; served Port of Spain, Geneva, Yaoundé, Tehran, Nuku'alofa, Kathmandu, Jedda, Cape Town, Havana, and Damascus; Chargé d'Affaires, Asmara, 2001–02; Deputy High Commissioner: Suva, 2002–03; Bandar Seri Begawan, 2003; Dep. COS, CPA (S) Basra, 2003–04; FCO, 2004–06. *Recreations:* archery, diving, tennis. *Address:* 28 Harrogate Road, Caversham, Reading RG4 7PN. *T:* (0118) 946 4873; *e-mail:* dysfam@beeb.net. *Club:* Civil Service.

DYSON, Rt Hon. Sir John (Anthony), Kt 1993; PC 2001; **Rt Hon. Lord Justice Dyson;** a Lord Justice of Appeal, since 2001; Deputy Head of Civil Justice, 2003–06; *b* 31 July 1943; *s* of late Richard Dyson and Gisella Dyson; *m* 1970, Jacqueline Carmel Levy; one *s* one *d*. *Educ:* Leeds Grammar Sch.; Wadham Coll., Oxford (Open Classics Scholar; MA; Hon. Fellow, 2001). Harmsworth Law Scholar, 1968, called to Bar, Middle Temple, 1968, Bencher, 1990; QC 1982; a Recorder, 1986–93; a Judge of the High Court of Justice, QBD, 1993–2001; Presiding Judge, Technology and Construction Court, 1998–2001. Dep. Chm., Civil Justice Council, 2003–06. Mem., Civil Procedure Rule Cttee, 2002–06. Member: Council of Legal Educn, 1992–96; Judicial Studies Bd, 1994–98. Vis. Prof., Queen Mary, Univ. of London, 2007–. Hon. Fellow: Soc. of Advanced Legal Studies, 1998–; Hebrew Univ. of Jerusalem, 2004. *Recreations:* piano playing, singing, gardening, walking. *Address:* Royal Courts of Justice, Strand, WC2A 2LL.

DYSON, John Michael; Chief Master of the Supreme Court of Judicature (Chancery Division), 1992–98 (a Master, 1973–98); a Recorder, 1994–98; *b* 9 Feb. 1929; *s* of late Eric Dyson, Gainsborough and Hope Patison (*née* Kirkland). *Educ:* Bradfield Coll.; Corpus Christi Coll., Oxford. 2nd Lieut, Royal Tank Regt, 1948. Admitted Solicitor, 1956; Partner, Field Roscoe & Co., 1957 (subseq. Field Fisher & Co. and Field Fisher & Martineau). *Address:* 20 Keats Grove, NW3 2RS. *T:* (020) 7794 3389. *Club:* Oxford and Cambridge.

DYSON, Prof. Kenneth Herbert Fewster, PhD; FRHistS; FBA 1997; AcSS; Distinguished Research Professor, School of European Studies, Cardiff University, since 2003; Visiting Professor of European Politics, University of Bradford, since 2002; *b* 10 Nov. 1946; *s* of Arthur Dyson and Freda Dyson; *m* 1971, Patricia Ann Holmes; two *s*. *Educ:* Scarborough Grammar Sch.; London Sch. of Econs (BSc Econ, MSc Econ); Univ of Liverpool (PhD 1980). FRHistS 1981. Lectr in Politics, 1969–79, Sen. Lectr, 1979–81 Univ. of Liverpool; Prof. of European Studies, 1982–2002, and Co-Dir, Europea Briefing Unit, 1987–2002, Univ. of Bradford. Visiting Professor: in Politics, Univ. o Konstanz, Germany, 1981–82; Inst d'Etudes Politiques de Lille, 2004. Chairman: Assoc for Study of German Politics, 1978–81; Standing Conf. of Heads of European Studies 1990–93; HEFCE Panel for European Studies, RAEs 1996 and 2001; British Academy Grants Officer, Politics Section, 1999–; Mem., Overseas Policy Cttee, and Res. Grant Cttee, 2003–. FRSA 1993; AcSS 2000. Hon. DLitt Aston, 2003. Federal Service Cros (1st Cl.) (Germany), 1990. *Publications include:* Party, State and Bureaucracy in Germany 1978; The State Tradition in Western Europe, 1980; (with S. Wilks) Industrial Crisis 1983; European Detente, 1986; The Politics of the Communications Revolution i Western Europe, 1986; Local Authorities and New Technologies, 1987; Broadcasting an New Media Policies in Western Europe, 1988; Combatting Long-Term Unemploymen 1989; Political Economy of Communications, 1990; Politics of German Regulation 1992; Elusive Union, 1994; Culture First, 1996; (with K. Featherstone) The Road t Maastricht, 1999; The Politics of the Euro-Zone, 2000; European States and the Euro 2002; (with K. Goetz) Germany, Europe and the Politics of Constraint, 2003; Enlargin the Euro Area: external empowerment and domestic transformation in East Centra Europe, 2006; The Euro at Ten, 2008; (with M. Marcussen) Central Banking in the Ag of the Euro, 2009. *Recreations:* Renaissance Florence, classical music, charity work for th disabled, walking, swimming. *Address:* School of European Studies, Cardiff University Cardiff CF10 3YQ.

DYSON, Nicholas Graham; Director, Analytical Data Integration for Government, HM Revenue and Customs, since 2007; *b* 29 Nov. 1945; *s* of Hugh Norman Dyson and Joyc Dyson (*née* Willan); one *s* two *d* by previous marriages. *Educ:* Brunel Univ. (BSc Maths) Work in private sector, 1967–74; statistician, Dept of Industry, 1974–82; Consultant European Stats Office, 1982–85; Course Dir, CS Coll., 1985–88; Nat. Statistician Solomon Is, 1988–91; Advr to OFT, 1991–94; Dir and Chief Statistician, Informatio Centre, DSS, later DWP, 1994–2002; Dir of Inf. and Analysis, DWP, 2002–05; Dir o Knowledge, Analysis and Intelligence, HMRC, 2005–07. *Recreations:* early music, jazz modern architecture, landscape gardening. *Address:* HM Revenue and Customs, Wes Wing, Somerset House, Strand, WC2R 1LB. *T:* (020) 7438 6604, *Fax:* (0191) 225 0894 *e-mail:* nick.dyson@hmrc.gsi.gov.uk. *Club:* Royal Commonwealth Society.

DYSON, Richard George, FCA; Partner, Ernst & Young LLP (formerly Ernst & Whinney), since 1983; *b* Huddersfield, 6 April 1949; *s* of George Hirst Dyson an Margaret Esther Dyson; *m* 1st, 1986, Valerie Anne Conlen (marr. diss. 1997); two *d*; 2nd 1998, Jane Veronica Kay. *Educ:* Clifton Coll.; Queens' Coll., Cambridge (BA 1971). ACA 1974. Articles with Whinney Murray & Co., London, 1971; Ernst & Whinney subsequently Ernst & Young: Head: Due Diligence Services in NW, 1983–97; Forensi Accounting Services, N of England, 1997–2001; Nat. Risk Mgt Partner, 2001–06. Mem Council, ICAEW, 2001– (Pres., 2006–08). Observer, Financial Reporting Counci 2005–06. Chm., Wythenshawe Hosp. Transplant Fund, 2008. *Recreations:* golf, opera *Address:* Portinscale, 45 Arthog Road, Hale, Cheshire WA15 0LU. *T:* (0161) 980 5552 *Fax:* (0161) 980 5558; *e-mail:* richard@portinscale.com. *Clubs:* Hawks (Cambridge); S James' (Manchester); Denham Golf, Formby Golf, Stockport Golf.

DYSON, Stephen John; Editor, Birmingham Mail, since 2005; *b* 5 March 1968; *s* of Rev Colin Dyson and Frances Dyson (*née* Ward); *m* 1992, Ruth Emma Lillywhite; three *Educ:* Primrose Hill Secondary Sch.; Matthew Boulton Coll., Birmingham; Lancaste Univ. (BA 1990). Trainee journalist, Caters News Agency, 1991; reporter: Birminghar Metro News, 1992; Sunday Mercury, Birmingham, 1993; Birmingham Evening Mai industrial corresp., 1994–96; Dep. News Ed., 1996–98; Features Ed., 1998–99; Hd o News, 1999–2001; Dep. Ed., 2001–02; Ed., Evening Gazette, Teesside, 2002–05. Chm Birmingham Mail Charity Trust, 2005–. Midland Business Journalist of Year, BT Re Awards, 1995; Ed., Newspaper of Year, NE Press Awards, 2003. *Publication:* (jtly) W Ain't Going Away!: the battle for Longbridge, 2000. *Recreations:* family, travelling walking, reading, meeting folk, drinking real ale, eating pork scratchings, learning fro mistakes. *Address:* Birmingham Mail, PO Box 78, Weaman Street, Birmingham B4 6AX *T:* (0121) 234 5688; *e-mail:* steve_dyson@mrn.co.uk. *Club:* Birmingham Press.

DYSON, Prof. Timothy Peter Geoffrey, FBA 2001; Professor of Population Studie London School of Economics, since 1993; *b* 1 Aug. 1949; *s* of Geoffrey Dyson an Maureen (*née* Gardner); *m* 1979, Susan Ann Borman; two *s*. *Educ:* Queen's Univ Kingston, Ont.; London Sch. of Econs (BSc Sociol. 1971, MSc Demography 1973). Re Officer, Inst. of Develt Studies, Univ. of Sussex, 1973–75; Res. Fellow, Centre fo Population Studies, LSHTM, 1975–80; Lectr in Population Studies, 1980–88, Reade 1988–93, LSE. *Publications:* (ed) India's Historical Demography, 1989; (ed) Sexua Behaviour and Networking, 1992; Population and Food: global trends and futu prospects, 1996. *Recreation:* gardening. *Address:* Development Studies Institute, Londo School of Economics, Houghton Street, WC2A 2AE. *T:* (020) 7955 7662.

DYTOR, Clive Idris, MC 1982; Head Master, Oratory School, since 2000; *b* 29 Oc 1956; *s* of (Cecil) Frederick Dytor and Maureen (Margaret) Dytor (*née* Owen); *m* 198 Sarah Louise Payler; one *s* one *d*. *Educ:* Trinity Coll., Cambridge (MA Hons Orient Studies); Wycliffe Hall, Oxford (MA Hons Theology). Served Royal Marines, 1980–8 officer trng, 1980–81; Troop Officer, 45 Cdo, 1981–82; Instructor, Officers' Trainin Wing, 1982–83; 2nd i/c Trng Team in Persian Gulf, 1983–84; Officer Recruiting Liaiso Officer, 1984–86; ordained deacon 1989, priest 1990; Curate, Rushall (dio. Lichfield 1989–92; Chaplain, Tonbridge Boys' Sch., 1992–94; received into RC Church, 199 Housemaster, St Edward's Sch., Oxford, 1994–2000. *Recreations:* sport, music, Hispani studies. *Address:* The Oratory School, Woodcote, Reading, Berks RG8 0PJ. *T:* (0149 683500. *Clubs:* East India; Pitt (Cambridge); Leander.

DYVIG, Peter; Comdr (1st cl.), Order of the Dannebrog, 1986; Chamberlain to He Majesty Queen Margrethe II of Denmark, 1999; *b* 23 Feb. 1934; *m* 1959, Karen Dyvi (*née* Møller); one *s* one *d*. *Educ:* Copenhagen Univ. (grad. in Law). Entered Danish Fo Service, 1959; bursary at Sch. of Advanced Internat. Studies, Washington, 1963–64; Fir Secretary: Danish Delegn to NATO, Paris, 1965–67; Brussels, 1967–69; Min. of Fo Affairs, Copenhagen, 1969–74; Minister Counsellor, Washington, 1974–76; Ambassado Asst Under-Sec. of State, Min. of For. Affairs, Copenhagen, 1976–79; Under-Sec. for Po Affairs, 1980; State Sec., 1983–86; Ambassador: to UK, 1986–89; to USA, 1989–95; t France, 1995–99. Chm. Exec. Bd, European Center for Minority Issues, Flensbur Germany, 1999–2005; Chm. Exec. Bd, La Maison du Danemark, Paris, 2000–04; Chm British Import Union, Copenhagen, 2000–06. Dir, various Danish cos. *Addres* Christiansgave 56, 2960 Rungsted Kyst, Denmark.

E

EADES, Robert Mark; His Honour Judge Eades; a Circuit Judge, since 2001; *b* 6 May 1951; *s* of John Robert Eades and Margaret Ursula Eades; *m* 1982, Afsaneh, (Sunny), Atri; two *d*. *Educ:* Moffats Sch., Bewdley, Worcs; Leighton Park Sch., Reading; Bristol Univ. (LLB). Called to the Bar, Middle Temple, 1974; in practice as barrister, specialising in criminal law, 1974–2001. *Recreations:* gardening, tennis, watching cricket, current affairs, English domestic architecture. *Address:* Stafford Combined Court Centre, Victoria Square, Stafford ST16 2QQ.

EADIE, Alexander, BEM 1960; JP; *b* 23 June 1920; *m* 1st, 1941, Jemima Ritchie (*d* 1981); one *s*; 2nd, 1983, Janice Murdoch. *Educ:* Buckhaven Senior Secondary Sch. Coal-miner from 1934. Chm., Fife County Housing Cttee, 9 yrs; Chm., Fife County Educn Cttee, 18 mths; Governor, Moray House Teachers' Training Coll., Edinburgh, 5 years; Exec. Committee: Scottish Council of Labour Party, 9 yrs; NUM Scottish Area, 2 yrs; Mem., Eastern Regional Hosp. Bd (Scotland), 14 yrs. Contested Ayr, 1959 and 1964; MP (Lab) Midlothian, 1966–92. Former PPS to Miss M. Herbison, MP, Minister of Social Security, and Mem. of Parly Select Cttee on Scottish Affairs; Opposition Front Bench Spokesman on Energy (incl. N Sea Oil), 1973–74; Parly Under-Sec. of State, Dept of Energy, 1974–79; Shadow Front Bench Spokesman on Energy, 1979–92. Chm., All Party Energy Studies Gp, 1991–92; Chm., Parly Labour Party Power and Steel Gp, 1972–74; Sec., Miners' Parly Gp, 1983–92; Vice-Chm., Parly Trade Union Group, 1972–74. JP Fife, 1951. *Recreations:* bowling, gardening. *Address:* Balkerack, The Haugh, East Wemyss, Fife KY1 4SB. *T:* (01592) 713636.

See also H. S. Eadie.

EADIE, Helen S.; Member (Lab) Dunfermline East, Scottish Parliament, since 1999; *b* 7 March 1947; *d* of James Jack Miller and Elizabeth Reid Stirling Miller; *m* 1967, Robert William Eadie, *s* of Alexander Eadie, *qv*; two *d*. *Educ:* Larbert High Sch.; Falkirk Tech. Coll.; LSE. Political researcher for Harry Ewing, MP and Alex Eadie, MP; Equal Opportunities and Political Officer, GMB. Mem. (Lab) Fife Regl Council, 1986–99. Contested (Lab) Roxburgh and Berwickshire, 1997. *Address:* Scottish Parliament, Edinburgh EH99 1SP; (office) 25 Church Street, Inverkeithing, Fife KY11 1LG. *T:* (01383) 412856, *Fax:* (01383) 412855; 3 Hopeward Mews, Dalgety Bay, Fife KY11 9TB.

EADY, family name of **Baron Swinfen**.

EADY, Hon. Sir David, Kt 1997; **Hon. Mr Justice Eady;** a Judge of the High Court of Justice, Queen's Bench Division, since 1997; *b* 24 March 1943; *s* of late Thomas William Eady and Kate Eady; *m* 1974, Catherine, *yr d* of J. T. Wiltshire; one *s* one *d*. *Educ:* Brentwood Sch.; Trinity Coll., Cambridge (Exhibnr; Pt I Moral Science Tripos, Pt II Law Tripos; MA, LLB). Called to the Bar, Middle Temple, 1966, Bencher, 1991; QC 1983; a Recorder, 1986–97. Mem., Cttee on Privacy and Related Matters (Calcutt Cttee), 1989–90. *Publication:* The Law of Contempt (with A. J. Arlidge), 1982, 3rd edn (ed with A. T. H. Smith), 2005. *Address:* Royal Courts of Justice, Strand, WC2A 2LL.

EADY, Jennifer Jane; QC 2006; a Recorder, since 2003; *b* 31 May 1965; *d* of Gordon James Eady and Theresa Alice Eady; *m* 2006, Paul Noordhof; one *s*. *Educ:* High Sch., Boston, Lincs; St Hugh's Coll., Oxford (BA Hons PPE 1986; Dip. Law). Called to the Bar, Inner Temple, 1989; in practice, specialising in employment law. Chm. (pt-time), Employment Tribunals, 2001–; Mem. Council, ACAS, 2008–. Trustee, Free Representation Unit. *Recreation:* my family. *Address:* Old Square Chambers, 10–11 Bedford Row, WC1R 4BU. *T:* (020) 7269 0300, *Fax:* (020) 7405 1387; *e-mail:* eadyq@oldsquare.co.uk.

EAGAR, (Edward) Patrick; freelance photographer, since 1965; *b* 9 March 1944; *s* of late Desmond Eagar and of Marjorie Eagar; *m* 1968, Annabel Trench (*d* 1996); one *s* one *d*. *Educ:* Magdalene Coll., Cambridge (BA 1965). Retrospective exhibn, Lord's Cricket Ground, 2005, 2006. *Publications:* (with John Arlott) An Eye for Cricket, 1979; (with Alan Ross) A Summer to Remember, 1981; Test Decade, 1982; Summer of the All Rounder, 1982; Summer of Speed, 1983; Kiwis and Indians, 1983; Botham, 1985; An Australian Summer, 1985; Summer of Suspense, 1986; West Indian Summer, 1988; Tour of Tours, 1989; (with Richard Wilson) Caught in the Frame, 1992; The Ashes in Focus, 2005. *Recreations:* wine, golf, gardening. *Address:* Queensberry Place, Richmond, Surrey TW9 1NW. *T:* (020) 8940 9269. *Clubs:* MCC; Royal Mid-Surrey Golf.

EAGLAND, (Ralph) Martin; Managing Director, Eagland Planning Associates (formerly Director, Martin Eagland Economic Development Consultancy), since 1995; *b* 1 May 1942; *s* of Norman Albert Eagland and Jessie Eagland; *m* 1963, Patricia Anne Norton; one *s* one *d*. *Educ:* Hipperholme Grammar Sch.; Leeds Sch. of Town Planning; Univ. of Bradford (MSc); Univ. of Birmingham. FRTPI, MIHT, CIMgt. Jun. planning posts, Huddersfield, Dewsbury and Halifax, 1959–67; Principal Planning Officer, City of Gloucester, 1967–72; Asst Co. Planning Officer, Northants CC, 1972–74; Chief Planner (Envmt), W Yorks CC, 1974–79, Head of Econ. Develt Unit, 1979–84; Chief Exec., Kettering Borough Council, 1984–88; Chief Exec. and Accounting Officer, Leeds Develt Corp., 1988–95. Director: Urban Regeneration Partnership, 1996–98; BURA, 2001– (Mem. Panel, 1995; Vice-Chm., 2002–04). Mem., W Yorks Cttee, CoSIRA, 1985–88; Sec., Kettering Enterprise Agency, 1986–88; Mem., Electricity Consumers' Cttee, Yorks Reg., 1997. Hon. Public Relns Officer, RTPI (Yorks Br. Exec. Cttee), 1990–92. Vice-Chm., Colne and Holme Valley Jt Cttee for the Blind, 1994–99; Mem., Rotary Club of Leeds, 1992–95. *Publications:* contribs to RTPI Jl, Instn of Highways and Transportation Jl and various property jls and publications. *Recreations:* environmental studies, music, history, gardening. *T:* (office) (01484) 686859. *Club:* Yorkshire Society (Leeds).

EAGLE, Angela; MP (Lab) Wallasey, since 1992; Exchequer Secretary to HM Treasury, since 2007; *b* 17 Feb. 1961; twin *d* of André and late Shirley Eagle. *Educ:* Formby High Sch.; St John's Coll., Oxford (BA PPE). Economic Directorate, CBI, 1984; Confederation of Health Service Employees: Researcher, 1984; Press Officer, 1986; Parly Officer, 1987–92. Parly Under-Sec. of State, DETR, 1997–98, DSS, 1998–2001, Home Office, 2001–02. Mem., Nat. Women's Cttee, 1989–, Nat. Exec. Cttee, Labour Party. Mem., BFI. *Recreations:* chess (Jun. Internat. Hons), cricket, cinema. *Address:* House of Commons, SW1A 0AA. *T:* (020) 7219 4074.

See also M. Eagle.

EAGLE, Maria; MP (Lab) Liverpool, Garston, since 1997; Parliamentary Under-Secretary of State, Ministry of Justice, since 2007, and Government Equalities Office, since 2008; *b* 17 Feb. 1961; twin *d* of André Eagle and late Shirley Eagle. *Educ:* Formby High Sch.; Pembroke Coll., Oxford (BA Hons); Coll. of Law, Lancaster Gate. Articles, Brian Thompson & Partners, Liverpool, 1990–92; Goldsmith Williams, Liverpool, 1992–95; Sen. Solicitor, Steven Irving & Co., Liverpool, 1994–97. Contested (Lab) Crosby, 1992. Parliamentary Under-Secretary of State: DWP, 2001–05; DfES, 2005–06; NI Office, 2006–07. *Address:* House of Commons, SW1A 0AA.

See also A. Eagle.

EAGLEN, Jane; international opera singer (soprano); *d* of late Ronald Arthur Eaglen and of Kathleen Eaglen; *m* 2000, Brian Lyson. *Educ:* Royal Northern Coll. of Music (vocal studies with Joseph Ward). Principal Soprano, ENO, 1983–91; major house débuts include: Donna Anna in Don Giovanni, Vienna State Opera, 1993; Brunnhilde in Die Walküre, La Scala, Milan, 1994; Norma, Seattle Opera, 1994; Amelia in Un Ballo in Maschera, Opéra National de Paris-Bastille, 1995; Brunnhilde in Ring Cycle, Lyric Opera, Chicago, 1996, Seattle, 2000–01, Metropolitan Opera, NY, 2000; Brunnhilde in Die Walküre, San Francisco Opera, 1995; Donna Anna, Metropolitan Opera, NY, 1996; Lady Macbeth, Macbeth, Vancouver Opera, 2006; Senta, Der Fliegende Holländer, Seattle Opera, 2007; other appearances include: La Gioconda, Chicago, 1999; Isolde, in Tristan and Isolde, Seattle and Chicago, 1999, Metropolitan Opera, NY, 2000; Julia, in La Vestale, ENO, 2002; Seattle Opera: Fidelio, 2003, Ariadne, in Ariadne auf Naxos, 2004 and 2005, Ortrud in Lohengrin, 2004, Brunnhilde in Ring Cycle, 2005, Rosalinda in Die Fledermaus, 2006; Brunnhilde in Ring Cycle, Chicago, 2005; Ariadne, Pittsburgh Opera, 2005. Recordings include Tosca, Norma, Tannhäuser and five solo discs of opera arias and song cycles. Hon. Dr McGill Univ. *Recreations:* computing, sport spectator. *Address:* c/o AOR Management, 6910 Roosevelt Way NE, PMB 221, Seattle, WA 98115, USA. *T:* (206) 7296160; *e-mail:* jennyrose@aormanagementuk.com. *Club:* Lady Taverners.

EAGLES, Lt-Col (Charles Edward) James, LVO 1988; Member, HM Body Guard of the Honourable Corps of Gentlemen-at-Arms, 1967–88 (Harbinger, 1981–86; Standard Bearer, 1986–88); *b* 14 May 1918; *o s* of late Major C. E. C. Eagles, DSO, RMLI and Esmé Field; *m* 1941, Priscilla May Nicolette, *d* of late Brig. A. F. B. Cottrell, DSO, OBE; one *s* three *d*. *Educ:* Marlborough Coll. 2nd Lieut RM, 1936; served: HMS Sussex, Mediterranean and S Atlantic, 1938–40; Mobile Naval Base Def. Orgn, UK, ME, Ceylon and India, 1940–43; 1 HAA Regt RM, India, UK and NW Europe, 1943–45; Asst Mil. Sec., 1945; Amphibious Trng Wing, 1945–47; Staff of Maj.-Gen. RM, Portsmouth, 1947–50; HMS Devonshire, 1951–52; RN Staff Course, 1952; DS, Amphibious Warfare Sch., 1952–55; HMS Afrikander, SO (Intell.), S Atlantic, 1955–57; Dep. Dir, PRORM, 1957–59; CSO, Plymouth Gp, 1960; AAG, Staff of CGRM, 1960–62; Dir, PRORM, 1962–65; retd 1965; Civil Service, MoD, 1965–83. Pres., T. S. Churchill Sea Cadet Corps, 1988–99. *Recreation:* genealogy. *Address:* The Old Brewery, Northleach, Glos GL54 3HB. *Club:* Army and Navy.

EAGLESTONE, Diana Barbara; Her Honour Judge Eaglestone; a Circuit Judge, since 1995; *b* 24 May 1949; *d* of Frank Nelson Eaglestone and Irene Eaglestone; *m* 1991, Michael Howard Redfern, *qv*; one *d*, two *d* by previous marriage, and one step *d*. *Educ:* Manchester Univ. (LLB). Called to the Bar, Gray's Inn, 1971; a Recorder, 1986–95. *Address:* Manchester Civil Justice Centre, 1 Bridge Street West, Manchester M60 9DJ.

EAGLETON, Prof. Terence Francis, PhD; FBA 2003; John Edward Taylor Professor of English Literature, University of Manchester, 2006–08; *b* 22 Feb. 1943; *s* of Francis Paul Eagleton and Rosaleen (*née* Riley); *m* 1st, 1966, Elizabeth Rosemary Galpin (marr. diss. 1976); two *s*; 2nd, 1997, Willa Murphy; one *s*. *Educ:* Trinity Coll., Cambridge (MA, PhD). Fellow in English, Jesus Coll., Cambridge, 1964–69; Oxford University: Tutorial Fellow, Wadham Coll., 1969–89; Lectr in Critical Theory, 1989–92; Fellow, Linacre Coll., 1989–92; Thomas Warton Prof. of English Lit., 1992–2001; Fellow, St Catherine's Coll., 1992–2001; Prof. of Cultural Theory and John Rylands Fellow, Univ. of Manchester, 2001–06. Hon. DLitt: Salford, 1993; NUI, 1997; Santiago di Compostela, 1999. *Publications:* Criticism and Ideology, 1976; Marxism and Literary Criticism, 1976; Literary Theory: an introduction, 1983; The Function of Criticism, 1984; The Ideology of the Aesthetic, 1990; Ideology: an introduction, 1993; Heathcliff and the Great Hunger: studies in Irish culture, 1995; Crazy John and the Bishop, and other Essays on Irish Culture, 1998; The Truth about the Irish, 1999; The Idea of Culture, 2000; The Gatekeeper: a memoir, 2002; Sweet Violence: a study of the tragic, 2002; After Theory, 2003; The English Novel: an introduction, 2004; Holy Terror, 2005; How to Read a Poem, 2006; The Meaning of Life, 2007; Trouble with Strangers, 2008. *Recreation:* Irish music. *Clubs:* Irish; United Arts (Dublin).

EAGLING, Wayne John; dancer and choreographer; Artistic Director, English National Ballet, since 2005; *s* of Eddie and Thelma Eagling. *Educ:* P. Ramsey Studio of Dance Arts; Royal Ballet Sch. Sen. Principal, Royal Ballet, 1975–91; Artistic Dir, Dutch Nat. Ballet, 1991–2003. Has danced lead rôles in major classics including Sleeping Beauty, Swan Lake,

Cinderella; first rôle created for him was Young Boy in Triad, 1972; subsequent created rôles include: Solo Boy in Gloria; Ariel in The Tempest; Woyzeck in Different Drummer. Choreographed: The Hunting of the Snark by Michael Batt; (for Royal Ballet) Frankenstein, The Modern Prometheus, 1985; Beauty and the Beast, 1986; The Wall, Berlin, 1990; (for Dutch Nat. Ballet) Ruins of Time, 1993, Symphony in Waves, 1994, Duet, 1995, Lost Touch, 1995, Holding a Balance (for opening of Vermeer exhibn in Mauritshuis), 1996, (with Toer van Schayk) Nutcracker and Mouseking, 1996, Magic Flute, 1999, Le sacré du printemps, 2000, Frozen, 2001; (for La Scala, Milan) Alma Mahler, 1994; choreographed, produced and directed various galas. *Publication:* (with Ross MacGibbon and Robert Jude) The Company We Keep, 1981. *Recreations:* golf, scuba diving, tennis, antique cars. *Address:* English National Ballet, Markova House, 39 Jay Mews, SW7 2ES.

EAMES, family name of **Baron Eames**.

EAMES, Baron *cr* 1995 (Life Peer), of Armagh, in the County of Armagh; **Rt Rev. Robert Henry Alexander Eames,** OM 2007; PhD; Archbishop of Armagh and Primate of All Ireland, 1986–2006; *b* 27 April 1937; *s* of William Edward and Mary Eleanor Thompson Eames; *m* 1966 Ann Christine Daly (*see* Lady Eames); two *s*. *Educ:* Belfast Royal Acad.; Methodist Coll., Belfast; Queen's Univ., Belfast (LLB (hons), PhD); Trinity Coll., Dublin. Research Scholar and Tutor, Faculty of Laws, QUB, 1960–63; Curate Assistant, Bangor Parish Church, 1963–66; Rector of St Dorothea's, Belfast, 1966–74; Examining Chaplain to Bishop of Down, 1973; Rector of St Mark's, Dundela, 1974–75; Bishop of Derry and Raphoe, 1975–80; Bishop of Down and Dromore, 1980–86. Select Preacher, Oxford Univ., 1987. Irish Rep., 1984, Mem. Standing Cttee, 1985, ACC; Chairman: Commn on Communion and Women in the Episcopate, 1988–90; Commn on Inter-Anglican Relations, 1988–91; Lambeth Commn on Communion, 2004 (Windsor Report). Co-Chm., Consultative Panel on the Past, NI, 2007–08. Governor, Church Army, 1985–90. Chairman: Armagh Observatory and Planetarium, 1986–2006; Bd, Royal Sch., Armagh, 1986–2006; Mem. Bd, St George's House, Windsor, 2008–. Hon. Bencher, Lincoln's Inn, 1998. Hon. LLD: QUB, 1989; TCD, 1992; Lancaster, 1994; Hon. DD Cambridge, 1994. *Publications:* A Form of Worship for Teenagers, 1965; The Quiet Revolution—Irish Disestablishment, 1970; Through Suffering, 1973; Thinking through Lent, 1978; Through Lent, 1984; Chains to be Broken, 1992; contribs to New Divinity, Irish Legal Quarterly, Criminal Law Review, The Furrow. *Address:* House of Lords, SW1A 0PW.

EAMES, Lady; Ann Christine Eames, OBE 2006; Member, Northern Ireland Human Rights Commission, 2001–07; *b* 21 Jan. 1943; *d* of Captain William Adrian Reynolds Daly and Olive Margaret Daly; *m* 1966, Rt Rev. Robert Henry Alexander Eames (*see* Baron Eames); two *s*. *Educ:* Ashleigh House Sch., Belfast; Queen's Univ., Belfast (LLB Hons, MPhil). World-Wide Pres., Mothers' Union, 1995–2000. Mem. Bd, Hunterhouse Sch., Belfast, 2008–. *Recreations:* sailing, reading. *Address:* 3 Downshire Crescent, Hillsborough, Co. Down BT26 6DD.

EAMES, Eric James; JP; Lord Mayor of Birmingham, 1974–75, Deputy Lord Mayor, 1975–76; *b* Highley, Shropshire, 13 April 1917; *s* of George Eames; *m* (marr. diss.); one *s*. *Educ:* Highley Sch., Highley, Shropshire. Member (Lab): Birmingham City Council, 1949–92; W Midlands CC, 1974–77. Mem., Governing Board, Internat. Center for Information Co-operation and Relationship among World's Major Cities. Dir, Assoc. for Neighbourhood Democracy (formerly Councils), 1992–. Governor, Harper Adams Agricl Coll., 1953–90. JP Birmingham, 1972. *Recreations:* gardening, do-it-yourself enthusiast.

EARDLEY-WILMOT, Sir Michael (John Assheton), 6th Bt *cr* 1821, of Berkswell Hall, Warwickshire; *b* 13 Jan. 1941; *o s* of Sir John Eardley-Wilmot, 5th Bt, LVO, DSC and Diana Elizabeth (*née* Moore); *S* father, 1995; *m* 1st, Wendy Wolstenholme (marr. diss. 1987); two *s* one *d*; 2nd, 1987, Diana Wallis; one *d*. *Educ:* Clifton. FRSA. *Recreations:* days in Barbados, nights in New York. *Heir:* *s* Benjamin John Eardley-Wilmot, *b* 24 Jan. 1974. *Address:* c/o Coutts Bank, 440 Strand, WC2R 0QS.

EARL, Belinda Jane; Chief Executive, Jaeger, since 2004; *b* 20 Dec. 1961; *d* of late Colin Lee and of Diana Lee; *m* 1985, David Mark Earl; two *s*. *Educ:* UCW, Aberystwyth (BScEcon (Econs and Business); Hon. Fellow, 2003). Controller, Fashion Div., Harrods, 1983–85; Debenhams Retail Plc: Merchandiser (Menswear), 1985–88; Controller (Children's), 1988–92; Dir (accessories, women's), 1992–97; Trading Dir, 1997–2000; Debenhams Plc: Dir, 1999–2003; Chief Exec., 2000–03. Chm., Skillsmart, 2002–04. FCGI 2006. *Address:* Jaeger, 57 Broadwick Street, W1F 9QS.

EARL, Christopher Joseph, MD; FRCP, FRCOphth; Hon. Consultant Physician to: Neurological Department, Middlesex Hospital, 1988 (Physician, 1971–88); National Hospital, Queen Square, 1988 (Physician, 1958–88); Moorfields Eye Hospital, 1988 (Physician, 1959–88); *b* 20 Nov. 1925; *s* of Christopher and Winifred Earl, Ashbourne, Derbyshire; *m* 1951, Alma Patience Hopkins, Reading; two *s* three *d*. *Educ:* Cotton Coll.; Guy's Hosp. (MB BS 1948). MRCP 1951, FRCP 1964; FRCOphth 1993. House phys. and house surg., Guy's Hosp., and MO, RAF, 1948–50. Lecturer in Chemical Pathology, Guy's Hosp., 1950–52; Research Fellow, Harvard Med. Sch., and Neurological Unit, Boston City Hosp., 1952–54; Resident MO, Nat. Hosp., Queen Square, 1954–56; Chief Asst, Neurological Dept, Guy's Hosp., 1956–58; Physician, Neurological Dept, London Hosp., 1961–71; Consultant Neurologist: King Edward VII Hosp. for Officers, 1966–95; Hosp. of St John and St Elizabeth, 1967–96. Civil Consultant in Neurol., RAF, 1976–88; Consultant Advr in Neurology to CMO, DoH, 1983–88. Director: Medical Sickness Annuity & Life Assce Soc. Ltd, 1981–95 (Chm., 1993–95); Permanent Insurance Co., 1985–95. Hon. Dir of Photography, Royal Society of Medicine, 1967–73. Hon. Sec., 1968–74, Pres., 1989–90, Assoc. British Neurologists; Mem. Council, 1967–91, Vice Chm. Bd of Management, 1993–96, Med. Defence Union; Censor, 1983–85, Chm., Cttee on Neurology, 1975–85, RCP. Corresp. Mem., Amer. Neurological Assoc., 1978. *Publications:* (ed jtly) Medical Negligence: the cranium, spine and nervous system, 1999; papers in learned jls on biochemistry and neurology. *Recreation:* reading history. *Address:* 23 Audley Road, Ealing, W5 3ES. *T:* (020) 8997 0380. *Club:* Garrick.

EARL, Eric Stafford; Clerk to the Worshipful Company of Fishmongers, 1974–88, retired; *b* 8 July 1928; *s* of late Alfred Henry Earl and Mary Elizabeth Earl; *m* 1951, Clara Alice Alston. *Educ:* SE Essex Technical Coll.; City of London Coll. Served with RA, 1946–48. Joined Fishmongers' Co. 1948: Accountant, 1961–68; Asst Clerk, 1969–73; Actg Clerk, 1973–74; Liveryman, 1977. Clerk to Governors of Gresham's Sch., 1974–88; formerly: Sec., City and Guilds of London Art School Ltd; Sec., Atlantic Salmon Res. Trust Ltd; Mem. Exec. and Mem. Council, Salmon and Trout Assoc.; Mem., Nat. Anglers' Council (Chm., 1983–85). Hon. Sec., Shellfish Assoc. of GB, 1974–88; Jt Hon. Sec., Central Council for Rivers Protection, 1974–88; Hon. Asst River Keeper of River Thames, 1968–88; Mem. Council, Anglers' Co-operative Assoc., 1974– (Vice Chm., 1988–). Director: Hulbert Property Co. Ltd, 1975–88; Hulbert Property Holdings Ltd, 1975–88. FZS 1988. Hon. Freeman, Watermen's Co., 1984. *Recreations:* fishing, gardening, tennis, cricket. *Address:* Dolphins, Watling Lane, Thaxted, Essex CM6 2RA. *T:* (01371) 830758. *Club:* Flyfishers'.

EARL, John, FSA; Consultant, Theatres Trust, since 1996 (Director, 1986–95); *b* 11 Apri 1928; *s* of Philip Haywood Earl and May Florence (*née* Walsh); *m* 1952, Valerie Atkins one *s* (one *d* decd). *Educ:* Roan Sch.; Brixton Sch. of Building. MRICS (ARICS 1952) FSA 1978. Nat. Service, RE, 1947–49. London County Council: Architect's Dept 1954–56; Historic Bldgs Section, 1956–61; MPBW (Special Services), 1961–65; Sectio Leader, GLC Historic Bldgs Div., 1965–86. Private consultancy, 1986–. Lectr, variou bldg conservation courses, 1970–2004; External Examiner for conservation courses at Heriot-Watt Univ., 1982–84; Architectl Assoc., 1984–86; RICS Coll. of Estate Mgt 1990–95 (Chm., Adv. Bd, 1996–2000); Tutor for SPAB William Morris Craft Fellows 1987–90. Pres., Frank Matcham Soc., 1999–. Trustee: Talawa Theatre Co., 1996–2000 Raymond Mander and Joe Mitchenson Theatre Collection, 1996–2004. FRSA 1992 IHBC 1998. Hon. Fellow, Coll. of Estate Mgt, 2001. *Publications:* (with J. Stanton Canterbury Hall and Theatre of Varieties, 1982; Philosophy of Building Conservation 1996, 3rd edn 2003; Dr Langdon-Down and the Normansfield Theatre, 1997 (architectural ed.) Theatres Trust Guide to British Theatres, 2000; British Theatres an Music Halls, 2005; conservation plans and historical reviews for a number of listed theatres contrib. numerous books and jls on building conservation and theatre buildings. *Recreation* avoiding organised sport.

EARL, Prof. Michael John, FBCS; Professor of Information Management, University o Oxford, 2002–07, now Emeritus; Dean, Templeton College, Oxford, 2002–08, nov Hon. Fellow, Green Templeton College; Pro-Vice-Chancellor, Development an External Affairs, University of Oxford, since 2008; *b* 11 Jan. 1944; *s* of late Vincent an Marjorie Earl; *m* 1969, Alison Jennifer Eades; one *s* one *d*. *Educ:* Univ. of Newcastle-upon Tyne (BA 1966); Univ. of Warwick (MSc 1971). FBCS 1992. Systems Analyst, Unite Steel Cos, 1966–68; Sen. Systems Analyst, Bowater Paper Corp., 1968–69; Gp System Manager, GEC Telecommunications Ltd, 1969–74; Lectr in Mgt Control, Mancheste Business Sch., 1974–76; Fellow in Information Mgt, Templeton Coll., Univ. of Oxford 1976–90; London Business School: Prof. of Information Mgt, 1991–2002; Dep. Principal 1996–98; Actg Principal, 1998. Non-executive Director: Shell Information Services BV 1997–98; Institut V, Stockholm Sch. of Economics, 2000–; Mem. European Adv. Bd EzGov. Inc., 2002–. Mem. Adv. Council, Oxford Philomusica, 2004–. Hon. Fellow Harris Manchester Coll., Oxford, 2008. *Publications:* (with A. M. McCosh) Accountin Control and Financial Strategy, 1978; (jtly) Developing Managerial Information Systems 1979; (jtly) Information Society: for richer, for poorer, 1982; Perspectives o Management, 1983; Information Management: the strategic dimension, 1989 Management Strategies for Information Technology, 1989; Information Management: th organizational dimension, 1996; articles in learned and professional jls. *Recreations:* golf music, tennis, travel. *Address:* Green Templeton College, University of Oxford, Oxfor OX2 6HG. *T:* (01865) 422722, *Fax:* (01865) 422726; *e-mail:* Michael.Earl@ templeton.ox.ac.uk. *Clubs:* Oxford and Cambridge; Frilford Heath Golf.

EARL, Stephen, TD 1992; a District Judge (Magistrates' Courts), since 2004; *b* 16 Apr 1958; *s* of Leslie Earl and Anne Earl; *m* 2002, Gillian Douglass; one *s* one *d*, and two ste *s* four step *d*. *Educ:* Beverley Grammar Sch.; Manchester Polytech. (BA Hons Law) Guildford Coll. of Law. Articled clerk, Hart Scales & Hodges, 1980–82; admitted solicito 1982; Asst Solicitor, Gibson & Co., 1983–90; sole practitioner, Earl Galpin, 1990–2004 A Dep. Dist Judge, 2000–04. VRSM 2001. *Recreations:* diving, reading, travel, family *Address:* Newcastle Magistrates' Court, Market Street, Newcastle upon Tyne NE99 1AU *T:* (0191) 232 7326, *Fax:* (0191) 221 0025.

EARL, Col Timothy James, OBE 2000; Private Secretary to HRH the Princess Royal 1999–2002; *b* 2 July 1943; *s* of Rowland William Earl and Elizabeth Sylvia Earl; *m* 1968 Elizabeth Mary Ghislaine de Pelet; two *s* one *d*. *Educ:* Brentwood Sch.; RMA Sandhurst Commnd 1st Bn King's Own Royal Border Regt, 1964; served British Guyana, Gu States, Cyprus, Gibraltar and Germany; transf. to Life Guards, 1974; served Germany Norway, Belize; CO, 1983–85; RCDS, 1985–87; MoD, 1987–90; HQ UKLF, 1990–93 Sec., Govt Hospitality Fund, 1993–99. *Recreations:* field sports, planting trees. *Address* Haddon Lodge, Stourton Caundle, Dorset DT10 2LB. *T:* (01963) 362241. *Clul* Flyfishers'.

EARLE, Arthur Frederick; management and economic consultant, since 1983; Toronto, 13 Sept. 1921; *s* of Frederick C. Earle and Hilda M. Earle (*née* Brown); *m* 1946 Vera Domini Lithgow; two *s* one *d*. *Educ:* Toronto; London Sch. of Economics (BS (Econ.), PhD; Hon. Fellow 1980). Royal Canadian Navy (Rating to Lieut Comdr) 1939–46. Canada Packers Ltd, 1946–48; Aluminium Ltd cos in British Guiana, Wes Indies and Canada, 1948–53; Treas., Alumina Jamaica Ltd, 1953–55; Aluminium Unior London, 1955–58; Vice-Pres., Aluminium Ltd Sales Inc., New York, 1958–61; Di 1961–74, Dep. Chm., 1961–65, Man. Dir, 1963–65, Hoover Ltd; Principal, Londo Graduate Sch. of Business Studies, 1965–72. Pres., Internat. Investment Corp. fc Yugoslavia, 1972–74; Pres., Boyden Consulting Group Ltd, 1974–82; Associate, 1974–82 Vice-Pres., 1975–82, Boyden Associates, Inc.; Advisor to the Pres., Canada Devel Investment Corp., 1983–86; Director: Rio Algom Ltd, 1983–92; National Sea Product Ltd, 1984–86; Bathpaul Ltd, UK, 1984–86; Monkwells Ltd, UK, 1984. Sen. Res. Fellow Nat. Centre for Management R & D, Univ. of Western Ontario, 1987–90. Membe Commn of Enquiry, Jamaican Match Industry, 1953; Consumer Council, 1963–68 NEDC Cttee on Management Educn, Training and Develt, 1967–69; NEDC fc Electrical Engineering Industry. Chm., Canadian Assoc. of Friends of LSE, 1975–96. Di Nat. Ballet of Canada, 1982–85. Governor: Ashridge Management Coll., 1962–65; LSE 1968–95; NIESR, 1968–74; Governor and Mem. Council, Ditchley Foundn, 1967 Fellow, London Business Sch., 1988. Thomas Hawksley Lecture, IMechE, 1968 *Publications:* numerous, on economics and management. *Recreations:* hill climbing, mode ship building. *Address:* 901–1230 Marlborough Court, Oakville, ON L6H 3K6, Canad *T:* (905) 3377977.

EARLE, Sir (Hardman) George (Algernon), 6th Bt *cr* 1869; *b* 4 Feb. 1932; *S* fathe 1979; *m* 1967, Diana Gillian Bligh, *d* of Col F. F. B. St George, CVO; one *s* one *d*. *Hei* *s* Robert George Bligh Earle, *b* 24 Jan. 1970.

EARLE, Joel Vincent, (Joe); Vice-President and Director, Japan Society Gallery, Nev York, since 2007; *b* 1 Sept. 1952; *s* of late James Basil Foster Earle and Mary Isabel Jessi Weeks; *m* 1980, Sophia Charlotte Knox; two *s*. *Educ:* Westminster Sch.; New Coll Oxford (BA 1st Cl. Hons Chinese). Far Eastern Department, Victoria & Albert Museum Res. Asst, 1974–77; Asst Keeper, 1977–82; Keeper, 1982–87; Head of Public Service V&A Mus., 1987–89; independent curator, 1990–2003; Chair, Dept of Art of Asi Oceania and Africa, Mus. of Fine Arts, Boston, 2003–07. Consultant, Christie' 1998–2003. Exhibns Co-ordinator, Japan Fest. 1991, 1990–91; *other exhibitions includ* Japan Style, V&A, 1980; Japanese Lacquer, V&A, 1980; Great Japan Exhibition, RA 1981; The Toshiba Gall. of Japanese Art, V&A, 1986; British Design, South Coast Plaz 1990; Visions of Japan, V&A, 1991–92; London Transport Posters, 1994; Da un antic castello inglese, Milan, 1994; Shibata Zeshin, Nat. Mus. of Scotland, 1997; Splendors c Meiji, USA, 1999; Netsuke, Mus. of Fine Arts, Boston, 2001; Serizawa: Master of Japanes

Textile Design, Nat. Mus of Scotland, 2001. *Publications:* An Introduction to Netsuke, 1980, 2nd edn 1982; An Introduction to Japanese Prints, 1980; (contrib.) Japan Style, 1980; (contrib.) The Great Japan Exhibition, 1981; (trans.) The Japanese Sword, 1983; The Toshiba Gallery: Japanese art and design, 1986; Flower Bronzes of Japan, 1995; (ed) Treasures of Imperial Japan: Lacquer, 1995; (ed) The Index of Inro Artists, 1995; Shibata Zeshin, 1996; Shadows and Reflections: Japanese lacquer art, 1996; Flowers of the Chisel, 1997; R. S. Huthart Collection of Netsuke, 1998; Splendors of Meiji, 1999; Infinite Spaces: the art and wisdom of the Japanese garden, 2000; Netsuke of Iwami Province, 2000; Japanese Lacquer: The Denys Eyre Bower Collection, 2000; Netsuke: fantasy and reality in Japanese miniature sculpture, 2001; Splendors of Imperial Japan, 2002; Lethal Elegance: the art of Samurai sword fittings, 2004; Contemporary Clay: Japanese ceramics for the new century, 2005; articles in learned jls. *Recreation:* reading Japanese fiction. *Address:* Japan Society Gallery, 333 East 47th Street, New York, NY 10017, USA. *T:* (212) 7151283; *e-mail:* jearle@japansociety.org.
See also T. F. Earle.

EARLE, John Nicholas Francis, (Nick); Headmaster, Bromsgrove School, 1971–85; *b* 14 Nov. 1926; *s* of John William Arthur Earle and Vivien Constance Fenton (*née* Davies); *m* 1959, Ann Veronica Lester; one *s* two *d*. *Educ:* Winchester Coll.; Trinity Coll., Cambridge. 1st cl. Maths Tripos pt 2, 1st cl. Theol. Tripos pt 1; MA. Deacon, 1952; Priest, 1953; relinquished Holy Orders, 1994. Curate, St Matthew, Moorfields, 1952–57; PARS Fellow, Union Theol Seminary, New York, 1957–58; Lectr, St Botolph, Aldgate, 1958–61; Asst Master, Dulwich Coll., 1961–71. *Publications:* What's Wrong With the Church?, 1961; Culture and Creed, 1967; Logic, 1973; Does God Make Sense?, 1998. *Recreations:* travel, gardening. *Address:* 1 Red Post Hill, Pond Mead, SE21 7BX.

EARLE, Prof. Thomas Foster, DPhil; King John II Professor of Portuguese Studies, University of Oxford, since 1996; Fellow, St Peter's College, Oxford, since 1996; *b* 5 April 1946; *s* of late James Basil Foster Earle and Mary Earle (*née* Weeks); *m* 1970, Gisèle Hilary Wilson; one *s* one *d*. *Educ:* Westminster Sch.; Wadham Coll., Oxford (BA 1967; DPhil 1976). University of Oxford: Lectr in Portuguese Studies, 1968–96; Fellow, Linacre Coll., 1968–96; Dir, Portuguese Studies, 1976–96; Chm., Centre for Study of Portuguese Discoveries, Linacre Coll., 1989–. Founder Mem., Associação Internacional de Lusitanistas, 1984. Grande oficial, Ordem do Infante D. Henrique (Portugal), 1995. *Publications:* Theme and Image in the Poetry of Sá de Miranda, 1980 (trans. Portuguese 1985); The Muse Reborn: the poetry of António Ferreira, 1988 (trans. Portuguese 1990); (ed) Castro de António Ferreira, 1990; (with J. Villiers) Albuquerque: Caesar of the East, 1990; (ed) Poemas Lusitanos de António Ferreira, 2000; O Livro de Eclesiastes, 2002; articles in collections, learned jls, etc. *Recreations:* music, gardening, walking. *Address:* Taylor Institution, St Giles', Oxford OX1 3NA. *T:* (01865) 270474.
See also J. V. Earle.

EARLES, Prof. Stanley William Edward, PhD, DScEng; FREng, FIMechE; Professor of Mechanical Engineering, King's College, University of London, 1976–94, Emeritus since 1994; *b* 18 Jan. 1929; *s* of late William Edward Earles and Winnifred Anne Cook; *m* 1955, Margaret Isabella Brown; two *d*. *Educ:* King's Coll., Univ. of London (BScEng, PhD, DScEng; AKC; FKC 1993). FIMechE 1976; FREng (FEng 1992). Nuffield Apprentice, Birmingham, 1944–50; King's Coll., Univ. of London, 1950–53; Scientific Officer, Royal Naval Scientific Service, 1953–55; University of London: Queen Mary College: Lectr in Mech. Engrg, 1955–69; Reader in Mech. Engrg, 1969–75; Prof. of Mech. Engrg, 1975–76; King's College: Head, Dept of Mech. Engrg, 1976–90, 1991–94; Dean of Engrg, 1986–90; Hd of Sch. of Phys. Scis and Engrg, 1990–91. James Clayton Fund prize, IMechE, 1967; Engineering Applied to Agriculture Award, IMechE, 1980. *Publications:* papers and articles in Proc. IMechE, Jl of Mech. Engrg Science, Jl of Sound and Vibration, Wear, Proc. ASME and ASLE, and Eng. *Recreations:* Real tennis, gardening, fell walking. *Address:* Woodbury, Church Lane, Wormley, Broxbourne, Herts EN10 7QF. *T:* (01992) 464616.

EARNSHAW, (Thomas) Roy, CBE 1978 (OBE 1971); Director and General Manager of Division, TBA Industrial Products Ltd, Rochdale, 1966–76; retired; *b* 27 Feb. 1917; *s* of Godfrey Earnshaw and Edith Annie (*née* Perry); *m* 1953, Edith Rushworth; two *d*. *Educ:* Marlborough Coll., Liverpool. MICS. Served War, Army, 1940–46: Major Lancs Fusiliers. Shipbroking, Liverpool, 1933–39; appts with subsid. cos of Turner & Newall Ltd: Turner Brothers Asbestos Co. Ltd, Rochdale (mainly Export Sales Manager), 1939–40 and 1946–53; Dir, AM&FM Ltd, Bombay, 1954–59; Export Dir, Ferodo Ltd, Chapel-en-le-Frith, 1959–66. British Overseas Trade Board: Mem. Adv. Council, 1975–82; Export Year Advr, 1976–77; Export United Advr, 1978–83. Director: Actair Holdings Ltd, 1979–83; Actair Internat. Ltd, 1979–83; Unico Finance Ltd, 1979–81. Formerly: Pres., Rochdale Chamber of Commerce; Chm., NW Region Chambers of Commerce; UK Delegate to European Chambers of Commerce. London Economic Adviser to Merseyside CC, 1980–82. Vis. Fellow, Henley Management Coll. (formerly ASC), 1981–90. Chm., Henley Crime Prevention Panel, 1992–94; Mem., Bd of Managers, Henley YMCA, 1989–91; Sec., Henley Wildlife Gp, 1994–99. *Publication:* Glad Hearts in Export Year, 1991. *Recreations:* gardening, oil painting, hill walking, cycling.

EARWICKER, Martin John, FREng, FInstP; Director, National Museum of Science & Industry, since 2006; *b* 11 May 1948; *s* of George Allen Earwicker and Joan Mary Earwicker (*née* West); *m* 1970, Pauline Ann Josey; two *s*. *Educ:* Farnborough Grammar Sch.; Univ. of Surrey (BSc Hons Physics 1970). FInstP 1999; FREng 2000. Various research posts, ARE, 1970–86; Dir, Science (Sea), MoD, 1986–89; Hd, Attack Weapons Dept, 1989–90, Hd, Flight Systems Dept, 1990–92, RAE; Dir, Operational Studies, 1992–93, Dir, Air Systems Sector, 1993–96, DRA; Dep. Chief Scientist (Scrutiny and Analysis), 1996–98, Dir Gen. (Scrutiny and Analysis), 1998–99, MoD; Man. Dir, Analysis, DERA, 1998–99; Hd of Science and Engrg Base Gp, OST, DTI, 1999–2001; Chief Exec., Defence Sci. and Technol. Lab., MoD, 2001–06. Vis. Prof., Faculty of Engrg, Imperial Coll., London, 2005–. Chm., Farnborough Coll. of Technol. Pres., Assoc. for Sci. Educn, 2008. *Recreations:* cycling, woodwork, music. *Address:* Science Museum, Exhibition Road, South Kensington SW7 2DD.

EASEN-THOMAS, Rita Margaret; *see* Donaghy, R. M.

EASMON, Prof. Charles Syrett Farrell, CBE 2000; MD, PhD; Deputy Chairman, Health Protection Agency, since 2003; *b* 20 Aug. 1946; *s* of Dr McCormack Charles Farrell Easmon and Enid Winifred Easmon; *m* 1977, Susan Lynn (*née* Peach). *Educ:* Epsom Coll.; St Mary's Hospital Med. Sch. (Open Schol.; MB BS; MD); PhD London. MRCP; FRCPath. Pathology trng, St Bartholomew's Hosp., 1970–71; St Mary's Hospital Medical School: Research Asst, 1971; Lectr, 1973; Sen. Lectr, 1976; Reader and Actg Head of Dept, 1980; Personal Chair, 1983; Fleming Prof. of Med. Microbiol., 1984–92; Dean of Postgrad. Med. for NW Thames, BPMF, Univ. of London, 1992–95; Dir of Educn and Trng, N Thames, then London, Reg., NHS Exec., 1994–2002; Clin. Dir, Directorate of Health and Social Care for London, DoH, 2002–03. Non-exec. Dir, SW London Strategic HA, 2003–06. Founder FMedSci 1998. *Publications:* (ed) Medical Microbiology, vol. 1 1982, vols 2 and 3 1983, vol. 4 1984; (ed) Infections in the Immunocompromised Host, 1983; (ed) Staphylococci and Staphylococcal Infections, 1983; numerous papers in learned jls. *Recreations:* music, history, fishing. *Address:* 21 Cranes Park Avenue, Surbiton, Surrey KT5 8BS. *Club:* Athenæum.

EASON, Anthony Gordon, CBE 1995; JP; Executive Director, Hong Kong Experts Consultancy Co. Ltd, 1997; *b* 30 May 1938; *s* of Aubrey Eason and Helen Eason (*née* Hajj); *m* 1962, Teresa Wong; two *d*. *Educ:* Chatham House Grammar Sch., Ramsgate; RMA, Sandhurst. Served RA, 1959–62. Hong Kong Civil Service: Exec. Officer, 1962–68; Admin. Service, 1968–89; Dir, Buildings and Lands, 1989–92; Sec. for Planning, Envmt and Lands, 1992–95. Mem., HK Housing Soc., 1989–. JP Hong Kong, 1996. *Recreations:* reading, walking, writing.

EASSIE, Rt Hon. Lord; Ronald David Mackay; PC 2006; a Senator of the College of Justice in Scotland, since 1997; Chairman, Scottish Law Commission, 2002–06; *b* 1945; *s* of Robert Ostler Mackay and Dorothy Lilian Johnson or Mackay; *m* 1988, Annette Frenkel; one *s*. *Educ:* Berwickshire High Sch.; Univ. of St Andrews (MA Hons); Univ. of Edinburgh (LLB). Admitted to Faculty of Advocates, 1972; Official of Court of Justice of European Communities, Luxembourg, 1979–82; QC (Scot.) 1986; Advocate Depute, 1986–90. *Recreations:* walking, ski-ing. *Address:* Parliament House, Parliament Square, Edinburgh EH1 1RQ. *Club:* New (Edinburgh).

EAST, David Albert, QPM 1982; Secretary, Welsh Rugby Union, 1989; *b* 5 June 1936; *s* of Albert East and Florence Emily East; *m* 1957, Gloria (*née* Swinden); one *d*. *Educ:* King Alfred Grammar Sch., Wantage, Berks; University Coll. London (LLB Hons). Berks Constabulary, 1958–65 (constable to sergeant); First Special Course, Police Coll., Bramshill, 1962 (Johnson Prize and Cert. of Distinction); Inspector, York City Police, 1965–68; UCL, 1965–68; Metropol. Police Chief Inspector to Chief Supt, 1968–75; Eight Sen. Comd Course, Bramshill, 1971; Asst Chief Constable, Avon and Somerset Constab., 1975–78; RCDS, 1978; Dep. Chief Constable, Devon and Cornwall Constab., 1978–82, Chief Constable, 1982–83; seconded to Cyprus, 1981 and to Singapore, 1982; Chief Constable, S Wales Constab., 1983–88. Chm., British Police Athletic Assoc. OStJ 1985. Police Long Service and Good Conduct Medal, 1980. *Recreations:* Rugby, cricket.

EAST, John Anthony, CBE 1996 (OBE 1982); Chief Executive, English Tourist Board, 1985–95; Chairman: Continuum Group (formerly Heritage Projects Ltd), since 1997; Valuelink Ltd, since 1998; Greenway LLP, since 2007; *b* 25 May 1930; *s* of John East and Jessie Mary East; *m* 1st, 1957, Barbara Collins (marr. diss. 1980); two *s* one *d*; 2nd, 1982, Susan Finch (marr. diss. 1996); two *d*. *Educ:* Bromley Grammar School. Reuter's, 1954–58; Notley Advertising, 1958–60; Director: French Government Tourist Office, 1960–70; English Tourist Bd, 1970–95. Chm., Watermark, 1995–97. *Publications:* History of French Architecture, 1968; Gascony and the Pyrenees, 1969; articles on France and French architecture. *Recreations:* walking, gardening, studying things French. *Address:* Continuum Group, St Edmunds House, Margaret Street, York YO10 4UX.

EAST, Kenneth Arthur, CMG 1971; HM Diplomatic Service, retired; Ambassador to Iceland, 1975–81; *b* 9 May 1921; *s* of H. F. East; *m* 1946, Katherine Blackley; two *s* three *d*. *Educ:* Taunton's Sch.; Southampton Univ. Served HM Forces, 1942–46. India Office/Commonwealth Relations Office, 1946–50; Asst Private Sec. to Sec. of State; First Secretary: Ottawa, 1950–53; Colombo, 1956–60; Head of East and General Africa Dept, CRO, 1961–63; Head of Personnel Dept, CRO, 1963–64; Counsellor, Diplomatic Service Administration, 1965; Counsellor and Head of Chancery, Oslo, 1965–70; Minister, Lagos, 1970–74. *Club:* Royal Commonwealth Society.

EAST, Rt Hon. Paul Clayton, CNZM 2005; PC 1998; QC (NZ) 1995; High Commissioner for New Zealand in the United Kingdom, 1999–2002; *b* 4 Aug. 1946; *s* of Edwin Cuthbert East and Edith Pauline Addison East; *m* 1972, Marilyn Kottman; three *d*. *Educ:* King's Coll., Auckland; Auckland Univ. (LLB 1970); Univ. of Virginia, USA (LLM 1972). Barrister and solicitor, Auckland, 1971; Graduate Fellow, Univ. of Va Sch. of Law, 1971–72; Partner, 1974–78, Consultant, 1978–90, East Brewster, Solicitors, Rotorua. City Councillor, and Dep. Mayor of Rotorua, 1974–79 (Chm., Finance Cttee, 1977–79). MP (N) New Zealand, 1978–99 (for Rotorua, 1978–96). Opposition Spokesman, NZ Parliament: for Commerce and Customs, 1984; on Justice, Attorney-Gen. and Constitutional Affairs, 1985–90; on Health, 1986; Attorney-Gen., 1990–97; Minister: for Crown Health Enterprises, 1991–96; of State Services, 1993–97; of Defence, and of Corrections, 1996–97. Leader of House of Representatives, 1990–93. Chm., Parly Select Cttee on Official Information, 1982; Member: Nat. Exec., NZ Nat. Party, 1985–87; NZ Delegn, Council of Europe and Eur. Parlt, 1985. Chm., Rotorua Airport Cttee, 1977–79; Mem. Exec., Airport Authorities of NZ, 1974–79. Director: Taylors Gp Ltd, 2002–; Benfield Gp (formerly Grieg) (NZ) Ltd, 2002–; Agriquality Ltd. Chm., Charity Gaming Assoc., 2002–. Trustee: NZ Antarctic Heritage Trust, 2002–. Fellow, Australia/NZ Foundn, 1983. *Publications:* numerous articles. *Recreations:* ski-ing, fishing, golf. *Address:* PO Box 608, Rotorua, New Zealand. *Club:* Northern (Auckland).

EAST, Ronald Joseph; Director, Kleinwort Charter Investment Trust PLC, 1987–97; formerly Director, Kleinwort Development Fund PLC; *b* 17 Dec. 1931; *s* of Joseph William and Marion Elizabeth Emma East; *m* 1955, Iris Joyce Beckwith; two *d*. *Educ:* Clare Coll., Cambridge Univ. (MA). Engineering Apprenticeship, Ford Trade Sch., Ford Motor Co. Ltd, 1945–52. Troop Comdr, RA (Lieut), 1953–55. Managerial posts in economics, product planning, finance, and engineering areas of Ford Motor Co. Ltd, 1959–65; Guest, Keen & Nettlefolds Ltd: Corporate Staff Dir of Planning, 1965–70; Planning Exec., Automotive and Allied Products Sector, 1972–73; Chairman: GKN Castings Ltd, 1974–77; GKN Kent Alloys Ltd, 1974–77; GKN Shotton Ltd, 1974–77; Dir, GKN (UK) Ltd, 1974–77; Corporate Staff Dir, Group Supplies, GKN Ltd, 1976–77. Dir, Programme Analysis and Review (PAR) and Special Advisor to Chief Sec. to the Treasury, 1971–72. Chairman: Hale Hamilton Hldgs, 1981–89; Hale Hamilton (Valves), 1981–89. *Recreation:* walking. *Address:* 12 Rutland Gate, SW7 1BB.

EAST, Trevor; Director of Sport, Setanta, since 2005; *b* Derby, 22 Oct. 1950; *s* of Ralph James and Hazel Jean East; *m* 1st, 1975, Penelope Anne McLean (marr. diss. 1987); two *s* one *d*; 2nd, 1995, Katharine Judith Brown; two *s* one *d*. *Educ:* Bemrose Grammar Sch., Derby. Trainee journalist, then journalist, Raymonds News Agency, 1967–72; Producer, ATV Sport, 1972–78; Presenter, Tiswas, 1973–78; Sports Ed., Central TV, 1978–84; Exec. Producer, 1984–92, Dep. Hd, 1992–94, Hd, 1994–95, ITV Sport; Dep. Man. Dir, Sky Sports, 1995–2005. Chm., Pitch Internat., 2005–. *Recreations:* sport, music, food, wine. *Address:* Setanta Sports, 8 Waterloo Place, SW1Y 4BE. *T:* (020) 7766 8484.

EAST ANGLIA, Bishop of, (RC), since 2003; **Rt Rev. Michael Evans;** *b* 10 Aug. 1951; *s* of Ralph and Jeannette Evans. *Educ:* St John's Seminary, Wonersh; Heythrop Coll., Univ. of London (MTh 1979). Ordained priest, 1975; Asst Priest, Richmond, Surrey, 1975–77; St John's Seminary, Wonersh: Lectr in Christian Doctrine, 1979–87, 1993–95; Vice-Rector, 1985–87, 1993–95; Chaplain to S London Univs, 1987–93; Parish Priest, Tunbridge Wells, 1995–2003. Member: Catholic Bps' Conf. Cttee for Ministerial

Formation, 1989–2003; British Methodist/Catholic Cttee, 1991–; Internat. Jt Commn for Dialogue between the RC Church and the World Methodist Council, 1996–; Chm., Cttee for Christian Unity, 2005–. Jt Pres., Christian-Muslim Forum, 2006–. *Publications:* Let My People Go, 1979; A Catholic Priest Today and Tomorrow, 1993; numerous booklets and articles. *Recreations:* listening to music, supporting Leeds United FC. *Address:* The White House, 21 Upgate, Poringland, Norwich NR14 7SH. *T:* (01508) 492202; *e-mail:* office@east-angliadiocese.org.uk.

EAST RIDING, Archdeacon of; *see* Butterfield, Ven. D. J.

EASTCOTT, Harry Hubert Grayson, MS; FRCS; FRCOG; Consulting Surgeon, St Mary's Hospital; Consultant in Surgery and Vascular Surgery to the Royal Navy, 1957–82, now Emeritus; *b* 17 Oct. 1917; *s* of Harry George and Gladys Eastcott; *m* 1941, Doreen Joy (*d* 2007), *e d* of Brenchley Ernest and Muriel Mittell; four *d. Educ:* Latymer Sch.; St Mary's Hosp. Medical School and Middlesex Hospital Medical Sch., University of London; Harvard Med. Sch. War of 1939–45, Junior surgical appts and service as Surgeon Lieut, RNVR up till 1946. Surg. Lieut Comdr RNVR, London Div., until 1957. MRCS; LRCP; MB, BS (Hons), 1941; FRCS 1946; MS (London), 1951. Sen. Registrar, 1950 as Hon. Cons. to St Mary's and Asst Dir Surgical Unit; Research Fellow in Surgery, Harvard Med. Sch., and Peter Bent Brigham Hosp., Boston, Mass, 1949–50; recognised teacher, 1953, and Examr, 1959, in surgery, University of London; Cons. Surgeon, St Mary's Hosp. and Lectr in Surgery, St Mary's Hosp. Med. Sch., 1955–82; Surgeon, Royal Masonic Hosp., 1964–80; Cons. Surgeon, King Edward VII Hosp. for Officers, 1965–87; Hon. Surg., RADA, 1959–; External Examr in Surgery: Queen's Univ., Belfast, 1964–67; Cambridge Univ., 1968–84; Univ. of Lagos, Nigeria, 1970–71. Editorial Sec., British Jl of Surgery, 1972–78. Royal College of Surgeons: Hunterian Prof., 1953; Mem. Court of Examrs, 1964–70; Mem. Council, 1971–83; Bradshaw Lectr, 1980; Vice-Pres., 1981–83; Cecil Joll Prize, 1984; RCS Visitor to RCOG Council, 1972–80; Mem. Court of Patrons, 1997–. FRSocMed (Hon. Sec., Section of Surgery, 1963–65, Vice-President, 1966, Pres., 1977; Pres., United Services Section, 1981–83, Hon. Mem., 1992). Fellow Medical Soc. of London (Hon. Sec., 1962–64, Vice-Pres. 1964, Pres., 1976, Fothergill Gold Medal, 1974, Trustee 1988). Pres., Assoc. of Surgeons of GB and Ireland, 1982–83. Mem., Soc. Apothecaries, 1967 (Galen Medal, 1993). Hon. FACS, 1977; Hon. FRACS, 1978; Hon. Fellow: Amer. Surgical Assoc., 1981; Amer. Heart Assoc.; Stroke Council, 1981; Hon. Member: Purkinje Med. Soc., Czechoslovakia, 1984; Internat. Union of Angiology, 1995; Europ. Soc. for Vascular Surgery, 1995. Leriche Prize, Internat. Surg. Soc., 2001. *Publications:* Arterial Surgery, 1969, 3rd edn 1992; A Colour Atlas of Operations on the Internal Carotid Artery, 1984; various articles on gen. and arterial surgery, Lancet, Brit. Jl of Surg., etc.; contrib. chap. of peripheral vascular disease, Med. Annual, 1961–80; various chaps in textbooks on these subjects. *Recreations:* music, travel, and a lifelong interest in aeronautics. *Address:* 16 White Cross Road, Haddenham, Bucks HP17 8BA. *T:* (01844) 290629. *Club:* Garrick.

EASTELL, Prof. Richard, MD; FRCP, FRCPE, FRCPath; Professor of Bone Metabolism, since 1995, and Hon. Consultant Physician, since 1989, University of Sheffield; *b* 12 Feb. 1953; *s* of Kenneth Eastell and Betty Eastell (*née* Hoare); *m* 1974, Joyce Rachel Noble; two *s* one *d. Educ:* Univ. of Edinburgh (BSc Hons 1974; MB ChB 1977; MD 1984). FRCP 1996; FRCPE 2000; FRCPath 2000. House Officer, Royal Infirmary and Western Gen. Hosp., Edinburgh, 1977–78; MRC Res. Fellow, 1978–80, Registrar, 1980–82, Western Gen. Hosp., Edinburgh; Registrar, Northwick Park Hosp., Harrow, 1982–84; Res. Associate and Sen. Clinical Fellow, Mayo Clinic, Rochester, Minn., 1984–89; University of Sheffield: Sen. Res. Fellow, 1989–92, Sen. Lectr, 1992–95, Dept of Human Metabolism and Clinical Biochemistry; Res. Dean, Sch. of Medicine and Biomed. Scis, 2002–05. Director: Div. of Clinical Scis (North), 1999–2003; R&D for Sheffield Teaching Hosps Trust, 2003–05. Visiting Professor in Endocrinology: Mayo Clinic, Rochester, USA, 1999; Univ. of Pittsburgh, 2002; Path West Vis. Lectr, Perth, Australia, 2005. Member: ARC Res. Cttee, 1998–2004; Res. Adv. Council, Res. into Ageing, 2001–04; MRC Physiological Systems and Clinical Scis Bd, 2003–06. President: Bone and Tooth Soc., 2002–05; Eur. Calcified Tissue Soc., 2006–; Chm., Nat. Osteoporosis Soc., 2007–. FMedSci 2000. Hon. FRCPI 1998. Randall G. Sprague Award, Mayo Clinic, 1989; Corrigan Medal, RCPI, 1998; Queen's Anniversary Award for Higher Educn, 2002; Kohn Award, Nat. Osteoporosis Soc., 2004; Soc. for Endocrinol. Medal, 2004. *Publications:* (ed jtly) Bone Markers: biochemical and clinical perspectives, 2001; 270 articles in med. literature. *Recreations:* golf, hill walking. *Address:* 289 Ringinglow Road, Bents Green, Sheffield, South Yorks S11 7PZ. *T:* (0114) 271 4705; *e-mail:* r.eastell@sheffield.ac.uk.

EASTER, Rev. Canon Ann Rosemarie; Chief Executive Officer, Renewal Programme, since 1995; Chaplain to the Queen, since 2007; *b* Upton Park, 9 Sept. 1947; *d* of Harry Easter and Audrey Easter (*née* Boater); *m* 1987, Rev. Christopher Owens; two *s* one *d. Educ:* George Green's Grammar Sch.; Queen's Coll., Birmingham (Dip. in Religious Studies 1979); Univ. of East London (Dip. in Mgt Studies 1994). Ordained deaconess, 1980, deacon, 1987, priest, 1994; Parish Minister, St John, St James and Christchurch, London, 1980–89; Manager, Newham Crossroads, 1990–95; Area Dean, Newham, 1996–2007. Hon. Canon, Chelmsford Cathedral, 2000–; Hon. Curate (part-time), All Saints, West Ham, 2008–. Regular contribs to Good Morning Sunday and Pause for Thought, BBC Radio 2. *Publication:* This Month We Celebrate, 1990. *Recreations:* playing the piano, entertaining and being entertained. *Address:* (office) 66B Sebert Road, E7 0NJ. *T:* (020) 8221 4420; *e-mail:* ann@renewalprogramme.org.uk. 67 Disraeli Road, E7 9JU. *T:* (020) 8555 6337.

EASTERLING, Prof. Patricia Elizabeth, FBA 1998; Regius Professor of Greek, Cambridge University, 1994–2001, and Fellow of Newnham College, Cambridge, 1994–2001 (Hon. Fellow, 1987–94 and since 2001); *b* 11 March 1934; *d* of Edward Wilson Fairfax and Annie Smith; *m* 1956, Henry John Easterling; one *s. Educ:* Blackburn High School for Girls; Newnham College, Cambridge (BA 1955, MA 1959). Asst Lectr, Univ. of Manchester, 1957–58; University of Cambridge: Asst Lectr, 1968; Lectr, 1969–87; Newnham College, Cambridge: Asst Lectr, 1958–60; Fellow and Lectr, 1960–87; Dir of Studies in Classics, 1979–87; Vice-Principal, 1981–86; Prof. of Greek, UCL, 1987–94. Townsend Lectr, Cornell Univ., 1990. Chm., Council of Univ. Classical Depts, 1990–93. President: Classical Assoc., 1988–89; Hellenic Soc., 1996–99. Mem., Academia Europaea, 1995. Corresp. étranger, Acad. des Inscriptions et Belles-Lettres, Inst de France, 2004. Hon. Fellow, UCL, 1997. Hon. DPhil: Athens, 1996; Uppsala, 2000; Ioannina, 2002; Hon. DLitt Bristol, 1999; Hon. DLit London, 1999. *Publications:* (with E. J. Kenney) Ovidiana Graeca, 1965; (ed) Sophocles, Trachiniae, 1982; (with B. M. W. Knox, ed and contrib.) Cambridge History of Classical Literature, vol. I, 1985; (ed with J. V. Muir) Greek Religion and Society, 1985; (ed) Cambridge Companion to Greek Tragedy, 1997; (ed with C. M. Handley) Greek Scripts, 2001; (ed with E. M. Hall) Greek and Roman Actors, 2002. *Recreation:* hill walking. *Address:* Newnham College, Cambridge CB3 9DF. *T:* (01223) 335700.

EASTHAM, Kenneth; *b* 11 Aug. 1927; *s* of late James Eastham; *m* 1951, Doris, *d* of Albe Howarth; one *d.* Planning engr, GEC, Trafford Park. Mem., Manchester CC, 1962–8 (Dep. Leader 1975–79; Chairman: Planning Cttee, 1971–74; Educn Cttee, 1978–79 Mem., NW Econ. Planning Council, 1975–79. MP (Lab) Manchester, Blackley, 1979–97 An Opposition Whip, 1987–92. *Address:* 12 Nan Nook Road, Manchester M23 9BZ.

EASTON, Carole, PhD; Chief Executive, CLIC Sargent, since 2006; *b* 13 July 1954; *d* c Laszlo Easton and late Naomi Easton. *Educ:* Brunel Univ. (BSc; PhD); Tavistock Clini (Child and Adolescent Psychotherapist). Child Psychotherapist, NHS, 1984–91 Counselling Manager, ChildLine, 1992–96; Hd, Clinical Services, The Place to Be 1996–98; Chief Exec., Cruse Bereavement Care, 1998–2001; ChildLine, 2001–06 *Address:* CLIC Sargent, Griffin House, 161 Hammersmith Road, W6 8SG. *T:* (020) 875 2828; *e-mail:* carole.easton@clicsargent.org.uk.

EASTON, David John; HM Diplomatic Service, retired; consultant on Arab and Sout Asian matters; *b* 27 March 1941; *o s* of Air Cdre Sir James Easton, KCMG, CB, CBE, an Anna, *d* of Lt-Col J. A. McKenna, Ottawa; *m* 1964, Alexandra Julie, *er d* of Kenneth W Clark (MBE 2000), London, W8; two *s* two *d. Educ:* Stone House, Broadstairs; Stow (Exhbnr); Balliol Coll., Oxford (Trevelyan Schol.; BA Hons Jurisprudence 1963, MA 1973). Apprentice, United Steel Cos, Workington, 1960. TA, 1959–65; 2nd Lieu Oxford Univ. OTC, 1962; Lieut, Inns of Court and City Yeo., 1964. Entered Foreig Office, 1963; Third Sec., Nairobi, 1965–66; Second Sec., UK Mission to UN, Genev 1967–70; MECAS, Lebanon, 1970–72; First Sec., FCO, 1972–73; First Se (Information), Tripoli, 1973–77; Defence Dept, FCO, 1977–80; First Sec. (Chancery later Political Counsellor, Amman, 1980–83; Counsellor, FCO, 1984–86; Counsello (Political), New Delhi, 1986–89; FCO, 1990–94; Gen. Manager, Network Security Mg Ltd, 1994–95; Dir (Internat. Affairs), ICAEW, 1995–97; Sec., RSAA, 1997–200 Director, Internat. Community Sch. (Jordan) Ltd, 1980–83 (Chm. 1981–83). Pres., Dell Diplomatic Assoc., 1988–89; Chm., Lansdowne Residents' Assoc., 1990–96. FRSA 199 FRGS 1998. *Recreations:* swimming, travel, antiques and antiquities.

EASTON, James, OBE 1986; HM Diplomatic Service, retired; Feature Write Accordion Times, since 1992; *b* 1 Sept. 1931; *s* of John Easton and Helen Easton (*n* Whitney); *m* 1960, Rosemary Hobbin (*d* 2006); one *s* two *d. Educ:* St John Cantiu Catholic Sch., Broxburn. Served 3rd Hussars, 1952–55. Admiralty, 1957–60; FO, 196 Prague, 1960–62; Paris, 1963–65; FO, 1965–68; Vice-Consul: Belgrade, 1968–71; La Pa 1971–74; Second Sec. (Commercial), New York, 1974–78; FCO, 1978–83; First Sec Rome, 1983–87; Counsellor (Admin) and Consul-Gen., Brussels, 1987–89. *Recreatio* music. *Address:* 6 Cedar Gardens, Sutton, Surrey SM2 5DD. *T:* (020) 8643 2432.

EASTON, Mark Richard Erskine; Home Editor, BBC News, since 2004; *b* 12 Marc 1959; *s* of Stephen and Fiona Easton; *m* 1987, Antonia Higgs; one *s* three *d. Educ:* Pete Symonds' Grammar Sch., Winchester. Southern Evening Echo, 1978–80; Radio Victor 1980–81; Radio Aire, 1981–82; LBC Radio, 1982–86; Corresp., BBC, 1986–96; Politic Ed., Channel 5, 1996–98; Home and Social Affairs Ed., Channel 4, 1998–200 *Recreations:* piano blues; Arsenal FC. *Address: e-mail:* mark.easton@bbc.co.uk.

EASTON, Robert Alexander, PhD; Chief Executive, Delta plc, 1989–96; *b* 24 Oc 1948; *s* of Malcolm Edward George Easton and Violet May Liddell Easton (*née* Taylor); 1983, Lynden Anne Welch; two *d. Educ:* St Lawrence Coll.; Univ. of Manchester (BS Hons); Univ. of Aston (PhD). Delta plc, 1974–96: Dir of Planning, 1980–83; Man. D Industrial Services Div., 1984–87; Dep. Chief Exec., 1988–89. Director: G. E. Crar (Holdings), 1986–91; Elementis (formerly Harrisons & Crosfield) plc, 1991–200 *Recreations:* golf, travel, medieval art and architecture.

EASTON, Sir Robert (William Simpson), Kt 1990; CBE 1980; CEng, FIMarES FRINA; Chairman: Yarrow Shipbuilders Ltd, 1979–94; GEC Scotland, 1989–99; *b* 3 Oct. 1922; *s* of James Easton and Helen Agnes (*née* Simpson); *m* 1948, Jean, *d* of H. F Fraser and Jean (*née* Murray); one *s* one *d. Educ:* Royal Technical Coll., Glasgow. Fairfie Shipbuilding Co., 1939–51; Manager, Yarrow & Co. Ltd, 1951–65; Yarrow Shipbuilde Ltd: Director, 1965; Dep. Managing Director, 1970; Managing Director, 1977–91; Ma Board Director, Yarrow & Co. Ltd, 1970–77. Vice Pres., Clyde Shipbuilders, 1972–7 Chm., Clyde Port Authy, 1983–93. Chm., GEC Naval Systems, 1991–94; Directo Genships (Canada), 1979–80; Supermarine Consortium Ltd, 1986–90; W of Scotlar Water Authy, 1995–97; Caledonian MacBrayne Ltd, 1997–2000. Chancellor, Paisl Univ., 1993–2003. President: Inst. of Welding, 1991–93; Inst. of Engineers ar Shipbuilders, Scotland, 1997–99; Member: Council, RINA, 1983–91 (Hon. Vice Pre 1991–); Worshipful Company of Shipwrights, 1982–96; Merchants House of Glasgo 1989–; Incorporation of Hammermen, 1989–. Hon. FIMechE 2000. *Recreations:* walkin golf, gardening. *Address:* Springfield, Stuckenduff, Shandon, Argyll & Bute G84 8NW. (01436) 820677. *Clubs:* Caledonian; Ross Priory Golf (Strathclyde).

EASTWOOD, Basil Stephen Talbot, CMG 1999; HM Diplomatic Service, retired; *b* March 1944; *s* of late Christopher Gilbert Eastwood, CMG and Catherine Emma (*n* Peel); *m* 1970, Alison Faith Hutchings; three *d* (and one *d* decd). *Educ:* Eton (KS); Merto College, Oxford. Entered Diplomatic Service, 1966; Middle East Centre for Arab Studie 1967–68; Jedda, 1968–69; Colombo, 1969–72; Cairo, 1972–76; Cabinet Office, 1976–7 FCO, 1978–80; Bonn, 1980–84; Khartoum, 1984–87; Athens, 1987–91; Dir of Res. a Analysis, FCO, 1991–96; Ambassador to Syria, 1996–2000; Project Dir, Middle East Ins 2000–01; Ambassador to Switzerland, 2001–04. *Address:* Church End, Church Stre Somerton, Oxon OX25 6NB.

EASTWOOD, Clinton, (Clint); actor, film director and producer; *b* San Francisco, May 1930; *s* of Clinton and Ruth Eastwood; *m* 1st, 1953, Maggie Johnson (marr. di 1978); one *s* one *d*; 2nd, 1996, Dina Ruiz; one *d*; one *d* with Frances Fisher; one *d* wi Roxanne Tunis; one *s* one *d* with Jacelyn Reeves. *Educ:* Oakland Tech. High Sch.; L City Coll. Actor, TV series, Rawhide, 1959–66. *Films include: actor:* A Fistful of Dolla 1964; For a Few Dollars More, 1965; The Good, The Bad and The Ugly, 1966; Ha 'Em High, 1968; Where Eagles Dare, Coogan's Bluff, 1968; Paint Your Wagon, 196 Kelly's Heroes, 1970; The Beguiled, Dirty Harry, 1971; Joe Kidd, 1972; Magnum Forc 1973; Thunderbolt and Lightfoot, 1974; The Enforcer, 1976; Every Which Way B Loose, 1978; Escape from Alcatraz, 1979; Tightrope (and prod.), City Heat, 1984; T Dead Pool, 1988; Pink Cadillac, 1989; In the Line of Fire, 1993; *actor and director:* Pl Misty for Me, 1971; High Plains Drifter, 1973; The Eiger Sanction, 1975; The Outla Josey Wales, 1976; Bronco Billy, 1980; The Rookie, 1990; *actor, director and produc* Firefox, Honkytonk Man, 1982; Sudden Impact, 1983; Pale Rider, 1985; Heartbre Ridge, 1986; White Hunter Black Heart, 1990; Unforgiven, 1992 (Academy Awards f Best Dir and Best Picture, 1993); A Perfect World, 1993; The Bridges of Madison Count 1995; Absolute Power, 1997; True Crime, 1999; Space Cowboys, 2000; Blood Wor 2002; Million Dollar Baby (Golden Globe Award for Best Dir; Academy Awards for Be Dir and Best Picture), 2005; *director and producer:* Bird, 1988 (Golden Globe Award for Be Dir, 1989); Midnight in the Garden of Good and Evil, 1997; Mystic River, 2003; Flags Our Fathers, 2006; Letters From Iwo Jima, 2007; L'Echange, 2008 (Special Prize, Cann

Film Fest., 2008). Founder and owner, Malpaso Prodns, 1969–. Proprietor: Mission Ranch, Carmel, Calif; Tehama Golf Club, Carmel Valley, Calif; co-founder, Tehama, clothing co., 1997. Mayor of Carmel, Calif, 1986–88.

EASTWOOD, Prof. David Stephen, DPhil; FRHistS; Chief Executive, Higher Education Funding Council for England, since 2006; *b* 5 Jan. 1959; *s* of Colin Eastwood and Elaine Clara Eastwood; *m* 1980, Jan Page; one *s* two *d. Educ:* Sandbach Sch., Cheshire; St Peter's Coll., Oxford (BA 1st Cl. Hons Modern Hist.; MA 1985; DPhil 1985; Hon. Fellow 2003). FRHistS 1991. Jun. Res. Fellow, Keble Coll., Oxford, 1983–87; Fellow and Tutor in Modern Hist., 1988–95, Sen. Tutor, 1992–95, Pembroke Coll., Oxford; Dep. Chair, Bd of Faculty of Modern Hist., Univ. of Oxford, 1994–95; University of Wales, Swansea: Prof. of Social Hist., 1995–2000; Hd, Dept of Hist., 1996–2000; Actg Hd, Dept of Philosophy, 1998–99; Dean, Faculty of Arts and Social Studies, 1997–99; Pro-Vice-Chancellor, 1999–2000; Chief Exec., AHRB, 2000–02; Vice-Chancellor, UEA, 2002–06, Emeritus Prof. of Hist., 2006. British Acad. Post-Doctoral Fellow, 1986–87. Literary Dir, RHistS, 1994–2000; Chm. Editl Bd, RHistS Studies in History series, 2000–04. Chair of Examrs, A Level Hist., UODLE, O&C, OCR, 1991–2000. Chair: Adv. Gp on Benchmarking, QAA, 2003–06; Assoc. of Univs in E of England, 2003–06; Member: RAE Review Gp, HEFCE, 2002–03; Res. Support Libraries Gp, 2002–03; 14–19 Wkg Gp, DfES, 2003–04; Res. Strategic Cttee, HEFCE, 2003–; Bd, QAA, 2004–06. Co-founder and non-exec. Chair, Nat. Centre for Public Policy, 1998–2000. Member: Gov. Council, John Innes Centre, 2003–06 (Dep. Chm., 2004–06); Council, Sainsbury Lab., 2003–06; Adv. Bd, Higher Educn Policy Inst., 2003–. Mem., Marshall Aid Meml Commn, 2003–. FRSA. Hon. DLitt: UWE, 2003; UEA, 2006. *Publications:* Governing Rural England: tradition and transformation in local government 1780–1840, 1994; Government and Community in the English Provinces 1700–1870, 1997; (ed with L. Brockliss) A Union of Multiple Identities: the British Isles *c* 1750–*c* 1850, 1997; (ed with N. Thompson) The Social and Political Writings of William Cobbett, 16 vols, 1998; numerous papers in scholarly jls, edited vols, etc. *Recreations:* music, collecting CDs, current affairs, walking, wine, watching sport. *Address:* Higher Education Funding Council for England, Northavon House, Coldharbour Lane, Bristol BS16 1QD. *T:* (0117) 931 7300, *Fax:* (0117) 931 7150. *Club:* Athenæum.

EASTWOOD, Noel Anthony Michael, MA; CEng, MRAeS; Chairman, InterData Group, 1981–93; *b* 7 Dec. 1932; *s* of Edward Norman Eastwood and Irene Dawson; *m* 1965, Elizabeth Tania Gresham Boyd, *d* of Comdr Thomas Wilson Boyd, CBE, DSO, DL and Irene Barbara Gresham; three *s. Educ:* The Leys School, Cambridge; Christ's College, Cambridge. Lieut RA, 1951–54; Pilot Officer, RAFVR, 1954–57; de Havilland Aircraft Co., 1956–60; Rio Tinto, 1960–61; AEI Group, 1961–64; Director: Charterhouse Development, 1964–69; Charterhouse Japhet, 1969–79 (Pres., Charterhouse Japhet Texas, 1974–77); Charterhouse Middle East, 1975–79; Burnett & Rolfe Ltd, 1964–69 (Chm.); Wharton Crane & Hoist, 1967–70 (Chm.); Daniel Doncaster & Son (International Nickel), 1971–81; The Barden Corp., 1971–82; Hawk Publishing (UAE), 1981–87; Oryx Publishing (Qatar), 1981–87; Falcon Publishing (Bahrain), 1981–84; Caribbean Publishing, 1981–84; IDP InterData (Australia), 1984–92 and 1995–96; European Public Policy Advisers Gp, 1987–97; Spearhead Communications, 1988–99; Seafish Falklands Ltd (Port Stanley), 1990–95. Sec., RAeS, 1983. Member: London Cttee, Yorkshire & Humberside Development Assoc., 1975–94; Management Cttee, Offshore Europe Conf. and Exhibn, 1990–2000; S Atlantic Council, 1991– (Hon. Treas., 1998–). Member: Much Hadham PCC, 1989–2007; Much Hadham Parish Council, 1995–97; St Albans Diocesan Synod, 1997–2006. Hon. Treas., 1992–99, Vice Chm., 2004–, Herts Soc.; Mem. Exec. Cttee, CPRE, 1995–98 (Chm., SE Reg., 1995–2000; Vice-Chm., E of England Cttee, 1999–2005); Chm., Thames NE Area Envmt Gp, 1997–2000; Mem. Exec. Cttee, E England Envmtl Forum, 1999–2006 (Chm., 1999); Mem., Thames and Chilterns Regl Cttee, 2001–02, E of England (formerly E Anglia) Regl Cttee, 2002–, Nat. Trust. Founder, Royal Artillery Heritage Campaign, 1991. *Recreations:* ski-ing, sailing, vintage sportscars, family picnics, desert travel. *Address:* Palace House, Much Hadham, Herts SG10 6HW. *T:* (01279) 842409. *Club:* Royal Thames Yacht.

EASTWOOD, Dr Wilfred, PhD; FREng, FICE, FIStructE, FIMechE; Senior Partner, Eastwood and Partners, Consulting Engineers, 1972–2000; *b* 15 Aug. 1923; *s* of Wilfred Andrew Eastwood and Annice Gertrude Eastwood; *m* 1947, Dorothy Jean Gover; one *s* one *d. Educ:* PhD Aberdeen 1949. Road Research Laboratory, 1945–46; University of Manchester, 1946–47; University of Aberdeen, 1947–53; University of Sheffield, 1954–70: Head, Dept of Civil Engrg, 1964–70; Dean, Faculty of Engrg, 1967–70. Pres., IStructE, 1976–77; Chairman: CEI, 1983–84; Commonwealth Engrg Council, 1981–85. Hon. DEng Sheffield, 1980. Médaille de la Ville de Paris, 1983. *Publications:* papers in Proc. ICE and Jl IStructE, etc. *Address:* 45 Whirlow Park Road, Sheffield S11 9NN. *T:* (0114) 236 4645.

EASTY, Prof. David Leonello, MD; FRCS, FRCOphth; Professor of Ophthalmology and Head of Department of Ophthalmology, University of Bristol, 1982–99, now Professor Emeritus; *b* 6 Aug. 1933; *s* of Arthur Victor Easty and Florence Margaret (*née* Kennedy); *m* 1963, Božana Martinović; three *d. Educ:* King's Sch., Canterbury; Univ. of Manchester. MD 1963; FRCS 1969; FRCOphth (FCOphth 1988). Capt., RAMC, 1959; Med. Officer, British Antarctic Survey, 1960. Moorfield's Eye Hospital: Resident, 1966–69; Lectr, 1969–72; Consultant, Bristol Eye Hosp., 1972–82. Dir, Corneal Transplant Service Eye Bank, 1986–99. Lectures: Lang, RSocMed, 1998; Doyne, Oxford Congress of Ophthalmol., 1999; Bowman, RCOphth, 2000; Castroviejo, Amer. Acad. of Ophthalmol., 2002. Nettleship Medal for Research, Ophthalmol Soc., 1999. Member: BMA; RSocMed (Pres., Sect. of Ophthalmol., 1998–2000). Member: Antarctic Club; Piscatorial Soc. *Publications:* Virus Disease of the Eye, 1985; (with G. Smolim) External Eye Disease, 1985; (ed) Current Ophthalmic Surgery, 1990; (with N. Ragge) Immediate Eye Care, 1990; Oxford Textbook of Ophthalmology, 1999. *Recreations:* fishing, running, opera, lawn tennis, Real tennis. *Address:* 42 Clifton Park Road, Clifton, Bristol BS8 3HN. *Clubs:* Army and Navy; Clifton (Bristol).

EATES, Edward Caston, CMG 1968; LVO 1961; QPM 1961; CPM 1956; Commissioner, The Royal Hong Kong Police, 1967–69, retired; re-employed at Foreign and Commonwealth Office, 1971–76; *b* London, 8 April 1916; *o s* of late Edward Eates and Elizabeth Lavinia Issac Eates (*née* Caston); *m* 1941, Maureen Teresa McGee (*d* 1987); no *c. Educ:* Highgate Sch.; King's Coll., London (LLB). Asst Examr, Estate Duty Office, 1935. Army, 1939–46 (RAC): Western Desert and NW Europe; Adjt 2nd Derby Yeo., 1943; Temp. Maj. 1944; Staff Coll. Quetta (sc), 1945. Apptd to Colonial Police Service, Nigeria, 1946; Sen. Supt, Sierra Leone, 1954; Comr, The Gambia, 1957; Asst Comr, 1963, Dep. Comr, 1966, Hong Kong. *Recreations:* cricket and association football, travel, motoring. *Address:* 2 Riverside Court, Colleton Crescent, Exeter EX2 4BZ. *T:* (01392) 436434. *Clubs:* Royal Commonwealth Society, East India; Surrey County Cricket.

EATOCK TAYLOR, Prof. (William) Rodney, FREng; Professor of Mechanical Engineering, University of Oxford, 1989–Sept. 2009 (Head of Department of Engineering Science, 1999–2004); Fellow of St Hugh's College, Oxford, since 1989; *b* 10 Jan. 1944; *s* of late William Taylor, Hadley Wood, Herts and Norah O'Brien Taylor (*née* Ridgeway); *m* 1971, Jacqueline Lorraine Cannon, *d* of late Desmond Cannon Brookes; two *s. Educ:* Rugby Sch.; King's Coll., Cambridge (BA, MA); Stanford Univ. (MS, PhD). FRINA 1986; FIMechE 1989; FREng (FEng 1990). Engineer, Ove Arup and Partners, 1968–70; University College London: Res. Asst, 1970; Lectr, 1972; Reader, 1980; Prof. of Ocean Engineering, 1984–89; Dean, Faculty of Engineering, 1988–89. Dir, Marine Technology Directorate Ltd, 1990–95; Chm., Marine Technology Trust, 1991–. Mem., Marine Technology Foresight Panel, OST, 1995–97. Mem. Council, 2003–07, Vice Pres., 2004–07, Royal Acad. of Engrg. Gov., Queenswood Sch., 1990–2003. Member, Editorial Boards: Engineering Structures, 1978–2008; Applied Ocean Research, 1984–; Jl of Fluids and Structures, 1990–; series: Ocean Technology, 1986–2001; Engineering Science, 1990–98. Hon. Fellow, UCL, 2008. *Publications:* numerous contribs to learned jls of structural dynamics and marine hydrodynamics. *Recreations:* walking, music. *Address:* St Hugh's College, Oxford OX2 6LE. *T:* (01865) 274900. *Club:* Athenæum.

EATON, Deborah Ann; QC 2008; a Recorder, since 2004; *b* Nottingham, 28 March 1962; *d* of Stanley Eaton and Margaret Ann Eaton. *Educ:* Univ. of Keele (BSocSci Hons 1983); City Univ., London (Dip. Law 1984). Called to the Bar, Inner Temple, 1983; in practice as a barrister, specialising in family law; Midland Circuit, 1985–. *Publication:* (author, and ed with Stephen Wildblood) Financial Provision in Family Matters, 1998. *Address:* 1 King's Bench Walk, Temple, EC4Y 7DB. *T:* (020) 7936 1500, *Fax:* (020) 7936 1590; *e-mail:* deaton@1kbw.co.uk.

EATON, Rt Rev. Derek Lionel, QSM 1985; Assistant Anglican Bishop of Egypt with North Africa and the Horn of Africa, since 2007; *b* 10 Sept. 1941; *s* of Henry Jackson Eaton and Ella Barbara (*née* McDouall); *m* 1964, Alice Janice Maslin; two *s* one *d. Educ:* Christchurch Boys' High Sch. (NZ); AG Graduate Sch., Missouri (MA *cum laude*); Christchurch Teachers' Coll. (Teacher Trng Cert); Switzerland (Cert. Française); Univ. of Tunis (Cert. Arabic and Islamics); Missionary Training Coll., Australia (DipTheol); Trinity Theol Coll., Bristol. School teacher, 1964. Missionary with Worldwide Evangelisation Crusade, Tunisia, 1968–78; ordained deacon and priest, 1971; Curate, St Luke's, Bristol, 1971–72; Vicar of Tunis, 1972–78; Hon. Chaplain, British Embassy, Tunis, 1972–78; Provost, Cairo Cathedral, Egypt, 1978–83 (Emeritus, 1984); Hon. Chaplain, British Embassy, Egypt, 1978–83; with Church Missionary Society, 1980–84; Associate Vicar, Papanui, Bishopdale, NZ, 1984–85; Vicar, Sumner, Redcliffs, NZ, 1985–90; Bishop of Nelson, NZ, 1990–2006. Hon. Canon, 1985, Episcopal Canon, 1992, Cairo Cathedral. *Publications:* What awaits us there: between reality and illusion (Arabic), 2002; Life After Death: welcome to the future, 2004; contrib. theol and missiological jls. *Recreations:* swimming, golf, reading, woodwork. *Address:* All Saints' Cathedral, PO Box 87, Zamalek 11211, Cairo, Egypt.

EATON, Duncan; *see* Eaton, N. D.

EATON, Fredrik Stefan, OC 1990; OOnt 2001; Chairman, White Raven Capital Corporation; *b* 26 June 1938; *s* of late John David Eaton and Signy Hildur Eaton (*née* Stephenson); *m* 1962, Catherine Howard (Nicky) Martin; one *s* one *d. Educ:* Univ. of New Brunswick (BA). T. Eaton Co. Ltd: joined 1962; positions in Victoria, London, England and Toronto, 1962–67; Dir, 1967–99; Pres. and CEO, 1979–88; Dir, Eaton's of Canada, 1969–; Chm., 1988–91; High Comr for Canada in the UK, 1991–94. Director: Hollinger, 1994–2003; Masonite (formerly Premdor), 1994–2005; former Director: Abitibi Consolidated; Argus Corp.; Norcen Energy; Maple Leaf Foods; Toronto-Dominion Bank; Bata Shoe Museum. Trustee: The Catherine and Fredrik Eaton Charitable Foundn; Canadian Mus. of Civilization (Chm., Bd of Trustees); Hon. Trustee, Univ. Health Network; Member: ICBP Rare Bird Club; Polite Soc. Patron, ESU of Canada. Pres., Toronto Club. FRSA. Chancellor, Univ. of New Brunswick, 1993–2003. Internat. Retailer of the Year Award, Nat. Retail Merchants Assoc., NY, 1978; McGill Univ. Management Award, 1987. Hon. LLD: New Brunswick, 1983; QUB, 1995. *Recreations:* sailing, fishing, golf. *Address:* (office) 55 St Clair Avenue West, Suite 260, Toronto, ON M4V 2Y7, Canada.

EATON, James Thompson, CBE 1992; TD 1963; Lord-Lieutenant, County Borough of Londonderry, 1986–2002; *b* 11 Aug. 1927; *s* of late J. C. Eaton, DL, and Mrs E. A. F. Eaton, MBE; *m* 1954, Lucy Edith Smeeton (OBE 1986); one *s* one *d. Educ:* Campbell Coll., Belfast; Royal Technical Coll., Glasgow. Man. Dir, Eaton & Co. Ltd, 1965–80. Mem., Londonderry Develt Commn, 1969–73 (Chm., Educn Cttee, 1969–73); Chm., Londonderry Port and Harbour Comrs, 1989–95 (Mem., 1977–95; Vice Chm., 1985). Served North Irish Horse (TA), 1950–67 (Major, 1961). Hon. Col, 1st (NI) Bn, ACF, 1992–98. High Sheriff, Co. Londonderry, 1982. *Recreations:* military history, gardening. *Address:* Cherryvale Park, Limavady, Co. Londonderry, Northern Ireland BT49 9AH.

EATON, Keith John, PhD; FRMetS; CEng, FIStructE; Chief Executive, Institution of Structural Engineers, since 1999; *b* 4 May 1945; *s* of John Ernest Eaton and Phyllis Marguerite (*née* Groom); *m* 1967, Janet Marion, *d* of Geoffrey and Winifred Allanson Walker; two *d. Educ:* Bishopshalt Grammar Sch., Hillingdon, Middx; Univ. of Birmingham (BSc Civil Engrg 1966); UCL (PhD Structural Engrg 1971). FRMetS 1971; CEng 1975; FIStructE 1986. Joined BRE, 1966; Head: Wind Loading Section, 1971–77; Overseas Develt Res. Unit, 1977–84; Structural Design Div., 1984–89; European Manager, 1989–91, Dep. Dir, 1991–99, Steel Construction Inst. Mem. Council, Hon. Sec. and Hon. Treas., IStructE, 1986–92. FCGI 2004. MASCE 1991; MIMMM (MIM 1994). *Publications:* Wind Loading Handbook, 1971; Wind Effects on Buildings and Structures, 1977; Buildings and Tropical Windstorms, 1981; A Comparative Environmental Life Cycle Assessment of Modern Office Buildings, 1998; technical papers on wind loading, earthquake engrg, sustainability and envmtl issues in learned jls. *Recreations:* social bridge, walking, travelling, competitive motoring, being a grandfather. *Address:* Institution of Structural Engineers, 11 Upper Belgrave Street, SW1X 8BH. *T:* (020) 7235 4535.

EATON, Adm. Sir Kenneth (John), GBE 1994; KCB 1990; FREng, FIET; Rear Admiral of the United Kingdom, 2001–07; Chairman, Mary Rose Trust, 2001–07; *b* 12 Aug. 1934; *s* of John and May Eaton; *m* 1959, Sheena Buttle; two *s* one *d. Educ:* Borden Grammar Sch.; Fitzwilliam Coll., Cambridge (BA). FIET (FIEE 1989); FREng (FEng 1994). HMS Victorious, 1959–61; ASWE, 1961–65; HM Ships Eagle, Collingwood and Bristol, 1965–71; Defence Communications Network, 1971–72; ASWE, 1972–76; HMS Ark Royal, 1976–78; MoD, 1978–81; ASWE, 1981–83; Dir Torpedoes, 1983–85; Dir-Gen. Underwater Weapons (Navy), 1985–87; Flag Officer, Portsmouth, and Naval Base Comdr, Portsmouth, 1987–89; Controller of the Navy, 1989–94. Chm., UKAEA, 1996–2002. Chairman: Guy's and St Thomas' NHS Trust, 1995–99; National Remote Sensing Centre (Infoterra Ltd), 1995–2001. Hon. DSc Aston, 2006. *Recreations:* countryside, theatre, opera, classical music. *Address:* c/o Naval Secretary, Fleet Headquarters, Whale Island, Portsmouth PO2 8BY.

EATON, Martin Roger, CMG 1993; HM Diplomatic Service, retired; Deputy Legal Adviser, Foreign and Commonwealth Office, 1991–2000; *b* 10 Nov. 1940; *m* 1972, Sylvia

White; two *s* one *d.* Admitted Solicitor, 1968; FCO, 1970; Bonn, 1977; FCO, 1981; Legal Counsellor: FCO, 1982; UKREP Brussels, 1987; FCO, 1991. Chm., Council of Europe Steering Cttee on Human Rights, 2003–04. *Recreations:* choral singing, gardening.

EATON, (Neil) Duncan, FCIPS; Chief Executive, NHS Purchasing and Supply Agency, 2000–06; *b* 28 May 1946; *s* of John and Bessie Eaton; *m* 1969, Ainsley Elizabeth Isles; two *d.* *Educ:* King Sch., Macclesfield; Manchester Coll. of Commerce (HND Business Studies); Dip. Inst. Healthcare Mgt; Dip. Chartered Inst. Purchasing and Supply. FCIPS (FInstPS 1985); MIHM 1972. Hosp. mgt and supply mgt posts, Manchester, Swindon and Wolverhampton, 1966–74; Area Supplies Officer: Tameside AHA, 1974–78; Northants AHA, 1978–83; Dir of Ops, NW Thames RHA, 1983–90; Chief Exec., Bedfordshire HA, 1990–2000. President: Chartered Inst. Purchasing and Supply, 1992–93; Health Care Supplies Assoc., 1996–2001. *Recreations:* amateur dramatics, Rugby, football. *Address:* 14 Knights Court, Linen Street, Warwick CV34 4DJ.

EATON, Robert James; Director, Chevron (formerly Texaco, then ChevronTexaco) Inc., since 2000; Chairman, Daimler Chrysler (formerly Chairman and Chief Executive, Chrysler Corporation), 1993–2000; *b* 13 Feb. 1940; *s* of Gene and Mildred Eaton; *m* 1964, Cornelia Cae Drake; two *s.* *Educ:* Univ. of Kansas (BS Mech Eng). Joined General Motors, 1963, transf. to English staff, 1971; Chevrolet Div., 1975; Oldsmobile, 1979; Vice-Pres. in charge of Tech. Staffs, 1986; Pres., General Motors Europe, 1988–92; Mem., Bd of Dirs, Lotus Group, 1986–2000; Chm., Saab Auto, 1990–2000. Member: Industrial Adv. Board, Stanford Univ.; Business Roundtable and Business Council. Mem. Bd, Dama. Former Chm., Nat. Acad. of Engrg; FSAE.

EATWELL, family name of **Baron Eatwell.**

EATWELL, Baron *cr* 1992 (Life Peer), of Stratton St Margaret in the County of Wiltshire; **John Leonard Eatwell;** President, Queens' College, Cambridge, since 1997; Professor of Financial Policy and Director, Cambridge Endowment for Research in Finance, Judge Business School (formerly Judge Institute of Management Studies), University of Cambridge, since 2002; *b* 2 Feb. 1945; *s* of Harold Jack and Mary Eatwell; *m* 1970, Hélène Seppain (marr. diss. 2002); two *s* one *d*; *m* 2006, Hon. Mrs Susan Elizabeth Digby (OBE 2007). *Educ:* Headlands Grammar Sch., Swindon; Queens' Coll., Cambridge (BA 1967; MA 1971); Harvard Univ. (PhD 1975). Teaching Fellow, Grad. Sch. of Arts and Scis, Harvard Univ., 1968–69; Res. Fellow, Queens' Coll., Cambridge, 1969–70; Fellow, Trinity Coll., Cambridge, 1970–96; Asst Lectr, 1975–77, Lectr, 1977–2002, Faculty of Econs and Politics, Cambridge Univ. Vis. Prof. of Economics, New Sch. for Social Res., NY, 1982–96. Econ. Advr to Rt Hon. Neil Kinnock, MP, Leader of the Labour Party, 1985–92. Opposition spokesman on Treasury affairs, and on trade and industry, H of L, 1992–93; Principal Opposition spokesman on Treasury and econ. affairs, H of L, 1993–97. Chm., British Screen Finance Ltd, 1997–2000; Dir, SFA, 1997–2002; Mem., Regulatory Decisions Cttee, FSA, 2001–06. Trustee, Inst. for Public Policy Res., 1988– (Sec., 1988–97; Chm., 1997–2000). Chm., Crusaid, 1993–98. Non-executive Director: Anglia Television Gp, 1994–2000; Cambridge Econometrics Ltd, 1996–2006; Rontech Ltd, 2003–. Chm., Commercial Radio Cos Assoc., 2000–04. Chm., Extemporary Dance Theatre, 1990; Governor: Contemporary Dance Trust, 1991–95; Royal Ballet Sch., 2003–06; Dir, Arts Theatre Trust, Cambridge, 1991–98; Mem. Bd, Royal Opera House, 1998–2006; Chm., British Library Bd, 2001–06. *Publications:* (with Joan Robinson) An Introduction to Modern Economics, 1973; Whatever Happened to Britain?, 1982; (ed with Murray Milgate) Keynes's Economics and the Theory of Value and Distribution, 1983; (ed with Murray Milgate and Peter Newman): The New Palgrave: A Dictionary of Economics, 4 vols, 1987; The New Palgrave Dictionary of Money and Finance, 3 vols, 1992; Transformation and Integration: shaping the future of central and eastern Europe, 1995; (ed) Global Unemployment: loss of jobs in the '90s, 1996; Not "Just Another Accession": the political economy of EU enlargement to the East, 1997; (with L. Taylor) Global Finance at Risk: the case for international regulation, 2000; Hard Budgets, Soft States, 2000; Social Policy Choices in Central and Eastern Europe, 2002; (with L. Taylor) International Capital Markets, 2002; articles in sci. jls and other collected works. *Recreations:* classical and contemporary dance, Rugby Union football. *Address:* Queens' College, Cambridge CB3 9ET. *T:* (01223) 335532, *Fax:* (01223) 335555; *e-mail:* president@queens.cam.ac.uk. *Club:* Harvard (New York).

EAVES, Prof. Laurence, CBE 2003; FRS 1997; Lancashire-Spencer Professor of Physics, University of Nottingham, since 2000 (Professor of Physics, 1986–2000); *b* 13 May 1948; *s* of Raymond Eaves and Margaret Eaves (*née* Howells); *m* 1985, Dr Ffiona Helen Gilmore. *Educ:* Rhondda Co. Grammar Sch.; Corpus Christi Coll., Oxford (BA 1st Cl. Hons Physics 1969; MA 1973; DPhil 1973). FInstP 1996. Res. Lectr, Christ Church, Oxford and Res. Fellow, Clarendon Lab., Univ. of Oxford, 1972–74; Miller Fellow, Univ. of Calif, Berkeley, 1974–75; Lectr, 1976–84, Reader, 1984–86, Dept of Physics, Univ. of Nottingham. Vis. Prof., Inst. for Solid State Physics, Univ. of Tokyo, 1995. Royal Soc. Leverhulme Sen. Res. Fellow, 1993–94; EPSRC Sen. Res. Fellow, 1994–99. Chm., Condensed Matter Div., Inst. of Physics, 1998–99; Member: Council, Royal Soc., 2002–04 (Mem., Sectional Cttee 2, 1999–2001, 2008–); HEFCE RAE Physics Subpanel, 2004–08. Mott Lectr, Inst. of Physics, 1988; European Physical Soc. Lectr., 1991. Guthrie Medal and Prize, Inst. of Physics, 2001. *Publications:* (jtly) numerous res. articles in Physical Rev., Physical Rev. Letters, Applied Physics Letters, etc. *Address:* School of Physics and Astronomy, University of Nottingham, Nottingham NG7 2RD. *T:* (0115) 951 5136.

EBADI, Dr Shirin; lawyer in private practice in Iran, specialising in human rights, since 1992; *b* 21 June 1947; *d* of late Mohammad Ali Ebadi; *m*; two *d.* *Educ:* Univ. of Tehran. Judge, 1969–79, Pres., 1975–79, Tehran City Court. Lectr in Law, Univ. of Tehran. Co-founder and President: Assoc. for Support of Children's Rights, 1995–2000; Human Rights Defence Centre, 2001–. Nobel Peace Prize, 2003. *Publications:* Criminal Laws, 1972; The Rights of the Child, 1987 (trans. English, 1993); Medical Laws, 1988; Young Workers, 1989; Copyright Laws, 1989; Architectural Laws, 1991; The Rights of Refugees, 1993; History and Documentation of Human Rights in Iran, 1993; (jtly) Tradition and Modernity, 1995; Children's Comparative Law, 1997 (trans. English, 1998); The Rights of Women, 2002; articles in learned jls. *Address:* No 19 Street 57, Seied Jamal eldin Asad Abadi Avenue, Tehran 14349, Iran.

EBAN, Anna Maeve; *see* Guggenheim, A. M.

EBBSFLEET, Bishop Suffragan of, since 2000; **Rt Rev. Andrew Burnham;** Provincial Episcopal Visitor, Province of Canterbury, since 2000; *b* 19 March 1948; *s* of David Burnham and Eileen Burnham (*née* Franks); *m* 1984, Cathy Ross; one *s* one *d.* *Educ:* New Coll., Oxford (BA 1969, 1971; MA 1973); Westminster Coll., Oxford (CertEd 1972); St Stephen's House, Oxford. ARCO(CHM). Ordained deacon, 1983, priest, 1984; Hon. Curate, Clifton, Southwell Dio., 1983–85; Curate, Beeston, 1985–87; Vicar, Carrington, 1987–94; Vice-Principal, St Stephen's House, Oxford, 1995–2000. Assistant Bishop: Dio. of Bath and Wells, 2001–; Dio. of Oxford, 2001–; Dio. of Exeter, 2001–; Dio. of Lichfield, 2001–. *Publication:* A Manual of Anglo-Catholic Devotion, 2000, pocket edn, 2004. *Recreations:* liturgy, music. *Address:* Bishop's House, Dry Sandford, Abingdon, Oxford OX13 6JP. *T:* (01865) 390746; *e-mail:* bishop.andrew@ebbsfleet.org.uk.

EBDON, Prof. Leslie Colin, PhD; CChem, FRSC; Vice-Chancellor and Chie[f] Executive, University of Bedfordshire (formerly University of Luton), since 2003; *b* 2[6] Jan. 1947; *s* of Harold and Doris Ebdon; *m* 1970, Judith Margaret Thomas; two *s* one [*d*] (and one *s* decd). *Educ:* Hemel Hempstead Grammar Sch.; Imperial Coll., Univ. o[f] London (BSc, PhD; ARCS, DIC). MCIWEM. Lectr in Chem., Makerere Univ., Uganda, 1971–73; Sen. Lectr, Sheffield City Poly., 1973–80; Plymouth Polytechnic, late[r] Polytechnic SouthWest, then Plymouth University: Reader in Analytical Chem., 1981–89; Hd, Dept of Envmtl Scis, 1989; Prof. of Analytical Chem., 1986–2003; Dep. Dir, 1989–92; Dep. Vice-Chancellor, 1992–2003. Mem., Measurement Adv. Cttee, DTI, 1999–. Mem. Council, RSC, 1996– (Chm., Strategy and Resources Bd, 2003–05). *Publications:* An Introduction to Analytical Atomic Spectroscopy, 1982, 2nd edn 1998; numerous contribs to refereed jls. *Recreations:* vegetable gardening, Baptist lay preacher. *Address:* University of Bedfordshire, Park Square, Luton LU1 3JU. *T:* (01582) 489255; *Fax:* (01582) 489362; *e-mail:* Les.ebdon@beds.ac.uk.

EBERLE, Adm. Sir James (Henry Fuller), GCB 1981 (KCB 1979); Vice Admiral o[f] the United Kingdom, 1994–97; President, Association of Masters of Harriers and Beagle[s] (Chairman, 1998); writer on international affairs and security; *b* 31 May 1927; *s* of lat[e] Victor Fuller Eberle and of Joyce Mary Eberle, Bristol; *m* 1950, Ann Patricia Thompso[n] (*d* 1988), Hong Kong; one *s* two *d.* *Educ:* Clifton Coll.; RNC Dartmouth and Greenwich. Served War of 1939–45 in MTBs, HMS Renown, HMS Belfast; subseq. in Far East; qua[l.] Gunnery Specialist 1951; Guided Missile Develt and trials in UK and USA, 1953–57; Naval Staff, 1960–62; Exec. Officer, HMS Eagle, 1963–65; comd HMS Intrepid, 1968–70; Asst Chief of Fleet Support, MoD (RN), 1971–74; Flag Officer Sea Training, 1974–75; Flag Officer Carriers and Amphibious Ships, 1975–77; Chief of Fleet Support, 1977–79; C-in-C, Fleet, and Allied C-in-C, Channel and Eastern Atlantic, 1979–81; C-in-C, Naval Home Comd, 1981–82, retired 1983. Rear Adm. of the UK, 1990–94. UK–Japan 2000 Gp, 1983–98. Vice-Pres., RUSI, 1979; Dir, RIIA, 1984–90. Di[r,] Countryside Alliance, 2000–07. Chm. Council, Clifton Coll., 1984–94; Chm., Devo[n] Rural Skills Trust, 1992–93. Freeman: Bristol, 1946; London, 1982. Hon. LLD: Bristol, 1989; Sussex, 1992. *Publications:* Management in the Armed Forces, 1972; Jim, First of th[e] Pack, 1982; Britain's Future in Space, 1988; Admiral Jim: a trilogy: Wider Horizons, Fro[m] Greenland's Icy Shore, Life on the Ocean Wave, 2007. *Recreations:* hunting (Master o[f] Britannia Beagles), tennis. *Address:* Homestead Farm, North Houghton, Stockbridge, Hants SO20 6LG. *Clubs:* Farmers'; Society of Merchant Venturers (Bristol); All Englan[d] Lawn Tennis.

EBERS, Prof. George Cornell, MD; FRCPC, FRCP; Action Research Professor o[f] Clinical Neurology, University of Oxford, since 1999 (Head, Department of Clinica[l] Neurology, 1999–2004); Fellow, St Edmund Hall, Oxford, since 1999; *b* Budapest, 2[?] July 1946; *s* of Cornell George Ebers and Leontine Amant Ebers; *m* 1997, Sharon Vital[;] one *s* one *d.* *Educ:* De La Salle Coll.; Univ. of Toronto (MD 1970); MA Oxon. FRCP[C] 1977. University of Western Ontario: Asst Prof., 1977–82; Associate Prof., 1982–87; Prof., Dept of Clinical Neurol Scis, 1987–99. Numerous vis. professorships and name[d] lectures. Member, Editorial Board: Jl Neuroimm., 1983–; Canadian Jl Neuro. Sci., 1985–; MS Res. Reports, 1987–; Jl Tropical Geog. Neurol., 1990–94; Neuroepidemiol., 1992–; Multiple Sclerosis, 1994–. FMedSci 2001. *Publications:* The Diagnosis of MS, 1984; Multiple Sclerosis, 1998; sole or jt author numerous scientific papers and articles. *Recreations:* book collecting, ornithology. *Address:* West Wing, John Radcliffe Hospital, Oxford OX3 9DU. *T:* (01865) 231903. *Club:* Osler.

EBERT, Peter; producer; *b* 6 April 1918; *s* of Carl Ebert, CBE, and Lucie Oppenheim; *m* 1st, 1944, Kathleen Havinden; two *d*; 2nd, 1951, Silvia Ashmole; five *s* three *d.* *Edu[c:]* Salem Sch., Germany; Gordonstoun, Scotland. BBC Producer, 1948–51; 1st oper[a] production, Mefistofele, Glasgow, 1951; Mozart and Rossini guest productions: Rome, Naples, Venice, 1951, 1952, 1954, 1955: Wexford Festival: 12 prods, 1952–65; 1st Glyndebourne Fest. prod., Ariecchino, 1954, followed by Seraglio, Don Giovanni, etc. 1st Edinburgh Fest. prod., Forza del Destino, 1955; Chief producer: Hannover Stat[e] Opera, 1954–60; Düsseldorf Opera, 1960–62; directed opera class, Hannover Stat[e] Conservatory, 1954–60; Head of Opera studio, Düsseldorf, 1960–62. Guest productio[ns] in Europe, USA, Canada. TV productions of Glyndebourne operas, 1955–64; 1st TV studio prod., 1963; Opera Adviser to BBC TV, 1964–65; Dir of Productions, 1965–77, Gen. Administrator, 1977–80, Scottish Opera Co. First drama prod., The Devil, Johannesburg, 1966; first musical, Houdini, London, 1966. Dir, Opera Sch., University o[f] Toronto, 1967–68; Intendant: Stadttheater, Augsburg, 1968–73; Stadttheater Bielefel[d,] 1973–75; Staatstheater Wiesbaden, 1975–77. Hon. DMus St Andrews, 1979. *Publicatio[n:]* In This Theatre of Man's Life: a biography of Carl Ebert, 1999. *Recreation:* family. *Addres[s:]* 12 Greater Paddock, Ringmer, East Sussex BN8 5LH.

EBERTS, John David, (Jake), OC 1992; Founder, and Chief Executive, since 198[5,] Allied Productions (formerly Allied Filmmakers); *b* 10 July 1941; *s* of Edmond Howar[d] Eberts and Elizabeth Evelyn MacDougall; *m* 1968, Fiona Louise Leckie; two *s* one *d.* *Edu[c:]* McGill Univ. (BChemEng 1962); Harvard Univ. (MBA 1966). Project Engr, L'A[ir] Liquide, Paris, 1962–64; Marketing Manager, Cummins Engine Co., Brussels, 1966–68; Vice Pres., Laird Inc., NY, 1968–71; Man. Dir, Oppenheimer and Co. Ltd, Londo[n,] 1971–76; Founder, 1976, and Chief Exec., 1976–83 and 1985–86, Goldcrest Films an[d] Television Ltd; Pres., Embassy Communications International, 1984–85. Directo[r,] Sundance Inst., 1993–; Sundance Channel, 1998–; Sundance Catalog Co., 2004–; Chm. National Geographic Feature Films, 2002–. Involved in prodn of many BAFTA an[d] Amer. Acad. award-winning films, including: Chariots of Fire; Gandhi; The Dresser; Th[e] Killing Fields; The Name of the Rose; Hope and Glory; Driving Miss Daisy; Dances wit[h] Wolves; A River Runs Through It; James and the Giant Peach; Chicken Run; Th[e] Legend of Bagger Vance. Film Producers' Award of Merit, 1986; Evening Standar[d] Special Award, 1987. Hon. DLitt McGill, 1998; Hon. DCL Bishop's Univ., 1999; Ho[n.] LLD Trent, 2005. *Publication:* (with Terry Ilott) My Indecision is Final, 1990. *Recreation[s:]* golf, tennis, ski-ing, photography. *Clubs:* North Hatley (Quebec); Golf de Fontainebleau.

EBRAHIM, Sir (Mahomed) Currimbhoy, (Sir Mohamed Currimbhoy), 4th Bt [cr] 1910; BA, LLB; Advocate, Pakistan; Member, Standing Council of the Baronetage, 196[?]; *b* 24 June 1935; *o s* of Sir (Huseinali) Currimbhoy Ebrahim, 3rd Bt, and Alhaja Lady Amir Khanum, *d* of Alhaj Cassumali Jairajbhoy; *S* father, 1952; *m* 1958, Dur-e-Mariam, *d* o[f] Minuchehir Ahmud Ghulamaly Nana; three *s* one *d.* *Recreations:* tennis (Karach[i] University No 1, 1957, No 2, 1958), cricket, table-tennis, squash, reading (literary), an[d] poetry writing, debate, quotation writing. *Heir:* *s* Zulfiqar Ali Currimbhoy Ebrahim [*b* ?] Aug. 1960; *m* 1984, Adila, *d* of Akhtar Halipota; one *s*].

EBRAHIM, Prof. Shaheen Brian John, FRCP, FFPH; Professor of Public Healt[h,] London School of Hygiene & Tropical Medicine, since 2005; *b* 19 July 1952; *s* of Dr Donald William Ebrahim and Marjorie Sybil (*née* Evans); *m* 1st, 1984, Julia Lesley Sha[w] (marr. diss. 2002); 2nd, 2004, Fiona Clair Taylor. *Educ:* King Henry VIII Sch., Coventr[y]

Nottingham Univ. Med. Sch. (BMed Sci; BM BS 1975; DM 1985). FRCP 1993; FFPH (FFPHM 1993). Wellcome Trust Clinical Epidemiology Trng Fellow, Nottingham Univ. Med. Sch., 1981–83; Lectr in Geriatric Medicine, Univ. of Nottingham, 1983–85; Wellcome Trust Lectr in Epidemiology, Dept of Social Medicine and Gen. Practice, St George's Hosp. Med. Sch., London, 1985–86; Cons. Physician and Sen. Lectr, Dept of Geriatric Medicine, Royal Free Hosp. Sch. of Medicine, 1987–89; Prof. of Geriatric Medicine, London Hosp. Med. Coll. and St Bartholomew's Hosp. Med. Coll., 1989–92; Prof. of Clinical Epidemiology, Royal Free Hosp. Sch. of Med., 1992–98; Prof. of Epidemiology of Ageing, Univ. of Bristol, 1998–2005. Vis. Prof., Christchurch Med. Sch., NZ, 1990; Nat. Heart Foundn of NZ Vis. Prof. in Stroke, 1991; Australian Veterans Vis. Prof., 1995; Vis. Prof., McMaster Univ., Canada, 1996; Vis. Prof., Sydney Univ., Australia, 2003; Hon. Prof., UCL 2003. *Publications:* Clinical Epidemiology of Stroke, 1990, 2nd edn 1999; (ed jtly) The Health of Older Women, 1992; (with G. Bennett) Essentials of Health Care in Old Age, 1992, 2nd edn 1995; (ed jtly) Epidemiology in Old Age, 1996; (ed jtly) Handbook of Health Research Methods, 2005; scientific papers on clinical epidemiology and geriatric medicine. *Recreations:* coarse fishing, music of Velvet Underground and Don Van Vliet. *Address:* Department of Epidemiology and Population Health, London School of Hygiene & Tropical Medicine, Keppel Street, WC1E 7HT. *Club:* Royal Society of Medicine.

EBRINGER, Prof. Alan Martin, MD; FRACP, FRCP, FRCPath; Professor of Immunology, King's College, London, since 1995; *b* 12 Feb. 1936; *s* of late Bernard Ebringer and Maria Ebringer; *m* 1960, Eva Marie Ernest; two *s* one *d*. *Educ:* Melbourne High Sch.; Univ. of Melbourne (BSc Maths 1961; MB BS 1962; MD 1971). FRACP 1967; MRCP 1970, FRCP 1987; FRCPath 1997. Prosector in Anatomy, Univ. of Melbourne, 1958–; Pathology Registrar, Geelong Hosp., 1964; Research Fellow: Walter and Eliza Hall Inst., Royal Melbourne Hosp., 1965–66; Austin Hosp., 1967–69; RACP Overseas Travelling Schol., Dept of Immunol., Middx Hosp., 1970; Berkeley Fellow, Middx Hosp. and Gonville and Caius Coll., Cambridge, 1971; King's College, London: Lectr, 1972–77; Sen. Lectr, 1977–82; Reader, 1982–95; Hon. Consultant Rheumatologist, UCL Hosps (formerly Middx Hosp.), i/c of Ankylosing Spondylitis Res. Clinic, 1980–. Appeared before Phillips Inquiry into BSE, 1998. Member: British Soc. Immunol., 1970; British Soc. Rheum., 1972; Amer. Coll. Rheumatol., 1996. Vis. Lectr, Melbourne, Edinburgh, Glasgow, Sheffield, Paris, Marseille, Brest, Madrid, Helsinki, Turku, Bratislava, Moscow, Suzdal, Innsbruck, San Antonio, Dallas, Uppsala. Life Mem., RSocMed, 2008. Hon. FRSH 2001. Donaldson Gold Medal, RSH, 2003. *Publications:* contrib. numerous papers dealing with autoimmune diseases produced by molecular mimicry to ext. agents, esp. ankylosing spondylitis (klebsiella), rheumatoid arthritis (proteus), bovine spongiform encephalopathy (acinetobacter), multiple sclerosis (acinetobacter) and Crohn's disease (Klebsiella). *Recreations:* languages, Karl Popper, walking. *Address:* 76 Gordon Road, W5 2AR.

EBSWORTH, Prof. Evelyn Algernon Valentine, CBE 1996; PhD, ScD; FRSC, FRSE; Chairman, Council for the Registration of Forensic Practitioners, 1998–2005; *b* 14 Feb. 1933; *s* of Brig. Wilfred Algernon Ebsworth, CB, CBE and late Cynthia (*née* Blech); *m* 1st, 1955, Mary Salter (*d* 1987); one *s* three *d*; 2nd, 1990, Rose Zuckerman. *Educ:* King's Coll., Cambridge (BA 1st Cl., 1954; PhD 1957; MA 1958; ScD 1967). FRSE 1969. Fellow, King's Coll., Cambridge, 1957–59; Res. Associate, Princeton Univ., 1958–59; Cambridge University: Demonstrator, 1959–63; Lectr, 1963–67; Fellow, 1959–67, Tutor, 1963–67, Christ's Coll.; Crum Brown Prof. of Chemistry, Edinburgh, 1967–90; Vice-Chancellor, Durham Univ., 1990–98. Chairman of Governors: The Leys Sch., Cambridge, 2002–; St Faith's Sch., Cambridge, 2002–. Corresp. Mem., Acad. of Scis, Göttingen. FRSA. Hon. DCL Durham, 2002. *Publications:* Volatile Silicon Compounds, 1963; (with S. Cradock and D. W. H. Rankin) Structural Methods in Inorganic Chemistry, 1988; papers in learned jls. *Recreations:* opera, gardening. *Address:* 16 Conduit Head Road, Cambridge CB3 0EY.

ECCLES, family name of **Viscount Eccles** and **Baroness Eccles of Moulton**.

ECCLES, 2nd Viscount, *cr* 1964, of Chute, co. Wilts; **John Dawson Eccles,** CBE 1985; Baron 1962; Chairman, The Bowes Museum, County Durham, since 2000; *b* 20 April 1931; *er s* of 1st Viscount Eccles, CH, KCVO, PC and Sybil (*d* 1977), *d* of 1st Viscount Dawson of Penn, GCVO, KCB, KCMG, PC; *S* father, 1999; *m* 1955, Diana Catherine Sturge (*see* Baroness Eccles of Moulton); one *s* three *d*. *Educ:* Winchester Coll.; Magdalen Coll., Oxford (BA). Commnd 1st 60th KRRC, 1950. Director: Glynwed International plc, 1972–96; Investors in Industry plc, 1974–88; Chairman: Head Wrightson & Co. Ltd, 1976–77 (Man. Dir, 1968); Chamberlin & Hill plc, 1982–2004; Acker Deboeck, corporate psychologists, 1994–2006; Courtaulds Textiles plc, 1995–2000 (Dir, 1992–2000); Director: The Nuclear Power Gp Ltd, 1968–74; Davy Internat. Ltd, 1977–81; Govett Strategic Investment Trust plc, 1996–2004. Member: Monopolies and Mergers Commn, 1976–85 (Dep. Chm., 1981–85); Industrial Develt Adv. Bd, 1989–93; Gen. Manager, subseq. Chief Exec., Commonwealth Develt Corp., 1985–94 (Mem., 1982–85). Chm., Bd of Trustees, Royal Botanic Gardens, Kew, 1983–91. Mem. Council, Eccles Centre for American Studies, BL, 2003–. Chm., Hosp. for Tropical Diseases Foundn, 2000–. Elected Mem., H of L, March 2005. Hon. DSc Cranfield Inst. of Technology, 1989. *Recreations:* gardening, theatre. *Heir:* *s* Hon. William David Eccles [*b* 9 June 1960; *m* 1984, Claire Margaret Alison Seddon (*d* 2001); two *s* one *d*]. *Address:* 5 St John's House, 30 Smith Square, SW1P 3HF. *T:* (020) 7222 4040; Moulton Hall, Richmond, N Yorks DL10 6QH. *T:* (01325) 377227. *Club:* Brooks's.

ECCLES OF MOULTON, Baroness *cr* 1990 (Life Peer), of Moulton in the County of North Yorkshire; **Diana Catherine Eccles, (Viscountess Eccles);** DL; Chairman, Ealing, Hammersmith and Hounslow Health Authority, 1993–2000 (Chairman, Ealing District Health Authority, 1988–93); *b* 4 Oct. 1933; *d* of late Raymond Sturge and Margaret Sturge; *m* 1955, John Dawson Eccles (*see* Viscount Eccles); one *s* three *d*. *Educ:* St James's Sch., West Malvern; Open Univ. (BA). Voluntary work, Middlesbrough Community Council, 1955–58; Partner, Gray Design Associates, 1963–77. Director: Tyne Tees Television, 1986–94; J. Sainsbury, 1986–95; Yorkshire Electricity Gp, 1990–97; National & Provincial Building Soc., 1991–96; Opera North, 1998–; Indep. Nat. Dir, Times Newspapers Holdings Ltd, 1998–. Member: North Eastern Electricity Bd, 1974–85; British Railways Eastern Bd, 1986–92; Teesside Urban Develt Corp., 1987–98; Yorkshire Electricity Bd, 1989–90. Member: Adv. Council for Energy Conservation, 1982–84; Widdicombe Inquiry into Local Govt, 1985–86; Home Office Adv. Panel on Licences for Experimental Community Radio, 1985–86; Unrelated Live Transplant Regulatory Authority, 1990–99. Vice Chairman: Nat. Council for Voluntary Orgns, 1981–87; Durham Univ. Council, 1985–2004 (Lay Mem., 1981–85); Chm., Tyne Tees Television Programme Consultative Council, 1982–84. Trustee: Charities Aid Foundn, 1982–89; York Minster Fund, 1989–99 and 2006–; London Clinic, 2003–. DL N Yorks, 1998. Hon. DCL Durham, 1995. *Address:* Moulton Hall, Richmond, N Yorks DL10 6QH. *T:* (01325) 377227; 5/30 Smith Square, SW1P 3HF. *T:* (020) 7222 4040.

ECCLES, (Hugh William) Patrick; QC 1990; **His Honour Judge Eccles;** a Circuit Judge, since 2000; *b* 25 April 1946; *s* of Gp Captain (retd) Hugh Haslett Eccles and Mary Eccles; *m* 1972, Rhoda Ann Eccles (*née* Moroney); three *d*. *Educ:* Stonyhurst Coll.; Exeter Coll., Oxford (MA). Called to the Bar, Middle Temple, 1968, Bencher, 1998; practising barrister, head of chambers, 1985–2000; a Recorder, 1987–2000; approved to sit as Dep. High Court Judge, QBD, 1997–2000, Chancery and Family Divs, 2002–. Asst Parly Boundary Comr, 1992; Legal Mem., Mental Health Review Tribunal (Restricted Patients), 2000–. Mem., County Court Rule Cttee, 1986–91. Trustee, Friends of Church of St Birinus, 2001–. Gov., Sch. of St Helen and St Katharine, Abingdon, 1992–. *Recreations:* playing tennis, supporting Rugby and soccer, listening to opera and rock, reading, gardening. *Address:* c/o Coventry Combined Court Centre, 140 Much Park Street, Coventry CV1 2SN.

ECCLES, Jack Fleming, CBE 1980; retired trade union official; *b* 9 Feb. 1922; *s* of Tom and Dora Eccles; *m* 1952, Milba Hartley Williamson; one *s* one *d*. *Educ:* Chorlton High Sch.; Univ. of Manchester. BA (Com). Gen. and Municipal Workers Union: District Organiser, 1948–60; Nat. Industrial Officer, 1960–66; Regional Sec. (Lancs), 1966–86. Trades Union Congress: Gen. Council, 1973–86; Chm., 1984–85; Pres., 1985. Non-Executive Director: Remploy Ltd, 1976–90; English Industrial Estates, 1976–92; Plastics Processing ITB, 1982–88 (Chm.); British Steel plc (formerly BSC), 1986–91. *Address:* Terange, 11 Sutton Road, Alderley Edge, Cheshire SK9 7RB. *T:* (01625) 583684.

ECCLES, Patrick; *see* Eccles, H. W. P.

ECCLES-WILLIAMS, Hilary a'Beckett, CBE 1970; *b* 5 Oct. 1917; *s* of late Rev. Cyril Eccles-Williams and Hermione (*née* Terrell); *m* 1941, Jeanne, *d* of W. J. Goodwin; two *s* four *d*. *Educ:* Eton; Brasenose Coll., Oxford (MA). Served War of 1939–45, Major RA (anti-tank), Dunkirk and Normandy (wounded). Consul: for Nicaragua, 1951–59; for Cuba, 1952–60; for Costa Rica, 1964–93; for Bolivia, 1965–82. Chairman of companies; Chm., 1978–82, non-exec. Dir, 1982–87, Rabone Petersen; has travelled 900,000 miles on export business. Chairman: Brit. Export Houses Assoc., 1958–59; Guardians of Birmingham Assay Office, 1979–88 (Guardian, 1970–); President: Birmingham Chamber of Commerce, 1965–66; Assoc. of Brit. Ch. of Commerce (93 Chambers), 1970–72. Comr of Income Tax, 1966–70. Chairman: Birmingham Cons. Assoc., 1976–79 (Pres., 1979–84); W Midlands Metropolitan Co. Co-ordinating Cttee, Cons. Party, 1980–86; European Parlt constituency of Birmingham S Cons. Assoc., 1978–82 (Pres., 1982–84); Latin Amer. Gp, Cons. Foreign and Overseas Council, 1986–89; President: Eur. Parlt constituency of Birmingham E Cons. Assoc., 1984–95; Sparkbrook Constituency Cons. Assoc., 1988–92; Anglo-Asian Cons. Soc., 1984–87; Cons. Party One Nation Forum, 1990–; Mem., National Union Exec. Cttee, Cons. Party, 1975–85. Mem., Brit. Hallmarking Council, 1976–88; Pres., Birmingham Consular Assoc., 1973–74; Chairman: Asian Christian Colls Assoc., 1960–66; Brit. Heart Foundn, Midland Counties, 1973–74; Golden Jubilee Appeal Cttee, Queen Elizabeth Hosp., Birmingham, 1987–90; W Midlands Macmillan Nurse Appeal, 1991–94; Mem., Nat. Council, Cancer Relief Macmillan Fund, 1992–94. Life Governor, Birmingham Univ., 1966; Trustee, Birmingham Centre for Drama, 1994–97. Liveryman, Worshipful Co. of Glaziers, 1974; Freeman, Goldsmiths' Co., 1988. Hon. Captain, Bolivian Navy, 1969. Numerous TV appearances. *Recreations:* walking, golf. *Address:* 49 Second Avenue, Frinton-on-Sea, Essex CO13 9LY. *Clubs:* Frinton Golf; Frinton Lawn Tennis.

ECCLESHARE, (Christopher) William; Chairman and Chief Executive Officer, BBDO Europe, Middle East and Africa, since 2005; *b* 26 Oct. 1955; *s* of late Colin Forster Eccleshare and of Elizabeth Eccleshare; *m* 1980, Carol Ann Seigel; two *s* one *d*. *Educ:* Fitzjohns Primary Sch.; William Ellis Sch.; Trinity Coll., Cambridge (BA Hist. 1978). Account Exec., 1978–89, Man. Dir, 1990–92, J. Walter Thompson; Chief Exec., PPGH/JWT Amsterdam, 1993–95; Global Strategy Dir, J. Walter Thompson, 1995–96; Chief Exec., Ammirati Puris Lintas, London, 1996–99; Partner, Leader Eur. Branding Practice, McKinsey & Co., 2000–02; Chm. and CEO, Young & Rubicam, Europe, 2002–05. Non-exec. Dir, Hays plc, 2004–. Mem., Mktg Gp of GB, 2006–. Mem. Council, University Coll. Sch., 2002–. FIPA 1998 (Mem. Council, 1998–2000; Judge, IPA Effectiveness Awards, 2002). *Publications:* (contrib.) The Timeless Works of Stephen King, ed J. Lannon, 2007; contribs to Campaign, Admap, Market Leader. *Recreations:* obsessively following Bruce Springsteen, British politics since 1964, the progress of a slow-growing hedge, and most other runners of the London Marathon. *Address:* BBDO EMEA, 151 Marylebone Road, NW1 5QE. *T:* (020) 7616 3498; *e-mail:* ecclesharew@bbdoeurope.com; 9 The Mount, NW3 6SZ. *Club:* Thirty.
See also J. J. Eccleshare.

ECCLESHARE, Julia Jessica; journalist and broadcaster; *b* 14 Dec. 1951; *d* of late Colin Forster Eccleshare and of Elizabeth Eccleshare; *m* 1977, John Lemprière Hammond, *s* of Prof. Nicholas Geoffrey Lemprière Hammond, CBE, DSO, FBA; three *s* one *d*. *Educ:* Camden Sch. for Girls; Girton Coll., Cambridge. Editorial assistant: TLS, 1973–78; Puffin Books, 1978–79; Fiction editor, Hamish Hamilton Children's Books, 1979–82; selector of Children's Books of Year for Book Trust, 1982–92; Children's Book corresp., Bookseller, 1993–97; Children's Books Editor, Guardian, 1997–. Co-dir, Centre for Literacy in Primary Educn, 2004–. Chm. Judges, Smarties Award, 1994–; Mem., Adv. Body, Reading is Fundamental (UK), 1996–; Trustee: Listening Books, 2000–; Volunteer Reading Help, 2003–06. Contributor to BBC Treasure Islands, Night Waves, Kaleidoscope, Woman's Hour and Open Book, 1985–. Eleanor Farjeon Award, 2000. *Publications:* The Woman's Hour Guide to Children's Books, 1987; A Guide to the Harry Potter Novels, 2002; Beatrix Potter to Harry Potter, 2002; The Rough Guide to Teenage Reading, 2003; ed numerous anthologies. *Address:* 21 Tanza Road, NW3 2UA. *T:* (020) 7431 1295; *e-mail:* julia.eccleshare@blueyonder.co.uk.
See also C. W. Eccleshare.

ECCLESHARE, William; *see* Eccleshare, C. W.

ECCLESTON, Christopher; actor; *b* 16 Feb. 1964; *s* of Joseph Ronald Eccleston and Elsie Lavinia Eccleston. *Educ:* Central Sch. of Speech and Drama. *Films include:* Let Him Have It, 1991; Shallow Grave, 1994; Jude, 1996; Elizabeth, A Price Above Rubies, 1998; Heart, Old New Borrowed Blue, eXistenZ, 1999; Gone in 60 Seconds, 2000; The Invisible Circus, The Others, 2001; I Am Dina, 28 Days Later, 2002; A Revenger's Tragedy, 2003. *Television includes:* Cracker (series), 1993–94; Hearts and Minds, 1995; Our Friends in the North (series), Hillsborough, 1996; Strumpet, 2001; Flesh and Blood, Othello, Sunday, 2002; The Second Coming, 2003; Doctor Who (series), 2005; Perfect Parents, 2006. *Theatre includes:* Miss Julie, Haymarket, 2000; Hamlet, 2002, Electricity, 2004, W Yorks Playhouse. *Address:* c/o Hamilton Hodell Ltd, 5th Floor, 66–68 Margaret Street, W1W 8SR.

ECCLESTON, Harry Norman, OBE 1979; PPRE (RE 1961; ARE 1948); RWS 1975 (ARWS 1964); RWA 1991; Artist Designer at the Bank of England Printing Works, 1958–83 (appointed first full-time bank-note designer, 1967); *b* 21 Jan. 1923; *s* of Harry Norman Eccleston and Kate Pritchard, Coseley, Staffs; *m* 1948, Betty Doreen Gripton (*d*

1995); two *d.* *Educ:* Sch. of Art, Bilston; Coll. of Art, Birmingham; Royal College of Art. ATD 1947; ARCA (1st Class) 1950. Studied painting until 1942. Served in Royal Navy, 1942–46; Temp. Commn, RNVR, 1943. Engraving Sch., Royal College of Art, 1947–51; engraving, teaching, free-lance graphic design, 1951–58. Pres., Royal Soc. of Painter-Etchers and Engravers, 1975–89. Hon. RBSA 1989; Hon. NEAC, 1995. Hon. PhD (DA) Wolverhampton, 2003. *Recreation:* reading. *Address:* 110 Priory Road, Harold Hill, Romford, Essex RM3 9AL. *T:* (01708) 340275. *Club:* Arts.

ECCLESTONE, Bernard, (Bernie); Chief Executive Officer: Formula One Administration Ltd; Formula One Management Ltd; *b* Suffolk, Oct. 1930; *m* 1st; one *d*; 2nd, Slavica; two *d.* *Educ:* Woolwich Polytechnic (BSc). Est. car and motorbike dealership, Midweek Car Auctions; racing car driver, F3; owner, Connaught racing team, 1957; Manager, Jochen Rindt; owner, Brabham racing team, 1970–90. Vice-Pres., Fed. Internat. de l'Automobile. Person of the Year, Motorsport Industry Assoc., Business Achievement Awards; inaugural Gold Medal, British Racing Drivers' Club. Keys to Cities of São Paulo and Rio de Janeiro. Medal (1st degree), Bahrain; Silver Medals, Monaco; Bandeirante Medal, Brazil. Grand Officer, Equestrian Order of St Agata, San Marino; Grand Decoration of Honour, Austria; Order of Merit, Hungary; Grand Officer, Order of Merit, Italy. *Address:* Formula One Administration Ltd, 6 Prince's Gate, SW7 1QJ. *T:* (020) 7584 6668, *Fax:* (020) 7589 0311; *e-mail:* lhibberd@fomltd.com, emarenghi@fomltd.com.

ECCLESTONE, Jacob Andrew; Assistant General Secretary, Writers' Guild, 1999–2001; *b* 10 April 1939; *s* of late Rev. Alan Ecclestone and Delia Reynolds Abraham; *m* 1966, Margaret Joan Bassett; two *s* one *d.* *Educ:* High Storrs Grammar Sch., Sheffield; Open Univ. (BA). Journalism: South Yorkshire Times, 1957–61; Yorkshire Evening News, 1961–62; The Times, 1962–66, 1967–81; Dep. Gen. Sec., NUJ, 1981–97 (Mem., 1977, Vice-Pres. 1978, Pres., 1979, Nat. Exec.). Member: Press Council, 1977–80; Exec., NCCL, 1982–86. *Recreations:* gardening, climbing, music. *Address:* 22 Robson Road, SE27 9LA. *T:* (020) 8670 8503.

ECHENIQUE, Prof. Marcial Hernan, DArch; Professor of Land Use and Transport Studies, since 1993, and Head, Department of Architecture, since 2004, University of Cambridge; Fellow, Churchill College, Cambridge, since 1972; *b* 23 Feb. 1943; *s* of Marcial Echenique and Rosa de Echenique (*née* Talavera); *m* 1963, Maria Luisa Holzmann; two *s* one *d.* *Educ:* Catholic Univ. of Chile; Univ. of Barcelona (DArch). MA Cantab 1972. MRTPI 1990; ARIBA 1997. Asst Lectr, Univ. of Barcelona, 1964–65; University of Cambridge: Research Officer, 1967–70; Lectr, 1970–80; Reader in Architecture and Urban Studies, 1980–93. Founder and Mem., Bd of Applied Res., Cambridge, 1969–83. Chm., Marcial Echenique & Partners Ltd, England, 1978–2001; Pres., Marcial Echenique y Compañía SA, Spain, 1988–2007; Member Board: Trasporti e Territorio SRL, Italy, 1992–2007; Autopista Vasco-Aragonesa SA, Spain, 1994–99; Tecnologica SA, Spain, 1994–96; Ferrovial-Agroman, Construcciones, Spain, 1995–2000; Dockways Ltd, Jersey, 1996–2000. Bank of Bilbao-Vizcaya of Spain: Mem. Bd, 1988–94; Trustee of Foundn, 1990–94. *Publications:* (ed jtly) La Estructura del Espacio Urbano, 1975; (ed jtly) Urban Development Models, 1975; (ed) Modelos Matematicos de la Estructura Espacial Urbana: aplicaciones en America Latina, 1975; (with L. Piemontese) Un Modello per lo Sviluppo del Sistema Grecia-Italia Meridionale, 1984; (jtly) Cambridge Futures, 1999; (ed jtly) Cities for the New Millennium, 2001; (jtly) Cities of Innovation: shaping places for high-tech, 2003. *Recreations:* music, reading, gardening. *Address:* Department of Architecture, University of Cambridge, 1 Scroope Terrace, Cambridge CB2 1PX. *T:* (01223) 332959; Farm Hall, Godmanchester, Cambs PE29 2HQ.

ECKERBERG, (Carl) Lennart, Hon. KCMG 1983; Officer of Royal Northern Star 1970; Swedish Ambassador to the Court of St James's, 1991–94; *b* 2 July 1928; *s* of late Enar Lars Eckerberg and of Dagmar Liljedahl; *m* 1965, Willia Fales; two *s* one *d.* *Educ:* Univ. of Stockholm (law degree 1953). Swedish Foreign Service in Stockholm, London, Warsaw and Washington, 1954–71; Disarmament Ambassador, Geneva, 1971; Minister Plenipotentiary, Washington, 1975; Ambassador, Dar es Salaam, 1977; Under Sec., Political Affairs, Stockholm, 1979; Ambassador, Bonn, 1983–91. Orders from Finland, Germany, Iceland, Spain and Mexico. *Recreations:* golf, tennis, bridge. *Address:* (summer) Martornsvägen 3, 230 11 Falsterbo, Sweden; (winter) 4101 Cathedral Avenue NW, Apt 1005, Washington, DC 20016, USA. *T:* (202) 9660594. *Clubs:* Chevy Chase (Washington); Falsterbo (Sweden).

ECKERSLEY, Sir Donald (Payze), Kt 1981; OBE 1977; farmer, since 1946; Inaugural President, National Farmers' Federation of Australia, 1979–81; *b* 1 Nov. 1922; *s* of Walter Roland Eckersley and Ada Gladys Moss; *m* 1949, Marjorie Rae Clarke; one *s* two *d.* *Educ:* Muresk Agricl Coll. (Muresk Diploma in Agriculture). Aircrew, RAAF, 1940–45. Pres., Milk Producers' Assoc., 1947–50; Farmers' Union of WA: Executive, 1962–67; Pres., Milk Sect., 1965–70; Vice-Pres., 1969–72; Gen. Pres., 1972–75; Pres., Australian Farmers' Fedn, 1975–79; Austr. Rep., Internat. Fedn of Agric., 1979–81. Pres., Harvey Shire Council, 1970–79; Director: Chamberlain John Deere, 1980–; Br. Bd. Australian Mutual Provident Soc., 1983–. Chairman: Leschenault Inlet Management Authority, 1977–80; Artificial Breeding Bd of WA, 1981–; SW Develt Authority, 1989–96; Bd, Muresk Inst. of Agric., 1984–88; Member: WA Waterways Commn, 1977–80; Nat. Energy Adv. Cttee, 1979–; Comr, WA State Housing Commn, 1982–. Mem., Senate, Univ. of WA, 1981–86. Mem., Harvey Rotary Club. JP WA, 1982–86. Hon. DTech Curtin, 1989. WA Citizen of Year award, 1976; Man of Year, Austr. Agriculture, 1979. *Publication:* (contrib.) Farm Focus: the '80s, 1981. *Recreations:* golf, fishing. *Address:* 323 Korijekop Avenue, WA 6220, Australia. *T:* (8) 97291472. *Clubs:* Weld (Perth); Harvey Golf.

ECKERSLEY-MASLIN, Rear Adm. David Michael, CB 1984; retired, RN; *b* Karachi, 27 Sept. 1929; *e s* of late Comdr C. E. Eckersley-Maslin, OBE, RN, Tasmania, and Mrs L. M. Lightfoot, Bedford; *m* 1955, Shirley Ann, *d* of late Captain H. A. Martin; one *s* one *d.* *Educ:* Britannia Royal Naval Coll. Qual. Navigation Direction Officer, 1954; rcds 1977. Navigating Officer, HMS Michael, Far East Malayan Campaign, 1950–53; Australian Navy, 1954–56; BRNC Dartmouth, 1959–61; commanded HM Ships Eastbourne, Euryalus, Fife and Blake, 1966–76; Captain RN Presentation Team, 1974; Dir, Naval Operational Requirements, 1977–80; Flag Officer Sea Training, 1980–82; ACNS (Operational Planning) (Falklands), 1982; ACDS (CIS), 1982–84; Asst Dir (CIS), IMS, NATO, Brussels, 1984–86; Dir Gen., NATO Communications and Inf. Systems Agency, 1986–91. ADC to the Queen, 1980. Vice Pres., AFCEA, 1987–90 (Gold Medal, 1991). Pres., Algerines Assoc., 1997–2000. Mem. Council, Shipwrecked Mariners Soc., 1992–97. Naval Gen. Service Decoration, Palestine, 1948, and Malaya, 1951. *Recreations:* tennis, cricket. *Address:* Dunningwell, Hall Court, Shedfield, near Southampton SO32 2HL. *T:* (01329) 832350. *Club:* MCC.

ECKERT, Neil David; Chief Executive, Climate Exchange plc, since 2006; *b* 20 May 1962; *s* of Clive and Mary Eckert; *m* 1986, Nicola Lindsay; three *d.* *Educ:* Merchant Taylors' Sch., Northwood, Middx. Reinsurance broker, 1980; joined Benfield Lovick & Rees & Co. Ltd, 1986; Mem. Bd, Benfield Gp plc, 1991–2000; Brit Insurance plc: Dir, 1995–2005; CEO, 1999–2005; non-exec. Dir, 2006–. Non-executive Chairman: Design Technology and Innovations Ltd; European Climate Exchange plc; Trading Emissions plc; non-executive Director: RI3K Ltd; Titan (Southwest) Ltd. *Recreations:* golf, sailing, tennis, other watersports in general, going to concerts, all types of music. *Address:* Climate Exchange plc, 62 Bishopsgate, EC2N 4AW. *T:* (020) 7382 7800, *Fax:* (020) 7382 781(*Clubs:* Royal Automobile, Hurlingham; St Enodoc Golf.

EDDERY, Patrick James John, Hon. OBE 2005; trainer; founder, Pat Eddery Racing 2003; *b* 18 March 1952; *s* of Jimmy and Josephine Eddery; *m* 1978, Carolyn Jane (*n*… Mercer); one *s* two *d.* Rode for Peter Walwyn, 1972–80; Champion Jockey, 1974, 197… 1976, 1977, 1986, 1988, 1989, 1990, 1991, 1993, 1996; Champion Jockey in Irelan… 1982; retired as jockey, 2003. Winner: Oaks, on Polygamy, 1974, on Scintillate, 1979, o… Lady Carla, 1996; Derby, on Grundy, 1975, on Golden Fleece, 1982, on Quest for Fam… 1990; Prix de l'Arc de Triomphe, on Detroit, 1980, on Rainbow Quest, 1985, o… Dancing Brave, 1986, on Trempolino, 1987; St Leger, on Moon Madness, 1986, o… Toulon, 1991, on Moonax, 1994, on Silver Patriarch, 1997 (his 4,000th win in GB… *Recreations:* swimming, golf, snooker. *Address:* Musk Hill Farm, Nether Winchendo… Aylesbury, Bucks HP18 0EB. *T:* (01844) 291980, *Fax:* (01844) 290282.

EDDINGTON, Sir Roderick Ian, (Sir Rod), Kt 2005; DPhil; non-executiv… Chairman, Australia and New Zealand, JPMorgan, since 2006; *b* 2 Jan. 1950; *s* of Gil an… April Eddington; *m* 1994, Young Sook Park; one *s* one *d.* *Educ:* Univ. of WA (BEng Hon… MEng Sci.); Lincoln Coll., Oxford (DPhil 1979). Res. Lectr, Pembroke Coll., Oxfor… 1978–79; John Swire & Sons, 1979–96 (on secondment to Cathay Pacific Airways as Ma… Dir, 1992–96); Director: Swire Pacific, 1992–96; John Swire & Sons Pty Ltd, 1997–… Exec. Chm., Ansett Australia, 1997–2000; Dir, News Ltd, 1997–2000; CEO, Britis… Airways plc, 2000–05. Non-executive Director: News Corp., 2000–; Rio Tinto pl… 2005–; CLP Holdings, 2006–; Chm., Victoria Major Events Co., 2006–. Commnd b… HM Treasury and DFT to provide long-term strategy for UK's transport infrastructur… 2005 (report, Eddington Transport Study, 2006). *Recreations:* cricket, bridge. *Addres…* JPMorgan, Level 31, 101 Collins Street, Melbourne, Vic 3000, Australia. *Clubs:* Vincent (Oxford); Melbourne; Hong Kong, Shek O (Hong Kong).

EDDLESTON, Prof. Adrian Leonard William Francis, DM; FRCP; Professor … Liver Immunology, London University, 1982–2000, now Emeritus, and Head of Guy'… King's College and St Thomas' School of Medicine of King's College Londo… 1998–2000; *b* 2 Feb. 1940; *s* of late Rev. William Eddleston and Kathleen Brenda (*n*… Jarman); *m* 1966, Hilary Kay Radford; three *s* one *d.* *Educ:* St Peter's Coll., Oxford (B… 1961; MB BCh, MA 1964; DM 1972); Guy's Hosp. Med. Sch., London. MRCS 196… LRCP 1965, MRCP 1967, FRCP 1979. House Surgeon, Casualty Officer, Hous… Physician, Sen. House Officer and Jun. Med. Registrar, Guy's Hosp., 1965–67; Me… Registrar, KCH, 1967–68; King's College School of Medicine and Dentistry: Res. Fello… and Hon. Lectr in Med., 1968–70, Hon. Sen. Lectr, 1972–78, Liver Unit; Dean, Facult… of Clinical Med., 1992–97; Dean, 1997–98; Hon. Consultant Physician, KC… 1982–2000. Mem., London Health Commn, 2000–04. MRC Vis. Res. Fellow, Cli… Immunol. Lab., Minnesota Univ., 1970–72. Non-exec. Dir, King's Healthcare NH… Trust, 1990–2000; Chm., Bromley Primary Care Trust, 2001–05. Vice-Chm., King… Fund Mgt Cttee, 2002–07 (Mem., 2000–07). Mem., Gen. Osteopathic Council, 2002 (Chm., 2008–). Trustee, St Christopher's Hospice, 2000–01. FKC 1996. Found… FMedSci 1998. *Publications:* Immune Reactions in Liver Disease, 1979; Interferons in th… Treatment of Chronic Virus Infection of the Liver, 1990; contrib. learned publications c… immunology of auto-immune and virus-induced liver diseases. *Recreations:* computin… choral singing. *Address:* Bridge End Farm, Threlkeld, Keswick, Cumbria CA12 4SX.

EDDY, Prof. Alfred Alan; Professor of Biochemistry, University of Manchester Institu… of Science and Technology, 1959–94, now Professor Emeritus and Honorary Visitin… Scientist, University of Manchester; *b* 4 Nov. 1926; Cornish parentage; *s* of late Alfred an… Ellen Eddy; *m* 1954, Susan Ruth Slade-Jones; two *s.* *Educ:* Devonport High Sch.; Ope… scholarship Exeter Coll., Oxford, 1944; BA 1st Class Hons, 1949. ICI Research Fellow 1950; DPhil 1951. Joined Brewing Industry Research Foundation, Nutfield, 195… *Publications:* various scientific papers. *Recreations:* walking, talking, wining and dinin… *Address:* Larchfield, Buxton Road, Disley, Cheshire SK12 2LH.

EDDY, Thomas Edward Dacombe, CBE 2002; Secretary, Royal Commission o… Environmental Pollution, since 2004; *b* 4 Aug. 1949; *s* of Thomas Charles Eddy an… Myrtle Constance Eddy (*née* Dacombe); *m* 1980, Cherry Eva; two *s.* *Educ:* Quee… Elizabeth Grammar Sch., Wimborne; Pembroke Coll., Cambridge (BA Natural Scis 197… MA 1973). Joined MAFF, 1973; Head of: Countryside Div., 1990–93, Animal Healt… Div., 1993–96, BSE Div., 1996–99, EU Div., 1999–2004, MAFF, subseq. DEFR… Mem., World Ship Soc. *Recreations:* commercial shipping history, reading. *Address:* Roy… Commission on Environmental Pollution, 5–8 The Sanctuary, SW1P 3JS. *T:* (020) 77… 8981; *e-mail:* tom.eddy@rcep.org.uk.

EDE, Anthony Roger; a District Judge (Magistrates' Courts), since 2006; *b* 20 Dec. 194… *s* of Hugh Geoffrey Ede and Rosalie Ede; *m* 1st (marr. diss.); 2nd, Jill Frances Drow… (marr. diss.); one *s* one *d*; 3rd, 2006, Akiyo Yamamoto. *Educ:* Hull Univ. (LLB Ho… 1968). Admitted as solicitor, 1971; Partner, Dundon, Ede & Studdert, solicitors, Lavend… Hill, 1975–88; Lectr in Law, Coll. of Law, Guildford, 1988–90; Dir, Practical Legal Trn… London, 1990–91; Law Society: Sec., Criminal Law Cttee, 1991–2000; Internat. Projec… Manager, 2000–06. Mem., Governing Council, Council for Registration of Forens… Practitioners, 1998–2005. *Publications:* (with E. Shepherd) Active Defence, 1997, 2nd ed… 2000; (with A. Edwards) Criminal Defence, 2000, 3rd edn 2007; (with L. Townle… Forensic Practice in Criminal Cases, 2003. *Recreations:* travelling to unusual and excitin… places, cooking and eating exotic food, world cinema, advising The Archers on crimin… storylines and scripts. *Address:* Brighton Magistrates' Court, The Law Courts, Edwa… Street, Brighton BN2 0LG. *T:* (01273) 670888.

EDE, Ven. Dennis; Archdeacon of Stoke-upon-Trent, 1990–97, now Emerit… permission to officiate, dioceses of Lichfield, Guildford and Southwark, since 2002; *b*… June 1931; *m* 1956, Angela Horsman; one *s* two *d.* *Educ:* Prebendal Choir Sch… Chichester; Ardingly Coll.; Portsmouth Tech. Coll.; Univ. of Nottingham (BA Theolo… 1955); Barnett House, Oxford (Cert. of Social Studies); Ripon Hall, Oxford; MSoc… Birmingham, 1972. Nat. Service, RAF, 1950–52; Pilot Officer, Admin. Branch. A… Curate, St Giles, Shelds, dio. Birmingham, 1957–60; Asst Curate-in-charge, St Philip a… St James, Hodge Hill, Birmingham, 1960–64, Priest-in-charge 1964–70, Team Rect… 1970–76; part-time Chaplain, East Birmingham Hosp., 1961–76; Vicar of All Saints Pari… Church, West Bromwich, dio. Lichfield, 1976–90; Rural Dean, W Bromwich, 1976–8… Hon. Priest i/c, All Saints, Tilford, dio. Guildford, 1997–2002. Mem., Gen. Synod of … of E, 1975–76, 1980–90. Diocese of Lichfield: Chm. House of Clergy, 1985–90; Chm. … Communications, 1983–97; Prebendary of Lichfield Cathedral, 1983–90; Hon. Cano… 1990–97. Chairman: Sandwell Volunteer, 1980–86; Faith in Sandwell, 1986–9… Shallowford House, 1990–97; Diocesan Clergy Retirement Cttee, 1990–97; Wido… (Diocesan) Officers Cttee, 1990–97; Surrey and Sussex Churches Broadcasting Ctte… 1997–. Co-ordinator for religious bodies in Staffs in major disasters, 1990–97. Broadcaste…

local radio, 1960–97; epilogian, ATV, 1961–73. *Recreations:* walking, cycling, table tennis. *Address:* Tilford, 13 Park Close, Carshalton, Surrey SM5 3EU. *T:* (020) 8647 5891; *e-mail:* dennisangelaede@aol.com.

EDELL, Stephen Bristow; Waterways Ombudsman, 1997–2005; *b* 1 Dec. 1932; *s* of late Ivan James Edell and late Hilda Pamela Edell; *m* 1958, Shirley Ross Collins; two *s* one *d*. *Educ:* St Andrew's Sch., Eastbourne; Uppingham; LLB London. Legal Mem., RTPI, 1971–92. Commnd RA, 1951. Articled to father, 1953; qual. Solicitor 1958; Partner, Knapp-Fishers (Westminster), 1959–75; Law Comr, 1975–83; Partner, Crossman Block and Keith (Solicitors), 1983–87; Building Societies Ombudsman, 1987–94; PIA Ombudsman, 1994–97. Mem. Cttee, 1973–85, Vice-Pres., 1980–82, Pres., 1982–83, City of Westminster Law Soc. Oxfam: Mem., Retailing and Property Cttee, 1984–93 (Chm., 1989–93); Mem. Council, 1985–93; Mem., Exec., 1987–93. Dir, Catholic Bldg Soc., 1998–2003. Chm. Council, Hurstpierpoint Coll., 1997–2002. Makers of Playing Cards' Company: Liveryman, 1955–; Mem., Ct of Assts, 1978–2000; Sen. Warden, 1980–81; Master, 1981–82. FRSA. *Publications:* Inside Information on the Family and the Law, 1969; The Family's Guide to the Law, 1974; articles in Conveyancer, Jl of Planning and Environmental Law, and newspapers. *Recreations:* family life; music, opera, theatre; early astronomical instruments; avoiding gardening; interested in problems of developing countries. *Address:* The Old Farmhouse, Twineham, Haywards Heath, Sussex RH17 5NP. *T:* (01273) 832058. *Club:* City Livery.

EDELMAN, Colin Neil; QC 1995; a Recorder, since 1996; Deputy High Court Judge, since 2008; *b* 2 March 1954; *s* of late Gerald Bertram Edelman and of Lynn Queenie Edelman (*née* Tropp); *m* 1978, Jacqueline Claire Seidel; one *s* one *d*. *Educ:* Haberdashers' Aske's Sch., Elstree; Clare Coll., Cambridge (MA). Called to the Bar, Middle Temple, 1977, Bencher, 2003; Asst Recorder, 1993–96; Head of Chambers, 2002–. *Publications:* (contrib.) Insurance Disputes, 1999, 2nd edn 2003; (ed) The Law of Reinsurance, 2005. *Recreations:* badminton, ski-ing, walking, Luton Town FC. *Address:* Devereux Chambers, Devereux Court, WC2R 3JJ. *T:* (020) 7353 7534, *Fax:* (020) 7353 1724.

EDELMAN, Prof. Gerald Maurice, MD, PhD; Director, Neurosciences Institute, La Jolla, since 1981; Chairman, Department of Neurobiology, Scripps Research Institute, since 1992; *b* NYC, 1 July 1929; *s* of Edward Edelman and Anna Freedman; *m* 1950, Maxine Morrison; two *s* one *d*. *Educ:* Ursinus Coll. (BS); University of Pennsylvania (MD); The Rockefeller University (PhD). Med. Hse Officer, Massachusetts Gen. Hosp., 1954–55; Asst Physician, Hosp. of The Rockefeller Univ., 1957–60; The Rockefeller University, NY: Asst Prof. and Asst Dean of Grad. Studies, 1960–63; Associate Prof. and Associate Dean of Grad. Studies, 1963–66; Prof., 1966–74; Vincent Astor Distinguished Prof. of Biochem., 1974–92. Trustee, Rockefeller Brothers Fund, 1972–82; Associate, Neurosciences Res. Program, 1965– (Scientific Chm., 1980–). Mem., Adv. Bd, Basel Inst. Immunology, 1970–77 (Chm., 1975–77); Member Emeritus, Weizmann Inst. of Science, 1987 (Mem., Bd of Governors, 1971–87); non-resident Fellow and Mem. Bd Trustees, Salk Inst. for Biol. Studies, 1973–85; Member: Biophysics and Biophys. Chem. Study Section, Nat. Insts of Health, 1964–67; Sci. Council, Center for Theoretical Studies, 1970–72; Bd of Overseers, Faculty Arts and Scis, Univ. of Pa, 1976–83; Board of Trustees, Carnegie Inst. of Washington (Mem., Adv. Cttee). Member: Nat. Acad. Scis; Amer. Acad. Arts Scis; Amer. Philosophical Soc.; Fellow: AAAS; NY Acad. Scis; NY Acad. of Medicine; Member: Amer. Soc. Biol Chemists; Amer. Assoc. Immunologists; Genetics Soc. of America; Harvey Soc. (Pres., 1975–76); Amer. Chem. Soc.; Amer. Soc. Cell Biol.; Soc. for Developmental Biol.; Sigma XI; Alpha Omega Alpha; Council of Foreign Relations. Hon. Member: Pharmaceutical Soc. of Japan; Japanese Biochem. Soc.; Foreign Mem., Academie des Sciences, Institut de France. Hon. DSc: Pennsylvania, 1973; Gustavus Adolphus Coll., Minn., 1975; Paris, Cagliari, Georgetown Univ. Sch. of Med., 1989; Univ. degli Studi di Napoli Federico II, 1990; Tulane, 1991; Adelphi, NY, 1995; Miami, 1995; Hon. ScD: Ursinus Coll., 1974; Williams Coll., 1976; Hon. MD Univ. Siena, 1974; Hon. Dr Bologna, 1998. Spencer Morris Award, Univ. of Pennsylvania, 1954; Eli Lilly Award in Biol Chem., Amer. Chem. Soc., 1965; Annual Alumni Award, Ursinus College, 1969; (jtly) Nobel Prize in Physiology or Medicine, 1972; Albert Einstein Commemorative Award, Yeshiva Univ., 1974; Buchman Meml Award, Caltech, 1975; Rabbi Shai Shacknai Meml Prize in Immunology and Cancer Res., Hebrew Univ. Hadassah Med. Sch., 1977; Regents Medal of Excellence, New York State, 1984; Hans Neurath prize, Washington Univ., 1986; Sesquicentennial Commem. Award, Nat. Liby of Medicine, 1986; Cécile and Oskar Vogt award, Dusseldorf Univ., 1988; Dist. Grad. Award, Pennsylvania Univ., 1990; Personnalité de l'année, Paris, 1990; Warren Triennial Prize, Massachusetts Gen. Hosp., Boston, 1992. *Publications:* Neural Darwinism, 1987; Topobiology, 1988; The Remembered Present, 1989; Bright Air, Brilliant Fire, 1992; (with Giulio Tononi) Consciousness: how matter becomes imagination, 2000; Wider Than the Sky: the phenomenal gift of consciousness, 2004; Second Nature: brain science and human knowledge, 2006. *Address:* Neurosciences Institute, 10640 John Jay Hopkins Drive, San Diego, CA 92121, USA.

EDELMAN, Keith Graeme; Managing Director, Arsenal Football Club, 2000–08; *b* 10 July 1950; *m* 1974, Susan Brown; two *s*. *Educ:* Haberdashers' Aske's Sch.; UMIST (BSc). IBM, 1971–73; Rank Xerox, 1973–78; Bank of America, 1978–83; Grand Metropolitan, 1983–84; Corporate Planning Dir and Chm., Texas Homecare, Ladbroke Group, 1984–91; Man. Dir, Carlton Communications, 1991–93; Chief Exec., Storehouse and BHS, 1993–99. Non-exec. Chm., Glenmorangie, 2002–05; non-executive Director: Eurotunnel plc, 1995–2004; Eurotunnel SA, 1995–2004; Channel Tunnel Gp Ltd, 1995–2004; France-Manche SA, 1995–2004; Qualcerum Shires plc, 2005–. *Recreations:* tennis, ski-ing. *Address:* Laurimar, 7 Linksway, Northwood, Middx HA6 2XA. *T:* (01923) 823990.

EDELSTEIN, Victor Arnold; painter; *b* 10 July 1945; *s* of Israel and Rebecca Edelstein; *m* 1973, Anna Maria Succi. Trainee Designer, Alexon, 1962–66; Asst Designer, Biba, 1966–68; formed own small dress designing co., 1968–72; Salvador, 1972–76; Designer, Christian Dior, 1976–78; founded Victor Edelstein Ltd, 1978, closed 1993. Ballet design, Rhapsody in Blue, 1989. One-man exhibitions: Sotheby's, 1996; Hopkins Thomas, Paris, 1999; Hazlitt, Gooden & Fox Gall., 2001; Didier Aaron, NY, 2004; (portraits) The Studio, Glebe Place, London, 2005. *Recreations:* walking, music. *Address:* Venice.

EDEN, family name of **Barons Auckland, Eden of Winton** and **Henley**.

EDEN OF WINTON, Baron *cr* 1983 (Life Peer), of Rushyford in the County of Durham; **John Benedict Eden;** PC 1972; Bt (E) 1672 and Bt (GB) 1776; Chairman, Lady Eden's Schools Ltd, 1974–2001 (Director, 1949–70); *b* 15 Sept. 1925; *s* of Sir Timothy Calvert Eden, 8th and 6th Bt and Patricia (*d* 1990), *d* of Arthur Prendergast; *S* father, 1963; *m* 1st, 1958, Belinda Jane (marr. diss. 1974), *o d* of late Sir John Pascoe; two *s* two *d*; 2nd, 1977, Margaret Ann, Viscountess Strathallan. Lieut Rifle Bde, seconded to 2nd KEO Goorkha Rifles and Gilgit Scouts, 1943–47. Contested (C) Paddington North, 1953; MP (C) Bournemouth West, Feb. 1954–1983. Mem. House of Commons Select Cttee on Estimates, 1962–64; Vice-Chm., Conservative Parly Defence Cttee, 1963–66 (formerly: Chm., Defence Air Sub-Cttee; Hon. Sec., Space Sub-Cttee); Vice-Chm., Aviation Cttee, 1963–64; Additional Opposition Front Bench Spokesman for Defence, 1964–66; Jt Vice-Chm., Cons. Parly Trade and Power Cttee, 1966–68; Opposition Front Bench Spokesman for Power, 1968–70; Minister of State, Min. of Technology, June–Oct. 1970; Minister for Industry, DTI, 1970–72; Minister of Posts and Telecommunications, 1972–74; Mem., Expenditure Cttee, 1974–76; Chairman: House of Commons Select Cttee on European Legislation, 1976–79; Home Affairs Cttee, 1981–83. Vice-Chm., Assoc. of Conservative Clubs Ltd, 1964–67, Hon. Life Vice-Pres., 1970–; President: Wessex Area Council, Nat. Union of Conservative and Unionist Assocs, 1974–77; Wessex Area Young Conservatives, 1978–80. UK Deleg. to Council of Europe and to Western European Union, 1960–62; Mem., NATO Parliamentarians' Conf., 1962–66. Chm., Royal Armouries, 1986–94. Chairman: WonderWorld plc, 1982–98; Gamlestaden plc, 1987–92; Bricom Gp, 1990–93. Pres., Independent Schs Assoc., 1969–71; a Vice-Pres., Nat. Chamber of Trade, 1974–86; Vice-Pres., Internat. Tree Foundn (formerly The Men of the Trees), 1953–98. Hon. Vice-Pres., Nat. Assoc. of Master Bakers, Confectioners & Caterers, 1978–82. Chm., British Lebanese Assoc., 1990–98. *Heir* (to baronetcies only): *s* Hon. Robert Frederick Calvert Eden, *b* 30 April 1964. *Address:* c/o House of Lords, SW1A 0PW. *Clubs:* Boodle's, Pratt's.

EDEN, Prof. Colin L., PhD; Professor of Management Science and Strategic Management, Associate Dean and Director, International Division, Strathclyde Business School, University of Strathclyde, since 2006; *b* 24 Dec. 1943; *s* of John and Connie Eden; *m* 1967, Christine. *Educ:* Univ. of Leicester (BSc); Univ. of Southampton (PhD). Operational Researcher, then Operational Res. Manager, then Mgt Cons., 1967–73; Lectr, then Sen. Lectr, then Reader, Sch. of Mgt, Univ. of Bath, 1974–87; Prof., Business Sch., 1988–99, Dir, Grad. Sch. of Business, 1999–2006, Univ. of Strathclyde. Advr, SHEFC; Mem., Mgt Bd, Scottish Exams Bd and Scottish Qualifications Authy. *Publications:* Management Decision and Decision Analysis, 1976; Thinking in Organizations, 1979; Messing About in Problems, 1983; Tackling Strategic Problems, 1990; Managerial and Organizational Cognition, 1998; Making Strategy, 1998; over 150 papers in learned jls. *Recreations:* sailing, ski-ing, walking. *Address:* 199 Cathedral Street, Glasgow G4 0QU. *Club:* Clyde Cruising.

EDEN, (Geoffrey) Philip, FRMetS; Trustee and Director, Chilterns Observatory Trust, since 2007; *b* 14 July 1951; *s* of late Edmund Benham Eden and of Céline Eden (*née* Malpeyre). *Educ:* Luton Grammar Sch.; Luton Sixth Form Coll.; Univ. of Birmingham (BA 1972; MSc 1973). FRMetS 1980. Meteorologist, Univ. of Birmingham, 1973–76; Forecaster, IMCOS Marine Ltd, 1976–81; Principal Meteorologist, Noble Denton and Associates, 1981–83; Proprietor, Philip Eden Weather Consultancy, 1983–; Weather Presenter: LBC, 1983–93; BBC Radio 5 Live, 1994–; Weather Correspondent: Daily Telegraph and Sunday Telegraph, 1986–; Wisden Cricketers' Almanack, 1999–. Royal Meteorological Society: Life Mem., 1993; Council Mem., 1987–90; Hon. Press Officer, 1990–2007; Vice-Pres., 2007–; Michael Hunt Award, 1993; Gordon Manley Weather Prize, 2001. Council Mem. and Hon. Meteorology Sec., Hampstead Scientific Soc., 1983–. *Publications:* Weatherwise, 1995; Weather Facts, 1995; The Secrets of the Weather, 1997; Flood, 2000; Daily Telegraph Book of the Weather, 2003; Change in the Weather, 2005; Great British Weather Disasters, 2008; contrib. meteorological jls. *Recreations:* cricket, classical music, musicals, France, cutting down trees. *Address:* Observatory Lodge, The Green, Whipsnade, Dunstable LU6 2LG. *T:* (01582) 872226; *e-mail:* philip@weather-uk.com. *Clubs:* Warwickshire County Cricket; MG Owners'.

EDEN, Prof. Osborn Bryan, (Tim), FRCPE, FRCP, FRCPath, FRCPCH, FRCR; Teenage Cancer Trust Professor of Teenage and Young Adult Cancer, since 2005, Hon. Consultant and Lead Clinician, Teenage Cancer Trust Young Oncology Unit, since 1994, Christie Hospital NHS Trust; Hon. Consultant, Central Manchester and Manchester Children's University Hospitals NHS Trust, since 1994; *b* 2 April 1947; *s* of late Eric Victor Eden and Gwendoline Eden (*née* Hambly); *m* 1970, Randi Forsgren; one *s* one *d*. *Educ:* University Coll. London (MB BS 1970). DRCOG 1972; FRCPE 1983; FRCP 1992 (MRCP 1974); FRCPath 1995; FRCPCH 1997; FRCR 2007. House physician, UCH, 1970–71; house surgeon, Portsmouth, 1971; Sen. House Officer appts, IoW, UCH, Simpson Meml Pavilion and Royal Hosp. for Sick Children, Edinburgh, 1971–73; Registrar, Paediatrics and Haematology, Royal Hosp. for Sick Children, Edinburgh, 1974–76; Fellow, Stanford Univ., Calif., 1976–77; Leukaemia Res. Fellow, Edinburgh, 1977–78; Lectr, Edinburgh Univ., 1978–79; Consultant Clinical Haematologist, Bristol Children's Hosp., 1979–82; Consultant Paediatric Haematologist, Royal Hosp. for Sick Children, Edinburgh, 1982–91; Prof. of Paediatric Oncology, St Bartholomew's Hosp., 1991–94; CRUK (formerly CRC) Prof. of Paediatric Oncology, Univ. of Manchester, 1994–2005; Lead Clinician, Paediatric Oncology, Royal Manchester Children's Hosp., 1994–2005. Chm., UK Children's Cancer Study Gp, 1989–92 (Chm., Haematology Oncology Div., 2000–06); Member: MRC Childhood Leukaemia Working Party, 1978– (Chm., 1991–2000); MRC Leukaemia Steering Cttee, 1991–2002; Cttee on Med. Effects of Radiation in the Envmt, 1991–2003; Clin. Trials Cttee, CRC, 1998–2002; Med. and Scientific Panel and Clin. Trials Cttee, Leukaemia Res. Fund, 2000–04; Clinical Trials Adv. and Awards Cttee, MRC/CRUK, 2002–04; CTRC, CRUK, 2007–. Pres., Internat. Soc. of Paediatric Oncology, 2004–07 (Chm., Scientific Cttee, 1996–99); Hon. Treas., Genetics Section, RSocMed, 2003–04 (Hon. Sec., 2001–03). Non-exec. Dir, Manchester Children's Hosps NHS Trust, 1996–2001. Med. Advr and Founding Mem., Over the Wall Gang Camp, 2001–. Trustee, Malcolm Sargent Cancer Fund, 1985–95; Founding Med. Trustee, World Childhood Cancer Fund, 2007. Mem., Adv. Bd, AFROX, 2008. Hon. Mem., Burma Med. Assoc., 1985. *Publications:* numerous scientific papers, editorials and chapters on paediatric haematology and oncology. *Recreations:* my family, hill-walking, photography, reading, urban wildlife, politics. *Address:* 5 South Gillsland Road, Edinburgh EH10 5DE. *T:* (0131) 447 8749.

EDEN, Philip; *see* Eden, G. P.

EDEN, Prof. Richard John, OBE 1978; Professor of Energy Studies, Cavendish Laboratory, University of Cambridge, 1982–89, now Emeritus; Fellow of Clare Hall, Cambridge, 1966–89, now Emeritus (Vice-President, 1987–89; Hon. Fellow, 1993); *b* 2 July 1922; *s* of James A. Eden and Dora M. Eden; *m* 1949, Elsie Jane Greaves; one *s* one *d* and one step *d*. *Educ:* Hertford Grammar Sch.; Peterhouse, Cambridge (BA 1943, MA 1948, PhD 1951). War service, 1942–46, Captain REME, Airborne Forces. Cambridge University: Bye-Fellow, Peterhouse, 1949–50; Stokes Student, Pembroke Coll., 1950–51; Clare College: Research Fellow, 1951–55; Official Fellow, 1957–66; Dir of Studies in Maths, 1951–53, 1957–62; Royal Soc. Smithson Res. Fellow, 1952–55; Sen. Lectr in Physics, Univ. of Manchester, 1955–57; Cambridge University: Lectr in Maths, 1957–64 (Stokes Lectr, 1962); Reader in Theoretical Physics, 1964–82; Head of High Energy Theoretical Physics Gp, 1964–74, Hd of Energy Res. Gp, 1974–89, Cavendish Lab. Mem., Princeton Inst. for Advanced Study, 1954, 1959, 1973, 1989; Vis. Scientist: Indiana Univ., 1954–55; Univ. of California, Berkeley, 1960, 1967; Vis. Professor: Univ. of Maryland, 1961, 1965; Columbia Univ., 1962; Scuola Normale Superiore, Pisa, 1964; Univ. of Marseilles, 1968; Univ. of California, 1969. Member: UK Adv. Council on Energy Conservation, 1974–83; Eastern Electricity Bd, 1985–93; Energy Adviser to UK

NEDO, 1974–75. Syndic, CUP, 1984–95. Chm., Cambridge Energy Res. Ltd, subseq. Caminus Energy Ltd, 1985–91. Companion, Inst. of Energy, 1985. Smiths Prize, Univ. of Cambridge, 1949; Maxwell Prize and Medal, Inst. of Physics, 1970; Open Award for Distinction in Energy Economics, BIEE, 1989. *Publications:* (jtly) The Analytic S Matrix, 1966; High Energy Collisions of Elementary Particles, 1967; Energy Conservation in the United Kingdom (NEDO report), 1975; Energy Prospects (Dept of Energy report), 1976; World Energy Demand to 2020 (World Energy Conf. report), 1977; (jtly) Energy Economics, 1981; (jtly) Electricity's Contribution to UK Energy Self Sufficiency, 1984; (jtly) UK Energy, 1984; Clare College and the Founding of Clare Hall, 1998; (jtly) Clare Hall 40, 2006; papers and review articles on nuclear physics and theory of elementary particles. *Recreations:* writing, painting, reading, gardening, travel. *Address:* Clare Hall, Cambridge CB3 9AL. *T:* (01223) 332360.

EDEN, Tim; *see* Eden, O. B.

EDER, (Henry) Bernard; QC 1990; *b* 16 Oct. 1952; *s* of Hans and Helga Eder; *m* 1976, Diana Levin (marr. diss. 2002); four *s* one *d*. *Educ:* Haberdashers' Aske's School, Elstree; Downing College, Cambridge (BA 1974). Called to the Bar, Inner Temple, 1975, Bencher, 2007; an Asst Recorder, 1996–2000; a Recorder, 2000–01. Vis. Prof., UCL, 1999–2003. *Recreations:* tennis, ski-ing. *Address:* Essex Court Chambers, 24–26 Lincoln's Inn Fields, WC2A 3EG. *T:* (020) 7813 8000; *e-mail:* beder@essexcourt.net.

EDES, (John) Michael, CMG 1981; HM Diplomatic Service, retired; Ambassador and Head, UK Delegation to Conventional Arms Control Negotiations, Vienna, 1989–90; *b* 19 April 1930; *s* of late Lt-Col N. H. Edes and Mrs Louise Edes; *m* 1978, Angela Mermagen; two *s*. *Educ:* Blundell's Sch.; Clare Coll., Cambridge (Scholar; BA); Yale Univ. (MA). HM Forces, 1948–49; Mellon Fellow, Yale Univ., 1952–54; FO, 1954; MECAS, 1955; Dubai, 1956–57; FO, 1957–59 (Moscow, 1959); Rome, 1959–61; FO, 1961–62; UK Delegn to Conf. on Disarmament, Geneva, 1962–65 (UK Mission to UN, NY, 1963); FO, 1965–68; Cabinet Office, 1968–69; FCO, 1969–71; Ambassador to Yemen Arab Republic, 1971–73; Mem., UK Delegn to CSCE, Geneva, 1973–74; FCO, 1974–77; RIIA, 1977–78; Paris, 1978–79; Ambassador to Libya, 1980–83; Hd, UK Delegn to Conf. on Confidence and Security Building Measures and Disarmament in Europe, Stockholm, 1983–86; Hd, UK team at conventional arms control mandate talks, 1987–89. Vis. Fellow, IISS, 1987. *Recreations:* listening to music, gardening. *Address:* c/o Lloyds TSB, 7 Pall Mall, SW1Y 5NA. *Clubs:* Athenæum; Hawks (Cambridge).

EDGAR, (Christopher) George; HM Diplomatic Service; Head, Consular Assistance Group, Foreign and Commonwealth Office, since 2007; *b* 21 April 1960; *s* of Dr William Macreadie Edgar and Dr Freda Elizabeth Edgar; *m* 1994, Elena Ryurikovna Nagornichnykh; two *d*. *Educ:* Trinity Coll., Cambridge Univ. (MA Philosophy); Open Univ. (MA Envmt, Policy and Society). FCO, 1981–83; Moscow, 1984–85; Lagos, 1986–88; FCO, 1988–92; resigned 1992, reinstated 1995; FCO, 1995–97; Ambassador to Cambodia, 1997–2000; Ambassador to Macedonia, 2001–04; Consul Gen., St Petersburg, 2004–06; Envoy for Climate Security in Africa, FCO, 2006–07. *Recreation:* music. *Address:* c/o Foreign and Commonwealth Office, King Charles Street, SW1A 2AH.

EDGAR, David Burman; author and playwright; Chair, MA in Playwriting Studies, 1989–99, Hon. Professor, since 1992, University of Birmingham; *b* 26 Feb. 1948; *s* of Barrie Edgar and late Joan (*née* Burman); *m* 1979, Eve Brook (*d* 1998); two *s*. *Educ:* Oundle Sch.; Univ. of Manchester (BA 1969). Fellow in Creative Writing, Leeds Polytechnic, 1972–74; Resident Playwright, Birmingham Rep. Theatre, 1974–75, Board Mem., 1985–; UK/US Bicentennial Arts Fellow, USA, 1978–79; Literary Consultant, 1984–88, Hon. Associate Artist, 1989, RSC; Hon. Sen. Res. Fellow, 1988–92, Prof. of Playwriting Studies, 1995–99, Birmingham Univ. Hon. Fellow, Birmingham Polytechnic, 1991; Judith E. Wilson Fellow, Clare Hall, Cambridge, 1996. Hon. MA Bradford, 1984; DUniv Surrey, 1993; Hon. DLitt Birmingham, 2002. *Plays:* The National Interest, 1971; Excuses Excuses, Coventry, 1972; Death Story, Birmingham Rep., 1972; Baby Love, 1973; The Dunkirk Spirit, 1974; Dick Deterred, Bush Theatre, 1974; O Fair Jerusalem, Birmingham Rep., 1975; Saigon Rose, Edinburgh, 1976; Blood Sports, incl. Ball Boys, Bush Theatre, 1976; Destiny, Other Place, 1976, Aldwych, 1977; Wreckers, 1977; Our Own People, 1977; (adaptation) The Jail Diary of Albie Sachs, Warehouse Theatre, 1978; (adaptation) Mary Barnes, Birmingham Rep., then Royal Court, 1978–79; (with Susan Todd) Teendreams, 1979; (adaptation) Nicholas Nickleby, Aldwych, 1980, Plymouth Theatre, NY, 1981; Maydays, Barbican, 1983; Entertaining Strangers, 1985, Nat. Theatre, 1987; That Summer, Hampstead, 1987; (with Stephen Bill and Anne Devlin) Heartlanders, Birmingham Rep., 1989; The Shape of the Table, NT, 1990; (adaptation) Dr Jekyll and Mr Hyde, Barbican, 1991; Pentecost, Other Place, 1994, Young Vic, 1995; (adaptation) Albert Speer, NT, 2000; The Prisoner's Dilemma, RSC, 2001; Continental Divide (2 play cycle, Daughters of the Revolution, and Mothers Against), Oregon Shakespeare Fest./ Berkeley Rep., 2003, Barbican, 2004; (trans.) The Life of Galileo, Birmingham Rep.; Playing with Fire, NT, 2005; Testing the Echo, Out of Joint (tour), 2008; *TV and radio:* The Eagle has Landed, 1973; Sanctuary, 1973; I know what I meant, 1974; Ecclesiastes, 1977; (with Neil Grant) Vote for Them, 1989; A Movie Starring Me, 1991; Buying a Landslide, 1992; Citizen Locke, 1994; Talking to Mars, 1996; (adaptation) The Secret Parts, 2000; Brave Faces, 2006; Something Wrong about the Mouth, 2007; *film:* Lady Jane, 1986. *Publications:* Destiny, 1976; Wreckers, 1977; The Jail Diary of Albie Sachs, 1978; Teendreams, 1979; Mary Barnes, 1979; Nicholas Nickleby, 1982; Maydays, 1983; Entertaining Strangers, 1985; Plays One, 1987; That Summer, 1987; The Second Time as Farce, 1988; Vote for Them, 1989; Heartlanders, 1989; Edgar Shorts, 1990; Plays Two, 1990; The Shape of the Table, 1990; Plays Three, 1991; Dr Jekyll and Mr Hyde, 1992; Pentecost, 1995; (ed) State of Play, 1999; Albert Speer, 2000; The Prisoner's Dilemma, 2001; Continental Divide, 2004; Playing with Fire, 2005; Testing the Echo, 2008. *Recreation:* correspondence. *Address:* c/o Alan Brodie Representation, 6th Floor, Fairgate House, 78 New Oxford Street, WC1A 1HB. *T:* (020) 7079 7990.

EDGAR, George; *see* Edgar, C. G.

EDGAR, William, CBE 2004; FREng, FIMechE; FRSE; Group Director, John Wood Group plc, 1995–2004; Chairman and Chief Executive, Wood Group Engineering Ltd, 1995–2004; Chairman, J. P. Kenny Engineering Ltd, 1995–2004; *b* 16 Jan. 1938; *s* of William Edgar and Alice Anderson McKerrell; *m* 1961, June Gilmour; two *s*. *Educ:* Royal Coll. of Science and Technology (Strathclyde Univ.); ARCST 1961; Birmingham Univ. (MSc 1962). CEng, FIMechE 1979. Develt Engr, BSC, Motherwell and Glasgow, 1954–62; Principal Aeromech. Engr, BAC, Warton, 1963–67; Chief Develt Engr, Gen. Manager Sales and Service, Gen. Works Manager, Weir Pumps, Glasgow, 1967–73; Chief Exec., Seaforth Engineering and Corporate Develt Dir, Seaforth Maritime, Aberdeen, 1973–86; Business Develt Dir, Vickers Marine Engineering, Edinburgh, 1986–88; Exec. Chm., Cochrane Shipbuilders, Yorks, 1988–90; Chief Exec., Nat. Engrg Lab., 1990–95. Chairman: European Marine Energy Centre, 2005–; Subsea UK Ltd, 2005–. Vis. Prof., Strathclyde Univ., 2001–. Chm., Offshore Contractors Assoc., 2000–03; Pres., IMechE, 2004–05 (Dep. Pres., 2002–04; Chm., Scottish Br., 1996–98). FREng 1999; FRSE 2003. Liveryman, Engineers' Co., 2006–. *Recreations:* golf, walking, reading, soccer. *Club:* Sloane.

EDGCUMBE, family name of **Earl of Mount Edgcumbe**.

EDGE, Geoffrey; Managing Director, Geonomics Ltd, since 2007; *b* 26 May 1943; single. *Educ:* London Sch. of Econs (BA); Birmingham Univ. Asst Lectr in Geography, Univ. of Leicester, 1967–70; Lectr in Geog., Open Univ., 1970–74. Member: Bletchley UDC, 1972–74 (Chm. Planning Sub-cttee 1973–74); Milton Keynes DC, 1973–76 (Vice-Chm. Planning Cttee, 1973–75); Bucks Water Bd, 1973–74; W Midlands CC, 1981–86 (Chm., Econ. Develt Cttee); Walsall MBC, 1983–90 (Leader, 1988–90). MP (Lab) Aldridge-Brownhills, Feb. 1974–1979; PPS to Minister of State for Educn, Feb.–Oct. 1974, 1976–77, to Minister of State, Privy Council Office, Oct. 1974–76. Research Fellow, Dept of Planning Landscape, Birmingham Polytechnic, 1979–80; Senior Research Fellow: Preston Polytechnic, 1980–81; NE London Polytechnic, 1982–84; Hon. Res. Fellow, Birmingham Polytechnic, 1980–81; New Initiatives Co-ordinator, COPEC Housing Trust, 1984–87; Sen. Associate, P-E Inbucon, then P-E Internat., 1987–97. Chm., West Midlands Enterprise Ltd, 1982–2007; Associate Dir, W. S. Atkins plc, 1997–99; Dir, Winning Pitch plc, 2007–. *Publications:* (ed jtly) Regional Analysis and Development, 1973; Open Univ. booklets on industrial location and urban development. *Recreations:* music, reading, touring. *Address:* 5 Sedgefield Close, Dudley DY1 2UU.

EDGE, Prof. Kevin Anthony, PhD, DSc; CEng, FREng, FIMechE; Professor of Mechanical Engineering, since 1991, and Pro-Vice-Chancellor (Research), since 2003, University of Bath; *b* 1 July 1949; *s* of George and Marion Edge; partner, Delyth Ann Davies. *Educ:* Univ. of Bath (BSc 1971; PhD 1975; DSc 1995). CEng 1982; FIMechE 1990. Sen. Control Systems Engr, Rolls Royce Ltd, 1974–76; University of Bath: Res. Officer, 1976; Lectr, 1976–87; Sen. Lectr, 1987–91; Reader, 1991; Dep. Dir, Centre for Power Transmission and Motion Control, 1993–. FREng 2003. *Publications:* papers in professional jls. *Recreations:* classical music, photography. *Address:* University of Bath, Claverton Down, Bath BA2 7AY. *T:* (01225) 386963, *Fax:* (01225) 386928; *e-mail:* k.a.edge@bath.ac.uk.

EDGE, Captain Sir (Philip) Malcolm, KCVO 1995; FNI; Deputy Master and Chairman, Board of Trinity House, 1988–96; *b* 15 July 1931; *s* of Stanley Weston Edge and Edith Edge (*née* Liddell); *m* 1st, 1967, (Kathleen) Anne Greenwood (*d* 1994); one *s* one *d*; 2nd, 2003, Carol Mann. *Educ:* Rockferry High School; HMS Conway. Master Mariner. Apprenticed to Shipping subsidiary of British Petroleum, 1949, and served in all ranks; in command, world wide, 1969–78. Elder Brother and Mem. Board, Trinity House, 1978; Mem., PLA, 1980–97. Dir, Standard Steamship Owners' Protection & Indemnity Assoc. Ltd, 1988–97 (Chm., 1992–97). Mem. Council, Internat. Assoc. of Lighthouse Authies, 1988–96 (Pres., 1988–90). Freeman, City of London, 1980; Liveryman: Hon. Co. of Master Mariners, 1980–; Shipwrights' Co., 1990–2006; Master, Watermen and Lightermen's Co., 1996–97. *Recreations:* sailing, family. *Address:* c/o Trinity House, Tower Hill, EC3N 4DH. *T:* (020) 7481 6900. *Clubs:* Royal Yacht Squadron (Hon.), Royal London Yacht, Royal Lymington Yacht.

EDGE, Stephen Martin; Corporate Tax Partner, Slaughter and May, since 1982; *b* Farnworth, Lancs, 29 Nov. 1950; *s* of late Harry Edge and of Mary Edge; *m* 1975, Melanie Lawler; two *d*. *Educ:* Canon Slade Grammar Sch., Bolton; Exeter Univ. (LLB Hons). Admitted solicitor, 1975; joined Slaughter and May, 1973 (Mem., Partnership Bd). Mem., Alumni and Develt Bd, Exeter Univ. Vice Pres., Lancs Cricket Fedn; Pres., Amberley CC. *Publications:* contrib. to tax pubns. *Recreations:* walking, golf, theatre, watching cricket and soccer. *Address:* Slaughter and May, 1 Bunhill Row, EC1Y 8YY. *T:* (020) 7600 1200, *Fax:* (020) 7090 5000; *e-mail:* steve.edge@slaughterandmay.com. *Club:* MCC.

EDGE, William, (3rd Bt *cr* 1937); *S* father, 1984, but does not use the title and his name does not appear on the Official Roll of the Baronetage. *Heir: s* Edward Knowles Edge.

EDGINGTON, Prof. Dorothy Margaret Doig, FBA 2005; Senior Research Fellow, School of Philosophy, Birkbeck, University of London, since 2006; *b* 29 April 1941; *d* of late Edward Milne and of Rhoda Milne (*née* Blair); *m* 1965, John Edgington; one *s* (one *d* decd). *Educ:* St Leonards Sch., St Andrews; St Hilda's Coll., Oxford (BA 1964; Hon. Fellow, 2004); Nuffield Coll., Oxford (BPhil 1967). Lectr in Philosophy, 1968–90, Sen. Lectr, 1990–96, Birkbeck Coll., London Univ.; Prof. of Philosophy, Oxford Univ., and Fellow of UC, Oxford, 1996–2001; Prof. of Philosophy, Birkbeck Coll., London Univ., 2001–03; Waynflete Prof. of Metaphysical Philosophy, Univ. of Oxford, 2003–06, now Emeritus, and Fellow of Magdalen Coll., Oxford, 2003–06. British Acad. Res. Reader in the Humanities, 1992–94; visiting posts: Univ. of British Columbia, 1974–75, 1990, 1992; Univ. Nacional Autónoma de México, 1985, 1988, 1990, 1995; Princeton Univ., 1986; Univ. of Calif, Berkeley, 1993. Hon. Sec., Aristotelian Soc., 1986–92 (Ed., Proc. of Aristotelian Soc., 1986–90). *Publications:* contrib. anthologies, and learned jls incl. Analysis, British Jl for Philos. of Sci., Crítica, Mind, Proc. of Aristotelian Soc., Revista Latinoamericana de Filosofía. *Address:* School of Philosophy, Birkbeck, University of London, Malet Street, WC1E 7HX.

EDINBURGH, Bishop of, since 2001; **Rt Rev. Brian Arthur Smith;** *b* 15 Aug. 1943; *s* of late Arthur and of Doris Marion Smith; *m* 1970, Elizabeth Berring (*née* Hutchinson); two *d*. *Educ:* George Heriot's School, Edinburgh; Edinburgh Univ. (MA Mental Philosophy 1966); Fitzwilliam Coll., Cambridge (BA Theology 1968; MA 1972); Westcott House, Cambridge; Jesus Coll., Cambridge (MLitt 1973). Curate of Cuddesdon, 1972–79; Tutor in Doctrine, Cuddesdon Coll., Oxford, 1972–75; Dir of Studies, Ripon Coll., Cuddesdon, 1975–78, Senior Tutor 1978–79; Diocese of Wakefield: Priest-in-charge of Cragg Vale, 1979–85; Dir of In-Service Training, 1979–81; Dir of Ministerial Trng, 1981–87; Warden of Readers, 1981–87; Sec. of Dio. Board of Ministry, 1979–87; Hon. Canon of Wakefield, 1981–87; Proctor in Convocation, 1985–87; Archdeacon of Craven, 1987–93; Bp Suffragan of Tonbridge, 1993–2001. Vice-Chairman, Northern Ordination Course, 1985–93. Chm., Churches Together in Kent, 1999–2001. Mem., Scotland Cttee, UNESCO, 2008–. A Director, Scottish Jl of Theology, 1977–81. *Recreations:* browsing in junk shops, walking, reading, music, short-wave radio listening. *Address:* 3 Eglinton Crescent, Edinburgh EH12 5DH; Diocesan Centre, 21A Grosvenor Crescent, Edinburgh EH12 5EL. *T:* (0131) 538 7044, *Fax:* (0131) 538 7088; *e-mail:* bishop@edinburgh.anglican.org.

EDINBURGH, Dean of; *see* Pearson, Very Rev. K.

EDINBURGH, (St Mary's Cathedral), Provost of; *see* Forbes, Very Rev. G. J. T.

EDINGTON, (George) Gordon, CBE 2007; FRICS; an Ambassador, Action for Children (formerly NCH, the Children's Charity) (a Vice-President, 1998; Chair of Trustees, 2001–07); *b* 7 Sept. 1945; *s* of George Adam Edington and Phyllis Mary (*née* Allan); *m* 1973, Jane Mary Adie (marr. diss.); four *s*. *Educ:* St Mary's Sch., Kenya; St Lawrence Coll., Kent. FRICS 1970. Man. Dir, Lynton plc, 1981–94; Director: BAA plc, 1991–99; Lend Lease Corp., 1999–; Chm., Earls Court and Olympia Gp Ltd, 2000–01.

Pres., British Property Fedn, 1998–99. Chairman: Michael Stuckey Trust, 1988–98; Public Art Develt Trust, 1992–98. Trustee, Tennis First Charitable Trust, 1999–. Gov., Wilson Centre, Cambridge Internat. Land Inst., 1993–98. FRSA 1992; Mem., Henley Royal Regatta. Freeman, City of London, 1994; Liveryman, Chartered Surveyors' Co., 1994–. *Publications:* The Clowes Family of Chester Sporting Artists, 1985; Property Management: a customer focused approach, 1997. *Recreations:* four sons, tennis, golf, fly fishing, hill walking, historic Thames rivercraft. *Address:* 78 Hotham Road, SW15 1QP; *e-mail:* gordonedington@snowshill.co.uk. *Clubs:* Flyfishers'; Royal Wimbledon Golf; Riverside Racquet.

EDINGTON, Martin George Ritchie; Sheriff of Lothian and Borders at Linlithgow, since 2007; *b* 28 Oct. 1955; *s* of George and Eva Edington; *m* 1979, Susan Jane Phillips; two *s*. *Educ:* Fettes Coll.; Dundee Univ. (LLB). NP 1981; WS 1985; Partner, Turnbull, Simson & Sturrock, WS, 1983–2001; Temp. Sheriff, 1999–2000; All-Scotland Floating Sheriff, 2001–03; Floating Sheriff at Linlithgow, 2003–07. *Recreations:* fine wines and whiskies, eating, travelling, curling, Rugby, cricket, making decisions. *Address:* Sheriff Court, High Street, Linlithgow EH49 7EQ. *T:* (01506) 842922, *Fax:* (01506) 848457.

EDIS, Andrew Jeremy Coulter; QC 1997; a Recorder, since 1999; a Deputy High Court Judge, since 2001; *b* 9 June 1957; *s* of late Dr Peter Marcus Edis and Barbara Louise Edis; *m* 1984, Sandy Wilkinson; one *s* two *d*. *Educ:* Liverpool Coll.; University Coll., Oxford (MA). Called to the Bar, Middle Temple, 1980, Bencher, 2004; Junior, Northern Circuit, 1983–84; Asst Recorder, 1994–99. Hd of Atlantic Chambers, 2000–06. *Recreations:* cricket, travel. *Address:* Atlantic Chambers, 4–6 Cook Street, Liverpool L2 9QU. *T:* (0151) 236 4421. *Club:* Oxford and Cambridge.

EDIS, (Angus) William (Butler); QC 2008; a Recorder, since 2003; *b* Liverpool, 15 June 1961; *s* of late Dr Peter Marcus Edis and Barbara Louise Edis; *m* 1996, Mary Elizabeth Pinder; two *s*. *Educ:* Liverpool Coll.; Trinity Coll., Oxford (BA Lit.Hum); City Univ. (Dip. Law). Called to the Bar, Lincoln's Inn, 1985; in practice, specialising in healthcare and disciplinary law. *Publications:* contribs to medico-legal jls. *Recreations:* family, football, bridge. *Address:* (chambers) 1 Crown Office Row, Temple, EC4Y 7HH. *T:* (020) 7797 7500, *Fax:* (020) 7797 7550. *Clubs:* Everton Football; Young Chelsea Bridge.
See also A. J. C. Edis.

EDLESTON, Rear Adm. Hugh Anthony Harold Greswell; defence consultant to International Defence and Non-Governmental Organisations, since 2004; *b* 24 Jan. 1949; *s* of late Tony Edleston and of Dorothy Edleston; *m* 1973, Lynne Taylor; one *s* one *d*. *Educ:* Wellington Coll.; BRNC, Dartmouth. Qualified Advanced Warfare Officer (A), 1980; Ops Officer, HMS Glamorgan, Falklands War, 1981–83; pce 1983; CO, HMS Glasgow, 1986–88; Asst Dir, ME, MoD, 1992–95; jsdc 1993; Commanding Officer: HMS Exeter, 1996; HMS Cardiff, and Capt., Fifth Destroyer Sqdn, 1996–98; Dir, Corporate Communications (RN), MoD, 1998–2001; hcsc 2001; Comdr, UK Task Gp, 2001. Mil. Advr to High Rep., Sarajevo, 2002–04. MNI 1991; ACMI (AMBIM 1991); AIPR 2000. Freeman, City of London, 2000; Liveryman, Co. of Carmen, 1998–. *Recreations:* blues and jazz music, cryptic crosswords, sundials. *Address:* *e-mail:* huedles@hotmail.com. *Club:* Liberal.

EDMONDS, David Albert, CBE 2003; Chairman, Legal Services Board, since 2008; *b* 6 March 1944; *s* of Albert and Gladys Edmonds; *m* 1966, Ruth Beech; two *s* two *d*. *Educ:* Helsby County Grammar School; University of Keele. BA Hons Political Institutions and History. Asst Principal, Min. of Housing and Local Govt, 1966–69; Private Sec. to Parly Sec., MHLG and DoE, 1969–71; Principal, DoE, 1971–73; Observer, CSSB, 1973–74; Vis. Fellow, Centre for Metropolitan Planning and Research, Johns Hopkins Univ., 1974–75; Private Sec. to Perm. Sec., DoE, 1975–77; Asst Sec., DoE, 1977–79; Principal Private Sec. to Sec. of State, DoE, 1979–83; Under Sec., Inner Cities Directorate, DoE, 1983–84; Chief Exec., Housing Corporation, 1984–91; Gen. Manager, then Man. Dir, Central Services, NatWest Gp, 1991–97; Dir Gen. of Telecommns, 1998–2003. Dir, Housing Finance Corp., 1988–91; Member: Bd, English Partnerships, 2000–03; Steering Bd, Radiocommunications Agency, 1998–2003; OFCOM, 2002–05; Bd, Legal Services Commn, 2004–08; Chairman: NHS Direct, 2004–08; NHS Shared Business Service, 2005–08. Non-executive Director: Hammerson PLC, 2003–; Wincanton plc, 2003–; William Hill plc, 2005–. Pres., Internat. New Town Assoc., 1987–91; Mem. Cttee, Notting Hill Housing Trust, 1991–94. Dep. Chm., New Statesman and Society, 1988–90 (Chm., New Society, 1986–88). Mem. Bd, Social Market Foundn, 2001–. Chair of Trustees, Crisis, 1996–2002. Mem. Council, Chm., Finance Cttee, and Univ. Treas., Keele Univ., 1997–2003. Hon. DLitt Keele, 2004. *Recreations:* theatre, opera, walking, golf. *Address:* 61 Cottenham Park Road, West Wimbledon, SW20 0DR. *T:* (020) 8946 3729. *Clubs:* Savile; Wimbledon Park Golf (Captain, 1997–98).

EDMONDS, John Christopher, CMG 1978; CVO 1971; HM Diplomatic Service, retired; *b* 23 June 1921; *s* of late Captain A. C. M. Edmonds, OBE, RN, and late Mrs Edmonds; *m* 1st, 1948, Elena Tornow (marr. diss., 1965); two *s*; 2nd, 1966, Armine Williams (*d* 2005). *Educ:* Kelly College. Entered Royal Navy, 1939; psc, 1946. Staff: of NATO Defence Coll., Paris, 1953–55; of C-in-C Home Fleet, 1956–57 (Comdr, 1957); of Chief of Defence Staff, 1958–59. Entered Diplomatic Service, 1959; Foreign Office, 1959–60; 1st Secretary (Commercial), Tokyo, 1960–62; FO, 1963–67; 1st Secretary and Head of Chancery, Ankara, 1967–68; Counsellor: Ankara, 1968–71; Paris, 1972–74; Head of Arms Control and Disarmament Dept, FCO, 1974–77; Leader, UK Delegn to Comprehensive Test Ban Treaty Negotiations, Geneva, with personal rank of Ambassador, 1978–81. Chm., Jt SDP-Liberal Alliance Commn on Defence and Disarmament, 1984–86. Vis. Fellow in Internat. Relations, Reading Univ., 1981–2000. Chm., Sonning Parish Council, 1984–90. *Recreations:* gardening, travel. *Address:* North Lodge, Sonning, Berks RG4 6ST.

EDMONDS, John Christopher Paul, CBE 1993; Chief Executive, Railtrack, 1993–97; *b* 22 April 1936; *s* of late Frank Winston Edmonds and Phyllis Mary Edmonds; *m* 1962, Christine Elizabeth Seago; one *s* one *d*. *Educ:* Lowestoft Grammar School; Trinity College, Cambridge. Nat. Service Commission, RAF, 1955–57. Joined British Rail, 1960; Chief Freight Manager, London Midland Region, 1981; Nat. Business Manager, Coal, 1982; Dir, Provincial, 1984; Gen. Manager, Anglia Region, 1987; Bd Mem., and Man. Dir, Gp Services, 1989–93. *Recreations:* gardening, music.

EDMONDS, John Walter; General Secretary, GMB (formerly General, Municipal, Boilermakers and Allied Trades Union), 1986–2003; *b* 28 Jan. 1944; *s* of Walter and Rose Edmonds; *m* 1967, Linden (*née* Callaby); two *d*. *Educ:* Brunswick Park Primary; Christ's Hosp.; Oriel Coll., Oxford (BA 1965, MA 1968). General and Municipal Workers' Union: Res. Asst, 1966; Dep. Res. Officer, 1967; Reg. Officer, 1968; Nat. Industrial Officer, 1972. Mem. Council, ACAS, 1992–2000. Pres., TUC, 1997–98. Chm., TU Adv. Cttee on Sustainable Develt, 1998–2003. Director: National Building Agency, 1978–82; Unity Trust Bank, 1986–2003 (Pres., 2001–03). Mem., Royal Commn on Environmental Pollution, 1979–89; a Forestry Comr, 1995–2001; Director: EA, 2002–; Carbon Trust, 2002–; Chm., Inland Waterways Adv. Council, 2002–. Dir, Salix Finance, 2004–. Vis. Fellow, Nuffield Coll., Oxford, 1986–94; Res. Fellow, KCL, 2003–. Mem. Council, Consumers' Assoc., 1991–96. Trustee: Inst. of Public Policy Research, 1988–2002; NSPCC, 1995–2002. Gov., LSE, 1986–95. Hon. LLD Sussex, 1994. *Recreations:* cricket, carpentry. *Address:* 50 Graham Road, Mitcham, Surrey CR4 2HA. *T:* (020) 8648 9991.

EDMONDS, Noel E.; DL; television presenter; *b* 22 Dec. 1948; *s* of Dudley Edmonds and Lydia Edmonds; *m* 1st, 1971, Gillian Slater (marr. diss.); 2nd, 1986, Helen Soby (marr. diss.); four *d*. *Educ:* Brentwood Sch. Newsreader, Radio Luxembourg, 1968–69; presenter, BBC Radio, 1969–2000, incl. Breakfast Show, 1973–78; BBC TV, 1970–2000; presenter, BBC TV series: Z Shed, 1975; Multicoloured Swap Shop, 1976–81; Lucky Numbers, 1978; The Late Late Breakfast Show, 1982–86; Time of Your Life, 1983; Telly Addicts, 1985–98; Saturday Roadshow, 1987; Noel's House Party, 1991–99; presenter: Channel 4 TV series, Deal or No Deal, 2005–; Sky One series, Are You Smarter Than a 10 Year Old?, 2007–. Chm., Unique Group, 1985. DL Devon, 2004. *Address:* Wood, Devon EX20 2LS.

EDMONDS, Robert Humphrey Gordon, CMG 1969; MBE 1944; writer; HM Diplomatic Service, retired; *b* 5 Oct. 1920; *s* of late Air Vice-Marshal C. H. K. Edmonds, CBE, DSO; *m* 1st, 1951, Georgina Combe (marr. diss.); three *s* (and one *s* decd); 2nd, 1976, Mrs Enid Balint (*d* 1994), *widow* of Dr Michael Balint; 3rd, 1998, Mrs Gillian Pawley. *Educ:* Ampleforth; Brasenose Coll., Oxford. Pres., Oxford Union, 1940. Served Army, 1940–46; attached to Political Div., Allied Commn for Austria, 1945–46. Entered Foreign Service, Dec. 1946; served Cairo, 1947; FO, 1949; Rome, 1953; Warsaw, 1957; FO, 1959; Caracas, 1962; FO, CO and FCO, 1966–69; Minister, Moscow, 1969–71; High Comr, Nicosia, 1971–72; Asst Under Sec. of State, FCO, 1974–77, retd 1978. Vis. Fellow, Glasgow Univ., 1973–74; Fellow, Woodrow Wilson Internat. Centre for Scholars, Washington, 1977; Leverhulme Res. Fellow, 1989–91; Hon. Fellow, Glasgow Inst. of Soviet and E European Studies, 1988–91. Adviser, Kleinwort Benson, 1978–83, consultant, 1984–86. Mem. Council, RIIA, 1986–92. *Publications:* Soviet Foreign Policy: the paradox of superpower, 1975; Soviet Foreign Policy: the Brezhnev years, 1983; Setting the Mould: the United States and Britain 1945–1950, 1986; The Big Three, 1990; (contrib.) Churchill, ed Blake and Louis, 1992; Pushkin: the man and his age, 1994; articles and review articles in International Affairs, TLS and Survival. *Club:* Turf.

EDMONDS-BROWN, (Cedric Wilfred) George; HM Diplomatic Service, retired; Executive Secretary, Canada-UK Colloquia, since 2001; *b* 24 April 1939; *s* of late Maj. W. R. E. Edmonds-Brown and E. M. Edmonds-Brown; *m* 1st, 1964, Everild A. V. Hardman (*d* 1988); one *s* two *d*; 2nd, 1990, Teiko Watanabe; one *s* one *d*. *Educ:* Dame Allan's Boys' Sch., Newcastle; King's Coll., Durham Univ. Joined CRO, 1962; Lagos, 1963; Karachi, 1964–68; Third Sec., Buenos Aires, 1968–73; FCO, 1973–76; Second Sec., Bucharest, 1976–80; First Sec. and HM Consul, Caracas, 1980–85; ODA, 1985–88; Head of Chancery, Ottawa, 1988; Dep. High Comr, Barbados, 1989–91; First Sec., Rome, 1991–95, Geneva, 1995–97; Consul, Geneva, 1997–99. *Recreations:* writing, art, travel, cricket. *Address:* 4 The Willows, Wootton, Oxon OX1 5LD.

EDMONDSON, family name of **Baron Sandford.**

EDMONDSON, Rt Rev. Christopher Paul; *see* Bolton, Bishop Suffragan of.

EDMONSTONE, Sir Archibald (Bruce Charles), 7th Bt *cr* 1774; *b* 3 Aug. 1934; *o* surv. *s* of Sir Charles Edmonstone, 6th Bt, and Gwendolyn Mary (*d* 1989), *d* of late Marshall Field and Mrs Maldwin Drummond; *S* father, 1954; *m* 1st, 1957, Jane (marr. diss. 1967), *er d* of Maj.-Gen. E. C. Colville, CB, DSO; two *s* one *d*; 2nd, 1969, Juliet Elizabeth, *d* of Maj.-Gen. C. M. F. Deakin, CB, CBE; one *s* one *d*. *Educ:* St Peter's Court; Stowe Sch. *Heir:* *s* Archibald Edward Charles Edmonstone [*b* 4 Feb. 1961; *m* 1988, Ursula (marr. diss. 1994), *e d* of late Benjamin Worthington]. *Address:* Duntreath Castle, Blanefield, Stirlingshire G63 9AJ.
See also Sir A. R. J. B. Jardine.

EDMONTON, Area Bishop of, since 1999; **Rt Rev. Peter William Wheatley;** *b* 7 Sept. 1947; *er s* of late William Nobes Wheatley and Muriel (*née* Ounsted). *Educ:* Ipswich Sch. (Queen's and Foundn Schol.); Queen's Coll., Oxford (Styring Schol., MA); Pembroke Coll., Cambridge (MA); Coll. of the Resurrection, Mirfield; Ripon Hall, Oxford. Deacon 1973, priest 1974; Asst Curate, All Saints, Fulham, 1973–78; Vicar: Holy Cross with St Jude and St Peter, St Pancras, 1978–82; St James, W Hampstead, 1982–95; Priest-in-charge: St Mary, Kilburn, 1982–90; St Mary with All Souls, Kilburn, 1990–95; Curate-in-charge, All Souls, S Hampstead, 1982–90; Archdeacon of Hampstead, 1995–99. Proctor in Convocation and Mem. Gen. Synod, C of E, 1975–95. *Recreation:* music. *Address:* 27 Thurlow Road, NW3 5PP. *T:* (020) 7435 5890.

EDMUNDS, Alan Geoffrey; Editor, Western Mail, since 2002; *b* 2 Aug. 1963; *s* of Geoffrey and Carol Edmunds; *m* 1988, Susanne; three *d*. *Educ:* Bristol Univ. (LLB Hons 1984); UC Cardiff (Postgrad. Dip. Journalism 1986). Ed., Wales on Sunday, 1997–2002. *Recreations:* football, tennis, Rugby Union, reading, coin collecting, children's TV trivia from the 1970s. *Address:* 10 Duffryn Avenue, Lakeside, Cardiff CF23 6LF. *T:* (029) 2049 5948; *e-mail:* alan.edmunds@mediawales.co.uk.

EDMUNDS, Martin James Simpson; QC 2006; a Recorder, since 1999; *b* 4 Dec. 1959; *s* of Brian Edmunds and Moira Edmunds. *Educ:* Brentwood Sch., Essex; Corpus Christi Coll., Cambridge (BA 1982). Called to the Bar, Middle Temple, 1983; barrister, Walnut House, Exeter, and Furnival Chambers, London. Chm., Barristers' Overseas Advocacy Cttee, 2000–. *Address:* Walnut House, 63 St David's Hill, Exeter EX4 4DW.

EDMUNDS, Prof. Michael Geoffrey, PhD; Professor of Astrophysics, Cardiff University, since 1997; *b* 18 June 1949; *s* of Geoffrey and Joyce Edmunds; *m* 1987, Margaret Morris; one *d*, and one step *d*. *Educ:* Woking Co. Grammar Sch.; Downing Coll., Cambridge (BA Natural Scis 1971; PhD 1976). FRAS 1975; FInstP, CPhys 2003. Bye-Fellow, Downing Coll., Cambridge, 1973–74; Cardiff University: Res. Fellow, 1974–76; Lectr, 1976–88; Sen. Lectr, 1988–96; Reader, 1996–97; Hd, Sch. of Physics and Astronomy, 2003–06. Royal Astronomical Society: Darwin Lectr, 2004; Mem. Council, 2007–. Member: PPARC, 2004–07 (Chm., Sci. and Soc. Adv. Panel, 2004–); Sci. and Technol. Facilities Council, 2007–. *Publications:* res. papers in Nature, Monthly Notices of RAS, Astrophysical Jl, etc. *Recreations:* walking, sailing, music, old railways. *Address:* School of Physics and Astronomy, Cardiff University, Queens Buildings, The Parade, Cardiff CF24 3AA. *T:* (029) 2087 4043, *Fax:* (029) 2087 4056; *e-mail:* mge@astro.cf.ac.uk; 3 Tyrwhitt Crescent, Roath Park, Cardiff CF23 5QP.

EDNAM, Viscount; William Humble David Jeremy Ward; *b* 27 March 1947; *s* and *heir* of Earl of Dudley, *qv* and of Stella Viscountess Ednam, *d* of M. A. Carcano, KCMG, KBE; *m* 1st, 1972, Sarah (marr. diss. 1976), *o d* of Sir Alastair Coats, Bt, *qv*; 2nd, 1976, Debra Louise (marr. diss. 1980), *d* of George Robert and Marjorie Elvera Pinney; one *d*. *Educ:* Eton; Christ Church, Oxford.

EDNEY, James David; public sector consultant and interim manager, since 2007; *b* 22 April 1953; *s* of late James William John Edney and of Alma Mary Edney; *m* 1974, Heather Anita Sayer; one *s* two *d*. *Educ:* Dr Morgan's Grammar Sch., Bridgwater; Univ. of Newcastle upon Tyne (BA Hons (Hist.)); New Coll., Durham (CPFA 1979). Asst Dir, Finance and Admin, Cambridgeshire CC, 1985–89; Deputy County Treasurer: Lincolnshire CC, 1989–91; Essex CC, 1991–2002; Chief Financial Officer, Essex CC, 2002–03; Dep. Chief Exec. and Exec. Dir of Resources, Lancashire CC, 2003–06. *T:* 07805 322721; *e-mail:* jim@edneyj.wanadoo.co.uk.

EDSON, Ven. Michael; Team Rector, Torridge Estuary Team Ministry, since 2002; *b* 2 Sept. 1942; *s* of Joseph Pratt and Elsie (*née* Edson); name changed to Edson, 1989; *m* 1968, (Ann) Frances Tuffley; three *s* one *d*. *Educ:* Univ. of Birmingham (BSc Hons 1964); Univ. of Leeds (BA Hons 1971); College of Resurrection, Mirfield. Management Consultant, 1966–68. Ordained deacon, 1972, priest, 1973; Curate, Barnstaple, Devon, 1972–77; Team Vicar, Barnstaple, 1977–82; Chaplain, N Devon Dist Hosp., 1976–82; Vicar, Roxbourne, Harrow, 1982–89; Area Dean of Harrow, 1985–89; Warden of Lee Abbey Fellowship, Devon, 1989–94; Archdeacon of Leicester, 1994–2002. Leicester Diocesan Evangelist, 1997–2002. *Publications:* The Renewal of the Mind, 1988; Loved into Life, 1993. *Recreations:* hill-walking, people, writing, spirituality, art. *Address:* The Rectory, Abbotsham Road, Bideford, Devon EX39 3AB. *T:* (01237) 470228.

EDUR, Agnes; *see* Oaks, A.

EDUR, Thomas; ballet dancer; teacher; choreographer, since 2000; *b* 20 Jan. 1969; *s* of Enn and Ludmilla Edur; *m* 1990, Agnes Oaks, *qv*. *Educ:* Estonian State Ballet Sch. Principal Dancer: Estonian Nat. Opera, 1988–90; English Nat. Ballet, 1990–96; Birmingham Royal Ballet, 1996–97; internat. freelance dancer, and with English Nat. Ballet, 1997–, with Zurich Ballet, 2000–. Guest Artist: La Scala, Milan, 1994–2001; Finnish Nat. Opera, 1999–2004; Berlin Staatsoper, 2000–02; Cape Town City Ballet, 2001–. Choreographed one-act ballets: Serenade de Florence, and Mozart, Estonian Th., Vanemuine, 2005; Anima, 2006; Fete Polonaise, 2008. Patron: British Ballet Orgn, 2004; English Nat. Ballet Sch., 2008. Evening Standard Award, 1994; Best Dancer Award and Unique Partnership Award (with Agnes Oaks), Critics Circle, 2003; Laurence Olivier Award for Outstanding Achievement in Dance (with Agnes Oaks), 2004. Order of White Star, 3rd Cl. (Estonia), 2001. *Recreations:* Formula 1, nature, reading, photography. *T:* and *Fax:* (020) 8674 1670; *e-mail:* mail@cclassics.co.uk; *web:* www.atballet.com.

EDWARD, Rt Hon. Sir David (Alexander Ogilvy), KCMG 2004 (CMG 1981); PC 2005; QC (Scotland) 1974; FRSE; Judge of the Court of Justice of the European Communities, 1992–2004 (Judge of the Court of First Instance, 1989–92); Temporary Judge, Court of Session, Scotland, since 2004; *b* 14 Nov. 1934; *s* of J. O. C. Edward, Travel Agent, Perth; *m* 1962, Elizabeth Young McSherry; two *s* two *d*. *Educ:* Sedbergh Sch.; University Coll., Oxford (Hon. Fellow, 1995); Edinburgh Univ. Sub-Lt RNVR (Nat. Service); HMS Hornet, 1956–57. Admitted Advocate, 1962; Clerk of Faculty of Advocates, 1967–70, Treasurer, 1970–77. Pres., Consultative Cttee of Bars and Law Societies, EC, 1978–80; Salvesen Prof. of European Instns, 1985–89, Hon. Prof., 1990, Univ. of Edinburgh. Trustee, Nat. Library of Scotland, 1966–95; Mem. Law Adv. Cttee, British Council, 1974–88; Specialist Advr, H of L Select Cttee on EC, 1985, 1986 and 1987. Mem., Panel of Arbitrators, Internat. Centre for Settlement of Investment Disputes, 1981–89 and 2004–. Director: Continental Assets Trust plc, 1985–89 (Chm.); Adam & Co. Group plc, 1983–89; Harris Tweed Association Ltd, 1984–89. Hon. Bencher, Gray's Inn, 1992. Member: Foundation Senate, Europa Universität Viadrina, Frankfurt/Oder, 1991–93; Bd of Trustees, Acad. of European Law, Trier, 1993–. Trustee: Industry and Parlt Trust, 1995–; Carnegie Trust for Univs of Scotland, 1996– (Chm., 2003–). Vice-President: British Inst. Internat. and Comparative Law, 2002–; Internat. Assoc. of Business and Parlt, 2004–. President: Johnson Soc., Lichfield, 1995; Franco-Scottish Soc., 1996–; Edinburgh Sir Walter Scott Club, 2001–02. FRSE 1990 (Royal Medal, 2005). Hon. LLD: Edinburgh, 1993; Aberdeen, 1997; Napier, 1998; Glasgow, 2003; DUniv Surrey, 2003; Dr (*hc*): Saarbrücken, 2001; Münster, 2001. Distinguished Cross, First Class, Order of St Raymond of Penafort, Spain, 1979. *Publications:* The Professional Secret, Confidentiality and Legal Professional Privilege in the EEC, 1976; (with R. C. Lane) European Community Law: an introduction, 1991, 2nd edn 1995; articles in legal jls, etc. *Address:* 32 Heriot Row, Edinburgh EH3 6ES. *Clubs:* Athenæum; New (Edinburgh).

EDWARDES, family name of **Baron Kensington**.

EDWARDES, Sir Michael (Owen), Kt 1979; Chairman: Tryhorn Investments Ltd, 1987–2007; Strand Partners, 1994–2007; Syndicated Services Co. Inc., 1995–2007; *b* 11 Oct. 1930; *s* of Denys Owen Edwardes and Audrey Noel (*née* Copeland); *m* 1st, 1958, Mary Margaret (*née* Finlay) (marr. diss.; she *d* 1999); three *d*; 2nd, 1988, Sheila Ann (*née* Guy). *Educ:* St Andrew's Coll., Grahamstown, S Africa; Rhodes Univ., Grahamstown (BA; Hon. LLD). Chairman: Chloride Gp PLC, 1969–77 and 1986; BL Ltd (formerly British Leyland), 1977–82; Mercury Communications Ltd, 1982–83; ICL PLC, 1984; Dunlop Hldgs plc, 1984–85; Charter PLC, 1988–96; Porth Gp, 1991–95; ARC Internat. Ltd (BVI), 1991–98; Dep. Chm., R K Carvill (Internat. Hldgs) Ltd, 1988–; Director: Hill Samuel Gp, 1980–87; Minorco SA, 1984–93; Standard Securities PLC, 1985–87; Delta Motor Corp. (Pty) Ltd, 1986–99; Flying Pictures Ltd, 1987–; Lansing Bagnall, 1987–88; Jet Press Hldgs BV, 1990–. Dir, Internat. Management Develt Inst., Washington, 1978–94. CCMI (Vice-Chm., BIM, 1977–80); Hon. FIMechE, 1981. President: Squash Rackets Assoc., 1991–95; Veterans Squash Club of GB, 1981–94. Trustee, Thrombosis Res. Inst., 1991–2001. *Publication:* Back From the Brink, 1983. *Recreations:* sailing, squash, water ski-ing, tennis. *Clubs:* Royal Automobile; Jesters; Rand and Country (Johannesburg).

EDWARDS, family name of **Baron Crickhowell**.

EDWARDS, Rev. Aled, OBE 2006; Chief Executive Officer, CYTÛN Churches Together in Wales, since 2006; *b* 4 Oct. 1955; *s* of David Samuel Edwards and Katie Olwen Edwards; *m* 1976, Susan Marie Ball; two *s* one *d*. *Educ:* St David's UC, Lampeter (BA Jt Hons Hist. and Theol. Wales 1977); Trinity Coll., Bristol. Ordained deacon, 1979, priest, 1980; Asst Curate, Glanogwen, 1979–82; Vicar: Llandinorwig with Penisa'rwaun, 1982–85; Botwnnog, 1985–93; Dewi Sant, Cardiff, 1993–99; CYTÛN Nat. Assembly Liaison Officer, 1999–2006. Wales Comr, Commn for Racial Equality, 2006–07; Mem. Cttee, Equality and Human Rights Commn, 2007–. *Publications:* Transforming Power: a Christian reflection on Welsh devolution, 2001; From Protest to Process: stories from the National Assembly for Wales, 2003. *Recreations:* supporting Llanelli Scarlets, watching West Wing. *Address:* CYTÛN, 58 Richmond Road, Cardiff CF24 3UR. *T:* (029) 2046 4378, *Fax:* (029) 2046 4371; *e-mail:* aled@cytun.org.uk.

EDWARDS, (Alfred) Kenneth, CBE 1989 (MBE 1963); Deputy Director-General, Confederation of British Industry, 1982–88; Director: Reliance Bank Ltd, since 1992; Salvation Army Trustee Co., since 1996; SATCOL Ltd, since 2003; *b* 24 March 1926; *s* of late Ernest Edwards and Florence Edwards (*née* Branch); *m* 1st, 1949, Jeannette Lilian (*d* 2002), *d* of David Speeks, MBE; one *s* two *d*; 2nd, 2004, Jenefer, *d* of John Nicholas. *Educ:* Latymer Upper Sch.; Magdalene Coll., Cambridge; University Coll. London. Served RAF, 1944–47; RAF Coll., Cranwell, 1945, FO (Pilot). Entered HMOCS, Nigeria, 1952; Provincial Administration, Warri and Benin, 1952–54; Lagos Secretariat, 1954; Sen. Asst Sec., Nigerian Min. of Communications and Aviation, 1959; retired, 1962. Secretary, British Radio Equipment Manufrs' Assoc., 1962; Gp Marketing Manager, Thorn Elec. Industries Ltd, 1965; Internat. Dir, Brookhirst Igranic Ltd (Thorn Gp), 1967; Gp Marketing Dir, Cutler Hammer Europa, 1972; Dep. Chm., BEAMA Overseas Trade Cttee, 1973; Chief Exec., BEAMA, 1976–82. CBI: Member: Council, 1974, 1976–82, Finance and Gen. Purposes Cttee, 1977–82; Vice-Chm., Eastern Reg. Council, 1974; Chm., Working Party on Liability for Defective Products, 1978–82; Mem., President's Cttee, 1979–82. Chm., Facilities & Properties Management Plc, 1989–91; Dir, Polar Electronics PLC, 1984–96. Member: Elec. Engrg EDC, 1976; Council, Elec. Res. Assoc. Ltd, 1976–82; Exec. Cttee, ORGALIME, 1976–82; Management Bd, Eur. Cttee for Develt of Vocational Training, 1988–; BSI Bd, 1978–82, 1984–89 (Chm., British Electrotechnical Cttee and Electrotechnical Divisional Council, 1981–82; Chm., Quality Policy Cttee, 1988–); BOTB, 1982–88; BTEC, 1983–89; BBC Consultative Gp on Indust. and Business Affairs, 1983–88; Bd and Exec. Cttee, Business in the Community, 1987–88; President: CENELEC, 1977–79; Liaison Cttee for Electrical and Electronic Industries, ORGALIME, 1979–82 (Chm., 1980–82); Mem. Exec. Cttee, 1982–89, and Chm. Finance Cttee, 1983–89, UNICE. Dep. Chm., Salvation Army Adv. Bd, 1995– (Mem., 1982; Mem., UK Bd of Trustees, 1998–). Mem. Court, Cranfield Inst. of Technol., 1970–75. *Publications:* contrib. technical jls; lectures and broadcasts on industrial subjects. *Recreations:* music, books, walking. *Address:* 51 Bedford Road, Rushden, Northants NN10 0ND. *Club:* Royal Air Force.

EDWARDS, Andrew John Cumming, CB 1994; public sector consultant, since 1995; conductor of music; *b* 3 Nov. 1940; *s* of John Edwards and Norah Hope Edwards (*née* Bevan); *m* 1st, 1969, Charlotte Anne Chilcot (marr. diss. 1987); one *s* two *d*; 2nd, 1994, Ursula Mary Richardson; one *s*. *Educ:* Fettes Coll., Edinburgh; St John's Coll., Oxford (MA); Harvard Univ. (AM, MPA). Asst master, Malvern Coll., 1962–63; HM Treasury. Asst Principal, 1963–67; Pvte Sec. to Jt Perm. Sec., 1966–67; Principal, 1967–75; Harkness Fellow, Harvard Univ., 1971–73; Asst Sec., 1975–83; RCDS, 1979; Asst Sec., DES, 1983–85; Under Sec., 1985–89, Dep. Sec., 1990–95, HM Treasury. Professional advr to Greenbury Cttee, 1995; conducted reviews of BM, 1996, Financial Regulation in Crown Dependencies, 1998, Finance Ministries of Bulgaria, 1999, Slovakia, 2000, Greece, 2002, and HM Land Registry, 2000–01; Mem., Financial Issues Adv. Gp for Scottish Parliament, 1998; Chm., Acacia Prog., 2002–05; Leader, OGC Gateway Reviews, 2003–. Gov., British Inst. of Recorded Sound, 1974–79; Sec., Bd of Dirs, Royal Opera House, 1988–2006 (Sec., Develt Bd, 1984–87). Conductor, Academy Choir and Orchs, Wimbledon, 1980–. *Publications:* Nuclear Weapons, the balance of terror, the quest for peace, 1986; reports; articles on European Community Budget, regulation of trusts and companies. *Recreations:* music, walking. *Address:* 15 Highbury Road, SW19 7PR.

EDWARDS, Prof. (Anthony) David, FRCP, FRCPCH, FMedSci; Weston Professor of Neonatal Medicine, since 1993, and Lead for Imaging Research, Imperial College of Science, Technology and Medicine (Chairman, Division of Paediatrics, Obstetrics and Gynaecology, 1998–2005); *b* 26 Nov. 1954; *s* of Raymond Edwards and Nora Edwards; *m* 1978, Catherine James; one *s* one *d*. *Educ:* St Peter's Coll., Oxford (MA; Univ. Boat Race winning crew, 1976); Harvard Univ.; Guy's Hosp. Med. Sch., Univ. of London (MB BS). FRCP 1993; FRCPCH 1997; FMedSci 2002. Sen. Lectr in Paediatrics, UCL, 1992–93; Associate Gp Hd, MRC Clin. Scis Centre, Hammersmith Hosp., 1999–. Assoc. Dir, UK Medicines for Children Res. Network. Visiting Professor: UCL, 1994; Univ. of Hong Kong, 2000. Member: Sci. Adv. Bd, Liggins Inst., Auckland, NZ, 2001–; INSERM, 2004–; MRC, 2004–05; Nat. Centre for Growth and Develt, NZ, 2005–. *Publications:* contrib. numerous papers to scientific jls. *Recreations:* Manouche jazz, the renaissance lute, sailing. *Address:* Department of Paediatrics, Imperial College London Faculty of Medicine, Hammersmith Hospital, Du Cane Road, W12 0NN. *T:* (020) 8383 3326; *e-mail:* david.edwards@imperial.ac.uk. *Clubs:* Athenæum; Royal Solent Yacht.

EDWARDS, Arthur Frank George; Vice-Chairman, Thames Water Authority, 1973–83; *b* 27 March 1920; *o s* of Arthur Edwards and Mabel (Elsie) Edwards; *m* 1946, Joyce May Simmons; one *s* one *d*. *Educ:* West Ham Grammar Sch.; Garnett Coll., London; West Ham Coll. of Technology; City of London Polytechnic (MSc 1990); King's College London (MPhil 2000). CEng, FIChemE; Hon. FIWM. Various posts with Ever Ready (GB) Ltd, 1936–50; Prodn Man., J. Burns & Co. Ltd, 1950–53; various lectrg posts, 1954–65; Organiser for science and techn. subjects, London Boroughs of Barking and Redbridge, 1965–83. Member: West Ham Co. Borough Council, 1946–65; Newham Council, 1964–86 (Mayor, 1967–68); GLC, 1964–86 (Dep. Chm., 1970–71; Chm., Public Services Cttee, 1973–77). Chm. of Governors, NE London Polytechnic, 1972–87. Hon. Alderman, London Borough of Newham, 2004. Hon. Prof., Moscow Univ. of Humanities, 1996. Mem., Fabian Soc. *Recreations:* reading, Association football (watching West Ham United). *Address:* 18 Wanstead Park Avenue, E12 5EN. *T:* (020) 8530 6436. *Clubs:* West Ham Supporters'; Aldersbrook Bowls.

EDWARDS, Barrie; *see* Edwards, G. B.

EDWARDS, Prof. Brian, CBE 1988; FHSM; Professor of Health Care Development, University of Sheffield, 1996–2002, now Emeritus (Foundation Dean, School of Health and Related Research, 1996–99); *b* 19 Feb. 1942; *s* of John Albert Edwards and Ethel Edwards; *m* 1964, Jean (*née* Cannon); two *s* two *d*. *Educ:* Wirral Grammar Sch. FHSM 1983. Jun. Administrator, Clatterbridge Hosp., 1958–62; Dep. Hosp. Sec., Cleaver Hosp., 1962–64; National Trainee, Nuffield Centre, Leeds, 1964–66; Administrator, Gen. Infirmary, Leeds, 1966–67; Hosp. Sec., Keighley Victoria Hosp., 1967–68; Administrator, Mansfield HMC, 1969–70; Lectr, Univ. of Leeds, 1970–72; Dep. Gp Sec., Hull A HMC, 1972–74; Nuffield Travelling Fellow, USA, 1973; Dist Administrator, Leeds AHA(T), 1974–76; Area Administrator, Cheshire AHA, 1976–81; Regional Administrator, 1981–84, Regl Gen. Man., 1984–93, Trent RHA; Chief Exec., W Midlands RHA, 1993–96; Regl Dir, NHS Exec., 1994–96. Chm., Clinical Pathology Accreditation Ltd, 1992–2000. Vis. Lectr, Health Care Studies, 1973–93, and Associate Fellow, Nuffield Inst., 1987–93, Univ. of Leeds; Vis. Prof., Health Care Studies, Univ. of Keele, 1989; Queen Elizabeth Nuffield Fellow, Nuffield Provincial Hosps Trust, 1991; Hon. Prof., Univ. of Keele, 1993. Adviser to WHO, 1982–; Chairman: NHS Manpower Planning Adv. Gp, 1983–86; Regional Gen. Managers Gp, 1986–87, 1991–94; NHS Patient Empowerment Gp, 1991–94; Patient's Charter Team, 1992; Council for the Professions Supplementary to Medicine, 1997–2002; Notts Health NHS Trust, 2001–07; Member: Steering Cttee on Future of Nursing, 1988; Standing Cttee on Medical Audit, RCP, 1989–94; Ashworth Inquiry, 1997–98; Leader: Sec. of State's Task Force on Quality in NHS, 1993; UK Delegn, Hosp. Cttee for Europe, 1994–2005 (Pres., 2005–08). Chm., ATM Consulting, 2007–; Director: Shirehall Gp, 1996–99; Health on the Box Ltd, 1999–2001. Institute of Health Service Administrators: Mem., 1964–; Pres., 1982–83; Mem. Editorial Cttee, Health Care in the UK: its organisation and management, 1982–83;

Pres., Assoc. of Health Service Supplies Officers, 2001–04. Patron, NHS Retirement Fellowship, 2002–07. Trustee: Marie Curie Trust, 1996–2000; Pharmacy Practice Res. Trust. Jt Editor, Health Services Manpower Review, 1970–91; Editor, Euro Hospital Yearbook, 1998–2005. CCMI (CBIM 1988); Hon. FRCPath 1996. DUniv UCE, 1998. *Publications:* Si Vis Pacem—preparations for change in the NHS, 1973; Profile for Change, 1973; Bridging in Health, Planning the Child Health Services, 1975; Industrial Relations in the NHS: managers and industrial relations, 1979; Manpower Planning in the NHS, 1984; Employment Policies for Health Care, 1985; Distinction Awards for Doctors, 1987; (contrib.) Doctors' Contracts, 1992; (contrib.) Public Sector Managers' Handbook, 1992; The NHS: a manager's tale, 1993, 2nd edn 1995; (contrib.) Management for Doctors, 1994; (contrib.) Managed Healthcare, 1998; (ed) NHS 50th Anniversary Lectures, 1999; The Executive Year of the NHS, 2005; An Independent NHS, 2007; Academic Health Science Centres, 2008; papers presented at numerous nat. and internat. confs; contrib. prof. jls. *Recreation:* golf. *Address:* 3 Royal Croft Drive, Baslow, Derbyshire DE45 1SN. *T:* (01246) 583459. *Clubs:* Athenæum; Bakewell Golf (Captain, 1991); La Manga (Spain).

EDWARDS, His Honour (Charles) Marcus; a Circuit Judge, 1986–2008; *b* 10 Aug. 1937; *s* of late John Basil Edwards, CBE; *m* 1st, 1963, Anne Louise Stockdale (*d* 1970), *d* of Sir Edmund Stockdale, 1st Bt; 2nd, 1975, Sandra Wates (*née* Mouroutsos); one *d* and three step *d*. *Educ:* Dragon Sch., Oxford; Rugby Sch.; Brasenose Coll., Oxford (scholar; BA Jurisprudence). Trooper, RAC, 1955; 2nd Lieut, Intelligence Corps, Cyprus, 1956–57. HM Diplomatic Service, 1960–65; Third Sec., 1960, Spain, 1961, FO, 1961–62, South Africa and High Commn Territories, 1962–63, Laos, 1964; Second Sec., FO, 1965, resigned. Called to the Bar, Middle Temple, 1962; practised, London, 1966–86; Mem., Midland and Oxford Circuit; a Recorder, 1985–86. Chm., Pavilion Opera, 1987–. *Recreations:* gardening, walking, talking, food and drink. *Address:* Mathon Lodge, Mathon, Herefordshire WR14 4DW. *T:* (01684) 564592; Menginolle, 32730 Malabat, France. *Clubs:* Beefsteak, Vincent's.

EDWARDS, Sir Christopher (John Churchill), 5th Bt *cr* 1866; Executive Vice-President and General Manager, RAM Electronics Corp., Fort Collins, Colorado, 1995–97; *b* 16 Aug. 1941; *s* of Sir (Henry) Charles (Serrell Priestley) Edwards, 4th Bt and of Lady (Daphne) Edwards (*née* Birt); *S* father, 1963; *m* 1972, Gladys Irene Vogelgesang; two *s*. *Educ:* Frensham Heights, Surrey; Loughborough, Leics; Regis Univ., Denver, USA (MSc). Gen. Manager, Kelsar Inc., American Home Products, San Diego, Calif, 1979–84; Vice-Pres., Valleylab Inc., Boulder, Colorado, 1981–89; Dir, Ohmeda BOC Group, Louisville, 1989–92. Pres., Intermed Consultants, Westminster, Colorado, 1992–. Affiliate Prof. of MSc in Mgt, Regis Univ., Denver, 1999–; Adjunct Prof. of MTech Mgt, Univ. of Denver, 1999–. Mem., Acad. of Mgt. *Heir:* *s* David Charles Priestley Edwards, *b* 22 Feb. 1974. *Address:* 11637 Country Club Drive, Westminster, CO 80234–2649, USA. *T:* (303) 4693156.

EDWARDS, Sir Christopher Richard Watkin, Kt 2008; MD; FRCP, FRCPE, FMedSci; FRSE; Chairman, Chelsea and Westminster NHS Foundation Trust, since 2007; Vice-Chancellor, University of Newcastle upon Tyne, 2001–07; *b* 12 Feb. 1942; *s* of Thomas Archibald Watkin Edwards and Beatrice Elizabeth Ruby Watkin Edwards; *m* 1968, Sally Amanda Kidd; two *s* one *d*. *Educ:* Marlborough Coll.; Christ's Coll., Cambridge (BA, MB, BChir, MA, MD). St Bartholomew's Hospital: Lectr in Medicine, 1969–75; Sen. Lectr in Medicine and MRC Sen. Res. Fellow, 1975–80; Hon. Consultant Physician, 1975–80; University of Edinburgh: Moncrieff Arnott Prof. of Clinical Medicine, 1980–95; Dean, Faculty of Medicine, 1991–95; Provost, Faculty Group of Medicine and Veterinary Medicine, 1992–95; Principal and Prof. of Medicine, ICSM, Univ. of London, 1995–2000. Non-executive Director: Celltech, 1997–2004; Argenta Discovery, 2000–04; One NorthEast, 2001–. Mem., MRC, 1991–95. Gov., Wellcome Trust, 1994–2005. Founder FMedSci 1998; FIC 2003. Hon. DSc Aberdeen, 2000. *Publications:* (ed) Clinical Physiology, 5th edn, 1984; (ed) Essential Hypertension as an Endocrine Disease, 1985; Endocrinology, 1986; (ed) Recent Advances in Endocrinology Metabolism, vol. 3, 1989; (ed) Davidson's Principles and Practice of Medicine, 17th edn, 1995; 421 scientific papers and communications. *Recreations:* running, reading, golf, ski-ing. *Address:* 4 Thomas Walk, SW11 3BG. *Club:* Athenæum.

EDWARDS, Rev. Canon Clare; *see* Edwards, Rev. Canon D. C.

EDWARDS, David; Director, John Laing plc, 1982–99; Chairman, Londondome Ltd, 1988–93; *b* 27 Oct. 1929; *s* of Col Cyril Edwards, DSO, MC, DL and Jessie Edwards; *m* 1966, Gay Clothier; two *s* one *d*. *Educ:* Felsted Sch.; Trinity Hall, Cambridge (MA, LLM). Called to the Bar, Middle Temple, 1952; Harmsworth Scholar, Middle Temple, 1955; admitted Solicitor, 1958. Partner, E. Edwards Son & Noice, 1959–75; Sec., Legal Aid, 1976–86, and Dep. Sec.-Gen., 1982–86, Law Soc. Dir, Laing Properties, 1988–90. Chm., Offshore Racing Council, 1970–78; Dep. Chm., Royal Yachting Assoc., 1976–81. *Recreation:* sailing. *Address:* Olivers, Colchester, Essex CO2 0HJ. *Clubs:* Royal Ocean Racing; Royal Yacht Squadron (Cowes).

EDWARDS, David; *see* Edwards, A. D.

EDWARDS, (David) Elgan (Hugh); His Honour Judge Elgan Edwards; DL; a Circuit Judge, since 1989, a Senior Circuit Judge, since 2002; *b* 6 Dec. 1943; *s* of Howell and Dilys Edwards; *m* 1982, Carol Anne Smalls; two *s* two *d*. *Educ:* Rhyl Grammar Sch.; University Coll. of Wales, Aberystwyth (LLB Hons 1966; Pres., Students Union, 1967; Hon. Fellow, 2005). Called to the Bar, Gray's Inn, 1967 (Bencher, 2004); a Recorder, Wales and Chester Circuit, 1983–89; Hon. Recorder, Chester, 1997; Resident Judge for Cheshire, 2006–. Contested (C): Merioneth, 1970; Stockport South, Feb. 1974. Freeman, City of London, 2002. Sheriff, City of Chester, 1977–78; DL Cheshire, 2000. *Recreations:* swimming, Manchester United FC, Chester Racer. *Address:* The Crown Court, Chester Castle, Chester CH1 2AN. *T:* (01244) 317606. *Club:* Chester City (Chester).

EDWARDS, Very Rev. David Lawrence, OBE 1995; Provost of Southwark Cathedral, 1983–94, Emeritus since 1994; *b* 20 Jan. 1929; *s* of late Lawrence Wright and Phyllis Boardman Edwards; *m* 1st, 1960, Hilary Mary (*née* Phillips) (marr. diss. 1984); one *s* three *d*; 2nd, 1984, Sybil, *d* of Michael and Kathleen Falcon. *Educ:* King's Sch., Canterbury; Magdalen Coll., Oxford. Lothian Prize, 1951; 1st cl. hons Mod. Hist., BA 1952; MA 1956. Fellow, All Souls Coll., Oxford, 1952–59. Deacon, 1954; Priest, 1955. On HQ staff of Student Christian Movement of Gt Brit. and Ireland, 1955–66; Editor and Man. Dir, SCM Press Ltd, 1959–66; Gen. Sec. of Movt, 1965–66. Curate of: St John's, Hampstead, 1955–58; St Martin-in-the-Fields, 1958–66; Fellow and Dean of King's College, Cambridge, 1966–70; Asst Lectr in Divinity, Univ. of Cambridge, 1967–70; Rector of St Margaret's, Westminster, 1970–78; Canon of Westminster, 1970–78; Sub-Dean, 1974–78; Speaker's Chaplain, 1972–78; Dean of Norwich, 1978–82. Exam. Chaplain: to Bp of Manchester, 1965–73; to Bp of Durham, 1968–72; to Bp of Bradford, 1972–78; to Bp of London, 1974–78; to Archbishop of Canterbury, 1975–78. Hulsean Lectr, 1967; Six Preacher, Canterbury Cathedral, 1969–76. Chairman: Churches' Council on Gambling, 1970–78; Christian Aid, 1971–78. Hon. Prof., King Alfred's Coll., Winchester, 1999. Hon. Fellow, South Bank Univ. (formerly Poly.), 1990. DD Lambeth, 1990. *Publications:* A History of the King's School, Canterbury, 1957; Not Angels But Anglicans, 1958; This Church of England, 1962; God's Cross in Our World, 1963; Religion and Change, 1969; F. J. Shirley: An Extraordinary Headmaster, 1969; The Last Things Now, 1969; Leaders of the Church of England, 1971; What is Real in Christianity?, 1972; St Margaret's, Westminster, 1972; The British Churches Turn to the Future, 1973; Ian Ramsey, Bishop of Durham, 1973; Good News in Acts, 1974; What Anglicans Believe, 1974; Jesus for Modern Man, 1975; A Key to the Old Testament, 1976; Today's Story of Jesus, 1976; The State of the Nation, 1976; A Reason to Hope, 1978; Christian England: vol. 1, Its story to the Reformation, 1981; vol. 2, From the Reformation to the Eighteenth Century, 1983; vol. 3, From the Eighteenth Century to the First World War, 1984; The Futures of Christianity, 1987; Essentials: a Liberal-Evangelical dialogue with John Stott, 1988; The Cathedrals of Britain, 1989; Tradition and Truth, 1989; Christians in a New Europe, 1990; The Real Jesus, 1992; What is Catholicism?, 1994; Christianity: the first two thousand years, 1997; A Concise History of English Christianity, 1998; After Death?: past beliefs and real possibilities, 1999; John Donne: a man of flesh and spirit, 2001; The Church That Could Be, 2002; What Anglicans Believe in the 21st Century, 2002; Poets and God, 2005; Yes: a positive faith, 2006; *edited:* The Honest to God Debate, 1963; Collins Children's Bible, 1978; Christianity and Conservatism, 1990; Robert Runcie: a portrait by his friends, 1990. *Address:* 19 Cripstead Lane, Winchester SO23 9SF. *T:* (01962) 862597. *Club:* Athenæum.

See also M. G. Falcon.

EDWARDS, David Leslie; QC 2006; *b* 8 Nov. 1966; *s* of Leslie Joseph Edwards and Angela Mary Edwards; *m* 1994, Caroline May Evans; three *s*. *Educ:* King's Sch., Chester; Peterhouse, Cambridge (BA 1988, MA 1991). Called to the Bar, Lincoln's Inn, 1989; in practice as barrister, 1990–, specialising in commercial law, incl. insurance, reinsurance, banking, internat. trade and professional negligence. *Recreations:* football, golf, ski-ing, reading, classical music. *Address:* 7 King's Bench Walk, Temple, EC4Y 7DS. *T:* (020) 7910 8300.

EDWARDS, David Michael, CMG 1990; international commercial mediator; Adjunct Faculty, Singapore Management University, since 2007; *b* 28 Feb. 1940; *s* of late Ernest William Edwards and Thelma Irene Edwards; *m* 1st, 1966, Veronica Margaret Postgate (marr. diss. 1996); one *s* one *d*; 2nd, 1996, Rain Ren; one *s* one *d*. *Educ:* The King's Sch., Canterbury; Univ. of Bristol (LLB Hons). Admitted to Roll of Solicitors, 1964. Solicitor of Supreme Court, 1964–67; Asst Legal Adviser, Foreign Office, 1967; Legal Adviser: British Military Govt, Berlin, 1972; British Embassy, Bonn, 1974; Legal Counsellor, 1977; Gen. Counsel and Dir, Legal Div., IAEA, Vienna, 1977–79; Legal Counsellor, FCO, 1979; Agent of the UK Govt in cases before European Commn and Court of Human Rights, 1979–82; Counsellor (Legal Adviser), UK Mission to UN, New York, and HM Embassy, Washington, 1985–88; Legal Counsellor, 1988–89, Dep. Legal Advr, 1989–90, FCO; Sen. Counsel, Bechtel Ltd, 1990; Law Officer (Internat. Law), Hong Kong Govt, 1990–95; Sen. Counsel, Bechtel Ltd, London, 1995–97; Asia Pacific Chief Counsel and Vice-Pres., Bechtel Internat. Inc., Singapore, 1997–2002; Proj. Legal Advr, Shell/CNOOC Nanhai USD 4 Billion Petrochemicals Complex, Daya Bay, SE China, 2002–05. *Recreations:* reading, travel, antique clocks. *Address:* 38A Jalan Mat Jambol, #02–04 Island View, Singapore 119519. *T:* 64721025, 81277543; *e-mail:* dmedward@singnet.com.sg. *Club:* Tanglin (Singapore).

EDWARDS, Prof. David Olaf, DPhil; FRS 1988; University Professor of Physics, Ohio State University, 1988–95, now Distinguished Professor Emeritus; *b* 27 April 1932; *s* of Robert Edwards and Margaret Edwina (*née* Larsen); *m* 1967, Wendy Lou Townsend; one *s* one *d*. *Educ:* Holt High Sch., Liverpool; Brasenose Coll., Oxford (BA 1st cl. Hons, 1953; Sen. Hulme Schol., 1953–56; MA; DPhil 1957). FAPS. Pressed Steel Co. Res. Fellow, Clarendon Lab., Oxford Univ., 1957–58; Ohio State University: Vis. Asst Prof., 1958–60; Asst Prof., 1960–62; Associate Prof., 1962–65; Prof., 1965–88. Visiting Professor: Imperial Coll., London, 1964; Sussex Univ., 1964, 1968; Technion, Israel, 1971–72; Ecole Normale Supérieure, Paris, 1978, 1982, 1986; Vis. Scientist, Brookhaven Nat. Lab., 1975. Consultant: Brookhaven Nat. Lab., 1975–77; Los Alamos Scientific Lab., 1979–81. Sir Francis Simon Prize, British Inst. of Phys, 1983; Dist. Schol. Award, Ohio State Univ., 1984; Special Creativity Awards, US Nat. Sci. Foundn, 1981, 1986; Oliver E. Buckley Condensed Matter Physics Prize, APS, 1990. Mem. Editl Bd, Jl of Low Temperature Physics, 1990–2004. *Publications:* (ed jtly) Proceedings of the Ninth International Conference on Low Temperature Physics (LT9), 1966; numerous articles on low temp. physics in scientific jls. *Recreations:* beagling (Master, Rocky Fork Beagles, 1975–90), snorkeling (Grand Cayman), crossword puzzles, reading detective stories. *Address:* 2345 Dorset Road, Columbus, OH 43221, USA. *T:* (614) 4864553; Department of Physics, Ohio State University, 174 W 18th Avenue, Columbus, OH 43210–1106, USA. *T:* (614) 2921771, *Fax:* (614) 2927557.

EDWARDS, David Stanley, OBE 2005; Chairman, zcargo, since 2005; Chief Executive, Cardiff and Vale NHS Trust, 1999–2004; *b* 5 Oct. 1943; *s* of Stanley and May Edwards; partner, Christine Baxter; two *s*. *Educ:* Coll. of Advanced Technol., Birmingham (HND Prodn and Mech. Engrg 1966); Coll. of Commerce, Birmingham (Dip. Mgt Studies 1969). DipHSM 1981. Tech. engr, then industrial engr, British Steel, Wednesbury (Tube Prodn), 1960–67; Sen. Industrial Engr, GKN (Birwelco) Ltd, Halesowen (Engrg), 1967–68; West Midlands Regional Health Authority: Orgn and Methods Assignment Officer, 1968–70; Mgt by Objectives Advr, 1970–72; Asst Regl Orgn and Methods Work Study Manager, 1972–74; West Birmingham Health Authority: Dist Support Services Manager, 1974–77; Dist Gen. Adminr (Planning), 1977–79; Central Birmingham Health Authority: Sector Adminr, Gen., Dental and Jaffray Hosp. and Community Services, 1979–82; Dep. Dist Adminr, 1982–85; Dir, Admin and Planning, 1985–86; Dist Gen. Manager, 1986–91; Chief Exec., Queen's Med. Centre, Nottingham Univ. Hosp. NHS Trust, 1991–99. Non-exec. Dir, James Paget Univ. Hosps NHS Foundn Trust, 2007–. Mem. Council, UEA, 2005– (Chm., Audit Cttee, 2006–). Fellow, Univ. of Nottingham, 1994. Companion IHM 2002; CCMI 2003. *Recreations:* two sons, two granddaughters, antique clocks and Victorian relief moulded jugs, classic cars, scuba diving (in warm water!), squash, running and all sport really, foreign travel, walking, reading for pleasure, music and playing the piano in private. *Address:* The Grove, Smee Lane, Great Plumstead, Norwich, Norfolk NR13 5AU. *T:* (01603) 717310.

EDWARDS, Rev. Canon (Diana) Clare; Residentiary Canon, Canterbury Cathedral, since 2004; *b* 14 Feb. 1956; *d* of Bryan Reginald Edwards and Vivienne Edwards. *Educ:* London Hosp., Whitechapel (SRN 1977); Hosp. for Sick Children, Gt Ormond St (RSCN 1981); London Univ. (DipN 1983); Nottingham Univ. (BTh 1986). Staff Nurse, London Hosp., Whitechapel, 1977–79; Community Mem., Scargill House, Yorks, 1979–80; Post Registration Student, Hosp. for Sick Children, Gt Ormond St, 1980–81; Staff Nurse, Mayday Hosp., Croydon, 1981–83; ordained deaconess, 1986, deacon, 1987, priest, 1994; Deaconess, 1986–87, Deacon, 1987–90, Holy Trinity & St Peter, S Wimbledon; Curate, St Peter & St Paul with St George, Crowhurst, and Chaplain, Lingfield Hosp. Sch., 1990–95; Rector, St Mary the Virgin, Bletchingley, 1995–2004; Rural Dean, Godstone, 1997–2004; Hon. Canon, 2001–04, Dean, Womens' Ministry,

2003–04, dio. of Southwark; Canon Pastor, Canterbury Cath., 2004–07. *Publication:* (contrib.) Human Rites. *Recreations:* swimming, windsurfing, embroidery, arts and crafts. *Address:* 22 The Precincts, Canterbury CT1 2EP. *T:* (01227) 865227; *e-mail:* canonclare@canterbury-cathedral.org.

EDWARDS, Prof. Dianne, CBE 1999; ScD; FRS 1996; FRSE; Distinguished Research Professor in Palaeobotany, University of Wales, Cardiff, since 1996; *b* 23 Feb. 1942; *d* of William John Edwards and Enid Edwards; *m* 1965, Thomas Geoffrey Morgan (*d* 1997); one *s*. *Educ:* Girton Coll., Cambridge (BA, MA; PhD 1968; ScD 1989). Res. Fellow, Girton Coll., Cambridge, 1967–70; Fellow, Univ. of Wales, 1970–72; University College, Cardiff: Lectr in Botany, 1972–82; Sen. Lectr, 1982–86; Reader in Plant Sci., 1986–92; Prof. of Palaeobotany, 1992–96. Royal Soc. Leverhulme Trust Sen. Res. Fellow, 1994–95. Mem., Countryside Council for Wales, 2001–07. Corresp. Mem., Botanical Soc. of America, 1994. Trustee: Nat. Botanic Garden of Wales, 1997–2006; Royal Botanic Garden, Edinburgh, 1999–2006; Natural Hist. Mus., 2003–. FRSE 2001. Hon. Fellow, Univ. of Wales, Swansea, 1997. Hon. ScD TCD, 2005. Ed., Botanical Jl of Linnean Soc., 1993–2006. *Publications:* contrib. to jls incl. Palaeontology, Rev. of Palaeobotany and Palynology, Botanical Jl Linnean Soc., Nature. *Recreations:* gardening, Mozart, opera. *Address:* School of Earth and Ocean Sciences, Cardiff University, Cardiff CF10 3YE. *T:* (029) 2087 4264.

EDWARDS, Duncan; *see* Edwards, J. D.

EDWARDS, Elgan; *see* Edwards, D. E. H.

EDWARDS, Elizabeth Alice; *see* Wilson, E. A.

EDWARDS, Very Rev. Erwyd; *see* Edwards, Very Rev. T. E. P.

EDWARDS, Frederick Edward, LVO 1992; RD 1968 and Clasp, 1977; CEnv; voluntary worker; Director of Social Work, Strathclyde Region, 1976–93; *b* 9 April 1931; *s* of Reginal Thomas Edwards and Jessie Howard Simpson; *m* 1st, 1957, Edith Jocelyn Price (marr. diss. 1990); two *s* one *d*; 2nd, 1990, Mary Olds (*née* Ellis). *Educ:* St Edward's Coll., Liverpool; Univ. of Glasgow (Dip. Applied Soc. Studies 1965). BA 1973, MA 2003, Open Univ. CEnv 2005. Merchant Navy Deck Officer, 1948–58; Perm. Commn, RNR, 1953, Lt-Comdr 1963; sailed Barque Mayflower to USA, 1957. Morgan Refractories, 1958–60; Probation Service, Liverpool, 1960–69; Dir of Social Work: Moray and Nairn, 1969–74; Grampian, 1974–76. Vis. Prof., Dept of Social Policy (formerly Social Admin.) and Social Work, Univ. of Glasgow, 1988–93. Member: Scottish Marriage Guidance Council, 1970– (Chm., 1980–83); Scottish Council on Crime, 1972–75; Adv. Council on Social Work, 1976–81; Bd, Scottish Envmt Protection Agency, 1999–2006. Chairman: Scottish Sen. Alliance Volunteering for the Envmt, 1989–2005; Carnegie Third Age Prog. Cttee, 1993–96; Capability Scotland, 1997–2005; President: Volunteer Develt Scotland, 1994–2000; Disability Scotland, 1995–99; Scottish Environment LINK, 2004–07. Trustee, New Lanark Trust, 1993–2008. FCMI; MIEEM 2004. MUniv Open, 1988; DUniv Paisley, 1993. *Recreations:* walking, natural history, reading. *Address:* Gardenfield, Ninemileburn, Midlothian EH26 9LT.

EDWARDS, Gareth Huw; Principal, George Watson's College, Edinburgh, since 2001; *b* Swansea, 9 April 1958; *s* of Roy and Gwyneth Edwards; *m* 1981, Jane Rees; one *d*. *Educ:* Tudor Grange Grammar Sch.; Solihull Sixth Form Coll.; Exeter Coll., Oxford (BA Hons Lit.Hum.); Univ. of Bristol (PGCE). Asst Classics Master, King Edward's Sch., Birmingham, 1981–85; Hd of Classics, Boys' Div., Bolton Sch., 1985–90; Vice-Principal, Newcastle-under-Lyme Sch., 1990–96; Rector, Morrison's Acad., Crieff, 1996–2001. *Recreations:* choral singing, Rugby refereeing, Welsh Rugby fan, Hellenophile. *Address:* George Watson's College, Colinton Road, Edinburgh EH10 5EG. *T:* (0131) 446 6002; *e-mail:* g.edwards@gwc.org.uk. *Club:* New (Edinburgh).

EDWARDS, His Honour Gareth Owen; QC 1985; a Circuit Judge, 1991–2006; *b* 26 Feb. 1940; *s* of Arthur Wyn Edwards and Mair Eluned Edwards; *m* 1967, Katharine Pek Har Goh; two *s* one *d*. *Educ:* Herbert Strutt Grammar Sch., Belper; Trinity Coll., Oxford (BA, BCL). Called to the Bar, Inner Temple, 1963; Army Legal Service, 1963–65; Commonwealth Office, 1965–67. Practised, Wales and Chester Circuit, 1967–91; Recorder, Crown Court, 1978–91. *Recreations:* climbing, chess. *Address:* 58 Lache Lane, Chester CH4 7LS. *T:* (01244) 677795. *Clubs:* Army and Navy; Athenæum (Liverpool).

EDWARDS, Gareth Owen, CBE 2007 (MBE 1975); retired 1978 as Welsh Rugby footballer; chairman of leisure company in S Wales; *b* 12 July 1947; *s* of Granville and Anne Edwards; *m* 1972, Maureen Edwards; two *s*. *Educ:* Pontardawe Tech. Sch.; Millfield Sch.; Cardiff College of Educn. Rugby Football: 1st cap for Wales, 1967 (*v* France); Captain of Wales on 13 occasions; youngest Captain of Wales (at 20 years), 1968; British Lions Tours: 1968, 1971, 1974; Barbarians, 1967–78. Member of Cardiff RFC, 1966–; a record 53 consecutive caps, to 1978. *Publications:* Gareth: an autobiography, 1978; (jtly) Rugby Skills, 1979; Rugby Skills for Forwards, 1980; Gareth Edwards on Fishing, 1984; Rugby, 1986; Gareth Edwards' 100 Great Rugby Players, 1987; (with Peter Bills) Gareth Edwards: the autobiography, 1999; (with Peter Bills) Tackling Rugby: the changing world of professional Rugby, 2002. *Recreations:* fishing, golf. *Address:* 211 West Road, Nottage, Porthcawl, Mid-Glamorgan CF36 3RT. *T:* (01656) 785669.

EDWARDS, Griffith; *see* Edwards, James G.

EDWARDS, Prof. (Gwilym) Barrie, CBE 2004; FRCVS; DVetMed; Professor of Equine Studies, 1987–2005, now Emeritus, and Head, Department of Veterinary Clinical Sciences, 2000–06, University of Liverpool; *b* 20 May 1938; *s* of William Idris and Glenys Edwards; *m* 1967, Nina Susan Kemble; one *s* one *d*. *Educ:* Grove Park Grammar Sch., Wrexham; Univ. of Liverpool (BVSc 1961); RVC, London Univ. (DVetMed 1991). FRCVS 1993. Lectr, Large Animal Surgery, Univ. of Liverpool, 1961–70; Sen. Lectr, RVC, London Univ., 1970–87. *Publications:* (jtly) An Atlas of Veterinary Surgery, 3rd edn 1995; (jtly) Handbook of Equine Colic, 1999; numerous contribs to textbooks and more than 120 articles in scientific jls. *Recreations:* classical music, photographing and drawing African wildlife, watching sport, playing golf. *Address:* The Hollies, 17 Tower Road North, Heswall, Wirral CH60 6RS. *T:* (0151) 342 4683; *e-mail:* g.b.edwards@liv.ac.uk. *Club:* Caldy Golf.

EDWARDS, Helen, CBE 2001; Director General, Criminal Justice and Offender Management Strategy, Ministry of Justice, since 2008; *b* 2 Aug. 1953; *d* of Charlton and Isobel Edwards; *m* 1987, David John Rounds; three *s*. *Educ:* Univ. of Sussex (BA Hons 1975); Univ. of Warwick (MA 1977; CQSW 1977). Social Worker, E Sussex CC, 1975–80; Dep. Project Dir, Save the Children Fund, 1980–83; National Association for Care and Resettlement of Offenders: Policy Develt Officer, 1983–85; Principal Officer, 1985–88; Asst Dir, 1988–93; Dir of Policy, Res. and Develt, 1993–96; Acting Chief Exec., 1996; Chief Exec., 1997–2001; Dir, Active Community Unit, 2002–04, Dir Gen., Communities Gp, 2004–05, Home Office; Chief Exec., Nat. Offender Mgt Service, Home Office, subseq. at MoJ, 2005–08. Member: Morgan Cttee on Safer Communities, Home Office, 1990–91; New Deal Adv. Task Force, 1997–2001; Working Gp reviewing prison Bds of Visitors, 2000–01; Learning and Skills Council, 2000–01; Nat. Employment Panel, 2001–. Mem. Council, Inst. of Employment Studies, 1998–. Trustee, Milton S. Eisenhower Foundn, USA, 2000–. FRSA 1997. *Publications:* articles in jls on crime, social exclusion and criminal justice. *Recreation:* family and friends. *Address:* Ministry of Justice, Selborne House, 54 Victoria Street, SW1E 6QW.

EDWARDS, Huw; Presenter, BBC Ten O'Clock News, since 2003; *b* 18 Aug. 1961; *s* of Prof. Hywel Teifi Edwards and Aerona Edwards (*née* Protheroe); *m*; five *c*. *Educ:* Llanelli Boys' Grammar Sch.; UWCC (BA French). Joined BBC as trainee journalist, 1984; Parly Corresp., BBC Wales, 1986–88; Political Corresp., then Chief Political Corresp., BBC TV News and BBC News 24, 1988–99; Presenter, BBC Six O'Clock News, 1999–2002. Presenter of BBC TV and radio progs incl. Trooping the Colour, Festival of Remembrance, State Opening of Parliament, D-Day 60, The Story of Welsh, Songs of Praise and progs on classical music. Hon. Prof. of Journalism, Cardiff Univ., 2006. Hon. Fellow: Cardiff Univ., 2003; Univ. of Wales, Lampeter, 2006; Univ. of Wales, Swansea, 2007; Univ. of Wales, Newport, 2007; Swansea Inst. of Higher Educn, 2007. Ambassador, Prince's Trust. Patron: Cancer Research, Wales; Nat. Coll. of Music; George Thomas Hospice, 2007. DUniv Glamorgan, 2007. Presenter of the Year, BAFTA Cymru/Wales, 2001, 2002, 2003, 2004.

EDWARDS, Huw William Edmund; Associate Lecturer, National School of Government; freelance political and training consultant; *b* 12 April 1953; *s* of Rev. Dr Ifor M. Edwards and Esme Edwards; *m* 2005, Tess Cooling; one step *d*. *Educ:* Eastfields High Sch., Mitcham; Manchester Polytechnic; Univ. of York (BA, MA, MPhil). Lecturer in Social Policy: Coventry (Lanchester) Poly., 1980–81; Univ. of Sheffield, 1983–84; Poly. of the South Bank, 1984–85; Manchester Poly., 1985–88. Res. Associate, Low Pay Unit, 1985–; Tutor with Open Univ., 1987–95; Sen. Lectr in Social Policy, Brighton Poly., later Univ. of Brighton, 1988–91, 1992–97. MP (Lab) Monmouth, May 1991–1992, 1997–2005; contested (Lab) same seat, 1992, 2005. Member: Select Cttee on Welsh Affairs, 1991–92, 1998–2001, and 2002–05; Modernisation Cttee, H of C, 1997–98. Chm., Welsh Parly Labour Gp, 2000–01; Sec., All Party Commons and Lords Rugby Club. Member: Labour campaign for Electoral Reform; Fabian Soc., 1992–. Pres., Chepstow Mencap, 1992–; Mem. Exec., Shelter Cymru, 1988–91; Mem. Monmouth Gp, Amnesty Internat., 1969–. Patron, Gwent ME Soc., 1997–. Mem., Boro' Welsh Congregational Chapel, London. Vice-Pres., Monmouth Rugby Club, 1997–. *Publications:* reports on low pay in Wales and a fair electoral system for the Welsh Assembly; articles in professional jls. *Recreations:* sport, football, Rugby, cricket, Welsh choral music (Member, Gwalia Male Voice Choir). *Address:* Wyefield House, The Paddocks, Monmouth NP25 3NP. *Club:* London Welsh Association.

EDWARDS, Ian Anthony; Regional Chairman of Industrial, subsequently Employment, Tribunals, Southampton, 1996–2003, a part-time Chairman, 2004–06; *b* 18 June 1940; *s* of Gordon Burrows Edwards and Florence Hilda Edwards; *m* 1976, Susan Joy Rooth; one *s* one *d*. *Educ:* Liverpool Inst.; Liverpool Univ. (LLB 1961); Southampton Univ. (LLM 1962). Admitted as solicitor, 1965; Partner, Paris Smith & Randall, Southampton, 1970–87; Chm., part-time, 1985–87, full-time, 1987–96, Industrial Tribunals, Southampton. *Publication:* (ed jtly) Mead's Unfair Dismissal, 5th edn, 1994. *Recreations:* leader of Urban Saints (formerly Crusaders), walking, music, railways.

EDWARDS, (Ifan) Prys; Director, Prys Edwards Consultancy, since 1986; *b* 11 Feb. 1942; *m* 1966, Catherine Williams; one *s* one *d*. *Educ:* Leighton Park Sch., Reading; Welsh Sch. of Architecture, Cardiff (DipArch). RIBA 1965. Principal Partner, Prys Edwards Partnership, 1966–86. Member: Wales and the Marches Postal Bd, 1974–76; Develt Bd for Rural Wales, 1976–84; BTA, 1984–92; Chairman: Wales Tourist Bd, 1984–92; Welsh Fourth Channel Authy, 1992–98. Dir, Wales Millennium Centre, 1997–2006. Pres., Welsh League of Youth, 1981–. *Recreations:* sailing, watching Rugby, golf. *Address:* Bryn Aberoedd, Caemelyn, Aberystwyth SY23 2HA. *T:* (01970) 623001.

EDWARDS, Prof. (James) Griffith, CBE 1989; DM, DSc; FRCP, FRCPsych, FMedSci; Professor of Addiction Behaviour, Institute of Psychiatry, University of London, 1979–94, Professor Emeritus since 1994; Hon. Director, Addiction Research Unit, 1970–94 (Principal Investigator, 1967–70); Hon. Consultant, Bethlem and Maudsley Hospitals, since 1967; *b* 3 Oct. 1928; *yr s* of late Dr J. T. Edwards and late Constance Amy (*née* McFadyean); *m* 1st, 1969, Evelyn Morrison (marr. diss. 1981); one *s* one *d* (and one *d* decd); 2nd, 1981, Frances Susan Stables. *Educ:* Andover Grammar Sch.; Balliol Coll., Oxford (BA Physiology 1952; MA; Theodore Williams Schol. in Anatomy); St Bartholomew's Hosp. (Kirkes Schol. and Gold Medal); DM Oxford, 1966; DPM London, 1962; DSc London, 1990; FRCP 1976; FRCPsych 1976 (Hon. FRCPsych 1998). Served RA, 1948–49 (2nd Lieut). Jun. hosp. appts, King George, Ilford, St Bartholomew's, Hammersmith and Maudsley Hosps, 1956–62; Inst. of Psychiatry: res. worker, 1962; Lectr, 1966; Sen. Lectr, 1967; Reader, 1973. Chm., RC Psych. Special Cttee on Drug Dependence, 1983–87 (on Alcohol and Alcoholism, 1975–78); Member: Home Office Working Party on Drunkenness Offenders, 1967–70; WHO Expert Adv. Cttee on Drug Dependence, 1969–2002; DoE Cttee on Drinking and Driving, 1974–75; Home Office Adv. Council on Misuse of Drugs, 1972–2000; DHSS Adv. Cttee on Alcoholism, 1975–78; ESRC (formerly SSRC), 1981–89; S African Adv. Cttee on Drug Abuse, 1995; Cabinet Office Adv. Gp on Alcohol Policy, 2002–03; Expert Advr, H of C Public Health Cttee, 2005. Consultant Advr on Alcoholism, DHSS, subseq. DoH, 1986–94; ODA Consultant in Bolivia, 1987. Chm., Nat. Addiction Centre, 1991–94; Med. Advr, Phoenix House, 1990–94; Patron, Clouds House, 1996. Jt contrib. report, Calling Time, Acad. Med. Scis, 2004. Editor, 1978–96, Editor-in-Chief, 1996–2004, Commng Ed., 2005–, Addiction (formerly British Jl of Addiction); Editor-in-Chief, Internat. Research Monographs on the Addictions, 1995–. Roche Vis. Prof., Aust. and NZ, 1982; Hon. Prof., Univ. of Chile, 1992–; Vis. Prof., Amer. Coll. of Neuropsychopharmacology, 1993. Steven's Lectr and Gold Medallist, RSM, 1971; Lectures: Dent, KCL, 1980; Pollak, 1988, Okey, 1995, Inst. of Psychiatry; Maudsley, RCPsych, 2001. FMedSci 1999; Dist. Fellow, Soc. for Study of Addiction, 2004. Jellinek Meml Award, 1980; Evian Award, 1986; Prize, Assoc. for Med. Educn and Res. on Substance Abuse, USA, 1990; Nathan B. Eddy Gold Medal, Coll. on Problems of Drug Dependence, USA, 1996; Auguste Forel Prize, Internat. Order of Good Templars, 1998. *Publications:* Unreason in an Age of Reason, 1971; (jtly) Alcohol Control Policies, 1975; (ed jtly) Drugs in Socio-Cultural Perspective, 1980; (jtly) Opium and the People, 1981; Treatment of Drinking Problems, 1982 (trans. into 6 langs), 4th edn 2003; (ed) Drug Scenes, 1987; (ed jtly) Nature of Dependence, 1990; (ed) Personal Influences and Scientific Movements, 1991; (ed) Nature of Alcohol and Drug Problems, 1992; (ed jtly) Drugs, Alcohol and Tobacco: strengthening the science and policy connections, 1993; (ed jtly) Addiction: processes of change, 1994; (ed jtly) Alcohol and Alcohol Problems, 1994; (jtly) Alcohol Policy and the Public Good, 1994; (jtly) Alcohol and Public Policy, Evidence and Issues, 1995 (trans. 8 langs); (jtly) Psychotherapy, Psychological Treatments and the Addictions, 1996; Alcohol: the ambiguous molecule, 2000 (US edn as Alcohol: the world's favorite drug, 2002); (ed) Addiction: evolution of a specialist field, 2002; (jtly) Alcohol and Policy: no ordinary commodity, 2003; Matters of Substance, 2004; articles in jls on scientific, historical and policy aspects of alcohol and drug dependence. *Recreations:* frequenting junk shops, putting the drink down, smoking the devils out. *Address:* 32 Crooms Hill, SE10 8ER. *T:* (020) 8858 5631; *e-mail:* (home) grifsu@crooms.freeserve.co.uk; (office) louisa@addictionjournal.org. *Club:* Athenæum.

EDWARDS, James Valentine, CVO 1978; MA; *b* 4 Feb. 1925; *s* of late Captain Alfred Harold Edwards, OBE, and Mrs Eleanor Edwards; *m* 1965, Barbara, Princess Cantacuzene, Countess Speransky, *d* of late Sir John Hanbury-Williams, CVO, and Lady Hanbury-Williams; two *d*, and one step *s* one step *d*. *Educ:* St Edmund's, Hindhead; Radley; Magdalen Coll., Oxford (MA). Served RN, 1943–47. Oxford, 1943 and 1947–49. *Address:* Wyndhams, Camel Street, Marston Magna, Yeovil, Somerset BA22 8DB. *T:* (01935) 851538. *Clubs:* MCC, Free Foresters; Vincent's (Oxford).

EDWARDS, Jeremy John Cary; Group Managing Director, Henderson Administration Group, 1989–95; *b* 2 Jan. 1937; *s* of late William Philip Neville Edwards, CBE, and Hon. Mrs Sheila Edwards (*née* Cary); *m* 1st, 1963, Jenifer Graham (*née* Mould) (decd); one *s* one *d*; 2nd, 1974, April Philippa Harding (marr. diss. 1993); one *s*; 3rd, 1994, Mrs Amanda Barber. *Educ:* Ridley Coll., Ontario; Vinehall Sch., Sussex; Haileybury and Imperial Service Coll. Unilever, 1955–57; Hobson Bates & Co., 1957–59; Overseas Marketing and Advertising, 1959–61; Courtaulds, 1961–63; Vine Products, 1963–66; Loewe SA, 1966–68; Jessel Securities, 1968–70; Man. Dir, Vavasseur Unit Trust Management, 1970–74; Henderson Admin Gp, 1974–95; Jt Man. Dir, 1983–89. Non-executive Director: College Hill Associates, 1996–2002; Tribune Trust, 1997–2006; Liontrust First UK Investment Trust, 1999–2004. Hon. Treas., WWF (UK), 1984–2002; Children's Society (formerly C of E Children's Society): Mem. Council, 1987–2002; Vice-Chm., 1996–2002; Chm., Jewson Associates (formerly E. Jewson Services to Charities) Ltd, 2000–06; Trustee, Breast Cancer Haven (formerly Haven Trust), 1998–. *Address:* 59 Dorothy Road, SW11 2JJ. *T:* (020) 7228 6055. *Club:* Boodle's.

EDWARDS, Rev. Joel; International Director, Micah Challenge, since 2009; *b* 15 Oct. 1951; *m* 1976, Carol Munroe-Edwards; one *s* one *d*. *Educ:* London Bible Coll. (BA Theology 1975). Probation Officer, 1978–88; Gen. Sec., African and Caribbean Evangelical Alliance, 1988–92; UK Dir, Evangelical Alliance, 1992–97; Gen. Dir, Evangelical Alliance UK, 1997–2008. Pastor, 1985–95, Associate Pastor, 1996–2003, Mile End New Testament Church of God. Comr, Equality and Human Rights Commn, 2007–. Hon. DD: Caribbean Grad. Sch. of Theol., Jamaica, 2006; St Andrews, 2007. Prime Minister's Award (Jamaica), 2003. *Publications:* Lord Make Us One—But Not All the Same!, 1999; The Cradle, The Cross and The Empty Tomb, 2000; Hope, Respect and Trust: valuing these three, 2004; Falling Back on God: a Lent group study on trust, 2006; (with D. Killingray) Black Voices: the shaping of our Christian experience, 2007; Advent Hope: a spiritual focus for personal or group use, 2007; An Agenda for Change: a global call for spiritual and social transformation, 2008. *Recreations:* gym, reading.

EDWARDS, John Charles; JP; Lord Mayor of Cardiff, 1980–81; *b* 3 April 1925; *s* of John Robert Edwards and Elsie Florence Edwards; *m* 1946, Cynthia Lorraine Bushell; one *s* two *d*. *Educ:* Lansdowne Road Sch., Cardiff. Served War of 1939–45, RM (1939–45 Star, France and Germany Star, War Medal 1939–45); TA, 1948–62, RASC (TEM). Postal Exec. Officer, GPO. Member: Cardiff CC, 1962–83 (Dep. Lord Mayor, 1978–79); S Glam CC, 1974–78; Associate Mem., Inst. of Transport Admin, 1982. Freeman of City of London, 1981. JP S Glam, 1979. Mem., St John's Council for S Glam; CStJ 1997 (OStJ 1980). *Recreations:* athletics, football. *Address:* 61 Cosmeston Street, Cathays, Cardiff CF2 4LQ. *T:* (029) 2022 1506. *Club:* Civil Service.

EDWARDS, John Coates, CMG 1989; HM Diplomatic Service, retired; Head of UK Delegation, EC Monitoring Mission in former Yugoslavia, April–Sept. 1995, April–Aug. 1996, May–Sept. 1997, April–July 1998 and March–June 1999; *b* 25 Nov. 1934; *s* of late Herbert John and Doris May Edwards; *m* 1959, Mary Harris (*d* 2006); one *s* one *d*. *Educ:* Skinners' Co. Sch., Tunbridge Wells, Kent; Brasenose Coll., Oxford (MA). Military Service, 1953–55: Lieut, RA. Asst Principal: Min. of Supply, 1958; Colonial Office, 1960; Private Sec. to Parly Under Sec. of State for the Colonies, 1961; Principal: Nature Conservancy, 1962; Min. of Overseas Develt, 1965; First Sec. (Develt), and UK Perm. Rep. to ECAFE, Bangkok, Thailand, 1968; Asst Sec., Min. of Overseas Develt, 1971; Head of E Africa Develt Div., Nairobi, Kenya, 1972; Asst Sec., Min. of Overseas Develt, 1976; Head of British Develt Div. in the Caribbean, Barbados, and UK Dir, Caribbean Develt Bank, 1978; Hd, West Indian and Atlantic Dept, FCO, 1981–84; Dep. High Comr, Kenya, 1984–88; High Commissioner: Lesotho, 1988–91; Botswana, 1991–94. Chm., Kenya Soc., 1997–. JP Kent, 2000. *Address:* Fairways, Back Lane, Ightham, Sevenoaks, Kent TN15 9AU. *Clubs:* Royal Over-Seas League (Mem. Central Council, 2003–); Muthaiga Country (Life Mem.) (Nairobi).

EDWARDS, (John) Duncan; Chief Executive (formerly Managing Director), National Magazine Co. Ltd, since 2002; *b* 28 March 1964; *s* of Dr Vernon A. Edwards, OBE, JP and Jean Edwards; *m* 1993, Sarah Kennedy; two *s*. *Educ:* Merchant Taylors' Sch., Northwood; Univ. of Sheffield (BA Hons Geog. and Politics 1985). With Media Week Ltd, 1985–89; Publisher, Company mag., 1989–93; Business Develt Dir, 1993–98, Dep. Man. Dir, 1998–2002, Nat. Mag. Co.; Chm., Comag Ltd, 2002–. *Recreations:* running, leading a full life! *Address:* The National Magazine Co., 72 Broadwick Street, W1F 9EP; *e-mail:* duncan.edwards@natmags.co.uk. *Clubs:* Soho House, George; Old Merchant Taylors' Rugby Football.

EDWARDS, Rear Adm. (John) Phillip, CB 1984; LVO 1972; CEng, FIMechE 1982; Fellow, Wadham College, Oxford, 1984–94, now Emeritus (Domestic Bursar, 1984–94; Development Director, 1994–99); *b* 13 Feb. 1927; *s* of Robert Edwards and Dilys (*née* Phillips); *m* 1951, Gwen Lloyd Bonner; two *d* (and one *d* decd). *Educ:* Brynhyfryd Sch., Ruthin, Clwyd; HMS Conway; Royal Naval Engrg Colls, Keyham and Manadon (King's Sword, 1947). MA 1984. Served, 1944–72: HMS King George V, Vengeance, Mauritius, Caledonia, Torquay, Lion, Diamond, Defender, HMCS Stadacona, and HMY Britannia; Mechanical Trng Estab., Portsmouth; Personnel Panel; Staff of C-in-C Fleet; SOWC; Dep. Dir, RN Staff Coll., 1972–74; Asst Dir, Dir Gen. Ships, 1974–76; RCDS, 1977; Captain of Portland Naval Base, 1978–80; Dir Gen., Fleet Support Policy and Services, 1980–83; ADC to the Queen, 1980. Comdr 1964, Captain 1971, Rear Adm. 1980. Mem. (non-exec.), Welsh Office Health Policy Bd, 1985–90. President: Oxford Royal Naval Assoc., 1984–90; Oxford Royal Naval and Royal Marine Assoc., 1994–; Midland Naval Officers Assoc., 1985–95 (Vice-Pres., 1995–); Vice-Pres., Oxfordshire SSAFA, 1984–. Trustee, Oxford Preservation Trust, 1994–2006 (Vice-Pres., 2006). Freeman, City of London, 1984; Liveryman, Co. of Engineers, 1984. FCMI (FBIM 1980). Hon. FISTC 1976. *Recreation:* golf. *Address:* Wadham College, Oxford OX1 3PN. *Club:* Frilford Heath Golf.

EDWARDS, John Reid, JD; attorney; US Senator from North Carolina, 1999–2005; *b* 10 June 1953; *s* of Wallace R. Edwards and Catherine Edwards; *m* 1977, (Mary) Elizabeth Anania; one *s* two *d* (and one *s* decd). *Educ:* NC State Univ. (BS 1974); Univ. of NC at Chapel Hill (JD 1977). Called to the Bar: NC, 1977; Tenn, 1978; Associate, Dearborn and Ewing, Nashville, Tenn, 1978–81; trial lawyer, Wade Smith, 1981; Associate, 1981–83, Partner, 1984–92, Tharrington Smith and Hargrove, Raleigh, NC; Partner, Edwards and Kirby, Raleigh, NC, 1993–99. Dir, Center on Poverty, Work and Opportunity, Univ. of N Carolina at Chapel Hill, 2005–06. Vice-Presidential cand. (Democrat), US elections, 2004. *Address:* (office) 410 Market Street, Suite 400, Chapel Hill, NC 27516, USA.

EDWARDS, Jonathan David, CBE 2001 (MBE 1996); athlete, retired 2003; broadcaster, BBC Sport; *b* 10 May 1966; *s* of Andrew David Edwards and Jill Edwards (*née* Caulfield); *m* 1990, Alison Joy Briggs; two *s*. *Educ:* Durham Univ. (BSc Hons). Triple jump athlete: English Schs Champion, 1984; Gold Medallist: World Cup, 1992, 2002; World Championships, Gothenburg, 1995 (estabd world record, 18.29m), Edmonton, 2001; Eur. Indoor Championships, Valencia, 1998; Eur. Championships, Budapest, 1998; Olympic Games, Sydney, 2000; Commonwealth Games, Manchester, 2002. Mem. Bd, London Organising Cttee, 2012 Olympic Games, 2005–. Mem. for England, Content Bd, Ofcom, 2003–. Sports Personality of Year Award, BBC, 1995. *Publication:* A Time to Jump, 2000. *Address:* c/o MTC (UK) Ltd, 20 York Street, W1U 6PU. *T:* (020) 7935 8000.

EDWARDS, Dame Julie Andrews; *see* Andrews, Dame J.

EDWARDS, Kenneth; *see* Edwards, A. K.

EDWARDS, Dr Kenneth John Richard; Vice-Chancellor, University of Leicester, 1987–99; *b* 12 Feb. 1934; *s* of John and Elizabeth May Edwards; *m* 1958, Janet Mary Gray; two *s* one *d*. *Educ:* Market Drayton Grammar Sch.; Univ. of Reading (BSc 1st class 1958); University Coll. of Wales, Aberystwyth (PhD 1961; Hon. Fellow). Nat. Service, RAF, 1952–54. Fellow, Univ. of California, 1961–62; ARC Fellow, Welsh Plant Breeding Station, Aberystwyth, 1962–63, Sen. Sci. Officer, 1963–66; Cambridge University: Lectr in Genetics, 1966–84; Head of Dept of Genetics, 1981–84; Sec. Gen. of Faculties, 1984–87; St John's College: Fellow, 1971–87; Lectr, 1971–84; Tutor, 1980–84. Vis. Lectr in Genetics, Univ. of Birmingham, 1965; Vis. Prof., INTA, Buenos Aires, 1973; Leverhulme Res. Fellow, Univ. of California, 1973. Chm., CVCP, 1993–95; Member: Marshall Aid Commemoration Commn, 1991–98; Council, ACU, 1994–99; Bd, CRE, 1994–2001 (Pres., 1998–2001). Mem. Bd, USS Ltd, 1994–97. Chm. Governing Body, Inst. of Grassland and Envmtl Res., 1994–99. Chm. Council, CRAC, 2001–; Chm. Govs, Perse Sch., Cambridge, 2002–. Hon. LLD: QUB, 1995; Leicester, 1999; Hon. DSc: Reading, 1995; Loughborough, 1995; Warwick, 2000; Hon. MA Nene Coll., 1997; Dr (*hc*) Babeş-Bolyai, Romania, 1998; Maribor, Slovenia, 2001; Olomouc, Czech Republic, 2002. *Publications:* Evolution in Modern Biology, 1977; articles on genetics in sci. jls. *Recreations:* music, gardening. *Address:* 10 Sedley Taylor Road, Cambridge CB2 8PW. *T:* (01223) 245680.

EDWARDS, Lionel Antony, (Tony), CEng, FRAeS; Head, Defence Export Services Organisation, 1998–2002; *b* 4 Nov. 1944; *s* of Lionel Victor and Marjorie Edwards. *Educ:* Abingdon Sch.; Univ. of Birmingham (BSc Hons 1966); Harvard Business Sch. (MBA 1972). CEng 1991; FRAeS 1991. Apprentice Engr, Rolls-Royce, Derby, 1962–68; Mfg Engr, General Electric, Lynn, Mass, 1968–71; Lectr, Harvard Univ., 1972–73; Manager/Dir, General Electric, Lynn and Cincinnati, Ohio, 1973–82; Gen. Manager, Storno A/S, Copenhagen, 1983–86; Corporate Vice-Pres., Motorola, Copenhagen, 1986–88; President: Challenger Exec. Jet Div., Montreal, 1988–89; Canadair Aerospace Gp, Montreal, 1989; Man. Dir, Lucas Aerospace Ltd, Solihull, 1989–92; Gp Man. Dir, Lucas Industries, 1992; Chief-Exec., Dowty, and Main Bd Dir, TI Gp PLC, 1992–98; Chm. and Chief Exec., Messier-Dowty, 1994–98. Chm., Defence and Aerospace Sector Panel, OST Technology Foresight Prog., 1995–97. Member: Council, SBAC, 1989–98 (Vice-Pres. 1990–91, Pres. 1991–92, Dep. Pres. 1992–93); DTI Aviation Cttee, 1992–98; Council, Air League, 1992–; Council, RAeS, 1992 (Pres., 1999–2000); NDIC, 1992–2001. Trustee: RAF Mus.; Swordfish Heritage Trust, subseq. Fly Navy Heritage Trust. *Recreations:* preservation of historic aircraft, shooting, classic cars, farming. *Address:* Wincott's Hill Farm, Long Compton Road, Whichford, Warwickshire CV36 5PQ.

EDWARDS, Hon. Sir Llewellyn (Roy), AC 1989; Kt 1984; FRACMA; Consultant, Jones Lang La Salle (formerly Jones Lang Wootton), Brisbane, since 1989; *b* 2 Aug. 1935; *s* of Roy Thomas Edwards and Agnes Dulcie Gwendoline Edwards; *m* 1st, 1958, Leone Sylvia Burley (decd); two *s* one *d*; 2nd, 1989, Jane Anne Brumfield, AM. *Educ:* Raceview State Sch.; Silkstone State Sch.; Ipswich Grammar Sch.; Univ. of Queensland (MB, BS 1965). Qualified Electrician, 1955. RMO and Registrar in Surgery, Ipswich Hosp., 1965–68; gen. practice, Ipswich, 1968–74. MLA (L) Ipswich, Qld Parlt, 1972–83; Minister for Health, Qld, 1974–78; Dep. Premier and Treasurer, Qld, 1978–83; Dep. Med. Supt, Ipswich Hosp., 1983–85. Chairman: Ansvar Australia Insurance Ltd, 1984–94; World Expo 88 Authority 1984–89; Australian Coachline Holdings Ltd, 1992–96; Micromedical Industries, 1993–96; Multi-Function Polis Develt Corp., SA, 1995–98; UQ Hldgs Pty Ltd, 1998–; Director: Westpac Banking Corp., 1984–; James Hardie Industries Pty Ltd, 1990–; Uniseed Pty Ltd, 2001–. Chm., Pacific Film and Television Commn, 1991–; Mem., Australia Japan Foundn Bd, 1992–. Chancellor, Univ. of Queensland, 1993– (Mem. Senate, 1984–). FRACMA 1984. Hon. FAIM 1988. Hon. LLD Queensland, 1988; DUniv Griffith, 1998. *Recreations:* tennis, walking, cricket, Rugby Union. *Address:* 8 Ascot Street, Ascot, Qld 4007, Australia. *Clubs:* Brisbane (Brisbane, Qld); United Services (Qld); Ipswich (Ipswich, Qld); Brisbane Polo.

EDWARDS, Malcolm John, CBE 1985; Chairman, Coal Investments Plc, 1993–96; founded Edwards Energy Ltd, 1992; Commercial Director, British Coal (formerly National Coal Board), 1985–92; Member of the Board, British Coal, 1986–92; *b* 25 May 1934; *s* of John J. Edwards and Edith (*née* Riley); *m* 1967, Yvonne, *d* of Mr and Mrs J. A. W. Daniels, Port Lincoln, S Australia; two *s*. *Educ:* Alleyn's Sch., Dulwich; Jesus Coll., Cambridge (MA). Joined NCB as trainee, 1956; Industrial Sales Manager, 1962; Dir of Domestic and Industrial Sales, 1969; Dir Gen. of Marketing, 1973; responsible for coal utilisation R & D, 1984–92; Chm., British Fuels Gp, 1988–92; Dep. Chm., Inter Continental Fuels, 1989–92. Chm., Finance Cttee, Southwark Diocesan Bd of Educn, 1992–. *Publication:* (with J. J. Edwards) Medical Museum Technology, 1959. *Recreations:* book collecting, arts and crafts movement, music, gardening. *Address:* Lodge Farm, Moot Lane, Downton, Salisbury, Wilts SP5 3LN.

EDWARDS, Marcus; *see* Edwards, C. M.

EDWARDS, Margaret Elizabeth; Chief Executive, Yorkshire and the Humber Strategic Health Authority, since 2006; *b* 21 May 1962; *d* of Bertie Arthur John Edwards and Christine Edwards (*née* Hamilton-Bell); partner, Michael Ramsden. *Educ:* UEA (BA Hons (Econs) 1983); Univ. of Plymouth (MBA 1993); Royal Soc. of Apothecaries (DPhilMed 1996); INSEAD (top mgt prog. 1998). Planning and Inf. Manager, Norwich HA, 1983–85; various mgt posts, Plymouth HA, 1985–94; Dir of Clin. Services, 1995–98, Chief Exec., 1998–2001, Heatherwood and Wexham Park NHS Trust; Dir of Performance, 2001–02, Dir of Access, 2002–06, DoH. *Recreations:* reading, travel, philosophy and ethics.

EDWARDS, Dr Michael Frederick, OBE 1993; FREng, FIChemE; Principal Engineer, Unilever, 1987–2001; *b* 27 April 1941; *s* of H. S. Edwards and J. Edwards (*née* Wallwork); *m* 1964, Margaret Roberta Thorne; one *s* one *d*. *Educ:* University Coll., Swansea (BSc, PhD). FIChemE 1980; FREng (FEng 1992). Lectr in Engrg Scis, Univ. of Warwick, 1966–69; Lectr, Sen. Lectr in Chem. Engrg, 1969–81, Prof. of Chemical Engrg, 1981–87, Bradford Univ. Mem., various research council bds and cttees. *Publication:* Mixing in the Process Industries, 1985, 2nd edn 1992. *Recreations:* hill-walking, classical music. *Address:* 44 Long Meadow, Gayton, Wirral CH60 8QQ. *T:* (0151) 342 5602.

EDWARDS, Prof. Michael Martin; JP; Joint Chairman, 2002–07, Chairman, 2007–08, Association of Governing Bodies of Independent Schools (Chairman, Governing Bodies Association, 1998–2002); *b* 19 July 1934; *s* of Charles Samuel and Lilian Edwards; *m* 1956, Dorothy Mildred Mayall; two *s*. *Educ:* London Sch. of Economics (BSc (Econ), PhD); London Univ. Inst of Education (PGCE); Univ. of Maryland (Fulbright Schol.). Hd of Econs Sch., Woolwich Poly., 1959–67; Hd of Dept of Mgt and Business Studies, Hendon Coll. of Technology, 1967–71; Asst Dir, Poly. of South Bank, 1971–73; Academic Dir and Dep. Chief Exec., Middlesex Poly., 1973–91. Lectured at summer schs and confs, Univs of Bremen, Cologne, Hamburg, Heidelberg, Munich, Poznan, Trondheim and Warsaw, 1975–92; leader of educn missions to Hong Kong, Malaysia and Singapore, 1990–94. Dir, ISC, 1998– (Mem., 1998–). Non-exec. Dir, Harrow Community NHS Trust, 1991–94. Chairman: Bishop of London's Industrial Adv. Council, 1970–84; Higher and Further Educn Cttee, London Dio., 1973–80; Fulbright Awards Selection Cttee, 1984–96 (Mem., Fulbright Commn, 1986–96); John Lyon Charity, 1993–; St Mark's Hosp. Academic Inst., 1995–2001; St Mark's Res. Foundn, 1998–. Mem., Wkg Gp, RNT Trust, 2002–. Chairman of Governors: Harrow Coll. of Higher Educn, 1981–85; John Lyon Sch., 1982–2002; Mem. Governing Council, Oak Hill Theol Coll., 1981–91; Governor: Harrow Sch., 1982–2004; Lancing Coll., 2004–; Council, Royal Alexandra and Albert Sch. Fellow, Woodard Corp., 2004–. FRSocMed 1999. JP Harrow, 1991. *Publications:* The Growth of the British Cotton Trade 1780–1815, 1967; Aspects of Capital Investment, 1971; N. J. Smelser and the Cotton Factory Family, 1971. *Recreations:* music, Victorian literature, theatre, golf. *Club:* Athenæum.

EDWARDS, Norman L.; *see* Lloyd-Edwards.

EDWARDS, Owen; Director, Sianel 4 Cymru (Welsh Fourth Channel Authority), 1981–89; *b* 26 Dec. 1933; *s* of Sir Ifan ab Owen Edwards and Eirys Mary Edwards; *m* 1st, 1958, Shân Emlyn (marr. diss. 1994); two *d*; 2nd, 1994, Rosemary Allen. *Educ:* Ysgol Gymraeg, Aberystwyth; Leighton Park, Reading; Lincoln Coll., Oxford (MA). Cataloguer, Nat. Library of Wales, 1958–60; BBC Wales: Compère, TV Programme Heddiw, 1961–66; Programme Organiser, 1967–70; Head of Programmes, 1970–74; Controller, 1974–81. Chairman: Assoc. for Film and TV in Celtic Countries, later Celtic Film and TV Assoc., 1983–85, 1989–91; Royal Nat. Eisteddfod of Wales, 1986–89 (Vice-Chm., 1985–86). Hon. LLD Wales, 1989. Gold Medal, RTS, 1989; BAFTA Cymru Special Award, 1995. *Address:* 2 Riversdale, Llandaff, Cardiff CF5 2QL. *T:* (029) 2055 5392.

EDWARDS, Patricia Anne, (Mrs Roger Cox); Legal Director, Office of Fair Trading, 1996–2004; *b* 29 May 1944; *d* of late Maurice James Edwards and of Marion Edwards (*née* Lewis); *m* 1970, Roger Charles Cox, *qv*. *Educ:* Barry and Purley County Grammar Schools; King's College London (LLB). Called to the Bar, Middle Temple, 1967, Bencher, 2003; Criminal Appeal Office, 1965–74; Law Officers' Dept, 1974–77; Home Office: Sen. Legal Asst, 1977–80; Asst Legal Adviser, 1980–88; Principal Asst Legal Advr, 1988–94; Dep. Parly Comr for Admin, 1994–96. *Recreations:* music, travel, reading, domestic pursuits.

EDWARDS, Prof. Paul Kerr, DPhil; FBA 1998; Professor of Industrial Relations, Warwick University, since 1992; *b* 18 March 1952; *s* of Ernest Edwards and Ida Vivienne Edwards (*née* Kerr); *m* 1975, Susan Jane Martin; one *s* one *d*. *Educ:* Magdalene Coll., Cambridge (BA 1973); Nuffield Coll., Oxford (BPhil 1975; DPhil 1977). Res. posts, 1977–88, Dep. Dir, 1988–98, Dir, 1998–2002, Indust. Relns Res. Unit, Warwick Univ.; Associate Dean, Warwick Business Sch., 2007–. Chm., Social Scis Gp, British Acad., 2006–. Fellow, AIM, 2004–07. Ed., Work, Employment and Society, 1996–98; Associate Ed., Human Relations, 2006–. *Publications:* Strikes in the United States, 1981; (jtly) The Social Organization of Industrial Conflict, 1982; Conflict at Work, 1986; Managing the Factory, 1987; (jtly) Attending to Work, 1993; (ed) Industrial Relations, 1995, 2nd edn 2003; (jtly) Managers in the Making, 1997; (ed jtly) The Global Economy, National States and the Regulation of Labour, 1999; (jtly) The Politics of Working Life, 2005; (ed jtly) Social Theory at Work, 2006. *Recreation:* cycling. *Address:* Cotswolds House, Newbold-on-Stour, Stratford-on-Avon, Warwicks CV37 8TS. *T:* (01789) 450547.

EDWARDS, Prof. Peter Philip, PhD; FRS 1996; Professor of Inorganic Chemistry, and Head of Inorganic Chemistry, University of Oxford, since 2003; Fellow of St Catherine's College, Oxford, since 2003; *b* 30 June 1949; *s* of late Ronald Goodlass and of Ethel Mary, who later *m* Arthur Edwards; *m* 1970, Patricia Anne Clancy; two *s* one *d*. *Educ:* Univ. of Salford (BSc; PhD 1974). Fulbright Scholar and NSF Fellow, Baker Lab. of Chem., Cornell Univ., 1975–77; SERC/NATO Fellow and Ramsay Meml Fellow, Inorganic Chem. Lab., Oxford Univ., 1977–79; Cambridge University: Demonstrator in Inorganic Chem., 1979–81, Lectr, 1981–91, Univ. Chem. Labs; Dir of Studies in Chem., Jesus Coll., 1979–91; Co-Founder and Co-Dir, IRC in Superconductivity, 1988; Nuffield Sci. Res. Fellow, 1986–87; BP Venture Res. Fellow, 1988–90; Birmingham University: Prof. of Inorganic Chem., 1991–2003, of Chem. and of Materials, 1999–2003; Hd, Sch. of Chem., 1996–99; Royal Soc. Leverhulme Sen. Res. Fellow, 1996–97. Vis. Prof., Cornell Univ., 1983–86. Mem., HEFCE Res. Assessment Panel, RAE for 1996 and 2001. FRSC 1988 (Vice-Pres., Dalton Div., 1995; Corday-Morgan Medal, 1985; Tilden Medal, 1992; Liversidge Medal, 1999). Hughes Medal, Royal Soc., 2003. *Publications:* (with C. N. R. Rao): The Metallic and Non-Metallic States of Matter, 1985; Metal-Insulator Transitions Revisited, 1995. *Address:* St Catherine's College, Oxford OX1 3UJ.

EDWARDS, Peter Robert; Director, Personal Investment Authority, 1992–2001; *b* 30 Oct. 1937; *s* of Robert and Doris Edith Edwards; *m* 1st, 1967, Jennifer Ann Boys; one *s*; 2nd, 1970, Elizabeth Janet Barrett; one *d*; 3rd, 2000, Marjorie Ann Edworthy. *Educ:* Christ's Hospital. Chartered Accountant. Ernst & Young (and predecessor firms), 1955–90; Chief Exec., Secretan, 1990–92. Indep. Mem. Council, FIMBRA, 1990–94. Dir, Blackwall Green Ltd, 1992–96. *Recreations:* ornithology, gardening. *Address:* Quince Cottage, The Street, Bury, Pulborough, West Sussex RH20 1PA. *T:* (01798) 831900.

EDWARDS, Prof. Philip Walter, PhD; FBA 1986; King Alfred Professor of English Literature, University of Liverpool, 1974–90, now Emeritus; *b* 7 Feb. 1923; *er s* of late R. H. Edwards, MC, and late Mrs B. Edwards; *m* 1st, 1947, Hazel Margaret (*d* 1950), *d* of late Prof. C. W. and late Mrs E. R. Valentine; 2nd, 1952, Sheila Mary, *d* of late R. S. and late Mrs A. M. Wilkes, Bloxwich, Staffs; three *s* one *d*. *Educ:* King Edward's High Sch., Birmingham; Univ. of Birmingham. MA, PhD Birmingham; MA Dublin. Royal Navy, 1942–45 (Sub-Lieut RNVR). Lectr in English, Univ. of Birmingham, 1946–60; Commonwealth Fund Fellow, Harvard Univ., 1954–55; Prof. of English Lit., TCD, 1960–66; Fellow of TCD, 1962–66; Prof. of Lit., Univ. of Essex, 1966–74; Pro-Vice-Chancellor, Liverpool Univ., 1980–83. Visiting Professor: Univ. of Michigan, 1964–65; Williams Coll., Mass, 1969; Otago Univ., NZ, 1980; Internat. Christian Univ., Tokyo, 1989; Visiting Fellow: All Souls Coll., Oxford, 1970–71; Huntington Liby, Calif., 1977, 1983. *Publications:* Sir Walter Ralegh, 1953; (ed) Kyd, The Spanish Tragedy, 1959; Shakespeare and the Confines of Art, 1968; (ed) Pericles Prince of Tyre, 1976; (ed with C. Gibson) Massinger, Plays and Poems, 1976; Threshold of a Nation, 1979; (ed jtly) Shakespeare's Styles, 1980; (ed) Hamlet Prince of Denmark, 1985; Shakespeare: a writer's progress, 1986; Last Voyages, 1988; The Story of the Voyage, 1994; Sea-Mark, 1997; Pilgrimage and Literary Tradition, 2005; numerous articles on Shakespeare and literature of his time in Shakespeare Survey, Proc. British Acad., etc. *Recreations:* gardening, calligraphy. *Address:* High Gillinggrove, Gillinggate, Kendal, Cumbria LA9 4JB.

EDWARDS, Rear Adm. Phillip; *see* Edwards, J. P.

EDWARDS, Prys; *see* Edwards, I. P.

EDWARDS, His Honour Quentin Tytler; QC 1975; a Circuit Judge, 1982–97; *b* 16 Jan. 1925; *s* of Herbert Jackson Edwards and Juliet Hester Edwards; *m* 1948, Barbara Marian Guthrie (*d* 2006); two *s* one *d*. *Educ:* Bradfield Coll.; Council of Legal Educn. Royal Navy, 1943–46. Called to Bar, Middle Temple, 1948; Bencher, 1972. A Recorder of the Crown Court, 1974–82; Chancellor: Dio. of Blackburn, 1977–90; Dio. of Chichester, 1978–99. Licensed Reader, Dio. of London, 1967–2003; Chm., Ecclesiastical Law Soc., 1990–96; Member: Legal Adv. Commn of General Synod of Church of England, 1973–2001; Dioceses Commn, 1978–96. Pres., Highgate Literary and Scientific Instn, 1988–93. Hon. MA (Archbp of Canterbury), 1961. *Publications:* (with Peter Dow) Public Rights of Way and Access to the Countryside, 1951; (with K. Macmorran, et al) Ecclesiastical Law, 3rd edn, Halsbury's Laws of England, 1955; What is Unlawful?, 1959 (with J. N. D. Anderson, et al) Putting Asunder, 1966. *Recreations:* the open air, architecture. *Club:* Athenæum.

EDWARDS, Richard, PhD; Member (Lab) Preseli Pembrokeshire, National Assembly for Wales, 1999–2003; *b* 1956. *Educ:* Queen Elizabeth Grammar Sch., Carmarthen; Univ. of Swansea; Univ. of Birmingham. Posts in local govt and political res. Mem., Carmarthen Town Council, 1991–99; Mayor of Carmarthen, 1997. Chair, Envmt, Planning and Transport Cttee, Nat. Assembly for Wales, 2000–03. Mem., ICSA. *Address:* c/o National Assembly for Wales, Cardiff Bay, Cardiff CF99 1NA.

EDWARDS, Prof. Richard Humphrey Tudor, FRCP; Professor of Research and Development for Health and Social Care, University of Wales College of Medicine, Cardiff, and Director of Research and Development for Health and Social Care in Wales, 1996–99, now Emeritus Professor; *b* 28 Jan. 1939; *s* of Hywel Islwyn Edwards and Menna Tudor Edwards (*née* Davies); *m* 1964, Eleri Wyn Roberts; one *d* (one *s* decd). *Educ:* Llangollen Grammar Sch.; Middlesex Hosp. Med. Sch., London (BSc, PhD, MB, BS). Ho. appts, Middlesex, National Heart and Hammersmith Hosps, 1964–65; Res. Fellow, Asst Lectr, then Lectr (Wellcome Sen. Res. Fellow in Clin. Science), Hon. Cons. Physician (Respiratory Med.), Royal Postgrad. Med. Sch., Hammersmith Hosp. 1966–76; Wellcome Swedish Res. Fellow, Karolinska Inst., Stockholm, 1970; Prof. of Human Metabolism, UCH Med. Sch., 1976–84; Hd of Dept of Medicine, UCL, 1982–84; University of Liverpool: Prof. and Head of Dept of Medicine, 1984–96; Dir, Magnetic Resonance Res. Centre, 1987–96; Dir., Muscle Res. Centre, 1986–96. Hon. Consultant Physician: Royal Liverpool Univ. Hosp., 1984–96; Robert Jones and Agnes Hunt Orthopaedic Hosp., Oswestry, 1979–96. *Publications:* Clinical Exercise Testing, 1975; sci. papers on human muscle in health and disease and on various fields of medicine in Jl of Physiology, Clinical Sci., Clinical Physiol., Muscle and Nerve, etc. *Recreations:* Wales—planting trees, mountain walking, gardening, music. *Address:* Berthlwyd, Nantgwynant, Caernarfon, Gwynedd LL55 4NL. *T:* (01766) 890364.

EDWARDS, Prof. Robert Geoffrey, CBE 1988; FRS 1984; Professor of Human Reproduction, Cambridge University, 1985–89, now Emeritus; Extraordinary Fellow, Churchill College, Cambridge; *b* 27 Sept. 1925; *s* of Samuel and Margaret Edwards; *m* 1956, Ruth Eileen Fowler; five *d*. *Educ:* Manchester Central High Sch.; Univs of Wales and Edinburgh. PhD (Edin) 1955; DSc (Wales) 1962; MA (Cantab). Service in British Army, 1944–48; commnd 1946. UC North Wales, Bangor, 1948–51; Univ. of Edinburgh, 1951–57; Res. Fellow at California Inst. of Tech., 1957–58; Scientist at Nat. Inst. of Medical Research, Mill Hill, NW7, 1958–62; Glasgow Univ. 1962–63; in Dept of Physiology, Cambridge Univ., 1963–89; Ford Foundation Reader in Physiology, 1969–85. Scientific Dir, Bourn Hallam Clinics, Cambridgeshire and London, 1988–91. Founder Chm., European Soc. of Human Reproduction and Embryology, 1984–86. Visiting Scientist: in Johns Hopkins Hosp., Baltimore, 1965; Univ. of N Carolina, 1966; Visiting Professor: Free Univ., Brussels, 1984; Univ. of Hong Kong, 1998. Hon. Pres., British Fertility Soc., 1988–; Patron, UK Nat. Gamete Donation Trust, 1999. Hon. FRCOG 1985; Hon. MRCP 1986; Hon. FIBiol 2007. Hon. Member: Assoc. of UK Clinical Embryologists, 1998; French Soc. for Infertility, 1983; Greek Fertility Soc., 1998; Middle East Fertility Soc., 1999. Life Fellow, Australian Fertility Soc., 1985; Hon. Fellow, Internat. Fedn of Fertility Socs, 1998. Hon. Citizen of Bordeaux, 1985. Hon. DSc: Hull, 1983; York; Dr *hc* Vrije Univ., Brussels. Spanish Fertility Soc. Gold Medal, 1985; King Faisal Award, 1989. Chief Editor, Human Reproduction, 1986–. *Publications:* A Matter of Life (with P. C. Steptoe), 1980; Conception in the Human Female, 1980; (with C. R. Austin) Mechanisms of Sex Differentiation in Animals and Man; (with J. M. Purdy) Human Conception in Vitro, 1982; (with J. M. Purdy and P. C. Steptoe) Implantation of the Human Embryo, 1985; (with M. Seppälä) In Vitro Fertilisation and Embryo Transfer, 1985; Life Before Birth, 1989; editor of several scientific textbooks on reproduction; numerous articles in scientific and medical jls, organiser of conferences, etc. *Recreations:* farming, politics, music. *Address:* Duck End Farm, Dry Drayton, Cambridge CB23 8DB. *T:* (01954) 780602.

EDWARDS, Robert John, CBE 1986; Deputy Chairman, Mirror Group Newspapers, 1985–86 (Senior Group Editor, 1984–85); *b* 26 Oct. 1925; *m* 1st, 1952, Laura Ellwood (marr. diss. 1972); two *s* two *d*; 2nd, 1977, Brigid Segrave. *Educ:* Ranelagh Sch., Bracknell. Editor, Tribune, 1951–54; feature writer, London Evening Standard, 1954–57; Dep. Editor, Sunday Express, 1957–59; Man. Editor, Daily Express, 1959–61; Editor: Daily Express, 1961, 1963–65; Evening Citizen, Glasgow, 1962–63; Sunday People, 1966–72; Sunday Mirror, 1972–84; Dir, Mirror Group Newspapers, 1976–88. Ombudsman to Today newspaper, 1990–95. Chm., Scoop of the Year Awards Panel, London Press Club, 1988–2003. *Publication:* Goodbye Fleet Street (autobiog.), 1988. *Address:* Tregeseal House, Nancherrow, St Just, Penzance, Cornwall TR19 7PW. *T:* (01736) 787060. *Clubs:* Garrick, Reform.

EDWARDS, Robert Septimus Friar, CVO 1964; CBE 1963; *b* 21 Oct. 1910; *y s* of late Augustus C. Edwards and Amy Edwards; *m* 1946, Janet Mabel Wrigley; one *s* two *d*. *Educ:* Hereford Cathedral Sch. Chief Engineering Asst, Hereford, until 1936; Min. of Transport,

Highway Engineering, 1936–43; Principal, Min. of War Transport, 1943; Mem. British Merchant Shipping Mission, Washington, DC, 1944–46. Sec. Gen. Internat. Conf. on Safety of Life at Sea, 1948; Principal Private Sec. to Minister of Transport, 1949–51; Shipping Attaché, British Embassy, Washington, DC, 1951–54; Dir of Sea Transport, 1954–57; Gen. Manager, London Airports, 1957–63; Gen. Manager, 1967–69, Dir-Gen., 1969–71, Mersey Docks and Harbour Board. Chm., Morris & David Jones Ltd, 1973–74. Called to the Bar, Middle Temple, 1941. *Address:* The Check House, Beer Road, Seaton, Devon EX12 2PR. *T:* (01297) 624000.

EDWARDS, Robin Anthony, CBE 1981; Partner with Dundas & Wilson, CS (formerly Davidson & Syme, WS), 1965–96; *b* 7 April 1939; *s* of Alfred Walton Edwards and Ena Annie Ruffell; *m* 1963, Elizabeth Alexandra Mackay (marr. diss.); one *s* one *d*; *m* 1986, Janet Cant Pow. *Educ:* Daniel Stewart's Coll., Edinburgh; Edinburgh Univ. (MA, LLB (distinction), Cl. Medallist). Former Lectr in Conveyancing, Edinburgh Univ.; Admitted Member, WS Society, 1964; Mem. Council, Law Society of Scotland, 1969–84, Vice-Pres., 1978–79, Pres., 1979–80 (youngest Pres. ever, at that time). Mem., Lands Tribunal for Scotland, 1991–2001. *Recreations:* French travel and cuisine. *Address:* 7/6 Rocheid Park, East Fettes Avenue, Edinburgh EH4 1RP.

EDWARDS, Prof. Sir Samuel Frederick, (Sir Sam Edwards), Kt 1975; FRS 1966; Cavendish Professor of Physics, 1984–95, Professor Emeritus since 1995 (John Humphrey Plummer Professor, 1972–84), and Pro-Vice-Chancellor, 1992–95, Cambridge University; Fellow, Gonville and Caius College, Cambridge, since 1972 (President, 1992–97); *b* 1 Feb. 1928; *s* of Richard and Mary Jane Edwards, Manselton, Swansea; *m* 1953, Merriell E. M. Bland; one *s* three *d*. *Educ:* Swansea Grammar Sch.; Gonville and Caius Coll., Cambridge (MA, PhD); Harvard University. Inst. for Advanced Study, Princeton, 1952; Univ. of Birmingham, 1953; Univ. of Manchester, 1958, Prof. of Theoretical Physics, 1963–72. Chief Scientific Adviser, Department of Energy, 1983–88. Chm., SRC, 1973–77. UK Deleg. to NATO Science Cttee, 1974–79; Mem., Planning Cttee, Max-Planck Gesellschaft, 1974–77. Vice-Pres., Institute of Physics, 1970–73 (Mem. Council, 1967–73); Mem. Council, Inst. of Mathematics and its Applications, 1976– (Vice-Pres., 1979, Pres., 1980–81). Member: Physics Cttee, SRC, 1968–73 (Chm. 1970–73); Polymer Cttee, SRC, 1968–73; Science Bd, SRC, 1970–73; Council, European Physical Soc., 1969–71 (Chm., Condensed Matter Div., 1969–71); UGC, 1971–73; Defence Scientific Adv. Council, 1973– (Chm., 1977–80); Metrology and Standards Req. Bd, Dept of Industry, 1974–77; AFRC, 1990–94; HEFCW, 1992–95. Chm., Adv. Council on R&D, Dept of Energy, 1983–88 (Mem., 1974–77); Member Council: European R&D (EEC), 1976–80; Royal Soc., 1982–83 (a Vice-Pres., 1982–83); Pres., BAAS, 1988–89 (Chm. Council, 1977–82). Non-exec. Director: Lucas Industries, 1981–93; Steetley plc, 1985–93; Chm., Sen. Adv. Gp, Unilever, 1992–95; Mem., Adv. Gp, BP, 1992–98. Hon. Mem., European Physical Soc., 1996; Foreign Member: Acad. des Scis, France, 1989; Nat. Acad. of Scis, USA, 1996; Russian Acad. of Sci., 2007. FIMA; FRSC. Hon. FInstP 1996; Hon. Fellow, French Physical Soc. Hon. DTech Loughborough, 1975; Hon. DSc: Salford, Edinburgh, 1976; Bath, 1978; Birmingham, 1986; Wales, 1987; Sheffield, 1989; Dublin, 1991; Leeds, 1994; UEA, 1995; Mainz, 2002; Tel Aviv, 2006; Hon. ScD Cambridge, 2001; DUniv Strasbourg, 1986. Hon. Fellow, UC Swansea, 1994. Maxwell Medal and Prize, Inst. of Physics, 1974; High Polymer Physics Prize, Amer. Phys. Soc., 1982; Davy Medal, Royal Soc., 1984; Gold Medal, Inst. of Maths, 1986; Guthrie Medal and Prize, Inst. of Physics, 1987; Gold Medal, Rheological Soc., 1990; Louis Vaillon Moët Hennessy Prize (Science pour l'Art), 1993; Boltzmann Medal, IUPAP, 1995; Founders Polymer Prize, Inst. of Physics, 2001; Royal Medal, Royal Soc., 2001; Dirac Medal, Internat. Centre for Theoretical Physics, 2006. *Publications:* Technological Risk, 1980; (with M. Doi) Theory of Polymer Dynamics, 1986; (with S. M. Aharoni) Networks of Liquid Crystal Polymers, 1994; contribs to learned jls. *Address:* 7 Penarth Place, Cambridge CB3 9LU. *T:* (01223) 366610. *Club:* Athenæum.

EDWARDS, Sian; freelance conductor; Music Director, English National Opera, 1993–95; *b* 27 Aug. 1959. *Educ:* Royal Northern Coll. of Music; Leningrad Conservatoire. Since 1985 has conducted many orchestras incl. LPO, RPO, Royal Scottish Orch., City of Birmingham SO, Hallé, English Chamber Orch. and Docklands Sinfonietta; conducted Orchestre de Paris and Philharmonique de Lille in France, and Pittsburgh Symphony, Philadelphia Orch., San Francisco Symphony, Los Angeles Philharmonic, Nat. Symphony, Atlanta Symphony, Minnesota Orch. in USA, and Ensemble Modern, Südwest funk Orchester, ND Radiofunkorchester in Germany; has also conducted orchestras in Canada, Belgium, Austria, Russia and Australia. Operatic début with Mahagonny (Weill), then Carmen, Scottish Opera, 1986; world première of Greek (Turnage), Munich Biennale and Edinburgh Fest., 1988; Glyndebourne: La Traviata, 1987; Katya Kabanova, 1988; New Year (Tippett), 1990; Royal Opera, Covent Garden: The Knot Garden (Tippett), 1988; Rigoletto, 1989; Il Trovatore, 1991; Madam Butterfly, 1992; English National Opera: The Gambler (Prokofiev), 1992; The Queen of Spades, 1993; La Bohème, Marriage of Figaro, Jenufa, The Mikado, Khovanshchina, 1995; Mahagonny, Carmen, Eugene Onegin, 1998; Peter Grimes, 2001; La Clemenza di Tito, Bordeaux, 1996; Clara (Gefors), Opéra Comique, Paris, 1997; Don Giovanni, Danish Royal Opera, 2001; The Death of Klinghoffer (John Adams), La Damnation de Faust, Finnish Nat. Opera, 2001. Recordings incl. orchestral works by Tchaikovsky, Prokofiev, Ravel, Britten, John Adams, and opera by Judith Weir. *Address:* c/o Ingpen & Williams Ltd, 7 St George's Court, 131 Putney Bridge Road, SW15 2PA. *T:* (020) 8874 3222.

EDWARDS, Dr Steven, MRCVS; Chief Executive, Veterinary Laboratories Agency, 2000–08, on secondment as interim Chief Executive, Animal Health, 2008, Department for Environment, Food and Rural Affairs (formerly Ministry of Agriculture, Fisheries and Food); *b* 9 March 1948; *s* of late William Edward Edwards and of Daisy May Edwards (*née* Candelent); *m* 1976, Virginia Elizabeth Marian Lynch Evans; two *s*. *Educ:* Wolverhampton Grammar Sch.; Trinity Hall, Cambridge (MA, VetMB); Edinburgh Univ. (MSc, DVMS). MRCVS 1972. General veterinary practice, Montgomery, Powys, 1972–76; Univ. of Edinburgh, 1976–77; MAFF Veterinary Investigation Centre, Aberystwyth, 1977–78; Tech. Co-op. Officer, ODM, El Salvador, 1978–80, Bolivia, 1980; MAFF Central Veterinary Laboratory: Vet. Research Officer, 1980–92; Head of Virology Dept, 1992–98; MAFF Veterinary Laboratories Agency: Dir of Lab. Services, 1998–99; Dir of Surveillance and Lab. Services, 1999–2000. Visiting Professor: Farm Animal Studies, Univ. of Liverpool, 2001–; Veterinary Infectious Diseases, RVC, London, 2002–. Sec. General, 1991–2000, Vice Pres., 2000–03, Pres., 2003–, Biological Standards Commn (formerly Standards Commn), Office Internat. des Epizooties, Paris. Founder Mem., European Soc. for Vet. Virology., 1987 (Sec., 1988–94; Hon. Mem., 1997); Pres., Vet. Res. Club, London, 1995–96. Co-founder, Sec. and Ed., Foundn for Medieval Genealogy, 2002–. Chm., St Lawrence Chobham Handbell Ringers, 2004–06. *Publications:* contribs and edtl for veterinary jls, text books and conf. proceedings, and for genealogy jls. *Recreations:* genealogy, railway preservation.

EDWARDS, Very Rev. (Thomas) Erwyd (Pryse); Dean of Bangor, 1988–98, now Emeritus; *b* 26 Jan. 1933; *s* of Richard and Gwladys Edwards; *m* 1961, Mair (*née* Roberts); two *s*. *Educ:* St David's University College, Lampeter (BA 1956); St Michael's College, Llandaff. Curate of Caernarfon, 1958–63; Asst Chaplain, St George's Hosp., London, 1963–66; Chaplain, King's College Hosp., London, 1966–72; Vicar: Penmon, Anglesey, 1972–75; Menai Bridge, 1975–61; St David's, Bangor, 1981–85; St David's and St James's, Bangor, 1985–88; Canon of Bangor Cathedral, 1988. *Address:* 61 Ffriddoedd Road, Bangor, Gwynedd LL57 2TT. *T:* (01248) 362108; *e-mail:* erwyd@erwyd.wanadoo.co.uk.

EDWARDS, Thomas Mowbray C.; *see* Charles-Edwards.

EDWARDS, Tony; *see* Edwards, L. A.

EDWARDS, Tracy Karen, MBE 1990; consultant on team-building, leadership and management; Project Manager, Child Exploitation and Online Protection Centre; *b* 5 Sept. 1962; *d* of Antony Herbert Edwards and Patricia Edwards; one *d*; *m* twice (both marrs diss.). *Educ:* Highlands Primary Sch., Berks; Arts Educnl, Tring; Gowerton Comprehensive Sch., Swansea. Assembled first all-female crew to compete in 1989 Whitbread Round the World Race (Maiden Project), 1987; set world fastest ocean record, 1997. Man. Dir, Tracy Edwards Associates Ltd, 1990–2002; CEO, Quest Series Ltd, 2003–05; managed Oryx Quest yacht race, Qatar, 2005. Presenter/Commentator, TV broadcasts, incl. 1993–94 Whitbread Race; Science of Sailing, 2001; On the Crest of a Wave, 2002. *Publications:* Maiden, 1990; Living Every Second (autobiog.), 2001. *Recreations:* riding, theatre, travel, reading, music, shooting, ski-ing. *Address:* c/o Lucas Alexander Whitley, 14 Vernon Street, W14 0RJ; *web:* www.tracyedwards.com. *Clubs:* Royal Ocean Racing, Mosimann's, Home House; Royal Yachting Association.

EDWARDS, Dr Victoria Mary, (Mrs R. M. Taylor), OBE 2004; FRICS; FAAV; Research Director, School of Environmental Design and Management, University of Portsmouth, since 2006; *b* 14 Aug. 1963; *d* of George Wade Brown Edwards and Betty Kathleen Edwards (*née* Mack); *m* 1999, Richard Michael Taylor; one step *s* one step *d*. *Educ:* Birkenhead High Sch.; Univ. of Reading (BSc; PhD 1995); Univ. of Canterbury, NZ (MSc Hons). FAAV 1985; FRICS 1986. Chartered Surveyor, Dreweatt-Neate, 1984–87; Commonwealth Schol., Univ. of Canterbury, NZ, 1987–89; Consultant (pt-time), QEII Nat. Trust, Wellington, NZ, 1988–89; Sen. Lectr, 1989–95, Principal Lectr, Faculty of Envmt, 1995–2006, Univ. of Portsmouth. Winston Churchill Travelling Fellow, 1991; Carthage Fellow, Pol Econ. Res. Center, Montana, 1991. Member: Countryside Commn, 1998–99; Bd, Countryside Agency, 1999–2004; Forestry Commn, 1999–2006. Mem., Burns Cttee for Inquiry into Hunting with Dogs, 1999–2000. Mem., Adv. Cttee, Sch. of Rural Econ. and Land Mgt, RAC, Cirencester, 1996–2001; Gov., Macaulay Land Res. Inst., 2001–03. Mem., Surveying Courses Bd, 1991–96, Educn and Membership Cttee, 1992–96, RICS. Trustee: Countryside Educn Trust, Beaulieu, Hants, 1998–2001; Habitat Res. Trust, 2003–; Ernest Cook Trust, 2007–. *Publications:* Dealing in Diversity: America's market for nature conservation, 1995; Corporate Property Management: aligning real estate with business strategy, 2004; contrib. articles to envmtl jls. *Recreations:* golf, ski-ing, riding, travel, cooking for friends, walking, West Highland Terriers, the New Forest. *Address:* Portland Building, Portland Street, Portsmouth, Hants PO1 3AH. *T:* (023) 9284 2918, *Fax:* (023) 9284 2913; *e-mail:* victoria.edwards@port.ac.uk.

EDWARDS-MOSS, (Sir) David John, (5th Bt *cr* 1868); *S* father, 1988, but does not use the title and his name does not appear on the Official Roll of the Baronetage.

EDWARDS-STUART, Antony James Cobham; QC 1991; a Recorder, since 1997; a Deputy High Court Judge, since 2003; *b* 2 Nov. 1946; *s* of late Lt-Col Ivor Arthur James Edwards-Stuart and Elizabeth Aileen Le Mesurier Edwards-Stuart (*née* Deck); *m* 1973, Fiona Ann, *d* of late Paul Weaver, OBE; two *s* two *d*. *Educ:* Sherborne Sch.; RMA Sandhurst; St Catharine's Coll., Cambridge. MCIArb. Called to the Bar, Gray's Inn, 1976; an Asst Recorder, 1991–97. Head of Chambers, 2005–. Chm., Home Office Adv. Cttee on Service Candidates, 1995–98. Commnd 1st RTR, 1966; Adjutant: 1st RTR, 1973–75; Kent and Sharpshooters Sqn, Royal Yeomanry, 1976–77. *Recreations:* woodwork, restoring property in France. *Address:* 4 Aberdeen Park, Highbury, N5 2BN. *T:* (020) 7359 7224; Crown Office Chambers, 2 Crown Office Row, Temple, EC4Y 7HJ; *e-mail:* edwards-stuart@crownofficechambers.com.

EDWARDSON, Prof. James Alexander, PhD; Professor of Neuroendocrinology, Newcastle University, since 1982; Director, Institute for Ageing and Health (formerly Institute for the Health of the Elderly), Newcastle University, 1994–2006; *b* 18 March 1942; *s* of James Thompson Hewson Edwardson and Isabel Ann Edwardson; *m* 1965, Caroline Hunter; one *s* two *d*. *Educ:* South Shields Grammar-Technical Sch. for Boys; Univ. of Nottingham (BSc Hons Zoology 1963); Inst. of Psychiatry, Univ. of London (PhD 1966). MRC Junior Res. Fellow, Inst. of Psychiatry, 1966–67; Lectr in Physiology, Aberdeen Univ., 1967–69; MRC Scientist and Lectr in Biochem., Imperial Coll., London, 1970–75; Sen. Lectr, then Reader, in Physiology, St George's Hosp. Med. Sch., 1975–79; Director: MRC Neurochem. Pathology Unit, 1979–2000; MRC-Newcastle Univ. Centre Develt for Clinical Brain Ageing, 2000–04. Chm., Years Ahead - NE Regl Forum on Ageing, 2005–. Vice-President: Alzheimer's Disease Soc., 1989–; Age Concern Newcastle, 2007–. Mem. Council, Natural Hist. Soc. of Northumbria, 2004–. *Publications:* numerous papers on brain biochem., physiology and behaviour and on Alzheimer's Disease and related neurodegenerative disorders. *Recreations:* allotment, bird watching, Labour Party, poetry. *Address:* 18 Leslie Crescent, Newcastle upon Tyne NE3 4AN. *T:* (0191) 285 0159, *Fax:* (0191) 284 2609.

EDZARD, Christine; film director; Managing Director, Sands Film Studios, since 1975; *b* 15 Feb. 1945; *d* of Dietz Edzard and Susanne Eisendieck, painters; *m* 1968, Richard Goodwin; one *d*, and one step *s* one step *d*. *Educ:* Ecole National de Science Politique, Paris (Econ degree). Asst designer to Lila de Nobili and Rostislav Doboujinsky, Paris; asst on Zefirelli's Romeo and Juliet, 1966; designer for Hamburg Opera, WNO and Camden Town Fest.; designer, costumes and sets and wrote (with Richard Goodwin) script of film, Tales of Beatrix Potter, 1971; directed short films, The Little Match Girl, The Kitchen and Little Ida, released as Tales from a Flying Trunk; dir, The Nightingale, 1979; wrote and directed: Biddy, 1981 (first feature film); Little Dorrit, 1987 (BAFTA Award, Best Screenplay; LA Critics Award, Best Film; Orson Welles Award, Best Director); The Fool, 1991; directed and produced, As You Like It, 1992; designed and directed, Menotti's Amahl and the Night Visitors, Spoleto Fest., 1996; wrote, designed and directed: The Nutcracker, 1997; The Children's Midsummer Night's Dream, 2000. *Address:* Sands Films, Grice's Wharf, 119 Rotherhithe Street, SE16 4NF. *T:* (020) 7231 2209, *Fax:* (020) 7231 2209; *e-mail:* CE@sandsfilms.co.uk.

EEKELAAR, John Michael, FBA 2001; Reader in Family Law, University of Oxford, 1990–2005; Academic Director, Pembroke College, Oxford, since 2005 (Tutorial Fellow, 1965–2005); *b* Johannesburg, 2 July 1942; *s* of John (Jan) Eekelaar and Delphine Eekelaar (*née* Stoughton); *m* 1978, Pia Nicole Lewis; two *d*. *Educ:* King's Coll., London (LLB);

University Coll., Oxford (BCL). Rhodes Schol., 1963–65; Vinerian Schol., 1965; University of Oxford: Lectr in Law, 1966–90; Res. Fellow, Centre for Socio-Legal Studies, 1976–2000; Co-Dir, Oxford Centre for Family Law and Policy, 2000–. Dist. Vis. Fellow, NZ Law Foundn, 2005. Pres., Internat. Soc. of Family Law, 1985–88. Gen. Ed., Oxford Jl Legal Studies, 1993–; Founding Co-ed., Internat. Jl Law Policy and the Family, 1987–. *Publications:* Family Security and Family Breakdown, 1971; Family Law and Social Policy, 1978, 2nd edn 1984 (trans German 1983); (ed jtly) Family Violence: an international and interdisciplinary study, 1978; (ed jtly) Marriage and Cohabitation in Contemporary Societies, 1982; (jtly) The Protection of Children: state intervention and family life, 1983; (ed jtly) The Resolution of Family Conflict: comparative legal perspectives, 1984; (jtly) Maintenance after Divorce, 1986; (ed jtly) Family, State and Individual Economic Security, 1988; (ed jtly) Divorce Mediation and the Legal Process, 1988; (ed jtly) An Aging World: dilemmas and challenges for law and social policy, 1989; (jtly) The Reform of Child Care Law, 1990; Regulating Divorce, 1991; (ed jtly) Parenthood in Modern Society: social and legal issues for the Twenty-First century, 1993; (ed jtly) A Reader on Family Law, 1994; (jtly) The Parental Obligation: a study of parenthood across households, 1997; (ed jtly) The Changing Family: family law and family forms in international perspective, 1998; (jtly) Family Lawyers: the divorce work of solicitors, 2000; (ed jtly) Cross Currents: family law and policy in the US and England, 2000; Family Law and Personal Life, 2006; contrib. articles to jls and chapters in books. *Recreation:* music. *Address:* Ridgeway Cottage, The Ridgeway, Boars Hill, Oxford OX1 5EX. *T:* (01865) 735485.

EFFINGHAM, 7th Earl of, *cr* 1837; **David Mowbray Algernon Howard;** DL; Baron Howard of Effingham 1554; Commander RN, retd; National President, The Royal British Legion, 2003–06; *b* 29 April 1939; *s* of Hon. John Algernon Frederick Charles Howard (*d* 1971), *yr s* of 5th Earl, and his 1st wife, Suzanne Patricia (*née* Macassey); *S* uncle, 1996; *m* 1st, 1964, Anne Mary Sayer (marr. diss. 1975); one *s*; 2nd, 1992, Mrs Elizabeth Jane Turner, former wife of Peter Robert Easton Turner; two step *s*. *Educ:* Fettes Coll., Edinburgh; Royal Naval Coll., Dartmouth. Royal Navy, 1961–91. DL Essex, 2006. *Recreations:* horse racing, fishing. *Heir: s* Lord Howard of Effingham, *qv*. *Address:* (home) Readings Farm House, Blackmore End, Essex CM7 4DH. *T:* (office) (01787) 460977. *Clubs:* Royal Navy, Army and Navy; Essex.
See also C. A. F. Howard.

EFFORD, Clive Stanley; MP (Lab) Eltham, since 1997; *b* 10 July 1958; *s* of Stanley Charles Efford and Mary Agnes Elizabeth Christina Caldwell; *m* 1981, Gillian Vallins; three *d*. *Educ:* Walworth Comprehensive Sch. Sen. Adventure Playground Leader; Asst to Warden, Pembroke Coll. Mission; former London taxi driver. Mem. (Lab) Greenwich LBC, 1986–98 (former Gp Sec.; Chief Whip; Chm., Social Services Select Cttee, Health and Envmt Cttee). Contested (Lab) Eltham, 1992. Mem., Procedure Select Cttee, 1997–2000, Transport Select Cttee, 2002–, H of C. Prelim. FA Coach's Badge. *Recreations:* sports, reading, cinema. *Address:* (office) 132 Westmount Road, Eltham, SE9 1UT. *T:* (020) 8850 5744. *Clubs:* Eltham Hill Working Man's, Woolwich Catholic.

EFSTATHIOU, Prof. George Petros, FRS 1994; Professor of Astrophysics, since 1997, and Director, Institute of Astronomy, 2004–08, University of Cambridge; Fellow, King's College, Cambridge, since 1997; *b* 2 Sept. 1955; *s* of Petros Efstathiou and Christina (*née* Parperi); *m* 1st, 1976, Helena Jane (*née* Smart) (marr. diss. 1997); one *s* one *d*; 2nd, 1998, Yvonne Nobis; two *s*. *Educ:* Somerset Comprehensive Sch.; Keble Coll., Oxford (BA); Univ. of Durham (Dept of Physics) (PhD). Res. Asst, Astronomy Dept, Univ. of California, Berkeley, 1979–80; SERC Res. Asst, Inst. of Astronomy, Univ. of Cambridge, 1980–83; Jun. Res. Fellow, 1980–84, Sen. Res. Fellow, 1984–88, King's Coll., Cambridge; Institute of Astronomy, Cambridge: Sen. Asst in Res., 1984–87; Asst Dir of Res., 1987–88; Head of Astrophysics, 1988–94; Savilian Prof. of Astronomy, and Fellow, New Coll., Oxford, 1988–97; PPARC Sen. Fellow, 1994–99. Mem., PPARC, 2001–04. Maxwell Medal and Prize, Inst. of Physics, 1990; Bodossaki Foundn Academic and Cultural Prize for Astrophysics, 1994; Robinson Prize in Cosmology, Univ. of Newcastle, 1997; Heineman Prize for Astrophysics, Amer. Inst. of Physics, 2005. *Publications:* articles in astronomical jls. *Recreations:* running, playing the guitar. *Address:* Institute of Astronomy, Madingley Road, Cambridge CB3 0HA. *T:* (01223) 337548.

EFUNSHILE, Althea; Executive Director, Arts Planning and Investment, Arts Council England, since 2007; *b* 20 Aug. 1956; *d* of Chas L. Barrett and Ena Louise Barrett; partner, David Reardon; one *s* one *d*. *Educ:* Univ. of Essex (BA Hons Sociol.); Goldsmiths' Coll., London (PGCE); Buckinghamshire Coll. (DMS). Teacher, Brent, 1980–83; Dir, Elimu Community Educn Centre, 1983–85; detached youth worker, 1987, Area Youth Worker, 1987–89, Bucks CC; Educn Officer, Harrow, 1989–93; Asst Dir of Educn, Merton, 1993–96; Exec. Dir, Educn and Culture, Lewisham, 1996–2001; Dir, Children and Young People's Unit, then Safeguarding Children Gp, subseq. Vulnerable Children Gp, DFES, 2001–06. *Recreations:* travel, reading, cinema. *Address:* Arts Council England, 14 Great Peter Street, SW1P 3NQ.

EGAN, Sir John (Leopold), Kt 1986; DL; Chairman, Severn Trent plc, since 2005; *b* 7 Nov. 1939; *m* 1963, Julia Emily Treble; two *d*. *Educ:* Bablake Sch., Coventry; Imperial Coll., London Univ., 1958–61 (BSc Hons; FIC 1985); London Business Sch., London Univ., 1966–68 (MScEcon). Petroleum Engineer, Shell International, 1962–66; General Manager, AC-Delco Replacement Parts Operation, General Motors Ltd, 1968–71; Managing Director, Leyland Cars Parts Div., Parts and Service Director, Leyland Cars, BLMC, 1971–76; Corporate Parts Director, Massey Ferguson, 1976–80; Chm. and Chief Exec., Jaguar Cars Ltd, 1980–85, Jaguar plc, 1985–90; Chief Exec., BAA plc, 1990–99; Chairman: MEPC plc, 1998–2000; Inchcape plc, 2000–05; Harrison Lovegrove Ltd, 2000–05; QinetiQ, 2001–02. Director: Foreign and Colonial Investment Trust, 1985–97; Legal & General Group, 1987–97 (Dep. Chm., 1993–97). Chm., 1993–97, Pres., 1998–, London Tourist Bd; Dir, BTA, 1994–97. Dep. Pres., 2001–02, Pres., 2002–04, CBI. Hon. Professor: Dept of Engrg, Warwick Univ., 1990; Aston Univ., 1990. Chancellor, Coventry Univ., 2007–. DL Warwicks, 1988. Sen. Fellow, RCA, 1987; FCIPS 1993; FRAeS 1994; FCIT 1994. Hon. FCIM 1989. Hon. Fellow: London Business Sch., 1988; Wolverhampton Poly., 1989. Dr *hc* Cranfield Inst. of Technology, 1986; Hon. DTech: Loughborough, 1987; Brunel, 1997; Hon. DBA Internat. Business Sch., 1988; Hon. LLD Bath, 1988; Hon. DSc Aston, 1992. Hon. Insignia for Technology, CGLI, 1987. Internat. Distinguished Entrepreneur Award, Univ. of Manitoba, 1989. MBA Award of the Year, 1988. *Recreations:* music, ski-ing, tennis. *Address:* Severn Trent Plc, 2297 Coventry Road, Birmingham B26 3PU. *Clubs:* Royal Automobile, MCC; Warwick Boat.

EGAN, Penelope Jane; Executive Director, Fulbright Commission, since 2007; *b* 18 July 1951; *d* of late Derek A. Morris and of June E. Morris; *m* 1975, David Anthony Egan; two *s*. *Educ:* St Paul's Girls' Sch.; Leicester Univ. (BA 1971). Mus. Asst, 1971–73, Press Officer, 1973–75, Victoria & Albert Mus.; Press Officer, Prime Minister's Office, 1975–77; Press and Publicity Officer, Crafts Council, 1977–82; Lecture Sec., 1986–95, Programme Develt Dir, 1995–97, Exec. Dir, 1998–2006, RSA. Mem., Design Council, 1999–. Trustee, Geffrye Mus., 2006–. Mem. Council, Warwick Univ., 2007–. *Recreations:* tennis, cooking, cinema. *Address:* 28 Glebe Road, Barnes, SW13 0EA. *T:* (020) 8876 1907; *e-mail* penny@pennyegan.com. *Club:* Roehampton.

EGAN, Rt Rev. Mgr Canon Thomas; Parish Priest of Our Lady of Lourdes, New Southgate, since 2001; *b* 15 Feb. 1942; *s* of Frank and Mary Egan. *Educ:* St Edmund's Coll., Ware; Inst. of Educn, London Univ. (BEd). Asst priest, Our Lady and St Joseph, Hanwell, 1967–72; Home Mission Team, 1972–73; asst priest, St Joan of Arc, Highbury, 1973–78; Parish Priest, St Pius X, St Charles Square, 1978–86; Pastoral Dir, Allen Hall Seminary, 1986–90; Parish Priest, Our Lady of Hal, Camden Town, 1990–93; VG, Archdio. Westminster, 1993–2001. Mem., Westminster Cath. Chapter of Canons, 2005–. *Recreations:* fishing, swimming, football. *Address:* 373 Bowes Road, New Southgate, N11 1AA.

EGDELL, Dr John Duncan; Consultant in Public Health Medicine (formerly Community Physician), Clwyd Health Authority, 1986–92, now Hon. Consultant, North Wales Health Authority; *b* 5 March 1938; *s* of late John William Egdell and Nellie (*née* Thompson); *m* 1963, Dr Linda Mary Flint; two *s* one *d*. *Educ:* Clifton Coll.; Univ. of Bristol. MB, ChB (Bristol) 1961; DipSocMed (Edin.) 1967; FFPH (FFPHM 1990; MFCM 1973; FFCM 1979). Ho. Phys. and Ho. Surg., Bristol Gen. Hosp., 1961–62; gen. practice, 1962–65; Med. Administration: with Newcastle Regional Hosp. Bd, 1966–69; with South Western Regional Hosp. Bd, 1969–74; Regional Specialist in Community Med., South Western Regional Health Authority, 1974–76; Regional Medical Postgrad. Co-ordinator, Univ. of Bristol, 1973–76; Regl MO, Mersey RHA, 1977–86; Hon. Lectr in Community Health, Univ. of Liverpool, 1980–86. *Recreations:* delving into the past, nature conservation. *Address:* Ravenswood, Glen Auldyn, Lezayre, Isle of Man IM7 2AQ. *T:* (01624) 818012.

EGERTON, family name of **Duke of Sutherland**.

EGERTON, Maj.-Gen. David Boswell, CB 1968; OBE 1956; MC 1940; *b* 24 July 1914; *s* of Vice-Admiral W. de M. Egerton, DSO, and Anita Adolphine (*née* David); *S* cousin, Sir John Grey Egerton, 15th Bt, 2008, but does not use the title; *m* 1946, Margaret Gillian, ARCM (*d* 2004), *d* of Canon C. C. Inge; one *s* two *d*. *Educ:* Stowe; RMA Woolwich. Commissioned Royal Artillery, Aug. 1934; served in India, 1935–39; ops in Waziristan, 1937; France and Belgium, 1940 (MC); Egypt 1942, Italy 1944 (wounded; lost left leg). Technical Staff course, RMCS, 1946; BJSM, Washington, DC, 1950–52; Asst Chief Engineer in charge of ammunition development, Royal Armament R&D Estabt, 1955–58; idc 1959; Army Mem., Defence Research Policy Staff, 1959–62; Comdt, Trials Estabt Guided Weapons, RA, 1962–63; Army Mem., Air Defence Working Party, 1963–64; Dir-Gen. of Artillery, Army Dept, 1964–67; Vice-Pres., Ordnance Board, 1967–69, President, 1969–70; retired 1970. Col Comdt, RA, 1970–74. Gen. Sec., Assoc. of Recognised Eng. Lang. Schs, 1971–79. *Recreations:* enjoying my family's progress, reading, keeping going! *Heir: s* William de Malpas Egerton [*b* 27 April 1949; *m* 1971, Ruth, *d* of late Rev. George Watson; two *s*]. *Address:* Bosworth Retirement Home, Preston, Dorset DT3 6HR.

EGERTON, Keith Robert, FRICS; *b* 26 June 1942; *s* of Harold and Doris Egerton; *m* 1968, Pauline Steele; one *s* one *d*. FRICS 1988 (ARICS 1966). Development Surveyor, Laing Properties, 1970–73; Commercial Union Properties: S Area Develt Manager, 1973–75; Dir, Belgian and Dutch projects, 1975–77; Dir, 1978–82; Dir, 1977–82, Chief Exec., 1978–82, Commercial Union Property Develts Ltd; Costain plc, 1982–91: Man. Dir, 1982–85, Chief Exec., 1985–91, County & District Properties; Director: resp. for Property, 1986–90; resp. for UK, Spanish and Calif Housing Ops and Property, 1990–91; joined Taylor Woodrow plc, 1991; Dir, 1992–2002; Gp Chief Exec., 1998–2002; Man. Dir, 1991–98, and Chm., 1992–99, Taylor Woodrow Property Co. Ltd; Director: Taywood Homes, 1996–98; Monarch Develt Corp., 1998–2002; non-exec. Dir, Rowlandson Orgn, 2002–. *Recreations:* cycling, gardening, hill walking, country pursuits, motorbikes, vintage and other interesting cars. *Address:* The White House, Run Common, Shamley Green, Guildford, Surrey GU5 0SY. *T:* (01483) 272944.

EGGAR, Rt Hon. Tim(othy John Crommelin); PC 1995; Chairman: Indago Petroleum plc, since 2005; Nitol Solar plc, since 2007; Director, Anglo-Asian Mining plc, since 2005; *b* 19 Dec. 1951; *s* of late John Drennan Eggar and of Pamela Rosemary Eggar; *m* 1977, Charmian Diana Minoprio; one *s* one *d*. *Educ:* Winchester Coll.; Magdalene Coll., Cambridge (MA). Called to the Bar, Inner Temple, 1976. European Banking Co. 1975–83; Director: Charterhouse Petroleum, 1984–85; LASMO plc, 1999–2000; Chairman: M W Kellogg, 1996–98; AGIP (UK) Ltd, 1997–98. Chm., Cambridge Univ. Cons. Assoc., 1972; Vice-Chm., Fedn of Cons. Students, 1973–74. MP (C) Enfield N, 1979–97. PPS to Minister for Overseas Develt, 1982–85; Parly Under-Sec. of State, FCO, 1985–89; Minister of State: Dept of Employment, 1989–90; DES, 1990–92; DTI (Minister for Energy, 1992–96, also for Industry, 1994–96). Chief Exec., Monument Oil and Gas PLC, 1998–99 (Dir, 1997–98); Vice-Chm., ABNAMRO Corporate Finance, 2000–05; Chm., Harrison Lovegrove & Co. Ltd, 2005–08. Pres., Russo-British Chamber of Commerce, 2004–. *Recreations:* ski-ing, simple gardening, shooting. *Address:* Nettlebed House, Nettlebed, Oxon RG9 5DD. *T:* (01491) 641148. *Club:* Carlton.

EGGINGTON, Dr William Robert Owen; Chief Medical Adviser, Department of Health and Social Security, later Department of Social Security, 1986–92; part-time Medical Adviser, Nestor Disability Alliance, 1999–2002; *b* 24 Feb. 1932; *s* of Alfred Thomas Eggington and Phyllis Eggington (*née* Wynne); *m* 1961, Patricia Mary Elizabeth, *d* of Henry David and Elizabeth Grant; one *s* one *d*. *Educ:* Kingswood School, Bath; Guy's Hosp. MB, BS 1955, DTM&H 1960, DPH 1962, DIH 1963; MFCM 1970. House Surgeon, Guy's Hosp., 1955; House Physician, St John's Hosp., Lewisham, 1956. RAMC, 1957–73, retired as Lt-Col, Senior Specialist Army Health. DHSS, later DSS, 1973–92. Medical Adviser: War Pensions Agency, 1994–98; Benefits Agency, 1998. *Recreations:* Goss heraldic china, military history, football spectator. *Address:* 33 Chestnut Road, Farnborough, Hants GU14 8LD.

EGGINTON, Anthony Joseph, CBE 1991; consultant; *b* 18 July 1930; *s* of Arthur Reginald Egginton and Margaret Anne (*née* Emslie); *m* 1957, Janet Leta, *d* of late Albert and Florence Herring; two *d*. *Educ:* Selhurst Grammar Sch., Croydon; University Coll. London (BSc 1951; Fellow, 1992). Res. Assoc., UCL, 1951–56; AERE Harwell (Gen. Physics Div.), 1956–61; Head of Beams Physics Gp, NIRNS Rutherford High Energy Lab., 1961–65; DCSO and Head of Machine Gp, SRC Daresbury Nuclear Physics Lab. 1965–72; Head of Engrg Div., 1972–74, Under Sec. and Dir of Engineering and Nuclear Physics, 1974–78, Dir of Science and Engrg Divs, 1978–83, SRC; Science and Engineering Research Council: Dir of Engrg, 1983–88; Dir Progs, and Dep. Chm. 1988–91. Vis. Prof., UCL, 1993–99. Head, UK Delegn, 1978–83, Chm., 1982–83, Steering Cttee, Inst. Laue-Langevin, Grenoble. *Publications:* papers and articles in jls and conf. proceedings on particle accelerators and beams. *Recreations:* sport, cinema, music. *Address:* 2 Millers Mews, Witney, Oxon OX28 1QT. *T:* (01993) 706738. *Club:* Lansdowne.

EGGLESTON, Anthony Francis, OBE 1968; Headmaster, Campion School, Athens, 1983–88, retired; *b* 26 Jan. 1928; *s* of late J. F. Eggleston and late Mrs J. M. Barnard, Harrow, Middx; *m* 1957, Jane Morison Buxton, JP, *d* of late W. L. Buxton, MBE and late Mrs F. M. M. Buxton, Stanmore, Middx; one *s* two *d*. *Educ:* Merchant Taylors' Sch., Northwood (Schol.); St John's Coll., Oxford (Sir Thomas White Schol.; BA 1949, MA 1953; 2nd cl. hons Chemistry). National Service, 1950–52; 2nd Lieut, RA, Suez Canal Zone. Asst Master, Cheltenham Coll., 1952–54; Sen. Science Master, English High Sch., Istanbul, 1954–56; Asst Master, Merchant Taylors' Sch., Northwood, 1956–62; Principal, English Sch., Nicosia, 1962–68; Headmaster, Felsted Sch., 1968–82. *Recreation:* looking at and lecturing about buildings of all periods. *Address:* Garden House, Chester Place, Norwich NR2 3DG. *T:* (01603) 616025.

EGGLESTON, Prof. James Frederick; Professor of Education, University of Nottingham, 1972–84, now Emeritus; *b* 30 July 1927; *s* of Frederick James and Anne Margaret Eggleston; *m* 1956, Margaret Snowden; three *s* two *d*. *Educ:* Appleby Grammar Sch.; Durham Univ. (King's Coll., Newcastle upon Tyne). BSc Hons Zoology; DipEd; FIBiol 1975. School teacher, 1953–64, Head of Biol., later Head of Sci., Hinckley Grammar Sch.; Res. Fellow, Res. Unit for Assessment and Curriculum Studies, Leicester Univ. Sch. of Educn, 1964; team leader, later consultant, Nuffield Sci. Teaching Project, 1964–68; Lectr in Educn, Leicester Univ. Sch. of Educn, 1966; apptd to Colls and Curriculum Chair of Educn, Nottingham Univ., 1973, Dean of Educn, 1975–81. *Publications:* A Critical Review of Assessment Procedures in Secondary School Science, 1965; Problems in Quantitative Biology, 1968; (with J. F. Kerr) Studies in Assessment, 1970; (jtly) A Science Teaching Observation Schedule, 1975; (jtly) Processes and Products of Science Teaching, 1976; contributions to: The Disciplines of the Curriculum, 1971; The Art of the Science Teacher, 1974; Frontiers of Classroom Research, 1975; Techniques and Problems of Assessment, 1976; (with Trevor Kerry) Topic Work in the Primary School, 1988; articles in professional jls. *Recreations:* fell walking, golf, photography. *Address:* The Old Chapel, Church Street, Fritchley, Derbys DE56 2FQ. *T:* (01773) 852870.

EGGLETON, Anthony, AO 1991; CVO 1970; Director, since 1996, Member of Advisory Council, since 2007, CARE Australia (National Director, 1995–96; Vice-Chairman, 2001–04; Chairman, 2004–07); Chairman, CARE International Strategy and Governance Committees, 2003–07; *b* 30 April 1932; *s* of Tom and Winifred Eggleton; *m* 1953, Mary Walker, Melbourne; two *s* one *d*. *Educ:* King Alfred's Sch., Wantage. Journalist, Westminster Press Group, 1948–50; Editorial Staff, Bendigo Advertiser, Vic, 1950–51; Australian Broadcasting Commn, 1951–60 (Dir of ABC-TV News Coverage, 1956–60); Dir of Public Relations, Royal Australian Navy, 1960–65; Press Sec. to Prime Ministers of Australia, 1965–71 (Prime Ministers Menzies, Holt, Gorton, McMahon); Commonwealth Dir of Information, London, 1971–74; Special Advr to Leader of Opposition, and Dir of Communications, Federal Liberal Party, 1974–75; Federal Dir, Liberal Party of Australia, 1975–90; Campaign Dir, Federal Elections, 1975, 1977, 1980, 1983, 1984, 1987, 1990. Sec.-Gen., 1991–95, Bd Mem., 2001–07, CARE Internat., Brussels; CEO, Centenary of Federation Council, 1997–2002. Chairman: Asia Pacific Democrat Union, 1998–2005 (Exec. Sec., 1982–84, 1985–87, Dep. Chm., 1987–90, Pacific Democrat Union); Australian Centre for Democratic Instns, 2007–. Mem., Australian Govt Aid Adv. Council, 2002–08. Mem. Bd, Nat. Stroke Foundn, 1997–2002. Chm., C. E. W. Bean (War Correspondents) Assoc., 2002–. Mem., Editl Adv. Bd, Australian Dept of Foreign Affairs, 1999–. Australian Public Relations Inst.'s 1st Award of Honour, 1968; Outstanding Service Award, Liberal Party of Australia, 1990; Centenary Medal, Australia, 2003. *Address:* 87 Buxton Street, Deakin, ACT 2600, Australia. *Clubs:* (Foundn Pres.) National Press (Canberra), Commonwealth (Canberra).

EGGLETON, Hon. Arthur C.; PC (Can.) 1993; Senator of Canada, since 2005; Director, Skylink Group of Companies Inc., since 2004; *b* 29 Sept. 1943; *m*; one *d*. Former accountant; consultant, urban mgt and policy issues. Toronto City Council: Mem., 1969–93; Budget Chief, 1973–80; Pres., 1975–76, 1978–80; Mayor of Toronto, 1980–91; former Member: Metropolitan Police Commn; Bd, Canadian Nat. Exhibn. MP (L) York Centre, Toronto, 1993–2004; Pres., Treasury Bd, and Minister responsible for Infrastructure, 1993–96; Minister: for Internat. Trade, 1996–97; of Nat. Defence, 1997–2002; Vice-Chm., Cabinet Cttee on Economic Policy, 1997–2002. Chm., Rebuilding Lives Campaign, St John's Rehabilitation Hosp. Civic Award of Merit, Toronto, 1992. *Address:* Senate of Canada, Suite 202, Victoria Building, Ottawa, ON K1A 0A6, Canada.

EGILSSON, Ólafur; attorney and diplomat; *b* 20 Aug. 1936; *s* of Egill Kristjánsson and Anna Margrjet Thuríður Ólafsdóttir Briem; *m* 1960, Ragna Sverrisdóttir Ragnars; one *s* one *d*. *Educ:* Commercial College, Iceland (grad. 1956); Univ. of Iceland, Faculty of Law (grad. 1963). Reporter on Vísir, 1956–58, Morgunblaðið, 1959–62; publishing Exec., Almenna bókafélagið, 1963–64; Head, NATO Regional Inf. Office, Iceland, 1964–66, and Gen. Sec., Icelandic Assoc. for Western Co-operation and Atlantic Assoc. of Young Political Leaders of Iceland; Icelandic Foreign Service, 1966; Foreign Ministry, 1966–69; First Sec., later Counsellor, Icelandic Embassy, Paris, and Dep. Perm. Rep. to OECD, UNESCO, 1969–71, and Council of Europe, Strasbourg, 1969–70; Dep. Perm. Rep., NATO and Dep. Head, Icelandic Delegn to EEC, Brussels, 1971–74; Counsellor, later Minister Counsellor, Political Div., Min. of Foreign Affairs, 1974–80; Chief of Protocol, with rank of Ambassador, 1980–83; Acting Principal Private Sec. to President of Iceland, Oct. 1981–June 1982; Dep. Perm. Under Sec. and Dir Gen. for Political Affairs, Min. of Foreign Affairs, 1983–87; Ambassador: to UK, 1986–89, and concurrently to the Netherlands, Ireland and Nigeria; to USSR, later Russia, 1990–94, and concurrently to Bulgaria, Japan, Romania and Ukraine; to Denmark, 1994–96, and also to Italy, Israel, Japan, Lithuania and Turkey; in charge of Arctic co-operation, 1996–98, also accredited to the Holy See, Turkey, Australia and NZ; Ambassador to China, and concurrently to Australia, Indonesia, Japan, Korea, Mongolia, New Zealand, Thailand and Vietnam, 1998–2002; Ambassador to Thailand, Singapore, Malaysia, Indonesia and Cambodia, 2003–06. Chm., Governing Bd, Icelandic Internat. Devlt Agency, 1982–87; Sec., Commn revising Foreign Service Act, 1968–69. President: Nat. Youth Council of Iceland, 1963–64; Acad. Assoc. of Reykjavík, 1967–68; Executive Member: Bible Soc., 1977–87 and 1996–; History Soc., 1982–88. Commander, Icelandic Order of the Falcon, 1981; holds numerous foreign orders. *Publications:* (jtly) Iceland and Jan Mayen, 1980; (ed) Bjarni Benediktsson: Contemporaries' views, 1983; (jtly) NATO's Anxious Birth: the prophetic vision of the 1940s, 1985. *Recreations:* walking, ski-ing, music (opera), history. *Address:* Valhusabraut 35, 170 Seltjarnarnes, Iceland. *T:* 6151121, *Fax:* 5515411; *e-mail:* olegice@simnet.is.

EGLIN, Philip Michael; ceramic artist; Senior Lecturer, Staffordshire University (formerly Staffordshire Polytechnic), since 1987; *b* Gibraltar, 29 Nov. 1959; *s* of Jack and Mary Eglin; *m* 1987, Jennet Walters; two *s*. *Educ:* Harlow Tech. Coll.; Staffordshire Poly. (BA 1982); Royal Coll. of Art. Mem., Selected Index Cttee, Crafts Council, 1997–2000. Fellow, Arts Foundn, 1993. Exhibitions include: Contemporary Applied Arts, London, 1986, 1988, 1989, 1992; (solo) Stafford Art Gall., 1990; (solo) Oxford Gall., 1991; Crafts Council, London, 1991, 1996, 1999; One from the Heart, Aberystwyth Arts Centre, 1995; The Nude in Clay, Chicago, 1995; (solo) New Work, Scottish Gall., Edinburgh, 2004; (solo) Franklin Parrasch Gall., NY; (solo) Barrett Marsden Gall., London, 2006, 2008; (solo) Borrowings, Nottingham Mus. and Art Gall., 2007; (solo) Dean Proj., Sculpture Objects and Functional Art Fair, NY, 2007; work in public collections, including: V&A Mus.; Brighton Mus.; Crafts Council, London; Portsmouth City Mus. and Art Gall.; Fitzwilliam Mus., Cambridge; York Mus.; Stedelijk Mus., Amsterdam; Gardiner Mus., Toronto; Mint Mus., N Carolina. Jerwood Prize for Applied Arts, Jerwood Foundn, 1996. *Publication:* Philip Eglin, 1997. *Recreations:* manager of football teams, Westpoint Wanderers (mini-soccer league, under 11s) and Shamblers FC (Potteries jun. youth league, under 13s).

EGLINGTON, Charles Richard John; Director, 1986–95, Vice-Chairman, 1990–95, S. G. Warburg Securities; *b* 12 Aug. 1938; *s* of late Richard Eglington and Treena Margaret Joyce Eglington. *Educ:* Sherborne. Dir, Akroyd & Smithers, 1978–86. Mem. Council, Stock Exchange, 1975–86, Dep. Chm., 1981–84 (Chairman: Quotations Cttee, 1978–81; Property and Finance Cttee, 1983–86). Governor: Sherborne Sch., 1979–; Twyford Sch., 1984–. *Recreations:* golf, cricket. *Address:* 2 Rectory Orchard, Church Road, Wimbledon, SW19 5AS. *Clubs:* MCC; Royal and Ancient Golf (St Andrews); Walton Heath Golf; Rye Golf.

EGLINTON and WINTON, 18th Earl of, *cr* 1507; **Archibald George Montgomerie;** Lord Montgomerie, 1448; Baron Seton and Tranent, 1859; Baron Kilwinning, 1615; Baron Ardrossan (UK), 1806; Earl of Winton (UK), 1859; Hereditary Sheriff of Renfrewshire; Chairman, Edinburgh Investment Trust plc, 1994–2003; *b* 27 Aug. 1939; *s* of 17th Earl of Eglinton and Winton and Ursula (*d* 1987), *er d* of Hon. Ronald Watson, Edinburgh; *S* father, 1966; *m* 1964, Marion Carolina, *o d* of John Dunn-Yarker; four *s*. *Educ:* Eton. Man. Dir, Gerrard & National Hldgs, 1972–92 (Dep. Chm., 1980–92); Chm., Gerrard Vivian Gray Ltd, 1992–94. Asst Grand Master, United Grand Lodge of England, 1989–95. *Heir: s* Lord Montgomerie, *qv*. *Address:* Balhomie, Cargill, Perth PH2 6DS.

EGLINTON, Prof. Geoffrey, PhD, DSc; FRS 1976; Professor of Organic Geochemistry, 1973–93, now Emeritus, and Senior Research Fellow, Biogeochemistry Research Centre, since 1995 (Director, 1991–96), University of Bristol; Adjunct Scientist: Woods Hole Oceanographic Institution, Massachusetts, since 1991; Dartmouth College, Hanover, New Hampshire, since 2003; *b* 1 Nov. 1927; *s* of Alfred Edward Eglinton and Lilian Blackham; *m* 1955, Pamela Joan Coupland; two *s* (one *d* decd). *Educ:* Sale Grammar Sch.; Manchester Univ. (BSc, PhD, DSc). Post-Doctoral Fellow, Ohio State Univ., 1951–52; ICI Fellow, Liverpool Univ., 1952–54; Lectr, subseq. Sen. Lectr and Reader, Glasgow Univ., 1954–67; Sen. Lectr, subseq. Reader, Bristol Univ., 1967–73. Mem., NERC, 1984–90. Hon. Fellow, Plymouth Polytechnic, 1981. Gold Medal for Exceptional Scientific Achievement, NASA, 1973; Hugo Müller Silver Medal, Chemical Soc., 1974; Alfred Treibs Gold Medal, Geochem. Soc., 1981; Coke Medal, 1985, Wollaston Medal, 2004, Geol Soc. of London; H. C. Urey Award, European Assoc. of Geochem., 1997; Royal Medal, Royal Soc., 1997; Martin Gold Medal, Chromatographic Soc., 1999; Goldschmidt Medal, Geochemical Soc., 2000; (jtly) Dan David Prize for Geoscis, 2008. *Publications:* Applications of Spectroscopy to Organic Chemistry, 1965; Organic Geochemistry: methods and results, 1969; 'Chemsyn', 1972, 2nd edn 1975; contrib. Nature, Geochim. Cosmochim. Acta, Phytochem., Chem. Geol., Sci. American. *Recreations:* gardening, walking, sailing. *Club:* Rucksack (Manchester).

EGMONT, 12th Earl of, *cr* 1733 (Ire.); **Thomas Frederick Gerald Perceval;** Bt 1661; Baron Perceval 1715; Viscount Perceval 1722; Baron Lovel and Holland (GB) 1762; Baron Arden 1770; Baron Arden (UK) 1802; *b* 17 Aug. 1934; *e s* of 11th Earl of Egmont and Ann Geraldine (*née* Moodie); *S* father, 2001. *Heir: b* Hon. Donald William Perceval [*b* 8 July 1954; *m* 1976, Nora Kindt; two *d*].

EGREMONT, 2nd Baron *cr* 1963, **AND LECONFIELD,** 7th Baron *cr* 1859; **John Max Henry Scawen Wyndham;** DL; FRSL, FSA; *b* 21 April 1948; *s* of John Edward Reginald Wyndham, MBE, 1st Baron Egremont and 6th Baron Leconfield, and of Pamela, *d* of late Captain the Hon. Valentine Wyndham-Quin, RN; *S* father, 1972; *m* 1978, Caroline, *er d* of A. R. Nelson, Muckairn, Taynuilt, Argyll, and Hon. Lady Musker; one *s* three *d*. *Educ:* Eton; Christ Church, Oxford (MA Modern History). Mem., Royal Commn on Historical MSS, 1989–2001. Chm., Friends of the Nat. Libraries, 1985–; Trustee: Wallace Collection, 1988–2000; British Museum, 1990–2000; Nat. Manuscripts Conservation Trust, 1995– (Chm., 2000–). Pres., ACRE, 1993–99. DL W Sussex, 1988. FRSL 2001; FSA 2005. *Publications:* (as Max Egremont) The Cousins: a biographical study of Wilfrid Scawen Blunt and George Wyndham, 1977 (Yorkshire Post First Book Award); Balfour: a life of Arthur James Balfour, 1980; Under Two Flags: the life of Major-General Sir Edward Spears, 1997; Siegfried Sassoon, 2005; *novels:* The Ladies' Man, 1983; Dear Shadows, 1986; Painted Lives, 1989; Second Spring, 1993. *Heir: s* Hon. George Ronan Valentine Wyndham, *b* 31 July 1983. *Address:* Petworth House, Petworth, West Sussex GU28 0AE. *T:* (01798) 342447; *e-mail:* egremont@dial.pipex.com.

EHRMAN, John Patrick William, FBA 1970; historian; *b* 17 March 1920; *o s* of late Albert and Rina Ehrman; *m* 1948, Elizabeth Susan Anne, *d* of late Vice-Adm. Sir Geoffrey Blake, KCB, DSO; four *s*. *Educ:* Charterhouse; Trinity Coll., Cambridge (MA). Served Royal Navy, 1940–45. Fellow of Trinity Coll., Cambridge, 1947–52; Historian, Cabinet Office, 1948–56; Lees Knowles Lectr, Cambridge, 1957–58; James Ford Special Lectr, Oxford, 1976–77. Hon. Treas., Friends of the National Libraries, 1960–77; Trustee of the Nat. Portrait Gall., 1971–85; Member: Reviewing Cttee on Export of Works of Art, 1970–76; Royal Commn on Historical Manuscripts, 1973–94; Chairman: Adv. Cttee to British Library Reference Div., 1975–84; Nat. Manuscripts Conservation Trust, 1989–94; Vice-Pres., Navy Records Soc., 1968–70, 1974–76. FSA 1958; FRHistS. *Publications:* The Navy in the War of William III, 1953; Grand Strategy, 1943–5 (2 vols, UK Official Military Histories of the Second World War), 1956; Cabinet Government and War, 1890–1940, 1958; The British Government and Commercial Negotiations with Europe, 1783–1793, 1962; The Younger Pitt, vol. 1, The Years of Acclaim, 1969, vol. 2, The Reluctant Transition, 1983, vol. 3, The Consuming Struggle (Yorkshire Post Book of the Year Award), 1996; contrib. Oxford DNB. *Address:* The Mead Barns, Taynton, near Burford, Oxfordshire OX18 4UH. *Clubs:* Army and Navy, Garrick.

See also W. G. Ehrman.

EHRMAN, Sir William (Geoffrey), KCMG 2007 (CMG 1998); HM Diplomatic Service; Ambassador to the People's Republic of China, since 2006; *b* 28 Aug. 1950; *s* of J. P. W. Ehrman, *qv* and Susan (*née* Blake); *m* 1977, Penelope Anne, *d* of late Brig. H. W. Le Patourel, VC and of Babette Le Patourel; one *s* three *d*. *Educ:* Eton; Trinity Coll., Cambridge (MA). Joined Diplomatic Service, 1973; language student, Hong Kong, 1975–76; Third/Second Sec., Peking, 1976–78; First Secretary: UK Mission to UN, NY, 1979–83; Peking, 1983–84; FCO, 1985–89; Pol Advr, Hong Kong, 1989–93; Head, Near East and N Africa Dept, FCO, 1993–94; UK Mem., Bosnia Contact Gp, 1994–95; Prin. Pvte Sec. to Sec. of State for Foreign and Commonwealth Affairs, 1995–97; seconded to Unilever (China) Ltd, 1997–98; Ambassador to Luxembourg, 1998–2000; Dir, Internat.

Security, 2000–02, Dir Gen., Defence and Intelligence, 2002–04, FCO; Chm., Jt Intelligence Cttee, and Hd, Intelligence and Security Secretariat, Cabinet Office, 2004–05. *Recreations:* sailing, walking, ski-ing. *Address:* c/o Foreign and Commonwealth Office, SW1A 2AH. *Club:* Royal Cruising.

EICHEL, Hans; Member (SPD), Bundestag, since 2002; Minister of Finance, Germany, 1999–2005; *b* Kassel, 24 Dec. 1941; *m*; two *c.* Secondary sch. teacher, Kassel, 1970–75. Mem., Kassel City Council, 1968–75; Mayor, Kassel, 1975–91; Mem. (SPD), Assembly, and Premier, Hesse Land, 1991–99. German Convention of Municipal Authorities: Mem., Presidium, 1981–91; Pres., 1985–87 and 1989–91. Joined SPD, 1964: Mem., Exec. Cttee, 1984–2005; Chm., Hesse, 1989–2005. *Address:* Deutscher Bundestag, Platz der Republik 1, 11011 Berlin, Germany.

EICHELBAUM, Rt Hon. Sir (Johann) Thomas, GBE 1989; PC 1989; Chief Justice of New Zealand, 1989–99; Judge of Appeal, Fiji, 1999–2007; non-permanent Judge, Court of Final Appeal, Hong Kong, since 2000; *b* 17 May 1931; *s* of Dr Walter and Frida Eichelbaum; *m* 1956, Vida Beryl Franz; three *s.* *Educ:* Hutt Valley High School; Victoria University College (LLB). Partner, Chapman Tripp & Co., Wellington, 1958–78; QC 1978; Judge of High Court of NZ, 1982–88. Pres., NZ Law Soc., 1980–82. Chm., Royal Commn on Genetic Modification, 2000–01. *Publications:* (Editor in Chief) Mauet's Fundamentals of Trial Techniques, NZ edn, 1989; (Consulting Editor) Advocacy in New Zealand, 2000. *Recreations:* reading, music, walking. *Address:* Raumati Beach, Kapiti Coast. *Club:* Wellington (Wellington).

EIGEN, Manfred; physicist, at Max-Planck-Institut für biophysikalische Chemie, Göttingen, since 1953 (Director, 1964); *b* 9 May 1927; *s* of Ernst and Hedwig Eigen (*née* Feld); *m* 1952, Elfriede Müller; one *s* one *d.* *Educ:* Göttingen Univ. Dr rer. nat. (Phys. Chem.) 1951. Research Asst, Inst. für physikal. Chemie, Göttingen Univ., 1951–53; Asst, Max-Planck-Institut für physikal. Chemie, 1953; Research Fellow, Max-Planck-Ges., 1958; Head of separate dept of biochemical kinetics, Max-Planck-Inst., 1962. Andrew D. White Prof. at Large, Cornell Univ., 1965; Hon. Prof., Technische Hochschule Braunschweig, 1965. For. Hon. Mem., Amer. Acad. of Arts and Sciences, 1964; Mem. Leopoldina, Deutsche Akad. der Naturforscher, Halle, 1964; Mem., Akad. der Wissenschaften, Göttingen, 1965; Hon. Mem., Amer. Assoc. Biol Chemists, 1966; For. Assoc., Nat. Acad. of Scis, Washington, 1966; For. Mem., Royal Soc., 1973. Dr of Science *hc* Washington, Harvard and Chicago Univs, 1966. Has won prizes, medals and awards including: Nobel Prize for Chemistry (jointly), 1967; Paul Ehrlich Award, 1996. *Publications:* numerous papers in learned jls on mechanics of biochemical reactions, molecular self-organisation and evolutionary biotechnology. *Address:* Max-Planck-Institut für biophysikalische Chemie, Am Fassberg 11, 37077 Göttingen, Germany.

EILLEDGE, Elwyn Owen Morris, CBE 2001; FCA; Chairman, Financial Reporting Advisory Board to HM Treasury, since 1996; Senior Partner, Ernst & Young, Chartered Accountants, 1989–95; *b* 20 July 1935; *s* of Owen and Mary Elizabeth Eilledge; *m* 1962, Audrey Ann Faulkner Ellis; one *s* one *d.* *Educ:* Merton College, Oxford (BA, MA). FCA 1968. Articled with Farrow, Bersey, Gain, Vincent & Co., later Binder Hamlyn, 1959–66; Whinney Murray & Co. subseq. Ernst & Whinney, now Ernst & Young, Liberia, 1966–68; Ernst & Whinney: Audit Manager, Hamburg, 1968–71; Partner, London, 1972; Managing Partner, London office, 1983–86; Dep. Sen. Partner, 1985; Sen Partner, 1986–89; Chairman: Ernst & Whinney Internat., 1988–89; Ernst & Young Internat., 1989–95. Chm., BTR, 1996–98; Dir, BG Group plc, 1997–2005. Member: Accounting Standards Bd, 1989–91; Financial Reporting Council, 1989–95. *Recreations:* gardening, swimming, tennis, listening to classical music. *Address:* Whitethorn House, Long Grove, Seer Green, Beaconsfield, Bucks HP9 2QH. *Club:* Brooks's.

EILON, Prof. Samuel, FREng; Professor of Management Science, Imperial College of Science, Technology and Medicine, University of London, 1963–89, Professor Emeritus, since 1989 (Senior Research Fellow, 1989–2002); industrial consultant on corporate performance and strategy; *b* 13 Oct. 1923; *s* of Abraham and Rachel Eilon; *m* 1946, Hannah Ruth (*née* Samuel); two *s* two *d.* *Educ:* Reali Sch., Haifa; Technion, Israel Inst. of Technology, Haifa; Imperial Coll., London. PhD London, 1955; DSc(Eng) London, 1963. FREng (Founder FEng 1976); FIMechE; FIET. Engr, Palestine Electric Co. Ltd, Haifa, 1946–48; Officer, Israel Defence Forces, 1948–52; CO of an Ordnance and workshop base depot (Major); Res. Asst, Imperial Coll., 1952–55; Lectr in Production Engrg, Imperial Coll., 1955–57; Associate Prof. in Industrial Engrg, Technion, Haifa, 1957–59; Imperial College: Head of Section, 1955–57; Reader, 1959–63; Head of Dept, 1959–87. Consultant and Lectr, European Productivity Agency, Paris, 1960–62. Professorial Research Fellow, Case Western Reserve Univ., Cleveland, Ohio, 1967–68. Vis. Fellow, University Coll., Cambridge, 1970–71. Mem., Monopolies and Mergers Commn, 1990–97. Past Mem. of several cttees of IProdE and DES; Member: Council, Operational Res. Soc., 1965–67; Council, Inst. of Management Scis, 1970–72, 1980–82; Exec. Cttee, British Acad. of Management, 1985–89. Adviser, P-E Consulting Gp, 1961–71; Principal and Dir, Spencer Stuart and Associates, 1971–74; Director: Amey Roadstone Corp., subseq. ARC, 1974–88; Campari Internat., 1978–80. Chief Editor, OMEGA, Internat. Jl of Management Science, 1972–94; Deptl Editor, Management Science, 1969–77. Hon. FCGI 1978. Two Joseph Whitworth Prizes for papers, IMechE, 1960; Silver Medal, ORS, 1982. *Publications:* Elements of Production Planning and Control, 1962; Industrial Engineering Tables, 1962; (jtly) Exercises in Industrial Management, 1966; (jtly) Industrial Scheduling Abstracts, 1967; (jtly) Inventory Control Abstracts, 1968; (jtly) Distribution Management, 1971; Management Control, 1971, 2nd edn 1979; (jtly) Applications of Management Science in Banking and Finance, 1972; (jtly) Applied Productivity Analysis for Industry, 1976; Aspects of Management, 1977, 2nd edn 1979; The Art of Reckoning: analysis of performance criteria, 1984; Management Assertions and Aversions, 1985; (jtly) The Global Challenge of Innovation, 1991; Management Practice and Mispractice, 1992; Management Science: an anthology, 1995; Management Strategies: a critique of theories and practices, 1999; some 300 papers and articles in the field of management. *Recreations:* theatre, walking. *Address:* 1 Meadway Close, NW11 7BA. *T:* (020) 8458 6650.

EISEN, Prof. Timothy George Quentin, PhD; FRCP; Professor of Medical Oncology, University of Cambridge, since 2006; *b* London, 13 Dec. 1963; *s* of Vuk and Phyl Eisen; *m* 2003, Julia Hardiman; one *s* one *d.* *Educ:* Arnold House Sch., London; Westminster Sch.; Middlesex Hosp. Med. Sch. (BSc); Gonville and Caius Coll., Cambridge (BChir 1986, MB 1987); Marie Curie Res. Inst., Surrey (PhD 1996). FRCP 2002. Clin. Res. Fellow, Marie Curie Res. Inst., 1990–94; Sen. Registrar, Royal Marsden Hosp., 1994–98; Senior Lecturer in Medical Oncology: UCL, 1998–2001; Inst. of Cancer Res., 2001–06. Chair: Lung Clin. Studies Gp, NCRI, 2004–; Med. Adv. Cttee, Macmillan Cancer Backup, 2006–. Trustee and Med. Advr, Balkans Relief, 1996–98; Trustee, Kidney Cancer UK, 2004–. *Publications:* (ed) Clinical Progress in Renal Cancer, 2007; contribs on kidney cancer, lung cancer and melanoma. *Recreations:* hill-bagging in Cambridgeshire (and beyond), tennis, trying to find a balance between unbridled optimism and pessimism. *Address:* Department of Oncology, Box 193, Addenbrooke's Hospital, Cambridge CB2 0QQ. *T:* (01223) 769312, *Fax:* (01223) 769313; *e-mail:* tgqe2@cam.ac.uk. *Club:* Athenæum.

EISENBERG, Neville; Managing Partner, Berwin Leighton Paisner LLP, Solicitors, since 1999 (Partner, 1996–99); *b* 12 April 1962; *s* of late Benjamin Elieser Eisenberg and of Masha Eisenberg. *Educ:* Paul Roos Primary Sch.; Paul Roos Gymnasium; Pretoria Boys High Sch.; Univ. of Witwatersrand (BCom 1982; LLB 1984); London Sch. of Econs and Pol Sci. (LLM 1988). Articled clerk, Werksmans Attorneys, 1985–87; solicitor, Berwin Leighton Paisner, 1989–95; admitted solicitor, England and Wales, 1991. Mem., London Council, CBI, 2002–. Chm., British Israel Law Assoc., 1996–. Nat. Chm., South African Union of Jewish Students, 1982–84; Comptroller, World Union of Jewish Students, 1986–89. Assoc. Gov., Hebrew Univ. of Jerusalem, 2004–. *Recreations:* current affairs, theatre, music, travel. *Address:* Berwin Leighton Paisner LLP, Adelaide House, London Bridge, EC4R 9HA. *T:* (020) 7760 1000, *Fax:* (020) 7760 1111; *e-mail:* neville.eisenberg@blplaw.com. *Club:* Home House.

EISENSTADT, Naomi, CB 2005; Director, Social Exclusion Task Force, Cabinet Office, since 2007; *b* 10 Feb. 1950; *d* of Berthold and Cecilia Leidner; *m* Prof. Marc Eisenstadt (marr. diss.); one *s*; partner, Michael Moutrie. *Educ:* Univ. of Calif, San Diego (BA; Post-grad. Dip. Early Childhood Educn); Cranfield Univ. (MSc Social Policy). Centre Leader, Moorlands Children's Centre, Milton Keynes, 1978–83; Lectr, Sch. of Educn, Open Univ., 1983–86; SCF, 1986–92; NCVO, 1992–96; Chief Exec., Family Service Units, 1996–99; Dir, Sure Start and Extended Schs, DfES, 1999–2006; Chief Advr on Children's Services to Sec. of State for Children, Schs and Families (formerly for Educn and Skills), 2006–07. Non-exec. Dir, Milton Keynes PCT. Mem., Editl Bd, Children and Society. *Recreations:* cooking, movies. *Address:* Cabinet Office, Admiralty Arch, The Mall, SW1A 2WH.

EISNER, Michael D(ammann); Founder, Tornante Company, 2005; Chief Executive Officer, 1984–2005, Director, 1984–2006, Walt Disney Co. (Chairman, 1984–2004); *b* 7 March 1942; *s* of Lester Eisner and Margaret Eisner (*née* Dammann); *m* 1967, Jane Breckenridge; three *s.* *Educ:* Lawrenceville Sch.; Denison Univ. (BA English Lit. and Theatre 1964). ABC Entertainment Corporation: Dir of Program Develt, East Coast, 1968–71; Vice President: Daytime Programming, 1971–75; Program Planning and Develt, 1975–76; Sen. Vice Pres., Prime-Time Production and Develt, 1976; Pres. and Chief Operating Officer, Paramount Pictures Corp., 1976–84. Jt Founder, Eisner Foundn, 1996. Host, TV show, Conversations with Michael Eisner, 2006–. Member of Board: California Inst. of the Arts; American Film Inst. Chevalier, Légion d'Honneur (France). *Publications:* Work in Progress (autobiog.), 1998; Camp (autobiog.), 2005. *Address:* c/o Eisner Foundation, 9401 Wilshire Boulevard, Suite 670, Beverly Hills, CA 90212, USA.

EKERS, Prof. Ronald David, PhD; FRS 2005; FAA; CSIRO Federation Fellow, Australia Telescope National Facility, since 2003 (Director, 1988–2003); *b* 18 Sept. 1941. *Educ:* Univ. of Adelaide (BSc 1963); Australian Nat. Univ. (PhD 1967). FAA 1993. Calif Inst. of Technol., 1967–70; Inst. of Theoretical Astronomy, Univ. of Cambridge, 1970–71; Kapteyn Lab., Groningen, 1971–80; Asst Dir, and Dir for Very Large Array Ops, Nat. Radio Astronomy Observatory, Socorro, USA, 1980–88. Pres., IAU, 2003–06. Flinders Medal, Aust. Acad. of Sci., 2005. Centenary Medal, Australia, 2003. *Publications:* articles in learned jls. *Address:* Australia Telescope National Facility, PO Box 76, Epping, NSW 1710, Australia.

EKERT, Prof. Artur Konrad, DPhil; FInstP; Professor of Quantum Physics, Oxford University, since 2007; Fellow of Merton College, Oxford, since 2007; *b* 19 Sept. 1961; *s* of Kazimierz and Janina Ekert; *m* 1990, Beata Wijowska. *Educ:* Jagiellonian Univ., Kraków, Poland (MSc); Wolfson Coll., Oxford (DPhil). FInstP 2004. Oxford University: Jun. Research Fellow, 1991–94, Res. Fellow, 1994–98, Merton Coll.; Prof. of Physics, 1998–2002; Fellow and Tutor, Keble Coll., 1998–2002; Leigh Trapnell Prof. of Quantum Physics, Cambridge Univ., 2002–07; Fellow, King's Coll., Cambridge, 2002–07. Howe Res. Fellow, Royal Soc., 1994–2000; Temasek Prof., Univ. of Singapore, 2002–05; Lee Kong Chian Centennial Prof., Nat. Univ. of Singapore, 2006–. Visiting Professor: Univ. of Innsbruck, 1994, 1998; Nat. Univ. of Singapore, 2001. Maxwell Medal and Prize, Inst. of Physics, 1995; (jtly) Descartes Prize, EU, 2004; Hughes Medal, Royal Soc., 2007. *Publications:* articles in scientific jls. *Recreations:* ski-ing, tennis, diving. *Address:* Mathematical Institute, 24–29 St Giles', Oxford OX1 3LB; *e-mail:* artur.ekert@qubit.org.

EKINS, Prof. Paul Whitfield, PhD; Professor of Energy and Environment Policy, King's College London, since 2008; *b* 24 July 1950; *s* of John Robert Ekins and Lydia Mary Ekins (*née* Daukes); *m* 1979, Susan Anne Lofthouse; one *s.* *Educ:* Imperial Coll., London (BSc Eng); Univ. of Bradford (MPhil); Birkbeck Coll., London (MSc Econ; PhD 1996). Res. Fellow, Birkbeck Coll., London, 1990–96; Sen. Lectr, then Reader, 1996–2000, Prof. of Sustainable Develt, 2000–02, Keele Univ.; Prof. of Sustainable Develt and Hd, Envmt Gp, Policy Studies Inst., Univ. of Westminster, 2002–07. Mem., Royal Commn on Envmtl Pollution, 2002–. Mem. Bd, NCC, 1996–2002. *Publications:* A New World Order, 1992; (ed jtly) Global Warming and Energy Demand, 1995; Economic Growth and Environmental Sustainability, 2000; contrib. numerous jl papers and articles. *Recreations:* music, theatre. *Address:* Department of Geography, King's College London, The Strand, WC2R 2LS. *T:* (020) 7848 1174, *Fax:* (020) 7848 2287; *e-mail:* paul.ekins@kcl.ac.uk.

EKINS, Prof. Roger Philip, PhD, DSc; FRS 2001; Professor of Biophysics, University of London, 1972–88, now Emeritus Professor; former Head, Department of Molecular Endocrinology, University College London Medical School (formerly at Middlesex Hospital Medical School); *b* 22 Sept. 1926; *s* of William Norman and Mathilde Therese Ekins; *m* 1st, 1947, Jane Woodger (marr. diss. 1963); two *d*; one *s* two *d*; 2nd, 1990, Marisa Antonietta Sgherzi. *Educ:* Westminster City Sch.; Emmanuel Coll., Cambridge (MA); Middx Hosp. Med. Sch. (PhD 1963; DSc 1990). Middlesex Hospital Medical School: Lectr in Physics Applied to Medicine, 1949–61; Lectr, then Sen. Lectr, 1961–68, Reader and Dep. Dir, 1968–72, Inst. of Nuclear Medicine; Dir, UK Supraregl Assay Service Centre, 1972–93 (Chm., SAS Dirs' Cttee, UK Supraregl Assay Service, 1974–77). Dr *hc* Univ. Claude Bernard, Lyons, 1993. Georg von Hevesy Medal, von Hevesy Foundn, Switzerland, 1984; Dist. Clin. Chemist Award, Internat. Fedn Clin. Chem., 1993; Inaugural Edwin F. Ullman Award, Amer. Assoc. Clin. Chem., 1998; Lifetime Achievement Award, DoH, 2006. *Publications:* contrib. numerous res. papers and book chapters relating to effects of maternal hormones on fetal brain develt, and develt of microarray and other microanalytical methods for sensitive measurement of substances of biol importance (eg hormones, DNA and RNA). *Recreations:* weaving rya rugs, potting, sailing, building houses, tasting fine wines, gardening, talking to attractive women. *Address:* Windeyer Institute, University College London, 46 Cleveland Street, W1T 4JF. *T:* (020) 7679 9410; Pondweed Place, Friday Street, Abinger Common, Dorking, Surrey RH5 6JR.

EKLUND, Graham Nicholas; QC 2002; barrister; *b* 23 Dec. 1950; *s* of Alan Nicholas Eklund and Mollie Jean (*née* Talbot); *m* 1987, Deborah Anne Bartley; one *s* one *d* (and one *s* decd). *Educ:* Auckland Univ. (BA; LLB Hons). Barrister and solicitor, Agar Keesing

McLeod & Co., NZ, 1975–78; solicitor, Herbert Smith, 1981–84; called to the Bar, Inner Temple, 1984; in practice as a barrister, 1984–. *Recreations:* wine, sport, song. *Address:* 4 New Square, Lincoln's Inn, WC2A 3RJ. *T:* (020) 7822 2000, *Fax:* (020) 7822 2001; *e-mail:* g.eklund@4newsquare.com.

EKSERDJIAN, Prof. David Patrick Martin, PhD; Professor of History of Art and Film, University of Leicester, since 2004; *b* 28 Oct. 1955; *s* of late Nubar Martin Ekserdjian and Mabel Brown Ekserdjian (*née* Angus); *m* 1990, Susan Moore; one *s* one *d*. *Educ:* Westminster Sch.; Trinity Coll., Cambridge (BA Modern and Medieval Langs 1977); Courtauld Inst. of Art, Univ. of London (MA 1979; PhD 1988). Christie's Jun. Res. Fellow, Balliol Coll., Oxford, 1983–86; Lectr, Courtauld Inst. of Art, 1986–87; Slade Fellow, Corpus Christi Coll., Oxford, 1987–91; with Christie, Manson & Woods, 1991–97; Editor, Apollo, 1997–2004. Guest Scholar, J. Paul Getty Mus., 2006. Member: Bd, Courtauld Inst. of Art, 1998–2002; Comitato Scientifico, Fondazione il Correggio, 2002–; Reviewing Cttee on Export of Works of Art, 2002–; Bd, MA course in history of design, V&A/RCA, 2003–; Adv. Bd, Bampton Opera, 2003–. Trustee: Nat. Gall., 2005–; Tate Gall., 2008–. Hon. Citizen, Correggio, 2004. *Publications:* (introd. and notes) Vasari, Lives of the Artists, 1996; Correggio, 1997; Parmigianino, 2006; Alle origini della natura morta, 2007; *exhibition catalogues:* (with D. Mahon) Guercino Drawings, 1986; Old Master Paintings from the Thyssen-Bornemisza Collection, 1987; Mantegna, 1992; contrib. to Macmillan Dictionary of Art, Saurs Allgemeine Künstlerlexicon, etc. *Recreations:* wine, Real tennis, opera, moths. *Address:* Department of History of Art and Film, University of Leicester, University Road, Leicester LE1 7RH. *T:* (0116) 252 2905. *Clubs:* Beefsteak, Queen's.

ELAM, Caroline Mary; Ruth and Clarence Kennedy Professor in Renaissance Studies, Smith College, Northampton, Mass, 2008; *b* 12 March 1945; *d* of John Frederick Elam and Joan Barrington Elam (*née* Lloyd). *Educ:* Colchester County High Sch.; Lady Margaret Hall, Oxford (BA); Courtauld Inst. of Art, Univ. of London. MA London and Cantab. Lectr, Fine Art Dept, Univ. of Glasgow, 1970–72; Jun. Res. Fellow, King's Coll., Cambridge, 1972–76 (Hon. Fellow, 1992); Lectr, History of Art Dept, Westfield Coll., Univ. of London, 1976–87; Editor, Burlington Mag., 1987–2002; Andrew W. Mellon Prof., Center for Advanced Study in the Visual Arts, Nat. Gall. of Art, Washington, 2002–04. Villa I Tatti, Florence: Fellow, Harvard Univ. Center for Renaissance Studies, 1981–82, 2002; Vis. Prof., 2005; Accademica, Accademia Raffaello, Urbino, 2005–. Member: Exec. Cttee, NACF, 1988–2002; Bd, Warburg Inst., 1992–97; Bd, Courtauld Inst. of Art, 1993–98; Syndic, Fitzwilliam Mus., Cambridge, 1993–2002. Agnes and Elizabeth Mongan Prize, 2004. *Publications:* Roger Fry and the Re-evaluation of Piero della Francesca, 2005; Roger Fry: Mantegna, 2006; Roger Fry: Giovanni Bellini, 2007; articles in Art History, Burlington Magazine, I Tatti Studies, Mitteilungen des Kunsthistorischen Insts in Florenz, Renaissance Studies, Jl of RSA, etc.

See also J. N. Elam.

ELAM, (John) Nicholas, CMG 1994; HM Diplomatic Service, retired; *b* 2 July 1939; *s* of John Frederick Elam, OBE and Joan Barrington Elam (*née* Lloyd); *m* 1967, Florence Helen, *d* of P. Lentz; two *s* one *d*. *Educ:* Colchester Royal Grammar Sch.; New Coll., Oxford (schol.). Frank Knox Fellow, Harvard Univ., 1961–62. Entered HM Diplomatic Service, 1962; served: Pretoria and Cape Town, 1964–68; Bahrain, 1971; Brussels, 1972–76; FCO, 1976–79, Dep. Head of News Dept, 1978–79; Counsellor and Dep. British Govt Rep., Salisbury, 1979; Dep. High Comr, Salisbury (later Harare), 1980–83; Consul-General, Montreal, 1984–87; Hd of Cultural Relations Dept, FCO, 1987–94; Ambassador to Luxembourg, 1994–98. Chm., Cultural Co-operation Council, Council of Europe, 1993–94. Administrator, Caine Prize for African Writing, 1999–; Dir, Dance Umbrella, 1999–2004; Consultant, Serious Internat. Music Producers, 1999–2002; Trustee, Triangle Arts Trust, 1998–; Chairman: Henri Oguike Dance Co., 2002–; Friends of UCL Art Collections, 2003–. Mem., British Council, 1994. Hon. Sen. Res. Fellow, Dept of History of Art, UCL, 2003–. *Recreations:* travel, the arts. *Address:* 86 Camberwell Church Street, SE5 8QZ. *Club:* Chelsea Arts.

See also C. M. Elam.

ELAND, Prof. John Hugh David, DPhil; FRS 2006; FRCS; Professor of Physical Chemistry, University of Oxford, 1997–2006; Fellow and Tutor in Chemistry, Worcester College, Oxford, 1983–2006, now Emeritus Fellow and Leverhulme Emeritus Fellow; *b* 6 June 1941; *s* of Rev.Thomas Eland and Verna Prosser Eland (*née* Reynolds); *m* 1967, Ieva Antonovics; three *s*. *Educ:* St John's Sch., Leatherhead; University Coll., Oxford (BA 1963; MA, DPhil, 1966). FRCS 2005. Physicist, Argonne Nat. Lab., USA, 1976–80; Lectr, Queen's Coll., Oxford, 1980–83. Visiting Professor: Univ. of Paris, 1981, 1995; Inst. Molecular Sci., Japan, 1989; Uppsala Univ., 1995; Tohoku Univ., Japan, 2002. *Publications:* Photoelectron Spectroscopy, 1972, 2nd edn 1984; contrib. numerous articles to learned jls. *Recreations:* astronomy, linguistics, walking. *Address:* Physical and Theoretical Chemistry Laboratory, University of Oxford, South Parks Road, Oxford OX1 3QZ. *T:* (01865) 275400, *Fax:* (01865) 275410; *e-mail:* eland@physchem.ox.ac.uk.

ELAND, Michael John, CB 2006; Commissioner, since 2000, and Director General, Law Enforcement and Compliance, since 2004, HM Revenue and Customs (formerly Customs and Excise); *b* 26 Sept. 1952; *s* of George and Betty Eland; *m* 1981, Luned Rhiannon Wynn Jones; one *s* one *d*. *Educ:* Worksop Coll.; Trinity Coll., Oxford (BA Jurisp, MA). Called to the Bar, Middle Temple, 1975. Administration Trainee, HM Customs and Excise, 1975; Private Sec. to Chm., 1979–81; Cabinet Office, 1982–87; Private Sec. to Lord President of the Council (Viscount Whitelaw), 1987–88; Asst. Sec., 1988–92, Comr, 1992–97, HM Customs and Excise; Dep. Dir-Gen., Policy, Immigration and Nationality Directorate, Home Office, 1997–2000; HM Customs and Excise: Dir Gen., Business Services and Taxes, 2000–03; Actg Chm., 2003–04. *Recreations:* walking, theatre. *Address:* HM Revenue and Customs, 100 Parliament Street, SW1A 2BQ.

ElBARADEI, Dr Mohamed Mostafa; Director General, International Atomic Energy Agency, since 1997; *b* Egypt, 17 June 1942; *s* of Mostafa and Aida ElBaradei; *m* 1975, Aida ElKachef; one *s* one *d*. *Educ:* Cairo Univ. Sch. of Law (Licence en droit 1962; Dip. Advanced Studies, Admin. Law, 1964); NY Univ. Sch. of Law (LLM 1971; JSD Internat. Law 1974). Dept of Internat. Orgns, Min. of Foreign Affairs, Egypt, 1964–67; Perm. Mission of Egypt to UN, NY, 1967–71; Sen. Fellow, Center for Internat. Studies, NY Univ., 1973–74; Special Asst to Foreign Minister, Min. of Foreign Affairs, Egypt, 1974–78; Perm. Mission of Egypt to UN, Geneva, and Alternate Rep., Cttee on Disarmament, 1978–80; Sen. Fellow and Dir, Internat. Law and Orgns Prog., UN Inst. for Trng and Res., NY, 1980–84; International Atomic Energy Agency: Rep. of Dir Gen. to UN, NY, 1984–87; Dir, Legal Div. and Legal Advr, Vienna, 1987–91; Dir, Ext. Relns, Vienna, 1991–93; Asst Dir Gen. for Ext Relns, 1993–97. Adjunct Prof. of Internat. Law, NY Univ. Sch. of Law, 1981–87. Rep. of Egypt or IAEA, to UN Gen. Assembly, UN Security Council, Cttee on Disarmament, Rev. Confs of Treaty on Non-Proliferation of Nuclear Weapons, OAU, UNDP, ILO and WHO. Has lectured widely on internat. law and orgns, arms control and non-proliferation and peaceful uses of nuclear energy. Nobel Peace Prize (jtly), 2005. *Publications:* The Right of Innocent Passage through Straits, 1974; (jtly) The International Law Commission: the need for a new direction, 1981; (jtly) Crowded Agendas, Crowded Rooms, 1981; Model Rules for Disaster Relief Operations, 1982; (jtly) The International Law of Nuclear Energy, 1993; contribs to NY Univ. Jl of Internat. Law and Politics, Leiden Jl of Internat. Law, etc. *Address:* International Atomic Energy Agency, Wagramerstrasse 5, PO Box 100, 1400 Vienna, Austria.

ELBORN, Peter Leonard, OBE 1990; Regional Director, East and Central Africa, and Director, Kenya, British Council, 2000–04; *b* 11 June 1945; *s* of Leonard and Joyce Elborn; *m* 1997, Sue Unsworth; three *s*. *Educ:* UC, Swansea (BA). British Council: Mexico, 1970–74; Croatia/Slovenia, 1977–82; Iraq, 1987–91; Zimbabwe, 1991–94; Kenya, 2000–04. Mem. Bd, Cultural Co-operation, 1998– (Chm., 2004–). FRSA 1998. *Recreations:* walking, swimming, reading. *Address:* 5 Well Road, NW3 1LH. *T:* (020) 7431 3179; *e-mail:* plelborn@yahoo.co.uk.

ELCOAT, Dame Catherine Elizabeth, DBE 2002; Director of Nursing and Patient Care, East Midlands Strategic Health Authority, since 2006; *b* 26 Feb. 1954; *d* of Derrick and Johanna Goulding; *m* 1975, Richard Thomas Elcoat. *Educ:* Birmingham Univ. (MScSoc); Darlington Meml Hosp. (RGN); Univ. of Teesside (DipHV). Student Nurse, 1972–75; North Tees Hospital: Staff Nurse, 1975–77; Ward Sister, 1977–82; Clinical Nurse Specialist, 1982–87; Health Visitor, 1987–90; Quality Manager, Darlington Meml Hosp., 1990–93; Exec. Dir of Nursing and Quality, S Durham Healthcare NHS Trust, 1993–96; Nursing Officer, NHS Exec., Leeds, 1996–97; Exec. Nurse Dir, City Hosp., Birmingham, 1997–99; Dep. Hd, NHS Clinical Governance Team, 1999–2001; Exec. Chief Nurse, Univ. Hosp. Birmingham NHS Trust, 2001–06. Nat. Clinical Advr, Health Care Commn, 2005–07. Mem., NHS Reconfiguration Panel, 2004–05. Special Prof., Univ. of Nottingham. *Publications:* Stoma Care Nursing, 1986, rev. edn 2003; contribs to various nursing, medical and professional jls. *Recreations:* egg decoration in the style of Fabergé, millinery, Feng Shui, craft work.

ELDER, Baron *cr* 1999 (Life Peer), of Kirkcaldy in Fife; **Thomas Murray Elder.** *Educ:* Kirkcaldy High Sch.; Edinburgh Univ. Bank of England, 1972–80; Res. Asst to Shadow Trade and Industry Sec., 1980–84; Gen. Sec., Scottish Labour Party, 1988–92; Chief of Staff to Leader of Labour Party, 1992–94; Political Advr to Leader of Labour Party, 1994; Special Advr, Scottish Office, 1997–99. Contested (Lab) Ross, Cromarty & Skye, 1983. *Address:* House of Lords, SW1A 0PW.

ELDER, Dorothy-Grace; political columnist, Scottish Daily Express, since 2002; *m* George Welsh; one *s* two *d*. Journalist; former campaigning columnist, Scotland on Sunday. MSP, Glasgow, 1999–2003 (SNP 1999–2002, Ind. 2002–03). Hon. Prof., Robert Gordon Univ., Aberdeen, 2006–, lectrg (pt-time) on investigative journalism. Oliver Brown Award, Scots Independent, 1995; UK Reporter of the Year, UK Press Awards, 1996. *Address: e-mail:* dg.elder@ntlworld.com.

ELDER, Sir Mark (Philip), Kt 2008; CBE 1989; conductor; Music Director, Hallé Orchestra, since 2000 (Music Director-Designate, 1999–2000); *b* 2 June 1947; *s* of John and late Helen Elder; *m* 1980, Amanda Jane Stein; one *d*. *Educ:* Bryanston Sch.; Corpus Christi Coll., Cambridge (Music Scholar, Choral Scholar; BA, MA). Music staff, Wexford Festival, 1969–70; Chorus Master and Asst Conductor, Glyndebourne, 1970–71; music staff, Covent Garden, 1970–72; Staff Conductor, Australian Opera, 1972–74; Staff Conductor, ENO, 1974, Associate Conductor, 1977, Music Dir, 1979–93; Music Dir, Rochester Philharmonic Orch., USA, 1989–94. Principal Guest Conductor: London Mozart Players, 1980–83; BBC Symphony Orchestra, 1982–85; CBSO, 1992–95. *Publication:* (with Peter Jonas and David Pountney) Power House, 1992. *Address:* c/o Ingpen and Williams Ltd, 7 St George's Court, 131 Putney Bridge Road, SW15 2PA.

ELDER, Prof. Murdoch George, MD, DSc; FRCS, FRCOG; Professor of Obstetrics and Gynaecology, University of London, at Institute of Obstetrics and Gynaecology, Royal Postgraduate Medical School, 1978–98, now Hon. Fellow and Professor Emeritus, Imperial College School of Medicine; Chairman, Division of Paediatrics, Obstetrics and Gynaecology, Imperial College School of Medicine, 1996–98; *b* 4 Jan. 1938; *s* of late Archibald James and Lotta Annie Elder; *m* 1964, Margaret Adelaide McVicker; two *s*. *Educ:* Edinburgh Acad.; Edinburgh Univ. (MB ChB 1961, MD 1973). DSc London, 1994. FRCS 1968; FRCOG 1978. Junior posts, Edinburgh and Bristol, 1961–68; Lectr, Inst. of Obst. and Gyn. and Royal Univ. of Malta, 1968–71; Sen. Lectr and Reader, Charing Cross Hosp. Med. Sch., Univ. of London, 1971–78; Dean, Institute of Obstetrics and Gynaecology, RPMS, 1985–95. Green Armytage Scholarship, RCOG, 1976; WHO Travelling Scholarship, 1977; Dir, Clinical Res. Centre, WHO, 1980–94; Member: Steering Cttee on Contraception, WHO, 1980–86; WHO Scientific Ethics Res. Cttee, 1996–2005. Mem., Hammersmith and Queen Charlotte's Special Health Authy, 1982–90. Mem. Council, RPMS, 1979–97. Visiting Professor: UCLA, 1984, 1986 and 1997; Singapore Univ., 1987; Natal Univ., 1988. Ext Examr for DSc, PhD, Masters and MB, BS degrees of 19 univs in several countries. Silver Medal, Hellenic Obstetrical Soc., 1983; Bronze Medal, Helsinki Univ., 1996. Mem., Editl Bds, Jl of Obst. and Gyn. and Clinical Reproduction, 1985–98. *Publications:* Human Fertility Control, 1979; (ed) Preterm Labour, 1980; (ed) Reproduction, Obstetrics and Gynaecology, 1988; Preterm Labour, 1997; Obstetrics and Gynaecology, 2001; chapters in books and learned articles on biochemistry in reproduction and pre term labour, clinical obstetrics, gynaecology and contraception. *Recreations:* travel, golf, curling. *Address:* Easter Calzeat, Broughton, Biggar ML12 6HQ. *T:* (01899) 830359. *Club:* 1942.

ELDER, Air Vice-Marshal Ronald David, CBE 1991; Managing Director, RED Partners LLP, since 2007; *b* 27 May 1946; *m* Sue; one *s* one *d*. *Educ:* RAF Coll., Cranwell. Commissioned RAF pilot, 1968; jun. appts and RAF Staff Coll., to 1981; Central Tactics and Trials Orgn, 1981–86; Comdr No 20 Sqdn, Laarbruch, 1986–88; Stn Comdr, Tri-National Tornado Trng Estabt, RAF Cottesmore, 1988–90; RAF Comdr, Tabuk, Saudi Arabia, 1990–91; RCDS 1991; Policy Area, Central Staff, MoD, 1991–93; Dir of Airspace Policy, CAA, 1993–98; RAF retd, 1999. Hd, Licensing Standards Div., CAA, 2003–07. FRAeS 1997. *Recreations:* Real tennis, golf, ski-ing. *Address:* Cramond, Upper Warren Avenue, Caversham, Berks RG4 7EB. *Club:* Royal Air Force.

ELDERFIELD, Prof. Henry, PhD, ScD; FRS 2001; Professor of Ocean Geochemistry and Palaeochemistry, University of Cambridge, since 1999; Fellow, St Catharine's College, Cambridge, since 1984; *b* 25 April 1943; *s* of late Henry Elderfield and Rhoda May Elderfield (*née* Risbrough); *m* 1st, 1965, Brenda Pauline Holliday (marr. diss.); two *d*; 2nd, 1992, Marlene Wrankle. *Educ:* Sir William Turner's Sch., Coatham; Eston Grammar Sch.; Liverpool Univ. (BSc; PhD 1970); MA, ScD 1989, Cantab. Res. Fellow, Imperial Coll., London, 1968–69; Lectr, Univ. of Leeds, 1969–82; Asst Dir in Res., 1982–89, Reader, 1989–99, Univ. of Cambridge. Visiting Professor: Univ. of RI, 1977–78; MIT, 1988–89 (Fulbright Schol., 1988); Lady Davis Vis. Prof., Hebrew Univ., Jerusalem, 1992; Vis. Schol., Woods Hole Oceanographic Instn, 1982; Vis. Scientist, Columbia Univ., 2004. Fellow: Geochem. Soc., 2000; Eur. Assoc. for Geochem., 2000; Amer. Geophysical Union, 2001; Hon. Fellow, Eur. Union of Geoscis, 2001. Prestwich Medal, 1993, Lyall Medal, 2003, Geol Soc.; Plymouth Medal, 1998; Patterson Medal, Geochem. Soc., 2002;

Urey Medal, Eur. Assoc. for Geochem., 2007. *Publications:* numerous contribs to scientific jls. *Recreation:* walking. *Address:* Department of Earth Sciences, University of Cambridge, Downing Street, Cambridge CB2 3EQ. *T:* (01223) 333400; St Catharine's College, Cambridge CB2 1RL. *T:* (01223) 338300.
See also J. Elderfield.

ELDERFIELD, John, PhD; Chief Curator of Painting and Sculpture, Museum of Modern Art, New York, 2003–08, now Emeritus; *b* 25 April 1943; *s* of late Henry Elderfield and Rhoda May Elderfield (*née* Risbrough); *m* 1st, 1965, Joyce Davey (marr. diss.); two *s*; 2nd, 1989, Jill Elizabeth Moser (marr. diss.); 3rd, 2005, Jeanne Collins. *Educ:* Univ. of Manchester; Univ. of Leeds (BA 1966; MPhil 1970); Univ. of London (PhD 1975). Lectr in Hist. of Art, Winchester Sch. of Art, 1966–70; Harkness Fellow, Yale Univ., 1970–72; John Simon Guggenheim Meml Fellow, 1972–73; Lectr in Hist. of Art, Univ. of Leeds, 1973–75; Museum of Modern Art, New York: Curator of Painting and Sculpture, 1975–93; Dir, Dept of Drawings, 1980–93; Chief Curator at Large, 1993–2003; Dep. Dir for Curatorial Affairs, 1996–99. Adjunct Prof. of Fine Arts, Inst. of Fine Arts, NY Univ., 1994. Vis. Scholar, Getty Res. Inst., Calif, 2001; Vis. Fellow, Amer. Acad. at Rome, 2006. Editor, Studies in Modern Art, 1991–2008. Member, Board of Directors: Dedalus Foundn, NY, 1996–; Master Drawings Assoc., 2000–; Members Bd, Phillips Collection, Washington, 2000–. Hon. Mem., Proyecto Armando Reverón, Caracas, 2007–. Hon. DLit Leeds, 2006. Commandeur des Arts et Lettres (France), 2006 (Chevalier, 1989). *Publications:* Hugo Ball: the flight out of time, 1974, 2nd edn 1996; The Wild Beasts: Fauvism and its affinities, 1976; European Master Paintings from Swiss Collections: Post Impressionism to World War II, 1976; The Cut-outs of Henri Matisse, 1978; Matisse in the Collection of the Museum of Modern Art, 1978; The Modern Drawing, 1983; The Drawings of Henri Matisse, 1984; Kurt Schwitters, 1985; Morris Louis, 1986; The Drawings of Richard Diebenkorn, 1988; Helen Frankenthaler, 1988; (jtly) Matisse in Morocco, 1990; Henri Matisse: a retrospective, 1992; Pleasuring Painting: Matisse's feminine representations, 1995; (jtly) Howard Hodgkin: paintings, 1995; The Language of the Body: drawings by Pierre-Paul Prud'hon, 1996; (jtly) The Art of Richard Diebenkorn, 1997; (jtly) Bonnard, 1998; (jtly) Modern Starts, 1999; (jtly) Bridget Riley: reconnaissance, 2001; (jtly) Matisse-Picasso, 2002; Modern Painting and Sculpture: 1880 to the present, 2004; (jtly) Against the Grain, 2006; Manet's "The Execution of the Emperor Maximilian", 2006; Armando Reverón, 2007; Martin Puryear, 2007. *Address:* Museum of Modern Art, 11 West 53 Street, New York, NY 10019–5498, USA. *T:* (212) 7089550. *Club:* Century (New York).
See also H. Elderfield.

ELDERFIELD, Maurice; Chairman and Chief Executive, Berfield Associates Ltd, 1980–92; Chairman: Midland Industrial Leasing Ltd, 1979–90; Saga Ltd, 1979–90; Sheldon & Partners Ltd, 1981–91; *b* 10 April 1926; *s* of Henry Elderfield and Kathleen Maud Elderfield; *m* 1953, Audrey June (*née* Knight); one *s* three *d*. *Educ:* Southgate Grammar Sch. FCA. Fleet Air Arm, 1944–47. Thomson, Kingdom & Co., Chartered Accountants (qual. 1949), 1947–49; Personal Asst to Man. Dir, Forrestell, Land, Timber & Railway Co., 1949–57; Group Chief Accountant, Stephens Group, 1957–60; various posts, Segas, culminating in Board Mem. and Dir for Finance, 1960–73; Dir of Finance, Southern Water Authority, 1973–75; PO Board Mem. for Finance and Corporate Planning, 1975–76; Dir of Finance, Ferranti Ltd, 1977; Finance Mem., British Shipbuilders, 1977–80. Director: S. P. International Ltd, Hong Kong, 1987–90; PV Ltd, 1987–90. Chairman: Throgmorton Trust, 1972–84; Throgmorton Investment Management, 1981–84; Capital for Industry Ltd, 1980–84. *Club:* Gravetye Manor Country.

ELDON, 5th Earl of, *cr* 1821; **John Joseph Nicholas Scott;** Baron Eldon 1799; Viscount Encombe 1821; *b* 24 April 1937; *s* of 4th Earl of Eldon, GCVO, and Hon. Magdalen Fraser, OBE (*d* 1969), *d* of 16th Baron Lovat; *S* father, 1976; *m* 1961, Comtesse Claudine de Montjoye-Vaufrey et de la Roche, Vienna; one *s* two *d*. *Educ:* Ampleforth; Trinity Coll., Oxford. 2nd Lieut Scots Guards (National Service). Lieut AER. *Heir: s* Viscount Encombe, *qv*.

ELDON, David Gordon, GBS 2004; CBE 2005; Senior Adviser, PricewaterhouseCoopers, since 2005; Chairman, Hongkong and Shanghai Banking Corporation Ltd, 1999–2005; Director, HSBC Holdings plc, 1999–2005; *b* Inverness, 14 Oct. 1945; *s* of late Leslie Gordon Eldon and of Mary Forbes Eldon (*née* Smith); *m* 1975, Maria Margarita Gaus; two *s* one *d*. *Educ:* Duke of York's Royal Mil. Sch. Union Internat. Co., 1963–64; Commercial Banking Co. of Sydney, 1964–67; with British Bank of the Middle East, later HSBC Group, 1968–2005: Dist Manager, Mongkok, 1982–84; Dep. Man. Dir, Saudi British Bank, 1984–87; CEO, Malaysia, 1988–92; Exec. Dir, Internat., 1993–95; CEO, Hongkong and Shanghai Banking Corp., 1996–98. Chm., Hang Seng Bank Ltd, 1996–2005; Director: Swire Pacific Ltd, 1996–2005; MTR Corp. Ltd, 1999–2008; Eagle Asset Management Ltd, 2006–; China Central Properties Ltd, 2007–. Chairman: Hong Kong Gen. Chamber of Commerce, 2005–07; Dubai Internat. Financial Centre, 2006–; Noble Group, 2007–; Founding Mem., Seoul Internat. Business Adv. Council, 2001– (Chm., 2002–05); Special Advr, Korea Nat. Competitiveness Council, Office of the President. Member: Council, Hong Kong Trade Develt Council, 1996–2007; Internat. Council, Bretton Woods Cttee, 2006–; Adv. Bd, Unisys, 2006–; Capital Adequacy Review Tribunal, 2007–; Advr, Southern Capital Gp. Vice Patron, Community Chest. JP Hong Kong, 2000. FCIB 1986; FCIB (Hong Kong) 1995. Hon. DBA Hong Kong City Univ., 2003. Businessman of the Year, DHL and S China Morning Post, 2003. *Recreations:* sports, music, reading, travel. *Address:* 22 Floor, Princes Building, 10 Chater Road, Hong Kong. *Clubs:* Hong Kong, Hong Kong Jockey (Steward, 1996–2008; Dep. Chm., 2006–08; Hon. Steward, 2008–), China, Shek O Country (Hong Kong).

ELDON, Stewart Graham, CMG 1999; OBE 1991; HM Diplomatic Service; UK Permanent Representative, UK Delegation to NATO, since 2006; *b* 18 Sept. 1953; *s* of John Hodgson Eldon and Rose Helen (*née* Stinton); *m* 1978, Christine Mary Mason; one *s* one *d*. *Educ:* Pocklington Sch.; Christ's Coll., Cambridge (BA Electrical Scis 1974; MSc 1976; MA 1977). MIET (MIEE 2002). Joined HM Diplomatic Service, 1976: UK Mission to UN, NY, 1976; FCO, 1977; Third, later Second Sec., Bonn, 1978–82; First Sec., FCO, 1982; Private Sec. to Minister of State, 1983–86; First Sec., UK Mission to UN, NY, 1986–90; Asst Hd, ME Dept, FCO (also Dep. Crisis Manager, Gulf War), 1990–91; Counsellor, Eur. Secretariat, Cabinet Office, 1991–93; Fellow, Center for Internat. Affairs, Harvard Univ., 1993–94; Counsellor (Political), UK Delegn to NATO, Brussels, 1994–97; Dir (Confs), FCO, 1997–98; Ambassador and Dep. Perm. Rep., UK Mission to UN, NY, 1998–2002; Ambassador to Ireland, 2003–06. Vis. Fellow, Yale Univ., 2002. *Publications:* contrib. RIIA paper, to RIIA jl and to Internat. Peace Acad. pubns. *Recreations:* music, travel, science fiction, breaking computers. *Address:* c/o Foreign and Commonwealth Office, King Charles Street, SW1A 2AH. *Club:* Athenæum.

ELEY, Bridget Katharine C.; *see* Cracroft-Eley.

ELEY, Prof. Daniel Douglas, OBE 1961; ScD, PhD Cantab; MSc, PhD Manchester; FRS 1964; CChem, FRSC; Professor of Physical Chemistry, University of Nottingham, 1954–80, now Emeritus; Dean of Faculty of Pure Science, 1959–62; *b* 1 Oct. 1914; *s* of Daniel Eley and Fanny Allen Eley (*née* Ross); *m* 1942, Brenda May Williams, MA, MB BChir (Cantab) (*d* 1992), 2nd *d* of Benjamin and Sarah Williams, Skewen, Glam; one *s*. *Educ:* Christ's Coll., Finchley; Manchester Univ.; St John's Coll., Cambridge; Manchester Univ. (Woodiwiss Schol. 1933, Mercer Schol. 1934, Darbishire Fellow 1936, DSIR Ser Award 1937; PhD 1937); PhD 1940, ScD 1954, Cambridge. Bristol University: Lectr in Colloid Chemistry, 1945; Reader in Biophysical Chemistry, 1951. Leverhulme Emeritus Fellow, 1981. Lectures: Reilly, Univ. of Notre Dame (USA), 1950; Royal Aust. Chem Inst., 1967; Sir Jesse Boot Foundn, Nottingham Univ., 1955, 1981; Sir Eric Rideal, Soc of Chem. Industry, 1975. Mem. Council of Faraday Soc., 1951–54, 1960–63; Vice-Pres 1963–66. Corresp. Mem., Bavarian Acad. of Sciences, 1971. Meetings Sec., British Biophysical Soc., 1961–63, Hon. Sec., 1963–65, Hon. Mem., 1983. Scientific Assessor to Sub-Cttee on Coastal Pollutions, House of Commons Select Cttee on Science and Technology, 1967–68. Medal of Liège Univ., 1950. *Publications:* (ed) Adhesion, 1961; papers in Trans Faraday Soc., Proc. Royal Soc., Jl Chem. Soc., Biochem. Jl, etc. *Recreations:* hill walking, gardening, reading. *Address:* Brooklands, 35 Brookland Drive, Chilwell, Nottingham NG9 4BD; Chemistry Department, Nottingham University, University Park, Nottingham NG7 2RD.

ELFER, His Honour David Francis; QC 1981; a Circuit Judge, 1996–2000; *b* 15 July 1941; *s* of George and Joy Elfer; *m* 1968, Karin Ursula Strub; two *s*; *m* 1988, Alexandra Smith-Hughes; one *s*. *Educ:* St Bede's Coll., Manchester; Emmanuel Coll., Cambridge (MA). Called to the Bar, Inner Temple, 1964, Bencher, 1989; a Recorder, 1978–96. Bar Col rep. for W Circuit, 1987–89. *Recreation:* music. *Address:* c/o Circuit Office, Ros Court, 2 Southwark Bridge, SE1 9HS.

ELGIN, 11th Earl of, *cr* 1633, **AND KINCARDINE,** 15th Earl of, *cr* 1647; **Andrew Douglas Alexander Thomas Bruce,** KT 1981; CD 1981; JP; Lord Bruce of Kinloss 1604, Lord Bruce of Torry, 1647; Baron Elgin (UK), 1849; 37th Chief of the Name of Bruce; Lord-Lieutenant of Fife, 1987–99; late Scots Guards; Captain; Royal Company of Archers, HM Body Guard for Scotland; Hon. Colonel, Elgin Regiment, Canada; *b* 17 Feb. 1924; *e s* of 10th Earl of Elgin, KT, CMG, TD and Hon. Katherine Elizabeth Cochrane (DBE 1938) (*d* 1989), *er d* of 1st Baron Cochrane of Cults; *S* father, 1968; *m* 1959, Victoria, *o d* of Dudley Usher, MBE and Mrs Usher of Larach Bhan, Kilchrennan, Argyll; three *s* two *d*. *Educ:* Eton; Balliol College, Oxford (BA Hons, MA Hons). Served War of 1939–45 (wounded). Dir, Royal Highland and Agricultural Soc., 1973–75; Pres. Scottish Amicable Life Assurance Soc., 1975–94. Chm., Nat. Savings Cttee for Scotland 1972–78; Mem., Scottish Post Office Bd (formerly Scottish Postal Bd), 1980–96. Chm Scottish Money Management Assoc., 1981–95. Lord High Comr, Gen. Assembly of Church of Scotland, 1980–81. Regent, RCSE, 1997–. County Cadet Commandant, Fife 1952–65. Hon. Col, 153(H) Regt RCT(V), TAVR, 1976–86. JP 1951, DL 1955, Fife Grand Master Mason of Scotland, 1961–65. Brigade Pres. of the Boys' Brigade, 1966–85 Pres., Royal Caledonian Curling Club, 1968–69. Hon. LLD: Dundee, 1977; Glasgow 1983; Hon. DLitt St Mary's, Halifax, NS. Freeman: Bridgetown, Barbados; Regina; Port Elgin; Winnipeg; St Thomas, Ont; Moose Jaw. Order of Merit (Norway), 1994. *Heir:* Lord Bruce, *qv*. *Address:* Broomhall, Dunfermline KY11 3DU. *T:* (01383) 872222, *Fax* (01383) 872904; *e-mail:* lord.elgin@virgin.net. *Clubs:* Beefsteak, Caledonian, Pratt's; New (Edinburgh).
See also Hon. J. M. E. Bruce.

ELIAS, Gerard; QC 1984; a Recorder of the Crown Court, since 1984; *b* 19 Nov. 1944; *s* of late Leonard Elias and Patricia Elias, JP; *m* 1970, Elisabeth Kenyon; three *s*. *Educ:* Cardiff High School; Exeter University (LLB). Barrister; called to the Bar, Inner Temple 1968, Bencher, 1993; Wales and Chester Circuit (Circuit Treasurer, 1990–92; Leader 1993–95); Asst Comr, Boundary Commission for Wales, 1981–83, 1985–; Chancellor dio. of Swansea and Brecon, 1999–. Mem., Bar Council, 1985–89, 1993–95; Dir, Bar Mutual Insurance Fund, 1987–97. Governor and Mem. Council, Malvern Coll., 1988–96 Mem. Governing Body, Ch in Wales, 2000–. Chairman: Disciplinary Commn, ECB (formerly TCCB), 1996–; Glam CCC, 1998–2003 (Mem. Exec. Cttee, 1986–93; Dep Chm., 1993–98); Sport Resolutions UK, 2007–. Pres., Tribunal, Church in Wales, 2007–. *Recreations:* music, cricket. *Address:* 13 The Cathedral Green, Llandaff, Cardiff, South Glamorgan CF5 2EB. *T:* (029) 2057 8857. *Club:* Cardiff and County.
See also Hon. Sir P. Elias.

ELIAS, Hon. Sir Patrick, Kt 1999; **Hon. Mr Justice Elias;** a Judge of the High Court Queen's Bench Division, since 1999; President, Employment Appeal Tribunal, since 2006; *b* 28 March 1947; *s* of late Leonard and Patricia Mary Elias; *m* 1970, Wendy Kinnersley-Haddock; three *s* one *d*. *Educ:* Cardiff High Sch.; Univ. of Exeter (LLB 1969) King's Coll., Cambridge (MA; PhD 1973). Called to the Bar, Inner Temple, 1973 Bencher, 1995; QC 1990. Fellow of Pembroke Coll., Cambridge, 1973–84; Lectr, Univ of Cambridge, 1975–84. Hon. LLD: Exeter, 2001; City, 2003. *Publications:* (jtly) Labour Law: cases and materials, 1979; Editor, Harvey on Industrial Relations and Employment Law, 1976; (with Keith Ewing) Trade Union Democracy, Members' Rights and the Law 1987. *Recreations:* reading, music, cricket, Rugby. *Address:* Royal Courts of Justice, Strand WC2A 2LL.
See also G. Elias.

ELIAS, Rt Hon. Dame Sian, GNZM 1999; PC 1999; Chief Justice of New Zealand since 1999; *b* 12 March 1949; *m* 1970, Hugh Alasdair Fletcher, *qv*; two *s*. *Educ:* Diocesan High Sch. for Girls; Auckland Univ. (LLB Hons 1972); Stanford Univ., Calif (JSM 1972) Admitted to Bar of NZ, 1970; Tutor, Law Sch., Univ. of Auckland, 1970; solicitor 1972–75; Barrister, 1975–95; QC 1988; Judge of the High Court of NZ, 1995. Mem. NZ Law Commn, 1985–89. Commemoration Medal (NZ), 1990. *Recreations:* chess piano. *Address:* Chief Justice's Chambers, High Court, PO Box 1091, Wellington, New Zealand. *T:* (4) 9143641. *Clubs:* Northern (Auckland); Wellington (Wellington).

ELIASSEN, Kjell, Hon. GCMG 1981; Commander with Star, Royal Order of Saint Olav 1982; Norwegian Ambassador to Germany, 1994–98; *b* 18 Aug. 1929; *s* of Carl August Eliassen and Bergljot (*née* Store); *m* 1953, Vesla Skretting; one *s* one *d*. *Educ:* Oslo Univ (law degree). Entered Norwegian Foreign Service 1953; served Belgrade, Moscow London; Counsellor, Min. of Foreign Affairs, 1963–67; Moscow, 1967–70; Dep. Dir Gen., Min. of Foreign Affairs, 1970–72; Dir-Gen., 1972–77; Ambassador to Yugoslavia 1977–80; Perm. Under-Sec., Min. of Foreign Affairs, 1980–84; Ambassador: to USA 1984–89; to UK, 1989–94. Numerous foreign decorations. *Address:* Generallunden 21 0381 Oslo, Norway.

ELIASSON, Jan; Special Envoy of UN Secretary General for Darfur, since 2006; *b* Göteborg, 1940; *m* 1967, Kerstin Englesson; one *s* two *d*. *Educ:* Swedish Naval Acad.; Sch of Econs, Göteborg (MEcons 1965). Harare, 1980; Diplomatic Advr to Swedish Prime Minister, 1982–83; Dir Gen. for Pol Affairs, Min. for For. Affairs, 1983–87; Swedish Ambassador to the UN, NY, 1988–92; UN Under-Sec.-Gen. for Humanitarian Affairs

1992; State Sec. for For. Affairs, 1994–2000; Swedish Ambassador to the USA, 2000–05; Foreign Minister, Sweden, 2006. Chm., UN Trust Fund for S Africa, 1988–92; Chm., working gp on emergency relief, 1991, Pres., 2005–06, UN Gen. Assembly; Vice Pres., ECOSOC, 1991–92. Vis. Prof., Uppsala Univ., 2006– Hon. Dr: American Univ., Washington, 1994; Göteborg, 2001; Bethany Coll., Kansas, 2005; Uppsala, 2006. *Address:* Ministry of Foreign Affairs, Gustav Adolfstorg 1, 10339 Stockholm, Sweden.

ELIBANK, 14th Lord *cr* 1643 (Scotland); **Alan D'Ardis Erskine-Murray;** Bt (Nova Scotia) 1628; personnel consultant; Deminex UK Oil and Gas, 1981–86; *b* 31 Dec. 1923; *s* of Robert Alan Erskine-Murray (*d* 1939) and Eileen Mary (*d* 1970), *d* of late John Percy MacManus; *S* cousin, 1973; *m* 1962, Valerie Sylvia (*d* 1997), *d* of late Herbert William Dennis; two *s*. *Educ:* Bedford Sch.; Peterhouse, Cambridge (MA Law). Barrister-at-Law. RE, 1942–47; Cambridge Univ., 1947–49; Practising Barrister, 1949–55; Shell International Petroleum Co., 1955–80. *Recreations:* golf, tennis. *Heir: s* Master of Elibank, *qv*. *Clubs:* Sloane, MCC.

ELIBANK, Master of; Hon. Robert Francis Alan Erskine-Murray; *b* 10 Oct. 1964; *s* and *heir* of 14th Lord Elibank, *qv*; *m* 1996, Antonia, *yr d* of Roger Carrington; two *d*. *Educ:* The Grove, Harrow School; Reading Univ. (BA (Hons) History and Politics, 1987). *Recreations:* golf, tennis.

ELIOT, family name of **Earl of St Germans**.

ELIOT, Lord; Albert Charger Eliot; *b* 2 Nov. 2004; *s* of Jago Nicholas Aldo Eliot, (Lord Eliot) (*d* 2006) and of Bianca Eliot (*née* Ciambriello); *g s* and *heir* of Earl of St Germans, *qv*.

ELIOT, Simon Flowerdew, MA; Headmaster, Sherborne School, since 2000; *b* 20 July 1952; *s* of late Geoffrey Philip Eliot and Margery Hope Eliot-Sutton; *m* 1983, Olivia Margaret Cicely Roberts; one *s* one *d*. *Educ:* Radley Coll.; Queens' Coll., Cambridge (MA). Sedgwick Forbes (Marine), 1974–75; Asst Master, Radley Coll., 1975–76; Winchester College: Asst Master, 1976–2000; Housemaster, 1988–2000. *Recreations:* history, theatre, music, horse racing. *Address:* Abbey Grange, Hospital Road, Sherborne, Dorset DT9 3JF. *T:* (01935) 810410.

ELIOTT of Stobs, Sir Charles (Joseph Alexander), 12th Bt *cr* 1666 (NS); *b* 9 Jan. 1937; *s* of Charles Rawdon Heathfield Eliott (*d* 1972) and Emma Elizabeth Harris (*d* 1999); *S* cousin, 1989; *m* 1959 (marr. diss. 1996); one *s* four *d* (and one *s* decd). *Educ:* St Joseph's Christian Brothers' College, Rockhampton. *Heir: s* Rodney Gilbert Charles Eliott [*b* 15 July 1966; *m* 1988 (marr. diss. 1998); one *s* two *d*]. *Address:* PO Box 402, Longreach, Qld 4730, Australia.

ELIS-THOMAS, family name of **Baron Elis-Thomas**.

ELIS-THOMAS, Baron *cr* 1992 (Life Peer), of Nant Conwy in the County of Gwynedd; **Dafydd Elis Elis-Thomas,** PC 2004; Member (Plaid Cymru) Dwyfor Meirionnydd, since 2007 (Meirionnydd Nant Conwy, 1999–2007) and Presiding Officer, since 1999, National Assembly for Wales; *b* 18 Oct. 1946; name changed from Thomas to Elis-Thomas by deed poll, 1992; *m* 1st, 1970, Elen M. Williams (marr. diss.); three *s*; 2nd, 1993, Mair Parry Jones. *Educ:* Ysgol Dyffryn Conwy; UC North Wales. Research worker, Bd of Celtic Studies, 1970; Tutor in Welsh Studies, Coleg Harlech, 1971; Lectr, Dept of English, UC North Wales, 1974. MP (Plaid Cymru) Merioneth, Feb. 1974–1983, Merionnydd Nant Conwy, 1983–92. Pres., Plaid Cymru, 1984–91. Mem., Arts Council for Wales; Chairman: Welsh Lang. Bd, 1993–99; Screen Wales; a Gov., BFI, 1997–2000. Part-time freelance broadcaster, BBC Wales, HTV, 1970–73; has also broadcast on S4C and Radio Wales. Pres., Univ. of Wales, Bangor, 2001–. Mem., Church in Wales. *Recreations:* hill walking, running, arts, Welsh literature. *Address:* 7 Bank Place, Porthmadog, Gwynedd LL49 9AA. *T:* (01766) 515028.

ELKAN, Prof. Walter; Professor of Economics, and Head of Economics Department, Brunel University, 1978–88, now Emeritus Professor; *b* Hamburg, 1 March 1923; *s* of Hans Septimus Elkan and Maud Emily (*née* Barden); *m* Susan Dorothea (*née* Jacobs) (marr. diss. 1982); one *s* two *d*. *Educ:* Frensham Heights; London Sch. of Economics. BSc (Econ), PhD. Army, 1942–47; Research Asst, LSE, 1950–53; Sen. Res. Fellow, E African Inst. of Social Research, 1954–58; Vis. Res. Assoc., MIT and Lectr, N Western Univ., 1958; Lectr in Econs, Makerere UC, 1958–60; Lectr in Econs, Durham Univ., 1960; Prof. of Econs, 1966–78, and rotating Head of Dept, 1968–78, Durham Univ. Vis. Res. Prof., Nairobi Univ., 1972–73. Member: Council, Overseas Develt Inst., 1978–2001; Econ. and Social Cttee, EEC, 1982–86; Bd of Management, Sch. of Hygiene and Trop. Med., 1982–86; Econ. and Social Cttee for Overseas Res., 1977–92; Associate, Inst. of Development Studies. Former Pres., African Studies Assoc.; former Member: Northern Economic Planning Council; REconS. Sometime consultant to Govts of Basutoland, Mauritius, Solomon Is, Fiji, Kenya and others. *Publications:* An African Labour Force, 1956; Migrants and Proletarians, 1960; Economic Development of Uganda, 1961; Introduction to Development Economics, 1973, 2nd edn 1995; articles mainly on contemp. African econ. history in econ. and other social science jls; ILO, UNESCO, IBRD and British Govt reports. *Recreation:* music. *Address:* 98 Boundary Road, NW8 0RH. *T:* (020) 7624 5102.

ELKES, Prof. Joel, MD, ChB; FACP, FAPA; psychiatrist and pharmacologist; Distinguished Service Professor Emeritus, The Johns Hopkins University, since 1975; Distinguished University Professor Emeritus, University of Louisville; Founding Fellow, 1989 and Senior Scholar-in-Residence, since 1993, Fetzer Institute, Kalamazoo; *b* 12 Nov. 1913; *s* of Dr Elchanan Elkes and Miriam (*née* Malbin); *m* 1st, 1943, Dr Charmian Bourne; one *d*; 2nd, 1975, Josephine Rhodes, MA; 3rd, 2001, Sally Ruth Lucke. *Educ:* private schools; Lithuania and Switzerland; St Mary's Hosp., London; Univ. of Birmingham Med. Sch. (MB, ChB 1947; MD Hons 1949). University of Birmingham: Sir Halley Stewart Research Fellow, 1942–45; Lectr, Dept of Pharmacology, 1945–48; Senior Lectr and Actg Head of Dept, 1948–50; Prof. and Chm., Dept of Experimental Psychiatry, 1951–57 (first dept of its kind in the world); Clinical Professor of Psychiatry, George Washington Univ. Med. Sch., Washington, 1957–63; Chief of Clinical Neuropharmacology Research Center, Nat. Inst. of Mental Health, Washington, 1957–63; Dir, Behavioral and Clinical Studies Center St Elizabeth's Hosp., Washington, 1957–63; Henry Phipps Prof. and Dir, Dept of Psychiatry and Behavioural Scis, Johns Hopkins Univ. Sch. of Medicine, and Psychiatrist-in-Chief, Johns Hopkins Hosp., 1963–74; Samuel McLaughlin Prof.-in-residence, McMaster Univ., 1975; Professor of Psychiatry: McMaster Univ., 1976–80; Univ. of Louisville, 1980–84 (Director: Div. of Behavioral Medicine, 1982; Arts in Medicine Prog.). Dir, Foundns Fund for Research in Psychiatry, 1964–68; Consultant, WHO, 1957. Vis. Fellow, New York Univ. and New England Med. Center, Boston, 1950; Benjamin Franklin Fellow, RSA, 1974. Lectures: Harvey, 1962; Salmon, 1963; Jacob Bronowski Meml, 1978, etc. President: (first) Amer. Coll. of Neuropsychopharmacology, 1962; Amer. Psychopathological Assoc., 1968; Chairman: Bd, Israel Inst. of Psychobiol., 1961–2004; Foundns Fund Prize Bd for Res. in Psychiatry, 1977–81; Board Member: Inst. for Advancement of Health, 1982; Govs, Hebrew Univ. of Jerusalem; Govs, Haifa Univ. Formerly Member: Council, Internat. Collegium N Psychopharm; Central Council, Internat. Brain Research Organisation, UNESCO (Chm., Sub-Cttee on Educn); RSM. (One-man show) In Praise of Trees, Selby Mus., Sarasota, Fla, 2008. Life Fellow, Amer. Psych. Assoc.; Charter Fellow, RCPsych, GB; Fellow: Amer. Acad. of Arts and Scis; Amer. Coll. of Psychiatry; Amer. Coll. of Neuropsychopharmacol (Joel Elkes Internat. Award estab. 1986); Amer. Acad. of Behavioral Medicine Res. and Soc. of Behavioral Medicine; Fetzer Inst., 1990; Fellow and Mem. Exec. Cttee, World Acad. of Art and Sci., 1985; Former Member: Physiological Soc., GB; Pharmacological Soc., GB; Amer. Soc. for Pharmacology and Experimental Therapeutics; Sigma Xi; Scientific Assoc.; Acad. of Psychoanalysis. Hon. DPhil Hebrew Univ. of Jerusalem, 1989. Hans Selye Internat. Award, 1994; (jtly) First Internat. Pioneer Award in Psychopharmacology, Glasgow Congress, 1998; Lifetime-Achievement Award, Louisville Cathedral Heritage Foundn, 2000. Two internat. symposia in his honour, 1984, 1985; Joel Elkes Res. Labs, Dept of Psychiatry, Johns Hopkins Univ., dedicated 1989; Elkes Cottage, Fetzer Inst., dedicated 1998. *Publications:* papers to various jls and symposia. *Recreation:* painting. *Address:* Fetzer Institute, 9292 WKL Avenue, Kalamazoo, MI 49009, USA. *Club:* Cosmos (Washington).

ELKIN, Sonia Irene Linda, OBE 1981 (MBE 1966); Director for Regions and Smaller Firms, Confederation of British Industry, 1985–92; *b* 15 May 1932; *d* of Godfrey Albert Elkin and Irene Jessamine Archibald. *Educ:* Beresford House Sch., Eastbourne. Association of British Chambers of Commerce, 1950–66; Lloyds Bank Overseas Dept, 1966–67; Confederation of British Industry, 1967–92. Commissioner, Manpower Services Commission, 1982–85. Non-executive Director: Greggs plc, 1992–2004; Kall Kwik Printing (UK), 1993–95. *Publications:* What about Europe?, 1967; What about Europe Now?, 1971. *Club:* Oxford and Cambridge (Lady Associate).

ELKINGTON, Prof. Andrew Robert, CBE 1996; FRCS; FRCOphth; Professor of Ophthalmology, University of Southampton, 1990–98, now Emeritus; Consultant Ophthalmic Surgeon, Southampton General Hospital, 1974–98; *b* 12 Dec. 1935; *s* of late Dr George Ernest Elkington, MC, FRCS, Newport, Salop and Kathleen Mary Elkington (*née* Budgen); *m* 1964, Patricia Kathleen Wright, *er d* of late R. M. Wright, MC and Bar and Joan Wright; four *s*. *Educ:* Repton Sch., Derbys; Clare Coll., Cambridge (MA); St Thomas' Hosp. (BChir, MB). FRCS 1969; FRCOphth 1988 (Hon. FRCOphth 1999); DRCOG 1965; DO 1968. Moorfields Eye Hospital: Hse Surgeon and Sen. Resident Officer, 1967–70; Chief Clinical Asst, 1970–74; Sen. Registrar in Ophthalmol., Westminster Hosp., 1970–74. European Vis. Prof., RSocMed, 1992–93. Examnr, DO, 1977–83 (Chm., Examng Bd, 1981–83); Mem., Ct of Examnrs (Ophthalmol.), RCS, 1984–89 (Chm., 1988–89); Ext. Examnr, RCPSG (Ophthalmol.), 1984–89; Examnr in ophthalmol., Univs. of Glasgow, 1991, Leicester, 1992, Bristol, 1987, London, 1988, Nottingham, 1993; Examnr to Ophthalmic Nursing Bd, 1980–98. Section of Ophthalmology, Royal Society of Medicine: Mem. Council, 1980–92; Hon. Sec., 1980–83; Vice Pres., 1983–86; Pres., 1990–92; Faculty of Ophthalmologists, subseq. Royal College of Ophthalmologists: Mem. Council, 1985–88; Hon. Sec., 1986–91; Vice-Pres., 1991–94; Pres., 1994–97; Ophthalmological Society of UK: Mem. Council, 1979–82; Vice Pres., 1987–88; Pres., British and Irish Orthoptic Soc., 2002–. Member: Council, RCS, 1994–96; GMC, 1994–98 (Mem., Educn Cttee, 1994–98). Chm., British Council for Prevention of Blindness, 2000–; Member: Council, Oxford Ophthalmol. Congress, 1982–98; Senate, Royal Surgical Colls, 1994–96; Conf. and Scottish Conf. of Med. Royal Colls and their Faculties, 1994–96; Standing Med. Adv. Cttee, 1994–97. Govt of Hong Kong Commnd Trainer in ophthalmol., 1991. Mem., Bd of Govs, Moorfields Eye Hosp., 1988–94. *Publications:* (jtly) Clinical Optics, 1984, 3rd edn 1999; Ophthalmology for Nurses, 1986; ABC of Eyes, 1988, 4th edn 2004; Aids to Ophthalmology, 1989; contribs on trauma, glaucoma and retinal detachment to ophthalmic jls. *Recreations:* wildlife, tending vegetables. *Club:* Travellers.

ELKINGTON, John Brett; environmentalist, entrepreneur, consultant, author, speaker; Co-Founder and Director, SustainAbility Ltd, since 1987 (Chairman, 1996–2006; Chief Entrepreneur, 2006–08); Founding Partner and Director, Volans Ventures Ltd, since 2008; *b* Padworth, Berks, 23 June 1949; *s* of John Francis Durham, (Tim), Elkington and Patricia Elkington; *m* 1973, Elaine Waite; two *d*. *Educ:* various schs in England, NI and Cyprus; Glencot Prep. Sch., Wookey Hole; Bryanston Sch.; Univ. of Essex (BA Hons 1970); University Coll. London (MPhil 1974). Associate and Sen. Planner, Transport and Envmt Studies, 1974–78; Environmental Data Services Ltd, 1978–83, Man. Dir, 1981–83, Editor, ENDS Report, 1981–83; Editor, Biotechnology Bulletin, 1983–98; Founder Dir, John Elkington Associates, 1983–. Chairman: Envmt Foundn, 1995–; Adv. Council, Export Credits Guarantee Dept, 2005–07; Member: EU Consultative Forum on the Envmt and Sustainable Develt, 1994–2001; Faculty, World Econ. Forum, 2002–; WWF-UK Council of Ambassadors, 2006–. Vis. Prof., Doughty Centre for Corporate Responsibility, Sch. of Mgt, Cranfield Univ., 2007–. Chm. Bd, Envmt Faculty, Herning Inst. of Business Admin and Technol., Denmark, 1995–98. Hon. Fellow, The Hub, 2008. FRSA. *Publications:* The Ecology of Tomorrow's World, 1980; Sun Traps: the renewable energy forecast, 1984; The Gene Factory, 1985; The Poisoned Womb, 1985; (with T. Burke) The Green Capitalists, 1987; (with J. Hailes and T. Burke) Green Pages: the business of saving the world, 1988; A Year in the Greenhouse, 1990; (with J. Hailes and P. Knight) The Green Business Guide: how to take up – and profit from – the environmental challenge, 1991; Cannibals with Forks: the triple bottom line of 21st century business, 1997; The Chrysalis Economy: how citizen CEOs and corporations can fuse values and value creation, 2001; (with P. Hartigan) The Power of Unreasonable People: how social entrepreneurs create markets that change the world, 2008; with Julia Hailes: The Green Consumer Guide: from shampoo to champagne, 1988; The Green Consumer's Supermarket Shopping Guide, 1989; The Young Green Consumer's Guide, 1990; Holidays That Don't Cost the Earth, 1992; Manual 2000: life choices for the future you want, 1998; The New Foods Guide: what's here, what's coming, what it means for us, 1999; author or jt author of over 40 reports; columnist for various pubns incl. China Dialogue, Director Mag., Época Negócios and Nikkei Ecology. *Recreations:* playing with ideas, thinking around corners, conversations with unreasonable people, reading an Alpine range of books (history to science fiction) and US business and science magazines, risking life and limb as a London cyclist, catch-it-as-you-can photography, art and design, writing all hours, pre-1944 aircraft, New World wines, 20th century popular music—and Johann Strauss II. *Address: e-mail:* johnelkington@mac.com, john@volans.com; *web:* www.johnelkington.com.

ELLACOMBE, Air Cdre John Lawrence Wemyss, CB 1970; DFC 1942 (Bar 1944); FCMI; *b* Livingstone, N Rhodesia, 28 Feb. 1920; *s* of Dr Gilbert H. W. Ellacombe; *m* 1951, Wing Officer Mary Hibbert, OBE, WRAF (*d* 2007); one *s* two *d*. *Educ:* Diocesan Coll., Rondebosch, Cape. War of 1939–45: RAF, 1939; Fighter Comd and Two ATA Force, 1940–45 (Pilot, Battle of Britain). Aden, 1946–48; RAF Staff Coll., 1948–49; Fighter Command, 1949–57; BJSM, Washington, 1959. JSSC, 1959–60; Gp Captain, CO RAF Linton on Ouse, to Nov. 1962; CFE, to Aug. 1965; Defence Operational Analysis Estabt, West Byfleet, 1965–68; Air Cdre, Commander Air Forces Gulf, 1968–70; Dir of Ops (Air Defence and Overseas), MoD (Air), 1970–73; St Thomas' Hospital: Dir,

Scientific Services, 1973–80; Administrator to Special Trustees, 1980–85. *Recreations:* photography, golf, cricket. *Address:* 33 The Drive, Northwood, Middlesex HA6 1HW. *Club:* Royal Air Force.

ELLAM, Michael James; Director of Communications and Prime Minister's Spokesman, Prime Minister's Office, since 2007; *b* London, 4 Oct. 1968; *s* of Brian and Kathleen Ellam; *m* 1995, Karina Saroukhanian; one *s* one *d*. *Educ:* Forest Hill Sch. for Boys; Peterhouse, Cambridge (BA 1990); London Sch. of Econs (MSc Econ 1991). Economist: Credit Suisse First Boston, 1992–93; HM Treasury, 1993–94; Pvte Sec. to Chancellor of the Exchequer, 1994–96; First Sec. (Econ.), Beijing, 1996–98; HM Treasury: Economist, EMU Policy Team, 1998–2000; Head: Debt and Reserves Mgt Team, 2000; Communications, 2000–03; Perf. and Efficiency Team, Public Services Directorate, 2004; Dir of Policy and Planning, 2004–07. *Recreations:* family, cinema, golf, watching football. *Address:* Prime Minister's Office, 10 Downing Street, SW1A 2AA. *Club:* West Ham United.

ELLAM, Prof. Robert Mark, PhD; Professor of Isotope Geochemistry, University of Glasgow, and Director of Research, Scottish Universities Environmental Research Centre, since 2007; *b* Shipley, W Yorks, 15 April 1962; *s* of Derek Ellam and Margaret Ellam (*née* Thomas); *m* 1985, Elspeth Rowena Wood; one *s* one *d*. *Educ:* Imperial Coll. London (BSc 1983); Open Univ. (PhD 1987). ARSM 1983. Post Doctoral Res. Asst, Univ. of Oxford, 1987–89; Lectr, 1990–2000, Reader, 2000–06, Univ. of Glasgow. *Publications:* more than 80 articles in learned jls. *Recreations:* playing 5-string banjo (badly), trying to learn Italian, listening to Radio 4. *Address:* Scottish Universities Environmental Research Centre, Rankine Avenue, East Kilbride G75 0QF. *T:* (01355) 270130, *Fax:* (01355) 229898; *e-mail:* r.ellam@suerc.gla.ac.uk, rob.ellam@blueyonder.co.uk.

ELLEN, Eric Frank, QPM 1980; LLB; Chairman and Director, First Approach Ltd, since 1999; Board Member, International Chamber of Commerce Commercial Crime Services, 1999–2001 (Executive Director, 1994–99; First Director: International Maritime Bureau, 1981–99; Counterfeiting Intelligence Bureau, 1985–99; Commercial Crime Bureau, 1992–99; Regional Piracy Centre, Kuala Lumpur, 1992–99); *b* London, 30 Aug. 1930; *s* of late Robert Frank Ellen and of Jane Lydia Ellen; *m* 1949, Gwendoline Dorothy Perkins; one *s* one *d*. *Educ:* Wakefield Central Sch., East Ham; Holborn Coll. of Law, Univ. of London (LLB Hons, London Univ. Certificate in Criminology). CCMI (FBIM 1978). Joined PLA Police, 1951; Sgt 1956; Inspector 1961; Chief Insp. 1972; Supt and Chief Supt 1973; attended 11th Sen. Comd Course, Bramshill Police Coll., 1974; Dep. Chief Constable 1975; Chief Constable, 1975–80. Adviser on security to Ports Div. of Dept of Environment; advised Barbados Govt on formation of Barbados Port Authy Police Force, 1983; reviewed port security at Jeddah and Dammam. Sec., Internat. Assoc. of Airport and Seaport Police, 1980–88 (Pres., 1977–78 and 1978–79); Founder, Chm. and Life Mem., EEC Assoc. of Airport and Seaport Police, 1975–78; Chm., Panel on Maritime Fraud, Commonwealth Secretariat, 1982–90; Consultant, Commercial Crime Unit. Member: Internat. Assoc. of Ports and Harbours Standing Cttee on Legal Protection of Port Interests, 1977–79 (Chm., Sub-Cttee on Protection of Ports against Sabotage and Terrorism, 1977–79); Cttee of Conservative Lawyers, 1985–; Shipbrokers Cttee on Maritime Fraud; British Acad. of Forensic Sciences; Hon. Soc. of Middle Temple. Police Long Service and Good Conduct Medal, 1974. Freeman of the City of London, 1978. Police Medal Republic of China, 1979. *Publications:* (co-author) International Maritime Fraud, 1981; (ed) Violence at Sea, 2nd edn, 1987; (ed) Piracy at Sea, 1989; (ed) Ports at Risk, 1993; (ed) Shipping at Risk: the rising tide of organised crime, 1997; A Guide to the Prevention of Money Laundering, 1998; professional articles on marine fraud and counterfeiting, terrorism, piracy and port policing, money laundering and fraud in commerce (has lectured on these topics at seminars in over 50 countries). *Recreations:* golf, swimming. *Address:* 38 Tyle Green, Hornchurch, Essex RM11 2TB.

ELLEN, Prof. Roy Frank, PhD; FBA 2003; FLS; Professor of Anthropology and Human Ecology, University of Kent, since 1988; *b* 30 Jan. 1947; *s* of Gerald Frank Ellen and Nancy Eileen (*née* Childs); *m* 1978, Nicola Jane Goward; two *d*. *Educ:* LSE (BSc; PhD); Univ. of Leiden. Lectr, LSE, 1972–73; Lectr, 1973–80, Sen. Lectr, 1980–86, Reader, 1986–88, Univ. of Kent, Canterbury. Vis. Fellow, Netherlands Inst. for Adv. Study, 1984. President: Anthropol. and Archaeol. Section, BAAS, 2004–05; RAI, 2007–. Lectures: Curl, RAI, 1987; Munro, Univ. of Edinburgh, 1994; Stirling, Univ. of Kent, 2007. FLS 2001. *Publications:* Nuaulu Settlement and Ecology, 1978; (ed with P. H. Burnham) Social and Ecological Systems, 1979; (ed with D. Reason) Classifications in Their Social Context, 1979; (ed) Environment, Subsistence and System, 1982, 2nd edn 2002; (ed) Ethnographic Research, 1984; (ed jtly) Malinowski Between Two Worlds, 1988; The Cultural Relations of Classification, 1993; Nuaulu Ethnozoology, 1993; (ed with C. W. Watson) Understanding Witchcraft and Sorcery in Southeast Asia, 1993; (ed with K Fukui) Redefining Nature, 1996, 2nd edn 2002; (ed jtly) Indigenous Environmental Knowledge and its Transformations, 2002; On the Edge of the Banda Zone, 2003; The Categorical Impulse, 2006; (ed) Ethnobiology and the Science of Humankind, 2006; (ed) Modern Crises and Traditional Strategies: local ecological knowledge in Island Southeast Asia, 2007. *Address:* Department of Anthropology, University of Kent, Canterbury, Kent CT2 7NS. *T:* (01227) 823421, *Fax:* (01227) 827289; *e-mail:* R.F.Ellen@kent.ac.uk.

ELLEN, Susan Caroline; Chairman, West Middlesex University Hospital NHS Trust, since 2002; *b* 15 Dec. 1948; *d* of late Albert John Davies and of (Winnifred) Ivy (Caroline) (*née* Emberton); *m* 1974, Simon Tudor Ellen; two *d*. *Educ:* Cardiff High Sch.; Malvern Girls' Coll.; Bristol Univ. (BSc Politics and Sociol.); Dip HSM. With NHS, 1970–77; joined BUPA, 1977: Dir, 1990–95; Man. Dir, BUPA Health Services, 1990–95; Man. Dir, United Racecourses (Hldgs) Ltd, 1996–2002; Non-executive Director: Asda Gp plc, 1992–98; Birmingham Midshires Building Soc., 1996–2000; Portman Building Soc., 2001–07; Nationwide Bldg Soc., 2007–. Member: Financial Reporting Rev. Panel, 1992–98; Financial Reporting Council, 1995–96. *Recreations:* family, racing, the arts. *Address:* West Middlesex University Hospital, Twickenham Road, Isleworth, Middx TW7 6AF. *T:* (020) 8565 5030.

ELLENA, Rt Rev. Richard; *see* Nelson, Bishop of.

ELLENBOROUGH, 8th Baron *cr* 1802; **Richard Edward Cecil Law;** *b* 14 Jan. 1926; *s* of 7th Baron and Helen Dorothy, *o d* of late H. W. Lovatt; *S* father, 1945; *m* 1st, 1953, Rachel Mary (*d* 1986), *o d* of late Major Ivor Hedley; three *s*; 2nd, 1994, Mrs Frances Kimberley (*d* 2004). *Educ:* Eton Coll.; Magdalene Coll., Cambridge. Partner, McAnally Montgomery, stockbrokers, 1969–78. Director: Towry Law & Co., 1958–96; Towry Law Gp, 1958–96. Pres., Nat. Union of Ratepayers' Associations, 1960–90. *Heir: s* Major the Hon. Rupert Edward Henry Law, Coldstream Guards, retd [*b* 28 March 1955; *m* 1981, Hon. Grania, *d* of Baron Boardman, MC, TD; two *s* one *d*]. *Address:* Withypool House, Observatory Close, Church Road, Crowborough, East Sussex TN6 1BN. *T:* (01892) 663139. *Club:* Turf.

ELLERAY, Anthony John; QC 1993; a Recorder, since 1999; *b* 19 Aug. 1954; *s* of late Alexander John Elleray and of Sheila Mary Elleray (*née* Perkins); *m* 1982, Alison Elizabeth Potter; one *s* one *d*. *Educ:* Bishop's Stortford Coll.; Trinity Coll., Cambridge (MA). Called to the Bar, Inner Temple, 1977. *Recreations:* pictures, garden, wine. *Address:* 7 Ralli Courts, West Riverside, Manchester M3 5FT. *T:* (0161) 833 2722. *Clubs:* Oxford and Cambridge; Manchester Tennis and Racquets.

ELLES, family name of **Baroness Elles**.

ELLES, Baroness *cr* 1972 (Life Peer), of the City of Westminster; **Diana Louie Elles;** *b* 19 July 1921; *d* of Col Stewart Francis Newcombe, DSO and Elisabeth Chaki; *m* 1945, Neil Patrick Moncrieff Elles (*d* 2008); one *s* one *d*. *Educ:* private Schs, England, France and Italy; London University (BA Hons). Served WAAF, 1941–45. Barrister-at-law. Care Cttee worker in S London, 1956–72. UK Delegn to UN Gen. Assembly, 1972; Mem., UN Sub-Commn on Prevention of Discrimination and Protection of Minorities, 1973–75; UN special rapporteur on Human Rights, 1973–75; Mem., British delegn to European Parlt, 1973–75. Mem., Cripps Cttee on legal discrimination against women; Chm., Sub-cttee of Women's Nat. Adv. Cttee (Conservative Party) on one-parent families (report publ. as Unhappy Families); Internat. Chm., European Union of Women, 1973–79; Chm., Cons. Party Internat. Office, 1973–78; Opposition front bench spokesman on foreign and Eur. affairs, H of L, 1975–79; Mem., H of L Europ. Communities Select Cttee, 1989–94 (Chm., Law and Institutions Sub-Cttee, 1992); Mem., 1996 IGC Sub-Cttee, 1995. European Parliament: MEP (C) Thames Valley, 1979–89; EDG spokesman on NI, 1980–87; Vice-Pres., 1982–87; Chm., Legal Affairs Cttee, 1987–89. Vice-Pres., UK Assoc. of European Lawyers, 1985–. Of Counsel, Van Bael and Bellis, Brussels, 1989–2002. Mem. Council, Caldecott Community, 1990–97; Mem. Res. Council, Europ. Univ. Inst., Florence, 1986–95; Trustee: Cumberland Lodge, 1982–96; Industry and Parlt Trust, 1985–96; Chm. Bd of Govs, British Inst., Florence, 1996 (Gov., 1986–96, Vice Chm., Bd of Govs, 1994–96, Life Gov., 1997); Gov., Reading Univ., 1986–96. Hon. Bencher, Lincoln's Inn, 1993. *Publications:* The Housewife and the Common Market (pamphlet), 1971; Human Rights of Aliens, 1980; articles, etc. *Address:* 75 Ashley Gardens, SW1P 1HG; Villa Fontana, Ponte del Giglio, Lucca, Italy.

See also J. E. M. Elles.

ELLES, James Edmund Moncrieff; Member (C) South East Region, England, European Parliament, since 1999 (Oxford and Buckinghamshire, 1984–94; Buckinghamshire and Oxfordshire East, 1994–99); *b* 3 Sept. 1949; *s* of late N. P. M. Elles and of Baroness Elles, *qv*; *m* 1977, Françoise Le Bail (marr. diss. 1997); one *s* one *d*. *Educ:* Ashdown House; Eton College; Edinburgh University. External Relations Div., EEC, 1976–80; Asst to Dep. Dir Gen. of Agriculture, EEC, 1980–83. European Parliament: EPP spokesman on the Budget, 1994–99; Vice-Pres., EPP-ED Gp, 1999– (Chm., Wkg Party C); Mem., Budget Cttee; Substitute Mem., Foreign Affairs Cttee and Budgetary Control Cttee; Mem., Jt Parly Cttee for Cyprus. Founder: Transatlantic Policy Network, 1992 (Chm., 1992–99); European Ideas Network, 2002. Co-founder, European Internet Foundn, 2002. Co-founder, EU Baroque Orch. *Address:* c/o European Parliament, Rue Wiertz, 1047 Brussels, Belgium. *T:* (2) 2845951, *Fax:* (2) 2849951; *e-mail:* jelles@europarl.eu.int. *Clubs:* Carlton; Royal and Ancient Golf (St Andrews).

ELLETSON, Harold Daniel Hope, PhD; *b* 8 Dec. 1960; *m* 1987, Fiona Margaret Ferguson; two *s*. *Educ:* Eton Coll.; Exeter Univ.; Voronezh Univ., USSR; Poly. of Central London; Bradford Univ. (PhD). Mem. (C) Lancashire CC, 1984–88; worked in journalism and public affairs, 1984–88; CBI and Illingworth Morris plc, 1988–90; public affairs adviser and consultant to cos trading in Eastern Europe, 1990–. Contested (C) Burnley, 1987. MP (C) Blackpool North, 1992–97; contested (C) Blackpool North and Fleetwood, 1997. Joined Liberal Democrats, 2002; Mem., Lib Dem foreign affairs team, 2003– (Chm.). Dir, NATO Forum on Business and Security, 2004. Associate, Centre for Defence and Internat. Security Studies. *Publication:* The General Against the Kremlin—Alexander Lebed: power and illusion, 1998.

ELLINGTON, Prof. Charles Porter, PhD; FRS 1998; Professor of Animal Mechanics, University of Cambridge, since 1999; Fellow of Downing College, Cambridge, since 1979; *b* 31 Dec. 1952; *s* of Dr Charles Porter Ellington and Margaret Moselle Ellington; *m* 1977, Dr Stephanie Katharine Lindsay Buckley; two *s*. *Educ:* Duke Univ. (BA 1973); Downing Coll., Cambridge (MA 1979; PhD 1982). Cambridge University: Demonstrator and Lectr in Zoology, 1979–97; Reader in Animal Mechanics, 1997–99. Editor, Jl of Experimental Biology, 1990–94. Scientific Medal, Zoological Soc., 1990. *Publications:* (ed with T. J. Pedley) Biological Fluid Dynamics, 1995; (ed with J. D. Altringham) Designs for Life: the science of biomechanics, 1999; papers on mechanics and physiology of insect flight. *Recreations:* gardening, wood- and metal-working. *Address:* Department of Zoology, University of Cambridge, Downing Street, Cambridge CB2 3EJ. *T:* (01223) 336668, 336600.

ELLINGTON, Marc Floyd, FSA; DL; communications and marketing consultant; *b* 16 Dec. 1945; *s* of late Homer Frank Ellington, Memsie, Aberdeenshire, and of Harriette Hannah Ellington (*née* Kellas); *m* 1967, Karen Leigh, *d* of Capt. Warren Sidney Streater; two *d*. Chm., Heritage Press (Scot.); Board Member: Soundcraft Audio Guides, 1979–; Aberdeen Univ. Res. Ltd, 1980–85; Gardenstown Estates Ltd, 1983–; Grampian Enterprises Ltd, 1992–96; Partner, Heritage Sound Recordings, 1981–. Composer and recording artiste; producer of documentary films and TV progs. Chm., Grampian Reg. Tourism Task Force, 1991–. Trustee, Nat. Galls of Scotland, 2002–; non-exec. Dir, Historic Scotland, 2005–; Member: Historic Bldg Council for Scotland, 1980–98; Cttee for Scotland, Heritage Lottery Fund, 1998–. Member: British Heritage Cttee, 1992–; HHA; PRS. FSA 1987. DL Aberdeenshire, 1984. Vice-Pres., Buchan Heritage Soc., 1986; Mem., Convention of Baronetage of Scotland. Patron, Banffshire Wildlife Rehabilitation Trust. Baron of Towie Barclay; Laird of Gardenstown and Crovie. OStJ 2004. Saltire Award, 1973; Eur. Architectural Heritage Award, 1975; Civic Trust Award, 1975, 1993. *Publications:* contribs to architectural and historic jls and periodicals. *Recreations:* sailing, historic architecture, art collecting, music. *Address:* Towie Barclay Castle, Auchterless, Turriff, Aberdeenshire AB53 8EP. *T:* (01888) 511347, *Fax:* (01888) 511522; *e-mail:* soundcraft@towiebarclay.co.uk.

ELLINGWORTH, Richard Henry; HM Diplomatic Service, retired; *b* 9 March 1926; *e s* of Vincent Ellingworth and Dora Ellingworth (*née* Church); *m* 1952, Joan Mary, *e d* of Sir Percival Waterfield, KBE, CB and Lady Waterfield; one *s* three *d*. *Educ:* Uppingham; Aberdeen Univ.; Magdalen Coll., Oxford (Demy); Exeter Univ. (certificates in French, 1989, Theology, 1991, and Russian, 1993). Served War of 1939–45: RA, and Intelligence Corps, 1944–47. Oxford, 1947–50 (first Lit. Hum.); HM Embassy, Japan, 1951–55; FO, 1955–59; HM Embassy: Belgrade, 1959–63; Japan, 1963–68 (Olympic Attaché, 1964); Head of Oil Dept., FCO, 1969–71; Research Associate, Internat. Inst. for Strategic Studies, 1971–72; Counsellor, Tehran, 1972–75; seconded to Dept of Energy, 1975–77. Course Dir (European Training), Civil Service Coll., 1978–83. Mem., Farningham Parish Council, 1979–83; pt-time Agent, Sevenoaks Liberal Assoc., 1983–84; Hon. Organiser, Farningham, Royal British Legion, 1982–87. *Publications:* (with A. N. Gilkes) An Anthology of Oratory, 1946; Japanese Economic Policy and Security, 1972. *Recreations:*

gardening, music. *Address:* Pullman House, 1 Church Street, Brixworth NN6 9BZ.
See also Sir J. C. King, Bt.

ELLIOT; *see* Elliot-Murray-Kynynmound, family name of Earl of Minto.

ELLIOT, Dr Alison Janet, OBE 2003; Associate Director, Centre for Theology and Public Issues, Edinburgh University, since 2001; Convener, Scottish Council for Voluntary Organisations, since 2007; *b* 27 Nov. 1948; *d* of Kenneth and Janet Macrae; *m* 1979, John Christian Elliot; one *s* one *d*. *Educ:* Bathgate Acad.; Edinburgh Univ. (MA 1970; PhD 1976); Sussex Univ. (MSc 1971). Lecturer in Psychology: Lancaster Univ., 1974–76; Edinburgh Univ., 1977–85. Elder, 1984, and Session Clerk, 2000–07, Greyfriars, Tolbooth and Highland Kirk, Edinburgh. Moderator of the Gen. Assembly, Church of Scotland, 2004–05; Convener: Church and Nation Cttee, Church of Scotland, 1996–2000; Action of Churches Together in Scotland, 2002–06; Mem., Central Cttee, Conf. of European Churches, 1997–. Hon. LLD TCD, 2004; Hon. DD: St Andrews, Edinburgh, Knox Coll., Toronto, 2005. *Publications:* Child Language, 1981; Scottish Churches and the Political Process Today, 1987; The Miraculous Everyday, 2005. *Recreations:* friends, family, food. *Address:* New College, Mound Place, Edinburgh EH1 2LX; *e-mail:* alisonelliot@btinternet.com.

ELLIOT, Sir Gerald (Henry), Kt 1986; FRSE; Chairman, Christian Salvesen plc, 1981–88; *b* 24 Dec. 1923; *s* of late Surg. Captain J. S. Elliot, RN, and Magda Salvesen; *m* 1950, Margaret Ruth Whale (MBE 1993), *d* of Rev. J. S. Whale; two *s* one *d*. *Educ:* Marlborough Coll.; New Coll., Oxford (BA PPE 1948). FRSE 1978. Captain FF Rifles, Indian Army, 1942–46. Christian Salvesen Ltd, 1948–88, Dep. Chm. and Man. Dir, 1973–81. Dir, Scottish Provident Instn, 1971–89, Chm., 1983–89; Chairman: Chambers and Fargus, 1975–79; Scottish Br., RIIA, 1973–77 (Sec., 1963–73); FAO Fishery Industries Develt Gp, 1971–76; Forth Ports Authority, 1973–79; Scottish Arts Council, 1980–86. Chairman: Scottish Unit Managers Ltd, 1984–88; Martin Currie Unit Trusts, 1988–90; Biotal, 1987–90. Sec., National Whaling Bd, 1953–62; Mem., Nat. Ports Council, 1978–81. Chm., Scottish Div., Inst. of Dirs, 1989–92; Vice-Chm., Scottish Business in the Community, 1987–89. Chairman: Prince's Scottish Youth Business Trust, 1987–94; Scottish Opera, 1987–92 (Vice-Pres., 1994–99). A Vice-Pres., RSE, 1988–91. Pres., UN 50 Scotland, 1993–95. Trustee: David Hume Inst., 1985–98 (Chm., 1985–95); Nat. Museums of Scotland, 1987–91; The Prince's Trust, 1992–94; Edinburgh Fest. Th., 1995–98; Pres., Edinburgh Univ. Develt Trust, 1990–94. Member Court: Edinburgh Univ., 1984–93; Regents, RCSE, 1990–99. Dr *hc* Edinburgh, 1989; Hon. LLD Aberdeen, 1991. Consul for Finland in Edinburgh, 1957–89; Dean, Consular Corps in Edinburgh-Leith, 1986–88. Kt 1st Cl., Order of White Rose of Finland, 1975. *Publications:* A Whaling Enterprise, 1998; papers on control of whaling and fishing, arts administration and economic management. *Address:* 39 Inverleith Place, Edinburgh EH3 5QD. *T:* (0131) 552 3005.

ELLIOT, Prof. Harry, CBE 1976; FRS 1973; Emeritus Professor of Physics, University of London; Professor of Physics at Imperial College, London, 1960–80 (Assistant Director of Physics Department, 1963–71); *b* 28 June 1920; *s* of Thomas Elliot and Hannah Elizabeth (*née* Littleton), Weary Hall, Cumberland; *m* 1943, Betty Leyman (*d* 2007); one *s* one *d*. *Educ:* Nelson Sch., Wigton; Manchester Univ. MSc, PhD. Served War, Signals Branch, RAF, incl. liaison duties with USAAF and USN, 1941–46. Manchester University: Asst Lectr in Physics, 1948–49; Lectr in Physics, 1949–54; Imperial College, London: Lectr in Physics, 1954–56; Sen. Lectr in Physics, 1956–57; Reader in Physics, 1957–60; Sen. Res. Fellow, 1982–87. Member: Science Research Council, 1971–77 (Chm., Astronomy, Space and Radio Bd, 1974–77); Council, Royal Soc., 1978–79; Science Adv. Cttee, ESA, 1979–80 (Chm., 1980–81). Hon. Prof., Universidad Mayor de San Andres, 1957; Hon. ARCS, 1965. Fellow, World Acad. of Arts and Scis, 1978. Holweck Prize and Medal, Inst. of Physics and Société Française de Physique, 1976. *Publications:* papers on cosmic rays, solar physics and magnetospheric physics in scientific jls; contrib. scientific reviews and magazine articles. *Recreation:* painting. *Address:* Rosan, Broadwater Down, Tunbridge Wells, Kent TN2 5PE.

ELLIOT, Iain Fleming, OBE 2000; PhD; Director, East-West Insight, since 2000; *b* 24 May 1943; *s* of John Darling Elliot and Isabel Elliot (*née* MacLean); *m* 1970, Dr Elisabeth Mary Robson; one *s* one *d*. *Educ:* Univ. of Glasgow (MA); Univ. of Sussex (MA); Univ. of Bradford (PhD 1974). Res. student, Univ. of Leningrad, 1967–68; res. asst and Lectr, Univ. of Bradford, 1969–70; Sen. Lectr, Univ. of Brighton, 1971–88; leader writer and specialist on Soviet affairs, The Times, 1982–86; Associate Dir, with responsibility for Russian broadcasting, Radio Liberty, subseq. also Chief Ed. and Dir, analytic research, RFE/RL Research Inst., Munich, 1987–93; Dir, Britain-Russia Centre, and British East-West Centre, 1993–2000. Ed., Soviet Analyst, 1972–88. *Publications:* The Soviet Energy Balance, 1974; (ed jtly) Demise of the USSR, 1995; contrib. books, jls and newspapers on Soviet and Russian affairs. *Address:* 42 Preston Park Avenue, Brighton, Sussex BN1 6HG. *T:* (01273) 556156. *Club:* Athenæum.

ELLIOT, (Robert) John, WS; Deputy Keeper of HM Signet, since 1999; Chairman, Lindsays WS, Edinburgh, since 1994; *b* 18 Jan. 1947; *s* of Robert Thomas Elliot and Barbara Elliot; *m* 1971, Christine Anne Glencross; one *s* one *d*. *Educ:* Craigflower Prep Sch., Dunfermline; Loretto Sch., Musselburgh; Edinburgh Univ. (LLB). WS 1971; Admitted solicitor, 1971; with Lindsays WS, Edinburgh, 1969–: Partner, 1973–; Man. Partner, 1988–94. Pres., Law Soc. of Scotland, 1997–98 (Mem. Council, 1990–99). Chm., Age Concern Edinburgh IT, 1995–. *Recreations:* golf, politics, argument, wine, literature. *Address:* Caldonian Exchange, 19A Canning Street, Edinburgh EH3 8HE. *T:* (0131) 656 5650.

ELLIOT, Virginia Helen Antoinette, MBE 1986; trainer of National Hunt jockeys and horses; former equestrian event rider; *b* 1 Feb. 1955; *d* of late Col Ronald Morris Holgate, RM and of Heather Holgate; *m* 1st, 1985, Hamish Julian Peter Leng (marr. diss. 1989), *s* of Gen. Sir Peter Leng, *qv*; 2nd, 1993, Michael Elliot. *Educ:* Bedgebury Park, Goudhurst, Kent. Three day event equestrian team trainer, 1996 Olympic Games. Three day event wins: Junior European Champion, 1973 (Dubonnet); Mini Olympics, 1975 (Jason); Burghley, 1983 (Priceless), 1984 (Nightcap), 1985 (Priceless), 1986 (Murphy Himself), 1989 (Master Craftsman); Badminton, 1985 (Priceless), 1989 (Master Craftsman), 1993 (Houdini); European Championship, 1985 (Priceless), 1987 (Nightcap), 1989 (Master Craftsman); World Championship, 1986 (Priceless); Team Silver Olympic Medal, 1984 and 1988; Bronze Individual Olympic Medal, 1984 (Priceless), and 1988 (Master Craftsman). *Publications:* (with Genevieve Murphy) Ginny, 1986; (with Nancy Roberts) Priceless, 1987; (with Genevieve Murphy) Ginny and Her Horses, 1987; (with Genevieve Murphy) Training the Event Horse, 1990; *novels for children:* Winning, 1995; Race against Time, 1996; High Hurdle, 1997. *Recreations:* ski-ing, cooking, art, theatre. *Address:* Holliers, Middle Barton, Oxon OX5 3QH.

ELLIOT-MURRAY-KYNYNMOUND, family name of **Earl of Minto**.

ELLIOTT, family name of **Baron Elliott of Morpeth**.

ELLIOTT OF MORPETH, Baron *cr* 1985 (Life Peer), of Morpeth in the County of Northumberland and of the City of Newcastle-upon-Tyne; **Robert William Elliott,** Kt 1974; DL; Vice-Chairman, Conservative Party Organisation, 1970–74; *b* 11 Dec. 1920; *s* of Richard Elliott; *m* 1956, Jane Morpeth; one *s* four *d* (of whom two are twin *d*). *Educ:* Morpeth Grammar Sch. Farmer, 1939–, at Low Heighley, Morpeth, Northumberland. MP (C) Newcastle-upon-Tyne North, March 1957–1983; Parliamentary Private Secretary: to joint Parliamentary Secs, Ministry of Transport and Civil Aviation, April 1958–Oct. 1959; to Under-Sec., Home Office, Nov. 1959–60; to Minister of State, Home Office, Nov. 1960–61; to Sec. for Technical Co-operation, 1961–63; Asst Govt Whip (unpaid), 1963–64; Opposition Whip, 1964–70; Comptroller of the Household, June–Sept. 1970. Chm., Select Cttee on Agric., Fisheries and Food, 1980–83. DL Northumberland, 1985. *Address:* Crown House, Kings Cliffe, Peterborough PE8 6XQ. *T:* (01780) 470888. *Clubs:* Carlton; Northern Counties (Newcastle upon Tyne).

ELLIOTT, Anthony Michael Manton, (Tony Elliott); Founder, 1968 and Chairman, Time Out Group; *b* 7 Jan. 1947; *s* of late Katherine and Alan Elliott; *m* 1st, 1976, Janet Street-Porter, *qv* (marr. diss. 1978); 2nd, 1989, Jane L. Coke; three *s* (incl. twins). *Educ:* Stowe Sch.; Keele Univ. Time Out Group publishing activities include: Time Out London; Time Out New York; Time Out Chicago; timeout.com; annual guides. Time Out Trust formed 1989. Director: Roundhouse Trust, 1998–; Somerset House Trust, 1999–; Photographers' Gall., 1999–2004; Soho Th. Co., 2000–03; Film London, 2003–. Gov., BFI, 1997–2003 (Chm., Production Bd, 1998–2000). Dir, Human Rights Watch, 2006– (Chm., London Cttee, 2003–). *Recreations:* travel, watching television, cinema going, eating out with friends, reading newspapers and magazines, being with family. *Address:* Time Out Group, Universal House, 251 Tottenham Court Road, W1T 7AB. *T:* (020) 7813 3000, *Fax:* (020) 7813 6001.

ELLIOTT, Brent; *see* Elliott, W. B.

ELLIOTT, Rev. Dr Charles Middleton; Fellow, Dean and Chaplain of Trinity Hall, 1990–2001, Affiliated Lecturer in Theology, 1991–2001, in Social and Political Sciences, 1993–2001, University of Cambridge; *b* 9 Jan. 1939; *s* of Joseph William Elliott and Mary Evelyn Elliott; *m* 1962, Hilary Margaret Hambling; three *s* (one *d* decd). *Educ:* Repton; Lincoln and Nuffield Colls, Oxford (MA, DPhil). Deacon, 1964; priest, 1965. Lectr in Econs, Univ. of Nottingham, 1963–65; Reader in Econs, Univ. of Zambia, 1965–69; Asst Sec., Cttee on Society, Develt and Peace, Vatican and World Council of Churches, 1969–72; Sen. Lectr in Develt Econs, Univ. of E Anglia, 1972–73; Dir, Overseas Develt Gp, UEA, 1973–77; Minor Canon, Norwich Cathedral, 1974–77; Prof. of Develt Policy and Planning, and Dir, Centre of Develt Studies, Univ. of Wales, 1977–82; Director of Christian Aid, 1982–84; Asst Gen. Sec., BCC, 1982–84; Benjamin Meaker Prof., Bristol Univ., 1985–86; Sen. Consultant, ODI, 1986–87. G. E. M. Scott Fellow, Univ. of Melbourne, 1984–85; Hon. Vis. Prof. of Christian Ethics, Univ. of Edinburgh, 1985–87; Vis. Prof. in Theology, KCL, 1986–88. Chm., Indep. Gp on British Aid, 1981–89. Prebendary of Lichfield Cathedral, 1987–95. *Publications:* The Development Debate, 1972; Inflation and the Compromised Church, 1973; Patterns of Poverty in the Third World, 1975; Praying the Kingdom: an introduction to political spirituality, 1985 (Biennial Collins Prize for Religious Lit., 1985); Comfortable Compassion, 1987; Praying through Paradox, 1987; Signs of Our Times, 1988; Sword and Spirit, 1989; Memory and Salvation, 1995; Strategic Planning for Churches: an appreciative approach, 1997; Locating the Energy for Change: an introduction to appreciative inquiry, 1999; articles in Jl of Develt Studies, Econ. Hist. Rev., Theology, World Health Forum, World Develt, Lancet, BMJ and in Proc. Royal Soc. *Recreations:* sailing, fly-fishing, walking, chatting to rural craftsmen.

ELLIOTT, (Charles) Thomas, CBE 1994; PhD; FRS 1988; Tom Elliott Consultancy Ltd, 1999–2006; *b* 16 Jan. 1939; *s* of Charles Thomas and Mary Jane Elliott; *m* 1962, Brenda Waistell; one *s* two *d*. *Educ:* Washington Grammar Sch.; Manchester Univ. (BSc 1960; PhD 1965). Univ. of Manchester: Research student, 1960–63; Asst Lectr/Lectr, 1963–67 (research on dielectric breakdown); joined RSRE 1967, to study electrical transport in semiconductors; SSO, 1967–73; Vis. Scientist, MIT, Lincoln Lab., USA, 1970–71; research into infrared detectors, infrared emitters, novel and ultra-high-speed semiconductor devices, 1972–2006; PSO, 1973–79, SPSO, 1979–86, DCSO, 1986–91, RSRE; CSO (Individual Merit), DRA, Electronics Sector, 1991–99; Chief Scientist, Electronics Sector, DERA, 1996–99. Part-time Prof. of Physics, 1999–2005, Vis. Prof. of Physics, 2005–, Heriot-Watt Univ. Hon. FRPS 2001. Rank Prize for optoelectronics and IEE Electronics Div. Premium Award, 1982; Churchill Medal, Soc. of Engineers, 1986; MacRobert Award for Engineering, 1991; Paterson Medal, Inst. of Physics, 1997; J. J. Thomson Medal, IEE, 1998; Progress Medal, RPS, 2001. *Publications:* numerous papers and patents. *Recreations:* reading, golf, music, motor caravanning. *Address:* Weardale, 8 Hall Green, Malvern, Worcs WR14 3QX. *T:* (01684) 562474.

ELLIOTT, Christine Anne; Chief Executive and Director, Society of Turnaround Professionals, since 2007; *b* 10 Oct. 1954; *d* of Charles Archbold Elliott and Geneviève Suzanne Marie Thérèse Elliott (*née* Colombé); marr. diss.; two *d*. *Educ:* Blyth Grammar Sch., Northumberland; Sheffield Univ. (BA Hons Law); Chambre de Commerce et d'Industrie, Paris (DS). Thomson Regl Press, 1977–78; NFWI, 1978–80; mkting and PR consultancy, 1980–93; Wiggins Gp plc and Hayklan Industries, 1994–97; Dir, Bletchley Park, 1998–2006; Chief Exec., Ramblers Assoc., 2006. Vis. Lectr, Univ. of Westminster, 1989–91; Expert Panellist, Cass Business Sch., 2005–. ARAeS. Mem., Poetry Soc. *Publications:* Bye Bye Belle (illustrated story book), 1996; Hijacking Enigma, 2003; Can You Keep a Secret?: children's codebreaking, 2004. *Recreations:* finding humour in hopeless situations, inflicting cello and piano on vicinity, learning languages, literature, opera, walking. *Address:* Society of Turnaround Professionals, 120 Aldersgate Street, EC1A 4JQ.

ELLIOTT, Maj.-Gen. Christopher Haslett, CVO 2004; CBE 1994; Director, Army Sport Control Board, since 2005; *b* 26 May 1947; *s* of late Lt-Col Blethyn Elliott and of Zara Elliott; *m* 1970, Annabel Melanie Emerson; four *d*. *Educ:* Kelly Coll., Tavistock; Mons Officer Cadet Sch.; Staff Coll., Camberley (psc). Commnd into S Wales Borderers, 1966: regtl duty appts, 1966–80 (despatches, NI, 1975); Army Staff Coll., Camberley, 1980; COS, Berlin Inf. Bde, 1981–83; Mem., Directing Staff, Army Staff Coll., Camberley, 1985–87; CO, 1st Bn, Royal Regt of Wales, 1987–90; Comdr, British Forces Belize, 1990–93; Dir, Army Recruiting, MoD, 1993–94; Comdr, Brit. Mil. Adv. and Trng Team, S Africa, 1994–97; GOC UKSC (Germany), 1997–2001; Defence Services Sec. and Dir Gen., Reserve Forces and Cadets, 2001–04. Col Comdt POW Div., 1999–; Col, Royal Regt of Wales, 1999–2004. Chm., Combined Services Sports Bd, 2006– (Mem., 2005); Mem. Council for S Africa, Royal Commonwealth Ex-Services League, 2006–. *Recreations:* fly-fishing, rough shooting, walking, watersports. *Club:* Army and Navy.
See also N. B. Elliott.

ELLIOTT, Maj. Gen. Christopher Leslie, CB 1999; MBE 1969; Chairman, Purple Secure Systems Ltd, since 2007; Director, Doctrine and Strategic Analysis, General

Dynamics UK Ltd, since 2002; *b* 18 March 1947; *s* of Peter Archibald Elliott and Evelyn Sarah (*née* Wallace); *m* 1970, Margaret Bennett; two *d*. *Educ:* Pocklington Sch., York; RMA, Royal Mil. Coll. of Sci. (BSc Hons Eng); Cranfield Inst. of Technol. (MPhil). Commnd RE, 1967; OC 48 Field Sqn RE, 1980; CO, 21 Engr Regt, 1986–88; ACOS 1 (BR) Corps, 1988–90; Comdr, 6th Armd Bde, 1990–91; Dir of Studies, Staff Coll., Camberley, 1991–92; Dir, Mil. Ops, 1993–95; UK Mil. Advr to Chm., Internat. Conf. on former Yugoslavia, 1995–96; Dir Gen. Army Trng and Recruiting, and Chief Exec., Army Trng and Recruiting Agency, 1996–99; COS, HQ QMG, 1999–2000; Dir-Gen. Develt and Doctrine, MoD, 2000–02. Comr, Royal Hosp., Chelsea, 1996–2002. Trustee, Army Central Fund, 1998–2000. Col Comdt, RE, 2000–. Consultant, Ove Arup and Partners, 2002–. Vis. Prof., Cranfield Univ., 2002–. Mem. Senate, Cranfield Univ., 1996–99; Mem. Adv. Council, RMCS, 2000–02; Pres., Instn of RE, 2002–07 (Fellow, 2007). Pres., Jt Services Paragliding and Hang-gliding Assoc., 1993–2002; Cdre, Army Sailing Assoc., 2001–02 (Vice-Cdre, 1993–94). Pres., Victim Support, Wilts, 2003–. Mem., Easton Royal Parish Council, 2003–. *Publication:* (contrib.) Blast Damage to Buildings, 1995. *Recreations:* sailing, paragliding, reading. *Address: e-mail:* cle@clelliott24.freeserve.co.uk. *Clubs:* Army and Navy, Royal Ocean Racing, Royal Cruising (Mem. Cttee, 2000–); Royal Engineer Yacht (Chatham) (Cdre, 1995–96); Royal Lymington Yacht.

ELLIOTT, Sir Clive (Christopher Hugh), 4th Bt *cr* 1917, of Limpsfield, Surrey; independent consultant on migratory pests in agriculture, since 2006; *b* Moshi, Tanganyika, 12 Aug. 1945; *s* of Sir Hugh Elliott, 3rd Bt, OBE and Elizabeth Margaret (*d* 2007), *d* of A. G. Phillipson; *S* father, 1989; *m* 1975, Marie-Thérèse, *d* of H. Rüttimann; two *s*. *Educ:* Dragon Sch., Oxford; Bryanston Sch., Dorset; University Coll., Oxford (BA Hons Zoology); Univ. of Cape Town, S Africa (PhD Zoology 1973). University of Cape Town: Research Officer, FitzPatrick Inst. of Ornithology, 1968–71; first Officer i/c National Unit for Bird-ringing Admin, 1972–75; Food and Agriculture Organization of the UN: ornithologist/ecologist, crop protectionist/project manager: Chad, 1975–78; Tanzania, 1978–86; Kenya, 1986–89; Country Projects Officer, Eastern and Southern Africa, 1989–95; Sen. Officer, Migratory Pests, 1995–2004; Sen. Officer, Locust and Other Migratory Pests Gp, Plant Protection Service, 2004–06. Mem., Field Staff Assoc. of FAO (Chm., 1992). *Publications:* (ed jtly with R. L. Bruggers) Quelea Quelea: Africa's Bird Pest, 1989; contrib. to books and jls on ornithology. *Recreations:* tennis, fishing, bird-watching, wildlife conservation. *Heir:* *s* Dr Ivo Antony Moritz Elliott, BSc(MedSci) St Andrews, MB ChB Manchester, MRCP, *b* 9 May 1978. *Address:* 173 Woodstock Road, Oxford OX2 7NB. *Club:* British Ornithologists' Union.

ELLIOTT, Sir David (Murray), KCMG 1995; CB 1987; Director General (Internal Market), General Secretariat of Council of European Union, 1991–95; *b* 8 Feb. 1930; *s* of late Alfred Elliott, ISM, and Mabel Kathleen Emily Elliott (*née* Murray); *m* 1956, Ruth Marjorie Ingram; one *d* (one *s* decd). *Educ:* Bishopshalt Grammar Sch.; London Sch. of Economics and Political Science (BScEcon); Kitchener Scholar. National Service, RAF, 1951–54; Gen. Post Office, 1954–57; seconded to Federal Ministry of Communications, Nigeria, 1958–62; GPO, 1962–69 (Clerk in Waiting, 1964–69); Asst Secretary: Min. of Posts and Telecommunications, 1969–74 (Dep. Leader, UK Delegn to Centenary Congress, UPU, Lausanne, 1974); Dept of Industry, 1974–75; Counsellor at UK Representation to the European Communities, Brussels, 1975–78; Under Sec., European Secretariat, Cabinet Office, 1978–82; Minister and Dep. UK Perm. Rep. to the Eur. Communities, Brussels, 1982–91. Advr on EU affairs under UK Know-How Fund and EU PHARE progs, 1995–98. Member Board: CARE UK, 1995–2001; CARE Internat., 1998–2001. *Address:* 31 Ailsa Road, St Margarets, Twickenham, Middlesex TW1 1QJ. *Club:* Travellers.

ELLIOTT, David Stewart Innes; Chief Executive, Royal Albert Hall, since 1998; *b* 6 April 1945; *s* of late John Innes Elliott, CBE and Edith Agnes Elliott; *m* 1978, Patricia Nicholson; two *s*. *Educ:* Whitgift Sch.; Oriel Coll., Oxford (MA). Commercial Evaluation Dept, 1966–68, Market and Commercial Analyst, 1969–70, Vickers Ltd; Corporate Finance Dept, Baring Brothers & Co. Ltd, 1970–80 (Asst Dir, 1978); Exec. Vice-Pres., Baring Brothers Inc., NY, 1981–84; Finance Dir, ENO, 1985–90; Dir of Finance and Admin, 1991–93, Dep. Chief Exec., 1994–97, Royal Albert Hall. Chm., Benesh Inst. of Choreology, 1997–2007; Mem. Exec. Cttee, Royal Acad. Dancing, 1997–2007. Hon. Treas., Lyric Th. Hammersmith, 1999–2006; Mem. Bd, English Touring Opera, 2007–. *Recreations:* opera, theatre, looking at pictures, sailing. *Address:* c/o Royal Albert Hall, Kensington Gore, SW7 2AP.

ELLIOTT, David Stuart; independent curator, writer and museum consultant, since 2008; Artistic Director, Sydney Biennale of Art, since 2008; Director, Istanbul Museum of Modern Art, 2007–08; *b* 29 April 1949; *s* of Arthur Elliott and May Elliott; *m* 1974, Julia Alison (marr. diss. 2006); two *d*. *Educ:* Loughborough Grammar Sch.; Durham Univ. (BA Hons Mod. Hist.); Univ. of London (MA Hist. of Art, Courtauld Inst.). Asst Stage Manager, Phoenix Theatre, Leicester, 1966; Asst, City Art Gallery, Leicester, 1971; Regional Art Officer, Arts Council, 1973–76; Director: Mus. of Modern Art, Oxford, 1976–96; Moderna Museet, Stockholm, 1996–2001; Mori Art Mus., Tokyo, 2001–06. Visitor, Ashmolean Mus., Oxford, 1992–2000. Rudolf Arnheim Guest Prof. of Art History, Humboldt Univ., Berlin, 2008; Guest Prof., Dept of Mus. Studies, Chinese Univ., Hong Kong, 2008. Pres., Internat. Cttee for Museums and Collections of Modern Art, ICOM, 1998–2004. President of Jury: La Biennale des Arts, Dakar, 2000; Internat. Architectural Competition for Tsunami Meml, Thailand, 2005. Contribs to radio and TV. Hon. DA Oxford Brookes, 1998. NACF Award, 1988. Orden de Mayo (Argentina), 2001. *Publications:* Alexander Rodchenko, 1979; José Clemente Orozco, 1980; New Worlds: Russian Art and Society 1900–1937, 1986; (ed jtly) Eisenstein at 90, 1988; (ed jtly) 100 Years of Russian Art 1889–1989, 1989; (ed jtly) Alexander Rodchenko: Works on Paper, 1991; (ed jtly) Engineers of the Human Soul: Soviet Socialist Realism, 1992; Photography in Russia 1840–1940, 1992; (ed) Art from Argentina 1920–1994, 1994; (ed jtly) Wounds: between democracy and redemption in contemporary art, 1998; (ed jtly) After the Wall: art and culture in post-Communist Europe, 1999; Organising Freedom: Nordic art of the '90s, 2000; (ed jtly) Happiness: a survival guide for art and life, 2003; (ed jtly) Hiroshi Sugimoto, 2005; contribs to arts magazines. *Recreations:* keeping fit, travelling. *Address: e-mail:* david@elliott.as.

ELLIOTT, Frank Alan, CB 1991; Permanent Secretary, Department of Health and Social Services, Northern Ireland, 1987–97; *b* 28 March 1937; *s* of Frank Elliott and Doreen Allen; *m* 1964, Olive Lucy O'Brien; one *s* two *d*. *Educ:* Royal Belfast Academical Inst.; Trinity Coll., Dublin (BA (Mod.) 1st cl.). Entered NI Civil Service, 1959; Principal, Min. of Health, 1966, Asst Sec., 1971; Sen. Asst Sec., Dept of Health and Social Services, 1975, Under Sec., 1981. Chm., Chief Execs' Forum, 1997–2001. Trustee, Leonard Cheshire Disability (formerly Leonard Cheshire Foundn), 2002– (Vice-Chm., 2005–). DUniv Ulster, 1998. *Publication:* Curing and Caring: 50 years of health and personal social services in NI, 1998. *Recreations:* music and the arts, motoring.

ELLIOTT, Rt Rev. George; *see* Elliott, Rt Rev. M. G. H.

ELLIOTT, George, FRICS; Senior Partner, Edmond Shipway and Partners, 1985–93; *b* 20 Aug. 1932; *s* of Harry Elliott and Nellie Elizabeth Elliott; *m* 1st, 1958, Winifred Joa (marr. diss. 1990); one *s* one *d*; 2nd, 1992, Hazel Ann Willis. *Educ:* Sir George Monou Grammar Sch.; SW Essex Technical Coll. FRICS 1966. Founder Partner, Edmon Shipway, 1963; Chief Exec., British Urban Develt Services Unit, 1975–78. Pres., Wester Australian Chapter, Naval Hist. Soc. of Australia, 2003–. *Recreations:* travel, naval history *Address:* 4 Langtry View, Mount Claremont, WA 6010, Australia. *T:* (8) 93842147.

ELLIOTT, Prof. (James) Keith, DPhil, DD; Professor of New Testament Textu Criticism, University of Leeds, 1997–2007; *b* 19 March 1943; *s* of James and Lillian Elliot *m* 1971, Carolyn Tull; one *d*. *Educ:* Liverpool Inst. High Sch.; University Coll. of N Wales, Bangor (BA 1st Cl. Hebrew and Biblical Studies 1964); St Peter's Coll., Oxfor (DPhil 1967); DD Wales 1988. Leeds University: Lectr in New Testament Lang. and Lit 1967–89; Sen. Lectr, 1989–93, Reader, 1993–97, Dept of Theol.; Warden, Charle Morris Hall, 1971–83. Ed., 1977–87, Sec., 1987–, Internat. Greek New Testamer Project; Asst Sec., Studiorum Novi Testamenti Societas, 1983–93; Book Rev. Ed., 1990– Pres., Editl Bd, 2008–, Novum Testamentum (Leiden). Mem. Cttee, Vacation Term fo Biblical Study, Oxford, 2003– (Vice-Chm., 2005–). Gov., Harrogate Grammar Sch 1989–93, 1996–2000. *Publications:* The Greek Text of the Epistles to Timothy and Titus 1968; Questioning Christian Origins, 1982; Codex Sinaiticus and the Simonides Affai 1982; A Survey of Manuscripts used in Editions of the Greek New Testament, 1987; Bibliography of Greek New Testament Manuscripts, 1989, 2nd edn 2000; Essays an Studies in New Testament Textual Criticism, 1992; The Apocryphal New Testamen 1993; The Apocryphal Jesus: legends of the Early Church, 1996; (with D. R. Cartlidge Art and the Christian Apocrypha, 2001; A Synopsis of the Apocryphal Nativity an Infancy Narratives, 2006. *Recreations:* walking in the Yorkshire Dales, cycling in Austri music (big bands, grand opera, especially Wagner). *Address:* 11 Cundall Way, Harrogat HG2 0DY; *e-mail:* j.k.elliott@leeds.ac.uk. *Club:* Army and Navy.

ELLIOTT, Prof. James Philip, PhD; FRS 1980; Professor of Theoretical Physic University of Sussex, 1969–94, now Professor Emeritus; *b* 27 July 1929; *s* of James Ellio and Dora Kate Smith; *m* 1955, Mavis Rosetta Avery; one *s* two *d*. *Educ:* Universit College, Southampton; London External degrees: BSc 1949, PhD 1952. FInstP. Senio Scientific Officer, AERE Harwell, 1951–58; Vis. Associate Prof., Univ. of Rocheste USA, 1958–59; Lecturer in Mathematics, Univ. of Southampton, 1959–62; Reader i Theoretical Physics, Univ. of Sussex, 1962–69. Rutherford Medal, Inst. of Physics, 1994 Lise Meitner Prize, Eur. Physical Soc., 2002. *Publications:* Symmetry in Physics, 1979 contribs include: The Nuclear Shell Model, Handbuch der Physik, vol 39, 1957; man papers, mostly published in Proc. Roy. Soc. and Nuclear Phys. *Recreations:* gardening sport and music. *Address:* 36 Montacute Road, Lewes, Sussex BN7 1EP. *T:* (01273 474783.

ELLIOTT, Prof. John, DLitt; Professor of Education, University of East Angli 1987–2002, Emeritus Professor, 2004 (Professorial Fellow, 2002–04); *b* 20 June 1938; *s* c Alfred George Lewis Elliott and Mary Doris Elliott (*née* Greason); *m* 1st, 1967, Jea Marion Walford (marr. diss. 1993); three *d*; 2nd, 1998, Anne Christine O'Hanlon. *Edu* Ashford Grammar Sch.; City of Portsmouth Trng Coll.; Bishop Otter Coll., Chicheste London Univ. Inst. of Educn (Dip. Phil. Ed. 1970; MPhil 1980); DLitt E Anglia, 2003 Horticultural researcher, E Malling Res. Stn, 1956–59; sch. teacher, 1962–67; Educr Researcher, Schs Council, 1967–72; Lectr in Applied Educnl Res., UEA, 1972–76; Tuto in Curriculum Studies, Cambridge Inst. of Educn, 1976–84; University of East Anglia Reader, 1984–87; Dean, Sch. of Educn and Professional Develt, 1992–95; Dir, Centre fo Applied Res. In Educn, 1996–99. Adv. Prof., Hong Kong Inst. of Educn, 2000–06. R an D Advr, Curriculum Develt Inst. of Hong Kong, 2000–07; Associate, Centre for Educn R and D, von Hügel Inst., St Edmund's Coll., Cambridge, 2004–. Indep. Acad. Adv Home Office, 2003–04. Visiting Professor: Manchester Metropolitan Univ., 2004– Sheffield Univ., 2004–. Mem., Norfolk Learning and Skills Council, 2001–08. FRS 1992. Hon. DEd Hong Kong Inst. of Educn, 2002; Hon. Dr Autonomous Univ. o Barcelona, 2003. *Publications:* Action Research for Educational Change, 1991; Th Curriculum Experiment, 1999; (ed with H. Altrichter) Images of Educational Change 2000; Reflecting Where the Action Is: selected works, 2007; contrib. numerous papers t learned jls. *Recreations:* golf, countryside, reading, cinema and theatre. *Address:* Centre fo Applied Research in Education, University of East Anglia, Norwich NR4 7TJ. *T:* (0160 592859.

ELLIOTT, John Dorman; Chairman, Australian Product Traders Pty Ltd, since 1992 Deputy Chairman, Foster's Brewing Group (formerly Elders IXL Ltd), 1990–9 (Chairman and Chief Executive, 1985–90); *b* 3 Oct. 1941; *s* of Frank Faithful Elliott an Anita Caroline Elliott; *m* 1st, 1965, Lorraine Clare (*née* Golder) (marr. diss. 1986); two one *d*; 2nd, 1987, Amanda Mary Drummond Moray (*née* Bayles); one *d*. *Educ:* Care Baptist Grammar School, Melbourne; BCom (Hons) 1962, MBA Melbourne 1965. Wit BHP, Melbourne, 1963–65; McKinsey & Co., 1966–72; formed consortium and raise $30 million to acquire Henry Jones (IXL), and became Man. Dir, 1972; Elder Smit Goldsbrough Mort merged with Henry Jones (IXL) to form Elders IXL, 1981; Elders IX acquired Carlton & United Breweries, 1983, largest takeover in Aust. history. Pres. Liberal Party of Australia, 1987–90. Pres., Carlton FC, 1983–2002. *Recreations:* footbal tennis, Royal tennis. *Address:* 39/108 Elgin Street, Carlton, Vic 3142, Australia. *T:* (3 996211411. *Clubs:* Melbourne, Australian, Savage (Melbourne).

ELLIOTT, Sir John (Huxtable), Kt 1994; FBA 1972; Regius Professor of Moder History, and Fellow of Oriel College, Oxford, 1990–97 (Hon. Fellow, Oriel College 1997); *b* 23 June 1930; *s* of late Thomas Charles Elliott and Janet Mary Payne; *m* 1958 Oonah Sophia Butler. *Educ:* Eton College; Trinity College, Cambridge (MA, PhD) Fellow of Trinity Coll., Cambridge, 1954–67, Hon. Fellow, 1991; Asst Lectr in History Cambridge Univ., 1957–62; Lectr in History, Cambridge Univ., 1962–67; Prof. o History: KCL, 1968–73; Inst. for Advanced Study, Princeton, NJ, 1973–90. Mem. Scientific Cttee, Prado Mus., 1996–. Chm., Adv. Council, Inst. for the Study of th Americas, Univ. of London, 2004–. King Juan Carlos Vis. Prof., New York Univ., 1988 Vis. Hon. Prof., Univ. of Warwick, 2003–07. Wiles Lectr, QUB, 1969; Trevelyan Lectr Cambridge Univ., 1982–83. Chm., Council, Omohundro Inst. of Early American Hist and Culture, Williamsburg, 2007–. FKC 1998. Corresp. Fellow, Real Academia de l Historia, Madrid, 1965; Fellow, Amer. Acad. Arts and Scis, 1977; Mem., Amer Philosophical Soc., 1982; Corresponding Member: Hispanic Soc. of America, 1975 (Hon Fellow, 1997); Real Academia Sevillana de Buenas Letras, 1976; Royal Acad. of Letters Barcelona, 1992; Nat. Acad. of History, Venezuela, 1992; Foreign Mem., Accademi Nazionale dei Lincei, 2003. Dr *hc*: Universidad Autónoma de Madrid, 1983; Genoa, 1992 Barcelona, 1994; Valencia, 1998; Lleida, 1999; Complutense, Madrid, 2003; Hon. DLitt Portsmouth, 1993; Warwick, 1995; London, 2007; Carlos III, Madrid, 2008; Hon. DHL Brown, 1996; Coll. of William and Mary, 2005. Medal of Honour, Universidad Internacional Menéndez y Pelayo, 1987; Medalla de Oro al Mérito en las Bellas Artes Spain, 1990; Premio Antonio de Nebrija, Univ. of Salamanca, 1993; Prince of Asturia Prize for Social Scis, 1996; Gold Medal, Spanish Inst., NY, 1997; Balzan Prize for History

1500–1800, Internat. Balzan Foundn, 1999. Visitante Ilustre de Madrid, 1983; Comdr, 1984, Grand Cross, 1988, Order of Alfonso X El Sabio; Comdr, 1987, Grand Cross, 1996, Order of Isabel la Católica; Cross of St George (Catalonia), 1999. *Publications:* The Revolt of the Catalans, 1963; Imperial Spain, 1469–1716, 1963; Europe Divided, 1559–1598, 1968; The Old World and the New, 1492–1650, 1970; (ed with H. G. Koenigsberger) The Diversity of History, 1970; (with J. F. de la Peña) Memoriales y Cartas del Conde Duque de Olivares, 2 vols, 1978–80; (with Jonathan Brown) A Palace for a King, 1980; Richelieu and Olivares, 1984 (Leo Gershoy Award, Amer. Hist. Assoc., 1985); The Count-Duke of Olivares, 1986 (Wolfson Lit. Prize for History); Spain and its World 1500–1700, 1989; (ed) The Hispanic World, 1991; (ed with Laurence Brockliss) The World of the Favourite, 1999; (ed with Jonathan Brown) The Sale of the Century, 2002; Empires of the Atlantic World (Francis Parkman Prize, Soc. of American Historians), 2006. *Recreation:* looking at paintings. *Address:* Oriel College, Oxford OX1 4EW; 122 Church Way, Iffley, Oxford OX4 4EG. *T:* (01865) 716703.

ELLIOTT, John Stanley; Chief Economist, Home Office, since 2007; *b* 26 March 1959; *s* of late Stanley Elliott and of Betty Elliott (*née* Cornish); partner, Shirley Ann McClune; (one *s* decd). *Educ:* Bemrose Sch., Derby; Jesus Coll., Oxford (MA PPE 1980; MPhil Econ. 1982). Econ. Asst, MSC, 1982–83; Sen. Econ. Asst, DES, 1983–86; Econ. Advr, MoD, 1986–89; Econ. Advr, 1989–92, Sen. Econ. Advr, 1992–95, Dept of Employment; Sen. Econ. Advr, DFEE, then DFES, 1995–2004; Chief Economist, DFES, then DCSF, 2004–07. Mem. Council, Inst. of Employment Studies, 2005–. Gov., Firth Park Community Arts Coll., 2006–. *Recreations:* hill-walking, crosswords, rowing. *Address:* Home Office, 2 Marsham Street, SW1P 4DF. *T:* (020) 7035 3391, *Fax:* 0870 336 9135; *e-mail:* john.elliott14@homeoffice.gsi.gov.uk. *Club:* City of Sheffield Rowing.

ELLIOTT, Keith; *see* Elliott, J. K.

ELLIOTT, Lawrence Brian; JP; Economics Editor, The Guardian, since 1995; *b* 29 Aug. 1955; *s* of Brian and Peggy Elliott; *m* 1980, Carol Ann Lelliott; two *d*. *Educ:* St Albans Sch.; Fitzwilliam Coll., Cambridge (BA Hist. 1977). Evening Post-Echo, Hemel Hempstead, 1978–83; Economics Correspondent: Press Assoc., 1983–88; The Guardian, 1988–95. Sen. Res. Fellow, Univ. of Herts. Council Mem., ODI. Mem., Scott Trust, 2001–08. JP Central Herts, 1992. *Publications:* with Dan Atkinson: The Age of Insecurity, 1998; Fantasy Island, 2007; The Gods that Failed, 2008. *Recreations:* soccer, golf, music, cooking, walking. *Address:* The Guardian, Kings Place, 90 York Way, N1 9AG; *e-mail:* larry.elliott@guardian.co.uk.

ELLIOTT, Margaret, CBE 1999; solicitor in private practice, since 1976; *b* 20 March 1951; *d* of Malachy and Kathleen Trainor; *m* 1973, Acheson Elliott; two *s* (twins) one *d*. *Educ:* Our Lady's Grammar Sch., Newry; Queen's Univ., Belfast (LLB Hons). Pres., Law Soc. of NI, 1989–90; Chm., Legal Aid NI, 1990–91. Non-executive Director: Ulsterbus/Citybus, 1990–95; Northern Bank Ltd, 1992–2005; National Irish Bank, 2001–05. Fair Employment Comr, 1993–96; Civil Service Comr, 1995–2006. Chm., Bd of Trustees, Nat. Mus and Galls NI, 1998–. Hon. LLD, 2002. *Recreations:* reading, cooking, travelling. *Address:* c/o The Elliott-Trainor Partnership, 3 Downshire Road, Newry, Co. Down BT34 1ED. *T:* (028) 3026 8116, *Fax:* (028) 3026 9208; *e-mail:* margaret.elliott@ elliotttrainorpartnership.co.uk.

ELLIOTT, Margaret Anne; *see* O'Brien, M. A.

ELLIOTT, Prof. Marianne, OBE 2000; DPhil; FBA 2002; Andrew Geddes and John Rankin Professor of Modern History, since 1993, and Director, Institute of Irish Studies, since 1997, University of Liverpool; *b* 25 May 1948; *d* of Terry Burns and Sheila Burns (*née* O'Neill); *m* 1975, Trevor Elliott; one *s*. *Educ:* Queen's University, Belfast (BA Hons History); Lady Margaret Hall, Oxford (DPhil 1975). Lectr II, W London Inst. of Higher Educn, 1975–77; Univ. Res. Fellow, 1977–79, Temp. Lectr, 1981–82, UC, Swansea; Univ. Res. Fellow, 1984–87, Hon. Fellow, 1987–93, Dept of History, Univ. of Liverpool; Simon Sen. Res. Fellow, Univ. of Manchester, 1988–89; Lectr in History, Birkbeck Coll., Univ. of London, 1991–93. Visiting Professor: Iowa State Univ., 1983; Univ. of S Carolina, 1984. Part-time Tutor: Balliol Coll., Oxford, 1974–75; Westminster Tutors, 1974–75; Dept of History and WEA/Dept of Educn, Univ. of Reading, 1974–75; Course Tutor, Open Univ., 1979–85; Tutor, Univ. of Warwick, 1980–81. Ford Lectr, Oxford, 2005. Mem., 1995–98, Chm., 1998, AHRB res. panel (hist. and archaeol.); Mem., Res. Cttee, British Acad., 2002–05. Mem., Opsahl Commn on NI, 1992–93. *Publications:* Partners in Revolution: the united Irishmen and France, 1982; Watchmen in Sion: the Protestant idea of Liberty, 1985; (trans.) The People's Armies, 1987; Wolfe Tone: prophet of Irish independence, 1989; (jtly) A Citizens' Inquiry: the report of the Opsahl Commission on Northern Ireland, 1993; The Catholics of Ulster: a history, 2000; (ed) The Long Road to Peace in Northern Ireland, 2002; Robert Emmet: the making of a legend, 2003; contribs to books and learned jls. *Recreations:* running, cycling, reading. *Address:* Institute of Irish Studies, University of Liverpool, Liverpool L69 3BX. *T:* (0151) 794 3831, *Fax:* (0151) 794 3836; *e-mail:* lindam@liv.ac.uk.

ELLIOTT, Marianne; Associate Director, National Theatre, since 2006; *b* London, 27 Dec. 1966; *d* of Michael Elliott and Rosalind Elliott (*née* Knight); *m* 2000, Nick Sidi; one *d*. *Educ:* St Hilary's Sch., Alderley Edge; Stockport Grammar Sch.; Hull Univ. (BA). An Artistic Dir, Manchester Royal Exchange Th.; Associate Dir, Royal Court Th. Productions include: Much Ado About Nothing, RSC, 2006; National Theatre: Pillars of the Community, 2005 (Evening Standard Award); Therese Raquin, 2006; St Joan, 2007 (Best Revival, Olivier Awards; South Bank Show Award); Warhorse, 2007. *Address:* National Theatre, Upper Ground, South Bank, SE1 9PX. *T:* (020) 7452 3347.

ELLIOTT, Mark, CMG 1988; HM Diplomatic Service, retired; *b* 16 May 1939; *s* of William Rowcliffe Elliott, CB, and Karin Tess Elliott (*née* Classen); *m* 1964, Julian Richardson; two *s*. *Educ:* Eton Coll. (King's Scholar); New Coll., Oxford. HM Forces (Intell. Corps), 1957–59. FO, 1963; Tokyo, 1965; FCO, 1970; Private Sec. to Perm. Under-Sec. of State, 1973–74; First Sec. and Head of Chancery, Nicosia, 1975–77; Counsellor, 1977–81, Head of Chancery, 1978–81, Tokyo; Hd of Far Eastern Dept, FCO, 1981–85; Under-Sec. on secondment to N Ireland Office, 1985–88; Ambassador to Israel, 1988–92; Dep. Under-Sec. of State, FCO, 1992–94; Ambassador to Norway, 1994–98. Grand Cross, Order of Merit (Norway), 1994. *Recreations:* fell walking, nature, music, photography.

ELLIOTT, Rt Rev. (Matthew) George (Holden); a Suffragan Bishop of Toronto (Area Bishop of York-Simcoe), since 2001; *b* 17 Feb. 1949; *s* of George and Phyllis Elliott; *m* 1977, Linda Ann Martinez; one *s* one *d*. *Educ:* Univ. of Toronto (BA 1972); George Brown Coll. (Dip. Food Services Mgt 1973); Wycliffe Coll. (MDiv 1979; Hon. DD 2002). Asst Curate, St Thomas à Becket, Toronto, 1979–80; Incumbent: Parish of Minden, 1981–88; All Saints', King City, 1989–2001. Regional Dean: Victoria/Haliburton, 1985–88; Holland, 1993–2000. Director: Toronto Parish Trng Prog., 1988–91; Wycliffe Coll. Internship Prog., 1992–94. *Recreations:* golf, cooking, gardening, reading. *Address:* (home) 28 Charles Street, King City, ON L7B 1J7, Canada. *T:* (905) 8334988; *e-mail:* bishopgeorge@sympatico.ca; (office) 2174 King Road, Unit 2, King City, ON L7B 1L5, Canada. *T:* (905) 8338327, *Fax:* (905) 8338329; *e-mail:* ysimcoe@ toronto.anglican.ca.

ELLIOTT, Michael Alwyn; actor, producer and director; *b* 15 July 1936; *s* of W. A. Edwards and Mrs J. B. Elliott (assumed stepfather's name); *m* Caroline Margaret McCarthy; two *s* one *d*. *Educ:* Raynes Park Grammar School. AMP INSEAD, 1976. Journalist, 1955–59; Public Relations, Avon Rubber Co. Ltd, 1959–63; Marketing, CPC International, 1963–68; Kimberly-Clark Ltd: Product Manager, 1968; Marketing Manager, 1969; Marketing and Development Manager, 1975; General Manager, 1976; Director, 1977; Gen. Administrator, Nat. Theatre, 1979–85; Dir of Admin, Denton, Hall, Solicitors, 1985–88; Head, Theatres Div., Bill Kenwright Ltd, 1992–93. Theatre Consultant: Gardner Arts Centre, 1988–99; Thorndike Th., 1992–95; Liverpool Playhouse, 1992–93; Yvonne Arnaud Th., 1994–97. Founder, Bitesize Lunchtime Theatre Co., 2002. Member: Executive Council, SWET, 1980–85; Council, The Actors Charitable Trust, 2003–07. Stage appearances incl: Anagnos in The Miracle Worker, Comedy, then Wyndhams, 1994; Dr Grimwig in Oliver, London Palladium, 1996; Corin in As You Like It, Shakespeare's Globe, 1997; O'Hara in Maddie, Lyric, 1997; television: The Bill, 1999; The Tenth Kingdom, 2000; Dogma, 2000; Baddiel Syndrome, 2001; Tales from the Tower, 2001; My Hero, 2003, 2005; Little Britain, 2004. *Recreations:* golfing, walking, ski-ing. *Address:* The Coach House, 51A Frant Road, Tunbridge Wells, Kent TN2 5LE. *T:* and *Fax:* (01892) 530615.

ELLIOTT, Michael Norman; Mayor of Ealing, 2005–06; *b* 3 June 1932; *m* 1979, Julia Perry. *Educ:* Brunel College of Technology. Formerly res. chemist in food industry. Mem., Ealing Borough Council, 1964–86 and 2002– (former Leader of Council and Chm., Educn Cttee). MEP (Lab) London W, 1984–99; contested (Lab) London Region, 1999. Formerly: Member: Civil Liberties Parly Cttee (Lab party spokesperson); Parly Cttee of Inquiry into Racism and Xenophobia; Parly Jt Cttees with Poland and with Malta; Substitute Mem., Econ. and Monetary Cttee; Pres., Parly Intergroup for Animal Welfare and Conservation. Pres., Local Authority Aircraft Noise Council. Member: CND, 1961–; Friends of the Earth, 1985–. Hon. Fellow, Ealing Coll. of Higher Educn, 1988. *Address:* 4 Fern Dene, Ealing, W13 8AN.

ELLIOTT, Michele, OBE 2008; Founder, and Director, Kidscape Children's Charity, since 1984; *b* 7 Jan. 1946; *d* of James Irmiter and Ivy (*née* Dashwood); *m* 1968, Edward Elliott; two *s*. *Educ:* Univ. of S Florida (MA *summa cum laude* 1967); Univ. of Florida (MA *cum laude* 1969). Educational Psychologist: Booker Washington Sch., Fla, 1969–71; Amer. Sch. in London, 1971–84. Winston Churchill Fellow, 1991. Chairman: Home Office Working Gp on prevention of sexual abuse, 1988; WHO Cttee on prevention of sexual abuse, 1989. Mem., Video Consultative Council, BBFC, 1992–99. Member: Hon. Adv. Bd, NSPCC, 1994–; Nat. Toy Council, 1996–; Bd, Internet Watch Foundn, 2003–. Mem., Soc. of Authors, 1990–. Hon. PhD Post Univ., Conn, 1993; Hon. DSc Birmingham, 2003. *Publications:* Preventing Child Sexual Assault: a practical guide to talking with children, 1985, 2nd edn 1987 (trans. Norwegian); Kidscape Primary Kit, 1986, 3rd edn 2001; Under Fives Programme, 1987, 4th edn 1999; Keeping Safe, 1988, 2nd edn 1995 (trans. German, French, Chinese, Czech, Norwegian, Polish, Slovenian, Russian); The Willow Street Kids, 1986, 2nd edn 1997; Dealing with Child Abuse, 1989; Teenscape, 1990, 3rd edn 2002; Feeling Happy Feeling Safe, 1991, 2nd edn 1999; Bullying: a practical guide to coping for schools, 1991, 3rd edn 2002; Protecting Children: a training package, 1992; Bullies Meet the Willow Street Kids, 1993, 2nd edn 1997; (ed) Female Sexual Abuse of Children: the ultimate taboo, 1993, 2nd edn 1997; (with J. Kilpatrick) How to Stop Bullying: a Kidscape training guide, 1994, 3rd edn 2002 (trans. Japanese); 501 Ways to be a Good Parent, 1996 (trans. Russian, Estonian, Chinese, Polish, German); 101 Ways to Deal with Bullying: a guide for parents, 1997 (trans. Japanese, Chinese); Bullying: wise guide, 1998; Bully Free, 1999; 601 Ways to be a Good Parent, 1999; The Anti-Bullying Pocketbook, 2005; numerous contribs to learned jls. *Recreations:* piano, cycling, walking, dancing. *Address:* Kidscape, 2 Grosvenor Gardens, SW1W 0DH. *T:* (020) 7730 3300.

ELLIOTT, Nicholas Blethyn; QC 1995; *b* 11 Dec. 1949; *s* of late Col Blethyn William Treharne Elliott, late South Wales Borderers, and of Zara Elliott; *m* 1976, Penelope, (Nemmy), Margaret Longbourne Browne; two *s*. *Educ:* Kelly Coll.; Bristol Univ. (LLB Hons). Called to the Bar, Gray's Inn, 1972, Bencher, 2003. Asst Boundary Comr, 2000–. *Publications:* (ed jtly) Banking Litigation, 1999, 2nd edn 2005; (ed) Byles on Bills of Exchange and Cheques, 28th edn 2007; (contrib.) Money Laundering and Financial Services, 2003. *Recreations:* tennis, cycling, swimming, bridge, rock and roll dancing. *Address:* Old Whistley Farmhouse, Potterne, Devizes, Wilts SN10 5TD.

See also Maj. Gen. C. H. Elliott.

ELLIOTT, Oliver Douglas; British Council Representative in Yugoslavia, 1979–85; *b* 13 Oct. 1925; *y s* of Walter Elliott and Margherita Elliott, Bedford; *m* 1954, Patience Rosalie Joan Orpen; one *s*. *Educ:* Bedford Modern Sch.; Wadham Coll., Oxford (MA); Fitzwilliam House, Cambridge. Served RNVR (Sub-Lt), 1944–47. Colonial Educn Service, Cyprus, 1953–59; joined British Council, 1959; served Lebanon, 1960–63; Dep. Rep., Ghana, 1963; Dir, Commonwealth I Dept, 1966; Dir, Service Conditions Dept, 1970; Dep. Educn Advr, India, 1973; Representative in Nigeria, 1976–79. *Recreation:* golf.

ELLIOTT, Paul; Clerk, Company of Scriveners, since 2007; Strategic Projects Officer, London Borough of Camden, 2003–04; *b* 27 Oct. 1949; *s* of John and Winifred Elliott; *m* 1995, Sharon Amanda Jordan; one *s* one *d*. *Educ:* Clare Coll., Cambridge (Hons Modern Langs). Joined MAFF, 1971; Private Secretary: to Perm. Sec., 1974–75; to Minister, 1975–76; First Sec. (Agriculture), Bonn, 1984–89; Head, Milk Div., 1989–94; Rural White Paper Team, 1994–95; Prin. Finance Officer, MAFF, then DEFRA, 1996–2001; Dir, Rural Economies and Communities Directorate, DEFRA, 2001–03. *Recreations:* music, photography, cricket, ICT, travel.

ELLIOTT, Prof. Paul, PhD; FRCP, FFPH, FMedSci; Professor of Epidemiology and Public Health Medicine, since 1995 and Head, Division of Primary Care and Population Health Sciences, Faculty of Medicine, since 1998, Imperial College London; *b* 21 April 1954; *s* of Dr Arnold Elliott, OBE and Esther Elliott; *m* Nina Gay; one *s* two *d*. *Educ:* Brentwood Sch., Essex; Christ's Coll., Cambridge (BA, MA Maths and Med. Scis); UCL (MB BS 1978); LSHTM (MSc 1983; PhD 1991). FFPH (FFPHM 1995); FRCP 1998; FMedSci 2000. Med. Registrar, Edgware Gen. Hosp., Middlesex, 1981–82; Wellcome Res. Fellow, St Mary's Hosp. Med. Sch. and LSHTM, 1982–87; Lectr, 1987–88, Sen. Lectr, 1988–93, Reader, 1993–95, in Epidemiology, LSHTM. Hon. Consultant Physician, Dept of Medicine, Hammersmith Hosp., London, 1990–; Hon. Consultant: in Public Health Medicine, Kensington and Chelsea PCT (formerly Kensington, Chelsea and Westminster HA), 1995–; St Mary's Hosp. NHS Trust, London, 1998–. Dir, UK Small Area Health Stats Unit, 1991–. *Publications:* (ed jtly) Geographical and Environmental Epidemiology: methods for small-area studies, 1992; (ed jtly) Coronary Heart Disease Epidemiology: from aetiology to public health, 1992, 2nd edn 2005; (ed jtly) Spatial Epidemiology: methods and applications, 2000; articles in learned jls on diet and blood pressure, epidemiology, small-area health statistics and methodology. *Recreations:* family, surfing, swimming. *Address:* Department of Epidemiology and Public Health, Faculty of Medicine, Imperial College London, St Mary's Campus, Norfolk Place, W2 1PG. *T:* (020) 7594 3328, *Fax:* (020) 7262 1034; *e-mail:* p.elliott@imperial.ac.uk.

ELLIOTT, Paul Richard; theatrical producer; Managing Director, Paul Elliott Ltd, since 1999; Joint Director, Triumph Entertainment Ltd, since 2000; Managing Director, E&B Productions, 1964–2000; *b* 9 Dec. 1941; *s* of late Lewis Arthur Elliott and Sybil Elliott; *m* 1st, 1971, Jenny Logan (marr. diss. 1986); one *s*; 2nd, 1987, Linda Hayden; one *s* one *d*. *Educ:* Bournemouth Sch. Actor, 1958–63; appeared in Dixon of Dock Green, 1961–62. *London productions* include: When We Are Married, Strand, 1970; The King and I, Adelphi, 1973; Grease, New London, 1973; The Pleasure of His Company, and I Do, I Do, Phoenix, 1974; Hedda Gabler, Aldwych, 1975; Hello Dolly, Theatre Royal, 1979; Run for Your Wife, Criterion, Whitehall, Aldwych, 1983–92; Buddy, Victoria Palace, Strand, 1989–2002; The Pirates of Penzance, Palladium, 1990; Jolson, Victoria Palace, 1996 (Olivier Award, Best Musical, 1996); The Goodbye Girl, Albery, 1997; Kat and the Kings, Vaudeville, 1998 (Olivier Award, Best Musical, 1999); Annie, Victoria Palace, 1998; Stones in His Pockets (Olivier and Evening Standard Awards, Best Comedy), Duke of York's, 2000, transf. NY, 2001; The Tempest, Old Vic, 2003; Thoroughly Modern Millie, Shaftesbury, 2004; The Philadelphia Story, Old Vic, 2005; As You Desire Me, Playhouse, 2006; The Last Confession, Haymarket, 2007; Macbeth, Gielgud, 2007, transf. NY, 2008; numerous pantomime prodns annually throughout UK; London *pantomimes* include: Aladdin, Shaftesbury, 1983; Snow White and the Seven Dwarfs, Strand, 1990; Jack and the Beanstalk, Piccadilly, 1991; Babes in the Wood, Sadler's Wells; Snow White and the Seven Dwarfs, Victoria Palace, 2004–05; *New York productions:* The Hollow Crown; Brief Lives; Run for Your Wife, 1989; Buddy, 1990; Private Lives (Tony Award), 2002; touring prodns in UK and overseas incl. USA, Canada, Australia, NZ, Japan, Hong Kong, Zimbabwe, India and Europe; writer of play, There's No Place Like a Home, 2006. Dir, SOLT, 1996–. Award for Contribution to Provincial Theatre, Theatre Managers Assoc., 1996. *Recreation:* watching sport! *Address:* 18 Exeter Street, WC2E 7DU. *T:* (020) 7379 4870. *Club:* Garrick.

ELLIOTT, Ven. Peter; Archdeacon of Northumberland, 1993–2005; *b* 14 June 1941; *s* of James Reginald and Hilda Elliott; *m* 1967, Evelyn Embleton; one *d*. *Educ:* Queen Elizabeth Grammar Sch., Horncastle; Hertford Coll., Oxford (MA Mod. History); Lincoln Theological Coll. Assistant Curate: All Saints, Gosforth, 1965–68; St Peter, Balkwell, 1968–72; Vicar: St Philip, High Elswick, 1972–80; North Gosforth, 1980–87; Embleton with Rennington and Rock, 1987–93. RD of Alnwick, 1989–93; Hon. Canon, Newcastle Cathedral, 1990–93. English Heritage: Member: Cathedrals and Churches Adv. Cttee, 1998–2001; Historic Built Envmt Cttee, 2001–03; Places of Worship Panel, 2001–05; Adv. Cttee, 2003–05. *Recreations:* genealogy, travel, railway timetables, food, wine, gardening. *Address:* 56 King Street, Seahouses, Northumberland NE68 7XS. *T:* (01665) 721133.

ELLIOTT, Sir Randal (Forbes), KBE 1977 (OBE 1976); President, New Zealand Medical Association, 1976; *b* 12 Oct. 1922; *s* of Sir James Elliott and Lady (Ann) Elliott (*née* Forbes), MBE; *m* 1949, Pauline June Young; one *s* six *d*. *Educ:* Wanganui Collegiate Sch.; Otago Univ. MB, ChB (NZ), 1947; DO, 1953; FRCS, FRACS. Group Captain, RNZAF. Ophthalmic Surgeon, Wellington Hospital, 1953–. Chm. Council, NZ Med. Assoc. GCStJ 1987 (KStJ 1978). *Publications:* various papers in medical jls. *Recreations:* sailing, ski-ing, mountaineering. *Address:* Highwic Apt 4, 32 Hobson Street, Wellington 6011, New Zealand. *T:* (4) 721375. *Club:* Wellington (NZ) (Life Mem.).

ELLIOTT, Robert Anthony K.; *see* Keable-Elliott.

ELLIOTT, Sir Roger (James), Kt 1987; FRS 1976; FInstP; Secretary to the Delegates and Chief Executive of Oxford University Press, 1988–93; Professor of Physics, Oxford University, 1989–96, now Emeritus; Fellow of New College, Oxford, 1974–96, now Emeritus; *b* Chesterfield, 8 Dec. 1928; *s* of James Elliott and Gladys Elliott (*née* Hill); *m* 1952, Olga Lucy Atkinson (*d* 2007); one *s* two *d*. *Educ:* Swanwick Hall Sch., Derbyshire; New Coll., Oxford (MA, DPhil; Hon. Fellow, 1999). FInstP (FPhysS 1960). Research Fellow, Univ. of California, Berkeley, 1952–53; Research Fellow, UKAEA, Harwell, 1953–55; Lectr, Reading Univ., 1955–57; Fellow of St John's College, Oxford, 1957–74, Hon. Fellow, 1988; University Reader, Oxford, 1964–74; Wykeham Prof. of Physics, 1974–89; Senior Proctor, 1969; Delegate, Oxford Univ. Press, 1971–88. Chm., Computer Bd for Univs and Research Councils, 1983–87; Vice-Chm., Parly Office of Sci. and Technol., 1990–93; Member: Adv. Bd for Res. Councils, 1987–90; (part-time) UKAEA, 1988–94; British Council Bd, 1990–98. Non-exec. Dir, Blackwell Ltd, 1996–2002 (Chm., 1999–2002); Chm., ICSU Press, 1997–2002. Chm., Disability Information Trust, 1998–2002. Physical Sec. and Vice-Pres., Royal Soc., 1984–88; Treas., ICSU, 2002–08. Pres., Publishers Assoc., 1993–94 (Treas., 1990–92). Visiting Prof., Univ. of California, Berkeley, 1961; Miller Vis. Prof., Univ. of Illinois, Urbana, 1966; Vis. Dist. Prof., Florida State Univ., 1981; Vis. Dist. Prof., Michigan State Univ., 1997–2000. Mem., Mexican Acad. of Scis, 2003. Hon. DSc: Paris, 1983; Bath, 1991; Essex, 1993. Maxwell Medal, 1968, Guthrie Medal, 1990, Inst. of Physics. *Publications:* Magnetic Properties of Rare Earth Metals, 1973; Solid State Physics and its Applications (with A. F. Gibson), 1973; papers in Proc. Royal Soc., Jl Phys., Phys. Rev., etc. *Address:* 11 Crick Road, Oxford OX2 6QL. *T:* (01865) 273997. *Club:* Athenæum.

See also R. C. Wilkin.

ELLIOTT, Thomas; *see* Elliott, C. T.

ELLIOTT, Thomas; Member (UU) Fermanagh and South Tyrone, Northern Ireland Assembly, since 2003; *b* 11 Dec. 1963; *s* of late John Elliott and of Noreen Elliott; *m* 1989, Anne; one *d*. *Educ:* Ballinamallard Primary Sch.; Duke of Westminster High Sch., Ballinamallard; Enniskillen Coll. of Agric. Self-employed farmer, 1981–. Mem. (pt-time), UDR/Royal Irish Regt, 1982–99. Mem. (UU), Fermanagh DC, 2001–. *Recreations:* community activity, sport, church. *Address:* 1 Regal Pass, Enniskillen, Co. Fermanagh BT74 7NT. *T:* (028) 6632 2028, *Fax:* (028) 6634 2846; *e-mail:* t.elliott6@btopenworld.com.

ELLIOTT, Timothy Stanley; QC 1992; *b* 2 April 1950; *s* of John Edwin Elliott and Annie Elizabeth Stanley (*née* Lowe); *m* 1973, Katharine Barbara Lawrance (*d* 2008); one *s* one *d*. *Educ:* Marlborough Coll.; Trinity Coll., Oxford (Exhibnr, MA Lit. Hum. 1973). Called to the Bar, Middle Temple, 1975. *Address:* 15 Essex Street, WC2R 3AA. *T:* (020) 7544 2600.

ELLIOTT, William, OBE 2003; HM Diplomatic Service; Consul-General, St Petersburg, since 2006; *b* Boston, Lincs, 16 March 1968; *s* of Roger Elliott and Rebecca Short (*née* Fernandez); *m* 2003, Daria Chrin; one *s* three *d*. *Educ:* Alderman Peel High Sch., Wells, Norfolk; Wymondham Coll.; Univ. of York (BA Eng. and Related Lit.). Lectr in English, Lodz and Tbilisi, 1991–92; entered HM Diplomatic Service, 1993; Second Sec., Warsaw, 1995–98; First Secretary: FCO, 1998; Kabul, 2001–02; Dep. Hd of Mission, Tallinn, 2002–06. *Recreations:* history and literature of Europe and S Asia, cricket, food and drink. *Address:* c/o Foreign and Commonwealth Office, King Charles Street, SW1A 2AH. *T:* (St Petersburg) (812) 3203200; *e-mail:* William.Elliott@fco.gov.uk. *Club:* English (St Petersburg).

ELLIOTT, (William) Brent, PhD; Historian, Royal Horticultural Society, since 2007; *b* 10 Jan. 1952; *s* of William Alfred and Annie Irene Elliott; *m* 1981, Dr Frances Margaret Clegg; one *s*. *Educ:* Univ. of BC (BA 1973; MA 1974); King's Coll., London (PhD 1978). Asst Librarian, 1977–82, Librarian and Archivist, 1982–2007, RHS. Ed., Garden Hist. (Jl Garden Hist. Soc.), 1984–88. English Heritage: Member: Gardens Cttee, 1985–89; Historic Landscapes Panel, 1989–93; Historic Parks and Gardens Adv. Cttee, 1994–. Member: Council, Garden Hist. Soc., 1979–89; Main Cttee, Victorian Soc., 1983–93 (Chm., Cemeteries Sub-cttee, 1980–89). FLS 1995. Veitch Meml Medal, RHS, 1994. *Publications:* Victorian Gardens, 1986; (with A. Clayton-Payne) Victorian Flower Gardens, 1988; (with C. Brooks) Mortal Remains, 1989; Waddesdon Manor: the gardens, 1994; Treasures of the Royal Horticultural Society, 1994; The Country House Garden, 1995; Flora: an illustrated history of the garden flower, 2001; The Royal Horticultural Society 1804–2004: a history, 2004; (with V. Buchan) Garden People, 2007; (vol. ed.) Flora: the Erbario Miniato and other drawings, in The Paper Museum of Cassiano dal Pozzo, 2007. *Recreations:* visiting parks, gardens and cemeteries, gardening, reading. *Address:* c/o Royal Horticultural Society, 80 Vincent Square, SW1P 2PE. *T:* (020) 7821 3050.

ELLIS, family name of **Baron Seaford**.

ELLIS, Dr Adrian Foss, CB 2004; FREng; Director of Field Operations, Health and Safety Executive, 1996–2003; *b* 15 Feb. 1944; *s* of Henry James Ellis and Marjorie Foss Ellis (*née* Smith); *m* 1st, 1968, Lesley Maxted Smith (*d* 1970); 2nd, 1973, Hilary Jean Miles; two *d* one *s*. *Educ:* Dean Close Sch., Cheltenham; Univ. of London (1st cl. Hons Chem. Eng.); Loughborough Univ. of Technology (PhD). FIChemE 1977; FInstE 1977; FREng (FEng 1995). Student Apprentice, Richard Thomas & Baldwins, 1962–66; British Steel Corp., 1966–71; DoE (Alkali and Clean Air), 1971–83; Health and Safety Executive: Major Hazards Assessment Unit, 1983–86; Dep. Chief Inspector (Chemicals), 1986; Reg. Dir, 1990; Dir of Technology and Dir of Hazardous Installations Policy, 1990; Dir of Technology and Health Scis Div., 1991–96. ILO Consultant on major hazards control in India, Pakistan, Thailand, Indonesia. Vis. Prof., Dept of Applied Energy, Cranfield Univ. (formerly Inst. of Technology), 1992–99. Pres., Internat. Assoc. of Labour Inspection, 2002–05 (Vice-Pres. and Sec. Gen., 1999–2002). Mem. Council, IChemE, 1993–97. *Publications:* papers on risk assessment and major hazards control. *Recreations:* bridge, Swindon Town FC, exploring car boot sales. *Address:* 1 Wootton Oast, Garlinge Green Road, Petham, Canterbury, Kent CT4 5RJ. *T:* (01227) 700137. *Club:* Athenæum.

ELLIS, Alexander Wykeham; HM Diplomatic Service; Ambassador to Portugal, since 2007; *b* London, 5 June 1967; *s* of Roger Wykeham Ellis, *qv*; *m* 1996, Teresa Adegas; one *s*. *Educ:* Dragon Sch., Oxford; Winchester Coll.; Magdalene Coll., Cambridge (BA Hons Mod. Hist. 1989). Teacher, St Edward's Sch., Oxford, 1989–90; FCO, 1990–92; Third, then Second Sec., Lisbon, 1992–96; First Sec. (Econ.), UK Repn to EU, Brussels, 1996–2001; FCO, 2001–03; Counsellor, EU, Madrid, 2003–05; Advr to Pres. of EC, 2005–07. *Recreations:* most ball games, music, theatre, history. *Address:* c/o Foreign and Commonwealth Office, King Charles Street, SW1A 2AH. *Clubs:* MCC; Denham Golf.

ELLIS, Andrew Steven, OBE 1984; international consultant/technical adviser on democracy and governance issues, since 1989; Director of Operations, International Institute for Democracy and Electoral Assistance, since 2006 (Head of Electoral Programmes, 2003–06; *b* 19 May 1952; *s* of late Peter Vernon Ellis and Kathleen Dawe; *m* 1st, 1975, Patricia Ann Stevens (marr. diss. 1987); 2nd, 1990, Helen Prudence Drummond. *Educ:* Trinity Coll., Cambridge (BA Mathematics); Univ. of Newcastle upon Tyne (MSc Statistics); Newcastle upon Tyne Polytechnic (BA Law). Proprietor, Andrew Ellis (Printing and Duplicating), Newcastle upon Tyne, 1973–81; freelance Election Agent/Organizer, 1981–84; Sec.-Gen., Liberal Party, 1985–88; Chief Exec., Social and Liberal Democrats, 1988–89; freelance political consultant, 1989–93; Dir, GJW Hldgs Ltd, 1993–99; Associate Dir, GJW, subseq. GJW-BSMG Worldwide, then GJW Europe-Weber Shandwick Worldwide, 1999–2002. Consultant Nat. Agent, Welsh Liberal Party, 1984–88. Contested (L): Newcastle upon Tyne Central, Oct. 1974, Nov. 1976, 1979; Boothferry, 1983; Leader, Liberal Gp, Tyne & Wear CC, 1977–81; Vice-Chm., Liberal Party, 1980–86. Tech. Advr to Chm., Palestine Central Election Commn, 1994–96; Co-ordinator, OSCE Observation Mission for Registration of Voters, Bosnia and Hercegovina, 1997; designer of Eur. Commn electoral assistance to Cambodia, 1997–98; Sen. Advr on constitutional, electoral and decentralisation issues, Nat. Democratic Inst., Indonesia, 1998–2003. *Publications:* Algebraic Structure (with Terence Treeby), 1971; Let Every Englishman's Home Be His Castle, 1978; (contrib.) Indonesia Matters, 2003; (contrib.) International Handbook of Electoral Systems, 2004; (jtly) Electoral System Design: the New International IDEA Handbook, 2006; (jtly) Electoral Management Design, 2006; (jtly) Voting Abroad, 2007. *Recreation:* travel. *Address:* (office) 10334 Strömsborg, Stockholm, Sweden; (home) Högomsvägen 11, 18350 Täby, Sweden. *Club:* National Liberal.

ELLIS, Arthur John, CBE 1986; Chairman, Fyffes Group Ltd, 1984–2008 (Chief Executive Officer, 1969–95); *b* 22 Aug. 1932; *s* of Arthur Ellis and Freda Jane Ellis; *m* 1956, Rita Patricia Blake; two *s* one *d*. *Educ:* Chingford Jun. High Sch.; South West Essex Technical Coll. FCCA; FCMA; FCIS; MBCS. Joined Fyffes Gp Ltd, Finance and Admin Dept, 1954; Chief Financial Officer, 1965; Financial Dir, 1967; Dir, Fyffes plc, 1991–2001. Chm., Nat. Seed Develt Organisation Ltd, 1982–87. Chm., Intervention Bd for Agricl Produce, later Intervention Bd Exec. Agency, 1986–95. *Recreations:* golf, reading, gardening. *Clubs:* Reform, Farmers'.

ELLIS, Bryan James; Under-Secretary, Department of Health and Social Security, later Department of Social Security, 1977–93; *b* 11 June 1934; *s* of late Frank and Renée Ellis; *m* 1960, Barbara Muriel Whiteley; one *s* one *d*. *Educ:* Merchant Taylors' Sch.; St John's Coll., Oxford (BA Lit.Hum. 1957; MA 1960); Open Univ. (BA Hist. 1998). Sec., Oxford Union Soc., 1956. Joined Min. of Pensions and National Insurance as Asst Principal, 1958; Principal, 1963; Asst Sec., DHSS, 1971; served in CSSB as Chm., 1986, and in OPCS as Dep. Dir, 1987–90. Chm., Assoc. of First Div. Civil Servants, 1983–85. Chm., Trustees of Leopardstown Park Hosp., Dublin, 1979–84. *Publications:* Pensions in Britain 1955–75, 1989; Walton Past, 2002. *Recreations:* theatre, cinema, bridge. *Address:* 8 The Chestnuts, Walton-on-Thames KT12 1EE. *Club:* MCC.

ELLIS, Carol Jacqueline, (Mrs Ralph Gilmore), CBE 1995; QC 1980; Consultant Editor, Road Traffic Reports, since 1970; *b* 6 May 1929; *d* of Ellis W. Ellis and Flora Bernstein; *m* 1957, Ralph Gilmore (*d* 1996); two *s*. *Educ:* Abbey Sch., Reading; La Ramée, Lausanne; Univ. of Lausanne; University Coll. London (LLB). Called to the Bar, Gray's Inn, 1951; supernumerary law reporter for The Law Reports, The Times, and other legal jls, 1952; law reporter to The Law Reports and Weekly Law Reports, 1954; Asst Editor, Weekly Law Reports, 1969; Managing Editor, The Law Reports and Weekly

Law Reports, 1970; Editor, 1976–90, Consultant Editor, 1990–99, Weekly Law Reports; Editor, 1976–96, Consultant Editor, 1996–99, The Law Reports. Mem., Inner London Probation Cttee, 1989–95. JP W Central Div. Inner London, 1972–98. *Recreations:* travel, music, theatre. *Address:* 11 Old Square, Lincoln's Inn, WC2A 3TS. *T:* (020) 7403 0341.

ELLIS, David Charles; Director of Business Improvement, National Trust, since 2006; *b* 29 Dec. 1960; *s* of Oswald David Ellis and Joyce Mary Ellis; *m* 1990, Yvonne (*née* Pauline); two *s*. *Educ:* Exeter Univ. (BSc Hons Physics). Overseas aid worker, Southern Sudan, 1984–87; with various UK disability charities, 1987–92; Regl Dir, British Red Cross, 1992–98; Dir of Services, Guide Dogs for the Blind, 1998–2001; Chief Exec., Cancer and Leukaemia in Childhood, then CLIC Sargent, 2001–05. *Recreations:* photography, gardening, reading. *Address:* c/o National Trust, Heelis, Kemble Drive, Swindon, Wilts SN2 2NA. *T:* (01793) 817400.

ELLIS, David Raymond; His Honour Judge Ellis; a Circuit Judge, since 1995; *b* 4 Sept. 1946; *s* of Raymond Ellis and Ethel Ellis (*née* Gordon); *m* 1974, Cathleen Margaret Hawe; one *s* one *d*. *Educ:* St Edward's Sch., Oxford; Christ Church, Oxford (MA Jurisprudence). Called to the Bar, Inner Temple, 1970; barrister, 1970–95; a Recorder, 1991–95. Chm., Lord Chancellor's SE London Adv. Cttee, 2000–05. *Recreations:* travel, theatre, boating, the garden. *Address:* Croydon Combined Court Centre, The Law Courts, Altyre Road, Croydon CR9 5AB. *Club:* Leander (Henley).

ELLIS, Diana; QC 2001; a Recorder, since 1998; *d* of Evan Henry Ellis and Irene Sarah Jeanette Ellis (*née* Behrens); *m* 2001, Geoffrey Keith Watts. *Educ:* London Sch. of Econs (Dip. Social Admin); LLB Hons London. Teacher, Italia Conti Stage Sch., 1971–74; called to the Bar, Inner Temple, 1978; in practice as barrister, SE Circuit, 1978–, specialising in criminal and internat. law. *Recreations:* reading, theatre, travel, walking, 'Italo-philia'. *Address:* 25 Bedford Row, WC1R 4HD.

ELLIS, Diana Margaret, CBE 2004; Chairman, Amateur Rowing Association Ltd, since 1989; *b* 11 April 1938; *d* of Robert and Mabel Helen Hall; *m* 1966, John David Ellis; one *d*. *Educ:* Guildford Coll. of Technol. MRSH 1994. Accounts manager, 1958–68; Dist Manager, Surrey CC, 1987–97. Steward, Henley Royal Regatta, 1997– (1st Lady Steward); Mem. Exec. Bd, British Olympic Assoc., 1997–; Director: Confedn of British Sport, 1999–; CCPR 2000– (Dep. Chm., 2005–); Sports Dispute Resolution Panel, 2001–; Skills Active, 2004–07. Trustee: British Olympic Med. Trust, 2000–; River and Rowing Mus., 2006–. FRSA. *Recreation:* rowing. *Address:* Amateur Rowing Association, The Priory, 6 Lower Mall, W6 9DJ. *T:* (020) 8237 6700, *Fax:* (020) 8237 6749. *Clubs:* Leander (Henley), Twickenham Rowing.

ELLIS, (Dorothy) June; Headmistress, The Mount School, York, 1977–86; Clerk to Central Committee, Quaker Social Responsibility and Education, 1987–90; *b* 30 May 1926; *d* of Robert Edwin and Dora Ellis. *Educ:* La Sagesse, Newcastle upon Tyne; BSc Pure Science, Durham; DipEd Newcastle upon Tyne. Assistant Mistress: Darlington High Sch., 1947–49; Rutherford High Sch., 1949–50; La Sagesse High Sch., 1950–53; Housemistress, 1953–61, Sen. Mistress, 1961–64, St Monica's Sch.; Dep. Head, Sibford Sch., 1964–77. Clerk, 1986–90, Mem., 1990–98, Swerford Parish Council; Mem., Milcombe PCC, 1999–2006. Mem. Cttee, Bray d'Oyley Housing Assoc., 1993–96. Mem. Council, Woodbrooke Coll., 1987–93; Governor: Ellerslie Sch., Malvern, 1987–92; Friends' Sch., Saffron Walden, 1990–93; St Mary's Primary Sch., Bloxham, 2000–04. *Recreations:* gardening, home-making. *Address:* Willowside, Swerford, Oxford OX7 4BQ. *T:* (01608) 737334.

ELLIS, Eileen Mary, RDI 1984; freelance textile designer; *b* 1 March 1933; *m* 1954, Julian Ellis; one *s* two *d*. *Educ:* Leicester, Central and Royal Colleges of Art. Des RCA 1957; FCSD (FSIAD 1976). Designer of contract and decorative woven furnishing fabrics, carpets and woven wall coverings; designed for Ascher & Co., 1957–59; Partner, Orbit Design Group, 1960–73; formed Weaveplan, to provide design and consultancy services, 1973–. Lecturer: Hornsey Coll. of Art/Middx Polytechnic, 1965–74; RCA, 1974–82. Director: Jamasque Ltd, 1982–96; Curragh Tintawn Carpets Ltd, 1987–95. Hon. Pres., Textile Soc., 2003–08. Textile Inst. Design Medal, 1985; Silver Medal, Weavers' Co., 2002. *Recreation:* country life. *Address:* Weaveplan, The Granary Studio, Holbeam Road, Stalisfield, Faversham, Kent ME13 0HS. *T:* (01795) 890852.

ELLIS, Prof. George Francis Rayner, PhD; FRS 2007; FRSSAf; Professor of Applied Mathematics, University of Cape Town, 1973–87 and 1989–2005, now Emeritus; President, Royal Society of South Africa, 1992–96; *b* 11 Aug. 1939; *s* of George Rayner Ellis and Gwendoline Hilda Ellis (*née* MacRobert); *m* 1st, 1963, Jane Mary Sue Parkes; one *s* one *d*; 2nd, 1978, Mary MacDonald Wheeldon. *Educ:* Univ. of Cape Town (BSc Hons 1960; Fellow, 1982); St John's Coll., Cambridge (PhD 1964). FRSSAf 1983 (Hon. FRSSAf, 2008). Lectr, Cambridge Univ., 1968–73; Prof., Scuola Internazionale Superiore di Studi Avanzati Trieste, 1987–89. Vis. Prof., Univs of Texas, Hamburg, Chicago, Alberta, and QMC London. Pres., Internat. Soc. of General Relativity and Gravitation, 1987–91. Clerk, S Africa Yearly Meeting of Quakers, 1982–86; Chairman: Quaker Service, W Cape, 1978–86; Quaker Peace Work Cttee, W Cape, 1989–. Hon. DSc: Haverford Coll., 1995; Natal Univ., 1998; London, 2001. Herschel Medal, Royal Soc. of S Africa, 1978; Medal, SA Assoc. for Advancement of Science, 1993; Gold Medal, SA Math. Soc., 2001. Star of S Africa Medal, 1999; Order of Mapungubwe, 2005. *Publications:* (with S. W. Hawking) The Large Scale Structure of Space-Time, 1973; (with D. Dewar) Low Income Housing Policy, 1979; Before the Beginning, 1993; (with N. Murphy) On the Moral Nature of the Universe, 1996; The Far Future Universe, 2001. *Recreations:* mountain climbing, gliding. *Address:* Department of Applied Mathematics, University of Cape Town, Rondebosch 7700, Cape Town, South Africa; 3 Marlow Road, Kenilworth, Cape Town 7700, South Africa. *T:* 7612313. *Club:* Mountain of South Africa (Cape Town).

ELLIS, Prof. Harold, CBE 1987; MA, MCh, DM; FRCS; FRCOG; Clinical Anatomist, University of London, at Guy's campus, since 1993; *b* 13 Jan. 1926; *s* of Samuel and Ada Ellis; *m* 1958, Wendy Mae Levine; one *s* one *d*. *Educ:* Queen's Coll. (State Scholar and Open Scholar in Natural Sciences), Oxford; Radcliffe Infirmary, Oxford. BM, BCh, 1948; FRCS, MA, 1951; MCh 1956; DM 1962; FRCOG *ad eundem*, 1987. House Surgeon, Radcliffe Infirmary, 1948–49; Hallett Prize, RCS, 1949. RAMC, 1949–51. Res. Surgical Officer, Sheffield Royal Infirm., 1952–54; Registrar, Westminster Hosp., 1955; Sen. Registrar and Surgical Tutor, Radcliffe Infirm., Oxford, 1956–60; Sen. Lectr in Surgery, 1960–62, Hon. Consultant Surgeon, 1960–89, Westminster Hosp.; Prof. of Surgery, Univ. of London, 1962–89; Clinical Anatomist, Univ. of Cambridge and Fellow, Churchill Coll., Cambridge, 1989–93. Hon. Consultant Surgeon to the Army, 1978–89. Mem. Council, RCS, 1974–86. Member: Association of Surgeons; British Soc. of Gastroenterol.; Surgical Research Soc.; Council: RSocMed; British Assoc. of Surgical Oncology; Associé étranger, L'Academie de Chirurgie, Paris, 1983. Hon. FACS 1989; Hon. FRCP 2004. *Publications:* Clinical Anatomy, 1960; Anatomy for Anaesthetists, 1963; Lecture Notes on General Surgery, 1965; Principles of Resuscitation, 1967; History of the Bladder Stone, 1970; General Surgery for Nurses, 1976; Intestinal Obstruction, 1982; Notable Names in Medicine and Surgery, 1983; Famous Operations, 1984; Wound Healing for Surgeons, 1984; Maingot's Abdominal Operations, 1985; Research in Medicine, 1990; Cross-sectional Anatomy, 1991; Surgical Case-Histories from the Past, 1994; (ed) French's Index of Differential Diagnosis, 1996; A History of Surgery, 2000; numerous articles on surgical topics in medical journals. *Recreation:* medical history. *Address:* 16 Bancroft Avenue, N2 0AS. *T:* (020) 8348 2720.

ELLIS, Herbert; *see* Ellis, W. H. B.

ELLIS, Jennifer; *see* Rowe, J.

ELLIS, John; Member, Local Government Planning Executive, 2000–03; Steel Worker, British Steel plc, Scunthorpe, 1980–89; *b* Hexthorpe, Doncaster, 22 Oct. 1930; *s* of George and Hilda Ellis; *m* 1953, Rita Butters; two *s* two *d*. *Educ:* Rastrick Gram. Sch., Brighouse. Laboratory technician, Meteorological Office, 1947–63; Vice-Chm., Staff side, Air Min. Whitley Council, 1961–63; Member Relations Offr, Co-op. Retail Services, Bristol/Bath Region, 1971–74. Member: Easthampstead RDC, 1962–66; Bristol City Council, 1971–74; Humberside County Council, 1987–96; N Lincs Council, 1995–2003 (Vice Chm., Housing Cttee, 1998–99; Chm., Planning Cttee, 1999–2003). Chairman: Humberside Social Service Council, 1992–94 (Vice-Chm., 1990–92); Social Services Children's Cttee, 1991–94; Member: Scunthorpe HA, 1988–91 (Chm., Jt Consultative Cttee, 1988–2000); NRA (formerly Lincs Land Drainage Cttee), 1988–96 (Member: Anglian Regl Flood Defence cttee; Lincs Flood Defence cttee). Contested (Lab) Wokingham, 1964; MP (Lab) Bristol North-West, 1966–70, Brigg and Scunthorpe, Feb. 1974–1979; PPS to Minister of State for Transport, 1968–70; an Asst Govt Whip, 1974–76. Formerly Mem., Select Cttee on Nationalised Industries. Chm., 1985–2002, Sec./Treas., 2002–05, Co-op. Party. JP North Riding Yorks, 1960–61. *Publication:* (jtly) Fabian pamphlet on MPs from Unions, 1974. *Recreations:* gardening, watching cricket. *Address:* 102 Glover Road, Scunthorpe DN17 1AS.

ELLIS, John, CB 1985; Head of Royal Armament Research and Development Establishment, Chertsey, 1984–85, retired; *b* 9 Jan. 1925; *s* of Frank William and Alice Ellis; *m* 1958, Susan Doris (*née* Puttock). *Educ:* Leeds Univ. BSc, 1st cl. hons. Mech. Eng; CEng, MIMechE. Hydro-Ballistic Research Estabt, Admty, 1945–47; David Brown & Sons Ltd, Huddersfield, 1948; RAE, Min. of Supply (Structures Dept, Armament Dept, Weapons Dept), 1948–68; MVEE (formerly FVRDE), MoD, 1968–84; Dir, MVEE, Chertsey, 1978–84, when MVEE and RARDE amalgamated. Ind. technical consultant, 1985–2001. *Recreations:* motoring, golf. *Address:* Foresters, 1 Kitchers Close, Sway, Lymington, Hants SO41 6DS. *T:* (01590) 682410.

ELLIS, John; *see* Ellis, Jonathan Richard.

ELLIS, John Norman, OBE 1995; industrial relations consultant, since 1995, Chairman, since 2000, Talking People Ltd; *b* 22 Feb. 1939; *s* of Margaret and Albert Ellis; *m* 1st; one *s* one *d*; 2nd, Diane; two step *s*. *Educ:* Osmondthorpe; Leeds Secondary Modern; Leeds College of Commerce. Post Office Messenger and Postman, 1954–58; Clerical Officer and Executive Officer, MPBW, 1958–67; Civil and Public Services Association: Asst Sec., 1968–82; Dep. Gen. Sec., 1982–86; Gen. Sec., 1986–92; Sec., CCSU, 1992–95. Member: Gen. Council, TUC, 1988–92 (Mem. Economic, Social Services, Industrial Welfare, Public Services and Pensions Specialists Cttees, 1988–92); Inst. of Employment Rights, 1989–; Industrial Tribunal Panel, 1992–; Exec. Cttee, Civil Service Pensioners' Alliance, 1996–2004; Exec. Cttee, London (South) Tribunal Members Assoc., 2001–. Mem., Bd and Vice Chm., Tandridge Leisure Ltd, 2000–. Chm., Caterham Br., Lab. Party, 1997–2004 (Vice-Chm., 1996). Mem., Caterham Valley Parish Council, 2002–04. *Recreations:* reading, watching sport, gardening, listening to music, dog walking, computer building. *Address:* 26 Harestone Valley Road, Caterham, Surrey CR3 6HD.

ELLIS, Prof. John Romaine; Professor of Automobile Engineering, 1960–82 and Director, 1960–76, School of Automotive Studies, Cranfield; *b* 30 Sept. 1922; *m* 1947, Madelaine Della Blaker; one *s* one *d*. *Educ:* Tiffin Sch., Kingston-on-Thames. Royal Aircraft Establishment, 1944–56; Fairey Aviation Company, 1946–48; Royal Military Coll. of Science, Shrivenham, near Swindon, Wilts, 1949–60. *Recreations:* golf, music.

ELLIS, John Russell, FCILT; transport consultant, since 1997; *b* 21 May 1938; *s* of Percy Macdonald Ellis and Winifred Maud (*née* Bunker); *m* 1962, Jean Eileen Taylor; two *d*. *Educ:* Rendcomb Coll., Cirencester; Pembroke Coll., Oxford (BA Hons PPE). FCILT 1997. Joined BR as Grad. Management Trainee, 1962; various posts, 1963–80; Chief Freight Manager, 1980–83, Divl Manager, 1983–84, Asst Gen. Manager, 1984–85, Eastern Region; Dep. Gen. Manager, Southern Region, 1985–87; Gen. Manager, ScotRail, 1987–90; Gen. Manager, Southern Region, 1990–91; Dep. Man. Dir, InterCity, 1992–93; Dir, Production, Railtrack, 1993–95; Man. Dir, ScotRail, 1995–97. Director: GB Railfreight, 2001–; Rail Estate Consultancy, 2002–. Trustee, Transport 2000 Trust, 2001–; Chm., Nat. Railway Heritage Awards, 2001–. *Recreations:* hockey, cricket, walking, gardening, music. *Address:* St Anne's, High Street, Chipping Campden, Glos GL55 6AL. *T:* (01386) 841253.

ELLIS, Dr Jonathan Richard, (John), FRS 1985; Senior Staff Physicist, Theoretical Studies Division, CERN, Geneva, since 1994 (Leader, 1988–94); *b* 1 July 1946; *s* of Richard Ellis and Beryl Lilian Ellis (*née* Ranger); *m* 1985, Maria Mercedes Martinez Rengifo; one *s* one *d*. *Educ:* Highgate Sch.; King's Coll., Cambridge (BA, PhD; Hon. Fellow, 2006). Postdoctoral research, SLAC, Stanford, 1971–72; Richard Chase Tolman Fellow, CIT, 1972–73; Staff Mem., CERN, Geneva, 1973–, Advr to Dir-Gen. for relns with non-member States. Member: PPARC, 2004–07; Sci. Bd, STFC, 2007–. FInstP. Maxwell Medal, Royal Soc., 1982. *Recreations:* movies, reading, travel, hiking in the mountains. *Address:* 5 Chemin du Ruisseau, Tannay, 1295 Mies, Vaud, Switzerland. *T:* (22) 7764858.

ELLIS, June; *see* Ellis, D. J.

ELLIS, Laurence Edward, MA; Rector, The Edinburgh Academy, 1977–92; *b* 21 April 1932; *s* of Dr and Mrs E. A. Ellis; *m* 1961, Elizabeth Ogilvie; two *s* one *d*. *Educ:* Winchester Coll.; Trinity Coll., Cambridge (MA). AFIMA. 2/Lieut Rifle Bde, 1950–52. Marlborough Coll., 1955–77 (Housemaster, 1968). Lay Reader, Salisbury, 1961–. FRSA. *Publications:* (part-author) texts on school maths, statistics, computing, and calculating; articles in jls. *Recreations:* writing, music. *Address:* Glendene, Wick Lane, Devizes, Wilts SN10 5DW.

ELLIS, Martin Arthur; costs mediator/costs consultant; Taxing Master of the Supreme Court, 1990–2000, Costs Judge, 1999–2000; *b* 10 Jan. 1933; *s* of Walter Ellis and Phoebe Alicia Ellis; *m* 1961, Moira Herbert; one *s* (and one *s* decd). *Educ:* Beckenham Grammar School. Solicitor, admitted 1956; 2nd Lieut, 4th Regt, Royal Horse Artillery, 1957–58; Partner, Simmons & Simmons, 1973–90. *Recreations:* sport, golf, cricket. *Address:* Field House, North Road, Sandwich Bay, Kent CT13 9PJ. *T:* and *Fax:* (01304) 619375. *Clubs:* MCC; Kent CC, Royal St George's Golf.

ELLIS, Michael Henry, OBE 2007; Group Finance Director, HBOS plc, 2001–04 and since 2008; *b* 4 Aug. 1951; *s* of late John Ellis and Joan (*née* Lawton); *m* 1973, Jeanette Booth; two *d*. *Educ:* Open Univ. (BA). CIPFA 1973; FCT 1990. Various posts in local govt sector, 1967–87; Halifax Building Society, later Halifax plc: Gp Treas., 1987–92; Gen. Manager, Treasury and Eur. Ops, 1992–95; Man. Dir, Treasury and Overseas Ops, 1995–96; Banking and Savings Dir, 1996–99; Financial Services Dir, 1999; Chief Operating Officer, 1999–2001. Fund Comr and Chm., Fund Distribution Ltd, 2005–06. Non-exec. Dir, W H Smith plc, 2005–. *Recreations:* travel, football, music, reading. *Address:* HBOS plc, The Mound, Edinburgh EH1 1YZ. *Club:* Royal Automobile.

ELLIS, Morag; *see* Ellis, R. M.

ELLIS, Nicholas St John; QC (Scot.) 2002; *b* 11 Nov. 1958; *s* of Anthony Brian Ellis and Pauline Ellis; *m* 1997, Victoria Craig; one *s* one *d*. *Educ:* Edinburgh Univ. (LLB). Admitted solicitor, 1981; WS 1985; called to the Scottish Bar, 1990. *Recreations:* hill-walking, fine wine. *Address:* The Old Manse, 3 Kaimes Road, Edinburgh EH12 6JR. *T:* (0131) 334 7557; *e-mail:* Nstje@aol.com.

ELLIS, Dr Norman David; Under Secretary, British Medical Association, 1980–2000 (Senior Industrial Relations Officer, 1978–82); *b* 23 Nov. 1943; *s* of late George Edward Ellis and late Annie Elsie Scarfe; *m* 1966, Valerie Ann Fenn, PhD; one *s*. *Educ:* Minchenden Sch.; Univ. of Leeds (BA); MA (Oxon), PhD. Research Officer, Dept of Employment, 1969–71; Leverhulme Fellowship in Industrial Relations, Nuffield Coll., Oxford, 1971–74; Gen. Sec., Assoc. of First Division Civil Servants, 1974–78. *Publications:* (with W. E. J. McCarthy) Management by Agreement, 1973; Employing Staff, 1984; (with J. Chisholm) Making sense of the Red Book, 1993, 3rd edn 1997; (ed with T. Stanton) Making sense of Partnerships, 1994; Making sense of General Practice, 1994; (with J. Lindsay) Making sense of Pensions and Retirement, 1995; General Practitioners' Handbook, 1997, 2nd edn (with D. Grantham), 2000; GP Employment Handbook, 1998; (with J. Lindsay) Staff Pensions in General Practice, 1998; various contribs to industrial relations literature. *Recreations:* maritime history, reading, travel, swimming. *Address:* 33 Foxes Dale, SE3 9BH. *T:* (020) 8852 6244.

ELLIS, Osian Gwynn, CBE 1971; harpist; Professor of Harp, Royal Academy of Music, London, 1959–89; *b* Ffynnongroew, Flints, 8 Feb. 1928; *s* of Rev. T. G. Ellis, Methodist Minister; *m* 1951, Rene Ellis Jones, Pwllheli; two *s*. *Educ:* Denbigh Grammar Sch.; Royal Academy of Music. Has broadcast and televised extensively. Has given recitals/concertos all over the world; shared poetry and music recitals with Dame Peggy Ashcroft, Paul Robeson, Burton, C. Day-Lewis, etc. Mem., Melos Ensemble; solo harpist with LSO, 1961–94. Former Mem., Music and Welsh Adv. Cttees, British Council. Works written for him include Harp Concertos by Hoddinott, 1957 and by Mathias, 1970, Jersild, 1972, Robin Holloway, 1985; chamber works by Gian Carlo Menotti, 1977; William Schuman, 1978; from 1960 worked with Benjamin Britten who wrote for him Harp Suite in C (Op. 83) and (for perf. with Sir Peter Pears) Canticle V, Birthday Hansel, and folk songs; from 1974 accompanied Sir Peter Pears on recital tours, Europe and USA; records concertos, recitals, folk songs, etc. Film, The Harp, won a Paris award; other awards include Grand Prix du Disque and French Radio Critics' Award. FRAM 1960. Hon. DMus Wales, 1970. *Publication:* Story of the Harp in Wales, 1991. *Address:* Arfryn, Ala Road, Pwllheli, Gwynedd LL53 5BN. *T:* (01758) 612501.

ELLIS, Prof. Reginald John, PhD; FRS 1983; Professor of Biological Sciences, University of Warwick, 1976–96, now Emeritus; *b* 12 Feb. 1935; *s* of Francis Gilbert Ellis and Evangeline Gratton Ellis; *m* 1963, Diana Margaret Warren; one *d*. *Educ:* Highbury County Sch.; King's Coll., London (BSc, PhD). ARC Fellow, Univ. of Oxford, 1961–64; Lectr in Botany and Biochemistry, Univ. of Aberdeen, 1964–70; Sen. Lectr, 1970–73, Reader, 1973–76, Dept of Biol Sciences, Univ. of Warwick; SERC Senior Res. Fellow, 1983–88. Sen. Vis. Fellow, St John's Coll., Oxford, 1992–93; Vis. Prof., Oxford Centre for Molecular Scis, 1997–2001. Mem. EMBO, 1986. LRPS 1987. Tate & Lyle Award (for contribs to plant biochem.), 1980; Internat. Gairdner Foundn Award, 2004; Internat. Medal, Cell Stress Soc., 2007. Research interests include chloroplast biogenesis, protein aggregation, and molecular chaperones. *Publications:* 160 papers in biochem. jls. *Recreations:* photography, hill walking.

ELLIS, Richard Marriott; Chairman, East of England Development Agency, since 2003; *b* 23 Jan. 1955; *s* of late Martin Beazor Ellis and of Janet Pamela Ellis (*née* Morgan); *m* 1987, Lesley Anne Smith; three *s* two *d*. *Educ:* Shene Grammar Sch.; Norwich City Coll. ACMA 1979. Financial Dir, Tucker Foods Ltd, 1984–92; Man. Dir, Norfolk Country Cottages, 1992–; Chief Exec., Kettle Foods Ltd, 1994–2000. Chairman: Arts and Business East, 2000–03; East of England Sustainable Develt Round Table, 2001–03. Chm., Earlham Early Years Centre, 2000–04; Trustee: Norwich Th. Royal, 1999–; The Forum Trust, 2002–; Norwich Heritage and Econ. Regeneration Trust, 2004–; Rothamsted Research, 2005–. FRSA. *Recreations:* travel, ski-ing badly, seeking adrenaline (bungee jumping, sky diving, etc.), finding things which aren't there, avoiding Who Was Who! *Address:* c/o East of England Development Agency, The Business Centre, Station Road, Histon, Cambridge CB4 9LQ. *T:* (01223) 484545, *Fax:* (01223) 713939; *e-mail:* richardellis@eeda.org.uk. *Club:* Norfolk.

ELLIS, Richard Peter; Principal Assistant Treasury Solicitor, Legal Advisory Division, Ministry of Defence, 1988–91; *b* 25 Oct. 1931; *s* of late Comdr Thomas Ellis, RN and Kathleen Mary Ellis (*nee* Lewis); *m* 1963, Penelope Jane, *yr d* of late Captain J. B. Hall, RN; two *s* two *d*. *Educ:* Sherborne; RMA Sandhurst. Commissioned Royal Irish Fusiliers, 1952; served 1st Bn, BAOR, Berlin, Korea, Kenya; resigned commission 1957. Called to the Bar, Lincoln's Inn, 1960; Practised Common Law Bar, 1960–65, Oxford Circuit; Treasury Solicitor's Dept, 1965–91. *Recreations:* country pursuits, travel, reading. *Address:* c/o Lloyds TSB, Somerton, Somerset TA11 7NB. *Club:* Army and Navy.

ELLIS, Prof. Richard Salisbury, CBE 2008; FRS 1995; Steele Professor, California Institute of Technology, since 2002 (Professor of Astronomy, since 1999); Royal Society Professor, Department of Astrophysics, University of Oxford, since 2008; Fellow, Merton College, Oxford, since 2008; *b* 25 May 1950; *s* of late Capt. Arthur Ellis, MBE and of Marion Ellis (*née* Davies); *m* 1972, Barbara Williams; one *s* one *d*. *Educ:* Abergele GS; University Coll. London (BSc Hons 1971; Fellow, 1998); Wolfson Coll., Oxford (DPhil 1974) FRAS 1974; FInstP 1998. Durham University: Sen. Demonstrator in Physics, 1974–77; Res. Asst, 1977–81; Lectr in Astronomy, 1981–83; Principal Res. Fellow, Royal Greenwich Observatory, 1983–85; Prof. of Astronomy, Durham Univ., 1985–93; SERC Sen. Res. Fellow, 1989–94; Cambridge University: Plumian Prof. of Astronomy and Exptl Philosophy, 1993–99; Dir, Inst. of Astronomy, 1994–99; Professorial Fellow, Magdalene Coll., 1994–99; Director: Palomar Observatory, 2000–02; Caltech Optical Observatories, 2002–05. Chm., SERC Large Telescope Panel, 1986–90; Mem., Anglo-Australian Telescope Bd, 1991–95. Associate, Canadian Inst. of Advanced Res., 1993–; Member: Space Telescope Science Inst. Council, 1995–2001; Gemini Telescopes Bd, 1996–98; Bd, W. M. Keck Observatory, 2000–05. Visiting Professor: Space Telescope Science Inst., 1985, 2006; Anglo-Australian Observatory, 1991; CIT, 1991, 1997; Princeton, 1992; Carnegie Observatory, 1998; UCL, 2005; Toronto, 2006; Oxford, 2007 Hon. Prof., Observational Astrophysics, Univ. of Cambridge, 2000–03. Lectures: J. L Bishop, Princeton, 1992; Halley, Oxford, 1993; Cormack, RSE, 1996; Lockyer, RAS 1997; Sackler, Harvard, 1998; Bakerian, Royal Soc., 1998; Poynting, Birmingham, 1998 Grubb Parsons, Durham, 1999; Rosenblum, Jerusalem, 1999; Lansdowne, Victoria, 2001 Allison-Levick, Astronomical Soc., Australia, 2004; J. Bahcall, NASA, 2006; J. L. Bishop NY, 2007; E. Spreadbury, UCL, 2008. Hon. DSc Durham, 2002. *Publications:* Epoch c Galaxy Formation, 1988; Observational Tests of Cosmological Inflation, 1991; Large Scal Structure in the Universe, 1999; numerous articles in astronomical jls. *Recreations* exploration, photography, music, ski-ing. *Address:* Astronomy Department, Mailsto 105–24, California Institute of Technology, Pasadena, CA 91125, USA. *T:* (626 3952598; Department of Astrophysics, Keble Road, Oxford OX1 3RH. *T:* (01865 273303.

ELLIS, (Robert) Thomas; *b* 15 March 1924; *s* of Robert and Edith Ann Ellis; *m* 1949 Nona Harcourt Williams; three *s* one *d*. *Educ:* Universities of Wales and Nottingham Works Chemist, ICI, 1944–47; Coal Miner, 1947–55; Mining Engineer, 1955–70 Manager, Bersham Colliery, N Wales, 1957–70. MP Wrexham, 1970–83 (Lab, 1970–81 SDP, 1981–83). Contested: Clywd South West (SDP) 1983, (SDP/Alliance) 1987 Pontypridd (SLD) Feb. 1989. Mem., European Parlt, 1975–79. *Publications:* Mines anc Men, 1971; Dan Loriau Maelor, 2003; After the Dust Has Settled, 2004. *Recreations:* golf reading, music. *Address:* 3 Old Vicarage, Ruabon, Wrexham LL14 6LG. *T:* (01978 821128.

ELLIS, Ven. Robin Gareth; Archdeacon of Plymouth, 1982–2000; *b* 8 Dec. 1935; *s* o Walter and Morva Ellis; *m* 1964, Anne Ellis (*née* Landers); three *s*. *Educ:* Worksop Coll. Notts; Pembroke Coll., Oxford (BCL, MA). Curate of Swinton, 1960–63; Asst Chaplain Worksop Coll., 1963–66; Vicar of Swaffham Prior and Reach, and Asst Director o Religious Education, Diocese of Ely, 1966–74; Vicar of St Augustine, Wisbech, 1974–82 Vicar of St Paul's, Yelverton, 1982–86. *Recreations:* cricket, theatre, prison reform. *Address* 24 Lyndhurst Road, Exmouth, Devon EX8 3DT. *T:* (01395) 272891.

ELLIS, Roger Wykeham, CBE 1984; Master of Marlborough College, 1972–86; *b* 3 Oct 1929; *s* of Cecil Ellis, solicitor, and Pamela Unwin; *m* 1964, Margaret Jean, *d* of Willian Hugh Stevenson; one *s* two *d*. *Educ:* St Peter's Sch., Seaford; Winchester Coll.; Trinity Coll., Oxford (Schol., MA). Royal Navy, 1947–49. Asst Master, Harrow Sch., 1952–67 and Housemaster of the Head Master's House, 1961–67; Headmaster of Rossall Sch. 1967–72. Graduate Recruitment Manager, Barclays Bank, 1986–91. Chm., HMC, 1983 Member: Harrow Borough Educn Cttee, 1956–60; Wilts County Educn Cttee, 1975–86 Governor: Campion Sch., Athens, 1981–2003; Cheam Sch., 1975–93 (Chm., 1987–93) Hawtreys Sch., 1975–86; Sandroyd Sch., 1982–86; Fettes Coll., 1983–94; St Edward' Sch., Oxford, 1985–2006 (Chm., 1992–99); Harrow Sch., 1987–97. Dir, Asquith Ct Sch Ltd, 1992–2000. Trustee, Hanover Foundn, 2001–05. *Publications:* Who's Who i Victorian Britain, 1997; (with Geoffrey Treasure) Britain's Prime Ministers, 2005 *Recreations:* golf, fishing. *Address:* 32 Hillcroft Crescent, Ealing, W5 2SQ. *Clubs:* East India Denham Golf.

See also A. W. Ellis, Dame E. A. Griffiths, H. A. Stevenson.

ELLIS, (Rosalind) Morag, (Mrs A. Bushell); QC 2006; *b* 5 June 1962; *d* of Ivor an Pamela Ellis; *m* 1985, Rev. Anthony Bushell; two *s* one *d*. *Educ:* Penrhos Coll., Colwyn Bay; St Catharine's Coll., Cambridge (BA 1983); Inns of Court Sch. of Law. Called to th Bar, Gray's Inn, 1984; in practice, specialising in law of planning, local government an village greens. Church of England Reader. *Publications:* (contrib.) Halsbury's Laws o England, 4th edn, 1998 reissue; articles in Jl Planning and Envmt Law. *Recreation:* music Member, Bach Choir, violin, viola. *Address:* 2–3 Gray's Inn Square, WC1R 5JH. *T:* (020 7242 4986, *Fax:* (020) 7405 1166; *e-mail:* chambers@2-3gis.co.uk.

ELLIS, Rt Rev. Timothy William; *see* Grantham, Bishop Suffragan of.

ELLIS, Tom; *see* Ellis, R. T.

ELLIS, Vernon James; International Chairman, Accenture (formerly Anderse Consulting), since 1999; *b* 1 July 1947; *s* of Norman and Phyllis Ellis; *m* 1972, Haze Marilyn Lucas; one *s* one *d*. *Educ:* Magdalen Coll. Sch., Oxford; Magdalen Coll., Oxfor (MA Hons PPE 1969). FCA 1982. Andersen Consulting: Partner, 1969; Man. Partne UK, 1986–89; Man. Partner, Europe, ME, Africa and India, 1989–99. Dir, World-Link Washington, 2002–06. Member: Bd, Prince of Wales Business Leaders Forum, 1997–200 (Chm. Bd, 2001–05); Adv. Bd, Centre for European Reform, 1998–; Council, Worl Economic Forum, 1999–2001; Mem., 2001–04, Dep. Chm., 2002–04, Mayor of Seoul' Internat. Adv. Council. UK private sector delegate, G8 Digital Opportunities Task Force 2000–02. Member: Develt Cttee, Magdalen Coll., Oxford, 1999–; Adv. Council, Saï Business Sch., Univ. of Oxford, 1996–2006; Foundn Bd, Internat. Inst. of Mgt Develt Lausanne, 1996–2004; Internat. Council, INSEAD, 2001–04; Bd, Arts & Business 2003–06. Mem. Bd, ENO, 2001– (Chm., 2006–); Chm. Bd, Classical Opera Co., 1996– Trustee: Florestan Trio, 2003–; Royal Coll. of Music, 2004–; Kathleen Ferrier Prize 2004–. Barclay Fellow, Templeton Coll., Oxford, 2002–06. *Recreations:* music, opera theatre, gardening, wine, cooking, photography. *Address:* Accenture, 20 Old Bailey EC4M 7AN; *e-mail:* vernon.j.ellis@accenture.com. *Club:* Athenaeum.

ELLIS, Dr (William) Herbert (Baxter), AFC 1954; MD; Medical Adviser, Departmen of Health and Social Security, 1972–92; Underwriting Member of Lloyd's; *b* 2 July 1921 *er s* of William Baxter Ellis and Georgina Isabella Ellis (*née* Waller); *m* 1st, 1948, Margare Mary Limb (marr. diss.); one *s* one *d*; 2nd, 1977, Mollie Marguerite Clarke (marr. diss.) 3rd, 1994, Jean Stanley Stawell Gross, *widow* of Ken Gross. *Educ:* Oundle Sch.; Durhan Univ. (BS, MD). Royal Navy, 1945–59: Surg. Comdr, Fleet Air Arm Pilot. Develope audio airspeed device to aid aircraft deck-landing, later used as car parking aid. Moto industry, 1960–71; research into human aspects of road traffic accidents, 1960–71; Dir Gen., Dr Barnardo's, 1971–73; dir of various companies. Industrial Medical Consultant Wellworthy, 1979–87; Telephone Manufacturing Co., 1980–87; Plessey Co., 1981–87 Part-time Mem., Employment Medical Adv. Service, 1973–81. Freeman, City of London 1994; Liveryman, Apothecaries' Soc., 1997. St John Ambulance: Chief Comdr, 1989–91 County Surgeon, 1979–87, Comdr, 1987–89, Glos Br.; Chm., St John Fellowship 2001–04, now Chm. Emeritus. KStJ 1989 (CStJ 1988). Gilbert Blane Medal, RCP, 1954 *Publications:* Physiological and Psychological Aspects of Deck Landings, 1954; Hippocrates RN—memoirs of a naval flying doctor (autobiog.), 1988; Why Not Live a Little Longer? 1997; various on the human factor in industrial management. *Recreations:* memories o walking, observing humanity, mending fences. *Address:* Littlecroft, 21 Buckswoo Grange, Rocks Road, Uckfield, East Sussex TN22 3PU. *T:* (01825) 767876. *Clubs:* Army and Navy, Naval and Military.

ELLIS-REES, Hugh Francis, CB 1986; Regional Director, West Midlands, Department of the Environment and Transport, 1981–89; *b* 5 March 1929; *s* of late Sir Hugh Ellis-Rees, KCMG, CB and Lady (Eileen Frances Anne) Ellis-Rees; *m* 1956, Elisabeth d

Mestre Gray; three *s* one *d. Educ:* Ampleforth Coll.; Balliol Coll., Oxford. Served Grenadier Guards, 1948–49. Joined War Office, 1954; DoE, 1970; Cabinet Office, 1972–74; Under Sec., DoE, 1974. Mem., Black Country Develt Corp., 1990–98. Chairman: Burford and Dist Soc., 2005–; Burford Fest., 2007–.

ELLISON, Dame Jillian Paula Anne, (Dame Jill), DBE 2001; Director of Nursing, Heart of England Foundation Trust (formerly East Birmingham Hospital, then Birmingham Heartlands and Solihull NHS Trust), since 1990; *b* 31 Jan. 1955; *d* of Joseph Ellison and Mollie Yvonne Ellison (*née* North). *Educ:* St Margaret's Sch., Bushey; Birmingham Poly. (HVCert 1980); MA UCE, 2001. Trained at Middx Hosp. Sch. of Nursing, 1973–76 (SRN); Staff Nurse: Middx Hosp., London, 1976–77; Hadassah Hosp., Israel, 1978–79; (Intensive Care) Charing Cross Hosp., 1979–80; Sandwell Health Authority: Health Visitor, 1980–85; Nurse Manager, 1985–87; Dist Sen. Nurse, 1987–90. Chm., Nurse Directors Assoc. *Recreation:* walking, cycling. *Address:* Birmingham Heartlands Hospital, Bordesley Green East, Birmingham B9 5SS. *T:* (0121) 424 1323.

ELLISON, Rt Rev. John Alexander; Bishop of Paraguay, 1988–2007; *b* 24 Dec. 1940; *s* of Alexander and Catherine Ellison; *m* 1964, Judith Mary Cox; one *s* two *d. Educ:* London College of Divinity (ALCD); Borough Road College (Teacher's Cert.). Secondary school teacher, 1961–64. Deacon 1967, priest 1968; Curate, St Paul, Woking, 1967–71; missionary, church planter, evangelist; Bible school/Bible institute lecturer, 1971–79; Asst to Archdeacon, St Saviour, Belgrano, Dio. Argentina, 1979–82; Rector, Aldridge, Dio. Lichfield, 1983–88. *Recreations:* walking, gardening, family, dining out, club. *Club:* Garden (Asunción).

ELLISON, Lawrence J., (Larry); Chief Executive Officer, Oracle Corporation, since 1977 (President, 1977–96; Chairman, 1996–2004); *b* New York City, 1944; *s* of Florence Spellman; adopted by Louis and Lillian Ellison; *m* 2003, Melanie Craft. *Educ:* High Sch., Chicago; Univ. of Illinois. Formerly computer programmer, Calif; posts with Amdahl Inc., 1967–71, and Ampex Corp., 1972–77; Founder (with Bob Miner), Oracle, 1977. Dir, Apple Computer Inc., 1997–2002. *Address:* Oracle Corporation, 500 Oracle Parkway, Redwood City, CA 94065, USA.

ELLISON, Mark Christopher; QC 2008; First Senior Treasury Counsel at the Central Criminal Court, since 2006; a Recorder, since 2000; *b* 8 Oct. 1957; *s* of late Anthony Ellison and of Arlette Maguire Ellison (*née* Blundell); *m* 1981, Kate Augusta (*née* Middleton); two *s* two *d. Educ:* Pocklington Sch.; Skinners' Sch.; UWIST (LLB). Called to the Bar, Gray's Inn, 1979; in practice at the Bar, 1980–; Treasury Counsel at CCC, 1994; Sen. Treasury Counsel, 2000–. *Recreations:* my children and dinghy sailing. *Address:* Queen Elizabeth Building, Temple, EC4Y 9BS. *T:* (020) 7583 5766; *e-mail:* barristers@qebholliswhiteman.co.uk.

ELLISON, Sir Ralph Harry C.; *see* Carr-Ellison, Sir R. H.

ELLISON, Robin Charles; Partner, Pinsent Masons, since 2002; *b* 3 Feb. 1949; *s* of Cecil Ellison and Vera Ellison (*née* Glicher); *m* 1986, Micheline Harris; two *s. Educ:* Manchester Grammar Sch. Cecil Ellison & Co., Manchester, 1973–75; Res. Fellow, Wolfson Coll., Cambridge, 1976–81; admitted Solicitor, 1979; Sen. Partner, Ellison Westhorp, Solicitors, 1981–94; Consultant, Hammond Suddards, 1994–97; Nat. Hd of Pensions, Eversheds, 1997–2002. Vis. Prof., Pensions Law and Econs, Cass Business Sch., City Univ., 2006. Chm., Nat. Assoc. of Pension Funds, 2005–07. Chairman: Magen David Adom UK, 2003–; Lung Cancer Res., 2004–. Mem. RSA. *Publications:* Pensions for Partners, 1978, 4th edn 1984; Private Occupational Pension Schemes, 1979; Pension Schemes for Controlling Directors, 1980, 3rd edn 1984; Pensions for Partners, 4th edn 1984; Pension Problems on Mergers and Acquisitions, 1984; Pensions Law and Practice (looseleaf), 1987–; Pensions and Divorce, 1991; Pensions: Europe and equality, 1993, 2nd edn 1995; Pension Disputes, 1995; Pension Trustees Handbook, 1995, 4th edn 2006; (jtly) Family Breakdown and Pensions, 1997, 3rd edn 2006; (jtly) Pensions and Insolvency, 1997; The Pocket Pensions Guide, 1998; Pensions and Investments, 2006. *Recreations:* walking, sailing, brutalist architecture. *Address:* 110 Frognal, NW3 6XU. *T:* (020) 7435 7330; *e-mail:* robin@pensionslaw.net. *Clubs:* Institute of Directors, Royal Society of Medicine.

ELLMAN, Louise Joyce; MP (Lab and Co-op) Liverpool Riverside, since 1997; *b* 14 Nov. 1945; *d* of late Harold and Annie Rosenberg; *m* 1967, Geoffrey David Ellman; one *s* one *d. Educ:* Manchester High Sch. for Girls; Hull Univ. (BA Hons); York Univ. (MPhil). Worked in further educn and on Open Univ., 1970–76. Member: Lancs CC, 1970–97 (Leader, Lab Gp, 1977–97; Leader, Council, 1981–97; Chm., 1981–85; Hon. Alderman, 1998–); W Lancs DC, 1974–87; Local Govt Adv. Cttee, Labour Party's NEC, 1977–; Regl Exec., NW Labour Party, 1985– (Chm., 1993–98). A Vice Pres., LGA, 1997–. Contested (Lab) Darwen, 1979. Member: Select Cttee on Envmt, Transport and Regl Affairs, 1997–2001; Select Cttee on Transport, 2002–; Vice Pres., All Pty Parly Cttee against Anti-semitism, 2007; Jt Sec., All Pty Gp against Trafficking, 2007–. Chm., PLP Regl Govt Gp, 1999–. Chair: Jewish Labour Movement, 2004–; Labour-Regeneration Gp, 2005–; Vice Chair: Labour Friends of Israel, 2004–; Parly Liverpool Capital of Culture Gp, 2006–. Vice-Chm., Lancashire Enterprises, 1982–97; Founder Mem., Co-operative Enterprises NW, 1979–; Founder Chm., NW Regl Assoc., 1992–93; Mem., NW Partnership, 1993–97. Youngest mem., Lancs CC, 1970; youngest mem. and first woman to be Chm., 1981. *Recreations:* theatre, travel. *Address:* House of Commons, SW1A 0AA.

ELLORY, Prof. (John) Clive, PhD; Professor of Physiology, University of Oxford, since 1996; Fellow of Corpus Christi College, Oxford, since 1985; *b* 16 April 1944; *s* of Ronald and Muriel Ellory; *m* 1969, Jane Metcalfe; one *s* one *d. Educ:* Latymer Upper Sch.; Univ. of Bristol (BSc Biochemistry 1964; PhD Zoology 1967); MA 1975, ScD 1995, Cantab; MA 1985, DSc 1996, Oxon. SO, 1967–71, SSO, 1971–75, PSO, 1975, Inst. of Animal Physiology, Babraham; Lectr, Dept of Physiology, Univ. of Cambridge, 1975–84; Fellow, Queens' Coll., Cambridge, 1975–84; Reader in Human Physiology, 1985–96, Hd of Physiology Dept, 1994–2006, Univ. of Oxford. Vis. Associate Prof., Yale, and Guest Fellow, Silliman Coll., 1971; Vis. Associate Prof., 1975, Vis. Prof., 1982, Univ. of Illinois; Investigator, US Antarctic Res. Program, McMurdo, Antarctica, 1980; Vis. Prof., Univ. of Nice, 1985, 1993; Royal Soc. Israel Res. Prof., Technion, Haifa, 1994. FMedSci 1999. *Publications:* jointly: Membrane Transport in Red Cells, 1977; Red Cell Membranes: a methodological approach, 1982; The Binding and Transport of Anions in Living Tissues, 1982; The Sodium Pump, 1985; Patronage and Plate at Corpus Christi College, Oxford, 1999; Red Cell Membrane Transport in Health & Disease, 2003. *Recreations:* food, antique silver, hill walking. *Address:* Corpus Christi College, Merton Street, Oxford OX1 4JF. *T:* (01865) 276760.

ELLSWORTH, Robert; Partner, Hamilton Bio Ventures LP, since 2000; *b* 11 June 1926; *s* of Willoughby Fred Ellsworth and Lucile Rarig Ellsworth; *m* 2002, Eleanor Bradford Lynch; one *s* one *d* from former marr. *Educ:* Univs of Kansas (BSME) and Michigan (JD). Active service, US Navy, 1944–46, 1950–53 (Lt-Comdr). Mem. United States Congress, 1961–67; Asst to President of US, 1969; Ambassador and Permanent Representative of US on N Atlantic Council, 1969–71; Asst Sec. of Defense (Internat. Security Affairs), 1974–75; Dep. Sec. of Defense, 1975–77. Vice Pres., IISS, 1998– (Mem., 1973–; Chm. Council, 1990–96). Licensed Lay Reader, Episcopal Dio. of Washington. Hon. LLD: Ottawa, 1969; Boston, 1970. Knight of Honour, Johanniter Orden, Berlin, 1996. *Recreations:* single sculling, swimming, music. *Address:* 2205 Caminito del Barco, Del Mar, CA 92014, USA. *Clubs:* Brook (New York); Cosmos (Washington).

ELLWOOD, Peter Brian, CBE 2001; DL; Chairman, Rexam PLC, since 2008; *b* 15 May 1943; *s* of Isaac and Edith Ellwood; *m* 1968, Judy Ann Windsor; one *s* two *d. Educ:* King's Sch., Macclesfield. FCIB. Barclays Bank, 1961–89; Chief Exec., Barclaycard, 1985–89; Chief Exec., Retail Banking, TSB, 1989–92; Gp Chief Exec., TSB Gp, 1992–95; Chm., Visa International, 1994–99; Dep. Gp Chief Exec., 1995–97, Gp Chief Exec., 1997–2003, Lloyds TSB Gp plc. Dep. Chm., 2003, Chm., 2004–08, ICI PLC. Non-exec. Dir, Royal Philharmonic Orchestra Ltd, 1996–2007. Chairman: The Work Foundn, 2001–07; Royal Parks Adv. Bd, 2003–07; Royal Parks Foundn, 2003–. Pres., Northampton Bach Choir, 2005–. Trustee, Royal Theatre, Northampton, 1982–99. Mem. Court, Univ. of Northampton (formerly Nene Coll., later UC Northampton), 1989–. FRSA. Hon. LLD Leicester, 1994; DUniv Central England, 1995. DL 2005, High Sheriff 2008, Northants. *Recreations:* theatre, music. *Address:* Rexam PLC, 4 Millbank, SW1P 3XR.

ELLWOOD, Peter David Roger, OBE 2002; Regional Director, Russia and North Europe, British Council, since 2007; *b* 17 Oct. 1948; *s* of John and Eileen Ellwood; *m* 1976, Susan Dianne Chester; one *s* two *d. Educ:* Trinity Hall, Cambridge (BA Hons English 1971, MA). Shell-Mex and BP, 1970–75; British Council, 1975–: Asst Rep., Nepal, 1975–79; Regl Officer, Middle East (based in London), 1979–81; Pvte Sec. to Dir Gen., 1981–83; Dep. Rep., Indonesia, 1983–86; Dir, Cameroon, 1986–89; Dep. Dir, France, 1989–94; Director: Sri Lanka, 1994–98; Pakistan, 1998–2002; Regional Director: Middle East, UAE, 2002–04; N and Central Europe, Sweden, 2004–07. *Recreations:* travel, birdwatching, theatre. *Address:* British Council, Bredovský dvůr, Politických vězňů 13, 110 00 Prague 1, Czech Republic.

ELLWOOD, Tobias; MP (C) Bournemouth East, since 2005; *b* 12 Aug. 1966; *s* of Peter Ellwood and Dr Caroline Ellwood; *m* 2005, Hannah Ryan. *Educ:* Vienna Internat. Sch.; Loughborough Univ. (BA Hons Design and Technol.); City Univ. Business Sch. (MBA). Served Army, RGJ, 1991–96. Researcher for Rt Hon. Tom King, 1996–97; Senior Business Develt Manager: London Stock Exchange, 1998–2002; Allen & Overy, 2002–04. *Recreations:* private pilot, wind-surfing, travel, diving, landscape gardening, military history. *Address:* House of Commons, SW1A 0AA. *T:* (020) 7219 3000; *e-mail:* Ellwoodt@parliament.uk.

ELLY, (Richard) Charles; His Honour Judge Elly; a Circuit Judge, since 1998; Partner, Reynolds, Parry-Jones & Crawford, solicitors, 1968–98; *b* 20 March 1942; *s* of Harold Elly and Dora Ellen Elly (*née* Luing); *m* 1967, Marion Rose Blackwell; one *s* one *d. Educ:* Sir William Borlase's Sch., Marlow; Hertford Coll., Oxford (MA); Coll. of Law, London. Admitted solicitor, 1966. Secretary: Southern Assoc. of Law Socs, 1975–82; Berks, Bucks and Oxon Law Soc., 1975–82 (Pres., 1988–89); Law Society: Mem. Council, 1981–97; Dep. Vice-Pres., 1992–93; Vice-Pres., 1993–94; Pres., 1994–95. Mem., Lord Chancellor's Adv. Cttee on Legal Educn and Conduct, 1997–98. Mem., Berks CC, 1980–81. Chairman: Maidenhead Deanery Synod, 1972–79; High Wycombe and Dist CAB, 1983–88. President: Cookham Soc., 1987–97; Hertford Coll. Lawyers Assoc., 1995–98; Criminal Law Solicitors Assoc., 1995–98. Governor: Coll. of Law, 1984–2000; Sir William Borlase's Sch., 1995– (Chm., 1996–2001). FRSA 1995. Hon. LLD Kingston, 1994. *Recreations:* bird-watching, theatre, walking, gardening. *Address:* Reading County Court, Friar Street, Reading, Berks RG1 1HE. *Club:* Oxford and Cambridge.

ELMES, Caroline Myfanwy Tonge, CMG 2001; HM Diplomatic Service, retired; *b* 20 Sept. 1948. Second Sec., FCO, 1975; First Secretary: Czechoslovakia, 1978–81; FCO, 1981–85; (Econ.), Rome, 1985–89; Dep. High Comr and Head of Chancery, Sri Lanka, 1989–92; Dep. Head of Mission, Czechoslovakia, 1992–95; Head of S Asia Dept, FCO, 1995–98; language trng, 1998; Ambassador to Angola, 1998–2002.

ELMS, Marsha Marilyn; JP; MA; Executive Head Teacher, Kendrick School and Reading Girls' School, since 2007; *b* 11 June 1946; *d* of James F. Carey and Carolyn M. Carey; *m* 1968, Richard A. Elms; one *s* one *d. Educ:* Tottenham County Grammar Sch.; Bedford Coll., London Univ. (BA); Brunel Univ. (PGCE 1969); Reading Univ. (MA 1988). Featherstone High School, Southall: teacher, 1969–90; Head, Liberal Studies Faculty, 1973–75; Dep. Head, 1990; Dep. Headteacher, Magna Carta Sch., Staines, 1990–93; acting Headteacher, Ashmead Sch., Reading, Summer term 1998; Headteacher, Kendrick Girls' Sch., 1993–2007. Mem., ACSL (formerly SHA), 1994–; Pres., Assoc. of Girls' Maintained Schs, 2002–03. JP Middx 1982. *Publications:* articles for ACSL and in educnl jls. *Recreations:* family, holidays, ski-ing, Spurs supporter, food. *Address:* Roseneath, Altwood Bailey, Maidenhead, Berks SL6 4PQ. *T:* (01628) 620085.

ELNASHAI, Prof. Amr Salah-Eldin, PhD; FREng; FASCE, FIStructE; University of Illinois at Urbana-Champaign: Professor of Earthquake Engineering, 2001; Director: Mid-America Earthquake Center, since 2004 (Associate Director, 2001–04); George E. Brown Network for Earthquake Engineering Simulation Laboratory, since 2004; William J. and Elaine F. Hall Professor of Civil and Environmental Engineering, since 2006; *b* 8 May 1954; *s* of Salah-Eldin Hamed Elnashai and Eitedal Rizk Agiz; *m* 1st, Maha Dabbous; one *s*; 2nd, Neveen Elnashai; one *s. Educ:* Cairo Univ. (BSc); Imperial Coll., London (MSc, DIC 1980; PhD 1984). FASCE 1997; FIStructE 1997; FREng 2001. Lectr, Cairo Univ., 1977–78; Res. Asst, Imperial Coll., London, 1980–84; Sen. Engr, Wimpey Offshore, 1984–85; Imperial College, London University: Lectr, 1985–89; Reader, 1989–92; Prof. of Earthquake Engrg, 1992–2001; Principal Consultant, EQE Internat. Ltd, 1995–2001. *Publications:* numerous refereed jl papers and keynote papers; also contrib. tech. magazine articles, book chapters and tech. reports, incl. earthquake field mission reports, on analysis, testing and design of structures subjected to earthquake loading. *Recreations:* squash, scuba diving. *Address:* Civil and Environmental Engineering Department, University of Illinois at Urbana-Champaign, Urbana, IL 61801, USA.

ELPHIN, Bishop of, (RC), since 1994; **Most Rev. Christopher Jones,** DD; *b* 3 March 1936; *s* of Christopher Jones and Christina Hanley. *Educ:* Maynooth Coll. (BA Classics 1958); UC Galway, NUI (Higher DipEd 1963); UC Dublin, NUI (DipSoc 1973). Ordained priest, 1962; Teacher, St Muireadach's, Ballina, 1962–65; Teacher, 1965–71, Spiritual Dir, 1972–79, Summerhill Coll., Sligo; Archivist, Diocesan Office, 1971–72; Dir, Sligo Social Service Council, 1973–87; Curate, Rosses Point, Sligo, 1979–87; Administrator, Cathedral Parish, Sligo, 1987–94. Freeman, Sligo City, 1995. *Publication:* Child, Adolescent and Adult in Family and Community, 1976, 2nd edn 1978. *Recreations:* walking, golfing, music, reading. *Address:* St Mary's, Sligo, Ireland. *T:* (71) 62670, (71) 50106. *Clubs:* Strandhill Golf; Co. Sligo Golf.

ELPHINSTONE, family name of **Lord Elphinstone**.

ELPHINSTONE, 19th Lord *cr* 1509; **Alexander Mountstuart Elphinstone;** Baron (UK) 1885; *b* 15 April 1980; *e s* of 18th Lord Elphinstone and of Willa Mary Gabriel, 4th *d* of Major David Chetwode; *S* father, 1994; *m* 2007, Nicola Jane, *yr d* of Michael Hall, Beaconsfield. *Educ:* Belhaven Hill Sch.; Eton Coll.; Univ. of Newcastle upon Tyne (MA 2005); Sch. of Oriental and African Studies, London (MSc Develt Studies 2006). *Heir: b* Hon. Angus John Elphinstone, *b* 7 July 1982.

ELPHINSTONE of Glack, Sir John, 11th Bt *cr* 1701, of Logie Elphinstone and Nova Scotia; Land Agent, retired; *b* 12 Aug. 1924; *s* of Thomas George Elphinston (*d* 1967), and of Gladys Mary Elphinston, *d* of late Ernest Charles Lambert Congdon; *S* uncle, 1970; *m* 1953, Margaret Doreen, *d* of Edric Tasker; four *s*. *Educ:* Eagle House, Sandhurst, Berks; Repton; Emmanuel College, Cambridge (BA). Lieut, Royal Marines, 1942–48. Chartered Surveyor; Land Agent with ICI plc, 1956–83; Consultant, Gandy & Son, Northwich, 1983–88. Past Pres., Cheshire Agricultural Valuers' Assoc.; Past Chm., Land Agency and Agric. Div., Lancs, Cheshire and IoM Branch, RICS; Mem., Lancs River Authority, 1970–74. *Heir: s* Alexander Elphinston [*b* 6 June 1955; *m* 1986, Ruth, *er d* of Rev. Robert Dunnett; three *s* one *d*].

ELPHINSTONE, Sir John (Howard Main), 6th Bt *cr* 1816, of Sowerby, Cumberland; *b* 25 Feb. 1949; *o s* of Sir Douglas Elphinstone, 5th Bt and of Helen Barbara Elphinstone (*née* Main); *S* father, 1995; *m* 1990, Diane Barbara Quilliam, *d* of Dr B. Q. Callow. *Educ:* Loretto Sch., Midlothian. *Heir: cousin* Henry Charles Elphinstone, *b* 7 July 1958. *Address:* Garden Cottage, 6 Amherst Road, Sevenoaks, Kent TN13 3LS. *T:* (01732) 459077.

ELRINGTON, Prof. Christopher Robin, FSA, FRHistS; Editor, Victoria History of the Counties of England, 1977–94; Professor of History, Institute of Historical Research, University of London, 1992–94, now Professor Emeritus; *b* 20 Jan. 1930; *s* of late Brig. Maxwell Elrington, DSO, OBE, and Beryl Joan (*née* Ommanney); *m* 1951, Jean Margaret (*née* Buchanan), RIBA; one *s* one *d*. *Educ:* Wellington Coll., Berks; University Coll., Oxford (MA); Bedford Coll., London (MA). FSA 1964; FRHistS 1969. Asst to Editor, Victoria County History, 1954; Editor for Glos, 1960; Dep. Editor, 1968. British Acad. Overseas Vis. Fellow, Folger Shakespeare Library, Washington DC, 1976. Mem., Adv. Bd for Redundant Churches, 1982–96. Pres., 1984–85, Hon. Gen. Ed., Glos Record Series, 1995–, Bristol and Glos Archaeol Soc.; Hon. Gen. Editor, 1962–72, Pres., 1983–, Wilts Record Soc. *Publications:* Divers Letters of Roger de Martival, Bishop of Salisbury, 2 vols, 1963, 1972; Wiltshire Feet of Fines, Edward III, 1974; articles in Victoria County History and in learned jls. *Address:* 34 Lloyd Baker Street, WC1X 9AB. *T:* (020) 7837 4971.

ELS, Theodore Ernest, (Ernie); South African golfer; *b* 17 Oct. 1969; *s* of Cornelius, (Nils), and Hester Els; *m* 1998, Liezl Wehmeyer; one *d*. *Educ:* Delville Sch.; Jan de Klerk Tech. Coll. Professional golfer, 1989–; winner: Jun. World Championship, USA, 1984; South African Open, 1992, 1996, 1998; US Open, 1994, 1997; World Match Play Championship, 1994, 1995, 1996, 2002, 2003, 2004, 2007; European Order of Merit, 1995; South African PGA Championship, 1995; Million Dollar Challenge, Sun City, 1999; Nedbank Golf Challenge, Sun City, 2000, 2002; Open, Muirfield, 2002. *Address:* 46 Chapman Road, Klippoortjie 1401, South Africa.

ELSE, Dame Jean, DBE 2001; MA; Headteacher, Whalley Range High School, Manchester, 1994–2006. Teacher: Counthill Sch., Oldham; various schs in Rochdale and Trafford. Co-ordinator for Manchester, DFES Excellence in the Cities, 1999. Trustee, Imperial War Mus., 2003–07.

ELSE, Martin Thomas; Chief Executive, Royal College of Physicians, since 2005; *b* 21 May 1953; *s* of late Richard Else and of Lilian Margaret Else (*née* Stickells); *m* 1978, Jennifer Louise Bridges; one *s* one *d*. *Educ:* Farnborough Grammar Sch.; Univ. of Salford (BSc Econ); Southampton Coll. of Technol.; London Business Sch. (Sloan Fellowship with Dist.). CPFA (IPFA 1979). Finance trainee, City and Hackney HA, 1975–79; Principal Finance Planning Manager, 1979–82, Principal Asst Treas., 1982–83, NE Thames RHA; Dep. Treas., 1983–86, Dir of Finance, 1986–90, Hampstead HA; Royal Free Hampstead NHS Trust: Dir of Finance and Dep. Chief Exec., 1990–94; Chief Exec., 1994–2005. Policy Advr, DoH, 2005; Director: RCP Regent's Park Ltd, 2005–; CORESS, 2006–. Treas., Alzheimer's Disease Internat., 2005–. Royal Free Hospital: Hon. Sec., Treas., and Special Trustee, 1986–2005; Trustee, Appeal Trust, 1988–92; Chm., Cancerkin Mgt Cttee, 1990–94; Trustee, Hampstead Wells and Campden Trust, 1996–2005. FRSM 2007. *Recreations:* football, golf, horseracing. *Address:* Royal College of Physicians, 11 St Andrews Place, Regent's Park, NW1 4LE. *T:* (020) 7935 1174.

ELSEY, Roger William; a District Judge (Magistrates' Courts), since 2004; *b* 12 June 1954; *s* of William Gattie Elsey and Rita Alillian Elsey; *m* 1985, Susan Coull; three *d*. *Educ:* Bede Sch.; Univ. of Newcastle upon Tyne (LLB Hons); Open Univ. (MA 2008). Called to the Bar, Gray's Inn, 1977; practised in criminal law, N Eastern Circuit. Actg Stipendiary Magistrate, 1999–2004. Jt Ed., Signpost mag., 2000–. Mem., Durham Diocesan Synod, 2003–. *Recreations:* cycling, theatre, walking, Anglican affairs. *Address:* Teesside Magistrates' Court, Victoria Square, Middlesbrough TS1 2AS. *T:* (01642) 240301.

ELSON, Anthony Kenneth; Local Government Adviser to the Department of Health, and independent consultant, since 2004; *b* 15 June 1948; *s* of William and Elsie Elson; *m* 1971, Joy Waterworth. *Educ:* Birmingham Univ. (BSc 1st cl. Hons Exptl Physics 1969); Liverpool Univ. (BPhil Applied Social Studies 1972); CQSW. Social Worker, 1972–76; Principal Lectr in Social Work, Worcester Coll. of Further Educn, 1976–78; Social Services, Birmingham City Council: Team Manager, 1978–81; Area Manager, 1981–83; Asst Dir, 1983–88; Kirklees Metropolitan Borough Council: Dir of Social Services, 1988–89; Exec. Dir (Housing and Social Services), 1989–97; Exec. Dir (Social Services and Educn), 1997–98; Chief Exec., 1998–2004. *Address:* Department of Health, Skipton House, 80 London Road, SE1 6LH; *e-mail:* tony.elson@dh.gsi.gov.uk, tony.elson@broomstileconsultants.co.uk.

ELSON, Prof. Diane Rosemary, PhD; Professor of Sociology, University of Essex, since 2000; *b* Bedworth, Warwickshire, 20 April 1946; *d* of Edwin and Vera Elson; one *s*. *Educ:* St Hilda's Coll., Oxford (BA Hons PPE 1968); Univ. of Manchester (PhD Econs 1994). Res. Asst, Inst. of Commonwealth Studies and St Antony's Coll., Oxford, 1968–71; Teaching Fellow, Dept of Economics, Univ. of York, 1971–75; Res. Officer, Inst. of Develt Studies, Univ. of Sussex, 1975–77; Temp. Lectr, Univ. of Manchester, 1978–79; part-time consultant and occasional lectr, 1979–84; University of Manchester: Hon. Res. Fellow, Internat. Develt Centre and Dept of Sociol., 1984–85; Lectr, 1985–91, Reader, 1992–95, in Develt Econs; Prof. of Develt Studies, 1995–98; Special Advr, UN Develt Fund for Women, 1998–2000. Member: UN Taskforce on Millennium Develt Goals, 1998–2000; Strategic Res. Bd, ESRC, 2008–. *Publications:* Male Bias in the Development Process, 1991, 2nd edn 1995; Progress of World's Women, 2000; Budgeting for Women's Rights, 2006. *Recreations:* gardening, bird watching, campaigning for women's rights. *Address:* Department of Sociology, University of Essex, Wivenhoe Park, Colchester CO4 3SQ. *T:* (01206) 873539, *Fax:* (01206) 873410; *e-mail:* drelson@essex.ac.uk.

ELSON, Graham Peel; Chief Executive, South West One, political and public affair company, since 1998; *b* 21 Aug. 1949; *s* of George Ernest Elson and Rhoda (*née* Atkinson *m* 1975, Jane Rosamunde Isaac. *Educ:* Palmers Endowed Sch. for Boys, Grays, Essex; N London Polytechnic (BA Business Studies). Brand Manager, Rank Hovis McDouga Foods, 1972–74; Gen. Manager, Wilkinson Sword Gp, 1974–85. Councillor (Lib Den and Leader, Oxfordshire CC, 1985–89; Councillor (Lib Dem), Mid Devon DC 1999–2003. Gen. Sec., Liberal Democrats, 1989–97. *Recreations:* boating, gardening supporting West Ham United FC. *Address:* 3 The Halt, Alphington, Exeter EX2 8FX.

ELSTEIN, David Keith; Chairman, DCD Media (formerly Digital Classics), since 2005 *b* 14 Nov. 1944; *s* of late Albert Elstein and Millie Cohen; *m*; one *s*. *Educ:* Haberdasher Aske's; Gonville and Caius Coll., Cambridge (BA, MA). BBC, 1964–68; ITV, 1968–82 founded Brook Prodns, 1982; Man. Dir, Primetime Television, 1983–86; Dir c Programmes, Thames Television, 1986–92; Hd of Programmes, BSkyB, 1993–96; Chie Exec., Channel 5 Broadcasting, 1996–2000. Chairman: British Screen Adv. Counci 1997–2008; Really Useful Theatres, 2001–06; Screen Digest Ltd, 2004–; Sparrowhaw Investments Ltd, 2004–07; Luther Pendragon Hldgs, 2006–; Vice-Chm., Hardt Gp (UK (formerly Kingsbridge Capital) Ltd, 2003–; non-executive Director: Virgin Medi (formerly NTL), 2003–08; Orion Holdings, 2006–. Chm., Broadcasting Policy Gp 2003–. *Recreations:* film, theatre, bridge, reading.

ELSTON, Christopher David; Chief Executive, London Bullion Market Associatior 1995–99; *b* 1 Aug. 1938; *s* of Herbert Cecil Elston and Ada Louisa (*née* Paige); *m* 1964 Jennifer Isabel Rampling; one *s* two *d*. *Educ:* University Coll. Sch., Hampstead; King Coll., Cambridge (BA Classics, 1960, MA 1980); Yale Univ. (MA Econs, 1967). Bank c England, 1960–95: seconded to Bank for Internat. Settlements, Basle, Switzerlanc 1969–71; Private Sec. to Governor of Bank of England, 1974–76; Asst to Chief Cashie 1976–79; seconded to HM Diplomatic Service, as Counsellor (Financial), British Embassy Tokyo, 1979–83; Advr, later Sen. Advr (Asia and Australasia), 1983–94. Advr, KorAr Bank London Br., 1995–2000. Ordinary Mem. Council and Chm. Business Gp, Japa Soc., 1997–2000. *Recreations:* music, golf, walking, garden. *Address:* 23 Grasmere Avenue Harpenden, Herts AL5 5PT. *T:* (01582) 760147.

ELTIS, Walter Alfred, DLitt; Emeritus Fellow of Exeter College, Oxford, since 1988; 23 May 1933; *s* of Rev. Martin Eltis and Mary (*née* Schnitzer); *m* 1959, Shelagh Mary, of Rev. Preb. Douglas Owen; one *s* two *d*. *Educ:* Wycliffe Coll.; Emmanuel Coll Cambridge (BA Econs 1956); Nuffield Coll., Oxford. MA Oxon 1960; DLitt Oxon 199(Nat. Service, Navigator, RAF, 1951–53. Res. Fellow, Exeter Coll., Oxford, 1958–6(Lectr in Econs, Exeter and Keble Colls, Oxford, 1960–63; Fellow and Tutor in Econs Exeter Coll., Oxford, 1963–88; National Economic Development Office: Econ. Di 1986–88; Dir Gen., 1988–92; Chief Economic Advr to Pres., BoT, 1992–95. Vis. Reade in Econs, Univ. of WA, 1970; Visiting Professor: Univ. of Toronto, 1976–77; Europea Univ., Florence, 1979; Reading Univ., 1992–2004; Gresham Prof. of Commerce Gresham Coll., 1993–96. Mem. Council, 1987–93, Chm., Social Scis Cttee, 1987–88 CNAA; Member Council: European Policy Forum, 1992–; Foundn for Manufacturin and Industry, 1993–96. Vice-Pres., European Soc. of Hist. of Econ. Thought, 2000–0 Gov., Wycliffe Coll., 1972–88. Gen. Ed., Oxford Economic Papers, 1975–81. *Publications* Economic Growth: analysis and policy, 1966; Growth and Distribution, 1973; (with R Bacon) The Age of US and UK Machinery, 1974; (with R. Bacon) Britain's Economi Problem: too few producers, 1976, 3rd edn (as Britain's Economic Problem Revisited 1996; The Classical Theory of Economic Growth, 1984, 2nd edn 2000; (with P. Sinclai Keynes and Economic Policy, 1988; Classical Economics, Public Expenditure an Growth, 1993; (ed with S. M. Eltis) Condillac, Commerce and Government, 199 Britain, Europe and EMU, 2000; contribs to econ. jls. *Recreations:* chess, music. *Addres* Danesway, Jarn Way, Boars Hill, Oxford OX1 5JF. *T:* (01865) 735440. *Club:* Reforn (Chm., 1994–95).

ELTON, family name of **Baron Elton**.

ELTON, 2nd Baron *cr* 1934, of Headington; **Rodney Elton,** TD 1970; Deputy Chairmar Andry Montgomery Ltd, 1978–79 and 1986–2001; *b* 2 March 1930; *s* of 1st Baron Elto and of Dedi (*d* 1977), *d* of Gustav Hartmann, Oslo; *S* father, 1973; *m* 1st, 1958, Ann Frances (separated 1973; marr. diss. 1979), *e d* of late Brig. R. A. G. Tilney, CBE, DSC TD; one *s* three *d*; 2nd, 1979, S. Richenda Gurney (CVO 1998), *y d* of late Sir Hug Gurney, KCMG, MVO, and Lady Gurney. *Educ:* Eton; New Coll., Oxford (MA Farming, 1954–64. Assistant Master: Loughborough Grammar Sch., 1964–67; Fairhar Comprehensive School for Boys, Nottingham, 1967–69; Lectr, Bishop Lonsdale Colleg of Education, 1969–72. Contested (C) Leics, Loughborough, 1966, 1970. Cons. Whip House of Lords, Feb. 1974–76, an Opposition spokesman, 1976–79; Parly Under Sec. c State, NI Office, 1979–81, DHSS, 1981–82, Home Office, 1982–84; Minister of State Home Office, 1984–85; DoE, 1985–86. House of Lords: Mem., Delegated Powe Scrutiny Cttee, 1993–96; a Dep. Chm. of Cttees, 1997–; elected Mem., 1999; a De Speaker, 1999–; Member: Lord Privy Seal's Cttee on Neill Report, 2001; Offices Selec Cttee, 2001–02; Select Cttee on the Constitution, 2002–; Jt Ecclesiastical Cttee, H of and H of C, 2002–. Mem. Exec. Cttee, Assoc. of Cons. Peers, 1986–93, 1994–9 2001–03 (Dep. Chm., 1991–93). Chm., FIMBRA, 1987–90; Mem., Panel on Takeove and Mergers, 1987–90. Formerly Director: Overseas Exhibition Services Ltd; Buildin Trades Exhibition Ltd. Dep. Sec., Cttee on Internat. Affairs, Synod of C of E, 1976–78 Licensed Lay Minister, Oxford dio., C of E, 1998–. Mem. Boyd Commn to evaluat elections in Rhodesia, 1979; Chm., Cttee of Enquiry into discipline in schools, 1988 Chm., Intermediate Treatment Fund, 1990–93; Vice-Pres., Inst. of Trading Standarc Administrators, 1990–; Member of Council: CGLI, 1987–91 (Chm., Quality an Standards Cttee, 1999–2005; Hon. FCGI 2005); Rainer Foundn, 1990–96; Foundin Chm., DIVERT Trust, 1993–2001; Pres., Building Conservation Trust, 1990–95 Trustee: City Parochial Foundn, 1990–97; Trust for London, 1990–97. Late Captair Queen's Own Warwickshire and Worcs Yeo.; late Major, Leics and Derbys (PAO) Yec Lord of the Manor of Adderbury, Oxon. *Heir: s* Hon. Edward Paget Elton, *b* 28 May 196(*Address:* House of Lords, SW1A 0PW. *Clubs:* Pratt's, Beefsteak, Cavalry and Guards.
See also Lord Gray.

ELTON, Sir Arnold, Kt 1987; CBE 1982; MS; FRCS; Consultant Surgeon, Northwic Park Hospital and Clinical Research Centre, 1970–85; *b* 14 Feb. 1920; *s* of late Max Elto and of Ada Elton; *m* 1952, Billie Pamela Briggs; one *s*. *Educ:* University Coll. Londo (exhibnr; MB BS 1943); UCH Med. Sch. (MS 1951); Jun. and Sen. Gold Medal i Surgery. LRCP 1943; MRCS 1943, FRCS 1946. House Surg., House Physician an Casualty Officer, UCH, 1943–45; Sen. Surgical Registrar, Charing Cross Hosp., 1947–5 (Gosse Res. Schol.); Consultant Surgeon: Harrow Hosp., 1951–70; Mount Vernon Hosp 1960–70; British Airways, 1981–95. First Chm., Med. Staff Cttee, Chm., Surgical Div and Theatre Cttee, Mem., Ethical Cttee, Northwick Park Hosp. Mem., Govt Wkg Part on Breast Screening for Cancer, 1985–. Mem., Tricare Europe Preferred Provide Network, 1997–. Med. Dir, 1997–2003, Dep. Chm., 2000–03, Medical Marketin Internat. Gp (formerly Management of Medical Innovation) plc; Chairman and Executiv

Director: Healthy Living (UK) Ltd, 1997–; Healthy Living (Durham) Ltd, 1998–; Universal Lifestyle Ltd, 1999–; Health Exec., Bovis Lend Lease, 2001–. Examiner: GNC; RCS, 1971–83; Surgical Tutor, RCS, 1970–82. Pres., Cons. Med. Soc., 1992–97, now President Emeritus (Nat. Chm., 1975–92; Eur. Rep., 1994–; Chm., Eur. Gp; Ed., Eur. Bull., 1994–); Mem., Cons. Central Council and Nat. Exec. Cttee, 1976–93. Chm., Internat. Med. and Science Fundraising Cttee, BRCS, 1998–. Founder Officer, British Assoc. of Surgical Oncology, 1972–; Member: Europ. Soc. of Surgical Oncology, 1994–; World Fedn Surgical Oncology Socs, 1994–; Ct of Patrons, RCS, 1986–; Dir and Co-ordinator, RCS Exchange of Surgeons with China, 1994–. Mem. and UK Chm., Internat. Med. Parliamentarians Orgn, 1996–. Chm., Med. and Sci. Div., World Fellowship Duke of Edinburgh's Award, 1997–. International Advisor: World Fedn Surgical Oncology Socs, 1998–; PPP/Colombia, subseq. HCA, Gp of Hosps, 1998–; Med. Advr, Virgin Active (Healthy Living Centres), 1997–; Health Consultant and Advr, Keltbray Ltd, 2003–. Fellow, Assoc. of Surgeons of GB; FRSocMed; FICS; Fellow, European Fedn of Surgeons. Freeman, City of London; Liveryman: Apothecaries' Soc.; Carmen's Co. Jubilee Medal, 1977. *Publications:* contribs to med. jls. *Recreations:* tennis, music, cricket. *Address:* 58 Stockleigh Hall, Prince Albert Road, NW8 7LB; The Consulting Rooms, Wellington Hospital, Wellington Place, NW8 9LE. *T:* (020) 7483 5275. *Clubs:* Carlton, Royal Automobile, MCC.

ELTON, Benjamin Charles; author and performer; *b* 3 May 1959; *s* of Prof. Lewis Richard Benjamin Elton, *qv* and Mary Elton (*née* Foster); *m* 1994, Sophie Gare; two *s* one *d* (of whom one *s* one *d* are twins). *Educ:* Godalming Grammar Sch.; S Warwicks Coll. of Further Educn; Manchester Univ. (BA Drama). First professional appearance, Comic Strip Club, 1981; writer for television: Happy Families, 1985; Filthy Rich and Catflap, 1986; The Thin Blue Line, 1995, 1996; Blessed, 2005; jointly: The Young Ones, 1982, 1984; Blackadder II, 1987; Blackadder the Third, 1988; Blackadder goes Forth, 1989; writer and performer: Friday Live, 1987–88; Saturday Live, 1987; The Man from Auntie, 1990, 1994; Stark, 1993; The Ben Elton Show, 1998; Get A Grip, 2007; writer and director: Gasping, Theatre Royal, Haymarket, 1990; Silly Cow, Theatre Royal, Haymarket, 1991; Popcorn, Apollo, 1997; Maybe Baby (film), 2000; Tonight's the Night (musical), Victoria Palace, 2003; writer: The Beautiful Game (musical), 2000; We Will Rock You (musical), 2002; actor: Much Ado About Nothing (film), 1993; numerous tours as a stand-up comic, 1986, 1987, 1989, 1993, 1996–97, 2005–06. Hon. Dr Manchester. *Publications: novels:* Stark, 1989; Gridlock, 1991; This Other Eden, 1993; Popcorn, 1996; Blast from the Past, 1998; Inconceivable, 1999; Dead Famous, 2001; High Society, 2002; Post Mortem, 2004; The First Casualty, 2005; Chart Throb, 2006; Blind Faith, 2007; *plays:* Gasping, 1990; Silly Cow, 1991; Popcorn, 1996; Blast from the Past, 1998. *Recreations:* walking, reading, socialising. *Address:* c/o Phil McIntyre, 2nd Floor, 35 Soho Square, W1D 3QX. *Club:* Groucho.

ELTON, Sir Charles (Abraham Grierson), 11th Bt *cr* 1717; film and television producer; *b* 23 May 1953; *s* of Sir Arthur Hallam Rice Elton, 10th Bt, and Margaret Ann (*d* 1995), *d* of Olafur Bjornson; *S* father, 1973; *m* 1990, Lucy Lauris (*see* L. L. Heller) (marr. diss. 2005), *d* of late Lukas Heller; one *s* one *d*. *Educ:* Eton Coll.; Reading Univ. Publishing, 1976–79; BBC, 1979–84; Director: Curtis Brown, 1984–91; First Choice Productions, 1991–2000; Exec. Producer, Carlton Television, subseq. ITV Productions, 2000–08. *Heir: s* Abraham William Elton, *b* 27 Sept. 1995. *Address:* Clevedon Court, Somerset BS21 6QU; 25 Dartmouth Park Hill, NW5 1HP. *Club:* Garrick.

ELTON, Dr George Alfred Hugh, CB 1983; consultant in biochemistry, since 1985; *b* 27 Feb. 1925; *s* of Horace and Violet Elton; *m* 1951, Theodora Rose Edith Kingham; two *d*. *Educ:* Sutton County Sch.; London Univ. (evening student). BSc 1944, PhD 1948, DSc 1956; FRSC (FRIC 1951); CChem 1974; Eur Chem 1993; FIFST 1968; FIBiol 1976; CBiol 1984. Mem. Faculty of Science, and Univ. Examnr in Chemistry, Univ. of London, 1951–58; Dir, Fog Res. Unit, Min. of Supply, 1954–58; Reader in Applied Phys. Chemistry, Battersea Polytechnic, 1956–58; Dir, British Baking Industries Res. Assoc., 1958–66; Dir, Flour Milling and Baking Res. Assoc., 1967–70; Ministry of Agriculture, Fisheries and Food: Chief Sci. Adviser (Food), 1971–85; Head of Food Science Div., 1972–73; Dep. Chief Scientist, 1972; Under-Sec. 1974; Chief Scientist (Fisheries and Food), 1981–85. Vis. Prof., Surrey Univ., 1982–97; Vis. Lectr, various overseas univs, 1952–92. Consultant: FAO, 1992; Internat. Life Scis Inst., USA, 1997–2001. Chairman: National Food Survey Cttee, 1978–85; Adv. Bd, Inst. of Food Res. (Bristol), 1985–88; Scientific Advr, BFMIRA, 1986–92; Scientific Governor: British Nutrition Foundn, 1971–2000; Internat. Life Scis Inst. (Europe), 1987–97; Vice-Chm., EEC Scientific Cttee for Food, 1987–92; Member: Cttee on Medical Aspects of Food Policy, 1971–85; UK Delegn, Tripartite Meetings on Food and Drugs, 1971–85; AFRC (formerly ARC), 1981–85; NERC, 1981–85; Fisheries Res. and Develt Bd, 1982–85; Adv. Bd for Research Councils, 1981–84; Council: Chemical Soc., 1972–75; BIBRA, 1990–2000 (Chm., 1993–95; Vice-Pres., 1996–2000). Co-inventor, Chorleywood Bread Process (Queen's Award to Industry 1966); Silver Medallist, Royal Soc. of Arts, 1969. Hon. DSc Reading, 1984; DUniv Surrey, 1991. *Publications:* research papers in jls of various learned societies. *Recreation:* golf. *Address:* Green Nook, Bridle Lane, Loudwater, Rickmansworth, Herts WD3 4JH. *Clubs:* MCC; Beaconsfield Golf.

ELTON, Sir Leslie (Norman), Kt 2004; DL; Chief Executive, Gateshead Council, 1984–2004; *b* 27 Feb. 1947; *s* of Harry Elton and Marjorie Elton; *m* 1969, Christine Mary Price; one *s* one *d*. *Educ:* Hulme Grammar Sch., Oldham; Univ. of Manchester (LLB 1968). Admitted solicitor, 1971; various posts with Salford, Nottingham, Stockport and Newcastle upon Tyne Councils, 1969–84; Clerk to Northumbria Police Authy, 1984–2004. Vis. Prof., Business Sch., 2004–, Mem. Council, 2004–07, Univ. of Newcastle upon Tyne. Chm., Northern Film and Media, 2007–; Dep. Chm., Port of Tyne Authy, 2004–. Gov., Northumbria Univ., 2007–. DL Tyne and Wear, 2005. *Recreations:* gardening, golf, family, good food. *Address:* The Hayway, Ovingham, Northumberland NE42 6DE. *T:* (01661) 836541; *e-mail:* les.elton@btinternet.com. *Clubs:* Matfen Hall Golf; Newcastle United Golf.

ELTON, Prof. Lewis Richard Benjamin, MA, DSc; CPhys; FSRHE; Visiting Distinguished Scholar, SCEPTrE, University of Surrey, since 2006; Visiting Professor of Higher Education, University of Gloucestershire, since 2008; Hon. College Professor of Higher Education, University College London, since 2003 (Professor of London University, 1994–99, College Professor, 1999–2003); *b* 25 March 1923; *yr s* of late Prof. Victor Leopold Ehrenberg, PhD, and Eva Dorothea (*née* Sommer); *m* 1950, Mary, *d* of late Harold William Foster and Kathleen (*née* Meakin); three *s* one *d*. *Educ:* Stepanska Gymnasium, Prague; Rydal Sch., Colwyn Bay; Christ's Coll., Cambridge (Exhibr; BA 1945, MA 1948); Univ. Correspondence Coll., Cambridge, and Regent Street Polytechnic (Certif.Ed Cantab 1945; BSc (External) 1st Cl. Hons Maths 1947); University Coll. London (Univ. Research Studentship; PhD 1950). Asst Master, St Bees Sch., 1944–46; Asst Lectr, then Lectr, King's Coll., London, 1950–57; Head of Physics Dept, Battersea Coll. of Technology, 1958–66; University of Surrey: Prof. of Physics, 1964–71; Head of Physics Dept, 1966–69; Prof. of Sci. Educn, 1971–86; Hd, Inst. of Educnl Develt (formerly Educnl Technol.), 1967–84; Associate Head, Dept of Educnl Studies, 1983–86; Prof. of Higher Educn, 1987–90, now Emeritus. Sen. Fulbright Award, 1955–56; Research Associate: MIT, 1955–56; Stanford Univ., 1956; Niels Bohr Inst., Copenhagen, 1962; Visiting Professor: Univ. of Washington, Seattle, 1965; UCL, 1970–77; Univ. of Sydney, 1971; Univ. of Sao Paulo, 1975; Univ. of Science, Malaysia, 1978, 1979; Univ. of Malaya, 1982, 1983; Asian Inst. of Technology, 1985, 1986; Fundaçao Armando Alvares Penteado, São Paulo, 1985–89; Univ. of Manchester, 2005–07. Higher Educn Advr, DfEE (formerly DoE), 1989–96. Member: Governing Body, Battersea Coll. of Technology, 1962–66; Council, Univ. of Surrey, 1966–67, 1981–83; Council for Educational Technology of UK, 1975–81; Army Educn Adv. Bd, 1976–80; Convener, Standing Conf. of Physics Profs, 1971–74; Chairman: Governing Council, Soc. for Research into Higher Educn, 1976–78 (Fellow, 1987). Vice-Pres., Assoc. for Educnl and Trng Technology, 1976–95. Fellow, Amer. Physical Soc., 1978. FRSA. Hon. Life Mem., Staff and Educnl Develt Assoc., 1994. Hon. LittD Kent, 1997; Hon. PhD Glos, 2003; Hon. DLitt London (ext), 2008. The Times Higher Lifetime Achievement Award, 2005. Univ. of Surrey Art Gall. named Lewis Elton Gall., 1997. *Publications:* Introductory Nuclear Theory, 1959, 2nd edn 1965 (Spanish edn 1964); Nuclear Sizes, 1961 (Russian edn 1962); Concepts in Classical Mechanics, 1971; (with H. Messel) Time and Man, 1978; Teaching in Higher Education: appraisal and training, 1987 (Japanese edn 1989); contribs to sci. jls on nuclear physics, higher education, science educn, med. educn, and educnl technology. Festschrift: (ed) P. Ashwin, Changing Higher Education: the development of learning and teaching, 2006. *Recreation:* words. *Address:* 3 Great Quarry, Guildford, Surrey GU1 3XN. *T:* (01483) 576548.

See also B. C. Elton.

ELTON, Michael Anthony; Director General, National Association of Pension Funds, 1987–95; *b* 20 May 1932; *s* of late Francis Herbert Norris Elton and Margaret Helen Elton (*née* Gray); *m* 1955, Isabel Clare, *d* of late Thomas Gurney Ryott and Clare Isabel Ryott; two *s* two *d*. *Educ:* Peter Symonds Sch.; Brasenose Coll., Oxford (Class. Mods 1952, BA 1st cl. Jurisp. 1954; MA, BCL 1955). Articled to Sir Andrew Wheatley, Clerk of Hants County Council, 1954; solicitor; Cumberland CC, 1958–61; Surrey CC, 1961–65; Asst Clerk, Bucks CC, 1965–70, Dep. Clerk of the Peace, 1967–70; Chief Exec., Assoc. of British Travel Agents, 1970–86; Dir Gen., European Fedn for Retirement Provision, 1987–91. FRSA; CCMI. *Publications:* (with Gyles Brandreth) Future Perfect: how to profit from your pension planning, 1988; Travelling to Retirement: plus ça change, plus c'est la même chose, 1989; Memories of Many Minds (autobiog.), 2005; articles in professional jls. *Recreations:* tennis, golf, music, oil painting, bridge, gardening. *Address:* 6 Royal Winchester Mews, Chilbolton Avenue, Chilbolton, Winchester, Hants SO22 5HX. *T:* (01962) 868470.

ELVEDEN, Viscount; Arthur Benjamin Jeffrey Guinness; *b* 6 Jan. 2003; *s* and *heir* of Earl of Iveagh, *qv*.

ELVERY, Nathan Dominic; Executive Director of Resources and Customer Services, and Deputy Chief Executive, London Borough of Croydon, since 2008; *b* 2 June 1969; *s* of Richard William Foote and Patricia Anne Foote; *m* 2003, Silke Anette Elvery; one *s* two *d*. *Educ:* Thomas Bennett Community Coll., Sussex; NE Surrey Coll. of Technol.; Lewes Tertiary Coll.; Brighton Coll.; CETEC. MAAT 1991; CIPFA 1995, CPD 2000. Principal consultant, Crawley BC, 1995–2000; Dep. Hd of Core Finance, GLA, 2000–02; Asst Dir, Finance and Business Mgt, Westminster CC, 2002–04; Dir of Finance, 2004–05, Dir of Finance and Resources, 2005–07, London Borough of Croydon. Chm., London Authorities Mutual Ltd, 2007 and 2008–. Member: Soc. of London Treasurers, 2004–; Soc. of Municipal Treasurers, 2004–. *Publications:* articles in Public Finance, Local Govt Chronicle, Municipal Jl, Accountancy Age, PQ Mag. and Public Servant. *Recreations:* my family, travelling, running. *Address:* Resources and Customer Services Department, London Borough of Croydon, Taberner House, Park Lane, Croydon CR9 1JL; *e-mail:* nathan.elvery@croydon.gov.uk.

ELVIDGE, Sir John (William), KCB 2006; Permanent Secretary, Scottish Government (formerly Scottish Executive), since 2003; *b* 9 Feb. 1951; *s* of Herbert William Elvidge and Irene Teresa Elvidge; *m* 2003, Maureen Margaret Ann McGinn. *Educ:* Sir George Monoux Sch., Walthamstow; St Catherine's Coll., Oxford (BA English Lang. and Lit.). Joined Scottish Office, 1973: Principal, 1978–84; Asst Sec., 1984–88; Dir, Scottish Homes, 1988–89 (on secondment); Asst Sec., 1989–93; Under Sec., 1993–98; Dep. Hd, Econ. and Domestic Secretariat, Cabinet Office, 1998–99 (on secondment); Hd, Educn Dept, 1999–2002, Finance and Central Services Dept, 2002–03, Scottish Exec. *Recreations:* painting, film, theatre, music, modern novels, food and wine. *Address:* Scottish Government, St Andrew's House, Edinburgh EH1 3DG.

ELVIN, David John; QC 2000; a Recorder, since 2002; *b* 30 April 1960; *s* of Walter and Margaret Elvin; *m* 1985, Helen Julia Shilling. *Educ:* A. J. Dawson Grammar Sch.; Hertford Coll., Oxford (BA 1st Cl. Hons Jurisprudence 1981, BCL 1982). Called to the Bar, Middle Temple, 1983. Asst Comr, Boundary Commn, 2000–. Mem. Council, RSCM, 2004–. *Publications:* Unlawful Interference with Land, 1995, 2nd edn 2002; (ed jtly) The Planning Encyclopaedia (loose-leaf); contrib. articles to Law Qly Rev., Judicial Rev., Jl of Planning and Envmt Law. *Recreations:* music (playing, singing, listening), opera, history. *Address:* Landmark Chambers, 180 Fleet Street, EC4A 2HG. *T:* (020) 7430 1221.

ELVIN, Joanne; Editor, Glamour magazine, since 2000; *b* Sydney, 21 Feb. 1970; *d* of Harry Elvin and Leonie Elvin; *m* 2000, Ross Jones; one *d*. *Educ:* Univ. of Western Sydney. Publicist, TV series, Neighbours, 1992; Dep. Editor, TV Hits mag., 1993–94; Editor: Sugar mag., 1994–96; B mag., 1996–98; New Woman mag., 1998–2000. *Address:* Glamour, 6–8 Old Bond Street, W1S 4PH. *T:* (020) 7499 9080. *Clubs:* Groucho, Soho House.

ELVIN, Violetta, (Violetta Prokhorova), (Signora Fernando Savarese); ballerina; a prima ballerina of Sadler's Wells Ballet, Royal Opera House, London (now The Royal Ballet), 1951–56; Director, Ballet Company, San Carlo Opera, Naples, 1985–87; *b* Moscow, 3 Nov. 1925; *d* of Vassilie Prokhorov, engineer, and Irena Grimouzinskaya, former actress; *m* 1st, 1944, Harold Elvin (divorced 1952), of British Embassy, Moscow; 2nd, 1953, Siegbert J. Weinberger, New York; 3rd, 1959, Fernando Savarese, lawyer; one *s*. *Educ:* Bolshoi Theatre Sch., Moscow. Trained for ballet since age of 8 by: E. P. Gerdt, A. Vaganova, M. A. Kojuchova. Grad, 1942, as soloist; made mem. Bolshoi Theatre Ballet; evacuated to Tashkent, 1943; ballerina Tashkent State Theatre; rejoined Bolshoi Theatre at Kuibishev again as soloist, 1944; left for London, 1945. Joined Sadler's Wells Ballet at Covent Garden as guest-soloist, 1946; later became regular mem. Has danced all principal rôles, notably, Le Lac des Cygnes, Sleeping Beauty, Giselle, Cinderella, Sylvia, Ballet Imperial, etc. Danced four-act Le Lac des Cygnes, first time, 1943; guest-artist Stanislavsky Theatre, Moscow, 1944, Sadler's Wells Theatre, 1947; guest-prima ballerina, La Scala, Milan, Nov. 1952–Feb. 1953 (Macbeth, La Gioconda, Swan Lake, Petrouchka); guest artist, Cannes, July 1954; Copenhagen, Dec. 1954; Teatro Municipal, Rio de Janeiro, May 1955 (Giselle, Swan Lake, Les Sylphides, Nutcracker, Don Quixote and The Dying Swan); Festival Ballet, Festival Hall, 1955; guest-prima ballerina in Giselle, Royal Opera House, Stockholm (Anna Pavlova Memorial), 1956; concluded stage career when appeared in Sleeping Beauty, Royal Opera House, Covent Garden, June 1956. *Appeared in films:* The Queen of Spades, Twice Upon a Time, Melba. Television appearances in Russia and England. Has toured with Sadler's Wells Ballet, France, Italy, Portugal, United States and Canada. *Recreations:* reading, painting, swimming.

ELWEN, Christopher; His Honour Judge Elwen; a Circuit Judge, since 1995; a Resident Judge, Truro Combined Courts, since 2008; *b* 14 Sept. 1944; *s* of Kenneth Spence Elwen and Joan Marie Elwen; *m* 1967, Susan Elizabeth Allan; one *s* one *d*. *Educ:* Quarry Bank High Sch., Liverpool; Univ. of Liverpool (LLB). Called to the Bar, Gray's Inn, 1969; Wm Brandts Sons & Co. Ltd, 1970–72; Cripps Warburg Ltd, 1972–75; Holman Fenwick & Willan, 1975–89; admitted solicitor, 1976; Stephenson Harwood, 1989–95; a Recorder, 1993–95. *Recreations:* painting, golf, mediaeval history, walking. *Address:* c/o Courts of Justice, Edward Street, Truro TR1 2PB. *T:* (01872) 267420. *Club:* Garrick.

ELWES, Henry William George; JP; Lord-Lieutenant of Gloucestershire, since 1992; *b* 24 Oct. 1935; *s* of John Hargreaves Elwes, MC, Major, Scots Guards (killed in action, N Africa, 1943) and late Isabel Pamela Ivy Beckwith, *g d* of 7th Duke of Richmond and Gordon, KG, GCVO, CB; *m* 1962, Carolyn Dawn Cripps; two *s* (and one *s* decd). *Educ:* Eton; RAC, Cirencester. Served Army, Lieut, Scots Guards, 1953–56. Member: Cirencester RDC, 1959–74; Glos CC, 1970–91 (Vice-Chm., 1976–83 and 1991; Chm., 1983–85). Regl Dir, Lloyds Bank, 1985–91. Mem., Nat. Jt Council for Fire Brigades, 1979–91; Director: Colesbourne Estate Co., 1969–; Cirencester Friendly Soc. (formerly Cirencester Benefit Soc. Trustee Co.) Ltd, 1974–2000. Pres., Western Woodland Owners Ltd, 1986–2003 (Chm., 1972–86). Patron, Pres. and Mem. of many Glos trusts and societies. Gloucestershire: High Sheriff, 1979–80; DL 1982; JP 1992; Hon. Alderman, 1992. Hon. Lay Canon, Gloucester Cathedral, 2001–. Hon. DPhil Gloucestershire, 2002; Hon. LLD UWE, 2006. Confrèrie des Chevaliers du Tastevin. KStJ 1992. *Address:* Colesbourne Park, near Cheltenham, Glos GL53 9NP.

ELWES, Sir Jeremy (Vernon), Kt 1994; CBE 1984; Chairman, St Helier NHS Trust, 1990–99; *b* 29 May 1937; *s* of late Eric Vincent Elwes and Dorothea Elwes, OBE (*née* Bilton); *m* 1963, Phyllis Marion Relf, 2nd *d* of late George Herbert Harding Relf and Rose Jane Relf (*née* Luery); one *s*. *Educ:* Wirral Grammar Sch.; Bromley Grammar Sch.; City of London Coll. ACIS 1963. Technical Journalist, Heywood & Co., 1958–62; Accountant and Co. Sec., Agricultural Press, 1962–70; Sec. and Dir, East Brackland Hill Farming Development Co., 1967–70; IPC Business Press: Pensions Officer, 1966–70; Divl Personnel Manager, 1970–73; Manpower Planning Manager, 1973–78; Exec. Dir (Manpower), 1978–82; Personnel Dir, Business Press Internat., then Reed Business Publishing, 1982–93; Human Resources Dir, Reed Publishing Europe, 1993–94. Director: Periodicals Trng Council, 1986–92; Sutton Enterprise Agency Ltd, 1987–94 (Chm., 1987–90). Chairman: Cons. Political Centre Nat. Adv. Cttee, 1981–84; Cons. SE Area, 1986–90; Mem., Nat. Union Exec. Cttee, 1972–94; Co-ordinator, Specialist Gps, Cons. Pty, 2000–; Hon. Sec., Cons. Med. Soc., 1996–2000. Mem. Exec. Cttee, GBGSA, 1996–99, 2000–03; Dir and Trustee, Eur. Sch. of Osteopathy, 1999–2007. Pres., Sevenoaks Div., 2000–, Dep. County Pres., Kent, 2001–, St John Ambulance. Chm. of Governors, Walthamstow Hall, 1984–2003. FRSA 1994. Liveryman: Stationers' and Newspapermakers' Co., 1991– (Master and Wardens Cttee, 1999–2002; Chm., Livery Cttee, 2000–02; Livery Rep., 2005–07; Mem. Ct Assts, 2007–; Chm., Hall and Heritage Cttee, 2008–); Chartered Secretaries' and Administrators' Co., 2003– (Sec., 2005–06, Chm., 2006–, Livery Liaison Gp). Member Council: Imperial Soc. of Kts Bachelor, 2002–; Printers' Charitable Corp., 2002–08 (Pres., 2004; Dep. Chm., 2005–06, Chm., 2006–08); Hospice in the Weald, 2003–; Foundn for Liver Res., 2005–. Chevalier, Ordre des Chevaliers Bretvins (Chancelier to 1992). *Recreations:* wine and food, reading, walking, golf. *Address:* Crispian Cottage, Weald Road, Sevenoaks, Kent TN13 1QQ. *T:* (01732) 454208. *Clubs:* Royal Over-Seas League; Knole; Admiralty Golf Soc.; Nizels Golf and Leisure (Captain, Veterans, 1998–99).

ELWOOD, Sir Brian (George Conway), Kt 1990; CBE 1985; Chairman, Kiwifruit New Zealand, since 2004; Chief Ombudsman of New Zealand, 1994–2003; *b* 5 April 1933; *s* of Jack Philip Elwood and Enid Mary Elwood; *m* 1956, Dawn Barbara Elwood (*née* Ward); one *s* two *d*. *Educ:* Victoria Univ., Wellington (LLB); Trinity Coll., London (ATCL). Barrister and Solicitor, 1957. Chairman: Local Govt Commn, NZ, 1985–92; Survey Industry Review Commn, 1990–92; Comr, Wellington Area Health Bd, 1991–92. Mayor, Palmerston North City, 1971–85. Internat. Pres., Internat. Ombudsman Inst., 1999–2002 (Regl Vice Pres., 1996–98). Chm., Age Concern (Wellington) Charitable Trust, 2004–; Trustee, Central Energy Trust, 2006–. Hon. Mem., NZ Inst. of Surveyors. Hon. DLitt Massey, 1994. Medal for Distinguished Public Service, Lions Club Internat., 1985. *Recreations:* golf, fishing, gardening. *Address:* Box 170, Waikanae, Kapiti Coast, New Zealand. *T:* (4) 2938113. *Club:* Wellington.

ELWORTHY, Air Cdre Hon. Sir Timothy (Charles), KCVO 2001 (CVO 1995); CBE 1986; Her Majesty's Senior Air Equerry, 1995–2001; Director of Royal Travel, 1997–2001; Extra Equerry to the Queen, since 1991; *b* 27 Jan. 1938; *e s* of Marshal of the RAF Baron Elworthy, KG, GCB, CBE, DSO, LVO, DFC, AFC and late Audrey Elworthy; *m* 1st, 1961, Victoria Ann (marr. diss.), *d* of Lt Col H. C. W. Bowring; two *d*; 2nd, 1971, Anabel, *d* of late Reginald Harding, OBE; one *s*. *Educ:* Radley; RAF Coll., Cranwell. CO 29 (Fighter) Sqn, 1975 (Wing Comdr); PSO to AO Commanding-in-Chief, Strike Comd, 1979; CO RAF Stn Leuchars, 1983 (Gp Capt.); RCDS, 1986; Dir, Operational Requirements, (Air), MoD, 1987 (Air Cdre); Captain of The Queen's Flight, 1989–95. Liveryman, GAPAN, 1995. QCVSA 1968. *Recreations:* country pursuits, wine, travel. *Address:* Coates House, Swyncombe, Henley-on-Thames, Oxon RG9 6EG. *Club:* Boodle's.

ELY, 9th Marquess of, *cr* 1801; **Charles John Tottenham;** Bt 1780; Baron Loftus 1785; Viscount Loftus 1789; Earl of Ely 1794; Baron Loftus (UK) 1801; Director of Admissions (formerly Head of French Department), Strathcona-Tweedsmuir School, Calgary, until 2004; *b* 2 Feb. 1943; *e s* of 8th Marquess of Ely and Katherine Elizabeth (*née* Craig); *S* father, 2006; *m* 1969, Judith Marvelle, *d* of Dr J. J. Porter, FRS, Calgary, Alberta; one *s* one *d*. *Educ:* Trinity Coll. Sch., Port Hope, Ont; Ecole Internationale de Genève; Univ. of Toronto (MA). *Heir:* *b* Lord Timothy Craig Tottenham [*b* 17 Jan.1948; *m* 1973, Elizabeth Jane McAllister; two *s*]. *Address:* 153 Chaparral Circle, Calgary, AB T2X 3M2, Canada.

ELY, Bishop of, since 2000; **Rt Rev. Anthony John Russell,** DPhil; *b* 25 Jan. 1943; *s* of Michael John William and Beryl Margaret Russell; *m* 1967, Sheila Alexandra, *d* of Alexander Scott and Elizabeth Carlisle Ronald; two *s* two *d*. *Educ:* Uppingham Sch.; Univ. of Durham (BA); Trinity Coll., Oxford (DPhil); Cuddesdon Coll., Oxford. Deacon 1970, Priest 1971; Curate, Hilborough Group of Parishes, 1970–73; Rector, Preston on Stour, Atherstone on Stour and Whitchurch, 1973–88; Chaplain, Arthur Rank Centre (Nat. Agricl Centre), 1973–82, Director, 1983–88; Canon Theologian, Coventry Cathedral, 1977–88; Chaplain to the Queen, 1983–88; Area Bp of Dorchester, 1988–2000. Entered H of L, 2007. Hulsean Preacher, Cambridge Univ., 2004. Mem., Gen. Synod, 1980–88. Royal Agricultural Society: Chaplain, 1982–91; Vice-Pres., 1991–2002; Vice-Patro 2002; Pres., 2004–05; Hon. Chaplain, RABI, 1983–2002. ARAgS 2003. Comr, Rur Develt Commn, 1991–99. Trustee, Rural Housing Trust, 1983–2006. Pres., Woodar Corp., 2003–. Gov., Radley Coll., 2003–. Visitor, Jesus Coll., St John's Coll., an Peterhouse, Cambridge, 2000–. Hon. Fellow: St Edmund's Coll., Cambridge, 200 Wolfson Coll., Cambridge, 2001; St Chad's Coll., Durham, 2007. *Publications:* Groups an Teams in the Countryside (ed), 1975; The Village in Myth and Reality, 1980; Th Clerical Profession, 1980; The Country Parish, 1986; The Country Parson, 1993. *Addres* The Bishop's House, Ely, Cambs CB7 4DW. *T:* (01353) 662749, *Fax:* (01353) 66947 *e-mail:* Bishop@ely.anglican.org.

ELY, Dean of; *see* Chandler, Very Rev. M. J.

ELY, Archdeacon of; *see* Beer, Ven. J. S., Archdeacon of Cambridge.

ELY, Keith; *see* Ely, S. K.

ELY, Philip Thomas, OBE 2003; Chairman, Legal Services Commission, 2003–04; *b* 2 March 1936; *s* of Eric Stanley Ely and Rose Josephine Ely; *m* 1966, Diana Mary (*n* Gellibrand); two *s* three *d*. *Educ:* Douai Sch.; LLB (external) London Univ. Admitte Solicitor, 1958. National Service, RN, 1958–60 (commnd, 1959). Articled Hephe Winstanley & Pugh, Southampton, 1953–58; joined Paris Smith & Randal Southampton, as Asst Solicitor, 1960; Partner, 1961–98, Sen. Partner, 1981–98. La Society: Mem. Council, 1979–93; Vice-Pres., 1990–91; Pres., 1991–92; Hampshi Incorporated Law Society: Asst Hon. Sec., 1961–66; Hon. Sec., 1966–74; Ho Treasurer, 1974–79; Pres., 1979. Appointed by HM Treasury to conduct enquiry in powers of Inland Revenue to call for papers of tax accountants, 1994. Mem., Leg Services Commn (formerly Legal Aid Bd), 1996–2004 (Chm., Regl Legal Services Cttee Reading, 1998–2002, London, 1998–2003); Chm., Police Disciplinary Appeals Tribuna 1996–2003. Hon. LLD Southampton, 1992. *Recreations:* fly-fishing, gardening, musi reading. *Address:* Orchard Cottage, Crawley, Winchester, Hants SO21 2PR. *T:* (0196 776379.

ELY, (Sydney) Keith; writer; *b* 17 April 1949; *s* of Charles Rodenhurst Ely and Doroth Mary Ely (*née* Rowlands); *m* 1st, 1970, Patricia Davies (marr. diss. 1994); three *d*; 2n 1994, Jo Ann Beroiz. *Educ:* Maghull Grammar Sch.; Open Univ. (BA). Journalis Liverpool Daily Post & Echo, 1968–78; Reuters, 1978–80; Daily Post, Liverpool: Busine Editor, 1980–84; Acting Asst Editor, 1984; Systems Develt, 1985–86; Features Edito 1987; Dep. Editor, 1987; Editor, 1989–95; Man. Dir, Trinity Weekly Newspapers Lt 1995–96; Editor and Gen. Manager, Channel One TV, Liverpool, 1996–97; Regl O Dir, Liverpool Daily Post & Echo Ltd, 1998–2000 (Dir, 1989–95 and 1998–2000); Ma Dir, Corporate Culture Plc, 2000–01 (Dir, 1988, 2000). *Recreations:* music, computin *Address:* 2481 Gardenbrook Court, Medford, OR 97504, USA.

ELYSTAN-MORGAN, family name of Baron Elystan-Morgan.

ELYSTAN-MORGAN, Baron *cr* 1981 (Life Peer), of Aberteifi in the County of Dyfe **His Honour Dafydd Elystan Elystan-Morgan;** a Circuit Judge, 1987–2003; *b* 7 De 1932; *s* of late Dewi Morgan and late Mrs Olwen Morgan; *m* 1959, Alwen (*d* 2006), *d* William E. Roberts; one *s* one *d*. *Educ:* Ardwyn Grammar Sch., Aberystwyth; UCW Aberystwyth. LLB Hons Aberystwyth, 1953. Research at Aberystwyth and Solicito Articles, 1953–57; admitted a Solicitor, 1957; Partner in N Wales (Wrexham) Firm Solicitors, 1958–68; Barrister-at-law, Gray's Inn, 1971; a Recorder, 1983–87. MP (La Cardiganshire, 1966–Feb. 1974; Chm., Welsh Parly Party, 1967–68, 1971–74; Par Under-Secretary of State, Home Office, 1968–70; front-bench spokesman on Hon Affairs, 1970–72, on Welsh Affairs, 1972–74, on Legal and Home Affairs, House of Lord 1981–85. Contested (Lab): Cardigan, Oct. 1974; Anglesey, 1979. President: Welsh Loc Authorities Assoc., 1967–73; Parlt for Wales Campaign, 1979. President: Univ. of Wale Aberystwyth, subseq. Aberystwyth Univ., 1998–2007; Welsh Sch. of Legal Studie 1998–. *Address:* Carreg Afon, Dolau, Bow Street, Dyfed SY24 5AE.

EMANUEL, David, FCSD; fashion designer; *b* 17 Nov. 1952; *s* of John Lawrence Mor Emanuel and late Elizabeth Emanuel; *m* 1975, Elizabeth Florence Weiner (*see* E. Emanuel) (separated 1990; marr. diss. 2008); one *s* one *d*. *Educ:* Cardiff Coll. of A (Diploma); Harrow Sch. of Art (Diploma); Royal College of Art (MA). Final Degree sho at RCA, 1977. Emanuel (couture business) commenced in Mayfair, W1, 1977, Jt Partne Dir, 1977–90; The Emanuel Shop (retail), London, SW3, 1986–90; ready-to-we business partnership in USA, 1988; formed David Emanuel Couture, 1990. Designe wedding gown for the Princess of Wales, 1981; ballet productions, incl. Frankenstein, th Modern Prometheus, Royal Opera House, Covent Garden, 1985 and La Scala, Mila 1987; uniforms for Virgin Atlantic Airways, 1990; prodns for theatre, film, TV an operatic recitals. Television presenter, fashion shows, 1994–. FCSD (FSIAD 1984). Ho FRWCMD (Hon. FWCMD 2000). *Publications:* (with Elizabeth Emanuel): Style for A Seasons, 1983; A Dress for Diana, 2006. *Recreations:* horse-riding, jet-ski-ing, tennis, oper *Address:* David Emanuel Couture, c/o Lanesborough Hotel, Lanesborough Place, SW1 7TA. *T:* (020) 7482 6486, *Fax:* (020) 7267 6627. *Clubs:* White Elephant; Royal Asc Tennis (Berks).

EMANUEL, Elizabeth Florence, FCSD; fashion designer; *b* 5 July 1953; *d* of Samu Charles Weiner and Brahna Betty Weiner; *m* 1975, David Emanuel, *qv* (separated 199 marr. diss. 2008); one *s* one *d*. *Educ:* City of London Sch. for Girls; Harrow Sch. of A (Diploma with Hons); Royal Coll. of Art (MA 1977; DesRCA 1977). FCSD 198 Emanuel (couture) commenced in Mayfair, W1, 1977; The Emanuel Shop (retai London, SW3, 1986–90; launched internat. fashion label, Elizabeth Emanuel, 1991; set u Elizabeth Emanuel Enterprises, 1999; designer, Luxury Brand Gp, 2001–02; started ne label, Art of Being, 2005–. Designed: wedding gown for the Princess of Wales, 198 range of wedding dresses for: Berkertex, 1995; BHS, 2008; ballet productions, inc Frankenstein, the Modern Prometheus, Royal Opera House, Covent Garden, 1985 an La Scala, Milan, 1987; costumes for films: The Changeling, 1995; RosBeef, 200 uniforms for: Virgin Atlantic Airways, 1990; Britannia Airways, 1995; prodns for theat and operatic recitals. *Publications:* (with David Emanuel): Style for All Seasons, 1983; Dress for Diana, 2006. *Recreations:* ballet, films, writing. *Address:* Garden Studio, 51 Maic Vale, Little Venice, W9 1SD.

EMBREY, Derek Morris, OBE 1986; CEng, FIET, FIMechE; Technical Directo Streamwatch Ltd, since 2004; Chairman, Turnock Ltd (formerly George Turnock Ltd 1998–2000; Group Technical Director, AB Electronic Products Group PLC, 1973–91; 11 March 1928; *s* of Frederick and Ethel Embrey; *m* 1st, 1951, Frances Margaret Stephe (marr. diss. 1995); one *s* one *d*; 2nd, 1999, Jean McKay Stevens, *d* of late Norman McK Fairgrieve. *Educ:* Wolverhampton Polytechnic (Hon. Fellow, 1987). Chief Design (Electronics), Electric Construction Co. Ltd, 1960–65, Asst Manager Static Plan 1965–69; Chief Engineer, Abergas Ltd, 1969–73. Member: Engineering Counc 1982–87; Welsh Industrial Develt Adv. Bd, 1982–85; NACCB, 1985–87; Council, IER

1984–88 (Vice Pres., 1985–88); National Electronics Council, 1985–99; Welsh Adv. Bd, 1986–90 (Chm., 1987–90). Vis. Prof., Univ. of Technology, Loughborough, 1978–84 (External Examr, Dept of Mechanical Engrg, 1984–88); Visiting Lecturer: Loughborough Univ., 1988–97; Birmingham Univ., 1989–2000. Member: Council, UWIST, Cardiff, 1984–88; Bd, Inst. of Transducer Technol., Southampton Univ., 1986–2000; Council, IEE, 1992–95 (Chm., Management and Design Divl Bd, 1993–94); Air Cadet Council, 1988–95; Regl Civilian Chm., ATC, Wales, 1988–95; Dir and Mem. Council, BTEC, 1993–96. Freeman, City of London, 1986; Liveryman, Scientific Instrument Makers' Co., 1986–; founder Liveryman, Welsh Livery Guild, 1994. Hon. Fellow UWIC, 1992. *Publications:* contribs to various jls. *Recreations:* remembering fondly flying and navigating powered aircraft and gliders; music, archaeology. *Address:* 21 Rockfield Glade, Penhow, Caldicot, Monmouthshire NP26 3JF. *T:* (01633) 400995. *Club:* Royal Air Force.

EMBUREY, John Ernest; Director of Cricket, Middlesex County Cricket Club, since 2006 (Director of Coaching, 2001–06); *b* 20 Aug. 1952; *s* of John Alfred Emburey and Rose Alice Emburey (*née* Roff); *m* 1980, Susan Elizabeth Anne Booth; two *d*. *Educ:* Peckham Manor. Professional cricketer: Middx CCC, 1971–95; England Test cricketer, 1978–95; 64 Test matches (Captain, 1988); 63 one-day internationals; Manager, England A Team tour to Pakistan, 1995; Chief Coach and Manager, Northants CCC, 1996–98; coach, England A Team tour, Zimbabwe and S Africa, 1999; player/coach, Berks CCC, 2000. *Publications:* Emburey (autobiog.), 1986; Spinning in a Fast World, 1989. *Recreations:* golf, reading. *Address:* c/o Middlesex County Cricket Club, Lord's Cricket Ground, NW8 8QZ. *Club:* MCC.

EMECHETA, Buchi, OBE 2004; writer and lecturer, since 1972; *b* 21 July 1944; *d* of Alice and Jeremy Emecheta; *m* 1960, Sylvester Onwordi; two *s* three *d*. *Educ:* Methodist Girls' High Sch., Lagos, Nigeria; London Univ. (BSc Hons Sociol.). Librarian, 1960–69; Student, 1970–74; Youth Worker and Res. Student, Race, 1974–76; Community Worker, Camden, 1976–78. Visiting Prof., 11 Amer. univs, incl. Penn. State, Pittsburgh, UCLA, Illinois at Urbana-Champaign, 1979; Sen. Res. Fellow and Vis. Prof. of English, Univ. of Calabar, Nigeria, 1980–81; lectured: Yale, Spring 1982; London Univ., 1982. Proprietor, Ogwugwn Afo Publishing Co. Included in twenty 'Best of Young British', 1983. Member: Arts Council of GB, 1982–83; Home Sec's Adv. Council on Race, 1979. Hon. DLitt Fairleigh Dickensons' Univ., NJ, 1992. *Publications:* In the Ditch, 1972; Second Class Citizen, 1975; The Bride Price, 1976; The Slave Girl, 1977; The Joys of Motherhood, 1979; Destination Biafra, 1982; Naira Power, 1982; Double Yoke, 1982; The Rape of Shavi, 1983; Head Above Water (autobiog.), 1984; Gwendolen, 1989; Kehinde, 1994; The New Tribe, 2000; *for children:* Titch the Cat, 1979; Nowhere to Play, 1980; The Moonlight Bride, 1981; The Wrestling Match, 1981; contribs to New Statesman, TLS, The Guardian, etc. *Recreations:* gardening, going to the theatre, listening to music, reading. *Clubs:* Africa Centre, PEN, International PEN (Trustee, 1993–98).

EMERSON, Michael Ronald, MA; FCA; Senior Research Fellow, Centre for European Policy Studies, Brussels, since 1998; *b* 12 May 1940; *s* of late James Emerson and Priscilla Emerson; *m* 1st, 1966, Barbara Brierley; one *s* two *d*; 2nd, 2000, Elena Prokhorova. *Educ:* Hurstpierpoint Coll.; Balliol Coll., Oxford (MA (PPE)). Price Waterhouse & Co., London, 1962–65; Organisation for Economic Cooperation and Development, Paris: several posts in Develt and Economics Depts, finally as Head of General Economics Div., 1966–73; EEC, Brussels: Head of Division for Budgetary Policy, Directorate-General II, 1973–76; Economic Adviser to President of the Commission, 1977; Dir for Nat. Economies and Economic Trends, 1978–81; Dir for Macroecon. Analyses and Policies, 1981–86; Dir, Economic Evaluation of Community Policies, Directorate-General II, 1987–90; Ambassador and Head of EC Delegn to CIS, 1991–96. Fellow, Centre for Internat. Affairs, Harvard Univ., 1985–86. Hon. DLitt Keele, 1993; Hon. DCL Kent, 1993. *Publications:* (ed) Europe's Stagflation, 1984; What Model for Europe, 1987; The Economics of 1992, 1988; One Market, One Money, 1991; Redrawing the Map of Europe, 1998; Wider Europe Matrix, 2004; contribs to various economic jls and edited volumes on internat. and European economics. *Address:* CEPS, 1 Place du Congrès, 1000 Brussels, Belgium.

EMERSON, Dr Peter Albert, MD; FRCP; Hon. Consultant Physician, Chelsea and Westminster Hospital (formerly Westminster and Charing Cross Hospitals), since 1988; *b* 7 Feb. 1923; *s* of Albert Emerson and Gwendoline (*née* Davy); *m* 1947, Ceris Hood Price; one *s* one *d*. *Educ:* The Leys Sch., Cambridge; Clare Coll., Univ. of Cambridge (MA); St George's Hosp., Univ. of London (MB, BChir 1947; MD 1954). FRCP 1964; Hon. FACP 1975. House Physician, St George's Hosp., 1947; RAF Med. Bd, 1948–52 (Sqdn Leader); Registrar, later Sen. Registrar, St George's Hosp. and Brompton Hosp., London, 1952–57; Asst Prof. of Medicine, Coll. of Medicine, State Univ. of New York, Brooklyn, USA, 1957–58; Consultant Phys., Westminster Hosp., 1959–88; Civilian Consultant Phys. in Chest Diseases to RN, 1974–88; Dean, Westminster Medical Sch., London, 1981–84. Hon. Consultant Phys., King Edward VII Hosp., Midhurst, 1969–88. Royal Coll. of Physicians: Asst Registrar, 1965–71; Procensor and Censor, 1978–80; Vice-Pres. and Sen. Censor, 1985–86; Mitchell Lectr, 1969. *Publications:* Thoracic Medicine, 1981; articles in med. jls and chapters in books on thoracic medicine and the application of decision theory and expert systems to clinical medicine. *Recreation:* managing/developing OPPASS (Out Patient Pre Admission Screening System). *Address:* 3 Halkin Street, SW1X 7DJ. *T:* (020) 7235 8529. *Club:* Royal Air Force.

EMERSON, Richard Martyn; Chief Inspector of Historic Buildings, Historic Scotland, 1999–2004; *b* 19 Dec. 1949; *s* of late Maj. Hugh Emerson and Keyna Emerson (*née* Parson); *m* 1st, 1971, Vanessa Leadam Andrews (marr. diss. 1990); two *s* one *d*; 2nd, 1991, Anne Grenfell Macdonald; one *s* one *d*. *Educ:* Wellington Coll.; Courtauld Inst. of Art, London Univ. (BA Hons). Dep. Conway Librarian, Courtauld Inst. of Art, 1971–73; Res. Asst, Nat. Monuments Record for Scotland, Royal Commn on Ancient and Historical Monuments of Scotland, 1973–78; Principal Inspector of Historic Bldgs, Historic Scotland, 1978–99. Hon. FRIAS 2006. *Address:* 2 Place Vieille, 06300 Nice, France.

EMERTON, Baroness *cr* 1997 (Life Peer), of Tunbridge Wells in the co. of Kent and of Clerkenwell in the London Borough of Islington; **Audrey Caroline Emerton,** DBE 1989; DL; RGN, RM, RNT; Chief Commander, St John Ambulance, 1998–2002; Chairman, Brighton Health Care NHS Trust, 1994–2000 (Vice Chairman, 1993–94); *b* 10 Sept. 1935; *d* of late George Emerton and of Lily (*née* Squirrell). *Educ:* Tunbridge Wells GS; St George's Hosp.; Battersea Coll. of Technol. Sen. Tutor, Experimental 2 year and 1 year Course, St George's Hosp., SW1, 1965–68; Principal Nursing Officer, Educn, Bromley HMC, 1968–70; Chief Nursing Officer, Tunbridge Wells and Leybourne HMC, 1970–73; Regl Nursing Officer, SE Thames RHA, 1973–91. St John Ambulance, Kent: Co. Nursing Officer, 1967–85; Co. Comr, 1985–88; St John Ambulance: Chief Nursing Officer, 1988–98; Chm. of Med. Bd, 1993–96; Chief Officer, Care in the Community, 1996–97; Chief Officer, Nursing and Social Care, 1997–98. Lay Mem., GMC, 1996–2001. Pres., Assoc. of Nurse Administrators, 1979–82; Hon. Vice Pres., RCN, 1994–99. Chairman: English Nat. Bd for Nursing, Midwifery and Health Visiting, 1983–85; UKCC, 1985–93; Assoc. of Hosp. and Community Friends, 2003–; Pres., Florence Nightingale Foundn, 2004–. Trustee: Kent Community Housing Trust, 1993–99; Defence Med. Welfare Service, 2001–. DL Kent, 1992. Hon. Fellow, Christ Church UC, Canterbury, 2003. Hon. DCL Kent, 1989; Hon. DSc Brighton, 1997; DUniv Central England, 1997; Hon. Dr of Science Kingston, 2001. GCStJ 2004. *Address:* House of Lords, SW1A 0PW.

EMERTON, Rev. Prof. John Adney, FBA 1979; Regius Professor of Hebrew, Cambridge, 1968–95, Emeritus Professor since 1995; Fellow of St John's College, since 1970; Honorary Canon, St George's Cathedral, Jerusalem, since 1984; *b* 5 June 1928; *s* of Adney Spencer Emerton and Helena Mary Emerton; *m* 1954, Norma Elizabeth Bennington; one *s* two *d*. *Educ:* Minchenden Grammar Sch., Southgate; Corpus Christi Coll., Oxford; Wycliffe Hall, Oxford. BA (1st class hons Theology), 1950; 1st class hons Oriental Studies, 1952; MA 1954. Canon Hall Jun. Greek Testament Prize, 1950; Hall-Houghton Jun. Septuagint Prize, 1951, Senior Prize, 1954; Houghton Syriac Prize, 1953; Liddon Student, 1950; Kennicott Hebrew Fellow, 1952. Corpus Christi Coll., Cambridge, MA (by incorporation), 1955; BD 1960; DD 1973. Deacon, 1952; Priest, 1953. Curate of Birmingham Cathedral, 1952–53; Asst Lecturer in Theology, Birmingham Univ., 1952–53; Lecturer in Hebrew and Aramaic, Durham Univ., 1953–55; Lecturer in Divinity, Cambridge Univ., 1955–62; Reader in Semitic Philology and Fellow of St Peter's Coll., Oxford, 1962–68. Visiting Professor: of Old Testament and Near Eastern Studies, Trinity Coll., Toronto Univ., 1960; of Old Testament, Utd Theol Coll., Bangalore, 1986; Fellow, Inst. for Advanced Studies, Hebrew Univ. of Jerusalem, 1982–83. Select Preacher before Univ. of Cambridge, 1962, 1971, 1986. President: Internat. Orgn for the Study of the Old Testament, 1992–95 (Sec., 1971–89); SOTS, 1979. Mem. Editorial Bd, Vetus Testamentum, 1971–97. Corresp. Mem., Akademie der Wissenschaften, Göttingen, 1990. Hon. DD Edinburgh, 1977. Burkitt Medal for Biblical Studies, British Acad., 1991. *Publications:* The Peshitta of the Wisdom of Solomon, 1959; The Old Testament in Syriac: Song of Songs, 1966; (ed) Studies in the Historical Books of the Old Testament, 1979; (ed) Prophecy: essays presented to Georg Fohrer, 1980; (ed) Studies in the Pentateuch, 1990; Editor, Congress Volumes (International Organization for Study of the Old Testament): Edinburgh 1973, 1974; Göttingen 1977, 1978; Vienna 1980, 1981; Salamanca 1983, 1985; Jerusalem 1986, 1988; Leuven 1989, 1991; Paris 1992, 1995; Cambridge 1995, 1997; articles in Journal of Semitic Studies, Journal of Theological Studies, Palestine Exploration Qly, Theology, Vetus Testamentum, Zeitschrift für die Alttestamentliche Wissenschaft. *Address:* 34 Gough Way, Cambridge CB3 9LN.

EMERY, Prof. Alan Eglin Heathcote, MD, PhD, DSc; FRSE, FRCP, FRCPE; FLS; Chief Scientific Advisor, European Neuromuscular Center, Baarn, The Netherlands, since 1999 (Research Director, and Chairman, Research Committee, 1989–99); Professor of Human Genetics, University of Edinburgh and Hon. Consultant Physician, Lothian Health Board, 1968–83, now Emeritus Professor and Hon. Fellow; Hon. Fellow, Green College, Oxford, 2006 (Hon. Visiting Fellow, 1986–2006); *b* 21 Aug. 1928; *s* of Harold Heathcote Emery and Alice Eglin; *m* 1988, Marcia Lynn (*née* Miller); three *s* three *d* from a previous marriage. *Educ:* Manchester Univ. (BSc (double 1st cl. Hons), MD, DSc; John Dalton Prize); Johns Hopkins Univ., Baltimore (PhD). FRIPH (FRIPHH 1965); FRCPE 1970; MFCM 1974; FRSE 1972; FLS 1985; FRCP 1985. Formerly Resident in Medicine and Surgery, Manchester Royal Infirmary; Fellow in Medicine, Johns Hopkins Hosp., Baltimore, 1961–64; Reader in Medical Genetics, Univ. of Manchester, 1964–68 and Hon. Consultant in Medical Genetics, United Manchester Hosps; Sen. Res. Fellow, Green Coll., Oxford, 1985–86. Hon. Vis. Prof., Peninsular Med. Sch., 2006–. Pres., British Clinical Genetics Soc., 1980–83; Council Mem., British Genetic Soc. (Mem. cttees on trng in genetics, 1976, 1979 and 1983 and NHS services, 1978, 1980, 1983 and 1989); Vice Pres., Musc. Dystrophy Campaign, GB, 1999–; Pres., Med. Genetics Sect., RSocMed, 2002–04. Hon. Member: Assoc. of British Neurologists, 1999; Netherlands Genetic Soc., 1999. FRSA 2002. Hon. FRSSAf 1989; Hon. FACMG 1993; Hon. FRSocMed 2006. Hon. MD: Naples, 1993; Würzburg, 1995. Nat. Foundn (USA) Internat. Award for Research, 1980; Gaetano Conte Award and Medal, Gaetano Conte Acad., Italy, 2000; Pro Finlandiae Gold Medal, Univ. of Helsinki, 2000; Elsevier Sci. Award, 2001; Assoc. Française Contre Les Myopathies Prize, 2001; Life-time Achievement Award, World Fedn of Neurology, 2002; Cockcroft Medal and Alumnus of the Year Award, Manchester Univ., 2006; Doubleday Medal in Medicine, 2007. Exec. Editor, Procs B, RSE, 1986–90. *Publications:* Elements of Medical Genetics, 1968, 13th edn as Emery's Elements of Medical Genetics (ed P. Turnpenny and S. Ellard), 2007; Methodology in Medical Genetics, 1976, 2nd edn 1986; Recombinant DNA—an introduction, 1984, 2nd edn (with S. Malcolm) 1995; Duchenne Muscular Dystrophy, 1987, 3rd edn 2003; Muscular Dystrophy: the facts, 1994, 3rd edn 2007; The History of a Genetic Disease, 1995; with M. Emery: Medicine and Art, 2002; Surgical and Medical Treatment in Art, 2005; Mother and Childcare in Art, 2007; editor: Modern Trends in Human Genetics, vol. 1, 1970, vol. 2, 1975; Antenatal Diagnosis of Genetic Disease, 1973; Registers for the Detection and Prevention of Genetic Disease, 1976; Principles and Practice of Medical Genetics, 1983, 5th edn as Emery & Rimoin's Principles and Practice of Medical Genetics, 2007; Psychological Aspects of Genetic Counselling, 1984; Diagnostic Criteria for Neuromuscular Disorders, 1994, 2nd edn 1997; Neuromuscular Disorders: clinical and molecular genetics, 1998; The Muscular Dystrophies, 2002; numerous scientific papers. *Recreations:* oil painting, medical and art history. *Address:* c/o Green Templeton College, Oxford OX2 6HG.

EMERY, Fred; author and broadcaster; Presenter, Panorama, BBC TV, 1978–80 and 1982–92; *b* 19 Oct. 1933; *s* of Frederick G. L. Emery and Alice May (*née* Wright); *m* 1958, E. Marianne Nyberg; two *s*. *Educ:* Bancroft's Sch.; St John's Coll., Cantab (MA). RAF fighter pilot, 266 & 234 Squadrons, National Service, 1953. Radio Bremen, 1955–56; joined The Times, 1958, Foreign Correspondent, 1961; served in Paris, Algeria, Tokyo, Indonesia, Vietnam, Cambodia, Malaysia and Singapore until 1970; Chief Washington Corresp., 1970–77; Political Editor, 1977–81; Home Editor, 1981–82; Exec. Editor (Home and Foreign), and Actg Editor, 1982. Reporter, Watergate (TV series), 1994 (Emmy Award, 1995). Press Officer, Crystal Palace Campaign, 1999–. *Publication:* Watergate: the corruption and fall of Richard Nixon, 1994. *Recreations:* ski-ing, hill walking, tennis. *Address:* 5 Woodsyre, SE26 6SS. *T:* (020) 8761 0076. *Club:* Garrick.

EMERY, George Edward, CB 1980; Director General of Defence Accounts, Ministry of Defence, 1973–80, retired; *b* 2 March 1920; *s* of late Frederick and Florence Emery; *m* 1946, Margaret (*née* Rice); two *d*. *Educ:* Bemrose Sch., Derby. Admiralty, 1938; Min. of Fuel and Power, 1946; Min. of Supply, 1951; Min. of Aviation, 1959; Min. of Technology, 1967; Principal Exec. Officer, 1967; Asst Sec., Min. of Aviation Supply, 1970; Ministry of Defence: Asst Sec., 1971; Exec. Dir, 1973; Under-Sec., 1973. *Address:* 3 The Orchard, Freshford, Bath BA2 7WX.

EMERY, Joyce Margaret; *see* Zachariah, J. M.

EMERY, Lina, (Mrs Ralph Emery); *see* Lalandi-Emery, L.

EMERY, Nicola Susan; *see* Clayton, N. S.

EMERY, Prof. Paul, MD; FRCP; ARC Professor of Rheumatology, and Head, Academic Section of Musculoskeletal Disease, University of Leeds, since 1995; Clinical Director, Leeds Teaching Hospitals Trust, since 1995; *b* 30 Nov. 1952; *s* of late Leonard Leslie Emery and Beryl Emery; *m* 1980, Shirley; two *d. Educ:* Cardiff High Sch.; Churchill Coll., Cambridge (BA, MA 1976); Guy's Hosp. Med. Sch.; MB BChir 1977, MD 1985 Cantab. MRCP 1979, FRCP 1992. Accredited Rheumatol. and Gen. (Internal) Medicine, JCHMT, 1985. Hse Officer and SHO rotation, Guy's Hosp., 1979; SHO, Brompton Hosp., 1980; Registrar, then Sen. Registrar in Gen. Medicine and Rheumatol., 1980–85; Hd of Rheumatol., Walter and Eliza Hall Inst., Melbourne and Hon. Consultant, Royal Melbourne Hosp., 1985–87; Sen. Lectr, Univ. of Birmingham, 1987–95. Licentiate Mem., Western Acad. Acupuncture, 1982. Treas., Eur. League Against Rheumatism, 2003. *Publications:* Visual Diagnosis Self-tests in Rheumatology, 1996, 2nd edn 2001; Clinician's Manual on COX-2 Inhibition, 1999, 2nd edn 2002; Adalimumab and Rheumatoid Arthritis, 2003; New Treatments in Arthritis, 2003; Early Rheumatoid Arthritis: rheumatic disease clinics of North America, 2006; chapters and editorials in rheumatol. pubns; articles in jls. *Recreations:* golf, walking, music. *Address:* Academic Section of Musculoskeletal Disease, Chapel Allerton Hospital, Chapeltown Road, Leeds LS7 4SA. *T:* (0113) 392 4884, *Fax:* (0113) 392 4991; *e-mail:* p.emery@leeds.ac.uk. *Clubs:* Pannal Golf, Newport Golf, Harrogate Academy Sports.

EMERY, Richard James; Chief Executive, UKTV Ltd, 1998–2006; *b* 21 July 1946; *s* of Frederick Harold Emery and Hilda Emery (*née* Newson); *m* 1st, 1978, Patricia Moore (marr. diss. 1993); one *s*, and one step *s*; 2nd, 1995, Hazel Susan Challis; one step *s* two step *d. Educ:* Reading Blue Coat Sch. Sales Controller: Anglia Television, 1976; TVS Ltd, 1982; Sales Dir, Central Independent Television Ltd, 1984; Jt Man. Dir and Founder, TSMS Ltd, 1989; Commercial Dir, ITN Ltd, 1991; Dir, Market Strategy, ITV Network Centre, 1993; Man. Dir, BBC Worldwide TV, 1994; Chief Operating Officer, BBC Worldwide Ltd, 1997. *Recreations:* Rugby, walking, reading, boating. *Address:* The Four Sycamores, Mill Road, Shiplake, Henley-on-Thames RG9 3LW. *T:* (0118) 940 3407.

EMERY, William Hubert; JP; PhD; Chief Executive, Office of Rail Regulation, since 2005; *b* 28 June 1951; *s* of Prof. John Lewis and Marjorie Rose Emery (*née* Mytton); *m* 1975, Celia Joan Abbott, PhD; one *s* one *d. Educ:* Univ. of Sheffield (BEng 1972; PhD 1976); Univ. of Bradford (MBA 1981). CEng, MICE 1978. Various posts, Yorkshire Water Authy, 1975–90; Office of Water Services: Hd, Engrg Intelligence, 1990–94; Asst Dir, 1994–98; Chief Engr and Dir of Costs and Performance, 1998–2005. JP S Yorks, 1981. *Address:* Office of Rail Regulation, One Kemble Street, WC2B 4AN. *T:* (020) 7282 2006, *Fax:* (020) 7282 2043; *e-mail:* bill.emery@orr.gsi.gov.uk.

EMERY-WALLIS, Frederick Alfred John, FSA; Member (C), 1973–2001, Chairman, 1999–2001, Hampshire County Council; Vice-President, Southern Tourist Board, 1988–2001 (Chairman, 1976–88); *b* 11 May 1927; *o s* of Frederick Henry Wallis and Lillian Grace Emery Coles; *m* 1960, Solange, *o d* of William Victor Randall, London, and Albertine Beaupère, La Guerche-sur-l'Aubois; two *d. Educ:* Blake's Academy, Portsmouth. Royal Signals SCU4 (Middle East Radio Security), 1945–48. Portsmouth City Council, 1961–74; Lord Mayor, 1968–69; Alderman, 1969–74; Vice-Chm., 1975–76, Leader, 1976–93 and 1997–99, Hants CC. Chm., Recreation Cttee, 1982–85, Mem., Exec. and Policy Cttees, ACC, 1974–93; Mem., LGA, 1997–2000. Chairman: Portsmouth Develt and Estates Cttee, 1965–74; Portsmouth Papers Editorial Bd, 1966–82; S Hampshire Plan Adv. Cttee, 1969–74; Portsmouth South Cons. and Unionist Assoc., 1971–79, 1982–85; Portsmouth Record Series Adv. Panel, 1982–2002; Hampshire Archives Trust, 1986–2001; Exec. Cttee, Hampshire Sculpture Trust, 1988–2001; Director: Warrior Preservation Trust, 1988–91; WNO, 1990–99; Learning Through Landscapes Trust, 1991–2001; Member: Economic Planning Council for the South East, 1969–74; SE Regl Cultural Consortium; British Library Adv. Council, 1979–84, 1986–91; Council, British Records Assoc., 1979–2004 (Vice-Pres., 1996–2004); Library and Information Services Council, 1980–83; Mary Rose Develt Trust, 1980–90; Arts Council of GB Reg. Adv. Bd, 1984–88; Hampshire Gardens Trust, 1984–99; Nat. Council on Archives, 1992–94; English Heritage Archives, Libraries and Information Adv. Cttee, 1999–2001; Victoria County History Cttee, 1993–2002. President: Hampshire Field Club, 1971–74; Hatrics, the Southern Information Network, 1978–2001. Gov., Univ. of Portsmouth, 1991–96 (Mem., 1961–92, Vice-Chm., 1967–75, Portsmouth Polytechnic); Chm. of Govs, Portsmouth High Sch. for Girls, 1982–92. Trustee: New Theatre Royal, Portsmouth, 1982–92; Royal Naval Mus., Portsmouth, 1987–2002; Royal Marines Mus., Portsmouth, 1993–94. Pres., Portsmouth YMCA, 1978–88. DL Hants 1988. Hon. Fellow, Portsmouth Polytechnic, 1972. FSA 1980. Hon. FRIBA 1985; Hon. FCLIP (Hon. FLA 1996). *Publications:* various publications concerning history and develt of Portsmouth and Hampshire. *Recreations:* book collecting, music. *Address:* Sussex House, 19 Sussex Road, Portsmouth PO5 3EX.

EMIN, Tracey, RA 2007; artist; *b* 1963. *Educ:* Maidstone Coll. of Art (BA 1986); Royal Coll. of Art (MA 1989). Solo exhibitions include: White Cube, 1993, 2001, 2005; S London Gall., 1997; Galerie Gebauer, Berlin, 2000; Stedelijk Mus., Amsterdam, 2002; Haus der Kunst, Munich, 2002; Modern Art Oxford, 2002; Art Gall. of NSW, 2003; Platform Garanti Contemp. Art Centre, Istanbul, 2004; Venice Biennale, 2007. Group exhibns incl. Sensation, RA, 1997. Set designer, Les Parents Terribles, Jermyn Street Th., 2004. Film, Top Spot, 2004. Founder, Tracey Emin Museum, London, 1995–98. *Publication:* Strangeland, 2005. *Address:* c/o White Cube, 48 Hoxton Square, N1 6PB.

EMLEY, Miles Lovelace Brereton; Chairman, St Ives plc, since 1993; *b* 23 July 1949; *s* of Col Derek Emley, OBE and late Mary Georgina Emley (*née* Lovelace); *m* 1976, Tessa Marcia Radclyffe Powell; two *s* one *d. Educ:* St Edward's Sch., Oxford; Balliol Coll., Oxford (MA). N. M. Rothschild & Sons Ltd, 1972–89 (Dir, 1982–89); Man. Dir, UBS Phillips & Drew, 1989–92. Non-exec. Dir, Marstons plc (formerly Wolverhampton & Dudley Breweries plc), 1998–. *Address:* St Ives plc, St Ives House, Lavington Street, SE1 0NX. *T:* (020) 7928 8844; *e-mail:* miles.emley@st-ives.co.uk. *Clubs:* White's, Brooks's.

EMLYN, Viscount; James Chester Campbell; *b* 7 July 1998; *s* and *heir* of Earl Cawdor, *qv.*

EMLYN JONES, John Hubert, CBE 1986 (MBE (mil.) 1941); FRICS; JP; Member of the Lands Tribunal, 1968–86; *b* 6 Aug. 1915; *s* of late Ernest Pearson Jones and Katharine Cole Jones (*née* Nicholas); *m* 1954, Louise Anne Montague, *d* of late Raymond Ralph Horwood Hazell; two *s* one *d. Educ:* Dulwich. FRICS 1939. Served War, RE, 1939–46: Major 1943. Partner, Rees-Reynolds and Hunt, and Alfred Savill & Sons, Chartered Surveyors, 1950–68. President: Rating Surveyors Assoc., 1965–66 (Hon. Mem. 1968); Climbers' Club, 1966–69 (Hon. Mem. 1970); Alpine Club, 1980–82 (Hon. Mem. 2006). Mem. Council, RICS, 1964–69. Mem. Bureau, 1964–72, Treasurer 1967–69, Fédération Internationale des Géomètres. Mem., expedns to Himalayas: Annapurna, 1950; Ama Dablam, 1959 (Leader). High Sheriff, Bucks, 1967–68, JP 1968. *Publications:* articles and revs in mountaineering jls. *Recreations:* mountaineering, music. *Address:* Ivinghoe Manor, Leighton Buzzard, Beds LU7 9EH. *T:* (01296) 668202. *Clubs:* Garrick, Alpine.

EMMERSON, David, CBE 1989; AFC 1982; Chairman, North Hampshire Hospita NHS Trust, 2002–05; *b* 6 Sept. 1939; *s* of late Alfred Robert and Sarah Helen Emmerson *m* 1961, Martha (Marie) Katherine Stuart. *Educ:* Colchester Royal Grammar Sch Operational and instructional flying, 1959–73; Canadian Staff Coll. and Air Staff Ottawa 1974–76; Policy Staff, MoD, 1976–77; Air Staff, Washington, 1978–80; OC 206 Sqn 1981–82; Gp Capt. Ops, Northwood, 1983; Stn Comdr, RAF Kinloss, 1984–85; RCDS 1986; Principal Staff Officer to CDS, 1987–88; Chief of Staff, HQ 18 Gp, Northwood 1989–90; retired in rank of Air Vice-Marshal. Chief Executive, Elizabeth FitzRoy Homes 1991–2000; Chm., Assoc. for Residential Care, 1995–2000. *Recreations:* travel, world politics, all sports. *Club:* Royal Air Force.

EMMETT, Bryan David; Chairman, EAGA Group, 1998–2000 (Director, EAGA Ltd 1991–2000); *b* 15 Feb. 1941; *m* 1960, Moira Miller (marr. diss. 1994); one *s. Edu* Tadcaster Grammar Sch. Clerical Officer, Min. of Labour, and National Service, 1958–59 Exec. Officer, War Dept, 1959–64; Asst Principal, MOP, 1965–69 (Asst Private Sec. t Ministers of Power, 1968–69); Principal, Electricity Div., DTI, 1969–74; Department c Energy: Principal, and Private Sec. to Minister of State, 1974–75; Asst Sec., and Principa Private Sec. to Sec. of State for Energy, 1975–76; Asst Sec., Petroleum Engrg Div 1977–80; Under Sec., and Principal Estab. Officer, 1980–81; Principal Estab. and Financ Officer, 1981–82; Chief Exec., Employment Div., MSC, 1982–85; Department o Energy: Head, Energy Policy Div., 1985–86; Head of Oil Div., 1986–87; Dir Gen Energy Efficiency Office, 1987–88; seconded as Chief Exec., Educn Assets Bd, Leed 1988–90; compulsorily retired, 1991. Subpostmaster, Greenham Court PO and Store Newbury, 1995–98. Adminr, EAGA Charitable Trust, 1993–95. Mem. (Lib Den 1997–2000, C, 2000), Newbury DC, later West Berks Council (Chm., Lib Dem Gp May–Sept. 1998). *Recreations:* National Hunt racing, horseriding, golf. *Address:* 31 Findo Avenue, Saltdean, Brighton BN2 8RF.

EMMOTT, William John, (Bill); author and consultant; *b* 6 Aug. 1956; *s* of Richar Anthony Emmott and Audrey Mary Emmott; *m* 1st, 1982, Charlotte Crowther (mar diss.); 2nd, 1992, Carol Barbara Mawer. *Educ:* Latymer Upper Sch., Hammersmith Magdalen Coll., Oxford (BA Hons PPE; Hon. Fellow, 2002); Nuffield Coll., Oxford. Th Economist: Brussels corresp., 1980–82; Economics corresp., 1982–83; Tokyo corresp 1983–86; Finance Editor, 1986–88; Business Affairs Editor, 1989–93; Editor-in-chie 1993–2006; Editorial Dir, Economist Intelligence Unit, May–Dec. 1992. Membe European Exec. Cttee, Trilateral Commn, 1999–; BBC World Service Governor Consultative Gp, 2000–06; Swiss Re Chairman's Adv. Panel, 2006–; Univ. of Toky President's Council, 2006–; Co-Chm., Canada-Europe Roundtable for Business, 2006– Non-exec. Dir, Development Consultants International, 2006–. Hon. LLD Warwic 1999; Hon. DLitt: City, 2001; Northwestern, 2008. *Publications:* The Pocket Economi (with Rupert Pennant-Rea), 1983; The Sun Also Sets, 1989; Japan's Global Reach, 199 Kanryo no Taizai, 1996; 20:21 Vision, 2003; The Sun Also Rises, 2006; Nihon n Sentaku, 2007; Rivals: how the struggle between China, India and Japan will shape ou next decade, 2008. *Recreations:* cricket, dogwalking, journalism. *Address:* PO Box 2 Dulverton, Somerset TA22 9WW. *T:* (01398) 323186; *web:* www.billemmott.com *Clubs:* Lansdowne, Walbrook.

EMMS, David Acfield, OBE 1995; MA; Director, The London Goodenough Tru (formerly London House) for Overseas Graduates, 1987–95; *b* 16 Feb. 1925; *s* of lat Archibald George Emms and Winifred Gladys (*née* Richards); *m* 1950, Pamela Bake Speed; three *s* one *d. Educ:* Tonbridge Sch.; Brasenose Coll., Oxford. BA Hons Mo Langs Oxford, 1950, Diploma in Education, 1951; MA 1954. Served War of 1939–4 RA, 1943–47. Undergraduate, 1947–50; Asst Master, Uppingham Sch. (Head of Mo Languages Dept, CO, CCF Contingent), 1951–60; Headmaster of: Cranleigh Schoo 1960–70; Sherborne School, 1970–74; Master, Dulwich Coll., 1975–86. Chm., HMC 1984; Pres., ISCO, 2001–06. Dep. Chm., E-SU, 1984–89; Chm., Jt Educnl Trus 1987–90; Mem. Cttee, GBA, 1989–92. Vice-Chm. Council and Dep. Pro-Chancello City Univ., 1989–91; Governor: Bickley Park, 1978–81; Feltonfleet, 1967–8 Brambletye, 1982–88; St Felix Sch., Southwold, 1981–88; Portsmouth Grammar Sch 1987–98; Tonbridge, 1988–2000; St. George's, Montreux, 1989–2000; St Dunstan Coll., 1992–97. President: Alleyn Club, 1985; Brasenose Soc., 1987. Mem. Counci Fairbridge Soc., 1984–96. FRSA 1988. Freeman, City of London; Master, Skinners' Co 1987–88. Hon. Col, 39th (City of London) Signal Regt (Special Communication (Volunteers), 1988–91. Chm., RNLI, Chichester, 1997–2005. Cdre, Alleynian Sailin Soc., 2008–. Played Rugby football: Oxford *v* Cambridge, 1949, 1950; Northampto 1951–56; Eastern Counties, 1951–57 (Capt. 1957); Barbarians, 1953. *Publication:* HM Schools and British Industry, 1981. *Recreations:* radical gardening, travel, putting names t faces. *Clubs:* East India, Devonshire, Sports and Public Schools, Pilgrims; Vincent (Oxford).

EMMS, Peter Fawcett; public administration consultant in former communist countrie since 1995; *b* 25 April 1935; *s* of late Reginald Emms and Hetty Emms; *m* 1960, Caro Wayne; three *d. Educ:* Derby Sch., Derby; Magdalen Coll., Oxford, 1956–59 (Ope Schol. in Mod. Langs; MA French and German). National Service, Jt Services Russia Course, 1954–56. Assistant Master: Abingdon Sch., 1959–62; Rugby Sch., 1962–74; Vi Master, Groton Sch., Mass, 1967–68; Hd of Mod. Langs 1969–71, Housemaster of Tow House 1971–74, Rugby Sch.; joined DoE as Principal, 1974, with posts in Road Safet Construction Industries and Housing; Asst Sec., 1979; Hd of Greater London Housin 1979–81; seconded to DES, Further and Higher Educn Br., 1981–83; Hd of Housin Management Div., and of Estate Action Unit, DoE, 1983–87; Nuffield Leverhulm Travelling Fellowship, 1987–88; Hd, Dept of Transport Internat. Transport Div., Mem Central Rhine Commn, 1988–89; Under Sec., 1989; Regl Dir, Eastern Reg., DoE an Dept of Transport, 1989–94; Leader, Know How Fund adv. team to Ukrainian gov 1994–95. *Publications:* Social Housing: a European dilemma?, 1990; (contrib.) Changin Housing Finance Systems, 1991. *Recreation:* travel. *Address:* 28 Sherard Court, 3 Man Gardens, N7 6FA; 71800 Vauban, France.

EMPEY, Prof. Duncan William, FRCP; Foundation Professor and Dean, Bedfordshir and Hertfordshire Postgraduate Medical School, since 2005; Consultant Physicia London Chest Hospital and Royal London Hospital, 1979–2004; *b* 9 Sept. 1946; *s* Henry Gordon Empey and Katherine Isobel (*née* Hooper); *m* 1972, Gillian Ma Charlesworth; three *d. Educ:* Christ's Coll., Finchley; University Coll. Londo Westminster Hosp. Med. Sch. (MB, BS). MRCS 1969; FRCP 1983 (LRCP 1969). NI Fogarty Internat. Res. Fellow, Cardiovascular Res. Inst., San Francisco, 1974–75; Ho Lectr, London Hosp. Med. Coll., 1975–79; Hon. Sen. Registrar, London Hosp 1975–79; Hon. Sen. Lectr, St Bartholomew's and Royal London Sch. of Medicine an Dentistry, 1995–; Hon. Consultant Physician, King Edward VII Hosp. for Officer 1995–; Hon. Prof., Univ. of Keele Centre for Health Planning and Mgt, 2002–0 Medical Director: Royal Hosps, then Barts and the London, NHS Trust, 1994–200 NHS Executive (N Thames) Trust Unit, 1997–98; Associate Dir, Rapid Response Uni subseq. Performance Develt Team, NHS Modernisation Agency, 2002–04. Ed., British of Diseases of the Chest, 1984–88. Sec.-Gen., European Soc. for Clinical Respirato

Physiol., 1979–84; Mem. Council, British Thoracic Soc., 2003–06. *Publications:* (jtly) Lung Function for the Clinician, 1981; papers on medical management, asthma, chronic bronchitis, pulmonary circulation, tuberculosis and cystic fibrosis. *Recreation:* equestrianism. *Address:* 18 Upper Wimpole Street, W1G 6LX. *T:* (020) 7935 2977, *Fax:* (020) 7935 2740. *Clubs:* Savage, Groucho.

EMPEY, Sir Reginald (Norman Morgan), Kt 1999; OBE 1994; Member (UU) Belfast East, Northern Ireland Assembly, since 1998; Minister for Employment and Learning, Northern Ireland, since 2007; Member, Belfast City Council, since 1985; Leader, Ulster Unionist Party, since 2005; *b* 26 Oct. 1947; *s* of Samuel Frederick Empey and Emily Winifred (*née* Morgan); *m* 1977, Stella Ethna Donnan (MBE 2007); one *s* one *d. Educ:* The Royal Sch., Armagh; Queen's Univ., Belfast (BSc (Econ)). Cons. & Unionist Assoc., QUB, 1967; Publicity Officer, 1967–68, Vice-Chm., 1968–72, Ulster Young Unionist Council; Chm., Vanguard Unionist Party, 1974–75; Mem., E Belfast, NI Constitutional Convention, 1975–76. Dep. Lord Mayor, 1988–89, Lord Mayor of Belfast, 1989–90 and 1993–94. Minister of Enterprise, Trade and Investment, NI, 1999–2002. Member: Belfast Harbour Comrs, 1985–89; Eastern Health and Social Services Bd, 1985–86; Ulster Unionist Council, 1987– (Hon. Sec., 1990–96; Vice-Pres., 1996–2004); Bd, Laganside Corp., 1992–98; Police Authy for NI, 1992–2001; European Cttee of the Regions for NI, Brussels, 1994–2002; Standing Adv. Commn on Human Rights, 1994–96. Contested (UU) Belfast East, 2005. *Recreations:* walking, gardening. *Address:* Knockvale House, 205 Sandown Road, Belfast BT5 6GX. *T:* (028) 9046 3900; Parliament Buildings, Stormont, Belfast BT4 3XX.

EMPEY, Rt Rev. Walton Newcombe Francis; Archbishop of Dublin and Primate of Ireland, 1996–2002; *b* 26 Oct. 1934; *m* 1960, Louise E. Hall; three *s* one *d. Educ:* Portora Royal School and Trinity College, Dublin. Curate Assistant, Glenageary, Dublin, 1958–60; Priest-in-charge, Grand Falls, NB, Canada, 1960–63; Parish Priest, Edmundston, NB, 1963–66; Incumbent, Stradbally, Co. Laois, Ireland, 1966–71; Dean of St Mary's Cathedral and Rector, Limerick City Parish, 1971–81; Bishop of Limerick and Killaloe, 1981–85; Bishop of Meath and Kildare, 1985–96; Bishop of Glendalough, 1996–2002. *Recreations:* reading, fishing, walking. *Address:* The Lodge, Rathmore, Tullow, Co. Carlow, Republic of Ireland.

EMSLEY, Dr John, FRSC; writer and broadcaster; *s* of Charles and Mary Emsley; *m* 1963, Joan Feather; one *s* one *d. Educ:* Manchester Univ. (BSc, MSc; PhD 1963); DSc London 1983. FRSC 1983. Lectr, 1966–84, Reader, 1984–90, KCL; Science Writer in Residence: Imperial Coll., London, 1990–97; Dept of Chem., Univ. of Cambridge, 1997–2002. Consultant, Broadcast Advertising Clearance Centre, 1996–2007. Columnist, Molecule of the Month, Independent, 1990–96. *Publications:* (with C. D. Hall) The Chemistry of Phosphorus, 1976; The Elements, 1989, 3rd edn 1998; The Consumer's Good Chemical Guide, 1994; Molecules at an Exhibition, 1998; (with P. Fell) Was it something you ate?, 1999; The Shocking History of Phosphorus, 2000; Nature's Building Blocks, 2001; Vanity, Vitality & Virility, 2004; Elements of Murder, 2005; Better Looking, Better Living, Better Loving, 2007; popular sci. books trans. into foreign langs, incl. German, French, Italian, Spanish, Portuguese, Polish, Finnish, Chinese and Japanese; original res. papers on phosphorus chem. and strong hydrogen-bonded systems; contrib. numerous sci. articles and features to jls incl. New Scientist, Independent, Guardian, Chem. in Britain, Chem Matters, Focus, Sci. Watch. *Recreation:* walking. *Address:* Alameda Lodge, 23A Alameda Road, Ampthill MK45 2LA. *T:* (01525) 404718; *e-mail:* JohnEmsley38@aol.com.

EMSLIE, Hon. Lord; Hon. George Nigel Hannington Emslie; a Senator of the College of Justice in Scotland, since 2001; *b* 17 April 1947; *s* of Rt Hon. Lord Emslie, PC, MBE; *m* 1973, Heather Ann Davis; one *s* two *d. Educ:* Edinburgh Acad.; Trinity Coll., Glenalmond; Gonville and Caius Coll., Cambridge (BA); Edinburgh Univ. (LLB). Admitted to Faculty of Advocates, 1972; Standing Junior Counsel: to Forestry Commn in Scotland and to Dept of Agric. and Fisheries for Scotland, 1981–82; to Inland Revenue in Scotland, 1982–86; QC (Scot.) 1986. Part-time Chm., Med. Appeal Tribunals, 1988–97. Dean, Faculty of Advocates, 1997–2001. *Address:* Court of Session, Parliament House, Edinburgh EH1 1RQ. *T:* (0131) 225 2595. *Clubs:* Hawks (Cambridge); New (Edinburgh).

See also Rt Hon. Lord Kingarth.

EMSLIE, Hon. Derek Robert Alexander; *see* Kingarth, Rt Hon. Lord.

EMSLIE, Donald Gordon; Chairman: Royal Lyceum Theatre Co., since 2004; Royal Zoological Society of Scotland, since 2008; Queuebay Ltd, since 2008; *b* 8 May 1957; *s* of Francis G. Emslie and Margaret Evelyn (*née* Campbell); *m* 1998, Sarah, *d* of Peter Gardner; two *d. Educ:* Jordanhill Coll., Glasgow (BEd Physical Educn). Teacher, Kingussie High Sch., 1979–82; with Bochringer Ingelheim Pharmaceuticals, 1982–85; sales, 1985–94, Commercial Dir, 1994–97, Scottish TV; Man. Dir, Broadcasting, SMG plc, 1997–99; Chief Executive: SMG Television, 1999–2006; SMG plc, 2006–07. Chm., GMTV Ltd, 2002–04. Chairman: ITV Council, 2002–07; Scottish Industry Skills Panel, 2004–. Non-exec. Dir, Scottish Water, 2008–. Member, Board: Scottish Screen, 2000–07; Skillset, 2004–; Screen Acad. Scotland, 2006– (Chm., Adv. Bd, 2006–); Jt Bd, Scottish Screen and Scottish Arts Council, 2007–. Jt Hon. Chm., BAFTA Scotland, 2004–07. *Recreations:* golf, tennis. *Address:* 32 Drumsheugh Gardens, Edinburgh EH3 7RM. *T:* (0131) 226 3938.

EMSLIE, Hon. George Nigel Hannington; *see* Emslie, Hon. Lord.

ENCOMBE, Viscount; John Francis Thomas Marie Joseph Columba Fidelis Scott; *b* 9 July 1962; *s* and *heir* of 5th Earl of Eldon, *qv; m* 1993, Charlotte, *d* of Bob de Vlaming; one *s* one *d.*

ENDERBY, Charles; *see* Enderby, S. C.

ENDERBY, Sir John (Edwin), Kt 2004; CBE 1997; FRS 1985; H. O. Wills Professor of Physics, 1981–96, now Emeritus, and Senior Research Fellow, since 1996, University of Bristol; *b* 16 Jan. 1931; *s* of late Thomas Edwin Enderby and Rheita Rebecca Hollinshead (*née* Stather); *m* Susan, *yr d* of late Harold Vincent Bowles, OBE and of Colleen Bessie Bowles; one *s* two *d*, and one *d* (one *s* decd) of previous marriage. *Educ:* Chester Grammar Sch.; London Univ. (BSc, PhD). Lecturer in Physics: Coll. of Technology, Huddersfield, 1957–60; Univ. of Sheffield, 1960–67; Reader in Physics, Univ. of Sheffield, 1967–69; Prof. in Physics and Head of the Dept, Univ. of Leicester, 1969–76; Prof. of Physics, Bristol Univ., 1976–81; Head of Dept of Physics, and Dir, H. H. Wills Physics Lab., Bristol Univ., 1981–94; Directeur-Adjoint, Institut Laue-Langevin, Grenoble, 1985–88. Fellow, Argonne Nat. Lab., Ill., USA, 1989–91; Visiting Fellow, Battelle Inst., 1968–69; Visiting Professor: Univ. of Guelph, Ont., 1978; Univ. of Leiden, 1989. Humphrey Davy Lectr, Royal Soc., 1997. Member: Physics Cttee, SRC, 1974–77; Neutron Beam Res. Cttee, SRC, 1974–80 and 1988–91 (Chm., 1977–80 and 1988–91); PPARC, 1994–98. Chm., Physics Panel, 2001 RAE, HEFCE, 1999–2001. Chm., Liquids Bd, Eur. Physical Soc., 1991–96. Member: Council, Institut Laue-Langevin, Grenoble,

1973–80; Council, Royal Soc., 1990–92 (Physical Sec. and Vice-Pres., 1999–2004). Chm., Melys Diagnostics Ltd, 2004–. MAE 1989. FInstP 1970 (Chm., SW Br., 1979–83; Guthrie Medal, 1995; Pres., 2004–06). Associate Editor, Philosophical Magazine, 1975–81; Editor, Proc. Royal Soc. A, 1989–94; Editor in Chief, Jl of Physics Condensed Matter, 1997–2002; Chief Sci. Advr, Inst of Physics Publishing, 2002–. Hon. Fellow, Birkbeck Coll., London, 1991. Hon. DSc: Loughborough, 1996; Leicester, 2006; Bristol, 2006; Sheffield, UEA, 2007. *Publications:* (jointly): Physics of Simple Liquids, 1968; Amorphous and Liquid Semiconductors, 1974; many publications on the structure and properties of liquids in: Phil. Mag. Adv. Phys, Jl Phys, Proc. Royal Soc., etc. *Recreations:* gardening, woodwork, watching Association football. *Address:* H. H. Wills Physics Laboratory, Tyndall Avenue, Bristol BS8 1TL. *T:* (0117) 928 8737; 7 Cotham Lawn Road, Bristol BS6 6DU. *T:* (0117) 973 3411. *Club:* Athenæum.

ENDERBY, Major (Samuel) Charles; JP; Lieutenant, Queen's Body Guard of the Yeoman of the Guard, since 2006; *b* 18 Sept. 1939; *s* of late Col Samuel Enderby, CVO, DSO, MC and of Pamela Enderby (*née* Hornby); *m* 1973, Mary Justina Compton; two *d. Educ:* Wellington Coll.; RMA, Sandhurst. Commnd 12th Royal Lancers, 1959; retd 1985, in rank of Major. Exon, Queen's Body Guard of Yeoman of the Guard, 1987–2006. Chm., Hexham Steeplechase Co. Ltd, 1991–. JP Tynedale, 1991. *Recreations:* gardening, reading, bird ringing, shooting. *Address:* The Riding, Hexham, Northumberland NE46 4PF. *Clubs:* Army and Navy, Pratt's.

ENDICOTT, Grattan, OBE 1998; Chief Executive and Secretary to the Trustees, Foundation for Sport and the Arts, 1991–2004; *b* 12 Jan. 1924; *s* of late Cecil George Endicott and Annette Rose Endicott; *m* 1st, 1944, Paolina Cicoria (marr. diss. 1955); two *s*; 2nd, 1961, Jean Thurgeson (marr. diss. 1981). *Educ:* Rhyl Co. Grammar Sch. Served RN, 1941–46; Principal Linguist, Navy Sub-Commn, Allied Commn, Rome, 1944–46. Personnel Asst, ICI, 1946–57; Littlewoods Pools: Asst Permutation Manager, 1957–66; Hd, Permutation Services, 1966–89. World Bridge Federation: Sec., Laws Cttee, 1997– (Vice-Chm., 1992–96); Co-ordinator, Laws Review Subcttee, 2001–07, Laws Drafting Subcttee, 2008–. Pres., Merseyside and Cheshire Contract Bridge Assoc. Gold Medal, World Bridge Fedn, 2005. *Publications:* European Bridge League Commentary on the Laws of Duplicate Contract Bridge 1987, 1992; (jtly) Draft Laws of Duplicate Bridge, 2006; (jtly) Laws of Duplicate Bridge, 2007. *Recreation:* competition (duplicate) bridge. *Address:* 14 Elmswood Court, Mossley Hill, Liverpool L18 8DJ. *T:* (0151) 724 1484. *Club:* Liverpool Bridge.

ENDICOTT, Prof. Timothy Andrew Orville, DPhil; Professor of Legal Philosophy, since 2006, and Dean, Faculty of Law, since 2007, University of Oxford; Fellow, Balliol College, Oxford, since 1999; *b* Golden, BC, 9 July 1960; *s* of Orville and Julianne Endicott; one *s* one *d. Educ:* Harvard Univ. (AB 1983); Univ. of Oxford (MPhil 1985; DPhil 1997); Univ. of Toronto (LLB 1988). Barrister and solicitor, Oslers, Toronto, 1988–91; Lectr in Law, Jesus Coll., 1994–95, St Anne's Coll., 1995–96, St Catherine's Coll., 1996–99 (Fellow, 1998–99), Oxford. *Publications:* Vagueness in Law, 2000; articles in law and philos. jls. *Address:* Balliol College, Oxford OX1 3BJ. *T:* (01865) 271564, *Fax:* (01865) 271493.

ENFIELD, Viscount; William Robert Byng; computer systems developer, CCP York, since 2002; *b* 10 May 1964; *s* and *heir* of 8th Earl of Strafford, *qv; m* 1994, Karen Elizabeth, *d* of S. Graham Lord, Leyland, Preston; twin *s* two *d. Educ:* Winchester Coll.; Durham Univ. *Heir: s* Hon. Samuel Peter Byng, *b* 17 July 1998. *Address:* 7 Church Street Villas, Durham DH1 3DW.

See also Hon. J. E. Byng.

ENFIELD, Harry; comedy actor and writer; *b* 30 May 1961; *m* 1997, Lucy Lyster; one *s* one *d. Educ:* York Univ. (BA Hons Politics). TV programmes include: Sir Norbert Smith: a life, 1989 (Silver Rose of Montreux, Emmy Award); Smashie and Nicey: the end of an era, 1994 (Silver Rose of Montreux); Norman Ormal, 1998; Kevin's Guide to Being a Teenager, 1999; Skins, 2007, 2008; series: Harry Enfield's Television Programme, 1990, 1992; Harry Enfield's Guide to the Opera, 1993; Harry Enfield and Chums, 1994 (Writers Guild Award) and 1997 (Silver Rose of Montreux); St Albion Parish Council, 1998, 1999; Harry Enfield's Brand Spanking New Show, 2000; Celeb, 2002; Ruddy Hell! It's Harry and Paul, 2007; Harry and Paul, 2008; also appeared regularly in: Saturday Night Live, 1986; Friday Night Live, 1988; Gone to the Dogs, 1991; Men Behaving Badly, 1992; films: Kevin and Perry Go Large, 2000; Churchill: the Hollywood Years, 2003; Tooth, 2004. Top BBC 1 Comedy Personality, British Comedy Awards, 1998. *Publication:* Harry Enfield and his Humorous Chums, 1997. *Address:* c/o PBJ Management Ltd, 7 Soho Street, W1D 3DQ. *T:* (020) 7287 1112, *Fax:* (020) 7287 1191; *e-mail:* general@pbjmgt.co.uk.

ENGEL, Matthew Lewis; Editor, Wisden Cricketers' Almanack, 1992–2000 and 2003–07; columnist, Financial Times, since 2004; *b* 11 June 1951; *s* of late Max David and Betty Ruth Engel; *m* 1990, Hilary Davies; one *d* (one *s* decd). *Educ:* Manchester Univ. (BA Econ). Reporter, Chronicle and Echo, Northampton, 1972–75; Reuters, 1977–79; The Guardian: journalist, 1979–2004; cricket corresp., 1982–87; feature writer, sports columnist, occasional political and foreign corresp., 1987–2001; columnist, 1998–2004; Washington corresp., 2001–03. Mem., Nothing Writers. Sports Writer of the Year, What the Papers Say, 1985; Sports Journalist of the Year, British Press Awards, 1991. *Publications:* Ashes '85, 1985; (ed) Guardian Book of Cricket, 1986; (ed) Sportswriter's Eye, 1989; (ed) Sportspages Almanac, 1990, 1991, 1992; (with A. Radd) History of Northamptonshire CCC, 1993; Tickle the Public, 1996; Extracts from the Red Notebooks, 2007; Eleven Minutes Late, 2009. *Recreation:* wishful thinking. *Address:* Fair Oak, near Bacton, Herefordshire HR2 0AT. *Clubs:* Cricket Writers'; Northamptonshire CCC (Vice-Pres.).

ENGEL, Natascha, (Mrs D. S. Jones); MP (Lab) Derbyshire North East, since 2005; *b* 9 April 1967; *d* of Achaz and Christina Engel; *m* 2001, David Salisbury Jones; two *s. Educ:* King's Coll., London (BA 1st Cl. Hons Mod. Langs); Westminster Press Dip. Journalism; Westminster Univ. (MA Tech. and Specialist Translation). Journalist, Dover Express, 1990; English and German teacher, Spain, 1990–92; teletext subtitler, 1992–97; GPMU Organiser, TUC Organising Acad., 1997–98; TU Liaison, Labour Party, 1998–2001; Prog. Dir, John Smith Inst., 2001–02; Co-ordinator, TU Political Fund Ballots, 2002–03. *Address:* House of Commons, SW1A 0AA. *T:* (020) 7219 3000; *e-mail:* engeln@parliament.uk.

ENGEL, Dame Sister Pauline Frances, DBE 1995 (CBE 1986); Vicar for Education, Diocese of Auckland (RC), New Zealand, 1994–2003; *b* 10 Sept. 1930; *d* of John Edmond Engel and Eileen Frances Engel (*née* McDavitt). *Educ:* St Mary's Coll., Wellington; Univ. of Auckland (MA Hons). Registered Teacher. Entered Sisters of Mercy Congregation, 1960; Dep. Principal, McAuley High Sch., 1978–79; Principal, Carmel Coll., 1983–91. Gen. Exec. Sec. to Major Superiors Conference, NZ, 1992–93. Sisters of Mercy Leadership Council, 1995–2000. *Publication:* The Abolition of Capital Punishment in New Zealand 1935–61, 1976. *Recreations:* classical music, reading. *Address:* Mount Carmel

Convent, Box 31142, Milford, Auckland 9, New Zealand; Sisters of Mercy Auckland Ltd, PO Box 6015, Wellesley Street, Auckland 1001, New Zealand.

ENGESET, Jetmund, Hon. LVO 2004; FRCSE; FRCSG; Consultant Surgeon, Grampian Health Board, 1987–2004; Surgeon to the Queen in Scotland, 1985–2004; *b* 22 July 1938; *s* of Arne K. Engeset and Marta Engeset; *m* 1966, Anne Graeme (*née* Robertson); two *d*. *Educ:* Slemdal and Ris Skole, Oslo, Norway; Oslo University; Aberdeen University (MB ChB, ChM Hons). House Officer (Surgical and Medical), Aberdeen Royal Infirmary, 1964–65; Aberdeen University: Res. Assistant, Dept of Surgery, 1965–67; Surgical Registrar, 1967–70; Lectr in Surgery, 1970–74; Sen. Lectr in Surgery, 1974–87; Head of Dept of Surgery, 1982–85 (seconded to Salgrenska Hosp. Surgical Unit, Gothenburg, Sweden, 1972–74). Golden Jubilee Medal, 2002. *Publications:* papers on microcirculation, vascular surgery, organ preservation and tissue transplantation. *Recreations:* ski-ing, angling, squash, gardening. *Address:* 66 Greystoke Park, Gosforth, Newcastle-upon-Tyne NE3 2DZ. *T:* (01912) 363223.

ENGLAND, Angela Catherine; *see* Finnerty, A. C.

ENGLAND, Prof. George Leslie, DScEng; CEng, FICE, FINucE; Professor of Mechanics and Structures, Imperial College, London, 1989–2000; *b* 9 Oct. 1935; *s* of John Edward Philip England and Rose Gladys England; *m* 1968, W. Margaret Landon. *Educ:* East Barnet Grammar Sch.; King's Coll., London (Sambrooke Schol.; BScEng 1st Cl. Hons; Jameson Prize (Eng); Eng. Soc. Centenary Prize, Tennant Medal (Geol); PhD 1961; DScEng 1974). King's College, London: Lectr, 1961; Reader in Engrg Mechanics, 1975; Dean, 1983–85; Vice-Dean, 1985–86; Prof. of Mechanics and Structures, 1986–89. Consultant to: HSE, NII, 1971; UN Develt Project, Central Soils and Materials Res. Station, India, 1992. Mem., British Orthop. Res. Soc.; MASCE. *Publications:* contribs to learned jls on time-dependent service-life performance of concrete structures and behaviour of structures at high temperatures. *Recreations:* landscape gardening, mountain walking. *Address:* Civil Engineering Department, Imperial College of Science, Technology and Medicine, SW7 2BU.

ENGLAND, Glyn, BSc(Eng); FREng, FIET, FIMechE; Chairman, RSA Sustainability Action Group Exchange, 1998–2003; *b* 19 April 1921; *m* 1942, Tania Reichenbach; two *d*. *Educ:* Penarth County Sch.; Queen Mary Coll., London Univ. (BSc (Eng)); London School of Economics. Department of Scientific and Industrial Research, 1939. War service, 1942–47. Chief Ops Engr, CEGB, 1966–71; Dir-Gen., SW Region, 1971–73; Chm., SW Electricity Bd, 1973–77; part-time Mem., 1975–77, Chm., 1977–82, CEGB. Director: F. H. Lloyd (Hldgs), 1982–87; Triplex Lloyd, 1987–90; The Wind Fund plc, 1994–2000; Chm., Windcluster Ltd, 1991–96. Consultant, World Bank, 1983–89. Mem., British Nat. Cttee, World Energy Conf., 1977–82; Vice-Pres., Internat. Union of Producers and Distributors of Electrical Energy, 1981–82. Mem., Bd of Dirs, UK CEED, 1984–96. Chairman: Council for Envmtl Conservation, 1983–88; Bd of Trustees, Silvanus Trust (formerly Dartington Action Res. Trust), 1985–94; Woodlands Initiatives, later Silvanus Services Ltd, 1988–96. Pres., Mendip Soc., 1999–2001. Sometime Labour Mem., Herts CC; Mem. Council, Magistrates' Assoc. JP Welwyn, Herts, 1962–71. FRSA 1965; CCMI (FBIM 1976). Hon. DSc Bath, 1981. *Publications:* (with Rex Savidge) Landscape in the Making; papers on: Economic Growth and the Electricity Supply Industry, Security of Electricity Supplies, Planning for Uncertainty, Railways and Power (IMechE Tritton Lecture), Efficiency Audits, Industrial Ecology. *Recreation:* actively enjoying the countryside. *Address:* Woodbridge Farm, Ubley, Bristol BS40 6PX. *T:* (01761) 462479.

ENGLAND, Prof. Philip Christopher, FRS 1999; Professor of Geology, Oxford University, since 2000; Fellow, University College, Oxford, since 2000; *b* 30 April 1951; *s* of Anthony Christopher England and Margaret Jean England; *m* 1978, Pamela Anne Shreeve; one *s* two *d*. *Educ:* Bristol Univ. (BSc Physics 1972); DPhil Geophysics, Oxford, 1976. NERC Research Fellow, 1977–79, IBM Res. Fellow, 1979–81, Dept Geodesy and Geophysics, Univ. of Cambridge; Asst, then Associate Prof., Harvard Univ., 1981–86; Lectr in Geophysics, Oxford Univ., 1986–99; Fellow, Exeter Coll., Oxford, 1986–2000. Fellow, Amer. Geophysical Union, 1996. *Publications:* contribs to earth science jls. *Recreations:* family, music.

ENGLAND, Rear-Adm. Timothy John, FIET; maritime and transport consultant, since 1997; Chief Staff Officer (Support) to Commander-in-Chief Fleet, 1992–94; *b* Llandudno, 6 Feb. 1942; *s* of late Wilfred James England and Kathleen Helen England (*née* Stacey); *m* 1966, Margaret Ann Cullen; one *s* one *d*. *Educ:* Trinity Sch. of John Whitgift, Croydon; RNEC Manadon. BScEng ext. London Univ. CEng. Joined RN at BRNC Dartmouth as Weapon Engineering specialist, 1960; served HM Ships Alert, Collingwood, London, Salisbury; Staff of DG Ships; HM Dockyard, Devonport; HMS Bristol; Staff of C-in-C Fleet; Directorate of Naval Operational Requirements, 1978–80; Weapon Engineer Officer, HMS Invincible, incl. Falklands Campaign, 1981–82; Staff Weapon Engineer Officer to FO Sea Training, 1982–84; Defence Operational Requirements, 1984–86; RCDS 1987; Fleet Weapon Engineer Officer, 1988–89; WRNS Sea Service Implementation Team Leader, 1990; Captain, RNEC, Manadon, 1990–92. Harbour Master, River Hamble, 1995–96. MInstD. *Publications:* articles in Naval and professional jls. *Recreations:* sailing/cruising, photography, information technology. *Address:* 14 East Hill Close, Fareham, Hants PO16 8SE.

ENGLE, Sir George (Lawrence Jose), KCB 1983 (CB 1976); QC 1983; First Parliamentary Counsel, 1981–86; *b* 13 Sept. 1926; *m* 1956, Irene, *d* of late Heinz Lachmann; three *d*. *Educ:* Charterhouse (scholar); Christ Church, Oxford (Marjoribanks and Dixon schols, MA). Served RA, 1945–48 (2nd Lt, 1947). Firsts in Mods and Greats; Cholmeley Schol., Lincoln's Inn, 1952. Called to Bar, Lincoln's Inn, 1953, Bencher, 1984. Joined Parly Counsel Office, 1957; seconded as First Parly Counsel, Fedn of Nigeria, 1965–67; Parly Counsel, 1970–80; with Law Commn, 1971–73; Second Parly Counsel, 1980–81. Pres., Commonwealth Assoc. of Legislative Counsel, 1983–86. Mem., Hansard Soc. Commn on the Legislative Process, 1992–93. Pres., Kipling Soc., 2001–. *Publications:* Law for Landladies, 1955; (ed jtly) Cross on Statutory Interpretation, 2nd edn 1987, 3rd edn 1995; contributor to: Ideas, 1954; O Rare Hoffnung, 1960; The Oxford Companion to English Literature, 1985; articles in Kipling Jl. *Recreations:* books, travel, theatre, bricolage. *Address:* 32 Wood Lane, Highgate, N6 5UB. *T:* (020) 8340 9750.

ENGLE, Prof. Robert Fry, PhD; Professor of Finance and Michael Armellino Professor in the Management of Financial Services, Leonard N. Stern School of Business, New York University, since 2000; *b* Nov. 1942; *m* 1969, Marianne Eger; one *s* one *d*. *Educ:* Williams Coll. (BS highest Hons (Physics) 1964); Cornell Univ. (MS (Physics) 1966; PhD (Econs) 1969). Asst Prof., 1969–74, Associate Prof., 1974–75, MIT; University of California, San Diego: Associate Prof., 1975–77; Prof., 1977; Chair, 1990–94; Chancellors' Associates Prof. of Econs, 1993; Prof. Emeritus and Res. Prof., 2003–. Principal, Robert F. Engle Econometric Services. Mem. Econ. Panel, NSF, 1979–81; Res. Associate, Nat. Bureau of Econ. Res., 1987–. Fellow: Econometric Soc., 1981 (Mem. Council, 1994; Mem., Nominating Cttee for Council, 1995); Amer. Acad. of Arts and Scis, 1995; Amer. Statistical Assoc., 2000. Associate Editor: Econometrica, 1975–81; Jl of Regl Sci., 1978–; Jl of Forecasting, 1985–; Jl of Applied Econometrics, 1988– (Co-Ed., 1985–89); Rev. o[f] Econs and Stats, 1992; Adv. Ed., Empirical Finance, 1992. Roger F. Murray Prize, Inst for Quantitative Res. in Finance, 1991; (jtly) Nobel Prize for Econs, 2003. *Publications:* (ed jtly) Long Run Economic Relations: readings in cointegration, 1991; (ed jtly) Handbook of Econometrics, vol. IV, 1994; (ed jtly) ARCH: selected readings, 1995; (ed jtly) Cointegration, Causality, and Forecasting: a festschrift in honor of Clive W. J. Granger 1999; contribs to Econometrica, Jl of Business and Econ. Stats, Jl of Econometrics, Jl o[f] Finance, Review of Financial Studies, Jl of Financial Economics, etc. *Address:* Leonard N Stern School of Business, New York University, 44 West Fourth Street, Suite 9–62, New York, NY 10012, USA. *T:* (212) 9980710, *Fax:* (212) 9954220; *e-mail:* rengle@stern.nyu.edu.

ENGLEHART, Robert Michael; QC 1986; a Recorder, since 1987; a Deputy High Court Judge, since 1994; *b* 1 Oct. 1943; *s* of G. A. F. and K. P. Englehart; *m* 1971 Rosalind Mary Foster; one *s* two *d*. *Educ:* St Edward's Sch., Oxford; Trinity Coll., Oxford (MA); Harvard Law School (LLM); Bologna Centre (Dip. in Internat. Relns). Assistente Univ. of Florence, 1968. Called to the Bar, Middle Temple, 1969 (Astbury Scholar Bencher, 1995); practising barrister, 1969–. Chairman: London Common Law and Commercial Bar Assoc., 1990–91; Jt Regulations Cttee, Inns of Court and Bar Council 2000–. Trustee, Free Representation Unit, 1991–. *Publication:* (contrib.) Il Controllo Giudiziario: a comparative study of civil procedure, 1968. *Recreations:* shooting, cricket windsurfing. *Address:* Blackstone Chambers, Blackstone House, Temple, EC4Y 9BW. *T:* (020) 7583 1770. *Clubs:* Garrick, MCC.

ENGLISH, Hon. Bill; *see* English, Hon. S. W.

ENGLISH, Gerald; Australian Artists Creative Fellow, 1994–99; *b* 6 Nov. 1925; *m* 1954 Jennifer Ryan; two *s* two *d*; *m* 1974, Linda Jacoby; one *s*. *Educ:* King's Sch., Rochester After War service studied at Royal College of Music and then began career as lyric tenor subsequently travelled in USA and Europe, appeared at Sadler's Wells, Covent Garden and Glyndebourne and recorded for major gramophone companies; Professor, Royal Coll. of Music, 1960–77; Director, Opera Studio, Victorian Coll. for the Arts, Melbourne 1977–89; Lectr, Music Dept, Newcastle Univ., 1990–94. Recorded all vocal music of Peggy Glanville-Hicks and all music written for him by Andrew Ford, 1994–99; retired from singing, 2004. Hon. DMus Sydney, 1989.

ENGLISH, Judith Frances, (Lady English); Principal, St Hilda's College, Oxford 2001–07; *b* 1 March 1940; *d* of Dr Kenneth James Grant Milne and Dr Constance Nellie Milne; *m* 1st, 1973, Ralph Talbot (marr. diss. 2001); two *d*; 2nd, 2002, Sir Terence English, *qv*. *Educ:* Notre Dame High Sch., Sheffield (State Schol.); Girton Coll. Cambridge (Crewdson Prize; MA 1963; Hon. Fellow 2004); University Coll. Hosp. Med Sch., London (MB BChir 1965). MRCP 1968; MRCPsych 1973, FRCPsych 2002 Medical house staff posts, Whittington Hosp., Brompton Hosp. and UCH, 1965–67 Lectr in Clinical Immunology, Inst. of Chest Diseases, London Univ., 1967–70; Registrar in Psychiatry, Maudsley Hosp., 1970–74; Fellow in Consultation-Liaison Psychiatry, then Staff Psychiatrist, UCLA, 1974–79; Director, Psychiatric Consultation Service: Boston Veterans' Affairs Med. Center, 1980–95; New England Med. Center, 1986–93; Chief of Staff, Boston Veterans' Affairs Med. Center, 1996–2000; Asst Prof. of Psychiatry, Tufts Univ., 1986–2000; Associate Clinical Prof. of Psychiatry, Boston Univ. Sch. of Medicine 1998–2000. *Publications:* contribs to med. and psychiatric jls. *Recreations:* reading, poetry dance, cooking. *Address:* 28 Tree Lane, Iffley Village, Oxford OX4 4EY.

ENGLISH, Michael; Chairman, London Network of NHS Patients' Forums, 2006–08; 24 Dec. 1930; *s* of late William Agnew English; *m* 1976, Carol Christine Owen; one *s* one *d*. *Educ:* King George V Grammar Sch., Southport; Liverpool Univ. (LLB). Employed until 1964 as Asst Manager of department concerned with management services in subsidiary of large public company. Joined Labour Party, 1949 (Hon. Life Mem.) Member: Rochdale County Borough Council, 1953–65 (Chairman Finance Cttee until 1964); Lambeth BC, 1990–2002. Mem., London Fire and Civil Defence Authy 1992–2000; Chm., Lambeth CHC, 1993–94. Pres., SE London Valuation Panel 1996–2002. Contested (Lab) Shipley Div., WR Yorks, 1959; MP (Lab) Nottingham West, 1964–83. Parly Private Sec., BoT, 1966–67. Chm., Gen. Sub-Cttee of H of C Expenditure Cttee, 1974–79; formerly Mem., Chairmen's Panel, Treasury and Civil Service, Procedure (Finance) and Sound Broadcasting Cttees. Chairman: Parly Affairs Gp PLP, 1970–76; E Midlands Gp, PLP, 1976–78; E Midlands Regl Lab. Party, 1979–80 *Recreation:* reading history. *Address:* 12 Denny Crescent, Kennington, SE11 4UY. *T:* (020) 7582 9970.

ENGLISH, Hon. Simon William, (Bill); MP (Nat.) Clutha-Southland, New Zealand since 1996; *b* 30 Dec. 1961; *s* of Mervyn English and Norah (*née* O'Brien); *m* 1987, Dr Mary Scanlon; five *s* one *d*. *Educ:* St Patrick's Coll., Silverstream; Otago Univ. (BCom) Victoria Univ. of Wellington (BA Hons English Lit.). Sheep farmer, Dipton, until 1987 Policy Analyst, NZ Treasury, 1987–89; MP (Nat.) Wallace, 1990–96; Parly Under-Sec for Health and Crown Health Enterprises, 1993–96; Minister for Crown Health Enterprises, Associate Minister of Educn and Mem., Cabinet, Feb.–Dec. 1996; Minister of Health, 1996–99; Associate Minister of Revenue, 1997–99; Associate Treas., 1998–99 Minister of Finance and Minister of Revenue, 1999; Opposition spokesman for educn 2003–06, on finance, 2006–. Dep. Leader, 2001–02 and 2006–, Leader, 2002–03, Nat Party. *Recreations:* Rugby, running. *Address:* Parliament Buildings, Wellington, New Zealand. *T:* (4) 4719999.

ENGLISH, Sir Terence (Alexander Hawthorne), KBE 1991; FRCS; FRCP; Master of St Catharine's College, Cambridge, 1993–2000; Consultant Cardiothoracic Surgeon Papworth and Addenbrooke's Hospitals, Cambridge, 1973–95; *b* 3 Oct. 1932; *s* of late Arthur Alexander English and Mavis Eleanor (*née* Lund); *m* 1st, 1963, Ann Dicey (marr diss. 2002); two *s* two *d*; 2nd, 2002, Judith Frances Milne (*see* J. F. English). *Educ:* Hilton Coll., Natal; Witwatersrand Univ. (Transvaal Chamber of Mines Scholarship, 1951–54 BSc(Eng) 1954); Guy's Hosp. Med. Sch. (MB, BS 1962); MA Cantab 1977. FRCSE 1967 FRCS 1967; FRCP 1990. House appointments, Guy's Hosp., 1962–63; Demonstrator Anatomy Dept, Guy's Hosp., 1964–65; Surgical Registrar: Bolingbroke Hosp., 1966 Brompton Hosp., 1967–68; Res. Fellow, Dept of Surgery, Univ. of Alabama, 1969; Sen Registrar, Brompton, National Heart and London Chest Hosps, 1968–72; Dir, Papworth Heart Transplant Res. Unit, 1980–88 (performed Britain's 1st successful heart transplant 1979); non-exec. Dir, Papworth Hosp. NHS Trust, 1997–2001. Chief Med. Advr BUPA, 1991–99. Mem., Audit Commn, 1993–98. Chm., Asia Healthcare plc, 1995–98 Member: British Cardiac Soc., 1973–; British Transplantation Soc., 1980–; Soc. of Thoracic and Cardiovascular Surgeons, 1972– (Exec. Council, 1975–77); Thoracic Soc. 1971– (Exec. Council, 1978–81). Member: Specialists Adv. Cttee in Cardiothoracic Surgery, 1980–87; Council, BHF, 1983–87; GMC, 1983–89; Standing Med. Adv. Cttee 1989–92; Jt Consultants Cttee, 1989–92; Supraregional Services Adv. Gp, 1990–92 Clinical Standards Adv. Gp, 1991–94. President: Internat. Soc. of Heart Transplantation 1984–85; Soc. of Perfusionists of GB and Ireland, 1985–86; RCS, 1989–92 (Mem Council, 1981–93; Court of Patrons, 1994; Trustee, Hunterian Mus., 1996–)

Cardiothoracic Sect., RSM, 1992–93; BMA, 1995–96; Vice Pres., British Lung Foundn, 2002–. Upjohn Lectr, Royal Soc., 1988. Capt., Guy's Hosp. RFC, 1959–60. Gov., Leys Sch., Cambridge, 1993–2001. Trustee: Northwick Park Inst. for Med. Res., 1996–2006; Comparative Clinical Science Foundn, 2003–. Member Council: Winston Churchill Meml Trust, 1995–; Univ. of Cambridge, 1998. Patron: Primary Trauma Care Foundn, 2006–; Emthonjeni Trust, 2006–. Hon. Freeman, Barbers' Co., 1993. DL Cambs, 1996–2001. FACC 1986. Hon. FRCSCan 1990; Hon. FRACS 1991; Hon. FCSSA 1991; Hon. FRCS (Thailand) 1991; Hon. FCP&S (Pakistan), 1991; Hon. FRCAnaes, 1991; Hon. FDSRCS 1992; Hon. FACS 1992; Hon. FRCSI 1992; Hon. FRCSGlas 1992; Hon. FCOphth 1993; Hon. FRSocMed 2007; Hon. Fellow: St Catharine's Coll., Cambridge, 1992; Hughes Hall, Cambridge, 1993; UMDS, Guy's and St Thomas' Hosps (now KCL), 1993; Worcester Coll., Oxford, 2003. Hon. DSc: Sussex, 1992; Hull, 1996; Hon. MD: Nantes, 1992; Mahidol, Thailand, 1993; Witwatersrand, 2008. Man of the Year, RADAR, 1980; Clement Price Thomas Award, RCS, 1986. *Publications:* (jtly) Principles of Cardiac Diagnosis and Treatment: a surgeons' guide, 1992; chapter on Surgery of the Thorax and Heart in Bailey and Love's Short Practice of Thoracic Surgery, 1980; numerous articles in medical jls on matters relating to the practice of heart transplantation and cardiothoracic surgery. *Recreations:* reading, 4 x 4 rallies, travel, classic cars. *Address:* 28 Tree Lane, Iffley Village, Oxford OX4 4EY; *e-mail:* tenglish@doctors.org.uk. *Clubs:* Athenæum; Hawks (Cambridge).

ENGLISH, Terence Michael; a District Judge (Magistrates' Courts) (formerly Metropolitan Stipendiary Magistrate), since 1986; *b* 3 Feb. 1944; *s* of John Robert English and Elsie Letitia English; *m* 1st, 1966, Ivy Joan Weatherley (*d* 1997); one *s* one *d*; 2nd, 2001, Clare Joanne Evans. *Educ:* St Ignatius' Coll., London N15; London Univ. (external LLB 1967). Admitted Solicitor of the Supreme Court, 1970. Assistant, Edmonton PSD, 1962–71; Dep. Clerk to Justices, Bullingdon, Bampton E, Henley and Watlington PSDs, 1972–76; Clerk to the Justices: Newbury and Hungerford and Lambourn PSDs, 1977–85; Slough and Windsor PSDs, 1985–86. A Recorder, 1994–97. Chairman: Family Panel, 1991–92; Inner London Juvenile Ct Panel, 1989–2002. *Recreations:* philately, music, travel, arts. *Address:* Reading Magistrates' Court, Castle Hill, Reading RG1 7RD.

ENNALS, Paul Martin, CBE 2002; Chief Executive, National Children's Bureau, since 1998; *b* 7 Nov. 1956; *s* of Baron Ennals, PC, and of Eleanor Maud Ennals (*née* Caddick); *m* 1996, Christine Reid. *Educ:* King's Coll. Sch., Wimbledon; New Coll., Oxford (BA Psychology). Director: Services, SENSE, 1983–89; Educn and Employment, RNIB, 1989–98. Chairman: Council for Disabled Children, 1991–98; Special Educnl Consortium, 1992–97; Independent Rev. of Pre-Schools, 1999; Interim Chm., 2004–05, Shadow Chm., 2006, Children's Workforce Develt Council; Chm., Children's Workforce Network, 2006–; Vice-Chm., Nat. Adv. Gp on Special Educnl Needs, 1997–2001; Mem., Children's Task Force, 2001–04. *Address:* National Children's Bureau, 8 Wakley Street, EC1V 7QE; *e-mail:* pennals@ncb.org.uk.

ENNIS, Catherine Mary, (Mrs J. A. Higham); concert organist; Organist, St Lawrence Jewry-next-Guildhall, EC2, since 1985; *b* 20 Jan. 1955; *d* of Séamus and Margaret Ennis; *m* 1988, John Arthur Higham, *qv*; two *s* one *d*, and one step *s* two step *d*. *Educ:* Christ's Hosp., Hertford; Kingsway Further Educn Coll.; St Hugh's Coll., Oxford (MA). Internat. concert organist; recitals, Europe and USA, 1977–; Dir of Music, St Marylebone Parish Church, 1978–90; Asst Organist, Christ Church Cathedral, Oxford, 1984–86; Professor: RAM, 1982–90; GSM, 1985–86; Mem. staff, Trinity Coll. of Music, 2001–. Estabd and Editor-in-Chief, London Organ Concerts Guide, 1995–. Pres., IAO, 2005–07; Mem. Council, RCO, 2006–08. Trustee, Nicholas Danby Trust, 1999–. Presenter, recitalist, concerto soloist and conductor on radio and TV; has made several commercial recordings. Prizewinner: GSM, 1973; Manchester Internat. Organ Comp., 1981 and 1983. *Publications:* contribs to organ jls. *Recreations:* opera, gardening, children. *Address:* c/o The Vestry, St Lawrence Jewry-next-Guildhall, EC2V 5AA; *e-mail:* cmennis@aol.com.

ENNIS, Jeffrey; MP (Lab) Barnsley East and Mexborough, since 1997 (Barnsley East, Dec. 1996–97); *b* 13 Nov. 1952; *s* of William Ennis and Jean Ennis; *m* 1980, Margaret Angela Knight; three *s*. *Educ:* Redland Coll.; Univ. of Bristol (BEd Hons). Teacher: Elston Hall Jun. Sch., Fordhouses, Wolverhampton, 1976–78; Burngreave Middle Sch., Sheffield, 1978–79; Hillsborough Primary Sch., Sheffield, 1979–96. Barnsley Metropolitan Borough Council: Councillor (Lab), 1980–97; Dep. Leader, 1988–95; Leader, 1995–96. PPS to Minister for Public Health, DoH, 1997–99, to Minister for Employment, 1999–2001. Mem., Educn and Skills Select Cttee, 2001–. Mem., British-Irish Inter-Parly Body, 1998–; Jt Chair, All Party Racing and Bloodstock Gp, 2001–; Treas., All Party China Gp; Sec., Lab back-bench Gp on Regeneration. Member: Co-op Party; TGWU; Chm., Brierley Lab. Pty Br., 1998–. *Recreations:* most sports, especially swimming, hill-walking, caravanning. *Address:* House of Commons, SW1A 0AA; (constituency office) Brierley Hall, Brierley, Barnsley S72 9HP.

ENNIS, Richard; Executive Director of Corporate Resources (formerly of Finance and Business Support), London Borough of Ealing, since 2005; *b* 9 Oct. 1965; *s* of Thomas and Wendy Ennis; *m* 1990, Theresa Dawn Jones; three *s*. *Educ:* W London Poly.; Harrow College (Finance and Business Studies degree 1989); Middlesex Poly. (Dip. Mgt Studies 1991); Thames Valley Univ. (ACMA 1995). Mgt Accountant, PO Ltd, 1986–90; Accountant, Slough BC, 1990–96; Finance and Systems Manager, Guildford Spectrum Leisure, 1996–98; Assistant Director, Finance: Slough Unitary Council, 1998–2000; Westminster CC, 2000–03; Exec. Dir of Finance, Lambeth LBC, 2003–05. *Recreation:* football coach. *Address:* Ealing Borough Council, Perceval House, 14–16 Uxbridge Road, Ealing, W5 2HL. *T:* (020) 8825 5269; *e-mail:* ennisr@ealing.gov.uk.

ENNISKILLEN, 7th Earl of, *cr* 1789 (Ire.); **Andrew John Galbraith Cole;** Baron Mountflorence 1760; Viscount Enniskillen 1776; Baron Grinstead (UK) 1815; pilot and company director; Captain Irish Guards, 1965; *b* 28 April 1942; *s* of 6th Earl of Enniskillen, MBE and Sonia (*d* 1982), *d* of Major Thomas Syers, RA; *S* father, 1989; *m* 1964, Sarah, *o d* of Maj.-Gen. J. Keith-Edwards, CBE, DSO, MC, Nairobi; three *d*. *Educ:* Eton. Man. Dir, Kenya Airways, 1979–81; CEO and Chm., AAR Health Services, 1991–2006. *Heir: cousin* Berkeley Arthur Cole [*b* 17 Dec. 1949; *m* 1978, Hon. Cecilia Anne Ridley (marr. diss. 2002), *e d* of 4th Viscount Ridley, *qv*; two *s*].

ENO, Brian Peter George St John Baptiste de la Salle; musician and artist; *b* 15 May 1948; *s* of William Arnold Eno and Maria Alphonsine Eno (*née* Buslot); *m* 1st, 1967, Sarah Grenville; one *d*; 2nd, 1988, Anthea Norman-Taylor; two *d*. *Educ:* Ipswich Sch. of Art; Winchester Coll. of Art. With Roxy Music, 1971–73. Vis. Prof., RCA, 1995–; Hon. Prof. of New Media, Berlin Univ. of Art, 1998–; Founder, Long Now Foundn, 1996–. Hon. DTech Plymouth, 1995. Brit Award, Best Producer, 1994. *Music:* solo recordings: Here Come the Warm Jets, 1974; Taking Tiger Mountain (By Strategy), 1974; Another Green World, 1975; Discreet Music, 1975; Before and After Science, 1977; Music for Films, 1978; Music for Airports, 1978; On Land, 1981; Thursday Afternoon, 1984; Nerve Net, 1992; The Shutov Assembly, 1992; Neroli, 1993; The Drop, 1997; Another Day on Earth, 2005; collaborative recordings: (with David Bowie) Low, 1977, Heroes, 1977, Lodger, 1979; (with David Byrne) My Life in the Bush of Ghosts, 1980; (with Daniel Lanois and Roger Eno) Apollo, 1983; (with J. Peter Schwalm) Drawn from Life, 2001; (with Paul Simon) Surprise, 2006; (with David Byrne) Everything that Happens Will Happen Today, 2008; *productions:* Talking Heads: More Songs about Buildings and Food, Fear of Music, Remain in Light, 1978–80; U2: Unforgettable Fire, The Joshua Tree, Rattle and Hum, Achtung Baby, Zooropa, All That You Can't Leave Behind (Grammy Award, Record of the Year: for track Beautiful Day, 2000, for track Walk On, 2001), 1984–2001; David Bowie: Outside, 1995; *visual:* over 80 exhibns of video artworks and audio-visual installations in museums and galleries worldwide, incl. Stedelijk Mus., Amsterdam, 1984; Venice Biennale, 1986; Marble Palace, St Petersburg, 1997; Hayward Gall., London, 2000; San Francisco Mus. of Modern Art, 2001; Lyon Biennial, 2005; Mus. für Abgüsse Klassischer Bildwerke, Munich, 2005. *Publications:* (with Peter Schmidt) Oblique Strategies (set of cards), 1975, 5th edn 2001; A Year with Swollen Appendices, 1996. *Recreation:* perfumery. *Address:* c/o Opal Ltd, 4 Pembridge Mews, W11 3EQ. *T:* (020) 7221 4933, *Fax:* (020) 7727 5404.

ENOCH, Dafydd Huw; QC 2008; a Recorder, since 2004; *b* Chelmsford, 24 April 1961; *s* of Dr Morgan David Enoch and late Margaret Joyce Enoch; *m* 1997, Naomi Jane Hartridge; one *s* two *d*. *Educ:* Univ. of Buckingham (LLB 1984); Univ. d'Aix-Marseille III (Diplôme d'Etudes Juridiques). Called to the Bar, Gray's Inn, 1985; in practice as barrister specialising in criminal and disciplinary law. *Recreations:* playing the guitar and drums, travelling, sport of all types. *Address:* 23 Essex Street, WC2R 3AA. *T:* (020) 7413 0353, *Fax:* (020) 7413 0374; *e-mail:* dafyddenoch@23es.com.

ENSOM, Donald, FRICS, FCIArb; Chartered Surveyor; Consultant, Debenham Tewson & Chinnocks, 1986–92 (Partner, 1962–86); *b* 8 April 1926; *s* of Charles R. A. W. Ensom and Edith (*née* Young); *m* 1951, Sonia (*née* Sherrard); one *s* one *d*. *Educ:* Norbury Manor Sch., Croydon. Qualified as Chartered Surveyor, 1951; FRICS 1958; FCIArb 1970. Served RA, 1943–47. Partner, Nightingale, Page & Bennett/Debenham Tewson & Chinnocks (after merger), 1958–86. Chm., Bldg Conservation Trust, 1981–83; Royal Institution of Chartered Surveyors: Pres., Bldg Surveyors Div., 1975–76; Chm., Professional Practice Cttee, 1978–83; Hon. Sec., 1983–90; Vice-Pres., 1988–90. Pres., Land Economy Soc., Univ. of Cambridge, 1990–91. Member: Pyramus and Thisbe Club (Chm. 1987–89); 1913 Wilderness Club (formerly Chartered Surveyors (1913) Club). *Publications:* (jtly) Party Walls, 1993; (jtly) The Party Wall Act Explained, 1997; numerous professional papers. *Recreations:* reading, opera and music, transport history, crossword puzzles, freemasonry. *Address:* 8 The Oast House, Grange Road, Cambridge CB3 9AP. *Club:* East India.

ENSOR, David, OBE 1986; Managing Director, Croydon Advertiser Ltd, 1979–85; *b* 2 April 1924; *s* of Rev. William Walters and Constance Eva Ensor; *m* 1947, Gertrude Kathleen Brown; two *s*. *Educ:* Kingswood Sch., Bath; London Coll. of Printing. Served Royal Signals, 1942–46, Captain; ADC to GOC Bengal Dist. Managing Director: George Reveirs, 1947–59; Charles Skipper & East, 1959–69; Knapp Drewett & Sons, 1969–79; Chairman: Methodist Newspaper Co., 1975–94; Methodist Publishing House, 1981–96. A Vice-Chm., Press Council, 1987–90 (Mem., 1982–90); Mem. Council, Newspaper Soc., 1979–94. Pres., London Printing Industries Assoc., 1976. Vice-Pres., Methodist Conf., 1981. *Address:* 2 Bemerton Farm, Lower Road, Bemerton, Salisbury, Wilts SP2 9NA. *T:* (01722) 417103.

ENSOR, His Honour George Anthony; a Circuit Judge, 1995–2008; *b* 4 Nov. 1936; *s* of George and Phyllis Ensor; *m* 1968, Jennifer Margaret Caile, MB, ChB; two *d*. *Educ:* Malvern College; Liverpool University (LLB). Solicitor, 1961 (Atkinson Conveyancing Medal, 1962; Rupert Bremner Medal, 1962); Partner, 1962–92, Sen. Partner, 1992–95, Rutherfords, later Weightman Rutherfords, Solicitors, Liverpool; a Recorder, 1983–95; Dep. Sen. Judge, Sovereign Base Area, Cyprus, 2005. Deputy Coroner, City of Liverpool, 1966–95; part-time Chairman, Industrial Tribunals, 1975–95; Asst Parly Boundary Comr, 1992–95. Mem., Judicial Studies Bd, 1987–89; President, Liverpool Law Society, 1982. Trustee, Empire Theatre (Merseyside) Trust, Ltd, 1986–. Dir, Liverpool FC, 1985–93. *Recreations:* golf, theatre. *Clubs:* Artists (Liverpool); Formby Golf; Waterloo Rugby Union.

ENSOR, Michael de Normann, CMG 1980; OBE 1958; Head, East Africa Development Division, Overseas Development Administration, 1975–80; *b* 11 June 1919; *s* of Robert Weld Ensor and Dr Beatrice Ensor; *m* 1945, Mona Irene Blackburn (*d* 2002); two *s*. *Educ:* Bryanston School; St. John's Coll., Oxford. Military service, 1940; Colonial Service, Gold Coast/Ghana Civil Service, 1940–58; Secretary, Foundation for Mutual Assistance in Africa South of the Sahara, 1958–64; Dept of Technical Cooperation/Min. of Overseas Development/Overseas Development Administration, 1964–80. Chairman: Paragon Management Co., 1983–86; Overseas Service Pensioners' Benevolent Soc., 1986–91. *Address:* Flat 1, 12 The Paragon, Blackheath, SE3 0NZ. *T:* (020) 8852 5345. *Club:* Travellers.

ENTWISTLE, George; Controller, Knowledge Commissioning, BBC TV, since 2008; *b* 8 July 1962; *s* of Philip and Wendy Entwistle; *m* 1992, Jane Porter; one *s* one *d*. *Educ:* Durham Univ. (BA Hons Philosophy and Politics 1983). Sub-ed. and Ed., Haymarket Magazines, 1984–89; joined BBC, 1989; broadcast journalism trainee, 1989–90; Asst Producer, Panorama, 1990–92; Producer, On The Record, 1993–94; Producer, 1994–97, Asst Ed., 1997–99, Newsnight; Dep. Ed., Tomorrow's World, 1999–2000; Dep. Ed., 2000–01, Ed., 2001–04, Newsnight; Ed., The Culture Show, 2004–05; Actg Controller, BBC Four, May–Dec. 2007; Hd of Current Affairs, BBC TV, 2005–07. *Recreations:* listening to music, reading, armchair Rugby Union. *Address:* c/o BBC White City, 201 Wood Lane, W12 7TS; *e-mail:* george.entwistle@bbc.co.uk.

ENTWISTLE, John Nicholas McAlpine, OBE 2005; Consultant Solicitor, Davies Wallis Foyster, 1992–2004; President, British Chambers of Commerce, 1998–2000; *b* 16 June 1941; *s* of Sir (John Nuttall) Maxwell Entwistle and Lady (Jean Cunliffe McAlpine) Entwistle; *m* 1968, Phillida Gail Sinclair Burgess; one *s* one *d*. *Educ:* Uppingham Sch. Admitted Solicitor, 1963. Asst Attorney, Shearman & Sterling, NY, 1963–64; Partner, Maxwell Entwistle & Byrne, Solicitors, 1966–91. Regl Dir, Midshires Building Soc., 1977–87; non-exec. Dir, Rathbone Brothers plc, 1992–98. Founder Dir, Merseyside TEC, 1990–91; Dep. Dist Chm., Appeals Service, 1999–2006 (pt-time Chm., Social Security Appeals Tribunal, 1992–99); pt-time Immigration Judge, 2000–. Member: Parole Bd, 1994–2000; Criminal Injuries Compensation Appeals Panel, 2000–; Disciplinary Cttee, Mortgage Code Compliance Bd, 1999–2004; Chancellor of Exchequer's Standing Cttee on Preparation for EMU, 1998–2000. Trustee: Nat. Museums and Galls on Merseyside, 1990–97 (Chm., Develt Trust, 1991–95); RA Trust, 2006–. Gen. Comr for Income Tax, 1978–83. Mem. (C), Liverpool CC, 1968–71. Contested (C) Huyton, 1970. DL Merseyside, 1992–2002. *Recreations:* collecting and painting pictures, gardening, shooting. *Address:* Low Crag, Crook, Cumbria LA8 8LE. *T:* (015395) 68268, *Fax:* (015395) 68769; *e-mail:* jentwistle@onetel.net. *Clubs:* Carlton (Mem., Political Cttee, 2004–), Lansdowne.

ENTWISTLE, Prof. Kenneth Mercer; Professor of Metallurgy and Materials Science, University of Manchester Institute of Science and Technology, 1962–90, now Emeritus;

b 3 Jan. 1925; *s* of William Charles and Maude Elizabeth Entwistle; *m* 1949, Alice Patricia Mary Johnson; two *s* two *d*. *Educ:* Urmston Grammar Sch.; Univ. of Manchester (BSc Elect. Eng. 1945, MSc 1946, PhD 1948). FIMMM, CEng. University of Manchester: Lectr in Metallurgy, 1948; Sen. Lectr, 1954; Reader, 1960; Dean, Faculty of Technology, 1976–77; Pro-Vice-Chancellor, 1982–85; Vice-Principal, UMIST, 1972–74. Adjunct Prof., Univ. of Canterbury, NZ, 2001–. Chairman: Materials Cttee, CNAA, 1972–74; Educn Cttee, Instn of Metallurgists, 1977–79; Metallics Sub-Cttee, SRC, 1979–81; Mem., UGC, 1985–89 (Chm., Technology Sub-Cttee, 1985–89); Engrg Advr to Chief Exec. of UFC, 1989–92. Comp. UMIST, 1991. Hon. Fellow, Sheffield Polytechnic, 1971. *Publications:* numerous papers in scientific jls. *Recreations:* Scottish dancing, choral singing. *Address:* Heronswood, 22 Castlegate, Prestbury, Macclesfield, Cheshire SK10 4AZ. *T:* (01625) 829269; *e-mail:* ken.entwistle@manchester.ac.uk. *Club:* Athenæum.

EÖTVÖS, Peter; composer and conductor; *m* 1st, 1968, Piroska Molnar (marr. diss. 1975); one *s*; 2nd, 1976, Pi-Hsien Chen (marr. diss. 1994); one *d*; 3rd, 1995, Maria Mezei. *Educ:* Acad. of Music, Budapest; Musik Hochschule, Cologne. Composer, chamber music, electronic music, opera and orchestral music; conductor and musical director, Ensemble Intercontemporain, Paris, 1979–91; principal guest conductor, BBC Symphony Orchestra, 1985–88; first Guest Conductor, Budapest Fest. Orch., 1992–95; Chief Conductor, Radio Chamber Orch. Hilversum, 1994–2005. Professor: Musikhochschule Karlsruhe, 1992–; Musikhochschule Köln, 1998–2001; Founder, Internat. Eötvös Inst., for young conductors and composers, 1991. *Recreations:* walking, pipe smoking, jazz. *Web:* www.eotvospeter.com.

EPHRAUMS, Maj.-Gen. Roderick Jarvis, CB 1977; OBE 1965; Major-General Royal Marines, Commando Forces, 1976–78, retired; *b* 12 May 1927; *s* of Hugh Cyril Ephraums and Elsie Caroline (*née* Rowden); *m* 1955, Adela Mary (*née* Forster); two *s* one *d*. *Educ:* Tonbridge. Commnd 2nd Lieut, RM, 1945; HMS Mauritius, 1946–48; 42 Commando, RM, 1952–54; RMFVR Merseyside, 1954–57; 42 Commando, RM, 1957–59, 1966–67; Staff Coll., Camberley, 1960; Bde Major, 3 Commando Bde, 1962–64; CO, 45 Commando RM, 1969–71; Royal Coll. of Defence Studies, 1972; Comdr, 3 Commando Bde, 1973–74; NATO Defense Coll., Rome, 1975. A Col Comdt, RM, 1985–, Rep. Col Comdt, 1987 and 1988. DL Angus, 1985–98. Silver Medal, RNLI, 1989. CStJ 1993. *Recreations:* painting, gardening. *Club:* Army and Navy.

EPSTEIN, Sir Anthony; *see* Epstein, Sir M. A.

EPSTEIN, Prof. David Bernard Alper, PhD; FRS 2004; Professor, Mathematics Institute, University of Warwick, 1969, now Professor Emeritus; *b* 16 May 1937; *s* of Dr Ben Epstein and Pauline Alper Epstein; *m* 1958, Rona; one *s* two *d*. *Educ:* Univ. of Witwatersrand (BSc Hons 1955); Churchill Coll., Cambridge (BA 1957); PhD Cantab 1960. Princeton Univ., 1960–61; Princeton Inst. for Advanced Study, 1961–62; Cambridge University: Fellow, Trinity Coll., 1960–62; Lectr, 1962–64; Dir, Studies in Maths, Churchill Coll., 1962–64; Reader in Maths, Univ. of Warwick, 1964–69. Scientific Dir, NSF Geometry Center, Minneapolis, 1990–91. Vis. Prof., Univ. of Paris, Orsay, 1974–75; Ordway Dist. Vis. Prof., Minnesota, 1986. *Publications:* (with N. E. Steenrod) Cohomology Operations, 1963; (jtly) Word Processing in Groups, 1992. *Recreations:* gardening, friends. *Address:* Mathematics Institute, University of Warwick, Zeeman Building, Coventry CV4 7AL. *T:* (024) 7652 2677; *e-mail:* dbae@maths.warwick.ac.uk.

EPSTEIN, Sir (Michael) Anthony, Kt 1991; CBE 1985; FRS 1979; Fellow, 1986–2001, Hon. Fellow, since 2001, Wolfson College, Oxford; Professor of Pathology, 1968–85 (now Emeritus), and Head of Department, 1968–82, University of Bristol; Hon. Consultant Pathologist, Bristol Health District (Teaching), 1968–82; *b* 18 May 1921; *yr s* of Mortimer and Olga Epstein; *m* 1950, Lisbeth Knight (separated 1965); two *s* one *d*. *Educ:* St Paul's Sch., London; Trinity Coll., Cambridge (Perry Exhibr, 1940); Middlesex Hosp. Medical Sch. MA, MD, DSc, PhD; FRCPath. Ho. Surg., Middlesex Hosp., London, and Addenbrooke's Hosp., Cambridge, 1944; Lieut and Captain, RAMC, 1945–47; Asst Pathologist, Bland Sutton Inst., Middx Hosp. Med. Sch., 1948–65, with leave as: Berkeley Travelling Fellow, 1952–53; French Govt Exchange Scholar at Institut Pasteur, Paris, 1952–53; Vis. Investigator, Rockefeller Inst., NY, 1956; Reader in Experimental Pathology, Middx Hosp. Med. Sch., 1965–68; Hon. Consultant in Experimental Virology, Middx Hosp., 1965–68. Member: Cttee, Pathological Soc. of GB and Ire., 1969–72 (Hon. Mem., 1987); Council, and Vice-Pres., Pathology Section of RSM, 1966–72 (Hon. Mem., 1988); Study Gp on Classification of Herpes Viruses, of Internat. Commn for Nomenclature of Viruses, 1971–81; Scientific Adv. Bd, Harvard Med. Sch.'s New England Regional Primate Center, 1972–96; Cancer Research Campaign MRC Jt Cttee, 1973–77, 1982–87 (Chm. 1983–87); Cttee, British Soc. for Cell Biology, 1974–77; MRC, 1982–86 (Mem. 1979–84, Chm. 1982–84, Cell Bd; Mem., 1984–85, Chm., 1985–88, Tropical Medicine Res. Bd); Council, Royal Soc., 1983–85, 1986–91 (Foreign Sec. and a Vice-Pres., 1986–91; Assessor on MRC, 1987–91); Medical and Scientific Panel, Leukaemia Research Fund, 1982–85; Scientific Adv. Cttee, Lister Inst., 1984–87; Expert Working Party on Bovine Spongiform Encephalopathy, DoH, 1988; Exec. Bd, ICSU, 1990–93 (Chm., Cttee on Sci. in Central and Eastern Europe, 1992–95); Exec. Council, ESF, 1990–93; Program Adv. Gp, World Bank China Key Studies Project, 1992–97; Special Rep. of Dir Gen. UNESCO for Sci. in Russia, 1992. Discovered in 1964 a new human herpes virus, now known as Epstein-Barr virus, which causes infectious mononucleosis and is also causally implicated in some forms of human cancer (esp. Burkitt's lymphoma, nasopharyngeal carcinoma and post-transplant lymphomas). Fellow, UCL, 1992. Founder FMedSci 1998. Mem., Academia Europaea, 1988. Mem. d'honneur, Belgian Soc. for Cancer Res., 1979. Hon. Professor: Sun Yat-Sen Med. Univ., Guangzhou, 1981; Chinese Acad. of Preventive Medicine, Beijing, 1988. Hon. Fellow: Queensland Inst. of Med. Research, 1983; CRUK, 2004; Bristol Univ., 2006; Hon. FRCP 1986; Hon. FRSE 1991; Hon. FRCPA 1995. Hon. MD: Edinburgh, 1986; Charles Univ., Prague, 1998; Hon. DSc Birmingham, 1996. Paul Ehrlich and Ludwig Darmstaedter Prize and Medal, Paul Ehrlich Foundn, W Germany, 1973; Markham Skerrit Prize, 1977; (jtly) Bristol-Myers Award, NY, 1982; Leeuwenhoek Prize Lectr, Royal Soc., 1983; Prix Griffuel, Assoc. pour la recherche sur le cancer, Paris, 1986; David Henderson Medal, PHLS, 1986; Samuel Weiner Distinguished Visitor Award, Univ. of Manitoba, 1988; John H. Lattimer Award, Amer. Urol Assoc., 1988; Internat. Award, Gairdner Foundn, Toronto, 1988; Jenner Medal, St George's Hosp. Med. Sch., 1989; Royal Medal, Royal Soc., 1992; Gold Medal, Charles Univ., Prague, 1998. *Publications:* over 240 scientific papers in internat. jls on tumour cell structure, viruses, tumour viruses, Burkitt's lymphoma, and the EB virus. Jt Founder Editor, The Internat. Review of Experimental Pathology (vols 1–28, 1962–86); (ed jtly) The Epstein-Barr Virus, 1979; (ed jtly) The Epstein-Barr Virus: recent advances, 1986; (ed jtly) Oncogenic γ-herpesviruses: an expanding family, 2001. *Address:* Nuffield Department of Clinical Medicine, University of Oxford, John Radcliffe Hospital, Oxford OX3 9DU. *T:* (01865) 221334, *Fax:* (01865) 222901.

EPSTEIN, Paul Jeremy; QC 2006; *b* London, 9 Aug. 1963; *s* of Maurice and Jill Epstein; partner, Laura Binns. *Educ:* Balliol Coll., Oxford (BA Hist. and Mod. Langs); City Univ., London (Dip. Law). Called to the Bar, Middle Temple, 1988; barrister, Cloisters chambers, 1990–. *Address:* Cloisters, 1 Pump Court, Temple, EC4Y 7AA. *T:* (020) 7827 4000, *Fax:* (020) 7827 4100; *e-mail:* clerks@cloisters.com.

ERAUT, Prof. Michael Ruarc, PhD; Professor of Education, University of Sussex, 1986–2006, now Emeritus; *b* 15 Nov. 1940; *s* of Lt-Col Ruarc Bertrand Sorel Eraut and Frances Mary (*née* Hurst); *m* 1964, (Mary) Cynthia Wynne; two *s*. *Educ:* Winchester Coll. (Scholar); Trinity Hall, Cambridge (Scholar; BA Nat. Sci.; PhD Chem.). Fulbright Scholar, 1965–67; Res. Assistant, 1965–66, Vis. Asst Prof., 1966–67, Univ. of Illinois, Chicago; University of Sussex: Fellow, 1967–71; Sen. Fellow, 1971–73; Dir, Centre for Educnl Technol., 1973–76; Reader in Educn, 1976–86; Dir, Inst. of Continuing and Professional Educn, 1986–91. Chm. of Corporation, Lewes Tertiary Coll., 1992–97. Ed.-in-Chief, Learning in Health and Social Care, 2002–06. *Publications:* (with N. Mackenzie and H. C. Jones) Teaching and Learning: new methods and resources in higher education, 1970, 3rd edn 1976 (trans. French, German, Spanish and Portuguese); In-Service Education for Innovation, 1972; The Analysis of Curriculum Materials, 1975 (trans. German 1976); Accountability in the Middle Years of Schooling, 1980; (with B. Connors and E. Hewton) Training in Curriculum Development and Educational Technology in Higher Education, 1980; (with T. Becher and J. Knight) Policies for Educational Accountability, 1981; Curriculum Development in Further Education, 1985; (with J. Burke) Improving the Quality of YTS, 1986; Local Evaluation of INSET, 1988; (ed) International Encyclopaedia of Educational Technology, 1989; (with G. Cole) Business Education: a handbook for schools, 1990; Education and the Information Society, 1991; (with C. Nash and M. Fielding) Flexible Learning in Schools, 1991; (with G. Cole) Assessing Competence in the Professions, 1993; Developing Professional Knowledge and Competence, 1994; Learning to Use Scientific Knowledge in Education and Practice Settings, 1995; Assessment of NVQs, 1996; Development of Knowledge and Skills in Employment, 1998; Evaluation of Vocational Training of Science Graduates in the NHS, 1998; (with B. Du Boulay) Developing the Attributes of Medical Professional Judgement and Competence, 1999; (with S. Steadman and J. James) Evaluation of Higher Level S/NVQs, 2001; (with W. Hirsch) The Significance of Workplace Learning for Individuals, Groups and Organisations, 2007; chapters in books and numerous conference papers. *Recreations:* music, travel. *Address:* 49 St Anne's Crescent, Lewes, E Sussex BN7 1SD. *T:* (01273) 475955.

ERECIŃSKA, Barbara; *see* Tuge-Erecińska.

EREMIN, Prof. Oleg, MD; FRCSE, FRACS, FMedSci; Special Professor in Surgery, University of Nottingham, at Queen's Medical Centre, Nottingham, since 1998; Consultant Breast Surgeon and Lead Clinician, since 1999, Director of Research and Development, since 2001, United Lincolnshire Hospitals (formerly Lincoln) NHS Trust; *b* 12 Nov. 1938; *s* of Theodor and Maria Eremin; *m* 1963, Jennifer Mary Ching; two *s* one *d*. *Educ:* Christian Brothers' Coll., St Kilda, Melbourne; Univ. of Melbourne. MB BS 1964; MD 1985. FRACS 1971; FRCSE 1983. Clinical posts: Royal Melbourne Hosp., 1965–72; Norfolk and Norwich Hosps, 1972–74; Research Asst-Associate, Dept of Pathology, Univ. of Cambridge, 1974–80; Sen. Lectr, Dept Clinical Surgery, Univ. of Edinburgh, 1981–85; Regius Prof. of Surgery, Univ. of Aberdeen, 1985–98. Clinical Dir, Trent Comprehensive Local Res. Network, 2007–. Hon. Professorial Fellow, Rowett Res. Inst., 1992. Founder FMedSci 1998; Hon. FRCST 2003. Hon. DSc Lincoln. *Publications:* articles in surgical, oncological and immunological jls. *Recreations:* music, sport, reading. *Address:* Orchard House, 51A Washdyke Lane, Nettleham, Lincoln LN2 2PX. *T:* (01522) 750669.

ERIKSSON, Sven-Göran; Head Coach, Mexico Football Team, since 2008; *b* Torsby, Sweden, 5 Feb. 1948; *s* of Sven and Ulla Eriksson; *m* Ann-Kristin (marr. diss.); one *s* one *d*. Former footballer (defender); clubs include Torsby IF, Sifhalla and KB Karlskoga (all Sweden); managerial posts: Asst Manager, 1976, Manager, 1977–78, Degerfors, Sweden; Manager: IFK Gothenburg, Sweden, 1979–82; Benfica, Portugal, 1982–84; AS Roma, Italy, 1984–87; AC Fiorentina, Italy, 1987–89; Benfica, 1989–92; Sampdoria, Italy, 1992–97; SS Lazio, Italy, 1997–2000 (winners: Italian Cup, 1998; Italian Super Cup, 1998; UEFA Cup Winners Cup, 1999; UEFA Super Cup, 1999; Italian Championship, 2000); Head Coach, England Football Team, 2001–06; Manager, Manchester City FC, 2007–08. *Address:* c/o Athole Still International Management, Foresters Hall, 25 Westow Street, SE19 3RY.

ERLEIGH, Viscount; Julian Michael Rufus Isaacs; *b* 26 May 1986; *s* and *heir* of Marquess of Reading, *qv*. *Address:* 7 Cecily Hill, Cirencester, Glos GL7 2EF.

ERMISCH, Prof. John Francis, FBA 1995; Professor of Economics, Institute for Social and Economic Research (formerly ESRC Research Centre on Micro-Social Change), University of Essex, since 1994; *b* 1 July 1947; *s* of Elmer and Frances Ermisch; *m* 1977, Dianne M. Monti. *Educ:* Univ. of Wisconsin (BSc); Univ. of Kansas (MA, PhD 1973). Res. Economist, US Dept of Housing and Urban Develt, 1974–76; Res. Fellow, Centres for Environmental Studies and for the Study of Social Policy, London, 1976–78; Sen. Res. Fellow, PSI, 1978–86; Sen. Res. Officer, NIESR, 1986–91; Bonar-Macfie Prof., Univ. of Glasgow, 1991–94. *Publications:* The Political Economy of Demographic Change, 1983; Lone Parenthood: an economic analysis, 1991; An Economic Analysis of the Family, 2003; contribs to economic and demographic jls. *Recreations:* films, tennis, golf. *Address:* Institute for Social and Economic Research, University of Essex, Wivenhoe Park, Colchester CO4 3SQ. *T:* (01206) 872335.

ERNE, 6th Earl of, *cr* 1789; **Henry George Victor John Crichton;** JP; Baron Erne 1768; Viscount Erne (Ireland), 1781; Baron Fermanagh (UK), 1876; Lord Lieutenant of Co. Fermanagh, Northern Ireland, since 1986; *b* 9 July 1937; *s* of 5th Earl and Lady Katharine Cynthia Mary Millicent (Davina) Lytton (who *m* 1945, Hon. C. M. Woodhouse, later 5th Baron Terrington, DSO, OBE; she *d* 1995), *yr d* of 2nd Earl of Lytton, KG, PC, GCSI, GCIE; *S* father, 1940; *m* 1958, Camilla Marguerite (marr. diss. 1980), *er d* of late Wing-Comdr Owen G. E. Roberts and Mrs Roberts; one *s* four *d*; *m* 1980, Mrs Anna Carin Hitchcock (*née* Bjork). *Educ:* Eton. Page of Honour to the Queen, 1952–54 (to King George VI, 1952). Lieut, North Irish Horse, 1959–66. Member: Royal Ulster Agricultural Society; Royal Forestry Society. JP Co. Fermanagh. *Recreations:* sailing, fishing, shooting. *Heir:* *s* Viscount Crichton, *qv*. *Address:* Crom Castle, Newtownbutler, Co. Fermanagh BT92 8AP. *T:* (028) 6773 8208. *Clubs:* White's; Lough Erne Yacht.

ERNEST, Most Rev. (Gerald James) Ian; *see* Indian Ocean, Archbishop of the.

ERNST, Prof. Edzard, MD, PhD; Professor of Complementary Medicine, Peninsula Medical School, Universities of Exeter and Plymouth, since 2000 (Professor of Complementary Medicine at University of Exeter, since 1993); *b* 30 Jan. 1948; *s* of Wolfgang Ernst and Erika (*née* Tillwichs); *m* 1983, Danielle Johnson (*née* Le Mignon). *Educ:* Maximilian Ludwig Univ., Munich (MD 1978; PhD 1985). FRCPE 1997; FRCP

2003. University of Munich: Sen. House Officer, 1977–79; Registrar, then Sen. Registrar, 1981–89; Res. Assistant, St George's Hosp., London, 1979–81; Prof. of Physical Medicine and Rehabilitation, Univ. of Hanover, 1989; Prof. of Physical Medicine and Rehabilitation, Univ. of Vienna, 1990–93. Visiting Professor: RCPS, Canada, 1999; UCLA, 2005. Member: Medicines Commn, British Medicines and Healthcare Products Regulatory Agency (formerly British Medicines Control Agency), 1993–2005; Scientific Cttee on Herbal Medicinal Products, Irish Medicines BD. Editor-in-Chief: Perfusion, 1987–; Focus on Alternative and Complementary Therapies, 1996–. HealthWatch Award, 2005, Amer. Botanical Council Annual Award, 2006, and 10 other scientific awards. *Publications include:* Meyler's Side Effects of Drugs, 2000; Desk Top Guide to Complementary and Alternative Medicine, 2001, 2nd edn 2006; (contrib.) Oxford Textbook of Medicine, 4th edn 2003; Oxford Handbook of Complementary Medicine, 2008; Trick or Treatment? Alternative Medicine on Trial, 2008; numerous articles in med. jls. *Recreations:* music, writing. *Address:* (office) 25 Victoria Park Road, Exeter EX2 4NT. *T:* (01392) 430802.

ERNST, Prof. Richard Robert; Professor of Physical Chemistry, Swiss Federal Institute of Technology (ETH-Z), 1976–98, now Emeritus; *b* 14 Aug. 1933; *s* of Prof. Robert Ernst, architect, and Irma Ernst (*née* Brunner); *m* 1963, Magdalena Kielholz; one *s* two *d*. *Educ:* Winterthur schools; ETH-Zentrum (DipChemEng 1956; PhD 1962). Mil. Service, 1956–57. Scientist, Instrument Div., Varian Associates, Calif., 1963–68; Swiss Federal Institute of Technology (ETH-Z): Lectr in Phys. Chem., 1968–70 (Group Leader in Magnetic Resonance Spectroscopy); Asst Prof., 1970; Associate Prof., 1972–76; Pres., Research Council, 1990. Mem. Bd, Spectrospin AG (Vice-Pres., 1989). Fellow, Amer. Phys. Soc.; For. Mem., Royal Soc., 1993; Member: internat. scientific bodies; editl bds of learned jls. Hon. doctorates: ETH Lausanne; Technical Univ., Munich; Zürich; Antwerp; Cluj-Napoca; Montpellier. Numerous medals and prizes, Swiss and foreign; Nobel Prize in Chemistry, 1991; Wolf Prize, 1991; Louisa Gross Horwitz Prize, 1991. *Address:* Laboratorium für Physikalische Chemie, Wolfgang Pauli Strasse 10, ETH Hönggerberg, HCI D 217, 8093 Zürich, Switzerland. *T:* (44) 6324368; *e-mail:* ernst@nmr.phys.chem.ethz.ch; Kurlistasse 24, 8404 Winterthur, Switzerland. *T:* (52) 2427807.

ERNSTING, Air Vice-Marshal John, CB 1992; OBE 1959; PhD; FRCP, FFOM, FRAeS; Hon. Civil Consultant in Aviation Medicine to RAF, since 1993; *b* 21 April 1928; *s* of late Reginald James Ernsting and Phyllis May Josephine Ernsting (*née* Allington); *m* 1st, 1952, Patricia Mary Woolford (decd); two *s* one *d*; 2nd, 1970, Joyce Marion Heppell. *Educ:* Chislehurst and Sidcup County Grammar Sch. for Boys; Guy's Hosp. Med. Sch. (BSc 1949; MB BS 1952; PhD 1964). MFOM 1981, FFOM 1993; MRCP 1985. Guy's Hosp., 1952–53; Guy's-Maudsley Neurosurgical Unit, 1953–54; RAF Medical Branch, 1954; Lectr in Physiology, Guy's Hosp. Med. Sch., 1961–85; RAF Consultant in Aviation Physiology, 1964; RAF Consultant Adviser in Aviation Medicine, 1971–89; Dep. Dir and Dir of Research, 1976–88, Comdt, 1988–92, RAF Inst. of Aviation Medicine; Dean of Air Force Medicine, 1990–91; Sen. Consultant (RAF) 1991–93, retd. QHS, 1989–93. Visiting Professor: KCL, 1987– (Head, Human Physiology and Aerospace Medicine, 1998–2004, Aerospace Medicine, 2004–); Imperial Coll., London, 1993–96. *Publications:* (ed) Aviation Medicine, 1978, 3rd edn 1999; papers and chapters in books on aviation physiology and aviation medicine. *Recreations:* music, reading, travel. *Address:* White Gables, 2A Greenways, Fleet, Hants GU52 7UG. *T:* (01252) 621788. *Club:* Royal Air Force.

ERRERA, Gérard, Hon. CVO 2004; Ambassador of France to the Court of St James's, 2002–07; *b* 30 Oct. 1943; *s* of Paul and Bella Errera; *m* Virginie Bedoya; two *s* one *d*. *Educ:* Institut d'Etudes Politiques, Paris; Ecole Nationale d'Administration. Joined Min. of Foreign Affairs, 1969; First Sec., Washington, 1971–75; Special Advr to Minister of Foreign Affairs, 1975–77; Political Counsellor, Madrid, 1977–80; Special Advr to Minister of Foreign Affairs, 1980–81; Consul General, San Francisco, 1982–85; Dir for Internat. Relns, French Atomic Energy Commn, and Governor for France, IAEA, 1985–90; Ambassador, Conf. on Disarmament, Geneva, 1991–95; Ambassador to NATO, Brussels, 1995–98; Political Dir, Min. of Foreign Affairs, 1998–2002. Chevalier de la Légion d'Honneur (France), 1992; Officier de l'Ordre National du Mérite (France), 1999; Officer: Order of the White Rose (Finland), 1976; Order of Civil Merit (Spain), 1980. *Recreations:* ski-ing, music, guitar. *Address:* c/o French Embassy, 58 Knightsbridge, SW1X 7JT.

ERRINGTON, Viscount; Alexander Rowland Harmsworth Baring; *b* 5 Jan. 1994; *s* and *heir* of Earl of Cromer, *qv*.

ERRINGTON, Col Sir Geoffrey (Frederick), 2nd Bt *cr* 1963; OBE 1998; Chairman, Harefield Hospital NHS Trust, 1991–98; *b* 15 Feb. 1926; *er s* of Sir Eric Errington, 1st Bt, JP, and Marjorie (*d* 1973), *d* of A. Grant Bennett; *S* father, 1973; *m* 1955, Diana Kathleen Forbes, *o d* of late E. Barry Davenport, Edgbaston, Birmingham; three *s*. *Educ:* Rugby Sch.; New Coll., Oxford. psc 1958. GSO 3 (Int.), HQ 11 Armd Div., 1950–52; GSO 3, MI3 (b), War Office, 1955–57; Bde Major 146 Inf. Bde, 1959–61; Coy Comdr, RMA Sandhurst, 1963–65; Military Assistant to Adjutant-General, 1965–67; CO 1st Bn, The King's Regt, 1967–69; GSO 1, HQ 1st British Corps, 1969–71; Col. GS, HQ NW District, 1971–74; AAG MI (Army), MoD, 1974–75; retired 1975. Col, The King's Regt, 1975–86; Chm., The King's and Manchester Regts Assoc., 1971–86. Director: Personnel Services, British Shipbuilders, 1977–78; Executive Appointments, 1979–90 (Chm., 1982–90). Employer Bd Mem., Shipbuilding ITB, 1977–78. Chm., Assoc. for Prevention of Addiction, Community Drug and Alcohol Initiatives, 1994–98 (Vice-Chm., 1991–94); Mem. Gen. Cttee, Not Forgotten Assoc., 1991–. Chm., Standing Council of the Baronetage, 2001–06 (Vice-Pres., 2006–). Dir-Gen., Britain-Australia Soc., 2006– (Hon. Dir, 1998–2006). Chm., Woodroffe's Club, 1988–94. Freeman, City of London, 1980; Liveryman: Broderers' Co.; Coachmakers' and Coach Harness Makers' Co. FRSA 1994. *Recreations:* music, travelling, gardening. *Heir: s* Robin Davenport Errington [*b* 1 July 1957; *m* 2001, Margerita Dudek; two *s*]. *Address:* Stone Hill Farm, Sellindge, Ashford, Kent TN25 6AJ; 203A Gloucester Place, NW1 6BU. *Clubs:* Boodle's, Oxford and Cambridge.

See also S. G. Errington.

ERRINGTON, Prof. Jeffery, PhD; FRS 2003; Professor of Cell and Molecular Biosciences and Director, Institute of Cell and Molecular Biosciences, University of Newcastle upon Tyne, since 2005; *b* 3 May 1956; *s* of Sidney Errington and Elizabeth Errington (*née* Wright); *m* 1982, Veronica Mary Geoghegan; two *d*. *Educ:* Blaydon Secondary Sch.; Univ. of Newcastle upon Tyne (BSc Hons Genetics/Zoology 1977); Thames Poly. (PhD 1981); MA Oxon 1989. Oxford University: Royal Soc. Univ. Res. Fellow, 1985–89; Lectr in Chemical Pathology, 1989–2000, Prof. of Microbiology, 2000–05, Sir William Dunn Sch. of Pathology; Fellow: Magdalen Coll., 1989–2001; Wadham Coll., 2001–06; BBSRC Sen. Res. Fellow, 1997–2002. Scientific Founder and Dir, Prolysis Ltd, 1998–. Mem., EMBO, 2004; FMedSci 2007. Trustee, EPA Cephalosporin Res. Fund, 1999–. *Publications:* over 100 peer-reviewed scientific papers; six patents. *Recreations:* soccer, snorkelling, ski-ing, walking. *Address:* Institute of Cell and Molecular Biosciences, Medical School, University of Newcastle, Newcastle upon Tyne NE2 4HH. *T:* (0191) 222 8126, *Fax:* (0191) 222 7424.

ERRINGTON, Sir Lancelot, KCB 1976 (CB 1962); Second Permanent Secretary, Department of Health and Social Security, 1973–76; *b* 14 Jan. 1917; *er s* of late Major L. Errington; *m* 1939, Katharine Reine, *o d* of late T. C. Macaulay; two *s* two *d*. *Educ:* Wellington Coll.; Trinity Coll., Cambridge. Entered Home Office, 1939. Served RNVR, 1939–45. Transferred to Ministry of National Insurance, 1945; Principal Private Sec. to Minister of National Insurance, 1951; Asst Sec., 1953; Under-Sec., 1957–65; Cabinet Office, 1965–68; Min. of Social Security, 1968; Asst Under-Sec. of State, DHSS, 1968–71, Dep. Under-Sec. of State, 1971–73. *Recreation:* sailing. *Address:* St Mary's, Fasnacloich, Appin, Argyll PA38 4BJ. *T:* (01631) 730331.

ERRINGTON, Stuart Grant, CBE 1994; JP; DL; Chairman, National Association of Citizens' Advice Bureaux, 1989–94; *b* 23 June 1929; *yr s* of Sir Eric Errington, 1st Bt and late Marjorie Lady Errington; *m* 1954, Anne, *d* of late Eric and Eileen Baedeker; two *s* one *d*. *Educ:* Rugby; Trinity College, Oxford (MA). National Service, 2nd Lieut Royal Artillery, 1947–49. Ellerman Lines, 1952–59; Astley Industrial Trust, 1959–70; Exec Dir, 1970, Man. Dir, 1977, Chm., 1985, Mercantile Credit Co., Chm. and Chief Exec., Mercantile Gp, 1988–89. Chairman: Equipment Leasing Assoc., 1976–78; European Fedn of Leasing Assocs, 1978–80; Finance Houses Assoc., 1982–84; Director: Barclays Merchant Bank, Barclays Bank UK, 1979–86; Kleinwort Overseas Investment Trust, 1982–98; Municipal Mutual Insurance, 1989–; Northern Electric, 1989–96; Nationwide Building Soc., 1989–97; Associated Property Owners Ltd, 1998–2002; Associated Property Hldgs Ltd, 2002–. Mem., 1989–, Vice-Chm., 1995–2005, Council, Royal Holloway (formerly RHBNC), London Univ. Chm., Sportsmatch England Award Panel, Dept of Culture, Media and Sport (formerly Dept of Heritage), 1992–2005. Chm., Berks and Oxfordshire Magistrates' Courts Cttee, 1999–2000. Hon. Fellow, RHUL, 2007. JP Windsor Forest, 1970; DL Berks, 2000. *Recreations:* fishing, golf, opera, travel. *Address:* Earleywood Lodge, Ascot SL5 9JP. *T:* (01344) 621977. *Club:* Boodle's.

ERROLL, 24th Earl of, *cr* 1452; **Merlin Sereld Victor Gilbert Hay;** Lord Hay, 1429; Baron of Slains, 1452; Bt 1685; 28th Hereditary Lord High Constable of Scotland, *cr* 1314; Celtic title, Mac Garadh Mor; 33rd Chief of the Hays (from 1171); Senior Great Officer, Royal Household in Scotland; computer consultant; *b* 20 April 1948; *er s* of 23rd Countess of Erroll and Sir Iain Moncreiffe of that Ilk, 11th Bt, CVO, QC; *S* mother, 1978 (and to baronetcy of father, 1985); *m* 1982, Isabelle Astell, *o d* of late T. S. Astell Hohler, MC; two *s* two *d*. *Educ:* Eton; Trinity College, Cambridge. Page to the Lord Lyon, 1956. Lieut, Atholl Highlanders, 1974. Chm., Cost Reduction Consultants Ltd, 1995–. Elected Mem., H of L, 1999; Member: Library and Computers Sub-Cttee, 1999–2001; Bd, POST, 2000–; Council, PITCOM, 2000–; Council, European Inf. Soc. Gp, 2000–; H of L Inf. Cttee, 2001–. Prime Warden, Fishmongers' Co., 2000–01. Hon. Col, RMP TA, 1992–97. OStJ 1977. Member, Queen's Body Guard for Scotland, Royal Company of Archers, 1978. Patron, Keepers of the Quaich. *Recreations:* country pursuits. *Heir: s* Lord Hay, *qv*. *Address:* Woodbury Hall, Sandy, Beds SG19 2HR; *e-mail:* errollm@parliament.uk. *Clubs:* White's, Pratt's; Puffin's (Edinburgh).

ERSHAD, Lt-Gen. Hussain Muhammad; Leader, Jatiya Party, Bangladesh; *b* 1 Feb. 1930; *s* of late Makbul Hussain, Advocate, and of Mojida Begum; *m* 1956, Begum Raushad Ershad; one *s* one adopted *d*. *Educ:* Carmichael Coll., Rangpur; Dhaka Univ. (BA 1st Div.). Staff Course, Defence Service Command and Staff Coll., Quetta, Pakistan, 1966; War Course, National Defence Coll., New Delhi, India, 1975. Infantry Regimental Service, 1953–58; Adjt, E Bengal Regimental Centre (Basic Inf. Trng Centre), 1960–62; E Pakistan Rifles, 1962–65; Bde Major/Dep. Asst Adjt and Quarter Master General, 1967–68; CO, Inf. Bn, 1969–71; Adjt General, Bangladesh Army, 1973–74; Dep. Chief of Army Staff, Bangladesh Army, Chm., Coordination and Control Cell for National Security, 1975–78; Chief of Army Staff, Bangladesh Army, 1978–86; C-in-C, Bangladesh Armed Forces, 1982; Chief Martial Law Administrator, Bangladesh, 1982–86; President: Council of Ministers, 1982–90; Bangladesh, 1983–90; Minister of Defence, Estabt, Health and Population Control, 1986–90. Chm., National Sports Control Bd. *Publications:* poems in Bengali contributed occasionally to literary jls. *Address:* Jatiya Dal, c/o Jatiya Sangsad, Dhaka, Bangladesh. *Club:* Kurmitola Golf (Dhaka).

ERSKINE; *see* St Clair-Erskine.

ERSKINE, family name of **Earls of Buchan** and **Mar and Kellie**.

ERSKINE, Sir Peter; *see* Erskine, Sir T. P. N.

ERSKINE, Peter Anthony; Chief Executive Officer, 2001–08, and Chairman, 2006–08, Telefónica O_2 Europe plc (formerly BT Wireless, later mmO_2, subsequently O_2); non-executive Director, Telefónica SA, since 2008 (Director, 2006–08); *b* 10 Nov. 1951; *s* of Stanley and Winifred Erskine; *m* 1975, Jan Green; three *s* one *d*. *Educ:* Bancroft's Sch., Woodford Green; Liverpool Univ. (BA Hons Psychology 1973). Various appointments at Polycell, Colgate and Palmolive; Sen. Vice-Pres. Sales and Marketing, Unitel, 1990–93; British Telecommunications: Man. Dir, BT Mobile, 1993–95; Pres. and CEO, Concert, USA, 1995–98; CEO, BT Cellnet, 1998–2000. Adv. Bd, Univ. of Reading Bus. Sch., 2003. Hon. LLD Reading, 2008. *Recreations:* football, family, cinema, curry. *Address:* c/o Telefonica Europe plc, Wellington Street, Slough SL1 1YP.

ERSKINE, Ralph; *see* Erskine, T. R.

ERSKINE, Sir (Thomas) Peter (Neil), 6th Bt *cr* 1821, of Cambo, Fife; DL; laird, Cambo Estate, since 1976; *b* 28 March 1950; *s* of Sir (Thomas) David Erskine, 5th Bt and of Ann Erskine (*née* Fraser-Tytler); *S* father, 2007; *m* 1972, Catherine Hewlett; two *s* two *d*. *Educ:* Birmingham Univ. (BSc Psychol.); Edinburgh Univ. (DipRuralAg). LBIPP. Cambo Estate: opened farm park, 1982, photo studio, 1990; gardens opened to public and holiday accommodation in mansion, 1993; opened Kingsbarns Golf Links, 2000. Founder, Scottish Organic Producers Assoc., 1986. *Recreations:* blues guitarist and singer, garden photography, cycling, reading, theatre and arts. *Heir: s* Thomas Struan Erskine, *b* 6 Feb. 1977. *Address:* Cambo House, Kingsbarns, St Andrews, Fife KY16 8QD. *T:* (01333) 450054, *Fax:* (01333) 450987; *e-mail:* peter@camboestate.com; *web:* www.camboestate.com. *Clubs:* New (Edinburgh); Royal & Ancient (St Andrews).

ERSKINE, (Thomas) Ralph, CB 1986; First Legislative Counsel, Northern Ireland, 1979–93; *b* 14 Oct. 1933; *m* 1966, Patricia Joan Palmer; one *s* one *d*. *Educ:* Campbell College; Queen's University, Belfast. Called to the Bar, Gray's Inn, 1962. *Publications:* (with Arthur Bauer and Klaus Herold) Funkpeilung als allierte Waffe gegen deutsche U-Boote 1939–1945, 1997; (ed with Michael Smith) Action This Day: Bletchley Park from the breaking of the Enigma code to the birth of the modern computer, 2001; contrib. Oxford DNB; contribs to Cryptologia, Annals of the History of Computing, legal jls, etc. *Recreations:* gardening, researching modern naval history. *Address:* c/o Office of the Legislative Counsel, Parliament Buildings, Belfast BT4 3SW.

ERSKINE CRUM, Douglas Vernon, CBE 1994; Chief Executive, Horserace Betting Levy Board, since 2008; *b* 31 May 1949; *s* of late Lt-Gen. Vernon Forbes Erskine Crum, CIE, MC and Rosemary (*née* Dawson); *m* 1980, Jacqueline Margaret Wilson; one *s* two *d*. *Educ*: Eton. Commissioned Scots Guards 1970; Staff Coll., Camberley, 1982; Brigade Major, Household Div., 1987–89; CO 2 SG, 1989–91; ACOS Ops, HQ N Ireland, 1991–92; Comdr 3 Inf. Brigade, 1992–94; Chief Exec., Ascot Racecourse, 1994–2007. *Recreations*: most sports, books.

ERSKINE-HILL, Sir (Alexander) Roger, 3rd Bt *cr* 1945, of Quothquhan, Co. Lanark; *b* 15 Aug. 1949; *s* of Sir Robert Erskine-Hill, 2nd Bt and of Christine Alison, *o d* of late Capt. (A) Henry James Johnstone of Alva, RN; *S* father, 1989; *m* 1st 1984, Sarah Anne Sydenham (marr. diss. 1994), *er d* of late Dr R. J. Sydenham Clarke and of Mrs Charles Clarke; one *s* one *d*; 2nd, 2000, Gillian Elizabeth Borlase Mitchell, *d* of David and Sheila Surgey. *Educ*: Eton; Aberdeen Univ. (LLB). Director: Map Marketing Ltd, 1986–2002; The Hillbrooke Partnership Ltd, 2002–. *Heir*: *s* Robert Benjamin Erskine-Hill, *b* 6 Aug. 1986. *Address*: Les Tissanderies, 24220 Le Coux et Bigaroque, Dordogne, France.

ERSKINE-HILL, Prof. (Henry) Howard, PhD, LittD; FBA 1985; Professor of Literary History, 1994–2003, now Emeritus, and Fellow of Pembroke College, 1980–2003, now Emeritus, Cambridge University; *b* 19 June 1936; *s* of late Henry Erskine-Hill and Hannah Lilian Poppleton. *Educ*: Ashville Coll.; Nottingham Univ. (BA, PhD); MA Cantab; LittD Cantab 1988. University of Wales, Swansea: Tutor, 1960; Asst Lectr, 1961; Lectr in Eng. Lit., 1962; Sen. Fellow, 1964–65; University of Cambridge: Lectr in English, 1969–84; Reader in Literary Hist., 1984–94; Fellow, 1969–80, Tutor, 1970–76, Jesus Coll.; Tutor for Graduates, Pembroke Coll., 1983–84. Olin Fellow, Nat. Humanities Center, NC, USA, 1988–89. Taught at British Council seminars in Britain, 1962–69; invited lectr, univs of Alberta, Adelaide, Berkeley (Calif), Bristol, Davis (Calif), Essex, Flinders (S Australia), Liverpool, London, Monash, Nantes, Oxford, Saskatchewan, Stanford, Singapore, Wales (Swansea), Victoria (BC), Warwick, W Australia and York; also at David Nichol Smith Seminar, Canberra, Inter-Univ. Centre, Dubrovnik, Inst. of Hist. Res., London, and Herzog-August Library, Wolfenbüttel. *Publications*: (ed) Alexander Pope: Horatian Satires and Epistles, 1964; Pope: The Dunciad, 1972; The Social Milieu of Alexander Pope, 1975; (ed with Anne Smith) The Art of Alexander Pope, 1978; (ed with Graham Storey) Revolutionary Prose of the English Civil War, 1983; The Augustan Idea, 1983; (ed with Alexander Lindsay) William Congreve: the critical heritage, 1989; Gulliver's Travels, 1993; (ed with Richard A. McCabe) Presenting Poetry, 1995; Poetry and the Realm of Politics, 1996; Poetry of Opposition and Revolution, 1996; (introd and ed) Alexander Pope: world and word, 1998; (ed) Alexander Pope, Selected Letters, 2000; (ed with Jonathan Clark) Samuel Johnson in Historical Context, 2002; (with Eveline Cruickshanks) The Atterbury Plot, 2004; contributions to: Renaissance and Modern Essays, ed G. R. Hibbard, 1966; English Drama: forms and development, ed Marie Axton and Raymond Williams, 1977; Ideology and Conspiracy, ed Eveline Cruickshanks, 1982; Samuel Johnson: new critical essays, ed Isobel Grundy, 1984; English Satire and the Satiric Tradition, ed Claude Rawson, 1984; The Enduring Legacy: Alexander Pope tercentenary essays, ed G. S. Rousseau and Pat Rogers, 1988; Lord Burlington: architect, art and life, ed Toby Barnard and Jane Clark, 1995; The Stuart Court in Exile and the Jacobites, ed Eveline Cruickshanks and Edward Corp, 1995; Enlightened Groves: essays in honour of Zenzo Suzuki, ed Eiichi Hara, Hiroshi Ozawa and Peter Robinson, 1996; Imagined Commonwealths, ed T. J. Cribb, 1999; John Dryden: tercentary essays, ed Paul Hammond and David Hopkins, 2000; That Second Bottle: essays on John Wilmot, Earl of Rochester, ed Nicholas Fisher, 2000; A Court in Exile, ed Edward Corp, 2004; John Dryden: his politics, his plays and his poets, ed Claude Rawson, 2004; Sustaining Literature, ed Greg Clingham, 2007; The Cambridge Companion to Alexander Pope, ed Pat Rogers, 2007; jls incl. Agenda, Age of Johnson, English Literary History, Essays in Criticism, Eighteenth-Century Studies, Jl of the Warburg and Courtauld Insts, Modern Language Review, Rev. of English Studies, Renaissance and Modern Studies, Yearbook of English Studies. *Recreation*: collecting. *Address*: Pembroke College, Cambridge CB2 1RF. *T*: (01223) 338100. *Club*: Oxford and Cambridge.

ERSKINE-HILL, Sir Roger; *see* Erskine-Hill, Sir A. R.

ERSKINE-MURRAY, family name of **Lord Elibank.**

ESAKI, Leo; Chairman, Science and Technology Promotion Foundation of Ibaraki, Japan, since 1998; Director-General, Tsukuba International Congress Centre, since 1998; President, Shibaura Institute of Technology, since 2000; *b* 12 March 1925; *s* of Soichiro Esaki and Niyoko Ito; *m* 1986, Masako Kondo; one *s* two *d* by previous *m*. *Educ*: Univ. of Tokyo. MS 1947, PhD 1959. Sony Corp., Japan, 1956–60; IBM Research, 1960–67; IBM Fellow, 1967–92. Dir, IBM-Japan, 1976–92. Pres., Univ. of Tsukuba, Japan, 1992–98. Research in tunnelling in semiconductor junctions which led to the discovery of the Esaki tunnel diode; subsequently research on man-made semiconductor superlattice in search of predicted quantum mechanical effect. Sir John Cass sen. vis. res. fellow, London Poly., 1982. Councillor-at-Large, Amer. Phys. Soc., 1971–75; Dir, Amer. Vacuum Soc., 1972–76; Member: Japan Academy, 1975; Max-Planck-Ges., 1989; For. Associate, Nat. Acad. of Sciences, USA, 1976; For. Associate, Nat. Acad. of Engineering, USA, 1977; Corresp. Mem., Academia Nacional De Ingenieria, Mexico, 1978. Nishina Meml Award, 1959; Asahi Press Award, 1960; Toyo Rayon Foundn Award, 1961; Morris N. Liebmann Meml Prize, 1961; Stuart Ballantine Medal, Franklin Inst., 1961; Japan Academy Award, 1965; (jtly) Nobel Prize for Physics, 1973; Science Achievement Award, US-Asia Inst., 1983; Centennial Medal, IEEE, 1984; Internat. Prize for New Materials, Amer. Physical Soc., 1985; Distinguished Foreign-born Individual Award, Internat. Center, NY, 1986; IEEE Medal of Honor, 1991; Japan Prize, 1998. Order of Culture (Japan), 1974; Grand Order of Rising Sun, First Class (Japan), 1998. *Publications*: numerous papers in learned jls. *Address*: Shibaura Institute of Technology, 3–9–14 Shibaura, Minato-ku, Tokyo 108–8548, Japan.

ESCHENBACH, Christoph; conductor and pianist; Music Director: Orchestre de Paris, since 2000; Philadelphia Orchestra, since 2003; *b* 20 Feb. 1940. *Educ*: Hamburg Conservatory; State Music Conservatory, Cologne. Chief Conductor, Tonhalle Orch., Zürich, and Artistic Dir, Tonhalle-Gesellschaft, Zürich, 1982–86; Music Director: Houston SO, 1988–99, now Conductor Laureate; Ravinia Fest., 1994–2003; NDR SO, 1998–2004; Artistic Dir, Schleswig-Holstein Music Fest., 1999–2002; Co-Artistic Dir, Pacific Music Fest., 1992–98. *As conductor*: studied with W. Bruckner Ruggeberg, George Szell; guest appearances include: NY Philharmonic, Boston Symphony, Chicago Symphony, Cleveland Orch., Pittsburgh Symphony, Los Angeles Philharmonic, London Symphony, BBC Philharmonia, Berlin Philharmonic, Bavarian Radio Symphony Munich, Munich Philharmonic, Vienna Symphonic, Czech Philharmonic, New Japan Philharmonic, Houston Grand Opera, and Metropolitan Opera. *As pianist*: studied with Eliza Hansen; winner: Internat. Piano Competition, Munich, 1962; Concours Clara Haskil, 1965; Canadian début, Montreal Expo, 1967; US début, Cleveland Orch., 1969; has toured Europe, N and S America, USSR, Israel, Japan; and has performed as pianist with leading orchs incl. Concertgebouw Amsterdam, Orch. de Paris, London Symphony, Berlin Philharmonic, and Cleveland Orch.; festivals incl. Salzburg, Lucerne, Bonn, and Aix-en-Provence. Officer's Cross with Ribbon, 1990, Commander's Cross, 1993, Order of Merit (Germany). *Address*: c/o Philadelphia Orchestra, Public Relations Department, 260 South Broad Street, 16th Floor, Philadelphia, PA 19102, USA.

ESCOTT COX, Brian Robert; *see* Cox.

ESCUDIER, Prof. Marcel Paul, PhD, DSc(Eng); FREng, FIMechE, FCGI; Harrison Professor of Mechanical Engineering, University of Liverpool, since 1989; *b* 17 July 1942; *s* of late Isabel Kate Escudier; *m* 1st, 1966, Sonja Kennedy Allen (marr. diss. 1973); 2nd, 1973, Agnes Margaret Simko; one *s*. *Educ*: Sir Walter St John's Grammar Sch., London; Imperial Coll., London Univ. (BScEng; DIC; PhD 1967); DSc(Eng) 1990. ACGI 1963; FIMechE 1995; FREng 2000; FCGI 2003. Res. Associate, MIT, 1967–69; Asst Prof. Univ. of Southern Calif, 1969–73; Mem., Plasmaphysics Res. Gp, 1973–74, Leader, Fluid Mechanics Res. Gp, 1974–86, Brown Boveri Res. Centre, Switzerland; Hd, Fluid Mechanics Res. Dept, Schlumberger Cambridge Res. Ltd, Cambridge, 1986–88; Hd Dept of Mech. Engrg, Univ. of Liverpool, 1990–97. *Publications*: The Essence of Engineering Fluid Mechanics, 1998; contrib. papers on vortex flows, non-Newtonian fluid flow, etc, to scientific jls. *Recreations*: gardening, cooking, erotic art, motor racing (non participatory), digital photography. *Address*: Silverburn, Park Road, Willaston, Neston CH64 1TJ. *T*: (0151) 327 2949.

ESDALE, Patricia Joyce, (Mrs G. P. R. Esdale); *see* Lindop, P. J.

ESER, Prof. Dr Günter Otto; Director General, International Air Transport Association, Montreal/Geneva, 1985–92; *b* 10 Sept. 1927; *s* of Ernst Eser and Martha Siering; *m* 1976, Florida Huisman; two *s*. *Educ*: Bonn Univ.; Federal Acad. of Finance, Siegburg; Harvard (Management Programme). Auditor, Fed. German Min. of Finance, 1953–55; Lufthansa German Airlines, 1955–84: Head, Persian subsidiary, Teheran; Head, Munich Dist Office for Southern Germany; Sales Dir, Germany; Gen. Man., N and Central America; Mem. Chief Exec. Bd. Member: Adv. Bd, Europäische Reiseversicherung, 1978–; Adv. Bd, Amer. Univ., 1982–. Vis. Prof., Pace Univ., NY, 1978. Bundesverdienstkreuz 1st Class (FRG), 1985; Commendatore Officiale (Italy), 1967. *Recreations*: trekking, ocean-fishing, literature, music. *Address*: La Bellangère, ch. de Sodome, 1271 Givrins, Vaud, Switzerland.

ESHER, 5th Viscount *cr* 1897; **Christopher Lionel Baliol Brett;** Baron 1885; *b* 23 Dec. 1936; *s* of 4th Viscount Esher and Christian (*née* Pike); *S* father, 2004; *m* 1st, 1962, Camilla Charlotte (marr. diss. 1970), *d* of Sir (Horace) Anthony Rumbold, 10th Bt, KCMG, KCVO, CB; one *s* two *d*; 2nd, 1971, Valerie Harrington; two *s* twin *d*. *Educ*: Eton; Magdalen Coll., Oxford. *Heir*: *s* Hon. Matthew Christopher Anthony Brett [*b* 2 Jan. 1963; *m* 1992, Hon. Emma Charlotte Denison-Pender, *e d* of Baron Pender, *qv*; one *s* two *d*]. *Address*: Beauforest House, Newington, Wallingford, Oxon OX10 7AG.

ESIRI, Prof. Margaret Miriam, DM; FRCPath; Professor of Neuropathology, Departments of Neuropathology and Neurology, Oxford University, 1996–2007, Professorial Fellow, St Hugh's College, Oxford, 1988–2007, now Emeritus; *b* 5 Oct. 1941; *d* of William Alfred Evans and Doreen Mary (*née* Bates); *m* 1963, Frederic Obukowho Uruemuowho Esiri; two *s* one *d*. *Educ*: Croydon High Sch. (GPDST); St Hugh's Coll., Oxford (BSc, MA, DM). FRCPath 1988. University of Oxford preregistration med. and surgical posts and scholarship for trng in research methods, 1967–69; Jun. Res. Fellow in Neuropathology, 1970–72; trng posts in Histopathology, 1973–79; MRC Sen. Clinical Fellow in Neuropathology, 1980–85; Consultant Neuropathologist, Radcliffe Infirmary, 1986–88; Clinical Reader in Neuropathology, 1988–96. *Publications*: (with J. Booss) Viral Encephalitis, 1986; (with D. R. Oppenheimer) Diagnostic Neuropathology, 1989, 2nd edn 1996, 3rd edn (with D. Perl) 2006; (ed with J. H. Morris) The Neuropathology of Dementia, 1997, 2nd edn (ed with V. M.-Y. Lee and J. Q. Trojanowski) 2004; (with J. Booss) Human Viral Encephalitis, 2003. *Recreation*: grandchildren. *Address*: Neuropathology Department, Level 1, West Wing, John Radcliffe Hospital, Headington, Oxford OX3 9DU. *T*: (01865) 234403; *e-mail*: margaret.esiri@clneuro.ox.ac.uk.

ESKENAZI, Giuseppe, (J. E. Eskenazi); Managing Director, Eskenazi Ltd, since 1969; *b* 8 July 1939; *s* of late Isaac Eskenazi and of Lea Eskenazi; *m* 1963, Laura (*née* Bandini); one *s* one *d*. *Educ*: King's School, Sherborne; The Polytechnic, Regent Street; University College London. Art dealer, primarily Chinese and Japanese, 1962–; Eskenazi Ltd founded by father in 1960. Mem., steering cttee to estab. Asian Art in London, 1997–98, Chm. 2002, 2003; Member: Exec. Cttee, Asia House, 1993–2007; Council, Oriental Ceramic Soc., 1998–2002, 2004–07; Adv. Bd, Bard Grad. Center for Studies in the Decorative Arts, NY, 2000–. Trustee, Asia House Trust (London), 2000–07. Adviser to Royal Academy for exhibitions: 100 Masterpieces of Imperial Chinese Ceramics from the Au Bak Ling Collection, 1998; Return of the Buddha, The Qingzhou Discoveries, 2002. Chevalier, Légion d'Honneur (France), 2006. *Publications*: numerous exhibition catalogues. *Recreations*: sailing, diving, opera. *Address*: 12 Carlyle Square, Chelsea, SW3 6EX. *T*: (020) 7352 7461; Eskenazi, 10 Clifford Street, W1S 2LJ. *T*: (020) 7493 5464.

ESLER, Gavin William James; presenter: BBC World, since 1998; BBC Radio Four, since 2000; Newsnight, since 2003; *b* 27 Feb. 1953; *s* of William John Esler and Georgena Esler; *m* 1979, Patricia Margaret Warner; one *s* one *d*. *Educ*: George Heriot's Sch. Edinburgh; Kent Univ. (BA English and American Lit); Leeds Univ. (MA Anglo-Irish Lit (Dist.)). Reporter, Belfast Telegraph, 1975–76; BBC: Reporter and Presenter, Northern Ireland, 1977–82; Reporter, Newsnight, 1982–88; Washington Corresp., 1989; Chief N America Corresp., 1989–97; presenter: Newsnight, 1997; BBC News 24, 1997–2002; Columnist, The Scotsman, 1998–2005. Hon. MA, 1995, Hon. DCL, 2005, Kent. RTS Award, 1989; Sony Gold Award, 2007. FRSA 2000. *Publications*: The United States of Anger: the people and the American dream, 1997; novels: Loyalties, 1990; Deep Blue, 1992; The Blood Brother, 1995; A Scandalous Man, 2008. *Recreations*: hiking, ski-ing, camping, especially in the American West. *Address*: Newsnight, BBC Television Centre, Wood Lane, Shepherds Bush, W12 7RJ.

ESLER, Prof. Philip Francis, DPhil, DD; Professor of Biblical Criticism, University of St Andrews, since 1995; Chief Executive, Arts and Humanities Research Council, since 2005; *b* 27 Aug. 1952; *s* of Patrick Joseph Esler and Evelyn Elizabeth Esler (*née* Flannery); *m* 1983, Patricia Kathryn Curran; two *s* one *d*. *Educ*: Sydney Univ. (BA Hons LLB, LLM), Magdalen Coll., Oxford (DPhil 1984); DD Oxford 2003. Associate to Justice W. H. Collins of NSW Supreme Court, 1977; articled clerk, then solicitor, Allen, Allen & Hemsley, Sydney, 1978–81 and 1984–86; barrister, NSW Supreme Court, 1986–92; University of St Andrews: Reader in New Testament, 1992–95; Vice-Principal for Res. and Provost, St Leonard's Coll., 1998–2001. Mem. Bd, Scottish Enterprise Fife, 1999–2003. *Publications*: Community and Gospel in Luke - Acts, 1987; The First Christians in their Social Worlds, 1994; Galatians, 1998; Conflict and Identity in Romans, 2003; (with J. Boyd) Velázquez and Biblical Text, 2004; New Testament Theology, 2005; (with R. A. Piper) Lazarus, Martha and Mary, 2006. *Recreations*: swimming, walking, tennis. *Address*: Kilninian House, Kemback, Cupar, Fife KY15 5TS. *T*: (01334) 654916.

ESMONDE, Sir Thomas (Francis Grattan), 17th Bt *cr* 1629 (Ire.), of Ballynastragh, Wexford; MD; Consultant Neurologist, Royal Victoria Hospital, Belfast, since 1996 (Senior Registrar in Neurology, 1992–96); *b* 14 Oct. 1960; *s* of Sir John Henry Grattan Esmonde, 16th Bt and of Pamela Mary, *d* of late Francis Stephen Bourke, FRCPI; *S* father, 1987; *m* 1986, Pauline Loretto Kearns; one *s* two *d*. *Educ:* Sandford Park Secondary School, Ranelagh, Dublin; Medical School, Trinity College, Dublin (MB, BCh, BAO 1984; MD 1995). MRCPI, MRCP (UK) 1987. Junior House Officer, Whiteabbey Hosp., 1984–85; SHO, Royal Victoria, Musgrave Park and Whiteabbey Hosps, 1985–87, Altnagelvin Hosp., Londonderry, 1987–88; Med. Registrar, Royal Gwent Hosp., Newport, 1988–89; Registrar in Neurology, Univ. Hosp. of Wales, 1989–90; Clinical Res. Fellow, Dept of Neurosci., Western General Hosp., Edinburgh, 1990–92. *Recreations:* chess, fishing. *Heir: s* Sean Vincent Grattan Esmonde, *b* 8 Jan. 1989.

ESOM, Steven Derek; Director of Food, Marks and Spencer, 2007–08; *b* 13 Nov. 1960; *s* of Derek Esom and Shirley Esom (*née* Beldom); *m* 1994, Fiona; one *s* one *d*. *Educ:* St Edward's Sch., Romford; Univ. of Wales, Swansea (BSc Hons Geog.). Sen. Manager, Buying, J. Sainsbury plc, 1982–93; with US subsidiary, Shaws, Boston, 1991–99; Buying and Merchandising Dir, Texas Homecare, Ladbroke Gp, 1994–95; Vice-Pres., Global Merchandising, Hilton Internat., 1995–96; Dir of Buying, 1996–2002, Man. Dir, 2002–07, Waitrose. Dir, CIES, 2004–07. Non-exec. Dir, Carphone Warehouse Gp plc, 2005–. FRSA; FIGD. *Recreations:* food & wine, ski-ing, fitness. *Address:* c/o Food Division, Marks and Spencer, Waterside House, 35 North Wharf Road, W2 1NW. *T:* (020) 7935 4422, *Fax:* (020) 7723 4924.

ESPEJO, Genefer D.; Headmistress, Nonsuch High School for Girls, Cheam, since 1995; *b* 17 July 1949; *d* of late Rev. D. G. Larkinson and of Mrs S. Larkinson; *m* 1972, Dr L. G. Espejo; one *s*. *Educ:* Queen's Univ., Belfast (BA Hons); Univ. of Sussex (PGCE). Dep. Hd, Kings' Sch., Winchester, 1985–92; Headmistress, Reading Girls' Sch., 1992–95. FRSA. *Recreations:* walking, visiting art galleries, theatre, contemporary fiction. *Address:* Nonsuch High School for Girls, Ewell Road, Cheam, Surrey SM3 8AB. *T:* (020) 8394 1308, *Fax:* (020) 8393 2307; *e-mail:* espejo-g@nonsuch.sutton.sch.uk.

ESPLEN, (Sir) John Graham, 3rd Bt *cr* 1921, of Hardres Court, Canterbury, but does not use the title; *b* 4 Aug. 1932; *s* of Sir William Graham Esplen, 2nd Bt and of Aline Octavia, *d* of late A. Octavius Hedley; *S* father, 1989; *m*; one *s* three *d*. *Educ:* Harrow; St Catharine's Coll., Cambridge. *Heir: s* William John Harry Esplen [*b* 24 Feb. 1967; *m* 1996, Helen Chesser; one *s* one *d*].

ESQUIVEL, Rt Hon. Manuel; PC 1986; Prime Minister of Belize, 1984–89 and 1993–98; Member, House of Representatives, Belize, 1984–98; Leader, United Democratic Party, 1982–98; *b* 2 May 1940; *s* of John and Laura Esquivel; *m* 1971, Kathleen Levy; one *s* two *d*. *Educ:* Loyola Univ., New Orleans (BSc Physics); Bristol Univ. (Cert Ed.). Instructor in Physics, St John's Coll., Belize City, 1967–82. Member: Belize City Council, 1974–80; Nat. Senate, 1979–84; Leader of the Opposition, Belize, 1989–93. Chm., Utd Democratic Party, 1976–82. Hon. DHL Loyola Univ., 1986. *Recreation:* electronics. *Address:* PO Box 1344, Belize City, Belize.

ESSAAFI, M'hamed; Grand Officier, Order of Tunisian Republic, 1963; Disaster Relief Co-ordinator and Under Secretary General, United Nations, 1982–92; *b* 26 May 1930; *m* 1956, Hedwige Klat; one *s* one *d*. *Educ:* Sadiki Coll., Tunis; Sorbonne, Paris. Secretariat of State for For. Affairs, 1956; 1st Sec., Tunisian Embassy, London, 1956; 1st Sec., Tunisian Embassy, Washington, 1957; Secretariat of State for For. Affairs, Tunis: Dir of Amer. Dept, 1960; America and Internat. Confs Dept, 1962; Ambassador to London, 1964–69; Ambassador to Moscow, 1970–74; Ambassador to Bonn, 1974–76; Sec.-Gen., Ministry of Foreign Affairs, Tunis, 1969–70 and 1976–78; Ambassador to Belgium and EEC, 1978–79; Permanent Rep. of Tunisia to the UN, and Special Rep. of the Sec.-Gen., 1980–81, Chef de Cabinet 1982. *Address:* rue de la Mosquée BH20, La Marsa, Tunis, Tunisia.

ESSAYAN, Michael; QC 1976; *b* 7 May 1927; *s* of late Kevork Loris Essayan and Rita Sirvarte (*née* Gulbenkian); *m* 1956, Geraldine St Lawrence Lee Guinness, *d* of K. E. L. Guinness, MBE; one *s* one *d*. *Educ:* France; Harrow; Balliol Coll., Oxford (1st Cl. Class. Hon. Mods 1949, 1st Cl. Lit. Hum. 1951, MA). Served with RA, 1945–48 (Palestine, 1947–48). Iraq Petroleum Co., London and ME, 1951–56. Called to the Bar, Middle Temple 1957 (Bencher 1983), joined Lincoln's Inn *ad eundem* 1958. Mem., Gen. Council of the Bar, 1987–88. Mem., Bd of Administration, Calouste Gulbenkian Foundn, Lisbon, 1981–2005, Hon. Pres., 1992–. Hon. FKC 2008. Comdr, Order of Merit (Portugal), 1993; Grand Cross, Order of Prince Henry the Navigator (Portugal), 2005. *Publications:* The New Supreme Court Costs (with M. J. Albery, QC), 1960; (ed with Hon. Mr Justice Walton) Adkin's Landlord and Tenant, 15th, 16th, 17th and 18th edns. *Recreations:* wine and wife. *Address:* 6 Chelsea Square, SW3 6LF. *T:* (020) 7352 6786. *Club:* Brooks's.

ESSER, Robin Charles; Executive Managing Editor, Daily Mail, since 1998; editorial and media consultant, since 1990; *b* 6 May 1935; *s* of late Charles and Winifred Eileen Esser; *m* 1959, Irene Shirley Clough (decd); two *s* two *d*; *m* 1981, Tui (*née* France); two *s*. *Educ:* Wheelwright Grammar School, Dewsbury; Wadham College, Oxford (BA Hons, MA). Edited Oxford Univ. newspaper, Cherwell, 1954. Commissioned, King's Own Yorkshire Light Infantry, 1956. Freelance reporter, 1957–60; Daily Express: Staff Reporter, 1960; Editor, William Hickey Column, 1963; Features Editor, 1965; New York Bureau, 1969; Northern Editor, 1970; Exec. Editor, 1985; Consultant Editor, Evening News, 1977; Editor, Sunday Express, 1986–89; Gp Editl Consultant, Express Newspapers, 1989–90. *Publications:* The Hot Potato, 1969; The Paper Chase, 1971. *Recreations:* lunching, shooting, tennis, reading. *Clubs:* Garrick, Hurlingham.

ESSERY, David James, CB 1997; Under Secretary, Scottish Office Home (formerly Home and Health) Department, 1991–97; *b* 10 May 1938; *s* of Lawrence and Edna Essery; *m* 1963, Nora Sim; two *s* one *d*. *Educ:* Royal High Sch., Edinburgh. Entered Dept of Health for Scotland, 1956; Private Sec. to Minister of State, Scottish Office, 1968; Principal, Scottish Develt Dept, 1969; Assistant Secretary: Scottish Economic Planning Dept, 1976; Scottish Develt Dept, 1981–85; Under Sec., Scottish Office Agric. and Fisheries Dept, 1985–91. Mem. Mgt Cttee, Hanover (Scotland) Housing Assoc., 2005–. *Recreations:* reading, music, golf, hill walking. *Address:* 110 Grange Loan, Edinburgh EH9 2EF.

ESSEX, 11th Earl of, *cr* 1661; **Frederick Paul de Vere Capell;** Baron Capell 1641; Viscount Malden 1661; Deputy Head Teacher, Skerton County Primary School, Lancaster, 1990–95 (Acting Head, 1992–93); *b* 29 May 1944; *s* of 10th Earl of Essex, and of Doris Margaret, *d* of George Frederick Tomlinson; *S* father, 2005. *Educ:* Skerton Boys' School; Lancaster Royal Grammar School; Didsbury College of Education, Manchester; Northern School of Music. ACP, LLCM(TD), ALCM. Assistant teacher, Marsh County Junior School, 1966–72; Deputy Head, 1972–75; Acting Head, 1975–77; Deputy Head Teacher, Marsh County Primary School, 1977–78; Head Teacher, Cockerham Parochial CE School, Cockerham, Lancaster, 1979–80; in charge of Pastoral Care, Curriculum Develt and Music, Skerton County Primary School, Lancaster, 1981–90. Patron: Morecambe Philharmonic Choir, 1990–; Friends of Cassiobury Park, Watford, 1998–. FRSA. *Recreation:* music. *Heir: kinsman* William Jennings Capell [*b* 9 Aug. 1952; *m* 1971, Sandra Elaine Matson; one *s* one *d*].

ESSEX, David Albert, OBE 1999; singer, actor and composer; *b* 23 July 1947; *s* of Albert Cook and Doris Cook (*née* Kemp); *m* 1971, Maureen Annette Neal; one *s* one *d*. *Educ:* Shipman Secondary Sch., E London. Music industry début, 1965; acting début, touring repertory co.; Jesus, in Godspell, Wyndhams, 1972 (Most Promising Newcomer Award, Variety Club of GB); Che Guevara, in Evita, Prince Edward, 1978; Byron, in Childe Byron, Young Vic, 1981; Fletcher Christian, in Mutiny, Piccadilly, 1985 (also wrote score); She Stoops to Conquer, Queen's, 1993; annual Christmas appearances in own musical version of Robinson Crusoe. Films include: That'll Be the Day, 1973; Stardust, 1974; Silver Dream Racer (also wrote score), 1979; Shogun Mayeda, 1991. Many best-selling singles and albums; first concert tour of UK, 1974; tours, 1975–, incl. Europe, USA, Australia, and a world tour; TV and radio appearances, incl. BBC TV series, The River, 1988. Mem. Council, VSO (Ambassador, 1990–92). *Publication:* (autobiography) A Charmed Life, 2002. *Address:* c/o Mel Bush Organisation, 26 Albany Park, Cabot Lane, Poole BH17 7BX; c/o MBO, PO Box 363, Bournemouth BH7 6LA.

ESSEX, Francis; author, producer and composer; *b* 24 March 1929; *s* of Harold and Beatrice Essex-Lopresti; *m* 1956, Jeanne Shires; one *s* (and one *s* decd). *Educ:* Cotton Coll., N Staffs. Light Entertainment Producer, BBC Television, 1954–60; Sen. Prod., ATV Network Ltd, 1960–65; Controller of Progs, Scottish Television, 1965–69; ATV Network Ltd: Prodn Controller, 1969–76; Mem., Bd of Dirs, 1974; Dir of Production, 1976–81. Chm., Children's Network Cttee, ITV, 1976–81. Chm., Conservatives Abroad, Javea, 1990–92. Wrote and presented, The Bells of St Martins, St Martin's Theatre, 1953; devised and directed, Six of One, Adelphi, 1964; author, Jolson, Victoria Palace, 1995; *television film scripts include:* Shillingbury Tales; Gentle Flame, Silent Scream; Cuffy series; *scores:* Luke's Kingdom; Seas Must Live; The Lightning Tree; Maddie With Love, etc; writer of plays and songs. Fellow, Royal Television Soc., 1974. British Acad. Light Entertainment Award, 1964; Leonard Brett Award, 1964, 1981; Olivier Award for Best Musical, 1996. *Publications:* Shillingbury Tales, 1983; Skerrymor Bay, 1984. *Recreations:* tennis, gardening. *Address:* Punta Vista, Buzon No 1, Aldea de las Cuevas, 19, 03759 Benidoleig, Prov. de Alicante, Spain.

ESSEX, Susan Linda, (Sue); Member (Lab) Cardiff North, National Assembly for Wales, 1999–2007; Minister for Finance, Local Government and Public Services, 2003–07; *b* 29 Aug. 1945; *m* 1967, Richard Essex; one *s* one *d*. *Educ:* Leicester Univ. (BA). MRTPI. Lectr in Planning, Univ. of Wales, Cardiff, 1992–99. Member (Lab): Cardiff City Council, 1983–96 (former Leader); Cardiff County Council, 1995–99. Sec., then Minister, for the Envmt, Nat. Assembly for Wales, 2000–03. Mem., Countryside Council for Wales, 1994–99. *Address:* 29 Lon-y-Dail, Rhiwbina, Cardiff CF14 6DZ.

ESSEX-CATER, Dr Antony John, LRCP, MRCS; FFPH; FRAI; Medical Officer of Health, States of Jersey, Channel Islands, 1974–88; Venereologist, General Hospital, Jersey, 1974–88; Vice President, National Association for Maternal and Child Welfare, since 1988 (Chairman, 1975–88); *b* 28 Sept. 1923; *s* of Herbert Stanley Cater and Helen Marjorie Essex; *m* 1947, Jane Mary Binning; three *s* one *d*. *Educ:* Solihull Sch.; King's Coll., Univ. of London; Charing Cross Hosp.; School of Hyg. and Trop. Med., Univ. of London. Bygott Postgrad. Schol., Univ. of London, 1952–53. DPH, DIH, DCH; FRSH; AFOM. Medical Br., RAF, 1948–50. Dep. MOH, Swansea, 1953–58; Admin. MOH, Birmingham, 1958–61; Dep. MOH, Manchester, 1961–68; County MOH, Monmouthshire, 1968–74. Part-time Lectr in Child Health, Univ. of Birmingham, 1958–61; Council of Europe Medical Fellow, 1968. Short-term Consultant, WHO, 1988–89. Mem. Exec. Cttee 1958, Vice-Chm. 1969, Nat. Assoc. for Maternal and Child Welfare; Member: Public Health Lab. Services Bd, 1969–75; Steering Cttee, Nat. Health Service Reorganization (Wales), 1971–72; Founder Fellow and Mem. First Bd, Fac. of Community Med., Royal Colls of Physicians of UK, 1972–73. Member: BMA; Med. Soc. for Study of Venereal Diseases. *Publications:* Synopsis of Public Health and Social Medicine, 1960, 2nd edn 1967; Manual of Public Health and Community Medicine, 3rd edn 1979; numerous papers on medical and allied subjects. *Recreations:* literary, music, sport. *Address:* Honfleur, La Vallette, Mont Cambrai, St Lawrence, Jersey, CI JE3 1JP. *T:* (01534) 872438. *Club:* Society of Authors.

ESSIG, Philippe Louis Charles Marie; Officier de l'Ordre National du Mérite, 1984; Commandeur de la Légion d'Honneur, 1994; international consultant, since 1991; Chairman, Board of Transmanche-Link, 1988–91; *b* 19 July 1933; *s* of Jean Essig and Germaine Olivier; *m* 1960, Isabelle Lanier; one *s* three *d*. *Educ:* Lycée Janson-de Sailly; Ecole Polytechnique; Engineer, Ponts et Chaussées. Engr, Dakar-Niger railway, 1957–59; Asst Dir, Régie du chemin de fer Abidjan-Niger, 1960–61; Dir, Régie des chemins de fer du Cameroun, 1961–66; Régie autonome des transports parisiens (RATP): Chief Engr, Research Dept, 1966–71; Chief Op. Officer, Ops Dept, 1971–73; Man. Dir, Railways, Paris, 1973–81; Gen. Man., 1982–85; Pres., SNCF, 1985–88. Sec. of State for Housing, 1988. Officier de l'Ordre de la Valeur Camerounaise, 1966. *Recreations:* walking, ski-ing, shooting. *Address:* 5 Avenue Fourcault de Pavant, 78000 Versailles, France.

ESSWOOD, Paul Lawrence Vincent; singer (counter-tenor); Professor of Baroque Vocal Interpretation, Royal Academy of Music, since 1985; *b* West Bridgford, Nottingham, 6 June 1942; *s* of Alfred Walter Esswood and Freda Garratt; *m* 1st, 1966, Mary Lillian Cantrill, ARCM (marr. diss.); two *s*; 2nd, 1990, Aimée Désirée Blattmann; one *s* one *d*. *Educ:* West Bridgford Grammar Sch.; Royal Coll. of Music (ARCM). Lay-Vicar, Westminster Abbey, 1964–71. Prof., RCM, 1973–85; Specialist in baroque performance; first broadcast, BBC, 1965; co-founder: Pro Cantione Antiqua; A Cappella Male Voice Ensemble for Performance of Old Music, 1967; joined The Musicke Companye, 1998; operatic début in Cavalli's L'Erismena, Univ. of California, Berkeley, 1968; début at La Scala, Milan with Zurich Opera in L'Incoronazione di Poppea and Il Ritorno d'Ulisse, 1978; Scottish Opera début in Dido and Aeneas, 1978; world premières: Penderecki's Paradise Lost, Chicago Lyric Opera, 1979; Philip Glass's Echnaton, Stüttgart Opera, 1984; Herbert Willi's Schlafes Bruder, Zurich Opera, 1996; performed in major festivals: Edinburgh, Leeds Triennial, English Bach, Vienna, Salzburg, Zurich, Hamburg, Berlin, Naples, Israel, Lucerne, Flanders, Wexford, Holland. Has made over 150 recordings for major cos, incl. solo recitals of Purcell, Schumann, English lute songs, Benjamin Britten folk songs and Canticle II (Abraham and Isaac). Début as conductor, Chichester Fest., 2000; conducted modern world première, Cavalli's Pompeo Magno, Varazdin Fest., Croatia, 2002. Hon. RAM 1990. *Recreations:* gardening (organic), apiculture. *Address:* Jasmine Cottage, 42 Ferring Lane, Ferring, West Sussex BN12 6QT. *T:* and *Fax:* (01903) 504480.

ESTEVE-COLL, Dame Elizabeth Anne Loosemore, DBE 1995; Vice-Chancellor, University of East Anglia, 1995–97; Chancellor, University of Lincoln, since 2001; *b* 14 Oct. 1938; *o d* of P. W. and Nora Kingdon; *m* 1960, José Alexander Timothy Esteve-Coll (*d* 1980). *Educ:* Darlington Girls High Sch.; Birkbeck Coll., London Univ. (BA 1976).

Head of Learning Resources, Kingston Polytechnic, 1977; University Librarian, Univ. of Surrey, 1982; Keeper, National Art Library, 1985, Dir, 1988–95, V&A Museum. *Recreations:* reading, music, foreign travel. *Address:* Coldham Hall, Tuttington, Aylsham, Norfolk NR11 6TA; c/o Le Colombier, Puylaurens, 81570 Semalens, Tarn, France.

ESTRIN, Prof. Saul, DPhil; Professor of Management and Head, Department of Management, London School of Economics and Political Science, since 2006; *b* 7 June 1952; *s* of Maurice Estrin and Irene Estrin (*née* Redhouse); *m* 1985, Jennifer Ann Lockwood; one *s* three *d. Educ:* St John's Coll., Cambridge (BA 1974; MA 1977); Univ. of Sussex (DPhil 1979). Lectr, Southampton Univ., 1977–84; Lectr, 1984–89, Sen. Lectr, 1989–90, in Econs, LSE, 1984–90; London Business School: Associate Prof. of Econs, 1990–94; Prof. of Economics, 1994–2006; Dir, CIS Middle Europe Centre, 1997–2000; Dep. Dean (Faculty and Academic Planning), 1998–2006; Res. Dir, Centre for New and Emerging Markets, 2000–06; Acting Dean, 2002. *Publications:* Self-Management: economic theory and Yugoslav practice, 1984; (jtly) Introduction to Microeconomics, 4th edn, 1993; (ed jtly) Competition and Competition Policy, 1993; Privatisation in Central and Eastern Europe, 1994; (ed jtly) Essential Readings in Economics, 1995; Foreign Direct Investment in Central and Eastern Europe, 1997; numerous academic papers. *Recreation:* family. *Address:* Department of Management, London School of Economics and Political Science, Houghton Street, WC2A 2AE. *T:* (020) 7955 6629; *e-mail:* s.estrin@lse.ac.uk.

ETCHELLS, (Dorothea) Ruth, MA, BD; Principal, St John's College with Cranmer Hall, University of Durham, 1979–88 (Hon. Fellow, St John's College, Durham, 1991); *b* 17 April 1931; *d* of late Walter and Ada Etchells. *Educ:* Merchant Taylor's School for Girls, Crosby, Liverpool; Universities of Liverpool (MA) and London (BD). Head of English Dept, Aigburth Vale High Sch., Liverpool, 1959; Lectr in English, 1963, Sen. Lectr in English and Resident Tutor, 1965, Chester College of Education; Trevelyan College, Univ. of Durham: Resident Tutor and part-time Lectr in English, 1968; Vice Principal, 1972; Sen. Lectr, 1973; Mem. Council, Durham Univ., 1985–88. Examining Chaplain to Bishop of Bath and Wells, 1984–88. Member: Gen. Synod, 1985–95; Doctrine Commn, 1986–91; Crown Appointments Commn, 1987–96; Bishop's Council and Standing Cttee of Durham Diocesan Synod, 1975–97 (Chm., House of Laity, 1988–94); Council, Durham Cathedral, 2002–. Vice-Chm., Durham FHSA, 1990–96 (Chm., Med. Services Cttee, 1990–96). Mem., Governing Council, Ridley Coll., Cambridge, 1988–2003; Mem., Governing Body, Durham High Sch., 1995–2002. Trustee, Anvil, 1983–92; Mem. Trustees, Hosp. of God, Greatham, 1995–99. Hon. Vice-Pres., CMS, 1992–. DD Lambeth, 1992; Hon. DLitt Liverpool, 2003. *Publications:* Unafraid To Be, 1969; The Man with the Trumpet, 1970; A Model of Making, 1983; (ed) Poets and Prophets, 1988; Praying with the English Poets, 1990; Just as I am: personal prayers for every day, 1994; Set My People Free: a lay challenge to the Churches, 1996; A Reading of the Parables of Jesus, 1998; Safer than a Known Way: personal prayers for every day, vol. 1, 2006, The Rainbow-coloured Cross: personal prayers for every day, vol. 2, 2007. *Recreations:* friends, quiet, country walking, painting and work in stained glass. *Address:* 12 Dunelm Court, South Street, Durham DH1 4QX. *T:* (0191) 3841497.

ETHERINGTON, David Charles Lynch; QC 1998; a Recorder, since 2000; *b* 14 March 1953; *s* of late Charles Henry Etherington and Beryl Etherington (*née* Croft). *Educ:* Keble Coll., Oxford (BA 1976, MA 2001; Special DPSA (Distinction) 1977). Called to the Bar, Middle Temple, 1979, Bencher, 2005; Asst Recorder, 1997–2000. Hd of Chambers, 2005–. Chm., Professional Practice Cttee, Bar Council, 2006–08. Dep. Chancellor, Dio. Norwich, 2005–. *Address:* 18 Red Lion Court, EC4A 3EB. *T:* (020) 7520 6000.

ETHERINGTON, Stuart James; Chief Executive, National Council for Voluntary Organisations, since 1994; *b* 26 Feb. 1955; *s* of late Ronald Etherington and of Dorothy Etherington (*née* West). *Educ:* Sondes Place Sch., Dorking; Brunel Univ. (BSc Politics 1977); Essex Univ. (MA Soc. Sci. Planning 1981); London Business Sch. (MBA 1992); SOAS (MA Internat. Relns and Diplomacy 1999). Social Worker, London Borough of Hillingdon, 1977–79; Sen. Res. Officer, Joseph Rowntree Meml Trust, Circle 33, 1980–82; Policy Advr, BASW, 1982–84; Dir, Good Practices in Mental Health, 1984–87; Dir, Public Affairs, 1987–91, Chief Exec., 1991–94, RNID. Mem. Council, ESRC, 1998–2003. Trustee: CAF, 1995–2004; BITC, 1995–; Civicus, 2001–07 (Treas., 2004–07). Member: RIIA, 1997; IISS. Member: Council, Open Univ., 2002–07; Court, Greenwich Univ., 2004–. Visiting Professor: London South Bank Univ., 2002–; City Univ., 2003–. FRSA 1995. Hon. DSocSc Brunel, 2000. *Publications:* Mental Health and Housing, 1984; Emergency Duty Teams, 1985; The Sensitive Bureaucracy, 1986; Social Work and Citizenship, 1987. *Recreations:* reading biographies, theatre, opera, watching cricket and Charlton Athletic. *Address:* National Council for Voluntary Organisations, Regents Wharf, 8 All Saints Street, N1 9RL. *T:* (020) 7713 6161; 40 Walnut Tree Road, Greenwich, SE10 9EU. *T:* (020) 8305 1379. *Clubs:* National Liberal, Reform; Surrey CC.

ETHERINGTON, William; MP (Lab) Sunderland North, since 1992; *b* 17 July 1941; *m* 1963, Irene; two *d. Educ:* Monkwearmouth Grammar Sch.; Durham Univ. Apprentice fitter, Austin & Pickersgill shipyard, 1957–63; fitter, Dawdon Colliery, 1963–83; full-time NUM official, 1983–92. Mem., NUM, 1963– (Vice-Pres., NE Area, 1988–92). Mem., 1997–, Dep. Leader, 2002–, UK delegn to Council of Europe and WEU. Secretary: Miners' Parly Gp, 1994–; All-Party Against Fluoridation Gp, 1998–2006. *Address:* House of Commons, SW1A 0AA.

ETHERTON, Rt Hon. Sir Terence (Michael Elkan Barnet), Kt 2001; PC 2008; **Rt Hon. Lord Justice Etherton;** a Lord Justice of Appeal, since 2008; Chairman, Law Commission, 2006–Aug. 2009 (on secondment); *b* 21 June 1951; *s* of Alan Kenneth Etherton and Elaine Myrtle (*née* Maccoby); civil partnership 2006, Andrew Howard Stone. *Educ:* Holmewood House Sch., Tunbridge Wells; St Paul's Sch., London (Sen. Foundn Schol.); Corpus Christi Coll., Cambridge (Open Exhibnr; MA (History and Law); LLM; Hon. Fellow, 2007). FCIArb 1993. Called to the Bar, Gray's Inn, 1974 (Uthwatt Schol., 1972; Holker Sen. Award, 1974; Arden Atkin and Mould Prize, 1975; Bencher 1998); in practice, 1975–2000; QC 1990; a Dep. High Court Judge, 2000; a Judge of the High Court, Chancery Div., 2001–08. Mem., Bar Council, 1978–81; Chm., Young Barristers' Cttee of Bar Council, 1980–81; Mem., Lord Rawlinson's Cttee on the Constitution of the Senate of the Inns of Court and the Bar, 1985–86; Vice Chm., Chancery Bar Assoc., 1999–2001. Mem., Mental Health Review Tribunal, 1994–99; Chairman: Broadmoor Hosp. Authy, 1999–2001; West London Mental Health NHS Trust, 2000–01; Dir (non-exec.), Riverside Mental Health NHS Trust, 1992–99 (Chm., Ethics Forum, 1994–99). Claims Adjudicator, Savings and Investment Bank (IOM) Depositors' Compensation Scheme, 1993–94. Chm., DoE/MAFF Indep. Review Panel on designation of nitrate vulnerable zones under EC Nitrate Directive, 1995 (report published, 1995). Mem. Council, RHBNC, 1992–2002 (Hon. Fellow, Royal Holloway, London Univ., 2005); Chm., City Law Sch. Adv. Bd, City Univ., 2006–08. Blundell Meml Lect., 1996. FRSA 2000. Hon. LLD City, 2009. Captain, Cambridge Univ. Fencing Team, 1971–72; Mem., GB Sen. Internat. Fencing Team (Sabre), 1977–80 (World Championships, 1977, 1978, 1979); England Sabre Team Gold Medal, Commonwealth Fencing Championships, 1978; selected for Moscow Olympics, GB Fencing Team, 1980. *Publications:* articles in various legal jls. *Address:* (until Aug. 2009) The Law Commission, Steel House, 11 Tothill Street, SW1H 9LJ; Royal Courts of Justice, Strand, WC2A 2LL. *Club:* Hawks (Cambridge).

ETHIOPIA AND THE HORN OF AFRICA, Area Bishop of, since 2007; **Rt Rev Andrew John Proud;** *b* 27 March 1954; *s* of late John Gascoigne Proud and of Joan Denise Proud; *m* 1977, Hon. (Fiona) Janice, PhD, *d* of Baron Brain, *qv*; one *s* one *d. Educ:* King's Coll., London (BD 1979, AKC); Sch. of Oriental and African Studies, Univ. of London (MA 2001). Ordained deacon, 1980, priest, 1981; Asst Curate, Stansted Mountfitchet, 1980; Team Vicar, Borehamwood, 1983; Asst Priest, Bishop's Hatfield, 1990; Rector, E Barnet, 1992; Chaplain, St Matthew's, Addis Ababa, 2002; Bishop's Asst for the Horn of Africa, 2004; Canon of Cairo, 2005. *Recreations:* cooking, music, bird watching, reading. *Address:* c/o Anglican Church Office, PO Box 14601, Addis Ababa, Ethiopia. *T:* (11) 6623578.

ETIANG, Paul Orono, BA London; Chairman, Uganda Railways Corporation, since 2003; *b* 15 Aug. 1938; *s* of late Kezironi Orono and Mirabu Achom Orono; *m* 1967, Zahra Ali Foum; two *s* two *d. Educ:* Makerere Univ. Coll. Uganda Admin. Officer, 1962–64; Asst Sec., Foreign Affairs, 1964–65; 3rd Sec., 1965–66, 2nd Sec., 1966–67, Uganda Embassy, Moscow; 1st Sec., Uganda Mission to UN, New York, 1968; Counsellor, 1968–69, High Commissioner, 1969–71, Uganda High Commission, London; Chief of Protocol and Marshal of the Diplomatic Corps, Uganda, 1971; Permanent Sec., Uganda Min. of Foreign Affairs, 1971–73; Minister of State for Foreign Affairs, 1973; Minister of State in the President's office, 1974; Minister of Transport and Communications, July 1976, of Transport, Communications and Works, Mar. 1977, of Transport and Works, 1978; an Asst. Sec.-Gen., OAU, Addis Ababa, 1978–87; Minister for Regl Co-operation, March–Dec. 1988; Minister: of Commerce, 1989–91; of Information, 1991–96; Third Dep. Prime Minister, 1996–98; Minister: of Labour and Social Services, 1996–98; for Disaster Preparedness and Refugees, 1998–99. *Recreations:* chess, classical music, billiards. *Address:* Kampala, Uganda.

ETTEDGUI, Joseph; fashion designer and retailer; Joint Founder, and Chairman until 2005, Joseph Ltd; *b* Casablanca; *m* Isabelle; one *d*. Came to London, 1960; with brother opened hairdressing salon and clothes shop, King's Road, Chelsea; has opened over 2[illegible] Joseph shops, incl. outlets in London, Manchester, Leeds, and in USA, France and Germany. Contemporary Collection Award, British Fashion Awards, 2000.

EUROPE, Suffragan Bishop in; *see* Gibraltar in Europe, Suffragan Bishop of.

EUSTACE, Dudley Graham, FCA; Chairman, Smith & Nephew plc, 2000–06; *b* 3 July 1936; *s* of Albert and Mary Eustace; *m* 1964, Carol Diane Zakrajsek; two *d. Educ:* Cathedral Sch., Bristol; Univ. of Bristol (BA Econ). FCA 1972. John Barritt & Son, Hamilton, Bermuda, 1962; Internat. Resort Facilities, Ont, 1963; Aluminium Securities Ltd, Montreal, 1964–65; Aluminium Co. of Canada Ltd, Vancouver, 1966–69, Montreal, 1969–73; Alcan Aluminio America Latina, Buenos Aires, 1973–76, Rio de Janeiro, 1976–79; Empresa Nacional del Aluminio, Madrid, 1979–83; Alcan Aluminium Ltd, Montreal, 1983–84; British Alcan Aluminium PLC, Gerrards Cross, Bucks, 1984–87; BAe, 1987–92 (Finance Dir, 1988–92); Chief Financial Officer, 1992–97, Vice Pres., 1992, Exec. Vice Pres. and Dep. Chm., 1992–99, Philips Electronics NV, Eindhoven; Chm., Sendo Hldgs PLC, 2000–05; Chief Financial Officer, Royal Ahold NV, 2003; Member, Advisory Council: Bayerische Landesbank, Munich, 1995–99; Rothschilds, 2005–; Member, Supervisory Board: Aegon NV, 1997– (Chm. Bd, 2005–); Hagemeyer NV, 1999–2006; KLM Royal Dutch Airlines, 1999–2004; Charterhouse Vermogensbeheer BV, 1999–; KPN NV, 2000–; Stork NV, 2007–08; Mem. Bd, sonae.com SGPS, 1999–2003. Member: Council, ECGD, 1988–92; Bd, Assoc. for Monetary Union in Europe, 1992–99; Bd, Amsterdam Inst. of Finance, 2001–05. Mem. Council, Univ. of Surrey, 2005– (Vice Chm., 2007). Liveryman, Chartered Accountants' Co., 1991. *Recreations:* gardening, reading. *Address:* Avalon, Old Barn Lane, Churt, Surrey GU10 2NA.

EUSTON, Earl of; James Oliver Charles FitzRoy, MA, FCA; *b* 13 Dec. 1947; *s* and *heir* of 11th Duke of Grafton, *qv*; *m* 1972, Lady Clare Kerr, MA, *d* of 12th Marquess of Lothian, KCVO; one *s* four *d. Educ:* Eton; Magdalene Coll., Cambridge (MA). Dir, Smith St Aubyn & Co. (Holdings) plc, 1980–86; Executive Director: Enskilda Securities, 1982–87; Jamestown Investments, 1987–91; Finance Director: Central Capital Hldgs, 1988–91; Capel-Cure Myers Capital Management, 1988–97. *Heir: s* Viscount Ipswich, *qv. Address:* The Racing Stables, Euston, Thetford, Norfolk IP24 2QT. *Club:* Turf (Chm.).

EVAN, Prof. Gerard Ian, PhD; FRS 2004; FMedSci; Gerson and Barbara Bass Bakar Distinguished Professor of Cancer Biology, University of California, San Francisco, since 1999; *b* 17 Aug. 1955; *s* of Robert Evan (*née* Ekstein) and Gwendoline Evan; *m* 1984, Jane Lindsay McLennan; one *s* one *d. Educ:* St Peter's Coll., Oxford (BA, MA); King's Coll., Cambridge (PhD 1982). Asst Mem., Ludwig Inst. for Cancer Res., Cambridge, 1984–88; Principal Scientist, ICRF, London, 1988–99; Royal Soc. Napier Res. Prof., UCL, 1996–99. Mem., EMBO, 1996. FMedSci 1999. Joseph Steiner Prize in Cancer Res., 1996. *Publications:* contrib. numerous res. pubns to learned jls. *Recreations:* hiking, music, mountain biking. *Address:* Cancer Research Institute, Comprehensive Cancer Center, University of California, 2340 Sutter Street, San Francisco, CA 94143–0875, USA; *e-mail:* gevan@cc.ucsf.edu.

EVANS; *see* Parry-Evans and Parry Evans.

EVANS, family name of **Baroness Blackstone** and **Barons Evans of Parkside, Evans of Temple Guiting, Evans of Watford** and **Mountevans**.

EVANS OF PARKSIDE, Baron *cr* 1997 (Life Peer), of St Helens, in the co. of Merseyside; **John Evans;** Chairman of Labour Party, 1991–92; *b* 19 Oct. 1930; *s* of late James Evans, miner and Margaret (*née* Robson); *m* 1959, Joan Slater; two *s* one *d. Educ:* Jarrow Central School. Apprentice Marine Fitter, 1946–49 and 1950–52; Nat. Service Royal Engrs, 1949–50; Engr, Merchant Navy, 1952–55; joined AUEW (later AEU), 1952; joined Labour Party, 1955; worked in various industries as fitter, ship-building and repairing, steel, engineering, 1955–65, 1968–74. Mem. Hebburn UDC, 1962, Leader 1969, Chm. 1972; Sec./Agent Jarrow CLP, 1965–68. MP (Lab) Newton, Feb. 1974–1983, St Helens, North, 1983–97. An Asst Govt Whip, 1978–79; Opposition Whip, 1979–80; PPS to Leader of Labour Party, 1980–83; opposition spokesman on employment, 1983–87. Mem., European Parlt, 1975–78; Chm., Regional Policy, Planning and Transport Cttee, European Parlt, 1976–78. Mem., Lab Party NEC, 1982–96. *Recreations:* watching football, reading, gardening. *Address:* 6 Kirkby Road, Culcheth, Warrington, Cheshire WA3 4BS. *Clubs:* Labour (Earlestown); Daten (Culcheth).

EVANS OF TEMPLE GUITING, Baron *cr* 2000 (Life Peer), of Temple Guiting in the co. of Gloucestershire; **Matthew Evans,** CBE 1998; Adviser to Chief Executive Officer

EFG Private Bank Ltd, since 2007; a Lord in Waiting (Government Whip), 2002–07; Chairman, Faber & Faber Ltd, 1981–2002 (Managing Director, 1972–93); *b* 7 Aug. 1941; *s* of late George Ewart Evans, and Florence Ellen Evans; *m* 1st, 1966, Elizabeth Amanda (*née* Mead) (marr. diss. 1991); two *s*; 2nd, 1991, Caroline (*née* Michel); two *s* one *d*. *Educ:* Friends' Sch., Saffron Walden; LSE (BScEcon). Bookselling, 1963–64; Faber & Faber, 1964–2002. Chairman: National Book League, 1982–84; English Stage Company, 1984–90; Library and Information Commn, 1995–99 (Chm. Working Gp on New Library: The People's Network, 1997); Re:source (Museums, Libraries and Archives Council), 2000–02. Dir, Which? Ltd, 1997–2000. Member: Council, Publishers Assoc., 1978–84; Literary Adv. Panel, British Council, 1986–97; DCMS Adv. Panel for Public Appts, 1996–2002; Arts Council Nat. Lottery Adv. Panel, 1997–99; Univ. for Industry Adv. Gp, 1997; Sir Richard Eyre's Working Gp on Royal Opera House, 1997; Arts and Humanities Res. Bd, 1998–2002. Mem., Franco-British Soc., 1981–95. Governor, BFI, 1982–97 (Vice Chm., 1996–97). FRSA 1990; Hon. FRCA 1999; Hon. FCLIP (Hon. FLA 1999). *Recreation:* cricket. *Address:* House of Lords, SW1A 0PW. *Club:* Groucho (Founder Mem., and Dir, 1982–97).

EVANS OF WATFORD, Baron *cr* 1998 (Life Peer), of Chipperfield in the co. of Hertfordshire; **David Charles Evans;** Chairman, Senate Consulting Ltd, since 2003; *b* 30 Nov. 1942; *s* of Arthur and Phyllis Evans; *m* 1966, June Scaldwell; one *s* one *d*; one *s*. *Educ:* Hampden Secondary Sch.; Watford Coll. Apprentice printer, Stone and Cox Ltd, 1957. Founded: Centurion Press Ltd, 1971; (with Susanne Lawrence) Personnel Publications Ltd, 1975; Centurion Press bv, 1975; Chairman: Centurion Press Gp, 1971–2002; Senate Media (formerly Centurion Media) Gp bv, 1974–; Personnel Publications Ltd, 1981–; Redactive Publishing (formerly Centurion Publishing) Ltd, 1995–; TU Ink Ltd, 2005–; MuTUal Ink, 2005–; Indigo Publishing Ltd; Evans Mitchell Books; non-executive Director: Partnership Sourcing Ltd, 2002–; Care Capital plc. Director: RAF Trading Co.; Watford Community Events; Dep. Chm., Internat. Medical Educn Trust; Mem. Develt Bd, UCL Hosp. Charitable Trust. Trustee, RAF Mus. Hon. Fellow, Cancer Research UK. Freeman, Marketors' Co., 1991. FCIM 1991; FCGI 2001. *Publications:* articles on marketing, print management and purchasing. *Recreations:* theatre, art, reading, travel. *Address:* 28 Eagle Wharf, 138 Grosvenor Road, Pimlico, SW1V 3JS. *T:* (020) 7233 6288; Senate Consulting Ltd, The Old Forge, Forge Mews, 16 Church Street, Rickmansworth, Herts WD3 1DH. *T:* (01923) 713030, *Fax:* (01923) 713040; *e-mail:* lordevans@senateconsulting.co.uk.

EVANS, Alun; *see* Evans, T. A.

EVANS, Alun Trevor Bernard; Director General, Transformation, Department for Communities and Local Government, since 2006; *b* 8 Dec. 1958; *s* of Thomas Francis Evans and late Marjorie Gladys Evans (*née* Macken); *m* 1986, Ingrid Elisabeth Dammers; two *d*. *Educ:* County Sch., Ashford, Middx; Essex Univ. (BA Hons); Birmingham Univ. (MPhil 1983). Civil Servant, Dept of Employment, subseq. DfEE, 1983–98: Private Sec. to Paymaster Gen. and Minister for Employment, 1986; Asst Regl Dir, Eastern Reg., 1992–93; Hd, Nuclear Safety Policy Div., HSE, 1993–94; Principal Private Sec. to Sec. of State for Employment, 1994–95, to Sec. of State for Educn and Employment, 1995–98; Hd, Strategic Communications Unit, Prime Minister's Office, 1998–2000; Dir of Communications, DETR, then DTLR, 2000–01; Sec. to Inquiry into lessons to be learned from foot and mouth disease outbreak, 2001–02; Cabinet Office, 2002–03; Dir of Civil Resilience, ODPM, subseq. of Fire and Resilience, DCLG, 2003–06. *Recreations:* political history, family, cricket, running, art, opera. *Address:* Department for Communities and Local Government, Eland House, Bressenden Place, SW1E 5DU. *Clubs:* Occasionals, Mandarins Cricket.

See also R. J. E. Evans.

EVANS, Amanda Louise Elliot, (Mrs A. S. Duncan); freelance writer, editor and editorial consultant, since 1997; *b* 19 May 1958; *d* of late Brian Royston Elliot Evans and of June Annabella (*née* Gilderdale); *m* 1989, Andrew Sinclair Duncan; one *s* two *d*. *Educ:* Tonbridge Girls' Grammar Sch. Editorial writer, Interiors magazine, 1981–83; Consultant Editor, Mitchell Beazley Publishers, 1983–84; freelance writer and stylist on A la carte, Tatler, Country Homes & Interiors, Sunday Times, 1984–86; Dep. Editor, April–Oct. 1986, Editor, 1986–96, Homes & Gardens. *Publications:* Homes and Gardens Bedrooms, 1997; Making the Most of Living Rooms, 1998. *Recreations:* mountain walking, opera, camping. *Address:* 98 Addison Gardens, W14 0DR. *T:* (020) 7603 1574.

EVANS, Anne Celia; *see* Segall, A. C.

EVANS, Dame Anne (Elizabeth Jane), DBE 2000; soprano; *b* 20 Aug. 1941; *d* of late David and Eleanor, (Nellie), Evans; *m* 1st, 1962, John Heulyn Jones (marr. diss. 1981); 2nd, 1981, John Philip Lucas. *Educ:* Royal Coll. of Music; Conservatoire de Genève. Début, Annina in La Traviata, Grand Théâtre, Geneva, 1967; UK début, Mimi in La Bohème, Coliseum, 1968; Principal soprano, ENO, 1968–78; subseq. major rôles at Metropolitan Opera House, NY, San Francisco Opera, Deutsche Oper, Berlin, Dresden State Opera, Vienna State Opera, Paris Opéra, Rome Opera, Théâtre de la Monnaie, Brussels, Teatro Colón, Buenos Aires, Royal Opera House, Covent Garden, WNO, Scottish Opera; rôles include: Brünnhilde in Der Ring des Nibelungen (incl. Bayreuth Fest., 1989–92), Isolde in Tristan und Isolde, Sieglinde in Die Walküre, Elsa in Lohengrin, Elisabeth in Tannhäuser, Senta in Der fliegende Holländer, Leonore in Fidelio, Cassandre in Les Troyens, Chrysothemis in Elektra, Marschallin in Der Rosenkavalier, Ariadne in Ariadne auf Naxos; recitals incl. Edinburgh Fest., Wigmore Hall; Last Night of the Proms, 1997. FRWCMD (FWCMD 1996). Hon. DMus Kent, 2005. *Recreations:* cooking, gardening. *Address:* c/o Ingpen & Williams Ltd, 7 St George's Court, 131 Putney Bridge Road, SW15 2PA.

EVANS, Anthony; *see* Evans, D. A.

EVANS, Sir Anthony (Adney), 2nd Bt *cr* 1920; *b* 5 Aug. 1922; *s* of Sir Walter Harry Evans, 1st Bt, and Margaret Mary, *y d* of late Thomas Adney Dickens; *S* father, 1954; *m*; two *s* one *d*. *Educ:* Shrewsbury; Merton Coll., Oxford.

EVANS, Anthony Clive Varteg, FCIL; Head Master, King's College School, Wimbledon, 1997–2008; *b* 11 Oct. 1945; *s* of Edward Varteg Evans and Doris Lilian Evans; *m* 1968, Danielle Jacqueline Nicole Bégasse (*d* 1997); two *s*. *Educ:* De la Salle Grammar Sch., London; St Peter's Coll., Oxford (MA); University Coll. London (MPhil); Inst. of Educn, London Univ. (Advanced DipEd). FCIL (FIL 1975). Assistant Master: Eastbourne Coll., 1967–72; Winchester Coll., 1972–77; Hd of Mod. Langs and Hd of Humanities, Dulwich Coll., 1977–83; Headmaster, Portsmouth Grammar Sch., 1983–97. Headmasters' and Headmistresses' Conference: Chm., 1996; Mem., 1985–94, Chm., 1990–94, Acad. Policy Cttee; Mem., Common Entrance Cttee, 1988–90; Mem., Cttee, 1989–97; Mem., HMC/GSA Univ. Cttee, 1993–2002 (Co-Chm., 1993–95). Member: Admiralty Interview Bd, 1985–97; Nat. Curriculum Council, 1989–91; ISC Council, 1996–2000; HEFCE, 1999–2002; Chm., ISC Adv. Council, 1997–99; Co-Chm., ISC Unity Cttee, 1997–99; Chm., Large Ind. Day Schs Gp, 2002–06. Fellow, Winchester Coll., Hants, 1997–2006; Governor: Mall Sch., Twickenham, 1997–2007; Sevenoaks Sch., 2000– (Chm., 2008–); Ecole Saint-Georges, Montreux, 2000–07; Perse Sch., Cambridge, 2003–05; Lancing Coll., 2008–; Marlborough Coll., 2008–. FKC 2008. *Publication:* Souvenirs de la Grande Guerre, 1985. *Recreations:* France, theatre, Southampton FC, avoiding dinner parties. *Address:* 3 Lewcos House, 57–63 Regency Street, SW1P 4AF; 27 rue de France, Nice 06000, France. *Club:* East India.

EVANS, Prof. Anthony Glyn, PhD; FRS 2001; FREng; Alcoa Chair and Professor of Materials and Mechanical Engineering, University of California, Santa Barbara, since 2001; *b* 4 Dec. 1942; *s* of William Glyn Evans and Annie May Evans; *m* 1967, Trisha Cross; three *d*. *Educ:* Imperial Coll., London (BSc 1964; PhD 1967). Member, Technical Staff, AERE, 1967–71; Nat. Bureau of Standards, 1971–74; Gp Leader, Rockwell Internat. Sci. Center, 1974–78; Prof., Dept of Materials Sci. and Mineral Engrg, Univ. of Calif, Berkeley, 1978–85; Alcoa Prof. and Chair, Materials Dept, UCSB, 1985–94; Gordon McKay Prof. of Materials Engrg, Div. of Applied Scis, Harvard Univ., 1994–98; Gordon Wu Prof. of Mechanical and Aerospace Engrg, and Dir, Princeton Materials Inst., Princeton Univ., 1998–2001. FREng 2006. Member: NAE, 1995; Amer. Acad. Arts and Scis, 2000; NAS, 2005. *Publications:* Metal Foams: a design guide, 2000; contribs to numerous scientific pubns in fields of materials and mechanical engrg. *Address:* Department of Materials, University of California, Santa Barbara, CA 93106–5050, USA. *T:* (805) 8937839, *Fax:* (805) 8938486; *e-mail:* agevans@engineering.ucsb.edu.

EVANS, Rt Hon. Sir Anthony (Howell Meurig), Kt 1985; RD 1968; PC 1992; arbitrator; a Justice of the Court of Appeal, Bermuda, since 2003; Chief Justice, DIFC Court, Dubai, since 2005; *b* 11 June 1934; *s* of late His Honour David Meurig Evans and Joy Diedericke (*née* Sander); *m* 1963, Caroline Mary Fyffe Mackie, *d* of late Edwin Gordon Mackie; one *s* two *d*. *Educ:* Bassaleg Sec. Grammar Sch., Mon; Shrewsbury Sch.; St John's Coll., Cambridge (BA 1957; LLB 1958). Nat. Service, RNVR, 1952–54 (Lt-Comdr RNR). Called to Bar, Gray's Inn, 1958 (Arden Scholar and Birkenhead Scholar; Bencher, 1979; Treas., 2000); QC 1971; a Recorder, 1972–84; a Presiding Judge, Wales and Chester Circuit, 1986–88; a Judge of the High Court of Justice, QBD, 1984–92; Judge in charge of the Commercial Court, 1991–92; a Lord Justice of Appeal, 1992–2000. Dep. Chm., Inf. Tribunal (Pres., Nat. Security Appeals), 2000–04; Vice-Pres., Internat. Cttee on Holocaust Era Insurance Claims Appeal Tribunal, 2000–06. Mem., Melbourne, Vic, Bar, 1975–84, Hon. Mem., 1985. Dep. Chm., Boundary Commn for Wales, 1989–92. Visitor: Cardiff Univ., 1999–; SOAS, 2002–. Pres., Bar Musical Soc., 1998–. Hon. Fellow, Internat. Acad. of Trial Lawyers, 1985; FCIArb 1986 (Patron, Wales Br., 1988–98; Hon. Pres., 1998–2001; Companion, 2007). A Vice President: British Maritime Law Assoc., 1992–; Assoc. of Average Adjusters, 1997–. Freeman, 2000, Liveryman, 2001, Shipwrights' Co. *Publication:* (Jt Editor) The Law of the Air (Lord McNair), 1964. *Recreations:* sailing, music. *Address:* Essex Court Chambers, 24 Lincoln's Inn Fields, WC2A 3EG. *Clubs:* Royal Yacht Squadron; Royal Welsh Yacht.

EVANS, Prof. Anthony John, PhD, FCLIP; Professor in Department of Information and Library Studies (formerly Library and Information Studies), 1973–95, now Emeritus Professor, and Director, Alumni Office, 1992–95, Loughborough University of Technology, now Loughborough University; *b* 1 April 1930; *s* of William John and Marian Audrey (*née* Young); *m* 1954, Anne (*née* Horwell); two *d*. *Educ:* Queen Elizabeth's Hosp., Bristol (Pres., Old Boys' Soc., 1999); Sch. of Pharmacy and University College, Univ. of London. BPharm, PhD. Lectr in Pharm. Eng. Sci., Sch. of Pharmacy, Univ. of London, 1954–58; Librarian, Sch. of Pharmacy, Univ. of London, 1958–63; University Librarian, 1964–91, and Dean, Sch. of Educnl Studies, 1973–76, Loughborough Univ. of Technology. Pres., IATUL, 1970–75 (Bd Mem. and Treasurer, 1968–70; Hon. Life Mem., 1976–); Mem. Exec. Bd, IFLA, 1983–89 (Treas., 1985–89; Consultative Cttee, 1968–76; Standing Cttee on Sci. and Tech. Libraries, 1977–87; Standing Cttee on Univ. Libraries, 1989–93; Chm., Cttee on Access to Information and Freedom of Expression, 1995–97); Pres., Commonwealth Library Assoc., 1994–96; ASLIB: Vice-Pres., 1985–88; Mem. Council, 1970–80, 1985–88; Internat. Relations Cttee, 1974–85; Annual Lecture, 1985; BSI: Mem. Bd, 1984–86; Chm., Documentation Standards Cttee, 1980–86 (Mem., 1976–86); Member: Inf. Systems Council, 1980–86. Member: Adv. Cttee, Sci. Ref. Library, 1975–83; Vice-Chancellors and Principals Cttee on Libraries, 1972–77; Jt UNESCO/ICSU Cttee for establishment of UNISIST, 1968–71; Internat. Cttee, LA, 1985–96; Adv. Council to Bd of Dirs of Engineering Information Inc., USA, 1986–91; Chm., Adv. Gp on Documentation Standards, ISO, 1983–85; consultancy work for British Council, ODA, UNESCO, UNIDO, World Bank in Africa, Asia and Latin America, especially China, Kenya and Mexico. Pres., Jaguars Wheelchair Basketball Club, 1997–2004. Hon. FCLIP (Hon. FLA 1990). Medal IFLA, 1989. *Publications:* (with D. Train) Bibliography of the tabletting of medicinal substances, 1964, suppl. 1965; (with R. G. Rhodes and S. Keenan) Education and training of users of scientific and technical information, 1977; articles in librarianship and documentation. *Recreations:* genealogy, sport, especially wheelchair basketball. *Address:* The Moorings, Mackleys Lane, North Muskham, Newark, Notts NG23 6EY. *T:* (01636) 700174.

EVANS, Anthony Thomas; a District Judge (Magistrates' Courts) (formerly Metropolitan Stipendiary Magistrate), since 1990; *b* 29 Sept. 1943; *s* of late Emlyn Roger Evans and Dorothy Evans; *m* 1st, 1965, Gillian Celia Mather (*d* 1988); one *s*; 2nd, 1991, Margaret Elizabeth Ryles (*née* Howorth); one step *s* one step *d*. *Educ:* Bishop Gore Grammar Sch., Swansea; Univ. of Manchester (LLB 1965; LLM 1968). Asst Lectr, Univ. of Manchester, 1965–68; admitted Solicitor, 1971; Partner: Haye & Reid, 1971–85; Evans & Co., 1985–89; sole practitioner, 1989–90. Chairman: Inner London Family Courts, 1991–2006; Inner London Youth Courts, 1993–2006. Mem., Criminal Procedure Rules Cttee, 2004–07. Mem., British Acad. of Forensic Scis, 1994. *Recreations:* reading, music, theatre. *Address:* c/o Chief Magistrate's Office, City of Westminster Magistrates' Court, 70 Horseferry Road, SW1P 2AX.

EVANS, Carole Denise M.; *see* Mills-Evans.

EVANS, Christina Hambley, (Lady Evans); *see* Brown, Tina.

EVANS, Christopher; radio and television presenter; Executive Producer and Writer, UMTV, since 2002; *b* 1 April 1966; *m* 1991, Carol McGiffen (marr. diss.); *m* 2001, Billie Piper (marr. diss. 2007); *m* 2007, Natasha Shishmanian; one *d* from a previous relationship. Started broadcasting career with Piccadilly Radio, Manchester; *radio:* producer and presenter, GLR; presenter: Radio One Breakfast Show, BBC, 1995–97; Virgin Radio Breakfast Show, 1997–2001; The Chris Evans Show, 2005–06, Drive Time Show, 2006–, BBC Radio 2; *televison:* presenter, Power Station, BSB Channel; Channel 4: co-presenter, The Big Breakfast, 1992–93; devised, wrote and presented, Don't Forget Your Toothbrush, 1993 (BAFTA Award, 1995); TFI Friday, 1997–2000. Chairman: Ginger Prodns, 1993–2000; Ginger Media Gp, 1997–2000; Virgin Radio, 1997–2001. Radio Personality of the Year, TRIC, 1997; Sony Radio Awards for Entertainment Personality and Music Radio Personality, 2007. *Address:* UMTV Ltd, Unit 315 First Floor, Highgate Studios, 53/79 Highgate Road, NW5 1TL.

EVANS, Christopher Charles, MD; FRCP, FRCPI; Consultant Physician, Cardiothoracic Centre and Royal Liverpool University Hospital, 1974–2003; President and Chairman, Medical Defence Union, since 2006 (Vice President and Vice Chairman, 2001–06); *b* 2 Oct. 1941; *s* of Robert Percy Evans and Nora Carson Evans; *m* 1966, Dr Susan Fuld; one *s* two *d*. *Educ:* Wade Deacon Grammar Sch., Widnes; Univ. of Liverpool Med. Sch. (MB ChB 1964; MD 1973). MRCP 1968, FRCP 1979; FRCPI 1997. Hon. Sen. Lectr, Univ. of Liverpool, 1974–2003. Consulting Medical Officer: Royal Sun Alliance, 1977–2005; Swiss Life, 1990–2005. Pres., Liverpool Med. Instn, 1991–92. Academic Vice Pres., RCP, 2001–03. Chm., NW Reg., British Lung Foundn, 1993–2000. *Publications:* (ed jtly) Symptoms and Signs in Clinical Medicine, 12th edn 1997; contrib. on general med. and thoracic topics, Thorax, BMJ, Lancet. *Recreations:* tennis, ski-ing, fell-walking, watching Liverpool FC. *Address:* Lagom, Glendyke Road, Liverpool L18 6JR. *T:* (0151) 724 5386; *e-mail:* christoffe58@hotmail.com. *Clubs:* Reform; XX, Artists (Liverpool).

EVANS, Rev. Prof. Christopher Francis, FBA 1991; MA; Professor of New Testament Studies, King's College, London, 1962–77, now Emeritus Professor, University of London; *b* 7 Nov. 1909; 2nd *s* of Frank and Beatrice Evans; *m* 1941, Elna Mary Pasco (*d* 1980), *d* of Walter and Elizabeth Burt; one *s*, and one step *d* (one step *s* decd). *Educ:* King Edward's Sch., Birmingham; Corpus Christi Coll., Cambridge. Asst Curate, St Barnabas, Southampton, 1934–38; Tutor Schol. Canc. Linc., 1938–44; Chaplain and Divinity Lecturer, Lincoln Training Coll., 1944–48; Chaplain, Fellow and Lecturer in Divinity, Corpus Christi Coll., Oxford, 1948–58, Emeritus Fellow, 1977; Lightfoot Prof. of Divinity in the University of Durham and Canon of Durham Cathedral, 1959–62; Vis. Fellow, Trevelyan Coll., Durham, 1982–83. Select Preacher, University of Oxford, 1955–57; Proctor in Convocation for University of Oxford, 1955–58; Exam. Chaplain: to Bishop of Bristol, 1948–58; to Bishop of Durham, 1958–62; to Archbishop of Canterbury, 1962–74; to Bishop of Lichfield, 1969–75. FKC, 1970. Hon. Fellow, Ripon Coll., Cuddesdon, 2005. Hon. DLitt Southampton, 1977; Hon. DD Glasgow, 1987. *Publications:* Christology and Theology, 1961; The Lord's Prayer, 1963; The Beginning of the Gospel, 1968; Resurrection and the New Testament, 1970; (ed jtly) The Cambridge History of the Bible: vol. I, From the Beginnings to Jerome, 1970; Is 'Holy Scripture' Christian?, 1971; Explorations in Theology 2, 1977; The Theology of Rhetoric, 1988; Saint Luke, 1990; contribs to Journal of Theological Studies, Theology and Religious Studies, to Studies in the Gospels and to Christian Faith and Communist Faith. *Recreation:* fishing. *Address:* 4 Church Close, Cuddesdon, Oxford OX44 9HD. *T:* (01865) 874406.

EVANS, Dr (Christopher) Paul; Strategic Director of Regeneration and Neighbourhoods, London Borough of Southwark, since 2001; *b* 25 Dec. 1948; *s* of Colwyn and late Margery Evans; *m* 1971, Margaret Beckett; two *d*. *Educ:* St Julian's High Sch., Newport; Trinity Coll., Cambridge (MA, DipArch, PhD). Department of the Environment, subseq. of the Environment, Transport and the Regions, then Department for Transport, Local Government and the Regions, later Office of the Deputy Prime Minister, 1975–2001: Private Sec. to Permanent Sec.,1978–80; Principal, 1980; Asst Sec., 1985; Under Sec., 1993; Dir, Urban Policy Unit, 1997–2001. *Address:* Regeneration Department, Council Offices, Chiltern House, Portland Street, SE17 2ES. *T:* (020) 7525 5501; *e-mail:* paul.evans@southwark.gov.uk.

EVANS, Sir Christopher (Thomas), Kt 2001; OBE 1995; PhD; CBiol, FIBiol; CChem, FRSC; Founder and Chairman, Merlin Biosciences Ltd, since 1996; *b* 29 Nov. 1957; *s* of Cyril and Jean Evans; *m* 1985, Judith Anne; two *s* two *d*. *Educ:* Imperial Coll., London (BSc 1979; ARCS 1979); Univ. of Hull (PhD). CBiol 1994, FIBiol 1994; CChem 1995; FRSC 1995. Postdoctoral Res., Univ. of Michigan, 1983; Alleix Inc., Toronto, 1984–86; Genzyme Biochemicals Ltd, Maidstone, 1986–87; Founder and Director: Enzymatix Ltd, 1987–; Chiroscience plc, 1992–; Celsis Internat. plc, 1992– (Chm., 1998–); Cerebrus Ltd, 1995–; Founder, Director and Chairman: Toad Innovations plc, 1993–; Merlin Scientific Services Ltd, 1995–; Enviros Ltd, 1995–; Cyclacel Ltd, 1996–; Dir, Microscience Ltd, 1997. Founder: Merlin Fund, 1996; Merlin Biosciences Fund. Mem., Prime Minister's Council for Sci. and Technol. FRSA 1995; FMedSci 2003; Fellow: Bath Univ.; Univ. of Wales, Aberystwyth. Hon. Prof., Univs of Manchester, Liverpool, Exeter and Bath, and Imperial Coll., London; Hon. Fellow: UWCC, 1996; Univ. of Wales Swansea, 1996; Hon. FREng 2005. Hon. DSc: Hull, 1995; Nottingham, 1995; East Anglia, 1998; Cranfield, 1998; Bath, 2000. Henderson Meml Medal, Porton Down, 1997; SCI Centenary Medal, 1998; RSC Interdisciplinary Medal, 1999. *Publications:* numerous scientific papers and patents. *Recreations:* wife, Rugby, gym, fly-fishing, electric guitar. *Address:* Merlin Biosciences, 33 King Street, St James's, SW1Y 6RJ. *T:* (020) 7811 4000.

EVANS, Air Vice-Marshal Clive Ernest, CBE 1982; DL; Senior Directing Staff (Air), Royal College of Defence Studies, 1988–91, retired; *b* 21 April 1937; *s* of Leslie Roberts Evans and Mary Kathleen Butcher; *m* 1963, Therese Goodrich; one *s* one *d*. *Educ:* St Dunstan's Coll., Catford. Flying training, RAF, 1955–56; graduated as pilot, 1956, as qualified flying instr, 1960; served on Vampires, Jet Provosts, Canberras, Lightnings and F111s (exchange tour with USAF), 1960–72; RAF Staff Coll., 1972; PSO to Controller Aircraft, 1973; OC No 24 Sqn (Hercules), 1974–76; Nat. Defence Coll., 1976–77; DS RAF Staff Coll., 1977–79; Head of RAF Presentation Team, 1979–81; OC RAF Lyneham, 1981–83; RCDS, 1984; COS and Dep. Comdr, British Forces Falkland Is, 1985; Dep. Air Sec., 1985–88. Pres., Surrey Wing, ATC. DL Greater London, 1997. *Recreations:* reading, cricket, golf, gardening. *Address:* 43 Purley Bury Close, Purley, Surrey CR8 1HW. *T:* (020) 8660 8115. *Club:* Royal Air Force.

EVANS, Colin Rodney; Director, Weapon Systems Research Laboratory, Defence Science and Technology Organisation, Adelaide, 1989–91; *b* 5 June 1935; *s* of John Evans and Annie (*née* Lawes); *m* 1963, Jennifer MacIntosh; two *d*. *Educ:* Bridlington Sch.; Woolwich Polytechnic; Imperial Coll., London. BSc(Eng); HND; MIMechE. Scientific Officer, ARDE (now RARDE), 1959–60; Lectr, RNC, Greenwich, 1960–61; Scientific Officer, then Sen. Scientific Officer and PSO, ARDE, 1961–69; SO to Chief Scientist (Army), MoD, 1969–71; British Defence Staff, Washington, 1971–73; SPSO, RARDE, 1973–79; Dep. Dir, Scientific and Technical Intell., MoD, 1979–81; seconded to Sir Derek Rayner's study team on efficiency in govt, 1981; RCDS, 1982; Dep. Dir (1), RARDE, 1983–84; Asst Under Sec. of State, MoD, Dep. Dir (Vehicles) and Hd of RARDE (Chertsey), 1985–89. President: Kent Squash Rackets Assoc., 1992–; Maudslay Soc., 1993–99. *Recreations:* travel, tennis, bird watching, stamp collecting. *Address:* c/o HSBC, 105 Mount Pleasant, Tunbridge Wells TN1 1QP.

EVANS, Dr (Daniel) John (Owen); President and Executive Director, Oregon Bach Festival, since 2007; editor, private diaries of Benjamin Britten; *b* 17 Nov. 1953; *s* of John Leslie Evans and Avis Evans (*née* Jones). *Educ:* Gowerton Boys' Grammar Sch.; University Coll., Cardiff (BMus 1975; MA 1976; PhD 1984). ATCL 1974. First Res. Schol., Britten-Pears Liby and Archive, Aldeburgh, Suffolk, 1980–84; Music Producer, BBC Radio 3, 1985–89; Sen. Producer, BBC Singers, 1989–92; Chief Producer, Series, BBC Radio 3, 1992–93; Head of Music Dept, BBC Radio 3, 1993–97; Head of Classical Music, BBC Radio, 1997–2000; Head of Music Programming, BBC Radio 3, 2000–06. Artistic Director: Volte Face Opera, 1986–89; Covent Garden Chamber Orch., 1990–94; Me South Bank Music Adv. Panel, 1994–96. Chm., IMZ Audio Gp, 1996–2000. Dir, T Britten Estate, 1999–; Chairman: Concentric Circles Theatre Co., 1999–20 DreamArts, 2005–07. Chairman: Opera Jury for Royal Phil. Soc. Awards, 2000– Radio Music Jury, Prix Italia, 2005; BBC Choir of the Year, 2005; Mem. Panel, Laure Olivier Awards, 2000–02; Juror: BBC Singer of the World, Cardiff, 2003 and 2005; Mu Broadcaster of the Year, Sony Radio Acad. Awards, 2006. Exec. Trustee, Peter Pe Award, 1989–92; Trustee: Masterprize Composing Competition, 1996–2001; Britte Pears Foundn, 1999–2007; Britten-Pears Will Trust, 2006–; Britten Family and Charita Settlement, 2006–. Vice Pres., Welsh Music Guild, 2005–. Prix Italia Award and Cha Heidsieck Award, 1989; Royal Philharmonic Soc. Award, 1994; Sony Radio Awa 1997. *Publications:* (with D. Mitchell) Benjamin Britten: pictures from a life 1913–19 1978; (ed) Benjamin Britten: his life and operas, by Eric Walter White, rev. edn 19 contributions to: A Britten Companion, 1984; A Britten Source Book, 1987; Leavi Home: the diaries of the young Benjamin Britten, 2009; ENO, Royal Opera Hse a Cambridge Opera guides on Britten's Peter Grimes, Gloriana, The Turn of the Screw a Death in Venice. *Recreations:* theatre, musicals, cooking, fine wines, entertaining, trav *Address:* Oregon Bach Festival, 1257 University of Oregon, Eugene, OR 97403–12 USA; *e-mail:* bachfest@oregon.edu.

EVANS, Dr David; *see* Evans, Dr W. D.

EVANS, David, CBE 1992; Director-General, National Farmers' Union, 1985– (Deputy Director-General, 1984–85); Director, Federation of Agricultural Co-operativ UK, 1995–2001; *b* 7 Dec. 1935; *yr s* of late William Price Evans and Ella Mary Evans; 1960, Susan Carter Connal, *yr d* of late Dr John Connal and Antoinette Connal; one *s* (o *d* decd). *Educ:* Welwyn Garden City Grammar Sch.; University Coll. London (BScEco Joined Min. of Agriculture, Fisheries and Food, 1959; Private Sec. to Parliamentary S (Lords), 1962–64; Principal, 1964; Principal Private Sec. to Ministers, 1970–71; Asst Se 1971; seconded to Cabinet Office, 1972–74; Under-Sec., MAFF, 1976–80; joined NF as Chief Economic and Policy Adviser, 1981. Mem., EU Econ. and Social Ctt 1998–2002. Director: ACT Ltd, 1996–2004; Drew Associates Ltd, 1997–2003. *Address* Orchard Rise, Kingston upon Thames, Surrey KT2 7EY. *T:* (020) 8336 5868.

EVANS, Rev. Canon David; Rector of Heyford with Stowe-Nine-Church 1989–2001, of Flore, 1996–2001, and Brockhall, 1997–2001; *b* Llanglydwe Carmarthenshire, 15 Feb. 1937; *o s* of late Rev. W. Noel Evans, JP, and Frances M. Eva *m* 1962, Jenifer Margaret (*née* Cross); three *s*. *Educ:* Sherborne; Keble Coll., Oxford (MA Wells Theological Coll. (BD London). 2nd Lieut, Royal Signals, 1956–57. Minor Canc Brecon Cath., and Asst Curate, Brecon St Mary with Battle, 1964–68; Bishop's Chapla to Students, UC, Swansea, and Asst Curate, Swansea St Mary with Holy Trinity, 1968–7 Bishop of Birmingham's Chaplain for Samaritan and Social Work, 1971–75; D Samaritans of Swansea, 1969–71, of Birmingham, 1971–75; Jt Gen. Sec., 1975–84, Ge Sec., 1984–89, The Samaritans; Licensed Priest, Dio. of Oxford, 1975–89; RD Daventry, 1995–2000. Chaplain, Northamptonshire Police, 1990–2001. No Residentiary Canon, Peterborough Cath., 1997–2001. Mem., Church in Wales Liturgi Commn, 1969–75. *Recreations:* music, railways, bird-watching. *Address:* Curlew Riv The Strand, Starcross, Exeter EX6 8PA. *T:* (01626) 891712.

EVANS, Prof. David Alan Price, FRCP; Senior Consultant Physician (forme Director of Medicine), Department of Medicine, Riyadh Armed Forces Hospital, Sau Arabia, since 1983; Emeritus Professor of Medicine, Liverpool University, since 1994; *b* March 1927; *s* of Owen Evans and Ellen (*née* Jones). *Educ:* Univ. of Liverpool (MD, Ph DSc); Johns Hopkins Univ. RAMC, Jun. Med. Specialist, BMH Kure, Field Hosp. Kore BMH Singapore and BMH Kinrara, Malaysia, 1953–55; Capt. RAMC, 1954–55. Hou Physician and House Surg. 1951–52, and Med. Registrar, 1956–58 and 1959–60, Unit Liverpool Hosps; Res. Fellow, Div. of Med. Genetics, Dept of Medicine, Johns Hopki Hosp., 1958–59; Lectr 1960–62, Sen. Lectr 1962–68, Personal Chair, 1968–72, Dept Medicine, Univ. of Liverpool; Prof. and Chm., Dept of Medicine and Dir, Nuffield U Medical Genetics, Univ. of Liverpool, 1972–83; Cons. Physician, Royal Liverpool Hos (formerly Royal Liverpool Infirmary) and Broadgreen Hosp., Liverpool, 1965–8 Visiting Professor: Karolinska Univ., Stockholm, 1968; Johns Hopkins Univ., 1972; Uni Michigan at Ann Arbor, 1981. Lectures: Poulson Meml, Oslo Univ., 1972; first Sir Hen Dale, and Medallist, Johns Hopkins Univ., 1972; first Walter Idris Jones, Univ. of Wal 1974; Watson Smith, RCP, 1976. Member: BMA, 1951; Assoc. of Physicians of GB a Ireland, 1964. University of Liverpool: Roberts Prize, 1959; Samuels Prize, 196 Thornton Prize, Eastern Psychiatric Assoc., 1964. Life Mem., Johns Hopkins Soc. Scholars, 1972. Scientific Ed., Saudi Med. Jl, 1983–93; Member, Editorial Board: Interna Jl of Clinical Pharmacology Res., 1980–; Jl of Saudi Heart Assoc., 1988–200 Pharmacogenetics, 1995–2001. *Publications:* Genetic Factors in Drug Therapy, 199 medical and scientific, principally concerned with genetic factors determining responses drugs. *Address:* 28 Montclair Drive, Liverpool L18 0HA. *T:* (0151) 722 3112; C1 Riyadh Armed Forces Hospital, PO Box 7897, Riyadh 11159, Saudi Arabia. *T:* (4791000; *e-mail:* dape28mont@yahoo.com.

EVANS, (David) Anthony; QC 1983; a Recorder of the Crown Court, 1980–2003; 15 March 1939; *s* of Thomas John Evans, MD and May Evans; *m* 1974, Angela Bewle *d* of John Clive Bewley, JP and Cynthia Bewley; two *d*. *Educ:* Clifton Coll., Bristo Corpus Christi Coll., Cambridge (BA). Called to the Bar, Gray's Inn, 1965, Benche 2004; in practice at the Bar, Swansea, 1965–84, London, 1984–; Hd of Chambe 1996–2003. DTI Inspector, 1988–92. Chm., Jt Disciplinary Scheme Tribunals, 2000– Mem., Accountancy Investigation and Disciplinary Bd Tribunal, 2005–. *Recreations:* spo of all kinds. *Address:* Carey Hall, Neath, W Glamorgan SA10 7AU. *T:* (01639) 643859; Coleherne Mews, SW10 9EA. *T:* (020) 7370 1025; 9–12 Bell Yard, WC2A 2JR. *T:* (02 7400 1800. *Clubs:* Turf, MCC; Cardiff and County (Cardiff); Swansea Cricket an Football (Swansea); Downhill Only (Wengen).

EVANS, Prof. (David) Ellis, DPhil; FBA 1983; Jesus Professor of Celtic, University Oxford, 1978–96, now Emeritus, and Fellow of Jesus College, 1978–96, now Emeritus; Llanfynydd, 23 Sept. 1930; *yr s* of David Evans and Sarah Jane (*née* Lewis); *m* 1957, Shei Mary, *er d* of David and Evelyn Jeremy; two *d*. *Educ:* Llandeilo Grammar Sch.; Universit Coll. of Wales, Aberystwyth (Hon. Fellow, 1992), and University Coll., Swansea (Ho Fellow, 1985) (BA Wales, 1952; MA Wales, 1954); Jesus Coll., Oxford (Meyricke Gra Scholar, 1952–54; DPhil 1962, MA 1978; Hon. Fellow, 1997). Hosp. porter, Swanse 1954–56; University College of Swansea: Asst Lectr in Welsh, 1957; Lectr, 1960; Reade 1968; Prof. of Welsh Lang. and Lit. and Head of Dept of Welsh, 1974; Hon. Prof., 199 Chm., Faculty of Medieval and Modern Langs, Oxford Univ., 1985–86. Lectures: Sir Joh Rhys Meml, British Acad., 1977; Rudolf Thurneysen Meml, Univ. of Bonn, 1979, 199 O'Donnell, Univ. of Wales, 1980; G. J. Williams Meml, UC Cardiff, 1986; Sir Thoma Parry-Williams Meml, UCW, Aberystwyth, 1990. Pres. and Organizing Sec., Sevent Internat. Congress of Celtic Studies, Oxford, 1983; President: Cymdeithas Dafydd a Gwilym, 1978–96; Irish Texts Soc., 1983–92 (Mem. Council, 1978–); Cambria

Archaeol Assoc., 1990–91; Vice President: N Amer. Congress of Celtic Studies, Ottawa, 1986; Nat. Liby of Wales, 1987–91 (Mem. Court and Council, 1974–91); Hon. Soc. of Cymmrodorion, 1999– (Mem. Council, 1984–98). Chairman: Welsh Dialect Studies Group, 1977–80; Council for Name Studies of GB and Ireland, 1980–84 (Mem. Council, 1962–); Member: Bd of Celtic Studies, Univ. of Wales, 1968–96; Internat. Cttee of Onomastic Sciences, 1975–; Welsh Arts Council, 1981–87; Royal Commn on Ancient and Hist. Monuments in Wales, 1984–96; Court, University of Wales, 1978–; Court, UC Swansea, 1980–; Court, Univ. of Wales Coll. of Cardiff, 1983–; UNESCO Internat. Cttee for the Study of Celtic Cultures, 1984– (Provisional Cttee, 1981–83); Celtic Commn, Austrian Acad. of Scis, 1987–98; Welsh Cttee, UFC, 1989–92. Editor, Lang. and Lit. Section, Bull. of Bd of Celtic Studies, 1972– (Editor-in-Chief, 1988–93); Editor-in-Chief, Studia Celtica, 1994–96; Mem. Editorial Bd: Geiriadur Prifysgol Cymru/A Dictionary of the Welsh Language, 1973–; Nomina, 1980–85; Welsh Acad. English-Welsh Dictionary, 1981–95. Hon. Mem., Druidic Order of Gorsedd of Bards, 1976–; Correspondant étranger, Etudes celtiques, 1982; For. Hon. Mem., Amer. Acad. of Arts and Scis, 1992; Hon. MRIA 2000. Hon. DLitt Wales, 1993. *Publications:* Gaulish Personal Names: a study of some continental Celtic formations, 1967; Gorchest y Celtiaid yn yr Hen Fyd, 1975; (ed) Cofiant Agricola, Rheolwr Prydain, 1975; Termau Gwleidyddiaeth, 1976; (ed) Proc. 7th Internat. Congress of Celtic Studies, Oxford (1983), 1986; (ed with R. Brinley Jones) Cofio'r Dafydd, 1987; (consultant ed.) Dictionary of Celtic Mythology, ed James MacKillop, 1998; *contributed:* Swansea and its Region, ed W. G. V. Balchin, 1971; Homenaje a Antonio Tovar, 1972; (contrib.) The Anatomy of Wales, ed R. Brinley Jones, 1972; Indogermanisch und Keltisch, ed K. H. Schmidt, 1977; Aufstieg und Niedergang der römischen Welt, ed H. Temporini and W. Haase, 1983; Proc. 6th Internat. Congress of Celtic Studies, Galway (1979), 1983; Geschichte und Kultur der Kelten, ed K. H. Schmidt, 1986; Y Gwareiddiad Celtaidd, ed Geraint Bowen, 1987; Cell Gymysg o'r Genedlaethol, 1989; Britain 400–600: Language and History, 1990; Cof Cenedl, 1992; Lengua y Cultura en la Hispania Prerromana, 1993; (jtly) The Celtic Languages, ed M. J. Ball, 1993; Indogermanica et Caucasica, ed R. Bielmeier, 1994; The World of the Celts, ed M. Aldhouse Green, 1995; Die grosseren altkeltischen Sprachdenkmäler, 1996; Irish Texts Society: the first hundred years, 1998; contrib. Proc. British Acad., colloquia and Festschriften; articles and revs in learned journals. *Recreations:* music, flowers. *Address:* 2 Price Close, Bicester, Oxon OX26 4JH. *T:* (01869) 246469.

EVANS, Air Chief Marshal Sir David (George), GCB 1979 (KCB 1977); CBE 1967 (OBE 1962); Bath King of Arms, 1985–99; Deputy Chairman, NAAFI, 1991–2001 (Director, 1984–2001; President of Council, 1981–83); *b* Windsor, Ont, Canada, 14 July 1924; *s* of William Stanley Evans, Clive Vale, Hastings, Sussex; *m* 1949, Denise Marson Williamson-Noble, *d* of late Gordon Till, Hampstead, London; two *d*, and two step *s*. *Educ:* Hodgson Sch., Toronto, Canada; North Toronto Collegiate. Served War, as Pilot, in Italy and NW Europe, 1944–45. Sqdn Pilot, Tactics Officer, Instructor, 1946–52; Sqdn Comdr, Central Flying Sch., 1953–55; RAF Staff Coll. course, 1955; OC No 11 (F) Sqdn, in Germany, 1956–57; Personal Staff Officer to C-in-C, 2nd Allied TAF, 1958–59; OC Flying, RAF, Coltishall, 1959–61; Coll. of Air Warfare course, 1961; Air Plans Staff Officer, Min. of Defence (Air), 1962–63; OC, RAF Station, Gutersloh, Germany, 1964–66; IDC, 1967; AOC, RAF Central Tactics and Trials Organisation, 1968–70; ACAS (Ops), 1970–73; AOC No 1 (Bomber) Group, RAF, 1973–76; Vice-Chief of Air Staff, 1976–77; C-in-C, RAF Strike Command, and UK NATO Air Forces, 1977–80; VCDS (Personnel and Logistics), 1981–83. Mil. Advr and Dir, BAe, 1983–92, and dir several BAe subsids; Chairman: BAe Canada Ltd, 1987–92; Arabian Gold, later Finngold Resources, plc, 1989–99; Dir, Intermin Resource Corp. Ltd, 1986 (Chm., 1989–93); Chairman: Officers Pensions Soc. Ltd; OPS Investment Co. Ltd; Trustees, OPS Widows' Fund; Dir, Airshow Canada. Queen's Commendation for Valuable Service in the Air (QCVSA), 1955. CCMI (CBIM 1978; Mem. Bd of Companions, 1983–; Dep. Chm., 1989–). *Recreations:* rep. RAF at Rugby football and winter sports (President: RAF Winter Sports Assoc.; Combined Services Winter Sports Assoc.); has rep. Gt Brit. at Bobsleigh in World Championships, Commonwealth Games and, in 1964, Olympic Games. *Address:* Royal Bank of Canada Europe Ltd, 71A Queen Victoria Street, EC4V 4DE. *Club:* Royal Air Force.

EVANS, David Howard; QC 1991; a Recorder, since 1992; *b* 27 July 1944; *s* of David Hopkin Evans and Phoebe Dora Evans (*née* Reading); *m* 1973, Anne Celia Segall, *qv*; two *s*. *Educ:* London Sch. of Economics (BSc Econ 1965; MSc 1967); Wadham Coll., Oxford (BA 1970; MA 2002). Asst Economic Adviser, HM Treasury, 1967–68; called to the Bar, Middle Temple, 1972, Bencher, 2004; Asst Recorder of the Crown Court, 1987. *Recreations:* tennis, swimming, listening to music. *Address:* Queen Elizabeth Buildings, Temple, EC4Y 9BS. *T:* (020) 7583 5766. *Clubs:* Lansdowne, Roehampton; Riviera Golf.

EVANS, David John; Chairman, Broadreach Group (formerly Broadreach Services) Ltd, 1990–2002; *b* 23 April 1935; *s* of Violet Edith Evans and Arthur Thomas Evans; *m* 1956, Janice Hazel (*née* Masters); two *s* one *d*. *Educ:* Raglan Road School; Tottenham Tech. College. Professional cricketer (Glos and Warwicks) and footballer (Aston Villa); founded Exclusive Office Cleaning Ltd, 1960; Chm. and Man. Dir, Brengreen (Holdings), first co. with contract for refuse collection and street cleansing services (Southend-on-Sea Borough Council), 1960–86 (Brengreen (Holdings) acquired by BET plc, 1986). MP (C) Welwyn, Hatfield, 1987–97; contested (C) same seat, 1997. Parliamentary Private Secretary: to Minister of State for Industry, DTI, 1990–91; to Minister for Corporate Affairs, DTI, 1991–92; to Minister of State for Local Govt and Inner Cities, DoE, 1992–93; to Sec. of State for Wales, 1993. Member: Select Cttee on Deregulation, 1995–97; Exec., 1922 Cttee, 1993–97; Cons. Party Bd of Treasurers, 1996–97. Chm., Luton Town Football and Athletic Co. Ltd, 1984–89 (Dir, 1977–90); Mem. Council, Lord's Taverners, 1978–96 (Chm., 1982–84; Chm., Finance Cttee, 1992–96). *Address:* Little Radley, Mackerye End, Harpenden, Herts AL5 5DS. *T:* (01582) 460302. *Clubs:* MCC, Lord's Taverners.

EVANS, David Julian; Director, Eastern India, British Council, 1999–2002; *b* 12 May 1942; *s* of David Thomas Evans and Brenda Muriel Evans (*née* Bennett); *m* 1967, Lorna Madeleine Jacques; three *s*. *Educ:* Fosters Sch., Sherborne; Queen Mary Coll., London Univ. (BA Hist. 1963). Teacher, Rajasthan, VSO, 1963–64; Mgt Trainee, J. Sainsbury Ltd, 1964–65; British Council: seconded to VSO, 1965–67; Sierra Leone, 1967–70; Dep. Rep., Wales, 1970–72; educn trng course, UC, Cardiff, 1972–73; Enugu, Nigeria, 1973–76; Dir, Istanbul, 1976–80; Dir Gen's Dept, 1980–81; Dep. Dir, Germany, 1981–85; Dir, Youth Exchange Centre, 1985–88; Dir, Drama and Dance, 1988–89; Dep. Dir, Arts Div., and Head, Arts Projects, 1989–94; Dir, USA, and Cultural Counsellor, British Embassy, Washington, 1994–98; Hd of Global Advice, Facilities Gp, 1999. Ind. Mem., Gen. Council, BUNAC, 2006–. *Recreations:* the arts, history, travel, walking. *Address:* The Garret, Old Probate House, 5 Duncombe Place, York YO1 7ED. *T:* (01904) 621125.

EVANS, David Lloyd C.; *see* Carey Evans.

EVANS, His Honour David Marshall; QC 1981; a Circuit Judge, 1987–2002, a Senior Circuit Judge, 2002–03; Designated Civil Judge, Liverpool Group, 1998–2003; *b* 21 July 1937; *s* of Robert Trevor and Bessie Estelle Evans; *m* 1961, Alice Joyce Rogers; two *s*. *Educ:* Liverpool Coll.; Trinity Hall, Cambridge (MA, LLM); Law Sch., Univ. of Chicago (JD). Called to the Bar, Gray's Inn, 1964. Teaching Fellow, Stanford University Law Sch., 1961–62; Asst Professor, Univ. of Chicago Law Sch., 1962–63; Lectr in Law, University Coll. of Wales, Aberystwyth, 1963–65; joined Northern Circuit, 1965; a Recorder, 1984–87. Mem., Vis. Cttee, Univ. of Chicago Law Sch., 1995–98. *Recreations:* walking, photography, visual arts, bird-watching, motorsport. *Address:* c/o Queen Elizabeth II Law Courts, Derby Square, Liverpool L2 1XA. *T:* (0151) 473 7373. *Clubs:* Athenæum, Artists' (Liverpool).

EVANS, David Morgan, FSA; General Secretary, Society of Antiquaries of London, 1992–2004; *b* 1 March 1944; *s* of David Morgan Evans and Elizabeth Margaret Evans (*née* Massey); *m* 1973, Sheena Gilfillan (*née* Milne); three *d*. *Educ:* Kings Sch., Chester; UC Cardiff (BA 1966). MIFA 1983 (Hon. MIFA 2002); FSA 1987. Insp. of Ancient Monuments, Wales, 1969–77, England, 1977–92, DoE and English Heritage. Chm., Butser Ancient Farm Trust, 2003–. Hon. Sec., All-Party Parly Archaeology Gp, 2004–. *Publications:* Rebuilding the Past: a Roman villa, 2003; articles on heritage and law, heritage management. *Recreations:* walking, gardening, Montgomeryshire, opera.

EVANS, Rt Rev. David Richard John; an Assistant Bishop, Diocese of Coventry and Associate Priest, Stourdene Group of Parishes, since 2003; *b* 5 June 1938; *s* of William Henry Reginald Evans and Beatrix Catherine Mottram; *m* 1964, Dorothy Evelyn Parsons; one *s* two *d*. *Educ:* Caius College, Cambridge (Hons degree in Mod. Langs and Theology, 1963; MA 1966). Curate, Christ Church, Cockfosters, 1965–68; Missionary Pastor and Gen. Sec., Argentine Inter-Varsity Christian Fellowship, in Buenos Aires, Argentina, 1969–77; Chaplain, Good Shepherd Church, Lima, Peru, 1977–82; Bishop of Peru, 1978–88 (with delegated jurisdiction of Bolivia from 1980); Assistant Bishop: dio. of Bradford, 1988–93; dios of Chichester, Canterbury and Rochester, 1994–97; dio. of Birmingham, 1997–2003; Gen. Sec., S Amer. Mission Soc., 1993–2003. Internat. Co-ordinator, Evangelical Fellowship of the Anglican Communion, 1989–2003. *Publication:* En Diálogo con Dios, 1976. *Recreations:* golf, philately. *Address:* The Vicarage, Alderminster, Stratford-upon-Avon CV37 8PE. *T:* (01789) 450198; *e-mail:* bishop.drjevans@virgin.net.

EVANS, Hon. Sir (David) Roderick, Kt 2001; **Hon. Mr Justice Roderick Evans;** a Judge of the High Court, Queen's Bench Division, since 2001; Presiding Judge: Wales and Chester Circuit, 2004–07; Wales, since 2007; *b* 22 Oct. 1946; *s* of Thomas James and Dorothy Evans; *m* 1971, Kathryn Rebecca Lewis; three *s* one *d*. *Educ:* Bishop Gore Grammar School, Swansea; University College London (LLB 1967; LLM 1968). Called to the Bar, Gray's Inn, 1970 (Bencher, 2001), Lincoln's Inn *ad eund.*, 2001; a Recorder, 1987–92; QC 1989; Resident Judge: Merthyr Tydfil Crown Ct, 1994–98; Swansea Crown Ct, 1998–99; Cardiff Crown Court, 1999–2001; Recorder of Cardiff, 1999–2001. Mem., Criminal Cttee, Judicial Studies Bd, 1998–2001. Hon. Mem., Gorsedd of Bards, 2002. Fellow: Univ. of Wales, Aberystwyth, 2003; Univ. of Wales, Swansea, 2007. *Recreations:* reading, walking, Welsh ceramics. *Address:* Royal Courts of Justice, Strand, WC2A 2LL.

EVANS, Delyth; media consultant; Member (Lab) Mid and West Wales, National Assembly for Wales, 2000–03; *b* 17 March 1958; *d* of David Gwynne Evans and Jean Margaret Evans; partner, Edward Charles Richards, *qv*; one *s* one *d*. *Educ:* Ysgol Gyfun Rhydfelen, Pontypridd; University Coll. of Wales, Aberystwyth (BA Hons French); Centre for Journalism Studies, Cardiff. Journalist, HTV Wales and BBC Radio 4, 1985–91; policy advr and speechwriter to John Smith, MP, Leader of Labour Party, 1992–94; Mgt Consultant, Adrian Ellis Associates, 1995–98; Special Advr to First Sec., Nat. Assembly for Wales, 1999–2000. *Recreations:* keeping fit, reading, the arts, family activities.

EVANS, Derek; *see* Evans, John D.

EVANS, Eben, OBE 1976; Controller, Books Division, British Council, 1976–80; *b* 1 Nov. 1920; *s* of John Evans and Mary Evans; *m* 1946, Joan Margaret Howells; two *s* two *d*. *Educ:* Llandovery Grammar Sch.; University Coll. of Wales, Aberystwyth (BA 1948). Served War, 1941–46 (Army, Captain). Appointed to British Council, 1948; Cardiff, 1948–55; Thailand, 1955–59; Gambia, 1959–62; Ghana, 1962–64; Personnel Dept, London, 1964–68; Representative: Algeria, 1968–73; Yugoslavia, 1973–76. *Recreations:* walking, music.

EVANS, (Elizabeth Gwendoline) Nerys; Member (Plaid Cymru) Wales Mid and West, National Assembly for Wales, since 2007; *b* 22 March 1980; *d* of Glanmor and Wendy Evans. *Educ:* Univ. of Manchester (BA Hons Govt and Pol Theory 2001); Cardiff Univ. (MSc Hons Welsh Politics 2004). Plaid Cymru: Organiser and Press Officer, Carmarthenshire CC, 2002–03; Pol Officer, Nat. Assembly for Wales, 2003–07. *Address:* National Assembly for Wales, Cardiff Bay, Cardiff CF99 1NA. *T:* (029) 2089 8286, *Fax:* (029) 2089 8288; *e-mail:* nerys.evans@wales.gov.uk.

EVANS, Ellis; *see* Evans, D. E.

EVANS, Ena Winifred; Headmistress, King Edward VI High School for Girls, Birmingham, 1977–96; *b* 19 June 1938; *d* of Frank and Leonora Evans. *Educ:* The Queen's Sch., Chester; Royal Holloway Coll., Univ. of London (BSc); Hughes Hall, Cambridge (CertEd). Asst Mistress, Bolton Sch. (Girls' Div.), 1961–65; Bath High School (GPDST): Head of Mathematics Dept, 1965–72; Second Mistress, 1970–72; Dep. Head, Friends' Sch., Saffron Walden, 1972–77. Pres., GSA, 1987–88. Mem., Central Birmingham DHA, 1988–90. Mem. Council: Aston Univ., 1989–98; Queen's Coll., Birmingham, 1996–; Birmingham Univ., 2000–05. FRSA 1986. Hon. DSc Aston, 1996. *Recreation:* music. *Address:* 26 Weoley Hill, Selly Oak, Birmingham B29 4AD.

EVANS, His Honour Fabyan Peter Leaf; a Circuit Judge, 1988–2005; *b* 10 May 1943; *s* of late Peter Fabyan Evans and Catherine Elise Evans; *m* 1967, Karen Myrtle (*née* Balfour), *g d* of 1st Earl Jellicoe; two *s* one *d*. *Educ:* Clifton College. Called to the Bar, Inner Temple, 1969. A Recorder, 1985–88. Resident Judge, Middx Guildhall Crown Court, 1995–2005. Chairman: Area Criminal Justice Liaison Cttee, London and Surrey, 1997–2000; London Area Criminal Justice Strategy Cttee, 2000–03. Mem., Parole Bd for England and Wales, 2005–. *Recreations:* golf, sailing, singing. *Club:* Brooks's.

EVANS, Hon. Gareth (John), AO 2001; QC (Vic and ACT) 1983; President and Chief Executive, International Crisis Group, since 2000; *b* 5 Sept. 1944; *m* 1969, Merran Anderson; one *s* one *d*. *Educ:* Melbourne High Sch.; Melbourne Univ. (law and arts); Oxford Univ. (PPE). Lectr in Law, 1971–74, Sen. Lectr, 1974–76, Melbourne Univ.; practising Barrister, 1977–78. Senator (Lab) for Victoria, 1978–96; Shadow Attorney-General, 1980–83; Attorney-General, 1983–84; Minister for Resources and Energy, 1984–87, for Transport and Communications, 1987–88, for Foreign Affairs, 1988–96; Dep. Leader of Govt in Senate, 1987–93, Leader, 1993–96; MP (ALP) Holt, Vic, 1996–99; Dep. Leader of Opposition and Shadow Treasurer, Australia, 1996–98. Co-

Chm., Internat. Commn on Intervention and State Sovereignty, 1999–2001; Chm., World Economic Forum Peace and Security Expert Gp, 2003–06; Member: Internat. Task Force on Global Public Goods, 2003–06; UN Sec.-Gen.'s High Level Panel on Threats, Challenges and Change, 2003–04; Commn on Weapons of Mass Destruction, 2004–06. Hon. Fellow, Magdalen Coll., Oxford, 2004. Hon. LLD: Melbourne, 2002; Carleton, Canada, 2005. *Publications:* (ed) Labor and the Constitution, 1972; (ed) Law, Politics and the Labor Movement, 1980; (ed) Labor Essays, 1980, 1981, 1982; (jtly) Australia's Constitution, 1983; (jtly) Australia's Foreign Relations, 1991, 2nd edn 1995; Co-operating for Peace, 1993. *Recreations:* reading, writing, football. *Address:* 149 Avenue Louise, Level 24, Brussels 1050, Belgium.

EVANS, Gareth Robert William; QC 1994; a Recorder, since 1993; *b* 19 Jan. 1947; *s* of late David M. J. Evans and Megan Evans; *m* 1971, Marion Green; one *s* one *d. Educ:* Caerphilly Grammar Tech. Sch.; Birmingham Poly.; LLB Hons London. Called to the Bar, Gray's Inn, 1973, Bencher, 2007. Head of No 5 Chambers (Birmingham, London, Bristol), 2002–07. *Recreations:* watching Rugby, reading poetry, sailing, cooking, golf, outdoor pursuits. *Address:* No 5 Chambers, Fountain Court, Steelhouse Lane, Birmingham B4 6DR. *T:* 0870 203 5555, *Fax:* (0121) 606 1501; *e-mail:* ge@no5.com.

EVANS, George James; Sheriff of Tayside, Central and Fife at Cupar, since 1997; *b* 16 July 1944; *s* of Colin Evans and Caroline Catherine Kennedy MacPherson Harris; *m* 1973, Lesley Jean Keir Cowie; two *d. Educ:* Ardrossan Acad.; Glasgow Univ. (MA Hons); Edinburgh Univ. (LLB). Advocate, 1973; Standing Jun. Counsel, Dept of Energy, Scotland, 1982; Sheriff of Glasgow and Strathkelvin at Glasgow, 1983–97. *Publications:* contribs to legal periodicals. *Recreations:* art, literature, history, choral and individual singing, visiting English cathedrals. *Address:* Catherine Bank, Bridgend, Ceres KY15 5LS. *T:* (01334) 652121.

EVANS, Georgina Mary; *see* Mace, G. M.

EVANS, Prof. Gillian Rosemary, FRHistS; Professor of Medieval Theology and Intellectual History, University of Cambridge, 2002–05; *b* Birmingham, 26 Oct. 1944; *d* of late Arthur Raymond Evans and Gertrude Elizabeth (*née* Goodfellow). *Educ:* King Edward VI High Sch. for Girls, Birmingham; St Anne's Coll., Oxford (MA 1966; DipEd 1967); Grad. Centre for Medieval Studies, Univ. of Reading (PhD 1974); DLitt Oxon 1983; LittD Cantab 1983. FRHistS 1978. Asst Mistress, Queen Anne's Sch., Caversham, 1967–72; Res. Asst, Univ. of Reading, 1974–78; Lectr in Theol., Univ. of Bristol, 1978–80; Lectr in Hist., Univ. of Cambridge, 1980–2002; British Acad. Res. Reader, 1986–88. Mem. Council, Univ. of Cambridge, 1997–2001. Called to the Bar, Gray's Inn, 2002. Vis. lectureships in USA and Canada and various European countries. Consulting Editor: Dictionary of Biblical Interpretation in English; Encyclopaedia of Medieval, Renaissance and Reformation Christian Thought; Jl Hist. of Biblical Interpretation; Jl of ADR, Mediation and Negotiation; Series Ed., I. B. Taurus History of the Christian Church, 2005–. Mem., Civil Mediation Council, 2005–. Member: Faith and Order Adv. Gp, Gen. Synod of C of E, 1986–96; Archbp's Gp on Episcopate, 1987–90; English Anglican-Roman Catholic Cttee, 1997–2002. Officer, Council for Acad. Freedom and Acad. Standards, 1994–2003; Mem., Cttee for Auctores Britannici Medii Aevi, Brit. Acad., 1980–2001. Co-Founder, Oxcheps Higher Educn Mediation Service, 2004; Project Leader, HEFCE-funded project on dispute resolution in higher educn, 2007–. Freeman, Guild of Educators, 2004. Hon. DLitt: Nottingham Trent, Southampton Inst. of Higher Educn, 2001. FRSA 1996. *Publications:* include: Anselm and Talking About God, 1978; Anselm and a New Generation, 1980; Old Arts and New Theology, 1980; The Mind of St Bernard of Clairvaux, 1983; Alan of Lille, 1983; Augustine on Evil, 1983; The Anselm Concordance, 1984; The Logic and Language of the Bible, 2 vols, 1984–85; The Thought of Gregory the Great, 1986; (ed) Christian Authority, 1988; Problems of Authority in the Reformation Debates, 1992; Philosophy and Theology in the Middle Ages, 1994; The Church and the Churches, 1994; Method in Ecumenical Theology, 1996; The Reception of the Faith, 1997; Calling Academia to Account, 1998; The Medieval Epistemology of Error, 1998; Discipline and Justice in the Church of England, 1999; Bernard of Clairvaux, 2000; (ed) Managing the Church, 2000; (ed) A History of Pastoral Care, 2000; (ed) The Medieval Theologians, 2001; (jtly) Universities and Students, 2001; Law and Theology in the Middle Ages, 2002; Academics and the Real World, 2002; Faith in the Medieval World, 2002; A Brief History of Heresy, 2002; (ed) The First Christian Theologians, 2004; Inside the University of Cambridge in the Modern World, 2004; Wyclif, a Biography, 2005; Belief, 2006; The Church in the Early Middle Ages, 2007; The Good, the Bad and the Moral Dilemma, 2007; A History of Christian Europe, 2008; contribs to jls, etc on medieval intellectual history, ecumenical theology, higher educn issues. *Recreation:* painting. *Address:* e-mail: gre1001@cam.ac.uk. *Clubs:* Nikaean, Royal Over-Seas League.

EVANS, Dame Glynne; *see* Evans, Dame M. G. D.

EVANS, Sir Harold (Matthew), Kt 2004; author and editor; *b* 28 June 1928; *s* of late Frederick and late Mary Evans; *m* 1st, 1953, Enid (marr. diss. 1978), *d* of late John Parker and of Susan Parker; one *s* two *d;* 2nd, 1981, Christina Hambley Brown (*see* Tina Brown); one *s* one *d. Educ:* St Mary's Road Central Sch., Manchester; Durham Univ. BA 1952, MA Dunelm 1966. Ashton-under-Lyne, Lancs, Reporter Newspapers, 1944–46 and 1949; RAF, 1946–49; Durham Univ., 1949–52; Manchester Evening News, 1952; Commonwealth Fund Fellow in Journalism, Chicago and Stanford Univs, USA, 1956–57; Asst Ed., Manchester Evening News, 1958–61; Ed., Northern Echo, 1961–66; Editor-in-Chief, North of England Newspaper Co., 1963–66; Sunday Times: Chief Asst to Editor, 1966; Managing Editor, 1966; Editor, 1967–81; Editor, The Times, 1981–82; Editor-in-Chief, Atlantic Monthly Press, NY, 1984–86; Founding Editor, Condé-Nast Traveler Magazine, 1986–90; Editl Dir, 1984–86, Contributing Editor, 1986–, US News and World Report, Washington; Vice-Pres. and Sen. Editor, Weidenfeld & Nicolson, NY, 1986–87; Pres. and Publisher, Random House Trade Gp, 1990–97; Editl Dir and Vice-Chm., NY Daily News Inc., US News & World Report, Atlantic Monthly, and Fast Company, 1998–99. Member, Executive Board: Times Newspapers Ltd, 1968–82 (Mem. Main Bd, 1978); International Press Inst., 1974–80; Director: The Sunday Times Ltd, 1968–82; Times Newspapers Ltd, 1978–82. Writer and presenter: Evans on Newspapers, BBC TV, 1981; A Point of View, BBC Radio 4, 2005. Hon. Vis. Prof. of Journalism, City Univ., 1978; Vis. Prof., Inst. of Public Affairs, Duke Univ., N Carolina, 1984. Fellow, Freedom Forum. Hon. FSIAD. Internat. Editor of the Year, 1975; Gold Medal Award, Inst. of Journalists, 1979; Hood Medal, RPS, 1981; Editor of the Year, 1982; Lotos Club Medal, NY, 1993. DUniv Stirling, 1982; Hon. DCL Durham, 1998. *Publications:* The Active Newsroom, 1961; Editing and Design (five volumes): vol. 1, Newsman's English, 1972; vol. 5, Newspaper Design, 1973; vol. 2, Newspaper Text, 1974; vol. 3, Newspaper Headlines, 1974; vol. 4, Pictures on a Page, 1977; Good Times, Bad Times, 1983, 3rd edn 1994; (jointly): We Learned To Ski, 1974; The Story of Thalidomide, 1978; (ed) Eye Witness, 1981; How We Learned to Ski, 1983; Front Page History, 1984; The American Century, 1998; They Made America, 2004. *Recreations:* swimming, music, chess, Sunday

in the park with George and Isabel. *Clubs:* Garrick, Royal Automobile; Century, Yale (New York).

EVANS, Sir Haydn T.; *see* Tudor Evans.

EVANS, (Henry) Nicholas; a District Judge (Magistrates' Courts) (formerly Metropolitan Stipendiary Magistrate), since 1994; *b* 7 Nov. 1945; 3rd *s* of Gilbert Arthur Evans and Muriel Elaine Evans (*née* Oxford); *m* 1980, Diana Claire Smith; one *s* one *d. Educ:* Highgate Sch. Called to the Bar, Middle Temple, 1971, Lincoln's Inn, *ad eundem,* 1975. *Address:* Westminster City Magistrates' Court, Horseferry Road, SW1P 2AX. *Clubs:* Garrick, Bar Yacht.

EVANS, Prof. (Hubert) Roy, CBE 2002; PhD; FREng; FICE, FIStructE; Vice-Chancellor, University of Wales, Bangor, 1995–2004; *b* 27 May 1942; *s* of David James Evans and Sarah Ann Evans; *m* 1966, Eira John; two *s* two *d. Educ:* Llandysul Grammar Sch.; University Coll. of Swansea (BSc, MSc; PhD 1967). Res. Fellow, University Coll. of Swansea, 1966–67; Asst Engr, Freeman Fox & Partners, 1967–69; University College, Cardiff, later University of Wales College of Cardiff: Lectr, 1969–75; Sen. Lectr, 1975–79; Reader, 1979–83; Prof. of Civil and Structural Engrg, 1983–95; Hd of Dept, 1984–95; Dean, 1987–88; Dep. Principal, 1990–93 and 1994–95. Vis. Prof., Univ. of W Virginia, 1983. FREng (FEng 1992). Hon. Fellow: UC, Swansea, 1995; Univ. of Wales, Cardiff, 1998. Telford Premium, 1976, 1979 and 1987, George Stephenson Medal, 1980, ICE; Henry Adams Bronze Medal, IStructE, 1976; Medal, Acad. of Scis, Czech Republic, 1995. *Publications:* numerous contribs in field of structural engrg and plate structures. *Recreations:* hill-walking, gardening, cricket, soccer. *Address:* Pwllcorn, Moylegrove, Cardigan, Pembrokeshire SA43 3BS. *T:* (01239) 881274.

EVANS, Iain Richard, FCA; Chairman, LEK Consulting, since 1991; *b* 17 May 1951; *s* of late Alan Caradog Crawshay Evans and Barr Hargreave Bell (*née* Dalglish); *m* 1st, 1973, Zoe Dorothy Valentine (*d* 2002); two *s;* 2nd, 1988, Jayne Doreen Almond; one *d. Educ:* John Lyon Sch.; Rotherham Sixth Form Coll.; Bristol Univ. (BSc Hons 1972); Harvard Univ. Grad. Sch. of Business Admin (MBA with High Distinction, Baker Scholar, Loeb Rhoades Fellow, 1978). ACA 1975, FCA 1977. Arthur Young McClelland Moores & Co., 1972–76; Bain & Co., 1978–83, Partner 1982; Founding Partner, L/E/K Partnership, subseq. LEK Consulting, 1983. Non-exec. Dir, Hyder (formerly Welsh Water Authy, then Welsh Water) plc, 1989–98 (Dep. Chm., 1992–93; Chm., 1993–98). *Recreations:* tennis, golf, fishing, marine paintings. *Address:* LEK Consulting LLP, 40 Grosvenor Place, SW1X 7JL. *T:* (020) 7389 7200.

EVANS, Dr (Ian) Philip, OBE 1999; FRSC; Head Master, Bedford School, 1990–2008; *b* 2 May 1948; *s* of Joseph Emlyn Evans and Beryl Evans; *m* 1972, Sandra Veronica Waggett; two *s. Educ:* Ruabon Boys' Grammar Sch.; Churchill College, Cambridge (BA 1970; MA 1973; 1st cl. hons Nat. Scis Tripos); Imperial College of Science and Technology (PhD, DIC). CChem, FRSC 1997. Post-Doctoral Fellow, Res. Sch. of Chemistry, ANU, 1973–75; Asst Master, St Paul's Sch., 1975–90 (Head of Chemistry Dept, 1984–90). Member: Schs Exams and Assessment Council, 1991–93; SCAA, 1993–97; Qualifications and Curriculum Authority, 1997–99. Chief Examr, A-level Chem., Univ. of London Schs Exam. Bd, 1987–90. Member Council: Nat. Trust, 1999–2001; RSC, 2007– (Trustee, and Chm. Educn Policy Bd, 2007–). *Publications:* (with S. V. Evans) Anyone for Science?, 1994; contribs to books; papers in learned jls. *Recreations:* music, cricket, poetry, wine. *Address:* Mon Hélie, Côte d'Or, 21900 Burgundy, France. *Club:* East India.

EVANS, James, CBE 1995; Chairman, Bristol United Press, 1997–2000; *b* 27 Nov. 1932; *s* of late Rex Powis Evans and Louise Evans; *m* 1961, Jette Holmboe; two *d. Educ:* Aldenham School; St Catharine's College, Cambridge (MA). Called to the Bar, Gray's Inn, 1959; admitted Solicitor, 1972; recalled to the Bar, Gray's Inn, 1991, Bencher, 1993. Commissioned 26th Field Regt RA, 1951–53. Legal Dept, Kemsley Newspapers Ltd, 1956–59; practised at Bar, 1959–65; Legal Adviser: Thomson Newspapers Ltd, 1965–73; Times Newspapers Ltd, 1967–73; Sec. and Mem. Exec. Bd, 1973–78, Dir, 1978–86, Thomson Organisation Ltd; Dir, 1977–81, Chm., 1980–81, Times Newspapers Ltd; Chm., Thomson Withy Grove Ltd, 1979–84; International Thomson Organisation plc: Dir, 1978; Jt Dep. Man. Dir, 1982–84; Man. Dir and Chief Exec., 1985–86; Chm., 1986; Chm. and Chief Exec., 1982–84, Dir, 1982–96, Thomson Regional Newspapers Ltd; Dir, Liverpool Daily Post and Echo Ltd, 1996–97. Dir, 1983–90, Chm., 1987–89, Press Assoc.; Dir, Reuters Holdings, 1984–92. Mem., Monopolies and Mergers Commn, 1989–97. Dir, Press Standards Bd of Finance, 1990–2000. Trustee, Visnews, 1985–95. Member: Council, Newspaper Soc., 1984–2001 (Vice-Pres., 1998–99; Pres., 1999–2000); Press Council, 1987–90; Council of Legal Educn, 1992–94. Mem., Home Office Deptl Cttee on Official Secrets Act (Franks Cttee), 1971. *Recreations:* various. *Address:* 6 Fishpool Street, St Albans, Herts AL3 4RT. *T:* (01727) 853064. *Club:* Garrick.

EVANS, James Humphrey R.; *see* Roose-Evans.

EVANS, Jane Elizabeth; *see* Collins, J. E.

EVANS, Jeremy David Agard; Director, Public Affairs, British Rail, 1990–97; *b* 20 June 1936; *s* of Arthur Burke Agard Evans and Dorothy (*née* Osborne); *m* 1964, Alison Mary (*née* White); one *s* two *d. Educ:* Whitgift Sch.; Christ's Coll., Cambridge (BA Hons). Ministry of Power, 1960–69; Sloan Fellow, London Business Sch., 1969–70; DTI, 1970–73; Asst Sec., DTI, 1973, Dept of Energy, 1974 (Offshore Supplies Office, 1973); seconded as Sec. to BNOC on its foundn, 1976–78; a Man. Dir, 1978; Man. Dir Corporate Develt and Sec., 1980–82, Mem. Bd 1981–82; Dir, Britoil plc, 1982–88. Mem., GDC, 1989–94. Gov., St Piers Sch., subseq. NCYPE, 1998–2001. *Recreations:* opera, ski-ing, walking, golf. *Address:* Dormans House West, Dormans Park, East Grinstead, West Sussex RH19 2LY. *T:* (01342) 870518.

EVANS, (Jeremy) Roger; Member (C) Havering and Redbridge, London Assembly, Greater London Authority, since 2000; *b* 23 June 1964; *s* of Ronald Evans and Doris Valentine Evans. *Educ:* Univ. of Sheffield (BSc Hons 1985); Westminster Univ. (CPE); Inns of Court School of Law. Various managerial rôles, Royal Mail, 1985–95; law student, 1995–98; called to Bar, Middle Temple, 1997; legal advr, Spring Gp, 1998–2000. Member (C): Waltham Forest LBC, 1990 (Leader, Cons. Gp, 1994–98); Havering LBC, 2006–. *Recreations:* badminton, swimming, public speaking. *Address:* Greater London Authority, City Hall, Queen's Walk, SE1 2AA.

EVANS, Jillian; Member (Plaid Cymru) Wales, European Parliament, since 1999; *b* 8 May 1959; *d* of Horace Burge and Valma Burge; *m* 1992, Syd Morgan. *Educ:* UCW, Aberystwyth (BA Hons Welsh); MPhil CNAA, 1986. Res. Asst, Poly. of Wales, Trefforest, 1980–85; self-employed administrator, 1986–89; Admin./Public Affairs Officer, 1989–93, Project Officer, 1994–97, NFWI Wales; Wales Regl Organiser, Child, Infertility Support Network, 1997–99. *Address:* 72 Tyntyla Road, Llwynypia, Rhondda CF40 2SR. *T:* (01443) 441395.

EVANS, John; *see* Evans, D. J. O.

EVANS, Dr John; *see* Evans, Dr N. J. B.

EVANS, Prof. John, PhD; Professor of Chemistry, University of Southampton, since 1990; *b* 2 June 1949; *s* of Leslie and Eleanor Evans; *m* 1972, Hilary Jane Fulcher; two *d*. *Educ:* Rutherford Grammar Sch., Newcastle upon Tyne; Imperial Coll. London (BSc 1970; ARCS); Sidney Sussex Coll., Cambridge (PhD 1973). Research Fellow, Princeton Univ., 1973–74; Cambridge University: ICI Res. Fellow, 1974–75; Royal Soc. Pickering Res. Fellow, 1975–76; Southampton University: Res. Fellow, 1976–78; Lectr, 1978–84; Sen. Lectr, 1984–87; Reader, 1987–90; Dean of Science, 1997–2000; Hd of School, 2007–. Science and Engineering Research Council: Chm., Synchrotron Radiation Cttee, 1991–94; UK Deleg. to Council of European Synchrotron Radiation Facility, 1991–94 (Mem., Scientific Adv. Cttee, 1995–98); Mem., Facilities Commn, 1993–94. Sci. Prog. Advr, Diamond Light Source Ltd, 2002–07 (Vice-Chm., Diamond Scientific Adv. Cttee, 2000–02). Royal Society of Chemistry: Sec. and Treas., Dalton Div., 1993–96; Council Mem., 1994–97. Tilden Lectr, RSC, 1994. Editor, Inorganic Chemistry Series, Oxford Chemistry Primers Text Book Series, 1991–2000. Meldola Medal, RSC, 1978. *Publications:* contrib. scientific jls, incl. Jl RSC. *Recreations:* cycling, watching football, travel. *Address:* School of Chemistry, University of Southampton, Southampton SO17 1BJ. *T:* (023) 8059 3307.

EVANS, John; *see* Evans, M. J.

EVANS, Maj.-Gen. John Alan Maurice, CB 1989; Vice-Chairman, AEI Cables, 1993–96 (Managing Director, 1992–93); *b* 13 Feb. 1936; *s* of John Arthur Mortimer Evans and Margaret (*née* Lewis); *m* 1958, Shirley Anne May; one *s* one *d*. *Educ:* Grammar schs in Wales and England; RMA Sandhurst; Trinity Coll., Cambridge (MA). Various Staff and RE appointments; CO, 22 Engr Regt, 1976–78; Comd, Berlin Inf. Bde, 1980–82; RCDS, 1983; Comdt, RMCS, Shrivenham, 1985–87; Sen. Army Mem., RCDS, 1988–90. Col Comdt, RE, 1991–96. With GEC Wire and Cables Gp, 1990. Pres., Inst. of Royal Engineers, 1990–93. *Recreations:* music, reluctant DIY, travel. *Address:* East Mead, Homington Road, Coombe Bissett, Salisbury SP5 4ND.

EVANS, John Alfred Eaton; Headmaster, Brentwood School, 1981–93; *b* 30 July 1933; *s* of John Eaton Evans and Millicent Jane Evans (*née* Righton); *m* 1958, Vyvyan Margaret Mainstone; two *s* one *d*. *Educ:* Bristol Grammar Sch.; Worcester Coll., Oxford. MA (Lit. Hum.). Nat. Service, 1952–54, commnd RAOC. Assistant Master: Blundell's Sch., 1958–63; Rugby Sch., 1963–73; Housemaster: Phillips Acad., Andover, Mass, USA, 1968–69; Rugby Sch., 1973–81. Chm., London Div., HMC, 1993. Member selection panels: CMS, 1983–91; Admiralty, 1985–96; Army Scholarship Bd, 1990–2002; ABM, 1992–2002. Chm. Trustees, Crescent Sch., Rugby, 1968–78; Governor: Colfe's Sch., 1993–2002; Prior Park Coll., 1998–2004; Mem. Adv. Bd, St Christopher's Sch., Burnham-on-Sea, 1994–97. FRSA 1983. *Publications:* various articles on community service in education. *Recreations:* cricket, Rugby fives, piano, singing, drama, walking. *Address:* Manor Farm House, Easton, near Wells, Somerset BA5 1EB. *Clubs:* Vincent's (Oxford); Savage (Bristol); Jesters; Cryptics Cricket.

EVANS, Prof. John Davies, OBE 1996; FBA 1973; Director, University of London Institute of Archæology, and Professor of Archæology in the University of London, 1973–89, now Professor Emeritus; *b* 22 Jan. 1925; *o s* of Harry Evans and Edith Haycocks; *m* 1957, Evelyn Sladdin. *Educ:* Liverpool Institute High Sch. (open schol. in English to Pemb. Coll.); Pembroke Coll., Cambridge. War Service, 1943–47. BA 1948, MA 1950, PhD 1956, LittD 1979; Dr *hc* Lyon 2, 1983. Fellow of British Institute of Archæology at Ankara, 1951–52; Research Fellow of Pembroke Coll., Cambridge, 1953–56; Prof. of Prehistoric Archæology, London Univ., 1956–73. President: Prehistoric Soc., 1974–78; Council for British Archæology, 1979–82; Member: Permanent Council, Internat. Union of Prehistoric and Protohistoric Scis, 1975– (Pres., 1982–86); Royal Commn on Historical Monuments (England), 1985–92; Chairman: Area Archaeol Adv. Cttee for SE England, 1975–79; Treasure Trove Reviewing Cttee, Dept of Nat. Heritage, 1988–96. FSA 1955 (Dir, 1975–80, 1983–84, Pres., 1984–87); Member: German Archaeological Inst., 1979– (Corr. Mem., 1968–79); Instituto Italiano di Preistoria e Protostoria, 1983–. *Publications:* Malta (Ancient Peoples and Places Series), 1959; (with Dr A. C. Renfrew) Excavations at Saliagos, near Antiparos, 1968; The Prehistoric Antiquities of the Maltese Islands, 1971; papers and reports in archæological journals. *Recreations:* walking, listening to music. *Address:* Melbury Cottage, 5 Love Lane, Shaftesbury, Dorset SP7 8BG.

EVANS, (John) Derek, CBE 2001; Chief Conciliator, Advisory, Conciliation and Arbitration Service, 1992–2001; *b* 11 Sept. 1942; *s* of late Leslie and Mary Evans; *m* 1964, Betty Wiseman; two *d*. *Educ:* Roundhay Sch., Leeds. FCIPD. Dept of Employment, 1962–74; Advisory, Conciliation and Arbitration Service: Midlands, 1974–78; Head Office, 1978–82; Dir, Wales, 1982–88; Dir, Adv. Services, 1988–91; Dir, Conciliation and Arbitration, 1991–92. Mem., Employment Appeal Tribunal, 2003–; Chm., Agricl Wages Bd, 2003–. Dir, URC (Wales) Trust, 2007–. Industrial Fellow, Kingston Univ., 1994–. Ind. Chm., Standards Cttee, Wokingham DC, 2002–04. *Recreations:* golf, driving, music. *Address:* 18 Everest Walk, Llanishen, Cardiff CF14 5AX. *T:* (029) 2076 6705. *Club:* Cardiff Golf.

EVANS, His Honour John Field; QC 1972; a Circuit Judge, 1978–93; *b* 27 Sept. 1928; 2nd *s* of late John David Evans, Llandaff, and Lucy May Evans (*née* Field). *Educ:* Cardiff High Sch.; Exeter Coll., Oxford (MA). Pilot Officer, RAF, 1948–49. Called to Bar, Inner Temple, 1953; Dep. Chm., Worcestershire QS, 1964–71; a Recorder of the Crown Court, 1972–78.

EVANS, Sir John G.; *see* Grimley Evans.

EVANS, John Kerry Q.; *see* Quarren Evans.

EVANS, John Robert, CC 1978; OOnt 1991; MD, DPhil; FRCP, FRCPC, FRSC; Vice Chairman, NPS-Allelix Inc. (formerly Allelix Inc. Biotechnology), 1999–2006; Chairman: Torstar Corporation, 1993–2006; Alcan Aluminium Ltd, 1995–2002; *b* 1 Oct. 1929; *s* of William Watson Evans and Mary Thompson; *m* 1954, Gay Glassco; four *s* two *d*. *Educ:* Univ. of Toronto (MD); University Coll., Oxford (Rhodes Schol.; DPhil; Hon. Fellow, 1990). MACP; FRCP 1980. Jun. interne, Toronto Gen. Hosp., 1952–53; Hon. Registrar, Nat. Heart Hosp., London, 1955; Asst Res.: Sunnybrook Hosp., Toronto, 1956; Toronto Gen. Hosp., 1957; Ontario Heart Foundn Fellow, Hosp. for Sick Children, Toronto, 1958; Chief Res. Physician, Toronto Gen. Hosp., 1959; Research Fellow, Baker Clinic Research Lab., Harvard Med. Sch., 1960; Markle Schol. in Acad. Med., Univ. of Toronto, 1960–65; Associate, Dept of Med., Faculty of Med., Univ. of Toronto, 1961–65; Asst Prof., 1965–66; Dean, Faculty of Med., McMaster Univ., 1965–72, Vice-Pres., Health Sciences, 1967–72; Pres., Univ. of Toronto, 1972–78 (Pres. Emeritus, 1995); Dir, Dept of Population, Health and Nutrition, IBRD, Washington, 1979–83; CEO, Allelix Inc. (Biotechnology), 1983–89. Member: Council RCP (Can.), 1972–78; Inst. of Medicine, Nat. Acad. Sci., USA, 1972– (Mem. Council, 1976–80); Adv. Cttee Med. Res., WHO, 1976–80. Chairman: Trustees, Rockefeller Foundn, 1987–95; Canada Foundn for Innovation, 1997–; Walter & Duncan Gordon Charitable Foundn, Toronto, 1997–2000; MaRS Discovery District, 2000–. Dir, MDS Health Gp Ltd, Toronto. Fellow, LSHTM, 1988. Hon. LLD: McGill, 1972; Dalhousie, 1972; McMaster, 1972; Queen's, 1974; Wilfred Laurier, 1975; York, 1977; Yale, 1978; Toronto, 1980; Calgary, 1996; Hon. DSc: Meml Univ. of Newfoundland, 1973; Montreal, 1977; Royal Mil Coll., Kingston, 1989; DU: Ottawa, 1978; Limbourg, 1980; Hon. DHL Johns Hopkins, 1978. *Recreations:* ski-ing, fishing, farming. *Address:* 58 Highland Avenue, Toronto, ON M4W 2A3, Canada.

EVANS, John Roger W.; *see* Warren Evans.

EVANS, Sir John (Stanley), Kt 2000; QPM 1990; DL; consultant in security and counter terrorism; Special Security Advisor: to the Football Association, since 2004; to the England and Wales Cricket Board, since 2008; *b* 6 Aug. 1943; *s* of late William Stanley and of Doris Evans; *m* 1965, Beryl Smith; one *s* one *d*. *Educ:* Wade Deacon Grammar Sch., Widnes; Liverpool Univ. (LLB Hons 1972). Liverpool City, then Merseyside Police, 1960–80; Asst Chief Constable, Greater Manchester Police, 1980–84; Dep. Chief Constable, Surrey Constabulary, 1984–88; Chief Constable, Devon and Cornwall Constabulary, 1989–2002. Pres., ACPO, 1999–2000. Chm., Police Athletic Assoc., 1996–2002 (Life Vice Pres.). Chm., Your Radio Ltd, 2003–06. Prince's Trust: Chm., SW England, 2001–; Mem., Nat. Trustees Council, 2005–07; Vice Chm., English Regions Council, 2005–07. Member: Public Inquiry into alleged sectarian murder of Robert Hamill, NI; several Police Appeal Tribunals. President: Devon and Cornwall Victim Support Schemes, 2002–07; Combined Community Watch Assoc., 2002–. Patron: Dream Away, 1990–; Wooden Spoon. Mem., Otter Valley Rotary Club, 2003–. DL Devon, 2000. *Recreations:* most sports (ran London Marathon, 1988, 1989), service and charitable activities. *Address:* c/o Woodbury Park Hotel, Golf & Country Club Ltd, Woodbury Castle, Woodbury, Exeter, Devon EX5 1JJ. *Club:* Woodbury Park Golf and Country (Pres., 2001–).

EVANS, Very Rev. (John) Wyn, FSA, FRHistS; Dean and Precentor of St Davids Cathedral, since 1994; Rector, Rectorial Benefice of Dewisland, since 2001; *b* 4 Oct. 1946; *o s* of late Ven. David Eifion Evans and Iris Elizabeth (*née* Gravelle); *m* 1997, Diane Katherine, *d* of George and Kathleen Baker. *Educ:* Ardwyn Grammar Sch., Aberystwyth; University Coll., Cardiff (BA); St Michael's Theol Coll., Llandaff (BD); Jesus Coll., Oxford. FSA 1989; FRHistS 1994. Deacon 1971, priest 1972; Curate, St Davids, 1971–75; Minor Canon, St Davids Cathedral, 1972–75; grad. student, Jesus Coll., Oxford, 1975–77, permission to officiate Oxford diocese, 1975–77; Diocesan Adviser on Archives, St Davids, 1976–83; Rector, Llanfallteg with Castell Dwyran and Clunderwen with Henllan Amgoed and Llangan, 1977–82; Exam. Chaplain to Bishop of St Davids, 1977; Diocesan Warden of Ordinands, 1978–83; Chaplain and Lectr, Trinity Coll., Carmarthen, 1982–90; Diocesan Dir of Educn, 1982–92; Hon. Canon, St Davids Cathedral, 1988–90, Canon (4th Cursal), 1990–94; Dean of Chapel, Trinity Coll., Carmarthen, 1990–94; Head, Dept of Theology and Religious Studies, 1991–94. Chairman: Deans of the Church in Wales, 2001–; Cathedral Libraries and Archives Assoc., 2001–07; Member: St Davids Diocesan Adv. Cttee, 1994– (Chm., 2006–); Cathedrals and Churches Commn, Church in Wales, 1995–; Exec., Friends of Friendless Churches, 1995–2006; Rep. Body, Church in Wales, 1999–2004. Mem. Governing Body, Trinity Coll., Carmarthen, 1994–2006; Member Court: Nat. Liby of Wales, 1998–; Univ. of Wales Cardiff, 2002–. Mem., Gorsedd of Bards (White Robe), 1997–. Hon. Fellow, Univ. of Wales, Lampeter, 2006. *Publications:* (with Roger Worsley) St Davids Cathedral 1181–1981, 1981; contribs to jls, including Jl Welsh Ecclesiastical History, Carmarthen Antiquary, Diwinyddiaeth. *Recreations:* reading, music, antiquities. *Address:* The Deanery, Cathedral Close, St Davids, Dyfed SA62 6RH. *T:* (01437) 720202. *Club:* Oxford and Cambridge.

EVANS, (John) Wynford, CBE 1995; Chairman: Bank of Wales, 1995–2002; South Wales Electricity plc (formerly South Wales Electricity Board), 1984–95; *b* 3 Nov. 1934; *s* of late Gwilym Everton and Margaret Mary Elfreda Evans; *m* 1957, Sigrun Brethfeld; two *s* (and one *s* decd). *Educ:* Llanelli Grammar Sch.; St John's Coll., Cambridge (MA). FBCS. Served RAF (Flying Officer), 1955–57. IBM, 1957–58; NAAFI, W Germany, 1959–62; Kayser Bondor, 1962–63; various posts, inc. Computer and Management Services Manager, S Wales Electricity Bd, 1963–76; ASC, Henley, 1968; Dep. Chm., London Electricity Bd, 1977–84. Dir, 1992 Nat. Garden Festival Ltd, 1987–88. Member: Milton Keynes IT Adv. Panel, 1982–84; Welsh Regional Council, CBI, 1984–99 (Chm., 1991–93); Council, CBI, 1988–97. Chm., SE Wales Cttee, Industry Year 1986. Dep. Chm., Prince of Wales Cttee, 1989–96. Mem., 1985–90, Dep. Chm., 1995–2001, Nat. Trust Cttee for Wales; Member: Hon. Soc. of Cymmrodorion, 1978–; Civic Trust Bd for Wales, 1984–88; Welsh Language Bd, 1988–89; Council, Nat. Mus. and Galls of Wales, 2000–07 (Chm., Pension Fund, 2000–06). Dir, Welsh Nat. Opera Ltd, 1988–93; Trustee and Dep. Chm., Cardiff Bay Opera House Trust, 1994–97; Trustee: Nat. Botanic Garden of Wales, 1998–2001; Gateway Gardens Trust, 2004–06. Mem. Council Europa Nostra, 1996–2008 (Chm., Heritage Awards Panel, 2001–05). Mem. Court, Cranfield Inst. of Technol., 1980–88; Governor, Polytechnic of Wales, 1987–88. Liveryman: Tin Plate Workers alias Wireworkers' Co.; Welsh Livery Guild. High Sheriff, S Glamorgan, 1995–96. Hon. Druid, Gorsedd of Bards of Island of Britain, 1999–. FInstD 1988; FRSA. *Recreations:* fishing, walking, reading. *Clubs:* London Welsh; Cardiff and County, Radyr Golf (Cardiff).

EVANS, John Yorath Gwynne; Deputy Director (Air), Royal Aircraft Establishment, 1972–76, retired; medical engineering consultant, 1980–88; *b* 10 Feb. 1922; *s* of Randell and Florence Evans, Carms; *m* 1948, Paula Lewis, *d* of late Roland Ford Lewis; two *s* one *d*. *Educ:* UCW Aberystwyth. Royal Aircraft Estabt, 1942; attached to RAF, Germany, 1945–46; Supt Wind Tunnels, RAE Bedford, 1958; Head of Aerodynamics Dept, RAE, 1971. *Publications:* contrib. various sci. and techn. jls. *Recreation:* reading.

EVANS, Jonathan, OBE 2005; Company Secretary of Royal Mail Group (formerly Secretary to the Post Office, then Consignia), since 1999; *b* 21 April 1952; *s* of Alec H. Evans and Beryl Evans; *m* 1978, Gillian Eileen Blundell; one *s* two *d*. *Educ:* King Edward VI Sch., Nuneaton; Durham Univ. (BSc Maths 1974). Joined Post Office, 1974; mgt trainee, 1974–76; Ops Exec., Midlands Postal Bd, 1976–82; Personal Asst to Chm., 1982–84; Asst Head Postmaster, Leicester, 1984–86; Asst Personnel Dir, PO Counters Ltd, 1986–92; Dir of Orgn, 1992–93; Gen. Manager, Midlands Region, 1993–95; Network Dir, 1995–99. Trustee Dir, Royal Mail Pension Plan, 2005–; Chm., Royal Mail Sen. Exec. Pension Plan, 2007–. Trustee, Rowland Hill Fund, 2007–. *Recreations:* music, campanology, cricket. *Address:* c/o Royal Mail Group, 148 Old Street, EC1V 9HQ. *T:* (020) 7250 2298.

EVANS, Jonathan; Director-General, Security Service, since 2007; *b* 1958. *Educ:* Sevenoaks Sch.; Bristol Univ. (BA Classical Studies). Joined Security Service, 1980; Dep. Dir-Gen., 2005–07. Mem. Council, RUSI, 2007. Hon. LLD Bristol, 2008. *Recreation:* town and country walks. *Address:* Security Service, PO Box 3255, SW1P 1AE.

EVANS, Jonathan Peter; solicitor; Member (C) Wales, European Parliament, since 1999; Chairman, Pearl Group Ltd, since 2005; *b* 2 June 1950; *s* of late David John Evans and Harriet Mary Drury; *m* 1975, Margaret Thomas; one *s* two *d*. *Educ:* Lewis Sch., Pengam; Howardian High Sch., Cardiff; Coll. of Law, Guildford and London. Admitted Solicitor of Supreme Court, 1974; Leo Abse & Cohen, Cardiff: Partner, 1974–92; Man. Partner, 1987–92; Dir of Insce, Eversheds, 1997–99, consultant, 1999–; Dir, NFU Mutual Insce Gp, 2000–. Dep. Chm., Tai Cymru (Welsh Housing Corp.), 1988–92. Contested (C): Ebbw Vale, Feb. and Oct., 1974; Wolverhampton NE, 1979; Brecon and Radnor, 1987. MP (C) Brecon and Radnor, 1992–97; contested (C) Brecon and Radnorshire, 1997. PPS to Minister of State, NI Office, 1992–94; Parly Under-Sec. of State, DTI, 1994–95 (Minister for Corporate Affairs, 1994–95, for Competition and Consumer Affairs, 1995); Parly Sec., Lord Chancellor's Dept, 1995–96; Parly Under-Sec. of State, Welsh Office, 1996–97; Chief Cons. Party Spokesman for Wales, 1997–98. Leader, Conservatives, EP, 2001–05; Pres., EP Delegn for Relns with US Congress, 2004–. Mem. Bd, Cons. Party, 2002–; Pres., Assoc. of Cons. Clubs, 2004–. Vice Pres., Catholic Union of GB, 2001–. Hon. Consultant on law and policy, NSPCC, 1991–94; Dep. Chm., Welsh NSPCC Council, 1991–94; Pres., Cardiff and Dist NSPCC, 1992–94. FRSA 1995. *Recreations:* watching Rugby Union and cricket, reading. *Address:* c/o European Parliament, Rue Wiertz, 1047 Brussels, Belgium. *Clubs:* Farmers; Cardiff and County (Cardiff).

EVANS, Julian Ascott; HM Diplomatic Service; Consul General, San Francisco, since 2007; *b* 5 July 1957; *s* of Frederick Evans and late Glenys Evans (*née* Williams); *m* 1991, Gayle Evelyn Louise (*née* Sperring); two *d*. *Educ:* Llanelli Grammar Sch.; Price's Coll., Fareham; University Coll. London (BA Hons Geog.). Joined HM Diplomatic Service, 1978; Russian lang. trng, RAEC, Beaconsfield, 1981; Third Secretary: (Scientific), Moscow, 1982–84; (Commercial), Zurich, 1985–86; Asst Private Sec. to Minister of State, FCO, 1987–89; FCO, 1989–91; Second, later First, Sec., UKMIS to UN, NY, 1991–95; FCO, 1996–2002; Deputy High Commissioner: Islamabad, 2002–03; Ottawa, 2003–07. *Recreations:* travel, gardening, cats. *Address:* c/o Foreign and Commonwealth Office, King Charles Street, SW1A 2AH. *Club:* Rideau (Ottawa).

EVANS, Kim, OBE 2007; Executive Director, Arts, Arts Council England (formerly Arts Council of England), 1999–2006; Member, Parole Board for England and Wales, since 2006; *b* 3 Jan. 1951; *d* of Jon Evans and Gwendolen (*née* McLeod); *m* 2001, David Hucker. *Educ:* Putney High Sch.; Our Lady of Sion Convent; Warwick Univ. (BA Hons Eng. and Amer. Lit.); Leicester Univ. (MA Hons Victorian Lit. and Society). Press Asst, Design Council, 1973–74; Asst Editor, Crafts mag., 1974–76; Chief Sub-Editor, Harpers & Queen, 1976–78; South Bank Show, LWT: researcher, 1978–82; Producer/Dir, 1982–89; BBC Television: Producer, Omnibus, 1989–92; Asst Hd, Music and Arts, 1992–93; Head of Music and Arts, subseq. of Arts, BBC TV, then of BBC Arts and Classical Music, 1993–99. Trustee, Nat. Heritage Meml Fund, 2008–. FRTS 1999. Hon. FRCA 2006. Huw Wheldon Award for Best Arts Prog., BAFTA, 1993. *Recreations:* travelling (particularly in Africa), dreaming, reading. *Address:* c/o Parole Board for England and Wales, Grenadier House, 99–105 Horseferry Road, SW1P 2DD.

EVANS, Leslie Elizabeth; Director, Europe, External Affairs and Culture, Scottish Government (formerly Scottish Executive), since 2007; *b* 11 Dec. 1958; *d* of Philip Charles Evans and Mary Elizabeth Nora Evans (*née* Else); *m* 1990, Derek George McVay; one *s*. *Educ:* Liverpool Univ. (BA Hons Music). Asst to Dir, Greenwich Fest., 1981; Entertainments Officer, London Bor. of Greenwich, 1981–83; Arts Co-ordinator, Sheffield CC, 1983–85; Sen. Arts Officer, Edinburgh DC, 1985–87; Principal Officer, Stirling CC, 1987–89; Asst Dir of Recreation, 1989–99, Strategic Projects Manager, 1999–2000, City of Edinburgh Council; Scottish Executive: Head: Local Govt, Constitution and Governance, 2000–03; Public Service Reform, 2003–05; Tourism, Culture and Sport, Scottish Exec. Educn Dept, 2006–07. Mem., Scotch Malt Whisky Soc. *Recreations:* the arts, Pilates and keeping fit, handbags. *Address:* Scottish Government, Victoria Quay, Edinburgh EH6 6QQ; *e-mail:* leslie.evans@scotland.gsi.gov.uk.

See also T. W. Evans.

EVANS, Lewis Jones; Chairman, Post Office Board, Wales and the Marches, 1997–2000; *b* 14 Feb. 1938; *s* of Evan Jones Evans and Jane Jones Evans (*née* Morgans); *m* 1961, Siân, *e d* of Rev. Harri Hughes, Penclawdd; two *s* one *d*. *Educ:* Tregaron County Sch.; Trinity Coll., Carmarthen (DipEd; Hon. Fellow, 2006). FCIB 1986. Schoolmaster, 1960–62; Lloyds Bank plc, 1962–90: branch and head office appts incl. Manager, Llanelli Br., 1970–73; Sen. Manager, Newcastle upon Tyne, 1982–84; Regl Dir and gen. mgt, 1984–90; Dir, Lloyds Develt Capital Ltd, Alex Lawrie Factors Ltd, and Internat. Factors Ltd, 1989–90; Dep. Man. Dir, 1990–91, Man. Dir, 1991–96, Girobank; Dir, Alliance and Leicester Building Soc., 1991–96. Mem. Council, British Bankers' Assoc., 1992–96. Member: Wales Tourist Bd, 1996–2004; Wales Adv. Bd, BITC, 1996–2000 (Chairman: Professional Firms Gp, Cardiff, 1996–99; Community Loan Fund for Wales, 1997–2000; Mem. Council, UK Local Investment Fund, 1997–2000); Wales Adv. Bd, Barclays Wealth (formerly Gerrard Ltd), 2000–; Panel of Ind. Assessors for Public Appts, 2000–04; Chairman: Cwlwm Busnes, Caerdydd, 1998–2006; GSL Farm and Pet Place Ltd, 2000–02. Member: Council, Royal Nat. Eisteddfod of Wales, 1999–2006 (Chm., Resources and Finance Cttee, 1999–2006); Council, CBI for Wales, 1997–2000; Dir, Cardiff Bay Opera Trust Ltd, 1994–97. Jt Chm., Action Res. Project on the Underachievement of Boys, 1996–98; Dep. Chm., NPFA, 2004–07 (Chm., NPFA Cymru, 2000–07). Hon. Vice-Pres., London Welsh Trust and Assoc., 1994–2000. Hon. Treas. and Mem. Council, Univ. of Wales, Lampeter, 1993–99; University of Wales: Member: Court, 1996–2002; Audit Cttee, 1997–2000; Council, 2004–07; Bd, Univ. of Wales Press, 2004–07. Governor: Univ. of Glamorgan, 1999–2002; Trinity Coll., Carmarthen, 2006–. CCMI (CIMgt 1994); FRSA 1994. Hon. Druid, Gorsedd of Bards, Isle of Britain, 1994. *Recreations:* family, music, sport. *T:* (01446) 773890, *Fax:* (01446) 775529. *Clubs:* Cardiff and County (Cardiff); Crawshays Rugby Football; Royal Porthcawl Golf.

EVANS, Lindsay; *see* Evans, W. L.

EVANS, Lloyd Thomas, AO 1979; DSc, DPhil; FRS 1976; FAA; Hon. Research Fellow, Commonwealth Scientific and Industrial Research Organization Division of Plant Industry, Canberra, Australia, since 1992; *b* 6 Aug. 1927; *s* of C. D. Evans and G. M. Fraser; *m* 1954, Margaret Honor Newell; two *s* one *d* (and one *d* decd). *Educ:* Wanganui Collegiate Sch., NZ; Univ. of NZ (BSc, MAgrSc, DSc); Univ. of Oxford (DPhil). FAA 1971. Rhodes Scholar, Brasenose Coll., Oxford, 1950–54; Commonwealth Fund Fellow, Calif Inst. of Technol., 1954–56; res. scientist, CSIRO Div. of Plant Industry, Canberra, 1956–92 (Chief, Div. of Plant Industry, 1971–78). National Acad. of Sciences (USA) Pioneer Fellow, 1963; Overseas Fellow, Churchill Coll., Cambridge, 1969–70; Vis. Fellow, Wolfson Coll., Cambridge, 1978. President: ANZAAS, 1976–77; Aust. Acad. of Science, 1978–82. Member, Board of Trustees: Internat. Foundn for Sci., Stockholm, 1982–87; Internat. Rice Res. Inst., Philippines, 1984–89; Internat. Center for Improvement of Wheat and Maize, 1990–95. Mem., Norwegian Acad. of Sci. and Letters, 1990; Foreign Fellow, Nat. Acad. of Agricl Scis, India, 1992. Hon. Member: Royal Soc., NZ, 1986; RASE, 1987. Hon. LLD Canterbury, 1978. Adolph E. Gude Award, Amer. Soc. of Plant Biol., 2004. *Publications:* Environmental Control of Plant Growth, 1963; The Induction of Flowering, 1969; Crop Physiology, 1975; Daylength and the Flowering of Plants, 1976; Wheat Science: today and tomorrow, 1981; Policy and Practice, 1987; Crop Evolution, Adaptation and Yield, 1993; Feeding the Ten Billion: plants and population growth, 1998; more than 200 scientific papers in jls. *Recreations:* tennis, chopping wood, Charles Darwin. *Address:* 3 Elliott Street, Canberra, ACT 2612, Australia. *T:* (2) 62477815.

EVANS, Dame (Madelaine) Glynne (Dervel), DBE 2000; CMG 1992; PhD; HM Diplomatic Service, retired; Senior Adviser, Olive Group Ltd, since 2006; *b* 23 Aug. 1944. *Educ:* Univ. of St Andrews (MA Hons 1st cl. Mediaeval and Modern Hist. 1966); University Coll. London (PhD 1971). Res. Fellow, Centre for Latin American Studies, Univ. of Liverpool, 1969–70; Vis. Lectr, Coll. of William and Mary, Williamsburg, 1970–71; Second Sec., FCO, 1971; Buenos Aires, 1972; First Sec., FCO, 1975; on loan to UN Secretariat, NY, 1978; First Sec., UKMIS NY, 1979; First Sec., subseq. Counsellor, FCO, 1982; Counsellor and Dep. Hd of Mission, Brussels, 1987; Head of UN Dept, FCO, 1990–96; Res. Associate, IISS, 1996–97; Ambassador to Chile, 1997–2000; Dist. Vis. Scholar, NATO Defense Coll., Rome, 2000–01; Ambassador to Portugal, 2001–04. Consultant, Defence Acad. of the UK, 2006–07. Associate Fellow, RUSI, 2004–. Advr, CAB, 2005–. *Publications:* The International Response to Crises in the African Great Lakes, 1997; articles on internat. peacekeeping and conflict management. *Address:* c/o Olive Group Ltd, PO Box 44780, SW1X 7YH.

EVANS, (Maldwyn) John; His Honour Judge John Evans; a Circuit Judge, since 2005; *b* 11 July 1950; *s* of late Cdre David Anthony Evans and of Margaret Evans; *m* 1998, Miriam Dorothy Swaddle (*née* Beaumont); one step *s* two step *d*, and two *s* one *d* from former marriage. *Educ:* Royal Hospital Sch., Holbrook; Newcastle upon Tyne Polytechnic (BA Hons 1972). Called to the Bar, Gray's Inn, 1973; a Recorder of the Crown Court, 1989; Hd, New Court Chambers, Newcastle, 1999–2005. Gov., King's Sch., Tynemouth, 2000–; Fellow, Woodard Corp., 2002. *Recreations:* sport, squash, skiing, sailing, cricket, Rugby in particular, holidays, walking, contemporary cinema. *Address:* c/o North Eastern Circuit Secretariat, 17th Floor, West Riding House, Albion Street, Leeds LS1 5AA.

EVANS, Prof. Margaret, PhD; FCLIP; Pro Vice-Chancellor, De Montfort University, 2000–02; *b* 29 April 1946; *d* of late Roderick McKay Campbell McCaskill and Gladys May McCaskill (*née* Ireland); *m* 1st, 1967, Anthony Howell (marr. diss.); two *d*; 2nd, 1978, Alan Fearn (marr. diss.); 3rd, 1985, Herbert Kinnell (marr. diss.); 4th, 1989, Gwynne Evans. *Educ:* Nottingham Poly. (BA CNAA); Leicester Poly. (MBA CNAA); Loughborough Univ. (PhD); Nottingham Univ. (PGCE). FCLIP (FLA 1994); FIInfSc 1995. Librarian, Nottingham City Libraries, 1964–65; Notts Co. Libraries, 1967–69; Sutton in Ashfield Libraries, 1971–73; antiquarian bookseller, 1973–75; Loughborough University: Lectr, 1979–88; Sen. Lectr, 1988–94; Prof. of Information Studies, 1994–2000; Hd of Dept of Information and Liby Studies, 1994–98; Dean, Sci. Faculty, 1998–2000. *Publications:* (jtly) Book acquisition and use by young people: a review of recent research initiatives, 1988; (ed) Planned Public Relations for Libraries, 1989; (ed) The Learning Experiences of Overseas Students, 1990; (ed) Managing Fiction in Libraries, 1991; All Change?: public library management strategies for the 1990's, 1991; (jtly) Managing Library Resources in Schools, 1994; (jtly) Meeting the marketing challenge: strategies for public libraries and leisure services, 1994; (jtly) Continuity and Innovation in the Public Library, 1996; (jtly) Marketing in the Not-for-profit Sector, 1997; (jtly) Learning support for special educational needs: potential for progress, 1997; (jtly) Adult reading promotion in UK public libraries, 1998; numerous other books, reports and articles. *Recreations:* Jamie, Lizzie, Flossie, animals.

EVANS, Mark; QC 1995; a Recorder, since 1996; *b* 21 March 1946; *s* of Rev. Clifford Evans and Mary (*née* Jones); *m* 1971, Dr Barbara Skew (marr. diss. 1995); one *s* one *d*; *m* 2001, Carolyn Poots, barrister. *Educ:* Christ Coll., Brecon; King's Coll., London (LLB Hons). Called to the Bar, Gray's Inn, 1971; practice in Bristol, 1973–; founded St John's Chambers, 1978. *Recreations:* music, vintage cars. *Address:* Temple Chambers, 12 Clytha Park Road, Newport, NP20 4PB; Grove Farm, Wapley BS37 8RW. *T:* (01454) 312150. *Club:* Savages (Bristol).

EVANS, Mark Armstrong, CVO 1994; Director, British Council, Austria, 1996–2000; *b* 5 Aug. 1940; *s* of late Charles Tunstall Evans, CMG, Birmingham, and Kathleen Armstrong, Newcastle; *m* 1965, Katharine, *d* of Alfred Bastable, Brecon; one *s* one *d*. *Educ:* Marlborough Coll.; Clare Coll., Cambridge (BA 1962; MA 1966); Moscow State Univ.; Bristol Univ. (PGCE 1964). Head, Russian and German, Chichester High Sch. for Boys, 1964–69; apptd to British Council, 1969; Bahrain, 1969–71; Frankfurt, 1971–73; MECAS, Lebanon, 1973–74; Dir, UAE in Dubai, 1974–77; temp. posting, Kabul, 1977; Asst Dir, Educnl Contracts, 1977–79; Dep. Rep. and Cultural Attaché, France, 1979–85; Head, Office Services, 1985–88; Dir, Canada, and Cultural Counsellor, Ottawa, 1988–92; Dir, and Cultural Counsellor, Russia, 1992–96. Chm., Chailey Parish Council, 2005–. Mem., E Sussex Valuation Tribunal, 2002–. Member: RSAA, 1972; Adv. Bd, Österreich Institut, 1999–2008. Gov., RNLI, 1995. Gov., Chailey Sch., 2004–. Mem., Bluebell Railway Preservation Soc., 1997–. *Recreations:* building models, gardening, household chores. *Address:* High Field, North Chailey, Sussex BN8 4JD. *Club:* Union (Cambridge).

EVANS, Sir Martin (John), Kt 2004; PhD, ScD; FMedSci; FRS 1993; Director, Cardiff School of Biosciences, and Professor of Mammalian Genetics, University of Cardiff, since 1999; *b* 1 Jan. 1941; *s* of Leonard Wilfred Evans and Hilary Joyce (*née* Redman); *m* 1966, Judith Clare Williams, MBE; two *s* one *d*. *Educ:* St Dunstan's Coll., Catford; Christ's Coll., Cambridge (BA Pt II in Biochem., MA); PhD London 1969; ScD Cambridge 1996. University College London: Res. Assistant, Dept of Anatomy and Embryology, 1963–66; Asst Lectr, 1966–69; Lectr, 1969–78; Cambridge University: Lectr, Dept of Genetics, 1978–91; Reader, 1991–94; Prof. of Mammalian Genetics, 1994–99. Discovered embryonic stem cells, 1981. Founder FMedSci 1998. Hon. Fellow, St Edmund's Coll., Cambridge, 2002. Hon. DSc Mount Sinai Sch. of Medicine, 2002. March of Dimes Prize in Develtl Biol., 1999; Albert Lasker Award for Basic Medical Research, 2001; Special Achievement Award, Miami Nature Biotechnol. Winter Symposium, 2003; (jtly) Nobel Prize for Medicine, 2007. *Publications:* numerous contribs to scientific works. *Recreations:* family, walking, golf. *Address:* Cardiff School of Biosciences, Biomedical Sciences Building, Cardiff University, Museum Avenue, PO Box 911, Cardiff CF10 3US. *T:* (029) 2087 4120.

EVANS, Michael; *see* Evans, T. M.

EVANS, Rt Rev. Michael; *see* East Anglia, Bishop of, (RC).

EVANS, Michael Stephen James; Defence Editor, The Times, since 1998; *b* 5 Jan. 1945; *s* of Reginald and Beatrix Evans; *m* 1971, Robyn Nicola Coles; three *s*. *Educ:* Christ's Hosp.; QMC, London Univ. (BA Hons English). Reporter, 1968–69, News Editor,

Loughton office, 1969–70, Express and Independent; Daily Express: Reporter, Action Line consumer column, 1970–72; Reporter, 1972–77; Home Affairs Correspondent, 1977–82; Defence and Diplomatic Correspondent, 1982–86; The Times: Whitehall Correspondent, 1986–87; Defence Correspondent, 1987–98. *Publications: fiction:* A Crack in the Dam, 1978; False Arrest, 1979; *non-fiction:* Great Disasters, 1981; South Africa, 1987; The Gulf Crisis, 1988. *Recreations:* cricket, golf, tennis, playing piano. *Address:* The Times, 1 Pennington Street, E98 1TA. *T:* (020) 7782 5921.

EVANS, Nerys; *see* Evans, E. G. N.

EVANS, Nicholas; *see* Evans, H. N.

EVANS, Nicholas Henry Robert; Director General Resources, Land Forces, Ministry of Defence, since 2006; *b* 21 July 1950; *s* of Ivor Robert Evans and Esther Jane Evans; *m* Sally Vera Carter; two *s*. *Educ:* Reading Sch.; St John's Coll., Oxford (MA Hons Modern History). Joined MoD, 1971; posts in RN, Army and Air Force policy, planning and finance, incl. Private Sec. to Under-Sec. of State for the Army, 1974–75, and Civil Advr to GOC NI, 1975–77; Asst Private Sec. to Sec. of State, 1981–84; Head: Naval Manpower and Trng, 1985–87; Mgt Services Div., 1987–90; Next Steps Implementation Team, 1990–92; Resources and Progs (Air), 1992–95; Asst Under-Sec. of State (Quartermaster), 1995–99; Exec. Dir (Finance), Defence Procurement Agency, 1999–2000; Dir Gen., Defence Logistics (Finance and Business Planning), then Resources, Defence Logistics Orgn, 2000–02; Dir Gen., Mgt and Orgn, 2003–06. *Recreations:* keeping the house up, the garden down and the children in. *Address:* Headquarters Land Command, Erskine Barracks, Wilson, Salisbury, Wilts SP2 0AG.

EVANS, Nigel Martin; MP (C) Ribble Valley, since 1992; *b* 10 Nov. 1957; *s* of late Albert Evans and of Betty Evans. *Educ:* Swansea Univ. (BA Hons). Retail Newsagent, family business, 1979–90. West Glamorgan County Council: Councillor (C), 1985–91; Dep. Leader, 1989. Chm., Welsh Cons. Candidates Policy Gp, 1990; Pres., Cons. NW Parly Gp, 1991. Contested (C): Swansea West, 1987; Pontypridd, Feb. 1989; Ribble Valley, March 1991. PPS to Sec. of State for Employment, 1993–94, to Chancellor of Duchy of Lancaster, 1994–95; Opposition front bench spokesman on Welsh and constitutional affairs, 1997–2001; Shadow Welsh Sec., 2001–03. Mem., Select Cttee on Transport, 1993, on Envmt, 1996–97, on Public Service, 1996–97, on Trade and Industry, 2003–05, on Culture, Media and Sport, 2005–; Secretary: NW Gp of Cons. MPs, 1992–; Manufacturing Cttee; All-Party Tourism Cttee; Chairman: All-Party Music Gp, 1996–97 (Vice-Chm., 2002–); All-Party Identity Fraud Gp, 2006–; All-Party Egypt Gp, 2007–; Co-Chm., All-Party Drugs Gp, 1997–. Vice-Chm., Cons. Party (Wales), 1999–2001. Director: Made in the UK Ltd; Small Business Bureau. *Recreations:* tennis, swimming, theatre, tourism, new technology, defence, broadcasting. *Address:* Brooklyn Cottage, Main Street, Pendleton, Clitheroe, Lancs BB7 1PT. *T:* (01200) 443875; House of Commons, SW1A 0AA. *Clubs:* Carlton, Royal Over-Seas League.

EVANS, Dr (Noel) John (Bebbington), CB 1980; Deputy Secretary, Department of Health and Social Security, 1977–84; *b* 26 Dec. 1933; *s* of William John Evans and Gladys Ellen (*née* Bebbington); *m* 1st, 1960, Elizabeth Mary Garbutt (marr. diss.); two *s* one *d*; 2nd, 1974, Eileen Jane McMullan. *Educ:* Hymers Coll., Hull (State scholar); Christ's Coll., Cambridge (scholar; 1st cl., Nat. Sci. Tripos); Westminster Medical Sch., London; London Sch. of Hygiene and Tropical Med. (Newsholme prize, Chadwick Trust medal and prize). MA, MB, BChir; FRCP, DPH (Dist.), FFPH. Called to Bar, Gray's Inn, 1965. House officer posts at: Westminster, Westminster Children's, Hammersmith, Central Middlesex and Brompton Hosps, 1958–60; Medical Registrar and Tutor, Westminster Hosp., 1960–61; Asst MoH, Warwickshire CC, 1961–65; Dept of Health and Social Security (formerly Min. of Health), 1965–84, DCMO 1977–82; Sir Wilson Jameson Travelling Fellowship, 1966. Chairman: Welsh Cttee on Drug Misuse, 1986–91; Nat. Biological Standards Bd, 1988–2002 (Mem., 1975–2002); UK Transplant Support Service Authority, 1991–98; Member: Welsh Cttee, Countryside Commn, 1985–89; Welsh Health Promotion Authority, 1987–89. Conducted Review of External Advice to DoH, reported 1995. Privy Council Mem., Council of Royal Pharmaceutical Soc., 1988–2003 (Hon. MRPharmS 2003). *Publications:* The Organisation and Planning of Health Services in Yugoslavia, 1967; Health and Personal Social Service Research in Wales, 1986; (with P. Benner) Isle of Man Health Services Inquiry, 1986; (with P. Cunliffe) Study of Control of Medicines, 1987; Postgraduate Medical and Dental Education in Wales, 1991; contribs to med. jls. *Recreations:* canals, photography. *Address:* Coach and Stables House, 21 Telegraph Street, Shipston-on-Stour, Warwickshire CV36 4DA. *T:* (01608) 664033.

EVANS, Ven. Patrick Alexander Sidney; Archdeacon of Canterbury, and a Canon Residentiary, Canterbury Cathedral, 2002–07, now Archdeacon Emeritus; *b* 28 Jan. 1943; *m* 1969, Jane Kemp; two *s* one *d*. *Educ:* Clifton College, Bristol; Lincoln Theological Coll. Curate: Holy Trinity, Lyonsdown, Barnet, 1973–76; Royston, 1976–78; Vicar: Gt Gaddesden, 1978–82; Tenterden, 1982–89; RD of West Charing, 1988–89; Archdeacon of Maidstone, 1989–2002; Diocesan Dir of Ordinands, Canterbury, 1989–94. Selector, ABM, 1992–95. Mem., Gen. Synod, 1996–2005; Chairman: Bd of Mission, 1994–95, and Pastoral Cttee, 1994–2002, dio. of Canterbury; Canterbury & Rochester Church in Society (formerly Council for Social Responsibility), 1997–2007. *Address:* 1 Streamside, Tolpuddle, near Dorchester, Dorset DT2 7FD.

EVANS, Paul; *see* Evans, C. P.

EVANS, Paul Anthony; Principal Clerk, Select Committees, House of Commons, since 2005; *b* 15 Oct. 1955; *s* of late John Evans and Cecilia Evans (*née* Monks); *m* 1991, Katharine Dufton; one *s* one *d*. *Educ:* St Peter's RC Primary Sch., Winchester; Peter Symonds, Winchester; Sevenoaks Sch.; King's Coll., Cambridge (BA 1977). Vis. Schol., Univ. of Siena; Vis. Fellow, Univ. of Heidelberg; Jun. Res. Fellow, St Edmund's House, Cambridge, 1980–81; Clerk, House of Commons, 1981–: Health Cttee, 1991–93; Defence Cttee, 1997–2001; Human Rights Cttee, 2001–04. Presidential Advr, Parly Assembly of Council of Europe, 2003–06. Chair, Study of Parlt Gp, 2005–07. *Publications:* (contrib.) Parliamentary Accountability, 1995; Dod's Handbook of House of Commons Procedure, 1997, 6th edn 2007; (contrib.) The Future of Parliament, 2005; (with Paul Silk) Parliamentarians Assembly of the Council of Europe: practice and procedure, 10th edn 2008. *Recreations:* Victorian and 20th century architecture, walking, silence and empty places, Wales. *Address:* Department of the Clerk of the House, House of Commons, SW1A 0AA. *T:* (020) 7219 1365; *e-mail:* evansp@parliament.uk.

EVANS, Paul Gareth; Master and Chief Executive, Royal Armouries, since 2003; *b* 9 Sept. 1963; *s* of Thomas Neville Evans and Rosamund Sheila Evans; *m* 1998, Barbara Shih Wen Chan; one *s* two *d*. *Educ:* Chilwell Comprehensive Sch.; Univ. of Surrey (BSc Hons); Univ. of Manchester (MBA). Project Manager, Kirin Beer, Tokyo, 1993; Area Manager, Whitbread Inns, 1994–98; Regl Ops Dir, Rank Holidays Div., Rank Orgn plc, 1998–2000; Chief Operating Officer, Royal Armouries, 2000–03. *Recreations:* most sports, fly fishing, research student at Manchester Business Sch. *Address:* Royal Armouries Museum, Armouries Drive, Leeds LS10 1LT. *T:* (0113) 220 1907, *Fax:* (0113) 220 1954; *e-mail:* paul@armouries.org.uk.

EVANS, Peter, CBE 1986; National Secretary, General Workers' Trade Group, Transport & General Workers' Union, 1974–90; *b* 8 Nov. 1929; *m* 1st, 1957, Christine Pamela (marr. diss.); one *d*; 2nd, 1975, Gillian Rosemary (decd); two *s* one *d*; 3rd, 1980, Joy Elizabeth (decd). *Educ:* Culvert Road Secondary School, Tottenham. London bus driver, 1955–62; District Officer, TGWU, 1962–66; Regional Trade Group Sec., Public Services, 1966–74. *Recreations:* talking, swimming in deep water, golf. *Address:* Flat 16, Gilwynes Court, Aldwick Felds, Aldwick, Bognor Regis, W Sussex PO21 3SQ. *T:* (01243) 821304. *Clubs:* Victoria, Players' Theatre; Selsey Golf.

EVANS, Prof. Peter Angus, DMus; FRCO; Professor of Music, University of Southampton, 1961–90; *b* 7 Nov. 1929; *y s* of Rev. James Mackie Evans and Elizabeth Mary Fraser; *m* 1953, June Margaret Vickery. *Educ:* West Hartlepool Grammar Sch.; St Cuthbert's Soc., University of Durham. BA (1st cl. hons Music), 1950; BMus, MA 1953; DMus 1958; FRCO 1952. Music Master, Bishop Wordsworth's Sch., Salisbury, 1951–52; Lecturer in Music, University of Durham, 1953–61. Conductor: Palatine Opera Group, 1956–61; Southampton Philharmonic Soc., 1965–90. Hon. GSM 1998. *Publications:* Sonata for Oboe and Piano, 1953; Three Preludes for Organ, 1955; Edns of 17th Century Chamber Music, 1956–58; The Music of Benjamin Britten, 1979, 3rd edn 1996; contributor to: Die Musik in Geschichte und Gegenwart; A Concise Encyclopædia of Music, 1958; New Oxford History of Music, 1974; New Grove Dictionary of Music, 1981; Blackwell History of Music in Britain, 1995; writer and reviewer, especially on twentieth-century music. *Address:* Pye's Nest Cottage. Parkway, Ledbury, Herefordshire HR8 2JD. *T:* (01531) 633256.

EVANS, Philip; *see* Evans, I. P.

EVANS, Dr Philip Richard, FRS 2005; Member of Scientific Staff, Medical Research Council Laboratory of Molecular Biology, Cambridge, since 1976; *b* 25 May 1946; *s* of Maurice Lionel Evans and Janette Marjorie (*née* Burridge); *m* 1969, Carol Ann Watkins; two *s* one *d*. *Educ:* Christ's Hosp.; Wadham Coll., Oxford (MA, DPhil 1974). IBM Res. Fellow, Oxford Univ., 1974. *Publications:* contrib. res. papers to scientific jls. *Recreations:* playing bassoon, walking. *Address:* MRC Laboratory of Molecular Biology, Hills Road, Cambridge CB2 0QH. *T:* (01223) 402211; *e-mail:* pre@mrc-lmb.cam.ac.uk.

EVANS, Sir Richard (Harry), Kt 1996; CBE 1986; Chairman: Samruk, Kazakhstan, since 2006; United Utilities, 2001–08 (non-executive Director, 1997–2008); *b* 1942; *m*; three *d*. *Educ:* Royal Masonic Sch. Joined Civil Aviation section, Min. of Transport, 1960; Min. of Technology, 1961; Govt Contracts Officer, Ferranti, 1967; British Aerospace (formerly British Aircraft Corporation): Contracts Officer, 1969, Commercial Dir, 1978, Asst Man. Dir, 1981, Dep. Man. Dir, 1983, Warton Div.; Mktg Dir, 1987; Chairman: British Aerospace (Dynamics), 1988; BAe (Military Aircraft), 1988; Chief Exec., 1990–98, Chm., 1998–2004, BAe plc, then BAE SYSTEMS. Chm., Royal Ordnance; Dir, Panavia, 1981. *Address:* 55 Grosvenor Street, W1K 3LJ.

EVANS, Richard Jeremy; *b* 28 June 1953; *s* of late George Evans and of Helen Maud Evans; *m* 1976, Alison Mary Thom. *Educ:* Ipswich Sch., Suffolk. Journalist: East Anglian Daily Times, 1974–78; Cambridge Evening News, 1978–79; with The Times, 1979–99 (Racing Correspondent, 1991–99); Racing Correspondent, Daily Telegraph, 1999–2005. Racing Journalist of the Year, Horserace Writers' Assoc., 1995. *Recreations:* golf, bridge, wine. *Address:* Old Village Hall, Stansfield, Suffolk CO10 8LP. *T:* (01284) 789478; *e-mail:* richard.j.evans@btinternet.com.

EVANS, Prof. Richard John, FBA 1993; FRHistS, FRSL; Regius Professor of Modern History, University of Cambridge, since 2008 (Professor of Modern History, 1998–2008); Fellow of Gonville and Caius College, Cambridge, since 1998; *b* 29 Sept. 1947; *s* of late Ieuan Trefor Evans and of Evelyn Evans (*née* Jones); *m* 1st, 1976, Elín Hjaltadóttir (marr. diss. 1993); 2nd, 2004, Christine L. Corton; two *s*. *Educ:* Forest Sch., London; Jesus Coll., Oxford (Open Schol.; 1st Cl. Hons Mod. Hist. 1969; Stanhope Hist. Essay Prize 1969; Hon. Fellow, 1998); St Antony's Coll., Oxford (MA, DPhil 1973); Hamburg Univ. (Hanseatic Schol.); LittD East Anglia, 1990. Lectr in History, Univ. of Stirling, 1972–76; University of East Anglia: Lectr, 1976; Prof. of European History, 1983–89; Birkbeck College, London: Prof. of History, 1989–98; Vice-Master, 1993–97; Acting Master, 1997. Vis. Associate Prof. of European History, Columbia Univ., 1980; Vis. Fellow, Humanities Res. Centre, ANU, Canberra, 1986; Alexander von Humboldt Fellow, Free Univ. of Berlin, 1981, 1985, 1989. FRHistS 1978; FRSL 2000. Wolfson Literary Award for History, 1987; William H. Welch Medal, Amer. Assoc. for Hist. of Medicine, 1989; Medaille für Kunst und Wissenschaft der Hansestadt Hamburg, 1993; Fraenkel Prize in Contemporary History, Inst. of Contemp. Hist., 1994. *Publications:* The Feminist Movement in Germany 1894–1933, 1976; The Feminists, 1977; (ed) Society and Politics in Wilhelmine Germany, 1978; Sozialdemokratie und Frauenemanzipation im deutschen Kaiserreich, 1979; (ed jtly) The German Family, 1981; (ed) The German Working Class, 1982; (ed jtly) The German Peasantry, 1986; (ed jtly) The German Unemployed, 1987; Comrades and Sisters, 1987; Rethinking German History, 1987; Death in Hamburg, 1987; (ed) The German Underworld, 1988; (ed) Kneipengespräche im Kaiserreich, 1989; In Hitler's Shadow, 1989; Proletarians and Politics, 1990; (ed jtly) The German Bourgeoisie, 1992; Rituals of Retribution, 1996; Rereading German History, 1997; In Defence of History, 1997; Tales from the German Underworld, 1998; Telling Lies About Hitler, 2002; The Coming of the Third Reich, 2003; The Third Reich in Power, 2005; The Third Reich at War, 2008. *Recreations:* playing the piano, opera, reading, gardening, cooking for friends. *Address:* Gonville and Caius College, Cambridge CB2 1TA.

EVANS, Richard Llewellyn; JP; Director of Social Services, Birmingham City Council, 1994–99; *b* 1 June 1949; *s* of Robert Ellis Evans and Sarah Christine (*née* Cassidy); *m*; one *s* one *d*. *Educ:* Chiswick Poly.; Dundee Univ. (Dip. Social Work; CQSW; Dip. TMHA). Aircraft engr, BAC, 1964–69; Surrey County Council: Instructor, 1969–72; Dep. Manager, 1972–73; Trng Officer, Lothian Regl Council, 1973–77; Manager, Emergency Duty Team, Wilts CC, 1977–79; Principal Officer, Lothian Regl Council, 1979–81; Develt Officer, London Boroughs' Regl Children's Planning Cttee, 1981–83; Avon County Council: Asst Dir of Social Services, 1983–90; Dir, Social Services, 1990–94. Chm., BBC Children in Need Appeal for South and West, 2004–06. JP Bristol and North Avon, 2006. *Recreations:* music, cinema, entertaining.

EVANS, Sir Richard (Mark), KCMG 1984 (CMG 1978); KCVO 1986; HM Diplomatic Service, retired; Emeritus Fellow, Wolfson College, Oxford (Senior Research Fellow, 1988–95); *b* 15 April 1928; *s* of late Edward Walter Evans, CMG; *m* 1960, Margaret Elizabeth Sessinger (marr. diss. 1970); *m* 1973, Rosemary Grania Glen Birkett; two *s*. *Educ:* Dragon Sch., Oxford; Repton Sch.; Magdalen Coll., Oxford (BA 1949; MA 1992). Joined HM Foreign (now Diplomatic) Service: Third Sec., London, 1952–55; Third Sec., Peking, 1955–57; Second Sec., London, 1957–62; First Sec.: Peking, 1962–64; Berne, 1964–68; London, 1968–70; Head of Near Eastern Dept, FCO, 1970–72, Head of Far

Eastern Dept, 1972–74; Fellow, Centre for Internat. Affairs, Harvard Univ., 1974–75; Commercial Counsellor, Stockholm, 1975–77; Minister (Economic), Paris, 1977–79; Asst Under-Sec. of State, 1979–82, Dep. Under-Sec. of State, 1982–83, FCO; Ambassador to People's Republic of China, 1984–88. Master, Ironmongers' Co., 1999–2000. *Publication:* Deng Xiaoping and the Making of Modern China, 1993. *Recreations:* travel, reading, music. *Address:* Sevenhampton House, Sevenhampton, near Highworth, Wilts SN6 7QA. *Club:* Oxford and Cambridge.

EVANS, Sir Robert, Kt 1994; CBE 1987; FREng; FIMechE, FInstE; Chairman, British Gas plc, 1989–93 (Chief Executive, 1983–92 and Member of the Board, 1983–89); *b* 28 May 1927; *s* of Gwilym Evans and Florence May Evans; *m* 1950, Lilian May (*née* Ward); one *s* one *d*. *Educ:* Old Swan Coll., Liverpool; Blackburn Coll.; City of Liverpool Coll. (Tech.). FREng (FEng 1991). D. Napier & Son Ltd, 1943–49; North Western Gas Bd, 1950–56; Burmah Oil Co., 1956–62; Dir of Engrg, Southern Gas Bd, 1962–70; Dep. Dir (Ops), Gas Council, 1972; Dir of Operations, British Gas, 1972–75; Dep. Chm., North Thames Gas, 1975–77; Chm., E Midlands Gas Region, 1977–82; Man. Dir, Supplies, British Gas Corp., 1982–83. President: Instn of Gas Engrs, 1981–82; Inst. of Energy, 1991–92; Pipeline Industries Guild, 1990–92. Chm., Nat. Council for Hospice and Specialist Palliative Care Services. FInstE (MInstE 1988); Hon. FIGasE 1961; CCMI (CBIM 1983); Hon. FCGI. Freeman, City of London, 1974; Mem., Engineers' Co., 1984. *Recreations:* reading, golf.

EVANS, Prof. Robert, PhD; FRS 2005; FInstP; H. O. Wills Professor of Physics, and Head of Department, University of Bristol, since 2005; *b* 7 April 1946; *s* of John David Evans and Mary Evans; *m* 1967, Margaret Hume; one *s*. *Educ:* A. J. Dawson Grammar Sch., Wingate; Univ. of Birmingham (BSc); Univ. of Bristol (PhD 1970). FInstP 1981. University of Bristol: Lectr, 1978–84; Reader, 1984–92; Prof. of Physics, 1992–2005. Res. Prof., Univ. of Wuppertal, 1997–98. *Publications:* contrib. numerous articles to learned jls. *Address:* H. H. Wills Physics Laboratory, University of Bristol, Tyndall Avenue, Bristol BS8 1TL.

EVANS, Robert John Emlyn; Member (Lab) London Region, European Parliament, since 1999 (London North West, 1994–99); *b* 23 Oct. 1956; *s* of T. F. Evans and late Marjorie Evans. *Educ:* County Sch., Ashford, Middlesex; Shoreditch Coll. of Educn; Inst. of Educn, London Univ. (BEd 1978; MA 1993). Teacher: Thames Ditton Middle Sch., 1978–83; Woodville Middle Sch., Leatherhead, 1983–85; Dep. Headteacher, Town Farm Middle Sch., 1985–89; Headteacher, Crane Jun. Sch., Hanworth, Hounslow, 1990–94. European Parliament: Member: Youth, Culture, Educn and Media Cttee, 1994–2001; Rules of Procedure Cttee, 1994–99 (Vice Pres., 1997–99); Cttee on Citizens' Freedoms and Rights, Justice and Home Affairs, 1999–2004 (Vice Pres., 1999–2004); Cttee on Transport and Tourism, 2004–; Mem. Delegn for Relns with Countries of S Asia, 1994–, with Romania, 1997–2006, with Georgia, Armenia and Azerbaijan, 2004–, with Moldova, 2005–; Chief EU Observer, Cambodian Elections, 2003; Rapporteur: mobility for students, volunteers, teachers and trainers, 2001; prevention of trafficking in human organs, 2003; certification of seafarers, 2004; access to aircraft for disabled people and passengers of reduced mobility, 2005. Contested (Lab): Berkshire East, 1987; Uxbridge, 1992; Brent E, Sept. 2003; London South and Surrey, European Parly election, 1989. Member: NUT (Pres., Leatherhead Br., 1984–85); GMB; Nat. Exec., Socialist Educnl Assoc., 1989–98; League Against Cruel Sports, 1976– (Hon. EP Consultant, 1997–). Trustee, Interact Worldwide, 2003–. Mem. Corp., Coll. of NW London, 2004–. DUniv Brunel, 1998. *Recreations:* cricket, hockey, swimming, cycling, ski-ing, cinema, psephology, mowing the lawn, theatre, travel, history of education. *Address:* European Parliament, Rue Wiertz, 1047 Brussels, Belgium; Labour European Office, 101 High Street, Feltham, Middx TW13 4HG. *T:* (020) 8890 1818, *Fax:* (020) 8890 1628; *e-mail:* robertevansmep@btclick.com. *Clubs:* MCC; Ruskin House Labour (Croydon); Ashford Hockey, Ashford Cricket (Middlesex); Middlesex County Cricket, Incogniti Cricket.
See also A. T. B. Evans.

EVANS, Prof. Robert John Weston, PhD; FBA 1984; Fellow, Oriel College, since 1997 and Regius Professor of Modern History, since 1997, Oxford; *b* 7 Oct. 1943; *s* of Thomas Frederic and Margery Evans (*née* Weston), Cheltenham; *m* 1969, Kati Róbert; one *s* one *d*. *Educ:* Dean Close School; Jesus College, Cambridge (BA 1st Cl. with distinction 1965, PhD 1968). Oxford University: Fellow, Brasenose Coll., 1968–97; Lectr, 1969–90; Reader in Modern History of E Central Europe, 1990–92; Prof. of European History, 1992–97. Mem., Inst. for Advanced Study, Princeton, 1981–82. Fellow: Hungarian Acad. of Scis., 1995; Austrian Acad. of Scis, 1997; Learned Soc. of Czech Republic, 2004. Hon. DPhil Charles Univ., Prague, 2005. František Palacký Medal, Czechoslovakia, 1991. Jt Editor, English Historical Review, 1985–95. *Publications:* Rudolf II and his World, 1973; The Wechel Presses, 1975; The Making of the Habsburg Monarchy, 1979 (Wolfson Literary Award for History, 1980; Anton Gindely Preis, Austria, 1986); (ed with H. Pogge von Strandmann) The Coming of the First World War, 1988; (ed with T. V. Thomas) Crown, Church and Estates: Central European politics, 1991; (ed with H. Pogge von Strandmann) The Revolutions in Europe, 1848–9, 2000; Austria, Hungary and the Habsburgs: essays on Central Europe *c* 1683–1867, 2006; (ed with M. Cornwall) Czechoslovakia in a Nationalist and Fascist Europe 1918–48, 2007. *Recreations:* music, walking, natural (and unnatural) history. *Address:* Oriel College, Oxford OX1 4EW; Rowan Cottage, 45 Sunningwell, Abingdon, Oxon OX13 6RD.

EVANS, Maj.-Gen. Robert Noel, CB 1981; Postgraduate Dean and Commandant, Royal Army Medical College, 1979–81; *b* 22 Dec. 1922; *s* of William Evans and Norah Moynihan; *m* 1950, Mary Elizabeth O'Brien (*d* 2007); four *s* one *d*. *Educ:* Christian Brothers Sch., Tralee, Co. Kerry; National University of Ireland (MB, BCh, BAO 1947). DTM&H 1961; FFARCS 1963. Commnd RAMC 1951; Consultant Anaesthetist, 1963; CO BMH Rinteln, 1969–71; ADMS 4th Div., 1971–73; DDMS HQ BAOR, 1973–75; Comdt, RAMC Trng Centre, 1975–77; DMS, HQ BAOR, 1977–79; QHP 1976–81. Col Comdt, RAMC, 1981–86. MFCM 1978. OStJ 1978. *Recreations:* gardening, walking, music. *Address:* 32 Folly Hill, Farnham, Surrey GU9 0BH. *T:* (01252) 726938.

EVANS, Robin Edward Rowlinson, FRICS; Chief Executive, British Waterways, since 2002; *b* 24 March 1954; *s* of Lt Col John and Connie Evans; *m* 1978, Hilary; two *s* one *d*. *Educ:* Reading Univ. (BSc Estate Mgt). FRICS 1990. Land Agent, NT, 1979–87; Dir, Landmark Trust, 1987–95; Palaces Dir, Historic Royal Palaces, 1995–99; Commercial Dir, British Waterways, 1999–2002. *Recreations:* family, walking, tennis. *Address:* British Waterways, 64 Clarendon Road, Watford WD17 1DA. *T:* (01923) 201286, *Fax:* (01923) 201455; *e-mail:* robin.evans@britishwaterways.co.uk.

EVANS, Hon. Sir Roderick; *see* Evans, Hon. Sir D. R.

EVANS, Roger; *see* Evans, J. R.

EVANS, Roger Kenneth; barrister; a Recorder, since 2000; *b* 18 March 1947; *s* of late G. R. Evans and Dr A. M. Evans; *m* 1973, June Rodgers, MA, barrister; two *s*. *Educ:* The Grammar Sch., Bristol; Trinity Hall, Cambridge (MA). President: Cambridge Union, 1970; Cambridge Georgian Gp, 1969; Chm., Cambridge Univ. Conservative Assoc. 1969. Called to the Bar: Middle Temple, 1970 (Astbury Schol.); Inner Temple, *ad eundem* 1979; in practice, 1970–94, 1997–; an Asst Recorder, 1998–2000. Contested (C): Warley West, Oct. 1974, 1979; Ynys Môn, 1987; Monmouth, May 1991. MP (C) Monmouth 1992–97; contested (C) same seat, 1997, 2001. Parly Under-Sec. of State, DSS, 1994–97 Member: Welsh Affairs Select Cttee, 1992–94; Ecclesiastical Cttee of Parlt, 1992–97 Chairman: Friends of Friendless Churches, 1998–; Prayer Book Soc., 2001–06 (Vice-Pres., 1995–2001); Mem., Ecclesiastical Law Soc., 1988–. Freeman, City of London 1976. *Recreations:* architectural and gardening history, building, gardening. *Address:* 2 Harcourt Buildings, Temple, EC4Y 9DB; *e-mail:* revans@harcourtchambers.law.co.uk *Clubs:* Carlton, Coningsby (Chm., 1976–77; Treas., 1983–87).

EVANS, Roger W.; *see* Warren Evans.

EVANS, Roy; *see* Evans, H. R.

EVANS, Roy Lyon, OBE 1993; General Secretary, Iron and Steel Trades Confederation 1985–93; *b* 13 Aug. 1931; *s* of David Evans and Sarah (*née* Lyon); *m* 1960, Brenda Jones one *s* two *d*. *Educ:* Gowerton Grammar Sch., Swansea. Employed in Tinplate Section o Steel Industry, 1948. Iron and Steel Trades Confederation: Divl Organiser, NW Area 1964–69; Divl Organiser, W Wales Area, 1969–73; Asst Gen. Sec., 1973–85. Mem., Gen Council, TUC, 1985–93. Jt Sec., Jt Industrial Council for the Slag Industry, 1975–85 Mem., ECSC Consultative Cttee, 1985–93 (Pres., 1986–88); Hon. Sec., British Section IMF, 1985–93 (Pres., Iron and Steel Dept (World), 1986). Member: Jt Acciden Prevention Adv. Cttee, 1974–93 (Chm., 1983); NEC of Labour Party, 1981–84. Bo Mem., British Steel (Industry) Ltd, 1986–94. *Recreations:* reading, walking.

EVANS, Russell Wilmot, MC 1945; Chairman, Rank Organisation, 1982–83; *b* 4 Nov 1922; *s* of William Henry Evans and Ethel Williams Wilmot; *m* 1956, Pamela Murie Hayward (*d* 1989); two *s* one *d*. *Educ:* King Edward's Sch., Birmingham; Birmingham Univ. LLB Hons. Served HM Forces, 1942–47; commnd Durham LI, 1942, Major, 1945 Admitted Solicitor, Birmingham, 1949; Solicitor with Shakespeare & Vernon Birmingham, 1949–50; Asst Sec., Harry Ferguson, 1951; Sec., Massey-Ferguson (Hldgs and UK subsids, 1955–62; Dir, gp of private cos in construction industry, 1962–67; joine Rank Organisation, 1967: Dep. Sec., 1967–68; Sec., 1968–72; Dir, 1972–83; Man. Dir 1975–82; Dep. Chm., 1981; Dir, principal subsid. and associated cos incl. Rank Xerox 1975–83; Fuji Xerox, 1976–83; Chm., Rank City Wall, 1976–83. Director: Eagle Sta Holdings, 1982–87; Oxford Economic Forecasting Ltd, 1986–96; Medical Cyclotron Ltd 1988–. *Recreations:* tennis, golf, photography. *Address:* Walnut Tree, Roehampton Gate SW15 5JR. *T:* (020) 8876 2433. *Clubs:* English-Speaking Union, Roehampton (Di 1971–87, Chm., 1984–87, Pres., 1991–).

EVANS, Ruth Elizabeth; Chairman, Bar Standards Board, since 2006; *b* 12 Oct. 1957; of Peter Evans and Dr Anne Evans; one *d*. *Educ:* Girton Coll., Cambridge (MA Hist.). Dir Maternity Alliance, 1981–86; Dep. Dir, then Actg Dir, Nat. Assoc. for Mental Healt (MIND), 1986–90; Gen. Sec., War On Want, 1990; Mgt Consultant, 1990–91; Dir, Nat Consumer Council, 1992–98; Chairman: Inquiry into Paediatric Cardiac Services, Roya Brompton and Harefield NHS Trust, 1999–2001; Ind. Inquiry into Drug Testing a Work, 2002–04. Non-executive Director: Financial Ombudsman Service, 1999–2002 Liverpool Victoria Gp, 1999–2002; Nationwide Bldg Soc., 2002–05; Mem. Adv. Bd ING Direct, UK, 2007–. Mem., Central R&D Cttee, NHS, 1995–99; Chm., Standin Adv. Gp on Consumer Involvement, NHS R&D Prog., 1995–99; Dep. Chm., Ofcor Consumer Panel, 2002–; Member: Ind. Rev. Panel for advertising of medicines for huma use, 1999–2003; Human Genetics Commn, 1999–2002; Medicines Commn, 2002–0 Law Soc. Governance Review Gp, 2003–04; non-exec. Mem., Tribunals for Users Prog Bd, LCD, 2003–05. Lay Mem., 1999–2007, and Chm., Standards and Ethics Cttee 2004–06, GMC. Member: UK Round Table on Sustainable Develt, 1995–99; Expe Panel on Sustainable Develt, DETR, 1998–99; Commn on Taxation and Citizenshi Fabian Soc., 1999–2000; BBC Licence Fee Review Panel, DCMS, 1999; Bd, Financia Services Ombudsman Scheme, subseq. Financial Ombudsman Service, 1999–2002; Pane of Ind. Assessors, Office of Comr for Public Appts, 1999–2005; Council, Britain i Europe, 1999–2004; Ind. Complaints Panel, Audit Commn, 2004–06; Queen's Counse Selection Panel, 2005–08; Customer Impact Panel, ABI, 2006–. Trustee, Money Advic Trust, 1994–2000 (Chm., Adv. Gp of UK money advice agencies, 1994–2000) *Recreations:* daughter, writing, music, swimming. *Address:* 24 Falkland Road, NW5 2PX *T:* (020) 7482 0420; *e-mail:* Reevans@btconnect.com.

EVANS, Sally Anne; Deputy Legal Adviser, Home Office, 1995–2000; *b* 20 March 1948 *d* of late Arthur Francis Gardiner Austin and Joy Austin (*née* Ravenor); *m* 1977, Richar Maurice Evans. *Educ:* High Sch. for Girls, Darlington; Univ. of Manchester (LLB Hon 1970). Called to the Bar, Gray's Inn, 1971; Barclays Bank DCO, then Barclays Ban Internat. Ltd, 1970–72; Western American Bank Ltd, 1972–73; Legal Adviser's Br., Hom Office, 1974–2000. Vice Chm., Friends of The Royal Marsden, 2006–. *Recreations* theatre, cooking, summer gardening.

EVANS, Sarah Hauldys; Headmistress, King Edward VI High School for Girls, sinc 1996; *b* 4 March 1953; *d* of Nancy and Wyndham Evans; *m* 1989, Andrew Romani Fowler; one *s*. *Educ:* King James' Grammar Sch., Knaresborough; Univ. of Sussex (BA Hons English); Univ. of Leicester (MA Victorian Studies); Univ. of Leeds (PGCE) English Teacher, Leeds Girls' High Sch., 1976–84; Dep. Head, Fulneck Girls' Sch 1984–89; Head, Friends' Sch., Saffron Walden, 1989–96. *Recreations:* the arts. *Address* King Edward VI High School for Girls, Edgbaston Park Road, Birmingham B15 2UB.

EVANS, Stephen Nicholas, CMG 2002; OBE 1994; HM Diplomatic Service; Hig Commissioner, Bangladesh, since 2008; *b* 29 June 1950; *s* of Vincent Morris Evans an late Doris Mary Evans (*née* Braham); *m* 1975, Sharon Ann Holdcroft; one *s* two *d*. *Edu* King's Coll., Taunton; Bristol Univ. (BA). Royal Tank Regt (Lieut), 1971–74; FCO 1974; language student (Vietnamese), SOAS, 1975; FCO, 1976; First Sec., Hano 1978–80; FCO, 1980–82; language training (Thai), Bangkok, 1982–83; First Sec Bangkok, 1983–86; FCO, 1986–90; First Sec. (Political), Ankara, 1990; Counsello (Econ., Commercial, Aid), Islamabad, 1993–96; seconded to UN Special Mission t Afghanistan, 1996–97; Counsellor and Head: OSCE and Council of Europe Dept, FCO 1997–98; S Asian Dept, FCO, 1998–2002; Chargé d'Affaires, Kabul, 2002; High Com Sri Lanka, 2002–06; Ambassador to Afghanistan, 2006–07; Dir, Afghanistan Inf. Strateg FCO, 2007–08. *Recreations:* military and naval history, golf, cycling. *Address:* c/o Foreig and Commonwealth Office, SW1A 2AH. *T:* (020) 7270 3000. *Club:* Athenæum.

EVANS, (Thomas) Alun, CMG 1994; HM Diplomatic Service, retired; Internationa Affairs Adviser, Cathay Pacific Airways, since 2002; *b* 8 June 1937; *s* of late Thomas Evan and Mabel Elizabeth (*née* Griffiths); *m* 1964, Bridget Elisabeth, *d* of late Peter Lloyd, CB and of Nora Kathleen Williams (*née* Patten); three *s*. *Educ:* Shrewsbury Sch.; Universit Coll., Oxford (MA). Army, 1956–58. Entered HM Foreign Service, 1961; Third Sec Rangoon, 1962–64; Second Sec., Singapore, 1964–66; FO, 1966–70; First Sec., Genev

1970–74; FCO, 1974–79; Counsellor: Pretoria, 1979–82; FCO, 1983–95. Internat. Risk and Internat. Affairs Advr, British Airways, 1995–2002; Director: Fleming, subseq. J. P. Morgan, Asian Investment Trust, 2001–; Sigma Internat. Ltd, 2002–04; Advr, Nimbus Trng, 2003–06; Chm., Lexicon Data Ltd, 2007–. Dir, British Iranian and Central Asian Assoc., 2000–01; Vice-Chm., British Iranian Chamber of Commerce, 2001–. Trustee, Pimpernel Trust, 1997–2005. *Recreations:* France, music, travel. *Club:* Travellers.

EVANS, His Honour (Thomas) Michael; QC 1973; a Circuit Judge, 1979–98; *b* 7 Sept. 1930; *s* of late David Morgan Evans, Barrister, and of Mary Gwynydd Lloyd; *m* 1957, Margaret Valerie Booker; one *s* four *d*. *Educ:* Brightlands Prep. Sch., Newnham, Glos; Marlborough Coll., Wilts; Jesus Coll., Oxford (MA (Juris.)). Called to the Bar, Gray's Inn, 1954; Wales and Chester Circuit, 1955; a Recorder of the Crown Court, 1972–79. Legal Chm., Mental Health Review Tribunal for Wales, 1970. Chancellor, Diocese of St Davids, 1986–2005; Pres., Provincial Court, Church in Wales, 1997–2007. Gov., Christ Coll., Brecon, 1992– (Chm. of Govs, 1999–2003). *Recreations:* walking, fishing, genealogy. *Address:* 7 Marine Walk, Maritime Quarter, Swansea SA1 1YQ.

EVANS, Timothy Hugh David; Apothecary to the Queen and to the Royal Household, since 2003; Private General Practitioner, since 1990; *b* 3 May 1955; *s* of David Lawrence Evans and late Betty Joan Evans; *m* 2000, Annabel Clare Blake; one *s* one *d*. *Educ:* Marlborough Coll.; Westminster Hosp. Med. Sch. (MB BS). MRCS 1979, LRCP 1979; DRCOG 1984; MRCGP 1985; DA 1987. House Officer, Westminster Hosp., 1979–80; SHO, Andrew Fleming Hosp., Harare, 1980–81; Dist MO, Kariba Hosp., Zimbabwe, 1981–83; SHO, Obstetrics, Cheltenham Gen. Hosp., 1984; GP Registrar, Tewkesbury, 1985; SHO, Anaesthetics, Cheltenham Gen. Hosp., 1986; RMO, London Clinic, Portland Hosp. for Women and Children, 1987–89. Mem., Chelsea Clinical Soc., 1993–. *Recreations:* golf, tennis, sailing, music, theatre. *Address:* 35 Henderson Road, Wandsworth Common, SW18 3RR; (practice) Westover House, 18 Earlsfield Road, SW18 3DW; *T:* (020) 8877 1877, *Fax:* (020) 8877 3664; *e-mail:* drtim@westoverhouse.com. *Clubs:* Hurlingham, Harbour; Royal Wimbledon Golf.

EVANS, Prof. Timothy William, MD, PhD, DSc; FRCP, FRCA; FMedSci; Professor of Intensive Care Medicine, Imperial College of Science, Technology and Medicine, University of London, since 1996; Head, Unit of Critical Care, National Heart and Lung Institute, since 1993; Consultant in Intensive Care and Thoracic Medicine, Royal Brompton Hospital, since 1987; *b* 29 May 1954; *s* of Philip Charles Evans and Mary Elizabeth Norah Evans (*née* Else); *m* 1987, Josephine Emer MacSweeney, Consultant in Neuroradiology, *d* of Prof. James MacSweeney; three *s* one *d*. *Educ:* High Storrs Grammar Sch., Sheffield; Univ. of Manchester (BSc Hons 1976; MB ChB Hons 1979; MD 1990); Univ. of Sheffield (PhD 1985; DSc 1997). MRCP 1982, FRCP 1993; FRCA 2000. House Officer, Univ. Dept of Neurosurgery, 1979–80, Renal and Gen. Medicine Dept, 1980, Manchester Royal Infirmary; Senior House Officer: Professorial Med. Unit, Royal Hallamshire Hosp., Univ. of Sheffield, 1980–81; in Gen. Medicine and Gastroenterology, Hammersmith Hosp./RPMS, 1981–82; in Thoracic Medicine, Brompton Hosp., 1982; Trent RHA Res. Fellow, and Hon. Med. Registrar, Acad. Div. of Medicine, Univ. of Sheffield, 1982–84; MRC Travelling Fellow, Cardiovascular Res. Inst., Univ. of Calif, San Francisco, 1984–85; Sen. Registrar in Thoracic and Gen. Medicine, Brompton and King's Coll. Hosps, 1985–86; Doverdale Fellow in Intensive Care and Hon. Sen. Registrar, Brompton Hosp., 1986–87; Cons. Physician, Chelsea and Westminster Hosp., 1988–. Hon. Consultant: in Intensive Care Medicine, HM Forces, 1998–; The Royal Hosp., Chelsea, 2004–. Member: Adv. Gp on Intensive Care Services, Nat. Audit Commn, 1998–99; Nat. Expert Gp, Adult Critical Care Services, NHS Exec., 1999–2000. Member: BMA Grants Cttee, 1989–94; British Lung Foundn Grants Cttee, 1992–95; BHF Grants Cttee, 2002–; Council, British Thoracic Soc., 1993–96; Council, European Intensive Care Soc., 1997–2005; Royal College of Physicians: Member: Thoracic Medicine Cttee, 1994–; Gen. Medicine Cttee, 1996–2005; Censor, 2003; Academic Registrar, 2005–. FMedSci 1999. Member, Editorial Board: Thorax, 1991–94; Intensive Care Medicine, 1996–99; Amer. Jl of Respiratory and Critical Care Medicine, 1997–2006; Amer. Jl of Physiology, 2000–03. *Publications:* jointly: Slide Interpretation for MRCP, 1988; Respiratory Medicine, 1989; The Drug Treatment of Respiratory Disease, 1994; Acute Respiratory Distress in Adults, 1996; Recent Advances in Critical Care 5, 1996; (ed jtly) Acute Lung Injury, 1997; (ed jtly) Tissue Oxygenation in Sepsis, 2001; more than 250 articles on scientific and clinical aspects of intensive care medicine. *Recreations:* flying, housework. *Address:* Department of Anaesthetics and Intensive Care Medicine, Royal Brompton Hospital, Sydney Street, SW3 6NP. *T:* (020) 7351 8523, *Fax:* (020) 7351 8524; *e-mail:* t.evans@rbht.nhs.uk.
See also L. E. Evans.

EVANS, Prof. Trevor, FRS 1988; Personal Professor, University of Reading, 1968–92, Emeritus Professor, 1992; *b* 26 April 1927; *s* of late Henry and Margaret Evans; *m* Patricia Margaret Booth (*née* Johnson); two *s*, and two step *s*. *Educ:* Bridgend Grammar Sch.; Univ. of Bristol (BSc, PhD, DSc). FInstP. Physicist: British Nylon Spinners, 1955–56; Tube Investments Res. Lab., 1956–58; Physics Department, University of Reading, 1958–92: Res. Physicist, 1958–61; successively, Lectr, Reader, Personal Prof., 1961–92; Hd of Dept, 1984–88; Warden of Wantage Hall, Reading Univ., 1971–84. For. Associate, RSSAf 1995. *Publications:* papers in Proc. Royal Soc. and Phil. Mag., almost entirely concerning synthetic and natural diamond. *Recreation:* gardening. *Address:* Aston, Tutts Clump, Reading, Berks RG7 6JZ. *T:* (0118) 974 4498.

EVANS, Dr Trevor John; Chief Executive, Ergonomics Society, since 2007; *b* 14 Feb. 1947; *o s* of late Evan Alban Evans and of Margaret Alice Evans (*née* Hilton); *m* 1973, Margaret Elizabeth (*née* Whitham); three *s* one *d*. *Educ:* King's Sch., Rochester; University Coll., London (BSc (Eng) 1968, PhD 1972; Fellow, 1997); CEng, FIChemE (Hon. FIChemE 2006); CSci. Res. Officer, CSIR, Pretoria, 1968–69; Ford Motor Co., Aveley, Essex, 1972–73; Institution of Chemical Engineers: Asst Sec., Technical, 1973–75; Dep. Sec., 1975–76; Gen. Sec., 1976–94; Chief Exec., 1994–2006. Member: Bd, Council of Science and Technology Institutes, 1976–87; Exec. Cttee, Commonwealth Engineers Council, 1976–2004; Steering Cttee, DTI Action for Engrg Prog., 1995–96, Bd, Science Council, 2001–06; Bd, Engrg Council (UK), 2002–06 (Dep. Chm., 2005–06); Engrg and Technology Bd, 2005–; Chm. Exec. Cttee, World Chem. Engrg Council, 2006–. Jt Hon. Sec., European Fedn of Chem. Engrg, 1976–2006. Mem. Ct, Imperial Coll., London, 1998–2006. FCMI; FRSA. Hon. Mem., Czech Soc. of Chemical Engrg, 2006. Kurnakov Meml Medal, USSR Acad. of Scis, 1991; Titanium Achema Plaque, 1997. *Publications:* scientific papers and general articles in Chemical Engrg Science, The Chem. Engr, etc. *Recreations:* home renovation, drama. *Address:* The Ergonomics Society, Elms Court, Elms Grove, Loughborough LE11 1RG. *T:* (01509) 234904.

EVANS, Very Rev. Trevor Owen; Dean of Bangor, 1998–2003; *b* 10 July 1937; *s* of John James Pierce Evans and Elizabeth Jane Evans; *m* 1962, Ann Christine Stephens; one *s* one *d*. *Educ:* Dolgellau Boys' Grammar Sch.; UCW, Aberystwyth (BSc); Coll. of the Resurrection, Mirfield. Ordained deacon, 1961, priest, 1962; Diocese of Bangor: Curate, Barmouth, 1961–64; Curate, 1964–70, Vicar, 1970–75, Llandudno; Vicar, Llanidloes, 1975–89; RD, Arwystli, 1976–89; Preb. and Canon of Bangor Cathedral, 1982–98; Rector of Trefdraeth, 1989–90; Dir of Ministry, 1989–98; Rector of Llanfair PG with Penmynydd, 1990–98, also with Llanddaniel-Fab and with Llanedwen, 1997–98; Surrogate, 1978–98. *Recreations:* hill-walking, wood-turning, ornithology, geology, geomorphology. *Address:* Hafan, 3 Coed y Castell, Bangor LL57 1PH.

EVANS, Valerie Jean, CBE 1991; FIBiol; Chair, Gender Statistics Users Group, since 2000; human rights activist; *b* 26 July 1930; *d* of Connie and Wilfred Evans. *Educ:* Wales; Bedford Coll., London Univ. (BSc). Science teacher, 1952–67; HM Inspectorate of Schools, 1967–90: specialist in science and develt of secondary school curriculum; Divl Staff Inspector, E and W Midlands Div., Birmingham, 1977–90. Soroptimist Internat. UK rep. on Women's Nat. Commn, 1994–97; Co-Chair, 1997–98, Chair, 1998–99, Women's Nat. Commn; Soroptimist Internat. Rep. to Econ. Commn of Europe reg. of UN, 1999–2002. Trustee or member, numerous educnl advisory bodies. *Recreations:* reading, music, china, paintings, cooking, gardens, wine. *Address:* Coombe, 84 Salisbury Road, Moseley, Birmingham B13 8JY.

EVANS, Maj.-Gen. William Andrew, CB 1993; DL; Secretary, Council of TAVRAs, 1993–2001; *b* 5 Aug. 1939; *s* of late Maj.-Gen. Roger Evans, CB, MC and Eileen Evans; *m* 1964, Virginia Susan, *e d* of late William Robert Tomkinson and Helen Mary Tomkinson, MBE; two *d*. *Educ:* Sherborne; RMA Sandhurst; Christ Church, Oxford (MA). Commnd 5th Royal Inniskilling Dragoon Guards, 1959; served in BAOR, Middle East, Cyprus, Libya, N Ireland; Staff Coll., Bracknell, 1971; Army Instructor, RAF Cranwell, 1974–75; Instructor, Army Staff Coll., 1978–80; CO 5th Royal Inniskilling Dragoon Guards, 1980–82 (despatches, 1981); Col, Asst Dir (Policy), Defence Policy Staff, 1982–83; Comdr 4 Armd Bde, 1983–85; RCDS 1986; DCS, HQ BAOR, 1987–89; GOC Eastern Dist, 1989–92, retired. Pres., Essex, Army Benevolent Fund, 1997–; Vice Chm., Royal Dragoon Guards Regtl Assoc., 1992–2002; Member Council: ACFA, 1993–2001; Union Jack Club, 1995–. Pres., Army Cricket Assoc., 1989–91; Chm., Combined Services Cricket Assoc., 1990. Trustee, Daws Hall Trust, 2000–. Mem., Court, Essex Univ., 1994–. Liveryman, Broderers' Co., 1992–. DL Essex, 1998. *Recreations:* fishing, birdwatching, golf, beekeeping. *Address:* Lyston House, Sudbury, Suffolk. *Club:* Essex.

EVANS, Dr (William) David; Director, Innovation, Department for Innovation, Universities and Skills (formerly Director, Technology and Innovation, Department of Trade and Industry), since 2006; *b* 20 April 1949; *s* of late Harold Evans and Gladys Evans (*née* Webber); *m* 1980, Elizabeth Crowe; three *s* one *d*. *Educ:* Haberdashers' Aske's School, Elstree; St Catherine's College, Oxford (BA 1971; DPhil 1974; Senior Scholar). FRAS 1975. Dept of Energy, 1974–80; First Sec., Science and Technology, British Embassy, Bonn, 1980–83; Asst Sec., 1984–89, Chief Scientist, 1989–92, Dept of Energy; Department of Trade and Industry: Hd of Envmt Div., 1992–94; Hd of Technology and Innovation Div., 1994–96; Director: Technol. and Standards, later Technol. and Standards Directorate, 1996–98; Competitiveness, 1998–2001; Dep. Chief Exec., Small Business Service, 2001–03; Dir, Finance and Resource Mgt, 2003–05; Acting Dir Gen., Services Gp, 2005–06. Member: NERC, 1989–92; EPSRC, 1994–98; PPARC, 1994–98; Assessor, SERC, ACORD, 1989–92. Interim Chief Exec., Technol. Strategy Bd, 2007. Senator, Engrg Council, 1996–98. *Publications:* scientific papers in professional jls. *Recreations:* music, reading, history of technology. *Address:* Department for Innovation, Universities and Skills, Kingsgate House, 66–74 Victoria Street, SW1E 6SW.

EVANS, (William) Lindsay; DL; freelance lecturer, television actor and presenter; Trustee, National Heritage Memorial Fund, 1992–99; Chairman, Committee for Wales, Heritage Lottery Fund, 1998–99; *b* 22 March 1933; *o s* of John Evans and Nellie (*née* Davies). *Educ:* Swansea GS; Univ. of Wales (BA, MA, DipEd); Jesus Coll., Oxford (MLitt 1961). School teacher, Middlesex CC, 1958–60; freelance newsreader, BBC, 1960–61; Asst Master, Llandovery Coll., 1961–65; Lectr in Drama, Bangor Normal Coll., 1965–67; Prin. Lectr and Hd of Drama Dept, Cartrefle Coll., Wrexham, 1967–91. Lectr, summer schools, Extra-Mural Dept, UCNW, Bangor, 1967–70; Standish Barry Lectr, Irish Georgian Soc., 2005. Member: Exec. Cttee, N Wales Arts Assoc., 1973–76; Welsh Arts Council, 1982–88; Historic Bldgs Council for Wales, 1977–99; Welsh Cttee, NT, 1984–90. Trustee, Patti Theatre Preservation Trust, 2004–. DL Clwyd, 1999. Author of numerous radio and television plays and documentaries in English and Welsh. *Publications:* Y Gelltydd (novel), 1980; The Castles of Wales, 1998; *contributed to:* Everyman's Guide to England & Wales, 2000; Treasures of Britain, 2002; The Twentieth Century Great House, 2002; articles on aspects of built envmt. *Recreations:* friends, music, discovering places and buildings. *Address:* 100 Erddig Road, Wrexham LL13 7DR.

EVANS, Very Rev. Wyn; *see* Evans, Very Rev. J. W.

EVANS, Wynford; *see* Evans, J. W.

EVANS-ANFOM, Emmanuel, FRCSE 1955; Commissioner for Education and Culture, Ghana, 1978–88; Member, Council of State, 1979; Chairman, National Education Commission, since 1984; *b* 7 Oct. 1919; *m* 1952, Leonora Francetta Evans (*d* 1980); three *s* one *d*; *m* 1984, Elise Henkel. *Educ:* Achimota School; Edinburgh University (MB ChB 1947; DTM&H; Alumnus of the Year Award, 1996). House Surgeon, Dewsbury Infirmary, 1948–49; Medical Officer, Gold Coast Medical Service, 1950–56, Specialist Surgeon, 1956–67; Senior Lecturer, Ghana Medical School, 1966–67; Vice-Chancellor, Univ. of Science and Technology, Kumasi, 1967–74. Mem., WHO Expert Panel on Med. and Paramed. Educn, 1972–; Chairman: Nat. Council for Higher Educn, 1974–78; W African Exams Council, 1991–94; Chairman: Med. and Dental Council; Akrofi-Christaller Centre for Mission Res. and Applied Theology, 1986–; Inter-church and Ecumenical Relations Cttee, Presbyterian Church of Ghana, 1990–. Titular Mem., Internat. Assoc. Surgeons; Past President: Ghana Medical Assoc.; Assoc. of Surgeons of W Africa; FICS. Fellow: Ghana Acad. Arts and Sciences, 1971 (Pres., 1987–91); African Acad. of Scis, 1986. Chm., Ghana Hockey Assoc. Pres., Ghana Boys' Brigade Council, 1987–. Hon. DSc: Salford, 1974; Kwame Nkrumah Univ. of Sci. and Technol., 2003. Life Achievement Award, Ghana Med. and Dental Council, 2004. Mem., Order of the Star of Ghana, 2006. *Publications:* Aetiology and Management of Intestinal Perforations, Ghana Med. Jl, 1963; Traditional Medicine in Ghana: practice problems and prospects, 1986; To the Thirsty Land: autobiography of a patriot, 2003. *Recreations:* hockey, music, art. *Address:* PO Box M135, Accra, Ghana.

EVANS-BEVAN, Sir Martyn Evan, 2nd Bt *cr* 1958; *b* 1 April 1932; *s* of Sir David Martyn Evans-Bevan, 1st Bt, and Eira Winifred, *d* of late Sidney Archibald Lloyd Glanley; *S* father, 1973; *m* 1957, Jennifer Jane Marion, *d* of Robert Hugh Stevens; four *s*. *Educ:* Uppingham. Entered family business of Evan Evans Bevan and Evans Bevan Ltd, 1953. High Sheriff of Breconshire, 1967; Liveryman, Worshipful Co. of Farmers; Freeman, City of London. *Recreations:* shooting and fishing. *Heir:* *s* David Gawain Evans-Bevan [*b* 16 Sept. 1961; *m* 1987, Philippa, *y d* of Patrick Sweeney; two *s* one *d*]. *Address:* Spring Valley, Rue de Creux, Baillot St Ouen, Jersey, CI. *Club:* Carlton.

EVANS-FREKE, family name of **Baron Carbery**.

EVANS-LOMBE, Hon. Sir Edward (Christopher), Kt 1993; a Judge of the High Court of Justice, Chancery Division, 1993–2008; *b* 10 April 1937; *s* of Vice-Adm. Sir Edward Evans-Lombe, KCB, and Lady Evans-Lombe; *m* 1964, Frances Marilyn MacKenzie, DL; one *s* three *d*. *Educ:* Eton; Trinity Coll., Cambridge (MA). National Service, 1955–57: 2nd Lieut Royal Norfolk Regt. Called to the Bar, Inner Temple, 1963, Bencher, 1985. Standing Counsel to Dept of Trade in Bankruptcy matters, 1971; QC 1978; a Recorder, 1982–93. Chm., Agricultural Land Tribunal, S Eastern Region, 1983–93. *Recreations:* fishing, ornithology, amateur archaeology. *Address:* c/o Royal Courts of Justice, Strand, WC2A 2LL. *Club:* Norfolk (Norwich).

EVANS-TIPPING, (Sir) David Gwynne, (5th Bt *cr* 1913, of Oaklands Park, Awre, Co. Gloucester); *b* 25 Nov. 1943; *e s* of Sir Francis Loring Gwynne-Evans, 4th Bt (who assumed name of Evans-Tipping, 1943–58), and of his 1st wife, Elisabeth Fforde, *d* of J. Fforde-Tipping; *S* father, 1993, but does not use the title. *Educ:* Trinity Coll., Dublin (BAgricSci). *Heir:* *b* Christopher Evan Evans-Tipping [*b* 27 Feb. 1946; *m* 1974, Fenella Catherine Morrison; one *s* one *d*].

EVATT, Hon. Elizabeth Andreas, AC 1995 (AO 1982); Member: World Bank Administrative Tribunal, 1998–2006; International Commission of Jurists, since 2003; *b* 11 Nov. 1933; *d* of Clive Raleigh Evatt, QC and Marjorie Hannah (*née* Andreas); *m* 1960, Robert J. Southan, *qv*; one *d* (one *s* decd). *Educ:* Sydney Univ. (LLB); Harvard Univ. (LLM). Called to the Bar: NSW, 1955; Inner Temple, 1958. Chief Judge, Family Court of Australia, 1976–88. Dep. Pres., Australian Conciliation and Arbitration Commn, 1973–89; Chairperson, Royal Commn on Human Relationships, 1974–77; Dep. Pres., Australian Ind. Relns Commn, 1989–94; Pres., Australian Law Reform Commission, 1988–93 (Mem., 1993–94). Member: UN Cttee on Elimination of Discrimination against Women, 1984–92 (Chairperson, 1989–91); UN Human Rights Cttee, 1993–2000; Human Rights and Equal Opportunity Commn, Australia, 1995–98. Chancellor, Univ. of Newcastle, 1988–94. Hon. LLD: Sydney, 1985; Macquarie, 1989; Queensland, 1992; Flinders, 1994; Univ. of NSW, 1996; Hon. Dr Newcastle, 1988. *Publication:* Guide to Family Law, 1986, 2nd edn 1991. *Recreation:* music. *Address:* Unit 2003, 184 Forbes Street, Darlinghurst, NSW 2010, Australia. *Club:* Royal Corinthian Yacht.

EVE, family name of **Baron Silsoe**.

EVE, Judith Mary, CBE 2005 (OBE 1998); Legal Chairman (part-time) for the Appeals Service, since 1984; *b* 13 April 1949; *d* of Edward Steele and Adele Steele (*née* Barnes); *m* 1st, 1971, Richard Eve (marr. diss. 1987); one *s*; 2nd, 1992, John McQuoid. *Educ:* Queen's Univ. of Belfast (LLB 1971). Called to the Bar, NI, 1973; Queen's University of Belfast: Lectr in Law, 1971–82; Sen. Lectr, 1982–92; Dean, Faculty of Law, 1986–89; Internat. Liaison Officer, 1989–2002. Member: Rent Assessment Panel for NI, 1985–91 and 1994–97; Mental Health Commn for NI, 1986–90; EOC for NI, 1992–98; Mem., 1993–2006, Chair, 1998–2006, CS Comrs for NI. Non-exec. Dir, N and W Belfast HSS Trust, 1993–2000. Mem., NI Council for Postgrad. Med. and Dental Educn, 2002–04; Mem. and Dep. Chm., NI Med. and Dental Trng Agency, 2004–. Ind. Assessor, OCPA (NI), 2004–. Mem., Bd of Visitors, Maghaberry Prison, 1990–92. Dir, BIH Housing Assoc., 1984– (Chm., 1985–87). *Recreation:* travel. *Address:* 47 Deramore Park South, Belfast BT9 5JY.

EVE, Trevor John; actor, since 1974; producer, since 1997; *b* 1 July 1951; *s* of Stewart Frederick Eve and Elsie (*née* Hamer); *m* 1980, Sharon Maughan; two *s* one *d*. *Educ:* Bromsgrove Sch.; Kingston Sch. of Architecture; Royal Acad. of Dramatic Art (Bancroft Gold Medal). *Theatre* includes: John, Paul, George, Ringo and Bert, 1975, Filumena, 1977, Lyric; A Bit of Rough, Soho Poly, 1977; Children of a Lesser God, Albery (Best Actor, Olivier Awards and Variety Club of GB), 1981; The Genius, Royal Court, 1983; High Society, Victoria Palace, 1986; Man Beast and Virtue, RNT, 1989; A Winter's Tale, Young Vic, 1991; Inadmissible Evidence, RNT, 1993; Uncle Vanya, Albery (Best Actor in Supporting Role, Olivier Awards and British Regl Th. Awards), 1997; *films* include: Dracula, 1979; Scandal, 1989; Aspen Extreme, 1993; The Tribe, Appetite, 1998; Possession, 2002; Troy, 2004; She's Out of My League, 2008; *television* includes: Shoestring, 1979–81 (Best TV Actor, Variety Club of GB, 1980); Jamaica Inn, 1983; A Wreath of Roses, 1986; Shadow of the Sun, 1987; A Sense of Guilt, 1988; Parnell and the Englishwoman, 1990; A Doll's House, 1992; Murder in Mind, Black Easter, The Politician's Wife, 1994; Heat of the Sun, 1997; An Evil Streak, 1998; David Copperfield, 1999; Waking the Dead, 2000–05, 2007; Lawless, 2004; The Family Man, 2006; Most Sincerely, 2008; *producer for television:* Alice Through the Looking Glass, 1998; Cinderella, 2000; Twelfth Night, 2003. Patron: Childhope Internat., 1998–; Amazon Co-op., 2004–. *Recreations:* tennis, ski-ing, golf, painting, architecture. *Address:* c/o Projector Pictures, 20–21 Newman Street, W1T 1PG. *T:* (020) 7861 8000, *Fax:* (020) 7861 8182; *e-mail:* film@projector.co.uk. *Clubs:* Chelsea Arts, Hurlingham, Queen's; Wentworth.

EVELEIGH, Rt Hon. Sir Edward Walter; PC 1977; Kt 1968; ERD; MA; a Lord Justice of Appeal, 1977–85; *b* 8 Oct. 1917; *s* of Walter William and Daisy Emily Eveleigh; *m* 1940, Vilma Bodnar; *m* 1953, Patricia Helen Margaret Bury (decd); two *s* (and one *s* decd); *m* 1996, Nell A. Cox. *Educ:* Peter Symonds; Brasenose Coll., Oxford (Hon. Fellow 1977). Commissioned in the Royal Artillery (Supplementary Reserve), 1936; served War of 1939–45 (despatches, 1940). Called to Bar, Lincoln's Inn, 1945, Bencher 1968, Treas., 1988; QC 1961. Recorder of Burton-on-Trent, 1961–64, of Gloucester, 1964–68; Chm., QS, County of Oxford, 1968–71 (Dep. Chm., 1963–68); a Judge of the High Court of Justice, Queen's Bench Div., 1968–77; Presiding Judge, SE Circuit, 1971–76. Mem., General Council of the Bar, 1965–67. Mem., Royal Commn on Criminal Procedure, 1978–80; Chm., Statute Law Soc., 1985–89; President: British-German Jurists' Assoc., 1974–85; Bar Musical Soc., 1980–89. Hon. Citizen: Texas, 1980; Austin, 1985; Dallas, 1985. *Club:* Garrick.

EVENNETT, David Anthony; MP (C) Bexleyheath and Crayford, since 2005; *b* 3 June 1949; *s* of late Norman Thomas Evennett and of Irene Evennett; *m* 1975, Marilyn Anne Smith; two *s*. *Educ:* Buckhurst Hill County High School for Boys; London School of Economics and Political Science (BSc (Econ) Upper Second Hons, MSc (Econ)). School Master, Ilford County High School for Boys, 1972–74; Marine Insurance Broker, Lloyd's, 1974–81; Mem., Lloyd's, 1976–92; Dir, Lloyd's Underwriting Agency, 1982–91; Commercial Liaison Manager, Bexley Coll., 1997–2001; mgt lectr and consultant, 2001–05. Consultant, J & H Marsh and McLennan (UK), then Marsh (UK), Ltd, 1998–2000. Redbridge Borough Councillor, 1974–78. Contested (C) Hackney South and Shoreditch, 1979; MP (C) Erith and Crayford, 1983–97; contested (C) Bexleyheath and Crayford, 1997, 2001. PPS to Minister of State, Dept of Educn, 1992–93, to Sec. of State for Wales, 1993–95, to Sec. of State for Educn and Employment, 1996–97; an Opposition Whip, 2005–. Member, Select Committee: on Educn, Science and the Arts, 1986–92; for Educn and Skills, 2005. Vice-Chm., H of C Motor Club, 1992–97 (Sec., 1985–86). Vice-Pres., Hackney S and Shoreditch Cons. Assoc., 1985–97; Dep. Chm. (Pol), Bexleyheath and Crayford Cons. Assoc., 2001–03. *Recreations:* my family, reading, history, music, cinema. *Address:* House of Commons, SW1A 0AA. *Club:* Bexleyheath Conservative.

EVENS, Rt Rev. Robert John Scott; *see* Crediton, Bishop Suffragan of.

EVERALL, Mark Andrew; QC 1994; **His Honour Judge Everall;** a Circuit Judge since 2006; *b* 30 June 1950; *s* of late John Everall, FRCP and of Pamela Everall; *m* 1978, Anne Perkins; two *d*. *Educ:* Ampleforth Coll., York; Lincoln Coll., Oxford (MA). Called to the Bar, Inner Temple, 1975, Bencher, 1998; Asst Recorder, 1993–96; a Recorder, 1996–2006. *Publication:* (ed jtly) Rayden and Jackson on Divorce and Family Matters, 17th edn 1997. *Recreations:* walking, music, architecture. *Address:* Circuit Office, Rose Court, 2 Southwark Bridge, SE1 9HS.

EVERARD, John Vivian; HM Diplomatic Service, retired; Ambassador to the Democratic People's Republic of Korea, 2006–08; *b* 24 Nov. 1956; *s* of William Ralph Everard and Margaret Nora Jennifer Everard (*née* Massey); *m* 1990, Heather Ann Starkey. *Educ:* King's Sch., Chester; King Edward VI Sch., Lichfield; Emmanuel Coll., Cambridge (BA 1978; MA 1986); Peking Univ.; Manchester Business Sch. (MBA 1986). Joined HM Diplomatic Service, 1979: FCO, 1979–81; Third (later Second) Sec., Peking, 1981–83; Second Sec., Vienna, 1983–84; Manchester Business Sch., 1984–86; Metapraxis Ltd, 1986–87; FCO, 1987–90; First Sec., Santiago, 1990–93; Chargé d'Affaires, Minsk, 1993; Ambassador, Belarus, 1993–95; OSCE Mission to Bosnia and Hercegovina, 1995–96; Dep. Hd, Africa (Equatorial) Dept, FCO, 1996–98; Counsellor (Political, Econ. and Develt), Peking, 1998–2000; Ambassador, Uruguay, 2001–05. *Recreations:* reading, travel, cats, cycling.

EVERARD, Richard Anthony Spencer; Vice Lord-Lieutenant of Leicestershire, since 2003; Chairman, Everards Brewery Ltd, since 1988 (Director, since 1983); *b* 31 March 1954; *s* of late Maj. Richard Peter Michael Spencer and Bettyne Ione (*née* Everard, formerly Lady Newtown-Butler); name changed to Everard by deed poll, 1971; *m* 1981, Caroline Anne Hill; one *s* one *d*. *Educ:* Eton; RMA Sandhurst. Commnd 1973, Lieut 1975, Royal Horse Guards 1st Dragoons, 1973–77. Pres., Age Concern Leics, 1992–. Trustee: Leics Police Charitable Trust, 1998–; County Air Ambulance, 1999–. Hon. Col, Leics, Northants and Rutland ACF, 2007–. Master, Co. of Brewers, 2004. DL 1997, High Sheriff, 2002–03, Leics. *Recreations:* shooting, ski-ing, flying helicopters, motorcycling, tennis, golf. *Address:* East Farndon Hall, Market Harborough, Leics LE16 9SE; Everards Brewery Ltd, Castle Acres, Narborough, Leics LE19 1BY. *T:* (0116) 201 4307, *Fax:* (0116) 281 4198. *Clubs:* MCC; Air Squadron; Eton Ramblers; Luffenham Heath Golf.

EVERARD, Sir Robin (Charles), 4th Bt *cr* 1911; *b* 5 Oct. 1939; *s* of Sir Nugent Henry Everard, 3rd Bt and Frances Audrey (*d* 1975), *d* of J. C. Jesson; *S* father, 1984; *m* 1963, Ariel Ingrid, *d* of late Col Peter Cleasby-Thompson, MBE, MC; one *s* two *d*. *Educ:* Sandroyd School; Harrow; RMA Sandhurst. Short service commn, Duke of Wellington's Regt, 1958–61. Money Broker; Jt Managing Director, P. Murray-Jones, 1962–76; Consultant, 1976–91. *Heir:* *s* Henry Peter Charles Everard [*b* 6 Aug. 1970; *m* 2003, Nicola Anne de Poher Wilkinson, *d* of late Geoffrey de la Poer Wilkinson; one *s* one *d*]. *Address:* Church Farm, Shelton, Long Stratton, Norwich NR15 2SB.

EVERARD, Timothy John, CMG 1978; HM Diplomatic Service, retired; Secretary General, Order of St John, 1988–93; *b* 22 Oct. 1929; *s* of late Charles M. Everard and Monica M. Everard (*née* Barford); *m* 1955, Josiane Romano; two *s* two *d*. *Educ:* Uppingham Sch.; Magdalen Coll., Oxford. BA (Mod. Langs). Banking: Barclays Bank DCO, 1952–62, in Egypt, Sudan, Kenya, Zaire. Entered Foreign (later Diplomatic) Service: First Sec., FO, 1962–63; First Sec., Commercial, Bangkok, 1964–66; resigned to take up directorship in Ellis & Everard Ltd, 1966–67. Rejoined Foreign and Commonwealth Office, Oct. 1967: First Sec., FO, 1967–68; Bahrain, 1969–72 (First Sec. and Head of Chancery, HM Political Residency); seconded to Northern Ireland Office, FCO, April–Aug. 1972; Consul-Gen., then Chargé d'Affaires, Hanoi, 1972–73; Economic and Commercial Counsellor, Athens, 1974–78; Commercial Counsellor, Paris, 1978–81; Minister, Lagos, 1981–84; Ambassador to GDR, 1984–88. Trustee, Dresden Trust, 1994–2005. KStJ 1988. *Recreations:* golf, tennis. *Address:* Leagues, Burnt Oak, Crowborough, Sussex TN6 3SD. *Club:* Reform.

EVERARD, William Fielding; His Honour Judge Everard; a Circuit Judge, Midland Circuit, since 2004; *b* 25 April 1949; *s* of Richard and Mary Everard; *m* 1980, Christine Bell. *Educ:* Repton; QUB (LLB 1972). Called to the Bar, Middle Temple, 1973; Hd of Chambers, KCH Barristers, Nottingham, 1996–2004; Asst Recorder, 1996–2000; Recorder, 2000–04. *Recreations:* flyfishing, shooting. *Address:* Leicester Crown Court, 90 Wellington Street, Leicester LE1 6HG. *Clubs:* Gentlemen of Leicestershire Cricket; Leicester Hockey.

EVERED, David Charles; Special Adviser, International Agency for Research on Cancer, World Health Organisation, 2001–03; *b* 21 Jan. 1940; *s* of late Thomas Charles Evered and Enid Christian Evered; *m* 1st, 1964, Anne Elizabeth Massey Lings, (Kit) (*d* 1998), *d* of John Massey Lings, Manchester; one *s* two *d*; 2nd, 2000, Sheila May Pusinelli, *d* of Charles Cecil Lennox Pusinelli and Margaret Chaloner Pusinelli, Thornton-le-Dale, Yorks. *Educ:* Cranleigh Sch., Surrey; Middlesex Hosp. Med. Sch. (BSc 1961, MB 1964; MRCP 1967, MD 1971). Junior hospital appointments, London and Leeds, 1964–70; First Asst in Medicine, Wellcome Sen. Res. Fellow and Consultant Physician, Univ. of Newcastle upon Tyne and Royal Victoria Infirmary, 1970–78; Dir, Ciba Foundn, 1978–88; Second Sec., MRC, 1988–96. Member: British Library Medical Information Review Panel, 1978–80; Council, St George's Hosp. Med. Sch. 1983–91; Cttee, Assoc. of Med. Res. Charities, 1981–84, 1987–88 (Vice-Chm., 1987–88); COPUS, Royal Soc. 1986–88; Media Resource Service Adv. Cttee, NY, 1986–; NW Thames RHA, 1988–90; Hammersmith & Queen Charlotte's SHA, 1989–94; Bd, Hammersmith Hosps NHS Trust, 1995–96; Council, Internat. Agency for Res. into Cancer (Lyon), 1988–96; Council, RPMS, 1994–96; Vice-Pres., Science Cttee, Louis Jeantet Fondation de Médecine, 1984–91; Chairman: Anglia & Oxford Res. Ethics Cttee, 1997–99; Nuffield Orthopaedic Centre NHS Trust, 1998–2001. FRCP 1978; FIBiol 1978; FRSocMed; Scientific Fellow, Zool Soc. of London (Mem. Council, 1985–89). Member: Soc. for Endocrinology; Eur. Thyroid Assoc. (Mem. Exec. Cttee, 1977–81, Sec.-Treas., 1983–89). *Publications:* Diseases of the Thyroid, 1976; (with R. Hall and R. Greene) Atlas of Clinical Endocrinology, 1979, 2nd edn 1990; (with M. O'Connor) Collaboration in Medical Research in Europe, 1981; numerous papers on medicine, education and science policy. *Recreations:* reading, history, tennis, Real tennis, gardening. *Address:* Old Rectory Farm, Rectory Road, Padworth Common, Berkshire RG7 4JD.

EVEREST, Prof. Kelvin Douglas, PhD; FEA; Andrew Cecil Bradley Professor of Modern Literature, University of Liverpool, since 1991; *b* 9 Sept. 1950; *s* of Les and Catherine Everest; *m* 1971, Faith Mary Rissen; three *d*. *Educ:* Reading Univ. (BA 1972; PhD 1977). Lectr, St David's UC Lampeter, 1975–79; Lectr, then Reader, Leicester Univ., 1979–91; Sen. Pro-Vice-Chancellor, Univ. of Liverpool, 2001–07. Mem., NW Regl Bd, NT, 2006–. Mem. Bd of Govs, RNCM, 2006–. An Associate Ed., Oxford

DNB, 1997–. Foundn FEA 1999. *Publications:* Coleridge's Secret Ministry, 1979; (ed) Shelley Revalued, 1983; (ed) The Poems of Shelley, vol. 1 1989, vol. 2 2000; English Romantic Poetry, 1990; (ed) Revolution in Writing, 1991; (ed) Bicentenary Essays on Shelley, 1992; (ed with A. Yarrington) Reflections of Revolution, 1993; Keats, 2002; contrib. numerous articles and chapters. *Recreations:* cricket, Liverpool FC, jazz guitar, wildlife, cooking, drinking. *Address:* School of English, University of Liverpool, Senate House, Liverpool L69 3BX. *T:* (0151) 794 2885, *Fax:* (0151) 794 2929; *e-mail:* k.d.everest@liverpool.ac.uk.

EVERETT, Bernard Jonathan, CVO 1999; HM Diplomatic Service, retired; Public Governor, Chesterfield Royal Hospital Foundation Trust, since 2007; *b* 17 Sept. 1943; *s* of late Arnold Edwin Everett and of Helene May Everett (*née* Heine); *m* 1970, Maria Olinda, *d* of Raul Correia de Albuquerque and Maria de Lourdes Gonçalves de Albuquerque; two *s* one *d* (and one *d* decd). *Educ:* King's Coll. Sch., Wimbledon; Lincoln Coll., Oxford (BA 1965). Researcher, Reader's Digest, 1965; entered HM Diplomatic Service, 1966; Third, later Second Sec., Lisbon, 1967; FCO, 1971; Consul, Luanda, 1975; FCO, 1976; Head of Chancery, Lusaka, 1978; Consul (Commercial), Rio de Janeiro, 1980; Asst Head, Information Dept, FCO, 1983; on secondment as Head, Sub-Saharan Africa Br., DTI, 1984; Ambassador to Guatemala, 1987–91; Consul-Gen., Houston, 1991–95; High Comr, Mozambique, 1996–2000; Consul-Gen., São Paulo and Dir of Trade and Investment for Brazil, 2000–03. *Recreations:* sport, performing arts, walking, gardening, family history, local issues.

EVERETT, Charles William Vogt; Chair, Hastings and Rother Primary Care Trust, since 2007; *b* 15 Oct. 1949; *s* of Dr Thomas Everett and Ingeborg Everett (*née* Vogt); *m* 1978, Elizabeth Vanessa Ellis; three *s*. *Educ:* Bryanston Sch.; Reading Univ. Admin. trainee, Lord Chancellor's Dept, 1971; Asst Private Sec. to Lord Chancellor, 1974–76; Dept of Transport, 1982–84; Lord Chancellor's Department: Asst Sec., 1984; Under Sec., 1991; Head of Policy and Legal Services Gp, 1991–94; Dir, Resource and Support Services, The Court Service, 1994–99; Home Office, 1999–2006: Director: Fire and Emergency Planning, 1999–2002; Corporate Develt and Services, 2002–06. Mem., Sussex Probation Bd, 2007–. *Address:* Hastings and Rother Primary Care Trust, Bexhill Hospital, Holliers Hill, Bexhill-on-Sea, E Sussex TN40 2DZ.

EVERETT, Christopher Harris Doyle, CBE 1988; MA; Director General and Secretary, Daiwa Anglo-Japanese Foundation, 1990–2000; *b* 20 June 1933; *s* of late Alan Doyle Everett, MBE, MS, FRCS, and Annabel Dorothy Joan Everett (*née* Harris); *m* 1955, Hilary (Billy) Anne (*née* Robertson); two *s* two *d*. *Educ:* Winchester College; New College, Oxford (MA 1st cl. Class. Mods and 1st cl. Lit. Hum.). Nat. Service, 2nd Lieut, Grenadier Guards, 1951–53. HM Diplomatic Service, 1957–70: posts included MECAS, Lebanon, Embassies in Beirut and Washington, and Foreign Office (Personnel Dept and Planning Staff); Headmaster: Worksop Coll., 1970–75; Tonbridge Sch., 1975–89. Chm., 1986, Vice-Chm., 1987, HMC. Pt-time Chm., CSSB, 1972–92; Mem., Extended Interview Bds for Police and Prison Services, and part-time assessor, Home Office Promotion and Selection Bds, 1974–. Hon. Liveryman, Skinners' Co., 1993– (Mem., Ct of Assts, 1997–; Master, 2002–03). JP Worksop, 1971–75, Tonbridge and W Malling, 1976–89. Hon. FCP 1988. *Recreations:* reading, walking, current affairs. *Address:* Lavender House, 12 Madeira Park, Tunbridge Wells, Kent TN2 5SX. *T:* (01892) 525624.

EVERETT, Eileen, (Mrs Raymond Everett); *see* Diss, E.

EVERETT, Katharine Winn; Director of Change, BBC, since 2004; *b* 3 July 1952; *d* of Comdr Peter Everett, OBE, RN retd and Penelope Everett (*née* Stapleton); *m* 1988, Horacio Queiro; one *s* one *d*. *Educ:* Lady Margaret Hall, Oxford (MA Eng. Lang. and Lit.). BBC Television: wardrobe asst, 1975–76; res. trainee, 1977–78; Producer, BBC Science, 1982–93; Finance Manager, BBC One, 1994–97; Hd of Programming, BBC Choice, 1997–99; Controller: Interactive TV, 1999–2001; BBC New Media, 2001–03. Vice-Chm., Relate Richmond, Kingston, Hounslow, 2006–. Mem., RTS, 2001. *Recreations:* walking, singing. *Address:* Media Centre, BBC White City, W12 7TQ.

EVERETT, Prof. Martin George, DPhil; Vice-Chancellor, University of East London, since 2007; *b* 25 May 1955; *s* of late Reginald Douglas Walter Everett and Joan Gladys Everett; *m* 1981, Vanessa Ann Kendrick; two *s*. *Educ:* Loughborough Univ. (BSc Maths 1976); Trinity Coll., Oxford (MSc Maths 1977; DPhil 1980). Thames Polytechnic, then University of Greenwich: Lectr, 1980–83; Sen. Lectr, 1983–86; Prin. Lectr, 1986–88; Reader, 1988–89; Prof., 1990–2003; Hd of Computing and Maths, 1991–2003; Campus Provost and Pro Vice-Chancellor, Univ. of Westminster, 2003–07. Vis. Hon. Fellow, Dept of Sociol., Univ. of Surrey, 1989–92. Treas., UK Heads of Depts of Mathematical Scis, 1999–2003. Mem., London Higher Bd, 2007–. Mem. Bd, Internat. Network of Social Network Analysts, 1994– (Pres., 2000–03). AcSS 2004. *Publications:* (jtly) Ucinet for Windows: software for social network analysis, 2002; papers on methods for social network analysis. *Recreations:* wine, theatre, Charlton Athletic FC. *Address:* University of East London, Docklands Campus, University Way, E16 2RD. *T:* (020) 8223 4000.

EVERETT, Oliver William, CVO 1991 (LVO 1980); Librarian, Windsor Castle and Assistant Keeper of The Queen's Archives, 1985–2002, Librarian Emeritus, since 2002; *b* 28 Feb. 1943; *s* of Charles Everett, DSO, MC and Judy Rothwell; *m* 1965, Theffania Vesey Stoney (separated 2003); two *s* two *d*. *Educ:* Felsted Sch.; Western Reserve Acad., Ohio, USA; Christ's Coll., Cambridge; Fletcher Sch. of Law and Diplomacy, Mass, USA. HM Diplomatic Service, 1967–81: First Sec., New Delhi, 1969–73; Head of Chancery, Madrid, 1980–81; Asst Private Sec. to HRH The Prince of Wales, 1978–80; Private Sec. to HRH The Princess of Wales, 1981–83. *Recreations:* lecturing, film, baseball. *Address:* 48 Egerton Gardens, SW3 2BZ. *T:* (020) 7581 3731; *e-mail:* olivereverett@royalcollection.org.uk. *Club:* Roxburghe.

EVERETT, Rupert; actor. *Educ:* Ampleforth Coll.; Central Sch. of Speech and Drama. Trained with Glasgow Citizens' Theatre, 1979–82; *stage* includes: Glasgow Citizens' Theatre: Waste of Time; Don Juan; Heartbreak House; The Vortex, 1988, transf. Garrick, 1989; The Picture of Dorian Gray, 1993; The Milk Train Doesn't Stop Here Anymore, 1994, transf. Lyric, Hammersmith, 1997; Another Country, Greenwich, transf. Queen's, 1982; Mass Appeal, Lyric, Hammersmith; L'importance d'être Constant, Théâtre de Chaillot, Paris, 1996; Some Sunny Day, Hampstead, 1996; *films* include: A Shocking Accident, 1982; Another Country, 1984; Dance with a Stranger, 1985; Duet for One, 1986; The Comfort of Strangers, 1990; Inside Monkey Zetterland, 1992; Prêt-à-Porter, 1994; The Madness of King George, 1995; My Best Friend's Wedding, 1997; B Monkey, 1998; An Ideal Husband, Shakespeare in Love, A Midsummer Night's Dream, 1999; The Next Best Thing, 2000; Unconditional Love, The Importance of Being Earnest, 2002; To Kill a King, 2003; Stage Beauty, 2004; Separate Lies, 2005; St Trinian's, 2007; *television* includes: The Far Pavilions, 1982. *Publications:* Hello Darling, Are You Working?, 1992; The Hairdressers of St Tropez, 1995; Red Carpets and Other Banana Skins (autobiog.), 2006. *Address:* c/o Independent, Oxford House, 76 Oxford Street, W1D 1BS.

EVERETT, Steven George; His Honour Judge Everett; a Circuit Judge, since 2007; *b* 21 July 1956; *s* of George and Jean Everett; *m* 1985, Melinda Birch; two *s*. *Educ:* Newport High Sch.; Lanchester Poly., Coventry (BA Business Law 1978). Admitted as solicitor, 1981; called to the Bar, Gray's Inn, 1989; criminal defence solicitor, 1981–83; prosecuting solicitor, 1983–86; Crown Prosecutor, 1986–89; barrister, Wales and Chester Circuit, 1989–2007; Asst Recorder, 1999–2000, Recorder, 2000–07. Bar Council: Member: Panel, Complaints Adv. Service, 1995–2007; Professional Conduct Cttee, 2005–07. *Recreations:* campanology, playing the piano (badly), visiting NT properties, supporting Everton FC and Newport County, watching any sport, eating decent meals in front of the TV, reading. *Address:* Bolton Combined Court Centre, Law Courts, Blackhorse Street, Bolton BL1 1SU.

EVERETT, Thomas Henry Kemp; Deputy Special Commissioner of Income Tax, 2000–03 (Special Commissioner of Income Tax, 1983–2000); *b* 28 Jan. 1932; *s* of late Thomas Kemp Everett and Katharine Ida Everett (*née* Woodward); *m* 1954, June (*née* Partridge); three *s*. *Educ:* Queen Elizabeth Hospital, Bristol; Univ. of Bristol (LLB Hons 1957). Solicitor (Hons), admitted 1960; Partner, Meade-King & Co., 1963–83. Clerk to General Commissioners, Bedminster Div., 1965–83. Chairman: Service 9, 1972–75; Bristol Council of Voluntary Service, 1975–80; St Christopher's Young Persons' Residential Trust, 1976–83; Mem., Governing Council, St Christopher's School, Bristol, 1983–89; Gov., Queen Elizabeth Hosp., 1974–92 (Vice-Chm. Govs, 1980–91); Pres., Queen Elizabeth Hosp. Old Boys' Soc., 1990–91. *Recreations:* music, motoring, gardening. *Address:* Dolebury Cottage, Dolberrow, Churchill, Winscombe, Som BS25 5NS. *T:* (01934) 852329.

EVERHART, Prof. Thomas Eugene, PhD; President, and Professor of Electrical Engineering and Applied Physics, California Institute of Technology, 1987–97, now President Emeritus and Professor Emeritus; *b* 15 Feb. 1932; *s* of William E. Everhart and Elizabeth A. Everhart (*née* West); *m* 1953, Doris A. Wentz; two *s* two *d*. *Educ:* Harvard Coll. (AB 1953); Univ. of California (MSc 1955); Clare Coll., Cambridge (PhD 1958). Department of Electrical Engineering and Computer Science, University of California, Berkeley: Asst Prof., 1958–62; Associate Prof., 1962–67; Prof., 1967–78; Dept Chm., 1972–77; Dean, Coll. of Engrg, Cornell Univ., 1979–84; Chancellor, Univ. of Illinois, Urbana-Champaign, 1984–87; Pro-Vice-Chancellor, Cambridge Univ., 1998. Director: General Motors Corp., 1989–2002; Hewlett-Packard Co., 1991–99; Reveo Inc., 1994–2003; Saint Gobain, 1996–; Raytheon Co., 1998–2006; Hughes Electronics Corp., 1999–2002; Agilent Technologies, 1999–2002. Trustee: CIT, 1998–; Harvard Bd of Overseers, 1999–2005 (Pres., 2004–05). Mem., NAE (USA), 1978; Foreign Mem., Royal Acad. of Engrg, 1990. Hon. LLD: Ill Wesleyan, 1990; Pepperdine, 1990; Hon. DEng Colo Sch. of Mines, 1990. Centennial Medal, 1984, Founders Medal, 2002, IEEE; Benjamin Garver Lamme Award, 1989, Centennial Medal, 1993, ASEE; Clark Kerr Award, Univ. of Calif., Berkeley, 1992. *Publication:* Microwave Communications, 1968. *Recreations:* hiking, fishing, ski-ing. *Address:* President Emeritus, Mail Code 202–31, California Institute of Technology, Pasadena, CA 91125, USA. *T:* (818) 3956303. *Clubs:* Athenæum (CIT), California (LA); Channel City (Santa Barbara).

EVERITT, Prof. Alan Milner, PhD; FRHistS; FBA 1989; Hatton Professor and Head of Department of English Local History, University of Leicester, 1968–82, now Professor Emeritus (Associate Professor, 1982–84); *b* 17 Aug. 1926; *s* of Robert Arthur Everitt and Grace Beryl Everitt (*née* Milner). *Educ:* Sevenoaks Sch.; Univ. of St Andrews (MA 1951); Inst. of Historical Res., London Univ. (Carnegie Scholar; PhD 1957). FRHistS 1969. Editorial Assistant, ACU, 1951–54; Department of English Local History, University of Leicester: Res. Assistant, 1957–59; Res. Fellow in Urban Hist., 1960–65; Lectr in Eng. Local Hist., 1965–68. Lectures: Gregynog, Univ. of Wales, 1976; Helen Sutermeister, UEA, 1982; James Ford Special, Univ. of Oxford, 1983; W. G. Hoskins, Univ. of Leicester, 1999. *Publications:* The County Committee of Kent in the Civil War, 1957; Suffolk and the Great Rebellion 1640–1660, 1960; The Community of Kent and the Great Rebellion 1640–60, 1966, 3rd edn 1986; Change in the Provinces: the seventeenth century, 1969; The Pattern of Rural Dissent: the nineteenth century, 1972; Perspectives in English Urban History, 1973; (with Margery Tranter) English Local History at Leicester 1948–1978, 1981; Landscape and Community in England, 1985; Continuity and Colonization: the evolution of Kentish settlement, 1986; (with John Chartres) Agricultural Markets and Trade 1500–1750, 1990; contribs to: The Agrarian History of England and Wales; Past and Present, Trans of RHistS, Agricl Hist. Rev., Urban History Yearbook, Jl of Histl Geog., Jl of Transport Hist., Archaeologia Cantiana, Local Historian, TLS, Nomina, Rural England, Landscapes, and other learned publications. *Recreation:* topographical research. *Address:* Fieldedge, Poultney Lane, Kimcote, Lutterworth, Leics LE17 5RX.

EVERITT, Anthony Michael; writer; Secretary-General, Arts Council of Great Britain, 1990–94 (Deputy Secretary-General, 1985–90); *b* 31 Jan. 1940; *s* of late Michael Anthony Hamill Everitt and Simone Dolores Cathérine (*née* de Vergriette; she *m* 2nd, John Brunel Cohen). *Educ:* Cheltenham Coll.; Corpus Christi Coll., Cambridge (BA Hons English, 1962). Lectured variously at National Univ. of Iran, Teheran, SE London Coll. of Further Educn, Birmingham Coll. of Art, and Trent Polytechnic, 1963–72; The Birmingham Post: Art Critic, 1970–75; Drama Critic, 1974–79; Features Editor, 1976–79; Director: Midland Gp Arts Centre, Nottingham, 1979–80; E Midlands Arts Assoc., 1980–85. Vis. Prof., Performing and Visual Arts, Nottingham Trent Univ., 1996–. Lead Reviewer, HK Arts Develt Council, 1998; Reviewer of Arts Councils: of NI, 2000; of Wales, 2001; of Ireland, 2001; of I of M, 2005. Chairman: Ikon Gall., Birmingham, 1976–79; Birmingham Arts Lab., 1977–79; Vice-Chm., Council of Regional Arts Assocs, 1984–85; Member: Drama Panel, 1974–78, and Regional Cttee, 1979–80, Arts Council of GB; Cttee for Arts and Humanities, 1986–87, Performing Arts Cttee, 1987–92, CNAA; General Adv. Council, IBA, 1987–90. Gov., Liverpool Inst. of Performing Arts, 2006– (Companion, 2003). Hon. Fellow, Dartington Coll. of Arts, 1995. *Publications:* Abstract Expressionism, 1974; in from the Margins, 1996; Joining In, 1997; The Governance of Culture, 1997; The Creative Imperative, 2000; Cicero: a turbulent life, 2001; New Voices, 2003; New Voices: an update, 2004; The First Emperor, Caesar Augustus and the Triumph of Rome, 2006; contribs to The Guardian, Financial Times, Studio Internat., Country Life, etc. *Address:* Westerlies, Anchor Hill, Wivenhoe, Essex CO7 9BL.

EVERITT, Prof. Barry John, PhD; ScD; FRS 2007, FMedSci; Master, Downing College, Cambridge, since 2003 (Fellow, 1976–2003); Professor of Behavioural Neuroscience, Department of Experimental Psychology, University of Cambridge, since 1997; *b* 19 Feb. 1946; *s* of Frederick John Everitt and Winifred Everitt; *m* 1st, 1966, Valerie Sowter (marr. diss. 1978); one *s*; 2nd, 1979, Dr Jane Carolyn Sterling; one *d*. *Educ:* Univ. of Hull (BSc Zool. 1967); Univ. of Birmingham (PhD 1970); MA, ScD 2004, Cantab. MRC Res. Fellow, Univ. of Birmingham Med. Sch., 1970–73; MRC Travelling Res. Fellow, Karolinska Inst., Sweden, 1973–74; Department of Anatomy, University of Cambridge: Demonstrator, 1974–79; Lectr, 1979–91; Reader in Neurosci., 1991–97; Dir of Studies in Medicine, Downing Coll., Cambridge, 1978–98. Ciba-Geigy Sen. Res. Fellow, Karolinska Inst., 1982–83; Vis. Prof., Univ. of Calif, San Francisco, 2000; Sterling

Vis. Prof., Univ. of Albany, NY, 2005; Internat. Dist. Scientist, Rikeu Inst., Tokyo, 2006; Lectures: EBBS Review, Madrid, 1993; Maudsley Bequest, 1997; Grass, Texas, 1997; Swammerdam, Amsterdam, 1999; Swedish Neurosci. Review, 1999; Hillarp, Miami, 1999; Soc. for Neurosci., Orlando, 2002; NIH Dir's, Washington, 2004; Internat. Narcotics, Kyoto, 2004; Spanish Psychobiol. Soc., 2004; Matarazzo, Univ. of Portland, Oregon, 2005; Dalbir Bindra, McGill, Canada, 2006; Grass Internat., UCLA, 2006; Johns Hopkins Univ., 2007; BMI Lausanne, 2007; Wallenberg, Stockholm, 2007; Elsevier, EBBS, Trieste, 2008; Internat. Basal Ganglia Soc., Amsterdam, 2008; President's, FENS, 2008. Editor-in-Chief: Physiol. and Behavior, 1994–99; European Jl Neurosci., 1997–; Reviewing Ed., Science, 2003–. Scientific Counsellor, Nat. Inst. on Drug Abuse, USA, 2002–06. Chairman: MRC Res. Studentships and Trng Awards Panel, 1995–97; Human Sci. Frontier Prog. Fellowships Cttee, 1994–96; Scientific Adv. Bd, Astra Arcus, Sweden, 1998–2001, Astra-Zeneca, 2001–04; Helsinki Neurosci. Centre, 2000–; Neurogenetics and Behavior Center, Johns Hopkins Univ., 2002–; Sci. Adv. Bd, Brain-Mind Inst., Lausanne, 2008–; Ecole des Neurosciences de Paris, 2008; Member: MRC Neurosci. and Mental Health Bd, 2001–05; Prog. Cttee, Soc. for Neuroscience, 2005–08. President: Brit. Assoc. Psychopharmacology, 1992–94; Eur. Brain and Behaviour Soc., 1998–2000; Eur. Behavioural Pharmacology Soc., 2003–05. Foreign Corresp. Mem., Amer. Coll. of Neuropsychopharmacology, 1999. FMedSci 2008. Highly Cited Neurosci. Researcher, Inst. Scientific Information, 2002–. *Publications:* Essential Reproduction, 1980, 5th edn 1999; over 400 papers in scientific jls. *Recreations:* opera, wine, cricket. *Address:* Downing College, Cambridge CB2 1DQ. *T:* (01223) 334806.

EVERITT, Caroline Mary; *see* Ludlow, C. M.

EVERITT, Father (Charles) Gabriel, OSB; Headmaster, Ampleforth College, since 2004; *b* 7 Jan. 1956; *s* of Prof. William Norrie Everitt and Katharine Elisabeth Everitt (*née* Gibson). *Educ:* Dundee High Sch.; Edinburgh Univ. (MA History 1978); Balliol Coll., Oxford (MA Theol. 1985; DPhil History 1986); St Stephen's House, Oxford. Asst Curate, St Aidan and St Columba, Hartlepool, 1986–89; recd into RC Church, 1989; entered Ampleforth Abbey, 1990, professed, 1991; ordained priest, 1994; Ampleforth College: Asst Master, 1992–97, Head, 1997–2003, Dept of Christian Theol.; Housemaster: St Aidan's, 1997–98; St Oswald's, 1998–2003; Third Master, 2000–03. *Recreations:* reading, cinema, weight training. *Address:* Ampleforth College, York YO62 4ER. *T:* (01439) 766800; *e-mail:* headmaster@ampleforth.org.uk.

EVERITT, Richard; Chief Executive, Port of London Authority, since 2004; *b* 22 Dec. 1948. Admitted solicitor; five yrs in private practice; joined legal dept, BAA, 1978, Head of Legal, 1984–90; Dir, Planning and Regulatory Affairs, 1990; Chief Exec., NATS Ltd, 2001–04. Non-exec. Dir, Air Partner plc, 2004–. *Address:* Port of London Authority, Bakers' Hall, 7 Harp Lane, EC3R 6LB.

EVERITT, William Howard, FREng; FIMechE, FIET; Group Managing Director, Technology, T & N plc, 1995–96; *b* 27 Feb. 1940; *s* of H. G. H. Everitt and J. S. Everitt; *m* Antha Cecilia; two *s*. *Educ:* Leeds Univ. (BSc). Director of Operations, IBM Europe, 1974; Managing Director: Wellworthy, AE, 1975–76; Bearings, AE, 1977–79; AE plc, 1983–86 (Dir, 1978); Dir, T & N plc, 1987–96; Man. Dir, Automotive, T & N, 1990–93. Non-exec. Dir, Domino Printing Services plc, 1997–. FREng (FEng 1988). *Recreation:* golf. *Address:* Horley House, Hornton Lane, Horley, near Banbury, Oxon OX15 6BL. *T:* (01295) 730603.

EVERSON, John Andrew; education consultant; *b* 26 Oct. 1933; *s* of Harold Leslie Everson and Florence Jane Stone; *m* 1961, Gilda Ramsden; two *s*. *Educ:* Tiffin Boys' Sch., Kingston-upon-Thames; Christ's Coll., Cambridge (MA); King's Coll., London (PGCE). Teacher: Haberdashers' Aske's Sch., Elstree, 1958–65; City of London Sch., 1965–68; Schools Inspectorate, DES, later Dept for Educn, 1968–92; Chief Inspector for Secondary Educn, 1981–89; seconded to Peat Marwick McLintock, 1989; Chief Inspector for Teacher Training, 1990–92. *Publications:* (with B. P. FitzGerald) Settlement Patterns, 1968; (with B. P. FitzGerald) Inside the City, 1972. *Recreations:* opera, walking, theatre, chess. *Address:* 74 Longdown Lane North, Epsom, Surrey KT17 3JF. *T:* (01372) 721556. *Club:* Athenæum.

EVERSON, Simon John; Headmaster, The Skinners' School, Tunbridge Wells, since 2006; *b* 31 Oct. 1965; *s* of John and Gilda Everson; *m* 2001, Virginia Murphy. *Educ:* St Alphege Jun. Sch.; Solihull Sch.; Fitzwilliam Coll., Cambridge (BA 1987; PGCE 1990); Nottingham Univ. (MA 1999). NPQH 2006. English teacher: Bretton Woods Community Coll., 1990–92 and 1993–94; Myokokogen Jun. High Sch., Japan, 1992–93; Nottingham High Sch. for Boys, 1994–99; Hd of English, Arnold Sch., 1999–2003; Dep. Headmaster, Westcliff High Sch. for Boys, 2003–06. *Recreations:* reading, music, philosophy, wine, exploring Neolithic sites. *Address:* The Skinners' School, St John's Road, Tunbridge Wells, Kent TN4 9PG.

EVERT, Christine Marie; American tennis player, retired 1989; founder, Chris Evert Charities Inc., 1989; *b* 21 Dec. 1954; *d* of James and Colette Evert; *m* 1st, 1979, John Lloyd (marr. diss. 1987); 2nd, 1988, Andy Mill (marr. diss.); three *s*; 3rd, 2008, Gregory John Norman, *qv*. *Educ:* St Thomas Aquinas High Sch., Fort Lauderdale. Amateur tennis player, 1970–72, professional player, 1972–89. Semi-finalist in US Open at age of 16; won numerous titles, including: Wimbledon: 1974, 1976, 1981 (doubles, 1976); French Open: 1974–75, 1979–80, 1983, 1985–86; US Open: 1975–78, 1980, 1982; Australian Open: 1982, 1984. Represented USA in Wightman Cup, 1971–73, 1975–82, and in Federation Cup, 1977–82. Pres., Women's Tennis Assoc., 1982–91. *Address:* c/o IMG, 1360 East 9th Street, Suite 100, Cleveland, OH 44114, USA; 7200 West Camino Real, Suite 310, Boca Raton, FL 33433, USA.

EVERTON, Timothy Charles; Dean of Educational Studies, 2001–06, and Head, Faculty of Education, 2002–06, University of Cambridge; Fellow, Homerton College, Cambridge, 2001–07, now Emeritus; *b* 28 March 1951; *s* of Charles John Everton and Patricia Anne Everton (*née* Sharpe); *m* 1974, Valerie Bates; three *d*. *Educ:* Queen Mary's Grammar Sch., Walsall; Keble Coll., Oxford (MA); Univ. of Keele (MSc). Teacher of maths in secondary schs in Walsall and Shrewsbury, 1974–81; Lectr in Maths Educn, NUU, 1981–83; Lectr, then Sen. Lectr in Educn, Univ. of Leicester, 1983–92; Homerton College, Cambridge: Dep. Principal, 1992–2001; Vice-Principal, 2001–05; Sen. Tutor, 1995–2001. Treasurer: British Curriculum Foundn, 1991–2007; UCET, 1999–2005. *Publications:* jointly: IT-INSET: partnership in training, 1989; Effective Learning: into a new ERA, 1990; 16–19 Mathematics: problem solving, 1991; 16–19: changes in education and training, 1992; 16–19 Mathematics: handbook for teachers, 1993; Mathematics for A and AS Level: Pure Mathematics, 1997. *Recreations:* watching sport, walking, reading, listening to jazz.

EVERY, Sir Henry (John Michael), 13th Bt *cr* 1641, of Egginton, Derbyshire; DL; Chairman, Derby Cathedral Council, since 2003; *b* 6 April 1947; *s* of Sir John Simon Every, 12th Bt and of Janet Marion, *d* of John Page; *S* father, 1988; *m* 1974, Susan Mary, *er d* of Kenneth Beaton, JP, Eastshotte, Hartford, Cambs; three *s*. *Educ:* Malvern College. FCA. Qualified as Chartered Accountant, 1970; worked in South Africa, 1970–7 Partner, Josolyne Layton-Bennett, Birmingham, 1979–81; merged with BDO Bind Hamlyn, 1982, then with Touche Ross, 1994, to form Deloitte & Touche; retired Partner, 2001. Chm., Burton Hosps NHS Trust, 2003–04. Pres., Birmingham and We Midlands Dist Soc. of Chartered Accountants, 1995–96 (Chm., Dist Trng Bd, 1991–93 Mem., Egginton Parish Council, 1987–2006. Mem. Cttee, Lunar Soc., 1993–2003. Gov Repton Sch., 2003–. Trustee: Nat. Meml Arboretum, 1996–2003; Repton Found 2002–04, 2006–. FRSA 1996. DL Derbys, 2006. *Recreations:* travel, National Trus gardening; supporter of Nottingham Forest FC. *Heir:* *s* Edward James Henry Every, *b* July 1975. *Address:* Cothay, Egginton, Derby DE65 6HJ.

EVES, David Charles Thomas, CB 1993; Associate Director, Sancroft International Lt since 2002; Deputy Director General, 1989–2002 and HM Chief Inspector of Factorie 1985–88 and 1992–2002, Health and Safety Executive; *b* 10 Jan. 1942; *s* of Harold Thom Eves and Violet Eves (*née* Edwards); *m* 1964, Valerie Ann Carter; one *d*. *Educ:* King's Sch Rochester; University Coll., Durham (BA). Teacher, Kent CC, 1963–64; HM Inspect of Factories, Min. of Labour, 1964; Health and Safety Executive: Under Sec., 1985–8 Dep. Sec., and Dep. Dir Gen., 1989–2002; Dir, Resources and Planning Div., 1988–8 International Association of Labour Inspection: Vice Pres., 1993–99; Sec. Gen., 1996–9 Technical Advr, 1999–2005. Ext. Examiner, Sch. of Law, Univ. of Warwick, 2007 Hon. Vice Pres., Safety Gps UK (formerly Nat. Health and Safety Gps Council), 2004 FIOSH (Hon. Vice Pres., 1992–). *Recreations:* sailing, fishing, music, reading, paintin gardening, wood turner. *Club:* Athenæum.

EVES, Ernest (Larry); Chairman, Jacob & Company Securities Inc., since 2007; Windsor, Ont, 17 June 1946; *s* of Harry Eves and Julie Eves (*née* Hawrelechko); *m*; one (one *s* decd). *Educ:* Vincent Massey High Sch.; Univ. of Toronto; Osgoode Law Sch. (LL 1970). Called to the Bar, Ont, 1972; QC (Ont) 1983. MPP (PC) Parry Sound, 1981–9 Parry Sound-Muskoka, 1999–2001, Dufferin-Peel-Wellington-Grey, Ontario, 2002–0 Government of Ontario: Parly Asst to Minister of Educn and Minister of Colls and Univ 1983; Minister: of Skills Develt, 1985; of Resource Develt and Provincial Sec. f Resources, 1985; of Community and Social Services, 1985; PC Party Chief Whi 1985–90, House Leader, 1990; Govt House Leader, 1995–96; Dep. Premier and Minist of Finance, 1995–2001; Vice-Chm., Policy and Priorities Bd, and Mgt Bd, Cabine 1995–2000; Premier of Ontario, Pres. of the Council, and Minister of Intergovtl Affai 2002–03; Leader of Opposition, 2003–04. Leader, PC Party, Ont, 2002–04. Partne Green and Eves, 1972–81; Vice Chm. and Sen. Advr, Credit Suisse First Bosto (Toronto), 2000–02; Lawyer, Borden, Ladner, Gervaise LLP, 2001–02. Chm., O Olympic Sports and Waterfront Develt Agency, 2000–01; Chm. and Special Adv Ontario Trade and Investment Adv. Council, 2006–; Dir, CB Richard Ellis Ltd (Canad 2006–. Founder and Chm., Justin Eves Foundn, 2005–. *Address:* 7th Floor, 56 Wellesl Street West, Toronto, ON M7A 2E7, Canada.

EVISON, Dame (Helen June) Patricia, DBE 1993 (OBE 1980); freelance actress stage, film, radio and television in New Zealand and Australia; *b* 2 June 1924; *d* of Re Ernest Oswald Blamires and Annie (*née* Anderson); *m* 1948, Roger Douglas Evison; tw *s* one *d*. *Educ:* Solway Coll., Masterton; Victoria Univ. (BA 1943); Auckland Teache Training Coll. (postgrad. course 1944); Auckland Univ. (DipEd 1944); LTCL (speec 1942). Directors course, Old Vic Theatre Centre, 1947–48 (first NZ bursary); Assistant Michel Saint-Denis, Young Vic Theatre Co., 1947–48; freelance director, Wellingto 1949–52; tutor for NZ Opera and NZ Ballet Schs, 1953–79. *Theatre includes:* Happy Day 1964, 1974; Father's Day, 1966; The Killing of Sister George, 1968; An Evening wi Katherine Mansfield (one-woman show), 1972; Awatea, 1974; Home, 1976; Juno and t Paycock, 1977; Hot Water, 1983; Last Days in Woolloomooloo, 1983; Ring Round t Moon, 1990; Steel Magnolias, 1991; Lettice and Lovage, 1993; The Cripple of Inishmaa 1999; *films:* Tim, 1979 (Best Supporting Actress, Aust. Film Inst., 1979); The Earthlin 1981; Starstruck, 1982; Bad Blood, 1982; The Silent One, 1983; The Clinic, 1983; Wh the Moon Saw, 1988; Moonrise, 1992; *television:* All Earth to Love, 1963; Pukeman 1971 (Cummings award for Best NZ Actress, 1972); Pig in a Poke, 1974 (Logie award f best individual acting perf., 1974); They Don't Clap Losers, 1974; Close to Home (serie 1975–82; The Emigrants, 1977; A Town Like Alice, 1982; Flying Doctors (serie 1984–87. Charter Member: Wellington Zonta Club; Zonta Club for Port Nicholso *Publication:* Happy Days in Muckle Flugga (autobiog.), 1998. *Recreations:* music, watchir cricket and soccer, reading, swimming, travel. *Address:* 11 Beerehaven Road, Seatou Heights, Wellington 6003, New Zealand. *T:* (4) 3888766.

EWANS, Sir Martin Kenneth, KCMG 1987 (CMG 1980); HM Diplomatic Servic retired; Chairman, Children's Aid Direct, 1996–2002; *b* 14 Nov. 1928; *s* of late Jo Ewans; *m* 1953, Mary Tooke; one *s* one *d*. *Educ:* St Paul's; Corpus Christi Col Cambridge (major scholar, MA). Royal Artillery, 1947–49, 2nd Lt. Join Commonwealth Relations Office, 1952; Second Sec., Karachi, 1954–55; First Se Ottawa, 1958–61; Lagos, 1962–64; Kabul, 1967–69. Counsellor, Dar-es-Salaa 1969–73; Head of East African Dept, FCO, 1973–77; Minister, New Delhi, 1978–8 Sen. Civilian Instructor, RCDS, 1982–83; High Commissioner: Zimbabwe, 1983–8 Nigeria, 1986–88. Chm., CSSB, 1989–95. Dir, Casalee SA, 1989–94. *Publication* Bharatpur, Bird Paradise, 1989; The Battle for the Broads, 1992; Afghanistan: a ne history, 2001; Afghanistan: a short history of its people and politics, 2002; Europe Atrocity, African Catastrophe, 2002; The Great Game: Britain and Russia in Central As 2003; Conflict in Afghanistan, 2005; Great Power Rivalry in Central Asia 1842–188 2005. *Recreations:* bird watching, writing. *Address:* 26 Gladstone Street, SE1 6EY.

EWART, David Scott; QC 2006; barrister; *b* 29 April 1964; *s* of David and Christi Ewart; one *s* one *d*. *Educ:* Hamilton Grammar Sch.; Trinity Coll., Oxford (BA 198 Called to the Bar, Gray's Inn, 1988. *Recreation:* bridge. *Address:* Pump Court T Chambers, 16 Bedford Row, WC1R 4EF. *T:* (020) 7414 8080. *Club:* Young Chels Bridge.

EWART, Dr Michael; Chief Executive, Scottish Prison Service, since 2007; *b* 9 Se 1952; *s* of James Ewart and late Joyce Goulden; partner, Dr Sally Anderson; one *s* one *Educ:* Jesus Coll., Cambridge (BA Hons 1974); York Univ. (DPhil 1977). Scottish Offic 1977–81; Asst Private Sec. to Sec. of State for Scotland, 1981–82; CS Fellow in Politi Univ. of Glasgow, 1982–83; Health Service Mgt Reform, 1983–86; Hd, Schs Div Scottish Educn Dept, 1986–91; Dep. Dir, Scottish Courts Admin, 1991–93; Chief Exe Scottish Court Service, 1993–99; Hd, Schs Gp, 1999–2002, Hd of Dept, 2002–0 Scottish Exec. Educn Dept. Member: Bd, Scottish Ballet, 2007–; Bd, Quality Scotlan 2007–. *Recreations:* music, books, military history, running, climbing (ice and rock), sk ing, geocaching. *Address:* Scottish Prison Service, Calton House, Redheughs Rig Edinburgh EH12 9HW. *T:* (0131) 244 8522; *e-mail:* mike.ewart@sps.gov.uk.

EWART, Sir (William) Michael, 7th Bt *cr* 1887, of Glenmachen, Co. Down and Glenbank, Co. Antrim; *b* 10 June 1953; *o s* of Sir (William) Ivan (Cecil) Ewart, 6th Bt ar Pauline Preston (*d* 1964); *S* father, 1995, but his name does not appear on the Official R of the Baronetage. *Educ:* Radley. *Recreations:* racing, ski-ing, travel. *Heir:* none. *Address:* Hill House, Hillsborough, Co. Down BT26 6AE. *Club:* Naval.

EWBANK, Sir Anthony (Bruce), Kt 1980; Judge of the High Court of Justice, Family Division, 1980–95; *b* 30 July 1925; *s* of late Rev. Harold Ewbank and Gwendolen Ewbank (*née* Bruce); *m* 1958, Moya McGinn; four *s* one *d. Educ:* St John's Sch., Leatherhead; Trinity Coll., Cambridge, Natural Sciences Tripos (MA). Sub Lieut RNVR, 1945–47. Maths Master, Stamford School, 1947–50; Physics Master, Epsom Coll., 1950–53. Permanent RNVR, 1951–56. Called to Bar, Gray's Inn, 1954; Bencher, 1980. Junior Counsel to Treasury in Probate matters, 1969; QC 1972; a Recorder of the Crown Court, 1975–80. Chm., Family Law Bar Assoc., 1978–80. *Address:* Beech Down, Elmhurst Road, Goring on Thames, Oxon RG8 9BN.

EWBANK, Ven. Walter Frederick; Archdeacon Emeritus and Canon Emeritus of Carlisle Cathedral; *b* Poona, India, 29 Jan. 1918; *er s* of late Sir Robert Benson Ewbank, CSI, CIE, and Frances Helen, *d* of Rev. W. F. Simpson; *m* 1st, 1941, Ida Margaret (*d* 1976), 3rd *d* of late John Haworth Whitworth, DSO, MC, Inner Temple; three *d;* 2nd, 1976, Mrs Josephine Alice Williamson (*née* Cartwright), MD, ChB, FRCOG (*d* 2003). *Educ:* Shrewsbury Sch.; Balliol Coll., Oxford (Classical Scholar, 1936; 1st, Classical Hon. Mods, 1938; 2nd, Hon. Sch. of Theology, 1946; BA and MA 1946); Bishops' Coll., Cheshunt, 1946; BD Oxon 1952. Friends' Ambulance Unit, 1939–42; agricl labourer, 1942–45; deacon, 1946; priest, 1947; Asst Curate, St Martin's, Windermere, 1946–49; Dio. Youth Chaplain and Vicar of Ings, 1949–52; Chap. to Casterton Sch. and Vicar of Casterton, 1952–62; Domestic Chap. to Bp of Carlisle, and Vicar of Raughtonhead, 1962–66; Vicar of St Cuthbert's, Carlisle, and Chap. to Corporation, 1966–71; Rural Dean of Carlisle, 1970–71; Archdeacon of Westmorland and Furness and Vicar of Winster, 1971–77; Archdeacon of Carlisle, 1977–84; Administrator of Church House, Carlisle and Chm., Diocesan Glebe Cttee, 1977–84; Canon Residentiary of Carlisle Cathedral, 1977–82; Hon. Canon, 1966–77 and 1982–84. Proctor in Convocation and Mem. Ch Assembly, 1957–70; Member: Canon Law Standing Commn, 1968–70; Faculty Jurisdiction Commn, 1979–83; Diocesan Director: of Ordinands, 1962–70; of Post Ordination Trng, 1962–66; Vice-Chm., Diocesan Synod, 1970–79; Chm., Diocesan Board of Finance, 1977–82. Chm., Carlisle Tithe Barn Restoration Cttee, 1968–70. Winter War Remembrance Medal (Finland), 1940. *Publications:* Salopian Diaries, 1961; Morality without Law, 1969; Charles Euston Nurse—A Memoir, 1982; Thomas Bloomer—A Memoir, 1984; Poems of Cumbria and of the Cumbrian Church, 1985; Ellen Margaret Cartwright—A Memoir, 1991; Memories of the Border Regiment in the First World War, 1991; Faith of Our Fathers, 1992; Characters and Occasions, 2002; articles in Church Quarterly Review. *Recreation:* classical studies. *Address:* 10 Castle Court, Castle Street, Carlisle CA3 8TP.

See also Baron Renfrew of Kaimsthorn, J. H. F. Fryer-Spedding.

EWENS, Prof. Warren John, PhD; FRS 2000; Professor of Biology, University of Pennsylvania, since 1972; *b* 23 Jan. 1937; *s* of John and Gwendoline Ewens; *m* 1st, 1961, Helen Wiley (marr. diss.); one *s* one *d;* 2nd, 1981, Kathryn Gogolin. *Educ:* Trinity Coll., Melbourne Univ. (MA); Australian Nat. Univ. (PhD 1964). Professor, Department of Mathematics: La Trobe Univ., 1967–72; Monash Univ., 1977–96. *Publications:* Population Genetics, 1969; Mathematical Population Genetics, 1979; Probability and Statistics in Bioinformatics, 2000. *Recreations:* tennis, bridge, reading. *Address:* c/o Department of Biology, University of Pennsylvania, PA 19104–6018, USA. *T:* (215) 8987109.

EWER, Graham Anderson, CB 1999; CBE 1991; President, European Logistic Association, 2004–06; *b* 22 Sept. 1944; *s* of late Robert and Maud Ewer; *m* 1969, Mary Caroline Grant; two *d. Educ:* Truro Cathedral Sch.; RMA, Sandhurst. FCILT (FILT 1999; FCIT 1999). Commnd RCT, 1965; served Germany, UK and ME, 1966–75; Army Staff Coll., 1976; Lt Col, Directing Staff, Army Staff Coll., 1984; CO, 8 Regt RCT, Munster, 1985–87; Col, DCS, G1/4 HQ 1st Armd Div., Verden, Germany and Gulf War, 1988–91; Comdt, Army Sch. of Transportation, 1991; Col, Logistic Support Policy Secretariat, 1992; Brig. 1993; Comd, Combat Service Support Gp, Germany and Guetersloh Garrison, 1993–94; Dir, Logistic Planning (Army), 1995; Maj. Gen. 1996; ACDS (Logistics), 1996–99; Chief Exec., Chartered Inst. of Logistics and Transport (UK), 1999–2004. Col Comdt, 2000, Rep. Col Comdt, 2007–08, RLC. FRSA 2004. *Publications:* contrib. Blackadder's War, ed M. S. White, 1995; contrib. to various jls. *Recreations:* sailing, military history. *Address:* c/o HSBC, 17 Boscawen Street, Truro, Cornwall TR1 2QZ. *Club:* Army and Navy.

EWING; *see Orr-Ewing and Orr Ewing.*

EWING, Annabelle Janet; solicitor; *b* 20 Aug. 1960; *d* of late Stewart Martin Ewing and of Winifred Margaret Ewing, *qv. Educ:* Craigholme Sch., Glasgow; Univ. of Glasgow (LLB Hons); Bologna Center, Johns Hopkins Univ.; Europa Inst., Amsterdam Univ. Apprentice lawyer, Ruth Anderson and Co., 1984–86; admitted solicitor, 1986; Legal Service, DG XIV, CEC, 1987; Associate, Lebrun de Smedt and Dassesse, Brussels, 1987–89; Associate, 1989–92, Partner, 1993–96, Akin Gump, Brussels; Special Counsel, McKenna and Cuneo, Brussels, 1996; EC lawyer, 1997; Associate, 1998–99, Partner, 1999–2001, Ewing & Co., solicitors, Glasgow; Consultant, Leslie Wolfson & Co., solicitors, Glasgow, 2001–03. MP (SNP) Perth, 2001–05; contested (SNP) Ochil and Perthshire South, 2005.

See also F. S. Ewing.

EWING, Bernadette Mary; *see Kelly, B. M.*

EWING, Fergus Stewart; Member (SNP) Inverness East, Nairn and Lochaber, Scottish Parliament, since 1999; Minister for Community Safety, since 2007; *b* 23 Sept. 1957; *s* of late Stewart Martin Ewing and of Winifred Margaret Ewing, *qv; m* 1983, Margaret McAdam (*d* 2006). *Educ:* Loretto Sch.; Glasgow Univ. (LLB). Solicitor, 1981; with Leslie Wolfson & Co., Solicitors, Glasgow, 1979–85; Partner, Ewing & Co., Solicitors, Glasgow, 1985–2000. Joined SNP, 1975; Mem., Nat. Exec., 1990–99, 2001–03. Contested (SNP) Inverness, Nairn and Lochaber, 1992, 1997. *Recreations:* reading, music, walking. *Address:* Burns Cottage, Tulloch's Brae, Lossiemouth, Morayshire IV31 6QY.

See also A. J. Ewing.

EWING, Maria Louise; soprano; *b* Detroit, 27 March 1950; *y d* of Norman Ewing and Hermina Ewing (*née* Veraar); *m* 1982, Sir Peter Reginald Frederick Hall, *qv* (marr. diss. 1990); one *d. Educ:* High School; Cleveland Inst. of Music. Studied with Marjorie Gordon, Eleanor Steber, Jennie Tourel, Otto Guth. First public performance, Meadowbrook, 1968 (Rigoletto); débuts Metropolitan Opera and La Scala, 1976; sings at Covent Garden, Glyndebourne, Salzburg, Paris, Metropolitan Opera, LA Opera, La Scala and other major venues; rôles include Blanche, Carmen, Cherubino, Dorabella, Lady Macbeth, Mélisande, La Périchole, Poppea, Rosina, Salomé, Susanna, Tosca, Zerlina; concerts and recitals. *Address:* e-mail: info@tomcroxonmanagement.co.uk.

EWING, Mrs Winifred Margaret; Member (SNP) Highlands and Islands, Scottish Parliament, 1999–2003; *b* 10 July 1929; *d* of George Woodburn and Christina Bell Anderson; *m* 1956, Stewart Martin Ewing, CA (*d* 2003); two *s* one *d. Educ:* Queen's Park Sen. Sec. Sch.; University of Glasgow (MA, LLB). Qual. as Solicitor, 1952. Lectr in Law, 1954–56; Solicitor, practising on own account, 1956–. Sec., Glasgow Bar Assoc., 1961–67, Pres., 1970–71. MP (SNP): Hamilton, Nov. 1967–70; Moray and Nairn, Feb. 1974–1979; contested (SNP) Orkney and Shetland, 1983. MEP (SNP), 1975–99, elected Mem. for Highlands and Is, 1979–99; Vice-Pres., Animal Welfare Intergp, EP, 1989–99. President: Scottish National Party, 1987–2005; European Free Alliance, 1991–; Mem., Lomé Assembly, 1981–. Pres., Glasgow Central Soroptimist Club, 1966–67. FRSA 1990. DUniv Open, 1993; Hon. LLD Glasgow, 1995; Hon. LLD Aberdeen, 2004. Freeman, City of Avignon, 1985; Comptroller of Scottish Privileges, Veere, Netherlands, 1997. *Address:* Bruaich Mhor, Barr's Lane, Kilmacolm, Renfrewshire PA13 4DE.

See also A. J. Ewing, F. S. Ewing.

EWINGTON, John, OBE 1996; General Secretary, Guild of Church Musicians, since 1979; Consultant, Carroll & Partners Ltd, 2001–03; *b* 14 May 1936; *s* of William and Beatrice Ewington; *m* 1967, Hélène Mary Leach; two *s. Educ:* South East Essex County Technical Sch., Dagenham. ACertCM 1968; Dip Church Music, Goldsmiths' Coll., 1988. Nat. Service, RN, 1954–56. Admin. Assistant, Inst. of London Underwriters, 1953–67; Underwriting Asst, P.C.W. Agencies, Lloyd's, 1967–86; Sen. Broker, 1986–97, Consultant, 1997–2000, HSBC Gibbs. Director of Music and Organist: Blechingley Parish Church, 1966–97; St Mary Woolnoth, 1970–93 (also Sen. Ch Warden, 1973–93); St Katharine Cree, 1998–; Dir, City Singers, 1976–. Freeman, City of London, 1980; Liveryman, Musicians' Co., 2002–. Hon. Associate and Conjoint Sen. Lectr, Conservatorium of Music and Drama, Faculty of Music and Arts, Univ. of Newcastle, NSW, 2004–. Governor: Stafford Sch., Caterham, 1980–85; Oxted Sch., 1985–2005 (Vice Chm. of Govs, 1993–2005). FGCM 1988. Hon. FCSM 1990; Hon. FFCM, Central Sch. of Religion, Indiana, 1998; Hon. RSCM 2002. MA Lambeth, 2003. KLJ 2007 (CLJ 2005). *Publications:* (with Canon A. Dobb) Landmarks in Christian Worship and Church Music, 2001; articles on church music in jls. *Recreations:* church music, cooking, eating out. *Address:* Hillbrow, Godstone Road, Bletchingley, Surrey RH1 4PJ. *T:* (01883) 743168; *e-mail:* JohnMusicsure@orbix.co.uk. *Club:* City Livery; Friday (Bletchingley).

EWINS, Prof. David John, FRS 2006; FREng, FIMechE; Professor of Vibration Engineering and Director, Bristol Laboratory for Advanced Dynamic Engineering, University of Bristol, since 2007; Professor of Vibration Engineering, Imperial College London (formerly Imperial College of Science, Technology and Medicine), since 1983; *b* 25 March 1942; *s* of W. J. and P. Ewins; *m* 1964, Brenda Rene (*née* Chalk) (marr. diss. 1997); three *d. Educ:* Kingswood Grammar Sch., Bristol; Imperial Coll., London (BScEng, ACGI, DScEng); Trinity Coll., Cambridge (PhD). FIMechE 1990; FREng (FEng 1995). Res. Asst for Rolls-Royce Ltd, Cambridge Univ., 1966–67; Imperial College, London University: Lectr, then Reader, in Mech. Engrg, 1967–83; formed Modal Testing Unit, 1981; Dir, Rolls-Royce sponsored Centre of Vibration Engrg, 1990–2002; Pro-Rector, Internat. Relations, 2001–05. Temasek Prof., and Dir, Centre for Mechanics of Microsystems, Nanyang Technol Univ., Singapore, 1999–2002. Sen. Lectr, Chulalongkorn Univ., Bangkok, 1968–69; Maître de Conférences, INSA, Lyon, 1974–75; Visiting Professor: Virginia Poly and State Univ., USA, 1981; ETH, Zürich, 1986; Inst. Nat. Polytechnique de Grenoble, 1990; Nanyang Technol Univ., Singapore, 1994, 1997; Hon. Professor: Nanjing Aero Inst., 1988; Shandong Polytechnic Inst., 1991. Partner, ICATS, 1989–. Consultant to: Rolls-Royce, 1969–; MoD, 1977–, and other organisations in Europe, S America and USA. Chm., then Pres., Dynamic Testing Agency, 1990–99. Governor: Cranleigh Sch., 1990–95; Parmiter's Sch., 1993–96. FCGI 2002. *Publications:* Modal Testing: theory and practice, 1984, 9th edn 1996; Modal Testing: theory, practice and application, 2000; (ed with D. J. Inman) Structural Dynamics, 2000; papers on vibration engrg in technical jls in UK, USA, France. *Recreations:* music (esp. piano duets), hill and moor walking, travel, good food, French, Italian. *Address:* Imperial College, Exhibition Road, SW7 2AZ. *T:* (020) 7594 7068.

EWINS, Peter David, CB 2001; FREng; FRAeS; Chief Executive, Meteorological Office, 1997–2004; *b* 20 March 1943; *s* of John Samuel Ewins and Kathleen Ewins; *m* 1968, Barbara Irene Howland; two *s* one *d. Educ:* Imperial College London (BSc Eng); Cranfield Inst. of Technology (MSc). FREng (FEng 1996); FRAeS 1996. Joined RAE Farnborough, 1966, research on structl applications of composite materials; section head, 1974; staff of Chief Scientist, RAF, MoD, 1978; Head of Helicopters Res. Div., RAE, 1981; seconded to Cabinet Office (Civil Service personnel policy), 1984; Dir, Nuclear Projects, MoD, 1987; Dir, ARE, MoD (PE), 1988; Man. Dir (Maritime and Electronics), 1991, Man. Dir, Command and Maritime Systems Gp, 1992, Man. Dir (Ops), 1993–94, DRA; Chief Scientist, MoD, 1994–97. Mem. Council, Royal Acad. of Engrg, 1999–. Hon. DSc Exeter, 2006. *Publications:* technical papers on structural composite materials in learned jls. *Recreations:* horticulture, bee-keeping, walking.

EWUSIE, Prof. Joseph Yanney; Chief Policy Adviser and Hon. Fellow, Ghana Council for Scientific and Industrial Research, since 1994; *b* 18 April 1927; *s* of Samuel Mainsa Wilson Ewusie and Elizabeth Dickson; *m* 1st, 1959, Stella Turkson (*d* 1989); five *s*, and one adopted *d;* 2nd, 1992, Emma (*née* Ghampson) (marr. diss. 1997); 3rd, 1998, Ruth (*née* Ohene Parry). *Educ:* Winneba Anglican Sch.; Mfantsipim Sch.; University Coll. of the Gold Coast; Univ. of Cambridge. BSc (London), PhD (Cantab). Lectr in Botany, Univ. of Ghana, 1957–62; Gen. Sec. (Chief Exec.), Ghana Academy of Sciences (highest learned and res. org. in Ghana), 1963–68; University of Cape Coast: Associate Prof. of Botany, 1969–72, Prof., 1973–79; Head, Dept of Botany, 1969–73; Dean, Faculty of Science, 1971–74; Pro-Vice Chancellor, 1971–73; Vice Chancellor, 1973–78. Vis. Prof./Prof., Univs of Nairobi and Ahmadu Bello, Nigeria, 1979–80; Sec.-Gen., Pan African Inst. for Development, 1980–83; Professor of Biology: Univ. of Swaziland, 1984–90; Univ. of Bophuthatswana, 1989–92. Mem. Exec. Cttee, ICSU, 1964–67. Founder and First Pres., Bophuthatswana Assoc. for Scientific Advancement, 1990; first Pres., Ghana Inst. of Biology, 1994 (Fellow 1995). Member: Bimillennium Foundn, Washington DC, 1984–; NY Acad. of Sciences, 1984–. FWA 1963. Co-Founder and First Editor, Swaziland Jl of Sci. and Technol. Hon. DSc Cape Coast, 1994. Medal (Govt of Hungary) for internat. understanding between Ghana and Hungary, 1964; Dipl. of Merit, Internat. Acad. of Science, Letters and Arts, Rome, 1968; Dipl. of Honour, Internat. Inst. of Community Service, 1975; Ghana Scientist of the Year, Ghana Science Assoc., 1985. *Publications:* School Certificate Biology for Tropical Schools, 1964, 4th edn 1974; Tropical Biological Drawings, 1973; Elements of Tropical Ecology, 1980; Phenology in Tropical Ecology, 1992. *Address:* PO Box LG 696, Legon-Accra, Ghana.

EXETER, 8th Marquess of, *cr* 1801; **William Michael Anthony Cecil;** Baron Burghley 1571; Earl of Exeter 1605; *b* 1 Sept. 1935; *s* of 7th Marquess of Exeter and Edith Lilian Csanady de Telegd (*d* 1954); *S* Father, 1988; *m* 1st, 1967, Nancy Rose (marr. diss. 1992), *d* of Lloyd Arthur Meeker; one *s* one *d;* 2nd, 1999, Barbara Anne, *d* of Eugene Magat. *Educ:* Eton. Rancher and businessman in 100 Mile House, BC, Canada, 1954–. *Publications:* (jtly) Spirit of Sunrise, 1979; The Long View, 1985; The Rising Tide of

Change, 1986; Living at the Heart of Creation, 1990. *Heir: s* Lord Burghley, *qv. Address:* 899 Timberlake Drive, Ashland, OR 97520–9090, USA. *T:* (541) 488 3646, *Fax:* (541) 488 0003; *e-mail:* mcecil@mind.net.

EXETER, Bishop of, since 2000; **Rt Rev. Michael Laurence Langrish;** *b* 1 July 1946; *s* of Douglas Frank and Brenda Florence Langrish; *m* 1968, Esther Vivien (*née* Rudd); one *s* two *d. Educ:* King Edward Sch., Southampton; Birmingham Univ. (BSocSc 1967; PGCE 1968); Fitzwilliam Coll., Cambridge (BA 1973; MA 1978); Ridley Hall, Cambridge. Lectr in Educn, Mid-West State Coll. of Educn, Nigeria, 1969–71. Ordained deacon, 1973, priest, 1974; Asst Curate, Stratford-upon-Avon with Bishopston, 1973–76; Chaplain, Rugby Sch., 1976–81; Vicar, Offchurch and Diocesan Dir of Ordinands, 1981–87; Team Rector, Rugby Team Ministry, 1987–93; Bishop Suffragan of Birkenhead, 1993–2000. Examining Chaplain to the Bishop of Coventry, 1982–89; Hon. Canon, Coventry Cathedral, 1990–93. Chairman: ACCM Vocations Cttee, 1984–91; House of Clergy, Coventry Diocesan Synod, 1988–93; Rural Strategy Gp (formerly Rural Affairs Cttee), C of E Bd of Mission, 2001–. Chairman: Devon Strategic Partnership, 2002–07; Melanesian Mission (UK), 2003–; Mem. Bd, Christian Aid, 2003–. Mem. Council, Univ. of Exeter, 2001–. Entered House of Lords, 2005. *Recreations:* walking, gardening, local history, theatre, railways, music. *Address:* The Palace, Exeter EX1 1HY. *T:* (01392) 272362. *Clubs:* Athenæum, Farmers'; Somerset CC.

EXETER, Dean of; *see* Meyrick, Very Rev. C. J.

EXETER, Archdeacon of; *see* Driver, Ven. P. M.

EXLEY, Margaret, CBE 2001; Chairman, Stonecourt Consulting, since 2007; *b* 9 Feb. 1949; *d* of Ernest and Elsie Exley; *m* 1984, Malcolm Grant; one *s* one *d. Educ:* Univ. of Manchester (BA Hons Econ); Univ. of Warwick (MSc). Res. Fellow, Manchester Business Sch., 1971–73; Principal, Cabinet Office, 1973–80; Dir, Hay Mgt Consultants, 1980–84; Chief Exec., Kinsley Lord Ltd, 1984–95; European Managing Partner, Towers Perrin, 1995–2001; Chm., Mercer Delta UK Ltd, 2001–07. Non-executive Director: Field Gp, 1997–99; HM Treasury, 1999–2005. Mem., Employment Appeal Tribunal, 1992–95. Mem., Charter Renewal Steering Gp, BBC, 2006–07. Mem., Adv. Bd, NPG, 2000–. FRSA 1996. *Publications:* various, on strategy and leadership, in learned and popular jls. *Recreation:* social history. *Address:* 11 Launceston Place, Kensington, W8 5RL. *T:* (020) 7376 1973, *Fax:* (020) 7376 0233; *e-mail:* margaret.exley@stonecourtconsulting.com. *Club:* Reform.

EXMOUTH, 10th Viscount *cr* 1816; **Paul Edward Pellew;** Bt 1796 (Pellew of Treverry); Baron 1814; Marqués de Olias (Spain *cr* 1652); *b* 8 Oct. 1940; *s* of 9th Viscount Exmouth and Maria Luisa (*d* 1994), *d* of late Luis de Urquijo, Marqués de Amurrio, Madrid; *S* father, 1970; *m* 1st, 1964, Krystina Garay-Marques (marr. diss. 1974); one *d*; 2nd, 1975, Rosemary Countess of Burford (marr. diss. 2000); twin *s. Educ:* Downside. Formerly cross bencher, House of Lords. *Heir: er* twin *s* Hon. Edward Francis Pellew, *b* 30 Oct. 1978. *Address: e-mail:* PaulExmouth@aol.com.

EXNER, Most Rev. Adam; Archbishop of Vancouver, (RC), 1991–2004, now Archbishop Emeritus; *b* 24 Dec. 1928. *Educ:* St Joseph's Coll., Yorkton, Sask; Gregorian Univ., Rome (LPH 1954; STB 1956 STL 1958). Ottawa Univ. (STD 1960). Entered novitiate, Oblates of Mary Immaculate, St Norbert, Manitoba, 1950; ordained Roviano, Rome, 1957; St Charles Scholasticate, Battleford, Saskatchewan: Prof., 1960–64 and 1971–72; Rector and Superior, 1965–71; Prof. of Moral Theology, Newman Theol Coll., Edmonton, Alberta, 1972–74; Bishop of Kamloops, BC, 1974–82; Archbishop of Winnipeg, 1982–91. Secretary: BC and Yukon Conf. of Bishops, 1974–79 (Chm., 1991–); Conf. of Catholic Bishops, 1974–80. Canadian Conference of Catholic Bishops: Mem., Admin. Bd, 1976–83; Rep. of Western Conf. of Bishops, 1981–83; Mem., Episcopal Commn for Christian Educn, 1983–88; Mem., Social Communications Commn, 1989–91; Rep. of W Reg. of Bishops on Permanent Council, 1989–93; Mem., Cttee on Sexual Abuse, 1990–92; Mem., Theol. Commn, 1991–93, 1995– (Pres., 1993–95); Mem., Working Gp Residential Schs, 1992–95; Mem., Progs and Priorities Cttee, 1993–95; Chm., Catholic Orgn for Life and Family, 1995–. Chm., Conf. of Bishops of Manitoba, 1983–91; Member: Sacred Congregation for Bishops, 1984–90; Nat. Catholic-Lutheran Dialogue, 1987–89. Chaplain, Knight of Columbus, 1974–82; Liaison Bp and Chaplain, Catholic Sch. Trustees Assoc. of BC, 1974–82; Mem., St Paul's Coll. Bd, Univ. of Manitoba, 1982. *Publications:* contrib. to Catholic Press, 1960–82. *Recreations:* playing piano and accordion, golf, working out, cross country ski-ing, jogging. *Address:* c/o 150 Robson Street, Vancouver, BC V6B 2A7, Canada.

EXON, Richard Douglas; Chief Executive Officer, Rainey Kelly Campbell Roalfe/Y&R, since 2007 (Managing Director, 2007); *b* Birmingham, 12 Aug. 1971; *s* of Dr and Mrs Peter Exon; *m* 2001, Melanie Copeland; one *d. Educ:* Yarlet Hall; Shrewsbury Sch.; Univ. of Durham (BA Hons 1993). Account Exec., Ogilvy & Mather, 1993; Account Manager to Global Business Develt Dir, Bartle Bogle Hegarty, 1994–2007. IPA Effectiveness Award, 1998. *Recreations:* winter sports, field sports, ball sports, cooking. *Address:* c/o Rainey Kelly Campbell Roalfe/Y&R, Greater London House, Hampstead Road, NW1 7QP. *T:* (020) 7611 6087. *Club:* Adam Street.

EXTON-SMITH, Jasmine; *see* Whitbread, J.

EYERS, Patrick Howard Caines, CMG 1985; LVO 1966; HM Diplomatic Service, retired; *b* 4 Sept. 1933; *s* of late Arthur Leopold Caines Eyers and Nora Lilian Eyers; *m* 1960, Heidi, *d* of Werner Rüsch, Dipl. Ing, and Helene (*née* Feil); two *s* one *d. Educ:* Clifton Coll.; Gonville and Caius Coll., Cambridge (BA Hons 1957); Institut Universitaire de Hautes Etudes Internationales, Geneva. RA, 1952–54. Asst Editor, Grolier Soc. Inc., New York, 1957; HM Foreign (now Diplomatic) Service, 1959; ME Centre for Arabic Studies, 1960; Dubai, 1961; Brussels, 1964; FO, 1966; Aden, 1969; Abidjan, 1970; British Mil. Govt, Berlin, 1971; FCO, 1974; Counsellor, Bonn, 1977; Head, Republic of Ireland Dept, FCO, 1981; RCDS, 1984; Ambassador: to Zaire, the Congo, Rwanda and Burundi, 1985–87; to Algeria, 1987–89; to GDR, 1990; to Jordan, 1991–93. Officer, Order of Leopold, Belgium, 1966. *Recreations:* music, ski-ing, sailing. *Address:* c/o Barclays Bank, 86 Queens Road, Bristol BS6 1RB. *Club:* Hurlingham.

EYRE, Brian Leonard, CBE 1993; DSc; FRS 2001; FREng; CPhys; Senior Visiting Fellow, University of Oxford, since 2006 (Visiting Professor, 1996–2006); Chairman, Council for the Central Laboratory of the Research Councils, 2000–01 (Member, 1998–2001); *b* 29 Nov. 1933; *s* of Leonard George and Mabel Eyre; *m* 1965, Elizabeth Caroline (*née* Rackham); two *s. Educ:* Greenford Grammar Sch.; Univ. of Surrey (BSc, DSc). FREng (FEng 1992); FIMMM; FInstP. Research Officer, CEGB, 1959–62; Gp Leader, UKAEA, Harwell, 1962–79; Prof., Materials Science, Univ. of Liverpool, 1979–84; United Kingdom Atomic Energy Authority: Dir, Fuel and Engrg Technology, Risley, 1984–87; Mem. Bd, 1987–96; Dep. Chm., 1989–96; Chief Exec., 1990–94; Dep. Chm., AEA Technology plc, 1996–97. Mem., PPARC, 1996–2000. Visiting Professor: Univ. of Illinois, 1969–70; Univ. of Wisconsin, 1976; Univ. of Liverpool, 1984–; UCL,

1995–; Vis. Fellow, Wolfson Coll., Oxford, 1996–2001. Mem. Council, Foundn of Sci and Technology, 1994–2001. *Publications:* over 150 papers in Procs Royal Soc. Philosophical Magazine, Acta Metallurgica, etc. *Recreations:* sailing, walking, mountaineering. *Address:* Materials Department, University of Oxford, Parks Road, Oxford OX1 3PH. *Club:* Athenæum.

EYRE, Prof. Deborah Mary; Professor of Education, University of Warwick, since 2002 (Director, National Academy for Gifted and Talented Youth, 2002–07); *b* 22 Jan. 1954; *d* of Philip and Mary Davis; *m* 1976, John Eyre; one *s* one *d. Educ:* Hunmanby Hall Sch., Filey; Westminster Coll., Oxford (Cert Ed); Univ. of Reading (MEd). Teacher, primary schs, 1976–83; educn consultant on gifted and talented, 1983–89; advr on gifted and talented, Oxon LEA, 1989–97; Oxford Brookes University: Dir, Res. Centre for Able Pupils, and Dep. Dean of Educn, 1997–2002; Prof. of Educn, 2002. Member Executive Board: Trng and Develt Agency for Schs; World Council for Gifted and Talented Children; Center for Talented Youth, Johns Hopkins Univ.; Adviser: Educn Select Cttee, H of C; Ministerial Task Force for Gifted and Talented, DfES. FRSA. *Publications:* Able Children in Ordinary Schools, 1997; Gifted and Talented International: international handbook for gifted education, 2007. *Recreations:* modern fiction, food and wine, family and friends. *Address:* University of Warwick, Coventry CV4 7AL. *T:* (02476) 574430; *e-mail:* Deborah.Eyre@warwick.ac.uk. 59 Linkside Avenue, Oxford OX2 8JE.

EYRE, James Henry Robert, OBE 2003; Director, Wilkinson Eyre Architects Ltd, since 1989; *b* 24 Jan. 1959; *s* of late Michael Robert Giles Eyre and of Susan Bennett; *m* 1983, Karen Fiona Turner; one *s* one *d. Educ:* Oundle Sch.; Liverpool Univ. (BA Hons 1980), AA Dip. 1983; RIBA 1985. Architect, Michael Hopkins & Partners, 1980–85; joined Chris Wilkinson Architects, subseq. Wilkinson Eyre Architects, 1985, Partner, 1986–; *projects include:* Stratford Market Depot for Jubilee Line Extension, 1996; South Dock Footbridge for LDDC, 1997; Hulme Arch, Manchester, 1997; Stratford Station for Jubilee Line Extension, 2000; Gateshead Millennium Bridge, 2001; Making the Modern World gall., Science Mus.; Floral Street bridge for Royal Ballet Sch., 2003; Mus. of London entrance and gall., 2003. *Publications:* (contrib.) The Architecture of Bridge Design, 1997; (jtly) Bridging Art and Science, 2001; contribs World Architecture, Architects Jl. *Recreations:* travel, game fishing, sketching. *Address:* (office) 24 Britton Street, EC1M 5UA. *T:* (020) 7608 7900.

EYRE, Major John Vickers; JP; DL; Vice Lord-Lieutenant of Gloucestershire, since 2007; *b* 30 April 1936; *s* of Nevill Cathcart Eyre and Maud Evelyn Eyre (*née* Truscott); *m* 1974, Sarah Margaret Aline Heywood; one *s* one *d. Educ:* Winchester; Staff Coll. Camberley. Commnd, 1955, RHA, 1957, 14th/20th Kings Hussars, 1962; retd, 1973; Asst to Chm., Savoy Hotel, 1973–75; Administrator, Brian Colquhoun and Partners, consulting engrs, 1975–79; Proprietor, Haresfield Garden Centre, 1981–86; Man. Dir, George Truscott Ltd, 1986–2003. Royal Glos Hussars, TA, 1980–83 (Patron, 1997–). Dis Comr, Berkeley Hunt Pony Club, 1986–95; Chm., Berkeley Hunt, 2005–. Gloucestershire: JP 1987; DL 2000; High Sheriff, 2000–01. Pres., Glos, RBL, 2008–. *Recreations:* country pursuits. *Address:* Boyts Farm, Tytherington, Wotton-under-Edge, Glos GL12 8UG. *T:* (01454) 412220; *e-mail:* jve@talktalk.net. *Clubs:* Boodle's, Army and Navy.

EYRE, Patrick Giles Andrew; Master of the Supreme Court, Queen's Bench Division, since 1992; *b* 11 March 1940; *s* of late Edward Joseph Eyre and Hon. Dorothy Elizabeth Anne Pelline Lyon-Dalberg-Acton; *m* 1977, Victoria Mary Bathurst Barthorp; one *s*, and one step *d. Educ:* Downside; Trinity Coll., Oxford (MA). Farmer, 1965–72. Called to the Bar, Inner Temple, 1974. *Publications:* articles on law, computers, horses and country pursuits. *Recreations:* books, horses, hunting, music. *Address:* Royal Courts of Justice, Strand, WC2A 2LL.

EYRE, Sir Reginald (Edwin), Kt 1984; President, Birmingham Heartlands Business Forum, 2004–05; Consultant, Eyre & Co., solicitors, 1992–2002; *b* 28 May 1924; *s* of late Edwin Eyre and Mary Eyre (*née* Moseley); *m* 1978, Anne Clements; one *d. Educ:* King Edward's Camp Hill Sch., Birmingham; Emmanuel Coll., Cambridge (MA). RNVR 1942–45 (Sub-Lt). Admitted a Solicitor, 1950; Senior Partner, Eyre & Co., solicitors, Birmingham, 1951–91. Chairman: Birmingham Heartlands Develt Corp. (formerly Birmingham Heartlands Ltd (East Birmingham Urban Develt Agency)), 1987–98; Birmingham Cable Corp. Ltd, 1988–99; Dep. Chm., Commn for New Towns, 1988–92. Hon. Consultant, Poor Man's Lawyer, 1948–58. Conservative Political Centre: Chm., W Midlands Area, 1960–63; Chm., National Advisory Cttee, 1964–66. Contested (C) Birmingham (Northfield) 1959; MP (C) Birmingham Hall Green, May 1965–87; Opposition Whip, 1966–70; a Lord Comr of the Treasury, June–Sept. 1970; Comptroller of HM Household, 1970–72; Parliamentary Under-Secretary of State: DoE, 1972–74; Dept of Trade, 1978–82; Dept of Transport, 1982–83. A Vice Chm., Cons. Party Organisation, 1975–79; Founder Chm., Cons. Parly Urban Affairs Cttee, 1974–79; Freeman, City of Birmingham, 1991. DUniv UCE, 1997. *Publication:* Hope for our Towns and Cities, 1977. *Address:* c/o Eyre & Co., 1041 Stratford Road, Hall Green, Birmingham B28 8AS.

EYRE, Richard Anthony; Chairman, RDF Media, since 2001; *b* 3 May 1954; *s* of Edgar Gabriel Eyre and Marjorie (*née* Corp); *m* 1977, Sheelagh Colquhoun; one *s* one *d. Educ:* King's Coll. Sch., Wimbledon; Lincoln Coll., Oxford (MA); Harvard Business Sch. (AMP). Media buyer, Benton & Bowles, 1975–79; TV airtime salesman, Scottish TV, 1979–80; media planner, Benton & Bowles, 1980–84; Media Director: Aspect, 1984–86; Bartle Bogle Hegarty, 1986–91; Chief Executive: Capital Radio plc, 1991–97; ITV, 1997–2000; Pearson Television, 2000–01; Dir, Strategy and Content, RTL Gp, 2000–01; Chairman: Signify Ltd, 2002–; I-Play Ltd, 2002–; Internet Advertising Bureau Ltd, 2003–; GCap Media, 2007–08; non-executive Director: Eden Project Ltd, 2003–; Guardian Media Gp, 2004–07. FRSA 1997. *Publication:* The Club (novel), 2005. *Recreations:* music, church, cooking. *Address:* RDF Media, The Gloucester Building, Kensington Village, Avonmore Road, W14 8RF. *Club:* Thirty.

EYRE, Sir Richard (Charles Hastings), Kt 1997; CBE 1992; theatre, film and TV director; Artistic Director, Royal National Theatre, 1988–97 (Associate Director, 1981–88); *b* 28 March 1943; *m* 1973, Susan Elizabeth Birtwistle, *qv*; one *d. Educ:* Sherborne Sch.; Peterhouse, Cambridge (BA; Hon. Fellow, 2001). Asst Dir, Phoenix Theatre, Leicester, 1966; Lyceum Theatre, Edinburgh: Associate Dir, 1967–70; Dir of Productions, 1970–72; freelance director: Liverpool; 7:84 Co.; West End; tours for British Council: W Africa, 1971; SE Asia, 1972; Artistic Dir, Nottingham Playhouse, 1973–78; Prod./Dir, Play for Today, BBC TV, 1978–80. A Gov., BBC, 1995–2003. Director: The Churchill Play, Nottingham, 1974; Comedians, Old Vic and Wyndhams, 1976; Touched, Nottingham, 1977; Hamlet, Royal Court, 1980; Edmond, Royal Court, 1985; Kafka's Dick, Royal Court, 1986; National Theatre: Guys and Dolls, 1982, revived 1996 (SWET Director of the Year, 1982, Standard Best Director, 1982, Critics' Circle Best Dir Award 1997); The Beggar's Opera, and Schweyk in the Second World War, 1982; The Government Inspector, 1985; Futurists, 1986 (Best Production Award, Time Out, 1986); The Changeling, Bartholomew Fair, 1988; Hamlet, The Voysey Inheritance, 1989;

Racing Demon, Richard III, 1990; White Chameleon, Napoli Milionaria, Murmuring Judges, 1991; Night of the Iguana, 1992; Macbeth, The Absence of War, 1993; Johnny on a Spot, Sweet Bird of Youth, 1994; La Grande Magia, 1995; Skylight, 1995, transf. Wyndham's, then NY, 1996, UK tour, then Vaudeville, 1997; The Prince's Play, John Gabriel Borkman (Critics' Circle Best Dir Award, 1997), 1996; Amy's View, 1997, NY, 1999; King Lear (Olivier Award, 1998), The Invention of Love (Evening Standard Award, 1997), 1997; Vincent in Brixton, transf. Wyndham's, 2002, NY, 2003 (Drama League Award); The Reporter, 2007; The Judas Kiss, Playhouse, transf. NY, 1998; (also trans.) The Novice, Almeida, 2000; The Crucible, NY, 2002; Mary Poppins, Prince Edward, 2004; (also trans.) Hedda Gabler, Almeida, transf. Duke of York's, 2005 (Olivier Award, 2006). Opera: La Traviata, Covent Gdn, 1994; Le Nozze di Figaro, Aix-en-Provence, 2001. Films: The Ploughman's Lunch (Evening Standard Award for Best Film, 1983), Loose Connections, 1983; Laughterhouse, 1984, released as Singleton's Pluck, USA, 1985 (TV Prize, Venice Film Fest.); Iris, 2002 (Humanitas Prize; Efebo d'Oro Award); Stage Beauty, 2004; Notes on a Scandal, 2007; for television: The Imitation Game, Pasmore, 1980; Country, 1981; The Insurance Man, 1986 (Special Prize, Tokyo TV Fest., 1986); Past Caring, 1986; Tumbledown, 1988 (BAFTA Award for best single drama, Italia RAI Prize, RTS Award, Press Guild Award, Tokyo Prize); v., 1988 (RTS Award); Suddenly Last Summer, 1992; The Absence of War, 1995; King Lear, 1998 (Peabody Award, 1999); writer and presenter, Changing Stages (series), 2000. Cameron Mackintosh Vis. Prof. of Contemporary Theatre, Oxford Univ., 1997. Hon. Fellow: Goldsmiths' Coll., 1993; KCL, 1994. Hon. DLitt: Nottingham Trent, 1992; South Bank, 1994; Liverpool, 2003; DUniv Surrey, 1998; Hon. DDra RSAMD, 2000; Hon. Dr Oxford Brookes, 2003. STV Awards for Best Production, 1969, 1970 and 1971; De Sica Award, Sorrento Film Fest., 1986; Laurence Olivier and South Bank Show Awards for Outstanding Achievement, 1997; Lifetime Achievement Awards, Critics' Circle, and Directors' Guild, 1997. Officier de l'ordre des Arts et des Lettres (France), 1998. Publications: Utopia and Other Places, 1993; The Eyre Review (report of inquiry into running of Royal Opera House), 1998; (with Nicholas Wright) Changing Stages: a view of British theatre in the twentieth century, 2000; Iris (screenplay), 2002; National Service, 2003 (Theatre Bk Award, 2004); Hedda Gabler (adaptation), 2005. Address: c/o Judy Daish Associates, 2 St Charles Place, W10 6EG. T: (020) 8964 8811.

EYRE, Very Rev. Richard Montague Stephens; Dean of Exeter, 1981–95; b 16 May 1929; s of Montague Henry and Ethel Mary Eyre; m 1963, Anne Mary Bentley; two d. Educ: Charterhouse; Oriel Coll., Oxford (MA); St Stephen's House, Oxford. Deacon 1956, priest 1957; Curate, St Mark's Church, Portsea, 1956–59; Tutor and Chaplain, Chichester Theological Coll., 1959–62; Chaplain, Eastbourne Coll., 1962–65; Vicar of Arundel, 1965–73; Vicar of Good Shepherd, Brighton, 1973–75; Archdeacon of Chichester, 1975–81; Treasurer of Chichester Cathedral, 1978–81; Priest i/c, St Andrew's, Pau, France, 2001–03. Mem., Gen. Synod of C of E, 1985–95. Publication: Faith in God?, 1990. Recreations: golf, music, travel, gardening. Address: Hathersage, Enmore Road, Enmore, Bridgwater, Som TA5 2DP. Club: Oxford and Cambridge.

EYRE, Susan Elizabeth, (Lady Eyre); see Birtwistle, S. E.

EYSENCK, Prof. Michael William; Professor of Psychology, Royal Holloway (formerly Royal Holloway and Bedford New College), University of London, since 1987 (Head of Department of Psychology, 1987–2005); b 8 Feb. 1944; s of late Prof. Hans Jürgen Eysenck and Margaret Malcolm Eysenck (née Davies); m 1975, Mary Christine Kabyn; one s two d. Educ: Dulwich Coll.; University College London (BA Psych, 1st cl. Hons; Rosa Morrison Medal for outstanding arts graduate, 1965); Birkbeck Coll., London (PhD Psych). Asst Lectr, Lectr and Reader in Psychology, Birkbeck Coll., Univ. of London, 1965–87. Vis. Prof., Univ. of S Florida, Tampa, 1980. Chm., Cognitive Psych. Section, BPsS, 1982–87; Pres., Internat. Soc. for Stress and Anxiety, 2006–08 (Pres.-elect, 2004–06; Past Pres., 2008–). Editor, European Jl of Cognitive Psych., 1989–91. Publications: Human Memory, 1977; (with H. J. Eysenck) Mindwatching, 1981; Attention and Arousal: cognition and performance, 1982; A Handbook of Cognitive Psychology, 1984; (with H. J. Eysenck) Personality and Individual Differences, 1985; (with J. T. Richardson and D. W. Piper) Student Learning: research in education and cognitive psychology, 1987; (with H. J. Eysenck) Mindwatching: why we behave the way we do, 1989; Happiness: facts and myths, 1990; (ed) The Blackwell Dictionary of Cognitive Psychology, 1990; International Review of Cognitive Psychology, 1990; (with M. T. Keane) Cognitive Psychology: a student's handbook, 1990; Anxiety: the cognitive perspective, 1992; (with M. Weller) The Scientific Basis of Psychiatry, 1992; (with A. Gale) Handbook of Individual Differences: biological perspectives, 1992; Principles of Cognitive Psychology, 1993; Perspectives on Psychology, 1994; Individual Differences:

normal and abnormal, 1994; Simply Psychology, 1996; Anxiety and Cognition: a unified theory, 1997; Psychology: an integrated approach, 1998; Psychology: a student's handbook, 2000; (with C. Flanagan) Psychology for A2 Level, 2001; Key Topics in A2 Psychology, 2003; Psychology for AS Level, 2003; Perspectives in Psychology, 2004; Fundamentals of Cognition, 2006; Fundamentals of Psychology, 2008; numerous book chapters and contribs to Qly Jl of Exptl Psychology, Jl of Exptl Psychology, Jl of Abnormal Psychology, British Jl of Clin. Psychology, Jl of Personality and Social Psychology, Psychol Bull., Emotion, and others. Recreations: travel, tennis, golf, walking, bridge, boules. Address: Department of Psychology, Royal Holloway, University of London, Egham Hill, Egham, Surrey TW20 0EX. T: (01784) 443530, Fax: (01784) 434347.

EYTON, Anthony John Plowden, RA 1986 (ARA 1976); RWS 1988 (ARWS 1985); RWA 1984; RCA 1993; NEAC 1985; b 17 May 1923; s of late Captain John Seymour Eyton, ICS, author, and Phyllis Annie Tyser, artist; m 1960, Frances Mary Capell, MA (marr. diss.); three d. Educ: Twyford Sch.; Canford Sch.; Dept of Fine Art, Reading Univ.; Camberwell Sch. of Art (NDD). Served War, 1939–45, Cameronians (Scottish Rifles), Hampshire Regt, and Army Educn Corps. Abbey Major Scholarship in Painting, 1950–51. Elected Mem., London Gp, 1958. One Man Exhibitions: St George's Gall., 1955; Galerie de Seine, 1957; New Art Centre, 1959, 1961, 1968; New Grafton Gall., 1973; William Darby Gall., 1975; Newcastle Polytechnic Art Gall., 1978; Browse & Darby, 1978, 1981, 1985, 1987, 1990, 1993, 1996, 2000, 2005; Austin Desmond Gall., 1990; A. T. Kearney Ltd, 1997; King's Road Gall., 2002; Woodlands Art Gall., 2003; Retrospective Exhibn, S London Art Gall., Towner Art Gall., Eastbourne, and Plymouth Art Gall., 1981; Hong Kong and the New Territories exhibn, Imperial War Museum, 1983 (subsequent to commission); work included in British Painting 1945–77, RA. Work in public collections: Tate Gall.; Arts Council; Plymouth Art Gall.; Towner Art Gall., Eastbourne; Carlisle Art Gall.; DoE; RA; Government Picture Coll.; BR; Contemp. Art Soc.; Guildhall Art Gall. Fellowship awarded by Grocers' Co. (for work and travel in Italy), 1974. Hon. Mem., Pastel Soc., 1986; Hon. ROI 1988. Prize, John Moore's Exhibn, Liverpool, 1972; First Prize, Second British Internat. Drawing Biennale, Middlesbrough, 1975; Charles Wollaston Award, RA, 1981. Relevant publication: Eyton's Eye, by Jenny Pery, 2005. Recreation: gardening. Address: c/o Browse & Darby Ltd, 19 Cork Street, W1X 1HB.

EZRA, family name of **Baron Ezra.**

EZRA, Baron cr 1983 (Life Peer), of Horsham in the County of West Sussex; **Derek Ezra,** Kt 1974; MBE 1945; President, National Home Improvement Council, 1986–2005 (Hon. Vice-President, since 2005); b 23 Feb. 1919; s of David and Lillie Ezra; m 1950, Julia Elizabeth Wilkins. Educ: Monmouth Sch.; Magdalene Coll., Cambridge (MA, Hon. Fellow, 1977). Army, 1939–47. Joined NCB, 1947; representative of NCB at Cttees of OEEC and ECE, 1948–52; Mem. of UK Delegn to High Authority of European Coal and Steel Community, 1952–56; Dep. Regional Sales Manager, NCB, 1956–58; Regional Sales Manager, 1958–60; Dir-Gen. of Marketing, NCB, 1960–65; NCB Bd Mem., 1965–67; Dep. Chm., 1967–71; Chm., 1971–82. Chairman: Associated Heat Services plc, 1966–99; J. H. Sankey & Son Ltd, 1977–82; Petrolex PLC, 1982–85; Throgmorton Trust PLC, 1984–91; Sheffield Heat and Power Ltd, 1985–2000; Associated Gas Supplies Ltd, 1987–95; Energy and Technical Services Gp plc, 1990–99; Micropower Ltd, 2000–05 (Patron, Micropower Council, 2005–); Director: British Fuel Co., 1966–82; Solvay SA, 1979–90; Redland PLC, 1982–89; Supervisory Bd, Royal Boskalis Westminster NV, 1982–85. Industrial Advr, Morgan Grenfell & Co. Ltd, 1982–88. Chm., NICG, 1972 and 1980–81; President: Nat. Materials Handling Centre, 1979; Coal Industry Soc., 1981–86 (Chm., 1961); W European Coal Producers' Assoc., 1976–79; BSI, 1983–86; Economic Res. Council, 1985–2000; Inst. of Trading Standards Admin, 1987–92; Vice-Pres., BIM, 1978 (Chm., 1976–78); Chm., British Iron and Steel Consumers' Council, 1983–86; Member: BOTB, 1972–82 (Chm., European Trade Cttee); Cons. Cttee, ECSC, 1973–82 (Pres., 1978–79); Adv. Council for Energy Conservation, 1974–79; Adv. Bd, Petrofina SA, 1982–90; Internat. Adv. Bd, Creditanstalt Bankverein, 1982–90; Energy Commn, 1977–79; Ct of Governors, Administrative Staff Coll., 1971–82; Internat. Adv. Bd, Banca Nazionale del Lavoro, 1984–94; Governor, London Business Sch., 1973–82. Pres., Keep Britain Tidy Gp, 1985–89 (Chm., 1979–85). Hon. Liveryman, Haberdashers' Co., 1982; Liveryman, Fuellers' Co., 1987. Hon. DSc Cranfield, 1979; Hon. LLD Leeds, 1982. Bronze Star (USA), 1945; Grand Officer, Italian Order of Merit, 1979; Comdr, Luxembourg Order of Merit, 1981; Officer of Légion d'Honneur, 1981. Publications: Coal and Energy, 1978; The Energy Debate, 1983. Address: House of Lords, Westminster, SW1A 0PW. T: (020) 7219 3180.

F

FABER, David James Christian; writer; *b* 7 July 1961; *s* of late Julian Tufnell Faber and of Lady (Ann) Caroline Faber, *e d* of 1st Earl of Stockton, OM, PC, FRS; *m* 1st, 1988, Sally Elizabeth Gilbert (marr. diss. 1996); one *s*; 2nd, 1998, Sophie Amanda Hedley; two *d*. *Educ:* Summer Fields, Oxford; Eton Coll.; Balliol Coll., Oxford (MA Mod. Langs). Conservative Central Office, 1985–87 (Personal Asst to Dep. Chm., 1985–86); Director: Sterling Marketing Ltd, 1987–2002; Freestream Aircraft Ltd, 1998–; Quintus Public Affairs Ltd, 2006–. Contested (C) Stockton North, 1987; MP (C) Westbury, 1992–2001. PPS to Min. of State, Foreign Office, 1994–96, to Sec. of State for Health, 1996–97; Opposition frontbench spokesman on foreign and commonwealth affairs, 1997–98. Member: Social Security Select Cttee, 1992–97; Culture, Media and Sport Select Cttee, 1998–2001; Public Accounts Cttee, 2000–01; Sec., Cons. back bench Educn Cttee, 1992–94. Trustee: Rehabilitation for Addicted Prisoners Trust, 1993–2001; Clouds House, 1992–2007 (Chm., 2003–07). Bd of Govs, Summer Fields Sch., Oxford, 2001–. *Publications:* Speaking for England, 2005; Munich, 2008. *Recreations:* Chelsea FC, cricket, golf. *Clubs:* White's, MCC (Mem. Cttee, 1997–2000, 2001–04, 2005–08); Vincent's (Oxford); Royal St George's Golf, Sunningdale Golf; Trevose Golf.

FABER, Diana; Her Honour Judge Faber; a Circuit Judge, since 2000; *b* 23 Oct. 1955; *d* of T. G. Faber and Mrs D. Swan. *Educ:* Putney High Sch.; University Coll. London (LLB Hons). Called to the Bar, Gray's Inn, 1977; practised at Common Law Bar, 1977–82; admitted solicitor, 1983; joined Richards Butler, 1982, Partner, 1988–94; a Law Comr, 1994–2000; a Recorder, 1998–2000. *Publications:* (General Ed.) Multimodal Transport: avoiding legal problems, 1997; numerous articles in legal and commercial jls and newspapers. *Recreations:* theatre, reading, walking.

FABER, Michael Leslie Ogilvie; Professor Emeritus, Institute of Development Studies, Sussex University (Director, 1982–87; Professorial Fellow, 1982–94); *b* 12 Aug. 1929; *s* of George and Kathleen Faber; *m* 1956, Diana Catriona Howard (*d* 2004); two *s* twin *d*. *Educ:* Avon Old Farms, USA; Eton; Magdalen Coll., Oxford (MA); Univ. of Michigan. MA Cantab. Served 11th Hussars, PAO, Germany, 1948–49. Merchant Seaman, 1953–54. Claims Adjuster, Amer. Internat. Underwriters, Japan and Korea, 1954; Foreign Correspondent for Sunday Times, Observer, and Economist in FE, ME, N and Central Africa, 1954–60; Lectr in Econs, UCRN, 1958–60; community develt worker with Danilo Dolci in Sicily, 1961; Lectr in Econs, UWI, 1962–63; Sen. Economist and Under-Sec., Govt of Zambia, 1964–67; Dept of Applied Econs, Cambridge, 1968; Overseas Develt Gp, UEA, 1969–78; Dir, Tech. Assistance Gp, Commonwealth Secretariat, 1972–75 and 1978–82. Member: Council, Overseas Develt Inst., 1982–2001; Bd, Commonwealth Develt Corp., 1988–97. Pres., UK Chapter, Soc. for Internat. Develt, 1986–91. Leader, UNDP/IBRD Mission to PNG, 1972; specialist negotiator of debt and resource agreements. *Publications:* Economic Structuralism and its Relevance, 1965; (with J. Potter) Towards Economic Independence, 1971; (ed with Dudley Seers) The Crisis in Economic Planning, 1972; (with R. Brown) Mining Agreements: law and policy, 1977; (with R. Brown) Changing the Rules of the Game, 1980; Conciliatory Debt Reduction: why it must come and how it could come, 1988; Beware of Debtspeak, 1988. *Address:* Rodmell Hill Cottage, Mill Lane, Rodmell, E Sussex BN7 3HS. *Club:* Brooks's.

FABER, Trevor Martyn; His Honour Judge Faber; a Circuit Judge, since 2001; *b* 9 Oct. 1946; *s* of Harry Faber and Millicent Faber (*née* Waxman); *m* 1985, Katrina Sally Clay. *Educ:* Clifton Coll.; Merton Coll., Oxford (MA; 3 boxing blues and Capt.). Called to the Bar, Gray's Inn, 1970; in practice, Midland and Oxford Circuit, 1970–2001; a Recorder, 1989–2001. *Recreations:* music, sport, theatre, literature, cooking. *Address:* The Crown Court, Queen Elizabeth II Law Courts, 1 Newton Street, Birmingham B4 7NA. *Club:* Vincent's (Oxford).

FABIAN, Prof. Andrew Christopher, OBE 2006; FRS 1996; Royal Society Professor, Institute of Astronomy, University of Cambridge, since 2002; Fellow of Darwin College, Cambridge, since 1983 (Vice-Master, since 1997); *b* 20 Feb. 1948; *s* of John Archibald and Daphne Monica Fabian; *m* 1st, 1971 (marr. diss. 1991); one *s* one *d*; 2nd, 1991, Dr Carolin Susan Crawford; two *s*. *Educ:* Daventry Grammar Sch.; King's Coll., London (BSc Physics); University Coll. London (PhD). SRC post doctoral research asst, University Coll. London, 1972–73; Institute of Astronomy, Cambridge: SRC post doctoral Fellow, 1973–75; SRC PDRA, 1975–77; Radcliffe Fellow in Astronomy, 1977–81; Royal Soc. Res. Prof., 1982–2002. (Jtly) Rossi Prize, AAS, 2001; Dannie Heineman Prize for Astrophysics, Amer. Inst. Physics and AAS, 2008. *Publications:* contribs to Monthly Notices RAS, Astrophys. Jl, Nature, etc. *Address:* Institute of Astronomy, Madingley Road, Cambridge CB3 0HA.

FABIAN, (Andrew) Paul; HM Diplomatic Service, retired; Chief Secretary, Turks and Caicos Islands, 1990–91; *b* 23 May 1930; *s* of late Andrew Taggart Fabian and Edith Mary Whorwell; *m* 1st, Elisabeth Vivien Chapman; one *s* two *d*; 2nd, 1983, Eryll Francesca Dickinson. *Educ:* Mitcham County School; Reading Sch.; St Paul's Sch.; Wadham College, Oxford (scholar; MA). Singapore Engineer Regt, 1953–54; Tanganyika, 1955–64 (on secondment to Foreign Office, serving at Usumbura, 1961–64); HM Diplomatic Service, 1964; served Lusaka, Ankara, New Delhi, FCO (Hd of Guidance), Islamabad, Karachi; High Comr, Nuku'alofa, Tonga, 1987–90. *Publication:* Delhi Post Bedside Book (ed), 1977. *Recreations:* chess, reading, bird-watching. *Address:* 5 Broadwater Court, Broadwater Down, Tunbridge Wells, Kent TN2 5PB. *Clubs:* Oxford and Cambridge; Tunbridge Wells Chess (Pres., 2006–).

FABIANI, Linda; Member (SNP) Central Scotland, Scottish Parliament, since 1999; Minister for Europe, External Affairs and Culture, since 2007; *b* 14 Dec. 1956; *d* of late Giovanni Aldo Fabiani and Claire Fabiani (*née* Smith, later Nutley). *Educ:* Napier Coll., Edinburgh (SHND); Glasgow Univ. (Dip Housing 1988). MCIH 1988. Admin. Sec., Yoker Housing Assoc., Glasgow, 1982–85; Housing Officer, Clydebank Housing Assoc. 1985–88; Develt Manager, Bute Housing Assoc., Rothesay, 1988–94; Dir, E Kilbrid Housing Assoc., 1994–99. Scottish Parliament: Dep. shadow spokesperson on socia justice, housing and urban regeneration, 1999–2003; SNP Dep. Business Manager an Whip, 2003–05; Convenor, European and External Relations Cttee, 2005–07. *Recreations* reading, theatre, music, holidays. *Address:* Scottish Parliament, Edinburgh EH99 1SP. *T* (0131) 348 5698.

FABIUS, Laurent; Deputy for Seine Maritime, French National Assembly, 1978–81, re elected 1981, 1986, 1993, 1997, 2002, 2007 (President, 1988–92, 1997–2000); *b* 20 Aug 1946; *s* of André Fabius and Louise Fabius (*née* Mortimer). *Educ:* Lycée Janson-de-Sailly Lycée Louis-le-Grand; Ecole Normale Supérieure, Paris; Institut d'Etudes Politiques, Pari (Agrégé des lettres); Ecole Nationale d'Administration. Conseil d'Etat, 1973–81; Nat Sec., Parti Socialiste (responsible for the press), 1979–81; Junior Minister, Ministry o Economy and Finance (responsible for the budget), 1981–83; Minister of Industry an Research, 1983–84; Prime Minister of France, 1984–86; MEP, 1989–92; Finance Ministe and Dep. Prime Minister, 2000–02; First Sec., Socialist Party, 1992–93; Pres., Socialist Gp Nat. Assembly, 1995–97. Mem., Conseil d'Etat, 1981–93. First Dep. Mayor, 1977–95 an 2000–, Mayor, 1995–2000, Grand Quevilly. *Publications:* La France inégale, 1975; L Coeur du Futur, 1985; C'est en allant vers la mer, 1990; Les Blessures de la Vérité, 1995 Cela commence par une balade, 2003; Une certaine idée de l'Europe, 2005. *Address:* 3 ru Aristide Briand, 75007 Paris, France.

FABRICANT, Michael Louis David; MP (C) Lichfield, since 1997 (Mid-Staffordshire 1992–97); *b* 12 June 1950; *s* of late Isaac Nathan Fabricant and of Helena (*née* Freed). *Educ* Loughborough Univ. (BA Law and Econs); Univ. of Sussex (MSc Systems). CEng, FIET Postgrad. doctoral res., mathematical econs, London Univ., Oxford Univ. and Univ. of California, LA. Formerly: Broadcaster, current affairs, BBC Radio; Man. Dir, Commercia Radio Gp; Founder Dir, Internat. Broadcast Electronics and Investment Gp, 1979–91 PPS to Financial Sec., HM Treasury, 1996–97; Opposition front-bench spokesman o economic affairs, 2003–05; an Opposition Whip, 2005–. Member, Select Committe Nat. Heritage, 1993–96, 1997–2005; Culture, Media and Sport, 1997–99, 2001–05 Home Affairs, 1999–2001; Information, 2001–03 (Chm., 2001–03); Member: Europea Legislation Scrutiny Cttee B, 1993–97; Finance and Services Cttee, 2001–03; Liaiso Cttee, 2001–03; Dep. Chm., All Party Cable and Satellite Gp, 1997–99 (Treas., 1995–97) Vice Chairman: All Party Gp on Smoking and Health, 1997–; All Party Anglo-Germa Gp, 1997–; All Party Gp on Film Industry, 1997–; Jt Chm., All Party Internet Gp 1998–2003; Chm., Royal Marines All Party Parly Gp, 2005– (Jt Chm., 1999–2005); Dep Chm., Cons. Parly Media Cttee, 1992–96. FCMI; FRSA. *Publications:* various newspape articles and pamphlets. *Recreations:* fell-walking, reading, music (Mozart to rock), ski-ing listening to the Archers. *Address:* House of Commons, SW1A 0AA. *Club:* Rottingdea (Sussex).

FACER, Roger Lawrence Lowe, CB 1992; Deputy Under-Secretary of State, Ministr of Defence, 1988–93; *b* 28 June 1933; *s* of late John Ernest Facer and Phyllis Facer; *m* 1960 Ruth Margaret, *o d* of late Herbert Mostyn Lewis, PhD, Gresford, Clwyd; three *d*. *Educ* Rugby; St John's Coll., Oxford (MA); Royal Holloway, Univ. of London (MA 2000) HM Forces, 2nd Lieut, East Surrey Regt, 1951–53. War Office, 1957; Asst Private Sec to Secretary of State, 1958; Private Sec. to Permanent Under-Sec., 1958; Principal, 1961 Cabinet Office, 1966; Ministry of Defence, 1968–93: Private Sec. to Minister of Stat (Equipment), 1970; Asst Sec., 1970; Internat. Inst. for Strategic Studies, 1972–73 Counsellor, UK Delegn, MBFR Vienna, 1973–75; Private Sec. to Sec. of State fo Defence, 1976–79; Asst Under-Sec. of State, 1979–81; Under Sec., Cabinet Office 1981–83; Rand Corporation, Santa Monica, USA, 1984; Asst Under-Sec. of State, MoD 1984–87. *Publications:* Weapons Procurement in Europe—Capabilities and Choices, 1975 Conventional Forces and the NATO Strategy of Flexible Response, 1985; articles i Alpine Garden Soc. Bulletin. *Recreations:* Alpine gardening, hill-walking, opera. *Address* Kennett Lodge, Hambledon, Hants PO7 4SA.

FACK, Robbert; Commander, Order of Orange-Nassau, 1979; Chevalier, Order o Netherlands Lion, 1971; Netherlands diplomat, retired; Ambassador of the Netherlands t the Court of St James's, 1976–82; also, concurrently, Ambassador to Iceland, 1976–82; 1 Jan. 1917; *m* 1943, Patricia H. Hawkins; four *s*. *Educ:* Univ. of Amsterdam. Militar service, 1937–45. Min. of Foreign Affairs, The Hague, 1945–46; New York (UN) 1946–48; Min. of Foreign Affairs, 1948–50; Rome, 1950–54; Canberra, 1954–58; Bonn 1958–63; Min. of Foreign Affairs, 1963–68; Ambassador-at-large, 1968–70; Perm. Rep to UN, New York, 1970–74. Holds various foreign decorations. *Publication:* Gedan Zaken (Finished Business), (reminiscences), 1984. *Address:* Widden Hill House, Horto near Chipping Sodbury, S Glos BS37 6QU. *Club:* Dutch.

FAGAN, Anne Marie, CBE 2000; Head Teacher, John Ogilvie High School, Hamilton 1991–2007; *b* 17 Dec. 1947; *d* of Edward Irons and Helen (née Muir); *m* 1969, Bernar Fagan; two *c*. *Educ:* St Patrick's High Sch., Coatbridge; Strathclyde Univ. (BA); Jordanhil Coll. (PGCE). Teacher of Business Educn, Columba High Sch., Coatbridge, 1969–79 Principal Teacher of Business Educn, Cardinal Newman High Sch., 1979–84; Asst H Teacher, Curriculum/Middle Sch., John Ogilvie High Sch., 1984–91. Pres., Catholi Headteachers Assoc. of Scotland, 2000–02 (Vice-Pres., 1998–2000); Mem. Exec., Hea Teachers Assoc. of Scotland. Member: Bd, Global Educn Centre, 2005–08; Nat. Adv. Gp Schs of Ambition Prog., 2005–. GTC Rep. on Bd of Govs, St Andrew's Coll. of Educn Bearsden, Glasgow. Mem., Lanarkshire Orchestral Soc., 1996–98. FRSA. *Recreations* singing (leading lady in light operatic society, 1986–96), playing piano, keep fit, running *Address:* c/o John Ogilvie High School, Farm Road, Burnbank, Hamilton ML3 9LA.

FAGAN, (Florence) Mary; JP; Lord-Lieutenant of Hampshire, since 1994; *b* 11 Sept. 1939; *o d* of Col George Vere-Laurie, JP, DL, Carlton Hall, Newark, Notts; *m* 1960, Capt. Christopher Fagan, Grenadier Guards; one *s* (and one *s* decd). *Educ:* Southover Manor, Sussex. Chm., Countess of Brecknock Hospice Trust and Home Care Service Appeal, Andover, 1989–. Former Mem., Sch. Adv. Cttee, N Hants; Chm., Hants Magistrates Adv. Cttee, 1994–. President: Hants Council of Community Service, 1994–; Hants and IoW Youth Options, 1994–; Hants Br., Army Benevolent Fund, 1994–; Vice-President: Southern Regl Assoc. for the Blind, 1994–; Mary Rose Trust, 1994–; Fortune Centre of Riding Therapy, 1994–; SSAFA; Patron: Rowans Hospice, Portsmouth, 1994–; Hants Music Trust, 1994–; Hants Br., BRCS, 1994–; Oakhaven Hospice, 1995–; The Children's Hospice, 1996–; Home-Start Eastleigh, 2002–; Marwell Zoo. Chm., Portsmouth Cathedral Develt Trust, 2004–; Trustee: Andover Med. Fund, 1994–; Hants Gardens Trust, 1994–. Chancellor, Univ. of Winchester, 2006–. Hon. Col, ACF, 1998–; Hon. Cdre, RNR, 2007– (Hon. Captain, 2001–07); Hon. Col, 457 Battery, RA, 1998–. Liveryman, Saddlers' Co., 1996–. JP Hants, 1994. Hon. DLitt Southampton, 1997; Hon. Dr jur Portsmouth, 2000. DStJ 1994 (Pres. Council, Hants, 1994–). *Recreations:* country activities. *Address:* Deane Hill House, Deane, near Basingstoke, Hants RG25 3AX. *T:* (01256) 780591.

FAGAN, Maj.-Gen. Patrick Feltrim, CB 1990; MBE (mil.) 1966; FRICS 1971; FRGS 1966; *b* 8 Dec. 1935; *s* of late Air Cdre Thomas Patrick Feltrim Fagan and Hon. Isabel Mairi, *yr d* of 15th Baron Arundell of Wardour; *m* 1967, Veronica Thompson (*née* Lorant) (*d* 2003), *widow* of Captain C. J. C. Thompson, RE; two *s*. *Educ:* Stonyhurst Coll.; RMA, Sandhurst; University Coll. London (MSc (Hons) 1969). Commnd RE, 1955; served in Gibraltar, Germany, Aden and Oman. Internat. Scientific Expedn to Karakoram, 1961–62; UAE-Oman Border Survey, 1964; Jt Services Expedn to S Georgia, 1964–65; Ordnance Survey, 1969–73; Geographic Advr, AFCENT, 1979–83; Chief Geographic Officer, SHAPE, 1983–85; Dir, Survey Operations and Prodn, 1985–87; Dir Gen. of Military Survey, 1987–90. Member: Council, RGS, 1987–92 and 1993–95 (Vice-Pres., 1990–92); Council, BSES, 1987–90; Cttee of Management, Mt Everest Foundn, 1989–95 (Chm., 1992–94); Nat. Cttee for Photogrammetry and Remote Sensing, 1987–91; Adv. Bd, Inst. of Engrg, Surveying and Space Geodesy, Nottingham Univ., 1987–91; Council, RICS Land Surveyors, 1988–91; RICS Pres.'s Disciplinary and Appeals Tribunal, 1989–95; Pres., Defence Surveyors' Assoc., 2004–. Dep. Pres., Army RU, 1989–91. Col Comdt, RE, 1991–96, Rep. Col Comdt, 1992. Chm., James Caird Soc., 2000–06. FCMI (FBIM 1971). *Publications:* articles on surveying and mapping in Geographical Jl, Photogrammetric Record, Survey Rev., Chartered Surveyor, and on ski mountaineering in subject jls. *Recreations:* mountain sports, cricket, reading, photography, opera, travel. *Clubs:* Royal Over-Seas League, Alpine (Vice Pres., 1999–2001), Alpine Ski (Pres., 1995–98), Eagle Ski (Pres., 1988–90), MCC, Geographical.

FAGGE, Sir John Christopher, 12th Bt *cr* 1660, of Wiston, Sussex; *b* 30 April 1942; *o s* of Sir John William Frederick Fagge, 11th Bt and Ivy Gertrude (*née* Frier); *S* father, 2000; *m* 1974, Evelyn Joy Golding.

FAHEY, Hon. John Joseph, AC 2002; MP (L) Macarthur (NSW), 1996–2001; Minister for Finance, 1996–2001, and for Administration, 1997–2001, Australia; *b* 10 Jan. 1945; *s* of Stephen Fahey and Annie (*née* Fahey); *m* 1968, Colleen Maree McGurren; one *s* two *d*. *Educ:* St Anthony's Convent, Picton, NSW; Chevalier Coll., Bowral, NSW; Univ. of Sydney Law Extension Cttee (Dip. Law). Practised law, Camden, NSW, 1971–86. New South Wales government: MP (L): Camden, 1984–88; Southern Highlands, 1988–96; Minister for Ind. Relns and Minister assisting the Premier, 1988–90; Minister for Ind. Relns, Further Educn, Trng and Employment, 1990–92; Premier, 1992–95; Treasurer, 1992–93; Minister for Econ. Develt, 1993–95. *Recreations:* tennis, Rugby, cricket, gardening, reading. *Address:* 39 Hurlingham Avenue, Burradoo, NSW 2576, Australia.

FAINT, John Anthony Leonard, CBE 2002; consultant on international development, since 2003; Director (International), Department for International Development, 1997–2002; *b* 24 Nov. 1942; *s* of Thomas Leonard Faint and Josephine Rosey Faint (*née* Dunkerley); *m* 1st, 1978, Elizabeth Theresa Winter (*d* 2002); 2nd, 2004, Dorothy Isobelle Rankin. *Educ:* Chigwell Sch.; Magdalen Coll., Oxford (BA Lit.Hum. 1965); MA Development Economics, Fletcher Sch., Mass, 1969. Ministry of Overseas Development (later Overseas Development Administration), London, 1965–71 (study leave in Cambridge, Mass, 1968–69); First Secretary (Aid), Blantyre, Malawi, 1971–73; ODM/ODA, London, 1974–80; Head of SE Asia Develt Div., Bangkok, 1980–83; Head of Finance Dept, ODA, FCO, 1983–86; Alternate Exec. Dir, World Bank, Washington, 1986–89; Head, E Asia Dept, 1989–90, Under Sec., Internat. Div., 1990–91, ODA; on secondment as UK Dir, EBRD, 1991–92; Under Sec. (Eastern Europe), ODA, 1991–93; Under Sec. (Eastern Europe and Western Hemisphere), ODA, later DFID, 1993–97. *Recreations:* music, bridge, walking, ski-ing, computers. *Address:* Hollow Way Cottage, Ardley Road, Somerton, Oxon OX25 6LP.

FAIRBAIRN, Alasdair Chisholm; Chief Executive, Sea Fish Industry Authority, 1997–2002; *b* 23 Jan. 1940; *s* of late Douglas Chisholm Fairbairn, CBE and Agnes Fairbairn (*née* Arnott); *m* 1964, Charlotte Henriette Tichelman; two *s* one *d*. *Educ:* Trinity Coll., Glenalmond, Perthshire; Corpus Christi Coll., Cambridge (MA Hons). Man. Dir, Conimex BV, Netherlands, 1975–78; Reckitt & Colman plc: Chief Manager, Planning and Evaluation, 1978–80; Regl Dir, 1980–84; Dir, LR Overseas Ltd, 1984–91; Chief Exec., Potato Mktg Bd, 1991–97. *Recreations:* walking, computers, dabbling in stock market. *Club:* Royal Over-Seas League.

FAIRBAIRN, Andrew Finlay, FRCPsych; Consultant in Old Age Psychiatry, Newcastle General Hospital, since 1989; Medical Director, Northumberland, Tyne and Wear NHS Trust, since 2006 (Acting Chief Executive, 2007–08); *b* 16 April 1950; *s* of Thomas Andrew Fairbairn and Pauline Mary Fairbairn; *m* 1971, Andrea Mary Hudson; one *s* two *d*. *Educ:* George Watson's Coll., Edinburgh; Newcastle upon Tyne Univ. (MB BS 1974). FRCPsych 1989. Consultant Psychiatrist, St Nicholas' Hosp., Newcastle upon Tyne, 1981–88. Medical Director: Newcastle Mental Health Trust, 1992–94; Newcastle City Health, 2000–01; Newcastle, N Tyneside and Northumberland Mental Health Trust, 2002–06 (Jt Med. Dir, 2001–02). Sen. Policy Advr (pt-time), 1994–98, Mem., Nat. Taskforce for Older People, 2000–04, DoH; Chm., Jt NICE/SCIE Guidelines Develt Gp on Dementia, 2004–06. Hon. Chm., Faculty for Psychiatry of Old Age, 1998–2002, Hon. Registrar, 2002–05, RCPsych. *Recreations:* house in France, collecting obscure Donizetti operas, 19th century history and biography. *Address:* 3 Killiebrigs, Heddon on the Wall, Northumberland NE15 0DD. *T:* (01661) 852686. *Club:* Royal Society of Medicine.

FAIRBAIRN, Sir Brooke; *see* Fairbairn, Sir J. B.

FAIRBAIRN, Carolyn Julie; Director of Group Development and Strategy, ITV, since 2007; *b* 13 Dec. 1960; *d* of David Ritchie Fairbairn, *qv*; *m* 1991, Peter Harrison Chittick; one *s* two *d*. *Educ:* Wycombe High Sch. for Girls; Bryanston (Schol.); Gonville and Caius Coll., Cambridge (Hon. Sen. Scholar, MA); Univ. of Pennsylvania (Thouron Schol., MA); INSEAD, Fountainebleau (MBA). Economist, World Bank, Washington, 1984–85; financial writer, The Economist, 1985–87; Mgt Consultant, McKinsey & Co., London and Paris, 1988–94; Mem., Prime Minister's Policy Unit, 1995–97; Dir of Strategy, BBC Worldwide, 1997–99; Dir of Strategy, then of Strategy and Distribution, BBC, 2000–04; Principal, McKinsey & Co., London, 2006–07. *Recreations:* tennis, travel. *Address:* 24 St Thomas Street, Winchester, Hants SO23 9HJ.

FAIRBAIRN, David Ritchie, OBE 1990; Chairman, Headstrong Inc., 2000–02; *b* 4 July 1934; *s* of G. F. Fairbairn; *m* 1958, Hon. Susan Hill, *d* of Baron Hill of Luton, PC; one *s* two *d*. *Educ:* Mill Hill Sch.; Gonville and Caius Coll., Cambridge (BAEcon). FBCS; FIDPM, FInstD. President, Cambridge Union Soc. Overseas Marketing Manager, Arthur Guinness Son & Co. Ltd, 1960; President, Guinness-Harp Corp., New York, 1964; Marketing Dir, Guinness Overseas Ltd, 1969; Man. Dir, Dataset Ltd (ICL), 1970; Manager, Retail and Distribution Sector, International Computers Ltd, 1975; Dir of Marketing, EMI Medical Ltd, 1976; Dir, Nat. Computing Centre, 1980–86; Man. Dir, James Martin Associates UK, 1985–89; Gp Man. Dir, James Martin Associates Ltd, 1989–92; Man. Dir, JMA Information Engineering Ltd, 1992–94; Vice-Chm., James Martin Holdings Ltd, 1994–99; Chm., James Martin Worldwide plc, 1999–2000; Vice Pres., Europe, Texas Instruments Inc., 1993–94. Pres., Inst. of Data Processing Management, 1982 (Vice-Pres., 1980–82). Vice-Chm., Parly IT Cttee, 1982. Member: Patent Office Steering Bd, 1989–2000; Telecommunications Panel, Monopoly and Mergers Commn, 1991–99. Freeman, City of London, 1990. FRSA. *Recreations:* sailing, water ski-ing, ski-ing. *Address:* 11 Oak Way, West Common, Harpenden, Herts AL5 2NT. *T:* (01582) 715820, *Fax:* (01582) 468339.

See also C. J. Fairbairn.

FAIRBAIRN, Sir (James) Brooke, 6th Bt *cr* 1869, of Ardwick; *b* 10 Dec. 1930; *s* of Sir William Albert Fairbairn, 5th Bt, and Christine Renée Cotton, *d* of late Rev. Canon Robert William Croft; *S* father, 1972; *m* 1st, 1960, Mary Russell (*d* 1992), *d* of late William Russell Scott, MB, ChB, FFARCS; two *s* one *d*; 2nd, 1997, Rosemary Anne Victoria, *d* of late Edwin Henderson, FRCSE. *Educ:* Stowe. Proprietor of J. Brooke Fairbairn & Co., textile converters and wholesalers dealing in furnishing fabrics. Upper Bailiff, Weavers' Co., 1992–93. *Heir: s* Robert William Fairbairn [*b* 10 April 1965; *m* 1990, Sarah, *e d* of Roger Griffin, BVSc, MRCVS; two *s* two *d*]. *Address:* Barkway House, Bury Road, Newmarket, Suffolk CB8 7BT. *T:* (01638) 662733; J. Brooke Fairbairn & Co., The Railway Station, Newmarket CB8 9WT. *T:* (01638) 665766.

FAIRBAIRN, John Sydney; Trustee, Esmée Fairbairn Foundation (formerly Esmée Fairbairn Charitable Trust), since 1966 (Chairman, 1988–2003); *b* 15 Jan. 1934; *s* of Sydney George Fairbairn, MC and Angela Maude Fairbairn (*née* Fane); *m* 1968, Mrs Camilla Fry (*d* 2000), *d* of late G. N. Grinling; one *s* two *d*, and two step *s* two step *d*; *m* 2001, Felicity, *widow* of 3rd Baron Milford; two step *s* three step *d*. *Educ:* Eton; Trinity College, Cambridge (MA). 2nd Lt, 17/21 Lancers, 1952–54. ACA 1960, FCA 1965. With M & G Group, 1961–99: Dep. Chm., 1979–89; non-exec. Dir, 1989–99. Chm., Unit Trust Assoc., 1989–91. Trustee: Monteverdi Trust, 1991–96; Royal Pavilion, Art Gall. and Museums of Brighton, 1993–2001; Comeback, 1993–99; Dulwich Picture Gall., 1994–97; Council Mem. and Treasurer, King's College London, 1972–84 (Fellow 1978); Council Member: Univ. of Buckingham, 1986–95; Policy Studies Inst., 1991–97. DL West Sussex, 1996–2001. Hon. Dr Buckingham, 1992. *Address:* The Old Vicarage, Powerstock, Dorset DT6 3TE.

FAIRBURN, Prof. Christopher James Alfred Granville; Wellcome Principal Research Fellow, and Professor of Psychiatry, University of Oxford, since 1996; *b* 20 Sept. 1950; *s* of Ernest Alfred Fairburn and Margaret Isabel Fairburn; *m* 1979, Susan Margaret Russam (marr. diss. 2007); one *s* one *d*. *Educ:* Malvern Coll.; Worcester Coll., Oxford (BM BCh). University of Oxford: Res. Psychiatrist, 1981–84; Wellcome Trust Sen. Lectr, 1984–96; Hon. Clinical Reader, 1991–96. Hon. Consultant Psychiatrist, Oxfordshire Mental Healthcare NHS Trust, 1984–. Gov., Wellcome Trust, 2008–. *Publications:* Binge Eating: nature, assessment and treatment, 1993; Eating Disorders and Obesity: a comprehensive handbook, 1995, 2nd edn 2002; Science and Practice of Cognitive Behaviour Therapy, 1997; Cognitive Behavior Therapy and Eating Disorders, 2008; contrib. numerous articles to learned jls. *Recreations:* garden design, wine, travelling off the beaten track.

FAIRCLOUGH, Anthony John, CMG 1990; Hon. Director General, European Commission (formerly Commission of the European Communities), since 1989; *b* 30 Aug. 1924; *m* 1957, Patricia Monks; two *s*. *Educ:* St Philip's Grammar Sch., Birmingham; St Catharine's Coll., Cambridge (Scholar 1944, BA Cantab 1945, MA 1950). Ministry of Aircraft Production and Ministry of Supply, 1944–48; Colonial Office, 1948–65; Secretary, Nyasaland Commn of Inquiry, 1959; Private Secretary to Minister of State for Commonwealth Relations and for the Colonies, 1963–64; Assistant Secretary, 1964; Head of Pacific and Indian Ocean Dept, Colonial Office, subseq. Commonwealth Office, 1964–68; Head of W Indian Dept, FCO, 1968–70; Head of New Towns 1 Div., DoE, 1970–72; Under-Sec., 1973; Head of Planning, Minerals and Countryside Directorate, 1973, of Planning, Sport and Countryside Directorate, 1973–74; Dir, Central Unit on Environmental Pollution, 1974–78; Dir, Internat. Transport, Dept of Transport, 1978–81; Dir for the Environment, CEC, 1981–85; Actg Dir Gen. for the Environment, Consumer Protection and Nuclear Safety, CEC, 1985–86; Dep. Dir-Gen. for Develt, CEC, 1986–89. Senior UK Commissioner at Sessions of South Pacific Commn, 1965–67; Minister's Deputy, European Conf. of Ministers of Transport, 1978–81; Chairman: Environment Cttee, OECD, 1976–79; British Channel Tunnel Co., 1978–81; British Co-Chm., Jt UK/USSR Cttee established under UK/USSR Agreement on cooperation in field of Environmental Protection, 1974–78; Special Advr, EC, 1989–94; Capacity 21 Advr, UNDP, 1993–95; Sen. Adviser, Envmtl Resources Mgt, 1989–99; Chm., Network for Envmtl Technology Transfer, asbl, Belgium, 1989–; Dir, Groundwork Foundn, 1989–95. Consultant to European Orgn for Res. and Treatment of Cancer, 1989–95. Member: Royal Soc.'s British Nat. Cttee on Problems of Environment, 1974–78; EDC for Internat. Freight Movement, 1978–80; Governing Body, Chiswick Sch., 1973–79. CompICE, 1989–93. FRSA. *Address:* 6 Cumberland Road, Kew, Richmond, Surrey TW9 3HQ; Appt 12, 32 Quai aux Briques, 1000 Brussels, Belgium.

FAIRCLOUGH, Oliver Noel Francis; Keeper of Art, Amgueddfa Cymru—National Museum Wales (formerly National Museums and Galleries of Wales), Cardiff, since 1998; *b* 27 March 1950; *s* of late Arthur Basil Rowland Fairclough and Jean McKenzie Fairclough (*née* Fraser); *m* 1977, Caroline Mary Latta; one *s* two *d*. *Educ:* Bryanston Sch.; Trinity Coll., Oxford (BA); Univ. of Keele (MA). AMA 1978. Asst, Liverpool Mus., 1971–74; Asst Keeper, Art, 1975–79, Dep. Keeper, Applied Art, 1979–86, Birmingham Museums and Art Gall.; Asst Keeper, Applied Art, Nat. Mus. of Wales, 1986–98. Lectr and author. Mem., various adv. bodies and learned socs. Ed., French Porcelain Soc., 2001–. *Publications:* (with E. Leary) Textiles by William Morris, 1981; The Grand Old Mansion, 1984; (with M. Evans) Companion Guide to the National Art Gallery, 1993, 2nd edn 1997; contribs to exhibn catalogues; contrib. to Burlington Mag. and other art Jls.

Recreations: walking, travel, architectural history, naval and military history. *Address:* Tyn y Llwyn, Partrishow, Crickhowell, Breconshire NP7 7LT. *T:* (01873) 890540.

FAIREY, Michael Edward; Deputy Group Chief Executive, Lloyds TSB Group plc, 1998–2008; *b* 17 June 1948; *s* of late Douglas and Marjorie Fairey; 1973, Patricia Ann Dolby; two *s. Educ:* King Edward VI Grammar Sch., Louth. ACIB 1974. Barclays Bank, 1967–92: Asst Dir, Watford Gp, 1986; Ops Dir, Barclaycard, 1986–88; Exec. Dir, Barclays Card Services, 1988–92; Dir, Retail Credit, and Gp Credit Dir, TSB Gp, 1992; Gp Dir, Credit and Ops, 1993–96; IT and Ops Dir, 1996–97, Gp Dir, Central Services, 1997–98, Lloyds TSB Gp. Non-executive Director: Energy Saving Trust; VTX Bidco. Chm., Race for Opportunity; Bd Mem., Business in the Community. Pres., British Quality Foundn. *Recreations:* tennis, opera, football.

FAIREY, Michael John, CB 1989; Chief Executive, The Royal London Hospital and Associated Community NHS Trust, 1991–94; *b* 20 Sept. 1933; *s* of late Ernest John Saunder Fairey and Lily Emily (*née* Pateman); *m* 1st, 1958 (marr. diss. 1989); two *s* one *d*; 2nd, 1990, Victoria Frances Hardman. *Educ:* Queen Elizabeth's Sch., Barnet; Jesus Coll., Cambridge (MA). Served RA, 1952–53. Jun. Administrator, St Thomas' Hosp., 1957–60; Gp Develt Sec., Westminster Hosp., 1960–62; Deputy House Governor, The London Hosp., 1962, House Governor 1972; Regional Administrator, NE Thames RHA, 1973; Dir, Planning and Inf., NHS Management Bd, DHSS, later Dept of Health, 1984–89; Dir of Information Systems, NHS Management Exec., Dept of Health, 1989–91. Sec., London Hospital Med. Coll., 1994–96. Gov., St Catherine's Sch., Ware, 1995– (Chm., 1997–2000). *Publications:* various articles in med. and computing jls. *Recreations:* church music, history of medieval exploration, Rugby football. *Club:* Athenæum.

FAIRFAX, family name of **Lord Fairfax of Cameron.**

FAIRFAX OF CAMERON, 14th Lord *cr* 1627; **Nicholas John Albert Fairfax;** Director: Sovcomflot (UK) Ltd, since 2005; Sovcomflot, 2007; *b* 4 Jan. 1956; *e s* of 13th Lord Fairfax of Cameron and of Sonia, *yr d* of late Capt. Cecil Gunston, MC; *S* father, 1964; *m* 1982, Annabel, *er d* of late Nicholas and of Sarah Gilham Morriss; three *s. Educ:* Eton; Downing Coll., Cambridge (LLB in international law subjects, 1981). Called to the Bar, Gray's Inn, 1977. Director: Thomas Miller P and I, and Thomas Miller Defence, 1987–90; Sedgwick Marine & Cargo Ltd, 1995–96; British-Georgian Soc. Ltd, 2006. Patron, AMUR Tiger and Leopard Charity, 2006. *Recreations:* sailing, motorcycling. *Heir:* *s* Hon. Edward Nicholas Thomas Fairfax, *b* 20 Sept. 1984. *Address:* 10 Orlando Road, SW4 0LF. *Club:* Royal Yacht Squadron (Cowes).

FAIRFAX, James Oswald, AO 1993; Chairman, John Fairfax Ltd, Sydney, 1977–87; *b* 27 March 1933; *s* of Sir Warwick Oswald Fairfax and late Marcie Elizabeth Fairfax (*née* Wilson). *Educ:* Geelong Grammar School; Balliol College, Oxford (MA; Hon. Fellow, 1992). Director, John Fairfax, 1957–87; Chm., Amalgamated Television Services Pty Ltd, 1975–87 (Dir, 1958); Chm., David Syme & Co., 1984–87 (Dir, 1977). Member: Bd of Management, Royal Alexandra Hosp. for Children, 1967–85 (Bd, Children's Med. Res. Foundn, 1986–88); Council, International House, Sydney Univ., 1967–79; Internat. Council, Museum of Modern Art, NY, 1971–99; Council, Australian Nat. Gallery, 1976–84; Dir, Art Exhibns Australia Ltd, 1994–98. Governor: Qld Art Gall. Foundn, 1995–; Art Gall. of WA Foundn, 2008; Life Governor: Art Gallery of NSW, 1991; Australian Nat. Gall. Foundn, 1992. Life Member: Nat. Trust of NSW, 1957; Nat. Gall. of Vic, 1992. *Publication:* My Regards to Broadway: a memoir, 1991. *Address:* Retford Park, Old South Road, Bowral, NSW 2576, Australia; Stanbridge Mill, Gussage All Saints, near Wimborne, Dorset BH21 5EP. *Clubs:* Garrick; Union, Australian (Sydney); Melbourne (Melbourne).

FAIRFAX-LUCY, Sir Edmund (John William Hugh Cameron-Ramsay-), 6th Bt *cr* 1836; painter, chiefly of still-life and interiors; *b* 4 May 1945; *s* of Sir Brian Fulke Cameron-Ramsay-Fairfax-Lucy, 5th Bt and Hon. Alice Caroline Helen Buchan (*d* 1993), *o d* of 1st Baron Tweedsmuir, PC, GCMG, GCVO, CH; *S* father, 1974; *m* 1994, Erica, *d* of Warren Loane, Crocknaerieve, Enniskillen; two *s. Educ:* City and Guilds of London Art Sch.; Royal Academy Schs of Art. Regular exhibitor, RA Summer Exhibn, 1967–; one-man shows, numerous mixed exhibitions. *Heir:* *s* Patrick Samuel Thomas Fulke Fairfax-Lucy, *b* 3 April 1995.

FAIRHAVEN, 3rd Baron *cr* 1929 and 1961 (new creation); **Ailwyn Henry George Broughton;** JP; Vice Lord-Lieutenant, Cambridgeshire, 1977–85; *b* 16 Nov. 1936; *s* of 2nd Baron Fairhaven and Hon. Diana Rosamond (*d* 1937), *o d* of late Captain Hon. Coulson Fellowes; *S* father, 1973; *m* 1960, Kathleen Patricia, *d* of late Col James Henry Magill, OBE; three *s* two *d* (and one *s* decd). *Educ:* Eton; RMA, Sandhurst. Royal Horse Guards, 1957–71. Mem., Jockey Club, 1977– (Steward, 1981–82, Sen. Steward, 1985–89). DL Cambridgeshire and Isle of Ely, 1973; JP South Cambridgeshire, 1975. KStJ 1992. *Recreations:* gardening, cooking. *Heir:* *s* Major Hon. James Henry Ailwyn Broughton [*b* 25 May 1963; *m* 1990, Sarah Olivia, *d* of late Harold Digby Fitzgerald Creighton; one *s* two *d*]. *Address:* Kirtling Tower, Cambs CB8 9PA. *Club:* White's.

FAIRLEY, John Alexander; Chairman: Highflyer Productions, since 1996; Channel 4 Racing, since 1997; Trainers House Enterprises, since 2004; *s* of Alexander Miller Fairley and Madge Irene Fairley; *m*; three *d. Educ:* Merchant Taylors' Sch., Crosby; Queen's Coll., Oxford (MA). Midshipman, RNVR. Journalist: Bristol Evening Post, 1963; London Evening Standard, 1964; Producer: BBC Radio, 1965–68; Yorkshire TV, 1968–78; freelance writer and broadcaster, 1979–84; Dir of Programmes, Yorkshire TV, 1984–92; Managing Director: Yorkshire TV Programmes, 1992–93; Yorkshire TV, 1993–95; Chief Exec., UK TV, 1995–96; Chairman: ITV Broadcast Bd, 1995; K Max Radio, 1995–97; Highfield Racing, 2006. Mem., British Horseracing Bd Stud and Stable Staff Commn, 2004. Trustee, Injured Jockeys Fund, 1999–. FRTS 1994; FRSA. *Publications:* (jtly) The Monocled Mutineer, 1978; (jtly) Arthur C. Clarke's Mysterious World, 1980, and subseq. vols, 1984, 1987; Great Racehorses In Art, 1984; Racing In Art, 1990; (jtly) The Cabinet of Curiosities, 1991; The Art of the Horse, 1995. *Recreations:* writing, racing, hunting. *Address:* Trainers House, Eddlethorpe, Malton, Yorks YO17 9QS.

FAIRLIE-CUNINGHAME, Sir Robert (Henry), 17th Bt *cr* 1630, of Robertland, Ayrshire; *b* 19 July 1974; *o s* of Sir William Henry Fairlie-Cuninghame, 16th Bt and of Janet Menzies, *d* of R. M. Saddington; *S* father, 1999; *m* 2005, Mary Louise, *d* of Captain Geoffrey Hugh Belasyse-Smith, Broadstairs; one *d. Heir:* cousin David Hastings Fairlie-Cuninghame [*b* June 1937; *m* 1963, Susan Gai White; one *s* one *d*]. *Address:* 29a Orinoco Street, Pymble, NSW 2073, Australia.

FAIRWEATHER, Clive Bruce, CBE 2003 (OBE 1990); HM Chief Inspector of Prisons for Scotland, 1994–2002; *b* 21 May 1944; *s* of George Fairweather and Helen Fairweather (*née* Henderson); *m* 1980, Ann Beatrice Dexter (marr. diss. 2003); one *s* one *d. Educ:* George Heriot's Sch.; RMA Sandhurst. Army Staff Coll., 1975–76; CO, Scottish Infantry Depot, 1984–87; Instr, RAF Staff Coll., 1987; CO, 1st Bn King's Own Scottish Borderers, 1987–89; Divl Col, Scottish Div., 1991–94. *Publications:* (jtly) Women Offenders: a safer

way, 1998; Punishment First – Verdict Later, 2000. *Recreation:* piano. *Address:* c/o Cox & King's, 7 Pall Mall, SW1Y 5NA. *Club:* Special Forces.

FAIRWEATHER, Prof. Denys Vivian Ivor, MD; FRCOG; Secretary-General International Federation of Gynaecology and Obstetrics, 1985–94; Professor and Head Department of Obstetrics and Gynaecology, 1966–90, and Vice-Provost, 1984–9 University College London; Pro-Vice-Chancellor for Medicine and Dentistry, University of London, 1989–92; *b* 25 Oct. 1927; *s* of late Albert James Ivor Fairweather and Gertrud Mary Forbes; *m* 1956, (Gwendolen) Yvonne Hubbard; one *s* two *d. Educ:* Forfar Acad Websters Seminary, Kirriemuir; St Andrews Univ. (MB, ChB 1949; MD 1966). FRCO 1967 (MRCOG 1958). Served RAF Med. Br., 1950–55, Sqn Leader. Sen. Lectr, Univ of Newcastle upon Tyne, 1959–66; Fulbright Scholar, Western Reserve Univ., USA 1963–64; Dean, Faculty of Clinical Science, UCL, 1982–84; Vice Provost (Medicine) and Head, University Coll. London Sch. of Medicine, later University Coll. and Middx Sch of Medicine of UCL, 1984–89; Hon. Fellow, UCL, 1985. Member: GMC, 1988–9 Internat. Med. Adv. Panel, IPPF, 1988–94; Vice Pres., FPA, 1985–98 (Patron, 1998– Hon. FAARM 1969; Hon. FACOG 1993. Freeman, City of Krakow, 1989. Dist. Servic Award, FIGO, 1997. *Publications:* Amniotic Fluid Research and Clinical Application 1973, 2nd edn 1978; Labour Ward Manual, 1985; over 160 pubns in scientific jls, perinatal mortality, rhesus disease, genetics, antenatal diagnosis, very low birthweight medical education. *Recreations:* gardening, fishing, do-it-yourself. *Address:* 37 Lyndhur Avenue, Mill Hill, NW7 2AD.

FAIRWEATHER, Eric John, FCIB; financial consultant; Head of Asset Finance, Co operative Bank PLC, 1999–2002; *b* 9 Nov. 1942; *s* of late John Walter Willia Fairweather and Lilian Emma Fairweather; *m* 1st, 1966, Frances Mary Ewer (marr. diss. two *d*; 2nd, 1991, Deborah Chubb; two *s. Educ:* Carlisle Grammar Sch. CeMAP 200 CeRGI 2006. Entered Midland Bank at Carlisle, 1961; Manager, Corporate Finance Div 1978–81; Sen. Asst Man., Poultry and Princes Street, 1981–84; on secondment as Di Industrial Develt Unit, DTI (Under Sec.), 1984–86; Manager, UK Business Secto Midland Bank, 1986; Manager, Central Management and Planning, 1986–87; Corporat Banking Area Manager, Manchester, 1987–93; Area Manager: Manchester, 1993–9 Sheffield, 1994–95; Regl Gen. Manager, NW, Co-operative Bank, 1995–98. Non executive Director: Cartel Mktg Ltd, 2004–07; Cartel Gp Hldgs plc, 2004–07; S Healthcare Ltd, 2008–. Director: Sheffield TEC, 1994–95; Wigan Borough Partnership 1996–2002. Gov., Bolton Sch., 2006–. *Recreations:* classical music, Association footba (Bolton Wanderers), golf. *Address:* 5 The Hamlet, Lostock, Bolton BL6 4QT.

FAIRWEATHER, Dr Frank Arthur; consultant in toxicology and pathology; *b* 2 Ma 1928; *s* of Frank and Maud Harriet Fairweather; *m* 1953, Christine Winifred Hobbs; tw *s. Educ:* City of Norwich Sch.; Middlesex Hospital. MB, BS 1954; MRCPath 196 FRCPath 1975; FIBiol 1972. Clinical house appts, Ipswich Gp of Hosps, 1955–5 Pathologist, Bland Sutton Inst. of Pathology, and Courtauld Inst. of Biochem., Middlese Hosp., Soho Hosp. for Women, 1956–60; Jt Sen. Registrar in Histopathology, Middlese and West Middlesex Hosps, 1961–62; Chief Med. Adviser and Cons. Pathologist, Beng Labs, 1962–63; Chief Pathologist and Nuffield Scholar, British Industrial Biological Re Assoc., Carshalton, and Hon. Sen. Lectr, RCS, 1963–65; Associate Res. Dir, Wyeth Lab Taplow, 1965–69; Sen. Med. Officer, DHSS, and Principal Med. Officer, Cttee on Safet of Medicines, 1969–72; SPMO, DHSS, 1972–82; Head of Safety and Envmt Res. Div Unilever, 1982–93. Mem., EEC Scientific Cttee for Food, 1976–84 (Chm., Sci. Cttee f Cosmetology); Consultant Adviser in Toxicology to DHSS, 1978–81; Dir, DHS Toxicological Lab., St Bartholomew's Hosp., 1978–82, Hon. Dir, 1982–84; Hon. Pro of Toxicology, Dept of Biochemistry, Univ. of Surrey, 1978–84; Hon. Prof. Toxicology and Pathology, Sch. of Pharmacy, Univ. of London, 1982–88. Chi Examiner in Toxicology, Inst. of Biology, 1989–2006. Chm., BIBRA, 1987–93. Hon FFOM 1991. QHP, 1977–80. *Publications:* various toxicological and medical paper *Recreations:* angling, gardening, water colours. *Address:* Fairland, Wayford, Stalham Norwich NR12 9LH. *T: and Fax:* (01692) 582588.

FAIRWEATHER, Sir Patrick (Stanislaus), KCMG 1992 (CMG 1986); HM Diplomatic Service, retired; Senior Adviser, Citigroup (formerly Schroders, then Schrode Salomon Smith Barney), since 1996; *b* 17 June 1936; *s* of John George Fairweather an Dorothy Jane (*née* Boanus); *m* 1962, Maria (*née* Merica); two *d. Educ:* Ottershaw Sch Surrey; Trinity Coll., Cambridge (Hons History). National Service in Royal Marines an Parachute Regt, 1955–57. Entered FCO, 1965; 2nd Secretary, Rome, 1966–69; FCC 1969–70; 1st Secretary (Economic), Paris, 1970–73; FCO, 1973–75; 1st Sec. and Head o Chancery, Vientiane, 1975–76; 1st Sec., UK Representation to EEC, Brussels, 1976–7 Counsellor (Economic and Commercial), Athens, 1978–83; Head of Europea Community Dept (Internal), FCO, 1983–85; Ambassador to Angola, 1985–87; As Under-Sec. of State, FCO, 1987–90; Dep. Under-Sec. of State (ME/Africa), FCC 1990–92; Ambassador to Italy and (non-resident) to Albania, 1992–96. Dir, Butrin Foundn, 1997–2004. *Recreations:* travel, gardening, photography, sailing. *Club:* Garrick.

FAIRWOOD, Ian Stuart; a District Judge, since 1996; a Recorder, since 2001; *b* 16 Ma 1951; *s* of George Centenus Fairwood and Kathleen Florence Fairwood; *m* 1976, Hila Joan Middleton; two *s. Educ:* Carlton Cavendish Secondary Modern; UCL (LLB). Ba Sch., 1974–75; called to the Bar, Middle Temple, 1974; Dep. Dist Judge, 1993–96; N. Circuit. *Recreations:* golf, tennis, ski-ing, gardening. *Address:* Pilmoor House, Pilmoo York YO61 2QF. *T:* (01423) 360395. *Club:* Notts County (Nottingham).

FAITH, (Irene) Sheila; JP; dental surgeon; *b* 3 June 1928; *yr d* of late I. Book; *m* 195 Dennis Faith. *Educ:* Central High School, Newcastle upon Tyne; Durham Univ. LD 1950. Practised as schools dental surgeon, Northumberland. Member: Northumberlan CC, 1970–74 (Mem., Health and Social Services Cttees; Rep., S Northumberland Your Employment Bd); Newcastle City Council, 1975–77 (Mem., Educn Cttee). Vice-Chm Jt Consultative Cttee on Educn for District of Newcastle during local govt reorganisation 1973–74. Mem., Parole Bd, 1991–94. Contested (C) Newcastle Central, Oct. 1974; M (C) Belper, 1979–83. Mem., Select Cttee on Health and Social Services, 1979–83; Se Conservative backbench Health and Social Services Cttee, 1982–83. MEP (C) Cumbr and Lancs N, 1984–89; Member: Transport Cttee, 1984–87; Cttee on Energy, Res. an Technol., 1987–89. Mem., Exec. Cttee, Cons. Medical Soc., 1981–84; Pres., Cumbr and Lancs N Cons. Euro Constituency Council, 1989–95; Dep. Chm., Hampstead an Highgate Cons. Assoc., 1991–92. Has served as Chm. or Mem. several school governin bodies and Manager of Community Homes and with CAB, Newcastle upon Tyne. JI Northumberland County, 1972–74; Newcastle upon Tyne, 1974–78; Inner London 1978–. *Recreations:* reading, music. *Address:* 52 Moor Court, Westfield, Gosforth Newcastle upon Tyne NE3 4YD. *T:* (0191) 285 4438. *Club:* Royal Society of Medicine

FAKLEY, Dennis Charles, OBE 1973; retired; *b* 20 Nov. 1924; *s* of Charles Frederic and Ethel May Fakley; *m* 1976, Louise Grace Swindell. *Educ:* Chatham House Grammar Sch., Ramsgate; Queen Mary Coll., Univ. of London (BSc Special Physics). Royal Nav Scientific Service, 1944–63; Min. of Defence, 1963–84. *Recreations:* reading, cricke *Address:* 14 Coval Gardens, SW14 7DG. *T:* (020) 8876 6856.

FALCON, David; international public management consultant, since 1992; *b* 3 Jan. 1946; *s* of Arnold and Barbara Falcon; *m* 1st, 1967 (marr. diss. 1991); two *s*; 2nd, 1998, Simoné Mondesir. *Educ:* Helston County Grammar Sch.; University College London (BSc); Lancaster Univ. (MA); Univ. of Pennsylvania. Research Associate, Univ. of Lancaster, 1969–72; Lectr, Leeds Polytechnic, 1972–74; Sen. Lectr, Sheffield Polytechnic, 1974–76; Asst Dir, Sen. Asst Dir, Dep. Dir of Education, Humberside CC, 1976–85; Dir of Education, ILEA, 1985–88; Dir-Gen., RIPA, 1988–92. *Publications:* articles in educn and management jls. *Recreations:* music, opera, photography, travel. *Address:* 45 rue du Pérou, 66500 Prades, France. *T:* (4) 68057458.

FALCON, Michael Gascoigne, CBE 1979; JP, DL; Chairman: Norwich Union Insurance Group, 1981–94 (Director, 1963–94; Vice Chairman, 1979–81); Norwich Winterthur Holdings Ltd, 1984–94; *b* 28 Jan. 1928; *s* of late Michael Falcon and Kathleen Isabel Frances Gascoigne; *m* 1954, April Daphne Claire Lambert; two *s* one *d*. *Educ:* Stowe Sch., Bucks; Heriot-Watt Coll., Edinburgh. National Service, Grenadier Gds and Royal Norfolk Regt, 1946–48. Head Brewer and Jt Man. Dir, E. Lacon & Co. Ltd, Great Yarmouth, 1952–68; Exec. Dir, Edgar Watts, Willow Merchants, 1968–73; Chairman: National Seed Develt Orgn Ltd, 1972–82; Pauls & Whites PLC, 1976–85 (Dir, 1973–85); Eastern Counties Regional Bd, Lloyds Bank Plc, 1979–91 (Dir, 1972–91); Director: Securicor (East) Ltd, 1969–72; Lloyds Bank UK Management Ltd, 1979–85; Matthew Brown plc, 1981–87; National Bus Properties Ltd, 1983–86; Greene King & Sons PLC, 1988–96; British Railways (Anglia) Bd, 1988–92. Chairman: Norwich HA, 1988–94; Norfolk and Norwich Health Care NHS Trust, 1994–97. Trustee, E Anglian Trustee Savings Bank, 1963–75. Chm., Trustees, John Innes Foundn, 1990–98. Mem., Norwich Prison Bd of Visitors, 1969–82. Chm., St John Council for Norfolk, 1980–89. JP 1967, High Sheriff 1979, DL 1981, Co. of Norfolk; High Steward, Great Yarmouth, 1984–. CStJ 1986. Hon. LLD Nottingham, 1988. *Recreation:* country pursuits. *Address:* Keswick Old Hall, Norwich, Norfolk NR4 6TZ. *T:* (01603) 454348. *Clubs:* Norfolk (Norwich); Royal Norfolk and Suffolk Yacht (Lowestoft).
See also Very Rev. D. L. Edwards.

FALCONER, family name of **Baron Falconer of Thoroton**.

FALCONER OF THOROTON, Baron *cr* 1997 (Life Peer), of Thoroton in the co. of Nottinghamshire; **Charles Leslie Falconer;** PC 2003; QC 1991; Secretary of State for Justice (formerly for Constitutional Affairs) and Lord Chancellor, 2003–07; *b* 19 Nov. 1951; *s* of John Leslie Falconer and late Anne Mansel Falconer; *m* 1985, Marianna Catherine Thoroton Hildyard, *qv*; three *s* one *d*. *Educ:* Trinity Coll., Glenalmond; Queens' Coll., Cambridge (Hon. Fellow, 2003). Called to the Bar, Inner Temple, 1974, Bencher, 1997. Solicitor-General, 1997–98; Minister of State: Cabinet Office, 1998–2001; for Housing, Planning and Regeneration, DTLR, 2001–02; for Criminal Justice, Sentencing and Law Reform, Home Office, 2002–03. *Address:* House of Lords, SW1A 0PW; *e-mail:* falconerc@parliament.uk.

FALCONER OF THOROTON, Lady; *see* Hildyard, M. C. T.

FALCONER, Alexander, (Alex); Secretary, Dunfermline and Coast Association of Community Councils, since 2000; *b* Dundee, 1 April 1940; *s* of John Falconer, labourer, and Margaret McFarlane Falconer, canteen assistant; *m* Margaret Cavell Falconer, chef; one *s* one *d*. Former foundry worker; served with RN, 1959–68; insulator, Rosyth dockyard, 1969–84. Shop Steward, TGWU, 1970–84; Chm., Fife Fedn of Trades Councils. MEP (Lab) Mid Scotland and Fife, 1984–99. Mem., CND. *Address:* Forthview, 2 Greenacres, Kingseat, Fife KY12 0RW.

FALCONER, Prof. Roger Alexander, FREng; Halcrow (formerly Hyder) Professor of Water Management, School of Engineering, Cardiff University, since 1997; *b* 12 Dec. 1951; *s* of late Cyril Thomas Falconer and Winifred Mary Matilda Falconer (*née* Rudge); *m* 1977, Nicola Jane Wonson; two *s* one *d*. *Educ:* King's Coll., London (BSc(Eng)); Univ. of Washington, USA (MScEng); Imperial Coll., London (PhD 1976; DIC 1976); Univ. of Birmingham (DEng 1992); Univ. of London (DSc(Eng) 1994). CEng 1982; Eur Ing 1990; FCIWEM 1990; FICE 1992; FREng (FEng 1997). Engr, Sir M. MacDonald and Partners, Cambridge, 1976–77; Lectr in Hydraulic Engrg, Dept of Civil Engrg, Univ. of Birmingham, 1977–86; University of Bradford: Prof. of Water Engrg and Dir, Envmtl Hydraulics Res. Gp, 1987–97; Dep. Hd, 1987–94, Hd, 1994–97, Dept of Civil and Envmtl Engrg. Adv. Prof., Tongji Univ., China, 1987–; Guest Prof., Tianjin Univ., China, 1999–. Co-Chm., Gp of Experts, Internat. Tribunal for Law of the Sea Malaysia *v* Singapore Land Reclamation Case, 2003–05. Member Council: CIWEM, 1997–2002; Internat. Assoc. for Hydraulic Res., 1999–; ICE, 2000–03. FASCE 1993; FCGI 1997. FRSA 1992. Ippen Award, Internat. Assoc. Hydraulic Res., 1991; Telford Premium, 1994, Robert Carr Prize, 2003, 2007, ICE; Silver Medal, Royal Acad. of Engrg, 1999; Hai He Award, China, 2004. *Publications:* *edited:* (jtly) Hydraulic and Environmental Modelling of Coastal, Estuarine and River Waters, 1989, 1992; (jtly) Wetland Management, 1994; over 250 papers on hydro-envmtl modelling of coastal, estuarine and river waters. *Recreations:* music, walking, travel. *Address:* School of Engineering, Cardiff University, The Parade, Cardiff CF24 0YB. *T:* (029) 2087 4280; *e-mail:* FalconerRA@cf.ac.uk; 3 Clos Cradog, Penarth, Vale of Glamorgan CF64 3RJ. *T:* (029) 2035 0250; *e-mail:* rogerfalconer@btinternet.com.

FALDO, Nicholas Alexander, MBE 1988; professional golfer; Chairman, Faldo Design, since 1991; *b* 18 July 1957; *s* of George and Joyce Faldo; *m*; one *s* three *d*. *Educ:* Welwyn Garden City. Won English Amateur Golf Championship, 1975; Professional golfer, 1976; Mem., Ryder Cup team, 1977–97, Captain, 2008; many championship titles include: Open, Muirfield, 1987, 1992, St Andrews, 1990; US Masters, 1989, 1990, 1996; French Open, 1983, 1988, 1989; GA Europ. Open, 1992; World Match Play Championship, 1992; Irish Open, 1991, 1992, 1993. *Publications:* Golf: the winning formula, 1989; In Search of Perfection, 1994; A Swing for Life, 1995; Life Swings, 2004. *Recreations:* helicopter flying, fly fishing, motor sports, cycling, photography. *Address:* *e-mail:* info@nickfaldo.com.

FALKENDER, Baroness *cr* 1974 (Life Peer), of West Haddon, Northants; **Marcia Matilda Falkender,** CBE 1970; Private and Political Secretary to Lord Wilson of Rievaulx, 1956–83 (at 10 Downing Street, 1964–70 and 1974–76); *b* March 1932; *d* of Harry Field. *Educ:* Northampton High School; Queen Mary Coll., Univ. of London. BA Hons Hist. Secretary to Gen. Sec., Labour Party, 1955–56. Member: Prime Minister's Film Industry Working Party, 1975–76; Interim Cttee on Film Industry, 1977–82; British Screen Adv. Council, 1985–. Chm., Canvasback Productions, 1989–91. Director: Peckham Building Soc., 1986–91; South London Investment and Mortgage Corp., 1986–91; General Mediterranean Holding Group (UK). Political columnist, Mail on Sunday, 1982–88. Trustee, Silver Trust, 1988–. Mem., External Relations Cttee, QMW (formerly QMC), London Univ., 1987–97; Governor, QMW, 1987–93. FRSA. *Publications:* Inside Number 10, 1972; Downing Street in Perspective, 1983. *Address:* House of Lords, SW1A 0PW.

FALKINER, Sir Benjamin (Simon) Patrick, 10th Bt *cr* 1778, of Annemount, Cork; *b* 16 Jan. 1962; *s* of Sir Edmond Charles Falkiner, 9th Bt and of his 1st wife, Janet Iris, *d* of Arthur Edward Bruce Derby; *S* father, 1997, but his name does not appear on the Official Roll of the Baronetage; *m* 1998, Linda Louise Mason (*d* 2006); one *s* one *d*. *Educ:* Queen Elizabeth's Grammar Sch. for Boys, Barnet. *Heir:* *b* Matthew Terence Falkiner, *b* 9 Jan. 1964. *Address:* 29 Glebeland, Hatfield, Herts AL10 8AA.

FALKLAND, 15th Viscount *cr* 1620 (Scot.), of Falkland, Co. Fife; **Lucius Edward William Plantagenet Cary;** Lord Cary 1620; Premier Viscount of Scotland on the Roll; *b* 8 May 1935; *s* of 14th Viscount Falkland, and Constance Mary (*d* 1995), *d* of late Captain Edward Berry; *S* father, 1984; *m* 1st, 1962, Caroline Anne (marr. diss. 1990), *o d* of late Lt-Comdr Gerald Butler, DSC, RN, and late Mrs Patrick Parish; one *s* two *d* (and one *d* decd); 2nd, 1990, Nicole, *o d* of late Milburn Mackey; one *s*. *Educ:* Wellington Coll.; Alliance Française, Paris. Late 2nd Lieut 8th Hussars. Export marketing consultant, formerly Chief Executive, C. T. Bowring Trading (Holdings) Ltd. Mem., H of L Select Cttee on Overseas Trade, 1984–85. Dep. Whip, Lib Dem, H of L, 1989–2002; spokesman on culture, media and sport (formerly nat. heritage), 1995–2005; elected Mem., H of L, 1999. *Recreations:* golf, motorcycling, racing, cinema. *Heir:* *s* Master of Falkland, *qv*. *Address:* c/o House of Lords, SW1A 0PW. *Clubs:* Brooks's; Sunningdale Golf.

FALKLAND, Master of; Hon. Lucius Alexander Plantagenet Cary; late Captain, 2nd Battalion, Scots Guards; *b* 1 Feb. 1963; *s* and *heir* of 15th Viscount Falkland, *qv*; *m* 1993, Linda, *d* of Raymond Purl, Colorado City, USA; one *s*. *Educ:* Loretto School; RMA Sandhurst. *Recreations:* ski-ing, golf. *Club:* Cavalry and Guards.

FALKNER, family name of **Baroness Falkner of Margravine**.

FALKNER OF MARGRAVINE, Baroness *cr* 2004 (Life Peer), of Barons Court in the London Borough of Hammersmith and Fulham; **Kishwer Falkner;** *b* 9 March 1955; *m* Robert Falkner; one *d*. *Educ:* St Joseph's Convent Sch., Karachi; LSE (BSc(Econ) 1992); Univ. of Kent (MA). Dir, Internat. Affairs, Lib Dems, 1993–99; Chief Prog. Officer, Political Affairs Div., Commonwealth Secretariat, 1999–2003; Chief Exec., Students Partnership Worldwide, 2003–04. Mem., H of L/H of C Jt Cttee on Human Rights. Contested (Lib Dem): Kensington and Chelsea, 2001; European Parlt, 2004. *Address:* House of Lords, SW1A 0PW.

FALL, Sir Brian (James Proetel), GCVO 1994; KCMG 1992 (CMG 1984); HM Diplomatic Service, retired; British Government Special Representative for the South Caucasus, since 2002; *b* 13 Dec. 1937; *s* of John William Fall, Hull, Yorkshire, and Edith Juliette (*née* Proetel); *m* 1962, Delmar Alexandra Roos; three *d*. *Educ:* St Paul's Sch.; Magdalen Coll., Oxford; Univ. of Michigan Law Sch. Served HM Forces, 1955–57. Joined HM Foreign (now Diplomatic) Service, 1962; served in Foreign Office UN Dept, 1963; Moscow, 1965; Geneva, 1968; Civil Service Coll., 1970; FO Eastern European and Soviet Dept and Western Organisations Dept, 1971; New York, 1975; Harvard Univ. Center for Internat. Affairs, 1976; Counsellor, Moscow, 1977–79; Head of Energy, Science and Space Dept, FCO, 1979–80; Head of Eastern European and Soviet Dept, FCO, 1980–81; Prin. Private Sec. to Sec. of State for Foreign and Commonwealth Affairs, 1981–84; Dir, Cabinet, Sec. Gen. of NATO, 1984–86; Asst Under-Sec. of State (Defence), FCO, 1986–88; Minister, Washington, 1988–89; High Comr to Canada, 1989–92; Ambassador to Russian Fedn, and to Republics of Armenia, Georgia, Moldova and Turkmenistan, 1992–95, also to Azerbaijan, Belarus, Kazakhstan, Kyrgyzstan and Uzbekistan, 1992–93; Principal, LMH, Oxford, 1995–2002 (Hon. Fellow, 2002). Advr, Rio Tinto, 1996–; Chm., MC Russian Market Fund, 1996–2002. Chm., ICC (UK) Cttee on Anti-Corruption, 2005–. Gov., ESU, 2002–. Dir, UK Foundn, Univ. of BC, 2005–. Gov., St Mary's Sch., Calne, 1996–2005. Hon. LLD York Univ., Toronto, 2002. *Recreation:* France. *Address:* 2 St Helena Terrace, Richmond, Surrey TW9 1NR. *Club:* Garrick.

FALL, David William, CMG 2007; HM Diplomatic Service, retired; Ambassador to Thailand, 2003–07; *b* 10 March 1948; *s* of George William Fall and Susan Fall; *m* 1973, Margaret Gwendolyn Richards; three *s*. *Educ:* St Bartholomew's Grammar Sch., Newbury; New Coll., Oxford (MA Mod. Hist.). VSO, Papua-New Guinea, 1970–71; joined FCO, 1971; language student, later 2nd then 1st Sec., Bangkok, 1973–77; seconded to Cabinet Office, 1977–78; FCO, 1978–80; 1st Sec., Cape Town and Pretoria, 1981–85; FCO, 1985–90; Counsellor, 1989; Head of Narcotics Control and AIDS Dept, FCO, 1989–90; Dep. Hd of Mission, Bangkok, 1990–93; Dep. High Comr, Canberra, 1993–97; Ambassador to Socialist Republic of Vietnam, 1997–2000; Estate Sales Prog., subseq. Estate Modernisation, Manager, FCO, 2000–03. Board Member: POWER International; Anglo-Thai Society. Internat. Trustee, British Red Cross. *Recreations:* cartooning, jogging, walking, golf, reading, Monty Python.

FALLAIZE, Prof. Elizabeth Anne, PhD; Professor of French, since 2002, and Pro-Vice-Chancellor, since 2005, University of Oxford; Fellow, St John's College, Oxford, since 1990; *b* 3 June 1950; *d* of John and Jill Fallaize; one *s* one *d*; *m* 1998, Alan Grafen. *Educ:* Univ. of Exeter (BA, MA; PhD). Lectr in French, Univ. of Birmingham, 1977–90; Lectr, Univ. of Oxford, 1990–2002. Trustee, Rhodes Trust, 2006–. Officier des palmes académiques (France), 2002. *Publications:* The Novels of Simone de Beauvoir, 1990; French Women's Writing: recent fiction, 1993; Simone de Beauvoir: a critical reader, 1998; French Fiction in the Mitterand Years, 2000; The Oxford Book of French Short Stories, 2002. *Address:* St John's College, Oxford OX1 3JP; *e-mail:* elizabeth.fallaize@sjc.ox.ac.uk.

FALLAS, Diana Elizabeth Jane; *see* Burrell, D. E. J.

FALLE, Sir Sam, KCMG 1979 (CMG 1964); KCVO 1972; DSC 1945; HM Diplomatic Service, retired; *b* 19 Feb. 1919; *s* of Theodore and Hilda Falle; *m* 1945, Merete Rosen; one *s* three *d*. *Educ:* Victoria Coll., Jersey, CI. Served Royal Navy, 1937–48; joined Foreign (subseq. Diplomatic) Service, 1948; British Consulate, Shiraz, Iran, 1949–51; British Embassy, Tehran, 1952; British Embassy, Beirut, 1952–55; FO, 1955–57; British Embassy, Baghdad, 1957–61; Consul-Gen., Gothenburg, 1961–63; Head of UN Dept, FO, 1963–67; with Lord Shackleton's mission to Aden, 1967; Deputy High Comr, Kuala Lumpur, 1967–69; Ambassador to Kuwait, 1969–70; High Comr, Singapore, 1970–74; Ambassador to Sweden, 1974–77; High Comr in Nigeria, 1977–78; Delegate, Commn of the European Communities, Algiers, 1979–82; carried out evaluation of EEC aid to Zambia, 1983–84, and Swedish aid to Swaziland, 1986. Hon. Fellow, Univ. of St Andrews, 1997. Kt Grand Cross, Order of Polar Star, Sweden, 1975. *Publication:* My Lucky Life (memoirs), 1996. *Recreations:* swimming, ski-ing. *Address:* Flat 44, Avondown House, Langdon Road, The Hollow, Twerton, Bath BA2 1ND. *T:* (01225) 337531.

FALLICK, Prof. Anthony Edward, PhD; FRSE; Professor of Isotope Geosciences, University of Glasgow, since 1996; *b* 21 April 1950; *s* of Edward Henry Fallick and Helen Fallick (*née* Murray); partner, Dr Charlotte Bryant; one *d*. *Educ:* Univ. of Glasgow (BSc Hons Natural Philosophy 1971; PhD Nuclear Geochem. 1975). Research Fellow,

McMaster Univ., 1975–78; Vis. Schol., Cambridge Univ., 1978–80; Res. Fellow, 1980–85, Lectr, 1985–90, Reader, 1990–96, Univ. of Glasgow; Dir, Scottish Univs Envmtl Res. Centre, 1999–2007. FRSE 1993; FRSA 1997; FMinSoc 1998 (Schlumberger Medal, 1998); Founding Fellow, Inst. of Contemp. Scotland, 2000. Richard A. Glenn Award, ACS, 2001; Coke Medal, Geol Soc., 2004. *Publications:* contrib. numerous articles and papers to peer-reviewed jls and symposia vols. *Recreations:* wine, song. *Address:* SUERC, Scottish Enterprise Technology Park, E Kilbride, Glasgow G75 0QF. *T:* (01355) 223332; *e-mail:* t.fallick@suerc.gla.ac.uk. *Club:* Four Forty Five (Hamilton, Ont.).

FALLON, Her Honour Hazel Rosemary; a Circuit Judge, 1978–96; *b* 7 Jan. 1931; *d* of late Arthur Henry Counsell and Elsie Winifred Counsell; *m* 1980, Peter Fallon, *qv*. *Educ:* Clifton High Sch.; Switzerland; Univ. of Bristol (LLB). Called to the Bar, Gray's Inn, 1956; Western Circuit, 1956–96; a Recorder of the Crown Court, 1976–77. Legal Dept, Min. of Labour, 1959–62. Mem. of Council, Univ. of Bristol, 1992–97. Hon. LLD UWE, 1996. *Recreations:* reading, swimming, travel, gardening. *Address:* c/o The Law Courts, Small Street, Bristol BS1 1DA.

FALLON, Ivan Gregory; Chief Executive Officer, Independent News & Media UK, since 2002; *b* 26 June 1944; *s* of Padraic and Dorothea Fallon; *m* 1st, 1967, Susan Mary Lurring (marr. diss. 1997); one *s* two *d*; 2nd, 1997, Elizabeth Rees-Jones. *Educ:* St Peter's Coll., Wexford; Trinity Coll., Dublin (BBS). Irish Times, 1964–66; Thomson Provincial Newspapers, 1966–67; Daily Mirror, 1967–68; Sunday Telegraph, 1968–70; Deputy City Editor, Sunday Express, 1970–71; Sunday Telegraph, 1971–84: City Editor, 1979–84; Dep. Editor, Sunday Times, 1984–94; Dir, Argus Gp, 1994–97; CEO, Ind. Newspapers of S Africa, then Ind. News & Media of SA, 1994–2002; Dep. Chief Exec. and Editl Dir, Independent Newspapers Hldgs Ltd, S Africa, 1994–97. Chm., iTouch plc, 2001–05; Director: N. Brown Group plc, 1994–; Independent Newspapers plc, Ireland, 1995–. Member: Council, Univ. of Buckingham, 1982–94; Council of Governors, United Med. and Dental Schs of Guy's and St Thomas's Hosps, 1985–94; Trustee: Project Trust, 1984–; Generation Trust, Guy's Hosp., 1985–. FRSA 1989. *Publications:* (with James L. Srodes) DeLorean: the rise and fall of a dream-maker, 1983; (with James L. Srodes) Takeovers, 1987; The Brothers: the rise and rise of Saatchi and Saatchi, 1988; Billionaire: the life and times of Sir James Goldsmith, 1991; Paper Chase, 1993; The Player: the life of Tony O'Reilly, 1994. *Recreations:* walking, tennis. *Address:* Independent House, 191 Marsh Wall, E14 9RS. *T:* (020) 7005 3800. *Clubs:* Garrick, Beefsteak, Political Economy; Rand (Johannesburg).
See also P. M. Fallon.

FALLON, Kieren; flat race jockey; *b* Crusheen, Co. Clare, 22 Feb. 1965; *s* of Frank and Maureen Fallon; *m* 1993, Julie Bowker; one *s* two *d*. With Lynda Ramsden stable, 1993–97; stable jockey for Henry Cecil, 1997–2000, for Michael Stoute, 2000–05, for Aidan O'Brien, 2005–; rode first British winner, 1988; rode 200 winners in season, 1997. Winner: Lincoln Handicap, on High Premium, 1993; 1,000 Guineas, on Sleepytime, 1997, on Wince, 1999, on Russian Rhythm, 2003, on Virginia Waters, 2005; Oaks, on Reams of Verse, 1997, on Ramruna, 1999, on Ouija Board, 2004; Grosser Preis von Baden, Germany, on Borgia, 1997; Prix de la Forêt, France, on Tomba, 1998; Derby, on Oath, 1999, on Kris Kin, 2003, on North Light, 2004; Irish Oaks, on Ramruna, 1999, on Ouija Board, 2004, on Alexandrova, 2006; Tattersalls Gold Cup, Ireland, on Shiva, 1999; 2,000 Guineas, on King's Best, 2000, on Golan, 2001, on Footstepsinthesand, 2005, on George Washington, 2006; King George VI and Queen Elizabeth Diamond Stakes, on Golan, 2002; Filly and Mare Turf, Breeders' Cup, on Islington, 2003, on Ouija Board, 2004; Irish Derby, on Hurricane Run, 2005, on Dylan Thomas, 2006; Prix de l'Arc de Triomphe, on Hurricane Run, 2005, on Dylan Thomas, 2007; French 2,000 Guineas, on Aussie Rules, 2006. Champion Jockey, 1997, 1998, 1999, 2001, 2002, 2003. *Address:* c/o Jockey Club, 42 Portman Square, W1H 0EM.

FALLON, Martin; *see* Patterson, Harry.

FALLON, Michael; MP (C) Sevenoaks, since 1997; *b* 14 May 1952; *s* of late Martin Fallon, OBE, FRCSI and of Hazel Fallon; *m* 1986, Wendy Elisabeth, *e d* of late Peter Payne, Holme-on-Spalding Moor, Yorks; two *s*. *Educ:* St Andrews Univ. (MA Hons 1974). European Educnl Res. Trust, 1974–75; Opposition Whips Office, House of Lords, 1975–77; EEC Officer, Cons. Res. Dept, 1977–79; Jt Man. Dir, European Consultants Ltd, 1979–81; Dir, Quality Care Homes plc, 1992–97; Chief Exec., Quality Care Develts Ltd, 1996–97; Man. Dir, Just Learning Ltd, 1996–2006; Director: Bannatyne Fitness Ltd, 1999–2000; Collins Stewart Tullett plc, 2004–06; Tullett Prebon plc, 2006–. Sec., Lord Home's Cttee on future of House of Lords, 1977–78; Assistant to Baroness Elles, 1979–83. MP (C) Darlington, 1983–92; contested (C) Darlington, 1992. PPS to Sec. of State for Energy, 1987–88; an Asst Govt Whip, 1988–90; a Lord Comr of HM Treasury, 1990; Parly Under-Sec. of State, DES, 1990–92; Opposition spokesman on trade and industry, 1997, on Treasury matters, 1997–98. Mem., Treasury Select Cttee, 1999–; Chm., All Party Classics Gp, 2005–. Mem., Exec., 1922 Cttee, 2005–07. Member: HEFCE, 1993–97; Adv. Council, Social Market Foundn, 1994–2001; Govt's Deregulation Task Force, 1994–97. Dir, Internat. Care and Relief, 1997–2003. Gov., Whitefield Schs, 1994–99. *Publications:* The Quango Explosion (jtly), 1978; Sovereign Members?, 1982; The Rise of the Euroquango, 1982; Brighter Schools, 1993; Social Mobility, 2007; contribs to journals. *Recreations:* books, ski-ing, visiting classical sites. *Address:* House of Commons, SW1A 0AA. *Club:* Academy.

FALLON, Padraic Matthew; Chairman, Euromoney Institutional Investor (formerly Euromoney Publications) PLC, since 1992; *b* 21 Sept. 1946; *s* of Padraic Fallon, poet and Dorothea (Don) (*née* Maher); *m* 1972, Gillian Elizabeth Hellyer; one *s* three *d*. *Educ:* St Peter's Coll., Wexford; Blackrock Coll., Co. Dublin; Trinity Coll., Dublin (BBS, MA). Reporter: Thomson Newspapers City office, 1969–70; Daily Mirror, 1970–72; Daily Mail City pages, 1972–74; Managing Editor, Middle East Money, Beirut, 1974; Editor, Euromoney, 1974–85; Euromoney Publications, subseq. Euromoney Institnl Investor, PLC: Dir, 1975–; Man. Dir, 1985–89; Chief Exec., 1989–92. Non-exec. Dir, Allied Irish Banks plc, 1988–2007; Dir, Daily Mail & General Trust plc, 1999–. Dir, TCD Foundn, 2000–. FRSA. *Publication:* A Hymn of the Dawn, 2003. *Recreation:* country sports. *Address:* Euromoney Institutional Investor PLC, Nestor House, Playhouse Yard, EC4V 5EX. *T:* (020) 7779 8888; 34 Abbotsbury Close, W14 8EQ. *T:* (020) 7602 1253. *Clubs:* Garrick, Flyfishers; Kildare Street and University (Overseas Member) (Dublin).
See also I. G. Fallon.

FALLON, Paul Michael; independent health and social care consultant, since 2007; Head of Children's Services and Director of Social Services, London Borough of Barnet, 2001–07; *b* 11 July 1952; *s* of Michael and Doreen Fallon; *m* 2003, Joanne (*née* Katz); one *s*. *Educ:* Barking Abbey Grammar Sch.; Redbridge Tech. Coll.; Southampton Univ. (BSc, CQSW, DASS). Youth and Community Worker, 1975–78, Sen. Social Worker and Team Leader, 1978–82, Solihull MBC; Principal Officer (Child Care), 1982–89, Operational Services Manager, 1989–94, Coventry CC; Asst Dir (Child Care), Islington LBC, 1994–99; Quality Protects Develt Officer, DoH, 1999–2000. Co-Chm., ADSS Children and Families Policy Cttee, 2005–. Non-exec. Dir, Pathway Care. *Recreation* playing the guitar. *Address:* *e-mail:* paulfallonuk@yahoo.co.uk.

FALLON, His Honour Peter; QC 1971; a Circuit Judge, 1979–96; a Senior Circui Judge, 1980–96; *b* 1 March 1931; *s* of Frederick and Mary Fallon; *m* 1st, 1955, Zina Mary (*née* Judd); one *s* two *d*; 2nd, 1980, Hazel Rosemary Counsell (*see* Her Honour H. R Fallon). *Educ:* Leigh Grammar Sch.; St Joseph's Coll., Blackpool; Bristol Univ. (LLB Hons). Called to Bar, Gray's Inn, 1953. Commissioned in RAF for three years. A Recorder of the Crown Court, 1972–79; Hon. Recorder of Bristol, 1995–96. Chm. Cttee of Inquiry into the Personality Disorder Unit, Ashworth Special Hosp., 1997–99 *Publications:* Crown Court Practice: Sentencing, 1974; Crown Court Practice: Trial, 1978 contrib. Proc. RSM. *Recreations:* golf, fishing, painting. *Address:* c/o The Law Courts Small Street, Bristol BS1 1DA.

FALLOWS, Albert Bennett, CB 1987; Hon. RICS; Chief Valuer, Inland Revenue Valuation Office and Commissioner of Inland Revenue, 1984–88; *b* 7 Dec. 1928; *s* o Bennett and May Fallows; *m* 1955, Maureen James; two *d*. *Educ:* Leek High School Private practice, surveying, 1945–56; local govt service, Staffs, 1956–63; joined CS, 1963 Dist Valuer, Basingstoke, 1973–75; Superintending Valuer, Liaison Officer, DoE/Dept o Transport, 1975–77; Board of Inland Revenue: Superintending Valuer, North West Preston, 1977–80; Asst Chief Valuer, 1980–83; Dep. Chief Valuer, 1983. *Address:* 1 Meadow Drive, Bude, Cornwall EX23 8HZ. *T:* (01288) 354434.

FALLOWS, Prof. David Nicholas, PhD; FBA 1997; Professor of Musicology University of Manchester, since 1997; *b* 20 Dec. 1945; *yr s* of late William John Fallow and Winifred Joan Fallows (*née* Sanderson); *m* 1976, Paulène Oliver (separated 1996); one *s* one *d*. *Educ:* Shrewsbury Sch.; Jesus Coll., Cambridge (BA 1967); King's Coll., London (MMus 1968); Univ. of Calif at Berkeley (PhD 1978). Assistant, Studio der Frühen Musik Munich, 1968–70; Lectr, Univ. of Wisconsin-Madison, 1973–74; Lectr, 1976–82, Sen Lectr, 1982–92, Reader in Music, 1992–97, Univ. of Manchester. Vis. Associate Prof. Univ. of N Carolina, Chapel Hill, 1982–83; Prof. invité de musicologie, Ecole Normale Supérieure, Paris, 1993; visiting posts: Univ. of Basel, 1996, 2004; Univ. of Vienna, 1999 Harvard Univ., 2002. Pres., Internat. Musicological Soc., 2002–07; Vice-Pres., Roya Musical Assoc., 2000–. Corresp. Mem., Amer. Musicol Soc., 1999. Reviews Editor, Early Music, 1976–95, 1999–2000; Gen. Editor and Founder, Royal Musical Assoc Monographs, 1982–98; Member, Editorial Board: Musica Britannica, 1985–; Jl of Roya Musical Assoc., 1986–88; Basler Jahrbuch für historische Musikpraxis, 1988–; Early Musi History, 1991–; Muziek en Wetenschap, 1992–2001; Early English Church Music, 1994– Chevalier, Ordre des Arts et des Lettres (France), 1994. *Publications:* Dufay, 1982, 2nd edn 1987; (jtly) Chansonnier de Jean de Montchenu, 1991; (ed jtly) Companion to Medieval and Renaissance Music, 1992, 2nd edn 1997; The Songs of Guillaume Dufay, 1995; (ed and introd) Oxford Bodleian Library MS Canon Misc. 213 (Late Medieval and Early Renaissance music in facsimile, vol. 1), 1995; Songs and Musicians in the Fifteenth Century, 1996; The Songbook of Fridolin Sicher, 1996; A Catalogue of Polyphonic Song 1415–1480, 1999; (ed) Josquin des Prez, Secular Works for Four Voices (New Josquin Edn vol. 28), 2005. *Address:* 10 Chatham Road, Manchester M16 0DR. *T:* (0161) 881 1188; *e-mail:* david.fallows@manchester.ac.uk.

FALLOWS, Geoffrey Michael; Headteacher, Camden School for Girls, 1989–2000; *b* 28 Sept. 1941; *er s* of late Rt Rev. William Gordon Fallows and of Edna (*née* Blakeman); *m* 1st, 1968, Carolyn (*d* 2000), *d* of late Dr William Brian Littler, CB and Pearl Littler; two *d*; 2nd, 2002, Johanna Koolhaas Revers, *d* of late Johann Koolhaas Revers and Maria Darley (*née* Buur). *Educ:* Shrewsbury Sch.; Wadham Coll., Oxford (MA); London Univ Inst. of Education (PGCE). Vis. Classics Fellow, Marlboro Coll., Vermont, 1964–65; Asst Master, Latymer Upper Sch., 1966–69; Head of Classics, Crown Woods Sch., 1969–75 Dep. Head, Camden Sch. for Girls, 1975–89. Dir, Huron Univ., USA, in London 1998–2005. Exec. Sec., 1978–81, Pres., 2003–05, JACT. Co-founder, Omnibu magazine, 1981. FRSA 1994. *Recreations:* theatre, gardening, Lake District. *Address:* 5 Byng Road, Barnet, Herts EN5 4NW. *T:* (020) 8449 2980, *Fax:* (020) 8440 7629; *e-mail* fallows@byngroad.co.uk.

FALMOUTH, 9th Viscount, *cr* 1720; **George Hugh Boscawen;** 26th Baron Le Despencer, 1264; Baron Boscawen-Rose, 1720; Lord-Lieutenant of Cornwall, 1977–94 *b* 31 Oct. 1919; 2nd but *e* surv. *s* of 8th Viscount Falmouth; *S* father, 1962; *m* 1953 Elizabeth Price Browne (*d* 2007), OBE 2002, DL; four *s*. *Educ:* Eton Coll.; Trinity Coll. Cambridge. Served War, 1939–46, Italy. Capt., Coldstream Guards. DL Cornwall, 1968 *Heir:* *s* Hon. Evelyn Arthur Hugh Boscawen [*b* 13 May 1955; *m* 1st, 1977, Lucia Vivian-Neal (marr. diss. 1995), *e d* of R. W. Vivian-Neal; one *s* one *d*; 2nd, 1995, Katharine Maley; two *s* one *d*].
See also Rt Hon. R. T. Boscawen.

FALSE BAY, Bishop of, since 2006; **Rt Rev. Merwyn Edwin Castle;** *b* 2 Nov. 1942 *s* of Ernest Edwin and Catherine Castle. *Educ:* Federal Theol Seminary, Alice (DipTh) Ordained deacon, 1969, priest, 1970; Rector, Christ the King, Coronationville, 1977–82 Dean, Johannesburg, 1982–87; Rector: Gambleville, Uitenhage, 1987–90 Matroosfontein, Cape Town, 1990–92; Chaplain, Archbishop of Cape Town, 1992–93 Rector, St Saviour's, Claremont, 1993–94; Bishop Suffragan of Cape Town, 1994–2006 Southern Reg., 1994–98, False Bay Reg., 1998–2006. Chm., Provincial Liturgical Cttee 2000–; Liaison Bishop, Council for the Religious Life, 2000–. Bishop Protector, African Province, Third Order of St Francis, 2005. *Recreations:* gardening, music, reading. *Address* Bishopsholme, 2 Slabbert Street, Somerset West, 7130, South Africa. *T:* (office) (21) 8525243; (home) (21) 8521686, *Fax:* (21) 8529430; *e-mail:* bishopm@ falsebaydiocese.org.za.

FALVEY, Dr David Alan, FGS; Executive Director, Physics, Chemistry and Geoscience Australian Research Council, since 2006; *b* Sydney, 19 Dec. 1945; *s* of late Keith Falvey and Ella Falvey (*née* Hendley); *m* 1969, Margaret Kaye (*d* 1984); one *s* one *d*; *m* 1986 Gillian Tidey. *Educ:* Univ. of Sydney (BSc Hons 1967); Univ. of New South Wales (PhD 1972). FGS 1998. Explorationist, Shell Develt, Australia, 1972–74; Lectr, then Sen. Lectr Univ. of Sydney, 1974–82; Chief, Marine Div., Bureau of Mineral Resources, 1982–89 Associate Dir, Petroleum and Marine Geoscis, Australian Geol Survey Orgn, 1989–94 Dir, Ocean Drilling Program, Jt Oceanographic Instns, Washington, 1994–98; Exec. Dir British Geological Survey, NERC, 1998–2006. CCMI 2003. Hon. DSc Nottingham Trent, 2001. *Publications:* numerous scientific contribs to learned jls. *Recreation:* golf *Address:* Australian Research Council, GPO 2702, Canberra, ACT 2601, Australia. *Clubs* Royal Canberra Golf; Cotgrave Place Golf (Notts).

FAME, Georgie; musician, vocalist, songwriter; *b* 26 June 1943; *s* of James and Mary Anne Powell; *né* Clive Powell, name changed by impresario Larry Parnes, 1960; *m* 1971 Nicolette (*d* 1993); two *s*. *Educ:* Leigh Central Co. Secondary Sch., Lancs. Professional musician, 1959–; toured with Eddie Cochran, Gene Vincent and Billy Fury, 1960; leader of own band, The Blue Flames, 1962–; toured with Count Basie Orch., 1967 and 1968 rep. UK, Fest. Internat. Da Cancao Popular, Brazil, 1967; in partnership with Alan Price

1970–73; collaborated with Van Morrison, 1988–98; Founder Mem., Bill Wyman's Rhythm Kings, 1998; hosted own series, BBC Radio 2, 2000; featured guest soloist with all of Europe's major jazz orchs; has composed and performed music for various feature films, television and radio commercials. Over 30 albums released under own name inc. Poet in New York, 2000 (Prix Billie Holiday, Acad. du Jazz de France); 13 hit singles, incl. 3 Number Ones: Yeh Yeh, 1965; Getaway, 1966; Ballad of Bonnie and Clyde, 1968. Hon. Mem. Swedish Exec. Jazz Soc., 2002. *Recreations:* aviation, crosswords.

FANCOURT, Timothy Miles; QC 2003; *b* 30 Aug. 1964; *s* of Dr Philip Fancourt and Georgina Mary Fancourt (*née* Brown); *m* 2000, Emily Windsor; one *d*. *Educ:* Whitgift Sch.; Gonville and Caius Coll., Cambridge (MA). Called to the Bar, Lincoln's Inn, 1987. Vice-Chm., Standards Cttee, Bar Standards Bd, 2006–. *Publications:* Enforceability of Landlord and Tenant Covenants, 1997, 2nd edn 2006; Megarry's Assured Tenancies, 2nd edn 1999. *Recreations:* cricket, classical music. *Address:* Falcon Chambers, Falcon Court, EC4Y 1AA. *T:* (020) 7353 2484, *Fax:* (020) 7353 1261; *e-mail:* fancourt@falcon-chambers.com.

FANE, family name of **Earl of Westmorland**.

FANE, Andrew William Mildmay, FCA; Chairman, Special Trustees, Great Ormond Street Hospital Children's Charity, 1999–2006 (Associate Trustee, since 2007); *b* 9 Aug. 1949; *s* of late Robert William Augustus Fane and of Elinor Valerie Fane (*née* Borthwick); *m* 1989, Clare Lucy Marx, CBE, FRCS. *Educ:* Radley Coll.; Emmanuel Coll., Cambridge (MA Law). FCA 1974. Chief Exec., Whitburgh Investments Ltd, 1982–92; Dir and Dep. Chm., Borthwicks plc, 1988–92. Non-exec. Dir, Gt Ormond St Hosp. for Children NHS Trust, 2001– (Chm., Audit Cttee, 2006–). Councillor, RBK&C, 1987–94 (Chm., Planning Cttee). Mem., Royal Commn on Histl Monuments of England, 1999–2003; English Heritage: Comr, 1995–2004; Dep. Chm., 2001–04; Chm., Audit Cttee, 2002–. Chairman: Historic Bldgs and Areas Adv. Cttee, 1995–2001; London Adv. Cttee, 1999–2004 (Mem., 1994–2004); Historic Built Envmt Adv. Cttee, 2001–02. Mem., E Anglia Regl Cttee, NT, 1994–2002. Chm., Bd of Govs, Framlingham Coll., Suffolk, 2001– (Gov., 1995–); Chm., Foundn Bd, 2002–, Mem. Council, 2003–, Radley Coll., Oxon. Mem., Develt Cttee, Emmanuel Coll., Cambridge, 1994–2001. Gov., 2005–, Trustee, 2007–, Coram (formerly Coram Family); Trustee, Foundling Mus., 2007–; Chm., Stowe House Preservation Trust, 2007–. *Recreation:* conservation. *Address:* Hoo House, Woodbridge, Suffolk; 64 Ladbroke Road, W11 3NR. *T:* (020) 7221 2748.

FANE TREFUSIS, family name of **Baron Clinton**.

FANELLI, Sara; artist and illustrator; *b* 20 July 1969; *d* of Giovanni Fanelli and Rosalia (*née* Bonito). *Educ:* Liceo Classico Michelangelo, Florence (Maturita Classica); Camberwell Coll. of Art (BA Hons Graphic Design); Royal Coll. of Art (MA Illustration). Projects include: stamp design for Royal Millennium Collection, 1999 (D&AD Silver Award); timeline 40 metres long and design of 4 gallery entrances at Tate Modern, 2005–; book jackets for Penguin, Orion, Bloomsbury, Random House, Pan MacMillan and Faber and Faber; magazine illustrations for: New Yorker, NY Times, New Scientist, Guardian, TES, Radio Times, Daily Telegraph, Independent on Sunday; work for: BBC English; BBC Worldwide; British Council; Amnesty; Virgin Classics; Orange; Edinburgh Fest.; Royal Exchange Th., Manchester; Lyric Th., London; Nat. Westminster Bank; Nickelodeon (US); Alessi; Issey Miyake; Ron Arad. Mem., AGI, 2000–. Hon. RDI 2006. Numerous awards including: Parallel Prize, 1995; Nat. Art Liby Illustration Award, V&A, 1995, Commended Winner, 1997, 1998, 2000; D&AD Silver Award for poster illustration, 2003; V&A Illustration Award, 2004. *Publications: written and illustrated:* Button, 1994 (MacMillan Prize for a Children's Picture Book, 1992); My Map Book, 1995, 2nd edn 2006; Cinderella: Picture Box, 1996; Pinocchio: Picture Box, 1996; Wolf!, 1997; A Dog's Life, 1998; It's Dreamtime, 1999; Dear Diary, 2000; First Flight, 2002; Mythological Monsters, 2002; *illustrated:* Dibby Dubby Dhu, 1997; The Folio Book of Short Novels, 1998; The New Faber Book of Children's Verse, 2001; Pinocchio, 2004; Sometimes I Think, Sometimes I Am, 2007. *Recreations:* film music, reading, travelling, flea markets, playing games, the moon. *Address:* c/o Walker Books, 87 Vauxhall Walk, SE11 5HJ; *web:* www.sarafanelli.com.

FANNER, His Honour Peter Duncan; a Circuit Judge, 1986–95; *b* 27 May 1926; *s* of late Robert William Hodges Fanner, solicitor, and Doris Kitty Fanner; *m* 1949, Sheila Eveline England; one *s* one *d*. *Educ:* Pangbourne Coll. Admitted Solicitor of the Supreme Court, 1951 (holder Justices' Clerks' Society's prize). Served War of 1939–45, Pilot in Fleet Air Arm, Lieut (A) RNVR, 1944–47. Asst Clerk to Bromley Justices, 1947–51; Dep. Clerk to Gore Justices, 1951–56; Clerk to Bath Justices, 1956–72; Metropolitan Stipendiary Magistrate, 1972–86; a Dep. Circuit Judge, 1974–80; a Recorder, 1980–86. Mem. Council of Justices' Clerks' Society, 1966–72; Assessor Mem. of Departmental Cttee on Liquor Licensing, 1971–72. Chairman: Bath Round Table, 1963–64; Claverton Parish Council, 1998–2005. *Publications:* Stone's Justices' Manual; contrib. to Justice of the Peace, The Magisterial Officer, The Lawyer's Remembrancer. *Recreations:* travel, railways. *Address:* c/o The Law Courts, Small Street, Bristol BS1 1DA. *T:* (0117) 976 3030.

FANSHAWE, Col David, LVO 2003; OBE 1977; Lieutenant, HM Body Guard of the Honourable Corps of Gentlemen-at-Arms, 2000–03; *b* 1 Nov. 1933; *s* of late Major Richard Gennys Fanshawe and Ruth Violet Mary, later Ruth, Baroness Dulverton, *o d* of Sir Walter Farquhar, 5th Bt; *m* 1963, Sheila McNeill; three *s*. *Educ:* Stowe; RMA Sandhurst. Commnd Grenadier Guards, 1954: served Europe, USA, Africa, Far East, and Middle East; Comdr, Guards Independent Parachute Co., 1967–70; Adjutant, RMA Sandhurst, 1970–73; CO 2nd Bn Grenadier Guards, 1974–76; Regtl Comdr, Grenadier Guards, 1978–80; Defence Attaché, Sudan and Somalia, 1981–83. Mem., HM Body Guard of Hon. Corps of Gentlemen-at-Arms, 1986–2003 (Clerk of Cheque and Adjt, 1998–2000). Dir, Hedley Foundn, 1983–98; Chm., Dulverton Trust, 2000–07. *Recreations:* sailing, ornithology. *Address:* Upper Mill, Sydling St Nicholas, Dorchester, Dorset DT2 9PD. *T:* (01300) 341230. *Club:* Cavalry and Guards.

FANTHORPE, Ursula Askham, CBE 2001; freelance writer, since 1989; *b* 22 July 1929; *d* of late His Honour Judge Richard Fanthorpe and Winifrid Elsie Askham (*née* Redmore); partner, Dr R. V. Bailey. *Educ:* St Catherine's Sch., Bramley; St Anne's Coll., Oxford (MA; Hon. Fellow 2003); Inst. of Educn, London (DipEd); Univ. of Swansea (Dip. Sch. Counselling). Cheltenham Ladies' College: Asst English Mistress, 1954–62; Hd of English, 1962–70; temp. clerical work, Bristol, 1973–74; clerk/receptionist, Burden Neurological Hosp., Bristol, 1974–89. Arts Council Writer-in-Residence, St Martin's Coll., Lancaster, 1983–85; Northern Arts Fellow, Durham and Newcastle Univs, 1987. FRSL 1988. Hawthornden Fellowship, 1987, 1997, 2002. Member: Poetry Soc.; Soc. of Authors (Travelling Fellowship, 1983); International PEN. Hon. Fellow, Sarum Coll., 2004. Hon. DLitt: UWE, 1995; Bath, 2006; Hon. PhD Gloucester, 2000. Queen's Gold Medal for Poetry, 2003. *Publications:* Side Effects, 1978; Standing To, 1982; Voices Off, 1984; Selected Poems, 1986; A Watching Brief, 1987; Neck-Verse, 1992; Safe as Houses, 1995; Consequences, 2000; Christmas Poems, 2002; Queueing for the Sun, 2003; Collected Poems, 2005; Homing In, 2006; From Me to You, 2007. *Recreations:* mediaeval parish churches, inland waterways. *Address:* Culverhay House, Wotton under Edge, Gloucestershire GL12 7LS. *T:* and *Fax:* (01453) 843105; *e-mail:* fanthorpe_bailey@yahoo.co.uk.

FANTONI, Prof. Barry Ernest; writer, performer, jazz musician; Member of editorial staff of Private Eye, since 1963; Professor of Communications and Media Studies, University of Salerno, since 1997; Director, All This Time Theatre Co., since 1998; *b* 28 Feb. 1940; *s* of late Peter Nello Secondo Fantoni and of Sarah Catherine Fantoni; became Italian citizen, 1997; *m* 1972, Teresa Frances, (Tessa), Reidy. *Educ:* Archbishop Temple Sch.; Camberwell Sch. of Arts and Crafts (Wedgwood Scholar). Cartoonist of The Listener, 1968–88; contrib. art criticism to The Times, 1973–77; record reviewer, Punch, 1976–77; Diary cartoonist, The Times, 1983–90; Dir, Barry Fantoni Merchandising Co., 1985–93; designer of film and theatre posters and illustrator of book jackets; mural for Queen Elizabeth II Conf. Centre, London, 1985; film and television actor; From the Dragon's Mouth (one-man show for stage), 1991–; plays: Jeanne, performed Battersea Arts Centre, 1997; Modigliani, My Love, Paris, 1999; Rooms of the House, 2001; The Piano Tuner, 2005, Extra Time, 2006, (with Barry Booth) Café de Paris, 2006, Lady Windermere's Fan, 2006, Death of an Elephant, 2007, Loving Art, 2008, Landor Th.; creator, Ronnie's Horns (perf. with O. T. Fagbenly), RADA, 2002; travelling act (with Dominic Alldis) An Evening with E.J. Thribb; presenter and writer, Barry Fantoni's Chinese Horoscopes, BBC Radio 4 series, 1986. One-man shows: Woodstock Gall., London, 1963; Comara Gall., LA, 1964; Brunel Univ., 1974; Times cartoon exhibition, Charlotte Lampard Gall., 1990; retrospective: Cadogan Contemporary Gall., 1991; Caricatures by Barry Fantoni, NPG, 2007; two-man shows (with Peter Fantoni): Langton Gall., London, 1977; Annexe Gall., London, 1978; Katherine House Gall., 1983; Fulford Cartoon Gall., 1983; New Grafton Gall., 1985; Green & Stone, Cirencester, 1986; work exhibited: AIA Gall., London, 1958, 1961 and 1964; D and AD Annual Exhibn, London, 1964; Royal Acad. Summer Exhibn, 1963 (as Stuart Harris, with William Rushton), 1964, 1975 and 1978 (with Richard Napper); Tate Gall., 1973; Bradford Print Biennale, 1974; National Theatre, 1977; Browse and Darby, 1977; Gillian Jason Gall., 1983; Three Decades of Art Schools, RA, 1983; Piers Feetham Gall., 2002. Collections of work at London Museum, 1980; V&A, 1984; Cartoon Museum, 1993; Univ. of Kent, 2005; BL, 2006; NPG, 2007 . Musical compositions include: popular songs (also popular songs with Marianne Faithfull and with Stanley Myers); The Cantors Crucifixion (musical improvisation for 13 instruments), 1977; (with John Wells) Lionel (musical), 1977; (with Barry Booth) We Are Your Future (official Unicef anthem), 1996; Mass of the Holy Spirit, 1999. Formed: (with John Butler) Barry Fantoni Duo, 1990–; Barry Fantoni's Jazz Circus, 1992 (a performance jazz trio). Patron, Landor Th., 2005–. Editor, St Martin's Review, 1969–74; weekly columnist on Chinese Horoscopes: Today, 1986–87; Woman, 1987–88; Plus magazine, 1989; The Guardian, 1990. Male TV Personality of the Year, 1966. *Publications:* (with Richard Ingrams) Private Pop Eye, 1968; (as Old Jowett, with Richard Ingrams) The Bible for Motorists, 1970; Tomorrow's Nicodemus, 1974; (as Sylvie Krin, with Richard Ingrams) Love in the Saddle, 1974; Private Eye Cartoon Library 5, 1975; (as E. J. Thribb, with Richard Ingrams) So Farewell Then…and Other Poems, 1978; Mike Dime, 1980; (as Sylvie Krin, with Richard Ingrams) Born to be Queen, 1981; Stickman, 1982; (ed) Colemanballs, 1982; (ed) Colemanballs 2, 1984; The Times Diary Cartoons, 1984; Barry Fantoni's Chinese Horoscope, annually 1985–, retitled Barry Fantoni's Complete Chinese Horoscope, 1991; (ed) Colemanballs 3, 1986; Barry Fantoni Cartoons: a personal selection from The Times and The Listener, 1987; The Royal Family's Chinese Horoscopes, 1988; (ed) Colemanballs 4, 1988; Chinese Horoscope Guide to Love, Marriage and Friendship, 1989; (ed) Colemanballs 5, 1990; (ed) Colemanballs 6, 1992; (ed) Colemanballs 7, 1994; (ed) A Hundred Years of Neasden Football Club, 1995; (ed) Colemanballs 8, 1996; (ed) Colemanballs 9, 1998; (ed) Colemanballs 10, 2000; (ed) Colemanballs 11, 2002; (ed) Colemanballs 12, 2004; (ed) Colemanballs 13, 2006; (ed) Colemanballs 14, 2008; Scenes You Seldom See, 2005; *illustrations for:* How To Be a Jewish Mother, 1966; The BP Festivals and Events in Britain, 1966; (with George Melly) The Media Mob, 1980; The Best of Barry Fantoni Cartoons, 1990. *Recreation:* animal welfare. *Address:* c/o The Marsh Agency, 11–12 Dover Street, W1X 3PD. *T:* (020) 7399 2800, *Fax:* (020) 7399 2801. *Clubs:* Arts, Chelsea Arts (Chm., 1978–80).

FARAGE, Nigel Paul; Member (UK Ind) South East Region, England, European Parliament, since 1999; *b* 3 April 1964; *s* of Guy Farage and Barbara Stevens; *m* 1st, 1988 (marr. diss. 1997); two *s*; 2nd, 1999, Kirsten Mehr; two *d*. *Educ:* Dulwich Coll. Commodity Broker: Drexel Burnham Lambert, 1982–86; Credit Lyonnais Rouse Ltd, 1986–93; Refco Overseas Ltd, 1994–2002; Natexis Metals, 2003–04. UK Independence Party: Founder Mem., 1993; Chm., 1998–2000; Spokesman, 2000–; Leader, 2006–. Co-Pres., Ind./Dem Gp, EP, 2004–. Contested (UK Ind): Eastleigh, June 1994; Salisbury, 1997; Bexhill & Battle, 2001; Itchen, Test & Avon, EP elecns, 1994. *Recreations:* military history 1914–18, sea angling, proper English pubs. *Address:* 1 Darwin Villas, Single Street, Berrys Green, Westerham, Kent TN16 3AA. *T:* (office) (01903) 885573. *Club:* East India.

FARDON, Prof. Richard Osborne, PhD; FBA 2004; Professor of West African Anthropology, since 1996, and Head of Department of Anthropology and Sociology, since 2006, School of Oriental and African Studies, University of London; *b* 16 Jan. 1952; *s* of Arthur Dennis Fardon and Hilda Fardon (*née* Davidson); partner, Prof. Catherine Davies; one *s*, and two step *d*. *Educ:* Sir Roger Manwood's Grammar Sch., Sandwich; UCL (BSc (Econs) 1973; PhD 1980). Lectr in Social Anthropol., Univ. of St Andrews, 1980–88; Lectr in W African and Caribbean Anthropol., 1988–91, Reader, 1991–96, SOAS; Chm., Centre of African Studies, Univ. of London, 1993–97 and 2001–05. Chair, Assoc. of Social Anthropologists of UK and Commonwealth, 2001–05. Hon. Ed., Africa: Jl of Internat. African Inst., 2001–07. *Publications:* (ed) Power and Knowledge, 1985; Raiders and Refugees: trends in Chamba political development 1750–1950, 1988; Localizing Strategies, 1990; Between God, the Dead and the Wild, 1991; (ed with P. T. Baxter) Voice, Genre, Text, 1991; (ed with Graham Furniss) African Languages, Development and the State, 1994; (ed) Counterworks: managing the diversity of knowledge, 1995; Mary Douglas: an intellectual biography, 1999; (ed and introd with Jeremy Adler) Franz Baermann Steiner: selected writings, vol. 1, Taboo, Truth and Religion, vol. 2, Orientpolitik, Value and Civilisation, 1999; (ed jtly) Modernity on a Shoestring, 1999; (ed with Graham Furniss) African Broadcast Culture, 2000; (ed jtly) From Prague Poet to Oxford Anthropologist Franz Baermann Steiner Celebrated: essays and translations, 2003; (with Christine Stelzig) Column to Volume, 2005; Lela in Bali: history through ceremony in Cameroon, 2006; Fusions: masquerades and thought style east of the Niger-Benue confluence, West Africa, 2007. *Recreations:* following opera and the fortunes of Tottenham Hotspur FC. *Address:* Department of Anthropology and Sociology, School of Oriental and African Studies, Thornhaugh Street, Russell Square, WC1H 0XG. *T:* (020) 7898 4406; *e-mail:* rf@soas.ac.uk.

FARHI, Nicole, (Lady Hare), Hon. CBE 2007; fashion designer; Founder, 1983 and Designer, Nicole Farhi Co.; *b* 25 July 1946; *d* of Ephraim Farhi and Marcelle (*née* Babani); one *d* by Stephen Marks; *m* 1992, Sir David Hare, *qv*. *Educ:* Lycée Calmette, Nice; Cours Berçot Art Sch., Paris. First designed for Pierre d'Albi, 1968; founded French Connection with Stephen Marks, 1973; launched Nicole Farhi For Men, 1989; opened Nicole's

Restaurant, 1994; opened Nicole Farhi US flagship store, NY, 1999. British Classics award, 1989, Best Contemporary Designer, 1995, 1996 and 1997, British Fashion Awards; Menswear Designer of the Year, FHM Awards, 2000; British Designer of the Year, Maxim Awards, 2001. *Recreation:* sculpture. *Address:* 16 Foubert's Place, W1F 7PJ. *T:* (020) 7399 7500.

FARINGDON, 3rd Baron *cr* 1916; **Charles Michael Henderson,** KCVO 2008; Bt 1902; Partner, Cazenove & Co., 1968–96; Chairman, Witan Investment Trust (formerly Witan Investment Company) plc, 1980–2003; a Lord in Waiting to the Queen, 1998–2008; *b* 3 July 1937; *s* of Hon. Michael Thomas Henderson (*d* 1953) (2nd *s* of Col Hon. Harold Greenwood Henderson, CVO, and *g s* of 1st Baron) and Oonagh Evelyn Henderson, *er d* of late Lt-Col Harold Ernest Brassey; *S* uncle, 1977; *m* 1959, Sarah Caroline, *d* of late J. M. E. Askew, CBE; three *s* one *d*. *Educ:* Eton College; Trinity College, Cambridge (BA). Treasurer, Nat. Art Collections Fund, 1984–91; Chm., RCHME, 1994–99; Comr, English Heritage, 1998–2001. Chm. Bd of Governors, Royal Marsden Hosp., 1980–85 (Mem., 1975–85); Chm., Bd of Management, 2001–05 (Mem., 1980–2000), Fellow, 2000, Inst. of Cancer Res. *Heir: s* Hon. James Harold Henderson [*b* 14 July 1961; *m* 1986, Lucinda, *y d* of late Desmond Hanson, Knipton, Lincs; two *s* one *d*]. *Address:* Buscot Park, Faringdon, Oxon SN7 8BU.

FARISH, William Stamps, III; Ambassador of the United States of America to the Court of St James's, 2001–04; *b* Houston, Tex, 1938; *m* Sarah Sharp; one *s* three *d*. *Educ:* Univ. of Virginia. Formerly: Stockbroker, Underwood, Neuhaus & Co., Houston; Pres., Navarro Exploration Co.; Founding Director: Eurus Inc., NY; Capital Nat. Bank, Houston; Pres., W. S. Farish & Co., Houston. Owner, Lane's End Farm, Versailles, Ky, 1980–; formerly Chairman: Churchill Downs Inc., Ky; Exec. Cttee, Breeders Cup Ltd; Vice-Chm., US Jockey Club; Dir, Thoroughbred Breeders and Owners Assoc.

FARLEY, Prof. Francis James Macdonald, FRS 1972; Professor Emeritus, Royal Military College of Science (Dean, 1967–82); *b* 13 Oct. 1920; *er s* of late Brig. Edward Lionel Farley, CBE, MC; *m* 1st, 1945, Josephine Maisie Hayden (marr. diss.); three *s* one *d*; 2nd, 1977, Margaret Ann Pearce (marr. diss.); 3rd, 2000, Irina Melyushina. *Educ:* Clifton Coll.; Clare Coll., Cambridge. MA 1945; PhD 1950; ScD Cantab 1967. FInstP. Air Defence Research and Development Establishment, 1941–45 (first 3cm ground radar, Doppler radar); Chalk River Laboratories, 1945–46; Research Student, Cavendish Lab., Cambridge, 1946–49; Auckland Univ. Coll., NZ, 1950–57; attached AERE, 1955; CERN, Geneva, 1957–67 (muon g-2 experiment). Vis. Lectr, Univ. of Bristol, 1965–66; Vis. Scientist, CERN, 1967– (muon storage ring, tests of relativity); Vis. Sen. Res. Physicist, Yale Univ., 1984–92; Visiting Professor: Swiss Inst. of Nuclear Research, 1976–77; Univ. of Reading, 1982–86; Consultant, Centre Antoine Lacassagne, Nice, 1986–92. Rep. NZ at UN Conf. on Atomic Energy for Peaceful Purposes, 1955. Governor: Clifton Coll., to 1994; Welbeck Coll., 1970–82; Member Court: Univ. of Bath, 1974–82; Cranfield Inst. of Technology, 1989–93. Hon. Mem., Instn of Royal Engineers. Hon. Fellow, TCD, 1986. Hughes Medal, Royal Soc., 1980. *Publications:* Elements of Pulse Circuits, 1955; Progress in Nuclear Techniques and Instrumentation, Vol. I, 1966, Vol. II, 1967, Vol. III, 1968; scientific papers on nuclear physics, electronics, high energy particle physics, wave energy. *Recreations:* gliding (FAI gold and diamond), ski-ing. *Address:* 8 chemin de Saint Pierre, 06620 Le Bar sur Loup, France. *T:* 0493424512; *e-mail:* fjmfarley@neuf.fr.

FARLEY, Henry Edward, (Rob); Group Deputy Chief Executive, Royal Bank of Scotland Group, 1986–90; Director, Nationwide Building Society, 1990–97; *b* 28 Sept. 1930; *s* of late William and Frances Elizabeth Farley; *m* 1955, Audrey Joyce Shelvey; one *s* one *d*. *Educ:* Harrow County Sch. for Boys. FCIB (FIB 1966). Entered National Bank, 1947; Head of UK Banking, 1978, Dir, 1981, Williams & Glyn's Bank; Chairman: Williams & Glyn's Bank (IOM) Ltd, 1973–76; Joint Credit Card Co. Ltd, 1982–84; Royal Bank of Scotland Gp Insce, 1988–90; Mem. Bd, Mastercard International Inc., 1982–84; Director: Royal Bank of Scotland Group plc, 1985–90; Royal Bank of Scotland, 1985–90 (Man. Dir, 1985–86); Charterhouse Japhet, 1985–86; Charterhouse Development, 1985–86; Charterhouse plc, 1986–90; Chm., Royscot Finance Gp, 1987–90; Dep. Chm., Supervisory Bd of CC Bank, Germany, 1989–90. Director: EFT-POS (UK) Ltd, 1986–88; A. T. Mays Gp, 1987–90; (Alternate) Citizens Financial Gp (USA), 1989–90; John Maunders Gp, 1989–99; Banque Rivaud, Paris, 1990–97; High Table Ltd, 1991–95; Davenham Gp, 1992–97. Mem. Develt Bd, Special Olympics, 1997–99. Member: Council, Inst. of Bankers, 1985–90; APACS Council, 1983–90; Exec. Cttee, British Bankers Assoc., 1983–90. UMIST: Gov., 1990–2000; Vice-Chm. Council, 1994–2000; Chm., Students Assoc., 2000–02; Dir, UMIST Foundn, 1999–2000; Mem., Gen. Assembly, 2004–, and Mem., Nominations Cttee, Manchester Univ.; Mem. Bd, Manchester Federal Sch. of Business and Management, 1994–99. Sen. Vice-Pres., Knutsford RFC, 2004–. FRSA 1995. Liveryman: Marketors' Co., 1987– (Dir, Marketors' Hall Ltd, 1992–95); Guild of Internat. Bankers, 2005–. *Publications:* The Clearing Banks and Housing Finance, 1983; Competition and Deregulation: branch networks, 1984; The Role of Branches in a Changing Environment, 1985; Deregulation and the Clearing Banks, 1986; The Happy Cookers (poetry), 2003; Cheshire Sets and Matches (poetry), 2003. *Recreations:* all forms of rough sport, travel, modern literature. *Address:* Sylvan Lodge, Leycester Road, Knutsford, Cheshire WA16 8QR. *Clubs:* Bankers', MCC; Pickwick Bicycle; St James, Racquets (Manchester).

FARLEY, Mary-Rose Christine, (Mrs R. D. Farley); *see* Bateman, M.-R. C.

FARLEY, Rob; *see* Farley, H. E.

FARMBROUGH, Rt Rev. David John; Bishop Suffragan of Bedford, 1981–93; Hon. Assistant Bishop, diocese of St Albans, since 1994; *b* 4 May 1929; 2nd *s* of late Charles Septimus and late Ida Mabel Farmbrough; *m* 1955, Angela Priscilla Hill, DL; one *s* three *d*. *Educ:* Bedford Sch.; Lincoln Coll., Oxford (BA 1951, MA 1953); Westcott House, Cambridge, 1951–53. Deacon, 1953, priest, 1954; Curate of Bishop's Hatfield, 1953–57; Priest-in-charge, St John's, Hatfield, 1957–63; Vicar of Bishop's Stortford, 1963–74; Rural Dean of Bishop's Stortford, 1973–74; Archdeacon of St Albans, 1974–81. Mem., Gen. Synod, 1972–81; Chm., and Treas., Clergy Orphan Corp., 1995–97. Chm. Govs, St Margaret's Sch., Bushey, 1999–2001. *Publications:* In Wonder, Love and Praise, 1966; Belonging, Believing, Doing, 1971. *Recreation:* gardening. *Address:* St Michael Mead, 110 Village Road, Bromham, Beds MK43 8HU. *T:* (01234) 825042.

FARMER, Bruce; *see* Farmer, E. B.

FARMER, Prof. David Malcolm, PhD; FRS 2006; FRSC; Professor of Oceanography and Dean, Graduate School of Oceanography, University of Rhode Island. *Educ:* McGill Univ. (MS 1969); Univ. of British Columbia (PhD 1972). FRSC 1993. Oceanographer, Inst. of Ocean Scis, Sidney, BC, now Scientist Emeritus. *Publications:* articles in learned jls. *Address:* Graduate School of Oceanography, University of Rhode Island, 19 Fish Building, 30 Fish Road, Narragansett, RI 02882, USA.

FARMER, Dr (Edwin) Bruce, CBE 1997; FREng; FIMMM; Chairman: Scottish & Southern Energy plc, 2000–05 (Deputy Chairman, 1999–2000); Southern Electric, 1998; *b* 18 Sept. 1936; *s* of Edwin Bruce Farmer and Doris Farmer; *m* 1962, Beryl Ann Griffiths; one *s* one *d*. *Educ:* King Edward's, Birmingham; Univ. of Birmingham (BSc, PhD). CEng 1994; FIMMM (FIM 1994); FREng (FEng 1997). Dir and Gen. Manager, Brico Metals, 1967–69; Man. Dir, Brico Engineering, 1970–76; Man. Dir, Wellworthy, 1976–81; The Morgan Crucible Co. plc: Dir, 1981–83; Chm., Thermal Ceramics Div., 1981–83; Man. Dir and Chief Exec., 1983–97; Chm., 1998–2003. Chairman: Allied Colloids Gp plc, 1996–98; Devro plc, 1998–2001; Bodycote Internat. plc, 1999–2002; Director: Scapa Gp plc, 1993–99; Foreign & Colonial Smaller Cos plc, 1999–2007 (Sen. Ind. Dir, 2005–07). Member: Council, CBI, 1990–2002; Adv. Bd, Imperial Coll. Management Sch., 1991–2003; Finance Cttee, Cancer Res. UK (formerly ICRF), 1997–; Court, Surrey Univ., 1998–2005. Pres., Inst. of Materials, 1999–2002 (Sen. Vice-Pres., 1997–99); Chm. Mgt Bd, 2002–04 (Platinum Medal, 2004), Chm., Communications Bd, 2006–, IMMM. CCMI (CIMgt 1984); FRSA 1995. Freeman, City of London, 1994; Liveryman, Scientific Instrument Makers' Co., 1995–. *Recreations:* music, cricket, hill walking. *Address:* Weston House, Bracken Close, Wonersh, Surrey GU5 0QS. *Club:* Athenæum.

FARMER, George Wallace; President, Immigration Appeal Tribunal, 1991–97 (Vice President, 1982–91); *b* 4 June 1929; *s* of George Lawrence Farmer and Blanche Amy (*née* Niccolls); *m* 1961, Patricia Mary Joyce; three *d*. *Educ:* The Lodge, Barbados; Harrison Coll., Barbados. Called to the Bar, Middle Temple, 1950. Private practice, Barbados, 1950–52; Magistrate, Barbados, 1952–56; Resident Magistrate, Uganda, 1956–63, Sen. Resident Magistrate, 1963–64; Dir of Public Prosecutions, Uganda, 1964–65; attached to Cottle Catford & Co., Solicitors, Barbados, 1965–67; Legal Manager, Road Transport Industry Trng Bd, 1967–70; Adjudicator, Immigration Appeals, 1970–82. *Recreation:* enjoying the company of grandchildren. *Address:* 40 South Croxted Road, West Dulwich, SE21 8BD. *T:* (020) 8670 4828.

FARMER, Michael; *see* Farmer, P. M.

FARMER, Paul David Charles; Chief Executive, Mind, since 2006; *b* 8 Oct. 1966; *s* of David and Ann Farmer; *m* 1994, Claire Dwyer; two *s*. *Educ:* Oratory Sch., Reading; St Peter's Coll., Oxford (BA Modern Hist.). Communications Manager, Samaritans, 1994–97; Dir, Public Affairs, Rethink, 1997–2006. Chm., Mental Health Alliance, 2000–06. Trustee: Samaritans, 1998–2001; Directory of Social Change, 2000– (Chm. 2003–05). FRSA. *Publications:* contribs to jls on anti-discrimination and stigma. *Recreations:* cricket, Rugby, film, cookery, listening. *Address:* c/o Mind, 15–19 Broadway, Stratford, E15 4BQ. *T:* (020) 8215 2262; *e-mail:* p.farmer@mind.org.uk.

FARMER, Paul Roy; a District Judge (Magistrates' Courts), Devon and Cornwall, since 2002; *b* 4 Dec. 1946; *s* of Charles Harry Farmer and Joan Farmer (*née* Mead); *m* 2nd, 1997, Christine Gillian Jago (*née* Pearce); one *d* from previous marriage. *Educ:* St Austell County Grammar Sch.; UWIST (LLB (ext.) London). Admitted Solicitor, 1971; articled Clerk, 1969–71, Asst Solicitor, 1971–74, Partner, 1974–78, Stephens and Scown, Solicitors; Dep. Justices' Clerk, 1978–86, Justices' Clerk, 1986–98, PSDs (Falmouth and Kerrier, Pydar, Truro, S Powder, 1986–98, E Penwith, Isles of Scilly, Penwith, 1991–98); acting Stipendiary Magistrate for Hampshire and Devon, 1994–98; Provincial Stipendiary Magistrate, subseq. a Dist Judge (Magistrates' Courts), Dorset, 1998–2002. Pres., Devon and Cornwall Justices' Clerks Soc., 1993–94. *Recreations:* golf, Rugby Union, cricket, music. *Address:* Magistrates' Court, St Andrews Street, Plymouth PL1 2DP. *Club:* Carlyon Bay Golf.

FARMER, Peter John; Member, Lord Chancellor's Advisory Committee on Justices of the Peace for Leeds, since 2005; Consultant, Office of the Legal Services Complaints Commissioner, since 2006; *b* 5 Nov. 1952; *s* of Alec and Norah Farmer; *m* 1986, Christine Ann Tetley. *Educ:* King Edward VI Sch., Southampton; Gonville and Caius College, Cambridge (Maths; MA); London Univ. (Cert. Psych.); Open Univ. (DipEcon). Joined HM Customs and Excise, 1975; HM Treasury, 1979; Lord Chancellor's Dept, 1981; Circuit Principal, Leeds, 1983; Asst Sec., 1987; Asst Public Trustee, 1988; Public Trustee and Accountant Gen. of Supreme Court, 1991; Circuit Administrator, NE Circuit, 1994–2002; Tribunal Appts Project Dir, LCD, 2002–03; Judicial Inf. and Planning Dir, Dept for Constitutional Affairs, 2003–04; Planning Dir, Office of the Legal Services Complaints Comr, 2004–05. Chm., Judicial Appts Panels, DCA, 2005–06; Panel Chm., Judicial Appts Commn, 2006–08. FCMI. *Recreations:* English folk dancing, hill walking, choral music. *Address:* Leeds Magistrates' Court, PO Box 97, Westgate, Leeds LS1 3JP.

FARMER, (Pryce) Michael; QC 1995; **His Honour Judge Farmer;** a Circuit Judge since 2001; *b* 20 May 1944; *er s* of Sarah Jane Farmer; *m* 1975, Olwen Mary, *d* of late Rev. Griffith John Roberts, MA, and of Margaret Morris Roberts; one *s* one *d*. *Educ:* Ysgol Dyffryn Nantlle, Penygroes; King's Coll., London (BA Hons); Inns of Court Sch. of Law. Schoolmaster, St David's Coll., Llandudno, 1968–71; called to the Bar, Gray's Inn, 1972, Bencher, 2005; practice, Wales and Chester Circuit, 1973–; Junior, Wales and Chester Circuit, 1992; Head of Chambers, Sedan House, Chester, 1995. Asst Recorder, 1993–95, a Recorder, 1995–2001; part-time Pres., Mental Health Review Tribunal, 2001–. Designated Family Judge, N Wales, 2004–; Dep. Liaison Judge for Welsh lang., Wales and Chester Circuit, 2004–; Dep. Sen. Judge, Sov. Base areas of Dhekelia and Akrotiri, Cyprus, 2004–. Wales and Chester Circuit Rep., Public Affairs Cttee, Bar Council, 1997–2001. Chm., Special Review Cttee, Ynys Môn CC, 1998–99. Contested (Plaid Cymru) Conwy, Feb. and Oct. 1974. *Recreations:* listening to classical music, reading, gardening, watching Rugby football. *Address:* Rhyl County Court, Clwyd Street, Rhyl LL18 3LA. *T:* (01745) 352940. *Clubs:* Reform; Rygbi yr Wyddgrug (Mold) (Pres. 2001–05).

FARMER, Sir Thomas, Kt 1997; CBE 1990; DL; Founder, Kwik-Fit, 1971; *b* 10 July 1940; *s* of John Farmer and Margaret (*née* Mackie); *m* 1966, Anne Drury Scott; one *s* one *d*. *Educ:* St Mary's Primary Sch., Edinburgh; Holy Cross Acad., Edinburgh. Chm. and Chief Exec., Kwik-Fit, 1984–2002. Chairman: Scottish BITC, 1990–2000; Investors in People Scotland, 1991–97; Mem. Bd, Scottish Enterprise, 1990–96. Chm., Bd of Trustees, Duke of Edinburgh Award. Chancellor, Queen Margaret Univ., Edinburgh, 2007–. DL Edinburgh, 1996. KCSG 1997. *Recreations:* tennis, swimming, ski-ing. *T:* (0131) 315 2830.

FARNELL, Graeme, FMA; Managing Director, Heritage Development Ltd, since 1996; Director: Heritage Business International, since 2005; Heritage Development International, since 2006; *b* 11 July 1947; *s* of Wilson Elliot Farnell and Mary Montgomerie Wishart Farnell (*née* Crichton); *m* 1969, Jennifer Gerda (*née* Huddlestone); one *s*. *Educ:* Loughborough Grammar Sch.; Edinburgh Univ. (MA); London Film Sch. (DipFilm Studies). FMA 1989; FSAScot 1976; MBIM. Asst Keeper, Mus. of East Anglian Life, 1973–76; Curator, Inverness Mus. and Art Gall., 1976–79; Dir, Scottish Museums Council, 1979–86; Dir Gen., Museums Assoc., 1986–89; Man. Dir, The Development (formerly Museum Development) Co. Ltd, 1989–94; Publishing Ed., IMS Publications, 1994–96; Publisher: New Heritage (formerly Heritage Development) magazine,

1996–2003; Heritage Business.net (formerly Heritage Insider, then Heritage Business) newsletter, 1998–; Heritage Retail mag., 1999–2003; Heritage Restoration mag., 2000–03; Heritage 365 mag., 2003–. *Publications:* (ed) The American Museum Experience, 1986; The Handbook of Grants, 1990, 2nd edn, 1993; (ed) The European Heritage Directory, 1998; (ed) New Museums in China, 2005; contribs to Museums Jl, Internat. Jl of Mus. Management and Curatorship, Museum (Unesco), Industrial Soc. *Recreations:* baroque opera, contemporary music, photography.

FARNELL, John Bernard Patrick; Director, Coordination and International Affairs, Enterprise and Industry Directorate-General, European Commission, since 2008 (Director, Competitiveness, 2006–07); *b* 24 Aug. 1948; *s* of James Farnell and Laura (*née* O'Connell); *m* 1976, Susan Mary Janus; two *s*. *Educ:* Downside Sch.; Christ's Coll., Cambridge (MA Hist.); London Sch. of Econs (MSc Econ). Economist, BEA, 1970–72; CBI, 1973–74; with European Commission, 1975–: Ext. Relns, 1975–77; Fisheries, 1977–82; Industry, 1982–93 (Internat. Questions Unit, 1982–87; Head: Standardisation and Certification Unit, 1987–93; Tech. Legislation Unit, 1993); Hd, Operation of Internal Mkt and Econ. Analysis Unit, Directorate-Gen. of Internal Mkt and Financial Services, 1993–97; Dir, Horizontal Measures and Markets, 1997–2001, Conservation Policy, 2001–06, Fisheries Directorate-General. *Publications:* Public and Private Britain, 1975; (with James Elles) In Search of a Common Fisheries Policy, 1984. *Recreations:* opera, fly-fishing, sailing. *Address:* 33 Rue du Châtelain, 1050 Brussels, Belgium.

FARNHAM, 13th Baron *cr* 1756; **Simon Kenlis Maxwell;** Bt (NS) 1627; *b* 12 Dec. 1933; *s* of late Hon. Somerset Arthur Maxwell, MP and Angela Susan (*née* Roberts); *S* brother, 2001; *m* 1964, Karol Anne, *d* of Maj.-Gen. G. E. Prior-Palmer, CB, DSO; two *s* one *d* (of whom one *s* one *d* are twins). *Educ:* Eton. Late Lt, 10th Royal Hussars. *Heir: s* Hon. Robin Somerset Maxwell [*b* 15 Sept. 1965; *m* 1993, Tessa Shepherd; two *s* one *d*]. *Address:* The Dower House, Westcote, near Chipping Norton, Oxon OX7 6SF.

See also Viscountess Knollys.

FARNISH, Christine, (Mrs J. Hayes); Director of Public Policy, Barclays PLC, since 2006; *b* 21 April 1950; *d* of Harry Farnish and Agnes Monica Farnish; *m* John Hayes; three *s* one *d*. *Educ:* Ipswich High Sch.; Manchester Univ. (BSc Botany and Geog. 1971); University Coll. London (MSc Conservation 1972). Asst Chief Exec., Cambridge CC, 1988–94; Consumer Dir, 1992–97, Actg Dep. Dir Gen., 1998, OFTEL; Consumer Dir, FSA, 1998–2002; Chief Exec., Nat. Assoc. of Pension Funds, 2002–06. Mem. Council, ASA, 2002–08; non-exec. Dir, OFT, 2003–06; Dir, NCC, 2008–. Non-exec. Dir, Papworth Hosp., 1998–2002. *Recreations:* singing, walking, ski-ing. *Address:* Flat 3, 3 Palmeira Square, Hove, East Sussex BN3 2JA. *T:* (020) 7116 6094. *Club:* Tottenham Hotspur Football.

FARNSWORTH, Ian Ross; Director, Coutts & Co., 1992–97 (Deputy Chairman and Chief Executive, 1992–95); *b* 15 Feb. 1938; *s* of Frederick Sutcliffe and Winifred Ruby Bryan; *m* 1964, Rosalind Amanda Baker; one *s* one *d*. *Educ:* Nottingham High Sch. ACIB. Westminster Bank, later National Westminster Bank: joined 1954; seconded Nat. Bank of N America, 1979–80; Exec. Vice-Pres., NatWest N America, 1981–84; Asst Gen. Manager, NatWest, 1987–88; Dir, European Businesses, 1988–90; Gen. Manager, NatWest, 1990–91; Dep. Chm., Coutts & Co. AG, Zürich, 1991–94; Mem., Supervisory Bd, F. van Lanschot Bankiers, Holland, 1991–95. Chm., Willowbrite Ltd, 1997–; Dir, Finsbury Foods plc, 1997–. Director: PEC Concerts Ltd, 1995–2000; New Sadler's Wells Ltd, 1996–2002; Gov., Sadler's Wells Foundn, 1995–2004. Mem., Develt Cttee, Univ. of Herts, 1996–. Liveryman, Information Technologists' Co., 1994–2005. *Recreations:* music, golf. *Address:* 15 Dellcroft Way, Harpenden, Herts AL5 2NQ. *T:* (01582) 712518.

FARNWORTH, His Honour John David; a Circuit Judge, 1991–2008; *b* 20 June 1935; *s* of George Arthur Farnworth and Mary Lilian Farnworth; *m* 1964, Carol Gay Mallett; one *s* two *d*. *Educ:* Bedford Sch.; St Edmund Hall, Oxford (BA). Bigelow Teaching Fellow, Univ. of Chicago Law Sch., 1958–59. Admitted Solicitor, 1962; a Recorder, 1986–91. *Recreations:* golf, cricket, snooker, art galleries. *Clubs:* MCC; Bedfordshire Golf.

FAROOKHI, Imtiaz; Chief Executive, National House-Building Council, since 1997; *b* 17 Jan. 1951; *s* of Mumtaz and Anwar Farookhi; *m*; two *s* one *d*. *Educ:* King Alfred Sch.; Acton Tech. Coll.; Univ. of Kent at Canterbury; Birkbeck Coll., London Univ. Asst Chief Exec., Hackney LBC, 1983–88; Head of Co-ordination, Wakefield MDC, 1988–89; Dir of Policy and Admin, Southwark LBC, 1988–91; Chief Exec., Leicester CC, 1991–96. Member: Bd, Envmt Agency, 1995–97; BURA, 1998–2004; British Bd of Agrément, 1999–; LSC, 2001–04; CITB Construction Skills Council, 2004–; SEEDA, 2004–; London Thames Gateway UDC, 2004–. Chm., Forum for Construction Skills, 2003–06. FRSA 1994. *Publications:* articles in jls. *Recreation:* family life. *Address:* (office) Buildmark House, Chiltern Avenue, Amersham, Bucks HP6 5AP. *T:* (01494) 434477. *Club:* QPR Supporters'.

FARQUHAR, Charles Don Petrie, OBE 1999; JP; DL; engineer; *b* 4 Aug. 1937; *s* of late William Sandeman Farquhar and Annie Preston Young Farquhar; *m*; two *d*. *Educ:* Liff Road and St Michael's Primary Schs, Dundee; Stobswell Secondary Sch., Dundee. Served with Royal Engineers (Trng NCO); subseq. supervisory staff, plant engrg, NCR Ltd, Area Manager, Community Industry, Dundee/Fife, 1972–91. City Councillor, Dundee, 1965–74 (ex-Convener, Museums, Works and Housing Cttees); Mem., Dundee DC, 1974–96 (Chm., Leisure and Recreation Cttees, 1992–96); Lord Provost and Lord Lieutenant of City of Dundee, 1975–77; Mem., Dundee City Council, 1995–2008 (Chm., Leisure Services Cttee). Chairman: Dundee Dist Licensing Bd, Dundee Dist Licensing Cttee, 1984–93; Cttee for Employment of Disabled People (formerly Disabled Adv. Cttee), Tayside and Fife, 1979–94. JP Dundee, 1974; DL Dundee, 1978. *Recreations:* fresh-water angling, gardening, numismatics, do-it-yourself. *Address:* 2 Killin Avenue, Dundee DD3 6EB.

FARQUHAR, Prof. Graham Douglas, PhD; FRS 1995; FAA; Distinguished Professor, since 2003, and Associate Director, Research School of Biological Sciences, since 2005, Australian National University, Canberra; *b* 8 Dec. 1947. *Educ:* Australian Nat. Univ. (BSc 1968; PhD 1973); Queensland Univ. (BSc Hons Biophysics 1969). FAA 1988. Dept of Energy Plant Res. Lab., Michigan State Univ., 1973–76; Australian National University: Res. Fellow, 1976–80; Sen. Res. Fellow, 1980–; Fellow, 1980–83; Sen. Fellow, 1983–88; Prof. of Biology, 1988–2003; Leader, Plant Envmtl Biology Gp, 1988–89, Envmtl Biology Gp, 1994–, Res. Sch. of Biological Scis. *Publications:* (ed jtly) Stomatal Function, 1987; (ed jtly) Perspectives of Plant Carbon and Water Relations for Stable Isotopes, 1993; numerous research texts. *Address:* Environmental Biology Group, Research School of Biological Sciences, Australian National University, GPO Box 475, Canberra, ACT 2601, Australia. *T:* (2) 61255052, *Fax:* (2) 61244919.

FARQUHAR, Margaret (Elizabeth), CBE 1999; JP; Lord Provost and Lord-Lieutenant of Aberdeen, 1996–99; *b* Aberdeen, 1930; *née* Burnett; *m* 1951, William Farquhar (*d* 1993); one *s* one *d*. *Educ:* Ruthrieston Secondary Sch., Aberdeen; Webster's Coll., Aberdeen. Clerical work: N of Scotland Coll. of Agric., 1947–48; Charles Michie, haulage contractor, 1948–51; Cordiners Sawmills, 1963–65; William Walker, haulage contractor, 1969–77. Member (Lab): Aberdeen DC, 1971–96 (Vice-Chm., 1994–96); Aberdeen CC, 1995–99. Mem., Planning Cttee, 1985–86, 1988–92, Aberdeen Council rep., 1992–99, COSLA. Dir, Grampian Enterprise, 1991–92. Member: Mgt Cttee, Aberdeen CAB, 1986–; Mgt Cttee, Northfield Community Centre, 1993–. Labour Party: Sec., Bridge of Don Br., 1980–81; Sec. and Chm., Cummings Pk Br., 1971–79; Chm., Aberdeen Women's Council, 1971–72. Hon. Pres., Grampian Girls' Bde, 1988–. Chm., Aberdeen Br., RNLI, 2003–. Chm., Friends of Gordon Highlanders Mus., 2001–. JP Aberdeen, 1972. Hon. LLD: Aberdeen, 1996; Robert Gordon, 1998. Paul Harris Fellowship, Rotary Internat., 1998. *Recreations:* working with the elderly and the young, bowling, driving, watching television.

FARQUHAR, Sir Michael (Fitzroy Henry), 7th Bt *cr* 1796, of Cadogan House, Middlesex; farmer; *b* 29 June 1938; *s* of Sir Peter Walter Farquhar, 6th Bt, DSO, OBE, and Elizabeth Evelyn (*d* 1983), *d* of Francis Cecil Albert Hurt; *S* father, 1986; *m* 1963, Veronica Geraldine Hornidge; two *s*. *Educ:* Eton; Royal Agricultural College. *Recreations:* fishing, shooting. *Heir: s* Charles Walter Fitzroy Farquhar [*b* 21 Feb. 1964; *m* 2004, Sarah Josephine Wynne-Williams; one *s* one *d*]. *Address:* Manor Farm, West Kington, Chippenham, Wilts SN14 7JG. *T:* (01249) 782671. *Club:* White's.

FARQUHAR MUNRO, John; *see* Munro.

FARQUHARSON of Invercauld, Captain Alwyne Arthur Compton, MC 1944; JP; Head of Clan Farquharson; *b* 1 May 1919; *er s* of late Major Edward Robert Francis Compton, JP, DL, Newby Hall, Ripon, and Torloisk, Isle of Mull, and Sylvia, *y d* of A. H. Farquharson; recognised by Lord Lyon King of Arms as Laird of Invercauld (16th Baron of Invercauld; *S* aunt 1941), also as Chief of name of Farquharson and Head of Clan, since 1949; assumed (surname) Compton as a third forename and assumed surname of Farquharson of Invercauld, by warrant granted in Lyon Court, Edinburgh, 1949; *m* 1st, 1949, Frances Strickland Lovell (*d* 1991), *d* of Robert Pollard Oldham, Seattle, Washington, USA; 2nd, 1993, Patricia Gabrielle Estelle Parry de Winton, *d* of Henry Norman Simms-Adams, Brancaster Hall, Norfolk. *Educ:* Eton; Magdalen Coll., Oxford. Joined Royal Scots Greys, 1940. Served War, 1940–45, Palestine, N Africa, Italy, France (wounded); Captain 1943. County Councillor, Aberdeenshire, 1949–75, JP 1951. *Address:* Valley Farm, Brancaster Staithe, King's Lynn, Norfolk PE31 8DB.

See also R. E. J. Compton.

FARQUHARSON, Angus Durie Miller, OBE 1995; Lord-Lieutenant of Aberdeenshire, since 1998 (Vice Lord-Lieutenant, 1987–98); *b* 27 March 1935; *s* of Dr Hugo Miller and Elsie (*née* Duthie); adopted surname of Farquharson, 1961; *m* 1961, Alison Mary Farquharson of Finzean, *o d* of W. M. Farquharson-Lang, CBE, 14th Laird of Finzean; two *s* one *d*. *Educ:* Glenalmond; Downing Coll., Cambridge (BA 1956; MA). Factor, farmer, forester, chartered surveyor. Member: Council, Scottish Landowners Fedn, 1980–88; Regl Adv. Cttee, Forestry Commn, 1980–94 (Chm., North Conservancy, 1993–94); Red Deer Commn, 1986–92; Nature Conservancy Cttee for Scotland, 1986–91; SNH NE Cttee, 1992–94. Elder, 1969–, and Gen. Trustee, 1994–2006, Church of Scotland. Hon. Pres., Kincardine Deeside Scouts, 1985; Dir, Lathallan Sch., 1982–98. Aberdeenshire: DL 1984; JP 1998. OStJ 2002. *Recreations:* gardening, walking, local history. *Address:* Glenferrick Lodge, Finzean, Banchory, Aberdeenshire AB31 6NG. *T:* (01330) 850229. *Club:* New (Edinburgh).

FARQUHARSON of Whitehouse, Captain Colin Andrew; JP; FRICS; chartered surveyor and land agent; Lord Lieutenant of Aberdeenshire, 1987–98 (Vice Lord-Lieutenant, 1983–87); *b* 9 Aug. 1923; *s* of late Norman Farquharson of Whitehouse; *m* 1st, 1948, Jean Sybil Mary (*d* 1985), *d* of late Brig.-Gen. J. G. H. Hamilton, Skene, DSO, JP, DL; two *d* (and one *d* decd); 2nd, 1987, Clodagh, *widow* of Ian Houldsworth, Dallas Lodge, Moray, and *d* of Sir Kenneth Murray, Geanies, Ross-shire; three step *s* two step *d*. *Educ:* Rugby. FLAS 1956, FRICS 1970. Served Grenadier Guards, 1942–48: ADC to Field Marshal Sir Harold Alexander (later (1st) Earl Alexander of Tunis), 1945. Member, Queen's Body Guard for Scotland (Royal Company of Archers), 1964–. Chartered surveyor and land agent in private practice in Aberdeenshire, 1953–; Director, MacRobert Farms (Douneside) Ltd, 1971–87. Member, Bd of Management for Royal Cornhill Hosps, 1962–74; Chm., Gordon Local Health Council, 1975–81; Mem., Grampian Health Bd, 1981–89. DL 1966, JP 1969, Aberdeenshire. *Recreations:* shooting, fishing. *Address:* Whitehouse, Alford, Aberdeenshire AB33 8DP. *Clubs:* MCC; Royal Northern and University (Aberdeen).

See also Master of Arbuthnott.

FARQUHARSON, Rt Hon. Sir Donald (Henry), Kt 1981; PC 1989; DL; a Lord Justice of Appeal, 1989–95; *b* 1928; *yr s* of Charles Anderson Farquharson, Logie Coldstone, Aberdeenshire, and Florence Ellen Fox; *m* 1960, Helen Mary, *er d* of Comdr H. M. Simpson, RN (retd), Abbots Brow, Kirkby Lonsdale, Westmorland; three *s* (one *d* decd). *Educ:* Royal Commercial Travellers Sch.; Keble Coll., Oxford (MA; Hon. Fellow, 1989). Called to Bar, Inner Temple, 1952; Bencher, 1979. Dep. Chm., Essex QS, 1970; a Recorder of the Crown Court, 1972–81; QC 1972; Judge, High Court of Justice, QBD, 1981–89; Presiding Judge, SE Circuit, 1985–88. A Legal Assessor to GMC and GDC, 1978–81; Chairman: Disciplinary Cttee of Bar, 1983–85; Judicial Studies Bd, 1992–94 (Mem., 1984–85); Criminal Justice Consultative Council, 1992–94. DL Essex, 1990. *Recreations:* opera, walking. *Address:* Bay Tree House, Bures, Suffolk CO8 5JG.

FARQUHARSON, Very Rev. Hunter Buchanan; Provost, St Ninian's Cathedral, Perth, since 1999; *b* 19 July 1958; *s* of Cameron Bruce Farquharson and Thelma Alice Buchanan Farquharson. *Educ:* Birmingham Sch. of Speech (ALAM, LLAM); Edinburgh Theol Coll. (General Ministerial Exams; Luscombe Scholar, 1989). Deacon 1988, priest 1989; Curate, West Fife Team, 1988–91; Rector, St Luke's, Glenrothes, 1991–97; Leader of Central Fife Team, 1995–97; Rector, Holy Trinity, Dunfermline and Leader of West Fife Team, 1997–99. Chm., Perth and Kinross Assoc. of Voluntary Services, 2000–. Chm., Scottish Flat-Coated Retriever Club, 2005– (Vice-Chm., 2002–05). Dir, 2005–, Vice-Chm., 2007–, Ochil Tower Sch. (Camphill), Auchterarder. *Recreations:* showing and breeding flat-coated retrievers and Toulouse Geese, fishing, hill-walking. *Address:* Upper Greenside, by Abernethy, Perthshire KY14 6EL. *T:* (01738) 850987; *e-mail:* huntfar@gmail.com. *Clubs:* Flat-coated Retriever Society; Scottish Kennel (Edinburgh).

FARQUHARSON, Jonathan, CBE 1997; Charity Commissioner, 1985–96; *b* 27 Dec. 1937; *s* of Alan George Farquharson and Winifred Mary Farquharson (*née* Wilson); *m* 1963, Maureen Elsie Bright; two *d*. *Educ:* St Albans School; Manchester Univ. (LLB). Solicitor, 1962; with D. Herbert, Banbury, 1962–64; Charity Commission, 1964–96. FRSA. *Recreations:* geology, photography, reading, record collecting, gardening. *Address:* 30 Ennerdale Road, Formby, Merseyside L37 2EA. *T:* (01704) 871820.

FARQUHARSON, Paul Hiram, QPM; High Commissioner of the Bahamas to the United Kingdom, and Ambassador to the European Union, Belgium, France, Germany and Italy, since 2008; *b* 10 Jan. 1949 *s* of late Ural Farquharson and Martha Deveaux; *m*

1969, Sharon Major; one s two d. Educ: Univ. of Louisiana (BAppSci); Univ. of Cambridge (Dip. Applied Criminol. and Police Studies); Atlanta Univ., Georgia (Cert. Criminal Justice, Admin and Principles of Mgt); Police Staff Coll., Bramshill (Strategic Comd Course; Overseas Comd Course). Enlisted Royal Bahamas Police Force, 1966: Corporal, 1971; Sergeant, 1974; Inspector, 1981; Chief Inspector, 1985; Asst Superintendent, 1988; Chief Superintendent, 1994; Asst Comr, 1998; Actg Comr of Police, 2000; Comr of Police, 2001–08. Aide-de-Camp: to Gov. Gen. of the Bahamas, 1984–88; to Rt Hon. Dr Robert Runcie, 1984–88; to Robert Mugabe, 1989; to HRH Duke of Edinburgh, 1993. Pres., Assoc. of Caribbean Comrs of Police, 2005; International Association of Chiefs of Police: Exec. Mem.; Mem., Firearms Cttee; Regl Chm. for Caribbean and Central America; Mem., Internat. Assoc. of Police Community Relns Officers. Mem., Bahamas Film and TV Commn. Salvation Army: Mem., Exec. Bd; Mem., Adv. Bd, Bahamas Div. Address: Bahamas High Commission, 10 Chesterfield Street, W1J 5JL. T: (020) 7659 0819, Fax: (020) 7499 9937; e-mail: info@bahamashclondon.net.

FARQUHARSON-ROBERTS, Surgeon Rear Adm. Michael Atholl, CBE 2001; FRCS; Medical Director General (Navy), 2003–07; b 23 Sept. 1947; s of Rev. Donald Arthur Farquharson–Roberts (Captain, RM) and Violet Farquharson-Roberts (née Crooks); m 1974, Jean Neilsen (née Harding); three s three d. Educ: Dorking County Grammar Sch.; Westminster Hosp. Sch. of Medicine (MB BS); RCDS/KCL (MA 2002); Exeter Univ. FRCS 1976. Orthopaedic trng, Nuffield Orthopaedic Centre, Oxford, Addenbrooke's Hosp., Cambridge and Royal Nat. Orthopaedic Hosp; Consultant Orthopaedic Surgeon, Royal Hosp. Haslar, 1983–84 and 1986–2000; Principal Med. Officer, HMS Illustrious, 1985–86; rcds, 2001; Change Manager, Defence Med. Trng Orgn, 2001–02; Dir Med. Ops (Navy), 2002–03. Defence Consultant Advr in Orthopaedics, 1996–2000; Mem., Intercollegiate Specialist Adv. Cttee in Orthopaedics, 1996–2000. QHS 1997–2007. Gov., Royal Star and Garter Homes, 2003–; Trustee, Help for Heroes, 2007–. OStJ 2002. Gulf War Medal, 1991. Publications: articles in learned jls incl. Jl of Bone and Joint Surgery and BMJ. Recreations: golf (badly), ship modelling. Address: 45 Bury Road, Gosport, Hants PO12 3UE; e-mail: mfr@globalnet.co.uk. Club: Army and Navy.

FARR, Clarissa Mary; High Mistress, St Paul's Girls' School, since 2006; b 30 June 1958; d of late Alan Farr and of Wendy Farr; m 1993, John Goodbody; one s one d. Educ: Bruton Sch. for Girls; Exeter Univ. (BA Hons Eng. Lit., MA); Bristol Univ. (PGCE). Teacher: Farnborough Sixth Form Coll., 1981–83; Filton High Sch., 1983–86; Head of Sixth Form, Shatin Coll., Hong Kong, 1986–89; Sen. Mistress, Leicester GS, 1990–92; Dep. Head, 1992–96, Principal, 1996–2006, Queenswood Sch., Hatfield. Chm., Boarding Schs' Assoc., 2001–02; Pres., GSA, 2005. Recreations: running, literature, theatre. Address: St Paul's Girls' School, Brook Green, W6 7BS. T: (020) 7603 2288.

FARR, David Charles; playwright; Artistic Director, Lyric Theatre, Hammersmith, since 2005; b 29 Oct. 1969; s of Martin and Maureen Farr; m 2000, Anne Siddons; two d. Educ: Trinity Hall, Cambridge (BA double 1st cl. Hons (English) 1991). Associate Dir, Gate Th., London, and freelance Dir, Almeida Opera, 1991–95; Artistic Director: Gate Th., 1995–98; (Jt) Bristol Old Vic, 2003–05. Director: Coriolanus, 2002, Julius Caesar, 2004, RSC; A Midsummer Night's Dream, 2003 (TMA Award for Best Dir), (also adapted) The Odyssey, 2005, Bristol Old Vic; writer/director: The Nativity, Young Vic, 1999; Crime and Punishment in Dalston, Arcola Th. and radio, 2002; Night of the Soul, RSC, 2002; The UN Inspector, NT, 2005; dir/adapter, Tamburlaine, Barbican/Young Vic, 2005. Publications: plays: Elton John's Glasses, 1998 (Writers' Guild Best Play); The Nativity, 1999; The Danny Crowe Show, 2001; Night of the Soul, 2001; Plays 1, 2005. Recreations: guitar, cinema, football, walking, Shamanism. Address: c/o United Agents, 12–26 Lexington Street, W1F 0LE. Club: Anorak.

FARR, Jennifer Margaret, MBE 2003; Vice Lord-Lieutenant of Nottinghamshire, 1999–2008; b 20 July 1933; d of late Charles Percival Holliday and Vera Margaret Emily (née Burchell); m 1956, Sydney Hordern Farr (d 1981); two s one d. Educ: Nottingham Girls' High Sch.; Middlesex Hosp.; Royal Victoria Hosp., Newcastle upon Tyne. Physiotherapist, Nottingham City Hosp., 1954–56. National Society for Prevention of Cruelty to Children: Mem., Nottingham & Dist Cttee, 1959–; Nat. Council Mem., 1973–94; a Nat. Vice-Pres., 1994–; Mem., Notts Centenary Appeal, 1983–85; Mem., Midlands Regions Bd, 2003–07; Chairman: Nottingham Br., 1983–98 (Pres., 1998–); Notts Full Stop Appeal, 1999–2004. Pres., League of Friends, Queen's Med. Centre, 1999–. Member: Nottingham Convent Council, 1992–98; Southwell 2000 Appeal, 1992–96; Public Catalogue Foundn, 2007–. Pres., Newark and Notts Agricl Soc., 2003. Gov., Nottingham High Sch. for Girls, 2001–. Pres., Thurgarton Cricket Club, 1981–99. JP Notts, 1979–89; DL 1993, High Sheriff 1998–99, Notts. Recreations: bridge, gardening, music, sports, theatre, family life. Address: Lanesmeet, Epperstone, Notts NG14 6AU. T: (0115) 966 4584. Club: Sloane.

FARR, Air Vice-Marshal Peter Gerald Desmond, CB 1968; OBE 1952; DFC 1942; retired; Director, Brain Research Trust, 1973–83; b 26 Sept. 1917; s of late Gerald Farr and Mrs Farr (née Miers); m 1949, Rosemarie (d 1983), d of late R. S. Haward; two s one d. Educ: Tonbridge Sch. Commnd in RAF, 1937; served War of 1939–45, Middle East, India and Burma; OC, No 358 Sqdn, 1944–45; OC, RAF Pegu, 1945–46; OC, 120 Sqdn, 1950–51; Dep. Dir, Jt Anti-Submarine Sch., 1952–54; OC, RAF Idris, 1954–55; Directing Staff, Jt Services Staff Coll., 1959; SASO, Malta, 1960–63; OC, RAF Kinloss, 1963–64; Air Officer Administration: RAF Germany, 1964–68; Strike Comd, 1969–72. Recreations: golf, music. Address: c/o Lloyds TSB, Great Missenden, Bucks HP16 0AT. Club: Royal Air Force.

FARRAN, Rt Rev. Brian George; see Newcastle, NSW, Bishop of.

FARRANCE, Roger Arthur, CBE 1988; Chief Executive, Electricity Association, 1990–93; Chairman: Electricity Association Services Ltd, 1991–93; Electricity Association Technology Ltd, 1991–93; b 10 Nov. 1933; s of Ernest Thomas Farrance and Alexandra Hilda May (née Finch); m 1956, Kathleen Sheila (née Owen); one d. Educ: Trinity School of John Whitgift, Croydon; London School of Economics (BScEcon). CCIPD; FIET (FIEE 2002). HM Inspector of Factories, Manchester, Doncaster and Walsall, 1956–64; Asst Sec., West of England Engineering Employers' Assoc., Bristol, 1964–67; Industrial Relations and Personnel Manager, Foster Wheeler John Brown Boilers Ltd, 1967–68; Dep. Director, Coventry and District Engineering Employers' Assoc., also Coventry Management Trng Centre, 1968–75; Electricity Council: Dep. Industrial Relations Adviser (Negotiating), 1975–76; Industrial Relations Adviser, 1976–79; Mem., 1979–88; Dep. Chm., 1989–90. Chm., Power Aid Logistics, 1993–94. Dir, Caswell Bay Court Mgt Co. Ltd, 2000–05 (Chm., 2002–05). Member Council: ACAS, 1983–89; CBI, 1983–93 (Chm., Health and Safety Policy Cttee, 1990–93); Mem., Directing Cttee, Union Internationale des Producteurs et Distributeurs d'Energie Electrique, 1991–94 (Chm., Human Factors Cttee, 1991–94). President: IPM, 1991–93; Electricity Supply Industry Ambulance Centre, St John's Amb. Assoc., 1979–93; St John's 210 (London Electricity) Combined Div., 1989–94. Chairman: Devonshire House Management Trustees, 1989–94; Management Bd, Electrical and Electronics Industry Benevolent Assoc.,

1987–93. Councillor (C), London Borough of Merton, 1994–98. Chm. Govs, Pentyrch Primary Sch., 2002–06. Freeman, City of London, 1985; Liveryman, Basketmakers' Co. 1986–98. FRSA 1985. OStJ 1983. Recreations: painting, woodwork, music, walking Address: The Rise, Heol-y-Parc, Pentyrch, Cardiff CF15 9NB.

FARRAND, Julian Thomas, LLD; Chairman, Leasehold Valuation Tribunals and RAC for London Area, Rent Assessment Panel, since 1984; b 13 Aug. 1935; s of J. and E. A Farrand; m 1st, 1957, Winifred Joan Charles (marr. diss. 1992); one s two d; 2nd, 1984 Brenda Marjorie Hoggett (see Baroness Hale of Richmond). Educ: Haberdashers' Aske Sch.; University Coll. London (LLB 1957, LLD 1966). Admitted Solicitor, 1960. As Lectr, then Lectr, KCL, 1960–63; Lectr, Sheffield Univ., 1963–65; Reader in Law, QMC 1965–68; Prof. of Law, 1968–88, Dean of Faculty of Law, 1970–72, 1976–78, Manchester Univ. Visiting Professor: UCL, 1990–2001; London Guildhall, subseq. Londo Metropolitan Univ., 2001–06. A Law Comr, 1984–88; Insce Ombudsman, 1989–94 Pensions Ombudsman, 1994–2001. Chairman: Gtr Manchester and Lancs Area, Ren Assessment Panel, 1973–84 (Vice-Pres., 1977–84); Supplementary Benefit Appeal Tribunal, 1977–80; Nat. Insce Local Tribunal, 1980–83; Social Security Appeal Tribunal 1983–88; Govt Conveyancing Cttee, 1984–85; Disciplinary Sub-Cttee, Banking Cod Standards Bd, 2001–05; Adjudicator, Indep. Cttee for Supervision of Standards o Telephone Inf. Services, 2001–. Chm., Pensions Compensation Bd, 1996–2001; Mem Adv. Cttee, English Longitudinal Study of Ageing, 2001–05. Non-exec. Dir, First Titl plc, 1996–2005. Mem., ADR Chambers (UK) Ltd, 2000–. Mem., Consumer Policy Adv Council, Brunel Univ., 2001–05. Ed., Emmet & Farrand on Title, 1967–. Hon. Prof. o Law, Essex Univ., 2000–. FCIArb 1994. Hon. QC 1994. Hon. LLD Sheffield, 1990 Publications: Contract and Conveyance, 1963–64, 4th edn 1983; (ed) Wolstenholme an Cherry, Conveyancing Statutes, 13th edn (vols 1–6) 1972, Consultant Ed., revd edn o vol. 6 as Wolstenholme and Cherry's Land Registration Act 2002, 2004; The Rent Ac and Regulations, 1978, 2nd edn (with A. Arden) 1981; (novel) Love at all Risks, 2001 Recreations: chess, bridge, wine, fiction. Address: 29 Morpeth Mansions, Morpeth Terrace SW1P 1ET.

FARRAR, Mark Jonathan, FCA; Corporate Services Director, ConstructionSkills, sinc 2007; b 14 Aug. 1961; s of Ronald and Doreen Farrar; m 2005, Francesca Ann Beckerleg one s one d, and two step s. Educ: Univ. of Wales, Swansea (BSc Hons). FCA 1988 Finance Dir, Corporate and Instns Gp, Barclays Bank, 1992–94; Asst Dir of Finance Allied Dunbar, 1994–95; Hd, Planning and Analysis, Norwich Union, 1995–2000 Finance and Resources Dir, 2000–04, Chief Exec., 2004–07, CEFAS. Mem., ACT Recreation: sailing (RYA Yachtmaster: Ocean). Address: ConstructionSkills, Birchan Newton, Norfolk PE31 6RH; e-mail: mark.farrar@cskills.org.

FARRAR-HOCKLEY, Maj.-Gen. (Charles) Dair, MC 1982; consultant i commercial dispute resolution, since 2006; Director General (formerly Secretary General Chartered Institute of Arbitrators, 1999–2006; b 2 Dec. 1946; s of Gen. Sir Anthon Farrar-Hockley, GBE, KCB, DSO, MC and Margaret Bernadette (née Wells); m 1969 Vicki King; two s one d. Educ: Exeter Sch. Commissioned Parachute Regt, 1967; Sta Coll., 1978–79; BM, Berlin, 1979–81; Co. Comdr, 2nd Para Bn, 1982, incl. Falklan Islands campaign; MA to Sec. to Chiefs of Staff Cttee, SHAPE, 1983; Directing Staff, Sta Coll., 1984; CO 3rd Para Bn, 1984–86; Special Briefer to COS, SHAPE, 1987; Highe Command and Staff Course, and Service Fellowship, KCL, 1988; Comdr 19 Inf. Bde 1989–91; RCDS, 1992; Comdr Inf. Training, 1993–95; British Liaison Officer to Czec Chief of Defence, 1995–96; GOC 2nd Div., 1996–99. Chm. of Trustees, Airborne Force Museum, 1993–; Trustee, Airborne Forces Security Fund, 1998–; Patron, Second Worl War Experience Centre, 1999–. Special Comr, Duke of York's Royal Mil. Sch., 2005– FCMI (FIMgt 1999); MCIArb 1999. Freeman, City of London, 1991. Publications: article on causes and effects of human migration. Recreations: cricket, cooking, wine photography. Address: c/o Personal Banking Office, National Westminster Bank Farnborough, Hants GU14 7YU. Club: Moulsford Cricket (Pres., 2007–).

FARRELL, David Anthony; QC 2000; a Recorder, since 2000; b 27 May 1956; s o Joseph Anthony Farrell and Valerie Mabel Farrell; m 1981, Sandra Nicole Hibble; four one d. Educ: Ashby-de-la-Zouch Grammar Sch.; Manchester Univ. (LLB Hons 1977) Called to the Bar, Inner Temple, 1978; Asst Recorder, 1996–2000. Recreations: tennis sailing, walking, music. Address: 36 Bedford Row, WC1R 4JH. T: (020) 7421 8000.

FARRELL, James Aloysius; Sheriff of Lothian and Borders at Edinburgh, since 1986; 14 May 1943; s of James Stoddart Farrell and Harriet Louise McDonnell; m 1st, 1967 Jacqueline Allen (marr. diss.); two d; 2nd, 1996, Patricia McLaren. Educ: St Aloysiu College; Glasgow University (MA); Dundee University (LLB). Admitted to Faculty o Advocates, 1974; Advocate-Depute, 1979–83; Sheriff: Glasgow and Strathkelvin, 1984; Strathclyde, Dumfries and Galloway, 1985. Recreations: sailing, hillwalking, cycling Address: 8B Merchiston Park, Edinburgh EH10 4PN.

FARRELL, Michael Arthur; b 27 April 1933; s of Herbert and Marjorie Farrell; m 1st 1957, Myra Shilton (d 1973); two d; 2nd, 1976, Beryl Browne. Educ: Beverley Gramma Sch., Yorks; Holly Lodge Grammar Sch., Birmingham. Design Draughtsman, 1949–51 Nat. Service, RASC, 1951–53; Planning Engineer, 1953–61; Representative, 1961–74 Sales Manager, Lillywhites Cantabrian, 1974–80; Sales Executive, En-Tout-Cas, 1980–82 Gen. Sec., AAA, subseq. British Athletic Fedn, 1982–91; Export Sales Dir, Cantabria Athletics Ltd, 1992–93; consultant, 1994–96; restaurateur, 1996–99. Recreations: painting walking, cycling.

FARRELL, Prof. Paul James, PhD; FMedSci; Professor of Tumour Virology, Imperia College, London, since 1994; Research Affiliate, Ludwig Institute for Cancer Research since 2005; b 10 July 1953; s of James Patrick Farrell and Audrey Winifred Farrell; m 1977 Diana Elizabeth Hamilton Kirby; one s one d. Educ: Churchill Coll., Cambridge (BA 1974); Clare Hall, Cambridge (PhD 1978). FRCPath 1995. Res. Fellow, Yale Univ 1977–80; Res. Scientist, MRC Lab. of Molecular Biology and Ludwig Inst., Cambridge 1980–86; Dir, St Mary's Br., Ludwig Inst. for Cancer Research, 1986–2005. FMedSc 2003. Publications: res. pubns on molecular biology of viruses and cancer, particularl Epstein–Barr virus. Recreations: sailing, gardening. Address: Department of Virology Faculty of Medicine, Imperial College, St Mary's Campus, Norfolk Place, W2 1PG. T (020) 7594 2005, Fax: (020) 7594 3973; e-mail: p.farrell@imperial.ac.uk.

FARRELL, Simon Henry; QC 2003; a Recorder, since 2006; b 17 Jan. 1960; s o Thomas and Joyce Farrell; m 1988, Kathryn Wood; three s one d. Educ: King's Sch. Canterbury; Gonville and Caius Coll., Cambridge (MA 1981). City Univ. (Dip. Law) Called to the Bar, Lincoln's Inn, 1983; barrister specialising in law of commercial fraud money laundering, tax evasion, civil and criminal confiscation of assets. Publications: (jtly The Proceeds of Crime Act 2002, 2002; (jtly) Asset Recovery, Criminal Confiscation an Civil Recovery, 2003; (jtly) The Fraud Act 2006, 2007. Recreations: squash, running watching Tottenham Hotspur FC, wine, family. Address: 3 Raymond Buildings, Gray' Inn, WC1R 5BH.

FARRELL, Sir Terence, (Sir Terry), Kt 2001; CBE 1996 (OBE 1978); Principal, Terry Farrell & Partners, since 1980; *b* 12 May 1938; *s* of Thomas and Molly Farrell (*née* Maguire); *m* 1st, 1960, Angela Rosemarie Mallam; two *d*; 2nd, 1973, Susan Hilary Aplin; two *s* one *d*. *Educ:* St Cuthbert's Grammar Sch., Newcastle; Newcastle Univ. (BArch, 1st class hons); Univ. of Pennsylvania (MArch, MCP). ARIBA 1963; MRTPI 1970; FCSD (FSIAD 1981). Harkness Fellow, Commonwealth Fund, USA, 1962–64. Partner in Farrell Grimshaw Partnership, 1965–80. Major projects include: redevelt of Charing Cross Station; Edinburgh Internat. Conf. Centre; British Consulate-Gen., Hong Kong; Vauxhall Cross (MI6), London; Kowloon Station, Hong Kong; Internat. Centre for Life, Newcastle; Deep Aquarium, Hull; Greenwich Peninsular masterplan; Home Office HQ, London; regeneration of Marylebone-Euston Road, London; Transportation Centre, Inchon Internat. airport, Seoul; Univ. of Newcastle masterplan; Manchester Southern Gateway masterplan; Manchester Univ. masterplan. *Exhibitions:* RIBA Heinz Gall., London, 1987; RIBA, London, 1995. Comr, English Heritage, 1990–96; Mem., Royal Parks Adv. Bd, 2003–. Chm., Walking Co-ordination Gp, Central London Partnership, 2003–. Vis. Prof., Univ. of Westminster, 1998–2001. Hon. FRIAS 1996; Hon. FAIA 1998. Hon. DCL Newcastle, 2000; Hon. DA Lincoln, 2003. *Publications:* Architectural Monograph, 1985; Urban Design Monograph, 1993; Place: a story of modelmaking, menageries and paper rounds (life and work: early years to 1981), 2004; articles in numerous British and foreign jls; *relevant publications:* Terry Farrell: selected and current works, 1994; Ten Years: Ten Cities: the work of Terry Farrell & Partners 1991–2001, 2002. *Recreations:* walking, swimming. *Address:* (office) 7 Hatton Street, NW8 8PL.

FARRELL, Timothy Robert Warwick; Organist, Liberal Jewish Synagogue, St John's Wood, since 1975; *b* 5 Oct. 1943; *m* 1st, 1975, Penelope Walmsley-Clark (marr. diss. 1995); one *s*; 2nd, 1996, Jane Emmanuel. *Educ:* Diocesan Coll., Cape Town; Royal Coll. of Music, London; Paris, etc. FRCO, ARCM (piano and organ). Asst Organist, St Paul's, Knightsbridge, 1962–66; Asst Organist, St Paul's Cath., 1966–67; Sub-organist, Westminster Abbey, 1967–74; Organ Tutor at Addington Palace, RSCM, 1966–73; Organist, Choirmaster and Composer, HM Chapels Royal, 1974–79. Broadcaster, recordings, electronic and orchestral music, etc. *Recreations:* golf, walking, sailing, flying. *Address:* Liberal Jewish Synagogue, 28 St John's Wood Road, NW8 7HA. *T:* (020) 7286 5181.

FARRELLY, (Christopher) Paul; MP (Lab) Newcastle-under-Lyme, since 2001; *b* Newcastle-under-Lyme, 2 March 1962; *s* of late Thomas Farrelly and of Anne Farrelly (*née* King); *m* 1998, Victoria Perry; one *s* two *d*. *Educ:* St Edmund Hall, Oxford (BA Hons PPE). Manager, Corporate Finance Div., Barclays de Zoete Wedd, 1984–90; Corresp., Reuters Ltd, 1990–95; Dep. City and Business Ed., Independent on Sunday, 1995–97; City Ed., The Observer, 1997–2001. Mem., Culture, Media and Sport Select Cttee, 2005–. *Recreations:* Rugby, football, writing. *Address:* House of Commons, SW1A 0AA. *T:* (020) 7219 8262. *Clubs:* Holy Trinity Catholic, Halmer End Working Men's (Newcastle-under-Lyme); Trentham Rugby Union Football, Finchley Rugby Football, Commons and Lords Rugby Union Football.

FARREN, Dr Sean; Member (SDLP) Antrim North, Northern Ireland Assembly, 1998–2007; *m* 1967, Patricia Clarke; one *s* three *d*. *Educ:* National Univ. of Ireland (BA 1960; HDE 1961); Essex Univ. (MA 1970); Univ. of Ulster (DPhil 1989). Teacher, Sierra Leone, Switzerland, Ireland, 1961–68; University Lectr in Educn, Univ. of Ulster, 1970–98. Fellow, Saltzburg Internat. Seminar, 1989. Minister of Higher and Further Educn, Trng and Employment, 1999–2001, of Finance and Personnel, 2001–02, NI. Contested (SDLP) Antrim N, 2001. *Publications:* The Politics of Irish Education 1920–1965, 1995; (with Robert Mulvihill) Paths to a Settlement in Northern Ireland, 1999; contributed to: Motivating the Majority—Modern Languages, Northern Ireland, 1991; Whose English, 1994; Irish Educational Documents, Vol. III, 1995; Language, Education and Society in a Changing World, 1996; A New History of Ireland, Vol. VII, 1998; Fiction, Multi-media and Intertextuality in Mother Tongue Education, 1998; contribs to Aspects of Educn, History of Educn, Etudes Irlandaises, Lang. Culture and Curriculum, Oxford Internat. Rev., Southeastern Pol Rev.; res. reports. *Recreations:* reading, swimming, cycling, theatre. *Address:* 3 Mill Square, Portstewart, Co. Derry BT55 7TB. *T:* (028) 7083 3042.

FARRER, (Arthur) Mark; DL; Partner, Farrer & Co., 1968–99; *b* 25 March 1941; *s* of Hugh Frederick Francis Farrer and Elizabeth Mary Cross; *m* 1969, Zara Jane Thesiger; one *d*. *Educ:* Eton. Served with Queen Victoria's Rifles, KRRC, 1959–65, subseq. transferred to TARO. Admitted solicitor, 1966. Chairman: Essex Water Co., 1992–96 (Dir, 1986–96; Dep. Chm., 1987); Suffolk Water Co., 1992–96 (Dir, 1990–96); Dir, Lyonnaise Europe, 1989–96. Mem. Council, Lloyd's, 1988–91; Chm., Assoc. of Lloyd's Members Ltd, 1991–92. Chm., N and W Salmon Fishery Dist Bd, 1999–2005. Pres., Old Etonian Assoc., 2005–06. DL Essex, 1996. *Publications:* articles in learned jls. *Recreations:* gardening, salmon fishing, the steam railway. *Address:* The Brick House, Finchingfield, Essex CM7 4LB. *T:* (01371) 810283; 56 Sangomore, Durness by Lairg, Sutherland IV27 4PZ. *Clubs:* Brooks's; Celer et Audax (Winchester).

FARRER, His Honour Brian Ainsworth; QC 1978; a Circuit Judge, 1985–2001; *b* 7 April 1930; *s* of A. E. V. A. Farrer and Gertrude (*née* Hall); *m* 1960, Gwendoline Valerie (*née* Waddoup), JP; two *s* one *d*. *Educ:* King's Coll., Taunton; University Coll., London (LLB). Called to the Bar, Gray's Inn, 1957. A Recorder, 1974–85. Chm., Standards Cttee, Coventry CC, 2000–08. *Recreations:* golf, music, chess, bridge. *Address:* 2 Badminton House, Chepstow Place, Streetly, Sutton Coldfield B74 3TL. *Club:* Aberdovey Golf.
See also P. A. Farrer.

FARRER, Sir (Charles) Matthew, GCVO 1994 (KCVO 1983; CVO 1973); Private Solicitor to the Queen, 1965–94; Partner in Messrs Farrer & Co., Solicitors, 1959–94; *b* 3 Dec. 1929; *s* of late Sir (Walter) Leslie Farrer, KCVO, and Hon. Lady Farrer; *m* 1962, Johanna Creszentia Maria Dorothea Bennhold; one *s* one *d*. *Educ:* Bryanston Sch.; Balliol Coll., Oxford (MA). A Trustee, British Museum, 1989–99; Comr, Royal Commn on Historical Manuscripts, 1991–2002; Mem., British Library Bd, 1994–2000. Trustee, Lambeth Palace Library, 1991–2002. Pres., Selden Soc., 2001–03. Mem., Ct of Assts, Fishmongers' Co., 1995– (Prime Warden, 2007–08). *Address:* 6 Priory Avenue, Bedford Park, W4 1TX. *T:* (020) 8994 6052.

FARRER, Rt Rev. David; *see* Farrer, Rt Rev. R. D.

FARRER, David John; QC 1986; a Recorder, since 1983; *b* 15 March 1943; *s* of John Hall Farrer and Mary Farrer; *m* 1969, Hilary Jean Bryson; two *s* one *d*. *Educ:* Queen Elizabeth's Grammar Sch., Barnet; Downing Coll., Cambridge (MA, LLB). Called to the Bar, Middle Temple, 1967, Bencher, 1998; in practice, 1968–. Dep. Chm., Information Tribunal, 2005. Mem., Bar Council, 1986–94; Chm., Bar Services Cttee, 1989–94. Contested (L): Melton, 1979; Rutland and Melton, 1983. *Recreations:* tennis, cricket, Liberal Party politics. *Address:* 7 Bedford Row, WC1R 4BU. *T:* (020) 7242 3555; The Grange, Hoby, Melton Mowbray, Leics LE14 3DT. *T:* (01664) 434232. *Club:* National Liberal.

FARRER, Mark; *see* Farrer, A. M.

FARRER, Sir Matthew; *see* Farrer, Sir C. M.

FARRER, Paul Ainsworth; QC 2006; a Recorder, since 2004; *b* 15 March 1965; *s* of Brian Ainsworth Farrer, *qv*; *m* 2004, Emma Louise Kelly; one *d*. *Educ:* Nottingham Univ. (LLB Hons 1986); Inns of Court Sch. of Law. Called to the Bar, Gray's Inn, 1988; in practice as barrister, 1988–, specialising in criminal law. *Recreations:* golf (handicap 2), skiing, tennis, travel. *Address:* St Philips Chambers, 55 Temple Row, Birmingham B2 5LS. *T:* (0121) 246 7000, *Fax:* (0121) 246 7001; *e-mail:* pfarrer@st-philips.com. *Clubs:* Little Aston Golf, Aberdovey Golf.

FARRER, Rt Rev. (Ralph) David; Vicar, St Nicholas, Arundel, with Tortington and South Stoke, since 2008; *b* 7 May 1944; *s* of Alexander John Farrer and Jacquelyn Mary Westacott Farrer (*née* Pattison); *m* 1969, Helen Belfield Walker; two *s*. *Educ:* Mentone Grammar Sch.; Ringwood High Sch.; St Barnabas Theol Coll. (ThL Hons; ThSchol Hons). Asst Curate, Good Shepherd, Plympton, SA, 1968–71; ordained priest, 1969; Priest i/c, St John the Baptist, Hillcrest, SA, 1971–73; Asst Priest, St Peter, Eastern Hill, Melbourne, 1973–75; Vicar: Christ Church, Brunswick, Vic, 1975–90; St Mary, Nottingham, 1988–89 (exchange); St Peter, Eastern Hill, 1990–98. Canon, St Paul's Cathedral, Melbourne, 1985–98; Archdeacon: La Trobe, Vic, 1994–96; Melbourne, 1996–98; Bishop of Wangaratta, Vic, 1998–2008. Dir, Inst. for Spiritual Studies, Melbourne, 1990–98. Chaplain to Parlt, Vic, 1992–98. CHLJ 1991; CMLJ 1996. *Publications:* Orthodoxy Down Under: tracts for our times, 1983; Wilderness Transformed, 1992. *Recreations:* reading, travel, golf. *Club:* Melbourne (Melbourne).

FARRIMOND, Herbert Leonard, CBE 1977; retired; Adviser, The Associated Octel Company Ltd, 1982–88; Chairman, H. L. Farrimond & Associates Ltd, 1978–88; *b* 4 Oct. 1924; *s* of late George and Jane Farrimond, Newcastle upon Tyne; *m* 1951, Patricia Sara (*née* McGrath); one *s*. *Educ:* St Cuthbert's Grammar Sch., Newcastle upon Tyne; Durham Univ. BA (Hons) Politics and Economics. Lieut RM, 1943–46. Australian Dept of Labour and Nat. Service, 1948–50; Imperial Chemical Industries Ltd, and Imperial Metal Industries Ltd, 1950–68; Upper Clyde Shipbuilders Ltd, 1968–69; Dir of Personnel, Dunlop Ltd, 1970–72; Mem., British Railways Bd, 1972–77. Director: British Rail Engineering Ltd; British Rail Shipping and Internat. Services Div.; Transmark Ltd (Chm.); Portsmouth and Sunderland Newspapers Ltd, 1978–80; Chm., British Transport Hotels, 1976–78. Adviser to industrial and commercial cos, 1978–88. Mem. Council, Advisory, Conciliation and Arbitration Service, 1974–78. Part-time Mem., British Waterways Bd, 1980–82. Governor, British Transport Staff Coll. Ltd, 1972–77. FCILT. *Recreations:* golf, gardening, music. *Address:* 9 Ardgare, Shandon, Helensburgh, Argyle and Bute G84 8NW. *T:* (01436) 820803.

FARRINGTON, family name of **Baroness Farrington of Ribbleton.**

FARRINGTON OF RIBBLETON, Baroness *cr* 1994 (Life Peer), of Fulwood in the County of Lancashire; **Josephine Farrington;** a Baroness in Waiting (Government Whip), since 1997; *b* 29 June 1940; *m* 1960, Michael James Farrington; three *s*. Lancashire County Council: Mem., 1977; Chm., 1992; Chm., Educn Cttee, 1981–91. Association of County Councils: Chm., Policy Cttee, 1993–94; Leader, Labour Gp, 1987–94; Vice-Chm., 1990–94; Chm., 1994–96. Mem., Consultative Council for Local Govt Finance, 1987–. UK Rep., Cttee of the Regions, 1994– (Chm., Educn and Trng Cttee, 1994–). Pres., Council of Europe Cttee for culture, educn and the media, 1989–94. UK European Woman of the Year, 1994. *Address:* 114 Victoria Road, Fulwood, Preston, Lancs PR2 4NN. *T:* (01772) 718836.

FARRINGTON, Rev. Canon Christine Marion; Associate Minister, Kirkwall Cathedral, Orkney, since 2007; Vicar of St Mark's, Cambridge, 1996–2002; Chaplain to the Queen, since 1998; *b* 11 June 1942; *d* of late Wilfred Bourne Farrington and Doris Violet Farrington. *Educ:* Cheshunt Grammar Sch.; Birkbeck Coll., London (BA Hons); Univ. of Nottingham (Dip. in Applied Social Studies); Univ. of Middlesex (MA in Deviancy and Social Policy); St Albans MTS. Ordained deaconess 1982, deacon, 1987, priest, 1994. Asst librarian, 1960–62; primary school teacher, 1962–65; probation officer, Hemel Hempstead, 1967–71; social work lectr, Middlesex Poly., 1971–79; sen. probation officer, Harrow, 1979–86; asst prison chaplain, 1986–87; Asst Dir of Pastoral Studies, Lincoln Theol Coll., 1986–87; Deacon, Salisbury Cathedral, 1987–93; Dir, Sarum Christian Centre, 1987–93; Co-Diocesan Dir of Ordinands and Dir of Women's Ministry, Dio. of Ely, 1993–2002; Hon. Canon, Ely Cathedral, 1993–2002, now Canon Emeritus; Chaplain, N Thames Ministerial Trng Course, 2003–07; RD, Wheathampstead, 2004–07. Hon. Chaplain: Wolfson Coll., Cambridge, 1993–2002; St John Ambulance Bde, Cambs, 2000–02. *Recreations:* gardening, walking, entertaining, reading, theatre and concerts. *Address:* 30 Lybury Lane, Redbourn, St Albans, Herts AL3 7HY.

FARRINGTON, Prof. David Philip, OBE 2004; PhD; FBA 1997; FMedSci; Professor of Psychological Criminology, University of Cambridge, since 1992; *b* 7 March 1944; *s* of William Farrington and Gladys Holden (*née* Spurr); *m* 1966, Sally Chamberlain; three *d*. *Educ:* Clare Coll., Cambridge (BA, MA, PhD Psychology). On staff of Cambridge Univ. Inst. of Criminology, 1969–: Reader in Psychol Criminology, 1988–92; Fellow, Darwin Coll., Cambridge, 1980–83. Mem., Parole Bd for England and Wales, 1984–87. Chm., Div. of Criminological and Legal Psychology, British Psychological Soc., 1983–85; President: British Soc. of Criminology, 1990–93; Europ. Assoc. of Psychology and Law, 1997–99; Amer. Soc. of Criminology, 1998–99; Acad. of Experimental Criminology, 2001–03. Vice-Chm., US Nat. Acad. of Scis Panel on Violence, 1989–92; Co-Chairman: US Office of Juvenile Justice and Delinquency Prevention Study Gp on Serious and Violent Juvenile Offenders, 1995–97, on Very Young Offenders, 1998–2000; High Security Psychiatric Services Commng Bd, Network on Primary Prevention of Adult Antisocial Behaviour, DoH, 1997; Chm., UK DoH Adv. Cttee, Nat. Prog. on Forensic Mental Health, 2000–03. FMedSci 2000. Sellin-Glueck Award, 1984, Sutherland Award, 2002, Amer. Soc. of Criminology; Amer. Sociol Assoc. Prize for Dist. Scholarship, 1988; Award for Dist. Contribns, US Office of Juvenile Justice and Delinquency Prevention, 1998; Joan McCord Award, Acad. of Experimental Criminology, 2005; Beccaria Gold Medal of Criminology, Soc. of German-Speaking Countries, 2005; Sen. Prize, Div. of Forensic Psychology, BPsS, 2007. *Publications:* Who Becomes Delinquent?, 1973; The Delinquent Way of Life, 1977; Behaviour Modification with Offenders, 1979; Psychology, Law and Legal Processes, 1979; Abnormal Offenders, Delinquency and the Criminal Justice System, 1982; Aggression and Dangerousness, 1985; Reactions to Crime, 1985; Prediction in Criminology, 1985; Understanding and Controlling Crime, 1986; Human Development and Criminal Behaviour, 1991; Offenders and Victims, 1992; Integrating Individual and Ecological Aspects of Crime, 1993; Psychological Explanations of Crime, 1994; Building a Safer Society, 1995; Understanding and Preventing Youth Crime, 1996; Biosocial Bases of Violence, 1997; Serious and Violent Juvenile Offenders, 1998; Antisocial Behaviour and Mental Health Problems, 1998; Evaluating Criminology and Criminal Justice, 1998; Sex and Violence, 2001; Offender Rehabilitation in Practice, 2001; Child Delinquents, 2001; Costs and Benefits of Preventing Crime, 2001; Evidence-

Based Crime Prevention, 2002; Early Prevention of Adult Antisocial Behaviour, 2003; Crime and Punishment in Western Countries, 2005; Integrated Developmental and Life-course Theories of Offending, 2005; Reducing Crime, 2006; Preventing Crime, 2006; Key Issues in Criminal Career Research, 2007; Saving Children from a Life of Crime, 2007; Violence and Serious Theft, 2008; Dictionary of Forensic Psychology, 2008. *Address:* Institute of Criminology, Sidgwick Avenue, Cambridge CB3 9DT. *T:* (01223) 335360.

FARRINGTON, Sir Henry (William), 8th Bt *cr* 1818, of Blackheath, Kent; *b* 27 March 1951; *s* of Sir Henry Francis Colden Farrington, 7th Bt and Anne, *e d* of Major W. A. Gillam, DSO; *S* father, 2004; *m* 1979, Diana Donne, *yr d* of Geoffrey Broughton; two *s*. *Educ:* Haileybury; RAC Cirencester. MRICS. *Heir: s* Henry John Albert Farrington, *b* 4 Jan. 1985. *Address:* Castle, Wiveliscombe, Taunton, Somerset TA4 2TJ.

FARRINGTON, Paul; freelance vocal consultant and remedial voice therapist; *b* 25 Feb. 1959; *s* of Brian and Mary Farrington. *Educ:* Birmingham Sch. of Music (GBSM, ABSM). Dir of Music, Birmingham Sch. of Speech and Drama, 1986–96; Opera Dir, Guildford Sch. of Acting, 1990–95; Vocal Tutor: Welsh Coll. of Music and Drama, 1990–97; RAM, 1994–99; Clinical Vocal Consultant, University Hosp., Birmingham, 1990–; Vocal Consultant: Samling Foundn, 1996–; Birmingham Sch. of Acting, 2001–; Internat. Vocal Tutor, NZ Opera Sch. for Emerging Artists, 2006–; Technical Vocal Coach, Young Artists Prog., Royal Opera, Covent Gdn, 2007–. *Recreations:* dining, gym, travel, theatre, fine wine, cooking, gardening, Pilates (keeping fit). *Address:* 16 Cramer House, 4 Cramer Street, W1U 4DZ. *T:* (020) 7935 2262; *e-mail:* farrynx.larynx@virgin.net.

FARRON, Timothy James; MP (Lib Dem) Westmorland and Lonsdale, since 2005; *b* 27 May 1970; *s* of Christopher Farron and Susan Farron (*née* Trenchard); *m* 2000, Rosemary Alison Cantley; two *s* two *d*. *Educ:* Univ. of Newcastle upon Tyne (BA Hons Politics 1991). Lancaster University: Adult Educn Officer, 1992–96; Special Needs Student Advr, 1996–98; Asst to Acad. Registrar, 1998–2002; Hd, Faculty Admin, St Martin's Coll., 2002–05. Member (Lib Dem): Lancs CC, 1993–2000; S Ribble BC, 1995–99; S Lakeland DC, 2004–. Mem., Amnesty Internat., 1993–. Mem., Cumbria Wildlife Trust, 2003–. Mem. PCC, Milnthorpe St Thomas, 2004–. Chm., Milnthorpe Youth Gp, 2004–. *Recreations:* walking, football (both playing and watching, respectively as an average goalkeeper and a Blackburn Rovers fan), music. *Address:* House of Commons, SW1A 0AA; Acland House, Smokehouse Yard, Strickland Gate, Kendal LA9 4ND. *T:* (01539) 723403, *Fax:* (01539) 740800; *e-mail:* tim@timfarron.co.uk. *Club:* Kendal and South Westmorland Liberal (Pres.).

FARROW, Christopher John; Chairman, Aga Foodservice Group, 2001–04; *b* 29 July 1937; *s* of late Thomas and Evangeline Dorothea Farrow; *m* 1961, Alison Brown; one *s* one *d*. *Educ:* Cranleigh Sch.; King's Coll., Cambridge (BA). Board of Trade, 1961; Harkness Fellowship and visiting scholar, Stanford Univ., USA, 1968–69; Private Sec. to Pres. of BoT and Minister for Trade, 1970–72; Dept of Trade and Industry, 1972–74; Cabinet Office, 1975–77; Dept of Industry, 1977–83; Asst Dir, Bank of England, 1983–87; Dir, Kleinwort, Benson Ltd, 1987–92; Dir-Gen., British Merchant Banking and Securities Houses, then London Investment Banking, Assoc., 1993–99. Director: London Metal Exchange Ltd, 1987–99 (Vice Chm., 1997–99); Glynwed International, 1993–2001 (Chm., 2000–01). Member: Engrg Council, 1984–86; Financial Reporting Review Panel, 1992–2002. *Recreation:* gardening.

FARROW, Christopher John; Chief Executive, Central Salford Urban Regeneration Co., since 2006; *b* 19 Nov. 1947; *s* of Sydney A. Farrow; *m* 1980, Susan Thomas; three *d*. *Educ:* Claysmore Sch., Dorset; Univ. of London (BA Hons); Polytechnic of Central London (DipTP Dist.). London Borough of Newham, 1974–81; Dir, LDDC, 1981–91; Chief Exec., Merseyside Develt Corp., 1991–98; Man. Dir, North, then Exec. Dir, N Wales, WDA, 1998–2006. Director: Greenland Dock Develt Co., 1985–90; Mersey Partnership, 1992–98. MRTPI. FRSA 1993. *Publications:* planning papers on urban develt and economy. *Address:* Central Salford URC, Digital World Centre, 1 Lowry Plaza, Salford Quays M50 3UB.

FARROW, Mia (Villiers); actress; *b* 9 Feb. 1945; *d* of late John Villiers Farrow and Maureen O'Sullivan; *m* 1st, 1966, Frank Sinatra (marr. diss. 1968; he *d* 1998); 2nd, 1970, André Previn, *qv* (marr. diss. 1979); three *s*, two adopted *d* (and one adopted *d* decd); one *s* by Woody Allen, *qv*; three adopted *s* three adopted *d* (and one adopted *d* decd). *TV series:* Peyton Place, 1965; A Girl Thing, 2001; *films:* Secret Ceremony, 1968; Rosemary's Baby, 1969; John and Mary, 1970; The Public Eye, 1972; The Great Gatsby, 1974; Full Circle, Death on the Nile, A Wedding, 1978; Hurricane, 1980; A Midsummer Night's Sex Comedy, 1982; Zelig, 1983; Broadway Danny Rose, 1984; The Purple Rose of Cairo, 1985; Hannah and her Sisters, 1986; Radio Days, 1987; September, 1988; Another Woman, 1989; Crimes and Misdemeanours, 1990; Alice, 1990; Husbands and Wives, 1992; Shadows and Fog, 1992; Widows' Peak, 1994; Miami Rhapsody, 1995; Reckless, 1995; Angela Mooney, 1996; Coming Soon, 1999; Purpose, 2002; The Omen, 2006; Be Kind Rewind, 2008; *stage:* The Importance of Being Earnest, NY, 1963; Mary Rose, Shaw, 1973; The Three Sisters, Greenwich, 1974; The House of Bernarda Alba, Greenwich, 1974; Peter Pan, 1975; The Marrying of Ann Leete, RSC, 1975; The Zykovs, Ivanov, RSC, 1976; A Midsummer Night's Dream, Leicester, 1976; Romantic Comedy, NY, 1979. David Donatello Award, Italy, 1969; Best Actress awards: French Academy, 1969; San Sebastian, 1969; Rio de Janeiro, 1970. *Publication:* What Falls Away (memoirs), 1997. *Address:* Bridgewater, CT, USA.

FARRY, Stephen Anthony, PhD; Member (Alliance) North Down, Northern Ireland Assembly, since 2007; *b* 22 April 1971; *s* of Vincent Farry and Margaret Farry (*née* Greer); *m* 2005, Wendy Watt, PhD. *Educ:* Queen's Univ., Belfast (BSocSc 1st Cl. Pols 1992; PhD Internat. Relns 2000). Mem. (Alliance), N Down BC, 1993– (Dep. Mayor, 2002–03; Mayor, 2007–08). Gen. Sec., Alliance Party of NI, 2000–07. Mem., Finance and Personnel Cttee, NI Assembly, 2007–. Sen. Fellow, US Inst. of Peace, 2005–06. *Publications:* various jl and newspaper articles. *Recreations:* travel, international affairs. *Address:* Parliament Buildings, Stormont, Belfast BT4 3XX; *e-mail:* stephen.farry@allianceparty.org.

FARTHING, Prof. Michael John Godfrey, MD; FRCP, FRCPE, FRCPGlas; Vice-Chancellor, University of Sussex, since 2007; *b* 2 March 1948; *s* of Dennis Jack Farthing and Joan Margaret Farthing (*née* Godfrey); *m* 1979, Alison Mary McLean; two *s*. *Educ:* Henry Thornton Sch., London; University Coll., London (BSc); UCH Med. Sch. (MB BS); MD London 1981; DSc (Med) London 2001. FRCP 1988; FRCPE 2001; FRCPGlas 2001. Res. Fellow, St Mark's Hosp., 1974; Med. Registrar, Addenbrooke's Hosp., 1975–77; Res. Fellow and Hon. Lectr, 1977–80, Wellcome Tropical Lectr, 1980–83, St Bart's Hosp.; Vis. Asst Prof., Tuft's Univ. Sch. of Medicine, 1981–83; St Bartholomew's Hospital Medical College, subseq. St Bartholomew's and Royal London Hospital School of Medicine and Dentistry, QMW: Wellcome Sen. Lectr, 1983–91; Prof. and Head of Dept of Gastroenterology, 1990–2000; Dir, Digestive Diseases Res. Centre, 1990–2000; Dean, Faculty of Clin. Medicine, 1995–97; Prof. of Medicine and Exec. Dean, Faculty of Medicine, Univ. of Glasgow, 2000–03; Prof. of Medicine and Principal, St George's Hosp. Med. Sch., subseq. St George's, Univ. of London, 2003–07; Pro-Vice-Chancellor for Medicine, Univ. of London, 2005–07. Hon. Cons. Gastroenterologist, St George's Healthcare NHS Trust, 2003–07; Hon. Consultant: St Mark's Hosp., 1987–; St Luke's Hosp. for Clergy, 1990–; to the Army, 1991–. Non-executive Director: E London and City HA, 1998–2000; Greater Glasgow NHS Bd, 2001–03; SW London Strategic HA, 2004–06. Editor, Gut, 1996–2002. Mem., GMC, 2001– (Mem., Educn Cttee, 2001–). Chairman: Cttee on Publication Ethics, 1997–2003; Scientific Cttee, United European Gastroenterology Fedn, 2004–; Hon. Sec., 1990–94, Pres., 2007–08, British Soc. of Gastroenterology; Pres., Eur. Assoc. of Gastroenterology and Endoscopy, 1998–2001; Vice-Pres., World Orgn of Gastroenterology, 2005–. Trustee, Digestive Disorders Foundn, 2003–. Founder FMedSci 1998. Mem. Ct of Assistants, Apothecaries' Soc., 2003–. *Publications:* Enteric Infection: mechanisms, manifestations and management, vol. 1 1989, vol. 2 1995; Clinical Challenges in Gastroenterology, 1996; Drug Therapy for Gastrointestinal and Liver Diseases, 2001; many papers on intestinal disorders. *Recreations:* theatre, modern literature, jazz, running, watersports. *Address:* University of Sussex, Sussex House, Falmer, Brighton BN1 9RH. *Club:* Glasgow Art.

See also S. F. G. Farthing.

FARTHING, Stephen Frederick Godfrey, RA 1998; Rootstein Hopkins Chair of Drawing, University of the Arts London, since 2004; *b* 16 Sept. 1950; *s* of Dennis Jack Farthing and Joan Margaret (*née* Godfrey); *m* 1975, Joni Elizabeth Jackson (marr. diss. 2004); one *d*. *Educ:* St Martin's Sch. of Art; Royal Coll. of Art; British Sch. at Rome. Lectr in Painting, Canterbury Coll. of Art, 1977–79; Tutor in Painting, RCA, 1980–85; Head of Painting, W Surrey Coll. of Art and Design, Farnham, 1985–90; Ruskin Master of Drawing, Oxford Univ., and Professorial Fellow, St Edmund Hall, Oxford, 1990–2000, now Emeritus Fellow; Exec. Dir, NY Acad. of Art, 2000–04. Artist in Residence, Hayward Gall., London, 1989. *One-man shows* include: Nat. Mus. of Modern Art, Kyoto; Museo Carrillo Gil, Mexico City; Arnolfini, Bristol; Edward Totah Gall., London. British School at Rome: Chm., Arts Faculty, 1996–2000; Mem., Council, 1998–. Mem., Bd of Dirs, MBNA Europe Bank Ltd, 2003–06. *Publications:* The Intelligent Persons Guide to Modern Art, 2000; (ed) 1001 Paintings You Must See Before You Die, 2006; (ed) 501 Artists, 2008. *Recreations:* watercolours, tennis. *Address:* Chelsea College of Art and Design, University of the Arts London, 16 John Islip Street, SW1P 4JU.

See also M. J. G. Farthing.

FASHAM, Dr Michael John Robert, FRS 2000; Hon. Professor, Southampton Oceanography Centre, University of Southampton, since 2002; *b* 29 May 1942; *s* of Ronald Henry Alfred Fasham and Hazel Grace Fasham (*née* Day); *m* 1967, Jocelyn Mary Hart; one *s*. *Educ:* Kilburn Grammar Sch.; Birmingham Univ. (BSc; PhD 1968). Sen. Geophysicist, Wimpey Labs, 1967–68; SSO, Nat. Inst. Oceanography, 1968–73; PSO, Inst. Oceanographic Scis, 1973–93; SPSO, Southampton Oceanography Centre, 1993–2002. Chm. Scientific Cttee, Jt Global Ocean Flux Study, 1998–2000. Silver Medal, Challenger Soc., 2002. *Publications:* (ed) Flows of Energy and Materials in Marine Ecosystems: theory and practice, 1984; (ed jtly) Towards a Model of Ocean Biogeochemical Processes, 1993; contrib. papers to oceanographic jls. *Recreations:* genealogy, British history, gardening. *Address:* White Cottage, Hill Road, Grayshott, Hindhead, Surrey GU26 6HL. *T:* (01428) 606119.

FASSETT, Kaffe; textile designer; *b* 7 Dec. 1937; *s* of William Elliot Fassett and Madeleine Fassett. Self-educated. Retrospective exhibitions: Tokyo, 1986; V&A Museum, 1989; Copenhagen, Stockholm, Oslo, Melbourne, Toronto and Helsinki, 1990; Vancouver, Holland, 1993; Osaka, Iceland, 1996; Minneapolis, 1997. *Publications:* Glorious Knitting, 1985; Glorious Needlepoint, 1987; Kaffe Fassett at the V & A, 1988, 4th edn, as Glorious Colour, 1991; Family Album, 1989; Glorious Inspiration, 1991; Kaffe's Classics, 1994; Glorious Interiors, 1995; Mosaics, 1997; Glorious Patchwork, 1999; Passionate Patchwork, 2001; Kaffe's Pattern Library, 2003; Kaffe Fassett's V & A Patchwork Quilts, 2005. *Address:* c/o Random Century, 20 Vauxhall Bridge Road, SW1V 2SA.

FATEH, Abul Fazal Muhammad Abul; Hon. Representative of Royal Commonwealth Society in Bangladesh, 1985–94; *b* 28 Feb. 1926; *s* of Abdul Gafur and Zohra Khatun; *m* 1956, Mahfuza Banu; two *s*. *Educ:* Dhaka, Bangladesh. MA (English Lit.); special course, LSE, 1949–50. Carnegie Fellow in Internat. Peace, 1962–63. Entered Pakistan Foreign Service, 1949; 3rd Secretary: Paris, 1951–53; Calcutta, 1953–56; 2nd Sec., Washington, DC, 1956–60; Dir, Min. of Foreign Affairs, Karachi, 1961–65; 1st Sec., Prague, 1965–66; Counsellor, New Delhi, 1966–67; Dep. High Comr for Pakistan, Calcutta, 1968–70; Ambassador of Pakistan, Baghdad, 1970–71; Adviser to Actg President of Bangladesh, Aug. 1971–Jan. 1972; Foreign Sec., Bangladesh, Oct. 1971–Jan. 1972; Ambassador of Bangladesh to France and Spain, 1972–75; Permanent Deleg. to UNESCO, 1972–76; High Comr for Bangladesh in London, 1976–77; Ambassador, Algeria, 1977–82. Leader, Bangladesh Delegation: Commonwealth Youth Ministers' Conf., Lusaka, 1973; Meeting of UN Council on Namibia, Algiers, 1980; Ministerial Meeting of Non-aligned Countries Co-ordination Bureau on Namibia, Algiers, 1981. Chm., Commonwealth Human Ecology Council Symposium, 1977. Mem., Poetry Soc., 1994–99. *Address:* 3 Hertford Lodge, 15 East End Road, Finchley Church End, N3 3NJ.

FATT, Prof. Paul, FRS 1969; Emeritus Professor, University of London, since 1989. Professor of Biophysics, University College, London, 1976–89 (Reader, 1956–76); Fellow, UCL, 1973. *Publications:* papers in various scientific jls. *Address:* 25 Tanza Road, NW3 2UA. *T:* (020) 7435 9802.

FAULKNER, family name of **Baron Faulkner of Worcester**.

FAULKNER OF DOWNPATRICK, Lady; Lucy (Barbara Ethel) Faulkner, CBE 1985; *b* 1 July 1925; *d* of William John Forsythe and Jane Ethel Sewell; *m* 1951, Arthur Brian Deane Faulkner (MP (NI) 1949–73; PC 1959; *cr* Baron Faulkner of Downpatrick, 1977) (killed in a hunting accident, 1977); two *s* one *d*. *Educ:* Aubrey House; Bangor Collegiate Sch.; Trinity College Dublin. BA (Hons History). Journalist, Belfast Telegraph, 1947; Personal Secretary to Sir Basil Brooke, Prime Minister of N Ireland, 1949. Nat. Governor for NI, BBC, 1978–85; Chm., Broadcasting Council for NI, 1981–85; Researcher, 1977, Trustee 1980–, Ulster Historical Foundation; Mem., NI Tourist Bd, 1985–91. Governor, Linenhall Library, 1982–. Hon. LLD QUB, 1994. *Recreations:* hunting and dressage, genealogy, book collecting. *Address:* Toberdoney, Farranfad, Downpatrick BT30 8NH. *T:* (028) 4481 1712.

FAULKNER OF WORCESTER, Baron *cr* 1999 (Life Peer), of Wimbledon in the London Borough of Merton; **Richard Oliver Faulkner;** Deputy Chairman, Cardiff Millennium Stadium plc, since 2004 (Director, 1997–2004); Strategy Adviser, Sportech Group plc (formerly Littlewoods Pools), since 1999; Alderney Gambling Control Commission, since 2005; Chairman, Railway Heritage Committee, since 2004 (Member, since 2002); Travel PR Ltd, since 2006; a Deputy Chairman, House of Lords, since 2007; *b* 22 March 1946; *s* of late Harold Ewart and Mabel Faulkner; *m* 1968, Susan Heyes; two *d*. *Educ:* Merchant Taylors' Sch., Northwood; Worcester Coll., Oxford (MA PPE; Hon.

Fellow, 2002). Research asst and journalist, Labour Party, 1967–69; PRO, Construction Ind. Trg Bd, 1969–70; Editor, Steel News, 1971; Account dir, F. J. Lyons (PR) Ltd, 1971–73; Dir, PPR International, 1973–76; communications advisor: to Leader of the Opposition and Labour Party (unpaid), gen. elections, 1987, 1992, 1997; to the Bishop at Lambeth, 1990; Govt relations adviser: rly trade unions, 1975–76; C. A. Parsons & Co., 1976–77; Pool Promoters Assoc., 1977–99; British Rlys Bd, 1977–97; Prudential Assurance Co., 1978–88; IPU, 1988–90; Southampton City Council, 1989–91; CAMRA, 1989; Barclays de Zoete Wedd, 1990–92; Standard Life Assurance, 1990–99; S Glam CC, 1991–96; Cardiff CC, 1996–99; Cardiff Bay Develt Corp., 1993–98; Littlewoods Orgn, 1994–99; FSA, 1998–99; Actg Hd of Communications, SIB, 1997; Jt Man. Dir, Westminster Communications Gp, 1989–97; Dep. Chm., Citigate, Westminster, 1997–99. Dept Liaison Peer, DETR, 2000–01, Cabinet Office, 2001–05; Member: Sub-cttee B, EC Select Cttee, H of L, 2000–03; Delegated Powers and Regulatory Reform Cttee, H of L, 2007–; Jt Scrutiny Cttee, Draft Gambling Bill, 2003–04; London Local Authy Private Bill Cttee, 2006; Chm., Inquiry into Betting on Sport, 2005. Treas., All Party Railways Gp, 2000–; Graduate Armed Forces Parly Scheme, attached to RN, 2002–07; Secretary: British-Norwegian Parly Gp, 2000–; British-Argentine Parly Gp, 2001–; British-Namibian Parly Gp, 2004–; Vice-Chairman: Football Gp, 2004–; British-Cyprus Gp, 2005–; Betting and Gaming Gp, 2005–; Abolition of Death Penalty Gp, 2007–; British Caribbean Gp, 2000–; British-S African Gp, 2002–; British-Danish Parly Gp, 2005–; British-Channel Islands Gp, 2007–; Jt Treas., British-Swedish Parly Gp, 2001–; Chairman: All Party War Graves and Battlefields Heritage Gp, 2002–; All Party Sustainable Aviation Gp, 2003–; Co-Chm., British-Taiwanese Parly Gp, 2005– (Sec., 2000–05). Football Trust: Foundn Trustee, 1979–82; Sec., 1983–86; First Dep. Chm., 1986–98; Chm., Sports Grounds Initiative, 1995–2000; Vice Chm., Govt's Football Task Force, 1997–99; Member: Sports Council, 1986–88; Football League enquiry into membership schemes, 1984, anti-hooliganism cttee, 1987–90; FIFA Wkg Gp on betting, 2006–; Chm., Women's Football Assoc., 1988–91; Dir, Football Assoc. of Wales, 2007–. Vice-Chm., 1986–99, Vice-Pres., 2000–, Campaign for Better Transport (formerly Transport 2000 Ltd). Pres., 2001–04, Vice Pres., 2004–, RoSPA; Vice-President: Football Conf., 2007–; Nat. Assoc. for Disabled Supporters, 2007–. Trustee: Foundn for Sport and the Arts, 2000–; Gamcare, 2005–; Nat. Mus. for Sci. and Industry, 2007–; Nat. Football Mus., 2007–; ASH, 2007–; Patron, Roy Castle Lung Cancer Foundn, 1999– (Trustee, 2003–07). Chairman: Worcester Coll. Appeal, 1996–2003; Adv. Cttee, Worcester Coll. Soc., 2003–; Mem. Ct, Bedfordshire Univ. (formerly Luton Univ.), 1999–; Vice-Pres., Old Merchant Taylors' Soc., 2006–. Mem., Merton Borough Council, 1971–78; contested (Lab) Devizes 1970, Feb. 1974, Monmouth, Oct. 1974, Huddersfield W, 1979. Co-founder, parly jl The House mag. (Mem., Editl Bd, 2003–). Hon. LLD Luton, 2003. Friendship Medal of Diplomacy (Taiwan), 2004; Order of the Brilliant Star with Grand Cordon (Taiwan), 2008. *Recreations:* collecting Lloyd George memorabilia, tinplate trains, watching Association Football, travelling by railway. *Address:* House of Lords, SW1A 0PW; *e-mail:* faulknerro@parliament.uk.

See also D. E. R. Faulkner.

FAULKNER, David Ewart Riley, CB 1985; Senior Research Associate, University of Oxford Centre for Criminology (formerly for Criminological Research), since 1992; *b* 23 Oct. 1934; *s* of Harold Ewart and Mabel Faulkner; *m* 1961, Sheila Jean Stevenson; one *s* one *d. Educ:* Manchester Grammar Sch.; Merchant Taylors' Sch., Northwood; St John's Coll., Oxford (MA Lit Hum). Home Office: Asst Principal, 1959; Private Sec. to Parly Under-Sec. of State, 1961–63; Principal, 1963; Jt Sec. to Inter-Party Conf. on House of Lords Reform, 1968; Private Sec. to Home Sec., 1969–70; Asst Sec., Prison Dept, 1970, Establishment Dept, 1974, Police Dept, 1976; Asst Under-Sec. of State, 1976; Under Sec., Cabinet Office, 1978–80; Home Office; Asst Under-Sec. of State, Dir of Operational Policy, Prison Dept, 1980–82; Dep. Under-Sec. of State, 1982; Head of Criminal and Res. and Statistical Depts, 1982–90; Principal Estab. Officer, 1990–92. Fellow, St John's Coll., Oxford, 1992–99. Chm., Howard League for Penal Reform, 1999–2002. Member: UN Cttee on Crime Prevention and Control, 1984–91; Adv. Bd, Helsinki Inst. for Crime Prevention and Control, 1988–93; Council, Magistrates' Assoc., 1992–98; Council, Justice, 1993–97; Commn on the Future of Multi-Ethnic Britain, 1998–2000. Trustee, Gilbert Murray Trust, Thames Valley Partnership, 1992–, and other charities. *Publications:* Darkness and Light, 1996; Crime, State and Citizen, 2001, 2nd edn 2006; Civil Renewal, Diversity and Social Capital in a Multi-Ethnic Britain, 2004; contribs to jls. *Recreations:* railways, birds. *Address:* c/o Centre for Criminology, Manor Road, Oxford OX1 3UR.

See also Baron Faulkner of Worcester.

FAULKNER, Sir Dennis; *see* Faulkner, Sir J. D. C.

FAULKNER, Prof. Douglas, WhSch, BSc, PhD; FREng, FRINA, FIStructE, FSNAME; RCNC; consulting structural engineer and naval architect, specialising in ship casualty investigations, since 1995; Head of Department of Naval Architecture and Ocean Engineering, University of Glasgow, 1973–95, now Emeritus Professor; *b* 29 Dec. 1929; *s* of Vincent and Florence Faulkner; *m* 1st, 1954, Jenifer Ann Cole-Adams (marr. diss. 1986); three *d*; 2nd, 1987, Isobel Parker Campbell. *Educ:* Sutton High Sch., Plymouth; HM Dockyard Technical Coll., Devonport; RNC, Greenwich. Aircraft Carrier Design, 1955–57; Production Engrg, 1957–59; Structural Research at NCRE, Dunfermline, 1959–63; Asst Prof. of Naval Construction, RNC, Greenwich, 1963–66; Structural Adviser to Ship Dept, Bath, 1966–68; Constructor Comdr att. to British Embassy, Washington DC, 1968–70, and Mem. Ship Research Cttee, Nat. Acad. of Scis, 1968–71; Res. Associate and Defence Fellow, MIT, 1970–71; Structural Adviser to Ship Dept, Bath, and to the Merrison Box Girder Bridge Cttee, 1971–73. UK Rep., Standing Cttee, Internat. Ship Structures Congress, 1973–85. Chm., Conoco-ABS cttee producing a design code for Tension Leg Platforms offshore, 1981–83; Dir, Veritec Ltd, 1985–88; Mem. Bd of Govs, BMT Quality Assessors Ltd, 1990–93. Technical Assessor, Lord Donaldson of Lymington's Assessment, MV Derbyshire, Dept of Transport, 1995–97; Ind. Expert Witness, re-opened formal investigation into loss of MV Derbyshire, 2000. President: Instn of Engrs and Shipbuilders in Scotland, 1995–97; Whitworth Soc., 1997–98. FREng (FEng 1981). FRSA 1983–99. Consulting Editor, Jl of Marine Structures, 1990–99 (Editor, 1987–90). Hon. DSc: Technical Univ. of Gdansk, 1993; Technical Univ. of Lisbon, 2001. David W. Taylor Medal, SNAME, 1991; William Froude Medal, RINA, 1993; Peter the Great Medal, St Petersburg Univ. of Ocean Technology, 1993. *Publications:* (ed jtly) Integrity of Offshore Structures, 1981; Integrity of Offshore Structures—3, 1987; Integrity of Offshore Structures—4, 1990; Integrity of Offshore Structures—5, 1993; chapters in Ship Structural Design Concepts (Cornell Maritime Press), 1975; papers related to structural design of ships, in Trans RINA, Jl of Ship Res., Behaviour of Offshore Structures, etc. *Recreations:* walking, music. *Address:* 4 Murdoch Drive, Milngavie, Glasgow G62 6QZ. *T:* (0141) 956 5071.

FAULKNER, Graham John; Chief Executive, National Society for Epilepsy, since 2000; *b* 26 Sept. 1948; *s* of William and Edna Faulkner; *m* 1st, 1975, Jennifer Barkway (marr. diss. 1998); one *s* one *d*; 2nd, 1999, Dorothy, (Dee), Napier (marr. diss. 2002). *Educ:* UC of Swansea (BSc Hons Psychol. 1970); Univ. of Leicester (postgrad. res.); Univ. of Birmingham (CQSW 1984; MSocSc). Local Govt O R Unit, RIPA, 1973–75; Planning Dept, 1975–77, Social Services Dept, 1977–85, Warwickshire CC; Dir, Retirement Security Ltd, 1985–92; Dir and Gen. Sec., Leonard Cheshire Foundn, 1992–98; Chief Exec., Rehab UK, 1999–2000. Gov., UCLH NHS Foundn Trust, 2004–. *Publications:* contributor to: White Media and Black Britain, 1975; Solving Local Government Problems, 1981; This Caring Business, 1988; contrib. jls and res. reports. *Recreations:* theatre, music, watching Coventry City! *Address:* National Society for Epilepsy, Chesham Lane, Chalfont St Peter, Bucks SL9 0RJ. *T:* (01494) 601300; *e-mail:* graham.faulkner@epilepsynse.org.uk.

FAULKNER, Gregory; *see* Faulkner, L. G.

FAULKNER, Sir (James) Dennis (Compton), Kt 1991; CBE 1980; VRD 1960; DL; Chairman, Marlowe Cleaners Ltd, 1973–2005; *b* 22 Oct. 1926; *s* of James and Nora Faulkner; *m* 1952, Janet Cunningham (*d* 1994); three *d. Educ:* College of St Columba, Co. Dublin. Served RNVR, 1946–71; UDR, 1971–92 (Col Comdt, 1986–92). Chairman: Belfast Collar Co. Ltd, 1957–63; Belfast Savings Bank, 1960–61; NI Develt Agency, 1978–82; Board Member: Gallaher NI, 1980–89 (Chm., 1982–89); Northern Bank Ltd, 1983–96; Chm., Ladybird (NI) Ltd, 1963–88; Dir, Giants Causeway and Bushmills Railway Co. Ltd, 1999–2005. Farming, 1946–. Mem., Strangford Lough Management Cttee, 1992–2004 (Chm., 1992–97); Chm., Ulster, North Down and Ards Hosp. Trust, 1993–94. President: Regtl Assoc. of UDR, 1986–2005 (Patron, 2005–); RBL NI, 1992–2000; Chm., UDR Benevolent Fund, 1986–; Trustee, Royal Irish Regtl Benevolent Fund, 1992–. DL County Down, 1988. *Recreations:* sailing, hunting, ocean racing. *Address:* Northern Ireland. *Clubs:* Royal Ocean Racing, Royal Cruising; Royal Yacht Squadron; Irish Cruising; Strangford Lough Yacht; Cruising Club of America (New York).

FAULKNER, John Richard Hayward; theatre and management consultant; international impresario; *b* 29 May 1941; *s* of Richard Hayward Ollerton and Lilian Elizabeth (*née* Carrigan), and step *s* of late Herbert Andrew Faulkner; *m* 1st, 1970, Janet Gill (*née* Cummings) (*d* 1994); two *d*, and two step *d*; 2nd, 2001, Christie Dickason; two step *s. Educ:* Archbishop Holgate's Sch., York; Keble Coll., Oxford (BA). Worked with a number of theatre companies, Prospect Productions, Meadow Players, Century Theatre, Sixty-Nine Theatre Co., Cambridge Theatre Co., toured extensively, UK, Europe, Indian Sub-Continent, Australia, 1960–72; Drama Director: Scottish Arts Council, 1972–77; Arts Council of GB, 1977–83; Head, Artistic Planning, Nat. Theatre, 1983–88. Associate, Prince Res. Consultants, 2001–. Mem., Assessors' Panel, Nat. Lottery Dept, Arts Council, 1995–2001. Director: Minotaur Films, 1988–; Visionhaven Ltd, 1991–2003; New Zoo Develts Ltd, 1992–. Proprietor, Ollerton Press, 2006–. Member: Pubns & Communication Commn, Orgn Internat. des Scénographes, Techniciens et Architectes de Théâtre, 1994– (Chm., 1999–2001); Internat. Soc. for the Performing Arts, 1997–; Council, Assoc. of British Theatre Technicians, 1998–2001 (sometime Chm.); Sec., Pleasance Theatre Trust, 1997–. Trustee: The Arts Educational Schools, 1986–92; The Arts for Nature, 1990–99; Performing Arts Labs, 1991–2001; Pension Scheme for Admin. and Tech. Staff in the Arts, 1996–; Orange Tree Th. Trust, 1998– (Jt Chm., 1999–2004, Chm., 2004–); Theatre Futures Ltd, 2003–. *Recreations:* intricacies and wildernesses. *Address:* 28 Ellesmere Road, Chiswick W4 4QH. *T:* (020) 8995 3041.

FAULKNER, (Leo) Gregory; HM Diplomatic Service, retired; Ambassador to Chile, 2000–03; *b* 21 Sept. 1943; *s* of late James and of Teresa Faulkner; *m* 1970, Fiona Hardie (*née* Birkett); three *d. Educ:* Manchester Univ. (BA Hons Spanish). FCO, 1968–72; Lima, 1972–76; Lagos, 1976–79; EC Internal Dept, FCO, 1979–82; Head of Chancery, Madrid, 1982–84; Head, Internat. Telecoms Br., DTI, 1984–86, on secondment; Commercial Counsellor, The Hague, 1986–90; Dep. Head of Mission, Buenos Aires, 1990–93; Head, Latin America Dept, FCO, 1993–96; High Commissioner, Trinidad and Tobago, 1996–99. *Recreations:* tennis, golf, watching cricket, football and Rugby. *Club:* Canning.

FAULKNER, Most Rev. Leonard Anthony; Archbishop of Adelaide, (RC), 1985–2001; *b* Booleroo Centre, South Australia, 5 Dec. 1926. *Educ:* Sacred Heart Coll., Glenelg; Corpus Christi Coll., Werribee; Pontifical Urban University, Rome. Ordained Propaganda Fide Coll., Rome, 1 Jan. 1950; Asst Priest, Woodville, SA, 1950–57; Administrator, St Francis Xavier Cathedral, Adelaide, 1957–67; Diocesan Chaplain, Young Christian Workers, 1955–67; Mem., Nat. Fitness Council of SA, 1958–67; Bishop of Townsville, 1967–83; Coadjutor Archbishop of Adelaide, 1983–85. Chairman: Aust. Catholic Bishops' Conf. Cttee for the Family and for Life, 1993–2001; S Australian Ministerial Adv. Bd on Ageing, 2002–06. *Address:* 11 Debra Court, Netley, SA 5037, Australia.

FAULKS, Edward Peter Lawless; QC 1996; a Recorder, since 2000; *b* 19 Aug. 1950; *s* of His Honour Peter Ronald Faulks, MC and Pamela Faulks (*née* Lawless); *m* 1990, Catherine Frances Turner, *d* of Lindsay Turner and Anthea Cadbury; two *s. Educ:* Wellington Coll.; Jesus Coll., Oxford (MA). FCIArb. Called to the Bar, Middle Temple, 1973, Bencher, 2002. Literary Agent, Curtis Brown, 1980–81; Asst Recorder, 1996–2000. Chm., Professional Negligence Bar Assoc., 2002–04. Special Advr to DCA on compensation culture, 2005–06. *Publication:* (contributing ed.) Local Authority Liabilities, 1998, 3rd edn 2005. *Recreations:* sports, the arts. *Address:* 33 Ladbroke Grove, W11 3AY; 1 Chancery Lane, WC2A 1LF. *T:* 0845 634 6666. *Club:* Garrick.

See also S. C. Faulks.

FAULKS, Esmond James; His Honour Judge Faulks; a Circuit Judge, since 1993; *b* 11 June 1946; *s* of Hon. Sir Neville Faulks, MBE, TD and Bridget Marigold (*née* Bodley); *m* 1972, Pamela Margaret Ives; one *s* one *d. Educ:* Uppingham Sch.; Sidney Sussex Coll., Cambridge (Exhibitioner; MA). Called to the Bar, Inner Temple, 1968; a Recorder, 1987–93. Mem., Parole Bd, 2003–. Hon. Vis. Prof. of Law, Samford Univ., Ala, 2005. *Recreations:* country pursuits. *Address:* c/o Combined Court Centre, Quayside, Newcastle upon Tyne NE1 2TH.

FAULKS, Sebastian Charles, CBE 2002; author; *b* 20 April 1953; *s* of His Honour Peter Ronald Faulks, MC and Pamela Faulks (*née* Lawless); *m* 1989, Veronica Youlten; two *s* one *d. Educ:* Wellington Coll.; Emmanuel Coll., Cambridge (Hon. Fellow). Editor, New Fiction Society, 1978–81; Daily Telegraph, 1978–82; feature writer, Sunday Telegraph, 1983–86; Literary Editor, Independent, 1986–89; Dep. Editor, 1989–90, Associate Editor, 1990–91, Independent on Sunday; columnist: The Guardian, 1992–98; London Evening Standard, 1997–99; Mail on Sunday, 1999–2000. Writer and presenter, Churchill's Secret Army (television), 2000. FRSL 1995. Hon. DLitt UEL, 2007. *Publications:* A Trick of the Light, 1984; The Girl at the Lion d'Or, 1989; A Fool's Alphabet, 1992; Birdsong, 1993; The Fatal Englishman, 1996; Charlotte Gray, 1998 (filmed 2002); (ed with Jörg Hensgen) The Vintage Book of War Stories, 1999; On Green Dolphin Street, 2001; Human Traces, 2005; Pistache, 2006; Engleby, 2007; Devil May Care, 2008; contribs to newspapers and magazines. *Address:* c/o Aitken Alexander Associates, 18–21 Cavaye Place, SW10 9PT.

See also E. P. L. Faulks.

FAULL, Jonathan Michael Howard; Director General, Justice, Freedom and Security (formerly Justice and Home Affairs), European Commission, since 2003; *b* 20 Aug. 1954; *s* of Gerald Faull and June Faull (*née* Shepherd); *m* 1979, Sabine Garrel; two *s*. *Educ:* Univs of Sussex and Geneva (BA); Coll. of Europe, Bruges (MA). European Commission, 1978–: Administrator, then Principal Administrator, various depts, 1978–87; Asst to Dir Gen., Directorate Gen. for Competition, 1987–89; Mem., Cabinet of Sir Leon Brittan, Vice-Pres., EC, 1989–92; Directorate General for Competition: Hd, Transport and Tourism Unit, 1992–93; Hd, Co-ordination and Gen. Policy Unit, 1993–95; Dir, Competition Policy, Co-ordination, Internat. Affairs and Relns with other Instns, 1995–99; Dep. Dir Gen. of Competition, 1999; Hd of Press and Communication Service, subseq. Dir Gen., Press and Communication, 1999–2003; Advr to British Chamber of Commerce, Belgium, 2003–. Prof. of Law, Free Univ. of Brussels, 1989–; Vis. Lectr, Inst. d'Etudes Politiques, Paris, 1992–95; Vis. Fellow, Centre for Eur. Legal Studies, Cambridge Univ., 1997–2001. Member: Bd, Inst. of European Studies, Brussels, 2005–; Adv. Bd, Security and Defence Agenda, Brussels, 2006–. Mem., editl or adv. boards of various law jls, incl. Common Market Law Reports, Eur. Business Law Rev., UK Competition Law Reports, and World Competition Review; EC corresp., Eur. Law Review, 1980–89. *Publications:* The EC Law of Competition, 1999, 2nd edn 2007; contrib. articles on various topics of EC law and policy. *Address:* European Commission, 1049 Brussels, Belgium. *T:* (322) 2958658.

FAULL, Very Rev. Vivienne Frances; Dean of Leicester, since 2000; *b* 20 May 1955; *d* of William Baines Faull and Pamela June Faull (*née* Dell); *m* 1993, Dr Michael Duddridge. *Educ:* Queen's Sch., Chester; St Hilda's Coll., Oxford; St John's Coll., Nottingham; Open Univ. Teacher, N India, 1977–79; youth worker, Everton, 1979. Ordained deaconess, 1982, deacon, 1987, priest, 1994; Deaconess, St Matthew and St James, Mossley Hill, 1982–85; Chaplain: Clare Coll., Cambridge, 1985–90; Gloucester Cathedral, 1990–94; Canon Pastor, 1994–2000, Vice Provost, 1995–2000, Coventry Cathedral. Mem., Gen. Synod of C of E, 2003–. *Address:* 21 St Martin's, Leicester LE1 5DE.

FAURE WALKER, Rev. Edward William; Vice Lord-Lieutenant, Hertfordshire, since 2001; farmer; Assistant Curate, All Saints, Pin Green, Stevenage, since 2004; *b* 14 Sept. 1946; *s* of Lt Col Henry W. Faure Walker and Elizabeth A. C. Faure Walker (*née* Fordham); *m* 1974, Louise Mary Robinson; two *s* one *d*. *Educ:* Eton; RMA, Sandhurst; St Albans and Oxford Ministry Course. Commnd Coldstream Guards, 1966–74 (C-in-C's Commendation for Courage and Leadership 1971). Farmer at Sandon Bury, 1974–. Chm., 1980–2000, Pres., 2000–, Herts Assoc. for Young People; Trustee, UK Youth, 1998–2007. Chm., Boxworth Exptl Husbandry Farm, 1988–93. Ordained deacon, 2004, priest, 2005. Agricl Chaplain for Herts, 2006–. Hon. Col, Herts ACF, 2002–. DL 1985, High Sheriff 2000–01, Herts. *Recreations:* country sports, mountaineering, reading, travelling, being at home with family. *Address:* Sandon Bury, Sandon, Buntingford, Herts SG9 0QY. *T:* (01763) 287224. *Club:* Alpine.

FAUSET, Ian David, CB 2002; aerospace consultant; *b* 8 Dec. 1943; *s* of late George William Fauset and Margaret Fauset (*née* Davies); *m* 1972, Susan, *d* of Donald and Gwendolen Best; two *s* one *d*. *Educ:* Chester City Grammar Sch.; King Edward VI Sch., Lichfield; University of London (BSc); UCW Aberystwyth (Dip. Statistics). CEng, FRAeS. Dept of Chief Scientist (RAF), MoD, 1968–78; Head of Air Studies, Defence Optl Analysis Orgn, Germany, 1978–82; fast jet aircraft and helicopter projects, MoD (PE), 1982–87; Civilian Management (Specialists), MoD, 1987–89; Project Dir, Tornado Aircraft, 1989, EH 101 Helicopter, 1989–91, MoD (PE); Asst Under-Sec. of State, Civilian Mgt (Personnel), MoD, 1991–96; Dir Gen. Aircraft Systems, MoD (PE), 1996–99; Exec. Dir, Defence Procurement Agency, MoD, 1999–2003. Non-exec. Dir, GEC Avery, 1991–94. *Recreations:* bridge, tennis, squash. *Club:* Royal Air Force.

FAVELL, Anthony Rowland; solicitor; *b* 29 May 1939; *s* of Arnold Rowland Favell and Hildegard Favell; *m* 1966, Susan Rosemary Taylor; one *s* one *d*. *Educ:* St Bees School, Cumbria; Sheffield University (LLB). MP (C) Stockport, 1983–92; PPS to Rt Hon. John Major, MP, 1986–90. Contested (C) Stockport, 1992. Chm., Tameside and Glossop Acute Services NHS Trust, 1993–97. Part-time Chairman: Mental Health Review Tribunals, 1995–; FHSA Appeal Tribunals, 1996–2002; Mem., Criminal Injuries Appeal Panel, 2000–. Member: High Peak BC, 2007–; Peak Dist Nat. Park Authy, 2007–. *Recreations:* music, gardening, hill walking, dry stone walling. *Address:* Skinners Hall, Edale, Hope Valley S33 7ZE. *T:* (01433) 670281. *Club:* Lansdowne.

FAWCETT, Amelia Chilcott, CBE 2002; Chairman, Pensions First LLP, since 2007; *b* 16 Sept. 1956; *d* of Frederick John Fawcett, II and Betsey Sargent Chilcott. *Educ:* Pingree Sch., Mass; Wellesley Coll. (BA 1978); Univ. of Virginia Sch. of Law (JD 1983). Admitted to New York Bar, 1984. Sullivan & Cromwell: NY, 1983–85; Paris, 1986–87; Morgan Stanley International, 1987–2007: Vice Pres., 1990; Exec. Dir, 1992; Man. Dir and Chief Admin Officer, 1996–2002; Mem., Eur. Exec. Cttee, 1996–2007; Vice Chm. and Chief Operating Officer, 2002–07. Non-executive Director: State St Corp., Boston, 2006–; Guardian Media Gp plc, 2007–. Mem. Court, Bank of England, 2004– (Chm., Audit Cttee, 2005–). Chm., Financial Services Subcttee, Amer. Chamber of Commerce, Brussels, 1995–96. Member: Competitiveness Subcttee on Investment, DTI, 1997–98; London Employers Coalition, 1998–2002; Practitioner Forum, FSA, 1998–2001; Competitiveness Council, DTI, 1999–2000; New Deal Task Force, 1999–2001; Dep. Chm., Nat. Employment Panel, 2001–04. Member: Adv. Bd, Community Links, 1992–2001; Board of Directors: Bright Red Dot Foundn, 1998–2001; London First, 1997–2002; BITC, 2005–. Trustee: Nat. Portrait Gall., 2003– (Chm., Develt Bd, 2002–; Dep. Chm., 2005–); Nat. Maritime Mus., Cornwall, 2004–06. Chm., London Internat. Fest. of Theatre, 2002–; Dir, Spitalfields Fest., 1998–2001. Mem. Council, Univ. of London, 2002– (Chm., Audit Cttee, 2003–). Hon. DIB American Univ., Richmond, 2006. Prince of Wales' Ambassador Award, 2004. *Recreations:* fly fishing, hill walking, sailing. *Address:* Pensions First LLP, 90 Long Acre, WC2E 9RA. *T:* (020) 7849 3496, *Fax:* (020) 7225 5021; *e-mail:* amelia@acfawcett.com. *Clubs:* Reform, Walbrook; Cradoc Golf; St Mawes Sailing.

FAWCETT, Prof. James William, PhD; FRCP; Chairman, Cambridge University Centre for Brain Repair, since 2001, and Merck Company Professor of Experimental Neurology, since 2002, University of Cambridge; Fellow, since 1986, and Director of Studies in Medicine, since 1999, King's College, Cambridge; *b* 13 March 1950; *s* of Edward Fawcett and Jane Fawcett; *m* 1980, Kay-Tee Khaw, *qv*; one *s* one *d*. *Educ:* Westminster Sch.; Balliol Coll., Oxford, (BA 1972); St Thomas's Hospital Med. Sch. (MB BS 1975); PhD London Univ. 1982. MRCP 1979, FRCP 2000. House Surgeon, St Thomas' Hosp., 1976; House Physician, Addenbrooke's Hosp., 1977; SHO Intensive Care, St Thomas' Hosp., 1977–78; SHO Immunology, Northwick Park Hosp., 1978–79; Scientist, NIMR, London, 1979–82; Asst Prof., Salk Inst., La Jolla, 1982–86; Lectr in Physiol., Cambridge Univ., 1986–2001. FMedSci 2003. *Publications:* (jtly) Formation and Regeneration of Nerve Connections, 1992; (jtly) Brain Damage, Brain Repair, 2002. *Recreations:* bagpiping, sailing, old machinery. *Address:* Cambridge University Centre for Brain Repair, Robinson Way, Cambridge CB2 2PY. *T:* (01223) 331160; *e-mail:* JF108@cam.ac.uk. *Clubs:* Pinstripe Highlanders; Brancaster Staithe Sailing.

FAWCETT, John Harold, CMG 1986; HM Diplomatic Service, retired; *b* 4 May 1929; *yr s* of late Comdr Harold William Fawcett, OBE, RN, and of late Una Isobel Dalrymple Fawcett (*née* Gairdner); *m* 1st, 1961, Elizabeth Shaw (*d* 2002); one *s*; 2nd, 2004, Linda Garnett. *Educ:* Radley (Scholar); University Coll., Oxford (Scholar). 1st cl. Hon. Mods 1951, 2nd cl. Lit. Hum. 1953. Nat. Service, RN (Radio Electrician's Mate), 1947–49. British Oxygen Co., 1954–63 (S Africa, 1955–57). Entered Foreign Service, 1963; FO, 1963–66; 1st Sec. (Commercial), Bombay, 1966–69; 1st Sec. and Head of Chancery, Port-of-Spain, 1969–70; Asst, Caribbean Dept, FCO, 1971–72; Head of Icelandic Fisheries Unit, Western European Dept, FCO, 1973; Amb. to Democratic Republic of Vietnam, 1974; Counsellor and Head of Chancery, Warsaw, 1975–78; Dep. High Comr, Wellington, 1978–86; Counsellor (Commercial and Economic, 1978–83, Political and Economic, 1983–86), and Head of Chancery 1983–86, Wellington; Amb. to Bulgaria, 1986–89. Mem., 1998–2002, Chm., 2000–02, Dent Parish Council. Mem., 1989–94, Lay Chm., 1994–99, Ewecross Deanery Synod, dio. of Bradford. Trustee: Bradford Dio. Church Buildings Fund, 1996–99; Sedbergh and Dist Community Trust, 1998–2005. Chm., Morecambe Bay Gp, CS Pensioners' Alliance, 1994–2000. Clerk, 1989–94, Chm. of Govs, 1994–2001, Dent Grammar Sch. Educnl Foundn; Governor, Dent C of E Primary Sch., 1994–99. Pres., Dent CC, 2001–05. *Recreations:* gardening, collecting books, mathematical models. *Address:* Strait End, Dent, Cumbria LA10 5QL. *Clubs:* Savile, MCC; Wellington Racing (Wellington); Royal Bombay Yacht.

FAWCETT, Kay-Tee; *see* Khaw, Kay-Tee.

FAWCUS, Maj.-Gen. Graham Ben, CB 1991; Chief of Staff and Head of UK Delegation, Live Oak, SHAPE, 1989–91, retired; *b* 17 Dec. 1937; *s* of late Col Geoffrey Arthur Ross Fawcus, RE and Helen Sybil Graham (*née* Stronach); *m* 1966, Diana Valerie, *d* of Dr P. J. Spencer-Phillips of Bildeston, Suffolk; two *s* one *d*. *Educ:* Wycliffe College; RMA Sandhurst (Sword of Honour); King's College, Cambridge (BA 1963, MA 1968). Commissioned RE, 1958; served UK, Cyprus, BAOR, MoD; OC 39 Field Squadron RE, BAOR, 1973–74; MoD, 1975–76; GSO1 (DS), Staff College, 1977–78; CO 25 Engineer Regt, BAOR, 1978–81; Cabinet Office, 1981; Comdt, RSME, 1982–83; ACOS, HQ 1 (Br) Corps, 1984–85; Chief, Jt Services Liaison Orgn, Bonn, 1986–89. Col Comdt RE, 1991–2000. Chm., RE Widows Soc., 1992–2000. Chm., Ipswich & Suffolk Small Business Assoc., 1996–99. Gov., 1995–2006, Chm. of Govs, 2006–, Wycliffe Coll. *Recreations:* ski-ing, tennis, Scottish country dancing, furniture restoration, bridge. *Address:* Flowton Hall, Flowton, Ipswich, Suffolk IP8 4LH.

FAWCUS, His Honour Simon James David; a Circuit Judge, 1985–2003; *b* 12 July 1938; *s* of late Ernest Augustus Fawcus and of Jill Shaw; *m* 1966, Joan Mary (*née* Oliphant); one *s* four *d*. *Educ:* Aldenham Sch.; Trinity Hall, Cambridge (MA). Called to the Bar, Gray's Inn, 1961; in practice on Northern Circuit, 1962–85; a Recorder, 1980–85. Pres., Council of Circuit Judges, 1996. *Recreations:* real tennis and other lesser sporting activities, music (listening). *Address:* Marton Oak House, Oak Lane, Marton, Macclesfield SK11 9HE. *Clubs:* MCC; Manchester Tennis and Racquet, Big Four (Manchester); Circuit Judges Golfing Soc.; Wilmslow Golf.

FAWKES, Wally; cartoonist, 1945–2005; *b* 21 June 1924; *m* 1st, 1949, Sandra Boyce-Carmichele (marr. diss. 1964; she *d* 2005); one *s* two *d* (and one *d* decd); 2nd, 1965, Susan Clifford; one *s* one *d*. *Educ:* Sidcup Central Sch.; Sidcup Sch. of Art; Camberwell Sch. of Art. Came from Vancouver, BC, to England, 1931. Joined Daily Mail, 1945; started Flook strip, 1949, transferred to The Mirror, 1984. Political cartoons for: Spectator, 1959; Private Eye, and New Statesman, 1965; Observer, 1965–95; Punch, 1971–92; Today, 1986–87; London Daily News, 1987; Times mag., 1995–96; Sunday Telegraph, 1996–2005; cartoons for Daily Express, 1994; caricatures for Oldie mag., 1996–2005; covers for The Week, 1997. Co-Founder, Humphrey Lyttelton Band, 1948. Hon. DLitt Kent, 2001. Cartoonist of the Year, British Press Awards, 2004. *Publications:* World of Trog, 1977; Trog Shots, 1984; Trog: 40 Graphic Years, 1987; collections of Flook strips. *Recreations:* playing jazz (clarinet and soprano saxophone), cooking, cricket. *Address:* 8 Glenhurst Avenue, NW5 1PS. *T:* (020) 7267 2979.

FAY, Dr Christopher Ernest, CBE 1999; FREng; Chairman: Expro International Group plc, since 1999; Tuscan Energy Group Ltd, 2002–05; *b* 4 April 1945; *s* of Harry Thomas Fay and Edith Margaret Fay (*née* Messenger); *m* 1971, Jennifer Olive Knight; one *s* two *d*. *Educ:* Leeds Univ. (BSc Civil Eng. 1967; PhD 1970). CEng 1974; FICE 1994 (MICE 1973; Hon. FICE 1998); FEI (FInstPet 1994); FREng (FEng 1996). Joined Shell Internat. Petroleum Co., 1970, as offshore design engr; Shell-BP Develt Co., Nigeria, 1971–74; Head, Engrg Planning and Design and Offshore Construction, Sarawak Shell Berhad, Malaysia, 1974–78; Develt Manager, Dansk Undergrunds Consortium, Copenhagen, on secondment from Dansk Shell, 1978–81; Technical Manager, Norske Shell Exploration and Production, Stavanger, 1981–84; Dir, Exploration and Production, Norway, 1984–86; Gen. Manager and Chief Exec., Shell Cos, Turkey, 1986–89; Man. Dir, Shell UK Exploration and Production and a Man. Dir, Shell UK, 1989–93; Chm. and Chief Exec., Shell UK, 1993–98. Chm., Brightside plc, 2008–; non-executive Director: BAA, 1998–2006; Stena Internat., 1999– (Chm.); Stena Drilling Ltd, 1999–; Anglo American plc, 1999–; Weir Gp plc, 2001–03; Conister Financial Gp plc, 2006–; Iofina plc, 2008–. Chm., Adv. Cttee on Business and the Envmt, 1999–2003. Member: CBI President's Cttee, 1993–98; INSEAD UK Cttee, 1993–95; British Cttee, Det. Norske Veritas, 1994–95 and 1996–2001; Bd, Oil, Gas and Petrochemicals Supplies (formerly Oil and Gas Projects and Supplies) Office, 1994–98; Exec. Cttee, British Energy Assoc., 1994–98; Chm., Oil Industries Emergency Cttee, 1993–98. Gov., Motability, 1999–2001 (Mem. Council, 1993–98). CCMI (CIMgt 1994); FRSE 1996; FRSA 1994. *Recreations:* gardening, ski-ing, golf, tennis. *Address:* Merrifield, Links Road, Bramley, Guildford GU5 0AL. *Clubs:* Sunningdale Golf, Bramley Golf.

FAY, His Honour Edgar Stewart; QC 1956; FCIArb; a Circuit Judge (formerly an Official Referee of the Supreme Court of Judicature), 1971–80; *b* 8 Oct. 1908; *s* of late Sir Sam Fay; *m* 1st, Kathleen Margaret, *e d* of late C. H. Buell, Montreal, PQ, and Brockville, Ont; three *s*; 2nd, Jenny Julie Henriette (*d* 1990), *yr d* of late Dr Willem Roosegaarde Bisschop, Lincoln's Inn; one *s*; 3rd, Eugenia Bishop, *yr d* of late Piero Biganzoli, Milan. *Educ:* Courtenay Lodge Sch.; McGill Univ.; Pembroke Coll., Cambridge (MA). FCIArb 1981. Called to Bar, Inner Temple, 1932; Master of the Bench, 1962. Recorder: of Andover, 1954–61; of Bournemouth, 1961–64; of Plymouth, 1964–71; Dep. Chm., Hants QS, 1960–71. Member: Bar Council, 1955–59, 1966–70; Senate of Four Inns of Court, 1970–72. Chm., Inquiry into Crown Agents, 1975–77. *Publications:* Why Piccadilly?, 1935; Londoner's New York, 1936; Discoveries in the Statute Book, 1937; The Life of Mr Justice Swift, 1939; Official Referees' Business, 1983. *Address:* 95 Highgate West Hill, N6 6NR. *T:* (020) 8348 5780.

FAY, Sir (Humphrey) Michael (Gerard), Kt 1990; Principal, Fay, Richwhite & Co. Ltd, Merchant Bankers, since 1974 (Joint Chief Executive, 1990–96); *b* 10 April 1949; *s* of James and Margaret Fay; *m* 1983, Sarah Williams; one *s* two *d*. *Educ:* St Patrick's Coll., Silverstream, Wellington; Victoria Univ., Wellington (LLB 1971). Jt Chief Exec., Capital Markets, 1986–90; Dir, Bank of New Zealand, 1989–92. Chairman: Australia/NZ Bicentennial Commn, 1988; Expo 1988 Commn, 1987–88; Expo 1992 Commn, 1989–; NZ Ireland Fund, 1995–98. Hon. Consul General for Thailand, 1996–98. Chm., NZ Americas Cup Challenges, 1987, 1988, 1992. Chm., Manu Samoa Rugby Club, 1997–. *Recreations:* horse breeding and racing, fishing, swimming, running, golf. *Clubs:* Royal New Zealand Yacht Squadron, Auckland Racing, Mercury Bay Boating.

FAY, Margaret, OBE 2004; Chairman, One NorthEast, since 2003; *b* 21 May 1949; *d* of Oswald and Joan Allen; *m* 1st, 1968, Matthew Stoker (marr. diss. 1978); one *s*; 2nd, 1982, Peter Fay (marr. diss. 1993). *Educ:* South Shields Grammar Sch. for Girls. Joined Tyne Tees TV, 1981; Dir of Ops, 1995–97; Man. Dir, 1997–2003. Dir, Newcastle Gateshead Initiative, 1999–; non-exec. Dir, Darlington Building Soc., 2000–. Gov., Teesside Univ., 1998–. *Recreations:* travel, theatre, wine. *Address:* One NorthEast, Stella House, Goldcrest Way, Newburn Riverside, Newcastle upon Tyne NE15 8NY. *T:* (0191) 229 6200.

FAY, Sir Michael; *see* Fay, Sir H. M. G.

FAY, Stephen Francis John; journalist and author; *b* 14 Aug. 1938; *s* of Gerard Fay and Alice (*née* Bentley); *m* 1964, Prudence Butcher; one *s* one *d*. *Educ:* Highgate Sch.; Univ. of New Brunswick, Canada (BA, MA). On editl staff: Glasgow Herald, 1961–64; Sunday Times, 1964–84; freelance writer, 1984–86, 1991–96; Ed., Business Mag., 1986–89; Dep. Ed., Independent on Sunday, 1989–91 and 1996–99; Ed., Wisden Cricket Monthly, 2000–03. *Publications:* Measure for Measure: reform in the Trade Unions, 1970; The Great Silver Bubble, 1980; The Ring: anatomy of an opera, 1984; Portrait of an Old Lady: turmoil at the Bank of England, 1987; Power Play: the life and times of Peter Hall, 1995; The Collapse of Barings, 1996; Tom Graveney at Lords, 2005. *Recreations:* theatre, galleries, watching sport. *Address:* 5A Furlong Road, N7 8LS. *T:* (020) 7607 8950, *Fax:* (020) 7619 9667; *e-mail:* sfay@cseisp.co.uk. *Clubs:* Garrick, Beefsteak, MCC.

FAYERS, Norman Owen; City Treasurer and Director of Financial Services, Bristol City Council, 1990–96; *b* 8 Jan. 1945; *s* of Claude Lance Fayers and Winifred Joyce (*née* Reynolds); *m* 1966, Patricia Ann Rudd; two *s*. *Educ:* Northgate Grammar Sch. for Boys, Ipswich; BA Open Univ. CPFA 1967; IRRV 1990; FMAAT 1999. Ipswich CBC, 1961–66; Eastbourne CBC, 1966–70; Group Accountant (Educn), Royal Borough of Kingston upon Thames, 1970–73; Chief Accountant, RBK & C, 1973–77; Chief Officer, Finance, London Borough of Ealing, 1977–90. Chartered Institute of Public Finance and Accountancy: Mem. Council, 1991–92; Pres., S Wales and W England Reg., 1993–95 (Vice Pres., 1991–93); Association of Accounting Technicians: Mem. Council, 1992–2001, 2004–07; Chm., Bristol Br., 2000–03. *Recreations:* golf, music, bridge. *Clubs:* Rotary (Bristol; Pres., 2008–June 2009); Kendleshire Golf.

FAYRER, Sir John (Lang Macpherson), 4th Bt *cr* 1896; Research Officer, University of Edinburgh, 1995–2001; *b* 18 Oct. 1944; *s* of Sir Joseph Herbert Spens Fayrer, 3rd Bt, DSC, and Helen Diana Scott (*d* 1961), *d* of late John Lang; *S* father, 1976. *Educ:* Edinburgh Academy; Scottish Hotel School, Univ. of Strathclyde. Res. Officer, Moray House Inst., 1991–95. *Publications:* Child Development from Birth to Adolescence, 1992; ed reports of Scotplay confs, 1993, 1994. *Heir:* none. *Address:* 21/2 Lady Nairne Crescent, Edinburgh EH8 7PE.

FAZIO, Antonio; Governor, Bank of Italy, 1993–2005; *b* 11 Oct. 1936; *m* Maria Cristina Rosati; one *s* four *d*. *Educ:* Univ. of Rome (BSc *summa cum laude* Econs and Business 1960); MIT. Asst Prof. of Demography, Univ. of Rome, 1961–66; Consultant to Res. Dept, Bank of Italy, 1961–66; Bank of Italy: Dep. Head, subseq. Head, Unit of Econometric Res., 1966–72; Dep. Dir, Monetary Sector, 1972, Head, 1973–79, Res. Dept; Central Manager for Economic Res., 1980–82; Dep. Dir Gen., 1982–93. Chm., Italian Foreign Exchange Office, 1993–2005; Member: Bd of Dirs, BIS, 1993–2005; Governing Council, Eur. Central Bank (formerly Eur. Monetary Inst.), 1993–2005. Hon. Dr Econs and Business Bari, 1994; Hon. DHL Johns Hopkins, 1995; Hon. Dr Pol Sci. Macerata, 1996; Hon. LLB Cassino, 1999; Hon. Dr Stats and Econs Milan, 1999; Hon. Dr Computer Engrg Lecce, 2000; Hon. Dr Banking Econs Verona, 2002; Hon. LLD St John's, 2002; Hon. DPhil Catania, 2002. Ezio Tarantelli Prize for most original theory in Economic Policy, 1995; Saint Vincent Prize for Economics, 1997; Pico della Mirandola Prize for Econs, Finance and Business, 1997–98; Internat. Award in the Humanities, Accad. di Studi Mediterranei, 1999; Keynes-Sraffa Prize, London, 2003. Kt Grand Cross, Order of Merit (Italy), 1993. *Publications:* scientific articles, mainly on monetary theory and monetary policy issues. *Address:* c/o Bank of Italy, Via Nazionale 91, 00184 Rome, Italy.

FEACHEM, Sir Richard (George Andrew), KBE 2007 (CBE 1995); PhD, DSc (Med); FREng; Professor of Global Health, University of California, San Francisco and Berkeley, and Director, Global Health Group, since 2007; *b* 10 April 1947; *s* of Charles George Paulin Feachem and Margaret Flora Denise Greenhow; *m* 1st, 1970, Zuzana Sedlarova (marr. diss. 1999); one *s* one *d*; 2nd, 1999, Neelam Sekhri. *Educ:* Wellington Coll.; Univ. of Birmingham (BSc 1969); Univ. of NSW (PhD 1974); DSc (Med) London, 1991. MICE 1980; FIWEM 1987; FICE 1990; FREng (FEng 1994). Volunteer, Solomon Is, 1965–66; Research Fellow: Univ. of NSW, 1970–74; Univ. of Birmingham, 1974–76; London School of Hygiene and Tropical Medicine: Lectr and Sen. Lectr, 1976–82; Reader, 1983–87; Prof. of Tropical Envmtl Health, 1987–95; Dean, 1989–95; Dir, Health, Nutrition and Population, World Bank, 1995–99; Prof. of Internat. Health, Univ. of Calif, San Francisco and Berkeley, and founding Dir, Inst. for Global Health; 1999–2002; founding Exec. Dir, Global Fund to Fight AIDS, Tuberculosis and Malaria, and Under Sec.-Gen., UN, 2002–07 (on leave of absence). Vis. Prof., LSHTM, 1995–; Adjunct Professor: Johns Hopkins Univ., 1996–2001; George Washington Univ., 1997–2001; Hon. Prof., Univ. of Qld, 2005–. Consultant, WHO, 1982–83; Principal Public Health Specialist, World Bank, 1988–89; Chairman: Adv. Cttee, World Develt Report, 1992–93; Adv. Cttee, TB Programme, WHO, 1992–95; Bd, Initiative on Public Private Partnerships for Health, 2000–02; Bd, Global Forum for Health Res., 2001–04; Member: Adv. Cttee, Caribbean Epidemiology Centre, 1990–95; Mgt Cttee, Inst. of Child Health, 1989–91; Bd on Internat. Health, US NAS, 1992–97, 2001–03; Bd, Internat. AIDS Vaccine Initiative, 1996–2003; Adv. Cttee, Aust. Nat. Centre for Epidemiology and Public Health, 1996–2001; Commn on Macroeconomics and Health, 2000–02; Commn on HIV/AIDS and Governance in Africa, 2003–. Member Council: RSTM&H, 1978–81; VSO, 1991–; Water Aid, 1994–95; Patron, Assoc. for Promotion of Healthcare in former Soviet Union, 1992–96. Trustee, Internat. Centre for Diarrhoeal Diseases Research, Bangladesh, 1985–89. Mem., Inst. of Medicine, 2002. Hon. FFPH (Hon. FFPHM 1990); Hon. Fellow, LSHTM, 2000. Dean's Medal, Johns Hopkins Sch. of Public Health, 2003. Member, Editorial Board: Transactions of the RSTM&H, 1979–88; Jl of Tropical Medicine and Hygiene, 1979–96; Current Issues in Public Health, 1993–2002; Health and Human Rights, 1993–2002; Tropical Medicine and Internat. Health, 1996–2001; Global Public Health, 2005–; Editor-in-Chief, WHO Bulletin, 1999–2002. *Publications:* Water, Wastes and Health in Hot Climates, 1977; Subsistence and Survival: rural ecology in the Pacific, 1977; Water, Health and Development, 1978; Evaluation for Village Water Supply Planning, 1980; Sanitation and Disease, 1983; Environmental Health Engineering in the Tropics, 1983; Evaluating Health Impact, 1986; Disease and Mortality in Sub-Saharan Africa, 1991; The Health of Adults in the Developing World, 1992; over 160 papers in scientific jls. *Recreations:* mountaineering, ski-ing. *Club:* Travellers.

FEAN, Sir (Thomas) Vincent, KCVO 2005; HM Diplomatic Service; Ambassador to Libya, since 2006; *b* 20 Nov. 1952; *s* of Joseph Peter Fean and Brigid Fean (*née* Walsh); *m* 1978, Anne Stewart; one *s* two *d*. *Educ:* St Theodore's RC Secondary Sch., Burnley; Sheffield Univ. (BA French and German 1975). Joined FCO, 1975; Second Sec., Baghdad, 1978; First Sec., Damascus, 1979–82; EU and Berlin issues, FCO, 1982–85; UK Repn to EU, Brussels, 1985–89; Personnel Mgt Dept, FCO, 1989–92; Counsellor, Press and Public Affairs, Paris, 1992–96; Head, Counter-Terrorism Policy Dept, FCO, 1996–99; Dir, Asia Pacific, Internat. Gp, Trade Partners UK, 1999–2002; High Comr, Malta, 2002–06. *Recreations:* supporting Burnley FC and Lancashire CCC, travel, walking, cycling, folk music. *Address:* c/o Foreign and Commonwealth Office, SW1A 2AH; *e-mail:* Vincent.Fean@fco.gov.uk. *Club:* Burnley Football.

FEARN, family name of **Baron Fearn**.

FEARN, Baron *cr* 2001 (Life Peer), of Southport in the County of Merseyside; **Ronald Cyril Fearn, (Ronnie),** OBE 1985; *b* 6 Feb. 1931; *s* of James Fearn and Martha Ellen Fearn; *m* 1955, Joyce Edna Dugan; one *s* one *d*. *Educ:* King George V Grammar School. FCIB. Banker with Williams Deacons Bank, later Williams & Glyn's Bank, later Royal Bank of Scotland. MP (L 1987–88, LibDem 1988–92 and 1997–2001) Southport; contested (Lib Dem) Southport, 1992. Lib Dem spokesman on health and tourism, 1988–89, on local govt, 1989–90, on transport, housing and tourism, 1990–92. Mem., Select Cttee on Culture, Media and Sport, 1997–2001. Councillor, Sefton MBC, 1974–. *Recreations:* badminton, amateur dramatics, athletics. *Address:* House of Lords, SW1A 0PW; Norcliffe, 56 Norwood Avenue, Southport, Merseyside PR9 7EQ. *T:* (01704) 228577.

FEARN, John Martin, CB 1976; Secretary, Scottish Education Department, 1973–76, retired; *b* 24 June 1916; *s* of William Laing Fearn and Margaret Kerr Fearn; *m* 1947, Isobel Mary Begbie, MA, MB, ChB (*d* 2006); one *d*. *Educ:* High Sch. of Dundee; Univ. of St Andrews; Worcester Coll., Oxford. Indian Civil Service, Punjab, 1940–47; District Magistrate, Lahore, 1946; Scottish Home Dept, 1947; Under-Sec., 1966; Under-Sec., Scottish Educn Dept, 1968. Chairmen's Panel, CSSB, 1977–85. *Recreation:* golf. *Address:* 10/8 St Margaret's Place, Edinburgh EH9 1AY. *T:* (0131) 447 5301. *Club:* New (Edinburgh).

FEARNLEY, David; Vice Lord-Lieutenant, West Yorkshire, 1992–2001; *b* 20 Dec. 1924; *s* of late Wilfred Fearnley and Elizabeth (*née* Walker); *m* 1947, Patricia Bentley; one *s* one *d*. *Educ:* Pocklington Sch., York; Univs of Bradford and Leeds. Served RN, War of 1939–45. Joined family firm, Walter Walker & Sons Ltd, 1945; Dir, 1955; Man. Dir, 1960; co. purchased by Allied Textiles, 1971; Dir, Allied Textiles plc, 1971–99. Chm., Louis Latour Ltd, 1990–; Director: WW Gp Ltd, 1990–99; Sharrow Bay Hotel, 1999–2004. Gen. Comr of Inland Revenue, Wakefield Div., 1973–2000 (Chm., 1987–99). Mem. Bd, Wakefield Prison, 1979–94. Fellow, Woodard Corp., 1989–95. High Sheriff, W Yorks, 1982–83. *Recreations:* fell walking, wine, tennis (playing), Rugby football (watching). *Address:* The Grange, Hopton, Mirfield, W Yorks WF14 8EL. *Club:* Garrick.

FEARNLEY-WHITTINGSTALL, Hugh Christopher Edmund; writer, broadcaster, cook and food campaigner, since 1989; *b* 14 Jan. 1965; *s* of Robert and Jane Fearnley-Whittingstall; *m* 2001, Marie Derôme; two *s*. *Educ:* Eton Coll.; St Peter's Coll., Oxford (BA Hons Philos. and Psychol.). Sous chef, River Cafe, 1989; journalist: Punch, 1989–92; Sunday Times, 1990–92; Daily Telegraph, 1993–98; Independent on Sunday, 2000–02; Observer, 2002–. Television includes series: Escape to River Cottage, 1998–99; Return to River Cottage, 2000; River Cottage Forever, 2002; Beyond River Cottage, 2004; The View from River Cottage, 2005. Mem., Devon Cattle Breeders' Assoc., 2004–. *Publications:* A Cook on the Wild Side, 1995; The River Cottage Cookbook, 2001; The River Cottage Year, 2003; The River Cottage Meat Book, 2004; The River Cottage Family Cookbook, 2005; Hugh Fearlessly Eats It All, 2007. *Recreations:* fishing, diving, growing vegetables, charcuterie. *Address:* c/o Antony Topping, Greene & Heaton, 37 Goldhawk Road, W12 8QQ. *Club:* Century.

FEARON, Prof. Douglas Thomas, MD; FRS 1999; FRCP; Sheila Joan Smith Professor of Immunology, University of Cambridge, since 2003; Fellow, Trinity College, Cambridge, since 2001; *b* 16 Oct. 1942; *s* of late Dr Henry Dana Fearon and of Frances Hudson (*née* Eubanks); *m* 1st, 1972, Margaret Andrews (marr. diss. 1975); 2nd, 1977, Clare MacIntyre (*née* Wheless); one *s* one *d*. *Educ:* Williams Coll. (BA 1964); Johns Hopkins Med. Sch. (MD 1968). FRCP 1994. Major, US Army Med. Corps, 1970–72 (Bronze Star and Army Commendation Medal, 1972). Med. Res., Johns Hopkins Hosp., 1968–70; Helen Hay Whitney Foundn Post-Doctoral Res. Fellow, 1974–77; Harvard Medical School: Res. Fellow in Medicine, 1972–75; Instr. in Medicine, 1975–76; Asst Prof., 1976–79, Associate Prof., 1979–84, Prof., 1984–87, of Medicine; Prof. of Medicine, and Director, Div. of Rheumatology and of Grad. Prog. in Immunology, Johns Hopkins Univ. Sch. of Medicine, 1987–93; Wellcome Trust Prof. of Medicine, Univ. of Cambridge, 1993–2003. Principal Res. Fellow, Wellcome Trust, 1993–; Hon. Consultant in Medicine, Addenbrooke's Hosp., 1993–. Member: Scientific Adv. Bd, Babraham Inst., 1998; Scientific Bd, Ludwig Inst. for Cancer Res., 1998–; Scientific Adv. Bd, Max Planck Institut für Immunobiologie, 2001; Scientific Adv. Cttee, Rita Allen Foundn, 2002–. Member: EMBO, 2001; NAS, USA, 2002; Hon. For. Mem., Amer. Acad. of Arts and Scis, 1999. Founder FMedSci 1998. Hon. MA Harvard, 1984. Merit Award, NIH, 1991. *Publications:* articles on immunology in learned jls. *Recreation:* golf. *Address:* Salix, Conduit Head Road, Cambridge CB3 0EY. *T:* (01223) 570067. *Club:* Country (Brookline, USA).

FEAST, Prof. William James, (Jim), CBE 2007; FRS 1996; CChem, FRSC; Courtaulds Professor of Polymer Chemistry, Durham University, 1989–2003, now Emeritus Professor; *b* 25 June 1938; *s* of William Edward Feast and Lucy Mary Feast (*née* Willis); *m* 1967, Jenneke Elizabeth Catherina van der Kuijl, Middleburg, Netherlands; two *d*. *Educ:* Sheffield Univ. (BSc 1960); Birmingham Univ. (PhD 1963). CChem, FRSC 1981; FIM 1994. Durham University: Lectr, 1965–76; Sen. Lectr, 1976–86; Prof., 1986–2003; Dir, IRC in Polymer Sci. and Technol., 1994–2002. Gillette Internation Res. Fellow, Leuven, Belgium, 1968–69; Vis. Prof., Max Planck Institut für Polymerforschungs, 1984–88. Pres., RSC, 2006–08. *Publications:* numerous res. papers, reviews in learned jls. *Recreations:* walking, gardening, theatre, fine arts. *Address:* Chemistry Department, Durham University, South Road, Durham DH1 3LE. *T:* (0191) 334 2105; *e-mail:* w.j.feast@durham.ac.uk.

FEATES, Prof. Francis Stanley, CB 1991; PhD; CEng, FIChemE; FRSC; CChem; Professor of Environmental Engineering, University of Manchester Institute of Science and Technology, 1991–95; *b* 21 Feb. 1932; *s* of Stanley James Feates and Dorothy Marguerite Jenny Feates (*née* Orford); *m* 1953, Gwenda Grace Goodchild; one *s* three *d*.

Educ: John Ruskin Sch., Croydon; Birkbeck Coll. London (BSc Special Chem.; PhD). FRSC 1972; FIChemE 1991; CEng 1991. Wellcome Res. Foundn, 1949–52; Chester-Beatty Cancer Res. Inst., Univ. of London, 1952–54. Chemistry Lectr, Goldsmiths' Coll., London, 1954–56; AERE, Harwell, UKAEA, 1956–78; Argonne Nat. Lab., Univ. of Chicago, Illinois, 1965–67; Department of the Environment: Dir, Nuclear Waste Management, 1978–83; Chief Radiochemical Inspector, 1983–86; Chief Inspector, Radioactive Substances, HM Inspectorate of Pollution, 1986–88; Dir and Chief Inspector, HM Inspectorate of Pollution, 1989–91. Consultant to EC (formerly EEC) on nuclear matters, 1991–. Director: Sir Alexander Gibb & Partners, 1991–94; Siemens Plessey Controls Ltd, 1991–92; Grundon Waste Management, 1991–92. Expert Mem., Scientific and Technical Cttee, EEC, Brussels, 1989–92; Member: Steering Cttee, Nuclear Energy Agency, OECD, Paris, 1988–91; Steering Bd, Lab. of Govt Chemist, 1991–94; Observer Mem., NRPB, 1988–91. Founder Editor, Jl of Hazardous Materials, 1975–85. *Publications:* Hazardous Materials Spills Handbook, 1982; Integrated Pollution Management, 1995; numerous scientific papers on pollution issues, nuclear power, electrochemistry, thermodynamics, waste management, electron microscopy. *Recreations:* walking, cycling, travel. *Address:* Rylands, 18 Mill Lane, Benson, Wallingford, Oxon OX10 6SA. *T:* (01491) 201180.

FEATHER, Prof. John Pliny, FCLIP; Professor of Information and Library Studies, since 1988, and Head, Department of Information Science (formerly Information and Library Studies), 1990–94 and 2003–06, Loughborough University; *b* 20 Dec. 1947; *m* 1971, Sarah, *d* of late Rev. A. W. Rees and Mrs S. M. Rees. *Educ:* Heath Sch., Halifax; Queen's Coll., Oxford (BLitt, MA); MA Cambridge, PhD Loughborough. FCLIP (FLA 1986). Asst Librarian, Bodleian Liby, Oxford, 1972–79; Munby Fellow in Bibliography, Cambridge Univ., 1977–78; Loughborough University: Lectr, then Sen. Lectr, 1979–88; Dean of Educn and Humanities, 1994–96; Pro-Vice-Chancellor, 1996–2000. Vis. Prof., UCLA, 1982. Pres., Oxford Bibliographical Soc., 1988–92. Mem., many nat. and internat. professional cttees; consultancy and teaching in many countries and for UNESCO, EEC and British Council, 1977–. FRSA 1994. *Publications:* The Provincial Book Trade in Eighteenth-Century England, 1985; A Dictionary of Book History, 1987; A History of British Publishing, 1988, 2nd edn 2005; Preservation and the Management of Library Collections, 1991, 2nd edn 1996; Index to Selected Bibliographical Journals 1971–1985, 1991; Publishing, Piracy and Politics: a history of copyright in the British book trade, 1994; The Information Society, 1994, 5th edn 2008; (with James Dearnley) The Wired World, 2001; Managing Preservation in Libraries and Archives, 2002; Publishing: communicating knowledge in the 21st century, 2003; articles and reviews in academic and professional jls, conf. procs, etc. *Recreations:* photography, music, travel, cooking. *Address:* 36 Farnham Street, Quorn, Leicestershire LE12 8DR. *Club:* Athenæum.

FEATHERBY, William Alan; QC 2008; a Recorder, since 2002; *b* Bristol, 16 May 1956; *s* of Joseph Alan Featherby and Patricia Annie Featherby (*née* Davies); *m* 1980, Clare Frances, JP, *d* of Ian Richard Posgate; five *s* five *d. Educ:* Ripley Court Sch., Ripley; Haileybury; Trinity Coll., Oxford (BA, Scholar). Called to the Bar, Middle Temple, 1978 (Astbury Law Scholar); practises in common law, esp. personal injury. Mem., Professional Conduct Cttee, Bar Council, 1995–2000. Mem., Southwark Dio. Synod, 2006–. *Publication:* A Yorkshire Furrow, 1992. *Recreations:* opera, Richard Strauss, reading, walking. *Address:* 12 King's Bench Walk, Temple, EC4Y 7EL. *Club:* Carlton.

FEATHERSTONE, Hugh Robert, CBE 1984 (OBE 1974); FCIS; Director-General, Freight Transport Association, 1969–84; *b* 31 March 1926; *s* of Alexander Brown Featherstone and Doris Olive Martin; *m* 1948, Beryl Joan Sly; one *s* one *d. Educ:* Minchenden Sch., Southgate, London. FCIS 1956. Served War, RNVR, 1943–46 (Sub-Lt). Assistant Secretary: Nat. Assoc. of Funeral Dirs, 1946–48; Brit. Rubber Develt Bd, 1948–58; Asst Sec. 1958–60, Sec. 1960–68, Traders Road Transport Assoc. *Publications:* contrib. to jls concerned with transport and admin. *Recreations:* golf, gardening, languages, travel, bridge, cookery.

FEATHERSTONE, Jane Elizabeth; Joint Managing Director, and Executive Producer, Kudos Film and Television, since 2002; *b* 24 March 1969; *d* of John Robert Featherstone and Elizabeth Ann Featherstone. *Educ:* Old Palace Sch., Croydon; Leeds Univ. (BA Jt Hons Hist. and German). PA, Paul Gascoigne Promotions, 1991–92; Producer: Hat Trick Prodns, 1992–95; United TV, 1995–97; Wall to Wall, 1998–99; Hd of Drama, Kudos Film and TV, 2000–02; Producer or Executive Producer: Touching Evil; Glasgow Kiss; Sex 'n' Death; Spooks (series 1–6); Hustle (series 1–4); Life on Mars (series 1–2); Tsunami, the Aftermath; Secret Life; Pleasureland; Wide Sargasso Sea; Ashes to Ashes. *Recreations:* family, friends, shops full of old things, ski-ing averagely, saying "quite frankly", good food and wine, the beach, wonderful writing. *Address:* c/o Kudos Film and Television, 12–14 Amwell Street, EC1R 1UQ. *T:* (020) 7812 3270.

FEATHERSTONE, Lynne (Choona); MP (Lib Dem) Hornsey and Wood Green, since 2005; *b* 20 Dec. 1951; *d* of Joseph and Gladys Ryness; *m* 1982, Stephen Featherstone (marr. diss. 2003); two *d. Educ:* South Hampstead High Sch.; Oxford Poly. (Dip. in Communications and Design). Various design posts, 1975–80; Man. Dir, own design co., Inhouse Outhouse Design, 1980–87; strategic design consultant, 1987–97. Dir, Ryness Electrical Supplies Ltd, 1991–2002. Member (Lib Dem): Haringey LBC, 1998– (Leader of the Opposition, 1998–2002); London Assembly, GLA, 2000–05. Lib Dem Shadow Sec. of State for Internat. Develt, 2006–; Lib Dem Spokesperson for Youth and Equalities, 2007–. Contested (LibDem) Hornsey and Wood Green, 2001. *Publication:* (as Lynne Choona Ryness) Marketing and Communication Techniques for Architects, 1992. *Recreations:* tennis, food, architecture, writing. *Address:* (office) 100 Uplands Road, N8 9BR. *T:* (020) 8340 5459.

FEATHERSTONE, Simon Mark; HM Diplomatic Service; Ambassador to Switzerland and to Liechtenstein, 2004–08; *b* 24 July 1958; *s* of David and Nora Featherstone; *m* 1981, Gail Teresa Salisbury; one *s* two *d. Educ:* Whitgift Sch., Croydon; Lincoln Coll., Oxford (BA Hons Law, MA). FCO, 1980; Chinese lang. trng, SOAS and Hong Kong, 1981–83; Second Sec., Peking, 1984; First Sec., FCO, 1987; on loan to Cabinet Office, 1988; First Sec. (Envmt), UK Perm. Rep. to EC, Brussels, 1990; Consul-Gen., Shanghai, 1994; Counsellor (Political), Peking, 1996; Hd, EU Dept (External), FCO, 1998–2003. *Recreations:* tennis, ski-ing, church activities. *Address:* c/o Foreign and Commonwealth Office, King Charles Street, SW1A 2AH.

FEATHERSTONE-WITTY, Mark; Founding Principal and Chief Executive Officer, Liverpool Institute for Performing Arts, since 1990; *b* 2 June 1946; *s* of Philip and Evy Featherstone-Witty; *m* 1972, Alison Thomas; one *s. Educ:* Univ. of Durham (BA, PGCE); Rollins Coll., Florida (MEd). Asst Ed., Macmillan Educnl Publishing, 1974–76; English teaching jobs in both private and maintained sector, 1976–80; Founder and Principal, Capital Coll., 1980–89; Chief Exec., London Sch. of Publishing, 1982–89; Co-founder and Principal, London Sch. of Insce, 1983–89; Co-founder, Rainbow Educn Prodns, 1983–86; Consultative Educn Ed., Quartet Books, 1984–86; Founder, and Sen. Educnl Advr, Brit Sch., 1989–91; Foundn Mem., Liverpool Coll., 2003–. Chair, Assoc. of Tutors, 1985–88. Founder Trustee, Schs for Performing Arts Trust, 1985–; Trustee: Liverpool

Royal Court Th. Foundn, 2000–; Nat. Acad. of Writing, 2003–; Mem. Bd, The Musi Lives Foundn, 2006–. Chm., Sefton Park Palm House Preservation Trust, 2004– *Publications:* Optimistic, Even Then, 2000; LIPA in Pictures: the first ten years, 2006 *Recreations:* reading comic crime books, entertainment, walking, projects. *Address* Liverpool Institute for Performing Arts, Mount Street, Liverpool L1 9HF. *T:* (0151) 33 3000; *e-mail:* m.featherstone-witty@lipa.ac.uk. *Club:* Lansdowne.

FEAVER, (Mary Frances) Clare; *see* Harvey, M. F. C.

FEAVER, William Andrew; writer, art critic and painter; *b* 1 Dec. 1942; *s* of Rt Rev Douglas Russell Feaver; *m* 1st, 1964, Victoria Turton (marr. diss.); one *s* three *d*; 2nd 1985, Andrea Rose; two *d. Educ:* St Albans School; Nottingham High School; Kebl College, Oxford. Teacher: South Stanley Boys' Modern Sch., Co. Durham, 1964–65 Newcastle Royal Grammar Sch., 1965–71; Sir James Knott Res. Fellow, Newcastl Univ., 1971–73; art critic: The Listener, 1971–75; Financial Times, 1974–75; art adviser Sunday Times Magazine, 1974–75; art critic, The Observer, 1975–98. Vis. Prof Nottingham Trent Univ., 1994–. Exhibitions curated include: George Cruikshank, V&A 1974; Thirties, Hayward Gall., 1979; The Ashington Gp, Beijing, 1980; Lucian Freuc Kendal, 1996, Tate Gall., and La Caixa, Barcelona, 2002, Mus. of Contemp. Art, LA 2002–03, Museo Correr, Venice, 2005; Michael Andrews: lights, Thyssen-Bornemisz Mus., Madrid, 2001; Michael Andrews, Tate Gall., 2001; John Constable, Grand Palais Paris, 2002. Trustee, Ashington Gp, 1989–. Critic of the Year, 1983, Commended, 1986 UK Press Awards. *Publications:* The Art of John Martin, 1975; When We Were Young 1976; Masters of Caricature, 1981; Pitmen Painters, 1988; James Boswell: unofficial wa artist, 2006; Lucian Freud, 2007. *Address:* 1 Rhodesia Road, SW9 9EJ. *T:* (020) 773 3386.

See also W. Horbury.

FEDDEN, (Adye) Mary, (Mrs J. O. Trevelyan), OBE 1997; RA 1992; RWA; painte *b* 14 Aug. 1915; *d* of Harry Vincent Fedden and Ida Margaret Fedden; *m* 1951, Julian Otte Trevelyan, Sen. Hon. RA (*d* 1988). *Educ:* Badminton Sch., Bristol; Slade Sch. of A (Schol). Exhibns yearly in London and provinces, 1948–; paintings in collections of th Queen, Prince Hassan of Jordan, Tate Gall., city art galls in UK, NZ, Malta, USA, and i private collections in England and overseas. Tutor: Royal College of Art, 1956–64 Yehudi Menuhin Sch., 1964–74. Pres., Royal West of England Acad., 1984–88. Hon DLitt Bath, 1996. *Publications:* books illustrated: The Green Man, by Jane Gardam, 1998 Birds, introd. Mel Gooding, 1999; *relevant publication:* Mel Gooding, Mary Fedden, 1995 *Recreation:* reading. *Address:* Durham Wharf, Hammersmith Terrace, W6 9TS.

FEDOTOV, Yury Viktorovich; Ambassador of the Russian Federation to the Court o St James's, since 2005; *b* 14 Dec. 1947; *m* 1973, Elena Fedotova; one *s* one *d. Edu* Moscow State Inst. of Internat. Relns. Joined USSR Diplomatic Service, 1971; served Algeria, 1974–80; Ministry of For. Affairs, Moscow, 1980–83; India, 1983–88; Ministr of For. Affairs, Moscow, 1988–94; Dep. Perm. Rep., then Actg First Dep. Perm. Rep. o Russian Fedn to UN, NY, 1994–99; Ministry of For. Affairs, Moscow, 1999–2002; Dep Minister of Foreign Affairs, 2002–05. Order of Friendship (Russia); Distinguished Mem of Diplomatic Service (Russia). *Address:* Embassy of Russia, 13 Kensington Palac Gardens, W8 4QX. *T:* (020) 7229 3620, *Fax:* (020) 7225 5804. *Club:* Athenæum.

FEENY, Patrick; External Relations (formerly Communications) Director, Departmen for Culture, Media and Sport, since 2005; *b* 27 June 1965; *s* of Victor Foy Feeny and Joa Aïda (*née* Dunbar-Stuart); partner, Alan Davey, *qv. Educ:* St Brendan's Coll., Bristol; King Coll., London (BD 1987). Asst Press Sec., Prime Minister's Office, 1993–96; Press. Sec. DFID, 1996–98; Policy and Commns Manager, Social Exclusion Unit, Cabinet Office 1998–2000; Commns Advr, Teenage Pregnancy Unit, DoH, 2000–01; Hd of News DCMS, 2001–05. *Recreations:* music, theatre, books. *Address:* Department for Culture Media and Sport, 2–4 Cockspur Street, SW1Y 5DH. *Club:* 2 Brydges.

FEESEY, Air Vice-Marshal John David Leonard, AFC 1977; retired, 1999; *b* 11 Oct 1942; *s* of Leonard Ewart Feesey and Maisie Veronica Lillian Feesey; *m* 1968, Glend Doris Barker; two *s. Educ:* Oldershaw Grammar Sch., Wallasey, Cheshire. RAF Office Cadet, 1961; commnd General Duties Br., 1962; RAF pilot (Hunter, Harrier), 1962–83 OC No 1 (Fighter) Sqdn (Harrier), 1983–86; Stn Comdr, RAF Wittering, 1986–88 Comnd Exec. Officer, HQ AAFCE, 1989–91; Dir Airspace Policy, 1991–93, Dir Gen Policy and Plans, 1993–96, HQ NATS; Dep. Comdr, Combined Air Ops Centre 4 1996–98. Vice-Pres., CCF Assoc., 1999–; Pres., No. 1 (Fighter) Sqdn Assoc., 2006– *Recreations:* hill walking, fishing, gardening. *Club:* Royal Air Force.

FEEST, Terry George, MD; FRCP; Consultant Nephrologist, Richard Bright Rena Unit, and Clinical Director, Renal and Transplant Services, Southmead Hospital, Nort Bristol NHS Trust, since 1991; *b* 16 Feb. 1944; *s* of Sydney George Feest and Doris Ma Feest; *m* 1991, Kathleen Alexis Blosick; two *s* one *d. Educ:* Sidney Sussex Coll., Cambridg (BA 1965; MB BChir 1968; MD 1980); King's Coll. Hosp., London. FRCP 1986 Consultant Physician and Nephrologist, Royal Devon and Exeter Hosp., 1978–91. Hon Prof. of Clinical Nephrology, Univ. of Bristol, 1995–. Chm., UK Renal Registry, Rena Assoc., 1990–2006; Mem. Appraisal Cttees, NICE, 2004–06. *Publications:* UK Rena Registry Annual Report, 1998–2005; papers in internat. renal and gen. med. jls *Recreations:* gardening, walking, ski-ing, theatre, music. *Address:* Richard Bright Rena Unit, Southmead Hospital, Bristol BS10 5NB. *T:* 07760 333890; *e-mail:* terry@ feest.co.uk.

FEILDEN, Sir Bernard (Melchior), Kt 1985; CBE 1976 (OBE 1969); FRIBA 1968 (ARIBA 1949); Consultant, Feilden and Mawson, Chartered Architects (Partner 1956–77); Member, Cathedrals Advisory Commission for England, 1981–90; *b* 11 Sept 1919; *s* of Robert Humphrey Feilden, MC, and Olive Feilden (*née* Binyon); *m* 1st, 1949 Ruth Mildred Bainbridge (*d* 1994); two *s* two *d*; 2nd, 1995, Christina Matilda Beatric Murdoch. *Educ:* Bedford Sch. Exhibr, Bartlett Sch. of Architecture, 1938 (Hon. Fellow UCL, 1985). Served War of 1939–45: Bengal Sappers and Miners. AA Diploma (Hons) 1949; Bratt Colbran Schol., 1949. Architect, Norwich Cathedral, 1963–77; Surveyor to the Fabric: York Minster, 1965–77; St Paul's Cathedral, 1969–77; Consultant Architect UEA, 1969–77. Dir, Internat. Centre for the Preservation and Restoration of Cultura Property, Rome, 1977–81. Hoffman Wood Prof. of Architecture, Leeds Univ., 1973–74 Member: Ancient Monuments Bd (England), 1964–77; Council, RIBA, 1972–77 Cathedrals Fabric Commn, 1990–95; Cathedrals Fabric Cttees, Bury St Edmunds and Ely 1990–2006. President: Ecclesiastical Architects' and Surveyors' Assoc., 1975–77; Guild o Surveyors, 1976–77. FSA 1969; FRSA 1973; Hon. FAIA 1987. Corresp. Mem. Architectes en Chef, France. DUniv York, 1973; Hon. DLitt: Gothenburg, 1988; Eas Anglia, 1989. Aga Khan Award for Architecture, 1986. Order of St William of York 1976. *Publications:* The Wonder of York Minster, 1976; Introduction to Conservation 1979; Conservation of Historic Buildings, 1982, 3rd edn 2003; Between Two Earthquakes, 1987; Guidelines for Conservation (India), 1989; Guidelines fo Management of World Cultural Heritage Sites, 1993; articles in Architectural Review Chartered Surveyor, AA Quarterly. *Recreations:* painting, fishing. *Address:* The Old Barn

Hall Farm Place, Bawburgh, Norwich, NR9 3LW. *T:* (01603) 747472. *Club:* Norfolk (Norwich).

FEILDEN, Sir Henry (Wemyss), 6th Bt *cr* 1846; *b* 1 Dec. 1916; *s* of Col Wemyss Gawne Cunningham Feilden, CMG (*d* 1943) (3rd *s* of 3rd Bt) and Winifred Mary Christian (*d* 1980), *d* of Rev. William Cosens, DD; *S* cousin, Sir William Morton Buller Feilden, 5th Bt, 1976; *m* 1943, Ethel May, 2nd *d* of John Atkinson, Annfield Plain, Co. Durham; one *s* two *d*. *Educ:* Canford Sch.; King's Coll., London. Served War, RE, 1940–46. Clerical Civil Service, 1960–79. *Recreations:* watching cricket, reading. *Heir: s* Henry Rudyard Feilden, BVetSc, MRCVS [*b* 26 Sept. 1951; *m* 1st, 1982, Anne Shepperd (marr. diss. 1996); one *s*; 2nd, 1998, Geraldine, *d* of Major G. R. Kendall; one *s* one *d*]. *Address:* Little Dene, Heathfield Road, Burwash, Etchingham, East Sussex TN19 7HN. *T:* (01435) 882205. *Club:* MCC.

FEILDING, family name of **Earl of Denbigh**.

FEILDING, Viscount; Peregrine Rudolph Henry Feilding; *b* 19 Feb. 2005; *s* and *heir* of Earl of Denbigh, *qv*.

FEINSTEIN, Elaine Barbara, FRSL; writer, since 1973; *b* 24 Oct. 1930; *d* of Isidore Cooklin and Fay Cooklin (*née* Compton); *m* 1956, Arnold Feinstein; three *s*. *Educ:* Wyggeston Grammar Sch. for Girls, Leicester; Newnham Coll., Cambridge (Exhibnr; English Tripos; MA). Mem., editl staff, CUP, 1959–62; Asst Lectr, Comparative Lit. Dept, Univ. of Essex, 1968–71. Rockefeller Foundn Fellow, Bellagio, 1998. Writer of reviews for The Times, Daily Telegraph, TLS, The Guardian and other newspapers, 1975–2002; Writer in Residence: for British Council, Singapore, 1993; Tromsø, 1995. Writer: *for television:* Breath, 1975; Lunch, 1981; The Edwardian Country Gentlewoman's Diary (12 part series), 1984; A Brave Face, 1985; *for radio:* Echoes, 1980; A Late Spring, 1981; A Day Off, 1983; Marina Tsvetayeva: a life, 1985; If I Ever Get On My Feet Again, 1987; The Man in Her Life, 1990; Foreign Girls (trilogy), 1993; A Winter Meeting, 1994; Lawrence's Women in Love (4 part adaptation), 1996; Cloudberries, 1999. Chm. Judges, T. S. Eliot Award, 1995. FRSL 1981. Hon. DLitt Leicester, 1990. Cholmondeley Award for Poetry, 1990; Soc. of Authors Travel Award, 1991. *Publications: novels:* The Circle, 1970; The Amberstone Exit, 1972; The Glass Alembic, 1973 (US edn as The Crystal Garden, 1974); Children of the Rose, 1975; The Ecstasy of Dr Miriam Garner, 1976; The Shadow Master, 1978; The Survivors, 1982; The Border, 1984; Mother's Girl, 1988; All You Need, 1989; Loving Brecht, 1992; Dreamers, 1994; Lady Chatterley's Confession, 1996; Dark Inheritance, 2001; The Russian Jerusalem, 2008; *poems:* In a Green Eye, 1966; The Magic Apple Tree, 1971; At the Edge, 1972; The Celebrants and Other Poems, 1973; Some Unease and Angels, 1977; Selected Poems, 1977; The Feast of Euridice, 1980; Badlands, 1987; City Music, 1990; Selected Poems, 1994; Daylight, 1997; (ed) After Pushkin, 1999; Gold, 2000; Collected Poems, 2002; Talking to the Dead, 2007; *poems in translation:* The Selected Poems of Marina Tsvetayeva, 1971, 5th revd edn 1999 (Arts Council Translation Awards, 1970, 1972); Three Russian Poets: Margarite Aliger, Yunna Morits, Bella Akhmadulina, 1976; *biography:* Bessie Smith, 1986; A Captive Lion: the life of Marina Tsvetayeva, 1987; Lawrence's Women, 1993 (US edn as Lawrence and The Women, 1993); Pushkin, 1998; Ted Hughes: the life of a poet, 2001; Anna of All the Russias: a life of Anna Akhmatova, 2005; *short stories:* Matters of Chance, 1972; The Silent Areas, 1980; *editor:* Selected Poems of John Clare, 1968; (with Fay Weldon) New Stories, 1979; New Poetry, 1988. *Recreations:* books, music, travel, the conversation of friends. *Address:* c/o Rogers Coleridge & White, 20 Powis Mews, W11 1JN. *T:* (020) 7722 3688; *e-mail:* ElaineFeinstein@compuserve.com. *Clubs:* Groucho, PEN.

FELDMAN, family name of **Baron Feldman**.

FELDMAN, Baron *cr* 1995 (Life Peer), of Frognal in the London Borough of Camden; **Basil Feldman,** Kt 1982; a Party Treasurer, Conservative and Unionist Party, since 1996; *b* 23 Sept. 1926; *s* of late Philip and Tilly Feldman; *m* 1952, Gita Julius; two *s* one *d*. *Educ:* Grocers' School. National Union of Conservative and Unionist Associations: Mem., 1975–98, Chm., 1991–96, Exec. Cttee; Vice-Chm., 1982–85, Chm., 1985–86; Vice-Pres., 1986–98; Jt Nat. Chm., Cons. Party's Impact 80s Campaign, 1982–87; Chm., Team 1000, 1989–93; Member: Policy Gp for London, 1975–81, 1984–87; Nat. Campaign Cttee, 1976 and 1978; Adv. Cttee on Policy, 1981–86; Cttee for London, 1984–87; Greater London area: Dep. Chm., 1975–78; Chm., 1978–81; Pres., 1981–85; Vice Pres., 1985–; Vice-Pres., Greater London Young Conservatives, 1975–77; President: Richmond and Barnes Cons. Assoc., 1976–84; Hornsey Cons. Assoc., 1978–82; Patron, Hampstead Cons. Assoc., 1981–86. Contested GLC Elections, Richmond, 1973; Member: GLC Housing Management Cttee, 1973–77; GLC Arts Cttee, 1976–81. Mem., Free Enterprise Loan Soc., 1977–84. Chairman: Martlet Services Gp Ltd, 1973–81; Solport Ltd, 1980–85; The Quality Mark, 1987–92. Chairman: Better Made in Britain Campaign, 1983–98 (organising 14 exhibns in 8 different countries); Market Opportunities Adv. Gp, DTI, 1991–93; Shopping Hours Reform Council, 1988–93 (Pres., 1993–95); Better Business Opportunities, 1990–96; Watchpost Ltd, 1983–; Dir, Young Entrepreneurs Fund, 1985–95. Underwriting Mem. of Lloyd's, 1979–96. Membre Consultatif, Institut Internat. de Promotion et de Prestige, Geneva (affiliated to Unesco), 1978–96. Member: Post Office Users National Council, 1978–81 (Mem., Tariffs Sub-Cttee, 1980–81); English Tourist Board, 1986–96; Chairman: Clothing EDC (NEDO), 1978–85; Maker/User Working Party (NEDO), 1988–89. Gov., Sports Aid Foundn, 1990–2002. Chairman: London Arts Season 1993–97; Festival of Arts and Culture, 1995; Salzburg Festival Trust, London, 2000–03 (Vice Chm., 1997–2000); Mem., Internat. Council, Los Angeles Philharmonic, 1995–. Chm., Fresh Hope Trust, 2003–. Freeman, City of London, 1984. FRSA 1987. Silver Decoration of Honour, Salzburg, 2003. *Publications:* Some Thoughts on Jobs Creation (for NEDO), 1984; Constituency Campaigning: a guide for Conservative Party workers; several other Party booklets and pamphlets. *Recreations:* golf, tennis, theatre, opera, travel, watching football. *Clubs:* Carlton, Garrick.

FELDMAN, Andrew Simon; Managing Director, Jayroma (London) Ltd, since 1995; Chief Executive, Conservative Party, since 2008; *b* London, 25 Feb. 1966; *s* of Malcolm and Marcia Feldman; *m* 1999, Gabrielle Gourgey; two *s* one *d*. *Educ:* Haberdashers' Aske's Sch., Elstree; Brasenose Coll., Oxford (BA 1st Cl. Juris.); Inns of Court Sch. of Law. Mgt Consultant, Bain & Co., 1988–90; commercial barrister, 1 Essex Court, 1991–95. *Recreations:* tennis, golf, reading. *Address:* Conservative Party Headquarters, 30 Milbank, SW1P 4DP. *Clubs:* George, Soho House.

FELDMAN, Prof. David John, FBA 2006; Rouse Ball Professor of English Law, since 2004, and Fellow of Downing College, since 2003, University of Cambridge; a Judge of Constitutional Court of Bosnia and Herzegovina, since 2002, a Vice-President, since 2006; *b* 12 July 1953; *s* of late Alec Feldman and of Valerie Feldman (*née* Michaelson); *m* 1983, Naomi Jill Newman; one *s* one *d*. *Educ:* Brighton, Hove and Sussex Grammar Sch.; Exeter Coll., Oxford (MA, DCL). Lectr in Law, 1976–89, Reader, 1989–92, Bristol Univ.; University of Birmingham: Barber Prof. of Jurisprudence, 1992–2000; Dean of Law, 1997–2000; Prof. of Law, 2000–04; Chm., Faculty Bd of Law, Univ. of Cambridge, 2006–March 2009. Vis. Fellow, ANU, 1989; Miegunyah Dist. Vis. Fellow, Univ. of Melbourne, 2006. Legal Advr to Jt Select Cttee on Human Rights, Houses of Parlt, 2000–04. FRSA. Hon. Bencher, Lincoln's Inn, 2003. Hon. QC 2008. *Publications:* Law Relating to Entry, Search and Seizure, 1986; Criminal Confiscation Orders: the new law, 1988; (ed) Criminal Investigation: reform and control, 1991; Civil Liberties and Human Rights in England and Wales, 1993, 2nd edn 2002; (ed jtly) Corporate and Commercial Law: modern developments, 1996; (ed) English Public Law, 2004; contrib. articles on public law, human rights and criminal procedure. *Recreations:* music, dog-walking, cooking, history, theatre. *Address:* Downing College, Cambridge CB2 1DQ. *T:* (01223) 334800.

FELDMAN, Sally Joy; Dean, School of Media, Arts and Design, University of Westminster, since 2003; *b* 10 March 1948; *d* of Reuben Feldman and Karola Landau; *m* 1981, Tony Russell; one *s* one *d*. *Educ:* Univ. of Reading (BA Hons English 1970); Univ. of Manitoba (MA English 1972). Freelance and editorial posts, 1970s; Press Officer, CRC and CRE, 1976–78; Editor, range of magazines: Love Affair, New Love, Loving, Woman's World, 1978–83; Woman's Hour, BBC Radio 4: Producer, 1983–86; Dep. Editor, 1986–89; Presenter, Weekend Edition, 1986; Editor, 1990–97, and Editor, range of other progs; Launch Editor, Treasure Islands; Dean, Sch. of Media, London Coll. of Printing, 1998–2002. Freelance broadcaster, and journalist and reviewer. Mem. Council, Media Soc. Associate Ed., New Humanist Mag. *Publications:* The Complete Desk Book, 1978; *novels for teenagers* (as Amber Vane): Hopelessly Devoted, 1995; Blazing Kisses, 1996; Freezing Heart, 1996; Follow the Sun, 1996; I Taught Him a Lesson He'll Never Forget, 1998. *Recreations:* voracious reading, talking, film, clothes, travel, friends and family. *Address:* 22 Cranbourne Road, N10 2BT. *T:* (020) 8444 2085, *Fax:* (020) 7911 5958; *e-mail:* feldmas@wmin.ac.uk, sally.feldman@virgin.net.

FELDMAN, Prof. Stanley, FRCA; Professor of Anaesthetics, Charing Cross and Westminster Medical School, University of London, 1989–95, now Emeritus; *b* 10 Aug. 1930; *s* of Israel and Lilly Feldman; *m* 1957, Carole Bowman; one *s* one *d*. *Educ:* London Univ. (BSc 1950); Westminster Med. Sch. (MB BS 1955). FRCA (FFARCS 1962). Fellow, Univ. of Washington, Seattle, 1957–58; Westminster Hospital: Registrar, 1958–62; Consultant Anaesthetist, 1962–89; Sen. Lectr, RPMS, 1963–66. Postgrad. Advr in Anaesthetics, RCS, 1966–72; Res. Consultant, Royal Nat. Orthopaedic Hosp. NHS Trust, 1995–98. Vis. Prof., Stanford Univ., 1967–68. Hon. Member: Australasian Soc. Anaesthetists; Spanish Portuguese Soc. Anaesth.; Belgian Soc. Anaesth.; Netherlands Soc. Anaesthetists; Israeli Soc. Anaesth. Editor, Review of Anaesthetic Pharmacology, 1992–97. *Publications:* Anatomy for Anaesthetists, 1963, 6th edn 1991; Scientific Foundations of Anaesthesia, 1971, 4th edn 1990; Muscle Relaxants, 1973, 2nd edn 1981; Drug Mechanisms in Anaesthesia, 1981, 2nd edn 1993; Neuromuscular Block, 1997; Organophosphates and Health, 2001; Poison Arrows, 2005; Panic Nation, 2005, 2nd edn 2006; Life Begins At..., 2007. *Recreations:* sailing, travel. *Address:* 28 Moore Street, SW3 2QW. *Club:* Royal Society of Medicine.

FELDMANN, Prof. Marc, PhD; FRCP, FRCPath; FMedSci; FRS 2006; FAA; Professor of Cellular Immunology, University of London, since 1985; Head, Kennedy Institute of Rheumatology Division, Faculty of Medicine, Imperial College London, since 2002 (Head, Cytokine Biology and Immunology, since 1992); *b* 2 Dec. 1944; *s* of Elie and Cyla Feldmann; *m* 1966, Tania Gudinski; one *s* one *d*. *Educ:* Univ. of Melbourne (MB BS 1967, BSc Med Hons 1970; PhD 1972). FRCPath 1984; FRCP 1998. Sen. Scientist, 1974–77, Principal Scientist, 1977–85, ICRF; Dep. Dir, Charing Cross Sunley Res. Centre, 1985–92. Pres., Internat. Cytokine Soc., 2002–03. FMedSci 2001; FAA 2005. (Jtly) Crafoord Prize, Royal Swedish Acad. of Sci., 2000; Albert Lasker Award for Clin. Med. Res., NY, 2003; Cameron Prize for Therapeutics, Edinburgh Univ., 2004. *Publications:* (ed with J. J. Oppenhaim) Cytokine Reference, 2001; (with R. N. Maini) Pocket Reference to TNFα Antagonist and Rheumatoid Arthritis, 2001; numerous contribs to scientific literature. *Recreations:* tennis, hiking, keeping fit, art, theatre. *Address:* Kennedy Institute of Rheumatology Division, Faculty of Medicine, Imperial College London, 1 Aspenlea Road, W6 8LH. *T:* (020) 8383 4444, *Fax:* (020) 8563 0399; *e-mail:* m.feldmann@imperial.ac.uk. *Club:* Queen's.

FELDSTEIN, Prof. Martin Stuart; Professor, Harvard University, since 1969; *b* 25 Nov. 1939; *m* Kathleen Foley; two *d*. *Educ:* Harvard Coll. (AB *summa cum laude* 1961); Oxford Univ. (BLitt 1963, MA 1964, DPhil 1967). Nuffield College, Oxford University: Research Fellow, 1964–65; Official Fellow, 1965–67; Hon. Fellow, 1998; Lectr in Public Finance, Oxford Univ., 1965–67; Harvard University: Asst Professor, 1967–68; Associate Professor, 1968–69. President, National Bureau of Economic Research, 1977–82 and 1984–2008; Chm., Council of Economic Advrs, 1982–84. Director: American International Gp; Eli Lilly. Pres., American Econ. Assoc., 2004. Member: Amer. Philosophical Soc.; Amer. Acad. of Arts and Scis; Trilateral Commn; Council on Foreign Relations. Corresp. FBA, 1998. *Publications:* (ed) The American Economy in Transition, 1980; Hospital Costs and Health Insurance, 1981; Inflation, Tax Rules, and Capital Formation, 1983; Capital Taxation, 1983; Effects of Taxation on Capital Formation, 1986; United States in the World Economy, 1988; International Economic Co-operation, 1988; American Economic Policy in the 1980s, 1994; International Capital Flows, 1999. *Address:* National Bureau of Economic Research, 1050 Massachusetts Avenue, Cambridge, MA 02138, USA.

FELL, Sir David, KCB 1995 (CB 1990); non-executive Chairman, Goldblatt McGuigan, since 2005; *b* 20 Jan. 1943; *s* of Ernest Fell and Jessie (*née* McCreedy); *m* 1967, Sandra Jesse (*née* Moore); one *s* one *d*. *Educ:* Royal Belfast Academical Instn; The Queen's University of Belfast (BSc: Pure and Applied Mathematics, also (1st Cl. Hons) Physics). Sales Manager, Rank Hovis McDougall Ltd, 1965–66; Teacher, 1966–67; Research Associate, 1967–69; Civil Servant, 1969–97: Dept of Agriculture (NI), 1969–72; Dept of Commerce (NI), 1972–82 (Under Secretary, 1981); Under Secretary, Dept of Economic Development (NI), 1982; Dep. Chief Exec., Industrial Develt Bd for NI, 1982–84; Permanent Sec., Dept of Economic Develt (NI), 1984–91; Hd of NICS, and Second Perm. Under Sec. of State, NI Office, 1991–97. Chairman: Northern Bank, 1998–2005; Boxmore Internat. plc, 1998–2000; Nat. Irish Bank, 1999–2005; Harland & Wolff Gp plc, 2001–02; Titanic Quarter Ltd, 2001–03; Titanic Properties Ltd, 2001–03; non-executive Director: Dunloe Ewart plc, 1998–2002; Nat. Australia Gp (Europe) Ltd, 1998–; Fred Olsen Energy ASA, 1999–2003; Chesapeake Corp. (USA), 2000– (Chm., 2005–). Chairman: Opera NI, 1998–99; Prince's Trust Volunteers (NI), 1998–99; Prince's Trust (NI), 1999–2005; Pres., Extern Orgn, 1998–. Mem. Council, Industrial Soc., 1998–2001. Pro-Chancellor, QUB, 2005–. CCMI; FRSA; FCIB. DUniv Ulster, 2003. *Recreations:* music, reading, golf, Rugby Union. *Address:* Goldblatt McGuigan, Alfred House, 19 Alfred Street, Belfast BT2 8EQ. *Club:* Old Instonians (Belfast).

FELL, Richard Taylor, CVO 1996; HM Diplomatic Service, retired; *b* 11 Nov. 1948; *s* of late Eric Whineray Fell and Margaret Farrer Fell (*née* Taylor); *m* 1981, Claire Gates; three *s*. *Educ:* Bootham Sch., York; Bristol Univ. (BSc); Univ. of London (MA). Joined HM Diplomatic Service, 1971; Ottawa, 1972–74; Saigon, 1974–75; Vientiane, 1975; First

Sec. and Chargé d'Affaires *ai*, Hanoi, 1979; First Sec., UK Delegn to NATO, 1979–83; First Sec. and Head of Chancery, Kuala Lumpur, 1983–86; FCO, 1986–88; on secondment to Thorn EMI, 1988–89; Counsellor, Ottawa, 1989–93; Dep. Hd of Mission, Bangkok, 1993–96; Counsellor, FCO, 1997–2000; Acting Consul-Gen., Toronto, 2000; RCDS, 2001; High Comr, New Zealand, Governor (non-res.) of Pitcairn, Henderson, Ducie and Oeno Is, and High Comr (non-res.), Samoa, 2001–06. *Publication:* Early Maps of South-East Asia, 1988. *Recreations:* antiques, reading, sport.

FELL, Robert, CB 1972; CBE 1966; Commissioner of Banking, Hong Kong, 1984–87; *b* 6 May 1921; *s* of Robert and Mary Ann Fell, Cumberland; *m* 1946, Eileen Wicks; two *s* one *d. Educ:* Whitehaven Grammar School. War Office, 1939; military service, 1940–46 (despatches); BoT, 1947; Trade Comr, Qld, 1954–59; Asst Sec., Tariff Div., 1961; Commercial Counsellor, Delhi, 1961–66; Under-Sec. i/c export promotion, 1967–71; Sec., ECGD, 1971–74; Chief Exec., The Stock Exchange, 1975–82; Comr for Securities, Hong Kong, 1981–84. Mem., British Overseas Trade Board, 1972–75; Pres., City Branch, BIM, 1976–82. FRSA. *Recreations:* Rugby football (watching), gardening. *Address:* 60 The Drive, Craigweil, Aldwick, Bognor Regis PO21 4DT. *Club:* Travellers.

FELL, William Varley, CMG 2002; International Risk Adviser, British Airways, since 2002; *b* 4 March 1948; *s* of John Richmond Fell and Cicely Juliet Fell (*née* Varley); *m* 1970, Jill Pauline Warren; two *s* one *d. Educ:* Charterhouse; Bristol Univ. (BA Hons). With Hambros Bank, 1969–71; entered HM Diplomatic Service, 1971; 3rd Sec., Vienna, 1973–75; 2nd Sec., Havana, 1976–78; 1st Secretary: Warsaw, 1979–82; FCO, 1982–88; Counsellor, Athens, 1988–92; FCO, 1992–2002. Gov., Skinners' Sch., Tunbridge Wells. Liveryman, 2003–, Extra Mem., Ct, 2006–, Skinners' Co. *Recreations:* walking, especially on Dartmoor and in Greece, history, travel. *Address:* c/o British Airways, Waterside (HDB2), PO Box 365, Harmondsworth UB7 0GB. *T:* (020) 8738 6892, *Fax:* (020) 8738 9930; *e-mail:* william.fell@ba.com. *Club:* Travellers.

FELLGETT, Prof. Peter Berners, PhD; FRS 1986; Professor of Cybernetics, University of Reading, 1965–87, now Emeritus; *b* 11 April 1922; *s* of Frank Ernest Fellgett and Rose, (Rowena), (*née* Wagstaffe); *m* 1947, Janet Mary (*d* 1998), *o d* of late Prof. G. E. Briggs, FRS and Mrs Nora Briggs; one *s* two *d. Educ:* The Leys Sch., Cambridge; Univ. of Cambridge (BA 1943, MA 1947, PhD 1952). Isaac Newton Student, Cambridge Observatories, 1950–51; Lick Observatory, Calif, 1951–52; Cambridge Observatories, 1952–59; Royal Observatory, Edinburgh, 1959–65. *Publications:* approx. 75 pubns in learned jls and 32 gen. articles. *Recreations:* making musical instruments, high quality audio, gardening, fun-running, not being interrupted and not being hurried. *Address:* Little Brighter Farm, St Kew Highway, Bodmin, Cornwall PL30 3DU.

See also T. R. Fellgett.

FELLGETT, (Terence) Robin, CB 2007; PhD; Deputy Head, Economic and Domestic Affairs Secretariat, Cabinet Office, since 2003; *b* 1 Oct. 1950; *s* of Prof. Peter Berners Fellgett, *qv* and late Mary Briggs; *m* 1976, Patti Douglas; one *s* one *d. Educ:* Univ. of Warwick (PhD Maths 1976); Birkbeck Coll., London Univ. (MSc Econs 1984); INSEAD (AMP 1995). BP Chemicals, 1969; Asst Prof., Univ. of Maryland, 1976–78; MSC, 1979; CSD 1979–83; joined HM Treasury, 1983: held posts in expenditure, privatisation and internat. finance; Dep. Dir, then Dir, Financial Sector, 1998–2003. *Recreations:* music, travel, relaxation. *Address:* Cabinet Office, 70 Whitehall, SW1A 2AS. *Clubs:* Jazz Café, Vortex.

FELLNER, Eric, CBE 2005; film producer; Co-Chairman, Working Title Films, since 1992; *b* 10 Oct. 1959; *m* (marr. diss.); three *s. Educ:* Cranleigh Sch.; Guildhall Sch. of Music and Drama. *Films include:* Sid and Nancy, 1986; Pascali's Island, 1988; The Rachel Papers, 1989; Hidden Agenda, 1990; A Kiss Before Dying, Liebestraum, 1991; Wild West, 1992; Posse, Romeo is Bleeding, 1993; Four Weddings and a Funeral, The Hudsucker Proxy, 1994; Loch Ness, French Kiss, Dead Man Walking, 1995; Fargo, 1996; Bean, The Borrowers, 1997; Elizabeth, The Big Lebowski, 1998; Notting Hill, Plunkett & Macleane, 1999; O Brother, Where Art Thou?, Billy Elliot, The Man Who Cried, 2000; Bridget Jones's Diary, Captain Corelli's Mandolin, The Man Who Wasn't There, Long Time Dead, 2001; 40 Days and 40 Nights, About A Boy, Ali G Indahouse, The Guru, My Little Eye, 2002; Love Actually, Calcium Kid, Ned Kelly, Shape of Things, Johnny English, Thirteen, 2003; Thunderbirds, Bridget Jones: The Edge of Reason, Shaun of the Dead, Wimbledon, Inside I'm Dancing, 2004; Mickybo and Me, Pride and Prejudice, Nanny McPhee, The Interpreter, 2005; Sixty Six, United 93, Hot Stuff, 2006; The Golden Age, Atonement, Mr Bean's Holiday, Hot Fuzz, Gone, Smokin' Aces, 2007. Four Academy Awards; twenty BAFTA awards. *Address:* Working Title Films, Oxford House, 76 Oxford Street, WID 1BS. *T:* (020) 7307 3000; Working Title Films, 4th Floor, 9720 Wilshire Boulevard, Beverly Hills, CA 90212, USA. *T:* (310) 777 3100.

FELLNER, Dr Peter John; Chairman, Vernalis (formerly British Biotech) plc, since 2002 (Director, 1988–90); *b* 31 Dec. 1943; *s* of late Hans Julius Fellner and Jessica (*née* Thompson); *m* 1st, 1969, Sandra Head (*née* Smith); one *d* and one step *s*; 2nd, 1982, Jennifer Mary Zabel (*née* Butler); two step *s. Educ:* Sheffield Univ. (BSc Biochem. 1965); Trinity Coll., Cambridge (PhD 1968). Post-doctoral Res. Fellow, 1968–70, Associate Prof., 1970–73, Strasbourg Univ.; Searle UK Research Laboratories: Sen. Res. Investigator, 1973–77; Dir of Chem., 1977–80; Dir of Res., 1980–84; Dir of Res., Roche UK Res. Centre, 1984–86; Man. Dir, Roche UK, 1986–90; Chief Exec., 1990–2003, Chm., 2003–04, Celltech, then Celltech Chirosci., subseq. Celltech Gp. Chairman: Astex Therapeutics (formerly Astex Technol.) Ltd, 2002–; Ionix Pharmaceuticals Ltd, 2002–05; Acambis plc, 2006–; Premier Research Gp plc, 2007–; non-executive Director: Colborn Dawes Ltd, 1986–90; Synaptica Ltd, 1999–2002; QinetiQ Gp plc, 2004–; UCB SA, 2005–; Evotec AG, 2005–; Bespak plc, 2005–. Mem., MRC, 2000–07. *Recreation:* country walking. *Address:* Vernalis plc, Oakdene Court, 613 Reading Road, Winnersh, Wokingham RG41 5UA. *T:* (0118) 977 3133, *Fax:* (0118) 989 9300.

FELLOWES, family name of **Barons De Ramsey** and **Fellowes**.

FELLOWES, Baron *cr* 1999 (Life Peer), of Shotesham in the county of Norfolk; **Robert Fellowes,** GCB 1998 (KCB 1991; CB 1987); GCVO 1996 (KCVO 1989; LVO 1983); QSO 1999; PC 1990; Chairman, Barclays Private Bank, since 2000 (Vice-Chairman, 1999–2000); Secretary and Registrar of the Order of Merit, since 2003; *b* 11 Dec. 1941; *s* of Sir William Fellowes, KCVO; *m* 1978, Lady Jane Spencer, *d* of 8th Earl Spencer, LVO; one *s* two *d. Educ:* Eton. Scots Guards (short service commission), 1960–63. Director, Allen Harvey & Ross Ltd, Discount Brokers and Bankers, 1968–77; Asst Private Sec. to the Queen, 1977–86, Dep. Private Sec., 1986–90; Private Sec. to the Queen and Keeper of the Queen's Archives, 1990–99. Non-exec. Dir, SABMiller (formerly South African Breweries), 1999–. Mem., UK Governing Body, Internat. Chamber of Commerce, 2004–. Vice-Chm., Commonwealth Educn Trust (formerly Commonwealth Inst.), 2000–; Chm., Prison Reform Trust, 2001–; Mem., British Liby Bd, 2007–. Trustee: Rhodes Trust, 2000–; Winston Churchill Meml Trust, 2001–; Mandela-Rhodes Trust, 2003–; Chm., Voices Foundn, 2004–. *Recreations:* reading, watching cricket, golf. *Address:* House of Lords, SW1A 0PW. *Clubs:* White's, Pratt's, Royal Over-Seas League, MCC.

FELLOWES, Julian Alexander K.; *see* Kitchener-Fellowes, J. A.

FELLOWS, Derek Edward, FIA; Executive Director, Securities and Investments Board 1989–91; *b* 23 Oct. 1927; *s* of late Edward Frederick Fellows and of Gladys Fellows; *m* 1948, Mary Watkins; two *d. Educ:* Mercers' Sch. FIA 1956. Entered Prudential Assurance Co. Ltd, 1943; Gp Pensions Manager, 1973–81; Chief Actuary, 1981–88; Man. Dir, Gp Pension Div., 1984–88; Dir, Prudential Corp. plc, 1985–88; non-exec. Dir, Countrywide Assured (formerly Hambro Guardian Assurance, then Hambro Assured), 1992–99. Mem. Occupational Pensions Bd, 1974–78; Chm., Bd of Trustees, South Bank Centre Retirement Plan, 1993–2001; Trustee, C of E Pensions Bd, 1998–2002. Church Comr 1996–2002 (Mem., Audit Cttee, 1994–2001). FPMI 1976; Vice Pres., Inst. of Actuaries 1980–83. *Publications:* contrib. Jl of Inst. of Actuaries. *Recreations:* music, theatre gardening, bridge. *Club:* Actuaries'.

FELLOWS, Edward Frank; Editorial Consultant, Fellows Media Ltd (formerly Fellow Associates), publishers, since 1999 (Managing Director, 1992–99); *b* 25 Sept. 1930; *s* o Edward Fellows and Gladys Nora Fellows; *m* 1962, Christine Woolmore; three *s. Educ* Ewell primary and secondary schs; Epsom Sch. of Art (schol.); Merrist Wood Agricl Inst Nat. Service, CRMP, 1949. Joined editorial staff of Farmer and Stockbreeder, 1957 Editor, Power Farming, 1974; Dep. Editor, Farmers Weekly, 1982; Editor, Crops, 1984 Editor, Farmers Weekly, 1987–90; Editor-in-Chief, Reed Farmers Publishing Group 1990–91; Features Editor, Shell Agriculture, 1993–94; Editor, Farming OPUS, 1995–97 Hon. Mem., Falkland Islands Assoc., 1983–. *Publication:* Tim Chooses Farming, 1962 *Recreations:* indoor rowing, Labrador dogs, walking, photography, gardening, reading *Address:* Manzanas, Orchard Mead, Painswick, Glos GL6 6YD. *T:* (01452) 814072; *e-mail* tedfellows@waitrose.com.

FELLOWS, Jeffrey Keith; Technical Consultant, BAE Systems, since 1999; *b* 17 Sept 1940; *s* of Albert and Hilda May Fellows; *m* 1965, Mary Ewins; one *s. Educ:* Handsworth Grammar Sch.; Birmingham Univ. (BSc (Phys) Hons 1962). Royal Aircraft Establishment joined Weapons Dept, 1962, Sect. Leader, 1973; Div. Leader, Systems Assessment Dept 1976; Head of: Combat Mission Systems Div., 1981; Flight Systems Dept, 1983; seconded to BNSC as Dir (Projects and Technol.), 1986; Dep. Dir (Mission Systems), RAE Farnborough, 1988–89; Asst Under Sec. of State, MoD, 1989–95; Technical Planning Dir, BAe plc, 1995–99; retired. *Publications:* various, for AGARD, IBA, US Nat. Space Foundn, etc. *Recreations:* tennis, aeromodelling.

FELLOWS, John Walter, CEng, FICE, FIHT; independent transportation consultant since 1996; *b* 27 July 1938; *s* of William Leslie Fellows and Lavinia Keziah (*née* Chilton) *m* 1964, Maureen Joyce Lewis; two *s. Educ:* Dudley Technical High Sch.; Wolverhampton Polytechnic; Birmingham Univ. (MSc). FICE 1990; FIHT 1989. Civil Engineer (pupil) Contractors Wilson Lovatt & Sons Ltd, 1954–59; Civil Engineer: CBs of Wolverhampton Coventry and Dudley, 1959–69; joined Department of Transport, 1969: Asst Sec. Highway Maintenance Div., 1984–88; Dir, SE, 1988–90; Regl Dir (SE), DoE/DoT 1990–94; Bd Dir, Highway Agency, 1994–96. *Publications:* papers to ICE and IHT *Recreations:* boating, sailing, golf, music, theatre. *Address:* 17 Chinthurst Park, Shalford Guildford, Surrey GU4 8JH.

FELLS, Prof. Ian, CBE 2000; FREng; FRSE; Professor of Energy Conversion, University of Newcastle upon Tyne, 1975–90, now Emeritus; *b* 5 Sept. 1932; *s* of late Dr Henry Alexander Fells, MBE and Clarice Fells, Sheffield; *m* 1957, Hazel Denton Scott; four *s Educ:* King Edward VII School, Sheffield; Trinity College, Cambridge. MA, PhD. FInstE FIChemE; FREng (FEng 1979); FRSE 1996. Chief Wireless Officer, British Troops in Austria, 1951–52; Lectr and Dir of Studies, Dept of Fuel Technology and Chem Engineering, Univ. of Sheffield, 1958–62; Reader in Fuel Science, King's Coll., Univ. of Durham, 1962; Public Orator, Univ. of Newcastle upon Tyne, 1970–73. Lectures Brough, Paisley Coll., 1977; Allerdale Wylde, Cumbria Science Socs, 1986; Fawley Southampton Univ., 1987; Robert Spence, RSC, 1988 and 1990; Charles Parsons' Meml Royal Soc., 1988; Clancey, City Univ., 1992; Erasmus Darwin, Lichfield Sci. and Engrg Soc., 1994; Hunter Meml, IEE, 1999; Higginson, Durham Univ., 2000; Idris Jones Meml Cardiff, 2000; Hawksley Meml, IMechE, 2001. Pres., Inst. of Energy, 1978–79; Scientific Advr, World Energy Council, 1990–98; Special Advisor: to H of L Select Cttee for the European Communities, 1991–92; to H of C Select Cttee on Envmt, 1993–94, and on Trade and Industry, 1995–96. Member: Electricity Supply Res. Council, 1979–90; Sci Consultative Gp, BBC, 1976–81; CNAA, 1987–93. Chm., New and Renewable Energy Centre, Blyth, Northumberland, 2002–05. Trustee, Internat. Centre for Life, 1995– Hatfield Meml Prize, 1974; Beilby Meml Medal and Prize, 1976; Faraday Award and Lect., 1993, Collier Medal and Lect., 1999, Royal Soc.; Melchett Medal and Lect., Royal Instn, 1999; Kelvin Medal, Royal Philosophical Soc. of Glasgow, 2002. Participator in TV series: Young Scientist of the Year, 1970; The Great Egg Race, 1970–85; Earth Year 2050, 1983; Men of Science, 1984; Take Nobody's Word For It, 1987, 1989; QED, 1987 1991; The Human Element, 1992; What If... the Lights Go Out?, 2004. *Publications* Energy for the Future, 1973, 2nd edn 1986; UK Energy Policy Post-Privatisation, 1991 Energy for the Future, 1995; World Energy 1923–98 and Beyond, 1998; contribs to professional jls. *Recreations:* sailing, cross-country ski-ing, energy conversation. *Address:* 29 Rectory Terrace, Newcastle upon Tyne NE3 1YB. *T:* (0191) 285 5343. *Club:* Naval and Military.

FELWICK, Wing Comdr David Leonard, CBE 2004; RAF retired; Deputy Chairman John Lewis Partnership, 2002–04 (Director of Trading (Food), 1991–2002); *b* 9 Nov. 1944; *s* of Leonard Felwick and Mary J. Felwick (*née* Rolling); *m* 1970, Lynne Margaret Yeardley; two *s. Educ:* Devonport High Sch., Plymouth; RAF Coll., Cranwell. Served RAF, 1962–82. Joined John Lewis Partnership, 1982; Man. Dir, John Lewis, Welwyn 1985–87; Dir of Selling, 1987–91, Man. Dir, 1991–2002, Waitrose Ltd. MInstD 1985 *Recreations:* ski-ing, shooting, tennis, golf. *Address:* Wood Farm Stables, Streatley, Berks RG8 9SU. *Club:* Royal Air Force.

FENBY, Jonathan Theodore Starmer, CBE 2000; author and journalist; *b* 11 Nov. 1942; *s* of late Charles Fenby and June (*née* Head); *m* 1967, Renée Wartski; one *s* one *d. Educ:* West House Sch., Birmingham; King Edward VI Sch., Birmingham; Westminster Sch.; New Coll., Oxford (BA). Reuters, 1963–77, Ed., Reuters World Service, 1973–77 correspondent in France and Germany, Economist, 1982–86; Asst Ed. and Home Ed., The Independent, 1986–88; Dep. Ed., The Guardian, 1988–93; Editor: The Observer, 1993–95; South China Morning Post and Sunday Morning Post, Hong Kong, 1995–99 Business Europe.com, 2000–01; Associate Ed., Sunday Business, 2000–01; Dir, China Research, Trusted Sources, 2007–; contrib. to press and broadcasting in UK, Europe, US Canada and Far East. Member Board: Journalists in Europe, 2000–02; European Journalism Centre, 2002–; British-Belgian Conf., 2006–. Chevalier, Ordre Nat. du Mérite (France), 1992. *Publications:* Fall of the House of Beaverbrook, 1979; Piracy and the Public, 1983; International News Services, 1986; On the Brink: the trouble with France, 1998 2nd edn 2002; Comment peut-on être français, 1999; Dealing with the Dragon: a year in the new Hong Kong, 2000; Generalissimo: Chiang Kai-shek and the China he lost, 2003; The Sinking of the Lancastria, 2005; Alliance, 2007; 70 Wonders of China, 2007; The

Dragon Throne, 2008; China's Journey, 2008; The Penguin History of Modern China, 2008. *Recreations:* walking, belote, jazz. *Address:* 101 Ridgmount Gardens, Torrington Place, WC1E 7AZ.

FENDALL, Prof. Neville Rex Edwards, MD; Professor of International Community Health, School of Tropical Medicine, University of Liverpool, 1971–81, now Emeritus Professor; Visiting Professor of Public Health, Boston University, since 1982; *b* 9 July 1917; *s* of Francis Alan Fendall and Ruby Inez Matthews; *m* 1942, Margaret Doreen (*née* Beynon). *Educ:* University College Hosp. (MD, BSc); London Sch. of Hygiene and Tropical Med. (DPH); FFPH. Colonial Medical Service, 1944–64, Nigeria, Malaya, Singapore, Kenya; Brit. Mil. Admin, 1945–46; Dir of Med. Services, Kenya; Staff Mem., Rockefeller Foundn, 1964–66; Regional Dir, Population Council Inc., New York, 1966–71. Mem., Panel of Experts, WHO, 1957–83; Consultant: World Bank; UN Fund for Population Activities; ODM; Cento; Internat. Develt Res. Centre, Canada; APHA; USAID; Overseas govts; Vis. Consultant, Univ. of Hawaii. Adjunct Prof. of Community Health, Univ. of Calgary, 1983–88; Visiting Lecturer: Harvard, 1966–83; Inst. of Tropical Medicine, Marseilles; Univ. of Glasgow; Univ. of Bradford; Commonwealth Foundn Travelling Lectr, 1976; Dist. Fellow, Boston Univ. Center for Internat. Health, 1992. Mem., Acad. of Med., Physical and Nat. Scis, Guatemala, 1986–. Patron, Commonwealth Human Ecology Council, 1994–. Langley Meml Prize, UNCAST, 1963; Gold Medal, Mrigendra Medical Trust, Nepal, 1983; Fendall Prize, Center for Internat. Health, Boston, USA, 1996. *Publications:* Auxiliaries in Health Care, 1972 (English, French, Spanish edns); (with J. M. Paxman and F. M. Shattock) Use of Paramedicals for Primary Health Care in the Commonwealth, 1979; (with F. M. Shattock) Restraints and Constraints to Development, 1983; contribs on primary health care, epidemiology, population dynamics, in various books and jls. *Recreations:* gardening, travel. *Address:* The Coach House, Mill Street, Ludlow, Shropshire SY8 1BB. *Club:* Royal Commonwealth Society (Life Mem.).

FENDER, Sir Brian (Edward Frederick), Kt 1999; CMG 1985; Chairman, BTG plc, 2003–08 (Board Member, British Technology Group, then BTG, 1992–2003); Chief Executive, Higher Education Funding Council for England, 1995–2001; *b* 15 Sept. 1934; *s* of late George Clements and of Emily Fender; *m* 1st, 1956; one *s* three *d*; 2nd, 1986, Ann Linscott. *Educ:* Carlisle Grammar Sch.; Sale County Grammar Sch.; Imperial College London (ARCS, BSc 1956; DIC, PhD 1959; FIC 1997); MA Oxon 1963. FRSC; FInstP. Research Instructor, Univ. of Washington, Seattle, 1959–61; Senior Research Fellow, Nat. Chem. Lab. (now NPL), 1961–63; University of Oxford: Dept Demonstrator in Inorganic Chemistry, 1963–65; Lectr, 1965–84; Senior Proctor, 1975–76; Mem., Hebdomadal Council, 1977–80; St Catherine's College: Fellow, 1963–84 (Hon. Fellow 1986); Sen. Tutor, 1965–69; Chm., Management Cttee, Oxford Colls Admissions Office, 1973–80; Vice-Chancellor, Univ. of Keele, 1985–95. Institut Laue-Langevin, Grenoble: Asst Dir, 1980–82; Dir, 1982–85; Mem., Steering Cttee, 1974–77; Mem., Scientific Council, 1977–80. Member: SERC, 1985–90; CERN Review Cttee, 1986–87; Chairman: Science Board, SERC, 1985–90 (Mem., 1974–77); Neutron Beam Res. Cttee, 1974–77 (Mem., 1969–71); Science Planning Group for Rutherford Lab. Neutron Scattering Source, 1977–80; Member: Defence Meteorol Bd, subseq. UK Meteorol Bd, 1991–2004; Adv. Cttee, Tate Gall., Liverpool, 1988–93; West Midlands Arts Bd, 1995–2002; Bd of Conservatoire for Dance and Drama, 2002–04; Dir, Higher Aims Ltd, 2002–; Chairman: Univs and Colls Employers Assoc., 1994–95; New Victoria Th. Trust, Staffs, 2003–; Nat. Council for Drama Trng, 2004–. Pres., NFER, 1999–2007; Pres. and Chm., Inst. of Knowledge Transfer, 2006–. Mem., HK UGC, 2003–07. CCMI (CBIM 1989). Hon. Fellow, Univ. of Wales, Cardiff, 1996; Hon. FRVC 2001; Hon. FTCL 2001; Hon. FRCA 2003. DUniv: Keele, 1996; Staffordshire, 2001; Hon. DSc Ulster, 2001; Hon. DCL Northumbria, 2001; Hon. Dr jur Lincoln, 2002; Hon. DEd UWE, 2002. *Publications:* scientific articles on neutron scattering and solid state chemistry. *Recreations:* theatre, modern art. *Address:* Bishops Offley Manor, Bishops Offley, Stafford ST21 6ET. *Club:* Athenæum.

FENECH-ADAMI, Hon. Dr Edward, KUOM 1990; LLD; President of Malta, since 2004; *b* Birkirkara, Malta, 7 Feb. 1934; *s* of late Luigi Fenech-Adami and Josephine (*née* Pace); *m* 1965, Mary (*née* Sciberras); four *s* one *d*. *Educ:* St Aloysius Coll., Malta; Royal Univ. of Malta (BA 1955, LLD 1958). Entered legal practice in Malta, 1959. Nationalist Party: Mem. Nat. Exec., 1961; Asst Gen. Sec., 1962–75; Pres., Gen. and Admin. Council, 1975–77; Leader, 1977–2004. MP Malta, 1969–2004; Shadow Minister for Labour and Social Services, 1971–77; Leader of the Opposition, 1977–82, 1983–87, 1996–98; Prime Minister, 1987–96, 1998–2004; Foreign Minister, 1989–90. Vice-Pres., European Union of Christian Democrat Parties, 1979–99. Editor, Il-Poplu (Party Newspaper), 1962–69. *Address:* (office) The Palace, Valletta, Malta.

FENHALLS, Richard Dorian; Chairman, Strand Partners Ltd, since 2007 (Chief Executive, 1993–2006; Deputy Chairman, 2006–07); *b* 14 July 1943; *s* of Roydon Myers and Maureen Rosa Fenhalls; *m* 1967, Angela Sarah Allen; one *s* one *d*. *Educ:* Hilton Coll., Univ. of Natal (BA); Christ's Coll., Cambridge (MA, LLM). Attorney, S Africa, 1969. Goodricke & Son, Attorney, S Africa, 1969–70; Citibank, 1970–72; Senior Vice President: Marine Midland Bank, 1972–77; American Express Bank, 1977–81; Dep. Chm. and Chief Exec., Guinness Mahon & Co. Ltd, 1981–85; Chief Exec., Henry Ansbacher Hldgs, 1985–93; Chm., Henry Ansbacher & Co. Ltd, 1985–93. *Recreations:* sailing, veteran cars, historic car rallying. *Address:* 26 Mount Row, W1K 3SQ. *Clubs:* Royal Ocean Racing, Royal Thames Yacht; Royal Southern Yacht (Hamble); Veteran Car of GB.

FENLON, Prof. Iain Alexander, FSA; Professor of Historical Musicology, University of Cambridge, since 2005; Fellow, King's College, Cambridge, since 1976; *b* 26 Oct. 1949; *s* of Albert Fenlon and Joan (*née* Rainey); *m* 1993, Nicoletta Guidobaldi. *Educ:* Reading Univ. (BA); Birmingham Univ. (MA); St Catharine's Coll., Cambridge; King's Coll., Cambridge (MA; PhD 1977). FSA 1989. Hayward Research Fellow, Birmingham Univ., 1974–75; Fellow, Villa I Tatti (Harvard Univ. Center for Italian Renaissance Studies), Florence, 1975–76; King's College, Cambridge: Jun. Res. Fellow, 1976–79; Sen. Res. Fellow, 1979–83; Vice-Provost, 1986–91; Sen. Tutor, 2005–; University of Cambridge: Asst Lectr, 1979–84; Lectr, 1984–96; Reader in Historical Musicology, 1995–2005. Vis. Scholar, Harvard Univ., 1984–85; Visiting Fellow: All Souls Coll., Oxford, 1991–92; New Coll., Oxford, 1992; British Acad. Res. Reader, 1996–98; Visiting Professor: Ecole Normale Supérieure, Paris, 1998–99; Univ. of Bologna, 1999–2000. Leverhulme Res. Award, 2000–03. Founding Ed., Early Music History, 1981–. Dent Medal, Internat. Musicological Soc./Royal Musical Assoc., 1984. *Publications:* Music and Patronage in Sixteenth-Century Mantua, 2 vols, 1980, 1982; (ed) Music in Medieval and Early Modern Europe, 1981; (with J. Haar) The Early Sixteenth-Century Italian Madrigal, 1988; (with P. Miller) The Song of the Soul: understanding Poppea, 1992; Music, Print and Culture in Early Sixteenth-Century Italy, 1995; Giaches de Wert: letters and documents, 1999; Music and Culture in Late Renaissance Italy, 2002; The Ceremonial City: history, memory and myth in Renaissance Venice, 2007; articles in various musicol jls, TLS, London Review of Books, etc. *Recreations:* travel, wine. *Address:* King's College, Cambridge CB2 1ST. *T:* (01223) 331100.

FENN, Prof. John Bennett, PhD; Professor of Analytical Chemistry, Virginia Commonwealth University, since 1993; *b* 15 June 1917; *s* of late Herbert Bennett Fenn and Jeanette Clyde Fenn (*née* Dingman); *m* 1939, Margaret Elizabeth Wilson; one *s* two *d*. *Educ:* Berea Coll. (AB 1937); Yale Univ. (PhD 1940). Research Chemist: Monsanto Chemical Co., 1940–43; Sharples Chemicals Inc., 1943–45; Vice-Pres., Experiment Inc., 1945–52; Dir, Project SQUID, 1952–62, Prof. of Mech. Engrg, 1959–63, Prof. of Aerospace Scis, 1963–66, Princeton Univ.; Prof. of Applied Sci. and Chemistry, 1967–80, Prof. of Engrg, 1980–87, Yale Univ., now Emeritus. Pres., Relay Develt Corp., 1975–. (Jtly) Nobel Prize in Chemistry, 2002. *Address:* Department of Chemistry, Virginia Commonwealth University, 1001 W Main Street, PO Box 842006, Richmond, VA 23284–2006, USA.

FENN, Sir Nicholas (Maxted), GCMG 1995 (KCMG 1989; CMG 1980); HM Diplomatic Service, retired; *b* 19 Feb. 1936; *s* of late Rev. Prof. J. Eric Fenn and of Kathleen (*née* Harrison); *m* 1959, Susan Clare (*née* Russell); two *s* one *d*. *Educ:* Kingswood Sch., Bath; Peterhouse, Cambridge (MA; Hon. Fellow, 2001). Pilot Officer, RAF, 1954–56. Third Sec., British Embassy, Rangoon, 1959–63; Asst Private Sec. to Sec. of State for Foreign Affairs, 1963–67; First Secretary: British Interests Sect., Swiss Embassy, Algiers, 1967–69; Public Relations, UK Mission to UN, NY, 1969–72; Dep. Head, Energy Dept, FCO, 1972–75; Counsellor, Peking, 1975–77; Head of News Dept and FCO Spokesman, 1979–82; Spokesman to last Governor of Rhodesia, 1979–80; Ambassador: Rangoon, 1982–86; Dublin, 1986–91; High Comr, India, 1991–96. Chief Exec., 1997–2000, Chm., 2000–06, Marie Curie Cancer Care. Jt Chm., Anglo-Irish Encounter, 1998–2003. Vice-Pres., Leprosy Mission, 1996–2002; Trustee: Sightsavers Internat., 1996–2005 (Vice Pres., 2006–); Guide Dogs for the Blind Assoc., 2002–06; Governor: Jawaharlal Nehru Meml Trust, 1997–2006; Kingswood Sch., Bath, 1996–2006. Churchwarden, Marden Parish Ch, 2001–06. *Recreation:* sailing. *Club:* Oxford and Cambridge.

See also R. D. R. Fenn.

FENN, Peter John; His Honour Judge Fenn; a Circuit Judge, since 2005; *b* 31 Oct. 1956; *s* of Eric Arthur William Fenn and Beryl Marjorie Fenn; *m* 2000, Maxine Helen Adams. *Educ:* Hertford Coll., Oxford (MA). Called to the Bar, Middle Temple, 1979; in practice as a barrister, Colchester, 1980–97, London, 1997–2005; a Recorder, 2003–05. Dir of Music, Stowmarket URC, 1995–2007. *Recreations:* travel, music, horse riding. *Address:* Chelmsford Crown Court, New Street, Chelmsford, Essex CM1 1EL. *T:* (01245) 603000, *Fax:* (01245) 603011.

FENN, Robert Dominic Russell; HM Diplomatic Service; Deputy High Commissioner, Nicosia, since 2004; *b* 28 Jan. 1962; *s* of Sir Nicholas Maxted Fenn, *qv*; *m* 2002, Julia Lloyd Williams; two *s*. *Educ:* Kingswood Sch., Bath; Peterhouse, Cambridge (BA 1st Cl. Hons Classics 1983). Entered FCO, 1983; Third Sec., The Hague, 1985–88; Second Sec., Lagos, 1988–89; First Secretary: S Africa Desk, FCO, 1989–92; Human Rights, UKMIS, NY, 1992–97; (EU/Econ.), Rome, 1997–2001; Dep. Hd, Southern Eur. Dept, later Team Leader, E Mediterranean (Cyprus/Greece/Turkey), FCO, 2001–04. *Recreations:* reading, poetry, armchair architecture. *Address:* British High Commission, Nicosia, BFPO 567. *T:* (2) 2861310, *Fax:* (2) 2861315; *e-mail:* rob.fenn@fco.gov.uk; c/o Foreign and Commonwealth Office, King Charles Street, SW1A 2AH.

FENNELL, Hon. Sir (John) Desmond (Augustine), Kt 1990; OBE 1982; a Judge of the High Court of Justice, Queen's Bench Division, 1990–92; *b* 17 Sept. 1933; *s* of late Dr A. J. Fennell, Lincoln; *m* 1966, Susan Primrose, *d* of late J. M. Trusted; one *s* two *d*. *Educ:* Ampleforth; Corpus Christi Coll., Cambridge. Served with Grenadier Guards, 1956–58. Called to the Bar, Inner Temple, 1959, Bencher, 1983; Dep. Chm., Bedfordshire QS, 1971; a Recorder of the Crown Court, 1972–89; QC 1974; Leader, Midland and Oxford Circuit, 1983–88; a Judge of the Court of Appeal of Jersey and Court of Appeal of Guernsey, 1984–89; a Judge of the Employment Appeal Tribunal, 1991–92. Vice-Chm., 1988, Chm., 1989, Gen. Council of the Bar. Inspector, King's Cross Underground fire, 1988. Pres., Stoke Mandeville Burns and Reconstructive Surgery Res. Trust, 2002– (Chm., 1994–2002). Chm., Buckingham Div. Cons. Assoc., 1976–79 (Pres., 1983–89). Hon. positions various local orgns. *Clubs:* Boodle's, Pilgrims.

FENNER, Prof. Frank John, AC 1989; CMG 1976; MBE 1944; FRCP, FRACP; FRS 1958; FAA; University Fellow, 1980–82, Visiting Fellow, 1983–2007, John Curtin School of Medical Research, Australian National University; *b* 21 Dec. 1914; *s* of Charles and Emma L. Fenner; *m* 1944, Ellen Margaret Bobbie Roberts (*d* 1995); one *d* (and one *d* decd). *Educ:* Thebarton Technical High Sch.; Adelaide High Sch.; Univ. of Adelaide (MB, BS 1938; MD 1942); DTM Sydney 1940. FAA 1954. Served as Medical Officer, Hospital Pathologist, and Malariologist, AIF, 1940–46; Francis Haley Research Fellow, Walter and Eliza Hall Inst. for Medical Research, Melbourne, 1946–48; Rockefeller Foundation Travelling Fellow, 1948–49; Prof. of Microbiology, 1949–67, Dir, John Curtin Sch. of Med. Research, 1967–73, Prof. of Environmental Studies and Dir, Centre for Resource and Environmental Studies, 1973–79, ANU; Overseas Fellow, Churchill Coll., Cambridge, 1961–62. Fogarty Schol., Nat. Insts of Health, USA, 1973–74, 1982–83. Chm., Global Commn for Certification of Smallpox Eradication, WHO, 1978–80. For. Associate, Nat. Acad. of Scis, USA, 1977. Harvey Lecture, Harvey Soc. of New York, 1957; Royal Society: Leeuwenhoek Lecture, 1961, Florey Lecture, 1983; Copley Medal, 1995; Australian Acad. of Science: Matthew Flinders Lecture, 1967; Burnet Lecture, 1985. Emeritus Mem., Amer. Soc. Virol., 1991. Fellow, World Acad. of Art and Sci., 1986. Hon. FRACP (FRACP 1959); Hon. FRCP (FRCP 1967); Hon. Fellow, University House, 2002. Hon. MD Monash, 1966; Dr *hc* Liège, 1992; Hon. DSc: Oxford Brookes Univ., 1995; ANU, 1996; DUniv Adelaide, 2007. David Syme Prize, Univ. of Melbourne, 1949; Mueller Medal, Australian and New Zealand Assoc. for the Advancement of Science, 1964; Britannica Australia Award for Medicine, 1967; ANZAC Peace Award, 1980; ANZAAS Medal, 1980; Stuart Mudd Award, Internat. Union of Microbiol Socs, 1986; Japan Prize (Preventive Medicine), Sci. & Technol. Foundn of Japan, 1988; Albert Einstein World Award for Science, 2000; Clunies Ross Nat. Sci. and Technol. Lifetime Contribution Award, 2002; Prime Minister's Prize for Science, 2002; Australian of the Year, 2003, Sen. Australian of the Year, 2006, ACT. *Publications:* The Production of Antibodies (with F. M. Burnet), 1949; Myxomatosis (with F. N. Ratcliffe), 1965; The Biology of Animal Viruses, 1968, 2nd edn 1974; Medical Virology (with D. O. White), 1970, 4th edn 1994; Classification and Nomenclature of Viruses, 1976; (with A. L. G. Rees) The Australian Academy of Science: the First Twenty-five Years, 1980; (jtly) Veterinary Virology, 1987, 2nd edn 1993; (jtly) Smallpox and its Eradication, 1988; (with Z. Jezek) Human Monkeypox, 1988; (with A. Gibbs) Portraits of Viruses: a history of virology, 1988; (jtly) The Orthopoxviruses, 1989; History of Microbiology in Australia, 1990; The Australian Academy of Science: the first forty years, 1995; (with B. Fantini) The Biological Control of Vertebrate Pests, 1999; (with D. R. Curtis) History of the John Curtin School of Medical Research 1948–1998, 2001; The Australian Academy of Science: the first fifty years, 2005; Nature, Nurture and Chance: the lives of Frank and Charles Fenner, 2006; numerous scientific papers, dealing with virology, epidemiology, bacteriology, environmental problems and history of science. *Recreation:* gardening. *Address:* 8 Monaro Crescent, Red Hill, Canberra, ACT 2603, Australia. *T:* (2) 62959176.

FENNER, Dame Peggy (Edith), DBE 1986; DL; *b* 12 Nov. 1922; *m* 1940, Bernard Fenner; (one *d* decd). *Educ:* LCC School, Brockley; Ide Hill, Sevenoaks. Contested (C) Newcastle-under-Lyme, 1966. MP (C) Rochester and Chatham, 1970–Sept. 1974 and 1979–83, Medway, 1983–97; contested (C) Medway, 1997. Parly Sec., MAFF, 1972–74 and 1981–86. Mem., British Delegn to European Parlt, Strasbourg, 1974; UK rep. to Council of Europe and WEU, 1987–97. Member: West Kent Divisional Exec. Educn Cttee, 1963–72; Sevenoaks Urban District Council, 1957–71 (Chairman, 1962 and 1963); Exec. of Kent Borough and Urban District Councils Assoc., 1967–71; a Vice-Pres., Urban District Councils Assoc., 1971. DL Kent, 1992. *Recreations:* reading, travel, theatre, gardening.

FENNESSY, Sir Edward, Kt 1975; CBE 1957 (OBE 1944); BSc; FIET, FRIN; *b* 17 Jan. 1912; *m* 1st, 1937, Marion Banks (*d* 1983); one *s* one *d;* 2nd, 1984, Leonora Patricia Birkett, *widow* of Trevor Birkett. *Educ:* Queen Mary Coll., London (Hon. Fellow, QMW, 1998). Telecommunications Research, Standard Telephones and Cables, 1934–38; Radar Research, Air Min. Research Station, Bawdsey Manor, 1938. War of 1939–45: commissioned RAFVR, 1940; Group Captain, 1945; staff No 60 Group, RAF, 1940–45; resp. for planning and construction radar systems for defence of UK, and Bomber Ops. Joined Bd of The Decca Navigator Co., 1946; Managing Director: Decca Radar Ltd, 1950–65; The Plessey Electronics Group, 1965–69. Chairman: British Telecommunications Research Ltd, 1966–69; Electronic Engineering Assoc., 1967–68; Man. Dir, Telecommunications, 1969–77, and Dep. Chm., 1975–77, Post Office Corp. Chairman: IMA Microwave Products Ltd, 1979–83; LKB Biochrom, 1978–87; British Medical Data Systems, 1981–91; Dep. Chm., LKB Instruments, 1978–87. Pres., Royal Institute of Navigation, 1975–78. DUniv Surrey, 1971. *Address:* Northbrook, Littleford Lane, Shamley Green, Surrey GU5 0RH. *T:* (01483) 892444.

FENNEY, Roger Johnson, CBE 1973 (MBE (mil.) 1945); Chairman, Special Trustees, Charing Cross Hospital, 1980–88; *b* 11 Sept. 1916; *s* of James Henry Fenney and Annie Sarah Fenney; *m* 1942, Dorothy Porteus (*d* 1989); two *d. Educ:* Cowley Sch., St Helens; Univ. of Manchester (BA Admin 1939). Served War, 1939–46: Gunner to Major, Field Artillery; served N Africa and Italy (mentioned in despatches). Secretary, Central Midwives Board, 1947–82; Governor, Charing Cross Hosp., 1958–74 (Chm., Clinical Res. Cttee, 1970–80; Mem. Council, Med. Sch., 1970–80); Governor, Hammersmith Hosp., 1956–74; Chm., W London Hosp., 1957–68; First Nuffield Fellow for Health Affairs, USA, 1968; Dep. Chm., Kennedy Inst. of Rheumatol., 1970–77. Member: Exec., Arthritis and Rheumatism Council, 1978–98; Ealing, Hammersmith and Hounslow AHA, 1974–79; Field Dir, Jt Study Gp (FIGO/ICM), Accra, Yaounde, Nairobi, Dakar, San José and Bogotá, 1972–76. *Address:* 11 Gilray House, Gloucester Terrace, W2 3DF. *T:* (020) 7262 8313.

FENTEM, Prof. Peter Harold, FRCP; Emeritus Professor, University of Nottingham, 1997 (Stroke Association Professor of Stroke Medicine, 1992–97); Hon. Consultant, Nottingham City Hospital NHS Trust (formerly Nottingham Health Authority), 1976–97; *b* 12 Sept. 1933; *s* of Harold and Agnes Fentem; *m* 1958, Rosemary Hodson; two *s* two *d. Educ:* Bury Grammar Sch.; Univ. of Manchester (BSc 1st cl. hons 1955; MSc 1956; MB ChB Hons 1959). FRCP 1989. Hosp. appts, Manchester Royal Inf., 1959–60; Demonstrator in Path., Univ. of Manchester, 1960–61; Manchester and Cardiff Royal Infs, 1961–64; Lectr in Physiol., St Mary's Hosp. Med. Sch., 1964–68; University of Nottingham: Sen. Lectr in Physiol., 1968; Reader, 1975; Prof. of Physiol., 1975–92; Dean of Medicine, 1987–93. Chm., BSI Tech. Sub-Cttee on Compression Hosiery, 1978–89; Sci. Sec., Fitness and Health Adv. Gp, Sports Council, 1981; Civil Consultant to RAF, 1983–2000; Hon. Consultant to Army, 1989–97; Member: Army Personnel Res. Cttee, 1983–93 (Chm., Applied Physiol. Panel, 1986–93); GMC, 1988–93; Trent RHA, 1988–90; DoH Physical Activity Task Force, 1993–96; Nat. Alliance for Physical Activity, 1997–99; Nat. Heart Forum, 1997–. Trustee: Age Concern Essex, 1999–; Stroke Assoc., 2000–. *Publications:* (jt author): Exercise: the facts, 1981; Work Physiology, in Principles and Practice of Human Physiology, 1981; The New Case for Exercise, 1988; Benefits of Exercise: the evidence, 1990; (Adv. Editor) Physiology Integrated Clinical Science, 1983. *Recreations:* gardening, walking.

FENTON, Prof. Alexander, CBE 1986; DLitt; Professor of Scottish Ethnology and Director, School of Scottish Studies, University of Edinburgh, 1990–94, now Professor Emeritus; Consultant, European Ethnological Research Centre, Edinburgh, since 2007 (Director, 1989–2007); *b* 26 June 1929; *s* of Alexander Fenton and Annie Stirling Stronach; *m* 1956, Evelyn Elizabeth Hunter; two *d. Educ:* Turriff Academy; Aberdeen Univ. (MA); Cambridge Univ. (BA); Edinburgh Univ. (DLitt). Senior Asst Editor, Scottish National Dictionary, 1955–59; Asst Keeper, Nat. Museum of Antiquities of Scotland, 1959–75, Dep. Keeper, 1975–78, Director, 1978–85; Res. Dir, Nat. Museums of Scotland, 1985–89. Mem., Ancient Monuments Bd for Scotland, 1979–94. Hon. Prof. of Antiquities to Royal Scottish Acad., 1996–. Member: Royal Gustav Adolf Acad., Uppsala, Sweden, 1978; Royal Danish Acad. of Scis and Letters, 1979; Soc. Royale des Lettres de Lund, Sweden, 1998; Jury, Europa Preis für Volkskunst (FVS Foundation, Hamburg) 1975–96. Hon. DLitt Aberdeen, 1989. Co-editor, Tools and Tillage (Copenhagen), 1968–2004; Editor: Review of Scottish Culture, 1984–2005; Scottish Studies, 1992–99. *Publications:* The Various Names of Shetland, 1973, 2nd edn 1977; Scottish Country Life, 1976, 3rd edn 1999; (trans.) S. Steensen Blicher, En Landsbydegns Dagbog (The Diary of a Parish Clerk, 1976); The Island Blackhouse, 1978; The Northern Isles: Orkney and Shetland, 1978, 2nd edn 1997; (with B. Walker) The Rural Architecture of Scotland, 1981; The Shape of the Past, 2 vols, 1985; (trans.) S. Weöres, Ha a Világ Rigó Lenne (If All the World were a Blackbird), 1985; Wird's an' Wark 'e Seasons Roon, 1987; Country Life in Scotland, 1987; The Turra Coo: a legal episode in the popular culture of NE Scotland, 1989; Scottish Country Life, 1989; Craiters—or Twenty Buchan Tales, 1995; Buchan Words and Ways, 2005; Scottish Life and Society: the food of the Scots, 2008; numerous articles in learned jls. *Address:* 132 Blackford Avenue, Edinburgh EH9 3HH. *T:* (0131) 667 5456. *Club:* New (Edinburgh).

FENTON, Ernest John; Director General, Association of Investment Trust Companies, 1993–97; *b* 14 Oct. 1938; *s* of Forbes Duncan Campbell Fenton and Janet Burnfield Fenton (*née* Easson); *m* 1965, Ann Ishbel Ramsay; one *s* two *d. Educ:* Harris Acad., Scotland. CA 1961; AIIMR 1972. Partner, W. Greenwell & Co., 1968–87; Chm. and Chief Exec., Greenwell Montagu Stockbrokers, 1987–92. Non-executive Director: Fleming Income & Capital Investment Trust PLC, 1991–2002; Cotesworth & Co. Ltd (Lloyd's Managing Agents), 1994–2001; Renaissance US Growth and Income Trust PLC, 1996– (Chm., 2004–); US Special Opportunities (formerly BFS US Special Opportunities) Trust plc, 2001–. Farmer, Kent and Sussex, 1973–. Proprietor, Fenton's Rink, Kent, 2004–. Mem. Investment Cttee, CRC, 1995–98. MSI 1986; MInstD 1994. FRSA 1993. *Recreations:* shooting, curling. *Address:* Dundale Farm, Dundale Road, Tunbridge Wells, Kent TN3 9AQ.

FENTON, James Martin, FRSL; FSA; writer; Professor of Poetry, University of Oxford, 1994–99; *b* 25 April 1949; *s* of Rev. Canon J. C. Fenton, *qv* and Mary Hamilton (*née* Ingoldby). *Educ:* Durham Choristers Sch.; Repton Sch.; Magdalen Coll., Oxford (MA, Hon. Fellow, 1999). FRSL 1983; FSA 2006. Asst Literary Editor, 1971, Editorial Asst, 1972, New Statesman; freelance correspondent in Indo-China, 1973–75; Political Columnist, New Statesman, 1976–78; German Correspondent, The Guardian, 1978–79; Theatre Critic, Sunday Times, 1979–84; Chief Book Reviewer, The Times, 1984–86; Far East Corresp., 1986–88, columnist, 1993–95, The Independent. Trustee, Nat. Gall., 2002–; Visitor, Ashmolean Mus., 2002–. FRSA 2003. Queen's Gold Medal for Poetry, 2007. *Publications:* Our Western Furniture, 1968; Terminal Moraine, 1972; A Vacant Possession, 1978; A German Requiem, 1980; Dead Soldiers, 1981; The Memory of War 1982; (trans.) Rigoletto, 1982; You Were Marvellous, 1983; (ed) The Original Michael Frayn, 1983; Children in Exile, 1984; Poems 1968–83, 1985; (trans.) Simon Boccanegra 1985; The Fall of Saigon, in Granta 15, 1985; The Snap Revolution, in Granta 18, 1986; (ed) Cambodian Witness: the autobiography of Someth May, 1986; (with John Fuller) Partingtime Hall (poems), 1987; All the Wrong Places: adrift in the politics of Asia, 1988; Manila Envelope, 1989; (ed) Underground in Japan, by Rey Ventura, 1992; Out of Danger (poems), 1993; Leonardo's Nephew, 1998; The Strength of Poetry, 2001; A Garden from a Hundred Packets of Seed, 2001; An Introduction to English Poetry, 2002; The Love Bomb (3 dramatic works for music), 2003; Selected Poems, 2006; Samuel Taylor Coleridge: poems selected by James Fenton, 2006; School of Genius: a history of the Royal Academy, 2006; (ed) The New Faber Book of Love Poems, 2006. *Address:* Peters Fraser & Dunlop, Drury House, 34–43 Russell Street, WC2B 5HA.

FENTON, Rev. Canon John Charles; Canon of Christ Church, Oxford, 1978–91, Hon. Canon, 1991–92, now Hon. Canon Emeritus and Emeritus Student; *b* 5 June 1921; *s* of Cornelius O'Connor Fenton and Agnes Claudina Fenton. *Educ:* S Edward's Sch., Oxford; Queen's Coll., Oxford (BA 1943, MA 1947, BD 1953); Lincoln Theol Coll. Deacon 1944, priest 1945. Asst Curate, All Saints, Hindley, Wigan, 1944–47; Chaplain Lincoln Theol Coll., 1947–51, Sub-Warden, 1951–54; Vicar of Wentworth, Yorks, 1954–58; Principal: Lichfield Theol Coll., 1958–65; S Chad's Coll., Durham, 1965–78 DD Lambeth, 2001. *Publications:* Preaching the Cross, 1958; The Passion according to John, 1961; Crucified with Christ, 1961; Saint Matthew (Pelican Commentaries), 1963; Saint John (New Clarendon Bible), 1970; What was Jesus' Message?, 1971; (with M. Hare Duke) Good News, 1976; Finding the Way through John, 1988; Sunday Readings, 1991; Affirmations, 1993; Finding the Way through Mark, 1995; The Matthew Passion, 1996 Galatians, 1996, with 1 & 2 Thessalonians, 1999 (People's Bible Commentary); More About Mark, 2001; contrib. Theol., Jl of Theol Studies, and Church Times. *Address:* 8 Rowland Close, Wolvercote, Oxford OX2 8PW. *T:* (01865) 554099.

FENTON, Mark Alexander, PhD; Headmaster, Dr Challoner's Grammar School Amersham, since 2001; *b* 20 Oct. 1965; *s* of Prof. George and Dr Sylvia Fenton. *Educ.* Peterhouse, Cambridge (MA); Anglia Poly. Univ. (MSc, PhD); Univ. of Buckingham (DipEd Law). Teacher of Hist., Boswells Sch., Chelmsford, 1988–91; Head of Hist. and Politics, 1991–97, Sen. Teacher, 1994–97, King Edward VI Grammar Sch., Chelmsford; Dep. Headteacher, Sir Joseph Williamson's Mathematical Sch., Rochester, 1997–2001. Bd Mem., Bucks Acad. of Sch. Leadership, 2004– (Chm., 2005–). Gov., The Beacon Sch., Chesham Bois, 2005–. Trustee, The Cricket Foundn, 2005–08. Dir, Ramsey Singers, 1987–; Manager, Bucks County U13 Cricket, 2001–06, U15 Cricket, 2005–; Schools' Rep., Bucks County Cricket Bd, 2002–; Chm., Bucks Schs Cricket Assoc., 2004– (on secondment to British Council SLANT Project (Trinidad and Tobago), 2006–). *Publications:* articles in educn mgt jls. *Recreations:* singing in and conducting choirs; playing, coaching, watching and talking about cricket. *Address:* Dr Challoner's Grammar School, Chesham Road, Amersham, Bucks HP6 5HA. *T:* (01494) 787500, *Fax:* (01494) 721862 *e-mail:* admin@challoners.com. *Club:* MCC.

FENWICK, Very Rev. Jeffery Robert; Dean of Guernsey, 1989–95; *b* 8 April 1930; *s* of Stanley Robert and Dorothy Fenwick; *m* 1955, Pamela Frances (*née* Galley); one *s* two *d. Educ:* Torquay and Selhurst Grammar Schools; Pembroke Coll., Cambridge (MA); Lincoln Theol Coll. Deacon 1955, priest 1956, Liverpool; Curate, St Thomas the Martyr, UpHolland, 1955; Priest-in-charge, Christ the King, Daramombe, Mashonaland, 1958; Secretary, USPG, Oxford, 1964; Rector, Gatooma 1965, Salisbury East 1967, Mashonaland; Dean, Bulawayo, Matabeleland, 1975; Canon Residentiary, Worcester Cathedral, 1978; Librarian and Treasurer, 1978–89. Examining Chaplain, Mashonaland and Matabeleland, 1966–78; Archdeacon of Charter, 1970–75, of Bulawayo 1975–78 Hon. Canon of Winchester Cathedral, 1989–95, now Emeritus. Chm., Cathedrals Finance Conf. for England, 1983–89. Chm., Britain-Zimbabwe Soc., 1996–. *Publications.* Chosen People, 1971; (contrib.) The Pattern of History, 1973. *Recreations:* painting, music, gardening, walking. *Address:* 3 Suid Street, Alexandria 6185, S Africa.

FENWICK, John James; Vice Lord-Lieutenant, Tyne and Wear, 2002–07; Deputy Chairman, Fenwick Ltd, 1972–79 and since 1997 (Managing Director, 1972–82; Chairman, 1979–97); Director, Northern Rock plc (formerly Northern Rock Building Society), 1984–99; *b* 9 Aug. 1932; *e s* of James Frederick Trevor Fenwick; *m* 1957, Muriel Gillian Hodnett; three *s. Educ:* Rugby Sch.; Pembroke Coll., Cambridge (MA). Chairman: Northumberland Assoc. of Youth Clubs, 1966–71; Retail Distributors Assoc., 1977–79; Vice Chm., National Assoc. of Citizens Advice Bureaux, 1971–79; Regional Dir, Northern Bd, Lloyds Bank, 1982–85. Member: Newcastle Diocesan Bd of Finance, 1964–69; Retail Consortium Council, 1976–79; Post Office Users' Nat. Council, 1980–82; Civic Trust for NE, 1979–96. Governor: Royal Grammar Sch., Newcastle upon Tyne, 1975–2000 (Chm. Govs, 1987–2000); St Paul's Girls' Sch., 1988–2001 (Chm. Govs, 1995–2001); Moorfields Eye Hosp., 1981–86; Royal Shakespeare Theatre, 1985–2002. Master, Mercers' Co., 1991–92. DL Tyne and Wear, 1986. Hon. DCL Northumbria, 1993. *Recreations:* travel, reading, walking. *Address:* 63 New Bond Street, W1A 3BS. *Clubs:* Garrick, MCC.

FENWICK, Justin Francis Quintus; QC 1993; a Recorder, since 1999; a Deputy High Court Judge, since 2003; *b* 11 Sept. 1949; *s* of David and Maita Fenwick; *m* 1975, Marcia Mary Dunn; one *s* three *d. Educ:* Ampleforth Coll., York; Clare Coll., Cambridge (MA Mod. Langs and Architectural Hist.). Commnd Grenadier Guards, 1968; Adjt, 2nd Battalion, 1977–79; Temp. Equerry to HRH the Duke of Edinburgh, 1979–81. Called to the Bar, Inner Temple, 1980, Bencher, 1997. Hd of Chambers, 4 New Square, 2000–05. Dir, 1997–, Chm., 1999–, Bar Mutual Indemnity Fund Ltd. *Recreations:* wine, shooting, reading. *Address:* 4 New Square, Lincoln's Inn, WC2A 3RJ. *T:* (020) 7822 2000. *Club:* Garrick.

FENWICK, Lex; Chief Executive Officer, Bloomberg LP, since 2002; *b* 21 March 1959; *s* of Benedict and Deirdre Fenwick; *m* 1990, Sophie Crichton-Stuart; two *d.* Bloomberg LP, 1996–: Man. Dir, Bloomberg Europe, ME and Africa, 1996–2000; Chief Operating Officer, 2001–02. *Recreations:* art, music. *Address:* Bloomberg LP, 731 Lexington Avenue, New York, NY 10022, USA.

FENWICK, Mary; *see* Nightingale, M.

FENWICK, Peter Brooke Cadogan, FRCPsych; Consultant Neuropsychiatrist, Maudsley Hospital, 1977–96, now Emeritus; President, Scientific and Medical Network, since 2003 (Chairman, 1987–2000); *b* 25 May 1935; *s* of Anthony Fenwick and Betty (*née* Darling); *m* 1963, Elizabeth Roberts; one *s* two *d*. *Educ:* Stowe Sch.; Trinity Coll., Cambridge (BA 1957; MB BChir 1960); DPM London 1966. FRCPsych 1986. House Officer, St Thomas' Hosp., 1960–62; SHO in Psychiatry, Middlesex Hosp., 1962–64; MRC Fellow, Nat. Hosp., 1964–66; Registrar, then Sen. Registrar, Maudsley Hosp., 1967–74; Consultant Neurophysiologist: Westminster Hosp., 1974–77; St Thomas' Hosp., 1974–96, now Hon. Consulting Neurophysiologist; Cons. Neuropsychiatrist, Radcliffe Infirmary, Oxford, 1989–2002, now Emeritus; Hon. Cons. Neurophysiologist, Broadmoor Special Hosp., 1972–; Hon. Sen. Lectr, Inst. of Psychiatry, London Univ., 1974–. Forensic expert on automatism and sleep disorders; has given expert neuropsychiatric evidence in many civil and criminal legal cases. Consultant, Music and the Brain documentary series, 1986. Ver Hayden de Lancey Prize, Cambridge Univ., 1987. *Publications:* with Elizabeth Fenwick: The Truth in the Light, 1995; The Hidden Door, 1997; Past Lives, 1999; over 200 contribs to learned jls. *Recreations:* flying, hill walking, wind and water turbines, the study of consciousness. *Address:* 42 Herne Hill, SE24 9QP. *T:* (020) 7274 3154.

FENWICK, Very Rev. Dr Richard David; Dean of Monmouth, since 1997; *b* 3 Dec. 1943; *s* of Ethel May and William Samuel Fenwick; *m* 1975, Dr Jane Elizabeth Hughes; one *s* one *d*. *Educ:* Glantâf Secondary Modern Sch.; Monkton House; Canton High Sch., Cardiff; Univ. of Wales, Lampeter (BA, MA, PhD); Trinity Coll., Dublin (MusB, MA); Fitzwilliam Coll., Cambridge; Ridley Hall, Cambridge. FLCM; FTCL. Ordained deacon, 1968, priest, 1969; Assistant Curate: Skewen, 1968–72; Penarth with Lavernock, 1972–74; Priest-Vicar, Succentor and Sacrist of Rochester Cathedral, 1974–78; Minor Canon, 1978–83, Succentor, 1979–83, Warden of the Coll. of Minor Canons, 1981–83, St Paul's Cathedral; Vicar, St Martin's, Ruislip, 1983–90; Priest-Vicar of Westminster Abbey, 1983–90; Canon Residentiary and Precentor, 1990–97, Sub-Dean, 1996–97, Guildford Cathedral. Chm., Liturgical Commn of the Church in Wales, 1998–. Warden, Guild of Church Musicians, 1998–. Liveryman, Musicians' Co.; Hon. Liveryman and Master's Chaplain, Co. of Gold and Silver Wyre Drawers. Hon. FVCM, 1990; Hon. FGCM, 2004. OStJ 2001. *Publications:* contribs to various musical and theol jls. *Recreations:* travel, reading, music. *Address:* The Deanery, Stow Hill, Newport, Monmouthshire NP20 4ED. *T:* (01633) 263338.

FERGUS, Prof. Sir Howard (Archibald), KBE 2001 (CBE 1995; OBE 1979); PhD; Deputy Governor, Montserrat, since 1976; Professor, University of West Indies, since 2001; *b* 22 July 1937; *s* of Simon and Priscilla Fergus; *m* 1970, Eudora Edgecombe; one *s* two *d*. *Educ:* Univ. of W Indies (BA, PhD 1984); Univ. of Bristol (CertEd); Univ. of Manchester (MEd). Primary sch. teacher, 1955–64; secondary sch. teacher, 1964–70; Chief Educn Officer, Montserrat, 1970–74; Lectr, 1974–81, Sen. Lectr, 1981–2001, Sch. of Continuing Studies, Univ. of WI. Mem. and Speaker, Legislative Council, Montserrat, 1975–2001. Supervisor of Elections, 1978–. *Publications:* Montserrat: history of a Caribbean colony, 1994; Gallery Montserrat: prominent people in our history, 1996; Montserrat Versus Volcano, 1996; Lara Rains and Colonial Rites (poetry), 1998; Volcano Song: poems of an island in agony, 2000; Montserrat in the Twentieth Century: trials and triumphs, 2001; contrib. several book chapters and articles to learned jls. *Recreations:* reading, writing, poetry. *Address:* University of West Indies, PO Box 256 Salem, Montserrat, W Indies. *T:* 4913924; (home) Olveston, Montserrat, W Indies. *T:* 4912414, *Fax:* 4918924.

FERGUSON, Sir Alexander Chapman, Kt 1999; CBE 1995 (OBE 1984); Manager, Manchester United Football Club, since 1986; *b* 31 Dec. 1941; *s* of Alexander and Elizabeth Ferguson; *m* 1966, Catherine Holding; three *s*. *Educ:* Govan High Sch., Glasgow. Footballer; played for: Queen's Park, 1958–60; St Johnstone, 1960–64; Dunfermline Athletic, 1964–67; Glasgow Rangers, 1967–69; Falkirk, 1969–73; Ayr United, 1973–74; numerous championship wins as Manager of St Mirren, 1974–78, of Aberdeen, 1978–86 (League Cup, 1985); wins with Manchester United: Premier Div., 1992–93, 1993–94, 1995–96, 1996–97, 1998–99, 1999–2000, 2000–01, 2002–03, 2006–07, 2007–08; FA Cup, 1990, 1994, 1996, 1999, 2004; European Cup Winners Cup, 1983, 1991; European Cup, 1999; Super Cup, 1983, 1991; League Cup, 1992; Charity Shield, 1990, 1993, 1994, 1996, 1997; FA Community Shield, 2007, 2008. *Publications:* A Light in the North, 1984; Six Years at United, 1992; Just Champion, 1993; A Year in the Life, 1995; (with David Meek) A Will to Win, 1997; (with Hugh McIlvanney) Managing My Life: my autobiography, 1999; The Unique Treble: achieving our goals, 2000. *Recreations:* golf, snooker. *Address:* Manchester United Football Club, Old Trafford, Manchester M16 0RA. *T:* (0161) 872 1661.

FERGUSON, Dr Archibald Thomas Graham, CPhys, FInstP; Nuclear Weapons Safety Advisor, Ministry of Defence, 1994–97; *b* 27 Dec. 1928; *s* of Francis Ferguson and Annie Orr Ferguson (*née* Graham); *m* 1956, Margaret Watson; two *d*. *Educ:* Irvine Royal Acad.; Glasgow Univ. (MA 1950; PhD 1954). CPhys 1974; FInstP 1974. United Kingdom Atomic Energy Authority, Harwell Laboratory, 1953–93: Nuclear Physics Div., 1953–65; Gp Leader, High Voltage Lab., 1961–81; on secondment to Neils Bohr Inst., Copenhagen, 1965–66; Head: Scientific Admin, 1982–85; Nuclear Physics Div., 1985–90; Safety, Culham and Harwell, 1990–93. *Publications:* contrib. numerous articles in learned jls; conf. proceedings. *Recreations:* sailing, gardening.

FERGUSON, Duncan George Robin, FIA; non-executive Chairman, Resolution Group Life Assurance Co., since 2003; *b* 12 May 1942; *s* of Dr R. L. Ferguson and K. I. Ferguson; *m* 1966, Alison Margaret Simpson; one *s* one *d* (and one *s* decd). *Educ:* Fettes Coll., Edinburgh; Trinity Coll., Cambridge (MA Maths and Econs 1964; DipAgSci (Agricl Econs) 1965). FIA 1970. Actuarial student, Bacon & Woodrow, 1965–69; Actuary and Asst Gen. Manager, Metropolitan Life, Cape Town, 1969–72; Actuary and Dir, Nation Life, 1972–75; Dir, Internat. Div., Eagle Star, 1975–88; Partner, 1988, Sen. Partner, 1994–2001, Bacon & Woodrow; Sen. Partner, B & W Deloitte, and Partner, Deloitte & Touche, 2001–03. Non-executive Director: HBOS Financial Services (formerly Halifax), 1994–2007; Illium Insce, 2003–05; Henderson, 2004–. Pres., Inst. of Actuaries, 1996–98. *Publications:* Unit Linked Life Assurance in South Africa, 1972; Life Assurance Solvency and Insolvency, 1976; Business Projections: a critical appraisal, 1980; Review of Law Relating to Insolvent Life Assurance Companies and Proposals for Reform, 1984; Reasonable Expectations of Policy Holders, 1984. *Address:* *e-mail:* dferguson@europe.com.

FERGUSON, Ernest Alexander; Under-Secretary and Accountant-General, Department of Employment, 1973–77; *b* 26 July 1917; *s* of William Henry and Lilian Ferguson; *m* 1940, Mary Josephine Wadsworth; two *s*. *Educ:* Priory Sch., Shrewsbury; Pembroke Coll., Cambridge (Scholar, 1935–39; MA 1944). Served War, RA (Captain), 1940–45. Entered Ministry of Labour, 1945; Principal, 1948; Asst Sec., 1962. Chm., Central Youth Employment Executive, 1967–69; Sec. to NEDC, 1971–73; Dep. Chm., Central Arbitration Cttee, 1977–87. *Recreations:* sport, hill walking, reading. *Address:* 164 Balcombe Road, Horley, Surrey RH6 9DS. *T:* (01293) 432138. *Club:* Civil Service.

FERGUSON, George Robin Paget; Director: Acanthus Ferguson Mann Architects, since 1988; Concept Planning Group, since 1991; President, Royal Institute of British Architects, 2003–05; *b* 22 March 1947; *s* of Robert Spencer Ferguson and Eve Mary Ferguson; *m* Lavinia (*née* Clerk); one *s* two *d*. *Educ:* Wellington Coll.; Univ. of Bristol (BA, BArch). RIBA. Mem. (L), Bristol CC, 1973–79. Contested (Lib/Alliance) Bristol West, 1983, 1987. Commenced own architectural practice as sole practitioner, 1971; Founder and Dir, Acanthus Associated Architectural Practices Ltd, 1986–; Founder and Owner, Tobacco Factory Arts Centre, S Bristol, 1995–. Presenter: The Architecture Show, TV, 1998; Demolition, C4, 2005–06. Chm., Bristol Exploratory, 1993–2001; Pres., Avon Youth Assoc., 1999–; Trustee: Greater Bristol Foundn, 1995–2001; Bristol Cathedral Trust, 1999–. Gov., UWE, 1995–99. Architect to RWA, 1997– (RWA, 1997–). High Sheriff, Bristol, 1996–97. Hon. MA Bristol, 1999; Hon. DDes UWE, 2003. RIBA Awards; Civic Trust Awards; RICS Awards. *Publication:* Races Against Time, 1983. *Recreations:* travel, people, ideas, challenging authority, making things happen. *Address:* Acanthus Ferguson Mann Architects, Royal Colonnade, 18 Great George Street, Bristol BS1 5RH. *T:* (0117) 929 9293, *Fax:* (0117) 929 9295; *e-mail:* george@afm-architects.com.

FERGUSON, Air Vice-Marshal Gordon MacArthur, CB 1993; CBE 1990; Chairman, Suffolk Probation Board, 2001–04; *b* 15 April 1938; *s* of James Miller Ferguson and late Elizabeth Thomson Ferguson (*née* Barron); *m* 1966, Alison Mary Saxby; one *s* one *d*. *Educ:* King Edward VI Sch., Southampton. Commissioned, RAF, 1960; served Mobile Air Movements, RAF Pergamos and Nicosia, HQ 38 Group, RAF Stafford and Fylingdales, MoD Supply Policy, HQ 2nd ATAF; RAF Staff Coll., 1977; OC Tac Supply Wing, 1977–79; MoD Supply Policy, 1979–81; Air Warfare Course, 1981; MoD Supply Policy, 1981–85; Dep. Dir, Supply Management, 1985–87, Dir, 1987–89; Dir, AMSO Reorgn Implementation Team, 1989–91; AOA, HQ Strike Comd, 1991–94. Man. Dir, Taylor Curnow Ltd, 1994–99. Trustee, Royal Patriotic Fund Corp., 1995–2004. *Recreations:* bridge, walking. *Address:* Calle Alhamilla 3, Aguadulce, 04720 Almeria, Spain. *Club:* Royal Air Force.

FERGUSON, Iain William Findlay; QC (Scot.) 2000; *b* 31 July 1961; *s* of James Thomas Ferguson and Catherine Doris (*née* Findlay); *m* 1992, Valérie Laplanche; two *s*. *Educ:* Univ. of Dundee (LLB Hons; DipLP). Admitted Faculty of Advocates, 1987; Standing Junior Counsel: MoD (Army), 1991–98; Scottish Exec., Planning, 1998–2000. *Recreations:* cycling, Rugby, cooking. *Address:* 16 McLaren Road, Edinburgh EH9 2BN. *T:* (0131) 667 1751.

FERGUSON, Sir Ian Edward J.; *see* Johnson-Ferguson.

FERGUSON, Ian Stewart, CBE 2005; Executive Chairman, Data Connection Ltd, since 1981; *b* 22 Feb. 1943; *s* of John Smith Ferguson and Victoria Alexandra Ferguson (*née* Luscombe); *m* 1st, 1967, Wilma Murray (marr. diss. 1991); one *s* one *d*; 2nd, 1995, Tessa Marston. *Educ:* High Sch. of Glasgow; Univ. of Glasgow (BSc Hons Maths 1965). Unilever, 1965–70; IBM, 1970–81. Dir, Business Link London, 1995–97. Member: Modern Apprenticeship Adv. Cttee, DfES, 2001; LSC, 2001– (Chm., Young Peoples' Learning Cttee, 2004–); 14–19 Govt Wkg Gp, 2003–04; Deputy Chairman: Apprenticeship Task Force, 2003–05; Apprenticeship Ambassadors Network, 2006–; Member, Board: QCA, 2003– (Chm., Qualifications and Skills Adv. Gp, 2003–); UK Skills, 2004–; Trng and Develt Agency for Schs, 2006–. Confederation of British Industry: Mem., Nat. Council, 1998–99; Mem., Educn and Trng Affairs Cttee, 2003–. FRSA 2006. *Recreations:* theatre, opera, music, ski-ing, food, wine, family, philosophy, human condition. *Address:* Data Connection Ltd, 100 Church Street, Enfield EN2 6BQ. *T:* (020) 8366 1177, *Fax:* (020) 8363 5062; *e-mail:* ian.ferguson@dataconnection.com.

FERGUSON, John Alexander; HM Senior Chief Inspector of Schools in Scotland, 1981–87, retired; *b* 16 Oct. 1927; *s* of George Ferguson and Martha Crichton Dykes; *m* 1953, Jean Stewart; two *s* one *d*. *Educ:* Royal Coll. of Science and Technology, Univ. of Glasgow (BSc Hons, Diploma). Teacher, Airdrie Central Sch., 1950–51; Lectr, 1951–55, Head of Dept of Engrg, 1955–61, Coatbridge Technical Coll.; HM Inspector of Schs, 1961–72, Asst Sec., 1972–75, Scottish Educn Dept; HM Depute Sen. Chief Inspector of Schs, 1975–81. *Recreations:* golf, bridge. *Club:* Craigmillar Park Lawn Tennis (Edinburgh).

FERGUSON, John McIntyre, CBE 1976; FREng; FIET, FIMechE; engineering consultant, 1973, retired 1986; *b* 16 May 1915; *s* of Frank Ferguson and Lilian (*née* Bowen); *m* 1941, Margaret Frances Tayler; three *s*. *Educ:* Armstrong Coll., Durham Univ. BScEng (1st Cl. Hons). English Electric Co., Stafford: Research, 1936; Chief Engr, 1953; Dir Engrg, Heavy Electric Products, 1965; Dir of Engrg, GEC Power Engrg Co., 1969. Member: Metrication Bd, 1969–76; Science Res. Council, 1972–76; UGC, 1977–82. President: IEE, 1977–78; IEETE, 1979–81. FREng (FEng 1978). Hon. FIEEIE. Hon. DSc Birmingham, 1983. *Recreations:* golf, sailing. *Address:* 11 Appledore Close, Baswich, Stafford ST17 0EW. *T:* (01785) 664700.

FERGUSON, Prof. Mark William James, CBE 1999; PhD; Professor, Faculty of Life Sciences (formerly School of Biological Sciences), University of Manchester, since 1984; Founder, 1998, and Chief Executive Officer, since 2000, Renovo Group plc (formerly Renovo Ltd); *b* 11 Oct. 1955; *s* of late James Ferguson and of Elenor Gwendoline Ferguson; *m* (marr. diss.); three *d*. *Educ:* Queen's Univ., Belfast (BSc 1st Cl. Hons Anatomy 1976; BDS 1st Cl. Hons Dentistry 1978; PhD Anatomy and Embryology 1982). FFDRCSI 1990; FDSRCSE 1997. Winston Churchill Travelling Fellow, 1978; Lectr in Anatomy, QUB, 1979–84; Head, Dept of Cell and Structural Biology, 1986–92, Dean, Sch. of Biol Scis, 1994–96, Univ. of Manchester. Founder and Chm. of Bd, Manchester Biotechnology Ltd, 1997–99. Chm., Health and Life Scis Panel, Tech. Foresight Prog., OST, 1994–99; Member: Lord Sainsbury's Biotech. Cluster Cttee, DTI, 1999; Biol Sub Cttee, Cttee of Safety of Medicines, 1999–2005; Genome Valley Steering Gp, DTI, 2000–01; Preclinical Medicine, Anatomy, Physiol. and Pharmacol. Panel, RAE 2001, HEFCE. President: Med. Scis Section, BAAS, 1997; Bd, BioIndustry Assoc., 2001–03; European Tissue Repair Soc., 2002–03 (Sec., 1996–2007). Gov., Res. into Ageing, 1995–2000. Steeger Vis. Prof. and Lectr, NY Univ. Med. Center, 1992; Lectures: Teale, RCP, 1994; Kelvin, IEE, 1995; Broadhurst, Harvard Med. Sch., 1996; Distinguished, Amer. Soc. of Human Genetics, 1998; Northcroft, British Orthodontic Soc., 2001; Langdon-Brown, RCP, 2002; Cairns, British Soc. Neurol Surgery, 2008; British Council lecture tours: India, 1999, China, 2002. Founder FMedSci 1998. Tech. Pioneer, World Econ. Forum, Davos, 2007–09. Hon. DMedSci QUB, 2002. John Tomes Prize and Medal, 1990, Charles Tomes Prize and Medal, 1998, RCS; Carter Medal, Clin. Genetics Soc., 1997; Internat. Assoc. for Dental Res. Award, 2000; Körber European Science Award, 2002; N. Rowe Lecture and Prize, BAOMS, 2003; Eur. Biotechnia Award, 2007. *Publications:* The Structure, Development and Evolution of Reptiles, 1984; Egg Incubation: its effects on embryonic development in birds and reptiles, 1991; (ed) Gray's Anatomy, 38th edn, 1995; more than 250 scientific papers and contribs to books on wound healing, prevention of scarring, cleft palate and sex determination. *Recreations:* travel, wildlife, reading, antiques, scientific research. *Address:* Renovo, Manchester Incubator Building, 48 Grafton Street, Manchester M13 9XX. *T:* (0161) 606 7222.

FERGUSON, Martin John, AM 1996; MP (ALP) Batman, Australia, since 1996; Minister for Resources and Energy, and Minister for Tourism, since 2007; *b* 12 Dec. 1953; *s* of Laurie John Ferguson and Mary Ellen Clare Ferguson (*née* Bett); *m* 1981, Patricia Jane Waller; one *s* one *d*. *Educ:* St Patrick's Convent, Guildford; St Patrick's Coll., Strathfield; Sydney Univ. (BEc Hons). Federated Miscellaneous Workers Union of Australia: Federal Research Officer, 1975–81; Asst Gen. Sec., 1981–84; Gen. Sec., 1984–90; Pres., ACTU, 1990–96. Asst to Ldr of Opposition on multicultural affairs, 1997–98; Opposition Shadow Minister, Australian Parliament: for employment and trng, 1996–98; for population, 1997–2001; for immigration, 1997–98; for regl devel and infrastructure, 1999–2002; for regl services, 1999–2001; for transport, 1999–2002; for urban devel, 2001–03; for regl devel, transport infrastructure and tourism, 2002–03; for urban and regl devel, transport and infrastructure, 2003–04; for resources, forestry and tourism, 2004–06, and for primary industries, 2005–06; for transport, roads and tourism, 2006–07. Mem., Governing Body, ILO, 1990–96. Member: Trade Develt Council, 1990–96; Econ. Planning Adv. Council, 1990–96; Australian Govt's Agric. Food Council, 1992–96; Exec. Bd, Construction Ind. Develt Agency, 1992–96. Mem. Bd, Nat. Liby of Australia, 1999–. *Address:* Parliament House, Canberra, ACT 2600, Australia. *T:* (2) 62774899, *Fax:* (2) 62778403.

FERGUSON, Prof. Michael Anthony John, CBE 2008; PhD; FRS 2000; FRSE; Professor of Molecular Parasitology, University of Dundee, since 1994; *b* 6 Feb. 1957; *s* of Dr Anthony John Alexander Ferguson and Pamela Mary (*née* Gray); *m* 1st, 1982, Sheila Duxbury (marr. diss. 1988); 2nd, 1992, Dr Maria Lucia Sampaio Güther; one *s*. *Educ:* St Peter's Sch., York; UMIST (BSc Hons Biochem. 1979); Charing Cross Hosp. Med. Sch., Univ. of London (PhD Biochem. 1982). Post-doctoral Research Fellow: Rockefeller Univ., NY, 1982–85; Oxford Univ., 1985–88; Res. Fellow, Pembroke Coll., Oxford, 1986–88; University of Dundee: Lectr, 1988–91; Reader, 1991–94. FRSE 1994; FMedSci 2007. Colworth Medal, Biochemical Soc., 1991. *Recreation:* travel. *Address:* Division of Biological Chemistry and Molecular Microbiology, Wellcome Trust Biocentre, University of Dundee, Dundee DD1 5EH. *T:* (01382) 384219.

FERGUSON, Prof. Niall Campbell Douglas, DPhil; Laurence A. Tisch Professor of History, Harvard University, since 2004; William Ziegler Professor of Business Administration, Harvard Business School, since 2006; Senior Fellow, Hoover Institution, Stanford University, since 2003; Senior Research Fellow, Jesus College, Oxford, since 2003; *b* 18 April 1964; *s* of Dr James Campbell Ferguson and Molly Archibald Ferguson (*née* Hamilton); *m* 1994, Susan Margaret Douglas (*see* S. M. Douglas Ferguson); adopted additional surname Douglas, 1994; two *s* one *d*. *Educ:* Glasgow Acad.; Magdalen Coll., Oxford (BA 1st Cl. Hons; DPhil 1989). Hanseatic Schol., Hamburg, 1986–88; Research Fellow, Christ's Coll., Cambridge, 1989–90; Official Fellow and Lectr, Peterhouse, Cambridge, 1990–92; University of Oxford: Lectr in Mod. Hist., 1992–2000; Prof. of Pol and Financial Hist., 2000–02; Vis. Prof. in Modern Eur. Hist., 2003–; John E. Herzog Prof. of Financial History, Leonard N. Stern Sch. of Business, NY Univ., 2002–04. Houblon-Norman Fellow, Bank of England, 1998–99. Presenter, TV series: Empire, 2003; American Colossus, 2004; War of the World, 2006. Ed., Jl of Contemp. History, 2004–; contributing ed., FT. *Publications:* Paper and Iron: Hamburg business and German politics in the era of inflation 1897–1927, 1995; (ed) Virtual History: alternatives and counterfactuals, 1997; The World's Banker: the history of the house of Rothschild, 1998; The Pity of War, 1998; The Cash Nexus, 2001; Empire: how Britain made the modern world, 2003; Colossus: the rise and fall of the American Empire, 2004; The War of the World: history's age of hatred, 2006; contrib. English Historical Rev., Past & Present, Econ. Hist. Rev., Jl of Econ. Hist. *Recreations:* double bass, journalism. *Address:* Minda de Gunzberg Center for European Studies, Harvard University, 27 Kirkland Street, Cambridge, MA 02138, USA; Jesus College, Oxford OX1 3DW. *Clubs:* Beefsteak, Savile, Royal Automobile; Gridiron (Oxford); Brook (New York).

FERGUSON, Nicholas Eustace Haddon; Chairman, SVG Capital plc, since 2006; *b* 24 Oct. 1948; *s* of Captain Derrick Ferguson, RN and Betsy Ferguson; *m* 1976, Margaret Jane Dura Collin; two *s* one *d*. *Educ:* Univ. of Edinburgh (BSc Econs 1970); Harvard Business Sch. (MBA 1975, Baker Scholar). CEO, Singapore Internat. Merchant Bankers, 1980–83; Chm., Schroder Ventures, 1983–2001; CEO, SVG Capital plc (formerly Schroder Ventures Internat. Investment Trust), 2001–06. Non-executive Director: Schroders plc, 1998–2001; BSkyB plc, 2004–. Chairman: Courtauld Inst. of Art, 2002–; Inst. for Philanthropy, 2003–. *Recreations:* collecting and studying Medieval art, country pursuits, ski-ing, gardening. *Address:* SVG Capital plc, 111 Strand, WC2R 0AG. *T:* (020) 7010 8911, *Fax:* (020) 7010 8912. *Club:* Brooks's.

FERGUSON, Patricia Josephine; Member (Lab) Glasgow Maryhill, Scottish Parliament, since 1999; *b* 24 Sept. 1958; *d* of John Ferguson and Andrewina Ferguson (*née* Power); *m* 1988, William Gerard Butler, *qv*. *Educ:* Garnethill Convent Secondary Sch., Glasgow; Glasgow Coll. of Technology (part-time) (SHNC Public Admin.). Greater Glasgow Health Board: Admin. Trainee, 1976–78; Administrator, 1978–83; Sec., Greater Glasgow SE Local Health Council, 1983–85; Administrator: Capital Services, Lanarkshire Health Bd, 1985–90; Scottish TUC, 1990–94; Organiser, South West of Scotland Lab. Party, 1994–96; Scottish Officer, Scottish Lab. Party, 1996–99. Scottish Parliament: Dep. Presiding Officer, 1999–2001; Minister: for Parly Business, and Govt Chief Whip, 2001–04; for Tourism, Culture and Sport, 2004–07; Shadow Minister for Europe, External Affairs and Culture, 2007. *Recreations:* reading, driving, travel, theatre. *Address:* 154 Raeberry Street, Maryhill, Glasgow G20 6EA. *T:* (0141) 946 1300, *Fax:* (0141) 946 1412.

FERGUSON, Ven. Paul John; Archdeacon of Cleveland, since 2001; *b* 13 July 1955; *s* of Thomas and Joyce Ferguson; *m* 1982, Penelope Hewitt-Jones; two *s* one *d*. *Educ:* Birkenhead Sch.; New Coll., Oxford (BA 1976, MA 1980); Westminster Coll., Oxford (PGCE); King's Coll., Cambridge (BA 1984, MA 1988); Westcott Hse, Cambridge. FRCO 1975. Ordained deacon, 1985, priest 1986; Curate, St Mary's Chester, 1985–88; Chaplain and Sacrist, 1988–92, Precentor, 1992–95, Westminster Abbey; Precentor and Residentiary Canon, York Minster, 1995–2001. *Publications:* (jtly) Sing His Glory, 1997; reviews, articles on music and liturgy. *Recreations:* cycling, swimming, flying. *Address:* 48 Langbaurgh Road, Hutton Rudby, Yarm TS15 0HL. *T:* (01642) 706095.

FERGUSON, Peter William; QC (Scot.) 2005; Advocate, since 1987; *b* 22 March 1961; *er s* of John Lambie Ferguson and Joyce Robertson Ferguson (*née* Carroll). *Educ:* Portobello High Sch., Edinburgh; Univ. of Edinburgh (LLB Hons 1983; MSc Dist. 1998); Univ. of Strathclyde (DipLP 1984). Admitted Advocate, 1987. *Publications:* Crimes Against the Person, 1989, 2nd edn 1998; contrib. legal pubns. *Address:* Advocates' Library, Parliament Square, Edinburgh EH1 1RF. *Club:* Scottish Arts (Edinburgh).

FERGUSON, Richard; QC 1986; QC (NI) 1973; SC (Ireland) 1983; *b* 22 Aug. 1935; *o s* of late Wesley Ferguson and Edith Ferguson (*née* Hewitt); *m* 1st, Janet Irvine Magowan (marr. diss.); three *s* one *d*; 2nd, Roma Felicity Whelan; one *s*. *Educ:* Rainey Sch. Magherafelt; Methodist Coll., Belfast; Trinity Coll., Dublin (BA); Queen's Univ. o Belfast (LLB). Called to NI Bar, 1956, to Bar of England and Wales, Gray's Inn, 197 (Bencher, 1994). Chairman: NI Mental Health Review Tribunal, 1973–84; Criminal Ba Assoc. of England and Wales, 1993–95. MP (OU) S Antrim, Nov. 1968–1970. Mem. Irish Sports Council, 1978–81. FRGS 1980. *Recreation:* watching the Arsenal. *Address* Carmelite Chambers, 9 Carmelite Street, EC4Y 0DR. *T:* (020) 7936 6300. *Club:* Garrick.

FERGUSON, Susan Margaret D.; *see* Douglas Ferguson.

FERGUSON, Veronica Mary Geneste, FRCS, FRCOphth; Consultant Ophthalmi Surgeon, Imperial College Healthcare NHS Trust (formerly Hammersmith Hospital NHS Trust and St Mary's Hospital NHS Trust), since 1996; Surgeon Oculist to HM Household, since 2002; *b* 18 May 1960; *d* of Geoffrey Crosby Ambrose and Dympna Mary Ambrose (*née* Bourke); *m* 1988, James Malcolm Ferguson, TD. *Educ:* Convent of Sacre Heart, Woldingham; Guy's Hosp. Med. Sch., London Univ. (MB BS 1983). FRCS 1987 FRCOphth 1989. Sen. House Officer, Guy's Hosp., Royal Free Hosp., Southampton Eye Hosp., and St Thomas' Hosp., 1984–89; Registrar, Southern Gen. Hosp., Glasgow 1989–91; Sen. Registrar, St George's Hosp. and Moorfields Eye Hosp., 1991–96 Consultant Ophthalmic Surgeon: King Edward VII's Hosp. (Sr Agnes), 1997–; St Luke' Hosp. for the Clergy, 2002–; Ophthalmologist, St Dunstan's Charity for Blind Ex-servicemen, 2004–. Hon. Sen. Lectr, Imperial Coll., London, 1996–. Mem. Council Royal Coll. Ophthalmologists, 1999–2005. *Publications:* contribs on cataract surgery ocular inflammation and strabismus to ophthalmic jls. *Recreations:* horses, gardening, bee-keeping, ski-ing. *Address:* 70 Harley Street, W1G 7HF. *T:* (020) 7580 0285, *Fax:* (020) 7580 0286; *e-mail:* v.ferguson@doctors.org.uk.

FERGUSON, William James, OBE 1996; FEAgS; farmer; Vice Lord-Lieutenant o Aberdeenshire, 1998–2005; Chairman, Aberdeen Milk Company, since 1994; *b* 3 April 1933; *s* of William Adam Ferguson and Violet (*née* Wiseman); *m* 1961, Carroll Isabella Milne; one *s* three *d*. *Educ:* Turriff Acad.; North of Scotland Coll. of Agriculture (Cert. o Agric.). Nat. Service, 1st Bn Gordon Highlanders, serving in Malaya, 1952–54. Chm. North of Scotland Coll. of Agric., 1986–91; Vice Chm., Scottish Agricl Colls, 1991–97 (Hon. Fellow, 1999). Former Chm., Grampian Farm Wildlife Adv. Gp; Member: Rowet Res. Inst., 1980–82; Technical Cttee, Crichton Royal Dairy Farm, Dumfries, 1980–83 Macaulay Inst. of Soil Res., 1983–85; Scottish Farm Bldgs Investigation Unit, 1984–86 Scottish Country Life Mus., 1986–96; Convenor, Land & Finance Cttee, Aberdee Endowments Trust, 2003–. FRAgS 1995. DL Aberdeenshire, 1988. *Recreations:* golf, ski-ing, field sports. *Address:* Nether Darley, Auchterless, Turriff, Aberdeenshire AB53 8LH *Club:* Farmers'.

FERGUSON DAVIE, Sir Michael, 8th Bt *cr* 1847, of Creedy, Devonshire; retire stockbroker; *b* 10 Jan. 1944; *er s* of Sir John Ferguson Davie, 7th Bt and (Joan) Zoë (Charlotte), *d* of Raymond Hoole, Vancouver, BC; *S* father, 2000; *m* 1st, 1968, (Margaret) Jean (marr. diss. 1992), *d* of Douglas Macbeth; one *s* decd; 2nd, 2001, Sarah, *d* of John Seyfried and Lady Cathleen Hudson (*née* Eliot), and former wife of Peter M. Smith; two step *s*. *Educ:* St Edward's Sch., Oxford. Grenfell & Co. (later Grenfell & Colegrave) 1961–79; Fielding Newson-Smith & Co., 1979–86; Dir, NatWest Markets, 1986–95 Consultant, Madoff Securities Ltd, 1995–2001; Partner, Footloose, 1997–2003. Trustee SCF Endowment, 2006–; Trustee and Treas., Somerset Community Foundn, 2007–. *Recreations:* writing, bridge, Real tennis. *Heir:* *b* Julian Anthony Ferguson Davie [*b* 6 July 1950; *m* 1976, Louise, *d* of John Marsden; three *s*]. *Address:* Sherston Lodge, Evercreech Somerset BA4 6LG. *T:* (01749) 830930. *Clubs:* Pratt's, City of London, MCC.

FERGUSON FLATT, Very Rev. Roy Francis; *see* Flatt.

FERGUSON-SMITH, Prof. Malcolm Andrew, FRS 1983; FRSE 1978; Professor o Pathology and Professorial Fellow, Peterhouse, University of Cambridge, 1987–98, now Emeritus Fellow; Director, Cambridge University Centre for Medical Genetics, 1989–98 *b* 5 Sept. 1931; *s* of John Ferguson-Smith, MA, MD, FRCP and Ethel May (*née* Thorne) *m* 1960, Marie Eva Gzowska; one *s* three *d*. *Educ:* Stowe Sch.; Univ. of Glasgow (MB ChB 1955). MRCPath 1966, FRCPath 1978; MRCPGlas 1972, FRCPGlas 1974; FRCOG 1993. Registrar in Lab. Medicine, Dept of Pathology, Western Infirmary, Glasgow 1958–59; Fellow in Medicine and Instructor, Johns Hopkins Univ. Sch. of Medicine 1959–61; Lectr, Sen. Lectr and Reader in Med. Genetics, Univ. of Glasgow, 1961–73 Prof. of Med. Genetics, 1973–87; Hon. Consultant: in Med. Paediatrics, Royal Hosp. for Sick Children, Glasgow, 1966–73; in Clin. Genetics, Yorkhill and Associated Hosps 1973–87; in Med. Genetics, Addenbrooke's NHS Trust, 1987–98; Director: W o Scotland Med. Genetics Service, 1973–87; E Anglian Regl Clin. Genetics Service 1987–95. President: Clinical Genetics Soc., 1979–81; Eur. Soc. of Human Genetics 1997–98; Internat. Soc. for Prenatal Diagnosis, 1998–2002; Assoc. of Clinica Cytogeneticists, 2002–05. Mem., Johns Hopkins Univ. Soc. of Scholars, 1983; For Mem., Polish Acad. of Scis, 1988; For. Corresp. Mem., Nat. Acad. of Medicine of Buenos Aires, 2002. Founder FMedSci 1998; Hon. ARCVS 2002. Hon. DSc: Strathclyde, 1992 Glasgow, 2002. Bronze Medal, Univ. of Helsinki, 1968; Makdougall-Brisbane Prize RSE, 1988; San Remo Internat. Prize for Genetic Res., 1990; Baschirotto Award, Eur Soc. of Human Genetics, 1996. Editor, Prenatal Diagnosis, 1980–2006. *Publications:* (ed) Early Prenatal Diagnosis, 1983; (jtly) Essential Medical Genetics, 1984, 5th edn 1997; (ed) Prenatal Diagnosis and Screening, 1992; papers on cytogenetics, gene mapping, human genetics and evolutionary biology in med. jls. *Recreations:* swimming, sailing, fishing *Address:* Department of Veterinary Medicine, Cambridge University, Madingley Road Cambridge CB3 0ES.

FERGUSSON, Adam (Dugdale); consultant on European affairs, since 1989; *b* 10 July 1932; *yr s* of Sir James Fergusson of Kilkerran, 8th Bt, LLD, FRSE, and Frances Dugdale *m* 1965, Penelope, *e d* of Peter Hughes, Furneaux Pelham Hall; two *s* two *d*. *Educ:* Eton Trinity Coll., Cambridge (BA History, 1955). Glasgow Herald, 1956–61: Leader-writer 1957–58; Diplomatic Corresp., 1959–61; Statist, 1961–67: Foreign Editor, 1964–67 Feature-writer for The Times on political, economic and environmental matters 1967–77. Special Advr on European Affairs, FCO, 1985–89. European Parliament Member (C) West Strathclyde, 1979–84; Spokesman on Political Affairs for European Democratic Gp, 1979–82; Vice-Chm., Political Affairs Cttee, 1982–84; Mem., Jt Cttee of ACP/EEC Consultative Assembly, 1979–84; contested (C) London Central, European elecn, 1984. Vice-Pres., Pan-European Union, 1981–; Mem., Scotland Says No Referendum Campaign Cttee, 1978–79. Dir, Murray International Trust PLC, 1995–2001. Gov., Howick Trust, 1976–2002; Vice-Pres., Bath Preservation Trust, 1997–. *Publications:* Roman Go Home, 1969; The Lost Embassy, 1972; The Sack of Bath, 1973; When Money Dies, 1975; Scone: a likely tale, 2004; *musical comedies:* book and lyrics for: State of Emergency, 1962; Gibbon Slept Here, 1964; various pamphlets; articles in national and internat. jls and magazines. *Address:* 15 Warwick Gardens, W14 8PH. *T:* (020) 7603 7900.

FERGUSSON, Alexander Charles Onslow; Member for Galloway & Upper Nithsdale, Scottish Parliament; Presiding Officer, Scottish Parliament, since 2007; *b* 8 April 1949; *s* of Lt Col Rev. Simon Charles David Fergusson and Auriole Kathleen Fergusson (*née* Hughes Onslow); *m* 1974, Jane Merryn Barthold; three *s*. *Educ:* Eton Coll.; West of Scotland Agricl Coll. (ONDA). Farmer, 1971–99. MSP, Scotland S, 1999–2003, Galloway & Upper Nithsdale, 2003– (C, 1999–2007, when elected Presiding Officer). JP S Ayrshire, 1997–99; DL Ayrshire and Arran, 1997–99. *Recreations:* curling, Rugby, folk music. *Address:* Grennan, Dalry, Kirkcudbrightshire DG7 3PL.

FERGUSSON of Kilkerran, Sir Charles, 9th Bt *cr* 1703; *b* 10 May 1931; *s* of Sir James Fergusson of Kilkerran, 8th Bt, and Frances (*d* 1988), *d* of Edgar Dugdale; *S* father, 1973; *m* 1961, Hon. Amanda Mary Noel-Paton, *d* of Lord Ferrier, ED; two *s*. *Educ:* Eton; Edinburgh and East of Scotland Coll. of Agriculture. *Heir: s* Adam Fergusson [*b* 29 Dec. 1962; *m* 1989, Jenifer, *yr d* of Adam Thomson; one *s* two *d*].

FERGUSSON, Rev. Prof. David Alexander Syme, DPhil; FRSE; Professor of Divinity, University of Edinburgh, since 2000; *b* Glasgow, 3 Aug. 1956; *s* of Thomas Fergusson and Charis Fergusson; *m* 1985, Margot Evelyn McIndoe; two *s*. *Educ:* Univ. of Glasgow (MA 1977); Univ. of Edinburgh (BD 1980); Univ. of Oxford (DPhil 1984). Licensed, 1980, ordained, 1984, C of S; Asst Minister, St Nicholas, Lanark, 1983–84; Associate Minister, St Mungo's, Cumbernauld, 1984–86; Lectr in Systematic Theol., Univ. of Edinburgh, 1986–90; Prof. of Systematic Theol., Univ. of Aberdeen, 1990–2000. Lectures: Cunningham, Univ. of Edinburgh, 1996; Bampton, Univ. of Oxford, 2001; Gifford, Univ. of Glasgow, 2008. FRSE 2004. *Publications:* Buttmann, 1992; Christ, Church and Society, 1993; John and Donald Baillie, 1997; The Cosmos and the Creator, 1998; Community, Liberation and Christian Ethics, 1998; John Macmurray: critical perspectives, 2002; Church, State and Civil Society, 2004; Scottish Philosophical Theology, 2007. *Recreations:* golf, football. *Address:* 23 Riselaw Crescent, Edinburgh EH10 6HN. *T:* (0131) 447 4022; *e-mail:* David.Fergusson@ed.ac.uk. *Clubs:* New, Mortonhall Golf (Edinburgh).

FERGUSSON, Sir Ewen (Alastair John), GCMG 1993 (KCMG 1987); GCVO 1992; HM Diplomatic Service, retired; King of Arms, Most Distinguished Order of St Michael and St George, 1996–2007; *b* 28 Oct. 1932; *er s* of late Sir Ewen MacGregor Field Fergusson; *m* 1959, Sara Carolyn, *d* of late Brig.-Gen. Lord Esmé Gordon Lennox, KCVO, CMG, DSO and *widow* of Sir William Andrew Montgomery-Cuninghame, 11th Bt; one *s* two *d*. *Educ:* Rugby; Oriel Coll., Oxford (MA; Hon. Fellow, 1988). Played Rugby Football for Oxford Univ., 1952 and 1953, and for Scotland, 1954. 2nd Lieut, 60th Rifles (KRRC), 1954–56. Joined Foreign (later Diplomatic) Service, 1956; Asst Private Sec. to Minister of Defence, 1957–59; British Embassy, Addis Ababa, 1960; FO, 1963; British Trade Development Office, New York, 1967; Counsellor and Head of Chancery, Office of UK Permanent Rep. to European Communities, 1972–75; Private Sec. to Foreign and Commonwealth Sec., 1975–78; Asst Under Sec. of State, FCO, 1978–82; Ambassador to S Africa, 1982–84; Dep. Under-Sec. of State (Middle East and Africa), FCO, 1984–87; Ambassador to France, 1987–92. Chairman: Coutts & Co. Gp, 1993–99; Savoy Hotel, 1995–98 (Dir, 1993–98; Co-Chm., Internat. Adv. Bd, Savoy Gp, 1999–2004). Director: British Telecom, 1993–99; Sun Alliance Gp, 1993–95. Chm., Govt Wine Adv. Cttee, 1993–2003. Governor, Rugby Sch., 1985–2002 (Chm. Govs, 1995–2002); Trustee: Nat. Gall., 1995–2002; Henry Moore Foundn, 1998–2007 (Chm., 2001–07). Hon. LLD Aberdeen, 1995. Grand Officier, Légion d'Honneur (France), 1992. *Address:* 111 Iverna Court, W8 6TX. *T:* (020) 7937 2240; Les Baumeriaux, 84340 Entrechaux, France. *T:* 490460496. *Clubs:* Royal Automobile, Beefsteak, Pratt's; Jockey (Paris).

FERGUSSON, George Duncan; HM Diplomatic Service; High Commissioner, New Zealand, Governor (non-resident) of Pitcairn, Henderson, Ducie and Oeno Islands, and High Commissioner (non-resident), Samoa, since 2006; *b* 30 Sept. 1955; *s* of Brig. Bernard Fergusson, later Baron Ballantrae, KT, GCMG, GCVO, DSO, OBE; *m* 1981, Margaret Sheila Wookey; three *d* (one *s* decd). *Educ:* Ballantrae Jun. Secondary Sch.; Hereworth Sch., NZ; Eton Coll.; Magdalen Coll., Oxford. Murray and Tait, Solicitors, 1977–78; joined Northern Ireland Office, 1978; seconded to NI Dept of Commerce, 1979–80; Private Sec. to Min. of State for NI, 1982–83; First Sec., Dublin, 1988–91; joined Diplomatic Service, 1990; FCO, 1991–93; First Sec., Seoul, 1994–96; FCO, 1996–99; Head: Republic of Ireland Dept, 1997–99; Devolved Admins Dept, 1999; Consul Gen., Boston, 1999–2003; Counsellor, Cabinet Office, 2003–06. *Address:* c/o Foreign and Commonwealth Office, King Charles Street, SW1A 2AH.

FERGUSSON, Kenneth James, CEng, FIMechE; Chief Executive, Coal Authority, 1997–2001; *b* 1938; *s* of Robert Brown Millar Fergusson and Agnes Tattersall Fergusson; *m* 1961, Beryl Foster; two *s* one *d*. *Educ:* Robert Gordon's Coll., Aberdeen; Harrow County Grammar Sch.; Imperial Coll., London (BSc 1st cl. Hons Engrg); Harvard Business Sch. (AMP). CEng 1966; FIMechE 1976; FIMMM (FIMM 1999). ICI Agricl Div., 1959–68; RTZ Gp 1968–86: Geschäftsführer, Duisburger Kupferhütte, 1981–85; Man. Dir, Rio Tinto Zimbabwe, 1985–86; Project Dir, European Transonic Windtunnel, Cologne, 1986–88; Man. Dir, Docklands Light Railway, 1988–90; Chief Exec., Hub Power Co., Karachi, 1992–93; Regl Dir, BESO, 1995–97. Trustee, Industrial Trust, 1998–. Pres., Combustion Engrg Assoc., 2002–06. FIMgt 1984–2002; MInstD 1987; FRSA 1998–2002. Freeman, City of London, 1990; Liveryman, Co. of Engineers, 1995. *Recreations:* advanced motoring and motorcycling, swimming, archaeology, gardening, music, current affairs, travel. *Address:* 24F Thorney Crescent, Morgans Walk, SW11 3TT. *T:* (020) 7585 1294.

FERLEGER BRADES, Susan Deborah; Director, Hayward Gallery, London, 1996–2004; *b* 7 July 1954; *d* of Alvin Ferleger and Beatrice Ferleger (*née* Supnick); *m* 1st, 1979, Peter Eric Brades (*d* 2001); one *s*; 2nd, 2006, Rhett Davies. *Educ:* Courtauld Inst. of Art (MA); Univ. of Mass, Amherst (BA 1976; magna cum laude; Phi Beta Kappa); Barnard Coll., Columbia Univ., NY. Curatorial Co-ordinator, Solomon R. Guggenheim Mus., NY, 1975–79; Nat. Endowment for Arts Fellowship, 1975–76; Researcher, British Sculpture in the Twentieth Century, Whitechapel Art Gall., London, 1979–80; Hayward Gallery: Exhibn Organiser, Arts Council of GB, S Bank Centre, 1980–88; Sen. Exhibn Organiser, Exhibns Dept, S Bank Centre, 1988–93 (Public Art Programme Co-ordinator, 1990); Dep. Dir, Hayward Gall., S Bank Centre, 1993–96. Purchaser, Arts Council Collection, 1983–2004; Visual Arts Advr, John Lyons Charity, 2004–. Trustee, IVAM Centro Julio Gonzalez, Valencia, 2000–04; Patron, Nat. Children's Art Day, 2001–. *Address: e-mail:* sferlegerbrades@hotmail.com.

FERMOR, Sir Patrick (Michael) Leigh, Kt 2004; DSO 1944; OBE (mil.) 1943; CLit 1991; author; Hon. Citizen of Herakleion, Crete, 1947, Gytheion, Laconia, 1966, and of Kardamyli, Messenia, 1967; *b* 11 Feb. 1915; *s* of late Sir Lewis Leigh Fermor, OBE, FRS, DSc, and Eileen, *d* of Charles Taaffe Ambler; *m* 1968, Hon. Joan Eyres-Monsell (*d* 2003), *d* of 1st Viscount Monsell, PC, GBE. *Educ:* King's Sch., Canterbury. After travelling for four years in Central Europe, Balkans and Greece, enlisted in Irish Guards, 1939; "I" Corps, 1940; Lieut, British Mil. Mission, Greece, 1940; Liaison Officer, Greek GHQ, Albania; campaigns of Greece and Crete; joined SOE, 1941; 2 years in German occupied Crete with Resistance, commanded some minor guerilla operations; team-commander in Special Allied Airborne Reconnaissance Force, N Germany, 1945. Dep.-Dir British Institute, Athens, till middle 1946; travelled in Caribbean and Central American republics, 1947–48. Corres. Mem., Athens Acad., 1980. Hon. DLitt: Kent, 1991; Amer. Sch. of Greece, 1993; Warwick Univ., 1996. Municipality of Athens Gold Medal of Honour, 1988; Prix Jacques Audiberti, Ville d'Antibes, 1992. Officier, l'Ordre des Arts et des Lettres (France), 1995; Commander, Order of the Phoenix (Greece), 2007. *Publications:* The Traveller's Tree (Heinemann Foundation Prize for Literature, 1950, and Kemsley Prize, 1951); trans. Colette, Chance Acquaintances, 1952; A Time to Keep Silence, 1953; The Violins of Saint Jacques, 1953; Mani, 1958 (Duff Cooper Meml Prize; Book Society's Choice); (trans.) The Cretan Runner (George Psychoundakis), 1955; Roumeli, 1966; A Time of Gifts, 1977 (W. H. Smith & Son Literary Award, 1978); Between the Woods and the Water, 1986 (Thomas Cook Travel Book Award, 1986; Internat. PEN/Time Life Silver Pen Award, 1986); Three Letters from the Andes, 1991; Words of Mercury, 2004. *Recreation:* travel. *Address:* c/o Messrs John Murray, 50 Albemarle Street, W1X 4BD. *Clubs:* White's, Travellers, Pratt's, Beefsteak, Special Forces, Puffins.

FERMOR-HESKETH, family name of **Baron Hesketh**.

FERMOY, 6th Baron *cr* 1856; **(Patrick) Maurice Burke Roche;** *b* 11 Oct. 1967; *s* of 5th Baron Fermoy and of Lavinia Frances Elizabeth, *o d* of late Captain John Pitman; *S* father, 1984; *m* 1998, Tessa Fiona Ledger, *d* of Major David Pelham Kayll; two *d*. *Educ:* Eton. A Page of Honour to the Queen Mother, 1982–85. Commnd, Blues and Royals, 1987–95; Capt. With Bass Taverns, 1996–99; Dir, Arrow Pubs Ltd, 1999–. Mem., Cherwell DC, 2000–04. *Recreations:* horses, scuba diving. *Heir: b* Hon. (Edmund) Hugh Burke Roche [*b* 5 Feb. 1972; *m* 2004, Phillipa Long; one *s* one *d*]. *Address:* Handywater Farm, Sibford Gower, Banbury, Oxon OX15 5AE.

FERNÁNDEZ, Mariano; Ambassador of Chile to the United States of America, since 2006; *b* Santiago, 21 April 1945; *s* of Mariano Fernández and María Angélica Amunategui; *m* 1969, María Angélica Morales; two *s* one *d*. *Educ:* Universidad Católica de Santiago (law degree 1970); Bonn Univ. (major in pol sociol.). Mem., Foreign Service, Chile, 1967–74; Third Sec., Embassy of Chile, Germany, 1971–74; in exile, Bonn, 1974–82: Ed., Develt and Co-opn Mag.; Chief Editor: IPS-Dritte welt Nachrichtenagentur (news agency); Handbuch der Entwicklungshilfe; returned to Chile, 1982; Researcher and Mem. Exec. Cttee, Centre of Studies for Develt, 1982–90; Ambassador: to EC, 1990–92; to Italy and (non-resident) to Malta, 1992–94; Vice Minister for Foreign Affairs, 1994–2000; Ambassador: to Spain and (non-resident) to Andorra, 2000–02; to UK, 2002–06, and (non-resident) to Libya, 2005–06. Board Member: Fintesa Financial Agency, 1982–84; Radio Cooperativa, 1982–90; Editorial Board Member: Mensaje, 1984–86; Fortin Mapocho, 1986–88; Apsi, 1986–89. President: European-Latin American Relations Inst., Madrid, 1992–93 (Vice-Pres., 1992); Internat. Council, Latin-American Centre for Relations with Europe, 1996–98; Vice-Pres., Italo-Latin American Inst., Rome, 1994; Mem. Exec. Cttee, Jacques Maritain Inst., Rome, 1994–96. Hd, Chilean Commn, Internat. Whaling Commn, 2003–07; Chilean Rep., IMO, 2006. Member: Pol Sci. Assoc. of Chile; Acad. Internat. du Vin; Cofradía del Mérito Vitivinícola de Chile; Jurade de St Emilion; Commanderie de Médoc et Graves; Europaische Weinritterschaft; Slow Food. Hon. Pres., Chilean Assoc. of Sommeliers. Grand Cross of: Argentina; Brazil; Colombia; Ecuador; Finland; Germany; the Holy See; Italy; Mexico; Panama; Peru; Spain; Grand Officer of: Croatia; Germany; Sweden. *Publications:* articles in mags and jls, mainly on internat. policy. *Address:* Embassy of Chile, 1732 Massachusetts Avenue NW, Washington, DC 20036, USA. *Clubs:* Travellers, Naval and Military.

FERNANDO, Most Rev. Nicholas Marcus; Archbishop of Colombo, (RC), 1977–2002, now Emeritus; *b* 6 Dec. 1932. *Educ:* St Aloysius' Seminary, Colombo; Universitas Propaganda Fide, Rome. BA (London); PhL (Rome); STD (Rome). Ordained priest, 1959. Pres., Catholic Bishops' Conf. of Sri Lanka, 1989–95. Mem., Sacred Congregation for Evangelization of Peoples. *Address:* c/o Archdiocese of Colombo, 976 Gnanartha Pradeepaya Mawatha, Colombo 8, Sri Lanka. *T:* (1) 695471/2/3, *Fax:* (1) 692009.

FERNEYHOUGH, Prof. Brian John Peter, FRAM; composer; William H. Bonsall Professor in Music, Stanford University, since 2000; *b* 16 Jan. 1943; *s* of Frederick George Ferneyhough and Emily May (*née* Hopwood); *m* 1990, Stephany Jan Hurtik. *Educ:* Birmingham Sch. of Music; RAM (FRAM 1998); Sweelinck Conservatory, Amsterdam; Musikakademie, Basle. Mendelssohn Schol., 1968; Stipend: City of Basle, 1969; Heinrich-Strobel-Stiftung des Südwestfunks, 1972; Composition teacher, Musikhochschule, Freiburg, 1973–86 (Prof., 1978–86); Principal Composition Teacher, Royal Conservatory, The Hague, 1986–87; Prof. of Music, UCSD, 1987–99. Guest Artist, Artists' Exchange Scheme, Deutsche Akad. Austauschdienst, Berlin, 1976–77; Lectr, Darmstadt Summer Sch., 1976–96 and 2004 (Comp. course co-ordinator, 1984–94); Guest Prof., Royal Conservatory, Stockholm, 1981–83, 1985; Vis. Prof., Univ. of Chicago, 1986; Fellow, Birmingham Conservatoire, 1996. Master Class, Civica Scuola di Musica di Milano, 1985–87. Mem., ISCM Internat. Jury, 1977, 1988. Prizes, Gaudeamus Internat. Comp., 1968, 1969; First Prize, ISCM Internat. Comp., Rome, 1974; Koussevitsky Prize, 1978; Royal Philharmonic Soc. Award, 1996. Chevalier, l'Ordre des Arts et des Lettres, 1984. Ernst von Siemens Music Prize, 2007. *Compositions include:* Sonatas for String Quartet, 1967; Epicycle, for 20 solo strings, 1968; Firecycle Beta, for large orch. with 5 conductors, 1971; Time and Motion Studies I–III, 1974–76; Unity Capsule, for solo flute, 1975; Funérailles, for 7 strings and harp, 1978; La Terre est un Homme, for orch., 1979; 2nd String Quartet, 1980; Lemma-Icon-Epigram, for solo piano, 1981; Carceri d'Invenzione, for various ensembles, 1981–86; 3rd String Quartet, 1987; Kurze Schatten II, for guitar, 1988; La Chute d'Icare, for clarinet ensemble, 1988; Trittico per G. S., 1989; 4th String Quartet, 1990; Bone Alphabet, for percussionist, 1991; Terrain, for violin and eight instruments, 1992; On Stellar Magnitudes, for voice and ensemble, 1994; String Trio, 1995; Incipits, for viola, percussion and small ensemble, 1996; Kranichtänze II, for piano, 1996; Maisons Noires, for ensemble, 1997; Unsichtbare Farben, for solo violin, 1999; Doctrine of Similarity, for choir and instruments, 2000; Opus Contra Naturam, for speaking pianist, 2000; Stele for Failed Time, for choir and electronics, 2001; Shadowtime, 1999–2004; Dum transisset I–IV, for string quartet, 2005–06; 5th String Quartet, 2006; Plötzlichkeit, for orch., 2006. *Publications:* Collected Writings, 1996; articles in Contrechamps, Musiktexte, and Contemp. Music Rev. *Recreations:* reading, wine, cats. *Address:* Department of Music, Braun Music Center, Stanford University, Stanford, CA 94305–3076, USA.

FERNIE, Prof. Eric Campbell, CBE 1995; FBA 2002; FSA; FRSE; Director, Courtauld Institute of Art, University of London, 1995–2003; *b* Edinburgh, 9 June 1939; *s* of Sydney Robert and Catherine Reid Fernie; *m* 1964, Margaret Lorraine French; one *s* two *d*. *Educ:* Univ. of the Witwatersrand (BA Hons Fine Arts); Univ. of London (Academic Diploma). FSA 1973; FSA (Scot.) 1984; FRSE 1993. Lectr, Univ. of the Witwatersrand, 1963–67; University of East Anglia: Lectr and Sen. Lectr, 1967–84; Dean, Sch. of Fine Art and Music, 1977–81; Public Orator, 1982–84; Watson Gordon Prof. of Fine Art, Univ. of

Edinburgh, 1984–95 (Dean, Faculty of Arts, 1989–92). Chm., Ancient Monuments Bd for Scotland, 1989–95; Trustee: Nat. Galleries of Scotland, 1991–97; Scotland Inheritance Fund, 1992–2005; Samuel Courtauld Trust, 1995–2003; Heather Trust for the Arts, 1997–2001; Comr, English Heritage, 1995–2001; Mem., RCHM of England, 1997–99. Pres., Soc. of Antiquaries of London, 2004–07 (Vice-Pres., 1992–95). *Publications:* An Introduction to the Communar and Pitcaner Rolls of Norwich Cathedral Priory (with A. B. Whittingham), 1973; The Architecture of the Anglo-Saxons, 1983; An Architectural History of Norwich Cathedral, 1993; Art History and its Methods, 1995; The Architecture of Norman England, 2000; contribs to British and overseas architectural jls. *Address:* 82 Bradmore Way, Old Coulsdon, Surrey CR5 1PB. *T:* (01737) 559553.

FEROZE, Sir Rustam Moolan, Kt 1983; MD; FRCS, FRCOG; retired; (first) President, European Association of Obstetrics and Gynaecology, 1985–88, now Hon. President; Consulting Obstetrician, Queen Charlotte's Maternity Hospital; Consulting Surgeon, Chelsea Hospital for Women; *b* 4 Aug. 1920; *s* of Dr J. Moolan-Feroze; *m* 1947, Margaret Dowsett; three *s* (one *d* decd). *Educ:* Sutton Valence Sch.; King's Coll. and King's Coll. Hospital, London. MRCS, LRCP 1943; MB, BS 1946; MRCOG 1948; MD (Obst. & Dis. Wom.) London 1952; FRCS 1952; FRCOG 1962; Hon. FRCSI 1984; Hon. FRACOG 1985; Hon. FACOG 1986. Surg.-Lt, RNVR, 1943–46. King's Coll. Hosp., 1946; RMO, Samaritan Hosp. for Women, 1948; Sen. Registrar: Hosp. for Women, Soho Sq., and Middlesex Hosp., 1950–53; Chelsea Hosp. for Women, and Queen Charlotte's Maternity Hosp., 1953–54; Consultant Obstetrician and Gynaecologist, King's Coll. Hosp., 1952–85. Dean, Inst. of Obstetrics and Gynaecology, Univ. of London, 1954–67; Dir, Postgrad. Studies, RCOG, 1975–80; Pres., RCOG, 1981–84; Chm., Conf. of Royal Colls and Faculties, 1982–84. McIlrath Guest Prof., Royal Prince Alfred Hosp., Sydney, 1970. Lectures: Soc. of Obstetrics and Gynaecology of Canada, Winnipeg, 1978; Bartholomew Mosse, Dublin, 1982; Shirodkar Meml, Bombay, 1982; Charter Day, National Maternity Hosp., Dublin, 1984. Past Examiner: RCOG; Univs of London, Cambridge, Birmingham and Singapore. *Publications:* contributor: Integrated Obstetrics and Gynaecology for Postgraduates, 1981; Gynaecological Oncology, 1981, rev. edn 1992; Bonney's Gynaecological Surgery, 1986; contribs to med. jls. *Recreations:* Bonsai, music. *Address:* 9 Arbor Close, Beckenham, Kent BR3 6TW. *Club:* Royal Automobile.

FERRAN, Brian; Chief Executive, Arts Council of Northern Ireland, 1991–2000; *b* 19 Oct. 1940; *s* of late Bernard and Susan Ferran; *m* 1963, Denise Devine; one *s* one *d*. *Educ:* St Columb's Coll., Derry (ATD); Courtauld Inst., London Univ. (BA 1973); Queen's Univ., Belfast (DBA 1975). Art Teacher, Derry, 1963–66; Visual Arts Dir, Arts Council of NI, 1966–91. Commissioner: Paris Biennale, 1980; São Paolo Biennial, 1985; Orgnr, exhibn of NI artists, Houston Internat. Fest. and US tour, 1990. HRUA 1980; HRHA 1998. Leverhulme European Award, 1969; Douglas Hyde Gold Medal for historical painting, 1965, 1976; Conor Prize, Royal Ulster Acad., 1979. *Publication:* Basil Blackshaw: painter, 1995. *Recreation:* visiting museums. *Address:* Goorey Rocks, Malin, Inishowen, Co. Donegal, Ireland. *T:* and *Fax:* 749370934.

FERRANTI, Sebastian Basil Joseph Ziani de; *see* de Ferranti.

FERRERO-WALDNER, Benita Maria; Member, European Commission, since 2004; *b* 5 Sept. 1948; *d* of Bruno and Emilie Waldner; *m* 1993, Prof. Francisco Ferrero Campos. *Educ:* Univ. of Salzburg (DIur). Export Dept, Paul Kiefel, Freilassing, Germany, 1971–72; Dir for Export Promotion, Gerns and Gahler, Freilassing, 1972–78; Sales Dir for Europe, P. Kaufmann Inc., NY, 1978–81; Chief Mgt Asst, Gerns and Gahler, 1981–83; Special Consultancy, Austrian Embassy, Madrid, 1984; Federal Ministry for Foreign Affairs, Austria: Depts of Econ. Affairs, Political Affairs and Consular Affairs, 1984–86; First Sec., Dakar, 1986; Dept for Devlt Co-operation, 1986–87; Counsellor for Econ. Affairs, 1987–90, Minister-Counsellor, Dep. Chief of Mission and Chargé d'Affaires, 1990–93, Paris; Dep. Chief of Protocol, 1993; Chief of Protocol, Exec. Office of Sec. Gen., UN Secretariat, NY, 1994–95; State Sec. for Foreign Affairs, 1995–2000; Minister for Foreign Affairs, Austria, 2000–04. Grand Decoration of Honour in Silver with Sash (Austria), 1999; holds numerous foreign decorations, including: Grand Cross: Order of Isabel la Católica (Spain), 1995; Royal Order of Merit (Norway), 1996; 2nd Cl., Order of Merit (FRG), 1997; SMO (Malta), 1999. *Publications:* Globale Ethik, 1998; Zukunft der Entwicklungszusammenarbeit, 1999. *Recreations:* reading, travelling, theatre, concerts, swimming, yoga. *Address:* European Commission, 200 Rue de la Loi, 1049 Brussels, Belgium.

FERRERS, 13th Earl *cr* 1711; **Robert Washington Shirley;** PC 1982; DL; Viscount Tamworth 1711; Bt 1611; High Steward of Norwich Cathedral, 1979–2007, now Emeritus; *b* 8 June 1929; *o s* of 12th Earl Ferrers and Hermione Morley (*d* 1969); *S* father, 1954; *m* 1951, Annabel Mary, *d* of late Brig. W. G. Carr, CVO, DSO; two *s* two *d* (and one *d* decd). *Educ:* Winchester Coll.; Magdalene Coll., Cambridge (MA (Agric.)). Lieut Coldstream Guards, 1949 (as National Service). A Lord-in-waiting, 1962–64, 1971–74; Parly Sec., MAFF, 1974; Jt Dep. Leader of the Opposition, House of Lords, 1976–79; Dep. Leader of House of Lords, 1979–83, 1988–97; Minister of State: MAFF, 1979–83; Home Office, 1988–94; DTI, 1994–95; DoE (Minister for the Envmt and Countryside), 1995–97; elected Mem., H of L, 1999. Mem., Armitage Cttee on political activities of civil servants, 1976. Chm., TSB of Eastern England, 1977–79; Mem., TSB Central Bd, 1977–79; Director: Central TSB, 1978–79; TSB Trustcard Ltd, 1978–79; Norwich Union Insurance Group, 1975–79 and 1983–88. Chairman: RCHM(Eng.), 1984–88; British Agricl Export Council, 1984–88; Mem. Council, Food From Britain, 1984–88; Director: Economic Forestry Gp, 1985–88; Chatham Historic Dockyard Trust, 1984–88. Pres., Assoc. of Cons. Peers, 2006–. Mem. Council, Hurstpierpoint Coll., 1959–68; Sub-Warden, Winchester Coll., 1998–2003 (Fellow, 1988–2003). DL Norfolk, 1983. Grand Prior, Order of St Lazarus of Jerusalem, 2002–. *Heir: s* Viscount Tamworth, *qv*. *Address:* Park Lodge, Hedenham, Norfolk NR35 2LE. *Club:* Beefsteak.

FERRIE, Dr John, CBE 2004; CEng, FREng; FRAeS; FIMechE; Company Officer, GE Aviation, since 2007; *b* 17 Jan. 1947; *s* of Hugh Ferrie and Barbara Ferrie (*née* Miller); *m* 1968, Helen Allan; two *s*. *Educ:* Univ. of Strathclyde (BSc 1st Cl. Hons Mech. Eng. 1970); Univ. of Warwick (DEng 1998). CEng, FREng 2000; FRAeS 1995; FIMechE 1996. With Rolls Royce, 1964–2000: Director: Manufacturing, 1992–96; Mil. Engines, 1996–98; Exec. Vice-Pres., Business Ops, 1998–2000; Exec. Dir and Gp Man. Dir, Aerospace, Smiths Gp plc, 2000–07. Non-exec. Dir, Westbury plc, 2004–06. *Recreations:* golf, music, hill walking. *Address:* GE Aviation, Bishops Cleeve, Cheltenham, GL52 8SF.

FERRIER, Prof. Robert Patton, FRSE 1977; Professor of Natural Philosophy, University of Glasgow, 1973–2002, now Emeritus, and Hon. Senior Research Fellow, since 2002; *b* 4 Jan. 1934; *s* of William McFarlane Ferrier and Gwendoline Melita Edwards; *m* 1961, Valerie Jane Duncan; two *s* one *d*. *Educ:* Glebelands Sch. and Morgan Academy, Dundee; Univ. of St Andrews (BSc, PhD). MA Cantab, FInstP. Scientific Officer, AERE Harwell, 1959–61; Res. Assoc., MIT, 1961–62; Sen. Asst in Res., Cavendish Lab., Cambridge, 1962–66; Fellow of Fitzwilliam Coll., Cambridge, 1965–73; Asst Dir of Res., Cavendish Lab. 1966–71; Lectr in Physics, Univ. of Cambridge, 1971–73; Guest Scientist, IBM Res. Labs San José, Calif, 1972–73. Chm., SER[C] Semiconductor and Surface Physics Sub-Cttee, 1979–. *Publications:* numerous papers i[n] Phil. Mag., Jl Appl. Physics, Jl Physics, etc. *Recreations:* do-it-yourself, tennis, gardening, reading novels. *Address:* Glencoe, 31 Thorn Road, Bearsden, Glasgow G61 4BS. *T:* (0141) 570 0769, *T:* (office) (0141) 330 5388.

FERRIS, Hon. Sir Francis (Mursell), Kt 1990; TD 1965; Judge of the High Court [of] Justice, Chancery Division, 1990–2003; Judge of Restrictive Practices Court, 1990–98; [b] 19 Aug. 1932; *s* of Francis William Ferris and Elsie Lilian May Ferris (*née* Mursell); *m* 1957 Sheila Elizabeth Hester Falloon Bedford; three *s* one *d*. *Educ:* Bryanston Sch.; Oriel Coll Oxford (BA (Modern History) 1955, MA 1979; Hon. Fellow, 2000). Served R[A] 1951–52; 299 Field Regt (RBY QOOH and Berks) RA, TA 1952–67, Major 1964 Called to the Bar, Lincoln's Inn, 1956, Bencher, 1987; practice at Chancery Bar, 1958–90 Standing Counsel to Dir Gen. of Fair Trading, 1966–80; QC 1980; a Recorder, 1989–90 Member: Bar Council, 1966–70; Senate of Inns of Court and the Bar, 1979–82. *Recreation[s]:* gardening without bending. *Address:* White Gables, New Road, Shiplake, Oxfordshi[re] RG9 3LB. *Club:* Marlow Rowing.

FERRIS, Paul Frederick; author and journalist; *b* 15 Feb. 1929; *o c* of late Frederic[k] Morgan Ferris and of Olga Ferris; *m* 1st, 1953, Gloria Moreton (marr. diss. 1995); one [s] one *d*; 2nd, 1996, Mary Turnbull. *Educ:* Swansea Gram. Sch. Staff of South Wales Evenin[g] Post, 1949–52; Womans Own, 1953; Observer Foreign News Service, 1953–5[4]. *Publications: novels:* A Changed Man, 1958; Then We Fall, 1960; A Family Affair, 196[3]; The Destroyer, 1965; The Dam, 1967; Very Personal Problems, 1973; The Cure, 197[4]; The Detective, 1976; Talk to Me About England, 1979; A Distant Country, 198[3]; Children of Dust, 1988; The Divining Heart, 1995; Infidelity, 1999; Cora Crane, 200[3]; *non-fiction:* The City, 1960; The Church of England, 1962; The Doctors, 1965; Th[e] Nameless: abortion in Britain today, 1966; Men and Money: financial Europe today, 196[8]; The House of Northcliffe, 1971; The New Militants, 1972; Dylan Thomas, 1977, rev. ed[n] 2006; Richard Burton, 1981; Gentlemen of Fortune: the world's investment banker[s], 1984; (ed) The Collected Letters of Dylan Thomas, 1986, rev. edn 2000; Sir Huge: th[e] life of Huw Wheldon, 1990; Sex and the British: a 20th century history, 1993; Caitli[n], 1993; Dr Freud, 1997; *television plays:* The Revivalist, 1975; Dylan, 1978; Nye, 1982; Th[e] Extremist, 1984; The Fasting Girl, 1984. *Address:* c/o Curtis Brown Ltd, Haymark[et] House, 28/29 Haymarket, SW1Y 4SP. *T:* (020) 7396 6600.

FERRIS, Rt Rev. Ronald Curry; *see* Algoma, Bishop of.

FERRIS, William Stephen; Chief Executive, Chatham Historic Dockyard Trust, sin[ce] 2000; *b* 3 June 1958; *s* of Harold Sydney Ferris and Grace Eileen Ferris; *m* 1982, Hon[or] Margaret Gregory; two *s*. *Educ:* Tavistock Comprehensive Sch.; Aston Univ. (BSc 1st C[l.] Hons Managerial and Admin. Studies). Self-employed baker, 1982–88; Commerci[al] Manager, Yorkshire Mining Mus., 1988–90; various posts, Heritage Projects (Mgt) Lt[d], 1990–2000 (Ops Dir, 1996–2000). Chm., Assoc. of Indep. Mus, 2002–. Mem. B[d], Tourism SE, 2003–. *Recreations:* trout fishing, mountain walking, ski-ing, Rugby footbal[l], gardening, family. *Address:* Chatham Historic Dockyard Trust, Historic Dockyar[d], Chatham ME4 4TZ. *T:* (01634) 823806, *Fax:* (01634) 823801; *e-mail:* bferris@chdt.org.uk. *Clubs:* Maidstone Rugby; Mid Kent Fisheries Fly Fishing.

FERRY, Bryan; musician; *b* 26 Sept. 1945; *s* of late Frederick Charles Ferry and Mary An[n] Ferry (*née* Armstrong); *m* 1982, Lucy Helmore (marr. diss. 2003); four *s*. *Educ:* Newcast[le] upon Tyne Univ. (BA Fine Art). Vocalist and founder mem., Roxy Music, 1971–8[3]; subseq. solo recording artist; *albums* include: (with Roxy Music): Roxy Music, 1972; Fo[r] Your Pleasure, 1973 (Grand Prix du Disque, Montreux, 1973); Stranded, 1973; Count[ry] Life, 1974; Siren, 1975; Viva Roxy Music, 1976; Manifesto, 1979; Flesh & Blood, 1980 Avalon, 1982; The High Road, 1983; Streetlife, 1986; (solo): These Foolish Things, 197[3]; Another Time Another Place, 1974; Let's Stick Together, 1976; In Your Mind, 1977; Th[e] Bride Stripped Bare, 1978; Boys and Girls, 1985; Bête Noire, 1987; Taxi, 199[3]; Mamouna, 1994; As Time Goes By, 2000; Frantic, 2002; Dylanesque, 2007; numerou[s] singles. *Recreations:* tennis, reading, shooting. *Address:* 65 New Cavendish Street, W1[G] 7LS; *e-mail:* bf@denejesmond.co.uk.

FERSHT, Sir Alan (Roy), Kt 2003; MA, PhD; FRS 1983; Herchel Smith Professor [of] Organic Chemistry, and Fellow, Gonville and Caius College, Cambridge since 198[8]; Hon. Director, Cambridge Centre for Protein Engineering (formerly MRC Unit fo[r] Protein Function and Design), since 1989; *b* 21 April 1943; *s* of Philip and Betty Fersh[t]; *m* 1966, Marilyn Persell; one *s* one *d*. *Educ:* Sir George Monoux Grammar Sch.; Gonvill[e] and Caius Coll., Cambridge (MA, PhD). Res. Fellow, Brandeis Univ., 1968; Scientifi[c] Staff, MRC Lab. of Molecular Biology, Cambridge, 1969–77; Fellow, Jesus Coll Cambridge, 1969–72; Eleanor Roosevelt Fellow, Stanford Univ., 1978; Wolfson Re[s.] Prof. of Royal Society, Dept of Chemistry, Imperial Coll. of Science and Technolog[y], 1978–89 (FIC 2004). Lectures: Smith Kline & French, Berkeley, 1984; Edsall, Harvar[d], 1984; B. R. Baker, Univ. of California at Santa Barbara, 1986; Frank Mathers, Univ. [of] Indiana, 1986; Cornell Biotechnol Program, 1987; Ferdinand Springer, FEBS, 1988–8[9]; Calvin, Berkeley, 1990; Walker, Edinburgh, 1990; Max Tishler Prize, Harvard Univ 1991–92; Jubilee, Biochemical Soc., E. Gordon Young Meml, Canada, and Brändströn[i], Gothenberg, 1993; Sternbach, Yale, 1994; Sunner Meml, Lund, 1994; Heatley, Oxfor[d]; Chan, Berkeley, Rudin, Columbia, and Hofmann, German Chemical Soc., 199[5]; Herriott, Johns Hopkins, Fritz Lipmann, German Biol Chem. Soc., and Merck-Fross[t], Montreal, 1996. Mem., EMBO, 1980; MAE 1989; FMedSci 2007. Hon. For. Mem[.] Amer. Acad. of Arts and Sci., 1988; For. Associate, Nat. Acad. of Scis, USA, 1993. Esse[x] County Jun. Chess Champion, 1961; Pres., Cambridge Univ. Chess Club, 1964 (Ha[lf] Blue, 1965). Hon. DPhil Uppsala, 1999; Dr *hc* Free Univ. of Brussels, 1999. FEB[S] Anniversary Prize, 1980; Novo Biotechnology Prize, 1986; Charmian Medal, 198[6]; Natural Products Award, 1999, RSC; Gabor Medal, 1991, Davy Medal, 1998, Roy[al] Medal, 2008, Royal Soc.; Harden Medal, Biochemical Soc., 1993; Feldberg Found[.] Prize, 1996; Distinguished Service Award, Miami, 1997; Anfinsen Award, 1999, Stein an[d] Moore Award, 2001, Protein Soc. *Publications:* Enzyme Structure and Mechanism, 197[7], 2nd edn 1984; papers in scientific jls. *Recreations:* chess, horology. *Address:* Universi[ty] Chemical Laboratory, Lensfield Road, Cambridge CB2 1EW. *T:* (01223) 336341, *Fa[x]:* (01223) 336445; 2 Barrow Close, Cambridge CB2 8AT.

FESTING, Andrew Thomas, MBE 2008; RP 1992; painter, since 1981; Presiden[t], Royal Society of Portrait Painters, since 2002; *b* 30 Nov. 1941; *s* of Field Marshal S[ir] Francis Wogan Festing, GCB, KBE, DSO and Mary Festing (*née* Riddell); *m* 196[8] Virginia Fyffe; one *d*. *Educ:* Ampleforth; RMA Sandhurst. Commnd Rifle Bde, 196[1]; Joined Sotheby & Co., 1969, Dir, English Picture Dept, 1977–81. Paintings in permane[nt] collections incl. Nat. Gall. of Ireland, Palace of Westminster, Royal Collection, NP[G] Notable commissions include HM the Queen, Queen Elizabeth the Queen Mothe[r], group portrait of whole Royal family; group picture of MPs in Library at Palace [of] Westminster, H of L in Session, Speakers Boothroyd and Martin; set of five pictures [of] famous cricketers for Lord's. *Recreations:* country sports, gardening. *Address:* 3 Hillsleig[h] Road, W8 7LE. *T:* (020) 7727 9287.

FETHERSTON-DILKE, Mary Stella, CBE 1968; RRC 1966; Organiser, Citizens' Advice Bureau, 1971–83, retired; *b* 21 Sept. 1918; *d* of late B. A. Fetherston-Dilke, MBE. *Educ:* Kingsley Sch., Leamington Spa; St George's Hospital, London (SRN). Joined QARNNS, 1942; Matron-in-Chief, QARNNS, 1966–70, retired. OStJ 1966. *Recreation:* antiques. *Address:* 12 Clareville Court, Clareville Grove, SW7 5AT.

FETHERSTONHAUGH, Guy Cuthbert Charles; QC 2003; *b* 29 Jan. 1955; *s* of Theobald Henry Robert Fetherstonhaugh and Genevieve Fetherstonhaugh (*née* Moreau); *m* 1991, Alexia Jane Musson Lees; two *s* one *d*. *Educ:* Stonyhurst Coll.; Bristol Univ. (BSc). Served 2nd Bn, RGJ, 1978–81. Called to the Bar, Inner Temple, 1983. *Publications:* (jtly) Handbook of Rent Review, 1991 and Supplements; (contrib.) The Litigation Practice, 1999–2003; Commonhold, 2004. *Recreations:* my family, woodwork, gardening, cycling. *Address:* Falcon Chambers, Falcon Court, EC4Y 1AA. *T:* (020) 7353 2484. *Club:* Rifles Officers'.

FETTIPLACE, Prof. Robert, FRS 1990; Professor of Physiology, University of Cambridge, since 2007; *b* 24 Feb. 1946; *s* of George Robert Fettiplace and Maisie Fettiplace (*née* Rolson); *m* 1977, Merriel Cleone Kruse. *Educ:* Nottingham High Sch.; Sidney Sussex Coll., Cambridge (BA 1968; MA 1972; PhD 1974). Research Fellow: Sidney Sussex Coll., Cambridge, 1971–74; Stanford Univ., 1974–76; Elmore Res. Fellow, Cambridge, 1976–79; Howe Sen. Res. Fellow, Royal Soc., 1979–90; Steenbock Prof. of Neural and Behavioral Scis, Univ of Wisconsin, 1991–2007. *Publications:* contribs to Jl Physiology, Jl Neuroscience and other learned jls. *Recreations:* bird watching, listening to music. *Address:* Department of Physiology, Development and Neuroscience, University of Cambridge, Downing Street, Cambridge CB2 3DY.

FEVERSHAM, 6th Baron *cr* 1826; **Charles Antony Peter Duncombe;** free-lance journalist; *b* 3 Jan. 1945; *s* of late Col Antony John Duncombe-Anderson and G. G. V. McNalty; *S* (to barony of) kinsman, 3rd Earl of Feversham (the earldom having become extinct), 1963; *m* 1st, 1966, Shannon (*d* 1976), *d* of late Sir Thomas Foy, CSI, CIE; two *s* one *d*; 2nd, 1979, Pauline, *d* of John Aldridge, Newark, Notts; one *s*. *Educ:* Eton; Middle Temple. Chairman: Standing Conf. of Regional Arts Assocs, 1969–76; Trustees, Yorkshire Sculpture Park, 1981–2004; President: Yorkshire Arts Assoc., 1987–91 (Chm., 1969–80); Soc. of Yorkshiremen in London, 1974; The Arvon Foundn, 1976–86; Yorks and Cleveland Local Councils Assoc., 1977–99; Nat. Assoc. of Local Councils, 1986–99. Governor, Leeds Polytechnic, 1969–76. *Publications:* A Wolf in Tooth (novel), 1967; Great Yachts, 1970. *Heir:* *s* Hon. Jasper Orlando Slingsby Duncombe, *b* 14 March 1968. *Address:* Duncombe Park, Helmsley, York YO62 5EB.

FEWSTER, Dr Kevin John, AM 2001; Director, National Maritime Museum, Greenwich, since 2007; *b* Perth, WA, 1 Dec. 1953; *s* of Geoffrey and Audrey Fewster; *m* 1996, Carol Scott; one *d*. *Educ:* Glyn Grammar Sch., Ewell; Haileybury Coll., Melbourne; Australian National Univ. (BA Hons); Univ. of New South Wales (PhD 1980). Teaching Fellow, Royal Mil. Coll. Duntroon, Univ. of NSW, 1976–80; Tutor, 1981–82, Sen. Tutor, 1983–84, History Dept, Monash Univ.; Director: S Australian Maritime Mus., Port Adelaide, 1984–89; Australian Nat. Maritime Mus., Sydney, 1989–2000; Powerhouse Mus., Sydney, 2000–07. Mem., Collections Council of Australia, 2004–07. Chm., Council of Australian Mus. Dirs, 2004–07. Vice Pres., 1993–96, Pres., 1996–99, Internat. Congress of Maritime Mus. Pres., Darling Harbour Business Assoc., 2000–02. FRSA. *Publications:* Gallipoli Correspondent: the frontline diary of C. E. W. Bean, 1983, 3rd edn 2007; (jtly) A Turkish View of Gallipoli: Canakkale, 1985, 2nd edn 2005. *Recreations:* tennis, football. *Address:* National Maritime Museum, Greenwich, SE10 9NF. *Club:* Sydney Cricket Ground.

FFOLKES, Sir Robert (Francis Alexander), 7th Bt *cr* 1774; OBE 1990; Save the Children UK, 1974–2003; *b* 2 Dec. 1943; *o s* of Captain Sir (Edward John) Patrick (Boschetti) ffolkes, 6th Bt, and Geraldine (*d* 1978), *d* of late William Roffey, Writtle, Essex; *S* father, 1960. *Educ:* Stowe Sch.; Christ Church, Oxford. *Recreations:* mountain ecology development and conservation, esp. in the Himalayas and Central Asia. *Address:* Coast Guard House, Morston, Holt, Norfolk NR25 7BH.

FFOWCS WILLIAMS, Prof. John Eirwyn, FREng; Rank Professor of Engineering, University of Cambridge, 1972–2002; Master, Emmanuel College, Cambridge, 1996–2002 (Professorial Fellow, 1972–96; Life Fellow, 2002); *b* 25 May 1935; *m* 1959, Anne Beatrice Mason; two *s* one *d*. *Educ:* Friends Sch., Great Ayton; Derby Techn. Coll.; Univ. of Southampton (BSc, PhD 1960); MA, ScD Cantab 1986. CEng, FREng (FEng 1988); FRAeS, FInstP, FIMA, FInstAcoust, Fellow Acoustical Soc. of America, FAIAA. Engrg Apprentice, Rolls-Royce Ltd, 1951–55; Spitfire Mitchell Meml Schol. to Southampton Univ., 1955–60 (Pres., Students' Union, 1957–58); Aerodynamics Div., NPL, 1960–62; Bolt, Beranek & Newman Inc., 1962–64; Reader in Applied Maths, Imperial Coll. of Science and Technology, 1964–69; Rolls Royce Prof. of Theoretical Acoustics, Imperial Coll., 1969–72. Chairman: Concorde Noise Panel, 1965–75; Topexpress Ltd, 1979–89; Dir, VSEL Consortium plc, 1987–95. Chm., Noise Research Cttee, ARC, 1969–76. FRSA. Honour Prof., Beijing Inst. of Aeronautics and Astronautics, 1992–. Foreign Hon. Mem., Amer. Acad. Arts and Scis, 1989; Foreign Associate, NAE, USA, 1995. Gov., Felsted Sch., 1980–94. Hon. ScD Southampton 2003. AIAA Aero-Acoustics Medal, 1977; Rayleigh Medal, Inst. of Acoustics, 1984; Silver Medal, Société Française d'Acoustique, 1989; Gold Medal, RAeS, 1990; Per Bruel Gold Medal, ASME, 1997; Sir Frank Whittle Medal, Royal Acad. Engrg, 2002; Aeroacoustics Award, Confedn of European Aerospace Socs, 2004. *Publications:* (with A. P. Dowling) Sound and Sources of Sound, 1983; articles in Philosophical Trans Royal Soc., Jl of Fluid Mechanics, Jl IMA, Jl of Sound Vibration, Annual Reviews of Fluid Mechanics, Random Vibration, Financial Times; (jtly) film on Aerodynamic Sound. *Recreations:* friends, research projects. *Address:* Emmanuel College, Cambridge CB2 3AP. *Club:* Athenæum.

FFRENCH, family name of **Baron ffrench**.

FFRENCH, 8th Baron *cr* 1798; **Robuck John Peter Charles Mario ffrench;** Bt 1779; *b* 14 March 1956; *s* of 7th Baron ffrench and of Sonia Katherine, *d* of late Major Digby Cayley; *S* father, 1986; *m* 1987, Dörthe Marie-Louise, *d* of Captain Wilhelm Schauer; one *d*. *Educ:* Blackrock, Co. Dublin; Ampleforth College, Yorks. *Heir:* *uncle* John Charles Mary Joseph Francis ffrench [*b* 5 Oct. 1928; *m* 1963, Sara-Primm, *d* of James A. Turner; three *d*].

FFRENCH-CONSTANT, Prof. Charles Kenvyn, PhD; FRCP; Professor of Medical Neurology, Director, Centre for Multiple Sclerosis Research and Deputy Director, MRC Centre for Regenerative Medicine, University of Edinburgh, since 2008; *b* 5 Nov. 1954; *m* Jennifer Wimperis, DM, FRCP, FRCPath; one *s* one *d*. *Educ:* Pembroke Coll., Cambridge (BA 1976; BChir 1979; MA 1980; MB 1980); University College London (PhD 1986). MRCP 1982, FRCP 1999. Lucille Markey Postdoctoral Fellow, MIT, 1986–88; Wellcome Trust Sen. Res. Fellow, Wellcome/CRC Inst. of Develtl Biol., 1991–96, Prof. of Neurological Genetics, 1999–2008, Univ. of Cambridge; Fellow, Pembroke Coll., Cambridge, 1999–2008. *Publications:* papers on develtl biol. *Recreation:* fishing. *Address:* Queen's Medical Research Institute, University of Edinburgh, 47 Little France Crescent, Edinburgh EH16 4TJ; 420 Unthank Road, Norwich NR4 7QH.

FFYTCHE, Timothy John, LVO 1997; FRCS; Surgeon-Oculist to the Queen, 1999–2001; Consultant Ophthalmologist: Moorfields Eye Hospital, 1975–2001; Hospital for Tropical Diseases, 1988–2006; Consultant Ophthalmic Surgeon to King Edward VIIth Hospital for Officers, 1980–2006; *b* 11 Sept. 1936; *s* of late Louis ffytche and Margaret (*née* Law); *m* 1961, Bärbl, *d* of late Günther Fischer; two *s*. *Educ:* Lancing Coll.; St George's Hosp., London. MB, BS; DO 1961; FRCS 1968. Registrar, Moorfields Eye Hosp., 1966–69; Wellcome Lectr, Hammersmith Hosp., 1969–70; Sen. Registrar, Middlesex Hosp., 1970–73; Ophthalmic Surgeon, St Thomas' Hosp., 1973–99; Surgeon-Oculist to HM Household, 1980–99. Sec., OSUK, 1980–82. Mem., Medical Adv. Bd, LEPRA, 1982–; Vice-Pres., Ophthalmol Sect., RSocMed, 1985–88; UK rep. to Internat. Fedn of Ophthalmic Socs, 1985–89; Mem., Adv. Cttee to Internat. Council of Ophthalmology, 1985–2002. Founder, Ophthalmic Aid to Eastern Europe, 1990–; Chm., European Sect., Internat. Agency for Prevention of Blindness, 1999– (Co-Chm., 1994–99); Pres., Med. Soc. of London, 2001–02. Clayton Meml Lectr, LEPRA, 1984. Editorial Committee: Ophthalmic Literature, 1968–82; Transactions of OSUK, 1984–89, Eye, 1989–96; European Jl of Ophthalmology, 1990–2006. *Publications:* articles on retinal diagnosis and therapy, retinal photography and the ocular complications of leprosy, in The Lancet, British Jl of Ophthalmol., Trans OSUK, Proc. Royal Soc. Med., Leprosy Review and other specialist jls. *Recreation:* occasional fishing. *Address:* (home) 1 Wellington Square, SW3 4NJ.

FIDDES, Rev. Prof. Paul Stuart, DPhil, DD; Professor of Systematic Theology, University of Oxford, since 2002; Professorial Research Fellow and Director of Research, Regent's Park College, Oxford, since 2007; *b* 30 April 1947; *s* of James Stuart Fiddes and Lois Sleeman Fiddes; *m* 1973, Marion Downing Anness; one *s* (and one *s* decd). *Educ:* Drayton Manor Grammar Sch.; St Peter's Coll., Oxford (BA Eng. Lang. and Lit. 1968; Theol 1970, MA 1972; Hon. Fellow 2004); Regent's Park Coll., Oxford (DPhil 1975; DD 2004). Ordained to Baptist Ministry, 1972; Regent's Park College, Oxford: Res. Fellow in OT, 1972–75; Tutorial Fellow in Christian Doctrine, 1975–89; Principal, 1989–2007, now Principal Emeritus; Lectr in Theol., St Peter's Coll., Oxford, 1979–85; Chm. Bd, Faculty of Theology, Oxford Univ., 1996–98. Gen. Ed., Regent's Study Guides; Jt Ed., Ecclesiology. Hon. Dr Bucharest, 2004. *Publications:* The Creative Suffering of God, 1988; Past Event and Present Salvation: the Christian idea of atonement, 1989; Freedom and Limit: a dialogue between literature and Christian doctrine, 1991; (ed) Reflections on the Water: understanding God and the world through the baptism of believers, 1996; (ed jtly) Pilgrim Pathways, 1999; The Promised End, 2000; Participating in God: a pastoral doctrine of the Trinity, 2000; (ed) The Novel, Spirituality and Modern Culture, 2000; (ed) Faith in the Centre: Christianity and culture, 2001; Tracks and Traces: baptist identity in church and theology, 2003; (ed jtly) Flickering Images: theology and film in dialogue, 2005. *Recreations:* music, literature, travel, inland waterways. *Address:* Regent's Park College, Oxford OX1 2LB; *e-mail:* paul.fiddes@regents.ox.ac.uk.

FIDDICK, Peter Ronald; journalist and broadcaster; *b* 21 Oct. 1938; *s* of Wing-Comdr Ronald Fiddick and Phyllis (*née* Wherry); *m* 1966, Jane Mary Hodlin; one *s* one *d*. *Educ:* Reading Sch.; Magdalen Coll., Oxford (BA English Lang. and Lit.). Journalist, Liverpool Daily Post, 1962–65; Leader writer, Westminster Press, 1965–66; Asst Editor, Nova, 1968; The Guardian: reporter, 1966–67 and 1969; Asst Features Editor, 1970–75; Television Columnist, 1971–84; Media Editor, 1984–88; Editor: The Listener, 1989–91; Television (RTS), 1991–2001; Research (Market Res. Soc.), 1992–99; RADA, The Magazine, 1993–; Media Columnist, Admap, 1997–2002. Newspaper Reviewer, BBC Breakfast News, 1989–99; Media Critic, BBC Radio Arts Programme, 1990–2001. Mem., Bd, George Foster Peabody Awards, USA, 2000–06 (Chm., 2005–06). FRTS 1992; Associate, RADA. Wrote and presented television series: Looking at Television, 1975–76; The Television Programme, 1979–80; Soviet Television – Fact and Fiction, 1985. *Publication:* (with B. Smithies) Enoch Powell on Immigration, 1969. *Recreations:* music, food, theatre, Saturdays.

FIDLER, John Allan, RIBA; FSA; Staff Consultant, Preservation Technology, Simpson Gumpertz & Heger Inc., Los Angeles, since 2006; *b* 1 Sept. 1952; *s* of late Eddie Fidler and Joan Margaret Fidler (*née* Edwards); *m* 1992, Jeanne Marie Teutonico. *Educ:* Sheffield Univ. (BA Hons; DipArch, MA Arch); Manchester Univ. (MA Conservation); Architectural Assoc., London (Grad. Dip. Conservation). RIBA 1979; IHBC 1998. Casework officer, Historic Bldgs Div., GLC, 1978–83; Historic Bldgs architect, City of London Corp., 1983–84; English Heritage: Conservation Officer for bldgs at risk, 1984–86; Superintending Architect, 1986–90; Head: Architectural and Survey Services, 1990–91; Bldg Conservation and Res., 1991–2002; Conservation Dir, 2002–06. Chm., Cttee B/209-7 drafting codes of practice, BSI, 2001–. Member: Council, ICCROM, 2001–05, 2005–07 (Vice Pres., 2005–07); Conservation Cttee, Getty Foundn (formerly J. P. Getty Trust Grants Prog.), 2001–. FAPT 2000; FSA 2002; FIIC 2006; FRICS 2007. FRSA 1980. *Publications:* (ed) English Heritage Directory of Building Sands and Aggregates, 2000; (ed) Stone, Vol. 2, 2002; contrib. technical papers to ASCHB Trans, Bull. Assoc. for Preservation Technol., English Heritage Trans. *Recreations:* hiking, visiting historic sites. *Address:* Simpson Gumpertz & Heger Inc., 1055 West 7th Street, Suite 2500, Los Angeles, CA 90017, USA. *T:* (213) 2711915, *Fax:* (213) 6170411; *e-mail:* jafidler@sgh.com.

FIDLER, Prof. (John) Kelvin, PhD; FREng, FIET; Vice-Chancellor and Chief Executive, University of Northumbria at Newcastle, since 2001; *b* 11 May 1944; *s* of Samuel Fidler and Barbara Fidler; *m* 1st, 1966, Jadwiga Sorokowska (marr. diss. 1995); one *s* one *d*; 2nd, 2002, Nadine Cleaver. *Educ:* Harrow Co. Sch. for Boys; King's Coll., Univ. of Durham (BSc); Univ. of Newcastle upon Tyne (PhD 1968). CEng 1972, FREng 2005; FIET (FIEE 1982). Sen. Res. Associate, Univ. of Newcastle upon Tyne, 1968–69; Lectr, 1969–74, Sen. Lectr, 1974–80, Reader, 1980–83, Univ. of Essex; Professor of Electronics: Open Univ., 1984–88; Univ. of York, 1989–2001. Chm., Engineering Council, 2005–. *Publications:* Computer Aided Circuit Design, 1978; Introductory Circuit Theory, 1980, 2nd edn 1989; Continuous Time Active Filter Design, 1998; numerous contribs on electronics to learned jls. *Recreations:* walking, ham radio, cooking. *Address:* Vice-Chancellor's Office, University of Northumbria at Newcastle, Ellison Place, Newcastle upon Tyne NE1 8ST. *T:* (0191) 227 4002.

FIDLER, Prof. Peter Michael, MBE 1993; DL; Vice-Chancellor and Chief Executive, University of Sunderland, since 1999. *Educ:* Univ. of Salford (MSc). Town planner. Formerly: Dean, Dept of Built Envmt, UWE; Dep. Vice-Chancellor (Academic Affairs), Oxford Brookes Univ. DL Tyne and Wear, 2005. *Address:* Office of the Vice-Chancellor, University of Sunderland, Edinburgh Building, City Campus, Chester Road, Sunderland SR1 3SD.

FIDLER-SIMPSON, John Cody; *see* Simpson.

FIELD, Brig. Anne, CB 1980; CBE 1996; Deputy Controller Commandant, Women's Royal Army Corps, 1984–92 (Director, 1977–82); Chairman of Council, 1991–97, and Life Vice President, 1999, WRAC Association (Vice President, 1984–97); *b* 4 April 1926; *d* of Captain Harold Derwent and Annie Helena Hodgson. *Educ:* Keswick Sch.; St George's, Harpenden; London Sch. of Economics. Joined ATS, 1947; commissioned: ATS, 1948; WRAC, 1949; Lt-Col, 1968; Col, 1971. Hon. ADC to the Queen, 1977–82. Dep. Col Comdt, AGC, 1992–94. Dir, London Regl Bd, Lloyds Bank, 1982–91 (Dep. Chm., 1990–91). Special Comr, Duke of York's Royal Mil. Sch., 1989–. Chm., ATS and WRAC Benevolent Fund, 1984–97. Patron, ATS Dinner Club, 1996–. Freeman, City of London, 1981; Liveryman, Spectacle Makers' Co., 1990. CCMI (FBIM 1978). *Address:* c/o Lloyds TSB, PO Box 1190, 7 Pall Mall, SW1Y 5NA. *Club:* Army and Navy.

FIELD, Barry John Anthony, TD 1984; *b* 4 July 1946; *s* of Ernest Field and late Marguerite Eugenie Field; *m* 1969, Jaqueline Anne Miller; one *s* one *d*. *Educ:* Collingwood Boys' Sch.; Mitcham Grammar Sch.; Bembridge Sch.; Victoria Street Coll. Chm., J. D. Field & Sons Ltd, 1993–94 (Dir, 1981–94); Dir, Great Southern Cemetery & Crematorium Co. Ltd, 1969–94. Councillor, Horsham Dist. Council, 1983–86 (Vice-Chm., Housing, 1984–85, Chm., Housing, 1985–86); Mem., IoW CC, 1986–89. MP (C) Isle of Wight, 1987–97. Chm., H of C Deregulation Cttee, 1995–97. Major RCT TA; Liveryman, Turners' Co.; Mem., Watermen and Lightermen's Co. *Recreations:* sailing, theatre, ski-ing. *Address:* Medina Lodge, 25 Birmingham Road, Cowes, Isle of Wight PO31 7BH. *T:* (01983) 292871. *Club:* Island Sailing (Cowes).

FIELD, Dr Clive Douglas, OBE 2007; FRHistS; FEA; Director of Scholarship and Collections, British Library, 2001–06; *b* 27 June 1950; *o s* of Joseph Stanley Field and Lily Field (*née* Battams); *m* 1972, Verena Duss; one *s*. *Educ:* Dunstable Grammar Sch.; Wadham Coll., Oxford (BA Modern History 1971; MA 1975; DPhil Modern History 1975); Westminster Coll., Oxford (PGCE 1975). FRHistS 2001; FEA 2008. SSRC Post-Doctoral Fellow, Wadham Coll., Oxford, 1975–77; Asst Librarian, 1977–87, Sub-Librarian, 1987–90, John Rylands Univ. Liby of Manchester; University of Birmingham: Dep. Librarian, 1990–95; Librarian and Dir of Inf. Services, 1995–2001; Associate Mem., 1992–2001, Hon. Res. Fellow, 2006–, Dept of Modern History. Project Director: Ensemble: towards a distributed nat. liby resource for music, 1999–2002; Revelation: unlocking research resources for 19th and 20th century church history and Christian theology, 2000–02. Co-Dir, Online Centre for British Data on religion, 2008–. Chairman: Internat. English Short Title Catalogue Cttee, 2001–06; Full Disclosure Implementation Gp, 2001–05; Jt Cttee on Voluntary Deposit, 2001–03; Jt Cttee on Legal Deposit, 2004–06; Member: Bd of Dirs, Consortium of Univ. Res. Libraries, 1996–2001, 2003–06 (Chm., 2000–01); Cttee on Electronic Inf., 1999–2001, Cttee for Content Services, 2002–05, and Cttee for Support of Research, 2003–04, Jt Inf. Systems Cttee; Midlands Metropolitan Area Network Mgt Cttee, 1999–2001; HEFCE Strategic Adv. Cttee for Res., 2003–06; Legal Deposit Adv. Panel, 2005–06; Adv. Council on Nat. Records and Archives, 2007–; Bd of Dirs, Birmingham Res. Park Ltd, 1999–2001. Pres., Religious Archives Gp, 2007–. Editor, The People Called Methodists microfiche project, 1988–98. Hon. DLitt Birmingham, 2006. *Publications:* Non-Recurrent Christian Data: reviews of UK Statistical Sources, 1987; Anti-Methodist Publications of the Eighteenth Century, 1991; Church and Chapel in Early Victorian Shropshire, 2004; Lutonian Odyssey, 2008; professional papers; articles, bibliographies and reviews on the social history of religion in Great Britain since 1689, with special reference to religious statistics, religious practice, and the history of Methodism. *Recreations:* historical research and writing, visiting (incl. virtually) secondhand bookshops. *Address:* 35 Elvetham Road, Edgbaston, Birmingham B15 2LZ; *e-mail:* c.d.field@bham.ac.uk.

FIELD, David Anthony; Zoological Director, Zoological Society of London, since 2006; *b* 9 Jan. 1967; *s* of Derek and Jean Field; *m* 1997, Dr Lesley Dickie. *Educ:* Foxyards Primary Sch.; Dudley Sch.; University Coll., Cardiff (BSc Hons Zool.); Open Univ. (MBA). SO, UFAW, 1988–90; Senior Zookeeper: Penscynor Wildlife Park, 1990–93; Edinburgh Zoo, 1993–98; Asst Dir, Dublin Zoo, 1998–2002; Curator, Whipsnade Zoo, 2002–03; Curator of Mammals, 2003–04, Hd of Animal Care, 2004–06, Zool Soc. of London. Member: Council, British and Irish Assoc. of Zoos and Aquaria, 2005–; Bd, Internat. Species Information Systems, 2008–; DEFRA Zoos Forum, 2008–. Trustee, Wild Vets Internat., 2006–07. *Recreations:* zoo history, golf, my dog, Mac. *Address:* Zoological Society of London, Regent's Park, NW1 4RY. *T:* (020) 7449 6500, *Fax:* (020) 7449 6283; *e-mail:* david.field@zsl.org.

FIELD, Douglas John; His Honour Judge Field; a Circuit Judge, since 2006; Resident Judge, Swindon Combined Court, since 2007; *b* 17 April 1947; twin *s* of Robert Henry Field and Ivy May Field (*née* Dicketts); *m* 1969, Karen Heather Strubbe; one *s* one *d*. *Educ:* Ottershaw Sch.; Coll. of Law, Guildford. Admitted solicitor, 1972; called to Bermuda Bar, 1974; in practice as barrister and attorney, Bermuda, 1974–77; a District Judge, 1995–2006. *Recreations:* watching cricket and Rugby, playing golf, cinema. *Address:* The Law Courts, Islington Street, Swindon, Wilts SN1 2HG. *T:* (01793) 69500, *Fax:* (01793) 690505.

See also Hon. Sir R. A. Field.

FIELD, (Edward) John, CMG 1991; HM Diplomatic Service, retired; High Commissioner, Sri Lanka, 1991–96; *b* 11 June 1936; *s* of late Arthur Field, OBE, MC, TD, and Dorothy Agnes Field; *m* 1960, Irene Sophie du Pont Darden; one *s* one *d*. *Educ:* Highgate Sch.; Corpus Christi Coll., Oxford; Univ. of Virginia. Courtaulds Ltd, 1960–62; FCO, 1963–96: 2nd, later 1st Sec., Tokyo, 1963–68; Amer. Dept, FCO, 1968–70; Cultural Attaché, Moscow, 1970–72; 1st Sec. (Commercial), Tokyo, 1973–76; Asst Head, S Asian Dept, FCO, 1976–77; Dept of Trade, 1977–79 (Head, Exports to Japan Unit); Counsellor: (Commercial), Seoul, 1980–83; at Harvard Univ., 1983–84; UK Mission to UN, 1984–87; Minister, Tokyo, 1988–91. Pres., Virginia Opera Assoc., 2003–05. Trustee, Chrysler Mus. of Art, Norfolk, Virginia, 2002–. *Recreations:* riding, listening to music. *Address:* 21 Dawson Place, W2 4TH; Jericho Farm, 19637 Governor Darden Road, Courtland, VA 23837, USA. *Club:* Travellers.

FIELD, Rt Hon. Frank; PC 1997; MP (Lab) Birkenhead, since 1979; *b* 16 July 1942; *s* of late Walter and of Annie Field. *Educ:* St Clement Danes Grammar Sch.; Univ. of Hull (BSc (Econ)). Director: Child Poverty Action Gp, 1969–79; Low Pay Unit, 1974–80. Minister of State (Minister for Welfare Reform), DSS, 1997–98. Chairman: Select Cttee on Social Services, 1987–90; Select Cttee on Social Security, 1991–97. Chm., Pensions Reform Gp, 1999– (reports: Universal Protected Pension: modernising pensions for the millennium, 2001; Universal Protected Pension: the following report, 2002). *Publications:* (ed jtly) Twentieth Century State Education, 1971; (ed jtly) Black Britons, 1971; (ed) Low Pay, 1973; Unequal Britain, 1974; (ed) Are Low Wages Inevitable?, 1976; (ed) Education and the Urban Crisis, 1976; (ed) The Conscript Army: a study of Britain's unemployed, 1976; (jtly) To Him Who Hath: a study of poverty and taxation, 1976; (with Ruth Lister) Wasted Labour, 1978 (Social Concern Book Award); (ed) The Wealth Report, 1979; Inequality in Britain: freedom, welfare and the state, 1981; Poverty and Politics, 1982; The Wealth Report—2, 1983; (ed) Policies against Low Pay, 1984; The Minimum Wage: its potential and dangers, 1984; Freedom and Wealth in a Socialist Future, 1987; The Politic of Paradise, 1987; Losing Out: the emergence of Britain's underclass, 1989; An Agenda fo Britain, 1993; (jtly) Europe Isn't Working, 1994; (jtly) Beyond Punishment: pathway from workfare, 1994; Making Welfare Work, 1995; How to Pay for the Future: buildin a stakeholders welfare, 1996; Stakeholder Welfare, 1997; Reforming Welfare, 1997 Reflections on Welfare Reform, 1998; The State of Dependency: welfare under Labou 2000; Making Welfare Work: reconstructing welfare for the millennium, 2001 Neighbours from Hell: the politics of behaviour, 2003; The Ethic of Respect: a left win cause, 2006. *Address:* House of Commons, SW1A 0AA. *T:* (020) 7219 5193.

FIELD, Maj.-Gen. Geoffrey William, CB 1993; CVO 2005; OBE 1983 (MBE 1976) Resident Governor and Keeper of the Jewel House, HM Tower of London, 1994–2006 Service Member, Pensions Appeal Tribunals, since 2005; *b* 30 Nov. 1941; *s* of Willian Edwin Field and Ellen Campbell Field (*née* Forsyth); *m* 1966, Janice Anne Olsen; one two *d*. *Educ:* Daniel Stewart's College, Edinburgh; RMA Sandhurst; RMCS Shrivenham Australian Staff College; RCDS. Commissioned RE 1961; OC 59 Indep. Cdo Sqn, RE 1976–78; CO 36 Engr Regt, 1980–83 (comd RE, Falkland Islands, 1982); Asst Di Defence Policy, MoD, 1983–85; Comd 11 Engr Gp, 1986–87; Dir Defence Programme MoD, 1989–90; Dir Gen., Logistic Policy (Army), 1990–93; Engr-in-Chief (Army) 1993–94. Colonel Commandant: RPC, 1991–93; RLC, 1993–96; RE, 1996–2006; Hon Col, RE Vols (Specialist Units), 1992–96. Comr, Royal Hosp., Chelsea, 1990–93. Dir Historic Royal Palaces Enterprises, 1998–2006. Trustee, Ulysses Trust, 1994–2005; Gov. St Katharine's and Shadwell Trust, 1999–2006. Freeman, City of London, 1995 *Recreation:* golf. *Address:* c/o Lloyds TSB, Cox's and King's Branch, 7 Pall Mall. SW1Y 5NA. *Club:* Rye Golf.

FIELD, Dr Ian Trevor, CBE 1994; Secretary General, World Medical Association 1994–97; *b* 31 Oct. 1933; *s* of late Major George Edward Field, MBE, IA, and Berth Cecilia Field; *m* 1960, Christine Mary Osman, OBE, JP; three *s*. *Educ:* Shri Shivaji School Poona; Bournemouth School; Guy's Hosp. Med. School. MB, BS; FFPH; FFOM. Roya Engineers, 1952–54; Med. Sch., 1954–60; house posts, 1960–62; general practice 1962–64; Asst Sec., later Under Sec., BMA, 1964–75; SMO, 1975–78, SPMO/Unde Sec., 1978–85, DHSS, (Internat. Health and Communicable Disease Control, later NH Regional Orgn); Chief Med. and Health Services Advr, ODA, 1978–83; Dep. Sec. 1985–89, Sec., 1989–93, BMA. Member: Council, Liverpool Sch. of Trop. Med 1979–83, 1993–96; Bd of Management, London Sch. of Hygiene and Trop. Med 1979–83; Council, Royal Vet. Coll., 1982–88; WHO Global Adv. Cttee on Malari Control, 1979–82 (Chm., 1981). Liveryman, Soc. of Apothecaries, 1971– (Ct o Assistants, 1986–; Master, 1998–99). *Publications:* contribs to medical jls. *Recreations* military history, opera, watching cricket and rugby. *Address:* Flat 2, Sturges Court, 7 Sturges Road, Wokingham, Berks RG40 2HE.

FIELD, Brig. Jill Margaret, CBE 1992; RRC 1988; Matron-in-Chief (Army) an Director of Defence Nursing Services, 1989–92; *b* 20 June 1934; *d* of late Major Charle Euston Field, Royal Signals, and Mrs Eva Gladys Field (*née* Watson). *Educ:* High Schoo for Girls, Southend-on-Sea; St Bartholomew's Hosp., London (SRN). Joined QARANC 1957; appointments include: service in Mil. Hosps in UK, BAOR, N Africa, Cyprus Singapore; Instructor, QARANC Trng Centre, 1971–74; Liaison Officer QARANC MoD, 1980–83; Matron, BMH Hannover, 1984–85; Dep. Medical (Nursing), BAOR 1985–87; Matron, Cambridge Mil. Hosp., Aldershot and Chief Medical (Nursing) SE an SW Dist, 1987–89. QHNS 1989–92. *Recreations:* gardening, reading, music.

FIELD, John; *see* Field, E. J.

FIELD, Prof. John Edwin, OBE 1987; PhD; FRS 1994; Professor of Applied Physics Department of Physics, University of Cambridge, 1994–2003, now Emeritus; Head o Physics and Chemistry of Solids Section, Cavendish Laboratory, Cambridge, 1987–2003 Fellow of Magdalene College, Cambridge, 1964–2003, now Emeritus; *b* 20 Sept. 1936; of William Edwin Field and Madge (*née* Normansell); *m* 1963, Ineke Tjan; two *s* one *d* *Educ:* Univ. of London (BSc); Univ. of Cambridge (PhD 1962). Graduate Tutor Magdalene Coll., Cambridge, 1974–87; Asst Lectr, 1966–71, Lectr, 1971–90, Reader 1990–94, Dept of Physics, Univ. of Cambridge. Hon. FRSSAf 2002. Hon. DSc: Univ. o Luleå, Sweden, 1989; Cranfield, 2002. Duddell Medal, Inst. of Physics, 1990. *Publications* (ed) The Properties of Diamond, 1979, 2nd edn 1991; (ed) The Properties of Natural an Synthetic Diamond, 1992; (ed) 3 conf. proc.; over 300 scientific papers. *Recreations* mountain walking, running, ski-ing. *Address:* 11A Church Street, Stapleford, Camb CB22 5DS. *T:* (01223) 846515.

FIELD, Sir Malcolm (David), Kt 1991; Chairman, Tube Lines Ltd, 2003–06; Externa Policy Adviser, Department for Transport, 2001–06; *b* 25 Aug. 1937; *s* of Stanley Herbe Raynor Field and Constance Frances (*née* Watson); *m* (marr. diss.); one *d*; *m* 2001, Ann Charlton. *Educ:* Highgate Sch.; London Business Sch. National Service, commnd Wels Guards (2nd Lieut), 1955–57 (served in Cyprus and Germany). PA to Dir, ICI (Pain Div.), 1957; joined family business, 1960 (taken over by W. H. Smith, 1963); Wholesal Dir, 1970–82, Man. Dir, Retail Gp, 1978–82, Gp Man. Dir, 1982–93, Chief Exec 1994–96, W. H. Smith. Chairman: Bd of Management, NAAFI, 1986–93 (Mem., Bd o Management, 1973–86; Dep. Chm., 1985–86); CAA, 1996–2001; Sofa Workshop 1998–2002; Aricom plc, 2004–06 (Sen. non-exec. Dir, 2006–); non-executive Director MEPC, 1989–99; Scottish & Newcastle Breweries, 1993–98; Phoenix Group Ltd 1995–97; Stationery Office, 1996–2001; Walker Greenbank, 1997–2002; Evolutio Beeson Gregory (formerly Beeson Gregory), 2000–04; Odgers, 2002–; Sen. non-exec Dir, Hochschild Mining plc, 2006–. Mem. Council, RCA, 1991–2001; Mem. Bd, Englis Nat. Ballet Sch., 1997–2007; Gov., Highgate Sch., 1994–2004 (Dep. Chm., 1999–2004) CCMI (CBIM 1988); CRAeS 1997; FRSA 1989. *Recreations:* watching cricket, tennis golf, restoring an orangery and garden in Devon, reading biographies, collecting moder art. *Address:* 21 Embankment Gardens, SW3 4LH. *Clubs:* Garrick, MCC.

FIELD, Mark Christopher; MP (C) Cities of London and Westminster, since 2001; *b* Oct. 1964; *s* of late Maj. Peter Field and of Ulrike Field (*née* Peipe); *m* 1st, 1994, Michel Louise Acton (marr. diss. 2006); 2nd, 2007, Victoria Margaret Philadelphia Elphicke; on *s*. *Educ:* Reading Sch.; St Edmund Hall, Oxford (MA Hons Juris.); Coll. of Law, Chester Trainee solicitor, Richards Butler, 1988–90; Solicitor, Freshfields, 1990–92; employmen consultant, 1992–94; Man. Dir, Kellyfield Consulting (publishing/recruiting firm) 1994–2001. Non-exec. Dir, Hoar Marshall, 2007–. Councillor (C), RBK&C, 1994–2002 An Opposition Whip, 2003–04; Shadow Minister for London, 2003–05; Shadov Financial Sec. to the Treasury, 2005; Shadow Minister for Culture, 2005–06. Mem. Select Cttee on LCD, 2003. Secretary, All Party Group: on Germany, 2002–05; o Venture Capital and Private Equity, 2002–. Member Standing Committee for: Procee of Crime Act, 2002; Enterprise Act, 2002; Finance Act, 2002; Licensing Act, 2003 Housing Act, 2004; Railways Act, 2005; Finance Act (No. 2), 2005; Regn of Financia Services (Land Transactions) Act, 2006; Nat. Insurance Contributions Act, 2006; Nationa Lottery Act, 2006; Crossrail Bill, 2007–08. Mem., Adv. Cttee, London Sch. o Commerce, 2005–. *Recreations:* cricket, soccer, researching local history, reading politica biographies and diaries, walking in London, listening to popular/rock music, visiting interesting places overseas. *Address:* House of Commons, SW1A 0AA. *T:* (020) 7219 8160, *T:* (office) (020) 7730 8181; 12 Evelyn Mansions, Carlisle Place, SW1P 1NH.

FIELD, Marshall Hayward, CBE 1985; Director, Phoenix Assurance, 1980–85 (Actuary, 1964–85, General Manager, 1972–85); *b* 19 April 1930; *s* of Harold Hayward Field and Hilda Maud Field; *m* 1960, Barbara Evelyn Harris (*d* 1998); two *d. Educ:* Dulwich College. FIA 1957. With Pearl Assce, 1948–58; joined Phoenix Assurance, 1958. Director: TSB Trust Co. Ltd, 1985–89; TSB Gp, 1990–95; Ark Life Assurance Co., Dublin, 1991–2003; Consultant, Bacon & Woodrow, 1986–2000. Institute of Actuaries: Hon. Sec., 1975–77; Vice-Pres., 1979–82; Pres., 1986–88; Vice Pres., International Actuarial Assoc., 1984–90; Chm., Life Offices' Assoc., 1983–85. Mem., Fowler Inquiry into Provision for Retirement, 1984; Consultant, Marketing of Investments Bd Organising Cttee, 1985–86. Mem., Dulwich Picture Gall. Cttee, 1985–94; Trustee, Dulwich Picture Gall., 1994–2002; Chm., Dulwich DFAS, 2002–05. Governor: Dulwich Coll. Estates, 1973–95 (Chm., 1988–90); Dulwich Coll., 1987–97; James Allen's Girls' School, 1981–95. Mem., Ct of Assistants, Actuaries' Co., 1989– (Master, 1996–97). *Recreations:* theatre, architecture. *Address:* 12 Gainsborough Court, College Road, SE21 7LT. *Club:* Bembridge Sailing.

FIELD, Hon. Michael Walter, AC 2003; consultant on organisational change; Chairman, Tasmanian Innovations Advisory Board, since 1999; *b* 28 May 1948; *s* of William Field and Blanche (*née* Burrows); *m* 1975, Janette Elizabeth Mary Fone; one *s* two *d. Educ:* Railton Primary Sch., Tasmania; Devonport High Sch., Tasmania; Univ. of Tasmania (BA Pol. Sci./History). Teacher, 1971–75; Community Develt Officer, 1975–76. Government of Tasmania: MHA (Lab) Braddon, 1976–97; Minister for Transport, Main Roads, Construction and Local Govt, 1979–82; Shadow Minister for: Transport, 1982–83; Education and Ind. Relns, 1982–86; State Development, 1992–97; Dep. Leader of Opposition and Shadow Minister for Forestry, Ind. Relns and Energy, 1986–88; Leader of the Opposition, 1988–89 and 1992–97; Premier, Treas. and Minister for State Develt and Finance, 1989–92; Shadow Minister for Educn, Trng, and Youth Affairs, 1996–97. Chm. Bd, Multiversity Digital Pty Ltd, 2002–05; Board Member: John Curtin House Ltd, 1997–; Leadership Adv. Gp, Ortus Star Inc., 1998–; Tasmanian Electricity Code Change Panel, 1999–2005. Dir, Port Arthur Historic Site Mgt Authy, 2005–. Life Mem. ALP, 2001. Hon. LLD Tasmania, 2000. *Recreations:* fishing, reading, music. *Address:* e-mail: mwField@bigpond.com.

FIELD, Patrick John; QC 2000; a Recorder, since 2001; *b* 19 March 1959; *s* of Michael Edward and Patricia Field; *m* Helen McCubbin; one *s* two *d. Educ:* Wilmslow Co. Grammar Sch.; King's Coll. London (LLB Hons). Called to the Bar, Gray's Inn, 1981, Bencher, 2007; Northern Circuit, 1982– (Junior, 1985). *Recreations:* fishing, travel. *Address:* Deans Court Chambers, 24 St John Street, Manchester M3 4DF. *T:* (0161) 214 6000.

FIELD, Hon. Sir Richard (Alan), Kt 2002; **Hon. Mr Justice Field;** a Judge of the High Court, Queen's Bench Division, since 2002; a Presiding Judge, Western Circuit, since 2009; *b* 17 April 1947; twin *s* of Robert Henry Field and Ivy May Field; *m* 1968, Lynne Hauskind (*d* 2007); two *s* two *d. Educ:* Ottershaw Sch.; Bristol Univ. (LLB); London School of Economics (LLM with Dist.). Asst Prof., Univ. of British Columbia, 1969–71; Lectr in Law, Hong Kong Univ., 1971–73; Associate Prof., McGill Univ., Montreal, 1973–77; called to the Bar, Inner Temple, 1977, Bencher, 1998. QC 1987; a Dep. High Court Judge, 1998–2001; a Recorder, 1999–2001. *Recreations:* cricket, leonburger dogs, opera, theatre. *Address:* Royal Courts of Justice, Strand, WC2A 2LL. *Club:* Garrick.
See also D. J. Field.

FIELD, Stuart, FRCR; Consultant Radiologist, Kent and Canterbury Hospital, 1974–2004; Director, Kent Breast Screening Programme, 1988–2004; *b* 22 June 1944; *s* of Walter Frederick William Field and Maisie Field (*née* Marlow); *m* 1968, Margaret Shirley Dawes; two *d. Educ:* Watford Grammar Sch. (Head Boy); Gonville and Caius Coll., Cambridge (BA 1st Cl. Hons Natural Sci. Tripos, MA, MB BChir). DMRD 1972; FRCR 1974. Houseman to Professorial Med. and Surgical Units, 1969–70, Registrar in Radiol., 1970–74, KCH. Royal College of Radiologists: Dean, Faculty of Clinical Radiology, 1991–93, Vice-Pres., 1993; Pres. Kent Postgrad. Med. Centre, 1994–2000; Hon. Prof., Kent Inst. of Medicine and Health Scis, Univ. of Kent at Canterbury, 1998–2007. Mem., DoH Adv. Cttee for Breast Cancer Screening, 1994–2003. Chairman: Breast Gp, 1997–99; League of Friends, Kent and Canterbury Hosp., 2007–. Hon. Mem., Romanian Radiol. Soc., 1993. President's Medal, RCR, 2002. *Publications:* numerous chapters in textbooks of radiol. on the plain abdominal radiograph in the acute abdomen; contrib. articles on breast cancer screening and other radiol topics to specialist radiol. jls. *Recreations:* gardening, walking, DIY, classical music, the family. *Address:* Bournes Corner, Bekesbourne Road, Bridge, Canterbury, Kent CT4 5AE.

FIELD-SMITH, Robin, MBE 1983; HM Inspector of Constabulary, since 2000; *b* Brighton, 24 Jan. 1948; *s* of John and Meriel Field-Smith; *m* 1970, Mary Paffett; two *s* one *d. Educ:* Manor House Sch.; Hurstpierpoint Coll.; Univ. of Liverpool (BA 1970); Churchill Coll., Cambridge (PGCE 1971); Open Univ. (MA 1993). FCIPD 1999. Commissioned: TA, 1970; RAEC, 1971; regtl duties, 1972–79; Staff Coll., 1980; SO2 HQ BAOR, 1981–82; BAOR and MoD, 1983–86; JSDC 1986; SO1 HQ AFCENT, 1987–89; Comd ETS, Berlin, 1990–92; SO1 HQ AGC, 1992–93; Comd ETS, BAOR, 1993–94; CO ASTS, 1995–97; Dep. Dir, ETS(A), 1997–99; Defence Trng Review, 1999–2000. Lay Chm., Army Synod, 1990–2000. Vice-Pres., Nat. Assoc. of Chaplains to the Police, 2008–. Dir, Wilts TEC, 1996–2000; Gov., Chippenham Coll., 1997–2001; Trustee, Royal Sch., Hampstead, 2003–. CCMI 2007. Freeman, City of London, 2008. Hon. MCGI 2004. *Publications:* over 60 inspection reports. *Recreations:* choral singing, family, ski-ing, gardening, steam railways. *Address:* HM Inspectorate of Constabulary, White Rose Court, Oriental Road, Woking, Surrey GU22 7PJ; *e-mail:* robin@field-smith.com. *Club:* Army and Navy.

FIELDER, Prof. Alistair Richard, FRCS, FRCP, FRCOphth; Professor of Ophthalmology, City University, 2005–07, now Emeritus; Hon. Consultant Ophthalmologist: St Mary's Hospital NHS Trust, 1995–2007; Hillingdon Hospital NHS Trust, 1996–2007; *b* 3 Sept. 1942; *s* of late Alfred Emmanuel Hugh Fielder and of Elizabeth Rachel Fielder (*née* Hutchinson); *m* 1965, Gillian Muriel Slough; one *s* three *d. Educ:* St George's Hosp. Med. Sch., London Univ. (MB BS 1966). FRCS 1974; FRCOphth (FCOphth 1988); MRCP 1991, FRCP 1994; FRCPCH 1999. RSO, Moorfields Eye Hosp., 1973–76; Consultant Ophthalmologist, Derby Hosps, 1977–82; Reader in Ophthalmology, Leicester Univ., 1982–88; Professor of Ophthalmology: Birmingham Univ., 1988–95; ICSTM, later ICL, 1995–2004. Vice Pres., 1995–99, Sen. Vice Pres., 1997–99, Royal Coll. of Ophthalmologists; British Rep., Societas Ophthalmologica Europæa, 1998–. Trustee: RNIB, 1990–2002 (Mem., Nat. Assembly, 2002–); Fight for Sight, 2003– (Sen. Scientific Advr, 2005–); Action for Blind People, 2006–; Chm. Trustees, Nat. Fedn of Families with Visually Impaired Children (LOOK), 2003–; Vice Chm. Trustees, Vision 2020 UK, 2002–07. *Publications:* scientific articles and contribs to books on the developing visual system and paediatric ophthalmology. *Recreation:* relaxing on narrow boat. *Address:* 18 Melrose Gardens, W6 7RW. *T:* (020) 7602 4790. *Club:* Royal Society of Medicine.

FIELDHOUSE, Brian; DL; Chief Executive, West Sussex County Council, 1990–95; *b* 1 May 1933; *s* of late Harry and Florence Fieldhouse; *m* 1959, Sonia J. Browne; one *s* one *d. Educ:* Barnsley Holgate Grammar Sch.; Keble Coll., Oxford (MA PPE). IPFA 1960. Formerly, Treasurer's Departments: Herts CC; Hants CC; Flints CC; County Treasurer: Lincs parts of Lindsey CC, 1970–73; W Sussex CC, 1973–90. Comr, Public Works Loans Bd, 1988–92. Principal Financial Advr, ACC, 1980–85. Pres., Soc. of Co. Treasurers, 1983. Dir, Chichester Fest. Theatre, 1995–97. Sec., Rees Jeffreys Road Fund, 1995–2005. DL West Sussex, 1996. FRSA 1984. *Recreations:* hill farming, theatre going. *Address:* 13 The Avenue, Chichester PO19 4PX. *Club:* Farmers'.

FIELDHOUSE, Prof. David Kenneth, FBA 1996; Vere Harmsworth Professor of Imperial and Naval History, Cambridge University, 1981–92; Fellow, Jesus College, Cambridge, 1981–92, subseq. Emeritus; *b* 7 June 1925; *s* of Rev. Ernest Fieldhouse and Clara Hilda Beatrice Fieldhouse; *m* 1952, Sheila Elizabeth Lyon; one *s* two *d. Educ:* Dean Close Sch., Cheltenham; Queen's Coll., Oxford (MA, DLitt). War Service: RN, Sub-Lt (A), 1943–47. History master, Haileybury Coll., 1950–52; Lectr in Modern History, Univ. of Canterbury, NZ, 1953–57; Beit Lectr in Commonwealth History, Oxford Univ., 1958–81; Fellow, Nuffield Coll., Oxford, 1966–81. *Publications:* The Colonial Empires, 1966, 2nd edn, 1982; The Theory of Capitalist Imperialism, 1967, 2nd edn 1969; Economics and Empire, 1973, 2nd edn 1984; Unilever Overseas, 1978; Colonialism 1870–1945, 1981; Black Africa 1945–80, 1986; Merchant Capital and Economic Decolonization, 1994; The West and the Third World, 1999; Kurds, Arabs and Britons, 2001; Western Imperialism in the Middle East, 1914–1958, 2006. *Recreations:* music, golf, sailing, reading fiction. *Address:* Jesus College, Cambridge CB5 8BL. *T:* (01223) 339339.

FIELDING, Sir Colin (Cunningham), Kt 1986; CB 1981; *b* 23 Dec. 1926; *s* of Richard Cunningham and Sadie Fielding; *m* 1953, Gillian Aerona (*née* Thomas) (*d* 2005); one *d. Educ:* Heaton Grammar Sch., Newcastle upon Tyne; Durham Univ. BSc Hons Physics. British Scientific Instruments Research Assoc., 1948–49; RRE Malvern, 1949–65; Asst Dir of Electronics R&D, Min. of Technology, 1965–68; Head of Electronics Dept, RRE Malvern, 1968–73; RCDS, 1973–74; Dir of Scientific and Technical Intelligence, MoD, 1975–77; Dir, Admiralty Surface Weapons Estabt, 1977–78; Dep. Controller, R&D Estabts and Res. A, and Chief Scientist (RN), MoD, 1978–80; Dep. Chief of Defence Procurement (Nuclear), and Dir, AWRE, MoD, 1980–82; Controller of R&D Estabts, Res. and Nuclear Progs, MoD, 1982–86. Dir, Cray Research (UK), 1988. *Publications:* papers in Proc. IEE, Proc. IERE, Nature. *Recreations:* yachting, tennis, music, golf.

FIELDING, Emma Georgina Annalies; actress; *b* 7 Oct. 1971; *d* of Johnny Fielding and Sheila Fielding (*née* Brown); *m* 2004, Michael Ashcroft. *Educ:* Royal Scottish Acad. of Music and Drama (Dip. Dramatic Art). BBC Radio Drama Co., 1991; Sheffield Crucible, 1992; Almeida Th., 1993, 1995, 1997, 2005; NT, 1993, 1999, 2005; RSC, 1994, 1998, 2003; *films* include: Pandaemonium, 2000; The Discovery of Heaven, 2001; Shooters, 2002; *television* includes: Tell Tale Hearts, 1992; The Maitlands, 1993; A Dance to the Music of Time, 1997; A Respectable Trade, 1998; Big Bad World, 1999; Other People's Children, 2000; My Uncle Silas, 2003; Beneath the Skin, The Government Inspector, The Ghost Squad, 2005; Cranford, 2007; many radio performances. London Critics' Circle Award, most promising newcomer, 1993. *Publication:* Twelfth Night: actors on Shakespeare, 2002. *Recreations:* walking, playing accordion in private. *Address:* c/o ARG, 4 Great Portland Street, W1W 8PA. *T:* (020) 7436 6400.

FIELDING, Fenella Marion; actress; *b* London, 17 Nov. 1934. *Educ:* North London Collegiate School. Began acting career in 1954; *plays include:* Cockles and Champagne, Saville, 1954; Pay the Piper, Saville, 1954; Jubilee Girl, Victoria Palace, 1956; Valmouth, Lyric, Hammersmith, 1958, Saville, 1959, and Chichester Fest., 1982; Pieces of Eight, Apollo, 1959; Five Plus One, Edinburgh Fest., 1961; Twists, Arts, 1962 (Best Revue Performance of the Year in Variety); Doctors of Philosophy, New Arts, 1962; Luv, New Arts, 1963; So Much to Remember—The Life Story of a Great Lady, Establishment, transf. to Vaudeville, 1963; Let's Get a Divorce, Mermaid, transf. to Comedy, 1966; The Beaux Stratagem and The Italian Straw Hat, Chichester Fest., 1967; The High Bid, Mermaid, 1967; Façade, Queen Elizabeth Hall, 1970; Colette, Ellen Stewart, NY, 1970 (first appearance in NY); Fish Out of Water, Greenwich, 1971; The Old Man's Comforts, Open Space, 1972; The Provok'd Wife, Greenwich, 1973; Absurd Person Singular, Criterion, 1974, transf. to Vaudeville, 1975; Fielding Convertible, Edinburgh Fest., 1976; Jubilee Jeunesse, Royal Opera House, 1977; Look After Lulu, Chichester Fest., transf. to Haymarket, 1978; A Personal Choice, Edinburgh Fest., 1978; Fenella on Broadway, W6, Studio, Lyric, Hammersmith, 1979; Wizard of Oz, Bromley, 1983; The Jungle Book, Adelphi, 1984; The Country Wife, Mermaid, 1990; A Dangerous Woman, New End Th., 1998; Blithe Spirit, Salisbury, 1999; *films include:* Drop Dead, Darling; Lock Up Your Daughters; Carry On Screaming; Carry On Regardless; Doctor in Clover; Doctor in Distress; Doctor in Trouble; No Love for Johnnie; Robin Hood; Guest House Paradiso; *television series:* That Was The Week That Was; A Touch of Venus; Ooh La La; Stories from Saki; Dean Martin and the Gold-Diggers; Comedy Tonight; Rhyme and Reason; numerous appearances in UK and USA. *Recreations:* reading, diarising. *Address:* c/o Barry Langford, 17 Westfields Avenue, SW13 0AT.

FIELDING, Sir Leslie, KCMG 1988; Vice-Chancellor, University of Sussex, 1987–92; *b* 29 July 1932; *o s* of late Percy Archer Fielding and of Margaret (*née* Calder Horry); *m* 1978, Dr Sally P. J. Harvey, FSA, FRHistS, sometime Fellow of St Hilda's Coll., Oxford; one *s* one *d. Educ:* Queen Elizabeth's Sch., Barnet; Emmanuel Coll., Cambridge (First in History; MA; Hon. Fellow 1990); School of Oriental and African Studies, London; St Antony's Coll., Oxford (MA; Vis. Fellow, 1977–78). Served with Royal Regt of Artillery, 1951–53; TA, 1953–56. Entered HM Diplomatic Service, 1956; served in: Tehran, 1957–60; Foreign Office, 1960–64; Singapore, 1964; Phnom Penh (Chargé d'Affaires), 1964–66; Paris, 1967–70; Dep. Head of Planning Staff, FCO, 1970–73; seconded for service with European Commn in Brussels, 1973; Dir (External Relns Directorate Gen.), 1973–77; permanent transfer 1979; Head of Delegn of Commn in Tokyo, 1978–82; Dir-Gen. for External Relns, Brussels, 1982–87. UK Mem., High Council of European Univ. Inst. in Florence, 1988–92. Chm., Nat. Curriculum Geography Wkg Gp, 1989–90. Adviser: IBM Europe, 1989–95; Panasonic Europe, 1990–96. Hon. Pres., Univ. Assoc. for Contemporary European Studies, 1990–2000; Founder Mem., Japan-EC Assoc., then Europe-Japan Business Forum, 1988–98; Mem., UK-Japan 2000 Gp, 1993–2001. Mem. Ct, Univ. of Sussex, 2000–. Mem., Gen. Synod, C of E, 1990–92. Admitted to office of Reader by Bishop of Exeter, 1981; served dios of Exeter, Tokyo, Gibraltar, Chichester and Hereford; Reader Emeritus, 2007. FRSA 1989; FRGS 1991 (Mem. Council, 1992–95). Hon. Fellow, Sussex European Inst., 1993. Hon. LLD Sussex, 1992. Grand Officer, Order of St Agatha (San Marino), 1987; Knight Commander Order of the White Rose (Finland), 1988; Grand Silver Medal of Honour with Star (Austria), 1989. *Publications:* Europe as a global partner: the external relations of the European Community,

1991; (contrib.) Travellers' Tales, 1999; (contrib.) More Travellers' Tales, 2005; Before the Killing Fields: witness to Cambodia and the Vietnam War, 2007; articles on internat. relations, higher educn and ecclesiastical matters. *Recreations:* life in the country, theology. *Address:* Wild Cherry Farm, Elton, Ludlow, Shropshire SY8 2HQ. *Club:* Travellers.

FIELDING, Dame Pauline, DBE 1999; PhD; Professional Adviser to the Healthcare Commission and the Health Ombudsman, since 2002; Director of Nursing: Preston Acute Hospitals NHS Trust, 1993–2003; Chorley and South Ribble NHS Trust, 1998–2003; *m* Rev. Michael Fielding. *Educ:* Univ. of Southampton (BSc; PhD 1981). Ward Sister, 1982, Sen. Nurse, then Dir of Clinical Nursing Res., Middx Hosp.; formerly Nursing Dir, Forest Healthcare Trust. Hon. Professor of Nursing: Univ. of Central Lancashire, 2000; Southampton Univ., 2003. Trustee, Smith & Nephew Foundn, 1999–. DUniv Southampton, 2003. *Address: e-mail:* paulinefielding@aol.com.

FIELDING, Richard Walter; Chairman, Richard Fielding Ltd, 1992–2000; *b* 9 July 1933; *s* of late Walter Harrison Fielding, MBE, and Marjorie Octavia Adair (*née* Roberts); *m* 1st, 1961, Felicity Ann Jones (*d* 1981); one *s* three *d*; 2nd, 1983, Jacqueline Winifred Digby (*née* Hussey). *Educ:* Clifton Coll., Bristol. National Service, Royal Engineers (Lieut), 1951–53. Broker to Dir, Bland Welch & Co. Ltd, 1954–68; Dir to Man. Dir, C. E. Heath & Co. Ltd, 1968–75; Founder and Chm., Fielding and Partners, 1975–86; Chairman: C. E. Heath PLC, 1987–92; Sharelink PLC, 1993–95. Chm., Syndicate Capital Trust, 1996–98 (Dir, 1993–96); Dir, Hambros Insurance Services, 1993–98. High Sheriff, Dorset, 1997. *Recreations:* hunting, country sports. *Address:* 104 Cambridge Street, SW1V 4QG.

FIELDS, Sir Allan (Clifford), KCMG 2005; Senator (Ind.) Barbados Parliament, since 2003; Chairman, Barbados Shipping & Trading, since 2005; *b* 19 Sept. 1942; *s* of James Percival Fields and Gwendolyn Fields; *m* 1964, Irene Elizabeth Smith; one *s* one *d*. *Educ:* Harrison Coll., Barbados; Stowe Coll. of Engrg, Glasgow. Engr, Barbados Light & Power, 1966–78; Managing Director: Neal & Massy, 1978–88; Banks Hldgs Ltd, 1988–99 (Chm.); Barbados Shipping & Trading, 1999–2005. Chm., Cable & Wireless (Barbados), 2002–. Chm., Private Sector Assoc., 1999–. *Recreations:* reading, gardening, cooking. *Address:* Morning Mist, Stepney, St George, Barbados. *T:* 4265195, *Fax:* 4294664; *e-mail:* afields@caribsurf.com.

FIELDSEND, Sir John (Charles Rowell), KBE 1998; Judge, Court of Appeal: St Helena, Falkland Islands and British Antarctic Territory, 1985–99; Gibraltar, 1985–97 (President, 1991–97); *b* 13 Sept. 1921; *s* of C. E. Fieldsend, MC, and Phyllis (*née* Brucesmith); *m* 1945, Muriel Gedling; one *s* one *d*. *Educ:* Michaelhouse, Natal; Rhodes University Coll., Grahamstown, SA (BA 1942, LLB 1947). Served RA, 1943–45. Called to the Bar, S Rhodesia, 1947; advocate in private practice, 1947–63; QC S Rhodesia, 1959; Pres., Special Income Tax Court for Fedn of Rhodesia and Nyasaland, 1958–63; High Court Judge, S Rhodesia, 1963, resigned 1968; Asst Solicitor, Law Commn, 1968–78, Sec., 1978–80; Chief Justice: of Zimbabwe, 1980–83; of Turks and Caicos Islands, 1985–87; of British Indian Ocean Territory, 1987–99 (Principal Legal Advr, 1984–87). *Recreations:* home-making, travel. *Address:* Great Dewes, Ardingly, Sussex RH17 6UP.

FIENNES, family name of **Baron Saye and Sele**.

FIENNES, Joseph Alberic; actor; *b* 27 May 1970; *s* of late Mark Fiennes and Jennifer Fiennes (*née* Lash). *Educ:* Guildhall Sch. of Music and Drama. *Theatre includes:* The Woman in Black, Fortune, 1993; A Month in the Country, Albery, 1994; A View from the Bridge, Strand, 1995; Real Classy Affair, Royal Court, 1998; Edward II, Crucible, Sheffield, 2001; Love's Labour's Lost, NT, 2003; Epitaph for George Dillon, Comedy, 2005; Unicorns, Almost (one-man play), Old Vic, 2006; 2,000 Feet Away, Bush Th., 2008; Royal Shakespeare Company: Son of Man, Les Enfants du Paradis, Troilus and Cressida, The Herbal Bed, 1996; As You Like It, 1997. *Television includes:* The Vacillations of Poppy Carew, 1995. *Films include:* Stealing Beauty, 1996; Elizabeth, Martha - Meet Frank, Daniel and Laurence, 1998; Shakespeare in Love, Forever Mine, 1999; Rancid Aluminium, 2000; Enemy at the Gates, Dust, 2001; Killing Me Softly, Leo, 2002; Luther, 2003; The Merchant of Venice, 2004; Man to Man, The Great Raid, 2005; The Darwin Awards, 2006; Running with Scissors, 2007; Goodbye Bafana, 2007; The Escapist, 2008; dir, The Spirit, 2008 (Best Short Film, Cinema for Peace). *Address:* c/o Ken McReddie, 36–40 Glasshouse Street, W1B 5DL.
See also R. N. Fiennes.

FIENNES, Very Rev. Hon. Oliver William Twisleton-Wykeham-; Dean of Lincoln, 1969–89, Dean Emeritus, since 1989; *b* 17 May 1926; *yr s* of 20th Baron Saye and Sele, OBE, MC, and Hersey Cecilia Hester, *d* of late Captain Sir Thomas Dacres Butler, KCVO; *m* 1956, Juliet (*d* 2005), *d* of late Dr Trevor Braby Heaton, OBE; two *s* two *d*. *Educ:* Eton; New College, Oxford; Cuddesdon College. Asst Curate, New Milton, Hants, 1954; Chaplain, Clifton College, Bristol, 1958; Rector of Lambeth, 1963. Church Comr, 1977–88. Chairman: Pilgrims Assoc., 1986–89; St Matthew Housing (formerly St Matthew Soc.), 1994–2001 (Vice Pres., 2001). World Fellow, Thanksgiving Square, Dallas, 1980; Vice Pres., Lincoln Br., Inst. of Advanced Motorists, 2002– (Pres., 1973–2002); Chm., Radio Lincolnshire Adv. Cttee, 1992–95. Governor, Marlborough Coll., 1970–89. Nat Patron, E-SU in USA, 1987. ChStJ 1971; KStJ 1996. *Recreations:* cricket, travel, country activities. *Address:* Home Farm House, Colsterworth, Grantham, Lincs NG33 5HZ. *T:* (01476) 860811.

FIENNES, Ralph Nathanial; actor; *b* 22 Dec. 1962; *s* of late Mark Fiennes and Jennifer Fiennes (*née* Lash). *Educ:* Bishop Wordsworth's Sch., Salisbury; RADA. *Theatre* includes: Open Air Theatre, Regent's Park: Twelfth Night, Ring Round the Moon, 1985; A Midsummer Night's Dream, 1985, 1986; Romeo and Juliet, 1986; Royal National Theatre: Six Characters in Search of an Author, Fathers and Sons, Ting Tang Mine, 1987; The Talking Cure, 2002; Royal Shakespeare Company: The Plantagenets, Much Ado About Nothing, 1988; Playing With Trains, 1989; Troilus and Cressida, King Lear, 1990; The Man Who Came to Dinner, 1991; Brand, transf. Th. Royal Haymarket, 2003; Almeida Theatre: Hamlet, 1995 (also Hackney Empire and Belasco, NY); Ivanov, 1997; Richard II, Coriolanus (transf. NY), 2000; Julius Caesar, Barbican, 2005; Faith Healer, Gate Th., Dublin, transf. NY, 2006; God of Carnage, Gielgud, 2008; *films:* Wuthering Heights, 1992; Baby of Macon, Schindler's List, 1993; Quiz Show, 1994; Strange Days, 1995; The English Patient, 1997; Oscar and Lucinda, The Avengers, 1998; Onegin, 1999 (also exec. producer); Sunshine, The End of the Affair, 2000; Red Dragon, Maid in Manhattan, 2002; Spider, 2003; Chromophobia, The Constant Gardener, Wallace and Gromit in the Curse of the Were-Rabbit, Harry Potter and the Goblet of Fire, 2005; The White Countess, Land of the Blind, 2006; Harry Potter and the Order of the Phoenix, Bernard and Doris, The Chumscrubber, 2007; In Bruges, The Duchess, 2008; *television* includes: A Dangerous Man, 1991; The Cormorant, 1992. *Recreation:* books. *Address:* c/o Dalzell & Beresford Ltd, 26 Astwood Mews, SW7 4DE. *T:* (020) 7341 9411.
See also J. A. Fiennes.

FIENNES, Sir Ranulph Twisleton-Wykeham-, 3rd Bt *cr* 1916; OBE 1993; *b* 7 Marc 1944; *s* of Lieut-Col Sir Ranulph Twisleton-Wykeham-Fiennes, DSO, 2nd Bt (died wounds, 1943) and Audrey Joan (*d* 2004), *yr d* of Sir Percy Newson, 1st Bt; *S* father 194 *m* 1st, 1970, Virginia Pepper (*d* 2004) (first female member of Antarctic Club, 1985; fi woman to be awarded Polar Medal, 1987); 2nd, 2005, Louise Millington; one *d*. *Edi* Eton. Liveryman, Vintners' Company, 1960. French Parachutist Wings, 1965. Lieu Royal Scots Greys, 1966, Captain 1968 (retd 1970). Attached 22 SAS Regt, 1966, Sulta of Muscat's Armed Forces, 1968 (Dhofar Campaign Medal, 1969; Sultan's Bravery Med 1970). T&AVR 1971, Captain RAC. Leader of British expeditions: White Nile, 196 Jostedalsbre Glacier, 1970; Headless Valley, BC, 1971; (Towards) North Pole, 1977; (wi Charles Burton) Transglobe (first surface journey around the world's polar axis), 1979–8 reached South Pole, 15 Dec. 1980, reached North Pole, 11 April 1982 (first man in histo to reach both Poles); North Polar Unsupported Expeditions: reached 84°48′N on 16 Ap 1986; reached 88°58′N on 14 April 1990 (Furthest North Unsupported record); (with I Mike Stroud) South Polar Unsupported Expedition: first crossing of Antarctic Contine and longest polar journey in history (1,345 miles), 1992–93; (with Dr Mike Stroud) La Rover 7x7x7 Challenge (7 marathons in 7 days on 7 continents), 2003; climbed Nor Face of Eiger, 2007. Hon. MRIN 1997. Hon. DSc: Loughborough, 1986; Portsmout 2000; Sheffield, 2005; Abertay Dundee, 2007; DUniv Birmingham, 1995; Hon. DL Glasgow Caledonian, 2002. Inst. of Navigation Award, 1977; elected to Guinness Hall Fame, 1987. Livingstone Gold Medal, RSGS, 1983; Explorers' Club of New York Mec (and Hon. Life Membership), 1983; Founder's Medal, RGS, 1984; Polar Medal, 198 clasp 1995; IITN Award, for the Event of the Decade, 1990; Millennium Award for Po Exploration, British Chapter, Explorers' Club; Oldies of the Year Award, 2004. *Fil* (cameraman) To the Ends of the Earth, 1983. *Publications:* A Talent for Trouble, 1970; I Fall in Norway, 1972; The Headless Valley, 1973; Where Soldiers Fear To Tread, 197 Hell on Ice, 1979; To the Ends of the Earth, 1983; (with Virginia Fiennes) Bothie, t Polar Dog, 1984; Living Dangerously (autobiog.), 1987, rev. and expanded 1994; T Feather Men, 1991; Atlantis of the Sands, 1992; Mind Over Matter, 1993; The Sett, 199 Fit for Life, 1998; Beyond the Limits, 2000; The Secret Hunters, 2001; Captain Sco 2003; Mad, Bad and Dangerous to Know: the autobiography, 2007. *Recreations:* langla photography. *Heir:* none. *Club:* Travellers (Hon. Mem.).

FIENNES-CLINTON, family name of **Earl of Lincoln**.

FIFE, 3rd Duke of, *cr* 1900; **James George Alexander Bannerman Carnegie;** Lo Carnegie of Kinnaird (Scot.), 1616; Earl of Southesk and Lord Carnegie of Kinnaird a Leuchars (Scot.), 1633; Bt (NS), 1663; Baron Balinhard, 1869; Earl of Macduff, 1900; 23 Sept. 1929; *o s* of 11th Earl of Southesk (*d* 1992), and Princess Maud (*d* 1945); *S* au HRH Princess Arthur of Connaught (Dukedom of Fife), 1959; *m* 1956, Hon. Caroli Cicely Dewar (marr. diss. 1966; she *m* 1980, Gen. Sir Richard Worsley), *er d* of 3rd Bar Forteviot, MBE; one *s* one *d*. *Educ:* Gordonstoun. Nat. Service, Scots Guards (Malay Campaign), 1948–50. Royal Agricultural College. Clothworkers' Company, and Freem City of London. Pres. of ABA, 1959–73, Vice-Patron, 1973–94; Ship's Pres., HMS Fi 1967–87; a Vice-Patron, Braemar Royal Highland Soc.; a Vice-Pres., British Olymp Assoc., 1973–2000. *Heir: s* Earl of Southesk, *qv*. *Address:* (seat) Kinnaird Castle, Brechi Angus DD9 6TZ; (home) Elsick House, Stonehaven, Kincardineshire AB39 3NT.

FIGEL, Ján; Member, European Commission, since 2004; *b* 20 Jan. 1960; *s* of Stefan Fig and Mária Figelova; *m* 1983, Maria; three *s* one *d*. *Educ:* Tech. Univ., Kosice (M Electronic Engrg); Georgetown Univ., Washington (Internat. Affairs); UFSIA, Antwe (European Econ. Integration). MP, Slovak Republic, 1992–98; State Sec., Min. Foreign Affairs, 1998–2002; Chm., Internat. Cttee, 2002–04. Mem., Parly Assembly Council of Europe, Strasbourg, 1993–98 (Vice Chm., Agric. and Rural Develt; Chn Internat. Econ. Relns). Chief Negotiator of Slovak Republic for accession to E 1998–2002. *Publications:* European Foreign Affairs Review: Slovakia's difficult b promising task, 1999; (jtly) Slovakia on the Road to the EU, 2002; (ed and contril Slovakia on the Road to the European Union, 2003. *Address:* European Commission, 2 rue de la Loi, 1049 Brussels, Belgium. *T:* (2) 2988719, *Fax:* (2) 2988088; *e-ma* Jan.Figel@cec.eu.int.

FIGES, Prof. Orlando Guy, PhD; Professor of History, Birkbeck College, Lond University, since 1999; *b* 20 Nov. 1959; *s* of John Figes and Eva Figes (*née* Unger); *m* 199 Stephanie Palmer; two *d*. *Educ:* Gonville and Caius Coll., Cambridge (BA History 198 Trinity Coll., Cambridge (PhD 1987). Fellow, 1984–99, Dir of Studies in Histo 1988–98, Trinity Coll., Cambridge; University Lectr in History, Cambridge, 1987–9 *Publications:* Peasant Russia Civil War: the Volga countryside in revolution 1917–21, 198 3rd edn 2000; A People's Tragedy: the Russian Revolution 1891–1924, 1996 (Wolfs History Prize, W. H. Smith Lit. Award, NCR Book Award, Los Angeles Times Bo Prize, 1997); (with B. Kolonitskii) Interpreting the Russian Revolution: the language a symbols of 1917, 1999; Natasha's Dance: a cultural history of Russia, 2002; T Whisperers: private life in Stalin's Russia, 2007. *Recreations:* soccer, music, gardenin wine. *Address:* Birkbeck College, Malet Street, WC1E 7HX.

FIGG, Sir Leonard (Clifford William), KCMG 1981 (CMG 1974); HM Diplomat Service, retired; *b* 17 Aug. 1923; *s* of late Sir Clifford Figg and late Lady (Eileen) Figg (*n* Crabb); *m* 1955, Jane Brown (*d* 2004), *d* of late Judge Harold Brown; three *s*. *Ed* Charterhouse; Trinity Coll., Oxford. RAF, 1942–46 (Flt-Lt). HM Diplomatic Servic 1947; served in: Addis Ababa, 1949–52; FO, 1952–58; Amman, 1958–61; FO, 1961–6 Counsellor, 1965; Deputy Consul-General, Chicago, 1967–69; DTI, 1970–73; Cons General and Minister, Milan, 1973–77; Asst Under Sec. of State, FCO, 1977–8 Ambassador to Ireland, 1980–83. Mem. Council, Cooperation Ireland, 1985–95. A Vic Chm., British Red Cross Soc., 1983–88; a Vice-Pres., Bucks Red Cross, 1988–9 President: Aylesbury Divl Conservative Assoc., 1985–95; Bucks Assoc. of Youth Clu 1987–2001; Chiltern Soc., 1990–2003; Bucks and Oxfordshire East Euro Constituen Cons. Assoc., 1998; Chm., Bucks Farming and Wildlife Adv. Gp, 1991–2000. *Recreatio* forestry, listening to tapes. *Address:* Little Hampden Farm, Great Missenden, Bucks HP1 9PS.

FIGGIS, Sir Anthony (St John Howard), KCVO 1996; CMG 1993; HM Diplomat Service, retired; HM Marshal of the Diplomatic Corps, 2001–08; *b* 12 Oct. 1940; *s* Roberts Richmond Figgis and Philippa Maria Young; *m* 1964, Miriam Ellen, (Mayell Hardt; two *s* one *d*. *Educ:* Rugby Sch.; King's Coll., Cambridge (Mod Langs). Joined H Foreign (later Diplomatic) Service, 1962; Third Sec., Belgrade, 1963–65; Commonweal Office, 1965–68; Second Sec., Polit. Residency, Bahrain, 1968–70; FCO, 1970–71; Fi Sec. (Commercial), Madrid, 1971–74; CSCE delegn, Geneva, 1974–75; FCO, 1975–7 Madrid: Head of Chancery, 1979–80; Commercial Counsellor, 1980–82; Counsello Belgrade, 1982–85; Head of E European Dept, FCO, 1986–88; Counsellor and Head Chancery, Bonn, 1988–89; Dir of Res., subseq. of Res. and Analysis, FCO, 1989–91; A Under-Sec. of State, FCO, and HM Vice-Marshal of the Diplomatic Corps, 1991–9 Ambassador to Austria, 1996–2000. Pres., Internat. Social Service (UK), 2001–0 Trustee, Guildhall Sch. Trust, 2001–; Gov., Goodenough Coll. for Overseas Graduat

2004–; Royal Over-Seas League: Mem., Central Council, 2004–, Exec. Cttee, 2006–; Vice-Chm., 2007–. Gentleman Usher of the Blue Rod, Order of St Michael and St George, 2002–. Freeman, City of London, 1996; Liveryman, Musicians' Co., 2007–. *Recreations:* family, fly-fishing, tennis, music (piano). *Address:* Brynllici, Pennorth, Brecon LD3 7PQ. *Club:* Royal Over-Seas League.

FIGGURES, Lt-Gen. Andrew Collingwood, CBE 1998; Deputy Chief of Defence Staff (Equipment Capability), 2006–May 2009; *b* 13 Nov. 1950; *s* of Colin Norman Figgures and Ethel Barbara Figgures (*née* Wilks); *m* 1978, Poppy Felicity Ann Ogley; one *d*. *Educ:* Loughborough Grammar Sch.; Welbeck Coll.; RMA Sandhurst; St Catharine's Coll., Cambridge (MA); Open Univ. (MBA). CEng 1991; MIEE 1991, FIET (FIEE 2005); FIMechE 1992. Commnd, REME, 1970; served UK, Cyprus, BAOR, Former Republic of Yugoslavia, Iraq; attended Army Staff Coll., HCSC and RCDS; Comdr, Equipment Support, Land Comd, 1995; DOR (Land), Defence Systems, MoD, 1999–2000; Capability Manager (Manoeuvre), MoD, 2000–03; Dep. Commanding Gen., Jt Task Force 7, Iraq, 2003–04; Master Gen. of the Ordnance, and Tech. Dir, Defence Procurement Agency and Defence Logistics Orgn, MoD, 2004–06. Col Comdt, REME, 2002–. MAPM 2005; FRAeS 2006. QCVS 2004. *Address:* Ministry of Defence, Main Building, Horse Guards Avenue, Whitehall, SW1A 2HB. *Clubs:* Royal Over-Seas League; Leander.

FILBEY, Air Vice-Marshal Keith David, CBE 1993; FRAeS; Chairman, AirTanker Services Ltd, since 2008 (Chief Executive, 2004–08); *b* 16 Dec. 1947; *s* of late Sqn Ldr Cecil Hayward Filbey and of Barbara Filbey; *m* 1982, Anne Feaver; one *s* one *d*. *Educ:* Brentwood Sch.; Royal Air Force Coll., Cranwell. Royal Air Force: Pilot, 214 Sqn, 1969–76; Flt Comdr 51 Sqn, 1976–78; Personnel Officer, 1978–79; RAF Staff Coll., 1980; Staff Officer, HQ 1 Gp, 1981–83; OC, 216 Sqn, 1983–86; staff appts, MoD and HQ 1 Gp, 1986–90; OC, RAF Brize Norton, 1990–92; RCDS, 1993; Dep. Chief of Assessments Staff, Cabinet Office, 1993–96; Dir, Air Ops, 1997; Sen. DS (Air), RCDS, 1998–99; AOC No 38 Gp, 2000; AOC No 2 Gp, 2000–02. Business Develt Advr, Cobham PLC, 2003–04. Mem., Air League, 1999–. Pres., RAF Cricket Assoc., 2000–02. Gov., Sherborne Sch. for Girls, 2005–. FRAeS 2000. Upper Freeman, GAPAN, 2000–. *Recreations:* walking, tennis, golf, choral music. *Clubs:* Royal Air Force, Innominate; Adastrian Cricket; Gents.

FILBY, Ven. William Charles Leonard; Archdeacon of Horsham, 1983–2002, now Emeritus; *b* 21 Jan. 1933; *s* of William Richard and Dorothy Filby; *m* 1958, Marion Erica, *d* of Prof. Terence Wilmot Hutchison, FBA; four *s* one *d*. *Educ:* Ashford County Grammar School; London Univ. (BA); Oak Hill Theological Coll. Curate, All Souls, Eastbourne, 1959–62; Curate-in-charge, Holy Trinity, Knaphill, 1962–65; Vicar, Holy Trinity, Richmond-upon-Thames, 1965–71; Vicar, Bishop Hannington Memorial Church, Hove, 1971–79; Rector of Broadwater, 1979–83; RD of Worthing, 1980–83; Hon. Canon of Chichester Cathedral, 1981–83. Proctor in Convocation, 1975–90. Chm., Redcliffe Missionary Trng Coll., Chiswick, 1970–91; Mem., Keswick Convention Council, 1973–93; Pres., Chichester Diocesan Evangelical Union, 1978–84; Chairman: Diocesan Stewardship Cttee, 1983–89; Sussex Churches Broadcasting Cttee, 1984–96; Diocesan Cttee for Mission and Renewal, 1989–93; Diocesan Industrial Mission Adv. Panel, 1989–2002; Diocesan Gp, Archbishops' Commn on Rural Areas, 1998–2002. Bishops Advr for Hosp. Chaplains, 1986–98. Governor: St Mary's Hall, Brighton, 1984–2002; UC, Chichester (formerly W Sussex Inst. of Higher Educn), 1985–2002. *Recreations:* sport, music. *Address:* Kymber Cottage, Hale Hill, West Burton, Pulborough, W Sussex RH20 1HE. *T:* (01798) 831269.

FILDES, (David) Christopher, OBE 1994; financial journalist; *b* 10 Nov. 1934; *s* of late David Garland Fildes and Shelagh Fildes (*née* Jones), Manley, Cheshire; *m* 1st, 1969, Susan Patricia Mottram (*d* 1978); one *d* decd; 2nd, 1986, Frederica Bement Lord (*d* 1992); one step *d*. *Educ:* Clifton; Balliol Coll., Oxford. Financial journalist, 1963–; columnist, editor and broadcaster (The Times, Spectator, Daily Mail, Euromoney, Evening News, Investors Chronicle, Business Prog.); financial columnist: Euromoney, 1969–98; Daily Telegraph, 1984–2005; Spectator, 1984–2006; Evening Standard, 2005–. Director: The Spectator (1828) Ltd, 1990–2004; London Mozart Players, 2000–. Member: Council, GDST, 1999–; Rly Heritage Cttee, 1999–. Hon. LittD Sheffield, 1999. Wincott Award for financial journalism, 1978 and 1986. *Publication:* A City Spectator, 2004. *Recreations:* racing, railways. *Address:* 4 Scarsdale Villas, W8 6PR. *Clubs:* Garrick, City of London.

FILER, Denis Edwin, CBE 1992; TD 1965 and 1977; FREng, FIMechE, FIChemE; Chairman, Board of Governors, University of Hertfordshire, 2004–07 (Governor, since 1996, Vice-Chairman, 2002–04); *b* 19 May 1932; *s* of Francis and Sarah Filer; *m* 1957, Pamela Armitage; one *s* two *d*. *Educ:* Manchester Central Grammar Sch.; Manchester Univ. (Hons BSc Mech. Eng.); BA Open 1987. Commissioned REME (Nat. Service); served in Germany; REME TA, 1955–: Col, 1975–77; Hon. Col, 1978–87. ICI: Works Maintenance Engineer, 1960–67; Project Manager, Manchester, 1967–71; Project Manager, Holland (ICI Europa), 1971–73; Div. Maintenance Advisor, Organics Div., 1973; Plastics Div., Wilton Works: Works Engineer, 1973–76; Engineering Manager, 1976–78; Engineering & Production Dir, 1978–81; Dir of Engrg, ICI, 1981–88; Dir.-Gen., Engrg Council, 1988–95 (Mem., 1986–88; Chm., Continuing Educn and Trng Cttee; Mem., Standing Cttee for Industry). Chairman: Rolinx, 1978–81; Adwest Gp, then Adwest Automotive plc, 1994–97 (Dir, 1991–97); Electra Innvotec Corporate Ventures Ltd, then Innvotec Corporate Ventures Ltd, 2000–01 (Dir, 1989–2001); Director: Bexford, 1978–80; Engineering Services Wilton, 1978–81; Eur. Adv. Dir, Callidus Technologies Inc., 1991–99. Member: Council, IMechE, 1983–89 (Vice-Pres., 1987–89, 1996–98; Dep. Pres., 1998–2000; Pres., 2000–01; Chm., Process Industries Div. Bd, 1985–87); Board, Lloyd's Register of Quality Assurance, 1986–88, Gen. Cttee, Lloyd's Register, 1988–95. Chm., F and GP Cttee, 2002–04. FREng (FEng 1985). Liveryman and Mem. Court, Engineers' Co., 1990–. Hon. DSc Herts, 1993. *Recreations:* tennis, sport, reading. *Address:* Brambles, Watton Green, Watton-at-Stone, Hertford SG14 3RB. *T:* (01920) 830207. *Club:* Army and Navy.

FILER, (Douglas) Roger, FCA; Managing Director, D & S Travel Supplies Ltd, since 1997; *b* 25 Feb. 1942; *s* of Horace Filer and Raie (*née* Behrman); *m* 1979, Vivienne Sara Green; one *s* one *d*. *Educ:* Clifton Coll.; St John's Coll., Oxford (MA); FCA 1970. Called to the Bar, Gray's Inn, 1979. Joined Association Television Group, 1967; Chief Accountant, Ambassador Bowling, 1967–69; Financial Controller, Bentray Investments, 1969–70; Financial Dir, M. Berman then Bermans & Nathans, 1971–73; Financial Controller, Stoll Theatres Corp./Moss Empires, 1974; Dir, 1982–92, Man. Dir, 1990–92, Stoll Moss Theatres; Man. Dir, Maybox Gp, subseq. Mayfair Theatres and Cinemas Ltd, 1993–96. *Recreations:* golf, history, walking. *Address:* Four Brim Hill, Hampstead Garden Suburb, N2 0HF. *T:* (020) 8455 7392.

FILKIN, family name of **Baron Filkin**.

FILKIN, Baron *cr* 1999 (Life Peer), of Pimlico in the City of Westminster; **David Geoffrey Nigel Filkin,** CBE 1997; *b* 1 July 1944; *s* of Donald Geoffrey and Winifred Filkin; *m* 1974, Elizabeth Tompkins (*see* Elizabeth Filkin) (marr. diss. 1994); three *d*; *m* 2005, Brigitte Paupy. *Educ:* King Edward VI Sch., Five Ways, Birmingham; Clare Coll., Cambridge (MA Hist.); Manchester Univ. (DipTP); Birmingham Univ. (postgrad. study). Formerly MRTPI. Teacher on VSO, Ghana, 1966–67; Planner, Redditch Develt Corp., 1969–72; Manager, Brent Housing Aid Centre, London Borough of Brent, 1972–75; Dep. Chief Exec., Merseyside Improved Houses, 1975–79; Borough Housing Officer, Ellesmere Port and Neston Council, 1979–82; Dir of Housing, London Borough of Greenwich, 1982–88; Chief Exec., Reading BC, 1988–91; Sec., ADC, 1991–97. Dir, New Local Govt Network, 1995–2001. A Lord in Waiting (Govt Whip), 2001–02; Parliamentary Under-Secretary of State: Home Office, 2002–03; DCA, 2003–04; DFES, 2004–05. Chairman: All Party Parly Business Services Gp, 2000; House of Lords Merits Cttee, 2005–; Founder and Chairman: The Parlt Choir, All Party Parly Gp, 2000–; Public Sector Res. Gp, 2005–. Non-executive Director: Accord, 2005–07; Serco (Civil Govt), 2006–. Chairman: Beacon Council Adv. Panel, 1999–2001; St Albans Cathedral Music Trust, 2006–. Adviser: on local govt, Joseph Rowntree Foundn, 1997–2001; H of C Envmt Cttee, 1998; Capgemini, 2005–; NCP, 2006–. *Publications:* pamphlets, papers and articles on housing and local govt policy. *Recreations:* music, walking, swimming. *Address:* c/o House of Lords, SW1A 0PW. *T:* (020) 7219 0640.

FILKIN, Elizabeth; Deputy Chairman, Regulatory Decisions Committee, Financial Services Authority, since 2005 (Member, since 2002); Chairman: Television (formerly Video) on Demand Association, since 2004; Advertising Advisory Committee, since 2005; *b* 24 Nov. 1940; *d* of Frances Trollope and John Tompkins; *m* 1974, David Geoffrey Nigel Filkin (marr. diss. 1994); three *d*; *m* 1996, Michael John Honey, *qv*. *Educ:* Birmingham Univ. (BSocSci). Organiser, Sparkbrook Assoc., 1961–64; Whyndham Deedes Fellowship, Israel, 1964; Res. Asst, Associate Lectr, Birmingham Univ., 1964–68; Lectr and Community Worker, Nat. Inst. for Social Work, 1968–71; Community Work Services Officer, London Borough of Brent, 1971–75; Lectr in Social Studies, Liverpool Univ., 1975–83; Chief Exec., Nat. Assoc. of CABx, 1983–88; Dir of Community Services, 1988–90, Asst Chief Exec., 1990–92, LDDC; Revenue Adjudicator, 1993–95; The Adjudicator, Inland Revenue, Customs and Excise, and Contribs Agency, 1995–99; Parly Comr for Standards, 1999–2002; Comr, Audit Commn, 1999–2004. Non-executive Director: Britannia Bldg Soc., 1992–98; Hay Management Consultants, 1992–98; Logica, 1995–98; Weatherall, Green & Smith, 1997–99; Jarvis plc, 2003–; Sen. Ind. non-exec. Dir, Stanelco plc, 2003– (Chm., 2002–03); Chm., HBS, 2005–. Chm., Lord Chancellor's Adv. Cttee on Legal Aid, 1991–94. Chairman: Rainer Foundn, 2004–; Appts Gp, RPSGB, 2005–. Dep. Chm. Council, Univ. of E London, 1999–2004. City Fellow, Hughes Hall, Cambridge Univ., 2003–06. *Publications:* The New Villagers, 1968; What a Community Worker Needs to Know, 1974; Community Work and Caring for Children, 1979; Caring for Children, 1979; (ed) Women and Children First, 1984. *Recreations:* walking, swimming.

FILLINGHAM, David James, CBE 2005; Chief Executive, Bolton Hospitals NHS Trust, since 2004; *b* 28 March 1960; *s* of Thomas Fillingham and Irene Fillingham (*née* Webster); *m* 1982, Janet Green; two *d*. *Educ:* Cowley High Sch.; Peterhouse, Cambridge (MA History 1982); Henley Coll. (MBA 1993). Personnel Officer, Pilkington plc, 1982–84; Personnel Manager, 1984–88, Product Develt Manager, 1988–89, Pilkington Glass; Regl Personnel Manager, Mersey RHA, 1989–91; Gen. Manager, Wirral FHSA, 1991–93; Chief Executive: St Helens and Knowsley HA, 1993–97; N Staffordshire Hosp. NHS Trust, 1997–2001; Dir, NHS Modernisation Agency, 2001–04. MIPM 1986. FRSA 2005. *Publications:* various articles in mgt jls and health service pubns. *Recreations:* going to the cinema, hill-walking, watching Rugby League. *Address:* Bolton Hospitals NHS Trust, Royal Bolton Hospital, Minerva Road, Farnworth, Bolton BL4 0JR; Springfield, Millbrow, St Helens, Merseyside WA10 4QQ. *T:* (01744) 29600.

FILLON, François Charles Amand; Prime Minister of France, since 2007; *b* Le Mans, 4 March 1954; *m* 1980, Penelope Clarke; four *s* one *d*. *Educ:* Univ. du Maine, Le Mans (Master's degree Public Law 1976); Univ. René Descartes, Paris (Dip. d'études appliquées Public Law 1977). Intern, Agence France-Presse, Paris, 1976; Parly Asst to Joël Le Theule, MP, 1976–77; Dep. Hd, private office of Joël Le Theule, 1976–78, 1980; Hd, legislation dept, private office of Michel Giraud, 1981. Sablé-sur-Sarthe: Mem. Municipal Council, 1981–2001; Dep. Mayor, responsible for econ. affairs, 1981; Mayor, 1983–2001; Sarthe General Council: Mem., 1981–98; Vice-Chm., responsible for econ. affairs, 1981; Chm., Cttee on Econ. Affairs and Tourism, 1985; Chm., 1992–98; Chm., Pays de la Loire Regl Council, 1998–2002; Pres., Community of Communes of Sablé sur Sarthe. MP (RPR) Sarthe, 1981–93, 1997–2002, 2007; Mem. of Senate for Sarthe, 2004–07. Minister: of Higher Educn and Res., 1993–95; for Information Technol. and the Post Office, 1995; Minister Delegate with responsibility for the Post Office, Telecommns and Space, 1995–97; Minister: of Social Affairs, Labour and Solidarity, 2002–04; for Nat. Educn, Higher Educn and Res., 2004–05. Pol Advr to Nicolas Sarkozy, UMP, 2004–07. Chm., France.9 think-tank, 2002; founder Mem., Union en Mouvement, 2002. Nat. Sec., 1997, Spokesman, 1998, RPR. *Publication:* La France peut supporter la vérité, 2006. *Recreations:* mountain climbing, ski-ing, hiking, motor racing, running, mountain biking, cinema, reading. *Address:* Office of the Prime Minister, 57 rue de Varenne, 75007 Paris, France.

FILMER-SANKEY, Dr William Patrick, FSA; Senior Associate, Alan Baxter & Associates, since 2005 (Senior Engineer, 2000; Associate, since 2002); *b* 13 Oct. 1957; *s* of late Patrick Hugh Filmer-Sankey and Josephine Filmer-Sankey; *m* 1981, Caroline Frances Sparrow; one *s* one *d*. *Educ:* Downside Sch.; New Coll., Oxford (BA Hons Mod. Hist. 1979); Inst. of Archaeology, Oxford (Dip. European Archaeol. 1981; DPhil 1989). Associate Archaeol Consultant, Oxford Archaeological Associates Ltd, 1990–93; Dir, Victorian Soc., 1993–2000. Dir, Snape Historical Trust, 1987–95; Hon. Sec., 1994–2000, Vice Pres., 2000–, British Archaeol Assoc.; Mem. Council, Soc. of Antiquaries, 2002–05. Vis. Fellow, Dept of Archaeol., Univ. of York, 2005–08. FSA 1997; FRSA 1998. Editor, Anglo-Saxon Studies in Archaeology and History, 1991–94. *Publications:* From the Dust of the Earth Returning: excavations of the Anglo-Saxon cemetery at Snape, Suffolk, 1990; (contrib.) Maritime Celts, Frisians and Saxons, 1991; (contrib.) The Age of Sutton Hoo, 1992; Snape Anglo-Saxon Cemetery: excavations and surveys 1824–1992, 2001; articles and papers. *Recreations:* archaeology, ornithology, sailing, deer stalking, Germany. *Address:* 57 Lavington Road, Ealing, W13 9LS. *T:* (020) 8579 0425.

FILOCHOWSKI, Julian, CMG 2004; OBE 1998; international development consultant, since 2005; Director, Catholic Agency for Overseas Development, 1982–2003; *b* 9 Dec. 1947; *s* of Tadeusz Filochowski and Jean Filochowski (*née* Royce). *Educ:* St Michael's Coll., Leeds; Churchill Coll., Cambridge (MA Econs). Economic Planning Advr, Min. of Finance, Belize, 1969–70; Central America Regl Co-ordinator, British Volunteer Prog., 1970–73; Co-ordinator, Educn Dept, Catholic Inst. for Internat. Relations, 1973–82. Dir, Tablet Publishing Co., 2003–. Vis. Fellow, Clare Coll., Cambridge, 2005. Chm., Archbp Romero Trust, 2005–; Trustee, Thomson Foundn, 2008–. Dr *hc*: Univ. Centroamericana, San Salvador, 2004; Roehampton, 2006. *Publications:* Reflections on Puebla, 1980; Archbishop Romero, Ten Years On, 1991; (ed jtly) Opening Up: speaking out in the

Church, 2005. *Recreations:* swimming, reading, walking. *Address:* 57 Lyme Grove, E9 6PX.

FINCH, Hilary Ann; Music Critic, The Times, since 1980; *b* 2 May 1951; *d* of Francis Richard Finch and Hilda Grace (*née* Davey). *Educ:* Univ. of Exeter (MA); Hughes Hall, Cambridge (PGCE). Asst to Arts Editor, TES, 1976–80; feature writer, The Times, 1980–; freelance writer and broadcaster, 1980–. *Recreations:* travel, walking in Iceland, Nordic art and literature. *Address:* 51 Victoria Road, Mortlake, SW14 8EX. *T:* (020) 8878 0957.

FINCH, Dame Janet Valerie, DBE 2008 (CBE 1999); DL; PhD; AcSS; Vice-Chancellor, Keele University, since 1995; *b* 13 Feb. 1946; *d* of Robert Bleakley Finch and Evelyn Muriel (*née* Smith); *m* 1st, 1967, Geoffrey O. Spedding (marr. diss. 1982); 2nd, 1994, David H. J. Morgan. *Educ:* Merchant Taylors' Sch. for Girls, Crosby; Bedford Coll., London (BA Hons Sociol.; Hon. Fellow, RHC, 1999); Univ. of Bradford (PhD Sociol. 1975). Lectr, Endsleigh Coll., Hull, 1974–76; Lancaster University: Lectr, then Sen. Lectr, 1976–88; Prof. of Social Relations, 1988–95; Pro-Vice-Chancellor, 1992–95. Non-executive Director: NW Regl HA, 1992–96; ONS, 1999–2008; Member: Bd, QAA, 1997–2004; Council for Science and Technology, 2004– (Ind. Co-Chm., 2007–); Indep. Panel, BBC Charter Review, 2004–05; Chm., Health Cttee, Universities UK, 2003–06. Chm., Preston CRC, 1980–85; Mem. Bd, Staffs Environmental Fund Ltd, 2000–04; Chm., Staffs Connexions Ltd, 2002–04. Non-exec. Dir, Identity and Passport Service, 2008–. Economic and Social Research Council: Mem., 1993–97; Chm., Res. Grants Bd, 1994–97. Chm. Exec., Brit. Sociol. Assoc., 1983–84. Governor: City of Stoke-on-Trent Sixth Form Coll., 1999–2002; Manchester Metropolitan Univ., 2002–. Trustee, Nat. Centre for Soc. Res., 2002– (Chm., 2007–). DL Staffs, 1999. AcSS 1999. Hon. Fellow, Liverpool John Moores Univ., 2001. Hon. DLitt UWE, 1997; Hon. DSc: Edinburgh, 2000; Southampton, 2001; Hon. DEd: Lincoln, 2002; Queen Margaret UC, Edinburgh, 2003. *Publications:* Married to the Job, 1983; Education as Social Policy, 1984; Research and Policy, 1986; Family Obligations and Social Change, 1989; Negotiating Family Responsibilities, 1993; Wills, Inheritance and Families, 1996; Passing On, 2000. *Recreations:* theatre-going, hill-walking in the Languedoc. *Address:* Vice-Chancellor's Office, Keele University, Staffs ST5 5BG. *Club:* Athenæum.

FINCH, (John) Russell, FCIArb; Judge, Royal Court of Guernsey, since 2005; Lieutenant-Bailiff and Judge of the Matrimonial Causes Division, since 1999; *b* 15 Feb. 1950; *s* of Reginald John Peter Fergusson Finch and Winifred Joan Finch (*née* Woods); *m* 1990, Anne Elizabeth Sergeant (*née* Lowe), *widow* of Peter Sergeant; one step *s*. *Educ:* Southern Grammar Sch. for Boys, Portsmouth; Queen Mary Coll., London (LLB); Univ. de Caen; Open Univ. (BA Hons, DipEurHum); Sheffield Hallam Univ. (MA 2004). FCIArb 1999. Articled to Clerk to Fareham and Gosport Justices, 1972–74; admitted solicitor, 1974; Court Clerk, 1974–75; Principal Asst, Aylesbury Gp of Magistrates' Courts, 1975–79; joined Dept of DPP, 1979; served on S, Metropolitan and Police Complaints Divs, 1979–86; Asst Br. Crown Prosecutor, Inner London CPS (Sen. Principal), 1986–88; joined Chambers of HM's Procureur (Attorney-Gen.) for Guernsey, 1988; Advocate, Royal Court of Guernsey, 1993; Crown Advocate, 1994; Stipendiary Magistrate and Coroner, 1997–2005, Sen. Magistrate, 2004–05, Guernsey. Chm., Guernsey Inf. Exchange, 1999–2005. Member: US Naval Inst., Annapolis; HMS Hood Assoc. *Publications:* Practical Police Prosecuting, 1977; contrib. articles to various jls on magisterial law and practice. *Recreations:* chess (mainly correspondence), history, listening to opera recordings. *Address:* Royal Court House, St Peter Port, Guernsey GY1 2PB. *T:* (01481) 726161; *e-mail:* russell.finch@gov.gg. *Clubs:* Royal Commonwealth Society, Royal Over-Seas League.

FINCH, Karen Solveig Sinding Møller, OBE 1976; FIIC; Founder, 1975, and Principal, 1975–86, Textile Conservation Centre, Hampton Court Palace, subseq. at Winchester College of Art, Southampton University; *b* 8 May 1921; *d* of Søren Møller and Ellen Sinding Møller, Viborg, Denmark; *m* 1946, Norman Frank Finch (*d* 1996); one *d*. *Educ:* Kunsthaandvarkerskolen, Copenhagen. FIIC 1962 (Hon. Fellow 2004). Royal Sch. of Needlework, 1946–48; conservation work, V&A Mus., 1954–59; Independent Textile Conservation Services (based on textiles as historic documents), 1960–75; teacher, hist. of textile techniques, Courtauld Inst. of Art, 1969–86 (jtly inaugurated postgrad. course in textile conservation, 1973), Hon. Sen. Lectr, 1975–86. Dedication of Karen Finch Liby and Ref. Collection, Winchester Coll., 1993. Mem. Council, Leather Conservation Centre, UC Northampton (formerly Nene Coll.), 1978–. Emeritus Mem., Embroiderers' Guild, 1980. Hon. DLitt Southampton, 1999. Award for Lifetime Service to the Arts, NACF, 1987; Festschrift from colleagues and friends, 1999. *Publications:* Caring for Textiles, 1977; The Care and Preservation of Textiles, 1985, 2nd edn 1991; contrib. papers and articles to textile related societies and to professional jls. *Recreations:* family and friends, reading, the arts, TV. *Address:* 37 Bisterne Avenue, Walthamstow, E17 3QR. *T:* (020) 8520 7680.

FINCH, Hon. Lance (Sidney George); Chief Justice of British Columbia and Yukon Courts of Appeal, Chief Justice of British Columbia, and Administrator of the Government, Province of British Columbia, since 2001; *b* 16 June 1938; *s* of Herbert George and Rita Muriel Finch; *m* 1963, Judith A. C. Jack; one *s* two *d*. *Educ:* Univ. of British Columbia (LLB 1962). Barrister and solicitor, 1963–83; Justice: Supreme Court of BC, 1983–93; BC and Yukon Courts of Appeal, 1993–2001. *Address:* The Law Courts, 800 Smithe Street, Vancouver, BC V6Z 2E1, Canada. *T:* (604) 6602710, *Fax:* (604) 6602833; *e-mail:* lance.finch@courts.gov.bc.ca. *Club:* Vancouver.

FINCH, Paul, OBE 2002; Editor, The Architectural Review, since 2005; *b* 2 March 1949; *s* of William and Nancy Finch; *m* 1973, Susanna Phillips; two *s*. *Educ:* Woolverstone Hall, Suffolk; Selwyn Coll., Cambridge (MA). Dep. Ed., Estates Times, 1976–83; Ed., Building Design, 1983–94; Jt Ed., Planning in London, qly jl, 1991–; Ed., Architects' Jl, 1994–99; Editorial Dir, Emap Construct, 1999–. Dep. Chm., Commn for Architecture and the Built Envmt, 1999–. Mem., Architectural Assoc. Hon. FRIBA 1994; Hon. Fellow, UCL, 2006. *Recreations:* cinema, novels, weekend cooking. *Address:* (office) Greater London House, Hampstead Road, NW1 7EJ; *e-mail:* paul.finch@emap.com. *Club:* Reform.

FINCH, Sir Robert Gerard, Kt 2005; DL; Chairman, Liberty International plc, since 2005; Lord Mayor of London, 2003–04; *b* 20 Aug. 1944; *s* of late Brig. J. R. G. Finch; *m* 1971, Patricia Ann Ross; two *d*. *Educ:* Felsted Sch. Articled Clerk, Monro Pennefather & Co., 1963; joined Linklaters & Paines (later Linklaters), 1969; Partner, 1974–2005; Head of Property Dept, 1996–99. Dir, IFSL, 2001–03. A Church Comr, 1999–. St Paul's Cathedral: Mem. Council, 2000–; Chm., Endowment Trust, 2006–. Member Court: HAC, 1992–; King Edward's Sch., Witley, 1992– (Vice-Pres., 2006–); Christ's Hosp., 1992–. Governor: Coll. of Law, 2000–06; St Paul's Sch., 2005–. Trustee, Morden Coll., 2002–. Mem., Corporate Bd, RA, 2005–. Hon. Mem., LSO, 2004– (Mem. Adv. Council, 2005–). Alderman, 1992, Sheriff, 1999–2000, City of London; Liveryman: Solicitors' Co., 1986– (Master, 1999–2000); Innholders' Co., 1991– (Mem. Ct Assts, 2001–); Hon. Freeman, Envmtl Cleaners' Co., 1998; Hon. Liveryman: Chartered Surveyors' Co., 2001; Leathersellers' Co., 2005. JP 1993, DL 2003, City of London. Hon. FRICS 1999. DCL *hc* City Univ., 2003. *Recreations:* sailing, ski-ing, climbing. *Address:* (office) 40 Broadwa SW1H 0BT. *Clubs:* Ski Club of GB, Alpine Ski, City Livery, East India; Itchenor Sailir (W Sussex).

FINCH, Russell; *see* Finch, J. R.

FINCH, Stephen Clark, OBE 1989; independent consultant, since 1989; *b* 7 March 192 *s* of Frank Finch and Doris Finch (*née* Lloyd), Haywards Heath; *m* 1975, Sarah Rosema Ann, *d* of Adm. Sir Anthony T. F. G. Griffin, GCB; two *d*. *Educ:* Ardingly; Sch. of Signal RMCS. FInstAM; FCMA. Commnd Royal Signals 1948; served Korea, UK and BAOR retired 1968. Joined British Petroleum Co. Ltd, 1968: Gp Telecommunications Manage 1968–81; Sen. Adviser, Regulatory Affairs, 1981–84; Asst Co-ordinator, Inf. Systen Admin, 1984–89. Member: Adv. Panel on Licensing Value Added Network Service 1982–87; Competition (formerly Monopolies and Mergers) Commn, 1985–200 Member: Inst. of Administrative Management, 1968– (Mem. Council, 1981–8 Medallist, 1985); Communications Mgt Assoc. (formerly Telecommunications Manage Assoc.), 1968– (Exec. Cttee, 1971–91; Chm., 1981–84; Regulatory Affairs Exec 1984–87; Dir, External Affairs, 1988–91); Council, Internat. Telecommunications Use Gp, 1981–94 (Chm., 1987–89). Member: City of London Deanery Synod, 1981– (La Chm., 1994–); London Diocesan Synod, 1994– (Bishop's Council, 1994–); Ci Churches Grants Cttee, 1994–; London DAC for Care of Churches, 1995–2006; Ci Churches Develt Gp, 1997–2002; Two Cities Area Council, 1997– (Vice-Chm 2001–07); Archdeacon of London's Finance Adv. Gp, 1999–; City Deanery Bishop's Adv Gp, 2003–. Trustee: Oxford Churches Trust, 1996– (Sec., 1997–); Dick Lucas Trus 1999– (Chm., 1999–). Churchwarden, St Martin Outwich. Freeman, City of Londo 1975. FCMI. *Publications:* occasional contribs to learned jls. *Recreations:* sailing, ski-in swimming, music. *Address:* 97 Englefield Road, Canonbury N1 3LJ. *T:* (020) 7226 280 *Club:* National.

FINCH, Stephen John; Partner, since 1989, Chairman, since 2005, Salans; *b* Carshalto 28 Nov. 1950; *s* of Harry John and Evelyn Louise Finch; three *s*. *Educ:* London Uni (LLB). Admitted solicitor, 1975; Solicitor: practising in Sydney and London, 1975–7 Lloyds Bowmaker, 1978–82; Citibank Internat., 1982–85; Partner, Mill Bailey, 1985–8 *Publication:* (contrib.) Practical Commercial Precedents. *Recreations:* anything involvin mainstream sports, spending time with family and friends, restaurant owner. *Address:* c/ Salans, Millennium Bridge House, 2 Lambeth Hill, EC4V 4AJ. *T:* (020) 7429 6000, *Fa* (020) 7429 6001; *e-mail:* sfinch@salans.com.

FINCH HATTON, family name of **Earl of Winchilsea and Nottingham**.

FINCH-KNIGHTLEY, family name of **Earl of Aylesford**.

FINCHAM, Peter Arthur; Director of Television, ITV, since 2008; *b* 26 July 1956; *s* Arthur and Joan Fincham; *m* 1995, Clare Lewthwaite; two *s* two *d*. *Educ:* Tonbridge Sch Churchill Coll., Cambridge (BA English 1977). Man. Dir, TalkBack Prodns, 1986–200 Chief Exec., talkbackThames, 2003–05. *Address:* ITV, 200 Gray's Inn Road, WC1X 8HF

FINDLATER, (John) Donald; child protection worker and commentator; Directo Research and Development, Lucy Faithfull Foundation, since 2007; *b* 23 March 1955; of Robert and Mary Findlater; *m* 1977, Jacqueline Durrant; four *s* one *d*. *Educ:* Kir George V Grammar Sch., Southport; Univ. of Kent, Canterbury (BA Hons Law 1976 Univ. of East Anglia (MA Soc. Work 1981; CQSW 1981). Probation Officer, Herefor and Worcester Probation Service, 1981–85; Probation Officer, then Sen. Probatio Officer, Surrey Probation Service, 1985–97; Manager, Wolvercote Clinic, 1995–200 Dep. Dir, Lucy Faithfull Foundn, 1997–2006; Manager, Stop it Now!, UK and Ir helpline, 2002–07. Consultant: to Home Office, DfES and DoH on sexual abus prevention; to RC, Anglican and Methodist Churches on sexual abuse prevention and se offender rehabilitation; Mem., Sir Roger Singleton's panel of child protection expert 2006–. Trustee: Langley House Trust, 2003–; Sanctuary, 2006–. FRSA. *Publication* contrib. to professional jls and ref. texts. *Recreations:* spending time with my family, DIY gardening, walking, visiting historic buildings, motorcycling, finding and sharing hop *Address:* Lucy Faithfull Foundation, Wolvercote Centre, 46 East Street, Epsom, Surre KT17 1HB. *T:* 07778 532851; *e-mail:* dfindlater@lucyfaithfull.org.

FINDLAY, Alastair Donald Fraser, FCIWEM; Chief Executive, North of Scotlan Water Authority, 1995–2000; *b* 3 Feb. 1944; *s* of late Rev. Donald Fraser Findlay an Isobel Ellis Findlay (*née* Louden); *m* 1969, Morag Cumming Peden; one *s* three *d*. *Edu* Pitlochry High Sch.; Kelso High Sch.; Univ. of Edinburgh (MA (Hons) Ment Philosophy). FCIWEM 1996. Asst Principal, Dept of Agriculture and Fisheries fo Scotland, 1966–70; Private Sec. to Jt Parly Under Sec. of State, Scottish Office, 1970–7 Principal, Scottish Office, 1971–74; on loan to FCO as First Sec. (Agric. and Food), Th Hague, 1975–78; Asst Sec., Higher Educn Div., Scottish Educn Dept, 1979–82; Fisheri Div., 1982–85, Livestock Products Div., 1985–88, Dept of Agric. and Fisheries fo Scotland; Under Sec., IDS, then Scottish Office Industry Dept, 1988–93; Fisheries Sec Scottish Office Agric. and Fisheries Dept, 1993–95. Advr to Scottish Fishermen's Org 2005–. Mem., Barnardo's Scottish Cttee, 2002–05. Trustee: Lloyds TSB Foundn fo Scotland, 1998–2004 (Dep. Chm., 2003–04); Univ. of Highlands and Islands Develt Tru (formerly Univ. of Highlands and Islands Millennium Inst. Develt Trust), 2003–08; Th Queen Mother's Memorial Fund for Scotland, 2003–08. Treas., Boroughmuir RFC 2001–. *Recreations:* walking, motor cars, Rugby spectating. *Club:* Royal Commonwealt Society.

FINDLAY, Donald Russell; QC (Scot.) 1988; *b* 17 March 1951; *s* of James Findlay an Mabel Findlay (*née* Muirhead); *m* 1982, Jennifer Edith (*née* Borrowman). *Educ:* Harr Academy, Dundee; Univ. of Dundee (LLB 1st cl. Hons); Univ. of Glasgow (MPhil Mem., Faculty of Advocates, 1975– (Chm., Faculty Services Ltd, 2003–05); Lectr in Law Heriot Watt Univ., 1976–77. Mem., Lothian Health Bd, 1987–91. Vice Chm., Glasgo Rangers FC, 1992–99 (Dir, 1991–99). Vice Chairman: N Cunninghame Cons. an Unionist Assoc., 1989–92; Leith Cons. and Unionist Assoc., 1985–88. Rector, S Andrews Univ., 1993–99. Vice Pres., Assoc. for Internat. Cancer Res., 1996–. Columnis Scottish Daily Express, 1995–97; radio and television broadcaster. FRSA 199 *Publications:* Three Verdicts (novel), 1998; contribs to Scots Law Times and variou medico-legal publications. *Recreations:* Glasgow Rangers FC, Egyptology, malt whisky photography, cooking, drinking claret, politics, ethics; challenging authority. *Addres* Faculty of Advocates, Parliament House, Edinburgh EH1 1RF. *T:* (0131) 226 288 *Clubs:* Glasgow Art (Glasgow); Glasgow Rangers Bond.

FINDLAY, James de Cardonnel; QC 2008; *b* Girvan, 27 June 1961; *s* of John Findla and Rosemary Findlay; *m* 1994, Caroline Pedersen; two *s* one *d*. *Educ:* Trinity Coll Glenalmond; Magdalene Coll., Cambridge (BA 1983). Called to the Bar, Middle Templ 1984; in practice as barrister specialising in administrative, planning and licensing law *Recreations:* walking, supporting Scottish Rugby. *Address:* 2–3 Gray's Inn Square, WC1 5JH. *T:* (020) 7242 4986; *e-mail:* jfindlay@2-3gis.co.uk. *Club:* Lansdowne.

FINDLAY, Ralph Graham; Chief Executive, Marston's plc (formerly The Wolverhampton & Dudley Breweries plc), since 2001; *b* 9 Jan. 1961; *s* of James Findlay and Margaret Findlay (*née* Teesdale); *m* 1990, Louise MacKenzie; one *s* one *d*. *Educ:* James Gillespie's High Sch., Edinburgh; Univ. of Edinburgh (BSc Hons 1983). FCA 1988; MCT (Dip). Price Waterhouse, 1984–90; Treasury Manager, Bass plc, 1990–92; Chief Accountant, Geest plc, 1992–94; joined Wolverhampton & Dudley Breweries plc, 1994, Gp Finance Dir, 1996–2001. *Recreations:* family, reading, music, running, sport. *Address:* Marston's plc, Marston's House, Brewery Road, Wolverhampton WV1 4JT. *T:* (01902) 329530, *Fax:* (01902) 778007; *e-mail:* ralph.findlay@marstons.co.uk. *Clubs:* South Staffordshire Golf (Wolverhampton); Wolverhampton and Newbridge Lawn Tennis and Squash.

FINDLAY, Richard Martin; Entertainment Law Partner, Tods Murray, LLP, since 1990; Lead Partner, T2M (Tods Total Media), since 2000; *b* 18 Dec. 1951; *s* of Ian Macdonald Semple Findlay and Kathleen Lightfoot or Findlay. *Educ:* Gordon Schs, Huntly; Univ. of Aberdeen (LLB). Trainee Solicitor, Wilsone & Duffus, Advocates, Aberdeen, 1973–75; Asst Solicitor, Maclay Murray & Spens, Glasgow, 1975–79; Partner, Ranken & Reid, SSC, Edinburgh, 1979–90. Mem., Business in the Arts Placement Scheme, 1994–; Associate Mem., 1996–2000, Mem., 2000–, Theatrical Management Assoc. Chm., Red FM Ltd, 2004–05; Director: Krazy Kat Theatre Co., 1984–86; Edinburgh Music Theatre Co. Ltd, 1985–88; Gallus Theatre Co. Ltd, 1996–98; Dance Base Ltd, 1997–98; Royal Lyceum Theatre Co. Ltd, 1999– (Vice-Chm., 2002–); Audio Description Film Fund Ltd, 2000–; Hill Adamson (formerly Scottish Nat. Photography Centre Ltd), 2002–; Scottish Screen, 2003–07; Scottish Screen Enterprises, 2003–07; Luxury Edinburgh Ltd, 2006–. Dir, Lothian Gay and Lesbian Switchboard Ltd, 1998–2002. Member: Internat. Assoc. of Entertainment Lawyers, 1990–; Internat. Entertainment & Multimedia Law & Business Network, 1995–; Scottish Media Lawyers Soc., 1995–; IBA, 1993–99; BAFTA, 1990– (Mem. Mgt Cttee, BAFTA (Scotland), 1998–2004); Writers' Guild, 1993–2002; New Producers Alliance, 1993–98; Inst. of Art and Law, 1996–98; RTS, 2003–05. Founder Mem., Screen Academy Scotland Adv. Bd, 2006–. Trustee: Peter Darrel Trust, 1996–2004; Frank Mullen Trust, 2004–08. Part-time Lectr on Law of Film, Napier Univ., then Screen Acad., Scotland, 1997–. Man. Editor, i-2-i–the business journal for the international film industry (formerly Internat. Film Business, Finance and Law Rev.), 1995–97; Scotland Ed., Methuen Amateur Theatre Handbook. *Recreations:* theatre, film, music, Highland Games, photography. *Address:* Tods Murray LLP, Edinburgh Quay, 133 Fountainbridge, Edinburgh EH3 9AG. *T:* (0131) 656 2000, *Fax:* (0131) 656 2023; *e-mail:* richard@richardfindlay.com.

FINE, Anne, OBE 2003; FRSL; writer; Children's Laureate, 2001–03; *b* 7 Dec. 1947; *d* of Brian Laker and Mary Baker; *m* 1968, Kit Fine (marr. diss. 1991); two *d*. *Educ:* Northampton High School for Girls; Univ. of Warwick (BA Hons History and Politics). Guardian Children's Fiction Award, 1990; Carnegie Medal, 1990, 1993; Children's Author of the Year, Publishing News, 1990, 1993. FRSL 2003. *Publications: for older children:* The Summer House Loon, 1978; The Other Darker Ned, 1978; The Stone Menagerie, 1980; Round Behind the Icehouse, 1981; The Granny Project, 1983; Madame Doubtfire, 1987; Goggle-Eyes, 1989; The Book of the Banshee, 1991; Flour Babies, 1992 (Whitbread Award, 1993); Step by Wicked Step, 1995; The Tulip Touch, 1996 (Whitbread Award, 1997); Very Different, 2001; Up on Cloud Nine, 2002; The Road of Bones, 2006; *for younger children:* Scaredy-Cat, 1985; Anneli the Art Hater, 1986; Crummy Mummy and Me, 1988; A Pack of Liars, 1988; Stranger Danger, 1989; Bill's New Frock, 1989; The Country Pancake, 1989; A Sudden Puff of Glittering Smoke, 1989; A Sudden Swirl of Icy Wind, 1990; Only a Show, 1990; Design-a-Pram, 1991; A Sudden Glow of Gold, 1991; The Worst Child I Ever Had, 1991; The Angel of Nitshill Road, 1991; Same Old Story Every Year, 1992; The Chicken Gave it to Me, 1992; The Haunting of Pip Parker, 1992; How To Write Really Badly, 1996; Press Play, 1996; Jennifer's Diary, 1997; Loudmouth Louis, 1998; Roll Over, Roly, 1999; Charm School, 1999; Bad Dreams, 2000; The More the Merrier, 2003; Return of The Killer Cat, 2003; Frozen Billy, 2004; Ivan the Terrible, 2007; *picture books:* Poor Monty, 1991; Ruggles, 2002; *novels:* The Killjoy, 1986; Taking the Devil's Advice, 1990; In Cold Domain, 1994; Telling Liddy, 1997; All Bones and Lies, 2001; Raking the Ashes, 2005; Fly in the Ointment, 2008. *Recreations:* reading, walking. *Address:* c/o David Higham Associates, 5–8 Lower John Street, W1R 4HA.

FINE, Prof. Leon Gerald, FRCP, FRCPGlas, FACP, FMedSci; Chairman, Department of Biomedical Sciences, Cedars-Sinai Medical Center and University of California, Los Angeles, since 2007; *b* 16 June 1943; *s* of Matthew Fine and Jeanette (*née* Lipshitz); *m* 1966, Brenda Sakinovsky; two *d*. *Educ:* Univ. of Cape Town, SA (MB, ChB). FACP 1978; FRCP 1986; FRCPGlas 1993. Internship and Residency in Internal Medicine, Tel Aviv Univ. Med. Sch., Israel, 1967–70; Asst Prof. of Medicine, Albert Einstein Coll. of Medicine, NY, 1975–76; University of Miami School of Medicine: Asst Prof., 1976–78; Associate Prof., 1978–82; Prof. of Medicine and Chief, Div. of Nephrology, UCLA, 1982–91; University College London: Prof. and Hd, Dept of Medicine, 1991–2002; Dean, Faculty of Clinical Sci., Royal Free and UC Med. Sch., 2002–06. Founder FMedSci 1998. Editor-in-Chief, Nephron, 2003–. *Publications:* contribs in professional jls on pathophysiology of chronic renal disease, renal growth control, renal growth responses to acute and chronic injury, genetic manipulation of the kidney, and history of medicine. *Recreations:* collecting rare books on the history of medicine, fine printing and photography, book-binding. *Address:* Department of Biomedical Sciences, Cedars-Sinai Medical Center, Davis Building, Room 5072, 8700 Beverly Boulevard, Los Angeles, CA 90048, USA. *T:* (310) 4236457; *e-mail:* leon.fine@cshs.org. *Club:* Athenæum.

FINER, Dr Elliot Geoffrey, CChem, FRSC; Director General, Chemical Industries Association, 1996–2002; *b* 30 March 1944; *s* of Reuben and Pauline Finer; *m* 1970, Viviane Kibrit; two *s*. *Educ:* Royal Grammar Sch., High Wycombe; Cheadle Hulme Sch.; East Barnet Grammar Sch.; St Catharine's Coll., Cambridge (BA 1965); Univ. of East Anglia (MSc 1966; PhD 1968). CChem, FRSC 1993. Unilever Research, Welwyn, 1968–75; Dept of Energy, 1975–90; Dir for Industry and Commerce, 1983–86, Dir Gen., 1988–90, Energy Efficiency Office; Under Secretary, 1988; Head of Management Develt Gp, Cabinet Office, 1990–92; Head of Chemicals and Biotechnology Div., DTI, 1992–95. Director: Spillers Foods Ltd, 1989–92; Vestry Court Ltd, 1997–. Dir, Enfield PCT, 2003–. Mem., BBSRC, 1994–95. Pres., Assembly of European Chemical Industry Fedns, 1998–2000. Mem. Council, RSC, 2002– (Hon. Treas., 2005–). Chm., Ramsay Meml Fellowship Trust, 2007–. *Publications:* scientific papers and articles in learned jls. *Recreations:* home and family, reading, DIY, music. *Club:* Athenæum.

FINESTEIN, His Honour Israel, MA; QC 1970; a Circuit Judge, 1972–87; *b* 29 April 1921; *y c* of late Jeremiah Finestein, Hull; *m* 1946, Marion Phyllis, *er d* of Simon Oster, Hendon, Middx. *Educ:* Kingston High School, Hull; Trinity Coll., Cambridge (Major Scholar and Prizeman; MA 1946). Called to the Bar, Lincoln's Inn, 1953. Former Pres., Mental Health Review Tribunal. President: Jewish Hist. Soc. of England, 1973–75, 1994–95; Bd of Deps of British Jews, 1991–94; former Chm., London Jewish Mus. Pres., Norwood Child Care, 1983–90. Hon. LLD Hull. *Publications:* Short History of the Jews of England, 1956; Jewish Society in Victorian England, 1993; Anglo-Jewry in Changing Times 1840–1914, 1999; Scenes and Personalities in Anglo-Jewry 1800–2000, 2002. *Recreation:* reading history. *Address:* 18 Buttermere Court, Boundary Road, NW8 6NR.

FINESTEIN, Jonathon Eli; a District Judge (Magistrates' Courts) (formerly Stipendiary Magistrate), Salford, since 2001; a Recorder, since 1996 (an Assistant Recorder, 1992–96); *b* 9 April 1950; *s* of Gustav Finestein and Esther Finestein; *m* 1985, Elaine March; one *d*. *Educ:* Hull Grammar Sch.; Leeds Univ. (LLB). Called to the Bar, Gray's Inn, 1973; practice in Hull; Asst Stipendiary Magistrate, 1989–92; Stipendiary Magistrate for Lancs and Merseyside, 1992–2001. *Recreations:* watching all sports, walking. *Address:* Salford Magistrates' Court, Bexley Square, Salford M3 6DJ. *T:* (0161) 834 9457.

FINGLETON, John, DPhil; Chief Executive Officer, Office of Fair Trading, since 2005; *b* 21 Sept. 1965. *Educ:* Trinity Coll., Dublin (BA Mod 1987); Nuffield Coll., Oxford (MPhil Econs 1989, DPhil 1991). Researcher, LSE, 1991; Lectr in Econs, Trinity Coll., Dublin, 1991–2000; Chm., Competition Authy of Ireland, 2000–05. Visiting Scholar: Université Libre de Bruxelles, 1995; Univ. of Chicago, 1998–2000. *Publications:* (jtly) Competition Policy and the Transformation of Central Europe, 1996; (jtly) The Dublin Taxi Market: re-regulate or stay queuing?, 1998; contrib. Global Agenda. *Address:* Office of Fair Trading, Fleetbank House, 2–6 Salisbury Square, EC4Y 8JX. *T:* (020) 7211 8920.

FINGRET, His Honour Peter; a Circuit Judge, 1992–2005; *b* 13 Sept. 1934; *s* of late Iser and Irene Fingret; *m* 1st, 1960, June Moss (marr. diss. 1980); one *s* one *d*; 2nd, 1980, Dr Ann Lilian Mary Hollingworth (*née* Field). *Educ:* Leeds Modern Sch.; Leeds Univ. (LLB Hons); Open Univ. (BA). President, Leeds Univ. Union, 1957–58. Admitted Solicitor, 1960. Partner: Willey Hargrave & Co., Leeds, 1964–75; Fingret, Paterson & Co., Leeds, 1975–82. Stipendiary Magistrate for Co. of Humberside sitting at Kingston-upon-Hull, 1982–85; Metropolitan Stipendiary Magistrate, 1985–92; a Recorder, 1987–92; a Pres., Mental Health Rev. Tribunal, 1993–. Mem., Parole Bd, 2003–. Chm., Lord Chancellor's Adv. Cttee on JPs for Cities of London and Westminster, 2005–07. Councillor, Leeds City Council, 1967–72; Member: Court, Univ. of Leeds, 1975–85; Cttee, Leeds Internat. Piano Competition, 1981–85. Freeman: Musicians' Co., 2002–; City of London, 2004–. *Recreations:* golf, music, theatre. *Address: e-mail:* peterfingret@hotmail.com. *Clubs:* Garrick, MCC.

FINK, Prof. George, FRCPE; FRSE; Professorial Research Fellow, University of Melbourne and Mental Health Research Institute of Victoria, Australia, since 2007 (Director, 2004–06; Director of Laboratory Research, 2003–04); *b* 13 Nov. 1936; *s* of John H. Fink and Therese (*née* Weiss); *m* 1959, Ann Elizabeth Langsam; one *s* one *d*. *Educ:* Melbourne High Sch.; Univ. of Melbourne (MB BS 1960; MD 1978); Hertford Coll., Univ. of Oxford (DPhil 1967). FRSE 1989; FRCPE 1998. Jun. and sen. house officer, Royal Melbourne and Alfred Hosps, Victoria, Australia, 1961–62; Demonstrator in Anatomy, Monash Univ., Victoria, 1963–64; Nuffield Dominions Demonstrator, Oxford Univ., 1965–67; Sen. Lectr in Anatomy, Monash Univ., 1968–71; Univ. Lectr 1971–80, Official Fellow in Physiology and Med., Brasenose Coll., 1974–80, Oxford Univ.; Dir, MRC Brain Metabolism Unit, 1980–99, Hon. Prof., 1984–, Univ. of Edinburgh; Vice-Pres. of Res., 1999–2003, consultant, 2003–04, Pharmos Corp. Royal Soc.-Israel Acad. Exchange Fellow, Weizmann Inst., 1979; Walter Cottman Fellow and Vis. Prof., Monash Univ., 1985, 1989; Arthur Fishberg Prof., Mt Sinai Med. Sch., NY, 1988. Prosector in Anatomy, Melbourne Univ., 1956; Wolfson Lectr, Univ. of Oxford, 1982; first G. W. Harris Lectr, Physiol Soc., Cambridge, 1987. Pres., European Neuroendocrine Assoc., 1991–95; Member: Council, European Neuroscience Assoc., 1980–82, 1994–98; Mental Health Panel, Wellcome Trust, 1984–89; Steering Cttee, British Neuroendocrine Group, 1984–88 (Trustee, BNG, 1990–); Co-ordinating Cttee, ESF Network on Neuroimmunomodulation, 1990–93. Chm., 5 Year Assessment Biomed. Prog., 1991–96; Monitor, EU Biomed. 2 Prog., 1995. Hon. Mem., British Neuroendocrine Soc., 2005. Lifetime Achievement Award, Internat. Soc. of Psychoneuroendocrinology, 2000. Trustee, Jl of Neuroendocrinology, 1990–2003. *Publications:* (ed with L. J. Whalley) Neuropeptides: Basic and Clinical Aspects, 1982; (ed with A. J. Harmar and K. W. McKerns) Neuroendocrine Molecular Biology, 1986; (ed with A. J. Harmar) Neuropeptides: A Methodology, 1989; (Ed. in Chief) Encyclopedia of Stress, 2000, 2nd edn 2007; numerous scientific publications mainly on neuroendocrinology and neuroendocrine molecular biology. *Recreations:* ski-ing, diving. *Address:* Mental Health Research Institute of Victoria, Locked Bag II, Parkville, Vic 3052, Australia. *T:* (3) 93881633, *Fax:* (3) 93875061; *e-mail:* gfink@mhri.edu.au.

FINK, Stanley; Director, 1987–2008, Deputy Chairman, 2007–08, Man Group plc; *b* 15 Sept. 1957; *s* of Louis and Janet Fink; *m* 1981, Barbara Paskin; two *s* one *d*. *Educ:* Manchester Grammar Sch.; Trinity Hall, Cambridge (MA Law). ACA. Qualified chartered accountant, Arthur Andersen, 1979–82; Financial Planning, Mars Confectionery, 1982–83; Vice Pres., Citibank NA, 1983–86; Man Group plc: Gp Finance Dir, 1992–96; Man. Dir, Asset Mgt, 1996–2000; Chief Exec., 2000–07; Chm., Man Investments, 2002–07. *Recreations:* golf, tennis, ski-ing.

FINKELSTEIN, Prof. Anthony Charles Wiener, PhD; CEng, FIET; CITP; FBCS; Professor of Software Systems Engineering, since 1997, and Head of Computer Science, since 2002, University College London; *b* London, 28 July 1959; *s* of Prof. Ludwik Finkelstein, *qv*; *m* 1985, Judith Fishman; two *s*. *Educ:* Univ. of Bradford (BEng); London Sch. of Econs and Pol Sci. (MSc); Royal Coll. of Art (PhD). Post-doctoral Res. Fellow, 1985–88, Lectr, 1988–94, Imperial Coll., London; Prof. of Computer Sci., 1994–97, Hd, Computer Sci., 1995–97, City Univ. Dist. Vis. Prof., Nat. Inst. of Informatics, Tokyo, 2007–. *Publications:* contrib. IEEE Transactions on Software Engrg, ACM Transactions on Software Engrg Methods, Internat. Conf. on Software Engrg and other learned jls. *Recreations:* reading, art, antiques, family life. *Address:* University College London, Department of Computer Science, Gower Street, WC1E 6BT; *e-mail:* a.finkelstein@cs.ucl.ac.uk. *Club:* Athenæum.

See also D. W. Finkelstein, T. M. Finkelstein.

FINKELSTEIN, Daniel William, OBE 1997; Associate Editor, since 2001, and Chief Leader Writer, since 2008, The Times (Comment Editor, 2004–08); *b* 30 Aug. 1962; *s* of Prof. Ludwik Finkelstein, *qv*; *m* 1993, Dr Nicola Ruth, *d* of Henry and Frances Connor; three *s*. *Educ:* Hendon Prep. Sch.; University College Sch.; London School of Economics (BSc Econs 1984); City Univ. (MSc 1986). Journalist, Network magazine, 1987–89; Editor, Connexion, 1989–92; Columnist, Jewish Chronicle, 2004–; Editor, Comment Central (weblog), Times Online, 2006–. Director: Social Market Foundn, 1992–95; Conservative Res. Dept, 1995–98; Policy Unit, Conservative Central Office, 1999–2001; Associate Editor, New Moon magazine, 1990–97. Res. Asst, RCA, 1984–87; Political Advr to Dr David Owen, MP, 1986–91. Contested: (SDP) Brent E, 1987; (C) Harrow W, 2001. Mem., Nat. Cttee, SDP, 1986–90. Founder and Bd Mem., Enterprise Europe, 1990– (Chm., 1990–95). *Publications:* (with Craig Arnall) The Open Network and its Enemies, 1990; Conservatives in Opposition: Republicans in the US, 1994. *Recreations:* US political memorabilia, Chinese food. *Address:* c/o The Times, 1 Pennington Street,

E98 1TT. *T:* (020) 7782 7188. *Club:* Reform.
    See also A. C. W. Finkelstein, T. M. Finkelstein.

FINKELSTEIN, Prof. Ludwik, OBE 1990; DSc, PhD; FREng; FIET; CPhys, FInstP; Professor of Measurement and Instrumentation, City University, 1980–97, now Emeritus; *b* 6 Dec. 1929; *s* of Adolf and Amalia Finkelstein; *m* 1957, Mirjam Emma, *d* of Dr Alfred and Dr Margarethe Wiener; two *s* one *d. Educ:* Univ. of London (BSc, MSc). DSc City Univ., 1989; Leo Baeck Coll. (MA 1996, PhD 2006, Open Univ.). Physicist, Technical Staff, Electronic Tubes Ltd, 1951–52; Scientist, Instrument Br., NCB Mining Res. Estabt, 1952–59; Northampton Coll., London, and City University, London: Lectr, 1959–61; Sen. Lectr, 1961–63; Principal Lectr, 1963–67; Reader, 1967–70; Prof. of Instrument and Control Engineering, 1970–80; Head of Dept of Systems Science, 1974–79; Head of Dept of Physics, 1980–88; Dean, Sch. of Electrical Engrg and Applied Physics, 1983–88; Dean, Sch. of Engrg, 1988–93; Pro-Vice-Chancellor, 1991–94. Visiting Prof., Delft Univ. of Technology, 1973–74. Pres., Inst. of Measurement and Control, 1980 (Vice-Pres., 1972–75, 1977–79; Hartley Silver Medal, 1980); Chm., Management and Design Div., IEE, 1984–85 (Management and Design Divl Premium (jtly), 1984). FREng (FEng 1986). Hon. FInstMC 1991. Hon. Dr St Petersburg Technical Univ., 1994; Hon. DCL City, 1999. *Publications:* papers in learned jls and conference procs. *Recreations:* books, conversation, Jewish studies. *Address:* City University, Northampton Square, EC1V 0HB; 9 Cheyne Walk, Hendon, NW4 3QH. *T:* (020) 8202 6966.
    See also A. C. W. Finkelstein, D. W. Finkelstein, T. M. Finkelstein.

FINKELSTEIN, Tamara Margaret, (Mrs M. Isaacs); Director, UK Border Agency Integration Programme, since 2008; *b* 24 May 1967; *d* of Prof. Ludwik Finkelstein, *qv; m* 1997, Michael Isaacs; one *s* two *d. Educ:* Haberdashers' Aske's Sch. for Girls; Balliol Coll., Oxford (BA Engrg Sci. 1989); London Sch. of Econs (MSc Econs 1992). HM Treasury: Economic Advr, 1992–97; Private Sec. and Speechwriter to Chancellor of the Exchequer, 1997–99; Sen. Advr, Gen. Expenditure Policy, 2000–01; Dep. Dir, Sure Start, 2001–04; HM Treasury: Hd, Permt Sec.'s Strategy Team, 2004; Dir of Ops, 2005; Dir, Govt Treasury Mgt, 2006–08. *Recreations:* family, book club, women's group. *Address:* UK Border Agency, 2 Marsham Street, SW1P 4DF. *T:* (020) 7035 3241; *e-mail:* tamara.finkelstein@homeoffice.gsi.gov.uk.
    See also A. C. W. Finkelstein, D. W. Finkelstein.

FINLAY OF LLANDAFF, Baroness *cr* 2001 (Life Peer), of Llandaff in the County of South Glamorgan; **Ilora Gillian Finlay,** FRCP, FRCGP; Hon. Professor in Palliative Medicine, since 1996, and Vice-Dean, School of Medicine, 2000–05, Cardiff University (formerly University of Wales College of Medicine); President, Royal Society of Medicine, 2006–08; *b* 23 Feb. 1949; *d* of Charles Beaumont Benoy Downman and Thaïs Hélène Downman (*née* Barakan); *m* 1972, Andrew Yule Finlay; one *s* one *d. Educ:* Wimbledon High Sch.; St Mary's Hosp. Med. Sch., Univ. of London (MB, BS 1972). DObstRCOG 1974; DCH 1975. FRCGP 1992; FRCP 1999. GP, 1981–86; first Med. Dir, Holme Tower Marie Curie Centre, Cardiff, 1987–2000. Consultant in Palliative Medicine, Velindre NHS Trust, Cardiff, 1994–. Course Dir, Dip. and MSc in Palliative Medicine, UWCM. Non-exec. Dir, Gwent HA, 1995–2001. Founder Mem., Cancer Res. UK, 2002–04 (Mem., Sci. and Educn Cttee). Mem., Internat. Scientific Expert Panel, Cicely Saunders Foundn. House of Lords: Mem., Select Cttee on Sci. and Technol., 2002–, and on Assisted Dying for Terminally Ill Bill, 2003–05; Chm., Allergy Inquiry, 2006–07. President: Medical Women's Fedn, 2001–02; CSP, 2002–. Governor, Howell's Sch., Llandaff, GDST, 2000–. Patron: Shalom Hospice, St David's, Pembrokeshire, 2001–; Coping and Living in Pain. Member, Editorial Board: Lancet Oncology, 2002–; Quality in Healthcare, 2002–; Medical Humanities, 2002–. Hon. Fellow, Cardiff Univ., 2002. Hon. Prof., Groningen Univ., 2006–. Hon. DSc Glamorgan, 2002. *Address:* House of Lords, SW1A 0PW; Velindre NHS Trust, Cardiff CF14 2TL.

FINLAY, Alexander William; retired; *b* 28 Nov. 1921; *s* of late Robert Gaskin Finlay and late Alice Finlay; *m* 1949, Ona Margaret Lewis; no *c. Educ:* Tottenham County School. Flt-Lt RAF, 1941–47; various posts, BOAC and British Airways, 1947–78, Planning Dir, 1971–78, retd. Chm., Soc. for Long Range Planning, 1978–79; Mem. Council, Sussex Trust for Nature Conservation, 1982–89; Trustee, Charitable Trust, 1983–2001. Active interest in support for crime victims, 1989–2001. FCILT. *Recreations:* conservation, photography, gardening. *Club:* Royal Air Force.

FINLAY, Amanda Jane, CBE 2001; Director, Legal Aid Strategy, Ministry of Justice (formerly Department for Constitutional Affairs), since 2005; *b* 3 Sept. 1949; *d* of John Alexander Robertson Finlay, QC (His Honour Judge Finlay) and late Jane Little Hepburn, CBE; *m* 1975, Richard Bevan Butt, *qv;* two *s. Educ:* Newnham Coll., Cambridge (BA English 1971). Lord Chancellor's Department, then Department for Constitutional Affairs, subseq. Ministry of Justice: fast stream entrant, 1971; Principal, 1976; Sec. to Legal Aid Adv. Cttee, 1981; Asst Sec., 1993; Sec. to Lord Woolf's inquiry, Access to Justice, 1994–96; implementation of Human Rights Act, 1997–99; Grade 3, 1999; Director: Public and Private Rights, 1999–2004; Legal Services and Civil and Administrative Justice, 2004–05. *Recreations:* gardening and cooking in France and England, travel, opera. *Address:* Ministry of Justice, Selborne House, 54–60 Victoria Street, SW1E 6QW.

FINLAY, Prof. Bland James, PhD; FRS 2004; Professor of Microbial Ecology, Queen Mary, University of London, since 2007; *b* 16 March 1952; *s* of Bland and Mabel Finlay; *m* 1996, Genoveva Esteban; one *s* one *d. Educ:* Univ. of Stirling (BA; PhD). Lectr in Biol., Univ. of Jos, Nigeria, 1977; PSO, Freshwater Biol Assoc., UK, 1984–92; NERC, 1992–2007 (Dep. CSO, 2005–07). Guest Prof., Univ. of Aarhus, 1982. Field work and expeditions in field of protozoology: Nigeria, 1977–78; Kenya (soda lakes), 1985; Spain (solution lakes), 1987 and 1990; Australia (volcanic crater lakes), 1997. Chm., Grant Cttee, Royal Soc., 2005–07. Fellow, Royal Danish Acad. of Scis and Letters. Scientific Medal, Zool Soc. of London, 1991. *Publications:* Ecology and Evolution in Anoxic Worlds (with T. Fenchel), 1995; over 200 scientific articles. *Recreations:* being on holiday with my wife, listening to J. S. Bach, continuously searching for my spectacles. *Address:* c/o The River Laboratory, Wareham, Dorset BH20 6BB. *T:* (01929) 401885; *e-mail:* b.j.finlay@qmul.ac.uk.

FINLAY, Sir David (Ronald James Bell), 2nd Bt *cr* 1964, of Epping, Co. Essex; *b* 16 Nov. 1963; *s* of Sir Graeme Bell Finlay, 1st Bt, ERD and of June Evangeline, *y d* of Col Francis Collingwood Drake, OBE, MC, DL; *S* father, 1987; *m* 1998, Camilla, *d* of Peter Acheson; one *s* one *d. Educ:* Marlborough College; Bristol Univ. (BSc Hons Economics/Philosophy). Peat Marwick McLintock, 1986–91; Hill Samuel Financial Services, 1992–94; Gerrard Vivian Gray, 1994–97; Greig Middleton, 1997; Cater Allen Asset Management, 1998–. Freeman, City of London, 1991. *Recreations:* ski-ing, shooting. *Heir: s* Tristan James Bell Finlay, *b* 5 April 2001.

FINLAY, Frank, CBE 1984; actor; *b* Farnworth, Lancs, 6 Aug. 1926; *s* of Josiah Finlay; *m* 1954, Doreen Shepherd; two *s* one *d. Educ:* St Gregory the Great, Farnworth; RADA (Sir James Knott Schol.). *Stage:* repertory, 1950–52 and 1954–57; Belgrade, Coventry, 1958; Epitaph for George Dillon, NY, 1958; Royal Court, 1958, 1959–62: Sugar in the

Morning; Sergeant Musgrave's Dance; Chicken Soup with Barley, Roots, I'm Talkin About Jerusalem; The Happy Haven; Platonov; Chips with Everything, Royal Cour transf. to Vaudeville Theatre, 1962 (Clarence Derwent Best Actor Award); Chicheste Festival, 1963: St Joan; The Workhouse Donkey; *with National Theatre Co.:* St Joan, 1963 Willie Mossop in Hobson's Choice, and Iago in Othello (both also Chichester Fest., 1964 Berlin and Moscow, 1965), The Dutch Courtesan (also Chichester Fest.), 1964; Gile Corey in The Crucible, Dogberry in Much Ado About Nothing, Mother Courage, 1965 Joxer Daly in Juno and the Paycock, Dikoy in The Storm, 1966; Peppino in Saturday Sunday, Monday, 1973; Sloman in The Party, 1973; Freddy Malone in Plunder, Be Prosser in Watch It Come Down, Josef Frank in Weapons of Happiness, 1976; Amadeus 1982; *other productions include:* Bernard in After Haggerty, Aldwych, Criterion, Jesus Chris in Son of Man, Leicester Theatre and Round House (first actor ever to play Jesus Chris on stage in English theatre), 1970; Kings and Clowns (musical), Phoenix, 1978; Filmena Lyric, 1978, US tour, 1979–80, and NY, 1980; The Girl in Melanie Klein, Palace Th Watford, 1980; The Cherry Orchard, tour and Haymarket, 1983; Mutiny (musical Piccadilly, 1985–86; Beyond Reasonable Doubt, Queen's, 1987, Australian tour 1988–89, UK tour, 1989–90; Black Angel, King's Head, Islington, 1990; A Sligh Hangover, 1991, The Heiress, 1992, Bromley and UK tour; The Woman in Black, U tour, 1993–94; Peter Pan, Chichester and UK tour; Gaslight, Richmond, 1995; Th Handyman, Chichester, 1996; The Cherry Orchard, Chichester, 2008; *films include* 1962–: The Longest Day, Private Potter, The Informers, A Life for Ruth, Loneliness c the Long Distance Runner, Hot Enough for June, The Comedy Man, The Sandwic Man, A Study in Terror, Othello (nominated for Amer. Acad. award; best actor awarc San Sebastian, 1966), The Jokers, I'll Never Forget What's 'Is Name, The Shoes of th Fisherman, Deadly Bees, Robbery, Inspector Clouseau, Twisted Nerve, Cromwell, Th Molly Maguires (in Hollywood), Assault, Victory for Danny Jones, Gumshoe, Shaft i Africa, Van Der Valk and the Girl, Van Der Valk and the Rich; Van Der Valk and th Dead; The Three Musketeers; The Ring of Darkness, The Wild Geese, The Thief c Baghdad, Sherlock Holmes—Murder by Decree; Enigma; Return of the Soldier; Th Ploughman's Lunch, 1982; La Chiave (The Key), Italy, 1983; Sakharov, 1983; Christma Carol, Arch of Triumph, 1919, 1984; Lifeforce, 1985; Casanova, 1986; The Return of th Musketeers, 1988; Cthulhu Mansion, 1992; Charlemagne, 1993; The Sparrow, 1993; Th Pianist, 2002; The Statement, 2003; *TV appearances include:* Julius Caesar, Les Misérable This Happy Breed, The Lie (SFTA Award), Casanova (series), The Death of Adolf Hitle Don Quixote (SFTA Award), Voltaire, Merchant of Venice, Bouquet of Barbed Wir (series) (Best Actor Award), 84 Charing Cross Road, Saturday Sunday Monday, Cou Dracula, The Last Campaign, Napoleon in Betzi, Dear Brutus, Tales of the Unexpectec Tales from 1001 Nights, Aspects of Love—Mona, In the Secret State, Verdict on Erebu (NZ), King of the Wind, Mountain of Diamonds (series), Stalin (US), Sherlock Holme How Do You Want Me (series), The Sins (series), The Lost Prince, Station Jim, Prim Suspect, Eroica, Life Begins (series), Johnny and the Bomb (series). Hon. Fellow, Bolto Inst., 1992. *Address:* c/o Ken McReddie, 36–40 Glasshouse Street, W1B 5DL. *Clut* Garrick.

FINLAY, Larry; Managing Director, Transworld Publishers, since 2001; *b* London, 20 Jar 1960; *s* of Harry Finlay and Tess Matz; *m* 2002, Claire Calman; one *s. Educ:* Universit College Sch., London; Univ. of Manchester (BA Econ. and Soc. Studies). Transworl Publishers: copywriter, 1983–86; Ad and Promotions Dir, 1986–90; Mktg Dir, 1990–9 Paperback Publisher, 1997–99; Dep. Publisher, 1999–2001. *Recreations:* reading gardening, reading to my son, arguing about God, eating my wife's wonderful food shouting at the TV, teaching my son to swim, unleashing nematodes on unsuspectin slugs. *Address:* Transworld Publishers, 61–63 Uxbridge Road, W5 5SA. *T:* (020) 857 2652.

FINLAY, Most Rev. Terence Edward; Archbishop of Toronto and Metropolitan of th Ecclesiastical Province of Ontario, 2000–04; *b* 19 May 1937; *s* of Terence John Finlay an Sarah McBryan; *m* 1962, Alice-Jean Cracknell; two *d. Educ:* Univ. of Western Ontari (BA); Huron Coll., London, Ont (BTh); Cambridge Univ., Eng. (MA). Deacon 196 priest 1962; Dean of Residence, Renison Coll., Waterloo, Canada; Incumbent: All Saints Waterloo, 1964–66; St Aidan's, London, Canada, 1966–68; Rector: St John th Evangelist, London, 1968–78; Grace Church, Brantford, 1978–82; Archdeacon of Bran 1978–82; Incumbent, St Clement's, Eglinton, Toronto, 1982–86; a Suffragan Bishop Diocese of Toronto, 1986; Coadjutor Bishop, 1987; Bishop of Toronto, 1989–2004. DL (*jure dignitatis*) Huron Coll., 1987; (*hc*) Wycliffe Coll., 1988; (*hc*) Trinity Coll., 1989 *Recreations:* music, ski-ing, travel. *Address:* 1602–62 Wellesley Street West, Toronto, ON M5S 2X3, Canada.

FINLAY, Thomas Aloysius; Chief Justice of Ireland, 1985–94; *b* 17 Sept. 1922; *s* c Thomas A. Finlay and Eva Finlay; *m* 1948, Alice Blayney; two *s* three *d. Educ:* Xavier Sch Dublin; Clongowes Wood Coll.; University Coll. Dublin. BA Legal and Political Scienc NUI. Called to the Bar, King's Inns, 1944 (Bencher, 1972); Hon. Bencher: Inn of Cour of NI, 1985; Middle Temple, 1986. Mem., Dáil Éireann, 1954–57; Sen. Counsel, 196 Judge of the High Court, 1972, Pres. of the High Court, 1974. *Recreations:* fishing shooting, conversation. *Address:* 22 Ailesbury Drive, Dublin 4, Ireland. *T:* (1) 693395.

FINLAY-MAXWELL, David Campbell, MBE 1994; PhD; CEng, MIET; FTI, FSDC Director, D. F. Maxwell Co., since 1991; *b* 2 March 1923; *s* of Luke Greenwood Maxwe and of Lillias Maule Finlay; *m* 1954, Constance Shirley Hood; one *s* one *d. Educ:* St Paul's Heriot-Watt Coll. (Edinburgh Univ.) (Electronic and Control Engrg). CEng 1950; MIE (MIEE 1950); FTI 1974; FSDC 1985. PhD Leeds, 1983. Major Royal Signals and SOE 1945. Harvard Univ. Advanced Management Programme, 1968. Man. Dir, 1946–8 Chm., 1960–89, Dir, 1993–98, John Gladstone & Co.; Chm. and Man. Dir, Joh Gladstone & Co. (Engrg), 1948–89. Chairman: Manpower Working Party, NEDC 1970–73; Wool Industries Res. Assoc., 1974–77; Textile Res. Council, 1977–82; Woo Textile EDC, 1977–79, UK Rep., Consultative Cttee for R&D, Brussels, 1979–84. EE(Reviewer, ESPRIT Prog., 1986–2001. Dir, Wool Foundn (Internat. Wool Secretariat 1985–. Member: Council, Textile Inst., 1972–74; British Textile Council, 1977–8 Textile Industry and Dyeing Adv. Cttee, Leeds Univ. Council, 1974–95; Soc. of Dyer and Colourists, 1950–. *Recreations:* radio propagation, satellite tracking. *Address:* D. F Maxwell Co., Tarrens, The Green, Pirbright, Surrey GU24 0JT. *Club:* Special Forces.

FINLAYSON, Sir Garet (Orlando), KCMG 2007; OBE 1999; Chairman and Chie Executive, Associated Bahamian Distillers & Brewers Ltd, since 1981; *b* Andros, Bahama 4 Aug. 1937; *s* of Hastings and Maud Finlayson; *m* 1963, Rowena Frances Rolle; two two *d. Educ:* Evelyn Wood Inst.; La Salle Univ., Chicago (home study course in business Bahamas Teachers' Coll., Nassau. Primary sch. teacher, 1949–52; tailor, 1950–61; waite 1961–68; car salesman, 1968–71; owner: car dealerships, 1972–92; Bahamas Catering Ltc 1972–; Davinci Restaurant, 1973–94; Atlantis Hotel and Night Club, 1974–93; Bethe Robertson & Co. Ltd, 1981–. Owner and Chairman: Burns House Ltd, 1980–; Bahama Distillers Ltd, 1981–; Butler & Sands Ltd, 2004–; Solomon's Mines Ltd, 2004–; Chairman Gen. Bahamian Cos Ltd, 1981–; Wholesale Wines & Spirits Ltd, 2004–; Todhunter Mitchell Co. Ltd, 2004–; Deputy Chairman: Bahamas In-Flight Ltd, 1972–

Commonwealth Brewery Ltd, 1988–. Mem., World Presidents Orgn. Silver Jubilee Award in Business, Bahamas, 1998. *Recreations:* reading, yachting, fishing. *Address:* PO Box N1019, Nassau, Bahamas. *T:* 3971498, *Fax:* 3233211; *e-mail:* gfinlayson@abdab.bs.

FINLAYSON, George; HM Diplomatic Service, retired; *b* 22 April 1943; *s* of late George Finlayson and Alison Boath (*née* Barclay); *m* 1966, Patricia Grace Ballantine; two *s*. *Educ:* Tynecastle High Sch., Edinburgh. Joined HM Diplomatic Service, 1965; Reykjavik, 1967–69; Prague, 1969–71; Lagos, 1971–75; FCO, 1975–78; 2nd Sec., New Delhi, 1978–81; 1st Sec., FCO, 1981–83; 1st Sec. and Head of Chancery, Montevideo, 1983–87; Consul (Commercial) and Dep. Dir for Trade Promotion, New York, 1987–90; Dep. High Comr, Dhaka, 1990–93; Consul-Gen., Melbourne, 1994–98; High Comr to Malaŵi, 1998–2001. Dep. Chm., Scots Australian Council, 2002–. Trustee: Malaŵi Tomorrow, 2005–; Scotland Malaŵi Business Gp, 2007–. Mem., Scottish Charity Appeals Panel, 2006–. *Recreations:* drawing, painting. *Address:* 12 Eglinton Crescent, Edinburgh EH12 5DD.

FINLAYSON, George Ferguson, CMG 1979; CVO 1983; HM Diplomatic Service, retired; *b* 28 Nov. 1924; *s* of late G. B. Finlayson; *m* 1st, 1951, Rosslyn Evelyn (*d* 1972), *d* of late E. N. James; one *d*; 2nd, 1982, Anthea Judith, *d* of late F. D. Perry. *Educ:* North Berwick High Sch. Royal Air Force, 1943–47. Apptd HM Foreign (later Diplomatic) Service, 1949; 2nd Sec. (Inf.), HM Embassy, Rangoon, 1952–54; FO, 1955–59; First Sec., 1959; HM Consul, Algiers, 1959–61; First Sec., HM Embassy, Bamako, 1961–63; HM Consul (Commercial), New York, 1964–68; Counsellor, 1968; Counsellor (Commercial), British High Commn, Singapore, 1969–72; Head of Trade Relations and Exports Dept, FCO, 1972–73; Counsellor (Commercial) Paris, 1973–78; Consul-General: Toronto, 1978–81; Los Angeles, 1981–84. *Recreations:* travel, walking, swimming. *Address:* 141b Ashley Gardens, SW1P 1HN. *T:* (020) 7834 6227. *Club:* Oriental.

FINLAYSON, Niall Diarmid Campbell, OBE 1998; PhD; FRCSE, FRCP, FRCPE; Consultant Physician, Centre for Liver and Digestive Disorders, Royal Infirmary Edinburgh, 1973–2003; Teaching Fellow, Edinburgh University, since 2004; *b* 21 April 1939; *s* of Duncan Iain Campbell Finlayson and Helen Rita Blackney; *m* 1972, Dale Kristin Anderson; one *s* one *d*. *Educ:* Loretto Sch., Musselburgh; Edinburgh Univ. (BSc (Hons) 1962; MB, ChB 1964; PhD 1972). FRCPE 1977; FRCP 1982; FRCSE 1999. Asst Prof. of Medicine, New York Hospital-Cornell Medical Center, NY, 1969–73; Hon. Sen. Lectr, Edinburgh Univ. Medical Sch., 1973–2003. CMO, Bright Gray Assurance Co., 2004–. Pres., RCPE, 2001–04. *Publications:* (ed jtly) Diseases of the Gastrointestinal Tract and Liver, 1982, 3rd edn 1997; about 100 publications in learned jls and as contributions to books. *Recreations:* music, history. *Address:* 10 Queens Crescent, Edinburgh EH9 2AZ. *T:* (0131) 667 9369; *e-mail:* ndc.finlayson@which.net.

FINLEY, Gerald Hunter, FRCM; baritone; *b* Montreal, 1960; *s* of Eric Gault Finley and Catherine Rae Finley; *m* 1990, Louise Winter, opera singer; two *s*. *Educ:* Glebe Collegiate Inst., Ottawa; Univ. of Ottawa; Royal Coll. of Music (ARCM 1980); King's Coll., Cambridge (BA 1983; MA 1986); Nat. Opera Studio. FRCM 2007. St Matthew's Church Choir, Ottawa, 1970–79; Ottawa Choral Soc., 1976–79; Ontario Youth Choir, 1977–78; King's Coll. Choir, 1981–83; Glyndebourne Chorus, 1986–88; *débuts:* Figaro in Le Nozze di Figaro, Downland Opera, 1984; Antonio in Le Nozze di Figaro, Nat. Arts Centre Opera, 1987; Graf Dominik in Arabella, Glyndebourne, 1989; Graf in Capriccio, Chicago Lyric Opera, 1994; Figaro in Le Nozze di Figaro, LA Music Centre, 1994, Royal Opera House, Covent Garden, 1995; Valentin in Faust, Opéra de Paris, 1997; Papageno in Die Zauberflöte, NY Met., 1998; Mr Fox in Fantastic Mr Fox, LA Opera, 1998; Harry Heegan in The Silver Tassie, ENO, 2000; Robert Oppenheimer in Doctor Atomic, San Francisco Opera, 2005; *other rôles include:* Forester in Cunning Little Vixen, title rôle in Don Giovanni, Royal Opera, 2003; Guglielmo in Così fan tutte, Salzburg, Olivier in Capriccio, Paris Opera, and Jaufre Rudel in L'amour de Loin (Sariaaho), Helsinki, 2004; Giorgio Germont in La Traviata, Royal Opera, and title rôle in Eugene Onegin, ENO, 2005; Count in Le Nozze di Figaro, Royal Opera, 2006; appears regularly at Glyndebourne Opera Fest. Vis. Prof., Royal Coll. of Music, 2000. Numerous opera and recital recordings. John Christie Award, Glyndebourne, 1989; Juno Award, Canadian Acad. of Recording Arts, 1998; Singer's Award, Royal Philharmonic Soc., 2000; Editor's Choice Award, Gramophone mag./Classic FM, 2006. *Recreations:* letterboxing, wine, cooking, Guitar Hero. *Address:* c/o IMG Artists Europe,The Light Box, 111 Power Road, Chiswick, W4 5PY. *T:* (020) 7957 5800; c/o IMG Artists, 159 W 57th Street, New York, NY 10019, USA. *T:* (212) 9943500. *Club:* Royal Commonwealth Society.

FINLEY, Michael John; Governor, International Press Foundation, 1988–97; *b* 22 Sept. 1932; *s* of late Walter Finley and Grace Marie Butler; *m* 1st, 1955, Sheila Elizabeth Cole (*d* 1992); four *s*; 2nd, 2001, Maureen Elizabeth Crocker. *Educ:* King Edward VII Sch., Sheffield. Editor, 1964–69, Sheffield Morning Telegraph (formerly Sheffield Telegraph); Editorial Dir, 1969–79, and Dir and Gen. Man., 1979–82, Kent Messenger Gp; Exec. Dir, Periodical Publishers Assoc., 1983–88; Dir, Internat. Fedn of Periodical Publishers, 1989–92. Hon. Mem. and Past Chm., Parly and Legal Cttee, Guild of British Newspaper Editors. Chm., Inst. of Dirs (Kent branch), 1980–83. Member: BBC Regional Adv. Council, 1967–69; BBC Gen. Adv. Council, 1971–77; Exec. Cttee, Internat. Fedn of Periodical Publishers, 1983–89; Bd, Fedn of Periodical Publishers in EEC, 1984–92; Bd, Internat. Press Centre, London, 1984–88; Gov., Cranbrook Sch., 1978–98. *Publication:* contrib. Advertising and the Community, 1968. *Recreations:* golf, Rugby (spectator), snooker, walking. *Address:* The Belvedere, Benenden, Kent TN17 4DB.

FINN, Benjamin James, OBE 2007; Co-founder and Director, Sibelius Software Ltd, 1993–2006; *b* 29 Nov. 1968; *s* of Timothy Finn and Anthea, (Widget), Finn (*née* Fox-Male). *Educ:* King's Coll. Choir Sch., Cambridge; King's Sch., Canterbury; Royal Coll. of Music; King's Coll., Cambridge (BA 1991; MPhil). *Recreations:* thinking, dabbling.

See also J. H. Finn.

FINN, Jonathan Humbert, OBE 2007; Co-Founder and Director, Sibelius Software Ltd, 1993–2006; *b* 29 Nov. 1968; *s* of Timothy Finn and Anthea, (Widget), Finn (*née* Fox-Male). *Educ:* King's Coll. Choir Sch., Cambridge; King's Sch., Canterbury; Christ Church, Oxford (BA Music 1990). Vis. Prof. of Notation Technol., Royal Acad. Music, 1995. *Publication:* The Scorpion Control Computer, 1987. *Recreations:* inventing, singing, trudging, speculating.

See also B. J. Finn.

FINN, Leo Peter; Chief Executive, Northern Rock PLC, 1997–2001; *b* 13 July 1938; *s* of Thomas Leo Finn and Jenny Finn (*née* Davison); *m* 1963, Alice Patricia Harold; two *s* two *d*. *Educ:* Carlisle Grammar Sch.; Newcastle upon Tyne Polytechnic (BA Hons). FCIB. Sec., 1982–89, Exec. Dir, 1989–91, Dep. Man. Dir, 1991–97, Northern Rock Building Soc.; Dir, Bellway plc, 1995–. Chairman: Newcastle/Gateshead Housing Market Restructure Pathfinder, 2002–05; Northern Recruitment Group PLC, 2005–; Dir, Eden Housing Assoc., 2005– (Vice Chm., 2008–). Lay Mem., Public Protection Panel Cumbria, 2002–. Chm., Joseph Rowntree Enquiry into home ownership 2010 and beyond, 2004–05. Chm., Newcastle Coll., 2001–06. Chm., Northern Rock Foundn, 2004–06 (Trustee, 1997–2006). Hon. DCL Northumbria, 2005. *Recreations:* walking, opera, cooking. *Address:* Eden House, Edenhall, Cumbria CA11 8SX. *T:* (01768) 881536.

FINNEGAN, Joseph; Hon. Mr Justice Finnegan; a Judge of the Supreme Court of Ireland, since 2006; *b* 1 Oct. 1942; *s* of Isaac Finnegan and Charlotte Finnegan (*née* Sheridan); *m* 1968, Kathleen Gilligan; one *s* three *d*. *Educ:* Marist Coll., Dundalk; University Coll., Dublin (BCL, LLB). Admitted solicitor, Ireland; called to the Bar, King's Inns, Dublin (Bencher, 1999); in practice as solicitor, 1966–68 and 1973–78; Asst Sec., Incorporated Law Soc. of Ireland, 1968–73; Jun. Counsel, 1978–90; Sen. Counsel, 1990–99; Judge of the High Court of Ireland, 1992–2001; Pres. of the High Court, 2001–06. Bencher, Middle Temple, 2006. *Recreations:* National Hunt racing, golf. *Address:* Ardara, Killarney Road, Bray, Co. Wicklow, Ireland. *T:* (1) 2866710; *e-mail:* josephfinnegan@courts.ie. *Clubs:* Blackrock College Rugby Football; Bray Golf, El Saler Golf (Valencia, Spain).

FINNEGAN, Kevin James; QC (NI) 1985; **His Honour Judge Finnegan;** a County Court Judge, Northern Ireland, since 2001; *b* 3 June 1947; *s* of James Finnegan and Sheila Finnegan; *m* 1976, Anne Frances Aubrey; six *s*. *Educ:* St Malachy's Coll., Belfast; Queen's Univ., Belfast (LLB Hons 1970). Called to the Bar, NI, 1973. *Recreations:* golf, reading, listening to the radio, sleeping, going to Van Morrison, John Pryne and Ray Davies concerts. *Address:* Royal Courts of Justice, Belfast BT1 3JF. *Club:* Malone Golf.

FINNEGAN, Prof. Ruth Hilary, OBE 2000; DPhil; FBA 1996; Visiting Research Professor, Open University, since 1999 (Professor in Comparative Social Institutions, 1988–99, Emeritus Professor, 2002); *b* 31 Dec. 1933; *d* of Tom Finnegan and Agnes (*née* Campbell); *m* 1963, David John Murray; three *d*. *Educ:* Mount Sch., York; Somerville Coll., Oxford (BA 1956; Dip in Anthropology 1959; BLitt 1960; Hon. Fellow, 1997); Nuffield Coll., Oxford (DPhil 1963). Teacher, Malvern Girls' Coll., 1956–58; Lectr in Social Anthropol., UC of Rhodesia and Nyasaland, 1963–64; Lectr in Sociol., 1965–67, Sen. Lectr, 1967–69, Ibadan Univ.; Open University: Lectr in Sociol., 1969–72; Sen. Lectr in Comparative Social Instns, 1972–75 and 1978–82; Reader, 1982–88; Reader in Sociol. and Head of Sociol. Discipline, Univ. of S Pacific, Suva, 1975–78. Vis. Prof., Univ. of Texas at Austin, 1989. Mem., Governing Body, SOAS, 1999–2007 (Vice-Chm., 2003–06). Trustee, Mass-Observation Archive, 1998–. Pres., Mount Old Scholars' Assoc., 2003–05. Associate Mem., Finnish Lit. Soc., 1989; Folklore Fellow, Finnish Acad. of Sci. and Letters, 1991; Hon. Mem., Assoc. of Social Anthropologists of UK and Commonwealth, 2002. *Publications:* Survey of the Limba people of Northern Sierra Leone, 1965; Limba Stories and Story-telling, 1967; Oral Literature in Africa, 1970, 1976; Oral Poetry, 1977, 2nd edn 1992; Literacy and Orality, 1988; The Hidden Musicians, 1989, 2nd edn 2007; Oral Traditions and the Verbal Arts, 1992; Tales of the City, 1998; Communicating: the multiple modes of human interconnection, 2002; The Oral and Beyond: doing things with words in Africa; *edited:* The Penguin Book of Oral Poetry, 1978, reissued as A World Treasury of Oral Poetry, 1982; Participating in the Knowledge Society: researchers beyond the university walls, 2005; *edited jointly:* Modes of Thought, 1973; Essays on Pacific Literature, 1978; Conceptions of Inquiry, 1981; New Approaches to Economic Life, 1985; Information Technology: social issues, 1987; From Family Tree to Family History, 1994; Sources and Methods for Family and Community Historians, 1994; South Pacific Oral Traditions, 1995; contrib. to learned jls. *Recreations:* singing in local choirs, walking, learning from grandchildren. *Address:* Faculty of Social Sciences, Open University, Milton Keynes MK7 6AA. *T:* (01908) 654458.

FINNERTY, Angela Catherine, (Mrs Mark England); Her Honour Judge Finnerty; a Circuit Judge, since 2000; *b* 22 March 1954; *d* of late Michael Peter Finnerty and of Mary Elizabeth Finnerty; *m* 1978, Mark England; one *s* one *d*. *Educ:* Bury Convent Grammar Sch.; Leeds Univ. (LLB 1st Cl. Hons); Coll. of Law, London. Called to the Bar, Middle Temple, 1976; in practice as barrister, 1976–2000; Head, Family Team, and child care specialist, Park Lane Chambers, Leeds, 1977–2000. *Recreations:* family life, travel. *Address:* Bradford Combined Court Centre, Exchange Square, Bradford BD1 1JA.

FINNEY, Albert; actor, stage and film; film director; *b* 9 May 1936; *s* of Albert Finney, turf accountant, and Alice (*née* Hobson); *m* 1st, 1957, Jane Wenham, actress (marr. diss.); one *s*; 2nd, 1970, Anouk Aimée (marr. diss.); 3rd, 2006, Pene Delmage. Associate Artistic Dir, English Stage Co., 1972–75; a Dir, United British Artists, 1983–86. *Stage:* London appearance in The Party, New, 1958; Cassio in Othello, and Lysander, Stratford-on-Avon, 1959; subsequently in: The Lily White Boys, Royal Court, 1960; Billy Liar, Cambridge Theatre, 1960; Luther, in Luther: Royal Court Theatre and Phoenix Theatre, 1961–62; New York, 1963; Armstrong in Armstrong's Last Goodnight, Miss Julie and Black Comedy, Chichester, 1965, Old Vic, 1966; A Day in the Death of Joe Egg, NY, 1968; Alpha Beta, Royal Court and Apollo, 1972; Krapp's Last Tape, Royal Court, 1973; Cromwell, Royal Court, 1973; Chez Nous, Globe, 1974; Uncle Vanya, and Present Laughter, Royal Exchange, Manchester, 1977; Orphans, Hampstead, transf. to Apollo, 1986; J. J. Farr, Phoenix, 1987; Another Time, Wyndham's, 1989, Chicago, 1991; Reflected Glory, Vaudeville, 1992; Art, Wyndham's, 1996; *National Theatre:* Love for Love, 1965; Much Ado About Nothing, 1965; A Flea in Her Ear, 1966; Hamlet, 1975; Tamburlaine, 1976; The Country Wife, 1977; The Cherry Orchard, Macbeth, Has "Washington" Legs?, 1978; *Directed for stage:* The Freedom of the City, Royal Court, 1973; Loot, Royal Court, 1975; *Directed for stage and appeared in:* The Biko Inquest, Riverside, 1984; Serjeant Musgrave's Dance, Old Vic, 1984; *Films include:* Saturday Night and Sunday Morning, 1960; Tom Jones, 1963; Night Must Fall, 1964; Two for the Road, 1967; Scrooge, 1970; Murder on the Orient Express, 1974; Loophole, 1980; Wolfen, 1981; Looker, 1981; Shoot the Moon, 1982; Annie, 1982; The Dresser, 1983; Under the Volcano, 1984; Orphans, 1987; Miller's Crossing, 1990; The Playboys, 1992; Rich in Love, 1992; The Browning Version, 1994; A Man of No Importance, 1994; The Run of the Country, 1995; Washington Square, 1997; Simpatico, 1999; Delivering Milo, 2000; Erin Brockovich, 2000; Breakfast of Champions, 2000; Big Fish, 2004; Amazing Grace, 2006; A Good Year, 2006; The Bourne Ultimatum, 2007; Before the Devil Knows You're Dead, 2008; founded Memorial Films, 1965: co-produced with Michael Medwin: Charlie Bubbles (also actor/dir); If…; Bleak Moments; Spring and Port Wine; Gumshoe (also actor); In Loving Memory; O Lucky Man; The Day; Alpha Beta (also actor); The Engagement; Law and Disorder; Memoirs of a Survivor; *TV films:* John Paul II, 1984; The Endless Game, 1990; The Image, 1990; A Rather English Marriage, 1998; The Gathering Storm, 2002; *serials:* The Green Man, 1990; Karaoke, 1996; Nostromo, 1997; My Uncle Silas, 2001. Hon. LittD: Sussex, 1965; Salford, 1979. *Address:* c/o Michael Simkins, Michael Simkins LLP, 45/51 Whitfield Street, W1T 4HB.

FINNEY, Prof. David John, CBE 1978; MA, ScD Cantab; FRS 1955; FRSE; consultant biometrician; Professor of Statistics, University of Edinburgh, 1966–84; Director, Agricultural and Food Research Council (formerly Agricultural Research Council) Unit of Statistics, 1954–84; *b* Latchford, Warrington, 3 Jan. 1917; *e s* of late Robert G. S. Finney and late Bessie E. Whitlow; *m* 1950, Mary Elizabeth Connolly (*d* 2006); one *s* two *d*. *Educ:* Lymm and Manchester Grammar Schools; Clare Coll., Cambridge; Galton Laboratory,

Univ. of London. Asst Statistician, Rothamsted Experimental Station, 1939–45; Lecturer in the Design and Analysis of Scientific Experiment, University of Oxford, 1945–54; Reader in Statistics, University of Aberdeen, 1954–63, Professor, 1963–66. Dir, ISI Res. Centre, Netherlands, 1987–88. Vis. Prof. of Biomathematics, Harvard Univ., 1962–63; Vis. Scientist, Internat. Rice Res. Inst., 1984–85. United Nations FAO expert attached to Indian Council of Agricultural Research, 1952–53; FAO Key Consultant, Indian Agricl Stats Res. Inst., 1984–90. Scientific Consultant, Cotton Research Corporation, 1959–75. Chm., Computer Bd for Univs and Research Councils, 1970–74 (Mem., 1966–74); Member: Adverse Reactions Sub-Cttee, Cttee on Safety of Medicines, 1963–81; BBC General Adv. Council, 1969–76. Trustee, Drug Safety Res. Trust, Bursledon Hall, Southampton, 1986–97. President of Biometric Society, 1964–65 (Vice-President, 1963, 1966); Fellow: Royal Statistical Soc. (Pres., 1973–74); American Statistical Assoc.; Mem., Internat. Statistical Inst.; Hon. Fellow Eugenics Society; Hon. Member: Société Adolphe Quetelet; Internat. Soc. of Pharmacovigilance, 2002. Weldon Memorial Prize, 1956; Paul Martini Prize, Deutsche Ges. für Medizinische Dokumentation und Statistik, 1971. Dr *hc*, Faculté des Sciences Agronomiques de l'Etat à Gembloux, Belgium, 1967; Hon. DSc: City, 1976; Heriot-Watt, 1981; Hon. Dr Math Waterloo (Ont), 1989. *Publications:* Probit Analysis, 1947 (3rd edn 1971); Biological Standardization (with J. H. Burn, L. G. Goodwin), 1950; Statistical Method in Biological Assay, 1952 (3rd edn 1978); An Introduction to Statistical Science in Agriculture, 1953 (4th edn 1972); Experimental Design and its Statistical Basis, 1955; Tecnica y Teoria en el diseño de Experimentos, 1957; An Introduction to the Theory of Experimental Design, 1960; Statistics for Mathematicians: An Introduction, 1968; Statistics for Biologists, 1980; Writings on Pharmacovigilance, 2006; over 300 papers in statistical and biological journals. *Recreations:* travel (active), music (passive), and the 3 R's. *Address:* 13 Oswald Court, South Oswald Road, Edinburgh EH9 2HY. *T:* (0131) 667 0135; *e-mail:* david.finney@freeuk.com.

FINNEY, Rt Rev. John Thornley; Bishop Suffragan of Pontefract, 1993–98; Hon. Assistant Bishop, diocese of Southwell and Nottingham (formerly diocese of Southwell), since 1998; *b* 1 May 1932; *s* of Arthur Frederick and Elaine Mary Finney; *m* 1959, Sheila Elizabeth Russell; three *d*. *Educ:* Charterhouse; Hertford College, Oxford (BA Jurisp.; Dip. Theol.). Ordained 1958; Curate, All Saints, Headington, 1958–61; Curate in Charge, Aylesbury, 1961–65; Rector, Tollerton, Notts, 1965–71; Vicar, St Margaret's, Aspley, Nottingham, 1971–80; Adviser in Evangelism to Bishop of Southwell, 1980–89; Officer for Decade of Evangelism, 1990–93. Manager, Research Project in Evangelism, BCC, 1989–92. Chm. Council, Lee Abbey, 1999–2003. *Publications:* Saints Alive!, 1983; Understanding Leadership, 1989; The Well Church Book, 1991; Church on the Move, 1992; Finding Faith Today, 1992; Stories of Faith, 1995; Recovering the Past: Celtic and Roman mission, 1996; Fading Splendour?, 2000; Emerging Evangelism, 2004. *Recreations:* golf, growing old gracefully. *Address:* Greenacre, Crow Lane, South Muskham, Newark, Notts NG23 6DZ. *T:* and *Fax:* (01636) 679791; *e-mail:* john.finney2@virgin.net.

FINNEY, Sir Thomas, Kt 1998; CBE 1992 (OBE 1961); *b* Preston, 5 April 1922; *s* of late Alf and Margaret Finney; *m* 1945, Elsie Noblett; one *s* one *d*. *Educ:* Deepdale County Primary Sch.; Deepdale Modern Sch. Joined plumbing firm of Pilkington's as apprentice, 1936. Professional footballer with Preston North End, 1940–42, 1946–60, for whom he played 433 league games and scored 187 goals; 76 appearances for England, 1946–58; Pres., Preston North End FC, 1975–76. Chm., Preston HA, 1985–88. Freeman, Borough of Preston, 1979. Hon. Fellow, Lancashire Poly., 1988. Hon. LLD Lancaster Univ., 1988. Footballer of the Year, Football Writers' Assoc., 1954, 1957. *Publication:* My Autobiography, 2003.

FINNIE, (James) Ross, CA; Member (Lib Dem) West of Scotland, Scottish Parliament, since 1999; *b* 11 Feb. 1947; *s* of late James Ross Finnie and Elizabeth Main Finnie; *m* 1971, Phyllis Sinclair; one *s* one *d*. *Educ:* Greenock Acad. Director: James Finlay Bank Ltd, 1975–86; Singer & Friedlander Ltd, 1986–91; Partner, Ross Finnie & Co., Chartered Accountants, 1991–99. Mem., Exec. Cttee, Scottish Council (Develt and Industry), 1976–87. Member (L then Lib Dem): Inverclyde DC, 1977–96; Inverclyde Council, 1995–99. Minister for Rural Affairs, then for Envmt and Rural Develt, Scottish Exec., 1999–2007; Lib Dem Shadow Cabinet Sec. for Health and Wellbeing, 2007–. Vice Convenor, Health and Sport Cttee, Scottish Parlt. Chm., Scottish Lib Party, 1982–86. Contested: (L) Renfrewshire W, 1979; (L/All) Stirling, 1983. *Address:* Scottish Parliament, Edinburgh EH99 1SP; (home) 91 Octavia Terrace, Greenock PA16 1PY. *T:* (01475) 631495, *Fax:* (01475) 636755.

FINNIGAN, Judith, (Judy); television presenter; *b* 16 May 1948; *d* of late John Finnigan and of Anne Finnigan; *m* 1986, Richard Holt Madeley, *qv*; one *s* one *d*, and two *s* from previous marriage. Researcher, Granada TV, 1971–73; reporter, Anglia TV, 1974–77; presenter: Granada TV, 1980–2001; Channel 4, 2001–; programmes include: This Morning, 1988–2001; Richard and Judy, 2001–08. *Publication:* (with R. Madeley) Richard & Judy: the autobiography, 2001. *Address:* c/o James Grant Management, 94 Strand on the Green, Chiswick, W4 3NN.

FINNIGAN, Stephen James, QPM 2006; Chief Constable, Lancashire Police Authority, since 2005; *b* Liverpool, 29 June 1957; *s* of James Francis Finnigan and late Veronica Finnigan (*née* Ramsey); *m* 1992, Jaqueline Marie Brammer; one *s* one *d*. *Educ:* Maricourt Comprehensive Sch.; St John's Coll., Cambridge (BA 1992); Univ. of Cambridge (Dip. Applied Criminol. and Police Studies 2000). Merseyside Police, 1976–2001: Sergeant, 1980–87; Inspector, 1987–93; Chief Inspector, 1993–96; Superintendent, 1996–2001; Lancashire Police Authority: Asst Chief Constable, 2001–02, Dep. Chief Constable, 2002–05. *Recreations:* running, watching football (Everton FC), spending time with young family. *Address:* Lancashire Constabulary, PO Box 77, Saunders Lane, Hutton, Preston PR4 5SB. *T:* (01772) 412221, *Fax:* (01772) 614916; *e-mail:* steve.finnigan@lancashire.pnn.police.uk.

FINNIS, Prof. John Mitchell, DPhil; FBA 1990; Professor of Law and Legal Philosophy, Oxford University, since 1989; Fellow and Praelector in Jurisprudence, since 1966, Stowell Civil Law Fellow, since 1973, Vice Master, since 2001, University College, Oxford; *b* 28 July 1940; *s* of Maurice and Margaret Finnis; *m* 1964, Marie Carmel McNally; three *s* three *d* (and one *d* decd). *Educ:* St Peter's Coll., Adelaide, SA; St Mark's Coll., Univ. of Adelaide (LLB 1961); University Coll., Oxford (Rhodes Scholar for SA, 1962; DPhil 1965). Called to the Bar, Gray's Inn, 1970. Associate in Law, Univ. of Calif at Berkeley, 1965–66; Rhodes Reader in Laws of British Commonwealth and United States, Oxford Univ., 1972–89; Prof. and Head of Dept of Law, Univ. of Malaŵi, 1976–78; Biolchini Prof. of Law, Univ. of Notre Dame, USA, 1995–. Huber Distinguished Vis. Prof., Boston Coll. Law Sch., 1993–94. Special Adviser to Foreign Affairs Cttee, House of Commons, on role of UK Parlt in Canadian Constitution, 1980–82; Consultor, Pontifical Commn, Iustitia et Pax, 1977–89; Member: Pontifical Council de Iustitia et Pace, 1990–95; Catholic Bishops' Jt Cttee on Bio-Ethical Issues, 1981–88; Internat. Theol Commn, The Vatican, 1986–92; Pontifical Acad. for Life, 2001–. Governor, Linacre Centre, London, 1981–96, 1998– (Vice-Chm., 1987–96, 2002–07). *Publications:* Commonwealth and Dependencies, in Halsbury's Laws of England, 4th edn, Vol. 6, 1974, revised 1991, 2003; Natural Law and Natural Righ 1980; Fundamentals of Ethics, 1983; (with Joseph Boyle and Germain Grisez) Nucle Deterrence, Morality and Realism, 1987; Moral Absolutes, 1991; Aquinas: mor political, and legal theory, 1998. *Address:* University College, Oxford OX1 4BH. (01865) 276602.

FINNISSY, Michael Peter; composer; Professor of Composition, University Southampton, since 1999; *b* 17 March 1946; *s* of George Norman Finnissy and Ri Isolene Finnissy (*née* Parsonson). *Educ:* Hawes Down Jun. Sch.; Bromley Tech. High Sch Beckenham and Penge Grammar Sch.; Royal Coll. of Music. Lectr, Music Dept, Londo Sch. of Contemporary Dance, 1969–74; Artist-in-Residence, Victorian Coll. of the Ar Melbourne, Australia, 1982–83; Lectr, Dartington Summer Sch., 1981, 1990, 1992 Consultant Tutor in Composition, Winchester Coll., 1988–; Res. Fellow in Music, Uni of Sussex, 1989–99; Mem., Composition Faculty, Royal Acad. of Music, 1990–200 KBC Prof. of New Music, Katholieke Univ., Leuven, 1999–2001. Pres., ISCM, 1990– (Hon. Mem., 1998–). Hon. FRCM. *Compositions include:* Eighteen Songs, 1963–7 World (vocal/orchestral), 1968–74; Tsuru-Kame (stage work), 1971–73; Mysteries (sta work), 1972–79; Verdi Transcriptions (piano), 1972–88; Cipriano (choral), 1974; Seve Piano Concertos, 1975–81; Pathways of Sun & Stars (orchestral), 1976; English Countr Tunes (piano), 1977; Alongside (orchestral), 1979; Sea and Sky (orchestral), 1979–8 Kelir (choral), 1981; The Undivine Comedy (stage work), 1985–88; Thérèse Raqu (stage work), 1992; Folklore (piano), 1993–94; Liturgy of S Paul (vocal), 1993–9 Shameful Vice (stage work), 1994; Speak its Name! (orchestral), 1996; The History Photography in Sound (piano), 1993–2000; This Church (choral), 2000–03; Six Se Minuets Three Trios (string quartet), 2003; Molly-House (open ensemble), 2004; Secon String Quartet, 2006–07; Grieg Quintettsatz, 2007; Mankind (stage work), 2007– *Address:* c/o Oxford University Press, Walton Street, Oxford OX2 6DP. *T:* (0186 556767.

FINUCANE, Brendan Godfrey Eamonn; QC 2003; a Recorder, since 2000; *b* March 1952; *s* of Raymond and Feardar Finucane; *m* 1998, Fiona Rosalie Horlick; two two *d* from former marriage. *Educ:* Bedford Coll., Univ. of London (BSc Hons Sociol. a Social Admin). Called to the Bar, Middle Temple, 1976, Bencher, 2006; in practic specialising in criminal law and medico-legal work. Member Council: Tate Membe 2001–; Friends of BM, 2002–. Chm., Equipment for Independent Living (Charity 1996–. Mem. Bd Dirs, City & Guilds of London Art Sch., 2006– (Chm., Develt Ctte 2004–). Trustee, Paintings in Hosps. *Recreations:* collecting art, architecture, theatr cinema, visiting art galleries, music. *Address:* 23 Essex Street, WC2R 3AA. *T:* (020) 741 0353, *Fax:* (020) 7413 0374; *e-mail:* BrendanFinucane@23es.com. *Clubs:* Athenæur Chelsea Arts.

FIORINA, Carleton S., (Carly); Director: Cybertrust, since 2005; Revolution Heal Group, since 2005; *b* Austin, Texas, 6 Sept. 1954. *Educ:* Stanford Univ. (BA 1976); Uni of Maryland (MBA 1980); Sloan Sch. of Mgt, MIT (MSc 1989); UCLA. Joined AT& 1980: posts included account exec., Sen. Vice-Pres. of Global Mktg, and Pres., Atlan and Canadian Region; Lucent Technologies (formerly subsid. of AT&T), 1996–99: Vic Pres. of Corp. Ops; Pres., Global Service Provider Business; Chm. and CEO, Hewle Packard Co., 1999–2005. Formerly Director: Kellogg Co.; Merck & Co. Inc.; non-exe Dir, Cisco Systems Inc., 2001. Mem., US China Bd of Trade. *Publication:* Tough Choice a memoir, 2006.

FIRNBERG, David; Principal, DFA Ltd, since 1989; *b* 1 May 1930; *s* of L. B. Firnbe and K. L. E. Firnberg; *m* 1957, Sylvia Elizabeth du Cros; one *s* three *d*. *Educ:* Mercha Taylors' Sch., Northwood. Went West, 1953–56; Television Audience Measurement Lt 1956–59; ICT/ICL, 1959–72; David Firnberg Associates Ltd, 1972–74; Dir, N Computing Centre Ltd, 1974–79; Eosys Ltd: Man. Dir, 1980–88; Chm., 1989–91; Chn The Networking Centre Ltd, 1985–91; Chief Exec., Strategic Planning Soc., 1985–8 President: UK Assoc. of Project Managers, 1978–84 (Hon. Fellow 1984); Briti Computer Soc., 1983–84 (Chm., IT Support for Disabled People project, 1989–9 Chairman: UK Council for Computing Devel̃t, 1990–91; Steering Cttee, RSA Desi Bursaries for Communications and Computing, 1989–94; Member: Foundn for Sci. a Technology, 1987–; Council, PITCOM, 1989–2002; Quality Audit Steering Counc Higher Educn Quality Council, 1992–97. Chm., Buckingham DFAS, 2004–08. Freema City of London, 1987. FBCS 1973; FInstD 1982; FRSA 1978. *Publications:* Compute Management and Information, 1973; Cassell's New Spelling Dictionary, 1976; Cassel Spelling Dictionary, 1984; (ed) The Blooding of Bourton, 2003; historical vignett *Address:* Mastings, Main Street, Preston Bissett, Buckingham MK18 4JR. *T:* (0128 848772; *e-mail:* david@firnberg.com.

FIRRELL, Lucy Morgan; *see* Theis, L. M.

FIRTH, Colin; actor; *b* 10 Sept. 1960; *s* of David and Shirley Firth; one *s* by Meg Tilly; 1997, Livia Guiggioli; two *s*. *Educ:* Montgomery of Alamein Sch., Winchester; Londo Drama Centre. *Stage* includes: Another Country, Queen's, 1983; The Lonely Road, O Vic, 1985; The Elms, Greenwich, 1987; The Caretaker, Almeida, 1991; Chatsk Almeida, 1993; Three Days of Rain, Donmar Warehouse, 1999; *films* include: Anoth Country, 1983; A Month in the Country, 1986; Valmont, 1988; Wings of Fame, 19 The Hour of the Pig, 1992; Circle of Friends, 1995; The English Patient, 1996; Fev Pitch, 1997; Shakespeare in Love, The Secret Laughter of Women, 1999; My Life So F Relative Values, 2000; Bridget Jones's Diary, 2001; The Importance of Being Earne 2002; Hope Springs, What A Girl Wants, Love Actually, 2003; Girl with a Pearl Earrin Trauma, Bridget Jones: The Edge of Reason, 2004; Nanny McPhee, Where the Tru Lies, 2005; And When Did You Last See Your Father?, The Last Legion, St Trinian 2007; The Accidental Husband, Mamma Mia!, 2008; *television* includes: Dutch Gir 1984; Tumbledown, 1987; Out of the Blue, 1990; The Deep Blue Sea, 1994; Pride a Prejudice, 1995; Nostromo, 1996; The Turn of the Screw, 1999; Donovan Quick, 200 *Address:* c/o Independent Talent Group Ltd, Oxford House, 76 Oxford Street, W1D 1B *T:* (020) 7636 6565.

FIRTH, Prof. David, PhD; FBA 2008; Professor of Statistics, University of Warwic since 2003; *b* Wakefield, Yorks, 22 Dec. 1957; *s* of Allan Firth and Betty Firth (*née* Bailey *m* 1987, Julie McCormack; one *s* two *d*. *Educ:* Trinity Hall, Cambridge (BA Maths 198 Imperial Coll. London (MSc 1982; PhD Stats 1987). Asst Prof., Univ. of Texas at Austi 1987–89; Lectr, Univ. of Southampton, 1989–93; Prof. of Social Stats, University Oxford, 1993–2003. Professorial Fellow, ESRC, 2003–06. *Publications:* contrib. articles learned jls incl. Biometrika, Jl Royal Statistical Soc., BMJ. *Recreations:* cycling, walkin *Address:* Department of Statistics, University of Warwick, Coventry CV4 7AL. *T:* (02 7657 2581, *Fax:* (024) 7652 4532; *e-mail:* d.firth@warwick.ac.uk.

FIRTH, (David) Colin; Headmaster, Cheadle Hulme School, 1977–89, retired; *b* 29 Ja 1930; *s* of Jack and Muriel Firth; *m* 1954, Edith Scanlan; three *s* one *d*. *Educ:* Rothw Grammar Sch.; Sheffield Univ. (BSc, DipEd). Royal Signals, 1952–54; Stand Gramm Sch., 1954–57; East Barnet Grammar Sch., 1957–61; Bristol Grammar Sch., 1961–73; T

Gilberd Sch., 1973–77. Treasurer: Penrith Music Club, 1995–; Penrith and Dist Probus Club; Watermillock Painting Gp. *Publications:* A Practical Organic Chemistry, 1966; Elementary Thermodynamics, 1969; (jtly) Introductory Physical Science, 1971. *Recreations:* golf, fell walking, talking about gardening, singing. *Address:* Hill House, Fell Lane, Penrith, Cumbria CA11 8BJ.

FIRTH, Mrs Joan Margaret, CB 1995; PhD; Chair, Bradford Health Authority, 1998–2000 (Vice Chair, 1996–98); Deputy Director of NHS Finance, Department of Health, 1990–95; *b* 25 March 1935; *d* of Ernest Wilson and Ann (*née* Crowther); *m* 1955, Kenneth Firth. *Educ:* Lawnswood High Sch., Leeds; Univ. of Leeds (1st Cl. BSc Colour Chemistry; PhD Dyeing of Wool). Research Asst, Leeds Univ., 1958–60; Head of Science, Selby High Sch., 1960–62; Sen. Lecturer in General Science, Elizabeth Gaskell Coll., Manchester, 1962–66; Lectr in Organic Chemistry, Salford Univ., 1966–67; joined Civil Service as Direct Entry Principal, 1967; Asst Sec., 1974; Under-Sec., DHSS, 1981; Under-Sec., Social Security Div. C, DHSS, later DSS, 1987–90. Member: ESRC, 1988–92; Training Bd, 1990–92. Mem., Audit Cttee, Inst. Cancer Res., 1994–98. *Publication:* contrib. Jl Textile Inst., 1958. *Recreations:* wine, walking.

FIRTH, Paul James; writer (part-time); a District Judge (Magistrates' Courts), Lancashire, 2001–05; *b* 2 June 1951; *s* of Albert and Violet Firth; *m* 1979, Ann Barbara Whitehead; one *s. Educ:* Bradford Grammar Sch.; Queen's Coll., Oxford (Hastings Exhibnr; MA 1973). Admitted solicitor, 1980; Trainee Court Clerk, Keighley Magistrates' Court, 1973–74; Trainee Court Clerk, Court Clerk, then Sen. Court Clerk, Leeds Magistrates' Court, 1975–81; Dep. Clerk to Justices (Legal), Manchester City Magistrates' Court, 1981–86; Clerk to Justices, Rotherham Magistrates' Court, 1986–95; Actg Stipendiary Magistrate, 1991–95; Stipendiary Magistrate, subseq. Dist Judge (Magistrates' Cts), Merseyside, 1995–2001. *Publications:* Four Minutes to Hell: the story of the Bradford City fire, 2005; contrib. The City Gent, New Law Jl, Yorkshire Post. *Recreations:* beginners' golf, various sports (reduced to watching, especially Bradford City), reading anything except law books. *Address: e-mail:* paulfirth@blueyonder.co.uk. *Club:* Yorkshire CC.

FIRTH, Rt Rev. Peter James; Bishop Suffragan of Malmesbury, 1983–94; Hon. Assistant Bishop, diocese of Gloucester, since 2003; *b* 12 July 1929; *s* of Atkinson Vernon Firth and Edith Pepper; *m* 1955, Felicity Mary Wilding; two *s* two *d* (and one long-term foster *d*). *Educ:* Stockport Grammar School; Emmanuel Coll., Cambridge (Open Exhibnr, MA, DipEd); Pres., Cambridge Footlights, 1953); St Stephen's House Theol Coll., Oxford. Ordained, 1955; Assistant Curate, St Stephen's, Barbourne in Worcester, 1955–58; Priest-in-charge, Church of the Ascension, Parish of St Matthias, Malvern Link, Worcs, 1958–62; Rector of St George's, Abbey Hey, Gorton in Manchester, 1962–66; Religious Broadcasting Assistant, North Region, BBC, 1966–67; Religious Broadcasting Organiser and Senior Producer, Religious Programmes, BBC South and West, Bristol, 1967–83. Religious Advr to HTV West, 1983–2003; Mem., W of England TV Council, 2003–. Pres., Religious Drama Soc. of GB, 1994–. Trustee, Bristol Cancer Help Centre, 1995–2007. Governor: Millfield Sch., 1994–2002. Clifton Coll., 1995–2007; Internat. Radio Festival winner, Seville, 1975. *Publications:* Lord of the Seasons, 1978; The Love that moves the Sun, 1996. *Recreations:* theatre, photography, music, travel, Manchester United. *Address:* Mill House, Silk Mill Lane, Winchcombe GL54 5HZ. *T:* (01242) 603669; *e-mail:* peter.united4@btinternet.com.

FIRTH, Tazeena Mary; designer; *b* 1 Nov. 1935; *d* of Denis Gordon Firth and Irene (*née* Morris). *Educ:* St Mary's, Wantage; Chatelard Sch. Theatre Royal, Windsor, 1954–57; English Stage Co., Royal Court, 1957–60; partnership in stage design with Timothy O'Brien estabd 1961; output incl.: The Bartered Bride, The Girl of the Golden West, 1962; West End prodns of new plays, 1963–64; London scene of Shakespeare Exhibn, 1964; Tango, Days in the Trees, Staircase, RSC, and Trafalgar at Madame Tussaud's, 1966; All's Well that Ends Well, As You Like It, Romeo and Juliet, RSC, 1967; The Merry Wives of Windsor, Troilus and Cressida (also Nat. Theatre, 1976), The Latent Heterosexual, RSC, 1968; Pericles (also Comédie Française, 1974), Women Beware Women, Bartholomew Fair, RSC, 1969; Measure for Measure, RSC, Madame Tussaud's in Amsterdam, and The Knot Garden, Royal Opera, 1970; Enemies, Man of Mode, RSC, 1971; La Cenerentola, Oslo, Lower Depths, and The Island of the Mighty, RSC, As You Like It, OCSC, 1972; Richard II, Love's Labour's Lost, RSC, 1973; Next of Kin, NT, Summerfolk, RSC, and The Bassarids, ENO, 1974; John Gabriel Borkman, NT, Peter Grimes, Royal Opera (later in Paris), The Marrying of Ann Leete, RSC, 1975; Wozzeck, Adelaide Fest., The Zykovs, RSC, and The Force of Habit, NT, 1976; Tales from the Vienna Woods, Bedroom Farce, NT, and Falstaff, Berlin Opera, 1977; The Cunning Little Vixen, Göteborg, Evita, London (later in USA, Australia, Vienna), A Midsummer Night's Dream, Sydney Opera House, 1978; Peter Grimes, Göteborg, The Rake's Progress, Royal Opera, 1979; Turandot, Vienna State Opera, 1983. Designed independently: The Two Gentlemen of Verona, RSC, 1969; Occupations, RSC, 1971; The Rape of Lucretia, Karlstad, 1982; Katherina Ismailova, Göteborg, 1984; La Traviata, Umeå, The Trojan Woman, Göteborg, and Bluebeard's Castle, Copenhagen, 1985; Il Seraglio, Göteborg, 1986; The Magic Flute, Rigoletto, Umeå, 1987; Romeo and Juliet, Malmö, 1988; The Rake's Progress, Göteborg, and, Dido and Aeneas, Copenhagen, 1989; From the House of the Dead, Göteborg, and, Barbarians, RSC, 1990; Macbeth, Göteborg, 1990; Lady Macbeth of Mtsensk, Copenhagen, La Bohème, Malmö, and Il Seraglio, Stockholm, 1991; Don Giovanni, Prague, 1991; Rigoletto, Oslo, and Carmen, Copenhagen, 1992; Carmen, Stockholm, Drot og Mask, Copenhagen, Magic Flute, Prague and Peter Grimes, Copenhagen, 1993; Vox Humana, Göteborg, 1994; Don Giovanni, Japan, Dido and Aeneas, and Oh Come Ye Sons of Art, Dröttningholm, Bluebeard's Castle, and Jenůfa, Göteborg, 1995; Peter Grimes, Göteborg and Finnish Nat. Opera, and Jenůfa, Copenhagen, 1998; Peter Grimes, New Israeli Opera, Tel Aviv, 2002. (Jtly) Gold Medal for Set Design, Prague Quadriennale, 1975. *Recreations:* sailing, walking. *Address:* Faraway, Keyhaven Marshes, Lymington SO41 0TR.

FISCHEL, David Andrew; Chief Executive, Liberty International (formerly TransAtlantic Holdings) plc, since 2001; *b* 1 April 1958. ACA 1983. Touche Ross & Co., 1980–85; with TransAtlantic Holdings, later Liberty International, 1985–: Man. Dir, 1992–2001. *Address:* c/o Liberty International plc, 40 Broadway, SW1H 0BT. *T:* (020) 7960 1200.

FISCHEL, Robert Gustav; QC 1998; proprietor, El Molino de la Cala hotel, Estepona; *b* 12 Jan. 1953; *s* of Bruno Rolf Fischel and Sophie Fischel (*née* Kruml); *m* 1st, 1989, Louise Kim Halsall (marr. diss. 1997); 2nd, 1999, Anna Louise, *d* of Patrick Landucci. *Educ:* City of London Sch.; Univ. of London (LLB). Called to the Bar, Middle Temple, 1975; in practice at the Bar, 1975–. *Recreations:* cooking, horse riding, ski-ing, travel. *Address:* Avenida de España 70–316, 29680 Estepona, Málaga, Spain.

FISCHER, August Antonios; Chairman and Chief Executive Officer, Axel Springer Verlag AG, Germany, 1998–2001; *b* 7 Feb. 1939; *s* of August Fischer and Elisabeth Fischer (*née* Zanola); *m* 1961, Gillian Ann Streete; one *s* one *d. Educ:* Univ. of Zurich, Switzerland (BA Business Admin). E. I. Du Pont de Nemours & Co., 1962–78; Napp Systems (Europe) Ltd, 1978–81; Napp Systems Inc., 1981–88; News International plc, 1989–95

(Chief Exec., 1994–95); Dir, Ringier AG, Switzerland, 1995–97; Dir, Ringier America Inc., USA, 1995. *Address:* 58 Egerton Crescent, SW3 2ED.

FISCHER, Dr Edmond Henri; Professor Emeritus, University of Washington, since 1990; *b* Shanghai, China, 6 April 1920; *s* of Oscar Fischer and Renee Tapernoux; *m* 1963, Beverley Bullock; two *s. Educ:* Univ. of Geneva (Licencié ès Sciences 1943; Diplôme d'Ingenieur 1944; DSc 1947). Asst, Labs of Organic Chem., Univ. of Geneva, 1946–47; Fellow, Swiss Nat. Foundn, 1948–50; Res. Fellow, Rockefeller Foundn, 1950–53; Res. Associate, Div. of Biol., CIT, 1953; University of Washington: Asst Prof. of Biochem., 1953–56; Associate Prof., 1956–61; Prof., 1961–90. Associate, Neurosciences Res. Prog., Neuroscience Res. Inst., La Jolla, Calif, 1995–. Member: Biochem. Section, NIH, 1959–64; Editl Adv. Bd, Biochemistry, Jl of ACS, 1961–66 (Associate Editor, 1966–92); Adv. Bd, ACS, 1962; Sci. Adv. Bd, Friedrich Miescher Inst. CIBA-GEIGY, 1976–84 (Chm., 1981–84); Council, Amer. Soc. Biol Chemists, 1980–83; Scientific Council on Basic Sci., Amer. Heart Assoc., 1977–80; Bd of Scientific Govs, Scripps Res. Inst., 1987–; Scientific Adv. Cttee, Muscular Dystrophy Assoc., 1980–89; Scientific Adv. Bd, Basel Inst. for Immunology, 1996–; Bd Govs, Weizmann Inst. of Sci., Israel, 1997–; Chm., Task Force, Muscular Dystrophy Assoc. Res. Centres, 1985–89. Member: Amer. Soc. Biol Chemists; ACS; Amer. Acad. of Arts and Scis, 1972; AAAS 1972; NAS 1973; Amer. Assoc. of Univ. Profs. Pres., Pole Universitaire de Montpellier, 1993–96. Hon. PhD: Montpellier 1985; Basel 1988; Med. Coll. of Ohio, 1993; Indiana, 1993; Ruhr-Univ., 1994. Numerous awards, medals and prizes; Nobel Prize in Physiology or Medicine, 1992. *Publications:* numerous. *Recreations:* playing classical piano, private pilot. *Address:* Department of Biochemistry, Box 357350, University of Washington, Seattle, WA 98195–7350, USA. *T:* (206) 5431741.

FISCHER, Iván; conductor; Founder and Music Director, Budapest Festival Orchestra, since 1983; *b* Budapest, 20 Jan. 1951; *s* of Sándor Fischer and Éva Boschán; two *d. Educ:* Béla Bartók Music Conservatory, Budapest; Wiener Hochschule für Musik; Mozarteum, Salzburg. Début in London with RPO, 1976; Music Director: Northern Sinfonia, Newcastle, 1979–82; Kent Opera, 1984–89; Lyons Opera House, 1999–2003; Principal Guest Conductor, Cincinnati SO, 1989–96; Principal Guest Conductor, 2006–08, Principal Conductor, 2008–, Nat. SO, Washington. Concert tours with LSO, to Spain, 1981, USA, 1982, world tour, 1983; concerts with orchestras, including: Berlin Philharmonic, Concertgebouw; Munich Philharmonic; Israel Philharmonic; Orch. de Paris; Orch. of Age of Enlightenment; LA and NY Philharmonics; Cleveland; Philadelphia; San Francisco Symphony; Chicago Symphony; opera prodns in London, Paris, Vienna. Has made recordings. Patron, British Kódaly Acad.; Founder, Hungarian Mahler Soc. Premio Firenze, 1974; Rupert Foundn Award, BBC, 1976; Gramophone Award for Best Orchestral Recording of Year, 1998; Crystal Award, World Econ. Forum, 1998. Golden Medal Award (Hungary), 1998. *Address:* Andrássy ut 27, 1061 Budapest, Hungary.

FISCHER, Joseph Martin, (Joschka); Visiting Lecturer, Woodrow Wilson School of Public and International Affairs, Princeton University, 2006–07; Minister of Foreign Affairs and Deputy Chancellor, Germany, 1998–2005; *b* 12 April 1948; *m* 1st, 1967, Edeltraud (marr. diss. 1984); 2nd, 1984, Inge (marr. diss. 1987); one *s* one *d*; 3rd, 1987, Claudia Bohm (marr. diss. 1999); 4th, 1999, Nicola Leske (marr. diss. 2003); 5th, 2005, Minu Barati. Mem., Green Party, Germany, 1982– (former Leader). State of Hesse: Minister for the Envmt and Energy, 1985–87; Mem., Landtag, 1987–91 (Chm., Green Party); Minister for the Envmt, Energy and Fed. Affairs, and Dep. to Minister-Pres., 1991–94; Mem., Bundestag, 1983–85, 1994–2006; Dep. Mem., Bundesrat, 1985–87; Parly spokesman, Alliance '90/Green Party, Bundestag, 1994–98. *Publication:* The Red-Green Years (autobiog.), 2007.

FISCHER, Hon. Timothy Andrew, AC 2005; Director, Australian Agricultural Co., since 2001; National Chairman, Royal Flying Doctor Service, since 2007; *b* 3 May 1946; *s* of J. R. Fischer; *m* 1992, Judy, *d* of Harry Brewer; two *s. Educ:* Xavier Coll., Melbourne. Platoon Comdr and Transport Officer, RAR, 1967; Nat. Service, S Vietnam, 1968–69. Primary producer, Boree Creek, 1964–65, 1970. MLA Sturt, 1971–80, Murray, 1980–84, NSW; Nat. Party Whip, NSW, 1981–84; MP (Nat.) Farrer, NSW, 1984–2001; Shadow Minister: for Veterans' Affairs, 1985–90; for Energy and Resources, 1990–93; for Trade, 1993–96; Dep. Prime Minister and Minister for Trade, 1996–99; Leader, Nat. Party of Australia, 1990–99. Chm., Tourism Australia, 2004–07. *Recreations:* chess, tennis, trekking, bushwalking in Bhutan. *Address:* Peppers, PO Box 10, Boree Creek, NSW 2652, Australia.

FISCHER BOEL, (Else) Mariann; Member, European Commission, since 2004; *b* 15 April 1943; *d* of Hans Boel and Valborg Boel; *m* 1967, Hans Fischer Boel. Mgt Sec., 1965–67, Finance Manager, 1967–71, export co., Copenhagen. Mem., Munkebo Municipal Council, 1982–91, 1994–97. MP (L) Denmark, 1990–2004; Minister for Food, Agriculture and Fisheries, 2001–04. *Address:* European Commission, Rue de la Loi 200, 1049 Brussels, Belgium.

FISCHER-DIESKAU, Dietrich; baritone; *b* Berlin, 28 May 1925; *s* of Dr Albert Fischer-Dieskau; *m* 1949, Irmgard Poppen (*d* 1963); three *s. Educ:* High Sch., Berlin; Music Academy, Berlin. First Baritone, Städtische Oper, Berlin, 1948–78; Hon. Mem., 1978–; Mem., Vienna State Opera, 1957–63. Extensive Concert Tours of Europe and USA; soloist in Festivals at Edinburgh, Salzburg, Bayreuth, Vienna, Berlin, Munich, Holland, Luzern, Prades, etc. Opera roles include: Wolfram, Jochanaan, Almaviva, Marquis Posa, Don Giovanni, Falstaff, Mandryka, Wozzeck, Danton, Macbeth, Hans Sachs. Many recordings. Prof., Music Acad., Berlin, 1983; Member: Acad. of Arts, Berlin; Acad. of Fine Arts, Munich; Hon. RAM, 1972; Honorary Member: Wiener Konzerthausgesellschaft, 1962; Königlich-Schwedische Akad., 1972; Acad. Santa Cecilia, Rome; Royal Philharmonic Soc., 1985. Hon. DMus Oxford, 1978; Dr *hc:* Sorbonne, 1980; Yale, 1980. Kunstpreis der Stadt Berlin, 1950; Internationaler Schallplattenpreis, since 1955 nearly every year; Orfeo d'oro, 1955 and 1966; Bayerischer Kammersänger, 1959; Edison Prize, 1961, 1964, 1966, 1970; Naras Award, USA, 1962; Mozart-Medaille, Wien, 1962; Berliner Kammersänger, 1963; Electrola Award, 1970; Léonie Sonning Music Prize, Copenhagen, 1975; Golden Gramophone Award, Germany, 1975; Ruckert-Preis, Schweinfurt, 1979; President's Prize, Charles Gros Acad., Paris, 1980; Ernst Von Siemens Prize, 1980; Artist of the Year, Phonoakademie, Germany, 1980; Gold Medal, Royal Philharmonic Soc., 1988. Bundesverdienstkreuz (1st class), 1958, Grosses Verdienstkreuz, 1974, Stern zum Grossen Bundesverdienstkreuz, 1986; Pour le mérite, Deutschland (FRG), 1984; Chevalier de la Légion d'Honneur (France), 1990. *Publications:* Texte Deutscher Lieder, 1968 (The Fischer-Dieskau Book of Lieder, 1976); Auf den Spuren der Schubert-Lieder, 1971; Wagner und Nietzsche, 1974; Robert Schumann—Wort und Musik, 1981; Töne sprechen, Worte klingen, 1985; Nachklang, 1987; Wenn Musik der Liebe Nahrung ist: Künstlerschicksale im 19 Jahrhundert, 1990; Weil nicht alle Blütenträume reifen (Reichardt), 1991; Johann Friedrich Reichardt: Kapellmeister dreier Preussenkönige, 1992; Fern die Klage des Fauns (Debussy), 1993; Carl Friedrich Zelter (biog.), 1997.

FISCHLER, Dr Franz; Member, European Commission, 1995–2004; b 23 Sept. 1946; s of Josef Fischler and Theodora Fischler; m 1973, Adelheid Hausmann; two s two d. Educ: Univ. for Soil Sci., Vienna (Dr in Natural Scis 1978). Univ. Asst, Dept of Regl Agricl Planning., Inst. for Farm Mgt, Vienna, 1973–79; Tyrol Chamber of Agriculture: Mem., 1979–84; Dir, 1985–89; elected Mem., Nationalrat, 1990, 1994; Fed. Minister of Agric. and Forestry, 1989–94. Grosse Goldene Ehrenzeichen am Bande (Austria), 1993. Address: Dörferstrasse 30B, 6067 Absam, Austria.

FISH, David John, PhD; Chairman, United Biscuits, since 2004; b 31 May 1948; s of George Henry and Edith Doreen Fish; m 1976, Linda Pamela Robinson; one s two d. Educ: Gateway Grammar Sch., Leicester; Univ. of Sheffield (BSc 1st cl. 1969, Mappin Medal; PhD Metal Physics 1972). Unilever, 1972–74; joined Mars, 1974; Operating Bd, Mars Inc., 1994–2001; Pres., European Snackfoods, 1998–2000; Jt Pres., Masterfoods Europe, 2000–01. Non-exec. Dir, Royal Mail, 2003–. Recreations: cricket, ski-ing, tennis, golf, music. Address: e-mail: David-j-fish@hotmail.com. Club: Wentworth.

FISH, Prof. David Royden, MD; FRCP; Medical Director (Specialist Hospitals), University College London Hospitals NHS Trust, since 2001; Professor of Clinical Neurophysiology and Epilepsy, University College London, since 2000; b 5 June 1956; s of George Henry Fish and Sadie Fish; m 1986, Glenda Joyce Parker; one s one d (twins). Educ: Selwyn Coll., Cambridge (BA 1978); King's Coll., London (MB BS 1981; MD 1989). FRCP 1994. Asst Prof., Neurology, McGill Univ., Montreal, 1988–89; Consultant Physician, Nat. Hosp. for Neurology and Neurosurgery, 1989–. Publications: contribs to learned jls and books on medical subjects incl. epilepsy, brain imaging, safety of video games and health care. Recreations: opera, trekking. Address: University College London Hospitals NHS Trust HQ, John Astor House, 3 Foley Street, W1W 6DN. T: (020) 7380 9750; e-mail: david.fish@UCLH.org.

FISH, David Stanley, CBE 2007; Director, East and Central Africa (formerly Africa), Department for International Development, since 2004; b 4 Oct. 1948; s of John and Phyllis Fish; m 1st, 1971, Sandra Templeton (marr. diss. 1990); two d; 2nd, 1992, Marion Fleming Semple; two d. Educ: Baines Grammar Sch., Poulton-le-Fylde. Department for International Development: Head: Develt Educn Unit, 1979–81; Manpower Policy Unit, 1981–84; Dependent Territories Section, British Develt Div. in the Caribbean, Barbados, 1985–86; Accounts Dept, 1986–88; Overseas Pensions Dept, 1988–93; Procurement, Appts and NGO Dept, 1993–97; Eastern Africa, Nairobi, 1997–99; Dir of Human Resources, 2000–04. Recreations: sport, politics, dog walking, supporting Blackpool and Crystal Palace. Address: 34 Shawton Road, Chapelton, Strathaven, Lanarkshire ML10 6RY; e-mail: dave-fish@dfid.gov.uk. Club: Chapelton Inn Racing.

FISH, David Thomas; QC 1997; a Recorder, since 1994; b 23 July 1949; s of Tom Fish and Gladys (née Durkin); m 1989, Angelina Brunhilde Dennett; one s one d. Educ: Ashton-under-Lyne Grammar Sch.; London Sch. of Econs (LLB). Called to the Bar, Inner Temple, 1973. Recreations: horse-racing, golf. Address: Deans Court Chambers, 24 St John Street, Manchester M3 4DF. T: (0161) 214 6000.

FISH, Prof. Francis, OBE 1989; BPharm, PhD; FRPharmS; Dean, School of Pharmacy, 1978–88 (Hon. Fellow, 1992), Professor of Pharmacy, 1988, Professor Emeritus, 1989, University of London; b 20 April 1924; s of William Fish and Phyllis (née Griffiths); m 1949, Hilda Mary Brown (d 2003); two s. Educ: Houghton-le-Spring Grammar Sch.; Technical Coll., Sunderland (now Univ. of Sunderland). BPharm (London) 1946; PhD (Glasgow) 1955. FPS 1946. Asst Lectr, 1946–48, Lectr, 1948–62, Royal Coll. of Science and Technology, Glasgow; University of Strathclyde: Sen. Lectr, 1962–69; Reader in Pharmacognosy and Forensic Science, 1969–76; Personal Prof., 1976–78; Dean, Sch. of Pharmaceutical Sciences, 1977–78; Supervisor, MSc course in Forensic Science, 1966–78. Mem. Editorial Bd, Jl Pharm. Pharmacol., 1964–70 and 1975–78. Member: Pharm. Soc. Cttee on Pharmacognosy, 1963–74; British Pharm. Codex Pharmacognosy Sub-Cttee A, 1968–73; Brit. Pharm. Conf. Sci. Cttee, 1973–78 (Science Chm., 1977); Brit. Pharmacopoeia Pharmacognosy Panel, 1974–77; Council, Forensic Science Soc., 1974–77 (Vice-Pres., 1981–82); Professional and Gen. Services Cttee, Scottish Council on Alcoholism, 1976–78; British Pharmacopœia Commn, 1980–91; Cttee on Safety of Medicines, 1980–83 (Mem., Herbal Sub-Cttee, 1978–80; Mem., Chemistry, Pharmacy and Standards Sub-Cttee, 1980–92); Univ. of London Senate, 1981–88; DHSS Standing Pharmaceutical Adv. Cttee, 1982–88; UGC Panel on Studies Allied to Medicine, 1982–89 (Chm., 1984–89); Nuffield Foundn Cttee of Inquiry into Pharmacy, 1983–86; Cttee on Review of Medicines, 1984–91; UGC Medical Subcttee, 1984–89. Chm., Post Qualification Educn Bd for NHS Pharmacists in Scotland, 1989–92. Mem., Governing Body, Wye College, 1985–88. Harrison Meml Medal, 1982; Charter Gold Medal, RPSGB, 1987. Publications: (with J. Owen Dawson) Surgical Dressings, Ligatures and Sutures, 1967; research pubns and review articles in Pharmaceut., Phytochem. and Forensic Sci. jls. Address: Grianan, Hazel Avenue, Crieff, Perthshire PH7 3ER.

FISH, Jocelyn Barbara, DCNZM 2001; CBE 1991; voluntary community worker, since 1959; farming partner, 1959–90; b 29 Sept. 1930; d of John Arthur Green and Edna Marion Green (née Garton); m 1959, Robert John Malthus Fish; one s two d. Educ: Hamilton High Sch., New Zealand; Auckland Univ. (BA); Auckland Teachers' College (cert.). Secondary school teacher, NZ and UK, 1953–59. Nat. Pres., Nat. Council of Women of NZ, 1986–90; (various offices) NZ Fedn of Univ. Women, and Anglican Women; Chm. Policy Cttee, survey, NZ Women—family, employment and education, Centre for Population Studies, Univ. of Waikato, 1995–98. NZ Deleg., UN Conf. on Women, Nairobi, 1985. Member: Film Censorship Bd of Review, 1981–84; Nat. Commn for Australian Bicentenary, 1987–88; Nat. Commn for UNESCO, 1989–94; Broadcasting Standards Authority, 1989–91; Transport Accident Investigation Commn, 1990–95; Hamilton Dist Legal Services Cttee, 1992–97; NZ Dental Council Complaints Assessment Cttee, 1995–2001. Member, Board: Waikato Br., Fedn of Univ. Women, 1991–99 (Chm.); Hamilton Community Law Centre Trust, 1994–2000 (Chm.); Hamilton Combined Christian Foodbank Trust, 1997–99; Waikato Anglican Social Services Trust, 2000–04 (Chm.). Councillor, Piako County Council, 1980–89. JP 1984. Hon. Fellow, Waikato Inst. of Technol., 2003. NZ Sesquicentenary Commemoration Medal, 1990; NZ Suffrage Commemoration Medal, 1993. Recreations: music, literature, family, travel, watching politics. Address: 63 Gilbass Avenue, Hamilton, New Zealand. T: (7) 839 1512.

FISH, John, OBE 1996; Under-Secretary, Head of Establishment General Services Division, Department of Industry, 1974–80; b 16 July 1920; m 1948, Frances; two s. Educ: Lincoln School. BA Open Univ., 1989. Entered Customs and Excise, 1937; Exchequer and Audit Dept, 1939; War service, Pilot in RAF, 1940–46; Exchequer and Audit Dept, 1946; BoT, 1949; Principal, 1950; Min. of Materials, 1951; Volta River Preparatory Commn, Accra, 1953; BoT, 1956; Asst Sec., 1960; Min. of Health, 1962; BoT, 1965; DTI, 1970; Under-Sec., 1973; Dept of Industry, 1974. Civil Service Retirement Fellowship: Mem. Cttee of Mgt, 1985–95; Trustee, 1998–2001; formerly Sec., Vice Chm., Chm. and Pres., Warwicks Br. Address: Galanos House, Banbury Road, Southam, Warwicks CV47 2BL. Club: Civil Service.

FISH, His Honour Peter Stuart; a Circuit Judge, 1994–2005; b 18 Dec. 1938; s of Geoffrey Chadwick Fish and Emma (née Wood); m 1963, Nola Ann Worrall; two s one (and one d decd). Educ: Rydal Sch.; Trinity Hall, Cambridge (MA). Admitted solicitor 1963; practised in Southport, 1964–87; Dist Registrar, subseq. Dist Judge, Manchester 1987–94; a Recorder, 1991–94. Recreations: music, gardening, golf.

FISHBURN, (John) Dudley; Director, HSBC Bank plc, since 2003; company director b 8 June 1946; s of John Eskdale Fishburn and Bunting Fishburn; m 1981, Victoria, y d o Sir Jack Boles, qv; two s two d. Educ: Eton Coll.; Harvard Univ. (BA). Exec. Editor, Th Economist, 1979–88. MP (C) Kensington, July 1988–1997. Parliamentary Privat Secretary: FCO, 1989–90; DTI, 1990–93. Chairman: HFC Bank, 1998–; Henderso Smaller Cos Investment Trust plc, 2003–; Espresso Broadband Ltd, 2007–. Non-executive Director: Altria Inc. (USA), 1999–; Beazley Gp plc, 2002–; Adviser: J. P. Morgan 1988–96; T. T. Internat., 1997–; Baring Private Equity, 1997–. Chm., Standing Cttee on Social Scis, 1993–96, Library Cttee, 1996–2006, Harvard Univ.; Mem., Bd of Overseer Harvard Univ., 1990–96; Pres., Harvard Club of London, 1970–90. Governor, English National Ballet, 1989–95; Chairman: Trustees, Open Univ., 1995–2001; Library Adv Cttee, Cambridge Univ., 2006–; Member of Council: Nat. Trust, 1993–2005 (Hon Treas., 1996–2002); Prison Reform Trust, 1993–2000; Foundn for Liver Res. (formerl Liver Res. Trust), 1995–; Dulwich Picture Gall. Council, 1997–2001; Royal Oak Foundn (USA), 1997–2004; Reading Univ. Council, 2002–; Gov., Peabody Trust, 2000–. Editor The Economist's World in 1993, and annually until 2003; Associate Editor, The Economist, 1989–2003. DUniv Open, 2002. Parly Radical of the Year, 1992. Recreation: sailing, cooking. Address: 7 Gayfere Street, SW1P 3HN; The Old Rectory, Englefiel RG7 5EP. Club: Brooks's.

FISHER, family name of **Baron Fisher**.

FISHER, 3rd Baron cr 1909, of Kilverstone; **John Vavasseur Fisher,** DSC 1944; JP Director, Kilverstone Latin-American Zoo and Wild Life Park, 1973–91; b 24 July 1921 s of 2nd Baron and Jane (d 1955), d of Randal Morgan, Philadelphia, USA; S father, 1955 m 1st, 1949, Elizabeth Ann Penelope (marr. diss. 1969), yr d of late Herbert P. Holt, MC two s two d; 2nd, 1970, Hon. Mrs Rosamund Anne Fairbairn, d of 12th Baron Cliffor of Chudleigh. Educ: Stowe; Trinity Coll., Cambridge. Member: Eastern Gas Bd, 1962–71 East Anglia Economic Planning Council, 1971–77. DL Norfolk, 1968–82; JP Norfolk 1970. Heir: s Hon. Patrick Vavasseur Fisher [b 14 June 1953; m 1977, Lady Karen Carnegie, d of 13th Earl of Northesk; three s four d (of whom one s one d are twins)] Address: Marklye, Rushlake Green, Heathfield, Sussex TN21 9PN. T: (01435) 830270.
See also Baron Clifford of Chudleigh.

FISHER, Adrian; maze designer, inventor and author; Chairman, Adrian Fisher Maze Ltd, since 1983; b 5 Aug. 1951; s of James Frederick Fisher and Rosemary (née Sterling-Hill); m 1st, 1975, Dorothy Jane Pollard (marr. diss. 1996); two d; 2nd, 1997, Marie Ann Butterworth; one s. Educ: Oundle Sch.; Portsmouth Poly. Over 500 mazes created in 30 countries, 1979–; designer: world's first cornfield maize maze, Pennsylvania, 1993, and subseq. over 200 maize mazes; hedge mazes, including: Leeds Castle; Blenheim Palace Scone Palace; pioneer: of mirror mazes, including mazes at: Wookey Hole Caves Longleat House; London Dungeon; Navy Pier, Chicago; Birmingham Sea Life Centre Absolut Amaze, mirror maze at Oxo Gall., London, 2002; of brick-path-in-grass mazes and foaming fountain water mazes; walk-through parting waterfalls, foaming fountain gates and wrought-iron maze gates in mazes; inventor: 7-sided Fisher Paver system for decorative brick paving; (jtly) Mitre Tile system for paving, tiling and decorative patterns designer of puzzles for 2000 and 2006 World Puzzle Championships; one-man show: At Amazing Art: Contemporary Labyrinths, Norton Mus. of Art, W Palm Beach, Florida 1997. Set 6 Guinness world records for progressively larger cornfield mazes in USA and England, 1993–2003. Dir, 1991—The Year of the Maze, British tourism campaign Mem., Dorset Gdns Trust, 2002–. Mem., Eur. Bd, Themed Entertainment Assoc., 2005– Liveryman: Soc. of Apothecaries, 1979–; Gardeners' Co., 1991–. Gold Medal for Beatles Maze, Liverpool Internat. Garden Fest., 1984; Risorgimento Award, Univ. of Tennessee at Knoxville, 2003. Publications: The Art of the Maze, 1990; Secrets of the Maze, 1997 Mazes and Follies, 2004; Mazes and Labyrinths, 2004; The Amazing Book of Mazes, 2006 Recreations: gardening, photography, water-colour painting, recreational mathematics keeping sheep. Address: Adrian Fisher Mazes Ltd, Portman Lodge, Durweston, Dorse DT11 0QA. T: (01258) 450033; e-mail: adrian@mazemaker.com; web www.fishermazes.com.

FISHER, Andrew Charles; Chief Executive, Towry Law Group, since 2006; b 22 June 1961; s of Harold Fisher and Jessie Fisher (now Stanley); m 1987, Bernadette Johnson; two s. Educ: Birmingham Univ. (BSc Hons Econs). Mktg Manager, Unilever PLC, 1982–87 Partner, Coopers & Lybrand Mgt Consultancy, 1987–91; Sales and Mktg Dir, Standard Chartered Bank, Equitor Div., 1991–94; Man. Dir, Rangeley Co. Ltd, 1994–97; Strategic Advr, NatWest Wealth Mgt, 1997–98; Gp Commercial Dir, Coutts NatWest Gp 1998–2000; Chief Exec., Coutts Gp, 2000–02; Partner, Carlyle Gp, 2002–03; Chief Exec., CPP Gp, 2003–04; Gp CEO, Cox Insurance, 2004; Exec. Chm., JS & P, 2005–06 Non-exec. Dir, Benfield Gp Ltd, 2003–. Recreations: ski-ing, golf, squash, scuba diving Address: (office) Towry Law House, Western Road, Bracknell RG12 1TL. Clubs Mosimann's; Wentworth Golf.

FISHER, Carol Ann; Chief Executive, COI Communications (formerly Central Office of Information), 1999–2002; b 13 April 1954; d of Joseph and Gladys Fisher. Educ: Univ. of Birmingham (BA Hons Medieval and Modern Hist.). Brand Manager, Bisto, RHM Foods, 1979–81; Sen. Mktg Manager and various other posts, Grand Metropolitan Brewing, 1982–88; Mktg Dir, Holsten Distributors, 1989–94; Gen. Manager, Mktg and Commercial, Courage Internat., 1994–95; Man. Dir, CLT-UFA UK Radio Sales 1996–98. Chief Advr to Govt on Mktg Commns, 2002. Member: Women in Advertising and Communications (Pres., 2000–01); Mktg Soc.; Mktg Gp GB. Recreations: walking long haul travel.

FISHER, (Christopher) Mark; Chief Executive, Sector Skills Development Agency 2005; b 8 Oct. 1960; s of late Christopher Forsyth Fisher and of (Nadia) Ruth Reeve Fisher (née Angel); m 1997, Helen, d of late Patrick Daniel Fitzgibbon and of Marie Fitzgibbon, Lymm, Cheshire. Educ: King Edward's Sch., Bath; Lady Margaret Hall, Oxford (BA Hons PPE). Jun. posts, DHSS, 1983–87; Principal: Social Security Policy Gp, DSS, 1988–90; Econ. Secretariat, Cabinet Office, 1990–92; speech writer for Sec. of State for Social Security, 1992; mgt posts, 1993–97; Personnel and Communications Dir, 1997–2000, Benefits Agency; Human Resources Dir, DSS, subseq. DWP, 2000–01; Dir, Performance and Product Mgt, then Business Strategy, Jobcentre Plus, DWP, 2001–05. Recreations: good company, railways, canals.

FISHER, David Paul; QC 1996; a Recorder, since 1991; b 30 April 1949; s of late Percy Laurence Fisher and Doris Mary Fisher; m 1st, 1971, Cary Maria Cicely Lamberton (d 1977); one d; 2nd, 1979, Diana Elizabeth Dolby. Educ: Felsted Sch. Called to the Bar, Gray's Inn, 1973, Bencher, 2003; Asst Recorder, 1987. Member: Gen. Council of the Bar,

1997–2000; Advocacy Studies Bd, 1997–2001; Criminal Procedure Rule Cttee, 2004–. *Recreations:* travel, sport, gardening, cinema. *Address:* 6 King's Bench Walk, Temple, EC4Y 7DR. *T:* (020) 7583 0410.

FISHER, David Richard; Strategy Director, EDS (on secondment from Ministry of Defence), 2001–07; *b* 13 May 1947; *s* of William Horace and Margaret Catherine Fisher; *m* 1970, Sophia Josephine Hibbard; two *d*. *Educ:* Reading Sch.; St John's Coll., Oxford (BA 1969, 1st cl. LitHum, 1st cl. Hon. Mods). Ministry of Defence, 1970–2007: Private Sec. to successive RAF Ministers, 1973–74; naval programme and budget, 1976–79; Defence Budget, 1981–83; Vis. Res. Fellow, Nuffield Coll., Oxford, 1983–84; Head, Resources and Progs (Air), 1984–88; Defence Counsellor, UK Delegn to NATO, Brussels (on loan to FCO), 1988–92; Asst Under-Sec. of State (Systems), MoD, 1992–97; Dep. Hd, Defence and Overseas Secretariat, Cabinet Office, 1997–99 (on secondment); Dir, Defence Trng Review, MoD, 1999–2001. Mem., Management Cttee, Council on Christian Approaches to Defence and Disarmament. *Publications:* Morality and the Bomb, 1985; (contrib.) Ethics and European Security, 1986; (contrib.) Just Deterrence, 1990; (contrib.) Some Corner of a Foreign Field, 1998; (contrib.) The Crescent and the Cross, 1998; (contrib.) Britain's Bomb—What Next?, 2006; (contrib.) The Price of Peace, 2007; contribs to jls on defence and ethical issues. *Recreations:* philosophy, gardening. *Address:* Department of War Studies, King's College, Strand, WC2R 2LS. *Club:* Royal Commonwealth Society.

FISHER, Desmond (Michael); Vice-Chairman, Provincial Publishers Ltd, since 2002; *b* 9 Sept. 1920; *e s* of Michael Louis Fisher and Evelyn Kate Shier; *m* 1948, Margaret Elizabeth Smyth; three *s* one *d*. *Educ:* St Columb's Coll., Derry; Good Counsel Coll., New Ross, Co. Wexford; University Coll., Dublin (BA (NUI)). Asst Editor, Nationalist and Leinster Times, Carlow, 1945–48; Foreign Editor, Irish Press, Dublin, 1948–51; Economic Correspondent, Irish News Agency, Dublin, 1951–54; London Editor, Irish Press, 1954–62; Editor, Catholic Herald, 1962–66; Radio Telefis Eireann: Dep. Head of News, 1967–73; Head of Current Affairs, 1973–75; Dir of Broadcasting Develt, 1975–83; Nationalist and Leinster Times, Carlow: Ed. and Man. Dir, 1984–89; Exec. Dir, 1989–92; Chm., 1992–2001. *Publications:* The Church in Transition, 1967; Broadcasting in Ireland, 1978; The Right to Communicate: a status report, 1981; The Right to Communicate: a new human right, 1983; contributor to The Economist, The Furrow, Irish Digest and to various Irish, US and foreign magazines. *Address:* Louvain 22, Dublin 14, Ireland. *T:* (1) 2884608.

FISHER, Donald, CBE 1987; County Education Officer, Hertfordshire, 1974–90; *b* 20 Jan. 1931; *s* of John Wilfred and Mabel Fisher; *m* 1953, Mavis Doreen (*née* Sutcliffe); one *s* two *d*. *Educ:* Heckmondwike Grammar Sch.; Christ Church, Oxford (MA). Teacher, Hull GS, 1954–59; Admin. Asst, Cornwall LEA, 1959–61; Asst Educn Officer, W Sussex LEA, 1961–64; Headmaster: Helston GS, 1964–67; Midhurst GS, 1967–72; Dep. Educn Officer, W Sussex LEA, 1972–74. Chm., Assoc. of Educn Officers, 1982; Pres., Soc. of Educn Officers, 1984. Hon. DEd Hatfield Polytechnic, 1989. *Publications:* (contrib.) Educational Administration, 1980, 3rd edn 1989; articles and book reviews in Education. *Recreations:* playing with grandchildren, reading. *Address:* 3 Scotchel Green, Pewsey, Wilts SN9 5AU. *T:* (01672) 562982.

FISHER, Dudley Henry, CBE 1990; DL; CPFA; Chairman, Wales Region, British Gas Corporation, 1974–87, retired; *b* 22 Aug. 1922; *s* of Arthur and Mary Fisher; *m* 1st, 1946, Barbara Lilian Sexton (*d* 1984); one *s* two *d*; 2nd, 1985, Jean Mary Livingstone Miller, *d* of late Dr and Mrs Robert Brown Miller, Cowbridge, S Glam. *Educ:* City of Norwich Sch. Various accountancy positions in Local Govt and Eastern Electricity Bd, 1938–53. War service, RAF, 1942–46 (pilot; Flt Lt). Northern Gas Bd, 1953; Wales Gas Board: Asst Chief Accountant, Dep. Chief Accountant, Chief Accountant, Dir of Finance, 1956–69; Dep. Chm., 1970. Member: Adv. Cttee on Local Govt Audit, 1979–82; Audit Commn for Local Authorities in England and Wales, 1983–88; Broadcasting Council for Wales, 1986–90; Hon. Treasurer, British National Cttee, 1980–89, and Chm., Admin. Cttee, 1986–89, World Energy Conf. Chairman: Welsh Council, CBI, 1987–89; Wales Festival of Remembrance Cttee, 1996–2007; Dep. Chm., Inst. of Welsh Affairs, 1991–95. Mem. Council, 1983–88, Treas., 1987–88, UC Cardiff; Member of Council: Univ. of Wales Cardiff (formerly Univ. of Wales Coll. of Cardiff), 1988–2002; Univ. of Wales Coll. of Medicine, 1992–2003; Chm., Audit Cttee, Univ. of Wales, 1994–96. Governor, United World Coll. of the Atlantic, 1988–96. Trustee, Help the Aged, 1987–97; Vice Chm., HelpAge Internat., 1993–97. Liveryman, Welsh Livery Guild, 1996–2007. High Sheriff, 1988–89, DL 1991, S Glam. *Recreations:* golf, gardening, reading. *Address:* Norwood Edge, 8 Cyncoed Avenue, Cardiff CF23 6SU. *T:* (029) 2075 7958. *Clubs:* Royal Air Force; Cardiff and County (Cardiff).

FISHER, Duncan Mark; Co-Founder and Chief Executive, Fatherhood Institute (formerly Fathers Direct), since 1999; *b* 3 Nov. 1961; *s* of Humphrey and Helga Fisher; *m* Clare; two *d*. *Educ:* Corpus Christi Coll., Cambridge (BA Natural Scis 1984; MPhil Theol 1986); School of Slavonic and East European Studies, London (MA Area Studies 1989). Founder and CEO, East West Environment, 1989–95; Founder and CEO, 1994–2003, Trustee, 2003–, Action for Conservation through Tourism, subseq. Travel Foundn. Mem., Equal Opportunities Commn, 2005–07. Member: Community Action Network, 1999–; Inst. of Fund Raising, 2002–. Mem., Amnesty Internat., 1995–. *Recreations:* making lists, eating very good chocolate (Mem., Chocolate Club), reading to children at local school, having fun with my children. *Address:* 37 Upper House Farm, Crickhowell, Powys NP8 1BZ. *T:* (01873) 810515; *e-mail:* duncan.fisher@btconnect.com.

FISHER, Elisabeth Neill; Her Honour Judge Fisher; a Circuit Judge, since 1989; *b* 24 Nov. 1944; *d* of late Kenneth Neill Fisher and Lorna Charlotte Honor Fisher. *Educ:* Oxford High Sch. for Girls (GPDST); Cambridge Univ. (MA). Called to the Bar, Inner Temple, 1968, Bencher, 2003. A Recorder, 1982–89. Mem. Senate, Inns of Court, 1983–86; Pres., Council of HM Circuit Judges, 2004. Member: Criminal Cttee, Judicial Studies Bd, 1995–98; Criminal Justice Consultative Council, 1992–99. Chm., Home Sec.'s Adv. Bd on Restricted Patients, 1998–2003. DUniv UCE, 1997. *Address:* Queen Elizabeth II Law Courts, Newton Street, Birmingham B4 7NA.

FISHER, Jacqueline, (Jackie), CBE 2005; Chief Executive and Principal, Newcastle College, since 2000; *b* 10 March 1956; *d* of Stanley and Anne Walton; *m* 1st, 1974, Thomas Fisher (marr. diss. 1978); two *s*; 2nd, 1996, David Collier. *Educ:* Leeds Univ. (BA Hons 1979; MA 1980; MSc 1989). Asst Principal, St Helen's Coll., 1989–94; Vice Principal, 1994–97, Chief Exec. and Principal, 1997–2000, Tameside Coll. Member: Bd, One North East, RDA, 2000–07; Council, HEFCE, 2001–08. *Recreations:* cinema, food, walking, travel in Central and Eastern Europe. *Address:* Newcastle College, Rye Hill Campus, Scotswood Road, Newcastle upon Tyne NE4 7SA. *T:* (0191) 2000 4015; *e-mail:* jackie.fisher@ncl-coll.ac.uk.

FISHER, Joan; Headteacher, King Edward VI Camp Hill School for Girls, Birmingham, 1992–2003; *b* 24 Sept. 1939; *d* of R. and A. R. Bowler; *m* 1969, Ronald William Fisher; four *d* (incl. triplets). *Educ:* Univ. of Leeds (BA Modern Langs); Univ. of York (Schoolteacher Fellowship); Inst. of Educn, London (MA). Teacher in comprehensive schs, Yorkshire and Surrey, 1962–89: Holme Valley GS, 1962–66; Middlesbrough Girls' High, 1966–69; Acklam High, 1970–72; Framwelgate Moor, 1972–73; Glebelands, 1974–82; Tomlinscote, 1982–89; Dep. Headteacher, Westcliff High Sch. for Girls, 1989–92. Chm. Govs, Northway Infant Sch., Tewkesbury, 2007–. FRSA 1997. *Publications:* teaching materials for German, including: Achtung! Achtung!, 1985; Begegnungen, 1985; Lesekiste, A, 1987, B, 1988; Pack's An!, 1991.

FISHER, Prof. John, PhD, DEng; CEng, FIMechE, FIPEM; Professor of Mechanical Engineering, since 1993, and Deputy Vice-Chancellor, since 2006, University of Leeds; *b* 10 Aug. 1955; *s* of James Fisher and Joan Fisher; *m* 1995, Eileen Ingham; two *d*. *Educ:* Univ. of Birmingham (BSc 1st Cl. Physics 1976); Univ. of Glasgow (PhD Bioengrg 1986); Univ. of Leeds (DEng 1996). CEng 1983; FIMechE 1995; FIPEM 1998; CSci 2005. Bioengr, Dept of Clinical Phys and Bioengrg, Greater Glasgow Health Bd, 1978–87; University of Leeds: Lectr, 1987–93; Dir, Inst. of Med. and Biol Engrg, 2001–; Pro-Vice-Chancellor, 2001–06. Chm., Tissue Regenix Ltd, 2007–; Dir, Bitecic Ltd, 2006–. *Publications:* 350 articles in jls. *Recreations:* walking, swimming, circuit training. *Address:* School of Mechanical Engineering, University of Leeds, Leeds LS2 9JT. *T:* (0113) 343 2128; *e-mail:* j.fisher@leeds.ac.uk.

FISHER, Jonathan Simon; QC 2003; *b* 24 Feb. 1958; *s* of Aubrey and Pauline Fisher; *m* 1980, Paula Goldberg; two *s* two *d*. *Educ:* Univ. of N London (BA 1st Cl. Hons); St Catharine's Coll., Cambridge (LLB). Called to the Bar, Gray's Inn, 1980; Lectr, Anglia Poly., 1981–82; in practice as barrister, specialising in white collar crime, serious organised crime and regulatory cases, 1982–; Standing Counsel to IR, CCC and London Crown Courts, 1991–2003. Member: Steering Gp, Assets Recovery Agency, 2003–06; Legal Panel, Accountancy Investigation and Disciplinary Bd, 2005–; Trustee Dir, Fraud Adv. Panel, 2006–. Hon. Mem., Steering Gp, London Fraud Forum, 2007–. Exec. Mem., 2005–06, Chm. of Res., 2006–, Soc. of Conservative Lawyers. Sen. Vis. Fellow, City Univ., 1986–2004; Visiting Professor: Cass Business Sch., City Univ., 2004–07; LSE, 2006– (Vis. Fellow, 2004–06). Gen. Ed., Lloyds Law Reports: Financial Crime, 2008–. *Publications:* (jtly) Pharmacy Law and Practice, 1995, 4th edn 2006; (jtly) Law of Investor Protection, 1997, 2nd edn 2003. *Recreations:* theatre, football, arts, history, travelling. *Address:* 23 Essex Street, WC2R 3AA. *T:* (020) 7413 0353, *Fax:* (020) 7413 0374; *e-mail:* jonathanfisher@23es.com. *Club:* Carlton.

FISHER, Mark, FSA; MP (Lab) Stoke-on-Trent Central, since 1983; *b* 29 Oct. 1944; *s* of Sir Nigel Fisher, MC and of Lady Gloria Flower; *m* 1971, Ingrid Geach (marr. diss. 1999); two *s* two *d*. *Educ:* Eton College; Trinity College, Cambridge (MA). Documentary film producer and script writer, 1966–75; Principal, Tattenhall Centre of Education, 1975–83. Mem., Staffs CC, 1981–85 (Chm., Libraries Cttee, 1981–83). Contested (Lab) Leek, 1979. An Opposition Whip, 1985–87; Opposition spokesman on the arts, 1987–92, 1993–97, on Citizen's Charter, 1992–93; Parly Under-Sec. of State, Dept for Culture, Media and Sport, 1997–98. Mem., Treasury and CS Select Cttee, 1983–85. Dep. Pro-Chancellor, Keele Univ., 1989–97. Vis. Fellow, St Antony's Coll., Oxford, 2000–01. Member: BBC Gen. Adv. Council, 1988–95; Council, PSI, 1989–95; Acceptance in Lieu Panel, 1998–; Museums and Galls Commn, 1999–. Trustee: Britten-Pears Foundn, 1998–2007; Estorick Collection of Modern Italian Art, 2000–; Hunterian Museum, 2005–; Friends of the Nat. Libraries, 2005–; Mem. Bd, Qatar Mus Authy, 2007–. FSA 2006. Hon. FRIBA 1992; Hon. FRCA 1993. Author of stage plays: Brave New Town, 1974; The Cutting Room, 1990. *Publications:* City Centres, City Cultures, 1988; (ed jtly) Whose Cities?, 1991; A New London, 1992; Britain's Best Museums and Galleries, 2004. *Address:* House of Commons, SW1A 0AA; 110 Victoria Street, Hartshill, Stoke-on-Trent ST4 6DU. *T:* (01782) 713813.

FISHER, Mark; *see* Fisher, C. M.

FISHER, Maurice, RCNC; General Manager, HM Dockyard, Rosyth, 1979–83; retired; *b* 8 Feb. 1924; *s* of William Ernest Fisher and Lily Edith (*née* Hatch); *m* 1955, Stella Leslie Sumsion; one *d*. *Educ:* St Luke's Sch., Portsmouth; Royal Dockyard Sch., Portsmouth; Royal Naval Coll., Greenwich. Constructor-in-Charge, HM Dockyard, Simonstown, 1956–60; Staff of Director of Naval Construction, 1960–63; Staff of C-in-C Western Fleet, 1963–65; Dep. Supt, Admiralty Experiment Works, Haslar, 1965–68; Dep. Prodn Manager, HM Dockyard, Devonport, 1968–72; Personnel Manager, HM Dockyard, Portsmouth, 1972–74; Planning Manager, 1974–77, Prodn Manager, 1977–79, HM Dockyard, Devonport. *Recreation:* game fishing. *Address:* 9 Roman Row, Bank Street, Bishops Waltham, Hants SO32 1RW.

FISHER, Prof. Michael Ellis, FRS 1971; Distinguished University Professor and Regents' Professor, Institute for Physical Science and Technology, University of Maryland, since 1993 (Wilson H. Elkins Distinguished Professor, 1987–93); *b* 3 Sept. 1931; *s* of Harold Wolf Fisher and Jeanne Marie Fisher (*née* Halter); *m* 1954, Sorrel Castillejo; three *s* one *d*. *Educ:* King's Coll., London. BSc 1951, PhD 1957, FKC 1981. Flying Officer (Educn), RAF, 1951–53; London Univ. Postgraduate Studentship, 1953–56; DSIR Sen. Research Fellow, 1956–58. King's Coll., London: Lectr in Theoretical Physics, 1958–62; Reader in Physics, 1962–64; Prof. of Physics, 1965–66; Cornell University: Prof. of Chemistry and Maths, 1966–73; Horace White Prof. of Chemistry, Physics and Maths, 1973–89; Chm., Dept of Chemistry, 1975–78. Guest Investigator, Rockefeller Inst., New York, 1963–64; Vis. Prof. in Applied Physics, Stanford Univ., 1970–71; Walter Ames Prof., Univ. of Washington, 1977; Vis. Prof. of Physics, MIT, 1979; Sherman Fairchild Disting. Scholar, CIT, 1984; Vis. Prof. in Theoretical Physics, Oxford, 1985; Lorentz Prof., Leiden, 1993; Vis. Prof., Nat. Inst. of Sci. and Technol., USA, 1994; Phi Beta Kappa Vis. Scholar, 1994. Lectures: Buhl, Carnegie-Mellon, 1971; 32nd Richtmyer Meml, 1973; 17th Fritz London Meml, 1975; Morris Loeb, Harvard, 1979; H. L. Welsh, Toronto, 1979; Bakerian, Royal Soc., 1979; Welch Foundn, Texas, 1979; Alpheas Smith, Ohio State Univ., 1982; Laird Meml, Univ. of Western Ontario, 1983; Fries, Rensselaer Polytechnic Inst., NY, 1984; Amos de-Shalit Meml, Weizmann Inst., Rehovoth, 1985; Cherwell-Simon, Oxford, 1985; Marker, Penn. State Univ., 1988; Nat. Sci. Council, Taiwan, 1989; Hamilton Meml, Princeton Univ., 1990; 65th J. W. Gibbs, Amer. Math. Soc., Condon, Univ. of Colorado, and M. S. Green Meml, Temple Univ., 1992; R. and B. Sackler, Tel Aviv, 1992; Lennard-Jones, RSC, 1995; G. N. Lewis, UC Berkeley, 1995; Hirschfelder, Wisconsin Univ., 1995; Baker, in Chemistry, Cornell Univ., 1997; F. G. Brickwedde, in Physics, Johns Hopkins Univ., 1998; Michelson, Case Western Reserve Univ., 1999; T. A. Edison Meml, Naval Res. Lab., Washington, 2000; J. R. Oppenheimer, Univ. of Calif, Berkeley, 2006; C. V. Raman Meml, Indian Inst. Sci., Bangalore, 2007; Homis Bhabha Meml, Tata Inst. Fundamental Res., Mumbai, 2007; E. L. Hudspeth Centennial, Univ. of Texas, Austin, 2007. Mem. Council and Vice-Pres., Royal Soc., 1993–95. Mem., Amer. Philos. Soc., 1993. John Simon Guggenheim Memorial Fellow, 1970–71, 1978–79; Fellow, Amer. Acad. of Arts and Scis, 1979; FAAAS 1986; For. Associate, National Acad. of Sciences, USA, 1983; Foreign Member: Brazilian Acad. of Scis, 1996; Royal Norwegian Soc. of Scis and Letters, 2003–. Hon. FRSE 1986; Hon. Fellow, Indian Acad. of Scis, Bangalore,

2000. Hon. DSc Yale, 1987; Hon. DPhil Tel Aviv, 1992. Irving Langmuir Prize in Chemical Physics, Amer. Phys. Soc., 1970; Award in Phys. and Math. Scis, NY Acad. of Scis, 1978; Guthrie Medal, Inst. of Physics, 1980; Wolf Prize in Physics, State of Israel, 1980; Michelson-Morely Award, Case-Western Reserve Univ., 1982; James Murray Luck Award, National Acad. of Sciences, USA, 1983; Boltzmann Medal, Internat. Union of Pure and Applied Physics, 1983; Lars Onsager Medal, Norwegian Inst. of Technol., 1993; Onsager Meml Prize, Amer. Phys. Soc., 1995; Hildebrand Award, Amer. Chem. Soc., 1995; Royal Medal, Royal Soc., 2005. *Publications:* Analogue Computing at Ultra-High Speed (with D. M. MacKay), 1962; The Nature of Critical Points, (Univ. of Colorado) 1964, (Moscow) 1968; contribs to Proc. Roy. Soc., Phys. Rev., Phys. Rev. Lett., Jl Sci. Insts, Jl Math. Phys., Arch. Rational Mech. Anal., Jl Chem. Phys., Commun. Math. Phys., Rept Prog. Phys., Rev. Mod. Phys., Physica, etc. *Recreations:* Flamenco guitar, travel. *Address:* Institute for Physical Science and Technology, University of Maryland, College Park, MD 20742–2431, USA. *T:* (301) 4054819.

FISHER, Peter Antony Goodwin, FRCP; Consultant Physician, since 1986, Director of Research, since 1996, and Clinical Director, since 1998, Royal London Homoeopathic Hospital; Physician to the Queen, since 2001; *b* 2 Sept. 1950; *s* of Antony Martin Fisher and Eve Fisher; *m* 1997, Nina Oxenham; two *d. Educ:* Tonbridge Sch.; Emmanuel Coll., Cambridge (BA 1972, MA 1975; MB BChir 1975); Westminster Hosp. Med. Sch. FFHom 1986 (Vice Pres., 1991 and 1999); FRCP 1997. Med. Dir, Royal London Homeopathic Hosp., 1998–99. FRSocMed 1984. Editor, Homeopathy (formerly British Homeopathic Jl), 1986–. Clin. Lead, Complementary and Alternative Medicine Specialist Liby, Nat. Liby for Health, 2005–. Chm., Wkg Gp on Homeopathy, WHO, 2005–. *Publications:* Alternative Answers to Arthritis and Rheumatism, 1999; numerous scientific articles on homeopathy. *Recreation:* gardening. *Address:* Royal London Homoeopathic Hospital, Great Ormond Street, WC1N 3HR. *T:* (020) 7391 8890.

FISHER, Rev. Canon Peter Timothy; Vicar, Maney, since 2002; *b* 7 July 1944; *s* of late Rev. James Atherton Fisher; *m* 1968, Elizabeth Lacey; two *s. Educ:* City of London Sch.; Durham Univ. (BA, MA); Cuddesdon Coll., Oxford. Ordained deacon, 1970, priest 1971; Curate, St Andrew's, Bedford, 1970–74; Chaplain, Surrey Univ., 1974–78; Sub-Warden, Lincoln Theol Coll., 1978–83; Rector, Houghton-le-Spring, 1983–94; Principal, The Queen's Coll., subseq. The Queen's Foundn for Ecumenical Theol Educn, Birmingham, 1994–2002. Mem., Faith and Order Commn, WCC, 2008–. Hon. Canon, Birmingham Cathedral, 2000–. *Recreations:* piano and water-colours, both strictly incognito. *Address:* The Vicarage, Maney Hill Road, Sutton Coldfield B72 1JJ. *T:* (0121) 354 2426.

FISHER, Richard, (Rick); lighting designer (freelance), since 1980; Chairman, Association of Lighting Designers, since 1995; *b* Pennsylvania, 19 Oct. 1954; *s* of Samuel M. Fisher and Helene K. Fisher. *Educ:* Dickinson Coll., Carlisle, PA (BA 1976). Lighting designs for theatre and dance productions include: An Inspector Calls, NT, 1992, transf. NY (Tony Award, Drama Desk Award, 1994); Matthew Bourne's Swan Lake, London, 1995, transf. Los Angeles and NY, and Cinderella, London, 1997, transf. Los Angeles; Via Dolorosa, Royal Court, transf. NY, 1998; Disney's The Hunchback of Notre Dame, Berlin, 1999; Blue/Orange, NT, 2000, Duchess, 2001; A Number, Royal Court, 2002; Far Away, NY, 2002; Honour, NT, 2003; A Woman of No Importance, Th. Royal Haymarket, 2003; Jerry Springer the Opera, NT, transf. Cambridge Th., 2003; Old Times, 2004, The Philanthropist, 2005, Donmar; Tin Tin, Barbican, 2005; Billy Elliot, Victoria Palace, 2005, transf. Sydney, 2007; Resurrection Blues, Old Vic, 2006; Landscape with Weapon, NT, 2007; opera productions include: Opera North: La Bohème, 1996; Gloriana, 1999; Bolshoi: Turandot, 2002; The Fiery Angel, 2004; Wozzeck, Royal Opera, 2002; A Midsummer Night's Dream, La Fenice, Venice, 2004; Santa Fe: La Sonnambula, 2004; Peter Grimes, 2005; Billy Budd, Radamisto, 2008; The Little Prince, Houston, 2003, NY, 2005; Betrothal in a Monastery, Glyndebourne, 2006. Olivier Award for Best Lighting Design, 1994 and 1998; Bronze Medal for Lighting Design, World Stage Design Expo, Toronto, 2005. *Recreations:* theatre going, travel, eating!, camping. *Address:* c/o Dennis Lyne Agency, 503 Holloway Road, N19 4DD.

FISHER, Robert Reginald James, AM 2003; JP; Agent General for Western Australia, 2001–05; *b* 13 Oct. 1942; *s* of Albert Reginald Fisher and Irene Fisher; *m* 1967, Lynette Fulford; one *s* one *d. Educ:* Univ. of Western Australia (BA, BEd). Member, Australian Trade Commissioner Service, 1970–80: Lima, 1971–73; Russian lang. trng, 1973–74; Moscow, 1974–76; New Delhi, 1976–77; San Francisco, 1977–80; Government of Western Australia, 1980–2005: Chief Executive: Dept of Industrial Develt, 1980–87; Countertrade Office, 1987–88; Dept of Trade Develt, 1988–91; Regl Develt, 1991–92; Family and Children's Services, 1993–2001. JP Western Australia, 2001. *Recreations:* swimming, golf. *Address:* 12 Sutcliffe Street, Dalkeith, WA 6009, Australia.

FISHER, Roger Anthony, FRCO(CHM); Organist and Master of Choristers, Chester Cathedral, 1967–96; *b* 18 Sept. 1936; *s* of Leslie Elgar Fisher and Vera Althea (*née* Salter); *m* 1st, 1967, Susan Mary Green (marr. diss. 1983); one *d*; 2nd, 1985, Gillian Rushforth (*née* Heywood). *Educ:* Bancroft's Sch., Woodford Green, Essex; Royal Coll. Music; Christ Church, Oxford (Organ schol.; MA). FRCO(CHM); ARCM; ATCL. Organist, St Mark's, Regent's Park, 1957–62; Asst Organist, Hereford Cathedral, 1962–67; Asst Lectr in Music, Hereford Coll. of Educn, 1963–67. Music Critic, Liverpool Echo, 1976–79; Associate Editor, Organists' Rev., 1996–2004. Recital tours incl. N America, Europe, Scandinavia, S Africa and Australia. Recordings in GB, Europe, USA and S Africa; BBC broadcasts as organist and with Chester Cathedral Choir. Conductor, choral socs and orchestras; Organ Consultant to churches and cathedrals. Geoffrey Tankard Prize for Solo Organ, RCM, 1959. *Publications:* Master Class with Roger Fisher, 2006; articles about the organ and related subjects in several periodicals. *Recreations:* railway interests, walking, motoring. *Address:* The Old Chapel, Trelogan, Holywell, Flintshire CH8 9BD.

FISHLOCK, Dr David Jocelyn, OBE 1983; Editor, R&D Efficiency, since 1991 (Publisher, 1992–2002); *b* 9 Aug. 1932; *s* of William Charles Fishlock and Dorothy Mary Turner; *m* 1959, Mary Millicent Cosgrove; one *s. Educ:* City of Bath Boys' Sch. (now Beechen Cliff Sch.); Bristol Coll. of Technol. FIBiol 1988; FEI (Comp. Inst. of Energy, 1987). National Service, REME, 1955–58. Westinghouse Brake & Signal Co. Ltd, 1948–55; McGraw-Hill, 1959–62; New Scientist, 1962–67; Science Editor, Financial Times, 1967–91. Columnist: Nuclear Europe Worldscan, 1981–2002; Business in East Anglia, 1997–; Erotic Review, 1998–; Chemistry World (formerly Chemistry in Britain), RSC, 2000–. Glaxo Travelling Fellow, 1978; Associate Fellow, Centre for Res. in Innovation & Competitiveness, 1998–2001. Member: R&D Soc., 1994–; Scientific Instrument Soc., 1994–. Hon. DLitt Salford, 1982; Hon. DSc Bath, 1993. Chemical Writer of the Year Award, BASF, 1982; Worthington Pump Award, 1982; British Press Award, 1986. Silver Jubilee Medal, 1977. *Publications:* The New Materials, 1967; Man Modified, 1969; The Business of Science, 1975; The Business of Biotechnology, 1982; (with Elizabeth Antébi) Biotechnology: strategies for life, 1986. *Recreations:* writing, reading, collecting old medical/pharmaceutical equipment. *Address:* Traveller's Joy, Copse Lane, Jordans, Bucks HP9 2TA. *T:* (01494) 873242. *Club:* Athenæum.

FISHLOCK, Trevor; journalist and author; roving foreign correspondent, The Dail Telegraph, 1986–89 and 1993–96; *b* 21 Feb. 1941; *m* 1978, Penelope Symon. *Edu* Churcher's Coll., Petersfield; Southern Grammar Sch., Portsmouth. Portsmouth Evenir News, 1957–62; freelance and news agency reporter, 1962–68; The Times: Wales and W England staff correspondent, 1968–77; London and foreign staff, 1978–80; S As correspondent, Delhi, 1980–83; New York correspondent, 1983–86; Mosco correspondent, Daily Telegraph, 1989–91; roving foreign correspondent, The Sunda Telegraph, 1991–93. Fellow, World Press Inst., St Paul, Minnesota, 1977–78. Mem Council for the Welsh Language, 1973–77. David Holden Award for foreign reportin (British Press Awards), 1983; Internat. Reporter of the Year (British Press Awards), 198 *Publications:* Wales and the Welsh, 1972; Talking of Wales, 1975; Discovering Britai Wales, 1979; Americans and Nothing Else, 1980; India File, 1983; The State of Americ 1986; Indira Gandhi (for children), 1986; Out of Red Darkness: reports from th collapsing Soviet Empire, 1992; My Foreign Country: Trevor Fishlock's Britain, 199 Cobra Road: an Indian journey, 1999; Conquerors of Time, 2004; In This Plac centenary vol. for Nat. Liby of Wales, 2007. *Recreation:* sailing. *Address:* 7 Teilo Stree Cardiff CF11 9JN. *Club:* Travellers.

FISHWICK, Avril, OBE 1997; Vice Lord-Lieutenant of Greater Manchester, 1988–98; 30 March 1924; *yr d* of Frank Platt and Charlotte Winifred Young; *m* 1950, Thom William Fishwick; two *d. Educ:* Woodfield; High Sch. for Girls, Wigan; Liverpool Uni (LLB 1946; LLM 1947). Admitted Solicitor 1949. War service, Foreign Office, Bletchle Park, 1942–45; Partner, Frank Platt & Fishwick, 1958–94. Chm., Envmtl Res. an Consultancy Unit (ERCU Ltd) Tidy Britain (formerly Tidy Britain Enterprises Ltd 1990–2000; Dir, Northern Adv. Bd, National Westminster Bank, 1984–92. Membe Wigan and Leigh HMC, 1960–73 (Mem., Exec. Council, 1966–73); NW RHA 1985–88; Chm., Wigan AHA, 1973–82. Local President: Civic Trust, 1976–91; RSPCA 1974–99; Little Theatre, 1985–91; Drumcroon Arts Centre, 1995–; Hon. Mem Soroptimists Internat., 1973–; Mem., Groundwork Trust, 1986–93. Trustee: Skelto Bounty, 1985–2003; Gtr Manchester Police Community Charity, 1986–98; Friends Rosie, 1995–. Hon. Associate Mem., Manchester Naval Officers Assoc., 2004–. Mem Court, Manchester Univ., 1984–2001. DL 1982, High Sheriff 1983–84, Gtr Mancheste Hon. MA Manchester, 1993. Paul Harris Fellow, Rotary Internat., 1995; Queen Mother Birthday Award for Envmtl Improvement, 1996. *Recreations:* family, natural histor *Address:* 6 Southfields, Richmond Road, Bowdon, Altrincham, Cheshire WA14 2TY. *T* (0161) 941 6660.

FISK, Prof. David John, CB 1999; ScD, PhD; FREng; Royal Academy of Engineerin Professor of Engineering for Sustainable Development, Imperial College London, sinc 2002; *b* 9 Jan. 1947; *s* of late John Howard Fisk and of Rebecca Elizabeth Fisk (*n* Haynes); *m* 1972, A. Anne Thoday; one *s* one *d. Educ:* Stationers' Company's Sch Hornsey; St John's Coll., Cambridge (BA, MA, ScD); Univ. of Manchester (PhD FCIBSE 1983 (Hon. FCIBSE 1998); FREng (FEng 1998); FInstP 1999. Joined Buildin Res. Estabt (traffic noise res.), 1972; Higher Sci. Officer, 1972–73; Sen. Sci. Offic (energy conservation res.), 1973–75; PSO, 1975–78; SPSO, Hd Mechanical and Ele Engrg Div., 1978–84; Department of the Environment: Asst Sec., Central Directorate Environmental Protection, 1984–87; Under Sec., 1987; Dep. Chief Scientist, 1987–8 Chief Scientific Advr, OPDM (formerly Dept of the Envmt, then DETR, later DTLR 1998–2006. Director: Air, Climate and Toxic Substances Directorate, 1990–95; Envmt Internat. Directorate, 1995–98; Central Strategy Directorate, DETR, then DTLR 1999–2002. Dir, Watford Palace Th., 2000–. *Publications:* Thermal Control of Building 1981; numerous papers on technical innovation, bldg sci., systems theory and economic *Recreations:* modern theatre, music. *Address:* Imperial College London, South Kensingto Campus, SW7 2AZ. *Club:* Athenæum.

FISON, Sir (Richard) Guy, 4th Bt *cr* 1905; DSC 1944; *b* 9 Jan. 1917; *er s* of Sir Williar Guy Fison, 3rd Bt; *S* father, 1964; *m* 1952, Elyn Hartmann (*d* 1987); one *s* one *d. Edu* Eton; New Coll., Oxford. Served RNVR, 1939–45. Entered Wine Trade, 1948; Maste of Wine, 1954; Dir, Saccone & Speed Ltd, 1952–82; Chairman: Saccone & Spee Internat., 1979–82; Percy Fox & Co. Ltd, 1982–83; Wine Develt Bd, 1982–83; Fir Vintage Wines Plc, 1985–95; Pres., Wine and Spirit Assoc., 1977–78. Hon. Freemar 1976, Renter Warden, 1981–82, Upper Warden, 1982–83, Master, 1983–84, Vintner Co. *Heir: s* Charles William Fison, *b* 6 Feb. 1954.

FITCH, Rodney Arthur, CBE 1990; PPCSD (FSIAD 1976); Chairman and Chie Executive, Fitch, worldwide design consultants, since 2003; *b* 19 Aug. 1938; *s* of la Arthur and Ivy Fitch; *m* 1965, Janet Elizabeth, *d* of Sir Walter Stansfield, CBE, MC, QPM one *s* four *d. Educ:* Willesden Polytechnic, Sch. of Building and Architecture; Centr School of Arts and Crafts (Theatre, TV Design, Interior and Furniture Design); Hornse Sch. of Art (Typography). Trainee designer, Hickman Ltd, 1956–58; National Servic RAPC, 1958–60; Charles Kenrick Associates, 1960–62; Conran Design Gp Ltd, 1962–6 C.D.G. (Design Consultants) Ltd, 1969–71; Founder, 1972 (resigned 1994), Fitch an Company, subseq. Fitch-RS and Fitch, a multi-discipline design practice; Founder an Chief Exec., Rodney Fitch, specialist design consultancy, 1994–2003; sometime Chm Fitch (Design Consultants). Mem., Design Council, 1988–94. Dir Bd, City of Londo Fest. of Arts, 1996–99. Member: Court of Govs, Univ. of the Arts, London (former London Inst.), 1989–2008 (Dep. Chm., 1989–2005); Council, RCA, 1989–94; Truste V&A Museum, 1991–2001; Chm., V&A Enterprises, 2003–. CSD (formerly SIAD): Pres 1985–87; Vice-Pres., 1982–84; Hon. Treas., 1984–87; Past Pres., DAAD, 1983. FRS 1976. Legion of Honor, Inst. of Store Planners, USA, 2006. *Publications:* (with L. Knobe Fitch on Retail Design, 1990; regular contributor to design publications. *Recreation* cricket, opera, theatre, his family. *Address:* (office) 121–141 Westbourne Terrace, W2 6JR

FITCHETT, Robert Duncan; HM Diplomatic Service; Deputy Head of Missior Mexico City, since 2008; *b* 10 June 1961; *s* of late John Charles Fitchett and of Sheila Mar Fitchett; *m* 1985, Adèle Thérèse Hajjar; one *s* two *d. Educ:* Northampton Sch. for Boys Univ. of Bradford (BA Hons Mod. Langs (French and German) 1983). Joined FCO, 198 Dakar, 1984–87; Bonn, 1987–90; FCO, 1990–93; Cabinet Office, 1993–94; First Sec Paris, 1994–98; FCO, 1998–2003; Dep. Hd of Mission, Manila, 2003–06; FCO, 2007–0 *Recreations:* horse racing, opera, classical music, reading, walking. *Address:* c/o Foreign an Commonwealth Office, King Charles Street, SW1A 2AH.

FITCHEW, Geoffrey Edward, CMG 1993; Chairman, Insolvency Practices Council since 2005; *b* 22 Dec. 1939; *s* of Stanley Edward Fitchew and Elizabeth Scott; *m* 196 Mary Theresa Spillane; two *s. Educ:* Uppingham School; Magdalen Coll., Oxford (MA London Sch. of Economics (MScEcon). Asst Principal, HM Treasury, 1964; Private Se to Minister of State, 1968–69; Principal, 1969; Gwilym Gibbon Research Fellow Nuffield Coll., Oxford, 1973–74; Asst Sec., Internat. Finance Div., HM Treasury 1975–77; Counsellor (Economics and Finance), UK Perm. Rep. to EEC, 1977–80; As Sec., HM Treasury, 1980–83; Under Sec., HM Treasury, 1983–86; Dir-Gen. (fo Banking, Financial Services and Company Law), Directorate Gen. XV, EC, Brussel 1986–93; Dep. Sec., Cabinet Office, 1993–94. Chm. and First Comr, Building Soc

Commn, and Chief Registrar of Friendly Socs, 1994–2001. Vice-Chm., Internat. Commn on Holocaust Era Insurance Claims, 1999–2003; Mem., Determinations Panel, Pensions Regulator, 2005–. *Recreations:* golf, theatre, opera, reading, armchair supporter of Manchester United. *Address:* (office) PO Box 698, Godalming, Surrey GU7 9AR.

FITTALL, Betty Daphne C.; *see* Callaway-Fittall.

FITTALL, William Robert; Secretary-General, Archbishop's Council and General Synod of the Church of England, since 2002; *b* 26 July 1953; *s* of Arthur Fittall and Elsie Fittall; *m* 1978, Barbara Staples; two *s*. *Educ:* Dover Grammar Sch.; Christ Church, Oxford (MA). Entered Home Office, 1975; Private Sec. to Minister of State, 1979–80; Principal, 1980; Ecole Nationale d'Administration, Paris, 1980–81; Broadcasting Dept, 1981–85; Private Sec. to Home Sec., 1985–87; Asst Sec., 1987; Sec., Review of Parole System, 1987–88; Prison Service HQ, 1988–91; Principal Private Sec. to Sec. of State for NI, 1992–93; Police Dept, Home Office, 1993–95; Asst Under Sec. of State, 1995; Chief of Assessments Staff, Cabinet Office, 1995–97; Dir, Crime Reduction and Community Progs, Home Office, 1997–2000; Associate Political Dir, NI Office, 2000–02. Anglican Lay Reader, 1977–. *Recreations:* playing church organs, watching sport, reading. *Address:* (office) Church House, Great Smith Street, SW1P 3AZ. *T:* (020) 7898 1360.

FITTER, Prof. Alastair Hugh, PhD; FRS 2005; Pro-Vice-Chancellor for Research, University of York, since 2004; *b* 20 June 1948; *s* of late Richard Sidney Richmond Fitter and Alice Mary, (Maisie), Fitter; *m* 1969, Rosalind Morris; two *s* one *d*. *Educ:* New Coll., Oxford (BA 1969); Univ. of Liverpool (PhD 1973). Lectr, Sen. Lectr, then Prof. of Ecology, 1972–2004, and Hd of Dept of Biol., 1997–2004, Univ. of York. Mem., NERC, 2005–. Jt Editor, Advances in Ecological Research, vols 18–30, 1987–99. Pres., British Ecol Soc., 2003–05. Hon. Member: British Naturalists' Assoc., 2006; Botanical Soc. of British Isles, 2007; British Mycol Soc., 2007. *Publications:* (with M. Blamey and R. Fitter) Wild Flowers of Britain and Northern Europe, 1974, 5th edn 1996; An Atlas of the Wild Flowers of Britain and Northern Europe, 1976; (with C. Smith) A Wood in Ascam: a study in wetland conservation, Askham Bog 1879–1979, 1979; Trees, 1980; (with R. K. M. Hay) Environmental Physiology of Plants, 1981, 3rd edn 2002; (with N. Arlott and R. Fitter) The Complete Guide to British Wildlife, 1981; (with R. Fitter and J. Wilkinson) Collins Guide to the Countryside, 1984; (with R. Fitter and A. Farrer) Grasses, Sedges, Rushes and Ferns of Britain and Northern Europe, 1984; (ed) Ecological Interactions in the Soil: plants, microbes and animals, 1985; (with R. Fitter) Collins Guide to the Countryside in Winter, 1988; (with M. Blamey and R. Fitter) Wild Flowers of Britain and Ireland, 2003. *Address:* Department of Biology, University of York, PO Box 373, York YO10 5YW.

FITTON, David John, CMG 2004; HM Diplomatic Service; Minister, Tokyo, since 2008; *b* 10 Jan. 1955; *s* of Jack and Joan Fitton; *m* 1989, Hisae Iijima; one *s* one *d*. *Educ:* Durham Univ. (BA Hons; MA). Entered FCO, 1980; appts in New Delhi, Tokyo and London, 1980–96; Political Counsellor, Tokyo, 1996–2000; Dep. Hd of Mission, Ankara, 2001–04; Actg Consul-Gen., Istanbul, 2003–04; Hd, Crisis Gp, Consular Directorate, FCO, 2004–07. *Recreations:* tennis, medieval French manuscripts, football, golf. *Address:* c/o Foreign and Commonwealth Office, SW1A 2AH. *T:* (020) 7008 1445; *e-mail:* david.fitton@fco.gov.uk. *Club:* Royal Commonwealth Society.

FITTON-BROWN, Edmund Walter; HM Diplomatic Service; Counsellor, Foreign and Commonwealth Office, since 2006; *b* 5 Oct. 1962; *s* of Anthony David and Daphne Mary Fitton-Brown; *m* 1995, Julie Ann Herring; two *s* one *d*. *Educ:* Wyggeston Boys' Sch., Leicester; Corpus Christi Coll., Cambridge (BA Hons Hist. 1984). Joined FCO, 1984; Third Sec., 1987–88, Second Sec., 1988–89, Helsinki; FCO, 1989–91; First Secretary: FCO, 1991–93; Cairo, 1993–96; FCO, 1996–98; Kuwait, 1998–2001; FCO, 2001–03; Counsellor: Cairo, 2003–05; Riyadh, 2005–06. *Recreations:* squash, football, tennis, golf, bridge. *Address:* c/o Foreign and Commonwealth Office, King Charles Street, SW1A 2AH; *e-mail:* edmund.fitton-brown@fco.gov.uk.

FITZALAN-HOWARD, family name of **Lady Herries of Terregles** and of **Duke of Norfolk**.

FITZGERALD, family name of **Duke of Leinster**.

FitzGERALD, Sir Adrian (James Andrew Denis), 6th Bt *cr* 1880, of Valencia, Co. Kerry; 24th Knight of Kerry; *b* 24 June 1940; *o s* of Major Sir George FitzGerald, 5th Bt, MC and of Angela Dora (*née* Mitchell); *S* father, 2001. *Educ:* Harrow. Editor, Monday World, political qly, 1967–74; hotelier, 1983–90. Mem. (C) Council, Royal Borough of Kensington and Chelsea, 1974–2002 (Mayor, 1984–85; Chief Whip, 1986–95; Chm., Educn and Libraries Cttee, 1995–98; Chm., Highways and Traffic Cttee, 1999–2001). Dep. Leader, London Fire and Civil Defence Authy, 1989–90. Pres., Anglo-Polish Soc., 2001– (Chm., 1989–92); Vice-Chm., London Chapter, Irish Georgian Soc., 1990; Pres., Benevolent Soc. of St Patrick, 1997–. Gov., Cardinal Vaughan Meml Sch., 1999– (Vice-Chm., 2002–03, Chm., 2003–). Kt of Honour and Devotion, SMO, Malta. *Publication:* (contrib.) Education, Church and State, ed M. R. O'Connell, 1992. *Heir: cousin* Anthony Desmond FitzGerald [*b* 24 Dec. 1953; *m* 1986, Janine Miller (marr. diss. 2003); one *s*]. *Clubs:* Beefsteak, Pratt's; Kildare Street and University (Dublin).

FitzGERALD, Christopher Francis; Chairman, Regulatory Decisions Committee, Financial Services Authority, 2001–04; *b* 17 Nov. 1945; *s* of late Lt Comdr Michael Francis FitzGerald, RN and of Anne Lise FitzGerald (*née* Winther); *m* 1st, 1968, Jennifer (*née* Willis) (marr. diss. 1984); one *s* two *d*; 2nd, 1986, Jill (*née* Freshwater); two step *d*. *Educ:* Downside Sch.; Lincoln Coll., Oxford (Classical Schol.; BA Juris.; MA 1967). Admitted solicitor, 1971; Partner, Slaughter and May, 1976–95; Gen. Counsel, and Mem., Exec. Dirs' Cttee, NatWest Gp, 1995–2000. Non-executive Director: Intercare Gp plc, 2001–03; City Merchants High Yield Trust, 2007–; Mimecast Ltd, 2007–; Textron Financial Ltd, 2008–. Member: Finance Cttee, Lincoln Coll., Oxford, 2003–; Review Panel, Financial Reporting Council, 2006–. Chm., Macfarlane Trust, 2007–. *Recreations:* travelling, opera, theatre and concert going, appreciating fine wines. *Address:* 21 Palace Gardens Terrace, W8 4SA.

FitzGERALD, Rev. (Sir) Daniel Patrick, SSC, (4th Bt *cr* 1903, of Geraldine Place, St Finn Barr, Co. Cork, but does not use the title); *b* 28 June 1916; *S* brother, Rev. (Sir) Edward Thomas FitzGerald (3rd Bt), 1988, but his name does not appear on the Official Roll of the Baronetage. Roman Catholic priest. *Heir: cousin* John Finnbarr FitzGerald [*b* 11 June 1918; *m* 1949, Margaret Hogg; one *s* one *d*].

FITZ-GERALD, Desmond John Villiers, (29th Knight of Glin); Consultant, Christie, Manson & Woods Ltd, since 2003 (Irish Agent, 1975–2003); *b* 13 July 1937; *s* of Desmond Windham Otho Fitz-Gerald, 28th Knight of Glin (*d* 1949), and Veronica (who *m* 2nd, 1954, Ray Milner, CC (Canada), QC, Edmonton, Alta, and Qualicum Beach, Vancouver Island, BC), 2nd *d* of late Ernest Amherst Villiers, MP, and of Hon. Elaine Augusta Guest, *d* of 1st Baron Wimborne; *m* 1st, 1966, Louise Vava Lucia Henriette (marr. diss. 1970), *d* of the Marquis de la Falaise, Paris; 2nd, 1970, Olda Ann, *o d* of T. V. W. Willes, 39 Brompton Sq., SW3; three *d*. *Educ:* Stowe Sch.; University of British Columbia (BA 1959); Harvard Univ. (MA 1961). FSA 1970; MRIAI 1996. Asst Keeper, 1965–72, Dep. Keeper, 1972–75, Dept of Furniture and Woodwork, V&A. Pres., Irish Georgian Soc., 1991–; Chm., Irish Georgian Foundn, 1990– (Dir, 1974–); Vice-President: Stowe House Restoration Trust, 1999–; Bath Preservation Trust, 1999–; Director: Castletown Foundn, 1979–; Irish Architectural Archive, 1987–. Hon. RHA 2003. Hon. DLitt TCD, 2002. *Publications:* (ed) Georgian Furniture, 1969; (with Maurice Craig) Ireland Observed, a handbook to the buildings and antiquities, 1970; The Music Room from Norfolk House, 1972; (with Edward Malins) Lost Demesnes: Irish Landscape Gardening 1660–1845, 1976; (with Anne Crookshank) The Painters of Ireland, 1978; Irish Furniture, 1978; (jtly) Vanishing Country Houses of Ireland, 1988; (jtly) The Watercolours of Ireland, 1994; (with Anne Crookshank) Ireland's Painters, 2002; (with J. Peill) Irish Furniture, 2007; *catalogues*, all jointly: Irish Houses and Landscapes, 1963; Irish Architectural Drawings, 1965; Irish Portraits 1660–1860, 1969; Mildred Anne Butler, 1981; articles and reviews on architecture and the decorative arts in many Art periodicals. *Address:* Glin Castle, Glin, Co. Limerick, Ireland. *T:* (068) 34077 and 34173, *Fax:* (068) 34364; 52 Waterloo Road, Dublin 4, Ireland. *T:* (1) 680765, *Fax:* (1) 680271; *e-mail:* knight@101.ie. *Clubs:* Beefsteak, Brooks's, Society of the Dilettanti; Kildare Street and University (Dublin).

FITZGERALD, Edward Hamilton, CBE 2008; QC 1995; a Recorder, since 2002; *b* 13 Aug. 1953; *s* of Carrol James Fitzgerald and Cornelia (*née* Claiborne); *m* 1988, Rebecca Fraser; three *d*. *Educ:* Downside; Corpus Christi Coll., Oxford (BA 1st cl. Hons Lit. Hum. 1975); MPhil Cantab 1979. Called to the Bar, Inner Temple, 1978, Bencher, 2002. Times Justice Award, 1998. *Recreations:* reading history and novels, visiting the seaside, travel. *Address:* (chambers) 11 Doughty Street, WC1N 2PL. *T:* (020) 7404 1313.

FITZGERALD, Frank, CBE 1989; PhD; FREng; consultant, since 1992; Director, Sheffield Forgemasters Ltd, 1993–98; *b* 11 Nov. 1929; *s* of George Arthur Fitzgerald and Sarah Ann (*née* Brook); *m* 1956, Dorothy Eileen Unwin; two *s* one *d*. *Educ:* Barnsley Holgate Grammar Sch.; Univ. of Sheffield (BScTech; PhD). FEI (FInstE 1965); FREng (FEng 1977); FIMMM (FIM 2000; Dedicatee, Frank Fitzgerald Medal and Travel Award, IMMM). Ministry of Supply, RAE, Westcott, Bucks, 1955; United Steel Cos, Swinden Laboratories, Rotherham, 1960–68; British Steel plc (formerly British Steel Corporation), 1968–92: Process Res. Manager, Special Steels Div., 1970; Head Corporate Advanced Process Laboratory, 1972; Director, R&D, 1977; Man. Dir, Technical, 1981–92; Dir, 1986–92; Chairman: British Steel Corp. (Overseas Services), subseq. British Steel Consultants, 1981–89; British Steel Stainless, 1989–91. Hon. Fellow, Queen Mary, Univ. of London, 2004. Hon. DEng Sheffield, 1993. Hadfield Medal, Iron and Steel Inst., for work on application of combustion and heat transfer science to industrial furnaces, 1972; Melchett Medal, Inst. of Energy, 1988; Bessemer Gold Medal, Inst. of Metals, 1991; Esso Energy Award, Royal Soc., 1991. *Publications:* papers in learned jls on heat and mass transfer and metallurgical processes. *Recreation:* rock climbing and mountaineering. *Clubs:* Alpine; Climbers'.

FITZGERALD, Garret, PhD; Barrister-at-Law; Member of the Dáil (TD) (FG) for Dublin South East, 1969–92; Taoiseach (Prime Minister of Ireland), June 1981–March 1982 and 1982–87; *b* Dublin, 9 Feb. 1926; *s* of late Desmond FitzGerald (Minister for External Affairs, Irish Free State, 1922–27, and Minister for Defence, 1927–32) and Mabel FitzGerald (*née* McConnell); *m* 1947, Joan (*d* 1999), *d* of late Charles O'Farrell; two *s* one *d*. *Educ:* St Brigid's Sch., Bray; Coláiste na Rinne, Waterford; Belvedere Coll., University Coll., and King's Inns (Hon. Bencher, 1993), Dublin. Called to the Bar, 1947. Aer Lingus (Irish Air Lines), 1947–58; Rockefeller Research Asst, Trinity Coll., Dublin, 1958–59; College Lectr, Dept of Political Economy, University Coll., Dublin, 1959–87. Member: Seanad Eireann (Irish Senate), 1965–69; Dáil Cttee on Public Accounts, 1969–73; Minister for Foreign Affairs, Ireland, 1973–77; Leader and President, Fine Gael Party, 1977–87; Leader of the Opposition, 1977–June 1981, and March–Dec. 1982. President: Council of Ministers, EEC, Jan.–June 1975; European Council, July–Dec. 1984; Irish Council of Eur. Movement, 1977–81 and March–Dec. 1982; Mem., Internat. Exec. Cttee of Eur. Movement, 1972–73; Vice-Pres., Eur. People's Party, 1979–87; Member: Trilateral Commission, 1977–81, 1987–; Adv. Bd, Centre for Economic Policy Res., 1992–97; Internat. Adv. Bd, RILA Inc., 1999–. Mem., Oireachtas Library Cttee, 1965–69; Governor, Atlantic Inst. of Internat. Relations, Paris, 1972–73; Mem. Bd, Internat. Peace Acad., NY, 1990–; Chm., Council of Patrons, Saferworld, 1992–; Member: Senate of National Univ. of Ireland, 1973– (Chancellor, 1997–); Authy, Radio Telefis Eireann, 1995–2000. Formerly: Irish Correspondent of BBC, Financial Times, Economist and other overseas papers; Economic Correspondent, Irish Times; also Managing Dir, Economist Intelligence Unit of Ireland; Economic Consultant to Fedn of Irish Industries and Construction Industry Fedn, and Rep. Body for Guards. Past Member: Exec. Cttee and Council, Inst. of Public Admin; Council, Statistical and Social Inquiry, Soc. of Ireland; Senate Electoral Law Commn; Workmen's Compensation Commn; Transport Advisory Cttee for Second Programme; Cttee on Industrial Organisation; Gen. Purposes Cttee of Nat. Industrial Economic Council. Director: Trade Develt Inst., Dublin, 1987–; Point Holdings Ltd, 1996–; Election.com, 1999–. Weekly columnist, Irish Times, 1991–. Lectures: Radcliffe, Warwick Univ., 1980; Richard Dimbleby, BBC, 1982; Heinz, Pittsburgh Univ., 1980; Dunbar, Tulane Univ., 1987; Bass, Univ. of Ulster, 1988; Gaitskell, Nottingham Univ., 1988; Centenary Reckitt, London, 1988; Boston Coll., 1988, 1989; Schumann, UC, Cork, 1989; Morrell, Univ. of York, 1989; Mackintosh, Edinburgh Univ., 1990; Williamson, Univ. of Stirling, 1990; White, QUB, 1990; 2500 Anniv. of Democracy, Manchester Univ., 1993; Lloyd George, Criccieth, 1996. Hon. LLD: New York, 1974; St Louis, 1974; St Mary's, Halifax, NS, 1985; Keele, 1986; Boston Coll., 1987; Westfield Coll., Mass, 1990; Hon. DCL: Oxon, 1987; NUI, 1991; Dublin, 1998; QUB, 2000. Grand Cordon, Order of Al-Kaubar Al-Undari (Jordan), 1975; Grand Officier, Ordre de la République (Tunisia), 1976; Grand Cross (1st Cl.), Order of Merit (FRG), 1986; Order of Christ (Portugal), 1986; Grand Cordon, Order of Rising Sun (Japan), 1989; Comdr, Légion d'Honneur (France), 1995. *Publications:* State-sponsored Bodies, 1959; Planning in Ireland, 1968; Towards a New Ireland, 1972; Unequal Partners (UNCTAD), 1979; Estimates for Baronies of Minimum Level of Irish Speaking Amongst Successive Decennial Cohorts 1771–1781 to 1861–1871, 1984; All in a Life: an autobiography, 1991; Reflections on the Irish State, 2002. *Address:* 37 Annavilla, Dublin 6, Ireland. *T:* 4962600, *Fax:* (1) 4962126; *e-mail:* garretfg@iol.ie. *Clubs:* Reform; Royal Irish Yacht (Dun Laoghaire).

FITZGERALD, Hon. Gerald Edward, (Hon. Tony), AC 1991; FCIArb, FIArbA; mediator, arbitrator, dispute resolution consultant; formerly: Chairman, Law and Justice Foundation; Director, Australian Research Alliance for Children and Youth; *b* Brisbane, 26 Nov. 1941; *m* 1968, Catherine Glynn-Connolly; one *s* two *d*. *Educ:* Univ. of Queensland (LLB). Admitted Queensland Bar, 1964; QC Queensland 1975 and subseq. QC NSW and Victoria; Judge of Federal Court of Australia, 1981–84; Judge of Supreme Court of ACT, 1981–84; Pres., Court of Appeal, Supreme Court of Qld, 1991–98; Judge of Ct of Appeal, Supreme Ct of NSW, 1998–2001. Presidential Mem., Administrative Appeals Tribunal, 1981–84; Mem., Australian Law Reform Commn, 1981–84; Chairman, Commission of Inquiry: into possible illegal activities and associated police misconduct, Qld, 1987–89; into the Conservation, Management and Use of Fraser Is. and the Gt Sandy Reg., Qld, 1990–91; Chairman: Litigation Reform Commn, Qld, 1991–92; Cape York Justice Study, 2001. Chm., Australian Heritage Commn, 1990–91. Chairman: Nat. Inst. for Law, Ethics and Public Affairs, 1992–95; Key Inst. for Ethics, Law, Justice and Governance, 1999– (Hon. Prof., 2003–); Vis. Scholar, New York Univ. Sch. of Law, 1997; Professorial Fellow, Univ. of Melbourne Law Sch., 1999–. Chancellor, Sunshine Coast UC, 1994–98. Dep. Chm., Gov. Bd, Mater Health Services, 1995–98. Mem., Adv. Bd, Legal Information Access Centre, State Liby of NSW, 2002–05. Fellow, Australian Centre for Internat. Commercial Arbitration Ltd; Inaugural Fellow, LEADR. Mem., List of Neutrals, Arbitration and Mediation Center, WIPO. DUniv: Qld Univ. of Technol., 1995; Sunshine Coast, 1999; Griffith, 2003. *Recreations:* tennis, reading, music. *Address:* Level 7, Wentworth Chambers, 180 Phillip Street, Sydney, NSW 2000, Australia. *T:* (2) 82243030, *Fax:* (2) 93571637; *e-mail:* tonyfitzgerald@pacific.net.au.

FITZGERALD, Gerard, (Ged); Chief Executive, Lancashire County Council, since 2008; *b* Liverpool, 26 Aug. 1961; *s* of Timothy and Patricia Fitzgerald; *m* 1999, Karen Morris; one *d*. *Educ:* Goldsmiths' Coll., Univ. of London (BA Hons); Univ. of Salford (MBA). ACIS 1986; DMS 1992. Sefton MBC, 1983–97; Eur. Officer, Knowsley MBC, 1987–88; Policy Officer, Sefton MBC, 1988–91; Econ. Develt Manager, Knowsley MBC, 1991–94; Exec. Dir, Bootle City Challenge, 1994–96; Hd, Econ. Develt and Eur. Affairs, Liverpool CC, 1996–98; Dep. Chief Exec., Calderdale MBC, 1998–2001; Chief Executive: Rotherham MBC, 2001–04; Sunderland CC, 2004–08. *Recreations:* family, football - Liverpool FC fan, travel. *Address:* Lancashire County Council, PO Box 78, County Hall, Preston, Lancs PR1 8XJ. *T:* (01772) 533354, *Fax:* (01772) 532885; *e-mail:* Ged.fitzgerald@lancashire.gov.uk.

FITZGERALD, Dr Michael; Senior Fellow, Strategic Initiatives, research and consultancy group, Washington, since 1999; Chief Executive, Learning Review.com; Director, mike fitzgerald associates Ltd; *b* 4 May 1951; *s* of Richard Michael Fitzgerald and Janet Kilpatrick Costine Fitzgerald; two *s*. *Educ:* St Mary's Coll., Liverpool; Selwyn Coll., Cambridge (MA); Univ. of Leicester (PhD). Univ. of Leicester, 1973–75; taught social sciences, and criminology, Open Univ., 1975–87; Coventry Polytechnic, 1987–91; Vice-Chancellor, Thames Valley Univ., 1991–98. Vice-Chair, CVCP, 1997–98. Trustee, Paul Hamlyn Foundn, 1996. FRSA. *Publications:* 8 books on criminology. *Recreations:* rock music, football, cricket, crime fiction, channel surfing. *Address:* *e-mail:* mike-fitzgerald@msn.com. *Clubs:* Reform, Chelsea Arts.

FitzGERALD, Michael Frederick Clive, OBE 2002; QC 1980; *b* 9 June 1936; *s* of Sir William James FitzGerald, MC, QC, and Mrs E. J. Critchley; *m* 1st, 1966, Virginia Grace Cave (marr. diss. 1992); one *s* three *d*; 2nd, 1999, Nicola Mary Rountree (*née* Norman-Butler). *Educ:* Downside; Christ's Coll., Cambridge, 1956–59 (MA). 2nd Lieut 9th Queen's Royal Lancers, 1954–56. Called to the Bar, Middle Temple, 1961, Bencher, 1987. Leader, Parly Bar, 1997–2002. Chm., Adv. Panel on Standards for Planning Inspectorate Exec. Agency, 1992–2000. *Recreations:* opera, field sports. *Address:* 49 Cheval Place, SW7 1EW. *Club:* Boodle's.

FitzGERALD, Niall William Arthur, Hon. KBE 2002; Chairman, Reuters PLC, since 2004 (non-executive Director, since 2003); *b* 13 Sept. 1945; *s* of William FitzGerald and Doreen Chambers; *m* 1st, 1970, Monica Cusack (marr. diss. 2003); two *s* one *d*; 2nd, 2003, Ingrid Van Velzen; one *d*. *Educ:* St Munchins Coll., Limerick; University College Dublin (MComm). FCT 1986. Unilever, 1968–2004: North America, 1978–80; Chief Exec. Officer, Foods, S Africa, 1981–85; Group Treasurer, 1985–86; Financial Dir, 1987–89; Exec. Dir, 1987–96; Vice-Chm., 1994–96; Chm., 1996–2004; Director: Unilever Foods, 1990–91; Unilever Detergents, 1992–96. Non-executive Director: Bank of Ireland, 1990–99; Prudential Corp., 1992–99; Ericsson, 2000–02; Merck, 2000–03. A Sen. Advr, Morgan Stanley International. Chairman: CBI Europe Cttee, 1995–2001; Conference Bd, 2003–05; Co-Chairman: Transatlantic Business Dialogue, 2004–05; Investment Climate Facility for Africa, 2005–. Chm., Internat. Business Council, 2006–08; Member: EU-China Business Council, 1997; US Business Council, 1998–2006; Trilateral Commn, 1999; Council: Co-operation Ireland; World Econ. Forum, 1999–; Mem., President of South Africa's Internat. Investment Adv. Council, 2000–07. Pres., Advertising Assoc., 2000–05. CCMI. Chm., Bd of Trustees, BM, 2006–. Gov., NIESR, 1997–. Chm., Nelson Mandela Legacy Trust (UK), 2005–08; Trustee, Leverhulme Trust, 1996–. FRSA. *Recreation:* observing humanity. *Address:* Reuters Group PLC, 30 South Colonnade, Canary Wharf, E14 5EP. *Clubs:* Royal Automobile; Wisley Golf.

FITZGERALD, Prof. Patrick John; Adjunct Professor of Law, Carleton University, Ottawa, since 1996 (Professor of Law, 1971–96); *b* 30 Sept. 1928; *s* of Dr Thomas Walter and Norah Josephine Fitzgerald; *m* 1959, Brigid Aileen Judge; two *s* one *d*. *Educ:* Queen Mary's Grammar Sch., Walsall; University Coll., Oxford. Called to the Bar, Lincoln's Inn, 1951; Ontario Bar, 1984. Fellow, Trinity Coll., Oxford, 1956–60. Professor of Law: Leeds Univ., 1960–66; Univ. of Kent at Canterbury, 1966–71. Visiting Prof., University of Louisville, 1962–63. Consultant, Law Reform Commn of Canada, 1973–92. *Publications:* Criminal Law and Punishment, 1962; Salmond on Jurisprudence (12th edn), 1966; This Law of Ours, 1977; Looking at Law, 1979, 4th edn 1994; (ed) Crime, Justice and Codification, 1986. *Recreations:* music, golf, bridge. *Address:* 246–3310 Southgate Road, Ottawa, ON K1V 8X4, Canada.

FitzGERALD, Presiley Lamorna, (Mrs R. K. FitzGerald); *see* Baxendale, P. L.

FitzGERALD, Rowanne; *see* Pasco, R.

FitzGERALD, Susanna Patricia; QC 1999; *d* of Frederick Patrick FitzGerald, FRCSI, PPICS and Zina Eveline FitzGerald (*née* Moncrieff), FRCP; *m* 1983, Wendell, (Nick), Clough; two *s*. *Educ:* Benenden Sch.; Bristol Univ. (LLB Hons). Called to the Bar, Inner Temple, 1973, Bencher, 2007; in practice at the Bar, 1973–; specialises in liquor, gaming, lotteries, betting and public entertainment licensing law. Dir, Business in Sport and Leisure. Dir, Inst. of Licensing. Trustee, Gamcare. *Publications:* (contributing ed.) Law of Betting, Gaming and Lotteries, 2nd edn; (contrib.) Gambling and Public Policy, 1991; contributing ed., Halsbury's Laws of England, vol. 4(1), Betting, Gaming and Lotteries, 4th edn reissue, 2002. *Recreations:* renovating old houses, ski-ing. *Address:* 1 Essex Court, Temple, EC4Y 9AR. *T:* (020) 7583 2000.

FitzGERALD, Sylvia Mary Denise, FLS; Head of Library and Archives (formerly Chief Librarian and Archivist), Royal Botanic Gardens, Kew, 1979–99; *b* 7 May 1939; *d* of Audoen Aengus FitzGerald and Doris Winifred (*née* Dickinson). *Educ:* Our Lady of Sion Sch., Worthing; Open Univ. (BA Hons 1977); Univ. Surrey (MA Pastoral Theology 2005). MCLIP (ALA 1962). Assistant: Science Mus. Liby, 1956–57; Brit. Mus. (Natural Hist.) Zool. Liby, 1957–63; Assistant Librarian: Patent Office Liby, 1963–65; MAFF, 1965–67; Librarian-in-charge: MAFF Food & Nutrition Liby, 1967–72; MAFF Tolworth Liby for State Vet. Service and Vertebrate Pest Control, 1972–78. Member, Library Committee: Linnean Soc. of London, 1985–2003; RHS, 1993–. FLS 1992. *Publications:* contrib. State Librarian, Aslib Prog., Archives, etc. *Recreations:* friends, music. *Address:* 13 London Road, Ewell, Epsom, Surrey KT17 2BT.

FITZGERALD, Hon. Tony; *see* Fitzgerald, Hon. G. E.

FITZGERALD-LOMBARD, Rt Rev. Charles, OSB, **(James Michael Hube[rt] Fitzgerald-Lombard);** Abbot of Downside, 1990–98; Parish Priest, St Edmun[d's] Bungay, since 2006; *b* 29 Jan. 1941; *s* of late Col James C. R. Fitzgerald-Lombard an[d] Winifred (*née* Woulfe Flanagan). *Educ:* Downside; Collegio Sant Anselmo, Rome; King['s] Coll., London (MPhil). Monk of Downside Abbey, 1962–; ordained priest, 1968; Teach[er] and Tutor, Downside Sch., 1968–75; Bursar and Sec. to the Trustees, 1975–90. De[p.] Chm., Union of Monastic Superiors, 1998. Titular Abbot of Glastonbury, 1999[–]. Governor: Downside Sch., 1999–2003; St Edmund's Sch., Bungay, 2006–. Ecclesiastic[al] CLJ, 1995–. *Publications:* Prayers and Meditations, 1967, 3rd edn 1974; A Guide to th[e] Church of St Gregory the Great, Downside Abbey, 1981, 4th edn 2000; English an[d] Welsh Priests 1801–1914, 1993. *Address:* St Edmund's Presbytery, St Mary's Stree[t], Bungay, Suffolk NR35 1AX.

FitzHARRIS, Viscount; James Hugh Carleton Harris; *b* 29 April 1970; *s* and *heir* [of] Earl of Malmesbury, *qv*; *m* 1997, Jemima, *e d* of Captain M. Fulford-Dobson, *qv*; two *s* o[ne] *d*. *Educ:* Eton; Christ Church, Oxford (MEng); RAC Cirencester (DipAgr). ACA 199[–]. *Heir:* *s* Hon. James Michael Oswald Harris, *b* 26 April 1999. *Address:* Sydling Cou[rt], Sydling St Nicholas, Dorchester, Dorset DT2 9PA.

FITZHARRIS, Ven. Robert Aidan; Archdeacon of Doncaster, since 2001; *b* 19 Au[g.] 1946; *s* of late John Joseph and Margaret Louisa Fitzharris; *m* 1971, Lesley Margaret Ma[rie] Rhind; three *d*. *Educ:* St Anselm's Coll., Birkenhead; Sheffield Univ. (BDS 1971); Linco[ln] Theol Coll. (Gen. Ministerial Exam. 1989). General dental practice, 1971–87; part-tim[e] Clinical Asst to Prof. of Child Dental Health, Charles Clifford Dental Hosp., Sheffiel[d], 1978–85. Ordained deacon, 1989, priest, 1990; Asst Curate, Dinnington, 1989–92; Vic[ar] of Bentley, 1992–2001; Substitute Chaplain, HMP Moorland, 1992–2001; Area Dea[n], Adwick-le-Street, 1995–2001. Hon. Associate Chaplain, Doncaster Royal Infirmary an[d] Mexbrough Montague Hosp. Trust, 1995–2001; Hon. Canon, Sheffield Cathedral, 199[8–]. Chairman: Sheffield Diocesan Strategy Gp, 1999–2001; Sheffield Diocesan Bd of Educ[.], 2001–; Sheffield Diocesan Parsonages Cttee, 2001–; Doncaster Minster Develt Ctte[e], 2005–07; Together for Regeneration Project, 2004–; Doncaster Refurnish Ltd, 2007[–]. Mem., Doncaster Adv. Gp, Common Purpose S Yorks, 2004–. Chm., Doncaster Canc[er] Detection Trust, 2003–. Chm., Wildwood Project (Bentley) Ltd, 1998–2004. Vic[e-] Patron, Doncaster and Dist Family Hist. Soc., 2006–. Hon. Freeman, Bor. of Doncaste[r], 2008. *Recreations:* travel, reading, cooking. *Address:* Fairview House, 14 Armthorpe Lan[e], Doncaster DN2 5LZ. *T:* (01302) 325787, (office) (01709) 309110; *e-ma[il]:* archdeacons.office@sheffield.anglican.org.

FITZHERBERT, family name of **Baron Stafford**.

FitzHERBERT, Giles Eden, CMG 1985; HM Diplomatic Service, retired; *b* Dublin, [–] March 1935; *e s* of late Captain H. C. FitzHerbert, Irish Guards, and Sheelah, *d* of J. X[.] Murphy; *m* 1st, 1962, Margaret Waugh (*d* 1986); two *s* three *d*; 2nd, 1988, Alexandra Eyr[e]; three *s* one *d*. *Educ:* Ampleforth Coll.; Christ Church Oxford; Harvard Business Sch. 2n[d] Lieut, 8th King's Royal Irish Hussars, 1957–58. Vickers da Costa & Co., 1962–66. Fir[st] Secretary: Foreign Office, 1966; Rome, 1968–71; FCO, 1972–75; Counsellor: Kuwa[it], 1975–77; Nicosia, 1977–78; Head of Eur. Community Dept (Ext.), FCO, 1978–82; c[–] sabbatical leave, LSE, 1982; Inspector, FCO, 1983; Minister, Rome, 1983–8[–]; Ambassador to Venezuela and concurrently (non-resident) to the Dominican Republi[c], 1988–93. Contested (L) Fermanagh and South Tyrone, Gen. Elect., 1964. *Addres[s]:* Woodbrook House, Killann, Co. Wexford, Ireland. *Clubs:* Beefsteak; Kildare Street an[d] University (Dublin).

FitzHERBERT, Sir Richard (Ranulph), 9th Bt *cr* 1784, of Tissington, Derbyshire; *b* [–] Nov. 1963; *s* of Rev. David Henry FitzHerbert, MC (*d* 1976) and of Charmia[n] Hyacinthe, *yr d* of late Samuel Ranulph Allsopp, CBE; *S* uncle, 1989; *m* 1993, Carolin[e] Louise (marr. diss. 2007), *d* of Major and Mrs Patrick Shuter; one *s* one *d*. *Educ:* Eto[n] College. President: Derbys Community Foundn, 1995–; Derbys Rural Communit[y] Council, 1996–; Derbys Scouts, 2004–; Chm., E Midlands HHA, 1999–; Mem., Bd, [–] Midlands Tourism, 2004–. Patron, Soc. of Derbys Golf Captains. *Recreations:* cricke[t], shooting, restoring family estate. *Heir:* *s* Frederick David FitzHerbert, *b* 23 March 199[–]. *Address:* Tissington Hall, Ashbourne, Derbys DE6 1RA; *e-mail:* tisshall@dircon.co.u[k]. *Clubs:* White's, MCC; I Zingari, Stansted Hall Cricket, Parwich Royal British Legio[n] Cricket.

FitzHUGH, (Edmund Francis) Lloyd, OBE 1995; JP; DL; landowner; Chairma[n], North East Wales NHS Trust, 1999–2005; *b* 2 Feb. 1951; *s* of late Godfrey Edmun[d] FitzHugh and Burness Grace FitzHugh (*née* Clemson); *m* 1975, Pauline Davison; two [–] *Educ:* Eton; Shuttleworth Agricl Coll. Chm., Bd of Mgt, Royal Welsh Agricl Soc[.], 1991–98. Dep. Chm., Local Govt Boundary Commn for Wales, 1995–2002. JP Wrexha[m] 1990; DL Clwyd 1996. *Recreations:* church music, wining and dining. *Address:* Garde[n] House, Plas Power, Bersham, Wrexham LL14 4LN. *T:* (01978) 263522.

FITZMAURICE; *see* Petty-Fitzmaurice, family name of Marquess of Lansdowne.

FITZPATRICK, Brian; advocate; *b* 9 June 1961; *s* of late Patrick Fitzpatrick and Kathlee[n] (*née* Strong); *m* 1986, Marie Macdonald; one *s* two *d*. *Educ:* Univ. of Glasgow (LLB Jur[.] 1984). Called to Scottish Bar, 1993; Solicitor, Glasgow, Edinburgh and London, 1984–9[–]. Mem., Faculty of Advocates, 1993–. Hd of Policy, First Minister's Policy Unit, Scottis[h] Parlt, 1999–2000. MSP (Lab) Strathkelvin and Bearsden, June 2001–2003. Conteste[d] (Lab) Strathkelvin and Bearsden, Scottish Parlt, 2003. *Recreations:* swimming, cinem[a], reading, poetry, travel, wine. *Address:* c/o Advocates' Library, Parliament Hous[e], Edinburgh EH1 1RF.

FITZPATRICK, James; MP (Lab) Poplar and Canning Town, since 1997; Parliamentar[y] Under-Secretary of State, Department for Transport, since 2007; *b* 4 April 1952; *s* of Jame[s] Fitzpatrick and Jean Fitzpatrick (*née* Stones). *Educ:* Holyrood Sch., Glasgow. Traine[e], Tytrak Ltd, Glasgow, 1970–73; driver, Mintex Ltd, 1973–74; Firefighter, London Fi[re] Brigade, 1974–97. PPS to Sec. of State for Health, 1999–2001; an Asst Govt Whi[p], 2001–02; a Lord Comr of HM Treasury (Govt Whip), 2002–03; Vice-Chamberlain [of] HM Household, 2003–05; Parliamentary Under-Secretary of State: ODPM, 2005–0[6]; DTI, 2006–07. Mem., NEC, Fire Bdes Union, 1988–97. Mem. Exec., Gtr London La[b] Party, 1988–2000 (Chm., 1991–2000). Fire Bde Long Service and Good Conduct Meda[l], 1994. *Recreations:* golf, cycling, reading, football (West Ham Utd), television and film[.] *Address:* House of Commons, SW1A 0AA. *T:* (020) 7219 5085.

FITZPATRICK, Air Marshal Sir John (Bernard), KBE 1984; CB 1982; Royal A[ir] Force, retired; *b* 15 Dec. 1929; *s* of Joseph Fitzpatrick and Bridget Fitzpatrick; *m* 195[–] Gwendoline Mary Abbott; two *s* one *d*. *Educ:* RAF Apprentice Sch., Halton; RAF Col[–]

Cranwell. Officer Commanding: No 81 Sqdn, 1966–68; No 35 Sqdn, 1971–72; Gp Captain Plans to AOC No 18 Gp, 1973; OC, RAF Scampton, 1974–75; RCDS, 1976; Dir of Ops (Strike), RAF, 1977–79; SASO, HQ Strike Command, 1980–82; Dir Gen. of Organisation, RAF, 1982–83; AOC No 18 Gp, RAF, and Comdr Maritime Air Eastern Atlantic and Channel, 1983–86. Ind. Panel Inspector, Depts of the Envmt and Transport, 1986–99. *Recreations:* good food, good company, DIY. *Club:* Royal Air Force.

FITZPATRICK, John Ronald; Solicitor and Parliamentary Officer, Greater London Council, 1977–85, Consultant, 1985–86; *b* 22 Sept. 1923; *s* of Henry Fitzpatrick and Mary Lister; *m* 1952, Beryl Mary Newton; two *s* one *d. Educ:* St Bede's Coll., Manchester; Univ. of Manchester (LLB). Served War, RAF, navigator (Flt Lt), 1942–46. Admitted Solicitor, 1947; LMRTPI 1951. Asst Solicitor: Burnley, 1947; Stockport, 1948–51; Asst/Principal Asst Solicitor, Middx CC, 1951–65; Asst Clerk/Asst Dir-Gen., GLC, 1965–69; Asst Dir, 1969–72, Dir, 1972–77, Planning and Transportation, GLC. *Recreations:* golf, bridge. *Address:* Courtlands, 2 Langley Grove, New Malden, Surrey KT3 3AL. *T:* (020) 8942 8652.

FitzPATRICK, Joseph Martin; Member (SNP) Dundee West, Scottish Parliament, since 2007; *b* 1 April 1967; *s* of Joseph K. FitzPatrick and Margaret M. FitzPatrick (*née* Crabb). *Educ:* Univ. of Abertay Dundee (BSc Hons). Mem., Dundee CC, 1999–2007. Contested (SNP) Dundee W, 2005. *Recreations:* hill-walking, trekking, scuba diving. *Address:* (office) 8 Old Glamis Road, Dundee DD3 8HP. *T:* (01382) 623200, *Fax:* (01382) 903205; *e-mail:* dundee@joefitzpatrick.net.

FITZPATRICK, Prof. Raymond Michael, PhD; Professor of Public Health and Primary Care, University of Oxford, since 1996; Fellow, Nuffield College, Oxford, since 1986; *b* 8 Oct. 1950; *s* of James Fitzpatrick and Maureen Fitzpatrick; *m* 1979, Mary Boulton. *Educ:* UC, Oxford (BA); Bedford Coll., London Univ. (MSc; PhD 1986). Lecturer: Bedford Coll., London Univ., 1978–86; Oxford Univ., 1986–. Mem., MRC, 1998–2003 (Chm., Health Services and Public Health Res. Bd, 1998–2003). *Publications:* (jtly) The Experience of Illness, 1984; (ed with G. Albrecht) Quality of Life in Health Care, 1994; (jtly) Understanding Rheumatoid Arthritis, 1995; (ed jtly) Health Services Research Methods, 1998. *Recreations:* music, theatre. *Address:* Nuffield College, Oxford OX1 1NF. *T:* (01865) 278500.

FitzROY, family name of **Duke of Grafton** and of **Baron Southampton**.

FitzROY NEWDEGATE, family name of **Viscount Daventry**.

FITZSIMONS, Anthony; *see* Fitzsimons, P. A.

FITZSIMONS, Prof. James Thomas, FRS 1988; Professor of Medical Physiology, University of Cambridge, 1990–95, now Emeritus Professor; Fellow of Gonville and Caius College, Cambridge, since 1961 (President, 1997–2005); *b* 8 July 1928; *s* of Robert Allen Fitzsimons, FRCS and Dr Mary Patricia (*née* McKelvey); *m* 1961, Aude Irène Jeanne, *d* of Gén. Jean Etienne Valluy, DSO and Marie (*née* Bourdillon); two *s* one *d. Educ:* St Edmund's Coll., Ware; Gonville and Caius Coll., Cambridge (1st cl. Pts I and II, Nat. Sci. Tripos; BA 1949; BChir 1953; MB 1954; MA 1954; PhD 1960; MD 1967, Sir Lionel Whitby Medal; ScD 1979); Charing Cross Hosp. House appts, Leicester Gen. and Charing Cross Hosps, 1954–55; RAF, Inst. of Aviation Medicine, 1955–57 (Flight Lieut); Cambridge University: MRC Scholar, Physiol. Lab., 1957–59; Univ. Demonstrator in Physiol., 1959–64, Lectr, 1964–76, Reader, 1976–90; Gonville and Caius College: Tutor, 1964–72; Coll. Lectr in Physiol, 1964–93; Dir of Studies in Medicine, 1978–93. Visiting Scientist: CNRS Lab. des Régulations Alimentaires, Coll. de France, 1967; Inst. of Neurol Scis, Univ. of Pennsylvania, 1968, 1972; CNRS Lab. de Neurobiol., Coll. de France, 1975; Lectures: Stevenson Meml, Univ. of Western Ontario, 1979; Halliburton, KCL, 1982. Royal Soc. rep., British Nat. Cttee for Physiol. Scis, 1976–82; Mem., Physiol. Soc. Cttee, 1972–76 (Chm., 1975–76); Mem., IUPS Commn on Physiol. of Food and Fluid Intake, 1973–80 (Chm., 1979–80). Member, Editorial Boards: Jl of Physiol., 1977–84; Neuroendocrinology, 1979–84; Editor, Biological Reviews, 1984–95. Hon. MD Lausanne, 1978. Dist. Career Award, Soc. for Study of Ingestive Behavior, 1998. *Publications:* The Physiology of Thirst and Sodium Appetite, 1979; scientific papers in professional jls. *Recreations:* Irish language and literature, cats, music, photography, grandchildren. *Address:* Physiological Laboratory, Downing Street, Cambridge CB2 3EG. *T:* (01223) 333813; 91 Thornton Road, Girton, Cambridge CB3 0NR. *T:* (01223) 276874.

FITZSIMONS, Lorna, (Mrs S. B. Cooney); Chief Executive Officer, Britain Israel Communications & Research Centre, since 2006; *b* 6 Aug. 1967; *d* of late Derek Fitzsimons and of Barbara Jean Taylor; *m* 2000, Stephen Benedict Cooney; one *s,* and one step *s* one step *d. Educ:* Wardle High Sch.; Rochdale Coll. of Art and Design; Loughborough Coll. of Art and Design (BA Hons Textile Design 1988; a Vice Pres., Students' Union, 1988–89). National Union of Students: part-time Nat. Exec. Officer, 1989–90; Vice Pres., Educn, 1990–92; Pres., 1992–94; Rowland Public Affairs: Account Manager, 1994–95; Account Dir, 1995–96; Associate Dir, 1996–97. Mem. Bd, Endsleigh Insce, 1992–94. Chair, Student Forum, EU, 1990–94; Mem., Quality Cttee, FEFC, 1993–94. Member National Executive: Fabian Soc., 1996–97; Lab. Co-ordinating Cttee, 1995–97, Campaign of Electoral Reform, 1997, Labour Party. MP (Lab) Rochdale, 1997–2005; contested (Lab) same seat, 2005. PPS to Minister of State, FCO, 2000–01, to Leader of H of C, 2001–03. Treas., 1997–2003, Chm., 2003–05, All Party Parly Gp on Kashmir. Chair, 1997–2001, Vice Pres., 2001–05, Women's Cttee, PLP. Supporter, Labour Friends of Israel, 1997–2005. Lorna Fitzsimons Consulting, 2005–06. Sen. Associate Fellow, UK Defence Acad. Advanced Res. and Assessment Gp, 2005. Governor: Wardle High Sch., 1982–83, 2003–; Loughborough Coll. of Art and Design, 1988–89; Sheffield Hallam Univ., 1995–96. *Recreations:* watching films, cooking, walking, travelling, dancing or listening to music. *Address: e-mail:* mail@lornafitzsimons.co.uk.

FITZSIMONS, P. Anthony; Chairman: Ruton Management Ltd, since 1994; Great Western Ambulance Service NHS Trust, since 2007; Gloucestershire Probation Service, since 2007; *b* 16 March 1946; two *s. Educ:* LSE (BSc Econ.). Rank Xerox: Australia, 1972–75; Southern Europe, 1975–76; Australasia, Middle East, 1976–79; Regional Control Dir, London, 1979–81; Grand Metropolitan: Finance Systems and Strategy Dir, Brewing and Retail Div., 1981–83; Man. Dir, Host Group, 1983–85; Man. Dir, Personal Banking, Citibank, 1985–89; Chief Exec. and Man. Dir, Bristol & West Bldg Soc., 1989–93. Chm., Avon TEC. *Recreations:* squash, riding, music, sailing. *Address:* Hill House, Hannington, Wilts SN6 7RS.

FITZWALTER, 22nd Baron *cr* 1295; **Julian Brook Plumptre;** *b* 18 Oct. 1952; *s* of 21st Baron Fitzwalter and of Margaret Melesina (*née* Deedes); *S* father, 2004; *m* 1988, Sally, *o d* of late I. M. T. Quiney; three *s. Educ:* Radley; Wye Coll., London Univ. *Heir: s* Hon. Edward Brook Plumptre, *b* 26 April 1989.

FIVET, Edmond Charles Paul, CBE 2008; FRCM; Principal, Royal Welsh College of Music and Drama, 1989–2007; *b* 12 Feb. 1947; *s* of Paul Fivet and Lorna (*née* Edwards);

m 1st, 1969, Christine Partington (marr. diss. 1976); one *s* one *d;* 2nd, 1978, Elizabeth Page. *Educ:* Royal Coll. of Music; Coll. of St Mark and St John; City Univ. (MA); Open Univ. (BA). FRCM 1988. Registrar, 1973–83, Dir, 1983–89, Jun. Dept, Royal Coll. of Music; Music Dir, Audi Jun. Musician, 1986–98. Member: Music Cttee, Welsh Arts Council, 1991–94; Steering Cttee, NYO of Wales, 1991–2002; Music Cttee, Cardiff Internat. Fest., 1992–95; Council, Arts Council of Wales, 2000–03; Vice-Pres., Richmond upon Thames Arts Council, 1986–98. Member: Assoc. of European Conservatoires, 1989–2007; Heads of Higher Educn, Wales, 1996–2007. FRSA 1990. Gov., Dartington Coll. of Arts, 1997–2004. Trustee, Millennium Stadium Charitable Trust, 2001–06. Hon. FBC 2006. Hon. Dr Glamorgan, 2007. *Recreations:* golf, music, theatre, reading, current affairs. *Address:* Fig Tree House, 15 Church Walk, Aldeburgh, Suffolk IP15 5DU. *Clubs:* Savile; Aldeburgh Golf.

FLACK, Bertram Anthony, CMG 1979; HM Diplomatic Service, retired; *b* 3 Feb. 1924; *y s* of Dr F. H. Flack and Alice Cockshut, Nelson, Lancs; *m* 1948, Jean W. Mellor; two *s* two *d. Educ:* Epsom Coll.; Liverpool Univ. (LLB Hons). Enlisted Gren. Gds, 1942; commissioned E Lancashire Regt, 1943; served in NW Europe (Captain). Joined Foreign Service, 1948; served Karachi, 1948–50; Alexandria, 1950–52; Stockholm, 1955–58; Accra, 1958–61; Johannesburg, 1964–67; Dep. High Comr, E Pakistan, 1967–68; Inspector, Diplomatic Service, 1968–70; Head of Communications Dept, FCO, 1971–73; Commercial Counsellor, Stockholm, 1973–75; Canadian Nat. Defence Coll., 1975–76; Dep. High Comr, Ottawa, 1976–79; High Comr, Repub. of Uganda, 1979–80. *Recreations:* cricket, golf. *Address:* Abbotswood House Nursing Home, Crossag Road, Ballasalla, Isle of Man IM9 3DZ.

FLACK, Rt Rev. John Robert; Priest-in-Charge, Nassington with Yarwell and Woodnewton, and of Apethorpe, since 2008; *b* 30 May 1942; *s* of Edwin John Flack and Joan Annie Flack; *m* 1968, Julia Clare Slaughter; one *s* one *d. Educ:* Hertford Grammar Sch.; Univ. of Leeds (BA 1964); Coll. of the Resurrection, Mirfield. Ordained, deacon, 1966, priest, 1967; Assistant Curate: St Bartholomew, Armley, Leeds, 1966–69; St Mary the Virgin, Northampton, 1969–72; Vicar: Chapelthorpe (Wakefield dio.), 1972–81; Ripponden with Rishworth and Barkisland with West Scammonden, 1981–85; Brighouse, 1985–92 (Team Rector, 1988–92); Rural Dean of Brighouse and Elland, 1986–92; Archdeacon of Pontefract, 1992–97; Bishop Suffragan of Huntingdon, 1997–2003; Dir, Anglican Centre in Rome, and Archbp of Canterbury's Rep. to the Holy See, 2003–08. Hon. Assistant Bishop: Peterborough Dio., 2003–; Dio. in Europe. Hon. Canon of Wakefield Cathedral, 1989–97. *Recreations:* cricket, Mozart. *Address:* The Vicarage, 34 Station Road, Nassington, Peterborough PE8 6QB. *T:* (01780) 782271; *e-mail:* johnrobertFlack@hotmail.com.

FLAGG, Rt Rev. John William Hawkins; General Secretary, South American Missionary Society, 1986–93; *b* 16 April 1929; *s* of Wilfred John and Emily Flagg; *m* 1954, Marjorie Lund (*d* 1999); two *s* four *d. Educ:* All Nations Christian Coll.; Clifton Theological Coll. Agricultural missionary, Chile, 1951; Chaplain and Missionary Superintendent, St Andrew's, Asunción, Paraguay, 1959–64; Archdeacon, N Argentine, 1964–69; Diocesan Bishop of Paraguay and N Argentine, 1969–73; Asst Bishop for Chile, Peru and Bolivia, 1973–77; Bishop, Diocese of Peru, 1977; Asst Bishop, Diocese of Liverpool, 1978–86; Vicar, St Cyprian's with Christ Church, Edge Hill, 1978–85; Priest-in-Charge of Christ Church, Waterloo, 1985–86; Hon. Assistant Bishop: of Rochester, 1986–92; of Southwell, 1992–97. Member of Anglican Consultative Council, 1974–79; Presiding Bishop of Anglican Council of South America (CASA), 1974–77. Diocesan Advr in rural ministry, and stewardship, 1993–96, and overseas relns, 1994–96, Southwell. *Publication:* From Ploughshare to Crook, 2000.

FLANAGAN, Andrew Henry; Chairman, Fleming Media, since 2007; *b* 15 March 1956; *s* of Francis Desmond Flanagan and Martha Donaldson Flanagan; *m* 1992, Virginia Walker; two *s* one *d. Educ:* Glasgow Univ. (BAcc). CA. Touche Ross, 1976–79; Price Waterhouse, 1979–81; Financial Control Manager, ITT, 1981–86; Finance Dir, PA Consulting Gp, 1986–91; Gp Finance Dir and Chief Financial Officer, BIS Ltd, 1991–94; Finance Dir, Scottish Television plc, 1994–96; Man. Dir, Scottish Television plc, 1996–97; Chief Exec., SMG (formerly Scottish Media Gp) plc, 1997–2006. Trustee, NESTA, 2006–. *Recreations:* golf, ski-ing, television. *Address:* 7 Collylinn Road, Bearsden, Glasgow G61 4PN. *Club:* Royal Automobile.

FLANAGAN, Barry, OBE 1991; RA 1991 (ARA 1987); sculptor; *b* 11 Jan. 1941. *Educ:* Birmingham Coll. of Arts and Crafts; St Martin's Sch. of Art. Teacher, St Martin's Sch. of Art and Central Sch. of Art and Design, 1967–71. One-man exhibitions include: Rowan Gall., 1966, 1968, 1970–74; Fischbach Gall., NY, 1969; Galleria del Leone, Venice, 1971; Mus. of Modern Art, NY, Mus. of Modern Art, Oxford, 1974; Hogarth Galls, Sydney, 1975; Centro de Arte y Communicación, Buenos Aires, 1976; (retrospective) Van Abbemuseum, Eindhoven, Arnolfini Gall., Bristol, Serpentine Gall. (tour), 1977–79; Galerie Durand-Dessert, Paris, 1980, 1982, 1988, 1992, 1996; Waddington Galls, 1980–81, 1983, 1985, 1990, 1994, 1998, 2001, 2004; Inst. of Contemporary Arts (prints and drawings), 1981–82; British Pavilion, XL Venice Biennale, and tour, 1982–83; Centre Georges Pompidou, Paris, 1983; Pace Gall., NY, 1983, 1990, 1994; Fuji Television Gall., Tokyo, 1985, 1991; Tate Gall., 1986; Laing Art Gall., Newcastle upon Tyne, Mus. of Contemporary Art, Belgrade, City Gall., Zagreb, Mus. of Modern Art, Ljubljana (tour), 1987–88; (retrospective) Madrid and Nantes, 1993–94; RHA Gallagher Gall., Dublin, 1995; Park Ave., NY, Grant Park, Chicago, 1995–96; Galerie Xavier Hufkens, Brussels, 1999; Tate, Liverpool, 2000; Kunsthalle Recklinghausen, Germany, Musée d'Art Moderne et d'Art Contemporaine, Nice (tour), 2002; Irish Mus. of Modern Art, Dublin, 2006. Work includes: outdoor sculpture for Sint Pietersplein, Ghent, 1980; Camdonian sculpture, Lincoln's Inn Fields, 1980; bronze sculptures: Baby Elephant and Hare on Bell, Equitable Life Tower West, NY, 1984; Nine Foot Hare, Victoria Plaza, London, 1984; The Boxing Ones, Capability Green, Luton Hoo Estate, Beds, 1986; Kouros Horse, Stockley Park, Uxbridge, 1987; The Cricketer, 1989, Jesus Coll., Cambridge; two bronze Leaping Hare sculptures for Kawakyo Co., Osaka, 1990. Choreographed two pieces for dance gp, Strider, 1972. Judge, Bath Sculpture Competition, 1985. *Address:* c/o Waddington Galleries, 11 Cork Street, W1S 3LT.

FLANAGAN, Caroline Jane; Partner, Ross & Connel, Solicitors, Dunfermline, since 1990; President, Law Society of Scotland, 2005–06; *b* 12 Jan. 1961; *d* of Leslie and Sheila Ebbutt; *m* 1986, Roy Flanagan; one *s* one *d. Educ:* Dollar Acad.; Edinburgh Univ. (LLB, DipLP). Trainee, then asst solicitor, 1982–90. Dean, Dunfermline and Dist Soc. of Solicitors, 2000–02; Vice-Pres., Law Soc. of Scotland, 2004–05. *Recreations:* ski-ing, walking, reading, music. *Address:* Ross & Connel, 18 Viewfield Terrace, Dunfermline KY12 7JH. *T:* (01383) 721156; *e-mail:* cflanagan@ross.connel.co.uk.

FLANAGAN, Michael Joseph; Director, Finance and Planning, Cheshire Constabulary, 1995–2000; Company Secretary, FFBA Ltd; *b* 21 Nov. 1946; *s* of Daniel and Margaret Constance Flanagan; *m* 1968, Patricia Holland; two *s* one *d. Educ:* St Joseph's Coll., Blackpool; Southampton Coll. of Higher Educn. IPFA 1972; DMS 1983. Trainee Accountant, Lancs CC, 1965–69; Preston County Borough, 1969–70; Southampton City

Council, 1970–72; Accountant, 1972, Asst Dir of Finance, 1981–87, Telford Develt Corp.; Dir of Finance and Tech. Services, 1987–90, Chief Exec., 1990–95, Develt Bd for Rural Wales. *Recreations:* sport, esp. football, golf, tennis; family activities. *Club:* Lancs CC.

FLANAGAN, Sir Ronald, GBE 2002 (OBE 1996); Kt 1999; QPM 2007; HM Chief Inspector of Constabulary, since 2005; *b* 25 March 1949; *s* of John Patrick Flanagan and Henrietta Flanagan; *m* 1968, Lorraine Nixon; three *s*. *Educ:* Belfast High Sch.; Univ. of Ulster (BA, MA); Graduate: FBI Nat. Acad., 1987; FBI Nat. Exec. Inst., 1996. Joined Royal Ulster Constabulary, as Constable, 1970: Sergeant, Belfast, 1973; Inspector, Londonderry, 1976, Belfast, 1977–81; Detective Inspector, 1981; Detective Chief Inspector, 1983; Detective Superintendent, Armagh, 1987; Chief Superintendent, Police Staff Coll., Bramshill, 1990; Asst Chief Constable, Belfast, 1992; Actg Dep. Chief Constable, 1995, affirmed Feb. 1996; Chief Constable, RUC, 1996–2002; HM Inspector of Constabulary, 2002–05. *Recreations:* walking, Rugby, reading (particularly Yeats' poetry), music (particularly Van Morrison), but very varied taste. *Address:* c/o Home Office, 2 Marsham Street, SW1P 4DF. *Club:* Royal Ulster Yacht (Bangor, Co. Down).

FLANDERS, Stephanie Hope; Economics Editor, BBC, since 2008; *b* 5 Aug. 1968; *d* of late Michael Flanders, OBE and Claudia Flanders, OBE; partner, John Arlidge; one *s*. *Educ:* St Paul's Girls' Sch., Hammersmith; Balliol Coll., Oxford (Schol.; BA 1st Cl. Hons PPE); John F. Kennedy Sch. of Govt, Harvard Univ. (Kennedy Schol.; MPA). Research Officer: London Business Sch., 1990–91; Inst. for Fiscal Studies, 1991–92; Teaching Fellow, Dept of Govt, Harvard Univ., and Kennedy Sch. of Govt, 1993–94; econs leader-writer and columnist, Financial Times, 1994–97; Sen. Advr and speechwriter to Lawrence H. Summers, US Treasury Dept, 1997–2001; reporter, NY Times, 2001; Econs Ed., Newsnight, BBC TV, 2002–08. Mem., Council on Foreign Relns, 2001–. Mem., Gen. Council, REconS, 2007–. FRSA 2006. *Publications:* Principal Editor: World Bank World Development Reports, 1996, 1997; UN Human Development Report, 2002. *Recreations:* cycling, collecting jokes. *Address:* Room 4220, BBC Television Centre, Wood Lane, W12 7RJ. *T:* (020) 8624 9820. *Club:* Soho House.

FLATHER, family name of **Baroness Flather**.

FLATHER, Baroness *cr* 1990 (Life Peer), of Windsor and Maidenhead in the Royal County of Berkshire; **Shreela Flather;** JP; DL; Councillor, Royal Borough of Windsor and Maidenhead, 1976–91 (first ethnic minority woman Councillor in UK), Mayor, 1986–87 (first Asian woman to hold this office); *b* Lahore, India; *née* Shreela Rai; *m* Gary Flather, *qv*; two *s*. *Educ:* University Coll. London (LLB; Fellow 1992). Called to the Bar, Inner Temple, 1962. Infant Teacher, ILEA, 1965–67; Teacher of English as a second lang., Altwood Comp. Sch., Maidenhead, 1968–74, Broadmoor Hosp., 1974–78. Chairman: Consortium for Street Children Charities, 1992–94; Disasters Emergency Cttee, 1993–96; Vice Chm., Refugee Council, 1991–94; Member: W Metropolitan Conciliation Cttee, Race Relations Bd, 1973–78; Cttee of Inquiry (Rampton, later Swann Cttee) into Educn of Children from Ethnic Minority Gps, 1979–85; Comr, CRE, 1980–86 (Chm., Educn, Housing and Services Cttee, and Welsh Consultative Cttee, 1980–86); UK Rep., EC Commn into Racism and Xenophobia, 1994–95. Member: Police Complaints Board, 1982–85; HRH Duke of Edinburgh's Inquiry into British Housing, 1984–85; Lord Chancellor's Legal Aid Adv. Cttee, 1985–88; Social Security Adv. Cttee, 1987–90; Econ. and Social Cttee, EC, 1987–90; Carnegie Inquiry into the Third Age, 1990–93; H of L Select Cttee on Med. Ethics, 1993–94; Equal Opportunities Cttee, Bar Council, 2002–03; Chm., Alcohol Educn and Res. Council, 1996–2002; Dir, Marie Stopes Internat., 1996–. President: Cambs, Chilterns and Thames Rent Assessment Panel, 1983–97; Community Council for Berks, 1991–98; Member: Thames and Chilterns Tourist Bd, 1987–88; Berks FPC, 1987–88; Jt Pres., FPA, 1995–98; Vice-Pres., BSA, 1988–91. Member: Cons. Women's Nat. Cttee (formerly Cons. Women's Nat. Adv. Cttee), 1978–89; Exec. Cttee, Anglo-Asian Cons. Soc., 1979–83; NEC, Cons. Party, 1989–90; Sec., Windsor and Maidenhead Cons. Gp, 1979–83. Chm., Star FM, 1992–97; Director: Daytime Television, 1978–79; Thames Valley Enterprise, 1990–93; Meridian Broadcasting, 1991–2001; Cable Corp., 1997–2000; Kiss FM, 2000–02; Pres., Global Money Transfer, 1997–2001. Member: BBC S and E Regl Adv. Cttee, 1987–89; Cttee of Management, Servite Houses Ltd, 1987–94; LWT Prog. Adv. Bd, 1990–94. Member: Bd of Visitors, Holloway Prison, 1981–83; Broadmoor Hosp. Bd, 1987–88 (Chm., Ethics Cttee, 1993–97; Equal Opportunities Cttee, 1994–97; Pres., League of Friends, 1991–98); Dir, Hillingdon Hosp. Trust, 1990–98. Vice President: Townswomen's Guilds; Servite Houses Housing Assoc.; Carers Nat. Assoc.; British Assoc. for Counselling and Psychotherapy, 1999–. Chm., Memorial Gates Trust, 1998–; Member Council: Winston Churchill Meml Trust, 1993–2008; St George's Hse, Windsor Castle, 1996–2002; Mem., UK Adv. Council, Asia House, 1996–; Chm., ClubAsia, 2002–07; Trustee: Berks Community Trust, 1978–90; Borlase Sch., Marlow, 1991–97; Rajiv Gandhi UK Foundn, 1993–2001; Bookpower (formerly Educational Low Priced Sponsored Texts), 2001–07; Pan African Health Foundn, 2004–. Governor: Commonwealth Inst., 1993–98; Altwood Comp. Sch., Maidenhead, 1978–86; Slough Coll. of Higher Educn, 1984–89; Mem. Council, Atlantic Coll., 1994–98. Pres., Alumni Assoc., 1998–2000, Lay Mem., Council, 2000–06, UCL. Sec./Organiser Maidenhead Ladies' Asian Club, 1968–78; Founder, LINK (club for Asian conservatives in H of L), 1994–98; Chm., New Star Boys' Club, 1969–79; Vice Chairman: Maidenhead CAB, 1982–88; Maidenhead CRC, 1969–72; formerly Vice Chairman: Maidenhead Police Consultative Cttee; Maidenhead Volunteer Centre. FRSA 1999. JP Maidenhead, 1971; DL Berks, 1994. DUniv Open, 1994. Asian of the Year, 1996. *Publication:* Stepping Stones (Adult English Training Scheme), 1973. *Recreations:* travel, cinema, swimming. *Address:* House of Lords, SW1A 0PW. *T:* (020) 7219 5353.

FLATHER, Gary Denis, OBE 1999; QC 1984; a Recorder, since 1986; a Deputy High Court Judge, since 1997; *b* 4 Oct. 1937; *s* of Denis Flather and Joan Flather; *m* 1965, Shreela Rai (*see* Baroness Flather); two *s*. *Educ:* Oundle Sch.; Pembroke Coll., Oxford (MA 1958). Called to the Bar, Inner Temple, 1962, Bencher, 1995 (Mem., Scholarships Cttee); first Hon. Mem. Bar, 2002. National Service, Second Lieut 1st Bn York and Lancaster Regt, 1956–58; Lieut Hallamshire Bn, TA, 1958–61. Asst Parly Boundary Comr, 1982–90; Asst Recorder, 1983–86. Mem., Panel of Chairmen: for ILEA Teachers' Disciplinary Tribunal, 1974–90 (Chm., Disciplinary ILEA Tribunal, William Tyndale Jun. Sch. teachers, 1976); for Disciplinary Tribunal for London Polytechnics, 1982–90; a Chairman: Police Disciplinary Appeals, 1987–; MoD (Police) Disciplinary Appeals, 1992–; Special Educnl Needs and Disability Tribunal, 2004–. Legal Mem., Mental Health Review Tribunal (restricted patients), 1987–; a Financial Services Act Inspector, employees of Coutts Bank, 1987–88; a legal assessor: GMC and GDC, 1987–95; RCVS, 2000–; a Comr, Royal Hosp. Chelsea, 2005–; Chairman: Statutory Cttee, RPharmS, 1990–2000 (Hon. MRPharmS 2001); Disciplinary Cttee, Chartered Inst. of Marketing, 1993–. Bar Council: Chm., Disability Panel, 1992–2002; Member: Chambers Arbitration Panel, 1995; Equal Opportunities Cttee, 1998–2002. Dir, W. Fearnehough (Bakewell) Ltd, 1991–2002. Pres., Maidenhead Rotary Club, 1990–91. Vice-Pres., Community Council for Berks, 1987–2001; Littlewick Green Show, 1997–. Trustee: ADAPT, 1995–2007; Disabled Living Foundn, 1997–2003. Escort to the Mayor of the Royal Borough of Windsor and Maidenhead, 1986–87. *Recreations:* travel, music, dogs, coping with multiple sclerosis, laughing with friends. *Address:* 4/5 Gray's Inn Square, Gray's Inn WC1R 5AY. *T:* (020) 7404 5252, *Fax:* (01628) 675355; *e-mail:* garyflather@yahoo.co.uk

FLATT, Rev. Roy Francis Ferguson; Dean of Argyll and the Isles, 1999–2005 (Hon Canon, since 2006); Rector of Christ Church, Lochgilphead, with St Columba's Poltalloch (Kilmartin), and All Saints, Inveraray, since 1983; *b* 4 Sept. 1947; *s* of Ray and Trixie Flatt; *m* 1978, Andrina Ferguson; two *s*. *Educ:* King Edward VI Grammar Sch. Bury St Edmunds; Scottish Sch. of Librarianship, Univ. of Strathclyde; Coates Hall Edinburgh. Deacon 1980, priest 1981; Curate, St Andrews, Elie and Earlsferry and Pittenweem, dio. St Andrews, 1980–82; Diocesan Supernumerary, 1982–83. *Recreations:* reading, sketching, playing solitaire on the PC, adding to the family semiopathy collection. *Address:* Bishopton House, Lochgilphead, Argyll PA31 8PY. *T:* (01546) 602315.

FLAUX, Hon. Sir Julian Martin, Kt 2007; **Hon. Mr Justice Flaux;** a Judge of the High Court, Queen's Bench Division, since 2007; *b* 11 May 1955; *s* of late Louis Michael Flaux and of Maureen Elizabeth Brenda Flaux; *m* 1983, Matilda Christian (*née* Gabb); three *s*. *Educ:* King's Sch., Worcester; Worcester Coll., Oxford (BCL, MA). Called to the Bar Inner Temple, 1978, Bencher, 2002; in practice, 1979–2007; QC 1994; a Recorder 2000–07; a Dep. High Ct Judge, 2002–07. *Recreations:* opera, reading, walking. *Address:* Royal Courts of Justice, Strand, WC2A 2LL.

FLAVELL, Prof. Richard Anthony, PhD; FRS 1984; Chairman, since 1988, and Sterling Professor of Immunobiology, since 2002 (Professor of Immunobiology, since 1988), Yale University School of Medicine; Professor of Biology, Yale University, and Investigator of the Howard Hughes Medical Institute, since 1988; *b* 23 Aug. 1945; *s* of John T. and Iris Flavell; *m* Madlyn (*née* Nathanson); one *d*; two *s* of former *m*. *Educ:* Dept of Biochemistry, Univ. of Hull (BSc Hons Biochem. 1967; PhD 1970). Royal Soc. Eur Fellow, Univ. of Amsterdam, 1970–72; EMBO Post-doctoral Fellow, Univ. of Zürich 1972–73; Wetenschappelijk Medewerker, Univ. of Amsterdam, 1973–79; Head, Lab. of Gene Structure and Expression, NIMR, Mill Hill, 1979–82; Pres., Biogen Res. Corp. 1982–88; Principal Res. Officer and CSO, Biogen Gp, 1984–88. Darwin Trust Vis. Prof. Univ. of Edinburgh, 1995. Mem., EMBO, 1978–. MRI 1984–; Mem., Amer. Assoc. of Immunologists, 1990–; FAAAS 2000; MNAS 2002; Mem., Inst. of Medicine, NAS, 2006 Anniversary Prize, FEBS, 1980; Colworth Medal, Biochem. Soc., 1980. *Publications:* *chapters in:* Handbook of Biochemistry and Molecular Biology, ed Fasman, 3rd edn 1976 McGraw-Hill Yearbook of Science and Technology, 1980; Eukaryotic Genes: their structure, activity and regulation, ed jtly with Maclean and Gregory, 1983; articles in numerous scientific jls, incl. Nature, Cell, Proc. Nat. Acad. Sci., EMBO Jl, Jl Exp. Med Sci., Science, and Immunity; contrib. Proceedings of symposia. *Recreations:* music, tennis horticulture. *Address:* Department of Immunobiology, Yale University School of Medicine, 300 Cedar Street, Suite S–569, New Haven, CT 06520–8011, USA; *e-mail:* richard.flavell@yale.edu.

FLAVELL, Dr Richard Bailey, CBE 1999; FRS 1998; Chief Scientific Officer, Ceres Inc., since 1998; *b* 11 Oct. 1943; *s* of Sidney Flavell and Emily Gertrude Flavell (*née* Bailey); *m* 1966, Hazel New; two *d*. *Educ:* Univ. of Birmingham (BSc 1964); Univ. of East Anglia (PhD 1967). Research Associate, Univ. of Stanford, California, 1967; Plant Breeding Institute, 1969–88 (Head, Molecular Genetics Dept, 1985–88); Dir, John Innes Inst., subseq. Centre, and John Innes Prof. of Biology, UEA, 1988–98; Chm. Mgt Cttee AFRC Inst. of Plant Sci. Res., 1990–94. Hon. Prof., King's College London, 1986–90 Fellow, EMBO, 1990; Pres., Internat. Soc. for Plant Molecular Biology, 1993–95 *Publications:* scientific papers and books. *Recreations:* music, gardening. *Address:* Ceres Inc. 1535 Rancho Conejo Boulevard, Thousand Oaks, CA 91320, USA. *T:* (805) 3766500 *e-mail:* rflavell@ceres-inc.com.

FLAXEN, David William; statistics consultant; *b* 20 April 1941; *s* of late William Henry Flaxen and Beatrice Flaxen (*née* Laidlow); *m* 1969, Eleanor Marie Easton; two *d*. *Educ:* Manchester Grammar Sch.; Brasenose Coll., Oxford (MA Physics); University Coll London (DipStat). Teacher, Leyton County High School for Boys, 1963; UK Government Statistical Service, 1963–96: Central Statistical Office and Min. of Labour 1964–71; UNDP Advr, Swaziland, 1971–72; Statistician, Dept of Employment, 1973–75 Chief Statistician: Dept of Employment, 1975–76; Central Statistical Office, 1976–77 and 1981–83; Inland Revenue, 1977–81; Asst Dir (Under-Sec.), Central Statistical Office 1983–89; Dir of Statistics, Dept of Transport, 1989–96. Creator of Tax and Price Index 1979. Stats consultant to overseas govts esp. in Central and Eastern Europe and Africa *Publications:* contribs to articles in Physics Letters, Economic Trends, Dept of Employment Gazette, etc. *Recreations:* bridge, wine, cooking, music. *Address:* 65 Corringham Road NW11 7BS. *T:* (020) 8458 5451, *Fax:* (020) 8731 6270; *e-mail:* dflaxen@easynet.co.uk.

FLECK, Prof. Norman Andrew, FRS 2004; PhD; CEng, FIMMM; Professor of Mechanics of Materials, Cambridge University, since 1997; Fellow of Pembroke College Cambridge, since 1982; *b* 11 May 1958; *s* of William and Roberta Fleck; *m* 1983, Vivien Christine Taylor; one *s* one *d*. *Educ:* Jesus Coll., Cambridge (BA 1979; MA 1981); PhD Cantab 1982. FIMMM (FIM 1997). Maudslay Res. Fellow, Pembroke Coll., Cambridge 1983–84; Lindemann Fellow, Harvard Univ., 1984–85; Cambridge University: Lectr in Engineering, 1985–94; Reader in Mechanics of Materials, 1994–97; Dir, Cambridge Centre for Micromechanics, 1996–. *Publications:* (jtly) Metal Foams: a design guide, 2000 numerous papers in mechanics and materials jls. *Recreations:* running, ski-ing, wine church. *Address:* Cambridge University Engineering Department, Trumpington Street Cambridge CB2 1PZ. *T:* (01223) 332650.

FLECKER, James William, MA; Founder/Director, European Language Year, since 2003; Headmaster, Ardingly College, 1980–98; *b* 15 Aug. 1939; *s* of Henry Lael Oswald Flecker, CBE, and Mary Patricia Flecker; *m* 1967, Mary Rose Firth; three *d*. *Educ:* Marlborough Coll.; Brasenose Coll., Oxford (BA, now MA Lit. Hum., 1962). Asst Master: Sydney Grammar Sch., 1962–63; Latymer Upper Sch., 1964–67; (and later Housemaster), Marlborough Coll., 1967–80. Recruitment Manager, Students Partnership Worldwide, 1998–2001 (Trustee, 2001–); Recruiter, BESO, 2001–05; Short Term Placement Advr, VSO, 2005–06. Trustee: Alive and Kicking, 2003– (Chm., 2005–) Good Earth Trust, 2006– (Chm., 2006–). Governor: Reed's Sch., Cobham, 1998–; Royal Masonic Sch. for Girls, Rickmansworth, 2007–. *Recreations:* hockey, cricket, flute playing children's operas. *Address:* 42 Church Street, Great Bedwyn, Wilts SN3 3PQ. *T:* (01672) 870079; *e-mail:* james@flecker.com.

FLEET, Dr Andrew James, FGS; Keeper of Mineralogy, Natural History Museum, since 1996; *b* 14 June 1950; *s* of late Rupert Stanley Fleet and of Margaret Rose Fleet (*née* Aitken); *m* 1976, Susan Mary Adamson; one *s* one *d*. *Educ:* Bryanston Sch.; Chelsea Coll. Univ. of London (BSc; PhD 1977). FGS 1976. UNESCO Fellow in Oceanography Open Univ., 1975–79; Lectr in Geochem., Goldsmiths' Coll., Univ. of London, 1979–80 Research and Exploration, BP, 1980–95, Head, Petroleum Geochem. Res., 1987–95. Vis Prof. in Geol., ICSTM, 1997–. Special Pubns Ed., 1993–2002, Mem. Council 1997–2000, 2002–05 and 2006–, Sec. (Publications), 2002–05, Treas., 2006–, Geol Soc *Publications:* edited jointly: Marine petroleum source rocks, 1987; Lacustrine petroleum source rocks, 1988; Petroleum migration, 1991; Coal and coal-bearing strata as oil-prone source rocks?, 1994; Muds and mudstones: physical and fluid flow properties, 1999; Petroleum Geology of Northwest Europe: proceedings of the 5th conference, 1999; contrib. papers in scientific jls on petroleum and sedimentary geochemistry and marine geology. *Recreations:* archaeology, cricket, family, cooking, wine. *Address:* Department of Mineralogy, Natural History Museum, Cromwell Road, SW7 5BD. *T:* (020) 7938 9226.

FLEGG, Dr James John Maitland, OBE 1997; FIHort; Director, External Affairs, Horticulture Research International, East Malling, 1995–97, now consultant, horticulture and environment; Chairman, Meiosis Ltd, since 2000; *b* Hong Kong, 23 April 1937; *s* of Jack Sydney Flegg and Lily Elizabeth (*née* Spooner); *m* 1976, Caroline Louise Coles; two *s. Educ:* Melbourne, Australia; Gillingham Grammar Sch.; Imperial Coll. of Science and Technol. (BSc, PhD). ARCS 1962; FIHort 1993. Nematologist, E Malling Res. Stn, 1956–66; MAFF, 1966–68; Dir, Brit. Trust for Ornithology, Tring, 1968–75; Hd, Zool. Dept, E Malling Res. Stn, 1976–87; Dir of Inf. Services, 1987–95, and Hd of Stn, 1990–95, Horticulture Res. Internat., East Malling. Presenter, Country Ways, Meridian TV. Sec., European Soc. of Nematologists, 1965–68; Mem. Council, RSPB, 1978–83; Pres., Kent Ornithol Soc., 1986–2004. MBOU 1966. Chm., Romney Marsh Res. Trust, 1990–2000. Freeman, City of London; Liveryman, Co. of Fruiterers. *Publications:* books include: In Search of Birds, 1983; Oakwatch, 1985; Birdlife, 1986; Field Guide to the Birds of Britain and Europe, 1990; Poles Apart, 1991; Deserts, 1993; Classic Birds (60 Years of Bird Photography): a biography of Eric Hosking, 1993; Photographic Field Guide to the Birds of Australia, 1996; Time to Fly: exploring bird migration, 2004; numerous papers and articles on nematological, ornithological and envmtl topics. *Recreations:* wildlife, rural history, environmental affairs, photography, gardening, music, communication. *Address:* Divers Farm, E Sutton, Maidstone, Kent ME17 3DT.

FLEISCHMANN, Prof. Martin, FRS 1986; FRSC 1980; Research Professor: Department of Chemistry, University of Southampton, since 1983; University of Utah, since 1988; *b* 29 March 1927; *s* of Hans Fleischmann and Margarethe Fleischmann (*née* Srb); *m* 1950, Sheila Flinn; one *s* two *d. Educ:* Worthing High School; Imperial College of Science and Technology. ARCS 1947; BSc 1948; PhD 1951. ICI Fellow, King's College, Univ. of Durham, 1952–57; Lectr, then Reader, Univ. of Newcastle upon Tyne, 1957–67; Electricity Council Faraday Prof. of Electrochemistry, Univ. of Southampton, 1967–77; Senior Fellowship, SERC, 1977–82. Pres., Internat. Soc. of Electrochemistry, 1970–72. Palladium Medal, US Electrochemical Soc., 1985. *Publications:* numerous papers and chapters in books. *Recreations:* ski-ing, walking, music, cooking. *Address:* Bury Lodge, Duck Street, Tisbury, Wilts SP3 6LJ. *T:* (01747) 870384.

FLELLO, Robert Charles Douglas; MP (Lab) Stoke-on-Trent South, since 2005; *b* 14 Jan. 1966; *s* of Douglas Flello and Valerie Swain; *m* 1990, Teresa (*née* Gifoli); one *d*, and one step *s. Educ:* University Coll. of N Wales, Bangor (BSc Hons). Consultant, Price Waterhouse, 1989–94; Manager, Arthur Andersen, 1994–99; Dir, Platts Flello Ltd, 1999–2003; CEO, Malachi Community Trust, 2003–04. Associate: Royal Inst. Taxation, 1990–; Soc. Financial Advrs, 1998–. *Recreations:* reading, running, ancient history, cooking, riding my motorbike. *Address:* House of Commons, SW1A 0AA; 2A Stanton Road, Stoke-on-Trent ST3 6DD. *T:* (01782) 593393, *Fax:* (01782) 593430.

FLEMING, Anne Elizabeth; film archive consultant, since 2005; *b* 12 Aug. 1944; *d* of Harry Gibb Fleming and Agnes Wilkie Fleming (*née* Clark); *m* 2003, Taylor Downing. *Educ:* Univ. of Edinburgh (MA Hons English Lit. and Lang.). Films Administrator, Edinburgh Film Fest., 1966, 1967, 1968, 1969; teacher of English as a foreign lang., Acad. of Langs, Catania, Sicily, 1967–68; Imperial War Museum; Res. Asst, Dept. of Film Programming, 1970–72; Res. Asst, Dept. of Film, 1972–73; Dep. Keeper, 1973–83, Keeper, 1983–90, Dept of Film; Dep. Curator, 1990–97, Curator, 1997–2000, BFI Nat. Film and TV Archive; Hd of Content, MAAS Media Online, British Univs Film and Video Council, 2001–05. *Publications:* contribs to catalogues and data-bases. *Recreations:* cinema, reading, walking, cooking, growing herbs. *Address:* 27 Malwood Road, SW12 8EN. *T:* (020) 8675 0674.

FLEMING, Ven. David; Chaplain-General to HM Prisons and Archdeacon of Prisons, 1993–2001; Chaplain to the Queen, 1995–2007; *b* 8 June 1937; *s* of John Frederick Fleming and Emma (*née* Casey); *m* 1966, Elizabeth Anne Marguerite Hughes; three *s* one *d. Educ:* Hunstanton County Primary School; King Edward VII Grammar School, King's Lynn; Kelham Theological Coll. National Service with Royal Norfolk Regt, 1956–58. Deacon 1963; Asst Curate, St Margaret, Walton on the Hill, Liverpool, 1963–67; priest 1964; attached to Sandringham group of churches, 1967–68; Vicar of Great Staughton, 1968–76; Chaplain of HM Borstal, Gaynes Hall, 1968–76; RD of St Neots, 1972–76; RD of March, 1977–82; Vicar of Whittlesey, 1976–85; Priest-in-Charge of Pondersbridge, 1983–85; Archdeacon of Wisbech, 1984–93; Vicar of Wisbech St Mary, 1985–88. Hon. Canon of Ely Cathedral, 1982–2001. Chm. of House of Clergy, Ely Diocesan Synod, 1982–85. *Recreations:* tennis, chess, extolling Hunstanton. *Address:* Fair Haven, 123 Wisbech Road, Littleport, Ely, Cambs CB6 1JJ. *Club:* Whittlesey Rotary.

FLEMING, Dr David, OBE 1997; Director, National Museums Liverpool (formerly National Museums and Galleries on Merseyside), since 2001; *b* 25 Dec. 1952; *s* of Jack and Doreen Fleming; *m* 2007, Alison Jane Hastings, *qv*; one *d*, and two *s* one *d* from a previous marriage. *Educ:* London Sch. of Econs; Leeds Univ. (BA Hons); Leicester Univ. (MA; PhD 1981). Curator: Yorkshire Mus. of Farming, 1981–83; Collection Services, Leeds Mus, 1983–85; Principal Keeper of Mus, Hull Mus, 1985–90; Asst Dir, 1990–91, Dir, 1991–2001, Tyne & Wear Museums. Mem. Exec. Bd, ICOM (UK), 1997–2000. Chairman: Social History Curators Gp, 1986–87; Museum Professionals Gp, 1986–90; Liverpool Culture Partnership, 2003–05; Liverpool Heritage and Regeneration Adv. Gp, 2005–06; Mem. Adv. Cttee on the Export of Works of Art, 1991–93; Convenor, Gp for Large Local Authority Museums, 1998–2001; Member: NW Cultural Consortium, 2003–04; Culture Cttee, UK Nat. Commn for UNESCO, 2005–; Creative Apprenticeship Task Force, 2005–. Trustee: Yorks and Humberside Museums Council, 1986–90; Nat. Mus. of Labour History, 1990–92; North of England Mus. Service, 1990–2001; Nat. Football Mus., 1996–2003; NE Cultural Consortium, 1999–2001; Cultural Heritage Nat. Trng Orgn, 2000–01; NE Museums, Libraries and Archives Council, 2001; NW Museums Service, 2001–02; Liverpool Capital of Culture Co., 2001–03; St George's Hall, 2001–08; Bluecoat Arts Centre, 2004–. President: Museums Assoc., 2000–02; Internat. Cttee on Mus. Mgt, 2004–. *Recreations:* my family, history, travel, literature, Leeds United, collecting CDs. *Address:* World Museum, William Brown Street, Liverpool L3 8EN. *T:* (0151) 478 4201; *e-mail:* david.fleming@liverpoolmuseums.org.uk.

FLEMING, Fergus Hermon Robert; writer, since 1991; *b* 13 Oct. 1959; *s* of Richard and Charm Fleming; partner, Elizabeth Hodgson; one *s* one *d. Educ:* Magdalen Coll., Oxford (MA); City Univ., London. Trainee accountant, Ernst & Whinney, 1981–82; acad. trng as barrister, 1982–83; furniture maker, Christopher Clark Workshops, 1984–85; writer and ed., Time-Life Books, 1985–91. Director: Ian Fleming Pubns Ltd; Queen Anne Press. *Publications:* Amaryllis Fleming, 1993; The Medieval Messenger, 1996; The

Greek Gazette, 1997; The Viking Invader, 1997; Stone Age Sentinel, 1998; Barrow's Boys, 1998; Killing Dragons, 2000; Ninety Degrees North, 2001; The Sword and the Cross, 2003; Tales of Endurance, 2004; (ed) The Explorer's Eye, 2005. *Address:* c/o Aitken Alexander Associates, 18–21 Cavaye Place, SW10 9PT. *T:* (020) 7373 8672. *Club:* Leander (Henley-on-Thames).

FLEMING, Prof. George, PhD; FREng, FICE; FCIWM; FRSE; Professor of Civil Engineering, University of Strathclyde, 1985–2003, now Emeritus; Managing Director, EnviroCentre, since 1993; *b* Glasgow, 16 Aug. 1944; *s* of Felix and Catherine Fleming; *m* 1966, Irene MacDonald Cowan; two *s* one *d. Educ:* Univ. of Strathclyde (BSc 1st cl. Hons; PhD 1969). FICE 1982; FREng (FEng 1987); FRSE 1992; FASCE 2000; FCIWM 2002 (MIWM 1987). Res. Fellow, Stanford Univ., 1967; University of Strathclyde: Res. Asst, 1966–69; Lectr, 1971–76; Sen. Lectr, 1976–82; Reader, 1982–85; Dir and Vice Pres., Hydrocomp Internat., 1969–77. Consultant, Watson Hawkesley, 1980–92; non-exec. Dir, WRAP, 2001–07. Member: Overseas Projects Bd, DTI, 1991–95; British Waterways Bd, 2001–07; Port of Tyne Bd, 2005–. Pres., ICE, 1999–2000; Mem., Smeatonian Soc. of Civil Engrs, 1998. Hon. Mem., British Hydrol Soc. *Publications:* Computer Simulation in Hydrology, 1971; The Sediment Problem, 1977; (ed) Recycling Derelict Land, 1991; (contrib.) Geochemical Approaches to Environmental Engineering of Metals, 1996; (contrib.) Energy and the Environment: geochemistry of fossil, nuclear and renewable resources, 1998. *Recreations:* farming, DIY, travelling. *Address:* EnviroCentre, Unit 2B, Craighall Business Park, Eagle Street, Glasgow G4 9XA.

FLEMING, Prof. Graham Richard, PhD; FRS 1994; Melvin Calvin Distinguished Professor of Chemistry, University of California, Berkeley, since 1997; Berkeley Director, Institute for Quantitative Biomedical Research (QB3), University of California, since 2001; *b* 3 Dec. 1949; *s* of Maurice Norman Henry Fleming and Lovima Ena Winter; *m* 1977, Jean McKenzie; one *s. Educ:* Bristol Univ. (BSc Hons); Royal Instn (PhD London). Res. Fellow, CIT, 1974–75; Univ. Res. Fellow, Univ. of Melbourne, 1975–76; Leverhulme Fellow, Royal Instn, 1977–79; University of Chicago: Asst Prof., 1979–83; Associate Prof., 1983–85; Prof., 1985–87; Arthur Holly Compton Dist. Service Prof., Dept of Chem., 1987–97; Dep. Dir, Lawrence Berkeley Nat. Lab., Univ. of Calif, Berkeley, 2005–07. Mem., NAS, 2007–. Fellow, Amer. Acad. of Arts and Scis, 1991. *Publications:* Chemical Applications of Ultrafast Spectroscopy, 1986; numerous articles in learned jls. *Recreation:* mountaineering. *Address:* Department of Chemistry, B84 Hildebrand #1460, University of California, Berkeley, CA 94720–1460, USA. *T:* (510) 6432735, *Fax:* (510) 6426340; *e-mail:* fleming@cchem.berkeley.edu.

FLEMING, Grahame Ritchie; QC (Scot.) 1990; Sheriff of Lothian and Borders, since 1993; *b* 13 Feb. 1949; *s* of Ian Erskine Fleming and Helen Ritchie Wallace or Fleming; *m* 1984, Mopsa Dorcas Robbins; one *d. Educ:* Forfar Acad.; Univ. of Edinburgh (MA, LLB). Admitted Faculty of Advocates, 1976. Standing Jun. Counsel to Home Office in Scotland, 1986–89. *Recreations:* food, travel, supporting the Scottish Rugby team. *Address:* Sheriff's Chambers, Sheriff Court House, Court Square, Linlithgow EH49 7EQ.

FLEMING, Prof. Ian, FRS 1993; Professor of Organic Chemistry, University of Cambridge, 1998–2002, now Emeritus (Reader in Organic Chemistry, 1986–98); Fellow of Pembroke College, Cambridge, 1964–2002; *b* 4 Aug. 1935; *s* of David Alexander Fleming and Olwen Lloyd Fleming (*née* Jones); *m* 1st, 1959, Joan Morrison Irving (marr. diss. 1962); 2nd, 1965, Mary Lord Bernard. *Educ:* Pembroke Coll., Cambridge (MA, PhD 1963; ScD 1982). Cambridge University: Res. Fellow, Pembroke Coll., 1962; Univ. Demonstrator, 1964–65; Asst Dir of Research, 1965–80; Univ. Lectr, 1980–86. *Publications:* (with D. H. Williams) Spectroscopic Methods in Organic Chemistry, 1966, 6th edn 2007; (with D. H. Williams) Spectroscopic Problems in Organic Chemistry, 1967; Selected Organic Syntheses, 1973; Frontier Orbitals and Organic Chemical Reactions, 1976; Pericyclic Reactions, 1998; 273 papers in chem. jls. *Recreations:* watching movies, reading, music. *Address:* Pembroke College, Cambridge CB2 1RF. *T:* (01223) 362862.

FLEMING, James Randolf G.; *see* Gibson Fleming.

FLEMING, John Bryden; retired; *b* 23 June 1918; *s* of W. A. Fleming, advocate, and Maria MacLeod Bryden; *m* 1st, 1942, Janet Louise Guthrie (*d* 1981); one *s* three *d*; 2nd, 1998, Valerie Howard (*née* Forbes). *Educ:* Edinburgh Academy; Univs of Edinburgh and London. MA Hons Geog. Edinburgh, BScEcon London. Army, 1940–46, RASC and REME. Planning Officer, Dept of Health for Scotland, 1946; Principal, 1956; Asst Sec., Scottish Develt Dept, 1963, Under Sec., 1974–78; Sec., Scottish Special Housing Assoc., 1978–83. *Recreations:* gardening, hill walking. *Address:* The Old Parsonage, Cambridge Street, Alyth, Perthshire PH11 8AW. *T:* (01828) 632027. *Club:* Royal Commonwealth Society.

FLEMING, John Marley; Vice President, Sales and Marketing, Saab Automobile, Sweden, 1993–94; *b* 4 April 1930; *s* of David A. Fleming and Mary L. Fleming (*née* Marley); *m* 1961, Jeanne (*née* Retelle); one *s* two *d. Educ:* Harvard Coll., Cambridge, Mass, USA (BA); Harvard Business Sch., Boston, Mass (MBA). Lieut US Navy, 1952–55. Dist Manager, Frigidaire Sales Corp., 1957–63; Sales Promotion Manager, Ford Motor Co., 1963–68; Vice-Pres., J. Walter Thompson Co., 1969; Dir of Marketing, Oldsmobile Div., GMC, 1970–76; Dir of Sales, Adam Opel AG, West Germany, 1977–79; Dir of Commercial Vehicles, 1980–81, and Chm. and Man. Dir, 1982–85, Vauxhall Motors Ltd; Vice Pres., Sales, General Motors, Europe, 1986–87; Gen. Dir, Marketing and Product Planning, Cadillac Motor Car Div., General Motors, 1988–91. *Recreations:* ski-ing, sailing, golf. *Clubs:* Abenaqui Country (New Hampshire); Lemon Bay Golf (Florida).

FLEMING, Kenneth Anthony, DPhil; FRCPath; Head of Medical Sciences Division, University of Oxford, since 2000; Fellow of Green Templeton College (formerly Green College), Oxford, since 1981; *b* 7 Jan. 1945; *s* of Thomas and Margaret Fleming; *m* 1969, Jennifer; two *s* one *d. Educ:* Univ. of Glasgow (MB ChB); Merton Coll., Oxford (DPhil; MA). FRCPath 1988. University of Glasgow: Sen. House Officer, 1969–70; Registrar in Pathology, 1970–72; Lectr in Pathology, 1972–78; Wellcome Res. Fellow in Pathology, Univ. of Oxford, 1978–80; MRC Travelling Fellow, Roche Inst. for Molecular Biology, USA, 1980–81; University of Oxford: Clinical Reader in Pathology, 1981–2000; Dir of Planning and Develt, 1995–97; Dean, Faculty of Clinical Medicine, 1997–2000. Hon. Consultant in Pathology, Oxford Radcliffe Hosps Trust, 1981–. Hon. FRCP. *Publications:* over 100 articles in learned jls on aspects of molecular biology and pathology. *Recreation:* golf. *Address:* Medical Sciences Office, University of Oxford, Level 3, John Radcliffe Hospital, Oxford OX3 9DU. *T:* (01865) 220548, *Fax:* (01865) 222951; *e-mail:* kenneth.fleming@admin.ox.ac.uk.

FLEMING, Prof. Peter John, CBE 2001; PhD; FRCP, FRCPC, FRCPCH; Professor of Infant Health and Developmental Physiology, University of Bristol, since 1995 (Head, Division of Child Health, 1996–2002); Consultant Paediatrician, Royal Hospital for Children, Bristol, since 1982; *b* 19 Aug. 1949; *s* of Nora Eileen Page and step *s* of Peter John Page; *m* 1973, Dr Josephine Olwen Allen; four *s. Educ:* Gillingham Grammar Sch., Kent; Univ. of Bristol (MB ChB 1972; PhD 1993). MRCP 1975, FRCP 1988; FRCPC

1981; FRCPCH 1997. Senior House Officer: Southmead Hosp., Bristol, 1974–75; Gt Ormond St Hosp., 1975–76; Sen. Resident, 1976–77, Fellow in Neonatal Medicine, 1977–78, Hosp. for Sick Children, Toronto; Sen. Registrar, Paediatrics, Royal Hosp. for Children, Bristol, 1978–81. Pres., Assoc. of Clinical Profs of Paediatrics, 2002–05; Member: Neonatal Soc., 1979–; British Assoc. Perinatal Medicine, 1980–; Paediatric Intensive Care Soc., 1987–. FRSA 1996. *Publications:* A Neonatal Vade Mecum, 1986, 3rd edn 1998; The Care of Critically Ill Children, 1993; Sudden Unexpected Death in Infancy, 2000; Unexpected Death in Childhood, 2007; contrib. numerous original and rev. articles on neonatal medicine, developmental physiology, the epidemiology and prevention of cot death and paediatric intensive care to learned jls. *Recreations:* being with my family, running marathons and half-marathons, listening to and playing music, reading. *Address:* Foundation for Study of Infant Deaths Research Unit, Level D, St Michael's Hospital, Southwell Street, Bristol BS2 8EG. *T:* (0117) 342 0172, *Fax:* (0117) 928 5154; *e-mail:* peter.fleming@bris.ac.uk.

FLEMING, Raylton Arthur; freelance journalist specialising in international affairs, music and Mallorca; editorial adviser, Majorca Daily Bulletin; *b* 1 Sept. 1925; *s* of Arthur and Evelyn Fleming; *m* 1967, Leila el Doweini; one *s*. *Educ:* Worksop Coll. Associate Producer, World Wide Pictures Ltd, 1952; Head of Overseas Television Production, Central Office of Information, 1957; Dep. Dir, Films/Television Div., COI, 1961; Asst Controller (Overseas) COI, 1968; Actg Controller (Overseas), 1969; Dir, Exhibns Div. COI, 1971; Controller (Home), COI, 1972–76; Controller (Overseas), COI, 1976–78; Dir of Inf., UN Univ., Japan, 1978–83; Dir, UN Univ. Liaison Office, NY, 1983–84; Liaison Officer, UN Univ., World Inst. for Develt Econs Res., Helsinki, 1984–86. *Recreations:* music, opera. *Address:* Camino del Castillo, 07340 Alaro, Mallorca, Spain.

FLEMING, Renée L.; soprano; *b* 14 Feb. 1959; *d* of Edwin Davis Fleming and Patricia (Seymour) Alexander; *m* 1989, Richard Lee Ross (marr. diss. 2000); two *d*. *Educ:* Potsdam State Univ. (BM Music Educn 1981); Eastman Sch. of Music (MM 1983). Studied at Juilliard American Opera Center, 1983–84, 1985–87; Fulbright Schol., Frankfurt, 1984–85. *Débuts* include: Spoleto Fest., Charleston and Italy, 1986; Houston Grand Opera, 1988; NYC Opera, 1989; Covent Garden, 1989; San Francisco Opera, 1991; Met. Opera, Paris Opera, Bastille, 1991; Teatro Colon, Buenos Aires, 1991; La Scala, Milan, 1993; Lyric Opera, Chicago, 1993. Winner, Met. Opera Nat. Auditions, 1988; George London Prize, 1988; Richard Tucker Award, 1990; Solti Prize, 1998; Grammy Award, 1999, 2003; Classical Brit Award, 2004. Hon. DMus Juilliard, 2003. Commandeur des Arts et des Lettres (France), 2002; Chevalier de la Légion d'Honneur (France), 2005. *Publication:* The Inner Voice, 2004. *Address:* c/o M. L. Falcone, Public Relations, 155 West 68th Street, Suite 1114, New York, NY 10023–5817, USA. *T:* (212) 5804302.

FLEMING, Robert, (Robin); DL; Chairman, Robert Fleming Holdings, 1990–97; *b* 18 Sept. 1932; *s* of late Major Philip Fleming and Joan Cecil Fleming (*née* Hunloke); *m* 1962, Victoria Margaret Aykroyd; two *s* one *d*. *Educ:* Eton College; Royal Military Academy, Sandhurst. Served The Royal Scots Greys, 1952–58. Joined Robert Fleming, 1958; Director: Robert Fleming Trustee Co., 1961– (Chm., 1985–91); Robert Fleming Holdings, 1974–97 (Dep. Chm., 1986–90). High Sheriff, 1980, DL 1990, Oxfordshire. *Recreations:* most country pursuits, most types of music. *Address:* Church Farm, Steeple Barton, Bicester, Oxon OX25 4QR. *T:* (01869) 347177.

FLEMING, Roderick John; Director: Fleming Family & Partners, 2000–08; Highland Star Group, since 2000; Chairman, Robert Fleming Holdings Ltd, 2000 (Director, 1994–2000; Deputy Chairman, 1999–2000); *b* 12 Nov. 1953; *s* of Richard Evelyn Fleming and Hon. Dorothy Charmian Fleming; *m* 1979, Diana Julia Wake; twin *d*. *Educ:* Eton Coll.; Magdalen Coll., Oxford (MA History). Trainee: Cazenove, 1974–75; Morgan Guaranty, NY, 1975–76; Corporate Finance Dept, Robert Fleming, 1976–80; joined Jardine Fleming, Singapore, 1980, Man. Dir, 1982–84; Dir, Jardine Fleming Internat. Ltd, with responsibility for internat. corporate finance, Jardine Fleming, Tokyo, 1984–86; International Portfolios Gp, Robert Fleming: joined, 1986; estbd Product Develt Gp, 1989; Product Develt Gp Dir, 1990–2000; Director: Capital Mkts, 1991–2000, Corporate Finance UK, 1993–2000, Robert Fleming; Robert Fleming Trustee Co. Ltd, 1991–; Dover Corp., 1995–2002; Ian Fleming (Glidrose) Pubns Ltd, 1996– (Chm., 2000–). *Recreation:* country pursuits. *Address:* Fleming Family & Partners (Liechtenstein) AG, AM Schrägen Weg 2, Postfach 740, 9490 Vaduz, Liechtenstein. *Clubs:* White's, Mark's.

FLEMING, Thomas Kelman, (Tom), CVO 1998; OBE 1980; *b* 29 June 1927; *s* of late Rev. Peter Fleming and Kate Ulla Fleming (*née* Barker). *Educ:* Daniel Stewart's Coll., Edinburgh. Actor, writer, producer and broadcaster; toured India with Edith Evans, 1945; RN, 1945–47; co-founder and Dir, Edinburgh Gateway Co., 1953–65; RSC, 1962–64, toured Europe, USA, USSR; founder and Dir, Royal Lyceum Theatre Co., 1965–66; Dir, Scottish Mil. Tattoo, Washington, 1976; Governor, Scottish Theatre Trust, 1980–82; Dir, Scottish Theatre Co., 1982–87; numerous Edinburgh Festival performances and productions. Member: Drama Adv. Panel, British Council, 1983–89; Lamp of Lothian Collegiate Trust, 1970–95; Scottish Internat. Educn Trust, 1996–. Pres., Edinburgh Sir Walter Scott Club, 2000. Hon. Mem., Royal Scottish Pipers' Soc.; Hon. Life Mem., Saltire Soc. Hon. FRSAMD 1986. DUniv Heriot-Watt, 1984; Hon. DLitt Queen Margaret UC, 1999. *Films* include: King Lear; Mary Queen of Scots; Meetings with Remarkable Men; *television:* title rôles include, 1952–: Redgauntlet; Rob Roy; Jesus of Nazareth; Henry IV; Weir of Hermiston; Reith; over 2000 broadcasts, 1944–; *television and radio:* BBC commentator, royal events, incl. Queen's Coronation, 1953, Silver Jubilee, 1977, and Queen's Birthday Parades, 1970–94; Cenotaph service, 1961, 1965–99; D Day, VE Day and VJ Day commems, 1994, 1995; also funeral services of HRH Duke of Windsor, King Frederick IX of Denmark, HRH Duke of Gloucester, Cardinal Heenan, Viscount Montgomery of Alamein, Pope John Paul I, Earl Mountbatten of Burma, President Tito, Princess Grace of Monaco, King Olav V of Norway, Diana, Princess of Wales and Queen Elizabeth, the Queen Mother. Proposed Immortal Memory of Robert Burns, Kremlin, 1991. Andrew Fletcher of Saltoun Award for services to Scotland, 2000. *Publications:* It's My Belief, 1953; So That Was Spring (poems), 1954; Miracle at Midnight (play), 1954; Voices out of the Air, 1981; (contrib.) BBC Book of Memories, 1991; (contrib.) A Scottish Childhood, 1998. *Recreations:* noticing, remembering and wondering. *Address:* c/o United Agents, 12–26 Lexington Street, W1F 0LE. *Clubs:* Royal Commonwealth Society; Scottish Arts (Hon. Mem.) (Edinburgh).

FLESCH, Michael Charles; QC 1983; *b* 11 March 1940; *s* of late Carl and Ruth Flesch; *m* 1972, Gail Schrire; one *s* one *d*. *Educ:* Gordonstoun Sch.; University College London (LLB 1st Cl. Hons). Called to the Bar, Gray's Inn, 1963 (Lord Justice Holker Sen. Schol.), Bencher, 1993. Bigelow Teaching Fellow, Univ. of Chicago, 1963–64; Lectr (part-time) in Revenue Law, University Coll. London, 1965–82. Practice at Revenue Bar, 1966–. Chairman: Taxation and Retirement Benefits Cttee, Bar Council, 1985–93; Revenue Bar Assoc., 1993–95. Governor of Gordonstoun Sch., 1976–96. *Publications:* various articles, notes and reviews concerning taxation, in legal periodicals. *Recreation:* all forms of sport. *Address:* (home) 38 Farm Avenue, NW2 2BH. *T:* (020) 8452 4547; (chambers) Gray's Inn Chambers, Gray's Inn, WC1R 5JA. *T:* (020) 7242 2642, *Fax:* (020) 7831 9017. *Club* MCC, Arsenal FC, Brondesbury Lawn Tennis and Cricket.

FLESHER, Timothy James, CB 2002; Chief of Corporate Services, Defence Equipme and Support Organisation, Ministry of Defence, since 2007; *b* 25 July 1949; *s* of Jam Amos Flesher and Evelyn May Flesher (*née* Hale); *m* 1986, Margaret McCormack; two *Educ:* Hertford Coll., Oxford (BA). Lectr, Cambridge Coll. of Arts and Techno 1972–74; Admin Trainee/HEO, Home Office, 1974–79; Sec. to Prisons Bd, 1979–8 Private Sec. to Prime Minister, 1982–86; Home Office: Head of: After Entry and Refuge Div., 1986–89; Personnel Div., 1989–91; Probation Service Div., 1991–92; Dir of Admi OFSTED, 1992–94; Dep. DG (Ops), Immigration and Nationality Directorate (former Dept), Home Office, and Chief Inspector, Immigration Service, 1994–98; a Com 1998–2003, a Dep. Chm., 1999–2003, Inland Revenue; Dep. Chief of Defence Logistic MoD, 2003–07. *Address:* Defence Equipment and Support Organisation, Maple 2, 2219, MoD Abbey Wood, Bristol BS34 8JH.

FLETCHER; *see* Aubrey-Fletcher.

FLETCHER, Andrew Fitzroy Stephen; QC 2006; *b* 20 Dec. 1957; *s* of Fitzroy Fletch and Brigid Fletcher (*née* Mahon); *m* 2004, Felicia Taylor; two *s*. *Educ:* Eton Col Magdalene Coll., Cambridge (BA 1980). 2nd Lieut, Welsh Guards, 1976. Called to th Bar, Inner Temple, 1980; in practice specialising in commercial litigation. Liveryma Grocers' Co., 1994–. *Recreations:* Real Tennis, travel, cricket, wine, reading. *Address:* Verulam Buildings, Gray's Inn, WC1R 5NT. *T:* (020) 7831 8441; *e-mail:* afletcher(3vb.com. *Clubs:* Pratt's, Boodle's, MCC.

FLETCHER, Dame Ann Elizabeth Mary; *see* Leslie, Dame A. E. M.

FLETCHER, Prof. Anthony John; Professor of English Social History, University London, at the Institute of Historical Research, 2001–03, now Emeritus; *b* 24 April 194 *s* of John Molyneux Fletcher and Delle Clare Chenevix-Trench; *m* 1st, 1967, Tresr Dawn Russell (marr. diss. 1999); two *s*; 2nd, 2006, Brenda Joan Lockhart-Smith (*n* Knibbs). *Educ:* Wellington Coll.; Merton Coll., Oxford (BA 1962). History Master, King Coll. Sch., Wimbledon, 1964–67; Lectr, Sen. Lectr, then Reader in History, Sheffiel Univ., 1967–87; Prof. of Modern History, Durham Univ., 1987–95; Prof. of Histor Essex Univ., 1995–2000; Dir and Gen. Ed., Victoria County History, Inst. of Histl Res Univ. of London, 2001–03. Auditor, QAA (formerly HEQC), 1994–2001. Pres Ecclesiast. Hist. Soc., 1996–97; Vice-Pres., RHistS, 1997–2001 (Mem. Counci 1992–96). Convenor, History at the Univs Defence Gp, 1997–2000; Chair, QAA Histo Subject Benchmarking Gp, 1998–99. *Publications:* Tudor Rebellions, 1967; A Coun Community in Peace and War, 1975; The Outbreak of the English Civil War, 1981; (e jtly) Order and Disorder in Early Modern England, 1985; Reform in the Provinces, 198 (ed jtly) Religion, Culture and Society in Early Modern Britain, 1994; Gender, Sex an Subordination in England 1500–1800, 1995; (ed jtly) Childhood in Question: childre parents and the state, 1999; Growing Up in England: the experience of childhoo 1600–1914, 2008; articles and reviews in learned jls. *Recreations:* theatre, opera, trave walking, gardening. *Address:* School House, South Newington, Banbury, Oxon OX1 4JJ.

FLETCHER, Dr Archibald Peter; Medical Director, IMS International; form Director, PMS International; Partner in Documenta Biomedica; *b* 24 Dec. 1930; *s* Walter Archibald Fletcher and Dorothy Mabel Fletcher; *m* 1972, Patricia Elizabe Samson (*née* Marr); three *s* two *d*. *Educ:* Kingswood Sch.; London Hosp. Med. Coll.; Mary's Hosp. Med. Sch., London Univ. MB, BS; PhD (Biochemistry). Sen. Lectr Chemical Pathology, St Mary's Hosp., London, 1961–69; Head of Biochemistr American Nat. Red Cross, USA, 1970–73; Med. Dir, Upjohn, Scandinavia; PMC Medicines Div., DHSS, 1977; Med. Assessor to Cttee on Safety of Medicines; Chief Sc Officer and SPMO, DHSS, 1978–79; Res. Physician, Upjohn International Inc., Brussel 1979. *Publications:* numerous papers in scientific and medical journals on glycoprotein physical chemistry, metabolism of blood cells and safety evaluation of new drug *Recreations:* gardening, golf. *Address:* Hall Corner Cottage, Little Maplestead, Halstea Essex CO9 2RU. *T:* (01787) 475465. *Club:* Royal Society of Medicine.

FLETCHER, Augustus James Voisey, OBE 1977; GM 1957; HM Diplomatic Servic retired; Foreign and Commonwealth Office, 1982–89; *b* 23 Dec. 1928; *s* of James Fletch and Naomi Fletcher (*née* Dudden); *m* 1956, Enyd Gwynne Harries; one *s* one *d*. *Edu* Weston-super-Mare Grammar Sch.; Oriental Language Institute, Malaya. Coloni Service, Palestine, 1946–48, Malaya, 1948–58; Min. of Defence, 1958–64; FCO, 1964– Hong Kong (seconded HQ Land Forces), 1966–70; FCO, 1970–73; Hong Kon 1973–76; FCO, 1976–79; Counsellor, New Delhi, 1979–82. *Recreations:* trout fishin walking, food/wine, theatre. *Club:* Travellers.

FLETCHER, Rt Rev. Colin William; *see* Dorchester, Area Bishop of.

FLETCHER, David Edwin, MBE 1986; Executive Director, Transpennine Campaig 1988–2005; environmental consultant and regional development specialist; *b* 15 July 193 *s* of Edwin and Winifred Fletcher; marr. diss. 1990; two *d*; *m* 2005, Hilary Darby. *Edu* Hebden Bridge Grammar Sch.; Calder High Sch.; Sheffield Univ. (BSc Jt Hons); Lee Univ. (PGCE); Bradford Univ. (MSc). Schoolmaster and Head of Biology, Bingley G 1957–60, Calder High Sch., 1960–69; Manchester Polytechnic: Sen. Lectr, 1970–7 Principal Lectr, 1974–80; Head, Envmt and Geographical Dept, 1980–88. Mem., Hebde Royd UDC, 1967–74 (Chm., Planning Cttee, 1969–74). Founder Chairman: Calde Civic Trust, 1965–75; Pennine Heritage Envmtl Trust, 1979–; Dir, Adv. Services, Civ Trust NW, 1970–76. Commissioner: Countryside Commn, 1988–96; Rural Deve Commn, 1993–2000. Chairman: Action for Market Towns, 1998–2005; Hebden Brid (formerly Hebden Royd Town) Partnership, 2002–; Dep. Chm., Upper Calder Valle Renaissance, 2003–07; Member: NW Council for Sport and Recreation, 1972–78; York and Humber Cttee, Heritage Lottery Fund, 2001–06. *Publications:* ASK - Amenit Society Knowhow, 1976; Industry Tourism, 1988; England's North West: a strateg vision for a European region, 1992; research and consultancy reports; contribs to acad. j environmental pamphlets. *Recreations:* walking, ski-ing, travel, meeting interesting peop in interesting situations, restoring and finding new uses for wonderful old mills in th Pennines. *Address:* c/o Birchcliffe, Hebden Bridge, W Yorks HX7 8DG. *T:* (0142 844450.

FLETCHER, Dr David John, CBE 2002; CEng, FREng, FIET; Chief Executive, Britis Waterways, 1996–2002; *b* 12 Dec. 1942; *s* of late John Fletcher and of Edna Fletcher; 1967, Irene Mary Luther; one *s* one *d*. *Educ:* The Crypt Grammar Sch., Gloucester; Uni of Leeds (BSc (Elect. Eng, High Frequency Electronics), DEng). FCIWEM; FREng 200 General Electric Company, 1965–95: GEC Applied Electronics Labs, Stanmore, 1965–8 Gen. Manager, Stanmore Unit, Marconi Space and Defence Systems, 1980–84; Man. Di Marconi Defence Systems, 1984–87; GEC Marconi, 1987–95 (Dep. Chm., 1993–95 Dir, Easynet Group PLC, 2001–06; Chm., Infrared Systems Ltd, 2004–06. Mem

Partnerships UK Adv. Council, 1999–2002. Chm., Assoc. of Inland Navigation Authorities, 1997–2003; Dir, Co. of Proprietors Stroudwater Navigation, 2003–. President: Sleaford Navigation, 2003–; Wendover Arm Trust, 2003–; Vice-President: Inland Waterways Assoc., 2002–; Cotswold Canal Trust, 2003–; Bedford/Milton Keynes Canal Trust, 2003–06; Trustee, Waterways Trust, 1999–. Director Trustee, Nat. Coal Mining Mus., 1997–. Member: Rare Breed Survival Trust; Nat. Trust. *Recreations:* boating, classic cars. *Address:* Beverley House, Nettleden Road, Little Gaddesden, Herts HP4 1PP.

FLETCHER, David Robert; His Honour Judge David Fletcher; a Circuit Judge, since 2004; *b* 6 May 1957; *s* of late Donald Fletcher and of Alice Fletcher (*née* Worrall); *m* 1982, Janet Powney; one *s* one *d*. *Educ:* Biddulph Grammar Sch.; Biddulph High Sch.; Univ. of Liverpool (LLB Hons 1978). Admitted solicitor, 1981; Higher Courts Advocate, 1999; Charltons, Solicitors: articled clerk, 1979–81; Asst Solicitor, 1981–84; Partner, 1984–96; Partner: Beswicks, Stoke-on-Trent, 1996–2001; Stevens, Stoke-on-Trent, Stafford and Wolverhampton, 2001–03. Actg Stipendiary Magistrate, 1998–2000; Dep. Dist Judge (Magistrates' Courts), 2000–03; a Dist Judge (Magistrates' Courts), Sheffield, 2003–04. Chm. Govs, Biddulph High Sch., 1996–2004. *Recreations:* swimming, hill walking, travel, cooking, music, speaking and learning Spanish, watching Port Vale FC. *Address:* Community Justice Centre, North Liverpool, Boundary Street, Liverpool L5 2QD.

FLETCHER, Hugh Alasdair; Chancellor, University of Auckland, since 2005 (Member of Council, since 2000); *b* 28 Nov. 1947; *s* of Sir James Muir Cameron Fletcher, ONZ and of Margery Vaughan Fletcher; *m* 1970, Sian Seerpoohi Elias (*see* Rt Hon. Dame Sian Elias); two *s*. *Educ:* Auckland Univ. (MCom Hons, BSc); Stanford Univ., USA (MBA 1972). Fletcher Holdings: Asst to Ops Res., 1969–70; PA to Man. Dir, 1972–76; Dep. Man. Dir, 1976–79; CEO, 1979–81; Fletcher Challenge Ltd: non-exec. Dir, 1981–2001; Man. Dir, 1981–87; CEO, 1987–97; Chairman: CGNU Australia Holdings Ltd (formerly CGU Insurance Australia), 1998–2003; New Zealand Insurance, 1998–2003. Non-exec. Chm., Air New Zealand Ltd, 1985–89; Director: Australasian Adv. Bd, Merrill Lynch, 1998–2000; Rubicon, 2001–; Fletcher Bldg, 2001–; Reserve Bank of NZ, 2002–; Ports of Auckland, 2002–06; IAG NZ, 2004–; IAG, 2007–. Chairman: NZ Thoroughbred Marketing, 1998–2000; Ministerial Inquiry into Telecommunications, 2000; Member: Prime Minister's Enterprise Council, 1992–97; Asia Pacific Adv. Cttee, New York Stock Exchange, 1995–2005; World Business Council for Sustainable Develt, Geneva, 1993–96; Adv. Cttee, UN Office for Project Services, 2000–07. *Recreations:* horse riding, horse breeding and racing, chess, Go. *Address:* PO Box 11468, Ellerslie, New Zealand.

FLETCHER, Ian Raymond; Chief Executive, UK Intellectual Property Office (Patent Office), since 2007; *b* New Zealand, 25 Aug. 1959; *s* of Raymond William Fletcher and Elizabeth Ruth (*née* Millin); *m* 1990, Lorna Windmill (marr. diss. 2007). *Educ:* Burnside High Sch., Christchurch, NZ; Canterbury Univ. (MA Hons 1982). NZ Diplomatic Service, 1982–89; Monopolies and Mergers Commn, UK, 1989–91; Department of Trade and Industry: general trade policy, 1992–94; telecommunications policy, 1994–95; EC, on secondment, 1996–98; DTI and British Trade Internat., 1998–99; Dir-Gen., UN Customs Service and Hd, Dept of Trade and Industry, UN Admin, Kosovo, 2000; Dir, Gas and Electricity, DTI, 2000–02; Principal Private Sec. to Sec. of the Cabinet, 2002–04; Dir, Internat. Trade Develt, UK Trade and Investment, 2004–07. *Address:* Patent Office, Concept House, Cardiff Road, Newport NP10 8QQ. *T:* (01633) 814500; *e-mail:* ian.fletcher@ipo.gov.uk.

FLETCHER, His Honour John Edwin; a Circuit Judge, 1986–2006; *b* 23 Feb. 1941; *s* of late Sydney Gerald Fletcher and Cecilia Lane Fletcher; *m* 1st, 1971, Felicity Jane Innes Dick (marr. diss.); 2nd, 1996, Mrs Susan Kennedy-Hawkes. *Educ:* Munro Coll., Jamaica; St Bees Sch., Cumbria; Clare Coll., Cambridge (MA). Called to the Bar, Inner Temple, 1964; Midland and Oxford Circuit, 1965–86; a Recorder, 1983–86. Mem. Panel of Chairmen, Medical Appeal Tribunals, 1981–86. *Recreations:* walking, photography.

FLETCHER, Kim Thomas; Chairman, National Council for the Training of Journalists, since 2004; Managing Director, Trinity Management Communications, since 2007; *b* 17 Sept. 1956; *s* of Jack Fletcher and Agnes Fletcher (*née* Coulthwaite); *m* 1991, Sarah Sands; one *s* one *d*, and one step *s*. *Educ:* Heversham Grammar Sch., Westmorland; Hertford Coll., Oxford (BA Law); UC Cardiff (Dip. Journalism Studies). Journalist: The Star, Sheffield, 1978–81; Sunday Times, 1981–86; Daily Telegraph, 1986–87; Sunday Telegraph, 1988–98: News Editor, 1991–95; Dep. Editor, 1995–98; Editor, Independent on Sunday, 1998–99; Editl Dir, Hollinger Telegraph New Media, 2000–03; Consultant Editor, Daily Telegraph, 2002–03; Editl Dir, Telegraph Gp Ltd, 2003–05. *Publication:* The Journalist's Handbook, 2005. *Recreation:* family life. *Address:* (home) 10 Caithness Road, W14 0JB. *T:* (020) 7602 4217; *e-mail:* kim.fletcher@dsl.pipex.com. *Club:* Groucho.

FLETCHER, Malcolm Stanley, MBE 1982; FREng; FICE; Consultant, Sir William Halcrow & Partners Ltd, Consulting Civil Engineers, since 1996; *b* 25 Feb. 1936; *s* of Harold and Clarice Fletcher; *m* 1965, Rhona Christina Wood; one *s* two *d*. *Educ:* Manchester Grammar Sch.; Manchester Univ. (MSc); Imperial Coll., London (DIC). FGS 1968; FICE 1976; FREng (FEng 1993). Pupil, Binnie & Partners, 1957–60; Sir William Halcrow & Partners, 1968–96: Partner, 1985–96; Chm., 1990–96. Resident Engineer: Jhelum Bridge, Pakistan, 1965–67; Giuliana Bridge, Libya, 1968–74; Design Team Leader, Orwell Bridge, Ipswich, 1976–82; Dir of Design, Second Severn Crossing, 1988–96; Adviser: Dartford River Crossing, 1985–90; Lantau Fixed Crossing, Hong Kong, 1990. *Recreation:* cycling. *Address:* Burderop Park, Swindon, Wilts SN4 0QD. *T:* (01793) 812479.

FLETCHER, Margaret Ann; *see* Cable, M. A.

FLETCHER, Comdt Marjorie Helen (Kelsey), CBE 1988; Director, Women's Royal Naval Service, 1986–88; *b* 21 Sept. 1932; *d* of late Norman Farler Fletcher and Marie Amelie Fletcher (*née* Adams). *Educ:* Avondale High Sch.; Sutton Coldfield High Sch. for Girls. Solicitor's Clerk, 1948–53; joined WRNS as Telegraphist, 1953; progressively, 3rd Officer to Chief Officer, 1956–76; Supt, 1981; served in Secretariat, Careers Advisor, Intelligence and Staff appts; ndc 1979; Directing Staff, RN Staff Coll., 1980–81; psc 1981; Internat. Mil. Staff, NATO HQ, 1981–84; Asst Dir, Dir Naval Staff Duties, 1984–85. ADC to the Queen, 1986–88. *Publication:* The WRNS, 1989. *Recreations:* reading, needlework.

FLETCHER, Martin Guy; Chief Executive, National Patient Safety Agency, since 2007; *b* Sydney, Australia, 3 April 1961; *s* of Brian and Beverley Fletcher; *m* 1988, Therese Hanna; two *s* one *d*. *Educ:* Univ. of Sydney (BSocStud); Macquarie Univ. (BA Hons); Univ. of Technol., Sydney (MMan). Manager, Care Plus (ACT) Pty Ltd, 1996–98; Dir, Australian Dept of Health and Ageing, 1998–2000; Dir, Australian Council for Safety and Quality in Health Care, 2000–03; Asst Dir, Nat. Patient Safety Agency, 2003–04; Hd, Patient Safety, WHO World Alliance for Patient Safety, 2004–07. *Publications:* contrib. articles on patient safety to jls incl. Med. Jl of Australia, Quality and Safety in Healthcare and Internat. Jl for Quality in Health Care. *Recreations:* swimming, reading, travel. *Address:* National Patient Safety Agency, 4–8 Maple Street, W1T 5HD; *e-mail:* martin.fletcher@npsa.nhs.uk. *Club:* Royal Society of Medicine.

FLETCHER, Michael John; Sheriff of Tayside Central and Fife, since 2000; *b* 5 Dec. 1945; *s* of Walter Fletcher and Elizabeth Fletcher (*née* Pringle); *m* 1968, Kathryn Mary Bain; two *s*. *Educ:* High Sch. of Dundee; Univ. of St Andrews (LLB). Admitted solicitor, 1968; apprenticeship, Kirk Mackie & Elliot, SSC, Edinburgh, 1966–68; Asst, then Partner, Ross Strachan & Co., Dundee, 1968–88; Partner, Hendry & Fenton, later Miller Hendry, Dundee, 1988–94; Sheriff of South Strathclyde, Dumfries and Galloway, 1994–99; Sheriff of Lothian and Borders, 1999–2000. Mem., Sheriff Court Rules Council, 2002–. Lectr (part-time) in Civil and Criminal Procedure, Univ. of Dundee, 1974–94. Editor, Scottish Civil Law Reports, 1999–. *Publication:* (jtly) Delictual Damages, 2000. *Recreations:* golf, badminton, gardening. *Address:* Sheriff Court House, Tay Street, Perth PH2 8NL. *T:* (01738) 620546.

FLETCHER, Neil; education consultant, since 2003; Head of Education, Local Government Association, 1998–2003; *b* 5 May 1944; *s* of Alan and Ruth Fletcher; *m* 1967, Margaret Monaghan; two *s*. *Educ:* Wyggeston Sch., Leicester; City of Leeds Coll. of Educn (Teachers' Cert.); London Univ. (BA Hons); London Business Sch. (MBA 1994). Charter FCP 1990. Schoolteacher, 1966–68; Lectr, 1969–76; Admin. Officer, 1976–91, Hd of Educn, 1991–94, NALGO; Hd of Strategic Projects, UNISON, 1994–95; mgt consultant, 1995–98. Member: Camden Bor. Council, 1978–86 (Dep. Leader, 1982–84); ILEA, 1979–90 (Chair, Further and Higher Educn Sub-Cttee, 1981–87; Leader, 1987–90); Chair: Council of Local Educn Authorities, 1987–88, 1989–90; Educn Cttee, AMA, 1987–90 (Vice-Chair, 1986–87). Advr, London Skills and Employment Bd, 2006–. Governor: Penn Sch., 1985–2006; London Inst., 1986–99; LSE, 1990–2001; City Literary Inst., 1996–2006 (Chair of Govs, 2003–06). FRSA 1989. *Recreations:* cricket, soccer, theatre, cookery, walking. *Address:* 42 Narcissus Road, NW6 1TH. *T:* (020) 7435 5306; *e-mail:* neil.fletcher5544@ukonline.co.uk.

FLETCHER, Philip John, CBE 2006; Chairman, Water Services Regulation Authority (Ofwat), since 2006 (Director General, Water Services, 2000–06); *b* 2 May 1946; *s* of late Alan Philip Fletcher, QC and Annette Grace Fletcher (*née* Wright); *m* 1977, Margaret Anne Boys; one *d* (and one *d* decd). *Educ:* Marlborough Coll.; Trinity Coll., Oxford (MA). Asst Principal, MPBW, 1968; Department of the Environment: Private Sec. to Permanent Sec., 1978; Asst Sec., Private Sector Housebuilding, 1980, local govt expenditure, 1982–85; Under Secretary: Housing, Water and Central Finance, 1986–90; Planning and Develt Control, 1990–93; Chief Exec., PSA Services, 1993–94, and Dep. Sec., Property Holdings, 1994; Dep. Sec., Cities and Countryside Gp, 1994–95; Receiver for the Metropolitan Police District, 1996–2000. Reader, Church of England; Mem., Archbishops' Council, 2007–. *Recreation:* walking. *Address:* Ofwat, Centre City Tower, 7 Hill Street, Birmingham B5 4UA. *T:* (0121) 625 1300, *Fax:* (0121) 625 1348; *e-mail:* philip.fletcher@ofwat.gsi.gov.uk.

See also Area Bishop of Dorchester.

FLETCHER, Richard George Hopper, CMG 1996; HM Diplomatic Service, retired; Senior Policy Adviser, EADS Defence and Security Systems, since 2005; *b* 8 Nov. 1944; *s* of late George Hopper Fletcher, CBE, FCA and Kathleen Mary Parsons; *m* 1967, Celia Rosemary Soord; two *d*. *Educ:* Leys Sch., Cambridge; Balliol Coll., Oxford. Joined Foreign Office, 1966–67; Athens, 1968; Nicosia, 1969–72; First Sec., Bucharest, 1973–76; FCO, 1977–83; Counsellor: Athens, 1984–88; FCO, 1989–98; Vice-Pres., Govt Relns and External Affairs, Europe, Nortel Networks, 1998–2001; Public Policy Advr, Cogent Defence and Security Networks Ltd, 2001–02; re-employed, FCO, 2003–05. *Recreations:* forestry, gardening, bridge, golf. *Clubs:* Athenæum; Wimbledon Park Golf (Dir, 2002–07; Capt., 2007); Dumfries and County Golf.

FLETCHER, Robin Anthony, OBE 1984; DSC 1944; DPhil; Warden of Rhodes House, Oxford, 1980–89; Professorial Fellow, Trinity College, Oxford, 1980–89, now Emeritus; *b* 30 May 1922; *s* of Philip Cawthorne Fletcher, MC, and Edith Maud Fletcher (*née* Okell); *m* 1950, Jinny May (*née* Cornish); two *s*. *Educ:* Marlborough Coll.; Trinity Coll., Oxford (MA, DPhil). Served Royal Navy (Lieut RNVR), 1941–46. University Lecturer in Modern Greek, 1949–79; Domestic Bursar, Trinity Coll., Oxford, 1950–74; Senior Proctor, 1966–67; Member, Hebdomadal Council, 1967–74. Represented England at hockey, 1949–55 and GB, 1952 Olympic Games (Bronze Medal). *Publications:* Kostes Palamas, Athens, 1984; various articles. *Recreations:* sport, music. *Address:* Binglea, Quoyloo, Stromness, Orkney KW16 3LU. *Clubs:* Naval; Vincent's (Oxford).

FLETCHER, Prof. Roger, PhD; FRS 2003; FRSE; Baxter Professor of Mathematics, 1993–2005, and Professor of Optimization, 1984–2005, University of Dundee, now Emeritus; *b* 29 Jan. 1939; *s* of Harry and Alice Fletcher; *m* 1963, Mary Marjorie Taylor; two *d*. *Educ:* Huddersfield Coll.; Selwyn Coll., Cambridge (MA); Univ. of Leeds (PhD 1963). FIMA 1971. Lectr, Leeds Univ., 1963–69; PSO, AERE Harwell, 1969–73; Sen. Lectr, then Reader, Univ. of Dundee, 1973–84. Hon. Prof., Univ. of Edinburgh, 2005–. FRSE 1988. *Publications:* Practical Methods of Optimization, Vol. 1, 1980, Vol. 2, 1981, 2nd edn as one vol. 1987; numerous contribs to jls. *Recreations:* hill-walking, bridge. *Address:* Department of Mathematics, University of Dundee, Dundee DD1 4HN. *T:* (01382) 384490, *Fax:* (01382) 385516; *e-mail:* fletcher@maths.dundee.ac.uk.

FLETCHER, Prof. Ronald Stanley, FRAeS; Professor of Thermal Power, 1972–2003, now Emeritus, and Deputy Vice-Chancellor, 1994–2003, Cranfield University (formerly Cranfield Institute of Technology); *b* 12 Dec. 1937; *s* of Reginald and Dorothy Fletcher; *m* 1965, Pamela Alys, *d* of Gwilym and Alys Treharne; one *s* twin *d*. *Educ:* Imperial College, London Univ. (PhD, DIC); UMIST (BSc Tech). FRAeS 1994. Senior Engineer, Northern Research & Engineering Corp., Cambridge, USA, 1965–70; Consultant, Northern Research & Engineering Corp., Herts, 1970–72; Cranfield Institute of Technology: Head of Mechanical Engineering, 1977–87; Dean of Engineering, 1982–85; Pro-Vice-Chancellor, 1985–93; Head of Cranfield Campus, 1989–94; Chairman: Cranfield Mgt Develt Ltd, 1993–2004; Cranfield Aerospace Ltd, 1996–98. Visiting Professor: Cairo, 1975; Brazil, 1977; China (Beijing Inst. of Aero. and Astro.), 1979. Member: ARC, 1974–77; Governing Body, AFRC Inst. of Engrg Res. (formerly Nat. Inst. of Agricl Engrg), 1978–93 (Chm., Finance Cttee, 1982–86); Council, British Hydro. Res. Assoc., 1979–89; AGARD (NATO) Propulsion and Energetics Panel, 1980–99 (Chm., 1997–98); Scientific Bd, Univ. de Technologie de Compiègne, 1989–94; Conseil Scientifique, Inst. Méditerranéen de Technologie, 1989–94. Governor, Bedford Modern Sch., 1986–89. Médaille Gustave Trasenster, Liège, 1990; Prix Formation Etranger, Acad. Nat. de l'Air et de l'Espace, France, 1991. Chevalier, 1990, Officier, 1994, Ordre des Palmes Académiques (France). *Publications:* papers on combustion. *Recreations:* sailing, music. *Address:* 34 Brecon Way, Bedford MK41 8DD. *T:* (01234) 358483. *Club:* Parkstone Yacht.

FLETCHER, Stuart Barron, OBE 2003; Chairman, Welsh Ambulance Services NHS Trust, since 2006; *b* 28 July 1945; *s* of Arthur Barron Fletcher and Bertha Fletcher; *m* 1970,

Dilys Roberts; two s one d. *Educ:* King George V Grammar Sch., Southport; Oriel Coll., Oxford (MA). MHSM, DipHSM. Entered Health Service as Nat. Trainee Administrator, 1968; NHS posts include: Hosp. Sec., Broadgreen Hosp., Liverpool, 1972–74; Area Gen. Administrator, St Helens and Knowsley HA, 1974–78; Dist Administrator, E Birmingham HA, 1978–82; Chief Exec., N Staffs HA, 1982–91; Regl Man. Dir, subseq. Chief Exec., W Midlands RHA, 1992–93; Chief Exec., Pembs, subseq. Pembs and Derwen, NHS Trust, 1994–2003; Chief Exec., Health Commn Wales, NHS Dept, Welsh Assembly Govt, 2003–05. Member: NHS Trng Authy, 1985–91; NHS Trng Adv. Bd, 1991–93. Pres., IHSM, 1991–92 (Mem., Nat. Council, 1981–95). *Recreations:* Rugby, fell walking, photography, theatre. *Address:* 5 Douglas James Close, Haverfordwest, Pembrokeshire SA61 2UF. *T:* (01437) 760103.

FLETCHER-VANE, family name of **Baron Inglewood.**

FLEW, Prof. Antony Garrard Newton; Emeritus Professor, University of Reading, since 1983; *b* 11 Feb. 1923; *o s* of Rev. Dr R. N. Flew; *m* 1952, Annis Ruth Harty; two d. *Educ:* St Faith's Sch., Cambridge; Kingswood Sch., Bath; Sch. of Oriental and African Studies, London; St John's Coll., Oxford (John Locke Schol., MA); DLitt Keele, 1974. Lecturer: Christ Church, Oxford, 1949–50; Univ. of Aberdeen, 1950–54; Professor of Philosophy: Univ. of Keele, 1954–71; Univ. of Calgary, 1972–73; Univ. of Reading, 1973–82; (part-time) York Univ., Toronto, 1983–85; Distinguished Res. Fellow (part-time), Social Philosophy and Policy Center, Bowling Green State Univ., Ohio, 1986–91. Many temp. vis. appts. Gavin David Young Lectr, Adelaide, 1963; Gifford Lectr, St Andrews, 1986. A Vice-Pres., Rationalist Press Assoc., 1973–88; Chm., Voluntary Euthanasia Soc., 1976–79. Fellow, Acad. of Humanism, 1983–. Phillip E. Johnson Award for Liberty and Truth, Biola Univ., 2006. *Publications:* A New Approach to Psychical Research, 1953; Hume's Philosophy of Belief, 1961; God and Philosophy, 1966; Evolutionary Ethics, 1967; An Introduction to Western Philosophy, 1971; Crime or Disease?, 1973; Thinking About Thinking, 1975; The Presumption of Atheism, 1976; Sociology, Equality and Education, 1976; A Rational Animal, 1978; Philosophy: an introduction, 1979; The Politics of Procrustes, 1981; Darwinian Evolution, 1984; Thinking About Social Thinking, 1985; Hume, Philosopher of Moral Science, 1986; (with G. Vesey) Agency and Necessity, 1987; The Logic of Mortality, 1987; Power to the Parents, 1987; Equality in Liberty and Justice, 1989; Atheistic Humanism, 1993; Shephard's Warning: setting schools back on course, 1994; Philosophical Essays of Antony Flew, 1998; How to Think Straight, 1998; Social Life and Moral Judgement, 2003; (with R. A. Varghese) There is No A God: how the world's most notorious atheist changed his mind, 2007; articles in philosophical and other jls. *Recreations:* walking, climbing, house maintenance. *Address:* 26 Alexandra Road, Reading, Berks RG1 5PD. *T:* (0118) 926 1848. *Club:* Union Society (Oxford).

FLEWITT, Neil; QC 2003; a Recorder, since 1998; *b* 3 July 1959; *s* of Robert Arthur Flewitt and Caroline Mary Flewitt; *m* 1987, Melanie Ann Carter; two s one d. *Educ:* St Edward's Coll., Liverpool; Liverpool Univ. (LLB 1980). Called to the Bar, Middle Temple, 1981; joined chambers, Liverpool, 1981; practises in criminal law (prosecution and defence). Mem., Criminal Bar Assoc. *Recreations:* films, food, football. *Address:* 7 Harrington Street, Liverpool L2 9YH. *T:* (0151) 242 0707, *Fax:* (0151) 236 2800; *e-mail:* neil.flewitt@7hs.co.uk.

FLIGHT, Howard Emerson; Chairman, Flight and Partners, since 2007; Director: Investec Asset Management Ltd, since 1999 (Joint Chairman, 1999–2003; Senior Director, since 2004; Consultant, Investec Group, since 2005); *b* 16 June 1948; *s* of late Bernard Thomas Flight and Doris Mildred Emerson Flight; *m* 1973, Christabel Diana Beatrice Norbury; one s three d. *Educ:* Brentwood Sch.; Magdalene Coll., Cambridge (MA Hist. Pt 1, Econs Pt 2); Univ. of Michigan (MBA 1971). Investment Adviser: N. M. Rothschild & Sons, 1970–73; Cayzer Ltd, 1973–77; Wardley Ltd (Hong Kong Bank), Hong Kong and India, 1977–79; Investment Dir, Guinness Mahon Co. Ltd, 1979–86; Jt Man. Dir, Guinness Flight Global Asset Mgt, 1986–99; Dep. Chm., Guinness Flight Hambro, 1997–98. Contested (C) Bermondsey, Feb. and Oct. 1974. MP (C) Arundel and South Downs, 1997–2005. Shadow Econ. Sec. to Treasury, 1999–2001; Shadow Paymaster Gen., 2001–02; Shadow Chief Sec. to HM Treasury, 2002–04. Mem., Envmt Select Cttee, 1997–98, Social Security Select Cttee, 1998–99. Jt Chm., All Party H of C Hong Kong Cttee, 1998–2005. Chairman: CIM Investment Mgt, 2006–; Loudwater Trust Ltd, 2007–; Director: Investec Global Strategy Fund, 1987–; Panmure Gordon & Co. (formerly Durlacher) plc, 2002–07; Speymill Group plc, 2005– (Chm.); St Helen's Capital, 2005–. Mem., Adv. Council, Financial Services Forum, 2005–; Mem., Guernsey Financial Services Commn, 2005–; Chm., Enterprise Investment Scheme Assoc., 2005–. Vice Pres., Elgar Foundn, 2005– (Trustee, 1979–2005); Trustee, Africa Res. Inst., 2006–; Governor, Brentwood Sch., 1989–. Liveryman, Carpenters' Co., 1999–. FRSA. *Publication:* All You Need to Know About Exchange Rates, 1988. *Recreations:* classical music, antiques, gardening, ski-ing. *Address:* 6 Barton Street, Westminster, SW1P 3NG; *e-mail:* hflight@btinternet.com. *Clubs:* Carlton, Pratt's, Boodle's.

FLINDALL, Jacqueline; Regional Nursing Officer, Wessex Regional Health Authority, 1983–85; *b* 12 Oct. 1932; *d* of Harry and Lilian Flindall. *Educ:* St David's Sch., Ashford, Middx; University Coll. Hosp., London (DipN). SRN, SCM, UCH, 1950–54; Midwifery, St Luke's Mat. Hosp., Guildford and Watford, 1955; exchange student, Mount Sinai Hosp., NY, 1956; Ward Sister and Clinical Teacher, UCH, 1957–63; Asst Matron, Wexham Park Hosp., 1964–66; Dep. Supt of Nursing, Prince of Wales and St Anne's, 1967–69; Chief Nursing Officer: Northwick Park Hosp., 1969–73; Oxfordshire HA, 1973–83. Associate Consultant, PA Management Consultants, 1986–94. Non-exec. Dir, Royal Nat. Orth. Hosp. NHS Trust, Stanmore, 1991–95. Vice Chm., Hosp. Chaplaincies Council, 1997–2003. Professional Organization Mem., RCN; Hon. FRCN 1983. JP Oxford, 1982, Salisbury, 1987–2002; Mem., Wilts Magistrates' Courts Cttee, 1995–2002. *Recreations:* painting, voluntary work.

FLINT, Prof. Anthony Patrick Fielding, PhD, DSc; FIBiol; Professor of Animal Physiology, School of Biosciences (formerly Department of Physiology and Environmental Science), University of Nottingham, since 1993; *b* 31 Aug. 1943; *s* of Maurice Fielding Flint and Patricia Joan (*née* Ince); *m* 1967, Chan Mun Kwun; two s. *Educ:* Hill Crest Sch., Swanage; King's Sch., Bruton; Univ. of St Andrews (Queen's Coll., Dundee) (BSc 1966); Univ. of Bristol (PhD 1969; DSc 1984). FIBiol 1982. Res. Fellow, Univ. of Western Ontario, 1969–72; Sen. Res. Biochemist in Obs and Gyn., Welsh Nat. Sch. of Medicine, Cardiff, 1972–73; Lectr, Nuffield Dept of Obs and Gyn., Oxford Univ., 1973–77; Staff Mem., AFRC Inst. of Animal Physiology and Genetics Res., Cambridge, 1977–87; Dir of Science and Dir of Inst. of Zool., Zool Soc. of London, 1987–93. Special Lectr, 1985–87, Special Prof. in Molecular Biol., 1987–93, Univ. of Nottingham Sch. of Agric.; Visiting Professor: Dept of Biology, UCL, 1989–; Biosphere Scis Div., KCL, 1989–. Member: Cttee, Soc. for Study of Fertility, 1981–89 (Sec., 1985–89); Steering Cttee, WHO Task Force on Plants for Fertility Regulation, 1982–87 (Chm., 1985). Member: Council of Management, Journals of Reproduction and Fertility Ltd, 1981–87 (Mem. Exec. Cttee, 1983–87); Bd of Scientific Editors, Jl of Endocrinology, 1983–87.

Medal, Soc. for Endocrinology, 1985. *Publications:* (ed jtly) Embryonic Diapause i Mammals, 1981; Reproduction in Domestic Ruminants, 1991; papers in physio endocrinol and biochemical jls. *Recreations:* playing Bach on the organ or cello, coasting i small ships. *Address:* School of Biosciences, University of Nottingham, Sutton Bonington Loughborough, Leics LE12 5RD.

FLINT, Rt Hon. Caroline Louise; PC 2008; MP (Lab) Don Valley, since 1997; Ministe of State (Minister for Europe), Foreign and Commonwealth Office, since 2008; *b* 20 Sep 1961; *d* of late Wendy Flint (*née* Beasley); *m* 1st, 1987 (marr. diss. 1990); one s one d; 2nd 2001, Phil Cole; one step s. *Educ:* Univ. of East Anglia (BA Hons American History an Lit.). Mgt Trainee, 1983–84, Policy Officer, 1984–86, GLC/ILEA; Head of Women Unit, NUS, 1988–89; Principal Officer, Lambeth, 1989–93; Sen. Researcher and Politica Officer, GMB, 1994–97. Parliamentary Private Secretary: to Minister of State, FCC 1999–2000 and 2001–02, Minister for Energy, DTI, 2001; to Minister without Portfoli and Labour Party Chair, 2003; Parly Under-Sec. of State, Home Office, 2003–05, DoH 2005–06; Minister of State, DoH, 2006–07, DWP, 2007–08; Minister for Yorks and th Humber, 2007–08; Minister for Housing, DCLG, 2008. *Recreations:* cinema, tap-dancing family and friends. *Address:* House of Commons, SW1A 0AA. *T:* (020) 7219 4407.

FLINT, Charles John Raffles; QC 1995. *Educ:* Trinity College, Cambridge (BA 1973 MA 1980). Called to the Bar, Middle Temple, 1975, Bencher, 2001; Junior Counsel t the Crown (Common Law), 1991–95. *Address:* Blackstone Chambers, Blackstone House Temple, EC4Y 9BW.

FLINT, Prof. David, TD; MA, BL, CA; Professor of Accountancy, 1964–85, (Johnston Smith Chair, 1964–75), and Vice-Principal, 1981–85, University of Glasgow; *b* 24 Fe 1919; *s* of David Flint, JP, and Agnes Strang Lambie; *m* 1953, Dorothy Mary Maclachla Jardine; two s one d. *Educ:* Glasgow High Sch.; University of Glasgow. Served with Roya Signals, 1939–46, Major (despatches). Awarded distinction final examination of Institut of Chartered Accountants of Scotland, 1948. Lecturer, University of Glasgow, 1950–6 Dean of Faculty of Law, 1971–73. Partner, Mann Judd Gordon & Co. Chartere Accountants, Glasgow, 1951–71. Hon. Prof. of Accountancy, Stirling Univ., 1988–91 Hon. Pres. Glasgow Chartered Accountants Students Soc., 1959–60; Chm., Assoc. c Univ. Teachers of Accounting (now British Accounting Assoc.), 1969. Mem. Council Scottish Business Sch., 1971–77; Vice-Pres., Scottish Economic Soc., 1977–99; Vice Pres., Inst. of Chartered Accountants of Scotland, 1973–75, Pres., 1975–76; Pres European Accounting Assoc., 1983–84; Member: Management and Ind. Rel. Cttee SSRC, 1970–72 and 1978–80; Commn for Local Authy Accounts in Scotland, 1978–80 DUniv Glasgow, 2001. BAA Lifetime Achievement Award, 2004. *Publications:* A Tru and Fair View in Company Accounts, 1982; Philosophy and Principles of Auditing: a introduction, 1988. *Recreation:* golf. *Address:* 16 Grampian Avenue, Auchterarde Perthshire PH3 1NY.

FLINT, Prof. Jonathan, FRCPsych; Michael Davys Professor of Neuroscience University of Oxford, since 2007; Fellow of Merton College, Oxford, since 2007; *b* Sutton, 22 Jan. 1958; *s* of Michael Frederick Flint, *qv*; *m* 1980, Alison Shaw; one s two *Educ:* Westminster Sch.; Merton Coll., Oxford (BM BCh 1988). FRCPsych 200 Registrar in Psychiatry, 1989–92, Sen. Registrar, 1992, Maudsley Hosp., London University of Oxford: Wellcome Trust Career Develt Fellow, 1992–97; Wellcome Trus Sen. Fellow, 1997–2007; Wellcome Trust Principal Fellow, 2007–; Prof. of Molecula Psychiatry, 2005–07; Hon. Consultant Psychiatrist, Warneford Hosp., Oxford, 1996– *Publications:* 200 articles in jls and contrib. to text books on the genetics of behaviour *Recreation:* work. *Address:* Wellcome Trust Centre for Human Genetics, Roosevelt Drive Oxford OX3 7BN. *T:* (01865) 287500, *Fax:* (01865) 287501; *e-mail:* jf@well.ox.ac.uk.

FLINT, Michael Frederick, FSA; consultant; *b* 7 May 1932; *s* of Frederic Nelson L Fargue Flint and Nell Dixon Smith; *m* 1st, 1954, Susan Kate Rhodes (marr. diss.) two one d; 2nd, 1984, Phyllida Margaret Medwyn Hughes. *Educ:* St Peter's Sch., York Kingswood Sch., Bath. Admitted Solicitor 1956; Denton Hall & Burgin, subseq. Dento Hall Burgin & Warrens, then Denton Wilde Sapte: Articled Clerk, 1951–56; Ass Solicitor, 1956–60; Partner, 1960–66 and 1972–93; Man. Partner, 1979–82; Chm 1990–93; Consultant, 1993–2000. Paramount Pictures Corporation: Asst Vice-Pres 1967; Vice-Pres., 1968–70; Consultant, Henry Ansbacher & Co., 1970; Chm., Londo Screen Enterprises, 1970–72 (Exec. Producer, feature film, Glastonbury Fayre, 1972). Dir Portman Entertainment Group Ltd, 1995–2001; Chm., Renaissance Films Ltd, 2002–04 Dir, and Chm. Council, 1995–99, Intellectual Property Inst. (formerly Council c Common Law Inst. of Intellectual Property; founder Mem.); Chm., Intellectual Property Entertainment and Telecommunications Cttee, Internat. Bar Assoc., 1985–90. Vice-Pres Brit. Archaeol Assoc., 1988–. Member: BAFTA, 1984–; British Screen Adv. Council 1991– (Dep. Chm., 1995–); Council, Aldeburgh Music, 1998–. Chairman: Orford Mus 1997–; Esmond House Day Care Centre, 2000–; Sudbourne Park Printmakers, 2003– FSA 1965. *Publications:* A User's Guide to Copyright, 1979, (jtly) 6th edn 2006; (jtly Television by Satellite: legal aspects, 1987; (jtly) Intellectual Property: the new law, 1989 *Recreations:* painting, etching, golf, opera. *Address:* Green Lane House, Castle Green Orford, Suffolk IP12 2NF. *Clubs:* Garrick; Aldeburgh Golf; Orford Sailing.
See also J. Flint.

FLINT, Rachael H.; see Heyhoe Flint.

FLINT, Simon Coleridge R.; see Russell Flint.

FLÖCKINGER, Gerda, CBE 1991; designer/lecturer/photographer; *b* Innsbruck, 8 Dec 1927; *d* of Karl Flöckinger and Anna (*née* Frankl); naturalised British citizen, 1946; *m* 1954 R. S. Houghton (marr. diss. 1962). *Educ:* Maidstone Girls' GS; Dorchester Co. High Sch for Girls; S Hampstead High Sch.; St Martin's Sch. of Art; Central Sch. of Arts and Craft Came to England, 1938. Lectr, Hornsey Coll. of Art, 1962–68 (created New Moder Jewellery course). *Solo shows:* British Crafts Centre, London, 1968; V&A Mus., 1971 an 1986; Bristol City Art Gall. and Mus., 1971; Dartington Cider Press Gall., 1977; Craf Council Shop at V&A, 1991; V&A, 2006; Electrum Gall., London, 2007; *numerous grou shows* including: ICA, 1954–64; V&A Mus.; Arnolfini Gall., Bristol; Goldsmiths' Hal Design Centre; Electrum Gall., London, Crafts Council, London; also in USA, Japan an Europe; work in *collections:* Bristol City Mus. and Art Gall.; Crafts Council; Nottingha Castle Mus.; Royal Scottish Mus., Edinburgh; Pompidou Centre, Paris Schmuckmuseum, Pforzheim, Germany; V&A Mus.; Goldsmiths' Co., London. Hon Fellow, Univ. of the Arts London, 2006. Freeman, Goldsmiths' Co., 1998. *Recreation* growing camellias, breeding Iris Germanica, pistol-shooting.

FLOISSAC, Rt Hon. Sir Vincent (Frederick), Kt 1992; CMG 1985; OBE 1973; PC 1992; Chief Justice and President of the Court of Appeal, Eastern Caribbean Suprem Court, 1991–96; *b* 31 July 1928; *m* 1954, Marilyn (*née* Bristol); twin d. *Educ:* St Mary' Coll., St Lucia; UCL (LLM 1953). Called to the Bar, Gray's Inn, 1952 (Hon. Bencher 1992); in practice, St Lucia, 1953–91; QC (St Lucia) 1969; Mem., Seychelles Ct of Appea 1988–91. Nominated Mem. and Dep. Speaker, St Lucia House of Assembly, 1969–75 first Pres., Senate of St Lucia, 1979; Acting Governor Gen., St Lucia, 1987–88. Mem., Judicial Cttee, Privy Council, 1992–. Chm., St Lucia Central Water Authority, 1965–72; Dir, St Lucia Co-op Bank Ltd, 1960–91. *Recreations:* football, table tennis, tennis. *Address:* c/o Floissac Fleming & Associates, PO Box 722, Castries, St Lucia, West Indies.

FLOOD, David Andrew; Organist and Master of the Choristers, Canterbury Cathedral, since 1988; *b* 10 Nov. 1955; *s* of Frederick Flood and June Flood (*née* Alexander); *m* 1976, Alayne Nicholas; two *s* two *d*. *Educ:* Royal Grammar School, Guildford; St John's Coll., Oxford (MA); Clare Coll., Cambridge (PGCE). FRCO(CHM). Assistant Organist, Canterbury Cathedral, 1978–86; Organist and Master of Choristers, Lincoln Cathedral, 1986–88. Mem., Royal Soc. of Musicians, 1996–; Hon. Sen. Mem., Darwin Coll., Univ. of Kent, 1989–. Hon. FGCM 2000. Hon. DMus Kent, 2002. *Recreations:* motoring, cooking, travel. *Address:* 6 The Precincts, Canterbury, Kent CT1 2EE. *T:* (01227) 865242; *e-mail:* davidf@canterbury-cathedral.org.

FLOOD, Prof. John Edward, OBE 1986; DSc, PhD; CEng, FIET; FInstP; Professor of Electrical Engineering, 1965–90, now Emeritus, and Head of Department of Electrical and Electronic Engineering, 1967–81 and 1983–89, University of Aston in Birmingham; *b* 2 June 1925; *s* of Sydney E. Flood and Elsie G. Flood; *m* 1949, Phyllis Mary Groocock; two *s*. *Educ:* City of London Sch.; Queen Mary Coll., Univ. of London (BSc 1945; PhD 1951; DSc 1965). CEng, FIET (FIEE 1959); FInstP 1987. Admiralty Signals Estab., 1944–46; Standard Telephone and Cables Ltd, 1946–47; PO Res. Stn, 1947–52; Siemens Brothers Ltd, 1952–57; Chief Engr, Advanced Develt Labs, AEI Telecommunications Div., 1957–65; Dean, Faculty of Engrg, 1971–74, and Sen. Pro-Vice-Chancellor, 1981–83, Univ. of Aston in Birmingham. Chairman: IEE Professional Gp on Telecommunications, 1974–77; IEE S Midland Centre, 1978–79; Univs Cttee on Integrated Sandwich Courses, 1981–82; BSI Cttee on Telecommunications, 1981–92; Member: British Electrotechnical Council, 1981–86; Monopolies and Mergers Commn, 1985–98. FCGI 1991 (CGIA 1962). Freeman, City of London, 1957. *Publications:* Telecommunication Networks, 1975, 2nd edn 1997; Transmission Systems, 1991; Telecommunications Switching, Traffic and Networks, 1995; papers in scientific and technical jls; patents. *Recreations:* swimming, wine-making. *Address:* 60 Widney Manor Road, Solihull, West Midlands B91 3JQ. *T:* (0121) 705 3604. *Club:* Royal Over-Seas League.

FLOOD, Prof. John Lewis, PhD; FRHistS; Senior Research Fellow, University of London Institute of Germanic Studies, since 2002 (Deputy Director, 1979–2002; Leverhulme Emeritus Research Fellow, 2002–04); Professor of German, University of London, 1993–2002, now Emeritus; *b* 22 Sept. 1938; *s* of late William Henry Flood and Ethel Mary Flood (*née* Daffern); *m* 1973, Ann Matthews, BA, MCLIP, *d* of late Edward Matthews; three *s*. *Educ:* Alderman Newton's Grammar Sch., Leicester; Univ. of Nottingham (BA 1961; MA 1963); Univ. of Munich; Univ. of Kiel; PhD London 1980. Lektor for English, Univ. of Erlangen-Nuremberg, 1963–64; Asst Lectr in German, Univ. of Nottingham, 1964–65; King's College London: Asst Lectr in German, 1965–67; Lectr, 1967–72; Sen. Lectr, 1972–79; Reader in German, Univ. of London, 1980–93. Chm., Panel for German, Dutch and Scandinavian Langs, RAEs 1996 and 2001, HEFCE; Mem., Coll. of Peer Review Assessors, AHRC (formerly AHRB), 2004–. Hon. Sec., Conf. of Univ. Teachers of German in GB and Ireland, 1971–92. Hon. Treas., 1984–2001, Vice-Pres., 2001–, Henry Sweet Soc. for Hist. of Linguistic Ideas; Vice-Pres., 1993–2004, Sen. Vice-Pres., 2002–04, Pres., 2004–06, Bibliographical Soc.; Member, Council: Philological Soc., 1998–2003; Viking Soc. for Northern Res., 2002–04. Adv. Ed., Oxford DNB, 2008–. Fellow, Centre for the Book, British Library, 1993–94. Corresp. Mem., Historical Commn, Börsenverein des Deutschen Buchhandels, Frankfurt am Main, 1995–. FRHistS 2002. Jacob und Wilhelm Grimm Prize, GDR, 1988. Officer's Cross, Order of Merit (FRG), 2002. *Publications:* (ed) Modern Swiss Literature, 1985; (ed) Ein Moment des erfahrenen Lebens, 1987; (ed) Mit regulu bithuungan, 1989; (ed) Kurz bevor der Vorhang fiel, 1990; (ed) Common Currency?, 1991; Die Historie von Herzog Ernst, 1992; (ed) The German Book 1450–1750, 1995; Johannes Sinapius 1505–1560, 1997; (with M. Davies) Proper Words in Proper Places: studies in lexicology and lexicography, 2001; Incunabula: German vernacular literature, 2003; Poets Laureate in the Holy Roman Empire: a bio-bibliographical handbook (4 vols), 2006; contrib. numerous essays in scholarly books and jls. *Recreation:* writing. *Address:* University of London Institute of Germanic and Romance Studies, Senate House, Malet Street, WC1E 7HU. *T:* (020) 7862 8966.

FLOOD, John Martin; non-executive Director, Hunting Engineering Ltd, 1994–99; *b* 3 Oct. 1939; *s* of late Harry Flood and Rita Flood (*née* Martin); *m* 1962, Irene Edwards; one *s*. *Educ:* Merchant Taylors' School, Crosby; Leeds Univ. (BSc Physics, 1st cl.). CEng 1991; FRAeS 1991. Graduate Apprentice, English Electric, Stevenage, 1962; joined RAE, 1963; Asst Dir, Dir Air Guided Weapons and on Army Chief Scientist staff, 1978–83; joined RAE, 1983; Head, Attack Weapons and Defensive Systems Depts, RAE, 1985–89; Dep. Dir (Mission Systems), RAE, 1989–91; Technical Dir, RAE, 1991–92; Dir, Weapon Systems Sector, 1991–93, Technical Dir, 1993–94, DRA. *Recreations:* bird watching, walking, theatre, reading (political biography). *Address:* Brandon, 38 Kings Road, Ilkley LS29 9AN.

FLOOD, Michael Donovan, (Mik); arts consultant, since 1997; *b* 7 May 1949; *s* of late Gp Capt. Donovan John Flood, DFC, AFC and of Vivien Ruth (*née* Alison); *m* 1975, Julie Ward (marr. diss. 1989); one *d*. *Educ:* St George's Coll., Weybridge; Llangefni County Sch., Anglesey. Founder and Artistic Dir, Chapter Arts Centre, Cardiff, 1970–81; Develt Dir, Baltimore Theater Project, USA, 1981–82; Administrator, Pip Simmons Theatre Gp, 1982–83; Arts consultancy, 1983–85; Dir, Watermans Arts Centre, Brentford, 1985–90; Dir, ICA, 1990–97. Producer of large-scale events: Woyzeck, Cardiff, 1976; Deadwood, Kew Gdns, 1986; Offshore Rig, River Thames, 1987. Member: Film Cttee, Welsh Arts Council, 1976–80; Exec. Cttee, SE Wales Arts Assoc., 1980–81; Co-Founder, Nat. Assoc. of Arts Centres, 1976. Exec. Bd, European Forum for Arts and Heritage, 2004–; Board of Directors: Pip Simmons Theatre Gp, 1977–83; Thames Fest., 2004–. Pres., Informal European Theatre Meeting, 1998–2002. Mem., Ct of Govs, RCA, 1990–97. Silver Jubilee Medal, 1977. *Publications:* book reviews in nat. newspapers; contribs on arts and cultural politics to British and European periodicals. *Recreations:* sailing, ichthyology, travel. *Address:* 1 Marshall House, Dorncliffe Road, SW6 5LF. *T:* (020) 7736 8668, *Fax:* (020) 7384 3770; *e-mail:* mik@mikflood.com. *Club:* Groucho.

FLOOD, Philip James, AO 1992; High Commissioner for Australia in the United Kingdom, 1998–2000; *b* 2 July 1935; *s* of Thomas and Maxine Flood; *m* 1990, Carole, *d* of Cuthbert and Nicole Henderson; two *s* one *d*. *Educ:* North Sydney Boys' High Sch.; Univ. of Sydney (BEc Hons). Australian Embassy and Mission to EC, Brussels, 1959–62; Australian Embassy and Mission to OECD, Paris, 1966–69; Asst Sec., Dept of Foreign Affairs, 1971–73; High Comr, Bangladesh, 1974–76; Minister, Washington, 1976–77; Special Trade Rep., 1977–80; First Asst Sec., Dept of Trade, 1981–84; Dep. Sec., Dept of Foreign Affairs and Trade, 1985–88; Ambassador to Indonesia, 1989–93; Director General: Australian Internat. Develt Assistance Bureau, 1993–95; Office of Nat. Assessments, 1995–96; Sec., Dept of Foreign Affairs and Trade, 1996–98. Mem., Minister's Foreign Affairs Council, 2004–07. Head: Inquiry into Immigration Detention, 2000–01; Inquiry into Australian Intelligence Agencies, 2004; Chm., Plasma Fractionation Review, 2006. Vis. Fellow, ANU, 2001–06. Mem., Commonwealth War Graves Commn, 1998–2000; Trustee, Imperial War Mus., 1998–2000. Chm., Australia Indonesia Inst., 2001–04; Dep. Chm., Asialink, 2005–. Dir and Dep. Chm., CARE Australia, 2003–. Order of Merit (Indonesia), 1993. *Publication:* Odyssey by the Sea, 2005. *Recreations:* reading, theatre, walking, swimming. *Address:* 96 Jervois Street, Deakin, ACT 2600, Australia. *Club:* Commonwealth (Canberra).

FLOOD, Thomas Oliver, CBE 2004; Chief Executive, BTCV (British Trust for Conservation Volunteers), since 2001 (Marketing Director, 1986–2001); *b* 21 May 1947; *s* of Thomas Joseph Flood and Elizabeth Gerard Flood (*née* Byrne); adopted British citizenship, 1999; civil partnership 2006, Paul Cornes. *Educ:* University Coll., Dublin (BA Eng, Metaphysics and Politics). Mkt res., W. S. Atkins Ltd, 1970–72; sales and mktg, 3M UK plc, 1972–86. Chm., Red Admiral Aids Charity, 1994–99. Mem. Bd, ACEVO, 2008–. FRSA 1995; FCMI 1995. *Recreations:* walking, cooking, opera, cinema. *Address:* British Trust for Conservation Volunteers, 80 York Way, N1 9AG. *T:* (020) 7843 4298, *Fax:* (020) 7278 8967; *e-mail:* T.Flood@btcv.org.uk.

FLOOK, Adrian John; Consultant, M:Communications, since 2005; *b* 9 July 1963; *s* of John Harold Julian Flook and late Rosemary Ann Flook (*née* Richardson); *m* 2003, Frangelica O'Shea; one *d*. *Educ:* King Edward's Sch., Bath; Mansfield Coll., Oxford (MA Hons Mod. Hist.). Stockbroker, Warburg Securities, and others, 1985–98; Financial Dynamics (business communications consultancy), 1998–2003. MP (C) Taunton, 2001–05; contested (C) same seat, 2005. *Address:* 37 Simpson Street, SW11 3HW.

FLORENCE, Prof. Alexander Taylor, CBE 1994; PhD, DSc; FRSE; FRPharmS, FRSC; Dean, School of Pharmacy, University of London, 1989–2006; *b* 9 Sept. 1940; *s* of late Alexander Charles Gerrard Florence and Margaret Florence; *m* 1st, 1964, Elizabeth Catherine McRae (marr. diss. 1995); two *s* one *d*; 2nd, 2000, Dr Florence Madsen, *d* of Bernard Madsen, Paris. *Educ:* Royal Coll. of Science and Technology, Glasgow and Univ. of Glasgow (BSc Hons 1962; PhD 1965); DSc Strathclyde, 1984. FRSC 1977; FRPharmS 1987. University of Strathclyde: MRC Jun. Res. Fellow, 1965–66; Lectr in Pharmaceutical Chemistry, 1966–72; Sen. Lectr in Pharm. Chem., 1972–76; J. P. Todd Prof. of Pharmacy, 1976–88. Member: Cttee on Safety of Medicines, 1983–98 (Mem., Sub-cttee on Chemistry, Pharmacy and Standards of Cttee on Safety of Medicines, 1972–98); Nuffield Inquiry into Pharmacy, 1984–86. Pres., Eur. Assoc. of Faculties of Pharmacy, 1997–2001; Vice Pres., Internat. Pharmaceutical Fedn, 1998–2000 (Høst-Madsen Medal, 1996); Pres., Controlled Release Soc., 2002–03 (Vice Pres., 2001–02). Co-Editor in Chief, Jl of Drug Targeting, 1993–97; Editor-in-Chief (Europe), Internat. Jl of Pharmaceutics, 1997–. FRSE 1987; FRSA 1989. DUniv: Hoshi, Tokyo, 2003; Strathclyde, 2004; Danish Univ. of Pharmaceutical Scis, 2006; UEA, 2007. British Pharmaceutical Conf. Science Award, 1972; Harrison Meml Medal, Royal Pharmaceutical Soc., 1986; Scheele Prize, Swedish Acad. of Pharmaceutical Scis, 1993; GlaxoSmithKline Internat. Achievement Award, 2001; Maurice-Marie Janot Award, Assoc. de Pharmacie Galenique Industrielle, France, 2006; Higuchi Prize, Acad. of Pharmaceutical Sci. and Technol., Japan, 2006. *Publications:* Solubilization by Surface Active Agents, 1968; Physicochemical Principles of Pharmacy, 1981, 4th edn 2006; Surfactant Systems, 1983; (ed) Materials Used in Pharmaceutical Formulation, 1985; (ed) Formulation Factors in Adverse Reactions, 1990; (ed jtly) Liposomes in Drug Delivery, 1992; (ed jtly) Modern Pharmaceutics, 2008; pubns on drug delivery and targeting, surfactants, dendrimers and nanotechnology. *Recreations:* music, writing, painting. *Address:* Newlands, 23 North Esk Road, Edzell, Angus DD9 7TW. *T:* (01356) 648833; La Providence, 7G rue Sincaire, 06300, Nice, France.

FLORENCE, Peter Kenrick, MBE 2005; Founder and Director, Hay Festival, since 1988; *b* 4 Oct. 1964, *s* of late Norman Samuel Florence and of Rhoda Lewis; *m* 1996, Becky Shaw; four *s*. *Educ:* Ipswich Sch.; Jesus Coll., Cambridge (BA Hons Mod. and Medieval Langs 1987, MA); Université Paris-Sorbonne (Paris IV). Designer: Festivaletteratura, Mantova, 1996; The Word, London, 1999; Festa Literaria Internacional de Parati (FLIP), Brazil, 2002; Hay Festival Cartagena, Colombia, 2005; Hay Festival Segovia, Spain, 2006. Hon. DLitt Glamorgan, 2004. *Recreations:* walking, food, family. *Address:* Hay Festival, 25 Lion Street, Hay HR3 5AD; *e-mail:* peter@litfest.com. *Clubs:* Groucho; Hawks (Cambridge).

FLOREY, Prof. Charles du Vé; Professor of Public Health Medicine (formerly Community Medicine), University of Dundee, 1983–99; *b* 11 Sept. 1934; *s* of Howard Walter Florey and Mary Ethel Florey; *m* 1966, Susan Jill Hopkins; one *s* one *d*. *Educ:* Univ. of Cambridge (MD); Yale Univ. (MPH). FFCM 1977; FRCPE 1986. Instructor, 1965, Asst Prof., 1966–69, Yale Univ. School of Medicine; Mem. Scientific Staff, MRC, Jamaica, 1969–71; St Thomas's Hospital Medical School, London: Sen. Lectr, 1971–78; Reader, 1978–81; Prof., 1981–83. Pres., Internat. Epidemiol Assoc., 1999–2002. *Publications:* (with S. R. Leeder) Methods for Cohort Studies of Chronic Airflow Limitation, 1982; (jtly) Introduction to Community Medicine, 1983; A European Concerted Action: maternal alcohol consumption and its relation to the outcome of pregnancy and child development at eighteen months, 1992; (ed) Epilex: a multilingual lexicon of epidemiological terms, 1993; (jtly) The Audit Handbook: improving health through clinical audit, 1993; (jtly) The Pocket Guide to Grant Applications, 1998. *Recreations:* photography, sailing, walking, computing. *Address:* 76 Alton Road, Poole, Dorset BH14 8SS.

FLÓREZ, Juan Diego; tenor; *b* Lima, Peru, 13 Jan. 1973; *s* of Ruben Flórez and Maria Teresa Flórez (*née* Salom, later French); *m* 2007, Julia Trappe. *Educ:* Conservatory of Lima; Curtis Inst., Philadelphia. Début in Matilde di Shabran, Rossini Opera Fest., 1996; has performed at: La Scala, Milan; Comunale of Florence; Rossini Opera Fest., Pesaro; Opera of Rome; Metropolitan Opera, NY; Staatsoper, Vienna; San Francisco Opera; Royal Opera Hse, Covent Gdn; Bayerische Staatsoper, Munich; Gran Teatre del Liceu, Barcelona; Paris Opera; Lyric Opera, Chicago; Deutsche Oper, Berlin. Abbiati Prize, Rossini d'Oro, Pesaro. *Address:* c/o Ernesto Palacio Artists Management, Via Donizetti 11, 24050 Lurano (BG), Italy; *e-mail:* ernestopalacio@tiscali.it.

FLOUD, Mrs Jean Esther, CBE 1976; MA, BSc(Econ); Principal, Newnham College, Cambridge, 1971–83, Hon. Fellow, 1983; *b* 3 Nov. 1915; *d* of Annie Louisa and Ernest Walter McDonald; *m* 1938, Peter Castle Floud, CBE (*d* 1960), *s* of late Sir Francis Floud, KCB, KCSI, KCMG, and formerly Keeper of Circulation, Victoria and Albert Museum; two *d* (one *s* decd). *Educ:* public elementary and selective secondary schools; London School of Economics (BScEcon), Hon. Fellow, 1972. Asst Dir of Educn, City of Oxford, 1940–46; Teacher of Sociology in the University of London (London School of Economics and Inst. of Educn), 1947–62; Official Fellow of Nuffield College, Oxford, 1961–72, Hon. Fellow, 1983; Hon. Fellow, Darwin Coll., Cambridge, 1986. Member: Franks Commission of Inquiry into the University of Oxford, 1964–66; University Grants Cttee, 1969–74; Social Science Research Council, 1970–73; Exec. Cttee, PEP, 1975–77; Adv. Bd for the Res. Councils, 1976–81; Council, Policy Studies Inst., 1979–83. Hon.

LittD Leeds, 1973; Hon. DLitt City, 1978; Hon. DLit London, 2003. *Publications:* (with A. H. Halsey and F. M. Martin) Social Class and Educational Opportunity, 1956; (with Warren Young) Dangerousness and Criminal Justice, 1981; papers and reviews in sociological jls. *Recreations:* books, music. *Address:* Elderwick House, The Ridings, Shotover, Oxford OX3 8TB.

FLOUD, Sir Roderick (Castle), Kt 2005; FBA 2002; Acting Dean, School of Advanced Study, University of London, since 2007; Vice-Chancellor, 2002–04, President, 2004–06, now President Emeritus, London Metropolitan University; *b* 1 April 1942; *s* of late Bernard Francis Castle Floud, MP and Ailsa (*née* Craig); *m* 1964, Cynthia Anne (*née* Smith); two *d*. *Educ:* Brentwood Sch.; Wadham Coll., Oxford (Hon. Fellow, 1999); Nuffield Coll., Oxford; MA, DPhil. Asst Lectr in Economic History, UCL, 1966–69; Lectr in Economic History, Univ. of Cambridge and Fellow of Emmanuel Coll., Cambridge, 1969–75 (Hon. Fellow, 2003); Prof. of Modern History, Birkbeck Coll., Univ. of London, 1975–88; Provost, City of London Poly., subseq. London Guildhall Univ., 1998–2002. Vis. Prof. of European History and of Economics, Stanford Univ., Calif, 1980–81. Research Associate, Nat. Bureau of Economic Research, USA, 1978–; Research Programme Dir, Centre for Economic Policy Research, 1983–88. Member: Council: ESRC, 1993–97; UUK (formerly CVCP), 1997–2005 (Pres., 2001–03); Convenor, London Higher Educn Consortium, 1999–2001; Mem. Bd, European Univ. Assoc., 2001–07 (Vice-Pres., 2005–07). Chair, Standing Cttee for Social Scis, ESF, 2007–. Mem., Lord Chancellor's Adv. Council on Public Records, 1978–84. Mem. Bd, London Develt Partnership, 1998–2001; Observer, London Develt Agency, 2001–06. Member: Tower Hamlets Coll. Corp., 1997–2001; Council, Gresham Coll., 1998– (Provost, 2008–). Trustee, Samaritans, 2006–. Treas., Oxford Union Soc., 1966. Freeman: City of London, 1995; Information Technologists' Co., 1996 (Liveryman, 2005); Guild of Educators, 2000 (Master, 2005–06). FCGI 2001. Hon. Fellow, Birkbeck Coll., 1994; Centenary Fellow, Historical Assoc., 2006. Hon. DLitt: City, 1999; Westminster, 2006. *Publications:* An Introduction to Quantitative Methods for Historians, 1973, 2nd edn 1980; (ed) Essays in Quantitative Economic History, 1974; The British Machine Tool Industry 1850–1914, 1976; (ed) The Economic History of Britain since 1700, 1981, 2nd edn 1994; (ed) The Power of the Past, 1984; (jtly) Height, Health and History, 1990; The People and the British Economy 1830–1914, 1997; (ed) Health and Welfare during Industrialisation, 1997; (ed) London Higher, 1998; (ed) The Cambridge Economic History of Modern Britain, 2004; articles in Economic History Review, Social Science History, etc. *Recreations:* family, walking, music. *Address:* School of Advanced Study, University of London, Senate House, Malet Street, WC1E 7HX. *T:* (020) 7862 8659; *e-mail:* roderick.floud@sas.ac.uk. 15 Flint Street, Haddenham, Bucks HP17 8AL. *T:* (01844) 291086. *Club:* Athenæum.

FLOWER, family name of **Viscount Ashbrook**.

FLOWER, Antony John Frank, (Tony), MA, PhD; Founding Chairman, The Young Foundation, 2005–07; *b* 2 Feb. 1951; *s* of late Frank Robert Edward Flower and Dorothy Elizabeth (*née* Williams). *Educ:* Chipping Sodbury Grammar Sch.; Univ. of Exeter (BA Hons Philosophy and Sociology; MA Sociology); Univ. of Leicester (PhD Mass Communications). Graphic Designer, 1973–76; Co-founder with Lord Young of Dartington, and first Gen. Sec., Tawney Soc., 1982–88; Dir, Res. Inst. for Econ. and Social Affairs, 1982–92. Co-ordinator, Argo Venture (Nat. Space Mus.), 1984–2002, Dir, Argo Trust, 1986–95; Director: Healthline Health Inf. Service, 1986–88; Health Information Trust, 1987–88 (Trustee, 1988–90); Environmental Concern Centre in Europe, 1990–92; Institute of Community Studies: Trustee, 1993–2005; Dep. Dir, 1994–96; Sen. Fellow, 1996–2001; Acting Dir, 2001; Chm., 2001–05; Dep. Dir, 1994–96, Chm., 2001–04, Mutual Aid Centre (Trustee, 1990–2004). Chm., ContinYou, 2003–05. Mem. Adv. Bd, The Earth Centre, 1990–2000; Sec., Ecological Studies Inst., 1990–92. Associate: Redesign Ltd, 1989–92; Nicholas Lacey & Partners (Architects), 1989–; Consultant: CIRIA, 1992–96; Rocklabs Geochemical Analysis CC, 1993–; Cambridge Female Educn Trust, 1999–. Co-ordinator, Campaign for Educnl Choice, 1988–89. Trustee: Gaia, 1988–2001; Educn Extra, 1995–2004 (Chm. of Trustees, 2001–03); Consultant, Joseph Rowntree Reform Trust Ltd, 1993–2003; Co-founder and Patron, Tower Hamlets Summer Univ. Trust, 1995–; Patron, Nat. Space Science Centre, 1996–. Mem., Council for Social Democracy, 1982–84; Dir of Develt, Green Alliance, 1991–92. Associate: Open Coll. of the Arts, 1988–2002; Inst. for Public Policy Res., 1989–95; Family Covenant Assoc., 1994–2000. Editor, Tawney Journal, 1982–88; Co-founder and Man. Editor, Samizdat Magazine, 1988–90. FRSA 1991. *Publications:* (with Graham Mort) Starting to Write: a course in creative writing, 1990; (ed jtly) The Alternative, 1990; (ed jtly) Young at Eighty: the prolific public life of Michael Young, 1995. *Recreations:* collecting junk, sailing, making and restoring musical instruments. *Address:* c/o 18 Victoria Park Square, E2 9PF.

FLOWER, Robert Philip; JP; HM Diplomatic Service, retired; Counsellor, Foreign and Commonwealth Office, 1994–96; *b* 12 May 1939; *s* of Philip Edward Flower and Dorothy Agnes Elizabeth (*née* Beukers); *m* 1964, Anne Daveen Tweddle; two *s*. *Educ:* Christ's Hosp.; Magdalene Coll., Cambridge (BA). Called to the Bar, Middle Temple, 1964. FCO, 1967–96; served in Malawi, Malaysia, UK Delegn to NATO, Bonn and London; Dep. Head of Mission, The Hague, 1990–93. Sec., Cumbria Br., Cambridge Soc., 2005–; Vice-Chm., Cumbria Decorative and Fine Arts Soc., 2006. JP Cumbria, 1998. *Recreations:* fell-walking, reading, music. *Address:* Lambfold, High Lorton, Cockermouth, Cumbria CA13 9UQ.

FLOWER, Prof. Roderick John, PhD, DSc; FMedSci; FRS 2003; Professor of Biochemical Pharmacology, and Joint Head, Department of Biochemical Pharmacology, William Harvey Research Institute, Barts and the London, Queen Mary's School of Medicine and Dentistry (formerly St Bartholomew's and the Royal London School of Medicine and Dentistry, Queen Mary and Westfield College), London, since 1994; *b* 29 Nov. 1945; *s* of Lesley Ralph Flower and Audrey Ellen Eckett; *m* 1994, Lindsay Joyce Riddell. *Educ:* Univ. of Sheffield (BSc 1st class Hons Physiol. 1971); PhD 1974, DSc 1985, London. Wellcome Res. Labs, Beckenham, 1973–84, Sen. Scientist, 1975–84; University of Bath: Prof. of Pharmacol., 1984–89; Hd, Sch. of Pharmacy and Pharmacol., 1987–89; Medical College of St Bartholomew's Hospital, London, then St Bartholomew's and Royal London Sch. of Medicine and Dentistry, QMW: Lilly Prof. of Biochem. Pharmacol., 1989–94; pt-time Actg Hd of Clinical Pharmacol., 1993–96; William Harvey Research Institute: a Dir and founding Mem., 1989–; Head of Inst., 1998–2002; Wellcome Trust Principal Res. Fellow, 1994–2007; a Dir and founding Mem., William Harvey Res. Ltd, 1989–. Pres., British Pharmacological Soc., 2000–01 (Fellow, 2005). *Publications:* (ed with N. J. Goulding) Glucocorticoids, 2001; (ed jtly) Rang & Dale's Pharmacology, 6th edn 2007; 280 peer reviewed articles and over 200 other publications incl. reviews, book chapters, abstracts, conf. procs, editorials and pubd correspondence. *Recreations:* the camera, history of science, travel. *Address:* Department of Biochemical Pharmacology, William Harvey Research Institute, Barts and the London School of Medicine, Charterhouse Square, EC1M 6BQ. *T:* (020) 7882 6073, *Fax:* (020) 7882 6076; *e-mail:* r.j.flower@qmul.ac.uk.

FLOWERS, family name of **Baron Flowers**.

FLOWERS, Baron *cr* 1979 (Life Peer), of Queen's Gate in the City of Westminster; **Brian Hilton Flowers,** Kt 1969; FRS 1961; Chancellor, Manchester University, 1994–2001; Chairman, Nuffield Foundation, 1987–98 (a Managing Trustee, 1982–98); *b* 13 Sept 1924; *o s* of late Rev. Harold J. Flowers, Swansea; *m* 1951, Mary Frances, *er d* of late Sir Leonard Behrens, CBE; two step *s*. *Educ:* Bishop Gore Grammar Sch., Swansea; Gonville and Caius Coll. (Exhibitioner), Cambridge (MA); Hon. Fellow, 1974; University of Birmingham (DSc). Anglo-Canadian Atomic Energy Project, 1944–46; Research in nuclear physics and atomic energy at Atomic Energy Research Establishment, Harwell, 1946–50; Dept of Mathematical Physics, University of Birmingham, 1950–52; Head of Theoretical Physics Div., AERE, Harwell, 1952–58; Prof. of Theoretical Physics, 1958–61, Langworthy Prof. of Physics, 1961–72, Univ. of Manchester; on leave of absence as Chm., SRC, 1967–73; Rector of Imperial Coll. of Sci. and Technol., 1973–85; Vice-Chancellor, Univ. of London, 1985–90. Chairman: Royal Commn on Environmental Pollution, 1973–76; Standing Commn on Energy and the Environment, 1978–81; Univ. of London Working Party on future of med. and dent. teaching resources, 1979–80; Cttee of Vice-Chancellors and Principals, 1983–85; Select Cttee on Science and Technology, H of L, 1989–93 (Mem., 1980–93, 1994–98, 1999–2002). Mem., AEA, 1970–80. President: Inst. of Physics, 1972–74; European Science Foundn, 1974–80; Nat. Soc. for Clean Air, 1977–79; Parly and Scientific Cttee, 1993–97. Chm., Computer Bd for Univs and Research Councils, 1966–70. Member: Council, RPMS, 1990–97 (Vice-Chm., 1991–97); Bd of Management, LSHTM, 1992–95 (Chm., 1994–95). Gov., Middx Univ., 1992–2001. Founding Mem. and Mem. Exec. Council, Academia Europaea, 1988. Founder Mem., SDP, 1981. FInstP 1961; Hon. FInstP 1996; Hon. FCGI, 1975; Hon. MRIA (Science Section), 1976; Hon. FIET (Hon. FIEE, 1975); Hon. FRCP 1992; Sen. Fellow, RCA, 1983; Hon. Fellow: UMIST, 1985; Royal Holloway, London Univ., 1996; Univ. of Wales, Swansea, 1996; Corresp. Mem., Swiss Acad. of Engrg Sciences, 1986. MA Oxon, 1956; Hon. DSc: Sussex, 1968; Wales, 1972; Manchester, 1973; Leicester, 1973; Liverpool, 1974; Bristol, 1982; Oxford, 1985; NUI, 1990; Reading, 1996; London, 1996; Hon. DEng Nova Scotia, 1983; Hon. ScD Dublin, 1984; Hon. LLD: Dundee, 1985; Glasgow, 1987; Manchester, 1995; DU Middlesex, 2001. Rutherford Medal and Prize, 1968, Glazebrook Medal and Prize, 1987, IPPS; Chalmers Medal, Chalmers Univ. of Technol., Sweden, 1980. Officier de la Légion d'Honneur, 1981 (Chevalier, 1975). *Publications:* (with E. Mendoza) Properties of Matter, 1970; An Introduction to Numerical Methods in C++, 1995; contribs to scientific periodicals on structure of the atomic nucleus, nuclear reactions, science policy, energy and the environment. *Recreations:* music, walking, computing, gardening. *Address:* 53 Athenaeum Road, N20 9AL. *T:* (020) 8446 5993.

FLOWERS, Angela Mary; Chairman, Angela Flowers Gallery plc, since 1989; *b* 19 Dec. 1932; *d* of Charles Geoffrey Holland and Olive Alexandra Holland (*née* Stiby); *m* 1st, 1952, Adrian Flowers (marr. diss. 1973); three *s* one *d*; 2nd, 2003, Robert Heller (partner, 1973–2003); one *d*. *Educ:* Westonbirt Sch., Glos; Wychwood Sch., Oxford; Webber Douglas Sch. of Singing and Dramatic Art. Posts in stage, film and advertising, until 1967; founded Angela Flowers Gallery, 1970: Lisle St, 1970–71; Portland Mews, 1971–78; Tottenham Mews, 1978–88; Richmond Rd, 1988–2001; Kingsland Rd, 2001–. Mem. Bd, Nat. Youth Jazz Orch., 1988–93. Trustee, John Kobal Foundn, 1992–97. Sen. Fellow, RCA, 1994. Hon. DArt, E London, 1999. *Recreations:* piano, singing, cooking, jazz, collecting contemporary art. *Address:* Flowers East, 82 Kingsland Road, E2 8DP. *T:* (020) 7920 7777, *Fax:* (020) 7920 7770; *e-mail:* angela@flowerseast.com.

FLOYD, Hon. Sir Christopher (David), Kt 2007; **Hon. Mr Justice Floyd;** a Judge of the High Court of Justice, Chancery Division, since 2007; *b* 20 Dec. 1951; *s* of David and Hana Floyd; *m* 1974, Rosalind Jane Arscott; one *s* two *d*. *Educ:* Westminster Sch.; Trinity Coll., Cambridge (MA Nat. Scis and Law). Called to the Bar, Inner Temple, 1975, Bencher, 2001; called to the Bar of Republic of Ireland, 1988. QC 1992; Asst Recorder, 1994–2000; a Dep. High Court Judge (Patents Court), 1998–2007; Recorder, 2000–07. Dep. Chm., Copyright Tribunal, 1995–2007. Member: Bar Council Chm.'s Arbitration/Conciliation Panel, 1996–2007; Bar Council Professional Conduct and Complaints Cttee, 1998–2002; Bar Council, 2000–04; Bar Council European Cttee, 2003–04; Litigation Accreditation Bd Appeal Panel, Chartered Inst. Patent Attorneys, 2005–07; Chm., Intellectual Property Bar Assoc., 1999–2004. *Recreations:* Austin Sevens, cricket, ski-ing, walking. *Address:* Royal Courts of Justice, Strand, WC2A 2LL.

FLOYD, Sir Giles (Henry Charles), 7th Bt *cr* 1816; Director, Burghley Estate Farms, since 1958; *b* 27 Feb. 1932; *s* of Sir John Duckett Floyd, 6th Bt, TD, and Jocelin Evadne (*d* 1976), *d* of late Sir Edmund Wyldbore Smith; *S* father, 1975; *m* 1st, 1954, Lady Gillian Moyra Katherine Cecil (marr. diss. 1978), 2nd *d* of 6th Marquess of Exeter, KCMG; two *s*; 2nd, 1985, Judy Sophia Lane, *er d* of late W. L. Tregoning, CBE, and D. M. E. Tregoning. *Educ:* Eton College. High Sheriff of Rutland, 1968. *Heir: er s* David Henry Cecil Floyd [*b* 2 April 1956; *m* 1981, Caroline, *d* of John Beckly, Manor Farm, Bowerchalke, Salisbury, Wilts; two *d*]. *Address:* Tinwell Manor, Stamford, Lincs PE9 3UF. *T:* (01780) 762676. *Club:* Turf.

FLOYD, Keith; cook, broadcaster; *b* 28 Dec. 1943; *s* of late Sydney Albert Floyd and of Winnifred Margaret Floyd; *m* 1995, Theresa Mary (*née* Smith); one *s* one *d* by prev. marriages. *Educ:* Wellington Sch. Commnd, 3rd RTR 1963; journalist, 1961–; broadcaster, 1986–. *Publications:* Floyd's Food, 1981; Floyd on Fish, 1985; Floyd on Fire, 1986; Floyd on France, 1987; Floyd on Britain and Ireland, 1988; Floyd in the Soup, 1988; A Feast of Floyd, 1989; Floyd's American Pie, 1989; Floyd on Oz, 1991; Floyd on Spain, 1992; Floyd on Hangovers, 1992; Far Flung Floyd, 1993; Floyd on Italy, 1994; The Best of Floyd, 1995; Floyd on Africa, 1996; Floyd's Barbies, 1997; Floyd's Fjord Fiesta, 1998; Floyd Uncorked, 1998; Floyd Around the Med, 1999; Out of the Frying Pan (autobiog.), 2000; Floyd's India, 2001; Flash Floyd, 2002; Floyd's Great Curries, 2004; Floyd's China, 2005; Splash and a Dash, 2006; Floyd's Thailand, 2006. *Recreations:* Rugby, fishing, drinking, gardening. *Address:* c/o Stan Green Management, PO Box 4, Dartmouth, Devon TQ6 0YD. *T:* (01803) 770046, *Fax:* (01803) 770075; *e-mail:* sgm@clara.co.uk.

FLUCK, Peter Nigel; freelance artist; sculptor of abstract kinetics, since 1994; founded (with Roger Law) Spitting Image, 1982; *b* 7 April 1941; *s* of Herbert William Fluck and Ada Margaret (*née* Hughes); *m* 1963, Anne-Cécile de Bruyne; one *d* one *s*. *Educ:* Cambs High Sch. for Boys; Cambridge Sch. of Art. Artist-reporter, illustrator, 1961–70; cartoonist and caricaturist, 1970–82; Luck & Flaw (with Roger Law), 1974–82; Spitting Image (18 TV series), 1982–94. Exhibitions: Chaotic Constructions (with Tony Myatt) Tate Gall., St Ives and Edin. Fest., 1997, (expanded) RIBA, 1999, Study Gall., Poole, 2004; Yew Tree Gall., Cornwall, 2004. *Recreations:* fly fishing, ceramics, print-making. *Address:* White Feather, Cadgwith, Cornwall TR12 7LB. *T:* (01326) 290546.

FLUGGE, Klaus; Founder, Publisher and Managing Director, Andersen Press Ltd, since 1976; *b* 29 Nov. 1934; *s* of Werner and Emmi Flügge; *m* 1964, Joëlle Dansac; one *s*. *Educ:* German Book Trade Sch., Leipzig (Dip.). Asst to Pres., Abelard-Schuman, NY, 1959–61; Man. Dir, Abelard-Schuman Ltd, 1963–76. Eleanor Farjeon Award for distinguished services to children's books, 1999. *Recreations:* book collecting, jazz, swimming. *Address:* c/o Andersen Press Ltd, 20 Vauxhall Bridge Road, SW1V 2SA. *T:* (020) 7840 8701. *Club:* Groucho.

FLYNN, Desmond James; Inspector General and Chief Executive, Insolvency Service, Department for Business, Enterprise and Regulatory Reform (formerly Department of Trade and Industry), 2001–07; *b* 21 March 1949; *s* of James Joseph Flynn and Kathleen Eithne Flynn (*née* Fagan); *m* 1975, Kumari Ramdewar; one *s* one *d*. *Educ:* Univ. of E Anglia (BA Hons 1974). Trainee examr, Official Receiver, London, 1968–71; Examr, Official Receiver, Birmingham, 1976–1980; Asst Official Receiver, Birmingham and London, 1980–86; Principal, Internat. Trade Policy Div., DTI, 1986–88; Principal Inspector of Official Receivers, 1988–89; Dep. Inspector Gen., Insolvency Service, DTI, 1989–2001. *Publication:* (contrib.) Insolvency Law: theory and practice, ed H. Rajak, 1993. *Recreations:* reading, golf. *Club:* Letchworth Golf.

FLYNN, Douglas Ronald; Chief Executive Officer, Rentokil Initial plc, 2005–08; *b* 8 June 1949; *s* of Ronald Norman Flynn and Rhona Ellen Flynn; *m* 1975, Lynne Cecily Harcombe; two *s*. *Educ:* Newcastle Boys' High Sch., Australia; Univ. of Newcastle, Australia (BEng Hons 1972); MBA Melbourne Univ. 1979. Australian Sales Manager, ICI Australia, Melbourne, 1975–80; Gen. Manager, ICI Explosives, Hong Kong, 1980–82; Regl Manager, Perth, 1982–85, Manager Strategic Planning, Melbourne, 1985–86, ICI Australia Ltd; Deloitte Haskins & Sells, 1986–87; Chief Exec., Hobart, Davies Bros Ltd, 1987–90; Man. Dir, News Ltd Suburban Newspapers, Sydney, 1990–94; Dep. Man. Dir, News Internat. Newspapers, London, 1994–95; Man. Dir, News Internat. plc, 1995–99; CEO, Aegis Gp, 1999–2005. *Recreation:* sailing. *Clubs:* Tasmanian (Hobart); Royal Corinthian Yacht, Royal Hong Kong Yacht, Royal Sydney Yacht Squadron.

FLYNN, Prof. Frederick Valentine, MD (Lond), FRCP, FRCPath; Professor of Chemical Pathology in University of London at University College School of Medicine, 1970–89, now Professor Emeritus; Civil Consultant in Chemical Pathology to Royal Navy, 1978–92; *b* 6 Oct. 1924; *e s* of Frederick Walter Flynn and Jane Laing Flynn (*née* Valentine); *m* 1955, Catherine Ann, *o d* of Dr Robert Walter Warrick and Dorothy Ann Warrick (*née* Dimock); one *s* one *d*. *Educ:* University Coll. London; University Coll. Hosp. Med. Sch. (Fellow, UCL, 1974). Obstetric Ho. Surg. and various posts, incl. Research Asst and Registrar, Dept of Clin. Pathology, UCH, 1947–60; Associate in Clin. Path., Pepper Laboratory of Clin. Medicine, Univ. of Pennsylvania, and British Postgrad. Med. Fedn Travelling Fellow, 1954–55; Consultant Chemical Pathologist, UCH, 1960–70. Chairman: Assoc. of Clin. Biochemists Sci. and Technical Cttee, 1968–70; Dept of Health's Adv. Gp on Scientific and Clinical Applications of Computers, 1971–76; Organising Cttee for 1st, 2nd and 3rd Internat. Confs on Computing in Clinical Labs, 1972–80; Research Cttee, NE Thames RHA, 1984–88; Member: Min. of Health Lab. Equipment and Methods Adv. Gp, 1966–71; Min. of Technol. Working Party on Lab. Instrumentation, 1966–67; BMA Working Party on Computers in Medicine, 1968–69; Dept of Health's Adv. Cttee on Med. Computing, 1969–76, and Laboratory Develts Adv. Gp, 1972–75; MRC Working Party on Hypogammaglobulinaemia, 1959–70; MRC Adv. Panel on Applications for Computing Facilities, 1973–77; NW Thames RHA Sci. Cttee, 1973–74; Med. Lab. Techns Bd, Council for Professions Supplementary to Medicine, 1984–88; NHS Supraregional Assay Services Bd, 1990–92; Sir Jules Thorn Charitable Trust: Mem. Med. Adv. Cttee, 1983–97; Trustee, 1988–2006; Section of Pathology, RSM: Mem. Council, 1968–72, 1986–93; Vice-Pres., 1971–72, 1989–91; Royal Coll. of Pathologists: Chm., Panel of Examrs in Chem. Path., 1972–82; Mem. Council, 1973–83 and 1984–87; Vice-Pres., 1975–78; Treas., 1978–83; Dir of Continuing Med. Educn, 1992–97; College Medal, 1995; Association of Clinical Pathologists: Chm., Working Party on Data Processing in Labs, 1964–67; Mem. Council, 1988–90; Pres.-elect, 1988–89; Pres., 1989–90. Mem. Editl Bd, Jl of Clin. Pathol., 1995–96. *Publications:* numerous contribs to med. and sci. books and jls. *Recreations:* photography, genealogy, gardening.

FLYNN, James Edward; QC 2003; barrister; *b* 21 June 1956; *s* of late Ronald Joseph Flynn and of Margaret Rose Flynn (*née* Crossland, now Harris); *m* 1983, Catherine Clare Gibson; one *s* one *d*. *Educ:* Loughborough Grammar Sch.; Brasenose Coll., Oxford (BA Jurisprudence 1977). Called to the Bar, Middle Temple, 1978; admitted solicitor, 1984; with Linklaters & Paines, London and Brussels, 1982–86 and 1989–96; Legal Sec., European Court of Justice, 1986–89; Partner, Linklaters & Paines, Brussels, 1993–96; in practice as a barrister, London and Brussels, 1996–. Mem. Cttee, Competition Law Assoc.; Co-Chm., European Cttee, Bar Council, 2006–; UK Mem., CCBE Perm. Delegn to European Cts. *Publications:* (jtly) Competition: understanding the 1998 Act, 1999; (jtly) The Law of State Aid in the EU, 2003; articles in jls and poems in literary reviews. *Recreations:* poetry, singing, music. *Address:* Brick Court Chambers, 7–8 Essex Street, WC2R 3LD. *T:* (020) 7379 3550; *e-mail:* james.flynn@brickcourt.co.uk.

FLYNN, John Gerrard, CMG 1992; HM Diplomatic Service, retired; Ambassador to Venezuela, and concurrently (non-resident) to the Dominican Republic, 1993–97; *b* 23 April 1937; *s* of late Thomas Flynn and Mary Chisholm; *m* 1973, Drina Anne Coates; one *s* one *d*. *Educ:* Glasgow Univ. (MA). Foreign Office, 1965; Second Sec., Lusaka, 1966; First Sec., FCO, 1968; seconded to Canning House as Asst Dir-Gen., 1970; First Sec. (Commercial) and Consul, Montevideo, 1971; FCO, 1976; Chargé d'Affaires, Luanda, 1978; Counsellor and Consul-Gen., Brasilia, 1979; Counsellor, Madrid, 1982; High Comr, Swaziland, 1987; Ambassador to Angola and (non-resident) to São Tomé and Príncipe, 1990–93. British Special Rep. for Sierra Leone, 1998. Chairman: Anglo Latin American Foundn, 1998–2003; Anglo-Venezuelan Soc., 1999–2005; British Venezuelan Chamber of Commerce, 1999–2003. *Recreations:* hill-walking, golf. *Address:* 27 Parthenia Road, SW6 4BE. *Clubs:* Travellers, Caledonian.

FLYNN, Padraig; Member, European Commission (formerly Commission of the European Communities), 1993–99; *b* 9 May 1939; *m* 1963, Dorothy Tynan; one *s* three *d*. *Educ:* St Gerald's Secondary Sch., Castlebar, Co. Mayo; St Patrick's Trng Coll., Dublin (DipEd). Mayo County Council: Mem., 1967–87; Vice-Chm., 1975–77. TD (FF), 1977–93; Minister of State, Dept of Transport and Power, 1980–81; Minister for: Gaeltacht, March–Oct. 1982; Trade, Commerce and Tourism, Oct.–Dec. 1982; spokesman on trade, commerce and tourism, 1982–87; Minister for: the Envmt, 1987–91; Justice, Feb.–Dec. 1992; Industry and Commerce, Nov.–Dec. 1992. Mem., Irish Nat. Teachers' Orgn, 1957. Mem., Gaelic Athletic Assoc., 1959–. *Recreations:* golf, reading, world affairs. *Address:* Carrowbrinogue Lodge, Castlebar, Co. Mayo, Ireland.

FLYNN, Paul Phillip; MP (Lab) Newport West, since 1987; *b* 9 Feb. 1935; *s* of late James Flynn and Kathleen Williams; *m* 1st, 1962, Anne Harvey (marr. diss. 1984); one *s* (one *d* decd); 2nd, 1985, Samantha Morgan, *d* of Douglas and Elsie Cumpstone; one step *s* one step *d*. *Educ:* St Illtyd's Coll., Cardiff. Steelworker, 1955–84; Researcher, 1984–87. Mem., Gwent CC, 1974–82. Contested (Lab) Denbigh, Oct. 1974. Frontbench spokesman on Wales, 1987, on social security, 1988–90. Mem., Gorsedd of Bards, 1991. Campaign for Freedom of Information Parly Award, 1991. *Publications:* Commons Knowledge: how to be a backbencher, 1997; Baglu 'Mlaen (autobiog.), 1998; Dragons led by Poodles, 1999. *Address:* House of Commons, SW1A 0AA. *Club:* Ringland Labour (Newport, Gwent).

FLYNN, Roger; President, International, SDI Media Group Inc., since 2007; *b* 4 Nov. 1962; *s* of Peter Flynn and late Shirley Flynn; *m* 1986, Lisa Eyre; two *d*. *Educ:* Imperial Coll., London (BSc 1st Cl. Hons Physics). ACA 1987. With Arthur Andersen, 1984–88; Corporate Finance Exec., Virgin Gp plc, 1988–91; Commercial Dir, Virgin Communications Ltd, 1991–95; Gen. Manager, World Sales and Distribution, BA plc, 1995–98; Man. Dir, Prudential Retail, 1998–2000; CEO, BBC Ventures Gp Ltd, 2001–04; CEO, Spring Board Gp Ltd, 2004–07. MInstP 1985; MRI 1985. Trustee, Youth Culture Television, 1994–2007. Mem., Magic Circle. *Recreations:* sport, reading. *Address:* St Audrey House, 4 Doneraile Street, Fulham, SW6 6EN. *T:* (020) 8237 7911; *e-mail:* rflynn@sdimediagroup.com.

FLYNN, Most Rev. Thomas; *see* Achonry, Bishop of, (RC).

FLYNN, Vernon James Hennessy; QC 2008; *b* London, 1 Sept. 1966; *s* of James and Alice Flynn; *m* 1996, Angela Porta; one *s* one *d*. *Educ:* Trinity Coll., Cambridge (BA 1989). Called to the Bar, Lincoln's Inn, 1991. Vis. Fellow, LSE, 2003–. *Address:* Essex Court Chambers, 24 Lincoln's Inn Fields, WC2A 3EG.

FO, Dario; Italian playwright and actor; *b* 24 March 1926; *s* of Felice Fo and Pina (*née* Rota); *m* 1954, Franca Rame; one *s*. *Educ:* Acad. of Fine Arts, Milan. Joined a small theatre gp, 1950; wrote satirical radio series, Poer nano (Poor Dwarf), 1951, and performed selections from it, Teatro Odeon, Milan; appeared in Cocorico, Teatro Odeon, Milan, 1952; jt founder and performer, Il Dito Nell'Occhio (revue co.), 1953–55 (toured nationally); screenwriter, Rome, 1955–58; performer and writer, theatre gp, Compagnia Fo-Rame, 1958–68; artistic dir, Chi l'ha visto? (TV musical revue), 1959; performer and writer, Canzonissima (TV variety show); returned to theatre work, 1962; jt founder, theatre co-operative, Nuova Scena, 1968 (toured, 1968–69); jt founder, theatre gp, la Comune, 1970; Tricks of the Trade (TV series), 1985. *Plays include:* Gli Arcangeli non Giocano a Flipper, 1959 (Archangels Don't Play Pinball); Isabella, Tre Caravelle e un Cacciabelle, 1963 (Isabella, Three Sailing Ships and a Con Man); Mistero Buffo, 1969; Morte Accidentale di un Anarchico, 1970 (Accidental Death of an Anarchist); Non Si Paga, Non Si Paga!, 1974 (Can't Pay! Won't Pay!); (with Franca Rame) Tutta Casa Letto e Chiesa, 1977; Storia Della Tigre ed Altre Storie, 1979 (Tale of a Tiger and Other Stories); Clacson, Trombette e Pernacchi, 1980 (Trumpets and Raspberries); (with Franca Rame) Coppia Aperta, 1983 (Open Couple); Il Papa e La Strega, 1989 (The Pope and the Witch); (with Franca Rame) L'Eroina—Grassa e' Bello, 1991; Johan Padan a la Descoverta de le Americhe, 1991; Discorsi sul Ruzzante, 1993; Il Diavolo con le Zinne, 1997; Da Tangentopoli all'Irrisistibile Ascesa di Ubu Bas, 2002; Ubu Bas Va alla Guerra, 2003; his plays have been translated into many languages and performed in many countries. Nobel Prize for Literature, 1997. *Publications:* The Tricks of the Trade, 1991; many plays. *Address:* CTFR Srl, Corso di Porta Romana 132, 20122 Milan, Italy.

FOAKES, Prof. Reginald Anthony; Professor of English, University of California at Los Angeles, 1983–93, now Emeritus; *b* 18 Oct. 1923; 2nd *s* of William Warren Foakes and Frances (*née* Poate); *m* 1st, 1951, Barbara (*d* 1988), *d* of Harry Garratt, OBE; two *s* two *d*; 2nd, 1993, Mary (*d* 1996), *d* of Albert White. *Educ:* West Bromwich Grammar Sch.; Birmingham Univ. (MA, PhD). Fellow of the Shakespeare Inst., 1951–54; Lectr in English, Durham Univ., 1954–62; Sen. Lectr, 1963–64; University of Kent at Canterbury: Prof. of Eng. Lit., 1964–82, now Emeritus Prof. of Eng. and Amer. Lit.; Dean, Faculty of Humanities, 1974–77. Commonwealth Fund (Harkness) Fellow, Yale Univ., 1955–56; Visiting Professor: University Coll., Toronto, 1960–62; Univ. of California, Santa Barbara, 1968–69; UCLA, 1981. *Publications:* (ed) Shakespeare's King Henry VIII, 1957; The Romantic Assertion, 1958; (ed with R. T. Rickert) Henslowe's Diary, 1961, 2nd edn 2002; (ed) The Comedy of Errors, 1962; (ed) The Revenger's Tragedy, 1966; (ed) Macbeth and Much Ado About Nothing, 1968; Romantic Criticism, 1968; Coleridge on Shakespeare, 1971; Shakespeare, the Dark Comedies to the Last Plays, 1971; (ed) The Henslowe Papers, 2 vols, 1977; Marston and Tourneur, 1978; (ed) A Midsummer Night's Dream, 1984; Illustrations of the English Stage 1580–1642, and Visitor's Guide, 1985; (ed) S. T. Coleridge, Lectures 1808–19: On Literature, 2 vols, 1987; (ed) Troilus and Cressida, 1987; (ed) Coleridge's Criticism of Shakespeare, 1989; Hamlet versus King Lear: cultural politics and Shakespeare's art, 1993; (ed) King Lear, 1997; (with Mary Foakes) The Columbia Dictionary of Quotations from Shakespeare, 1998; Shakespeare and Violence, 2003; Inventing Parents, 2003; Imagined Places, 2005. *Address:* Department of English, University of California at Los Angeles, 405 Hilgard Avenue, Los Angeles, CA 90095, USA.

FOALE, Air Cdre Colin Henry; *b* 10 June 1930; *s* of late William Henry Foale and Frances M. (*née* Muse); *m* 1954, Mary Katherine Harding, Minneapolis, USA; one *s* one *d* (and one *s* decd). *Educ:* Wolverton Grammar Sch.; RAF Coll., Cranwell. 1951–74: 13 Sqdn Pilot, Egypt; 32 Sqdn Flt Comdr; Fighter Flt, RAF Flying Coll., Manby; Officer and Aircrew Selection, Hornchurch; OC 73 Sqdn, Cyprus (Sqdn Ldr); Staff Coll., Bracknell; Air Staff, HQ RAF Germany (Wing Comdr); Jt Services Staff Coll., Latimer; OC 39 Sqdn, Malta; SO Flying, MoD (PE) (Gp Captain); Stn Comdr, Luqa, Malta, 1974–76; RCDS, 1977 (Air Cdre); Dir of Public Relations (RAF), 1977–79; retired at own request, 1979. Trng Advr to Chm., Conservative Party, 1980–81; Pilot to Cttee for Aerial Photography, Univ. of Cambridge, 1981–90. Member: St Catharine's Coll., Cambridge; Selwyn Coll., Cambridge; Univ. Air Sqdn, Cambridge; RAF Histl Soc.; Anglo Zulu War Histl Soc. FCMI; FIWM. *Publication:* Waystation to the Stars, 1999. *Recreations:* drama, writing. *Address:* 37 Pretoria Road, Cambridge CB4 1HD; St Catharine's College, Cambridge. *Club:* Royal Air Force.

See also C. M. Foale.

FOALE, (Colin) Michael, CBE 2005; PhD; Astronaut, US National Aeronautics and Space Administration; *b* 6 Jan. 1957; dual UK/US nationality; *s* of Air Cdre Colin Henry Foale, *qv*; *m* 1987, Rhonda Butler; one *s* one *d*. *Educ:* King's Sch., Canterbury; Queens' Coll., Cambridge (1st Cl. Hons Nat. Sci. Tripos 1978; PhD Lab. Astrophysics 1982; Hon. Fellow, 1998). National Aeronautics and Space Administration (US): Payload Officer, 1983–87; Astronaut, 1987–; Space Shuttle Missions: Atlas 1, 1992; Atlas 2, 1993; Space Suit Test, 1995; Russian Space Station Mir, May–Oct. 1997; Hubble Telescope Repair, 1999; Asst Dir (Technical), 1998; Chief of Expedn Corps, Astronaut Office, Johnson Space Center, 1999; Comdr, Internat. Space Stn Expedn 8, 2003–04; Dep. Assoc. Adminr, Exploration Ops, NASA HQ, 2005–06. Hon. FRAeS 1997. DUniv: Kent, 2000; Lincs and Humberside, 2000. Founder's Medal, Air League, 1993; Barnes Wallis Award, GAPAN, 1994. *Recreations:* flying, wind surfing, diving, ski-ing, theoretical physics. *Address:* c/o NASA JSC, Houston, TX 77058, USA.

FOALE, Rodney Alan, FRCP, FACC, FESC, FCSANZ; Consultant Cardiologist, since 1985, and Clinical Director of Surgery, Cardiovascular Science and Clinical Care, since 1999, St Mary's Hospital, London; *b* 11 Sept. 1946; *s* of Maurice Foale; *m* 1981, Emma Gordon (marr. diss. 2007); two *s*; partner, Dr Samina Showghi; one *d*. *Educ:* Univ. of

Melbourne (MB BS 1971). FACC 1985; FESC 1990; FRCP 1994; FCSANZ 2003. Sen. Clin. Fellow, Harvard Univ. and Massachusetts Gen. Hosp., 1980–82; Sen. Registrar (Cardiol.), Hammersmith Hosp., 1982–85. *Recreations:* a variety of indoor and outdoor pursuits. *Address:* 66 Harley Street, W1G 7HD. *T:* (020) 7323 4687, *Fax:* (020) 7631 5341; *e-mail:* raf@smht-foale.co.uk. *Clubs:* Flyfishers', Chelsea Arts.

FOCKE, His Honour Paul Everard Justus; QC 1982; a Circuit Judge, 1997–2007; *b* 14 May 1937; *s* of late Frederick Justus Focke and Muriel Focke; *m* 1973, Lady Tana Marie Alexander, *er d* of 6th Earl of Caledon; two *d*. *Educ:* Downside; Exeter Coll., Oxford; Trinity Coll., Dublin. National Service, 1955–57; Territorial Army, 1957–66, Cheshire Yeomanry (Captain). Called to the Bar, Gray's Inn, 1964 (Bencher, 1992), to the Bar of NSW and to the NZ Bar, 1982; QC NSW 1984; a Recorder, 1986–97. Dir, Bar Mutual Indemnity Fund, 1988–97. *Recreations:* travelling, aeroplanes. *Clubs:* Pratt's, Turf, Beefsteak, Cavalry and Guards.

FODEN, (Arthur) John; Chairman, PA Consulting Group, 1986–95; *b* 4 Oct. 1939; *s* of Air Vice-Marshal Arthur Foden, CB, CBE and Constance Muriel Foden (*née* Corkill); *m* 1963, Virginia Caroline Field; two *d*. *Educ:* Abingdon Sch., Oxon. Joined Whitbread and Co. Ltd, 1959, Industrial Relns Manager, 1967; PA Consulting Group, 1967–95: Gp Human Resources Dir, 1975–79; Chief Exec. of PA Germany, 1979–80, of PA Personnel Services, 1980–85; Chief Exec., 1985–92; Chm., 1986–95. Chm., Scottish Provident Instn, 1998–2001 (non-exec. Dir, 1995–2001); non-executive Director: Media Audits Ltd, 1992–2001; Scottish Mutual Assce plc, 2001–03. *Publication:* Paid to Decide, 1991. *Recreations:* house restoration, surfing, cooking.

FOËX, Prof. Pierre, DPhil; FRCA, FANZCA, FMedSci; Nuffield Professor of Anaesthetics, 1991–2002, and Fellow, 1991–2002, Supernumerary Fellow, since 2002, Pembroke College, University of Oxford; *b* 4 July 1935; *s* of Georges and Berthe Foëx; *m* 1958, Anne-Lise Schürch; two *s*. *Educ:* Univ. of Geneva (DM); professional qualifying Swiss State Exam. in Medicine and Surgery, 1960; DPhil Oxon 1973. FRCA (FFARCS 1985); FANZCA 1993. University Hospital, Geneva: Asst, 1961–62 and Chef de Clinique, 1962–63, Dept of Neurology; Asst, 1963–65, Chef de Clinique-adjoint, 1966–68 and Chef de Clinique, 1969–70, Dept of Medicine; Nuffield Department of Anaesthetics, University of Oxford: Res. Fellow, 1970–71; Lectr, 1971–73; Univ. Lectr, 1973–76; Clinical Reader and Hon. Consultant (Clinical Physiology), 1976–91; Emer. Fellow, Worcester Coll., Oxford, 1993 (Fellow, 1976–91). Mem., Exec. Cttee, Anaesthetic Res. Soc., 1982–86; Senator, European Acad. of Anaesthesiology, 1988–99 (Vice-Pres., 1991–93); Mem. Council, RCAnaes, 1996–2002. Vis. Prof., univs in Australia, Canada, Europe, NZ, USA. Founder FMedSci 1998. *Publications:* Anaesthesia for the Compromised Heart, 1989; Principles and Practice of Critical Care, 1997; Cardiovascular Drugs in the Perioperative Period, 1999; chapters and papers on cardiac physiology, cardiovascular physiology applied to anaesthesia, myocardial ischaemia, cardiovascular pharmacology, anaesthesia and hypertension. *Recreations:* walking, foreign travel. *Address:* 26 Jack Straw's Lane, Oxford OX3 0DW. *T:* (01865) 761771.

FOGDEN, Michael Ernest George, CB 1994; Chairman, Accountancy Investigation and Disciplinary Board, since 2004; *b* 30 May 1936; *s* of late George Charles Arthur and of Margaret May Fogden; *m* 1957, Rose Ann Diamond; three *s* one *d*. *Educ:* High Sch. for Boys, Worthing. Nat. Service, RAF, 1956–58. Ministry of Pensions and National Insurance, later Department of Health and Social Security: Clerical Officer, 1958–59; Exec. Officer, 1959–67; Private Sec. to Parly Sec., 1967–68; Asst Private Sec. to Sec. of State for Social Services, 1968–70; Principal, 1970–76; Asst Sec., 1976–83; Under Sec., 1983–84; Under Sec., Dept of Employment, then DFEE, 1984–96 (Chief Exec. Employment Service, 1987–96). Chm., Nat. Blood Authy, 1998–2005. Dep. Chm., Civil Service Appeal Bd, 1999–2006. Chm., First Div. Assoc. of Civil Servants, 1980–83. Chairman: London Council, RIPA, 1989–93; Public Management Forum (formerly London Inst. of Public Admin), 1994–98; Exec. Cttee, Public Mgt and Policy Assoc., 1998–2003; Investigation and Disciplinary Bd, Accountancy Foundn, 2001–03. FRSA. *Recreations:* gardening, talking, music. *Address:* 59 Mayfield Avenue, Orpington, Kent BR6 0AH. *T:* (01689) 77395. *Club:* Royal Commonwealth Society.

FOGEL, Prof. Robert William; Charles R. Walgreen Distinguished Service Professor of American Institutions, University of Chicago, since 1981; *b* 1 July 1926; *s* of Harry G. Fogel and Elizabeth (*née* Mitnik); *m* Enid C. Morgan; two *s*. *Educ:* Cornell Univ. (AB 1948); Columbia Univ. (AM 1960); Johns Hopkins Univ. (PhD 1963). Instructor, Johns Hopkins Univ., 1958–59; Asst Prof., Univ. of Rochester, 1960–64; Assoc. Prof., Univ. of Chicago, 1964–65; Prof., Econs and History, Univ. of Chicago, 1965–75, Univ. of Rochester, 1968–75. Taussig Research Prof., Harvard Univ., 1973–74; Pitt Prof. of Amer. History and Instns, Cambridge Univ., 1975–76; Harold Hitchings Burbank Prof. of Econs and Prof. of History, Harvard Univ., 1975–81. President: Economic History Assoc., 1977–78; Social Sci. Hist. Assoc., 1980–81; American Econ. Assoc., 1998–99; Mem., Europ. Acad. of Sci., 1994. Fellow: Econometric Soc., 1971; Amer. Acad. of Arts and Scis, 1972; Nat. Acad. of Scis, 1973; Amer. Philosophical Soc., 2000; FAAAS, 1978; FRHistS 1975; Corresponding FBA, 1991. Hon. DSc: Rochester, 1987; Palermo, 1994; Brigham Young, 1995; SUNY Binghampton, 1999; Torino, 2000. Phi Beta Kappa, 1963; Arthur H. Cole Prize, Economic History Assoc., 1968; Schumpeter Prize, Harvard Univ., 1971; Bancroft Prize, Columbia Univ., 1975; Gustavus Myers Prize, 1990; (jtly) Nobel Prize for Economics, 1993; Distinguished Alumnus Prize, Johns Hopkins, 2001. *Publications:* The Union Pacific Railroad: a case in premature enterprise, 1960; Railroads and American Economic Growth: essays in econometric history, 1964 (Spanish edn 1972); (jtly) The Reinterpretation of American Economic History, 1971 (Italian edn 1975); (jtly) The Dimension of Quantitative Research in History, 1972; (jtly) Time on the Cross: the economics of American Negro slavery, 1974 (Japanese edn 1977, Spanish edn 1981); Ten Lectures on the New Economic History, 1977; (jtly) Which Road to the Past? Two Views of History, 1983; Without Consent or Contract: the rise and fall of American slavery, vol. 1, 1989, vols 2–4 (jtly), 1992; The Fourth Great Awakening and the Future of Egalitarianism, 2000; The Slavery Debates 1952–1990: a retrospective, 2003; The Escape from Hunger and Premature Death 1700–2100: Europe, America and the Third World, 2004; numerous papers in learned jls. *Address:* (office) Center for Population Economics, University of Chicago, Graduate School of Business, 5807 S Woodlawn Avenue, Chicago, IL 60637, USA.

FOGG, Alan, MBE 1994; Chairman, Royal Philanthropic Society, 1982–90; former Director, PA International; *b* 19 Sept. 1921; *o s* of John Fogg, Dulwich; *m* 1948, Mary Marsh; two *s* one *d*. *Educ:* Repton; Exeter Coll., Oxford (MA, BSc). Served with RN, 1944–47. *Publications:* (with Barnes, Stephens and Titman) Company Organisation: theory and practice, 1970; various papers on management subjects. *Recreations:* travel, gardening, youth charities. *Address:* 124 Nutfield Road, Merstham, Redhill, Surrey RH1 3HG. *T:* (01737) 642023.

FOGG, Cyril Percival, CB 1973; Director, Admiralty Surface Weapons Establishment, Ministry of Defence (Procurement Executive), 1973–75, retired; *b* 28 Nov. 1914; *s* of Henry Fogg and Mabel Mary (*née* Orton); *m* 1st, 1939, Margaret Amie Millican (*d* 1982); two *d*; 2nd, 1983, June Adele McCoy. *Educ:* Herbert Strutt Sch., Belper; Gonville ar Caius Coll., Cambridge (MA, 1st cl. Mechanical Sciences Tripos). Research Staff, Gener Electric Co., 1936–37; various positions in Scientific Civil Service from 1937 with A Ministry, Ministries of Aircraft Production, Supply, Aviation and Technology. Head Ground Radar Dept, RRE Malvern, 1956–58; Dir Electronics R&D (Ground), 1959–6 Imperial Defence Coll., 1961; Dir of Guided Weapons Research, 1963–64; Dir-Gen. Electronics R&D, Min. of Aviation, 1964–67; Dep. Controller of Electronics, Min. Technology, later MoD (Procurement Executive), 1967–72. *Address:* 10 Miles Cottage Taylors Lane, Bosham, Chichester, West Sussex PO18 8QG.

FOGLE, Bruce, MBE 2004; DVM; veterinary surgeon, writer, broadcaster; *b* 17 Fel 1944; *s* of Morris Fogle and Aileen (*née* Breslin); *m* 1973, Julia Foster; one *s* two *d*. *Edu* Ontario Vet. Coll., Univ. of Guelph (DVM 1970). MRCVS 1970. Clinical Veterinar Surgeon, Portman Vet. Clinic, London, 1973–; Founder and Partner, Emergency Ve Clinic, London, 1980–; Partner, Elizabeth Street Vet. Clinic, London, 1980–. Co Founder and Vice Chm., Hearing Dogs for Deaf People, 1982–. Television: Presente Petwatch, 1986; Good Companions, 1987; London Walkies, 1988; People and Pet 1989–90; radio: Resident Vet, The Jimmy Young Prog., 1992–2003, The Jeremy Vir Show, 2003–, Radio 2; columnist: Today, 1986–89; Prima mag., 1986–92; Dogs Toda mag., 1990–; Daily Telegraph, 1992–97; feature writer, The Times. Consultant t internat. pet food ind. cos, Pet Plan, Encyclopedia Britannica, Microsoft Encart Member: BVA, 1970; British Small Animal Vet. Assoc., 1970. Consumer Writer of Yea PPA, 1991. *Publications:* Interrelations Between People and Pets (ed and contrib.), 198 Pets and their People, 1983; Games Pets Play, 1986; Paws Across London, 1989; Th Dog's Mind, 1990; The Cat's Mind, 1991; People and Pets, 1991; Know Your Cat, 199 Know Your Dog, 1992; The Complete Dog Care Manual, 1993; 101 Questions Your Ca Would Ask its Vet if Your Cat Could Talk, 1993; 101 Questions Your Dog Would As its Vet if Your Dog Could Talk, 1993; The Complete Dog Training Manual, 1994; 10 Essential Tips: caring for your dog, 1995; First Aid for Cat Owners, 1995; First Aid fo Dog Owners, 1995; The Encyclopedia of the Dog, 1995; The Cocker Spaniel Handbook 1996; The Golden Retriever Handbook, 1996; The Labrador Retriever Handbook, 199 The German Shepherd Handbook, 1996; The Dachshund Handbook, 1997; The Pood Handbook, 1997; The Secret Life of Cat Owners, 1997; The Secret Life of Dog Owner 1997; 101 Essential Tips: training your dog, 1997; 101 Essential Tips: caring for you puppy, 1997; The Encyclopedia of the Cat, 1997; Cat's Christmas, 1998; Natural Do Care, 1999; Natural Cat Care, 1999; The New Encyclopedia of the Dog, 2000; The Nev Encyclopedia of the Cat, 2001; The New Complete Dog Training Manual, 2001; What' up with my Dog?, 2001; What's up with my Cat?, 2001; The Dog Owner's Manual, 200 The Cat Owner's Manual, 2002; Caring for your Dog, 2003; Dialogues with Dogs, 200 Travels with Macy, 2005; If Only They Could Talk, 2006; A Dog Abroad, 200 Eyewitness Companions: Dogs, 2006; Cats, 2006; *contributions to:* New Perspectives on ou Lives with Companion Animals, 1983; The Veterinary Annual, 1986; Eye to Eye: th psychology of relationships, 1988; Animals and People Sharing the World, 1988; contrib to learned jls in Eur. and N America, and to many newspapers and magazines. *Recreations* stalking painted Gustavian furniture in rural Sweden, acting as putty in my dog's paws *Address:* 86 York Street, W1H 1QS. *T:* (020) 7723 2068, *Fax:* (020) 7723 9009; *e-mai* bruce.fogle@clara.co.uk. *Club:* Garrick.

FOISTER, Dr Susan Rosemary; Curator of Early Netherlandish, German and Britis Paintings, since 1990, and Director of Collections, since 2004, National Gallery; *b* 12 Ma 1954; *d* of late Philip and Pamela Foister; *m* 1985, Richard Bulkeley Ritchie; two *s* one *d* *Educ:* Hastings High Sch.; St Anne's Coll., Oxford (BA English 1975); Courtauld Inst. o Art (MA 1977; PhD 1982). Jun. Res. Fellow, Warburg Inst., 1979–81; Curator, Victorian Portraits, NPG, 1983–89; Hd, Curatorial Dept, Nat. Gall., 2000–04. Dir, Nat. Gall. Co Ltd, 2005–. Member: Adv. Bd, Renaissance Studies, 1997–; Adv. Panel, Public Catalogue Foundn, 2003–. Chm., Soc. of Renaissance Studies, 1992–95. *Publications:* Drawings by Holbein from the Royal Library, Windsor Castle, 1983; Cardinal Newman, 1990; (jtly Giotto to Dürer, 1991; (ed jtly) Robert Campin: new directions in scholarship, 1996; (jtly Making and Meaning: Holbein's Ambassadors, 1997; (jtly) Dürer to Veronese, 1999; (ec jtly) Investigating Jan van Eyck, 2000; (jtly) Art in the Making: Renaissance underdrawing 2002; Dürer and the Virgin in the Garden, 2004; Holbein and England, 2004; Holbein in England, 2006; Art of Light: German Renaissance stained glass, 2007; (jtly) Renaissance Faces: Van Eyck to Titian, 2008; contrib. articles to Burlington Mag., Apollo. *Address* National Gallery, Trafalgar Square, WC2N 5DN. *T:* (020) 7839 3321, *Fax:* (020) 7742 2472.

FOKAS, Prof. Athanasios Spyridon, MD; PhD; Professor of Nonlinear Mathematica Science, University of Cambridge, since 2002; Fellow, Clare Hall, Cambridge, since 2005 *b* 30 June 1952; *s* of Spyridon and Anastasia Fokas; *m* 1996, Regina Karousou; one *s* two *d*. *Educ:* Imperial Coll., London (BS 1975); CIT (PhD 1979); Sch. of Medicine, Univ. of Miami (MD 1986). Saul Kaplun Res. Fellow in Applied Maths, CIT, 1979–80; Asst Prof., 1980–82, Prof. and Chm., 1986–93, Dept of Maths and Computer Sci., Clarkson Univ.; Prof., Dept of Maths, Univ. of Loughborough, 1993–95; Prof. of Applied Maths, Dept of Maths, Imperial Coll., London, 1996–2001. Vis. Prof., Dept of Maths, Stanford Univ., 1987–88. Member, Editorial Board: Jl Nonlinear Science, 1991–; Selecta Mathematica, 1998–; Proc. Royal Soc., 2002–; Jl Math. Physics, 2002–. Mem., Acad. of Athens, 2004. Hon. DSc: Tech. Univ. of Crete, 2004; Athens, 2006; Hon. Dr Applied Maths and Phys. Scis, Tech. Univ. of Athens, 2004; Hon. Dr Maths Patras, 2005. Naylor Prize, LMS, 2000; Aristeion Prize: Acad. of Athens, 2004; Bodossaki Foundn (Greece), 2006. Comdr, Order of the Phoenix (Greece), 2005. *Publications:* (with M. J. Ablowitz) Introduction and Applications of Complex Variables, 1997; (jtly) Painlevé Transcendents, the Riemann-Hilbert Approach, 2006; edited jointly: Important Developments in Soliton Theory, 1993; Nonlinear Processes in Physics, 1993; Algebraic Aspects of Integrable Equations, 1996; conference procs; about 200 papers. *Address:* Department of Applied Mathematics and Theoretical Physics, University of Cambridge, Wilberforce Road, Cambridge CB3 0WA. *T:* (01223) 339733, *Fax:* (01223) 765900; *e-mail:* t.fokas@damtp.cam.ac.uk.

FOKINE, Yuri Evgenievich; Adviser to Rector, Diplomatic Academy, Ministry of Foreign Affairs, Russian Federation (Rector, 2000); *b* 2 Sept. 1936; *s* of Evgeni G. Fokine and Ekaterina I. Fokine; *m* 1958, Maya E. Klimova; one *s* (one *d* decd). *Educ:* Moscow State Inst. for Internat. Relations (grad 1960). Entered Diplomatic Service, 1960; posts in USSR Perm. Mission to UN, Dept of Internat. Orgns, USSR Foreign Min., and Secretariat, USSR Foreign Min.; Dep. Perm. Rep. to UN, 1976–79; Ministry of Foreign Affairs: Dep. Sec.-Gen., 1979–80; Sec.-Gen. and Mem. of Collegium, 1980–86; Ambassador to Cyprus, 1986–90; Dir, 2nd Eur. Dept, Min. of Foreign Affairs, 1990–95; Ambassador to Norway, 1995–97, to UK, 1997–2000. Mem., Editl Council, Internat. Affairs Mag., Moscow, 2000–. Grand Gold Cross, Order of Merit (Austria), 1995; Royal Order of Merit (Norway), 1997; also national decorations. *Publications:* (ed) Diplomatic Yearbook (annually), 2001–; A. Akaev: president, 2004; articles in jls. *Recreations:* art, ballet, reading, tennis. *Address:* Diplomatic Academy, 53/2 Ostozhenka, Moscow 119021, Russia.

FOLDES, Prof. Lucien Paul; Professor of Economics, University of London, at London School of Economics and Political Science, 1979–96, then Emeritus; *b* 19 Nov. 1930; *s* of Egon and Marta Foldes; *m* Carol Rosalind Hewlett. *Educ:* Bunce Court Sch.; Monkton Wyld Sch.; London School of Economics (BCom, MScEcon, DBA). National Service, 1952–54. London School of Economics and Political Science: Asst Lecturer in Economics, 1954–55; Lectr, 1955–61; Reader, 1961–79. Rockefeller Travelling Fellow, 1961–62. *Publications:* articles in Rev. of Economic Studies, Economica, Jl of Mathematical Economics, Stochastics, Mathematical Finance, Jl of Economic Dynamics and Control, and others. *Recreation:* mathematical analysis. *Address:* London School of Economics, Houghton Street, WC2A 2AE. *T:* (020) 7405 7686.

FOLEY, family name of **Baron Foley**.

FOLEY, 8th Baron *cr* 1776; **Adrian Gerald Foley;** *b* 9 Aug. 1923; *s* of 7th Baron and Minoru (*d* 1968), *d* of late H. Greenstone, South Africa; *S* father, 1927; *m* 1st, 1958, Patricia Meek (marr. diss. 1971); one *s* one *d*; 2nd, 1972, Ghislaine Lady Ashcombe (*d* 2000); *m* 2003, Hannah, (Bebe), Steinberg. *Heir: s* Hon. Thomas Henry Foley, *b* 1 April 1961. *Club:* White's.

FOLEY, Rt Rev. Graham; *see* Foley, Rt Rev. R. G. G.

FOLEY, Hugh Smith; Principal Clerk of Session and Justiciary, Scotland, 1989–97. *Educ:* Dalkeith High Sch. (Joint Dux). Student Actuary, Standard Life Assce Co., 1956–59; nat. service, RAF, 1959–61; entered Scottish Court Service, Court of Session Br., 1962; Asst Clerk of Session, 1962–71; Depute Clerk of Session, 1972–80; seconded to Sheriff Court, Edinburgh, 1980–81; Prin. Sheriff Clerk Depute, Glasgow, 1981–82; Sheriff Clerk, Linlithgow, 1982; Dep. Prin. Clerk of Session, 1982–86; Sen. Dep. Principal Clerk, 1986–89. Member: Lord President's Cttee on Procedure in Personal Injuries Litigation in Court of Session, 1978–79; Lothian Valuation Appeal Panel, 1997–2007. *Recreations:* walking, painting, golf.

FOLEY, Johanna Mary, (Jo); journalist; *b* 8 Dec. 1945; *d* of John and Monica Foley. *Educ:* St Joseph's Convent, Kenilworth; Manchester Univ. (BA Jt Hons English and Drama, 1968). Sen. Asst Editor, Woman's Own, 1978; Woman's Editor, The Sun, 1980; Editor, Woman, 1982; Exec. Editor (Features), The Times, 1984–85; Man. Editor, The Mirror, 1985–86; Editor: Observer Magazine, 1986–87; Options, 1988–91. Editor of the Year, British Soc. of Magazine Editors, 1983. *Recreations:* eating, reading, cinema, opera.

FOLEY, John Dominic; His Honour Judge Foley; a Circuit Judge, since 1994; *b* 17 Jan. 1944; *s* of Cyril Patrick Foley and Winifred Hannah (*née* McAweeny); *m* 1978, Helena Frances McGowan (marr. diss. 1986); two *d*. *Educ:* St Brendan's Coll., Bristol; Exeter Univ. (LLB Hons). Called to the Bar, Inner Temple, 1968; Western Circuit, 1969–; Attorney-Gen. Special Prosecutor, NI, 1971–73; Asst Recorder, 1986–89; Recorder, 1990–93; an Investigating Judge (Judicial Discipline), 2006–. Vice-Pres., Immigration Appeal Tribunal, 1998–2005; Mem., Special Immigration Appeal Commn, 2002–05. Ind. Arbitrator (Discipline), RFU and Internat. Rugby Bd, 2005–. Pres., Bracton Law Soc., Exeter Univ. *Recreations:* Rugby (formerly 1st XV, Exeter Univ.), cricket, travel, rock. *Clubs:* Clifton Rugby Football, Bristol Rugby Football; Somerset County Cricket; Carlton Cricket (Barbados), Barbados Cricket Assoc.

FOLEY, Lt-Gen. Sir John (Paul), KCB 1994 (CB 1991); OBE 1979; MC 1976; DL; Lieutenant Governor and Commander-in-Chief, Guernsey, Channel Islands, 2000–05; *b* 22 April 1939; *s* of Henry Thomas Hamilton Foley, MBE and Helen Constance Margaret Foley (*née* Pearson); *m* 1972, Ann Humphries; two *d*. *Educ:* Bradfield College; Mons OCS; Army Staff College (psc). Lieut, Royal Green Jackets, 1959; RMCS and Army Staff Coll., 1970–71; Regimental Duty, 1972–74; Chief of Staff, 51 Inf. Bde, Hong Kong, 1974–76; Instructor, Army Staff Coll., 1976–78; CO 3rd Bn RGJ, 1978–80; Comdt Jun. Div., Staff Coll., 1981–82. Arms Dir, MoD, 1983–85; RCDS 1986; Chief, British Mission to Soviet Forces in Germany, 1987–89; ACDS, MoD, 1989–92; Comdr, British Forces Hong Kong, and Maj.-Gen. Brigade of Gurkhas, 1992–94; Chief of Defence Intelligence, MoD, 1994–97. Col Comdt, 1st Bn, Royal Green Jackets, 1991–94, The Light Div., 1994–97. Chm., British Greyhound Racing Bd, 1999–2000. Mem., Royal Patriotic Fund Corp., 2000–01. Pres., BRIXMIS Assoc., 2002–. Liveryman, Skinners' Co., 1972– (Mem. Court, 1995–2000). DL Herefords, 2006; High Sheriff, Herefords and Worcs, 2006–07. KSJ 2000. Officer, Legion of Merit (USA), 1997. *Recreations:* tennis, walking, shooting, reading, golf. *Club:* Boodle's.

FOLEY, Prof. Robert Andrew, PhD, ScD; FBA 2007; Professor of Human Evolution, since 2003, and Director, Leverhulme Centre for Human Evolutionary Studies, since 2001, University of Cambridge; Fellow, King's College, Cambridge, since 1987; *b* 18 March 1953; *s* of late Nelson Foley and of Jean Foley; *m* 2003, Marta Mirazon Lahr; two *s*, and two step *s*. *Educ:* Peterhouse, Cambridge (BA 1974; PhD 1980); King's Coll., Cambridge (ScD 1996). Lectr in Anthropology, Univ. of Durham, 1977–85; Lectr in Biol Anthropology, 1986–98, Reader in Evolutionary Anthropology, 1998–2003, Univ. of Cambridge. *Publications:* Off-Site Archaeology, 1981; Hominid Evolution and Community Ecology, 1984; Another Unique Species, 1987; Comparative Socioecology of Humans and Other Mammals, 1989; The Origins of Human Behaviour, 1991; Humans Before Humanity, 1995; (with P. Donnelly) Genes, Fossils and Behaviour, 2001; (with R. Lewin) Principles of Human Evolution, 2003; many scientific papers. *Recreations:* reading, travel, cricket. *Address:* King's College, Cambridge CB2 1ST. *T:* (01223) 331459, *Fax:* (01223) 335460.

FOLEY, Rt Rev. (Ronald) Graham (Gregory); appointed Bishop Suffragan of Reading, 1982, Area Bishop, 1985, retired 1989; Assistant Bishop, Diocese of York, 1989–2007; *b* 13 June 1923; *s* of Theodore Gregory Foley and Cessan Florence Page; *m* 1944, Florence Redman; two *s* two *d*. *Educ:* King Edward's Grammar Sch., Aston, Birmingham; Wakefield Grammar Sch.; King's Coll., London; St John's Coll., Durham. BA Hons Theol., LTh. Curate, South Shore, Blackpool, 1950; Vicar, S Luke, Blackburn, 1954; Dir of Educn, Dio. of Durham, and Rector of Brancepeth, 1960; Chaplain, Aycliffe Approved Sch., 1962; Vicar of Leeds, 1971–82; Chaplain to the Queen, 1977–82. Hon. Canon: Durham Cathedral, 1965–71; Ripon Cath., 1971–82. Dir, Yorks Electricity Bd, 1976–82. Chm. of Trustees, Dorothy Kerin Trust, Burrswood, 1983–89. *Publication:* (jtly) Religion in Approved Schools, 1969. *Recreations:* journalism, reading detective stories, watching other people mow lawns. *Address:* Ramsey Cottage, 3 Poplar Avenue, Kirkbymoorside, York YO6 6ES. *T:* (01751) 432439.

FOLEY, Thomas Stephen, Hon. KBE 1995; Partner, Akin, Gump, Strauss, Hauer & Feld, 1995–97 and since 2001; Chairman, North American Trilateral Commission, since 2001; *b* 6 March 1929; *s* of Ralph E. Foley and Helen Marie (*née* Higgins); *m* 1968, Heather Strachan. *Educ:* Gonzaga High Sch.; Gonzaga Univ.; Washington Univ. (BA 1951; LLB 1957). Partner, Higgins and Foley, 1957–58; Lectr in Law, Gonzaga Univ., 1958–60; Dep. Prosecuting Attorney, Spokane County, 1958–60; Asst Attorney Gen., Washington State, 1960–61; Special Counsel, Senate Interior and Insular Affairs Cttee, 1961–64; Mem. of 89th–101st Congresses from 5th Dist Washington (Democrat), 1964–95. Chm., 1975–80, Vice-Chm., 1981–86, Agriculture Cttee. Chm., House Democratic Caucus, 1976–80; House Majority Whip, 1981–87; Majority Leader, 1987–89; Speaker, US House of Representatives, 1989–95; American Ambassador to Japan, 1997–2001. Mem., Bd of Advrs, Yale Univ. Council; Dir, Council on Foreign Relations. *Address:* (office) 1333 New Hampshire Avenue NW, Washington, DC 20036, USA.

FOLJAMBE, family name of **Earl of Liverpool**.

FOLKESTONE, Viscount; Jacob Pleydell-Bouverie; *b* 7 April 1999; *s* and *heir* of Earl of Radnor, *qv*.

FOLLETT, Barbara; *see* Follett, D. B.

FOLLETT, Sir Brian (Keith), Kt 1992; DL; FRS 1984; Chairman, Training and Development Agency for Schools (formerly Teacher Training Agency), since 2003; *b* 22 Feb. 1939; *m* 1961, Deb (*née* Booth); one *s* one *d*. *Educ:* Bournemouth Sch.; Univ. of Bristol (BSc 1960, PhD 1964); Univ. of Wales (DSc 1975). Res. Fellow, Washington State Univ., 1964–65; Lectr in Zool., Univ. of Leeds, 1965–69; Lectr, subseq. Reader and Prof. of Zool., University Coll. of N Wales, Bangor, 1969–78; Bristol University: Prof. of Zool., 1978–93, AFRC Res. Prof., 1989–93; Hd of Dept of Zool., 1978–89; Chm., Sch. of Biol Scis, 1989–93; Vice-Chancellor, Warwick Univ., 1993–2001; Chm., AHRB, then AHRC, 2001–07. Vis. Prof., Dept of Zoology, Univ. of Oxford, 2001–. Chm., Infectious Diseases Inquiry, Royal Soc., 2001–02. Chairman: ESRC-British Acad. Working Party on the Future of Funding Res. in the Humanities, 1992; Adv. Bd, British Library, 2000–07; Res. Support Librarians Review Gp, 2001–03; Adv. Forum, STEM Strategy Gp, DfES, 2007–; Member: Biol Sci. Cttee, SERC, 1981–84; AFRC, 1984–88 (Mem., Animals Cttee, 1984–88); Biol Sci. Cttee, UGC, 1985–88; UFC, 1989–93; HEFCE, 1992–96 (Chairman: Libraries Review Gp, 1992–97; Strategic Subjects Adv. Gp, 2007–); Council, BBSRC, 1994–2001 (Chm., Sci. and Engrg Bd, 1994–97); Royal Commn on Envmtl Pollution, 2000–05. Trustee, BM (Natural Hist.), 1989–98. Biol Sec. and Vice-Pres., Royal Soc., 1987–93; Member of Council: Soc. for Study of Fertility, 1972–87 (Prog. Sec., 1976–78; Treas., 1982–87); Soc. for Endocrinology, 1974–77; Bristol Zoo, 1978–93; Wildfowl Trust, Slimbridge, 1983–86; Zool Soc. of London, 1983–86. Pres. ASE, 1997. Lectures: Amoroso, Soc. for Study of Fertility, 1985; Annual Zool., Liverpool Univ., 1991; Barrington Meml, Nottingham Univ., 1992. Gov., RSC, 2007–. Mem., Academia Europaea, 1988. DL West Midlands, 2000. Hon. FCLIP (Hon. FLA 1997); Hon. FZS 2004. Hon. Fellow: UCNW, Bangor, 1990; Worcester, 2008. Hon. LLD: Wales, 1992; Calgary, 2001; St Andrews, 2002; Bristol, 2005; Hon. DSc: Univ. Teknologi, Malaysia, 1999; Leicester, 2001; Warwick, 2002; East Anglia, 2003; London, 2004; Hon DLitt Oxford, 2002. Scientific Medal, 1976, Frink Medal, 1993, Zool Soc. of London; Dale Medal, Soc. of Endocrinology, 1988. Editorial Bds: Jl of Endocrinology, 1971–78; Gen. & Comparative Endocrinology, 1974–82; Jl of Biol Rhythms, 1986–2000; Proc. of Royal Soc., 1987–90. *Publications:* over 260 scientific papers on biol clocks and reproductive physiology. *Address:* Training and Development Agency for Schools, 151 Buckingham Palace Road, SW1W 9SZ. *T:* (020) 7023 8814; *e-mail:* brian.follett@tda.gov.uk; Department of Zoology, University of Oxford, Oxford OX1 3PS; *e-mail:* brian.follett@zoo.ox.ac.uk; 120 Tiddington Road, Stratford-upon-Avon, Warwicks CV37 7BB.

FOLLETT, (Daphne) Barbara; MP (Lab) Stevenage, since 1997; Parliamentary Under-Secretary of State, Department for Culture, Media and Sport, since 2008; Minister for the East of England, since 2007; *b* 25 Dec. 1942; *d* of late William Vernon Hubbard and Charlotte Hubbard (*née* Goulding); *m* 1st, 1963, Richard Turner (marr. diss. 1971); two *d*; 2nd, 1971, Gerald Stonestreet (marr. diss. 1974); 3rd, 1974, Leslie Broer (marr. diss. 1985); one *s*; 4th, 1985, Ken Follett, *qv*; one step *s* one step *d*. *Educ:* London Sch. of Economics (BSc Econ); Open Univ. Teacher, Berlitz Sch. of Language, Paris, 1963–64; Jt Manager, fruit farm, Stellenbosch, S Africa, 1966–77; acting Regl Sec., S African Inst. of Race Relations, Cape Town, 1970; Regl Manager (Cape and Namibia), 1971–74, Nat. Health Educn Dir, 1975–78, Kupugani; Asst Course Orgnr and Lectr, Centre for Internat. Briefing, Farnham, 1980–84; freelance lectr and consultant, 1984–92. Vis. Fellow, Inst. of Public Policy Research, 1993–95. Contested (Lab): Woking, 1983; Epsom and Ewell, 1987. Parliamentary Under-Secretary of State: DWP, 2007; Govt Equalities Office, 2008. Founder Member: EMILY's List UK, 1992– (also Dir); Women's Movt for Peace, S Africa, 1976; Labour Women's Network (Mem., Steering Cttee, 1988–); Member: Fawcett Soc., 1993; Nat. Alliance of Women's Orgns, 1993; Nat. Women's Network, 1993. *Recreations:* photography, Scrabble, Star Trek. *Address:* House of Commons, SW1A 0AA. *T:* (020) 7219 2649, *Fax:* (020) 7219 1158.

FOLLETT, Ken; author, since 1977; *b* 5 June 1949; *s* of Martin Dunsford Follett and late Lavinia Cynthia (Veenie) Follett (*née* Evans); *m* 1st, 1968, Mary Elson (marr. diss. 1985); one *s* one *d*; 2nd, 1985, Barbara Broer (*see* D. B. Follett). *Educ:* Harrow Weald Grammar Sch.; Poole Tech. Coll.; University Coll. London (BA; Fellow 1994). Trainee journalist, S Wales Echo, 1970–73; Reporter, London Evening News, 1973–74; Everest Books: Editl Dir, 1974–76; Dep. Man. Dir, 1976–77. Dir, Stevenage Leisure Ltd, 1997–2005. Mem. Council, Nat. Literary Trust, 1996– (Trustee, 2005–); Chm., Nat. Year of Reading, 1998–99; Bd Dir, Nat. Acad. of Writing, 2003–. Pres., Dyslexia Inst., 1998–. Vice-President: Stevenage Bor. FC, 2000–02; Stevenage Community Trust, 2002– (Pres., 2005–); Patron, Stevenage Home-Start, 2000–. Chm. Govs, Roebuck Primary Sch. and Nursery, 2001–05. Mem., Yr Academi Gymreig. Hon. DLitt: Glamorgan, 2007; Saginaw Valley State, 2007; Exeter, 2008. Olaguibel Prize, Colegio Oficial de Arquitectos Vasco-Navarro, 2008. *Publications include:* Eye of the Needle (Edgar Award, Mystery Writers of Amer.), 1978; Triple, 1979; The Key to Rebecca, 1980; The Man from St Petersburg, 1982; On Wings of Eagles, 1983; Lie down with Lions, 1986; The Pillars of the Earth, 1989; Night over Water, 1991; Mrs Shiblak's Nightmare (pamphlet), 1992; A Dangerous Fortune, 1993; A Place Called Freedom, 1995; The Third Twin, 1997; The Hammer of Eden, 1998; Code to Zero, 2000; Jackdaws, 2001 (Corine Buchpreis, 2003); Hornet Flight, 2002; Whiteout, 2004; World Without End, 2007; various articles, screenplays and short stories. *Recreations:* bass guitarist in a blues band; Labour Party supporter and campaigner. *Address:* The Old Rectory, Old Knebworth Lane, Stevenage, Herts SG3 6PT. *Clubs:* Athenæum, Groucho.

FONAGY, Prof. Peter, PhD; FBA 1997; Freud Memorial Professor of Psychoanalysis, University of London, at University College, since 1992; Chief Executive, Anna Freud Centre, 2003 (Director of Research, 1989–2003); Director of Research, Menninger Clinic, Kansas, since 1995; *b* 14 Aug. 1952; *s* of Ivan Fonagy and Judith (*née* Barath); *m* 1990, Dr Anna Higgitt; one *s* one *d*. *Educ:* UCL (BSc Hons 1974; PhD 1980). Dip. Clin. Psych. 1980. Lectr, 1977–88, Sen. Lectr, 1988–92, in Psychology, Univ. of London; Dir, Sub-Dept of Clin. Health Psychology, UCL, 1995–; Adjunct Prof. of Clin. Psychology, Kansas Univ., 1995–; Menninger Clinic: Co-ordinating Dir, Child and Family Center, 1995, Clin. Protocols and Outcome Center, 1996–; Vorhees Distinguished Prof., 1995. Visiting Professor: Hebrew Univ. of Jerusalem, 1993; Univ. of Haifa, 1993, 1995; Cornell

Med. Coll., NY, 1994; Marie and Scott S. Smith Chair in Child Develt, Karl Menninger Sch. of Psychiatry and Mental Health Scis, Kansas, 1999–2003. Mem., 1988–, and Trng and Supervising Analyst, 1995–, British Psycho-Analytical Soc. *Publications:* (with A. Higgitt) Personality Theory and Clinical Practice, 1985; (with A. D. Roth) What Works for Whom?, 1996; Attachment Theory and Psychoanalysis, 2001; (jtly) What Works for Whom? A Critical Review of Treatments for Children and Adolescents, 2002; (jtly) Affect Regulation, Mentalization and the Development of the Self, 2002; (with M. Target) Psychoanalytic Theories: perspectives from developmental psychopathology, 2002; (jtly) Social Cognition and Developmental Psychopathology, 2008; papers, contribs books. *Recreations:* ski-ing, theatre, gardening. *Address:* Sub-Department of Clinical Health Psychology, University College London, Gower Street, WC1E 6BT. *T:* (020) 7679 1943; *e-mail:* p.fonagy@ucl.ac.uk.

FONTAINE, André Lucien Georges; Managing Editor and Publisher, le Monde, 1985–91; *b* 30 March 1921; *s* of Georges Fontaine and Blanche Rochon Duvigneaud; *m* 1943, Belita Cavaillé; two *s* one *d*. *Educ:* Paris Univ. (diplomes études supérieures, droit public et économie politique, lic.lettres). Joined Temps Présent, 1946; le Monde, 1947: Foreign Editor, 1951; Chief Editor, 1969. Editorialist, Radio Luxemburg, 1980–91. Chm. Adv. Gp, Internat. Strategy for the 9th Plan, 1982–84; Mem. Bd, Institut Français des Relations Internationales, 1982–92; Vice-Chm., French section, Franco-British Council, 2000–02. Mem. Bd, Bank Indosuez, 1983–85. Grand Officer, Order of Dom Enrique (Portugal); Commander: German Merit; Italian Merit; Greek Phoenix; Officer, Orders of Vasa (Sweden), Leopold (Belgium) and Lion (Finland); Kt, Danebrog (Denmark) and Crown of Belgium; Order of Tudor Vladimirescu (Romania). Atlas' Internat. Editor of the Year, 1976. *Publications:* L'Alliance atlantique à l'heure du dégel, 1960; Histoire de la guerre froide, vol. 1 1965, vol. 2 1966 (English trans., History of the Cold War, 1966 and 1967); La Guerre civile froide, 1969; Le dernier quart du siècle, 1976; La France au bois dormant, 1978; Un seul lit pour deux rêves, 1981; (with Pierre Li) Sortir de l'Hexagonie, 1984; L'un sans l'autre, 1991; Après eux, le déluge, 1995; La tache rouge, 2004. *Address:* 80 Boulevard Auguste Blanqui, 75707 Paris Cedex 13, France.

FONTAINE, Barbara Janet; Master of the Supreme Court, Queen's Bench Division, since 2003; *b* 29 Dec. 1953; *d* of late John Fontaine and Brenda Fontaine (*née* Taylor); *m* 1990, Trevor John Watkins; twin *s*. *Educ:* Stockport High Sch. for Girls; KCL (LLB). Admitted solicitor, 1978; articled Bird & Bird, 1976–78; Solicitor: Hill, Dickinson, London, 1978–83; Coward Chance, later Clifford Chance, 1983–87; Baker & McKenzie, Hong Kong, 1987–93 (Partner, 1989); Dep. Queen's Bench Master, 1997–2003. *Recreations:* theatre, reading, cooking, ski-ing, travel. *Address:* Royal Courts of Justice, Strand, WC2A 2LL.

FONTAINE, Nicole Claude Marie; Member (EPP), European Parliament, since 2004; *b* 16 Jan. 1942; *d* of Jean Garnier and Geneviève Garnier (*née* Lambert); *m* 1964, Jean-René Fontaine; one *d*. *Educ:* Faculté de Droit, Paris (law degree, 1962); Inst. d'Etudes Politiques, Paris (Dip. 1964); DenD 1969. Teacher, 1963–64; Catholic Education Secretariat, France: Legal Advr, 1965; Dep. Sec.-Gen., 1972–81; Chief Rep., 1981–84. Member: Nat. Educn Council, France, 1975–81; Economic and Social Council, France, 1980–84. European Parliament: Mem. (UDF), 1984–2002; Vice Pres., 1989–94; First Vice Pres., 1994–99; Pres., 1999–2002; Member: Legal Affairs and Citizens' Rights Cttee, 1984–89; Women's Rights Cttee, 1984–89; Culture, Youth, Educn, Media and Sport Cttee, 1989–2002; Israel Delegn, 1989–97; Perm. Mem., Conciliation Cttee, 1994–99; Chm., Delegn to COSAC. Minister for Industry, France, 2002–04. Mem., Union pour un Mouvement Populaire (Mem., Founding Council and Exec. Cttee). *Publications:* Les établissements d'enseignement privé associés à l'Etat par contrat, 1980; Les députés européens: qui sont-ils? que font-ils?, 1994; L'Europe de vos initiatives, 1997; Le traité d'Amsterdam, 1998; Mes combats à la présidence du Parlement européen, 2002. *Address:* European Parliament, Rue Wiertz, 1047 Brussels, Belgium; 45 rue du Bois de Boulogne, 92200 Neuilly/Seine, France.

FOOKES, Baroness *cr* 1997 (Life Peer), of Plymouth in the co. of Devon; **Janet Evelyn Fookes,** DBE 1989; DL; *b* 21 Feb. 1936; *d* of late Lewis Aylmer Fookes and Evelyn Margery Fookes (*née* Holmes). *Educ:* Hastings and St Leonards Ladies' Coll.; High Sch. for Girls, Hastings; Royal Holloway Coll., Univ. of London (BA Hons; Hon. Fellow, 1998). Teacher, 1958–70. Councillor for County Borough of Hastings, 1960–61 and 1963–70 (Chm. Educn Cttee, 1967–70). MP (C): Merton and Morden, 1970–74; Plymouth, Drake, 1974–97. Mem., Speaker's Panel of Chairmen, 1976–97; Second Dep. Chm. of Ways and Means and Dep. Speaker, H of C, 1992–97. Sec., Cons. Parly Educn Cttee, 1971–75; Chairman: Educn, Arts and Home Affairs Sub-Cttee of the Expenditure Cttee, 1975–79; Parly Gp for Animal Welfare, 1985–92 (Sec., 1974–82); Member: Unopposed Bills Cttee, 1973–75; Services Cttee, 1974–76; Select Cttee on Home Affairs, 1984–92. A Dep. Speaker, H of L, 2002–; a Dep. Chm. of Cttees, H of L, 2002–; Chm., Refreshment Cttee, H of L, 2003–; Member: Jt Select Cttee on Draft Mental Capacity Bill (formerly Mental Incapacity Bill), 2003–; Select Cttee on Crossrail Bill, 2008–. Chm., Cons. West Country Mems Cttee, 1976–77, Vice-Chm., 1977. Fellow, Industry and Parlt Trust, 1978. Pres., Hastings and Rye Cons. Assoc., 1998–. Member: Council, RSPCA, 1975–92 (Chm., 1979–81; Vice-Pres., 1992–); Nat. Art Collections Fund; Council, SSAFA, 1980–98 (Vice-Pres., 1998–); Council, Stonham Housing Assoc., 1980–92; Commonwealth War Graves Commn, 1987–97; Council of Mgt, Coll. of St Mark and St John, 1989–2004. President: Hastings, St Leonards on Sea, Bexhill and Dist Br., NSPCC, 2000–; War Widows Assoc., 2005–. Patron, Plymouth Workroute, 1998–. Gov., Kelly Coll., 2002–. Member: RHS; Nat. Trust. DL E Sussex, 2001. Hon. DLitt Plymouth, 1993. *Recreations:* theatre, gardening, scuba diving, swimming, yoga. *Address:* House of Lords, SW1A 0PW.

FOOT, David Lovell, CB 1998; FICFor; Head of Forestry Authority, 1995–99; *b* 20 May 1939; *s* of late John Bartram Lovell Foot, MBE and of Bertha Lilian Foot; *m* 1964, Verena Janine Walton; one *s* one *d*. *Educ:* John Lyon Sch., Harrow; Edinburgh Univ. (BSc Hons 1961). FICFor 1980. Dist Officer, Forestry Commn, 1961–64; Silviculturist, Dept of Forestry and Game, Govt of Malawi, 1964–70; Forestry Commission: various appts in S Scotland, N Wales and E Scotland, 1970–86; Comr, 1986–99. Trustee, Woodland Trust, 1999–. *Recreations:* walking, fishing, photography. *Address:* The Warren, Chalk Lane, East Horsley, Surrey KT24 6TH. *T:* (01483) 280756.

FOOT, Sir Geoffrey (James), Kt 1984; Chairman and Commissioner, Hydro Electric Commission of Tasmania, 1987–89 (Associate Commissioner, 1984–87); *b* 20 July 1915; *s* of James P. Foot and Susan J. Foot; *m* 1940, Mollie W. Snooks; two *s* one *d*. *Educ:* Launceston High Sch. AASA; ACIS. MLC, Tasmania, 1961–72 (Leader for Govt, 1969–72). Chairman: Tasmania Permanent Bldg Soc., 1982–85; Launceston Gas Co., 1982–84; Gas Corp. of Tasmania, 1984–87. Mem., Lilydale Commn—Local Govt, 1983–85. Mem. Council, Univ. of Tasmania, 1970–85. Freeman, City of Launceston, 1990. Hon. LLD Tasmania, 1988. *Recreations:* reading, music. *Address:* Manor Complex, Guy Street, Kings Meadows, Tas 7250, Australia. *T:* (03) 63431143.

FOOT, Rt Hon. Michael; PC 1974; *b* 23 July 1913; *s* of late Rt Hon. Isaac Foot, PC; *m* 1949, Jill Craigie (*d* 1999). *Educ:* Forres Sch., Swanage; Leighton Park Sch., Reading; Wadham Coll., Oxford (Exhibitioner). Pres. Oxford Union, 1933; contested (Lab) Mon 1935; MP (Lab): Devonport Div. of Plymouth, 1945–55; Ebbw Vale, Nov. 1960–1983; Blaenau Gwent, 1983–92; Sec. of State for Employment, 1974–76; Lord President of the Council and Leader of the House of Commons, 1976–79; Leader of the Opposition 1980–83. Mem., Labour Party Nat. Exec. Cttee, 1971–83; Deputy Leader of the Labour Party, 1976–80, Leader of the Labour Party 1980–83. Asst Editor, Tribune, 1937–38; Acting Editor, Evening Standard, 1942; Man. Dir, Tribune, 1945–74, Editor, 1948–52, 1955–60; political columnist on the Daily Herald, 1944–64; former Book Critic, Evening Standard. Hon. Fellow, Wadham Coll., Oxford, 1969. *Publications:* Guilty Men (with Frank Owen and Peter Howard), 1940; Armistice 1918–39, 1940; Trial of Mussolini, 1943; Brendan and Beverley, 1944; Still at Large, 1950; Full Speed Ahead, 1950; Guilty Men (with Mervyn Jones), 1957; The Pen and the Sword, 1957; Parliament in Danger, 1959; Aneurin Bevan: Vol. I, 1897–1945, 1962; Vol. II, 1945–60, 1973; Debts of Honour, 1980; Another Heart and Other Pulses, 1984; Loyalists and Loners, 1986; The Politics of Paradise, 1988; H. G.: the history of Mr Wells, 1995; Dr Strangelove, I Presume, 1999; The Uncollected Michael Foot, 2003. *Recreations:* Plymouth Argyle supporter, chess, reading, walking. *Address:* c/o Tribune, 9 Arkwright Road, NW3 6AN.

FOOT, Michael Colin, OBE 1984; part-time Tutor, International Academy, University of Essex, since 2007; *b* 3 Feb. 1935; *s* of William Reginald Foot and Elsie (*née* Collins); *m* 1964, Heather Pearl Foot (*née* Beaton); two *s* two *d*. *Educ:* Taunton's Sch., Southampton; University Coll., Leicester (BA London); Leicester Univ. (PGCE); Univ. of Essex (MA 1994). Lycée Champollion, Grenoble, 1959–60; Ashlyn's Sch., Berkhamsted, 1960–63. Served RAF, 1963–66. British Council: Asst Rep., Chile, 1966–71; Hd of Overseas Recruitment, Personnel Div., 1971–75; Dep. Rep., Nigeria, 1975–78; Dep. Dir, Personnel, 1978–81; Rep., Bangladesh, 1981–83; Dir, Personnel, 1984–85; Controller, Personnel, 1986–89; Dir, Australia, 1989–93; retd 1993. *Recreations:* reading, theatre, music, botany, swimming. *Address:* c/o HSBC, Bitterne, Southampton SO9 3RZ. *Club:* Royal Air Force.

FOOT, Michael David Kenneth Willoughby, CBE 2003; Chairman (London), Promontory Financial Group, since 2007; *b* 16 Dec. 1946; *s* of Kenneth Willoughby Foot and Ruth Joan (*née* Cornah); *m* 1972, Michele Annette Cynthia Macdonald; one *s* two *d*. *Educ:* Pembroke Coll., Cambridge (MA); Yale Univ., USA (MA). Joined Bank of England, 1969; manager, 1978; sen. man., 1985; seconded to IMF, Washington, as UK Alternate Exec. Dir, 1985–87; Head: Foreign Exchange Div., 1988–90; European Div., 1990–93; Banking Supervision Div., 1993–94; Dep. Dir, Supervision and Surveillance, 1994–96; Exec. Dir, Bank of England, 1996–98; Man. Dir, Deposit Takers and Mkts, FSA, 1998–2004; Inspector of Banks, Central Bank of the Bahamas, 2004–07. *Publications:* contrib. essays on monetary econs to books and jls. *Recreations:* choral singing, tennis, voluntary youth work.

FOOT, Michael Richard Daniell, CBE 2001; TD 1945; historian; *b* 14 Dec. 1919; *s* of late R. C. Foot and Nina (*née* Raymond); *m* twice; one *s* one *d*; 3rd, 1972, Mirjam Michaela Romme (*see* M. M. Foot). *Educ:* Winchester (scholar); New Coll., Oxford (scholar). Served in Army, 1939–45 (Major RA, parachutist, wounded). Taught at Oxford, 1947–59; research, 1959–67; Prof. of Modern Hist., Manchester, 1967–73; Dir of Studies, European Discussion Centre, 1973–75. Fellow, St Deiniol's Liby, Hawarden, 2001. Hon. Vice-Pres., RHistS, 2004–. French Croix de Guerre, 1945; Officer, Order of Orange Nassau (Netherlands), 1989; Chevalier, Legion of Honour (France), 2005. *Publications:* Gladstone and Liberalism (with J. L. Hammond), 1952; British Foreign Policy since 1898, 1956; Men in Uniform, 1961; SOE in France, 1966, new edn 2004; (ed) The Gladstone Diaries: vols I and II, 1825–1839, 1968; (ed) War and Society, 1973; (ed with Dr H. C. G. Matthew) The Gladstone Diaries: vols III and IV, 1840–1854, 1974; Resistance, 1976; Six Faces of Courage, 1978, 2nd edn 2003; (with J. M. Langley) MI9, 1979; SOE: an outline history, 1984, 3rd edn 1995; Art and War, 1990; (ed) Holland at war against Hitler, 1990; (ed with I. C. B. Dear) Oxford Companion to World War II, 2001, 2nd edn 2005; SOE in the Low Countries, 2001; *festschrift:* (ed. K. G. Robertson) War, Resistance and Intelligence: collected essays in honour of M. R. D. Foot, 1999. *Recreations:* reading, talking. *Address:* Martins Cottage, Nuthampstead, Royston, Herts SG8 8ND. *Clubs:* Savile, Special Forces.

See also S. R. I. Foot.

FOOT, Prof. Mirjam Michaela, DLitt; FSA; Professor of Library and Archive Studies, University College London, 2000–06, now Emeritus; *b* 11 Oct. 1941; *d* of Carl Paul Maria Romme and Anthonia Maria Wiegman; *m* 1972, Michael Richard Daniell Foot, *qv*. *Educ:* Amsterdam Univ. (BA, MA, DLitt 1979). FSA 1986. Asst Lectr, Bedford Coll., Univ. of London, 1965–66; British Library: Asst Keeper, Rare Book Collection, 1966–84; Curator, Preservation Service, 1984–87; Dep. Dir, Hd of W European Collections and Hd of Acquisitions, 1987–90; Dir of Collections and Preservation, 1990–99. Associate, Clare Hall, Cambridge, 1970–72; Sandars Reader in Bibliography, Univ. of Cambridge, 2002–03; Hon. Sen. Res. Fellow, Sch. of Advanced Study, Univ. of London, 2006–. Ed. British Liby Jl, 1977–85. Bibliographical Society: Hon. Sec., 1975–94; Vice-Pres. 1990–2000; Pres., 2000–02. Vice-Pres., Soc. of Antiquaries, 2001–05. Hon. Fellow, Designer Bookbinders, 1986. *Publications:* The Henry Davis Gift: Vol I: Studies in the History of Bookbinding, 1978; Vol II: North European Bindings, 1983; Pictorial Bookbindings, 1986; (with H. M. Nixon) The History of Decorated Bookbinding in England, 1992; Studies in the History of Bookbinding, 1993; The History of Bookbinding as a Mirror of Society, 1998; The Decorated Bindings in Marsh's Library, Dublin, 2004; (ed) Eloquent Witnesses: bookbindings and their history, 2004; Bookbinders at Work: their roles and methods, 2005; contrib. articles in Book Collector, The Liby, British Liby Jl, Revue française d'histoire du livre, Proc. and Bulletins of Assoc. Internat. de Bibliophilie, Paper Conservator. *Recreations:* music, reading, walking. *Address:* Martins Cottage, Bell Lane, Nuthampstead, Herts SG8 8ND.

FOOT, Prof. Philippa Ruth, FBA 1976; Griffin Professor, University of California at Los Angeles, 1988–91, now Emeritus (Professor of Philosophy, 1974–91); *b* 3 Oct. 1920; *d* of William Sydney Bence Bosanquet, DSO, and Esther Cleveland Bosanquet, *d* of Grover Cleveland, Pres. of USA; *m* 1945, Michael Richard Daniell Foot, *qv* (marr. diss. 1960); no *c*. *Educ:* St George's Sch., Ascot; privately; Somerville Coll., Oxford (BA 1942, MA 1946). Somerville College, Oxford: Lectr in philosophy, 1947; Fellow and Tutor, 1950–69; Vice-Principal, 1967–69; Sen. Res. Fellow, 1970–88; Hon. Fellow, 1988. Formerly Vis. Prof., Cornell Univ., MIT, Univ. of California at Berkeley, Princeton Univ., City Univ. of NY; Fellow, Center for Advanced Studies in Behavioral Scis, Stanford, 1981–82. Pres. Pacific Div., Amer. Philos. Assoc., 1982–83. Fellow, Amer. Acad. of Arts and Scis, 1983. Hon. Dr Sofia, 2000. *Publications:* Theories of Ethics (ed), 1967; Virtues and Vices, 1978; Natural Goodness, 2001; Moral Dilemmas, 2002; articles in Mind, Aristotelian Soc. Proc. Philos. Rev., New York Rev., Philosophy and Public Affairs. *Address:* 15 Walton Street, Oxford OX1 2HG. *T:* (01865) 557130.

FOOT, Prof. Rosemary June, PhD; FBA 1996; John Swire Senior Research Fellow in International Relations, St Antony's College, Oxford, since 1990; Professor of International Relations, University of Oxford, since 1997; *b* 4 June 1948; *d* of Leslie William Foot, MBE and Margaret Lily Frances Foot; *m* 1996, Timothy C. S. Kennedy. *Educ:* Univ. of Essex (BA Hons Govt 1972); SOAS, London Univ. (MA Area Studies (Far East) 1973); LSE (PhD Internat. Relns 1977). Lectr in Internat. Relns, Univ. of Sussex, 1978–90. Fulbright Scholar and American Council of Learned Socs Fellow, E Asian Inst., Columbia Univ., NY, 1981–82. *Publications:* The Wrong War: American policy and the dimensions of the Korean conflict 1950–1953, 1985; A Substitute for Victory: the politics of peacemaking at the Korean Armistice talks, 1990; (ed jtly) Migration: the Asian experience, 1994; The Practice of Power: US relations with China since 1949, 1995; (ed jtly) Hong Kong's Transitions 1842–1997, 1997; Rights Beyond Borders: the global community and the struggle over human rights in China, 2000; (ed jtly) Order and Justice in International Relations, 2003; (ed jtly) US Hegemony and International Organisations, 2003; Human Rights and Counter-terrorism in America's Asia Policy, 2004; (ed jtly) Does China Matter?: a reassessment, 2004; Framing Security Agendas: US counter-terrorist policies and Southeast Asian responses, 2008. *Recreations:* walking, music, sailing. *Address:* St Antony's College, Oxford OX2 6JF. *T:* (01865) 432031.

FOOT, Prof. Sarah Rosamund Irvine, PhD; FRHistS, FSA; Regius Professor of Ecclesiastical History, University of Oxford, since 2007; *b* 23 Feb. 1961; *d* of Michael Richard Daniell Foot, *qv*, and Elizabeth Mary Irvine Foot (*née* King); *m* 1st, 1986, Geoffrey Martin Kenneth Schrecker (marr. diss. 1999); one *s*; 2nd, 2002, Prof. Michael John Bentley. *Educ:* Withington Girls' Sch., Manchester; Newnham Coll., Cambridge (BA 1984, MA 1986; PhD 1990). FSA 2001; FRHistS 2001. Res. Fellow, Gonville and Caius Coll., Cambridge, 1989–93; University of Sheffield: Lectr, 1993–2001; Sen. Lectr, 2001–04; Prof. of Early Medieval Hist., 2004–07. Lay Canon, Christ Ch, Oxford, 2007–. *Publications:* Veiled Women: the disappearance of nuns from Anglo-Saxon England, 2 vols, 2000; Monastic Life in Anglo-Saxon England *c* 600–900, 2006. *Recreations:* music, fiction, travel, Pilates. *Address:* Christ Church, Oxford OX1 1DP. *T:* (01865) 276150; *e-mail:* sarah.foot@chch.ox.ac.uk.

FOOTE, Prof. Peter Godfrey; Emeritus Professor of Scandinavian Studies, University of London; *b* 26 May 1924; 4th *s* of late T. Foote and Ellen Foote, Swanage, Dorset; *m* 1951, Eleanor Jessie McCaig, *d* of late J. M. McCaig and Margaret H. McCaig; one *s* two *d*. *Educ:* Grammar Sch., Swanage; University Coll., Exeter; Univ. of Oslo; University Coll., London. BA London 1948; MA London 1951; Fil. dr *hc* Uppsala, 1972; dr phil. *hc* Univ. of Iceland, 1987. Served with RNVR, 1943–46. University College London: Asst Lectr, Lectr and Reader in Old Scandinavian, 1950–63; Prof. of Scandinavian Studies, 1963–83; Fellow, 1989. Jt Sec., Viking Soc., 1956–83 (Pres., 1974–76; 1990–92; Hon. Life Mem., 1983). Member: Royal Gustav Adolfs Academy, Uppsala, 1967; Kungliga Humanistiska Vetenskapssamfundet, Uppsala, 1968; Vísindafélag Islands, 1969; Vetenskapssocieteten, Lund, 1973; Kungliga Vetenskaps-samhället, Göteborg; Det kongelige Norske Videnskabers Selskab, 1977; Societas Scientiarum Fennica, 1979; Det norske Videnskapsakademi, 1986; Hon. Member: Islenska Bókmenntafélag, 1965; Thjóðvinafélag Íslenska í Vesturheimi, 1975; Félag íslenzkra fræða, 1995; Corresp. Mem., Kungliga Vitterhets Hist. och Antikvitets Akad., Stockholm, 1971. Crabtree Orator, 1968. Commander with star, Icelandic Order of the Falcon, 1984 (Comdr, 1973); Knight, Order of Dannebrog (Denmark); Comdr, Royal Order of North Star (Sweden), 1977; Comdr, Royal Order of Merit (Norway), 1993. *Publications:* Gunnlaugs saga ormstungu, 1957; Pseudo-Turpin Chronicle in Iceland, 1959; Laing's Heimskringla, 1961; Lives of Saints: Icelandic manuscripts in facsimile IV, 1962, and XIX, 1990; (with G. Johnston) The Saga of Gisli, 1963; (with D. M. Wilson) The Viking Achievement, 1970, 2nd edn 1980; (jt trans. and ed) Laws of Early Iceland, vol. I, 1980, vol. II, 2000; Aurvandilstá (selected papers), 1984; (ed) Olaus Magnus: a description of the Northern Peoples, vol. I, 1996, vols II and III, 1998; (ed) Jóns saga Hólabyskups ens helga, 2003; Kreddur (more selected papers), 2004; papers in Saga-Book, Arv, Studia Islandica, Islenzk Tunga, etc. *Recreations:* bell-ringing, walking. *Address:* 18 Talbot Road, N6 4QR. *T:* (020) 8340 1860.

FOOTMAN, John Richard Evelegh; an Executive Director, Bank of England, since 2003; *b* 6 Sept. 1952; *s* of Jack and Joyce Footman; *m* 1983, Elaine Watkiss; two *s* three *d*. *Educ:* Clifton Coll., Bristol. Joined Bank of England, 1969; Private Sec. to Gov., 1986–89; Head of Information, 1989–94; Sec., 1994–97; Dep. Dir, 1997–99; Dir of Personnel, 1999–2003. *Address:* Bank of England, EC2R 8AH. *T:* (020) 7601 5765.

FOOTS, Sir James (William), Kt 1975; AO 1992; mining engineer; Chairman: MIM Holdings Ltd, 1970–83 (Director, 1956–87); Westpac Banking Corporation, 1987–89 (Director, 1971–89); *b* 12 July 1916; *m* 1939, Thora H. Thomas; one *s* two *d*. *Educ:* Melbourne Univ. (BME). President: Austr. Inst. Mining and Metallurgy, 1974; Austr. Mining Industry Council, 1974 and 1975; 13th Congress, Council of Mining and Metallurgical Instns, 1986. Fellow, Australian Acad. of Technol Scis. University of Queensland: Mem. Senate, 1970–92; Chancellor, 1985–92. Hon. DEng Univ. of Qld, 1982. *Address:* c/o 53 Royston Street, Brookfield, Qld 4069, Australia.

FOOTTIT, Rt Rev. Anthony Charles; Bishop Suffragan of Lynn, 1999–2003; *b* 28 June 1935; *s* of Percival Frederick and Mildred Foottit; *m* 1977, Rosamond Mary Alyson Buxton; one *s* two *d*. *Educ:* Lancing Coll.; King's Coll., Cambridge (MA). Asst Curate, Wymondham, 1961–64; Vicar, Blakeney Group, 1964–71; Rector, Camelot Group, 1971–81; RD of Cary, 1979–81; St Hugh's Missioner for Lincolnshire, 1981–87; Hon. Canon of Lincoln Cathedral, 1986–87; Archdeacon of Lynn, 1987–98. *Publications:* Mission and Ministry in Rural France, 1967; A Gospel of Wild Flowers, 2006. *Recreations:* gardening, botany, rambling. *Address:* Ivy House, Whitwell Street, Reepham, Norfolk NR10 4RA. *T:* (01603) 870340.

FOPP, Dr Michael Anton; Director General, Royal Air Force Museum, since 1988; *b* 28 Oct. 1947; *s* of late Sqdn Ldr Desmond Fopp, AFC, AE and of Edna Meryl Fopp; *m* 1968, Rosemary Ann Hodgetts; one *s*. *Educ:* Reading Blue Coat Sch.; City Univ., London (MA 1984; PhD 1989). FMA; FRAeS. Dep. Keeper 1979–82, Keeper 1982–85, Battle of Britain Mus.; Co. Sec., Hendon Mus. Trading Co. Ltd, 1983–85; Dir, London Transport Mus., 1985–88. Hon. Sec. 1976–86, Chm. 1986–88, Soc. of Friends of RAF Mus. President: London Underground Rly Soc., 1987–88; Internat. Assoc. of Transport Museums, 1992–98. Chairman: Museums' Documentation Assoc., 1995–98; London Transport Flying Club Ltd, 1986–97. Freeman, City of London, 1984; Liveryman, 2002–, Warden, 2006–, GAPAN. *Publications:* The Boeing Washington, 1980; The Battle of Britain Museum Guide, 1980; The Bomber Command Museum Guide, 1982; The RAF Museum Guide, 1985; (ed) A Junior Guide to the RAF Museum, 1985; (ed) Battle of Britain Project Book, 1989; Royal Air Force Museum, 1992, 2nd edn 2003; (ed) High Flyers, 1993; Managing Museums and Galleries, 1997; The Implications of Emerging Technologies for Museums and Galleries, 1997; The Tradition is Safe, 2003; various articles on aviation, museums and management, in magazines and jls. *Recreations:* flying, computers, Chinese cookery. *Address:* Royal Air Force Museum, Hendon, NW9 5LL. *T:* (020) 8205 2266. *Clubs:* Royal Air Force; Air Squadron.

FORBES, family name of **Lord Forbes** and of **Earl of Granard.**

FORBES, 22nd Lord *cr* 1445 or before; **Nigel Ivan Forbes,** KBE 1960; JP, DL; Premier Lord of Scotland; Representative Peer of Scotland, 1955–63; Major (retired) Grenadier Guards; Chairman, Rolawn Ltd, 1975–98; *b* 19 Feb. 1918; *o s* of 21st Lord and Lady Mabel Anson (*d* 1972), *d* of 3rd Earl of Lichfield; *S* father, 1953; *m* 1942, Hon. Rosemary Katharine Hamilton-Russell, *o d* of 9th Viscount Boyne; two *s* one *d*. *Educ:* Harrow; RMC Sandhurst. Served War of 1939–45 (wounded); Adjt, Grenadier Guards, Staff Coll. Military Asst to High Comr for Palestine, 1947–48. Minister of State, Scottish Office, 1958–59. Member: Inter-Parly Union Delegn to Denmark, 1956; Commonwealth Parly Assoc. Delegn to Canada, 1961; Parly Delegn to Pakistan, 1962; Inter-Parly Union Delegn to Hungary, 1965; Inter-Parly Union Delegn to Ethiopia, 1971. Director: Grampian Television PLC, 1960–88; Blenheim Travel Ltd, 1981–88; Dep. Chm., Tenant Caledonian Breweries Ltd, 1964–74. Mem., Aberdeen and District Milk Marketing Bd, 1962–72; Mem. Alford District Council, 1955–58; Chm., River Don District Bd, 1962–73. Pres., Royal Highland and Agricultural Society of Scotland, 1958–59; Member: Sports Council for Scotland, 1966–71; Scottish Cttee, Nature Conservancy, 1961–67; Chm., Scottish Br., Nat. Playing Fields Assoc., 1965–80; Pres., Scottish Scout Assoc., 1970–88. Pres., Books Abroad, 1982–; Chm., Alford Car Transport Service, 2000–. Patron, Friends of Insch Hosp., 1992–. JP 1955, DL 1958, Aberdeenshire. *Recreations:* wildlife, travel, photography. *Heir:* *s* Master of Forbes, *qv*. *Address:* Balforbes, Alford, Aberdeenshire AB33 8DR. *T:* (01975) 562516, *Fax:* (01975) 562438. *Club:* Army and Navy.

FORBES, Viscount; Jonathan Peter Hastings Forbes; *b* 24 Dec. 1981; *e s* and *heir* of Earl of Granard, *qv*.

FORBES, Master of; Hon. Malcolm Nigel Forbes; DL; landowner; *b* 6 May 1946; *s* and *heir* of 22nd Lord Forbes, *qv*; *m* 1st, 1969, Carole Jennifer Andrée (marr. diss. 1982), *d* of N. S. Whitehead, Aberdeen; one *s* one *d*; 2nd, 1988, Jennifer Mary Gribbon, *d* of I. P. Whittington, Tunbridge Wells. *Educ:* Eton; Aberdeen Univ. Director, Instock Disposables Ltd, 1974–; Chm., Castle Forbes Collection Ltd, 1996–. DL Aberdeenshire, 1996. *Address:* Castle Forbes, Alford, Aberdeenshire AB33 8BL. *T:* (01975) 562574; 3 Steeple Close, SW6 3LE. *T:* (020) 7736 0730.

FORBES, Major Sir Andrew (Iain Ochoncar), 13th Bt *cr* 1630 (NS), of Craigievar, Aberdeenshire and of Corse; *b* 28 Nov. 1945; *s* of Lt-Col Patrick Walter Forbes of Corse, OBE and Margaret Hawthorne Forbes (*née* Lydall); *S* kinsman, 2000, but his name does not appear on the Official Roll of the Baronetage; *m* 1984, Jane Elizabeth Dunbar-Nasmith; two *s* two *d*. *Educ:* Trinity Coll., Glenalmond; RMA Sandhurst; St Catherine's Coll., Oxford (BA 1969); Cranfield Sch. of Mgt (MBA 1979). Major, Gordon Highlanders, retired. *Heir:* *s* James Patrick Ochoncar Forbes, *b* 1 Nov. 1986.

FORBES, Anthony David Arnold William; Joint Senior Partner, Cazenove & Co., 1980–94; *b* 15 Jan. 1938; *s* of late Lt-Col D. W. A. W. Forbes, MC, and Diana Mary (*née* Henderson), later Marchioness of Exeter; *m* 1st, 1962, Virginia June Ropner; one *s* one *d*; 2nd, 1973, Belinda Mary Drury-Lowe. *Educ:* Eton. Served Coldstream Guards, 1956–59. Joined Cazenove & Co., 1960; Member of Stock Exchange, subseq. MSI, 1965–2003. Director: Carlton Communications Plc, 1994–2002; The Merchants Trust PLC, 1994–2002; Royal & Sun Alliance Insurance Gp (formerly Royal Insurance Hldgs plc), 1994–2002 (Dep. Chm., 1998–2002); RTZ Pension Investment Ltd, 1994–2000; Watmoughs (Hldgs) PLC, 1994–98; Phoenix Group Ltd, 1995–97; Rio Tinto Pension Fund Trustees Ltd, 2000–06. Chairman: Hospital and Homes of St Giles, 1975–; Wellesley House Educnl Trust, 1983–94; Hon. Trustee, Royal Botanic Gardens Kew Foundn, 1992–; Trustee, Botanic Gardens Conservation Internat., 1992–2005. Governor: Cobham Hall, 1975–94; Royal Choral Soc., 1979–. FRSA 1993. Hon. DBA De Montfort Univ., 1994. *Recreations:* music, gardening. *Address:* Wakerley Manor, Wakerley, Oakham, Rutland LE15 8PA. *T:* (01572) 747549.

FORBES, Bryan, CBE 2004; film director and author; *b* 22 July 1926; *m* 1955, Nanette Newman, *qv*; two *d*. *Educ:* West Ham Secondary Sch. Studied at RADA, 1941; entered acting profession, 1942, and (apart from war service) was on West End stage, then in films here and in Hollywood, 1948–60. Formed Beaver Films with Sir Richard Attenborough, 1959; wrote and co-produced The Angry Silence, 1960. Subseq. wrote, dir. and prod. numerous films; *films include:* The League of Gentlemen, Only Two Can Play, Whistle Down the Wind, 1961; The L-Shaped Room, 1962; Séance on a Wet Afternoon, 1963; King Rat (in Hollywood), 1964; The Wrong Box, 1965; The Whisperers, 1966; Deadfall, 1967; The Madwoman of Chaillot, 1968; The Raging Moon, 1970; The Tales of Beatrix Potter, 1971; The Stepford Wives, 1974 (USA); The Slipper and the Rose, 1975 (Royal Film Perf., 1976); International Velvet, 1978; (British segment) The Sunday Lovers, 1980; Better Late Than Never, 1981; The Naked Face, 1983; (narrator and co-dir) I am a Dancer, 1971. *Stage:* directed: Macbeth, Old Vic, 1980; Killing Jessica, Savoy, 1986; The Living Room, Royalty, 1987; One Helluva Life, Dublin Fest., 2002, (renamed Barrymore) Th. Royal, Windsor, 2004; directed and acted in Star Quality, Th. Royal, Bath, 1983. *Television:* produced and directed: Edith Evans, I Caught Acting Like the Measles, Yorkshire TV, 1973; Elton John, Goodbye Norma Jean and Other Things, ATV 1973; Jessie, BBC, 1980; The Endless Game, C4, 1989; acted in: December Flower, Granada, 1984; First Among Equals, Granada, 1986. Man. Dir and Head of Production, ABPC Studios, 1969–71; Man. Dir and Chief Exec., EMI-MGM, Elstree Studios, 1970–71; Dir, Capital Radio Ltd, 1973–97. Member: BBC Gen. Adv. Council, 1966–69; BBC Schs Council, 1971–73; President: Beatrix Potter Soc., 1982–96; Nat. Youth Theatre, 1984–2005; Writers' Guild of GB, 1988–91. Hon. DLit London, 1992; Hon. DLitt Sussex, 1999. Won British Acad. Award, 1960; Writers' Guild Award (twice); London Film Critics' Circle Award for Excellence in Film, 2005; Lifetime Achievement Award, BAFTA, 2007; numerous internat. awards. *Publications:* Truth Lies Sleeping, 1950; The Distant Laughter, 1972; Notes for a Life, 1974; The Slipper and the Rose, 1976; Ned's Girl: biography of Dame Edith Evans, 1977; International Velvet, 1978; Familiar Strangers, 1979; That Despicable Race, 1980; The Rewrite Man, 1983; The Endless Game, 1986; A Song at Twilight, 1989; A Divided Life, 1992; The Twisted Playground, 1993; Partly Cloudy, 1995; Quicksand, 1996; The Memory of All That, 1999; The Fatal Trinity, 2002; The Choice, 2007; contribs to: The Spectator, and other periodicals. *Recreations:* reading, landscape gardening, photography. *Address:* Pinewood Studio, Iver Heath, Bucks SL0 0NH.

See also Sir John Leon, Bt.

FORBES, Prof. Charles Douglas, MD, DSc; Professor of Medicine, University of Dundee, 1987–2004, now Emeritus; *b* 9 Oct. 1938; *s* of late John Forbes and Dr Annie Forbes (*née* Stuart); *m* 1965, Jannette MacDonald Robertson; two *s*. *Educ:* Univ. of Glasgow (MB ChB 1961; MD 1972; DSc 1986). Trng grades, Dept of Materia Medica, Univ. of Glasgow, 1961–65; Lectr in Medicine, Makerere Univ., Uganda, 1965–66; Registrar in Haemophilia, Royal Infirmary, Glasgow, 1966–68; American Heart Fellow/Fulbright Fellow, Cleveland, Ohio, 1968–70; Sen. Lectr, then Reader, Univ. of Glasgow, 1970–87. *Publications:* (with W. F. Jackson) Colour Atlas and Text of Clinical Medicine,

1993; (jtly) Haemophilia, 1997; articles and research papers on blood coagulation and thrombosis. *Recreations:* gardening, walking, DIY. *Address:* East Chattan, 108 Hepburn Gardens, St Andrews, Fife KY16 9LT. *T:* (01334) 472428.

See also J. S. Forbes.

FORBES, Colin, RDI 1974; Consulting Partner, Pentagram Design AG, since 1993; *b* 6 March 1928; *s* of Kathleen and John Forbes; *m* 1961, Wendy Schneider; one *s* two *d. Educ:* Sir Anthony Browne's, Brentwood; LCC Central Sch. of Arts and Crafts. Design Asst, Herbert Spencer, 1952; freelance practice and Lectr, LCC Central Sch. of Arts and Crafts, 1953–57; Art Dir, Stuart Advertising, London, 1957–58; Head of Graphic Design Dept, LCC Central Sch. of Arts and Crafts, 1958–61; freelance practice, London, 1961–62; Partner: Fletcher/Forbes/Gill, 1962–65; Crosby/Fletcher/Forbes, 1965–72; Pentagram Design Ltd, 1972–78; Pentagram Design Inc., NY, 1978–93. Mem., Alliance Graphique Internationale, 1965– (Internat. Pres. 1976–79); Pres., Amer. Inst. Graphic Arts, 1984–86. *Publications:* Graphic Design: visual comparisons, 1963; A Sign Systems Manual, 1970; Creativity and Communication, 1971; New Alphabets A to Z, 1973; Living by Design, 1978; Pentagram: the compendium, 1993. *Address:* Forbes Farm, 2879 Horseshoe Road, Westfield, NC 27053, USA. *T:* (336) 3513941.

FORBES, Very Rev. Graham John Thomson, CBE 2004; Provost, St Mary's Cathedral, Edinburgh, since 1990; *b* 10 June 1951; *s* of J. T. and D. D. Forbes; *m* 1973, Jane T. Miller; three *s. Educ:* George Heriot's School, Edinburgh; Univ. of Aberdeen (MA); Univ. of Edinburgh (BD). Curate, Old St Paul's Church, Edinburgh, 1976–82; Provost, St Ninian's Cathedral, Perth, 1982–90. Dir, Theol Inst. of Scottish Episcopal Ch, 2002–04. HM (Lay) Inspector of Constabulary, 1995–98. Member: Parole Bd for Scotland, 1990–95; Scottish Consumer Council, 1995–98; GMC, 1996–; Scottish Criminal Cases Rev. Commn, 1999– (Chm., 2002–); Clinical Standards Bd for Scotland, 1999–2002; NHS Quality Improvement Scotland, 2002–05; Chairman: MMR Expert Gp, Scottish Exec., 2001–02; UK Cttee on Ethical Aspects of Pandemic Influenza, 2006–. Mem., Historic Bldgs Council (Scotland), 2000–02. DUniv Napier. *Recreations:* running, fly-fishing. *Address:* 8 Lansdowne Crescent, Edinburgh EH12 5EQ. *T:* (home) (0131) 225 2978, *T:* (office) (0131) 225 6293.

FORBES, Adm. Sir Ian (Andrew), KCB 2003; CBE 1994; Deputy Supreme Allied Commander Transformation, 2003–04; *b* 24 Oct. 1946; *s* of late James and Winifred Forbes; *m* 1975, Sally, *d* of late Ronald Statham and Cynthia Statham; two *d. Educ:* Eastbourne Coll.; BRNC. Sea-going appointments, 1969–83: HM Ships Hermes, Upton, HM Yacht Britannia, USS W. H. Stanley; RAF Staff Coll., 1982–83; HM Ships Whitby, Kingfisher (CO), Apollo, Juno, Glamorgan, Diomede (CO), 1984–86; Chatham (CO), 1989–91; MoD, 1991–94; RCDS 1994; HMS Invincible (CO), 1995–96; MA to UN High Rep., Sarajevo, 1996–97; Comdr, UK Task Gp and Comdr, Anti-Submarine Warfare Striking Force, 1997–2000; Flag Officer Surface Flotilla, 2000–01; Dep. SACLANT, 2002; SACLANT, 2002–03. Chm., Naval Review, 2007–. Sen. Advr, Booz Allen Hamilton, 2006–. Chm. Council, Eastbourne Coll., 2005–; Gov., Portsmouth High Sch., 2001–; Mem. Adv. Bd, Occidental Coll., Calif., 2001–. Associate FRUSI, 2005–. Hon. Citizen, City of Norfolk, Va, 2004. QCVS 1996; Legion of Merit (US); NATO Meritorious Service Medal. *Recreations:* tennis, history, gardening. *Clubs:* Army and Navy, Pilgrims.

FORBES, James, FCA; Chairman, Tate & Lyle Group Pension Fund, 1978–85; Forestry Commissioner, 1982–88; *b* 2 Jan. 1923; *s* of Donald Forbes and Rona Ritchie Forbes (*née* Yeats); *m* 1948, Alison Mary Fletcher Moffat; two *s. Educ:* Christ's Hospital; Officers' Training School, Bangalore. Commissioned Indian Army, 1942; 15 Punjab Regt, 1943–44, Capt. CO Mobile Army Inspection Unit; Maj. DADOS AHQ, 1945–46; released 1947, Hon. Major. Peat Marwick Mitchell Co., 1952–58; Chief Accountant, L. Rose, 1958; Group Operational Research Manager, Schweppes, 1960, Group Chief Accountant, 1963 (Dir, subsid. cos); Sec. and Financial Adviser, Cadbury Schweppes (on formation), 1969, Main Board Dir, 1971, Group Finance Dir to April 1978; Senior Exec. Dir, Tate & Lyle, 1978, Vice-Chm., 1980–84. Non-executive Director: British Transport Hotels, 1978–83; British Rail Investments, 1980–84; Steetley plc, 1984–89; Compass Hotels, 1984–99; Lautro Ltd, 1986–90. Mem. Council, Inst. of Chartered Accountants, 1971–88 (Treasurer, 1984–86). Gov., Christ's Hosp., 1983– (Chm. and Treas., Council of Almoners, 1987–96). Mem., Highland Society. *Recreation:* golf. *Address:* 31 Rosemary Court, Church Road, Haslemere, Surrey GU27 1BH. *Clubs:* Caledonian, Royal Commonwealth Society.

FORBES, James Alexander, CBE 2003; CEng; non-executive Director, FirstGroup plc, since 2000; *b* 6 Aug. 1946; *s* of James A. Forbes and Verna Kelman; *m* 1969, Jean Clark; four *s. Educ:* Paisley Coll. of Tech. (BSc (1st cl. hons) Elect. Engrg); Loughborough Univ. of Tech. (MSc Electro-heat). MIEE. Scottish Power: Student Apprentice, 1964; Commercial Engr, 1973–84; Area Commercial Officer, 1984–86; Mktg Manager, 1986–89; Northern Electric: Commercial Dir, 1989–90; Distrib. Dir, 1990–91; Southern Electric: Ops Dir, 1991–94; Man. Dir, Electricity, 1994–96; Chief Operating Officer, 1996; Chief Exec., 1996–98; Chief Exec., Scottish and Southern Energy plc, 1998–2002. Non-exec. Chm., Thames Water, 2006. *Recreation:* golf.

FORBES, Sir James Thomas Stewart, 8th Bt *cr* 1823, of Newe, Aberdeenshire; *b* 28 May 1957; *o s* of Major Sir Hamish Stewart Forbes, 7th Bt, MBE, MC and Jacynthe Elizabeth Mary (*née* Underwood); *S* father, 2007, but his name does not appear on the Official Roll of the Baronetage; *m* 1986, Kerry Lynne, *o d* of Rev. Lee Toms, Sacramento; two *d. Educ:* Eton; Bristol Univ. (BA).

FORBES, Vice-Adm. Sir John Morrison, KCB 1978; *b* 16 Aug. 1925; *s* of late Lt-Col R. H. Forbes, OBE and Gladys M. Forbes (*née* Pollock); *m* 1950, Joyce Newenham Hadden (*d* 2004); two *s* two *d. Educ:* RNC, Dartmouth. Served War: HMS Mauritius, Verulam and Nelson, 1943–46. HMS Aisne, 1946–49; Gunnery course and staff of HMS Excellent, 1950–51; served in RAN, 1952–54; Staff of HMS Excellent, 1954–56; HMS Ceylon, 1956–58; Staff of Dir of Naval Ordnance, 1958–60; Comdr (G) HMS Excellent, 1960–61; Staff of Dir of Seaman Officers' Appts, 1962–64; Exec. Officer, Britannia RN Coll., 1964–66; Operational Comdr and 2nd in Comd, Royal Malaysian Navy, 1966–68; Asst Dir, Naval Plans, 1969–70; comd HMS Triumph, 1971–72; comd Britannia RN Coll., Dartmouth, 1972–74; Naval Secretary, 1974–76; Flag Officer, Plymouth, Port Adm., Devonport, Comdr, Central Sub Area, Eastern Atlantic, and Comdr, Plymouth Sub Area, Channel, 1977–79. Naval ADC to the Queen, 1974. Kesatria Manku Negara (Malaysia), 1968. *Recreation:* country pursuits. *Address:* c/o National Westminster Bank, Waterlooville, Portsmouth, Hants. *Clubs:* Army and Navy, RN Sailing Association.

FORBES, John Stuart; Sheriff of Tayside, Central and Fife at Dunfermline, 1980–2002; part-time Sheriff, whole of Scotland, 2003–05; *b* 31 Jan. 1936; *s* of late John Forbes and Dr A. R. S. Forbes; *m* 1963, Marion Alcock; one *s* two *d. Educ:* Glasgow High Sch.; Glasgow Univ. (MA, LLB). RA, TA, 1958–63 (Lieut). Solicitor, 1959–61; Advocate, Scottish Bar, 1962–76; Standing Jun. Counsel, Forestry Commn, 1972; Sheriff of Lothian and Borders, 1976–80. Pres., Glasgow Juridical Soc., 1963–64. Life Trustee, Carnegie,

Dunfermline and Hero Fund Trusts, 1985–2002; Trustee, Carnegie UK Trust, 1990–2002. *Recreations:* tennis, golf, curling, shooting, fishing. *Address:* Inglewood, Old Perth Road, Milnathort, Kinross KY13 9YA. *Clubs:* Royal Scots (Edinburgh), Edinburgh Sports.

See also C. D. Forbes.

FORBES, Nanette; *see* Newman, N.

FORBES, Hon. Sir Thayne (John), Kt 1993; a Judge of the High Court of Justice, Queen's Bench Division, 1993–2009; *b* 28 June 1938; *s* of late John Thomson Forbes and Jessie Kay Robertson Stewart; *m* 1960, Celia Joan; two *s* one *d. Educ:* Winchester College (Quirister); Wolverton Grammar Sch.; University College London (LLB, LLM). Served Royal Navy (Instructor Lieutenant), 1963–66. Called to Bar, Inner Temple, 1966, Governing Bencher, 1991; QC 1984; a Recorder, 1986–90; a Circuit Judge (Official Referee), 1990–93; Presiding Judge, Northern Circuit, 1995–99; Judge i/c Technology and Construction Ct, 2001–04. *Recreations:* music, reading, sailing, bird watching, astronomy, beekeeping. *Address:* c/o Royal Courts of Justice, Strand, WC2A 2LL. *Club:* Garrick.

FORBES, Sir William (Daniel) Stuart-, 13th Bt *cr* 1626 (NS), of Pitsligo and of Monymusk, Aberdeenshire; *b* 21 Aug. 1935; *s* of William Kenneth Stuart-Forbes (*d* 1946) 3rd *s* of 10th Bt, and of Marjory Gilchrist; *S* uncle, 1985; *m* 1st, 1956, Jannette (*d* 1997), *d* of late Hori Toki George MacDonald; three *s* two *d*; 2nd, 2001, Betty Dawn Ward, *d* of William Henry Gibson and Ellen Dorothy Neilson. *Heir: s* Kenneth Charles Stuart-Forbes [*b* 26 Dec. 1956; *m* 1981, Susan, *d* of Len Murray; one *s* two *d*]. *Address:* 169 Budge Street, Blenheim, Marlborough, New Zealand.

FORBES, Captain William Frederick Eustace; Vice Lord-Lieutenant of Stirling and Falkirk, 1984–96; Forestry Commissioner, 1982–88; *b* 6 July 1932; *er s* of late Lt-Col W. H. D. C. Forbes of Callendar, CBE and Elizabeth Forbes; *m* 1st, 1956, Pamela Susan (*d* 1993), *er d* of Lord McCorquodale of Newton, KCVO, PC; two *d*; 2nd, 1995, Venetia, Hon. Lady Troubridge, *widow* of Sir Peter Troubridge, 6th Bt. *Educ:* Eton. Regular soldier, Coldstream Guards, 1950–59; farmer and company director, 1959–. Chairman: Scottish Woodland Owners' Assoc., 1974–77; Nat. Playing Fields Assoc., Scottish Branch, 1980–90. *Recreations:* country pastimes, golf, cricket, travel. *Address:* Earlstoun Lodge, Dalry, Castle Douglas, Kirkcudbrightshire DG7 3TY. *T:* (01644) 430213. *Clubs:* MCC; New (Edinburgh); Royal and Ancient Golf.

FORBES-LEITH of Fyvie, Sir George Ian David, 4th Bt *cr* 1923, of Jessfield, co. Midlothian; *b* 26 May 1967; *e s* of Sir Andrew George Forbes-Leith, 3rd Bt and Jane Kate (*née* McCall-McCowan); *S* father, 2000; *m* 1995, Camilla Frances Ely; two *s* one *d. Educ:* RAC, Cirencester. *Recreations:* shooting, ski-ing, fishing. *Heir: s* Alexander Philip George Forbes-Leith, *b* 4 Feb. 1999. *Address:* Tifty, Fyvie, Turiff AB53 8JT.

FORBES-MEYLER, John William, OBE 1990; HM Diplomatic Service, retired; Ambassador to Ecuador, 1997–2000; *b* 3 July 1942; *s* of late J. J. C. Forbes and of Moira Patricia (*née* Garvey, who later *m* James Robert Meyler (now decd)); changed name by Deed Poll, 1963 to Forbes-Meyler; *m* 1st, 1964, Margaret Goddard (marr. diss. 1979); one *d*; 2nd, 1980, Mary Read (*née* Vlachou); one step *s. Educ:* grammar sch., etc. Joined HM Diplomatic Service, 1962: CRO, 1962–64; Lagos, 1964–68; Chicago, 1968–69; Boston, 1969–70; FCO, 1970–71; NY, 1971–72; FCO, 1972–75; Athens, 1975–80; FCO, 1980–83; 1st Sec. (Econ.), Bonn, 1983–86; on loan to MoD, 1986–88; Deputy Head of Mission: Bogota, 1988–92; Vienna, 1992–96. *Recreations:* walking, music, reading. *Address: e-mail:* jfmconsultants@acn.gr. *Club:* Special Forces.

FORBES SMITH, Michael; *see* Smith, M. F.

FORBES WATSON, Anthony David; Chief Executive, Penguin Group (UK), 1996–2005; *b* 25 Sept. 1954; *s* of Ian and Evelyn Forbes Watson; *m* 1983, Jennifer Ann Curnow; one *s* one *d. Educ:* Charterhouse Sch.; York Univ. (BA English and Related Lit.). Internat. Sales, OUP, 1977–80; Harper Collins: Internat. Sales Mgt, 1980–86; Sales and Mktg Dir, 1986–90; Managing Director: Pitman Publishing, 1990–91; Ladybird Books Ltd, 1991–96. Pres., Publishers' Assoc. of UK, 2002–03. Governor, Loughborough Coll. of Art and Design, 1993–95. *Recreations:* tennis, ski-ing, golf. *Address:* Saffron House, Ewelme, Wallingford, Oxon OX10 6HP. *Clubs:* Garrick; Huntercombe Golf.

FORD, family name of **Baroness Ford.**

FORD, Baroness *cr* 2006 (Life Peer), of Cunninghame in North Ayrshire; **Margaret Anne Ford;** Managing Director, Royal Bank of Canada Capital Markets, since 2007; *b* 16 Dec. 1957; *d* of Edward and Susan Garland; *m* 1990, David Arthur Bolger; one *s* one *d* by a previous marriage. *Educ:* Glasgow Univ. (MA Hons, MPhil). Scottish Organiser, BIFU, 1982–87; Managing Consultant, Price Waterhouse & Co., 1987–90; Dir, Scottish Homes, 1990–93; Man. Dir, 1993–2000, Chm., 2000–02, Eglinton Mgt Centre; Chm., English Partnerships, 2002–07. Chm., Lothian Health Bd, 1997–2000; Chief Exec., 2000–04, Dep. Chm., 2004–05, Good Practice Ltd; Chm., Irvine Bay URC, 2006–. Non-executive Director: Scottish Prison Service, 1994–98; Ofgem, 2000–03; Thus plc, 2002–05; Serco plc, 2003–. Mem., Scottish Economic Council, 1997–2000. Hon. Prof., Urban Studies Dept, Univ. of Glasgow. Hon. MRICS. *Recreations:* family, sport, fine art, travel. *Address:* House of Lords, SW1A 0PW.

FORD, Rev. Adam; Chaplain, St Paul's Girls' School, London, 1976–2001 (Head of Lower School, 1986–92); *b* 15 Sept. 1940; *s* of John Ford and Jean Beattie Ford (*née* Winstanley); *m* 1969, Veronica Rosemary Lucia Verey (marr. diss. 1993); two *s* two *d. Educ:* Minehead Grammar Sch.; King's Coll., Univ. of London (BD Hons, AKC 1964); Lancaster Univ. (MA Indian Religion 1972). Asst, Ecumenical Inst. of World Council of Churches, Geneva, 1964; Curate, Cirencester Parish Church, Glos, 1965–69; Vicar of Hebden Bridge, W Yorkshire, 1969–76; Priest-in-Ordinary to the Queen, 1984–90. Regular contributor to Prayer for the Day, Radio 4, 1978–; writer and narrator, Whose World?, series of TV progs on sci. and religion, 1987. Hon. FRAS 1960. *Publications:* Spaceship Earth, 1981; Weather Watch, 1982; Star Gazers Guide to the Night Sky (audio guide to astronomy), 1982; Universe: God, Man and Science, 1986; The Cuckoo Plant, 1991; Mr Hi-Tech, 1993; Faith and Science, 1999; articles in The Times and science jls on relationship between science and religion, also on dialogue between religions; regular contrib. Church Times. *Recreations:* dry stone walling, astronomy, searching for neolithic flints. *Address:* 55 Bolingbroke Road, Hammersmith, W14 0AH. *T:* (020) 7602 5902.

FORD, Lt Col Andrew Charles; Comptroller, Lord Chamberlain's Office, since 2006; *b* 5 Feb. 1957; *s* of Charles and Irmgard Ford; *m* 1985, Rosalind Birkett; two *s. Educ:* King's Coll., Taunton; RMA Sandhurst; JSDC Greenwich. Commnd Grenadier Guards, 1977; Comd, 1st Bn Welsh Guards, 1999–2002; Extra Equerry to the Queen, 2005. *Address:* c/o Buckingham Palace, SW1A 1AA. *Clubs:* Turf, Pratt's.

FORD, Sir Andrew (Russell), 3rd Bt *cr* 1929, of Westerdunes, Co. of East Lothian; Head of Sport and Leisure, 1974–96, Senior Lecturer in English, 1996–2003, Wiltshire College (formerly Chippenham College); *b* 29 June 1943; *s* of Sir Henry Russell Ford, 2nd Bt, TD and Mary Elizabeth (*d* 1997), *d* of late Godfrey F. Wright; *S* father, 1989; *m* 1968, Penelope Anne, *d* of Harry Relph; two *s* one *d*. *Educ:* Winchester; New Coll., Oxford (half-blue, athletics, 1962); Loughborough Coll. (DLC); London Univ. (BA external); Birmingham Univ. (MA external). Schoolmaster: Blairmore Sch., Aberdeens, 1967–71; St Peter's Sch., Cambridge, NZ, 1971–74. *Heir: s* Toby Russell Ford, *b* 11 Jan. 1973. *Address:* 20 Coniston Road, Chippenham, Wilts SN14 0PX. *T:* (01249) 655442.

FORD, Anna; broadcaster, BBC, 1989–2006; *b* 2 Oct. 1943; *d* of John Ford and Jean Beattie Winstanley; *m* 1st, 1970, Dr Alan Holland Bittles (marr. diss. 1976); 2nd, 1981, Charles Mark Edward Boxer (*d* 1988); two *d*. *Educ:* Manchester Univ. (BA Hons Econ 1966; DipAdultEd 1970). Work for students' interests, Manchester Univ., 1966–69; Lectr, Rupert Stanley Coll. of Further Educn, Belfast, 1970–72; Staff Tutor, Social Sci., and Staff Tutor, NI Reg., Open Univ., 1972–74; presenter and reporter: Granada TV, 1974–76; BBC Man Alive, 1976–77; BBC Tomorrow's World, 1977–78; newscaster, ITN, 1978–80; TV am, 1980–82; freelance broadcasting and writing, 1982–86; BBC news and current affairs, 1989–2006; presenter, The Garden Quiz, R4, 2008. Non-executive Director: Sainsbury's, 2006–; Amazing Gp, 2006–. Chair, Index on Censorship, 2005. Trustee: Royal Botanic Gardens, Kew, 1995–2002; Forum for the Future, 2006–. Chancellor, 2001–, Co-Chancellor, 2004–, Univ. of Manchester. FRGS 1990. Hon. Bencher, Middle Temple, 2002. Hon. LLD Manchester, 1998; DUniv Open, 1998. *Publication:* Men: a documentary, 1985. *Recreations:* gardening, music, walking, drawing.
See also Rev. Adam Ford.

FORD, Anthony; *see* Ford, J. A.

FORD, Antony, CMG 1997; HM Diplomatic Service, retired; Ambassador to Austria, 2000–03; *b* Bexley, 1 Oct. 1944; *s* of late William Ford and Grace Ford (*née* Smith); *m* 1970, Linda Gordon Joy; one *s* one *d*. *Educ:* St Dunstan's Coll., Catford; UCW, Aberystwyth (BA). Joined HM Diplomatic Service, 1967; Third, later Second, Sec., Bonn, 1968–71; Second Sec., Kuala Lumpur, 1971–73; First Secretary: FCO, 1973–77; Washington, 1977–81; FCO, 1981–84; Counsellor: East Berlin, 1984–87; FCO, 1987–90; Consul-Gen., San Francisco, 1990–94; Chm., CSSB, on secondment to RAS Agency, 1994–96; Minister, Berlin, 1996–99; on secondment to Andersen Consulting, 1999–2000. *Recreations:* reading, golf, cricket. *Club:* Morgan Sports Car.

FORD, Benjamin Thomas; DL; *b* 1 April 1925; *s* of Benjamin Charles Ford and May Ethel (*née* Moorton); *m* 1950, Vera Ada (*née* Fawcett-Fancet); two *s* one *d*. *Educ:* Rowan Road Central Sch., Surrey. Apprenticed as compositor, 1941. War Service, 1943–47, Fleet Air Arm (Petty Officer). Electronic Fitter/Wireman, 1951–64; Convener of Shop Stewards, 1955–64. Pres., Harwich Constituency Labour Party, 1955–63; Mem., Clacton UDC, 1959–62; Alderman Essex CC, 1959–65; JP Essex, 1962–67. MP (Lab) Bradford N, 1964–83; contested (Lab Ind.) Bradford N, 1983. Mem., H of C Select Cttee (Services), 1970–83 (Chm., Accom. and Admin Sub-Cttee, 1979–83); Chm., Jt Select Cttee on Sound Broadcasting, 1976–77; Chairman: British-Portuguese Parly Gp, 1965–83; British-Argentinian Parly Gp, 1974–81; British-Brazilian Parly Gp, 1974–79; British-Malaysian Parly Gp, 1975–83; British-Venezuelan Parly Gp, 1977–83; All-Party Wool Textile Parly Gp, 1974–83; Vice-Chairman: British-Latin American Parly Gp, 1974–79; PLP Defence Cttee, 1979–82; Mem. Exec. Cttee, IPU British Gp, 1971–83 (Chm., 1977–79); Sec., British-Namibian Parly Gp, 1980–83. Chm., Leeds NW Lib Dems, 1988–91; Pres., Leeds Fedn of Lib Dems, 1991–97. Bd Mem., Bradford & Northern Housing Assoc., 1975–95 (Chm., Yorks and Humberside Regl Cttee). President: English Shooting Council, 1996–2001 (Chm., 1982–96); English Target Shooting Fedn, 2001–04; Yorks Rifle Assoc., 2004– (Chm., 1999–2004); Vice-Pres., British Assoc. for Shooting and Conservation, 1983–; Mem. Council, Nat. Rifle Assoc., 1968–94 (Vice-Pres., 1984–). President: Yorks and Humberside Region, Mencap, 1986–91; Bradford Civic Soc., 1988–96. Freeman, City of London, 1979; Liveryman, Gunmakers' Co., 1978–99. DL W Yorks, 1982. Hon. FAIA 1983. Grand Officer, Order of the Southern Cross (Brazil), 1976. *Publication:* Piecework, 1960. *Recreations:* music, shooting, family, reading. *Address:* 9 Wynmore Crescent, Bramhope, Leeds LS16 9DH. *Clubs:* Idle Working Men's; East Ward Labour (Bradford).

FORD, Colin John, CBE 1993; lecturer, writer and broadcaster on films, theatre and photography; exhibition organiser; Chairman: Partnership Events & Entertainment, since 1999; Kraszna-Krausz Foundation, since 2003; *b* 13 May 1934; *s* of John William and Hélène Martha Ford; *m* 1st, 1961, Margaret Elizabeth Cordwell (marr. diss.); one *s* one *d*; 2nd, 1984, Susan Joan Frances Grayson; one *s*. *Educ:* Enfield Grammar Sch.; University Coll., Oxford (MA). Manager and Producer, Kidderminster Playhouse, 1958–60; Gen. Man., Western Theatre Ballet, 1960–62; Vis. Lectr in English and Drama, California State Univ. at Long Beach and UCLA (Univ. Extension), 1962–64; Dep. Curator, Nat. Film Archive, 1965–72. Organiser, 30th Anniv. Congress of Internat. Fedn of Film Archives, London, 1968; Dir, Cinema City Exhibn, 1970; Programme Dir, London Shakespeare Film Festival, 1972; Keeper of Film and Photography, Nat. Portrait Gall., 1972–81; founding Hd, Nat. Mus. of Photography, Film and Television, 1982–93; Dir, Nat. Mus. of Wales, then Nat. Museums & Galls of Wales, 1993–98. Vice-Pres., Julia Margaret Cameron Trust, 2005–. Hon. FRPS 1999. Hon. MA Bradford, 1989. *Film:* Masks and Faces, 1966 (BBC TV version, Omnibus, 1968). *Publications:* (with Roy Strong) An Early Victorian Album, 1974, 2nd edn 1977; The Cameron Collection, 1975; (principal contrib.) Oxford Companion to Film, 1975; (ed) Happy and Glorious: Six Reigns of Royal Photography, 1977; Rediscovering Mrs Cameron, 1979; People in Camera, 1979; (with Brian Harrison) A Hundred Years Ago (Britain in the 1880s), 1983; Portraits (Gallery of World Photography), 1983; (ed) The Story of Popular Photography, 1988; Lewis Carroll, 1998; André Kertész and the Avant Garde, 1999; (ed) Performance!, 2000; (with Julian Cox) Julia Margaret Cameron: the complete photographs, 2003; Julia Margaret Cameron: 19th century photographer of genius, 2003; (with Karl Steinorth): You Press the Button, We Do the Rest: the birth of snapshot photography, 1988; Lewis Carroll: photographs, 1991; Ferenc Berko: 60 Years of Photography, 1991; articles in many jls. *Recreations:* travel, music, small boats. *Address:* 7 Gentleman's Row, Enfield EN2 6PT.

FORD, Prof. David Frank, PhD; Regius Professor of Divinity and Fellow of Selwyn College, Cambridge University, since 1991; *b* 23 Jan. 1948; *s* of George Ford and Phyllis (*née* Woodman); *m* 1982, Deborah Perrin Hardy, *d* of late Rev. Prof. Daniel Wayne Hardy; one *s* two *d* (and one *d* decd). *Educ:* Trinity Coll. Dublin (BA (Mod) 1970); St John's Coll., Cambridge (MA 1976; PhD 1977); Yale Univ. (STM 1973); Tübingen Univ. Lectr in Theology, Birmingham Univ., 1976–91; Cambridge University: Chairman: Faculty Bd of Divinity, 1993–95; Mgt Cttee, Centre for Advanced Religious and Theol Studies, 1995–; Dir, Cambridge Inter-faith Prog., 2002–; Member: Arts and Humanities Personal Promotions Cttee, 2003–; Gen. Bd Adv. Cttee on Sen. Appts, 2005–. Mem., CUP Syndicate, 1993–2004. Pres., Soc. for Study of Theology, 1997–98. Member: World Econ. Forum Council of 100 Leaders, 2003–; AHRC Peer Review Coll., 2005–. Trustee, Center of Theological Inquiry, Princeton, 2007–; Mem., Bd of Advrs, John Templeton Foundn, 2008–. Hon. DD Birmingham, 2000. *Publications:* Barth and God's Story: biblical narrative and the theological method of Karl Barth in the Church Dogmatics, 1981; (with Daniel W. Hardy) Jubilate: Theology in praise, 1984; (with Frances M. Young) Meaning and Truth in 2 Corinthians, 1987; (ed) The Modern Theologians, vols I and II, 1989, 3rd edn 2005; (ed jtly) Essentials of Christian Community, 1996; The Shape of Living, 1997; Self and Salvation: being transformed, 1999; Theology: a very short introduction, 1999; (ed jtly) Jesus, 2002; (ed jtly and contrib.) Scripture and Theology: reading texts, seeking wisdom, 2003; (ed jtly) Fields of Faith: theology and religious studies for the twenty-first century, 2005; (ed jtly) The Promise of Scriptural Reasoning, 2006; Christian Wisdom: desiring God and learning in love, 2007; (ed jtly) Musics of Belonging: the poetry of Michael O'Siadhail, 2007; Shaping Theology: engagements in a religious and secular world, 2007. *Recreations:* gardening, poetry, drama, sports (especially ball games). *Address:* Faculty of Divinity, West Road, Cambridge CB3 9BS. *T:* (01223) 763031.

FORD, Sir David (Robert), KBE 1988 (OBE 1976); LVO 1975; Chief Secretary, Hong Kong Government, 1986–93; Chairman, PCCW (Europe), since 2003; Chairman, UK Broadband, since 2004; *b* 22 Feb. 1935; *s* of William Ewart and Edna Ford; *m* 1st, 1958, Elspeth Anne (*née* Muckart) (marr. diss. 1987); two *s* two *d*; 2nd, 1987, Gillian Petersen (*née* Monsarrat). *Educ:* Tauntons School. National Service, 1953–55; regular commn, RA, 1955; regimental duty, Malta, 1953–58; Lieut, UK, 1958–62; Captain, Commando Regt, 1962–66; active service: Borneo, 1964; Aden, 1966; Staff Coll., Quetta, 1967; seconded to Hong Kong Govt, 1967; retired from Army (Major), 1972. Dep. Dir, Hong Kong Govt Information Service, 1972–74, Dir, 1974–76; Dep. Sec., Govt Secretariat, Hong Kong, 1976; Under Sec., NI Office, 1977–79; Sec. for Information, Hong Kong Govt, 1979–80; Hong Kong Comr in London, 1980–81 and 1994–97; RCDS, 1982; Hong Kong Government: Dir of Housing, 1983–84; Sec. for Housing, 1985; Sec. for the Civil Service, 1985–86. Chm., Council for Protection of, subseq. Campaign to Protect, Rural England, 1998–2003. Vice-Pres., Rare Breeds Survival Trust, 2004–07. Chm., Hong Kong Soc., 2003–06. *Recreation:* rare breeds. *Address:* Culverwell Farm, Branscombe, Devon EX12 3DA.

FORD, Prof. Gary Ashley, FRCP; Professor of Pharmacology of Old Age, since 2000, and Director, Newcastle Clinical Research Centre, since 2005, Newcastle University; Director, UK Stroke Research Network, since 2005; *b* Coventry, 18 Nov. 1958; *s* of Ashley Greg Ford and Eileen Mary Ford (*née* Painter); *m* 1987, Angela Mary Lewis; two *s* one *d*. *Educ:* King Henry VIII Sch., Coventry; Clare Coll., Cambridge (BA 1979); King's Coll. Hosp. Med. Sch., London (BA Hons; MB BChir 1983). MRCP 1985; FRCP 1996. Sen. House Officer, Addenbrooke's Hosp., Cambridge, 1983–85; Registrar, Glos Royal Hosp., 1985–87; Post-doctoral Res. Fellow in Clin. Pharmacol., Stanford Univ., Calif, 1987–89; Sen. Registrar in Geriatric and Gen. Medicine (Clin. Pharmacol.), Freeman Hosp., Newcastle upon Tyne, 1989–92; Sen. Lectr and Cons. Physician in Clin. Pharmacol. and Geriatric Medicine, 1992–2000, Hon. Consultant Physician in Stroke Medicine, 2000–, Univ. of Newcastle upon Tyne and Freeman Hosp. *Recreations:* music, cooking, travel. *Address:* Clinical Research Centre, 4th Floor Leazes Wing, Royal Victoria Infirmary, Newcastle upon Tyne NE1 4LP. *T:* (0191) 222 7744, *Fax:* (0191) 282 0064.

FORD, Geoffrey; *see* Ford, M. G.

FORD, Dr Gillian Rachel, (Mrs N. I. MacKenzie), CB 1981; FRCP, FFPH; Medical Director, Marie Curie Cancer Care (formerly Marie Curie Memorial Foundation), 1990–97; *b* 18 March 1934; *d* of Cecil Ford and Grace Ford; *m* 1988, Prof. Norman I. MacKenzie. *Educ:* Clarendon Sch., Abergele; St Hugh's Coll., Oxford; St Thomas' Hosp., London. MA, BM, BCh; FFCM 1976; FRCP 1985. Junior hospital posts, St Thomas', Oxford, Reading, 1959–64; Medical Officer, Min. of Health, 1965, Sen. Med. Officer, 1968; SPMO, 1974–77, Dep. Chief MO (Dep. Sec.), 1977–89, DHSS, later Dept of Health; on secondment as Dir of Studies, St Christopher's Hospice, Sydenham, 1985–88; Med. Sec., Standing Cttee on Postgrad. Med. Educn, 1989–90. Vice Pres., St Christopher's Hospice, 1999–; Vice Chm., Hospice in the Weald, 1999–2003. *Publications:* papers on health services research, terminal care, audit, palliative medicine and care in sundry med. publications. *Recreations:* music, ski-ing, children's literature, gardening. *Address:* 20 Winterbourne Mews, Lewes, E Sussex BN7 1HG. *T:* (01273) 479206.

FORD, Glyn; *see* Ford, J. G.

FORD, Harrison; actor; *b* Chicago, 13 July 1942; *m* 1st, Mary Ford (marr. diss. 1978); two *s*; 2nd, 1983, Melissa Mathison (marr. diss. 2004), screenwriter; one *s* one *d*. *Educ:* Ripon Coll., Wis. *Films* include: Dead Heat on a Merry-Go-Round, 1966; Journey to Shiloh, 1968; Getting Straight, 1970; The Conversation, 1974; American Graffiti, 1974; Star Wars, 1977; Force 10 from Navarone, 1978; Apocalypse Now, 1979; The Frisco Kid, 1979; The Empire Strikes Back, 1980; Raiders of the Lost Ark, 1981; Blade Runner, 1982; Return of the Jedi, 1983; Indiana Jones and the Temple of Doom, 1984; Witness, 1985; Mosquito Coast, 1986; Frantic, 1988; Indiana Jones and the Last Crusade, 1989; Presumed Innocent, 1990; Regarding Henry, 1991; The Fugitive, 1992; Patriot Games, 1992; Clear and Present Danger, 1994; Sabrina, 1995; Devil's Own, 1996; Air Force One, 1997; Six Days, Seven Nights, 1998; Random Hearts, 1999; What Lies Beneath, 2000; K-19: The Widowmaker, 2002; Hollywood Homicide, 2003; Firewall, 2006; Indiana Jones and the Kingdom of the Crystal Skull, 2008; numerous TV appearances, including The Virginian, Gunsmoke, Ironside. *Address:* 10279 Century Woods Drive, Los Angeles, CA 90067, USA.

FORD, Prof. Sir Hugh, Kt 1975; FRS 1967; FREng; Professor of Mechanical Engineering, 1969–80, Professor Emeritus, since 1980, Pro-Rector, 1978–80, University of London (Imperial College of Science and Technology); Chairman, Sir Hugh Ford & Associates Ltd, since 1982; *b* 16 July 1913; *s* of Arthur and Constance Ford; *m* 1st, 1942, Wynyard (*d* 1991), *d* of Major F. B. Scholfield; two *d*; 2nd, 1993, Mrs Thelma Jensen. *Educ:* Northampton Sch.; City and Guilds Coll., Univ. of London. DSc (Eng); PhD. Practical trng at GWR Locomotive Works, 1931–36; researches into heat transfer, 1936–39; R&D Engrg, Imperial Chemical Industries, Northwich, 1939–42; Chief Engr, Technical Dept, British Iron and Steel Fedn, 1942–45, then Head of Mechanical Working Div., British Iron and Steel Research Assoc., 1945–47; Exec. Dir, Paterson Engrg Ltd, 1947–48; Reader in Applied Mechanics, Univ. of London (Imp. Coll. of Science and Technology), 1948–51, Prof., 1951–69; Head of Dept of Mech. Engineering, 1965–78. Mem. Bd of Governors, Imperial Coll., 1982–89. Technical Dir, Davy-Ashmore Group, 1968–71; Director: Ford & Dain Research Ltd, 1972–93; Alfred Herbert Ltd, 1972–79; Air Liquide UK Ltd, 1979–95; Ricardo Consulting Engrs Ltd, 1980–88; Chm., Adv. Bd, Prudential Portfolio Managers, 1985–88; Mem., Adv. Bd, Brown and Root (UK), 1983–92. John Player Lectr, 1973, Hugh Ford Management Lectr, 1988, IMechE. First Pres., Inst. of Metals, 1985–87 (merger of Inst. of Metallurgists and Metals Soc.); President: Section 6, British Assoc., 1975–76; Welding Inst., 1983–85; Founder Fellow, Fellowship (later Royal Acad.) of Engineering, 1976 (Vice-Pres., 1981–83, Mem. Council, 1986–92); Member: Council, IMechE (Vice-Pres., 1972, 1975, Sen. Vice-Pres., 1976, Pres., 1977–78); SRC, 1968–72 (Chm. Engineering Bd); Council, Royal Soc., 1973–74; ARC, 1976–81. FICE; Whitworth Schol.; FCGI; FIC 1982; Sen. Fellow, RCA, 1987. Foreign Mem., Finnish Acad. of Technology, 1979. Hon. MASME, 1980; Hon. FIMechE 1984; Hon. FIChemE 1987. Hon. DSc: Salford, 1976; QUB, 1977; Aston, 1978; Bath, 1978; Sheffield, 1984; Sussex, 1990. Thomas Hawksley Gold Medallist, IMechE, 1948, for researches into rolling of metals; Robertson Medal, Inst. of Metals, 1954; James Alfred Ewing Gold Medal, ICE, 1982; James Watt Internat. Gold Medal, 1985. *Publications:* Advanced Mechanics of Materials, 1963; papers to Royal Soc., IMechE, Iron and Steel Inst., Inst. of Metals, foreign societies, etc. *Recreations:* gardening, music, model engineering. *Address:* 18 Shrewsbury House, Cheyne Walk, SW3 5LN; Shamley Cottage, Stroud Lane, Shamley Green, Surrey GU5 0ST. *Club:* Athenæum.

FORD, James Allan, CB 1978; MC 1946; *b* 10 June 1920; 2nd *s* of Douglas Ford and Margaret Duncan (*née* Allan); *m* 1948, Isobel Dunnett; one *s* one *d. Educ:* Royal High School, Edinburgh; University of Edinburgh. Served 1940–46, Capt. Royal Scots. Entered Civil Service, 1938; Asst Sec., Dept of Agriculture and Fisheries for Scotland, 1958; Registrar Gen. for Scotland, 1966–69; Principal Establishment Officer, Scottish Office, 1969–79. A Trustee, Nat. Lib. of Scotland, 1981–91. *Publications:* The Brave White Flag, 1961; Season of Escape, 1963; A Statue for a Public Place, 1965; A Judge of Men, 1968; The Mouth of Truth, 1972. *Address:* 6 Hillpark Court, Edinburgh EH4 7BE. *T:* (0131) 336 5398. *Club:* Royal Scots (Edinburgh).

FORD, (James) Glyn; Member (Lab) South West Region, England, European Parliament, since 1999 (Greater Manchester East, 1984–99); *b* 28 Jan. 1950; *s* of late Ernest Benjamin Ford and Matilda Alberta Ford (*née* James); *m* 1st, 1973, Hazel Nancy Mahy (marr. diss. 1992); one *d*; 2nd, 1992, Daniela Zannelli (marr. diss. 2005); one *s. Educ:* Marling; Reading Univ. (BSc Geol. with Soil Sci.); UCL (MSc Marine Earth Sci.); Manchester Univ. Undergraduate Apprentice, BAC, 1967–68; Course Tutor in Oceanography, Open Univ., 1976–78; Teaching Asst, UMIST, 1977–78; Res. Fellow, Sussex Univ., 1978–79; Manchester University: Res. Asst, 1976–77; Res. Fellow, 1979; Lectr, 1979–80; Sen. Res. Fellow, Prog. of Policy Res. in Engrg Sci. and Technol., 1980–84; Hon. Vis. Res. Fellow, 1984–. Vis. Prof., Tokyo Univ., 1983. Mem., Lab Party NEC, 1989–93 (Member: Sci. and Technol. Policy Sub-Cttee, 1981–83; Review Gp on Trade Union/Labour Party Links, 1992–93). European Parliament: Chm., Cttee of Inquiry into Growth of Racism and Fascism in Europe, 1984–86; Vice-Chm., Sub-Cttee on Security and Disarmament, 1987–89; first Vice-Pres., Group of Party of European Socialists, 1989–93; Vice Chm., Delgn, Japanese Diet, 1992–94, 1996–99; Leader, 1989–93, Dep. Leader, 1993–94, Eur. PLP. Mem., Consultative Cttee on Racism and Xenophobia, Council of Ministers of EU, 1994–98. EU Chief Observer: Indonesian elections, 2004; Aceh, 2006–07. Treas., Anti Nazi League. Mem., Steering Cttee, UNITE Against Fascism. Contested (Lab), Hazel Grove, 1987. *Publications:* (with C. Niblett and L. Walker) The Future for Ocean Technology, 1987; Fascist Europe, 1992; The Evolution of a European, 1994; Changing States, 1996; Making European Progress, 2002. *Recreation:* Asia. *Address:* (office) Belle Vue Centre, Belle Vue Road, Cinderford GL14 2AB. *T:* (01594) 827193. *Clubs:* Groucho, Soho House.

FORD, John; *see* Ford, S. J.

FORD, (John) Anthony, OBE 1998; Director, Crafts Council, 1988–99 (Deputy Director, 1985–88); *b* 28 April 1938; *s* of Frank Everatt Ford and Dorothy Mary Ford; *m* 1st, 1963, Caroline Rosemary Wharrad (marr. diss.); one *d*; 2nd, 1984, Sandra Edith Williams. *Educ:* Epsom Coll.; St Edmund Hall, Oxford (MA). Admitted Solicitor, 1963. Dir, Art Services Grants, 1974–79; Crafts Council, 1979–99. Mem., Visual Arts Adv. Cttee, British Council, 1988–99. Vice-Pres. for Europe, World Crafts Council, 1987–93 (Advr, 1993–). Mem., Fabric Adv. Cttee, Rochester Cathedral, 1990–2004. Member: Court, RCA, 1989–99; Court of Govs, London Inst., 1993–2000; Board of Governors: Kent Inst. of Art and Design, 2001–05 (Dep. Chm., 2002–05); Univ. (formerly UC) for the Creative Arts at Canterbury, Epsom, Farnham, Maidstone and Rochester, 2005–. Trustee: Craft Pottery Charitable Trust, 1991– (Chm., 2004–); Idlewild Trust, 2000–. *Recreations:* theatre, cinema. *Address:* 64 Wood Vale, SE23 3ED. *T:* (020) 8693 4837.

FORD, Sir John (Archibald), KCMG 1977 (CMG 1967); MC 1945; HM Diplomatic Service, retired; *b* 19 Feb. 1922; *s* of Ronald Mylne Ford and Margaret Jesse Coghill, Newcastle-under-Lyme, Staffs; *m* 1956, Emaline Burnette (*d* 1989), Leesville, Virginia; two *d. Educ:* St Michael's Coll., Tenbury; Sedbergh Sch., Yorks; Oriel Coll., Oxford. Served in Royal Artillery, 1942–46 (temp. Major); demobilised, 1947. Joined Foreign (subseq. Diplomatic) Service, 1947. Third Sec., British Legation, Budapest, 1947–49; Third Sec. and a Resident Clerk, FO, 1949–52; Private Sec. to Permanent Under-Sec. of State, FO, 1952–54; HM Consul, San Francisco, 1954–56; seconded to HM Treasury, 1956–59; attended Course at Administrative Staff Coll., 1959; First Sec. and Head of Chancery, British Residency, Bahrain, 1959–61; Asst, FO Personnel Dept, 1961–63; Asst, FO Establishment and Organisation Dept, 1963; Head of Diplomatic Service Establishment and Organisation Dept, 1964–66; Counsellor (Commercial), Rome, 1966–70; Asst Under-Sec., FCO, 1970–71; Consul-Gen., New York, and Dir-Gen., British Trade Develt in USA, 1971–75; Ambassador to Indonesia, 1975–78; British High Comr in Canada, 1978–81. Lay Administrator, Guildford Cathedral, 1982–84. Mem., Exec. Cttee, VSO, 1982–87; Chm. of Trustees, Voluntary and Christian Service, 1985–88; Chm., AIDS Care Educn and Trng, 1989–93; Trustee: World in Need, 1987–95; Opportunity Trust, 1991–96; Opportunity Internat. (USA), 1994–95. *Publications:* Honest to Christ, 1988; The Answer is the Christ of AD 2000, 1996; Introducing the Young to the Christ of AD 2000, 1999; Searching for the Christ of AD 2000 in Saint John's Gospel, 1999; Seeking the Christ of AD 2000 through Francis of Assisi and Brother Lawrence, 1999; Praying in the Mystical Body of the Christ of AD 2000, 1999; Spiritual Exercises for AD 2000, 1999; Looking for the Christ of AD 2000 in the Recorded Sayings of Jesus, 2000; God's Project People, 2002. *Recreations:* walking, gardening, sailing. *Address:* Admiral 633, 8750 South Ocean Drive, Jensen Beach, FL 34957–2128, USA; 51 Forest Avenue #133, Old Greenwich, CT 06870, USA.

FORD, Rt Rev. John Frank; *see* Plymouth, Bishop Suffragan of.

FORD, (Martin) Geoffrey; Librarian, 1990–2002, and Director of Information Services, 1999–2002, University of Bristol; *b* 24 Jan. 1942; *s* of George Frederick Ford and Muriel (*née* Dowding); *m* 1974, Elizabeth Jill Barker. *Educ:* Sir Joseph Williamson's Mathematical Sch., Rochester; Leicester Univ. (BSc 1963); Sheffield Univ. (DipLib 1965; MSc 1973). MCLIP (ALA 1967). Liby Asst, Leicester Univ., 1963–64; Durham University: Asst Librarian, 1965–67; Sen. Res. Asst, 1968–69; Res. Associate, Bristol Univ., 1969–72; Asst Dir, Liby Res. Unit, Lancaster Univ., 1972–75; Sen. Res. Officer and Dir, Centre for Res. on User Studies, Sheffield Univ., 1976–78; Southampton University: Sub-librarian, 1978–87; Dep. Librarian, 1987–89. Member: Adv. Council, British Library, 1995–2000 (Member: Res. Cttee, 1990–94; Adv. Cttee on Bibliographical Services, 1991–94); SCONUL Council, 1992–2001 (Vice Chm., 1996–98; Chm., 1998–2000); Vice-Chm.,

SW Regl Liby System, 1999–2002 (Chm., 1998–99). (Jtly) Robinson Medal, LA, 197? *Publications:* Review of Methods for Determining the Use of Library Stock, 1990; re reports, articles and reviews in learned jls. *Recreations:* travelling on trains, gentle walking listening to jazz, naval and transport history. *Address:* 21 Redland Grove, Bristol BS6 6PT

FORD, Peter George Tipping; Secretary, Medical Protection Society, 1983–90; *b* 1 Sept. 1931; *s* of late Raymond Eustace Ford, CBE; *m* 1958, Nancy Elizabeth Procter; fou *d. Educ:* Epsom Coll.; St Bartholomew's Hosp. Med. Coll., Univ. of London (MB, BS MRCGP, DObstRCOG. Nat. Service, RAMC, 1957–59. Gen. practice, Hyth 1960–68; Asst Sec., Med. Protection Soc., 1968–72; Dep. Sec., 1972–83. Sec., Jt Cc ordinating Cttee, UK Defence Organizations, 1985–89. Mem., Soc. of Apothecarie FRSocMed. Medal of Honour, Med. Defence Soc. of Queensland, 1984. *Publication* contribs to medico-legal periodicals. *Recreations:* baroque choral music, gardening, bridg *Address:* Braeside Cottage, Cannongate Road, Hythe, Kent CT21 5PT. *T:* (0130? 267896.

FORD, Peter John, CBE 1998; Chairman: Reliance Integrated Services, 2000–02 London Transport, 1994–98; *b* 21 Nov. 1938; *s* of John Frederick Arthur Ford and Haze Mary Ford; *m* 1966, Olivia Mary Temple; two *s* two *d. Educ:* King's Sch., Canterbury Christ Church, Oxford (MA Chem.); Harvard Business Sch. (MBA). With Shell Chemic Co., 1961–65; McKinsey & Co., NY, 1967–70; Exec. Dir, Sterling Guarantee Trus 1970–85; Exec. Dir, P&OSNCo., 1985–93. Director: Countrywide Assured Gi 1994–2002; Palliser Furniture, Winnipeg, Canada, 2001–; Cambridge Biostability Lte 2004–. Pres., Sheffield Chamber of Commerce, 1985–86; Dep. Pres., London Chambe of Commerce and Industry, 1998–2000. Governor: Kingston Univ., 1993–98 Collingwood Coll., 2001–. *Recreations:* walking, music. *Address:* 16 The Drive Wimbledon, SW20 8TG. *T:* (020) 8944 7207. *Club:* Royal Automobile.

FORD, Peter William; HM Diplomatic Service; Ambassador to Syria, 2003–06; *b* 27 Jun 1947; *s* of Alec and Gertrude Ford; *m* 1st, 1974, Aurora Garcia Mingo (marr. diss. 1992 2nd, 1992, Alganesh Haile Beyene. *Educ:* Helsby Grammar Sch.; Queen's Coll., Oxfor (BA Hons). FCO, 1971–72; Beirut, 1972–73; Second, then First, Sec., Cairo, 1974–78 Eur. Integration Dept, FCO, 1978–80; First Sec., Paris, 1980–85; Asst Hd, EC Dep FCO, 1985–87; Counsellor (Commercial), Riyadh, 1987–90; Vis. Fellow, Harvard Univ 1990–91; Dep. High Comr and Counsellor (Econ. and Commercial), Singapore 1991–94; Hd, Near East and N Africa Dept, FCO, 1994–99; Ambassador to Bahrain 1999–2003. Internat. Fellow, Brandeis Univ., 2001–03. *Recreations:* sport, reading, trave *Address:* c/o Foreign and Commonwealth Office, King Charles Street, SW1A 2AH.

FORD, Gen. Sir Robert (Cyril), GCB 1981 (KCB 1977; CB 1973); CBE 1971 (MBI 1958); Vice-Chairman, Commonwealth War Graves Commission, 1989–9 (Commissioner, 1981–93); *b* 29 Dec. 1923; *s* of late John Stranger Ford and Gladys Ford Yealmpton, Devon; *m* 1st, 1949, Jean Claudia Pendlebury (*d* 2002), *d* of late Gp Capt Claude Pendlebury, MC, TD; one *s*; 2nd, 2003, Caroline Margaret Peerless (*née* Leather *Educ:* Musgrave's Coll. War of 1939–45: commissioned into 4th/7th Royal Dragoo Guards, from Sandhurst, 1943; served with Regt throughout NW European campaigr 1944–45 (despatches) and in Egypt and Palestine, 1947–48 (despatches). Instructor, Mor OCS, 1949–50; Training Officer, Scottish Horse (TA), 1952–54; Staff Coll., Camberley 1955; GSO 2 Mil. Ops, War Office, 1956–57; Sqdn Ldr 4/7 RDG, 1958–59; Bde Majo 20th Armoured Bde, 1960–61; Brevet Lt-Col, 1962; Sqdn Ldr, 4/7 RDG, 1962–63 GSO1 to Chief of Defence Staff, 1964–65; commanded 4/7 RDG in S Arabia an N Ireland, 1966–67; Comdr, 7th Armd Bde, 1968–69; Principal Staff Officer to Chief o Defence Staff, 1970–71; Cmdr Land Forces, N Ireland, 1971–73; Comdt, RMA Sandhurst, 1973–76; Military Secretary, 1976–78; Adjutant-General, 1978–81; ADC General to the Queen, 1980–81; Governor, Royal Hosp., Chelsea, 1981–87. Colone Commandant: RAC, 1980–82; SAS Regt, 1980–85; Col 4th/7th Royal Dragoon Gds 1984–88. President: Services Kinema Corp., 1978–81; Army Boxing Assoc., 1978–8 Chm., 1981–87, and Pres., 1986–97, Army Benevolent Fund; Chm., Royal Cambridg Home for Soldiers' Widows, 1981–87; Nat. Pres., Forces Help Soc. and Lord Rober Workshops, 1981–91. Governor, Corps of Commissionaires, 1981–94. Freeman, City c London, 1981. CCMI. *Recreations:* watching cricket, tennis, war studies, theatre. *Clubs* Cavalry and Guards, MCC.

FORD, Robert Stanley; HM Diplomatic Service, retired; *b* 30 Nov. 1929; *s* of lat Robert Hempstead Ford and Janet Mabel Elliot; *m* 1957, Cynthia Valerie Arscott, *d* of lat Ronald Prowse Arscott, Bexhill-on-Sea, Sussex; one *s* two *d. Educ:* Daniel Stewart's Coll Edinburgh; Univ. of Edinburgh (MA). Joined HM Diplomatic Service, 1949; HM Force 1949; FCO, 1951; Third Sec., Moscow, 1955; Consul, Dakar, 1958; FCO, 1959 Information Officer, NY, 1963; First Sec., Managua, 1965; Consul, Naples, 1968; FCO 1972; Consul-Gen., Madrid, 1978; FCO, 1982; Counsellor (Admin), Paris, 1984–86 *Recreations:* music, photography, gardening, travel. *Address:* 20 Heatherbank, Hayward Heath, W Sussex RH16 1HY. *T:* (01444) 455321.

FORD, Robert Webster, CBE 1982; HM Diplomatic Service, retired; *b* 27 March 1923 *s* of late Robert Ford; *m* 1956, Monica Florence Tebbett; two *s. Educ:* Alleyne's Sch Served RAF, 1939–45. Served with British Mission, Lhasa, Tibet and Political Agency i Sikkim and Bhutan, 1945–47; joined Tibetan Govt Service, 1947; advised on and installe Tibet's first radio communication system and broadcasting stn; travelled extensively i Northern and Eastern Tibet, 1947–50; taken prisoner during Chinese Occupation o Tibet, 1950; imprisoned in China, 1950–55; freelance writer and broadcaster on Chines and Tibetan affairs, 1955; entered Foreign Service, 1956; 2nd Sec., Saigon, 1957–58; 1s Sec. (Information), Djakarta, 1959; Washington, 1960–62; FO, 1962–67; Consul-Gen. Tangier, 1967–70; Counsellor, 1970; Consul-General: Luanda, 1970–74; Bordeaux 1974–78; Gothenburg, 1978–80; Geneva, 1980–83. *Publication:* Captured in Tibet, 1956 repr. 1990. *Recreations:* ski-ing, gardening, travelling. *Address:* Cedar Garth, Latimer Road Monken Hadley, Barnet, Herts EN5 5NU. *Clubs:* Royal Commonwealth Society, Roya Geographical Society.

FORD, Roy Arthur, MA; Director of Visits, Canterbury Cathedral, 1986–90; *b* 10 Ma 1925; *s* of Arthur Ford and Minnie Elizabeth Ford; *m* 1965, Christine Margaret Moore two *s. Educ:* Collyer's Sch., Horsham; Corpus Christi Coll., Cambridge (Scholar; 1st Cl Pts I and II, History Tripos; BA 1949, MA 1971). Asst Master: Uppingham Sch., 1951–54 Tonbridge Sch., 1954–66; Uppingham Sch., (also Head of History and Sixth Form Master), 1966–71; Headmaster: Southwell Minster Grammar Sch., 1971–75; King's Sch. Rochester, 1975–86. *Recreations:* walking, travel, music. *Address:* North Street Farmhouse Sheldwich, Kent ME13 0LN. *T:* (01795) 537614.

FORD, (Sydney) John, CBE 1999; PhD; Chief Executive, Driver and Vehicle Licensin Agency 1995–2000; *b* 23 Aug. 1936; *s* of Sidney James Ford and Barbara Ford (*née* Essenhigh); *m* 1st, 1960, Beryl Owen (marr. diss. 1990); two *s*; 2nd, 1990, Morag Munro *Educ:* Bromsgrove High Sch.; Swansea Grammar Sch.; UC Swansea, Univ. of Wales (BS Maths; PhD Maths; Hon. Fellow, 1999). British Aluminium Co. plc, 1966–82 (Dir 1977–82; Man. Dir, 1982); Dep. Man. Dir, British Alcan Aluminium plc, 1982–85; UK

Ops Dir, Williams Hldgs plc, 1985–88; Dir, European Distrib., Christian Salvesen plc, 1988–93; Chief Exec., Driving Standards Agency, 1993–94. Chm., Ofwat CSC Wales, subseq. WaterVoice Wales, 2001–05; Mem., Consumer Council for Water, Midlands, 2005–07. *Recreations:* watercolour and pastel painting, qualified Rugby referee and coach. *Address:* Shenval, 1 Evertons Close, Droitwich Spa WR9 8AE. *T:* (01905) 776000.

FORD, William Clay, Jr; Executive Chairman, Ford Motor Company, since 2006 (Director, since 1988; Chairman, 1999; Chief Executive, 2001–06); *b* Detroit, 3 May 1957; *m*. *Educ:* Princeton Univ. (BA 1979); MIT (Alfred P. Sloan Fellow, 1983–84, MBA 1984). Ford Motor Company: Product Planning Analyst, Advanced Vehicle Develt, Design Center, then Manufg Engr, Automobile Assembly Div., subseq. NY Zone Manager, Ford Div., 1979–82; Mktg Strategy Analyst, N Amer. Automobile Ops, and Advertising Specialist, Ford Div., 1982–83; Internat. Finance Specialist, 1984–85; Planning Manager, Car Product Develt, 1985–86; Dir, Commercial Vehicle Mktg, Ford of Europe, 1986–87; Chm. and Man. Dir, Ford of Switzerland, 1987–89; Manager, Heavy Truck Engrg and Manufg, Ford Truck Ops, 1989–90; Dir, 1990–91, Exec. Dir, 1991–92, Business Strategy, Ford Auto Gp; Gen. Manager, Climate Control Div., 1992–94; Vice Pres., Commercial Truck Vehicle Center, Ford Automotive Ops, 1994–95; Chm., Finance Cttee, 1995–99. Chm., Bd of Trustees, Henry Ford Mus. and Greenfield Village; Trustee, Henry Ford Health System; Chairman: Detroit Renaissance Exec. Commn; Economic Club of Detroit; Vice Chm., Detroit Lions (prof. football team); Member: Global Leaders for Tomorrow, World Econ. Forum; NFL Finance Cttee; NFL Properties Cttee. *Address:* Ford Motor Company, One American Road, Dearborn, MI 48126–2798, USA. *T:* (313) 3223000.

FORDE, Helen, PhD; FSA; archivist; lecturer; *b* Oxford, 26 May 1941; *d* of Antony Andrewes and Alison Andrewes (*née* Hope); *m* 1962, Thomas Middleton Forde; one *s* one *d*. *Educ:* Oxford High Sch. for Girls; University Coll. London (BA Hist. 1962); Univ. of Liverpool (DAA 1968); Univ. of Leicester (PhD 1977). FSA 2001. Archivist, Nottingham City, 1970–73; Urban Res. Asst, Council for British Archaeol., 1973–75; Archivist, Liby of the Soc. of Friends, 1978–79; Public Record Office: Asst Keeper, 1979–2001; Head: Liby and Mus., 1979–82; Conservation Dept, 1982–92; Preservation Services, 1992. Extra mural tutor: Nottingham Univ., 1970–73; London Univ., 1975–89; Lectr, Sch. of Liby, Archive and Inf. Studies, 1989–2007, Vis. Prof., 2008, UCL. Society of Archivists: Chm., 1993–95; Pres., 2002–05; Vice Pres., 2005–. Chm., Preservation Cttee, 1992–2000, Mem., Cttee of Prog. Mgt, 2000–04, Internat. Council on Archives; Museums, Libraries and Archives Council: Chm., Designation Panel, 2004–; Chm., E Midlands, 2005–; Mem. Bd, 2007–; Member: Northants Archives Panel, 1994; (and Vice Chm.) Lincoln Cath. Liby Council, 2001–06; (and Chm.) Expert Panel for Mus, Libraries and Archives, Heritage Lottery Fund, 2001–05; British Postal Mus. and Archive, 2001– (Vice Chm., 2007–); Documentary Heritage Review of C of E, 2004–05; Trustee, Marc Fitch Fund, 2001–. Chm., Banbury Histl Soc., 2008–. *Publications:* Domesday Preserved, 1986; Preserving Archives, 2007; contrib. archive and liby jls; ed professional works and online information sources. *Recreations:* music, gardening, travelling. *Address:* Lovells, The Square, Kings Sutton, Banbury OX17 3RE. *T:* (01295) 811247; *e-mail:* helen.forde@lovells-online.co.uk.

FORDE, Martin Andrew; QC 2006; *b* 1961; *s* of Ralph and Cynthia Forde; *m* 2004, Nadège Vidal; one *s* one *d*. *Educ:* Langley Grammar Sch.; Brasenose Coll., Oxford (BA Hons Juris). Called to the Bar, Middle Temple, 1984 (Harmsworth Exhibnr, 1983); in practice, specialising in professional negligence, employment, professional regulatory and public law. *Recreations:* sport, music, travel. *Address:* 1 Crown Office Row, Temple, EC4Y 7HH; *e-mail:* martin.forde@1cor.com.

FORDE, (Mary Marguerite) Leneen, AC 1993; Chancellor, Griffith University, Queensland, since 2000; Governor of Queensland, 1992–97; *b* 12 May 1935; *d* of John Alfred Kavanagh and Evlyn Philomena Kavanagh (*née* Bujold); *m* 1st, 1955, Francis Gerard Forde (*d* 1966), *s* of Rt Hon. Francis Michael Forde, PC; three *s* two *d*; 2nd, 1983, (Albert) Angus McDonald (*d* 1999). *Educ:* Lisgar Collegiate, Ottawa (Dip.); Univ. of Queensland (LLB). Student Med. Lab. Technician, Ottawa Gen. Hosp., 1952–53; Med. Lab. Technician, Drs Rousell and Gagne, Ottawa, 1953–54; Haematol. Dept, Royal Brisbane Hosp., 1954–56; medical lab. work, 1956–58; articled Law Clerk, Alexander McGillivray, 1969–70; Solicitor, Cannan & Peterson, 1971–74; Partner, Sly, Weigall, Cannan & Peterson, subseq. Deakins, 1974–92. Comr, Royal Commn of Inquiry into Abuse of Children in Queensland Instns, 1998–99; Nat. Chm., Australian Defence Reserves Support Council, 2002–05. Board Member: St Leo's Coll., 1998–2000; Brisbane Coll. of Theol., 1999–2000; Brisbane City Council Arts and Envmt Trust, 1999–2000; Qld Ballet, 2000–; Qld Govt Forde Foundn, 2000–07; Qld Community Foundn, 2008–; All Hallow's Sch., 2008–. Founder, Qld Women Lawyers' Assoc., 1976; Member: Qld Law Soc., 1971–; Women Chiefs of Enterprises Internat., 1989–; Zonta Club of Brisbane Inc., 1971–; President: Zonta Internat., 1990–92; Scout Assoc. of Aust., 1997–2003 (Vice-Pres., 2003–). Patron, Nat. Pioneer Women's Hall of Fame, 1999–. Paul Harris Fellow, Rotary Club of Brisbane, 1990; Woman of Substance Award, Qld Girl Guides' Assoc., 1990; Queenslander of the Year, 1991; Queensland Great, 2007. DUniv: Griffith, 1992; Qld Univ. of Technology, 1993; Australian Catholic, 2000; Southern Qld, 2000; Hon. DLitt Queensland, 1996. DStJ 1992. *Publication:* Queensland Annual Law Review, 1991, 1992. *Recreations:* theatre, art, music, ballet, surfing. *Address:* Griffith University, Kessels Road, Nathan, Qld 4111, Australia.

FORDER, Ven. Charles Robert; Archdeacon Emeritus, Diocese of York, since 1974; *b* 6 Jan. 1907; *s* of late Henry Forder, Worstead, Norfolk; *m* 1933, Myra, *d* of late Harry Peat, Leeds; no *c*. *Educ:* Paston Sch., North Walsham; Christ's Coll., Cambridge (Exhibnr and Prizeman, 1926; 1st Cl. Math. Trip. Part I, 1926, BA (Sen. Opt. Part II) 1928, MA 1932); Ridley Hall, Cambridge. Curate: St Peter's, Hunslet Moor, 1930–33; Burley, 1933–34; Vicar: Holy Trinity, Wibsey, 1934–40; St Clement's, Bradford, 1940–47; Organising Sec., Bradford Church Forward Movement Appeal, 1945–47; Vicar of Drypool, 1947–55; Rector of Routh and Vicar of Wawne, 1955–57; Canon, and Prebendary of Fenton, York Minster, 1957–76; Rector of Sutton-on-Derwent, 1957–63; Rector of Holy Trinity, Micklegate, York, 1963–66; Archdeacon of York, 1957–72. Chaplain to HM Prison, Hull, 1950–53; Proctor in Convocation, 1954–72; Organising Sec., Diocesan Appeal, 1955–76; Church Comr, 1958–73. *Publications:* A History of the Paston Grammar School, 1934, 2nd edn 1975; The Parish Priest at Work, 1947; Synods in Action, 1970; Churchwardens in Church and Parish, 1976; contrib. to Encyclopædia Britannica. *Recreations:* reading and writing. *Address:* Dulverton Hall, Esplanade, Scarborough YO11 2AR. *T:* (01723) 340112.

FORDHAM, His Honour (John) Jeremy; a Circuit Judge, 1986–99; *b* 18 April 1933; *s* of John Hampden Fordham, CBE and Rowena Langran; *m* 1962, Rose Anita (*née* Brandon), *d* of Philip Brandon, Wellington, New Zealand; one *s* one *d*. *Educ:* Gresham's Sch.; Univ. of New Zealand. LLB (NZ). Merchant Navy, 1950–55 (2nd Mate (Foreign Going) Cert.); labourer, fireman etc, 1955–60; Barrister and Solicitor, New Zealand, 1960–64; called to Bar, Inner Temple, 1965; practised 1965–71, 1976–78; Sen. Magistrate, Gilbert and Ellice Islands, 1971–75; a Metropolitan Stipendiary Magistrate, 1978–86; a Recorder, 1986; a Dep. Circuit Judge, 1999–2001. Legal Chm., Immigration Appeal Tribunal, 1999–; Asst Surveillance Comr, 2001–07. *Recreations:* boats, games. *Club:* Garrick.

FORDHAM, Michael John; QC 2006; *b* 21 Dec. 1964; *s* of John and Margaret Fordham; *m* 1993, Alison Oxley; one *s* two *d*. *Educ:* Spalding Grammar Sch.; Hertford Coll., Oxford (BA Hons, BCL); Univ. of Virginia (LLM). Called to the Bar, Gray's Inn, 1990 (Prince of Wales Schol., Karmel Schol., Mould Schol., 1989); Lectr, Hertford Coll., Oxford, 1989–; in practice as barrister, 1990–. Mem., Adv. Bd, British Inst. Internat. and Comparative Law, 2003–. Co-Ed., Judicial Rev., 1996–. *Publication:* Judicial Review Handbook, 1994, 4th edn 2004. *Recreations:* St Albans Hockey Club (Captain, Veterans' Team), Marlborough Road Methodist Church, St Albans (Youth Music Co-ordinator). *Address:* Blackstone Chambers, Temple, EC4Y 9BW. *T:* (020) 7583 1770; *e-mail:* michaelfordham@blackstonechambers.com.

FOREMAN, Michael, RDI 1985; AGI; writer and illustrator; *b* 21 March 1938; *s* of Walter and Gladys Mary Foreman; *m* 1st, 1959, Janet Charters (marr. diss. 1966); one *s*; 2nd, 1980, Louise Phillips; two *s*. *Educ:* Notley Road Secondary Modern Sch., Lowestoft; Royal College of Art, London (ARCA 1st Cl. Hons and Silver Medal). Freelance, 1963–; six animated films produced, 1967–68. Hon. DArts Plymouth, 1998. Awarded Aigle d'Argent, Festival International du Livre, Nice, 1972; (jtly) Kurt Maschler Award, 1982; Graphics Prize, Bologna, 1982; Kate Greenaway Medal, Library Assoc., 1983 and 1989. *Publications:* author and illustrator: The Perfect Present, 1966; The Two Giants, 1966; The Great Sleigh Robbery, 1968; Horatio, 1969; Moose, 1971; Dinosaurs and all that Rubbish, 1972 (Francis Williams Prize, 1972); War and Peas, 1974; All The King's Horses, 1976; Panda and his Voyage of Discovery, 1977 (Francis Williams Prize, 1977); Trick a Tracker, 1980; Panda and the Odd Lion, 1981; Land of Dreams, 1982; Panda and the Bunyips, 1984; Cat and Canary, 1984; Panda and the Bushfire, 1986; Ben's Box, 1986; Ben's Baby, 1987; The Angel and the Wild Animal, 1988; War Boy (autobiog.), 1989; Oneworld, 1990; World of Fairytales, 1990; The Boy Who Sailed with Columbus, 1991; Jack's Fantastic Voyage, 1992; War Game, 1993; Grandfather's Pencil, 1993; Dad, I Can't Sleep, 1994; Surprise, Surprise, 1994; After the War Was Over, 1995; Seal Surfer, 1996; The Little Reindeer, 1996; Look! Look!, 1997; Angel and the Box of Time, 1997; Jack's Big Race, 1998; Chicken Licken, 1998; Little Red Hen, 1999; Rock-a-Doodle Do, 1999; Cat in the Manger, 2000; Saving Sinbad, 2001; Wonder Goal, 2002; Dinosaur Time, 2002; Playtime Rhymes, 2002; Evie and the Man who Helped God, 2003; Cat on the Hill, 2003; Hello World, 2003; Can't Catch Me, 2005; Classic Fairy Tales, 2005; Norman's Ark, 2006; Fox Tale, 2006; Mia's Story, 2006; Soggy the Bear, 2006; Say Hello, 2007; The Littlest Dinosaur, 2007; Soggy to the Rescue, 2007; illustrator of many books by other authors. *Recreations:* football, travelling. *Address:* 11 Howards Lane, SW15 6NX. *Club:* Chelsea Arts.

FOREMAN, Sir Philip (Frank), Kt 1981; CBE 1972; DL; FREng, FIAE, FIMechE; Member Council, 1986–98, Chairman, 1988–91, and President, 1994–98, British Standards Institution; *b* 16 March 1923; *s* of late Frank and Mary Foreman; *m* 1971, Margaret Cooke; one *s*. *Educ:* Soham Grammar Sch., Cambs; Loughborough Coll., Leics. (DLC (Hons)). Royal Naval Scientific Service, 1943–58. Short Bros, 1958–88: Man. Dir, 1967–88; Chm., 1983–88. Director: Simon Engrg Ltd, 1987–94 (Dep. Chm., 1992; Chm., 1993); Progressive Bldg Soc., 1987–2000 (Chm., 1990–2000); Ricardo Group (formerly Ricardo International) plc, 1988–97 (Chm., 1992–97); Consultant, Foreman Associates, 1988–2001. Member: Design Council, 1986–92; NI Economic Council, 1972–88; Chm., Teaching Co. Management Cttee, 1987–90; Trustee, Scotch-Irish Trust, 1980–. Mem. Senate, QUB, 1993–2002. Pres., IMechE, 1985–86. FREng (FEng 1982); FIAE 1997; Fellow: Irish Management Inst., 1986; Irish Inst. of Engrs, 1987; MInstD 1987; CCMI. FRSA 1978. A Freeman, City of London, 1980; Liveryman, Engineers' Co., 1992–. DL Belfast, 1975. Hon. FRAeS 1983. Hon. DSc QUB, 1976; Hon. DTech Loughborough, 1983; DUniv Open, 1985. *Publications:* papers to: Royal Aeronautical Soc.; Instn of Mechanical Engineers. *Recreation:* gardening. *Address:* Ashtree House, 26 Ballymenoch Road, Holywood, Co. Down BT18 0HH. *T:* (028) 9042 5673.

FORESTER; *see* Weld Forester, family name of Baron Forester.

FORESTER, 9th Baron *cr* 1821; **Charles Richard George Weld Forester;** land agent, since 2004; *b* 8 July 1975; *o s* of 8th Baron Forester and of Catherine Elizabeth Weld Forester; *S* father, 2004. *Educ:* Harrow; RAC Cirencester. *Recreations:* sport (cricket, tennis ski-ing), bridge, reading, countryside pursuits. *Heir: cousin* Wolston William Weld Forester, *b* 19 March 1941. *Address:* 21a Wix's Lane, Clapham, SW4 0AL. *T:* (020) 7380 1287.

FORESTIER-WALKER, Sir Michael (Leolin), 6th Bt *cr* 1835; General Manager, Leatherhead Theatre, since 2003 (Development Manager, 2002–03); *b* 24 April 1949; *s* of Lt-Col Alan Ivor Forestier-Walker, MBE (*d* 1954) (*g s* of 2nd Bt), and Margaret Joan Forestier-Walker (*née* Marcoolyn) (*d* 1988); *S* cousin, 1983; *m* 1988, Elizabeth Hedley, *d* of Joseph Hedley, Bellingham, Northumberland; one *s* one *d*. *Educ:* Wellington College, Crowthorne; Royal Holloway College, London Univ. (BA Hons). Teacher, Feltonfleet Sch., 1975–2002. *Heir: s* Joseph Alan Forestier-Walker, *b* 2 May 1992. *Address:* Bibury, 116 Hogshill Lane, Cobham, Surrey KT11 2AW.

FORFAR, Prof. John Oldroyd, MC; Professor of Child Life and Health, University of Edinburgh, 1964–82, now Professor Emeritus; *s* of Rev. David Forfar, MA and Elizabeth Campbell; *m* 1942, Isobel Mary Langlands Fernback, MB, ChB, DPH, AFOM; two *s* one *d*. *Educ:* Perth Acad.; St Andrews Univ. BSc 1938, MB, ChB 1941, St Andrews; DCH (London) 1948; FRCPE 1953 (MRCPE 1948); MD (Commendation) St Andrews, 1958; FRCP 1964 (MRCP 1947); FRSE 1975; FRCPGlas 1979 (MRCPGlas 1978). House Officer, Perth Royal Infirmary, 1941; RAMC, 1942–46: Med. Off., 47 Royal Marine Commando, 1943–45 (MC 1944; despatches, 1945); Registrar and Sen. Registrar, Dundee Royal Infirmary, 1946–48; Sen. Lectr in Child Health, St Andrews Univ., 1948–50; Sen. Paediatric Phys., Edinburgh Northern Gp of Hosps, and Sen. Lectr in Child Life and Health, Edinburgh Univ., 1950–64; Consultant Paediatrician, Royal Hosp. for Sick Children and Royal Infirm., Edinburgh, 1964–82. Chairman: Scottish Assoc. of Voluntary Child Care Organisations, 1965–69; Medical Gp, Assoc. of British Adoption Agencies, 1966–76; Jt Paediatric Cttee of Royal Colls of Physicians and British Paediatric Assoc., 1979–85; President: Scottish Paediatric Soc., 1972–74; Assoc. of Clinical Professors and Heads of Departments of Paediatrics, 1980–83; Pres., BPA, 1985–88. Vice-President: Gt Ormond St Wishing Well Appeal, 1987–89; Royal Hosp. for Sick Children Appeal, 1992–95; Trustee, Malcolm Sargent Cancer Fund for Children, 1975–84. Fellow, Amer. Coll. of Nutrition, 1977; Hon. Member: Australian Coll. of Paediatrics, 1986; Faculty of Paediatrics, RCPI, 1986. Hon. FRCPCH 1997. James Spence Medallist, BPA, 1983. *Publications:* (ed) Textbook of Paediatrics, 1973, 6th edn 2006; Child Health in a Changing Society, 1988; The British Paediatric Association 1928–1988, 1989; From Omaha to the Scheldt: the story of 47 Royal Marine Commando, 2001 (Royal Marine

Histl Soc. Award, 2005); contribs to general medical and to paediatric jls and books. *Recreations:* walking, writing.

FORGAN, Dame Elizabeth (Anne Lucy), DBE 2006 (OBE 1999); writer and broadcaster; Chair, Scott Trust, since 2004; *b* 31 Aug. 1944; *d* of late Thomas Moinet Forgan and of Jean Margaret Muriel. *Educ:* Benenden Sch.; St Hugh's Coll., Oxford (BA). Journalist: Teheran Journal, 1967–68; Hampstead and Highgate Express, 1969–74; Evening Standard, 1974–78; The Guardian, 1978–81; Channel Four TV: Sen. Commissioning Editor, 1981–86; Dep. Dir of Progs, 1987; Dir of Progs, 1988–93; Man. Dir, Network Radio BBC, 1993–96. Director: Most Media Ltd, 1998–; Guardian Media Gp, 1998–2004. Non-exec. Dir, DCMS, 2008–. Member: HFEA, 1990–98; Churches Conservation Trust, 1998–2001 (Chm., 1999–2001); Chair, NHMF and HLF, 2001–08. Trustee, Conservatoire for Dance and Drama, 2002–. Patron, St Giles Trust, 2007–. FRTS 1988; FRSA 1989. Hon. DLitt Keele, 1994; Hon. MA Salford, 1995. Chevalier de l'ordre des arts et des lettres (France), 1990. *Recreations:* church music, cheap novels, Scottish islands. *Address:* Most Media Ltd, 112 Regent's Park Road, NW1 8UG. *Club:* Reform.

FORMAN, Sir Denis, Kt 1976; OBE 1956; Chairman, Granada Television, 1974–87; Deputy Chairman, Granada Group, 1984–90 (Director, 1964–90); *b* 13 Oct. 1917; *s* of late Rev. Adam Forman, CBE, and Flora Smith; *m* 1st, 1948, Helen de Mouilpied (*d* 1987); two *s*; 2nd, 1990, Moni, *widow* of James Cameron, CBE; one step *s* one step *d*. *Educ:* at home; Loretto; Pembroke Coll., Cambridge. Served War, 1940–45: Argyll and Sutherland Highlanders; Commandant, Orkney and Shetland Defences Battle Sch., 1942 (wounded, Cassino, 1944). Chief Production Officer, Central Office of Information Films, 1947; Dir, British Film Inst., 1948–55 (Chm., Bd of Governors, 1971–73); Granada TV Ltd, 1955–87: Dir, 1959; Jt Man. Dir, 1965–81; Chm., Novello & Co., 1971–88. Dep. Chm., Royal Opera Hse, Covent Gdn, 1983–91 (Dir, 1981–91); Chm., Scottish Film Production Fund, 1990–93; Mem. Council, RNCM, 1975–84 (Hon. Mem., RNCM, 1981; Hon. FRNCM 1993). Fellow, BAFTA, 1977. DUniv: Stirling, 1982; Keele, 1990; DU Essex, 1986; Hon. LLD: Manchester, 1983; Lancaster, 1989; Hon. Dr Manchester Metropolitan, 1990. Ufficiale dell'ordine Al Merito della Repubblica Italiana. *Publications:* Mozart's Piano Concertos, 1971; Son of Adam (autobiog.), 1990; To Reason Why (autobiog.), 1991; (ed) The Good Opera Guide, 1994; Persona Granada: some memories of Sidney Bernstein and the early days of Independent Television (autobiog.), 1997; The Good Wagner Guide, 2000. *Recreation:* music. *Address:* Flat 2, 15 Lyndhurst Gardens, NW3 5NT. *Clubs:* Garrick, Savile, Oriental; New (Edinburgh).

FORMAN, (Francis) Nigel; Hon. Senior Research Fellow, Constitution Unit, University College London, since 2002; *b* 25 March 1943; *s* of late Brig. J. F. R. Forman and Mrs P. J. M. Forman; *m*. *Educ:* Dragon Sch., Oxford; Shrewsbury Sch.; New Coll., Oxford; College of Europe, Bruges; Kennedy Sch. of Govt, Harvard; Sussex Univ. Information Officer, CBI, 1970–71; Conservative Research Dept, 1971–76. Contested (C) Coventry NE, Feb. 1974. MP (C) Carshalton, March 1976–1983, Carshalton and Wallington, 1983–97; contested (C) Carshalton and Wallington, 1997. PPS to Lord Privy Seal, 1979–81 and to Minister of State, FCO, 1979–83, to Chancellor of the Exchequer, 1987–89; Parly Under Sec. of State, Dept for Educn, 1992. Member: Select Cttee on Science and Technology, 1976–79; Select Cttee on Foreign Affairs, 1990–92; Vice-Chairman: Cons. Finance Cttee, 1983–87; All Party Social Sci. and Policy Cttee, 1984–97; Secretary: Cons. Education Cttee, 1976–79; Cons. Energy Cttee, 1977–79. Mem. Exec., 1922 Cttee, 1990–92. Director: HFC Bank plc, 1995–; Prospects Services Ltd, 2001–03. Mem., ESRC, 1991–92. Chm., GB-E Europe Centre, 1990–92; Hon. Dir, Job Ownership Ltd, 1993–2001; Mem. Council, Federal Trust, 1995–. Mem. Council, Tavistock Inst., 1993–2005. *Publications:* Towards a More Conservative Energy Policy, 1977; Another Britain, 1979; Mastering British Politics, 1985, 4th edn 1999; (with John Maples) Work to be Done, 1985; Constitutional Change in the United Kingdom, 2002.

FORMAN, Air Vice-Marshal Graham Neil, CB 1989; Director of Legal Services, Royal Air Force, 1982–89; *b* 29 Nov. 1930; *s* of Stanley M. Forman and Eva Forman (*née* Barrett); *m* 1957, Valerie Fay (*née* Shaw); one *s* two *d*. *Educ:* Boston Grammar School; Nottingham Univ. Law School; Law Society's School of Law; admitted solicitor 1953. Commissioned RAF Legal Branch, 1957; served HQ Far East Air Force, Singapore, 1960–63 and 1965–68; Dep. Dir, RAF Legal Services, HQ Near East Air Force, Cyprus, 1971–72 and 1973–76; Dep. Dir, RAF Legal Services, HQ RAF Germany, 1978; Dep. Dir, Legal Services (RAF), 1978–82. *Clubs:* Royal Air Force, MCC, Middlesex CC (Life Mem.).

FORMAN, Sir John Denis; *see* Forman, Sir Denis.

FORMAN, Miloš; film director; *b* Čáslav, 18 Feb. 1932; *m* Martina; four *s*. *Educ:* Acad. of Music and Dramatic Art, Prague. Director: Film Presentations, Czechoslovak Television, 1954–56; Laterna Magika, Prague, 1958–62. Co-chm. and Prof., Film Div., Columbia Univ. Sch. of Arts, 1978–. Films directed include: Talent Competition; Peter and Pavla, 1963 (Czech. Film Critics' Award; Grand Prix, Locarno, 1964; Prize, Venice Festival, 1965); A Blonde in Love (Grand Prix, French Film Acad., 1966); The Fireman's Ball, 1967; Taking Off, 1971; (co-dir) Visions of Eight, 1973; One Flew Over the Cuckoo's Nest, 1975 (Academy Award, 1976; BAFTA Award, 1977); Hair, 1979; Ragtime, 1982; Amadeus, 1985 (Oscar Award, 1985); Valmont, 1988; The People vs Larry Flynt, 1996 (Golden Globe Award, 1997); Man on the Moon, 2000; Goya's Ghosts, 2006. *Publication:* Turnaround: a memoir, 1993.

FORMAN, Nigel; *see* Forman, F. N.

FORMAN, Roy; Managing Director and Chief Executive, Private Patients Plan Ltd, 1985–94; *b* 28 Dec. 1931; *s* of Leslie and Ena Forman; *m* 1954, Mary (*née* Nelson); three *s* one *d*. *Educ:* Nunthorpe Grammar Sch., York; Nottingham Univ. (BA Hons). RAF, 1953–56. Business economist, 1956–61; electricity supply industry, 1961–80: Chief Commercial Officer, S Wales Elec. Bd, 1972–76; Commercial Adviser, Electricity Council, 1976–80; Private Patients Plan Ltd: Gen. Manager, Marketing and Sales, 1980–81; Marketing Dir, 1981–85; Man. Dir, Age Concern Enterprises Ltd, 1995–96; Director: General Healthcare Group PLC, 1994; Reliastar Reinsurance Group (UK) Ltd, 1997. FRSA 1992. *Recreations:* music, walking, reading.

FORRES, 4th Baron *cr* 1922; **Alastair Stephen Grant Williamson,** MARAC; Bt 1909; Chairman, Agriscot Pty Ltd; Director, Jaga Trading Pty Ltd; *b* 16 May 1946; *s* of 3rd Baron Forres and of Gillian Ann Maclean, *d* of Major John Maclean Grant, RA; *S* father, 1978; *m* 1969, Margaret, *d* of late G. J. Mallam, Mullumbimby, NSW; two *s*. *Educ:* Eton. Alderman, Orange City Council, 1987. Pres., Big Brother Movt, 1986–. Patron, Sydney Scottish Week, 1981–. *Heir:* *s* Hon. George Archibald Mallam Williamson [*b* 16 Aug. 1972; *m* 2002, Charlotte, *e d* of Timothy and Sara Barrett]. *Clubs:* Union, Australian Jockey, Sydney Turf (Sydney).

FORREST, Prof. (Alexander) Robert (Walker), FRCP, FRCPE, FRCPath; CChem, FRSC; Hon. Consultant in Clinical Chemistry and Forensic Toxicology, Royal Hallamshire Hospital, and Hon. Professor of Forensic Chemistry, University of Sheffield, since 2005; *b* 5 July 1947; *s* of Alexander Muir Forrest and Rose Ellen Forrest (*née* Ringham); *m* 1999, Dr Wendy Susan Phillips; two *s*. *Educ:* Stamford Sch.; Univ. of Edinburgh (BSc Hons 1970; MB ChB 1973); Cardiff Law Sch. (LLM). DObstRCOG 1975; MCB 1981; CChem, FRSC 1983; FRCPE 1989; FRCP 1992; FRCPath 1992; RFP 2004. Sen. Registrar, Royal Infirmary, Glasgow, 1979–81; Consultant in Clin. Chem. and Toxicol., Sheffield Univ. Hosps NHS Trust at Royal Hallamshire Hosp., Sheffield, 1981–98 (Hon. Consultant, 1998–2005); Prof. of Forensic Toxicol., Sheffield Univ., 1998–2005. Asst Dep. Coroner, S Yorks W, 1989–. Mem., Sec. of State for Transport's Hon. Medical Adv. Panel for Alcohol, Drugs and Substance Misuse and Driving. Ed., Science and Justice, 1999–2006. Pres., Forensic Sci. Soc., 2005–07. *Publications:* numerous contribs to med. and scientific literature on forensic toxicology and related subjects. *Recreations:* family, cats, computers, books. *Address:* 37 Marlborough Road, Sheffield S10 1DA. *T:* and *Fax:* (0114) 266 7423; *e-mail:* toxicologist@mac.com. *Club:* Athenæum.

FORREST, Prof. Sir (Andrew) Patrick (McEwen), Kt 1986; Regius Professor of Clinical Surgery, University of Edinburgh, 1970–88, now Professor Emeritus; *b* 25 March 1923; *s* of Rev. Andrew James Forrest, BD, and Isabella Pearson; *m* 1955, Margaret Beryl Hall (*d* 1961); one *s* one *d*; *m* 1964, Margaret Anne Steward; one *d*. *Educ:* Dundee High Sch.; Univ. of St Andrews. BSc 1942; MB, ChB 1945; ChM hons, University Gold Medal, 1954; MD hons, Rutherford Gold Medal, 1958; FRCSE 1950; FRCS 1952; FRCSGlas 1962; FRSE 1976; FIBiol 1986; FRCPE 1999. Surg.-Lt RNVR, 1946–48. Mayo Foundation Fellow, 1952–53; Lectr and Sen. Lectr, Univ. of Glasgow, 1955–62; Prof. of Surgery, Welsh Nat. Sch. of Medicine, 1962–70. Hon. Consultant Surgeon, Royal Inf. of Edinburgh, until 1988; Royal Prince Alfred Hosp., Sydney; Civilian Consultant to RN, 1977–88. Chief Scientist (pt-time), SHHD, 1981–87. McIlrath Vis. Prof., Royal Prince Alfred Hosp., Sydney, 1969; Nimmo Vis. Prof., Royal Adelaide Hosp., 1973; McLauchlin-Gallie Prof., RCP of Canada, 1974; numerous other visiting professorships; Vis. Scientist, Nat. Cancer Inst., 1989–90; Associate Dean, Internat. Med. Coll., Kuala Lumpur, 1993–96. Eponymous lectures include: Lister Meml, Canadian Med. Assoc., 1970; Inaugural Bruce Wellesley Hosp., Toronto, 1970; Inaugural Peter Lowe, RCP Glas., 1980. Member: Medical sub-cttee, UGC, 1967–76; MRC, 1974–79; Scientific Adv. Cttee, Cancer Res. Campaign, 1974–83; ABRC, 1982–85. Asst Editor and Editor, Scottish Med. Jl, 1957–61; Hon. Secretary: Scottish Soc. for Experimental Medicine, 1959–62; Surgical Research Soc., 1963–66, Pres., 1974–76; Chairman: British Breast Gp, 1974–77; Working Gp on Breast Cancer Screening (reported, 1986); Scottish Cancer Foundn, 1998–2003. Member Council: Assoc. of Surgeons of GB and Ireland, 1971–74 (Pres., 1988–89); RCSE, 1976–84, 1986–89; Member: Internat. Surgical Gp, 1963–; James IV Assoc. of Surgeons Inc., 1981–; Scottish Hosp. Endowments Res. Trust, 1990–94. Mem., Kirk Session, St Giles' Cathedral. Hon. Fellow, Amer. Surgical Assoc., 1981; Hon. FACS 1978; Hon. FRACS 1987; Hon. FRCR 1988; Hon. FRCSCan 1989; Hon. FFPH (Hon. FFPHM 2001). Hon. DSc: Wales, 1981; Chinese Univ. of Hong Kong, 1986; Hon. LLD Dundee, 1986; Hon. MD Internat. Medical Univ., 2007. Lister Medal, RCS, 1987; Gold Medal, Netherlands Surgical Assoc., 1988; Gimbernat Prize, Catalan Soc. of Surg., 1996; Breast Cancer Award, European Inst. of Oncology, 2000. *Publications:* (ed jtly) Prognostic Factors in Breast Cancer, 1968; (jtly) Principles and Practice of Surgery, 1985; Breast Cancer: the decision to screen, 1991; various papers in surgical jls, mainly on gastro-intestinal disease and breast cancer. *Address:* 19 St Thomas Road, Edinburgh EH9 2LR. *T:* (0131) 667 3203.

FORREST, John Richard, CBE 2002; DPhil; FREng; FIET; Deputy Chairman: Surrey Satellite Technology Ltd, since 2006; Omniglobe Networks Ltd, since 2006; *b* 21 April 1943; *s* of late John Samuel Forrest, FRS and Ivy May Olding; *m* 1st, 1973, Jane Patricia Robey Leech (marr. diss. 2000); two *s* one *d*; 2nd, 2006, Diane Martine James. *Educ:* Sidney Sussex Coll., Cambridge (MA); Keble Coll., Oxford (DPhil). Research Associate and Lectr, Stanford Univ., Calif, 1967–70; Lectr, later Prof., Electronic and Elect. Engrg Dept, UCL, 1970–84; Technical Dir, Marconi Defence Systems Ltd, 1984–86; Dir of Engrg, IBA, 1986–90; Chief Exec., 1990–94, Dep. Chm., 1994–96, National Transcommunications Ltd; Chairman: Brewton Group, 1994–99; Human IT Ltd, 2000–03; CDS Ltd, 2003–05; Adv. Bd., Interregnum plc, 2003–06. Director: Ega Internat., 1994–; Drake Automation, 1996–99; Loughborough Sound Images, 1996–98; Screen, 1997–2000; Tricorder Technology, 1997–2001; 3i Gp, 1997–2004; Blue Wave Systems Inc., 1998–2001 (Chm., 2000–01); Globecast (Northern Europe) Ltd, 1998–2000; Printable Field Emitters Ltd, 1999–2000; Morgan Howard Internat. Gp Ltd, 1999–2000; Cellular Design Services Ltd, 2001–02; System C Healthcare, 2005–. Chm., UK Govt Spectrum Mgt Adv. Gp, 1998–2003; Member: UK Adv. Bd, Stanford Res. Inst. Internat., 1996–98; EC IT Rev. Bd, 1995–99; Steering Bd, Eur. Digital Video Broadcast Initiative, 1995–97. Sen. Vice-Pres., Royal Acad. of Engrg, 1999–2002 (FEng 1985; Hon. Sec. for Electrical Engrg, and Mem. Council, 1995–97; Vice-Pres., 1997–99); Vice-President: IEE, 1992–95; RTS, 1994–97. Pro-Chancellor, Surrey Univ., 2005–. Mem. Council, Brunel Univ., 1996–99. FRSA 1986; FRTS 1990; FInstD 1991. Hon. Fellow, BKSTS. Hon. DSc City, 1992; Hon. DTech Brunel, 1995. Chevalier de l'ordre des arts et des lettres (France), 1990. *Publications:* papers and contribs to books on phased array radar, satellite communications, broadcasting and optoelectronics. *Recreations:* travel, sailing, mountain walking, literature, study of mankind. *T:* 07785 251734; *e-mail:* johnrforrest1@btinternet.com.

FORREST, Prof. Sir Patrick; *see* Forrest, Prof. Sir A. P. M.

FORREST, Peter; Director, 1994–2001, Deputy Chairman, 2000–01, Dawson International plc; *b* 2 May 1938; *s* of Leonard and Dora Jane Forrest; *m* 1st, 1963, Jo Thornton (marr. diss. 1992); three *s*; 2nd, 1994, Evie Tindal; two step *s*. *Educ:* Batley Grammar Sch.; Dewsbury Technical Coll. ATI. Man. Dir, Dundee Textiles Ltd, 1975–80; Director: Courtaulds Northern Weaving Div., 1975–80; Legler Industria Tessile, Bergamo, Italy, 1980–91; Dawson International plc: Premier Fibres & Yarns Div., 1991–95; Man. Dir, Todd & Duncan Ltd, 1991–95; Man. Dir, 1995–98; Chief Exec., 1998–2000. *Recreations:* sailing, reading, classical music. *Address:* Whinfield House, The Muirs, Kinross KY13 8AU. *Club:* Royal Highland Yacht.

FORREST, Robert; *see* Forrest, A. R. W.

FORREST, Rev. Canon Robin Whyte; Dean of Moray, Ross and Caithness, 1992–98; Canon of St Andrew's Cathedral, Inverness, 1986–98, now Hon. Canon; Rector of Forres, 1979–98; *b* 1933. *Educ:* Edinburgh Theol Coll., 1958. Ordained deacon, 1961, priest, 1962; Asst Curate, St Mary, Glasgow, 1961–66; Rector: Renfrew, 1966–70; Motherwell, 1970–79, with Wishaw, 1975–79; Nairn, 1979–92. Synod Clerk, Moray, 1991–92. *Address:* Landeck, Cummingston, Elgin, Moray IV30 5XY. *T:* (01343) 835539.

FORRESTER, David Michael; education consultant; Director, Further Education and Youth Training, Department for Education and Employment, 1995–2001; *b* 22 June

1944; *s* of late Reginald Grant Forrester and Minnie Forrester (*née* Chaytow); *m* 1st, 1978, Diana Douglas (marr. diss. 1983); 2nd, 1993, Helen Mary Williams, *qv*; one *s* one *d*. *Educ:* St Paul's Sch.; King's Coll., Cambridge (BA Hons 1st Cl. 1966, MA); Kennedy Sch. of Govt, Harvard Univ. (an inaugural Kennedy Scholar, 1966–67). DES, 1967; Private Sec. to Parly Under Sec., 1971–72; Principal, DES, 1972–76; HM Treasury, 1976–78; Asst Sec., DES, 1979–85; DTI, 1985–87; Under Sec., DES, subseq. DFE, then DFEE, 1988; Hd of Further Educn Br., 1994–95. FRSA 1999. *Recreations:* cricket, squash, music, esp. opera, mountain walking. *Address:* 340 Liverpool Road, N7 8PZ. *T:* (020) 7607 1492. *Club:* Pretenders'.

FORRESTER, Rev. Prof. Duncan Baillie; Professor of Theology and Public Issues, 2000–01, Professor of Christian Ethics and Practical Theology, 1978–2000, and Dean, Faculty of Divinity, 1996–99, University of Edinburgh (Principal, New College, 1986–96); Director, Edinburgh University Centre for Theology and Public Issues, 1984–2000; *b* 10 Nov. 1933; *s* of Rev. Prof. William Forrester and Isobel McColl or Forrester; *m* 1964, Rev. Margaret R. McDonald or Forrester (former Minister of St Michael's Parish Church, Edinburgh); one *s* one *d*. *Educ:* Madras Coll., St Andrews; Univ. of St Andrews (MA Hons Mod. Hist. and Pol Sci.); Univ. of Chicago (Grad., Dept of Politics); Univ. of Edinburgh (BD); DPhil Sussex. Part-time Asst in Politics, Univ. of Edinburgh, 1957–58; Asst Minister, Hillside Church and Leader of St James Mission, 1960–61; Church of Scotland Missionary to S India, 1962, Lectr, then Prof. of Politics, Madras Christian Coll., Tambaram, 1962–70; ordained as Presbyter of Church of S India; part-time Lectr in Politics, Univ. of Edinburgh, 1966–67; Chaplain and Lectr in Politics and Religious Studies, Sch. of African and Asian Studies, Univ. of Sussex, 1970–78. Lectures: Lee, Edinburgh, 1980; Hensley Henson, Oxford, 1988; Bernard Gilpin, Durham, 1992; F. D. Maurice, KCL, 1995; Bishop Butler, Bristol, 1996; Richard Hooker, Exeter, 1999; Von Hügel, Cambridge, 2000; Ferguson, Manchester, 2002; Eric Abbott, Westminster, 2003; Boutwood, Cambridge, 2004. Chm., Edinburgh Council of Social Service, 1983–87. President: Soc. for the Study of Theol., 1991–93; Soc. for the Study of Christian Ethics, 1991–94; Church Service Soc., 1999–2001; Vice-Pres., Council on Christian Approaches to Defence and Disarmament, 1998–. Member: Faith and Order Commn, WCC, 1983–96; Center of Theol Inquiry, Princeton, 1992–; Nuffield Council on Bioethics, 1996–2002. FRSA 2000; FRSE 2007. Hon. Fellow, Harris Manchester Coll., Oxford, 2000. Hon. DTheol Univ. of Iceland, 1997; Hon. DD: Glasgow, 1999; St Andrews, 2000. Templeton UK Award, 1999. *Publications:* chapters on Luther, Calvin and Hooker, in History of Political Philosophy, ed Strauss and Cropsey, 1963, 3rd edn 1986; Caste and Christianity, 1980; (with J. I. H. McDonald and G. Tellini) Encounter with God, 1983; (ed with D. Murray) Studies in the History of Worship in Scotland, 1984; Christianity and the Future of Welfare, 1985; (ed with D. Skene and co-author) Just Sharing, 1988; Theology and Politics, 1988; Beliefs, Values and Policies: conviction politics in a secular age, 1989; (ed jtly) Worship Now, Book 2, 1989; (ed) Theology and Practice, 1990; The True Church and Morality, 1997; Christian Justice and Public Policy, 1997; Truthful Action: explorations in practical theology, 2000; On Human Worth: a Christian vindication of equality, 2001; Apocalypse Now? reflections on faith in a time of terror, 2005; Theological Fragments: explorations in unsystematic theology, 2005; articles on Indian politics and religion, ethics and political theology. *Recreations:* hill-walking, ornithology. *Address:* 25 Kingsburgh Road, Edinburgh EH12 6DZ. *T:* (0131) 337 5646.

FORRESTER, Giles Charles Fielding; His Honour Judge Forrester; a Circuit Judge, since 1986; a Senior Circuit Judge and Permanent Judge at the Central Criminal Court, since 1995; *b* 18 Dec. 1939; *s* of late Basil Thomas Charles Forrester and Diana Florence Forrester (*née* Sandeman); *m* 1966, Georgina Elizabeth Garnett; one *s* one *d*. *Educ:* Rugby School; Grenoble Univ.; Trinity College, Oxford (MA Jurisp.). Account Exec., Pritchard Wood and Partners, 1962–66. Called to the Bar, Inner Temple, 1966; practised, SE Circuit, 1966–86; a Recorder of the Crown Court, 1986. Judicial Mem., Parole Bd, 2002–07. Mem., HAC Infantry Bn, 1963–67, Veteran Mem., 1994–; Pres., HAC RFC, 1994–98. Mem. Council, Magistrates' Assoc., 1998– (Pres., SW London Br., 1991–2007). FRGS 2004. Freeman, City of London, 1997; Freedom, Weavers' Co., 1998. *Recreations:* a wide variety, mainly sporting. *Address:* c/o The Central Criminal Court, City of London, EC4M 7EH. *T:* (020) 7248 3277. *Clubs:* Boodle's, Roehampton; Royal Western Yacht; St Enodoc Golf; New Zealand Golf (Weybridge).

FORRESTER, Helen Mary; see Williams, H. M.

FORRESTER, Ian Stewart; QC (Scot.) 1988; *b* 13 Jan. 1945; *s* of late Alexander Roxburgh Forrester and Elizabeth Richardson Forrester (*née* Stewart); *m* 1981, Sandra Anne Therese Keegan, Louisiana lawyer; two *s*. *Educ:* Kelvinside Acad., Glasgow; Univ. of Glasgow (MA 1965; LLB 1967); Tulane Univ. of Louisiana (MCL 1969). Mem., British Univs debating team, 1966; Commonwealth expedn to India, 1967. Admitted Faculty of Advocates, Scots Bar, 1972; admitted Bar of State of NY, following order of NY Court of Appeals, 1977; admitted English Bar, Middle Temple, 1996. With Maclay, Murray & Spens, 1968–69; Davis Polk & Wardwell, 1969–72; Cleary Gottlieb Steen & Hamilton, 1972–81; estab. indep. chambers, Brussels, 1981; co-founder, Forrester & Norall, 1981 (Forrester Norall & Sutton, 1989; White & Case, 1998), practising before European Commn and Courts. Chm., British Conservative Assoc., Belgium, 1982–86. Hon. Vis. Prof., European Law, Univ. of Glasgow, 1991–. Mem., Eur. Adv. Bd, 1992–2006, Dean's Adv. Bd, Law Sch., 2006–, Tulane Univ. Trustee, EU Baroque Orch., 2005–. Elder, St Andrew's Church of Scotland, Brussels, 1992–. *Publications:* numerous articles on EEC customs, dumping and trade law, competition law, German civil and commercial codes. *Recreations:* politics, wine, cooking, restoring old houses. *Address:* White & Case, 62 Rue de la Loi, 1040 Brussels, Belgium; Advocates' Library, Parliament House, Edinburgh EH1 1RF. *Clubs:* Athenæum; International Château Ste-Anne (Brussels); Royal Yacht Club of Belgium.

FORRESTER, James William; Director, Imperial War Museum North, since 2002; *b* 25 Feb. 1952; *s* of Dr Sam Forrester and Dr Marion Forrester; *m* 1988, Caroline Slinger; one *s* one *d*. *Educ:* Univ. of Durham (BA Hons English Lit. and Lang. 1973); Univ. of Leicester (Mus Dip.). Apprentice boatbuilder, 1974–76; journeyman boatbuilder, 1976–84; Ship and Boat Conservator, 1984–88; Public Progs Officer, 1988–96, Merseyside Maritime Mus.; Gen. Manager, NMGM Trading Co., 1996–2001. *Recreations:* boats, tuba and euphonium, cooking, travel and fun with family, life's unfolding tapestry. *Address:* Imperial War Museum North, The Quays, Trafford Wharf Road, Manchester M17 1TZ. *T:* (0161) 836 4010; *e-mail:* jforrester@iwm.org.uk.

FORRESTER, John Stuart; *b* 17 June 1924; *s* of Harry and Nellie Forrester; *m* 1945, Gertrude H. Weaver. *Educ:* Eastwood Council Sch.; City Sch. of Commerce, Stoke-on-Trent; Alsager Teachers' Training Coll. Teacher, 1946–66. MP (Lab) Stoke-on-Trent, N, 1966–87. Sec., Constituency Labour Party, 1961–84. Mem., Speaker's Panel of Chairmen, 1982–87; Member: NUT, 1949–87; APEX, 1942–43, 1946–49, 1984–. Councillor, Stoke-on-Trent, 1970–2000. Freedom of Stoke-on-Trent, 1992. *Address:* 13 Cadeby Grove, Milton, Stoke-on-Trent ST2 7BY.

FORRESTER, Prof. John Vincent, MD; FRCSE, FRCOphth, FRCSGlas, FRCPE, FMedSci, FRSE; Cockburn Professor of Ophthalmology, University of Aberdeen, since 1984; *b* 11 Sept. 1946; *m* Anne Gray; two *s* two *d*. *Educ:* St Aloysius Coll., Glasgow; Glasgow Univ. (MD Hons 1980). FRCSE 1975; FRCSGlas 1985; FRCOphth 1990; FRCPE 1996. Various hosp. appts, Glasgow, 1971–78; MRC Travelling Fellow, Columbia Univ., NY, 1976–77; Consultant Ophthalmologist, Southern Gen. Hosp., Glasgow, 1979–83. Spinoza Prof., Univ. of Amsterdam, 1997. Master, Oxford Ophthalmol Congress, 2000–02. Pres., European Assoc. of Eye and Vision Res., 2001–02. Ed., British Jl Ophthalmol., 1992–2000. FMedSci 1998; FRSE 2003. *Recreation:* family. *Address:* Department of Ophthalmology, University of Aberdeen Institute of Medical Sciences, Foresterhill, Aberdeen AB25 2ZD. *T:* (01224) 553782.

FORRESTER-PATON, His Honour Douglas Shaw; QC 1965; a Circuit Judge (formerly a Judge of County Courts), 1970–86; *b* 22 June 1921; 3rd *s* of late Alexander Forrester-Paton, JP; *m* 1948, Agnete, *d* of Holger Tuxen; one *s* two *d*. *Educ:* Gresham's Sch., Holt; Queen's Coll., Oxford (BA). Called to Bar, Middle Temple, 1947; North East Circuit. Served RAF, 1941–45. Recorder: Middlesbrough, 1963–68; Teesside, 1968–70. *Address:* 11 The Dorkings, Great Broughton, Middlesbrough TS9 7NA. *T:* (01642) 712301; 5 King's Bench Walk, Temple, EC4Y 7DB.

FORSHAW, Sarah Anne; QC 2008; *b* Gloucester, 2 July 1964; *d* of late Brig. Peter Forshaw, CBE and of Helen Forshaw (*née* Cliff); *m* 1991 (marr. diss. 2002); two *s*. *Educ:* King's Coll., Taunton; King's Coll. London (LLB). Called to the Bar, Middle Temple, 1987; in practice as barrister specialising in crime. *Address:* 5 King's Bench Walk, Temple, EC4Y 7DN. *T:* (020) 7353 5638.

FORSTER, Donald, CBE 1988; Managing Director, 1945–81, and Chairman, 1981–86, B. Forster & Co. Ltd, Leigh (textile manufacturing company); *b* 18 Dec. 1920; *s* of Bernard and Rose Forster; *m* 1942, Muriel Steinman; one *s* two *d*. *Educ:* N Manchester Grammar School. Served War, RAF pilot (Flt Lieut), 1940–45. Mem., Skelmersdale Develt Corp., 1980–82; Chairman: Warrington/Runcorn Develt Corp., 1982–86; Merseyside Develt Corp., 1984–87. *Recreations:* golf, music, paintings. *Address:* 72A Elizabeth Street, SW1W 9PD. *Clubs:* Whitefield Golf, Dunham Forest Country; The Lakes (USA).

See also L. C. Goldstone.

FORSTER, Jilly, (Mrs R. A. Lamond); Founder and Chair, The Forster Co., since 1996; *b* 8 Dec. 1955; *d* of Dr Matthew Forster and Dr Margaret Forster; *m* 1979, Robert Andrew Lamond; two *s*. *Educ:* N London Collegiate Sch.; The Priory, Lewes. Founding Dir, Munro & Forster, 1984–89; Dir, Body Shop Internat. plc, 1989–96; Dir, Big Issue, 1991–93. Trustee: Children on the Edge, 2004–; Forgiveness Project, 2004–; Royal Parks Foundn, 2004–. *Recreations:* slow food, semiology, social enterprise. *Address:* The Forster Co., 49 Southwark Street, SE1 1RU. *T:* (020) 7403 2230; *e-mail:* jilly@forster.co.uk.

FORSTER, Margaret; author; *b* 25 May 1938; *d* of Arthur Gordon Forster and Lilian (*née* Hind); *m* 1960, Edward Hunter Davies, *qv*; one *s* two *d*. *Educ:* Carlisle and County High Sch. for Girls; Somerville Coll., Oxford (BA). FRSL. Teacher, Barnsbury Girls' Sch., Islington, 1961–63. Member: BBC Adv. Cttee on Social Effects of Television, 1975–77; Arts Council Literary Panel, 1978–81. Chief non-fiction reviewer, Evening Standard, 1977–80. *Publications: non-fiction:* The Rash Adventurer: the rise and fall of Charles Edward Stuart, 1973; William Makepeace Thackeray: memoirs of a Victorian gentleman, 1978; Significant Sisters: grassroots of active feminism 1839–1939, 1984; Elizabeth Barrett Browning: a biography, 1988; (ed, introd. and prefaces) Elizabeth Barrett Browning: selected poems, 1988; Daphne du Maurier, 1993; Hidden Lives (memoir), 1995; Rich Desserts and Captains Thin: a family and their times 1831–1931, 1997; Precious Lives, 1998; Good Wives? Mary, Fanny, Jennie and Me, 1845–2001, 2001; *novels:* Dames' Delight, 1964; Georgy Girl, 1965 (filmscript with Peter Nichols, 1966); The Bogeyman, 1965; The Travels of Maudie Tipstaff, 1967; The Park, 1968; Miss Owen-Owen is At Home, 1969; Fenella Phizackerley, 1970; Mr Bone's Retreat, 1971; The Seduction of Mrs Pendlebury, 1974; Mother, can you hear me?, 1979; The Bride of Lowther Fell, 1980; Marital Rites, 1981; Private Papers, 1986; Have the Men Had Enough?, 1989; Lady's Maid, 1990; The Battle for Christabel, 1991; Mothers' Boys, 1994; Shadow Baby, 1996; The Memory Box, 1999; Diary of an Ordinary Woman 1914–1995, 2003; Is There Anything You Want?, 2005; Keeping the World Away, 2006; Over, 2007. *Recreations:* walking on Hampstead Heath, reading contemporary fiction. *Address:* 11 Boscastle Road, NW5 1EE. *T:* (020) 7485 3785; Grasmoor House, Loweswater, near Cockermouth, Cumbria CA13 0RU. *T:* (01900) 85303.

FORSTER, Rt Rev. Peter Robert; see Chester, Bishop of.

FORSYTE, Charles; see Philo, G. C. G.

FORSYTH, family name of **Baron Forsyth of Drumlean.**

FORSYTH OF DRUMLEAN, Baron *cr* 1999 (Life Peer), of Drumlean in Stirling; **Michael Bruce Forsyth,** Kt 1997; PC 1995; *b* 16 Oct. 1954; *s* of John T. Forsyth and Mary Watson; *m* 1977, Susan Jane Clough; one *s* two *d*. *Educ:* Arbroath High School; St Andrews University (MA). Pres., St Andrews Univ. Cons. Assoc., 1972–75; Nat. Chm., Fedn of Cons. Students, 1976–77; Dir, Flemings, 1997–99; Vice-Chm., Investment Banking Europe, JP Morgan, 1999–2001; Dep. Chm., JP Morgan UK, 2002–05; Sen. Advr, 2006–07; Sen. Man. Dir, 2007–; Evercore Partners Ltd; non-executive Director: J & J Denholm Ltd, 2005–; Denholm Industrial Services (Hldgs) Ltd, 2006–; Denholm Brown Brothers, 2007–. MP (C) Stirling, 1983–97; contested (C) same seat, 1997. PPS to Sec. of State for Foreign and Commonwealth Affairs, 1986–87; Parly Under-Sec. of State, 1987–90, Minister of State, 1990–92, Scottish Office; Minister of State: Dept of Employment, 1992–94; Home Office, 1994–95; Sec. of State for Scotland and Lord Keeper of the Great Seal of Scotland, 1995–97. Chm., Scottish Cons. Party, 1989–90. Mem., Westminster City Council, 1978–83. Mem. Develt Bd, Nat. Portrait Gall., 1999–2003. Dir, Centre for Policy Studies, 2006–. Patron, Craighalbert Centre, 1999–. *Recreations:* photography, gardening, fly-fishing, mountaineering, ski-ing, amateur astronomy. *Address:* House of Lords, SW1A 0PW.

FORSYTH OF THAT ILK, Alistair Charles William; JP; FSCA, FSAScot; FInstPet; Baron of Ethie; Chief of the Name and Clan of Forsyth; *b* 7 Dec. 1929; *s* of Charles Forsyth of Strathendry, FCA, and Ella Millicent Hopkins; *m* 1958, Ann, OStJ, *d* of Col P. A. Hughes, IA; four *s*. *Educ:* St Paul's Sch.; Queen Mary Coll., London. FInstPet 1973; FSCA 1976; FSAScot 1979. National Service, 2nd Lieut The Queen's Bays, 1948–50; Lieut The Parachute Regt, TA, 1950–54. Chm., Hargreaves Reiss & Quinn Ltd, 1981–99. Mem., Standing Council of Scottish Chiefs, 1978–. Freeman, City of London, 1993; Liveryman, Scriveners' Co., 1993–. CStJ 1982 (OStJ 1974). JP NSW, 1965; JP Angus, 1987. KHS 1992. *Address:* Chateau de Monteleone, 32100 Condom, France. *Club:* New (Edinburgh).

FORSYTH, Bill; film director and script writer; *b* Glasgow, 1947; one *s* one *d*. *Educ:* National Film Sch. *Films directed:* That Sinking Feeling, 1980; Gregory's Girl, 1981; Local

Hero, 1983; Comfort and Joy, 1984; Housekeeping, 1988; Breaking In, 1990; Being Human, 1993; Gregory's Two Girls, 1999. TV film, Andrina, 1981. BAFTA Award: best screenplay, 1982; best dir, 1983. Hon. DLitt Glasgow, 1984; DUniv Stirling, 1989. *Address:* c/o Peters Fraser and Dunlop, Drury House, 34–43 Russell Street, WC2B 5HA.

FORSYTH, Bruce; *see* Forsyth-Johnson, B. J.

FORSYTH, Frederick, CBE 1997; author; *b* 25 Aug. 1938; *m* 1st, 1973, Carole Cunningham; two *s*; 2nd, 1994, Sandy Molloy. *Educ:* Tonbridge Sch. RAF, 1956–58. Reporter, Eastern Daily Press, Norfolk, 1958–61; joined Reuters, 1961: Reporter, Paris, 1962–63; Chief of Bureau, E Berlin, 1963–64; joined BBC, 1965; radio and TV reporter, 1965–66; Asst Diplomatic Correspondent, BBC TV, 1967–68; freelance journalist, Nigeria and Biafra, 1968–69. *Publications: non fiction:* The Biafra Story, 1969, 2nd edn 1977; *fiction:* The Day of the Jackal, 1971 (filmed, 1973); The Odessa File, 1972 (filmed, 1975); The Dogs of War, 1974 (filmed, 1981); The Shepherd, 1975; The Devil's Alternative, 1979; No Comebacks (short stories), 1982; Emeka, 1982; The Fourth Protocol, 1984 (filmed, 1987); The Negotiator, 1988; The Deceiver, 1991; (ed) Great Flying Stories, 1991; The Fist of God, 1993; Icon, 1996; The Phantom of Manhattan, 1999; The Veteran and Other Stories, 2001; Avenger, 2003; The Afghan, 2006. *Address:* c/o Bantam Books, 62/63 Uxbridge Road, W5 5SA.

FORSYTH, Prof. Murray Greensmith, FRHistS; Professor of Politics, University of Leicester, 1990–94, now Emeritus; *b* 30 Oct. 1936; *s* of Maj. Henry Russell Forsyth and Marie Elaine Forsyth; *m* 1964, Marie Denise Edelin de la Praudière; one *s* two *d*. *Educ:* Wellington Coll.; Balliol Coll., Oxford (BA Mod. Hist. 1959; MA 1964); College of Europe, Bruges. FRHistS 1991. Research Officer, Political and Econ. Planning, London, 1960–64; University of Leicester: Lectr in Politics, 1964–70; Reader in Internat. Politics, 1971–90; Dir, Centre for Federal Studies, 1988–94; Prof. of Govt and Pol Sci., Hong Kong Baptist Univ., 1995–97. British Acad. Wolfson Fellow, Paris, 1977; Bradlow Fellow, S African Inst. of Internat. Affairs, 1983; Vis. Prof., Coll. of Europe, Bruges, 1993–94; Robert Schuman Vis. Prof., Fudan Univ., Shanghai, 1998. Pres., European Consortium for Regl and Federal Studies, 1993–94. *Publications:* The Parliament of the European Communities, 1964; (jtly) Economic Planning and Policies in Britain, France and Germany, 1968; (ed jtly) The Theory of International Relations, 1970; Unions of States: the theory and practice of confederation, 1981; Reason and Revolution: the political theory of the Abbé Sieyes, 1987; (ed jtly) The Political Classics: Plato to Rousseau, 1988; (ed) Federalism and Nationalism, 1989; (trans.) The Spirit of the Revolution of 1789, 1989; (ed jtly) The Political Classics: Hamilton to Mill, 1993, Green to Dworkin, 1996. *Recreations:* collecting prints and watercolours, browsing in second-hand bookshops. *Address:* Blackmore House, Blackmore Park Road, Malvern, Worcs WR14 3LF. *T:* (01684) 560901.

FORSYTH, Rt Rev. Robert Charles; Bishop of South Sydney and an Assistant Bishop, Diocese of Sydney, since 2000; *b* 8 June 1949; *m* 1970, Margaret Diane Shelley; two *s* two *d*. *Educ:* Meadowbank Boys' High Sch.; Sydney Univ.; Moore Coll. Assistant Minister: Glenbrook, 1976–77; Holy Trinity, Adelaide, 1978–83; Rector, St Barnabas', Broadway and Chaplain, Sydney Univ., 1983–2000. Sydney Gen. Synod Rep., 1990– (Mem., Strategic Issues Adv. Panel, 1999–); Member: Sydney Standing Cttee, 1990–; Archbishop's Liturgical Panel, 1993–; St Andrew's Cathedral Chapter, 1993–; Sydney Doctrine Commn, 1994–; Archbishop's Selection Panel, 1996– (Examining Chaplain, 1991–94). Sydney Anglican Cursillo Spiritual Dir, 1995–97. Chairman: EU Graduates Fund, 1995–; Langham Partnership Australia, 2000–. Columnist, Southern Cross newspaper, 1989–2000; co-author and developer, LifeWorks evangelism prog. *Address:* PO Box Q190, QVB Post Office, NSW 2000, Australia. *Club:* Australian (Sydney).

FORSYTH-JOHNSON, Bruce Joseph, (Bruce Forsyth), CBE 2006 (OBE 1998); entertainer and comedian; *b* 22 Feb. 1928; *m* 1st, 1953, Penny Calvert (marr. diss.); three *d*; 2nd, 1973, Anthea Redfern (marr. diss. 1982); two *d*; 3rd, 1983, Wilnelia Merced; one *s*. *Educ:* Higher Latimer Sch., Edmonton. Started stage career as Boy Bruce—The Mighty Atom, 1942; after the war, appeared in various double acts and did a 2 yr spell at Windmill Theatre; first television appearance, Music Hall, 1954; resident compère, Sunday Night at the London Palladium, 1958–60; own revue, London Palladium, 1962; leading role, Little Me, Cambridge Theatre, 1964; début at Talk of the Town (played there 7 times); compèred Royal Variety Show, 1971, and on subseq. occasions; London Palladium Show, 1973 (also Ottawa and Toronto) and 1980; commenced Generation Game, BBC TV series, 1971 (completed 7 series), and 1990–95; compèred Royal Windsor to mark BBC Jubilee Celebrations, 1977; One Man Show, Theatre Royal, Windsor, and Lakeside, 1977; Bruce Forsyth's Big Night, ITV, 1978; Play Your Cards Right, ITV, 1980–87, 1994–2000; Slinger's Day, ITV, 1986, 1987; You Bet!, 1988; Takeover Bid, BBC, 1990–91; Bruce's Guest Night, BBC, 1992–93; Bruce's Price is Right, 1996–2000; Strictly Come Dancing, BBC, 2004–07. Films include: Star; Can Hieronymous Merkin Ever Forget Mercy Humppe and Find True Happiness?; Bedknobs and Broomsticks; The Magnificent 7 Deadly Sins; Pavlova. Numerous records. Fellow, BAFTA, 2008. Show Business Personality of the Year, Variety Club of GB, 1975; TV Personality of the Year, Sun Newspaper, 1976 and 1977; Male TV Personality of the Year, TV Times, 1975, 1976, 1977 and 1978; Favourite Game Show Host, TV Times, 1984; BBC TV Personality of the Year, 1991; Lifetime Achievement Award, Comic Heritage, 2002. *Publication:* Bruce: the autobiography, 2001. *Recreation:* golf (handicap 10, Wentworth Golf Club). *Address:* c/o Billy Marsh Associates, 76a Grove End Road, St John's Wood, NW8 9ND.

FORSYTHE, Air Cdre James Roy, (Paddy), CBE 1966; DFC; Director of Development, 1976–81, Joint Chief Executive, 1981–86, Look Ahead Housing Association Ltd; *b* 10 July 1920; *s* of W. R. and A. M. Forsythe; *m* 1st, 1946, Barbara Mary Churchman (*d* 1983); two *s* two *d*; 2nd, 1989, Mrs W. P. Newbery. *Educ:* Methodist Coll., Belfast; Queen's Univ., Belfast. Bomber Comd, 1944–45; OC, Aberdeen Univ. Air Sqdn, 1952–54; psa 1955; Principal Staff Officer to Dir-Gen. Orgn (RAF), 1956–58; OC, 16 Sqdn, 1958–60; Directing Staff, Coll. of Air Warfare, Manby, 1960–62; Head of RAF Aid Mission to India, 1963; Stn Comdr, RAF Acklington, 1963–65; Dep. Dir Air Staff Policy, MoD, 1965–68; Dir Public Relations, Far East, 1968–70; Dir Recruiting, RAF, 1971–73; Dir, Public Relations, RAF, 1973–75. Chm., RAF RU, 1972, 1973, 1974; Chm., Combined Services RU, 1974; Vice-Pres., 1979, Chm., 1988–90, Pres., 1990–92, London Irish RFC. Chm., League of Friends, Royal Brompton Hosp., 1992–98. MCIPR. *Recreations:* Rugby, golf. *Address:* 104 Earls Court Road, W8 6EG. *T:* (020) 7937 5291. *Club:* Royal Air Force.

FORSYTHE, John Leslie Robert, FRCS, FRCSE; Consultant Transplant Surgeon, since 1995, and Clinical Director (formerly Lead Clinician), Transplant Service, since 1999, Royal Infirmary of Edinburgh; Reader in Surgery, School of Clinical Sciences and Community Health, University of Edinburgh, since 2006; *b* 27 Feb. 1958; *s* of Rev. Canon John Leslie Forsythe and Margaret Forsythe; *m* 1982, Jo-ann E. G. Harvey (marr. diss. 2007); one *s* two *d*. *Educ:* Univ. of Newcastle upon Tyne (MB BS 1981); Edinburgh Univ. (MD 1991); FRCSE 1986; FRCS 2001. Surgical trng, Newcastle upon Tyne; Consultant Transplant Surgeon and Hon. Sen. Lectr, Royal Victoria Infirmary, Newcastle upon Tyne, 1991–95. Specialist Advr to CMO, Scotland, 2000–07. Chairman: Scottish Transplant Gp, 2001; Kidney Pancreas Adv. Gp, UK Transplant SHA, 2002–06 (Mem. 1996–2001); Adv. Cttee on Safety of Blood, Tissues and Organs, DoH, 2007–. Member: Bd, NHS Quality Improvements Scotland, 2003–08; Bd, NHS Blood and Transplant, 2006–. Pres., British Transplantation Soc., 2005–07 (Vice-Pres., 2003–05). *Publications:* A Companion to Specialist Surgical Practice, Vol. VII, 1997, 3rd edn 2005; Principles and Practice in Surgery, 2002; numerous reviewed contribs to learned jls. *Address:* Transplant Unit, Royal Infirmary of Edinburgh, 51 Little France Crescent, Old Dalkeith Road, Edinburgh EH16 4SA. *T:* (0131) 242 1715, *Fax:* (0131) 242 1739; *e-mail:* john.forsythe@luht.scot.nhs.uk.

FORSYTHE, Dr (John) Malcolm; Chairman, South West Kent Primary Care Trust (formerly Tunbridge Wells Primary Care Group), 1998–2004; *b* 11 July 1936; *s* of late Dr John Walter Joseph Forsythe and Dr Charlotte Constance Forsythe (*née* Beatty); *m* 1961, Delia Kathleen Moore (marr. diss. 1984); one *s* three *d*; *m* 1985, Patricia Mary Barnes. *Educ:* Repton Sch., Derby; Guy's Hosp. Med. Sch., London Univ. BSc(Hons), MB, BS, MSc; DObstRCOG, FRCP; FFPH. Area Medical Officer, Kent AHA, 1974–78; SE Thames Regional Health Authority: Dir of Planning, 1985–89; Regl MO, 1978–92; Regl Dir of Public Health and Service Develt, 1989–92; Professorial Fellow in Public Health, Kent Univ., 1992–2001; Sen. Lectr, King's Coll. Sch. of Medicine and Dentistry, 1992–2001. Hon. Consultant, Univ. of Kent Health Services Res. Unit, 1977–92. Vis. Prof., Univ. of N Carolina, Chapel Hill, 1973, 1976, 1993; Adjunct Prof., Univ. of St Georges, Grenada, 1995–; Jack Masur Fellow, Amer. Hosp. Assoc., 1976. Head, UK Deleg., Hospital Cttee, EEC, 1980–85, 1989–90; Consultant, Urwick Orr Ltd; Chm., GMC Wkg Pty on Performance Assessment in Public Health Medicine, 1995–97; Member: Resource Allocation Wkg Pty and Adv. Gp on Resource Allocation, 1975–78; Technical Sub Gp, Review of Resource Allocation Working Party Formula, 1986–87; DHSS Med. Manpower Planning Review, 1986–88; NHS Computer Policy Cttee, 1981–85; Standing Med. Adv. Cttee to Sec. of State, 1982–86; PHLS Bd, 1986–95; Central Council for Postgrad. Med. Educn, 1986–88; Health Services Res. Cttee, MRC, 1988–91; Bd of Governors, UMDS of Guy's and St Thomas', 1982–92; Delegacy, King's Coll. Hosp. Med. and Dental Schs, 1978–95. External Examiner to Univ. of London, 1987–89. Member: Bd of Management, Horder Centre for Arthritis, Crowborough, 1992– (Chm., 1996–2000); Tech. Bd, BUPA Ltd, 1992–2007. Trustee, Sick Doctors Trust, 1996–. Vice-Pres., Epidemiology Sect., RSM, 2001–04 (Pres., 1998–2000); Mem. Editl Bd, RCP, 1999–2003. Member: Hyde Housing Assoc., 1999–; Bd, Chichester Diocesan Housing Assoc., 2001–07; Bd, In Touch, 2006–. Chm., Ind. Remuneration Panel, Tonbridge & Malling BC, Sevenoaks DC and Tunbridge Wells BC, 2001–07. Council of Europe Fellowship, 1975; Silver Core Award, IFIP, 1977. *Publications:* (ed jtly) Information Processing of Medical Records, 1969; Proceedings of First World Conference on Medical Informatics, 1975. *Recreations:* tennis, music, ornithology. *Address:* Buckingham House, 1 Royal Chase, Tunbridge Wells, Kent TN4 8AX. *T:* (01892) 522359. *Clubs:* Royal Society of Medicine (Hon. Sec., Retired Fellows Section, 2006–); Chasers.

FORSYTHE, Air Cdre Paddy; *see* Forsythe, Air Cdre J. R.

FORSYTHE, William; choreographer; Director: Theater am Turm, since 1999 (Artistic Director, 1996–99); The Forsythe Company, since 2005; *b* NYC, 1949; *m*; one *s* one *d*. *Educ:* Jacksonville Univ., Florida; Joffrey Ballet Sch., NY. Joined Stuttgart Ballet as dancer, 1973, subseq. choreographer; Dir, Frankfurt Ballet, 1984–2004. *Works choreographed* include: Urlicht, 1976; Flore Subsimplici, 1978; Orpheus, 1979; Gänge, 1983; Artifact, 1984; Steptext, 1985; Impressing the Czar, 1988; Limb's Theorem, 1991; The Loss of Small Detail, 1991; Herman Schmerman, 1992; Firstext, 1995; Eidos: Telos, 1995; In The Middle, Somewhat Elevated, 1987; The The, 1998; Work within Work, 1998; Quartette, 1998; Woundwork, 1999; Endless House, 1999; Die Befragung des Robert Scott, 2000; Kammer Kammer, 2000; Woolf Phrase, 2001; works performed by NYC Ballet, San Francisco Ballet, Nat. Ballet of Canada, Royal Ballet, Royal Swedish Ballet, etc. *Address:* The Forsythe Company, Bockenheimer Depot, Bockenheimer Warte, 60325 Frankfurt am Main, Germany.

FORT, Mrs Jean; Headmistress of Roedean School, Brighton, 1961–70; *b* 1915; *d* of G. B. Rae; *m* 1943, Richard Fort (*d* 1959), MP Clitheroe Division of Lancs; four *s* one *d*. *Educ:* Benenden Sch.; Lady Margaret Hall, Oxford (MA, DipEd). Asst Mistress, Dartford County Sch. for Girls, 1937–39; WVS Headquarters staff, 1939–40; Junior Civil Asst, War Office, 1940–41; Personal Asst to Sir Ernest Gowers, Sen. Regional Comr for Civil Def., London, 1941–44. *Address:* 6 King's Close, Henley-on-Thames, Oxon RG9 2DS.

FORT, Dame Maeve (Geraldine), DCMG 1998 (CMG 1990); DCVO 1999; HM Diplomatic Service, retired; High Commissioner, South Africa, 1996–2000; *b* 19 Nov. 1940; *d* of late F. L. and R. E. Fort. *Educ:* Trinity College, Dublin (MA); Sorbonne, Paris. Joined Foreign Service, 1963; UKMIS, NY, 1964; CRO, 1965; seconded to SEATO, Bangkok, 1966; Bonn, 1968; Lagos, 1971; Second, later First Sec., FCO, 1973; UKMIS, NY, 1978; Counsellor, FCO, 1982; RCDS, 1983; Counsellor, Hd of Chancery and Consul-Gen., Santiago, 1984–86; Head of W African Dept, FCO, 1986–89, and Ambassador (non-resident) to Chad, 1987–89; Ambassador to: Mozambique, 1989–92; Lebanese Republic, 1992–96. Trustee: Beit Trust, 2000–; BRCS, 2001–07. *Address:* 5 Simon Close, Portobello Road, W11 3DJ.

FORTE, Hon. Sir Rocco (John Vincent), Kt 1995; FCA; Chairman, Rocco Forte Hotels (formerly RF Hotels Ltd), since 1996; *b* 18 Jan. 1945; *s* of Baron Forte; *m* 1986, Aliai, *d* of Prof. Giovanni Ricci, Rome; one *s* two *d*. *Educ:* Downside Coll.; Pembroke Coll., Oxford (MA). Trusthouse Forte, subseq. Forte: Dir of Personnel, 1973–78; Dep. Chief Exec., 1978–82; Jt Chief Exec., 1982–83; Chief Exec., 1983–92; Chm., 1992–96. Pres., BHA. Dir, BTA, 1986–97. *Recreations:* triathlon, golf, country pursuits. *Address:* (office) 70 Jermyn Street, SW1 6NY.

See also Hon. O. Polizzi.

FORTESCUE, family name of **Earl Fortescue**.

FORTESCUE, 8th Earl *cr* 1789; **Charles Hugh Richard Fortescue;** Baron Fortescue, 1746; Viscount Ebrington, 1789; *b* 10 May 1951; *s* of 7th Earl and his 1st wife, Penelope Jane (*d* 1959), *d* of Robert Evelyn Henderson; *S* father, 1993; *m* 1974, Julia, *er d* of Air Commodore J. A. Sowrey; three *d*. *Heir: cousin* John Andrew Francis Fortescue [*b* 27 March 1955; *m* 1990, Phoebe Anne Cecilia, *d* of late Rev. John Eustace Burridge; two *s* one *d*].

FORTESCUE, Hon. Seymour Henry; Chief Executive, Banking Code Standards Board, 1999–2006; *b* 28 May 1942; *s* of 6th Earl Fortescue, MC, TD and late Sybil, *d* of 3rd Viscount Hardinge, CB; *m* 1st, 1966, Julia Mary Blair Pilcher (marr. diss. 1990); one *s* one *d*; 2nd, 1990, Jennifer Ann Simon; one *d*. *Educ:* Eton Coll.; Trinity Coll., Cambridge (MA); London Business Sch. (MSc). With Barclays Bank plc, 1964–91: Local Dir, Luton, 1972–77; Hd, Mktg, 1977–80; Chief Exec., Barclaycard, 1980–85; Dir, UK Personal

Sector, 1986–91; Dir, Voluntary Income, ICRF, 1991–96; Chief Exec., HEA, 1996–99. Chm., UK Remittances Task Force, 2006–. Hon. Treas., LEPRA, 1985–96; Chm., BookPower (formerly Educnl Low-Priced Sponsored Texts), 2001–07. Mem. Council, London Univ., 2006–; Governor, Oundle Sch., 1999–2004. Mem., Court of Assistants, Grocers' Co., 1987– (Master, 1997–98). *Recreations:* gardening, travel, opera, country activities. *Address:* Flat 2, 11 Chelsea Embankment, SW3 4LE. *T:* (01235) 868592.

FORTESCUE, Trevor Victor Norman, (Tim), CBE 1984; Secretary-General, Food and Drink Industries Council, 1973–83; *b* 28 Aug. 1916; *s* of Frank Fortescue; *m* 1st, 1939, Margery Stratford (marr. diss. 1975), *d* of Dr G. H. Hunt; one *s* one *d* (and one *s* decd); 2nd, 1975, Anthea Maureen, *d* of Robert M. Higgins. *Educ:* Uppingham Sch.; King's Coll., Cambridge. BA 1938; MA 1945. Colonial Administrative Service, Hong Kong, 1939–47 and Kenya, 1949–51 (interned by Japanese, 1941–45); FAO, UN, Washington, DC, 1947–49 and Rome, 1951–54; Chief Marketing Officer, Milk Marketing Bd of England and Wales, 1954–59; Manager, Nestlé Gp of Cos, Vevey, Switz., 1959–63 and London, 1963–66. MP (C) Liverpool, Garston, 1966–Feb. 1974; an Asst Govt Whip, 1970–71; a Lord Comr of HM Treasury, 1971–73. Chairman: Conference Associates Ltd, 1978–87; Standing Cttee, Confedn of Food and Drink Industries of European Community (CIAA), 1982–84; Pres., British Food Manufg Industries Res. Assoc., 1984–92; Member: Meat Promotion Rev. Body, 1984; Council, British Industrial Biol. Res. Assoc., 1980–83. Develt Manager (with A. M. Fortescue), Winchester Cathedral, 1989–90; Dir, Winchester Cathedral Enterprises Ltd, 1990–2000. Trustee, Uppingham Sch., 1957–63; Patron and Trustee, The Quest Community, Birmingham, 1971–85. *Publications:* Lovelines, 1987; Lovelines from Winchester, 1996. *Recreation:* marriage to Anthea. *Address:* 4 Compton Road, Winchester, Hants SO23 9SL. *T:* (01962) 854693.

FORTEVIOT, 4th Baron *cr* 1917 of Dupplin, Perthshire; **John James Evelyn Dewar;** Bt 1907; farmer, landowner; *b* 5 April 1938; *s* of 3rd Baron Forteviot, MBE, and Cynthia Monica Starkie (*d* 1986); *S* father, 1993; *m* 1963, Lady Elisabeth Waldegrave (*d* 2003), 3rd *d* of 12th Earl Waldegrave, KG, GCVO; one *s* three *d. Educ:* Eton. Nat. Service, Black Watch (RHR), 1956–58. John Dewar & Sons Ltd, 1959–62; ADC to Governor General of NZ, 1962–63; John Dewar & Sons, 1963–98. *Recreations:* fishing, shooting, birdwatching, travel. *Heir: s* Hon. Alexander John Edward Dewar [*b* 4 March 1971; *m* 1997, Donryn (*née* Clement); two *s* one *d*]. *Clubs:* Boodle's, Royal Perth Golfing and Country and City.

FORTEY, Dr Richard Alan, FRS 1997; Merit Researcher, since 1986, Research Associate, since 2006, Natural History Museum; *b* 15 Feb. 1946; *s* of Frank Allen Fortey and Margaret Fortey (*née* Wilshin); *m* 1st, 1968, Bridget Elizabeth Thomas (marr. diss.); one *s;* 2nd, 1977, Jacqueline Francis; one *s* two *d. Educ:* Ealing Grammar Sch.; King's Coll., Cambridge (BA, MA; PhD 1971; ScD 1986). Res. Fellow, 1970–73, SSO, 1973–77, BM (Natural Hist.); PSO, Natural Hist. Mus., 1978–86. Howley Vis. Prof., Meml Univ. of Newfoundland, 1977–78; Vis. Prof. of Palaeobiology, Univ. of Oxford, 2000–08; Collier Prof. of Public Understanding of Sci. and Technol., Univ. of Bristol, 2002–03. Pres., Geol Soc. of London, 2006–08 (Mem., 1972–); Mem., Brit. Mycological Soc., 1980–. Lyell Medal, Geol Soc., 1996; Frink Medal, Zool Soc. of London, 2001; Lewis Thomas Prize, Rockefeller Univ., 2003; Linnean Medal for Zoology, 2006; Michael Faraday Prize, Royal Soc., 2006. *Publications:* Fossils: the key to the past, 1982, 3rd edn 2002; The Hidden Landscape, 1993; Life: an unauthorized biography, 1997; Trilobite!, 2000; The Earth: an intimate history, 2004; Dry Store Room No 1: the secret life of the Natural History Museum, 2008; (as Roderick Masters) The Roderick Masters Book of Money Making Schemes, 1981. *Recreations:* mushrooms and toadstools, East Anglia, cacti, conviviality. *Address:* Natural History Museum, South Kensington, Cromwell Road, SW7 5BD. *T:* (020) 7942 5493.

FORTUNE, John; scriptwriter and actor; *b* 30 June 1939; *s* of Hubert William George Wood and Edna Maude Fortune; *m* 1st, 1962, Susannah Waldo (marr. diss. 1976); one *s* one *d;* 2nd, 1995, Emma Burge. *Educ:* Cathedral Sch., Bristol; King's Coll., Cambridge (MA). Has worked in theatre and television since 1961; *television* includes: writer and performer: Not So Much a Programme, More a Way of Life; BBC3; The Late Show; Rory Bremner; Rory Bremner… Who Else?; Bremner, Bird and Fortune; writer: Roger Doesn't Live Here Anymore; Round and Round. *Publications:* (with John Wells) A Melon for Ecstasy, 1971; (with Eleanor Bron) Is Your Marriage Really Necessary?, 1972; (with John Bird) The Long Johns, 1996; (with John Bird and Rory Bremner) You Are Here, 2004. *Recreation:* lounging about. *Address:* c/o Richard Stone Partnership, 2 Henrietta Street, WC2E 8PS. *T:* (020) 7497 0849.

FORTUNE, Robert Andrew; QC 2003; *b* 4 July 1953; *s* of Hamish Campbell Fortune and Hazel Phoebe Fortune. *Educ:* Millfield Sch.; London Sch. of Econs (LLB Hons). Called to the Bar, Middle Temple, 1976, in practice, specialising in criminal law. *Recreations:* travel, reading, archaeology. *Address:* 9 Bedford Row, WC1R 4AZ. *T:* (020) 7489 2727, *Fax:* (020) 7489 2828.

FORTY, Prof. Arthur John, CBE 1991; PhD, DSc; FRSE; FRSA; Principal and Vice-Chancellor, Stirling University, 1986–94; *b* 4 Nov. 1928; *s* of Alfred Louis Forty and Elisabeth Forty; *m* 1950, Alicia Blanche Hart Gough; one *s. Educ:* Headlands Grammar Sch.; Bristol Univ. (BSc; PhD 1953; DSc 1967). FRSE 1988, FRSA 1989. Served RAF, 1953–56. Sen. Res. Scientist, Tube Investments Ltd, 1956–58; Lectr, Univ. of Bristol, 1958–64; University of Warwick: Foundn Prof. of Physics, 1964–86; Pro-Vice-Chancellor, 1970–86. Visiting scientist: Gen. Electric Co., USA; Boeing Co.; Nat. Bureau of Standards, Washington, USA. Member: SRC Physics Cttee, 1969–73; SRC Materials Cttee, 1970–73; Computer Bd, 1982–85; University Grants Committee: Mem., 1982–86, Vice-Chm., 1985–86; Chairman: Physical Sciences Sub-cttee, 1985–86; Equipment Sub-cttee, 1985–86; Chairman: Jt ABRC, Computer Bd and UGC Working Party on Future Facilities for Advanced Res. Computing (author, Forty Report), 1985; Management Cttee for Res. Councils' Supercomputer Facility, 1986–88; UFC Cttee for Information Systems (formerly Computer Bd for Univs and Res. Councils), 1988–91; Jt Policy Cttee for Advanced Res. Computing, 1988–94; Cttee of Scottish Univ. Principals, 1990–92; Edinburgh Parallel Computing Centre, 1994–97; Adv. Cttee, Scottish Science Liby, 1995–2001; Member: British Library Bd, 1987–94; Bd of Trustees, Nat. Liby of Scotland, 1995–2001; Academic Adv. Bd, Univ. of the Highlands and Islands, 1999–. Chm., ICIAM 99 Ltd, 1995–96. Hon. Fellow, Edinburgh Univ., 1994. Hon. LLD St Andrew's, 1989; DUniv Stirling, 1995; Hon. DSc Warwick, 2005. *Publications:* papers in Proc. Royal Soc., Phil Magazine and other learned jls. *Recreations:* sailing, gardening, the ancient metallurgy of gold. *Address:* Port Mor, St Fillans, by Crieff, Perthshire.

FORWELL, Prof. George Dick, OBE 1993; PhD; FRCP; Chief Administrative Medical Officer, 1973–93, and Director of Public Health, 1989–93, Greater Glasgow Health Board; *b* 6 July 1928; *s* of Harold C. Forwell and Isabella L. Christie; *m* 1957, Catherine F. C. Cousland; two *d. Educ:* George Watson's Coll., Edinburgh; Edinburgh Univ. (MB, ChB 1950; PhD 1955). MRCPE 1957, DIH 1957, DPH 1959, FRCPE 1967, FFCM 1972, FRCPGlas 1974, FRCP 1985. House Officer and Univ. Clin. Asst, Edinburgh Royal Infirm., 1950–52; RAF Inst. of Aviation Med., 1952–54; MRC and RCPE grants,

1954–56; pneumoconiosis field res., 1956–57; Grad. Res. Fellow and Lectr, Edinburgh Univ. Dept of Public Health and Social Med., 1957–60; Asst Dean, Faculty of Med., Edinburgh Univ., 1960–63; Dep. Sen. and Sen. Admin. MO, Eastern Reg. Hosp. Bd, Dundee, 1963–67; PMO, Scottish Home and Health Dept, 1967–73. Vis. Prof., Dept of Public Health, Glasgow Univ., 1990–93; Hon. Prof., Sch. of Biol and Med. Scis, St Andrews Univ., 1993–98. QHP, 1980–83. Mem., GMC, 1984–89. *Publications:* papers on clin. res. and on health planning and services, in med. and other jls. *Recreation:* running. *Address:* 20 Irvine Crescent, St Andrews, Fife KY16 8LG. *Club:* Royal Air Force.

FORWOOD, family name of **Baroness Arlington**.

FORWOOD, Nicholas James; QC 1987; **Hon. Judge Forwood;** Judge, Court of First Instance, European Community, since 1999; *b* 22 June 1948; *s* of Lt-Col Harry Forwood and late Wendy Forwood (*née* French-Smith); *m* 1971, Sally Diane Gerrard, *e d* of His Honour Basil Harding Gerrard; one *s* three *d. Educ:* Stowe Sch.; St John's Coll., Cambridge (Open Schol., MA, Pt I Mechanical Scis, Pt II Law). Called to the Bar, Middle Temple, 1970, Bencher, 1998. Member: Law Adv. Cttee, British Council, 1985–91; Internat. Relations (formerly Internat. Practice) Cttee, Bar Council, 1994–99. Chm., Permanent Delegn of CCBE to European Courts, 1997–99. *Recreations:* ski-ing, golf, walking across Europe, opera. *Address:* Court of First Instance of the EC, rue du Fort Niedergrünewald, 2925 Luxembourg. *T:* 43031; 14 rue de Bourglinster, 6112 Junglinster, Luxembourg. *Club:* Oxford and Cambridge.

FORWOOD, Sir Peter Noel, 4th Bt *cr* 1895; *b* 15 Oct. 1925; *s* of Arthur Noel Forwood, 3rd *s* of 1st Bt, and Hyacinth Forwood (*née* Pollard); *S* cousin, 2001; *m* 1950, Roy Murphy; six *d. Educ:* Radley. Served 1939–45 War, Welsh Guards. *Heir:* none. *Address:* Newhouse Farm, Shillinglee, Chiddingfold Godalming, Surrey GU8 4SZ.

FOSKETT, Hon. Sir David (Robert), Kt 2007; **Hon. Mr Justice Foskett;** a Judge of the High Court of Justice, Queen's Bench Division, since 2007; *b* 19 March 1949; *s* of Robert Frederick Foskett and Ruth (*née* Waddington); *m* 1975, Angela Bridget Jacobs; two *d. Educ:* Warwick Sch.; King's Coll., London (LLB Hons; Pres., Faculty of Laws, 1969–70; Pres., Union Soc., 1970–71; Mem., Delegacy, 1970–72). FCIArb 1992. Called to the Bar, Gray's Inn, 1972, Bencher, 1999; Mem., Midland Circuit; QC 1991; Asst Recorder, 1992–95; Recorder, 1995–2007; a Dep. High Ct Judge, 1998–2007. Mem., Civil Procedure Rule Cttee, 1997–2001; Chm., Law Reform Cttee, Bar Council, 2005–07. President: KCL Assoc., 1997–2000; Old Warwickian Assoc., 2000. *Publications:* The Law and Practice of Compromise, 1980, 6th edn 2005; Settlement Under the Civil Procedure Rules, 1999; various articles. *Recreations:* theatre, music, poetry, cricket, golf. *Address:* Royal Courts of Justice, Strand, WC2A 2LL. *Clubs:* Athenæum, MCC; Woking Golf.

FOSTER, family name of **Barons Foster of Bishop Auckland** and **Foster of Thames Bank**.

FOSTER OF BISHOP AUCKLAND, Baron *cr* 2005 (Life Peer), of Bishop Auckland in the County of Durham; **Derek Foster;** PC 1993; DL; *b* 25 June 1937; *s* of Joseph and Ethel Maud Foster; *m* 1972, Florence Anne Bulmer; three *s* one *d. Educ:* Bede Grammar Sch., Sunderland; Oxford Univ. (BA Hons PPE). In industry and commerce, 1960–70; Youth and Community Worker, 1970–73; Further Educn Organiser, Durham, 1973–74; Asst Dir of Educn, Sunderland Borough Council, 1974–79. Councillor: Sunderland Co. Borough, 1972–74; Tyne and Wear County Council, 1973–77 (Chm. Econ. Develt Cttee, 1973–76). Chm., North of England Develt Council, 1974–76. MP (Lab) Bishop Auckland, 1979–2005. North Regional Whip, 1981–82; opposition front bench spokesman on social security, 1982–83; PPS to Leader of Opposition, 1983–85; Opposition Chief Whip, 1985–95; opposition front bench spokesman on the Duchy of Lancaster, 1995–97. Member: Select Cttee on Trade and Industry, 1980–82, on Employment, 1997–2005 (Chm., 1997–2001), on Educn and Employment, 1997–2005 (Jt Chm., 1997–2001); Standards and Privileges Select Cttee, 2003–05. Member: H of C Liaison Cttee, 1997–2005; Parly Ecclesiastical Cttee, 1997–2005; Registration of Political Parties Adv. Gp, 1998–2005; Exec. Mem., British American Parly Gp, 1997–2005. Chairman: PLP Employment Cttee, 1980–81; PLP Econ. and Finance Cttee, 1981–82. Mem. (ex officio) Lab. Party NEC, 1985–95. Fellow, Industry and Parlt Trust. Chm., Bishop Auckland Develt Co., 2001–; Mem., Co. Durham Develt Co., 2006–. Chairman: Manufg Industry Gp, 1998–; N Regl Electronic Economy Prog.; non-executive Director: Northern Informatics, 1998–; Walker Hall Associates, 2006–; HB Innovations, 2006–; Pres., SW Durham Engrg Training Ltd, 2003–. Vice Chm., Youthaid, 1979–86; Chairman: Northern Region Information Soc. Initiative, 1996; Pioneering Care Partnership, 1997–; Nat. Prayer Breakfast, 1997–99; former Vice-Pres., Christian Socialist Movt; Mem., Nat. Adv. Bd, Salvation Army. Chm., Heritage Lottery Fund NE, 2006–. Trustee: Auckland Castle, 1996–; Nat. e² Learning Foundn, 2001– (Chm., e² Learning Foundn NE, 2004–). Mem., Fabian Soc. CompILE 2001. DL Durham, 2001. Hon. DCL Durham, 2005. *Recreations:* brass bands, choirs, uniformed member Salvation Army. *Address:* 3 Linburn, Rickleton, Washington, Tyne and Wear NE38 9EB. *T:* (0191) 4171580.

FOSTER OF THAMES BANK, Baron *cr* 1999 (Life Peer), of Reddish in the county of Greater Manchester; **Norman Robert Foster,** OM 1997; Kt 1990; RA 1991 (ARA 1983); RWA 1994; RDI 1988; RIBA, FCSD, FAIA; architect; Chairman Partner, Foster + Partners, London, Berlin, Singapore; *b* Reddish, 1 June 1935; *s* of late Robert Foster and Lilian Smith; *m* 3rd, 1996, Dr Elena Ochoa; one *s* one *d. Educ:* Univ. of Manchester Sch. of Architecture (DipArch 1961, CertTP); Yale Univ. Sch. of Architecture (Henry Fellow, Jonathan Edwards Coll., March 1962). Founded: Foster Associates, 1967; Foster and Partners, 1992; in collab. with Dr Buckminster Fuller, 1968–83; Cons. Architect, UEA, 1978–87. Mem. Council: AA, 1969–70, 1970–71 (Vice Pres., 1974); RCA, 1981. Taught at: Univ. of Pennsylvania; AA, London; Bath Acad. of Arts; London Polytechnic; Visiting Professor: Bartlett Sch. of Architecture, 1998; Harvard Univ. Grad. Scholar of Design, 2000. External Examr, 1971–73 and Mem. Visiting Bd of Educn, RIBA. Major projects include: Head Office for Willis Faber & Dumas, Ipswich, 1975 (First Trustees', Medal, RIBA, 1990); Sainsbury Centre for Visual Arts, UEA, Norwich, 1977; UK headquarters for Renault, 1983; Nomos Furniture System, 1985; new HQ, Hongkong and Shanghai Banking Corp., Hong Kong, 1986; King's Cross London Master Plan, 1988; Stockley Park, Uxbridge, 1989; Millennium Tower, Tokyo, 1990; RA Sackler Galls, 1991; Terminal Zone, Stansted Airport, 1991; ITN HQ, 1991; Century Tower, Tokyo, 1991; inner harbour, Duisburg, 1991–; Barcelona Telecoms Tower, 1992; Micro-Electronics Centre, Duisburg, 1993–97; Arts Centre, Nîmes, 1993; school, Fréjus, 1993; German Parlt bldg (Reichstag), Berlin, 1993 and 1999; Bilbao Metro System, 1995; Univ. of Cambridge Faculty of Law, 1996; American Air Mus., Duxford, 1997; HQ for Commerzbank, Frankfurt, 1997; Hong Kong Internat. Airport, 1998; Congress Centre, Valencia, 1998; BM redevelt, 2000; City Hall, London, 2002; Swiss Re Tower, London (RIBA Stirling Prize), 2004; TAG McLaren HQ, Woking, 2004; Sage Centre, Gateshead, 2004; Wembley Stadium, 2006. Work exhibited: Antwerp, Barcelona, Berlin, Bordeaux, Hanover, London, Lyon, Manchester, Madrid, Milan, Munich, NY, Nîmes, Paris, Seville,

Tokyo, Valencia, Zurich; permanent collections: MOMA, NY, Centre Georges Pompidou, Paris. IBM Fellow, Aspen Conference, 1980; Hon. Prof., Buenos Aires, 1997; Hon. FAIA 1980; Hon. FREng; Hon. FIStructE; Hon. FRIAS 2000; Hon. Fellow, Inst. of Art and Design, Kent; Hon. Mem., Bund Deutscher Architekten, 1983; Member: Internat. Acad. of Architecture, Sofia; French Order of Architects; Eur. Acad. of Scis and Arts; Foreign Member: Royal Acad. of Fine Arts, Sweden; Amer. Acad. of Arts and Scis; Associate, Académie Royale de Belgique, 1990. Hon. Dr: E Anglia, Bath, Valencia, Humberside, Manchester, RCA, Eindhoven, Oxford, London, Negev, London Inst. Practice awards: over 200 for design excellence, including: R. S. Reynolds Internat. Awards, USA, 1976, 1979, 1986; 23 RIBA Awards and Commendations; 8 Financial Times Awards for outstanding Industrial Architecture; 9 Structural Steel Awards; Internat. Design Award; RSA Award, 1976; Ambrose Congreve Award, 1980; 5 Civic Trust Awards; 2 IStructE Special Awards; Premio Compasso d'Oro Award, 1987; 5 Interiors Awards (USA); 8 British Construction Industry Awards; 4 Aluminium Imagination Awards; Best Building of the Year Award, Royal Fine Art Commn/Sunday Times, 1992, 1993, Royal Fine Art Commn/BSkyB, (jtly) 1998; 3 BCO Awards; Queen's Award for Export, 1995; Regl Arch. Award, AIA, 1995. Personal awards include: RIBA Gold Medal, 1983; Kunstpreis, Berlin, 1989; Japan Design Foundn Award, 1987; Mies van der Rohe Award, Barcelona, 1991; Gold Medal, French Acad. of Arch., 1991; Brunner Meml Award, AAIL, 1992; Gold Medal, AIA, 1994; MIPIM Man of the Year, 1996; Building Award Personality of the Year, 1996; Best Internat. Promotion of Barcelona Award, 1997; Silver Medal, CSD, 1997; Berliner Zeitung Kultur-preis, 1998; special prize for positive contribution to British-German relations, German-British Forum, 1998; Pritzker Architecture Prize, 1999; special prize, 4th Internat. Biennial of Architecture, São Paulo, 1999; Visual Arts Award, South Bank Show, 2001. Officer, Order of Arts and Letters (France), 1994; Order of North Rhine Westphalia. *Relevant publications:* The Work of Foster Associates, 1979; Norman Foster, 1988; Norman Foster Foster Associates Buildings and Projects, vol. 2, 1971–78, 1989, vol. 3, 1978–85, 1989, vol. 1, 1964–73 (Norman Foster Team Four and Foster Associates Buildings and Projects), 1991, vol. 4, 1985–89, 1996; (by Kenneth Powell) Stansted: Norman Foster and the architecture of flight, 1992; Norman Foster Sketches, 1992; Foster Associates, 1992; Foster and Partners, 1996; Sir Norman Foster, 1997; The Master Architect Series II: Norman Foster, 1997; Norman Foster 30 Colours, 1998; The Norman Foster Studio, 2000; On Foster...Foster On, 2000. *Recreations:* running, flying, ski-ing. *Address:* (office) Riverside Three, 22 Hester Road, SW11 4AN. *T:* (020) 7738 0455, *Fax:* (020) 7738 1107; *e-mail:* enquiries@fosterandpartners.com.

FOSTER, Alicia Christian, (Jodie); American film actress and director; *b* 19 Nov. 1962; *d* of Lucius Foster and Evelyn Foster (*née* Almond); two *s*. *Educ:* Yale Univ. (BA Eng. Lit. 1985). *Films* include: Napoleon and Samantha, 1972; Kansas City Bomber, 1972; Tom Sawyer, 1973; Alice Doesn't Live Here Anymore, 1975; Taxi Driver, 1976; Bugsy Malone, 1976; The Little Girl Who Lives Down the Lane, 1977; Candleshoe, 1977; Foxes, 1980; Carny, 1980; Hotel New Hampshire, 1984; Siesta, 1987; Five Corners, 1988; The Accused, 1988 (Academy Award for Best Actress, 1989); Little Man Tate, 1991 (also dir); The Silence of the Lambs, 1991 (Academy Award for Best Actress, 1992); Shadows and Fog, 1991; Sommersby, 1993; Maverick, 1994; Nell, 1994 (also prod.); dir and prod., Home for the Holidays, 1995; Contact, 1997; Anna and the King, 1999; Panic Room, 2002; Flight Plan, 2005; Inside Man, 2006; The Brave One, 2007; *television* includes: Mayberry, 1969; Bonanza; Paper Moon, 1974–75.

FOSTER, Alison Lee Caroline, (Lady Havelock-Allan); QC 2002; *b* 22 Jan. 1957; *o d* of Leslie Francis Foster and Marie Anne Foster (*née* Mackintosh Hudson); *m* 1986, (Anthony) Mark (David) Havelock-Allan (*see* Sir A. M. D. Havelock-Allan, Bt); one *s* two *d*. *Educ:* Bexhill Grammar Sch. for Girls; Jesus Coll., Oxford (BA Hons English 1979); Courtauld Inst. of Art, London Univ. (MPhil 1981); City Univ. (Dip. Law 1983). Called to the Bar, Inner Temple, 1984, Bencher, 2002; in practice, specialising in administrative law. Pt-time Legal Mem., Mental Health Rev. Tribunal, 2001–. *Recreations:* painting, gardening, fishing. *Address:* c/o 39 Essex Street, WC2R 3AT. *T:* (020) 7832 1111, *Fax:* (020) 7353 3978. *Club:* Groucho.

FOSTER, Prof. Allan (Bentham); Professor of Chemistry, University of London, 1966–86, now Emeritus; *b* 21 July 1926; *s* of late Herbert and Martha Alice Foster; *m* 1949, Monica Binns; two *s*. *Educ:* Nelson Grammar Sch., Lancs; University of Birmingham. Frankland Medal and Prize, 1947; PhD, 1950; DSc, 1957. University Res. Fellow, University of Birmingham, 1950–53; Fellow of Rockefeller Foundn, Ohio State Univ., 1953–54; University of Birmingham: ICI Res. Fellow, 1954–55; Lectr, 1955–62; Sen. Lectr, 1962–64; Reader in Organic Chemistry, 1964–66; Institute of Cancer Research: Head of Chemistry Div., Chester Beatty Res. Inst., 1966–82; Head, Drug Metabolism Team, Drug Develt Sect., 1982–86. Sec., British Technol. Gp, New Cancer Product Develt Adv. Bd, 1986–91. FChemSoc (Mem. Coun., 1962–65, 1967–70); Corresp. Mem., Argentinian Chem. Soc. Editor, Carbohydrate Research, 1965–92. *Publications:* numerous scientific papers mainly in Jl Chem. Soc., Carbohydrate Research and cancer jls. *Recreations:* golf, theatre. *Address:* 3 Wingfield Court, High Street, Banstead, Surrey SM7 2GD. *T:* (01737) 360780. *Club:* Banstead Downs.

FOSTER, Andrew Kevin, CBE 2005; Chief Executive, Wrightington, Wigan and Leigh NHS Trust, since 2007; *b* 3 March 1955; *s* of Kevin William Foster and late Doreen Foster; *m* 1981, Sara Gillian Daniels; one *s* two *d*. *Educ:* Millfield Sch.; Keble Coll., Oxford (BA Hons PPE, MA). Mktg Manager, Rowntree Mackintosh plc, 1976–81; Dir, Worldcrest Ltd, 1981–. Chairman: W Lancs NHS Trust, 1993–96; Wigan & Leigh NHS Trust, 1996–2001; Policy Dir, NHS Confedn, 1998–2001; Dir of Human Resources, then of Workforce, DoH, 2001–06; Dir of HR and Organisational Develt, Blackpool, Fylde and Wyre Hosps NHS Trust, 2006–07. *Recreations:* hockey, golf. *Address:* Wrightington, Wigan and Leigh NHS Trust Headquarters, Royal Albert Edward Infirmary, The Elms, Wigan Lane, Wigan WN1 2NN. *T:* (01942) 822196.

FOSTER, Sir Andrew (William), Kt 2001; Deputy Chairman, Royal Bank of Canada, since 2003; *b* 29 Dec. 1944; *s* of George William and Gladys Maria Foster; *m* 1st, 1967, Christine Marquiss (marr. diss. 2000); one *s* one *d*; 2nd, 2001, Jadranka Porter. *Educ:* Abingdon School; Newcastle Polytechnic (BSc Sociol.); LSE (Postgrad. Dip. Applied Social Studies). Social Worker, London, 1966–71; Area Social Services Officer, 1971–75; Asst Dir of Social Services, Haringey, 1975–79; Dir of Social Services, Greenwich, 1979–82, N Yorks, 1982–87; Regional Gen. Manager, Yorks RHA, 1987–91; Dep. Chief Exec., NHS Management Exec., 1991–92; Controller, Audit Commn, 1992–2003. Non-executive Director: Nestor Healthcare, 2004–; Nat. Express Gp, 2004–; Prudential Health Ltd, 2004–. Chair: Foster Review Group Athletics, 2004; Further Education Review Gp, 2005; Commonwealth Games England, 2007–; 2020 Public Services Commn, 2008–. Non-exec. Dir, Sport England, 2003–. Hon. DCL Northumbria at Newcastle, 1996. *Recreations:* golf, walking, travel, theatre, food, wine. *Address:* 269 Lauderdale Mansions, Lauderdale Road, Maida Vale, W9 1LZ.

FOSTER, Angiolina; Chief Executive, Communities Scotland, since 2004; *b* 1 Feb. 1956; *d* of Andrew Seath and Vera Seath; *m* 1983, Michael Foster; one *s* one *d*. *Educ:* Univ. of Glasgow (MA Hons); Glasgow Caledonian Univ. (Dip. Mgt Studies). Glasgow DC, 1979–85; Chief Housing Benefits Officer, Edinburgh DC, 1985–87; Depute Dir, Housing, City of Edinburgh Council, 1987–2001; Dir, Regulation and Inspection, Communities Scotland, 2001–02; Actg Chief Exec., Glasgow Housing Assoc., 2002–03. *Recreations:* long distance walks, charity runs, food and wine with good friends, cinema, theatre. *Address:* Communities Scotland, Thistle House, 91 Haymarket Terrace, Edinburgh EH12 5HE. *T:* (0131) 479 5200, *Fax:* (0131) 313 4527; *e-mail:* angiolina.foster@communitiesscotland.gsi.gov.uk.

FOSTER, Ann; *see* Knowles, P. A.

FOSTER, Arlene Isobel; Member (DemU) Fermanagh and South Tyrone, Northern Ireland Assembly, since 2003; Minister of the Environment, since 2007; *b* 17 July 1970; *d* of John William Kelly and Julia Georgina Kelly (*née* Sills); *m* 1995, William Brian Johnston Foster; two *s* one *d*. *Educ:* Collegiate Grammar Sch. for Girls, Enniskillen; Queen's Univ. Belfast (LLB Hons 1993; CPLS 1996). Solicitor, private practice, 1996–2005, pt-time 2005–07. Mem. (DemU), Fermanagh DC, 2005–07. Mem., NI Policing Bd, 2006–07. *Recreations:* reading (especially political and historical biographies), listening (and singing along to) music of all types. *Address:* (constituency office) 54 Belmore Street, Enniskillen BT74 6AA. *T:* (028) 0632 0722, *Fax:* (028) 0632 0123; *e-mail:* arlene.foster.co@niassembly.gov.uk.

FOSTER, Brendan, CBE 2008 (MBE 1976); television athletics commentator, since 1981; Managing Director, Nova International Ltd, since 1987; *b* 12 Jan. 1948; *s* of Francis and Margaret Foster; *m* 1972; one *s* one *d*. *Educ:* St Joseph's Grammar Sch., Hebburn, Co Durham; Sussex Univ. (BSc); Carnegie Coll., Leeds (DipEd). School Teacher, St Joseph's Grammar Sch., Hebburn, 1970–74; Sports and Recreation Manager, Gateshead Metropolitan Bor. Council, 1974–81; UK Man. Dir, Nike Internat., 1981–87; Chm. Nike (UK), 1981–86; Man. Dir, Nike Europe, 1985–87; Vice Pres. Marketing, Nike Inc Oregon, USA, 1986–87. Commonwealth Games: Bronze medal: 1500m, 1970; 5000m, 1978; Silver medal, 5000m, 1974; Gold medal, 10,000m, 1978; European Games: Bronze medal, 1500m, 1971; Gold medal, 5000m, 1974; Olympic Games: Bronze medal, 10,000m, 1976; World Records: 2 miles, 1973; 3000m, 1974. BBC Sports Personality of the Year, 1974. Hon. Fellow, Sunderland Polytechnic, 1977; Hon. MEd Newcastle, 1978; Hon. DLitt Sussex, 1982. *Publications:* Brendan Foster, 1978; Olympic Heroes 1896–1984, 1984. *Recreations:* running (now only a recreation), sport (as spectator). *Address:* Nova International Ltd, Newcastle House, Albany Court, Monarch Road, Newcastle upon Tyne NE4 7YB.

FOSTER, Prof. Brian, OBE 2003; DPhil; FRS 2008; CPhys, FInstP; Professor of Experimental Physics, University of Oxford, since 2003; Fellow of Balliol College, Oxford, since 2003; *b* 4 Jan. 1954; *s* of John and Annie Foster; *m* 1983, Sabine Margot Koch; two *s*. *Educ:* Wolsingham Secondary Sch.; Queen Elizabeth Coll., Univ. of London (BSc 1975); St John's Coll., Oxford (DPhil 1978); MA Oxon 2003. CPhys, FInstP 1992. Research Associate: Rutherford Appleton Lab., 1978–82; Imperial Coll. of Science and Technology, 1982–84; Bristol University: Lectr, 1984–92; SERC, subseq. PPARC Advanced Fellow, 1991–97; Reader, 1992–96; Prof. of Experimental Physics, 1996–2003, Emeritus, 2004. Chm., Nuclear and Particle Physics Div., Inst. of Physics, 1989–93; Recorder, Physics Section, BAAS, 1994–97; Mem., PPARC, 2001–06 (Mem., 1995, and Chm., 1996–99, Particle Physics Cttee; Jt Chm., 1996–99, Mem., 2001–07, Science Cttee); Mem., Physics Sub-Panel, 2008 RAE. Member: various adv. cttees, CERN, 1993–2000; Extended Scientific Council, Deutsches Elektronen-Synchrotron, 1998–; Evaluation Commn, Sci. Council of Germany, 2001–07; Scientific Policy Cttee, CERN Council, 2002–05; Chm., European Cttee for Future Accelerators, 2002–05. Spokesman, ZEUS Collaboration, 1999–2003; European Dir, Global Design Effort for the Internat. Linear Collider, 2005–. Alexander von Humboldt-Stiftung Res. Prize, 1999–2000; Max Born Medal, Inst. of Physics and German Physical Soc., 2003. *Publications:* (ed) Topics in High Energy Particle Physics, 1988; (ed jtly) Forty Years of Particle Physics, 1988; (ed and contrib.) Electron-Positron Annihilation Physics, 1990; numerous papers in learned jls; articles on science in popular press. *Recreations:* squash, violin playing, history and politics, hill walking. *Address:* Denys Wilkinson Building, Keble Road, Oxford OX1 3RH; Hillview Cottage, Blackford, near Wedmore, Somerset BS28 4NL. *T:* (01934) 712699.

FOSTER, Sir Christopher (David), Kt 1986; MA; Chairman, Better Government Initiative, since 2006; Vice-President: RAC, since 2003 (Vice-Chairman, 1998–99; non-executive Director, 1994–98); RAC Foundation, since 2003 (Chairman, 1999–2003); *b* 30 Oct. 1930; *s* of George Cecil Foster and Phyllis Joan Foster (*née* Mappin); *m* 1958, Kay Sheridan Bullock; two *s* three *d*. *Educ:* Merchant Taylors' Sch.; King's Coll., Cambridge (Scholar) (History Tripos Pt I, Economics Tripos Pt II, 1954; MA 1959). Commnd into 1st Bn Seaforth Highlanders, Malaya, 1949. Hallsworth Research Fellow, Manchester Univ., 1957–59; Senior Research Fellow, 1959–64, Official Fellow and Tutor, 1964–66, Hon. Fellow, 1992, Jesus Coll., Oxford; Dir-Gen. of Economic Planning, MoT, 1966–70; Head of Unit for Res. in Urban Economics, LSE, 1970–76; Prof. of Urban Studies and Economics, LSE, 1976–78; a Dir and Head of Econ. and Public Policy Div., Coopers & Lybrand Associates, 1978–84; a Dir, Public Sector Practice Leader and Economic Adviser, Coopers & Lybrand, 1984–86; Commercial Adviser to British Telecom, 1986–88; Sen. Public Sector and Econs Partner, Coopers & Lybrand Deloitte, later Coopers & Lybrand Associates, 1988–94; Advr to Chm., Coopers & Lybrand Associates, 1994–99. Governor, 1967–70, Dir, 1976–78, Centre for Environmental Studies; Visiting Professor: of Economics, MIT, 1970; LSE, 1978–86. Special Economic Adviser (part time), DoE, 1974–77; Special Advr on BR Privatisation to Sec. of State for Transport, 1992–94; Mem. Bd, Railtrack, 1994–2000. Member: (part time), PO Bd, 1975–77; Audit Commn, 1983–88; ESRC, 1985–89; Chm., NEDO Construction Industry Sector Gp, 1988–92; Chm., Cttee of Inquiry into Road Haulage Licensing, 1977–78; Mem., Cttee of Inquiry into Civil Service Pay, 1981–82; Economic Assessor, Sizewell B Inquiry, 1982–86. Member: Econ. and Financial Cttee, CBI, 1987–94; LDDC, 1988–96. Chairman: Circle 33 Housing Assoc., 1986–90; Construction Round Table, 1993–97. Gov., RSC, 1991–. *Publications:* The Transport Problem, 1963; Politics, Finance and the Role of Economics: an essay on the control of public enterprise, 1972; (with R. Jackman and M. Perlman) Local Government Finance, 1980; Privatisation, Public Ownership and the Regulation of Natural Monopoly, 1993; (with F. J. Plowden) The State Under Stress, 1996; British Government in Crisis, 2005; papers in various economic, political and other journals. *Address:* 6 Holland Park Avenue, W11 3QU. *T:* (020) 7727 4757. *Clubs:* Reform, Royal Automobile.

FOSTER, Christopher Norman; consultant on horseracing matters, since 2006; Keeper of the Match Book, The Jockey Club, since 1983; *b* 30 Dec. 1946; *s* of Maj.-Gen. Norman Leslie Foster, CB, DSO; *m* 1981, Anthea Jane Sammons; two *s*. *Educ:* Westminster Sch. ACA 1969, FCA 1979. Cooper Brothers & Co., Chartered Accountants, 1965–73; Weatherbys, 1973–90; The Jockey Club: Sec., 1983–90; Exec. Dir, 1993–2006. Vice

Chm., Internat. Fedn of Horseracing Authorities, 2000–08. Director: Wincanton Racecourse, 2006–; The National Stud, 2008–. Governor, Westminster Sch., 1990–. *Recreations:* racing, shooting, fishing, gardening. *Address:* The Old Vicarage, Great Durnford, Salisbury, Wilts SP4 6AZ. *Club:* MCC.

FOSTER, Rt Rev. Christopher Richard James; *see* Hertford, Bishop Suffragan of.

FOSTER, Prof. Christopher Stuart, MD; PhD, DSc; FRCPath; George Holt Professor of Pathology, and Director of Cellular Pathology and Molecular Genetics, University of Liverpool, since 1994; *b* Pilling, Lancs, 22 Oct. 1947; *s* of Geoffrey Stuart Foster and Dilys Joan Foster (*née* Hughes); *m* 1992, Joan Elizabeth Hardie; one *s* one *d*. *Educ:* Midsomer Norton Grammar Sch.; Dover Boys' Grammar Sch.; University Coll. London (BSc Physiol. and Biochem. 1966); Westminster Med. Sch. (MB BS 1974); Ludwig Inst. for Cancer Res., London (PhD 1983); Children's Hosp. of Philadelphia (MD 1987); Inst. of Cancer Res. (DSc 2002). LRCP, MRCS 1973; MRCPath 1984, FRCPath 1995. Exptl Officer, RN Physiol Lab., Alverstoke, 1966–68; SHO, Royal Marsden Hosp., Sutton, 1975–76; Registrar: in Gen. Medicine, Redhill Gen. Hosp., 1976–77; in Histopathol., Greenbank Hosp., 1977–79; Clin. Scientist, Ludwig Inst. for Cancer Res., London, 1979–83; Res. Fellow, ICRF and Sen. Registrar in Pathol., St Bartholomew's Hosp., London, 1983–85; Sen. Res. Fellow, Children's Hosp. of Philadelphia, 1985–87; Sen. Lectr in Pathol., RPMS and Hammersmith Hosp., London, 1987–94; Hd, Sch. of Clin. Lab. Scis, Univ. of Liverpool, 2004–06. Visiting Professor: Medunsa Univ., S Africa, 1990; Al Quds Med. Univ., Palestine, 1998; Univ. of Beijing, 2003–04. European Editor: Human Pathol., 1995–2005; Amer. Jl Clin. Pathol., 1999–2005. Chm., NHS-NW Reg. Pathol. Modernisation Cttee, 2000–01; Mem., Nat. Steering Cttee, Pathol. Modernisation, DoH, 2001–06. Reference Pathologist, WHO Prostate Cancer, 1999–; Co-Chm., Pathol. Section, WHO Internat. Consultation on Prostate Cancer, 1999; Chm., Pathol. Section, WHO Cttee on Benign Prostatic Hyperplasia, 2000; Sen. Pathologist, Transatlantic Prostate Gp, 2004–. Dir, Workforce Planning, RCPath, 2004–07. Mem. Council, ACP, 1995–98. *Publications:* Diagnostic Liver Pathology, 1993; Pathology of the Prostate, 1997; Pathology of the Urinary Bladder, 2004; Molecular Oncology of Prostate Cancer, 2007; contrib. papers on tumour pathology, particularly develt of novel biomarkers applied to diagnosis and prognosis of cancer. *Recreations:* ski-ing, sailing, fly-fishing, cooking. *Address:* Division of Pathology, School of Cancer Studies, University of Liverpool, Sixth Floor Duncan Building, Daulby Street, Liverpool L69 3GA. *T:* (0151) 706 4484, *Fax:* (0151) 706 5883; *e-mail:* csfoster@liv.ac.uk. *Club:* Athenæum.

FOSTER, Donald Michael Ellison; MP (Lib Dem) Bath, since 1992; *b* 31 March 1947; *s* of late Rev. J. A. Foster and Iris Edith (*née* Ellison); *m* 1968, Victoria, 2nd *d* of late Major Kenneth Pettegree, OBE, TD and Jean Pettegree; one *s* one *d*. *Educ:* Lancaster Royal Grammar Sch.; Univ. of Keele (BA Hons; Cert Ed 1969); Univ. of Bath (MEd 1982). CPhys, MInstP. Science teacher, Sevenoaks Sch., Kent, 1969–75; Science Curriculum Proj. Dir, Avon LEA, 1975–81; Science Educn Lectr, Bristol Univ., 1981–89: Head, Science Educn Centre; teacher trainer; organiser of link with Univ. of Zambia; Managing Consultant, Pannell Kerr Forster, 1989–92. Mem., Avon CC, 1981–89 (Leader, Liberal Gp; Chm., Educn Cttee, 1987–89). Mem. Exec. Cttee, ACC, 1985–89. Contested (L/All) Bristol East, 1987. Lib Dem spokesman: on educn, 1992–99; on envmt, transport and the regions, 1999–2001; on transport, local govt and the regions, 2001–02; on transport, 2002–03; on culture, media and sport, 2003–. Mem., Select Cttee on Educn and Employment, 1996–99. Treas., All-Party Yugoslav Gp, 1994–97. Vice-Chm., British Assoc. for Central and Eastern Europe, 1994–97. Pres., Nat. Campaign for Nursery Educn, 1999–2001 (Vice-Chm., 1993–99); Hon. Pres., British Youth Council, 1992–99; Trustee: Open Sch., 1992–99; Educn Extra, 1992–99. Hon. Fellow, Bath Coll. of Further Educn, 1994. *Publications:* Resource-based Learning in Science, 1979; Science with Gas, 1981; (jtly) Aspects of Science, 1984; (jtly) Reading about Science, 1984; (jtly) Nuffield Science, 1986; (ed) Teaching Science 11–13, 1987; From the Three Rs to the Three Cs, 2003; science curriculum resources and educn papers. *Recreations:* watching all forms of sport (former rower and Rugby player), reading, films, music. *Address:* House of Commons, SW1A 0AA. *T:* (020) 7219 5001; Myrtle Cottage, Northend, Bath BA1 8ES. *T:* (01225) 858093.

FOSTER, Ian Hampden; a Master of the Supreme Court, Queen's Bench Division, since 1991; a Recorder, since 1998; *b* 27 Feb. 1946; *s* of Eric Hampden Foster and Irene Foster (*née* Warman); *m* 1975, Fiona Jane, *d* of Rev. J. N. and Mrs Robertson-Glasgow; one *s* one *d*. *Educ:* Battersea Grammar Sch.; Univ. of Exeter (LLB Hons 1968). Called to the Bar, Inner Temple, 1969; practice at common law bar, 1969–91. Adv. Editor, Atkin's Court Forms, 1991–2003; Jt Editor, Supreme Court Practice, 1993–98. *Recreations:* gardening, watching cricket. *Address:* Royal Courts of Justice, Strand, WC2A 2LL. *Clubs:* Travellers; Norfolk (Norwich).

FOSTER, Jacqueline; aerospace consultant, Brussels, since 2006; *b* 30 Dec. 1947; *d* of late Samuel and Isabella Renshaw; *m* 1975, Peter Laurance Foster (marr. diss. 1981). *Educ:* Prescot Girls' Grammar Sch., Lancashire. Cabin Services, BEA, then British Airways, 1969–81; Area Manager, Austria, Horizon, 1981–85; Cabin Services, British Airways, 1985–99; Founder Mem. and Exec. Officer, Cabin Crew '89 (Airline Trade Union), 1989–99; Man. Dir, Foster Jay Ltd, Aviation Consultants, 2004–06. MEP (C) NW Reg., England, 1999–2004; Chm., Cons. backbench cttee, 1999–2004; Mem. Industry and Transport (Aviation) Cttees, 1999–2004; Cons. spokesman on transport, 2001–04. Mem., Eur. Aviation Club. *Recreations:* ski-ing, travel. *Club:* Carlton.

FOSTER, Joan Mary; Under Secretary, Department of Transport, Highways Planning and Management, 1978–80, retired; *b* 20 Jan. 1923; *d* of John Whitfield Foster and Edith Foster (*née* Levett). *Educ:* Northampton School for Girls. Entered Civil Service (HM Office of Works), Oct. 1939; Ministry of Transport, 1955; Asst Secretary, 1970. *Recreations:* gardening, cooking, good wine. *Address:* 3 Hallfields, Shouldham, King's Lynn, Norfolk PE33 0DN. *T:* (01366) 347809.

FOSTER, Joanna Katharine, CBE 2002; Chair: Nuffield Orthopaedic Centre NHS Trust, since 2001; Crafts Council, since 2006; *b* 5 May 1939; *d* of late Michael and of Lesley Mead; *m* 1961, Jerome Foster (marr. diss. 2002); one *s* one *d*. *Educ:* Benenden School; Univ. of Grenoble. Sec. and Editl Asst, Vogue Magazine, London and NY, 1958–59; journalist, San Francisco Chronicle, 1959; Management Adviser, Industrial Soc., 1966–72; Dir, Centre Actif Bilingue, Fontainebleau, 1972–79; Press Attachée and Editor, INSEAD, Fontainebleau, 1972–79; Educn and Trng Dir, Corporate Services, Western Psychiatric Inst. and Clinic, Univ. of Pittsburgh, 1980–82; Management Adviser, 1982–85, Head of Pepperell Unit, 1985–88, Mem. Council, 1990–2000, Industrial Soc.; Chair: Equal Opportunities Commn, 1988–93; UK Council, UN Internat. Year of the Family 1994, 1993–95; Dir, 1995–97, Chm., 1997–2001, BT Communication Forum; Chm., Nat. Work-Life Forum, 1998–2002. Pres., European Commn Adv. Cttee on Equal Opportunities, 1991–92 (Vice Pres., 1990, 1991, 1993); Member: Nat. Adv. Council for Careers and Educnl Guidance, 1993–94; Sec. of State for Employment's Women's Issues Adv. Gp, 1991–93; Target Team for Business in the Community's Opportunity 2000 Initiative, 1992–99; Govt Adv. Gp on Work-Life Balance, 2000–02. Chair, Adv. Cttee, European Public Policy Inst., Warwick Univ., 1993–95. Chm., Lloyds TSB (formerly TSB) Foundn, 1997–2003 (Dep. Chm., 1991–97). Dir, WNO, 1990–94; Mem., Central TV Adv. Bd, 1991–95; Mem., Adv. Bd, Econ. Regl Analysis, 1997–; Dir, Pennell Initiative for Women's Health, 1997– (Chm., 2003–). Pres., Relate, 1993–96. Trustee: Employment Policy Inst., 1995–98; Open Univ. Foundn, 2004–. Governor: Oxford Brookes Univ., 1993– (Dep. Chm., 1998–2003); Birkbeck Coll., Univ. of London, 1996–98. Hon. Fellow, St Hilda's Coll., Oxford, 1988. Hon. DLitt Kingston, 1993; DU Essex, 1993; Hon. LLD: Oxford Brookes, 1993; West of England, 1993; Strathclyde, 1994; Salford, 1994; Bristol, 1996. *Recreations:* family, friends, food. *Address:* Meadow House, Mill Street, Islip, Oxford OX5 2SZ. *Clubs:* Reform, Forum UK.

FOSTER, Jodie; *see* Foster, A. C.

FOSTER, John Edward, CBE 2008; Chief Executive, London Borough of Islington, since 2008; *b* 30 Dec. 1948; *s* of John and Ethel Foster; *m* 2003, Pauline de Silva; one *s* three *d* from a former marriage. *Educ:* Univ. of London (BSc Hons ext. 1970); Univ. of Durham. Community worker, Northumberland CC, 1971; Community Develt Officer, Durham CC, 1972; Community Develt Project, Home Office, 1973–92; various rôles with N Tyneside MBC and NALGO, 1979–92; Exec. Dir, North Tyneside MBC, 1992–97; Chief Executive: Middlesbrough Council, 1998–2002; City of Wakefield MDC, 2003–08. Director: Wakefield First, 2003; Solace Enterprises, 2004. Trustees, New Local Govt Network, 2002. *Recreations:* weekends away from it all, Friends of the Royal Academy. *Address:* Islington Borough Council, Town Hall, Upper Street, N1 2UD.

FOSTER, John Graham; District Judge (Magistrates' Court), South Yorkshire, since 2001; *b* 28 April 1947; *s* of James Beaumont Foster and Margaret Foster; *m* 1971, Susan Boothroyd; three *s*. *Educ:* Woodhouse Grove Sch.; Sheffield Univ. (LLB Hons). Admitted Solicitor, 1973; in private practice with Morrish & Co., Solicitors, Leeds, 1970–2001 (Partner 1975–2001); Dep. Dist Judge, 1997–2001. *Recreations:* after dinner speaking, theatre, films, music, sport, especially badminton and cricket. *Address:* c/o Rotherham Magistrates' Court, The Statutes, PO Box 15, Rotherham S60 1YW. *T:* (01709) 839339.

FOSTER, (John) Peter, OBE 1990; Surveyor of the Fabric of Westminster Abbey, 1973–88, now Emeritus; *b* 2 May 1919; *s* of Francis Edward Foster and Evelyn Marjorie, *e d* of Sir Charles Stewart Forbes, 5th Bt of Newe; *m* 1944, Margaret Elizabeth Skipper; one *s* one *d*. *Educ:* Eton; Trinity Hall, Cambridge. BA 1940, MA 1946; ARIBA 1949. Commnd RE 1941; served Norfolk Div.; joined Guards Armd Div. 1943, served France and Germany; Captain SORE(2) 30 Corps 1945; discharged 1946. Marshall Sisson, Architect: Asst 1948, later Partner; Sole Principal 1971; Surveyor of Royal Academy of Arts, 1965–80. Partner with John Peters of Vine Press, Hemingford Grey, 1957–63. Member: Churches Cttee for Historic Building Council for England, 1977–84; Adv. Bd for Redundant Churches, 1979–91; Exec. Cttee, Georgian Gp, 1983–91; Fabric Cttee, Canterbury Cathedral, 1987–91 (Chm., 1990); Council, Ancient Monuments Soc., 1988–; Fabric Cttee, Ely Cathedral, 1990–. Chm., Cathedral Architects Assoc., 1987–90; President: Cambridge Antiquarian Soc., 1968–70; Assoc. for Studies in Conservation of Historic Buildings, 2001. Art Workers' Guild: Mem., 1971; Master, 1980; Trustee, 1985–2002. Pres., Surveyors Club, 1980. Governor, Suttons Hosp., Charterhouse, 1982–2000. FSA 1973; FRSA 1994. CStJ 1987. *Publication:* Holiday Painter: watercolours 1935–1998, 2000. *Recreations:* painting, books, travel. *Address:* Harcourt, Hemingford Grey, Huntingdon, Cambs PE28 9BJ. *T:* (01480) 462200. *Club:* Athenæum.

FOSTER, Jonathan Rowe; QC 1989; **His Honour Judge Foster;** a Circuit Judge, since 2004; *b* 20 July 1947; *s* of Donald Foster and Hilda Eaton; *m* 1978, Sarah Ann Mary da Cunha; four *s*. *Educ:* Oundle Sch.; Keble Coll., Oxford (Exhibr). Called to the Bar, Gray's Inn, 1970, Bencher, 1998; a Recorder, 1988–2004; a Dep. High Ct Judge, 1994–; Hd of Chambers, 1997–2004. Treas., Northern Circuit, 1992–97. Mem., Appeal Panel, Criminal Injuries Compensation Bd, 1995–2004. Gov., Ryleys' Sch., 1990–2006. *Recreations:* outdoor pursuits, bridge. *Address:* Minshull Street Crown Court, Manchester M1 3FS. *Club:* St James's (Manchester).

FOSTER, Lawrence; conductor; Music Director, Gulbenkian Orchestra, Lisbon, since 2002; *b* Los Angeles, 23 Oct. 1941; *s* of Thomas Foster and Martha Wurmbrandt; *m* 1972, Angela Foster; one *d*. *Educ:* Univ. of California, LA; studied under Fritz Zweig, Bruno Walter and Karl Böhm. Asst Conductor, Los Angeles Philharmonic, 1965–68; British début, Royal Festival Hall, 1968; Covent Garden début, Troilus and Cressida, 1976; Chief Guest Conductor, Royal Philharmonic Orchestra, 1969–74; Music Dir and Chief Conductor, Houston Symphony Orchestra, 1971–78; Chief Conductor, Orchestre National (later Orchestre Philharmonique) of Monte Carlo, 1978–95; Gen. Music Dir, Duisberg concert series, 1982–86; Prin. Guest Conductor, Düsseldorf Opera, 1982–86; Music Director: Lausanne Chamber Orch., 1985–90; Aspen Fest., 1991–96; Barcelona S0 and Nat. Orch. of Catalonia, 1996–2002; Orch. and Nat. Opera of Montpellier, 2009–; Artistic Dir, Georg Enescu Fest., 1998–2001; Guest Conductor: Deutsche Oper Berlin; LA Music Centre Opera; LA Philharmonic Orch.; Hallé Orch.; Pittsburgh, Chicago, Montreal, and Jerusalem Symphony Orchs; Orchestre de Paris. *Recreations:* reading European history, films. *Address:* c/o HarrisonParrott, 12 Penzance Place, W11 4PA.

FOSTER, Michael George; Chief Executive, Charter plc, since 2006 (Commercial Director, 2005–06); *b* 17 Feb. 1953; *s* of Brian and Betty Foster; *m* 1977, Marion Frances Chambers; one *s* one *d*. *Educ:* Nottingham High Sch.; Peterhouse, Cambridge (BA 1975, MA 1979); Council for Legal Educn. Called to the Bar, Inner Temple, 1977; barrister in private practice, 1977–85; admitted solicitor, 1989; GKN plc: Sen. Commercial Lawyer, 1985–88; Asst Gp Treas., 1988–93; Dep. Hd, Corporate Finance, 1993–94; Gp Treas., Trafalgar House plc, 1994–95; Chief Executive: Kvaerner Metals (Davy), 1995–98; Kvaerner Engrg & Construction Div., 1998–2000; Exec. Dir, RMC plc, 2000–04. Non-exec. Dir, Charter plc, 2001–04. Mem., ACT. *Recreations:* family, theatre and film, opera, blues, rock and roll, literature, travel, clay pigeon shooting. *Address:* Charter plc, 52 Grosvenor Gardens, SW1W 0AU. *T:* (020) 781 7800, *Fax:* (020) 7259 9343.

FOSTER, Michael Jabez; DL; MP (Lab) Hastings and Rye, since 1997; *b* Hastings, 26 Feb. 1946; *s* of Dorothy Foster; *m* 1969, Rosemary, *d* of Eric and Hilda Kemp; two *s*. *Educ:* Hastings Secondary Sch.; Hastings Grammar Sch.; Leicester Univ. (LLM). Admitted Solicitor, 1980; ACIArb 1997. Partner, 1980–99, Consultant, 1999–, Fynmores, solicitors, Bexhill-on-Sea; specialist in employment law. Member: Hastings CBC, 1971–74 (Ldr, Lab. Gp, 1973); Hastings BC, 1973–79, 1983–87 (Ldr, Lab. Gp and Dep. Ldr of Council, 1973–79); E Sussex CC, 1973–77, 1981–97 (Dep. Leader, Lab Gp, 1984–93); Mem., Sussex Police Authy, 1991–96; Mem., E Sussex AHA, later Hastings HA, 1974–91. Contested (Lab) Hastings, Feb. and Oct. 1974, 1979. PPS to Attorney General, 1999–2003. DL E Sussex, 1993. *Address:* House of Commons, SW1A 0AA; *e-mail:* mp@1066.net.

FOSTER, Michael John; MP (Lab) Worcester, since 1997; Parliamentary Under-Secretary of State, Department for International Development, since 2008; *b* 14 March

1963; *s* of Brian and Edna Foster; *m* 1985, Shauna Ogle; one *s* two *d*. *Educ:* Great Wyrley High Sch., Staffs; Wolverhampton Poly. (BA Hons Econs 1984); Univ. of Wolverhampton (PGCE 1995). ACMA. Management Accountant, Jaguar Cars, 1984–91; Lectr, Worcester Coll. of Technology, 1991–97. Department of Education and Skills: PPS to Minister of State for Lifelong Learning and Higher Educn, 2001–03, for Children, 2003–04; Departmental PPS, 2004–05; PPS to Sec. of State for NI, 2005–06; an Asst Govt Whip, 2006–08. Mem., Educn Select Cttee, 1999–2001. *Recreations:* most sports, gardening. *Address:* House of Commons, SW1A 0AA. *T:* (020) 7219 6379. *Club:* Worcestershire County Cricket.

FOSTER, Peter; *see* Foster, J. P.

FOSTER, Richard John Samuel; His Honour Judge Foster; a Circuit Judge, since 2004; a Deputy High Court Judge, since 2003; *b* 28 May 1954; *s* of late Samuel Geoffrey Foster and of Beryl Foster; *m* 1st, 1980, Ann Scott (*d* 2002); one *d*; 2nd, 2004, Susan Claire Sansome; one step *s* one step *d*. *Educ:* Bromsgrove Sch.; Coll. of Law, Guildford. Qualified solicitor, 1979; Partner, 1987–97, Jt Sen. Partner, 1997–98, Vizards, London; Sen. Partner, Vizard Oldham, London, 1998–2002; Partner and Hd, Health Care Law, Weightman Vizards, subseq. Weightmans Solicitors, 2002–04. Asst Recorder, 1997–2000; Recorder, 2000–04. Mem., Beds Probation Bd, 2006–. Chm. Trustees, Royal British Legion Pension Fund, 2004. *Publication:* (ed) Morrell and Foster on Local Authority Liability, 1998, 3rd edn 2005. *Recreations:* golf, gardening. *Address:* c/o Luton Crown Court, 7 George Street, Luton LU1 2AA. *Clubs:* Reform; Berkhamsted Golf; Andratx Golf (Mallorca).

FOSTER, Richard Scot, CBE 2007; Chief Executive, Crown Prosecution Service, 2002–07; *b* 26 March 1950; *s* of Frank Walter Foster and Betty Lilian Foster; *m* 1997, Susan Warner Johnson; one *s* one *d*. *Educ:* Devonport High Sch.; Pembroke Coll., Cambridge (MA Hons Moral Scis). Joined Dept of Employment, 1973; Sec., MSC, 1975–77; Private Sec. to Minister, 1977–78; on secondment to FCO, Stockholm, 1981–84; Industrial Relations legislation, 1984–86; Head of Deptl Strategy Unit, 1986–88; Director: Finance and Planning, Employment Service, 1988–90; Trng Commn, 1990–92; Employment Service, 1992–98; Dir, Welfare to Work, DFEE, subseq. at DWP, 1998–2001. Trustee, Refugee Council of GB, 2007–. *Recreations:* ski-ing, climbing, opera, theatre, tennis. *Address:* Torrens, Cavendish Road, Weybridge, Surrey KT13 0JW. *T:* (01932) 855672.

FOSTER, Robert; Commissioner, and Chair of Licence Project Board, National Lottery Commission, since 2005; *b* 12 May 1943; *s* of David and Amelia Foster; *m* 1967, Judy Welsh; one *s* one *d*. *Educ:* Oundle Sch.; Corpus Christi Coll., Cambridge (BA 1964; MA 1967). CEng, FIET (FIEE 1993); FRAeS 1996. Parkinson Cowan, 1964–66; Automation Ltd, 1966–71; Exec. Engineer, Post Office Telecommunications, 1971–76; DTI, 1977–92; Under Sec., OST, Cabinet Office, 1992–93, DTI, 1993–2000; Chief Exec. and Sec., Competition Commn, 2001–04. Non-exec. Dir, Jersey Competition Regulatory Authy, 2004–; Vice Chair, KCH NHS Foundn Trust, 2004–. *Recreations:* theatre, tennis, music. *Address:* 9 Holmdene Avenue, Herne Hill, SE24 9LB.

FOSTER, Prof. Robert Fitzroy, (Roy), PhD; FRSL; FRHistS; FBA 1989; Carroll Professor of Irish History, University of Oxford, since 1991; *b* 16 Jan. 1949; *s* of Frederick Ernest Foster and Elizabeth (*née* Fitzroy); *m* 1972, Aisling O'Conor Donelan; one *s* one *d*. *Educ:* Newtown Sch., Waterford; St Andrew's Sch., Middletown, Delaware, USA; Trinity Coll., Dublin (MA; PhD 1975). FRHistS 1979; FRSL 1992. Lectr, 1974, Reader, 1983, Professor of Modern British Hist., 1988–91, Hon. Fellow, 2005, Birkbeck Coll., London Univ. Alistair Horne Fellow, St Antony's Coll., Oxford, 1979–80; British Acad. Res. Reader in the Humanities, 1987–89; Fellow, IAS, Princeton, and Vis. Fellow, Dept of English, 1988–89, Whitney J. Oates Fellow, 2002, Princeton Univ. Wiles Lectr, QUB, 2004. Hon. DLitt: Aberdeen, 1997; QUB, 1998; TCD, 2003; NUI, 2004; Hon. DLaws Queen's Univ., Ontario, 2007. Irish Post Community Award, 1982; Sunday Independent/Irish Life Arts Award, 1988; M. L. Rosenthal Award, Yeats Soc. of NY, 2003. *Publications:* Charles Stewart Parnell: the man and his family, 1976, 2nd edn 1979; Lord Randolph Churchill: a political life, 1981, 3rd edn 1987; Political Novels and Nineteenth Century History, 1983; Modern Ireland 1600–1972, 1988; (ed) The Oxford Illustrated History of Ireland, 1989; (ed) The Sub-Prefect Should Have Held His Tongue and other essays, by Hubert Butler, 1990; Paddy and Mr Punch: connections in English and Irish history, 1993; The Story of Ireland, 1995; W. B. Yeats: a life, Vol. 1 The Apprentice Mage 1865–1914, 1997 (James Tait Black Prize for biog., 1998), Vol. 2 The Arch-Poet 1915–1939, 2003; The Irish Story: telling tales and making it up in Ireland, 2001 (Christian Gauss Award for literary criticism, 2004); (with Fintan Cullen) Conquering England: Ireland in Victorian London, 2005; Luck and the Irish, 2007; numerous essays and reviews. *Recreation:* recreation. *Address:* Hertford College, Oxford OX1 3BW. *Club:* Kildare Street and University (Dublin).

FOSTER, Roy; *see* Foster, Robert Fitzroy.

FOSTER, Prof. Russell Grant, PhD; FRS 2008; Professor of Circadian Neuroscience, since 2006, and Chair, Nuffield Laboratory of Ophthalmology, since 2007, University of Oxford; Nicholas Kurti Senior Fellow, Brasenose College, Oxford, since 2006; *b* Aldershot, 19 Aug. 1959; *s* of Donald and Doreen Foster; *m* 1984, Elizabeth Ann Downes; one *s* two *d*. *Educ:* Heron Wood Sch., Aldershot; Farnborough 6th Form Coll.; Univ. of Bristol (BSc 1980; PhD 1984). Asst Prof., Dept of Biol., Univ. of Va, 1988–95; Imperial College London: Governor's Lectr, Dept of Biol., 1995–97, Reader in Zool., 1997–99; Prof., Dept of Integrative and Molecular Neurosci., 2000–03; Dep. Chair, Dept of Visual Neurosci., 2003–06. Visiting Professor: Dept of Biomed. and Molecular Scis, Univ. of Surrey, 1999–; Dept of Biol Scis, Imperial Coll. London, 2006–; Dept of Biol Scis, Univ. of WA, 2007–. Chm., Animal Scis Cttee, 2002–06, Mem., Strategy Bd, 2007–, BBSRC. Mem., UK Panel for Res. Integrity in Health and Biomed. Scis, 2006–. Mem. Faculty, Lundbeck Internat. Neurosci. Foundn, Denmark, 2007–. *Publications:* (with L. Kreitzman) Rhythms of Life: the biological clocks that control the daily lives of every living thing, 2005 (multiple trans); contrib. to research-related jls. *Recreations:* listening to opera, Wagner when possible, to compensate doing anything that involves laughter, hunting for fossils, being in or near the sea, food and wine with family and friends. *Address:* Nuffield Laboratory of Ophthalmology, Level 5 and 6 West Wing, John Radcliffe Hospital, Headley Way, Headington, Oxford OX3 9DU. *T:* (01865) 234777; *e-mail:* Russell.foster@eye.ox.ac.uk.

FOSTER, Samuel, CBE 2002; Member (UU) Fermanagh and South Tyrone, Northern Ireland Assembly, 1998–2003; *b* 7 Dec. 1931; *s* of late Samuel and Margaret Foster; *m* 1952, Dorothy Claire Brown; two *s* one *d*. *Educ:* Enniskillen Tech. Coll.; Ulster Poly., Belfast (CQSW). Compositor and proof reader, 1946–66; Sen. Educn Welfare Officer, Western Educn and Liby Bd, 1967–78; Social Worker: Wirral Social Services, 1979; Western Health and Social Services, 1980–96. Co. Comdr, UDR, 1970–78 (Major). Mem. (UU), Fermanagh DC, 1981–2001 (Chm., 1995–97). Mem. for Fermanagh and S Tyrone, NI Forum for Political Dialogue, 1996–98. Minister for the Envmt, NI Assembly, 1999–2002. Member: Police Authy for NI, 1982–85; NI Policing Bd, 2002–06. *Publication:* Recall: a little history of Orangeism and Protestantism in Fermanagh—King William Prince of Orange and all that … (booklet), 1990. *Recreations:* sport, especially soccer, table tennis, historical aspects, debate. *Address:* 35 Derrychara Road, Enniskillen, Co. Fermanagh BT74 6JF. *T:* (028) 6632 3594. *Club:* Fermanagh Unionist (Enniskillen).

FOSTER, Sir Saxby Gregory, 4th Bt *cr* 1930, of Bloomsbury, co. London; *b* 3 Sept. 1957; *s* of Sir John Gregory Foster, 3rd Bt, and of Jean Millicent, *d* of late Elwin Watts; father, 2006; *m* 1989, Rowen Audrey, *d* of late Reginald Archibald Ford; two *s*. *Heir:* Thomas James Gregory Foster, *b* 1 May 1991.

FOSTER, Simon Ridgeby; farmer; *b* 1 Sept. 1939; *s* of Sir Ridgeby Foster and of Lady Nancy Foster (*née* Godden); *m* 1st, 1966, Mairi Angela Chisholm (marr. diss.); one *s* two *d*; 2nd, 1990, Philippa Back. *Educ:* Shrewsbury Sch.; Jesus Coll., Cambridge (MA Hist.); London Business Sch. (Sloane Fellow); Wye Coll., London Univ. (MSc Sustainable Agric 1995). Pres. and Dir Gen., Dunlop France, 1983–88; Dir, SMMT, 1988–91; Man. Dir Toyota GB, 1991–93. Médaille d'Allier, 1987. *Publication:* Politique Industrielle, 1990. *Recreations:* farming, Dutch sailing barges.

FOTHERBY, Gordon; Senior Manager for Legal Services, KPMG, since 2008; *b* 15 Nov. 1950; *m* 1974, Victoria Eloise. *Educ:* Hull GS; Sheffield Univ. (LLB Hons 1972). Called to the Bar, Inner Temple, 1973; Capt., Army Legal Corps, 1973–77; Solicitor's Office HM Customs and Excise, later HM Revenue and Customs, 1977–2005: Asst Sec., Legal 1986–93; on secondment to EC, 1989–91; Dep. Solicitor and Hd of Advisory and European, 1993–99, Hd of Prosecutions, 1999–2005; Sen. Legal Counsellor, Internat Policy, 2005; with The Khan Partnership, LLP, 2006–08.

FOTHERGILL, Alastair David William; Series Producer, BBC Natural History Unit since 1998; *b* 10 April 1960; *s* of David and Jaqueline Fothergill; *m* 1994, Melinda Jan Barker; two *s*. *Educ:* Harrow Sch.; St Andrews Univ.; Durham Univ. (BSc). Joined BBC Natural History Unit, 1983, Head, 1992–98. Director: Deep Blue (film), 2004; Earth (film), 2007. *Publications:* Life in the Freezer, 1993; The Blue Planet, 2001; Planet Earth 2006. *Recreations:* fly-fishing, walking, diving. *Address:* 5 Caledonia Place, Clifton, Bristol BS8 4DH. *T:* (0117) 973 1312.

FOTHERGILL, Dorothy Joan; Director, Postal Pay and Grading, 1974–83, retired; *b* 31 Dec. 1923; *d* of Samuel John Rimington Fothergill and Dorothy May Patterson. *Educ* Haberdashers' Aske's Sch., Acton; University Coll. London (BA (Hons) History). Entered Civil Service as Asst Principal, 1948; Principal, Overseas Mails branch, GPO, 1953; UPU Congress, Ottawa, 1957; Establishments work, 1958–62; HM Treasury, 1963–65; Asst Sec., Pay and Organisation, GPO, 1965; Director: Postal Personnel, 1970; London Postal Region, 1971. *Recreations:* gardening, walking, theatre. *Address:* 5 Meadway, Rustington, Littlehampton, West Sussex BN16 2DD.

FOU TS'ONG; concert pianist; *b* 10 March 1934; *m* 1st, 1960, Zamira Menuhin (marr. diss. 1970); one *s*; 2nd, 1973, Hijong Hyun (marr. diss. 1976); 3rd, 1987, Patsy Toh; one *s*. *Educ:* Shanghai and Warsaw. Debut, Shanghai, 1953. Concerts all over Eastern Europe including USSR up to 1958. Arrived in Great Britain, Dec. 1958; London debut, Feb. 1959, followed by concerts in England, Scotland and Ireland; subsequently has toured all five Continents. Recordings include: Chopin, Mozart, Schumann, Debussy, Scarlatti, Handel, Haydn and Bach. Hon. DLitt Hong Kong, 1983. *Recreations:* bridge, Scrabble, watching sport, Chinese painting. *Address:* 62 Aberdeen Park, N5 2BL. *T:* (020) 722 9589, *Fax:* (020) 7704 8896.

FOUBISTER, Stuart Russell; Head of Food and Environment Division, Scottish Government Legal Directorate, since 2008; *b* 12 Oct. 1958; *s* of late John and Yvonne Foubister; *m* 2006, Kirsten Rosemary Davidson; one *s*. *Educ:* Stewart's Melville Coll., Edinburgh; Edinburgh Univ. (LLB Hons 1980). Admitted solicitor, 1983. Joined Office of Solicitor to Sec. of State for Scotland, 1985; Divl Solicitor, 1997–2001; Scottish Executive, later Scottish Government: Dep. Solicitor, 2001–03; Legal Sec. to Lord Advocate, 2003–05; Scottish Legislative Counsel, 2005–07. *Recreations:* hill-walking, golf, cricket, reading. *Address:* (office) Victoria Quay, Edinburgh EH6 6QQ. *T:* (0131) 24 1408, *Fax:* (0131) 244 0591; *e-mail:* stuart.foubister@scotland.gsi.gov.uk.

FOULDS, (Hugh) Jon; Chairman: L Huntsworth plc, 2000–08; Fauchier Partners Ltd since 1995; Halifax plc (formerly Halifax Building Society), 1990–99 (Director, 1986–99); *b* 2 May 1932; *s* of late Dr E. J. Foulds and Helen Shirley (*née* Smith); *m*; two *s*. *Educ* Bootham Sch., York. Dir and Chief Exec., 1976–88, Dep. Chm., 1988–92, Investors in Industry, subseq. 3i Gp plc; Director: Brammer plc, 1980–91 (Chm., 1988–90); London Smaller Companies (formerly London Atlantic) Investment Trust, 1983–95; Pan-Holding SA, 1986–; Eurotunnel plc, 1988–96; Mercury Asset Management Gp plc, 1989–98; Mem. Bd of Banking Supervision, Bank of England, 1993–96. Hon. MA Salford, 1987. *Recreations:* tennis, ski-ing, shooting, pictures. *Address:* 28 Grosvenor Crescent Mews, SW1X 7EX. *Clubs:* Garrick, Hurlingham.

FOULGER, Keith, BSc(Eng); CEng, MIMechE; FRINA, RCNC; Chief Naval Architect, Ministry of Defence, 1983–85, retired; *b* 14 May 1925; *s* of Percy and Kate Foulger; *m* 1951, Joyce Mary Hart; one *s* one *d*. *Educ:* Univ. of London (Mech. Eng.) Royal Naval Coll., Greenwich. Asst Constructor, 1950; Constructor, 1955; Constructor Comdr, Dreadnought Project, 1959; Staff Constructor Officer to C-in-C Western Fleet 1965–66; Chief Constructor, 1967; Asst Director, Submarines, 1973; Deputy Director Naval Construction, 1979; Naval Ship Production, 1979–81; Submarines, Ship Dept 1981–83; Asst Under-Sec. of State, 1983. *Recreations:* enjoying grandfatherhood, travel gardening, photography. *Address:* Lindley, North Road, Bathwick, Bath BA2 6HW.

FOULIS, Lindsay David Robertson; Sheriff of Tayside, Central and Fife at Perth, since 2001; *b* 20 April 1956; *s* of Henry Edwards Foulis and Mary Robertson Foulis; *m* 1981 Ellenore Brown; two *s* one *d*. *Educ:* High Sch. of Dundee; Univ. of Edinburgh (LLB Hons 1978). Legal apprentice, 1978–80, legal asst, 1980–81, Balfour and Manson, Edinburgh asst, 1981–84, Partner, 1984–2000, Reid Johnston Bell and Henderson, subseq Blackadder Reid Johnston, Dundee; Temp. Sheriff, 1998–99; All Scotland Floating Sheriff, Perth, 2000–01. Dundee University: Lectr (pt-time), 1994–2000; Hon. Prof. in Scots Law, 2001–. Mem. Council, Sheriff Court Rules, 1996–2000. *Publications:* (jtly) Civil Court Practice materials for Diploma in Legal Practice, 2001; contrib. articles on civil procedure to Jl Law Soc. of Scotland. *Recreations:* sport, now mainly golf (played badly) music. *Address:* Sheriff's Chambers, Sheriff Court House, Tay Street, Perth PH2 8NL.

FOULIS, Michael Bruce; Director, Housing and Regeneration, Scottish Government (formerly Scottish Executive), since 2007; *b* 23 Aug. 1956; *s* of Kenneth Munro Foulis and Edith Lillian Sommerville (*née* Clark); *m* 1981, Gillian Margaret Tyson; one *s* one *d*. *Educ* Kilmarnock Acad.; Edinburgh Univ. (BSc Geog.). Joined Scottish Office, 1978: Private Sec. to Parly Under Sec. of State, 1987–89; on secondment to Scottish Financial Enterprise as Asst Dir, 1989–91; Scottish Educn Dept, 1991–93; Principal Private Sec. to Sec. of State for Scotland, 1993–95; Hd of Div., Agric., Envmt and Fisheries Dept, 1995–97; or secondment to Cabinet Office as Dep. Hd, Devolution Team, Constitution Secretariat, 1997–98; Hd of Gp, Educn and Industry Dept, 1998–99; Scottish Executive: Hd of Gp, Enterprise and Lifelong Learning Dept, 1999–2001; Hd, Envmt Gp, Envmt and Rural Affairs Dept, 2001–05; on secondment to Mining (Scotland) Ltd, subseq. Scottish Resources Gp, to work on corp. strategy, 2006–07. Bd Mem., Children 1st, 2002–. *Recreations:* playing cello, appreciating lithographs, moderate exercise. *Address:* Scottish Government, Victoria Quay, Edinburgh EH6 6QQ.

FOULKES, family name of **Baron Foulkes of Cumnock**.

FOULKES OF CUMNOCK, Baron *cr* 2005 (Life Peer), of Cumnock in East Ayrshire; **George Foulkes;** PC 2002; JP; Member (Lab) Lothians, Scottish Parliament, since 2007; *b* 21 Jan. 1942; *s* of late George and Jessie M. A. W. Foulkes; *m* 1970, Elizabeth Anna Hope; two *s* one *d*. *Educ:* Keith Grammar Sch., Keith, Banffshire; Haberdashers' Aske's Sch.; Edinburgh Univ. (BSc 1964). President: Edinburgh Univ. SRC, 1963–64; Scottish Union of Students, 1965–67; Manager, Fund for Internat. Student Cooperation, 1967–68. Scottish Organiser, European Movement, 1968–69; Director: European League for Econ. Co-operation, 1969–70; Enterprise Youth, 1970–73; Age Concern, Scotland, 1973–79. Councillor: Edinburgh Corp., 1970–75; Lothian Regional Council, 1974–79; Chairman: Lothian Region Educn Cttee, 1974–79; Educn Cttee, Convention of Scottish Local Authorities, 1975–78. MP (Lab and Co-op) S Ayrshire, 1979–83, Carrick, Cumnock and Doon Valley, 1983–2005. Opposition spokesman on European and Community Affairs, 1984–85, on Foreign Affairs, 1985–92, on Defence, 1992–93, on Overseas Develt, 1994–97; Parly Under-Sec. of State, DFID, 1997–2001; Minister of State, Scotland Office, 2001–02. Mem., Select Cttee on Foreign Affairs, 1981–83. Jt Chm., All Party Pensioners Cttee, 1983–97 (Sec./Treasurer 1979–83). UK Delegate to Parly Assembly of Council of Europe, 1979–81, 2002–05; Mem., Parly Assembly, WEU, 2002–05. Member: Sub Cttee F, European Scrutiny Cttee, H of L, 2006–; Intelligence & Security Cttee, H of L, 2007–. Treas., Parliamentarians for Global Action, 1993–97 (Mem. Council, 1987–97); Member: UK Exec., CPA, 1987–97, 2002–05; IPU, 1989–97 (Mem., British Cttee, 2002–08). Member: Scottish Exec. Cttee, Labour Party, 1981–89; Exec., Socialist Internat., 2003–08; Chm., Labour Movt for Europe in Scotland, 2002–. Pres., Caribbean-Britain Business Council, 2002–; Vice-Chm., Cuba Initiative, 2005–. Rector's Assessor, Edinburgh Univ. Court, 1968–70, Local Authority Assessor, 1971–79. Chairman: Scottish Adult Literacy Agency, 1976–79; John Wheatley Centre, 1990–97. Mem. Exec., British/China Centre, 1987–93. Director: St Cuthbert's Co-op. Assoc., 1975–79; Co-op. Press Ltd, 1990–97. JP Edinburgh, 1975. Wilberforce Medal, City of Hull, 1998. *Publications:* Eighty Years On: history of Edinburgh University SRC, 1964; (contrib.) A Claim of Right, ed Owen Dudley Edwards, 1989. *Recreations:* boating, watching Heart of Midlothian FC (Chm., 2004–05). *Address:* House of Lords, SW1A 0PW. *T:* (020) 7219 3474; Scottish Parliament, Edinburgh EH99 1SP.

FOULKES, Sir Arthur (Alexander), KCMG 2001; Deputy Governor-General of the Bahamas, since 2008; *b* 11 May 1928; *s* of late Dr William Alexander Foulkes and Julie Blanche Foulkes (*née* Maisonneuve); *m* 1st, Naomi Louise Higgs; 2nd, Joan Eleanor Bullard. *Educ:* Public Sch., Inagua, Bahamas; Western Central Sch., Nassau, Bahamas; privately tutored in journalism. News Editor, The Tribune, 1950–62; Editor, Bahamian Times, 1962; Founder/Chm., Diversified Services (PR), 1967. MP Bahamas, 1967; Chm., Bahamas Telecommunications Corp., 1967; Cabinet Minister, 1968; Co-Founder, Free Nat. Movement, 1970; Mem., Senate, 1972. Delegate: Bahamas Petition to UN Cttee on Decolonization, 1965; Bahamas Constitutional Conf., London, 1972. High Comr to UK and Ambassador to France, Italy, Germany, Belgium and the EC, 1992–99; Ambassador (non-resident) to China and to Cuba, 1999–2002. Chairman: Bahamas Broadcasting Corp., 2001–02; Bahamas Parly Salaries Commn, 2001–; Bahamas Order of Merit Cttee, 2001–; Dir, Bahamas Information Services, 2007–. *Recreations:* theatre, music, art, literature. *Address:* Government House, Government Hill, PO Box N8301, Nassau, Bahamas.

FOULKES, Sir Nigel (Gordon), Kt 1980; Chairman: ECI International Management Ltd, 1987–91; ECI Management (Jersey) Ltd, 1986–91; Equity Capital Trustee Ltd, 1983–90; *b* 29 Aug. 1919; *s* of Louis Augustine and Winifred Foulkes; *m* 1948, Elisabeth Walker (*d* 1995), *d* of Ewart B. Walker, Toronto; one *s* one *d* of former marr. *Educ:* Gresham's Sch., Holt; Balliol Coll., Oxford (Schol., MA). RAF, 1940–45. Subsequently executive, consulting and boardroom posts with: H. P. Bulmer; P. E. Consulting Gp; Birfield; Greaves & Thomas; International Nickel; Rank Xerox (Asst Man. Dir 1964–67, Man. Dir 1967–70); Charterhouse Group Ltd (Dir, 1972–83); Dir, Charterhouse J. Rothschild plc, 1984–85; Chm., Equity Capital for Industry, 1983–86 (Vice-Chm., 1982); Dir, Bekaert Gp (Belgium), 1973–85. Chairman: British Airports Authority, 1972–77; Civil Aviation Authority, 1977–82. CCMI; FRSA. *Club:* Royal Air Force.

FOULKES, Brig. Thomas Howard Exton, CEng; FICE, FIMechE; Director General, Institution of Civil Engineers, since 2002; Secretary-General, Commonwealth Engineers Council, since 2002; *b* 31 Aug. 1950; *s* of late Maj.-Gen. Thomas Herbert Fischer Foulkes, CB, OBE and of Delphine Foulkes (*née* Exton Smith); *m* 1976, Sally Winter; two *d*. *Educ:* Clifton Coll.; RMA Sandhurst; RMCS Shrivenham (BSc); Open Univ. (MBA). FIMechE 1997; FICE 1998. Commnd RE, 1971; Troop Comdr, Ind. Field Troop, AMFL, 1976–79; OC, 1st Field Sqn RE, 1985–87; CO, 28 Amphibious Engr Regt, 1989–92; Project Manager, Gen. Engr Equipment, MoD PE, 1992–95; Col ES42, HQ QMG, 1995–98; rcds, 1998; Dir, Army Estates Orgn, 1999–2002. Member: Public Monuments & Sculpture Assoc., 1985–; Friends of Mt Athos, 2002–; Smeatonian Soc., 2004–. Liveryman, Engineers' Co., 2005. *Publications:* contribs to RE Jl, chiefly on military bridging and walks in Whitehall. *Recreations:* monuments in Whitehall, history of ideas, obituaries, football, photography, gardening, cycling. *Address:* Institution of Civil Engineers, One Great George Street, SW1P 3AA. *T:* (020) 7665 2002. *Clubs:* Athenæum; Royal Engineers Assoc. Football (Pres., 1992–2002).

FOULSHAM, Richard Andrew, CMG 2006; HM Diplomatic Service, retired; Chief Executive, Hope and Homes for Children, since 2006; *b* 24 Sept. 1950; *s* of William Foulsham and Lilian Elizabeth Foulsham (*née* Monro); *m* 1982, Deirdre Elizabeth Strathairn; one *s* one *d*. *Educ:* Univ. of St Andrews (MA Hons 1973). Argyll and Sutherland Highlanders, 1973–79; joined FCO, 1982; Second Sec., FCO, 1982–84; First Secretary: Brunei, 1984–86; Lagos, 1986–90; FCO, 1990–95; Counsellor (Political), Rome, 1995–99; Counsellor: FCO, 1999–2001; Ottawa, 2001–03; FCO, 2003–05. *Recreation:* walking in mountains. *Address:* Hope and Homes for Children, East Clyffe, Salisbury, Wilts SP3 4LZ.

FOUNTAIN, Alan; Founder, Mondial Television, 1994; Chairman, Mondialonline.com, since 1995; *b* 24 March 1946; *s* of Harold Fountain and Winifred Cecily Brown. *Educ:* Nottingham Univ. (BA Hons Philosophy). Film Officer, E Midlands Arts, 1976–79; producer, 1979–81; Channel Four TV, 1981–94 (Sen. Commissioning Editor, 1982–94); Head, Northern Media Sch., 1995–97; Programme Dir, Alfa TV, 1997–98. Professor of Cultural Industries, Middlesex Univ., 2001; Head of Studies, EAVE, 1999. *Publications:* (ed) Ruff's Guide to the Turf, 1972; contrib. film and TV pubns. *Recreations:* family, golf, watching sports. *Address:* 72 Sydney Road, N10 2RL.

FOUNTAIN, Hon. Sir Cyril (Stanley Smith), Kt 1996; Chief Justice, Supreme Court of Bahamas, 1996, retired; *b* 26 Oct. 1929; *s* of Harold Jackson Fountain and Winifred Olive Helen Fountain (*née* Smith); *m* 1954, Dorothy Alicia Hanna; two *s* one *d*. *Educ:* St Benedict's Coll., Atchison, Kansas (BA *cum laude* Econs); King's Coll. London (LLB Hons 1962). Head Teacher, Bd of Educn, Bahamas, 1955–58; articled law student to Sir Leonard J. Knowles, 1958–59; called to the Bar: Gray's Inn, 1963; Bahamas, 1963; Partner, Cash, Fountain & Co., 1963–93; Supreme Court of Bahamas: Actg Judge, April 1985 and April–Aug. 1990; Justice, 1993–94; Sen. Justice, 1994–96. MP (FNM) Long Island, Rum Cay and San Salvador, 1972–77. *Recreations:* swimming, historical reading. *Address:* PO Box N 476, Nassau, Bahamas. *T:* (home) 3936493; (office) 3222956/7.

FOURCADE, Jean-Pierre; Officier de l'ordre national du Mérite; Senator, French Republic, for Hauts-de-Seine, since 1977; *b* 18 Oct. 1929; *s* of Raymond Fourcade (Médecin) and Mme Fourcade (*née* Germaine Raynal); *m* 1958, Odile Mion; one *s* two *d*. *Educ:* Collège de Sorèze; Bordeaux Univ. Faculté de Droit, Institut des Etudes politiques (Dip.); Ecole nationale d'administration; higher studies in Law (Dip.). Inspecteur des Finances, 1954–73. Cabinet of M. Valéry Giscard d'Estaing: Chargé de Mission, 1959–61; Conseiller technique, 1962, then Dir Adjoint to chef de service, Inspection gén. des Finances, 1962; Chef de service du commerce, at Direction-Gén. du Commerce intérieur et des Prix, 1968–70; Dir-gén. adjoint du Crédit industriel et commercial, 1970; Dir-gén., 1972, and Administrateur Dir-gén., 1973; Ministre de l'Economie et des Finances, 1974–76; Ministre de l'Equipement et de l'Aménagement du Territoire, 1976–77. Senate: Pres., 1983–98, Mem., 1998–2004, Commn des Affaires Sociales; Mem., Commn des Affaires Etrangères, de la Défense et des Forces Armées, 2004–. Mayor of Saint-Cloud, 1971–92; Conseiller général of canton of Saint-Cloud, 1973–89; Conseiller régional d'Ile de France, 1976– (Vice-Président, 1982–95); Mayor of Boulogne-Billancourt, 1995–2007. Président: Clubs Perspectives et Réalités, 1975–82; Comité des Finances Locales, 1980–2004; Commn Consultative d'Evaluation des Changes, 2005–. Vice-Pres., Union pour la Démocratie Française, 1978–86 (Mem. Bureau, 1986); Mem., UMP, 2002–. *Publications:* Et si nous parlions de demain, 1979; La tentation social-démocrate, 1985; Remèdes pour l'Assurance-Maladie, 1989. *Address:* Palais du Luxembourg, 75291 Paris cedex 06, France; 8 Parc de Béarn, 92210 Saint-Cloud, France.

FOURNIER, Bernard; non-executive Chairman, Xerox Ltd, 1998–2001 (Chief Executive Officer, 1995–98); *b* 2 Dec. 1938; *s* of Jean Fournier and Solange Hervieu; *m* 1st; two *s*; 2nd, 1980, Françoise Chavailler; one *s*. *Educ:* Philo Lycée (Baccalauréat); Louis Le Grand, Paris; Ecole des Hautes Etudes Commerciales, Lille. Joined: Publiart SA, 1964; Sanglier SA, 1965; Rank Xerox, 1966: Regional Manager Africa, Eastern Europe, 1980; Gen. Manager, RX France, 1981; Pres., Amer. Ops, Xerox, 1988; Man. Dir, Rank Xerox Ltd, 1989–95. Non-exec. Dir, AEGIS, 2001–. Chm., Ecole des Hautes Etudes Commercial du Nord. *Recreations:* cooking, oenology, stamps, antiques, golf.

FOURNIER, Jean, OC 1987; CD 1972; retired diplomat; *b* Montreal, 18 July 1914; *s* of Arthur Fournier and Emilie Roy; *m* 1942, May Coote; five *s*. *Educ:* High Sch. of Québec; Laval Univ. (BA 1935, LLB 1938). Admitted to Bar of Province of Quebec, 1939. Royal Canadian Artillery (NPAM) (Lieut), 1935; Canadian Active Service Force Sept. 1939; served in Canada and overseas; discharged 1944, Actg Lt-Col. Joined Canadian Foreign Service, 1944; Third Sec., Canadian Dept of External Affairs, 1944; Second Sec., Canadian Embassy, Buenos Aires, 1945; Nat. Defence Coll., Kingston, 1948 (ndc); Seconded: to Privy Council Office, 1948–50; to Prime Minister's Office, Oct. 1950–Feb. 1951; First Sec., Canadian Embassy, Paris, 1951; Counsellor, 1953; Consul Gen., Boston, 1954; Privy Council Office (Asst Sec. to Cabinet), 1957–61; Head of European Division (Political Affairs), Dept of External Affairs, 1961–64; Chm., Quebec Civil Service Commn, 1964–71; Agent Gen. for the Province of Quebec in London, 1971–78. Mem., Canadian Metric Commn, 1981–85. Pres., Inst. of Public Administration of Canada, 1966–67; Pres., Centre Québecois de Relations Internationales; Chm. Bd, Canadian Human Rights Foundn, 1982–90; Member: Canadian Inst. of Strategic Studies; Canadian Inst. of Internat. Affairs. Freedom, City of London, 1976. Pres., Canadian Veterans Assoc. of the UK, 1976–77. *Address:* Apt 615, 4430 Ste-Catherine 0, Westmount, QC H3Z 3E4, Canada. *T:* (514) 9328633.

FOUYAS, Metropolitan Methodios, of Pisidia; former Archbishop of Thyateira and Great Britain; Greek Orthodox Archbishop of Great Britain, 1979–88; *b* 14 Sept. 1925. *Educ:* BD (Athens); PhD (Manchester), 1962. Vicar of Greek Church in Munich, 1951–54; Secretary-General, Greek Patriarchate of Alexandria, 1954–56; Vicar of Greek Church in Manchester, 1960–66; Secretary, Holy Synod of Church of Greece, 1967–78; Archbishop of Aksum (Ethiopia), 1968–79. Founder, Harmony of Otherness, 2000. Member, Academy of Religious Sciences, Brussels, 1974–. Dist. Lectr, Univ. of Berkeley, 1992. Estabd Foundn for Hellenism in GB, 1982; Editor, Texts and Studies: a review of the Foundn for Hellenism in GB, Vols I–X, 1982–91; Founder-Editor, Abba Salama Review of Ethio-Hellenic Studies, 10 Volumes; Editor: Ekklesiastikos Pharos (Prize of Academy of Athens), 11 Volumes; Ecclesia and Theologia, vols I-XII, 1980–93. Hon. DD: Edinburgh, 1970; Gr. Th. School of Holy Cross, Boston, 1984. Grand Cordon: Order of Phoenix (Greece); of Sellassie (Ethiopia). *Publications:* Orthodoxy, Roman Catholicism and Anglicanism, 1972, 2nd edn 1984, 3rd edn in Greek 1996; The Person of Jesus Christ in the Decisions of the Ecumenical Councils, 1976, 2nd edn in Greek 1997; History of the Church in Corinth, 1968, 2nd edn 1997; Christianity and Judaism in Ethiopia, Nubia and Meroe, 1st Vol., 1979, 2nd Vol., 1982; Theological and Historical Studies, Vols 1–18, 1979–2003; Greeks and Latins, 1990, 2nd edn 1994; Hellenism, the Pedestal of Christianity, 1992; Contemporary History of the Church of Alexandria, 1993; Hellenism, the Pedestal of Islam, 1994, 2nd edn 1995; Hellenism and Judaism, 1995; The Hellenistic Jewish Tradition, 1996; Hellenic Problems, 1997; Letters of Meletius Pegas, Pope and Patriarch of Alexandria 1590–1601, 1976, 2nd edn 1998; Hellenism, the Pedestal of European Civilisation, 1999; The World Wise Spreading of the Hellenic Civilization, 2001; contrib. to many other books and treatises. *Recreation:* gardening. *Address:* 9 Riga Feraiou Street, Khalandri, 15232 Athens, Greece. *T:* (210) 6824793.

FOWDEN, Sir Leslie, Kt 1982; FRS 1964; Director of Arable Crops Research, Agricultural and Food Research Council, 1986–88; *b* Rochdale, Lancs, 13 Oct. 1925; *s* of Herbert and Amy D. Fowden; *m* 1949, Margaret Oakes; one *s* one *d*. *Educ:* University Coll., London. PhD Univ. of London, 1948. Scientific Staff of Human Nutrition Research Unit of the MRC, 1947–50; Lecturer in Plant Chemistry, University Coll. London, 1950–55, Reader, 1956–64, Prof. of Plant Chemistry, 1964–73; Dean of Faculty of Science, UCL, 1970–73; Dir, Rothamsted Exptl Station, 1973–86. Rockefeller Fellow at Cornell Univ., 1955; Visiting Prof. at Univ. of California, 1963; Royal Society Visiting Prof., Univ. of Hong Kong, 1967. Consultant Dir, Commonwealth Bureau of Soils, 1973–88. Chm., Agric. and Vet. Adv. Cttee, British Council, 1987–95; Member: Advisory Board, Tropical Product Inst., 1966–70; Council, Royal Society, 1970–72; Radioactive Waste Management Adv. Cttee, 1983–91. Royal Botanic Gardens, Kew:

Mem., Scientific Adv. Panel, 1977–83; Trustee, 1983–93; Trustee, Bentham-Moxon Trust, 1994–. Foreign Member: Deutsche Akademie der Naturforscher Leopoldina, 1971; Lenin All-Union Acad. of Agricultural Sciences of USSR, 1978–92; Acad. of Agricl Scis of GDR, 1986–91; Russian Acad. of Agricl Scis, 1992–; Corresponding Mem., Amer. Soc. Plant Physiologists, 1981; Hon. Mem., Phytochemical Soc. of Europe, 1985. Hon. DSc Westminster, 1993. *Publications:* contribs to scientific journals on topics in plant biochemistry.

FOWELLS, Joseph Dunthorne Briggs, CMG 1975; DSC 1940; Deputy Director General, British Council, 1976–77, retired; *b* 17 Feb. 1916; *s* of late Joseph Fowells and Maud Dunthorne, Middlesbrough; *m* 1st, 1940, Edith Agnes McKerracher (marr. diss. 1966); two *s* one *d*; 2nd, 1969, Thelma Howes (*d* 1974). *Educ:* Sedbergh Sch.; Clare Coll., Cambridge (MA). School teaching, 1938; service with Royal Navy (Lt-Comdr), 1939–46; Blackie & Son Ltd, Educnl Publishers, 1946; British Council, 1947: Argentina, 1954; Representative Sierra Leone, 1956; Scotland, 1957; Dir Latin America and Africa (Foreign) Dept, 1958; Controller Overseas B Division (foreign countries excluding Europe), 1966; Controller Planning, 1968; Controller European Div., 1970; Asst Dir Gen. (Functional), 1972; Asst Dir Gen. (Regional), 1973–76. *Recreations:* golf, sailing. *Address:* The Manor, Edward Gardens, Old Bedhampton, Havant, Hants PO9 3JJ. *T:* (023) 9249 8317.

FOWKE, Sir David (Frederick Gustavus), 5th Bt *cr* 1814, of Lowesby, Leics; *b* 28 Aug. 1950; *s* of Lt-Col Gerrard George Fowke (*d* 1969) (2nd *s* of 3rd Bt) and of Daphne (*née* Monasteriotis); *S* uncle, 1987. *Educ:* Cranbrook School, Sydney; Univ. of Sydney (BA 1971). *Heir:* none.

FOWLER, family name of **Baron Fowler**.

FOWLER, Baron *cr* 2001 (Life Peer), of Sutton Coldfield in the County of West Midlands; **Peter Norman Fowler,** Kt 1990; PC 1979; Chairman, Aggregate Industries, 2000–06; *b* 2 Feb. 1938; *s* of late N. F. Fowler and Katherine Fowler; *m* 1979, Fiona Poole, *d* of John Donald; two *d*. *Educ:* King Edward VI Sch., Chelmsford; Trinity Hall, Cambridge (MA). Nat. Service commn, Essex Regt, 1956–58; Cambridge, 1958–61; Chm., Cambridge Univ. Conservative Assoc., 1960. Joined staff of The Times, 1961; Special Corresp., 1962–66; Home Affairs Corresp., 1966–70; reported Middle East War, 1967. Mem. Council, Bow Group, 1967–69; Editorial Board, Crossbow, 1962–69; Vice-Chm., North Kensington Cons. Assoc., 1967–68; Chm., E Midlands Area, Cons. Political Centre, 1970–73. MP (C): Nottingham S, 1970–74; Sutton Coldfield, Feb. 1974–2001. Chief Opposition spokesman: Social Services, 1975–76; Transport, 1976–79; Opposition spokesman, Home Affairs, 1974–75; PPS, NI Office, 1972–74; Sec. of State for Transport, 1981 (Minister of Transport, 1979–81), for Social Services, 1981–87, for Employment, 1987–90; Opposition front bench spokesman on the envmt, transport and the regions, 1997–98, on home affairs, 1998–99. Mem., Parly Select Cttee on Race Relations and Immigration, 1970–74; Jt Sec., Cons. Parly Home Affairs Cttee, 1971–72, 1974 (Vice-Chm., 1974); Chairman: Cons Parly Cttee on European Affairs, 1991–92; H of L Select Cttee on BBC, 2005; H of L Select Cttee on Communication, 2007–. Special Advr to Prime Minister, 1992 Gen. Elecn; Chm., Cons. Party, 1992–94; Mem. Exec., Assoc. of Cons. Peers, 2001–04 (Vice Chm., 2004–). Chairman: Midland Independent Newspapers, 1991–98; Regl Independent Media (Yorks Post gp of newspapers), 1998–2002; Numark Ltd, 1998–; Thomson Foundn, 2007–; Director: NFC plc, 1990–97; Holcim Ltd, 2006–. Chm., NHBC, 1992–98. *Publications:* After the Riots: the police in Europe, 1979; political pamphlets including: The Cost of Crime, 1973; The Right Track, 1977; Ministers Decide: a memoir of the Thatcher years, 1991. *Address:* House of Lords, SW1A 0PW.

FOWLER, Prof. Alastair David Shaw, FBA 1974; Professor of English, University of Virginia, 1990–98; Regius Professor of Rhetoric and English Literature, University of Edinburgh, 1972–84, now Emeritus (University Fellow, 1985–87 and since 2007); *b* 17 Aug. 1930; *s* of David Fowler and Maggie Shaw; *m* 1950, Jenny Catherine Simpson; one *s* one *d*. *Educ:* Queen's Park Sch., Glasgow; Univ. of Glasgow; Univ. of Edinburgh; Pembroke Coll., Oxford. MA Edin. 1952 and Oxon 1955; DPhil Oxon 1957; DLitt Oxon 1972. Junior Res. Fellow, Queen's Coll., Oxford, 1955–59; Instructor, Indiana Univ., 1957–58; Lectr, UC Swansea, 1959–61; Fellow and Tutor in English Lit., Brasenose Coll., Oxford, 1962–71. Visiting Professor: Columbia Univ., 1964; Univ. of Virginia, 1969, 1979, 1985–90; Mem. Inst. for Advanced Study, Princeton, 1966, 1980; Visiting Fellow: Council of the Humanities, Princeton Univ., 1974; Humanities Research Centre, Canberra, 1980; All Souls Coll., Oxford, 1984. Lectures: Witter Bynner, Harvard, 1974; Churchill, Bristol Univ., 1979; Warton, British Acad., 1980; Ballard Matthews, Univ. of Wales, 1981; Coffin, UCL, 1984; Read-Tuckwell, Bristol Univ., 1991; Shakespeare, British Acad., 1995; Croston, Oxford, 2003; Bateson, Oxford, 2008. Mem., Agder Akademi, 2003. Mem., Scottish Arts Council, 1976–77. Adv. Editor, New Literary History, 1972–2003; Gen. Editor, Longman Annotated Anthologies of English Verse, 1977–80; Member, Editorial Board: English Literary Renaissance, 1978–2003; Word and Image, 1984–91, 1992–97; The Seventeenth Century, 1986–2003; Connotations, 1990–98; Translation and Literature, 1990–; English Review, 1990–. *Publications:* (trans. and ed) Richard Wills, De re poetica, 1958; Spenser and the Numbers of Time, 1964; (ed) C. S. Lewis, Spenser's Images of Life, 1967; (ed with John Carey) The Poems of John Milton, 1968; Triumphal Forms, 1970; (ed) Silent Poetry, 1970; (ed with Christopher Butler) Topics in Criticism, 1971; Seventeen, 1971; Conceitful Thought, 1975; Catacomb Suburb, 1976; Edmund Spenser, 1977; From the Domain of Arnheim, 1982; Kinds of Literature, 1982; A History of English Literature, 1987; The New Oxford Book of Seventeenth Century Verse, 1991; The Country House Poem, 1994; Time's Purpled Masquers, 1996; (ed) Paradise Lost, 1998; Renaissance Realism, 2003; How to Write, 2006; contribs to jls and books. *Address:* 11 East Claremont Street, Edinburgh EH7 4HT.

FOWLER, Beryl, (Mrs Henry Fowler); *see* Chitty, M. B.

FOWLER, Prof. (Christine) Mary Rutherford, PhD; Professor of Geophysics, since 2003 and Head of Department of Earth Sciences, since 2002, Royal Holloway, University of London; *b* 1950; *d* of Peter and Rosemary Fowler; *m* 1975; one *s* two *d*. *Educ:* Girton Coll., Cambridge (BA 1st Cl. Maths 1972); Darwin Coll., Cambridge (PhD 1976). Royal Soc. Eur. Fellow, ETH Zürich, 1977–78; University of Saskatchewan: Professional Res. Associate, 1981–82, 1983–91; Asst Prof., 1982–83; Adjunct Prof., 1991–2001; Lectr, then Sen. Lectr (pt-time), Royal Holloway Coll., Univ. of London, 1992–2003. Associate Editor: Reviews of Geophysics, 1991–94; Jl Geophysical Res., 1998–2004. Dir, Sask Energy, 1992. Mem. Council, 1998–2002, Vice-Pres., 2000–02, RAS; Mem. Council, Geol Soc., 2007–. Member: Bureau, Internat. Lithosphere Prog., 1997–2002; Governing Bd, Sch. of Cosmic Physics, Dublin Inst. for Advanced Studies, 2006–. Prestwich Medal, Geol Soc., 1996. *Publications:* (ed with E. G. Nisbet) Heat Metamorphism and Tectonics, 1988; The Solid Earth: an introduction to global geophysics, 1990, 2nd edn 2005; (ed jtly) The Early Earth: physical, chemical and biological development, 2002; contrib. learned jls. *Address:* Department of Earth Sciences, Royal Holloway, University of London, Egham, Surrey TW20 0EX. *T:* (01784) 443582, *Fax:* (01784) 471780.

FOWLER, Christopher B.; *see* Brocklebank-Fowler.

FOWLER, Prof. David, CBE 2005; PhD; FRS 2002; FRSE; Science Directo Biogeochemistry, Centre for Ecology and Hydrology, Natural Environment Resear Council, Edinburgh, since 2003; *b* 1 June 1950; *s* of late Roy Fowler and of Phyllis Jo Fowler (*née* Lee); *m* 1976, Annette Francesca Odile Rossetti; one *s* two *d*. *Educ:* City Sch Lincoln; Univ. of Nottingham (BSc 1972; PhD 1976). Institute of Terrestrial Ecolog subseq. Centre for Ecology and Hydrology, Edinburgh: HSO, 1975–78; SSO, 1978–8 PSO, 1985; Section Hd, Air Pollution, 1986; Grade 6, 1991; Grade 5, 1998; H Atmospheric Scis Div., 2002–03. Hon. Lectr, Univ. of Edinburgh, 1988; Special Prof. Envmtl Sci., Univ. of Nottingham, 1991. Chairman: UK Photochemical Oxidants Re Gp, 1990–98; UK Nat. Expert Gp on Transboundary Air Pollution, 1999. FRSE 199 Member Editorial Board: Tellus, 1995; Environmental Pollution, 2000. *Publications:* (wi M. H. Unsworth) Acid Deposition at High Elevation, 1988; Ozone in the Unit Kingdom, 1997; Acidification, Eutrophication and Ozone in the UK, 2001; (with C. R. Pitcairn and J. W. Erisman) Air-Surface Exchange of Gases and Particles; ma scientific papers in Qly Jl RMetS, Atmospheric Envmt, Envmtl Pollution, Tellus, Ne Phytologist and Nature. *Recreations:* hill walking, gardening, music, photography, natu history, cycling. *Address:* Centre for Ecology and Hydrology, Bush Estate, Penicui Midlothian EH26 0QB. *T:* (0131) 445 4343, *Fax:* (0131) 445 3943; *e-mail:* dfo ceh.ac.uk.

FOWLER, Dennis Houston, OBE 1979 (MBE 1963); HM Diplomatic Service, retire *b* 15 March 1924; *s* of Joseph Fowler and Daisy Lilian Wraith Fowler (*née* Houston); 1944, Lilias Wright Nairn Burnett; two *s* one *d*. *Educ:* Alleyn's Sch., Dulwich. Coloni Office, 1940; RAF, 1942–46; India Office (subseq. CRO), 1947; Colombo, 1951; Seco Secretary, Karachi, 1955; CRO, 1959; First Secretary, Dar es Salaam, 1961; Diploma Service Administration (subseq. FCO), 1965; First Sec. and Head of Chancery, Reykjavi 1969; FCO, 1973; First Sec., Head of Chancery and Consul, Kathmandu, 197 Counsellor and Hd of Claims Dept, FCO, 1980–83. *Recreations:* golf, music, do- yourself. *Address:* 25 Dartnell Park Road, West Byfleet, Surrey KT14 6PN. *T:* (0193 341583. *Clubs:* West Byfleet Golf; Royal Nepal Golf (Kathmandu).

FOWLER, Sir (Edward) Michael (Coulson), Kt 1981; Mayor of Wellington, Ne Zealand, 1974–83; architectural consultant, since 1989; former company chairman a director; *b* 19 Dec. 1929; *s* of William Coulson Fowler and Faith Agnes Netherclift; 1953, Barbara Hamilton Hall; two *s* one *d*. *Educ:* Christ's Coll., Christchurch, N Auckland Univ. (MArch). Architect, London office, Ove Arup & Partners, 1954–55; ow practice, Wellington, 1957–59; Partner, Calder Fowler Styles and Turner, 1959–8 Wellington buildings designed and supervised: Overseas Passenger Terminal, 1963; T Reserve Bank, 1970; Dalmuir House, 1971; Church of the Immaculate Conceptio Taumarunui, 1975; St Andrew's Presbyterian Church, Blenheim, 1976; Greenock Hous 1978; alterations and additions, Old St Mary's Convent, Blenheim, 1986; Highfie Winery, Marlborough, 1995–2000; many country and urban houses. Director: Ne Zealand Sugar Co., 1983–95; Cigna Insurance New Zealand Ltd, 1985–89. Chm., Que Elizabeth II Arts Council, 1983–87. Wellington City Councillor, 1968–74. Nat. Pre YHA of NZ, 1984–87. Medal of Honour, NZIA, 1983; Alfred O. Glasse Award, NZ In of Planning, 1984. *Publications:* Wellington Sketches: Folio I, 1971, Folio II, 197 Country Houses of New Zealand, 1972, 2nd edn 1977; The Architecture and Planning Moscow, 1980; Eating Houses in Wellington, 1980; Wellington Wellington, 1981; Eati Houses of Canterbury, 1982; Wellington—A Celebration, 1983; The New Zeala House, 1983; Buildings of New Zealanders, 1984; Michael Fowler's University Auckland, 1993. *Recreations:* sketching, reading, writing, history, politics. *Address:* Goring Street, Thorndon, Wellington, New Zealand; *e-mail:* michael.fowler@xtra.co.n *Club:* Wellington (Wellington, NZ).

FOWLER, John Francis, DSc, PhD; FInstP; Professor, Department of Human Oncolo and Medical Physics, University of Wisconsin, USA, 1988–94 and 1999–2004, no Emeritus; Director of Cancer Research Campaign's Gray Laboratory, at Mount Vern Hospital, Northwood, 1970–88; *b* 3 Feb. 1925; *er s* of Norman V. Fowler, Bridpo Dorset; *m* 1st, 1953, Kathleen Hardcastle Sutton, MB, BS (marr. diss. 1984); two *s* five 2nd, 1992, Anna Edwards, BSc, MCSP, SRP. *Educ:* Bridport Grammar Sch.; Universi Coll. of the South-West, Exeter. BSc 1st class Hons (London) 1944; MSc (London) 194 PhD (London) 1955; DSc (London) 1974; FInstP 1957. Research Physicist: Newa Insulation Co., 1944; Metropolitan Vickers Electrical Co., 1947; Newcastle upon Ty Regional Hosp. Board (Radiotherapy service), 1950; Principal Physicist at King's Co Hosp., SE5, 1956; Head of Physics Section in Medical Research Coun Radiotherapeutic Res. Unit, Hammersmith Hosp., 1959 (later the Cyclotron Uni Reader in Physics, London Univ. at Med. Coll. of St Bartholomew's Hosp., 1962; Pr of Med. Physics, Royal Postgraduate Med. Sch., London Univ., Hammersmith Hosp 1963–70, Vice-Dean, 1967–70. Visiting Professor: in Oncology, Middx Hosp. Med. Sc 1977–88; Dept. of Oncol., University Hosp. of Leuven, Belgium, 1994–99; Bush V Prof., Ontario Cancer Inst., Toronto, 1991. President: Hosp. Physicists Assoc., 1966–6 Europ. Soc. Radiat. Biol., 1974–76; British Inst. Radiol., 1977–78. Hon. Fellow: Ame Coll. of Radiology, 1981; Amer. Coll. of Radiation Oncology, 1994; RCR, 1999. Ho Member: Amer. Assoc. of Med. Physicists, 1983; Inst. of Physics & Engrg in Medicin 1994. Hon. MD Helsinki, 1981; Hon. DSc Med. Coll. Wisconsin, 1989. Roentg Award, BIR, 1965; Röntgen Plakette, Deutsches Röntgen Museum, 1978; Heath Me Award, Univ. of Texas, Houston, 1981; Breur Medal, European Soc. Therapeut Radiology and Oncology, 1983; Barclay Medal, BIR, 1985; Marie Sklodowska-Cur Medal, Polish Radiation Res. Soc., 1986; Gold Medal, Amer. Soc. Therapeutic Radi and Oncol., 1995; Failla Award, US Radiation Res. Soc., 2003. *Publications:* Nucle Particles in Cancer Treatment, 1981; papers on radiobiology applied to radiotherapy, Brit. Jl Radiology, Clinical Oncology, Radiotherapy and Oncology, Internat. Jl Radiati Oncology Biol. Physics, etc. *Recreations:* theatre, ballroom dancing, getting into t countryside. *Address:* 150 Lambeth Road, SE1 7DF; *e-mail:* jackfowler@btinternet.com

FOWLER, Mary Rutherford; *see* Fowler, C. M. R.

FOWLER, Sir Michael; *see* Fowler, Sir E. M. C.

FOWLER, Neil Douglas; Editor, Which? magazine, since 2006; *b* 18 April 1956; *s* of la Arthur Vincent Fowler and Helen Pauline Fowler; *m* 1989, Carol Susan (*née* Cherry); o *d*, and one step *s*. *Educ:* Southend High Sch. for Boys; Univ. of Leicester (BA Social Sci Reporter, Leicester Mercury, 1978–81; Dep. News Editor, then Asst Chief Sub-edit Derby Evening Telegraph, 1981–84; Asst to Editor, Asst Editor, then Editor, Lincolnshi Echo, 1984–87; Editor: Derby Evening Telegraph, 1987–91; The Journal, Newcast upon Tyne, 1991–94; The Western Mail, 1994–2002; Proprietor, Neil Fowl Communications, 2002–03; CEO and Publisher, Toronto Sun, 2003–05. Dir, Publishi NTO, 2000–03. FRSA 1999. Pres., Society (formerly Guild) of Editors, 1999–20 (Vice-Pres., 1998–99). Regional Editor of Year, Newspaper Focus magazines, 1994; B Welsh Journalist, 1999. *Recreations:* cricket, cinema, music of Frank Zappa. *Addres*

Which?, 2 Marylebone Road, NW1 4DF. *T:* (020) 7770 7237; *e-mail:* neil.fowler@ which.co.uk.

FOWLER, Peter James, CMG 1990; HM Diplomatic Service, retired; International Adviser, Cairn Energy PLC, since 2002 (Director, 1996–2001); *b* 26 Aug. 1936; *s* of James and Gladys Fowler; *m* 1962, Audrey June Smith; one *s* three *d. Educ:* Nunthorpe Grammar Sch., York; Trinity Coll., Oxford (BA). Army service, 1954–56. FCO, 1962–64; Budapest, 1964–65; Lisbon, 1965–67; Calcutta, 1968–71; FCO, 1971–75; East Berlin, 1975–77; Counsellor, Cabinet Office, 1977–80; Comprehensive Test Ban Delegn, Geneva, 1980; Counsellor, Bonn, 1981–85; Head of N America Dept, FCO, 1985–88; Minister and Dep. High Comr, New Delhi, 1988–93; High Comr to Bangladesh, 1993–96. Vice-Chm., Diplomatic Service Appeal Bd, 1997–2003. Chm., Charles Wallace Trust (Bangladesh), 1996–; Hon. Pres., Bangladeshi-British Chamber of Commerce, 1998–. *Recreations:* reading, South Asia, opera. *Address:* 33 Northdown Street, N1 9BL. *Club:* Royal Over-Seas League.

FOWLER, Peter Jon, PhD; world heritage consultant, since 2000; Emeritus Professor, University of Newcastle upon Tyne, since 1996; *b* 14 June 1936; *s* of W. J. Fowler and P. A. Fowler; *m* 1959, Elizabeth (*née* Burley) (marr. diss. 1993); three *d. Educ:* King Edward VI Grammar Sch., Morpeth, Northumberland; Lincoln Coll., Oxford (MA 1961); Univ. of Bristol (PhD 1977). Investigator on staff of RCHM (England), Salisbury office, 1959–65; Staff Tutor in Archaeology, Dept of Extra-Mural Studies, 1965–79, and Reader in Arch., 1972–79, Univ. of Bristol; Sec., Royal Commn on Historical Monuments (England), 1979–85; Prof. of Archaeology, 1985–96, and Leverhulme Fellow, 1996–99, Univ. of Newcastle upon Tyne. Member: Historic Bldgs and Ancient Monuments Adv. Cttees, Historic Buildings and Monuments Commn, 1983–86 (Ancient Monuments Bd, 1979–83); Council, National Trust, 1983–2000; Pres., Council for British Archaeol., 1981–83 (Vice-Pres., 1979–81). Archaeological consultant, Forestry Commn, 1988–2000; Mem., Landscape Adv. Cttee, DoT, 1990–95. Chm., Jarrow 700AD Ltd, 1991–2000. *Publications:* Regional Archaeologies: Wessex, 1967; (ed) Archaeology and the Landscape, 1972; (ed) Recent Work in Rural Archaeology, 1975; (ed with K. Branigan) The Roman West Country, 1976; Approaches to Archaeology, 1977; (ed with H. C. Bowen) Early Land Allotment in the British Isles, 1978; (with S. Piggott and M. L. Ryder) Agrarian History of England and Wales, I, pt 1, 1981; The Farming of Prehistoric Britain, 1983; Farms in England, 1983; (with P. Boniface) Northumberland and Newcastle upon Tyne, 1989; (jtly) Who Owns Stonehenge?, 1990; (with M. Sharp) Images of Prehistory, 1990; The Past in Contemporary Society: then, now, 1992; (jtly) Cadbury Congresbury 1968–73: a late/post-Roman hilltop settlement in Somerset, 1992; (with P. Boniface) Heritage and Tourism in 'the global village', 1993; (jtly) The Experimental Earthwork Project 1960–1992, 1996; (with I. Blackwell) The Land of Lettice Sweetapple, 1998; Landscape Plotted and Pieced: landscape history and local archaeology in Fyfield and Overton, Wiltshire, 2000; (with I. Blackwell) An English Countryside Explored, 2000; Farming in the First Millennium AD, 2002; World Heritage Cultural Landscapes, 1992–2002, 2003; Landscapes for the World, 2004; (jtly) Inventory of Cultural and National Heritage Sites of Potential Outstanding Universal Value in Palestine, 2005; contribs to learned jls. *Recreations:* writing, painting, sport. *T:* and *Fax:* (020) 7837 5818.

FOWLER, Robert Asa, Owner and Chairman, Fowler International, since 1986; Consul General for Sweden, 1989–99; *b* 5 Aug. 1928; *s* of Mr and Mrs William Henry Fowler; *m* 1987, Monica Elizabeth Heden; three *s* one *d* by a previous marriage. *Educ:* Princeton Univ. (BA Econs); Harvard Business Sch. (MBA). Lieut USNR, 1950–53. Various appts with Continental Oil, 1955–75; Area Manager, Northwest Europe, Continental Oil Co., 1975–78; Chm. and Man. Dir, Conoco Ltd, 1979–81; Vice-Pres., Internat. Marketing, Conoco Inc., 1981–85. An Hon. Consul Gen. for Sweden. *Recreations:* tennis, ski-ing. *Address:* 2 Azalea Court, Princeton, NJ 08540, USA. *T:* (609) 5141511. *Clubs:* Hurlingham; River, Knickerbocker (NY); Allegheny Country (Pa); Chagrin Valley Hunt (Ohio).

FOWLER, Prof. Robert Louis Herbert, DPhil; Henry Overton Wills Professor of Greek, since 1996, and Dean of Arts, since 2004, University of Bristol; *b* 19 May 1954; *s* of Rev. Dr Louis Heath Fowler and Helen Minto Fowler (*née* Wilson); *m* 1976, Judith Lee Evers; two *s. Educ:* Univ. of Toronto Schs; Univ. of Toronto (BA 1976, MA 1977); Wadham Coll., Oxford (DPhil 1980). Fellow, Calgary Inst. for the Humanities, 1980; Department of Classical Studies, University of Waterloo, Canada: Asst Prof., 1981–86; Associate Prof., 1986–94; Chm. of Dept, 1988–96; Prof., 1994–96. Chm. Council, Classical Assoc., 2002–07. Ed., Jl Hellenic Studies, 2001–05. *Publications:* The Nature of Early Greek Lyric, 1987; (ed) Early Greek Mythography, vol. I, 2000; (ed) The Cambridge Companion to Homer, 2004; contrib. articles to learned jls. *Recreation:* piano. *Address:* Department of Classics and Ancient History, University of Bristol, 11 Woodland Road, Bristol BS8 1TB. *T:* (0117) 331 7349.

FOWLER, Prof. Robert Stewart, OBE 2001; Principal and Chief Executive, Central School of Speech and Drama, 1986–2001; *b* 1 Feb. 1932; *s* of William Fowler and Breta Bell Fowler (*née* Stewart); *m* 1965, Penelope Jessie Hobbs; two *s* one *d. Educ:* Queen's Coll., Oxford (MA); Queen's Univ., Belfast (DipEd); Guildhall Sch. of Music and Drama (LGSM). Served RAEC, 1950–52. Asst in English, Drama and Latin, Royal Belfast Acad. Instn, 1955–58; Hd of Dept, Forest Gate Sch., 1958–60; Warden, Bretton Hall Coll., Wakefield, 1960–66; Dep. Principal and Principal Elect, Sittingbourne Coll. of Educn, 1966–76; HMI with resp. for theatre, the arts in teacher trng and staff inspector, teacher trng, 1976–86. Chief Ext. Examr (Theatre Design), Nottingham Trent Univ., 1996–98. Vis. Prof., Birmingham City Univ. (formerly Univ. of Central England), 1995–. Vice-Pres., European League Inst. of Arts, 1998–2002; Member: Bd, Univs and Colls Employers' Assoc., 1996–2000; Nat. Council for Drama Trng, 1996–2000. Panel Chm., Hong Kong Council for Academic Accreditation, 1996–. Chm. Govs, Keswick Sch., 2007– (Foundn Gov., 2004–; Trustee, 2007). Sec., Oxford Univ. Soc. Cumbria, 2005–. FRSA 1990. NW Vision Film Writing Award, 2003. *Publications:* Themes in Life and Literature, 1967; (jtly) English 11/16, 5 books, 1971–73; The Hobbit Introduced for Schools, 1973; (jtly) English: a literary foundation course, 1975. *Recreations:* living, loving, life-saving, laughing, Lake District, Provence, family, friends, writing. *Address:* Gutherscale, Newlands, Keswick, Cumbria CA12 5UE.

FOWLER, Sarah Hauldys; see Evans, S. H.

FOWLIE, John Kay; JP; Vice Lord-Lieutenant of Banffshire, since 2003; *b* 28 Jan. 1936; *s* of late Spencer Stephen Fowlie, MC and Agnes Howatson (*née* Kay); *m* 1960, Catherine Ann Coull Flett; one *s* one *d* (and one *s* decd). *Educ:* Buckie High Sch.; Jordanhill Coll. of Educn, Glasgow (Teaching Dip. in PE 1960). Nat. Service, 3rd Bn Parachute Regt, Cyprus and Suez, 1955–57; served TA 3rd Bn Gordon Highlanders, 1964–68. Teacher, then Principal Teacher of PE, Keith Grammar Sch., 1960–77; Principal Teacher (Guidance), Buckie High Sch., 1977–96. Mem., then Chm., Moray Children's Panel Adv. Cttee, 1985–96. RNLI: fundraising, 1970–; Station Hon. Sec., Launch Authy, Buckie Lifeboat, 1985–2003; Member: Steering Gp Cttee for RNLI Family Assoc., 2002–03; Scottish Lifeboat Council, 1999–2003; Cttee Mem., Buckie & District Fishing Heritage

Mus., 2002–. Elder, Buckie S & W Church, 1975–; Sec., Buckie & District Seamen's Meml Chapel, 1998–. JP Moray, 1995; DL Banffshire, 1998. *Publication:* The Times, the People, and the Buckie Fishermen's Choir, 2005. *Recreations:* walking, gardening, local history, reading. *Address:* Dunedin, 16 Titness Street, Buckie, Banffshire AB56 1HR. *T:* (01542) 832429.

FOX, Dr Alan Martin; Clerk to Trustees, St Marylebone Almshouses, since 1998; *b* 5 July 1938; *s* of Sidney Nathan Fox and Clarice Solov; *m* 1965, Sheila Naomi Pollard; one *s* two *d. Educ:* Bancroft's Sch., Essex; Queen Mary Coll., London (BSc Hons II1, Physics 1959; PhD Math. Phys. 1963). ACIArb 1997, MCIArb 1999. Home Civil Service by Open Competition, 1963; Ministry of Aviation: Private Sec. to Parly Sec., 1965–67; 1st Sec. (Aviation and Defence) on loan to FCO, Paris, 1973–75; MoD, 1975–78; RCDS, 1979; MoD, 1980–98; Asst Under Sec. of State (Ordnance), 1988–92; Vis. Fellow, Center for Internat. Affairs, Harvard, 1992–93; Asst Under-Sec. of State (Quartermaster), 1994–95, (Export Policy and Finance), 1995–98. Lectr (part-time), UCL, 1998–2000. Member: London Rent Assessment Panel, 1999–; Compliance and Supervision Cttee, 2000–01; Adjudication Panel, 2002–, SRA (formerly Office for the Supervision of Solicitors); Review Cttee on Non-Competitive Contracts, 2000–07. Clerk to Governors: Henrietta Barnett Sch., 1998–2003; Jews Free Sch., 2000–02. *Recreations:* grandchildren, playing chess, computer games, watching Rugby, cricket, TV. *Address:* 4 Woodside Avenue, N6 4SS.

FOX, Dr (Anthony) John, FFPH; Strategic Advisor, Research, Information Centre for Health and Social Care (formerly Director, Customer and Stakeholder Engagement, NHS Health and Social Care Information Centre), since 2005; *b* 25 April 1946; *s* of Fred Frank Fox, OBE, and Gertrude Price; *m* 1971, Annemarie Revesz; one *s* two *d. Educ:* Dauntsey's School; University College London (BSc); Imperial College London (PhD, DIC). FFPH (FFPHM 2000). Statistician: Employment Medical Adv. Service, 1970–75; OPCS, 1975–79; Prof. of Social Statistics, City Univ., 1980–88; Chief Medical Statistician, OPCS, 1988–96; Dir, Census, Population and Health Gp, ONS, 1996–99; Dir of Statistics, DoH, 1999–2005. Visiting Professor: LSHTM, 1990–; UCL, 2006–. Hon. DSc City, 1997. *Publications:* Occupational Mortality 1970–72, 1978; Socio-Demographic Mortality Differentials, 1982; Health Inequalities in European Countries, 1989; (jtly) Health and Class: The early years, 1991. *Recreations:* family, tennis, bridge, theatre. *Address:* Information Centre for Health and Social Care, Harmsworth House, 13–15 Bouverie Street, EC4Y 8DP.

FOX, Brian Michael, CB 1998; Head of Civil Service Corporate Management (Grade 2), Cabinet Office, 1998–2000; *b* 21 Sept. 1944; *s* of Walter Frederick and Audrey May Fox; *m* 1966, Maureen Ann Shrimpton; one *d. Educ:* East Ham Grammar School for Boys. Joined CS, HM Treasury, 1963–98: Private Sec. to Financial Sec., 1967–69; secondment to 3i Gp, 1981–82; Dep. Estabt Officer, 1983–87; Head of Defence Policy and Materiel Div., 1987–89; Principal Estabt and Finance Officer, 1989–93; Dir (Grade 3), Sen. and Public Appts Gp, later Sen. CS Gp, Cabinet Office (on loan), 1994–98. Trustee, Help The Aged, 1998–; Property Trustee, Civil Service Benevolent Fund, 2001–. Chm., Anim-Mates, 2006–. *Recreations:* bowls, badminton, soccer. *Club:* Elm Park Bowls.

FOX, Sir Christopher, Kt 2006; QPM 1996; Managing Director, Chris Fox Consulting Ltd, since 2006; *b* 21 July 1949; *s* of Douglas Charles Fox and Olive Eileen Fox (*née* Vigar); *m* 1972, Carol Ann Wortley; one *s* two *d. Educ:* Broomhill Primary Sch.; Robert Gordon's Coll., Aberdeen; W Bridgeford GS, Nottingham; Loughborough Univ. (BSc Physics and Electronic Engrg; DIS). Joined Notts Constabulary, 1972; detective and uniform duties, 1972–83; Superintendent, Mansfield, 1984–87; Chief Supt, Nottingham N Div., 1987–90; Actg Asst Chief Constable, Nottingham, 1990–91; Asst Chief Constable, 1991–94, Dep. Chief Constable, 1994–96, Warwickshire; Chief Constable, Northants, 1996–2003; Pres., ACPO, 2003–06. Trustee, Endeavour Trng, 1995–. *Recreations:* played Rugby at first class level (Nottingham), cricket player and coach (still active), laid back cruiser sailing. *T:* 07714 689219; *e-mail:* chris@chrisfoxconsulting.com.

FOX, Claire; Founder Director, Institute of Ideas, since 2000; *b* 5 June 1960; *d* of late John Fox and of Maura Fox. *Educ:* Warwick Univ. (BA Hons English and American Lit.); Thames Poly. (PGCE 1992). Mental health social worker for variety of orgns in voluntary sector, incl. Cyrenians and MIND, 1981–87; Lectr and Tutor in English Lang. and Lit., Thurrock Tech. Coll., 1987–90 and W Herts Coll., 1992–99; Publisher, Living Marxism, subseq. LM mag., 1997–2000. *Publications:* A Lecturer's Guide to Further Education, 2006; contributed chapters to: Debating Education: issues for the new millennium, 1996; Dumbing Down, 2000; The McDonaldisation of Higher Education, 2002; The Routledge Falmer Guide to Key Debates in Education, 2004; The Lottery Debate, 2006; Panic Attack, 2006. *Recreations:* putting my head above the parapet, saying the unsayable and stirring up intellectual debate. *Address:* Institute of Ideas, Signet House, 49–51 Farringdon Road, EC1M 3JP. *T:* (020) 7269 9223, *Fax:* (020) 7269 9235; *e-mail:* clairefox@instituteofideas.com.

FOX, Colin; Member (Scot Socialist) Lothians, Scottish Parliament, 2003–07; *b* 17 June 1959; *s* of John Fox and Agnes Fox (*née* Mackin); partner, Zillah Jones; one *s* one *d. Educ:* Our Lady's High Sch., Motherwell; Bell Coll., Hamilton (SHND Accounting). Political organiser (militant), 1983–95; Scottish Socialist Alliance organiser, 1995–98; Scottish Socialist Party: Founder Mem., 1998; Organiser, 1998–2003; Nat. Convenor, 2005–. Co-organiser, Edinburgh Mayday Fest., 1998–; Founder/Organiser, Edinburgh People's Fest., 2002–. *Publication:* Motherwell is Won for Moscow, 1991. *Recreations:* golf, reading.

FOX, Edward, OBE 2003; actor; *b* 13 April 1937; *s* of late Robin and Angela Muriel Darita Fox; *m* 1st, 1958, Tracy (*née* Pelissier) (marr. diss. 1961); one *d*; 2nd, 2004, Joanna David; one *s* one *d. Educ:* Ashfold Sch.; Harrow Sch. RADA training, following National Service, 1956–58; entry into provincial repertory theatre, 1958, since when, films, TV films and plays, and plays in the theatre, have made up the sum of his working life. *Theatre includes:* Knuckle, Comedy, 1973; The Family Reunion, Vaudeville, 1979; Anyone for Denis, Whitehall, 1981; Quartermaine's Terms, Queen's, 1981; Hamlet, Young Vic, 1982; Interpreters, Queen's, 1985; Let Us Go Then, You and I, Lyric, 1987; The Admirable Crichton, Haymarket, 1988; (also dir) Another Love Story, Leicester Haymarket, 1990; The Philanthropist, Wyndham's, 1991; The Father, tour, 1995; A Letter of Resignation, Comedy, 1997; The Chiltern Hundreds, Vaudeville, 1999; The Browning Version, and The Twelve-Pound Look, Th. Royal, Bath, 2002; The Winslow Boy, tour, 2002; The Old Masters, Comedy, 2004; You Never Can Tell, Th. Royal, Bath, 2005, Garrick, 2005–06; Legal Fictions, tour, 2007. *Films include:* The Go-Between, 1971 (Soc. of Film and Television Arts Award for Best Supporting Actor, 1971); The Day of the Jackal, A Doll's House, 1973; Galileo, 1976; The Squeeze, A Bridge Too Far (BAFTA Award for Best Supporting Actor, 1977), The Duellists, The Cat and the Canary, 1977; Force Ten from Navarone, 1978; The Mirror Crack'd, 1980; Gandhi, 1982; Never Say Never Again, The Dresser, 1983; The Bounty, 1984; The Shooting Party, 1985; A Month by the Lake, 1996; Stage Beauty, 2004. *Television series include:* Hard Times, 1977; Edward and Mrs Simpson, 1978 (BAFTA Award for Best Actor, 1978; TV Times Top Ten Award for Best Actor, 1978–79; British Broadcasting Press Guild TV Award for Best

Actor, 1978; Royal TV Soc. Performance Award, 1978–79); They Never Slept, 1991; A Dance to the Music of Time, 1997; Daniel Deronda, 2002; Oliver Twist, 2007. *Recreations:* music, reading, walking. *Club:* Savile.

See also J. Fox, R. M. J. Fox, Viscount Gormanston.

FOX, Hazel Mary, (Lady Fox), CMG 2006; Director, British Institute of International and Comparative Law, 1982–89; General Editor, International and Comparative Law Quarterly, 1987–98; *b* 22 Oct. 1928; *d* of J. M. B. Stuart, CIE; *m* 1954, Rt Hon. Sir Michael Fox, PC (*d* 2007); three *s* one *d*. *Educ:* Roedean Sch.; Somerville Coll., Oxford (1st Cl. Jurisprudence, 1949; MA). Called to the Bar, Lincoln's Inn, 1950 (Buchanan Prize; Bencher, 1989); practised at the Bar, 1950–54 and 1994–; Fellow of Somerville Coll., Oxford, 1976–81, Hon. Fellow 1988. Chairman: London Rent Assessment Panel, 1977–98; London Leasehold Valuation Tribunal, 1981–98; Mem., Home Office Deptl Cttee on Jury Service, 1963–65. Mem., Institut de droit international, 2001 (Associate, 1997–99). Hon. QC 1993. JP London, 1959–77; Chm., Tower Hamlets Juvenile Court, 1968–76. *Publications:* (with J. L. Simpson) International Arbitration, 1959; (ed) International Economic Law and Developing States, vol. I 1988, vol. II 1992; (ed) Joint Development of Offshore Oil and Gas, vol. I 1989, vol. II 1990; (ed jtly) Armed Conflict and the New Law, vol. II: Effecting Compliance, 1993; The Law of State Immunity, 2002, 2nd edn 2008. *Address:* 4/5 Grays Inn Square, WC1R 5JP. *T:* (020) 7404 5252; *e-mail:* (020) 7242 7803.

FOX, James; actor; *b* 19 May 1939; *s* of late Robin and Angela Fox; changed forename from William to James, 1962; *m* 1973, Mary Elizabeth Piper; four *s* one *d*. *Educ:* Harrow Sch.; Central Sch. of Speech and Drama. National Service, 1959–61. Entered acting as child, 1950; left acting to pursue Christian vocation, 1970–79; returned to acting, 1980. Main *films* include: The Servant, 1963; King Rat, 1964; Thoroughly Modern Millie, 1965; The Chase, 1966; Isadora, 1968; Performance, 1969; A Passage to India, 1984; Runners, 1984; Farewell to the King, 1987; Finding Mawbee (video film as The Mighty Quinn), 1988; She's Been Away, 1989; The Russia House, 1990; Afraid of the Dark, 1991; The Remains of the Day, 1993; Anna Karenina, 1997; Mickey Blue Eyes, 1999; Up the Villa, 1999; Sexy Beast, 1999; The Golden Bowl, 1999; The Prince and Me, 2004; Charlie and the Chocolate Factory, 2005; Mr Lonely, 2006; *theatre* includes: Uncle Vanya, NY, 1995; Resurrection Blues, Old Vic, 2006; *television* includes: The Choir (serial), 1995; Gulliver's Travels, 1996; The Lost World, 2001; The Falklands (play), 2002; Suez, 2006. *Publication:* Comeback: an actor's direction, 1983. *Recreation:* Russian language and culture. *Address:* c/o United Agents, 12–26 Lexington Street, W1F 0LE.

See also E. Fox, R. M. J. Fox.

FOX, John; see Fox, A. J.

FOX, John Rupert Anselm; a Vice President, Immigration Appeal Tribunal, 2000–04 (Legal Member, 1996–2005); an Adjudicator, Immigration and Asylum Appeals, 1990–2005; *b* 10 Dec. 1935; *s* of John Arnold Fox, MBE (mil.) and Eleanor Margaret Fox (née Green); *m* 1965, Isabel June Mary Jermy Gwyn; three *s* one *d* (and two *s* one *d* decd). *Educ:* Stonyhurst Coll. 2nd Lieut, RASC, 1954; transf. to Cheshire Yeo., 1958; Capt. 1959; RAC Reserve of Officers, 1966. Admitted solicitor, 1960; articled to Simpson North Harley & Co., London and Liverpool, 1953, Solicitor, Liverpool, 1960–62; Partner, Whatley Weston & Fox, Worcester, Malvern and Hereford, 1963–76; Asst Dir/ Legal Advr, Foreign Investment Agency of Canada, 1976–78; Partner, John Fox Solicitors, Broadway, Worcs, 1978–91. Mem., Special Immigration Adv. Commn, 1999–2005. Under Sheriff, City of Worcester, 1965–76. Jt Sec., Liverpool River Pilots' Assoc., 1960–62. KM 1975 (Officer of Merit, Civil Div., 1980). *Recreations:* gardening, painting. *Address:* Regina Cottage, Belle Orchard, Ledbury, HR8 1DD. *Club:* Cavalry and Guards.

FOX, Prof. Keith Alexander Arthur, FRCPE; Duke of Edinburgh Professor of Cardiology, since 1989, and Head, Division of Medical and Radiological Sciences, University of Edinburgh; Hon. Consultant Cardiologist, Royal Infirmary of Edinburgh; *b* 27 Aug. 1949; *m* Aileen Fox; one *s* one *d*. *Educ:* Falcon Coll.; Univ. of Edinburgh (BSc 1972; MB ChB 1974). FRCPE 1987. Asst Prof. of Medicine, Univ. of Washington, 1980–85; Sen. Lectr in Cardiol. and Hon. Cons. Cardiologist, UWCM, 1985–89. FESC 1988; FMedSci 2001. *Address:* Centre for Cardiovascular Science, Chancellor's Building, 49 Little France Crescent, Edinburgh EH16 4SB; 13 Cumin Place, Edinburgh EH9 2JX.

FOX, Kenneth Lambert, FCIPS; public sector consultant, since 1986; *b* 8 Nov. 1927; *s* of J. H. Fox, Grimsby, Lincolnshire; *m* 1959, P. E. Byrne; one *d*. *Educ:* City of London Coll.; Univ. of London. BSc (Hons); MIIM. Plant Manager, Rowntree Gp, 1950–63; Supply Manager, Ford Motor Co. (UK), 1963–67; Sen. Management Conslt, Cooper & Lybrand Ltd, 1967–70; Manager of Conslts (Europe), US Science Management Corp., 1971–72; Supply Management, British Gas Corp., 1972–75; Dir of Supplies, GLC, 1975–86. *Recreations:* tennis, painting, bird watching, DIY. *Address:* 9 Dolphin Lane, Melbourn, Royston, Herts SG8 6AF. *T:* (01763) 206573.

FOX, Dr Liam; MP (C) Woodspring, since 1992; *b* 22 Sept. 1961; *s* of William Fox and Catherine Young; *m* 2005, Dr Jesmé Baird. *Educ:* St Bride's High Sch., E Kilbride; Univ. of Glasgow (MB ChB 1983). MRCGP 1989. General Practitioner, Beaconsfield, 1987–91; Army MO (civilian), RAEC, 1981–91; Divl Surgeon, St John's Ambulance, 1987–91. Contested (C) Roxburgh and Berwickshire, 1987. PPS to Home Sec., 1993–94; an Asst Govt Whip, 1994–95; a Lord Comr of HM Treasury (Govt Whip), 1995–96; Parly Under-Sec. of State, FCO, 1996–97; Opposition spokesman on constitutional affairs, 1997–99, on health, 1999–2001; Shadow Health Sec., 2001–03; Co-Chm., Cons. Party, 2003–05; Shadow Foreign Sec., 2005; Shadow Defence Sec., 2005–. Mem., Select Cttee on Scottish Affairs, 1992; Secretary: Cons. back bench Health Cttee, 1992–93; Cons. West Country Members Group, 1992–93. *Publications:* Making Unionism Positive, 1988; (contrib.) Bearing the Standard, 1991; contrib. to House of Commons Magazine. *Recreations:* tennis, swimming, cinema, theatre. *Address:* House of Commons, SW1A 0AA. *T:* (020) 7219 4086.

FOX, Ven. Michael John; Archdeacon of West Ham, 1996–2007; *b* 28 April 1942; *s* of John and Dorothy Fox; *m* 1966, Susan Cooper; one *s* one *d*. *Educ:* Barking Abbey GS; Hull Univ. (BSc); Coll. of the Resurrection, Mirfield. Ordained deacon, 1966, priest, 1967; Curate: St Elizabeth, Becontree, 1966–70; Holy Trinity, S Woodford, 1970–72; Vicar: Ch. of the Ascension, Victoria Docks, and Missioner, Felsted Sch., 1972–76; All Saints, Chelmsford, 1976–88; Asst RD and RD, Chelmsford, 1982–88; Rector, St James, Colchester, 1988–93; Archdeacon of Harlow, 1993–96. Hon. Canon, Chelmsford Cathedral, 1991–. *Recreations:* walking, photography, West Ham. *Address:* 17A Northgate Street, Colchester, Essex CO1 1EZ. *T:* (01206) 710701.

FOX, Sir Paul (Leonard), Kt 1991; CBE 1985; Managing Director, BBC Television Network, 1988–91; *b* 27 Oct. 1925; *m* 1948, Betty Ruth (née Nathan); two *s*. *Educ:* Bournemouth Grammar Sch. Served War, Parachute Regt, 1943–46. Reporter, Kentish Times, 1946; Scriptwriter, Pathé News, 1947; joined BBC Television, 1950: Scriptwriter, Television Newsreel; Editor, Sportsview, 1953, Panorama, 1961; Head, Public Affairs,

1963, Current Affairs, 1965; Controller, BBC1, 1967–73; Dir of Progs, 1973–84, Ma Dir, 1977–88, Yorkshire Television. Chairman: ITN, 1986–88 (Dir, 1980–86); BB Enterprises Ltd, 1988–91; Stepgrades Consultants, 1991–2002; Director: Tride Television, 1973–80; Channel Four, 1985–88; World Television News, 1986–8 Thames Television, 1991–95; Barnes Television Trust, 1997–2000. Sports columnist, T Daily Telegraph, 1991–2003. Chm., Racecourse Assoc. Ltd, 1993–97; Director: Brit Horseracing Bd, 1993–97; Horseracing Betting Levy Bd, 1993–97. Chm., Disaste Emergency Cttee, 1996–99; Member: Royal Commn on Criminal Procedure, 1978–8 Inquiry into Police Responsibilities and Rewards, 1992–93. Pres., RTS, 1985–92; Mer Cttee, Nat. Mus. of Film, Photography and TV, 1985–95; Trustee, Cinema an Television Benevolent Fund, 1987–90 and 1995–2002 (Pres., 1992–95). BAFTA Fellow 1990. CCMI (CBIM 1987). Hon. LLD Leeds, 1984; Hon. DLitt Bradford, 1991. Cy Bennett Award, for outstanding television programming, 1984; Founders Award, Intern Council, US Nat. Acad. of TV Arts and Scis, 1989; RTS Gold Medal, for outstandi services to television, 1992. *Recreations:* travel, theatre, films. *Address:* c/o F. W. Stephe and Co., 3rd Floor, 24 Chiswell Street, EC1Y 4YX. *Club:* Garrick.

FOX, Peter Kendrew; University Librarian, University of Cambridge, and Fellow Selwyn College, Cambridge, since 1994; *b* 23 March 1949; *s* of Thomas Kendrew Fox a Dorothy Fox; *m* 1983, Isobel McConnell; two *d*. *Educ:* Baines GS, Poulton-le-Fylc King's Coll., London (BA, AKC 1971); Sheffield Univ. (MA 1973); MA Cantab 197 MA Dublin, 1984. ALA 1974; ALAI 1989. Cambridge University Library: grad. traine 1971–72; Asst Liby Officer, 1973–77; Asst Under-Librarian, 1977–78; Under-Librariа 1978–79; Trinity College Dublin: Dep. Librarian, 1979–84; Librarian and Coll. Archivi 1984–94. Chairman: SCONUL Adv. Cttee on Inf. Services, 1987–90; Bd of Di Consortium of Univ. Res. Libraries, 1997–2000; Brotherton Collection Adv. Cttee 1999–2002 (Mem., 1995–2002); Wellcome Trust Liby Adv. Cttee, 2000–05 (Mem 1996–2005); Bd, Nat. Preservation Office, 2002–05 (Mem., Mgt Cttee, 1996–2002 Gen. Sec., LIBER, 2003–06 (Vice-Pres., 2007–08); Member: An Chomhai Leabharlanna, Dublin, 1982–94; Cttee on Liby Co-operation in Ireland, 1983–94; N Preservation Adv. Cttee, 1984–95; Adv. Cttee for Document Supply, 1991–95, Ar Humanities and Social Scis Adv. Cttee, 2000–02, British Liby; Lord Chancellor's Ad Council on Nat. Records and Archives (formerly Public Records), 2001–06; Leg Deposit Adv. Panel, DCMS, 2005–. *Publications:* Reader Instruction Methods in Briti Academic Libraries, 1974; Trinity College Library, Dublin, 1982; *edited:* Treasures of tl Library: Trinity College Dublin, 1986; Book of Kells: commentary vol. to facsimile ed 1990; Cambridge University Library: the great collections, 1998; Proc. Internat. Confs Library User Education, 1980, 1982, 1984; contrib. learned jls. *Address:* Universi Library, West Road, Cambridge CB3 9DR. *T:* (01223) 333045.

FOX, Prof. Renée Claire, PhD; FAAAS; Annenberg Professor of the Social Science University of Pennsylvania, 1969–98, now Emerita (also Professor of: Sociology Psychiatry, 1969–98; Sociology in Medicine, 1972–98; Sociology, School of Nursin 1978–98); Senior Fellow, Center for Bioethics, University of Pennsylvania, 1999–200 now Emerita; *b* 15 Feb. 1928; *d* of Paul Fred Fox and Henrietta Gold Fox. *Educ:* Smi Coll., Northampton, Mass (BA *summa cum laude* 1949); Harvard Univ. (PhD Socio 1954). Teaching Fellow, Harvard Univ., 1950–51; Columbia University: Res. Ass Bureau of Applied Social Res., 1953–55; Res. Associate, 1955–58; Barnard College, Ne York: Lectr in Sociol., 1955–58; Asst Prof., 1958–64; Associate Prof., 1964–66; Harva University: Lectr in Sociol., 1967–69; Res. Fellow, Center for Internat. Affairs, 1967–6 Res. Associate, Program on Technol and Soc., 1968–71; Consultant, Social Sc Curriculum, Lincoln Center Coll., Fordham Univ., NY, 1968–70; University Pennsylvania: Faculty Asst to Pres., 1971–72; Chm., Dept of Sociol., 1972–78. Re Associate, Queen Elizabeth House, Internat. Develt Centre, Univ. of Oxford, 1999–200 Numerous distinguished visiting appointments and lectureships; George Eastman V Prof., Oxford Univ., 1996–97. Fellow, Amer. Acad. of Arts and Scis, 1971; FAAAS 197 Mem. Inst. of Med., US NAS, 1975. Hon. Mem., Alpha Omega Alpha Honor Med. Soc 2004. Chevalier, Order of Leopold II (Belgium), 1995. *Publications:* (with W. de Craeme The Emerging Physician: a sociological approach to the development of a Congole medical profession, 1968; Experiment Perilous: physicians and patients facing th unknown, 1974, repr. with new epilogue, 1997; (with J. P. Swazey) The Courage to Fa a social view of organ transplants and dialysis, 1974, rev. edn 1978; Essays in Medic Sociology: journeys into the field, 1979, 2nd edn 1988; (ed) The Social Meaning of Deat 1980; L'Incertitude Médicale, 1988; (jtly) Spare Parts: organ replacement in America society, 1992 (trans. Japanese 1999); The Sociology of Medicine: a participant observer view, 1989 (trans. Korean 1993); In the Belgian Château: the spirit and culture European society in the age of change, 1994 (French edn, with new epilogue, 1997); (jtly) Meanings and Realities of Organ Transplantation, 1996; (ed jtly) After Parsons: theory of social action for the twenty-first century, 2005; contrib. numerous articles c medical sociology, incl. articles on organ donation and transplantation, bioethics, med. re and educn, and med. humanitarian action, to scientific and learned jls worldwide. *Addre* Sociology Department, University of Pennsylvania, 3718 Locust Walk, Philadelphia, P 19104–6299, USA; The Wellington # 1104, 135 South 19th Street, Philadelphia, P 19103, USA. *T:* (215) 5634912.

FOX, Prof. Robert, FSA; FRHistS; Professor of the History of Science, University Oxford, and Fellow of Linacre College, 1988–2006; *b* 7 Oct. 1938; *s* of Donald Fox an Audrey Hilda Fox (née Ramsell); *m* 1964, Catherine Mary Lilian Roper Power; three *Educ:* Doncaster Grammar Sch.; Oriel Coll., Oxford (BA 1961; MA 1965; DPhil 196 Hon. Fellow 2006). Asst Master, Tonbridge Sch., 1961–63; Clifford Norton Junior Re Fellow, Queen's Coll., Oxford, 1965–66; University of Lancaster: Lectr, 1966; Sen. Lect 1972; Reader, 1975; Prof. of History of Science, 1987. Mem., Inst. for Advanced Stud Princeton, 1974–75 and 1985; Vis. Prof. and Mem., Davis Center for Historical Studie Princeton Univ., 1978–79; Visiting Professor: Ecole des Hautes Etudes en Scis Sociale Paris, 1984 and 2000; Johns Hopkins Univ., Baltimore, 2007; Dir, Centre de Recherch en Histoire des Sciences et des Techniques, Cité des Sciences et de l'Industrie, Paris, an Dir de recherche associé, Centre Nat. de la Recherche Scientifique, 1986–88; Asst Di Science Museum, 1988. President: IUHPS, 1995–97 (Pres., Div. of History of Scienc 1993–97); European Soc. for History of Science, 2004–06. Chevalier de l'Ordre de Palmes Académiques (France), 1998; Chevalier de l'Ordre des Arts et des Lettres (France 2005. *Publications:* The Caloric Theory of Gases from Lavoisier to Regnault, 1971; Sa Carnot: Réflexions sur la puissance motrice du feu, 1978 (trans. English 1986, Germa 1987, Italian 1992); (ed jtly) The Organization of Science and Technology in Franc 1808–1914, 1980; The Culture of Science in France 1700–1900, 1992; (ed jtly Education, Technology and Industrial Performance in Europe 1850–1939, 1993; Science Technology, and the Social Order in Post-revolutionary France, 1995; (ed) Technologic Change: methods and themes in the history of technology, 1996; (ed jtly) Luxury Trade and Consumerism in Ancien Régime Paris, 1998; (ed jtly) Natural Dyestuffs and Industri Culture in Europe 1750–1880, 1999; (jtly) Laboratories, Workshops and Sites, 1999; (e Thomas Harriot: an Elizabethan man of science, 2000; (ed jtly) Physics in Oxfor

1839–1939, 2005. *Address:* Museum of the History of Science, Broad Street, Oxford OX1 3AZ. *T:* (01865) 512787. *Club:* Athenæum.

FOX, Dr Robert McDougall, FRCP, FRCPE; Editor: The Lancet, 1990–95; Journal of the Royal Society of Medicine, 1996–2005; *b* 28 Dec. 1939; *s* of Sir Theodore Fortescue Fox and Margaret Evelyn McDougall; *m* 1969, Susan Clark; two *s* one *d.* *Educ:* Univ. of Edinburgh (MB ChB). MRCP 1993, FRCP 1996; FRCPE 1990. House physician, Western Gen. Hosp., Edinburgh; house surgeon, Royal Infirmary, Edinburgh; joined staff of The Lancet, 1968, Dep. Editor, 1976–90. Associate Editor, Circulation, 1995–2005. *Recreation:* words. *Address:* Green House, Rotherfield, Crowborough, East Sussex TN6 3QU. *T:* (01892) 852850.

FOX, Robert Michael John; theatre, film and television producer; Managing Director, Robert Fox Ltd, since 1980; *b* 25 March 1952; *s* of late Robin Fox and Angela Fox; *m* 1st, 1975, Celestia Sporborg (marr. diss. 1990); one *s* two *d*; 2nd, 1990, Natasha Richardson, *qv* (marr. diss. 1994); 3rd, 1996, Fiona Golfar; one *s* one *d.* *Educ:* Harrow. Asst Dir, Royal Court Th., 1971–73; PA, Michael White Ltd, 1973–80. *Productions* include: *theatre:* Goose Pimples, Garrick, 1981; Anyone For Denis?, Whitehall, 1981; Another Country, Queen's, 1982; The Seagull, Queen's, 1985; Chess, Prince Edward, 1986; Lettice and Lovage, Globe, 1987, NY, 1990; A Madhouse In Goa, Apollo, 1989; Anything Goes, Prince Edward, 1989; Burn This, Lyric, 1990; The Big Love, NY, 1991; When She Danced, Globe, 1991; The Ride Down Mount Morgan, Wyndham's, 1991; The Importance of Being Earnest, Aldwych, 1993; Vita & Virginia, Ambassadors, 1992, NY, 1994; Three Tall Women, Wyndham's, 1994; Burning Blue, Haymarket, 1995; Skylight, Wyndham's, 1995, NY, 1996, Vaudeville, 1997; Who's Afraid of Virginia Woolf?, Almeida, transf. Aldwych, 1996; Master Class, Queen's, 1997; A Delicate Balance, Haymarket, 1997; Amy's View, RNT, transf. Aldwych, 1997, NY 1999; Closer, RNT, transf. Lyric, 1998, NY 1999; The Judas Kiss (co-producer), Almeida, transf. Playhouse, NY, 1998; The Boy from Oz (co-producer), Australia, 1998; The Lady in the Van, Queen's, 1999; The Blue Room, NY, 1999; The Caretaker, Comedy, 2000; The Breath of Life, Haymarket, 2002; Salome: the reading, NY, 2003, LA, 2006; Gypsy, NY, 2003; The Boy From Oz, NY, 2003, arena tour, 2006; The Pillowman, NY, 2005; Hedda Gabler, Almeida, transf. Duke of York's, 2005; Frost/Nixon, Gielgud, 2006, NY, 2007; The Vertical Hour, NY, 2006; The Lady from Dubuque, Haymarket, 2007; *films:* A Month by the Lake, 1996; Iris, 2001; The Hours, 2002; Closer, 2004; Notes on a Scandal, 2006; Atonement, 2007; *television:* Oscar's Orchestra, 1996; Working with Pinter, 2007. *Address:* (office) 6 Beauchamp Place, SW3 1NG. *T:* (020) 7584 6855, *Fax:* (020) 7225 1638.

See also E. Fox, J. Fox.

FOX, Robert Trench, (Robin), CBE 1993; Chairman, Lombard Risk Consultants, since 2000; *b* 1 Jan. 1937; *s* of Waldo Trench Fox and Janet Mary Kennedy Fox (*née* Bassett); *m* 1962, Lindsay Garrett Anderson; two *s* two *d.* *Educ:* Winchester Coll.; University Coll., Oxford (MA). FCIB. Kleinwort Benson Group, 1961–99; Vice-Chm., Kleinwort Benson Gp, 1989–97; Pres., Kleinwort Benson Asia Ltd, 1997–99. Chairman: Whiteaway Laidlaw Bank, 1997– (Dir, 1992–); Boyer Allan Pacific Fund, 1998–; Boyer Allan Japan Fund, 2000–; Boyer Allan India Fund, 2003–; Boyer Allan Greater China Fund, 2006–; Boyer Allan Pacific Opportunities Fund, 2006–. Chm., Export Guarantees Adv. Council, 1992–98; Mem., Overseas Projects Bd, 1988–98. Chm. Council, City Univ. Business Sch., 1991–99. *Recreations:* sailing, shooting, theatre, reading. *Address:* Lombard Risk Consultants, 21st Floor, Empress State Building, 55 Lillie Road, SW6 1TR. *T:* (020) 7384 5000. *Clubs:* Brooks's; Royal Cornwall Yacht.

FOX, Robin James L.; *see* Lane Fox.

FOX, Roy, CMG 1980; OBE 1967; HM Diplomatic Service, retired; consultant with various companies; *b* 1 Sept. 1920; *s* of J. S. and A. Fox; *m* 1st, 1943, Sybil Verity; two *s* one *d*; 2nd, 1975, Susan Rogers Turner. *Educ:* Wheelwright Grammar Sch., Dewsbury; Bradford Technical Coll. Served in RNVR, 1940–46. Bd of Trade, 1947–58; British Trade Commissioner: Nairobi, 1958–60; Montreal, 1960–62; Winnipeg, 1962–64; Dep. Controller, Bd of Trade Office for Scotland, 1964–65. First Sec. Commercial, Karachi, 1965–68; Deputy High Comr, E Pakistan, 1968–70; Consul-Gen. and Comm. Counsellor, Helsinki, 1970–74; promoted to Minister, 1977; Consul-Gen., Houston, 1974–80. *Recreations:* golf, reading, tennis. *Address:* 21 Alexandra Court, Ellerthwaite Road, Windermere, Cumbria LA23 2PR.

FOX, Ruth W.; *see* Winston-Fox.

FOX, Prof. Wallace, CMG 1973; MD, FRCP, FFPH; Professor of Community Therapeutics, Cardiothoracic Institute, Brompton Hospital, 1979–86, now Emeritus; Director, Medical Research Council Tuberculosis and Chest Diseases Unit, Brompton Hospital, 1965–86; Hon. Consultant Physician, Brompton Hospital, 1969–86; WHO Consultant, since 1961; *b* 7 Nov. 1920; *s* of Samuel and Esther Fox; *m* 1956, Gaye Judith Akker; three *s.* *Educ:* Cotham Grammar Sch., Bristol; Guy's Hosp. MB, BS (London) 1943; MRCS, LRCP, 1943; MRCP 1950; MD (Dist.) (London) 1951; FRCP 1962; FFPH (FFCM 1976). Ho. Phys., Guy's USA Hosp., 1945–46; Resident Phys., Preston Hall Sanatorium, 1946–50; Registrar, Guy's Hosp., 1950–51; Asst Chest Physician, Hammersmith Chest Clinic, 1951–52; Mem. Scientific Staff of MRC Tuberculosis and Chest Diseases Unit, 1952–56, 1961–65; seconded to WHO, to establish and direct Tuberculosis Chemotherapy Centre, Madras, 1956–61; Dir, WHO Collaborating Centre for Tuberculosis Chemotherapy and its Application, 1976–87. Lectures: Marc Daniels, RCP, 1962; First John Barnwell Meml, US Veterans Admin, 1968; Philip Ellman, RSocMed, 1976; Martyrs Meml, Bangladesh Med. Assoc., 1977; first Quezon Meml, Philippine Coll. of Chest Physicians, 1977; Morriston Davies Meml, BTA, 1981; Mitchell, RCP, 1982; E. Merck Oration, Indian Chest Soc., 1983; A. J. S. McFadzean, Univ. of Hong Kong, 1986; Ranbaxy-Robert Koch Oration, Tuberculosis Assoc. of India, 1989. Waring Vis. Prof. in Medicine, Univ. of Colorado and Stanford Univ., 1974. Mem. Tropical Med. Research Bd, 1968–72; Mem., several MRC Cttees; Member: WHO Expert Adv. Panel on Tuberculosis, 1965–91; BCG Vaccination Sub-Cttee, Min. of Health, 1968–; Mem. Council, Chest, Heart & Stroke Assoc., 1974–90; International Union Against Tuberculosis: Mem., later Chm., Cttee of Therapy, 1964–71; Associate Mem., Scientific Cttees, 1973; Mem., Exec. Cttee, 1973–85 (Chm., 1973–77). Chm., Acid Fast Club, 1971–72. Editor, Advances in Tuberculosis Research. Life Mem., BMA, 1994; Elected Corresp. Mem., Amer. Thoracic Soc., 1962; Mem., Mexican Acad. of Medicine, 1976; Hon. Life Mem., Canadian Thoracic Soc., 1976; Corresp. Mem., Argentine Nat. Acad. of Medicine, 1977; Corresp. For. Member: Argentine Soc. of Phthisiol. and Thoracic Pathol., 1977; Coll. of Univ. Med. Phthisiologists of Argentine, 1978; Hon. Member: Argentine Med. Assoc., 1977; Singapore Thoracic Soc., 1978. Sir Robert Philip Medal, Chest and Heart Assoc., 1969; Weber Parkes Prize, RCP, 1973; Carlo Forlanini Gold Medal, Fedn Ital. contra la Tubercolosi e le Malattie Polmonari Sociali, 1976; Hon. Medal, Czech. Med. Soc., 1980; Robert Koch Centenary Medal, Internat. Union against Tuberculosis, 1982; Presidential Citation Award, Amer. Coll. of Chest Physicians, 1982; Presidential Commendation, Amer. Thoracic Soc., 1989. *Publications:* Reports on tuberculosis services in Hong Kong to Hong Kong Government: Heaf/Fox, 1962; Scadding/Fox, 1975; Fox/Kilpatrick, 1990; contribs to med. jls: on methodology of controlled clinical trials, on epidemiology and on chemotherapy, particularly in tuberculosis, and carcinoma of the bronchus. *Address:* 28 Mount Ararat Road, Richmond, Surrey TW10 6PG. *T:* (020) 8940 9662. *Club:* Athenæum.

FOX, Winifred Marjorie, (Mrs E. Gray Debros); Under-Secretary, Department of the Environment, 1970–76; *d* of Frederick Charles Fox and Charlotte Marion Ogborn; *m* 1953, Eustachy Gray Debros (*d* 1954); one *d.* *Educ:* Streatham County Sch.; St Hugh's Coll., Oxford. Unemployment Assistance Board, 1937; Cabinet Office, 1942; Ministry of Town and Country Planning, 1944; Ministry of Housing and Local Govt, 1952 (Under-Sec., 1963); Dept of the Environment, 1970; seconded to CSD as Chm., CS Selection Bd, 1971–72. *Address:* West Dalling, Rock's Lane, High Hurstwood, Uckfield, E Sussex TN22 4BN.

FOX BASSETT, Nigel; Commissioner, Building Societies Commission, 1993–2001; Member Council: London First, since 1998; London Chamber of Commerce and Industry, 1993–99; *b* 1 Nov. 1929; *s* of Thomas Fox Bassett and Catherine Adriana Wiffen; *m* 1961, Patricia Anne Lambourne; one *s* one *d.* *Educ:* Taunton Sch.; Trinity Coll., Cambridge (MA Hons History and Law). Articled, Coward Chance, 1953; admitted Solicitor, 1956; Partner, Coward Chance, later Clifford Chance, 1960–93 (Sen. Partner, 1990–93). Dir, London First, later London First Centre, 1993–98. Member: Council, British Inst. of Internat. and Comparative Law, 1977–2005 (Chm., Exec. Cttee, 1986–96; Hon. Mem., 2004; Mem. Adv. Bd, 2005–); Council, British Gp, Internat. Assoc. for Protection of Indust. Property, 1984–89; Council, British Branch, Internat. Law Assoc., 1971–86 (Chm., Cttee on Internat. Securities Regulation, 1989–93); Business Section, Internat. Bar Assoc., 1969–93; European Gp, Law Soc., 1969–93; Cttee, Amer. Bar Assoc., 1979–93; Deleg., Banking and Finance Mission to Poland, 1989. Liveryman, City of London Solicitors' Co. Pres. Council, Taunton Sch., 1994–97 (Mem. Council, 1985–97; Hon. Life Vice-Pres., 2005). Mem., charitable, sports, opera concerns. *Publications:* (contrib.) Branches and Subsidiaries in the European Common Market, 1976; (contrib.) Business Law in Europe, 1982, 2nd edn 1990; articles in law professional jls. *Recreations:* shooting, painting, cricket, art, opera. *Address:* 10 Upper Bank Street, E14 5JJ. *T:* (020) 7006 1000. *Clubs:* Garrick, Pilgrims, MCC; Seaview Yacht.

FOX-PITT, William; international three day event rider, since 1993; *b* 2 Jan. 1969; *s* of Oliver and Marietta Fox-Pitt; *m* 2003, Alice Plunkett; two *s.* *Educ:* Eton Coll.; Goldsmiths' Coll., London Univ. (BA Hons French 1993). Three day event rider, first competed at jun. level, 1984, also trainer, 1993–; winner: Burghley Horse Trials, 1994, 2002, 2005, 2007; British Open Championships, 1995, 2000, 2005; Badminton Horse Trials, 2004; Open European Championships: team Gold Medal, 1995; team Gold and individual Bronze Medal, 1997; team Gold Medal, 2001, 2003; team Gold and individual Silver Medal, 2005; World Championships: team Bronze Medal, 2002; team Silver Medal, 2006; team Silver Medal, Olympic Games, Athens, 2004; represented GB in team at Atlanta Olympics, 1996; ranked World No 1, 2002, World No 2, 2003, 2004, 2005 and 2006. Board Director: Professional Event Riders' Assoc., 1998–; British Eventing (formerly British Horse Trials Assoc.), 2000–. *Publications:* Schooling for Success, 2004; What Will Be: the autobiography, 2007. *Recreations:* ski-ing, jogging, travel.

FOX-STRANGWAYS, family name of **Earl of Ilchester.**

FOXALL, Colin, CBE 1995; reinsurance consultant, since 1997; Director, Radian Asset Assurance Ltd, since 2003; *b* 6 Feb. 1947; *s* of Alfred George Foxall and Ethel Margaret Foxall; *m* 2003, Diane Linda Price. *Educ:* Gillingham Grammar Sch., Kent. MIEx; FICM. Joined ECGD, 1966; Dept of Trade, 1974; ECGD, 1975–91: Underwriter, Eastern Bloc, 1975; Dep. Hd, For. Currency Branch, 1977; Hd, Financial Planning, 1979; Asst Sec., ME Project Gp, 1982; Under Sec., and Dir of Comprehensive Guarantee, subseq. Insce Services, Gp, 1986–91; Man. Dir and Chief Exec., NCM Credit Insurance Ltd, 1991–97; Vice-Chm., NCM (Hldg) NV, 1996–97; Bd Advr, Classic Construction, 2003–04. Chm., Passenger Focus, 2005–; Member: Rail Passengers Council, 2004–05; British Transport Police Authy, 2005–. *Recreations:* clay target shooting, farming. *Address:* Brynglas Cottage, Devauden, Chepstow, Mon NP16 6NT.

FOXELL, Clive Arthur Peirson, CBE 1987; FREng; consultant; Managing Director, Engineering and Procurement, and Board Member, British Telecom, 1986–89; *b* 27 Feb. 1930; *s* of Arthur Turner Foxell and Lillian (*née* Ellerman); *m* 1956, Shirley Ann Patey Morris; one *d.* *Educ:* Harrow High Sch.; Univ. of London. (BSc). FREng (FEng 1985); FIET, FInstP (Hon. FInstP 2002), FCIPS. GEC Res. Labs, 1947–68; Man., GEC Semiconductor Labs, 1968–71; Man. Dir, GEC Semiconductors Ltd, 1971–75; Dep. Dir of Research, PO, 1975–78; Dep. Dir, Procurement Exec., 1978–79; Dir of Purchasing, PO, 1980; British Telecom: Dir of Procurement, 1981–84; Senior Dir, 1984; Chief Exec., Procurement, 1984–86; Dir, British Telecommunications Systems Ltd, 1982–89. Chairman: Fulcrum Communications Ltd, 1985–86; TSCR Ltd, 1986–88; Phonepoint Ltd, 1989–93; Dir, BT&D Technologies Ltd, 1986–88. Institution of Electrical Engineers: Mem. Council, 1975–78, 1982–85, 1987–90; Vice-Pres., 1996–99; Chm., Electronics Div., 1983–84. Member: SERC (formerly SRC) Engrg Bd, 1977–80 (Chm., Silicon Working Party, 1980–81; Chm., Microelectronics, 1982–86); SERC, 1986–90; NEDC (electronics), 1987–90; ACARD Working Party on IT, 1981; Council, Foundn for Sci. and Technol., 1996–2002. Senator, Engrg Council, 1999–2002. Pres., Mobile Radio Trng Trust, 1991–95. President: IBTE, 1987–90; Inst. of Physics, 1992–94. Hon. Treas., Nat. Electronics Council, 1994–99. Bulgin Premium, IERE, 1964. Liveryman, Engineers' Co. Hon. DSc Southampton, 1994. *Publications:* Low Noise Microwave Amplifiers, 1968; Chesham Shuttle, 1996; Chesham Branch Album, 1998; The Met & GC Joint Line, 2000; Memories of the Met & GC Joint Line, 2002; Rails to Metro-Land, 2005; articles and papers on electronics. *Recreations:* photography, steam railways. *Address:* 4 Meades Lane, Chesham, Bucks HP5 1ND. *T:* (01494) 785737.

FOXON, Prof. (Charles) Thomas (Bayley), PhD; FRS 2006; Research Professor, School of Physics and Astronomy, University of Nottingham. *Educ:* BSc, PhD. Sen. Principal Scientist, Philips Res. Labs, until 1991; Prof. of Physics, Univ. of Nottingham, 1991–. *Publications:* articles in learned jls. *Address:* School of Physics and Astonomy, University of Nottingham, University Park, Nottingham NG7 2RD.

FOXTON, David Andrew; QC 2006; PhD; *b* 14 Oct. 1965; *s* of Adrian and Catherine Foxton; *m* 1992, Heather Crook; two *s* two *d.* *Educ:* Glasgow Acad.; Magdalen Coll., Oxford (MA, BCL); King's Coll. London (PhD). Called to the Bar, Gray's Inn, 1989; in practice, specialising in commercial law. Vis. Prof., Univ. of Nottingham, 2007–. Mem. Cttee, Church Urban Fund, 2006–. Freeman, City of London, 2007. *Publications:* Scrutton on Charterparties, 19th edn 1996; Revolutionary Lawyers: Sinn Fein and Crown Courts in Britain and Ireland 1916–1923, 2008; articles in legal jls. *Recreations:* Irish history, sport (especially cricket and football), dog walking, child-ferrying and other forms of travel. *Address:* Essex Court Chambers, 24 Lincoln's Inn Fields, WC2A 3EG. *T:* (020) 7813 8000, *Fax:* (020) 7813 8080.

FOY, John Leonard; QC 1998; a Recorder, since 2000; *b* 1 June 1946; *s* of late Leonard James Foy and Edith Mary Foy; *m* 1972, Colleen Patricia Austin (*d* 2006); one *s*. *Educ:* Dartford GS; Birmingham Univ. (LLB Hons 1967). Called to the Bar, Gray's Inn, 1969, Bencher, 2004; in practice at the Bar, 1969–. Mem., Mental Health Review Tribunal, 2003–. *Publications:* contribs to various legal books and jls. *Recreations:* watching West Bromwich Albion, football, Rugby, reading modern literature. *Address:* 9 Gough Square, EC4A 3DG. *T:* (020) 7832 0500.

FRACKOWIAK, Prof. Richard Stanislaus Joseph, MD, DSc; FRCP, FMedSci; Vice-Provost, University College London, since 2002; Director, Département d'Etudes Cognitives, Ecole Normale Supérieure, Paris, since 2005; *b* 26 March 1950; *s* of Joseph Frackowiak and Wanda (*née* Majewska); *m* 1st, 1972, Christine Jeanne Françoise Thepot (marr. diss. 2004); one *s* two *d*; 2nd, 2004, Laura Frances Spinney. *Educ:* Latymer Upper Sch.; Peterhouse, Cambridge (Wilhelm Brauer Open Schol.; MA); Middlesex Hosp. Med. Sch. (MB BChir; MD 1983); DSc London 1996. FRCP 1987. Sen. Lectr, 1984–90, Prof. of Neurology, 1990–94, RPMS and Hammersmith Hosp.; Consultant Neurologist: Hammersmith Hosp., 1984–95; Nat. Hosp. for Neurology and Neurosurgery, 1984–; MRC Trng Fellow, 1980–81; MRC Clinical Scientist, 1984–94; Wellcome Principal Res. Fellow, 1994–; Institute of Neurology, London University: Prof. and Chm., Wellcome Dept of Cognitive Neurol., 1994–2002; Dir, Leopold Muller Functional Imaging Lab., 1994–2002; Dean, 1998–2002. Adjunct Prof. of Neurology, Cornell Univ. Med. Sch., NY, 1990; Visiting Professor: Wellcome Lab. of Neurobiol., UCL, 1991–95; Cath. Univ., Louvain, Belgium, 1996–97; Harvard Med. Sch., 1999; Yale Med. Sch., 2001. Non-exec. Dir, UCLH NHS Foundn Trust Bd, 2003–. Member: Assoc. of British Neurologists, 1984; American Neurological Assoc., 1988 (Hon. Mem., 2000); Soc. Française de Neurologie, 1993; Academia Europaea, 1995; L'Academie Royale de Médecine de Belgique, 1995. Foreign Associate, Acad. Nat. de Médecine de France, 2000. Founder FMedSci 1998 (Mem. Council, 2000–). Hon. Dr Liège 1999. Wilhelm Feldberg Foundn Prize, 1996; (jtly) Ipsen Prize for Neuronal Plasticity, Ipsen Foundn, Paris, 1997; Klaus Joachim Zulch Prize, Gertrud Reemtsma Foundn and Max Planck Soc., 2004. *Publications:* (jtly) Human Brain Function, 1997, 2nd edn 2004; Brain Mapping: the disorders, 2000; numerous on functional anatomy and organisation of the human brain using non-invasive monitoring techniques. *Recreations:* motorcycling, reading. *Address:* Wellcome Trust Centre for Neuroimaging, Institute of Neurology, 12 Queen Square, WC1N 3AR. *T:* (020) 7833 7458. *Clubs:* Athenæum, Hurlingham.

FRAENKEL, Prof. Ludwig Edward, FRS 1993; Professor of Mathematics, School of Mathematical Sciences, University of Bath, since 1988; *b* 28 May 1927; *s* of Eduard David Mortier Fraenkel and Ruth (*née* von Velsen); *m* 1954, Beryl Jacqueline Margaret Currie; two *d*. *Educ:* Dragon Sch., Oxford; Univ. of Toronto Schs; Univ. of Toronto (BASc 1947; MASc 1948); MA Cantab 1964. SO, RAE, Farnborough, 1948–52; Res. Fellow, Univ. of Glasgow, 1952–53; Imperial College, London: Lectr, Aeronautics Dept, 1953–58, Reader 1958–61; Reader, Mathematics Dept, 1961–64; Lectr in Applied Maths, Univ. of Cambridge, 1964–75; Fellow, Queens' Coll., Cambridge, 1964–68; Prof., Maths Div., Univ. of Sussex, 1975–88. Sen. Whitehead Prize, London Math. Soc., 1989. *Publications:* An Introduction to Maximum Principles and Symmetry in Elliptic Problems, 2000; some 60 papers in jls ranging from Aeronautical Qly to Acta Mathematica. *Recreations:* ski-ing, cycling. *Address:* School of Mathematical Sciences, University of Bath, Bath BA2 7AY. *T:* (01225) 826249. *Club:* Ski of Great Britain.

FRAENKEL, Peter Maurice, FREng, FICE, FIStructE, FIHT; Founder and Senior Partner, Peter Fraenkel & Partners, since 1972 (Chairman, 1995–2006); Director, Peter Fraenkel BMT Ltd, 1990–95 (Chairman, 1990–93); Chairman, Peter Fraenkel Maritime Ltd, 1995–2007; *b* 5 July 1915; *s* of Ernest Fraenkel and Luise (*née* Tessmann); *m* 1946, Hilda Muriel, *d* of William Norman; two *d*. *Educ:* Battersea Polytechnic; Imperial Coll., London. BSc(Eng). FICE 1954, FIStructE 1954; FREng (FEng 1984); FIHT 1992. Asst Engr with London firm of contractors, engaged on design and construction of marine and industrial structures, 1937–40; served in Army, 1941–42; Works Services Br., War Dept, 1942–45; Rendel, Palmer & Tritton, Cons. Engineers: Civil Engr, 1945; Sen. Engr, 1953; Partner, 1961–72. Dir, British Maritime Technology, 1990–96. Has been responsible for, or closely associated with, technical and management aspects of many feasibility and planning studies, and planning, design and supervision of construction of large civil engrg projects, incl. ports, docks, offshore terminals, inland waterways, highways, power stations and tunnels in Gt Britain, Middle East, India, Far East and Australia, including: new Oil port at Sullom Voe, Shetland; new Naval Dockyard, Bangkok; Shatin to Tai Po coastal Trunk Road, Hong Kong; comprehensive study for DoE, of maintenance and operational needs of canals controlled by Brit. Waterways Bd (Fraenkel Report), and new port at Limassol, Cyprus. James Watt Medal, 1963, Telford Gold Medal, 1971, ICE. *Publications:* (jtly) papers to Instn of Civil Engrs: Special Features of the Civil Engineering Works at Aberthaw Power Station, 1962; Planning and Design of Port Talbot Harbour, 1970. *Address:* Little Paddock, Rockfield Road, Oxted, Surrey RH8 0EL. *T:* (01883) 712927. *Club:* Athenæum.

FRAGA-IRIBARNE, Manuel; President, Government of Galicia, 1989–2005; Member for Galicia, Senate of Spain; *b* 23 Nov. 1922; *m* 1948, María del Carmen Estévez (*d* 1996); two *s* three *d*. *Educ:* Insts of Coruña, Villalba and Lugo; Univs of Santiago de Compostela and Madrid. Joined Legal Corps, Spanish Parlt, 1945, Diplomatic Sch., 1947; Prof. of Polit. Law, Univ. of Valencia, 1948; Prof. of Polit. Sci. and Constit. Law, Univ. of Madrid, 1953–87; Sec.-Gen., Instituto de Cultura Hispánica, 1951; Sec.-Gen. in Min. of Educn, 1953; Head, Inst. of Polit. Studies, 1961; Minister of Information and Tourism, 1962–69; Ambassador to UK, 1973–75; Govt Vice-Pres. and Interior Minister, Spain, 1975–76; Mem., Cortés, 1977–87; Leader of the Opposition, 1982–86; MEP (EDG), 1987–89. Founder Mem., 1976, Pres., 1979–86 and 1989, Popular Alliance, subseq. Popular Party, Spain. Hon. Dr of 19 nat. and internat. univs. Holds numerous foreign orders. *Publications:* more than 90 books on law, polit. sci., history and sociology, incl. one on British Parlt. *Recreations:* shooting, fishing. *Address:* Palacio del Senado, Plaza de la Marina Española No 8, 28013 Madrid, Spain.

FRAME, David William; Member, Baltic Exchange, since 1961 (Chairman, 1987–89); *b* 26 July 1934; *s* of William and Ursula Frame; *m* 1963, Margaret Anne Morrison; two *d*. *Educ:* Wellington College. Commissioned Royal Artillery, National Service. Qualified Chartered Accountant, 1960; joined Usborne & Son (London), 1961, Dir 1962; Dir, Usborne and Feedex subsid. cos and other cos. *Recreation:* golf (played for GB and Ireland in Walker Cup, 1961, for England, 1958–63). *Address:* Green Glades, Frensham Vale, Lower Bourne, Farnham, Surrey GU10 3HT. *T:* (01252) 793272. *Clubs:* Royal and Ancient, Worplesdon Golf, Trevose Golf, Old Thorns Golf, Plettenberg Bay Golf.

FRAME, Frank Riddell; Deputy Chairman, Hongkong and Shanghai Banking Corporation, 1986–90; *b* 15 Feb. 1930; *s* of late William Graham Frame; *m* 1958, Maureen Willis Milligan; one *s* one *d*. *Educ:* Hamilton Academy; Univ. of Glasgow (MA, LLB); admitted solicitor, 1955. North of Scotland Hydro-Electric Board, 1955–60; UK Atomic Energy Authority, 1960–68; Weir Group plc, 1968–76 (Dir, 1971–76); joined Hongkong and Shanghai Banking Corp., as Gp Legal Advr, 1977, Exec. Dir, 1985–90; Advr to Bo HSBC Hldgs plc, 1990–98. Chairman: South China Morning Post Ltd, 1981–87; Fa Eastern Economic Review Ltd, 1981–87; Wallem Group Ltd, 1992–2004; Directo Marine Midland Banks Inc., 1986–90; The British Bank of the Middle East, 1986–91 Swire Pacific Ltd, 1986–90; Consolidated Press Internat. Ltd, 1988–91; Securities an Futures Commn, Hong Kong, 1989–90; Baxter Internat. Inc., 1992–2001; Edinburg Dragon Trust plc, 1994–; Northern Gas Networks Ltd, 2004–. DUniv Glasgow, 200 *Publication:* (with Prof. Harry Street) The Law relating to Nuclear Energy, 1966. *Addres* The Old Rectory, Bepton, Midhurst, W Sussex GU29 0HX. *T:* (01730) 813140. *Clul* Brooks's.

FRAME, Rt Rev. John Timothy, DD; Dean of Columbia and Rector of Christ Churc Cathedral, Victoria, BC, 1980–95; *b* 8 Dec. 1930; *m*; three *d*. *Educ:* Univ. of Toronto Burns Lake Mission, Dio. Caledonia, 1957; Hon. Canon of Caledonia, 1965; Bishop c Yukon, 1968–80. *Address:* 2173 Tull Avenue, Courtenay, BC V9N 7S1, Canada.

FRAME, Ronald William Sutherland; author; *b* 23 May 1953; *s* of Alexander D. Fram and Isobel D. Frame (*née* Sutherland). *Educ:* High Sch. of Glasgow; Univ. of Glasgow (M Hons); Jesus Coll., Oxford (MLitt). Full-time author, 1981–; first Betty Trask Prize (jtly) 1984; Samuel Beckett Prize, 1986; Television Industries' Panel's Most Promising Write New to TV Award, 1986. *Television* films: Paris, 1985; Out of Time, 1987; Ghost City 1994; A Modern Man, 1996; M. R. James (Ghost Stories for Christmas), 2000; Darier Disaster in Paradise, 2003; Cromwell, 2003; (contrib.) The Two Loves of Anthon Trollope, 2004; *radio* drama includes: Winter Journey, 1984; Cara, 1989; The Lanter Bearers, 1997; The Hydro (serial), 1997, 2nd series 1998, 3rd series 1999; Havisham, 1998 Maestro, 1999; Pharos, 2000; Sunday at Sant' Agata, 2001; Greyfriars, 2002; The She House, 2008; Blue Marvel, 2008; (adaptations): Don't Look Now, 2001; The Servan 2005; The Razor's Edge, 2005; A Tiger for Malgudi, 2006; The Blue Room, 2007 Monsieur Monde Vanishes, 2009. *Publications:* Winter Journey, 1984; Watching Mr Gordon, 1985; A Long Weekend with Marcel Proust, 1986; Sandmouth People, 1987; A Woman of Judah, 1987; Paris, 1987; Penelope's Hat, 1989; Bluette, 1990; Underwoo and After, 1991; Walking My Mistress in Deauville, 1992; The Sun on the Wall, 1994 The Lantern Bearers, 1999 (Scottish Book of the Year, Saltire Soc., 2000; Stonewall Barbara Gittings Honor Prize in Fiction, Amer. Liby Assoc., 2003); Permanent Violet 2002; Time in Carnbeg, 2004; contrib. weekly Carnbeg story, The Herald, 2008 *Recreations:* swimming, walking. *Address:* c/o Blake Friedmann Ltd, 122 Arlington Road NW1 7HP. *T:* (020) 7284 0408, *Fax:* (020) 7284 0442; *e-mail:* info@ blakefriedmann.co.uk; *web:* www.carnbeg.com.

FRAME, Rt Rev. Prof. Thomas Robert, PhD; Director, St Mark's Nationa Theological Centre, since 2007; Professor and Head, School of Theology, Charles Stur University, since 2007; *b* 7 Oct. 1962; *s* of Robert and Doreen Catherine Frame; *m* 1983 Helen Mary (*née* Bardsley); two *d*. *Educ:* Royal Austalian Naval Coll. HMAS Creswell Univ. of NSW (BA Hons 1985, PhD 1992); Univ. of Melbourne (DipEd 1986); MT Sydney Coll. of Divinity 1993; Univ. of Kent at Canterbury (Lucas Tooth Schol. 1996–97; MA Hons 1997). Officer, RAN, 1979–92; ordained deacon, 1993, priest, 1994 Asst Priest, Wagga Wagga, 1993–95; Rector: Binda, 1995–99; Bungendore, 1999–2001 Anglican Bishop to Australian Defence Force, 2001–07. Res. Fellow, Mt Stroml Observatory, ANU, 1999–2003; Lectr in Public Theol., St Mark's Nat. Theol Centre 2000–02; Vis. Fellow, Sch. of Humanities, Charles Sturt Univ., 2000–06. W. J. Liu Priz for Excellence in Chinese Studies, Univ. of NSW, 1985. *Publications:* First In Last Out the Navy at Gallipoli, 1990; (with G. Swinden) The Garden Island, 1990; (ed jtly Reflections on the RAN, 1991; Where Fate Calls: the HMAS Voyager tragedy, 1992 Pacific Partners: a history of Australian-American naval relations, 1992; HMAS Sydney loss and controversy, 1993; Where the Rivers Run: a history of the Anglican parish o Wagga Wagga, 1995; (with G. Webster) Labouring in Vain: a history of Bishopthorpe 1996; (with G. Webster) The Seven Churches of Binda, 1998; Binding Ties: a experience of adoption and reunion in Australia (autobiog.), 1999; The Shores o Gallipoli: naval aspects of the Anzac campaign, 2000; A Church for a Nation, 2000; (wit K. Baker) Mutiny!: naval insurrections in Australia and New Zealand, 2001; (with D Faulkner) Stromlo: an Australian observatory, 2003; Living by the Sword?: the ethics o armed intervention, 2004; 'No Pleasure Cruise': the story of the Royal Australian Navy 2004; The Cruel Legacy: the tragedy of HMAS Voyager, 2005; The Life and Death o Harold Holt, 2005; (ed) Agendas for Australian Anglicanism, 2006; Church and State Australia's imaginary wall, 2006; Anglicans in Australia, 2007; Children on Demand: th ethics of defying nature, 2008. *Recreations:* Rugby, reading biographies. *Address:* St Mark' National Theological Centre, 15 Blackall Street, Barton, ACT 2600, Australia. *T:* (2 62731592; *e-mail:* tframe@csu.edu.au.

FRANCE, Sir Christopher (Walter), GCB 1994 (KCB 1989; CB 1984); Permanen Secretary, Ministry of Defence, 1992–95; *b* 2 April 1934; *s* of W. J. and E. M. France; *m* 1961, Valerie (*née* Larman) (*see* V. E. France); one *s* one *d*. *Educ:* East Ham Grammar Sch. New College, Oxford (MA (PPE), DipEd). CDipAF. HM Treasury, 1959–84: Principa Private Secretary to the Chancellor of the Exchequer, 1973–76; Principal Establishmen Officer, 1977–80; on secondment to Electricity Council, 1980–81; Dep. Sec., 1981; or secondment to MoD, 1981–84; Dep. Sec., 1984–86, Second Perm. Sec., 1986, Perm Sec., 1987–92, DHSS, subseq. DoH. Staff Counsellor for Security and Intelligence Services, 1995–99. Bd Mem., Macmillan Cancer Relief, 1995–2004 (Vice-Pres., 2004–) Trustee, Nuffield (formerly Nuffield Provincial Hosps) Trust, 1998–2004. Chm. Council QMW, 1995–2003. Founder FMedSci 1998. Liveryman, Drapers' Co., 2003–. Hon. Col RMR (City of London), 1996–99. Hon. DMSc London, 2004. *Address:* c/o Barclays Premier Banking, 80 High Street, Sevenoaks, Kent TN13 1LR. *Club:* Reform.

FRANCE, Elizabeth Irene, CBE 2002; Chief Ombudsman, The Ombudsman Service Ltd, since 2008 (Telecommunications Ombudsman, since 2002; Energy Supply Ombudsman, since 2006; Surveyors Ombudsman, since 2007); *b* 1 Feb. 1950; *d* of Ralph Salem and Elizabeth Joan Salem (*née* Bryan); *m* 1971, Dr Michael William France; two *s* one *d*. *Educ:* Beauchamp Sch., Leics; UCW, Aberystwyth (BScEcon Pol. Sci.). Home Office: Admin Trainee, 1971; Principal, 1977; Asst Sec., 1986; Police Dept, Criminal Justice and Constitutional Dept, IT and Pay Services, 1986–94; Data Protection Registrar, subseq. Comr, then Inf. Comr, 1994–2002. Non-exec. Dir, Serious and Organised Crime Agency, 2005–. Member: Commn for control of Interpol's files, 2001–05; Compliance Cttee, Aarhus Convention, 2003–05. Mem. Court, Univ. of Manchester, 2002–; Vice-Pres., Aberystwyth Univ., 2008–. Fellow, Univ. of Wales, Aberystwyth, 2003. FRSA 1995. Hon. FICM 1999; Hon. Fellow, Inst. for Mgt of Inf. Systems, 2003. Hon. DSc De Montfort, 1996; Hon. DLitt Loughborough, 2000; Hon. LLD Bradford, 2002. *Address:* (office) Wilderspool Park, Greenall's Avenue, Warrington WA4 6HL. *T:* (01925) 430049; *e-mail:* enquiries@tosl.org.uk.

FRANCE, Prof. Peter, DPhil; FBA 1989; FRSE; Professor of French, University of Edinburgh, 1980–90, now Emeritus (University Endowment Fellow, 1990–2000); *b* 19 Oct. 1935; *s* of Edgar France and Doris Woosnam Morgan; *m* 1961, Siân Reynolds; three

d. Educ: Bridlington Sch.; Bradford Grammar Sch.; Magdalen Coll., Oxford (MA; DPhil). FRSE 2003. Lectr, then Reader, in French, Univ. of Sussex, 1963–80. French Editor, MLR, 1979–85. Jt Gen. Editor, Oxford History of Literary Translation in English (5 vol. series), 2005–. Mem., Chuvash Nat. Acad., 1991. Dr *hc* Chuvash State Univ., 1996. Officer de l'Ordre des Palmes Académiques (France), 1990; Chevalier, Légion d'Honneur (France), 2001. *Publications:* Racine's Rhetoric, 1965; Rhetoric and Truth in France, 1972; Poets of Modern Russia, 1982; Racine: Andromaque, 1977; Diderot, 1983; Rousseau: Confessions, 1987; trans., An Anthology of Chuvash Poetry, 1991; Politeness and its Discontents, 1992; (ed) New Oxford Companion to Literature in French, 1995; trans., Gennady Aygi, Selected Poems, 1997; (ed) Oxford Guide to Literature in English Translation, 2000; (ed) Mapping Lives: the uses of biography, 2002; (ed jtly) Oxford History of Literary Translation in English, vol. 4: 1790–1900, 2006; trans., Gennady Aygi, Field-Russia, 2007. *Address:* 10 Dryden Place, Edinburgh EH9 1RP. *T:* (0131) 667 1177.
See also Rev. R. T. France.

FRANCE, Rev. Richard Thomas; Rector, Wentnor with Ratlinghope, Myndtown, Norbury, More, Lydham and Snead, diocese of Hereford, 1995–99; *b* 2 April 1938; *s* of Edgar and Doris Woosnam France; *m* 1965, Barbara Wilding; one *s* one *d. Educ:* Bradford Grammar School; Balliol Coll., Oxford (MA); BD London; PhD Bristol. Asst Curate, St Matthew's Church, Cambridge, 1966–69; Lectr in Biblical Studies, Univ. of Ife, Nigeria, 1969–73; Librarian, Tyndale House, Cambridge, 1973–76; Sen. Lectr in Religious Studies, Ahmadu Bello Univ., Nigeria, 1976–77; Warden, Tyndale House, Cambridge, 1978–81; London Bible College: Senior Lectr, 1981–88; Vice-Principal, 1983–88; Principal, Wycliffe Hall, Oxford, 1989–95. Hon. Canon Theologian, Ibadan Cathedral, 1994–. Hon. Res. Fellow, Dept of Theol. and Religious Studies, Univ. of Wales, Bangor, 2004–. *Publications:* Jesus and the Old Testament, 1971; (ed with D. Wenham) Gospel Perspectives, vols 1–3, 1980–83; The Gospel According to Matthew: an introduction and commentary, 1985; The Evidence for Jesus, 1986; Matthew: evangelist and teacher, 1989; Divine Government, 1990; (ed with A. E. McGrath) Evangelical Anglicans, 1993; Women in the Church's Ministry, 1995; The Gospel of Mark: a commentary on the Greek text, 2002; The Gospel of Matthew (New International Commentary on the New Testament), 2007. *Recreations:* mountains, wildlife, travel, music. *Address:* Ty'n-y-Twll, Llangelynin, Llwyngwril, Gwynedd LL37 2QL. *T:* (01341) 250596.
See also P. France.

FRANCE, Valerie Edith, (Lady France), OBE 1994; MA; Headmistress, City of London School for Girls, 1986–95; *b* 29 Oct. 1935; *d* of Neville and Edith Larman; *m* 1961, Sir Christopher Walter France, *qv*; one *s* one *d. Educ:* St Hugh's Coll., Oxford (MA); CertEd Cantab. Deputy Headmistress, Bromley High Sch., GPDST, 1984–86; Acting Hd, Atherley Sch., Oct.–Dec. 1996. Mem., Eco-Schs Adv. Panel, 1996–2000. Member Council: Cheltenham Ladies' Coll., 1995–98; Francis Holland Schs Trust, 1997–2005 (Chm. Council, 1999–2005); Mem. Court, Whitgift Foundn, 1994–97; Gov., Trinity Sch., 1997–2003. FRGS 1959; FRSA 1991. Freeman, City of London, 1988; Liveryman, Needlemakers' Co., 1992–. *Recreations:* family, friends, places. *Address:* c/o Barclays Premier Banking, 80 High Street, Sevenoaks, Kent TN13 1LR.

FRANCES DOMINICA, Sister; *see* Ritchie, Sister F. D. L.

FRANCIES, Michael Shaul; Managing Partner, London Office, Weil, Gotshal & Manges, since 1998; *b* Tiberius, Israel, 14 Oct. 1956; *s* of Anthony and Iris Francies; *m* 1979, Claire Heather Frome; three *s. Educ:* Kingsbury High Sch.; Manchester Univ. (LLB Hons); Coll. of Law, Lancaster Gate. Clifford Turner, subseq. Clifford Chance: articled clerk, 1979–81; Asst Solicitor, 1981–83 and 1984–86; Partner, 1986–98; Asst Dir and Co. Sec., Carlton Communications, 1983–84. *Recreations:* family, football, Rugby, reading, music. *Address:* Weil, Gotshal & Manges, 1 South Place, EC2M 2WG. *T:* (020) 7903 1000, *Fax:* (020) 7903 0990; *e-mail:* michael.francies@weil.com.

FRANCIS, Arthur; *see* Francis, F. A. S.

FRANCIS, Clare Mary, MBE 1978; writer; *b* 17 April 1946; *d* of late Owen Francis, CB and Joan St Leger (*née* Norman); *m* 1977, Jacques Robert Redon (marr. diss. 1985); one *s. Educ:* Royal Ballet Sch.; University Coll. London (BScEcon; Fellow, 1978). Crossed Atlantic singlehanded, Falmouth to Newport, in 37 days, 1973; Observer Transatlantic Singlehanded Race: women's record (29 days), 1976; Whitbread Round the World Race (fully-crewed), first woman skipper, 1977–78. Chm., Soc. of Authors, 1997–99. Chm., Govt Adv. Cttee on PLR, 2000–03. Pres., Action for ME, 1990–. Hon. Fellow, UMIST, 1981. *Publications: non-fiction:* Come Hell or High Water, 1977; Come Wind or Weather, 1978; The Commanding Sea, 1981; *novels:* Night Sky, 1983; Red Crystal, 1985; Wolf Winter, 1987; Requiem, 1991; Deceit, 1993 (televised, 2000); Betrayal, 1995; A Dark Devotion, 1997; Keep Me Close, 1999; A Death Divided, 2001; Homeland, 2004; Unforgotten, 2008. *Recreation:* opera. *Address:* c/o Johnson & Alcock Ltd, 45–47 Clerkenwell Green, EC1R 0HT.

FRANCIS, (David) Hywel, PhD; MP (Lab) Aberavon, since 2001; *b* 6 June 1946; *s* of late David Francis and of Catherine Francis (*née* Powell); *m* 1968, Mair Georgina Price; one *s* one *d* (and one *s* decd). *Educ:* UC, Swansea (BA 1968; PhD 1978). Admin. Asst, TUC, 1971–72; University College, Swansea, subseq. University of Wales Swansea: Sen. Res. Officer, 1972–74; Tutor/Lectr, Contg Educn, 1974–87; Dir, Contg Educn, 1987–99; Prof., Contg Educn, 1992–99; Prof. Emeritus, 2006. Chm., Wales Congress in Support of Mining Communities, 1984–86; Nat. Convenor, Yes for Wales Campaign, 1997; Special Policy Advr, Sec. of State for Wales, 1999–2000. Chair: Select Cttee on Welsh Affairs, 2005– (Mem., 2001–); All-Party Parly Steel Gp, 2005– (Sec., 2002–05); All-Party Carers Gp, 2005–. Introd Private Mem.'s Bill, Carers (Equal Opportunities), which received Royal Assent in 2004. Chm., Paul Robeson Wales Trust, 2001–; Trustee and Vice-Chm., Bevan Foundn, 2001–. Chm., Adv. Bd, Richard Burton Centre, Swansea Univ., 2005–. Mem., Gorsedd of Bards, 1986. FRSA 1987. *Publications:* (with David Smith) The Fed: a history of the South Wales miners in the twentieth century, 1980, 2nd edn 1998; Miners against Fascism: Wales and the Spanish Civil War, 1984, 2nd edn 2004; Wales: a learning country, 1999; contrib. hist. and educnl articles in learned jls. *Recreations:* photography, walking, reading. *Address:* House of Commons, SW1A 0AA. *T:* (020) 7219 8121; (office) Eagle House, 2 Talbot Road, Port Talbot, West Glam SA13 1DH. *Clubs:* Côr Meibion Aberafan (Pres.); Port Talbot Cricket (Pres.); Aberavon Rugby Football (Vice-Pres.).

FRANCIS, Dick, (Richard Stanley), CBE 2000 (OBE 1984); FRSL; author; *b* 31 Oct. 1920; *s* of George Vincent Francis and Catherine Mary Francis; *m* 1947, Mary Margaret Brenchley (*d* 2000); two *s. Educ:* Maidenhead County Boys' School. Pilot, RAF, 1940–45 (Flying Officer). Amateur National Hunt jockey, 1946–48, Professional, 1948–57; Champion Jockey, season 1953–54. Racing Correspondent, Sunday Express, 1957–73. Mem., CWA. FRSL 1998. Hon. LHD Tufts, 1991. Edgar Allan Poe Grand Master Award, 1996. *Publications:* Sport of Queens (autobiog.), 1957, 3rd updated edn, 1982; Dead Cert, 1962; Nerve, 1964; For Kicks, 1965; Odds Against, 1965; Flying Finish, 1966; Blood Sport, 1967; Forfeit, 1968 (Edgar Allan Poe Award, 1970); Enquiry, 1969; Rat Race, 1970; Bonecrack, 1971; Smoke Screen, 1972; Slay-Ride, 1973; Knock Down, 1974; High Stakes, 1975; In the Frame, 1976; Risk, 1977; Trial Run, 1978; Whip Hand, 1979 (Golden Dagger Award, Crime Writers' Assoc., 1980; Edgar Allan Poe Award, 1980); Reflex, 1980; Twice Shy, 1981; Banker, 1982; The Danger, 1983; Proof, 1984; Break In, 1985; Lester, the official biography, 1986; Bolt, 1986; Hot Money, 1987; The Edge, 1988; Straight, 1989; Longshot, 1990; Comeback, 1991; (ed jtly) Great Racing Stories, 1989; Driving Force, 1992; Decider, 1993; Wild Horses, 1994; Come to Grief, 1995 (Edgar Allan Poe Award, 1996); To the Hilt, 1996; 10lb Penalty, 1997; Field of Thirteen, 1998; Second Wind, 1999; Shattered, 2000; Under Orders, 2006; (with Felix Francis) Dead Heat, 2007; (with Felix Francis) Silks, 2008. *Recreations:* boating, travel. *Address:* c/o Johnson and Alcock Ltd, 45/47 Clerkenwell Green, EC1R 0HT. *Club:* Garrick.

FRANCIS, Prof. (Edward) Howel, DSc; FRSE; CGeol; FGS; Professor of Earth Sciences, University of Leeds, 1977–89; *b* 31 May 1924; *s* of Thomas Howel Francis and Gwendoline Amelia (*née* Richards); *m* 1952, Cynthia Mary (*née* Williams) (*d* 1997); one *d. Educ:* Port Talbot County Sch.; Univ. of Wales, Swansea (BSc, DSc; Hon. Fellow 1989). FGS 1948; FRSE 1962. Served Army, 1944–47. Geological Survey of Great Britain (now incorporated in British Geol Survey): Field Geologist, Scotland, 1949–62; Dist Geologist, NE England, 1962–67, N Wales, 1967–70; Asst Dir, Northern England and Wales, 1971–77. Geological Society of London: Murchison Fund, 1963; Mem. Council, 1972–74; Pres., 1980–82; Pres., Section C (Geol.), BAAS, 1976; Mem., Inst. of Geol., 1978. Clough Medal, Edinburgh Geol Soc., 1983; Sorby Medal, Yorks Geol Soc., 1983; Major John Sacheverell A'Deane Coke Medal, Geol Soc. of London, 1989. *Publications:* memoirs, book chapters and papers on coalfields, palaeovolcanic rocks and general stratigraphy, mainly of Britain. *Recreations:* opera, golf. *Address:* 3 Manor Farm Barn, Newton, Porthcawl, Bridgend, Glam CF36 5SP. *Club:* Grove Golf.

FRANCIS, Elizabeth Ann, (Lisa); Member (C) Wales Mid & West, National Assembly for Wales, 2003–07; *b* 29 Nov. 1960; *d* of Thomas Foelwyn and Dilys Olwen Francis. *Educ:* Ardwyn Grammar Sch.; W London Inst. of Higher Educn. PA to Gp Chief Exec., Lead Industries Gp Ltd; Managerial Sec., African Dept, Glaxo Gp; Manager, Queensbridge Hotel, Aberystwyth, 1985–2002; Dir, Mid Wales Tourism Co., 2002–. *Recreations:* reading, travel, theatre, opera, swimming in the sea, cooking for friends.

FRANCIS, Prof. (Frederick) Arthur (Stratton); Professor of Management and Dean, Bradford University School of Management, since 1998; *b* 16 Dec. 1944; *s* of late Arthur James Stratton Francis and Jessie Margery Francis; *m* 1969, Janice Mary Taylor; one *s* two *d. Educ:* Warwick Sch.; Imperial Coll., London (BSc Eng). Res. student and Res. Officer, Imperial Coll., London, 1967–73; Res. Officer, Nuffield Coll., Oxford, 1973–76; Lectr, then Sen. Lectr, Imperial Coll. Sch. of Mgt, 1976–92; University of Glasgow: Prof. of Corporate Strategy, Business Sch., 1992–98; Associate Dean (Res.), Faculty of Soc. Scis, 1992–98. Sen. Res. Fellow, ESRC, 1986–91; Member: ESRC Cttee on Mgt Res., 1991–93; ESRC Res. Progs Bd, 1991–94. Vis. Prof., Kobe Univ., 1989. Nat. Rep., European Gp for Organizational Studies, 1973–90; Chm., EC COST A3 Action on Mgt and New Technol., 1993–96. Vice Chm., then Chm., Assoc. of Business Schs, 2002–06. Chm. Council, Bradford Cathedral, 2000–; Hon. Lay Canon, Bradford Cathedral, 2008–. FRSA 1993; Fellow British Acad. of Mgt, 1997; CCMI 2000. *Publications:* (ed jtly) Power, Efficiency and Institutions, 1982; (jtly) Office Automation, Organisation and the Nature of Work, 1984; (jtly) Innovation and Management Control: labour relations at BL Cars, 1985; New Technology at Work, 1986; (ed jtly) New Technologies and Work: capitalist and socialist perspectives, 1989; (ed jtly) The Competitiveness of European Industry, 1989; (jtly) The Structure of Organizations, 1992; (ed jtly) Design, Networks and Strategies, 1995; articles in Sociology, Cambridge Jl of Econs, Organization Studies, Strategic Mgt Jl and Internat. Jl of Ops and Prodn Mgt. *Recreations:* music, local history, cars, family. *Address:* Bradford University School of Management, Emm Lane, Bradford BD9 4JL. *T:* (work) (01274) 234371, (home) (01943) 830264; *e-mail:* a.francis@bradford.ac.uk.

FRANCIS, Gwyn Jones, CB 1990; Director-General and Deputy Chairman, Forestry Commission, 1986–90, retired; *b* 17 Sept. 1930; *s* of Daniel Brynmor Francis and Margaret Jane Francis; *m* 1st, 1954, Margaretta Meryl Jeremy (*d* 1985); one *s* one *d* (and one *s* decd); 2nd, 1986, Audrey Gertrude (*née* Gill). *Educ:* Llanelli Grammar Sch.; University Coll. of N Wales, Bangor (BSc Hons 1952); Univ. of Toronto (MSc 1965). Served RE, 1952–54. Forestry Commission: Dist Officer, 1954; Principal, Forester Training Sch., 1962; Asst Conservator, 1969; Head, Harvesting and Marketing Div., 1976; Comr, 1983–86. Mem. Council, 1992–98, and Chm., Scottish Cttee, 1992–98, RSPB. FICFor 1982; FIWSc 1984. Hon. Fellow, Univ. of Wales, 1991. *Recreations:* bird-watching, painting. *Address:* 2/16 Succoth Court, Succoth Park, Edinburgh EH12 6BZ. *T:* (0131) 337 5037. *Club:* New (Edinburgh).

FRANCIS, Sir (Horace) William (Alexander), Kt 1989; CBE 1976; FREng; FICE; Director, British Railways Board, 1994–97; *b* 31 Aug. 1926; *s* of Horace Fairie Francis and Jane McMinn Murray; *m* 1949, Gwendoline Maud Dorricott; two *s* two *d. Educ:* Royal Technical Coll., Glasgow. Dir, Tarmac Civil Engineering Ltd, 1960; Man. Dir, Tarmac Construction Ltd, 1963; Dir, Tarmac Ltd, 1964, Vice-Chm., 1974–77; Director: Trafalgar House Ltd, 1978–85; Trafalgar House Construction Hldgs, 1979–85; Trafalgar House Oil and Gas, 1986–88; Mining (Scotland) Ltd, 1995–98; Barr Holdings Ltd, 1994–2000; Chairman: Fitzpatrick Internat. Ltd, 1993–99; Enhanced Recovery Systems, 1999–. Member: Export Guarantees Adv. Council, 1974–80; British Overseas Trade Bd, 1977–80; Chairman: Overseas Projects Bd, 1977–80; Black Country UDC, 1987–94; Midlands Enterprise Fund, 1996–99. Mem., Engrg Council, 1995–96. Pres., ICE, 1987–88 (Vice-Pres., 1984–87). Lt-Col, Engr and Transport Staff Corps, TA, 1982. FREng (FEng 1977). FRSA 1989. Hon. LLD Strathclyde, 1988; Hon. DSc Aston, 1990. *Recreations:* golf, shooting, fishing, construction. *Address:* The Firs, Cruckton, near Shrewsbury, Shropshire SY5 8PW. *T:* (01743) 860796, *Fax:* (01743) 860969, *T:* and *Fax:* (020) 7930 5008. *Clubs:* Army and Navy, Livery, Royal Over-Seas League.

FRANCIS, Howel; *see* Francis, E. H.

FRANCIS, Hywel; *see* Francis, D. H.

FRANCIS, Jennifer; freelance consultant in public and media affairs, since 1992; *b* 13 July 1959; *d* of Luke Faure and Clytie Jean Francis; *m* 1981; two *s. Educ:* St Augustine's C of E Sch., London; City Univ. DipCAM. MCIPR (MIPR 1989). Br. Manager, Brook Street Bureau, 1980–83; PR, Cannons Sports Club, 1983–85; freelance PR, 1985–86; Man. Dir, Networking Public Relations, then Head of African, Caribbean, Asian and Pacific Gp, Pielle Public Relations, 1986–92; PR, LAPADA, 1999; Mktg Dir and Fest. Organiser, Carriacou Maroon Music. Fest., 2000–; Diversity Project Manager, London Tourist Bd, 2003; Dir of Communications, The Drum, 2003–. Actg Hd of Media Relations, V&A Mus., 1998; Actg Dir of Public Relations—The Show, RCA, 1999. Member: Media Adv. Gp, CRE, 1990–91; Nat. Consumer Council, 1991–94; ITC Advertising Adv. Cttee, 1992–; Prince's Youth Business Trust Ethnic Minority Adv. Gp, 1993–; Radio Authority, 1994–99; Chm., Women's Enterprise Develt Agency, 1990–93. Black Business Woman of the Year, 1989. *Publications:* contrib. to periodicals. *Recreations:* watercolours, travel, current affairs, music.

FRANCIS, Dr John Michael, FRSE; Consultant and Adviser, UNESCO (Chair: UK National Commission, 1999–2003; Sustainable Development, Peace and Human Rights, UK UNESCO, 1999–2003; Deputy Chair, Scotland Committee, since 2007); Chair, Governing Board, UNESCO Centre for Water Law, Policy and Science, University of Dundee, since 2008; *b* 1 May 1939; *s* of late William Winston Francis and Beryl Margaret Francis (*née* Savage); *m* 1963, Eileen Sykes, Cyncoed, Cardiff; two *d*. *Educ:* Gowerton County Grammar Sch.; Royal Coll. of Sci., Imperial Coll. of Sci. and Tech., Univ. of London (BSc, ARCS, PhD, DIC). FRIC 1969; FRSGS 1990; FRSE 1991; FRZSScot 1992. Res. Officer, CEGB, R&D Dept, Berkeley Nuclear Labs, 1963–70; First Dir, Society, Religion and Tech. Project, Church of Scotland, 1970–74; Sen. Res. Fellow in Energy Studies, Heriot-Watt Univ., 1974–76; Scottish Office, Edinburgh, 1976–84; Dir Scotland, Nature Conservancy Council, 1984–91 (Mem., Adv. Cttee for Scotland, 1974–76); Chief Exec., NCC for Scotland, 1991–92; Asst Sec., Envmt Dept, 1992–95, Sen. Policy Advr, Home Dept, 1995–99, Scottish Office. Member: Oil Develt Council for Scotland, 1973–76; Indep. Commn on Transport, 1974; Adv. Cttee on Marine Fishfarming Crown Estate Commn, 1989–92. Chm., Francis Group (Consultants), 1992–99. Consultant on Sci., Tech. and Social Ethics, WCC, Geneva, 1971–83; Church of Scotland: Chm., Cttee on Society, Religion and Technol., 1980–94; Trustee, Society, Religion and Technol. Project Trust, 1998–2007; Member: Church and Nation Cttee, 2000–05; Church and Society Council, 2005–. Chm., Edinburgh Forum, 1984–93. Mem. Council, Nat. Trust for Scotland, 1985–92. Mem., St Giles' Cathedral, Edinburgh. Associate, Scottish Inst. of Human Relations, 1974–94; Member: Scottish Univs Policy, Res. and Advice Network, 1999–; Internat. Develt Gp, Scottish Parlt, 2001–; Steering Gp, Scottish Sustainable Develt Forum, 2004–; Exec. Bd, Centre for Theology and Public Issues, Univ. of Edinburgh, 2005–. Trustee, RSE Scotland Foundn, 2004–07. Fellow, Inst. for Advanced Studies in the Humanities, Edinburgh Univ., 1988; Hon. Fellow, Edinburgh Univ., 2000; Vis. Fellow, Centre for Values and Social Policy, Univ. of Colorado at Boulder, 1991; UK Rep., Millennium Proj., UN Univ., 1992–2004. Professional Mem., World Futures Soc., Washington DC, 1991–; Mem., UNA, 2004– (Convener, UNA Edinburgh, 2006–07). Mem., John Muir Trust, 1994–. *Publications:* Scotland in Turmoil, 1973; (jtly) Changing Directions, 1974; (jtly) The Future as an Academic Discipline, 1975; Facing up to Nuclear Power, 1976; (jtly) The Future of Scotland, 1977; (jtly) North Sea Oil and the Environment, 1992; (jtly) Democratic Contracts for Sustainable and Caring Societies, 2000; (jtly) Conserving Nature, 2005; contribs to scientific and professional jls and periodicals, and to RSE programmes on public understanding of science. *Recreations:* writing on environmental values and the ethics of science and technology, ecumenical travels, hill walking, theatre. *Address:* 49 Gilmour Road, Newington, Edinburgh EH16 5NU. *T:* (0131) 667 3996; *e-mail:* john.m.francis@btinternet.com.

FRANCIS, Rev. Canon Prof. Leslie John, PhD, ScD, DD; CPsychol, FBPsS; Professor of Religions and Education, Institute of Education, University of Warwick, since 2007; *b* 10 Sept. 1947; *s* of Ronald Arthur Francis and Joan Irene Francis. *Educ:* Colchester Royal Grammar Sch.; Pembroke Coll., Oxford (BA (Theol.) 1970, MA 1974); Westcott House, Cambridge; Queens' Coll., Cambridge (PhD (Educn) 1976); Univ. of Nottingham (MTh 1976); Inst. of Educn, Univ. of London (MSc (Psychol.) 1977); Oxford Univ. (BD (Theol.) 1990; DD 2001); Univ. of Cambridge (ScD 1997); Univ. of Wales, Bangor (DLitt 2007). FBPsS 1988; CPsychol 1989. Ordained deacon, 1973, priest, 1974; Curate, St Mary's, Haverhill, 1973–77; Leverhulme Res. Fellow, London Central YMCA/Westminster Med. Sch., 1977–82; non-stipendiary Priest-in-charge, St Mary's, Gt Bradley and Holy Trinity, Little Wratting, Suffolk, 1978–82; Res. Officer, 1982–86, Sen. Res. Officer, 1986–88, Culham Coll. Inst.; non-stipendiary Priest-in-charge, All Saints, N Cerney and St Margaret's, Bagendon, Glos, 1982–85; non-stipendiary priest, dio. Oxford, 1985–88; Trinity College, Carmarthen: Mansel Jones Fellow, 1989–99; Principal Lectr in Religious Studies, 1989–91; Dir, Centre for Theol. and Educn and Dir of Res., 1992–99; Asst Chaplain, 1989–94; Dean of Chapel, 1994–99; D. J. James Prof. of Pastoral Theol., Univ. of Wales, Lampeter, 1992–99; Prof. of Practical Theol. and Dir, Welsh Nat. Centre for Religious Educn, Univ. of Wales, Bangor, 1999–2007; non-stipendiary priest, dio. Bangor, 1999–. Hon. Canon, St Davids Cathedral, 1998–99; Hon. Canon and Canon Theologian, Bangor Cathedral, 2006–. Chairman: Census 2001 Wkg Party, CCBI, 1995–2001; Religious Affiliation Subgp, Census Content Wkg Gp, ONS, 1996–98; Religious Affiliation Gp, 2001 Census, 1998–. Church in Wales: Chairman: Continuing Ministerial Educn Cttee, 1992–2001; Children's Sector, 1995–; Mem., Governing Body, 1997–2001. National Council of YMCAs: Mem., Wkg Party on use and abuse of alcohol, 1983–84; Chm., Educn and Prog. Develt, 1985–90; Mem., Exec. Cttee and Nat. Bd, 1985–90. Consultant, Archbps' Commn on Rural Areas, 1989–90. British Psychological Society: Mem., Standing Cttee on teaching psychol. to other professional gps, 1990–2000; Trustee, Welfare Fund, 1992–. Trustee: Alister Hardy Trust, 1999– (Chm., 2002–; Chm., Res. Cttee, 1999–2002); St Deiniol's Liby, Hawarden, 2002–; Network for the Study of Implicit Religion, 2002–; Internat. Seminar for Religious Educn and Values, 2003–; Intereuropean Commn on Church and School, 2005–. FCP 1994. *Publications:* Youth in Transit, 1982; Experience of Adulthood, 1982; Young and Unemployed, 1984; Teenagers and the Church, 1984; Rural Anglicanism: a future for young Christians?, 1985; Partnership in Rural Education: church schools and teacher attitudes, 1986; Religion in the Primary School, 1987; (with K. Williams) Churches in Fellowship: local councils of churches in England, 1991; (with W. K. Kay) Teenage Religion and Values, 1995; (with W. K. Kay) Drift from the Churches: attitudes towards Christianity during childhood and adolescence, 1996; Church Watch: Christianity in the countryside, 1996; (with J. Martineau) Rural Praise, 1996; Personality Type and Scripture: exploring Mark's Gospel, 1997; (with P. Richter) Gone but not Forgotten: church leaving and returning, 1998; (with M. Robbins) The Long Diaconate 1987–1994: women deacons and the delayed journey to priesthood, 1999; (jtly) Rural Ministry, 2000; (with P. Atkins) Exploring Luke's Gospel: a guide to the gospel readings in the Revised Common Lectionary, 2000; The Values Debate: a voice from the pupils, 2001; (with J. Martineau) Rural Visitors, 2001; (with J. Martineau) Rural Youth, 2001; (with P. Atkins) Exploring Matthew's Gospel: a guide to the gospel readings in the Revised Common Lectionary, 2001; (with J. Martineau) Rural Mission, 2002; (with J. Astley) Children, Churches and Christian Learning, 2002; (with P. Atkins) Exploring Mark's Gospel: an aid for readers and preachers using year B of the Revised Common Lectionary, 2002; (with S. H. Louden) The Naked Parish Priest: what priests really think they're doing, 2003; Faith and Psychology: personality, religion and the individual, 2005; (with M. Robbins and J. Astley) Fragmented Faith: exposing the fault-lines in the Church of England, 2005; (with M. Robbins) Urban Hope and Spiritual Health: the adolescent voice, 2005; (with J. M. Haley) British Methodism: what circuit ministers really think, 2006; (with P. Richter) Gone for Good?: church-leaving and returning in the 21st century, 2007; *edited books:* (with A. Thatcher) Christian Perspectives for Education: a reader in the theology of education, 1990; (with J. Astley) Christian Perspectives on Faith Development: a reader, 1992; (with D. W. Lankshear) Christian Perspectives on Church Schools: a reader, 1993; (with J. Astley) Critical Perspectives on Christian Education, 1994; (jtly) Fast-moving Currents in You Culture, 1995; (with J. Astley) Christian Theology and Religious Education, 1996; (wi S. H. Jones) Psychological Perspectives on Christian Ministry: a reader, 1996; (jtl Research in Religious Education, 1996; (jtly) Theological Perspectives on Christia Formation: a reader on theology and Christian education, 1996; (with W. K. Ka Religion in Education: vol. 1, 1997, vol. 2, 1998, vol. 3, 2000, vol. 4 (also with Watson), 2003; (with J. Francis) Tentmaking: perspectives on self-supporting ministr 1998; Sociology, Theology and the Curriculum, 1999; (with Y. J. Katz) Joining ar Leaving Religion: research perspectives, 2000; (jtly) The Fourth R for the Thi Millennium: education in religion and values for the global future, 2001; (with J. Astle Psychological Perspectives on Prayer: a reader, 2001; (jtly) Changing Rural Life: Christian response to key rural issues, 2004; (jtly) Making Connections: a reader c preaching, 2005; (jtly) The Idea of a Christian University: essays on theology and high education, 2005; (jtly) Religion, Education and Adolescence: international empiric perspectives, 2005; (jtly) Peace or Violence: the ends of religion and education, 2007; h also written 14 bks for teachers and clergy, and over 30 bks for children, incl. (with N. M Slee) Teddy Horsley Bible Books series. *Recreations:* music, the countryside an architecture, holder of licence to drive coaches and buses. *Address:* Warwick Religions an Education Research Unit, Institute of Education, University of Warwick, Coventry CV 7AL. *T:* (024) 7652 2539, *Fax:* (024) 7657 2638; *e-mail:* leslie.francis@warwick.ac.uk.

FRANCIS, Lisa; *see* Francis, E. A.

FRANCIS, Mary Elizabeth, CBE 2005; LVO 1999; senior independent Directo Centrica plc, since 2006 (non-executive Director, since 2004); non-executive Directo Aviva plc, since 2005; St Modwen Properties Plc, since 2005; Alliance & Leicester pl since 2007; *b* 24 July 1948; *d* of Frederick Henry George and Barbara Henrietta Georg (*née* Jeffs); *m* 1st, Dr Roger John Brown, *qv* (marr. diss.); 2nd, 1991, Prof. Peter Willia Francis (*d* 1999); 3rd, 2001, Ian Campbell Ferguson Rodger. *Educ:* James Allen's Girl Sch., Dulwich; Newnham Coll., Cambridge (MA Hist.). Res. Asst to Prof. Max Belo All Souls Coll., Oxford, 1970–72; Admin. Trainee, then Principal, CS Dept and HM Treasury, 1972–82; Private Sec. to Lord Privy Seal and Minister for the Arts, 1982–8 seconded to Hill Samuel & Co. Ltd, 1984–86; Asst Sec., HM Treasury, 1986–9 Economic Counsellor, British Embassy, Washington, 1990–92; Private Sec. to Prim Minister, 1992–95; Asst Private Sec. to the Queen, 1996–99, Dep. Private Sec., Feb.–Jun 1999; Dir-Gen., ABI, 1999–2005. Non-exec. Dir, Bank of England, 2001–07. Membe Press Complaints Commn, 2001–05; Adv. Bd, NCC, 2002–; Adv. Bd, Cambridge Uni Centre for Business Res., 2006–; Sen. Advr, RIIA, 2008–. Gov., Pensions Policy Inst 2002–. Trustee, Almeida Th., 2002–. Associate Fellow, Newnham Coll., Cambridg 1995–98. Gov., James Allen's Girls' Sch., Dulwich, 1992–2001. *Recreations:* readin swimming, ballet, walking. *Address:* 115 Ashley Gardens, SW1P 1HJ.

FRANCIS, Nicholas; *see* Francis, P. N.

FRANCIS, Norman; *see* Francis, W. N.

FRANCIS, Paul Richard, FRICS, PPISVA; Surveyor Member, Lands Tribunal, sinc 1998; *b* 14 Feb. 1948; *o s* of Richard Francis and Pamela Francis (*née* Rouse); *m* 200 Mollie Labercombe. *Educ:* King's Sch., Harrow. FSVA 1974; FRICS 2000. Midlan Marts (Banbury), 1967–70; E. J. Brooks & Son, Chartered Surveyors, 1970–75; Partne A. C. Frost & Co., 1975–86; Nat. Survey and Valuation Dir, Prudential Property Servic Ltd, 1986–98. Pres., ISVA, 1994–95. Chm. Adv. Bd, Cert. in Residential Estate Agenc Coll. of Estate Mgt, 1997–2000; Vice-Chm., RICS Dispute Resolution Faculty Bo 2001–07. *Recreations:* motor sailing, golf, shooting. *Address:* Lands Tribunal, Processio House, 55 Ludgate Hill, EC4M 7JW. *Club:* Royal Southampton Yacht.

FRANCIS, Very Rev. Peter Brereton; Warden and Chief Librarian, St Deiniol Library, Hawarden, since 1997; *b* 18 June 1953; *s* of Richard and Pauline Francis; *m* 1s 1976, Denise Steele (marr. diss. 1997); 2nd, Helen Grocott; one step *d*. *Educ:* Malver Coll.; St Andrews Univ. (MTh 1977); Queen's Coll., Birmingham. Ordained deaco 1978, priest, 1979; Curate, Hagley, Worcs, 1978–81; Chaplain, QMC, 1981–87; Recto Holy Trinity, Ayr, 1987–92; Provost and Rector, St Mary's Cathedral, Glasgow, 1992–9 Dir, Gladstone Project, 1997–. *Publications:* The Grand Old Man, 2000; The Gladston Umbrella, 2001; (ed jtly) Changing Rural Life, 2004; (ed Jtly) Cinema Divinité, 2005; (ed Rebuilding Communion, 2007. *Recreations:* cinema, theatre, cricket. *Address:* Th Warden's Lodge, St Deiniol's Library, Hawarden, Flintshire CH5 3DF. *T:* (0124 532350, 531659, *Fax:* (01244) 520643.

FRANCIS, (Peter) Nicholas; QC 2002; a Recorder, since 1999; *b* 22 April 1958; *s* c Peter and Jean Francis; *m* 2000, Penny Seguss; two *s*, and one *d* from previous marriag *Educ:* Radley Coll.; Downing Coll., Cambridge (MA). Called to the Bar, Middle Templ 1981; in practice, specialising in family law; Asst Recorder, 1997–99; Head of Chamber 29 Bedford Row, 2002–. *Recreations:* sailing, theatre, wine. *Address:* 29 Bedford Row WC1R 4HE. *T:* (020) 7404 1044, *Fax:* (020) 7831 0626; *e-mail:* nfrancis@ 29bedfordrow.co.uk. *Clubs:* Royal London Yacht, Royal Solent Yacht.

FRANCIS, Richard Mark; barn restorer and art historian; *b* 20 Nov. 1947; *s* of Ralp Lawrence and Eileen Francis; *m* 1976, Tamar Janine Helen Burchill; one *d*. *Educ:* Oakha Sch.; Cambridge Univ.; Courtauld Inst. Walker Art Gall., Liverpool, 1971–72; Ar Council of GB, 1973–80; Asst Keeper, Tate Gall., London, 1980–86; Curator, Tate Gall Liverpool, 1986–90; Chief Curator, Mus. of Contemp. Art, Chicago, 1993–97; Christie' NY, 1997–2002. *Publication:* Jasper Johns, 1984.

FRANCIS, Richard Stanley; *see* Francis, Dick.

FRANCIS, Robert Anthony; QC 1992; a Recorder, since 2000; *b* 4 April 1950; *s* of lat John Grimwade Francis and of Jean Isobel Francis; *m* 1st, 1976, Catherine Georgievsk (marr. diss. 2005); one *s* two *d*; 2nd, 2007, Alison Meek. *Educ:* Uppingham Sch.; Exete Univ. (LLB Hons). Pres., Exeter Univ. Guild of Students, 1971–72. Called to the Ba Inner Temple, 1973, Bencher, 2002. Asst Recorder, 1996–2000. Legal Assesso Chartered Soc. of Physiotherapists, 1991. Mem. Exec. Cttee, Professional Negligence Ba Assoc., 2000–06 (Vice Chm., 2002; Chm., 2004). Trustee, Peper Harow Orgn 1992–2002. Churchwarden, St John's Parish Church, Milford, Surrey, 1984–92 Consultant Ed., LS Law Medical (formerly Lloyd's Law Reports: Medical), 1999– *Publication:* (jtly) Medical Treatment Decisions and the Law, 2001. *Recreation:* cricket *Address:* 3 Serjeants' Inn, EC4Y 1BQ. *T:* (020) 7423 5000. *Club:* Travellers.

FRANCIS, Sheena Vanessa; *see* Wagstaff, S. V.

FRANCIS, Stewart Alexander Clement, MA; Headmaster, Colchester Royal Gramma School, 1985–2000; *b* 25 Feb. 1938; *s* of Clement Francis and Patricia Francis (*né* Stewart); *m* 1965, Valerie Stead; one *s* one *d*. *Educ:* St Andrew's Sch., Eastbourne; S Edward's Sch., Oxford; St John's Coll., Cambridge (MA Classics, Cert Ed). Assistan Master: Mill Hill Sch., London, 1963; Maidenhead GS, 1963–66; temp. teaching posts i

S Africa and England, 1966–67; Hd, Lower Sch., Maidenhead GS, 1967–69; Hd of English and Hd of Sixth Form, William Penn Sch., Rickmansworth, 1969–74; Dep. Head, Southgate Sch., London, 1974–79; Headmaster, Chenderit Sch., Middleton Cheney, Northants, 1979–84. OFSTED sch. inspector, 2005–; sch. improvement partner, 2006–. Pres., NE Essex Headteachers' Assoc., 1987–88. Trustee, Colchester Blue Coat Sch. Foundn, 1985–. Mem. Court, Univ. of Essex, 1996–2000. FRSA 1995. Mem., Cricket Soc., 2005–; Men's squash champion, Bucks, 1970. Friend, Rotary Club of Colchester, 2008–. Chevalier du Sacavin d'Anjou, 2008. *Publication:* contrib. Cricket Qly. *Recreations:* cricket and other sports, reading, writing, theatre, painting, visiting art galleries. *Address:* Willow Springs, 32 The Lane, West Mersea, Essex CO5 8NT. *T:* (01206) 386084. *Clubs:* MCC, Jesters Cricket, Cricketers.

FRANCIS, Sir William; *see* Francis, Sir H. W. A.

FRANCIS, His Honour (William) Norman; a Circuit Judge (formerly Judge of County Courts), 1969–93; *b* 19 March 1921; *s* of Llewellyn Francis; *m* 1951, Anthea Constance (*née* Kerry); one *s* one *d*. *Educ:* Bradfield; Lincoln Coll., Oxford (BCL, MA). Served War of 1939–45, RA. Called to Bar, Gray's Inn, 1946. Dep. Chm., Brecknock QS, 1962–71. Member: Criminal Law Revision Cttee, 1977–; Policy Adv. Cttee on Sexual Offences, 1977–85; County Court Rule Cttee, 1983–88 (Chm., 1987–88). Pres., Council of HM Circuit Judges, 1987. Chancellor, dio. of Llandaff, 1979–99. Fellow, Woodard Corp. (Western Div.), 1985–91. *Address:* 2 The Woodlands, Lisvane, near Cardiff CF14 0SW. *T:* (029) 2075 3070.

FRANCOIS, Mark Gino; MP (C) Rayleigh, since 2001; *b* London, 14 Aug. 1965; *m* 2000, Karen Thomas (marr. diss. 2006). *Educ:* Nicholas Comprehensive Sch., Basildon; Univ. of Bristol (BA 1986); King's Coll. London (MA 1987). Mgt trainee, Lloyds Bank, 1987; Consultant and Dir, Market Access Internat. Public Affairs Consultancy, 1988–95; Public Affairs Consultant, Francois Associates, 1996–2001. Mem. (C) Basildon DC, 1991–95. Opposition Jun. Whip, 2002; Shadow Econ. Sec., HM Treasury, 2004; Shadow Paymaster Gen., 2005–07; Opposition spokesman on Europe, 2007–. Mem., Envmtl Audit Cttee, H of C, 2001–05. Contested (C) Brent East, 1997. Served TA, 1983–89 (Lieut). Mem., RUSI. Fellow, Huguenot Soc. of GB and Ire., 2001–. Freeman, City of London, 2004; Liveryman, Co. of Wheelwrights, 2005–. Pres., Palace of Westminster Lions Club, 2006–. *Recreations:* reading, travel, walking, history (including military history). *Address:* (office) 25 Bellingham Lane, Rayleigh, Essex SS6 7ED; c/o House of Commons, SW1A 0AA. *T:* (020) 7219 3000. *Clubs:* Carlton; Rayleigh Conservative.

FRANÇOIS-PONCET, Jean André; Member of the French Senate (Lot-et-Garonne), since 1983 (Chairman of the Economic Committee, since 1986); *b* 8 Dec. 1928; *s* of André François-Poncet, Grand'Croix de la Légion d'Honneur, and Jacqueline (*née* Dillais); *m* 1959, Marie-Thérèse de Mitry; two *s* one *d*. *Educ:* Paris Law Sch.; Ecole Nationale d'Administration; Wesleyan Univ.; Fletcher Sch. of Law and Diplomacy. Joined Ministry of Foreign Affairs, 1955; Office of Sec. of State, 1956–58; Sec. Gen. of French delegn to Treaty negotiations for EEC and Euratom, 1956–58; Dep. Head, European Orgns, Ministry of Foreign Affairs, 1958–60; Head of Assistance Mission, Morocco, 1961–63; Dep. Head, African Affairs, 1963–65; Counsellor, Tehran, 1969–71. Professor, Institut d'Etudes Politiques, Paris, 1960–. Chm. 1971, Vice-Pres. 1972, Pres. and Chief Exec. 1973–75, Carnaud SA. Sec. of State for Foreign Affairs, Jan.–July 1976; Sec.-Gen. to Presidency of France, 1976–78; Minister for Foreign Affairs, 1978–81. Vice-Chm., Foreign Relns Cttee, French Senate, 2004–. Co-Chm., Indo-French Forum, 1998–. Mem., Internat. Adv. Bd, Chase Manhattan. Pres., Comité du Bassin Adour-Garonne, 1980–. *Publication:* The Economic Policy of Western Germany, 1970. *Address:* 53 rue de Varenne, 75007 Paris, France; (office) Palais du Luxembourg, 15 rue de Vaugirard, 75291 Paris cedex 06, France; (office) Préfecture de Lot-et-Garonne, Place de Verdun, 47920 Agen cedex 9, France.

FRANCOME, John, MBE 1986; writer; racing presenter, Channel 4 Television; first jockey to F. T. Winter, 1975–85; *b* 13 Dec. 1952; *s* of Norman and Lillian Francome; *m* 1976, Miriam Strigner. *Educ:* Park Senior High School, Swindon. First ride, Dec. 1970; Champion Jockey (National Hunt), 1975–76, 1978–79, 1980–81, 1981–82, 1982–83, 1983–84, 1984–85; record number of jumping winners (1,036), May 1984; retired March 1985 (1,138 winners). *Publications:* Born Lucky (autobiog.), 1985; How to Make Money Betting—or at least how not to lose too much, 1986; Twice Lucky: the lighter side of steeplechasing, 1988; *novels*: Blood Stock, 1989; Stud Poker, 1990; Stone Cold, 1991; Rough Ride, 1992; Outsider, 1993; Break Neck, 1994; Dead Ringer, 1995; False Start, 1996; High Flyer, 1997; Safe Bet, 1998; Tip Off, 1999; Lifeline, 2000; Dead Weight, 2001; Inside Track, 2002; Stalking Horse, 2003; Back Hander, 2004; Cover Up, 2005; (with James MacGregor): Eavesdropper, 1986; Riding High, 1987; Declared Dead, 1988. *Recreations:* tennis, music. *Address:* c/o Channel 4 Television, 124 Horseferry Road, SW1P 2TX; Beechdown Farm, Sheepdrove, Lambourn, Berks RG17 7UN.

FRANK, Sir Andrew; *see* Frank, Sir R. A.

FRANK, David; Chief Executive, RDF Media, since 1993; *b* 24 Sept. 1958; *s* of late Peter James Frank and of Joyce Miriam Frank (*née* Sollis); *m* 1983, Isabelle Turquet de Beauregard; two *s* one *d*. *Educ:* Trinity Coll., Oxford (BA Juris.). Manager: Hill Samuel & Co. Ltd, 1982–85; Swiss Bank Corp. Internat., 1985–87; freelance journalist, 1987–89; reporter, BBC TV, 1989–92. *Recreations:* football, scuba-diving, golf, tennis, fly-fishing. *Address:* RDF Media, Gloucester Building, Kensington Village, W14 8RF; *e-mail:* david.frank@rdfmedia.com. *Club:* Roehampton.

FRANK, Sir (Robert) Andrew, 4th Bt *cr* 1920, of Withyham, Co. Sussex; freelance event management and training consultant, since 2000; *b* 16 May 1964; *s* of Sir Robert John Frank, 3rd Bt, FRICS, and Margaret Joyce (*d* 1995), *d* of Herbert Victor Truesdale; *S* father, 1987; *m* 1990, Zoë, *er d* of S. A. Hasan. *Educ:* Ludgrove Prep. School; Eton College. *Recreations:* travel, theatre, cinema. *Heir:* none.

FRANKEL, Dr Hans Ludwig, OBE 1993; FRCP; Consultant in Spinal Injuries, National Spinal Injuries Centre, Stoke Mandeville Hospital, 1966–2002, now Honorary Consultant; *b* 7 April 1932; *s* of late Dr Paul Frankel, CBE and Helen Frankel; *m* 1956, Mavis Anne Richardson; two *s*. *Educ:* Dauntsey's Sch.; University Coll. London; University Coll. Hosp. Med. Sch. (MB BS 1956). MRCS 1956; LRCP 1956, MRCP 1964, FRCP 1977. Casualty officer, Hampstead Gen. Hosp., 1957; Stoke Mandeville Hospital, 1957–: Hse Physician, 1957–58; National Spinal Injuries Centre: Registrar, 1958–62; Sen. Registrar, 1962–66; Dep. Dir, 1969–77; Mem., Exec. Bd, 1991–98; Clin. Dir, 1993–98. Hon. Consultant, Star & Garter Home, Richmond, 1979–. Vis. Prof., ICSTM, 2000–. Member: Editorial Board: Paraplegia; Annales de Readaptation et de Médecine Physique; Clinical Autonomic Res.; Editl Adv. Bd, Annals of Sports Medicine. Buckinghamshire Area Health Authority: Vice-Chm., 1976–77, Chm., 1978–80, Med. Adv. Cttee. International Medical Society of Paraplegia: Hon. Treas., 1966–78; Hon. Sec., 1976–87; Vice Pres., 1987–91; Pres., 1996–2000; Chm., Scientific Cttee, 1992–96. President: Brit. Cervical Spine Soc., 1990–92; Chiltern Gp, Spinal Injuries Assoc., 1989–98. Mem., Exec. Cttee, Brit. Paraplegic Sports Soc., 1977–91. Chm. Trustees, Internat. Spinal Res. Trust, 1983–97; Mem., Mgt Council, Brit. Neurol Res. Trust, 1989–. Numerous lectures in UK, Europe, USA and throughout the world, incl. Arnott Demonstrator, RCS 1987, Sandoz Lectr, Inst. of Neurol., London, 1988 and 1992. *Publications:* (ed) volume on Spinal Cord Injuries in Handbook of Clinical Neurology, 1992; contrib. chapters on spinal cord injuries to text books. *Recreations:* ski-ing, opera. *Address:* National Spinal Injuries Centre, Stoke Mandeville Hospital, Mandeville Road, Aylesbury, Bucks HP21 8AL. *T:* (01296) 315852.

FRANKEL, Prof. Stephen John, DM, PhD; FRCP, FFPH; Professor of Epidemiology and Public Health, University of Bristol, 1993–2007, now Emeritus; establishing a carbon-neutral and self-sufficient small-holding; *b* 4 Nov. 1946; *s* of Eric and Constance Frankel; *m* 1st, 1972, Hermione Jane Dennis (marr. diss. 2003); one *s* one *d*; 2nd, 2004, Elizabeth-Jane Grose. *Educ:* Corpus Christi Coll., Oxford (BM BCh 1970; MA 1970; DM 1983); Corpus Christi Coll., Cambridge (PhD 1981). MFPHM 1985, FFPH (FFPHM 1991); FRCP 2000. District Medical Officer, Papua New Guinea, 1972–74; Res. Officer, Dept of Social Anthropology, Cambridge Univ., 1977–81; Res. Fellow, Clare Hall, Cambridge, 1981–84; Senior Lecturer in Epidemiology: Univ. of Wales Coll. of Medicine, 1985–89; Univ. of Bristol, 1989–92. Consultant, WHO, 1985–2001; Director: Health Care Evaluation Unit, Univ. of Bristol, 1989–93; R&D, South Western Reg., NHS, 1992–96; NHS Cancer Res. Prog., 1993–96; MRC Health Services Res. Collaboration, 1996–97. *Publications:* The Huli Response to Illness, 1986; (ed jtly) A Continuing Trial of Treatment, 1988; (ed) The Community Health Worker, 1992; (ed jtly) Rationing and Rationality in the National Health Service: the persistence of waiting lists, 1993; (ed jtly) Priority Setting: the health care debate, 1996; numerous articles in med. and sci. jls concerning the aetiology of disease, disease prevention and health service research. *Recreations:* the usual things, plus windsurfing, Danny the dog, and bluegrass. *Address:* Carhart Mill, Wadebridge, Cornwall PL27 7HZ. *T:* (01208) 816818.

FRANKL, Peter; pianist; *b* Hungary, 2 Oct. 1935; *s* of Laura and Tibor Frankl; adopted British nationality, 1967; *m* 1958, Annie Feiner; one *s* one *d*. *Educ:* Liszt Ferenc Acad. of Music, Budapest. First Prize, several internat. competitions; London début, 1962; New York début, with Cleveland Orch. under George Szell, 1967; performances with Berlin Philharmonic, Amsterdam Concertgebouw, Israel Phil., Leipzig Gewandhaus, Orchestre de Paris, and with all London and major Amer. orchs (Chicago, Philadelphia, Boston, Washington, Los Angeles, San Francisco, Pittsburg, etc); many tours in Japan, Australia, NZ and SA, playing with orchs, in recitals and chamber music concerts; over 20 appearances, BBC Promenade Concerts, London; regular participant at Edinburgh, Cheltenham, Aldeburgh, Verbier and Kuhmo Fests; regular guest artist at summer fests in Aspen, Chautauqua, Hollywood Bowl, Marlboro, Norfolk, Ravinia and Santa Fé. Vis. Prof. of Piano, Yale Univ. Sch. of Music, 1987–. Hon. Prof., Liszt Acad., Budapest, 2006. Recordings include: complete solo works for piano by Schumann and Debussy; complete works for piano and orch. by Schumann; (with ECO) Mozart concerti; (with Tamás Vásáry) complete 4-hand works by Mozart; (with Lindsay Quartet) Brahms, Schumann, Dvorak and Martinu quintets. Officer's Cross, Order of Merit (Hungary), 1995. *Recreations:* football, opera, theatre. *Address:* 5 Gresham Gardens, NW11 8NX. *T:* (020) 8455 5228.

FRANKLAND, family name of **Baron Zouche**.

FRANKLAND, (Anthony) Noble, CB 1983; CBE 1976; DFC 1944; MA, DPhil; historian and biographer; *b* 4 July 1922; *s* of late Edward Frankland, Ravenstonedale, Westmorland; *m* 1st, 1944, Diana Madeline Fovargue (*d* 1981), *d* of late G. V. Tavernor, of Madras and Southern Mahratta Rly, India; one *s* one *d*; 2nd, 1982, Sarah Katharine, *d* of His Honour the late Sir David Davies, QC and late Lady Davies (Margaret Kennedy). *Educ:* Sedbergh; Trinity Coll., Oxford. Served Royal Air Force, 1941–45 (Bomber Command, 1943–45). Air Historical Branch Air Ministry, 1948–51; Official Military Historian, Cabinet Office, 1951–58. Rockefeller Fellow, 1953. Deputy Dir of Studies, Royal Institute of International Affairs, 1956–60; Dir, Imperial War Museum (at Southwark, 1960–82, Duxford Airfield, 1976–82, and HMS Belfast, 1978–82). Lees Knowles Lecturer, Trinity Coll., Cambridge, 1963. Historical advisor, Thames Television series, The World At War, 1971–74. Vice-Chm., British Nat. Cttee, Internat. Cttee for Study of Second World War, 1976–82. Mem., Council, Morley Coll., 1962–66; Trustee: Military Archives Centre, KCL, 1963–82; HMS Belfast Trust, 1971–78 (Vice-Chm., 1972–78); HMS Belfast Bd, 1978–82. *Publications:* Documents on International Affairs: for 1955, 1958; for 1956, 1959; for 1957, 1960; Crown of Tragedy, Nicholas II, 1960; The Strategic Air Offensive Against Germany, 1939–1945 (4 vols) jointly with Sir Charles Webster, 1961; The Bombing Offensive against Germany, Outlines and Perspectives, 1965; Bomber Offensive: the Devastation of Europe, 1970; (ed jtly) The Politics and Strategy of the Second World War (8 vols), 1974–78; (ed jtly) Decisive Battles of the Twentieth Century: Land, Sea, Air, 1976; Prince Henry, Duke of Gloucester, 1980; general editor and contributor, Encyclopaedia of 20th Century Warfare, 1989; Witness of a Century: the life and times of Prince Arthur Duke of Connaught, 1993; History at War: the campaigns of an historian, 1998; The Unseen War (novel), 2007; Belling's War (novel), 2009; historical chapter in Manual of Air Force Law, 1956; contrib. to Encyclopaedia Britannica; other articles and reviews; broadcasts on radio and TV. *Address:* 26/27 River View Terrace, Abingdon, Oxfordshire OX14 5AE. *T:* (01235) 521624. *Club:* Royal Over-Seas League.

See also M. D. P. O'Hanlon.

FRANKLIN, Andrew Cecil; Publisher and Managing Director, Profile Books Ltd, since 1996; *b* 6 March 1957; *s* of Norman Albert Jessel Franklin and Jill (*née* Leslie); *m* 1981, Caroline Elton; two *s* one *d*. *Educ:* Leighton Park Sch.; Balliol Coll., Oxford (MA PPE). HM Factory Inspector, 1979–81; bookseller, Hatchards Bookshop, 1981–82; editl asst, Faber and Faber, 1982–83; editor: Methuen, 1983–84; Penguin Books, 1984–89; Publishing Dir, Hamish Hamilton, and Dir, Penguin Books, 1989–95. Chm., Jewish Community Centre for London, 2004–. Fellow, Jerusalem Book Fair, 1985; Aspen Fellow, 1987. Trustee and Director: Jewish Literary Trust, 1987– (Chm., 1994–96); Edinburgh Internat. Book Fest., 2006–. Stanley Unwin Fellowship Award, Publishers Assoc., 1986; Friend of Jerusalem Award, City of Jerusalem, 2005. *Publications:* contrib. various newspapers. *Recreations:* my family and making trouble (separately and together). *Address:* Profile Books, 3A Exmouth House, Pine Street, Exmouth Market, EC1R 0JH. *T:* (020) 7841 6300, *Fax:* (020) 7833 3969; *e-mail:* andrew.franklin@profilebooks.com.

FRANKLIN, Daniel, PhD; Executive Editor, The Economist, and Editor in Chief, economist.com, since 2006; *b* London, 27 Nov. 1955; *s* of Colin and Charlotte Franklin; *m* 1987, Gaby; one *s* one *d*. *Educ:* University College Sch., London; St John's Coll., Oxford (MA French and Russian); Aston Univ., Birmingham (PhD). Joined The Economist, 1983; Europe Ed., 1986–92; Britain Ed., 1992–93; Washington Bureau Chief, 1993–97; Editl Dir, Economist Intelligence Unit, 1997–2006; Ed., "The World In", 2003–. *Recreations:* travel, learning languages. *Address:* The Economist, 25 St James's Street,

SW1A 1HG. *T:* (020) 7576 1185, *Fax:* (020) 7925 0651; *e-mail:* danielfranklin@economist.com.

FRANKLIN, George Henry; Consultant, Third World planning and development; *b* 15 June 1923; *s* of late George Edward Franklin, RN, and Annie Franklin; *m* 1950, Sylvia D. Franklin (*née* Allen); three *s* one *d.* *Educ:* Hastings Grammar Sch.; Hastings Sch. of Art; Architectural Assoc. Sch. of Arch. (AADipl); Sch. of Planning and Research for Regional Develt, London (SPDip); RIBA, FRTPI. Served War of 1939–45: Parachute Sqdn; RE, Europe; Bengal Sappers and Miners, RIE, SE Asia. Finchley Bor. Council, 1952–54; Architect, Christian Med. Coll., Ludhiana, Punjab, India, 1954–57; Physical Planning Adviser (Colombo Plan) to Republic of Indonesia, 1958–62, and Govt of Malaysia, 1963–64; Physical Planning Adviser, Min. of Overseas Develt, later Overseas Develt Admin, FCO, 1966–83 (Overseas Div., Building Research Station, 1966–73, ODM, later ODA, 1973–83). Hon. Prof., Dept of Town Planning, UWIST, 1982–88; Sen. Advr, Develt Planning Unit, UCL, 1983–. Chm., Overseas Sch., Town and Country Planning Summer Sch., 1970–75. Commonwealth Assoc. of Planners: Mem. Exec. Cttee, 1970–80; Pres., 1980–84; Hon. Sec., 1984–88; Member: Exec. Cttee, Commonwealth Human Ecology Council, 1970–90; Internat. Adv. Bd, Centre for Develt and Environmental Planning, Oxford Polytechnic, 1985–92; World Service Cttee, United Bible Socs, 1968–77. Chm., Warminster Bible Soc. Action Gp, 1991–; Vice Chm., W Wilts, Leonard Cheshire Care-at-Home (formerly Family Support) Service, 1994–96 (Chm., Warminster and Westbury Dist, 1990–94). Co-ordinator, Christian Aid, Warminster Dist, 1991–2006. Member Editorial Board: Third World Planning Review, 1979–91; Cities, 1983–91. FRSA; AIIA, 1955; AITP India, 1956. *Publications:* papers to internat. confs and professional jls concerning planning, building and housing in the Third World. *Recreations:* family, Christian, Third World, human rights and environmental issues and interests, fly-fishing. *Address:* The Manse, Sutton Veny, Warminster, Wilts BA12 7AW. *T:* (01985) 840072. *Club:* Victory Services.

FRANKLIN, Gordon Herbert, CVO 1989 (LVO 1976; MVO 1965); a Serjeant-at-Arms to HM the Queen, 1990–93; Personnel Officer, Royal Household, 1988–93, retired; *b* 1 Sept. 1933; *s* of late Herbert and Elsie Franklin; *m* 1959, Gillian Moffett; three *d.* *Educ:* Windsor County Boys' Sch. Barclays Bank, 1950. 2nd ATAF, Germany, 1952–54. Royal Household, 1956–93: Chief Clerk, Master of the Household's Dept, 1975; Chief Accountant of Privy Purse, 1982. Member: Central Finance Board and Council of Methodist Church, 1984–96; Methodist Council Exec., 1993–97. Vice-Pres., Friends of Wesley's Chapel, 1989–. Foundn Gov., Royal Sch., Great Park, Windsor, 1997–2007; Gov., Brigidine Sch., Windsor, 1999–2003. Chm., Windsor and Eton Soc., 1998–2004. Methodist local preacher, 1955–. Freeman, City of London, 1982; Liveryman, Painter Stainers' Co., 1983–. *Recreations:* theatre, walking, travel. *Address:* 10 Cumberland Lodge Mews, The Great Park, Windsor, Berks SL4 2JD. *Club:* Royal Over-Seas League.

FRANKLIN, John; *see* Franklin, W. J.

FRANKLIN, John Richard; Head Master, Christ's Hospital, since 2007; *b* 17 May 1953; *s* of late Richard Franklin and of Jean Franklin; *m* 1980, Kim Gillespie. *Educ:* Lockyer High Sch.; Ipswich Grammar Sch.; Univ. of Southern Qld (Dip. Teaching; BA); Univ. of New England, Australia (MEd Admin). Teacher: of English and Drama, Qld Educn Dept, 1976–79; and Housemaster and Hd of Sen. Sch., Toowoomba GS, 1980–88; Sedbergh Sch., 1989; Marlborough Coll., 1989–92; Dep. Headmaster, St Peter's Coll., Adelaide, 1993–98; Headmaster, Ardingly Coll., 1998–2007. *Recreations:* theatre, travel, golf. *Address:* Christ's Hospital, Horsham, W Sussex RH13 7LS. *T:* (01403) 211293. *Clubs:* East India; Naval, Military and Air Force (S Australia).

FRANKLIN, Sir Michael (David Milroy), KCB 1983 (CB 1979); CMG 1972; Permanent Secretary, Ministry of Agriculture, Fisheries and Food, 1983–87; *b* 24 Aug. 1927; *o s* of late Milroy Franklin; *m* 1951, Dorothy Joan Fraser; two *s* one *d.* *Educ:* Taunton Sch.; Peterhouse, Cambridge (1st cl. hons Economics). Served with 4th RHA, BAOR. Asst Principal, Min. of Agric. and Fisheries, 1950; Economic Section, Cabinet Office (subseq. Treasury), 1952–55; Principal, Min. of Agric., Fisheries and Food, 1956; UK Delegn to OEEC (subseq. OECD), 1959–61; Private Sec. to Minister of Agric., Fisheries and Food, 1961–64; Asst Sec., Head of Sugar and Tropical Foodstuffs Div., 1965–68; Under-Sec. (EEC Gp), MAFF, 1968–73; a Dep. Dir Gen., Directorate Gen. for Agric., EC, Brussels, 1973–77; Dep. Sec., Head of the European Secretariat, Cabinet Office, 1977–81; Permanent Sec., Dept of Trade, 1982–83. Director: Agricultural Mortgage Corp., 1987–93; Barclays Bank, 1988–93; Barclays PLC, 1988–93; Whessoe plc, 1988–97; Whitbread plc, 1991–98; Co-Chm., UK Adv. Bd, Rabobank, 1996–2006. Pres., West India Cttee, 1987–95; Chm., Europe Cttee, British Invisibles (formerly BIEC), 1993–98 (Dep. Chm., 1988–93); Member: Council, Royal Inst. for Internat. Relations, 1988–95; Internat. Policy Council on Agric., Food and Trade, 1988–98; Chm., Jt Consultative Cttee, Potato Marketing Bd, 1990–97. Governor, Henley Management Coll. (formerly Henley Administrative Staff Coll.), 1983–93; Chm., Charlemagne Inst., 1996–99; Co-Chm., Wyndham Place Charlemagne Trust, 1999–2001. *Publications:* Rich Man's Farming: the crisis in agriculture, 1988; Britain's Future in Europe, 1990; The EC Budget, 1992; (with Jonathan Ockenden) European Agriculture: making the CAP fit the future, 1995. *Address:* 15 Galley Lane, Barnet, Herts EN5 4AR. *Club:* Oxford and Cambridge.

FRANKLIN, Prof. Raoul Norman, CBE 1995; FREng; FInstP, FIMA; FIET; Visiting Professor, Open University, since 1998; Vice Chancellor, 1978–98, and Professor of Plasma Physics and Technology, 1986–98, The City University, London; *b* 3 June 1935; *s* of Norman George Franklin and Thelma Brinley Franklin (*née* Davis); *m* 1st, 1961, Faith (*d* 2004), *d* of Lt-Col H. T. C. Ivens and Eva (*née* Gray); two *s*; 2nd, 2005, Christine Penfold, *d* of Henry Harold and Irene Josephine (*née* Matthews). *Educ:* Howick District High Sch.; Auckland Grammar Sch., NZ; Univ. of Auckland (ME, DSc); Christ Church, Oxford (MA, DPhil, DSc). FInstP 1968; FIMA 1970; FIET (FIEE 1986); FREng (FEng 1990). Officer, NZ Defence Scientific Corps, 1957–75. Sen. Res. Fellow, RMCS, Shrivenham, 1961–63; University of Oxford: Tutorial Fellow, 1963–78, Dean, 1966–71, Hon. Fellow, 1980, Keble Coll.; Univ. Lectr in Engrg Science, 1966–78; Mem., Gen. Bd, 1967–74 (Vice Chm., 1971–74); Mem., Hebdomadal Council, 1971–74, 1976–78. Chairman: Associated Examining Bd, 1994–98; Assessment and Qualifications Alliance, 1998–2003. Consultant, UKAEA Culham, 1968–2001. Dep. Editor, Jl of Physics D, 1986–90. Member: UGC Equipment Sub Cttee, 1975–78; Plasma Physics Commn, IUPAP, 1971–79; Science Bd, SERC, 1982–85; Exec. Council, Business in the Community, 1982–90; Management Cttee, Spallation Neutron Source, 1983–86; Technology Educn Project, 1986–88; UK-NZ 1990 Cttee, 1988–90; Internat. Scientific Cttee, Eur. Sectional Conf. on Atomic and Molecular Processes in Ionized Gases, 1993–97. Chairman: Internat. Science Cttee, Phenomena in Ionized Gases, 1976–77; City Technology Ltd, 1978–93 (Queen's Award for Technol., 1982, 1985, for Export, 1988, 1991). Mem., London Pensions Fund Authority, 1989–95. Trustee: Ruskin School of Drawing, 1975–78; Lloyds Tercentenary Foundn, 1990–2007. Member Council: Gresham Coll., 1981–98; C&G, 1994–2000. Governor: Ashridge Management Coll., 1986–99; Univ. of Buckingham, 2000–06. Freeman, City of London, 1981. Liveryma Curriers' Co., 1984– (Master, 2002–03); Master, Guild of Educators (former Preceptors), 1999–2002. Hon. Mem. RICS, 1992; Hon. GSMD 1993. CCMI (CBI 1986); FRSA. Hon. DCL City, 1999. *Publications:* Plasma Phenomena in Gas Discharge 1976; papers on plasmas, gas discharges and granular materials. *Recreations:* walkin gardening. *Address:* 12 Moreton Road, Oxford OX2 7AX; Open University, Oxfo Research Unit, Foxcombe Hall, Boars Hill, Oxford OX1 5HR. *Club:* Athenæum.

FRANKLIN, Prof. Simon Colin, DPhil; Professor of Slavonic Studies, University Cambridge, since 2004; Fellow, Clare College, Cambridge, since 1980; *b* 11 Aug. 195 *s* of Colin and Charlotte Franklin; *m* 1975, Natasha Gokova; one *s* one *d.* *Educ:* Universi Coll. Sch.; King's Coll., Cambridge (BA 1976); St Antony's Coll., Oxford (DPhil 1981 Jun. Fellow, Dumbarton Oaks Center for Byzantine Studies, Washington, 1979–8 University of Cambridge: Res. Fellow, Clare Coll., 1980–83; Univ. Lectr in Russia 1983–99; Reader, 1999–2003; Prof. of Russian Studies, 2003–04. Chm., Pushkin Hou Trust, 2004–. *Publications:* (trans with A. Boyars) The Face Behind the Face: new poen by Yevgeny Yevtushenko, 1979; (with A. Kazhdan) Studies in Byzantine Literature of th Eleventh and Twelfth Centuries, 1984; Sermons and Rhetoric of Kievan Rus, 1991; (wit J. Shepard) The Emergence of Rus 750–1200, 1996; Writing, Society and Culture in Ear Rus c950–1300, 2002; (ed with E. Widdis) National Identity in Russian Culture: a introduction, 2004. *Recreations:* old books, watching football. *Address:* Clare Colleg Cambridge CB2 1TL. *T:* (01223) 333263; *e-mail:* scf1000@cam.ac.uk.

FRANKLIN, Thomas Gerald; Chief Executive, Ramblers' Association, since 2007; *b* 2 June 1969; *s* of Gerald Joseph Franklin and Jillian Ruth Franklin. *Educ:* King Edward V Upper Sch., Bury St Edmunds; Univ. of Hull (BA Politics). Account Dir, Rowland Publ Affairs, 1996–2000; Chief Exec., Living Streets (The Pedestrians Assoc.), 2002–07. Mem (Lab) Lambeth BC, 1994–06 (Leader, 2000–02). *Recreations:* cycling, walking, cinem travelling. *Address:* Ramblers' Association, 2nd Floor, Camelford House, 87–90 Albe Embankment, SE1 7TW. *T:* (020) 7339 8500, *Fax:* (020) 7339 8501; *e-ma* tom.franklin@ramblers.org.uk. *Club:* Constituency Labour (Streatham).

FRANKLIN, (William) John; DL; Deputy Chairman, Chartered Trust plc, 1986–9 (Director, 1982–97); Chairman: Howells Motors Ltd, 1986–89; Powell Duffryn Wago 1986–89; *b* 8 March 1927; *s* of late William Thomas Franklin and Edith Hannah Frankli *m* 1951, Sally (*née* Davies) (*d* 2003); one *d.* *Educ:* Monkton House Sch., Cardiff. W. P Gresty, Chartered Accountants, 1947–50; Peat Marwick Mitchell, Charter Accountants, 1950–55; Powell Duffryn, 1956–86: Director, Cory Brothers, 1964; Ma Dir, Powell Duffryn Timber, 1967–70; Dir, 1970–86; Man. Dir and Chief Exec 1976–85; Dep. Chm., Jan.–July 1986. Treas., UC of Swansea, 1989–92. DL M Glamorgan, 1989. *Recreation:* golf. *Address:* 80 South Road, Porthcawl, Bridgend CF3 3DA. *Club:* Royal Porthcawl Golf.

FRANKLYN, Prof. Jayne Agneta, (Mrs Michael Gammage), MD, PhD; FRC Professor of Medicine, since 1995, and Head, School of Clinical and Experiment Medicine, College of Medical and Dental Sciences, since 2008, University Birmingham; Consultant Physician, Queen Elizabeth Hospital, Birmingham, since 198 *b* Birmingham, 7 July 1956; *d* of late Ivor George Franklyn and Joyce Helen Franklyn; 1980, Dr Michael Gammage; one *s* one *d.* *Educ:* Univ. of Birmingham (MB ChB Ho 1979; MD 1985; PhD 1988). MRCP 1982, FRCP 1991. University of Birminghan MRC Trng Fellow, 1994–95; Wellcome Trust Sen. Res. Fellow in Clin. Sci., 1988–8 Sen. Lectr, then Reader in Medicine, 1989–95. Chm., Specialist Adv. Cttee i Endocrinol. and Diabetes, JRCPTB, 2006–. Pres., British Thyroid Assoc., 2008– FMedSci 2000. *Publications:* contrib. papers on thyroid disease pathogenesis, treatment an long term effects. *Recreations:* gardening, enjoying the Devon coast and sea. *Addres* Institute of Biomedical Research, The Medical School, University of Birminghan Edgbaston, Birmingham B15 2TH. *T:* (0121) 415 8811, *Fax:* (0121) 415 8712; *e-ma* j.a.franklyn@bham.ac.uk.

FRANKLYN, Rear-Adm. Peter Michael, CB 1999; MVO 1978; Chief Executiv Royal Hospital for Neuro-disability, since 2000; *b* 10 Sept. 1946; *s* of late Roy Verno Bolton Franklyn and Yvonne Beryl Franklyn (*née* Hooper); *m* 1977, Caroline Barba Anne Jenks; one *s* one *d.* *Educ:* King's Coll., Taunton. Joined RN, 1963; Comdr, 198 CO, HMS Active, 1980–82; Trng Comdr, BRNC, Dartmouth, 1982–84; SO Ops F 3rd Flotilla, 1984–86; Captain, 1986; Naval Asst to 1st Sea Lord, 1986–88; CO, HM Bristol, 1988–90; RCDS, 1991; Capt., Sch. of Maritime Ops, 1992–93; Dir Nav Officers' Appts (Seaman), 1993–94; Rear-Adm., 1994; Comdr, UK Task Gp, 1994–9 Flag Officer, Sea Training, 1996–97; Flag Officer, Surface Flotilla, 1997–2000. Mem RNSA, 1993–. Younger Brother, Trinity House, 1996. *Recreations:* family, outdo activities, antique furniture, old houses. *Address:* Royal Hospital for Neuro-disabilit West Hill, Putney, SW15 3SW.

FRANKS, Sir Arthur Temple, (Sir Dick Franks), KCMG 1979 (CMG 1967); H Diplomatic Service, retired; *b* 13 July 1920; *s* of late Arthur Franks, Hove; *m* 1945, Rach Marianne (*d* 2004), *d* of late Rev. A. E. S. Ward, DD; one *s* two *d.* *Educ:* Rugby; Queen Coll., Oxford. HM Forces, 1940–46 (despatches). Entered Foreign Service, 1949; Britis Middle East Office, 1952; Tehran, 1953; Bonn, 1962; FCO, 1966–81. *Address:* Roefiel Alde Lane, Aldeburgh, Suffolk IP15 5DZ. *Clubs:* Travellers; Aldeburgh Golf.

FRANKS, Cecil Simon; solicitor; company director; Chairman, Pryde Investments Lt residential property, since 1960; *b* 1 July 1935; *m* (marr. diss. 1978); one *s.* *Edu* Manchester Grammar Sch.; Manchester Univ. (LLB). Admitted solicitor, 1958. Membe Salford City Council, 1960–74 (Leader, Cons. Gp); Manchester City Council, 1975–8 (Leader, Cons. Gp). Mem., North West RHA, 1973–75. MP (C) Barrow and Furnes 1983–92; contested (C) Barrow and Furness, 1992. Indep. Mem., Parole Bd, 1994–9 *Recreations:* theatre, literature. *Address:* Oak Cottage, 3 Church Brow, Bowdon, Cheshir WA14 2SF. *T:* (0161) 928 7561.

FRANKS, His Honour Desmond Gerald Fergus; a Circuit Judge, 1972–93; *b* 24 Ja 1928; *s* of F. Franks, MC, late Lancs Fus., and E. R. Franks; *m* 1952, Margaret Leigh (*n* Daniel); one *d.* *Educ:* Cathedral Choir Sch., Canterbury; Manchester Grammar Sch University Coll., London (LLB). Called to Bar, Middle Temple, 1952; Northern Circui Asst Recorder, Salford, 1966; Deputy Recorder, Salford, 1971; a Recorder of the Crow Court, 1972. Pres., SW Pennine Br., Magistrates' Assoc., 1977–93. Chm., Selcare (G Manchester) Trust, 1978–84. *Recreations:* gardening, music, photography.

FRANKS, Sir Dick; *see* Franks, Sir A. T.

FRANKS, Jeremy Christopher Reynell; Deputy Chairman, DAKS Simpson Group pl 2002–04; *b* 26 April 1937; *s* of late Geoffrey Charles Reynell Franks and Molly (*n* McCulloch); *m* 1959, Elizabeth Brown; one *d.* *Educ:* Lancing Coll. 2nd Lt, 1st King Dragoon Guards, 1956–57, Aide de Camp to British High Comr for Fedn of Malay Man. Dir, Simpson (Piccadilly) Ltd, 1985–86; Dir, DAKS Simpson Gp plc, 1986–8

Man. Dir, DAKS Simpson Ltd, 1987–91; Gp Man. Dir, 1991–92, Chief Exec. and Man. Dir, 1992–2002, DAKS Simpson Gp plc; Dir, Sankyo Seiko Co. Ltd, Japan, 1992–2002. Chm., British Menswear Guild, 1989–91 and 1993–95. Chm., Walpole Cttee, 1994–2000. Dir, Pony Club (GB), 2008–. *Recreations:* Rugby, cricket, antiques, theatre. *Club:* Mark's.

FRANKS, Simon; Founder and Chairman, Redbus (media group), since 1998; Chairman, Lions Gate UK, since 2005; *b* 23 Aug. 1971; *s* of David and Brenda Franks. *Educ:* UMIST (BSc Hons). Executive: J. P. Morgan, 1992–95; BNP Paribas, 1995–97; Co-Founder and Chief Exec., Redbus Film Distribution, 1998–2005. *Recreations:* politics, film. *Address:* Redbus Group, 74A Charlotte Street, W1T 4QJ; *e-mail:* sfassist@redbus.com.

FRANSMAN, Laurens François, (Laurie); QC 2000; *b* 4 July 1956; *s* of Henri Albert, (Harry), Fransman and Hannah Lena, (Helen), Fransman (*née* Bernstein); *m* 1st, 1977, Claire Frances Goodman (marr. diss. 1985); one *s*; 2nd, 1994, Helena Mary Cook; two *s*. *Educ:* King David High Sch., Johannesburg; Jerusalem Univ.; Leeds Univ. (LLB 1978). Called to the Bar, Middle Temple, 1979; in practice at the Bar, 1979–. Co-Founder, 1983 and Mem. Exec. Cttee, Immigration Law Practitioners' Assoc.; Member: Bar European Gp; Justice; Liberty. Member, Editorial Board: Immigration and Nationality Law and Practice, 1987–; Immigration and Internat. Employment Law, 1999–2001. *Publications:* British Nationality Law and the 1981 Act, 1982; (jtly) Tribunals Practice and Procedure, 1985; (UK contrib. Ed.) Immigration Law and Practice Reporter, 1985; (jtly) Immigration Emergency Procedures, 1986; Fransman's British Nationality Law, 1989, 2nd edn 1998; (contrib.) The Constitution of the United Kingdom, 1991; Halsbury's Laws of England, 4th edn, cons., Nationality sect., 1991, Ed., and principal contrib., British Nationality, Immigration and Asylum, 2002; (contrib.) Strangers and Citizens, 1994; (contrib.) Citizenship and Nationality Status in the New Europe, 1998; (ed jtly and contrib.) Immigration, Nationality and Asylum under the Human Rights Act 1998, 1999; (contrib.) Immigration Law and Practice, 2001; (contrib.) Immigration Law and Practice in the United Kingdom, 6th edn 2005; (contrib.) Max Planck Encyclopedia of Public International Law, 2008; numerous articles on law practice, procedure and policy. *Recreations:* family, guitar, ski-ing, theatre, travel. *Address:* Garden Court Chambers, 57–60 Lincoln's Inn Fields, WC2A 3LS. *T:* (020) 7993 7600.

FRANZ, Kevin Gerhard; General Secretary, Quaker Peace and Social Witness, since 2007; *b* 16 June 1953; *m* 1976, Veda Fairley; one *s* one *d*. *Educ:* Univ. of Edinburgh (MA 1974; BD 1979; PhD 1992); Edinburgh Theol Coll. Ordained deacon, 1979, priest 1980; Curate, St Martin, Edinburgh, 1979–83; Rector, St John's, Selkirk, 1983–90; Provost, St Ninian's Cathedral, Perth, 1990–99, Canon, 2000–05; Gen. Sec., Action of Churches Together in Scotland, 1999–2007. Chm., Scottish Religious Adv. Cttee, BBC, 2002–05. Chm., Perth and Kinross Assoc. of Voluntary Services, 1995–2001. *Address:* Friends House, 173 Euston Road, NW1 2BJ. *T:* (020) 7663 1069; *e-mail:* kevinf@quaker.org.uk.

FRASER, family name of **Barons Fraser of Carmyllie** and **Lovat, Lady Saltoun** and **Baron Strathalmond**.

FRASER OF CARMYLLIE, Baron *cr* 1989 (Life Peer), of Carmyllie in the District of Angus; **Peter Lovat Fraser;** PC 1989; *b* 29 May 1945; *s* of Rev. George Robson Fraser and Helen Jean Meiklejohn or Fraser; *m* 1969, Fiona Macdonald Mair; one *s* two *d*. *Educ:* St Andrews Prep. Sch., Grahamstown, S Africa; Loretto Sch., Musselburgh; Gonville and Caius Coll., Cambridge (BA Hons; LLM Hons); Edinburgh Univ. Called to Scottish Bar, 1969; QC (Scot.) 1982. Lectr in Constitutional Law, Heriot-Watt Univ., 1972–74; Standing Jun. Counsel in Scotland to FCO, 1979. Director: Total Exploration and Production (UK), 1997–; Carnoustie Golf Course Hotel, 1998–2006; Alkane Energy, 2001–; Chairman: JKX Oil and Gas plc, 1997–; Ram Energy, 2002–. Director: ICE Futures (formerly Internat. Petroleum Exchange), 1997– (Chm., 1999); London Metal Exchange, 1997–. Contested (C): N Aberdeen, Oct. 1974; Angus E, 1987; MP (C): S Angus, 1979–83; Angus E, 1983–87. PPS to Sec. of State for Scotland, 1981–82; Solicitor Gen. for Scotland, 1982–89; Lord Advocate, 1989–92; Minister of State: Scottish Office, 1992–95; DTI, 1995–97 (Minister for Energy, 1996–97); Dep. Leader of the Opposition, H of L, 1997–98. Chm., Scottish Conservative Lawyers Law Reform Group, 1976. Chm., Statutory Cttee, RPSGB, 2000–07. Hon. Vis. Prof. of Law, Dundee Univ., 1986. Hon. Bencher, Lincoln's Inn, 1989. Hon. President: Attend (formerly Nat. Assoc. of Leagues of Hosp. Friends, then Nat. Assoc. of Hosp. and Community Friends), 1983–; CIArb, 2003–06. Patron, Queen Margaret UC, 1999–. *Recreations:* ski-ing, golf. *Address:* Slade House, Carmyllie, by Arbroath, Angus DD11 2RE. *T:* (01241) 860215. *Clubs:* Pratt's; New (Edinburgh); Hon. Co. of Edinburgh Golfers (Muirfield).

FRASER, Sir Alasdair (MacLeod), Kt 2001; CB 1992; QC 1989; Director of Public Prosecutions for Northern Ireland, since 1989; *b* 29 Sept. 1946; *s* of late Rev. Dr Donald Fraser and Ellen Hart McAllister; *m* 1975, Margaret Mary Glancy; two *s* one *d*. *Educ:* Sullivan Upper School, Holywood; Trinity College Dublin (BA (Mod.); LLB); Queen's Univ., Belfast (Dip. Laws). Called to the Bar of Northern Ireland, 1970, Bencher, 1999. Director of Public Prosecutions for Northern Ireland: Court Prosecutor, 1973; Asst Dir, 1974; Senior Asst Dir, 1982; Dep. Dir, 1988. *Address:* Belfast Chambers, 93 Chichester Street, Belfast BT1 3JR. *T:* (028) 9089 7181.

FRASER, Alex; *see* Fraser, J. A.

FRASER, (Alexander) Malcolm; Founder, 1993, and Director, since 2006, Malcolm Fraser Architects; *b* 21 July 1959; *s* of William Fraser and Margaret (*née* Watters); *m* 1998, Helen Lucas; one *s* two *d*. *Educ:* George Watson's Coll., Edinburgh; Edinburgh Univ. (MA Hons; DipArch 1985). ARB. Vis. Prof., UWE, 2003–. Dep. Chm., Architecture+Design Scotland, 2005–07. Principal buildings completed: Scottish Poetry Liby, Edinburgh, 1999; Dance Base, Edinburgh, 2001; Dance City, Newcastle, 2005; Scottish Storytelling Centre, Edinburgh, 2006; HBOS HQ, Edinburgh, 2006. *Address:* Malcolm Fraser Architects, North Bridge Studios, 28 North Bridge, Edinburgh EH1 1QG. *T:* (0131) 225 2585, *Fax:* (0131) 226 1895; *e-mail:* malcolm.fraser@malcolmfraser.co.uk.

FRASER, Andrew John, CMG 2001; Senior Adviser, Mitsubishi Corporation, since 2000; *b* 23 Oct. 1950; *s* of John and Mary Fraser; *m* 1st, 1976, Julia Savell (marr. diss. 1987); two *d*; 2nd, 1996, Jane Howard. *Educ:* Univ. of Sussex (BA); ESU Schol., Harvard Sch.; exchange schol., UCLA. Account Dir, Young and Rubicam, London, 1972–76; Man. Dir, McCann Erickson, Thailand, 1976–80; Exec. Vice Pres., Dir of Business Develt, Saatchi and Saatchi Worldwide, 1981–92; Man. Dir, cdp Europe (Dentsu Worldwide), 1992–94; Chief Exec., Invest in Britain Bureau, later INVEST.UK, 1994–2000. Dir, UK-Japan 21st Century Gp, 1998–2004; non-exec. Dir, English Partnerships, 1999–2000; Mem., Internat. Adv. Bd, Financial Dynamics, 2003–. Dir, Think London (formerly London First Centre), 2002–. Advr, Arup Gp, 2001–05. Pres., Worldaware, 2002–05; Member: Develt Council, 2001–06, Trust Bd, 2006–, Shakespeare's Globe; Council, Chatham House (RIIA), 2006–; Council, Japan Soc., 2006– (Chm., Business Gp, 2006–). *Recreations:* sports, theatre, food and drink, conversation. *Clubs:* Royal Automobile, MCC; V&A Cricket; Woking Golf.

FRASER, Dr Andrew Kerr, FRCPE, FRCPGlas, FFPH; Director of Health and Care, Scottish Prison Service, since 2006; *b* 10 Dec. 1958; *s* of Sir William (Kerr) Fraser, *qv* and of Lady Marion Fraser, *qv*; *m* 1985, Geraldine Mary Martin (separated); three *s* one *d*. *Educ:* George Watson's Coll.; Univ. of Aberdeen (MB ChB 1981); Univ. of Glasgow (MPH 1990). FRCPE 1998; FFPH (FFPHM 1999); FRCPGlas 2001. Med. Dir, Nat. Services Div., CSA, 1993–94; Dir of Public Health, Highland Health Bd, 1994–97; Dep. CMO, Scottish Office, subseq. Scottish Exec., 1997–2003; Head of Health, Scottish Prison Service, 2003–06. *Recreations:* music, mountain walking. *Address:* Scottish Prison Service, Calton House, 5 Redheughs Rigg, Edinburgh EH12 9HW. *T:* (0131) 244 6998.

FRASER, Angus Robert Charles, MBE 1999; Cricket Correspondent, Independent, since 2002; *b* 8 Aug. 1965; *s* of Donald and Irene Fraser; *m* 1996, Denise Simmonds; one *s* one *d*. *Educ:* Gayton High Sch.; Orange Hill Sen. High Sch. Played for Middlesex CCC, 1984–2002 (Captain, 2000–02); England Test Cricketer, 1989–99: 46 Test matches (took 177 Test wickets); 42 One-day Internationals. Sponsorship consultant, Whittingdale, 1991–93 (whilst injured). *Publication:* Fraser's Tour Diaries, 1998. *Recreations:* golf, wine, Liverpool FC, watching children play sport. *Address:* Independent News Media, 191 Marsh Wall, E14 9RS. *Clubs:* MCC, Stanmore Cricket, Middlesex County Cricket.

FRASER, Angus Simon James; Chairman, Alpha Plus (formerly DLD) Holdings Ltd, 2002–07; *b* 28 Feb. 1945; *s* of Baron Fraser of Kilmorack, CBE and Elizabeth Chloë Fraser (*neé* Drummond); *m* 1970, Jennifer Ann, *d* of Colin McKean Craig, FRCS and Irene Joan Craig (*née* Yeldham); two *s* one *d*. *Educ:* Fettes Coll., Edinburgh; Selwyn Coll., Cambridge (MA); European Inst. of Business Admin (INSEAD), France (MBA); Dip. Finance Houses Assoc. Dunlop Co. Ltd, 1968–70; Mercantile Credit Co. Ltd, 1971–76; Chloride Group PLC, 1976–2006: Chm., Chloride Europe, 1983–85; Main Bd Mem., 1984; Exec. Dir, Industrial Operations, 1985–87, Corporate Operations, 1987–88; non-exec. Dir, 1988–2006; Man. Dir, Imperial Coll. of Sci., Technol. and Medicine, 1989–94 (Gov., 1990–94); Chief Exec., Scruttons plc, 1995–97; Chm., Benitec Ltd, 1998–2002. Non-executive Director: Davies, Laing and Dick Ltd, 1998–2002 (Chm., 2000–02); Technology Enterprise Kent, 1998–2005; Singapore Para Rubber Estates plc, 1999–2001; Bertam Hldgs plc, 2001–05 (Dep. Chm., 2001–05); Shepherd Bldg Gp Ltd, 2002–07; Caldecott Foundn Ltd, 2004– (Dep. Chm., 2006–); IdaTech plc, 2007–. *Recreations:* opera, golf, fly-fishing, painting, walking. *Address:* Applecote, Pilgrims Way, Boughton Aluph, Ashford, Kent TN25 4EX.

FRASER, Air Cdre Anthony Walkinshaw; company director; *b* 15 March 1934; *s* of late Robert Walkinshaw Fraser and Evelyn Elisabeth Fraser; *m* 1st, 1955, Angela Mary Graham Shaw (marr. diss. 1990); one *s* three *d*; 2nd, 1990, Grania Ruth Eleanor Stewart-Smith. *Educ:* Stowe Sch. MIL. RAF Pilot and Flying Instructor, 1952–66; sc Camberley, 1967; MA/VCDS, MoD, 1968–70; Chief Instructor Buccaneer OCU, 1971–72; Air Warfare Course, 1973; Directing Staff, National Defence Coll., 1973; Dep. Dir, Operational Requirements, MoD, 1974–76; Comdt, Central Flying Sch., 1977–79. ADC to the Queen, 1977–79. Dir, SMMT, 1980–88. Chairman: Personal Guard, 1992–94; Chlorella Products Ltd (formerly Nature's Balance Marketing), 1994–; Enhanced Office Environments Ltd, 2001–07; Dir, Nissan UK Ltd, 1989–91. President: Comité de Liaison de la Construction Automobile, 1980–83; Organisation (formerly Bureau Perm.) Internat. des Constructeurs d'Automobiles, 1983–87 (Vice-Pres., 1981–83). FCMI. *Recreations:* shooting, golf, fishing, languages. *Address:* 31 Grove End Road, NW8 9LY. *T:* (020) 7286 0521. *Clubs:* Royal Air Force, Sunningdale.

FRASER, Lady Antonia, (Lady Antonia Pinter), CBE 1999; FRSL; writer; *b* 27 Aug. 1932; *d* of 7th Earl of Longford, KG, PC, and late Elizabeth, Countess of Longford, CBE; *m* 1st, 1956, Rt Hon. Sir Hugh Charles Patrick Joseph Fraser, MBE, MP (marr. diss. 1977, he *d* 1984); three *s* three *d*; 2nd, 1980, Harold Pinter, *qv*. *Educ:* Dragon School, Oxford; St Mary's Convent, Ascot; Lady Margaret Hall, Oxford (MA; Hon. Fellow, 2007). General Editor, Kings and Queens of England series. Mem., Arts Council, 1970–72; Chairman: Soc. of Authors, 1974–75; Crimewriters' Assoc., 1985–86; Vice Pres., English PEN, 1990– (Mem. Cttee, 1979–88; Pres., 1988–89; Chm., Writers in Prison Cttee, 1985–88, 1990). Goodman Lecture, 1997. FRSL 2003; Centenary Fellow, Histl Assoc., 2006. Norton Medlicott Medal, Histl Assoc., 2000. Hon. DLitt: Hull, 1986; Sussex, 1990; Nottingham, 1993; St Andrews, 1994. *Publications:* (as Antonia Pakenham): King Arthur and the Knights of the Round Table, 1954 (reissued, 1970); Robin Hood, 1955 (reissued, 1971); (as Antonia Fraser): Dolls, 1963; A History of Toys, 1966; Mary Queen of Scots (James Tait Black Memorial Prize, 1969), 1969 (reissued illus. edn, 1978); Cromwell Our Chief of Men, (in USA, Cromwell the Lord Protector), 1973; King James: VI of Scotland, I of England, 1974; (ed) Kings and Queens of England, 1975 (reissued, 1988); (ed) Scottish Love Poems, a personal anthology, 1975 (reissued, 1988), new edn 2002; (ed) Love Letters: an anthology, 1976, rev. edn 2002; Quiet as a Nun (mystery), 1977, adapted for TV series, 1978; The Wild Island (mystery), 1978 (reissued as Tartan Tragedy, 2005); King Charles II, (in USA, Royal Charles), 1979; (ed) Heroes and Heroines, 1980; A Splash of Red (mystery), 1981 (basis for TV series Jemima Shore Investigates, 1983); (ed) Mary Queen of Scots: poetry anthology, 1981; (ed) Oxford and Oxfordshire in Verse: anthology, 1982; Cool Repentance (mystery), 1982; The Weaker Vessel: woman's lot in seventeenth century England, 1984 (Wolfson History Award, 1984; Prix Caumont-La Force, 1985); Oxford Blood (mystery), 1985; Jemima Shore's First Case (mystery short stories), 1986; Your Royal Hostage (mystery), 1987; Boadicea's Chariot: the Warrior Queens, 1988 (paperback, The Warrior Queens, 1989, in USA The Warrior Queens, 1989); The Cavalier Case (mystery), 1990; Jemima Shore at the Sunny Grave (mystery short stories), 1991; The Six Wives of Henry VIII, 1992, reissued illus. edn, 1996 (Schloss Bauverein Preis, 1997; USA, as The Wives of Henry VIII); (ed) The Pleasure of Reading, 1992; Political Death (mystery), 1994; The Gunpowder Plot: terror and faith in 1605, 1996 (CWA Non Fiction Gold Dagger, 1996) (in USA, Treason and Faith: the story of the gunpowder plot; St Louis Literary Award, 1996); Marie Antoinette: the Journey, 2001 (Enid McLeod Lit. Award, Franco-British Soc., 2002); First Jemima Shore Anthology (Quiet as a Nun, Tartan Tragedy, A Splash of Red), 2005; Second Jemima Shore Anthology (Oxford Blood, Cool Repentance, Your Royal Hostage), 2006; Love and Louis XIV: the women in the life of the Sun King, 2006; various mystery stories in anthols, incl. Have a Nice Death, 1983 (adapted for TV, 1984); TV plays: Charades, 1977; Mister Clay, Mister Clay (Time for Murder series), 1985. *Recreations:* cats, swimming, grandchildren. *Address:* c/o Curtis Brown, Haymarket House, 28–29 Haymarket, SW1Y 4SP; *web:* www.antoniafraser.com. *Clubs:* PEN; Literary Society.

See also F. Fraser.

FRASER, Sir Charles (Annand), KVCO 1989 (CVO 1985; LVO 1968); WS; non-executive Vice Chairman, United Biscuits (Holdings), 1986–95 (Director, 1978–95); Partner, W & J Burness, WS, Edinburgh, 1956–92; *b* 16 Oct. 1928; *o s* of late Very Rev. John Annand Fraser, MBE, TD; *m* 1957, Ann Scott-Kerr; four *s*. *Educ:* Hamilton Academy; Edinburgh Univ. (MA, LLB). Purse Bearer to Lord High Commissioner to

General Assembly of Church of Scotland, 1969–88. Chairman: Morgan Grenfell (Scotland), 1985–86; Adam & Co., 1989–98; Lothian & Edinburgh Enterprise Ltd, 1991–94; NSM, 1992–94; Director: Scottish Widows' Fund, 1978–94; British Assets Trust, 1969–; Scottish Media Group plc (formerly Scottish Television Ltd), 1979–98, and other companies. Chm., Sec. of State for Scotland's Adv. Cttee on Sustainable Develt, 1995–98. Trustee, WWF (UK), 1998–2000. Mem. Council, Law Society of Scotland, 1966–72; Governor of Fettes, 1976–86; Mem. Court, Heriot-Watt Univ., 1972–78. WS 1959; DL East Lothian, 1984–2003. Dr *hc* Edinburgh, 1991; Hon. LLD Napier, 1992. *Recreations:* gardening, ski-ing, piping. *Address:* Shepherd House, Inveresk, Midlothian EH21 7TH. *T:* (0131) 665 2570. *Clubs:* New, Hon. Co. of Edinburgh Golfers (Edinburgh); Royal and Ancient (St Andrews).

FRASER, Christopher James; MP (C) Norfolk South West, since 2005. Chm., Internat. Communications Gp. Mem., Three Rivers DC, 1992–96. MP (C) Mid Dorset and N Poole, 1997–2001. PPS to Leader of the Opposition, H of L, 1999–2001. Member: Culture, Media and Sports Select Cttee, 1997–2001; NI Select Cttee, 2005–; Vice Chm., All-Party Forestry Gp, 1997–2001; Mem., Parly Inf. and Technol. Cttee, 1997–2001; Chm., Parly Mgt Consultancy Gp, 2000–01; Vice Chm., Cons. Trade and Industry Cttee, 2000–01. Member: IPU, 1997–; CPA, 1997–; Council of Europe, 2005–07; WEU, 2005–07. Director: Small Business Bureau, 1997–2005; Genesis Foundn. Patron, Firmlink, 1995–2001. Appeals Chm., Pramacare, 1996–2007; Mem., County Cttee, Holton Lee Charity Appeal, 1997–2001. Mem., Soc. of Dorset Men, 1997–2001. Freeman, City of London, 1992. *Address:* House of Commons, SW1A 0AA.

FRASER, Gen. Sir David (William), GCB 1980 (KCB 1973); OBE 1962; retired; Vice Lord-Lieutenant of Hampshire, 1988–96; *b* 30 Dec. 1920; *s* of Brig. Hon. William Fraser, DSO, MC, *y s* of 18th Lord Saltoun and Pamela, *d* of Cyril Maude and *widow* of Major W. La T. Congreve, VC, DSO, MC; *m* 1st, 1947, Anne Balfour; one *d*; 2nd, 1957, Julia de la Hey; two *s* two *d*. *Educ:* Eton; Christ Church, Oxford. Commnd into Grenadier Guards, 1941; served NW Europe; comd 1st Bn Grenadier Guards, 1960–62; comd 19th Inf. Bde, 1963–65; Dir, Defence Policy, MoD, 1966–69; GOC 4 Div., 1969–71; Asst Chief of Defence Staff (Policy), MoD, 1971–73; Vice-Chief of the General Staff, 1973–75; UK Mil. Rep. to NATO, 1975–77; Commandant, RCDS, 1978–80; ADC General to the Queen, 1977–80. Col, The Royal Hampshire Regt, 1981–87. DL Hants, 1982. Hon. DLitt Reading, 1992. *Publications:* Alanbrooke, 1982; And We Shall Shock Them, 1983; The Christian Watt Papers, 1983; August 1988, 1983; A Kiss for the Enemy, 1985; The Killing Times, 1986; The Dragon's Teeth, 1987; The Seizure, 1988; A Candle for Judas, 1989; In Good Company, 1990; Adam Hardrow, 1990; Codename Mercury, 1991; Adam in the Breach, 1993; The Pain of Winning, 1993; Knight's Cross: a life of Field Marshal Erwin Rommel, 1993; Will: a portrait of William Douglas Home, 1995; Frederick the Great, 2000; Wars and Shadows, 2002. *Address:* Vallenders, Isington, Alton, Hants GU34 4PP. *T:* (01420) 23166. *Clubs:* Turf, Pratt's.

FRASER, Prof. Derek, FRHistS; Vice-Chancellor, University of Teesside, 1992–2003; Chairman, Standards Verification UK, since 2005; Independent Football Ombudsman, since 2008 (Chairman, Independent Football Commission, 2001–08); *b* 24 July 1940; *s* of Jacob and Dorothy Fraser; *m* 1962, Ruth Spector; two *s* one *d*. *Educ:* Univ. of Leeds (BA, MA, PhD). Schoolteacher, 1962–65; Lectr, Sen. Lectr, Reader and Prof. of Modern History, Univ. of Bradford, 1965–82; Prof. of English History, UCLA, 1982–84; HMI (History and Higher Educn), 1984–88; Staff Inspector (Higher Educn), DES, 1988–90; Asst/Dep. Principal, Sheffield City Polytechnic, 1990–92. Chm., Univ. Vocational Awards Council, 1999–2001; Member: NACETT, 1999–2001; One NorthEast RDA, 1999–2001; Educn Cttee, RICS, 2006–. Hon. LLD Teesside, 2003. *Publications:* The Evolution of the British Welfare State, 1973, 4th edn 2009; Urban Politics in Victorian England, 1976; Power and Authority in the Victorian City, 1979; (ed) A History of Modern Leeds, 1980; (ed jtly) The Pursuit of Urban History, 1980; (ed) Municipal Reform and the Industrial City, 1982; (ed) Cities, Class and Communication: essays in honour of Asa Briggs, 1990; The Welfare State, 2000. *Recreations:* cruising, bridge, music, football and other spectator sports. *Address:* Office of the Independent Football Ombudsman, Suite 49, 57 Great George Street, Leeds LS1 3AJ.

FRASER, Donald Hamilton, RA 1985 (ARA 1975); artist; Member, Royal Fine Art Commission, 1986–99; *b* 30 July 1929; *s* of Donald Fraser and Dorothy Christiana (*née* Lang); *m* 1954, Judith Wentworth-Sheilds; one *d*. *Educ:* Maidenhead Grammar Sch.; St Martin's Sch. of Art, London; Paris (French Govt Scholarship). Tutor, Royal Coll. of Art, 1958–83, Fellow 1970, Hon. FRCA 1984. Has held 70 one-man exhibitions in Britain, Europe, N America and Japan. Work in public collections includes: Museum of Fine Arts, Boston; Albright-Knox Gall., Buffalo; Carnegie Inst., Pittsburgh; City Art Museum, St Louis; Wadsworth Athenaeum, Hartford, Conn; Hirshhorn Museum, Washington, DC; Yale Univ. Art Museum; Palm Springs Desert Museum; Nat. Gall. of Canada, Ottawa; Nat. Gall. of Vic, Melbourne; many corporate collections and British provincial galleries; Arts Council, DoE, etc. Designed Commonwealth Day issue of postage stamps, 1983. Vice-Pres. Artists Gen. Benevolent Inst., 1981– (Chm., 1981–87); Vice-Pres., Royal Over-Seas League, 1986–. Trustee: British Instn Fund, 1982–93; Royal Acad., 1993–99 (Hon. Curator, 1992–99). *Publications:* Gauguin's 'Vision after the Sermon', 1969; Dancers, 1989. *Address:* Bramham Cottage, Remenham Lane, Henley-on-Thames, Oxon RG9 2LR. *T:* (01491) 574253. *Club:* Leander (Henley).

FRASER, Dame Dorothy (Rita), DBE 1987; QSO 1978; JP; Australasian Chairman, Community Systems Foundation Australasia, 1991–94 (New Zealand Director, 1975–91); *b* 3 May 1926; *d* of Ernest and Kate Tucker; *m* 1947, Hon. William Alex Fraser; one *s* one *d*. *Educ:* Gisborne High Sch. Chm., Otago Hosp. Bd, 1974–86 (Mem., 1953–56, 1962–86); Member: Nursing Council of NZ, 1981–87; Grading Review Cttee (Health Service Personnel Commn), 1984–87; Hosps Adv. Council, 1984–86; NZ Health Service Personnel Commn, 1987–88; Otago Plunket-Karitane Hosp. Bd, 1979–87; NZ Lottery Bd, 1985–90; Vice-Pres., NZ Hosp. Bds Assoc., 1981–86; Chairman: Southern Region Health Services Assoc., 1984–86; Hosp. and Specialist Services Cttee, NZ Bd of Health, 1985–88. Consultant, ADT Ltd Australasia, later Command Pacific Group, 1988–91. Chm., Otago Jt Tertiary Educn Liaison Cttee, 1988–99; Panel Chm., NZ Colls of Educn Accreditation Cttee, 1996–2004; Member: Council, Univ. of Otago, 1974–86; Otago High Schs Bd of Governors, 1964–85. Chm., Dunedin Airport Cttee, 1971–74; Member: Dunedin CC, 1970–74; NZ Exec. Marr. Guidance, 1969–75. Chairman: Montecillo Trust, 2001–08; Montecillo Veterans' Home and Hospital Ltd, 2001–08. Life Mem., NZ Labour Party; Gold Badge for Service to Labour Party. JP 1959. Hon. LLD Otago, 1994. Silver Jubilee Medal, 1977. *Recreations:* gardening, golf, reading. *Address:* 21 Ings Avenue, St Clair, Dunedin, New Zealand. *T:* (3) 4558663.

FRASER, Edward; *see* Fraser, J. E.

FRASER, Flora, (Mrs P. R. Soros); writer; *b* 30 Oct. 1958; *d* of Rt Hon. Sir Hugh Charles Patrick Joseph Fraser, MBE, MP, and of Lady Antonia Fraser, *qv*; *m* 1st, 1980, Robert James Powell-Jones (marr. diss. 1989); one *d*; 2nd, 1997, Peter Ross Soros; two *s*. *Educ:* St Paul's Girls' Sch.; British Inst., Florence; Wadham Coll., Oxford (BA Lit. Hum.). Mem., Exec. Cttee, Friends of Nat. Libraries, 1999–2003. Trustee, NPG, 1999–. Co Founder: Elizabeth Longford Prize for Historical Biog., 2003; Elizabeth Longford Gran for Historical Biographers, 2003. *Publications:* Tamgar, 1981; Double Portrait, 198 Maud: the diaries of Maud Berkeley, 1985; Beloved Emma: the life of Emma, Lad Hamilton, 1986; The English Gentlewoman, 1987; The Unruly Queen: the life of Quee Caroline, 1996; Princesses: the six daughters of George III, 2004. *Recreation:* family *Address:* 15 Kensington Park Gardens, W11 3HD.

FRASER, Rev. Dr Giles Anthony; Team Rector, Parish of Putney, since 200 columnist, Church Times, since 2003; *b* 27 Nov. 1964; *s* of Wing Comdr Anthony Fras and Gillian Fraser; *m* 1993, Sally Aagaard; one *s* two *d*. *Educ:* Uppingham Sch.; Univ. c Newcastle-upon-Tyne (BA Hons Philosophy 1984); Ripon Coll., Cuddesdon (BA Hor Theol. (Oxon) 1992; MA (Oxon) 1997); Univ. of Lancaster (PhD 1999). Ordaine deacon, 1993, priest, 1994; Curate, All Saints, Streetly, 1993–97; Chaplain, Univ. Churc of St Mary the Virgin, Oxford, 1997–2000; Wadham College, Oxford: Chaplai 1997–2000; Lectr in Philosophy, 2000–07. Mem., Gen. Synod, C of E, 2003–. Founde 2003–, Pres., 2005–, Inclusive Church. Regular contrib. to Radio 4's Thought for th Day, Guardian. *Publications:* Christianity and Violence, 2001; Redeeming Nietzsch 2002; Christianity with Attitude, 2007. *Recreations:* golf, food, politics. *Address:* 45 S John's Avenue, Putney, SW15 6AL. *T:* (020) 8788 4575; *e-mail:* giles.fraser@ btinternet.com.

FRASER, Helen Jean Sutherland; Managing Director, Penguin, since 2001; *b* 8 Jun 1949; *d* of George Sutherland Fraser and Paddy Fraser; *m* 1982, Grant McIntyre; two *a* and two step *d*. *Educ:* St Anne's Coll., Oxford (BA Eng. Lang. and Lit. 1970, MA). Edito Methuen Academic, 1972–74; Open Books, 1974–77; Editor, then Editl Dir, Willian Collins, 1977–87; Publisher, then Man. Dir, Reed Trade Books, 1987–97; Man. Di Penguin General, 1997–2001. *Recreations:* opera, ballet, theatre, concerts. *Address* Penguin, 80 Strand, WC2R 0RL. *T:* (020) 7010 3000, *Fax:* (020) 7010 6713; *e-mai* helen.fraser@penguin.co.uk.

FRASER, Sir Iain (Michael Duncan), 3rd Bt *cr* 1943, of Tain, co. Ross; owner of Th Elephant House chain of café/bistros, Edinburgh, since 1994; *b* 27 June 1951; *er s* of Pro Sir James David Fraser, 2nd Bt and of Edith Maureen, *d* of Rev. John Reay, MC; *S* fathe 1997; *m* 1st, 1981, Sherylle Ann Gillespie (marr. diss. 1991), Wellington, NZ; one *s* on *d*; 2nd, 2004, Mrs Anne Ferguson (*née* Sim). *Educ:* Glenalmond; Edinburgh Univ. (BS Business Studies 1974). Sales manager, Edinburgh and Hong Kong, Ben Line Containe Ltd, 1974–80; internat. traffic manager, Asia, Amerex International, 1980–84; sales marketing management, Hong Kong, Singapore, New York and San Francisco, America President Lines, 1984–94. *Recreations:* photography, historical tourism, coffee. *Heir:* Benjamin James Fraser, *b* 6 April 1986.

FRASER, (James) Edward, CB 1990; Secretary of Commissions for Scotland, 1992–94 an Assistant Local Government Boundary Commissioner for Scotland, since 1997; *b* 1 Dec. 1931; *s* of late Dr James F. Fraser, TD, Aberdeen, and late Dr Kathleen Blomfield *m* 1959, Patricia Louise Stewart; two *s*. *Educ:* Aberdeen Grammar Sch.; Univ. of Aberdee (MA); Christ's Coll., Cambridge (BA). FSAScot. RA, 1953; Staff Captain 'Q', Tel-el Kebir, 1954–55. Asst Principal, Scottish Home Dept, 1957–60; Private Sec. to Permane Under Sec. of State, 1960–62, and to Parly Under-Sec. of State, 1962; Principal: SHHD 1962–64; Cabinet Office, 1964–66; HM Treasury, 1966–68; SHHD, 1968–69; Asst Sec. SHHD, 1970–76; Asst Sec., 1976, Under Sec., 1976–81, Local Govt Finance Gp, Scottis Office; Under Sec., SHHD, 1981–91. Pres., Scottish Hellenic Soc. of Edinburgh an Eastern Scotland, 1987–93. Pres., Former Pupils' Club, Aberdeen GS, 1997–98 (Hon Vice-Pres., 1998–). *Recreations:* reading, music, walking, Greece ancient and modern DIY. *Address:* 59 Murrayfield Gardens, Edinburgh EH12 6DH. *T:* (0131) 337 2274. *Club* Scottish Arts (Edinburgh).

FRASER, James Owen Arthur; a Sheriff of Grampian, Highland and Islands, 1984–2002 *b* 9 May 1937; *s* of James and Effie Fraser; *m* 1961, Flora Shaw MacKenzie; two *s*. *Edu* Glasgow High Sch. (Classical Dux 1954); Glasgow Univ. (MA 1958; LlB 1961). Qualifie as Solicitor, 1961; employed as solicitor, Edinburgh, 1961–65, Glasgow, 1965–66 Partner, Bird Son & Semple, later Bird Semple & Crawford Herron, Solicitors, Glasgow 1967–84. Part-time Lectr in Evidence and Procedure, Glasgow Univ., 1976–83. Temp Sheriff, 1983–84. *Recreation:* golf. *Address:* Ardmara, 18 Marine Terrace, Rosemarkie Ross-shire IV10 8UL. *T:* (01381) 621011.

FRASER, Hon. John Allen; PC (Can.) 1979; OC 1995; OBC 1995; CD 1962; QC (Can.) 1983; Chairman, BC Pacific Salmon Forum, Canada, since 2005; *b* Japan, 15 Dec 1931; *m* 1960, Catherine Findlay; three *d*. *Educ:* Univ. of British Columbia (LLB 1954) Law practice, Victoria, Powell River, Vancouver, 1955–72. MP (PC) Vancouver S 1972–94; Opposition Critic, Environment, 1972–74, Labour, 1974–79; Minister o Environment and Postmaster General, 1979–80; Opposition Critic, Environment Fisheries, Post Office, and Solicitor-General, 1980–84; Minister of Fisheries and Oceans 1984–85; Speaker of H of C, Canada, 1986–94; Ambassador for the Envmt, Dept o Foreign Affairs and Internat. Trade, Canada, 1994–98. Chm., Pacific Fisheries Resourc Conservation Council, 1998–2005. Chairman: Nat. Defence Minister's Monitoring Cttee on Change, 1998–2005; Parly Precinct Oversight Adv. Cttee, 2000–. Hon. LLD: S Lawrence Univ., 1999; Simon Fraser Univ., 1999; British Columbia, 2004. Hon. Lt-Col Seaforth Highlanders of Canada, 1994– (Hon. Col). *Address:* (office) L-427 Fitzwillian Street, Nanaimo, BC V9R 3A9, Canada. *T:* (205) 7553036, *Fax:* (205) 7553037.

FRASER, John Denis; *b* 30 June 1934; *s* of Archibald and Frances Fraser; *m* 1960, Ann Hathaway; two *s* one *d*. *Educ:* Sloane Grammar Sch., Chelsea; Co-operative Coll. Loughborough; Law Soc. Sch. of Law (John Mackrell Prize). Entered Australia & New Zealand Bank Ltd, 1950; Army service, 1952–54, as Sergt, RAEC (educnl and resettlement work). Solicitor, 1960; practised with Lewis Silkin. Mem. Lambeth Borough Council, 1962–68 (Chm. Town Planning Cttee; Chm. Labour Gp). MP (Lab) Norwood 1966–97. PPS to Rt Hon. Barbara Castle, 1968–70; Opposition front bench spokesmar on Home Affairs, 1972–74; Parly Under-Sec. of State, Dept of Employment, 1974–76 Minister of State, Dept of Prices and Consumer Protection, 1976–79; oppositior spokesman on trade, 1979–83, on housing and construction, 1983–87, on legal affairs 1987–94. *Recreations:* athletics, football, music. *Address:* 24 Turney Road, SE21 8LU.

FRASER, Rt Hon. (John) Malcolm, AC 1988; CH 1977; PC 1976; MA Oxon; Prime Minister of Australia, 1975–83; *b* 21 May 1930; *s* of late J. Neville Fraser; *m* 1956, Tamara *d* of S. R. Beggs; two *s* two *d*. *Educ:* Melbourne C of E Grammar Sch.; Magdalen Coll., Oxford (MA 1952; Hon. Fellow, 1982). MHR (L) for Wannon, Vic, 1955–83; Mem. Jt Party Cttee on Foreign Affairs, 1962–66; Minister: for the Army, 1966–68; for Educn and Science, 1968–69, 1971–72; for Defence, 1969–71; Leader of Parly Liberal Party, 1975–83; Leader of the Opposition, 1975. Sen. Adjunct Fellow, Center for Strategic and Internat. Studies, Georgetown Univ., Washington, 1983–86. Chairman: UN Sec. Gen's Expert Gp on African Commodity Problems, 1989–90; CARE Australia, 1987–2001; Vice-Pres., CARE Internat., 1995–99 (Pres., 1990–95). Co-Chm., Commonwealth

Eminent Persons Gp on S Africa, 1986. Member: InterAction Council for Former Heads of Govt (Chm., 1996–); ANZ Internat. Bd of Advice, 1987–93. Distinguished Internat. Fellow, Amer. Enterprise Inst. for Public Policy Res., 1984–86; Fellow, Center for Internat. Affairs, Harvard Univ., 1985. Mem. Council, Aust. Nat. Univ., 1964–66. Hon. Vice President: Oxford Soc., 1983; Royal Commonwealth Soc., 1983. Hon. LLD: Univ. of SC, 1981; UTS, 2002; Murdoch Univ., 2002; Univ. of NSW, 2003; Hon. DLitt Deakin Univ., 1989. Grand Cordon, Order of the Rising Sun, Japan, 2006. *Publication:* Common Ground: issues that bind and divide us, 2002. *Recreations:* fishing, photography, vintage cars, golf. *Address:* Level 32, 101 Collins Street, Melbourne, Vic 3000, Australia. *Club:* Melbourne.

FRASER, John Stewart; Chairman and Chief Executive, Ciba-Geigy plc, 1990–96; *b* 18 July 1931; *s* of Donald Stewart Fraser and Ruth (*née* Dobinson); *m* 1st, 1955, Diane Louise Witt (marr. diss. 1996); two *s* one *d*; 2nd, 1996, Lynette Ann Murray. *Educ:* Royal Melbourne Inst. of Technology. ARACI. Technical Rep., Australian Sales Manager and Australian Marketing Manager, Monsanto Australia Ltd, 1953–68; Marketing Manager, Ilford (Australia) Pty Ltd, 1968–73; Ilford Ltd, UK: Marketing Dir, 1973–78; Man. Dir and Chief Exec., 1978–84; Corporate Man. Dir, Ciba-Geigy Plastics and Additives Co., UK, 1982–84; Ciba-Geigy plc, UK: Gp Man. Dir, 1984–87; Gp Man. Dir and Chief Exec., 1987–90. Non-exec. Dir, Westminster Health Care, 1993–99. Chm., Assoc. for Schools' Sci., Engrg and Technol. (formerly Standing Conf. on Schools' Sci. and Technol.), 1996–2000. Pres., Chemical Industries Assoc., 1994–95. *Recreation:* golf. *Address:* 2009 The Boulevarde, The Aspects, Royal Pines Riverside, Ashmore Road, Benowa, Qld 4217, Australia.

FRASER, Julian Alexander, (Alex); Director, Logistics, HM Customs and Excise, 2000–03; *b* 23 July 1959; *s* of Peter Marshall Fraser, MC, FBA and Ruth Fraser. *Educ:* Abingdon Sch., Oxon; Manchester Univ. (BA Hons Classics 1987). Teacher, Latin and Computer Studies, Lawrence House Sch., St Annes on Sea, Lancs, 1978–84; Database Researcher, CEDIM srl, Ancona, 1987–89; Information Consultant, Atefos SpA, Turin, 1989–90; Manager, Inf. Resource Centre, Merrill Lynch Europe Ltd, 1990–93; Asst Dir and Head of Inf. Systems, Western Merchant Bank Ltd, 1993–95; J. Henry Schroder & Co. Ltd: Manager, Inf. Centre, 1995–96; Head of Ops, European Corporate Finance Div., 1996–97; Dir and Global Head, Corporate Finance Support Services, 1997–2000. *Recreations:* equine.

FRASER, Kenneth John Alexander; international marketing consultant; *b* 22 Sept. 1929; *s* of Jack Sears Fraser and Marjorie Winifred (*née* Savery); *m* 1953, Kathleen Grace Booth; two *s* one *d*. *Educ:* Thames Valley Grammar Sch., Twickenham; London School of Economics (BScEcon Hons). Joined Erwin Wasey & Co. Ltd, 1953, then Lintas Ltd, 1958; Managing Director, Research Bureau Ltd, 1962; Unilever: Head of Marketing Analysis and Evaluation Group, 1965; Head of Marketing Division, 1976–79, 1981–89; Hd of Internat. Affairs, 1985–89; Hd of External Affairs, 1989–90; seconded to NEDO as Industrial Dir, 1979–81. Advr, European Assoc. of Branded Goods Manufacturers, 1991–93. Member: Consumer Protection Adv. Cttee, Dept of Prices and Consumer Protection, 1975; Management Bd, ADAS, MAFF, 1986–92; Chairman: CBI Marketing and Consumer Affairs Cttee, 1977; Internat. Chamber of Commerce Marketing Commn, 1978; Vice Chm., Advertising Assoc., 1981–90; Dir, Direct Mail Services Standards Bd, 1991–94. Mem., Advocacy Cttee, Nat. Children's Home, 1987–95. FRSA 1980. *Recreations:* walking, music, reading. *T:* (office) (020) 8949 3760.

FRASER, Rt Hon. Malcolm; *see* Fraser, Rt Hon. J. M.

FRASER, Malcolm; *see* Fraser, A. M.

FRASER, Lady Marion Anne, LT 1996; Chair of the Board, Christian Aid, 1990–97; Lord High Commissioner, then HM High Commissioner, General Assembly, Church of Scotland, 1994–95; *b* 17 Oct. 1932; *d* of Robert Forbes and Elizabeth Taylor Watt; *m* 1956, Sir William (Kerr) Fraser, *qv*; three *s* one *d*. *Educ:* Hutchesons' Girls' Grammar Sch.; Univ. of Glasgow (MA); Royal Scottish Academy of Music. LRAM, ARCM. Chm., Scottish Internat. Piano Comp., 1995–99. Director: Friends of Royal Scottish Academy (Founder Chm., 1986–89); Scottish Opera, 1990–94; St Mary's Music School, 1989–95. Chm., Scottish Assoc. for Mental Health, 1995–99. Pres., Scotland's Churches Scheme, 1997–. Trustee: Scottish Churches Architectural Heritage Trust, 1989–; Lamp of Lothian Collegiate Trust, 1996–2005; Gov., Laurel Bank Sch. for Girls, 1988–95. Hon. Mem., Co. of Merchants of City of Edinburgh, 1998. FRCPSGlas 2002. Hon. LLD Glasgow, 1995; DUniv Stirling, 1998. *Recreations:* family, friends, people and places. *Address:* Broadwood, Edinburgh Road, Gifford, East Lothian EH41 4JE. *Club:* New (Edinburgh).
See also A. K. Fraser.

FRASER, Murdo Mackenzie; Member (C) Scotland Mid and Fife, Scottish Parliament, since Aug. 2001; Deputy Leader, Scottish Conservative and Unionist Party, since 2005; *b* 5 Sept. 1965; *s* of Sandy Fraser and Barbara Fraser (*née* MacPherson); *m* 1994, Emma Jarvis. *Educ:* Inverness Royal Acad.; Univ. of Aberdeen (LLB 1986; Dip. Legal Studies). Admitted solicitor, 1988; practised in Aberdeen and Edinburgh; Associate Partner, Ketchen and Stevens WS, Edinburgh, 1994–2001. Chairman: Scottish Young Conservatives, 1989–92; Nat. Young Conservatives, 1991–92; former Dep. Chm., Edinburgh Central Cons. Assoc. Contested (C): East Lothian, 1997; N Tayside, 2001; N Tayside, Scottish Parlt, 1999, 2003 and 2007. *Recreations:* climbing, hillwalking, travel, Scottish history, classic cars, Rangers FC. *Address:* Scottish Parliament, Edinburgh EH99 1SP. *T:* (0131) 348 5293; (office) Control Tower, Perth Airport, Scone, Perth PH2 6PL. *T:* (01738) 553990; *e-mail:* murdo.fraser.msp@scottish.parliament.uk.

FRASER, Dr Nicholas Campbell; Keeper of Natural Sciences, National Museums Scotland, since 2007; *b* Nottingham, 14 Jan. 1956; *s* of Hugh Mckenzie Fraser and Patricia Margaret Fraser; *m* 1982, Christine Mary; two *d*. *Educ:* Univ. of Aberdeen (BSc Zool. 1978; PhD Geol. 1984). Res. Fellow, Girton Coll., Cambridge, 1985–90; Curator of Vertebrate Paleontol., 1990–2007, Dir of Res. and Collections, 2004–07, Virginia Mus. of Natural Hist. Adjunct Professor of Geology: Virginia Tech, 1993–; N Carolina State Univ., 2007–. Ed., Memoirs Series, Soc. Vertebrate Paleontol. Hon. MA Cantab 1985. *Publications:* (ed with Hans-Dieter Sues) In the Shadow of the Dinosaurs, 1994; Dawn of the Dinosaurs, 2006; contrib. peer-reviewed jls. *Recreations:* soccer, hill-walking, travel. *Address:* Royal Museums Scotland, Chambers Street, Edinburgh EH1 1JF. *T:* (0131) 247 4007, *Fax:* (0131) 220 4819; *e-mail:* nick.fraser@nms.ac.uk.

FRASER, Robert William, MVO 1994; **His Honour Judge Fraser;** a Circuit Judge, since 2007; *b* Birkenhead, 23 Sept. 1955; *s* of Gordon Smith Fraser and Kathleen Mary Fraser; *m* 1990, Isobel Patricia Mary Clapham; two *d*. *Educ:* Birkenhead Sch.; Univ. of Liverpool (LLB Hons). Called to the Bar, Gray's Inn, 1984; Recorder, 2000–07. Royal Navy, 1974–2007: HMS Yarmouth, 1985–86; HMS Battleaxe, 1986–87; Equerry to the Prince of Wales, 1991–94; Briefing Officer to First Sea Lord, 1997–98; Dir of Staff, NATO HQ, Naples, 2000–02; rcds, 2002; Sec. to Chiefs of Staff Cttee, 2004–05; Cdre, 2005; Dir Naval Legal Services, 2005–07. *Publication:* (contrib.) Seaford House Papers, 2002. *Recreations:* sailing, ski-ing, motor cars. *Address:* c/o Inner London Crown Court, Sessions House, Newington Causeway, SE1 6AZ.

FRASER, Simon James; HM Diplomatic Service; Director General for Europe and Globalisation, Foreign and Commonwelath Office, since 2008; *b* 3 June 1958; *s* of late James Stuart Fraser and of Joan Fraser; two *d*. *Educ:* St Paul's Sch.; Corpus Christi Coll., Cambridge (MA). Joined FCO, 1979; Second Secretary: Baghdad, 1982–84; Damascus, 1984–86; First Sec., FCO, 1986–88; Private Sec. to Minister of State, FCO, 1989–90; Policy Planning Staff, FCO, 1991–92; Asst Head, Non-Proliferation and Defence Dept, FCO, 1992–93; First Sec., Financial and Eur. Affairs, Paris, 1994–96; Dep. Chef de Cabinet of Vice-Pres. of EC, 1996–99; Pol Counsellor, Paris, 1999–2002; Dir for Strategy and Innovation, FCO, 2002–04; Dir, Middle East and N Africa, FCO, 2004; Chief of Staff to Peter Mandelson, EC, 2004–08. *Recreations:* ski-ing, football, opera, art. *Address:* c/o Foreign and Commonwealth Office, King Charles Street, SW1A 2AH.

FRASER, Simon Joseph, CBE 2003; Chairman, 1984–2003, Director, 1990–2005, Fibrowatt Ltd; *b* 13 March 1929; *s* of late Maj. Hon. Alastair Thomas Joseph Fraser and Lady Sibyl Fraser (*née* Grimston); *m* 1956, E. Jane Mackintosh; one *s* five *d*. *Educ:* Ampleforth Coll.; Magdalen Coll., Oxford (BA, MA Hist.). Man. Dir, Internat. Janitor, 1964–70; Dir, S. G. Warburg & Co. Ltd, 1970–75; Chm., Kirkhill Investment & Mgt Co. Ltd, 1975–84; Founder, Fibrowatt Ltd (gp of cos which developed UK's first 3 biomass fired power stations), 1984. *Recreations:* music, early church history, tackling environmental challenges. *Address:* 38 Clarendon Road, W11 3AD.

FRASER, Simon William Hetherington; Sheriff of North Strathclyde at Dumbarton, since 1989; *b* 2 April 1951; *s* of late George MacDonald Fraser, OBE and of Kathleen Margarette (*née* Hetherington); *m* 1979, Sheena Janet Fraser; one *d*. *Educ:* Glasgow Acad.; Glasgow Univ. (LLB). Solicitor, 1973–89 (Partner, Flowers & Co., Glasgow, 1976–89). Temp. Sheriff, 1987–89. Pres., Glasgow Bar Assoc., 1981–82. *Recreations:* watching Partick Thistle, cricket. *Address:* Sheriff Court, Church Street, Dumbarton G82 1QR. *T:* (01389) 763266. *Club:* Avizandum (Glasgow).

FRASER, Prof. Thomas Grant, MBE 2006; PhD; FRHistS; Professor of History, 1991–2006, now Professor Emeritus and Hon. Professor of Conflict Research, University of Ulster (Provost of Magee Campus, 2002–06); *b* 1 July 1944; *s* of Thomas Fraser and Annie Grant Alexander; *m* 1970, Grace Frances Armstrong; one *s* one *d*. *Educ:* Univ. of Glasgow (MA Medieval and Modern Hist. 1966; Ewing Prize); London Sch. of Economics (PhD 1974). New University of Ulster, subseq. University of Ulster: Lectr, 1969–85; Sen. Lectr, 1985–91; Hd, Dept of Hist., 1988–94; Hd, Sch. of Hist., Philosophy and Politics, 1994–98. Fulbright Scholar-in-Residence, Indiana Univ. South Bend, 1983–84. Chm., NI Museums Council, 1998–2006; Trustee, Nat. Museums and Galls of NI, 1998–2002. Dir, Playhouse Community Arts Centre, Derry, 2002–. FRHistS 1992; FRSA 2000. *Publications:* Partition in Ireland, India and Palestine, 1984; The USA and the Middle East since World War 2, 1989; The Arab Israeli Conflict, 1995, new edn 2007 (Italian edn 2002); Ireland in Conflict 1922–1998, 2000; (with D. Murray) America and the World since 1945, 2002. *Recreations:* travel, cooking. *Address:* INCORE, Magee Campus, University of Ulster, Northland Road, Londonderry BT48 7JL. *T:* (028) 7137 5575; 45 Blackthorn Manor, Londonderry BT47 5ST. *T:* (028) 7131 2290.

FRASER, Veronica Mary; Diocesan Director of Education, Diocese of Worcester, 1985–93; *b* 19 April 1933; *o d* of late Archibald Fraser. *Educ:* Richmond County Sch. for Girls; St Hugh's Coll., Oxford. Head of English Department: The Alice Ottley Sch., Worcester, 1962–65; Guildford County Sch. for Girls, 1965–67 (also Librarian); Headmistress, Godolphin Sch., Salisbury, 1968–80; Adviser on Schools to Bishop of Winchester, 1981–85. Pres., Assoc. of Sen. Members, St Hugh's Coll., Oxford, 1994–98. Gov., SPCK, 1994–98.

FRASER, Vincent; QC 2001; a Recorder, since 2002; *b* 18 Oct. 1958; *s* of Martin and Monica Fraser; *m* 1994, Mary Elizabeth Sweeney; one *s* three *d*. *Educ:* St Mary's Coll., Crosby; University Coll., Oxford (Open Schol.; MA Juris.; Sweet & Maxwell Prize). Called to the Bar, Gray's Inn, 1981. *Publication:* Planning Decisions Digest, 1987, 2nd edn 1992. *Recreations:* literature, music, football. *Address:* Kings Chambers, 36 Young Street, Manchester M3 3FT. *T:* (0161) 832 9082, *Fax:* (0161) 835 2139; *e-mail:* vfraser@kingschambers.com.

FRASER, Prof. William Irvine, CBE 1998; MD; FRCPE, FRCPsych, FMedSci; Professor of Developmental Disability, University of Wales College of Medicine, 1989–2002, now Emeritus; *b* 3 Feb. 1940; *s* of late Duncan Fraser and Muriel (*née* Macrae); *m* 1964, Joyce Carrol; two *s*. *Educ:* Greenock Acad.; Glasgow Univ. (MBChB 1963; DPM 1967; MD (with commendation) 1969). FRCPsych 1979; FRCPE 2000. Physician Superintendent, Mental Handicap Service, Fife, 1974–78; Hon. Sen. Lectr in Psychology, Univ. of St Andrews, 1973–89; pt-time Sen. Lectr, Psychiatry, Univ. of Edinburgh, 1973–89; Consultant Psychiatrist, Royal Edinburgh Hosp., 1978–89. Ed., Jl of Intellectual Disability Research, 1982–2003. Trustee: Bailey Thomas Charitable Fund, 1999–; Autism Cymru, 2001–. Res. Medallist, Burden Inst., 1989; Fellow, Internat. Assoc. for Scientific Study of Intellectual Disability, 1997 (Dist. Achievement Award, 1996); FMedSci 2001. *Publications:* (with R. McGillivray) Care of People with Intellectual Disabilities, 1974, 9th edn, 1998; (with R. Grieve) Communicating with Normal and Retarded Children, 1981; (with M. Kerr) Seminars in Learning Disabilities, 2003. *Recreation:* sailing. *Address:* 146 Wenallt Road, Cardiff CF14 6TQ. *T:* (029) 2052 1343.

FRASER, William James; JP; Lord Provost of Aberdeen, 1977–80; Member, City of Aberdeen District Council, 1974–96; *b* 31 Dec. 1921; *s* of late William and Jessie Fraser; *m* 1961, Mary Ann; three *s* one *d*. *Educ:* York Street Sch., Aberdeen; Frederick Street Sch., Aberdeen. Mem., Scottish Exec., Labour Party, 1949–74 (Chm., 1962–63). Pres., Aberdeen Trades Council, 1952. JP Aberdeen, 1950. Hon. LLD Aberdeen, 1995. *Address:* Thorngrove House, 500 Great Western Road, Aberdeen AB10 6PF.

FRASER, Sir William (Kerr), GCB 1984 (KCB 1979; CB 1978); Chancellor, University of Glasgow, 1996–2006 (Principal and Vice-Chancellor, 1988–95); *b* 18 March 1929; *s* of A. M. Fraser and Rachel Kerr; *m* 1956, Marion Anne Forbes (*see* Lady Marion Fraser); three *s* one *d*. *Educ:* Eastwood Sch., Clarkston; Glasgow Univ. (MA, LLB). Joined Scottish Home Dept, 1955; Private Sec. to Parliamentary Under-Sec., 1959, and to Secretary of State for Scotland, 1966–67; Civil Service Fellow, Univ. of Glasgow, 1963–64; Asst Sec., Regional Development Div., 1967–71; Under Sec., Scottish Home and Health Dept, 1971–75; Dep. Sec., 1975–78, Permanent Under-Sec. of State, 1978–88, Scottish Office. Chm., Scottish Mutual Assce, 1999 (Dir, 1990–99). Chm., Royal Commn on the Ancient and Historical Monuments of Scotland, 1995–2000. Gov., Caledonian Res. Foundn, 1990–99. FRSE 1985. FRCPS (Hon.) 1992; FRSAMD 1995. Hon. LLD: Glasgow, 1982; Strathclyde, 1991; Aberdeen, 1993; Dr *hc* Edinburgh, 1995. *Address:* Broadwood, Edinburgh Road, Gifford, East Lothian EH41 4JE. *T:* (01620) 810319. *Club:* New (Edinburgh).
See also A. K. Fraser.

FRATTINI, Franco; Member, European Commission, since 2004; *b* 14 March 1957. *Educ:* La Sapienza Univ., Rome (LLB). State Attorney, 1981; Attorney, State Attorney-Gen.'s Office, 1984; Magistrate, Regl Admin. Tribunal, Piedmont, 1984–86; Council of State Judge, 1986; Legal Adviser: to Minister of Treasury, 1986–90; to Dep. Prime Minister, 1990–91; to Prime Minister, 1992; Dep. Sec.-Gen., 1993, Sec.-Gen., 1994–95, Prime Minister's Office; Minister for the Civil Service and Regl Affairs, 1995–96; MP (Forza Italia), 1996–2004; Minister for Civil Service and for Co-ordination of Intelligence and Security Services, 2001–02; Minister for Foreign Affairs, 2002–04. Mem., Rome CC, 1997–2000. *Address:* European Commission, Rue de la Loi 200, 1049 Brussels, Belgium.

FRAWLEY, Carolyn; *see* McCall, C.

FRAWLEY, Thomas Jude, CBE 2008; Assembly Ombudsman for Northern Ireland and Northern Ireland Commissioner for Complaints, since 2000; *b* Limerick, 4 Feb. 1949; *s* of Joseph and Bride Frawley; *m* 1983, Marie Mallon; two *s* one *d*. *Educ:* St Mary's Grammar Sch., Belfast; Trinity Coll., Dublin (BA). Grad. Trainee, NHS, 1971–73; Unit Administrator, Ulster Hosp., Dundonald, 1973–77; Asst Dist Administrator, Lisburn, 1977–80; Dist Administrator for Londonderry, Limavady and Strabane Dist, 1980; Chief Admin. Officer, 1980–85, Gen. Manager, 1985–2000, Western Health and Social Services Bd. Dir-Gen., Co-operation and Working Together Initiative, 1990–2000; led project to support health system in Zimbabwe, 1994. King's Fund Travel Bursary, 1983; King's Fund Internat. Fellowships, 1988 and 1992; Eisenhower Fellowship, 1989. Mem., Ministerial Adv. Bd on Health Estates, NI, 1998–2000; Chairman: Expert Panel on Review of Public Admin, 2002–; Gp on Review of Ambulance Service, NI, 1998–2000. Trustee, NHS Confedn, 1998–2000. Vice Pres., World Bd, Internat. Ombudsman Inst., 2006–. Mem., BITC, 1998–2000. Gov., Lumen Christi Coll., 1998–2000. Rep. of Ire., Alumni Adv. Council, Eisenhower Fellowship, 2004. DUniv Ulster, 2003. *Recreations:* current affairs, sport (played Rugby and Gaelic football). *Address:* Office of the Ombudsman for Northern Ireland, 33 Wellington Place, Belfast BT1 6HN.

FRAY, Prof. Derek John, FRS 2008; FREng; Professor of Materials Chemistry, Cambridge University, 1996–2007, now Emeritus (Head, Department of Materials Science and Metallurgy, 2001–05); Professorial Fellow, Fitzwilliam College, Cambridge, 1996–2007, now Life Fellow; *b* 26 Dec. 1939; *s* of Arthur Joseph Fray and Doris Lilian Fray; *m* 1965, Mirella Christine Kathleen Honey (marr. diss. 2004); one *s* one *d*. *Educ:* Emanuel Sch.; Imperial Coll., Univ. of London (BSc Eng, ARSM 1961; PhD, DIC 1965). FIMMM; FREng (FEng 1989); FRSC 2003. Asst Prof. of Metallurgy, MIT, 1965–68; Gp Leader, Imperial Smelting Corp., Bristol, 1968–71; Cambridge University: Lectr, Dept of Materials Sci. and Metallurgy, 1971–91; Fitzwilliam College: Fellow, 1972–90; Tutorial and Estates Bursar, 1974–86; Bursar, 1986–88; Investment and Estates Bursar, 1988–90; Prof. of Mineral Engrg, Univ. of Leeds, 1991–96 (Head of Dept). Hon. Professor: Beijing Univ. of Sci. and Technol., 1995–; Hubei Poly. Univ., 2006–; Vis. Prof., Univ. of Leeds, 1996–. Director: Cambridge Advanced Materials, 1989–; Ion Science, 1989–; Ion Science Messtechnik, 1994–; British Titanium plc, 1998–; EMC Ltd, 2000–; Metalysis Ltd, 2002–04; Inotec AMD Ltd, 2005–; Camfridge Ltd, 2005–. Numerous medals and awards, UK and overseas. *Publications:* (jtly) Worked Examples in Mass Heat Transfer in Materials Technology, 1983; numerous papers and patents on extractive metallurgy and allied subjects. *Recreations:* reading, cinema, sailing. *Address:* 7 Woodlands Road, Great Shelford, Cambridge CB2 5LW. *T:* (01223) 842296.

FRAYLING, Sir Christopher (John), Kt 2001; MA, PhD; Professor of Cultural History, 1979–summer 2009, Rector and Vice-Provost, 1996–summer 2009, Royal College of Art, London; Chairman, Arts Council England, since 2004; *b* 25 Dec. 1946; *s* of late Arthur Frederick Frayling and Barbara Kathleen (*née* Imhof); *m* 1981, Helen Snowdon. *Educ:* Repton Sch.; Churchill Coll., Cambridge (BA, MA, PhD). FCSD 1994. Churchill Research Studentship, 1968–71; Lectr in Modern History, Univ. of Exeter, 1971–72; Tutor, Dept of General Studies, Royal College of Art, 1972–73, Vis. Lectr, 1973–79; Research Asst, Dept of Information Retrieval, Imperial War Mus., 1973–74; Lectr in the History of Ideas and European Social History, Univ. of Bath, 1974–79; Royal College of Art: founder, 1979, and Head of Dept, 1979–96, Dept of Cultural History (ex General Studies); founded courses: History of Design, 1982; Conservation, 1987; Visual Arts Admin, subseq. Curating Contemporary Art, 1991; Pro-Rector, 1993–96. Vis. Prof., Shanghai Univ. of Technol., 1991. Historian, lectr, critic; regular contributor, as writer and presenter, to radio (incl. Kaleidoscope, Stop the Week, Meridian, Critics' Forum, Third Opinion, Third Ear, Nightwaves, Front Row, Back Row, The Film Programme; series: The American Cowboy; America: the movie (Silver Medal, NY Internat. Radio Fest., 1989); Britannia: the film; Print the Legend; Cinema Cities) and TV (incl. series Scene, Art of Persuasion (Gold Medal, NY Internat. Film and TV Fest., 1985), Busting the Block—or the Art of Pleasing People, Design Classics, Design Awards, Timewatch, Movie Profiles, The Face of Tutankhamun, Strange Landscape, and Nightmare: the birth of horror). Curator of exhibitions: Once Upon a Time in Italy, Autry Nat. Center, LA, 2005 (Humanities Prize for scholarship); (co-curator) Gothic Nightmares—Fuseli, Blake and the Romantic Imagination, Tate Britain, 2006. Chm., Design Council, 2000–04; Mem., Crafts Council, 1982–85. Arts Council of England (formerly of GB): Mem., 1987–2000; Mem., Art Panel, 1983–94 (Dep. Chm., 1984–87; Chm., 1987–94); Chm., Film, Video and Broadcasting Panel, 1994–97; Chm., Educn and Trng Panel, 1996–98; Chm., Combined Arts Cttee, 1989–95; Chm., New Collaborations Cttee, 1990–94. Chairman: Curriculum Develt Bd, Arts Technol. Centre, 1989–94; Design Sub-Gp, Liturgical Publishing Commn, 1999–2000; Royal Mint Adv. Cttee, 2000–. Chm. of Trustees, Crafts Study Centre, Bath, 1982–2004; Foundn Trustee, Holburne of Menstrie Mus., Bath, 1985–2000; Chm., Free Form Arts Trust, 1984–88; Trustee: V&A Museum, 1984– (Member: Adv. Council, 1981–83; Sen. Staff Appts Cttee, 1987–91; S Kensington Jt Planning Cttee, 1989–95; Educn and Res. Cttees, 1990–97; Chm., Bethnal Green Mus. Cttee, 1995–99; Chm., Contemporary Projects Cttee, 1999–2002; Chm., S Kensington Cultural Gp, 1999–2004); Koestler Trustees for Art in Prisons, 1992–99; Member: Litmus Gp for Millennium Dome, 1998–2000; Bd, Design Mus., 1999–2004; AHRB, 1999–2004; Council, Catalyst, 2004–. Governor, BFI, 1982–87 (Mem., 1982–86, Chm. 1984–86, Educn Cttee); Member: Art and Design Sect., Leverhulme Team on Arts in Higher Educn, 1982; Working Party on art and design advising NAB, 1985–87. Chm., Soc. of Designer-Craftsmen, 1997–2004. Patron: Guild of Handicraft Trust, 1989–; Parnham Trust for Makers in Wood, 1989–2003. FRSA 1984 (Bicentennial Medal, 2001; Hon. Life Fellowship, 2006). Hon. FRIBA 2005; Hon. RCM 2007. Hon. DLitt NSW, 1999; DUniv Staffordshire, 2002; Hon. DArts: UWE, 2003; Bath, 2003; Hon. DHL Richmond, 2005; Hon Dr Lancaster, 2008. Sir Misha Black Medal, CSD, 2003; Maitland Medal, IStructE, 2006. Radio play, The Rime of the Bounty (Sony Radio Award, 1990). *Publications:* Napoleon Wrote Fiction, 1972; (ed) The Vampyre—Lord Ruthven to Count Dracula, 1978; Spaghetti Westerns: Cowboys and Europeans, from Karl May to Sergio Leone, 1981; The Schoolmaster and the Wheelwrights, 1983; The Royal College of Art: one hundred and fifty years of art and design, 1987; Vampyres, 1991; (ed) Beyond the Dovetail: essays on craft, skill and imagination, 1991; Clint Eastwood, 1992; The Face of Tutankhamun, 1992; (with Helen Frayling) The Art Pack, 1992; Research in Art and Design, 1994; Strange Landscape: a journey through the Middle Ages, 1995; Things to Come: a classic film, 1995; (ed jtly) Design of the Times: one hundred years of the Roya[l] College of Art, 1996; Nightmare: the birth of horror, 1996 (Hamilton Deane Award 1997); Tim Mara: the complete prints, 1998; Art and Design: 100 years at the Roya[l] College of Art, 1999; Sergio Leone: something to do with death, 2000; (ed) The Hound of the Baskervilles, 2001; Ken Adam: the art of production design, 2005; Once Upon a Time in Italy, 2005; Mad, Bad and Dangerous?: images of the scientist in film, 2005; contribs to: Reappraisals of Rousseau—studies in honour of R. A. Leigh, 1980; Cinema, Politics and Society in America, 1981; Rousseau et Voltaire en 1978, 1981; Rousseau After Two Hundred Years: Proc. of Cambridge Bicentennial Colloquium, 1982; Eduardo Paolozzi: perspectives and themes, 1984; Rape: an interdisciplinary study, 1987; The Cambridge Guide to the Arts in Britain, Vol. IX (post 1945), 1988; BFI Companion to the Western, 1988; Craft Classics since the 1940s, 1988; Eduardo Paolozzo: Noah's Ark, 1990; Ariel at Bay: reflections on broadcasting and the arts, 1990; Objects and Images: essay on design and advertising, 1992; BFI Companion to Horror, 1996; Fear: essays on the meaning and experience of fear, 2007; articles on film, popular culture and the visual arts/crafts in Cambridge Rev., Cinema, Film, Sight & Sound, London Magazine, New Statesman & Society, Crafts, Burlington Magazine, Art and Design, Designer, Design Week, Design, THES, TLS, Time Out, Punch, Designer, Craft History, Creative Review, Blueprint, Independent Magazine, Independent on Sunday, Culture Magazine, Listener, Times, Sunday Times, Guardian, Daily Telegraph, and various learned jls. *Recreation:* finding time. *Address:* (until summer 2009) Royal College of Art, Kensington Gore, SW7 2EU. *T:* (020) 7590 4101.

See also Very Rev. N. A. Frayling.

FRAYLING, Very Rev. Nicholas Arthur; Dean of Chichester, since 2002; *b* 29 Feb. 1944; *s* of late Arthur Frederick Frayling, OBE and Barbara Kathleen (*née* Imhof). *Educ:* Repton Sch.; Exeter Univ. (BA Theology 1969); Cuddesdon Theol Coll., Oxford. Management training, retail trade, 1962–64; Temp. Probation Officer (prison welfare), Inner London Probation and After-Care Service, 1965–66, pt-time, 1966–71. Deacon 1971; priest, 1972; Asst Curate, St John, Peckham, 1971–74; Vicar, All Saints, Tooting Graveney, 1974–83; Canon Residentiary and Precentor, Liverpool Cathedral, 1983–87; Hon. Canon, 1989–2002; Rector of Liverpool, 1987–2002. Chaplain: St Paul's Eye Hosp., Liverpool, 1987–90; Huyton Coll., 1987–91; to High Sheriff of Merseyside 1992–93, 1997–98 and 1999–2000; Hon. Chaplain, British Nuclear Tests Veterans Assoc., 1988–. Chairman: Southwark Diocesan Adv. Cttee for Care of Churches 1980–83; Religious Adv. Panel, BBC Radio Merseyside, 1988–2002; Welfare Orgn Cttee, Liverpool CVS, 1992–2002; Mersey Mission to Seafarers, 2000–02. Hon. Fellow Liverpool John Moores Univ., 2003. Hon. LLD Liverpool, 2001. *Publication:* Pardon and Peace: a reflection on the making of peace in Ireland, 1996. *Recreations:* music, friends. *Address:* The Deanery, Chichester, W Sussex PO19 1PX. *T:* (01243) 812494, (office) (01243) 812485, *Fax:* (01243) 812499; *e-mail:* dean@chichestercathedral.org.uk. *Clubs:* Royal Commonwealth Society, Oriental.

See also Sir C. J. Frayling.

FRAYN, Claire, (Mrs Michael Frayn); *see* Tomalin, C.

FRAYN, Michael, CLit 2007; writer; *b* 8 Sept. 1933; *s* of late Thomas Allen Frayn and Violet Alice Lawson; *m* 1st, 1960, Gillian Palmer (marr. diss. 1989); three *d*; 2nd, 1993, Claire Tomalin, *qv*. *Educ:* Kingston Gram. Sch.; Emmanuel Coll., Cambridge (Hon. Fellow, 1985). Reporter, Guardian, 1957–59; Columnist, Guardian, 1959–62; Columnist, Observer, 1962–68. Foreign Hon. Mem., Amer. Acad. of Arts and Scis, 2000. Hon. DLitt Cambridge, 2001. *Television:* plays: Jamie, 1968 (filmed as Remember Me?, 1997); Birthday, 1969; First and Last, 1989 (Internat. Emmy Award, 1990); A Landing on the Sun, 1994; *documentaries:* Imagine a City Called Berlin, 1975; Vienna—the Mask of Gold, 1977; Three Streets in the Country, 1979; The Long Straight, 1980; Jerusalem, 1984; Prague—the Magic Lantern, 1993; Budapest: written in water, 1996; *stage plays:* The Two of Us, 1970; The Sandboy, 1971; Alphabetical Order, 1975 (Evening Standard Drama Award for Best Comedy); Donkeys' Years, 1976 (SWET Best Comedy Award); Clouds, 1976; Liberty Hall, 1980; Make and Break, 1980 (New Standard Best Comedy Award); Noises Off, 1982 (Standard Best Comedy Award; SWET Best Comedy Award); Benefactors, 1984 (Standard Best Play Award; Laurence Olivier (formerly SWET) Award for Play of the Year; Plays and Players London Theatre Critics' Best New Play); Look Look, 1990; Here, 1993; Now You Know, 1995; Copenhagen, 1998 (Evening Standard Best Play, South Bank Show Award for Theatre, Critics' Circle Best New Play, 1998; Prix Molière, 1999; Tony Award, Best Play, 2000); Alarms and Excursions, 1998; Democracy, 2003 (Best Play, Evening Standard, 2003; South Bank Show Award, 2003; Best New Play, Critics' Circle Awards, 2004); The Crimson Hotel, 2007; Afterlife, 2008; *opera:* La Belle Vivette, 1995; *filmscripts:* Clockwise, 1986; Remember Me?, 1997. Nat. Press Award, 1970; Golden PEN Award, 2003; Saint Louis Literary Award, 2006; McGovern Award, Cosmos Club Foundn, 2006. Bundesverdienstkreuz (Germany), 2004. *Publications:* collections of columns: The Day of the Dog, 1962; The Book of Fub, 1963; On the Outskirts, 1964; At Bay in Gear Street, 1967; The Original Michael Frayn, 1983; Speak After the Beep, 1995; The Additional Michael Frayn, 2000; *non-fiction:* Constructions, 1974; (with David Burke) Celia's Secret, 2000; The Human Touch, 2006; *novels:* The Tin Men, 1965 (Somerset Maugham Award); The Russian Interpreter, 1966 (Hawthornden Prize); Towards the End of the Morning, 1967; A Very Private Life, 1968; Sweet Dreams, 1973; The Trick of It, 1989; A Landing On the Sun, 1991 (Sunday Express Book of the Year Award, 1991); Now You Know, 1992; Headlong, 1999; Spies, 2002 (Whitbread Novel of the Year, 2003); *translations:* Tolstoy, The Fruits of Enlightenment, 1979 (prod. 1979); Anouilh, Number One, 1984; Chekhov: The Cherry Orchard, 1978 (prod. 1978, 1989); Three Sisters, 1983 (prod. 1985); Wild Honey, 1984 (prod. 1984); The Seagull, 1986 (prod. 1986); Uncle Vanya, 1988 (prod. 1988); The Sneeze (adapted from one-act plays and short stories), 1989 (prod. 1988); Trifonov, Exchange, 1986 (prod. 1986, 1990). *Address:* c/o Greene & Heaton Ltd, 37a Goldhawk Road, W12 8QQ.

FRAYNE, Very Rev. David; Dean (formerly Provost) of Blackburn, 1992–2001, now Emeritus; *b* 19 Oct. 1934; *s* of late Philip John Frayne and Daisy Morris Frayne (*née* Eade), *m* 1961, Elizabeth Ann Frayne (*née* Grant); one *s* two *d*. *Educ:* Reigate Grammar Sch.; St Edmund Hall, Oxford (BA 1958 (2nd cl. Hons PPE); MA 1962); The Queen's Coll., Birmingham (DTh 1960). Pilot Officer, RAF, 1954–55. Ordained deacon, 1960, priest, 1961; Asst Curate, St Michael, East Wickham, 1960–63; Priest-in-charge, St Barnabas, Downham, Lewisham, 1963–67; Vicar of N Sheen, Richmond, 1967–73; Rector of Caterham, 1973–83; Vicar of St Mary Redcliffe with Temple, Bristol and St John the Baptist, Bedminster, 1983–92. Rural Dean of Caterham, 1980–83; Hon. Canon, Southwark Cathedral, 1982, Emeritus, 1983; Rural Dean of Bedminster, 1986–92; Proctor in Convocation, 1987–90; Hon. Canon of Bristol Cathedral, 1991. A Church Comr, 1994–98; Mem., Redundant Churches Cttee, 1995–2001. *Recreations:* walking, camping, music. *Address:* Newlands Cottage, Crown Lane, Peacemarsh, Gillingham, Dorset SP8 4HD. *T:* and *Fax:* (01747) 824065; *e-mail:* davidandliz@newlands2002.fsnet.co.uk. *Club:* Oxford Society.

FRAZER, Prof. Malcolm John, CBE 1992; PhD, FRSC; education consultant; *b* 7 Feb. 1931; *m* 1st, 1957, Gwenyth Ida Biggs (marr. diss. 1990), JP, MA; three *s*; 2nd, 1991, Aleksandra Kornhauser. *Educ:* Univ. of London (BSc 1952, PhD 1955). Royal Military Coll. of Science, 1956–57; Lecturer and Head of Dept of Chemistry, Northern Polytechnic, London, 1965–72; Prof. of Chemical Educn, 1972–86, and Pro-Vice Chancellor, 1976–81, Univ. of East Anglia, Norwich; Chief Executive: CNAA, 1986–93; HEQC, 1992–93; Chm., CATE, 1993–94. Vis. Prof., Open Univ., 1993–. Vice-President: RSC, 1973–74; Royal Instn, 1988–91; SHRE, 1993–; Gen. Sec./Vice-Pres. Chm. Council, BAAS, 1978–91. Hon. Fellow: N London Poly., 1988; SCOTVEC, 1990; Poly. South West, 1991; Brighton Poly., 1992; Manchester Metropolitan Univ., 1993; Bolton Inst., 1994; Cardiff Inst. of Higher Educn, 1994. Hon. FCollP, 1988. Hon. Dr Leuven, 1985; Hon. DSc: Leicester, 1993; Luton, 1993; Hon. DEd: CNAA, 1992; Heriot-Watt, 1993; Bath, 2002; Hon. DLitt Glasgow Caledonian, 1993; DUniv Open, 1994. Nyholm Medal, RSC, 1982. *Publications:* textbooks on chemistry, chemical educn, and problem solving; contribs to Jl Chem. Soc., etc. *Address:* Sora, Abingdon Road, Tubney, Oxon OX13 5QQ.

FREAN, Jennifer Margaret, (Jenny), RDI 1998; Founder, and Head, First Eleven Studio, since 1986; *b* 17 April 1947; *d* of Theodore Farbridge and Isobel Farbridge (*née* Reid-Douglas); *m* 1970 (Christopher) Patrick Frean; one *d. Educ:* City of London Sch. for Girls; Hornsey Coll. of Art (BA Hons); Royal Coll. of Art (MA 1972). Design Consultant, Centro Design Montefibre, Milan, 1974; set up Jenny Frean Associates, textile design studio, 1975; portraitist, 1984–86; founded First Eleven Studio; working with textile manufacturers worldwide on every aspect of colour and surface decoration, 1986. *Recreations:* music (especially opera), all art forms, gardening. *Address:* Christmas Cottage, Ingrams Green, Midhurst, W Sussex GU29 0LJ. *T:* (01730) 812337.

FREARS, Stephen Arthur; film director; *b* 20 June 1941; *s* of late Dr Russell E. Frears and Ruth M. Frears; *m* 1st, 1968, Mary-Kay Wilmers, *qv* (marr. diss. 1974); two *s*; 2nd, 2002, Anne Rothenstein; one *s* one *d. Educ:* Gresham's Sch., Holt; Trinity Coll., Cambridge (BA Law). Director: Gumshoe, 1971; Bloody Kids, 1980; Going Gently, 1981; Walter, 1982; Saigon, 1983; The Hit, 1984; My Beautiful Laundrette, 1985; Prick Up Your Ears, 1986; Sammy and Rosie Get Laid, 1987; Dangerous Liaisons, 1989; The Grifters, 1990; Accidental Hero, 1992; The Snapper, 1993; Mary Reilly, 1996; The Van, 1996; The Hi-Lo Country, 1999; High Fidelity, 2000; Liam, 2001; Dirty Pretty Things, 2002; Mrs Henderson Presents, 2005; The Queen, 2006; television: Fail Safe, 2000; The Deal, 2003. *Recreation:* reading. *Address:* c/o Casarotto Co. Ltd, 7–12 Noel Street, W1F 8GQ. *T:* (020) 7287 4450.

FRÉCHETTE, Louise, OC 1999; Deputy Secretary-General, United Nations, 1998–2006; Distinguished Fellow, Centre for International Governance Innovation, Canada, since 2006; *b* 16 July 1946. *Educ:* Collège Basile Moreau (BA 1966); Univ. of Montreal (LèsL Hist. 1970); Coll. of Europe, Bruges (Post-grad Dip. Econ. Studies 1978). With Dept of External Affairs, Govt of Canada, 1971–; Ambassador to Argentina and Uruguay, 1985–88; Assistant Deputy Minister: for Latin America and Caribbean, Min. of Foreign Affairs, 1988–91; for Internat. Econ. and Trade Policy, 1991–92; Ambassador to UN, 1992–94; Associate Dep. Minister, Dept of Finance, 1994–95; Dep. Minister of Defence, Canada, 1995–98. Hon. LLD St Mary's Univ., Halifax, 1993. *Recreations:* golf, reading. *Address:* Centre for International Governance Innovation, 57 Erb Street West, Waterloo, ON N2L 6C2, Canada.

FREDERICK, Sir Christopher (St John), 11th Bt *cr* 1723, of Burwood House, Surrey; *b* 28 June 1950; *s* of Sir Charles Frederick, 10th Bt and of Rosemary, *er d* of Lt-Col R. J. H. Baddeley, MC; *S* father, 2001; *m* 1990, Camilla Elizabeth, *o d* of Sir Derek Gilbey, 3rd Bt; one *s* one *d. Heir: s* Benjamin St John Frederick, *b* 29 Dec. 1991.

FREDMAN, Prof. Sandra Debbe, FBA 2005; Professor of Law, University of Oxford, since 1999; Fellow and Lecturer in Law, Exeter College, Oxford, since 1988; barrister; *b* 28 July 1957; *d* of Michael Geoffrey Fredman and Naomi Pauline Fredman (*née* Greenstein); *m* 1985, Alan Leslie Stein; two *s* one *d. Educ:* Univ. of Witwatersrand (BA 1st Cl. Maths and Philosophy 1977); Wadham Coll., Oxford (Rhodes Schol., 1979–82; BA 1st Cl. Hons Jurisp. 1981; BCL 1st Cl. Hons 1982). Political and econs journalist, Financial Mail, S Africa, 1978–79; articled clerk, Lawford & Co., Gray's Inn, 1983–84; Lectr in Law, KCL, 1984–88. Leverhulme Major Res. Fellow, 2004–07. Scientific Dir, European Network of Legal Experts in the Non-Discrimination Field, 2005–07. *Publications:* (with M. Nell and P. Randall) The Narrow Margin: how black and white South Africans view change in South Africa, 1983; (with B. Hepple) Labour Law and Industrial Relations in Great Britain, 1986, 2nd edn 1992; (with G. Morris) The State as Employer: labour law in the public services, 1989; Women and the Law, 1997; (ed) Discrimination and Human Rights, 2001; Discrimination Law, 2002; (ed with S. Spencer) Age as an Equality Issue, 2003; Human Rights Transformed: positive rights and positive duties, 2008; articles in legal jls. *Recreations:* outdoor activities, literature, theatre, travel. *Address:* Exeter College, Oxford OX1 3DP. *T:* (01865) 279600; Old Square Chambers, 1 Verulam Buildings, Gray's Inn, WC1R 5LQ.

FREE STATE, Bishop of the Diocese of the, since 1997 (formerly Bishop of Bloemfontein); **Rt Rev. (Elistan) Patrick Glover;** *b* 1 Feb. 1944; *s* of Rev. Chirho Glover and Sylvia Glover; *m* 1971, Kirsteen Marjorie Bain; two *s* two *d. Educ:* King Edward VII High Sch., Johannesburg; Rhodes Univ. (BA); Keble Coll., Oxford (BA Theol 1968; MA 1978); St Paul's Theol Coll., Grahamstown. Deacon 1969, priest 1970; Curate: St Peter's Church, Krugersdorp, 1969–71; St Martin's-in-Veld, Johannesburg, 1971–74; Rector: St Catherine's, Johannesburg, 1975–83; St George's, Johannesburg, 1983–86; Dean of Bloemfontein, 1987–94; Suffragan Bishop of Bloemfontein, 1994–97. *Recreations:* squash, scuba diving, jogging, cycling. *Address:* Bishop's House, 16 York Road, Waverley, Bloemfontein 9300, OFS, S Africa. *T:* (office) (51) 4476053, (home) (51) 4364351.

FREEDBERG, Prof. David Adrian; Professor of Art History, since 1984, and Director, Italian Academy for Advanced Studies in America, since 2000, Columbia University; *b* 1 June 1948; *s* of William Freedberg and Eleonore Kupfer; one *s* one *d. Educ:* S African Coll. High Sch., Cape Town; Yale Univ. (BA); Balliol Coll., Oxford (DPhil). Rhodes Scholar, Oxford, 1969–72; Lectr in History of Art: Westfield Coll., Univ. of London, 1973–76; Courtauld Inst. of Art, Univ. of London, 1976–84; Slade Prof. of Fine Art, Univ. of Oxford, 1983–84. Baldwin Prof., Oberlin Coll., Ohio, 1979; Andrew W. Mellon Prof. of Fine Art, Nat. Gall. of Art, Washington, 1996–98; Vis. Mem., Inst. for Advanced Study, Princeton, NJ, 1980–81; Gerson Lectr, Univ. of Groningen, 1983; VUB–Leerstoel, Brussels Univ., 1988–89. Fellow: Amer. Acad. of Arts and Scis, 1997; Amer. Philosophical Soc., 1997. *Publications:* Dutch Landscape Prints of the Seventeenth Century, 1980; The Life of Christ after the Passion (Corpus Rubenianum Ludwig Burchard, VII), 1983; Iconoclasts and their Motives, 1985; Iconoclasm and Painting in the Revolt of the Netherlands 1566–1609, 1988; The Power of Images, 1989; (ed) The Prints of Pieter Bruegel the Elder, 1989; (ed with Jan De Vries) Art in History/History in Art: studies in seventeenth century Dutch culture, 1991; Joseph Kosuth: The Play of the Unmentionable,

1992; Peter Paul Rubens: paintings and oil sketches, 1995; (with Enrico Baldini) The Paper Museum of Cassiano dal Pozzo: citrus fruit, 1997; (with Andrew Scott) The Paper Museum of Cassiano dal Pozzo: fossils and fossil woods, 2001; The Eye of the Lynx: Galileo, his friends, and the beginnings of modern natural history, 2003; (with David Pegler) The Paper Museum of Cassiano dal Pozzo: fungi, 2006; articles in Burlington Magazine, Revue de l'Art, Gentse Bijdragen, Art Bulletin, Münchner Jahrbuch der Bildenden Kunst, Jl of Warburg and Courtauld Insts, Print Quarterly, Quaderni Puteani, Trends in Cognitive Science. *Address:* Department of Art History, Columbia University, Schermerhorn Hall, New York, NY 10027, USA.

FREEDLAND, Jonathan Saul; Columnist and Policy Editor, The Guardian, since 1997; *b* 25 Feb. 1967; *s* of Michael and Sara Freedland; *m* 2000, Sarah Peters; two *s. Educ:* University Coll. Sch., London; Wadham Coll., Oxford (BA Hons PPE). Reporter, Sunday Correspondent, 1989–90; news trainee, BBC, 1990; reporter, BBC News and Current Affairs, 1991–93; Laurence Stern Fellow, as staff writer, Washington Post, 1992; Washington Corresp., The Guardian, 1993–97. Monthly Columnist: Jewish Chronicle, 1998–; Daily Mirror, 2002–04; Presenter, The Long View, Radio 4, 1999–. Dir and Trustee, Index on Censorship, 2002–. Columnist of the Year, What the Papers Say Awards, 2002. *Publications:* Bring Home the Revolution, 1998 (Somerset Maugham Award for Non-fiction); Jacob's Gift: a journey into the heart of belonging, 2005. *Recreations:* family, music, movies. *Address:* The Guardian, Kings Place, 90 York Way, N1 9AG; *e-mail:* freedland@guardian.co.uk.

FREEDLAND, Prof. Mark Robert, DPhil; FBA 2002; Professor of Employment Law, University of Oxford, since 1996; Fellow and Tutor in Law, St John's College, Oxford, since 1970; *b* 19 April 1945; *s* of Nathaniel Freedland and Esther (*née* Bendas); *m* 1st, 1973, Lalage Lewis (*d* 1976); one *s* one *d*; 2nd, 1997, Geraldine Field. *Educ:* Hendon Co. Grammar Sch.; University Coll. London (LLB); Brasenose Coll., Oxford (MA; DPhil 1970). Called to the Bar, Gray's Inn, 1971, Bencher, 1998; University of Oxford: Lectr, 1971–94; Reader, 1994–96; Dir, Inst. of European and Comparative Law, 2001–04; Leverhulme Major Res. Fellow, 2005–. Visiting Professor: European Univ. Inst., Florence, 1995; Univ. of Paris I, 1996–98; Univ. of Paris II, 1999–2002. Dr *hc* Paris II, 2000. *Publications:* The Contract of Employment, 1976; (with P. L. Davies) Labour Law Text and Materials, 1979, 2nd edn 1983; (ed with P. L. Davies) Kahn-Freud's Labour and the Law, 1983; (with P. L. Davies) Labour Legislation and Public Policy, 1993; (jtly) Public Services and Citizenship in European Law, 1998; The Personal Employment Contract, 2003; contrib. articles to Public Law, Industrial Law Jl. *Recreation:* living village life in France. *Address:* St John's College, Oxford OX1 3JP. *T:* (01865) 277387; *e-mail:* mark.freedland@sjc.ox.ac.uk.

FREEDMAN, Amelia, (Mrs Michael Miller), CBE 2006 (MBE 1989); FRAM; Artistic Director and Founder, Nash Ensemble, since 1964; Head of Classical Music, South Bank Centre, 1995–2006; *b* 21 Nov. 1940; *d* of Miriam Freedman (*née* Claret) and Henry Freedman; *m* 1970, Michael Miller; two *s* one *d. Educ:* St George's Sch., Harpenden; Henrietta Barnet, London; RAM (LRAM (piano), ARCM (clarinet); ARAM 1977, FRAM 1986). Music teacher, 1961–72: King's Sch., Cambridge; Perse Sch. for Girls, Cambridge; Chorleywood College for the Blind; Sir Philip Magnus Sch., London. Artistic Director: Bath Internat. Fest., 1984–93; Bath Mozartfest, 1995–; Musical Adviser, Israel Fest., 1989–90; Programme Adviser, Philharmonia Orch., 1993–95; chamber music consultant for various projects at South Bank Centre and Barbican, and for LSO; has commnd 140 new works for Nash Ensemble. Trustee, Nash Concert Soc., 1968–. Freeman, City of London, 2003. FRSA 2004. Hon. DMus Bath, 1993. Walter Wilson Cobbett Gold Medal, Musicians' Co., 1996; Leslie Boosey Award, PRS/Royal Philharmonic Soc., 2000. Chevalier, l'Ordre des Arts et des Lettres (France), 1983; Czech Govt Medal for services to Czech music in UK, 1984; Chevalier, l'Ordre National du Mérite (France), 1996. *Recreations:* theatre, cinema, ballet, opera; spectator sport—cricket, rugger, football (supporting Arsenal); children. *Address:* 14 Cedars Close, Hendon, NW4 1TR. *T:* (020) 8203 3025, *Fax:* (020) 8203 9540.

FREEDMAN, (Benjamin) Clive; QC 1997; a Recorder, since 2000; a Deputy High Court Judge, since 2003; *b* 16 Nov. 1955; *s* of Lionel and Freda Freedman; *m* 1980, Hadassa Helen Woolfson; one *s* three *d. Educ:* Manchester Grammar Sch.; Pembroke Coll., Cambridge (MA). Called to the Bar, Middle Temple, 1978, Bencher, 2005; Mem., Northern Circuit, 1980–; an Asst Recorder, 1997–2000. *Recreations:* Manchester City FC, Test Match Special. *Address:* Littleton Chambers, 3 King's Bench Walk North, Temple, EC4Y 7HR.

FREEDMAN, Charles, CB 1983; Commissioner, Customs and Excise, 1972–84; *b* 15 Oct. 1925; *s* of late Solomon Freedman, OBE, and Lilian Freedman; *m* 1949, Sarah Sadie King; one *s* two *d. Educ:* Westcliff High Sch.; Cheltenham Grammar Sch.; Trinity Coll., Cambridge (Sen. Schol., BA). Entered HM Customs and Excise, 1947; Asst Sec., 1963. *Address:* 10 Cliff Avenue, Leigh-on-Sea, Essex SS9 1HF. *T:* (01702) 473148.

FREEDMAN, Clive; *see* Freedman, B. C.

FREEDMAN, Her Honour Dawn Angela, (Mrs N. J. Shestopal); a Circuit Judge, 1991–2007; *b* 9 Dec. 1942; *d* of Julius and Celia Freedman; *m* 1970, Neil John Shestopal. *Educ:* Westcliff High Sch. for Girls; University Coll., London (LLB Hons). Called to the Bar, Gray's Inn, 1966; Metropolitan Stipendiary Magistrate, 1980–91; a Recorder, 1989–91. Mem. Parole Bd, 1992–96. Chm., Jewish Marriage Council, 1998–2002. Mem. Council, London Sch. of Jewish Studies, 1998–2002. *Recreations:* theatre, television, cooking. *Address:* c/o Harrow Crown Court, Hailsham Drive, Harrow HA1 4TU.

FREEDMAN, Prof. Judith Anne, (Lady Freedman); KPMG Professor of Tax Law, and Fellow of Worcester College, University of Oxford, since 2001; *b* 10 Aug. 1953; *d* of Harry Hill and Estella Hill; *m* 1974, Lawrence David Freedman (*see* Sir Lawrence Freedman); one *s* one *d. Educ:* North London Collegiate Sch.; Lady Margaret Hall, Oxford (BA 1st Class Hons Jurisprudence, MA). Articled Clerk, Stanleys & Simpson North, 1976–78; Solicitor of Supreme Court, 1978; Solicitor, Corporate Tax Dept, Freshfields, 1978–80; Lectr in Law, Univ. of Surrey, 1980–82; London School of Economics: Lectr, Law Dept, 1982–91; Sen. Lectr, 1991–96; Reader in Law, 1996–2000; Prof. of Law, 2000–01; Sen. Res. Fellow in Company and Commercial Law, Inst. of Advanced Legal Studies, 1989–92. Mem., Tax Law Review Cttee, 1994–. Mem. Council, Inst. for Fiscal Studies, 2003–. European Editor, Palmer's Company Law, 1991–2003; Jt Editor, British Tax Review, 1997– (Asst Ed., 1988–97); Mem. Editorial Cttee, Modern Law Review, 1987–. *Publications:* (jtly) Property and Marriage: an integrated approach, 1988; (ed jtly) Law and Accounting: competition and co-operation in the 1990s, 1992; Employed or Self-employed? tax classification of workers and the changing labour market, 2001. *Recreations:* family, friends, doodling. *Address:* Worcester College, Oxford OX1 2HB.

FREEDMAN, Prof. Sir Lawrence (David), KCMG 2003; CBE 1996; DPhil; FBA 1995; Professor of War Studies, since 1982, and Vice-Principal (Research), since 2003, King's College, London; *b* 7 Dec. 1948; *s* of late Lt-Comdr Julius Freedman and Myra

Freedman; *m* 1974, Judith Anne Hill (*see* J. A. Freedman); one *s* one *d*. *Educ:* Whitley Bay Grammar Sch.; BAEcon Manchester; BPhil York; DPhil Oxford. Teaching Asst, York Univ., 1971–72; Research Fellow, Nuffield Coll., Oxford, 1974–75; Research Associate, IISS, 1975–76 (Mem. Council, 1984–92 and 1993–2002); Research Fellow, 1976–78, Head of Policy Studies, 1978–82, RIIA. Hon. Dir, Centre for Defence Studies, 1990–. Chm., Cttee on Internat. Peace and Security, Social Science Res. Council (US), 1993–98. Trustee, Imperial War Mus., 2001–. FKC 1992. FRSA 1991; FRHistS 2000. AcSS 2001. Chesney Gold Medal, RUSI, 2006. *Publications:* US Intelligence and the Soviet Strategic Threat, 1977, 2nd edn 1986; Britain and Nuclear Weapons, 1980; The Evolution of Nuclear Strategy, 1981, 2nd edn 2003; (jtly) Nuclear War & Nuclear Peace, 1983; (ed) The Troubled Alliance, 1983; The Atlas of Global Strategy, 1985; The Price of Peace, 1986; Britain and the Falklands War, 1988; (jtly) Signals of War, 1990; (ed) Population Change and European Security, 1991; (ed) Britain in the World, 1991; (jtly) The Gulf Conflict 1990–1991, 1993; War: a Reader, 1994; (ed) Military Intervention in Europe, 1994; (ed) Strategic Coercion, 1998; The Politics of British Defence, 1999; Kennedy's Wars, 2000; The Cold War, 2001; (ed) Superterrorism, 2002; Deterrence, 2004; The Official History of the Falklands Campaign, vols I and II, 2005; A Choice of Enemies, 2008. *Recreations:* tennis, political caricature. *Address:* c/o Office of the Principal, King's College London, James Clerk Maxwell Building, 57 Waterloo Road, SE1 8WA. *T:* (020) 7848 3984.

FREEDMAN, Susan Rachel; *see* Prevezer, S. R.

FREELAND, Henry John, FSA; RIBA; Partner, Freeland Rees Roberts Architects, 1981–2005; Director, Freeland Rees Roberts Architects Ltd, since 2005; *b* 16 Jan. 1948; *s* of Lt-Gen. Sir Ian Henry Freeland, GBE, KCB, DSO and of Mary Freeland; *m* 1971, Elizabeth Margaret Sarel Ling; one *s* three *d*. *Educ:* Eton Coll.; Bristol Univ. (BA 1st Cl. Hons Architecture 1970; BArch 1st Cl. Hons 1973). ARCUK, RIBA 1975; AABC. Twist and Whitley, Architects, Cambridge, 1972–74; Cecil Bourne, Architects, Cambs, 1974–77; Whitworth & Hall, Architects, Bury St Edmunds, 1977–81. Surveyor to the Fabric, King's Coll. Chapel, Cambridge, 1987–; Architect and Surveyor: Guildford Cath., 1995–; Norwich Cath., 1996–. Member: Ely DAC, 2001–; Fabric Adv. Cttee, Cath. and Abbey Ch of St Alban, 2006–. Member: Ecclesiastical Architects' and Surveyors' Assoc., 1978–; Cathedral Architects' Assoc., 1995–; Life Mem., SPAB, 1970. FSA 2006. Freeman, City of London, 1985; Liveryman, Co. of Chartered Architects, 1986–. Trustee, D'Oyly Carte Trust, 2001–. *Recreations:* family, painting, cricket, archaeology, fossils. *Address:* Freeland Rees Roberts Architects, 25 City Road, Cambridge CB1 1DP. *T:* (01223) 366555, *Fax:* (01223) 312882; *e-mail:* hf@frrarchitects.co.uk. *Club:* Surveyors'.

FREELAND, Sir John Redvers, KCMG 1984 (CMG 1973); QC 1987; HM Diplomatic Service, retired; Judge, Arbitral Tribunal and Mixed Commission for Agreement on German External Debts, since 1988; Judge, European Court of Human Rights, 1991–98; *b* 16 July 1927; *o s* of C. Redvers Freeland and Freda Freeland (*née* Walker); *m* 1952, Sarah Mary, *er d* of late S. Pascoe Hayward, QC; one *s* one *d*. *Educ:* Stowe; Corpus Christi Coll., Cambridge. Royal Navy, 1945 and 1948–51. Called to Bar, Lincoln's Inn, 1952, Bencher, 1985; Mem. *ad eundem*, Middle Temple. Asst Legal Adviser, FO, 1954–63, and 1965–67; Legal Adviser, HM Embassy, Bonn, 1963–65; Legal Counsellor, FCO (formerly FO), 1967–70; Counsellor (Legal Advr), UK Mission to UN, NY, 1970–73; Legal Counsellor, FCO, 1973–76; Second Legal Advr, 1976–84, Legal Advr, 1984–87, FCO. Agent of UK govt, cases before European Commn of Human Rights, 1966–70. Mem., US-Chile Internat. Commn of Investigation, 1989–. Member: Exec. Cttee, David Davies Meml Inst. of Internat. Studies, 1974–2001; Council of Management, British Inst. of Internat. and Comparative Law, 1984–87; Cttee of Management, Inst. of Advanced Legal Studies, 1984–87; Bd of Govs, British Inst. of Human Rights, 1992–2004.

FREELAND, Simon Dennis Marsden; QC 2002; **His Honour Judge Freeland;** a Circuit Judge, since 2007; *b* 11 Feb. 1956; 2nd *s* of Dennis Marsden Freeland and Rosemary Turnbull Tarn; *m* 2000, Anne Elizabeth, *y d* of Sir (Robert) Kynaston Studd, 3rd Bt, and of Anastasia, Lady Studd; one *s* one *d*. *Educ:* Malvern Coll.; Manchester Univ. (LLB Hons). Called to the Bar, Gray's Inn, 1978, Bencher, 2007; in practice at the Bar, 1978–2007, specialising in police law and civil liberties; Head of Chambers, 5 Essex Court, 2002–07; Recorder, 2000–07. *Recreations:* horse-racing, walking, good food and fine wine, family. *Address:* Snaresbrook Crown Court, 75 Hollybush Hill, E11 1QW. *T:* (020) 8530 0000.

FREELING, Laurel Claire P.; *see* Powers-Freeling.

FREEMAN, family name of **Baron Freeman**.

FREEMAN, Baron *cr* 1997 (Life Peer); **Roger Norman Freeman;** PC 1993; MAFCA; Chairman: UK Advisory Panel (formerly Corporate Finance Advisory Board), PricewaterhouseCoopers, since 1999; Thales UK plc, since 1999; Metalysis Ltd, since 2003; Skill Force Development Ltd, since 2004; Cambridge Enterprise Ltd (formerly Cambridge University Venture Board), since 2005; Parity Group plc, since 2007; Director: Thales SA, since 1999; Chemring Group PLC, since 2006; *b* 27 May 1942; *s* of Norman and Marjorie Freeman; *m* 1969, Jennifer Margaret Watson (*see* Lady Freeman); one *s* one *d*. *Educ:* Whitgift Sch., Croydon; Balliol Coll., Oxford (MA PPE). Chartered Accountant, 1969; FCA 1979. Articled with Binder Hamlyn & Co., 1964–69 (Hons Prize, 1968); General Partner, Lehman Brothers, 1969–86. MP (C) Kettering, 1983–97; contested (C) same seat, 1997. Parliamentary Under-Secretary of State: for the Armed Forces, 1986–88; DoH, 1988–90; Minister of State: Dept of Transport, 1990–94; MoD, 1994–95; Chancellor of the Duchy of Lancaster, 1995–97. Partner, PricewaterhouseCoopers, 1997–99. A Vice-Chm., Cons. Party, 1997–2001. President: British Internat. Freight Assoc., 1999–2002; RFCA (formerly TAVRA) Council, 1999–. *Publications:* Professional Practice, 1968; Fair Deal for Water, 1985; (ed) UK Rail Privatisation 1992–1997, 2000; (ed) University Spin-out Technology Companies, 2004. *Address:* House of Lords, SW1A 0PW. *Club:* Carlton.

FREEMAN, Lady; Jennifer Margaret Freeman, FSA; architectural historian, writer and specialist developer; Director, Historic Chapels Trust, since 1993; Chairman, Freeman Historic Properties Ltd, since 1992; *b* 28 Oct. 1944; *d* of Malcolm Woodward Watson and Margaret Hannah Watson; *m* 1969, Roger Norman Freeman (*see* Baron Freeman); one *s* one *d*. *Educ:* Withington Girls' Sch., Manchester; Univ. of Manchester (BA Hons); Architectural Assoc. (Dip. Building Conservation); Inst. of Historic Bldg Conservation. Project Co-ordinator, Save the City: a conservation study of the City of London, report published 1976, 2nd edn 1979. Member: Cttee, Save Britain's Heritage, 1977–; London Adv. Cttee, English Heritage, 1986–2001; Council for the Care of Churches, 1991–2001; Develt Bd, Bodleian Liby, 2003–. Chm., Fabric Cttee, Friends of Kensal Green Cemetery, 1987– (Pres., 2004–); Vice-President: Friends of the City Churches, 1996–; Nat. Churches Trust (formerly Historic Churches Preservation Trust), 2003–. Sec., Victorian Soc., 1982–85. Trustee: Heritage Link, 2002–; Constable Trust, 2003–. Pres., Kettering Civic Soc., 2004–. Hon. Life Mem., Rothwell Preservation Trust, 1997. Assessor, City Heritage Award, 1978–. FRSA 2003; FSA 2005. Freeman, City of London, 1998. Hon. DArts De Montfort, 1997. *Publications:* (jtly) Kensal Green Cemetery, 2001; W. D. Caröe (1857–1938): his architectural achievement, 1990; contrib. various articles to learned jls. *Recreations:* embroidery, art gallery and museum-going, country walking, riding, theatre, reading, travel. *Address:* *e-mail:* freemanr@parliament.uk.

FREEMAN, Catherine; Director, Dove Productions, since 1989; *b* 10 Aug. 1931; *d* of Harold Dove and Eileen Carroll; *m* 1st, 1958, Sir Charles (Cornelius-) Wheeler, CMG; 2nd, 1962, Rt Hon. John Freeman, *qv*; two *s* one *d*. *Educ:* Convent of the Assumption; St Anne's Coll., Oxford (MA Hons). Joined BBC as trainee producer, 1954; Producer/director: Panorama, Brains Trust, Monitor, Press Conference, 1954–58; joined Thames Television as Sen. Producer in Features Dept, 1976; Editor, Daytime progs, 1976–82; originator and series producer of Citizen 2000 for Channel 4; Controller, Documentaries, Features and Religion, 1982–86; Controller, Features and Religion, 1986–89. Member, Devlin Cttee on Identification Procedures, 1974–76; Literature Panel, Arts Council, 1981–84; Broadcasting, Film and Video panel, Arts Council, 1986–88; Council, ICA, 1983–93. Dir, One World Broadcasting Trust, 1990–95. *Address:* Davis Cottage, Torriano Cottages, NW5 2TA.

See also M. J. A. Freeman.

FREEMAN, David Charles; Founder/Director of Opera Factory; freelance opera and theatre director; *b* 1 May 1952; *s* of Howard Wilfred Freeman and Ruth Adair Nott; *m* 1985, Marie Angel; one *s* one *d*. *Educ:* Sydney Univ., NSW (BA Hons). Opera Factory Sydney, 1973–76; Opera Factory Zürich, 1976–95: directed 20 prodns, appearing in 5, writing the text of 4; Opera Factory London, 1981–98: directed 21 prodns (8 televised by Channel Four), writing text of two; founded Opera Factory Films, 1991; Associate Artist, ENO, 1981–95: prodns include world première of The Mask of Orpheus, 1986; directed Goethe's Faust, Pts I and II, Lyric, Hammersmith, 1988; (also adapted) Malory's Morte d'Arthur, Lyric, Hammersmith, 1990; The Winter's Tale, Shakespeare's Globe (opening prodn), 1997; Madam Butterfly, 1998 and 2003, Tosca, 1999, Carmen, 2002, Royal Albert Hall; Magic Flute, Sydney Opera House, 2006; Gadaffi (world première), ENO, 2006; Sweeney Todd, RFH, 2007; opera prodns in New York, Houston, Paris, Germany and St Petersburg. Chevalier de l'Ordre des Arts et des Lettres, France, 1985.

FREEMAN, David John; Founder, 1952, Senior Partner, 1952–92, Consultant, 1992–2003, D. J. Freeman, Solicitors (name changed to Kendall Freeman, 2003, then Edwards Angell Palmer and Dodge UK LLP, 2008); *b* 25 Feb. 1928; *s* of late Meyer Henry and Rebecca Freeman; *m* 1st, 1950, Iris Margaret Alberge (*d* 1997); two *s* one *d*; 2nd, 2001, Connie Levy. *Educ:* Christ's Coll., Finchley. Lieut, Army, 1946–48. Admitted Solicitor, 1952. Dept of Trade Inspector into the affairs of AEG Telefunken (UK) Ltd, and Credit Collections Ltd, 1977. Chairman: Trustees and Exec. Cttee, Holocaust Conference, Remembering for the Future, Oxford, 2000; UCL Inquiry into the provenance of 654 Aramaic incantation bowls, 2005–06; UCL Inquiry to recommend sound principles for the future treatment of cultural objects, 2005–. Governor, Royal Shakespeare Theatre, 1979–96. *Recreations:* reading, theatre, gardening, golf. *Address:* 6 Hyde Park Gardens, W2 2LT. *Clubs:* Athenæum; Huntercombe Golf.

FREEMAN, Dr Ernest Allan, CEng, FIET; CMath, FIMA; Director, Trent Polytechnic, 1981–83; *b* 16 Jan. 1932; *s* of William Freeman and Margaret Sinclair; *m* 1954, Mary Jane Peterson; two *d*. *Educ:* Sunderland Technical Coll.; King's Coll., Univ. of Durham (Mather Scholarship, 1955–57). BSc, PhD, Durham; DSc Newcastle upon Tyne; MA (Oxon) 1972. Sunderland Forge & Engineering Co. Ltd. 1949–55; English Electric Co., 1957–58; Ferranti Ltd (Edinburgh), 1958–59; Sunderland Polytechnic: Dir of Research, 1959–65; Head of Control Engrg Dept, 1965–72; Rector, 1976–80; Tutor and Fellow in Engrg, St Edmund Hall, Oxford Univ., 1972–76. FRSA. *Publications:* contribs mainly in the fields of control engrg, systems theory and computing, to Wireless Engr, Proc. IEE (Heaviside Prize, 1974), Jl of Electronics and Control, Trans AIEE, Electronic Technol., Control, Jl of Optimisation Theory and Application, Trans Soc. of Instrument Technol., Proc. Internat. Fedn for Analogue Computation, Internat. Jl of Control. *Recreations:* swimming, browsing around antique shops, playing bridge. *Address:* 12 Rolfe Place, Headington, Oxford OX3 0DS.

FREEMAN, Prof. Ernest Michael, PhD; FREng; Professor of Applied Electromagnetics, Imperial College of Science, Technology and Medicine, London University, 1980–2003, now Emeritus Professor of Electromagnetics; *b* 10 Nov. 1937; *s* of Ernest Robert Freeman and Agnes Maud Freeman; *m* 1987, Helen Anne Rigby. *Educ:* Colfe's Grammar Sch., Lewisham; King's Coll., London (BScEng; PhD 1964). Lectr, King's Coll., London, 1960–63 and 1966–70; Engrg Designer, AEI, Rugby, 1964–65; Reader: Brighton Polytechnic, 1970–73; Imperial Coll. of Science and Technology, 1973–80. Chm., Infolytica Ltd, 1978–; Vice Pres., Infolytica Corp., 1978–. FREng (FEng 1987). *Publications:* papers in learned society jls on magnetics. *Recreations:* architecture, military history, art, aristology. *Address:* Electrical Engineering Department, Imperial College of Science, Technology and Medicine, Exhibition Road, SW7 2BT. *T:* (020) 7594 6166; *e-mail:* e.freeman@ic.ac.uk.

FREEMAN, Frank Gerard, FRAD; international freelance classical ballet teacher, lecturer, examiner, adjudicator, writer and choreographer; *b* Bangalore, India, 16 July 1945; *s* of Frank James and Amber Theresa Freeman. *Educ:* Royal Ballet Sch., White Lodge; Royal Ballet Upper Sch.; Royal Acad. of Dance (Professional Dancers' Teaching Dip. (Dist.) 1976). FRAD 2000. With Royal Ballet, 1963–71; Royal Ballet Educnl Unit, Ballet for All, 1971; soloist, Festival Ballet, 1971–72; teacher: Hirofumi Inoue Ballet Co., 1977, Bangkok, 1978 (under auspices of British Council); Kobayashi Ballet Theatre and Sch., Tokyo, 1978–80; at major British vocational schs, 1976–, incl. Royal Ballet Schs, English Nat. Ballet Sch., Arts Educnl Schs, Rambert Sch. of Ballet and Contemp. Dance, Central Sch. of Ballet, Elmhurst Sch. for Dance, Northern Ballet Sch., Ballet West, Doreen Bird Coll., Bush Davies Sch., Performers Coll., Laine Th. Arts and Guildford Sch. of Acting Conservatoire; Lectr on Professional Dancers' Teaching Dip. for RAD, 1977–2007; introduced RAD syllabus in Japan, 1978. Vocational Grades Examr, RAD, 1976–; trained Vocational Grades Examrs for RAD, 2001–05; interviewer for Voices of British Ballet Sound Archive, 2006–. Member: Artistic Cttee, RAD, 2001– (Trustee, 2008–); Dance Panel, Laurence Olivier Awards, 2001 and 2002; Judging Panel, Young British Dancer of Year, 2007 and 2008. Founder Patron, Nat. Youth Ballet of GB, 1988–. Gov., Royal Ballet Cos, 2007–. Choreographer: Puccini's opera, Le Villi for London Univ. Opera, 1982; Massenet's opera, Cendrillon for RNCM, 1984; Set Dances for GCSE O Level dance syllabus, 1984. *Publications:* (jtly) The Foundations of Classical Ballet Technique, 1997; (jtly) The Progressions of Classical Ballet Technique, 2002; contrib. articles on ballet to Dancing Times, Dance Now, Dance Expression and Dance Gazette. *Recreations:* music, opera, ballet, reading, collecting antique glass and 19th century watercolours. *Address:* c/o Royal Academy of Dance, 36 Battersea Square, SW11 3RA.

FREEMAN, George Vincent; Under-Secretary (Legal), Treasury Solicitor's Department, 1973–76, retired; *b* 30 April 1911; *s* of Harold Vincent Freeman and Alice Freeman; *m* 1945, Margaret Nightingale; one *d*. *Educ:* Denstone Coll., Rocester. Admitted Solicitor, 1934; in private practice Birmingham until 1940. Served RN, 1940–46, Lieut RNVR.

Legal Asst, Treasury Solicitor's Dept, 1946; Sen. Legal Asst 1950; Asst Treasury Solicitor 1964. *Recreation:* gardening. *Address:* 8 Shelley Close, Ashley Heath, Ringwood, Hants BH24 2JA. *Clubs:* Civil Service; Conservative (Ringwood).

FREEMAN, Hugh Lionel, FRCPsych; FFPH; Hon. Consultant Psychiatrist, Salford Mental Health Trust (formerly Health Authority), University of Manchester School of Medicine, since 1988 (Consultant Psychiatrist, 1961–88); *b* Salford, 4 Aug. 1929; *s* of late Bernard Freeman, FBOA and Dora Doris Freeman (*née* Kahn); *m* 1957, Sally Joan Casket (*see* S. J. Freeman); three *s* one *d*. *Educ:* Altrincham Grammar Sch.; St John's Coll., Oxford (open schol.; BM BCh 1954; MA; DM 1988); MSc Salford 1980. DPM 1958; FFPH (FFCM 1989). Captain, RAMC, 1956–58. House Surg., Manchester Royal Inf., 1955; Registrar, Bethlem Royal and Maudsley Hosps, 1958–60; Consultant Psychiatrist, Salford Royal Hosp., 1961–70; Hon. Consultant Psychiatrist: Salford Health Dept, 1961–74; Salford Social Services Dept, 1974–88. Hon. Med. Consultant, NAMH, 1963–74. Med. Advisor, NW Fellowship for Schizophrenia, 1980–88; Professional Advr, SANE, 1998–. Chairman: Psychiatric Sub-Cttee, NW Reg. Med. Adv. Cttee, 1978–83; Area Med. Cttee and Med. Exec. Cttee, Salford AHA, 1974–78. University of Manchester: Hon. Lectr, 1973–99; Mem., Univ. Court, 1989–94; Hon. Res. Fellow, UC and Middlesex Sch. of Medicine, 1989; Centre for Psychoanalytic Studies, Kent Univ., 1993. Visiting Professor: Univ. of WI, 1970; Univ. of WA, 1990; Univ. of Bern, 1995; Hungarian Medical Schools, 1996; Rockefeller Foundn Vis. Fellow, Italy, 1980; Vis. Fellow, 1986–97, Hon. Vis. Fellow, 1997, Green Coll., Oxford. Delta Omega Lectr, Tulane Univ., 1977; Linacre Lectr, Linacre Coll., Oxford, 1996. Examiner: Univ. of Manchester, United Examg Bd, 1993–2001; RCPsych. Med. Mem., Mental Health Rev. Tribunal, 1982–93. Member: Sex Educn Panel, Health Educn Council, 1968–72; Working Party on Behaviour Control, Council for Sci. and Society, 1973–76; Minister of State's Panel on Private Practice, DHSS, 1974–75; UK Delgn to EC Conf. on Mental Health in Cities, Milan, 1980; Mental Health Act Commn, 1983–84; Home Sec's Wking Party on Fear of Crime, 1989; Historic Building Panel, City of Manchester, 1981–89. WHO Consultant: Grenada, 1970; Chile, 1978; Philippines, 1979; Bangladesh, 1981; Greece, 1985; Rapporteur: WHO Conf. on Mental Health Services in Pilot Study Areas, Trieste, 1984; WHO Workshop on Nat. Mental Health Progs, Rwanda, 1985. Editor, British Jl of Clin. and Social Psych., 1982–84; Dep. Editor, Internat. Jl of Social Psych., 1980–83; Editor: British Jl of Psych., 1983–93 (Asst Editor, 1978–83); Current Opinion in Psychiatry, 1988–93; Co-Editor, Psychiatric Bulletin, 1983; Associate Editor, Internat. Jl of Mental Health, 1981–; Asst Editor, History of Psychiatry, 1993–. Mem. Internat. Res. Seminars, US National Inst. of Mental Health: Washington, 1966; Pisa, 1977; has lectured to and addressed univs, confs and hosps worldwide; advr on and participant in radio and TV progs. Mem. Exec. Cttees, Royal Medico-Psychol Assoc., 1965–69. Royal College of Psychiatrists: Foundn Mem., 1971; Fellow 1971, Hon. Fellow 1998; Mem. Council, 1983–93; Chm., Journal Cttee; Vice-Chm., Social and Community Gp; Maudsley Lectr, 1993. FRSH (Hon. Sec., Mental Health Gp, 1973–76); Vice-Chm., 1983–87, Mem., Council, 1987–91, MIND. Corresp. Fellow, Amer. Psychiatric Assoc., 1993; Corresp. Member: US Assoc. for Clinical Psychosociol Res.; US Assoc. for Behavioral Therapies; Hon. Member: Chilean Soc. of Psych., Neurol. and Neurosurgery; Egyptian Psychiatric Assoc.; Polish Psychiatric Assoc., 1986; Hungarian Psychiatric Soc., 1991; Bulgarian Soc. for Neuroscis, 1991; Sen. Common Room, Pembroke Coll., Oxford, 1981. Mem., Hon. Cttee, European Assoc. for History of Psychiatry, 2003–. Vice-Chm., Manchester Heritage Trust, 1983–89; Mem., Mercian Regional Cttee, NT, 1986–92. Hon. Professorial Fellow, Salford Univ., 1986. Freeman, City of London; Liveryman, Soc. of Apothecaries, 1984 (Mem., Livery Cttee, 1987). Hon. Editor, The Apothecary, 2007. Distinguished Service Commendation, US Nat. Council of Community Mental Health Centers, 1982; 650 Anniversary Medal of Merit, Charles Univ., Prague, 1999. *Publications:* (ed jtly) Trends in the Mental Health Services, 1963; (ed) Psychiatric Hospital Care, 1965; (ed jtly) New Aspects of the Mental Health Service, 1968; (ed) Progress in Behaviour Therapy, 1969; (ed) Progress in Mental Health, 1970; (ed) Pavlovian Approach to Psychopathology, 1971; (ed jtly) Dangerousness, 1982; Mental Health and the Environment, 1985; (jtly) Mental Health Services in Europe, 1985; (ed jtly) Mental Health Services in Britain: the way ahead, 1985; (ed jtly) Interaction between Mental and Physical Illness, 1989; (ed jtly) Community Psychiatry, 1991; (ed jtly) 150 Years of British Psychiatry, 1991; La Malattie del Potere, 1994; (ed jtly) 150 Years of British Psychiatry: the aftermath, 1996; (ed jtly) Quality of Life in Mental Disorders, 1997, 2nd edn 2005; (ed) A Century of Psychiatry, 1999; (ed jtly) Psychiatric Cultures Compared, 2006; (ed jtly) Impact of the Environment on Psychiatric Disorders, 2008; contribs to national press and learned jls. *Recreations:* architecture, travel, music. *Address:* 21 Montagu Square, W1H 2LF. *Club:* Oxford and Cambridge.

FREEMAN, Sir James (Robin), 3rd Bt *cr* 1945; *b* 21 July 1955; *s* of Sir (John) Keith (Noel) Freeman, 2nd Bt and Patricia Denison (*née* Thomas); *S* father, 1981, but his name does not appear on the Official Roll of the Baronetage. *Heir:* none.

FREEMAN, Jennifer Margaret; *see* Freeman, Lady.

FREEMAN, Joan; *see* Freeman, S. J.

FREEMAN, Rt Hon. John, MBE 1943; PC 1966. *Educ:* Westminster Sch.; Brasenose College, Oxford (Hon. Fellow, 1968). Active service, 1940–45. MP (Lab) Watford Div. of Herts, 1945–50; Borough of Watford, 1950–55; PPS to Sec. of State for War, 1945–46; Financial Sec., War Office, 1946; Parly Under Sec. of State for War, April 1947; Leader, UK Defence Mission to Burma, 1947; Parly Sec., Min. of Supply, 1947–51, resigned. Asst Editor, New Statesman, 1951–58; Deputy Editor, 1958–60; Editor, 1961–65. British High Commissioner in India, 1965–68; British Ambassador in Washington, 1969–71. Chairman: London Weekend Television Ltd, 1971–84; LWT (Holdings) plc, 1976–84; Page & Moy (Holdings) Ltd, 1976–84; Hutchinson Ltd, 1978–82 (Director, until 1984); ITN, 1976–81. Vis. Prof. of Internat. Relns, Univ. of California, Davis, 1985–90. Governor, BFI, 1976–82. Vice-Pres., Royal Television Soc., 1975–85 (Gold Medal, 1981).

See also M. J. A. Freeman.

FREEMAN, John; a Senior Immigration Judge, Asylum and Immigration Tribunal (formerly a Vice-President, Immigration Appeal Tribunal), since 2000; a Recorder, since 2003; *b* 13 July 1951; *s* of late E. A. Freeman, FRCS and Joan (*née* Horrell). *Educ:* Winchester Coll.; Corpus Christi Coll., Cambridge (MA); Univ. of Warwick (LLM). Practised at Bar, Midland and Oxford Circuit, 1976–83, 1986–89; Resident Magistrate, Registrar and Commissioner of High Court and Court of Appeal, actg Dir of Public Prosecutions, Solomon Islands, 1983–86; consultant, ODA and UNHCR, 1987–92; Immigration Appeal Adjudicator, 1989–90, 1991–2000. Part-time Legal Mem., Special Immigration Appeals Commn, 2001–. *Recreation:* breeding Staffordshire bull terriers. *Address:* (office) Field House, 15–25 Bream's Buildings, EC4A 1DZ. *Club:* Royal Geographical Society.

FREEMAN, John Anthony, FCA; Managing Director, Home Service Division, Prudential Corporation plc, 1984–94; *b* 27 May 1937; *o s* of late John Eric Freeman and Dorothy Mabel Freeman; *m* 1st, 1964, Judith Dixon (marr. diss. 1984); one *s* one *d*; 2nd, 1986, Margaret Joyce (*née* Langdon-Ellis). *Educ:* Queen Elizabeth Grammar Sch., Mansfield; Birmingham Univ. (BCom). FCA 1961; FCMA 1974. Mellors Basden & Mellors, Chartered Accountants, 1958–62; Peat Marwick Mitchell, Chartered Accountants, 1962–73; National Freight Corp., 1973–77; Prudential Corp., 1977–94. *Recreations:* golf, gardening, music.

FREEMAN, Prof. Kenneth Charles, PhD; FRS 1998; Duffield Professor, Research School of Astronomy and Astrophysics, since 2000 (Professor, Mount Stromlo and Siding Spring Observatories, 1987–2000), Institute of Advanced Studies, Australian National University; *b* 27 Aug. 1940; *s* of Herbert and Herta Freeman; *m* 1963, Margaret Leigh Cook; one *s* three *d*. *Educ:* Scotch Coll.; Univ. of Western Australia (BSc Hons Mathematics 1962); Trinity Coll., Cambridge (PhD 1965). FAA 1981. Res. Fellow, Trinity Coll., Cambridge, 1965–69; McDonald Postdoctoral Fellow in Astronomy, Univ. of Texas, 1966; Mount Stromlo and Siding Spring Observatories, Australian National University: Queen Elizabeth Fellow, 1967–70; Fellow, 1970–74; Sen. Fellow, 1974–81; Professorial Fellow, 1981–87. Sen. Scientist, Kapteyn Lab., Univ. of Groningen, 1976; Vis. Mem., IAS, Princeton, 1984, 1988; Distinguished Vis. Scientist, Space Telescope Science Inst., Baltimore, 1988–; Oort Prof., Univ. of Leiden, 1994; Vis. Fellow, Merton Coll., Oxford, 1997; Tinsley Prof., Univ. of Texas, 2001; Blaauw Prof., Univ. of Groningen, 2003; de Vaucouleurs Lectr, Univ. of Texas, 2003. Chm., Nat. Cttee on Astronomy, Australian Acad. of Science, 1984–86 (Pawsey Medal, 1972). ARAS 2002. Hon. DSc WA, 1999. Heineman Prize, Amer. Inst. of Physics and Amer. Astronomical Soc., 1999; Citation Laureate Award, Thomson ISI, 2001. *Publications:* (with G. McNamara) In Search of Dark Matter, 2006; more than 750 articles in learned astronomical jls. *Recreations:* bushwalking, birdwatching, classical music. *Address:* Mount Stromlo Observatory, Cotter Road, Weston Creek, ACT 2611, Australia. *T:* (2) 61250264.

FREEMAN, Dr Marie Joyce, FFCM; Health Service Management Consultant, 1988–95; *b* 14 April 1934; *d* of Wilfrid George Croxson and Ada Mildred (*née* Chiles); *m* 1958, Samuel Anthony Freeman (decd); one *s*. *Educ:* Royal Free Hospital Sch. of Medicine (MB BS, DPH). Specialist in Community Medicine, Avon AHA, 1974; District MO, Southmead HA, 1982; Actg Regl MD, SW RHA, 1986–88. *Recreations:* patchwork and quilting, making miniatures, living in Provence. *Address:* Wingfield House, Darlington Place, Bath BA2 6BY. *T:* (01225) 466670; Hameau de la Lauze, 84570 Blauvac, Vaucluse, France.

FREEMAN, Dr Matthew John Aylmer, FRS 2006; Member, Permanent Scientific Staff, since 1992, and Joint Head of Division of Cell Biology, since 2007, Medical Research Council Laboratory of Molecular Biology, Cambridge; *b* 16 June 1961; *s* of Rt Hon. John Freeman, *qv* and Catherine Freeman, *qv*; *m* 1990, Rose Taylor; one *s* one *d*. *Educ:* King Alfred's Sch.; Pembroke Coll., Oxford (BA Hons); Imperial Coll., London (PhD 1987). Postdoctoral Fellow, Univ. of Calif, Berkeley, 1987–92. Chairman: British Scientists Abroad, 1990–92; British Soc. for Develtl Biology, 2004–; Member: Exec., Campaign for Sci. and Engrg (formerly Save British Sci.), 1992–; Agric. and Envmt Biotechnol. Commn, 2000–05; Dir, Co. of Biologists, 2003–. Ed., Develtl Biol., 2003–. Mem., EMBO, 1999– (Gold Medal, 2001). Hooke Medal, British Soc. for Cell Biology, 2003. *Publications:* contrib. primary res. articles and reviews in specialist and gen. sci. jls. *Recreation:* sailing. *Address:* MRC Laboratory of Molecular Biology, Hills Road, Cambridge CB2 0QH. *T:* (01223) 248011.

FREEMAN, Michael Alexander Reykers, MD; FRCS; Consultant Orthopaedic Surgeon, The London Hospital, 1968–96; Hon. Consultant, Royal Hospitals NHS Trust, since 1996; *b* 17 Nov. 1931; *s* of Donald George and Florence Julia Freeman; *m* 1st, 1951, Elisabeth Jean; one *s* one *d*; 2nd, 1959, Janet Edith; one *s* one *d*; 3rd, 1968, Patricia; one *d* (and one *s* decd). *Educ:* Stowe Sch.; Corpus Christi Coll., Cambridge (open scholarship and closed exhibn); London Hospital Med. Coll. BA (1st cl. hons), MB BCh, MD (Cantab). FRCS 1959. Trained in medicine and surgery, London Hosp., and in orthopaedic and traumatic surgery, London, Westminster and Middlesex Hosps; co-founder, Biomechanics Unit, Imperial Coll., London, 1964; Cons. Surg. in Orth. and Traum. Surgery, London Hosp., also Res. Fellow, Imperial Coll., 1968; resigned from Imperial Coll., to devote more time to clinical activities, 1979. Special surgical interest in field of reconstructive surgery in lower limb, concentrating on joint replacement; originator of new surgical procedures for reconstruction and replacement of arthritic hip, knee, ankle and joints of foot; has lectured and demonstrated surgery, Canada, USA, Brazil, Japan, China, Australia, S Africa, continental Europe; guest speaker at nat. and internat. profess. congresses. Robert Jones Lectr, RCS, 1989. Visiting Professor: Sch. of Engrg Sci., Univ. of Southampton, 2001; Inst. of Orthopaedics, UCL, 2001. Mem., Editl Adv. Bd, 1986–97, Eur. Ed.-in-Chief, 1997–2001, Jl of Arthroplasty. Past Member: Scientific Co-ordinating Cttee, ARC; MRC; Clin. Res. Bd, London Hosp. Bd of Governors; Brent and Harrow AHA; DHSS working parties. President: Internat. Hip Soc., 1982–85; British Hip Soc., 1989–91; British Orthopaedic Assoc., 1992–93; Eur. Fedn of Nat. Assocs of Orthopaedics and Traumatol., 1994–95. Member: BMA; Amer. Acad. Orth. Surgs; Orth. Res. Soc.; SICOT; RSM; Health Unit, IEA; SIROT; European Orth. Res. Soc. Hon. Member: Danish Orth. Assoc.; Soc. Française de Chirurg. Orth. et Traum.; Canadian Orth. Assoc. Hon. Fellow, Soc. Belge de Chirurg. Orth. et de Traum. Bacon and Cunning Prizes and Copeman Medal, CCC; Andrew Clark and T. A. M. Ross Prize in Clin. Med., London Hosp. Med. Coll.; Robert Jones Medal, Brit. Orth. Assoc. *Publications:* editor and part-author: Adult Articular Cartilage, 1973, 2nd edn 1979; Scientific Basis of Joint Replacement, 1977; Arthritis of the Knee, 1980; chapters in: Bailey and Love's Short Practice of Surgery; Mason and Currey's Textbook of Rheumatology; papers in Proc. Royal Soc., Jl Bone and Joint Surgery, and med. jls. *Recreations:* gardening, reading, surgery. *Address:* 79 Albert Street, NW1 7LX. *T:* (020) 7387 0817.

FREEMAN, Paul, DSc (London), ARCS, FRES; Keeper of Entomology, British Museum (Natural History), 1968–81; *b* 26 May 1916; *s* of Samuel Mellor Freeman and Kate Burgis; *m* 1942, Audrey Margaret Long; two *d*. *Educ:* Brentwood Sch., Essex; Imperial Coll., London. Demonstrator in Entomology, Imperial Coll., 1938. Captain, RA and Army Operational Research Group, 1940–45. Lecturer in Entomology, Imperial Coll., 1945–47. Asst Keeper, Dept of Entomology, British Museum (Nat. Hist.), 1947–64, Dep. Keeper, 1964–68. Royal Entomological Soc. of London: Vice-Pres., 1956, 1957; Hon. Sec., 1958–62; Hon. Fellow, 1984. Sec., XIIth Internat. Congress of Entomology, London, 1964. *Publications:* Diptera of Patagonia and South Chile, Pt III–Mycetophilidae, 1951; Simuliidae of the Ethiopian Region (with Botha de Meillon), 1953; numerous papers in learned jls, on taxonomy of Hemiptera and Diptera. *Recreations:* gardening, natural history. *Address:* Briardene, 75 Towncourt Crescent, Petts Wood, Orpington, Kent BR5 1PH. *T:* (01689) 827296.

FREEMAN, Paul Illife, CB 1992; PhD; Controller and Chief Executive of HM Stationery Office, and the Queen's Printer of Acts of Parliament, 1989–95; *b* 11 July 1935; *s* of late John Percy Freeman and Hilda Freeman; *m* 1959, Enid Ivy May Freeman; one *s* one *d. Educ:* Victoria University of Manchester (BSc (Hons) Chemistry, PhD). Post Doctoral Fellow, Nat. Research Council of Canada, 1959–61; Research Scientist, Dupont De Nemours Co. Ltd, Wilmington, Del, USA, 1961–64; Nat. Physical Laboratory: Sen. Scientific Officer, 1964–70; Principal Scientific Officer, 1970–74; Exec. Officer, Research Requirements Bds, DoI, 1973–77; Director: Computer Aided Design Centre, 1977–83; National Engrg Lab., 1980–83; Central Computer and Telecommunications Agency, HM Treasury, 1983–88. Member: CS Coll. Adv. Council, 1983–88; Bd, NCC, 1983–88; Bd, DVLA, 1990–92; Council, UEA, 1994–2003. Vis. Prof. Univ. of Strathclyde, 1981–86. CCMI (CIMgt 1995). *Publications:* scientific papers. *Recreations:* fishing, reading, walking, gardening.

FREEMAN, Peter David Mark, CBE 2001; Principal Finance Officer, Department for International Development, 2000–01; *b* 8 Dec. 1947; *s* of Dr Victor Freeman and Ethel (*née* Halpern); *m* 1980, Anne Tyndale; two *d. Educ:* Merton Coll., Oxford (BA Hons); Univ. of Toronto (MA). Asst Private Sec. to Minister for Overseas Develt, 1973–75; Office of UK Exec. Dir, World Bank, 1975–78; British High Commn, Zimbabwe, 1980–83; Overseas Development Administration, then Department for International Development: Head: EC Dept, 1984–88; Central and Southern Africa Dept, 1988–90; Aid Policy Dept, 1990–91; Internat. Div., 1991–93; Personnel, Orgn and Services Div., 1993–96; Dir, Africa Div., 1996–99. Non-exec. Dir, Shared Interest Soc. Ltd, 2003–. Mem., Audit Cttee, Sightsavers Internat., 2001–. Trustee: Internat. HIV/AIDS Alliance, 2002–; Shared Interest Foundn, 2005–; IDS, 2006–. Governor: Stanford Jun. Sch., Brighton, 1988– (Chm., 1992–96); Dorothy Stringer High Sch., Brighton, 1996–99; Brighton, Hove and Sussex Sixth Form Coll., 2001– (Chm., 2005–); Chm., Brighton and Hove Schs Forum, 2003–. Chm., Brighton Pavilion Labour Party, 2003–. *Address:* 18 Montpelier Crescent, Brighton BN1 3JF.

FREEMAN, Peter John; Member, since 2003, and Chairman, since 2006, Competition Commission (Deputy Chairman, 2003–05); *b* 2 Oct. 1948; *s* of Comdr John Kenneth Herbert Freeman, LVO, RN retd and Jean Forbes Freeman (*née* Irving); *m* 1972, Elizabeth Mary Rogers; two *s* two *d. Educ:* King Edward's Sch., Bath; Kingswood Sch., Bath; Goethe Inst., Berlin; Trinity Coll., Cambridge (Exhibnr; MA); Univ. Libre de Bruxelles (Licence Spéciale en Droit Européen). Called to the Bar, Middle Temple, 1972; admitted solicitor, 1977; Simmons & Simmons: asst, 1973; Partner, 1978–2003; Hd, EC and Competition Gp, 1987–2003; Managing Partner, Commercial and Trade Law Dept, 1994–99. Chm., Regulatory Policy Inst., Oxford, 1998–2007. Jt Gen. Ed., 1991–2005, Cons. Ed., 2005–, Butterworth's Competition Law. Member of Advisory Board: ESRC Res. Centre for Competition Policy, 2007–; Competition Law Jl, 2007–; Internat. Competition Law Forum (St Gallen), 2007–. *Publications:* (with R. Whish) A Guide to the Competition Act 1998, 1999; articles on competition law. *Recreations:* studying naval history, painting in oils, playing the piano. *Address:* Competition Commission, Victoria House, Southampton Row, WC1B 4AD. *T:* (020) 7271 0114, *Fax:* (020) 7271 0203; *e-mail:* peter.freeman@cc.gsi.gov.uk. *Clubs:* Oxford and Cambridge, Reform.

FREEMAN, Prof. Raymond, MA, DPhil, DSc (Oxon); FRS 1979; John Humphrey Plummer Professor of Magnetic Resonance, and Fellow of Jesus College, Cambridge University, 1987–99, now Emeritus Professor; *b* 6 Jan. 1932; *s* of late Albert and Hilda Frances Freeman; *m* 1958, Anne-Marie Périnet-Marquet; two *s* three *d. Educ:* Nottingham High Sch. (scholar); Lincoln Coll., Oxford (open scholar). Ingénieur, Centre d'Etudes Nucléaires de Saclay, Commissariat à l'Energie Atomique, France, 1957–59; Sen. Scientific Officer, Nat. Phys. Lab., Teddington, Middx, 1959–63; Man., Nuclear Magnetic Resonance Research, Varian Associates, Palo Alto, Calif, 1963–73; Lectr in Physical Chemistry, 1973–82, Aldrichian Praelector in Chemistry, 1982–87, and Fellow, Magdalen Coll., 1973–87, Oxford Univ. Chem. Soc. Award in Theoretical Chem. and Spectroscopy, 1978; Leverhulme Medal, Royal Soc., 1990; Longstaff Medal, RSC, 1999; Queen's Medal, Royal Soc., 2002. Hon. DSc Durham, 1988. *Publications:* A Handbook of Nuclear Magnetic Resonance, 1987; Spin Choreography: basic steps in high resolution NMR, 1997; Magnetic Resonance in Chemistry and Medicine, 2003; articles on nuclear magnetic resonance spectroscopy in various scientific journals. *Recreations:* swimming, traditional jazz. *Address:* Department of Chemistry, University of Cambridge, Lensfield Road, Cambridge CB2 1EW; Jesus College, Cambridge CB5 8BL; 29 Bentley Road, Cambridge CB2 8AW. *T:* (01223) 323958.

FREEMAN, Ven. Robert John; Archdeacon of Halifax, since 2003; *b* 26 Oct. 1952; *s* of Ralph and Constance Freeman; *m* 1974, Christine Weight; three *d. Educ:* Durham Univ. (BSc Psychol. 1974); Fitzwilliam Coll., Cambridge (MA Theol. 1976). Ordained deacon, 1977, priest, 1978; Asst Curate, Blackpool Parish Ch, 1977–81; Team Vicar, Chigwell (St Winifred), 1981–85; Vicar, Ch of the Martyrs, Leicester, 1985–99; Nat. Evangelism Advr, Archbishops' Council, 1999–2003. RD, Christianity South (Leicester), 1994–98; Hon. Canon, Leicester Cathedral, 1994–2003. Vice-Chm. and Dir, Leicester City Challenge, 1992–94; Dir, Just Fair Trade, 2000–03; Director and Chairman: rejesus.co.uk, 2001–; Christian Enquiry Agency, 2006–; Dir, Active Faith Communities, 2005–. Chm. and Trustee, Agenda and Support Cttee, Gp for Evangelisation of Churches Together in England, 1999–2003; C of E rep., Leicester Standing Adv. Cttee on Religious Educn, 1997–99; Mem., Churches Regional Commn Yorks and Humberside, 2004–. Editor: Good News, 2000–03; www.evangelism.uk.net, 2000–03. *Publications:* (jtly) 20 from 10: insights from the Decade of Evangelism, 2000; Mission-shaped Church, 2004. *Recreations:* Motown, R & B, air guitar, puddings, web design, computer games, adventure novels, cats, QVC. *Address:* 2 Vicarage Gardens, Rastrick, Brighouse HD6 3HD. *T:* (01484) 714553, *Fax:* (01484) 711897; *e-mail:* frmn@frmn.com.

FREEMAN, Dr (Sally) Joan, PhD; CPsychol, FBPsS; FCP; Visiting Professor, School of Lifelong Learning and Education, Middlesex University, since 1992; *b* 17 June 1935; *d* of late Phillip Casket and Rebecca (*née* Goldman); *m* 1957, Hugh Lionel Freeman, *qv*; three *s* one *d. Educ:* Broughton High Sch.; Univ. of Manchester (BSc, PhD 1980, MEd, DipEdGuidance). FBPsS 1985; CPsychol 1988; FCP 1990. Sen. Lectr in Applied Psychol., Preston Poly., 1975–81; Hon. Tutor, Dept of Educn, Univ. of Manchester, 1975–89; Hon. Lectr, Inst. of Educn, Univ. of London, 1988–94. Private psychology practice, London, 1989–. Ed., High Ability Studies, 1995–98. Dir, Gulbenkian Res. Project on Gifted Children, 1973–88. Founder Pres., European Council for High Ability, 1987–92. Mem., various cttees and projects on the educn of children of high ability, incl. Adv. Bd on Exceptionally Able Pupils, SCAA, 1994–, and Govt Adv. Gp, Gifted and Talented Children, 1998–. Vis appts, scholarships and consultancies, Italy, Bulgaria, Canada, SA, Hong Kong and Australia. College of Preceptors, now College of Teachers: Member: Bd of Examnrs, 1987–; Council, 1995–; Exec. Cttee, 1999–; Sen. Vice-Pres., 2002–; Chm., Publications Bd, 1998–; Hon. Fellow, 2006; British Psychological Society: Mem., Nat. Council, 1975–86; Chm., Northern Br., 1978–86; Mem., Standing Press Cttee, 1980–85; Lifetime Achievement Award, 2007. Chm., Tower Educn Gp; Mem., Strategic Thinking Forum, Centre for British Teachers. Mem., Fawcett Soc., 1984–. Hon. FCollT 2006. *Publications:* Human Biology and Hygiene, 1968, 2nd edn 1981; In and Out of School: an introduction to applied psychology in education, 1975 (trans. Portuguese, Hebrew and Spanish); Gifted Children: their identification and development in a social context, 1979;

Clever Children: a parents' guide, 1983 (trans. German, Finnish and Thai); (ed) The Psychology of Gifted Children: perspectives on development and education, 1985 (trans. Spanish); Gifted Children Growing Up, 1991; Bright as a Button: how to encourage your children's talents 0–5 years, 1991 (trans. Indonesian); Quality Basic Education: the development of competence, 1992 (trans. French); (with S. Ojanen) The Attitudes and Experiences of Headteachers, Class-teachers and Highly Able Pupils Towards the Education of the Highly Able in Finland and Britain, 1994; (ed jtly) Actualising Talent: a lifelong challenge, 1995; Highly Able Girls and Boys, 1996; How to Raise a Bright Child, 1996 (trans. Russian and Chinese); Educating the Very Able: current international research, 1998 (trans. Thai); International Out-of-school Education for the Gifted and Talented, 1998; (with Z. C. Guenther) Educando os Mais Capazes: idéias e ações comprovadas, 2000; Gifted Children Grown Up, 2001; numerous academic papers and chapters in books; contrib. numerous articles and book reviews on child develt, psychol and educn for both professional and lay jls. *Recreations:* photography, reading, travel. *Address:* 21 Montagu Square, W1H 2LF. *T:* (020) 7486 2604; *e-mail:* joan@joanfreeman.com.

FREEMAN-ATTWOOD, Prof. Jonathan; Principal, Royal Academy of Music, since 2008 (Vice-Principal, 1995–2008); Professor, University of London, since 2001; *b* Woking, 4 Nov. 1961; *s* of Harold Warren Freeman-Attwood and Marigold Diana Sneyd (*née* Philips); *m* 1990, Henrietta Christian Paula Parham; one *s* one *d. Educ:* Univ. of Toronto (BMus Hons); Christ Church, Oxford (MPhil). Royal Academy of Music: GRSM Tutor, 1990–91; Associate Dean, 1991–92, Dean, 1992–95, of Undergraduate Studies; Dir of Studies, 1995–96. Vis. Prof., KCL, 2007–. Pres., RAM Club, 2006–07. Critic, Gramophone, 1992–; freelance writer on Bach performances and traditions, etc; regular contrib. to CD Review, BBC Radio 3, 1992–. Trumpet player for many ensembles; solo recordings: Albinoni for Trumpet, 1993; Bach Connections, 1999; The Trumpets that Time Forgot, 2003; La Trompette Retrouvée, 2007; Trumpet Masque, 2008. Producer of over 100 CDs (6 Gramophone Awards). Hon. RAM 1997. *Publications:* (contrib.) The New Grove Dictionary of Music and Musicians, 2nd edn 2000; (contrib.) The Cambridge Companion to Recorded Music, 2009. *Recreations:* lots of Bach, playing cricket, French wine châteaux, Liverpool FC, reading, singing to the dog. *Address:* c/o Royal Academy of Music, Marylebone Road, NW1 5HT. *T:* (020) 7873 7377; *e-mail:* j.freeman-attwood@ram.ac.uk.

FREEMAN-GRENVILLE, family name of **Lady Kinloss.**

FREEMANTLE, Andrew, CBE 2007 (MBE 1982); Chief Executive, Royal National Lifeboat Institution, since 1999; *b* 26 Sept. 1944; *s* of Lt-Col Arthur Freemantle and Peggy Frances Freemantle (*née* Wood); *m* 1972, Patricia Mary Thompson; four *d. Educ:* Framlingham Coll.; RMCS; RCDS; Sheffield Univ. Commnd Royal Hampshire Regt, 1965; Australian Army, 1969–72; Royal Hampshire Regt, 1972–76; sc, Camberley, 1978; Directing Staff, Staff Coll. Camberley, 1983–84; CO 1st Bn Royal Hampshire Regt, 1985–87 (despatches 1987); Brigadier 1987; Comd 19 Infantry Bde, 1987–89; Mem., RCDS, 1990. Chief Exec., Scottish Ambulance Service NHS Trust, 1991–99. Freeman, City of London, 2001. CCMI 2003. *Recreations:* running, cooking. *Address:* Royal National Lifeboat Institution, West Quay Road, Poole, Dorset BH15 1HZ. *T:* (0845) 122 6999, *Fax:* (0845) 126 1999; *e-mail:* afreemantle@rnli.org.uk. *Club:* Army and Navy.

FREER, Maj. Gen. Adrian Robert, OBE 1994; Co-ordinator, Kosovo Protection Corps, 2004–05; *b* 17 April 1952; *s* of Air Chief Marshal Sir Robert William George Freer, *qv*; *m* 1983, Caroline Mary Henderson; two *d. Educ:* Trent Coll., Long Eaton, Notts. Commnd Parachute Regt, 1972; served 1 Para, 1972–80; Instructor, NCO Tactical Wing, Brecon, 1980–81; served 3 Para, 1982–83; Army Staff Coll., 1984; COS, 48 Gurkha Bde, 1985–86; Co. Comd 3 Para, 1987–88; Chief Instructor, RMA Sandhurst, 1989–90; Directing Staff, Army Staff Coll., 1990–91; CO 2 Para, 1992–94; Comdt, Inf. Trng Centre, 1994–97; Comd 5 Airborne Bde, 1997–99; rcds 2000; ACOS, J7 PJHQ, 2001–02; Comd Internat. Military Adv. Team, Sierra Leone, 2003–04. *Recreations:* all sports, particularly golf! *Address: e-mail:* arfreer@hotmail.com. *Clubs:* MCC; New (Edinburgh); Crieff Golf.

FREER, Maj. Gen. Ian Lennox, CB 1994; CBE 1988 (OBE 1985); Principal, Lennox Freer and Associates Pty Ltd, 1997; Director, since 2004, and Executive Chairman, since 2007, Ocean Software Pty Ltd (Managing Director, 2004–07); *b* 18 May 1941; *s* of late Lt-Col George Freer, OBE and Elizabeth (*née* Tallo), Edinburgh; *m* 1970, Karla Thwaites; one *s* two *d. Educ:* George Watson's Coll., Edinburgh; RMA Sandhurst. Commnd Staffordshire Regt (Prince of Wales's), 1961; served UK, Kenya, Germany, Gulf States, Belize, Gibraltar; Staff Capt. to QMG, 1972–73; MA to COS, BAOR, 1975–77; SO1, Instr Staff Coll., 1980–81; CO 1st Bn, Staffords Regt, 1982–84; Div. Col, Staff Coll., 1985; Comdr, 39 Inf. Bde (NI), 1986–87; Chief, BRIXMIS (Berlin), 1989–91; Comdr, Land Forces, NI, 1991–94; GOC Wales and Western Dist, later 5th Div., 1994–96. Col, Staffords Regt, 1990–96; Col Comdt, POW Div., 1993–96. Dir, Woodleigh Sch., Vic, 1999–; Mem. Council, RUSI, Vic, 1999–; Rep., Beacon Foundn. Mem., Pacific Inst. of Aust. *Recreations:* sailing, gardening. *Address:* 15 Mann Road, Mount Eliza, Vic 3930, Australia. *Clubs:* Melbourne; Royal Brighton Yacht, Flinders Yacht.

FREER, Air Chief Marshal Sir Robert (William George), GBE 1981 (CBE 1966); KCB 1977; Commandant, Royal College of Defence Studies, 1980–82, retired; Director, Pilatus Britten-Norman Ltd, 1988–96; *b* Darjeeling, 1 Sept. 1923; *s* of late William Freer, Stretton, Cirencester, Glos; *m* 1950, Margaret, 2nd *d* of late J. W. Elkington and Mrs M. Elkington, Ruskington Manor, near Sleaford, Lincs; one *s* one *d. Educ:* Gosport Grammar Sch. Flying Instructor, S Africa and UK, 1944–47; RAF Coll., Cranwell, 1947–50; served 54 and 614 Fighter Sqdns, 1950–52; Central Fighter Estabt, 1952–54; commanded 92 Fighter Sqdn, 1955–57 (Queen's Commendation, 1955); psa 1957; Directing Staff, USAF Acad., 1958–60; pfc 1960; Staff of Chief of Defence Staff, 1961–63; Station Comdr, RAF Seletar, 1963–66; DD Defence Plans (Air), MoD, 1966–67; idc 1968; Air ADC to the Queen, 1969–71; Dep. Comdt, RAF Staff Coll., 1969–71; SASO, HQ Near East Air Force, 1971–72; AOC 11 Group, 1972–75; Dir-Gen., Organisation (RAF), April-Sept. 1975; AOC No 18 Group, RAF, 1975–78; Dep. C-in-C, Strike Command, 1978–79. Director: Rediffusion, 1982–88; British Manufg & Res. Co., 1984–88; Rediffusion Simulation, 1985–88. Mem. Council, RAF Benevolent Fund and Chm. Mgt Bd, Princess Marina House, Rustington, 1993–96. Pres., RAF LTA, 1975–81; Mem., Sports Council, 1980–82. CCMI (FBIM 1977); FRSA 1988–94; FRAeS 1995. *Recreations:* golf, tennis, hill-walking. *Address:* Cotterstock House, Clumps Road, Lower Bourne, Farnham, Surrey GU10 3HF. *Clubs:* Royal Air Force; All England Lawn Tennis and Croquet; Hankley Common Golf.

See also Maj. Gen. A. R. Freer.

FREER, Dame Yve Helen Elaine; *see* Buckland, Dame Y. H. E.

FREETH, Denzil Kingson, MBE 1997; *b* 10 July 1924; *s* of late Walter Kingson and late Vera Freeth. *Educ:* Highfield Sch., Liphook, Hants; Sherborne Sch. (Scholar); Trinity Hall, Cambridge (Scholar). Served War, 1943–46: RAF (Flying Officer). Pres. Union

Soc., Cambridge, 1949; Chm. Cambridge Univ. Conservative Assoc. 1949; debating tour of America, 1949, also debated in Ireland; Mem. Exec. Cttee Nat. Union, 1955. MP (C) Basingstoke Division of Hants, 1955–64. PPS to Minister of State, Bd of Trade, 1956, to Pres. of the Bd of Trade, 1957–59, to Minister of Educn, 1959–60; Parly Sec. for Science, 1961–63. Mem. Parliamentary Cttee of Trustee Savings Bank Assoc., 1956–61. Mem. Select Cttee on Procedure, 1958–59. Employed by and Partner in stockbroking firms, 1950–61 and 1964–89; Mem. of Stock Exchange, 1959–61, 1965–91. Chm. Finance Cttee, London Diocesan Fund, 1986–94. Churchwarden, All Saints' Church, Margaret St, W1, 1977–96. *Recreations:* good food, wine and conversation. *Address:* 3 Brasenose House, 35 Kensington High Street, W8 5BA. *T:* (020) 7937 8685. *Clubs:* Carlton; Pitt (Cambridge).

FREETH, Peter Stewart, RA 1991 (ARA 1990); RE 1991 (ARE 1987); Tutor, Etching, Royal Academy Schools, since 1966; *b* 15 April 1938; *s* of Alfred William Freeth and Olive Walker; *m* 1967, Mariolina Meliadó; two *s*. *Educ:* King Edward's Grammar School, Aston, Birmingham; Slade School, London (Dip Fine Art). Rome Scholar, Engraving, British Sch., Rome, 1960–62; teacher of Printmaking, Camden Inst., 1979–2007. One man shows: Christopher Mendez Gall., London, 1987–89; Friends' Room, Royal Acad., 1991; S Maria a Gradillo, Ravello, Italy, 1997; Word Play, RA, 2001; Christchurch Coll. Gall., Oxford, 2006; North House Gall., Manningtree, 2006; represented in collections: British Museum; V&A; Fitzwilliam Mus., Cambridge; Arts Council; Metropolitan Mus., NY; Nat. Gall., Washington; Hunterian Mus., Glasgow. Mem., Royal Soc. of Painter Printmakers. *Recreations:* music, books, yet more work. *Address:* 83 Muswell Hill Road, N10 3HT.

FREI, Matt; Chief Washington Correspondent, BBC TV, since 2002; *b* 26 Nov. 1963; *s* of Peter and Anita Frei; *m* 1996, Penny Quested; one *s* three *d*. *Educ:* Westminster Sch.; St Peter's Coll., Oxford (MA Hist. and Spanish). Joined BBC, 1988; BBC Television: Southern Europe Corresp., 1991–96; Asia Corresp., 1996–2002. RTS Award, 2000. *Publication:* Italy: the unfinished revolution, 1996, 2nd edn 1998. *Recreation:* painting. *Address:* Suite 800, 2000 M Street NW, Washington, DC 20036, USA. *T:* (202) 2232050, *Fax:* (202) 7751395; e-mail: Matt.Frei@bbc.co.uk.

FREIER, Most Rev. Philip Leslie; see Melbourne, Archbishop of.

FREMANTLE, family name of **Baron Cottesloe.**

FRÉMAUX, Louis Joseph Felix; conductor; *b* 13 Aug. 1921; *m* 1st, 1948, Nicole Petibon (*d* 1999); four *s* one *d*; 2nd, 1999, Cecily Hake. *Educ:* Conservatoire National Supérieur de Musique de Paris. Chef d'Orchestre Permanent et Directeur, l'Orchestre National de l'Opéra de Monte Carlo, 1956–66; Principal Conductor, Orchestre de Lyon, 1968–71; Musical Dir and Principal Conductor, City of Birmingham Symphony Orch., 1969–78; Music Dir and Principal Conductor, 1979–81, Principal Guest Conductor, 1982–85, Sydney Symph. Orch. First concert in England, with Bournemouth Symph. Orch., 1964. Guest appearances with all symph. orchs in GB; many recordings. Hon. RAM, 1978. Hon. DMus Birmingham, 1978. Croix de Guerre, 1945, 1947; Chevalier de la Légion d'Honneur, 1969. *Recreations:* walking, photography.

FRENCH, family name of **Baron De Freyne.**

FRENCH, Prof. Anthony Philip, PhD; Professor of Physics, Massachusetts Institute of Technology, 1964–91, now Emeritus; *b* 19 Nov. 1920; *s* of Sydney James French and Elizabeth Margaret (*née* Hart); *m* 1st, 1946, Naomi Mary Livesay (*d* 2001); one *s* one *d*; 2nd, 2002, Dorothy Ada Jensen. *Educ:* Varndean Sch., Brighton; Sidney Sussex Coll., Cambridge (major schol.; BA Hons 1942, MA 1946, PhD 1948). British atomic bomb project, Tube Alloys, 1942–44; Manhattan Project, Los Alamos, USA, 1944–46; Scientific Officer, AERE, Harwell, 1946–48; Univ. Demonstrator in Physics, Cavendish Laboratory, Cambridge, 1948–51, Lectr 1951–55; Dir of Studies in Natural Sciences, Pembroke Coll., Cambridge, 1949–55, Fellow of Pembroke, 1950–55; Visiting research scholar: California Inst. of Technology, 1951; Univ. of Michigan, 1954; Prof. of Physics, Univ. of S Carolina, 1955–62 (Head of Dept, 1956–62); Guignard Lectr, 1958; Vis. Prof., MIT, 1962–64; Vis. Fellow of Pembroke Coll., Cambridge, 1975. Member, Internat. Commn on Physics Educn, 1972–84 (Chm., 1975–81); Pres., Amer. Assoc. of Physics Teachers, 1985–86. FInstP 1986; Fellow, Amer. Physical Soc., 1987. Hon. ScD Allegheny Coll., 1989. Bragg Medal, Institute of Physics, 1988; Oersted Medal, 1989, Melba Newell Phillips Award, 1993, Amer. Assoc. of Physics Teachers. *Publications:* Principles of Modern Physics, 1958; Special Relativity, 1968; Newtonian Mechanics, 1971; Vibrations and Waves, 1971; Introduction to Quantum Physics, 1978; Einstein: a centenary volume, 1979; Niels Bohr: a centenary volume, 1985; Introduction to Classical Mechanics, 1986; Physics in a Technological World, 1988; Physics History from AAPT Journals II, 1995. *Recreations:* music, squash, reading, writing. *Address:* c/o Physics Department, Room 6C–435, Massachusetts Institute of Technology, Cambridge, MA 02139, USA.

FRENCH, Cecil Charles John, FREng; Group Technology Director, Ricardo International, 1990–92, retired; *b* 16 April 1926; *s* of Ernest French and Edith Hannah French (*née* Norris); *m* 1st, 1956, Olive Joyce Edwards (*d* 1969); two *d*; 2nd, 1971, Shirley Frances Outten; one *s* one *d*. *Educ:* King's Coll., Univ. of London (MScEng; DSc Eng 1987); Columbia Univ., New York. FIMechE, FIMarEST; FREng (FEng 1982). Graduate apprentice, CAV Ltd, 1948–50; Marshall Aid scholar, MIT, USA (research into combustion in engines), 1950–52; Ricardo Consulting Engineers, subseq. Ricardo Internat., 1952–92, Director, 1969, Vice-Chm., 1982, Man. Dir, 1989; Man. Dir, 1979–83, Chm., 1984–87, G. Cussons Ltd. President, Instn of Mechanical Engineers, 1988–89 (Vice-Pres, 1981–86, Dep. Pres., 1986–88). Hon. DSc Brighton, 2006. *Publications:* numerous articles on diesel engines in learned soc. jls world wide. *Recreations:* folk dancing, photography. *Address:* 303 Upper Shoreham Road, Shoreham-by-Sea, Sussex BN43 5QA. *T:* (01273) 452050.

FRENCH, David; Chief Executive, Westminster Foundation for Democracy, since 2003; *b* 20 June 1947; *s* of late Captain Godfrey Alexander French, CBE, RN, and Margaret Annis French; *m* 1974, Sarah Anne, *d* of Rt Rev. H. D. Halsey, *qv*; four *s*. *Educ:* Sherborne Sch.; Durham Univ. (BA). MCIPD. Nat. Council of Social Service, 1971–74; Hd of Social Services Dept, RNID, 1974–78; Dir of Services, C of E Children's Soc., 1978–87; Dir, Nat. Marriage Guidance Council, then Relate, 1987–95; consultant on family policy, 1995–97; Dir Gen., subseq. Chief Exec., Commonwealth Inst., 1997–2002. Chairman: London Corrymeela Venture, 1973–76; St Albans Internat. Organ Fest., 1985–87; Twenty First Century Foundn, 1996–2001. Trustee: Charity Appts, 1984–91; British Empire and Commonwealth Mus., 1999–2003; The Round Table: Commonwealth Jl of Internat. Affairs, 2001–. Mem. Governing Council, Family Policy Studies Centre, 1989–2001. Mem., St Albans Cathedral Council, 1996–2000. Liveryman, Glaziers' Co., 1990–. MRSocMed 1988. FRSA 1993. *Recreation:* challenging projects. *Address:* 21 Prospect Road, St Albans, Herts AL1 2AT. *T:* (01727) 860520.

FRENCH, Air Vice-Marshal David Rowthorne, CB 1993; MBE 1976; engineering consultant, since 1994; *b* 11 Dec. 1937; *s* of Norman Arthur French and late Edna Mary French (*née* Rowthorne); *m* 1st, 1963, Veronica Margaret Mead (marr. diss. 1982); two *s* one *d*; 2nd, 1984, Philippa Anne Pym, *d* of Sir Alexander Ross; one *s* one *d*. *Educ:* Gosport County Grammar Sch.; RAF Technical Coll., Henlow. CEng, MRAeS 1969. Commnd Engr Br., RAF, 1960; various engrg appts, 1960–69; Sen. Engrg Officer, No 14 Sqn, RAF Bruggen, 1970–71; OC Airframe Systems Sqn, CSDE, RAF Swanton Morley, 1971–72; RAF Staff Coll., Bracknell, 1973; Sen. Engrg Officer, No 54 Sqn, RAF Coltishall, 1974–76; OC Engrg Wg, RAF Lossiemouth, 1976–79; Air Warfare Coll., RAF Cranwell, 1979; SO for Offensive Support Aircraft, HQ Strike Comd, 1980; Dep. Dir of Engrg Policy, MoD, 1981–82; Comd Mech. Engr, HQ RAF Germany, 1983–86; Dir of Policy, Directorate Gen., Defence Quality Assurance, MoD (PE), 1986–87; AO Wales and Stn Comdr, RAF St Athan, 1988–90; Comd Mech. Engr, HQ Strike Comd, 1990–91; AO Maintenance and Chief Exec. Maintenance Gp Defence Support Agency, RAF Support Comd, 1991–94, retd. Chairman: RAF Germany Golf, 1983–86; RAF Support Comd Golf, 1988–90; Capt., RAF Germany Golf Club, 1985–86. *Recreations:* golf, ski-ing, gardening, wine. *Address:* Milestone Piece, Yarmouth Road, Blofield, Norwich, Norfolk NR13 4LQ. *Clubs:* Royal Air Force; Royal Norwich Golf.

FRENCH, Douglas Charles; Chairman, Westminster and City Programmes, since 1997; *b* London, 20 March 1944; *s* of Frederick Emil French and late Charlotte Vera French; *m* 1978, Sue, *y d* of late Philip Arthur Phillips; two *s* one *d*. *Educ:* Glyn Grammar Sch., Epsom; St Catharine's Coll., Cambridge (MA). Called to the Bar, Inner Temple. Exec., then Dir, P. W. Merkle Ltd, 1966–87. Asst to Rt Hon. Sir Geoffrey Howe, Shadow Chancellor, 1976–79; Special Advr to Chancellor of the Exchequer, 1981–83. Contested (C) Sheffield, Attercliffe, 1979; MP (C) Gloucester, 1987–97; contested (C) same seat, 1997. PPS to Minister of State, FCO, 1988–89, ODA, 1989–90, MAFF, 1992–93, DoE, 1993–94, to Sec. of State for the Envmt, 1994–97. Chm., All Party Cttee on Building Socs, 1996–97. Initiated Building Socs (Jt Account Holders) Act 1995, and Building Socs (Distributions) Act 1997. Chm., Bow Gp, 1978–79. Pres., Gloucester Conservative Club, 1989–97. Pres., Glyn Old Boys' Assoc., 2005–. Gov., Glyn Technol. Coll., Epsom, 2000– (Vice-Chm., 2003–05; Chm., 2006–). *Publications:* articles and reviews. *Recreations:* gardening, renovating period houses, ski-ing, squash. *Address:* 231 Kennington Lane, SE11 5QU. *Club:* Royal Automobile.

FRENCH, Air Chief Marshal Sir Joseph Charles, (Sir Joe), KCB 2003; CBE 1991 (OBE); FRAeS; Commander-in-Chief Strike Command, 2006–07; Air Aide-de-Camp to the Queen, 2006–07; *b* 15 July 1949. Joined RAF, 1967; rcds; psa; postings in ME, Germany, Hong Kong and UK; ADC to CDS; Central Trials and Tactics Orgn; Hd, RAF Presentation Team; PSO to AOC-in-C Strike Comd, 1986–88; RAF Staff Coll., Bracknell, 1988; Station Comdr, RAF Odiham, Hants, 1989–91; Dir, Air Force Staff Duties, MoD, 1992–95; ACDS (Policy), 1995–97; Dir Gen. Intelligence and Geographic Resources, MoD, 1997–2001; Chief of Defence Intelligence, 2001–03; Air Mem. for Personnel and C-in-C PTC, 2003–06.

FRENCH, Philip Neville; writer and broadcaster; Film Critic, The Observer, since 1978; *b* Liverpool, 28 Aug. 1933; *s* of late John and Bessie French; *m* 1957, Kersti Elisabet Molin; three *s*. *Educ:* Bristol Grammar Sch.; Exeter Coll., Oxford (BA Law) (editor, The Isis, 1956); Indiana Univ. Nat. Service, 2nd Lieut Parachute Regt, 1952–54. Reporter, Bristol Evening Post, 1958–59; Producer, BBC N Amer. Service, 1959–61; Talks Producer, BBC Radio, 1961–67; New Statesman: Theatre Critic, 1967–68; Arts Columnist, 1967–72; Sen. Producer, BBC Radio, 1968–90: editor of The Arts This Week, Critics' Forum and other series, writer-presenter of arts documentaries, Radio 3. Vis. Prof., Univ. of Texas, 1972. Mem., BFI Prodn Bd, 1968–74; Jury Mem., Cannes Film Fest., 1986. Hon. Life Mem., BAFTA, 2008. Hon. DLitt Lancaster, 2006. *Publications:* Age of Austerity 1945–51 (ed with Michael Sissons), 1963; The Movie Moguls, 1969; Westerns: aspects of a movie genre, 1974, 3rd expanded edn as Westerns and Westerns Revisited, 2005; Three Honest Men: Edmund Wilson, F. R. Leavis, Lionel Trilling, 1980; (ed) The Third Dimension: voices from Radio Three, 1983; (ed with Deac Rossell) The Press: observed and projected, 1991; (ed) Malle on Malle, 1992; (ed with Ken Wlaschin) The Faber Book of Movie Verse, 1993; (with Kersti French) Wild Strawberries, 1995; (with Karl French) Cult Movies, 1999; numerous articles and essays in magazines, newspapers and anthologies. *Recreations:* woolgathering in England, picking wild strawberries in Sweden. *Address:* 62 Dartmouth Park Road, NW5 1SN. *T:* (020) 7485 1711.

FRENCH, Roger; HM Diplomatic Service, retired; Counsellor (Management) and Consul-General, Tokyo, 2003–07; *b* 3 June 1947; *s* of Alfred Stephen George French and Margaret (*née* Brown); *m* 1969, Angela Cooper; one *s* one *d*. *Educ:* County Grammar Sch., Dagenham. Joined Foreign and Commonwealth Office, 1965; Havana, 1970; Vice-Consul: Madrid, 1971–73; Puerto Rico, 1973–76; FCO, 1977–80; Second, later First, Sec., (Chancery), Washington, 1980–84; First Sec. (Commercial), Muscat, 1985–88; Dep. Hd of N America Dept, FCO, 1988–92; Dep. Consul-Gen., Milan, 1992–96; Counsellor (Mgt) and Consul-Gen., Washington, 1997–2001; Actg Dep. High Comr, Nigeria, 2001; Hd of Inf. Mgt Gp, FCO, 2001–03. Commnd Kentucky Col, 1998. *Recreation:* music. *Address:* e-mail: angrog1969@hotmail.co.uk.

FRENK, Prof. Carlos Silvestre, PhD; FRS 2004; Ogden Professor of Fundamental Physics and Director, Institute for Computational Cosmology, University of Durham, since 2002; *b* 27 Oct. 1951; *s* of Silvestre Frenk and Alicia Mora de Frenk; *m* 1978, Susan Frances Clarke; two *s*. *Educ:* Nat. Autonomous Univ. of Mexico (BSc Theoretical Physics 1976); King's Coll., Cambridge (Math. Tripos Part III 1977); Inst. of Astronomy, Univ. of Cambridge (PhD 1981). Postdoctoral Research Fellow: Dept of Astronomy, Univ. of Calif at Berkeley, 1981–83; Astronomy Centre, Univ. of Sussex, 1983–85; Asst Res. Physicist, Inst. for Theoretical Physics, Univ. of Calif at Santa Barbara, 1984; University of Durham: Lectr in Astronomy, Dept of Physics, 1985–91; Reader in Physics, 1991–93; Prof. of Astrophysics, 1993–2002. Occasional broadcasts, radio and television, 1988–. Member: IAU, 1985; AAS, 1993. FRAS 1981. Wolfson Res. Merit Award, Royal Soc., 2006; Daniel Chalonge Medal, Internat. Sch. of Astrophysics, 2007. *Publications:* (ed) The Epoch of Galaxy Formation, 1989; (ed) Observational Tests of Cosmological Inflation, 1991; more than 300 scientific papers in prof. jls, incl. Nature, Astrophys. Jl, Astronomical Jl. *Recreations:* literature, ski training. *Address:* Department of Physics, Ogden Centre for Fundamental Physics, University of Durham, Science Laboratories, South Road, Durham DH1 3LE. *T:* (0191) 334 3641.

FRENKEL, Prof. Daniel, PhD; Professor of Theoretical Chemistry, University of Cambridge, since 2007; Fellow, Trinity College, Cambridge, since 2008; *b* Amsterdam, 27 July 1948; *s* of Maurits Frenkel and Herta G. Tietz; *m* 1st, 1986, Alida H. Bolliger (*d* 1995); two *d*; 2nd, 2004, Dr Erika Eiser. *Educ:* Barlaeus Gymnasium, Amsterdam; Univ. of Amsterdam (Masters degree in Phys. Chem. 1972; PhD 1977). Post-doctoral Res. Fellow, UCLA, 1977–80; Res. Scientist, Shell Res., Amsterdam, 1980–81; University of Utrecht: Lectr, then Reader, Dept of Physics, 1981–86; Prof. of Computational Chem. (pt-time), 1987–; Prof. of Macromolecular Simulations (pt-time), Univ. of Amsterdam,

1998–2007; Gp Leader, 1987–2007, Scientific Advr, 2007–, Inst. for Atomic and Molecular Physics, Foundn for Fundamental Res. on Matter, Amsterdam. Hon. Prof., Beijing Univ. of Chem. Technol., 2005–. Chm., Amsterdam Centre for Multiscale Modelling, 2007–. Member: Royal Dutch Acad. of Scis, 1998; Hollandsche Maatschappij der Wetenschappen, Netherlands, 2002. Foreign Mem., Royal Soc. (London), 2006; Foreign Hon. Mem., Amer. Acad. Arts and Scis, 2008. Hon. DSci Edinburgh, 2007. *Publications:* (jtly) Simulation of Liquids and Solids, Molecular Dynamics and Monte Carlo Methods in Statistical Mechanics, 1987; (jtly) Understanding Molecular Simulation: from algorithms to applications, 1996, 2nd edn 2002; contrib. internat. jls. *Address:* Department of Chemistry, University of Cambridge, Lensfield Road, Cambridge CB2 1EW. *T:* (01223) 336376; *e-mail:* df246@cam.ac.uk.

FRERE, Vice-Adm. Sir Richard Tobias, (Sir Toby), KCB 1994; Chairman, Prison Service Pay Review Body, 2001–05; Member, Armed Forces Pay Review Body, 1997–2002; *b* 4 June 1938; *s* of late Alexander Stewart Frere and Patricia Frere; *m* 1968, Jane Barraclough; two *d.* *Educ:* Eton College; Britannia Royal Naval College. Joined RNVR as National Serviceman; transf. RN 1956; commissioned 1958; submarines 1960; served Canada, 1961–62, Australia, 1966–67, 1973; commanded HM Submarines Andrew, Odin and Revenge and Frigate HMS Brazen. JSSC Canberra, 1973; RCDS London, 1982; Dir Gen. Fleet Support, Policy and Services, 1988–91; Flag Officer Submarines, and Comdr Submarines Eastern Atlantic, 1991–93; Chief of Fleet Support and Mem., Admiralty Bd, 1994–97. Chm. Govs, Oundle Sch., 2007–. Master, Grocers' Co., 2004–05. *Recreation:* sailing. *Address:* c/o Naval Secretary, Fleet Headquarters, Whale Island, Portsmouth PO2 8BY. *Clubs:* Garrick, Naval, MCC.

FRERE, Prof. Sheppard Sunderland, CBE 1976; FSA 1944; FBA 1971; Professor of the Archæology of the Roman Empire, and Fellow of All Souls College, Oxford University, 1966–83, now Professor Emeritus and Emeritus Fellow; *b* 23 Aug. 1916; *e s* of late N. G. Frere, CMG; *m* 1961, Janet Cecily Hoare; one *s* one *d.* *Educ:* Lancing Coll.; Magdalene Coll., Cambridge. BA 1938, MA 1944, LittD 1976, DLitt 1977. Master, Epsom Coll., 1938–40. National Fire Service, 1940–45. Master, Lancing Coll., 1945–54; Lecturer in Archæology, Manchester Univ., 1954–55; Reader in Archæology of the Roman Provinces, London Univ. Inst. of Archæology, 1955–62; Prof. of the Archæology of the Roman Provinces, London Univ., 1963–66. Dir, Canterbury Excavations, 1946–60; Dir, Verulamium Excavations, 1955–61. Vice-Pres., Soc. of Antiquaries, 1962–66; President: Oxford Architectural and Historical Soc., 1972–80; Royal Archæological Inst., 1978–81; Soc. for Promotion of Roman Studies, 1983–86. Hon. Corr. Mem. German Archæological Inst., 1964, Fellow, 1967; Member: Royal Commn on Hist. Monuments (England), 1966–83; Ancient Monuments Board (England), 1966–82. Hon. LittD: Leeds, 1977; Leicester, 1983; Kent, 1985. Gold Medal, Soc. of Antiquaries, 1989. Editor, Britannia, 1969–79. *Publications:* (ed) Problems of the Iron Age in Southern Britain, 1961; Britannia, a history of Roman Britain, 1967, 4th edn 1999; Verulamium Excavations, vol. I, 1972, vol. II, 1983, vol. III, 1984; Excavations on the Roman and Medieval Defences of Canterbury, 1982; Excavations at Canterbury, vol. VII, 1983; (with J. K. St Joseph) Roman Britain from the Air, 1983; (with F. A. Lepper) Trajan's Column, 1988; (with J. J. Wilkes) Strageath: excavations within the Roman fort, 1989; (ed with R. Tomlin) The Roman Inscriptions of Britain, vol. II, fasc. 1, 1990, fascs 2–3, 1991, fasc. 4, 1992, fasc. 5, 1993, fasc. 6, 1994, fascs 7–8, and Epigraphic Indexes, 1995; Excavations at the Roman Fort at Bowes, 2008; papers in learned jls. *Recreation:* gardening. *Address:* Netherfield House, Marcham, Abingdon, Oxon OX13 6NP.

FRERE, Vice-Adm. Sir Toby; *see* Frere, Vice-Adm. Sir R. T.

FRESKO, Adrienne Sheila, CBE 2003; Director, Foresight Partnership, since 2004; *b* 22 Feb. 1957; *d* of Mendal and Esther Marcus; *m* 1979, Marc Marcos Fresko; two *d.* *Educ:* Manchester High Sch. for Girls; St Anne's Coll., Oxford (MA Exptl Psychol.); Birkbeck Coll., London (MSc Occupational Psychol.). Mem., BPsS, 1998. Vice-Pres., Human Resources, Citibank, 1985–86; Principal, Adrienne Fresko Consulting, 1989–97; Audit Commission: Mem., 1996–2000; Dep. Chair, 2000–03; Actg Chair, 2001–02; Hd, Centre for Public Governance, Office of Public Mgt, 2000–04. Chairman: Croydon Dist HA, 1992–96; Croydon HA, 1996–2000; Lead Chm., Croydon Health Commng Agency, 1994–96. Dir, Accountancy Foundn, 1999–2003. MCIPD (MIPD 1991); FRSA 2000. *Publication:* Making a Difference: women in public appointments, 2001. *Recreations:* family, travel, community. *Address:* Foresight Partnership, 12 Welcomes Road, Kenley, Surrey CR8 5HD. *T:* (020) 8660 6465; *e-mail:* adrienne@foresight-partnership.co.uk.

FRETWELL, Sir (Major) John (Emsley), GCMG 1987 (KCMG 1982; CMG 1975); HM Diplomatic Service, retired; Political Director and Deputy to the Permanent Under-Secretary of State, Foreign and Commonwealth Office, 1987–90; *b* 15 June 1930; *s* of late Francis Thomas and Dorothy Fretwell; *m* 1959, Mary Ellen Eugenie Dubois (OBE 2001); one *s* one *d.* *Educ:* Chesterfield Grammar Sch.; Lausanne Univ.; King's Coll., Cambridge (MA). HM Forces, 1948–50. Diplomatic Service, 1953; 3rd Sec., Hong Kong, 1954–55; 2nd Sec., Peking, 1955–57; FO, 1957–59; 1st Sec., Moscow, 1959–62; FO, 1962–67; 1st Sec. (Commercial), Washington, 1967–70; Commercial Counsellor, Warsaw, 1971–73; Head of European Integration Dept (Internal), FCO, 1973–76; Asst Under-Sec. of State, FCO, 1976–79; Minister, Washington, 1980–81; Ambassador to France, 1982–87. Specialist Advr, H of L, 1992–93; Specialist Assessor, HEFC, 1995–96. Mem., Council of Lloyd's, 1991–92. Chm., Franco-British Soc., 1995–2005. *Recreations:* history, walking, wine. *Club:* Brooks's.

FREUD, Anthony Peter, OBE 2006; General Director and Chief Executive Officer, Houston Grand Opera, since 2006; *b* 30 Oct. 1957; *s* of Joseph Freud and Katalin Lowi. *Educ:* King's Coll. London (LLB 1978); Inns of Court Sch. of Law. Called to the Bar, Gray's Inn, 1979; Th. Manager, Sadler's Wells Th., 1980–84; Gen. Manager and Dir, Opera Planning, WNO, 1984–92; Exec. Producer, Philips Classics, 1992–94; Gen. Dir, WNO, 1994–2005. Vice-Chm., Opera America, 2007–. Honorary Fellow: Cardiff University, 2005; RWCMD, 2006. *Address:* Houston Grand Opera, 510 Preston Street, Houston, TX 77002, USA. *T:* (713) 5460260, *Fax:* (713) 2470906; *e-mail:* anthony_freud@houstongrandopera.org.

FREUD, Sir Clement (Raphael), Kt 1987; writer, broadcaster, caterer; *b* 24 April 1924; *s* of late Ernst and Lucie Freud; *m* 1950, June Beatrice, (Jill), 2nd *d* of H. W. Flewett, MA; three *s* two *d.* Apprenticed, Dorchester Hotel, London. Served War, Royal Ulster Rifles; Liaison Officer, Nuremberg war crimes trials, 1946. Trained, Martinez Hotel, Cannes. Proprietor, Royal Court Theatre Club, 1952–62. Sports writer, Observer, 1956–64; Cookery Editor: Time and Tide, 1961–63; Observer Magazine, 1964–68; Daily Telegraph Magazine, 1968–. Sports Columnist, Sun, 1964–69; Columnist: Sunday Telegraph, 1963–65; News of the World, 1965; Financial Times, 1964–; Daily Express, 1973–75; Saga magazine, 1987–2002; Radio Times, 1992–; Independent, 1997–; Times Diarist, 1988–98, Columnist, 1992–96. Consultant: Intercity, 1990–97; Rail Gourmet, 1998–; Compass Gp, 1999–. Contested (L) Cambridgeshire NE, 1987. MP (L): Isle of Ely, July 1973–1983; Cambridgeshire NE, 1983–87. Liberal spokesman on education, the arts and broadcasting; sponsor, Official Information Bill. Chm., Standing Cttee, Liberal Party, 1982–86. Rector: Univ. of Dundee, 1974–80; St Andrews Univ., 2002–06. Pres., Down's Children Assoc., 1988. £5,000 class winner, Daily Mail London-NY air race, 1969; line honours, Cape Town-Rio yacht race, 1971. Award winning petfood commercial: San Francisco, Tokyo, Berlin, 1967. BBC (sound) Just a Minute, 1968–. MUniv Open, 1989; Hon. LLD St Andrews, 2005. *Publications:* Grimble, 1968; Grimble at Christmas, 1973; Freud on Food, 1978; Clicking Vicky, 1980; The Book of Hangovers, 1981; Below the Belt, 1983; No-one Else has Complained, 1988; The Gourmet's Tour of Great Britain and Ireland, 1989; Freud Ego (autobiog.), 2001; contributor to, New Yorker, etc (formerly to Punch). *Recreations:* racing, backgammon, pétanque. *Address:* 14 York House, Upper Montagu Street, W1H 1FR. *T:* (020) 7724 5432; Westons, Walberswick, Suffolk IP18 6UH; Casa de Colina, Praia da Luz, Algarve. *Clubs:* MCC, Lord's Taverners', Groucho.
See also R. W. A. Curtis, L. Freud, M. R. Freud.

FREUD, Elisabeth; *see* Murdoch, E.

FREUD, Lucian, OM 1993; CH 1983; painter; *b* 8 Dec. 1922; *s* of late Ernst and Lucie Freud; *m* 1st, 1948, Kathleen Garman (marr. diss. 1952), *d* of Jacob Epstein; two *d*; 2nd, 1953, Lady Caroline Maureen Blackwood (marr. diss. 1957; she *d* 1996), *d* of 4th Marquess of Dufferin and Ava. *Educ:* Central Sch. of Art; East Anglian Sch. of Painting and Drawing. Worked on merchant ship SS Baltrover as ordinary seaman, 1942. Teacher, Slade Sch. of Art, 1948–58; Vis. Asst, Norwich Sch. of Art, 1964–65. Painted mostly in France and Greece, 1946–48; Cyclamen bathroom, 1959, Thornhill bedroom, Chatsworth House, Derbyshire. Hon. Mem., Amer. Acad. and Inst. of Arts and Letters, 1988. Hon. DLitt Glasgow, 2003. Jerg-Ratgeb Prize, Reutlingen, 2002. *Exhibitions:* Lefevre Gall., 1944, 1946; London Gall., 1947, 1948; British Council and Galérie René Drouin, Paris, 1948; Hanover Gall., 1950, 1952; British Council and Vancouver Art Gall., 1951; British Council, Venice Biennale, 1954; Marlborough Fine Art, 1958, 1963, 1968, 2005; Anthony d'Offay, 1972, 1978 (subseq. Davis & Long, NY), 1982; Nishimura Gall., Tokyo, 1979, 1991; Thos Agnew & Sons, 1983; Scottish Nat. Gall. of Modern Art, 1988; Berggruen Gall., Paris, 1990; Saatchi Collection, 1990; Thomas Gibson Fine Art Ltd, 1991; Palazzo Ruspoli, Rome, 1991; Castello Sforzesca, Milan, 1991; Art Gall. of NSW, 1992; Tochigi Prefectural Mus. of Fine Arts, Otani Meml Art Mus., Nishinomiya, and Setagaya Art Museum, Tokyo, Japan, 1992; Whitechapel Art Gall., 1993; Metropolitan Mus. of Art, New York, 1993; Museo Nacional Centro de Arte Reina Sofia, Madrid, 1994; Astrup Fearnley Museet for Moderne Kunst, Oslo, 1994; Dulwich Picture Gall., 1994; Fondation Maeght, St Paul de Vence, 1995; Abbot Hall Art Gall., Kendal, 1996; Acquavella Contemp. Art, NY, 1996; Tel Aviv Mus. of Art, 1996; Nat. Gall. of Scotland, 1997; Tate Gall., 1998; Yale Center for British Art, 1999; Nat. Gall., 2000; Timothy Taylor Gall., 2003; Hunterian Gall., Glasgow, 2003; Wallace Collection, 2004; Aquavella Gall., NY, 2004, 2006; *retrospectives:* Hayward Gall., 1974 (subseq. Bristol, Birmingham and Leeds), 1988 (also Washington, Paris and Berlin, 1987–88); Works on Paper, Ashmolean Mus., Oxford, 1988 (subseq. other towns in provinces and in USA); Tate Gall., Liverpool, 1992; Tate Britain, 2002; Fundacion la Caixa, Barcelona, 2002; Mus. of Contemp. Art, LA, 2003; Scottish Nat. Gall. of Modern Art, 2004; Museo Correr, Venice, 2005; Irish Mus. of Modern Art, Dublin, 2007; Louisiana Mus., Copenhagen, 2007; Mus. of Modern Art, NY, 2007–08; Gemeente Mus., The Hague, 2008. *Works included in public collections:* London: Tate Gall.; Nat. Portrait Gall.; V & A Museum; Arts Council of GB; British Council; British Mus.; DoE; provinces: Cecil Higgins Museum, Bedford; Fitzwilliam Mus., Cambridge; Nat. Mus. of Wales, Cardiff; Scottish Nat. Gall. of Mod. Art, Edinburgh; Hartlepool Art Gall.; Walker Art Gall., Liverpool; Liverpool Univ.; City Art Gall. and Whitworth Gall., Manchester; Ashmolean Mus. of Art, Oxford; Harris Mus. and Art Gall., Preston; Rochdale Art Gall.; Southampton Art Gall.; Australia: Queensland Art Gall., Brisbane; Art Gall. of S Australia, Adelaide; Art Gall. of WA, Perth; France: Musée National d'Art Moderne, Centre Georges Pompidou, Paris; Beaverbrook Foundn, Fredericton, New Brunswick; USA: Art Inst. of Chicago; Mus. of Mod. Art, NY; Cleveland Mus. of Art, Ohio; Mus. of Art, Carnegie Inst., Pittsburgh; Achenbach Foundn for Graphic Arts and Fine Arts Mus. of San Francisco; Art Mus., St Louis; Hirshhorn Musum and Sculpture Garden, Smithsonian Instn, Washington. Rubenspreis, City of Siegen, 1997. *Relevant publications:* Lucian Freud, by Lawrence Gowing, 1982; Lucian Freud, Paintings, by Robert Hughes, 1987; Lucian Freud, works on paper, by Nicholas Penney and Robert Flynn Johnson, 1988; The Etchings of Lucian Freud: a catalogue raisonné, by Craig Hartley, 1995; Lucian Freud, introd. by Bruce Bernard, 1996; Lucian Freud 1996–2005, introd. by Sebastian Smee, 2005; Lucian Freud, by William Feaver, 2007. *Address:* c/o Diana Rawstron, Goodman Derrick LLP, 90 Fetter Lane, EC4A 1PT.
See also Sir C. R. Freud.

FREUD, Matthew Rupert; Chairman, Freud Communications (formerly Freud Associates), since 1985; *b* 2 Nov. 1963; *s* of Sir Clement Raphael Freud, *qv*; *m* Caroline Victoria Hutton (marr. diss.); two *s*; *m* Elisabeth Murdoch, *qv*; one *s* one *d.* *Educ:* St Anthony's, Westminster. Dir, Prince's Trust Trading. Vice-Chm., NSPCC Full Stop campaign, 1999–; Trustee, Comic Relief, 2000–. *Address:* (office) 55 Newman Street, W1T 3EB. *T:* (020) 3003 6300.

FREYBERG, family name of **Baron Freyberg**.

FREYBERG, 3rd Baron *cr* 1951, of Wellington, New Zealand and of Munstead, Co. Surrey; **Valerian Bernard Freyberg;** *b* 15 Dec. 1970; *o s* of 2nd Baron Freyberg, OBE, MC, and of Ivry Perronelle Katharine, *d* of Cyril Harrower Guild, Aspall Hall, Debenham, Suffolk; *S* father, 1993; *m* 2002, Dr Harriet Atkinson, *d* of late John Atkinson and of Jane (who *m* 2nd, John Watherston, *qv*); one *s.* *Educ:* Eton Coll.; Camberwell Coll. of Art; Slade Sch. of Fine Art (MA Fine Art 2006). Elected Mem., H of L, 1999. Mem., Design Council, 2001–04. *Heir:* *s* Hon. Joseph John Freyberg, *b* 21 March 2007. *Address:* House of Lords, SW1A 0PW.

FRICKER, His Honour (Anthony) Nigel; QC 1977; a Deputy Circuit Judge, 2001–05 (a Circuit Judge, 1984–2001); Member, Mental Health Review Tribunal, since 2001; *b* 7 July 1937; *s* of late Dr William Shapland Fricker and Margaret Fricker; *m* 1960, Marilyn Ann, *d* of late A. L. Martin, Pa, USA; one *s* two *d.* *Educ:* King's School, Chester; Liverpool Univ. (LLB 1958). President of Guild of Undergraduates, Liverpool Univ., 1958–59. Called to Bar, Gray's Inn, 1960. Conf. Leader, Ford Motor Co. of Australia, Melbourne, 1960–61. Recorder, Crown Court, 1975–84; Prosecuting Counsel to DHSS, Wales and Chester Circuit, 1975–77; an asst comr, Boundary Commn for Wales, 1981–84; Mem. Bd, Children and Family Court Adv. and Support Service, 2001. Member: Bar Council, 1966–70; Senate and Bar Council, 1975–78; County Court Rule Cttee, 1988–92; Family Proceedings Rule Cttee, 1997–2001. Pres., Council of HM Circuit Judges, 1997. Fellow, Internat. Acad. of Trial Lawyers, 1979–. Mem. Court: Liverpool Univ., 1977–2007; York Univ., 1984–2007. Confrérie des Chevaliers du Tastevin. *Publications:* (jtly) Family Courts: Emergency Remedies and Procedures, 1990, 3rd edn (loose-leaf) as Emergency Remedies in the Family Courts (Gen. Ed., 1990–99, Consulting Ed., 1999–2002); (with David Bean) Enforcement of Injunctions and Undertakings, 1991; (consulting ed.) The Family Court Practice, (annually) 1993–2002; contrib. legal periodicals in UK and USA (Family and

Conciliation Courts Rev.). *Address:* 6 Park Square, Leeds LS1 2LW; Farrar's Building, Temple, EC4Y 7BD.

FRICKER, Rt Rev. Joachim Carl; a Suffragan Bishop of Toronto (Bishop of Credit Valley), 1985–95; *b* Zweibrucken, Germany, 1 Dec. 1927; *s* of Carl and Caroline Fricker; *m* 1952, Shirley Joan (*née* Gill); three *s* two *d. Educ:* Niagara Falls Public Schools; Univ. of Western Ontario (BA); Huron College (LTh). Ordained deacon and priest, 1952; Rector: St Augustine's, Hamilton, 1952–59; St David's, Welland, 1959–65; St James, Dundas, 1965–73; Canon of Christ's Church Cathedral, Hamilton, 1964–73; Dean of Diocese of Niagara and Rector, Christ's Church Cathedral, 1973–85. Chm., Nat. Doctrine and Worship Cttee (Anglican Church of Canada), 1989–92. Hon. DD: Huron Coll., 1974; Trinity Coll., 1987; Hon. DSL, Wycliffe Coll., 1987. *Recreations:* theatre, gardening, reading, walking. *Address:* 233 Oak Crescent, Burlington, ON L7L 1H3, Canada.

FRIEDBERGER, Maj.-Gen. John Peter William, CB 1991; CBE 1986 (MBE 1975); Administrator, Sovereign Base Areas and Commander, British Forces, Cyprus, 1988–90; *b* 27 May 1937; *s* of late Brig. John Cameron Friedberger, DSO, DL and Phyllis Grace Friedberger, JP; *m* 1966, Joanna Mary, *d* of Andrew Thorne, ERD; one *s* two *d. Educ:* Red House School, York; Wellington College; RMA Sandhurst. Commissioned, 10th Royal Hussars (PWO), 1956; seconded to Northern Frontier Regt, Sultan's Armed Forces, Oman, 1961–63; Australian Army Staff Coll., 1969; CO The Royal Hussars (PWO), 1975–78; RCDS, 1978–79; Comdr, Royal Brunei Armed Forces, 1982–86; ACOS, HQ Northern Army Group, 1986–88. Chief Exec., British Helicopter Adv. Bd, 1992–2002. Hon. Colonel: The Royal Hussars (PWO), 1991–92; The King's Royal Hussars, 1992–97. Mem., Rail Passengers' Cttee, S England, 1997–2005. FRGS 1990. Dato, DPKT (Negara Brunei Darussalam) 1984. *Recreation:* travel. *Address:* c/o Home HQ, The King's Royal Hussars, Peninsula Barracks, Winchester, Hants SO23 8TS. *Club:* Cavalry and Guards.

FRIEDMAN, David Peter; QC 1990; *b* 1 June 1944; *s* of Wilfred Emanuel Friedman and Rosa Lees; *m* 1972, Sara Geraldine Linton. *Educ:* Tiffin Boys' School; Lincoln College, Oxford (BCL, MA). Called to the Bar, Inner Temple, 1968, Bencher, 1999; a Recorder, 1998–2005. *Recreations:* good food (cooked by others), reading. *Address:* 4 Pump Court, Temple, EC4Y 7AN. *T:* (020) 7842 5555. *Club:* Lansdowne.

FRIEDMAN, Prof. Jerome Isaac, PhD; Professor of Physics, Massachusetts Institute of Technology, since 1967; *b* 28 March 1930; *m* Tania Baranovsky Friedman; two *s* two *d. Educ:* Univ. of Chicago (AB 1950; MS 1953; PhD Physics 1956). Research associate; Univ. of Chicago, 1956–57; Stanford Univ., 1957–60; MIT: Asst Prof. and Associate Prof., 1960–67; Dir, Nuclear Science Lab., 1980–83; Head of Dept of Physics, 1983–88. Fellow: Amer. Phys. Soc.; Nat. Acad. of Scis; Amer. Acad. of Arts and Scis. (Jtly) W. H. K. Panofsky Prize for Physics, 1989; (jtly) Nobel Prize for Physics, 1990. *Publications:* numerous papers in learned jls on particle physics, esp. the division of protons and neutrons into smaller particles, leading to different types of quarks. *Address:* Department of Physics, Massachusetts Institute of Technology, Cambridge, MA 02139, USA.

FRIEDMAN, Sonia Anne Primrose; Producer, Sonia Friedman Productions, since 2002; *b* 19 April 1965; *d* of Leonard and Clair Friedman; partner, Jasper Rees. *Educ:* St Christopher's Sch., Letchworth; Central Sch. of Speech and Drama (HND Stage Mgt). Hd of Mobile Prodns, RNT, 1990–93; Producer and Co-Founder, Out of Joint Theatre Co., 1993–98; Producer, Ambassador Theatre Gp, 1998–2002. *Recreations:* classical music, walking, reading. *Address:* Duke of York's Theatre, 104 St Martins Lane, WC2N 4BG. *T:* (020) 7854 7050, *Fax:* (020) 5854 7059; *e-mail:* mail@soniafriedman.com.

FRIEDMANN, Jacques-Henri; Grand Officier, Légion d'Honneur, 2006 (Commandeur, 1996); Chevalier, Ordre du Mérite, 1970; Honorary Chairman, Musée du Quai Branly, since 2005 (Chairman, Planning Committee, 1999–2005); *b* Paris, 15 Oct. 1932; *s* of André Friedmann and Marie-Louise Bleiweiss; *m* 1962, Cécile Fleur; two *s* one *d. Educ:* Inst. d'Etudes Politiques, Paris (law degree). Student, Ecole Nat. d'Admin, 1957–58; Inspector of Finance, 1959; Lectr, Inst. d'Etudes Politiques, 1964–68; Special Asst 1964, Tech. Advr 1965–66, Deptl Staff of Valéry Giscard d'Estaing, Minister of Finance; Special Asst, Gen. Directorate of Domestic Trade and Pricing, 1966; Actg Dep. Sec. Gen., Interministerial Cttee on Europ. Econ. Co-op., 1966–67; Hd, Finance Dept, French Planning Org., 1967–68; Chief Executive Secretary: to Jacques Chirac, Sec. of State for Econ. Affairs and Finance, 1969–70, and Minister responsible for liaison with Parlt, 1971; Hd of Dept of Gen. Inspectorate of Finances and of Central Dept of Gen. Inspectorate for the Nat. Economy, 1971–72; Advr on Econ. and Financial Affairs to Pierre Messmer, Prime Minister, then Chief Exec. Sec., 1972–74; Special Asst to Jacques Chirac, Prime Minister, 1974; Chm., Co. Générale Maritime, 1974–82; Inspector Gen. of Finance, 1980; Chm. and Man Dir, Co. Parisienne de Chauffage Urbaine, 1983–87; Special Asst to Edouard Balladur, Minister of Econ. Affairs, Finance and Privatisation, 1986–87; Chairman: Caisse d'Epargne de Paris, 1985–95; Air France, 1987–88; SAGI, 1989–93; UAP, 1993–97; Supervisory Bd, AXA, 1997–2000. *Address:* 80 avenue de Breteuil, 75015 Paris, France. *T:* (1) 47340459; 222 Rue de l'Université, 75343 Paris, Cedex 07, France. *T:* (1) 56617001.

FRIEDMANN, Prof. Peter Simon, MD; FRCP, FMedSci; Professor of Dermatology, University of Southampton, since 1998; *b* 18 Nov. 1943; *s* of Charles Aubrey Friedmann and Atersia Friedmann (*née* Le Roux); *m* 1967, Bridget Ann Harding; one *s* one *d. Educ:* Trinity Coll., Cambridge (BA 1966); University Coll. Hosp., London (MB BChir 1969; MD 1977). FRCP 1984. Wellcome Trng Fellow, RCS, 1973–77; University of Newcastle upon Tyne: Lectr in Dermatology, 1977–81; Sen. Lectr, 1981–90; University of Liverpool: Prof. of Dermatology, 1990–97; Actg Hd, Dept of Medicine, 1996–97. Hon. Res. Fellow, Tufts Univ., Boston, 1985–86. Med. Advr to All-Party Parly Gp on Skin, 1996–. Chm., Scientific Cttee, Nat. Eczema Soc., 1995–2001. Founder FMedSci 1998. *Publications:* contrib. book chapters; numerous scientific papers. *Recreations:* music (playing flute), bird-watching, tennis, ski-ing. *Address:* Dermatology Unit, Southampton General Hospital, Tremona Road, Southampton SO16 6YD. *T:* (023) 8079 6142.

FRIEL, Brian; writer; *b* 9 Jan. 1929; *s* of Patrick Friel and Christina Friel (*née* MacLoone); *m* 1954, Anne Morrison; one *s* four *d. Educ:* St Columb's Coll., Derry; St Patrick's Coll., Maynooth; St Joseph's Trng Coll., Belfast. Taught in various schools, 1950–60; writing full-time from 1960. Lived in Minnesota during first season of Tyrone Guthrie Theater, Minneapolis. Member: Irish Acad. of Letters, 1972; Aosdana, 1983–; Amer. Acad. of Arts and Letters. FRSL 1998. Hon. DLitt: Chicago, 1979; NUI, 1983; NUU, 1986. *Publications: collected stories:* The Saucer of Larks, 1962; The Gold in the Sea, 1966; *plays:* Philadelphia, Here I Come!, 1965; The Loves of Cass McGuire, 1967; Lovers, 1968; The Mundy Scheme, 1969; Crystal and Fox, 1970; The Gentle Island, 1971; The Freedom of the City, 1973; Volunteers, 1975; Living Quarters, 1976; Aristocrats, 1979; Faith Healer, 1979; Translations, 1981 (Ewart-Biggs Meml Prize, British Theatre Assoc. Award); (trans.) Three Sisters, 1981; The Communication Cord, 1983; (trans.) Fathers and Sons, 1987; Making History, 1988; London Vertigo, 1989; Dancing at Lughnasa, 1990; A Month in the Country, 1990; Wonderful Tennessee, 1993; Molly Sweeney, 1995; Give Me Your Answer, Do!, 1997; (trans.) Uncle Vanya, 1998; (trans.) The Bear, 2002; The Yalta Game, 2002; Afterplay, 2002; Performances, 2003; The Home Place, 2005 (Best Play, Evening Standard Th. Awards, 2005); (trans.) Hedda Gabler, 2008. *Address:* Drumaweir House, Greencastle, Co. Donegal, Ireland.

FRIEL, (Michael) John; District Judge (Magistrates' Courts) (formerly Stipendiary Magistrate), Derbyshire, since 1997; *b* 3 Sept. 1942; *s* of Hugh and Madeline Friel; *m* 1980, Elizabeth Mary Jenkins; two *s* one *d. Educ:* Leeds Univ. (LLB). Admitted solicitor, 1969; Nottingham Magistrates' Court: Court Clerk, 1965–71; Dep. Clerk to the Justices, 1972–73; Clerk to the Justices: Isle of Ely, Cambs, 1973–76; Mansfield, Notts, 1976–97; also Clerk to: Worksop and E Retford Justices, 1977–97; Newark and Southwell Justices, 1986–97; Nottingham Justices, 1996–97. *Recreations:* sports (tennis, cricket, football, squash, ski-ing). *Address:* The Court House, Tapton Lane, Chesterfield S41 7TW. *T:* (01246) 224040.

FRIEND, Andrew Erskine; Strategic Adviser, India Infrastructure plc, since 2008; *b* 25 June 1952; *s* of Philip Friend and Eileen (*née* Erskine); *m* 1985, Jennifer Elizabeth Keating; one *s* two *d. Educ:* Christ's Hosp.; Peterhouse, Cambridge (BA 1973). MAICD 1994; CCMI 2006. Policy Advr, GLC, 1982–84; City of Melbourne: Dir, Econ. Develt, 1985–89; Corporate Manager, 1990–95; Chief Exec., 1995–97; Associate Dir, Macquarie Bank, 1997–99; Man. Dir, Laing Investments, 1999–2003; Chief Exec., John Laing plc, 2003–06; Commercial Advr, DfT, 2006–08. Non-executive Director: ING European Infrastructure Fund, 2006–; Partnerships UK, 2007–. Trustee, Oxfam, 2007–; Financial Security Assurance (UK) Ltd, 2007–. *Publications:* Slump City: the politics of mass unemployment, 1981; res. pubns on housing, econ. and urban develt. *Recreations:* golf, walking, reading history, lino-cuts, growing vegetables.

FRIEND, Rev. Frederick James; Non-Stipendiary Minister, Hughenden, diocese of Oxford, since 1982; Hon. Director, Scholarly Communication, University College London, since 2002 (Librarian, 1982–97; Director, 1997–2002); *b* 7 April 1941; *s* of James Frederick Friend and Emily Mary Friend (*née* Giddens); *m* 1969, Margaret Rusholme; one *s* one *d. Educ:* Dover Grammar Sch. for Boys; King's Coll., London (BA 1963); University Coll. London (DipLib 1965); Oak Hill Coll. Asst Librarian, Manchester Univ. Library, 1965–71; Sub-Librarian, Leeds Univ., 1971–76; Dep. Librarian, Nottingham Univ., 1976–78; Librarian, Essex Univ., 1978–82; various consultancies, 2002–. Mem. Council, 1985–88, Chm. Scholarly Communication Cttee, 1996–2000, Sec., 2000–04, SCONUL; Treas., Consortium of Univ. Res. Libraries, 1996–98. Deacon 1982, priest 1983. *Publications:* various articles in learned jls. *Recreations:* walking the dogs, prayer. *Address:* The Chimes, Cryers Hill Road, High Wycombe, Bucks HP15 6JS.

FRIEND, John Richard, DM; FRCOG; Consultant Obstetrician and Gynaecologist, Plymouth General Hospital, 1973–2000 (Medical Director, 1999–2000); Senior Vice President, Royal College of Obstetricians and Gynaecologists, 1995–98; *b* 31 Jan. 1937; *s* of George Chamings Friend and Gwendoline Mary Lewis Friend; *m* 1971, Diana Margaret Fryer; one *s* two *d* (incl. twin *s* and *d*). *Educ:* St Edward's Sch. (schol.); St Edmund Hall, Oxford (MA; BM, BCh, DM); St Thomas' Hosp. MRCOG 1968, FRCOG 1987; MRCP 1999. Queen Charlotte's Hosp. and Chelsea Hosp., 1965–66; MRC Fellow, 1969–70; Hammersmith Hosp., 1966–67; KCH, 1967–73. Hon. Consultant Gynaecologist, RN, 1987–. *Publications:* articles in jls. *Recreations:* golf, tennis. *Address:* Holme House, Stoke Hill Lane, Crapstone, Yelverton, Devon PL20 7PP. *T:* (01822) 852527. *Clubs:* Royal Western Yacht; Yelverton Golf.

FRIEND, Lionel; conductor; *b* 13 March 1945; *s* of Moya and Norman A. C. Friend; *m* 1969, Jane Hyland; one *s* two *d. Educ:* Royal Grammar School, High Wycombe; Royal College of Music; London Opera Centre. LRAM; ARCM. Glyndebourne Opera, 1969–72; Welsh National Opera, 1969–72; Kapellmeister, Staatstheater, Kassel, Germany, 1972–75; Staff Conductor, ENO, 1978–89; Musical Dir, New Sussex Opera, 1989–96; Conductor-in-residence, Birmingham Conservatoire, 2003–. Guest Conductor: BBC orchestras; Philharmonia; Royal Ballet; Oper Frankfurt; Opera Australia; Opéra National, Brussels; State Symphony, Hungary; Nash Ensemble, etc. *Recreations:* reading, theatre. *Address:* 136 Rosendale Road, SE21 8LG. *T:* (020) 8761 7845.

FRIEND, Prof. Peter John, MD; FRCS; Professor of Transplantation, University of Oxford, since 1999; Fellow, Green Templeton College (formerly Green College), Oxford, since 1999; Hon. Consultant Surgeon, Oxford Radcliffe NHS Trust, since 1999; *b* 5 Jan. 1954; *s* of late John Friend and (Dorothy) Jean Friend (*née* Brown); *m* 2001, Dr Laurie Elizabeth Maguire. *Educ:* Rugby Sch.; Magdalene Coll., Cambridge (MA, MB, BChir, MD); St Thomas's Hosp. Med. Sch. FRCS 1983. St Thomas' Hosp., London, W Norwich Hosp., Bedford Gen. Hosp., Addenbrooke's Hosp., Cambridge, 1978–88; Vis. Asst Prof., Indiana Univ., USA, 1988–89; Lectr in Surgery, Univ. of Cambridge and Hon. Consultant Surgeon, Addenbrooke's Hosp., 1989–99; Fellow, Magdalene Coll., Cambridge, 1993–99. Pres., British Transplantation Soc., 2007–09. *Publications:* papers on transplantation and surgery in scientific jls. *Address:* Nuffield Department of Surgery, University of Oxford, John Radcliffe Hospital, Headington, Oxford OX3 9DU. *Club:* Oxford and Cambridge.

FRIEND, Dame Phyllis (Muriel), DBE 1980 (CBE 1972); Chief Nursing Officer, Department of Health and Social Security, 1972–82; *b* 28 Sept. 1922; *d* of late Richard Edward Friend. *Educ:* Herts and Essex High Sch., Bishop's Stortford; The London Hospital (SRN); Royal College of Nursing (RNT). Dep. Matron, St George's Hospital, 1956–59; Dep. Matron, 1959–61, Matron, 1961–68, Chief Nursing Officer 1969–72, The London Hospital. *Address:* Barnmead, Start Hill, Bishop's Stortford, Herts CM22 7TA. *T:* (01279) 654873.

FRIEND, Sir Richard (Henry), Kt 2003; FRS 1993; FREng, FIET, FInstP; Cavendish Professor of Physics, University of Cambridge, since 1995; Fellow, St John's College, Cambridge, since 1977; *b* 18 Jan. 1953; *s* of John Henry Friend and Dorothy Jean (*née* Brown); *m* 1979, Carol Anne Maxwell (*née* Beales); two *d. Educ:* Rugby Sch.; Trinity Coll., Cambridge (MA, PhD; Hon. Fellow, 2004). FInstP 1999; FREng 2002; FIET (FIEE 2002). Res. Fellow, St John's Coll., Cambridge, 1977–80; University of Cambridge: Demonstrator in Physics, 1980–85; Lectr, 1985–93; Reader in Experimental Physics, 1993–95. R&D Dir, 1996–98, Chief Scientist, 1998–, Cambridge Display Technology; Chief Scientist, Plastic Logic Ltd, 2000–. Vis. Prof., Univ. of Calif, Santa Barbara, 1986–87; Vis. Fellow, Royal Instn, 1992–99; Nuffield Science Res. Fellowship, 1992–93; Mary Shepard B. Upson Vis. Prof., Cornell Univ., 2003. Lectures: Mott, Inst. of Physics, 1994; Kelvin, IEE, 2004; Holst Meml, Tech. Univ. of Eindhoven and Philips Res., 2004. Hon. FRSC 2004. Hon. DSc: Linköping, 2000; Mons, 2002. C. V. Boys Prize, Inst. of Physics, 1988; Interdisciplinary Award, RSC, 1991; Hewlett-Packard Prize, European Physical Soc., 1996; Rumford Medal and Prize, Royal Soc., 1998; Italgas Prize for res. and technol innovation, 2001; Silver Medal, 2002, MacRobert Prize, 2002, Royal Acad. of Engrg; Faraday Medal, IEE, 2003; Gold Medal, Eur. Materials Res. Soc., 2003; Descartes Prize, Eur. Commn, 2003; Jan Rachmann Prize, Soc. for Information Displays, 2005. *Publications:* papers on chem. physics and solid-state physics in scientific jls. *Address:*

Cavendish Laboratory, J. J. Thomson Avenue, Cambridge CB3 0HE. *T:* (01223) 337218; *e-mail:* rhf10@cam.ac.uk.

FRIES, Richard James; Chief Charity Commissioner, 1992–99; Visiting Fellow, Centre for Civil Society, London School of Economics, 2000–06; *b* 7 July 1940; *s* of late Felix Theodore Fries and Joan Mary Fries (subseq. Mrs John Harris); *m* 1970, Carole Anne Buick; one *s* two *d. Educ:* King's Coll., Cambridge. Home Office, 1965–92. Chm. Bd. Internat. Center for Not-for-Profit Law, Washington, 1999–2005. *Recreations:* chess, walking.

FRINDALL, William Howard, (Bill), MBE 2004; freelance cricket statistician, broadcaster, writer, and editor, since 1965; *b* 3 March 1939; *s* of late Arthur Howard Frindall and Evelyn Violet Frindall (*née* McNeill); *m* 1st, 1960, Maureen Doris Wesson (marr. diss. 1970); two *s* one *d*; 2nd, 1970, Jacqueline Rose Seager (marr. diss. 1980); 3rd, 1992, Deborah Margaret Brown; one *d. Educ:* Reigate Grammar Sch.; Kingston upon Thames Sch. of Art. Asst Prodn Manager, Lutterworth Press, 1958; Royal Air Force, 1958–65; commnd Secretarial Br., 1964. BBC cricket statistician, 1966–; Editor, Playfair Cricket Annual, 1986–; Cricket Corresp., Mail on Sunday, 1987–89; cricket statistician, the Times, 1994–; cricket archivist to Sir Paul and Lady Getty, 1996–. President: British Blind Sport, 1984–2004; BBC Cricket Club, 1998–. Patron: German Assoc. of Cricket Umpires and Scorers, 2005–; German Cricket Bd, 2006–. Hon. DTech Staffordshire, 1998. Statistician of the Year, Assoc. of Cricket Statisticians and Historians, 1996. *Publications:* The Wisden Book of Test Cricket, 1979, 5th edn 2000; The Wisden Book of Cricket Records, 1981, 4th edn 1998; The Guinness Book of Cricket Fact and Feats, 1983, 4th edn 1996; England Test Cricketers, 1989; Ten Tests for England, 1989; Gooch's Golden Summer, 1991; A Tale of Two Captains, 1992; Playfair Cricket World Cup Guide, 1996; Limited-Overs International Cricket: the complete record, 1997; NatWest Playfair Cricket World Cup, 1999; Bearders - My Life in Cricket, 2006. *Recreations:* cricket, sketching, painting, photography, philately, elementary gardening (under supervision from my wife). *Address:* Urchfont, Wiltshire. *Clubs:* MCC, Lord's Taverners; Cricket Writers'; Forty; Master's.

FRISBY, Audrey Mary; *see* Jennings, A. M.

FRISBY, Terence; playwright, actor, producer, director, author; *b* 28 Nov. 1932; *s* of William and Kathleen Frisby; *m* 1963, Christine Vecchione (marr. diss.); one *s. Educ:* Dobwalls Village Sch.; Dartford Grammar Sch.; Central Sch. of Speech Training and Dramatic Art. Substantial repertory acting and directing experience, also TV, films and musicals, 1957–63; appeared in A Sense of Detachment, Royal Court, 1972–73 and X, Royal Court, 1974; Clive Popkiss, in Rookery Nook, Her Majesty's, 1979, and many since. Productions: Once a Catholic (tour), 1980–81; There's a Girl in My Soup (tour), 1982; Woza Albert!, Criterion, 1983; The Real Inspector Hound/Seaside Postcard (tour), 1983–84; Comic Cuts, 1984. Has written: many TV scripts, incl. series Lucky Feller, 1976; That's Love, 1988–92 (Gold Award, Houston Film Festival); film, There's A Girl in My Soup, 1970 (Writers Guild Award, Best British Comedy Screenplay); stage musical, Just Remember Two Things..., 2004. *Publications:* Outrageous Fortune (an autobiog. story), 1998; *plays:* The Subtopians, 1964; There's a Girl in My Soup, 1966; The Bandwagon, 1970; It's All Right if I Do It, 1977; Seaside Postcard, 1978; Just Remember Two Things: It's Not Fair And Don't Be Late, 1989 (radio play; Giles Cooper Award, 1988); Rough Justice, 1995; Funny About Love, 2002. *Address:* c/o The Agency, 24 Pottery Lane, Holland Park, W11 4LZ. *T:* (020) 7727 1346. *Club:* Richmond Golf.

FRISCHMANN, Wilem William, CBE 1990; PhD; FREng; FICE; FIStructE; FCGI; Chairman: Pell Frischmann Group; Pell Frischmann Consulting Engineers Ltd, since 1985; Pell Frischmann Consultants Ltd, since 1986; Pell Frischmann Milton Keynes Ltd, since 1988; Pell Frischmann Engineering, since 1988; Pell Frischmann Water Ltd, since 1990; Conseco International, since 1985; *s* of Lajos Frischmann and Nelly Frischmann; *m* 1957, Sylvia Elvey; one *s* one *d. Educ:* Hungary; Hammersmith College of Art and Building; Imperial Coll. of Science and Technology (DIC); City University (PhD). MASCE, MSISdeFr. FIStructE 1964; FREng (FEng 1985); FCGI 1988; FConsE 1993; FICE 2004. Engineering training with F. J. Samuely and Partners and W. S. Atkins and Partners; joined C. J. Pell and Partners, 1958, Partner, 1961. Dep. Chm., Building & Property Management Services Ltd, 1993–. Structural Engineer for Nat. Westminster Tower (ICE Telford Premium Award), Centre Point, Drapers Gardens tower (IStructE Oscar Faber Prize) and similar high buildings, leisure buildings, hotels and hospitals; Engineer for works at Bank of England, Mansion House and Alexandra Palace; particular interest and involvement in tall economic buildings, shear walls and diaphragm floors, large bored piles in London clay, deep basements, lightweight materials for large span bridges, monitoring and quality assurance procedures for offshore structures; advisory appts include: Hong Kong and Shanghai Bank HQ, Malayan Banking Berhad, Kuala Lumpur. Hon. DSc. *Publications:* The use and behaviour of large diameter piles in London clay (IStructE paper), 1962; papers to learned socs and instns, originator of concepts: English Channel free-trade port; industrial complex based on Varne and Colbart sandbanks; two-mile high vertical city. *Recreations:* ski-ing, jogging, chess, architecture, design. *Address:* (office) 5 Manchester Square, W1A 1AU. *T:* (020) 7486 3661, *Fax:* (020) 7487 4153; Haversham Grange, Haversham Close, Twickenham, Middx TW1 2JP. *Club:* Arts.

FRISK, Monica Gunnel Constance C.; *see* Carss-Frisk.

FRISTON, Prof. Karl John, FRS 2006; Professor of Neuroscience, since 1998, and Wellcome Principal Research Fellow, Wellcome Trust Centre for Neuroimaging (formerly Wellcome Department of Imaging Neuroscience), since 1999, Institute of Neurology, University College London; *b* 12 July 1959; *s* of Anthony Harpen Friston and Audrey Agnes Friston (*née* Brocklesby); *m* 1997, Ann Elisabeth Leonard; three *s. Educ:* Gonville and Caius Coll., Cambridge (Exhibnr; BA Med. Scis Tripos 1980); King's Coll. Med. Sch., Univ. of London (MB BS 1983); MA Cantab 1985. MRCPsych 1988. Pre-registration, Surgery, Bromley Hosp. and Medicine, Farnborough Hosps, 1984–85; Post-registration, Rotational Trng Scheme in Psychiatry, Dept of Psychiatry, Univ. of Oxford, 1985–88; Hon. Senior Registrar: Dept of Psychiatry, Charing Cross and Westminster Med. Sch., 1988–91; RPMS, 1991–94 (Hon. Lectr, 1991–92); Sen. Lectr, 1994–97, Reader, 1997–98, Inst. Neurol., UCL. Research: Wellcome Trust Fellow, MRC Clin. Neuropharmacol. Unit, Oxford Univ., 1987–88; Wellcome Trust Res. Fellow, 1988–91, MRC Clin. Scientist (Sen. Grade), 1991–92, MRC Cyclotron Unit, Hammersmith Hosp.; W. M. Keck Foundn Fellow in Theoretical Neurobiol., Neuroscis Inst., La Jolla, Calif, 1992–94; Wellcome Sen. Res. Fellow in Clin. Sci., Inst. of Neurol., 1994–99. Hon. Consultant, Nat. Hosp. for Neurol. and Neurosurgery, Queen Sq., 1999–. FMedSci 1999. *Publications:* (ed jtly) Human Brain Function, 1997, 2nd edn 2004; (ed jtly) Statistical Parametric Mapping and Causal Models for Brain Imaging, 2006; contrib. numerous peer-reviewed articles to acad. lit. *Recreation:* painting. *Address:* Wellcome Trust Centre for Neuroimaging, 12 Queen Square, WC1N 3BG. *T:* (020) 7833 7457, *Fax:* (020) 7813 1445; *e-mail:* k.friston@fil.ion.ucl.ac.uk.

FRITCHIE, family name of **Baroness Fritchie.**

FRITCHIE, Baroness *cr* 2005 (Life Peer), of Gloucester in the county of Gloucestershire; **Irene Tordoff Fritchie,** DBE 1996; Commissioner for Public Appointments 1999–2005; Civil Service Commissioner, 1999–2005; *b* 29 April 1942; *d* of Charles Fredrick Fennell and Eva (*née* Tordoff); *m* 1960, Don Jamie Fritchie; one *s* (and one decd). *Educ:* Ribston Hall Grammar Sch. for Girls. Admin. Officer, Endsleigh Insce Brokers, 1970–73; Sales Trng Officer, Trident Insce Ltd, 1973–76; Head of Trng Conf and Specialist Trng Advr on Women's Develt, Food and Drink ITB, 1976–80; Consultant, Social Ecology Associates, 1980–81; Dir, Transform Ltd, 1981–85; Rennie Fritchie Consultancy, 1985–89; Man. Dir, Working Choices Ltd, 1989–91; Consultant Mainstream Develt Consultancy, 1991–; Vice Chair, Stroud and Swindon Bldg Soc. 2002–08 (Bd Mem., 1995–2008). Chair: Gloucester HA, 1988–92; South-Western RHA 1992–94; S and W Region, NHS Executive (formerly S and W RHA), 1994–97; 2gether Glos NHS Foundn Trust, 2008–. Member: NHS Policy Bd, 1994–97; GMC, 1996–99 Board, British Quality Foundn, 1994–99; Selection Panel, Glos Police Authy, 1994–99 Chair: Ind. Appts Selection Bd, RICS, 2006–; Adv. Bd, Web Sci. Res. Initiative Southampton/MIT, 2006–; Vice-Chm., Audit Cttee, Scottish Public Service Ombudsman, 2007–. Mem., Forum UK, IHSM, 1993. Pres., Pennell Initiative for Women's Health in Later Life, 1999–2006 (Chair, 1997–99); Chm., Chronic Pain Policy Coalition, 2006–08; Vice-Chm., British Lung Foundn, 2006–. Patron: Healing Arts 1995–2002; SHARE young persons counselling service, 1997–2002; Meningitis Trust 1998–2002; Westbank League of Friends, 1998–2002; Bart's Cancer Centre, 1998–2000 Effective Intelligence, 2000–02; SPACE, 2000–02; Swindon Arts Foundn, 2000–02; Lord Mayor's Appeal, 2000–01; Pied Piper Appeal, 2002–; Winston's Wish (grief support charity for children), 2002– (Pres., 1996–2000). Vis. Associate Prof., York Univ., 1996–; Pro-Chancellor, Southampton Univ., 1998–2008 (Chm. Council, 1998–2000). Mem. British and Irish Ombudsman Assoc., 2002–. Mem., Editl Adv. Bd, Revans Inst., 2002–; CCMI (CIMgt 2000). Fellow: Glos Univ. (formerly Cheltenham & Gloucester Coll. of Higher Educn), 1996–; Sunningdale Inst., Nat. Sch. of Govt, 2006–; FCGI, 2002. Hon PhD Southampton, 1996; DUniv: York, 1998; Oxford Brookes, 2001; Open, 2003 QUB, 2005; Hon. LLD St Andrews, 2002; Hon. DLitt Hull, 2006. *Publications:* Working Choices, 1988; The Business of Assertiveness, 1991; Resolving Conflicts in Organisations 1998. *Recreations:* family, reading, gardening, swimming, theatre, cooking, the 'Archers'. *Address:* Mainstream Development, 51 St Paul's Road, Gloucester GL1 5AP. *T:* (01452) 414542.

FRITH, Anthony Ian Donald; Board Member, Bristol Water Holdings plc, 1989–99; *b* 11 March 1929; *s* of Ernest and Elizabeth Frith; *m* 1952, Joyce Marcelle Boyce; one *s* one *d. Educ:* various grammar schs and techn. colls. CEng. Various appts in North Thames Gas Bd and Gas Light & Coke Co., 1945–65; Sales Man. 1965–67, Dep. Commercial Man 1967–68, North Thames Gas Bd; Marketing Man., Domestic and Commercial Gas, Gas Council, 1968–72; Sales Dir, British Gas Corp., 1972–73; Chm., SW Region, British Gas 1973–90; Mem. Bd, Bath Dist HA, 1990–94; non-exec. Dir, Wilts and Bath Health Commn, 1992–94. *Publications:* various techn. and prof. in Gas Engineering and other jls *Recreations:* fishing, golf. *Address:* Greenacres, Hayeswood Road, Timsbury, Bath BA2 0HH.

FRITH, Prof. Christopher Donald, PhD; FRS 2000; FBA 2008; Professor in Neuropsychology, Institute of Neurology, University College London, 1994–2008, now Emeritus; Niels Bohr Visiting Professor, University of Aarhus, Denmark; *b* 16 March 1942; *s* of Donald Alfred Frith, OBE; *m* 1966, Uta Aurnhammer (*see* U. Frith); two *s. Educ:* Leys Sch., Cambridge; Christ's Coll., Cambridge (MA 1963); Inst. of Psychiatry, London Univ. (Dip. Psych. 1965; PhD 1969). Res. Asst, Inst. of Psychiatry, 1965–75; MRC Scientific Staff: Clin. Res. Centre, Div. of Psychiatry, Northwick Park Hosp. 1975–92; MRC Cyclotron Unit, Hammersmith Hosp., 1992–94; Wellcome Principal Res. Fellow, Wellcome Trust Centre for Neuroimaging (formerly Wellcome Dept of Cognitive Neurology), Inst. of Neurology, UCL, 1994–2008. FRSA 1996; FMedSci 1999; FAAAS 2000. Kenneth Craik Award, St John's Coll., Cambridge, 1999. *Publications:* Cognitive Neuropsychology of Schizophrenia, 1992; Schizophrenia: a very short introduction, 2003; Making up the Mind, 2007; papers on cognitive neuropsychology in various scientific jls. *Recreations:* music, study of consciousness. *Address:* Wellcome Trust Centre for Neuroimaging, 12 Queen Square, WC1N 3BG. *T:* (020) 7833 7457.

FRITH, David Edward John; cricket author and journalist; Founder, 1979, Editor and Editorial Director, 1979–96, Wisden Cricket Monthly; *b* 16 March 1937; *s* of Edward Frith and Patricia Lillian Ethel Frith (*née* Thomas); *m* 1957, Debbie Oriel Christina Pennell; two *s* one *d. Educ:* Canterbury High Sch., Sydney. First grade cricket, Sydney, 1960–64. Editor, The Cricketer, 1972–78. Cricket Soc. Literary Award, 1970, 1987 and 2003; Cricket Writer of the Year, Wombwell Cricket Lovers Soc., 1984; Magazine Sports Writer of the Year, Sports Council, 1988. *Publications:* Runs in the Family (with John Edrich), 1969; (ed) Cricket Gallery, 1976; My Dear Victorious Stod, 1977; (with Greg Chappell) The Ashes '77, 1977; The Golden Age of Cricket 1890–1914, 1978; The Ashes '79, 1979; Thommo, 1980; The Fast Men, 1981; The Slow Men, 1984; (with Gerry Wright) Cricket's Golden Summer, 1985; (ed) England v Australia Test Match Records 1877–1985, 1986; Archie Jackson, 1987; Pageant of Cricket, 1987; Guildford Jubilee 1938–1988, 1988; England v Australia: A Pictorial History of the Test Matches since 1877, 1990; By His Own Hand, 1991; Stoddy's Mission, 1995; (ed) Test Match Year, 1997; Caught England, Bowled Australia (autobiog.), 1997; The Trailblazers, 1999; Silence of the Heart, 2001; Bodyline Autopsy, 2002; The Ross Gregory Story, 2003; The Battle for the Ashes, 2005; The Battle Renewed 2006–07, 2007; Inside Story: unlocking Australian cricket's archives, 2007. *Recreations:* collecting cricketana, watching documentaries. *Address:* 6 Beech Lane, Guildford, Surrey GU2 4ES. *T:* (01483) 532573. *Club:* MCC.

FRITH, Air Vice-Marshal Edward Leslie, CB 1973; *b* 18 March 1919; *s* of late Charles Edward Frith, ISO. *Educ:* Haberdashers' Askes School. Gp Captain, 1961; Air Cdre, 1968; Dir of Personal Services (2) RAF, MoD, 1969–71; Air Vice-Marshal, 1971; Air Officer Administration, Maintenance Comd, later Support Comd, 1971–74. *Recreations:* lawn tennis, bridge. *Clubs:* All England Lawn Tennis and Croquet, International Lawn Tennis of GB.

FRITH, Mark; Editor-in-Chief, heat magazine, 1999–2008; *b* 22 May 1970; *s* of John and Monica Frith; partner, Gaby; one *s. Educ:* Norton Free Primary Sch., Sheffield; Gleadless Valley Secondary Sch., Sheffield; Univ. of E London. Editor: Overdraft mag. (UEL mag.), 1989–90; Smash Hits mag., 1994–95; Sky mag., 1995–97; presenter, Liquid News, BBC TV, 2002–03. *Publications:* (ed) The Best of Smash Hits: the eighties, 2006; The Celeb Diaries, 2008. *Recreations:* music, cinema, Sheffield UFC, talking too fast, clumsiness, finding things to read in other people's recycling bins, Dostoyevsky (not really!).

FRITH, Rt Rev. Richard Michael Cokayne; *see* Hull, Bishop Suffragan of.

FRITH, Prof. Simon Webster, PhD; Tovey Professor of Music, University of Edinburgh, since 2006; *b* 25 June 1946; *s* of Donald Frith and Mary Frith (*née* Tyler); *m* 1999, Jenny McKay; one *d. Educ:* Balliol Coll., Oxford (BA PPE); Univ. of Calif, Berkeley (MA; PhD Sociol. 1976). Lectr, then Sen. Lectr in Sociol., Warwick Univ., 1972–87;

Professor: of English Studies, Univ. of Strathclyde, 1987–99; of Film and Media, Univ. of Stirling, 1999–2005. Dir, Media Econs and Media Culture Res. Prog., ESRC, 1995–2000. Chair of Judges, Mercury Music Prize, 1992–. *Publications:* Sound Effects, 1983; Music for Pleasure, 1988; Performing Rites, 1996; Music and Copyright, 2004; Taking Popular Music Seriously, 2007. *Recreation:* music. *Address:* Music Department, University of Edinburgh, Alison House, 12 Nicolson Street, Edinburgh EH8 9DF. *T:* (0131) 650 2426; *e-mail:* simon.frith@ed.ac.uk.

FRITH, Prof. Uta, PhD; FMedSci; FRS 2005; FBA 2001; Professor of Cognitive Development, Institute of Cognitive Neuroscience, University College London, 1996–2006, now Emeritus (Deputy Director, 1998–2006); Guest Professor, Niels Bohr Project on Interacting Minds, Aarhus University, since 2007; *b* 25 May 1941; *d* of Wilhelm Aurnhammer and Anne (*née* Goedel); *m* 1966, Prof. Christopher Donald Frith, *qv*; two *s*. *Educ:* Univ. des Saarlandes (Vordiplom. Psychol. 1964); Inst. of Psychiatry, Univ. of London (Dip. Abnormal Psychol. 1966; PhD Psychol. 1968). CPsychol. MRC Scientific Staff: Scientist, 1968–80; Sen. Scientist, 1980–98; Special Appt, 1998–. FMedSci 2001. Hon. FBPsS 2006. Hon. Fellow, UCL, 2007. Hon. DPhil: Göteborg, 1998; St Andrews, 2000; Palermo, 2005; York, 2005; Nottingham, 2007. *Publications:* Autism: explaining the enigma, 1989, 2nd edn 2003; Autism and Asperger's Syndrome, 1991; Autism in History, 2000. *Recreations:* collecting art and antiques, tidying and polishing, enjoying my husband's cooking. *Address:* Institute of Cognitive Neuroscience, University College London, Alexandra House, 17 Queen Square, WC1N 3AR. *T:* (020) 7679 1177.

FRITSCH, Elizabeth, CBE 1995; potter; *b* Shropshire, 1940; *d* of Welsh parents; one *s* one *d*. *Educ:* Royal Acad. of Music; Royal Coll. of Art (Silver Medallist, 1970). Established own workshop, E London, 1985. Mem., Crafts Council (Bursary awarded, 1980). *One-woman exhibitions include:* Crafts Council, 1974; CAA, 1976; Leeds City Art Galls, 1978, touring to Glasgow, Bristol, Bolton and Gateshead City Art Galls; V & A, 1980; RCA, 1984; Besson Gall., London, 1989; Royal Mus. of Scotland, 1990; Hetjens Mus., Dusseldorf, 1990; touring to British City Art Galls, 1992; NY Crafts Council, 1993; Crafts Council, 1994; *group exhibitions include:* Oxford Gall., 1974; ICA, 1985; Kunstler Haus, Vienna, 1986; Fischer Fine Art, London, 1987; Kyoto and Tokyo Nat. Museums of Modern Art, 1988; Crafts Council, touring to Amsterdam, 1988; Sotheby's, 1988; 35 Connaught Square, London (Lord Queensberry), 1991; Stuttgart, 1991; Oriel Gall., Cardiff, 1991; *works in public collections:* V & A; Crafts Council; Lotherton Hall, Leeds City Art Galls; Royal Mus. of Scotland; Glasgow, Bolton, Bristol and Birmingham City Art Galls. Judge, Fletcher Challenge Internat. Ceramics Competition, NZ, 1990. Major influences on work: music, fresco painting, topology. Sen. Fellow, RCA, 1995. Herbert Read Meml Prize, 1970; Winner, Royal Copenhagen Jubilee Competition, 1972; Gold Medal, Internat. Ceramics Competition, Sopot, Poland, 1976. *Recreations:* music, mountains, theatre.

FRIZZELL, Edward William, CB 2000; Head, Scottish Executive Enterprise, Transport and Lifelong Learning (formerly Enterprise and Lifelong Learning) Department, 1999–2006; *b* 4 May 1946; *s* of late Edward Frizzell, CBE, QPM and Mary McA. Russell; *m* 1969, Moira Calderwood; two *s* one *d*. *Educ:* Paisley Grammar School, Glasgow Univ. (MA Hons). Scottish Milk Marketing Board, 1968–73; Scottish Council (Develt and Industry), 1973–76; Scottish Office, 1976–78; First Sec., Fisheries, FCO UK Rep. Brussels, 1978–82; Scottish Office, then Scottish Executive, 1982–2006: SED, 1982–86; Finance Div., 1986–89; Industry Dept/SDA (Dir, Locate in Scotland), 1989–91; Under Sec., 1991; Chief Exec., Scottish Prison Service, 1991–99. *Recreations:* running, mountain biking, painting. *Club:* Mortonhall Golf.

FROGGATT, Anthony Grant; Chief Executive Officer, Scottish & Newcastle PLC, 2003–07; *b* 9 June 1948; *s* of Sir Leslie Trevor Froggatt, *qv*, *m* 1999, Chris Bulmer; three *s*. *Educ:* Queen Mary Coll., Univ. of London (LLB Hons); Columbia Business Sch., NY (MBA). Man. Dir, Swift & Moore, Sydney, Australia, 1983–88; CEO, Cinzano Internat., Geneva, 1988–92; President: Asia Pacific, 1992–95, Europe, 1995–98, Internat. Distillers & Vintners; Europe and Africa, Seagram, 1999–2002. Consultant Dir, Rothschild Australia, 2003. Non-executive Director: Brambles Ltd, 2006–; Billabong Ltd, 2008–. *Recreations:* tennis, travel, autograph collection. *Address:* 7 Eastbourne Road, Darling Point, Sydney, NSW 2027, Australia.

FROGGATT, Sir Leslie (Trevor), Kt 1981; Chairman, Ashton Mining Ltd, 1981–94; *b* 8 April 1920; *s* of Leslie and Mary Helena Froggatt (*née* Brassey); *m* 1945, Jessie Elizabeth Grant; three *s*. *Educ:* Birkenhead Park Sch., Cheshire. Joined Asiatic Petroleum Co. Ltd, 1937; Shell Singapore, Shell Thailand, Shell Malaya, 1947–54; Shell Egypt, 1955–56; Dir of Finance, Gen. Manager, Kalimantan, Borneo, and Dep. Chief Rep., PT Shell Indonesia, 1958–62; Shell International Petroleum Co. Ltd: Area Co-ordinator, S Asia and Australia, 1962–63; assignment in various Shell cos in Europe, 1964–66; Shell Oil Co., Atlanta, 1967–69; Chm. and Chief Exec. Officer, Shell Gp in Australia, 1969–80; non-exec. Dir, Shell Australia Ltd, 1981–87. Chairman: Pacific Dunlop, 1986–90 (Vice-Chm., 1981; Dir, 1978–90); BRL Hardy, 1992–95; Director: Australian Industry Develt Corp., 1978–90; Australian Inst. of Petroleum Ltd, 1976–80, 1982–84 (Chm., 1977–79); Moonee Valley Racing Club Nominees Pty Ltd, 1977–92; Tandem Australia, 1989–98 (Chm., 1992–98). Member: Australian Nat. Airlines Commn (Australian Airlines), 1981–87 (Vice-Chm., 1984–87); Internat. Bd of Advice, ANZ Banking Gp, 1986–91; Internat. Adv. Council, Tandem Computers Inc., USA, 1988–98; Bd, CARE Australia, 1989– (Vice Chm., 1995–2002). Chm., Co-op. Res. Centre for Cochlear Implant. *Recreations:* reading, music, racing, golf. *Address:* 3 Teringa Place, Toorak, Vic 3142, Australia. *T:* (3) 9827 2362. *Clubs:* Melbourne, Australian, Victoria Racing, Victoria Amateur Turf, Moonee Valley Racing, Commonwealth Golf (Melbourne).
     See also A. G. Froggatt.

FROGGATT, Sir Peter, Kt 1985; MD; FRCP, FRCPI; Trustee, National Museums and Galleries of Northern Ireland, 1998–2003; Pro-Chancellor, University of Dublin, 1985–2003 (Senior Pro-Chancellor, since 1999); President and Vice-Chancellor, Queen's University of Belfast, 1976–86; *b* 12 June 1928; *s* of Albert Victor and Edith (*née* Curran); *m* 1958, Norma Cochrane; four *s* (and one *s* decd). *Educ:* Royal Belfast Academical Institution; Royal Sch., Armagh (Schol.); Trinity Coll., Dublin (BA; MB; BCh; BAO 1952; MA 1956; MD 1957; Welland Prize; Cunningham Medal; Begley Schol.); Queen's Univ., Belfast (DPH 1956; PhD 1967; Carnwath Prize). MRCPI 1972; FRCPI 1973; FFPH (FFCM 1973); MRCP 1974; FFOMI 1975; FFCMI 1976; MRIA 1978; FRCP 1980. House Surgeon and Physician, Sir Patrick Dun's Hosp., Dublin, 1952–53; Nuffield Res. Student, 1956–57; Med. Officer, Short Bros and Harland Ltd, 1957–59; Queen's University, Belfast: Lectr, 1959–65; Reader, 1965–68; Prof. of Epidemiology, 1968–76; Dean, Faculty of Medicine, 1971–76; Consultant, Eastern Health and Social Services Board, 1960–76. Hon. Prof., St Bartholomew's Hosp. Med. Sch., 1986–94. Chairman: Independent Scientific Cttee on Smoking and Health, 1980–91 (Mem., 1977–80); Tobacco Products Res. Trust, 1981–97; ASME, 1987–92; Central Ethical Compliance Gp, Unilever, 1991–97. Director: AIB Gp plc, 1984–95; TSB Bank (Northern Ireland), later First Trust Bank, 1991–98. President: Biol Scis Section, British Assoc., 1987–88;

BMA, 1999–2000; Member: Bd, 1983–85, Adv. Cttee, NI, 1988–94, British Council; Gen. Adv. Cttee, BBC, 1986–88; Supervisory Bd, NHS NI, 1986–92; British Occupational Health Res. Foundn, 1991–2000. Hon. Member: Soc. for Social Medicine; Soc. of Occupational Medicine. Lectures: Robert Adams, 1977, Kirkpatrick, 1984, Abrahamson, 1986, RCSI; Apothecaries, SOM, 1978; Freyer, NUI, 1984; Bayliss, RCP, 1989; Smiley, FOMI, 1989; Bartholomew Mosse, Rotunda Hosp., 1992; John Snow, Assoc. of Anaesthetists, 2001; Doctors Award Redistribution Enterprise, FPHM, 2001. Trustee, Mater Infirmorum Hosp., Belfast, 1994–2002; Chm., Scotch-Irish Trust of Ulster, 1990–. Freeman, City of London, 1990. FSS 1963; Hon. FRCSI 1988; Hon. Fellow, Royal Acad. of Medicine in Ireland; CCMI (CBIM 1986). Hon. LLD: Dublin, 1981; QUB, 1991; Hon. DSc NUI, 1982. Dominic Corrigan Gold Medal, RCPI, 1981. *Publications:* (jtly) Causation of Bus-driver Accidents: Epidemiological Study, 1963; (ed jtly) Nicotine, Smoking and the Low Tar Programme, 1988; articles in jls on human genetics, occupational medicine, med. history, med. educn, epidemiology and smoking policies. *Recreations:* golf, music, travel. *Address:* Rathganley, 3 Strangford Avenue, Belfast BT9 6PG.

FROSSARD, Sir Charles (Keith), KBE 1992; Kt 1983; Bailiff of Guernsey, 1982–92; Judge of the Court of Appeal, Jersey, 1983–92; a Judge of the Courts of Appeal of Jersey and Guernsey, 1992–95; *b* 18 Feb. 1922; *s* of late Edward Louis Frossard, CBE, MA, Hon. CF, Dean of Guernsey, 1947–67, and Margery Smith Latta; *m* 1950, Elizabeth Marguerite, *d* of late J. E. L. Martel, OBE; two *d*. *Educ:* Elizabeth Coll., Guernsey; Univ. de Caen (Bachelier en Droit; *Dhc* 1990). Enlisted Gordon Highlanders, 1940; commnd 1941, 17 Dogra Regt, Indian Army; seconded to Tochi Scouts and Chitral Scouts; served India and NW Frontier, 1941–46. Called to Bar, Gray's Inn, 1949, Hon. Bencher, 2000; Advocate of Royal Court of Guernsey, 1949; People's Deputy, States of Guernsey, 1958–67; Conseiller, States of Guernsey, 1967–69; HM Solicitor General, Guernsey, 1969–73; HM Attorney General, Guernsey, 1973–76; Dep. Bailiff of Guernsey, 1977–82. Member, Church Assembly and General Synod, Church of England, 1960–82. Pres., Indian Army Assoc., 1993–; Member Council: British Assoc. of Cemeteries in SE Asia, 1998–; Royal (formerly British) Commonwealth Ex-Services League, 1999–. KStJ 1985. Médaille de Vermeil, Paris, 1984. *Recreations:* hill walking, fishing. *Address:* Les Lierres, Rohais, St Peter Port, Guernsey. *T:* (01481) 722076. *Clubs:* Naval and Military; United (Guernsey).

FROST, Abraham Edward Hardy, CBE 1972; Counsellor, Foreign and Commonwealth Office, 1972–78; *b* 4 July 1918; *s* of Abraham William Frost and Margaret Anna Frost; *m* 1972, Gillian (*née* Crossley); two *d*. *Educ:* Royal Grammar Sch., Colchester King's Coll., Cambridge (MA); London Univ. (BScEcon). FCIS. RNVR, 1940–46 (Lieut). ILO, Geneva, 1947–48; HM Treasury, 1948–49; Manchester Guardian, City Staff, 1949–51; FO (later FCO), 1951–78. *Publication:* In Dorset Of Course (poems), 1976. *Address:* Hill View, Buckland Newton, Dorset DT2 7BS. *T:* (01300) 345415.

FROST, Alan John, FIA; Chairman, Teachers' Building Society, since 2004 (non-executive Director, since 2001); *b* 6 Oct. 1944; *s* of Edward George Frost and Ellen Lucy Jamieson; *m* 1973, Valerie Jean Bennett; two *s*. *Educ:* Stratford County Grammar Sch., London; Manchester Univ. (BSc Hons). FIA 1970. Pearl Assurance Co., 1966–67; Australian Mutual Provident Soc., 1967–72; Laurie, Milbank & Co., 1972–74; London & Manchester Assurance Gp, 1974–84; Sun Life Assurance Soc., 1984–86; Man. Dir, Abbey Life Assurance Co., 1986–98; Gp Chief Exec., United Assce Gp plc, 1998–2000; Dep. Chief Exec., Royal London Gp, 2000–01; Chm., Queen Mab Consultancy Ltd, 2001–04. Non-executive Director: INVESCO Pensions Ltd, 2001–; Bournemouth Univ., 2001– (Chm., 2004–); NFU Mutual Insce Co., 2002–; Car Crash Line Gp, 2002–06; Hamworthy plc, 2004–. Chm., Dorset Opera, 2004–. Liveryman, Co. of Actuaries, 1986– (Master, 2004–05). FCMI (FIMgt 1990); MInstD. *Publications:* (with D. P. Hager) A General Introduction to Institutional Investment, 1986; (with D. P. Hager) Debt Securities, 1990; A Light Frost, 2005; actuarial papers. *Recreations:* opera, shooting. *Address:* e-mail: mail@alanfrost.co.uk. *Club:* Reform.

FROST, Albert Edward, CBE 1983; Director, Marks & Spencer Ltd, 1976–87; Chairman: Remploy, 1983–87; Trustees, Remploy Pension Fund, 1989–98; *b* 7 March 1914; *s* of Charles Albert Frost and Minnie Frost; *m* 1942, Eugénie Maud Barlow. *Educ:* Oulton Sch., Liverpool; London Univ. Called to the Bar, Middle Temple (1st Cl. Hons). HM Inspector of Taxes, Inland Revenue, 1937; Imperial Chemical Industries Ltd: Dep. Head, Taxation Dept, 1949; Dep. Treasurer, 1957; Treasurer, 1960; Finance Dir, 1968; retd 1976. Director: British Airways Corp., 1976–80; BL Ltd, 1977–80; S. G. Warburg & Co., 1976–83; British Steel, 1980–83 (Chm., Audit and Salaries Cttees); Guinness Peat Gp, 1983–84; Chairman: Guinness Mahon Hldgs Ltd, 1983–84; Guinness Mahon & Co., 1983–84; Billingsgate City Securities, 1989–90. Mem. Council, St Thomas's Med. Sch., London, 1974– (Chm., Finance Cttee, 1978–85); Governor, United Med. Schs of Guy's and St Thomas's Hosps, 1982–98 (Dep. Chm. of Govs, 1989–97); Chm., Finance and Investment Cttees, 1982–85; Hon. Fellow, 1994). Member: Council and Finance Cttee, Morley Coll., London, 1975–85; Exec. Cttee for Develt Appeal, Royal Opera House, Covent Garden, 1975–87; Arts Council of GB, 1982–84; Vice-Pres., ABSA, 1992– (Mem. Council, 1976–93; Jt Dep. Chm., 1985–92); Chairman: Robert Mayer Trust for Youth and Music, 1981–90 (Dir, 1977–90); Jury, and of Org. Cttee, City of London Carl Flesch Internat. Violin Competition, 1984–92. Trustee and Treas., Loan Fund for Mus. Instruments, 1980–2006; Dir, City Arts Trust, 1982–93. FRSA. *Publications:* (contrib.) Simon's Income Tax, 1952; (contrib.) Gunns Australian Income Tax Law and Practice, 1960; articles on financial matters affecting industry and on arts sponsorship. *Recreations:* violinist (chamber music); swimming (silver medallist, Royal Life Saving Assoc.); athletics (county colours, track and cross country); walking; arts generally. *Club:* Royal Automobile.

FROST, (Angela) Jane; Director, Individual Customers, HM Revenue and Customs, since 2006; *b* 14 July 1957; *d* of Dr William Derek Walsh and Julia Margaret Walsh; *m* 1981, Martin John Frost; one *s* one *d*. *Educ:* New Hall, Cambridge (BA 1978). Trainee manager to Product Gp Manager, Lever Brothers Ltd, 1978–85; Hd of Mktg, Shell Middle East Ltd (Dubai), 1985–88; Shell International Trading Company plc: Brand Coordinator Lubricants, 1988–91; Internat. Brand Coordinator, 1991–94; Planning and Mktg Dir (Far East and Australasia), 1995; Controller, Brand Mktg, BBC, 1995–2000; Dir, Mktg and Strategy, BBC Technol. Ltd, 2000–01; Dir, Greystones Consulting, 2001–02; Dir, Consumer Strategy, subseq. Strategy, DCA, 2003–06. Mem. Supervisory Bd, Wolters Kluwer NV, 2000–. Dir, BBC Children in Need Ltd, 1997–. Non-exec. Dir, 2003–, Trustee, 2005–, Lowry Arts Centre; Mem. Council of Trustees, Heads, Teachers and Industry, 2003–; Chm., Heads, Teachers and Industry Trust, 2005–. FCIM; FRSA. *Recreations:* my children, my dogs, Georgian glass. *Address:* HM Revenue and Customs, 100 Parliament Street, SW1A 2BQ. *T:* (020) 7147 2168; *e-mail:* jane.frost@hmrc.gsi.gov.uk. *Club:* Women in Advertising and Communications London.

FROST, Christopher Ian; Chief Executive, Rathbone (education and training for disadvantaged young people), 2001–04; *b* 17 April 1949; *s* of Joffre and late Emily Frost; partner, Sandra Lomax; one *s* two *d*. *Educ:* Lewes County Grammar Sch. for Boys;

Nottingham Univ. (MEd). Teacher, subseq. Hd of Dept, Sir William Nottidge Sch., 1970–77; Hd, Community Educn, Wigan, 1977–81; Dep. Educn Officer, Notts LEA, 1981–84; Educn Officer, Leics LEA, 1984–91; NVQ Development Officer, Home Office, 1991–93; Dir, City Coll., Manchester, 1994–2001. *Publications:* reports and newspaper articles on supporting develt of democracy for offenders and of new trng initiatives for prison governors in Russia. *Recreations:* musical theatre, travel. *Address:* 21 Coronet Avenue, Kingsmead, Northwich CW9 8FX.

FROST, David George Hamilton, CMG 2006; HM Diplomatic Service; Ambassador to Denmark, 2006–08; *b* 21 Feb. 1965; *s* of George Leonard Frost and Margaret Elsie Frost; *m* 1993, Jacqueline Elizabeth Dias; one *s* one *d*. *Educ:* St John's Coll., Oxford (BA Hons). Entered FCO, 1987: London, 1987–89; Third Sec. (Political), Nicosia, 1989–90; KPMG Peat Marwick (on secondment), 1990–92; FCO, 1992–93: First Secretary (Economic): UK Repn to EU, 1993–96; UKMIS to UN, NY, 1996–98; Private Sec. to Perm. Under Sec., FCO, 1998–99; Dep. Hd, EU Dept, FCO, 1999–2001; Counsellor (Econ. and EU), Paris, 2001–03; Dir, EU (Internal) (formerly Dep. Dir, Europe), FCO, 2003–06. *Recreations:* Medieval history, art, architecture. *Address:* c/o Foreign and Commonwealth Office, King Charles Street, SW1A 2AH; *e-mail:* david.frost@fco.gov.uk.

FROST, Sir David (Paradine), Kt 1993; OBE 1970; interviewer, author, producer, columnist, and television presenter; Chairman and Chief Executive, David Paradine Ltd, since 1966; *b* 7 April 1939; *s* of late Rev. W. J. Paradine Frost, Tenterden, Kent; *m* 1983, Lady Carina Fitzalan-Howard, 2nd *d* of 17th Duke of Norfolk, KG, GCVO, CB, CBE, MC; three *s*. *Educ:* Gillingham Grammar Sch.; Wellingborough Grammar Sch.; Gonville and Caius Coll., Cambridge (MA). Sec., The Footlights; Editor, Granta. Jt Founder, LWT, 1967–68; Jt Founder and Dir, TV-am, 1981–93. BBC Television series: That Was the Week That Was, 1962–63 (in USA, 1964–65); A Degree of Frost, 1963, 1973; Not So Much a Programme, More a Way of Life, 1964–65; The Frost Report, 1966–67; Frost Over England, 1967; Frost Over America, 1970; Frost's Weekly, 1973; The Frost Interview, 1974; We British, 1975–76; Forty Years of Television, 1976; The Frost Programme, 1977; The Guinness Book of Records Hall of Fame, 1986, 1987, 1988; Breakfast with Frost, 1993–2005; Through the Keyhole, 1997–; The Frost Interviews, 2005–06; single programmes: Margaret Thatcher: the path to power and beyond, 1995; Nick Leeson: the man who broke the bank, 1995; Norma Major Behind Closed Doors, 1996; Prince Charles, Why it Matters to Me, 1997; Forty Years with Frost, 2000; BBC Radio: David Frost at the Phonograph, 1966, 1972; Frost on Thursday, 1974; series, Pull the Other One, 1987, 1988, 1990; ITV series and programmes: The Frost Programme, 1966–67, 1967–68, 1972, 1973, 1993–95; Frost on Friday, 1968–69, 1969–70; The Sir Harold Wilson Interviews, 1976; A Prime Minister on Prime Ministers, 1977–78; Are We Really Going to be Rich?, 1978; David Frost's Global Village, 1979, 1980, 1982; The 25th Anniversary of ITV, The Begin Interview, and Elvis—He Touched Their Lives, 1980; The BAFTA Awards, and Onward Christian Soldiers, 1981; A Night of Knights: a Royal Gala, 1982; The End of the Year Show, 1982, 1983; Frost on Sunday (TV-am), 1983–92; David Frost Presents Ultra Quiz, 1984; Twenty Years On, 1985, 1986; Through the Keyhole, 1987–96; Beyond Belief, 1995, 1996, 1997; Live for Peace, 1995; A Royal Gala, 1996; A Gala Comedy Hour, 1996; The Easter Enigma, 1996; Masters of Talk, 1996–97; Frost's Century, 1997–98; The Alpha Series, 2001; Hitler and Hess, 2001; Muhammad Ali—Then and Now, 2003; Inside Elton's World, 2005; The Frost Years, 2006; Frost Tonight, 2006; series, The World's Greatest Sporting Legends (Sky One), 2005. Al Jazeera English TV series, Frost Over the World, 2006–. US programmes include: That Was The Week That Was, 1964–65; David Frost's Night Out in London, 1966–67; The Next President, 1968; Robert Kennedy the Man, 1968; The David Frost Show, 1969–70, 1970–71, 1971–72; The David Frost Revue, 1971–72, 1972–73; That Was the Year That Was, 1973, 1985; David Frost Presents the Guinness Book of Records, 1973–76; Frost over Australia, 1972, 1973, 1974, 1977; Frost over New Zealand, 1973, 1974; The Unspeakable Crime, 1975; Abortion—Merciful or Murder?, 1975; The Beatles—Once Upon a Time, 1975; David Frost Presents the Best, 1975; The Nixon Interviews with David Frost, 1976–77; The Crossroads of Civilization, 1977–78; Headliners with David Frost, 1978; A Gift of Song—MUSIC FOR UNICEF Concert, The Bee Gees Special, and The Kissinger Interview, 1979; The Shah Speaks, and The American Movie Awards, 1980; Show Business, This Is Your Life 30th Anniversary Special, The Royal Wedding (CBS), 1981; David Frost Presents The Internat. Guinness Book of World Records, annually 1981–86; The American Movie Awards, Rubinstein at 95, and Pierre Elliott Trudeau, 1982; Frost over Canada, 1982, 1983; David Frost Live by Satellite from London, 1983; The Search for Josef Mengele, 1985; Spitting Image: Down and Out in the White House, 1986; The Spitting Image Movie Awards, 1987; The Spectacular World of Guinness Records, 1987–88; Entertainment Tonight, 1987, 1988; The Next President with David Frost, 1987–88; ABC Presents a Royal Gala, 1988; The President and Mrs Bush Talking with David Frost, 1989; Talking with David Frost (USA), 1991–98; Interviews I'll Never Forget, 1998; David Frost, One-on-One, 1999–; The Complete Nixon, 2002; In Their Own Words, 2003; The Strategic Humor Initiative, 2003; President George W. Bush Talking with David Frost, 2003; Decisive Battles of the Ancient World, 2004–05. Stage: An Evening with David Frost (Edinburgh Fest.), 1966; An Audience with David Frost, 2004–. Produced films: The Rise and Rise of Michael Rimmer, 1970; Charley One-Eye, 1972; Leadbelly, 1974; The Slipper and the Rose, 1975; James A. Michener's Dynasty, 1975; The Ordeal of Patty Hearst, 1978; The Remarkable Mrs Sanger, 1979; Rogue Trader, 1999. Mem., British/USA Bicentennial Liaison Cttee, 1973–76; Pres., Lord's Taverners, 1985, 1986. Companion, TRIC, 1992. Hon. Prof., Thames Valley Univ., 1994. Golden Rose, Montreux, for Frost Over England, 1967; Royal Television Society's Silver Medal, 1967; Richard Dimbleby Award, 1967; Emmy Award (USA), 1970, 1971; Religious Heritage of America Award, 1970; Albert Einstein Award, Communication Arts, 1971; MOMI Award, NY, 1998; Mus. of TV and Radio Salute, 1999; Bernard Delfont Award, Variety Club, 2005; Man of the Year Award, Media Soc., 2005; BAFTA Fellowship, 2005. LLD Emerson Coll., USA; Hon. DLitt Sussex, 1994. *Publications:* That Was the Week That Was, 1963; How to Live under Labour, 1964; Talking with Frost, 1967; To England With Love, 1967; The Presidential Debate 1968, 1968; The Americans, 1970; Whitlam and Frost, 1974; I Gave Them a Sword, 1978; I Could Have Kicked Myself, (David Frost's Book of the World's Worst Decisions), 1982; Who Wants to be a Millionaire?, 1983; (jtly) The Mid-Atlantic Companion, 1986; (jtly) The Rich Tide, 1986; (jtly) If You'll Believe That; The World's Shortest Books, 1987; David Frost: an autobiography: part one: From Congregations to Audiences, 1993; Billy Graham: thirty years of conversations with David Frost, 1997. *Address:* David Paradine Productions Ltd, The Penthouse, 346 Kensington High Street, W14 8NS. *T:* (020) 7371 3111, *Fax:* (020) 7602 0411.

FROST, David Stuart; Director-General, British Chambers of Commerce, since 2002; *b* 22 Feb. 1953; *s* of George William Stuart Frost and Winifred Leslie Frost; *m* 1981, Mari Doyle; two *d*. *Educ:* Thames Poly. (BA Hons Pol Economy); Poly. of the South Bank (Dip Internat. Financial Studies). Economist, London Chamber of Commerce, 1976–79; Dir of Services, Walsall Chamber of Commerce, 1979–86; Chief Executive: Walsall Chamber of Commerce and Industry, 1986–96; East Mercia Chamber of Commerce, 1996–2000; Coventry and Warwickshire Chamber of Commerce, 2000–02. Liveryman, Co. Loriners, 1986. DUniv 2008. *Recreations:* cycling, motorcycling, sailing. *Address:* 5 Norfo Gardens, Sutton Coldfield, West Midlands B75 6SS. *T:* (0121) 355 7788, *Fax:* (0121) 3 5084; *e-mail:* david@dsfrost.com.

FROST, Ven. George; Archdeacon of Lichfield and Canon Treasurer of Lichfie Cathedral, 1998–2000; *b* 4 April 1935; *s* of William John Emson Frost and Emily Dai Frost; *m* 1959, Joyce Pratt; four *s*. *Educ:* Hatfield Coll., Durham Univ. (BA 1956, M 1961); Lincoln Theological Coll. Schoolmaster, Westcliff High School, 1956–5 labourer, Richard Thomas and Baldwin Steelworks, Scunthorpe, 1958–59; Asst Curat St Margaret, Barking Parish Church, 1960–64; Minister, Ecclesiastical District of St Mar Marks Gate, 1964–70; Vicar: St Matthew, Tipton, 1970–77; St Bartholomew, Pen Wolverhampton, 1977–87; RD of Trysull, 1984–87; Archdeacon of Salop, 1987–9 Vicar of Tong, 1987–98. Prebendary of Lichfield Cathedral, 1985–87, Hon. Cano 1987–98. *Recreations:* walking, wild flowers, photography. *Address:* 23 Darnford Lan Lichfield, Staffs WS14 9RW. *T:* (01543) 415109.

FROST, Gerald Philip Anthony; author and journalist; Editor, eurofacts, since 200 General Director, Caspian Information Centre, since 2004; *b* 8 Nov. 1943; *s* of Sidney ar Flora Frost; *m* 1970, Margaret Miriam Freedman; two *s*. *Educ:* Univ. of Sussex (BA Hon mature student). Junior reporter, Ilford and East London newspapers, 1960–64; reporte Recorder Newspapers, Ilford, 1964–65; Yorkshire Post, 1965–67; Chief reporte Morning Telegraph, 1967–68; Sub-editor: Daily Express, Manchester, 1968–69; Pre Assoc., 1969–71; research staff, Centre for Policy Studies, 1974–80 (Sec. and Mem B 1977–80); Chief Leader Writer, Evening Standard, 1979–80; Director: Inst. for Europea Defence and Strategic Studies, 1980–92; Centre for Policy Studies, 1992–95; Trade an Welfare Unit, IEA, 1997–2001. Consultant Dir, New Atlantic Initiative, 1996–9 *Publications:* Protest and Perish: a critique of unilateralism (with P. Towle and I. Eliot 1983; Antony Fisher: champion of liberty, 2002; (with John Blundell) Friend or Foe what Americans should know about the European Union, 2004; *editor and contributo* Europe in Turmoil, 1991; In search of Stability, 1992; Hubris: the tempting of mode conservatives, 1992; Loyalty Misplaced, 1997; Unfit to Fight: the cultural subversion the armed forces in Britain and America, 1999; contribs to British and US newspapers an jls. *Recreations:* family pursuits, reading, wine. *Address:* 36 Victoria Avenue, Surbito Surrey KT6 5DW. *Club:* Reform.

FROST, Jane; *see* Frost, A. J.

FROST, Jeffrey Michael Torbet; Executive Director, London & Continental Banker 1983–89 (Associate Director, 1982–83); *b* 11 June 1938; *s* of late Basil Frost and Doroth Frost. *Educ:* Diocesan Coll., Cape, South Africa; Radley Coll.; Oriel Coll., Oxfor Harvard Univ. Admin. Asst, Brazilian Traction, Light and Power Co., Toronto and Brazi 1965–70; Economics Dept, Bank of London and S America, 1971–73; Asst Dir, 1974–7 Exec. Dir, 1976–81, Cttee on Invisible Exports. Hon. Sec., Anglo-Brazilian Soc 1977–84. Liveryman, Worshipful Co. of Clockmakers. FRSA. *Recreations:* bridge, balle walking. *Address:* 34 Paradise Walk, SW3 4JL. *T:* (020) 7352 8642; The Parish Roon Kintbury, near Hungerford, Berks RG17 9UP. *Clubs:* White's; Leander (Henley-on Thames).

FROST, Michael Edward, LVO 1983; HM Diplomatic Service, retired; Consul-Genera San Francisco, 1998–2001; *b* 5 July 1941; *s* of Edward Lee Frost and Ivy Beatrice (*ne* Langmead); *m* 1964, Carole Ann Beigel; three *s*. *Educ:* Torquay Grammar Sch. FCC 1959–62; Algiers, 1962–67; Commercial Officer, Kuala Lumpur, 1967–71; 3rd Sec., late 2nd Sec. Commercial, Bucharest, 1972–75; FCO, 1975–78; Consul (Commercial Seattle, 1978–83; FCO, 1983–84; on secondment to ICI, 1984–87; Dep. Head of Missior Sofia, 1987–90; Dep. Consul Gen. and Dir (Investment), British Trade and Investmer Office, NY, 1991–95; Head of Migration and Visa Dept, FCO, 1995–97. *Recreation* watercolours, golf, travel. *Address:* 25 Waldens Park Road, Woking, Surrey GU21 4RN

FROST, Ronald Edwin; Chairman, Hays plc, 1989–2001; *b* 19 March 1936; *s* of Charle Henry Frost and Doris (*née* Foggin); *m* 1959, Beryl Ward; one *s* two *d*. Founde Farmhouse Securities, 1965, Chm., 1979–81; Farmhouse Securities purchased by Hay Gp, 1981: Chief Exec., Distribn Div., 1981–83; Chief Exec. and Man. Dir, 1983–8 MInstD 1975; CIMgt (CBIM 1989). Freeman, City of London, 1983; Liveryman, Co. c Watermen & Lightermen, 1983–. *Recreations:* farming, game shooting, sailing. *Addres* The Grove, Le Mont Cambrai, St Lawrence, Jersey JE3 1JN. *Clubs:* Carlton, Roya Thames Yacht; Royal Channel Islands Yacht.

FROST, Thomas Pearson, FCIB; Group Chief Executive, National Westminster Bank 1987–92; *b* 1 July 1933; *s* of James Watterson Frost and Enid Ella Crawte (*née* Pearson); 1958, Elizabeth (*née* Morton); one *s* two *d*. *Educ:* Ormskirk Grammar Sch. FCIB (FI 1976). Joined Westminster Bank, 1950; Chief Exec. Officer and Vice Chm., NBNA (late National Westminster Bank USA), 1980; National Westminster Bank: Gen. Man Business Develt Div., 1982; Dir, 1984–93; Dep. Gp Chief Exec., 1985–87; Dep. Chm 1992–93; Chm., London Clearing House Ltd, 1993–96. Chairman: Five Oak Investments PLC, 1995–98 (non-exec. Dir, 1993–95); WSPA (UK), 2003–07 (Adv Council, 2007–); non-executive Director: Freedom Food Ltd, 1994–2003; Fenchurc PLC, 1993–97. Member: BOTB, 1986–93; UK Adv. Bd, British-American Chamber o Commerce, 1987–93; Business in the Cities, 1988–91; Policy Adv. Cttee, Tidy Britai Gp, 1988–92; Adv. Bd, World Economic Forum, 1990–93; Chairman: CBI Business & Urban Regeneration Task Force, 1987–88; Exec. Cttee, British Bankers' Assoc., 1991–92 Trustee, British Sports Trust, 1988–92; Gov., Royal Ballet Sch., 1988–98. Fellow, Worl Scout Foundn, 1984. Freeman, City of London, 1978. FCIM 1987; CompOR 1987 CCMI (CIMgt 1987); Companion, BITC, 1993; FRSA 1993. OStJ 1991. *Recreations* orchids, theatre. *Clubs:* Carlton, MCC.

FROST, Vince; Graphic Designer, Creative Director and Chief Executive Officer, Fros Design, since 1994; *b* 23 Nov. 1964; *s* of Alan Frost and Irene Frost; *m* 1997, Sonia Dell Grazia-Frost; two *s* one *d*. *Educ:* W Sussex Coll. of Art and Design. Joined Pentagram 1989, Associate Dir, 1992; founded own practice, Frost Design, 1994. Exhibns incl Frost*bite: Graphic Ideas by Vince Frost, Sydney Opera House Exhibn Hall, 2006 Member: D&AD; Chartered Soc. of Designers; Internat. Soc. of Typographic Designers Aust. Graphic Design Assoc.; AGI. Over 300 design awards. *Publication:* Frost*(sorry trees), 2006. *Recreations:* surfing, walking, playing with my kids. *Address:* Frost Design Level 1, 15 Foster Street, Surry Hills, Sydney, NSW 2010, Australia. *T:* (2) 92804233 *Fax:* (2) 92804266; *e-mail:* vince@frostdesign.com.au.

FROUDE, Andrew Christopher Haysom; Chairman, Jackson-Stops & Staf Consortium, since 1992; *b* 17 Oct. 1936; *s* of Robert and Dorothy Froude; *m* 1998 Patricia Elizabeth Roberts; two *s*. *Educ:* Leighton Park Sch., Reading; Coll. of Estate Management, London. FRICS 1969. Dir, Jackson-Stops & Staff Ltd, 1982–92; Chm., Jackson-Stops & Staff (North West) Ltd, 1992–2008. *Recreations:* golf, gardening, country pursuits. *Address:* The Riddings, Clotton Common, Tarporley, Cheshire CW6 0HQ. *Clubs:* Chester City; Chartered Surveyors Golfing Society (Capt., 1990).

FROW, Prof. John Anthony, PhD; Professor of English, University of Melbourne, since 2004; *b* 13 Nov. 1948; *s* of Anthony Gaunt Frow and Nola Marjorie Frow; *m* 1970, Mayerlene Engineer (marr. diss. 1985); one *s*; partner, 1978, Christine Alavi; one *d*; partner, 2001, Sandra Hawker. *Educ:* Australian National Univ. (BA); Cornell Univ. (MA 1974; PhD 1977). Lectr in American Lit., Universidad del Salvador, Buenos Aires, 1970; Lectr in English Lit., then Sen. Lectr, Murdoch Univ., WA, 1975–88; Visiting Professor: Univ. of Minnesota, 1988–89; Univ. of Qld, 1989–2000; Regius Prof. of Rhetoric and English Lit., Univ. of Edinburgh, 2000–04. FAHA 1998. *Publications:* Marxism and Literary History, 1986; Cultural Studies and Cultural Value, 1995; Time and Commodity Culture, 1997; (jtly) Accounting for Tastes, 1999; Genre, 2006. *Address:* Department of English, University of Melbourne, Vic 3010, Australia.

FROY, Prof. Martin; Professor of Fine Art, University of Reading, 1972–91, now Emeritus; *b* 9 Feb. 1926; *s* of late William Alan Froy and Helen Elizabeth Spencer. *Educ:* St Paul's Sch.; Magdalene Coll., Cambridge (one year); Slade Sch. of Fine Art. Dipl. in Fine Art (London). Visiting Teacher of Engraving, Slade Sch. of Fine Art, 1952–55; taught at Bath Acad. of Art, latterly as Head of Fine Art, 1954–65; Head of Painting Sch., Chelsea Sch. of Art, 1965–72. Gregory Fellow in Painting, Univ. of Leeds, 1951–54; Leverhulme Research Award, six months study in Italy, 1963; Sabbatical Award, Arts Council, 1965. Mem., Fine Art Panel, 1962–71, Mem. Council, 1969–71, Nat. Council for Diplomas in Art and Design; Trustee: National Gall., 1972–79; Tate Gall., 1975–79. Fellow, UCL, 1978. *One-Artist Exhibitions:* Hanover Gall., London, 1952; Wakefield City Art Gall., 1953; Belgrade Theatre, Coventry, 1958; Leicester Galls, London, 1961; Royal West of England Acad., Bristol, 1964; Univ. of Sussex, 1968; Hanover Gall., London, 1969; Park Square Gall., Leeds, 1970; Arnolfini Gall., Bristol, 1970; City Art Gall., Bristol (seven paintings), 1972; Univ. of Reading, 1979; New Ashgate Gall., Surrey, 1979; Serpentine Gall., 1983. *Other Exhibitions:* Internat. Abstract Artists, Riverside Mus., NY, 1950; ICA, London, 1950; Ten English Painters, Brit. Council touring exhibn in Scandinavia, 1952; Drawings from Twelve Countries, Art Inst. of Chicago, 1952; Figures in their Setting, Contemp. Art Soc. Exhibn, Tate Gall., 1953; Beaux Arts Gall., London, 1953; British Painting and Sculpture, Whitechapel Art Gall., London, 1954; Le Congrès pour la Liberté de la Culture Exhibn, Rome, Paris, Brussels, 1955; Pittsburgh Internat., 1955; Six Young Painters, Arts Council touring Exhibn, 1956; ICA Gregory Meml Exhibn, Bradford City Art Gall., Leeds, 1958; City Art Gall., Bristol, 1960; Malerei der Gegenwart ans Sudwestengland, Kunstverein, Hanover, 1962; Corsham Painters and Sculptors, Arts Council Touring Exhibn, 1965; Three Painters, Bath Fest. Exhibn, 1970; Park Square Gall., Leeds, 1978; Ruskin Sch., Univ. of Oxford, 1978; Newcastle Connection, Newcastle, 1980; Homage to Herbert Read, Canterbury, 1984. *Commissions, etc:* Artist Consultant for Arts Council to City Architect, Coventry, 1953–58; mosaic decoration, Belgrade Th., Coventry, 1957–58; two mural panels, Concert Hall, Morley Coll., London, 1958–59. *Works in Public Collections:* Tate Gall.; Mus. of Mod. Art, NY; Chicago Art Inst.; Arts Council; Contemp. Art Soc.; Royal W of England Acad.; Leeds Univ.; City Art Galls of Bristol, Carlisle, Leeds, Southampton and Wakefield; Reading Mus. and Art Gall.

FRUTIGER, Adrian; typeface designer; *b* 24 May 1928; *m* 1956, Simone Bickel; one *s*. *Educ:* compositor at Schlaefli Printer's, Interlaken; School of Applied Art, Zurich (Dip. in Type Design 1951). Typeface Designer and Artistic Manager, Deberny & Peignot, Paris, 1952–60; typeface designer and Studio Manager, Arcueil, Paris, 1960–92; Lecturer in type design, hist. of type and type drawing, Ecole Estienne, Paris, 1952–60; Ecole Nat. Supérieure des Arts Décoratifs, Paris, 1954–68; has designed more than 30 alphabets, incl. Univers, Frutiger, Centennial, OCR-B, Meridien, and Indian alphabet, Devanagari. Gutenberg Preis, City of Mainz, 1986; Medal, Type Dirs Club, NY, 1987; Grand Prix Nat. des Arts Graphiques, France, 1993. Officier de l'Ordre des Arts et des Lettres (France), 1993. *Publications:* Der Mensch und seine Zeichen, 1978; Signs and Symbols, 1998; Forms and Counterforms, 1998; Life Cycle, 1999. *Recreations:* walking through forest, drawing, wood cutting. *Address:* Kunoweg 15, 3047 Bremgarten, Switzerland. *T:* and *Fax:* (31) 3026875; c/o Erich Alb, Lindenbühl 33, 6330 Cham, Switzerland; *e-mail:* erich.alb@bluewin.ch.

FRY, Sir Graham (Holbrook), KCMG 2006; HM Diplomatic Service, retired; Ambassador to Japan, 2004–08; *b* 20 Dec. 1949; *s* of Wing Comdr Richard Holbrook Fry and Marjorie Fry; *m* 1st, 1977, Mayko Iida (marr. diss. 1991); two *s*; 2nd, 1994, Toyoko Ando. *Educ:* Brasenose Coll., Oxford (BA 1972). Entered HM Diplomatic Service, 1972; Third, later Second, Sec., Tokyo, 1974–78; seconded to Invest in Britain Bureau, DoI, 1979–80; FCO, 1981–83; First Sec., Paris, 1983–87; FCO, 1987–88; Political Counsellor, Tokyo, 1989–93; Head, Far Eastern Dept, later Far Eastern and Pacific Dept, FCO, 1993–95; Dir, Northern Asia and Pacific, FCO, 1995–98; High Comr, Malaysia, 1998–2001; Dep. Under-Sec. of State, FCO, 2001–03; Dir Gen., Econ., FCO, 2003–04. *Recreation:* bird-watching.

FRY, Gregory John; Executive Director: St George PLC, since 1986; The Berkeley Group plc, since 1996; *b* 29 April 1957; *s* of Wilfred John Fry, Freeman of the City of London. *Educ:* Lord Wandsworth Coll., Hants. ACA 1983. Joined Berkeley Homes, 1983. Gov., Richmond upon Thames Coll., 2000–04. FInstD 1990. *Recreation:* Rugby. *Address:* St George PLC, St George House, 76 Crown Road, Twickenham TW1 3EU. *T:* (020) 8917 4000, *Fax:* (020) 8917 4120; *e-mail:* Greg.Fry@stgeorgeplc.com. *Club:* Harlequins Rugby.

FRY, Dr Ian Kelsey, DM, FRCP, FRCR; Dean, Medical College of St Bartholomew's Hospital, 1981–89; Consultant Radiologist, St Bartholomew's Hospital, 1966–87; *b* 25 Oct. 1923; *s* of Sir William and Lady Kelsey Fry; *m* 1951, Mary Josephine Casey; three *s* (one *d* decd). *Educ:* Radley Coll.; New Coll., Oxford; Guy's Hosp. Medical Sch. BM BCh 1948, DM Oxon 1961; MRCP 1956, FRCP 1972; DMRD 1961; FFR 1963; FRCR 1975. RAF Medical Services, 1949–50 (Sqdn Ldr). Director, Dept of Radiology, BUPA Medical Centre, 1973–86; Dir of Radiology, London Independent Hosp., 1986–94; Mem. Council, Royal College of Radiologists, 1979–82; Pres. and Chm. Bd, Med. Defence Union, 1993–97 (Mem. Bd, 1991–93); President, British Institute of Radiology, 1982–83. Gov., Charterhouse Sch., 1984–94. *Publications:* chapters and articles in books and jls. *Recreations:* golf, hill walking, racing. *Address:* 8 Kingsmere, 43 Chislehurst Road, Chislehurst, Kent BR7 5LE. *T:* (020) 8467 4150.

FRY, Jonathan Michael; Chairman, Control Risks Holdings Ltd, 2000–07; *b* 9 Aug. 1937; *s* of late Stephen Fry and Gladys Yvonne (*née* Blunt); *m* 1st, 1970, Caroline Mary Dunkerly (marr. diss. 1997); four *d*; 2nd, 1999, Marilyn Diana Russell. *Educ:* Repton Sch.; Trinity Coll., Oxford (Lit. Hum., MA). Engagement Manager and Consultant, McKinsey & Co., 1966–73; Unigate Foods Division: Man. Dir, 1973–76; Chm., 1976–78; Gp Planning Dir, Burmah Oil Trading Ltd, 1978–81; Chief Executive: Burmah Speciality Chemicals Ltd, 1981–87; Castrol Internat., 1987–93; Burmah Castrol: Man. Dir, 1990–93; Chief Exec., 1993–98; Chm., 1998–2000. Chm., Christian Salvesen plc, 1997–2003; non-executive Director: Northern Foods plc, 1991–2002 (Dep. Chm., 1996–2002); Elementis (formerly Harrisons & Crosfield), 1997–2004 (Chm., 1997–2004). Mem. Council, RIIA, 1998–2002. Chm. Govs, Repton Sch., 2004–. *Recreations:* cricket, ski-ing, archaeology. *Address:* Beechingstoke Manor, Pewsey, Wilts SN9 6HQ. *Clubs:* Beefsteak, MCC; Vincent's (Oxford).

FRY, Dame Margaret (Louise), DBE 1989 (OBE 1982); Chairman, National Union of Conservative and Unionist Associations, 1990–91 (a Vice-Chairman, 1987–90); *b* 10 March 1931; *d* of Richard Reed Dawe and Ruth Dora Dawe; *m* 1955, Walter William John Fry; three *s*. *Educ:* Tavistock Grammar School. Conservative Women's Advisory Committee (Western Area): Vice-Chm., 1975–78; Chm., 1978–81; Conservative Women's National Committee: Vice-Chm., 1981–82; Chm., 1984–87; Chm., W Devon Cons. Assoc., 1982–85; Patron, Torridge and W Devon Cons. Assoc., 1999– (Pres., 1992–99; Pres., Women's Cttee, 1988–93); Pres., Western Area Cons, 1995–99. Chairman of Trustees: Peninsula Med. Sch. of Univs of Exeter and Plymouth, 2001–; Primrose Foundn for Breast Care, Derriford Hosp., Plymouth, 2001–. *Recreations:* farming, conservation, church, sport (former member, Devon County Hockey XI). *Address:* Thorne Farm, Launceston, Cornwall PL15 9SN. *T:* (01566) 784308.

FRY, Sir Peter (Derek), Kt 1994; *b* 26 May 1931; *s* of Harry Walter Fry and late Edith Fry; *m*; one *s* one *d*; *m* 1982, Helen Claire Mitchell. *Educ:* Royal Grammar School, High Wycombe; Worcester College, Oxford (MA). Tillotsons (Liverpool) Ltd, 1954–56; Northern Assurance Co., 1956–61; Political Education Officer, Conservative Central Office, 1961–63. Member Bucks County Council, 1961–67. Consultant to Parly Monitoring Services Ltd, 1992–. Contested (C) North Nottingham, 1964, East Willesden, 1966. MP (C) Wellingborough, 1969–97; contested (C) same seat, 1997. Mem., Select Cttee on Transport, 1979–92; Joint Chairman: All-Party Roads Study Gp, 1974–97; Parly Road Passenger Gp, 1992–97; All-Party Aviation Gp, 1992–97; Parly Transport Forum, 1992–97; Vice. Chm., Cons. Aviation Cttee, 1994–97; Chairman: All-Party Footwear and Leather Gp, 1979–87; Anglo-Bahamas Parly Gp, 1980–97; British Slovenia Gp, 1993–97; British Macedonia Gp, 1993–97; formerly Chm., British Yugoslav Parly Gp; Vice-Chairman: British Bosnia Gp, 1993–95; British Croatia Gp, 1993–95; All-Party CSA Monitoring Gp, 1995–97; Jt Chm., All-Party Recreation and Leisure Gp, 1994–97; Vice Pres., British Southern Slav Soc. Formerly Mem., Delegn to Council of Europe/WEU. Non-exec. Chm., Bingo Assoc., 1998–; Pres., EUBingo, 2006–. Played Rugby for Bucks County, 1956–58, Hon. Secretary, 1958–61. *Recreations:* watching Rugby football, reading history and biographies. *Address:* Glebe Farm House, Church Lane, Cranford, Kettering, Northants NN14 4AE.

FRY, Lt-Gen. Sir Robert (Alan), KCB 2005; CBE 2001 (MBE 1981); Vice-President, EDS Corporation, since 2007; Deputy Commanding General, Multinational Force, Iraq, 2006; *b* 6 April 1951; *s* of Raymond and Elizabeth Fry; *m* 1977, Elizabeth Woolmore; two *d*. *Educ:* Bath Univ. (BScEcon); King's Coll., London (MA). Worked in commerce, NY, 1972–73; joined Royal Marines, 1973: COS, 3 Commando Bde, 1989–91; CO 45 Commando, 1995–97; Dir Naval Staff, MoD, 1997–99; Comdr 3 Commando Bde, 1999–2001; Comdt-Gen., Royal Marines, 2001–02; COS, Perm. Jt HQ, 2002–03; DCDS (Commitments), MoD, 2003–06. Director: McKinney Rogers, NY; Injazat Data Services, Abu Dhabi; Meeza Corp., Doha. Officer, Legion of Merit (USA), 2006. *Publications:* contrib. to RUSI J1, US Naval Inst. Proc., Bull. d'Etudes de la Marine. *Recreations:* Welsh Rugby, cinema, photography, history. *Address:* EDS, Lansdowne House, Berkeley Square, W1J 6ER. *Club:* Special Forces.

FRY, Sarah McC.; *see* McCarthy-Fry.

FRY, Stephen John; writer, actor, comedian; *b* 24 Aug. 1957; *s* of Alan John Fry and Marianne Eve (*née* Newman). *Educ:* Uppingham Sch.; Queens' Coll., Cambridge (MA; Hon. Fellow, 2005). *TV series:* Blackadder, 1987–89; A Bit of Fry and Laurie, 1989–95; Jeeves in Jeeves and Wooster, 1990–92; Gormenghast, 2000; Absolute Power, 2003, 2005; Kingdom, 2007–08; presenter, QI, 2003–; *TV documentary:* Stephen Fry: the secret life of a manic depressive, 2006 (Emmy Award, 2007); *theatre:* Forty Years On, Queen's, 1984; The Common Pursuit, Phoenix, 1988; *films:* Peter's Friends, 1992; I.Q., 1995; Wilde, 1997; Cold Comfort Farm, 1997; The Tichborne Claimant, 1998; Whatever Happened to Harold Smith?, 2000; Relative Values, 2000; Gosford Park, 2002; (dir) Bright Young Things, 2003; Tooth, 2004; The Life and Death of Peter Sellers, 2004; V for Vendetta, 2006; St Trinian's, 2007; (for television) Tom Brown's Schooldays, 2005. Columnist: The Listener, 1988–89; Daily Telegraph, 1990–. *Publications:* Me and My Girl, 1984 (musical performed in West End and on Broadway); A Bit of Fry and Laurie: collected scripts, 1990; Moab is My Washpot (autobiog.), 1997; The Ode Less Travelled, 2005; *novels:* The Liar, 1991; The Hippopotamus, 1994; Making History, 1996; The Stars' Tennis Balls, 2000. *Recreations:* smoking, drinking, swearing, pressing wild flowers. *Address:* c/o Hamilton Hodell Ltd, 5th Floor, 66–68 Margaret Street, W1W 8SR. *Clubs:* Savile, Oxford and Cambridge, Groucho, Chelsea Arts, Garrick.

FRY, William Norman H.; *see* Hillier-Fry.

FRYAR, Rt Rev. Godfrey Charles; *see* Rockhampton, Bishop of.

FRYE, Michael John Ernest, CBE 1997; President and Director-General, Swiss Digital Technologies, since 1999; *b* 2 June 1945; *s* of late Jack Frye, CBE and Daphne Page-Croft; *m* 1st, 1970, Geraldine Elizabeth Kendall; one *s*; 2nd, 1989, Valerie Patricia Harfield-Simpson; one *d*. *Educ:* Marlborough Coll.; MIT (SB Business Management, Mech. Eng. Minor). B. Elliott and subsidiaries, 1967–99; Dir, Goldfields Industrial, 1973–76; Overseas Dir, B. Elliott, 1974–76, non-exec. Dir, 1976–87, Chm., 1987–92, Chief Exec., 1988–99; Chm. and Chief Exec., Rotaflex Gp of Cos, 1975–87; Chm., Concord Lighting, 1976–87; non-exec. Dir, Thorn Lighting Group, 1993–99. Chairman: Deltadot, 2000–04; Water & Waste plc, 2001–04. Chm. and Founder, Light and Health Res. Council, 1978; Member: NEDC Sub-Cttee, exports for luminaire manufrs, 1980–81; Council, Lighting Industry Fedn, 1980–87 (Vice-Pres., 1987); Illuminating Eng. Soc. of N America, 1979–; Chairman: Cttee to establish nat. lighting award, 1984–87; Lighting Div., CIBSE, 1987–88. Chairman: West London Leadership, 1990–2002; Business Link London, 1995–96; Creative London, 2003–; London Sci. and Industry Council, 2003–05; Dep. Chm., Park Royal Partnership, 1993–95 (Chm., 1991–92); Director: London First, 1992–2002 (a Dep. Chm., 1996–2002); London Develt Partnership, 1998–2001 (Chm., Skills Taskforce, 1998–2001); Member Board: London Develt Agency, 2001–; London Climate Change Agency, 2005–. Chm., CBI London Reg., 1997–99 (Vice-Chm., 1996–97). Mem., Public Services Productivity Panel, 2000–, Public Services and Public Expenditure Cttee, 2001–, HM Treasury. Chm. and Mem., numerous technical and arts organisations. Hon. Prof., Thames Valley Univ., 1995. Liveryman, Turners' Co. and Lightmongers' Co. FRAeS 1994; Fellow, RSPB, 1987; FRSA 1978 (Vice Pres., 1990–; Chm., 1991–93; Dep. Chm., 1993–94). Hon. Fellow, RCA, 1987. DUniv Brunel, 2001; Hon. DEng London Metropolitan, 2004. *Recreations:* golf, tennis, chess, bird watching, collecting old or rare bird books. *Address:* Lynara (Management) Ltd, Crown House, 72

Hammersmith Road, W14 8TH. *Clubs:* Boodle's, City Livery, Royal Automobile; Royal Worlington and Newmarket Golf.

FRYER, Dr Geoffrey, FRS 1972; Deputy Chief Scientific Officer, Windermere Laboratory, Freshwater Biological Association, 1981–88; *b* 6 Aug. 1927; *s* of W. and M. Fryer; *m* 1953, Vivien Griffiths Hodgson; one *s* one *d. Educ:* Huddersfield College. DSc, PhD London. Royal Navy, 1946–48. Colonial Research Student, 1952–53; HM Overseas Research Service, 1953–60: Malawi, 1953–55; Zambia, 1955–57; Uganda, 1957–60; Sen., then Principal, then Sen. Principal Scientific Officer, Freshwater Biological Assoc., 1960–81. H. R. Macmillan Lectr, Univ. of British Columbia, 1963; Distinguished Vis. Schol., Univ. of Adelaide, 1985; Distinguished Lectr, Biol Scis Br., Dept. Fisheries and Oceans, Canada, 1987; Hon. Prof., Inst. of Environmental and Natural (formerly Biol) Scis, Lancaster Univ., 1988–. Mem. Council, Royal Soc., 1978–80. Mem., Adv. Cttee on Science, Nature Conservancy Council, 1986–91. Pres., Yorks Naturalists' Union, 1993. Frink Medal, Zool Soc. of London, 1983; Linnean Medal for Zoology, Linnean Soc., 1987; Elsdon-Dew Medal, Parasitological Soc. of Southern Africa, 1998. *Publications:* (with T. D. Iles) The Cichlid Fishes of the Great Lakes of Africa: their biology and evolution, 1972; A natural history of the lakes, tarns and streams of the English Lake District, 1991; The Freshwater Crustacea of Yorkshire: a faunistic and ecological survey, 1993; (ed with V. R. Alexeev) Diapause in the Crustacea, 1996; numerous articles in scientific jls. *Recreations:* natural history, history of science, walking, church architecture, photography. *Address:* Elleray Cottage, Windermere, Cumbria LA23 1AW.

FRYER-SPEDDING, John Henry Fryer, CBE 2003 (OBE 1982); Vice Lord-Lieutenant of Cumbria, since 2006; *b* 23 Jan. 1937; *s* of Lieut Col James Eustace Spedding, OBE and Mary Catherine Spedding (*née* Fryer); *m* 1968, Clare Caroline Ewbank, *d* of Ven. Walter Ewbank, *qv*; two *s. Educ:* Trinity Coll., Cambridge (BA 1958, MA 1961). Royal Green Jackets, 1958–68: served Germany, Cyprus and Borneo; retd Maj. 1968. Called to the Bar, Gray's Inn, 1970; a Recorder, 1990–97. Mem., Lake Dist Nat. Park Authy, 1997–2001. Pres., Royal Forestry Soc., 2003–05. Vice-President: Calvert Trusts (for disabled people), 2005– (Trustee, 1976–2006; Chm. Council, 2002–06); Cumbria Community Foundn, 2007– (Trustee, 1997–2007; Chm., 1997–2002). Fellow, Wordsworth Trust, 2000– (Trustee, 1978–2000); Vice-Pres., Tennyson Soc., 1984–. DL 1985, High Sheriff, 1997–98, Cumbria. DLI (TA), 1969–78: CO 7th Bn, 1976–78; retd Lt Col, 1978. *Recreations:* forestry, bee-keeping. *Address:* West Mirehouse, Keswick, Cumbria CA12 4QE. *T:* (01768) 775356, *Fax:* (01768) 775356. *Club:* Lansdowne.

FUAD, Kutlu Tekin, CBE 1993; SPMB 1999; President, Court of Appeal, Negara Brunei Darussalam, 1993–2000; a non-permanent Judge, Court of Final Appeal, Hong Kong, since 1997; *b* 23 April 1926; *s* of Mustafa Fuad Bey, CMG, and Belkis Hilmi; *m* 1952, Inci Izzet; two *s* one *d. Educ:* Temple Grove; Marlborough Coll.; St John's Coll., Cambridge (MA). Called to the Bar, Inner Temple, 1952, Hon. Bencher, 1993. Mil. Service, Lieut KRRC, 1944–48 (Palestine 1946–48). Colonial Legal Service, 1953–62: Magistrate, Cyprus; Resident Magistrate, Sen. Crown Counsel, Legal Draftsman, and Dir of Public Prosecutions, Uganda; Judge of the High Court, Uganda, 1963–72 (Pres., Industrial Court; Chm., Law Reform Cttee); Dir, Legal Div., Commonwealth Secretariat, 1972–80; Judge, High Court of Hong Kong, 1980–82; Justice of Appeal, 1982–88, Vice-Pres., 1988–93, Court of Appeal, Hong Kong. Comr, Supreme Ct of Negara Brunei Darussalam, 1983–86, 1988–92. Nominated by Turkey as *ad hoc* judge for case brought to ECHR, 2000. Mem., Law Reform Commn, Hong Kong, 1983–89. Pres., Hong Kong Family Law Assoc., 1986–93. Formerly Chm., Visitation Cttee, Makerere University Coll. *Recreations:* music, Rugby football, gardening. *Address:* PO Box 415, Lefkoşa, Mersin 10, Turkey. *T:* (392) 2283299; 76 Abingdon Villas, Kensington, W8 6XB. *T:* (020) 7937 8646.

FUENTES, Prof. Carlos; Professor at Large, Brown University, since 1995; *b* 11 Nov. 1928; *s* of Ambassador Rafael Fuentes and Berta Fuentes; *m* 1st, 1957, Rita Macedo; one *d*; 2nd, 1973, Sylvia Lemus; one *s* one *d. Educ:* Law School, Nat. Univ., Mexico; Inst. des Hautes Etudes Internat., Geneva. Sec., Mexican Deleg. to ILO, Geneva, 1950; Under Director of Culture, Nat. Univ., Mexico, 1952–54; Head, Cultural Relations Dept, Min. of Foreign Affairs, Mexico, 1955–58; Ambassador to France, 1975–77; Prof. of English and Romance Languages, Univ. of Pennsylvania, 1978–83; Prof. of Comparative Literature, Harvard, 1984–86; Simón Bolivar Prof., Cambridge, 1986–87; Robert F. Kennedy Prof. of Latin American Studies, Harvard, 1987–90. Member: El Colegio Nacional, Mexico, 1974–; Mexican Nat. Commn on Human Rights, 1989–; Fellow, Wilson Center, Washington DC, 1974; Mem., Amer. Acad. and Inst. of Arts and Letters, 1986; Trustee, NY Public Library, 1987. Hon. DLitt: Wesleyan, 1982; Warwick, 1992; Hon. LLD Harvard, 1983; Hon. LittD Cambridge, 1987; DUniv Essex, 1987; Dr *hc* Tufts, 1993; UCLA, 1993; Salamanca, 2002. Nat. Prize for Literature, Mexico, 1985; Miguel de Cervantes Prize, 1987; Menéndez Pelayo Prize, Univ. of Santander, 1992; Delaware Commonwealth Award, 2002. Légion d'Honneur (France), 1992; Order Cruzeiro do Sul (Brazil), 1997. *Publications:* Where the Air is Clear, 1958; The Good Conscience, 1959; The Death of Artemio Cruz, 1962; Aura, 1962; A Change of Skin, 1967 (Biblioteca Breve Prize, Barcelona); Terra Nostra, 1975 (Rómulo Gallegos Prize); Distant Relations, 1980; Burnt Water, 1982; The Old Gringo, 1984 (filmed, 1989); Cristóbal Nonato, 1987; Myself with Others: selected essays, 1988; The Campaign, 1991; Valiente Mundo Nuevo: essays, 1991; Constancia and other stories for virgins, 1991; The Buried Mirror, 1992 (televised); El Naranjo (The Orange Tree) (novellas), 1993; Geography of the Novel: essays, 1993; A New Time for Mexico, 1997; Diana, 1997; Por un Progreso Incluyente, 1997; The Crystal Frontier: a novel in nine stories, 1997; Portraits in Time (photo essay), 1998; The Years with Laura Diaz, 1999; (ed jtly) The Picador Book of Latin American Stories, 1999; Los Cinco Solesda México, 2000; Inez, 2003; The Eagle's Throne, 2003; This I Believe, 2004. *Address:* c/o Brandt & Brandt, 1501 Broadway, New York, NY 10036, USA.

FUGARD, Athol; playwright, director, actor; *b* 11 June 1932; *s* of Harold David Fugard and Elizabeth Magdalene Potgieter; *m* 1956, Sheila Meiring; one *d. Educ:* Univ. of Cape Town. Directed earliest plays, Nongogo, No Good Friday, Johannesburg, 1960; acted in The Blood Knot, touring S Africa, 1961; Hello and Goodbye, 1965; directed and acted in The Blood Knot, London, 1966; Boesman and Lena, S Africa, 1969; directed Boesman and Lena, London, 1971; directed Serpent Players in various prodns, Port Elizabeth, from 1963, directed co-authors John Kani and Winston Ntshona in Sizwe Bansi is Dead, SA, 1972, The Island, 1973, and London, 1973–74; acted in film, Boesman and Lena, 1972; directed and acted in Statements after an Arrest under the Immorality Act, in SA, 1972, directed in London, 1973; wrote Dimetos for Edinburgh Fest., 1975; directed and acted in, A Lesson from Aloes, SA, 1978, London, 1980 (directed, NY 1981, winning NY Critics Circle Award for Best Play); directed: Master Harold and the Boys, NY, 1982 (Drama Desk Award), Johannesburg, 1983, Nat. Theatre, 1983 (Standard award for Best Play); The Road to Mecca, Yale Repertory Theatre, 1984; (also wrote) My Children! My Africa!, NY, 1990; (also wrote) Playland, SA, 1992, NY and London, 1993; (also wrote and acted in) Valley Song, Royal Court, 1996; (also wrote and acted in) The Captain's Tiger, NY, 1999, London, 2000; (also wrote and dir.) Sorrows and Rejoicings, London, 2002. Hon. DLitt: Natal, 1981; Rhodes, 1983; Cape Town, 1984; Emory, 1992; Port Elizabeth, 1993; Hon. DFA Yale, 1983; Hon. DHL Georgetown, 1984. *Films:* Boesman and Lena, 1973; The Guest, 1977; (acted in) Meetings with Remarkable Men (dir, Peter Brook), 1979; (wrote and acted in) Marigolds in August (Silver Bear Award, Berlin), 1980; (acted in) Gandhi, 1982; (co-dir and acted in) Road to Mecca, 1991. *Publications:* The Blood Knot, 1962; People Are Living There, Hello and Goodbye, 1973; Boesman and Lena, 1973; (jtly) Three Port Elizabeth Plays: Sizwe Bansi is Dead, The Island, Statements after an Arrest under the Immorality Act, 1974; Tsotsi (novel), 1980 (also USA) (filmed 2005); A Lesson from Aloes, 1981 (also USA); Master Harold and the Boys, US 1982, UK 1983; Notebooks 1960–1977, 1983 (also USA); Road to Mecca, 1985; A Place with the Pigs, 1988; Cousins: a memoir, 1994. *Recreations:* angling, skin-diving, bird-watching. *Address:* c/o William Morris, 1325 Avenue of the Americas, New York, NY 10019, USA.

FUGGER, Prof. Lars, MD, PhD, DMSc; Professor of Neuroimmunology, University of Oxford, since 2007; Fellow of Oriel College, Oxford, since 2007; Honorary Consultant, Department of Clinical Immunology, John Radcliffe Hospital, Oxford, since 2003; *b* Copenhagen, 15 Aug. 1960; *s* of Henrik Fugger and Inger Fugger; *m* 1991, Astrid Kristine Nagel Iversen, MD, PhD; two *s* two *d. Educ:* Rungsted Gymnasium (BA Maths 1979); Univ. of Copenhagen (MD 1987; PhD 1990, DMSc 1993). Internships and residencies, various hosps, Denmark, 1987–90; Postdoctoral Fellow, Dept of Microbiol. and Immunol., Stanford Univ., 1990–94; Clin. Fellow, Dept of Clin. Immunol. Rigshospitalet, Copenhagen Univ. Hosp., 1994–96; Prof. of Clin. Immunology, Aarhus Univ. Hosp., 1996–; Sen. Clin. Fellow, MRC Human Immunol. Unit, Weatherall Inst of Molecular Medicine, John Radcliffe Hosp., Oxford, 2002–07; Prof. of Clin. Immunol. Univ. of Oxford, 2004–. Chm., Danish MRC, 2007–. Gold Medal, Univ. of Aarhus 1985; Anders Jahre Nordic Med. Res. Prize for young scientists, 1998; Descartes Prize EC, 2002; August Krogh Prize, Danish Med. Soc., 2003; Award for Excellence in Clin Sci., Eur. Soc. of Clin. Investigation, 2005. *Address:* Department of Clinical Neurology and MRC Human Immunology Unit, Weatherall Institute of Molecular Medicine, John Radcliffe Hospital, University of Oxford, Oxford OX3 9DS. *T:* (01865) 222498, *Fax* (01865) 222502; *e-mail:* lars.fugger@imm.ox.ac.uk.

FUHR, Michael John, OBE 1999; Director, Major Projects, Department for Transport since 2003; *b* 5 June 1949; *s* of late Max Fuhr and of Betty Fuhr (*née* Neuman); *m* 1975, Susan Harrington; two *d. Educ:* Bradford Grammar Sch.; Univ. of Surrey (BSc Hons 1973). Admin trainee, 1974, Principal, 1978, DoE; Department of Transport, then DETR, subseq. DTLR, 1979–2001; Asst Sec., 1989; Project Dir, Channel Tunnel Rail Link, 1996–99; Dir, London Underground Task Gp, 1999–2001; Dir of Corporate Strategy, Treasury Solicitor's Dept, 2001–03. Dir, Cross London Rail Links Ltd, 2004–. *Recreations:* most sports, photography, technology, following the variable fortunes of Bradford City AFC. *Address:* Department for Transport, 76 Marsham Street, SW1P 4DR.

FUJII, Hiroaki; Chairman, Mori Arts Center, Tokyo, since 2004; Adviser, Japan Foundation, Tokyo, since 2003 (President, 1997–2003); *b* 21 Aug. 1933; *m* 1963, Kiyoko Shimoda; three *d. Educ:* Tokyo Univ.; Amherst Coll., USA (BA 1958). Entered Min. of Foreign Affairs, Japan, 1956; Dir, Econ. Affairs Div., UN Bureau, 1971–72; Private Sec to Minister for Foreign Affairs, 1972–74; Dir, 2nd Econ. Co-operation Div., Econ. Co-operation Bureau, 1974–75; Dir, 1st N American Div., American Affairs Bureau 1975–76; Fellow, Center for Internat. Affairs, Harvard Univ., 1976; Counsellor, Embassy of Japan, Washington, 1977–79; Ministry of Foreign Affairs: Dir, Personnel Div. Minister's Secretariat, 1979–81; Dep. Dir Gen., Asian Affairs Bureau, 1981–83; Consul-Gen., Hong Kong, 1983–85; Ministry of Foreign Affairs: Dir Gen., N American Affairs Bureau, 1985–88; Dep. Vice-Minister, 1988–89; Ambassador to: OECD, Paris, 1989–92 Thailand, 1992–94; Court of St James's, 1994–97. Hon. DCL: Durham, 1997; UEA 1999; Hon. LLD Birmingham, 1997. Kt Grand Cross (1st Cl.), Most Exalted Order of White Elephant (Thailand), 1994. *Address:* Mori Arts Center, Roppongi Hills Mori Tower, 6–10–1 Roppongi, Minato-ku, Tokyo 106–6150, Japan. *T:* (3) 64066133, *Fax* (3) 64066518.

FULBROOK, Prof. Mary Jean Alexandra, PhD; FRHistS; FBA 2007; Professor of German History, since 1995, and Director, Centre for European Studies, since 1991 University College London; *b* 28 Nov. 1951; *d* of Prof. Arthur J. C. Wilson and Dr Harriett C. Wilson (*née* Friedeberg); *m* 1973, Dr Julian Fulbrook; two *s* one *d. Educ:* Sidcot Sch., Somerset; King Edward VI High Sch., Birmingham; Newnham Coll., Cambridge (BA 1973 Double 1st Cl. Hons; Schol., Sen. Schol., Helen Gladstone Meml Schol.; MA 1977); Harvard Univ. (AM 1975; PhD 1979). FRHistS 1987. Harvard Center for European Studies Krupp Fellow, LSE, 1976–77; Temporary Lecturer: LSE, 1977–78 Brunel Univ., 1978–79; Lady Margaret Res. Fellow, New Hall, Cambridge, 1979–82 Res. Associate, KCL, 1982–83; University College London: Lectr, 1983–91, Reader 1991–95, in German Hist.; Hd, German Dept, 1995–2006; Mem., Council, 2003–07. Vis Fellow, Forschungsschwerpunkt Zeithistorische Studien, Potsdam, 1994; Vis. Bye-Fellow, Newnham Coll., Cambridge, 1994. Jt Founding Ed., German History, 1984–94 Member: Jt Cttee on W Europe of ACLS/SSRC, 1990–94; Adv. Bd, German Historical Inst., London, 2003–; AHRC (formerly AHRB) Res. Panel for Hist., 2004–07; Adv. Bd Stiftung Gedenkstätten Buchenwald und Mittelbau-Dora, 2007–; Adv. Bd Bundeskanzler-Willy-Brandt-Stiftung, 2008–. Chm., German Hist. Soc., 1996–99. Vice-Chairman of Governors: Great Ormond Street Hosp. Sch. for Sick Children, 1980–85 Haverstock Sch., 1999–2001; Chm. Govs, S Camden Community Sch., 1992–94 Mayoress, London Bor. of Camden, 1985–86. *Publications:* Piety and Politics: religion and the rise of absolutism in England, Württemberg and Prussia, 1983; A Concise History of Germany, 1990, 2nd edn 2004 (trans. Hungarian, Spanish, Swedish, Korean, Romanian Chinese, Japanese); The Divided Nation: Germany 1918–1990, 1991 (trans. Italian), 2nd edn as A History of Germany 1918–2000: the divided nation, 2002; The Two Germanies 1945–1990: problems of interpretation, 1992, 2nd edn as Interpretations of the Two Germanies 1945–1990, 2000; (ed) National Histories and European History, 1993 Anatomy of a Dictatorship: inside the GDR 1949–89, 1995; (ed with D. Cesarani) Citizenship, Nationality and Migration in Europe, 1996; (ed with J. Breuilly) German History since 1800, 1997; German National Identity after the Holocaust, 1999 (trans Hungarian); (ed) The Short Oxford History of Europe 1945–2000, 2000 (trans. Spanish and Polish); (ed with M. Swales) Representing the German Nation, 2000; (ed) Twentieth-century Germany: politics, culture and society 1918–1990, 2001; Historical Theory, 2002 Hitler, Book 1, 2004, Book 2, 2005; The People's State: East German Society from Hitler to Honecker, 2005; (ed) Uncivilising Processes? Excess and Transgression in German Society and Culture, 2006; numerous articles in jls and chapters in books. *Recreations:* swimming, running very slowly (London marathon 2002), reading novels, spending time with my family. *Address:* Department of German, University College London, Gower Street, WC1E 6BT. *T:* (020) 7679 7120; *e-mail:* m.fulbrook@ucl.ac.uk.

FULFORD, Hon. Sir Adrian Bruce, Kt 2002; **Hon. Mr Justice Fulford;** a Judge of the High Court, Queen's Bench Division, since 2002; a Judge of the International Criminal Court, The Hague, since 2003; a Presiding Judge, South Eastern Circuit, since 2009; *b* 8 Jan. 1953; *s* of Gerald John Fulford and Marie Bettine (*née* Stevens). *Educ.*

Elizabeth Coll., Guernsey; Southampton Univ. (BA Hons). Housing Advr, Shelter's Housing Aid Centre, 1974–75; called to the Bar, Middle Temple, 1978, Bencher, 2002; QC 1994; a Recorder, 2001–02. Ed., UK Human Rights Reports, 2000–. *Publications:* (contrib.) Atkin's Court Forms, 1987; (ed) Archbold Criminal Pleadings and Practices, 1992; (jtly) A Criminal Practitioner's Guide to Judicial Review and Case Stated, 1999; (jtly) Judicial Review: a practical guide, 2004; (ed jtly) Archbold International Criminal Courts, 2005. *Recreations:* riding, golf. *Address:* Royal Courts of Justice, Strand, WC2A 2LL; International Criminal Court, Maanweg 174, 2516 AB The Hague, Netherlands. *Club:* Garrick.

FULFORD, Prof. Michael Gordon, PhD; FSA; FBA 1994; Professor of Archaeology, University of Reading, since 1993; *b* 20 Oct. 1948; *s* of Comdr E. G. J. D. Fulford, RN (retd) and E. Z. Fulford (*née* Simpson); *m* 1972, Charlotte Jane Hobbs; one *s* one *d.* *Educ:* St Edwards Sch., Oxford; Univ. of Southampton (BA Hons 1970; PhD 1975). DES Res. Student, 1970; Research Assistant: Univ. of Southampton, 1971–72; Univ. of Oxford, 1972–74; University of Reading: Lectr in Archaeol., 1974–85; Reader, 1985–88; Leverhulme Res. Fellow, 1987; Personal Prof., 1988–93; Dean, Faculty of Letters and Social Scis, 1994–97; Pro-Vice-Chancellor, 1998–2004; Leverhulme Major Res. Fellow, 2004–07. Chm., Archaeol. Panel, RAE 2001, Main Panel H, RAE 2008, HEFCE. Dalrymple Lectr, Glasgow Univ., 1996. Pres., Soc. for Promotion of Roman Studies, 2005–08 (Editor, Britannia, 1994–99). English Heritage: Chm., Hadrian's Wall Adv. Panel, 1989–97 (Mem., 1985–97); Mem., Ancient Monuments Adv. Cttee, 1991–97; Comr, RCHM, 1993–99; Member: Archaeology Adv. Cttee, Nat. Mus. of Wales, 1991–99; SE Mus., Library and Archive Council, 2002–06. Vice-President: Royal Archaeol Inst., 1996–2001; British Acad., 2006– (Mem. Council, 2003–; Mem., Humanities Res. Bd, 1995–98; Chm., Acad.-Sponsored Insts and Socs Bd, 2005–); Mem. Council, British Sch. at Rome, 2003–05. Chm., Aimhigher, Berks, 2004. FSA 1977. *Publications:* New Forest Roman Pottery, 1975; (with B. Cunliffe) CSIR Great Britain I: Bath and the Rest of Wessex, 1982; Silchester Defences, 1984; (with D. Peacock) Excavations at Carthage: The British Mission, The Pottery and other Ceramics, Vol. 1, 1984, Vol. 2, 1994; The Silchester Amphitheatre, 1989; Excavations at Sabratha 1948–1951, Vol. 2, pt i (ed with M. Hall), 1989, pt ii (ed with R. Tomber), 1994; (ed jtly) Developing Landscape of Lowland Britain: the archaeology of the British gravels, 1992; (ed jtly) England's Coastal Heritage, 1997; (with J. R. Timby) Late Iron Age and Roman Silchester: excavations on the site of the Forum-Basilica 1977 and 1980–86, 2000; (jtly) Life and Labour in Late Roman Silchester: excavations in Insula IX since 1997, 2006; (jtly) Iron Age and Romano-British Settlements and Landscapes of Salisbury Plain, 2006. *Recreations:* music, walking, sailing. *Address:* Department of Archaeology, University of Reading, PO Box 227, Reading, Berks RG6 6AB. *T:* (0118) 378 8048.

FULFORD, Robert John; Keeper, Department of Printed Books, British Library (formerly British Museum), 1967–85; *b* 16 Aug. 1923; *s* of John Fulford, Southampton; *m* 1950, Alison Margaret Rees (*d* 1996); one *s* one *d.* *Educ:* King Edward VI Sch., Southampton; King's Coll., Cambridge; Charles Univ., Prague. Asst Keeper, Dept of Printed Books, British Museum, 1945–65; Dep. Keeper, 1965–67 (Head of Slavonic Div., 1961–67); Keeper, 1967–85. *Address:* 7 Tulip Tree Close, Tonbridge, Kent TN9 2SH. *T:* (01732) 350356; Maumont, 24390 Hautefort, France. *T:* (5) 53505007.

FULFORD-DOBSON, Captain Michael, CVO 1999; OBE 2008; JP; RN; Lord-Lieutenant of Dorset, 1999–2006; *b* 6 April 1931; *e s* of late Lt-Col Cyril Fulford-Dobson, OBE and Betty Bertha Fulford-Dobson (*née* Bendelack-Hudson-Barmby); *m* 1966, Elizabeth Barbara Mary Rose Tate; three *d.* *Educ:* Pangbourne Coll.; RN Coll., Dartmouth. Royal Navy, 1949–84 (served Korean War, Suez Operation, first Cod War; 3 Sea Comds); Gentleman Usher to the Queen, 1985–99, Extra Gentleman Usher, 1999–. Chm., W Dorset Hosps NHS Trust, 1991–98. Chm., Dorset Trust, 1991–2000; Pres., Dorset Br., CPRE, 1995–2008; Trustee, Cancer Care Dorset, 1998–2007. Dir, In and Out Ltd, 1993–96. Member of Court: Exeter Univ., 1999–2007; Southampton Univ., 1999–2007; Governor, Sherborne Sch., 1999–2007. High Sheriff of Dorset, 1994–95; JP Dorset, 1999. KStJ 1999 (Pres., St John Council for Dorset, 1999–). Hon. Dr Arts Bournemouth, 2007. *Recreations:* restoration of historic buildings, cross country ski-ing, field sports. *Address:* Cerne Abbey, Dorset DT2 7JQ. *T:* (01300) 341284, *T:* and *Fax:* (01300) 341948; *e-mail:* mfd@ukonline.co.uk. *Club:* White's.

See also Viscount Fitzharris.

FULHAM, Bishop Suffragan of, since 1996; **Rt Rev. John Charles Broadhurst;** *b* 20 July 1942; *s* of late Charles Harold Broadhurst and of Dorothy Sylvia (*née* Prince); *m* 1965, Judith Margaret Randell; two *s* two *d.* *Educ:* Owen's Sch., Islington; King's Coll., London (AKC 1965); St Boniface Coll., Warminster; STh Lambeth, 1982. Ordained deacon, 1966, priest, 1967; Asst Curate, St Michael-at-Bowes, 1966–70; Priest-in-charge, 1970–75, Vicar, 1975–85, St Augustine, Wembley Park; Team Rector, Wood Green, 1985–96. Area Dean: Brent, 1982–85; E Haringey, 1985–91. Member: Gen. Synod of C of E, 1972–96 (Mem., Standing Cttee, 1988–96); ACC, 1991–96. Chm., Forward in Faith, 1992–; Vice-Chm., Church Union, 1997. Hon. DD Nashotah House, Wisconsin, 2003. *Publications:* (ed and contrib.) Quo Vaditis, 1996; numerous contribs to jls. *Recreations:* gardening, history, travel. *Address:* 26 Canonbury Park South, N1 2FN. *T:* (020) 7354 2334, *Fax:* (020) 7354 2335; *e-mail:* bpfulham@aol.com.

FULLER, Anne Rosemary, OBE 2000; JP; Chairman of Council, Magistrates' Association, 1996–99 (Deputy Chairman, 1993–96); *b* 27 Sept. 1936; *d* of Ronald Clifford Dent and Clara Vera Dent (*née* Murray); *m* 1960, John Acland Fuller (*d* 2006); two *s* one *d.* *Educ:* St Anne's Sch., Windermere; Royal Holloway Coll., Univ. of London (BA Hons 1957); KCL and LSE (Dip. in Law 1992). Market Research Executive: McCann Erickson, then Marplan, 1958–60; Bureau of Commercial Research, 1960–65; freelance market res. consultant, 1965–. Member: Nat. Forum, SCAA, 1996–97; Home Secretary's Task Force on Youth Justice, 1997–98; Compliance and Supervision Cttee, Office for Supervision of Solicitors, 1998–2001; Sentencing Adv. Panel, 1999–; Adjudication Panel: Law Soc., 2001–07; SRA, 2007–; Tribunal Mem., Disciplinary Cttee, ICAEW, 2000–. Dir and Trustee, Soc. of Voluntary Associates, 2000–04. JP Kingston-upon-Thames, 1975 (Dep. Chm., 1991–95); Chm., Betting Licensing Cttee, 1986–89; Mem., Magistrates' Courts Cttee, 1987–96; Chm., Youth Panel, 1990–93; Vice Pres., Magistrates' Assoc., 1999– (Mem. Council, 1984–; Vice Chm., Sentencing Cttee, 1991–93); Mem., Magistrates' Courts Consultative Council, 1993–99 (Mem., Trial Issues Gp, 1996–99); Nat. Co-ordinator, Magistrates in Community Project, 1993–97. FRSA 1997. *Publications:* (ed jtly) International Directory of Market Research Organisations, 1974, 11th edn 1994; numerous articles on magisterial matters. *Recreations:* music, theatre, cookery. *Address:* White Ridge, Ruxley Crescent, Claygate, Surrey KT10 0TX. *T:* (01372) 462609.

FULLER, Brian Leslie, CBE 1989; QFSM 1981; Commandant Chief Executive, Fire Service College, 1990–94; *b* 18 April 1936; *s* of Walter Leslie Victor Fuller and Eliza May Fuller; *m* 1957, Linda Peters; three *s.* *Educ:* St Albans County Grammar Sch. for Boys. FIFireE 1975. Station Officer: Herts Fire Brigade, 1960–66; Warwicks Fire Brigade, 1966–68; Asst Divl Officer, Notts Fire Brigade, 1968–69; Divl Commander, Essex Fire Brigade, 1969–72; Dep. Chief Fire Officer, Glamorgan Fire Brigade, 1972–74; Chief Fire Officer: Mid Glamorgan Fire Brigade, 1974–80; Notts Fire Brigade, 1980–81; W Midlands Fire Service, 1981–90. Gen. Manager and Principal, Fire Safety Engrg Coll., Oman, 1997–2001. Hon. DSc South Bank, 1993. *Recreations:* cricket, music, reading. *Address:* Newlands, Aqueduct Lane, Alvechurch, Birmingham B48 7BP.

FULLER, Eleanor Mary; HM Diplomatic Service; Permanent Representative of the United Kingdom to the Council of Europe, Strasbourg, since 2007; *b* Aldershot, 31 Dec. 1953; *d* of Peter and Ruth Breedon; *m* 1984, Simon William John Fuller, *qv*; three *s.* *Educ:* Somerville Coll., Oxford (MA Modern Langs). Joined FCO, 1975; FCO, 1975–77; Paris, 1978–81; FCO, 1981–83; on loan to ODA, 1983–86; Second, later First Sec., FCO, 1990–93; UNRWA for Palestine refugees in Near East, Vienna, 1993–96; First Sec., UK Delegn to OSCE, Vienna, 1998–99; First Sec., UK Mission to UN and WTO, Geneva, 2000–04; on loan to DFID, 2004–06; FCO, 2006–07. *Recreations:* gardens, music. *Address:* c/o Foreign and Commonwealth Office, King Charles Street, SW1A 2AH; *e-mail:* eleanor.fuller@fco.gov.uk.

See also T. J. Breedon.

FULLER, Geoffrey Herbert, CEng, FRINA, FIMarEST; RCNC; defence and maritime consultant; Director, British Maritime Technology Ltd, Teddington, 1985–2000 (Deputy Chairman, 1985–95); *b* 16 Jan. 1927; *s* of late Major Herbert Thomas Fuller and Clarice Christine Fuller; *m* 1952, Pamela-Maria Quarrell; one *d.* *Educ:* Merchant Taylors', Northwood, Middx; Royal Naval Engrg Coll., Keyham; Royal Naval Coll., Greenwich. FRINA 1965; FIMarEST (FIMarE 1974). Constructor Commander: Staff of Flag Officer (Submarines), 1958; British Navy Staff, Washington, 1960; RCDS, 1973; Support Manager Submarines, 1976; Dep. Dir, Submarines/Polaris, Ship Dept, MoD, 1979; Dir of Naval Ship Production, 1981–82; Dir, Manpower and Productivity, HM Dockyards, 1982–83; Mem. Bd, and Man. Dir, Warship Div., British Shipbuilders, 1983–85; Exec. Chm., 1984–86, Technical Adviser, 1986–87, Vickers Shipbuilding and Engrg Ltd, Barrow. Vice-Pres., RINA, 2004–07 (Chm. Council, 1994–96; Treas., 1999–2004). FRSA 1995. *Address:* Casa Feliz, Weston Park, Bath BA1 4AL. *T:* (01225) 466054; *e-mail:* casafuller@btinternet.com.

FULLER, Sir James (Henry Fleetwood), 4th Bt *cr* 1910, of Neston Park, Corsham, Wiltshire; manager, Neston Park; *b* 1 Nov. 1970; *e s* of Major Sir John William Fleetwood Fuller, 3rd Bt and of Lorna Marian (*née* Kemp-Potter); *S* father, 1998; *m* 2000, Venetia, *d* of Col Robin Mactaggart; two *s.* *Educ:* Milton Abbey Sch. Commnd The Life Guards, 1991; Belize, 1993; Bosnia, 1994; Knightsbridge, 1995–98; with Fuller Smith & Turner plc, 1998–2003. *Heir:* *s* Archie Mungo Fleetwood Fuller, *b* 7 Aug. 2001. *Address:* Neston Park, Corsham, Wiltshire SN13 9TG. *T:* (01225) 810211.

FULLER, Hon. Sir John (Bryan Munro), Kt 1974; President: Arthritis Foundation of Australia, 1980–91 (Emeritus Vice-President, since 1991); Barnardo's Australia, 1985–95 (Member, Management Committee, 1980–85); *b* 22 Sept. 1917; *s* of late Bryan Fuller, QC; *m* 1940, Eileen, *d* of O. S. Webb; one *s* one *d.* *Educ:* Knox Grammar Sch., Wahroonga. Chm., Australian Country Party (NSW), 1959–64; MLC, NSW, 1961–78; Minister for Decentralisation and Development, 1965–73; NSW Minister for Planning and Environment, 1973–76; Vice-Pres. of Exec. Council and Leader of Govt in Legis. Council, 1968–76; Leader of Opposition, 1976–78; Leader, various NSW Govt trade missions to various parts of the world. Pres., Assoc. of Former Mems of NSW Parlt, 1988–92. Australian Institute of Export: Federal Pres., 1986–91; Mem., Federal Council, 1985–92; Pres., NSW, 1985; Fellow, 1969; Hon. Life Fellow, 1991. Vice-Pres., Graziers Assoc. of NSW, 1965; Member: Council, Univ. of NSW, 1967–78; Cttee, United World Colls Trust, NSW, 1978–88; Bd, Foundn for Res. and Treatment Alcohol and Drug Dependence, 1980–85; Council, Nat. Heart Foundn, NSW, 1980–. Chm., Rushcutters Bay Maritime Reserve Trust, 1993–96. Nat. Patron, Australian Monarchist League, 1997–. *Recreations:* tennis, bowls. *Address:* 54/8 Fullerton Street, Woollahra, NSW 2025, Australia. *Clubs:* Australian (Sydney); Royal Sydney Golf, Australian Jockey.

FULLER, John Leopold, FRSL 1980; writer; Fellow of Magdalen College, Oxford, and Tutor in English, 1966–2002, now Fellow Emeritus; *b* 1 Jan. 1937; *s* of late Roy Broadbent Fuller, CBE, FRSL; *m* 1960, Cicely Prudence Martin; three *d.* *Educ:* St Paul's School; New Coll., Oxford (BLitt, MA). Vis. Lectr, State Univ. of NY at Buffalo, 1962–63; Asst Lectr, Univ. of Manchester, 1963–66. *Publications:* Fairground Music, 1961; The Tree that Walked, 1967; A Reader's Guide to W. H. Auden, 1970; The Sonnet, 1972; Cannibals and Missionaries, 1972, and Epistles to Several Persons, 1973 (Geoffrey Faber Meml Prize, 1974); Squeaking Crust, 1973; The Last Bid, 1975; The Mountain in the Sea, 1975; Lies and Secrets, 1979; The Illusionists (Southern Arts Lit. Prize), 1980; The Extraordinary Wool Mill and other stories, 1980; Waiting for the Music, 1982; Flying to Nowhere (Whitbread Prize for a First Novel), 1983; The Beautiful Inventions, 1983; (ed) The Dramatic Works of John Gay, 1983; Come Aboard and Sail Away, 1983; The Adventures of Speedfall, 1985; Selected Poems 1954–1982, 1985; (with James Fenton) Partingtime Hall, 1986; Tell It Me Again, 1988; The Grey Among the Green, 1988; The Burning Boys, 1989; (ed) The Chatto Book of Love Poetry, 1990; The Mechanical Body, 1991; Look Twice, 1991; The Worm and the Star, 1993; Stones and Fires, 1996 (Forward Prize, Forward Poetry Trust, 1997); Collected Poems, 1996; A Skin Diary, 1997; W. H. Auden: a commentary, 1998; (ed) The Oxford Book of Sonnets, 2000; The Memoirs of Laetitia Horsepole, 2001; Now and for a Time, 2002; Ghosts, 2004; Flawed Angel, 2005; The Space of Joy, 2006; Song & Dance, 2008. *Recreations:* correspondence chess, music. *Address:* Magdalen College, Oxford OX1 4AU.

FULLER, Jonathan Paul; QC 2002; a Recorder of the Crown Court, since 1999 and of the County Court, since 2004; *b* 27 Feb. 1954; *s* of Edward and Joan Fuller; *m* 1988, Karon J. Quinn; two *s* one *d.* *Educ:* Ampleforth; Liverpool Poly. (LLB Lond. (ext.)); Inns of Court Sch. of Law. Called to the Bar, Lincoln's Inn, 1977. *Address:* Chambers of Andrew Trollope, QC, 187 Fleet Street, EC4A 2AT.

FULLER, Rev. Canon Dr Michael Jeremy; Pantonian Professor, since 2000, and Provincial Ministerial Development Officer, since 2004, Theological Institute of the Scottish Episcopal Church; *b* 7 Jan. 1963; *s* of Peter Roy Fuller and Mary Eileen Fuller; *m* 1993, Sue Rigby; two *s.* *Educ:* King Edward VI Grammar Sch., Chelmsford; Worcester Coll., Oxford (BA 1985, MA 1989; DPhil 1989); Westcott House and Queens' Coll., Cambridge (BA 1991). Ordained deacon 1992, priest 1993; Curate, All Saints', High Wycombe, 1992–95; Associate Rector, St John's, Princes Street, Edinburgh, 1995–99; Principal, 2000–02, Initial Ministerial Educn Officer, 2002–04, Theol Inst. of Scottish Episcopal Ch. Canon, St Mary's Cathedral, Edinburgh, 2000–. Hon. Vis. Fellow, New Coll., Edinburgh, 1998–. *Publications:* Atoms and Icons, 1995; articles and reviews in Theology, Modern Believing, New Blackfriars, Musical Times, etc. *Recreations:* opera, reading, writing. *Address:* Theological Institute of the Scottish Episcopal Church, Forbes House, 21 Grosvenor Crescent, Edinburgh EH12 5EE. *T:* (0131) 225 6357. *Club:* New (Edinburgh).

FULLER, Michael John; Director and Chief Executive Officer, Bank of Kuwait and Middle East, 2003–06; Chairman, ais>BrandLab, since 2007; *b* 20 July 1932; *s* of Thomas Frederick and Irene Emily Fuller; *m* 1st, 1955, Maureen Rita Slade (marr. diss. 1989); two *s* two *d*; 2nd, 1990, Elizabeth Frost. *Educ:* Wallington County Grammar Sch. FCIB 1980. National Service, commnd RAF, 1950–52. Midland Bank, 1948–90: various branch, regl and head office posts; Gp Public Affairs Advr, 1977–79; Regl Dir, Southampton, 1979–81; Gen. Manager, Midland and Wales, 1981–82; Gen. Manager, Business Develt Div., 1982–85; UK Operations Dir, 1985–87; Dep. Chief Exec., 1987–89, Chief Exec., 1989–90, UK Banking Sector; Gen. Man., Nat. Bank of Abu Dhabi, 1991–92; Dir and CEO, Al Ahli Commercial Bank BSC, subseq. Ahli United Bank (Bahrain) BSC(c), 1992–2002. FRSA 1994. *Recreations:* reading, travelling, rough golf, ski-ing. *Club:* Royal Air Force.

FULLER, Simon; Founder and Chief Executive Officer, 19 Entertainment Ltd, since 1985; *b* 17 May 1960. Chrysalis Music, 1981–85; founder of 19 Entertainment, comprising management, merchandising, music recording and TV production operations; manager of artists incl. Annie Lennox, Cathy Dennis, Spice Girls, Emma Bunton, S Club 7, S Club Juniors, Will Young, Gareth Gates, David and Victoria Beckham. Director: Popworld Ltd, 2000–; CKX, 2005–. Creator and producer, TV series, Pop Idol, 2001, American Idol, 2002. *Address:* 19 Entertainment Ltd, 33 Ransomes Dock, 35–37 Parkgate Road, SW11 4NP.

FULLER, Simon William John, CMG 1994; HM Diplomatic Service, retired; UK Permanent Representative to the Office of the United Nations and other international organisations, Geneva, 2000–03; *b* 27 Nov. 1943; *s* of late Rowland William Bevis Fuller and Madeline Fuller (*née* Bailey); *m* 1984, Eleanor Mary Breedon (*see* E. M. Fuller); three *s*. *Educ:* Wellington College; Emmanuel College, Cambridge (BA Hist.). Served Singapore and Kinshasa, 1969–73; First Sec., Cabinet Office, 1973–75; FCO, 1975–77; UK Mission to UN, New York, 1977–80; FCO, 1980–86 (Counsellor, 1984); Dep. Hd of Mission, Tel Aviv, 1986–90; Hd of NE and N African Dept, FCO, 1990–93; Hd of UK Delegn to CSCE, then OSCE, Vienna, 1993–99. *Recreations:* cooking, golf. *Address:* 27 Carlisle Mansions, Carlisle Place, SW1P 1EZ. *T:* (020) 7828 5484. *Clubs:* Brooks's, MCC.

FULLERTON, Hance, OBE 1995; Chairman: Grampian University Hospitals NHS Trust, 1996–2002; Angle plc (formerly AngleTechnology Ltd), 1996–2007; *b* 6 Dec. 1934; *s* of late Robert Fullerton and Jessie Fullerton (*née* Smith); *m* 1958, Jeannie Reid Cowie; three *d*. *Educ:* Anderson Educnl Inst., Lerwick; Aberdeen Univ. (BSc). Technical, producn and operational mgt in paper industry, 1958–78; Gen. Manager, Aberdeen, 1978–81, Divl Dir, 1981–86, Wiggins Teape Ltd; Gen. Manager, Grampian Health Bd, 1986–91; Chief Exec., Grampian Enterprise Ltd, 1991–96. Chairman: Aberdeen Univ. Res. and Industrial Services Ltd, 1996–2000; Cordah Ltd, 1996–99. Hon. LLD Aberdeen, 1996. *Recreations:* golf, walking, reading, theatre. *Club:* Royal Northern and University (Aberdeen).

FULLERTON, William Hugh, CMG 1989; HM Diplomatic Service, retired; Ambassador to Morocco and Mauritania, 1996–99; *b* 11 Feb. 1939; *s* of late Major Arthur Hugh Theodore Francis Fullerton, RAMC, and of Mary (*née* Parker); *m* 1968, Arlene Jacobowitz; one *d*. *Educ:* Cheltenham Coll.; Queens' Coll., Cambridge (MA Oriental Langs). Shell Internat. Petroleum Co., Uganda, 1963–65; FO, 1965; MECAS, Shemlan, Lebanon, 1965–66; Information Officer, Jedda, 1966–67; UK Mission to UN, New York, 1967; FCO, 1968–70; Head of Chancery, Kingston, Jamaica, 1970–73, and Ankara, 1973–77; FCO, 1977–80; Counsellor (Economic and Commercial), 1980–83 and Consul-Gen., 1981–83, Islamabad; Ambassador to Somalia, 1983–87; on loan to MoD, 1987–88; Gov., Falkand Is, and Comr for S Georgia and S Sandwich Is, 1988–92; High Comr, British Antarctic Territory, 1988–89; Ambassador to Kuwait, 1992–96. Trustee, Arab-British Centre, London, 2002– (Dir, 2000–02; Chm., 2002–07). Member: Friends of Kuwait; Falkland Is Assoc. Trustee: Soc. for Protection of Animals Abroad, 2000–; Lord Caradon Lectures Trust, 2004–. Kuwait Medallion, First Class, 1995; Comdr, Ouissam Alaouite (Morocco), 1999. *Recreations:* travelling in remote areas, sailing, reading, walking. *Club:* Travellers.

FULTON, Andrew; *see* Fulton, R. A.

FULTON, Prof. John Francis; Secretary, Northern Ireland Fund for Reconciliation, since 1999; *b* 21 Sept. 1933; *s* of Robert Patrick Fulton and Anne Fulton (*née* McCambridge); *m* 1958, Elizabeth Mary Brennan; one *s* one *d*. *Educ:* St Malachy's College, Belfast; QUB (BA 1954, DipEd 1958, MA 1964); Univ. of Keele (PhD 1975). Lectr and Principal Lectr, St Joseph's Coll. of Educn, Belfast, 1961–73; Queen's University of Belfast: Lectr, Inst. of Educn, 1973–76; Prof. and Head of Dept of Educnl Studies, 1977–85; Dir, Sch. of Educn, 1985–93; Pro-Vice-Chancellor, 1987–92; Provost, Legal, Social and Educnl Scis, 1993–97; Dir of Develt, 1997–98; Prof. Emeritus, 1997. Mem., IBA, subseq. ITC, 1987–94. Mem., Trng and Employment Agency, 1993–98; Chairman: Strategy Gp for Health Services R&D, 1999–2003; Central Services Agency, Dept of Health and Social Services and Public Safety, NI, 2004– (non-exec. Dir, 1999–2003). FRSA. Hon. LLD QUB, 2000. *Publications:* contribs to: Education in Great Britain and Ireland, 1973; Educational Research and Development in Great Britain, 1982; Willingly to School, 1987; articles in learned jls. *Recreations:* golf, music. *Address:* Northern Ireland Fund for Reconciliation, c/o Queen's University of Belfast, BT7 1NN. *T:* (028) 9027 3773.

FULTON, (Paul) Robert (Anthony); Chairman: Ducane Housing Association, since 2004; CHAS (Central London), since 2006 (Treasurer, 2004–06); Vice Chairman, Society of Voluntary Associates, since 2004; *b* 20 March 1951; *s* of George Alan Fulton and Margaret Fulton (*née* Foxton); *m* 1981, Lee Hong Tay. *Educ:* Nunthorpe Grammar Sch., York; Churchill Coll., Cambridge (BA Hons French and Russian). Home Office, 1973–2003: Private Sec. to Perm. Sec., 1977–78; Radio Regulatory Dept, 1978–83; Police Dept, 1984–88; Prison and Criminal Policy Depts, 1988–91; Dir of Prison Service Industries and Farms, 1991–96; Principal Finance Officer, 1996–2000; Dir, Strategy and Performance, 2000–02; Implementation Dir, Assets Recovery Agency, 2002–03. *Recreations:* learning new things, re-learning old things. *Address:* 1 Meadow Close, Hinchley Wood, Esher, Surrey KT10 0AY. *Club:* Royal Commonwealth Society.

FULTON, (Robert) Andrew; HM Diplomatic Service, retired; Chairman, Scottish Conservative and Unionist Party, since 2008; *b* 6 Feb. 1944; *s* of late Rev. Robert M. Fulton and of Janet W. Fulton (*née* Mackenzie); *m* 1970, Patricia Mary Crowley; two *s* one *d*. *Educ:* Rothesay Academy; Glasgow University (MA, LLB). Foreign and Commonwealth Office, 1968; Third later Second Secretary, Saigon, 1969; FCO, 1972; First Sec., Rome, 1973; FCO, 1977; First Sec., E Berlin, 1978; FCO, 1981; Counsellor, Oslo, 1984; FCO, 1987; UK Mission to UN, NY, 1989; FCO, 1992; Counsellor: Washington, 1995–99; FCO, 1999. Dir, Scotland, Control Risks Gp, 2002–06; Internat. Business Advr, Memex Technology, 2003–; Global Business Adviser: Dynamic Knowledge Corp., 2005–; Armor Gp, 2006–. Chairman: Scottish N American Business Council, 2000–; Adv. Bd, Proudfoot Consulting, 2003–; Edo Midas, 2004–; nation 1 2005–; gpw ltd, 2006–; Huntswood, 2006–. Vis. Prof., Univ. of Glasgow Sch. of Law 1999–2003. *Recreations:* golf, racing, reading, cinema. *Address:* 7 Crown Road South Glasgow G12 9DJ.

FULTON, Lt-Gen. Sir Robert (Henry Gervase), KBE 2005; Governor and Commander-in-Chief, Gibraltar, since 2006; *b* 21 Dec. 1948; *s* of late James Fulton and Cynthia Fulton (*née* Shaw); *m* 1975, Midge Free; two *s*. *Educ:* Eton Coll.; Univ. of East Anglia (BA Hons). Entered RM, 1972: 42 Commando, 1973–75; 40 Commando 1976–78; Instructor, Sch. of Signals, Blandford, 1978–80; student, Army Staff Coll. Camberley, 1980–81; Instructor, Jun. Div. Staff Coll., 1981–83; 42 Commando, 1983–85 SO2 Ops, HQ Training, Reserve and Special Forces, 1985–87; SO2 Commitments, Dep of Comdt Gen., 1987–90; SO1 DS, Army Staff Coll., Camberley, 1990–92; CO, 42 Commando, 1992–94; Asst Dir, CIS Operational Requirements, MoD, 1994–95; RCDS 1996; Comdr, 3 Commando Bde, 1997–98, Comdt Gen., 1998–2001, RM; Capability Manager (Inf. Superiority), 2001–03; DCDS (Equipment Capability), 2003–06 *Recreations:* playing and watching sport, military history. *Address:* The Convent, Main Street, Gibraltar. *Clubs:* Army and Navy, MCC.

FUNNELL, Christina Mary; Director, Christina Funnell (formerly Funnell Associates) Consultancy, since 1997; *b* 24 Aug. 1947; *d* of Joanna Christina Beaumont (*née* Lenes) and Norman Beaumont; *m* 1970 (marr. diss. 1994); one *s* one *d*. *Educ:* Hull Univ. (BA Spec Hons Soc. Admin. 1968). W Riding CC Social Services, 1964; Methodist Assoc. of Youth Clubs, 1965–68; London Council of Social Service, 1971; Herts CC Youth Service, 1973 Nat. Eczema Soc., 1982–96 (Dir, 1987–96; Chief Exec., Skin Care Campaign, 1995–96) Mem., Standing Adv. Gp on consumer involvement in NHS R&D prog., 1996–98 Chm., Consumer Health Inf. Centre, 1997–99; Organising Sec., Health Coalition Initiative, 1997–; Sec. and Co-ordinator, Patient Information Forum, 2001–03; Patient and Public Involvement Consultant, Perf. Develt Team, NHS Modernisation Agency 2003–05; Patient Consultant, N and E Yorks and N Lincs Strategic Health Authy 2005–07; Patient Engagement Officer, Patient Opinion, 2007–. Lay Member: Nat. Clin Assessment Authy, 2001–05; Nursing and Midwifery Council, 2002–; Health Technol Devices Prog., DoH, 2002–. Panel Mem., Richard Neale Inquiry, 2005. Feasibility Consultant to North Bank Estate, Muswell Hill, London, 1998–99. Vice-Chm., Socialist Health Assoc.; Trustee, Pharmacy Practice Res. Trust, 2005–. Mem., City of York Council, 2007– (Chm., Health Overview and Scrutiny Cttee). Member: Wesley's Chapel 1996–; Exec., Christian Socialist Movt, 1998–2003; Associate Mem., Iona Community 1997–. *Publications:* (contrib.) Clinical and Experimental Dermatology, 1993; (contrib. Developing New Clinical Roles: a guide for health professionals, 2000. *Recreations* gardening, travel, social and political history, current affairs. *Address:* 6 Upper Price Street off Scarcroft Road, York YO23 1BJ. *T:* and *Fax:* (01904) 613041; *e-mail:* tinafunnell@btopenworld.com. *Club:* New Cavendish.

FUNNELL, Philippa Rachel, MBE 2005; event rider; *b* 7 Oct. 1968; *d* of George and Jennifer Nolan; *m* 1993, William Funnell. *Educ:* Wadhurst Coll. Young Rider Gold Medallist, 1987; British Open Champion, 1992 and 2002; European Championships Team and Individual Champion, 1991 and 2001; Team Champion and Individual Bronze Medallist, 2003; Olympic Games: Team Silver Medallist, Sydney, 2000; Team Silver and Individual Bronze Medallist, Athens, 2004; winner: Badminton Horse Trials, 2002, 2003 2005; Rolex Grand Slam (Badminton, Burghley and Kentucky), 2003. *Publications* Training the Young Horse, 2002; My Story (autobiog.), 2004. *Recreations:* tennis, cooking *Address:* c/o British Eventing, Stoneleigh Park, Kenilworth, Warwicks CV8 2RN.

FURBER, (Frank) Robert; retired solicitor; *b* 28 March 1921; *s* of late Percy John Furber and Edith Furber; *m* 1948, Anne Wilson McArthur; three *s* one *d*. *Educ:* Willaston Sch. Berkhamsted Sch.; University College London. LLB. Articled with Slaughter and May solicitor 1945; Partner, Clifford-Turner, 1952–86. Mem., Planning Law Cttee, Law Society, 1964–69. Chairman: Blackheath Soc., 1968–89; Blackheath Preservation Trust 1972–2000; Film Industry Defence Organization, 1968–89; Governor: Yehudi Menuhin Sch., 1964–91; Live Music Now!, 1977–87; Berkhamsted Sch., and Berkhamsted Sch. for Girls, 1976–91 (Chm., 1986–91); Board Member: Trinity Coll. of Music, 1974–91; Nat Jazz Centre, 1982–87; Common Law Inst. of Intellectual Property, 1982–87; Chm., Rules of Golf Cttee, Royal and Ancient Golf Club, 1976–80; Trustee, Robert T. Jones Mem. Trust, 1982–86; Mem. and Hon. Sec., R & A Golf Amateurism Commn of Inquiry 1984–85; Mem., CCPR Cttee of Enquiry into Amateurism in Sport, 1986–88. Hon Fellow, Trinity College, London. *Publication:* A Course for Heroes, 1996. *Recreations:* golf music, books. *Address:* 8 Pond Road, Blackheath, SE3 9JL. *T:* (020) 8852 8065. *Clubs* Buck's; Royal Blackheath Golf, Royal St George's Golf, Royal and Ancient, Honourable Company of Edinburgh Golfers; Pine Valley (USA).

See also S. A. Coakley, R. J. Furber, W. J. Furber.

FURBER, James; *see* Furber, W. J.

FURBER, (Robert) John; QC 1995; *b* 13 Oct. 1949; *s* of (Frank) Robert Furber, *qv*, and Anne Wilson Furber (*née* McArthur); *m* 1977, Amanda Cherry Burgoyne Varney; one *s* two *d*. *Educ:* Westminster Sch.; Gonville and Caius Coll., Cambridge (MA). Called to the Bar, Inner Temple, 1973. Chm., Field Lane Foundn, 2004–06. *Publications:* (ed jtly) Halsbury's Laws of England: Landlord and Tenant, 4th edn 1981, Compulsory Acquisition of Land, 4th edn reissue 1996; (ed jtly) Hill and Redman's Landlord and Tenant, 17th edn 1982, 18th edn (looseleaf) 1988–; (jtly) Guide to the Commonhold and Leasehold Reform Act, 2002. *Address:* Wilberforce Chambers, 8 New Square, Lincoln's Inn, WC2A 3QP *T:* (020) 7306 0102; 1 Hallgate, Blackheath Park, SE3 9SG. *T:* (020) 8852 7633. *Clubs* Buck's, Beefsteak, Pratt's.

See also S. A. Coakley, W. J. Furber.

FURBER, Prof. Stephen Byram, CBE 2008; FRS 2002; FREng; ICL Professor of Computer Engineering, University of Manchester, since 1990 (Head, Department of Computer Science, 2001–04); *b* 21 March 1953; *s* of Benjamin Neil Furber and Margaret Furber (*née* Schofield); *m* 1977, Valerie Margaret Elliott; two *d*. *Educ:* St John's Coll. Cambridge (BA Maths 1st Cl. 1974; PhD Aerodynamics 1980). FREng 1999. Rolls Royce Res. Fellow, Emmanuel Coll., Cambridge, 1978–81; Hardware Design Engr, then Design Manager, Acorn Computers Ltd, Cambridge, 1981–90. Non-executive Director Manchester Informatics Ltd, 1994–; Cogency Technology Inc., 1997–99; Cogniscience Ltd, 2000–; Transitive Technologies Ltd, 2001–04; Silistix Ltd, 2004–06. *Publications* VLSI RISC Architecture and Organization, 1989; (ed jtly) Asynchronous Design Methodologies, 1993; ARM System Architecture, 1996; ARM System-on-Chip Architecture, 2000; (ed jtly) Principles of Asynchronous Circuit Design: a systems perspective, 2001; over 50 conf. and jl papers. *Recreations:* 6-string and bass guitar (Church music group), badminton. *Address:* School of Computer Science, The University of Manchester, Oxford Road, Manchester M13 9PL. *T:* (0161) 275 6129, *Fax:* (0161) 275 6236; *e-mail:* steve.furber@manchester.ac.uk.

FURBER, (William) James; Partner, since 1985, Senior Partner, since 2008, Farrer & Co.; *b* 1 Sept. 1954; *s* of (Frank) Robert Furber, *qv*; *m* 1982, Rosemary Elizabeth Johnston; two *s* one *d*. *Educ:* Westminster Sch.; Gonville and Caius Coll., Cambridge (BA 1975, MA 1979). Admitted solicitor, 1979; joined Farrer & Co. (Solicitors), 1976, Associate Partner, 1981. Solicitor to Duchy of Cornwall, 1994–. Trustee: Leonard Cheshire Foundn, 2000–06; Arvon Foundn, 2000–07; Trinity Coll. of Music, 2003–06; Trinity Coll. of Music Trust, 2006–; Secretary: St Bartholomew's Med. Coll. Charitable Trust, 1996–; Art Workers Guild Trust, 2007–. Reader, C of E, 1991–. Treas., Lowtonian Soc., 2003–. *Publication:* (contrib.) Encyclopedia of Forms and Precedents, vol. 36, 1990. *Recreation:* golf. *Address:* c/o Farrer & Co., 66 Lincoln's Inn Fields, WC2A 3LH. *T:* (020) 7242 2022, *Fax:* (020) 7917 7556; *e-mail:* wjf@farrer.co.uk. *Clubs:* Athenæum; Hawk's (Cambridge); Royal & Ancient Golf (St Andrews), Royal St George's Golf (Sandwich), Royal West Norfolk Golf (Brancaster), Royal Blackheath Golf.

See also S. A. Coakley, R. J. Furber.

FURCHGOTT, Prof. Robert Francis, PhD; Emeritus Professor of Pharmacology, State University of New York Health Science Center, Brooklyn, since 1990; *b* Charleston, SC, 4 June 1916; *m* 1941; three *d*. *Educ:* Univ. of N Carolina (BS 1937); Northwestern Univ. (PhD Biochem. 1940). Medical College, Cornell University: Res. Fellow in Medicine, 1940–43; Res. Associate, 1943–47; Instructor in Physiol., 1943–48; Asst Prof. of Med. Biochem., 1947–49; Asst Prof., then Associate Prof. of Pharmacol., Med. Sch., Washington Univ., 1949–56; SUNY Health Science Center, Brooklyn: Chm., Dept of Pharmacol., 1956–83; Prof., 1956–88; Univ. Dist. Prof., 1988–90. Visiting Professor: Univ. of Geneva, 1962–63; Univ. of Calif., San Diego, 1971–72; Med. Univ., SC, 1980; UCLA, 1980; Adjunct Prof. of Pharmacol., Sch. Medicine, Univ. of Miami, 1989–2001; Vis. Dist. Prof., Med. Univ., SC, 2002–. Member: ACS, 1937; AAAS, 1940; Amer. Soc. Biochem., 1948; Amer. Soc. Pharmacol. and Exptl Therapeutics, 1952 (Pres., 1971–72; Goodman and Gilman Award, 1984); NAS, 1991; Harvey Soc. Hon. degrees from Univs of Lund, N Carolina, Ghent, Ohio State, Autonomous Univ. of Madrid, Mt Sinai Med. Sch., Med. Univ. of S Carolina, Med. Coll. of Ohio, Northwestern Univ., UCL and Charles Univ., Prague. Awards include: Res. Achievement Award, Amer. Heart Assoc., 1990; Bristol-Myers Squibb Award for Achievement in Cardiovascular Res., 1991; Medal, NY Acad. Medicine, 1992; Wellcome Gold Medal, Brit. Pharmacol. Soc., 1995; Gregory Pincus Award for Res., 1996; Lasker Award for Med. Res., 1996; Nobel Prize for Physiology or Medicine, 1998. *Address:* One Garden Way, Apt 252, Charleston, SC 29412, USA.

FURLONG, Prof. (Vivian) John, PhD; Professor of Educational Studies and Director, Department of Education (formerly of Educational Studies), University of Oxford, since 2003; Fellow of Green Templeton College (formerly Green College), Oxford, since 2003; *b* 7 May 1947; *s* of late William James Furlong and of Ann Furlong; *m* 1972, Ruth Roberts; two *s*. *Educ:* Hertford Grammar Sch.; Middx Poly. (BA 1968); City Univ. (PhD 1978); Corpus Christi Coll., Cambridge (MA 1984). Teacher, Paddington Sch., London, 1971–74; Lectr in Educn, Univ. of Cambridge, 1981–92; Professor and Head: Dept of Educn, Univ. of Swansea, 1992–95; Grad. Sch. of Educn, Univ. of Bristol, 1995–2000; Prof., Sch. of Social Scis, Cardiff Univ., 2000–03. Pres., British Educnl Res. Assoc., 2003–05. FRSA 1995; AcSS 2003. Member, Editorial Board: Cambridge Jl of Educn; Oxford Rev. of Educn. *Publications:* The Language of Teaching (with A. D. Edwards), 1978; The Deviant Pupil: sociological perspectives, 1985; (jtly) Initial Teacher Training and the Role of the School, 1988; (with T. Maynard) Mentoring Student Teachers: the growth of professional knowledge, 1995; (ed jtly) The Role of Higher Education in Initial Teacher Education, 1996; (jtly) Teacher Education in Transition: re-forming professionalism?, 2000; (ed jtly) Education, Reform and the State: policy, politics and practice, 2001; (jtly) Screenplay: children and computing in the home, 2003; (jtly) Adult Learning in the Digital Age, 2005; over 100 articles in educnl jls and books. *Recreations:* gardening, keeping chickens, cooking, travel, entertaining. *Address:* Department of Education, University of Oxford, 15 Norham Gardens, Oxford OX2 6PY. *T:* (01865) 274024, *Fax:* (01865) 274027; *e-mail:* john.furlong@education.ox.ac.uk.

FURLONGER, Robert William, CB 1981; retired public servant, Australia; *b* 29 April 1921; *s* of George William Furlonger and Germaine Rose Furlonger; *m* 1944, Verna Hope Lewis; three *s* one *d*. *Educ:* Sydney High Sch.; Sydney Univ. (BA). Served War, AMF, 1941–45. Australian Dept of External (later Foreign) Affairs, 1945–69 and 1972–77 (IDC, 1960; Dir, Jt Intell. Org., Dept of Def., 1969–72); appointments included: High Comr, Nigeria, 1961; Aust. Perm. Rep. to the European Office of the UN, 1961–64; Minister, Aust. Embassy, Washington, 1965–69; Ambassador to Indonesia, 1972–74, and to Austria, Hungary and Czechoslovakia, 1975–77; Dir-Gen., Office of National Assessments, Canberra, 1977–81. *Address:* PO Box 548, Belconnen, ACT 2616, Australia. *T:* (2) 62531384. *Clubs:* Canberra; Royal Canberra Golf.

FURMSTON, Prof. Michael Philip, TD 1966; Professor of Law, University of Bristol, 1978–98, now Emeritus; Professor of Law and Dean, School of Law, Singapore Management University, since 2007; *b* 1 May 1933; *s* of late Joseph Philip Furmston and Phyllis (*née* Clowes); *m* 1964, Ashley Sandra Maria Cope; three *s* seven *d*. *Educ:* Wellington Sch., Somerset; Exeter Coll., Oxford (BA 1st Cl. Hons Jurisprudence, 1956; BCL 1st Cl. Hons 1957; MA 1960). LLM Birmingham, 1962. Called to the Bar, Gray's Inn, 1960 (1st Cl. Hons), Bencher, 1989. National Service, RA, 1951–53 (2nd Lieut); Major, TA, 1966–78, TAVR. Lecturer: Univ. of Birmingham, 1957–62; QUB, 1962–63; Fellow, Lincoln Coll., Oxford, 1964–78 (Sen. Dean, 1967–68; Sen. Tutor and Tutor for Admissions, 1969–74); Univ. Lectr in Law, 1964–78, Curator, University Chest, 1976–78, Oxford; Lectr in Common Law, Council of Legal Educn, 1965–78; Dean, Faculty of Law, 1980–84 and 1995–98, Pro-Vice-Chancellor, 1986–89, Univ. of Bristol. Chm., COMEC, 1996–2000. Visiting Professor: City Univ., 1978–82; Katholieke Universiteit, Leuven, 1980, 1986, 1992 and 1999; Nat. Univ. of Singapore, 1987, 1999; Singapore Mgt Univ., 2006; McWilliam Vis. Prof. of Commercial Law, Univ. of Sydney, 2005. Sen. Fellow, Univ. of Melbourne, 2003–05. Liveryman, Arbitrators' Co. Jt Editor, 1985–97, Editor, 1997–, Construction Law Reports. *Publications:* (ed) Cheshire, Fifoot and Furmston's Law of Contract, 8th edn 1972, to 15th edn 2006; Contractors Guide to ICE Conditions of Contract, 1980; Misrepresentation and Fraud, in Halsbury's Law of England, 1980, 1998; Croner's Buying and Selling Law, 1982; (ed jtly) The Effect on English Domestic Law of Membership of the European Communities and Ratification of the European Convention on Human Rights, 1983; (jtly) A Building Contract Casebook, 1984, 4th edn 2006; (jtly) Cases and Materials on Contract, 1985, 5th edn 2007; (ed) The Law of Tort: policies and trends in liability for damage to property, 1986; (ed) You and the Law, 1987; Croner's Model Business Contracts, 1988; (jtly) 'A' Level Law, 1988, 4th edn 2002; Sale of Goods, 1990; Sale and Supply of Goods, 1994, 3rd edn 2000; (jtly) Commercial Law, 1995, 2nd edn 2001; Contract Formation and Letters of Intent, 1998; (ed) The Law of Contract, 1999, 3rd edn 2007. *Recreations:* chess (Member, English team, Postal Olympiads), watching cricket, dogs. *Address:* 5 Priory Court, Bridgwater, Somerset TA6 3NR. *T:* (01278) 421676; Faculty of Law, University of Bristol, Wills Memorial Building, Queen's Road, Bristol BS8 1RJ. *T:* (0117) 928 9000, 928 7441; School of Law, Singapore Management University, 60 Stamford Road, Singapore 178900. *Clubs:* Reform, Naval and Military, MCC.

FURNESS, Alan Edwin, CMG 1991; HM Diplomatic Service, retired; Ambassador of the Order of Malta to Senegal, since 2000; *b* 6 June 1937; *s* of late Edwin Furness and Marion Furness (*née* Senton); *m* 1971, Aline Elizabeth Janine Barrett; two *s*. *Educ:* Eltham Coll.; Jesus Coll., Cambridge (BA, MA). Commonwealth Relations Office, 1961; Private Sec. to Parliamentary Under-Secretary of State, 1961–62; Third, later Second Secretary, British High Commn, New Delhi, 1962–66; First Secretary, DSAO (later FCO), 1966–69; First Sec., UK Delegn to European Communities, Brussels, 1969–72; First Sec. and Head of Chancery, Dakar, 1972–75; First Sec., FCO, 1975–78; Counsellor and Head of Chancery, Jakarta, 1978–81; Counsellor and Head of Chancery, Warsaw, 1982–85; Head of S Pacific Dept., FCO, 1985–88; Dep. High Comr, Bombay, 1989–93; Ambassador to Senegal and, concurrently, to Cape Verde, Guinea, Guinea Bissau and Mali, 1993–97. Knight of Magistral Grace, 1999, Grand Officer pro Merito Melitensi, 2005, Order of Malta. *Recreations:* music, literature, gardening. *Address:* 40 Brunswick Court, 89 Regency Street, SW1P 4AE. *Club:* Oxford and Cambridge.

FURNESS, (Hugh) Jonathan; QC 2003; a Recorder, since 1998; *b* 8 Nov. 1956; *s* of Thomas Hogg Batey Furness and Hilda Anita Furness; *m* 1984, Anne Margaret Jones; three *s* one *d*. *Educ:* St John's Coll., Cambridge (MA). Called to the Bar, Gray's Inn, 1979; in practice, specialising in divorce and child care work. *Recreations:* golf, cricket, music. *Address:* 30 Park Place, Cardiff CF10 3BS. *T:* (029) 2039 8421. *Clubs:* Mitres Cricket (Llandaff); Whitchurch Golf.

FURNESS, Mark Richard; His Honour Judge Furness; a Circuit Judge, since 1998; *b* 28 Nov. 1948; *m* 1974, Margaretta Trevor Evans; one *s* one *d*. *Educ:* Hereford Cathedral Sch.; St John's Coll., Cambridge (BA 1970; MA 1972). Called to the Bar, Lincoln's Inn, 1970; an Asst Recorder, 1992–96; a Recorder, 1996–98. Chairman: Social Security Appeal Tribunal, 1987–94; Disability Appeal Tribunal, 1991–98. Chairman: Marie Curie Cttee for Wales, 2001–07; Trustees and Managing Cttee, Swansea Children Contact Centre, 2002–. *Recreations:* gardening, motoring, literature, music, DIY, travel. *Address:* Newport (Gwent) County Court, The Concourse, Clarence House, Clarence Place, Newport, S Wales NP19 7AA. *Club:* Cardiff and County (Cardiff).

FURNESS, Michael James; QC 2000; a Deputy High Court Judge, since 2004; *b* 2 Sept. 1958; *s* of late Harry Furness and of Rosemary Nancy Furness. *Educ:* Emmanuel Coll., Cambridge (MA); St Edmund Hall, Oxford (BCL). Called to the Bar, Lincoln's Inn, 1982; First Standing Jun. Counsel to Inland Revenue, 1998–2000. *Recreations:* acting (Hon. Sec., Bar Theatrical Soc.), walking. *Address:* Wilberforce Chambers, 8 New Square, Lincoln's Inn, WC2A 3QP. *T:* (020) 7306 0102.

FURNESS, Robin; *see* Furness, Sir S. R.

FURNESS, Col Simon John; Vice Lord-Lieutenant of Berwickshire, since 1990; *b* 18 Aug. 1936; 2nd *s* of Sir Christopher Furness, 2nd Bt and Violet Flower Chipchase Furness, OBE (*d* 1988), *d* of Lieut-Col G. C. Roberts, Hollingside, Durham. *Educ:* Charterhouse; RMA Sandhurst; Royal Naval Staff College. Commissioned 2nd Lieut Durham Light Infantry, 1956; served Far East, UK, Germany; active service, Borneo and NI; Comd 5th Bn LI, 1976–78, retired 1978. Dep. Col (Durham), LI, 1989–93. DL Berwickshire, 1984. SBStJ 2003. *Recreations:* gardening, country sports, fine arts. *Address:* The Garden House, Netherbyres, Eyemouth, Berwickshire TD14 5SE. *T:* (01890) 750337. *Club:* Army and Navy.

FURNESS, Sir Stephen (Roberts), 3rd Bt *cr* 1913, of Tunstall Grange, West Hartlepool; farmer and sporting/landscape artist (as Robin Furness); *b* 10 Oct. 1933; *e s* of Sir Christopher Furness, 2nd Bt, and Flower, Lady Furness, OBE (*d* 1988), *d* of late Col G. C. Roberts; *S* father, 1974; *m* 1961, Mary, *e d* of J. F. Cann, Cullompton, Devon; one *s* one *d*. *Educ:* Charterhouse. Entered RN, 1952; Observer, Fleet Air Arm, 1957; retired list, 1962. NCA, Newton Rigg Farm Inst., 1964. Member: Armed Forces Art Soc.; Darlington Art Soc. *Recreations:* looking at paintings, foxhunting, racing. *Heir:* *s* Michael Fitzroy Roberts Furness [*b* 12 Oct. 1962; *m* 1998, Katrine Oxtoby]. *Address:* Stanhow Farm, Great Langton, Northallerton, Yorks DL7 0TJ. *T:* (01609) 748614.

See also S. J. Furness.

FURNHAM, Prof. Adrian Frank, DSc, DPhil, DLitt; Professor of Psychology, University College London, since 1992; *b* 3 Feb. 1953; *s* of late Leslie Frank Furnham and of Lorna Audrey (*née* Cartwright); *m* 1990, Dr Alison Clare Green; one *s*. *Educ:* Natal Univ. (BA Hons, MA; DLitt 1997); LSE (MSc Econ 1976; DSc 1991); Strathclyde Univ. (MSc 1977); Wolfson Coll. and Pembroke Coll., Oxford (DPhil 1982). Oxford University: Res. Officer, Dept Exptl Psychol., 1979–81; Lectr in Psychol., Pembroke Coll., 1980–82; University College London: Lectr, 1981–87; Reader, 1988–92. Visiting Lecturer: Univ. of NSW, 1984; Univ. of WI, 1986; Univ. of Hong Kong, 1994–96; Vis. Prof., Henley Mgt Coll., 1999–2001. Founder Dir, ABRA, business consultancy, 1986–2002. Ext. Examr at various univs. Mem., Internat. Adv. Council, Social Affairs Unit, 1995–. Dir, Internat. Soc. for Study of Individual Differences, 1996–2001 (Pres., 2003–05). Mem., editl bd of 11 internat. scientific jls. *Publications:* books include: Culture Shock, 1986; Lay Theories, 1988; The Protestant Work Ethic, 1990; Personality at Work, 1992; Corporate Assessment, 1994; All in the Mind, 1996, 2nd edn 2001; The Myths of Management, 1996; The Psychology of Behaviour at Work, 1997; Complementary Medicine, 1997; The Psychology of Money, 1998; The Psychology of Managerial Incompetence, 1998; Children as Consumers, 1998; Personality and Social Behaviour, 1999; Body Language at Work, 1999; The Hopeless, Hapless and Helpless Manager, 2000; Designing and Analysing Questionnaires and Surveys, 2000; Children and Advertising, 2000; The Psychology of Culture Shock, 2001; Assessing Potential, 2001; The 3D Manager: dangerous, derailed and deranged, 2001; Mad, Sad and Bad Management, 2003; The Incompetent Manager, 2003; Management and Myths, 2004; The Dark Side of Behaviour at Work, 2004; Personality and Intellectual Competence, 2005; The People Business, 2005; Learning at Work, 2005; Just for the Money, 2005; Management Mumbo-Jumbo, 2006; The Body Beautiful, 2007; Dim Sum Management, 2008; The Psychology of Physical Attractiveness, 2008; Head and Heart Management, 2008; Personality and Intelligence at Work, 2008; 700 scientific papers; contrib. articles and columns to newspapers, incl. Daily Telegraph, Sunday Times. *Recreations:* travel, theatre, arguing at dinner parties. *Address:* 45 Thornhill Square, Islington, N1 1BE. *T:* (020) 7607 6265; *e-mail:* ucjtsaf@ucl.ac.uk.

FURNISS, Prof. Graham Lytton, PhD; Professor of African-Language Literature, School of Oriental and African Studies, University of London, since 1999; *b* 21 June 1949; *s* of Alfred Lytton and Margaret Elizabeth Furniss; *m* 1977, Wendy Jane de Beer; one *s* two *d*. *Educ:* Sch. of Oriental and African Studies, Univ. of London (BA; PhD 1977). Lectr, Dept of Langs and Linguistics, Univ. of Maiduguri, Nigeria, 1977–79; School of Oriental and African Studies, University of London: Lectr, then Sen. Lectr in Hausa, 1979–96; Reader in Hausa Cultural Studies, 1996–99; Hd, Lang. Centre, 1995–98; Dean: of Langs,

1995–97; Faculty of Langs and Cultures, 2002–04. Chm., Africa sub-panel, 2001 RAE Panel 46: African and ME Studies. Vice-Chm., Royal African Soc., 2000–; President: Internat. Soc. for Oral Lit. in Africa, 1998–2002; African Studies Assoc. of UK, 2004–06. *Publications:* (ed with R. Fardon) African Languages, Development and the State, 1994; (ed with E. Gunner) Power, Marginality and African Oral Literature, 1995; Ideology in Practice: Hausa poetry as exposition of values and viewpoints, 1995; Poetry, Prose and Popular Culture in Hausa, 1996; (ed with R. Fardon) African Broadcast Cultures: radio in transition, 2000; Orality: the power of the spoken word, 2004. *Recreations:* hill-walking, beach-combing, pottery, painting, tropical plants, gardening, cooking. *Address:* Faculty of Languages and Cultures, School of Oriental and African Studies, University of London, Thornhaugh Street, Russell Square, WC1H 0XG. *T:* (020) 7898 4366; *e-mail:* gfl@soas.ac.uk.

FURNISS, (Mary) Jane; Chief Executive, Independent Police Complaints Commission, since 2006; *b* 28 March 1954; *d* of Eric Richard Sanders and Catherine Lilly Sanders; *m* 1977, David Kenneth Furniss. *Educ:* Burton-on-Trent Girls' High Sch.; Bradford Univ. (BSc Hons 1975); York Univ. (MSW 1978). West Yorkshire: Probation Officer, 1975–76, 1978–85; Sen. Probation Officer, 1985–90; Asst Chief Probation Officer, 1990–95; Home Office: HM Inspector of Probation, 1995–97; HM Dep. Chief Inspector, 1997–2001; Hd, Justice and Victims Unit, 2001–02; Dir, Criminal Policy, then Criminal Justice, Gp, 2002–05; Dir, Criminal Justice, Office for Criminal Justice Reform, 2005–06. *Recreations:* music (listening), art (viewing), the world (exploring). *Address:* Indepedent Police Complaints Commission, 90 High Holborn, WC1V 6BH; *e-mail:* Jane.Furniss@ipcc.gsi.gov.uk.

FURNIVALL, Barony *cr* 1295; in abeyance. *Co-heiresses:* Hon. Rosamond Mary Dent (Sister Ancilla, OSB); *b* 3 June 1933; Hon. Patricia Mary Dent [*b* 4 April 1935; *m* 1st, 1956, Captain Thomas Hornsby (marr. diss., 1963; he *d* 1967); one *s* one *d*; 2nd, 1970, Roger Thomas John Bence; one *s* one *d*].

FURSDON, (Edward) David; DL; a Crown Estate Commissioner, since 2008; Strategic Consultant, Smiths Gore, since 2008; *b* Sevenoaks, 20 Dec. 1952; *s* of Maj. Gen. (Francis William) Edward Fursdon, CB, MBE and late Joan Fursdon; *m* 1978, Catriona Margaret McCreath; three *s*. *Educ:* Sherborne Sch.; St John's Coll., Oxford (BA 1975); RAC, Cirencester. FRICS 1998. Owner/manager, Fursdon Estate, 1981–; Officer, 6th QEO Gurkha Rifles, 1971–72; civil servant, MoD and UN, Geneva, 1975–79; Teacher, Blundell's Sch., 1979–84; RAC, Cirencester, 1984–86; Land agent, 1986–94; Partner, Stags, 1994–2007. Chm., 2003–05, Pres., 2005–07, CLA. Gov., Blundell's Sch., 1984– (Chm., 2000–). FAAV 1988; ARAgS 2007. DL Devon, 2004. *Recreations:* planting trees, appreciating landscape, buildings and gardens, moving from playing to watching sport. *Address:* c/o The Crown Estate, 16 New Burlington Place, W1S 2HX. *T:* (020) 7851 5000; *e-mail:* david.fursdon@smithsgore.co.uk. *Clubs:* Farmers, MCC; Vincent's (Oxford).

FURSE, Dame Clara (Hedwig Frances), DBE 2008; Chief Executive, London Stock Exchange plc, since 2001; *b* 16 Sept. 1957; 2nd *d* of Herman Werner Siemens and Cornélie Siemens-Gravin Schimmelpenninck; *m* 1981, Richard Furse; two *s* one *d*. *Educ:* St James's Sch., W Malvern; London Sch. of Econs (BScEcon). Joined UBS, 1983, Man. Dir, 1995–98; Gp Chief Exec., Credit Lyonnais Rouse, 1998–2000. Dep. Chm., LIFFE, 1997–99. *Address:* London Stock Exchange, 10 Paternoster Square, EC4M 7LS.

FURST, David Anthony, FCA; President, Institute of Chartered Accountants in England and Wales, 2008–June 2009; Chairman, Horwath Clark Whitehill LLP, since 2004; Member Board, Horwath International, since 2002; *b* London, 4 Sept. 1950; *s* of Arthur Gerald Furst and Aline Verity Furst; *m* 1987, Anne Elizabeth Fleming; two *s* two *d*. *Educ:* Leighton Park Sch., Reading. FCA 1973. Horwath Clark Whitehill: Partner, 1984–; Chief Exec., 1998–2004. Founder Mem. Cttee, Assoc. of Partnership Practitioners, 1998–2004. *Publications:* Essential Guide to Self Assessment, 1994; regular contrib. to legal and accountancy jls. *Recreations:* bridge, ski-ing, watching motor racing, Rugby, cricket and football. *Address:* c/o Horwath Clark Whitehill, St Bride's House, 10 Salisbury Square, EC4Y 8EH. *Clubs:* MCC; Goodwood Road Racing, Silverstone Racing.

FURST, Stephen Andrew; QC 1991; a Recorder, since 1999; *b* 8 Feb. 1951; *s* of Herbert and Viviane Furst; *m* 1979, Bridget Collins; one *s* one *d*. *Educ:* Edinburgh Academy; St Edmund Hall, Oxford (BA Hons); Leeds Univ. (LLB Hons). Called to the Bar, Middle Temple, 1975, Bencher, 2000. An Asst Recorder, 1993–99. Joint Editor, Construction Law Yearbook, 1994–. *Publication:* (ed jtly) Keating on Building Contracts, 8th edn 2006. *Recreations:* bee-keeping, watercolour painting. *Address:* Keating Chambers, 15 Essex Street, WC2A 3AA. *T:* (020) 7544 2600.

FURTADO, Peter Randall, FRHistS; Editor, History Today, since 1997; *b* 20 May 1952; *s* of Robert Audley Furtado and Marcelle Elizabeth Furtado (*née* Whitteridge); *m* 1st, 1977, Roberta Jane Day (marr. diss.); 2nd, 1983, (Margaret Elizabeth) Ann Swoffer; three *d*. *Educ:* Whitgift Sch., Croydon; Oriel Coll., Oxford (BA 1st Cl. Hons 1973; Dip. Hist. Art 1974). Sen. ed., Hamlyn Books, 1977–83; freelance ed., 1983–87; sen. ed., Equinox Books, 1987–91; Exec. Ed., Andromeda Books, 1991–97. Managing Editor: The Ordnance Survey Atlas of Great Britain, 1981; The Illustrated History of the 20th Century, 10 vols, 1989–92; The Cassell Atlas of World History, 1996. Chm., Bd of Dirs, Shintaido Foundn, 1994–97, 2002–; Dir, Internat. Shintaido Foundn, 2003–. FRHistS 2002. *Recreations:* life, liberty, pursuit of happiness. *Address:* 1 Marlborough Court, Duke Street, Oxford OX2 0QT. *T:* (01865) 251234; *e-mail:* p.furtado@historytoday.com.

FYFE, family name of **Baron Fyfe of Fairfield**.

FYFE OF FAIRFIELD, Baron *cr* 2000 (Life Peer), of Sauchie in Clackmannanshire; **George Lennox Fyfe;** Chairman, Unity Trust Bank, since 2000; Chief Executive, Midlands Co-operative Society, 1995–2000 (Leicestershire Co-operative Society, 1975–95); *b* 10 April 1941; *s* of late George L. and Elizabeth S. Fyfe; *m* 1965, Ann Clark Asquith (*d* 1999); one *d* (one *s* decd). *Educ:* Alloa Acad.; Co-operative Coll., Loughborough. Gen. Manager, Kirriemuir Co-operative Soc., 1966–68; Regl Manager, Scottish Co-operative Soc., 1968–72; Gp Gen. Manager, CWS, 1972–75. Director: Shoefayre Ltd, 1981–2000 (Chm., 1984–2000); CWS, 1981–2000 (Vice-Chm., 1986–89; Chm., 1989–2000); Co-operative Insce Soc. Ltd, 1982–2000; Central TV-East, 1983–92; Co-operative Bank plc, 1986–2000 (Dep. Chm., 1996–2000). Mem. Central Cttee Internat. Co-op. Alliance, 1989–2000; Pres., Co-op. Congress, 2001. Mem., E Midland Econ. Planning Council, 1976–79. Member: EU Sub-Cttee D, Envmt, Agric., Publi Health and Consumer Protection, H of L, 2000–03; EU Sub-Cttee B, Internal Mkt, H o L, 2005–. Mem. Court, Leicester Univ. JP Perthshire, 1972–75. CCMI. *Recreation* observing human nature. *Address:* House of Lords, SW1A 0PW. *Clubs:* Reform, Farmers' Royal Automobile.

FYFE, Maria; Vice-Chair, Glasgow Housing Association, 2001–06; *b* 25 Nov. 1938; *d* o James O'Neill and Margaret Lacey; *m* 1964, James Joseph Fyfe (decd); two *s*. *Edu* Strathclyde Univ. (BA Hons. Economic History 1975). Senior Lecturer, Trade Unio Studies Unit, Glasgow Central College of Commerce, 1978–87. Mem., Labour Party 1960–, Scottish Exec., 1981–88; Mem., Glasgow District Council, 1980–87 (Vice Convener, Finance Cttee, 1980–84; Convener, Personnel Cttee, 1984–87). MP (Lab Glasgow, Maryhill, 1987–2001. Dep. Shadow Minister for Women, 1988–91; Convene Scottish Gp of Labour MPs, 1991–92; Scottish front bench spokesperson, 1992–95. Chai Labour Deptl Cttee on Internat. Devélt, 1997–2001; Labour Gp, UK Delegn to Counc of Europe, 1997–2001. DUniv Glasgow, 2002. *Address:* 10 Ascot Avenue, Glasgow G1 0AX. *T:* (0141) 334 6737.

FYFE, Prof. William Sefton, CC (Canada) 1989; FRS 1969; Professor of Geology University of Western Ontario, since 1972 (Dean of Science, 1986–90); *b* 4 June 1927; of Colin and Isabella Fyfe; *m* 1968; two *s* one *d*. *Educ:* Otago Univ., New Zealand. BSc 1948, MSc 1949, PhD 1952; FRSC 1980. Univ. of California, Berkeley: Lecturer i Chemistry, 1952, Reader, 1958; Prof. of Geology, 1959; Royal Soc. Res. Prof (Geochemistry), Univ. of Manchester, 1967–72. Guggenheim Fellow, 1983. Pres., IUGS 1992–. Hon. Fellow, Geological Soc. Amer.; Corresponding Member: Brazilian Acad. o Science; Russian Acad. of Scis; Indian Acad. of Scis. Hon. DSc: Meml Univ. o Newfoundland, 1989; Lisbon, 1990; Lakehead, 1990; Guelph, 1991; Otago, 1995 Western Ontario, 1996. Mineralogical Soc. of Amer. Award, 1964; Logan Medal, Geolog Assoc. of Canada, 1982; Willet G. Miller Medal, Royal Soc. of Canada, 1985; Arthu Holmes Medal, European Union of Geoscientists, 1989; Day Medal, Geol Soc. o America, 1990; Canada Gold Medal for Science and Engineering, 1992; Roebling Medal Mineralogical Soc. of America. Commemoration Medal, New Zealand, 1990, Canada 1992; Ordem Nacional do Merito Cientifico (Brazil), 1996; Wollaston Medal, Geol Soc. London, 2000. *Publications:* Metamorphic Reactions and Metamorphic Facies, 1958; The Geochemistry of Solids, 1964; Fluids in the Earth's Crust, 1978; also numerous scientifi papers. *Address:* Department of Earth Sciences, University of Western Ontario, London ON N6A 5B7, Canada; *e-mail:* pjfyfe@uwu.ca.

FYFE, William Stevenson, CBE 1992 (OBE 1987); FIIM; Chairman, Greater Glasgow Health Board, 1993; *b* Glasgow, 10 June 1935; *s* of Dr Andrew Fyfe and Janet Isabella Fyfe (*née* Soutar), New Cumnock; *m* 1986, Margaret H. H. Auld; one *s* one *d*. *Educ:* Dolla Acad.; Scottish Coll. of Commerce. FIIM 1985. Town Councillor (C), Prestwick 1967–73; Co. Councillor (C), Ayrshire, 1970–73; Ayrshire and Arran Health Board Financial Convener, 1973–81; Chm., 1981–93. Exec. Officer, Minerva Housing Assoc. Prestwick, 1997–2004. Chm., Scottish Health Services Adv. Council, 1989–93; Mem. General Whitley Council, 1989–93. *Recreation:* gardening. *Address:* Les Granges du Quercy, 47120 Auriac sur Dropt, France.

FYFIELD, Frances; novelist; solicitor; *b* 8 Nov. 1948; *d* of Dr Andrew George Hegarty and Winifred Doris Hegarty (*née* Fyfield). *Educ:* convent and grammar schools, Newcastle upon Tyne; Newcastle upon Tyne Univ. (BA English Lit. 1970); Coll. of Law. Admitted solicitor, 1973; a solicitor: for Metropolitan Police, 1973–80; for DPP, 1980–86; CPS 1986–97; lawyer and novelist, 1987–2000. Registrar, Royal Literary Fund. Presenter Tales from the Stave, Radio 4, 2007–08. *Publications:* A Question of Guilt, 1988 (televise 1994); Shadows on the Mirror, 1989; Trial by Fire, 1990 (televised 1999); Deep Slee (Silver Dagger Award, CWA), 1990; Shadow Play, 1991; Perfectly Pure and Good, 1992 A Clear Conscience, 1994 (Grand Prix de Literature Policière, 1998); Without Consent 1996; Blind Date, 1998 (televised 2000); Staring at the Light, 1999; Undercurrents, 2000 Helen West Omnibus, 2002 (televised, as Helen West, 2002); The Nature of the Beast 2001; Seeking Sanctuary, 2003; Looking Down, 2004; Safer Than Houses, 2005; The Ar of Drowning, 2006; Blood from Stone, 2008; *as Frances Hegarty:* The Playroom, 1990 Half Light, 1992; Let's Dance, 1995. *Recreations:* tobacco and fine wine, paintings company, watching the sea. *Address:* c/o Rogers Coleridge White, 20 Powis Mews, W11 1JN.

FYJIS-WALKER, Richard Alwyne, CMG 1980; CVO 1976; HM Diplomatic Service retired; Chairman, Commonwealth Institute, 1988–93; *b* 19 June 1927; *s* of Harold and Marion Fyjis-Walker; *m* 1st, 1951, Barbara Graham-Watson (marr. diss.); one *s*; 2nd 1972, Gabrielle Josefi; one *s*. *Educ:* Bradfield Coll.; Magdalene Coll., Cambridge (MA) Army (KRRC), 1945–48. Joined Foreign (subseq. Diplomatic) Service, 1955; served Amman, 1956; FO, 1957–61; Paris, 1961–63; Cairo, 1963–65; FCO, 1966–71 Counsellor, 1970; Ankara, 1971–74; Counsellor (Information), Washington, 1974–78 Counsellor, UK Mission to UN, NY, 1978–79; Ambassador to the Sudan, 1979–84 Ambassador to Pakistan, 1984–87. *Address:* 17 Stonefield Street, N1 0HW.

FYSH, (Robert) Michael; QC 1989; QC (NI) 1990; **His Honour Judge Fysh;** a Circuit Judge, Patents County Court, since 2001; *b* 2 Aug. 1940; *s* of Dr Leslie Fysh and Margaret Fysh, Ashford, Kent; *m* 1971, Mary Bevan; three *s*. *Educ:* Downside Sch.; Exeter Coll., Oxford (MA). Called to the Bar, Inner Temple, 1965, Bencher, 1999; NI, 1974 NSW, 1975; Ireland, 1975; India, 1982; Pakistan, 1987; SC Trinidad and Tobago Bar 1990; SC Dublin, 1994. A Dep. High Court Judge, Chancery Div., 1997–; an Additional Judge, Technol. and Construction Court, 2002–. Chm., Copyright Tribunal, 2006–. Vis Prof., Intellectual Property Inst., New Delhi, 2002. Hon. LLD Wolverhampton, 2005 *Publications:* Russell-Clarke on Registered Designs, 4th edn 1974; The Industrial Property Citator, 1982, 2nd edn 1996; (ed) The Spycatcher Cases, 1989. *Recreations:* forestry swimming, travel. *Address:* Patents County Court, Field House, 15–25 Bream's Buildings EC4A 1DZ. *Club:* Kildare Street and University (Dublin).

FYSON, Anne Elizabeth; *see* Howells, A. E.

G

GABATHULER, Prof. Erwin, OBE 2001; FRS 1990; FInstP; Sir James Chadwick Professor of Physics, Liverpool University, 1991–2001, now Emeritus Professor (Professor of Experimental Physics, 1983–91); *b* 16 Nov. 1933; *s* of Hans and Lena Gabathuler; *m* 1962, Susan Dorothy Jones, USA; two *s* one *d*. *Educ:* Queen's University Belfast (BSc 1956; MSc 1957); Univ. of Glasgow (PhD 1961). Research Fellow, Cornell Univ., 1961–64; Group Leader, Research, SERC, Daresbury Lab., 1964–73; CERN (European Organisation for Nuclear Research): Vis. Scientist, EMC Experiment, 1974–77; Leader, Exp. Physics Div., 1978–80; Dir of Research, 1981–83; Hd of Physics Dept, Liverpool Univ., 1986–91 and 1996–99. Chm., Particle Physics Cttee, SERC, 1985–88; Member: Nuclear Physics Bd, 1985–88; NATO Collaborative Research Grants Panels, 1990–93; Educn and Trng Cttee, PPARC, 1994–96. Dr *hc* Univ. of Uppsala, 1982; Hon. DSc QUB, 1997. Rutherford Medal, Inst. of Physics, 1992. *Publications:* articles in research jls. *Recreations:* music, walking. *Address:* 3 Danebank Road, Lymm, Cheshire WA13 9DQ. *T:* (01925) 752753.

GABBANA, Stefano; President, Dolce & Gabbana; *b* 14 Nov. 1962. Asst in design studio, Milan; with Domenico Dolce opened fashion consulting studio, 1982; Co-founder, Dolce & Gabbana, 1985; first major women's collection, 1986; knitwear, 1987; beachwear, lingerie, 1989; men's collection, 1990; women's fragrance, 1992; D&G line, men's fragrance, 1994; eyewear, 1995; opened boutiques in major cities in Europe, America and Asia. *Publications:* (with Domenico Dolce): 10 Years Dolce & Gabbana, 1996; Wildness, 1997; Mémoires de la Mode, 1998; Animal, 1998; Calcio, 2004; Music, 2005; 20 Years Dolce & Gabbana, 2005; (with Eve Claxton and Domenico Dolce) Hollywood, 2003. *Address:* Dolce & Gabbana, Via Santa Cecilia 7, 20122 Milan, Italy.

GABBITAS, Peter; Director of Health and Social Care, Edinburgh City Council, since 2005; *b* 15 Aug. 1961; *s* of Robert and Mary Gabbitas; *m* 1986, Karen Brown; one *d*. *Educ:* St Thomas Aquinas RC Grammar Sch.; Durham Univ. (BA Gen. Arts 1984); Warwick Univ. (MBA Dist. 1994). DipHSM 1987. NHS gen. mgt trainee, 1984–86; Director: of Service Develt, Solihull Acute Trust, 1989–91; of Ops, Dudley Gp of Hosps, 1991–97; Chief Executive: E and Midlothian NHS Trust, 1997–99; W Lothian Healthcare NHS Trust, 1999–2005. *Recreations:* golf, gardening, swimming, stained and fused glass. *Address:* City of Edinburgh Council/NHS Lothian, Waverley Court, 4 East Market Street, Edinburgh EH8 8BG; *e-mail:* peter.gabbitas@edinburgh.gov.uk. *Club:* Glen Golf.

GABITASS, Jonathan Roger, MA; Head Master, Merchant Taylors' School, 1991–2004; *b* 25 July 1944; *s* of William Gabitass and Nell Gabitass (*née* Chaffe); *m* 1967, Fiona Patricia Hoy; two *d*. *Educ:* Plymouth Coll.; St John's Coll., Oxford (MA English Lang. and Lit., PGCE). Asst English teacher, Clifton Coll., Bristol, 1967–73; Head of English, 1973–78, Second Master, 1978–91, Abingdon Sch., Oxon. *Recreations:* Rugby football, Cornish coastal path walking, 18th and 19th Century caricature, art galleries and theatre. *Clubs:* East India; Vincent's (Oxford).

GABRIEL, Peter; singer, musician and songwriter; *b* 13 Feb. 1950; *m* 1st, 1971, Jill Moore (marr. diss.); two *d*; 2nd, 2002, Meabh Flynn; one *s*. *Educ:* Charterhouse. Mem., Genesis, 1966–75; solo artist, 1975–. Founder: World of Music, Arts and Dance (annual festivals), 1982; Real World Gp, 1985; Real World Studios, 1986; Real World Records, 1989; Real World Multimedia, 1994; Jt Founder, Witness (human rights programme), 1992. *Albums* include: *with Genesis:* From Genesis to Revelation, 1969; Nursery Crime, 1971; Foxtrot, 1972; Selling England by the Pound, 1973; The Lamb Lies Down on Broadway, 1974; *solo:* Peter Gabriel I, 1977, II, 1978, III, 1980, IV, 1982; So, 1986; Us, 1992; Ovo, 2000; Up, 2002; *film soundtracks:* Birdy, 1984; Last Temptation of Christ, 1988; Rabbit-Proof Fence, 2002. *Address:* Real World, Box Mill, Box, Wilts SN13 8PL.

GADD, (John) Staffan; Hon. Chairman, Gadd & Co. AB, Stockholm, since 2005; Hon. Vice President, Swedish Chamber of Commerce for UK, since 1996 (Chairman, 1993–96); Chairman, Saga Securities Ltd, 1985–98; *b* 30 Sept. 1934; *s* of John Gadd and Ulla Olivecrona; *m* 1st, 1958, Margaretha Löfborg (marr. diss.); one *s* one *d*; 2nd, 1990, Kay McGreeghan. *Educ:* Stockholm Sch. of Econs. MBA. Sec., Confedn of Swedish Industries, 1958–61; Skandinaviska Banken, Stockholm, 1961–69 (London Rep., 1964–67); Dep. Man. Dir, Scandinavian Bank Ltd, London, 1969–71, Chief Exec. and Man. Dir, 1971–80; Chief Exec., 1980–84, Chm., 1982–84, Samuel Montagu & Co. Ltd; Chm., Montagu and Co. AB, Sweden, 1982–86; Dir, Guyerzeller Zurmont Bank AG, Switzerland, 1983–84; Chm., J. S. Gadd Cie SA, Geneva, 1989–98; Mem. Bd, Carta Corporate Advisors AB, 1990–98. *Recreations:* shooting, ski-ing, the arts, walking, travel. *Address:* Locks Manor, Hurstpierpoint, West Sussex BN6 9JZ.

GADD, Ruth Maria; *see* Kelly, R. M.

GADDES, (John) Gordon; Director, DENS Ltd (formerly Dacorum Emergency Night Shelter), since 2003 (Chairman, 2003–07); *b* 22 May 1936; *s* of late James Graham Moscrop Gaddes and of Irene Gaddes (*née* Murray; who married E. O. Kine); *m* 1958, Pamela Jean (*née* Marchbank); one *s* one *d*. *Educ:* Carres Grammar Sch., Sleaford; Selwyn Coll., Cambridge (MA Hons Geography); London Univ. (BScEcon Hons 1966; MA Philosophy and Religion 2005). Asst Lectr in Business Studies, Peterborough Technical Coll., 1960–64; Lectr in Business Studies, later Head of Business Studies, then Vice-Principal, Dacorum Coll. of Further Educn, Hemel Hempstead, 1964–69; Head of Export Services: British Standards Instn, 1969–72; Quality Assurance Dept, 1972–73; Dir, BSI Hemel Hempstead Centre, 1973–77; Commercial Dir, BSI, 1977–81; Dir, Information, Marketing and Resources, BSI, 1981–82; Dir Gen., BEAMA, 1982–97; UK Deleg., 1997, Sec. Gen., 1998–2001, Pres., 2001–03, European Orgn for Testing and Certification, subseq. for Conformity Assessment. Dir, Gaddes Associates Ltd, 1998–2007. Gov., Adeyfield Sch., 2001– (Vice-Chm., 2005–). Vice-Chm., Parish of St Mary and St Paul,

Hemel Hempstead, 2005–. *Recreations:* golf, swimming, family, church and community affairs. *Clubs:* Athenæum; Whipsnade Park Golf.

GADHIA, Jitesh; Managing Director, Global Head of Advisory, Barclays Capital, since 2008; *b* Kampala, Uganda, 27 May 1970; *s* of Kishore and Hansa Gadhia; *m* 2001, Angeli Saujani. *Educ:* Fitzwilliam Coll., Cambridge (BA Hons Econs 1991); London Business Sch. (Sloan Fellow; MSc Mgt). Baring Bros, 1991–98; Manek Investment Mgt, 1998–99; ABN AMRO, 2001–08. Trustee: Guy's and St Thomas' Charity, 1999–; NESTA, 2007–. *Recreations:* reading, walking, cinema, travel. *Address:* c/o Barclays Capital, 5 The North Colonnade, Canary Wharf, E14 4BB. *T:* (020) 7623 2323; *e-mail:* jitesh.gadhia@barclayscapital.com.

GADNEY, Jane Caroline Rebecca; *see* Parker-Smith, J. C. R.

GADSBY, Prof. David Christopher, PhD; FRS 2005; Professor and Head, Laboratory of Cardiac/Membrane Physiology, Rockefeller University, since 1991. *Educ:* Trinity Coll., Cambridge (BA 1969, MA 1973); University Coll. London (PhD 1978). Asst Prof., 1978–84, Associate Prof., 1984–91, Lab. of Cardiac Physiol., Rockefeller Univ. *Publications:* contrib. learned jls. *Address:* Laboratory of Cardiac/Membrane Physiology, Rockefeller University, 1230 York Avenue, New York, NY 10065, USA.

GAFFNEY, James Anthony, CBE 1984; FREng; FICE; *b* Bargoed, Glam, 9 Aug. 1928; *s* of James Francis and Violet Mary Gaffney; *m* 1953, Margaret Mary, 2nd *d* of E. and G. J. Evans, Pontypridd; one *s* two *d*. *Educ:* De La Salle Coll.; St Illtyd's Coll., Cardiff; UWIST; UC, Cardiff (Fellow, 1984). BSc (Eng) London. FR.Eng (FEng 1979); FICE 1968; FInstHE 1970. Highway Engr, Glam CC, 1948–60; Asst County Surveyor, Somerset CC, 1960–64; Deputy County Surveyor, Notts CC, 1964–69; County Engr and Surveyor, WR Yorks, 1969–74; Dir Engrg Services, W Yorks MCC, 1974–86. President: County Surveyors' Soc., 1977–78; Instn of Highway Engrs, 1978–79; ICE, 1983–84; Vice-Pres., Fellowship of Engrg, 1989–92. Hon. DSc: Wales, 1982; Bradford, 1984. *Recreations:* golf, travel, supporting Rugby. *Address:* Drovers Cottage, 3 Boston Road, Wetherby, W Yorks LS22 5HA. *Club:* Alwoodley Golf (Leeds).

GAFFNEY, John Campion B.; *see* Burke-Gaffney.

GAGE, family name of **Viscount Gage**.

GAGE, 8th Viscount *cr* 1720 (Ire.); **Henry Nicholas Gage;** DL; Bt 1622; Baron Gage (Ire.) 1720; Baron Gage (GB) 1790; *b* 9 April 1934; *yr s* of 6th Viscount Gage, KCVO and his 1st wife, Hon. Alexandra Imogen Clare Grenfell (*d* 1969), *yr d* of 1st Baron Desborough, KG, GCVO; *S* brother, 1993; *m* 1974, Lady Diana Adrienne Beatty (marr. diss. 2002); two *s*. *Educ:* Eton; Christ Church, Oxford. 2nd Lt Coldstream Guards, 1953. DL East Sussex, 1998. *Recreations:* country and other pursuits. *Heir: s* Hon. Henry William Gage, *b* 25 June 1975. *Address:* Firle Place, Lewes, East Sussex BN8 6LP. *T:* (01273) 858535, *Fax:* (01273) 858188.

GAGE, Rt Hon. Sir William (Marcus), Kt 1993; PC 2004; a Lord Justice of Appeal, 2004–08; *b* 22 April 1938; *s* of late His Honour Conolly Gage; *m* 1962, Penelope Mary Groves; three *s*. *Educ:* Repton; Sidney Sussex Coll., Cambridge. MA. National Service, Irish Guards, 1956–58. Called to the Bar, Inner Temple, 1963, Bencher, 1991; QC 1982; a Recorder, 1985–93; a Judge of the High Court of Justice, QBD, 1993–2004. Presiding Judge, S Eastern Circuit, 1997–2000. Chancellor, diocese of Coventry, 1980–, of Ely, 1989–. Member: Criminal Injuries Compensation Bd, 1987–93; Parole Bd, 2001–04. *Recreations:* shooting, fishing, travel. *Address:* c/o Royal Courts of Justice, Strand, WC2A 2LL.

GAGEBY DENHAM, Susan; *see* Denham.

GAGEN, Heather Jacqueline; *see* Yasamee, H. J.

GAGGERO, Joseph James, CBE 1989; President, Bland Group of Shipping, Aviation and Travel Companies; *b* 20 Nov. 1927; *s* of Sir George Gaggero, OBE, JP and Mabel Andrews-Speed; *m* 1st, 1958, Marilys Healing (marr. diss. 1987); one *s* one *d*; 2nd, 1994, Christina Russo (marr. diss. 2008). *Educ:* Downside Sch. Dir, Gibraltar Chamber of Commerce, 1951–56; Head, Gibraltar Govt Tourist Dept, 1955–59; served on or led other Gibraltar Govt Cttees and Gibraltar Trading Assocs, 1948–. Hon. Consul Gen. for Sweden in Gibraltar, 1971–95. Director: Hovertravel; Cadogan Holidays; President: Rock Hotel; Gibraltar Airways. Dep. Pres., Moroccan-British Business Council, 2008–. Pres., British Moroccan Soc., 2005–. Freeman, City of London, 1997; Liveryman, GAPAN, 1997–. Patron: Hispanic British Foundn, Madrid; Gibraltar Philharmonic Orch. Air League Founders' Medal, 2007. KHS. Comdr, Royal Order of the Polar Star (Sweden), 1991; Comdr, Royal Order Al Alaoui (Morocco), 2006. *Publication:* Running with the Baton (autobiog.), 2005. *Recreations:* travel, painting. *Address:* Cloister Building, Gibraltar. *T:* 78456. *Clubs:* Travellers; Valderrama Golf.

GAHAGAN, Michael Barclay, CB 2000; Director, Housing (formerly Housing, Private Policy and Analysis) Directorate, Office of the Deputy Prime Minister (formerly Department for the Environment, Transport and the Regions, then Department for Transport, Local Government and the Regions), 1997–2003; *b* 24 March 1943; *s* of Geoffrey and Doris Gahagan; *m* 1967, Anne Brown; two *s*. *Educ:* St Mary's Coll., Southampton; Univ. of Manchester (MA Econ, BA). MRICS. W. H. Robinson & Co., Chartered Surveyors, Manchester, 1964–66; DEA (NW), 1966–69; Min. of Housing and Local Govt (NW), 1969–71; DoE, Central Res. and Inner Cities Directorates, NW, SE and London Regl Offices, 1971–88; seconded to DTI Inner Cities Unit, 1988–91; Dir, Inner Cities, subseq. Cities and Countryside Policy, then Regeneration, Directorate, DoE,

1991–96. Pres., Internat. Urban Develt Assoc., 1995–99. Chm., S Yorks Housing Market Renewal Pathfinder, 2003–; Mem. Bd, Paradigm Housing Gp, 2003–. *Recreations:* soccer, bridge.

GAIMSTER, Dr David Richard Michael, FSA; General Secretary and Chief Executive, Society of Antiquaries of London, since 2004; *b* 3 Jan. 1962; *s* of late Rev. Leslie Rayner Gaimster and of Mareike Gaimster (*née* Döhler); *m* 1st 1990, Märit Thurborg (marr. diss. 2004); one *s* one *d*; 2nd, 2005, Amy Clarke; one *d*. *Educ:* Longsands Sch., St Neots, Cambs; Durham Univ. (BA Hons Archaeol. 1984); University Coll. London (PhD Medieval Archaeol. 1991). Asst Keeper, Dept of Medieval and Later Antiquities, BM, 1986–2001; Sen. Policy Advr, Cultural Property Unit, DCMS, 2002–04. Vis. Prof. in Historical Archaeol., Dept of Cultural Scis, Univ. of Turku, Finland, 2000–; Hon. Res. Fellow, Inst. of Archaeol., UCL, 2000–. Member: Culture Cttee, UK Commn for UNESCO, 2005–; Guild of Arts Scholars, Dealers and Collectors, 2007–; IoD, 2008. Vice-Chm., City of London Archaeol Trust, 2006–. FSA 1996; AMA 2001; MIFA 1987. OM, Soc. of Historical Archaeol of N America, 2005. *Publications:* German Stoneware 1200–1900: archaeology and cultural history, 1997; (ed jtly) The Age of Transition: the archaeology of English culture 1400–1600, 1997; (ed jtly) Pottery in the Making: world ceramic traditions, 1997; Maiolica in the North: the archaeology of tin-glazed earthenware in NW Europe *c* 1500–1600, 1999; (ed jtly) Novgorod: the archaeology of a Russian medieval city and its hinterland, 2001; (ed jtly) The Archaeology of Reformation 1480–1580, 2003; The Historical Archaeology of Pottery Supply and Demand in the Lower Rhineland, AD 1400–1800, 2006; contribs to archaeol and historical monographs and learned jls. *Recreations:* antiques, historic buildings and interiors, travel in Europe. *Address:* Society of Antiquaries of London, Burlington House, Piccadilly, W1J 0BE. *T:* (020) 7479 7080, *Fax:* (020) 7287 6967; *e-mail:* dgaimster@sal.org.uk.

GAINFORD, 3rd Baron *cr* 1917; **Joseph Edward Pease;** *b* 25 Dec. 1921; *s* of 2nd Baron Gainford, TD, and Veronica Margaret (*d* 1995), *d* of Sir George Noble, 2nd Bt; *S* father, 1971; *m* 1953, Margaret Theophila Radcliffe, *d* of late Henry Edmund Guise Tyndale; two *d*. *Educ:* Eton, Gordonstoun; Open Univ. (Dip. in Eur. Humanities, 1995; BA Hons, 1997). FRGS; TechRICS. RAFVR, 1941–46. Hunting Aerosurveys Ltd, 1947–49; Directorate of Colonial Surveys, 1951–53; Soil Mechanics Ltd, 1953–58; London County Council, 1958–65; Greater London Council, 1965–78. UK Delegate to UN, 1973. Mem., Coll. of Guardians, Nat. Shrine of Our Lady of Walsingham, 1979–. Mem., Plaisterers' Co., 1976. *Recreations:* Association football, music, veteran and vintage aviation. *Heir: b* Hon. George Pease [*b* 20 April 1926; *m* 1958, Flora Daphne, *d* of late Dr N. A. Dyce Sharp; two *s* two *d*]. *Address:* 1 Dedmere Court, Marlow, Bucks SL7 1PL. *T:* (01628) 484679. *Clubs:* MCC; Phyllis Court (Henley-on-Thames).

GAINS, Sir John (Christopher), Kt 2003; CEng, FICE; Chairman: Aktrion Holdings Ltd, since 2005; CCS Group plc, since 2008; Chief Executive, Mowlem (formerly John Mowlem & Co.) PLC, 1995–2004 (Director, 1992–2005); *b* 22 April 1945; *s* of Albert Edward Gains and Grace (*née* Breckenridge); *m* 1969, Ann Murray (*d* 1999); one *s* one *d*. *Educ:* King Henry VIII Sch., Coventry; Loughborough Univ. (BSc). CEng 1970; FICE 1992. Joined John Mowlem & Co. PLC, 1966; Dir, Mowlem Civil Engineering, 1983–95. Non-executive Director: SGB plc, 1997–2000; Heiton Gp plc, 2002–05; Thames Water Utilities Ltd, 2005–06. Mem. Council, Loughborough Univ., 2006–. Hon. DTech Loughborough, 2004. *Recreations:* golf, sailing, walking. *Address:* Longridge, Farm Lane, East Markham, Newark, Notts NG22 0QH. *T:* (01777) 870616. *Clubs:* Reform; Lincoln Golf.

GAINSBOROUGH, 5th Earl of, (2nd) *cr* 1841; **Anthony Gerard Edward Noel;** JP; Bt 1781; Baron Barham, 1805; Viscount Campden, Baron Noel, 1841; *b* 24 Oct. 1923; *s* of 4th Earl and Alice Mary (*d* 1970), *e d* of Edward Eyre, Gloucester House, Park Lane, W1; *S* father, 1927; *m* 1947, Mary, *er d* of late Hon. J. J. Stourton, TD and Mrs Kathleen Stourton; four *s* three *d*. *Educ:* Georgetown, Garrett Park, Maryland, USA. Chairman: Oakham RDC, 1952–67; Executive Council RDC's Association of England and Wales, 1963 (Vice-Chairman 1962, Pres., 1965); Pres., Assoc. of District Councils, 1974–80; Vice-Chm. Rutland CC, 1958–70, Chm., 1970–73; Chm., Rutland Dist Council, 1973–76. Chm., Bd of Management, Hosp. of St John and St Elizabeth, NW8, 1970–80 (Pres., 1995–). Chm., Hosp. Mgt Trust, 1985–2002. Mem. Court of Assistants, Worshipful Co. of Gardeners of London, 1960 (Upper Warden, 1966; Master, 1967). Hon. FICE (Hon. FIMunE 1969). JP Rutland, 1957, Leics, 1974. Knight of Malta, 1948; Bailiff Grand Cross Order of Malta, 1958; Pres. Br. Assoc., SMO, Malta, 1968–74. KStJ 1970. *Recreations:* shooting, sailing. *Heir: s* Viscount Campden, *qv*. *Address:* Horn House, Exton Park, Oakham, Rutland LE15 7QU. *T:* (office) (01780) 460772. *Clubs:* Brooks's, Pratt's; Bembridge Sailing.

See also Earl of Liverpool, Hon. G. E. W. Noel.

GAINSBOROUGH, George Fotheringham, CBE 1973; PhD, FIET; Barrister-at-law; Secretary, Institution of Electrical Engineers, 1962–80; *b* 28 May 1915; *o s* of late Rev. William Anthony Gainsborough and of Alice Edith (*née* Fennell); *m* 1937, Gwendoline (*d* 1976), *e d* of John and Anne Berry; two *s*. *Educ:* Christ's Hospital; King's Coll., London; Gray's Inn. Scientific Staff, Nat. Physical Laboratory, 1938–46; Radio Physicist, British Commonwealth Scientific Office, Washington, DC, USA, 1944–45; Administrative Civil Service (Ministries of Supply and Aviation), 1946–62. Imperial Defence College, 1960. Hon. Sec., Commonwealth Engineering Conf., 1962–69; Hon. Sec.-General, World Fedn of Engineering Organizations, 1968–76. *Publications:* papers in Proc. Instn of Electrical Engineers. *Address:* c/o 3 Methley Street, SE11 4AL. *Club:* Athenæum.

See also Michael Gainsborough.

GAINSBOROUGH, Michael; Commissioner, Royal Hospital, Chelsea, 2001–07 (Secretary, 1994–2001); *b* 13 March 1938; *s* of George Fotheringham Gainsborough, *qv*; *m* 1962, Sally (*née* Hunter); one *s* two *d*. *Educ:* St Paul's Sch.; Trinity Coll., Oxford. Air Ministry, 1959–64; Ministry of Defence, 1964–78; Defence Counsellor, UK Delegn to NATO, Brussels, FCO, 1978–81; Dir, Resources and Programmes (Strategic Systems), MoD, 1981–83; Asst Under-Sec. of State (Naval Staff), 1984, (Programmes), 1985–86, MoD; Center for Internat. Affairs, Harvard Univ., 1986–87; Asst Under-Sec. of State (Adjutant Gen.), 1987–91, (Service Personnel), 1992, MoD. Mem., Royal Patriotic Fund Corp., 1987–2000. Trustee and Gov., Royal Sch., Hampstead, 1997–2004. *Recreations:* various. *Address:* 3 Methley Street, SE11 4AL.

GAINSFORD, Sir Ian (Derek), Kt 1995; FDSRCS, FDSRCSE; Dean of King's College School of Medicine and Dentistry, King's College London, 1988–97; Vice-Principal, King's College London, 1994–97; *b* 24 June 1930; *s* of late Rabbi Morris Ginsberg, MA, PhD, AKC, and Anne Freda; *m* 1957, Carmel Liebster; one *s* two *d*. *Educ:* Thames Valley Grammar Sch., Twickenham; King's Coll. and King's College Hosp. Med. Sch., London (BDS; FKC 1984); Toronto Univ., Canada (DDS Hons). FDSRCS 1967; FDSRCSE 1998. Junior Staff, King's College Hosp., 1955–57; Member staff, Dept of Conservative Dentistry, London Hosp. Med. Sch., 1957–70; Sen. Lectr/Consultant, Dept of Conservative Dentistry, King's College Hosp., 1970–97; Dep. Dean of Dental Studies, 1973–77; Dir of Clinical Dental Services, KCH, 1977–87 (Dean of Dental Studies, KCHMS, 1977–83); Dean, Faculty of Clinical Dentistry, KCL, 1983–87. President British Soc. for Restorative Dentistry, 1973–74; Member: BDA, 1956– (Pres Metropolitan Br., 1981–82); Internat. Dental Fedn, 1966–; American Dental Soc. c London, 1960– (Pres., 1982); Amer. Dental Soc. of Europe, 1965– (Hon. Treas. 1971–77 Pres., 1982); GDC, 1986–94 (Chm., Educn Cttee, 1990–94; Chm., Specialist Trng Adv Cttee, 1996–2000). Examiner for Membership in General Dental Surgery, RCS, 1979–8 (Chm., 1982–84); External Examiner: Leeds Univ. Dental Sch., 1985–87; Hong Kon Dental Sch., 1988–90; Fellow, and Mem., 1967–, Hon. Mem., 1996, Pres., 1993–94 Odontological Sect., RSM; a Regent, RCSE, 2002–. Non-exec. Dir, SE Thames RHA 1988–93. President: Western Marble Arch Synagogue, 1998–2000; The Maccabaeans 2000–07; St Marylebone Soc., 2001–04. Hon. Pres., British Friends of Magen David Adom, 1995–. Hon. Mem., Amer. Dental Assoc., 1983. Hon. Scientific Advr, British Dental Jl, 1982. FICD 1975; MGDS RCS 1979; FACD 1988. Hon. FRCSE 2006 *Publication:* Silver Amalgam in Clinical Practice, 1965, 3rd edn 1992. *Recreations:* theatre canal cruising. *Address:* 31 York Terrace East, NW1 4PT. *T:* (020) 7935 8659. *Clubs* Athenæum, Royal Society of Medicine.

GAIR, Hon. George Frederick, CMG 1994; QSO 1988; former New Zealand politician; *b* 13 Oct. 1926; *s* of Frederick James Gair and Roemer Elizabeth Elphege (*née* Boecking); *m* 1951, Esther Mary Fay Levy; one *s* two *d*. *Educ:* Wellington Coll.; Wairarap Coll.; Victoria and Auckland Univ. Colls (BA 1949). Journalist: NZ Herald, 1945–47 BCON, Japan, 1947–48; Sun News Pictorial, Melbourne, 1949–50; Auckland Star 1950–52; Auckland PRO, 1952–57; Staff Leader of Opposition, NZ, 1958; Press Office and Personal Asst to Chief Exec., TEAL (later Air NZ), 1960–66. MP (Nat.) North Shore 1966–90; Parly Under-Sec. to Minister of Educn, 1969–71; Minister of: Customs, and Associate Minister of Finance, 1972; Housing, and Dep. Minister of Finance, 1975–77 Energy, 1977–78; Health, and of Social Welfare, 1978–81; Transport, Railways, and Civil Aviation, 1981–84; Dep. Leader of Opposition, 1986–87; retd 1990. High Comr for NZ in UK, 1991–94, concurrently High Comr in Nigeria and Ambassador to Republic c Ireland. Mayor, North Shore City, NZ, 1995–98. Chm., NZ Ambulance Bd, 1995–2001 President: Alumni Assoc., Univ. of Auckland, 1994–96; Assoc. of Former MPs of NZ 2002–03. *Recreation:* walking. *Address:* Villa 59 Mayfair Village, 14 Oteha Valley Road Browns Bay, Auckland 1311, New Zealand.

GAISFORD, Rt Rev. John Scott; Bishop Suffragan of Beverley, 1994–2000; Episcopal Visitor for the Province of York, 1994–2000; Hon. Assistant Bishop of Ripon 1996–2000; *b* 7 Oct. 1934; *s* of Joseph and Margaret Thompson Gaisford; *m* 1962, Gillian Maclean; one *s* one *d*. *Educ:* Univ. of Durham (Exhibnr, St Chad's Coll., Durham; BA Hons Theol. 1959, DipTh with Distinction 1960, MA 1976). Deacon 1960, priest 1961 Manchester; Assistant Curate: S Hilda, Audenshaw, 1960–62; S Michael, Bramhall 1962–65; Vicar, S Andrew, Crewe, 1965–86; RD of Nantwich, 1974–85; Hon. Canon of Chester Cathedral, 1980–86; Archdeacon of Macclesfield, 1986–94. Proctor in Convocation, Mem. Gen. Synod, 1975–95; Church Commissioner, 1986–94; Member Church of England Pensions Bd, 1982–97; Churches Conservation Trust (formerly Redundant Churches Fund), 1989–98. *Recreation:* fell walking. *Address:* 5 Trevone Close Knutsford, Cheshire WA16 9EJ. *T:* (01565) 633531; *e-mail:* jandg.gaisford@tiscali.co.uk *Club:* Athenæum.

GAISMAN, Jonathan Nicholas Crispin; QC 1995; a Recorder, since 2000; *b* 10 Aug 1956; *o s* of Peter and Bea Gaisman; *m* 1982, Tessa Jardine Paterson (MBE 1990); one two *d*. *Educ:* Summer Fields; Eton College (King's Scholar); Worcester Coll., Oxford (BCL; MA 1st cl Hons Jurisp.). Called to the Bar, Inner Temple, 1979, Bencher, 2004 Asst Recorder, 1998–2000. Director: English Chamber Orchestra and Music Soc. Ltd 1992–96; Internat. Musicians' Seminar, Prussia Cove, 1994–; Streetwise Opera, 2002–. FRSA 1997. *Recreations:* the arts, travel, country pursuits. *Address:* 7 King's Bench Walk Temple, EC4Y 7DS. *T:* (020) 7910 8300. *Clubs:* Beefsteak; I Zingari.

GAITSKELL, Robert; QC 1994; PhD; CEng, FIET, FIMechE; FCIArb; a Recorder since 2000; Vice President, Institution of Electrical Engineers, 1998–2001; *b* 19 April 1948; *s* of late Stanley Gaitskell and late Thelma Phyllis Gaitskell (*née* Holmes); *m* 1974 Dr Deborah Lyndall Bates; one *d*. *Educ:* Hamilton High Sch., Bulawayo, Zimbabwe Univ. of Cape Town (BSc Eng); KCL (PhD 1998; AKC 1998). CEng 1993; FIET (FIEE 1993); FCIArb 1995; FIMechE 1998. CEDR Accredited and Registered Mediator, 1999 Grad. trainee, Reyrolle Parsons, 1971–73; Engr, Electricity Dept, Bulawayo CC Zimbabwe, 1973–75; Electrical Engr, GEC (South Africa), 1975–76; called to the Bar Gray's Inn, 1978, Bencher, 2003; in practice at Bar in construction cases; arbitrator; Asst Recorder, 1997–2000. Lectr, Centre of Construction Law and Mgt, KCL, 1993–2003, for LLM, on Internat. Infrastructure Arbitration, KCL, 2006–, and other professional bodies Institution of Electrical Engineers: Mem. Council, 1994–2001; Chairman: Bd of Mgt and Design Div., 1995; Professional Gp on Engrg and the Law, 1994; Internat. Bd, 1998–99 Public Affairs Bd, 1999–2000; Professional Bd, 2000. Mem., Heilbron Cttee on Civil Procedure, 1993; Chm., IET/IMechE Jt Cttee on Model Forms, 2001–. Senator, Engrg Council, 1998–2002 (Chairman: Election Cttee, 1999–2001; Code of Conduct Cttee 1999–2001). Mem., Arbitration Panel, Dubai Internat. Arbitration Centre, 2006–. Member Committee: London Common Law and Commercial Bar Assoc., 1987–2000 Official Referees Bar Assoc., 1987–93; Gray's Inn Barristers, 2002–03. Legal columnist Engrg Mgt Jl, 1994–2003; Mem. Editl Bd, Construction and Engrg Law Jl, 1998–2005 Methodist local preacher. Liveryman: Engineers' Co., 1997–; Arbitrators' Co., 2002–. *Publications:* (ed) Engineers' Dispute Resolution Handbook, 2006; papers and articles on law and engrg. *Recreations:* walking, theatre, travel. *Address:* Keating Chambers, 15 Essex Street, WC2R 3AA.

GAJDUSEK, Daniel Carleton, MD; Director of Program for Study of Child Growth and Development and Disease Patterns in Primitive Cultures, and Laboratory of Slow Latent and Temperate Virus Infections, National Institute of Neurological Disorders (formerly of Neurological and Communicative Disorders and Stroke), National Institutes of Health Bethesda, Md, 1958–97; Chief, Central Nervous System Studies Laboratory, NINDS 1970–97; *b* Yonkers, NY, 9 Sept. 1923; *s* of Karol Gajdusek and Ottilia Dobroczki; sixty-seven adopted *s* and *d* (all from New Guinea and Micronesia). *Educ:* Marine Biological Lab., Woods Hole, Mass; Univ. of Rochester (BS *summa cum laude*); Harvard Medical Sch (MD); California Inst. of Technology (Post-Doctoral Fellow). Residencies: Babies Hosp. NY, 1946–47; Children's Hosp., Cincinatti, Ohio, 1947–48; Children's Hosp., Boston Mass, 1949–51; Sen. Fellow, Nat. Research Council, Calif Inst. of Tech., 1948–49 Children's Hosp., Boston, Mass, 1949–51; Research Fellow, Harvard Univ. and Sen Fellow, Nat. Foundn for Infantile Paralysis, 1949–52; Walter Reed Army Medical Center 1952–53; Institut Pasteur, Tehran, Iran and Univ. of Maryland, 1954–55; Vis Investigator, Nat. Foundn for Infantile Paralysis and Walter and Eliza Hall Inst., Australia 1955–57. Adjunct Prof., Inst. of Human Virology, Baltimore, 1996–97; Guest Scientist CNRS, Institut Alfred Fessard, Gif-sur-Yvette, France, 1998–; Visiting Professor: Human Retrovirus Lab., Univ. of Amsterdam, 1998–; Univ. of Tromsø, 1998–. Member: Nat. Acad. of Sciences, 1974; Amer. Philos. Soc., 1978; Amer. Acad. of Arts and Scis, 1978; Amer. Acad. of Neurol.; Infectious Dis. Soc. of America; Amer. Pediatric Soc.; Amer

Epidemiological Soc.; Amer. Soc. for Virology; Deutsche Akademie der Naturforscher Leopoldina, 1982; Czechoslovak, Portuguese, Australian, Russian, Sakha and Korean Acads of Science; Mexican Nat. Acad. of Medicine; Nat. Acad. of Medicine, Colombia; Royal Acad. of Medicine of Belgium. Mem., Scientific Council, Fondn pour l'Etude du Système Nerveux, Geneva, 1983–96. Discovered slow virus infections of man; studied child growth and develt and disease patterns in primitive and isolated populations, virus encephalitides, hemorrhagic fevers, hantavirus and human retrovirus infections, chronic degenerative brain diseases, cerebral amyloidoses, and aging, spontaneous generation of infectious agents by nucleating induction of infectious conformation of host precursor proteins, molecular casting. E. Meade Johnson Award, Amer. Acad. Pediatrics, 1963; DHEW Superior Service Award, 1970; DHEW Distinguished Service Award, 1975; Lucien Dautrebande Prize, Belgium, 1976; shared with Dr Baruch Blumberg Nobel Prize in Physiology or Medicine, for discoveries concerning new mechanisms for the origin and dissemination of infectious diseases, 1976; George Cotzias Meml Prize, Amer. Acad. of Neurol., 1978; Huxley Medal, RAI, 1988; Gold Medal, Slovak Acad. of Scis, 1996; Premio Gargano, Inst. di Cultura, Manfredouia, 2000; Qi Liu Friendship Prize, Shandong, 2000. Hon. Curator, Melanesian Ethnography, Peabody Mus., Salem, Mass; Hon. Pres., World Hantavirus Soc., 1994–; Hon. Advr, Shandong Acad. Scis, 2000–. Hon. Prof., many med. colls and univs in China, incl. Beijing, 1987, Ningxia Med. Coll., 2001, Youjiang Med. Coll. for Nationalities, Baise, 2003, and Sichuan, 2006. Hon. DSc: Univ. of Rochester, 1977; Med. Coll. of Ohio, 1977; Washington and Jefferson Coll., 1980; Harvard Med. Sch. (Bicentennial), 1982; Hahnemann Univ., 1983; Univ. of Medicine and Dentistry of NJ, 1987; Hon. LHD: Hamilton Coll., 1977; Univ. of Hawaii, 1986; Comenius Univ., Bratislava, 1996; Docteur hc: Univ. of Marseille, 1977; Univ. of Lisbon, 1991; Univ. of Ust-Kamenogorsk, 1995; Univ. of Kharkov, 1995; Univ. of Las Palmas, 1996; Hon. LLD Aberdeen, 1980; Laurea hc Univ. of Milan, 1992. *Publications:* Acute Infectious Hemorrhagic Fevers and Mycotoxicoses in the USSR, 1953; (ed with C. J. Gibbs, Jr and M. P. Alpers) Slow, Latent and Temperate Virus Infections, 1965; Journals 1937–2005, 75 vols, 1958–2005; Smadel-Gajdusek Correspondence 1955–1958; (ed with J. Farquhar) Kuru, 1981; Viliuisk Encephalitis, 1996; over 1000 papers in major jls of medicine, microbiology, immunology, pediatrics, neurology, developmental biology, psychosexual development, neurobiology, genetics, evolution, anthropology and linguistics.

GALASKO, Prof. Charles Samuel Bernard; Professor of Orthopaedic Surgery, University of Manchester, 1976–2004, now Professor Emeritus; Consultant Orthopaedic Surgeon, Hope Hospital, 1976–2004 (Medical Director, 1993–96); Director of Education and Training, Salford Royal Hospitals NHS Trust, 2003–05; *b* 29 June 1939; *s* of David Isaac Galasko and Rose Galasko; *m* 1967, Carol Freyda Lapinsky; one *s* one *d. Educ:* King Edward VII Sch., Johannesburg; Univ. of Witwatersrand (MB BCh 1st Cl. Hons 1962; ChM 1969); MSc Manchester 1980. FRCS 1966; FRCSEd 1966. Med., surg. and orth. trng, Johannesburg Gen. Hosp. and Univ. of Witwatersrand, 1963–66; House Surgeon and Surg. Registrar, Hammersmith Hosp. and RPMS, 1966–69; Lord Nuffield Schol. in Orthopaedic Surgery, Univ. of Oxford, 1969; Orth. and Trauma Registrar and Sen. Registrar, Radcliffe Infirmary and Nuffield Orth. Centre, Oxford, 1970–73; Cons. Orth. Surgeon, Dir of Orth. Surgery, and Asst Dir, Div. of Surgery, RPMS and Hammersmith Hosp., 1973–76; Cons. Orth. Surgeon, Royal Manchester Children's Hosp., 1976–2002. Member, Management Board: Royal Manchester Children's Hosp., 1989–92; Salford Royal Hosps NHS Trust, 1989–96. Hunterian Prof., RCS, 1971; Sir Arthur Sims Commonwealth Prof., 1998. Lectures: Hunterian, 1972; Annandale, 1979; Batson, 1979; Stanford Cade, 1993; Malkin, 1996; David Fuller, 1996; Chatterjee, 1997; Francois P. Fouche, 1999; Robert Jones, 1999; Hunterian Orator, 2003. Chm., Jt Cttee on Higher Surgical Trng, UK and Ire., 1997–2000. Member: Med. Sub-Cttee, British Olympic Assoc., 1988–2002; Internat. Cttee, 1990–93; Internat. Adv. Bd, 1994–96, SICOT (A. O. Internat. Award, 1981); President: SIROT, 1990–93; British Orthopaedic Assoc., 2000–01 (Vice Pres., 1999–2000; Mem. Council, 1988–91, 1998–2003); Faculty of Sport and Exercise Medicine, 2006– (Chm., Intercollegiate Academic Bd of Sport and Exercise Medicine, 2002–05); Vice President: Sect. of Oncology, RSM, 1987 (Mem. Council, 1980–87); RCS, 1999–2001 (Mem. Council, 1991–2003; Chm., Hosp. Recognition Cttee, 1992–95; Chm., Trng Bd, 1995–99). Vice Pres., British Amateur Wrestling Assoc., 1996–2002 (Chm., 1992–96; Med. Advr, 1987–2002); Vice-Chm., English Olympic Wrestling Assoc., 1998–2000 (Med. Advr, 1987–2000). SICOT Fellow, 1972; ABC Fellow, 1978; Aust. Commonwealth Fellow, 1982. Hon. Member: S African Orth. Assoc.; Amer. Fracture Assoc.; Emeritus Mem., Amer. Orth. Assoc.; Corresp. Mem., Columbian Soc. of Orth. Surgery and Traumatology. FMedSci 2002; FFSEM (Ireland) 2003; FFSEM (UK) 2006. Hon. FCMSA 2002. Moynihan Prize, Assoc. of Surgeons, 1969. *Publications:* (ed jtly) Radionuclide Scintigraphy Orthopaedics, 1984; (ed) Principles of Fracture Management, 1984; Skeletal Metastases, 1986; (ed) Neuromuscular Problems in Orthopaedics, 1987; (ed jtly) Recent Developments in Orthopaedic Surgery, 1987; (ed jtly) Current Trends in Orthopaedic Surgery, 1988; (ed jtly) Imaging Techniques in Orthopaedics, 1989; (jtly) Competing for the Disabled, 1989; articles and contribs to books on aspects of orthopaedics and trauma. *Recreations:* sport, opera, music. *Address:* 72 Gatley Road, Gatley, Cheadle, Cheshire SK8 4AA. *T:* (0161) 428 0316.

GALBRAITH, family name of **Baron Strathclyde.**

GALBRAITH, Colin Archibald, PhD; Director of Policy and Advice, Scottish Natural Heritage, since 2007; *b* 4 Feb. 1959; *s* of Lorne Galbraith; *m* 1987, Maria; one *s* one *d. Educ:* Minard Primary Sch.; Lochgilphead Sec. Sch.; Oban High Sch.; Paisley Univ. (BSc Hons Biol. 1981); Univ. of Aberdeen (PhD Zool. 1987). Joint Nature Conservation Committee: Hd, Vertebrate Ecology, 1991–96; Hd, Biodiversity Service, 1996–97; Scottish Natural Heritage: Hd, Adv. Services, 1997–2001; Dir, Scientific and Adv. Services, 2001–07. Hon. Prof., Univ. of Stirling, 2002–. Chm., 1999–2005, Vice Chm., 2005–, Scientific Council, Convention on Migratory Species; Mem. Bd, Millennium Ecosystem Assessment, 2002–05. *Publications:* (ed jtly) Mountains of Northern Europe, 2005; (ed jtly) Farming, Forestry and the Natural Heritage, 2006; (ed jtly) Waterbirds around the World, 2006. *Recreations:* bird watching, hill walking, photography, travel, antiques. *Address:* Scottish Natural Heritage, Silvan House, 231 Corstorphine Road, Edinburgh EH12 7AT. *T:* (0131) 446 2404; *e-mail:* colin.galbraith@snh.gov.uk.

GALBRAITH, James Hunter, CB 1985; Under Secretary, Department of Employment Industrial Relations Division, 1975–85; *b* 16 July 1925; *o s* of late Prof. V. H. Galbraith, FBA, and Dr G. R. Galbraith; *m* 1954, Isobel Gibson Graham; two *s. Educ:* Dragon Sch.; Edinburgh Academy; Balliol Coll., Oxford. 1st Cl. Litt Hum. Fleet Air Arm (pilot), 1944–46. Entered Ministry of Labour, 1950; Private Sec. to Permanent Sec., 1953–55; Jun. Civilian Instructor, IDC, 1958–61; Private Sec. to Minister of Labour, 1962–64; Chm. Central Youth Employment Exec., 1964–67; Sen. Simon Research Fellow, Manchester Univ., 1967–68; Asst Under-Sec. of State, Dept of Employment and Productivity (Research and Planning Div.), 1968–71; Dir, Office of Manpower Economics, 1971–73; Under-Sec., Manpower Gen. Div., Dept of Employment, 1973–74; Sec., Manpower Services Commn, 1974–75. Mem., Employment Appeal Tribunal, 1986–96. Chm., Bd of Govs. Volunteer Centre UK, 1989–93. *Recreations:*

Rugby (Oxford Blue), golf, fishing. *Address:* The Orangery, Alde House, Aldeburgh, Suffolk IP15 5EE. *T:* (01728) 452594.
  See also G. M. Moore.

GALBRAITH, Samuel Laird; *b* 18 Oct. 1945. *Educ:* Glasgow Univ. (BSc Hons 1968; MB ChB Hons 1971; MD 1977); FRCSGlas 1975. Consultant in Neurosurgery, Gtr Glasgow Health Bd, 1978–87. MP (Lab) Strathkelvin and Bearsden, 1987–2001. Opposition spokesman on Scottish affairs and health, 1988–92, on employment, 1992–93; Parly Under-Sec. of State, Scottish Office, 1997–99. Scottish Parliament: Mem. (Lab) Strathkelvin and Bearsden, 1999–2001; Minister: for Children and Educn, Culture and the Arts and Sport, 1999–2000; for the Envmt, 2000–01. *Publication:* An Introduction to Neurosurgery, 1983.

GALE, Baroness *cr* 1999 (Life Peer), of Blaenrhondda in the county of Mid Glamorgan; **Anita Gale;** General Secretary, Wales Labour Party, 1984–99; *b* 28 Nov. 1940; *d* of late Arthur and Lillian Gale; *m* 1959 (marr. diss. 1983); two *d. Educ:* Pontypridd Tech. Coll.; University Coll., Cardiff (BSc Econ). Clothing factory machinist and shop asst, 1955–69; returned to full-time educn, 1969–76; Women's Officer and Asst Organiser, Wales Labour Party, 1976–84. Member: Inf. Select Cttee, H of L, 2001–04; Jt Cttee on Statutory Instruments, 2004–07; (co-opted) Sub Cttee G, EU Select Cttee, 2006–; Parly Delegn, Council of Europe, 2008–. All Party Parliamentary Groups: Member: British/Taiwan, 2002–; Penal Affairs, 2007–; Jt Sec., Children in Wales; Vice-Chm., Smoking and Health, Belize, 2007–; Chm., Parkinson's Disease, 2008–; Mem., Associate Parly Gp on animal welfare, 2000– (Vice-Chm., 2000–01; Jt Sec., 2001–). Vice-Chm., Labour Animal Welfare Soc., 1999–. Mem., IPU, 1999–. Comr for Wales, Women's Nat. Commn, 2004–. Pres., Treherbert and Dist Br., RBL, 2000–; Patron, Kidney Wales Foundn, 2008–. *Recreations:* walking, swimming, gardening. *Address:* House of Lords, SW1A 0PW. *T:* (020) 7219 8511; *e-mail:* galea@parliament.uk.

GALE, Audrey Olga Helen; *see* Sander, A. O. H.

GALE, Prof. Edwin Albert Merwood, FRCP; Professor of Diabetic Medicine, Bristol University, since 1997; *b* 21 March 1945; *s* of George Edwin Gale and Carole Fisher Gale; *m* 1982, Lone Brogaard; one *s* two *d. Educ:* Sevenoaks Sch.; Sidney Sussex Coll., Cambridge (MA, MB BChir). Sen. Lectr, 1984–92, Prof. of Diabetes, 1992–97, St Bartholomew's Hosp. *Publications:* (with R. B. Tattersall) Diabetes: clinical management, 1990; papers on causes, prediction and possible prevention of type 1 diabetes. *Recreations:* ancient coins, fossils. *Address:* 9 Carnarvon Road, Bristol BS6 7DR. *T:* (0117) 924 3123.

GALE, (Gwendoline) Fay, AO 1989; PhD; FASSA; President: Association of Asian Social Science Research Councils, 2001–03; Academy of the Social Sciences in Australia, 1998–2000; *b* 13 June 1932; *d* of Rev. George Jasper Gilding and Kathleen Gertrude Gilding; one *s* one *d. Educ:* Adelaide Univ. (BA 1952, Hons I 1954; PhD 1962). University of Adelaide: Lectr, 1966–71; Sen. Lectr, 1972–74; Reader, 1975–77; Prof., 1978–89; Pro-Vice-Chancellor, 1988–89; Vice-Chancellor, Univ. of WA, 1990–97. Pres., Australian Vice-Chancellors' Cttee, 1996–97. Comr, Australian Heritage Commn, 1989–95. Mem. Nat. Cttee, UNESCO, 1999–2005. Elin Wagner Fellow, 1971; Catherine Helen Spence Fellow, 1972. FASSA 1978. Hon. Life Fellow, Inst. of Australian Geographers, 1994 (Pres., 1989). DUniv Adelaide, 1994; Hon. DLitt WA, 1998. British Council Award, 1972; John Lewis Gold Medal, RGS, SA, 2000; Griffith Taylor Medal, Inst. of Aust. Geographers, 2001. *Publications:* Race Relations in Australia: the Aboriginal situation, 1975; Urban Aborigines, 1972; Poverty among Aboriginal families in Adelaide, 1975; Adelaide Aborigines, a case study of urban life 1966–81, 1982; We are bosses ourselves: the status and role of Aboriginal women today, 1983; Tourists and the National Estate: procedures to protect Australia's heritage, 1987; Aboriginal youth and the criminal justice system: the injustice of justice, 1990; Changing Australia, 1991; Inventing Places: studies in cultural geography, 1992; Juvenile Justice: debating the issues, 1993; Tourism and the Protection of Aboriginal Cultural Sites, 1994; (ed) Cultural Geographics, 1999; (ed) Youth in Transition: the challenges of generational change in Asia, 2005. *Recreations:* bush walking, music, theatre. *Address:* c/o Vice Chancellory, University of Adelaide, North Terrace, Adelaide, SA 5005, Australia.

GALE, John, OBE 1987; theatre producer; *b* 2 Aug. 1929; *s* of Frank Haith Gale and Martha Edith Gale (née Evans); *m* 1950, Liselotte Ann (née Wratten); two *s. Educ:* Christ's Hospital; Webber Douglas Academy of Dramatic Art. Formerly an actor; presented his first production, Inherit the Wind, London, 1960; has since produced or co-produced, in London, British provinces, USA, Australia, New Zealand and S Africa, over 80 plays, including: Candida, 1960; On the Brighter Side, 1961; Boeing-Boeing, 1962; Devil May Care, 1963; Windfall, 1963; Where Angels Fear to Tread, 1963; The Wings of the Dove, 1963; Amber for Anna, 1964; Present Laughter, 1964, 1981; Maigret and the Lady, 1965; The Platinum Cat, 1965; The Sacred Flame, 1966; An Evening with G. B. S., 1966; A Woman of No Importance, 1967; The Secretary Bird, 1968; Dear Charles, 1968; Highly Confidential, 1969; The Young Churchill, 1969; The Lionel Touch, 1969; Abelard and Héloïse, 1970; No Sex, Please—We're British, 1971; Lloyd George Knew My Father, 1972; The Mating Game, 1972; Parents' Day, 1972; At the End of the Day, 1973; Birds of Paradise, 1974; A Touch of Spring, 1975; Separate Tables, 1977; The Kingfisher, 1977; Sextet, 1977; Cause Célèbre, 1977; Shut Your Eyes and Think of England, 1977; Can You Hear Me at the Back?, 1979; Middle Age Spread, 1979; Private Lives, 1980; A Personal Affair, 1982. The Secretary Bird and No Sex, Please—We're British set records for the longest run at the Savoy and Strand Theatres respectively; No Sex, Please—We're British is the longest running comedy in the history of World Theatre and passed 6,000 performances at the Garrick Theatre in Nov. 1985. Chichester Festival Theatre: Exec. Producer, 1983–84; Director, 1984–89. Director: John Gale Productions Ltd, 1960–90; Gale Enterprises Ltd, 1960–90; West End Managers Ltd, 1972–89; Lisden Productions Ltd, 1975–90. President, Soc. of West End Theatre Managers, 1972–75; Chm., Theatres National Cttee, 1979–85. Governor, 1976–, and Almoner, 1978–95, Christ's Hospital; Chm. of Govs, Guildford Sch. of Acting, 1989–2000. Member, Amicable Soc. of Blues, 1981–. Liveryman, Gold and Silver Wyredrawers Company, 1974. FRSA 1990. *Recreations:* travel, Rugby. *Address:* East Dean Cottage, East Dean, near Chichester, W Sussex PO18 0JA. *T:* (01243) 811407. *Clubs:* Garrick; London Welsh Rugby Football (Richmond) (Chairman, 1979–81).

GALE, Michael; QC 1979; a Recorder of the Crown Court, 1977–97; *b* 12 Aug. 1932; *s* of Joseph Gale and Blossom Gale; *m* 1963, Joanna Stephanie Bloom; one *s* two *d. Educ:* Cheltenham Grammar Sch.; Grocers' Sch.; King's Coll., Cambridge (Exhibnr; BA History and Law, 1954, MA 1958). National Service, Royal Fusiliers and Jt Services Sch. for Linguists, 1956–58. Called to the Bar, Middle Temple, 1957, Bencher, 1988; Harmsworth Law Scholar, 1958. Mem., Gen. Council of the Bar, 1987–94; Legal Assessor: GMC, 1995–; GDC, 1995–; Gen. Osteopathic Council, 1998–; CIPFA, 2000–; Chm., Review and Complaints Cttee, Nat. Heritage Meml Fund and Heritage Lottery Fund, 1996–2001. *Publications:* jointly: A Guide to the Crime (Sentences) Act, 1997; Fraud and the PLC, the Criminal Justice and Police Act 2001: a guide for practitioners, 1999. *Recreations:* the arts and country pursuits. *Address:* 1 King's Bench Walk, Temple, EC4Y 7DB. *T:* (020) 7936 1500. *Clubs:* Garrick, MCC.

GALE, Michael Denis, PhD; FRS 1996; John Innes Professor, University of East Anglia, 2000–03, now Professorial Fellow, School of Biological Sciences; Associate Research Director, John Innes Centre, Norwich, 1994–98, 1999–2003, now John Innes Foundation Emeritus Fellow (Research Director, 1999); *b* 25 Aug. 1943; *s* of Sydney Ralph Gale and Helen Mary (*née* Johnson); *m* 1979, Susan Heathcote Rosbotham; two *d. Educ:* W Buckland Sch., Barnstaple; Birmingham Univ. (BSc Hons); UCW, Aberystwyth (PhD). Plant Breeding Institute, subseq. AFRC Institute of Plant Science Research, Cambridge: Researcher, 1968–86; Head, Cereals Res. Dept, and Individual Merit SPSO, Cambridge Lab., 1986–92; Head of Cambridge Lab., Norwich, 1992–94. Mem., Consultative Gp on Internat. Agricultural Res., Science Council, 2004–. Farrer Meml Bicentennial Fellow, NSW Dept of Agric., 1989; Hon. Res. Prof., Inst. of Crop Germplasm Resources, Acad. Sinica, 1992. Advr, Inst. of Genetics, Beijing, 1992; Chm., Internat. Adv. Bd, Chinese Acad. of Agricl Sci., 2007–. Foreign Fellow, Chinese Acad. of Engrg, 1999. Hon. DSc Birmingham, 2005; Hon. Dr, Norwegian Univ. of Life Scis, Ås, Norway, 2005. Res. Medal, RASE, 1994; Rank Prize for Nutrition, 1997; Darwin Medal, Royal Soc., 1998. *Publications:* 300 scientific papers and articles on plant genetics and cytogenetics, esp. dwarfism, quality and genome res. in wheat. *Recreations:* golf, poker (Dropsy Champion, Llangollen, 2002, 2004). *Address:* John Innes Centre, Norwich Research Park, Colney, Norwich NR4 7UH. *T:* (01603) 450000. *Club:* Royal Norwich Golf.

GALE, Roger James; MP (C) North Thanet, since 1983; *b* Poole, Dorset, 20 Aug. 1943; *s* of Richard Byrne Gale and Phyllis Mary (*née* Rowell); *m* 1st, 1964, Wendy Dawn Bowman (marr. diss. 1967); 2nd, 1971, Susan Sampson (marr. diss.); one *d*; 3rd, 1980, Susan Gabrielle Marks; two *s. Educ:* Southbourne Prep. Sch.; Hardye's Sch., Dorchester; Guildhall Sch. of Music and Drama (LGSM). Freelance broadcaster, 1963–72; freelance reporter, BBC Radio, London, 1972–73; Producer, Current Affairs Gp, BBC Radio (progs included Newsbeat and Today), 1973–76; Producer/Dir, BBC Children's Television, 1976–79; Producer/Dir, Thames TV, and Editor, teenage unit, 1979–83. Joined Conservative Party, 1964; Mem., Cttee, Greater London Young Conservatives, 1964–65. PPS to Minister of State for Armed Forces, 1992–94. Member: Select Cttee on Televising of Proceedings of the House, 1988–91; Home Affairs Select Cttee, 1990–92; Broadcasting Select Cttee, 1997–2005; All Party Parly Gp, Fund for Replacement of Animals in Med. Experiments, 1983–86; Chm., All Party Animal Welfare Gp, 1992–98; Mem., Chairman's Panel, 1997–. Vice Chm., Cons. Party, 2001–03. Founding Mem., Police and Parlt Scheme, 1996. Delegate, Council of Europe, 1987–89. Contested Birmingham, Northfield, Oct. 1982 (Lab. majority, 289). Mem., Gen. Council, BBC, 1992–94. Founder, East Kent Development Assoc., 1984–86. Fellow: Industry and Parlt Trust, 1985; Parlt and Armed Forces Fellowship, 1992; Postgrad. Fellowship, Parlt Armed Forces Scheme, 2001–02. Pres., Cons. Animal Welfare Gp, 2003–. Special Constable, British Transport Police, 2003–06. *Recreations:* swimming, sailing. *Address:* House of Commons, Westminster, SW1A 0AA; *e-mail:* galerj@parliament.uk. *Clubs:* Farmers, Lord's Taverners; Kent County Cricket.

GALE, William Stuart; QC (Scot) 1993; *b* 10 June 1955; *s* of William Grimshaw Gale and Patricia Sheila (*née* Nicol); *m* 1981, Michele Marie Keklak (marr. diss.); one *d. Educ:* Univ. of Dundee (LLB Hons 1977); Tulane Univ., New Orleans (LLM 1978). Advocate of Scottish Bar, 1980–93; Standing Jun. Counsel to FCO in Scotland, 1987–93. *Recreation:* modern jazz. *Address:* Dalshian, Western Road, Auchterarder, Perthshire PH3 1JJ.

GALIONE, Prof. Antony Giuseppe, PhD; Professor of Pharmacology and Head, Department of Pharmacology, University of Oxford, since 2006; Fellow, Lady Margaret Hall, Oxford and Extraordinary Lecturer in Biochemical Pharmacology, New College, Oxford, since 2006; *b* Chelmsford, 13 Sept. 1963; *s* of Angelo and Margaret Galione; *m* 1992, Angela Clayton. *Educ:* Felsted (Lord Butler of Saffron Walden Schol.); Trinity Coll., Cambridge (Sen. Schol.; BA 1985; PhD 1989). Harkness Fellow, 1989–91, Dmitri d'Arbeloff Fellow in Biol., 1990–91, John Hopkins Univ.; University of Oxford: Beit Meml Fellow for Med. Res., Dept of Pharmacol., 1991–94; Hayward Jun. Res. Fellow, Oriel Coll., 1992–95; Lectr in Med. Scis, St Hilda's Coll., 1993–95; Wellcome Trust Career Develt Fellow, Dept of Pharmacol., 1994–97; Staines Med. Res. Fellow, Exeter Coll., 1995–98; Lectr in Molecular and Cellular Biochem., St Catherine's Coll., 1997–98; Wellcome Trust Sen. Fellow in Basic Biomed. Sci., Dept of Pharmacol., 1997–2005; Fellow and Tutor in Biochem. Pharmacol., New Coll., 1998–2005; Titular Prof. of Pharmacol., 2002–05. Herbert Rand Vis. Fellow, Marine Biol Lab., Woods Hole, Mass, 1993. Ed., Biochem. Jl, 1997–2006; Mem., Editl Bd, Zygote, 1998–. Mem., Physiol. and Pharmacol. Panel, 2002–05, Basic Sci. Interest Cttee, 2006–, Wellcome Trust. Member: Amer. Biophysical Soc., 1995–; British Marine Biol Assoc., 1995–; British Pharmacol Soc., 1997–; British Neurosci. Assoc., 1997–. Novartis Prize, British Pharmacol Soc., 2001. *Publications:* contrib. scientific papers on cell signalling to jls incl. Nature, Science and Cell. *Recreations:* Egyptology, cats, Jack Russell terriers, gardening. *Address:* Department of Pharmacology, Oxford University, Mansfield Road, Oxford OX1 3QT. *T:* (01865) 271862, *Fax:* (01865) 271850; *e-mail:* antony.galione@pharm.ox.ac.uk.

GALL, Anthony Robert S.; *see* Scott-Gall.

GALL, Henderson Alexander, (Sandy), CBE 1988; freelance writer and broadcaster; Foreign Correspondent, Independent Television News, 1963–92 (Newscaster, 1968–90); *b* 1 Oct. 1927; *s* of Henderson Gall and Jean Begg; *m* 1958, Eleanor Mary Patricia Ann Smyth; one *s* three *d. Educ:* Glenalmond; Aberdeen Univ. (MA). Foreign Correspondent, Reuters, 1953–63, Germany, E Africa, Hungary, S Africa, Congo; joined ITN, 1963, working in Middle East, Africa, Vietnam, Far East, China, Afghanistan; Newscaster on News at Ten, 1970–90; Producer/Presenter/Writer, documentaries on: King Hussein, 1972; Afghanistan, 1982, 1984, 1986; Cresta Run, 1984; George Adamson: lord of the lions, 1989; Richard Leakey, the man who saved the animals, 1995; Empty Quarter, 1996; Veil of Fear (Taliban rule in Afghanistan), 1996; Imran's Final Test, 1997; Sandy's War: face of the Taliban, 2001; Afghanistan: war without end, 2004. Chm., Sandy Gall's Afghanistan Appeal, 1983–. Rector, Aberdeen Univ., 1978–81 (Hon. LLD, 1981). Sitara-i-Pakistan, 1986; Lawrence of Arabia Medal, RSAA, 1987. *Publications:* Gold Scoop, 1977; Chasing the Dragon, 1981; Don't Worry About the Money Now, 1983; Behind Russian Lines, 1983; Afghanistan: Agony of a Nation, 1988; Salang, 1989; Lord of the Lions, 1991; News from the Front, 1994; The Bushmen of Southern Africa: slaughter of the innocent, 2001. *Recreations:* golf, gardening, swimming. *Address:* Doubleton Oast House, Penshurst, Tonbridge, Kent TN11 8JA. *Clubs:* Turf, Saints and Sinners; Rye Golf; St Moritz Tobogganing (Hon. Mem.).

GALLACHER, Bernard, OBE 1996; professional golfer; golf professional, Wentworth Golf Club, 1975–96; *b* 9 Feb. 1949; *s* of Bernard and Matilda Gallacher; *m* 1974, Lesley Elizabeth Wearmouth; one *s* two *d. Educ:* St Mary's Academy, Bathgate. Golf tournaments won: Scottish Open Amateur Championship, 1967; PGA Schweppes, W. D. & H. O. Wills Open, 1969; Martini Internat., 1971, 1982; Carrolls Internat., 1974; Dunlop Masters, 1974, 1975; Spanish Open, 1977; French Open, 1979; Tournament Playe Championship, 1980; Gtr Manchester Open, 1981; Jersey Open, 1982, 1984. Har Vardon Trophy, 1969. Scottish Professional Champion, 1971, 1973, 1974, 1977, 198 Ryder Cup Team, 1969, 1971, 1973, 1975, 1977, 1979, 1981, 1983, European Captai 1991, 1993, 1995. Pres., Golf Foundn, 1996–2001. *Publications:* (with Mark Wilso Teach Yourself Golf, 1988; (with Renton Laidlaw) Captain at Kiawah, 1991. *Recreatio* walking dogs, reading. *Address:* c/o Wentworth Club, Virginia Water, Surrey GU25 4L

GALLACHER, John; HM Diplomatic Service, retired; *b* 16 July 1931; *s* of John Gallach and Catherine Gallacher (*née* Crilly); *m* 1956, Eileen Agnes (*née* McGuire); one *s. Ed* Our Lady's High School, Motherwell. Nat. Service, RAF, 1950–52. Kenya Polic 1953–65 (retired as Supt of Police, 1965); Libyan Govt (attached to Min. of Interio 1965–67; FCO, 1967–70; Lagos, 1970–73; FCO, 1973–74; Kuwait, 1974–77; FCO 197 Counsellor, FCO, 1983–84. Gp Security Advr, Gallaher Ltd, 1985–91; Rep. (Scotlan Control Risks Gp, 1992–98. *Recreations:* reading, golf, travel, gardening. *Address:* 1 Lochend Road, Gartcosh, Glasgow G69 8BB.

GALLAGHER, Ann; Head of Collections (British Art), Tate, since 2006; *b* Nottingha 14 May 1957; *d* of Eugene Gallagher and Diana Gallagher (*née* Greaves); *m* 2001, Dav Batchelor. *Educ:* Mackie Acad., Stonehaven; Bedford Coll., Univ. of London (BA Hon Nigel Greenwood Gall., London, 1984–89; Dir, Anthony Reynolds Gall., Londo 1989–94; Sen. Curator, Visual Arts Dept, British Council, London, 1994–2005; H British Art Post 1900, Tate Collection, London, 2005–06. Mem. of Faculty, British Sc at Rome, 2005–. Trustee, Whitechapel Art Gall., London, 2008–. *Publications:* (ed) Rach Whiteread, 1997; Landscape, 2000; (ed) Mark Wallinger, 2001; Still Life, 2002; Sodio Asfalto, 2004; Chris Ofili: the Upper Room, 2006. *Recreations:* architecture and desig film, literature. *Address:* c/o Tate, Millbank, SW1P 4RG.

GALLAGHER, Edward Patrick, CBE 2001; FREng, FIET, FCIWEM; Cha Energywatch, 2004–March 2009; Renewable Fuels Agency, since 2008; *b* 4 Aug. 1944; 1969, Helen Wilkinson; two *s. Educ:* Univ. of Sheffield (BEng Hons; Diploma in Busine Studies; Mappin Medal, 1966; John Brown Award, 1966). MRI 1992. Systems Analy Vauxhall Motors, 1963–68; Corporate Planning Manager, Sandoz Products, 1968–7 Computer Services Manager, Robinson Willey, 1970–71; with Black and Decke 1971–86: Director: Marketing Services, 1978–79; Service and Distribn, 1979–81; Busine Analysis, 1981–83; Market and Product Develt, 1983–86; Amersham International: Dir Corporate Develt, 1986–88; Divl Chief Exec., 1988–90; Mfg Dir, 1990–92; Chi Executive and Board Member: NRA, 1992–95; EA, 1995–2001. Dir, ECUS Ltd, 2001 Chm., Enviro-fresh Ltd, 2003–06. Vice-Pres., Council for Envmtl Educn, 1997–200 Mem. Bd and Chm. Audit Cttee, English Nature, 2001–06; Mem., NCC, 2008–. Chn Pesticides Forum, DEFRA, 2003–06. A CS Comr, 2001–06. Middlesex University: V Prof., Business Sch. and Faculty of Technol., 1994–97, Sch. of Health, Biol and Envm Sci., 1997–; Mem., Faculty of Technol. Adv. Gp, 1994–97; Gov., 1994–2004 (Chm., F of Govs, 2001–04); Chairman: Audit Cttee, 1995–2000; Planning and Resources Ctte 2000–01; Governance Cttee, 2000–01; Bristol University: Mem. Council, 1994–9 Mem. Finance Adv. Gp, 1994–2001; Chm. Adv. Bd, Centre for Social and Econ. Res. Global Envmt, UEA, 2004–08 (Mem., 2001–04). Mem. Council, 1998–2001, Mem Envmt and Energy Policy Cttee, 1999–2002 (Chm., 2002–04), IEE; Royal Academy Engineering: Mem., Sustainable Develt Educn Panel, 1999–2003; Mem., Awards Ctte 2001–04; Chm., Health, Safety and Envmt Cttee, EEF, 2001–04. Patron, Envm Industries Commn, 2001–. Trustee: Living Again Trust, Royal Hosp. for Neurodisabili (formerly Royal Hosp. and Home, Putney), 1993–2003; Envmtl Vision, 2001– (Chn 2004–). FRSA 1995–2007; CCMI (CIMgt 1996). Freeman, City of London; Liveryma Co. of Water Conservators (Mem., Ct of Assistants, 1999–2001). Hon. DEng Sheffiel 1996; Hon. DSc: Tomsk, 1998; Plymouth, 1998; Brunel, 1999; DUniv Middx, 200 *Recreations:* tennis, theatre, walking, guitar, clocks. *Address:* Renewable Fuels Agenc Ashdown House, Sedlescombe Road North, Hastings, East Sussex TN37 7GA.

GALLAGHER, Eileen Rose; Co-owner, co-founder, and Chief Executive, Sh Productions plc, since 1998; *b* 26 Nov. 1959; *d* of Mathew Gallagher and Christir McAvoy. *Educ:* Glasgow Univ. (MA Hons Politics); UC Cardiff (Dip. Journalism Freelance journalist, 1980–84; Scottish Television: Press Officer, 1984–87; Head Programme Planning, 1987–91; Head of Broadcasting Div., 1991–92; Dir Broadcasting, 1992–94; Man. Dir, Granada/LWT Broadcasting, then Man. Dir, LWT an Dep. Man. Dir, Granada UK Broadcasting, 1994–98; Man. Dir, Ginger TV, 199 Director: Granada, 1995–98; LWT, 1995–98. *Address:* Shed Productions, 2 Holford Yar WC1X 9HD.

GALLAGHER, (Francis George) Kenna, CMG 1963; HM Diplomatic Service, retire *b* 25 May 1917; *er s* of late George and Johanna Gallagher. *Educ:* St Joseph's Coll.; King Coll., University of London (LLB (Hons)). Served in HM Forces, 1941–45; apptd Mem., HM Foreign (subseq. Diplomatic) Service, 1945; Vice-Consul Marseille 1946–48; HM Embassy, Paris, 1948–50; FO, 1950–53; First Sec., HM Embass Damascus, 1953–55; FO, 1955; appointed Counsellor and Head of European Econom Organisations Dept, 1960; Counsellor (Commercial), HM Embassy, Berne, 1963–6 Head of Western Economic Dept, CO, 1965–67, of Common Market Dept, 1967–6 Asst Under-Sec. of State, FCO, 1968–71; Ambassador and Head of UK Delegn to OECI 1971–77. Consultant on Internat. Trade Policy, CBI, 1978–80. *Recreations:* musi reading. *Address:* 37 Howard Terrace, Morpeth, Northumberland NE61 1HT. *T:* (0167 504384.

GALLAGHER, Francis Xavier, OBE 1986; HM Diplomatic Service, retired; Head Panel 2000 Unit, Foreign and Commonwealth Office, 1998; *b* 28 March 1946; *s* of F. H. Gallagher and Carmen Gallagher (*née* Wilson); *m* 1981, Marie-France Martine Guille one *d. Educ:* Oxford Univ. (Chancellor's Essay and Matthew Arnold Meml Prizes; BA BPhil). Tutor, Villiers Park Educnl Trust, Oxon, 1970; joined FCO, 1971: MECAS Lebanon, 1972–74; served FCO, Beirut, Khartoum, Kuwait, NY, 1974–95; Dep. Hd Mission, Copenhagen, 1995–98. Officier, Ordre National du Lion (Senegal), 198 *Recreations:* music, walking. *Address:* 23 Queen's Gate Terrace, SW7 5PR.

GALLAGHER, James Daniel, CB 2005; FRSE; Director General, Devolution, Minist of Justice and Cabinet Office, since 2007; Visiting Professor of Government, Universit of Glasgow; *s* of William Gallagher and Bridget Gallagher (*née* Hart); *m* 1978, Una Ma Green; one *s* two *d. Educ:* Glasgow Univ. (BSc Hons Chemistry and Nat. Phil. 1976 Edinburgh Univ. (MSc Public Policy 1986). Joined Scottish Office, 1976: Private Sec. t Minister for Home Affairs, 1979; Head of Criminal Policy and Procedure Brs, 1981–8 Sec., Mgt Gp, 1985–88; Head of Urban Policy Div., 1988–89; Private Sec. to successiv Secs of State for Scotland, 1989–91; Dir (Human Resources), Scottish Prison Servic 1991–96; Hd, Local Govt Finance Gp, later Local Govt and Europe Gp, Scottish Offic 1996–99; Dep. Head of Economic and Domestic Secretariat, Cabinet Office, 1999; Polic Advr, Prime Minister's Policy Unit, 1999–2000; Hd, Scottish Exec. Justice Dep 2000–04; Prof. of Govt, Univ. of Glasgow, 2005–07 (on secondment). Vis. Prof., Centr for Ethics in Public Policy and Corporate Life, Glasgow Caledonian Univ., 2005–

Director: Scottish Mutual Assurance, 1999–2003; Abbey National Life, 1999–2003; Scottish Provident Life Assurance, 2001–03; Chm., Supervisory Cttee, Scottish Provident, 2003–; Mem., Abbey Nat. Policy Holder Review Cttee, 2003–06. FRSE 2007. *Address:* Ministry of Justice, Selborne House, 54 Victoria Street, SW1E 6QW.

GALLAGHER, Kenna; *see* Gallagher, F. G. K.

GALLAGHER, Sister Maire Teresa, CBE 1992 (OBE 1987); SND; Sister Superior, Convent of Notre Dame, Dumbarton, 1987–94, retired; *b* 27 May 1933; *d* of Owen Gallagher and Annie McVeigh. *Educ:* Notre Dame High Sch., Glasgow; Glasgow Univ. (MA Hons 1965); Notre Dame Coll. of Educn (Dip. 1953). Principal Teacher of History, Notre Dame High Sch., Glasgow, 1965–72; Lectr in Secondary Educn, Notre Dame Coll., 1972–74; Head Teacher, Notre Dame High Sch., Dumbarton, 1974–87. Chair, Scottish Consultative Council (formerly Scottish Consultative Cttee) on the Curriculum, 1987–91 (Mem., 1976–91; Chair, Secondary Cttee, 1983–87); Mem., Sec. of State's Cttee of Enquiry into Teachers' Pay and Conditions of Service, (Main Cttee), 1986; Pres., Scottish Br., Secondary Heads Assoc., 1980–82. Member: Central Council, Action of Churches Together in Scotland, 1990–2003 (Convener, 1999–2003); Assembly, CCBI, 1990–2002; Steering Cttee, CTBI, 2004–06. Fellow: SCOTVEC, 1989; Scottish Qualifications Authority, 1997. Hon. MEd CNAA, 1992. *Publications:* papers and articles in jls on teaching and management of schools. *Recreations:* homemaking skills, reading. *Address:* Sisters of Notre Dame, 65/67 Moorpark Avenue, Penilee, Glasgow G52 4ET. *T:* (0141) 810 4214.

GALLAGHER, Michael; consultant, Bellway Homes Ltd; *b* 1 July 1934; *s* of Michael and Annie Gallagher; *m* 1959, Kathleen Mary Gallagher; two *s* three *d*. *Educ:* Univ. of Nottingham; Univ. of Wales. Dip. General Studies. Branch Official, NUM, 1967–70; day release, Univ. of Nottingham, 1967–69; TUC scholarship, Univ. of Wales, 1970–72; Univ. of Nottingham, 1972–74. Councillor: Mansfield Borough Council, 1970–74; Nottinghamshire CC, 1973–81. Contested (Lab) Rushcliffe, general election, Feb. 1974; Member (Lab) Nottingham, European Parlt, 1979–83, (SDP) 1983–84; contested (SDP) Lancs Central, European elecn, 1984. *Recreations:* leisure, sports. *Address:* 4 Mansfield Road, Mansfield Woodhouse, Mansfield, Notts NG19 9JN.

GALLAGHER, Dame Monica (Josephine), DBE 1976; *m* 1946, Dr John Paul Gallagher, OAM, KCSG, KM; two *s* two *d*. Mem., Friends of St Mary's Cathedral, Sydney, 1994–2001 (Chm., 1984–87 and 1998–2001; Dep. Chm., 1988–93); Pres., Flower Festival Cttee, 1987–95, Dir, Flower Fest., 1996–97, St Mary's Cathedral; Mem. Cttee, Order of British Empire Assoc., NSW, 1995– (Vice-Pres., 1985–89; Pres., 1989–92); Vice-Pres., SCF, NSW, 1992–94; Member: Dr Horace Nowland Travelling Scholarship; Australian Church Women, NSW Div.; Adv. Bd, Fest. of Light; former Mem., Nursing Adv. Cttee, Australian Catholic Univ. (formerly Catholic Coll. of Educn), Sydney. Tour Guide, St Mary's Cathedral. State Pres., NSW, and Gen. Pres., Sydney Archdiocese, Catholic Women's League, Aust., 1972–80 (Nat. Pres., 1972–74); Past President: Catholic Central Cttee for Care of Aged; Catholic Women's Club, Sydney; Associated Catholic Cttee; Catholic Inst. of Nursing Studies. Former Member: Austcare; NSW Div., UNA; UN Status of Women Cttee; Exec. Bd, Mater Misericordiae Hosp., N Sydney; Bd, Gertrude Abbott Nursing Home; Selection Cttee, Queen Elizabeth II Silver Jubilee Trust; former Chm., YWCA Appeal Cttee, Sydney. Patron, Flower Club of NSW, 1999–. Good Citizen Award, Festival of Light, 1979; Papal Honour, Augustae Crucis Insigne pro Ecclesia et Pontifice, 1981; DCSG 2001. *Address:* Unit 92/2 Artarmon Road, Willoughby, NSW 2068, Australia.

GALLAGHER, Paul, CBE 1996; General Secretary, Amalgamated Engineering and Electrical Union, 1995–96; *b* 16 Oct. 1944; *s* of Joe and Annie Gallagher; *m* 1974, Madeleine. *Educ:* St Anne's, Droylesden, Manchester. Electrical, Electronic, Telecommunication and Plumbing Union: full-time officer, 1966–78; Exec. Councillor for Manchester and N Wales, 1978–91; Pres., 1986–91; Gen. Sec., 1992–95. Mem., HSC, 1990–96. *Recreations:* gardening, music, reading.

GALLAGHER, Thomas Joseph; Member (SDLP) Fermanagh and South Tyrone, Northern Ireland Assembly, since 1998; *b* 17 Aug. 1942; *s* of Thomas and Nellie Gallagher; *m* 1968, Eileen Carty; two *s* one *d*. *Educ:* St Joseph's Coll.; Queen's Univ., Belfast. Mem., NI Forum, 1996. Mem. (SDLP), Fermanagh DC, 1989. Contested (SDLP) Fermanagh and S Tyrone, 2001, 2005. Mem., Western Educn and Library Bd, 1989–. *Recreations:* Gaelic games, horse racing. *Address:* Keenaghan, Belleek, Co. Fermanagh BT93 3ES. *T:* (028) 6865 8355. *Club:* Erne Gaels Gaelic Football.

GALLEN, Hon. Sir Rodney (Gerald), KNZM 2000; QC 1976; High Court Judge, New Zealand, 1983–99; *b* 12 Aug. 1933; *s* of Gerald Collins Gallen and Eva Susan Ann Gallen. *Educ:* Victoria UC, Wellington (LLB). *Recreations:* gardening, music, reading. *Address:* Birchwood RD2, Hastings, New Zealand. *T:* (6) 8778499. *Clubs:* Wellington, Hawkes Bay.

GALLEY, Roy; Director, Planning, Post Office Property Holdings, 1998–2006; *b* 8 Dec. 1947; *s* of late Kenneth Haslam Galley and Letitia Mary Chapman; *m* 1976, Helen Margaret Butcher; one *s* one *d*. *Educ:* King Edward VII Grammar Sch., Sheffield; Worcester Coll., Oxford (MA). North-East Postal Bd, 1969–83: started as management trainee; Asst Controller, Projects (regional manager), 1980–83; Head of Project Control, London Building and Estates Centre, Royal Mail Letters, 1987–91; Royal Mail, London: Dir, Facilities, 1992–95; Dir, Restructuring, 1995–96; Dir, Operations, 1996–98. Chm., Kingston and Richmond (formerly Kingston and Esher) DHA, 1989–98. Member: Calderdale MBC, 1980–83; Maresfield Parish Council, 2006–; Wealden DC, 2007–. Conservator, Ashdown Forest, 2008. Chm., Yorks Young Conservatives, 1974–76; contested (C): Dewsbury, 1979; Halifax, 1987. MP (C) Halifax, 1983–87. Sec., Cons. Backbench Health Cttee, 1983–87; Mem., Social Services Select Cttee, 1984–87. Chm., Kingston and St George's Coll. of Nursing, 1993–96. Fellow, British Inst. of Facilities Mgt, 1997. *Recreations:* history, European literature, theatre, music, gardening, riding. *Address:* Fairplace Farm, Nutley, Uckfield, East Sussex TN22 3HE.

GALLI, Paolo; Italian Ambassador to the Court of St James's, 1995–99; *b* 10 Aug. 1934; *s* of Carlo Galli and Bianca Metral-Lambert; *m* 1959, Maria Giuliana Calioni; two *d*. *Educ:* Univ. of Padua (law degree). Entered Italian Diplomatic Service, 1958; Minister of State's Private Office, 1958–61; Vice Consul, Cardiff, 1961–63; Second Sec., Washington, 1963–65; First Sec., Co-ordination Dept, Sec.-Gen's Office, Min. for Foreign Affairs, 1965–68; First Sec., later Counsellor and First Counsellor, London, 1968–72; First Counsellor, Warsaw, 1972–75; Min. for Foreign Affairs, Econ. Affairs Dept, 1975–79; Foreign Minister's Private Office, 1979–80; Minister-Counsellor, Dep. Perm. Rep. to EEC, Brussels, 1980–85; promoted to rank of Minister, 1985; Ambassador to Warsaw, 1986–88; Dir-Gen., Aid and Co-operation Dept, Min. for Foreign Affairs, 1988–91; promoted to rank of Ambassador, 1989; Ambassador to Tokyo, 1992–95. Cavaliere di Gran Croce, Ordine al Merito della Repubblica Italiana, 1997. *Recreations:* classical music, the arts, fencing. *Address:* Zattere 1404, 30123 Venice, Italy.

GALLIANO, John Charles, CBE 2001; RDI 2002; Company Director and Couturier for Maison John Galliano, since 1984; Designer of Haute Couture and Prêt-à-Porter for Dior, since 1996; *b* 28 Nov. 1960. *Educ:* Wilson's Grammar Sch. for Boys; St Martin's Sch. of Art and Design (BA; Hon. Fellow, London Inst., 1997). Regular seasonal collections, 1985–. Designer of Haute Couture and Prêt-à-Porter for Givenchy, 1995–96. British Designer of the Year, British Fashion Council, 1987, 1994, 1995, 1997 (jtly); Telva Award for Best Internat. Designer, Mejor Creador International, 1995; VH1 Best Women's Wear Designer Award, 1998; Internat. Designer Award, Council of Fashion Designers of America, 1998. *Address:* 60 rue d'Avron, 75020 Paris, France. *T:* (1) 55251111, *Fax:* (1) 55251112.

GALLIE, Prof. Duncan Ian Dunbar, DPhil; FBA 1995; Professor of Sociology, University of Oxford, since 1996; Official Fellow, Nuffield College, Oxford, since 1985; *b* 16 Feb. 1946; *s* of Ian Gallie and Elsie (*née* Peers); *m* 1971, Martine Josephine Jurdant. *Educ:* St Paul's Sch., London (Scholar); Magdalen Coll., Oxford (Demyship; BA 1st Cl. Hons History); LSE (MSc); St Antony's Coll., Oxford (DPhil). Research Fellow, Nuffield Coll., Oxford, 1971–73; Lectr in Sociology, Univ. of Essex, 1973–79; Reader in Sociology, Univ. of Warwick, 1979–85; Dir, ESRC Social Change and Economic Life Initiative, 1985–90. Advr, Comité Nat. d'Evaluation de la Recherche, 1991; Member, Scientific Committee: IRESCO, 1989–93; IFRESI, 1993–98; Mem., EU Adv. Gp on Social Scis and Humanities in European Res. Area, 2002–. Vice-Pres., 2004–, and Foreign Sec., 2006–, British Acad. Dist. Contrib. to Scholarship Award, Amer. Sociol. Assoc., 1985. *Publications:* In Search of the New Working Class, 1978; Social Inequality and Class Radicalism in France and Britain, 1983; (ed jtly) New Approaches to Economic Life, 1985; (ed) Employment in Britain, 1988; (ed jtly) Social Change and the Experience of Unemployment, 1994; (ed jtly) Trade Unionism in Recession, 1996; (jtly) Restructuring the Employment Relationship, 1998; (ed jtly) Welfare Regimes and the Experience of Unemployment in Europe, 2000; (ed) Resisting Marginalization, 2004; articles in learned jls. *Recreations:* travelling, music, museum gazing. *Address:* Nuffield College, Oxford OX1 1NF. *T:* (01865) 278586; 149 Leam Terrace, Leamington Spa, Warwickshire CV31 1DF. *T:* (01926) 314941.

GALLIE, Philip Roy; Member (C) Scotland South, Scottish Parliament, 1999–2007; Managing Consultant, PG Business Advice, 1998–2007; *b* 3 June 1939; *s* of George Albert Gallie and Ivy Edith Gallie (*née* Williams); *m* 1964, Marion Wands Whyte; one *s* one *d*. *Educ:* Dunfermline High Sch.; Kirkcaldy Tech. Coll. MIPlantE; TE. Apprentice elect. fitter, HM Dockyard, Rosyth, 1955–60; Elect. Engineer, Ben Line Steamers, 1960–64; Electricity Supply Industry; Kincardine, Ironbridge and Inverkip Power Stations; SSEB Central Maint. Orgn; Galloway and Lanark Hydros and Inverkip Power Station (Manager, 1989–92). Dist Councillor, Cunninghame, 1980–84. Contested (C): Cunninghame South, 1983; Dunfermline West, 1987. MP (C) Ayr, 1992–97; contested (C) same seat, 1997, 2001. Vice-Chm., Scottish Cons. and Unionist Party, 1995–97; party spokesman on industry and economy, 1997–99, on justice and home affairs, 1999–2001, on constitutional and European affairs, 2001–07. Assoc. Mem., Prestwick Br., RAFA. *Recreations:* politics, sports. *Club:* Ayr Rugby Football.

GALLIFORD, Rt Rev. David George; Assistant Bishop, Diocese of York, since 1991; *b* 20 June 1925; *s* of Alfred Edward Bruce and Amy Doris Galliford; *m* 1st, 1954, Enid May Drax (*d* 1983); one *d*; 2nd, 1987, Claire Margaret Phoenix. *Educ:* Bede Coll., Sunderland; Clare Coll., Cambridge (Organ Scholar, 1942, BA 1949, MA 1951); Westcott House, Cambridge. Served 5th Royal Inniskilling Dragoon Guards, 1943–47. Curate of St John Newland, Hull, 1951–54; Minor Canon of Windsor, 1954–56; Vicar of St Oswald, Middlesbrough, 1956–61; Rector of Bolton Percy and Diocesan Training Officer, 1961–70; Canon of York Minster, 1969; Canon Residentiary and Treasurer of York Minster, 1970–75; Bishop Suffragan of Hulme, 1975–84; Bishop Suffragan of Bolton, 1984–91. SBStJ 1992. *Publications:* God and Christian Caring, 1973; Pastor's Post, 1975; (ed) Diocese in Mission, 1968. *Recreations:* music, composition, water colours. *Address:* 10 St Mary's Mews, Wigginton, York YO32 2SE. *T:* (01904) 761489.

GALLIGAN, Prof. Denis James, DCL; Professor of Socio-Legal Studies, and Director, Centre for Socio-Legal Studies, University of Oxford, since 1993; Fellow, Wolfson College, Oxford, since 1993; *b* 4 June 1947; *s* of John Felix Galligan and Muriel Maud Galligan; *m* 1972, Martha Louise Martinuzzi; one *s* one *d*. *Educ:* Univ. of Queensland (LLB 1970); Univ. of Oxford (BCL 1974; MA 1976; DCL 2000). Barrister, Supreme Court of Qld, 1970; called to the Bar, Gray's Inn, 1996. Rhodes Scholar, Magdalen Coll., Oxford, 1971–74; Lectr, Faculty of Law, UCL, 1974–76; Fellow, Jesus Coll., and CUF Lectr, Oxford Univ., 1976–81; Sen. Lectr, Univ. of Melbourne, 1982–84; Prof. of Law, Univ. of Southampton, 1985–92 (Dean, Law Faculty, 1987–90); Prof. of Law, Univ. of Sydney, 1990–92. Visiting Professor: Central European Univ., 1993–2004; Princeton Univ., 2002–; Jean Monnet Prof., Univ. of Siena, 2003–. AcSS 2000. *Publications:* Essays in Legal Theory, 1984; Law, Rights and the Welfare State, 1986; Discretionary Powers, 1986; Australian Administrative Law, 1993; Socio-Legal Readings in Administrative Law, 1995; Socio-Legal Studies in Context, 1995; Due Process and Fair Procedures, 1996; Administrative Justice in the New Democracies, 1998; Western Concepts of Administrative Law, 2002; Law and Informal Practices, 2003; Law and Modern Society, 2006. *Recreations:* reading, gardening. *Address:* Wolfson College, Linton Road, Oxford OX2 6UD; The Rosery, Beckley, Oxford OX3 9UU. *T:* (01865) 284220 and 351281.

GALLOP, Prof. Hon. Geoffrey (Ian), AC 2008; DPhil; Professor and Director, Graduate School of Government, University of Sydney, since 2006; *b* 27 Sept. 1951; *s* of Douglas and Eunice Gallop; *m* 1975, Beverley Jones; two *s*. *Educ:* Univ. of Western Australia (BEc); Murdoch Univ. (MPhil); St John's and Nuffield Colls, Oxford (MA, DPhil). Res. Fellow, Nuffield Coll., Oxford, 1979–81; Lectr in Social and Political Theory, Murdoch Univ., 1981–86. MLA (ALP) Victoria Park, WA, 1986–2006; Minister: for Educn, and Parly and Electoral Reform, 1990–91; for Fuel and Energy, Microecon. Reform, Parly and Electoral Reform, and Assisting the Treas., 1991–93; Leader of the Opposition, WA, 1996–2001; Premier of WA, 2001–06. FIPAA. Hon. DLitt Murdoch. *Publications:* (ed) Pigs' Meat: selected writings of Thomas Spence, 1982; A State of Reform: essays for a better future, 1998. *Recreations:* swimming, cricket, football. *Address:* Graduate School of Government, University of Sydney, Sydney, NSW 2006, Australia. *Clubs:* Swan Districts Football, West Coast Eagles.

GALLOWAY, 13th Earl of, *cr* 1623; **Randolph Keith Reginald Stewart;** Lord Garlies, 1607; Bt 1627, 1687; Baron Stewart of Garlies (GB), 1796; *b* 14 Oct. 1928; *s* of 12th Earl of Galloway, and Philippa Fendall (*d* 1974), *d* of late Jacob Wendell, New York; *S* father, 1978; *m* 1975, Mrs Lily May Budge, DLJ (*d* 1999), *y d* of late Andrew Miller, Duns, Berwickshire. *Educ:* Harrow. KLJ. *Heir: cousin* Andrew Clyde Stewart [*b* 13 March 1949; *m* 1977, Sara, *o d* of Brig. Patrick Pollock; one *s* two *d*]. *Address:* Castle Douglas, Kirkcudbrightshire.

GALLOWAY, Bishop of, (RC), since 2004; **Rt Rev. John Cunningham,** JCD; *b* 22 Feb. 1938. *Educ:* Blairs Coll.; St Peter's Coll., Cardross; Pontifical Scots Coll., Rome; Pontifical Gregorian Univ. (JCD). Ordained priest, 1961; Asst, Our Lady of Lourdes,

Bishopton, 1964–69; Chaplain, Moredun Convent, 1969–74; Asst Priest, St Columba's, Renfrew, 1974–86; Officialis, Scottish Nat. Tribunal, 1986–92; Parish Priest, St Patrick's, Greenock, 1992–2004; VG Paisley, 1997. Prelate of Honour, 1999. *Address:* Candida Casa, 8 Corsehill Road, Ayr KA7 2ST.

GALLOWAY, Alexander Kippen, CVO 2006; Clerk to the Company of Glaziers and Painters of Glass, since 2007; *b* 29 April 1952; *s* of late Alexander Kippen Galloway and Vera Eleanor Galloway; *m* 1st, 1973, Elaine Margaret Watkinson (marr. diss. 2005); three *s*; 2nd, 2006, Suzanne Lesley Phillips. *Educ:* Birkenhead Sch.; Jesus Coll., Oxford (MA Lit.Hum.); LLB Hons Open Univ. 2006. Department of the Environment: Exec. Officer, 1974; Principal, 1982; Private Sec. to Chancellor of Duchy of Lancaster, 1982–84, to Paymaster Gen., 1982–83 and 1984–85; Secretariat, Cabinet Office, 1992–93; Asst Sec., DoE, 1994–98; Clerk of the Privy Council, 1998–2006. Member: Architects' Registration Bd, 2007–; Professional Regulation Exec. Cttee (formerly Affairs Bd), Actuarial Profession, 2007–. Trustee, Projects in Partnership, (Chm., 1999–2004). Liveryman, Co. of Glaziers and Painters of Glass, 2006–. FRSA 2002. Hon. FSE 2004. *Recreations:* playing the cello, choral singing, ski-ing. *Address:* 19 Frythe Close, Kenilworth, Warwickshire CV8 2SY. *T:* (01926) 777569.

GALLOWAY, Prof. David Malcolm, PhD; FBPsS; Professor of Education, University of Durham, 1992–2001, now Emeritus (Head of School of Education, 1993–2000); *b* 5 July 1942; *s* of late Malcolm Ashby Galloway and Joan Dorah Frances Galloway (*née* Slater); *m* 1971, Christina Mary King; two *s* one *d*. *Educ:* St Edmund Hall, Oxford (BA Psychol., Phil. and Physiol. 1970; MA 1974); UCL (MSc Educnl Psychol. 1972); Sheffield City Poly (PhD 1980). FBPsS 1983. Educnl Psychologist and Sen. Educnl Psychologist, Sheffield LEA, 1972–79; Sen. Lectr, Victoria Univ. of Wellington, NZ, 1980–83; Lectr, UC Cardiff, 1983–87; Lectr and Reader in Educnl Res., Lancaster Univ., 1987–91. Chm., Assoc. for Child Psychology and Psychiatry, 1999–2001. *Publications:* books include: Schools and Persistent Absentees, 1985; (with C. Goodwin) The Education of Disturbing Children: pupils with learning and adjustment difficulties, 1987; (with A. Edwards) Primary School Teaching and Educational Psychology, 1991; (jtly) The Assessment of Special Educational Needs: whose problem?, 1994; (jtly) Motivating the Difficult to Teach, 1998; numerous articles in acad. and professional jls. *Recreations:* bee-keeping, fell search and mountain rescue (Chm., Kirkby Stephen Mountain Rescue Team, 2002–07). *Address:* Leases, Smardale, Kirkby Stephen, Cumbria CA17 4HQ.

GALLOWAY, George; MP (Respect) Bethnal Green and Bow, since 2005 (Glasgow, Hillhead, 1987–97, Glasgow Kelvin, 1997–2005; Lab 1987–2003, Ind Lab 2003–04, Respect 2004–05); *b* 16 Aug. 1954; *s* of George and Sheila Galloway; *m* 1st, 1979, Elaine Fyffe (marr. diss. 1999); one *d*; 2nd, Dr Amineh Abu-Zayyad (separated 2005); one *s* by Rima Husseini. *Educ:* Charleston Primary Sch.; Harris Acad., Dundee. Engrg worker, 1973; organiser, Labour Party, 1977; Gen. Sec., War on Want, 1983–87. Contested (Respect) London reg., EP elections, 2004. HQA (Pakistan), 1990; HPK (Pakistan), 1995. *Publications:* (jtly) Downfall: the Ceausescus and the Romanian revolution, 1991; I'm Not the Only One, 2004. *Recreations:* boxing, football, films, music. *Address:* House of Commons, SW1A 0AA. *T:* (020) 7219 4084.

GALLOWAY, Maj.-Gen. Kenneth Gardiner, CB 1978; OBE 1960; Director Army Dental Service, 1974–78; *b* 3 Nov. 1917; *s* of David and Helen Galloway, Dundee and Oban; *m* 1949, Sheila Frances (*née* Dunsmor); two *d* (one *s* decd). *Educ:* Oban High Sch.; St Andrews Univ. LDS 1939, BDS 1940. Lieut Army Dental Corps, 1940; Captain 1941; Major 1948; Lt-Col 1955; Col 1963; Brig. 1972; Maj.-Gen. 1974. Served in Egypt, Palestine, Syria and Iraq, 1942–46; Chief Instructor and 2nd in comd, Depot and Training Establishment, RADC, 1956–60; Malta and BAOR, 1960–67; Asst Dir Dental Service, MoD, 1967–71; Dep. Dir Dental Service: Southern Comd, 1971–72; BAOR, 1972–74. QHDS 1971–78. Col Comdt, RADC, 1980–83. OStJ 1960. *Recreations:* tennis, golf, gardening. *Address:* Berwyn Court, Avenue Road, Farnborough, Hants GU14 7BH. *T:* (01252) 544948.

GALLOWAY, Peter George, CBE 2006; Rector, Trinity Academy, Edinburgh, since 1983; *b* 21 March 1944; *s* of John and Mary Galloway; *m* 1971, Elizabeth Taylor; one *d*. *Educ:* Buckhaven High Sch.; Heriot-Watt Univ. (Dip Commerce 1966; BA 1970); Moray House Coll. Asst Rector, Royal High Sch., Edinburgh, 1976–80; Depute Head, James Gillespie's High, Edinburgh, 1980–83. Chm., Partnership Planning Gp, Enterprise in Educn, 2004–; Member: UK Council for European Educn, 1995–2000; Determined to Succeed Gp, 2001; Smith Gp, 2005–. Dir, Schools Enterprise Scotland Ltd, 2003–05. FRSA. *Recreations:* all sports, particularly Rugby, cricket and football as a spectator, golf as a player, travel, cooking. *Address:* 32 Bramdean Rise, Braids, Edinburgh EH10 6JR. *T:* (home) (0131) 447 3070, (office) (0131) 474 5050; *e-mail:* peter.galloway@trinity.edin.sch.uk. *Club:* Motonhall Golf.

GALLOWAY, Rev. Dr Peter John, OBE 1996; JP; Chaplain of the Queen's Chapel of the Savoy and of the Royal Victorian Order, since 2008; Visiting Professor in Politics and History, Brunel University, since 2008; *b* 19 July 1954; *s* of late Henry John Galloway and of Mary Selina (*née* Beshaw). *Educ:* Westminster City Sch.; Goldsmiths' Coll., Univ. of London (BA); King's Coll., London (PhD); St Stephen's House, Oxford. Ordained deacon, 1983; priest, 1984; Curate: St John's Wood, 1983–86; St Giles-in-the-Fields, 1986–90; Priest-in-charge, 1990–95, Vicar, 1995–2008, Emmanuel Church, W Hampstead; Warden of Readers, London Episcopal Area, 1987–92; Area Dean, N Camden, 2002–07; Surrogate, 2006–. Member: London Dio. Synod, 1997–2000; London Dio. Adv. Cttee, 2007–. St John Ambulance: Asst Dir-Gen., 1985–91; Dep. Dir-Gen., 1991–99; Chm., Nat. Publications Cttee, 1988–95; Order of St John: Mem., Chapter Gen., 1996–99; Mem., Priory of England Chapter, 1999–; Sub Dean, Priory of England, 1999–2007; Registrar, 2007–. Mem., Lord Chancellor's Adv. Cttee, 1994–2000 and 2005–. London University: Mem. Council, 1999–2008; Vice Chm. Convocation, 1999–2003 (Acting Chm., 2001–03); Chm., Convocation Trust, 2005–; Mem. Council, Goldsmiths' Coll., 1993–99 (Hon. Fellow, 1999); Chm., Goldsmiths' Soc., 1997–2007 (Vice-Chm., 1991–97); Mem. Council, Heythrop Coll., 2006–. Gov., Soho Parish Sch., 1989–91; Chm. of Governors, Emmanuel Sch., W Hampstead, 1990–2008; Patron, English Schs Orch., 1998–. Trustee, St Gabriel's Trust, 2001–04. Provost (formerly Chaplain), Imperial Soc. of Knights Bachelor, 2006–. Freeman, City of London, 1995; Liveryman, Glaziers' Co., 1998– (Freeman, 1997). JP City of London, 1989 (Dep. Chm., 2000, Chm., 2001–04, Bench); Dep. Chm., 2003, Chm., 2004, Gtr London Bench Chairmen's Forum. FSA 2000. KStJ 1997. *Publications:* The Order of St Patrick 1783–1983, 1983; Henry Falconar Barclay Mackay, 1983; (with Christopher Rawll) Good and Faithful Servants, 1988; The Cathedrals of Ireland, 1992; The Order of the British Empire, 1996; (jtly) Royal Service, 1996; The Most Illustrious Order, 1999; A Passionate Humility: Frederick Oakeley and the Oxford movement, 1999; The Cathedrals of Scotland, 2000; The Order of St Michael and St George, 2000; Companions of Honour, 2002; The Order of the Bath, 2006. *Recreations:* reading, writing, book collecting, solitude. *Address:* The Queen's Chapel of the Savoy, Savoy Hill, Strand, WC2R 0DA. *Club:* Athenæum.

GALPIN, Rodney Desmond; Chairman, Alpha Airports Group PLC, 1994–2002; *b* Feb. 1932; *s* of Sir Albert James Galpin, KCVO, CBE; *m* 1956, Sylvia Craven; one *s* one *d*. *Educ:* Haileybury and Imperial Service Coll. Joined Bank of England, 1952; Sec. t Governor (Lord Cromer), 1962–66; Dep. Principal, Discount Office, 1970–74; Dep Chief Cashier, Banking and Money Markets Supervision, 1974–78; Chief c Establishments, 1978–80; Chief of Corporate Services, 1980–82; Associate Dir, 1982–84 Exec. Dir, Bank of England, 1984–88; Chairman and Group Chief Executive: Standar Chartered plc, 1988–93; Standard Chartered Bank, 1988–93. Director: Cater Alle Holdings PLC, 1993–97; Capital Shopping Centres PLC, 1994–2000; Ascot (formerl Ascot Holdings) PLC, 1995–2001; P&O, 1996–2005; Abbey National Treasury Service PLC, 1997–2002. Chm., Independent Review Body (formerly Code of Banking Practi Review Cttee), 1994–99. Mem. Council, Foundn for Management Educn, 1984–86 Chm., Look Ahead Housing Assoc. Ltd, 1994–2003. Life Gov., 1973, and Council Mem 1973–2004, Haileybury; Mem. Council, Scout Assoc., 1972–. CCMI (FBIM 1979); FCI 1988. Freeman, City of London, 1981. OStJ. *Recreations:* tennis, gardening, music. *Addres* Alderman's Cottage, Lutmans Haven, Knowl Hill, Reading, Berks RG10 9YN. *Clu* Bankers' (Pres., 1992–93).

GALSWORTHY, Sir Anthony (Charles), KCMG 1999 (CMG 1985); HM Diplomati Service, retired; Adviser, Standard Chartered Bank, since 2002; Director, Bekaert SA since 2004; *b* 20 Dec. 1944; *s* of Sir Arthur Norman Galsworthy, KCMG, and Margar Agnes Galsworthy (*née* Hiscocks); *m* 1970, Jan Dawson-Grove; one *s* one *d*. *Educ:* St Paul Sch.; Corpus Christi Coll., Cambridge (MA). FCO, 1966–67; Hong Kong (languag training), 1967–69; Peking, 1970–72; FCO, 1972–77; Rome, 1977–81; Counsello Peking, 1981–84; Head of Hong Kong Dept, FCO, 1984–86; Principal Private Sec. t Sec. of State for Foreign and Commonwealth Affairs, 1986–88; seconded to RIIA 1988–89; Sen. British Rep., Sino-British Jt Liaison Gp, Hong Kong, 1989–93; Chief c Assessments Staff, Cabinet Office, 1993–95; Dep. Under Sec. of State, FCO, 1995–97 Ambassador to People's Republic of China, 1997–2002. Scientific Associate, Natural His Mus., 2001–. Member Council: British Trust for Ornithology, 2002–06; Wildfowl an Wetlands Trust, 2002–. Dir, Earthwatch (Europe), 2002–06. Hon. Prof., Kunming Ins of Botany, Chinese Acad. of Scis. Hon. Fellow, Royal Botanic Gdns, Edinburgh, 2001 *Recreations:* bird-watching, wildlife. *Club:* Oxford and Cambridge.

GALSWORTHY, (Arthur) Michael (Johnstone), CVO 2002; CBE 1999; Chairman Trewithen Estates Management Co., since 1979; Vice Lord-Lieutenant, Cornwall, sinc 2002; *b* 10 April 1944; *s* of Sir John Galsworthy, KCVO, CMG and late Jennifer Rut Johnstone; *m* 1st, 1972, Charlotte Helena Prudence Roberts (*d* 1989); one *s* two *d*; 2nd 1991, Sarah Christian Durnford; one *s* one *d*. *Educ:* Radley; St Andrews Univ. (MA Hons) International Harvester Corp., 1967–69; English China Clays PLC, 1970–82; Man. Di Hawkins Wright Associates, 1982–86. Local Adv. Dir, Barclays Bank, 1987–98. Mem Prince of Wales Council, 1985–2002; Dir, CoSIRA, 1985–88; a Develt Comr, 1987–92 Trustee, Rural Housing Trust, 1986–92; Chairman: Cornwall Rural Housing Assoc 1985–95; Royal Cornwall Hosps NHS Trust, 1991–93; Chm., In Pursuit of Excellenc Partnership for Cornwall, 1994–2000. Chm., Cornwall Co. Playing Fields, 1978–96; Di Woodard Corp. (W Region), 1983–87. Vice Pres., Royal Cornwall Agricl Assoc., 1987– FRAgS 2007; FZS 2008. Mem., Court of Assts, Goldsmiths' Co., 1998–. Chm. Counci Order of St John for Cornwall, 1995–99. DL Cornwall, 1993; High Sheriff, Cornwal 1994. *Publications:* In Pursuit of Excellence: testimonial of business in Cornwall, 1994; Th IPE Business Journal, 1996; The IPE Green Book Testimonial, 1997; A Wealth of Talen the best of crafts in Cornwall, 1998. *Recreations:* gardening, fishing, shooting, walkin *Address:* Trewithen, Grampound Road, near Truro, Cornwall TR2 4DD. *T:* (0172 882418. *Clubs:* Brooks's, Farmers.

GALTON, Bernard John; Director, Human Resources Group, Welsh Assembl Government, since 2004; *b* 5 July 1956; *s* of Roy and Kathleen Galton; *m* 1978, Susa Fox; two *s*. *Educ:* City of Bath Boys' Sch. Ministry of Defence, 1973–2004: Dir, HI Policy, 1996–98; HR Dir, Defence Aviation Repair Agency, 1998–2004. Chartere FCIPD (FCIPD 2001); Mem., BPsS. *Recreations:* reading, travelling, gym, good food an wine, family. *Address:* Welsh Assembly Government, Cathays Park, Cardiff CF10 3NQ *T:* (029) 2082 3695, *Fax:* (029) 2082 5021; *e-mail:* bernard.galton@wales.gsi.gov.uk.

GALTON, Raymond Percy, OBE 2000; author and scriptwriter, since 1951; *b* 17 Jul 1930; *s* of Herbert and Christina Galton; *m* 1956, Tonia Phillips (*d* 1995); one *s* two *d* *Educ:* Garth Sch., Morden. *Television:* with Alan Simpson: Hancock's Half Hour, 1954–6 (adaptation and translation, Fleksnes, Scandinavian TV, film and stage); Comed Playhouse, 1962–63; Steptoe and Son, 1962–74 (adaptations and translations: Sanford an Son, US TV; Stiefbeen and Zoon, Dutch TV; Albert och Herbert, Scandinavian TV, filn and stage); Galton-Simpson Comedy, 1969; Clochemerle, 1971; Casanova '74, 1974 Dawson's Weekly, 1975; The Galton and Simpson Playhouse, 1976–77; Paul Merton i Galton and Simpson's…, 1996, 1997; Fleksnes Fataliteter, Scandinavian TV, 2002; wit Johnny Speight: Tea Ladies, 1979; Spooner's Patch, 1979–80; with John Antrobus: Roon at the Bottom, 1986–87 (Banff TV Fest. Award for Best Comedy, 1987); Get Well Soon 1997; *films:* with Alan Simpson: The Rebel, 1960; The Bargee, 1963; The Spy with a Col Nose, 1966; Loot, 1969; Steptoe and Son, 1971; Steptoe and Son Ride Again, 1973; De Siste Fleksnes (Scandinavia), 1974; Die Skraphandlerne (Scandinavia), 1975; with Ala Simpson and John Antrobus: The Wrong Arm of the Law, 1963; with Andrew Galton Camping (Denmark), 1990; *theatre:* with Alan Simpson: Way Out in Piccadilly, 1966; Th Wind in the Sassafras Trees, 1968; Albert och Herbert (Sweden), 1981; Fleksne (Norway), 1983; Mordet på Skolgatan 15 (Sweden), 1984; with John Antrobus: Whe Did You Last See Your Trousers?, 1986, UK tour, 1994; Steptoe and Son in Murder a Oil Drum Lane, Comedy Th., 2006. Awards, with Alan Simpson: Scriptwriters of th Year, 1959 (Guild of TV Producers and Directors); Best TV Comedy Series, Steptoe an Son, 1962/3/4/5 (Screenwriters Guild); John Logie Baird Award (for outstandin contribution to Television), 1964; Best Comedy Series (Steptoe and Son, Dutch TV) 1966; Best comedy screenplay, Steptoe and Son, 1972 (Screenwriters Guild); Lifetim Achievement Award, Writers' Guild of GB, 1997. *Publications:* (with Alan Simpson) Hancock, 1961; Steptoe and Son, 1963; The Reunion and Other Plays, 1966; Hancoc Scripts, 1974; The Best of Hancock, 1986; The Best of Steptoe and Son, 1988. *Recreations* reading, worrying. *Address:* The Ivy House, Hampton Court, Middx KT8 9DD. *T:* (020 8977 1236; Tessa Le Bars Management, 54 Birchwood Road, Petts Wood, Kent BR 1NZ. *T:* (01689) 837084.

GALVIN, Bernard Vincent Joseph, CB 1991; Secretary to the Treasury, New Zealand 1980–86; *b* 15 March 1933; *s* of Eustace Bartholemew Galvin and Margaret Jean (*né* Lenihan); *m* 1st, 1960, Beverly Ann Snook (marr. diss. 1977); three *s* one *d*; 2nd, 1980 Margaret Clark. *Educ:* Univ. of NZ (BSc 1954); Victoria Univ. of Wellington (BA Hon 1959); Harvard Univ. (MPA 1961). Joined Treasury, NZ, 1955; Harkness Fellow, USA 1960–61; Econ. Counsellor, NZ High Commn, London, 1965–68; Treasury Dir, 1969 Asst Sec., 1972; Dep. Sec., 1974; Perm. Head of PM's Dept, 1975–80. Chm., Econ Develt Commn, 1986–89. Alternate Gov., World Bank, 1976–86. Chm., Ministeria Wkg Pty on Disability and Accident Compensation, 1991. Vis. Fellow, Inst. of Polic

Studies, 1989–98. Mem. Council, Victoria Univ. of Wellington, 1989–98 (Treas., 1990–96). *Publications:* Policy Co-ordination, Public Sector and Government, 1991; chapters in books on NZ government; articles in public admin jls. *Recreations:* beach house, gardening, reading, walking. *Address:* 10 Jellicoe Towers, 189 The Terrace, Wellington, New Zealand. *T:* (4) 4728143. *Club:* Wellington (Wellington, NZ).

GALVIN, John Rogers; General, United States Army, retired; Supreme Allied Commander, Europe, and Commander-in-Chief, US European Command, Stuttgart, 1987–92; Dean, Fletcher School of Law and Diplomacy, Tufts University, 1995–2000, now Emeritus; *b* 13 May 1929; *s* of John J. Galvin and Mary Josephine Logan; *m* 1961, Virginia Lee Brennan; four *d*. *Educ:* US Mil. Acad. (BS); Columbia Univ. (MA); US Army Command and General Staff Coll.; Univ. of Pennsylvania; US Army War Coll.; Fletcher Sch. of Law and Diplomacy (US Army War Coll. Fellowship). Platoon Leader, I Co., 65 Inf. Regt, Puerto Rico, 1955–56; Instructor, Ranger Sch., Colombia, 1956–58; Co. Comdr, 501 Airborne Battle Group, 101 Airborne Div., 1958–60; Instructor, US Mil. Acad., 1962–65; DACOS, Plans, 1st Cavalry Div., Vietnam, 1966–67; MA and Aide to Sec. of US Army, 1967–69; Comdr, 1st Bn, 8th Cavalry, 1st Cavalry Div., Vietnam, 1969–70; Dep. Sec., Jt Staff, US European Comd, Stuttgart, 1973–74; MA to SACEUR, 1974–75; Comdr, Div. Support Comd, 1975–77; COS, 3rd Inf. Div. (Mechanized), Würzburg, 1977–78; Asst Div. Comdr, 8th Inf. Div. (Mechanized), Mainz, 1978–80; Asst DCOS for Training, US Army Training and Doctrine Comd, 1980–81; Comdg Gen., 24 Inf. Div. (Mechanized), and Fort Stewart, 1981–83; Comdg Gen., VII Corps, Stuttgart, 1983–85; C-in-C, US Southern Comd, Panama, 1985–87. Olin Dist. Prof. of Nat. Security, W Point, 1992–94; Dist. Policy Analyst, Mershon Center, Ohio State Univ., 1994–95. Defense DSM, Army DSM, Navy DSM, Air Force DSM, Silver Star, Legion of Merit (with 2 Oak Leaf Clusters), DFC, Soldier's Medal, Bronze Star (with 2 Oak Leaf Clusters), Combat Infantryman Badge, Ranger Tab, foreign decorations. *Publications:* The Minute Men, 1967; Air Assault: the development of airmobility, 1969; Three Men of Boston, 1975. *Recreations:* walking, jogging. *Address:* 2714 Lake Jodeco Circle, Jonesboro, GA 30236, USA.

GALWAY, 12th Viscount *cr* 1727; **George Rupert Monckton-Arundell;** Baron Killard, 1727; Lieut Comdr RCN, retired; *b* 13 Oct. 1922; *s* of Philip Marmaduke Monckton (*d* 1965) (*g g s* of 5th Viscount) and Lavender, *d* of W. J. O'Hara; *S* cousin, 1980; *m* 1944, Fiona Margaret, *d* of late Captain P. W. de P. Taylor; one *s* three *d*. *Heir: s* Hon. John Philip Monckton [*b* 8 April 1952; *m* 1st, 1980, Deborah Holmes (marr. diss. 1992); 2nd, 2002, Tracey Jean Black; one *s* two *d*]. *Address:* 787 Berkshire Drive, London, ON N6J 3S5, Canada.

GALWAY, Sir James, Kt 2001; OBE 1977; FRCM 1983; fluteplayer; *b* 8 Dec. 1939; *s* of James Galway and Ethel Stewart Clarke; *m* 1st, 1965; one *s*; 2nd, 1972; one *s* twin *d*; 3rd, 1984, Jeanne Cinnante. *Educ:* St Paul's Sch., and Mountcollyer Secondary Modern Sch., Belfast; RCM, and Guildhall Sch. of Music, London; Conservatoire National Supérieur de Musique, Paris. First post in wind band of Royal Shakespeare Theatre, Stratford-upon-Avon; later worked with Sadler's Wells Orch., Royal Opera House Orch. and BBC Symphony Orch.; Principal Flute, London Symphony Orch., 1966, Royal Philharmonic Orch., 1967–69; Principal Solo Flute, Berlin Philharmonic Orch., 1969–75; international soloist, 1975–. Principal Guest Conductor, London Mozart Players, 1999–. Recordings of works by C. P. E. Bach, J. S. Bach, Beethoven, Corigliano, Debussy, Franck, Handel, Khachaturian, Mancini, Mozart, Nielsen, Prokoviev, Reicha, Reincke, Rodrigo, Schubert, Stamitz, Telemann and Vivaldi; also albums of flute showpieces, Australian, Irish and Japanese collections. Grand Prix du Disque, 1976, 1989. Hon. FGSM 2003. Hon. MA Open, 1979; Hon. DMus: QUB, 1979; New England Conservatory of Music, 1980; St Andrews, 2003. Officier des Arts et des Lettres (France), 1987. *Publications:* James Galway: an autobiography, 1978; Flute (Menuhin Music Guide), 1982; James Galway's Music in Time, 1983 (TV series, 1983); Masterclass: performance editions of great flute literature, 1987; Flute Studies, 2003. *Recreations:* music, walking, swimming, films, theatre, TV, chess, backgammon, computing, talking to people.

GAMBETTA, Prof. Diego, PhD; FBA 2000; Professor of Sociology, University of Oxford, since 2002; Official Fellow, Nuffield College, Oxford, since 2003; *b* 30 Jan. 1952; *s* of Carlo Gambetta and Giovanna (*née* Giavelli); *m* 1992, Dr Valeria Pizzini; one *s* one *d*. *Educ:* Chieri, Turin; Univ. of Turin (BA Philosophy); King's Coll., Cambridge (PhD 1983). Civil servant, Regl Admin, Piedmont, Italy, 1978–84; Jun. Res. Fellow, 1984–88, Sen. Res. Fellow, 1988–91, King's Coll., Cambridge; University of Oxford: Fellow, St Anne's Coll. and Lectr in Sociology, 1991–95 (*ad hominem* Reader, 1993); Reader in Sociology, 1995–2002; Fellow, All Souls Coll., 1995–2003. Vis. Prof. in Social Orgn, Grad. Sch. of Business and Dept of Sociol., Univ. of Chicago, 1994; Vis. Prof., Sciences Po, Paris, 2005; Guest Lectr, Collège de France, Paris, 2007. Inaugural Fellow, Italian Acad. for Advanced Studies, Columbia Univ., 1996–97. *Publications:* Were they pushed or did they jump?: individual decision mechanisms in education, 1987 (trans. Italian 1990), 2nd edn 1996; (ed) Trust: making and breaking co-operative relations, 1988 (trans. Italian 1989); The Sicilian mafia: the business of private protection (Premio Iglesias), 1993 (trans. Italian, 1992, German, 1994, Spanish, 2007), 2nd edn 1996 (Premio Borsellino, 2003); (with S. Warner) La retorica della riforma: fine del sistema proporzionale in Italia, 1994; (ed) Making Sense of Suicide Missions, 2005; (with H. Hamill) Streetwise: how taxi drivers establish the trustworthiness of their customers, 2005; contribs to anthologies and social scientific jls. *Recreations:* mountaineering, ski-ing, yoga, cinema. *Address:* Nuffield College, Oxford OX1 1NF.

GAMBLE, Alan James; Social Security and Child Support Commissioner, since 2008; *b* Glasgow 29 April 1951; *s* of Frank Gamble and Nancy Gamble (*née* Johnston); *m* 1977, Elizabeth Rodger Waugh; two *s* one *d*. *Educ:* High Sch. of Glasgow; Univ. of Glasgow (LLB); Harvard Law Sch. (LLM). Advocate, 1978; Lectr, 1976–86, Sen. Lectr, 1986–93, in Private Law, Univ. of Glasgow; District Chm., Appeal Tribunals, 1993–2008; Dep. Social Security and Child Support Comr, 1994–2008; Convener, Mental Health Tribunal for Scotland, 2005–. *Publications:* (contrib.) Legal Issues in Medicine, 1981; (contrib.) The Law of Property in Scotland, 1996; (ed) Obligations in Context, 2000; articles on legal topics. *Recreations:* reading, hill walking. *Address:* (office) George House, 126 George Street, Edinburgh EH3 7PW. *T:* (0131) 271 4310, *Fax:* (0131) 271 4398.

GAMBLE, Prof. Andrew Michael, PhD; FBA 2000; AcSS; Professor of Politics, University of Cambridge, and Fellow of Queens' College, Cambridge, since 2007; *b* 15 Aug. 1947; *s* of Marcus Elkington Gamble and Joan (*née* Westall); *m* 1974, Christine Jennifer Rodway; one *s* two *d*. *Educ:* Brighton Coll.; Queens' Coll., Cambridge (BA Econs 1968); Univ. of Durham (MA Pol Theory 1969); Gonville and Caius Coll., Cambridge (PhD Social and Pol Scis 1975). University of Sheffield: Lectr in Politics, 1973–82; Reader, 1982–86; Prof. of Politics, 1986–2006; Pro-Vice-Chancellor, 1994–98; Dir, Pol Economy Res. Centre, 1999–2004; Leverhulme Res. Fellow, 2004–07. Visiting Professor: Univ. of Kobe, 1990; Univ. of Hitotsubashi, 1992; Univ. of Chuo, 1994; ANU, 2005. Mem. Exec., 1988–91, Vice-Chair, 1989–91, Political Studies Assoc. Joint Editor: New Political Economy, 1996–; Political Qly, 1997–. FRSA 1999; AcSS 2002. Mitchell Prize, 1977; Sir Isaiah Berlin Prize for Lifetime Contrib. to Pol Studies, Pol Studies Assoc., 2005. *Publications:* (jtly) From Alienation to Surplus Value (Isaac Deutscher Meml Prize), 1972; The Conservative Nation, 1974; (jtly) Capitalism in Crisis, 1976; Britain in Decline, 1981, 4th edn 1994; An Introduction to Modern Social and Political Thought, 1981; (ed jtly) Developments in British Politics, vol. 1, 1983, vol. 2, 1986, vol. 3, 1990, vol. 4, 1993, vol. 5, 1997, vol. 6, 2000, vol. 7, 2003; (jtly) The British Party System and Economic Policy, 1984; (ed jtly) The Social Economy and the Democratic State, 1987; The Free Economy and the Strong State, 1988, 2nd edn 1994; (ed jtly) Thatcher's Law, 1989; Hayek: the iron cage of liberty, 1996; (ed jtly) Regionalism and World Order, 1996; (ed jtly) Stakeholder Capitalism, 1997; (ed jtly) Fundamentals in British Politics, 1999; (ed jtly) Marxism and Social Science, 1999; (ed jtly) The New Social Democracy, 1999; Politics and Fate, 2000; (ed jtly) The Political Economy of the Company, 2000; Between Europe and America: the future of British politics, 2003 (W. J. M. Mackenzie Prize, Pol Studies Assoc., 2005); (ed jtly) Restating the State, 2004; articles in learned jls. *Recreations:* music, growing tomatoes. *Address:* Queens' College, Cambridge CB3 9ET.

See also C. S. Gamble.

GAMBLE, Dr Christine Elizabeth; Consultant on equality and diversity issues, since 2005; *b* 1950; *d* of late Albert Edward Gamble and Kathleen Laura (*née* Wallis); *m* 1989, Edward Barry Antony Craxton. *Educ:* Royal Holloway Coll., London Univ. (BA 1st Cl. Hons; PhD 1977). English-French Cultural Orgn, 1974–75; served British Embassy, Moscow, 1975–76; with British Council, 1977–98: New Delhi, 1977–79; Stratford-on-Avon, 1979–80; Harare, 1980–82; Regl Officer for Soviet Union in London, 1982–85; Dep. Dir, Athens, 1985–87; Dir General's Dept (Corporate Planning), 1988–90; Head, Project Pursuit Dept and Dir, Chancellor's Financial Sector Scheme for Former Soviet Union, 1991–92; Dir, Visitors' Dept, 1992–93; Gen. Manager, Country Services Gp, 1993–95 and Hd, European Series, 1994–96; Cultural Counsellor, Paris and Dir, France, 1996–98; Dir, RIIA, 1998–2001; Co. Sec., Ind. Football Commn, 2002–05. Dir, Japan 21st Century Gp, 1999–2005; Mem., Franco-British Council, 2000–06. *Recreations:* collecting books, football, reading, music, theatre, gardening. *Address:* Syke Fold House, Dent, Sedbergh LA10 5RE.

GAMBLE, Prof. Clive Stephen, PhD; FBA 2000; FSA; Professor of Geography, Royal Holloway, University of London, since 2004; *b* 10 March 1951; *s* of Marcus Elkington Gamble and Joan Gamble (*née* Westall); *m* 1981, Dr Elaine Lisk Morris. *Educ:* Brighton Coll.; Jesus Coll., Cambridge (BA 1972, MA 1975; PhD 1978). FSA 1981; MIFA 1987. Department of Archaeology, University of Southampton: exptl officer, 1975; Lectr, 1976–86; Sen. Lectr, 1986–90; Reader, 1990–95; Prof. of Archaeol., 1995–2004; British Acad. Res. Reader, 2000–02; Dir, Centre for Archaeol. of Human Origins, 1999–2004. *Publications:* The Palaeolithic Settlement of Europe, 1986; Timewalkers: the prehistory of global colonisation, 1993; (with C. Stringer) In Search of the Neanderthals, 1993; The Palaeolithic Societies of Europe, 1999; Archaeology: the basics, 2001; Origins and Revolutions, 2007. *Recreations:* cats, cricket, gardening. *Address:* Department of Geography, Royal Holloway, University of London, Egham, Surrey TW20 0EX. *T:* (01784) 441 4673.

See also A. M. Gamble.

GAMBLE, Sir David (Hugh Norman), 6th Bt *cr* 1897, of Windlehurst, St Helens, Co. Palatine of Lancashire; *b* 1 July 1966; *s* of Sir David Gamble, 5th Bt and of Dawn Adrienne, *d* of late David Hugh Gittins; *S* father, 1984. *Educ:* Shiplake College, Henley-on-Thames. *Heir: cousin* Hugh Robert George Gamble [*b* 3 March 1946; *m* 1989, Rebecca Jane, *d* of Lt Comdr David Odell, RN; one *s* one *d*]. *Address:* Keinton House, Keinton Mandeville, Somerton, Somerset TA11 6DX. *T:* (01458) 223964.

GAMBLE, Richard Arthur; non-executive Chairman, Highway Insurance Group plc, since 2007 (Executive Chairman, 2006–07; non-executive Director, since 2003); *b* 19 Sept. 1939; *s* of late Arthur Gamble and of Grace Emily Gamble (*née* Little); *m* 1966, Elizabeth Ann, *d* of Edward Godwin-Atkyns; two *s*. *Educ:* Raynes Park Co. Grammar Sch. FCA 1962. Articled clerk, W. J. Gilbert & Co., London, 1957–62; Asst Manager, Turquand Youngs & Co., 1962–66; Dir and Co. Sec., Lee Davy Gp Ltd, 1966–68; Dir and Sec., Hamilton Smith, Lloyd's Brokers, 1968–70; Finance Dir, Lowndes Lambert Internat., Lloyd's Brokers, 1970–76; European Finance Dir, Data100/Northern Telecom Systems, 1976–80; Finance Dir, McDonnell Douglas Inf. Systems and Dir, McDonnell Douglas UK, 1980–84; Dep. Chief Financial Officer, British Airways, 1984–89; Royal Insurance Holdings PLC: Gp Finance Dir, 1989–91; Gp Chief Operating Officer, 1991; Gp Chief Exec., 1992–96; Gp Chief Exec., Royal & Sun Alliance Insurance Gp plc, 1996–97. Non-executive Chm., Denne Gp Ltd, 2001–03 (Advr, 1999–2001); non-executive Dir, Excel Airways Gp plc, 2003–05. Mem. Bd, ABI, 1994–96; Chm., Policy Holders Protection Bd, 1994–98. Mem., Adv. Cttee on Business in the Envmt and Chm., Financial Services Working Gp, 1993–96. Mem., Educnl Nat. Leadership Team, BITC, 1995–97. Trustee, Crimestoppers, 1995–; Pres., GB Wheelchair Basketball Assoc., 1997–; Gov., RSC, 1997–2002. CCMI (CIMgt 1992). *Recreations:* all sport, particularly golf, walking with dogs, theatre, family. *Address:* Chart Hall Farm, Green Lane, Chart Sutton, Kent ME17 3ES. *T:* (01622) 842526.

GAMBLING, Prof. (William) Alex(ander), PhD, DSc; FRS 1983; FREng; *b* 11 Oct. 1926; *s* of George Alexander Gambling and Muriel Clara Gambling; *m* 1st, 1952, Margaret Pooley (marr. diss. 1994); one *s* two *d*; 2nd, 1994, Barbara Colleen O'Neil. *Educ:* Univ. of Bristol (BSc, Alfred Fry Prize, DSc); Univ. of Liverpool (PhD). FIERE 1964; CEng, Hon. FIET (FIEE 1967); FREng (FEng 1979); FHKAES 2000. Lectr in Electric Power Engrg, Univ. of Liverpool, 1950–55; National Res. Council Fellow, Univ. of BC, 1955–57; Univ. of Southampton: Lectr, Sen. Lectr, and Reader, 1957–64; Prof. of Electronics, 1964–80; Dean of Engrg and Applied Science, 1972–75; Hd of Dept, 1974–79; BT Prof. of Optical Communication, 1980–95; Dir, Optoelectronics Res. Centre, 1989–95; Royal Soc. Kan Tong Po Prof. and Dir, Optoelectronics Res. Centre, City Univ., Hong Kong, 1996–2001. Dir, York Ltd, 1980–97. Vis. Professor: Univ. of Colo, USA, 1966–67; Bhabha Atomic Res. Centre, India, 1970; Osaka Univ., Japan, 1977; City Univ. of Hong Kong, 1995; Hon. Professor: Huazhong Univ. of Sci. and Technol., Wuhan, China, 1986–; Beijing Univ. of Posts and Telecommunications, 1987–; Shanghai Univ., 1991–; Shandong Univ., 1999–; Hon. Dir, Beijing Optical Fibre Inst., 1987–. Member: Electronics Res. Council, 1977–80 (Mem., Optics and Infra-Red Cttee, 1965–69 and 1974–80); Board, Council of Engrg Instns, 1974–79; National Electronics Council, 1977–78, 1984–95; Technol. Sub-Cttee of UGC, 1973–83; British Nat. Cttee for Radio Science, 1978–87; Nat. Adv. Bd for Local Authority Higher Educn, Engrg Working Gp, 1982–84; Engineering Council, 1983–88; British Nat. Cttee for Internat. Engineering Affairs, 1984–88; Council, Royal Acad. of Engrg, 1989–92; Chairman: Commn D, Internat. Union of Radio Science, 1984–87 (Vice-Chm., 1981–84); Nat. DTI/SERC Optoelectronics Cttee, 1988–91. Pres., IERE, 1977–78 (Hon. Fellow 1983); Vice Pres., Hong Kong Acad. of Engrg Scis, 2004–08. Selby Fellow, Australian Acad. of Science, 1982; For. Mem., Polish Acad. of Scis, 1985. Freeman, City of London, 1987; Liveryman, Worshipful Co. of Engrs, 1988. Dr *hc* Univ. Politècnica de Madrid, 1994; Hon. DSc: Aston, 1995; Southampton, 2005. Hon. DEng Bristol, 1999. Bulgin Premium,

IERE, 1961, Lord Rutherford Premium, IERE, 1964, Electronics Div. Premium, IEE, 1976 and 1978, Oliver Lodge Premium, IEE, 1981, Heinrich Hertz Premium, IERE, 1981, for research papers; J. J. Thomson Medal, IEE, 1982, Faraday Medal, IEE, 1983, Churchill Medal, Soc. of Engineers, 1984 and Simms Medal, Soc. of Engineers, 1989, for research innovation and leadership; Academic Enterprise Award, 1982; Micro-optics Award, Japan, 1989; Dennis Gabor Award, Internat. Soc. for Optical Engrg, USA, 1990; Rank Prize for Optoelectronics, 1991; Medal and Prize, Foundn for Computer and Communications Promotion, Japan, 1993; Mountbatten Medal, Nat. Electronics Council, 1993; James Alfred Ewing Medal, ICE/Royal Soc., 2002. *Publications:* 300 papers on electronics and optical fibre communications. *Recreations:* music, reading. *Address:* Los Grillos MG26, Calle Carrasca 4, 03737 Jávea, Alicante, Spain. *T:* and *Fax:* (96) 5795455.

GAMBON, Sir Michael (John), Kt 1998; CBE 1990; actor; *b* 19 Oct. 1940; *s* of Edward and Mary Gambon; *m* 1962, Anne Miller; one *s*; one *c* by Philippa Hart. *Educ:* St Aloysius School for Boys, Somers Town, London. Served 7 year apprenticeship in engineering; first appeared on stage with Edwards/MácLiammoir Co., Dublin, 1962; Nat. Theatre, Old Vic, 1963–67; Birmingham Rep. and other provincial theatres, 1967–69 (title rôles incl. Othello, Macbeth, Coriolanus); RSC Aldwych, 1970–71; Norman Conquests, Globe, 1974; Otherwise Engaged, Queen's, 1976; Just Between Ourselves, Queen's 1977; Alice's Boys, Savoy, 1978; King Lear and Antony and Cleopatra (title rôles), RSC Stratford and Barbican, 1982–83; Old Times, Haymarket, 1985; Uncle Vanya, Vaudeville, 1988; Veterans Day, Haymarket, 1989; Man of the Moment, Globe, 1990; Othello and Taking Steps, Scarborough, 1990; Tom and Clem, Aldwych, 1997; The Unexpected Man, Barbican Pit, transf. Duchess, 1998; Juno and the Paycock, Gaiety, Dublin, 1999; Cressida, Albery, 2000; The Caretaker, Comedy (Variety Club Best Actor, Critics' Circle Best Actor), 2000; A Number, Royal Court, 2002; Endgame, Albery, 2004; Eh Joe, Duke of York's, 2006; National Theatre: Galileo, 1980 (London Theatre Critics' Award, Best Actor); Betrayal, 1980; Tales From Hollywood, 1980; Chorus of Disapproval, 1985 (Olivier Award, Best Comedy Performance); Tons of Money, 1986; A View from the Bridge, 1987, transf. Aldwych (Best Actor, Evening Standard Awards, Olivier Awards, and Plays and Players London Theatre Critics' Awards; Best Stage Actor, Variety Club Awards); A Small Family Business, 1987; Mountain Language, 1988; Skylight, transf. Wyndhams, then NY, and Volpone (Best Actor, Evening Standard Awards), 1995; Henry IV, Parts 1 and 2, 2005. *Television* includes: The Singing Detective, 1986 (BAFTA Award, Best Actor, 1987); Maigret, 1992, 1993; Faith, 1994; Wives and Daughters, 1999 (BAFTA Award, Best Actor, 2000); Longitude, 2000 (BAFTA Award, Best Actor, 2001); Perfect Strangers, 2001 (BAFTA Award, Best Actor, 2002); The Lost Prince, 2003; Angels in America, 2004; Cranford, 2007. *Films* include: The Cook, The Thief, His Wife and Her Lover, The Heat of the Day, Paris by Night, 1989; A Dry White Season, 1990; Mobsters, Toys, 1992; The Browning Version, 1993; A Man of No Importance, Midnight in Moscow, 1994; The Innocent Sleep, All Our Fault, 1995; Mary Reilly, Two Deaths, Nothing Personal, The Gambler, 1996; The Wings of the Dove, Dancing at Lughnasa, 1997; Plunkett and Macleane, 1999; The Last September, Sleepy Hollow, The Insider, 2000; End Game, High Heels and Low Lifes, 2001; Gosford Park, Charlotte Gray, Ali G Indahouse, Path to War, 2002; The Actors, 2003; Sylvia, Being Julia, Layer Cake, Open Range, Harry Potter and the Prisoner of Azkaban, Sky Captain and the World of Tomorrow, 2004; The Life Aquatic with Steve Zissou, Harry Potter and the Goblet of Fire, 2005; Amazing Grace, 2006; The Good Shepherd, Harry Potter and the Order of the Phoenix, 2007. Trustee, Royal Armouries, 1995–. Liveryman, Gunmakers' Co. Hon. DLitt Southampton, 2002. *Recreations:* flying, gun collecting, clock making. *Address:* Independent Talent Group Ltd, Oxford House, Oxford Street, W1D 1BS. *Club:* Garrick.

GAME, Amanda, (Mrs A. O. E. Raven); Co-Founder, 2005, Lead Director, since 2008, IC: Innovative Craft; *b* 22 Aug. 1958; *d* of John Game and Margaret Newman Game (*née* Smith); *m* 1987, Andrew Owen Earle Raven, OBE (*d* 2005). *Educ:* Open Univ. (BA 1st Cl. Hons Humanities Art Hist. and Lit.). Asst, Oxford Gall., 1984–86; Scottish Gallery, Edinburgh: Manager for Contemporary Craft, 1986–95; Dir of Applied Art, 1995–2007. Curator, Jewellery Moves, 1997–99, Res. Associate, 1998–, Nat. Mus of Scotland. Crafts Advr, Scottish Arts Council, 1995–2001; Advisor: Inches Carr Trust, Edinburgh, 1999–; Goldsmiths' Trust, Edinburgh, 2002–. Freeman, 1995, Liveryman, 2007, Goldsmiths' Co. Chair, Judging Panel, Jerwood Applied Arts Prize, Textiles, 1997; Judge: Young Designer Silversmith Award, Goldsmiths' Hall, 1994–2004; Leonardo Prize, 2004. *Publication:* Jewellery Moves, 1998, 3rd edn 2001. *Recreations:* hill-walking, classical music, opera, literature, film, gardens, architecture.

GAMMAGE, Jayne Agneta; *see* Franklyn, J. A.

GAMMELL, Sir William Benjamin Bowring, (Sir Bill), Kt 2006; Chief Executive, Cairn Energy PLC, since 1989; *b* 29 Dec. 1952; *s* of James Gilbert Sidney Gammell and Patricia Bowring Gammell (*née* Toms). *Educ:* Stirling Univ. (BA Econ). Founded Cairn Energy Mgt, 1980, Man. Dir, 1980–89. Director: Scottish Inst. of Sport, 1998–; Artemis Aim VCT Trust, 2001–; Chm., Scottish Inst. of Sport Foundn, 2006–. *Recreations:* Rugby (Scotland Rugby Internat., 1977–78), squash, football, golf, ski-ing. *Address:* Cairn Energy plc, 50 Lothian Road, Edinburgh EH3 9BY; *e-mail:* bill.gammell@cairn-energy.plc.uk. *Clubs:* New (Edinburgh); Golf House (Elie, Fife).

GAMMIE, Malcolm James, CBE 2005; QC 2002; *b* 18 Feb. 1951; *s* of Maj. James Ian Gammie, MC, and Florence Mary Gammie (*née* Wiggs); *m* 1974, Rosalind Anne Rowe; one *s* three *d*. *Educ:* Edge Grove Sch., Aldenham; Merchant Taylors' Sch.; Sidney Sussex Coll., Cambridge (MA). Linklaters & Paines: articled clerk, 1973–75; solicitor, Tax Dept, 1975–78 and 1985–87; Partner, 1987–97; Dep. Hd, Tax Dept, CBI, 1978–79; Director: Nat. Tax Office, Thomson McLintock & Co., 1979–84; Nat. Tax Services, KMG Thomson McLintock, 1984–85; called to the Bar, Middle Temple, 1997; in practice as barrister, 1997–. Dep. Special Comr and pt-time VAT and Duties Tribunal Chm., 2002–. Vis. Professorial Fellow, Centre for Commercial Law Studies, QMW, 1997–; Res. Fellow, Inst. for Fiscal Studies, 1997–; Unilever Prof. of Internat. Business Law, Leiden Univ., 1998; Visiting Professor: of Tax Law, LSE, 2000–; of Internat. Tax Law, Sydney Univ., 2000 and 2002. Editor: Law and Tax Rev., 1982–88; Land Taxation, 1985–; Consulting Ed., Butterworth's Tax Handbook, 1994–2004. Cabinet Office: Member: Taxation Deregulation Gp, 1993–97; Fiscal Studies Wkg Party Adv. Council on Sci. and Technol., 1993; Mem., 1994–97, Res. Dir, 1997–, Tax Law Rev. Cttee; Mem., Special Cttee of Tax Law Consultative Bodies, Taxation Cttee, IOD, 1987–97. Chartered Institute of Taxation: Mem. Council, 1985–2001; Chm., Capital Taxes Wkg Party, 1986–92; Chm., Exec. Cttee, 1991–97. London Chamber of Commerce and Industry: Mem., 1976–; Mem. Council, 1989–92; Chm., Taxation Cttee, 1989–92. Chm., Revenue Law Cttee, Law Soc., 1996–97; Mem., Soc. for Advanced Legal Studies, 1997–. Mem., Perm. Scientific Cttee, Internat. Fiscal Assoc., 1998– (Vice-Chm., British Br. Cttee). FRSA 1993. *Publications:* (with S. Ball) Taxation Publishing, Tax on Company Reorganisations, 1980, 2nd edn 1982; Tax Strategy for Companies, 1981, 3rd edn 1986; (with D. Williams) Stock Relief, 1981; (with D. Williams) Tax Focus on Interest and Discounts, 1983; Tax Strategy for Directors, Executives and Employees, 1983, 2nd edn 1985; (jtly) Whiteman on Capital Gains Tax, 1988; The Process of Tax Reform in the United Kingdom, 1990. *Recreations:* music, church architecture. *Address:* (chambers) 1 Essex Court, Temple, EC4Y 9AR. *T:* (020) 7583 2000, *Fax:* (020) 7583 0118; *e-mail:* mgammie@oeclaw.co.uk.

GAMON, Hugh Wynell, CBE 1979; MC 1944; formerly Partner, Winckworth & Pemberton (incorporating Sherwood & Co., 1991); HM Government Agent, 1970–89; *b* 31 March 1921; *s* of Judge Hugh R. P. Gamon and E. Margaret Gamon; *m* 1949, June Elizabeth (*d* 2003), *d* of William and Florence Temple; one *s* three *d*. *Educ:* St Edward's Sch., Oxford; Exeter Coll., Oxford, 1946–48. MA 1st Cl. Hons Jurisprudence; Law Society Hons; Edmund Thomas Childe Prize. Served War, 1940–46: Royal Corps of Signals, N Africa, Italy and Palestine, with 1st Division. Articled to Clerk of Cumberland CC, 1949–51; joined Sherwood & Co., 1951; Parly Agent, 1954; Sen. Partner, Sherwood & Co., 1972; retd from Winckworth & Pemberton, 1995. *Recreation:* gardening. *Address:* Claygate, Shipbourne, Kent TN11 9RL. *T:* (01732) 810308.

GAMON, Maj.-Gen. John Anthony, CBE 2003; Special Project Officer Deputy Chief of Defence Staff (Health), 2005–06; *b* 13 March 1946; *s* of James Davidson Gamon and Dorothy Gamon (*née* Radford); *m* 1968, Mary Patricia Medicke; one *s* one *d*. *Educ:* Penlan Multilateral Sch., Swansea; Royal Dental Hosp., London (BDS 1969); Eastman Dental Inst., London (MSc 1978). MGDSRCS 1982; DRD RCSEd 1983. Gen. clinical appts, Army Dental Service, 1970–92; Deputy Director: Defence Dental Services, 1993–96; Army Dental Service, 1996–97; Director: Army Dental Service, 1997–2001; Clinical Services, 1997–99; Corporate Develt, 1999–2001, Defence Dental Agency; Dir Gen., Defence Dental Services and Chief Exec., Defence Dental Agency, 2001–05. QHDS, 1997–2006. Pres., British Soc. for Gen. Dental Surgery, 2001–02. FInstD 2002. *Recreations:* fly fishing, hill walking, gardening, reading. *Address:* 1 Bushmead Close, Whitchurch, Aylesbury, Bucks HP22 4SH. *Club:* Naval and Military.

GANDHI, Hon. Gopalkrishna; Governor of West Bengal, India, since 2004; *b* 22 April 1945; *s* of Devadas Mohandas Gandhi and Lakshmi Rajagopalachami; *m* Tara Ananth; two *d*. *Educ:* St Stephen's Coll., Delhi Univ. (BA Hons 1964; MA English Lit 1964). Member, Indian Administrative Service, 1968–92: various positions, Tamil Nadu, 1969–77; First Sec., Asst High Commn of India, Kandy, Sri Lanka, 1978–82; Dir of Handlooms and Textiles, Govt of Tamil Nadu, 1982–83; Sec. to Governor of Tamil Nadu, 1983–85; Sec. to Vice-Pres. of India, 1985–87; Jt Sec. to Pres. of India, 1987–92; voluntary retirement, 1992; Minister (Culture) and Dir, Nehru Centre, London, 1992–96; High Comr in S Africa, 1996–97; Sec. to Pres. of India, 1997–2000; High Comr in Sri Lanka, 2000–02; Ambassador to Norway, 2002–04. Hon. LLD Natal, 1999; Hon. DLitt Peradeniya, Kandy, 2001. *Publications:* Saranam (novel), 1985, reprinted as Refuge, 1987; Dara Shukoh (play), 1993; trans. Hindustani, Seth, A Suitable Boy, 1998. *Address:* Raj Bhavan, Kolkata 700062, India. *Club:* India International Centre (New Delhi).

GANDHI, Sonia; President: Congress Party, India, since 1998; Indian National Congress, since 2005; MP (Congress) Raebareli, UP, Lok Sabha, 2004–March 2006 and since May 2006 (MP for Amethi, 1999–2004); *b* Italy, 9 Dec. 1947; adopted Indian nationality, 1983; *d* of Stefano and Paola Maino; *m* 1968, Rajiv Gandhi (*d* 1991); one *s* one *d*. *Educ:* language sch., Cambridge; Art restoration course, Nat. Gall. of Modern Art, New Delhi. Pres., Rajiv Gandhi Foundn. Mem., Congress Party, 1997–. Leader of the Opposition, Lok Sabha, 1999–2004. *Publications:* (ed) Freedom's Daughter, 1989; (ed) Two Alone, Two Together, 1992; Rajiv, 1992; Rajiv's World, 1994. *Address:* 10 Janpath, New Delhi 110011, India; All India Congress Committee, 24 Akbar Road, New Delhi 110011, India.

GANDY, Christopher Thomas; HM Diplomatic Service, retired; *b* 21 April 1917; *s* of late Dr Thomas H. Gandy and late Mrs Ida Gandy (authoress of A Wiltshire Childhood, Around the Little Steeple, etc); unmarried. *Educ:* Marlborough; King's Coll., Cambridge. On active service with Army and RAF, 1939–45. Entered Foreign Office, Nov. 1945; Tehran, 1948–51; Cairo, 1951–52; FO, 1952–54; Lisbon, 1954–56; Libya, 1956–59; FO, 1960–62; apptd HM Minister to The Yemen, 1962, subsequently Counsellor, Kuwait; Minister (Commercial) Rio de Janeiro, 1966–68. Sen. Common Room Mem., St Antony's Coll., Oxford, 1973–. *Publications:* articles in Asian Affairs, Middle East International, The New Middle East, The Annual Register of World Events, Art International, Arts of Asia, Jl of Royal Asiatic Soc., British Jl of Middle Eastern Studies, and Financial Times. *Recreations:* music, gardening. *Address:* c/o G. M Gandy, 65 High Street, Barrington, Cambridge CB2 5QX. *Club:* Travellers.

GANDY, David Stewart, CB 1989; OBE 1981; Consultant, Pannone and Partners, solicitors, since 1993; Deputy Director of Public Prosecutions and Chief Executive, Crown Prosecution Service, 1987–93; *b* 19 Sept. 1932; *s* of Percy Gandy and Elizabeth Mary (*née* Fox); *m* 1956, Mabel Sheldon; one *s* one *d*. *Educ:* Manchester Grammar Sch.; Manchester Univ. Nat. Service, Intell. Corps (Germany and Austria), 1954–56. Admitted Solicitor, 1954; Asst Solicitor, Town Clerk, Manchester, 1956–59; Chief Prosecuting Solicitor: Manchester, 1959–68; Manchester and Salford, 1968–74; Gtr Manchester, 1974–85; Head of Field Management, Crown Prosecution Service, 1985–87; Acting DPP, Oct. 1991–May 1992. Mem., Home Office Assessment Consultancy Unit, 1993–2005. Mem. Council, Criminal Law Solicitors Assoc., 1992–2001. Lect. tour on English Criminal Justice System, for Amer. Bar Assoc., USA and Canada, 1976; Lecturer: UN Asia and FE Inst. for Prevention of Crime and Treatment of Offenders, Tokyo, 1990, 1995; Internat. Congress of Criminal Lawyers on Penal Reform, La Plata, 1995. Law Society: Mem., Criminal Law Standing Cttee, 1969–97 (Vice Chm., 1995–96); Mem., Council, 1984–96; Prosecuting Solicitors' Society of England and Wales: Mem., Exec. Council, 1966–85; Pres., 1976–78; Chm., Heads of Office, 1982–83; President: Manchester Law Soc., 1980–81; Manchester and Dist Medico-Legal Soc., 1982–84; Manchester Trainee Lawyers Gp, 1982–84. Non-exec. Dir, Mancunian Community Health NHS Trust, 1993–98. Mem. Council, Order of St John, 1978–85. *Recreations:* cricket, theatre, bridge, walking. *Address:* The Ridgeway, Broad Lane, Hale, Altrincham, Cheshire WA15 0DD.

GANE, Barrie Charles, CMG 1988; OBE 1978; HM Diplomatic Service, retired; Director Group Research, Group 4 Securitas, 1993–2000; *b* 19 Sept. 1935; *s* of Charles Ernest Gane and Margaret Gane; *m* 1974, Jennifer Anne Pitt; two *d* of former marriage. *Educ:* King Edward's School, Birmingham; Corpus Christi College, Cambridge. MA. Foreign Office, 1960; served Vientiane, Kuching and Warsaw; First Sec., Kampala, 1967; FCO, 1970; First Sec., later Counsellor, seconded to HQ British Forces, Hong Kong, 1977; Counsellor, FCO, 1982–92. *Recreations:* walking, reading. *Club:* Brooks's.

GANE, Michael, DPhil, MA; economic and environmental consultant; *b* 29 July 1927; *s* of late Rudolf E. Gane and Helen Gane; *m* 1954, Madge Stewart Taylor; one *d*. *Educ:* Colyton Grammar Sch., Devon; Edinburgh Univ. (BSc Forestry 1948); London Univ. (BSc Econ 1963); Oxford Univ. (DPhil, MA 1967). Asst Conservator of Forests, Tanganyika, 1948–62; Sen. Research Officer, Commonwealth Forestry Inst., Oxford, 1963–69; Dir, Project Planning Centre for Developing Countries, Bradford Univ., 1969–74; Dir, England, Nature Conservancy Council, 1974–81. *Publications:* Forest Strategy, 2007; various contribs to scientific and technical jls. *Recreations:* natural history, gardening. *Address:* Coast Watchers Cottage, 6 Avalanche Road, Southwell, Portland, Dorset DT5 2DJ.

GANELLIN, Charon Robin, PhD, DSc; FRS 1986; CChem, FRSC; Smith Kline and French Professor of Medicinal Chemistry, University College London, 1986–2002, now Emeritus; *b* 25 Jan. 1934; *s* of Leon Ganellin and Beila Cluer; *m* 1st, 1956, Tamara Greene (*d* 1997); one *s* one *d*; 2nd, 2003, Dr Monique Garbarg (*née* Lehmann). *Educ:* Harrow County Grammar School for Boys; Queen Mary Coll., London Univ. (BSc, PhD, DSc; Fellow, QMW, 1992). Res. Associate, MIT, 1960; Res. Chemist, then Dept Hd in Medicinal Chem., Smith Kline & French Labs Ltd, 1958–59, 1961–75; Smith Kline & French Research Ltd: Dir, Histamine Res., 1975–80; Vice-President: Research, 1980–84; Chem. Res., 1984–86. Hon. Lectr, Dept of Pharmacol., UCL, 1975–86; Hon. Prof. of Medicinal Chem., Univ. of Kent at Canterbury, 1979–89. Tilden Lectr and Medal, 1982, Adrien Albert Lectr and Medal, 1999, RSC. Pres., Section on Medicinal Chemistry, 2000–01, Chm., Subcttee on Medicinal Chem. and Drug Devlt, IUPAC, 2002–; Chm., Soc. for Drug Res., 1985–87; Hon. Mem., Soc. Española de Quimica Terapeutica, 1982; Corresp. Academician, Real Académia Nacional de Farmacia, Spain, 2006. Hon. DSc Aston, 1995. Medicinal Chem. Award, RSC, 1977; Prix Charles Mentzer, Soc. de Chimie Therap., 1978; Div. of Medicinal Chem. Award, ACS, 1980; Messel Medal, SCI, 1988; Award for Drug Discovery, Soc. for Drug Res., 1989; USA Nat. Inventors' Hall of Fame, 1990; Nauta Prize for Pharmacochem., European Fedn for Medicinal Chem., 2004; Pratesi Gold Medal, Medicinal Chem. Div., Italian Chem. Soc., 2006. *Publications:* Pharmacology of Histamine Receptors, 1982; Frontiers in Histamine Research, 1985; Dictionary of Drugs, 1990; (jtly) Medicinal Chemistry, 1993; Dictionary of Pharmacological Agents, 1997; Analogue-based Drug Discovery, 2006; res. papers and reviews in various jls, incl. Jl Med. Chem., Jl Chem. Soc., Brit. Jl Pharmacol. *Recreations:* music, sailing, walking. *Address:* Department of Chemistry, University College London, 20 Gordon Street, WC1H 0AJ.

GANI, Prof. David, DPhil; CChem, FRSC; FRSE; Director of Research Policy and Strategy, Scottish Further and Higher Education Funding Council (formerly Director of Research Policy, Scottish Funding Councils for Further and Higher Education), since 2002; Hon. Professor of Organic Chemistry, Birmingham University, since 2001; *b* 29 Sept. 1957; *m* Jo-Ann Margaret; one *s* two *d*. *Educ:* Sussex Univ. (BSc; DPhil 1983). Technician, Wellcome Res. Labs, 1974–76; Southampton University: Royal Soc. Res. Fellow and Lectr in Organic Chem., 1983–89; Sen. Lectr, 1989–90; St Andrews University: Prof. of Chemistry, 1990–98, Purdie Prof., and Res. Dir, Sch. of Chemistry, 1997–98; Dir, Centre for Biomolecular Scis, 1995–98; Prof. of Organic Chem., Birmingham Univ., 1998–2001. Mem., Strategy Bd, BBSRC, 1997–2002. *Publications:* (jtly) Enzymic Catalysis, 1991; contrib. to learned jls. *Address:* Scottish Funding Council, 97 Haymarket Terrace, Edinburgh EH12 5HD. *T:* (0131) 313 6632.

GANT, Andrew John, PhD; Organist, Choirmaster and Composer, Chapels Royal, since 2000; composer; *b* 6 Aug. 1963; *s* of John Gant and Vivien Gant (*née* Christian); *m* 1992, Dr Katherine Willis; two *s* one *d*. *Educ:* Radley Coll.; St John's Coll., Cambridge (Choral Schol.; BA 1984; MA 1994); Royal Acad. of Music (MMus 1993; ARAM 2003); PhD Goldsmiths Coll., London 2000. Lay Vicar, Westminster Abbey, 1988–90; Dir of Music in Chapel, Selwyn Coll., Cambridge, 1993–98; Organist and Master of Choir, Royal Military Chapel, Wellington Barracks, 1997–2000. Tutor in Music, Univ. of Oxford, 1998–. *Compositions include:* May We Borrow Your Husband (opera), 1999; (with Andrew Motion) A Hymn for the Golden Jubilee, 2002; The Vision of Piers Ploughman (oratorio), 2002; A Good-Night (anthem), 2002. *Recreations:* golf, walking, cycling. *Address:* 55 Middle Way, Summertown, Oxford OX2 7LE. *T:* (01865) 558841; Chapel Royal, St James's Palace, SW1A 1BG. *T:* (020) 7930 4832; *e-mail:* andrew.gant@btopenworld.com.

GANT, Diana Jillian; Headmistress, Mount School, York, since 2001; *b* 25 April 1948; *d* of John Edward Wakeham Scutt and Lucy Helen Scutt; *m* 1969, Rev. Canon Brian Leonard Gant; two *d*. *Educ:* Harrow Co. Grammar Sch. for Girls; King's Coll. London (BD Hons 1970); Christ Ch Coll., Canterbury (PGCE 1973). Various teaching posts, 1973–84; Hd of Religious Studies, King's Sch., Worcester, 1984–89; Hd of Careers and Dep. Hd of 6th Form, Tonbridge GS for Girls, 1989–95; Dep. Headmistress, Norwich High Sch for Girls (GDST), 1995–2000. Gov., York St John Univ. (formerly Coll., then UC), 2005–. *Recreations:* walking, cooking, reading. *Address:* The Mount School, Dalton Terrace, York YO24 4DD. *T:* (01904) 667508, *Fax:* (01904) 667524; *e-mail:* head@mount.n-yorks.sch.uk. *Club:* University Women's.

GANT, John, CB 2003; Chairman, Leicestershire County and Rutland Primary Care Trust, since 2006; *b* 25 Feb. 1944; *s* of William and Barbara Gant; *m* 1967, Annette Sonia Cobb; two *s*. *Educ:* Univ. of Newcastle upon Tyne (BA Hons French and German). Inland Revenue: Inspector of Taxes, 1966; Dist Inspector, 1972–74; Head Office Adviser, 1974–77; Dist Inspector, 1977–81; Group Controller, 1981–83; Asst Dir, Ops, 1983–88; Regl Controller, 1988–90; Dep. Dir, Ops, 1990–92; Dir of Human Resources, 1992–2000; Dir of Finance, 2000–03. Mem., Audit Cttee, Statistics Commn, 2004–08. Chm., Melton, Rutland and Harborough PCT, 2003–06. *Recreations:* music, theatre, ballet, travel, horse racing. *Address:* (office) Lakeside House, Grove Park, Enderby, Leicester LE19 1SS.

GAO XINGJIAN; writer; *b* Ganzhou, Jiangxi Province, China, 4 Jan. 1940. Formerly translator: China Reconstructs mag.; Chinese Writers' Assoc. Left China, 1987; now a French citizen. Nobel Prize for Literature, 2000. Chevalier de l'Ordre des Arts et des Lettres (France), 1992. *Publications:* A Preliminary Discussion of the Art of Modern Fiction, 1981; A Pigeon Called Red Beak, 1985; In Search of a Modern Form of Dramatic Representation, 1987; *novels:* Soul Mountain, 1999; One Man's Bible; *stories:* Buying a Fishing Rod for My Father, 2004; *plays:* Signal Alarm, 1982; Bus Stop, 1983; Wild Man, 1985; Collected Plays, 1985; The Other Shore, 1986; Fugitives; Summer Rain in Peking; articles in jls. *Address:* c/o HarperCollins Publishers Ltd, 77–85 Fulham Palace Road, W6 8JB.

GAPES, Michael John; MP (Lab and Co-op) Ilford South, since 1992; *b* 4 Sept. 1952; *s* of Frank William Gapes and Emily Florence Gapes (*née* Jackson). *Educ:* Staples Road Infants' Sch., Loughton; Manford County Primary Sch., Chigwell; Buckhurst Hill County High Sch., Essex; Fitzwilliam Coll., Cambridge (MA Hons Econs 1975); Middlesex Polytechnic (Dip. Indust. Relations and Trade Union Studies 1976). VSO teacher, Swaziland, 1971–72; Sec., Cambridge Students' Union, 1973–74; Chm., Nat. Orgn of Labour Students, 1976–77. Admin. Officer, Middlesex Hosp., 1977; Nat. Student Organiser, Lab. Party, 1977–80; Res. Officer, Internat. Dept, Lab. Party, 1980–88; Sen. Internat. Officer, Lab. Party, 1988–92. Contested (Lab) Ilford North, 1983. PPS to Minister of State: NI Office, 1997–99; Home Office, 2001–02. Mem., 1992–97, Chm., 2005–, Foreign Affairs Select Cttee; Mem., Defence Select Cttee, 1999–2001, 2003–05; Chm., UN All Party Parly Gp, 1997–2001; Vice-Chm., All Party Parly Gp against Anti-Semitism, 1992–; Mem., All Party Pakistan Gp, 1998–; Chm., PLP Children and Families' Cttee, 1994–95; Vice-Chm., PLP Defence Cttee, 1992–95 and 1996–97. Dep. Chm., Labour Friends of Israel, 1997–2005; Member: Labour Nat. Policy Forum, 1998–2005; Labour Friends of India, 1999–; Labour ME Council, 2002–. Mem., NATO Parly Assembly, 2002–05. Chm., Westminster Foundn for Democracy, 2002–05. Member, Council: RIIA, 1996–99; VSO, 1997–. Vice Pres., Valentines Park Conservationists, 1998–. *Publications:* co-author of books on defence policy; Labour Party and Fabian Society pamphlets. *Recreations:* blues and jazz music, supporting West Ham United FC. *Address:* House of Commons, SW1A 0AA.

GARBETT, Mark Edward; Headteacher, Latymer School, since 2005; *b* 14 May 1957; *s* of Edward and Mary Garbett; two *d*. *Educ:* Tividale Sch.; Selwyn Coll., Cambridge (BA Maths 1978; PGCE); Open Univ. (MEd). NPQH. Hd of Maths and Housemaster, Framlingham Coll., 1986–91; Hd of Maths and ICT, Royal Belfast Academical Instn, 1991–97; Dep. Head, Skegness GS, 1997–2000; Head, Stretford GS, 2000–05. *Recreations:* creek crawling on the East coast, running, playing piano. *Address:* Latymer School, Haselbury Road, Edmonton, N9 9TN. *T:* (020) 8807 4037, *Fax:* (020) 8887 8111; *e-mail:* gar@latymer.co.uk.

GARBUTT, Graham Bernard; Chief Executive, Commission for Rural Communities, since 2006; *b* 16 June 1947; *s* of Alfred Garbutt and Rhoda Garbutt (*née* Jones); *m* 1986, Lyda Patricia Jadresić, MD; one *s* two *d*. *Educ:* Grove Sch., Market Drayton; Univ. of Bath (BSc 1970; BArch (1st cl.) 1972); Univ. of Sheffield (MA Town and Regl Planning 1974). Urban Renewal Co-ordinator, Haringey BC, 1974–80; Policy and Prog. Planning Officer, Hackney BC, 1980–87; Dir, S Canning Town and Custom House Project, Newham BC, 1987–90; Chief Exec., Gloucester CC, 1990–2001; Regl Dir, Govt Office for W Midlands, ODPM, 2001–05 (Chairman: Europ. Prog. Monitoring Cttee, 2001–05; Regl Housing Bd, 2004–05; Regl Resilience Forum, 2004–05) ; Chief Exec., Countryside Agency, 2005–06. Planning and housing consultant, Nigeria, 1976–77. Vis. Lectr, AA Grad. Sch., London, 1976–82. England rep., 2002–, Pres., 2004–05, European Assoc. of State Territorial Reps; Advr to OECD territorial review of Chile, 2008. *Recreations:* family, visual arts, architecture, travel, garden. *Address:* (office) John Dower House, Crescent Place, Cheltenham, Glos GL50 3RA. *T:* (01242) 533307; *e-mail:* graham.garbutt@ruralcommunities.gov.uk.

GARCIA, Arthur, CBE 1989; JP; Judge of the High Court, Hong Kong, 1979–89; Commissioner for Administrative Complaints, Hong Kong, 1989–94, retired; *b* 3 July 1924; *s* of late F. M. Garcia and of Maria Fung; *m* 1948, Hilda May; two *s*. *Educ:* La Salle Coll., Hong Kong; Inns of Court Sch. of Law. Called to the Bar, Middle Temple, 1957. Jun. Clerk, Hong Kong Govt, 1939–41; Staff Mem., British Consulate, Macao, 1942–45; Clerk to Attorney Gen., Hong Kong, 1946–47; Asst Registrar, 1951–54; Colonial Devlt and Welfare Scholarship, Inns of Court Sch. of Law, 1954–57; Legal Asst, Hong Kong, 1957–59; Magistrate, 1959; Sen. Magistrate, 1968; Principal Magistrate, 1968; Dist Judge, 1971. Member: Preliminary Working Cttee, HKSAR, 1994–95; Preparatory Cttee, HKSAR, 1996–97. JP Hong Kong, 1991. *Recreations:* photography, swimming. *Address:* 15 Briar Avenue, Hong Kong. *Club:* Hong Kong Jockey (Hong Kong).

GARCÍA MÁRQUEZ, Gabriel; *see* Márquez.

GARCÍA-PARRA, Jaime; Gran Cruz, Orden de San Carlos, Colombia, 1977; Gran Cruz de Boyacá, Colombia, 1981; President, J. García P. y Cía, Consultants, since 1993; *b* 19 Dec. 1931; *s* of Alfredo García-Cadena and Elvira Parra; *m* 1955, Lillian Duperly; three *s*. *Educ:* Gimnasio Moderno, Bogotá, Colombia; Univ. Javeriana, Bogotá; Univ. la Gran Colombia, Bogotá; Syracuse Univ., USA (MA); LSE, London (MSc). Lawyer. Minister (Colombian Delegn) to Internat. Coffee Org., 1963–66; Finance Vice-Pres., Colombian Nat. Airlines AVIANCA, 1966–69; Consultant in private practice, 1969–74; Actg Labour and Social Security Minister and Minister of Communications, 1974–75; Minister of Mines and Energy, 1975–77; Ambassador of Colombia to UK, 1977–78; Minister of Finance, Colombia, 1978–81; Exec. Dir, World Bank, 1981–82; Senator, Colombia, 1982; Pres. and Chief Exec. Officer, Acerías Paz del Río, steel and cement, 1982–90; Ambassador to USA, 1990–93. Mem., several delegns to UNCTAD and FAO Confs at Geneva, 1964, New Delhi, 1968, Rome, 1970, 1971. Hon. Fellow, LSE, 1980. Gran Cruz, Orden del Baron de Rio Branco, Brasil, 1977. *Publications: essays:* La Inflación y el Desarrollo de América Latina (Inflation and Development in Latin America), 1968; La Estrategia del Desarrollo Colombiano (The Strategy of Colombian Development), 1971; El Problema Inflacionario Colombiano (Colombia's Inflationary Problem), 1972; Petróleo un Problema y una Política (Oil—a Problem and a Policy), 1975; El Sector Eléctrico en la Encrucijada (The Electrical Sector at the Cross-Roads), 1975; Una Política para el Carbón (A Policy for Coal), 1976; La Cuestión Cafetera (The Coffee Dilemma), 1977; Política Agraria (Agrarian Policy), 1977. *Recreations:* walking, reading, poetry, tennis, cooking. *Clubs:* Jockey, Country (Bogotá).

GARDAM, David Hill; QC 1968; *b* 14 Aug. 1922; *s* of late Harry H. Gardam, Hove, Sussex; *m* 1954, Jane Mary Gardam, *qv*; two *s* one *d*. *Educ:* Oundle Sch.; Christ Church, Oxford. MA 1948. War Service, RNVR, 1941–46 (Temp. Lieut). Called to the Bar, Inner Temple, 1949; Bencher 1977. *Recreations:* painting, etching, printing. *Address:* 1 Atkin Building, Gray's Inn, WC1R 5BQ. *T:* (020) 7404 0102; Haven House, Sandwich, Kent CT13 9ES.

See also T. D. Gardam.

GARDAM, Jane Mary; novelist; *d* of William Pearson, Coatham Sch., Redcar and Kathleen Mary Pearson (*née* Helm); *m* 1954, David Hill Gardam, *qv*; two *s* one *d*. *Educ:* Saltburn High Sch. for Girls; Bedford Coll., London Univ. Red Cross Travelling Librarian, Hospital Libraries, 1951; Sub-Editor, Weldon's Ladies Jl, 1952; Asst Literary Editor, Time and Tide, 1952–54. FRSL 1976. Hon. DLitt Teesside, 2003. Heywood Hill Award for lifetime's contrib. to enjoyment of books, 2000. *Publications:* A Long Way From Verona, 1971 (Phoenix Award, Childrens' Literature Assoc., 1991); The Summer After The Funeral, 1973; Bilgewater, 1977; God on the Rocks, 1978 (Prix Baudelaire, 1989; televised, 1992); The Hollow Land (Whitbread Literary Award), 1981; Bridget and William, 1981; Horse, 1982; Kit, 1983; Crusoe's Daughter, 1985; Kit in Boots, 1986; Swan, 1987; Through the Doll's House Door, 1987; The Queen of the Tambourine (Whitbread Novel Award), 1991; Faith Fox, 1996; Tufty Bear, 1996; The Green Man, 1998; The Flight of the Maidens, 2000; Old Filth, 2004; *non-fiction:* The Iron Coast, 1994; *short stories:* A Few Fair Days, 1971; Black Faces, White Faces (David Higham Award, Winifred Holtby Award), 1975; The Sidmouth Letters, 1980; The Pangs of Love, 1983 (Katherine Mansfield Award, 1984); Showing the Flag, 1989; Going into a Dark House, 1994; Missing the Midnight, 1997; The People on Privilege Hill, 2007. *Address:* Haven House, Sandwich, Kent CT13 9ES. *Club:* PEN.

See also T. D. Gardam.

GARDAM, Timothy David; Principal, St Anne's College, Oxford, since 2004; *b* 14 Jan. 1956; *s* of David Hill Gardam, *qv* and Jane Mary Gardam, *qv*; *m* 1982, Kim Scott Walwyn (*d* 2002); one *d*. *Educ:* Westminster Sch.; Gonville and Caius Coll., Cambridge (MA). Joined BBC as trainee researcher, 1977; Asst Producer, Nationwide, 1977–79; Producer, Newsnight, 1979–82; Executive Producer: Timewatch, 1982–85; Bookmark, 1984–85; Dep. Editor, Election Programmes, 1985–87; Editor: Panorama, 1987–90; Newsnight,

1990–93; Hd, Weekly Programmes, BBC News and Current Affairs, 1993–96; Controller, News, Current Affairs and Documentaries, Channel Five, 1996–98; Dir of Programmes, 1998–2002, Dir of Television, 2002–03, Channel 4. Non-exec. Dir, OFCOM, 2008–. Chm., Reuters Inst. for Study of Journalism, Univ. of Oxford, 2006–. Dir, Oxford Playhouse, 2005–. Chm., Voltaire Foundn, 2005–. *Recreations:* history, gardens. *Address:* The Principal's Lodgings, St Anne's College, Oxford OX2 6HS.

GARDEN, family name of **Baroness Garden of Frognal**.

GARDEN OF FROGNAL, Baroness *cr* 2007 (Life Peer), of Hampstead, in the London Borough of Camden; **Susan Elizabeth Garden;** *b* 22 Feb. 1944; *d* of late Henry George Button, author, and Edith Margaret Heslop; *m* 1965, Timothy Garden (later Baron Garden (Life Peer), KCB) (*d* 2007); two *d*. *Educ:* Westonbirt Sch., Glos; St Hilda's Coll., Oxford (BA 1965; MA 1982). Secondary sch. teacher in UK and Germany, 1977–79; City and Guilds of London Institute, later C&G, 1988–: Manager, 1990–2000; consultant, 2000–. Educn Ed., The Source, 2000–02. Chm., ASM, St Hilda's Coll., Oxford, 1996–2000; Trustee, Oxford Univ. Soc., 2001–05 (Vice-Chm., 2005–08). Contested (Lib Dem) Finchley and Golders Green, 2005. Mem., Lib Dem Federal Conf. Cttee, 2004–. Vice Pres., Inst. of Export, 2005–. Mem., Co. of World Traders, 2000– (Master, 2008–Oct. 2009). CAB Advr, 1982–87; Pres., Relate, Central Middx, 1997–2002; SSAFA Caseworker, 2001–05. Vice Chm., RBL City of London Poppy Appeal, 2006–. FRSA 1993. *Address:* House of Lords, SW1A 0PW; *e-mail:* sue.garden@blueyonder.co.uk. *Clubs:* National Liberal, Royal Air Force.

GARDEN, Ian Harrison; barrister; *b* 18 June 1961; *s* of late Norman Harrison Garden and of Jean Elizabeth Garden; *m* 1986, Alexandra Helen Grounds; two *s*. *Educ:* Sedbergh Sch.; UC Wales, Aberystwyth (LLB Hons 1982). Barrister in private practice, 1989–. Dep. Chancellor, Dio. of Sheffield, 1999–. Mem., Gen. Synod, C of E, 1995–2005 (Member: Legislative Cttee, 1996–2000; Legal Adv. Commn, 2001–); Member: Bishop's Council and Standing Cttee, Dio. of Blackburn, 1996–2004; Crown Appts, then Crown Nominations, Commn, 1997–2005; Archbishops' Council, 2000–05; C of E Appts Cttee, 2001–05; Chm., Dio. of Blackburn Vacancy-in-See Cttee, 2001–. Lay Canon, Blackburn Cathedral, 2003–. Member, Appeals Tribunal Panels, 1996–2001: Pastoral Measure (1983); Incumbents (Vacation of Benefices) Measure (1977); Ordination of Women (Financial Provisions) Measure (1993). Director: Walsingham Coll. Trust Assoc., 1999–; Walsingham Coll. (Yorks Properties) Ltd, 2001–; Mem. Bd Dirs, Manchester Camerata Ltd, 2003–. Guardian, Shrine of Our Lady of Walsingham, 1996–. Gov., Quainton Hall Sch., Harrow, 1999–2001. *Recreations:* orchestral and choral conducting, organ playing, driving classic cars on the continent. *Address:* Old Church Cottage, 29 Church Road, Rufford, near Ormskirk, Lancs L40 1TA. *T:* (chambers) (0151) 236 7191, (home) (01704) 821303. *Clubs:* East India; Athenæum (Liverpool).

GARDEN, Malcolm; Sheriff of Grampian Highland and Islands at Peterhead, since 2001; *b* 7 Aug. 1952; *s* of George Garden and Phillippa Mary Hills or Garden; *m* 1984, Sandra Moles; two *s* one *d*. *Educ:* Robert Gordon's Coll., Aberdeen; Univ. of Aberdeen (LLB). NP 1976. Apprentice, then Asst Solicitor, Watt and Cumine, Aberdeen, 1973–76; Asst Solicitor, 1976–79, Partner, 1979–2001, Clark-Wallace, Aberdeen; Temp. Sheriff, 1994–99; Sheriff (pt-time), 2000–01. Tutor (pt-time), Univ. of Aberdeen, 1980–85. Mem., Aberdeen and NE Legal Aid Cttee, 1984–86; Reporter to Scottish Legal Aid Bd, 1986–96. Member: Law Soc. of Scotland, 1976–; Soc. of Advocates, Aberdeen, 1978–. *Recreations:* family, golf, football, tennis. *Address:* Sheriff Court House, Queen Street, Peterhead, Aberdeenshire AB42 6TP. *T:* (01779) 476676; *e-mail:* Sheriff.MGarden@scotcourts.gov.uk.

GARDEN, Prof. (Olivier) James, MD; FRCSE, FRCSGlas, FRCPE; Regius Professor of Clinical Surgery, since 2000, and Head, School of Clinical Sciences and Community Health, 2003–06, University of Edinburgh; Surgeon to the Queen in Scotland, since 2004; *b* 13 Nov. 1953; *s* of late James Garden and of Marguerite Marie Jeanne Garden (*née* Vourch); *m* 1977, Amanda Gillian Merrills; one *s* one *d*. *Educ:* Lanark Grammar Sch.; Univ. of Edinburgh (BSc 1974; MB ChB 1977; MD 1988). FRCSGlas 1981; FRCSE 1994; FRCPE 2003. Lectr in Surgery, Univ. of Glasgow, 1985; Chef de Clinique, Univ. de Paris-Sud, 1986–88; University of Edinburgh: Sen. Lectr in Surgery, 1988–98; Prof. of Hepatobiliary Surgery, 1998–2000; Head, Dept of Clin. and Surgical Scis, 1999–2003. Hon. Consultant Surgeon: Royal Infirmary of Edinburgh, 1988–; and Head, Scottish Liver Transplant Unit, 1992–. Ext. Examr, univs incl. Glasgow, Newcastle, Bristol, Hong Kong and Dublin. Member: James IV Assoc. of Surgeons, 1996– (Hon. Sec., 1999–); Assoc. Upper Gastrointestinal Surgeons, 1996– (Pres., 2002–04); Internat. Hepato Pancreato Biliary Assoc., 1998–2006. Company Sec., British Jl of Surgery Soc. Ltd, 2003–. Hon. FRACS 2007; Hon. FRCP&S (Canada) 2009. *Publications:* Principles and Practice of Surgical Laparoscopy, 1994; Intraoperative and Laparoscopic Ultrasonography, 1995; Color Atlas of Surgical Diagnosis, 1995; A Companion to Specialist Surgical Practice (7 vols), 1997, 3rd edn 2005; Liver Metastasis: biology, diagnosis and treatment, 1998; Principles and Practice of Surgery, 2000, 5th edn 2007; numerous contribs to surgical and gastroenterological jls. *Recreations:* ski-ing, golf, food, wine. *Address:* 22 Moston Terrace, Edinburgh EH9 2DE. *T:* (0131) 667 3715.

GARDINER, Barry Strachan; MP (Lab) Brent North, since 1997; *b* 10 March 1957; *s* of late John Flannegan Gardiner and Sylvia Jean Strachan; *m* 1979, Caroline Anne Smith; three *s* one *d*. *Educ:* Haileybury; St Andrews Univ. (MA Hons). Corpus Christi Coll., Cambridge. ACII. Scottish Sec., SCM, 1979–81. John F. Kennedy Schol., Harvard Univ., 1983; General Average Adjuster, 1987–97. Parliamentary Under-Secretary of State:, NI Office, 2004–05; DTI, 2005–06; DEFRA, 2006–07. *Publications:* articles in Philosophical Qly, Lloyd's List, Insurance Internat. *Recreations:* music, bird watching, hill walking. *Address:* House of Commons, SW1A 0AA.

GARDINER, Elizabeth Anne Finlay; Parliamentary Counsel, since 2003; *b* 19 March 1966; *m* 1990, Alan Gardiner; one *s* one *d*. *Educ:* Edinburgh Univ. (LLB 1987; DLP). Admitted as solicitor, Scotland, 1990, England and Wales, 1991; Asst Parly Counsel, 1991–95; Sen. Asst Parly Counsel, 1995–2000; Dep. Parly Counsel, 2000–03. *Address:* Office of the Parliamentary Counsel, 36 Whitehall, SW1A 2AY. *T:* (020) 7210 0952.

GARDINER, George; Senior Civil Servant, since 2002; *b* 25 Oct. 1955; *s* of George Gardiner and Isabella Colquhoun Gardiner; *m* 1981, Colleen May Holbrow; three *d*. *Educ:* Paisley Grammar Sch. MoD, 1974–. *Recreations:* listening to and creating electronic music, studying the detection techniques of Lord Peter Wimsey, day-dreaming.

GARDINER, Sir John Eliot, Kt 1998; CBE 1990; conductor; Founder and Artistic Director, English Baroque Soloists, Monteverdi Choir, Monteverdi Orchestra, and Orchestre Révolutionnaire et Romantique; Chef fondateur, Opéra de Lyon Orchestra, since 1988 (Musical Director, 1983–88); *b* 20 April 1943; *s* of Rolf Gardiner and late Marabel Gardiner (*née* Hodgkin); *m* 1981, Elizabeth Suzanne Wilcock (marr. diss. 1997); three *d*; *m* 2001, Isabella de Sabata. *Educ:* Bryanston Sch.; King's Coll., Cambridge (MA History); King's Coll., London (Certif. of Advanced Studies in Music, 1966; Hon. FKC 1992). French Govt Scholarship to study in Paris and Fontainebleau with Nadia Boulanger, 1966–68. Founded: Monteverdi Choir, following performance of Monteverdi's Vespers of 1610, King's Coll. Chapel, Cambridge, 1964; Monteverdi Orchestra, 1968; English Baroque Soloists (period instruments), 1978; Orchestre Révolutionnaire et Romantique, 1990. Début: (concert), Wigmore Hall, 1966; (operatic), Sadler's Wells Opera, London Coliseum, 1969; Royal Opera House, Covent Garden, 1973; Royal Festival Hall, 1972; Glyndebourne, 1997; Guest engagements conducting major orchestras in Paris, Brussels, Geneva, Frankfurt, Dresden, Leipzig, London, Vienna, Boston, Cleveland, Pittsburgh, NY; European Music Festivals: Aix-en-Provence, Aldeburgh, Bath, Berlin, Edinburgh, Flanders, Holland, Salzburg, City of London, etc; concert revivals in London of major dramatic works of Purcell, Handel and Rameau; world première: (staged) of Rameau's opera Les Boréades, Aix-en-Provence, 1982; Berlioz, Messe Solennelle, Westminster Cath., 1993; Bach Cantata Pilgrimage, 1999–2001. Principal Conductor: CBC Vancouver Orchestra, 1980–83; NDR Symphony Orch., Hamburg, 1991–94. Artistic Director: Göttingen Handel Fest., 1981–90; Veneto Music Fest., 1986; residency at Le Châtelet, Paris, 1999–2004. Has made over 200 records ranging from Monteverdi and Mozart to Massenet, Rodrigo and Central American Percussion Music. Hon. FRAM 1992. DUniv Univ. Lumière Lyon, 1987. Grand Prix du Disque, 1978, 1979, 1980, 1992; Gramophone Awards for early music and choral music records, 1978, 1980, 1986, 1988, 1989, 1990, 1991 (Record of the Year), 1994 (Artist of the Year); Prix Caecilia, 1982, 1983, 1985; Edison Award, 1982, 1986, 1987, 1988, 1989, 1996, 1997; Internat. Record Critics Award, 1982, 1983; Deutscher Schallplattenpreis, 1986, 1994, 1997; Arturo Toscanini Music Critics Award, 1985, 1986; IRCA Prize, Helsinki, 1987; Best Choir of the Year for Monteverdi Choir, Internat. Classical Music Awards, 1992. Commandeur, Ordre des Arts et des Lettres (France), 1997 (Officier, 1988). *Publications:* (ed) Claude le Jeune Hélas! Mon Dieu, 1971; contrib. to opera handbook on Gluck's Orfeo, 1980. *Recreations:* forestry, organic farming. *Address:* c/o Askonas Holt, Lincoln House, 300 High Holborn, WC1V 7JH.

GARDINER, Prof. John Graham, PhD; FIET; FREng; Professor of Electronic Engineering, 1986–94, and Dean of Engineering and Physical Sciences, 1996–2002, University of Bradford; Director, Wireless Technologies CIC, since 2006; *b* 24 May 1939; *s* of William Clement Gardiner and Ellen (*née* Adey); *m* 1962, Sheila Joyce Andrews; one *s* two *d*. *Educ:* Univ. of Birmingham (BSc 1st Cl. Hons; PhD 1964). FIET (FIEE 1988); FREng (FEng 1994). Software designer, Racal Res. Ltd, 1966–68; University of Bradford: Lectr, 1968–72; Sen Lectr, 1972–78; Reader, 1978–86; Hd, Dept of Electronic and Electrical Engrg, 1994–96. SMIEE 1995; FRSA 1997. *Publications:* (with J. D. Parsons) Mobile Communication Systems, 1989; (with B. West) Personal Communication Systems and Technologies, 1995. *Recreation:* music. *Address:* 1 Queen's Drive Lane, Ilkley, W Yorks LS29 9QS. *T:* (01943) 609581.

GARDINER, John Ralph; QC 1982; *b* 28 Feb. 1946; *s* of late Cyril Ralph Gardiner and Mary Gardiner (*née* Garibaldi); *m* 1976, Pascal Mary Issard-Davies; one *d*. *Educ:* Bancroft's Sch., Woodford; Fitzwilliam Coll., Cambridge (BA (Law Tripos), MA, LLM). Called to the Bar, Middle Temple, 1968 (Harmsworth Entrance Scholar and Harmsworth Law Scholar; Bencher, 1992); practice at the Bar, 1970–; Mem., Senate of Inns of Court and Bar, 1982–86 (Treasurer, 1985–86); Chm., Taxation and Retirement Benefits Cttee, Bar Council, 1982–85. FRSA 2001. *Publications:* contributor to Pinson on Revenue Law, 6th to 15th (1982) edns. *Recreation:* tennis. *Address:* 11 New Square, Lincoln's Inn, WC2A 3QB. *T:* (020) 7242 3981; Admiral's House, Admiral's Walk, Hampstead, NW3 6RS. *T:* (020) 7435 0597.

GARDINER, Juliet; writer and historian; *b* 24 June 1943; *d* of Charles and Dorothy Wells; *m* 1st, 1961, George Arthur Gardiner (later Sir George Gardiner) (marr. diss. 1980; he *d* 2002); two *s* one *d*; 2nd, 1990, Henry Horwitz. *Educ:* Berkhamsted Sch. for Girls; University Coll. London (BA 1st Cl. Hons Hist.). Ed., History Today, 1981–85; Acad. Dir, then Publisher, Weidenfield & Nicolson, 1985–89; Middlesex University: Principal Lectr, 1992–97; Acad. Chair, Communication, Cultural and Media Studies, 1997–2000; Hd, Publishing Studies, Oxford Brookes Univ., 2000–01. Res. Fellow, Inst. Histl Res., Univ. of London, 1979–81; Hon. Vis. Prof., Sch. of Arts, Middlesex Univ. 2004–07. Consultant, Atonement (film), 2006. *Publications:* Over Here: GIs in wartime Britain 1942–45, 1992; The World Within: the Brontës at Haworth, 1992; (ed) Women's Voices: the new woman 1880–1914, 1993; Picture Post Women, 1994; (ed) The History Today Companion to British History, 1995; Oscar Wilde: a life in letters, writings and wit, 1995; Queen Victoria, 1997; From the Bomb to the Beatles: the changing face of post-war Britain 1945–65, 1999; The Penguin Dictionary of British History, 2000; The History Today Who's Who in British History, 2000; The 1940s House, 2000; The Edwardian Country House, 2002; Wartime: Britain 1939–1945, 2004; The Children's War, 2005; The Animals' War, 2006; War on the Home Front, 2007. *Recreation:* London. *Address:* *e-mail:* juliet@julietgardiner.com.

GARDINER, Air Vice-Marshal Martyn John, OBE 1987; FRAeS; Military Advisor to High Representative for Bosnia and Herzegovina, 2001–02; *b* 13 June 1946; *s* of late John Glen Gardiner and Edith Eleanor Gardiner (*née* Howley); *m* 1971, Anne Dunlop Thom; two *s* one *d*. *Educ:* Frimley and Camberley Grammar Sch.; Southampton Univ. (BScEng Aeronautics and Astronautics 1967). FRAeS 2000. Flying and staff appointments include: Coll. of Air Warfare, 1969–71; No 99 Sqdn, Brize Norton, 1971–75; Dept of Air Warfare, Gen. Duties Aero-Systems Course, 1976; No 72 Sqdn, Odiham, 1977–80; HQ 2 Armd Div., Germany, 1980–82; RAF Staff Coll., Bracknell, 1983; OC 32 Sqdn, RAF Northolt, 1984–87; HQ STC, 1987–88; Defence Policy and Commitments Staffs, MoD, 1988–91; OC RAF Northolt, 1991–93; SASO, HQ 38 Gp, 1994–96; COS Reaction Force Air Staff Kalkar, 1996–98; Dep. Comdr, Combined Air Ops Centre 4, Messstetten, 1998–2001. Chairman: NE Lincs Aircrew Assoc., 2004–; Louth RAFA, 2004–. Dir, Grimsby Corp., 2004–; Dir and Trustee, Katherine Martin Charitable Trust, 2006–; Chm. of Govs, Duke of Kent Sch., Ewhurst, 2002–; Chm., Alexander Duckham Meml Schs Trust, 2004–. *Recreations:* golf, ski-ing, walking, Rugby-watching. *Address:* Heronsbrook, Stewton Lane, Louth, Lincolnshire LN11 8SB. *Club:* Royal Air Force.

GARDINER, Peter Dod Robin; First Deputy Head, Stanborough School, Hertfordshire, 1979–92, retired; *b* 23 Dec. 1927; *s* of late Brig. R. Gardiner, CB, CBE; *m* 1959, Juliet Wright; one *s* one *d*. *Educ:* Radley College; Trinity Coll., Cambridge. Asst Master, Charterhouse, 1952–67, and Housemaster, Charterhouse, 1965–67; Headmaster, St Peter's School, York, 1967–79. *Publications:* (ed) Twentieth-Century Travel, 1963; (with B. W. M. Young) Intelligent Reading, 1964; (with W. A. Gibson) The Design of Prose, 1971. *Recreations:* reading, music, walking, acting. *Address:* Willows, Stream Road, Upton, Didcot, Oxfordshire OX11 9JG.

GARDINER, Victor Alec, OBE 1977; Director and General Manager, London Weekend Television, 1971–87; *b* 9 Aug. 1929; *m*; one *s* two *d*. *Educ:* Whitgift Middle Sch., Croydon; City and Guilds (radio and telecommunications). Techn. Asst, GPO Engrg, 1947–49; RAF Nat. Service, 1949–51; BBC Sound Radio Engr, 1951–53; BBC TV Cameraman, 1953–55; Rediffusion TV Sen. Cameraman, 1955–61; Malta TV Trng

Man., 1961–62; Head of Studio Prodn, Rediffusion TV, 1962–67; Man. Dir, GPA Productions, 1967–69; Production Controller, London Weekend Television, 1969–71; Director: LWT (Hldgs) Ltd, 1976–87; London Weekend Services Ltd, 1976–87; Richard Price Television Associates, 1981–87; Chairman: Dynamic Technology Ltd, 1972–87; Standard Music Ltd, 1972–87; LWT Internat., 1981–87. Mem., Royal Television Soc., 1970– (Vice-Chm. Council, 1974–75; Chm. Papers Cttee, 1975; Chm. Council, 1976–77; Fellow, 1977). *Recreations:* music, building, gardening, narrow boating.

GARDNER, family name of **Baroness Gardner of Parkes**.

GARDNER OF PARKES, Baroness *cr* 1981 (Life Peer), of Southgate, Greater London, and of Parkes, NSW; **(Rachel) Trixie (Anne) Gardner,** AM 2003; JP; dental surgeon; Chairman, Plan International (UK) Ltd, 1990–2003; *b* Parkes, NSW, 17 July 1927; eighth *c* of late Hon. J. J. Gregory McGirr and Rachel McGirr, OBE, LC; *m* 1956, Kevin Anthony Gardner (*d* 2007), *o s* of late George and Rita Gardner, Sydney, Australia; three *d*. *Educ:* Monte Sant Angelo Coll., N Sydney; East Sydney Technical Coll.; Univ. of Sydney (BDS 1954; Hon. Fellow 2005). Cordon Bleu de Paris, Diplôme 1956. Came to UK, 1955. Member: Westminster City Council, 1968–78 (Lady Mayoress, 1987–88); GLC, for Havering, 1970–73, for Enfield-Southgate, 1977–86. Contested (C) Blackburn, 1970; N Cornwall, Feb. 1974. House of Lords: a Dep. Speaker, 1999–2002; Dep. Chm. of Cttees, 1999–2002. Chm., Royal Free Hampstead NHS Trust, 1994–97; Vice-Chm., NE Thames RHA, 1990–94; Member: Inner London Exec. Council, NHS, 1966–71; Standing Dental Adv. Cttee for England and Wales, 1968–76; Westminster, Kensington and Chelsea Area Health Authority, 1974–82; Industrial Tribunal Panel for London, 1974–97; N Thames Gas Consumer Council, 1980–82; Dept of Employment's Adv. Cttee on Women's Employment, 1980–88; Britain–Australia Bicentennial Cttee, 1984–88; London Electricity Bd, 1984–90. British Chm., European Union of Women, 1978–82; UK Rep., UN Status of Women Commn, 1982–88. Director: Gateway Building Soc., 1987–88; Woolwich Building Soc., 1988–93. Chm., Suzy Lamplugh Trust, 1993–97. Governor: Eastman Dental Hosp., 1971–80; Nat. Heart Hosp., 1974–90. Hon. Pres., War Widows Assoc. of GB, 1984–87; Hon. Vice-Pres., Women's Sect., RBL, 2000–06. JP North Westminster, 1971. DUniv Middlesex, 1997. *Recreations:* gardening, reading, travel, needlework. *Address:* House of Lords, SW1A 0PW.

GARDNER, Antony John; Registrar, Central Council for Education and Training in Social Work, 1988–92 (Principal Registration Officer, 1970–88), retired; *b* 27 Dec. 1927; *s* of David Gardner, head gardener, and Lillian Gardner; *m* 1956, Eveline A. Burden (*d* 2003). *Educ:* elem. school; Co-operative Coll.; Southampton Univ. (Pres. Union, Southampton, 1958–59; BSc (Econ) 1959). Apprentice toolmaker, 1941–45; National Service, RASC, 1946–48; building trade, 1948–53. Tutor Organiser, Co-operative Union, 1959–60; Member and Education Officer, Co-operative Union, 1961–66. Contested (Lab): SW Wolverhampton, 1964; Beeston, Feb. and Oct. 1974; MP (Lab) Rushcliffe, 1966–70. Contested (Lab) Dorset and E Devon, Eur. Parly elecns, 1994. *Recreations:* angling, gardening and the countryside generally. *Address:* 12 Heath Avenue, Poole, Dorset BH15 3EJ. *T:* (01202) 676683. *Club:* Parkstone Trades and Labour (Poole).

GARDNER, Brigid Catherine Brennan, OBE 2002; Principal, St George's British International (formerly English) School, Rome, 1994–2004; *b* 5 May 1941; *d* of John Henthorn Cantrell Brennan and Rosamond Harriet Brennan (*née* Gardner); *m* 1963, Michael Henry Davies (marr. diss. 1980); three *d*. *Educ:* The Alice Ottley Sch., Worcester; Girton Coll., Cambridge (MA). English and History teacher, Harrogate High Sch., 1963–66; English teacher, Hong Kong, 1967–69; James Allen's Girls' School: Head of History, 1976–83; Dep. Head, 1981–83; Headmistress, 1984–94. Governor: Oundle Sch., 1992–94; Whitgift Foundn, 1992–94. *Recreations:* gardening, wine-making, travelling, walking, reading. *Address:* Ash Cottage, Court Lane, Dulwich Village, SE21 7DH.

GARDNER, Christopher James Ellis; QC 1994; **Hon. Chief Justice Gardner;** Chief Justice of the Turks and Caicos Islands, since 2004; *b* 6 April 1945; *s* of James Charles Gardner and Phillis May Gardner (*née* Wilkinson); *m* 1972, Arlene Sellers; one *s* one *d*. *Educ:* Rossall Sch., Lancs; Fitzwilliam Coll., Cambridge (MA). Called to the Bar, Gray's Inn, 1968; a Recorder, 1993–. FCIArb 1999; Chartered Arbitrator, 2003; Accredited Mediator, 2000. Liveryman, Arbitrators' Co., 2003. Fellow, Soc. for Advanced Legal Studies, 1999; FRSocMed 2000. *Recreations:* theatre, ballet, bell ringing, golf, cooking curries. *Address:* Supreme Court, Grand Turk, Turks and Caicos Islands, West Indies. *Club:* Dartmouth Yacht.

GARDNER, Prof. David Pierpont, PhD; President, The William and Flora Hewlett Foundation, 1993–99; President, University of California, 1983–92; Professor of Education, University of California at Berkeley, 1983–92; *b* 24 March 1933; *s* of Reed S. Gardner and Margaret (*née* Pierpont); *m* 1st, 1958, Elizabeth Fuhriman (*d* 1991); four *d*; 2nd, 1995, Sheila S. Rodgers. *Educ:* Brigham Young Univ. (BS 1955); Univ. of Calif, Berkeley (MA 1959, PhD 1966). Dir, Calif Alumni Foundn, Calif Alumni Assoc., Univ. of Calif, Berkeley, 1962–64. University of California, Santa Barbara: Asst Prof. of Higher Educn, 1964–69; Associate Prof. of Higher Educn, 1969–70; Prof. of Higher Educn (on leave), 1971–73; Asst to the Chancellor, 1964–67; Asst Chancellor, 1967–69; Vice Chancellor and Exec. Asst, 1969–70; Vice Pres., Univ. of Calif, 1971–73; Pres., and Prof. of Higher Educn, Univ. of Utah, 1973–83, Pres. Emeritus, 1985. Vis. Fellow, Clare Hall, Univ. of Cambridge, 1979 (Hon. Fellow, 2002). Fellow, Nat. Acad. of Public Administration; Member: Amer. Philosophical Soc.; Nat. Acad. of Educn. Board of Dirs, Fluor Corp.; Chm., J. Paul Getty Trust, 2000–04. Trustee, Tanner Lectures on Human Values, 1975–2004. Fulbright 40th Anniversary Distinguished Fellow, Japan, 1986; Fellow, Amer. Acad. of Arts and Scis, 1986. Hon. LLD: Univ. of The Pacific, 1983; Nevada, Las Vegas, 1984; Westminster Coll., 1987; Brown, 1989; Notre Dame, 1989; Hon. DH Brigham Young, 1981; Hon. DLitt Utah, 1983; Hon. HHD Utah State, 1987; Hon. Dr Bordeaux II, 1988; Hon. DHL Internat. Christian Univ. Benjamin P. Cheney Medal, Eastern Washington Univ., 1984; James Bryant Conant Award, Educn Commn of the States, 1985; Hall of Fame Award, Calif. Sch. Bd Res Foundn, 1988. Chevalier, Légion d'Honneur (France), 1985; Knight Commander, Order of Merit (Germany), 1992. *Publications:* The California Oath Controversy, 1967; Earning My Degree: memoirs of an American university president, 2005; contrib. articles to professional jls. *Address:* (office) Center for Studies in Higher Education, South Hall Annex, University of California, Berkeley, CA 94720, USA.

GARDNER, Douglas Frank; Chairman, Board of Governors, Nuffield Hospitals, since 2001 (Governor, since 1995); *b* 20 Dec. 1943; *s* of late Ernest Frank Gardner and Mary Gardner; *m* 1978, Adèle (*née* Alexander); one *s* two *d*. *Educ:* Woolverstone Hall; College of Estate Management, London Univ. (BSc). FRICS. Chief Exec., Properties Div., Tarmac plc, 1976–83; Man. Dir, 1983–93, Chm., 1993–2000, Brixton Estate plc. Chairman: Industrial Realisation plc, 2000–; Industrial Develt Partnership, 2000–07; GPT Halverton Ltd, 2004–; Director: Invesco UK Property Income Trust, 2004–; Hirco plc, 2006–; Mem., Investment Cttee, Eur. Industrial Property Fund, 2001–04. *Recreations:* tennis, theatre. *Address:* 20 Cottesmore Gardens, Kensington, W8 5PR. *T:* (020) 7937 7127.

GARDNER, Francis Rolleston, OBE 2005; BBC Security Correspondent, since 2002; *b* 31 July 1961; *s* of Robert Neil Gardner and Grace Rolleston Gardner; *m* 1997, Amanda Jane Pearson; two *d*. *Educ:* Marlborough Coll.; Exeter Univ. (BA Hons Arabic and Islamic Studies 1984). Marketing Manager, Gulf Exports, 1984–86; Trading and Sales, Saudi Internat. Bank, 1986–90; Dir, Robert Fleming, 1990–95; joined BBC News, 1995: World TV, 1995–97; Gulf Corresp., 1997–99; ME Corresp., 1999–2002. Commnd 4th (V) Bn, RGJ, 1984–90. FRGS 2006. Hon. LLD: Staffordshire, 2006; Nottingham, 2006; Exeter, 2007. El Mundo Internat. Journalism Prize, 2006; McWhirter Award for Bravery, 2006; Zayed Medal for Journalism, UAE, 2007; Al-Rawabi Prize for Saudi-British Relns, 2008. *Publication:* Blood and Sand, 2006. *Recreations:* ski-ing, scuba diving, birdwatching, exploring. *Address:* BBC TV Centre, 87 Wood Lane, W12 7RJ. *Clubs:* Travellers, Rifles Officers London.

GARDNER, James Jesse, CVO 1995; CBE 1986; DL; consultant, since 1986; Chairman, OFWAT National Consumer Council, 1993–98; *b* 7 April 1932; *s* of James and Elizabeth Rubina Gardner; *m* 1st, 1955, Diana Sotheran (*d* 1999); three *s* one *d*, 2nd, 2002, Joan Adamson. *Educ:* Kirkham Grammar Sch.; Victoria Univ., Manchester (LLB). Nat. Service, 1955–57. Articled to Town Clerk, Preston, 1952–55; Legal Asst, Preston Co. Borough Council, 1955; Crosby Borough Council: Asst Solicitor, 1957–59; Chief Asst Solicitor, 1959–61; Chief Asst Solicitor, Warrington Co. Borough Council, 1961–65; Stockton-on-Tees Borough Council: Dep. Town Clerk, 1966; Town Clerk, 1966–68; Asst Town Clerk, Teesside Co. Borough Council, 1968; Associate Town Clerk and Solicitor, London Borough of Greenwich, 1968–69; Town Clerk and Chief Exec. Officer, Co. Borough of Sunderland, 1970–73; Chief Exec., Tyne and Wear CC, 1973–86; Chm., Tyne and Wear PTE, 1983–86. Chief Exec., Northern Develt Co. Ltd, 1986–87; Chairman: Sunderland DHA, 1988–90; Northumbrian Water Customer Services Cttee, 1990–2001; North East Television, 1991–92; Dir, Birtley Enterprise Action Management (BEAM) Ltd, 1989–93; Sec., Northern Region Councils Assoc., 1986. Clerk to Lieutenancy, Tyne and Wear, 1974–91. Dir, Garrod Pitkin (1986) Ltd, 1991–93. Chairman: Prince's Trust Trustees, 1986–94; Prince's Trust and Royal Jubilee Trust Management Bd, 1989–93 (former Chm., Northumbria Cttee, Royal Jubilee and Prince's Trusts); Prince's Trust Events Ltd, 1987–94; Director: Threshold (formerly Prince's Trust Training & Employment Ltd), 1991–95 (Chm., 1992); NE Civic Trust, 1986–92. Chairman: Century Radio, 1993–2000; St Benedict's Hospice, Sunderland, 1993–2008; Royalty Theatre, 2001–05; Trustee: Tyne Tees Telethon Trust, 1988–91; Great North Air Ambulance Service Appeal, 1991–95. DL Tyne and Wear, 1976. FRSA 1976; CCMI (CIMgt 1987). Hon. Fellow, Sunderland Polytechnic, 1986. *Recreations:* golf, music, theatre, food and drink. *Address:* Wayside, 121 Queen Alexandra Road, Sunderland, Tyne and Wear SR2 9HR.

GARDNER, (James) Piers; barrister; *b* 26 March 1954; *s* of Michael Clement Gardner and Brigitte Elsa Gardner (*née* Ekrut); *m* 1978, Penelope Helen Chloros; three *s* one *d*. *Educ:* Bryanston Sch.; Brasenose Coll., Oxford (MA Jurisp. 1st Class). Solicitor of the Supreme Court, 1979–2000; called to the Bar, Gray's Inn, 2000. Articled and in private practice as solicitor, with Stephenson Harwood, London, 1977–80; Secretariat, European Commn of Human Rights, Council of Europe, Strasbourg, 1980–87; Exec. Dir, 1987–89, Dir, 1989–2000, British Inst. of Internat. and Comparative Law. *Recreations:* foreign property, arguing. *Address:* Monckton Chambers, 1–2 Raymond Buildings, Gray's Inn, WC1R 5NR. *T:* (020) 7405 7211. *Club:* Athenæum.

GARDNER, Prof. John, DPhil; Professor of Jurisprudence, University of Oxford, since 2000; Fellow, University College, Oxford, since 2000; *b* 23 March 1965. *Educ:* New Coll., Oxford (BA 1986; Vinerian Schol.; BCL 1987); Inns of Court Sch. of Law; All Souls Coll., Oxford (DPhil 1993). Called to the Bar, Inner Temple, 1988, Bencher, 2003; Fellow, All Souls Coll., Oxford, 1986–91; Fellow and Tutor, Brasenose Coll., Oxford, 1991–96; Reader in Legal Philosophy, KCL, 1996–2000; Fellow, All Souls Coll., Oxford, 1998–2000. Visiting Professor: Columbia Univ. Sch. of Law, NY, 2000; Yale Law Sch., 2002–03, 2005; Univ. of Texas, 2006; Princeton Univ., 2008. *Publications:* Action and Value in Criminal Law, 1993; Relating to Responsibility, 2001; Offences and Defences, 2007; contrib. jls incl. Oxford Jl Legal Studies, Cambridge Law Jl, Univ. of Toronto Law Jl. *Recreations:* cooking, web design. *Address:* University College, Oxford OX1 4BH. *T:* (01865) 276638.

GARDNER, John Linton, CBE 1976; composer; *b* 2 March 1917; *s* of late Dr Alfred Gardner, Ilfracombe, and Muriel (*née* Pullein-Thompson); *m* 1955, Jane (*d* 1998), *d* of late N. J. Abercrombie; one *s* two *d*. *Educ:* Eagle House, Sandhurst; Wellington Coll.; Exeter Coll., Oxford (BMus). Served War of 1939–45: RAF, 1940–46. Chief Music Master, Repton Sch., 1939–40. Staff, Covent Garden Opera, 1946–52; Tutor: Morley Coll., 1952–76 (Dir of Music, 1965–69); Bagot Stack Coll., 1955–62; London Univ. (extra-mural) 1959–60; Dir of Music, St Paul's Girls' Sch., 1962–75; Prof. of Harmony and Composition, Royal Acad. of Music, 1956–86. Conductor: Haslemere Musical Soc., 1953–62; Dorian Singers, 1961–62; European Summer Sch. for Young Musicians, 1966–75; Bromley YSO, 1970–76. Brit. Council Lecturer: Levant, 1954; Belgium, 1960; Iberia, 1963; Yugoslavia, 1967. Adjudicator, Canadian Festivals, 1974, 1980. Chm., Composers' Guild, 1963; Member: Arts Council Music Panel, 1958–62; Cttee of Management, Royal Philharmonic Soc., 1965–72; Brit. Council Music Cttee, 1968. Dir, Performing Right Soc., 1965–92 (Dep. Chm., 1983–88). Worshipful Co. of Musicians: Collard Fellow, 1962–64; elected to Freedom and Livery, 1965. Hon. RAM 1959; Hon. Mem., Royal Philharmonic Soc., 1998. Bax Society's Prize, 1958. *Works include: orchestral:* Symphony no 1, 1947; Variations on a Waltz of Carl Nielsen, 1952; Piano Concerto no 1, 1957; Sinfonia Piccola (strings), 1960; Occasional Suite, Aldeburgh Festival, 1968; An English Ballad, 1969; Three Ridings, 1970; Sonatina for Strings, 1974; Divertimento, 1977; Symphony no 2, 1984; Symphony no 3, 1989; Concerto for Oboe and Strings, 1990; Concerto for Flute and Strings, 1995; Irish Suite, 1996; Concerto for Bassoon and Strings, 2004; *chamber:* Concerto da Camera (4 insts), 1968; Partita (solo 'cello), 1968; Chamber Concerto (organ and 11 insts), 1969; English Suite (harpsichord), 1971; Sonata Secolare for organ and brass, 1973; Sonata da Chiesa for two trumpets and organ, 1976; String Quartet no 2, 1979; Hebdomade, 1980; Sonatina Lirica for brass, 1983; Triad, 1984; Quartet for Saxes, 1985; Oboe Sonata no 2, French Suite for Sax. 4tet, 1986; String Quartet no 3, 1987; Octad, 1987; Piano Sonata no 3, 1988; Larkin Songs, 1990; Organ Sonata, 1992; Sextet for piano and wind, 1995; Easter Fantasy for organ and brass, 1997; *ballet:* Reflection, 1952; *opera:* A Nativity Opera, 1950; The Moon and Sixpence, 1957; The Visitors, 1972; Bel and the Dragon, 1973; The Entertainment of the Senses, 1974; Tobermory, 1976; *musical:* Vile Bodies, 1961; *choral:* Cantiones Sacrae 1973; (sop., chor. and orch.), 1952; Jubilate Deo (unacc. chor.), 1957; The Ballad of the White Horse (bar., chor. and orch.), 1959; Herrick Cantata (ten. solo, chor. and orch.), 1961; A Latter-Day Athenian Speaks, 1962; The Noble Heart (sop., bass, chor and orch.), Shakespeare Quatercentenary Festival, 1964; Cantor popularis vocis, 18th Schütz Festival Berlin, 1964; Mass in C (unacc. chor.), 1965; Cantata for Christmas (chor. and chamb. orch.), 1966; Proverbs of Hell (unacc. chor.), 1967; Cantata for Easter (soli, chor., organ and percussion), 1970; Open Air (chor. and brass band), 1976; Te Deum for Pigotts, 1981; Mass in D, 1983; Cantata for St Cecilia, 1991; Stabat Mater (sop., chor., organ and timpani), A Burns Sequence (chor. and orch.), 1993; Seven Last Words, 1996; many smaller pieces and music for films, Old Vic and Royal Shakespeare Theatres, BBC. *Publications:* Robert Schumann, the man and his music, 1972; The Musical Companion, 1978; contributor to: Dublin Review, Musical Times, Tempo, Composer, Listener, Music in Education, DNB. *Recreations:* jazz, bore-watching. *Address:* 20 Firswood Avenue, Epsom, Surrey KT19 0PR. *T:* (020) 8393 7181.

GARDNER, Norman Keith Ayliffe; *b* 2 July 1925; *s* of late Charles Ayliffe Gardner and Winifred Gardner; *m* 1951, Margaret Patricia Vinson; one *s* one *d*. *Educ:* Cardiff High Sch.; University Coll., Cardiff (BScEng); College of Aeronautics, Cranfield; Univ. of London Commerce Degree Bureau (BScEcon Hons). CEng. Flight Test Observer, RAE, 1944; Test Engr, Westland Aircraft Ltd, 1946; Development Engr, Handley Page Ltd, 1950; Engr, Min. of Aviation, 1964; Economic Adviser, Min. of Technology, 1970; Asst Dir (Engrg), DTI, 1973; Sen. Economic Adviser, 1974, Under Secretary: DoI, 1977; Dept of Employment, 1979; DTI, 1984–85. *Publications:* The Economics of Launching Aid, in The Economics of Industrial Subsidies (HMSO), 1976; Decade of Discontent: the changing British economy, 1987; A Guide to United Kingdom and European Community Competition Policy, 1990, 2nd edn as A Guide to United Kingdom and European Union Competition Policy, 1996, 3rd edn 2000; Mistakes: how they have happened and how some might be avoided, 2007; papers in Jl Instn Prodn Engrs and other engrg jls. *Recreation:* music. *Address:* 15 Chanctonbury Way, N12 7JB. *T:* (020) 8922 0847.

GARDNER, Ven. Paul Douglas, PhD; Senior Minister, Christ Church Presbyterian Church, Atlanta, Georgia, since 2005; *b* 28 May 1950; *s* of Rev. David Gardner and Dr Joy M. Gardner; *m* 1971, Sharon Anne Bickford; two *s* one *d*. *Educ:* Leeds Grammar Sch.; KCL (BA 1972, AKC 1972); Reformed Theol Seminary, USA (MDiv 1979); Ridley Hall, Cambridge; Sidney Sussex Coll., Cambridge (PhD 1989). Company dir, 1972–77. Ordained deacon, 1980, priest, 1981; Curate, St Martin's, Cambridge, 1980–83; Lectr in NT and Acad. Registrar, Oak Hill Theol Coll., 1983–90; Vicar, St John the Baptist, Hartford, Cheshire, 1990–2003; Archdeacon of Exeter, 2003–05. RD, Middlewich, 1994–99. *Publications:* The Gifts of God and the Authentication of a Christian, 1994; The Complete Who's Who in the Bible, 1995; (ed and contrib.) New International Encyclopedia of Bible Characters, 1995, 4th edn 2002; Focus on the Bible series: 2 Peter and Jude, 1998; Revelation, 2001; Ephesians, 2006. *Recreations:* alpine walking, ski-ing, writing, photography. *Address:* 143 Ridgeland Way, Atlanta, GA 30305, USA.

GARDNER, Piers; *see* Gardner, J. P.

GARDNER, Sir Richard (Lavenham), Kt 2005; PhD; FRS 1979; Royal Society Edward Penley Abraham Research Professor, Department of Zoology, University of Oxford, since 2003; Student of Christ Church, Oxford, since 1974; *b* 10 June 1943; *s* of late Allan Constant and Eileen May Gardner; *m* 1968, Wendy Joy Cresswell; one *s*. *Educ:* St John's Sch., Leatherhead; North East Surrey Coll. of Technology; St Catharine's Coll., Cambridge (BA 1st Cl. Hons Physiol., 1966; MA; PhD 1971; Hon. Fellow, 2008). Res. Asst, Physiological Lab., Cambridge, 1970–73; Oxford University: Lectr in Developmental and Reproductive Biology, Dept of Zoology, 1973–77; Res. Student, Christ Church, 1974–77; Royal Soc. Henry Dale Res. Prof., Dept of Zool., 1978–2003; Hon. Dir, ICRF Develtl Biol. Unit, 1986–96. Indep. Mem., ABRC, 1990–93. Pres., Inst. Biol., 2006–08. Scientific Medal, Zoological Soc. of London, 1977; March of Dimes Prize in Develtl Biology, 1999; Royal Medal, Royal Soc., 2001; Albert Brachet Prize, Royal Acad. of Belgium, 2004. *Publications:* contribs to Jl of Embryology and Experimental Morphology, Nature, Jl of Cell Science, and various other jls and symposia. *Recreations:* ornithology, music, sailing, painting, gardening. *Address:* Christ Church, Oxford OX1 1DP.

GARDNER, Dr Rita Ann Moden, CBE 2003; Director and Secretary, Royal Geographical Society (with the Institute of British Geographers), since 1996; *b* 10 Nov. 1955; *d* of John William Gardner and Evelyn Gardner (*née* Moden); partner, 1982, Dr Martin Eugene Frost. *Educ:* Huntingdon Grammar Sch.; Hinchingbrooke Sch.; University Coll. London (BSc 1st cl. Hons Geog.); Wolfson Coll., Oxford (DPhil 1981). Lectr in Physical Geog., St Catherine's Coll., Oxford, 1978–79; Lectr in Geog., KCL, 1979–94; Dir, Envmtl Sci. Unit and Reader in Envmtl Sci., QMW, 1994–96. Mem., Archives TaskForce, DCMS, 2002–03. Ed., Geographical Jl, 1989–93. Hon. Sec., RGS, 1991–96. Trustee, WWF-UK, 2000–04. Busk Medal, RGS, 1995. *Publications:* Landscape in England and Wales, 1981, 2nd edn 1994; Mega-geomorphology, 1981; Land Shapes, 1986; numerous academic papers in learned jls specialising in geomorphology, physical geog., sedimentology and Quaternary envmtl change. *Recreations:* restoration of historic vernacular buildings, contemporary architecture and furniture, gardening, travel, good food and wine. *Address:* Royal Geographical Society (with IBG), 1 Kensington Gore, SW7 2AR. *T:* (020) 7591 3010; *e-mail:* director@rgs.org.

GARDNER, Sir Robert Henry B.; *see* Bruce-Gardner.

GARDNER, Sir Roy Alan, Kt 2002; FCCA; Chairman, Compass Group PLC, since 2006 (non-executive Director, since 2005); Senior Advisor, Credit Suisse, since 2006; *b* 20 Aug. 1945; *s* of Roy Thomas Gardner and Iris Joan Gardner; *m* 1969, Carol Ann Barker; one *s* two *d*. *Educ:* Strode's Sch., Egham. FCCA 1980. Works Acct, later Concorde Project Acct, BAC Ltd, 1963–75; Chief Acct, Asst Finance Dir, then Finance Dir, Marconi Space & Defence Systems, 1975–84; Finance Dir, Marconi Co. Ltd, 1984–85; STC plc: Finance Dir, 1986–89; Dir, 1986–91; Man. Dir, STC Communications Ltd, 1989–91; Chief Operating Officer, Northern Telecom Europe Ltd, 1991–92; Man. Dir, GEC-Marconi Ltd, 1992–94; Dir, GEC plc, 1994; Exec. Dir, British Gas plc, 1994–97; Chief Exec., Centrica plc, 1997–2006. Non-exec. Dir, 1999–2005, Chm., 2002–05, Manchester United plc; non-exec. Director: Laporte plc, 1997–2001; Willis Gp Hldgs Ltd, 2006–. Chairman: Employers' Forum on Disability, 2000–03; Modern Apprenticeship Task Force, 2002–05; Apprentices Ambassadors Network UK, 2006–; British Olympic Appeal for Beijing Games 2008, 2007. Mem., Council for Ind. and Higher Educn, 1996–99. Member Council: RUSI, 1992–96; Brunel Univ., 1998–2001. Pres., Carers UK (formerly Carers Nat. Assoc.), 1998–. Trustee, Develt Trust, 1997–. CCMI; FRSA 1995. *Recreations:* golf, running. *Address:* c/o Compass Group PLC, Compass House, Guildford Street, Chertsey, Surrey KT16 9BQ. *Clubs:* Brooks's, Annabel's, Mark's.

GARDOM, Hon. Garde Basil; QC (Canada) 1975; Lieutenant-Governor of British Columbia, 1995–2001; *b* 17 July 1924; *s* of Basil Gardom and Gabrielle Gwladys (*née* Bell); *m* 1956, Theresa Helen Eileen Mackenzie; one *s* four *d*. *Educ:* Univ. of British Columbia (BA, LLB). Called to Bar of British Columbia, 1949; elected to BC Legislature as Mem. for Vancouver-Point Grey, 1966; re-elected, 1969, 1972, 1975, 1979, 1983; Govt House Leader, 1977–86; Attorney Gen. of BC, 1975–79; Minister of Intergovtl Relns, 1979–86; Chairman: Constitution Cttee, 1975–86; Legislation Cttee, 1975–86; Mem., Treasury Bd and Planning and Priorities Cttee, 1983–86; Minister responsible, Official Visits to Expo '86; Policy Cons., Office of the Premier, 1986–87; Agent General for BC in the UK and Europe, 1987–92; Director: Crown Life Insurance Co., 1993–95; Brouwer Claims Canada Ltd, 2001–. Member: Canadian Bar Assoc., 1949–; Vancouver Bar Assoc., 1949–; British Columbia Sports Hall of Fame, 1995; Phi Delta Theta Fraternity, 1943. Director: Canadian Club, BC, 2003; Justice Inst. of BC, 2004. Hon. Patron: Nature Conservancy Canada, 2001; BC Alcohol and Drug Educn Services, 2002; BCAA Traffic Foundn, 2004; Heraldry Soc. of Canada; RUSI Vancouver Is.; Pacific Alzheimer Res. Foundn, 2007. Hon. Col, BC Regt (Duke of Connaught's Own), 1997. Freeman, City of London, 1992. Hon. LLD: Vancouver, 2002; Victoria, 2003. Lifetime Achievement Award, Univ. of British Columbia, 2002. KStJ 1996. *Recreation:* fishing. *Address:* 2122 SW Marine Drive, Vancouver, BC V6P 6B5, Canada. *Clubs:* Royal Over-Seas League, Royal Commonwealth Society; Vancouver, Union Club of BC, Vancouver Lawn Tennis and Badminton (British Columbia).

GAREL-JONES, family name of **Baron Garel-Jones**.

GAREL-JONES, Baron *cr* 1997 (Life Peer), of Watford in the co. of Hertfordshire; **William Armand Thomas Tristan Garel-Jones;** PC 1992; Managing Director, UBS Investment Bank (formerly Warburg Dillon Read), since 1999; *b* 28 Feb. 1941; *s* of Bernard Garel-Jones and Meriel Garel-Jones (*née* Williams); *m* 1966, Catalina (*née* Garrigues); four *s* one *d*. *Educ:* The King's Sch., Canterbury. Principal, Language Sch., Madrid, Spain, 1960–70; Merchant Banker, 1970–74; worked for Cons. Party, 1974–79 (Personal Asst to Party Chm., 1978–79). Contested (C): Caernarvon, Feb. 1974; Watford, Oct. 1974. MP (C) Watford, 1979–97. PPS to Minister of State, CSD, 1981; Asst Govt Whip, 1982–83; a Lord Comr of HM Treasury, 1983–86; Vice-Chamberlain of HM Household, 1986–88; Comptroller of HM Household, 1988–89; Treasurer of HM Household and Dep. Chief Whip, 1989–90; Minister of State, FCO, 1990–93. *Recreation:* collecting books. *Address:* House of Lords, SW1A 0PW.

GARFITT, His Honour Alan; a Circuit Judge, 1977–92, and Judge, Cambridge County Court and Wisbech County Court, 1978–92; *b* 20 Dec. 1920; *s* of Rush and Florence Garfitt; *m* 1st, 1941, Muriel Ada Jaggers; one *s* one *d*; 2nd, 1973, Ivie Maud Hudson; 3rd, 1978, Rosemary Lazell; one *s* one *d*. *Educ:* King Edward VII Grammar Sch., King's Lynn; Metropolitan Coll. and Inns of Court Sch. of Law. Served War of 1939–45, RAF, 1941–46. LLB London 1947; called to the Bar, Lincoln's Inn, 1948. Hon. Fellow, Faculty of Law, Cambridge, 1978. *Publications:* Law of Contracts in a Nutshell, 4 edns 1949–56; The Book for Police, 5 vols, 1958; jt ed, Roscoe's Criminal Evidence, Practice and Procedure, 16th edn, 1952; contribs to Jl of Planning Law, Solicitors' Jl and other legal pubns. *Recreations:* farming, gardening, DIY activities, horse riding and, as a member since 1961 and President 1978–93 of the Association of British Riding Schools (Fellow, 1989), the provision of good teaching and riding facilities for non-horse owners, dinghy sailing, boat building. *Address:* Leap House, Barcham Road, Soham, Ely, Cambs CB7 5TU.

GARLAND, Basil; Registrar, Family Division of High Court of Justice (formerly Probate, Divorce and Admiralty Division), 1969–85; *b* 30 May 1920; *o c* of late Herbert George Garland and Grace Alice Mary Martha Garland; *m* 1942, Dora Mary Sudell Hope (*d* 2008); one *s*. *Educ:* Dulwich Coll.; Pembroke Coll., Oxford (MA). Served in Royal Artillery, 1940–46: commnd 1941; Staff Officer, HQ RA, Gibraltar, 1943–45; Hon. Major 1946. Called to Bar, Middle Temple, 1948; Treasury Junior Counsel (Probate), 1965; Registrar, Principal Probate Registry, 1969. *Publications:* articles in Law Jl. *Recreations:* sailing, drama, painting. *Address:* Christmas Cottage, Blyth's Lane, Wivenhoe, Colchester, Essex CO7 9BG. *T:* (01206) 827566. *Club:* Bar Yacht.

GARLAND, Nicholas Withycombe, OBE 1998; Political Cartoonist, The Daily Telegraph, 1966–86 and since 1991; *b* 1 Sept. 1935; *s* of Tom and late Peggy Garland; *m* 1st, 1964, Harriet Crittall (marr. diss. 1968); 2nd, 1969, Caroline Beatrice (marr. diss. 1994), *d* of Sir Peter Medawar, OM, CH, CBE, FRS; three *s* one *d*; 3rd, 1995, Priscilla Roth (*née* Brandchaft). *Educ:* Slade School of Fine Art. Worked in theatre as stage man. and dir, 1958–64; Political Cartoonist: New Statesman, 1971–78; The Independent, 1986–91; has drawn regularly for The Spectator, 1979–; with Barry Humphries created and drew comic strip, Barry McKenzie, in Private Eye. *Publications:* (illustrated) Horatius, by T. B. Macaulay, 1977; An Indian Journal, 1983; Twenty Years of Cartoons by Garland, 1984; Travels with my Sketchbook, 1987; Not Many Dead, 1990; (illustrated) The Coma, by Alex Garland, 2004; I Wish..., 2007. *Address:* The Daily Telegraph, 111 Buckingham Palace Road, SW1W 0DT.

GARLAND, Patrick Ewart; director and producer of plays, films, television; writer; Artistic Director, Chichester Festival Theatre, 1980–84 and 1991–94; *b* 10 April 1935; *s* of late Ewart Garland and Rosalind, *d* of Herbert Granville Fell, editor of The Connoisseur; *m* 1980, Alexandra Bastedo. *Educ:* St Mary's Coll., Southampton; St Edmund Hall, Oxford (MA; Hon. Fellow, 1997). Actor, Bristol Old Vic, 1959; Age of Kings, BBC TV, 1961; lived in Montparnasse, 1961–62; writing—two plays for ITV, 1962; Research Asst, Monitor, BBC, 1963; Television interviews with: Stevie Smith, Philip Larkin, Sir Noel Coward, Sir John Gielgud, Sir Ralph Richardson, Dame Ninette de Valois, Claire Bloom, Tito Gobbi, Marcel Marceau, 1964–78. Director and Producer, BBC Arts Dept, 1962–74; Stage Director: *West End:* 40 Years On, 1968, 1984; Brief Lives, 1968; Getting On, 1970; Cyrano, 1971; The Doll's House (New York and London), 1975; Billy, the Musical, 1976; Under the Greenwood Tree, 1978; Look After Lulu, 1978; Beecham, 1980; Hair (Israel), 1972; York Mystery Plays, 1980; My Fair Lady (US), 1980; Kipling (Mermaid and New York), 1984; Canaries Sometimes Sing, Albery, 1987; The Secret of Sherlock Holmes, Wyndham's, 1988; A Room of One's Own, Hampstead, 1989, 2002, New York, 1991; Song in the Night, Lyric, Hammersmith, 1989; The Dressmaker, Windsor and tour, 1990; Tovarich, Piccadilly, 1991; Vita and Virginia, Ambassadors, 1993; The Tempest, Regent's Park Open Air, 1996; The Importance of Being Oscar, Savoy, 1997; The Mystery of Charles Dickens, Comedy, 2000, Albery and NY, 2002; The Woman in Black, San Diego and NY, 2001; Full Circle, UK tour, 2004; Visiting Mr Green, UK tour, 2007–08, Trafalgar Studio, 2008; Mr Chops and Doctor Marigold, Edinburgh, 2008; Brief Lives, UK tour, 2008; co-author, Underneath the Arches, Chichester, and Prince of Wales, 1982–83; Director, *Chichester Festival Theatre:* The Cherry Orchard, 1981; The Mitford Girls, 1981 (also London, 1981); On the Rocks, 1982; Cavell, 1982; Goodbye, Mr Chips, 1982; As You Like It, 1983; Forty Years On, Merchant of Venice, 1984; Victory (adapted from The Dynasts by Thomas Hardy), 1989; Tovarich, 1991; Pickwick, 1993; Pygmalion, 1994; Beatrix, 1996; Chimes at Midnight, 1998; produced: Fanfare for Elizabeth, the Queen's 60th birthday gala, Covent Garden, 1986; Celebration of a Broadcaster, for Richard Dimbleby Cancer Fund at Westminster Abbey, 1986; Thanksgiving service for Lord Olivier, 1989; *television:* prod Christmas Glory, ITV, annually 1997–; Director: Talking Heads, 1998; Telling Tales, 2000. *Films:* The Snow Goose, 1974; The Doll's House, 1976. Creative Writing Fellowship, Bishop Otter Coll., Chichester, 1984–85. Hon. DLitt Southampton, 1994. *Publications:* Brief Lives, 1967; The Wings of the Morning (novel), 1989; Oswald the Owl (for children), 1990; Angels in the Sussex Air: an anthology of Sussex poems, 1995; The Incomparable Rex: a memoir of Rex Harrison in the 1980s, 1998; poetry in: London Magazine, 1954; New Poems, 1956; Sussex Seams, 1996; Poetry West; Encounter; short stories in:

Transatlantic Review, 1976; England Erzählt, Gemini, Light Blue Dark Blue. *Recreations:* reading Victorian novels, walking in Corsica. *Club:* Garrick.

GARLAND, Sir Patrick (Neville), Kt 1985; a Judge of the High Court, Queen's Bench Division, 1985–2002; Senior Trial Judge, England and Wales, 2000–02; *b* 22 July 1929; *s* of Frank Neville Garland and Marjorie Garland; *m* 1955, Jane Elizabeth Bird; two *s* one *d*. *Educ:* Uppingham Sch. (Scholar); Sidney Sussex Coll., Cambridge (Exhibnr and Prizeman; MA, LLM; Hon. Fellow, 1991). Called to the Bar, Middle Temple, 1953, Bencher, 1979. Asst Recorder, Norwich, 1971; a Recorder, 1972–85; QC 1972; Dep. High Court Judge, 1981–85; a Judge of the Employment Appeal Tribunal, 1986–95; Presiding Judge, SE Circuit, 1989–93. Mem., Judges' Council, 1993–94. President: Central Probation Council (formerly Central Council of Probation Cttees), 1986–2001; Technol. and Construction Bar Assoc., 1985–2002; Mem., Parole Bd, 1988–2002 (Vice-Chm., 1989–91). *Publications:* articles in legal and technical jls. *Recreations:* shooting, gardening, industrial archaeology. *Address:* 9 Ranulf Road, NW2 2BT. *Clubs:* Savage, Royal Over-Seas League; Norfolk (Norwich); Cumberland Lawn Tennis.

GARLAND, Prof. Peter Bryan, CBE 1999; PhD; FRSE; Professor of Biochemistry, Institute of Cancer Research, University of London, 1992–99, now Emeritus Professor (Chief Executive, 1989–99); *b* 31 Jan. 1934; *s* of Frederick George Garland and Molly Kate Jones; *m* 1959, Ann Bathurst; one *s* two *d*. *Educ:* Hardye's Sch., Dorchester; Downing Coll., Cambridge (BA 1st Class Hons in Physical Anthropol., 1955; BChir 1958, MB 1959; PhD 1964); King's Coll. Hosp. Med. Sch. (Burney Yeo Schol.). MRC Res. Schol., Chem. Pathol. Dept, KCH Med. Sch., and Biochem. Dept, UCL, 1959–61; British Insulin Manufacturers' Fellow, Biochem. Dept, Cambridge Univ., 1961–64; Lectr, 1964–68, Reader, 1969–70 in Biochem., Bristol Univ.; Prof. of Biochem., Dundee Univ., 1970–84; Principal Scientist and Hd, Biosciences Div., Unilever Research, 1984–87; Dir of Research, Amersham Internat., 1987–89. Vis. Prof., Johnson Res. Foundn, Philadelphia, 1967–69; Vis. Fellow, ANU, 1983. Member: MRC, 1980–84 (Chm., Cell Biol.-Disorders Bd, 1980–82); EMBO, 1981; CRC Scientific Policy Cttee, 1985–92. Director: CRC Technology Ltd, 1988–96 (Chm., 1988–91); CAT plc, 1990–2004 (Chm., 1995–2004). FRSE 1977. Hon. Fellow, UCL, 1999. Hon. LLD Dundee, 1990. Colworth Medal, Biochem. Soc., 1970. *Publications:* numerous articles in biochemistry and biophysics. *Recreations:* sport (athletics blue, Cambridge, 1954–55), ski-ing, sailing, windsurfing, reading. *Address:* Hope Cottage, Sunny Way, Bosham, W Sussex PO18 8HQ. *Clubs:* Athenæum; Bosham Sailing.

GARLAND, Peter Leslie, CB 2002; Director, Health and Social Care (Northern), Department of Health, 2002–03; *b* 21 Sept. 1946; *s* of Leslie and Stella Garland; *m* 1979, Janet Rosemary Prescott; three *d*. *Educ:* Bristol Cathedral Sch.; Manchester Univ. Joined DHSS, 1974; Asst Sec. 1989; Under Sec. and Dep. Dir of Finance, 1993–99, Regl Dir, Northern and Yorks Reg., 1999–2002, NHS Exec., DoH. *Recreations:* family, gardening. *Address:* 140 Curly Hill, Ilkley, W Yorks LS29 0DS.

GARLAND, Hon. Sir (Ransley) Victor, KBE 1982; Chairman: Henderson Far East Income Trust PLC, 1990–2006 (Director, 1984–2006); Fidelity Asian Values PLC, since 2000 (Director, since 1996); Director: Throgmorton Trust PLC, 1985–2006; Vice-Chairman, South Bank Board, 1985–2000; Director, South Bank Foundn, 1996–2001; *b* 5 May 1934; *m* 1960, Lynette Jamieson, BMus (Melb.); two *s* one *d*. *Educ:* Univ. of Western Australia. BA(Econ); FCA. Practised as Chartered Accountant, 1958–70. Director: Prudential Corp., 1984–93; Mitchell Cotts PLC, 1984–86; Govett Funds Inc., 1991–2000 (Pres., 1997–2000). MP for Curtin, Australian Federal Parliament, 1969–81; Minister for Supply, 1971–72; Executive Councillor, 1971; Minister Asstg Treasurer, 1972; Chief Opposition Whip, 1974–75; Minister for Special Trade Representations, also Minister Asstg Minister for Trade and Resources, 1977–79; Minister for Business and Consumer Affairs, 1979–80; High Comr for Australia in UK, 1981–83. Govt Representative Minister: at Commonwealth Ministerial Meeting for Common Fund, London, 1978; at Ministerial Meetings of ESCAP, New Delhi, 1978; Minister representing Treas., at Ministerial Meeting of OECD, Paris, 1978; Leader, Aust. Delegn to UNCTAD V and Chm. Commonwealth Delegns to UNCTAD V, Manila, 1979; attended, with Premier, Commonwealth Heads of Govt meeting, Lusaka, 1979. Parly Adviser, Aust. Mission to UN Gen. Assembly, New York, 1973; Chairman: House of Reps Expenditure Cttee, 1976–77; Govt Members' Treasury Cttee, 1977. Councillor, UK, Royal Commonwealth Society for the Blind, 1988. Freeman, City of London, 1982. *Recreations:* music (chorister, St George's Cathedral, 1942–46), reading, shooting, ski-ing.

GARLAND, William George; Editor, Official Report (Hansard), House of Commons, 2002–05; *b* 9 March 1946; *s* of George and Evelyn Garland; *m* 1st, 1969, Sally Doyle (marr. diss. 1985); one *s* one *d*; 2nd, 1993, Mary Frances Finch. *Educ:* Sir Joseph Williamson's Mathematical Sch., Rochester. Jun. Cttee Clerk, Northfleet Council, 1963–65; News Reporter, Kent Messenger Gp, 1965–70; Parly Reporter, Press Assoc., 1970–75; Hansard, 1975–2005. Sec., Commonwealth Hansard Editors Assoc., 2002–05. *Recreations:* theatre, watching cricket and football.

GARLICK, Rev. Preb. Kathleen Beatrice, (Kay); Rector, Wormelow Hundred Group of Parishes, since 2003; Member, Archbishop's Council, since 2006; *b* 26 Feb. 1949; *d* of Arthur and Beatrice Harris; *m* 1973, Dr Peter Garlick; one *s* three *d*. *Educ:* Prendergast Grammar Sch.; Leeds Univ. (BA Hons Music); Birmingham Univ. (PGCE); Gloucester Sch. for Ministry. Music teacher, Kidbrooke Comprehensive Sch., 1973–75; mother and housewife, 1975–87; ordained priest, 1990; NSM, Birch Gp of parishes, Hereford dio., 1990–96; Chaplain, Hereford Sixth Form Coll., 1996–2002. Mem., Gen. Synod of C of E, 1995– (Chair, Business Cttee, 2006–). *Recreations:* playing and singing Early Music (Medieval and Renaissance), directing choirs and persuading and encouraging even the least confident to sing. *Address:* The Rectory, Birch Lodge, Much Birch, Herefordshire HR2 8HT. *T:* (01981) 540666; *e-mail:* kaygarlick@hotmail.com.

GARLICK, Kenneth John; Keeper of Western Art, Ashmolean Museum, Oxford, 1968–84; Professorial Fellow of Balliol College, Oxford, 1968–84, now Emeritus; *b* 1 Oct. 1916; *s* of late D. E. Garlick and Annie Hallifax. *Educ:* Elmhurst Sch., Street; Balliol Coll., Oxford; Courtauld Inst. of Art, London. MA Oxon, PhD Birmingham; FMA. RAF Signals, 1939–46. Lectr, Bath Academy of Art, 1946–48; Asst Keeper, Dept of Art, City of Birmingham Museum and Art Gallery, 1948–50; Lectr (Sen. Lectr 1960), Barber Inst. of Fine Arts, Univ. of Birmingham, 1951–68. Governor, Royal Shakespeare Theatre, 1978–95. FRSA. Hon. DLitt Birmingham, 1996. *Publications:* Sir Thomas Lawrence, 1954; Walpole Society Vol. XXXIX (Lawrence Catalogue Raisonné), 1964; Walpole Society Vol. XLV (Catalogue of Pictures at Althorp), 1976; (ed with Angus Macintyre) The Diary of Joseph Farington, Vols I–II, 1978, III–VI, 1979; Sir Thomas Lawrence, 1989; Portraits in the Bodleian Library Catalogue, 2004; numerous articles and reviews. *Recreations:* travel, music. *Address:* The Cotswold Home, Bradwell Village, Burford OX18 4XA.

GARLICK, Paul Richard; QC 1996; a Recorder, since 1997; *b* 14 Aug. 1952; *s* of late Arthur Garlick and of Dorothy Garlick (*née* Allan). *Educ:* Liverpool Univ. (LLB 1973). Called to the Bar, Middle Temple, 1974, Bencher, 2005; Standing Counsel to HM Customs and Excise, 1990–96; Asst Recorder, 1993–97. Internat. Judge, War Crimes Chamber of State Court of Bosnia and Herzegovina, 2005–06. Trustee, Redress, 2004–. Mem., Justice, 2003–. *Recreations:* music, cooking, ski-ing, walking, travel. *Address:* Outer Temple Chambers, 222 Strand, WC2R 1BA. *T:* (020) 7353 6381, *Fax:* (020) 7583 1786; *e-mail:* paul.garlickqc@outertemple.com.

GARLING, David John Haldane, (Ben), ScD; Reader in Mathematical Analysis, Cambridge University, 1978–99, now Emeritus; Fellow of St John's College, Cambridge, since 1963; *b* 26 July 1937; *s* of Leslie Ernest Garling and Frances Margaret Garling; *m* 1963, Anthea Mary Eileen Dixon; two *s* one *d*. *Educ:* Highgate Sch.; St John's Coll., Cambridge (BA, MA, PhD; ScD 1978). Cambridge University: Asst Lectr, 1963–64; Lectr, 1964–78; Head of Dept of Pure Maths and Math. Stats, 1984–91; Pro-Proctor, 1995–96, Sen. Proctor, 1996–97, Dep. Proctor, 1997–98; Tutor, 1971–78, Pres., 1987–91, St John's Coll. Mem., SERC Mathematics Cttee, 1983–86. Exec. Sec., London Mathematical Soc., 1998–2002 (Mem. Council, 1986–88 and 1995–98; Meetings and Membership Sec., 1995–98). *Publications:* A Course in Galois Theory, 1987; Inequalities, 2007; papers in sci. jls. *Address:* St John's College, Cambridge CB2 1TP. *T:* (01223) 338600.

GARMOYLE, Viscount; Hugh Sebastian Frederick Cairns; *b* 26 March 1965; *s* and *heir* of Earl Cairns, *qv*; *m* 1991, Juliet, *d* of Andrew Eustace Palmer, *qv*; one *s* two *d*. *Educ:* Eton; Edinburgh Univ. (MA Hons); London Coll. of Law. With Freshfields, solicitors, 1990–94; with Cazenove, stockbrokers, 1994–. *Heir:* *s* Hon. Oliver David Andrew Cairns, *b* 7 March 1993.

GARNER, Alan, OBE 2001; FSA; author; *b* 17 Oct. 1934; *s* of Colin and Marjorie Garner; *m* 1st, 1956, Ann Cook; one *s* two *d*; 2nd, 1972, Griselda Greaves; one *s* one *d*. *Educ:* Alderley Edge Council Sch.; Manchester Grammar Sch.; Magdalen Coll., Oxford. Writer and presenter, documentary films: Places and Things, 1978; Images, 1981 (First Prize, Chicago Internat. Film Fest.). Mem. Internat. Editl Bd, Detskaya Literatura Publishers, Moscow, 1991–. Co-Founder, Blackden Trust, 2004. FSA 2007. Karl Edward Wagner Special Award, British Fantasy Soc., 2003. *Publications:* The Weirdstone of Brisingamen, 1960 (Lewis Carroll Shelf Award, USA, 1970); The Moon of Gomrath, 1963; Elidor, 1965; Holly from the Bongs, 1966; The Old Man of Mow, 1967; The Owl Service, 1967 (Library Assoc. Carnegie Medal 1967, Guardian Award 1968); The Hamish Hamilton Book of Goblins, 1969; Red Shift, 1973 (with John Mackenzie, filmed 1978); (with Albin Trowski) The Breadhorse, 1975; The Guizer, 1975; The Stone Book, 1976 (Phoenix Award, Children's Lit. Assoc. of Amer., 1996); Tom Fobble's Day, 1977; Granny Reardun, 1977; The Aimer Gate, 1978; Fairy Tales of Gold, 1979; The Lad of the Gad, 1980; Alan Garner's Book of British Fairy Tales, 1984; A Bag of Moonshine, 1986; Jack and the Beanstalk, 1992; Once Upon a Time, 1993; Strandloper, 1996; The Voice That Thunders, 1997; The Little Red Hen, 1997; The Well of the Wind, 1998; Grey Wolf, Prince Jack and the Firebird, 1998; Approach to the Edge, 1998; Thursbitch, 2003; *plays:* Lamaload, 1978; Lurga Lom, 1980; To Kill a King, 1980; Sally Water, 1982; The Keeper, 1983; *dance drama:* The Green Mist, 1970; *libretti:* The Bellybag, 1971 (music by Richard Morris); Potter Thompson, 1972 (music by Gordon Crosse); Lord Flame, 1995; *screenplay:* Strandloper, 1992. *Recreation:* work. *Address:* Blackden, Cheshire CW4 8BY. *Club:* Portico Library (Manchester).

GARNER, Sir Anthony (Stuart), Kt 1984; parliamentary and public affairs consultant, since 1988; Director of Organisation, Conservative Central Office, 1976–88; *b* 28 Jan. 1927; *s* of Edward Henry Garner, MC, FIAS, and Dorothy May Garner; *m* 1967, Shirley Taylor; two *s*. *Educ:* Liverpool Coll. Grenadier Guards, 1945–48. Young Conservative Organiser, Yorks Area, 1948–51; Conservative Agent, Halifax, 1951–56; Nat. Organising Sec., Young Conservative Org., 1956–61; Conservative Central Office Agent for: London Area, 1961–64; Western Area, 1964–66; North West Area, 1966–76. Chm., Conservative Agents' Examination Bd, 1976–88. Pres., Conservative Agents' Benevolent Assoc., 1976–88. Director: Carroll Anglo-American Corp., 1989–94; Clifton Court Residents Ltd, 1990– (Chm., 1996–); Farnborough Aerospace Develt Corp., 1994–95; Carroll Aircraft Corp., 1994–95; British-Iranian Chamber of Commerce, 1996–2000 (Vice Chm., 1996–2000). Trustee, Old Sessions Hse Charitable Trust, 2004–. Life Governor, Liverpool Coll., 1980. Pres., Old Lerpoolian Soc., 1995–97. *Recreations:* travelling, theatre. *Address:* The Beeches, Bottom Lane, Seer Green, Beaconsfield, Bucks HP9 2UH. *Clubs:* Carlton, St Stephen's.

GARNER, Prof. (Christopher) David, PhD; FRS 1997; CChem, FRSC; Professor of Biological Inorganic Chemistry, University of Nottingham, since 1999; *b* 9 Nov. 1941; *s* of Richard Norman Garner and Chrystabel (*née* Potts); *m* 1968, Pamela Eva Kershaw; one *s* one *d*. *Educ:* Cheadle Hulme Warehousemen & Clerk's Orphans' Sch.; Nottingham Univ. (BSc 1st Cl. Hons Chem. 1963; PhD 1966). CChem 1982; FRSC 1982. Post-doctoral Res. Fellow, CIT, 1966–67; ICI Res. Fellow, Univ. of Nottingham, 1967–68; University of Manchester: Lectr in Chemistry, 1968–78; Sen. Lectr, 1978–84; Prof. of Inorganic Chemistry, 1984–99; Hd of Chemistry, 1988–96; Mem. Court, 1995–99; Mem. Council, 1996–99. Vis. Prof., Univ. of Lausanne, 1977; Frontiers in Chem. Res. Vis. Prof., Texas A&M Univ., 1987; Visiting Professor: Strasbourg Univ., 1990–92; Univ. of Florence, 1995; Univ. of Arizona, 1998; Sydney Univ., 2000; Wilsmore Fellow, Univ. of Melbourne, 1994; Bye Fellow and Fellow, Robinson Coll., Cambridge, 1997. Chm., Metbio Prog., ESF, 1994–98. Royal Society of Chemistry: Tilden Medal, 1985; Chatt Lectr, 1999; Pres., Dalton Div., 2001–04; Mem. Council, 2005–; Ludwig Mond Lectr, 2007–08. Founding Pres., Soc. Biol Inorganic Chem., 1996–98. Elder, URC, Bramhall, and Chm., Develt Gp, 1990–98. *Publications:* original res. papers and reviews, primarily concerned with roles of transition metals in biological systems and develt of chemical analogues for centres which occur in nature. *Recreations:* listening to classical music, theatre, dining out and in, watching sport. *Address:* School of Chemistry, Nottingham University, Nottingham NG7 2RD. *T:* (0115) 951 4188.

GARNER, John Donald, CMG 1988; CVO 1991 (LVO 1979); HM Diplomatic Service, retired; *b* 15 April 1931; *s* of late Ronald Garner and Doris Ethel Garner (*née* Norton); *m* Karen Maria Conway; two *d*. *Educ:* Trinity Grammar Sch., N22. Royal Navy, National Service, 1949–51. Foreign Office, 1952–55; Third Secretary: Seoul, 1955; Bangkok, 1957; Foreign Office, 1959–63; Second Secretary: Benghazi and Tripoli, 1963–67; Sydney, 1967–69; First Sec., Tel Aviv, 1969–73; FCO, 1973–76; NDC 1976; Dep. High Commissioner, Lilongwe, 1977–80; Chargé d'affaires, Kabul, 1981–84; High Comr, The Gambia, 1984–87; Consul-Gen., Houston, 1988–91. Rep. of Sec. of State for Foreign and Commonwealth Affairs, 1996–. *Recreation:* golf. *Address:* 30 The Green, N14 6EN. *T:* (020) 8882 6808. *Club:* South Herts Golf.

GARNER, Maurice Richard; formerly specialist in the structure and governmental control of public enterprises; *b* 31 May 1915; *o s* of Jesse H. Garner; *m* 1943, Joyce W. Chapman; one *s* one *d*. *Educ:* Glendale County Sch.; London Sch. of Economics and Political Science. Royal Armoured Corps, 1942–45 (despatches). Inland Revenue (Tax Inspectorate), 1938–46; BoT, Asst Principal and Principal, 1947; Commercial Sec. and

UK Trade Comr in Ottawa, 1948–55; transf. to Min. of Power, 1957; Asst Sec. 1960; Under-Sec., Electricity Div., Min. of Technology, 1969, later DTI, retired 1973. Vis. Prof., Dept of Govt, LSE, 1981–85. *Recreations:* reading, oenology. *Address:* 52 Brook Court, Burcot Lane, Bromsgrove, Worcs B60 1AD. *T:* (01527) 870242.

GARNER, His Honour Michael Scott; a Circuit Judge, 1988–2004; *b* 10 April 1939; *s* of William Garner and Doris Mary (*née* Scott); *m* 1st, 1964, Sheila Margaret (*d* 1981) (*née* Garland); one *s* one *d*; 2nd, 1982, Margaret Anne (*née* Senior). *Educ:* Huddersfield Coll.; Manchester Univ. (LLB). Admitted Solicitor, 1965. Asst Recorder, 1978–85; a Recorder, 1985–88. *Recreations:* reading, walking, gardening, motoring, cooking.

GARNETT, Ven. David Christopher; Archdeacon of Chesterfield, since 1996; Priest-in-charge, Beeley and Edensor, since 2007; *b* 26 Sept. 1945; *s* of Douglas and Audrey Garnett; *m* 1974, Susanne Crawford; two *s*. *Educ:* Giggleswick Sch.; Nottingham Univ. (BA Hons); Fitzwilliam Coll., Cambridge (BA Hons); Westcott House, Cambridge; MA Cantab. Curate of Cottingham, E Yorks, 1969–72; Chaplain, Fellow, Tutor, Selwyn Coll. and Pastoral Advr, Newnham Coll., Cambridge, 1972–77; Rector of Patterdale and Diocesan Dir of Ordinands, Carlisle, 1977–80; Vicar of Heald Green, Dio. Chester and Chaplain, St Ann's Hospice, 1980–87; Rector of Christleton and Chm., Bishop's Theol Adv. Gp, 1987–92; Team Rector, Ellesmere Port, 1992–96; Canon of Derby Cathedral, 1996–. Mem. Gen. Synod, 1990–96, 2000–05. *Recreations:* poultry breeding, genetics. *Address:* The Vicarage, Edensor, Bakewell, Derbys DE45 1PH. *Club:* Poultry of Great Britain.

GARNETT, Adm. Sir Ian (David Graham), KCB 1998; Commandant, Royal College of Defence Studies, 2005–08; *b* 27 Sept. 1944; *s* of late Capt. Ian Graham Hartt Garnett, DSC, RN and Barbara Anne Langrishe (*née* Hackett); *m* 1973, Charlotte Mary Anderson; one *s* two *d*. *Educ:* Canford Sch.; BRNC, Dartmouth. Entered RN, 1962; Lt 1967; flying trng, 1968–69; HMS Hermes, 814 Sqdn, 1969–70; Loan Service, RAN, 1971–72; HMS Tiger, 826 Sqdn, 1973–74; Warfare Officer, 1974–76; HMS Blake, Sen. Pilot, 820 Sqdn, 1977–78; Dep. Dir, JMOTS, 1978–80; in comd, HMS Amazon, 1981–82; RN staff course, 1983; Asst Dir, Operational Requirements, 1983–86; Captain Fourth Frigate Sqdn (HMS Active), 1986–88; RN Presentation Team, 1988–89; Dir Operational Requirements, 1989–92; FO Naval Aviation, 1993–95; Dep. SACLANT, 1995–98; Chief of Jt Ops, MoD, 1999–2001; COS SHAPE, 2001–04. Chm., Chatham Historic Dockyard Trust, 2005–; Mem., Commonwealth War Graves Commn, 2006–. Mem., Fleet Air Arm Officers Assoc., 1992–. *Recreations:* my family and other matters. *Address:* Haslemere, Surrey. *Clubs:* Royal Navy of 1765 and 1785, Army and Navy.

GARNETT, Dame Julia Charity; *see* Cleverdon, Dame J. C.

GARNETT, Kevin Mitchell; QC 1991; Legal Member, Boards of Appeal, European Patent Office, since 2005; *b* 22 June 1950; *s* of Frank Raymond Garnett and Cynthia Ruby Eberstein; *m* 1980, Susan Jane Louise (*née* Diboll); one *s*. *Educ:* Bradfield Coll., Berks; University Coll., Oxford (MA). Called to the Bar, Middle Temple, 1975; Bencher, Lincoln's Inn, 2000. Asst Recorder, 1996–2000; Recorder, 2000–05; a Dep. High Court Judge, 2000–05. Vice-Chm., Cartoon Art Trust, 1994–2005. *Publications:* (ed jtly) Williams, Mortimer and Sunnucks on Executors, Administrators and Probate, 16th edn 1982, 17th edn 1993; (ed jtly) Copinger and Skone James on Copyright, 13th edn 1991 to 15th edn 2005; (contrib.) Copyright and Free Speech, 2005. *Recreations:* singing, tennis, ski-ing, mountain walking. *Club:* National Liberal.

GARNHAM, Diana Anjoli; Chief Executive, Science Council, since 2006; *b* 17 Nov. 1954; *d* of George Leslie John Garnham and Monisha Vida (*née* Mander); *m* 2003, Rodney Stewart Buse. *Educ:* Christ's Hosp., Hertford; Lady Margaret Sch., London; Univ. of Leicester (BSocSc (Politics)); King's Coll. London (MA War Studies); University Coll. of Wales, Aberystwyth. Admin. Sec., Council on Christian Approaches to Defence and Disarmament, 1983–87; Association of Medical Research Charities: Exec. Officer, 1987–89; Asst Sec.-Gen., 1989–91; Gen. Sec., then Chief Exec., AMRC, 1991–2005. Member: BBC Appeals Cttee, 1992–98; Bd, Groundwork Southwark, 1995–2002; NHS Standing Cttee (formerly Adv. Gp) on Consumer Involvement in NHS R&D, 1997–2002; Chief Scientist Cttee, Scottish Exec., 1999–2005; COPUS, Royal Soc., 2001–03; HEFCE Res. Strategy Cttee, 2003–06; Panel, UK Stem Cell Initiative, 2005; Nat. Adv. Gp, UK Resource Centre for Women in SET, 2006–; Forensic Sci. Occupational Cttee, 2006–; Nat. Scis Cttee, UK Nat. Commn for UNESCO; Chm., Mgt Bd, Coalition for Med. Progress, 2003–05. Member: Adv. Cttee, Inst. of Psychiatry, 2003–; Council, Nottingham Univ., 2003–. Trustee: Sense about Science, 2003–; Internat. Spinal Res. Trust; Mem., Bd, Benevolent Soc. of Blues, 2000–; Patron, Cae Dai Trust, 2008–; also involved in other charity sector gps. *Recreations:* music, needlework, food and drink, travel. *Address:* Science Council, 32–36 Loman Street, SE1 0EH. *T:* (020) 7922 7888; *e-mail:* d.garnham@sciencecouncil.org. *Clubs:* Royal Commonwealth Society.

GARNHAM, Neil Stephen; QC 2001; barrister; a Recorder, since 2001; *b* 11 Feb. 1959; *s* of Geoffrey Arthur Garnham and Cynthia Avril Rose Garnham; *m* 1991, Gillian Mary Shaw; two *s*. *Educ:* Ipswich Sch.; Peterhouse, Cambridge (MA). Called to the Bar, Middle Temple, 1982; a Jun. Counsel to the Crown, 1995–2001. *Address:* 1 Crown Office Row, Temple, EC4Y 7HH. *T:* (020) 7797 7500.

GARNIER, Edward Henry; QC 1995; MP (C) Harborough, since 1992; barrister; a Recorder, since 2000; *b* 26 Oct. 1952; *s* of late Col William d'Arcy Garnier and of Hon. Lavender Hyacinth (*née* de Grey); *m* 1982, Anna Caroline Mellows; two *s* one *d*. *Educ:* Wellington Coll.; Jesus Coll., Oxford (BA, MA). Called to the Bar, Middle Temple, 1976, Bencher, 2001; Asst Recorder, 1998–2000. Vice-Pres., Hemsworth Assoc., 1987–. Contested: Wandsworth BC by-election, 1984; Tooting ILEA election, 1986; (C) Hemsworth, Gen. Election, 1987. PPS to Ministers of State, FCO, 1994–95; PPS to Attorney General and to Solicitor General, 1995–97, and to Chancellor of the Duchy of Lancaster, 1996–97; Opposition spokesman, Lord Chancellor's Dept, 1997–99; Shadow Attorney-Gen., 1999–2001; Opposition frontbench spokesman on home affairs, 2005–07; Shadow Minister for Justice, 2007–. Mem., Home Affairs Select Cttee, 1992–95; Sec., Cons. Foreign Affairs Cttee, 1992–94. Mem., Exec. Cttee, 1922 Cttee, 2001–05. UK Election Observer: Kenya, 1992; Bosnia, 1996. Vis. Parly Fellow, St Antony's Coll., Oxford, 1996–97. Mem., Leics and Rutland Cttee, 1992–, Legal and Parly Cttee, 1994–2000, CLA. *Publications:* (contrib.) Halsbury's Laws of England, 4th edn, 1985; (contrib.) Bearing the Standard, 1991; (contrib.) Facing the Future, 1993. *Recreations:* cricket, shooting, opera. *Address:* House of Commons, SW1A 0AA. *T:* (020) 7219 3000. *Clubs:* White's, Pratt's.

GARNIER, Jean-Pierre, PhD; Chief Executive, GlaxoSmithKline, 2000–08; Member, Advisory Board, Dubai International Capital, since 2008; *b* 31 Oct. 1947; *m* Danyele; three *d*. *Educ:* Univ. of Louis Pasteur, France (MS, PhD); Stanford Univ., Calif (Fulbright Scholar; MBA 1974). Schering Plough: Gen. Manager of overseas subsidiaries, 1975–83; Sen. Dir of Mktg, 1983–84, Vice-Pres. of Mktg, 1984–85, Sen. Vice-Pres. and Gen. Manager for Sales and Mktg, 1987–88, Pres., 1989–90, US Pharmaceutical Products Div SmithKline Beecham: Pres., pharmaceutical business in N America, 1990–93; Exec. Di 1992–2000; Exec. Vice-Pres., 1993–94, Chm., 1994–95, Pharmaceuticals; Chie Operating Officer, 1995–2000; Chief Exec., 2000. Officier de la Légion d'Honneu (France), 2007 (Chevalier, 1997).

GARNIER, Rear-Adm. Sir John, KCVO 1990 (LVO 1965); CBE 1982; Extra Equerr to the Queen, since 1988; *b* 10 March 1934; *s* of Rev. Thomas Vernon Garnier and Hele Stenhouse; *m* 1966, Joanna Jane Cadbury; two *s* one *d*. *Educ:* Berkhamsted School Britannia Royal Naval College. Joined RN 1950; served HM Yacht Britannia, 1956–57 HMS Tyne (Suez Operation) 1956; qualified navigation specialist, 1959; Naval Equerr to HM Queen, 1962–65; Comd HMS Dundas, 1968–69; Directorate of Naval Ops an Trade, 1969–71; Comd HMS Minerva, 1972–73; Defence Policy Staff, 1973–75; HM Intrepid, 1976; Asst Dir, Naval Manpower Planning, 1976–78; RCDS 1979; Comd HM London, 1980–81; Dir, Naval Ops and Trade, 1982–84; Commodore Amphibiou Warfare, 1985; Flag Officer Royal Yachts, 1985–90. Private Sec. and Comptroller t HRH Princess Alexandra, 1991–95. Younger Brother of Trinity House, 1974. Mem Council, Shipwrecked Fishermen and Mariners' Royal Benevolent Soc., 1996–2004 Gov., Sherborne Sch. for Girls, 1985–2004. Freeman of City of London, 1982. *Recreations* sailing, golf, gardening, opera. *Address:* Bembury Farm, Thornford, Sherborne, Dors DT9 6QF.

GARNOCK, Viscount; William James Lindesay-Bethune; *b* 30 Dec. 1990; *s* and *he* of Earl of Lindsay, *qv*.

GARNON, Tudor Mansel; Employment Judge (formerly Chairman of Employmen Tribunals), Newcastle Region, since 2002; *b* 19 Oct. 1953; *s* of David Carey Garnon an Marian Garnon; *m* 1976, Jean Davina Hewet; one *d*. *Educ:* Trinity Hall, Cambridge (MA) Admitted as solicitor, 1978; Partner, Richard Reed and Co., Solicitors, 1980–92; sol practitioner, Garnon and Co., 1993–99; Partner, McArdles, Solicitors, 2000–01; Chm Employment Tribunals, London NW, 2001–02. *Recreations:* various sports. *Address:* 13 Priors Grange, High Pittington, Durham DH6 1DF. *T:* (0191) 327 0367.

GARNSEY, Prof. Peter David Arthur, FBA 1993; Fellow of Jesus College, Cambridge 1974–2006, now Emeritus; *b* 22 Oct. 1938; *m* 1967, Elizabeth Franklin; one *s* two *d*. *Edu* Sydney Univ. (BA); Rhodes Scholar, 1961; MA 1967, DPhil 1967, Oxon; PhD Cantal 1974. Jun. Fellow, University Coll., Oxford, 1964–67; Asst, then Associate, Prof., Univ of Calif, Berkeley, 1967–73; Cambridge University: Lectr, 1974–90; Reader in Ancien History, 1990–97; Prof. of the Hist. of Classical Antiquity, 1997–2006; Dir of Res 2006–07. Hon. FAHA 2001. *Publications:* Social Status and Legal Privilege in the Roma Empire, 1970; (ed jtly) Imperialism in the Ancient World, 1978; (ed jtly) Trade an Famine in Classical Antiquity, 1983; (ed) Nonslave Labour in the Graeco-Roman World 1980; (jtly) Early Principate: Augustus to Trajan, 1982; (ed jtly) Trade in the Ancier Economy, 1983; (jtly) Roman Empire: economy, society and culture, 1987; Famine an Food Supply in the Graeco-Roman World, 1988; (ed) Food, Health and Culture i Classical Antiquity, 1989; Ideas of Slavery from Aristotle to Augustine, 1996; (ed jtly Hellenistic Constructs: essays in culture, history and historiography, 1997; (ed jtly Cambridge Ancient History XIII: the Late Empire AD325–425, 1998; Cities, Peasants an Food in Classical Antiquity, 1998; Food and Society in Classical Antiquity, 1999; (ed jtly Cambridge Ancient History XI: the High Empire AD70–192, 2000; (jtly) The Evolutio of the Late Antique World, 2001; (jtly) Lactantius, Divine Institutes (trans. wit introduction and notes), 2003; Thinking about Property: from antiquity to the age o revolution, 2007. *Address:* Jesus College, Cambridge CB5 8BL.

GARRARD, Rt Rev. Richard; an Hon. Assistant Bishop: Diocese of Europe, since 2001 Diocese of Norwich, since 2003; Hon. Assisting Bishop, American Episcopa Convocation of Churches, since 2001; *b* 24 May 1937; *s* of Charles John Garrard an Marjorie Louise (*née* Pow); *m* 1961, Elizabeth Ann Sewell; one *s* one *d*. *Edu* Northampton Grammar Sch.; King's Coll., Univ. of London (BD, AKC). Ordaine deacon, 1961, priest, 1962; Assistant Curate: St Mary's, Woolwich, 1961–66; Great S Mary's, Cambridge, 1966–68; Chaplain/Lectr, Keswick Hall Coll. of Educn, Norwich 1968–74; Principal, Church Army Training Coll., 1974–79; Canon Chancello Southwark Cathedral and Dir of Training, dio. of Southwark, 1979–87; Cano Residentiary, St James's Cathedral, Bury St Edmunds and Advr for Clergy Training, dio of St Edmundsbury and Ipswich, 1987–91; Archdeacon of Sudbury, 1991–94; Suffraga Bp of Penrith, 1994–2001; Dir, Anglican Centre in Rome, and Archbp of Canterbury' Rep. to the Holy See, 2001–03. *Publications:* Lent with St Mark, 1992; A Time to Pray 1993; Love on the Cross, 1995. *Recreations:* cats, crosswords, Italy, the fells. *Address:* 2 Carol Close, Stoke Holy Cross, Norwich, Norfolk NR14 8NN.

GARRETT, Sir Anthony (Peter), Kt 1997; CBE 1992; General Secretary, Associatio of British Dispensing Opticians, since 1999; *b* Jersey, 28 Nov. 1952; *m* 1st, 1974 (marr diss. 1985); twin *d*; 2nd, 1989, Jane Wight Scott; two *d*. *Educ:* Canterbury Tech. High Sch for Boys. Conservative Party Organisation, 1971–98: Constituency Agent, Rochester an Chatham, 1973–79; Cons. Central Office, 1979–98: SE Area Office, 1979–86; Asst Di Campaigning, 1986–92; Dir of Campaigning, 1992–98; Mem., Cons. Bd of Mgt 1993–98. Pres., Cons. Agents' Benevolent Fund, 1992–98 (Trustee, 2001–); Trustee Cons. Agents' Superannuation Fund, 1992–98. *Recreations:* cricket, travel. *Address:* c/ Association of British Dispensing Opticians, 199 Gloucester Terrace, W2 6HX. *Clubs* Carlton; Kent County Cricket (Life Mem.).

GARRETT, Godfrey John, OBE 1982; HM Diplomatic Service, retired; consultant o Central and Eastern Europe, since 1996, and on Global Conflict Prevention Policy to HM Government, 2004–06; *b* 24 July 1937; *s* of Thomas and May Garrett; *m* 1963, Elisabet Margaret Hall; four *s* one *d*. *Educ:* Dulwich Coll.; Cambridge Univ. (MA). Joined FO 1961; Third Sec., Leopoldville (later Kinshasa), 1963; Second Sec. (Commercial), Prague 1965; FCO, 1968; First Sec., Buenos Aires, 1971; FCO, 1973; First Sec., later Counsello Stockholm, 1981; Counsellor: Bonn, 1983; FCO, 1988; E Berlin, 1990; Prague, 1990–92 FCO, 1992–93; Head of UK Delegn to EC Monitoring Mission, Zagreb, 1993–94; Hd OSCE Mission to Ukraine, 1995. Consultant, Control Risks Group Ltd, 1996–98. Orde of the Northern Star, Sweden, 1983. *Recreations:* all outdoor activities, especially ski-ing travel, gardening, languages. *Address:* White Cottage, Henley, Haslemere, Surrey GU2 3HQ. *T:* (01428) 652172; Mains of Glenlochy, Bridge of Brown, Tomintoul Ballindalloch, Banff AB37 9HR. *T:* (01807) 580257.

GARRETT, Maj.-Gen. Henry Edmund Melvill Lennox, CBE 1975; *b* 31 Jan. 1924 *s* of John Edmund Garrett and Mary Garrett; *m* 1973, Rachel Ann Beadon; one step *s* on step *d*. *Educ:* Wellington Coll.; Clare Coll., Cambridge (MA). Commnd 1944; psc 1956 DAAG, HQ BAOR, 1957–60; US Armed Forces Staff Coll., 1960; OC 7 Field Sqdn RE 1961–63; GSO2 WO, 1963–65; CO 35 Engr Regt, 1965–68; Col GS MoD, 1968–69 Comdr 12 Engr Bde, 1969–71; RCDS, 1972; Chief of Staff HQ N Ireland, 1972–75 Maj.-Gen. i/c Administration, HQ UKLF, 1975–76; Vice Adjutant General, MoD 1976–78; Dir of Security (Army), MoD, 1978–89. Chm., Forces Help Soc. and Lor

Roberts Workshops, 1991–96; Vice-President: SSAFA, 1991–96; SSAFA/Forces Help, 1997–; Lady Grover's Hosp. Fund for Officers' Families, 2002–. Col Comdt RE, 1982–90. Chm., RE Assoc., 1989–93. Chm. Governors, Royal Soldiers' Daughters Sch., 1983–86. *Recreations:* reading, walking. *Address:* c/o National Westminster Bank, 7 Hustlegate, Bradford, W Yorkshire BD1 1PP. *Club:* Army and Navy.

GARRETT, Lesley, CBE 2002; FRAM; Principal Soprano, English National Opera, 1984–98; *b* 10 April 1955; *d* of Derek Arthur Garrett and Margaret Garrett (*née* Wall); *m* 1991; one *s* one *d*. *Educ:* Thorne Grammar Sch.; Royal Acad. of Music (FRAM 1995); Nat. Opera Studio (Post-grad.). Winner, Kathleen Ferrier Meml Competition, 1979. Performed with WNO, Opera North and at Wexford and Buxton Fests and Glyndebourne; joined ENO, 1984; début with Royal Opera, 1997; has appeared in opera houses in Geneva, São Paulo, Boboli Gdns, Florence, Bolshoi Theatre, Moscow and Kirov Theatre, St Petersburg; major roles include: Susanna in Marriage of Figaro; Despina in Così Fan Tutte; Musetta in La Bohème; Jenny in The Rise and Fall of The City of Mahaggony; Atalanta in Xerxes; Zerlinda in Don Giovanni; Yum-Yum in The Mikado; Adèle in Die Fledermaus; Oscar in A Masked Ball; Dalinda in Ariodante; Rose in Street Scene; Bella in A Midsummer Marriage; Eurydice in Orpheus and Eurydice; Rosina in The Barber of Seville; title rôles in The Cunning Little Vixen, La Belle Vivette, and The Merry Widow; Mother Superior in The Sound of Music; concert hall appearances in UK and abroad include: Royal Variety Performance, 1993, Last Night of the Proms, Royal Albert Hall, Royal Fest. Hall, Centre Pompidou, Paris; numerous recordings and TV and radio appearances. Hon. DArts Plymouth, 1995. Best selling classical artist, Gramophone award, 1996. *Recreation:* watching cricket. *Address:* The Music Partnership Ltd, New Broad Street House, New Broad Street, EC2M 1NH.

GARRETT, Richard Anthony, CBE 1987; company director; Chairman, National Association of Boys' Clubs, 1980–87, retired; *b* 4 July 1918; 3rd *s* of Charles Victor Garrett and Blanche Michell; *m* 1st, 1946, Marie Louise Dalglish (*d* 1999); one *s* two *d* (and one *d* decd); 2nd, 2000, Nancy Rae Wise. *Educ:* King's Sch., Worcester. Served War, 1939–45 (despatches, 1945). Joined W.D. & H.O. Wills, 1936; Chm., ITL, retd 1979; Chm. and Man. Dir, John Player & Sons, 1968–71; Chm., Dataday Ltd, 1978–83; Director: HTV Gp plc, 1976–89 (Vice-Chm., 1978–83); Standard Commercial (formerly Standard Commercial Tobacco) Corp., 1980–95. Vice Pres., (Founder), Arts & Business (formerly Assoc. of Business Sponsorship of the Arts). Chm., Bath Festival, 1986–87; Trustee, Glyndebourne Arts Trust, 1976–88. Liveryman, Worshipful Co. of Tobacco Pipe Makers and Tobacco Blenders. MInstD; CCMI (CBIM 1979). *Recreations:* golf, gardening, music, opera, reading. *Address:* Marlwood Grange, Thornbury, Bristol BS35 3JD. *T:* (01454) 412630. *Clubs:* Naval and Military, MCC, XL; Bristol and Clifton Golf.

GARRETT, Terence, CMG 1990; CBE 1967; Assistant Secretary (International Affairs), Royal Society, 1991–94; *b* 27 Sept. 1929; *e s* of late Percy Herbert Garrett and Gladys Annie Garrett (*née* Budd); *m* 1960, Grace Elizabeth Bridgman Braund, *yr d* of Rev. Basil Kelly Braund; two *s* three *d*. *Educ:* Alleyn's Sch.; Gonville and Caius Coll., Cambridge (Scholar; 1st Cl. Hons, Mathematics). DipMathStat. Instructor Lieut RN, 1952–55. Lecturer, Ewell County Technical Coll., 1955–56; Sen. Lectr, RMCS, Shrivenham, 1957–62; Counsellor (Sci. and Technol.), Moscow, 1962–66 and 1970–74; Programmes Analysis Unit, Min. of Technology, 1967–70; Internat. Technological Collaboration Unit, Dept of Trade, 1974–76; Sec. to Bd of Governors and to Gen. Conf. of Internat. Atomic Energy Agency, Vienna, 1976–78; Counsellor (Science and Technology), Bonn, 1978–82; DCSO, Research and Technology Policy Div., DTI, 1982–87; Counsellor (Sci. and Technol.), Moscow, 1987–91. *Recreation:* travel. *Address:* Lime Tree Farmhouse, Chilton, Didcot, Oxon OX11 0SW. *Club:* Hawks (Cambridge).

GARRICK, Sir Ronald, Kt 1994; CBE 1986; DL; FREng; FRSE; Deputy Chairman, HBOS plc, since 2003 (Director, since 2001); *b* 21 Aug. 1940; *s* of Thomas Garrick and Anne (*née* McKay); *m* 1965, Janet Elizabeth Taylor Lind; two *s* one *d*. *Educ:* Royal College of Science and Technology, Glasgow; Glasgow University (BSc MechEng, 1st cl. hons). FIMechE; FREng (FEng 1984); FRSE 1992. Joined G. & J. Weir Ltd, 1962; Weir Pumps: Dir, Industrial Div., 1973; Dir Production Div., 1976; Managing Dir, 1981; Dir, 1981, Man. Dir and Chief Exec., 1982–99, Chm., 1999–2002, Weir Group. Vis. Prof., Dept of Mech. Engrg, Univ. of Strathclyde, 1991–96. Member: Scottish Council, CBI, 1982–90; Gen. Convocation, 1985–96, Court, 1990–96, Univ. of Strathclyde; Restrictive Practices Court, 1986–96; Offshore Industry Adv. Bd, 1989–97; Scottish Economic Council, 1989–98; Scottish Business Forum, 1998–99; Dep. Chm., Scottish Enterprise Bd, 1991–96; Dearing Cttee of Inquiry into Higher Educn, 1996–97 (Chm., Scottish Cttee). Non-executive Director: Supervisory Bd, NEL, 1989–92; Strathclyde Graduate Business Sch., 1990–96; Scottish Power PLC, 1992–99; Shell UK Ltd, 1993–98; Bank of Scotland, 2000–01. DL Renfrewshire, 1996. DUniv: Paisley, 1993; Strathclyde, 1994; Hon. DEng Glasgow, 1998. *Recreations:* golf, reading. *Address:* 14 Roddinghead Road, Giffnock, Glasgow G46 6TN.

GARROD, Lt-Gen. Sir (John) Martin (Carruthers), KCB 1988; CMG 1999; OBE 1980; DL; UN Regional Administrator of Mitrovica, Kosovo, 1999; *b* 29 May 1935; *s* of Rev. William Francis Garrod and Isobel Agnes (*née* Carruthers); *m* 1963, Gillian Mary, *d* of late Lt-Col R. G. Parks-Smith, RM; two *d*. *Educ:* Sherborne School. Joined Royal Marines, 1953; served Malta, Cyprus, DS Officers' Training Wing, RM School of Music, Malaya, Borneo, 1955–66; Staff Coll., Camberley, 1967; HQ 17 Div., Malaya, 1968–69; HQ Farelf, Singapore, 1970–71; 40 Commando RM (Co. Comdr, Plymouth and N Ireland), 1972–73 (despatches); GSO2 Plans, Dept of CGRM, 1973–76; GSO1, HQ Commando Forces RM, 1976–78; CO 40 Commando RM, 1978–79 (OBE operational, NI); Col Ops/Plans, Dept of CGRM, 1980–82; Comdr 3 Commando Bde RM, 1983–84; ADC to the Queen, 1983–84; COS to Comdt Gen. RM, 1984–87; Comdt Gen., RM, 1987–90. Mem., EC Monitor Mission in Bosnia, 1993–94; COS to EU Adminr, Mostar, 1994–96; EU Special Envoy, Mostar, 1996; Head, 1997–98, a Dep. High Rep., 1998, Regl Office of High Representative resp. for Southern Bosnia and Hercegovina. Dep. Dir, Maastricht Referendum Campaign, 1993. Freeman, City of London, 1990. DL Kent, 1992. *Recreation:* portrait photography. *Address:* c/o Lloyds TSB, 2 High Street, Deal, Kent CT14 7AD. *Club:* East India.

GARSIDE, Charles Alexander; Assistant Editor, Daily Mail, since 2006 (Managing Editor, 2004–06); Proprietor, Miller Howe Hotel and Restaurant, Windermere, 1998–2006; Managing Director, 649 Service Ltd, since 1997; *b* 9 April 1951; *s* of John Robert Garside and Florence Garside (*née* Wilson); *m* 1st, 1972, Shirley May Reynolds (marr. diss.); 2nd, 1984, Carole Anne Short (marr. diss.); one *s* one *d*; partner, Gail Graham. *Educ:* Queen Elizabeth's Grammar Sch., Blackburn; Harris Coll., Preston. News Editor, London Evening News, 1979–80; News Editor, 1981–85, Asst Editor, 1986, Evening Standard; Dep. News Editor, The Times, 1987; Dep. Editor, Sunday Express, 1988–89; Asst Editor, The Times, 1989–90; Dep. Editor, 1991–92, Editor and Gen. Manager, 1992–94, Editor in Chief, 1994–97, The European. *Recreations:* fly fishing, theatres, classic cars. *Address:* The Daily Mail, 2 Derry Street, W8 5TT. *T:* (020) 7938 6125; *e-mail:* managingeditor@dailymail.co.uk.

GARSIDE, Charles Roger; QC 1993; a Recorder, since 1994; *b* 13 Aug. 1948; *s* of Richard Murray Garside and Jane Garside (*née* Boby); *m* 1973, Sophie Shem-Tov; two *s* one *d*. *Educ:* Tonbridge Sch. Called to the Bar, Gray's Inn, 1971. Mem., Manchester Pedestrian Club, 1993–. *Recreations:* gardening, cricket, Rugby. *Address:* 9 St John Street, Manchester M3 4DN. *T:* (0161) 955 9000. *Clubs:* Lancashire County Cricket; Manchester Pedestrian.

GARSIDE, Prof. John, CBE 2005; PhD, DSc(Eng); FREng, FIChemE; Professor of Chemical Engineering, 1982–2004, now Emeritus, and Principal and Vice-Chancellor, 2000–04, University of Manchester Institute of Science and Technology; *b* 9 Oct. 1941; *s* of Eric and Ada Garside; *m* 1965, Patricia Louise Holtom; one *s* one *d*. *Educ:* Christ's Coll., Finchley; University Coll. London (BSc(Eng), PhD, DSc(Eng); Fellow, 1994). FIChemE 1986; FREng (FEng 1988). ICI Agricl Div., 1966–69; Lectr, later Reader, UCL, 1969–81; Vice-Principal, UMIST, 1985–87. Vis. Prof., Iowa State Univ., 1976–77. Mem., various cttees and Engrg Bd, SERC, 1989–93. Institution of Chemical Engineers: Mem. Council, 1992–; Pres., 1994–95. Exec. Vice-Pres., EFCE, 2006–. *Publications:* (ed) Advances in Industrial Crystallization, 1991; Precipitation: basic principles and industrial application, 1992; From Molecules to Crystallizers, 2000; papers in Chem. Engrg Sci., Trans IChemE, Amer. Instn Chem. Engrs, Jl Crystal Growth, etc. *Recreations:* music, sailing, gardening. *Address:* Bryham House, Low Knipe, Askham, Penrith CA10 2PU.

GARSIDE, (Pamela) Jane, CBE 1995; JP; Chief Commissioner, The Guide (formerly Girl Guides) Association of the United Kingdom and the Commonwealth, 1990–95; *b* 20 Aug. 1936; *d* of Ronald and Nellie Whitwam; *m* 1958, Adrian Fielding Garside; two *s* (two *d* decd). *Educ:* Royds Hall Grammar Sch., Huddersfield; Yorkshire Trng Coll. of Housecraft, Leeds Inst. of Educn (Teaching Dip. 1957). Teacher, Deighton Secondary Sch., 1957–58; Co. Sec. 1959–, Dir 1964–, Highfield Funeral Service Ltd. Girl Guides: Dist Comr, Huddersfield N, 1973–77; County Comr, W Yorks S, 1977–83 (County Pres., 1996–2001); Chief Comr, NE England, 1984–89 (Vice-Pres., 1990–2000; Pres., 2000–05). Nat. Pres., Trefoil Guild, 2004–08. *Recreations:* reading, gardening, music.

GARSIDE, Roger Ramsay; Executive Chairman, GMA Capital Markets Ltd (formerly Garside, Miller Associates), advisers to emerging financial markets, 1990–2000; *b* 29 March 1938; *s* of late Captain F. R. Garside, RN and Mrs Peggie Garside; *m* 1st, 1969, Evelyne Guérin (marr. diss. 2001); three *d*; 2nd, 2004, Mariota Rosanna Theresa, *d* of Keith and Oona Kinross. *Educ:* Eton; Clare Coll., Cambridge (BA EngLit, MA); Sloan Fellow in Management, Massachusetts Inst. of Technology. 2nd Lieut, 6th Gurkha Rifles, 1958–59; entered HM Foreign Service, 1962; served, Rangoon, 1964–65; Mandarin Chinese Lang. Student, Hong Kong, 1965–67; Second Secretary, Peking, 1968–70; FCO, 1970–71, resigned 1971; World Bank, 1972–74; rejoined Foreign Service, 1975; served FCO, 1975; First Sec., Peking, 1976–79; on leave of absence, as Vis. Professor of East Asian Studies, US Naval Postgrad. Sch., Monterey, Calif, 1979–80; Dep. Head, Planning Staff, FCO, 1980–81; seconded, HM Treasury, 1981–82; Financial and Commercial Counsellor, Paris, 1982–87, resigned 1987; Dir, Public Affairs, Internat. Stock Exchange of UK and Rep. of Ireland (now London Stock Exchange), 1987–90. *Publication:* Coming Alive: China after Mao, 1981. *Recreations:* reading, writing, walking. *Address:* 7 East Street, Hambledon, Hants PO7 4RX. *Club:* Reform.

GARTHWAITE, Sir (William) Mark (Charles), 3rd Bt *cr* 1919, of Durham; Director, Willis Ltd (formerly Willis Faber), Lloyds Brokers, since 1997; *b* 4 Nov. 1946; *s* of Sir William Francis Cuthbert Garthwaite, 2nd Bt, DSC and Bar and of his 2nd wife, Patricia Beatrice Eden (*née* Neate); *S* father, 1993; *m* 1979, Victoria Lisette Hohler, *e d* of Gen. Sir Harry Tuzo, GCB, OBE, MC; one *s* two *d*. *Educ:* Dragon Sch.; Gordonstoun; Univ. of Pennsylvania (Wharton Sch.; BSc Econ.). Seascope Insurance Services, Lloyds Brokers, 1970–87 (Man. Dir, 1980–87); Brandram and Garthwaite Ltd, 1987–88; Director: Regis Low Ltd, Lloyds Brokers, 1988–92; Steel Burrill Jones Ltd, Lloyds Brokers, 1992–97. Chm., London Market Insurance Brokers Cttee Marine, 2000–02. *Recreations:* sailing, skiing, trekking. *Heir:* *s* William Tuzo Garthwaite, *b* 14 May 1982. *Address:* 3 Hazlewell Road, SW15 6LU. *Clubs:* Turf; Royal Southampton Yacht (Southampton); Royal Yacht Squadron.

GARTON, George Alan, PhD, DSc; FRSE 1966; FRS 1978; Hon. Professorial Fellow, Rowett Research Institute, Bucksburn, Aberdeen, since 1992; Hon. Research Fellow, University of Aberdeen, since 1987; *b* 4 June 1922; *o s* of late William Edgar Garton, DCM, and Frances Mary Elizabeth Garton (*née* Atkinson), Scarborough, N Yorks; *m* 1951, Gladys Frances Davison, BSc; two *d*. *Educ:* Scarborough High Sch.; Univ. of Liverpool (BSc (War Service) 1944, (Hons Biochem.) 1946; PhD 1949, DSc 1959). Experimental Asst, Chemical Inspection Dept, Min. of Supply, 1942–45; Johnston Research and Teaching Fellow, Dept of Biochem., Univ. of Liverpool, 1949–50; Rowett Research Inst., Bucksburn, Aberdeen: Biochemist, 1950; Dep. Dir, 1968–83; Head of Lipid Biochem. Dept, 1963–83; Hon. Res. Associate, 1983–92; Hon. Res. Associate, Univ. of Aberdeen, 1966–86. Sen. Foreign Fellow of Nat. Science Foundn (USA), and Vis. Prof. of Biochem., Univ. of N Carolina, 1967. Chm., British Nat. Cttee for Nutritional and Food Sciences, 1982–87; Pres., Internat. Confs on Biochem. Lipids, 1982–89. Scientific Gov., British Nutrition Foundn, 1982–2003, Gov. Emeritus, 2004–; a Dir, The Mother and Child Foundn, 1995–2000. SBStJ 1985. *Publications:* papers, mostly on aspects of lipid biochemistry, in scientific jls. *Recreations:* gardening, golf, foreign travel. *Address:* 2 St Devenick's Mews, Cults, Aberdeen AB15 9LH. *T:* (01224) 867012. *Club:* Deeside Golf (Aberdeen).

GARTON, Rt Rev. John Henry; Bishop Suffragan of Plymouth, 1996–2005; Hon. Assistant Bishop, diocese of Oxford, since 2006; *b* 3 Oct. 1941; *s* of Henry and Dorothy Garton; *m* 1969, Pauline (*née* George); two *s*. *Educ:* RMA Sandhurst; Worcester Coll., Oxford (MA); Cuddesdon Coll., Oxford. Commissioned in Royal Tank Regt, 1962. Ordained, 1969; CF, 1969–73; Lectr, Lincoln Theol Coll., 1973–78; Rector of Coventry East Team Ministry, 1978–86; Principal, Ripon Coll., Cuddesdon, 1986–96; Vicar, All Saints, Cuddesdon, 1986–96. Hon. Canon of Worcester Cathedral, 1988–96. *Address:* 52 Clive Road, Cowley, Oxford OX4 3EL. *T:* (01865) 771093.

GARTON ASH, Prof. Timothy John, CMG 2000; writer; Professor of European Studies, University of Oxford, since 2004; Fellow, St Antony's College, Oxford, since 1989 (Director, European Studies Centre, 2001–06); *b* 12 July 1955; *s* of John Garton Ash and Lorna (*née* Freke); *m* 1982, Danuta Maria Brudnik; two *s*. *Educ:* Sherborne; Exeter Coll., Oxford (BA 1st Cl. Hons Mod. Hist., MA); St Antony's Coll., Oxford; Free Univ., W Berlin; Humboldt Univ., E Berlin. Foreign Editor, Spectator, 1984–90; editl writer on Central Europe, The Times, 1984–86; Fellow, Woodrow Wilson Center, Washington, 1986–87; columnist: Independent, 1988–90; Guardian, 2002–; Sen. Fellow, Hoover Instn, Stanford Univ., 2001–. Gov., Westminster Foundn for Democracy, 1992–2000. FRSA; FRHistS; FRSL; Fellow: Berlin-Brandenburg Acad. of Scis, European Acad. of Scis; Institut für die Wissenschaften vom Menschen, Vienna. Hon. DLitt: St Andrews, 2004; Sheffield Hallam, 2005. Commentator of Year, What the Papers Say awards, 1989; David Watt Meml Prize, RTZ, 1990; Premio Napoli, 1995; OSCE Prize for Journalism and Democracy, 1998; George Orwell Prize, 2006. Order of Merit (Poland), 1992;

Bundesverdienstkreuz (FRG), 1995; Order of Merit (Czech Republic), 2003. *Publications:* 'Und willst Du nicht mein Bruder sein …' Die DDR heute, 1981; The Polish Revolution: Solidarity, 1983, 3rd edn 1999 (Somerset Maugham Award, 1984); The Uses of Adversity, 1989, 2nd edn 1991 (Prix Européen de l'Essai, 1989); We the People, 1990, 2nd edn 1999; In Europe's Name: Germany and the divided continent, 1993; The File: a personal history, 1997; History of the Present, 1999, 2nd edn 2000; Free World, 2004. *Address:* St Antony's College, Oxford OX2 6JF. *T:* (01865) 274474, *Fax:* (01865) 274478.

GARTRY, David Stanley, MD; FRCS, FRCOphth; Consultant Ophthalmic Surgeon, Moorfields Eye Hospital, London, since 1995; *b* 23 June 1956; *s* of Stanley and Phyllis Gartry; *m* 1980, Lily Giacoman; three *s*. *Educ:* Glasgow Coll. of Technol. (BSc 1st Cl. Hons Optometry 1978); University Coll. London (Suckling Prize in Neuroanatomy, 1981; Duke-Elder undergrad. prize in Ophthalmol., 1983; MB BS 1984); MD London 1995. FCOptom 1979; FRCS 1988; FRCOphth 1988. Sen. Lectr, UCL, 1995–. Discourse Lectr, Royal Instn, 1995; Vis. Lectr, 1997–2006, Vis. Prof., 2006–, City Univ. Ext. Examnr, City Univ., 2006; Examnr, RCOphth. First surgeon in UK to perform laser refractive surgery, 1989. Pres., British Soc. for Refractive Surgery, 1999–2002. Master's (SMC), Colebrook and Porter Prizes, BOA, 1979; Honor Award, Amer. Acad. Ophthalmol., 1999. *Publications:* Excimer Lasers in Ophthalmology, 1997; Cataract Surgery, 2003; numerous scientific contribs and book chapters. *Recreations:* formerly enthusiastic squash player (quite good, Middlesex ranked, Cumberland Cup), guitar (not bad), piano (poor!), car/driving enthusiast. *Address:* The London Clinic, 149 Harley Street, W1G 6DE. *T:* (020) 7486 3112; *e-mail:* david@gartry.com. *Club:* Cumberland Lawn Tennis and Squash.

GARVAGH, 5th Baron *cr* 1818; **Alexander Leopold Ivor George Canning;** Accredited Representative, Trade and Industry, The Cayman Islands, 1981; *b* 6 Oct. 1920; *s* of 4th Baron and Gladys Dora May (*d* 1982), *d* of William Bayley Parker; *S* father, 1956; *m* 1st, 1947, Christine Edith (marr. diss. 1974), *d* of Jack Cooper; one *s* two *d*; 2nd, 1974, Cynthia Valerie Mary, *d* of Eric E. F. Pretty, CMG, Kingswood, Surrey. *Educ:* Eton; Christ Church, Oxford. Commissioned Corps of Guides Cavalry, Indian Army, 1940; served Burma (despatches). Founder Dir, Internat. Business Services Ltd, 1947; Director: Stonehaven Tankers Ltd; Campden Research & Sales Ltd; Independent Chartering Ltd; AODC (UK) Ltd; Camco Machinery Ltd; Telomex (New York) Inc. Founder Mem., Instituto de Proprietarios Extranjeros (Spain), 1985. Mem., Baltic Exchange, 1978. Mem., British Inst. of Exports, 1957; MCMI (MBIM 1962); FInstD 1964. Past Mem. Court, Painter Stainers Co. Consultant and contributor, Spanish Property Gazette, 1987–88. *Publication:* contrib. to The Manufacturing Optician, 1949. *Recreations:* travel, motoring, and motor sport; writing articles, short stories, etc. *Heir: s* Hon. Spencer George Stratford de Redcliffe Canning [*b* 12 Feb. 1953; *m* 1979, Julia Margery Morison Bye, *er d* of Col F. C. E. Bye, Twickenham; one *s* two *d*]. *Address:* The Courtyard, Water Street, Deal, Kent CT14 6DJ.

GARVEY, Arnold James; Editor, Horse and Hound, 1995–2001; *b* 7 Aug. 1946; *s* of late James Adamson Garvey and Esme Muriel (*née* Noble); *m* 1st, 1969, Kathleen Gordon (marr. diss. 1996); two *d*; 2nd, 1997, Marta-Lisà Conversi; two *s* one *d*. *Educ:* Bramston, Witham, Essex; Braintree Coll., Essex. Joined Horse and Hound, as sub-editor, 1971: Dep. Ed., 1987–94; Actg Ed., 1994–95. *Recreations:* horse riding, theatre, walking. *Address:* 27 Cornel Close, Witham, Essex CM8 2XH. *Club:* Farmers.

GARVEY, Thomas, (Tom); Deputy Director General (Environment, Nuclear Safety and Civil Protection), European Commission, 1992–98; *b* 27 May 1936; *s* of Thomas and Brigid Garvey; *m* 1961, Ellen Devine; two *s* two *d*. *Educ:* University Coll., Dublin (MA Econ). Fellow, Management Inst. Ireland. Various marketing and internal trade appts, 1958–69; Chief Exec., Irish Export Bd, 1969–76; EEC Delegate, Nigeria, 1977–80; Chief Exec., An Post (Irish Postal Service), 1980–84; Dir, Internal Market and Ind. Affairs, EEC, 1984–89; Dir, DG1 (External Relns), EC, 1990–92. Mem. Gen. Assembly and Life Fellow, Regl Envmt Centre, Budapest, 1996; Chm., Regl Envmt Centre, Moldova, 1999. Visiting Lecturer: Univ. of Pittsburgh, 1998; Univ. of Cape Town; Internat. Univ., Venice. Life FRSA 1990. *Publications:* (jtly) Where to Now?: ideas on the future of the EU, 2005; various, in industrial, trade and academic jls. *Recreations:* golf, music.

GARVIN, Clifton Canter, Jr; Chairman of the Board and Chief Executive Officer, Exxon Corporation, 1975–86, retired; *b* 22 Dec. 1921; *s* of Clifton C. Garvin, Sr, and Esther Ames; *m* 1943, Thelma Volland; one *s* three *d*. *Educ:* Virginia Polytechnic Inst. and State Univ. MS (ChemEng) 1947. Exxon: Process Engr, subseq. Refining Operating Supt, Baton Rouge, Louisiana Refinery, 1947–59; Asst Gen. Manager, Supply Dept, Exxon Corp., 1959–60; Gen. Manager, Supply Dept, 1960–61; Manager, Production, Supply & Distribution Dept, Exxon Co., USA, 1961–62, subseq. Vice-Pres., Central Region, 1963–64; Exec. Asst to Pres. and Chm., Exxon Corp., NY, 1964–65; Pres., Exxon Chemical (US), subseq. Pres. Exxon Chemical (Internat.), 1965–68; Dir, subseq. Exec. Vice-Pres., subseq. Pres., Exxon Corp., 1968–75. Dir, Saudi Arabian Oil Co.; former Director: Citicorp and Citibank; Hosp. Corp. of America; PepsiCo, Inc.; Johnson & Johnson; J. C. Penney Co., Inc.; TRW Inc.; Americas Soc.; Member: Amer. Inst. of Chem. Engrs; Business Roundtable; Council on Foreign Relns; Business Council; Nat. Associate, White Burkett Miller Center of Public Affairs, Univ. of Virginia. Virginia Polytechnic Institute and State University: Mem. Cttee of 100—Coll. of Engrg Corporate Develt; Bd of Visitors. *Recreations:* golf, bird watching.

GARWOOD, Air Vice-Marshal Richard Frank, CBE 2002; DFC 1991; Air Officer Commanding 22 (Training) Group, since 2007; *b* 10 Jan. 1959; *s* of Sidney Richard Garwood and Queenie Blanche May Garwood (*née* Bradfield); *m* 1981, Susan Ann Trendell; one *s*. *Educ:* Smithdon High Sch., Hunstanton; Norfolk Coll. of Arts and Technol.; King's Coll. London (MA Defence Studies). Pilot, RAF, grad. RAF Coll., Cranwell, 1979; Fighter Reconnaissance pilot, 41 (Fighter) Sqdn, 1982–85; Instructor pilot, 234 Sqdn, RAF Brawdy, 1985–87; exchange pilot, USAF, 1987–90; Flight Comdr, No II (AC) Sqdn, 1990–93; Staff Officer, Operational Requirements, MoD, 1993–96; Army Comd and Staff Coll., 1995; OC II (AC) Sqdn, 1996–98; SO, PJHQ, Northwood, 1998–2000; CO, RAF Marham, 2000–02; rcds 2003; HQ 1Gp, 2003–04; HQ 1 Gp SO, Dir of Air Staff, 2004–07; CDS Liaison Officer to US Chm. of Jt Chiefs of Staff, 2007. *Recreations:* game fishing, shooting, falconry. *Address:* c/o 22 (Training) Group, HQ RAF Air Command, High Wycombe, Bucks HP14 4UE. *Club:* Royal Air Force.

GASCOIGNE, Bamber; author and broadcaster; Editor-in-Chief: www.historyworld.net, since 2000; www.timesearch.info. since 2007; *b* 24 Jan. 1935; *s* of late Derick Gascoigne and Midi (*née* O'Neill); *m* 1965, Christina Ditchburn. *Educ:* Eton; Magdalene Coll., Cambridge (Hon. Fellow, 1996). Commonwealth Fund Fellow, Yale, 1958–59. Theatre Critic, Spectator, 1961–63, and Observer, 1963–64; Co-editor, Theatre Notebook, 1968–74. Founded Saint Helena Press, 1977; Chm., Ackermann Publishing, 1981–85; Co-founder and Chm., HistoryWorld, 2000. Trustee: Nat. Gall., 1988–95; Tate Gall., 1993–95; Chm., Friends of Covent Garden, 1991–95; Member: Bd of Dirs, Royal Opera House, Covent Garden, 1988–95; Council, Nat. Trust, 1989–94. Sandars Lectr in Bibliography, Cambridge, 1993–94. FRSL 1976. *Theatre:* Share My Lettuce, London, 1957–58; Leda Had a Little Swan, New York, 1968; The Feydeau Farce Festival of Nineteen Nine, Greenwich, 1972; Big in Brazil, Old Vic, 1984. *Television:* presenter of: University Challenge, (weekly) 1962–87; Cinema, 1964; (also author) The Christians, 1977; Victorian Values, 1987; Man and Music, 1987–89; The Great Moghuls, 1990; Brother Felix and the Virgin Saint, 1992; deviser and presenter of Connoisseur, 1988–89; author of: The Four Freedoms, 1962; Dig This Rhubarb, 1963; The Auction Game, 1968. *Publications:* (many with photographs or watercolour illustrations by Christina Gascoigne): Twentieth Century Drama, 1962; World Theatre, 1968; The Great Moghuls, 1971; Murgatreud's Empire, 1972; The Heyday, 1973; The Treasures and Dynasties of China, 1973; Ticker Khan, 1974; The Christians, 1977; Images of Richmond, 1978; Images of Twickenham, 1981; Why the Rope went Tight, 1981; Fearless Freddy's Magic Wish, 1982; Fearless Freddy's Sunken Treasure, 1982; Quest for the Golden Hare, 1983; Cod Streuth, 1986; How to Identify Prints, 1986; Amazing Facts, 1988; Encyclopedia of Britain, 1993; Milestones in Colour Printing, 1997. *Address:* Saint Helena Terrace, Richmond, Surrey TW9 1NR.

GASCOYNE-CECIL, family name of **Marquess of Salisbury**.

GASH, Haydon Boyd W.; *see* Warren-Gash.

GASH, Prof. Norman, CBE 1989; FBA 1963; FRSL 1973; FRSE 1977; FRHistS; Professor of History, St Salvator's College, University of St Andrews, 1955–80, now Emeritus; *b* 16 Jan. 1912; *s* of Frederick and Kate Gash; *m* 1st, 1935, Ivy Dorothy Whitehorn (*d* 1995); two *d*; 2nd, 1997, Mrs Ruth Frances Jackson. *Educ:* Reading Sch.; St John's Coll., Oxford (Hon. Fellow 1987). Scholar, St John's Coll.; 1st cl. Hons Mod. Hist., 1933; BLitt, 1934; MA 1938. FRHistS 1953. Temp. Lectr in Modern European History, Edinburgh, 1935–36; Asst Lectr in Modern History, University Coll., London, 1936–40. Served War, 1940–46: Intelligence Corps; Capt. 1942; Major (Gen. Staff), 1945. Lectr in Modern British and American History, St Salvator's Coll., University of St Andrews, 1946–53; Prof. of Modern History, University of Leeds, 1953–55; Vice-Principal, 1967–71, Dean of Faculty of Arts, 1978–80, St Andrews Univ. Hinkley Prof. of English History, Johns Hopkins Univ., 1962; Ford's Lectr in English History, Oxford Univ., 1963–64; Sir John Neale Lectr in English Hist., UCL, 1981; Wellington Lectr, Southampton Univ., 1992. Vice-Pres., Hist. Assoc. of Scotland, 1963–64. Hon. DLitt: Strathclyde, 1984; St Andrews, 1985; Southampton, 1988. *Publications:* Politics in the Age of Peel, 1953; Mr Secretary Peel, 1961; The Age of Peel, 1968; Reaction and Reconstruction in English Politics, 1832–1852, 1966; Sir Robert Peel, 1972; Peel, 1976; (jtly) The Conservatives: a history from their origins to 1965, 1978; Aristocracy and People: England 1815–1865, 1979; Lord Liverpool, 1984; Pillars of Government, 1986; (ed) Wellington: studies in the military and political career of the first Duke of Wellington, 1990; Robert Surtees and Early Victorian Society, 1993; (ed) W. B. Ferrand "The Working Man's Friend" 1809–1889, by John Ward, 2002; articles and reviews in Eng. Hist. Review, Trans. Royal Historical Society, and other learned jls. *Recreations:* gardening, swimming. *Address:* Old Gatehouse, Portway, Langport, Som TA10 0NQ. *T:* (01458) 250334.

GASKELL, Dr Colin Simister, CBE 1988; FREng; Chairman, Ferranti Technologies Ltd, 2000–05; *b* 19 May 1937; *s* of James and Carrie Gaskell; *m* 1961, Jill (*née* Haward); one *s* one *d*. *Educ:* Manchester Grammar Sch.; Manchester Univ. (BSc); St Edmund Hall, Oxford (DPhil). CEng, FREng (FEng 1989); FIET (Hon. Treas., IEE, 1996–99). Research Fellow, Oxford Univ., 1960–61; Central Electricity Res. Labs, 1961–62; Microwave Associates, 1962–67; Chief Engineer, Microwave Div., Marconi Instruments, 1967–71; Technical Dir, Herbert Controls, 1971–74; Marconi Instruments: Technical Management, 1974–77; Technical Dir, 1977–79; Man. Dir, 1979–90; Gp Man. Dir, 1990–96, Chief Exec., 1996–97, 600 Group plc; Chm., Telemetrix plc, 1997–2003. *Recreations:* reading, walking, theatre, family pursuits.

GASKELL, Joseph William; His Honour Judge Gaskell; a Circuit Judge, since 1996; *b* 5 June 1947; *s* of Joseph Gerald Gaskell and Maureen Elizabeth Jane Gaskell (*née* Thomas); *m* 1970, Rowena Gillian Case; one *s* one *d*. *Educ:* Harrow Sch.; Clare Coll., Cambridge. Called to the Bar, Inner Temple, 1970; in private practice, Cardiff, 1971–96; Asst Recorder, 1990; Recorder, 1993–96; Asst Parly Boundary Comr, 1994. *Recreations:* the arts, sailing, dog walking. *Address:* The Crown Court, Cathays Park, Cardiff CF1 3PG. *Clubs:* Cardiff and County; Penarth Yacht.

GASKELL, Sir Richard (Kennedy Harvey), Kt 1989; Consultant, TLT Solicitors (formerly Lawrence Tucketts), since 1997 (Partner, 1963–89; Senior Partner, 1989–97); President of the Law Society, 1988–89; *b* 17 Sept. 1936; *o s* of late Dr Kenneth Harvey Gaskell, MRCS, LRCP, DMRD and Jean Winsome Gaskell; *m* 1965, Judith Poland; one *s* one *d*. *Educ:* Marlborough Coll. Admitted solicitor, 1960. Chm., Nat. Cttee, Young Solicitors' Gp, 1964–65; Law Society: Mem. Council, 1969–92; Dep. Vice-Pres. 1986–87; Vice Pres., 1987–88; President: Bristol Law Soc., 1978–79; Assoc. of South Western Law Socs, 1980–81. Member: Crown Court Rules Cttee, 1977–83; Security Service Tribunal, 1989–2000; Intelligence Services Tribunal, 1994–2000; Criminal Justice Consultative Council, 1991–94; Criminal Injuries Compensation Bd, 1992–2000; Criminal Injuries Compensation Appeals Panel, 1997–2004; Investigatory Powers Tribunal, 2000–; Professional Conduct Cttee, GMC, 2001–06. Director: Law Society Trustees Ltd, 1974–92; Bristol Waterworks Co., 1989–91; Bristol Water Gp plc, 1991–2005 (Dep. Chm., 1998–2005). Mem., Adv. Council, PYBT, 1988–2000. Dir, Wildfowl Trust (Hldgs) Ltd, 1980–2005; Mem. Council, Wildfowl and Wetlands (formerly Wildfowl) Trust, 1980–92 (Chm., 1983–87; Vice-Pres., 1992–); Vice-Pres., SS Great Britain Project Ltd, 2000– (Chm., 1992–2000; Chm. Exec. Cttee and Council, SS Great Britain, 1992–). Trustee: Frenchay and Southmead Med. Trust, 1968–99; Laura Ashley Foundn, 1990–97; CLIC (UK), 1991–95. Kt Pres., Imperial Soc. of Kts Bachelor, 2007– (Mem. Council, 1995–2006; Chm., 1999–2000; Kt Principal, 2000–06). Mem. Court, Bristol Univ., 1973–2000. Liveryman, Farmers' Co., 2002–; Hon. Freeman, Butchers' Co., 2002. Hon. LLD Bristol, 1989; Hon. LLM Bristol Polytechnic, 1989. *Address:* Grove Farm, Yatton Keynell, Chippenham, Wilts SN14 7BS. *T:* (01249) 782289, *Fax:* (01249) 783267. *Club:* Farmers'.

GASKELL, Vincent; Chief Executive, Criminal Records Bureau, since 2003; *b* 17 June 1952; *s* of late John Rigby Gaskell and of Eilleen Winnifred Gaskell; *m* 1972, Anne Frances Neil; one *s* two *d*. *Educ:* W Park Grammar Sch., St Helens; Salford Univ.; Open Univ. (BA). Area Dir, Benefits Agency, 1994–96; Prog. Dir, DSS, 1996–99; Mem. Bd, CSA, 1999–2003. *Recreations:* mountaineering, mountain biking. *Address:* Criminal Records Bureau, Shannon Court, 10 Princes Parade, Princes Dock, Liverpool L3 1QY. *T:* (0151) 676 1556; *e-mail:* Vince.Gaskell@crb.gsi.gov.uk. *Club:* Pannal Wheelers.

GASKILL, William; freelance stage director; *b* 24 June 1930; *s* of Joseph Linnaeus Gaskill and Maggie Simpson. *Educ:* Salt High Sch., Shipley; Hertford Coll., Oxford. Asst Artistic Dir, English Stage Co., 1957–59; freelance Dir with Royal Shakespeare Co., 1961–62; Assoc. Dir, National Theatre, 1963–65, and 1979; Artistic Director, English Stage Company, 1965–72, Mem. Council, 1978–87; Dir, Joint Stock Theatre Gp, 1973–83.

Publication: A Sense of Direction: life at the Royal Court (autobiog.), 1988. *Address:* 124A Leighton Road, NW5 2RG.

GASKIN, Catherine; author; *b* Co. Louth, Eire, 2 April 1929; *m* 1955, Sol Cornberg (*d* 1999). *Educ:* Holy Cross Coll., Sydney, Australia; Conservatorium of Music, Sydney. Brought up in Australia; lived in London, 1948–55, New York, 1955–65, Virgin Islands, 1965–67, Ireland, 1967–81, Isle of Man, 1981–2000. *Publications:* This Other Eden, 1946; With Every Year, 1947; Dust In Sunlight, 1950; All Else Is Folly, 1951; Daughter of the House, 1952; Sara Dane, 1955; Blake's Reach, 1958; Corporation Wife, 1960; I Know My Love, 1962; The Tilsit Inheritance, 1963; The File on Devlin, 1965; Edge of Glass, 1967; Fiona, 1970; A Falcon for a Queen, 1972; The Property of a Gentleman, 1974; The Lynmara Legacy, 1975; The Summer of the Spanish Woman, 1977; Family Affairs, 1980; Promises, 1982; The Ambassador's Women, 1985; The Charmed Circle, 1988. *Recreations:* music, reading. *Address:* Villa 139, The Manors, 15 Hale Road, Mosman, NSW 2088, Australia.

GASKIN, John Martin; Managing Director, Education Bradford, since 2005; *b* 27 Jan. 1951; *s* of Les and Gwen Gaskin; *m* 1980, Rosemary (marr. diss. 2005); two *d*; *m* 2005, Jean Samuel. *Educ:* City Coll. of Educn, Sheffield (CertEd); Sheffield City Poly. (BEd Hons); Univ. of Sheffield (AdvDipEd). Headteacher: Swavesey Primary Sch., Cambs, 1984–86; Concord Middle Sch., Sheffield, 1986–89; Advr, 1989–92, Chief Advr, 1992–95, Hd, Educn Services, 1995–97, Barnsley LEA; HM Inspector of Schs, 1997–98; City Educn Officer, Portsmouth LEA, 1998–2002; Dir of Educn and Lifelong Learning, Bristol CC, 2002–04; Dir, Learning Services, Prospects Services, 2004. *Recreations:* late comer to running, fishing, but not often enough, wondering why and concentrating on why not! *Address:* Education Bradford, Bolling Road, Bradford BD4 7EB.

GASKIN, Prof. Maxwell, DFC 1944 (and Bar 1945); Jaffrey Professor of Political Economy, Aberdeen University, 1965–85, now Professor Emeritus; *b* 18 Nov. 1921; *s* of late Albert and Beatrice Gaskin; *m* 1952, Brenda Patricia, *yr d* of late Rev. William D. Stewart; one *s* three *d*. *Educ:* Quarry Bank Sch., Liverpool; Liverpool Univ. (MA). Lever Bros Ltd, 1939–41. Served War, RAF Bomber Comd, 1941–46. Economist, Raw Cotton Commn, 1949–50; Asst Lectr, Liverpool Univ., 1950–51; Lectr and Sen. Lectr, Glasgow Univ., 1951–65; Visiting Sen. Lectr, Nairobi Univ., 1964–65. Consultant to Sec. of State for Scotland, 1965–87. Member, Committee of Inquiry: into Bank Interest Rates (N Ire.), 1965–66; into Trawler Safety, 1967–68; Member and Chairman: Wages Councils, 1967–93; Bd of Management for Foresterhill and Associated Hosps, 1971–74; Independent Member: Scottish Agricl Wages Bd, 1972–90; EDC for Civil Engineering, 1978–84; Chm., Industry Strategy Cttee for Scotland (Building and Civil Engrg EDCs), 1974–76. Director: Offshore Med. Support Ltd, 1978–85; Aberdeen Univ. Research & Industrial Services, 1981–85. President: Section F, British Assoc., 1978–79; Scottish Economic Soc., 1981–84. *Publications:* The Scottish Banks, 1965; (co-author and ed) North East Scotland: a survey of its development potential, 1969; (jtly) The Economic Impact of North Sea oil on Scotland, 1978; (ed) The Political Economy of Tolerable Survival, 1981; articles in economic and banking jls; reports on the international coal trade. *Recreations:* music and country life. *Address:* 22 North Mill Place, Halstead, Essex CO9 2FA. *T:* (01787) 478062.

See also C. J. Butcher.

GASPARINI, Robert Lincoln; Chairman, Chief Executive Officer and President, Drake Beam Morin Inc., since 2007; Partner, President and Managing Director, Monticello Partners LLC, since 2003; *b* 22 Oct. 1950; *s* of late Baron Carlo Gasparini, sometime Italian Ambassador to Nato, and Gloria Gasparini, *d* of Marquis A. Ferrante di Ruffano and Virginia MacVeagh; *m* 1979, Marilyn Varnell Murphy; one *s*. *Educ:* French Baccalaureat, Brussels; Univ. of Rome (BA Pol Scis); Columbia Univ. (MBA 1977). Product Mgt, Colgate Palmolive, NY, 1977–79; Management Consultant: Booz Allen & Hamilton, London, 1979–83; Strategy Res. Associates, London, 1983–85; Man. Dir, European Ops, Fort Howard Corp., London, 1985–88; Williams plc: Man. Dir, Europe, Paris, 1988–91; Man. Dir, Consumer & Building Products, NY, 1992–94; Man. Dir, Global Systems & Services, NY, 1994–2000; Main Bd Dir, 1999–2000; CEO, Chubb plc, 2000–03. Dir, Compass Partners Internat. *Recreations:* tennis, sailing, cinema. *Address:* (office) DBM, 750 Third Avenue, 28th Floor, New York, NY 10017, USA. *T:* (212) 2993298. *Club:* La Caccia (Rome).

GASS, Elizabeth Periam Acland Hood, (Lady Gass); JP; Lord-Lieutenant of Somerset, since 1998 (Vice Lord-Lieutenant, 1996–98); *b* 2 March 1940; *d* of late Hon. John Acland-Hood, barrister, *yr s* of 1st Baron St Audries, PC and of Dr Phyllis Acland-Hood (*née* Hallett); *m* 1975, Sir Michael Gass, KCMG (*d* 1983). *Educ:* Cheltenham Ladies' Coll.; Girton Coll., Cambridge (MA). Somerset County Council: Member, 1985–97; Chm., Exmoor Nat. Park Cttee, 1989–93; Vice-Chm., Social Services Cttee, 1989–93. Dir, Avalon NHS Trust, 1993–96. Comr, English Heritage, 1995–2001. Member: Rail Users' Consultative Cttee for Western England, 1992–99; Nat. Trust Wessex Cttee, 1994–2002; Nat. Exec. Cttee, CLA, 1998–2003; Wessex Cttee, HHA, 1998–; Wells Cathedral Council, 2004–. Member, Council: Cheltenham Ladies' Coll., 1992–2001; Bath Univ., 1999–2002. Trustee, West of England Sch. for Children with Little or no Sight, 1996–2008. Pres., Royal Bath and W of England Soc., 2002–03. High Sheriff 1994, DL 1995, JP 1996, Somerset. *Recreations:* gardening, music, archaeology. *Address:* Fairfield, Stogursey, Bridgwater, Somerset TA5 1PU. *T:* (01278) 732251, *Fax:* (01278) 732277.

GASS, James Ronald, CMG 1989; Consultant, European Economic Commission, since 1989; *b* 25 March 1924; *s* of Harold Amos Gass and Cherry (*née* Taylor); *m* 1950, Colette Alice Jeanne Lejeune; two *s* one *d*. *Educ:* Birkenhead Park High Sch.; Liverpool Univ. (BA Hons); Nuffield and Balliol Colls, Oxford. Flight Lieut Pilot, RAF, service in US, India and Burma, 1942–46. PSO, DSIR Intelligence Div., 1951–57; Special Asst to Chm., Task Force on Western Scientific Co-operation, NATO, Paris, 1957; OEEC, subsequently OECD, Paris: Head of Div., Scientific and Tech. Personnel, 1958–61; Dep. Dir for Scientific Affairs, 1961–68; Director: Centre for Educnl Res. and Innovation, 1968–89; Social Affairs, Manpower and Educn, 1974–89; retired 1989. *Recreations:* restoration of antiques, gymnastics, philosophy. *Address:* 2 avenue du Vert Bois, Ville d'Avray, 92410 Paris, France. *T:* 47095481.

GASS, Simon Lawrance, CMG 1998; CVO 1999; HM Diplomatic Service; Ambassador to Greece, 2004–08; *b* 2 Nov. 1956; *s* of late Geoffrey Gass and of Brenda Gass (*née* Lawrance); *m* 1980, Marianne Enid Stott; two *s* one *d*. *Educ:* Eltham Coll.; Reading Univ. (LLB 1977). Joined FCO, 1977; Lagos, 1979–83; Athens, 1984–87; FCO, 1987–90; Asst Private Sec. to Foreign Sec., 1990–92; Rome, 1992–95; Counsellor, FCO, 1995–98; Dep. High Comr, S Africa, 1998–2001; Dir, Resources, then Finance, FCO, 2001–04. *Address:* c/o Foreign and Commonwealth Office, King Charles Street, SW1A 2AH.

GASSON, (Gordon) Barry, OBE 1985; RSA; Principal, Barry Gasson, Architects; *b* 27 Aug. 1935; *s* of late Gladys Godfrey (previously Gasson) and Stanley Gasson; *m* Rosemary Mulligan; one *s* two *d*. *Educ:* Solihull Sch.; Birmingham Sch. of Architecture (Dip. Arch. 1958); RIBA (Owen Jones Student); Columbia Univ., NY (MS 1961); Q. W. Boese English Speaking Fellowship; MA Cantab 1963. ARIAS, RIBA. Lectr, Univ. of Cambridge, 1963–73; visiting critic: University Coll., Dublin, 1969–72; California State Poly., 1969; Mackintosh Sch. of Arch., 1978–85; Edinburgh Coll. of Art, 1986–92; Vis. Prof., Univ. of Manchester, 1987–95. Former Mem., Royal Fine Art Commn for Scotland. Assessor, Civic Trust Awards, RIBA student medals, nat. competitions; Chm., RIBA regional awards. Farmer (biodynamic). Designed galleries for Burrell Collection, Glasgow (won in open comp., 1972); awards: Stone Fedn, 1983; Arch. Design; RA Premier Arch., 1984; Museum of the Year; British Tourist Trophy; Sotheby Fine Art; Services in Building; Civic Trust; Eternit Internat., 1985; RIBA 1986; RSA Gold Medal, 1983; World Biennale of Arch. Gold Medal, 1987. *Publication:* contrib. to The Burrell Collection, 1983.

GASSON, John Gustav Haycraft, CB 1990; Head of Policy and Legal Services Group, Lord Chancellor's Department, 1987–91; *b* 2 Aug. 1931; *s* of late Dr and Mrs S. G. H. Gasson; *m* 1964, Lesley, *d* of L. L. Thomas, Nyamandhlovu, Zimbabwe; two *s* one *d*. *Educ:* Diocesan Coll., Rondebosch, Cape Town; Cape Town Univ. (BA); Pembroke Coll., Oxford (Rhodes Schol. Rhodesia 1953; MA, BCL). Called to the Bar, Gray's Inn, 1957; Advocate of High Court of S Rhodesia, 1959; Lord Chancellor's Dept, 1964; Sec., Law Commn, 1982–87. *Recreations:* cycling, gardening. *Address:* The White House, Candys Lane, Blandford Road, Shillingstone, Dorset DT11 0SF. *Club:* Bulawayo (Zimbabwe).

GASTON, Prof. John Stanley Hill, PhD; FRCP, FMedSci; Professor of Rheumatology, University of Cambridge, since 1995; Fellow, St Edmund's College, Cambridge, since 2000; *b* 24 June 1952; *s* of John Gaston, CBE and Elizabeth Gaston (*née* Gordon); *m* 1975, Christine Mary Arthur; one *s* one *d*. *Educ:* Royal Belfast Academical Instn; Lincoln Coll., Oxford (MA); Oxford Univ. Med. Sch. (BM BCh); Univ. of Bristol (PhD 1983). FRCP 1995. SHO, then Registrar posts at Hammersmith Hosp., Bristol Hosps and Torbay, 1977–80; Sir Michael Sobell Cancer Res. Fellow, Univ. of Bristol, 1980–83; MRC Travelling Fellowship, Stanford Univ. Med. Centre, 1983–85; University of Birmingham: MRC Res. Trng Fellow, 1985–87; Wellcome Sen. Res. Fellow in Clinical Sci., 1987–92; Sen. Lectr, then Reader in Rheumatology, 1992–95. Hon. Consultant in Rheumatology, S Birmingham HA, 1987–95. FMedSci 2001. *Publications:* papers on immunology and immunological aspects of rheumatic diseases. *Recreations:* music, reading biographies. *Address:* University of Cambridge School of Clinical Medicine, Box 157, Level 5, Addenbrooke's Hospital, Hills Road, Cambridge CB2 2QQ. *T:* (01223) 330161; *e-mail:* jshg2@medschl.cam.ac.uk; 6 Parsonage Court, Whittlesford, Cambs CB2 4PH.

GASTON, Prof. Kevin John, DPhil; Professor of Biodiversity and Conservation, University of Sheffield, since 2000; *b* 5 Nov. 1964; *s* of Mervyn John and Ann Grace Gaston; *m* 1987, Sian Roberts; one *d*. *Educ:* Tunbridge Wells Tech. High Sch.; Univ. of Sheffield (BSc 1986); Univ. of York (DPhil 1989). Department of Entomology, Natural History Museum, London: Jun. Res. Fellow, 1989–91; Sen. Res. Fellow, 1991–93; Principal Res. Fellow, 1993–94; Hon. Res. Fellow, 1999–2005; Royal Society University Research Fellow: Dept of Biol., Imperial Coll., London, 1994–95; Dept of Animal and Plant Scis, Univ. of Sheffield, 1995–2002; Royal Soc. Wolfson Res. Merit Award, 2006–. Prof. Extraordinary in Zool., Univ. of Stellenbosch, 2002–. Internat. Recognition of Professional Excellence Prize, Ecology Inst., 1999. *Publications:* Perspectives on Insect Conservation (ed jtly), 1993; Rarity, 1994; (ed) Biodiversity: a biology of numbers and difference, 1996; (ed jtly) The Biology of Rarity: causes and consequences of rare-common differences, 1987; (jtly) Biodiversity: an introduction, 1998, 2nd edn 2004; (jtly) Physiological Diversity and its Ecological Implications, 1999; (jtly) Pattern and Process in Macroecology, 2000; The Structure and Dynamics of Geographic Ranges, 2003; (ed jtly) Macroecology: concepts and consequences, 2003; (jtly) Gough Island: a natural history, 2005; (jtly) Endemic plants of the Altai mountain country, 2008; over 300 sci. papers in peer-reviewed jls. *Recreations:* natural history, reading, travel, walking. *Address:* Department of Animal and Plant Sciences, University of Sheffield, Sheffield S10 2TN. *T:* (0114) 222 0030, *Fax:* (0114) 222 0002; *e-mail:* k.j.gaston@sheffield.ac.uk.

GATEHOUSE, Graham Gould; Director, Orchard Lane Initiatives Ltd, since 1995; *b* 17 July 1935; *s* of G. and G. M. Gatehouse; *m* 1960, Gillian M. Newell; two *s* one *d*; one *d* by Wanda Kwilecka. *Educ:* Crewkerne Sch., Somerset; Exeter Univ., Devon (DSA); London School of Economics (Dip. Mental Health). Served Royal Artillery, 1954–56. Somerset County Council, 1957–67; Worcestershire CC, 1967–70; Norfolk CC, 1970–73; West Sussex CC, 1973–81; Dir of Social Services, Surrey CC, 1981–95. FRSA 1987. *Recreations:* Rugby football, cricket, theatre. *Address:* Fir Tree Farm, Doncaster Road, Darfield, Barnsley, S Yorks S73 9JB.

GATENBY, Michael Richard Brock, FCA; Vice Chairman, Charterhouse Bank Ltd, 1989–95; *b* 5 Oct. 1944; *s* of Arthur Duncan Gatenby and Dora Ethel (*née* Brock); *m* 1990, Lesley Ann Harding; two step *s*. *Educ:* Haileybury; Trinity Hall, Cambridge (BA 1966). ACA 1970. With Peat Marwick Mitchell, 1966–71; Hill Samuel & Co. Ltd, 1971–85 (Dir, 1975–85); Charterhouse Bank Ltd, 1985–95: Man. Dir, 1986–89; Director: Staveley Industries plc, 1980–96; Bridport plc, 1980–99; Scholl plc, 1996–98; Philip Harris plc, 1996–97; SGB Gp plc, 1997–2000; Protherics (formerly Proteus International) plc, 1997–2004; Powell Duffryn plc, 1997–2000; Tarmac plc, 1999–2000; SRS Technology Gp plc, 2002–06; Porvair plc, 2002–; Johnson Service Gp plc, 2002–; Cobra Biomanufacturing plc, 2003–; Chm., Alliance Pharma plc, 2004–. *Recreations:* golf, skiing. *Address:* 11 Norland Square, W11 4PX. *T:* (020) 7221 9420.

GATES, Hon. Robert M.; Secretary of Defense, USA, since 2006; *b* Kansas, 25 Sept. 1943; *m* Becky; two *c*. *Educ:* Coll. of William and Mary (BA 1965); Indiana Univ. (MA History, 1966); Georgetown Univ. (PhD Russian and Soviet History, 1974). Joined CIA, 1966; intelligence analyst; Asst. Nat. Intell. Officer for Strategic Programs; staff, Nat. Security Council, 1974–79; rejoined CIA, 1979: admin. posts; Nat. Intell. Officer for Soviet Union; Dep. Dir for Intell., 1982–86; Chm., Nat. Intell. Council, 1983–86; Dep. Dir, 1986–89, Actg Dir, 1986–87, Dir, 1991–93, Central Intelligence; Asst to the President, and Dep. for Nat. Security Affairs, Nat. Security Council, 1986–91. Presidential Citizens Medal; Nat. Intell. Distinguished Service Medal; Distinguished Intell. Medal, CIA; Intell. Medal of Merit; Arthur S. Flemming Award. *Publication:* From the Shadows, 1996. *Address:* (office) 1000 Pentagon, Washington, DC 20301, USA.

GATES, Emeritus Prof. Ronald Cecil, AO 1978; FASSA; Vice-Chancellor, University of New England, 1977–85; *b* 8 Jan. 1923; *s* of Earle Nelson Gates and Elsie Edith (*née* Tucker); *m* 1953, Barbara Mann; one *s* two *d* (and one *s* decd). *Educ:* East Launceston State Sch., Tas; Launceston C of E Grammar Sch., Tas; Univ. of Tas (BCom Econs and Commercial Law); Oxford Univ. (MA PPE). FASSA 1968. Served War, 1942–45: Private, AIF. Clerk, Aust. Taxation Office, Hobart, 1941–42; Rhodes Scholar (Tas), Oxford, 1946–48; Historian, Aust. Taxation Office, Canberra, 1949–52; Univ. of Sydney: Sen. Lectr in Econs, 1952–64; Associate Prof., 1964–65; Rockefeller Fellow in Social Sciences, 1955; Carnegie Travel Grant, 1960; Prof. of Econs, Univ. of Qld, 1966–77 (Pres., Professorial Bd, 1975–77). Pres., Econ. Soc. of Australia and NZ, 1969–72. Chairman: statutory Consumer Affairs Council of Qld, 1971–73; Aust. Inst. of Urban Studies, 1975–77. Comr, Commonwealth Commn of Inquiry into Poverty, 1973–77.

Chairman: Aust. Nat. Commn for Unesco, 1981–83 (Vice-Chm., 1979); Adv. Council for Inter-govt Relations, 1979–85; Internat. Relations Cttee, Cttee of Australian Vice-Chancellors, 1981–84; Local Govt Trng Council (formerly Nat. Local Govt Industry Trng Cttee), 1983–92; Armidale-Dumaresq Jt Planning Cttee, 1992–97. Pres., Australian Esperanto Assoc., 1998–2001 (Vice-Pres., 1995–98). Hon. FRAPI 1976; Hon. Fellow, Aust. Inst. of Urban Studies, 1979. Hon. DEcon Qld, 1978; Hon. DLitt New England, 1987. *Publications:* (with H. R. Edwards and N. T. Drane) Survey of Consumer Finances, Sydney 1963–65: Vol. 2, 1965; Vols 1, 3 and 4, 1966; Vols 5, 6 and 7, 1967; (jtly) The Price of Land, 1971; (jtly) New Cities for Australia, 1972; (jtly) Land for the Cities, 1973; (with P. A. Cassidy) Simulation, Uncertainty and Public Investment Analysis, 1977; *in Esperanto:* detective novels: La Septaga Murdenigmo, 1991; Kolera Afero, 1993; Morto de Sciencisto, 1994; Mortiga Ekskurso, 2006; La Vidvino kaj la Profesoro (romantic novel), 1997; short stories: Sep Krimnoveloj, 1993; Refoje Krimnoveloj Sep, 1994; Tria Kolekto da Krimnoveloj, 1996; chapters in books and articles in learned jls. *Recreations:* music, Esperanto, bridge. *Address:* Wangarang, 182 Kelly's Plains Road, Armidale, NSW 2350, Australia.

GATES, William Henry, III, Hon. KBE 2004; Chairman, since 1976, and Chief Software Architect, 2000–08, Microsoft Corp.; *b* 28 Oct. 1955; *s* of William Henry and Mary Maxwell Gates; *m* 1994, Melinda French; one *s* two *d. Educ:* Lakeside High Sch., Seattle; Harvard Univ. Co-founder, Micro Soft, later Microsoft Corp., 1975. *Publications:* The Road Ahead, 1995; (with C. Hemingway) Business @ the Speed of Thought: using a digital nervous system, 1999. *Address:* Microsoft Corp., 1 Microsoft Way, Redmond, WA 98052–8300, USA.

GATFORD, Ven. Ian; Archdeacon of Derby, 1993–2005; *b* 15 June 1940; *s* of Frederick Ernest and Chrissie Lilian Gatford; *m* 1965, Anne Maire (*née* Whitehead); one *s* three *d. Educ:* King's Coll. London (AKC 1965); St Boniface Coll., Warminster. Management Trainee, Taylor Woodrow Gp, 1959–62; Accounts and Admin, Farr's (Construction) Ltd, 1965–66; ordained deacon 1967, priest 1968; Curate, St Mary, Clifton, Nottingham, 1967–71; Team Vicar, Holy Trinity, Clifton, 1971–75; Vicar, St Martin, Sherwood, 1975–84; Canon Residentiary, Derby Cathedral, 1984–2000; Sub-Provost, Derby Cathedral, 1990–93. Presenter of weekly help-line programmes, BBC Radio Nottingham, 1972–84; presenter of religious affairs programmes, BBC Radio Derby, 1984–93; Chairman: BBC Local Adv. Council, 1998–2001; Derbys Area Cttee, RSCM, 2007–. *Recreations:* playing the piano, classical music, German and French literature and conversation, walking, cycling and cycle training with Cycle Derby from 2006. *Address:* 9 Poplar Nook, Derby DE22 2DW.

GATHERCOLE, Ven. John Robert; Archdeacon of Dudley, 1987–2001; *b* 23 April 1937; *s* of Robert Gathercole and Winifred Mary Gathercole (*née* Price); *m* 1963, Claire (*née* London); one *s* one *d. Educ:* Judd School, Tonbridge; Fitzwilliam Coll., Cambridge (BA 1959, MA 1963); Ridley Hall, Cambridge. Deacon 1962, priest 1963; Curate: St Nicholas, Durham, 1962–66; St Bartholomew, Croxdale, 1966–70; Social and Industrial Adviser to Bishop of Durham, 1967–70; Industrial Chaplain, Redditch, dio. Worcester, 1970–87; RD of Bromsgrove, 1978–85; Team Leader, and Sen. Chaplain, Worcs Industrial Mission, 1985–91. Member: General Synod of C of E, 1995–2001; Council for the Care of Churches, 1998–2001. *Publication:* The Riley Imp: histories and profiles, 2008. *Recreations:* vintage sports cars, music. *Address:* Wisteria Cottage, Main Road, Ombersley, Worcs WR9 0EL. *T:* (01905) 676128.

GATHORNE-HARDY, family name of **Earl of Cranbrook**.

GATT, Colin, CMG 1993; Director, Managed Projects, Commonwealth Development Corporation, 1989–94; *b* 16 Aug. 1934; *s* of late William John Sim Gatt and Margaret Whyte-Hepburn; *m* 1st, 1957, Sheena Carstairs (*d* 1996); two *s* one *d*; 2nd, 1998, Susan Tessa Jennifer (*née* Lewis-Antill). *Educ:* state schs in Scotland. Engineer, 1955–71: manager, gen. manager and consultant, agricl businesses in Africa and Asia; Commonwealth Development Corporation, 1971–94: managed businesses in third world countries in Asia, Africa and Pacific regions, 1971–88. Independence Medal (Solomon Is), 1978. *Recreations:* reading, golf, wine, basic survival cookery. *Address:* The Barn House, Moreton, Thame, Oxon OX9 2HR. *Club:* Oxfordshire Golf (Thame).

GATT, Ian Andrew; QC 2002; a Recorder of the Crown Court, since 2000; Partner, Herbert Smith LLP, since 2005; *b* 21 April 1963; *s* of John Alexander Gatt and Marie Gatt; *m* 1987, Nicola Jane Gatt (*née* Cherry); one *s* two *d. Educ:* Hertford Coll., Oxford (BA (Hons) Jurisprudence 1st cl.). Called to the Bar, Lincoln's Inn, 1985. *Publications:* (jtly) Arlidge and Parry on Fraud, 2nd edn, 1996; (with John Bowers) Procedure in Courts and Tribunals, 2nd edn 2000. *Recreations:* family, friends, Rugby, rallying, cars. *Address:* Herbert Smith LLP, Exchange House, Primrose Street, EC2A 2HS. *T:* (020) 7466 3576, *Fax:* (020) 7374 0888; *e-mail:* ian.gatt@herbertsmith.com. *Club:* Goodwood Road Racing.

GATTI, Daniele; conductor; Music Director: Royal Philharmonic Orchestra, 1996–Sept. 2009; Orchestre National de France, since 2008; *b* Milan, 6 Nov. 1961; *m* 1990, Silvia Chiesa. *Educ:* Milan Conservatory. Founder and Music Dir, Stradivari Chamber Orch., 1986–92; débuts: La Scala, Milan, 1987–88; in USA with American Symphony Orch., Carnegie Hall, NY, 1990; Covent Gdn, 1992; Metropolitan Opera, NY, 1994–95; with RPO, 1994; with NY Philharmonic, 1995; Music Dir, Accad. di Santa Cecilia, Rome, 1992–97; Principal Guest Conductor, Covent Gdn, 1994–96; Music Dir, Teatro Communale, Bologna, 1997–2007; has worked with leading opera cos incl. Lyric Opera, Chicago, Staatsoper, Berlin; has conducted leading internat. orchestras incl. Toronto Symphony and LA Philharmonic, 1991; Orchestre Symphonique de Montreal, LSO, Philadelphia Orch., 1993; Cincinnati Symphony, Chicago Symphony, LPO, 1994; Berlin Philharmonic, 1997. Has toured extensively and made numerous recordings. *Recreations:* reading, walking, football, chess. *Address:* c/o Royal Philharmonic Orchestra, 16 Clerkenwell Green, EC1R 0DP.

GATTING, Michael William, OBE 1987; Managing Director, Cricket Partnerships, England and Wales Cricket Board, since 2007; *b* 6 June 1957; *s* of William Alfred Gatting and Vera Mavis Gatting; *m* 1980, Elaine Mabbott; two *s. Educ:* John Kelly Boys' High Sch. Middlesex County Cricket team, 1975–98: début, 1975; county cap, 1977; Captain, 1988–97; retired from 1st XI, 1998; scored 77 hundreds, 8 double hundreds, 1000 runs in a season 17 times; highest score 258, 1984; also took 129 wickets and 393 catches. Test début, 1977; England Captain, 1986–88; overseas tours with England: NZ and Pakistan, 1977–78, 1983–84; W Indies, 1980–81, 1985–86; India and Sri Lanka, 1981–82, 1992–93; India, 1984–85; Australia, 1986–87; Australia and NZ, 1987–88; Australia, 1994–95; also, World Cup, 1987–88, *v* India, Pakistan, Australia and NZ; scored ten Test centuries; highest score 207, 1984–85. England A team coach, Australia tour, 1996–97, Kenya and Sri Lanka tour, 1997–98; Dir of Coaching, Middx CCC, 1998–2000; Manager: England Under 19 team, NZ tour, 1999; England A team, NZ tour, 1999. Mem., Selection Panel, ECB, 1997–99. Dir, Ashwell Leisure Group, 2001. Pres., Lord's Taverners, 2004–06. *Publications:* Limited Overs, 1986; Triumph in Australia, 1987; Leading from the Front, 1988. *Recreations:* golf, swimming, reading, music. *Address:* c/o Middlesex County Cricket Club, Lord's Cricket Ground, St John's Wood Road, NW8 8QN.

GATTY, Trevor Thomas, OBE 1974; HM Diplomatic Service, retired; international business consultant, arbitrator and mediator; President, TGC Group (formerly MGT International), since 1989; *b* 8 June 1930; *s* of Thomas Alfred Gatty and Lillian Gatty (*née* Wood); *m* 1st, 1956, Jemima Bowman (marr. diss. 1983); two *s* one *d*; 2nd, 1989, Myrna Saturn; one step *s* one step *d. Educ:* King Edward's Sch., Birmingham. Served Army, 1948–50, 2/Lieut Royal Warwickshire Regt, later Lieut Royal Fusiliers (TA), 1950–53. Foreign Office, 1950; Vice-Consul, Leopoldville, 1954; FO, 1958–61; Second (later First) Sec., Bangkok, 1961–64; Consul, San Francisco, 1965–66; Commercial Consul, San Francisco, 1967–68; FCO, 1968–73; Commercial Consul, Zürich, 1973–75; FCO, 1975–76; Counsellor (Diplomatic Service Inspector), 1977–80; Head, Migration and Visa Dept, FCO, 1980–81; Consul-General, Atlanta, 1981–85. Protocol Advr, Atlanta Organising Cttee for Olympic Games, 1996; Co-founder and Bd Mem., Internat. Soc. of Protocol and Etiquette Professionals, 2002–. Hon. British Consul for N Carolina, 1994–2001. *Address:* 229 North Poplar Street (#15), Charlotte, NC 28202, USA. *T:* (704) 3381372, (UK) (020) 7993 6587; *e-mail:* tgatty@earthlink.net.

GATWARD, (Anthony) James; Deputy Chairman, Premium TV Ltd, 2000–03; *b* 4 March 1938; *s* of George James Gatward and Lillian Georgina (*née* Strutton); *m* 1969, Isobel Anne Stuart Black, actress; three *d. Educ:* George Gascoigne Sch., Walthamstow; South West Essex Technical Coll. and Sch. of Art (drama course). Entered TV industry, 1957; freelance drama producer/director: Canada and USA, 1959–65; BBC and most ITV cos, 1966–70; partner in prodn co., acting as Exec. Prod. and often Dir of many internat. co-prodns in UK, Ceylon, Australia and Germany, 1970–78; instigated and led preparation of application for S and SE England television franchise, 1979–80 (awarded Dec. 1980); Man. Dir, 1979–84, Chief Exec., 1984–91, Television South, subseq. TVS Entertainment PLC; Dep. Chm. and Chief Exec., 1984–90, Chm., 1990–91, TVS Television; Chief Exec., 1993–96, Chm., 1996–2000, Complete Media Mgt Ltd; Chm., Digital Television Network Ltd, 1996–99. Director: Southstar, Scottish and Global TV, 1971–78; Indep. TV Publications Ltd, 1982–88; Oracle Teletext Ltd, 1982–88; Solent Cablevision Ltd, 1983–89; Channel 4 TV Co., 1984–89; Indep. TV News Ltd, 1986–91; Super Channel Ltd, 1986–88; ITV Super Channel Ltd, 1986–89; Chm., TVS Production, 1984–89; Chm. and Chief Exec., TVS N American Hldgs, 1988–91; Pres., Telso Communications Inc., 1987–90; Chairman: Telso Communications Ltd, 1987–91; Telso Overseas Ltd, 1987–91; Midem Orgn SA, 1987–89; MTM Entertainment Inc., 1988–91 (Chief Exec. Officer, 1989–91); Redgrave Theatre, 1995–98. Member: Council, Operation Raleigh; Court of the Mary Rose. Pres., SE Agricl Soc., 1992; Governor, S of England Agricl Soc. *Recreations:* sailing, music. *Clubs:* Royal Thames Yacht; Porquerolles Yacht (Hyères).

GAU, John Glen Mackay, CBE 1989; independent television producer; Managing Director, 1981–88, Chief Executive, 1990–2002, John Gau Productions; *b* 25 March 1940; *s* of late Cullis William Gau and Nan Munro; *m* 1966, Susan Tebbs; two *s. Educ:* Haileybury and ISC; Trinity Hall, Cambridge; Univ. of Wisconsin. BBC TV: Asst Film Ed., 1963; Current Affairs Producer, 24 Hours, Panorama, 1965–72; Dep. Ed., Midweek, 1973–74; Ed., Nationwide, 1975–78; Head of Current Affairs Progs, 1978–81; Dep. Chief Exec. and Dir of Progs, British Satellite Broadcasting, 1988–90. Dir, Channel 4, 1984–88. Chm., Indep. Programme Producers' Assoc., 1983–86. FRTS 1986 (Chm. Council, 1986–88; Hon. Sec., 1993–2002; Gold Medal, 2003). *Publications:* (jtly) Soldiers, 1985; Lights, Camera, Action!, 1995. *Address:* 15 St Albans Mansion, Kensington Court Place, W8 5QH. *T:* (020) 7937 4033.

GAUKE, David Michael; MP (C) Hertfordshire South West, since 2005; *b* 8 Oct. 1971; *s* of Jim Gauke and Susan Gauke (now Hall); *m* 2000, Rachel Katherine Rank; two *s. Educ:* Northgate High Sch., Ipswich; St Edmund Hall, Oxford; Chester Coll. of Law. Trainee solicitor and solicitor, Richards Butler, 1995–98; admitted, 1997; solicitor, Macfarlanes, 1999–2005. *Recreations:* cricket, football, walking, reading, family. *Address:* House of Commons, SW1A 0AA. *T:* (020) 7219 3000; *e-mail:* david@davidgauke.com. *Clubs:* Rickmansworth Conservative; Tring Conservative.

GAULIN, Jean, OQ 2004; Chairman, President and Chief Executive Officer, Ultramar Diamond Shamrock Corporation, 2000–02; a Director, National Bank of Canada, since 2001; *b* 9 July 1942; *m* 1981, Andrée LeBoeuf; two *s* one *d. Educ:* Univ. of Montreal (degrees in appl. scis and chem. eng.). Vice-Pres., Ultramar Canada, 1977–79; President: Nouveler Inc., 1980–82; Gaz Metropolitan Inc., 1982–85 (and Chief Exec.); Ultramar Canada, 1985–89; CEO, Ultramar plc, 1989–92; Chm. and CEO, Ultramar Corp., 1992–96; Vice-Chm., Pres. and Chief Operating Officer, Ultramar Diamond Shamrock, 1997–99. *Address:* c/o National Bank of Canada, 600 rue de La Gauchetière ouest, Montreal, QC H3B 4L2, Canada.

GAULT, David Hamilton; Executive Chairman, Gallic Management Co. Ltd, 1974–93; *b* 9 April 1928; *s* of Leslie Hamilton Gault and Iris Hilda Gordon Young; *m* 1950, Felicity Jane Gribble; three *s* two *d. Educ:* Fettes Coll., Edinburgh. Nat. Service, commnd in RA, 1946–48; Clerk, C. H. Rugg & Co. Ltd, Shipbrokers, 1948–52; H. Clarkson & Co. Ltd, Shipbrokers: Man. 1952–56; Dir 1956–62; Jt Man. Dir 1962–72; Gp Man. Dir, Shipping Industrial Holdings Ltd, 1972–74; Chm., Jebsen (UK) Ltd, 1962–81; Chm., Seabridge Shipping Ltd, 1965–73. *Recreations:* gardening, walking. *Address:* Kent House, East Harting, near Petersfield, Hants GU31 5LS. *T:* (01730) 825206. *Club:* Boodle's.

GAULT, David Thomas, FRCS; Consultant Plastic Surgeon, The Portland Hospital, since 2006; Founder, London Centre for Ear Reconstruction, Portland Hospital, 2006; *b* 21 March 1954; *s* of William and Irene Mabel Bebe Gault; *m* 1989, Debra Hastings-Nield; two *s* two *d. Educ:* Edinburgh Univ. (MB ChB 1977). FRCS 1982. MRC French Exchange Fellow, 1987; Craniofacial Fellow, Hôpital des Enfants Malades, Paris, 1987; Sen. Registrar, Plastic Surgery, St Thomas' Hosp., Gt Ormond St Hosp. for Sick Children and Royal Marsden Hosp., 1988–91; Consultant Plastic Surgeon: Mt Vernon Hosp., 1991–2006; Gt Ormond St Hosp. for Sick Children, 2000–06; Consultant: Bishops Wood Hosp., 1991–; Wellington Hosp., 1992–. Hon. Sen. Lectr, UCL, 1999–; Vis. Prof., Chinese Univ. of Hong Kong, 2004–05. Ethicon Foundn Travelling Schol., 1987; Wellington Foundn Schol., 1989; BAPS Travelling Bursary, 1990. *Publications:* contribs to books and articles on laser and plastic surgery, particularly on ear reconstruction and depilation laser treatment. *Recreations:* rowing, painting, sculpting, planting. *Address:* The Portland Hospital, Great Portland Street, W1W 5AH. *T:* 0870 766 1066. *Club:* Cliveden (Taplow).

GAULT, Michael, OBE 2008; pistol shooter; Test and Measuring Equipment Controller, Ministry of Defence, since 1997; *b* 2 May 1954; *s* of Elizabeth Gault; *m* 1974, Janet Mary Manning; one *s* two *d. Educ:* St Bede's Jun. Sch.; St Newman's Sch., Carlisle. RAF, 1969–96: trained as electronics technician, RAF Cosford; served with 29 Sqn (Lightnings), 57 Sqn (Victors), 14 and 20 Sqns (Jaguars). Pistol shooter: British Champion, annually, 1992–96, 1998–99, and 2001–07; Commonwealth Games medals: Victoria, 1994: Gold,

Free Pistol; Silver, Men's 25m Centre Fire Pistol; Bronze, Free Pistol pairs (with P. Leatherdale); Kuala Lumpur, 1998: Gold: Free Pistol; Free Pistol pairs (with N. Baxter); Men's 10m Air Pistol; 10m Air Pistol pairs (with N. Baxter); Manchester, 2002: Gold: Men's 10m Air Pistol; Men's 50m Pistol; Men's 10m Air Pistol pairs (with N. Baxter); Bronze, Men's 25m Standard Pistol; Melbourne, 2006: Gold, Men's 25m Standard Pistol; Silver: Men's 10m Air Pistol pairs (with N. Baxter); Men's 50m Pistol; Bronze, 50m Pistol pairs (with N. Baxter). Hon. Life Member: London and Middlesex Rifle Assoc.; Norwich City Pistol and Rifle Club; British Pistol Club; Holt and District Rifle and Pistol Club (Hon. Life Pres.); Nat. Small-bore Rifle Assoc. (Gold Medal, 2006). Dereham Citizen of the Year, 2006–07. RAF Long Service and Good Conduct Medal, 1987. *Recreations:* qualifying as a pistol coach, looking for spare time. *Address:* 105 Boyd Avenue, Toftwood, Dereham, Norfolk NR19 1ND. *T:* (01760) 337261, ext. 7152; *e-mail:* mickey.g@talktalk.net.

GAULT, Rt Hon. Thomas Munro, DCNZM 2001; PC 1992; Judge of the Supreme Court of New Zealand, 2004–06; *b* 31 Oct. 1938; *s* of Thomas Gordon Gault and Evelyn Jane Gault (*née* Paulmeir); *m* 1963, Barbara Pauline Stewart; one *s*. *Educ:* Wellington Coll.; Victoria University Coll. (LLB); Victoria Univ. of Wellington (LLM). Solicitor of Supreme Court of NZ, 1961; A. J. Park & Son, 1961–81; practised at NZ Bar, 1981–87; QC 1984; Judge of High Court of NZ, 1987–91; Judge, 1991–2004, Pres., 2002–04, Court of Appeal, NZ. Mem. of Honour, Internat. Assoc. for Protection of Industrial Property, 1990. *Recreation:* golf (Capt., Royal and Ancient Golf Club of St Andrews, 2005–06). *Address:* 25a Benbow Street, Auckland, New Zealand. *T:* (9) 5757695.

GAULTER, Derek Vivian, CBE 1978; Chairman, Construction Industry Training Board, 1985–90; *b* 10 Dec. 1924; *s* of late Jack Rudolf Gaulter, MC and Muriel Gaulter (*née* Westworth); *m* 1st, 1949, Edith Irene Shackleton (*d* 1996); one *s* three *d*; 2nd, 2000, Marion Bowker. *Educ:* Denstone College; Peterhouse, Cambridge (MA). RNVR, Sub Lieut MTBs/Minesweepers, 1943–46. Lord Justice Holker Sen. Scholarship, Gray's Inn; called to the Bar, Gray's Inn, 1949; Common Law Bar, Manchester, 1950–55. Federation of Civil Engineering Contractors: Legal Sec., General Sec., Dep. Dir Gen., 1955–67; Dir Gen., 1967–86. Trustee, Woodland Trust, 1995–2000. *Recreations:* gardening, travel, opera. *Address:* 4 Abbotts Lea Cottages, Worthy Road, Winchester SO23 7HB.

GAULTIER, Jean-Paul; fashion designer; *b* 24 April 1952; *s* of Paul Gaultier and Solange Gaultier (*née* Garrabe). *Educ:* Lycée, Arcueil, Paris. Assistant: to Pierre Cardin, 1970; to Jacques Esterel, 1971–73; designer of US collections for Pierre Cardin, 1974–75; ind. designer, 1976–82; founder, Jean-Paul Gaultier SA, 1978. Début collection, 1976; first collection for men, 1984, for children, 1988; also perfumes, 1993, 1995, 1999 and 2006. Designed costumes: for ballet, Le Défilé de Régine Chopinot, 1985; for films: The Cook, the Thief, His Wife and her Lover, 1989; Kika, 1994; La Cité des Enfants Perdus, 1995; The Fifth Element, 1996; for Madonna's Blond Ambition tour, 1990. Chevalier des Arts et des Lettres (France); Chevalier de la Légion d'Honneur (France). *Address:* Jean-Paul Gaultier SA, 325 rue Saint-Martin, 75003 Paris, France.

GAUMOND, Most Rev. Mgr André; *see* Sherbrooke, Archbishop of (RC).

GAUNT, Jonathan Robert; QC 1991; a Deputy High Court Judge, since 2002; *b* 3 Nov. 1947; *s* of late Dr Brian Gaunt and Dr Mary Gaunt (*née* Hudson); *m* 1975, Lynn Dennis; one *d*. *Educ:* St Peter's Coll.; Radley; University Coll., Oxford (BA). Called to the Bar, Lincoln's Inn, 1972, Bencher, 1998. Jt Head, Falcon Chambers, 1993–. *Publications:* (ed) Halsbury's Laws of England, Vol. 27, 4th edn 1981, rev. 1994; (ed) Gale on Easements, 16th edn 1996, 17th edn 2002. *Recreations:* golf, sailing. *Address:* Falcon Chambers, Falcon Court, EC4Y 1AA. *T:* (020) 7353 2484. *Club:* North Middlesex Golf.

GAUTIER-SMITH, Peter Claudius, FRCP; Consultant Neurologist, National Hospitals for Nervous Diseases, Queen Square and Maida Vale, 1962–89; *b* 1 March 1929; *s* of late Claudius Gautier-Smith and Madeleine (*née* Ferguson); *m* 1960, Nesta Mary Wroth; two *d*. *Educ:* Cheltenham Coll. (Exhibnr); King's Coll., Cambridge; St Thomas's Hosp. Med. Sch. MA, MD. Casualty Officer, House Physician, St Thomas' Hosp., 1955–56; Medical Registrar, University Coll. Hosp., 1958; Registrar, National Hosp., Queen Square, 1960–62; Consultant Neurologist, St George's Hosp., 1962–75; Dean, Inst. of Neurology, 1975–82. Mem., Bd of Governors, Nat. Hosps for Nervous Diseases, 1975–89. Hon. Neurologist, Dispensaire Français, London, 1983–89. *Publications:* Parasagittal and Falx Meningiomas, 1970; papers in learned jls on neurology; (as Peter Conway) over 25 novels incl.: Locked In, 2006; Evil Streak, 2006; Unwillingly to School, 2007; Deserving Death, 2007; Deadly Obsession, 2008. *Recreations:* literary; French language; squash (played for Cambridge v Oxford, 1951; Captain, London Univ., 1954); tennis (played for King's Coll., Cambridge, 1952, St Thomas' Hosp., 1953–55). *Clubs:* MCC; Hawks (Cambridge); Jesters.

GAUTREY, Peter, CMG 1972; CVO 1961; DK (Brunei) 1972; HM Diplomatic Service, retired; High Commissioner in Guyana, 1975–78, concurrently Ambassador (non-resident) to Surinam, 1976–78; *b* 17 Sept. 1918; *s* of late Robert Harry Gautrey, Hindhead, Surrey, and Hilda Morris; *m* 1947, Marguerite Etta Uncles; one *s* one *d*. *Educ:* Abbotsholme Sch., Derbys. Joined Home Office, 1936. Served in Royal Artillery, (Capt.), Sept. 1939–March 1946. Re-joined Home Office; Commonwealth Relations Office, 1948; served in British Embassy, Dublin, 1950–53; UK High Commission, New Delhi, 1955–57 and 1960–63; British Deputy High Commissioner, Bombay, 1963–65; Corps of Diplomatic Service Inspectors, 1965–68; High Commissioner: Swaziland, 1968–71; Brunei, 1972–75. FRSA 1972. *Recreations:* walking, music, art. *Address:* 24 Fort Road, Guildford, Surrey GU1 3TE.

GAVASKAR, Sunil Manohar; Padma Bhushan; cricketer; business executive; Chairman, Cricket Committee, International Cricket Council, 2000–08; *b* 10 July 1949; *s* of Manohar Keshav Gavaskar and Meenal Manohar Gavaskar; *m* 1974, Marshniel Mehrotra; one *s*. *Educ:* St Xavier's High Sch.; St Xavier's Coll.; Bombay Univ. (BA). Represented India in cricket, 1971–88; Captain, Indian Team, 1978, 1979–80, 1980–82 and 1984–85; made 10,122 runs, incl. 34 centuries, in 125 Test matches; passed world records for no of runs in Test matches, 1983, and no of Test centuries, 1984; first batsman to score over 10,000 Test runs, 1987. Sheriff of Mumbai, 1994–95. *Publications:* Sunny Days, 1976; Idols, 1983; Runs 'n Ruins, 1984; One-day Wonders, 1985. *Clubs:* Cricket Club of India, Bombay Gymkhana.

GAVIN, (Alexander) Rupert; Chairman, Incidental Colman, since 1996; Chief Executive, Odeon and UCI Cinema Group, since 2005; *b* 1 Oct. 1954; *s* of late David Maitland Gavin and Helen Gavin (who *m* 1991, Sir Hugh Hambling, Bt, *qv*); *m* 1991, Ellen Janet Miller; two *d*. *Educ:* Magdalene Coll., Cambridge (BA Hons 1975; MA). Dir and Partner, Sharps Advertising, 1981–85; Dir, Saatchi & Saatchi Gp, 1985–87; Dep. Man. Dir, Dixons Stores Gp, 1987–94; Man. Dir, Consumer Div., British Telecom, 1994–98; Chief Exec., BBC Worldwide, 1998–2004; Chm., Contender Entertainment Gp, 2004–06; Chief Exec., Kingdom Media, 2005–06 (Dir, 2004–06). Dir, Ambassador Theatre Gp, 1999–; non-exec. Dir, Virgin Mobile, 2004–06. Liveryman, Grocers' Co., 1986–. FRTS 2005 (Vice-Pres., 1997–2006); CCMI 2007. Olivier Awards: for Best Entertainment, 1999, 2000 and 2002; for Best New Play, 2003. *Recreations:* commercial theatre, songwriting, garden design. *Clubs:* Pratt's, Royal Automobile, Thirty, Two Brydges.

GAVRON, family name of **Baron Gavron**.

GAVRON, Baron *cr* 1999 (Life Peer), of Highgate in the London Borough of Camden; **Robert Gavron,** CBE 1990; Chairman, Folio Society Ltd, since 1982; Chairman, St Ives plc, 1964–93; Proprietor, Carcanet Press Ltd, since 1983; *b* 13 Sept. 1930; *s* of Nathaniel and Leah Gavron; *m* 1955, Hannah Fyvel (*d* 1965); one *s* (and one *s* decd); *m* 1967, Felicia Nicolette Coates (*see* F. N. Gavron) (marr. diss. 1987); two *d*; *m* 1989, Katharine Gardiner (*née* Macnair) (*see* Lady Gavron). *Educ:* Leighton Park Sch.; St Peter's Coll., Oxford (MA; Hon. Fellow, 1992). Called to the Bar, Middle Temple, 1955. Entered printing industry, 1955; founded St Ives Gp, 1964 (public co., 1985). Director: Octopus Publishing plc, 1975–87; Electra Management Plc, 1981–91; Chm., Guardian Media Group plc, 1997–2000; Dir, National Gallery Company (formerly National Gallery Publications) Ltd, 1996–2001 (Chm., 1996–98). Chm., Open Coll. of the Arts, 1991–96 (Trustee, 1987–96); Dir, Royal Opera House, 1992–98. Trustee: Nat. Gall., 1994–2001; Scott Trust, 1997–2000; IPPR, 1991– (Treas., 1994–2000). Gov., LSE, 1997–2002. Hon. Fellow: RCA, 1990; RSL 1996. *Publication:* (jtly) The Entrepreneurial Society, 1998. *Address:* 44 Eagle Street, WC1R 4FS. *T:* (020) 7400 4300. *Club:* MCC.

GAVRON, Lady; Katharine Susan Gavron, (Kate), PhD; Chair, Carcanet Press Ltd, since 1989; *b* 19 Jan. 1955; *d* of His Honour (Maurice John) Peter Macnair and of Vickie Macnair; *m* 1st, 1975, Gerrard Gardiner (marr. diss. 1982); 2nd, 1989, Robert Gavron (*see* Baron Gavron). *Educ:* Francis Holland Sch.; London Sch. of Econs (BSc; PhD 1997). William Heinemann Ltd, 1974–88 (Dir, 1984–88); Director: Secker & Warburg Ltd, 1984–88; Virago Press Ltd, 1994–96. Dir, Mutual Aid Centre, 1996–2005; Trustee and Research Fellow: Inst. Community Studies, 1992–2005; Young Foundn, 2005–. Trustee: Runnymede Trust, 1997–; The Poetry Archive, 2001–; George Piper Dances, 2001–. *Publications:* (with G. Dench and T. Flower) Young at Eighty: the prolific public life of Michael Young, 1995; (with G. Dench and M. Young) The New East End: kinship, race and conflict, 2006. *Address:* c/o Young Foundation, 18 Victoria Park Square, E2 9PF. *Club:* Groucho.

GAVRON, Felicia Nicolette, (Nicky); Member (Lab), London Assembly, Greater London Authority, since 2000 (Member for Enfield and Haringey, 2000–04); Deputy Mayor of London, 2000–03 and 2004–08; *d* of Clayton English Coates and Elisabet Charlotta Horstmeyer; *m* 1967, Robert Gavron (*see* Baron Gavron) (marr. diss. 1987); two *d*. *Educ:* Worcester Girls' Grammar Sch.; Courtauld Inst. Lectr, Camberwell Sch. of Art and St Martin's Sch. of Art. Mem. (Lab) Haringey BC, 1986–2002 (former Chm., Planning and Envmt Services Cttees). Mem., and Leader, Lab Gp, London Planning Adv. Cttee, 1989–97 and 1998–2000 (Dep. Chm., 1989–94; Chm., 1994–97 and 1998–2000); Chm., LGA Planning Cttee, 1997–99 (Vice Chm., 1999–2000); Member: Exec., GLAA, 1986–92 (Vice Chm., London Arts Bd, 1992–2000); SE Regl Planning Conf., 1989–2001 (Leader, Lab Gp, 1993–97; Vice Chm., 1997–2000); Bd, London First, 1997–2001. Chairman: Nat. Planning Forum, 1999–2002; Commn for Integrated Transport, 1999–2002; London Hydrogen Partnership, 2004–; Dep. Chm., London Climate Change Agency, 2006–; Member: Metropolitan Police Authy, 2000–; Sustainable Develt Commn, 2001–03; Advr, Urban Task Force, 1998–2000. Founding Trustee, Jackson's Lane Community Centre, 1975–. Hon. FRIBA 2001. Hon. Dr London Guildhall, 2001. *Address:* Greater London Authority, City Hall, More London, Queen's Walk, SE1 2AA.

GAY, Mark Edward; Partner and Head, Sports Group, DLA Piper LLP, since 2005; *b* London, 25 June 1962; *s* of Eamon and Hannah Gay; *m* 1997, Susan Elizabeth Holmes; two *d*. *Educ:* Clapham Coll., London; Lady Margaret Hall, Oxford (BA Juris. 1984). Trainee solicitor, 1985–88, Associate, 1988–91, Linklaters & Paines; Associate, 1991–95, Partner, 1995–99, Herbert Smith; Partner, Denton Hall, 1999; Solicitor Advocate, 2007. *Recreations:* chauffeuring my children, fine wine, Buffy the Vampire Slayer. *Address:* DLA Piper LLP, 3 Noble Street, EC2V 7EE. *T:* (020) 7796 6025, *Fax:* (020) 7796 6592; *e-mail:* mark.gay@dlapiper.com. *Club:* Richmond Football.

GAYMER, Janet Marion, CBE 2004; Commissioner for Public Appointments, since 2006; a Civil Service Commissioner, since 2006; *b* 11 July 1947; *d* of late Ronald Frank Craddock and Marion Clara Craddock (*née* Stringer); *m* 1971, John Michael Gaymer; two *d*. *Educ:* Nuneaton High Sch. for Girls; St Hilda's Coll., Oxford (MA Jurisprudence; Hon. Fellow 2002); LSE (LLM). Simmons & Simmons: admitted solicitor, 1973; Head, Employment Law Dept, 1973–2001; Partner, 1977–2001; Sen. Partner, 2001–06. Chm., Employment Tribunal System Taskforce, 2001–02 and 2003–06; Member: Justice Cttee, Industrial Tribunals, 1987; Council, ACAS, 1995–2001; Steering Bd, Employment Tribunals Service, 2001–06. Chairman: Employment Law Sub Cttee, City of London Law Soc., 1987; Employment Law Cttee, Law Soc., 1993–96; Founder Chm. and Life Vice-Pres., Employment Lawyers Assoc., 1993; Founder Chm. and Hon. Chm., European Employment Lawyers Assoc., 1998; Mem., Exec. Bd, 1995–2003, Council, 1995–, Justice. Mem. Bd, RSC, 1999–2006. Member Editorial Advisory Board: Sweet & Maxwell's Encyclopedia of Employment Law, 1987; Tolley's Health and Safety at Work, 1995–2006. Patron: Assoc. of Women Solicitors, 2000–; City Women's Network, 2006–. Hon. QC 2008. Hon. LLD Nottingham, 2004; DUniv Surrey, 2006. The Times Woman of Achievement in the Law Award, 1997. *Publication:* The Employment Relationship, 2001. *Recreations:* watercolour painting, music, theatre, opera, swimming. *Address:* Office of the Commissioner for Public Appointments, 3rd Floor, 35 Great Smith Street, SW1P 3BQ. *T:* (020) 7276 2603, *Fax:* (020) 7276 2633; *e-mail:* ocpa@gtnet.gov.uk. *Clubs:* Athenæum, Arts, Royal Air Force.

GAYOOM, Maumoon Abdul, Hon. GCMG 1997; President and Commander-in-Chief of the Armed Forces and of the Police, Republic of Maldives, since 1978; *b* 29 Dec. 1937; *s* of late Abdul Gayoom Ibrahim and Khadeeja Moosa; *m* 1969, Nasreena Ibrahim; two *s* twin *d*. *Educ:* Al-Azhar Univ., Cairo. Res. Asst, Amer. Univ. of Cairo, 1967–69; Lectr in Islamic Studies and Philosophy, Abdullahi Bayero Coll., Ahmadu Bello Univ., 1969–71; teacher, Aminiya Sch., 1971–72; Manager, Govt Shipping Dept, 1972–73; writer and translator, President's Office, 1972–74; Under-Sec., Telecommunications Dept, 1974; Special Under-Sec., Office of the Prime Minister, 1974–75; Dep. Ambassador to Sri Lanka, 1975–76; Under-Sec., Dept of External Affairs, 1976; Dep. Minister of Transport, 1976; Perm. Rep. to UN, 1976–77; Minister of Transport, 1977–78; Governor, Maldives Monetary Authy, 1981–2004; Minister: of Defence and Nat. Security, 1982–2004; of Finance, 1989–93; of Finance and Treasury, 1993–2004. Numerous hon. degrees. *Publication:* The Maldives: a nation in peril, 1998. *Recreations:* reading, poetry, astronomy, calligraphy, photography, badminton, cricket. *Address:* Ma. Ki'nbigasdhoshuge, Malé 20229, Republic of Maldives; Presidential Palace, Orchid Magu, Malé 20208, Republic of Maldives. *T:* 3322100, 3322200; The President's Office, Boduthakurufaanu Magu, Malé 20113, Republic of Maldives.

GAZDAR, Prof. Gerald James Michael; Professor of Computational Linguistics, University of Sussex, 1985–2002, now Emeritus; *b* 24 Feb. 1950; *s* of John and Kathleen Gazdar. *Educ:* Heath Mount; Bradfield Coll.; Univ. of East Anglia (BA Phil with Econ); Reading Univ. (MA Linguistics, PhD). Sussex University: Lectr 1975–80; Reader 1980–85; Dean, Sch. of Cognitive and Computing Scis, 1988–93. Fellow, Center for Advanced Study in the Behavioral Sciences, Stanford Univ., California, 1984–85. Vis. Prof., Univ. of Brighton, 2007–. FBA 1988–2002. *Publications:* (with Klein, Pullum) A Bibliography of Contemporary Linguistic Research, 1978; Pragmatics, 1979; (with Klein, Pullum) Order, Concord, and Constituency, 1983; (with Klein, Pullum, Sag) Generalized Phrase Structure Grammar, 1985; (with Coates, Deuchar, Lyons) New Horizons in Linguistics II, 1987; (with Franz, Osborne, Evans) Natural Language Processing in the 1980s, 1987; (with Mellish): Natural Language Processing in Prolog, An Introduction to Computational Linguistics, 1989; Natural Language Processing in LISP, An Introduction to Computational Linguistics, 1989; Natural Language Processing in POP-11, An Introduction to Computational Linguistics, 1989. *Address:* Department of Informatics, University of Sussex, Brighton BN1 9QH. *T:* (01273) 678030.

GAZE, Dr (Raymond) Michael, FRS 1972; FRSE 1964; Head, Medical Research Council Neural Development and Regeneration Group, Edinburgh University, 1984–92, Hon. Professor, since 1986; *b* 22 June 1927; *s* of late William Mercer Gaze and Kathleen Grace Gaze (*née* Bowhill); *m* 1957, Robinetta Mary Armfelt; one *s* two *d. Educ:* at home; Sch. of Medicine, Royal Colleges, Edinburgh; Oxford Univ. (MA, DPhil). LRCPE, LRCSE, LRFPSG. House Physician, Chelmsford and Essex Hosp., 1949; National Service, RAMC, 1953–55; Lectr, later Reader, Dept of Physiology, Edinburgh Univ., 1955–70; Alan Johnston, Lawrence and Moseley Research Fellow, Royal Soc., 1962–66; Head, Div. of Developmental Biol., 1970–83, Dep. Dir 1977–83, Nat. Inst. for Med. Research. Visiting Professor: of Theoretical Biology, Univ. of Chicago, 1972; of Biology, Middlesex Hosp. Med. Sch., 1972–74. *Publications:* The Formation of Nerve Connections, 1970; Editor, 1975–88, and contrib., Development (formerly Jl Embryology and Exper. Morphology); various papers on neurobiology in Jl Physiology, Qly Jl Exper. Physiology, Proc. Royal Soc., etc. *Recreations:* drawing, hill-walking, music. *Address:* 37 Sciennes Road, Edinburgh EH9 1NS. *T:* (0131) 667 6915.

GAZZARD, Prof. Brian George, FRCP; Clinical Research Director, HIV Unit, Chelsea and Westminster Hospital, since 1978; Professor of HIV Medicine, Imperial College, University of London, since 1998; *b* 4 April 1946; *s* of Edward George Gazzard and Elizabeth (*née* Hill); *m*; three *s. Educ:* Queens' Coll., Cambridge (MA); King's Coll. Hosp., London (MD 1976). FRCP 1983. Senior Registrar: Liver Unit, KCH, 1974–76; Gastroenterology Unit, St Bartholomew's Hosp., 1976–78; Consultant Physician, Westminster and St Stephen's Hosps, 1978–. Prin. UK Investigator, various collaborative AIDS studies incl. MRC Delta Trial, 1978–. *Publications:* Treatment of Peptic Ulcer, 1989; Common Symptoms in Gastroenterology, 1990; Gastroenterological Manifestations in AIDS Patients, 1992. *Recreation:* gardening. *Address:* 11 Kempson Road, SW6 4PX.

GAZZARD, Roy James Albert, FRIBA; FRTPI; Pro-Director, 1982–84, Director, 1984–86, Hon. Fellow, 1987, Centre for Middle Eastern and Islamic Studies, Durham University; *b* 19 July 1923; *s* of James Henry Gazzard, MBE, and Ada Gwendoline Gazzard (*née* Willis); *m* 1947, Muriel Joy Morgan; one *s* two *d* (and one *s* decd). *Educ:* Stationers' Company's Sch.; Architectural Assoc. Sch. of Architecture (Dip.); School of Planning and Research for Reg. Develt (Dip.). Commissioned, Middx Regt, 1943; service Palestine and ME (Hon. Major). Acting Govt Town Planner, Uganda, 1950; Staff Architect, Barclays Bank Ltd, 1954; Chief Architect, Peterlee Develt Corp., 1960; Dir of Develt, Northumberland CC, 1962; Chief Professional Adviser to Sec. of State's Environmental Bd, 1976; Under Sec., DoE, 1976–79. Prepared: Jinja (Uganda) Outline Scheme, 1954; Municipality of Sur (Oman) Develt Plan, 1975. Renter Warden, Worshipful Co. of Stationers and Newspaper Makers, 1985–86. Captain, Durham City Mayoral Bodyguard, 2007–08. Govt medals for Good Design in Housing; Civic Trust awards for Townscape and Conservation. *Publications:* Durham: portrait of a cathedral city, 1983; contribs to HMSO pubns on built environment. *Recreations:* Islamic art and architecture, fortifications, dry-stone walling.

GEACH, Prof. Peter Thomas, FBA 1965; Professor of Logic, University of Leeds, 1966–81; *b* 29 March 1916; *o s* of Prof. George Hender Geach, IES, and Eleonora Frederyka Adolfina Sgonina; *m* 1941, Gertrude Elizabeth Margaret Anscombe, FBA (*d* 2001); three *s* four *d. Educ:* Balliol Coll., Oxford (Domus Schol.; Hon. Fellow, 1979). 2nd cl. Class. Hon. Mods, 1936; 1st cl. Lit. Hum., 1938. Gladstone Research Student, St Deiniol's Library, Hawarden, 1938–39; philosophical research, Cambridge, 1945–51; University of Birmingham: Asst Lectr in Philosophy, 1951; Lectr, 1952; Sen. Lectr, 1959; Reader in Logic, 1961. Vis. Prof., Univ. of Warsaw, 1985. Lectures: Stanton, in the Philosophy of Religion, Cambridge, 1971–74; Hägerström, Univ. of Uppsala, 1975; O'Hara, Univ. of Notre Dame, 1978. Forschungspreis, A. Von Humboldt Stiftung, 1983; Aquinas Medal, Amer. Catholic Philosophical Assoc., 2000. Papal medal, Pro Ecclesia et Pontifice, 1999. *Publications:* Mental Acts, 1957; Reference and Generality, 1962, 4th edn 2006; (with G. E. M. Anscombe) Three Philosophers, 1961; God and the Soul, 1969; Logic Matters, 1972; Reason and Argument, 1976; Providence and Evil, 1977; The Virtues, 1977; Truth, Love, and Immortality: an introduction to McTaggart's philosophy, 1979; Truth and Hope, 2001; articles in Mind, Philosophical Review, Analysis, Ratio, etc. *Recreations:* reading stories of detection, mystery and horror; collecting and annotating old bad logic texts. *Address:* 3 Richmond Road, Cambridge CB4 3PP. *T:* (01223) 353950. *Club:* Union Society (Oxford).

GEAKE, Jonathan Richard Barr; His Honour Judge Geake; a Circuit Judge, Northern Circuit, since 1994; *b* 27 May 1946; *s* of late Michael and of Margaret Geake; *m* 1978, Sally Louise Dines; three *s. Educ:* Sherborne Sch.; Fitzwilliam Coll., Cambridge (BA). Called to the Bar, Inner Temple, 1969; practised on Northern Circuit; a Recorder, 1989; Standing Counsel for Customs & Excise, 1989. *Recreations:* golf and various other sporting activities, gardening. *Address:* Crown Court, Manchester M3 3FL. *Clubs:* Knutsford Golf, St Enodoc Golf; Alderley Edge Cricket.

GEAR, Alan, MBE 2003; Director, Gear Changes Ltd, independent consultancy in organic gardening, farming and food, since 2003; *b* 12 June 1949; *s* of Harold Archibald Gear and Nora Esme Gear; *m* 1971, Jacqueline Anne Parker (*see* J. A. Gear). *Educ:* University Coll. of Wales, Swansea (BSc Hons 1970, MSc Civil Engrg 1971). Graduate Engr, West Glamorgan Water Bd, 1971–74; Deputy Dir, 1974–85, Chief Exec., 1985–2003, Henry Doubleday Res. Assoc. Mem., Adv. Cttee on Organic Standards, DEFRA, 2003–05. Hon. MRHS 2006. *Publications:* The Organic Food Guide, 1983, repr. as The New Organic Food Guide, 1986; (ed jtly) Thorsons Organic Consumer Guide, 1990; *contributions to:* Thorsons Organic Wine Guide, 1991; A Future for the Land: organic practice from a global perspective, 1992; Environmental Issues and the Food Industry, 1994, 2nd edn 1999. *Recreations:* listening to classical music, reading, gardening, model-making. *Address:* 23 Styleman Way, Snettisham, Norfolk PE31 7NT. *T:* (01485) 543695.

GEAR, Jacqueline Anne, MBE 2003; Director and Secretary, Gear Changes Ltd, independent consultancy in organic gardening, farming and food, since 2003; *b* 18 Dec. 1949; *d* of Stephen Edward Parker and Phyllis Mary Parker; *m* 1971, Alan Gear, *qv. Educ:* University Coll. of Wales, Swansea (BSc Hons Zoology 1971). Biologist, Gower RDC, 1971–74; Dir, Analytical Res., Henry Doubleday Res. Assoc., 1974–80; R&D Manager, F. H. Nash Ltd, 1981–84; Exec. Dir, Henry Doubleday Res. Assoc., 1985–2003. Hon. MRHS 2006. *Publications:* (jtly) Ryton Gardens Recipe Book, 1988; (jtly) Thorsons Organic Consumer Guide, 1990; (jtly) Thorsons Organic Wine Guide, 1991; (jtly) Organic Gardening: your questions answered, 1993; (jtly) The Chilli and Pepper Cookbook, 1995; (contrib.) Encyclopaedia of Organic Gardening, 2001. *Recreations:* classical music, reading, cooking, walking, the countryside. *Address:* 23 Styleman Way, Snettisham, Norfolk PE31 7NT. *T:* (01485) 543695.

GEAR, Rt Rev. Michael Frederick; Bishop Suffragan of Doncaster, 1993–99; Hon. Assistant Bishop: Diocese of Rochester, since 1999; Diocese of Canterbury, since 2000; *b* 27 Nov. 1934; *s* of Frederick Augustus and Lillian Hannah Gear; *m* 1961, Daphne, *d* of Norman and Millicent Earl; two *d. Educ:* St John's College and Cranmer Hall, Durham. BA Social Studies, 1st cl., 1959; DipTh 1961. Assistant Curate: Christ Church, Bexleyheath, 1961–64; St Aldate, Oxford, 1964–67; Vicar of St Andrew, Clubmoor, Liverpool, 1967–71; Rector, Avondale, Salisbury, Rhodesia, 1971–76; Tutor, Wycliffe Hall, Oxford, 1976–80; Team Rector, Macclesfield, 1980–88; Archdeacon of Chester, 1988–93. Hon. Chaplain, Mothers' Union, 1996–99. Chairman: Cranmer Hall Cttee, St John's Coll., Durham, 1994–98; Northern Ordination Course, 1995–99; Member: Scargill Council, 1993–99; Bd, Church Army, 1993–99. *Recreations:* photography, golf, history and contemporary politics of Southern Africa. *Address:* 10 Acott Fields, Yalding, Maidstone ME18 6DQ.

GEATER, Sara; Chief Operating Officer, talkbackThames, since 2007; *b* Coventry, 18 March 1955; *d* of Jack and Patricia Geater; civil partnership 2007, Felicity Milton; one *s* one *d. Educ:* Farnham Common CP Sch.; Beaconsfield High Sch.; Leamington Coll. for Girls; City of London Poly.; Holborn Law Sch. (LLB). Called to the Bar, Middle Temple, 1998. CEDR Accredited Mediator, 2006. Prodn Accountant, LWT, 1977–84; producer, Business as Usual (film), 1985; line producer, Mr Pye (film), 1986; Head: of Production, Drama and Film, Channel 4, 1987–97; of Production, HAL/Miramax, 1997–98; of Film and TV, Avalon, 1998–2000; Dir, Rights and Business Affairs, BBC, 2000–04; Hd, Commercial Affairs, Channel 4, 2004–07. Chm., Women in Film and TV, 1994–97. Chm., BAFTA Prodns, 2007–. Gov., London Film Sch., 2007–. Mem., RTS. FRSA 2006. *Recreations:* eating, drinking with friends, gardening, reading, flying, being with family. *Address:* c/o talkbackThames, 21 Newman Street, W1T 1PG. *T:* (020) 7861 8363, *Fax:* (020) 7861 8141; *e-mail:* sara.geater@talkbackthames.tv. *Clubs:* Groucho, Soho House.

GEDDES, family name of **Baron Geddes**.

GEDDES, 3rd Baron *cr* 1942; **Euan Michael Ross Geddes;** Company Director, since 1964; *b* 3 Sept. 1937; *s* of 2nd Baron Geddes, KBE, and Enid Mary, Lady Geddes (*d* 1999), *d* of late Clarance H. Butler; *S* father, 1975; *m* 1st, 1966, Gillian (*d* 1995), *d* of late William Arthur Butler; one *s* one *d*; 2nd, 1996, Susan Margaret Hunter, *d* of late George Harold Carter. *Educ:* Rugby; Gonville and Caius Coll., Cambridge (MA 1964); Harvard Business School. Elected Mem., H of L, 1999; a Dep. Speaker, 2000–; Mem., Procedure Cttee, 2002–07. Treas., Assoc. of Cons. Peers, 2000–. *Recreations:* golf, bridge, music, gardening, shooting. *Heir:* *s* Hon. James George Neil Geddes [*b* 10 Sept. 1969; *m* 2004, Alice Arabella Alexander; two *s*]. *Address:* House of Lords, SW1A 0PW. *T:* (020) 7219 6400. *Clubs:* Brooks's; Hong Kong (Hong Kong); Noblemen and Gentlemen's Catch; Aldeburgh Golf, Hong Kong Golf.

GEDDES, Prof. Alexander MacIntosh, (Alasdair), CBE 1996; FRCP, FRCPE, FRCPath, FFPH, FMedSci; Professor of Infection, 1991–99, and Deputy Dean, Faculty of Medicine and Dentistry, 1994–99, University of Birmingham (Professor of Infectious Diseases, 1982–91; Associate Dean, 1999–2002); *b* 14 May 1934; *s* of Angus and Isabella Geddes; *m* 1984, Angela Lewis; two *s. Educ:* Fortrose Acad.; Univ. of Edinburgh (MB ChB). FRCPE 1971; FRCP 1981; FRCPath 1995; FFPH (FFPHM 1998). Served RAMC, Captain, 1958–60. Med. Registrar, Aberdeen Hosps, 1961–63; Sen. Registrar, City Hosp. and Royal Infirmary, Edinburgh, 1963–67; Cons. Phys., E Birmingham Hosp., 1967–91; Hon. Cons. Phys., S Birmingham Health Dist, 1991–99. Examiner: MRCP (UK), 1972–99; Final MB, Univs of Birmingham, Glasgow, London, Sheffield, 1975–99. Forbes Vis. Fellow, Fairfield Hosp., Melbourne, Aust., 1988; Sir Edward Finch Vis. Prof., Univ. of Sheffield, 1989. Chairman: Sub-Cttee on Communicable and Trop. Diseases, Jt Cttee on Higher Med. Trng, 1984–94; Isolation Beds Working Party, DoH, 1989–95; Member: Birmingham AHA, 1977–81; Health Educn Authority, 1987–98; Sub-Cttee on Efficacy and Adverse Reactions, Cttee on Safety of Medicines, 1978–85; DHSS Expert Adv. Gp on AIDS, 1985–92; DoH (formerly DHSS) Jt Cttee on Vaccination and Immunization, 1986–95; Trop. Med. Res. Bd, MRC, 1984–88; Ministerial Inquiry into the Public Health Function, 1985–87; DoH Cttee on Safety of Medicines, 1993–96; Consultant Advr in Infectious Diseases, DoH, 1990–94; Civilian Consultant, Infectious Diseases and Tropical Medicine, RN, 1991–. Non-exec. Dir, City Hosp. NHS Trust, 1999–. Chm., Brit. Soc. for Antimicrobial Therapy, 1982–85; Chm., Communicable and Tropical Diseases Cttee, 1983–93, Censor, 1987–89, RCP; Mem., Assoc. of Physicians of GB and Ire., 1976–; President: Internat. Soc. for Infectious Diseases, 1994–96; 21st Internat. Chemotherapy Congress, 1999. Lectures: Honeyman-Gillespie, Univ. of Edinburgh, 1975; Public, Univ. of Warwick, 1980; Davidson, RCPE, 1981; Watson-Smith, 1988; Lister, RCPE, 1990. FMedSci 2000. Chm., Editorial Bd, Jl of Antimicrobial Therapy, 1975–85; Ed.-in-Chief, Internat. Jl of Antimicrobial Agents, 2005–. *Publications:* (ed) Control of Hospital Infection, 1975, 5th edn 2000; (ed) Recent Advances in Infection, 1975, 3rd edn 1988; (contrib.) Davidson, Principles and Practice of Medicine, 16th edn 1991, 17th edn 1995; (contrib.) Kumar and Clark, Clinical Medicine, 6th edn 2005; papers on infectious diseases, immunology, antibiotic therapy and epidemiology in learned jls. *Recreations:* gardening, reading. *Address:* 34 The Crescent, Solihull, West Midlands B91 1JR. *T:* (0121) 705 8844, *Fax:* (0121) 705 2314; *e-mail:* a.m.geddes@bham.ac.uk. *Club:* Athenæum.

GEDDES, Andrew Campbell; His Honour Judge Geddes; a Circuit Judge, since 1994; Designated Civil Judge, Worcester (formerly Coventry) Group of Courts, since 1998; *b* 10 June 1943; *s* of Hon. Alexander Campbell Geddes, OBE, MC, TD and Hon. Margaret Kathleen Geddes (*née* Addis); *m* 1st, 1974, Jacqueline Tan Bunzl; two *s*; 2nd, 1985, Bridget Bowring; one *s* one *d. Educ:* Stowe; Christ Church, Oxford (MA). Founder, Building Products Index, 1965. Called to the Bar, Inner Temple, 1972; a Recorder, 1990; authorised to sit as High Court Judge, 1995. *Publications:* Product and Service Liability in the EEC, 1992; Public Procurement, 1993; Protection of Individual Rights under EC Law, 1995; Public and Utility Procurement, 1996; contribs to learned jls. *Recreations:* music, walking, reading, writing, gardening. *Address:* 4 Essex Court, Temple, EC4Y 9AJ. *T:* (020) 7797 7970.

GEDDES, Prof. Duncan Mackay, MD, FRCP; Professor of Respiratory Medicine, Imperial College School of Medicine, since 1996; Consultant Physician, Royal Brompton Hospital, 1978–2007; *b* 6 Jan. 1942; *s* of Sir Reay Geddes, KBE and Lady Geddes (Imogen, *d* of late Captain Hay Matthey); *m* 1968, Donatella Flaccomio Nardi Dei; two *s* one *d*. *Educ:* Eton Coll.; Magdalene Coll., Cambridge (MA); Westminster Hosp. Med. Sch. (MB, BS 1971; MD 1978). FRCP 1982. Hon. Consultant: Royal London Hosp., 1982–2007; Royal Marsden Hosp., 1990–2007; Civilian Consultant in chest disease to the Army and Navy, 1986–2007. Director: Finsbury Worldwide Pharmaceutical Trust, 1995–; SR Pharma plc, 2000–02; India Pharma Fund, 2005–. Chm. Council, Nat. Asthma Campaign, 1996–2003. Mem., Med. Adv. Bd, Transgene, France, 1997–2002. Pres., British Thoracic Soc., 2000–01 (Vice-Pres., 1999–2000). *Publications:* Practical Medicine, 1976; Airways Obstruction, 1981; Respiratory Medicine, 1990; Cystic Fibrosis, 1995; numerous papers in med. and scientific jls. *Recreations:* tennis, golf, painting. *Address:* 57 Addison Avenue, W11 4QU. *Clubs:* Boodle's, Queen's.

GEDDES, Prof. John Richard, MD; FRCPsych; Professor of Epidemiological Psychiatry, University of Oxford, since 2002 (Senior Clinical Research Fellow, since 1995); *b* 28 Oct. 1961; *s* of William Watt Geddes and Carol Geddes (*née* Blomerley); partner, Jane O'Grady; one *d*. *Educ:* Manchester Grammar Sch.; Leeds Univ. (MB ChB 1985; MD 1994). FRCPsych 2000. Registrar, Sheffield Hosps, 1986–90; Sen. Registrar, Royal Edinburgh Hosp., 1990–95; Clinical Lectr, Dept of Psychiatry, Univ. of Oxford, 1995. Hon. Fellow, Amer. Coll. of Psychiatrists, 2008. *Publications:* (jtly) Psychiatry, 2nd edn 1999, 3rd edn 2005; (jtly) Lecture Notes on Psychiatry, 8th edn 1998, 9th edn 2005; (jtly) New Oxford Textbook of Psychiatry, 2nd edn 2008; papers in gen. and specialist med. jls on clinical epidemiol. and psychiatry. *Recreations:* walking, gardening, music. *Address:* Department of Psychiatry, University of Oxford, Warneford Hospital, Oxford OX3 7JX. *T:* (01865) 226480, *Fax:* (01865) 793101; *e-mail:* john.geddes@psych.ox.ac.uk.

GEDDES, Keith Taylor, CBE 1998; Policy Director, Pagoda PR (formerly P. S. Communication Consultants) Ltd, since 1999; *b* 8 Aug. 1952. *Educ:* Galashiels Acad.; Edinburgh Univ. (BEd 1975); Moray House Coll. of Educn (Cert. in Youth and Community work 1977); Heriot-Watt Univ. (Dip. in Housing 1986). Worker, Shelter Housing Aid (Scotland), 1977–84. Lothian Regional Council: Mem. (Lab), 1982–96; Chair, Educn Cttee, 1987–90; Leader, Labour Gp, 1990–96; Leader, City of Edinburgh Council, 1995–99. Bd Mem., Accounts Commn, 2002–08. Sen. Vice Pres., 1994–96, Pres., 1996–99, COSLA. Chm., Greenspace Scotland, 2003–. Contested (Lab) Tweeddale, Ettrick and Lauderdale, 2001. Dep. Chm. Bd, Scottish Natural Heritage, 2005– (Mem., 2001–). *Recreations:* hill walking, golf. *Address:* 7 Howard Street, Edinburgh EH3 5JP. *T:* (0131) 624 2365.

GEDDES, Michael Dawson; Executive Director, Milton Keynes Economic Partnership, 1995–2003; *b* 9 March 1944; *s* of late David Geddes and Audrey Geddes; *m* 1966, Leslie Rose Webb; two *s*. *Educ:* Sherborne Sch., Dorset; Univ. of BC (Goldsmith's Exhibitioner) (BA). Cranfield Institute of Technology: Admin. Asst, 1968–71; Planning Officer, 1971–77; Develt and Estates Officer, 1977–83; Financial Controller, RMCS, 1983–84; Sec., Ashridge (Bonar Law Meml) Trust; Dir, Admin, Ashridge Management Coll. and Dir, Ashridge subsids, 1984–90; Chief Exec., Recruitment and Assessment Services Agency, 1990–95; Civil Service Comr, 1990–97. Gov., Arts Educnl Sch., Tring, 2006–. *Publications:* (with W. Briner and C. Hastings) Project Leadership, 1990; Making Public Private Partnerships Work, 2005; papers on resource allocation in univs and on project management. *Recreations:* golf, bridge. *Address:* 2 Tidbury Close, Woburn Sands, Milton Keynes MK17 3QW. *T:* (01908) 282830.

GEDLING, Raymond, CB 1969; Deputy Secretary, Department of Health and Social Security, 1971–77; *b* 3 Sept. 1917; *s* of late John and Mary Gedling; *m* 1956, Joan Evelyn Chapple (*d* 2000); one *s*. *Educ:* Grangefield Grammar Sch., Stockton-on-Tees. Entered Civil Service as Executive Officer, Min. of Health, 1936; Asst Principal, 1942, Principal, 1947. Cabinet Office, 1951–52; Principal Private Sec. to Minister of Health, 1952–55; Asst Sec., 1955; Under-Sec., 1961; Asst Under-Sec. of State, Dept of Educn and Science, 1966–68; Dep. Sec., Treasury, 1968–71. *Recreations:* walking, chess. *Address:* 27 Wallace Fields, Epsom, Surrey KT17 3AX. *T:* (020) 8393 9060.

GEE, Anthony Hall; QC 1990; His Honour Judge Anthony Gee; a Circuit Judge, since 2004; *b* 4 Nov. 1948; *s* of late Harold Stephenson Gee and Marjorie Gee (*née* Hall); *m* 1975, Gillian Pauline Glover, St Annes-on-Sea; one *s* two *d*. *Educ:* Cambs High School for Boys; Chester City Grammar Sch.; Inns of Court School of Law. Called to the Bar, Gray's Inn, 1972; Mem., Northern Circuit, 1972–; a Recorder, 1985–2004. Mem., Probation Bd, 2004–. Mem., Medico-Legal Soc., 1996–. *Recreations:* golf, cricket, tennis, fly-fishing, fell walking. *Address:* Manchester Crown Court, Crown Square, Manchester M3 3FL. *Clubs:* Bramhall Golf; Lancashire County Cricket; Northern Lawn Tennis (Didsbury).

GEE, David Charles Laycock; Co-ordinator, Emerging Issues and Scientific Liaison, European Environment Agency, Copenhagen, since 1995; consultant, environmental and occupational risk, since 1992; Partner, WBMG Environmental Communications, since 1992; *b* 18 April 1947; *s* of Charles Laycock Gee and Theresa Gee (*née* Garrick); *m* 1974, Vivienne Taylor Gee; four *d*. *Educ:* Thomas Linacre and Wigan Grammar Schs; York Univ. (BA Politics). MIOSH 1985. Res. Dept, AUEW, 1970–73; Educn Service, TUC, 1973–78; Nat. Health/Safety Officer, GMB, 1978–88; Occupational/Environmental Cons., 1988–89; Campaign Co-ordinator, 1989–90, Dir, 1990–91, Friends of the Earth. Fellow, Collegium Ramazzini, Italy, 1984; FRSA 1990. *Publications:* (with John Cox and Dave Leon) Cancer and Work, 1982; (with Lesley Doyal et al) Cancer in Britain, 1983; Eco-nomic Tax Reform: a primer, 1994; *contributions to:* Radiation and Health—Biological Effects of Low Level Exposure to Ionising Radiation, 1987; Transport and Health, ed Fletcher and McMichael, 1995; Ecotaxation, ed O'Riordan, 1997; The Market and the Environment, ed Sterner, 1999; The Daily Globe: environmental change, the public and the media, ed Smith, 2000; Late Lessons from Early Warnings: the precautionary principle 1896–2000, 2002; pubns for EEA and MSF. *Recreations:* family, swimming, tennis, running, entertaining, theatre, music. *Address:* European Environment Agency, Kongens Nytorv 6, 1050 Copenhagen, Denmark. *T:* 33367142, *Fax:* 33367128; *e-mail:* david.gee@eea.eu.int.

GEE, His Honour David Stephenson; a Circuit Judge, 1992–2007; *b* 16 Dec. 1944; *s* of William and Marianne Gee; *m* 1972, Susan Margaret Hiley; two *s* two *d*. *Educ:* William Hulme's Grammar Sch., Manchester; Leeds Univ. (LLB Hons). Admitted Solicitor, 1970; Registrar, Manchester County Court and Dist Registry, 1982–90; Dist Judge, 1991–92; a Recorder of the Crown Court, 1991; Designated Family Judge: Blackburn Care Centre, 1994–95; Lancs, 2005–07. Chairman: Selcare (Greater Manchester) Trust, 1989–95; Rhodes Foundn Scholarship Trust, 1989–2005. Adv. Editor, Atkins' Court Forms, 1989–2003; Editor, Butterworth's Family Law Service, 1990–98. *Recreations:* music, walking, reading. *Address:* c/o Regional Director, 1 Bridge Street, Manchester M60 1TE.

GEE, James; Director of Fraud Services, KPMG Forensic, since 2007; *b* 1 Oct. 1957; *m* 1992, Lesley Ann White. *Educ:* London Sch. of Econs (BSc Econs 1978); CPE Law 1995. Civil servant, 1978–90; Counter Fraud Manager, London Boroughs of: Islington, 1990–94; Haringey, 1994–96; Lambeth, 1996–98. Advr to Social Security Select Cttee, H of C, 1995–97; Counter Fraud Advr to Minister of State for Welfare Reform, 1997–98; Dir, Counter Fraud Services, DoH, 1998–2002; Chief Exec., NHS Counter Fraud and Security Mgt Service, 2003–06. *Recreations:* military history, chess, gardening. *Address:* KPMG Forensic, 8 Salisbury Square, EC4Y 8BB. *T:* (020) 7694 5614; *e-mail:* jim.gee@kpmg.co.uk. *Club:* Manchester United Football.

GEE, Dr Maggie Mary, FRSL; writer; Vice President, Royal Society of Literature, since 2008 (Chair, 2004–08); *b* 2 Nov. 1948; *d* of Victor Gee and Aileen Gee (*née* Church); *m* 1983, Nicholas Rankin; one *d*. *Educ:* Somerville Coll., Oxford (BA, MA, BLitt); Wolverhampton Polytech. (PhD 1980). FRSL 1994. Writing Fellow, UEA, 1982; Northern Arts Writer-in-Residence, 1996. Vis. Fellow, Sussex Univ., 1986–; Hawthornden Fellow, 1989, 2002; Vis. Prof., Sheffield Hallam Univ., 2006–. Mem., Govt PLR Cttee, 1999–. Member: Council, RSL, 1999–; Mgt Cttee, Soc. of Authors, 1991–94. Judge, Booker Prize, 1989. Best of Young British Novelists, Granta, 1982. *Publications:* Dying in Other Words, 1981, 3rd edn 1993; The Burning Book, 1983, 2nd edn 1993; Light Years, 1985, 3rd edn 2004; Grace, 1988; Where Are the Snows, 1991, 2nd edn 2006; Lost Children, 1994; The Ice People, 1998, 2nd edn 1999; The White Family, 2002; The Flood, 2004; My Cleaner, 2005; The Blue: short stories, 2006; My Driver, 2009. *Recreations:* music, walking, swimming, looking at pictures, dancing. *Address:* c/o Karolina Sutton, Curtis Brown, 5th Floor, Haymarket House, 28–29 Haymarket, SW1Y 4SP. *Club:* Ronnie Scott's.

GEE, Mark Norman K.; *see* Kemp-Gee.

GEE, Nigel Ian, RDI 2007; FREng; Innovator-in-residence, Curtin University of Technology, Perth, WA, 2008–09; Managing Director, BMT Nigel Gee and Associates, 2003–06 (Founder and Managing Director, Nigel Gee and Associates, 1986–2003); *b* 30 July 1947; *s* of Saville and Betty Gee; *m* 1969, Susan Margaret Campbell Stewart; one *s* one *d*. *Educ:* Univ. of Newcastle upon Tyne (BSc Hons (Naval Architecture) 1969). CEng 1974, FREng 2006; FRINA 1993. Engrg Manager, Hovermarine, 1976–79; Sen. Lectr in Naval Architecture, Southampton Inst., 1979–83; Technical Gen. Manager, Vosper Hovermarine, 1983–86. Pres., RINA, 2004–07. FRSA 2008. Hon. DEng Southampton Solent, 2005. *Publications:* 21 papers on fast ships and boats for a variety of worldwide confs. *Recreations:* cruising under sail, painting, solving the Saturday Guardian crossword with assistance from my mother-in-law. *Address:* Ashlake Farmhouse, Ashlake Farm Lane, Wootton Bridge, Ryde, Isle of Wight PO33 4LF; *e-mail:* nigelgee@btopenworld.com. *Clubs:* Cruising Association; Royal Victoria Yacht.

GEE, Richard; a Circuit Judge, 1991–99; *b* 25 July 1942; *s* of John and Marie Gee; *m* 1st, 1965; three *s*; 2nd, 1995, Mrs Marilyn Gross. *Educ:* Kilburn Grammar School; University College London (LLB Hons). Admitted Solicitor, 1966; Assistant Recorder, 1983; Recorder, 1988. Mem., Main Board, Judicial Studies Board, 1988–93 (Mem., Ethnic Minorities Adv. Cttee, 1991–93). *Recreations:* golf, the arts.

GEE, Ruth; Director, Hong Kong, British Council, since 2003; *b* 21 May 1948; *d* of late George Gaskin and Florence Ann Gaskin; *m* 1972 (marr. diss. 2003); one *s* one *d*. *Educ:* Stoneraise Primary Sch., Cumbria; Whitehouse Sch., Brampton, Cumbria; Manchester Polytech. (London Univ. ext. BA Gen. Arts); Newcastle upon Tyne Univ. (Postgrad. DipEd). Teacher of English in comprehensive schs, 1970–80; Asst Dir, Polytech. of N London, 1986–89; Dir/Chief Exec., Edgehill Coll. of Higher Educn, 1989–93; Chief Executive: Assoc. for Colls, 1993–96; British Trng Internat., 1997–2000; British Council, London, 2000–03. Mem. (Lab) Hackney LBC, 1978–86. Co-opted Mem., 1980, Mem., 1981–86, ILEA (Dep. Leader, 1983–86). Non-executive posts: Basic Skills Agency, 1993–2003; Consumers' Assoc., 1996–2003. Mem., Hong Kong Women's Commn, 2006–08. *Recreations:* health farm addict and aspiring pilates teacher, who likes exploring quiet parts of Hong Kong on foot in winter, and walking to work whenever possible; dreaming of equality of opportunity in education and contributing less than I would like, for example, to Univ. of Fort Hare Develt Trust, S Africa. *Address:* British Council, 3 Supreme Court Road, Admiralty, Hong Kong; *e-mail:* ruth.gee@britishcouncil.org.hk. *Clubs:* China, Helena May (Hong Kong).

GEE, Steven Mark; QC 1993; a Recorder, since 2000; *b* 24 Aug. 1953; *yr s* of Dr Sidney Gee and Dr Hilda Elman; *m* 1999, Meryll Emilie Bacri; two *s*. *Educ:* Tonbridge Sch.; Brasenose Coll., Oxford (Open Scholar; MA 1st Cl. Hons Jurisprudence; Gibbs Prize for Law). Called to the Bar, Middle Temple, 1975 (Inns of Court Prize, Harmsworth Scholar); admitted NY Bar, 1999. Standing Jun. Counsel, ECGD, DTI, 1986–93. Hd of Chambers. *Publications:* Mareva Injunctions and Anton Piller Relief, 1995, 4th edn 1998; Commercial Injunctions, 5th edn, 2004. *Recreations:* marathon running, bridge. *Address:* 4 Field Court, Gray's Inn, WC1R 5EA. *T:* (020) 7440 6900. *Club:* MCC.

GEEKIE, Charles Nairn; QC 2006; a Recorder, since 2006; *b* 7 Feb. 1962; *s* of David Nairn Geekie and Gillian Mary Geekie (*née* Dind); *m* 1993, Geeta Manglani; one *s* one *d*. *Educ:* Hawford Lodge; Malvern Coll.; Bristol Univ. (LLB). Called to the Bar, Inner Temple, 1985; in practice as barrister, 1985–, specialising in family law. *Recreations:* cycling, hill walking, theatre. *Address:* 1 Garden Court, Temple, EC4Y 9BJ. *T:* (020) 7797 7900; *e-mail:* geekie@1gc.com.

GEERING, Ian Walter; QC 1991. *Educ:* Bedford Sch.; Univ. of Edinburgh (BVMS). Called to the Bar, Inner Temple, 1974. *Recreations:* walking, reading, sailing, photography. *Address:* 3 Verulam Buildings, Gray's Inn, WC1R 5NT.

GEERING, Rev. Prof. Lloyd George, ONZ 2007; PCNZM 2001; CBE 1989; Foundation Professor of Religious Studies, Victoria University of Wellington, 1971–84, now Professor Emeritus; *b* 26 Feb. 1918; *s* of George Frederick Thomas Geering and Alice Geering; *m* 1st, 1943, Nancy McKenzie (*d* 1949); one *s* one *d*; 2nd, 1951, Elaine Parker (*d* 2001); one *d*; 3rd, 2004, Shirley White. *Educ:* Univ. of Otago (MA 1st Cl. Hons Maths; BD Hons OT); Melbourne Coll. of Divinity. Presbyterian Parish Minister, 1943–55; Professor of Old Testament: Emmanuel Coll., Brisbane, 1956–59; Theol Hall, Knox Coll., Dunedin, 1960–71 (Principal, 1963–71). Hon. DD Otago, 1976. *Publications:* God in the New World, 1968; Resurrection: a symbol of hope, 1971; Faith's New Age, 1981; In the World Today, 1988; Tomorrow's God, 1994; The World to Come, 1999; Christianity without God, 2002; Wrestling with God, 2006. *Address:* 5B Herbert Gardens, 186 The Terrace, Wellington 6011, New Zealand. *T:* (4) 4730188.

GEFFEN, Dr Terence John; Medical Adviser, Capsticks Solicitors, 1990–99; *b* 17 Sept. 1921; *s* of late Maximilian W. Geffen and Maia Geffen (later Reid); *m* 1965, Judith Anne Steward; two *s*. *Educ:* St Paul's Sch.; University Coll., London; UCH. MD, FRCP. House Phys., UCH, 1943; RAMC, 1944–47; hosp. posts, Edgware Gen. Hosp., Hampstead Gen. Hosp., UCH, 1947–55; Min. of Health (later DHSS), 1956–82, SPMO, 1972–82;

Consultant in Public Health Medicine, NW Thames RHA, 1982–90. FRSocMed 1991. *Publications:* various in BMJ, Lancet, Clinical Science, etc. *Recreations:* music, reading, bridge. *Address:* 2 Stonehill Close, SW14 8RP. *T:* (020) 8878 0516.

GEHRELS, Jürgen Carlos, Hon. KBE 1997; non-executive Chairman, Siemens Holdings plc, 1998–2007 (Chief Executive, 1986–98); *b* 24 July 1935; *s* of Dr Hans Gehrels and Ursula (*née* da Rocha); *m* 1963, Sigrid Kausch; one *s* one *d*. *Educ:* Technical Univs, Berlin and Munich (Dipl. Ing.). Siemens AG, Germany, 1965–79; Pres., General Numeric Corp., Chicago, USA, 1979–82; Dir, Factory Automation, Siemens AG, Germany, 1982–86. Chairman: Siemens Communication Systems Ltd, 1986–92; Siemens Financial Services Ltd, 1988–92; Siemens Controls Ltd, 1990–98; Siemens-Nixdorf Inf. Systems Ltd, 1990–98; Director: Siemens Domestic Appliances Ltd, 1987–98; Comparex Ltd, 1988–92; Alfred Engelmann Ltd, 1989–98; Plessey UK, 1989–98; Plessey Overseas, 1989–98; Siemens Business Communication Systems Ltd, 1996–98; non-executive Director: Nammo AS, Norway, 1989–2003; Management Engineers, Germany, 1997–2006; Plus Plan (UK) Ltd, 2001–2003. Pres., German-British Chamber of Industry and Commerce in UK, 1997–2002 (Chm., 1992–97). Gov., Henley Mgt Coll., 1998–2003. FIET (FIEE 1991). FRSA 1993. *Recreations:* golf, gardening, architecture. *Address:* Al Ruscello, Via Panoramica 32, 22010 Piano Di, Porlezza, Italy. *Club:* Reform.

GEHRY, Frank Owen, CC 2002; architect; Principal, Frank O. Gehry & Associates, since 1962; *b* Toronto, 28 Feb. 1929; *s* of late Irving and Thelma Gehry; *m* 1975, Berta Aguilera; two *s*, and two *d* by a previous marriage. *Educ:* Univ. of Southern Calif (BArch 1954); Grad. Sch. of Design, Harvard Univ. Designer, 1953–54, Planning, Design and Project Dir, 1958–61, Victor Gruen Associates, LA; Project Designer and Planner, Pereira & Luckman, LA, 1957–58. Projects include: Loyola Law Sch., 1981–84; Calif Aerospace Mus., 1984; Inf. and Computer Sci./Engrg Res. Lab., Univ. of Calif, Irvine, 1986–88; Centre for Visual Arts, Univ. of Toledo, 1992; Frederick R. Weisman Art Mus., Minneapolis, 1993; American Centre, Paris, 1994; Vitra Internat. HQ, Basel, 1994; EMR Communication and Tech. Centre, Bad Oeynhausen, Germany, 1995; Nationale Nederlanden bldg, Prague, 1996; Guggenheim Mus., Bilbao, 1997; Experience Music Project, Seattle, 2000; Weatherhead Sch. of Mgt, Case Western Reserve Univ., 2001; Walt Disney Concert Hall, LA, 2003; Maggie's Cancer Care Centre, Ninewells Hosp., Dundee, 2003 (Royal Fine Art Commn Trust Bldg of Year, 2004); Jay Pritzker Pavilion, Chicago, 2004; Serpentine Gall. Pavilion, Kensington, 2008. Charlotte Davenport Prof. of Architecture, Yale Univ., 1982, 1985, 1987–89; Eliot Noyes Prof. of Design, Harvard Univ., 1984. FAIA 1974. Hon. RA 1998. Prizes include: Arnold W. Brunner Meml Prize in Architecture, 1983; Gold Medal, RIBA, 2000. *Publications:* (with Thomas Hines) Franklin D. Israel: buildings and projects, 1992; (with L. William Zahner) Architectural Metals: a guide to selection, specification and performance, 1995; Individual Imagination and Cultural Conservatism, 1995.

GEIDT, Rt Hon. Christopher, CVO 2007; OBE 1997; PC 2007; Private Secretary to The Queen and Keeper of The Queen's Archives, since 2007; *b* 1961; *s* of Mervyn Bernard Geidt and Diana Cecil, *d* of Alexander John MacKenzie, OBE, DSC (and 2 bars); *m* Emma, *d* of Baron Neill of Bladen, *qv*; two *d*. *Educ:* Dragon Sch., Oxford; Trinity Coll., Glenalmond; King's Coll. London; Trinity Hall, Cambridge. RMA Sandhurst (invalided), 1982–83; small business, 1983–86; RUSI, 1987–90; Army (commnd Intelligence Corps), 1990–94; Foreign and Commonwealth Office: Political Liaison Officer, EC Monitor Mission, Sarajevo, 1994–95; Political Advr, Internat. Conf. on former Yugoslavia, Geneva, 1995–96; Political Advr, later Sen. Advr, Office of High Rep., Sarajevo and Brussels, 1996–99; Private Sec. to UN Sec.-Gen.'s Special Envoy for the Balkans, Geneva, 1999–2001; Magdalen Coll., Oxford, 2001–02; Asst Private Sec. to The Queen, 2002–05, Dep. Private Sec., 2005–07. *Address:* Buckingham Palace, SW1A 1AA.

GEIM, Prof. Andre Konstantin, PhD; FRS 2007; Professor of Physics, since 2001, Langworthy Professor of Physics, since 2008, and Director, Manchester Centre for Mesoscience and Nanotechnology, since 2003, Manchester University; *b* 21 Oct. 1958. *Educ:* Moscow Phys-Tech. Univ. (MSc 1982); Inst. of Solid State Physics, Moscow (PhD Physics 1987). Research Scientist: Russian Acad., 1987–90; Univs of Copenhagen, Bath, and Nottingham, 1990–94; Associate Prof., Nijmegen Univ., Netherlands, 1994–2000. Ig Nobel Prize for levitation, 2000; Mott Medal and Prize for discovery of graphene, Inst. Physics, 2007. *Publications:* contrib. Science, Nature and other jls. *Recreation:* hiking in high mountains.

GELDER, Prof. Michael Graham; W. A. Handley Professor of Psychiatry, University of Oxford, 1969–96, now Emeritus Professor; Fellow of Merton College, Oxford, 1969–96, now Emeritus Fellow (Subwarden, 1992–94); *b* 2 July 1929; *s* of Philip Graham Gelder and Margaret Gelder (*née* Graham); *m* 1954, Margaret (*née* Anderson); one *s* two *d*. *Educ:* Bradford Grammar Sch.; Queen's Coll., Oxford. Scholar, Theodore Williams Prize 1949 and first class Hons, Physiology finals, 1950; MA, DM Oxon, FRCP, FRCPsych; DPM London (with distinction) 1961. Goldsmit Schol., UCH London, 1951. House Physician, Sen. House Physician, UCH, 1955–57; Registrar, Maudsley Hosp., 1958–61; MRC Fellow in Clinical Research, 1962–63; Sen. Lectr, Inst. of Psychiatry, 1965–67 (Vice-Dean, 1967–68); Physician, Bethlem Royal and Maudsley Hosps, 1967–68. Hon. Consultant Psychiatrist, Oxford RHA, later DHA, 1969–96; Mem., Oxford DHA, 1985–92; Dir, Oxford Mental Health Care NHS Trust, 1993–97. Dir, WHO Collaborating Centre, 1994–96. Mem., MRC, 1978–79 (Chm., 1978–79, Mem., 1975–78 and 1987–90, Neurosciences Bd). Chm., Wellcome Trust Neuroscience Panel, 1990–95 (Mem., 1984–88). Chairman: Assoc. of Univ. Teachers of Psychiatry, 1979–82; Jt Cttee on Higher Psychiatric Trng, 1981–85. Europ. Vice-Pres., Soc. for Psychotherapy Research, 1977–82. Advisor, WHO, 1992–2001. Mem., Assoc. of Physicians, 1983–2007. Mem. Council, RCPsych, 1981–90 (Vice Pres. 1982–83; Sen. Vice-Pres., 1983–84; Chm. Res. Cttee, 1986–91). Founder FMedSci 1998. Mayne Guest Prof., Univ. of Queensland, 1990. Lectures: Malcolm Millar, Univ. of Aberdeen, 1984; Yap Meml, Hong Kong, 1987; Guze, Univ. of Washington, 1993; Curran, St George's Hosp. Med. Sch., 1996; Sargant, RCPsych, 1996. Gold Medal, Royal Medico-Psychol Assoc., 1962. *Publications:* (jtly) Agoraphobia: nature and treatment, 1981; (jtly) The Oxford Textbook of Psychiatry, 1983 (Russian edn 1997), 5th edn as Shorter Oxford Textbook of Psychiatry, 2006 (Chinese and French edns 2005); (jtly) Concise Oxford Textbook of Psychiatry, 1994; Psychiatry: an Oxford core text, 1999 (Portuguese edn 2002, Japanese edn 2007), 3rd edn 2005; (ed jtly) New Oxford Textbook of Psychiatry, 2 vols, 2000 (Spanish edn 2003); chapters in books and articles in medical jls. *Recreations:* photography, gardening, travel. *Address:* Merton College, Oxford OX1 4JD.

GELDOF, Bob, Hon. KBE 1986; singer; songwriter; initiator and organiser, Band Aid, Live Aid, Live 8 and Sport Aid fund-raising events; *b* Dublin, 5 Oct. 1951; *m* 1986, Paula Yates (marr. diss. 1996; she *d* 2000); three *d*. *Educ:* Black Rock Coll. Sometime journalist: Georgia Straight, Vancouver; New Musical Express; Melody Maker. Jt Founder, Boomtown Rats, rock band, 1975; *albums:* Boomtown Rats: Boomtown Rats, 1977; A Tonic for the Troups, 1978; The Fine Art of Surfacing, 1979; Mondo Bongo, 1980; V Deep, 1982; In the Long Grass, 1984; Loudmouth, 1994; solo: Deep in the Heart of Nowhere, 1986; The Vegetarians of Love, 1990; The Happy Club, 1992; Sex, Age and Death, 2001. Acted in films: Pink Floyd—The Wall, 1982; Number One, 1985. Organised Band Aid, 1984, to record Do They Know It's Christmas, sales from which raised £8 million for famine relief in Ethiopia; organised simultaneous Live Aid concerts in London and Philadelphia to raise £50 million, 1985; organised Sport Aid to raise further £18 million, 1986. Chm., Band Aid Trust, 1985–; Founder, Live Aid Foundn, USA, 1985–. Freeman: Borough of Swale, 1985; Newcastle. Hon. MA Kent, 1985; Hon. DSc(Econ) London, 1987; Hon. DPh Ghent. TV film: The Price of Progress, 1987. Awards include: UN World Hunger Award, FAO Medal; EEC Gold Medal; Irish Peace Prize; music awards include: Ivor Novello (four times); Brit Award for Outstanding Contribution to Music, 2005; several gold and platinum discs. Order of Two Niles (Sudan); Cavalier, Order of Leopold II (Belgium). *Publications:* Is That It? (autobiog.), 1986; Geldof in Africa, 2005.

GELL-MANN, Murray; Professor and Distinguished Fellow, Santa Fe Institute, since 1993; Robert Andrews Millikan Professor of Theoretical Physics at the California Institute of Technology, 1967–93, now Emeritus; *b* 15 Sept. 1929; *s* of Arthur and Pauline Gell-Mann; *m* 1st, 1955, J. Margaret Dow (*d* 1981); one *s* one *d*; 2nd, 1992, Marcia Southwick (marr. diss. 2005); one step *s*. *Educ:* Yale Univ.; Massachusetts Inst. of Technology. Mem., Inst. for Advanced Study, Princeton, 1951; Instructor, Asst Prof., and Assoc. Prof., Univ. of Chicago, 1952–55; Assoc. Prof. 1955–56, Prof. 1956–66, California Inst. of Technology. Vis. Prof., Collège de France and Univ. of Paris, 1959–60. Overseas Fellow, Churchill Coll., Cambridge, 1966. Member: President's Science Adv. Cttee, 1969–72; President's Council of Advrs on Sci. and Technol., 1994–2001. Regent, Smithsonian Instn, 1974–88; Chm. of Bd, Aspen Center for Physics, 1973–79; Dir, J. D. and C. T. MacArthur Foundn, 1979–2002; Vice-Pres. and Chm. of Western Center, Amer. Acad. of Arts and Sciences, 1970–76; Member: Nat. Acad. of Sciences, 1960–; Sci. and Grants Cttee, Leakey Foundn, 1977–90; Sci. Adv. Cttee, Conservation Internat., 1993–. Santa Fe Institute: Founding Trustee, 1982–; Chm., Bd of Trustees, 1982–85; Co-Chm., Sci. Bd, 1985–2000. Member Board: California Nature Conservancy, 1984–93; Wildlife Conservation Soc., 1993–. Foreign Mem., Royal Society, 1978. Hon. ScD: Yale, 1959; Chicago, 1967; Illinois, 1968; Wesleyan, 1968; Utah, 1970; Columbia, 1977; Southern Illinois, 1993; (Nat. Resources), Florida, 1994; Southern Methodist, 1999; Hon. DSc: Cantab, 1980; Oxon, 1992; Hon. Dr, Turin, 1969. Listed on UN Envmtl Program Roll of Honor for Envmtl Achievement (Global 500), 1988. Dannie Heineman Prize (Amer. Phys. Soc.), 1959; Ernest O. Lawrence Award, 1966; Franklin Medal (Franklin Inst., Philadelphia), 1967; John J. Carty Medal (Nat. Acad. Scis), 1968; Research Corp. Award, 1969; Nobel Prize in Physics, 1969; Erice Science for Peace Prize, 1990; Procter Prize for Scientific Achievement, Sigma Xi, 2004; Albert Einstein Medal, Einstein Soc., 2005. *Publications:* (with Yuval Ne'eman) The Eightfold Way, 1964; The Quark and the Jaguar, 1994; various articles in learned jls on topics referring to classification and description of elementary particles of physics and their interactions. *Recreations:* walking in wild country, study of natural history, languages. *Address:* Santa Fe Institute, 1399 Hyde Park Road, Santa Fe, NM 87501, USA. *T:* (505) 9848800; *e-mail:* mgm@santafe.edu. *Clubs:* Cosmos (Washington) Explorers', Century (New York); Athenæum (Pasadena).

GELLING, Donald James, CBE 2002; Member of the Legislative Council, Isle of Man, 2002–07; Chief Minister, Isle of Man, 1996–2001 and 2004–06; *b* 5 July 1938; *s* of John Cyril Gelling and Gladys Gelling (*née* Maddrell); *m* 1960, Joan Frances Kelly; three *s* one *d*. *Educ:* Santon Primary Sch.; Murrays Road Junior; Douglas High Sch. for Boys. Comr, Santon Parish, 1961–86. MHK, 1986–2002; Minister: of Agriculture and Fisheries, 1987–89; of the Treasury, 1989–1996. Mem., British-Irish Council, 2004–. Captain of the Parish, Santan, 2004–. Mem., Rushen and Western Mann Past Rotarians Club. *Recreations:* golf, travel, DIY. *Address:* Grenaugh Beg, Santon, Isle of Man IM4 1HF. *T:* (01624) 823482, *Fax:* (01624) 827178. *Club:* Castletown Golf.

GELLING, Margaret Joy, OBE 1995; PhD; FBA 1998; FSA; President, English Place-Name Society, 1986–98; *b* 29 Nov. 1924; *d* of Lucy and William Albert Midgley; *m* 1952, Peter Stanley Gelling (*d* 1983). *Educ:* Chislehurst Grammar Sch.; St Hilda's Coll., Oxford (BA 1945; MA 1951; Hon. Fellow, 1993); University Coll. London (PhD 1957). FSA 1986. Temp. Civil Servant, 1945–46; Res. Asst, English Place-Name Soc., 1946–53. Hon. Reader, Univ. of Birmingham, 1981–. Vice-Pres., Internat. Council for Onomastic Scis, 1993–99. Hon. DLitt: Nottingham, 2002; Leicester, 2003. *Publications:* English Place-Name Society volumes: Oxfordshire, part 1, 1953, part 2, 1954; Berkshire, part 1, 1973, part 2, 1974, part 3, 1976; Shropshire, part 1, 1990, part 2, 1995, part 3, 2001, part 4, 2004, part 5, 2006; (jtly) The Names of Towns and Cities in Britain, 1970; Signposts to the Past, 1978, 3rd edn 1997; The Early Charters of the Thames Valley, 1979; Place-Names in the Landscape, 1984; The West Midlands in the Early Middle Ages, 1992; (jtly) The Landscape of Place-Names, 2000; papers in Medieval Archaeology, Anglo-Saxon England, etc. *Recreation:* gardening. *Address:* 31 Pereira Road, Harborne, Birmingham B17 9JG. *T:* (0121) 427 6469.

GEM, Dr Richard David Harvey, OBE 2002; FSA; Secretary, Cathedrals Fabric Commission for England, 1991–2002; *b* 10 Jan. 1945. *Educ:* Eastbourne Coll.; Peterhouse, Cambridge (MA, PhD). Inspector of Ancient Monuments, DoE, 1970–80; Res. Officer, Council for Care of Churches, 1981–88; Dep. Sec., then Sec., Cathedrals Adv. Commn for England, 1988–91. Mem., RCHM, 1987–99. President: British Archaeol Assoc., 1983–89; Soc. for Church Archaeol., 2006–; Bucks Archaeol Soc., 2008–. *Publications:* numerous papers on early medieval architecture in British and foreign learned jls. *Recreations:* gardening, theatre, music, foreign travel, philosophy and theology. *Address:* The Bothy, Mentmore, Leighton Buzzard, Beds LU7 0QG.

GEMMELL, Campbell; *see* Gemmell, J. C.

GEMMELL, Gavin John Norman, CBE 1998; CA; Chairman, Archangels, since 2008; *b* 7 Sept. 1941; *s* of late Gilbert A. S. Gemmell and of Dorothy M. Gemmell; *m* 1967, Kathleen Fiona Drysdale; one *s* two *d*. *Educ:* George Watson's Coll., Edinburgh. CA 1964. Baillie Gifford & Co., 1964–2002: investment trainee, 1964–67; Partner, 1967; Partner, Pension Funds, 1973–89; Sen. Partner, 1998–2001. Chairman: Scottish Widows, 2002–07 (Dep. Chm., 1995–2002); Gyne Ideas, 2006–; Mpathy Medical Devices, 2007–; non-executive Director: Scottish Enterprise Edinburgh and Lothian, 1995–2003; Scottish Financial Enterprise, 1998–2002; Archangel Informal Investments, 2001–; Lloyds TSB Gp, 2002–07. Trustee, Nat. Galls of Scotland, 1999–2007. Chm., Standing Cttee, Scottish Episcopal Ch, 1997–2002. Chm. Ct, Heriot-Watt Univ., 2002–08. *Recreations:* golf, foreign travel. *Address:* 14 Midmar Gardens, Edinburgh EH10 6DZ. *T:* (0131) 466 6367; *e-mail:* gavingemmell@blueyonder.co.uk. *Clubs:* Hon. Co. of Edinburgh Golfers (Muirfield); Gullane Golf.

GEMMELL, Dr (James) Campbell; Chief Executive, Scottish Environment Protection Agency, since 2003; *b* 24 Jan. 1959; *s* of late James Stewart Gemmell and Agnes Campbell Little; *m* 1992, Avril Gold. *Educ:* High Sch. of Stirling; Univ. of Aberdeen (BSc 1st cl. Hons; PhD 1985); MA Oxon 1985. Res. Lectr in Glaciol., Christ Church, Oxford, 1985–89; Exec., Scottish Develt Agency, Glasgow, 1988–90; Sen. Consultant, Ecotec

Res. and Consulting Ltd, 1990–91; Policy Manager, then Strategist, Scottish Enterprise, 1991–94; Chief Exec., Central Scotland Countryside Trust, 1994–2001; Dir, Strategic Planning, SEPA, 2001–03. Chm., Dounreay Particles Adv. Gp, 2001–03. Mem., Minister's Rural Focus Gp, Scottish Office, 1992–96. Chm., Landwise, and Mem. Gp Bd, Wise, 1999–2001. Hon. Prof., Faculties of Phys. and Mathematical Scis, Univ. of Glasgow, 2007–. *Publications:* earth science papers in glaciol. and glacial geomorphology (winner, Wiley Earth Sci. Paper, 1991). *Recreations:* walks with our Collie, eating fine seafood and drinking fine wines, combined, if possible, with visits to California and New Zealand; passionate about Norway and Belgian beers, writing. *Address:* *e-mail:* jcgemmell@aol.com, campbell.gemmell@sepa.org.uk.

GEMMELL, Roderick, OBE 2002; HM Diplomatic Service, retired; *b* 19 Aug. 1950; *s* of Matthew and Ethel Gemmell; *m* 1975, Janet Bruce Mitchell; one *d.* *Educ:* Craigbank Secondary Sch., Glasgow. PO Savings Bank, 1966; joined FCO, 1967; Bahrain, 1971–72; Washington, 1972–74; The Hague, 1975–79; FCO, 1979–82; Mbabane, 1982–84; Stockholm, 1984–87; Second Sec. (Commercial/Econ), Ankara, 1987–91; Second Sec., FCO, 1991–94; First Sec. (Mgt), Kampala, 1994–97; First Sec. (Consular/Immigration), then Dir of Entry Clearance, Lagos, 1998–2002; High Comr, Bahamas, 2003–05. *Recreations:* travel, reading, golf. *Address:* *e-mail:* gemmellrj@ntlworld.com. *Club:* Rutherglen Bowling.

GEMS, Iris Pamela, (Pam); playwright; *b* 1 Aug. 1925; *d* of late James Price and Elsie Mabel Price; *m* 1949, Keith Leopold Gems; two *s* two *d.* *Educ:* Brockenhurst Grammar Sch.; Manchester Univ. *Plays* include: Dusa, Fish, Stas and Vi, 1976; Queen Christina, 1977; Piaf, 1978, revival, 2008; Franz into April, 1978; The Treat, 1979; Pasionaria, 1981; Aunt Mary, 1982; Camille, 1985; The Danton Affair, 1986; The Blue Angel, 1991; Deborah's Daughter, 1994; I Wish You Love, 1995; Stanley, 1995 (Evening Standard Award, Best Play; Olivier award for best play, 1997); Marlene, 1997; The Snow Palace, 1998; Natalya Ivanovna, 1998; Nelson, 2005; Mrs Pat, 2006; plays performed RSC, RNT, Hampstead, West End and Broadway; (adapted): Yerma, Royal Exchange, Manchester, 2003; The Lady from the Sea, Almeida, 2003; The Little Mermaid, Greenwich, 2004; The Cherry Orchard, Crucible, Sheffield, 2007. *Publications:* (novels) Mrs Frampton, 1986; Bon Voyage, Mrs Frampton, 1988. *Recreation:* working. *Address:* c/o Rose Cobbe, United Agents, 12–26 Lexington Street, W1F 0LE.

GENGE, Rt Rev. Kenneth Lyle; Bishop of Edmonton (Alberta), 1988–96; Chaplain, St George's College, Jerusalem, 1996; *b* 25 Oct. 1933; *s* of Nelson Simms Genge and Grace Winifred Genge; *m* 1959, Ruth Louise Bate; two *s* one *d.* *Educ:* Univ. of Saskatchewan (BA 1958); Emmanuel Coll., Saskatoon (LTh 1957; BD 1959). Parish priest, 1959–85; Conference Retreat Centre Director, 1985–88. Hon. DD Emmanuel Coll. and St Chad, 1989. *Recreations:* sports, physical fitness, music.

GENGE, Rt Rev. Mark; Bishop of Central Newfoundland, 1976–90; Pastoral Associate, St John's, Yorkmills, Ontario, 1990–92; *b* 18 March 1927; *s* of Lambert and Lily Genge; *m* 1959, Maxine Clara (*née* Major); five *d.* *Educ:* Queen's Coll. and Memorial Univ., Newfoundland; Univ. of Durham (MA); BD Gen. Synod of Canada. Deacon, Corner Brook, Newfoundland, 1951; priest, Stephenville, 1952; Durham, 1953–55; Vice-Principal, Queen's Coll., St John's, Newfoundland, 1955–57; Curate, St Mary's Church, St John's, 1957–59; Rector: Foxtrap, 1959–64; Mary's Harbour, 1964–65; Burgeo, 1965–69; Curate, Marbleton, PQ, 1969–71; Rector, South River, Port-de-Grave, 1971–73; District Sec., Canadian Bible Soc., 1973–76. Chaplain, Queen's Coll., Newfoundland, 1993–98. *Recreations:* badminton, swimming, rollerblading. *Address:* 6 Maypark Place, St John's, Newfoundland A1B 2E3, Canada.

GENN, Dame Hazel (Gillian), DBE 2006 (CBE 2000); LLD; FBA 2000; Professor of Socio-Legal Studies, University College London, since 1994; *b* 17 March 1949; *d* of Lionel Isaac Genn and Dorothy Rebecca Genn; *m* 1973, Daniel David Appleby; one *s* one *d.* *Educ:* Univ. of Hull (BA Hons 1971); CNAA (LLB 1985); Univ. of London (LLD 1992). Res. Asst, Cambridge Inst. of Criminology, 1972–74; Sen. Res. Officer, Oxford Univ. Centre for Socio-Legal Studies, 1974–85; Lectr, 1985–88, Reader, 1988–91, Prof. and Head of Law Dept, 1991–94, Queen Mary and Westfield Coll., London Univ. Member: Cttee on Standards in Public Life, 2003–07; Judicial Appts Commn, 2006–. Hon. QC 2006. *Publications:* Surveying Victims, 1978; Hard Bargaining, 1987; Personal Injury Compensation: how much is enough?, 1994; Mediation in Action, 1999; Paths to Justice, 1999; Paths to Justice Scotland, 2001; Tribunals for Diverse Users, 2006. *Recreations:* music, walking, spending time with my family. *Address:* Faculty of Laws, University College London, Bentham House, Endsleigh Gardens, WC1H 0EG. *T:* (020) 7679 1436.

GENSCHER, Hans-Dietrich; lawyer, with Büsing, Müffelmann & Theye, Berlin, since 1999; Managing Partner, Hans-Dietrich Genscher Consult GmbH, since 2000; Federal Minister for Foreign Affairs and Deputy Chancellor, Federal Republic of Germany, 1974–92 (in government of Helmut Schmidt, to Oct. 1982, then in government of Helmut Kohl);; *b* Reideburg/Saalkreis, 21 March 1927; *m* Barbara; one *d.* *Educ:* Higher Sch. Certif. (Abitur); studied law and economics in Halle/Saale and Leipzig Univs, 1946–49. Served War, 1943–45. Mem., state-level org. of LDP, 1946. Re-settled in W Germany, 1952: practical legal training in Bremen and Mem. Free Democratic Party (FDP); FDP Asst in Parly Group, 1956; Gen. Sec.: FDP Parly Group, 1959–65; FDP at nat. level, 1962–64. Mem., Bundestag, 1965–98. A Parly Sec., FDP Parly Group, 1965–69; Hon. Chm., FDP, 1992 (Dep. Chm., 1968–74; Chm., 1974–85); Federal Minister of the Interior, Oct. 1969 (Brandt-Scheel Cabinet); re-apptd Federal Minister of the Interior, Dec. 1972. He was instrumental in maintaining pure air and water; gave a modern structure to the Federal Police Authority; Federal Border Guard Act passed; revised weapons laws, etc; in promoting relations between West and East, prominent role in CSCE, Helsinki, 1975, Madrid, 1980–83, Stockholm, 1984–86 and in setting up conferences on Conventional Armed Forces, Confidence and Security Building Measures, Vienna, 1989; an initiator of reform process that led to the inclusion of the Single European Act 1986. Co-initiator: 'Eureka' initiative; independence process in Namibia. Promotes co-operation between EC and other regional gps, ASEAN, Central Amer. States, (San José Conferences), Golf Co-operation Council. Chm., Bd of Trustees, Franckesche Stiftungen, Halle, 1992–94. Chm., Assoc. of Friends and Patrons, State Opera, Berlin. Hon. Prof., Free Univ., Berlin, 1994. Hon. Dr: Madras, 1977; Salamanca, Athens, Seoul, Budapest, 1988; Georgetown, Washington, Heidelberg, Maryland, 1990; Columbia, S Carolina, Ottawa, 1991; Kattowitz, 1992; Essex, Moscow, Warsaw, Medford, Massachusetts, Durham, 1993; Tiflis, 1998; Szczecin, 2002; Hon. Master, German Handicrafts 1975. Hon. citizen Costa Rica, 1987. Grand Fed. Cross of Merit 1973, 1975 with star and sash; Wolfgang-Döring Medal 1976; numerous foreign decorations. *Publications:* Umweltschutz: Das Umweltschutzprogramm der Bundesregierung, 1972; Bundestagsreden, 1972; Aussenpolitik im Dienste von Sicherheit und Freiheit, 1975; Deutsche Aussenpolitik, 1977, 3rd edn 1985; Bundestagsreden und Zeitdokumente, 1979; Zukunftsverantwortung, 1990; Erinnerungen, 1995. *Recreations:* reading, walking, swimming. *Address:* PO Box 200655, 53136 Bonn, Germany.

GENT, Sir Christopher (Charles), Kt 2001; Chairman, GlaxoSmithKline, since 2005; Senior Adviser, Bain & Co. Inc.; *b* 10 May 1948; *s* of late Charles Arthur Gent and of Kathleen Dorothy Gent; *m* 1st, Lynda Marion Tobin (marr. diss. 1999); two *d*; 2nd, 1999, Kate Elisabeth Lock; two *s.* *Educ:* Archbishop Tennison Grammar Sch. With Nat West Bank, 1967–71; Schroder Computer Services, 1971–79; Man. Dir, Baric Computing Services, 1979–84; Dir, Network Services Div., ICL, 1983–84; Man. Dir, Vodafone, 1985–97; Dir, Racal Telecom plc, 1988–91; Dir, 1991–97, Chief Exec., 1997–2003, Vodafone Gp plc; Chm., Supervisory Bd, Vodafone AG. Mem. Bd Reps, Verizon Wireless Partnership; non-executive Director: China Mobile (Hong Kong) Ltd; Lehman Brothers Holdings Inc., 2003–08; Ferrari SpA. Vice-Pres., Council, Computer Services Assoc., 1984. Mem., Adv. Bd, Reform (Chm., 2003). Nat. Chm., Young Conservatives, 1977–79. *Recreations:* family, cricket, politics, horseracing. *Clubs:* Carlton, MCC; Goodwood (Sussex); Royal Ascot Racing; Lord's Taverners.

GENT, (John) David (Wright), FIMI; Director General, Retail Motor Industry Federation, 1985–95; *b* 25 April 1935; *s* of late Reginald Philip Gent and Stella Eva Parker; *m* 1970, Anne Elaine Hanson. *Educ:* Lancing Coll. Admitted a Solicitor, 1959. Joined Soc. of Motor Manufacturers as Legal Advr, 1961; Asst Sec., 1964; Sec., 1965; Dep. Dir, 1971–80; joined Lucas Industries as Gen. Man., Lucas Service UK, 1981; Gp PR Man., 1982–83; Dir, British Road Fedn, 1983–84. Director: DC Cook Hldgs, 1995–2001; Autofil Properties Ltd, 2002–05. Member: Road Transport ITB, 1985–91; Vehicle Security Installation Bd, 1994–95. FRSA 1995. Freeman, City of London, 1985; Liveryman, Coach Makers and Coach Harness Makers' Co., 1985. *Recreations:* golf, gardening. *Address:* 44 Ursula Street, SW11 3DW. *T:* (020) 7228 8126.

GENTLEMAN, David (William), RDI 1970; artist and designer; *b* 11 March 1930; *s* of late Tom and Winifred Gentleman; *m* 1st, 1953, Rosalind Dease (marr. diss. 1966; she *d* 1997); one *d*; 2nd, 1968, Susan, *d* of late George Ewart Evans; two *d* one *s.* *Educ:* Hertford Grammar Sch.; St Albans Sch. of Art; Royal College of Art. Work includes: painting in watercolour, illustration, graphic design, lithography and wood engraving; commissions include Eleanor Cross mural designs for Charing Cross underground station, 1979; illustrations for many publishers; postage stamps for the Royal Mail, including, 1962–: Shakespeare, Churchill, Darwin, Ely Cathedral, Abbotsbury Swans, Millennium, etc; coins for Royal Mint: Entente Cordiale, 2004; Slave Trade Abolition, 2007; posters for London Transport, National Trust, and Stop the War Coalition; symbols for British Steel, Bodleian Library, etc. Solo exhibitions: at Mercury Gallery: watercolours of: India, 1970; S Carolina, 1973; Kenya and Zanzibar, 1976; Pacific, 1981; Britain, 1982; London, 1985; British coastline, 1988; Paris, 1991; India, 1994; Italy, 1997; City of London, 2000; watercolours and designs, RCA, 2002; watercolours, Fine Art Soc., 2004 (retrospective), 2007. Editions of lithographs of architecture and landscape, 1967–2005. Work in public collections incl. Tate Gall., V&A, BM, Fitzwilliam Mus., and Nat. Maritime Mus., and also in private collections. Member: Nat. Trust Properties Cttee, 1985–2005; Alliance Graphique Internat.; Council, Artists' Gen. Benevolent Instn. Master of Faculty, RDI, 1989–91. Hon. Fellow, RCA, 1981; Hon. FRIBA 1996. *Publications:* author and illustrator: Design in Miniature, 1972; David Gentleman's Britain, 1982; David Gentleman's London, 1985; A Special Relationship, 1987; David Gentleman's Coastline, 1988; David Gentleman's Paris, 1991; David Gentleman's India, 1994; David Gentleman's Italy, 1997; The Wood Engravings of David Gentleman, 2000; Artwork, 2002; *for children:* Fenella in Greece, 1967; Fenella in Spain, 1967; Fenella in Ireland, 1967; Fenella in the South of France, 1967; *illustrator:* Plats du Jour, 1957; Bridges on the Backs, 1961; Swiss Family Robinson, 1963 (USA); The Shepherd's Calendar, 1964; Poems of John Keats, 1966 (USA); The Pattern Under the Plough, 1966; covers for New Penguin Shakespeare, 1968–78; The Jungle Book, 1968 (USA); Robin Hood, 1977 (USA); The Dancing Tigers, 1979; Westminster Abbey, 1987; The Illustrated Poems of John Betjeman, 1995; Inwards where all the battle is, 1997; The Key Keeper, 2001; *illustrator and editor:* The Crooked Scythe, 1993. *Address:* 25 Gloucester Crescent, NW1 7DL. *T:* (020) 7485 8824; *e-mail:* d@gentleman.demon.co.uk.

GEOGHEGAN, Hugh; Hon. Mr Justice Geoghegan; a Judge of the Supreme Court of Ireland, since 2000; *b* 16 May 1938; *s* of late Hon. James Geoghegan (a Judge of the Supreme Court of Ireland, 1936–50) and Eileen Geoghegan (*née* Murphy); *m* 1981, Mary Finlay Geoghegan, Judge of High Court of Ireland, *d* of Thomas Aloysius Finlay, *qv*; one *s* two *d.* *Educ:* Clongowes Wood Coll.; University Coll., Dublin (BCL, LLB). Called to the Bar: King's Inns, 1962 (Bencher, 1992); Middle Temple, 1975 (Bencher, 2006); Northern Ireland, 1989; SC 1977; Judge of High Court, Dublin, 1992–2000. Arbitrator of Public Service staff claims, 1984–92. Former Mem., Bar Council. Mem. Council, Royal Victoria Eye and Ear Hosp., Dublin. Mem. Council, Irish Legal Hist. Soc. Gov., Clongowes Wood Coll., 1995–2002. *Recreations:* history, genealogy, music. *Address:* The Supreme Court, Four Courts, Dublin 7, Ireland. *Clubs:* Kildare Street and University, Royal Dublin Society, Fitzwilliam Lawn Tennis (Dublin).

GEOGHEGAN, Michael Francis, CBE 2003; Group Chief Executive, HSBC Holdings plc, since 2006 (an Executive Director, since 2004); *b* 4 Oct. 1953; *m*; two *s.* Joined HSBC Gp, 1973; Gen. Manager, Brazil, 1997–2000; Hd, S America, 2000; Pres., HSBC Investment Bank Brazil, 2000–03; Chief Exec., HSBC Bank plc, 2004–06. Chm., Young Enterprise UK, 2004–. *Address:* HSBC Holdings plc, 8 Canada Square, E14 5HQ.

GEORGALA, Prof. Douglas Lindley, CBE 1986; PhD; FIFST; Director of Food Research, Agricultural and Food Research Council, 1988–94; External Professor, University of Leeds, since 1993; independent scientific consultant, 1994–2002; *b* 2 Feb. 1934; *s* of late John Michael Georgala and of Izetta Iris Georgala; *m* 1959, Eulalia Catherina Lochner; one *s* one *d.* *Educ:* South African College Sch., Cape Town; Univ. of Stellenbosch (BScAgric); Univ. of Aberdeen (PhD). FIFST 1987. Research Officer, Fishing Research Inst., Univ. of Cape Town, 1957–60; Research Microbiologist, 1960–69, Division Manager, 1969–72, Head of Laboratory, 1977–86, Unilever Colworth Laboratory; Technical Member, Unilever Meat Products Co-ordination, 1973–77; Mem., Unilever Res. Div., 1987–88; Indust. Consultant, Biotechnology Unit, DTI, 1987–88. Chairman: Fisheries Res. Bd, 1980–84; Adv. Cttee of Food Science Dept, Leeds Univ., 1984–88; Scientific and Technical Cttee, Food and Drink Fedn, 1986–88; Adv. Cttee on Microbiological Safety of Food, 1996–2004 (Mem., 1991–; Acting Chm., 1994–95); Member: ACARD, 1980–83; Food Cttee, 1984–88, Strategy Bd, 1991–93, AFRC; Co-ordinating Cttee for Marine Science and Technol., 1988–89; Food Adv. Cttee, 1989–94; Council, Inst. of Food Science and Technology, 1992–94; Ownership Bd, Centre for Envmt, Fisheries and Agric. Sci., 1997–2001. Vis. Prof., UEA, Leeds and Reading Univs, 1988–94. Scientific Governor, British Nutrition Foundn, 1992–2002. Trustee, World Humanity Action Trust, 1999–2000. FRSA 1984. *Publications:* papers in jls of general microbiology, applied bacteriology, hygiene, etc. *Recreations:* gardening, recorded music.

GEORGE; *see* Lloyd George and Lloyd-George.

GEORGE; *see* Passmore, G.

GEORGE, family name of **Baron George**.

GEORGE, Baron *cr* 2004 (Life Peer), of St Tudy in the County of Cornwall; **Edward Alan John George,** GBE 2000; PC 1999; DL; Governor, Bank of England, 1993–2003; *b* 11 Sept. 1938; *s* of Alan George and Olive Elizabeth George; *m* 1962, Clarice Vanessa Williams; one *s* two *d. Educ:* Dulwich Coll.; Emmanuel Coll., Cambridge (BAEcon 2nd Cl. (i); MA). Joined Bank of England, 1962; worked initially on East European affairs; seconded to Bank for International Settlements, 1966–69, and to International Monetary Fund as Asst to Chairman of Deputies of Committee of Twenty on Internat. Monetary Reform, 1972–74; Adviser on internat. monetary questions, 1974–77; Dep. Chief Cashier, 1977–80; Asst Dir (Gilt Edged Div.), 1980–82; Exec. Dir, 1982–90; Dep. Gov., 1990–93. DL Cornwall, 2006. Hon. DSc: (Econ) Hull, 1993; City, 1995; Cranfield, 1997; UMIST, 1998; Buckingham, 2000; Hon. DLitt: Loughborough, 1994; Sheffield, 1999; Hon. DPhil London Guildhall, 1996; Hon. LLD: Exeter, 1997; Bristol, 1999; Herts, 1999; Cantab, 2000; DUniv London Metropolitan, 2002. *Recreations:* family, sailing, bridge.

GEORGE, Andrew Henry; MP (Lib Dem) St Ives, since 1997; *b* Mullion, Cornwall, 2 Dec. 1958; *s* of Reginald Hugh George and Diana May (*née* Petherick); *m* 1987, Jill Elizabeth, *d* of William and Margery Marshall; one *s* one *d. Educ:* Helston Grammar (subseq. Comprehensive) Sch.; Sussex Univ. (BA); University Coll., Oxford (MSc). Rural Officer, Notts Rural Community Council, 1981–85; Dep. Dir, Cornwall Rural Community Council, 1986–97. Contested (Lib Dem) St Ives, 1992. Lib Dem spokesman: on fisheries, 1997–2005; on disabilities, 2000–01; on rural affairs, 2002–05; on internat. develt, 2005–06; PPS to Leader of Lib Dem Party, 2001–02. *Publications:* The Natives are Revolting Down in the Cornwall Theme Park, 1986; (jtly) Cornwall at the Crossroads, 1989; A Vision of Cornwall (Cornwall Blind Assoc.), 1995; A view from the bottom left hand corner, 2002; housing and planning pubns and res. reports. *Recreations:* football, Rugby, cricket, gardening, cycling, walking, singing, poetry. *Address:* House of Commons, SW1A 0AA. *T:* (020) 7219 4588; Knights' Yard, Belgravia Street, Penzance, Cornwall TR18 2EL. *T:* (01736) 360020. *Clubs:* Commons Football, Commons and Lords Rugby, Commons and Lords Cricket; Penzance and Newlyn Rugby, Leedstown Cricket, Hayle Rugby (Vice-Pres.).

GEORGE, Andrew Neil; HM Diplomatic Service; Governor of Anguilla, since 2006; *b* 9 Oct. 1952; *s* of Walter George and late Madeleine George (*née* Lacey); *m* 1977, Watanalak Chaovieng; one *s* one *d. Educ:* Royal High Sch., Edinburgh; Univ. of Edinburgh (MA Politics and Modern History 1974). Entered HM Diplomatic Service, 1974; W Africa Dept, FCO, and Third Sec., Chad, 1974–75; SOAS, London Univ., 1975–76; Third, subseq. Second, Sec., Bangkok, 1976–80; S America Dept, 1980–81, W Africa Dept, 1981–82, Perm. Under-Sec.'s Dept, 1982–84, FCO; First Sec., Canberra, 1984–88; First Sec. and Head of Chancery, Bangkok, 1988–92; Republic of Ireland Dept, 1993–94, Eastern Dept, 1994–95, Non-Proliferation Dept, 1995–98, FCO; Ambassador to Paraguay, 1998–2001; Counsellor (Commercial Develt), Jakarta, 2002; Asst Dir, Medical and Welfare, HR Directorate, FCO, 2003–06. *Recreations:* reading, golf, watching football. *Address:* c/o Foreign and Commonwealth Office, King Charles Street, SW1A 2AH.

GEORGE, Prof. Andrew Robert, PhD; FBA 2006; Professor of Babylonian, School of Oriental and African Studies, University of London, since 2000; *b* 3 July 1955; *s* of Eric and Frances George; *m* 1996, Junko Taniguchi; three *s. Educ:* Christ's Hosp., Horsham; Univ. of Birmingham (BA; PhD 1985). School of Oriental and African Studies, University of London: Lectr in Ancient Near Eastern Studies, 1985–94; Reader in Assyriology, 1994–2000. Hon. Res. Fellow, 1995–98, Hon. Lectr, 1998–2002, Hon. Prof., 2002–, Inst. of Archaeol., UCL. Vis. Prof., Univ. of Heidelberg, 2000. Mem., Inst. for Advanced Study, Princeton, 2004–05. Jt Ed., Iraq jl, 1994–. *Publications:* Babylonian Topographical Texts, 1992; House Most High: the temples of Ancient Mesopotamia, 1993, 2nd edn 2004; The Epic of Gilgamesh: a new translation, 1999, 3rd edn 2003; The Babylonian Gilgamesh Epic: introduction, critical edition and cuneiform texts, 2003, 2nd edn 2004. *Recreation:* trying to make time. *Address:* School of Oriental and African Studies, University of London, Russell Square, WC1H 0XG. *T:* (020) 7898 4335; *e-mail:* ag5@soas.ac.uk.

GEORGE, Sir Arthur (Thomas), AO 1987; Kt 1972; solicitor and company director; *b* 17 Jan. 1915; *s* of late Thomas George; *m* 1939, Renee (AM 1998), *d* of Anthony Freeleagus; one *d. Educ:* Sydney High Sch., NSW. Chm. and Man. Dir, George Investment Pty Ltd Group, 1943; Chm., Australia Solenoid Holdings Ltd, 1967. Chm., Assoc. for Classical Archæology, of Sydney Univ., 1966–2002. Chm., Australian Soccer Fedn., 1969–88; Comr, Australian Sports Commn, 1986–89; Member: Exec., FIFA, 1981–94; Organising Cttee, 1983 World Youth Championship. Founder, The Arthur T. George Foundation Ltd, 1972. Fellow, Confedn of Australian Sport, 1985; Hon. Fellow, Senate of Univ. of Sydney, 1985. Gold Order of Merit, FIFA, 1994. Coronation Medal; Silver Jubilee Medal, 1977; Centenary Medal, Australia, 2003. Grand Commander (Keeper of the Laws), Cross of St Marks, and Gold Cross of Mount Athos, Greek Orthodox Church; Order of Phoenix (Greece). *Recreations:* interested in sport, especially Association football, etc. *Address:* Unit 15, 51 William Street, Double Bay, NSW 2028, Australia.

GEORGE, Rt Hon. Bruce Thomas; PC 2001; MP (Lab) Walsall South, since Feb. 1974; *b* 1 June 1942; *m* 1992, Lisa Toelle. *Educ:* Mountain Ash Grammar Sch.; UCW Swansea (Hon. Fellow, 2001); Univ. of Warwick. BA Politics Wales 1964, MA Warwick 1968. Asst Lectr in Social Studies, Glamorgan Polytechnic, 1964–66; Lectr in Politics, Manchester Polytechnic, 1968–70; Senior Lectr, Birmingham Polytechnic, 1970–74. Vis. Lectr, Univ. of Essex, 1985–86. Member: Select Cttee on Violence in the Family; Select Cttee on Defence, 1979– (Chm., 1997–2005); Chm., All Party Parly Maritime Gp. Mem., North Atlantic Assembly, 1981– (Chm., Mediterranean Special Gp). OSCE Parliamentary Assembly: Mem., 1992–; Gen. Rapporteur, 1992–95; Chm., 1996–99; Vice Pres., 1999–2002; Pres., 2002–04; Pres. Emeritus, 2004–; Hd, Election Observation Missions, Office of Democratic Instns and Human Rights, OSCE. Member: RIIA; IISS; RUSI (Mem. Council). Hon. Advr, Royal British Legion, 1997. Co-founder, Sec., House of Commons FC. Fellow, Parliament and Industry Trust, 1977–78. Ed., Jane's NATO Handbook, 1988–91. *Publications:* numerous books and articles on defence and foreign affairs. *Recreations:* Association football, snooker, student of American Indians, eating Indian food. *Address:* 42 Wood End Road, Walsall, West Midlands WS5 3BG. *T:* (01922) 627898; House of Commons, SW1A 0AA.

GEORGE, Sir Charles (Frederick), Kt 1998; MD; FRCP, FFPM; Chairman, Board of Science and Education, British Medical Association, since 2005; Emeritus Professor of Clinical Pharmacology, University of Southampton, since 1999; *b* 3 April 1941; *s* of William and Evelyn George; *m* 1969, Rosemary Moore (marr. diss. 1973). *Educ:* Univ. of Birmingham Med. Sch. (BSc 1962; MB ChB 1965; MD 1974). MRCP 1968; FRCP 1978; FFPM 1989. Med. Registrar, United Birmingham Hosps, 1967–69; Hammersmith Hospital, London: Med. Registrar, 1969–71; Sen. Registrar, 1971–73; University of Southampton: Sen. Lectr, 1973–75; Prof. of Clinical Pharmacology, 1975–99; Dean, Faculty of Medicine, Health and Biol Scis, 1993–98; Med. Dir, BHF, 1999–2004. Non-exec. Chm., Fulcrum Pharma plc, 2000–08; non-exec. Dir, BMJ Publishing Gp, 2006–08. Pres., BMA, 2004–05. Founder FMedSci 1998. FRSA 1993; FESC 2000, Emeritus FESC 2005; Hon. FFPH 2004; Hon. FBPharmacolS 2006. Hon. DSc: Birmingham, 2003; Leicester, 2007; Hon. DM Southampton, 2004. *Publications:* Topics in Clinical Pharmacology, 1980; (ed) Presystemic Drug Metabolism, 1982; (ed) Clinical Pharmacology and Therapeutics, vol. 1, 1982; (ed) Drug Therapy in the Elderly, 1998. *Recreations:* music, walking, wind surfing. *Address:* 15 Westgate Street, Southampton SO1 2AY.

GEORGE, Charles Richard; QC 1992; a Recorder, since 1997; *b* 8 June 1945; *s* of Hugh Shaw George, CIE and Joan George (*née* Stokes); *m* 1976, Joyce Tehmina Barnard; two *d. Educ:* Bradfield Coll.; Magdalen Coll., Oxford (MA 1st Cl. Hons Modern History); Corpus Christi Coll., Cambridge. Asst Master, Eton Coll., 1967–72; called to the Bar, Inner Temple, 1974, Bencher, 2001; called to Irish Bar, King's Inns, Dublin, 1995; speciality, Parly, Envmtl and Admin. Law; an Asst Recorder, 1994–97. Chancellor, dioc of Southwark, 1996–; Mem., Legal Adv. Commn, Gen. Synod of C of E, 2003–. Mem. Council, St Stephen's House, Oxford, 1999–. *Publication:* The Stuarts: an age of experiment, 1973. *Recreations:* tennis, architecture, travel. *Address:* Ashgrove Farm, Ashgrove Road, Sevenoaks, Kent TN13 1SU. *T:* (01732) 451875; Francis Taylor Building, Inner Temple, EC4Y 7BY. *T:* (020) 7353 8415. *Clubs:* Athenæum, Garrick.

GEORGE, Prof. Donald William, AO 1979; Vice-Chancellor and Principal, University of Newcastle, New South Wales, 1975–86; *b* 22 Nov. 1926; *s* of late H. W. George, Sydney; *m* 1950, Lorna M. Davey, Parkes, NSW; one *s* one *d. Educ:* Univ. of Sydney (BSc, BE, PhD). FTSE, FIET, FIMechE, FIEAust, FAIP. Lectr, Elec. Engrg, NSW Univ. of Technology, 1949–53; Exper. Officer, UKAEA, Harwell, 1954–55; Res. Officer, Sen. Res. Officer, AAEC, Harwell and Lucas Heights, 1956–59; Sen. Lectr, Elec. Engrg, Univ. of Sydney, 1960–66; Associate Prof., Elec. Engrg, Univ. of Sydney, 1967–68; P. N. Russell Prof. of Mech. Engrg, Univ. of Sydney, 1969–74. Chairman: Australian-American Educational Foundn, 1977–84; Australian Atomic Energy Commn, 1976–83. Hon. Life Trustee, Asian Inst. of Technology, 1998 (Trustee, 1978–98). Hon. DEng Newcastle NSW, 1986; Hon. DTech Asian Inst. of Technol., Bangkok, 1999. *Publications:* numerous sci. papers and techn. reports. *Address:* Villa 932, Henry Kendall Village, Wyoming, NSW 2250, Australia. *T:* (2) 43255079.

GEORGE, Henry Ridyard, CBE 1979; Director of Petroleum Engineering, Department of Energy, 1973–81; retired; *b* 14 May 1921; *s* of Charles Herbert George and Mar Ridyard; *m* 1st, 1948, Irene May Myers (*d* 1981); one *s*; 2nd, 1985, Gwen (*née* Gooderham) (*d* 2004), *widow* of Prof. E. O'Farrell Walsh. *Educ:* George Dixon's Secondary Sch., Birmingham; Univ. of Birmingham (1st Cl. Hons degree, Oil Engrg and Refining and Petroleum Technol., 1941). Served War, REME/IEME, 1941–46 (2nd Lieut, later Captain). Pet. Engr with Royal Dutch/Shell Gp, 1947–68: service in USA, Holland, Brunei, Nigeria and Venezuela in a variety of positions, incl. Chief Pet. Engr in last countries; Dept of Energy, 1968–81. *Recreation:* gardening. *Address:* Flat 3, 269 Dyke Road, Hove, E Sussex BN3 6PB. *T:* (01273) 540297.

GEORGE, Hywel, CMG 1968; OBE 1963; Fellow, Churchill College, Cambridge, since 1971 (Bursar, 1972–90); *b* 10 May 1924; *s* of Rev. W. M. George and Catherine M George; *m* 1955, Edith Pirchl; three *d. Educ:* Llanelli Grammar. Sch.; UCW Aberystwyth; Pembroke Coll., Cambridge; SOAS, London. RAF, 1943–46. Cadet, Colonial Admin Service, N Borneo, 1949–52; District Officer, 1952–58; Secretariat, 1959–62; Resident, Sabah, Malaysia, 1963–66; Administrator, 1967–69, Governor, 1969–70, St Vincent; Administrator, British Virgin Is, 1971. Mem. Court and Council, Univ. of Wales, Bangor, 1999–2007. Panglima Darjah Kinabalu (with title of Datuk), Sabah, 1964; JMN, Malaysia, 1966. CStJ 1969. *Recreation:* walking. *Address:* 46 St Margaret's Road, Girton, Cambridge CB3 0LT. *T:* (01223) 563766; Tu Hwnt ir Afon, The Close, Llanfairfechan LL33 0AG. *T:* (01248) 681509.

GEORGE, Rt Rev. Ian Gordon Combe, AO 2001 (AM 1989); Archbishop of Adelaide and Metropolitan of South Australia, 1991–2004; *b* 12 Aug. 1934; *s* of late Gordon Frank George and Kathleen Mary George (*née* Combe); *m* 1964, Barbara Dorothy (*née* Peterson); one *d* (one *s* decd). *Educ:* St Peter's Coll., Adelaide; Univ. of Adelaide (LLB 1957); Gen. Theol Seminary, NY (MDiv 1964). Judges' Associate, Supreme Court of S Australia, 1955–57; barrister and solicitor, S Australia, 1957–61. Ordained deacon and priest, New York, 1964; Assistant Curate: St Thomas', Mamaroneck, NY, USA, 1964–65; St David's, Burnside, SA, 1966–67; Priest-in-charge, St Barbara's, Woomera, SA and Chaplain and Welfare Officer, Australian Regular Army, 1967–69; Sub-Warden and Chaplain, St George's Coll., 1969–73, Lectr in History, 1969–73, Univ. of W Australia; Dean of Brisbane, Qld, 1973–81; Senior Chaplain (Army), Qld, 1975–81; Lectr in Theol., Univ. of Queensland, 1975–81; Archdeacon of Canberra, 1981–89; Rector, St John's Church, Canberra, 1981–89; Lectr in Theol., St Mark's Coll., 1982–91; Asst Bp, Dio. of Canberra and Goulburn, 1989–91. Chairman: Christian World Service Commn, Nat. Council of Chs of Australia, 1994–2002; Anglican Communion Internat. Migrant and Refugee Network, 1998–; Minister for For. Affairs, Overseas Aid Adv. Council, 1996–2002; Mem., Adv. Council, Burmese Border Consortium, 2000–02. Art Critic, The News, Adelaide, 1965–67. Vice-Pres., Qld Fest. of the Arts, 1975–81. Trustee, Qld Art Gall., 1974–81. Founding Pres., Alcohol and Drug Problems Assoc. of Qld, 1975–81. Hon. DD Gen. Theol Seminary, NY, 1990. ChStJ 1992; ChLJ 1995 (Dep. Nat. Chaplain, 2002–07; Nat. Chaplain, 2007–). *Publications:* Meditations on the Life of Jesus, 1991; Making Worship Work, 1992; many articles in theol, church and aesthetics jls on art and religion. *Recreations:* gardening, reading, the Arts, wine, tennis. *Address:* 3/21 Park Terrace, Gilberton, SA 5081, Australia.

GEORGE, Prof. Kenneth Desmond; Professor of Economics, 1988–98, now Emeritus, and Pro Vice-Chancellor (formerly Vice-Principal), 1993–98, University of Wales Swansea (formerly University College of Swansea); *b* 11 Jan. 1937; *s* of Horace Avor George and Dorothy Margaret (*née* Hughes); *m* 1959, Elizabeth Vida (*née* Harries); two *s* one *d. Educ:* Ystalyfera Grammar Sch.; University Coll. of Wales, Aberystwyth (MA). Res. Asst, then Lectr in Econs, Univ. of Western Australia, 1959–63; Lectr in Econs, University Coll. of N Wales, Bangor, 1963–64; Univ. Asst Lectr, Univ. of Cambridge, 1964–66; Univ. Lectr, 1966–73; Fellow and Dir of Studies in Econs, Sidney Sussex Coll., Cambridge, 1965–73; Prof. and Head of Dept of Econs, 1973–88, and Dep. Principal, 1980–83, UC, Cardiff; Head of Dept of Economics, 1988–95 and Dean, Faculty of Econ. and Soc. Studies, 1992–93, UC Swansea. Vis. Prof., McMaster Univ., 1970–71. Part-time Mem., Monopolies and Mergers Commn, 1978–86; Member: Ind. panel on public appointments, Welsh Office, 1996–; Parly Boundary Commn for Wales, 1998–2006; Editor, Jl of Industrial Economics, 1970–83; Mem. Adv. Bd, Antitrust Law and Econ. Rev., 1988–92. *Publications:* Productivity in Distribution, 1966; Productivity and Capital Expenditure in Retailing, 1968; Industrial Organisation, 1971, 4th edn (with C. Joll and E. Lynk), 1992; (with T. S. Ward) The Structure of Industry in the EEC, 1975; (ed with C. Joll) Competition Policy in the UK and EEC, 1975; (with J. Shorey) The Allocation of Resources, 1978; (ed with L. Mainwaring) The Welsh Economy, 1988; articles in Econ. Jl, Oxford Econ. Papers, Aust. Econ. Papers, Jl Indust. Econs, Rev. of Econs and

Stats, Oxford Bull., Scottish Jl Polit. Econ., and British Jl Indust. Relations. *Recreations:* walking, music.

GEORGE, L(esley) Anne; *see* Glover, L. A.

GEORGE, Michael; freelance classical singer, bass-baritone; *b* 10 Aug. 1950; *s* of late John James George and Elizabeth (*née* Holmes, now Clayton); *m* 1972, Julie Elizabeth Kennard; one *s* two *d*. *Educ:* King's Coll. Choir Sch., Cambridge; Oakham Sch.; Royal Coll. of Music (ARCM Hons). Opera appearances with ENO, Buxton Opera and Scottish Opera incl. Fidelio, Semele and Orfeo, and St John Passion. Has performed in concerts worldwide and worked with leading conductors. Numerous recordings incl. Dream of Gerontius, The Creation, St Matthew Passion, Messiah, complete sacred works of Purcell. *Recreations:* golf, dog walking. *Address:* c/o Hazard Chase Ltd, 25 City Road, Cambridge CB1 1DP. *Club:* Royal Mid-Surrey Golf.

GEORGE, Patrick Herbert; artist; Emeritus Professor of Fine Art, University of London, since 1988; *b* 28 July 1923; *s* of A. H. George and N. George (*née* Richards); *m* 1st, 1953, June Griffith (marr. diss. 1980); four *d*; 2nd, 1981, Susan Ward (marr. diss. 2008). *Educ:* Downs Sch.; Bryanston Sch.; Edinburgh Coll. of Art; Camberwell Sch. of Art (NDD). Served War, RNVR, 1942–46. Asst, Slade Sch. of Fine Art, London, 1949–. Head, Dept of Fine Art, Nigerian Coll. of Art, Zaria, 1958–59; Slade School of Fine Art: Lectr, 1962; Reader in Fine Art, 1976; Prof. of Fine Art, Univ. of London, 1983; Slade Prof. of Fine Art, 1985–88. Works in public collections in GB and USA; one-man exhibn, Gainsborough's House, Sudbury, 1975; retrospective exhibn, Serpentine Gall., London, 1980; exhibn, Browse & Darby, 1984, 1989, 1994, 1998 and 2003; dealer, Browse & Darby. *Recreation:* make do and mend. *Address:* 33 Moreton Terrace, SW1 2NS. *T:* (020) 7828 3302; Grandfathers, Great Saxham, Bury St Edmunds, Suffolk IP29 5JW. *T:* (01284) 810997.

GEORGE, Sir Richard (William), Kt 1995; CVO 1998; Director, 1972–2008, Chairman, 1982–2008, Weetabix Ltd (Managing Director, 1982–2004); *b* 24 April 1944; *m* Patricia Jane Ogden; two *s* one *d*. *Educ:* Repton Sch.; Kansas State Univ. (BSc). Joined Weetabix Ltd, 1968: Dep. Man. Dir, 1976–82; Chm., Whitworths Holdings Ltd, 1987–97. Dep. Chm., Envmt Agency, 1995–98. Member: Exec. Cttee, Assoc. of Cereal Food Mfrs, 1977–2005 (Chm., 1983–85); Council, Food and Drink Fedn (formerly Food Mfrs Fedn), 1982–2004 (Mem., Exec. Cttee, 1984–2001 and 2003–04); Dep. Pres., 1990–92; Pres., 1993–95; Vice-Pres., 2001–02); Exec. Cttee, Ceereal (European Breakfast Cereal Assoc.), 1992–96 (Pres., 1994–96). Chm., Governing Body, Inst. of Food Res. (formerly Adv. Bd, Inst. of Food Res.), 1993–98; Mem., Food from Britain Council, 1993–98. Mem., Council, Royal Warrant Holders' Assoc., 1983– (Pres., 1993; Hon. Treas., 1998–2003). Prince's Trust: Mem., Mgt Bd, 1993–99 (Vice Chm., 1996–99); Mem., Northants Cttee, 1985–94 (Chm., 1985–88, 1991–94); Pres., Northants Prince's Youth Business Trust, 1998– (Vice-Chm., 1986–98). Chm., RAF Benevolent Fund, 2001–05. Hon. Air Cdre, 504 (Co. of Nottingham) Sqn (formerly Offensive Support Role Support Sqn), RAF Cottesmore, 1998–. FIGD 1983; FInstD 1981; FRSA 1991. Freeman, City of London, 2001; Liveryman, GAPAN, 2001– (Freeman, 1982). Hon. LLD Leicester, 1997. *Recreations:* family, golf. *Clubs:* Saints and Sinners; Royal and Ancient (St Andrews).

GEORGE, Prof. Stephen Alan; Professor, Department of Politics, University of Sheffield, 1994–2004, now Emeritus; *b* 14 Oct. 1949; *s* of Arthur George and Florence Lilian George (*née* Jefferson); *m* 1970, Linda Margaret Booth; one *s* one *d*. *Educ:* Univ. of Leicester (BA 1st cl. Hons Social Scis 1971; MPhil 1974). Res. Asst in European Affairs, Huddersfield Poly., 1971–72; Lectr, 1973–90, Sen. Lectr, 1991–92, Reader, 1992–94, in Politics, Univ. of Sheffield. Chair, Univ. Assoc. for Contemporary European Studies, 1996–2000. Dir, S Yorks Neighbourhood Watch Assoc., 2007–. *Publications:* Politics and Policy in the European Community, 1985, 3rd edn, as Politics and Policy in the European Union, 1996; An Awkward Partner: Britain in the European Community, 1990, 3rd edn 1998; (jtly) Politics in the European Union, 2001, 2nd edn 2006. *Recreations:* walking, reading history, poetry and novels. *Address:* 33 St Quentin Drive, Bradway, Sheffield S17 4PN. *T:* (0114) 236 4564.

GEORGE, Timothy John Burr, CMG 1991; HM Diplomatic Service, retired; *b* 14 July 1937; *s* of late Brig. J. B. George, late RAMC and M. Brenda George (*née* Harrison); *m* 1962, Richenda Mary, *d* of late Alan Reed, FRIBA and Ann Reed (*née* Rowntree); one *s* two *d*. *Educ:* Aldenham Sch.; Christ's Coll., Cambridge (MA). National Service, 2nd Lieut RA, 1956–58; Cambridge Univ., 1958. FCO, 1961; 3rd Secretary: Hong Kong, 1962; Peking, 1963; 2nd, later 1st Sec., FCO, 1966; 1st Sec. (Economic), New Delhi, 1969; Asst Political Adviser, Hong Kong, 1972; Asst European Integration Dept (Internal), FCO, 1974; Counsellor and Head of Chancery, Peking, 1978–80; Res. Associate, IISS, 1980–81; Counsellor and Hd of Chancery, UK Perm. Delegn to OECD, 1982–86; Hd, Republic of Ireland Dept, FCO, 1986–90; Ambassador to Nepal, 1990–95; FCO, 1996–99. Mem. Bd, CARE Internat. UK, 1998–2004. Gov., Ogbourne Sch., 2004– (Chm., 2006–). Lay Reader, C of E, 2002–. *Publication:* (jtly) Security in Southern Asia, 1984. *Address:* Martlets, Ogbourne St George, Marlborough, Wilts SN8 1SL. *T:* (01672) 841278.

GEORGE, William; His Honour Judge George; a Circuit Judge, since 1995; *b* 28 Sept. 1944; *s* of William Henry George and Elizabeth George; *m* 1973, Susan Isabel Pennington; two *d*. *Educ:* Herbert Strutt Grammar Sch.; Victoria Univ. of Manchester (LLB, LLM). Called to the Bar, Lincoln's Inn (Mansfield Scholar), 1968, Bencher, 2003; Chancery Bar, Liverpool, 1968–95; Head, Chancery Chambers, Liverpool, 1985–95; Asst Recorder, 1990–93; Recorder, 1993–95. Chm., Northern Chancery Bar Assoc., 1992–94. *Recreations:* history (military history and the American Civil War), contemporary British art, gardening. *Address:* Queen Elizabeth II Law Courts, Derby Square, Liverpool L2 1XA. *Club:* Athenæum (Liverpool).

GEORGE, Prof. William David, CBE 2008; FRCS; Regius Professor of Surgery, University of Glasgow, 1999–2006 (Professor of Surgery, 1981–99), now Honorary Professor, Faculty of Medicine; *b* 22 March 1943; *s* of William Abel George and Peggy Eileen George; *m* 1st, 1967, Helen Marie (*née* Moran) (*d* 1986); one *s* three *d*; 2nd, 1990, Pauline (*née* Mooney). *Educ:* Reading Bluecoat Sch.; Henley Grammar Sch.; Univ. of London (MB, BS 1966; MS 1977). FRCS 1970. Jun. surgical jobs, 1966–71; Registrar in Surgery, Royal Postgrad. Med. Sch., 1971–73; Lectr in Surg., Univ. of Manchester, 1973–77; Sen. Lectr in Surg., Univ. of Liverpool, 1977–81. *Publications:* articles in BMJ, Lancet, British Jl of Surg. *Recreations:* veteran rowing, fishing, squash. *Address:* 30 Highburgh Road, Glasgow G12 9DZ. *T:* (0141) 339 7497. *Club:* Clyde Amateur Rowing (Glasgow).

GEORGY, Orla; *see* Guerin, O.

GERARD, family name of **Baron Gerard**.

GERARD, 5th Baron *cr* 1876; **Anthony Robert Hugo Gerard;** Bt 1611; *b* 3 Dec. 1949; *er s* of Maj. Rupert Charles Frederick Gerard, MBE (*g g s* of 1st Baron), and of Huguette Reiss-Brian; *S* cousin, 1992; *m* 1976, Kathleen (marr. diss. 1997), *e d* of Dr Bernard Ryan, New York; two *s*. *Educ:* Harvard. *Heir: s* Hon. Rupert Bernard Charles Gerard, *b* 17 Dec. 1981. *Address:* PO Box 2308, East Hampton, NY 11937, USA.

GERARD, Ronald, OBE 1987; businessman and philanthropist; *b* 30 Oct. 1925; *s* of Samuel and Caroline Gerard; *m* 1952, Patricia Krieger; one *s* one *d*. *Educ:* Regent Street Polytechnic; College of Estate Management. FRICS 2000 (FSVA 1968). Royal Engineers, 1943–47, Italy and Egypt; articled to a City Chartered Surveyor, 1947–50; Principal, R. P. Gerard & Co., Surveyors and Valuers, 1952–59; Jt Man. Dir, 1959–87, Chm., 1982–87, London & Provincial Shop Centres Plc (created regional HQ buildings for many well-known public cos). Chm., Ronald Gerard Charitable Trust, 1983–95; has also funded many charitable enterprises, several of them eponymous, incl. medical research, facilities for the handicapped and the general public. Funded restoration of works of art incl. Barry murals at RSA and Verrio mural at Royal Hosp., Chelsea. Has a special interest in mil. charitable orgns, incl. Army Benevolent Fund, and Not Forgotten Assoc.; donated Sovereign's Mace, 2002 and Carved Crest, by Sarah Berry, 2005 to Royal Hosp., Chelsea. Hon. Benefactor, William Shipley Gp for RSA Hist., 2005. Work in youth cricket includes: President: London Community Cricket Assoc., 1992–94; London Cricket Coll., 1992–94; Middlesex Cricket Union, 1992–95; Middlesex Colts Assoc., 1995–97; Middlesex CCC, 1999–2001 (Life Vice-Pres., 1992; Trustee, Youth Centenary Trust, 1984–94); Vice-President: English Schools Cricket Assoc., 1981–; Seaxe Club, 2001–; Patron, Wilf Slack Young Cricketers Develt Trust, 1999; Hon. Mem., Middlesex Cricket Bd, 2002; Mem. Council, Lord's Taverners, 1984–90 (Hon. Benefactor). Patron, Brooklands Club, Brooklands Motor Mus., 1991. Liveryman, Glass Sellers' Co., 1990; Freeman, City of London, 1990. FRSA (Hon. Benefactor). KStJ 1992. Granted Arms, 1989. Barry Medal, 2005. *Clubs:* Carlton, MCC (Life Mem.).

GERARD-PEARSE, Rear-Adm. John Roger Southey, CB 1979; Group Personnel Manager, Jardine Matheson Co. Ltd, Hong Kong, 1980–84; *b* 10 May 1924; *s* of Dr Gerard-Pearse; *m* 1955, Barbara Jean Mercer; two *s* two *d*. *Educ:* Clifton College. Joined RN, 1943; comd HM Ships Tumult, Grafton, Defender, Fearless and Ark Royal; Flag Officer, Sea Training, 1975–76; Asst Chief, Naval Staff (Ops), 1977–79. *Recreations:* sailing, carpentry. *Address:* Hope House, The Green, Offham, Kent ME19 5NN. *T:* (01732) 842375.

GERE, Richard Tiffany; actor; *b* 31 Aug. 1949; *s* of Homer and Doris Gere; *m* 1st, 1991, Cindy Crawford (marr. diss. 1995); 2nd, 2002, Carey Lowell; one *s*. *Educ:* Univ. of Massachusetts. Played trumpet, piano, guitar and bass and composed music with various gps; stage performances: with Provincetown Playhouse, Seattle Rep. Theatre; Richard Farina, Long Time Coming and Long Time Gone, Back Bog Beat Bait, off-Broadway; Soon, Habeas Corpus and Grease on Broadway; A Midsummer Night's Dream, Lincoln Center; Taming of the Shrew, Young Vic, London; Bent, on Broadway (Theatre World Award); *films* include: Report to the Commissioner, 1975; Baby Blue Marine, 1976; Looking for Mr Goodbar, 1977; Days of Heaven, Blood Brothers, 1978; Yanks, American Gigolo, 1979; An Officer and a Gentleman, 1982; Breathless, Beyond the Limit, 1983; The Cotton Club, 1984; King David, 1985; Power, No Mercy, 1986; Miles From Home, 1989; Pretty Woman, Internal Affairs, 1990; Rhapsody in August, 1991; Final Analysis, 1992; Mr Jones, Sommersby, 1993; And the Band Played On, Intersection, 1994; First Knight, 1995; Primal Fear, 1996; The Jackal, Red Corner, 1998; The Runaway Bride, 1999; Autumn in New York, Dr T and the Women, 2000; The Mothman Prophecies, Unfaithful, Chicago, 2002; Shall We Dance?, 2005; Bee Season, 2006; The Hoax, I'm Not There, 2007. Founding Chm. and Pres., Tibet House, NY. *Publication:* Pilgrim, 1997. *Address:* c/o ICM, 40 West 57th Street, New York, NY 10019, USA.

GERGIEV, Valery Abesalovich; Artistic Director and Principal Conductor, Kirov Opera, since 1988; Director, Mariinsky Theatre, St Petersburg, since 1996; Principal Conductor, London Symphony Orchestra, since 2007; *b* Moscow, 2 May 1953. *Educ:* studied conducting under Ilya Musin, Rimsky-Korsakov Conservatory, Leningrad. Asst Conductor, Kirov Opera, 1977–88 (début, War and Peace, 1978); Chief Conductor, Armenian State Orch., 1981–85; has appeared with numerous major internat. orchs, incl. Bayerische Rundfunk, Berlin Philharmonic, Boston SO, LPO, LSO, BBC Symphony, Philharmonia, NY Philharmonic, Vienna Philharmonic; tours with Kirov Opera. Principal Conductor, Rotterdam Philharmonic Orch., 1995–2008; Principal Guest Conductor, Metropolitan Opera, NY, 1997–2008; Artistic Director: Stars of the White Nights Fest., St Petersburg, 1993–; Rotterdam Philharmonic/Gergiev/Philips Fest., 1996–; Director and Founder: Mikkeli Internat. Fest., Finland, 1992–; Peace to the Caucasus Fest., 1996–; Red Sea Internat. Music Fest., Eilat, Israel, 1996–. Has made numerous recordings. Winner, Herbert von Karajan Conductors Competition, Berlin; Dmitri Shostakovich Award; Golden Mask Award; People's Artist of Russia. *Address:* c/o Columbia Artists Management Inc., 1790 Broadway, New York, NY 10019–1412, USA.

GERHOLD, Dorian James, FRHistS, FSA; Principal Clerk of Select Committees, House of Commons, since 2006; *b* 7 March 1957; *s* of late Peter Kenneth Gerhold and of Nancy Melinda Gerhold (*née* Jones). *Educ:* King's Coll. Sch., Wimbledon; Merton Coll., Oxford (MA Hist.). Clerk, House of Commons, 1978–: Energy Cttee, 1989–92; Trade and Industry Cttee, 1992–96; Table Office, 1996–2000; Eur. Scrutiny Cttee, 2000–05; Hd, Scrutiny Unit, 2005–06. Presidential Advr, Parly Assembly of Council of Europe, 2001–04. Hon. Res. Fellow, Roehampton Univ., 2005–. Mem. Editl Bd, Jl Transport Hist., 1992–. Chm., Transport Hist. Res. Trust, 1997–2000. FRHistS 1996; FSA 2006. Fellow, Industry and Parlt Trust, 1992. *Publications:* Road Transport Before the Railways: Russell's London flying waggons, 1993; (with T. Barker) The Rise and Rise of Road Transport 1700–1990, 1993, 2nd edn 1995; (ed) Putney and Roehampton Past, 1994; (ed) Road Transport in the Horse-drawn Era, 1996; Wandsworth Past, 1998; Westminster Hall, 1999; Carriers and Coachmasters: trade and travel before the turnpikes, 2005 (Transport Book of the Year, 2006); The Putney Debates 1647, 2007; articles in Econ. Hist. Rev., Jl Transport Hist., Local Historian. *Recreations:* historical research, travel, walking. *Address:* Committee Office, House of Commons, 7 Millbank, SW1P 3JA; *e-mail:* gerholddj@parliament.uk.

GERKEN, Ian, LVO 1992; HM Diplomatic Service, retired; Ambassador to Ecuador, 2000–03; *b* 1 Dec. 1943; *s* of late Alfred Gerken and Esther Mary (*née* Chesworth); *m* 1976, Susana Drucker; two *s*, and one step *d*. *Educ:* Liverpool Collegiate. Entered Foreign Office, 1962: served in Budapest, 1965; Buenos Aires, 1966–68; FCO, 1968–71; Caracas, 1971–75; FCO, 1975–79; Lima, 1979–84; UN Gen. Assembly, 1984; FCO, 1985–88; Dep. High Comr, Valletta, 1988–92; Counsellor and Dep. Head, Perm. Under Sec's Dept, FCO, 1992–95; Ambassador to El Salvador, 1995–99.

GERKEN, Vice-Adm. Sir Robert William Frank, KCB 1986; CBE 1975; DL; Royal Navy, retired 1987; *b* 11 June 1932; *s* of Francis Sydney and Gladys Gerken; *m* 1st, 1966, Christine Stephenson (*d* 1981); two *d*; 2nd, 1983, Mrs Ann Fermor. *Educ:* Chigwell Sch.; Royal Naval Coll., Dartmouth. Sea service as Lieut and Lt-Comdr, 1953–66; RN Staff

Course, 1967; in command HMS Yarmouth, 1968–69; Commander Sea Training, 1970–71; Naval Staff, 1972–73; in command: Sixth Frigate Sqdn, 1974–75; HMS Raleigh, 1976–77; Captain of the Fleet, 1978–81; Flag Officer Second Flotilla, 1981–83; Dir Gen., Naval Manpower and Trng, 1983–85; Flag Officer Plymouth, Port Admiral Devonport, Comdr Central Sub Area Eastern Atlantic, Comdr Plymouth Sub Area Channel, 1985–87. Chm., Plymouth Develt Corp., 1993–96; Dir, 1988–2001, Chm., 1994–2001, Corps of Commissionaires. Chm., China Fleet Club (UK) Charitable Trust, 1987–. President: British Korean Veterans' Assoc. (Devon and Cornwall); Plymouth Lifeboat, RNLI, 1988–2007; SSAFA Forces Help Plymouth, 1998–. Governor, Chigwell Sch., 1987–2000. DL Devon, 1995. Hon. DSc Plymouth, 1993. *Recreations:* travel and family. *Address:* 22 Custom House Lane, Mill Bay, Plymouth, Devon PL1 3TG. *T:* (01752) 665104. *Clubs:* Naval; Royal Western Yacht (Cdre, 1993–97).

GERMAN, Lt-Col David John Keeling, TD 1972; JP; Vice Lord-Lieutenant of Staffordshire, 1995–2007; *b* 25 May 1932; *s* of Col Guy German, DSO and Rosemary German (*née* Keeling), MBE; *m* 1961, Anita Blanche Jupp; one *s* one *d. Educ:* Winchester; RMA, Sandhurst. Served Grenadier Guards, 1952–59; Keeling & Walker Ltd, Stoke on Trent, Chem. Mfrs, 1959–90, Man. Dir, 1974–90. Served Staffs Yeomanry, 1960–70, commanded QO Mercian Yeomanry, 1972–75. Freeman, City of London, 1983. JP 1972, DL 1979, High Sheriff 1982–83, Staffs. *Recreations:* yachting, field sports, France. *Address:* Ridgecombe, Penton Grafton, Andover SP11 0RR. *Clubs:* Army and Navy; Royal Yacht Squadron, Household Division Yacht.

GERMAN, Michael James, OBE 1996; Member (Lib Dem) South Wales East, and Leader of Welsh Liberal Democrats, National Assembly for Wales, since 1999; *b* 8 May 1945; *s* of Arthur Ronald German and Molly German; *m* 1970 (marr. diss. 1996); two *d. Educ:* St Mary's Coll., London (CertEd 1966); BA Open Univ. 1972; Bristol Poly. (Postgrad. Dip. in Educn Mgt 1973). Primary sch. teacher, 1966–67; Secondary sch. teacher, Mostyn High Sch., 1967–70; Head of Music: Lady Mary High Sch., Cardiff, 1970–86; Corpus Christi High Sch., Cardiff, 1986–91; Dir, European Div., Welsh Jt Educn Cttee, 1991–99. Mem., Cardiff CC, 1983–96 (Jt Leader, 1987–91; Leader, Liberal Democrats, 1983–96). National Assembly for Wales: Sec., subseq. Minister, for Econ. Develt, 2000–01; Dep. First Minister, 2000–01 and 2002–03; Minister for Rural Develt and Wales Abroad, 2002–03; Chm., Legislation Cttee, 1999–2000. *Publications:* articles in political and educnl jls. *Recreations:* music, travel. *Address:* 12 Cwm Road, Argoed, Blackwood NP12 0HJ. *T:* (01495) 221979.

GERMOND, Rt Rev. Brian Charles; *see* Johannesburg, Bishop of.

GEROSA, Peter Norman; Trustee, Tree Council, 1991–2003 (Secretary, 1983–91); *b* 1 Nov. 1928; *s* of late Enrico Cecil and Olive Doris Gerosa; *m* 1955, Dorothy Eleanor Griffin; two *d. Educ:* Whitgift Sch.; London Univ. (Birkbeck). BA (Hons) 1st Cl., Classics. Civil Service, 1945–82; Foreign Office, 1945; Home Office, 1949; HM Customs and Excise, 1953; Min. of Transport, 1966; DoE, 1970; Under Secretary: DoE, 1972; Dept of Transport, 1977; Dir of Rural Affairs, DoE, 1981–82. *Recreations:* singing, gardening, walking. *Address:* Sunnyside, Chart Lane, Reigate, Surrey RH2 7BW.

GERRARD, Ven. David Keith Robin; Archdeacon of Wandsworth, 1989–2004, now Emeritus; *b* 15 June 1939; *s* of Eric Henry and Doris Jane Gerrard; *m* 1963, Jennifer Mary Hartley; two *s* two *d. Educ:* Royal Grammar School, Guildford; St Edmund Hall, Oxford (BA); Lincoln Theol Coll. Curate: St Olave, Woodberry Down, N16, 1963–66; St Mary, Primrose Hill, NW3, 1966–69; Vicar: St Paul, Lorrimore Square, SE17, 1969–79; St Andrew and St Mark, Surbiton, Surrey, 1979–89; RD of Kingston upon Thames, 1983–88. *Publication:* (co-author) Urban Ghetto, 1976. *Recreations:* embroidery, Proust, Yorkshire, statistics. *Address:* 15 Woodbourne Drive, Claygate, Surrey KT10 0DR.

GERRARD, Neil Francis; MP (Lab) Walthamstow, since 1992; *b* 3 July 1942; *m* 1968, Marian Fitzgerald (marr. diss. 1983); two *s. Educ:* Manchester Grammar Sch.; Wadham Coll., Oxford (BA Hons); Chelsea Coll., London (MEd). Teacher, Queen Elizabeth's Sch., Barnet, 1965–68; Lectr in Computing, Hackney Coll., 1968–92. Mem. (Lab) Waltham Forest BC, 1973–90 (Leader of Council, 1986–90). Contested (Lab) Chingford, 1979. *Address:* House of Commons, SW1A 0AA.

GERRARD, Peter Noël, CBE 1991; General Counsel, London Stock Exchange, 1991–94; *b* 19 May 1930; *o c* of Sir Denis Gerrard and of Hilda Goodwin (*née* Jones, who *m* 2nd, Sir Joseph Cantley, OBE); *m* 1957, Prudence Lipson-Ward; one *s* two *d. Educ:* Rugby; Christ Church, Oxford (MA). 2nd Lieut, XII Royal Lancers, Malaya, 1953–54. Solicitor, 1959; Partner, Lovell, White & King, 1960, Sen. Partner, 1980–88; Sen. Partner, Lovell White Durrant, 1988–91. Member: Bd of Banking Supervision, 1990–2001; City Capital Markets Cttee, 1974–91. Member: Council, Law Society, 1972–82; Bd, Inst. of Advanced Legal Studies, 1985–96; Council, St George's Hosp. Med. Sch., 1982–94. *Recreations:* music, walking. *Address:* Pightle Cottage, Ashdon, Saffron Walden, Essex CB10 2HG. *T:* (01799) 584374.

GERRARD, Ronald Tilbrook, FREng, FICE, FCIWEM; Senior Partner, Binnie & Partners, Consulting Engineers, 1974–83, retired; *b* 23 April 1918; *s* of Henry Thomas Gerrard and Edith Elizabeth Tilbrook; *m* 1950, Cecilia Margaret Bremner; three *s* (one *d* decd). *Educ:* Imperial Coll. of Science and Technology, Univ. of London. BSc(Eng). FCGI; FICE 1957; FIWE 1965; FREng (FEng 1979); MEIC. Served War, RE, 1939–45. Resident Engr, sea defence and hydro-electric works, 1947–50; Asst Engr, design of hydro-power schemes in Scotland and Canada, 1951–54; Binnie & Partners: Sen. Engr, 1954; Partner, 1959; resp. for hydro-power, water supply, river engrg, coast protection and indust. works in UK and overseas. Chm., Assoc. of Cons. Engrs, 1969–70; Mem. Council, ICE, 1974–77. Telford Silver Medal, ICE, 1968. *Publications:* (jtly) 4 papers to ICE. *Address:* 6 Ashdown Road, Epsom, Surrey KT17 3PL. *T:* (01372) 724834. *Club:* Athenæum.

GERRARD-WRIGHT, Maj.-Gen. Richard Eustace John, CB 1985; CBE 1977 (OBE 1971; MBE 1963); DL; Director, Territorial Army and Cadets, 1982–85, retired; *b* 9 May 1930; 2nd *s* of Rev. Robert Lancelot Gerrard-Wright; *m* 1960, Susan Kathleen, *d* of Lt-Col Frederick Walter Young, MBE, Royal Lincolnshire Regt; two *s* one *d* (and one *d* decd). *Educ:* Christ's Hospital; RMA Sandhurst. Commnd Royal Lincolnshire Regt, 1949; served Egypt, Germany and UK, 1950–55; Malaya, 1955–58 (despatches, 1958); Instructor, RMA Sandhurst, 1958–62 (2nd E Anglian Regt, 1960); Staff Coll., India, 1962–63; served Kenya, Aden, Malta, Malaya, 1963–70 (Royal Anglian Regt, 1964); Bn Comdr, UK, Germany, NI, 1970–73 (despatches 1973); Comdr, 39 Inf. Bde, Belfast, 1975–77; Nat. Defence Coll., Canada, 1977–78; Chief of Staff, 1 (Br) Corps, 1978–79; GOC Eastern District, 1980–82. Dep. Col, Royal Anglian Regt, 1975–80; Col Comdt, Queen's Div., 1981–84. Pres., SSAFA Forces Help, Lincs, 1998–. Chief Exec. and Sec., Hurlingham Club, 1985–87. DL Cambs, 1993–97; DL Lincs 1997–. *Address:* 21 Market Place, Folkingham, Sleaford, Lincs NG34 0SE. *Clubs:* Army and Navy, MCC; Free Foresters.

GERSHON, Sir Peter (Oliver), Kt 2004; CBE 2000; FREng; Chairman: Premier Farne plc, since 2005; Symbian Ltd, since 2004; General Healthcare Group, since 2006; Verte Data Sciences, since 2007; *b* 10 Jan. 1947; *s* of late Alfred Joseph Gershon and Ger Gershon; *m* 1971, Eileen Elizabeth Walker; one *s* two *d. Educ:* Reigate Grammar Sch Churchill Coll., Cambridge (MA). FIEE 1998, Hon. FIET (Hon. FIEE 2005); FRAe 2000; FCIPS 2000; FREng 2001. Joined ICL, 1969; Mem. Mgt Bd, and Dir of Netwo Systems, 1985; Managing Director: STC Telecommunications Ltd, 1987–90; GPT Lt 1990–94; Marconi Electronic Systems Ltd, 1994–99; Chief Operating Officer, BA Systems, 1999–2000; Chief Exec., Office of Govt Commerce, 2000–04. Mem. Ct an Council, Imperial Coll., London, 2002–. CCMI (CIMgt 1996); FBCS 2005. Ho Fellow, Cardiff Univ., 2007. Hon. DTech Kingston, 2005. *Publications:* Review of Civ Procurement in Central Government, 1999; Independent Review of Public Sect Efficiency, 2004; Independent Review of Royal Family and Ministerial Air Travel, 200 *Recreations:* swimming, reading, theatre, ski-ing. *T:* (01494) 729127.

GERSHUNY, Prof. Jonathan Israel, DPhil; FBA 2002; Professor of Sociolog University of Oxford, since 2006; Fellow of St Hugh's College, Oxford, since 2006; *b* 1 Sept. 1949; *s* of Charles and Cynthia Gershuny; *m* 1974, Esther Gershuny; one *s* one *Educ:* Loughborough Univ. (BSc Econs and Politics 1971); Strathclyde Univ. (MSc 1972 Sussex Univ. (DPhil 1977). Res. Officer, Dept of Transport Technology, Loughboroug Univ., 1973–74; Science Policy Research Unit, Sussex University: Fellow, 1974–81; Se Fellow, 1981–84; Vis. Professorial Fellow, 1986–91; on secondment as pt-time Re Fellow, Res. Unit on Ethnic Relations, Univ. of Bristol, 1978–79; University of Bat Prof. of Sociology, 1984–89; Head: Sociology and Social Policy Gp, 1984–88; Sch. Social Scis, 1988–89; Univ. Lectr, Dept of Social and Admin. Studies, and Fellow Nuffield Coll., Univ. of Oxford, 1990–93; Prof. of Econ. Sociology and Dir, ESRC Re Centre on Micro-social Change, subseq. Inst. for Social and Econ. Res., Univ. of Esse 1993–2006. Chm., Sect. S4 (Sociol., Demography, Social Stats), British Acad., 2006 Silver Medal, Market Res. Soc., 1986. *Publications:* After Industrial Society?, 1978 (tran German, 1981, Italian, 1985); Social Innovation and the Division of Labour, 1983 (tran Swedish, 1986); (with I. D. Miles) The New Service Economy, 1983 (trans. Japanes 1983, Spanish, 1988); (ed jtly) Time Use Studies World Wide, 1991; L'innovazior Sociale: tempo, produzione e consumi, 1993; (jtly) Changing Households, 1994; (ed jtl The Social and Political Economy of the Household, 1994; Changing Times: the soci and political economy of post industrial society, 2000; (ed jtly) Seven Years in the Liv of British Households, 2000; (ed jtly) Information and Communication Technologies Society, 2007. *Recreations:* coarse gardening, ski-ing, opera. *Address:* Department Sociology, Manor Road Building, Manor Road, Oxford OX1 3UQ. *T:* (01865) 28617 *e-mail:* jonathan.gershuny@sociology.ox.ac.uk.

GERSON, John Henry Cary, CMG 1999; Group Political Adviser, BP plc, since 200 *b* 25 April 1945; *s* of late Henry and of Benedicta Joan Gerson; *m* 1968, Mary Alison, *d* late George Ewart Evans; one *s* one *d. Educ:* Bradfield; King's Coll., Cambridge (MA HM Diplomatic Service, 1968–99: Third Sec., FCO, 1968; language student, Hor Kong, 1969–71; Second Secretary: Singapore, 1971–73; FCO, 1973–74; First Sec. ar HM Consul, Peking, 1974–77; First Sec., FCO, 1978; on loan to Home CS, 1978–7 First Sec., later Counsellor, FCO, 1979–87; Counsellor, Hong Kong, 1987–92; V Fellow, Princeton Univ., 1992; Counsellor, FCO, 1992–99. Mem. Simuri Trib Manokwari, Irian Jaya, 2001. *Recreations:* ornithology, sinology, literature. *Address:* BP pl 1 St James's Square, SW1Y 4PD. *Club:* Athenæum.

GERSTENBERG, Frank Eric, MA; Principal, George Watson's College, Edinburg 1985–2001; *b* 23 Feb. 1941; *s* of late Eric Gustav Gerstenberg and Janie Willis Gerstenber *m* 1966, Valerie Myra (*née* MacLellan); one *s* twin *d. Educ:* Trinity College, Glenalmon Clare College, Cambridge (MA); Inst. of Education, Univ. of London (PGCE). As History Teacher, Kelly Coll., Tavistock, 1963–67; Housemaster and Head of Histor Millfield School, 1967–74; Headmaster, Oswestry School, 1974–85. Chm. of Gov Glenalmond Coll., 2005–; Gov., Compass Sch., Haddington. *Recreations:* ski-ing, gol *Address:* Craigmore, Whim Road, Gullane, East Lothian EH31 2BD. *Club:* Ne (Edinburgh).

GERSTLE, Prof. (C.) Andrew, PhD; Professor of Japanese Studies, since 1993 ar Director, AHRC (formerly AHRB) Centre for Asian and African Studies, since 200 School of Oriental and African Studies, University of London; *b* 18 June 1951. *Edu* Columbia Univ. (BA 1973); Waseda Univ., Tokyo (MA 1979); Harvard Univ. (Ph 1980). Lectr, 1980–89, Prof. of Japanese, 1989–93, ANU. Guest Curator, Kabuki Hero on the Osaka Stage 1780–1830 (special exhibn), BM, 2005. *Publications:* Circles of Fantas convention in the plays of Chikamatsu, 1986, 2nd edn 1996; (ed) Eighteenth Centu Japan: culture and society, 1989; (with K. Inobe and W. Malm) Theatre as Music: th Bunraku play 'Mt Imo and Mt Se: An Exemplary Tale of Womanly Virtue', 1990; (with A. Milner) Recovering the Orient: artists, scholars, appropriations, 199 Chikamatsu: five late plays, 2001; Kabuki Heroes on the Osaka Stage 1780–1830, 200 *Address:* School of Oriental and African Studies, University of London, Russell Squar WC1H 0XG; *e-mail:* ag4@soas.ac.uk.

GERSTNER, Louis Vincent, Jr; Hon. KBE 2001; Chairman, Carlyle Group, since 200 *b* NY, 1 March 1942. *Educ:* Dartmouth Coll. (BA Engrg 1963); Harvard Business Sc (MBA 1965). Dir, McKinsey & Co., Inc., 1965–78; Pres., American Express Co 1978–89; Chairman and Chief Executive Officer: RJR Nabisco Inc., 1989–93; IBM 1993–2002. Director: NY Times Co., 1986–97; Bristol-Myers Squibb Co. Dir, Ne American Schs Develt Corp. Dir, Japan Soc., 1992–. Mem. Bd, Lincoln Center f Performing Arts, 1984–2002. *Publication:* Who Says Elephants Can't Dance: inside IBM historic turnaround, 2002. *Address:* Carlyle Group, 520 Madison Avenue, 41st Floor, Ne York, NY 10022, USA.

GERTYCH, Prof. Zbigniew; Professor, Botanical Garden, Polish Academy of Science Warsaw, since 1990; *b* 26 Oct. 1922; *s* of Tadeusz Gertych and Maria Gertych (*n* Marecka); *m* 1st, 1945, Roza (*née* Skrochowska) (decd); one *s* two *d*; 2nd, 1970, Zofia (*n* Dobrzanska). *Educ:* Uniw. Jagiellonski, Krakow. MA eng 1946, DAgric 1950. Joine Army as volunteer and participated in September campaign, 1939; during Nazi occupatic took part in clandestine activities, was detained in camps and Gestapo prisons; after escap served Home Army (AK) to 1945 (wounded in partisan combat). Polish Academy Sciences (PAN), 1946–83: Head of Pomology Dept, Dendrology Research Centr Kórnik, 1947–53; Dir Exp. Fruit Growing Research Centre, Brzeźna, 1953–64; Di Research Centre, Agric. and Forestry Econ. Science, 1964–78; Vice-Dir and Di Vegetable Growing Inst., Skierniewice, 1964–82; Vice-Sec. and Sec., Agric. and Forest Scis Dept, 1964–87; First Dep. Gen. Sec., 1981–83; Mem., PAN, 1976; Mem., Presidiu of PAN, 1978–86; Asst Prof., 1963, Associate Prof., 1969, Prof., 1979, Jagiellonian Univ Cracow and Polish Acad. of Scis. MP, Nowy Sacz, 1957–89; Dep. Speaker, Sejn 1982–85 (Chm., Budget Commn, Social and Economic Council and Main Cttee, Na Action for School Assistance); Dep. Chm., Council of Ministers, 1985–87; Ambassador Poland to the Court of St James's and to Republic of Ireland, 1987–90. Pres., Homo

Planta Foundn, 1991–; Mem., Supreme Council and Exec. Cttee, Internat. Soc. of Hort. Scis. Hon. Dr, Acad. of Agric. Scis, Berlin, 1974; DAgr *hc* Szczecin Univ., 1989. Cross of Valour, 1944; Comdr's Cross, Order of Polonia Restituta, 1984; other Polish decorations; numerous foreign honours and awards. *Publications:* contribs to sci. jls. *Recreations:* music, art, travels. *Address:* Botanical Garden, Polish Academy of Sciences, vl. Prawdziwka 2, POB 84, 02–973 Warsaw 34, Poland. *Club:* Rotary.

GERVAIS, Most Rev. Marcel; Archbishop of Ottawa, (RC), 1989–2007; *b* 21 Sept. 1931; *s* of Frédéric Pierre Gervais and Marie-Louise Beaudry. *Educ:* St Peter's Seminary, London, Ont.; Angelicum Athenæum Pontifical Inst., Rome; Pontifical Biblical Inst., Rome; Ecole Biblique et Archéologique Française de Jérusalem. Ordained priest, 1958; Prof. of Sacred Scriptures, St Peter's Seminary, London, 1962–76; Dir of Divine Word Internat. Centre of Religious Educn, London, 1974–80; Auxiliary Bishop of London, Ontario, 1980–85; Bishop of Sault Sainte-Marie, 1985–89; Coadjutor Archbishop of Ottawa, June–Sept. 1989. Pres., Canadian Conf. of Catholic Bishops, 1991–93. *Address:* c/o Archdiocese of Ottawa, 1247 Kilborn Place, Ottawa, ON K1H 6K9, Canada. *T:* (613) 7385025.

GERVIS MEYRICK; *see* Meyrick.

GERY, Sir Robert Lucian W.; *see* Wade-Gery.

GESTETNER, David; President, Gestetner Holdings PLC, 1987–95; *b* 1 June 1937; *s* of late Sigmund Gestetner and Henny Gestetner, OBE; *m* 1st, 1961, Alice Floretta Sebag-Montefiore (*d* 2000); one *s* three *d*; 2nd, 2006, Mrs Angela Howard. *Educ:* Midhurst Grammar Sch.; Bryanston Sch.; University Coll., Oxford (MA). Gestetner Holdings: Dir, 1967–2005; Jt Chm., 1972–86; Man. Dir, 1982–86; Jt Pres., 1986–87. Director: Alphameric PLC, 1994–2000; Nipson Digital Printing Systems PLC, 2004–. *Recreations:* sailing, book collecting. *Clubs:* Reform, MCC; Grolier (New York).

See also J. Gestetner.

GESTETNER, Jonathan; Chairman, Marlborough Rare Books Ltd, since 1990; *b* 11 March 1940; *s* of late Sigmund Gestetner and Henny Gestetner, OBE; *m* 1965, Jacqueline Margaret Strasmore; two *s* one *d*. *Educ:* Bryanston Sch.; Massachusetts Institute of Technology (BScMechEngrg). Joined Gestetner Ltd, 1962; Jt Chm., Gestetner Hldgs PLC, 1972–87; Director: DRS, USA, 1987–89; Klein Associates, USA, 1987–90. Member: Executive Council, Engineering Employers' London Assoc., 1972–77 (Vice-Pres., 1975–77); Maplin Development Authority, 1973–74; SSRC, 1979–82; Dir, Centre for Policy Studies, 1982–96. Mem., Educnl Council, MIT, 1973–. *Recreation:* the visual arts. *Clubs:* Brooks's, MCC.

See also Gestetner, D.

GETHIN, Sir Richard (Joseph St Lawrence), 10th Bt *cr* 1665, of Gethinsgrott, Cork; civil engineer; *b* 29 Sept. 1949; *s* of Sir Richard Patrick St Lawrence Gethin, 9th Bt and of Fara, *y d* of late J. H. Bartlett; *S* father, 1988; *m* 1974, Jacqueline Torfrida, *d* of Comdr David Cox; three *d*. *Educ:* The Oratory School; RMA Sandhurst; RMCS Shrivenham; Cranfield Inst. of Technology (BSc(Eng), MSc). Joined first unit, 1971; served in Germany and UK; retd in rank of Major, 1990. *Recreations:* gardening, woodwork. *Heir:* cousin Antony Michael Gethin [*b* 10 Jan. 1939; *m* 1965, Vanse, *d* of late Col C. D. Barlow, OBE, KSLI; two *s* one *d*]. *T:* (01474) 814231.

GETTY, Hon. Donald Ross; PC (Can.) 1985; OC 1998; President and Chief Executive Officer, Sunnybank Investments Ltd, since 1993; Premier of Alberta, 1985–93; MLA Edmonton Whitemud, 1967–79, 1985–93; *b* 30 Aug. 1933; *s* of Charles Ross Getty and Beatrice Lillian Getty; *m* 1955, Margaret Inez Mitchell; four *s*. *Educ:* Univ. of Western Ontario (BBA 1955). MLA Alberta 1967; Minister of Federal and Intergovernmental Affairs, 1971; Minister of Energy and Natural Resources, 1975; resigned 1979; re-elected MLA, 1985. Joined Imperial Oil, 1955; Midwestern Industrial Gas, 1961; formed Baldonnel Oil & Gas, 1964 (Pres. and Man. Dir); Partner, Doherty Roadhouse & McCuaig, 1967; Pres., D. Getty Investments, 1979; Chm., Ipsco, 1981–85; former Chm. and Chief Exec., Nortek Energy Corp.; director of other cos. Played quarterback for Edmonton Eskimos Canadian Football team for 10 years. *Recreations:* horse racing, golf, hunting. *Address:* 1273 Potter Greens Drive NW, Edmonton, AB T5T 5Y8, Canada.

GETTY, Mark Harris; Chairman, Getty Images Inc., since 1995; *b* 9 July 1960; *s* of Sir (John) Paul Getty, KBE and of Gail Harris Getty; *m* 1982, Domitilla Lante Harding; three *s*. *Educ:* Taunton Sch.; St Catherine's Coll., Oxford (BA). Kidder, Peabody, Inc., 1984–88; Hambros Bank, 1990–93; Getty Images Inc., 1994–. Chm., John Wisden & Co., 2006–. Trustee, Nat. Gall., 2001– (Chm. Trustees, 2008–).

GHAFFUR, (Mohammed) Tarique, CBE 2004; QPM 2001; an Assistant Commissioner, since 2001, and Head of Central Operations and Olympics Security, since 2006, Metropolitan Police (a Deputy Assistant Commissioner, 1999–2001); Director, Specialist Crime, since 2003; *b* 8 June 1955; *m* 1990, Shehla (*née* Aslam); one *s* one *d*. *Educ:* Uganda; Manchester Poly. (BA); Keele Univ. (MA). Greater Manchester Police: uniform and CID posts, 1974–78; Sergeant, 1978; Inspector, 1982; Chief Inspector, 1988; Superintendent, Leics Constabulary, 1989–96; Asst Chief Constable, Lancs Constabulary, 1996–99; Dep. Chief Constable, Police Inf. Technol. Orgn, 1999. *Publications:* articles on crime, diversity, security and IT. *Address:* Metropolitan Police, New Scotland Yard, Broadway, SW1H 0BG.

GHAHRAMANI, Prof. Zoubin, PhD; Professor of Information Engineering, University of Cambridge, since 2006; *b* 8 Feb. 1970; *s* of Ghahraman Ghahramani and Manijeh Dabiri. *Educ:* American Sch. of Madrid, Spain; Univ. of Pennsylvania (BA Cognitive Sci. 1990; BSE Computer Sci. 1990); Massachusetts Inst. of Technol. (PhD 1995). Postdoctoral Fellow, Univ. of Toronto, 1995–98; Lectr, Gatsby Unit, 1998–2003, Reader, 2003–06, Adjunct Faculty, Gatsby Unit, 2006–, UCL. Associate Res. Prof., Carnegie Mellon Univ., 2003–. *Publications:* (ed) Advances in Neural Information Processing Systems, 2002; 10th International Workshop on Artificial Intelligence and Statistics, 2005; (ed) Proceedings of the International Conference on Machine Learning, 2007; contrib. to Science, Nature, Jl Machine Learning Res., Phil. Trans, Royal Soc. B, Neural Computation, Bioinformatics. *Recreation:* adventure travel. *Address:* Department of Engineering, University of Cambridge, Trumpington Street, Cambridge CB2 1PZ; *e-mail:* zoubin@eng.cam.ac.uk.

GHALI, Boutros B.; *see* Boutros-Ghali.

GHEORGHIU, Angela; soprano; *b* 1965; *m* 1st, 1988, Andrei Gheorghiu (marr. diss.); 2nd, 1996, Roberto Alagna, *qv*; one step *d*. *Educ:* Bucharest Acad. Débuts: Nat. Opera, Cluj, 1990; Royal Opera, Covent Garden, 1992; Vienna State Opera, 1992; Metropolitan Opera, NY, 1993. Rôles include: Mimi in La Bohème; Violetta in La Traviata; Micaela in Carmen; title rôle in Turandot; Adina in L'elisir d'amore; Juliette in Roméo et Juliette; Amelia in Simon Boccanegra; Marguerite in Faust. Film, Tosca, 2002. Performs worldwide and has made numerous recordings. *Address:* c/o Royal Opera House, Covent

Garden, WC2E 9DD; c/o Alexander Gerdanovits, Seenstrasse 28a, 9081 Reifnitz, Austria; *e-mail:* agerdanovits@gmx.net.

GHERAIEB, Abdelkrim; Ambassador of Algeria to Saudi Arabia, 1986–89 and since 2001; *b* 30 July 1935; *m* Fizia Gheraieb; one *s* three *d*. *Educ:* Univ. of Algiers (LèsL); Inst. of Pol Scis, Univ. of Algiers (Diploma). Hd of Legal Services, First Nat. Assembly, 1962–65; Chm., Assoc. of Algerians in Europe, 1965–79; Ambassador to: Teheran, 1979–82; Peking, 1982–84; Beirut, 1984–86; UK, 1989–91; Ambassador Councillor, Min. of For. Affairs, Algeria, 1992–93; Mediator, Touareg dispute, North Mali, 1993; Ambassador to Mali, 1996–2001. Member: Assemblée Nationale Populaire, 1977; (nominated) Central Cttee, FLN Party, 1979. Médaille de la Résistance, Algerian war of liberation, 1982. Kt, Order of Cedar (Lebanon), 1986; Order of HM King Abdul Aziz (Saudi Arabia), 1989; Nat. Order (Mali), 2001. *Address:* Algerian Embassy, PO 94388, Riyadh 11693, Saudi Arabia; c/o Ministry of Foreign Affairs, 6 rue 16n-Batran, el-Mouradia, Algiers, Algeria.

GHODSE, Prof. (Abdol) Hamid, Hon. CBE 1999; MD, PhD, DSc; FRCP, FRCPsych; Professor of Psychiatry and Addictive Behaviour, 1987–2003, now Professor Emeritus of International Drug Policy, and Director, International Centre for Drug Policy (formerly Centre for Addiction Studies), since 1992, University of London at St George's Hospital Medical School; Hon. Consultant Psychiatrist: St George's Hospital, since 1978; Springfield University Hospital, since 1978; *b* 30 April 1938; *s* of Abdol Rahim Ghods and Batool Daneshmand; *m* 1973, Barbara Bailin; two *s* one *d*. *Educ:* Esfehan, Tabriz and Tehran; American Univ., Beirut (Schol. 1958); MD Iran 1965; DPM 1974; PhD 1976, DSc 2002, London. FRCPsych 1985; FRCP 1992; MFPHM 1996, FFPH (FFPHM 1997); FRCPE 1997. Lieut, Iranian Health Corps, 1965–67. Postgrad. trng, Morgannwg Hosp., Wales, and St Bartholomew's and Maudsley Hosps, London, 1968–74; res. psychiatrist, Inst. of Psychiatry, Univ. of London, 1974–78; Consultant Psychiatrist, St Thomas' Hosp., 1978–88; Hon. Consultant, Public Health, Wandsworth PCT (formerly Merton, Sutton and Wandsworth HA), 1987–. Vis. Prof., Keele Univ., 2002–05. Mem. Council, St George's Hosp. Med. Sch., 1993–96. Co-ordinator, Higher Degrees in Psychiatry, Univ. of London, 1993– (Chm., Subject Panel in Psychiatry, 2003–; Mem., Medical Studies Cttee, 2003–). Director: Regl Drug and Alcohol Team, SW Thames RHA, 1991–97; Medical Council on Alcoholism, 1996–2003; Addiction Resource Agency for Comrs, 1997–2004; Nat. Clinical Assessment Authy, 2001–05; Nat. Patient Safety Agency, 2005–. Member: WHO Adv. Panel, 1979–; WHO Prog. Planning Wkg Gp, 1986–89; Scientific Cttee on Tobacco and Health, 2000–; Vice-Chm., London S Sub-Cttee, NHS Clinical Excellence Awards, 2004–06; Med. Dir, Adv. Cttee on Clin. Excellence Awards, DoH, 2006–; Convenor, Mem., Rapporteur and Chm. of various WHO Expert Cttees and Wkg Gps on Drug Dependence, 1980–. Advr, BNF, 1984–; Clinical Advr, Parly and Health Service Ombudsman, 2004–06. Editor: Internat. Jl Social Psychiatry, 1982–2000; Substance Misuse Section, Current Opinion in Psychiatry, 1994–2001; Internat. Psychiatry, 2003–. Royal College of Psychiatrists: Mem., Exec. Cttee, Substance Misuse Faculty, 1981–95; Chm., Substance Misuse Sect., 1990–94; Mem. Council, 1990–94, 2000–; Mem., Court of Electors, 1993–99; Vice-Pres., 2000–02; Dir, Bd of Internat. Affairs, 2001–07; Clin. Honours Cttee, 2004–; President: Assoc. for Prevention of Addiction, 1984–90; Internat. Narcotics Control Bd, 1993–95, 1997–99, 2000–02, 2004–06 (Mem., 1992–); European Collaborating Centres for Addiction Studies, 1995–. Hon. Sec., Assoc. of Profs of Psychiatry, 1990–2002 (Chm., 2002–); Convenor, Assoc. of European Profs of Psychiatry, 1996–; Mem., Fedn of Assocs of Clinical Profs. McLeod Prof., SA, 1990; Hon. Professor: Beijing Med. Univ., 1997; Peking Univ., 2000. Devised Ghodse Opiate Addiction Test (US, German, French and UK patents); invented pupillometer for measuring anisocoria (European, Canadian and US patents). *Publications:* (jtly) Misuse of Drugs, 1986, 3rd edn 1996; (jtly) Psychoactive Drugs: improving prescribing practices, 1988 (trans. 8 langs); Drugs and Addictive Behaviour: a guide to treatment, 1989, 3rd edn 2002; (ed jtly) Substance Abuse and Dependence, 1990; (ed jtly) Drug Misuse and Dependence, 1990; (ed jtly) Doctors and their Health, 2000; (ed jtly) Young People and Substance Misuse, 2004; Addiction at Work, 2005; numerous articles on self-poisoning, substance misuse and med. educn. *Recreations:* reading, cycling. *Address:* St George's Hospital Medical School, Cranmer Terrace, SW17 0RE. *T:* (020) 8725 5719. *Club:* Athenæum.

GHOSH, Dame Helen Frances, DCB 2008; Permanent Secretary, Department for Environment, Food and Rural Affairs, since 2005; *b* 21 Feb. 1956; *d* of William and Eileen Kirkby; *m* 1979, Peter Robin Ghosh; one *s* one *d*. *Educ:* St Hugh's Coll., Oxford (BA Mod. Hist.) 1976); Hertford Coll., Oxford (MLitt (6th century Italian Hist.) 1980). Admin trainee, DoE, 1979; variety of posts in local govt finance, housing, urban regeneration, 1979–95, inc. Prin. Private Sec. to Minister of State for Housing, 1986–88; Dep. Dir, Efficiency Unit, Cabinet Office, 1995–97; Dir of Regeneration for E London, Govt Office for London, 1997–99; Dir Children's Gp, DSS, subseq. DWP, 1999–2001; Dir Gen., Machinery of Govt Secretariat, Cabinet Office, 2001–03; Dir Gen. for Corporate Services, 2003–05, and a Comr, 2003–05, Bd of Inland Revenue, later HM Revenue and Customs. Chm., Blackfriars Overseas Aid Trust, 1999–. *Publication:* (contrib.) Boethius: his life, thought and influence, 1981. *Recreations:* family life, ballet, gardening. *Address:* Department for Environment, Food and Rural Affairs, Nobel House, 17 Smith Square, SW1P 3JR.

GHOSH, (Indranil) Julian, DPhil; QC 2006; *m* 1994, Catherine Elizabeth Waring. *Educ:* Univ. of Edinburgh (LLB); London Sch. of Econs (LLM); Birkbeck Coll., London (MA); St Edmund Hall, Oxford (DPhil). Called to the Bar, Lincoln's Inn, 1993; a Dep. Special Comr, 2002–. Sen. Vis. Fellow, Queen Mary and Westfield Coll., London, 1994–2006; Vis. Prof., Univ. of Leiden, 2005–. *Publications:* Taxation of Loan Relationships and Derivatives, 1996; Principles of the Internal Market and Direct Taxation, 2007. *Recreations:* music, chess, fencing, cricket. *Address:* Pump Court Tax Chambers, 16 Bedford Row, WC1R 4EF. *Clubs:* Athenæum, Arts, Lansdowne, Two Brydges; New (Edinburgh).

GHOSH, Shaks; Chief Executive, Private Equity Foundation, since 2007; *b* 17 Jan. 1957; *d* of Samir Ghosh and Maria Rheinhold. *Educ:* Frank Anthony Public Sch.; Calcutta Univ. (BA 1st cl. Hons Geog. 1978); Salford Univ. (MSc Urban Studies 1980). Urban Renewal Officer, Leicester CC, 1980–84; Improvement Officer, Islington LBC, 1984–86; Supported Housing Officer, Community Housing Assoc., Camden and Westminster, 1986–89; Asst Dir, Centrepoint, 1989–92; Supported Housing Manager, NFHA, 1992–94; Head of London Region, Nat. Housing Fedn, 1994–97; Chief Exec., Crisis, 1997–2006. *Recreations:* gardening, travel, current affairs. *Address:* Private Equity Foundation, CAN Mezzanine, 1 London Bridge, SE1 9BG.

GHOSN, Carlos, Hon. KBE 2007; President, since 2000, and Chief Executive Officer, since 2001, and Co-Chairman, Board of Directors, since 2003, Nissan Motor Co. Ltd; Co-Chairman, Board of Directors, President and Chief Executive Officer, Renault, since 2005; *b* Brazil, 9 March 1954; *s* of late Jorges Ghosn and of Rose Ghosn; *m* 1985, Rita; one *s* three *d*. *Educ:* Ecole Poytechnique, Paris (engrg degree 1974); Ecole des Mines de

Paris (engrg degree 1978). Michelin: joined, 1978; Plant Manager, Le Puy Plant, France, 1981–84; Hd, R&D for industrial tyres, 1984; Chief Op. Officer, S Amer. Ops, Brazil, 1985–90; Chm. and CEO, N America, 1990–96; Exec. Vice Pres., Renault, 1996–99; Chief Op. Officer, Nissan Motor Co. Ltd, 1999–2001. Mem. Bd of Dirs, Alcoa. Légion d'Honneur (France), 2002; Ordem de Rio Branco (Brazil), 2002; Medal of Blue Ribbon, Emperor of Japan, 2004. *Publications:* Renaissance (autobiog.), 2001; Shift: inside Nissan's historic revival (autobiog.), 2005. *Recreations:* swimming, playing tennis, reading, playing contract bridge. *Address:* Nissan Motor Co. Ltd, 17–1 Ginza 6-chome, Chuo-ku, Tokyo 104–8023, Japan. *T:* (3) 35435523.

GHURBURRUN, Sir Rabindrah, Kt 1981; Vice-President, Republic of Mauritius, 1992–97; *b* 27 Sept. 1929; *s* of Mrs Sookmeen Ghurburrun; *m* 1959; one *s* one *d. Educ:* Keble Coll., Oxford. Called to the Bar, Middle Temple; QC Mauritius, 1991; practised as Lawyer, 1959–68; High Comr for Mauritius in India, 1968–76; MLA 1976; Minister of Justice, 1976; Minister of Economic Planning and Development, 1977–82. Member: Central Board; Bar Council (Chm., 1991–92). Former President: Mauritius Arya Sabha; Mauritius Sugar Cane Planters' Assoc.; Hindu Educn Authority; Nat. Congress of Young Socialists. Patron, Commonwealth ESU in Mauritius. Grand Order of the Star and Key, Mauritius, 1993. *Address:* 18 Dr Lesur Street, Cascadelle, Beau Bassin, Mauritius. *T:* 4546421.

GIACCONI, Prof. Riccardo; President, Associated Universities Inc., 1999–2004; *b* 6 Oct. 1931; *s* of Antonio Giacconi and Elsa Canni Giacconi; *m* 1957, Mirella Manaira; one *s* two *d. Educ:* Univ. of Milan (Doctorate in Physics 1954). Asst Prof. of Physics, Univ. of Milan, 1954–56; Res. Associate (Fulbright Fellow), Indiana Univ., 1956–58; Res. Associate, Cosmic Ray Lab., Princeton Univ., 1958–59; American Science & Engineering Inc., Cambridge, Mass., 1959–73: Sen. Scientist and Mem. Bd of Dirs, 1966–73; Exec. Vice Pres., 1969–73; Associate Dir, High Energy Astrophysics Div., Harvard-Smithsonian Center for Astrophysics, 1973–81; Prof. of Astronomy, Harvard Univ., 1973–82; Johns Hopkins University: Prof. of Astronomy, 1981–99; Res. Prof., 1999–; Dir, Space Telescope Sci. Inst., Baltimore, 1981–92. Chm. Bd, Instituto Donegani, Italy, 1987–88; Prof. of Physics and Astronomy, Univ. of Milan, 1991–99; Dir Gen., European Southern Observatory, Germany, 1993–99. Prin. Investigator on NASA progs including: SAS-A (UHURU), 1960–81; SO-54 (SKYLAB); HEAO-2 (Einstein); AXAF Interdisciplinary Scientist (Chandra), 1986–. Hon. DSc: Chicago, 1983; Warsaw, 1996; Laurea *hc:* in Astronomia, Padua, 1984; in Physics, Rome, 1998; Hon. DScTech Uppsala, 2000. Helen B. Warner Award, AAS; Como Prize, Italian Physical Soc., 1967; Röntgen Prize in Astrophysics, Physikalisch-Medizinische Ges., Wurzburg, 1971; NASA Medal for Exceptional Scientific Achievement, 1971, 1980; NASA Distinguished Public Service Award, 1972, 2003; Richtmyer Meml Lectr, American Assoc. of Physics Teachers, 1975; Space Sci. Award, AIAA, 1976; Elliott Cresson Medal, Franklin Inst., Philadelphia, 1980; Catherine Wolfe Bruce Gold Medal, Astronomical Soc. of the Pacific, 1981; Dannie Heineman Prize for Astrophysics, AAS/AIP, 1981; Henry Norris Russell Lectr, AAS, 1981; Gold Medal, RAS, 1982; A. Cressy Morrison Award in Natural Scis, NY Acad. of Scis, 1982; Wolf Prize in Physics, 1987; Targhe d'Oro della Regione Puglia, 1996; (jtly) Nobel Prize in Physics, 2002; Nat. Medal of Science, USA, 2003. Cavaliere di Gran Croce Ordine al Merito (Italy), 2003. *Publications:* (ed jtly) X-ray Astronomy, 1974; (ed jtly) Physics and Astrophysics of Neutron Stars and Black Holes, 1978; (ed jtly) A Face of Extremes: the X-ray universe, 1985; contrib. more than 300 articles in prof. jls. *Recreation:* painting. *Address:* Department of Physics and Astronomy, Johns Hopkins University, 3400 N Charles Street, Baltimore, MD 21218–2686, USA. *Clubs:* Cosmos (Washington); Johns Hopkins (Baltimore).

GIACHARDI, Dr David John, FRSC; Secretary General and Chief Executive, Royal Society of Chemistry, 2000–06; *b* 17 May 1948; *o s* of Thomas and Kathleen Giachardi; *m* 1971, Helen Margaret Fraser; one *d. Educ:* Watford Boys' Grammar Sch.; Merton Coll., Oxford (BA Chem. 1971); St John's Coll., Oxford (MA, DPhil 1974). FRSC 1990. Boston Consulting Group, 1975–79; Courtaulds, 1979–98: Dir of Research, 1982–94; Exec. Dir, 1987–98; Human Resources Dir, 1994–98; Dir of Policy and Assoc. Affairs, EEF, 1998–2000. Member: Nat. Commn on Educn, 1991–93; European Science and Technology Assembly, 1994–97; EPSRC, 1994–99; Quality Assurance Cttee, HEFCE, 1999–2003; Vice-Chm., Industrial R&D Adv. Cttee to Commn for EC, 1991–94. Chm. Adv. Council, ASE, 1996–2001 (Pres., 1994); Mem. Council, Royal Instn of GB, 1995–98 (Chm., 1997–98). *Recreations:* science, golf. *Address:* Laburnum, Cheverells Green, Markyate, St Albans, Herts AL3 8RN. *Clubs:* Athenæum, Oxford and Cambridge; Brocket Hall Golf.

GIAEVER, Prof. Ivar; Institute Professor, Physics Department, Rensselaer Polytechnic Institute, Troy, New York, 1988–2005; Professor-at-large, University of Oslo, Norway, since 1988; *b* 5 April 1929; *s* of John A. Giaever and Gudrun (*née* Skaarud); *m* 1952, Inger Skramstad; one *s* three *d. Educ:* Norwegian Inst. of Tech.; Rensselear Polytechnical Inst. ME 1952; PhD 1964. Norwegian Army, 1952–53; Norwegian Patent Office, 1953–54; Canadian General Electric, 1954–56; General Electric, 1956–58; Staff Mem., Gen. Electric R&D Center, 1958–88. Fellow, Amer. Phys. Soc.; Member: Nat. Acad. of Sciences; Nat. Acad. of Engineering; Amer. Acad. of Arts and Scis; Norwegian Acad. of Scis; Norwegian Acad. of Technology; Norwegian Profl Engrs; Swedish Acad. of Engrg. Hon. DSc: RPI, 1974; Union Coll., 1974; Clarkson, Potsdam, NY, 1983; Trondheim, Norway; Hon. DEng, Michigan Tech. Univ., 1976; Hon. DPhys: Oslo, 1976; State Univ. of NY, 1984. Oliver E. Buckley Prize, 1964; Nobel Prize for Physics, 1973; Zworykin Award, 1974. *Publications:* contrib. Physical Review, Jl Immunology. *Recreations:* ski-ing, tennis, camping, hiking. *Address:* c/o Physics Department, Rensselaer Polytechnic Institute, Troy, NY 12180–3590, USA. *T:* (518) 2766429, *Fax:* (518) 2762825; *e-mail:* giaevi@rpi.edu.

GIBB, Andrew Thomas Fotheringham; Partner, Balfour and Manson, Solicitors, Edinburgh, since 1975 (Chairman, 1996–2005); President, Law Society of Scotland, 1990–91; *b* 17 Aug. 1947; *s* of Thomas Fotheringham Gibb and Isabel Gow McKenzie or Gibb; *m* 1971, Mrs Patricia Anne Eggo or Gibb; two *s. Educ:* Perth Acad.; Edinburgh Univ. (LLB Hons). Temporary Sheriff, 1989–99. Member: Lothian and Borders Legal Aid Cttee, 1977–84; Legal Aid Central Cttee, 1984–86; Council, Law Soc. of Scotland, 1981–94. Chm. Management Cttee, Lothian Allellon Soc., 1984–97 (Mem., Bd of Govs, 1984–2001). Accredited family law specialist. Session Clerk, St Ninian's Church, Corstorphine, Edinburgh. *Recreations:* music, church organist, golf. *Address:* 58 Frederick Street, Edinburgh EH2 1LS. *Club:* New (Edinburgh); Royal Burgess Golfing Soc.

GIBB, Frances Rebecca; Legal Editor, The Times, since 1999; *b* 24 Feb. 1951; *d* of late Matthew Gibb and of Bettina Mary Gibb (*née* Dawson); *m* 1978, Joseph Cahill; three *s. Educ:* St Margaret's Sch., Bushey; Univ. of E Anglia (BA 1st Cl. Hons English). News researcher, Visnews, 1973; reporter, THES, 1974–78; Art Sales corresp., Daily Telegraph, 1978–80; The Times: reporter, 1980–82; Legal Corresp., 1982–99. Vis. Prof., QMC. Gov., King's College Sch., Wimbledon. MUniv Open, 2000. *Recreations:* my family, gardening, theatre. *Address:* The Times, 1 Pennington Street, E98 1XY. *Club:* Reform.

GIBB, Sir Francis Ross, (Sir Frank Gibb), Kt 1987; CBE 1982; BSc; FREng; FICE; Chairman and Chief Executive, Taylor Woodrow Group, 1985–89 (Joint Managing Director, 1979–85, and a Joint Deputy Chairman, 1983–85); President, Taylor Woodrow Construction, since 1985 (Chairman, 1978–85); *b* 29 June 1927; *s* of Robert Gibb and Violet Mary Gibb; *m* 1st, 1950, Wendy Marjorie Fowler (*d* 1997); one *s* two *d*; 2nd, 2000, Kirsten Harwood. *Educ:* Loughborough Coll. BSc(Eng); CEng. Dir, 1963–70, Man. Dir, then Jt Man. Dir, 1970–84, Taylor Woodrow Construction; Director: Taylor Woodrow Internat., 1969–85; Taylor Woodrow plc, 1972–89; Chm., Taywood Santa Fe, 1975–85. Jt Dep. Chm., Seaforth Maritime Ltd, 1986–89; Director: Seaforth Maritime Hldgs, 1978–89; (indep.) Energy Saving Trust Ltd, 1992–99 (Chm., 1995–98); non-executive: Eurotunnel plc, 1986–87; Babcock Internat. Group, 1989–97; Steetley plc, 1990–92; Nuclear Electric plc, 1990–94; H. R. Wallingford, 1995–; AMCO Corporation plc, 1995–99. Member: Construction Industry Adv. Cttee, HSE, 1978–81; Gp of Eight, 1979–81; Board, British Nuclear Associates, 1980–88 (Chm., Agrément Bd, 1980–82); Chm., Nat. Nuclear Corp., 1981–88. Mem. Council, CBI, 1979–80, 1985–90. Dir, Holiday Pay Scheme, 1980–84 and Trustee, Benefits Scheme, 1980–84, Building and Civil Engrg Trustees. Federation of Civil Engineering Contractors: Vice-Chm., 1978–79; Chm., 1979–80; Vice Pres., 1980–84; Pres., 1984–87; Vice-Pres., ICE, 1988–90. Freeman, City of London, 1978. Hon. FINucE 1984; Hon. FCGI 1990. Hon. DTech Loughborough, 1989. *Recreations:* ornithology, gardening, walking, music. *Address:* Ross Gibb Consultants, 11 Latchmoor Avenue, Gerrards Cross, Bucks SL9 8LJ. *Club:* Arts.

GIBB, Ian Pashley; Director of Public Services, Planning and Administration, British Library (Humanities and Social Sciences), 1985–87; *b* 17 April 1926; *s* of late John Pashley Gibb and Mary (*née* Owen); *m* 1953, Patricia Mary Butler (*d* 1993); two *s. Educ:* Latymer Upper Sch.; UCL (BA). MCLIP. Sen. Library Asst, Univ. of London, 1951–52; Asst Librarian, UCL, 1952–58; Dep. Librarian, National Central Library, 1958–73; British Library: Dep. Dir, Science Reference Library, 1973–75; Head of Divl Office, Reference Div., 1975–77; Dir and Keeper, Reference Div., 1977–85. Part-time Lectr, UCL, 1967–77, Hon. Research Fellow, 1977–85, Examiner, 1985–87. Hon. Treasurer, Bibliographical Soc., 1961–67; Member Council: Library Assoc., 1980–82; Friends of British Library, 1989–2001 (Dep. Chm., 1989–93). Chm., Dacorum NT Assoc., 1993–97. *Publications:* (ed) Newspaper Preservation and Access, 2 vols, 1988; various articles. *Recreations:* music, watching cricket, wine-tasting, travel especially to Austria and Greece, cruising. *Address:* The Old Cottage, 16 Tile Kiln Lane, Leverstock Green, Hemel Hempstead, Herts HP3 8ND. *T:* (01442) 256352.

GIBB, Moira, CBE 2001; Chief Executive, London Borough of Camden, since 2003; *d* of James Bogan and Catherine Bogan (*née* McTaggart); *m* 1990, Henry Blythe; one *s. Educ:* Glasgow Univ. (MA); Edinburgh Univ. (Dip. Soc. Admin; CQSW); Univ. of Newcastle upon Tyne (PQCCC). Social worker and teacher, 1970–80; Lectr, Preston Polytech., 1980–81; Child Care Inspector, Surrey CC, 1981–84; Asst Dir, London Bor. of Ealing, 1984–88; Royal Borough of Kensington and Chelsea: Dep. Dir, 1988–91, Dir, 1991–2000, Social Services; Exec. Dir, Housing and Social Services, 2000–03. Mem., Adv. Bd, UK CeMGA, ONS, 2005–; non-exec. Mem., UK Statistics Authy, 2008–. Vis. Lectr, LSE, 1982–84. Pres., Assoc. of Dirs of Social Services, 2000–01. Governor: Our Lady of Victories Sch., SW15, 1996–2004; Coram Family, 2002–05. Dir, London Marathon. *Recreations:* cycling, running, detective fiction. *Address:* London Borough of Camden, Town Hall, Judd Street, WC1H 9JE; *e-mail:* moira.gibb@camden.gov.uk.

GIBB, Nicolas John; MP (C) Bognor Regis and Littlehampton, since 1997; *b* 3 Sept. 1960; *s* of late John McLean Gibb and Eileen Mavern Gibb. *Educ:* Maidstone Grammar Sch.; Roundhay Sch., Leeds; Thornes House Sch., Wakefield; Univ. of Durham (BA Hons). ACA 1987. Chartered Accountant, KPMG, 1984–97. Opposition spokesman: on HM Treasury, 1998–99; on trade and industry, 1999–2001; on education, 2005–. Member: Social Security Select Cttee, 1997–98; Public Accounts Cttee, 2001–03; Educn and Skills Select Cttee, 2003–05. Contested (C): Stoke-on-Trent Central, 1992; Rotherham, May 1994. *Address:* House of Commons, SW1A 0AA.

GIBBENS, Barnaby John, OBE 1989; Chairman, Skin Treatment and Research Trust, since 1991; *b* 17 April 1935; *s* of late Dr Gerald Gibbens and Deirdre Gibbens; *m* 1st, 1960, Sally Mary Stephenson (marr. diss. 1990); one *s* two *d*; 2nd, 1990, Kristina de Zabala. *Educ:* Winchester College. FCA 1972. Founder, 1962, Dep. Chm., 1962–81, Chm., 1981–90, Computer Analysts & Programmers (later CAP Group, then SEMA Group); Chairman: Enterprise Systems Group Ltd, 1989–96; The Royal Tennis Court, Hampton Court Palace, 1995–2001; Mercator Systems Ltd, 2000–02. Chairman: Computing Services Industry Trng Council, 1984–93; IT Industry Lead Body, 1987–93; IT Trng Accreditation Council, 1991–94; IT Industry Trng Orgn, 1992–95; a Director: National Computing Centre, 1987–90; UK Skills, 1990–2001; Member: Nat. Cttee on Computer Networks, 1978; NCVQ, 1989–92; NCET, 1991–94. Pres., Computing Services Assoc., 1975. Chm., Young IT Technician of the Year, 1993–2000. Founding Master, Co. of Information Technologists, 1987. Hon. Mem., C & G, 1993. FRSA 1993. *Recreations:* golf, Real tennis, music, gardening. *Address:* 12 Kings Road, Wimbledon, SW19 8QN. *T:* (020) 8542 3878. *Clubs:* MCC; Wisley Golf.

GIBBINGS, Sir Peter (Walter), Kt 1989; Chairman, Radio Authority, 1995–99; *b* 25 March 1929; *s* of late Walter White Gibbings and Margaret Russell Gibbings (*née* Torrance); *m* 1st, Elspeth Felicia Macintosh; two *d*; 2nd, Hon. Louise Barbara, *d* of 2nd Viscount Lambert, TD; one *s. Educ:* Rugby; Wadham Coll., Oxford. Called to the Bar, Middle Temple, 1953. Served in 9th Queen's Royal Lancers, 1951–52. The Observer, 1960–67 (Deputy Manager and Dir, 1965–67); Man. Dir, Guardian Newspapers Ltd, 1967–73; Dir, Manchester Guardian and Evening News Ltd, 1967–73; Chm., Guardian and Manchester Evening News plc, 1973–88; Anglia Television Gp: Dir, 1981–94; Dep. Chm., 1986–88; Chm., 1988–94. Director: Press Assoc. Ltd, 1982–88 (Chm., 1986–87); Reuters Holdings PLC, 1984–88; The Economist, 1987–99; Rothschild Trust Corp. Ltd, 1989–96; Council, UEA, 1989–96. Mem., Press Council, 1970–74; Pres., CPU, 1989–91. *Recreations:* fishing, music. *Address:* 10 The Vale, SW3 6AH.

GIBBINS, Rev. Dr Ronald Charles; Methodist Minister; Superintendent Minister, Wesley's Chapel, London, 1978–88; *s* of Charles and Anne Gibbins; *m* 1949, Olive Ruth (*née* Patchett); one *s* two *d. Educ:* London Univ. (BScSociol); Wesley Theological Coll., Bristol; Eden Theological Seminary, US (DMin). Methodist Minister: Bradford, 1948–49; Spennymoor, 1949–50; Middlesbrough, 1950–57; Basildon, 1957–64; East End Mission, London, 1964–78. *Publications:* Mission for the Secular City, 1976; The Lumpen Proletariat, 1979; The Stations of the Resurrection, 1987. *Recreations:* travel, journalism.

GIBBON, Gary; Political Editor, Channel 4 News, since 2005; *b* 15 March 1965; *s* of Robert Philip Gibbon and Elizabeth Mary Gibbon (*née* Harries); *m* 1994, Laura Kate Pulay; two *s. Educ:* John Lyon Sch., Harrow; Balliol Coll., Oxford (BA). Researcher, Viewpoint Productions, 1987–89; Producer, BBC Business Breakfast, 1989–90; Political Prod., 1990–94, Political Corresp., 1994–2005, Channel 4 News. Home News Award, RTS, 2006. *Address:* c/o Channel 4 News, Parliamentary Press Gallery, House of Commons, SW1A 0AA. *T:* (020) 7430 4990; *e-mail:* gary.gibbon@itn.co.uk.

GIBBON, His Honour Michael; QC 1974; a Senior Circuit Judge, 1993–99 (a Circuit Judge, 1979–99); *b* 15 Sept. 1930; 2nd *s* of late Frank and Jenny Gibbon; *m* 1956, Malveen Elliot Seager (*d* 2007); two *s* one *d*. *Educ:* Brightlands; Charterhouse; Pembroke Coll., Oxford (MA). Commnd in Royal Artillery, 1949. Called to the Bar, Lincoln's Inn, 1954. A Recorder of the Crown Court, 1972–79; Hon. Recorder, City of Cardiff, 1986–99; Resident Judge, Cardiff Crown Court, 1993–99. Chairman: Electoral Adv. Cttee to Home Sec., 1972; Local Govt Boundary Commn for Wales, 1978–79 (Dep. Chm., 1974–78); Lord Chancellor's Adv. Cttee for S Glam, 1990–2000; Criminal Justice Area Liaison Cttee for S and SW Wales, 1992–99; Mem., Parole Bd, 1986–88. A Chm., Bar Disciplinary Tribunal, 1988. *Recreations:* music, golf. *Clubs:* Cardiff and County (Cardiff); Royal Porthcawl Golf, Cardiff Golf.

GIBBONS, Brian Joseph, FRCGP; Member (Lab) Aberavon, National Assembly for Wales, since 1999; Minister for Social Justice and Local Government, since 2007; *b* 25 Aug. 1950. *Educ:* National Univ. of Ireland (MB BCh, BAO 1974). DRCOG 1979; Cert. FPA 1979; MRCGP 1980, FRCGP 1995. Jun. hosp. doctor, Galway, Roscommon and Sheffield, 1974–76; Calderdale GP Vocation Trng Scheme, 1977–80; GP, Blaengwynfi, 1980–99. Sec., W Glamorgan/Morgannwg LMC, 1994–99. National Assembly for Wales: Dep. Minister for Health and Social Services, 2000–03, for Economic Develt and Transport, 2003–05; Minister for Health and Social Services, 2005–07, for the Econ. and Transport, 2007. *Address:* National Assembly for Wales, Cardiff Bay, Cardiff CF99 1NA. *T:* (029) 2089 8382. *Club:* Gwynfi Social and Athletic.

GIBBONS, Hon. Sir David; *see* Gibbons, Hon. Sir J. D.

GIBBONS, Prof. Gary William, PhD; FRS 1999; Professor of Theoretical Physics, since 1997, and Fellow of Trinity College, since 2002, University of Cambridge; *b* 7 July 1946; *s* of Archibald Gibbons and Bertha Gibbons (*née* Bunn); *m* 1972, Christine Howden; two *s*. *Educ:* Purley County Grammar Sch.; St Catharine's Coll., Cambridge (BA 1968; MA 1972); Clare Coll., Cambridge (PhD 1973). University of Cambridge: Lectr in Maths, 1980–90; Reader in Theoretical Physics, 1990–97. *Publication:* (with S. W. Hawking) Euclidean Quantum Gravity, 1993. *Recreations:* listening to music, looking at paintings. *Address:* 52 Hurst Park Avenue, Cambridge CB4 2AE. *T:* (01223) 363036.

GIBBONS, Prof. Ian Read, FRS 1983; Research Cell Biologist, University of California, Berkeley, since 1997; *b* 30 Oct. 1931; *s* of Arthur Alwyn Gibbons and Hilda Read Cake; *m* 1961, Barbara Ruth Hollingworth; one *s* one *d*. *Educ:* Faversham Grammar School; Cambridge Univ. (BA, PhD). Research Fellow, 1958–63, Asst Prof., 1963–67, Harvard Univ.; Associate Prof., 1967–69, Prof. of Biophysics, 1969–97, Univ. of Hawaii. *Publications:* contribs to learned jls. *Recreations:* gardening, computer programming, music. *Address:* Department of Molecular and Cell Biology, University of California, Berkeley, 335 LSA–3200, Berkeley, CA 94720–3200, USA. *T:* (510) 6422439.

GIBBONS, Jeremy Stewart; QC 1995; a Recorder, since 1993; *b* 15 July 1949; *s* of Geoffrey Gibbons and Rosemary Gibbons (*née* Stewart); *m* 1st, 1974, Mary Mercia Bradley; two *s* one *d* (and one *d* decd); 2nd, 1998, Sarah Valerie Jenkins. *Educ:* Oakmount Sch., Southampton; St Edward's Sch., Oxford. Called to the Bar, Gray's Inn, 1973; Asst Recorder, 1989–93. *Recreations:* cooking, gardening, ski-ing, carpentry. *Address:* 12 College Place, Southampton SO15 2FE. *T:* (023) 8032 0320.

GIBBONS, Hon. Sir (John) David, KBE 1985; JP; Chairman, Colonial Insurance Co. Ltd, Bermuda, since 1986; *b* 15 June 1927; *s* of late Edmund G. Gibbons, CBE, and Winifred G. Gibbons, MBE; *m* 1958, Lully Lorentzen; three *s* (and one *d* by former *m*). *Educ:* Saltus Grammar Sch., Bermuda; Hotchkiss Sch., Lakeville, Conn; Harvard Univ., Cambridge, Mass (BA). Mem. Govt Boards: Social Welfare Bd, 1949–58; Bd of Civil Aviation, 1958–60; Bd of Educn, 1956–59 (Chm., 1973–74); Trade Develt Bd, 1960–74. MP Bermuda, 1972–84; Minister of Health and Welfare, 1974–75, of Finance, 1975–84; Premier of Bermuda, 1977–82. Chm., Bank of N. T. Butterfield & Son Ltd, Bermuda, 1986–97. Chairman: Bermuda Monetary Authy, 1984–86; Economic Council, Bermuda, 1984–86. Mem., Law Reform Cttee, 1969–72. Mem. Governing Body, subseq. Chm., Bermuda Technical Inst., 1956–70. Trustee, Massachusetts Financial Services, 1988–2002. CCMI. JP Bermuda, 1974. *Recreations:* tennis, golf, ski-ing, swimming. *Address:* Leeward, 5 Leeside Drive, Pembroke HM 05, Bermuda. *T:* (441) 2952396. *Clubs:* Phoenix (Cambridge, Mass); Harvard (New York); Royal Bermuda Yacht, Royal Hamilton Amateur Dinghy, Mid-Ocean, Riddells Bay Golf, Spanish Point Boat (Bermuda); Lyford Cay (Bahamas).

GIBBONS, Dr John Ernest, CBE 2000; Architectural Adviser, Scottish Parliament, since 2001; *b* Halesowen, Worcs, 20 April 1940; *s* of late John Howard Gibbons and Lilian Alice Gibbons (*née* Shale); *m* 1963, Patricia Mitchell; one *s* two *d*. *Educ:* Oldbury Grammar Sch.; Birmingham Sch. of Architecture; Edinburgh Univ. PhD; DipArch; DipTP; ARIBA; ARIAS; FSA(Scot). In private practice, 1962–65; Lectr, Birmingham Sch. of Architecture and Univ. of Aston, 1964–66; Res. Fellow, 1967–69, Lectr, 1969–72, Edinburgh Univ.; Scottish Development Department: Prin. Architect, 1972–78; Asst Dir, Building Directorate, 1978–82; Dep. Dir and Dep. Chief Architect, 1982–84; Dir of Building and Chief Architect, Scottish Office, 1984–99; Chief Architect, Scottish Exec., 1999–2005. Vis. Res. Scientist, CSIRO, Melbourne, 1974–75; Vis. Prof., Mackintosh Sch. of Architecture, 2000–. Member, Council: EAA and RIAS, 1977–80; ARCUK, 1984. FRSA 1979. DUniv UCE, 1999. *Publications:* contribs on architectural and planning matters to professional and technical jls. *Recreations:* reading, photography, music, travel. *Club:* New (Edinburgh).

GIBBONS, Ven. Kenneth Harry; Archdeacon of Lancaster, 1981–97, now Emeritus; *b* 24 Dec. 1931; *s* of Harry and Phyllis Gibbons; *m* 1962, Margaret Ann Tomlinson; two *s*. *Educ:* Blackpool and Chesterfield Grammar Schools; Manchester Univ. (BSc); Cuddesdon Coll., Oxford. RAF, 1952–54. Ordained, 1956; Assistant Curate of Fleetwood, 1956–60; Secretary for Student Christian Movement in Schools, 1960–62; Senior Curate, St Martin-in-the-Fields, Westminster, 1962–65; Vicar of St Edward, New Addington, 1965–70; Vicar of Portsea, 1970–81; RD of Portsmouth, 1973–79; Priest-in-charge of Weeton, 1981–85; Vicar, St Michael's-on-Wyre, 1985–97; Diocesan Dir of Ordinands, Blackburn, 1982–90; Priest i/c, St Magnus the Martyr, Lower Thames St with St Margaret, Fish St, and St Michael, Crooked Lane, 1997–2003, St Clement, Eastcheap, 1999–2007, City of London. Acting Chaplain to HM Forces, 1981–85. *Address:* 112 Valley Road, Kenley, Surrey CR8 5BU. *T:* (020) 8660 7502. *Club:* Reform.

GIBBONS, Michael Gordon, MBE 2002; PhD; Director, Science and Technology Policy Research, University of Sussex, 2004–06; Secretary General, Association of Commonwealth Universities, 1996–2004; *b* 15 April 1939; *m* 1968, Gillian Monks; one *s* one *d*. *Educ:* Concordia Univ., Montreal (BSc Maths and Physics); McGill Univ., Montreal (BEng); Queen's Univ., Ont (MSc Radio Astronomy); Manchester Univ. (PhD 1967). Department of Science and Technology Policy, University of Manchester: Lectr, 1967–72; Sen. Lectr, 1972–75; Prof., 1975–92; Hd of Dept, 1975–92; Dir, Univ./UMIST Pollution Res. Unit, 1979–86; Chm. and Founding Dir, Policy Res. in Engrg, Sci. and Technol., 1979–92; Dir, Res., Exploitation and Develt, Vice-Chancellor's Office, 1984–92; University of Sussex: Dean, Grad. Sch. and Dir, Science Policy Res. Unit, 1992–96; Mem., Senate and Mgt Cttee, 1992–96; Mem., Court and Council, 1994–96; Hon. Prof., 1994. Visiting Professor: Univ. of Montreal, 1976 and 1977–81; Univ. of Calif, Berkeley, 1992. Chm., Marinetech NW, 1981–91. Special Advr, H of C Sci. and Technol. Cttee, 1993–. Mem. Council, ESRC, 1997–2001 (Mem., 1994–97, Chm., 1997–2001, Res. Priorities Bd). Consultant, Cttee of Sci. and Technol. Policy, OECD, Paris, 1979–. Founding Bd Mem., Quest Univ., Canada (Chm., Bd of Govs, 2006–). Fellow, Royal Swedish Acad. of Engrg Scis, 2000. Member, Editorial Board: Technovation, 1984–; Prometheus, 1992–. Hon. LLD: Ghana, 1999; Concordia, 2004; DUniv Surrey, 2005. Golden Jubilee Medal (Canada), 2002. *Publications:* (jtly) Wealth from Knowledge, 1972; (jtly) Future of University Research, 1981; (ed jtly) Science Studies Today, 1983; (jtly) New Forms of Communication and Collaboration between Universities and Industry, 1985; (jtly) Post-Innovation Performance: technological development and competition, 1986; (with L. Georghiou) The Evaluation of Research: a synthesis of current practice, 1987; (jtly) The New Production of Knowledge: the dynamics of science and research in contemporary societies, 1994; (jtly) Re-Thinking Science: knowledge and the public in an age of uncertainty, 2001; contrib. numerous papers and articles on science policy. *Address:* 24 Fletsand Road, Wilmslow, Cheshire SK9 2AB.

GIBBONS, Sir William Edward Doran, 9th Bt *cr* 1752; JP; Director, Passenger Shipping Association, since 1994; Marketing Director, European Cruise Council, since 2004; *b* 13 Jan. 1948; *s* of Sir John Edward Gibbons, 8th Bt, and of Mersa Wentworth, *y d* of late Major Edward Baynton Grove Foster; *S* father, 1982; *m* 1st, 1972, Patricia Geraldine Archer (marr. diss. 2004), *d* of Roland Archer Howse; one *s* one *d*; 2nd, 2004, Maggie Moone. *Educ:* Pangbourne; RNC Dartmouth; Bristol Univ. (BSc); Southampton Univ. Management Sch. (MBA 1996). Asst Shipping and Port Manager, Sealink UK, Parkeston Quay, 1979–82; Service Manager (Anglo-Dutch), Sealink UK Ltd, 1982–85; Ferry Line Manager (Harwich-Hook), 1985–87, Gen. Manager, IoW Services, 1987–90, Sealink British Ferries. Transport and management consultant, 1990–94. Chm., Council of Travel and Tourism, 1996–2001 (Vice Chm., 1995–96); Mem. Bd, Duty Free Confedn, 1996–2000. Non-Exec. Mem., IoW DHA, 1990–94. Mem., Manningtree Parish Council, 1981–87 (Chm., 1985–87). JP: Portsmouth, 1990–94; Westminster Div., Inner London, 1994– (Probation Liaison Justice, 1998–2006). *Heir:* *s* Charles William Edwin Gibbons, *b* 28 Jan. 1983. *Address:* 1 West Walks, Dorchester, Dorset DT1 1RE.

GIBBS, family name of **Barons Aldenham** and **Wraxall**.

GIBBS, Barbara Lynn; education consultant, since 2006; Head Teacher, British School in The Netherlands, 2001–06; *b* 8 Nov. 1945; *d* of William Newill and Mabel Till; *m* 1967, John Colin Gibbs; two *d*. *Educ:* Bromley Grammar Sch. for Girls; Univ. of Hull (BSc Hons Chem.); Univ. of E Anglia (MA; PGCE). Teaching and lecturing, mainly on chem. and maths, in various educnl estabts in Yorks, Notts, Norfolk and Barnet, 1967–86; Sen. Teacher, Henrietta Barnett Sch., 1986–90; Vice Principal, Havering Sixth Form Coll., 1990–94; Head Teacher, Newstead Wood Sch. for Girls, 1994–2001. OFSTED Inspector, 1998–2002; Strategic Dir, Prospects Educn Services, 1999–2001; ISI Inspector, 2003–; NPQH tutor. FRSA 1994; MInstD 1999. *Recreations:* music, literature, travel, swimming, Rugby Union. *Clubs:* Royal Automobile; Royal Scots (Edinburgh).

GIBBS, Air Vice-Marshal Charles Melvin, CB 1976; CBE 1966; DFC 1943; RAF retd; Recruiting Consultant with Selleck Associates, Colchester, 1977–86; *b* 11 June 1921; American father, New Zealand mother; *m* 1947, Emma Pamela Pollard (*d* 1991); one *d*; *m* 1999, Adrienne Ryan. *Educ:* Taumarunui, New Zealand. MECI 1980. Joined RNZAF, 1941; service in Western Desert and Mediterranean, 1942–44; Coastal Comd, 1945; India, 1946–47; commanded Tropical Experimental Unit, 1950–52; RAF Staff Coll., 1953; commanded No 118 Squadron, 1954–55; Directing Staff, RAF Staff Coll., 1956–58; Pakistan, 1958–61; Chief Instructor, RAF Chivenor, 1961–63; CO, Wattisham, 1963–66; idc 1967; Defence Policy Staff, 1968–69; Dir of Quartering, 1970–72; AOA, Germany, 1972–74; Dir-Gen. Personal Services, RAF, 1974–76. *Recreations:* fishing, golf. *Address:* 5 Kew Place, Taupo, New Zealand. *T:* (7) 3771957.

GIBBS, Marion Olive; Headmistress, James Allen's Girls' School, Dulwich, since 1994; *b* 16 Sept. 1951; *d* of Harry Norman Smith and Olive Mabel (*née* Lewis). *Educ:* Pate's Grammar Sch. for Girls, Cheltenham; Bristol Univ. (BA 1st cl. Hons Classics 1973; PGCE 1974; MLitt 1981). Assistant Mistress: City of Worcester Girls' Grammar Sch., 1974–76; Chailey Comprehensive Sch., 1977; Hd of Sixth Form, Dir of Studies and Hd of Classics, Burgess Hill Sch. for Girls, 1977–89; Hd of Sixth Form and Classics, Haberdashers' Aske's Girls' Sch., Elstree, 1989–91; HMI of Schools, 1992–94. Tutor, Open Univ., 1979–91. Member Council: Classical Assoc., 1984–87, 1995–98 (Hon. Jt Sec., 1989–92); Hellenic Soc., 1997–2000; Chm. Council, JACT, 2001–04. Columnist, SecEd, 2004–. FRSA 1997. *Publications:* Greek Tragedy: an introduction, 1989; (contrib.) Two Sectors, One Purpose, 2002; (contrib.) The Teaching of Classics, 2003; (contrib.) Heads: leading schools in the 21st century, 2007. *Recreations:* music, gardening, drama, keeping informed about the developing world. *Address:* James Allen's Girls' School, East Dulwich Grove, SE22 8TE. *T:* (020) 8693 1181.

GIBBS, Patrick Michael Evan; QC 2006; *b* 24 April 1962; *s* of Michael Edmund Hubert Gibbs and Helen Antonia Gibbs; *m* 1989, Catherine Clare Barroll; one *s* one *d*. *Educ:* Eton; Christ Church, Oxford; City Univ. Called to the Bar, Middle Temple, 1986. *Address:* 3 Raymond Buildings, Gray's Inn, WC1R 5BH.

GIBBS, Dr Richard John; management consultant, Tribal Group (formerly Secta Ltd), since 2002; Chief Executive, Kingston and Richmond (formerly Kingston and Esher) Health Authority, 1990–2002; *b* 15 May 1943; *s* of Leslie and Mary Gibbs; *m* 1968, Laura Wanda Olasmi; one *d*. *Educ:* Merchant Taylors' Sch., Northwood; Pembroke Coll., Cambridge (BA 1965); Warwick Univ. (PhD 1974). Teacher, City of London Sch. for Boys, 1965; Scientific Officer, Home Office, 1968; Sen. Scientific Officer, 1970, PSO, 1972, DHSS; Res. Schol., Internat. Inst. for Applied Systems Analysis, Austria, 1977; SPSO, DHSS, 1978; Central Policy Review Staff, 1980; Dir of Operational Res. (DCSO), 1982, CSO, 1985, DHSS; Under Sec. and Dir of Stats and Management, DHSS, then DoH, 1986–90. Vis. Prof., UCL, 1985. Non-exec. Dir, Southwark PCT, 2007–. *Publications:* contribs to Jl of ORS. *Recreations:* windsurfing, cooking. *Address:* *e-mail:* rjgibbs@dircon.co.uk.

GIBBS, Hon. Sir Richard (John Hedley), Kt 2000; a Judge of the High Court of Justice, Queen's Bench Division, 2000–08; Presiding Judge, Midland Circuit, 2004–07; *b* 2 Sept. 1941; *s* of Brian Conaway Gibbs and Mabel Joan Gibbs; *m* 1965, Janet (*née* Whittall); one *s* two *d* (and one *d* decd). *Educ:* Oundle Sch.; Trinity Hall, Cambridge (MA). Called to the Bar, Inner Temple, 1965, Bencher, 2000; a Recorder, 1981–90; QC 1984; a Circuit Judge, 1990–2000. *Address:* c/o Royal Courts of Justice, Strand, WC2A 2LL.

GIBBS, Sir Roger (Geoffrey), Kt 1994; Director: Fleming Family & Partners, 2000–07 (Chairman, 2000–03); Gerrard & National Holdings PLC (formerly Gerrard & National Discount Co. Ltd), 1971–94 (Chairman, 1975–89); Chairman, The Wellcome Trust, 1989–99 (Governor, 1983–99); *b* 13 Oct. 1934; 4th *s* of Hon. Sir Geoffrey Gibbs, KCMG, and Hon. Lady Gibbs, CBE; *m* 2005, Mrs Jane Patricia Lee. *Educ:* Eton; Millfield. Jessel Toynbee & Co. Ltd, 1954–64, Dir 1960; de Zoete & Gorton, later de Zoete & Bevan, Stockbrokers, 1964–71, Partner 1966. Chm., London Discount Market Assoc., 1984–86. Director: Arsenal FC, 1980–2006; Colville Estate Ltd, 1989–; Howard de Walden Estates Ltd, 1989–2001 (Chm., 1993–98). Member: Council, Royal Nat. Pension Fund for Nurses, 1975–2002; Finance and Invest Cttee, 1985–2002, Council, 1982–2002, ICRF. Chm., St Paul's Cathedral Foundn, 2000–; Trustee, Winston Churchill Meml Trust, 2001–. Governor, London Clinic, 1983–93; Special Trustee, Guy's Hosp., 1983–92. Freeman, City of London; Liveryman, Merchant Taylors' Co. Trustee, Arundel Castle Cricket Foundn, 1987– (Chm., 1987–95). *Publication:* The Cresta Run 1885–1985, 1984. *Recreations:* travel, sport. *Clubs:* Boodle's, Pratt's, Queen's, MCC; Swinley Forest Golf (Chm., 1993–97).

GIBRALTAR, Archdeacon of; *see* Sutch, Ven. C. D.

GIBRALTAR IN EUROPE, Bishop of, since 2001; **Rt Rev. Dr (Douglas) Geoffrey Rowell;** *b* 13 Feb. 1943; *s* of late Cecil Victor Rowell and Kate (*née* Hunter). *Educ:* Eggar's Grammar Sch., Alton, Hants; Winchester Coll.; Corpus Christi Coll., Cambridge (MA, PhD); MA, DPhil, DD Oxon; Cuddesdon Theol Coll. Ordained deacon, 1968, priest 1969; Hastings Rashdall Student and Asst Chaplain, New Coll., Oxford, 1968–72; Hon. Asst Curate, St Andrew's, Headington, 1968–71; University of Oxford: Fellow, Chaplain and Tutor in Theology, Keble Coll., 1972–94 (Emeritus Fellow, 1994–); Lectr in Theology, 1977–94; Leader, expedn to Ethiopia, 1974; Pro-Proctor, 1980–81; Suffragan Bishop of Basingstoke, 1994–2001. Canon, Chichester Cathedral, 1981–2002; Vis. Canon-Theologian, St James' Episcopal Cathedral, Chicago, 1988. Member: C of E Liturgical Commn, 1981–91; C of E Doctrine Commn, 1991–96, 1998–2005 (Consultant, 1996–98); Inter-Anglican Standing Commn on Ecumenical Relations, 2000– (Vice-Chm., 2003–); Anglican Co-Chm., Anglican-Oriental Orthodox Jt Doctrinal Commn, 2001– (Mem., Anglican-Oriental Orthodox Internat. Forum, 1985, 1989, 1993, 1996); Chm., Churches Funerals Gp (formerly Churches Gp on Funeral Services in Cemeteries and Crematoria), 1997–. Examining Chaplain to: Bp of Leicester, 1979–90; Bp of Winchester, 1991–93. Hon. Dir, Archbp's Exam. in Theol., 1985–2001; Conservator, Mirfield Cert. in Pastoral Theol., 1987–94; Mem., Theol Colls Assessment Gp, 1993. Gov., SPCK, 1984–94, 1997–2004 (Vice-Pres., 1994–). Member: Council of Almoners, Christ's Hosp., 1979–89; Council of Mgt, St Stephen's Hse, Oxford, 1986– (Chm., 2003–); Governor: Pusey Hse, Oxford, 1979– (Pres., Govs, 1996–); Eggar's Sch., Alton, 1994–98; Chm. Council, Hse of St Gregory and St Macrina, Oxford, 1987–94. Vis. Prof., UC, Chichester (formerly Chichester Inst. of Higher Educn), 1996–2003. Trustee, Scott Holland Lectureship, 1979– (Chm., 1992–); Louise Ward Haskin Lectr, St Paul's, Washington, 1995. Hon. Consultant, Nat. Funerals Coll., 1995–2001. Contrib., Credo column, The Times, 1992–. Mem., Internat. Editl Bd, Mortality, 1995–; Jt Ed., Internat. Jl for Study of the Christian Church, 2001–. FRSA 1989. Hon. DD Nashotah House, Wisconsin, 1996. *Publications:* Hell and the Victorians: a study of the 19th century theological controversies concerning eternal punishment and the future life, 1974; (ed with B. E. Juel Jensen) Rock-Hewn Churches of Eastern Tigray, 1976; The Liturgy of Christian Burial: an historical introduction, 1977; The Vision Glorious: themes and personalities of the Catholic Revival in Anglicanism, 1983; (ed) Tradition Renewed: the Oxford Movement Conference Papers, 1986; (ed and contrib.) To the Church of England, by G. Bennett, 1988; (ed with M. Dudley) Confession and Absolution, 1990; (ed) The English Religious Tradition and the Genius of Anglicanism, 1992; (ed with M. Dudley) The Oil of Gladness: anointing in the Church, 1993; The Club of Nobody's Friends 1800–2000, 2000; (contrib.) History of the University of Oxford: Nineteenth Century Oxford, pt 2, 2000; (with J. Chilcott-Monk) Flesh, Bone, Wood: entering into the mysteries of the cross, 2001; (ed jtly) Love's Redeeming Work: the Anglican quest for holiness, 2001; (with J. Chilcott-Monk) Come, Lord Jesus!: daily readings for Advent, Christmas and Epiphany, 2002; (ed jtly and contrib.) The Gestures of God: explorations in sacramentality, 2004; (contrib.) Glory Descending: Michael Ramsey and his writings, 2005; (contrib.) Death Our Future, 2008; contributor to various books on theol subjects, to Oxford DNB, and Oxford Dict. of the Christian Church (3rd edn); articles in Jl Theol Studies, English Hist. Rev., Jl Ecclesiastical Hist., Church Hist., Anglican and Episcopal Hist., Internationale Cardinal-Newman Studien, Studia Urbania, etc. *Recreations:* travel in remote places, reading, music, examining graduate theses. *Address:* Bishop's Lodge, Church Road, Worth, Crawley, W Sussex RH10 7RT. *T:* (01293) 883051, *Fax:* (01293) 884479; *e-mail:* bishop@dioceseineurope.org.uk.

GIBRALTAR IN EUROPE, Suffragan Bishop of, since 2002; **Rt Rev. David Hamid;** *b* 18 June 1955; *s* of Ebrahim Hamid and Patricia (*née* Smith); *m* 1978, Colleen Gwen Moore; two *s*. *Educ:* Nelson High Sch., Burlington, Canada; McMaster Univ. (BSc Hons); Univ. of Trinity Coll., Toronto (MDiv 1981). Ordained deacon, 1981, priest, 1982; Asst Curate, St Christopher's, Burlington, 1981–83; Rector, St John's, Burlington, 1983–87; Mission Co-ordinator for Latin Amer. and Caribbean, Anglican Ch of Canada, 1987–96; Dir, Ecumenical Affairs and Studies, ACC, 1996–2002. Canon, Santo Domingo, 1992–. Hon. Asst Bishop, dio. of Rochester, 2003–. Member: Faith and Order Adv. Gp, C of E, 1996–2002; Anglican-Old Catholic Internat. Co-ordinating Council, 2005– (Co-Sec., 1999–2002); Porvoo Panel, 2005–; Co-Sec., Internat. Anglican-Baptist Conversations, 2000–02; Consultant: Jt Working Gp, WCC and RC Ch, 1998–; Internat. Anglican-RC Commn for Unity and Mission, 2002–. Secretary: Metropolitical Council, Cuba, 1987–96; Inter Anglican Theol Doctrinal Commn, 2000–02; Inter Anglican Standing Cttee on Ecumenical Relns, 2000–02; Co-Secretary: ARCIC, 1996–2002; Internat. Commn of Anglican Orthodox Theol Dialogue, 1996–2002; Anglican-Lutheran Internat. Working Gp, 1999–2002. Treasurer: Anglican Council of N America and Caribbean, 1983–87; Canadian Interch Cttee on Human Rights in Latin America, 1987–96. Mem. Council, USPG: Anglicans in World Mission (formerly USPG), 2002–. Adv. Gp, Older People Residing Abroad, 2007–. Hon. DD Trinity Coll., Univ. of Toronto, 2005. *Publications:* (contrib.) Beyond Colonial Anglicanism: the Anglican Communion in the Twenty-First Century, ed I. Douglas, 2001; contrib. to Ecclesiastical Law Jl, Unité des Chrétiens. *Recreations:* music, languages, history, travel. *Address:* Diocese in Europe, 14 Tufton Street, SW1P 3QZ. *T:* (020) 7898 1160, *Fax:* (020) 7898 1166; *e-mail:* david.hamid@europe.c-of-e.org.uk. *Club:* Royal Commonwealth Society.

GIBSON, family name of **Baron Ashbourne**.

GIBSON OF MARKET RASEN, Baroness *cr* 2000 (Life Peer), of Market Rasen in the Co. of Lincolnshire; **Anne Bartell,** OBE 1998; National Secretary, (Union for) Manufacturing, Science, Finance, 1987–2000; *b* 10 Dec. 1940; *d* of Harry Tasker and Jessie Tasker (*née* Roberts); *m* 1st, 1962, John Donald Gibson (marr. diss. 1985); one *d*; 2nd, 1988, John Bartell; one step *d*. *Educ:* Market Rasen C of E Sch.; Caistor Grammar Sch., Lincs; Chelmsford Coll. of Further Educn, 1970–71; Univ. of Essex, 1972–76 (BA Hons II1, Govt). Sec., Penney and Porter Engrg Co., Lincoln, 1956; Cashier, Midland Bank, Market Rasen, 1959–62. Organiser, Saffron Walden Labour Party, 1966–70; Asst Sec., Organisation and Industrial Relns Dept, TUC, 1977–87. Member: TUC Gen. Council, 1989–2000; EOC, 1991–98; Dept of Employment Adv. Gp on Older Workers, 1993–96; HSC, 1996–2000; Chm., DTI Wkg Gp on Bullying at Work, 2005–. Mem., Lab. Party Nat. Constitutional Cttee, 1997–2000. EC Mem., RoSPA, 2000– (Pres., 2004–) Member Council: Air League, 2005–; ATC, 2005–. Hon. Pres., Yeadon Sqdn Air Cadets 2002–. *Recreations:* Francophile, embroidery, reading, theatre. *Address:* House of Lords, SW1A 0PW.

GIBSON, Charles Andrew Hamilton; His Honour Judge Gibson; a Circuit Judge, since 1996; *b* 9 July 1941; *s* of late Rev. Preb. Leslie Andrew Gibson and Kathleen Anne Frances Gibson; *m* 1969, Susan Judith Rowntree; two *d*. *Educ:* Sherborne Prep. Sch.; Sherborne Sch.; Hertford Coll., Oxford (MA). Called to the Bar, Lincoln's Inn, 1966; practised at the Bar, 1966–96; Asst Recorder, 1987–91; a Recorder, 1991–96. Mem., Mental Health Review Tribunal, 2002–. Chm., Southwark Diocesan Pastoral Cttee, 1993–2003. Chm., Hertford Soc., 2004–. *Publication:* (with Prof. M. R. A. Hollis) Surveying Buildings, 1983, 5th edn 2005. *Recreations:* music, theatre, wine. *Address:* c/o Lambeth County Court, Cleaver Street, SE11 4DZ. *T:* (020) 7091 4410. *Club:* Oxford and Cambridge.

GIBSON, Charles Anthony Warneford; QC 2001; a Recorder, since 2001; *b* 25 Sept. 1960; *s* of Philip Gaythorne Gibson and Margaret Elizabeth (*née* Mellotte, now Sim); *m* 1989, Mary Ann Frances, *e d* of Sir John (Albert Leigh) Morgan, *qv*; three *s* one *d*. *Educ:* Wellington Coll.; Durham Univ. (BA Hons Classics); Dip. Law, Central London. Called to the Bar, Inner Temple, 1984, Bencher, 2008. *Recreations:* family, sport, ballet, boxing, theatre, food, comedy. *Address:* 2 Harcourt Buildings, Temple, EC4Y 9DB. *T:* (020) 7583 9020.

GIBSON, Christopher Allen Wood; QC 1995; a Recorder, since 2002; *b* 5 July 1953; *s* of Rt Hon. Sir Ralph Brian Gibson and of Ann Gibson; *m* 1984, Alarys Mary Calvert Eaton; two *d*. *Educ:* St Paul's Sch.; Brasenose Coll., Oxford. FCIArb 1992. Called to the Bar, Middle Temple, 1976, Bencher, 2003. *Recreations:* Whitstable, motorcycles, family. *Address:* Doughty Street Chambers, 10–11 Doughty Street, WC1N 2PL. *T:* (020) 7404 1313.

GIBSON, Rev. Sir Christopher (Herbert), 4th Bt *cr* 1931, of Linconia, Argentina, and of Faccombe, Southampton; CP; *b* 17 July 1948; *o s* of Sir Christopher Herbert Gibson, 3rd Bt and Lilian Lake Young, *d* of Dr George Byron Young; *S* father, 1994, but his name does not appear on the Official Roll of the Baronetage. Ordained priest, 1975. *Heir: cousin* Robert Herbert Gibson [*b* 21 Dec. 1966; *m* 1992, Catherine Grace, *d* of E. W. Pugh; one *s* one *d*].

GIBSON, David, CB 1997; Secretary, Northern Ireland in Europe, 2002–04; *b* 8 Sept 1939; *s* of Frank Edward Gibson and Nora Jessie Gibson (*née* Gurnhill); *m* 1963, Roberta Alexandra (*née* McMaster); one *s* two *d*. *Educ:* King Edward VI Grammar Sch., Retford. FCCA. GPO, 1958–63; MAFF, 1963–68; Belfast City Council, 1968–72; Dept of Commerce, NI, 1972–82; Dir of Accountancy Services, 1982–85, Asst Sec., 1985–87, Under Sec., then Dep. Sec., 1987–99, Dept of Economic Develt, NI; Dep. Chm., NI Sci Park Foundn, 1999–2002. Pres., Irish Region, Assoc. of Chartered Certified Accountants, 1982–83. Trustee, The Bytes Project, 2000–05. *Recreations:* reading, music, walking. *Address:* 14 Bramble Grange, Newtownabbey, Co. Antrim BT37 0XH. *T:* (028) 9086 2237.

GIBSON, Lt-Col Edgar Matheson, (Gary), MBE 1986; TD 1975; DL; self-employed artist - painting and sculpture, since 1990; Vice Lord-Lieutenant of Orkney, since 2007; *b* Kirkwall, Orkney, 1 Nov. 1934; *s* of James Edgar Gibson and Margaret Johnston Gibson (*née* Matheson); *m* 1960, Jean McCarrick; two *s* two *d*. *Educ:* Kirkwall Grammar Sch.; Gray's Coll. of Art, Aberdeen (DA 1957); Teachers' Training Coll., Aberdeen. National Service, Army (Lt-Col), 1958–60. Principal Art Master, 1974–88, Asst Headmaster, 1988–90, Kirkwall Grammar Sch. Examiner in Higher Art and Design, Scottish Cert. of Educn Examn Bd, Dalkeith, 1978–93. Mem., Orkney Health Bd, 1991–99. TA and TAVR, Lovat Scouts, 1961–85, JSLO, Orkney, 1980–85; Cadet Comdt, Orkney Lovat Scouts ACF, 1979–86; Hon. Col, Orkney Lovat Scouts, 1986–2004; Chm., N Area Highland TAVRA, 1987–93. Pres., Orkney Br., SSAFA, 1997– (Chm., 1990–97). Mem., Selection Cttee, 1983–91, County Co-ordinator, 1991–93, Operation Raleigh. Chairman: St Magnus Cathedral Fair, 1982–2004; Preservation Cttee, Italian POW Chapel, 2006 (Mem., 1976–); Hon. President: Soc. of Friends of St Magnus Cathedral, 1994–; Orkney Craftsmen's Guild, 1997–2002 (Chm., 1962–82). DL Orkney, 1976. Hon. Sheriff, Grampian, Highland and Is, 1992–. *Recreations:* ba playing (old Norse game), whisky tasting. *Address:* Transcona, New Scapa Road, Kirkwall, Orkney KW15 1BN. *T:* (01856) 872849. *Club:* Highland and Lowland Brigades'.

GIBSON, Prof. Frank William Ernest, AM 2004; FRS 1976; FAA; Emeritus Professor of Biochemistry, Australian National University, since 1989 (Visiting Fellow, 1989); *b* 22 July 1923; *s* of John William and Alice Ruby Gibson; *m* 1st, 1949, Margaret Isabel Nancy (marr. diss. 1979); two *d*; 2nd, 1980, Robin Margaret; one *s*. *Educ:* Queensland Univ.; Melbourne Univ. (BSc, DSc); DPhil Oxon. Research Asst, Melbourne and Queensland Univs, 1938–47; Sen. Demonstrator, Melbourne Univ., 1948–49; ANU Scholar, Oxford, 1950–52. Melbourne University: Sen. Lectr, 1953–58; Reader in Chem. Microbiology, 1959–65; Prof. of Chem. Microbiology, 1965–66; Australian National University: Prof. of Biochem., 1967–88; Hd of Biochem. Dept, 1967–76, Chm., Div. of Biochemical Scis, 1988, John Curtin Sch. of Medical Res.; Howard Florey Prof. of Medical Res., and Dir, John Curtin Sch. of Med. Res., 1977–79. Newton-Abraham Vis. Prof. and Fellow of Lincoln Coll., Oxford Univ., 1982–83. David Syme Research Prize, Univ. of Melb., 1963. FAA 1971. *Publications:* scientific papers on the biochemistry of bacteria, particularly the biosynthesis of aromatic compounds, energy metabolism. *Recreations:* tennis, ski-ing. *Address:* 7 Waller Crescent, Campbell, ACT 2612, Australia.

GIBSON, Gary; *see* Gibson, Lt-Col E. M.

GIBSON, Ven. (George) Granville; Archdeacon of Auckland, Diocese of Durham, 1993–2001, now Archdeacon Emeritus; *b* 28 May 1936; *s* of late George Henry Gibson and of Jessie Gibson (*née* Farrand); *m* 1958, Edna (*née* Jackson); two *s* one *d* (and one *s* decd). *Educ:* Queen Elizabeth Grammar Sch., Wakefield; Barnsley Coll. of Technology; Cuddesdon Coll., Oxford. Mining Surveyor, NCB, 1952–62; Field Officer, The Boys' Brigade, 1962–69. Ordained deacon, 1971, priest, 1972; Curate, St Paul, Cullercoats, 1971–73; Team Vicar, Cramlington, 1973–77; Vicar, St Clare, Newton Aycliffe, 1977–85; Rector of Bishopwearmouth and RD of Wearmouth, 1985–93; Hon. Canon of Durham, 1988–2001, now Emeritus. Proctor in Convocation, 1980–2000; Church Comr, 1991–98 (Mem., Bd of Govs., 1993–98). Stavrofor, Romanian Orthodox Church, 1997–. Trustee, Church Urban Fund, 1991–2003. Chm., Governing body, Eastbourne C of E Acad., Darlington, 2007–. *Recreations:* gardening, cactus plants, cookery, grandchildren. *Address:* 12 West Crescent, Darlington DL3 7PR. *T:* (01325) 462526; *e-mail:* gib65@aol.com.

GIBSON, Prof. (Gerald) John, MD; FRCP, FRCPE; Professor of Respiratory Medicine, University of Newcastle upon Tyne, 1993–March 2009, then Emeritus; Consultant Physician (Respiratory Medicine), Freeman Hospital, Newcastle upon Tyne, 1978–March 2009; *b* 3 April 1944; *s* of Maurice Gibson and Margaret Gibson (*née* Cronin); *m* 1977, Dr Mary Teresa Cunningham; three *s*. *Educ:* St Michael's Coll., Leeds; Guy's Hosp. Med. Sch., Univ. of London (BSc 1st Class Hons Physiol. 1965; MB BS Hons 1968; MD 1976). FRCP 1982; FRCPE 2000. Hse Physician, Guy's Hosp., 1968; Hse Surgeon, Leeds Gen. Infirmary, 1969; Resident Physician, McMaster Univ., Ont, 1970–71; Registrar and Sen. Registrar, Hammersmith Hosp. and RPMS, 1971–77. Mem. Council, RCP, 2000–03; President: Brit. Thoracic Soc., 2004–05 (Hon. Sec., 1986–88; Chm., 1997–99); Eur. Respiratory Soc., 2002–03. *Publications:* Clinical Tests of Respiratory Function, 1984, 3rd edn 2009; Respiratory Medicine, 1990, 3rd edn 2003; contrib. papers on several aspects of respiratory medicine, sleep apnoea and clinical respiratory physiology. *Recreations:* photography, opera and singers. *Address:* (until March 2009) Department of Respiratory Medicine, Freeman Hospital, Newcastle upon Tyne NE7 7DN. *T:* (0191) 233 6161, *Fax:* (0191) 213 7087; *e-mail:* g.j.gibson@ncl.ac.uk.

GIBSON, Ven. Granville; *see* Gibson, Ven. G. G.

GIBSON, Ian, PhD; MP (Lab) Norwich North, since 1997; *b* 26 Sept. 1938; *s* of late William and Winifred Gibson; *m* 1974, Elizabeth Frances (*née* Lubbock); two *d*. *Educ:* Dumfries Acad.; Edinburgh Univ. (BSc, PhD). Indiana Univ., 1963–64; Univ. of Washington, 1964–65. Lectr, 1968–71, Sen. Lectr, and Dean, Sch. of Biol Scis, 1991–97, Hon. Prof., 2003, UEA. Contested (Lab) Norwich N, 1992. Chm., Select Cttee on Sci. and Technol., 2001–05. Chairman: Parly OST, 1998–2001; All Party Parly Gp on Cancer, 1998–; All Party Parly Gp on Cuba, 2004–; All Party Parly Writers Gp, 2008. Non-executive Director: Inst. of Food Res., 2001–06; Stem Cell Foundn, 2005–; Chm., Nanotechnology Taskforce. Jt Manager, Parly football squad, 1999–2005. Governor: Hellesdon High Sch., 1992–97; Sprowston High Sch., 1995–97 (Chm.). Macmillan Cancer Relief Champion, 2003; Parly Award, Royal Soc. Chemistry, 2004. *Publication:* Anti-sense Technology, 1997. *Recreations:* football coaching, watching, listening and questioning. *Address:* House of Commons, SW1A 0AA. *T:* (020) 7219 1100.

GIBSON, Sir Ian, Kt 1999; CBE 1990; FInstP; Chairman: Trinity Mirror plc, since 2006; William Morrison Supermarkets plc, since 2008 (Deputy Chairman 2007–08); *b* 1 Feb. 1947; *s* of Charley Gibson and Kate Gibson (*née* Hare); *m* 1st, 1969, Joy Musker (marr. diss.); two *d*; 2nd, 1988, Susan Wilson; one *s*. *Educ:* UMIST (BSc Physics 1969). FInstP 1999. Ford Motor Co. and Ford Werke AG: various posts in industrial relns and gen. mgt, 1969–79; General Manager: Halewood Ops, 1979–82; Saarlouis, 1982–83; Nissan Motor Manufacturing: Dir, 1984–2000; Dep. Man. Dir, 1987–89; Man. Dir, 1989–98; Chm., UK, 1999–2000; Vice-Pres., 1994–98, Pres., 1999–2000, Nissan Europe; Sen. Vice-Pres., Nissan Motor Co. Ltd and Supervisory Bd Mem., Nissan Europe NV, 2000–01. Dep. Chm., ASDA plc, 1994–99; non-exec. Dir, 2001–05, Dep. Chm., 2003–04, Chm., 2004–05, BPB plc. Mem. Court, Bank of England, 1999–2004. Non-executive Director: GKN plc, 2002–07; Northern Rock plc, 2002–08. CCMI (CBIM 1990; Gold Medal, 2001). Hon. DBA Sunderland Poly., 1990. Mensforth Gold Medal, IEE, 1998. *Recreations:* sailing and working on my boat, ski-ing, reading. *Club:* Royal Automobile.

GIBSON, John; *see* Gibson, G. J.

GIBSON, John Peter; Chief Executive, Seaforth Maritime, 1986–88 (Deputy Chairman, 1978–83; Chairman, 1983–86); *b* 21 Aug. 1929; *s* of John Leighton Gibson and Norah Gibson; *m* 1954, Patricia Anne Thomas; two *s* three *d*. *Educ:* Caterham Sch.; Imperial Coll., London (BSc (Hons Mech. Engrg), ACGI). Post-grad. apprenticeship Rolls Royce Derby, 1953–55; ICI (Billingham and Petrochemicals Div.), 1955–69; Man. Dir, Lummus Co., 1969–73; Dir Gen. Offshore Supplies Office, Dept of Energy, 1973–76. Dir, Taylor Woodrow Construction Ltd, 1989–90. *Recreations:* gardening, handyman. *Address:* Little Stapleton, Haytor, Ilsington, Newton Abbot, Devon TQ13 9RR.

GIBSON, Joseph, CBE 1980; PhD; CChem, FRSC; FREng, FEI; Coal Science Adviser, National Coal Board, 1981–83 (Member for Science, 1977–81); *b* 10 May 1916; *m* 1944, Lily McFarlane Brown; one *s* one *d*. *Educ:* King's Coll. (now Univ. of Newcastle upon Tyne; MSc, PhD). Res., Northern Coke Res. Lab. 1938; Head of Chemistry Dept, Sunderland Technical Coll., and Lectr, Durham Univ., 1948; Chief Scientist, Northern Div., 1958, and Yorks Div., 1964, NCB; Director: Coal Res. Estab., 1968; Coal Utilisation Res., 1975. President: Inst. of Fuel, 1975–76; BCURA, 1977–81 and 1992– (Chm. 1972–77). Lectures: Cadman Meml, 1980, 1983; Prof. Moore Meml, 1981; Brian H. Morgans Meml, 1983. Coal Science Lecture Medal, 1977; Carbonisation Sci. Medal, 1979. Hon. FIChemE. Hon. DCL Newcastle, 1981. *Publications:* jointly: Carbonisation of Coal, 1971; Coal and Modern Coal Processing, 1979; Coal Utilisation: technology, economics and policy, 1981; papers on coal conversion and utilisation. *Recreations:* bridge, gardening. *Address:* 31 Charlton Close, Charlton Kings, Cheltenham, Glos GL53 8DH. *T:* (01242) 517832.

GIBSON, Kenneth James; Member (SNP) Cunninghame North, Scottish Parliament, since 2007; *b* Paisley, 8 Sept. 1961; *s* of Kenneth George Gibson and Iris Gibson; *m* 1st, 1989, Lynda Dorothy Payne (marr. diss. 2006); two *s* one *d*; 2nd, 2007, Patricia Duffy. *Educ:* Bellahouston Acad., Glasgow; Univ. of Stirling (BA Econs). Member (SNP): Glasgow DC, 1992–96; Glasgow CC, 1995–99 (Leader of Opposition, 1998–99). Scottish Parliament: MSP (SNP) Glasgow, 1999–2003; Shadow Minister for Local Govt, 1999–2001, for Social Justice, Housing, Urban Regeneration and Planning, 2001–03; Mem., Local Govt Cttee; Deputy Convenor: Social Justice Cttee, 2001–03; Local Govt and Communities Cttee, 2007–; contested (SNP) Glasgow, Pollok, 2003. Mem., SNP Nat. Exec. Cttee, 1997–99. *Recreations:* cinema, theatre, swimming, classical history. *Address:* Scottish Parliament, Edinburgh EH99 1SP; (constituency office) 15 Main Street, Dalry KA24 5DL.

GIBSON, Madeline; Regional Nursing Officer, Oxford Regional Health Authority, 1973–83; retired; *b* 12 March 1925; *d* of late James William Henry Davis, JP, and Mrs Edith Maude Davis; *m* 1977, Comdr William Milburn Gibson, RN (*d* 1991). *Educ:* Haberdashers' Aske's Hatcham Girls' Sch.; Guy's Hosp. (SRN); British Hosp. for Mothers and Babies, Woolwich; Bristol Maternity Hosp. (SCM). Ward Sister, then Dep. Night Supt, Guy's Hosp., 1949–53; Asst Matron, Guy's Hosp., 1953–57; Admin. Sister then Dep. Matron, St Charles' Hosp., London, 1957–61; Asst Nursing Officer, 1962–68, Chief Regional Nursing Officer, 1968–73, Oxford Regional Hosp. Bd. Formerly Mem., Central Midwives Board. *Recreations:* village community work, theatre, golf. *Address:* Cherry Holt, Middle Street, Islip, Oxon OX5 2SF.

GIBSON, Mark, CB 2005; Director General, Enterprise and Business Group (formerly Business Group), Department for Business, Enterprise and Regulatory Reform (formerly Department of Trade and Industry), since 2002; *b* 2 Jan. 1953; *m* 1981, Jane Norma Lindley. *Educ:* University Coll., Oxford (BA 1974); London Business Sch. (MSc). Entered Department of Trade and Industry, 1974: Dep. Project Manager, Next Steps team, Cabinet Office, 1990–92; Asst Sec. Competitiveness Unit, 1992–94; Principal Private Sec. to Pres., BoT, and Dep. Prime Minister, 1994–97; Dir, British Trade Internat., 1997–2000; Dir-Gen., Enterprise and Innovation, DTI, 2000–02. *Address:* Department for Business, Enterprise and Regulatory Reform, 151 Buckingham Palace Road, SW1W 9SS. *T:* (020) 7215 4178.

GIBSON, Mel Columcille Gerard, AO 1997; actor, director and producer; *b* Peekskill, NY, 3 Jan. 1956; *s* of Hutton Gibson and late Anne Gibson; *m* 1980, Robyn Moore; six *s* one *d* (incl. twin *s*). *Educ:* Nat. Inst. of Dramatic Art, Univ. of NSW. Joined State Theatre Co. of SA, 1977; theatre includes: Waiting for Godot, Sydney, 1979; Death of a Salesman, Nimrod Th., Sydney, 1982; No Names, No Pack Drill; Romeo and Juliet. Co-founder and Partner, Icon Entertainment Internat., 1989–. *Films include:* Summer City, 1977; Mad Max, Tim, 1979; The Z Men, 1980; Gallipoli, Mad Max 2: The Road Warrior, 1981; The Year of Living Dangerously, 1982; The Bounty, The River, Mrs Soffell, 1984; Mad Max: Beyond Thunderdome, 1985; Lethal Weapon, 1987; Tequila Sunrise, 1988; Lethal Weapon 2, 1989; Bird on a Wire, Air America, 1990; Hamlet, 1991; Lethal Weapon 3, Forever Young, 1992; The Man Without a Face (also dir), 1993; Maverick, 1994; Braveheart (also dir and co-prod.), 1995 (Academy, Golden Globe and BAFTA Awards for best dir, 1996); Ransom, 1997; Conspiracy Theory, 1997; Lethal Weapon 4, 1998; Payback, 1999; The Million Dollar Hotel, The Patriot, 2000; What Women Want, 2001; We Were Soldiers, Signs, 2002; The Singing Detective (also prod.), 2004; dir, prod. and writer, The Passion of the Christ, 2004; dir and prod., Apocalypto, 2007. *Address:* c/o Shanahan Management Pty Ltd, PO Box 1509, Darlinghurst, NSW 1300, Australia.

GIBSON, Air Vice-Marshal Michael John, CB 1994; OBE 1979; FRAeS; Head of Aviation Regulation Enforcement, Civil Aviation Authority, 1996–99; *b* 2 Jan. 1939; *m* 1961, Dorothy Russell; one *s* one *d*. *Educ:* Imperial Coll., London (BSc); Selwyn Coll., Cambridge; National Defense Univ., Washington, DC. ACGI; FRAeS. Commnd RAFVR, 1959; commnd RAF, 1961; various appointments as fighter pilot and instructor; Personal Air Sec. to Air Force Minister, 1972–73; Officer Commanding: 45 Sqdn (Hunter), 1974–76; 20 Sqdn (Jaguar), 1976–79; RAF Brawdy, 1982–84; RAF Stanley, 1984–85; Air Officer Plans, HQ Strike Comd, 1987–88; Dir, Airspace Policy, 1988–91, Dir Gen. of Policy and Plans, 1991–94, Head of Mgt Support Unit, 1994–96, NATS. *Recreation:* music (singing and church organ playing). *Address:* 12 Watling Street, Radlett, Herts WD7 7NH. *Club:* Royal Air Force.

GIBSON, Paul Alexander; Founder, 1973, Partner, 1973–2001, now Consultant, Sidell Gibson Partnership, Architects; *b* 11 Oct. 1941; *s* of Wing-Comdr Leslie Gibson and Betty Gibson (later Betty Stephens); *m* 1969, Julia Atkinson. *Educ:* Kingswood Sch., Bath; King's Coll., London; Canterbury Sch. of Architecture; Regent Street Polytechnic Sch. of Architecture (DipArch 1968). Worked for Farrell Grimshaw Partnership, 1968–69; Lectr, North Dakota State Univ., 1969; worked for Foster Associates, 1970–73. 3 RIBA awards, Good Housing, 1986; won open competition for redevelt of Grand Buildings, Trafalgar Square, 1986; won competition for redevelt of Winchester Barracks, 1988; expansion of Jewel House, HM Tower of London, 1992–94. *Recreations:* struggling pianist, keen gardener. *Address:* Sidell Gibson Architects, The Canal Building, 37 Kentish Town Road, NW1 8NX. *T:* (020) 7784 9005.

GIBSON, Rt Hon. Sir Peter (Leslie), Kt 1981; PC 1993; a Lord Justice of Appeal, 1993–2005; *b* 10 June 1934; *s* of late Harold Leslie Gibson and Martha Lucy Gibson (*née* Diercking); *m* 1968, Katharine Mary Beatrice Hadow, PhD (*d* 2002); two *s* one *d*. *Educ:* Malvern Coll.; Worcester Coll., Oxford (Scholar; Hon. Fellow, 1993). 2nd Lieut RA, 1953–55 (National Service). Called to the Bar, Inner Temple, 1960; Bencher, Lincoln's Inn, 1975; Treas., Lincoln's Inn, 1996. 2nd Jun. Counsel to Inland Revenue (Chancery), 1970–72; Jun. Counsel to the Treasury (Chancery), 1972–81; a Judge of the High Court of Justice, Chancery Div., 1981–93. A Judge of the Employment Appeal Tribunal, 1984–86. A Judge of Qatar Financial Centre Civil and Commercial Court, 2007–. Chairman: Law Commn, 1990–92; Trust Law Cttee, 2004–. Intelligence Services Comr, 2005–. *Address:* c/o Royal Courts of Justice, Strand, WC2A 2LL.

GIBSON, Prof. Quentin Howieson, FRS 1969; Professor of Biochemistry and Molecular Biology, Cornell University, Ithaca, NY, 1966–90, now Emeritus; *b* 9 Dec. 1918; *s* of William Howieson Gibson, OBE, DSc; *m* 1951, Audrey Jane, *yr d* of G. H. S. Pinsent, CB, CMG, and Katharine Kentisbeare, *d* of Sir George Radford, MP; one *s* three *d*. *Educ:* Repton. MB, ChB, BAO, Belfast, 1941, MD 1944, PhD 1946, DSc 1951. Demonstrator in Physiology, Belfast, 1941–44; Lecturer in Physiology: Belfast, 1944–46; Sheffield Univ., 1946–55; Professor of Biochem., Sheffield Univ., 1955–63; Prof. of Biophys. Chem., Johnson Research Foundn, University of Pennsylvania, 1963–66. Dist. Faculty Fellow, Rice Univ., Houston, 1996–. Fellow, Amer. Acad. of Arts and Sciences, 1971; MNAS 1982. *Recreation:* sailing. *Address:* 3 Woods End Road, Etna, NH 03750, USA.

GIBSON, Prof. Robert Dennis, AO 2002; PhD, DSc; FTS, FAICD; Chancellor, Royal Melbourne Institute of Technology, since 2003; *b* 13 April 1942; *m*; one *s* two *d*; *m* 1994, Catherin Bull. *Educ:* Hull Univ. (BSc Hons); Newcastle upon Tyne Univ. (MSc, PhD); DSc CNAA 1987. FAIM 1982; FTS 1993. Asst Lectr, Maths Dept, Univ. of Newcastle upon Tyne, 1966–67; Scientific Officer, Culham Plasma Lab., UKAEA, 1967–68; Lectr in Maths, Univ. of Newcastle upon Tyne, 1968–69; Sen. Lectr, Maths and Statistics, Teesside Polytechnic, 1969–77; Head, Dept of Maths, Stats and Computing (later Sch. of Maths, Stats and Computing), Newcastle upon Tyne Polytechnic, 1977–82; Queensland Institute of Technology: Dep. Dir then Actg Dir, 1982–83; Dir, 1983–88; first Vice-Chancellor, Qld Univ. of Technol., 1989–2003. Mem., 1988–92, Dep. Chm., 1991–92, Aust. Res. Council; Chm., Grad. Careers Council of Aust., 2000–06. Chairman: M & MD Pty Ltd, 2003–; RDDT Pty Ltd, 2007–. Mem. Council, Bond Univ., 2005–. FAICD 1995. DUniv: USC, 1999; Qld Univ. of Technol., 2003. *Publications:* numerous research papers on various aspects of mathematical modelling. *Recreations:* jogging, cricket. *Address:* Royal Melbourne Institute of Technology, 124 La Trobe Street, Melbourne, Vic 3000, Australia. *Club:* Brisbane.

GIBSON, Prof. Robert Donald Davidson, AO 2002; PhD; Professor of French, University of Kent at Canterbury, 1965–94, now Emeritus (Master of Rutherford College, 1985–90); *b* Hackney, London, 21 Aug. 1927; *o s* of Nicol and Ann Gibson, Leyton, London; *m* 1953, Sheila Elaine, *o d* of Bertie and Ada Goldsworthy, Exeter, Devon; three *s*. *Educ:* Leyton County High Sch. for Boys; King's Coll., London; Magdalene Coll., Cambridge; Ecole Normale Supérieure, Paris. BA (First Class Hons. French) London, 1948; PhD Cantab. 1953. Asst Lecturer, St Salvator's Coll., University of St Andrews, 1954–55; Lecturer, Queen's Coll., Dundee, 1955–58; Lecturer, Aberdeen Univ., 1958–61; Prof., Queen's Univ. of Belfast, 1961–65. *Publications:* The Quest of Alain-Fournier, 1953; Modern French Poets on Poetry, 1961; (ed) Le Bestiaire Inattendu, 1961; Roger Martin du Gard, 1961; La Mésentente Cordiale, 1963; (ed) Brouart et le

Désordre, 1964; (ed) Provinciales, 1965; (ed) Le Grand Meaulnes, 1968; The Land Without a Name, 1975; Alain-Fournier and Le Grand Meaulnes, 1986; (ed) Studies in French Fiction, 1988; Annals of Ashdon, 1988; The Best of Enemies, 1995, 2nd edn 2004; The End of Youth, 2005; reviews and articles in: French Studies, Modern Language Review, The London Magazine, Times Literary Supplement, Encyclopædia Britannica, Collier's Encyclopædia. *Recreations:* reading, writing, talking. *Address:* Thalassa!, Cliff Road, Sidmouth, Devon EX10 8JN.

GIBSON, Robert McKay; Member (SNP) Highlands and Islands, Scottish Parliament, since 2003; *b* 16 Oct. 1945; *s* of John and Elsie Gibson; partner, Dr Eleanor Roberta Scott, *qv*. *Educ:* Dundee Univ. (MA Hons Modern Hist.); Dundee Coll. of Educn (DipEd 1973; Secondary Teaching Dip. 1973). Teacher, Geog. and Modern Studies, 1973–74, Asst Principal Teacher of Guidance, 1974–77, Invergordon Acad.; Principal Teacher of Guidance, Alness Acad., 1977–95; writer and researcher, 1995–2003. Vice-Pres., Brittany Scotland Assoc., 2005–; Hon. Pres., Kilt Soc. of France, 2006–. *Publications:* The Promised Land, 1974; Highland Clearances Trail, 1983, new edn 2006; Toppling the Duke: outrage on Ben Bhraggie, 1996; Plaids and Bandanas, 2003. *Recreations:* traditional music singer, organic gardener, hill walker, traveller. *Address:* Scottish Parliament, Edinburgh EH99 1SP; *e-mail:* rob.gibson.msp@scottish.parliament.uk; Tir Nan Oran, 8 Culcairn Road, Evanton, Ross-shire IV16 9YT. *T:* (01349) 830388; *e-mail:* robgibson273@btinternet.com.

GIBSON, Robin Warwick, OBE 2001; art historian and writer; Chief Curator, National Portrait Gallery, 1994–2001; *b* 3 May 1944; *s* of Walter Edward Gibson and Freda Mary Yates (*née* Partridge). *Educ:* Royal Masonic Sch., Bushey; Magdalene Coll., Cambridge (BA 1966). Asst Keeper, City Art Gall., Manchester, 1967–68; National Portrait Gallery: Asst Keeper, 1968–83; Curator, Twentieth Century Collection, 1983–94. Mem. Cttee, NT Foundn for Art, 1991–2000. *Publications:* The McDonald Collection, 1970; (jtly) British Portrait Painters, 1971; Flower Painting, 1976; The Clarendon Collection, 1977; 20th Century Portraits, 1978; Glyn Philpot, 1984; John Bellany: new portraits, 1986; (jtly) Madame Yevonde, 1990; John Bratby Portraits, 1991; The Portrait Now, 1993; (jtly) The Sitwells, 1994; (jtly) Glenys Barton, 1997; The Face in the Corner, 1998; (jtly) Painting the Century, 2000; contrib. to Oxford DNB; various catalogue essays; articles and reviews for Burlington Mag., Museums Jl, The Independent, Folio, Modern Painters. *Recreations:* composing music, village organist, plants, my dog, paintings other than portraiture. *Address:* Maple Cottage, 1 The Bull Ring, Thaxted, Essex CM6 2PL; *e-mail:* robline@btinternet.com.

GIBSON, Roy; aerospace consultant, since 1980; Director General, British National Space Centre, 1985–87; *b* 4 July 1924; *s* of Fred and Jessie Gibson; *m* 1st, 1946, Jean Fallowes (marr. diss. 1971); one *s* one *d*; 2nd, 1971, Inga Elgerus. *Educ:* Chorlton Grammar Sch.; Wadham College, Oxford; SOAS. Malayan Civil Service, 1948–58; Health and Safety Br., UKAEA, 1958–66; European Space Research Orgn, 1967–75 (Dir of Admin, 1970–75); Dir Gen., European Space Agency, 1975–80. DSC (Kedah, Malaysia), 1953; Das Grosse Silberne Ehrenzeichen mit Stern (Austria), 1977. *Publications:* Space, 1992; numerous articles in aerospace technical jls. *Recreations:* music, chess, walking. *Address:* Résidence les Hespérides, 51 Allée J. de Beins, Montpellier 34000, France. *T:* 467648181.

GIBSON, Prof. Susan Elizabeth, DPhil; Professor of Chemistry, Imperial College, London, since 2003; *b* 3 Nov. 1960; *d* of late Arnold Sutcliffe Thomas and of Kathleen Thomas; *m* 1994, Vernon Charles Gibson, *qv*; one *s* one *d*. *Educ:* Darwen Vale High Sch.; Sidney Sussex Coll., Cambridge (BA 1981); New Coll., Oxford (DPhil 1984). Lecturer: Univ. of Warwick, 1985–90; ICSTM, London, 1990–99; Daniell Prof. of Chemistry, KCL, 1999–2003. Mem. Council, EPSRC, 2003–06. Rosalind Franklin Award, Royal Soc., 2003–04. *Publications:* Organic Synthesis: the roles of boron and silicon, 1991; more than 130 articles in learned jls. *Recreations:* scooting, launching stomp rockets, learning to read. *Address:* Department of Chemistry, Imperial College, London, South Kensington Campus, SW7 2AZ. *T:* (020) 7594 1140; *e-mail:* s.gibson@imperial.ac.uk.

GIBSON, Ven. Terence Allen; Archdeacon of Ipswich, 1987–2005, now Archdeacon Emeritus; *b* 23 Oct. 1937; *s* of Fred William Allen and Joan Hazel Gibson. *Educ:* Jesus Coll., Cambridge (MA); Cuddesdon Coll., Oxford. Curate of St Chad, Kirkby, 1963–66; Warden of Centre 63, Kirkby C of E Youth Centre, 1966–75; Rector of Kirkby, Liverpool, 1975–84; RD of Walton, Liverpool, 1979–84; Archdeacon of Suffolk, 1984–87. *Address:* 5 Berry Close, Purdis Farm, Ipswich IP3 8SP. *T:* (01473) 714756.

GIBSON, Prof. Vernon Charles, DPhil; FRS 2004; Sir Edward Frankland BP Professor of Inorganic Chemistry, Imperial College London, since 2001; *b* 15 Nov. 1958; *s* of Dennis Charles Gibson and Pamela Gibson (*née* Lambley); *m* 1994, Susan Elizabeth Thomas (*see* S. E. Gibson); one *s* one *d*. *Educ:* Huntingtower Rd County Primary Sch.; King's Sch., Grantham; Univ. of Sheffield (R. D. Haworth Medal, 1980; BSc); Balliol Coll., Oxford (DPhil 1984). Lectr in Inorganic Chem., 1986–93, Prof. of Chem., 1993–95, Univ. of Durham; Imperial College London: Prof. of Polymer Synthesis and Catalysis, 1995–98; Sir Geoffrey Wilkinson Chair of Chem., 1998–2001. Royal Society of Chemistry: BP Chemicals Young Univ. Lectr Award, 1990–93; Sir Edward Frankland Prize Fellowship, 1992–93; Corday-Morgan Medal and Prize, 1993–94; Monsanto Organometallic Chemistry Award, 1999; Joseph Chatt Lectr, 2001–02; Tilden Lectr, 2004–05. *Publications:* numerous book chapters; more than 250 papers in learned jls and 30 published patents. *Recreations:* jogging around Hyde Park and Kensington Gardens, ski-ing, reading, old vintage claret. *Address:* *e-mail:* v.gibson@imperial.ac.uk. *Club:* Athenæum.

GIBSON-CRAIG-CARMICHAEL, Sir David Peter William, 15th Bt *cr* 1702 (Gibson Carmichael) and 8th Bt *cr* 1831; *b* 21 July 1946; *s* of Sir Archibald Henry William Gibson-Craig-Carmichael, 14th Bt and Rosemary Anita (*d* 1979), *d* of George Duncan Crew, Santiago, Chile; *S* father, 1969; *m* 1973, Patricia, *d* of Marcos Skarnic, Santiago, Chile; one *s* one *d*. *Educ:* Queen's Univ., Canada (BSc Hons Geology, 1971). *Heir:* *s* Peter William Gibson-Craig-Carmichael, *b* 29 Dec. 1975.

GIBSON FLEMING, James Randolf; Vice Lord-Lieutenant of Dorset, since 2006; *b* 27 July 1958; *s* of late Maj. William H. Gibson Fleming and of Selina Littlehales Gibson Fleming (*née* Baker); *m* 1986, Fiona Lucy Don; two *s* one *d*. *Educ:* Eton; RMA Sandhurst; RAC Cirencester. SSC, Royal Hussars, PWO, 1977–81; served NI and W Berlin. Partner/dir, farming, property and asset mgt firms/cos, 1981–; Chief Exec., Hanford plc, 1987–93. Chm., CLA Game Fair Bd, 1992–97. Trustee: Talbot Village Trust, 1991–; Cancercare Dorset, 1994–2004 (Chm., 2000–04); Joseph Weld and Trimar Hospice and Cancercare Dorset, 2004–06 (Vice-Chm., 2004–06). DL Dorset, 2005–06. *Recreations:* field sports, flying, ski-ing, holidaying on Isle of Mull. *Address:* Ranston, Blandford, Dorset DT11 8PU. *Clubs:* Cavalry and Guards, Air Squadron, MCC.

GIBSON-SMITH, Christopher Shaw, PhD; Chairman: London Stock Exchange, since 2003; The British Land Company PLC, since 2006; *b* 8 Sept. 1945; *s* of John and Winifred Agnes Gibson-Smith; *m* 1969, Marjorie Hadwin Reed; two *d*. *Educ:* Durham Univ. (BSc Geol); Newcastle Univ. (PhD Geochem 1970); Stanford Univ. (MSc Business Sci). Joined BP, 1970; CEO Europe, BP Exploration, 1992–95; Chief Operating Officer, BP Chemicals, 1995–97; Gp Man. Dir, BP, 1997–2001. Chm., NATS, 2001–05. Non-executive Director: Lloyds TSB, 1999–2005; Powergen, 2000–01; Sen. Ind. Dir, British Land plc, 2003–06. *Recreations:* art, music, opera, ski-ing, golf, tennis. *Address:* Lansdowne, White Lane, Guildford, Surrey GU4 8PR. *T:* (01483) 572400, *Fax:* (01483) 455548. *Club:* Athenæum.

GIDDENS, Baron *cr* 2004 (Life Peer), of Southgate in the London Borough of Enfield; **Anthony Giddens,** PhD; Director, London School of Economics, 1997–2003; *b* 18 Jan. 1938; *s* of T. G. Giddens; *m* 1963, Jane M. Ellwood. *Educ:* Hull Univ. (BA); LSE (MA); MA 1970, PhD 1974, Cantab. Cambridge University: Lectr in Sociology, subseq. Reader, 1969–85; Prof. of Sociology, Faculty of Econs and Politics, 1985–96; Fellow, King's Coll., 1969–96. Reith Lectr, BBC, 1999. *Publications:* Capitalism and Modern Social Theory, 1971; (ed) Sociology of Suicide, 1972; Politics and Sociology in the Thought of Max Weber, 1972; (ed and trans) Emile Durkheim: Selected Writings, 1972; (ed) Positivism and Sociology, 1974; New Rules of Sociological Method, 1976; Studies in Social and Political Theory, 1976; Central Problems in Social Theory, 1979; Class Structure of the Advanced Societies, 2nd edn 1981; Contemporary Critique of Historical Materialism: vol. 1, Power, Property and State, 1981, vol. 2, Nation, State and Violence, 1985; (jtly) Classes, Power and Conflict, 1982; Profiles and Critiques in Social Theory, 1983; (ed jtly) Social Class and the Division of Labour, 1983; Constitution of Society, 1984; Durkheim, 1985; Sociology: a brief but critical introduction, 1986; Social Theory and Modern Sociology, 1987; (ed jtly) Social Theory Today, 1987; Sociology, 1989; The Consequences of Modernity, 1990; Modernity and Self-Identity, 1991; The Transformation of Intimacy, 1992; Beyond Left and Right, 1994; In Defence of Sociology, 1996; Third Way, 1998; Runaway World (Reith Lectures), 1999; (with Will Hutton) On the Edge: living with global capitalism, 2000; The Third Way and its Critics, 2000. *Recreations:* theatre, cinema, playing tennis, supporting Tottenham Hotspur. *Address:* House of Lords, SW1A 0PW.

GIDDINGS, Anthony Edward Buckland, MD; FRCS; Consultant Surgeon in General and Vascular Surgery, Guy's, King's and St Thomas' Hospitals, 1997–2004; *b* 8 Feb. 1939; *s* of Edward Walter Giddings and Doris Margaret Giddings; *m* 1966, Maureen Ann Williams; one *s* one *d*. *Educ:* Cathedral Sch., Bristol; Univ. of Bristol (MB ChB 1966; MD 1978). FRCS 1971. Consultant Surgeon, Royal Surrey Co. Hosp., 1979–97. Non-exec Dir, Nat. Clinical Assessment Authy, 2001–05. MRCS Course Dir, St Thomas' Hosp., 2003–05. Founding Pres., Assoc. of Surgeons in Training, 1976; President: Sect. of Surgery, RSM, 1994; Assoc. of Surgeons of GB and Ireland, 1997–98; Dir, James IV Assoc. of Surgeons Inc., 1998–2001; Chairman: Specialist Adv. Cttee in Gen. Surgery, 1998–2001; Fedn of Surgical Specialist Assocs, 1998–2001; Mem. Council, RCS, 2001–07. Hunterian Prof., RCS, 1978; James IV Assoc. of Surgeons Inc. Travelling Fellow, 1979; Visiting Professor: Univ of Texas, 1980; Oregon Health Scis Univ., 1996. Lectures: A. B. Mitchell, QUB, 1996; Moynihan, RCS, 2007. Work on med. perf. and assessment, Nat. Clinical Assessment Authy, GMC and RCS, 1997–2007; work on org. of surgical services, NHS Modernization Agency and DoH, 2001–08; clinical res. and educn and trng develt in safety and leadership for surgeons, 1997–2008; Surgical Advisor, Performance Support Team, DoH, 2006–08; Nat. Clinical Adv. Team, DoH, 2007–. Mem., Editl Bd, British Jl of Surgery, 1994–2000. *Publications:* contrib. papers and book chapters on surgical science, the safety of patients and the orgn of surgical services. *Recreations:* theatre, music, flying light aircraft. *Address:* 6 Fairway, Guildford, Surrey GU1 2XG. *T:* (01483) 561826; *e-mail:* tonygiddings@btinternet.com. *Club:* Royal Automobile.

GIDDINGS, Air Marshal Sir (Kenneth Charles) Michael, KCB 1975; OBE 1953; DFC 1945; AFC 1950 and Bar 1955; *b* 27 Aug. 1920; *s* of Charles Giddings and Grace Giddings (*née* Gregory); *m* 1946, Elizabeth McConnell; two *s* two *d*. *Educ:* Ealing Grammar Sch. Conscripted, RAF, 1940; Comd, 129 Sqdn, 1944; Empire Test Pilots Sch., 1946; Test pilot, RAE, 1947–50; HQ Fighter Command, 1950–52; RAF Staff Coll., 1953; OC, Flying Wing, Waterbeach, 1954–56; CFE, 1956–58; OC, 57 Sqdn, 1958–60; Group Captain Ops, Bomber Command, 1960–62; Supt of Flying, A&AEE, 1962–64; Dir Aircraft Projects, MoD, 1964–66; AOC, Central Reconnaissance Estabt, 1967–68; ACAS (Operational Requirements), 1968–71; Chief of Staff No 18 (M) Group, Strike Command, RAF, 1971–73; Dep. Chief of Defence Staff, Op. Requirements, 1973–76; Dir, Nat. Counties Building Soc., 1982–85. Indep. Panel Inspector, DoE, 1979–91. *Recreations:* golf, gardening, music. *Address:* 16 Grasmere Court, Wordsworth Road, Worthing, W Sussex BN11 3JE. *T:* (01903) 205731.

GIDDINGS, Dr Philip James; Senior Lecturer in Politics, since 1998, and Head, School of Sociology, Politics and International Relations, since 2006, University of Reading; *b* April 1946; *s* of Albert Edward Robert Giddings and Irene Trustrail Giddings (*née* Dunstan); *m* 1st, 1970, Margaret Anne Mulrenan (*d* 1978); one *d*; 2nd, 1979, Myfanwy Hughes; one *s*. *Educ:* Sir Thomas Rich's Sch., Gloucester; Worcester Coll., Oxford (BA Hons PPE); Nuffield Coll., Oxford (DPhil 1970). Lectr in Public Admin, Univ. of Exeter, 1970–72; Lectr in Politics, Reading Univ., 1972–98. Member: Crown Appointments Commn, 1992–97; Archbishops' Council, 1999– (Chairman: Church and World Div., 1999–2002; Mission and Public Affairs Div., 2003–). Mem., Gen. Synod of C of E, 1985– (Vice-Chm., House of Laity, 1995–2000, 2006–; Dep. Chm., Legislative Cttee, 2005–); Lay Vice-Pres., Oxford Diocesan Synod, 1988–2000. Convenor, Anglican Mainstream UK, 2003–. *Publications:* Marketing Boards and Ministers, 1974; Parliamentary Accountability, 1995; (with G. Drewry) Westminster and Europe, 1996; (with R. Gregory) Righting Wrongs: the ombudsman in six continents, 2000; (with R. Gregory) The Ombudsman, the Citizen and Parliament, 2002; Britain in the European Union, 2004; The Future of Parliament, 2005; (with M. Rush) The Palgrave Review of British Politics 2005, 2006; (with M. Rush) The Palgrave Review of British Politics 2006, 2007. *Recreations:* light gardening, short walks. *Address:* 5 Clifton Park Road, Caversham, Reading, Berks RG4 7PD. *T:* (0118) 954 3892.

GIDLEY, Sandra Julia; MP (Lib Dem) Romsey, since May 2000; *b* 26 March 1957; *d* of Frank Henry and Maud Ellen Rawson; *m* 1979, William Arthur Gidley; one *s* one *d*. *Educ:* Eggars Grammar Sch., Alton; AFCENT Internat., Brunssum, Netherlands; Windsor Girls Sch., Hamm, Germany; Bath Univ. (BPharm). MRPharmS 1979, FRPharmS 2008. Pharmacist, Cheltenham, 1979–80; Pharmacy Manager, Gloucester, then Cheltenham, 1980–82; locum pharmacist, 1982–92; Pharmacy Manager: Safeway, 1992–99; Tesco, 1999–2000. Mem. (Lib Dem) Test Valley BC, 1995–2003; Mayor of Romsey, 1997–98. Lib Dem spokesman for women, 2002–06, for older people, 2003–06, for health, 2006–. *Recreations:* food, photography, badminton. *Address:* House of Commons, SW1A 0AA; 15 Sycamore Close, Romsey, Hants SO51 5SB. *T:* (01794) 517652.

GIDOOMAL, Balram, (Ram), CBE 1998; Chairman: Winning Communications Partnership Ltd, since 1992; Citylife Ltd, since 2005; *b* 23 Dec. 1950; *s* of late Gagandas Gidoomal and of Vasanti Gidoomal; *m* 1976, Sunita Shivdasani; two *s* one *d*. *Educ:* Aga Khan Sch., Mombasa; Christopher Wren Sch., London; Imperial Coll., London (BSc

Hons Physics). ARCS 1972. Inlaks Group: Dep. Gp Chief Exec., Head Office, France, then Geneva, 1978–85; UK Gp Chief Exec. and Vice Chm., 1985–92. Non-exec. Director: Amsphere Ltd, 2006– (Chairman: Audit Cttee; Remuneration Cttee); Nirmaan Bharati SAAVS, 2007–; non-exec. Adv. Bd Mem., Six Senses BVI, 2007–. Board Member: Covent Gdn Mkt Authy, 1998–2004; English Partnerships, 2000–03; Think London (formerly London First Centre), 2001–; Postmaster.net, 2003–06; Dir, Far Pavilions Ltd, 1998–. Member: Better Regulation Task Force, Cabinet Office, 1997–2002; Complaints Audit Cttee, UK Border Agency (formerly Immigration Nationality Directorate, then Border and Immigration Agency), Home Office, 2006–. Mem., Royal Mail Stamp Adv. Cttee, 2002–. Mem., Nat. Leadership Team and Chm., London Exec., Race for Opportunity, 1993–99; Founder Chm., Business Links London South, 1995–98; Director: Business Links-Nat. Accreditation Adv. Bd, 1995–2000; Business Links London, 1995–98 (Chm., CEO's Gp, 1996–98); Mem., SRI Adv. Cttee, Hendersons Global Investments, 2004– (Chm.). Patron, Small Business Bureau, 1998–. Mem. Council, Britain in Europe, 1999–2005. Chm., S Asian Develt Partnership, 1991–. Vis. Prof., Middx Univ., 2001–. Member: Council, RSA, 1993–2002, 2004– (Trustee, 1999–2002); Council, Inst. of Employment Studies, 2001– (Bd Mem., 2003–). Chairman: Christmas Cracker Trust, 1989–2000; London Sustainability Exchange, 2001–07; London Community Foundn, 2001–03. Leader, Christian Peoples Alliance, 2001–04; Pres., Nat. Information Forum, 2003–; Vice President: Leprosy Mission, 1999–; Shaftesbury Soc., 2003–. Member: Adv. Bd for ethics in the workplace, Inst of Business Ethics, 2002–06; Adv. Council for Clinical Excellence Awards, 2004–06; Adv. Council, Friends of the Elderly, 2003–; Internat. Health Partners, 2006–. Gov., Health Foundn (formerly PPP Medical Healthcare Trust, subseq. PPP Foundn), 2000–05. Trustee: Inst. of Citizenship, 2000–05; Employability Forum, 2000– (Chm., 2003–); Timebank, 2001–04; Forum for the Future, 2001–; Trng for Life, 2001–04. Mem. Ct of Govs, Luton Univ., 2001–; Gov. and Mem., Ct and Council, Imperial Coll. London, 2002– (Chairman: Res. Ethics Cttee, 2006–; Student Trustee Bd, 2007–); Lay Mem. Council, St George's, Univ. of London (formerly St George's Hosp. Med. Sch.), 2002– (Vice-Chm., 2007–; Chairman: Audit Cttee, 2006–; Estates Project Bd, 2006–). Governor: James Allen's Girls' Sch., Dulwich, 1997–2002; King's Coll. Sch., Wimbledon, 1998–. Freeman, City of London, 1997; Liveryman, Co. of Inf. Technologists, 2003– (Mem., 1998–; Mem., Court of Assistants, 2003–05). CCMI (CIMgt 2001; Mem. Bd of Companions, 2002–); FRSA 1993; FCGI 2008. Hon. Mem., Faculty of Divinity, Cambridge Univ., 1998–. Dehejia Fellow, Sidwell Friends Sch., Washington, DC, 2008. Hon. LLD Bristol, 2002; Hon. DLitt Nottingham Trent, 2003; DUniv Middlesex, 2003. *Publications:* Sari 'n' Chips, 1993; Karma 'n' Chips, 1994; Chapatis for Tea, 1994; Lions, Princesses and Gurus, 1996; The UK Maharajahs, 1997; Hinduism: a way of life, 1997; Building on Success: the South Asian contribution to UK competitiveness, 1997; (jtly) How Would Jesus Vote?, 2001; The British and How to Deal With Them: doing business with Britain's ethnic communities, 2001; various reports and lectures. *Recreations:* music, current affairs, swimming. *Address:* 14 The Causeway, Sutton, Surrey SM2 5RS.

GIELGUD, Maina; free-lance ballerina; ballet producer; guest répétiteur; *b* 14 Jan. 1945; *d* of late Lewis Gielgud and Elisabeth Grussner, (stage name, Zita Sutton). *Educ:* BEPC (French). Ballet du Marquis de Cuevas, 1962–63; Ballet Classique de France, 1965–67; Ballet du XXème Siècle, Maurice Béjart, 1967–72; London Festival Ballet, 1972–77; Royal Ballet, 1977–78; free-lance, 1978–; rehearsal director, London City Ballet, 1981–82; Artistic Dir, Australian Ballet, 1983–96; Dir, Royal Danish Ballet, Copenhagen, 1997–99; Artistic Associate, Houston Ballet, 2003–05. Guest Répétiteur: English National Ballet; Tokyo Ballet; Béjart Ballet, Lausanne; Ballet du Rhin; Boston Ballet; Australian Ballet. Hon. AO 1991. *Address:* 1/9 Stirling Court, 3 Marshall Street, W1V 1LQ. *T:* (020) 7734 6612.

GIESKE, Dr Friedhelm; Member, Supervisory Board, RWE AG, 1995–2001 (Chairman, Managing Board, 1989–95); *b* Schwege/Bohmte, near Osnabrück, 12 Jan. 1928. *Educ:* Göttingen (Dr jur 1954). Joined RWE (Rheinisch-Westfälisches Elektrizitätswerk), 1953; Dep. Mem., 1968, Mem. (Finance), 1972, Bd of Management; Bd spokesman, 1988; Chairman, Supervisory Board: Karstadt Quelle AG, Essen; MAN AG, München; National-Bank AG, Essen. *Address:* c/o RWE AG, Opernplatz 1, 45128 Essen, Germany.

GIEVE, Sir (Edward) John (Watson), KCB 2005 (CB 1999); Deputy Governor, Bank of England, 2006–spring 2009; *b* 20 Feb. 1950; *s* of late David Watson Gieve, OBE and Susan Gieve; *m* 1972, Katherine Vereker; two *s*. *Educ:* Charterhouse; New Coll., Oxford (BA PPE, BPhil). Dept of Employment, 1974–78; HM Treasury: Principal, Industrial Policy Div., 1979–81; Energy Div., 1981–82; Private Sec., 1982–84; Investment Controller, Investors in Industry, 1984–86 (on secondment); Public Expenditure Survey Div., 1986–88; Press Sec., 1988–89; Principal Private Sec. to Chancellor of the Exchequer, 1989–91; Under Sec., Banking Gp, 1991–94; Dep. Dir, then Dir, Budget and Public Finances, 1994–98; Dir, then Man. Dir, Public Services, 1998–2001; Man. Dir, Finance, Regulation and Industry, 2001; Permanent Under-Sec. of State, Home Office, 2001–05. *Recreations:* golf (playing), football (mainly watching). *Address:* c/o Bank of England, Threadneedle Street, EC2R 8AH.

GIFFARD, family name of **Earl of Halsbury**.

GIFFARD, Adam Edward; *b* 3 June 1934; *o s* of 3rd Earl of Halsbury, FRS; *S* father as 4th Earl, 2000, but does not use the title; *m* 1976, Joanna Elizabeth, *d* of late Frederick Harry Cole; two *d*. *Educ:* Jesus Coll., Cambridge (MA 1961); BSc Open Univ. 1995.

GIFFARD, Sir (Charles) Sydney (Rycroft), KCMG 1984 (CMG 1976); HM Diplomatic Service, retired; *b* 30 Oct. 1926; *s* of Walter Giffard and Minna Giffard (*née* Cotton); *m* 1st, 1951, Wendy Vidal (marr. diss. 1976); one *s* one *d*; 2nd, 1976, Hazel Roberts, OBE. *Educ:* Repton Sch.; Wadham Coll., Oxford (Hon. Fellow, 1991). Served in Japan, 1952; Foreign Office, 1957; Berne, 1961; Tokyo, 1964; Counsellor, FCO, 1968; Royal Coll. of Defence Studies, 1971; Counsellor, Tel Aviv, 1972; Minister in Tokyo, 1975–80; Ambassador to Switzerland, 1980–82; Dep. Under-Sec. of State, FCO, 1982–84; Ambassador to Japan, 1984–86. Grand Cordon, Order of the Rising Sun (Japan), 2003. *Publications:* Japan Among the Powers 1890–1990, 1994; (ed) Guns, Kites and Horses, 2003. *Address:* Winkelbury House, Berwick St John, Wilts, near Shaftesbury, Dorset SP7 0EY. *Club:* Lansdowne.

GIFFARD, John William, CBE 2003; QPM 1997; DL; Chief Constable, Staffordshire Police, 1996–2006; *b* 25 March 1952; *s* of late Peter Richard de Longueville Giffard and of (Mary) Roana (Borwick) Giffard; *m* 1978, Crescent Vail; two *s*. *Educ:* Eton; Univ. of Southampton (BA Hons 1973). With Staffordshire Police, 1973–91: Grad. Entrant 1973; Chief Supt, 1991; Asst Chief Constable, N Yorks Police, 1991–96. DL Staffs, 1999. *Recreations:* cricket, shooting, bridge. *Address:* Chillington Hall, Codsall Wood, Wolverhampton WV8 1RE. *T:* (01902) 850236. *Clubs:* MCC, I Zingari; Staffs Gents Cricket, Yorks Gents Cricket.

GIFFARD, Sir Sydney; *see* Giffard, Sir C. S. R.

GIFFORD, family name of **Baron Gifford**.

GIFFORD, 6th Baron *cr* 1824; **Anthony Maurice Gifford;** QC 1982; Barrister at Law, practising since 1966; Attorney-at-Law, Jamaica, since 1990; *b* 1 May 1940; *s* of 5th Baron Gifford and Lady Gifford (*née* Margaret Allen) (*d* 1990), Sydney, NSW; *S* father, 1961; *m* 1st, 1965, Katherine Ann (marr. diss. 1988), *o d* of Dr Mundy; one *s* one *d*; 2nd, 1988, Elean Roslyn (marr. diss. 1998), *d* of Bishop David Thomas, Kingston, Jamaica; one *d*; 3rd, 1998, Tina Natalia Goulbourne, Kingston, Jamaica. *Educ:* Winchester Coll. (scholar); King's Coll., Cambridge (scholar; BA 1961). Student at Middle Temple, 1959–62, called to the Bar, 1962. Chairman: Cttee for Freedom in Mozambique, Angola and Guiné, 1968–75; Mozambique Angola Cttee, 1982–90. Chairman: N Kensington Neighbourhood Law Centre, 1974–77 (Hon. Sec., 1970–74); Legal Action Gp, 1978–83; Vice-Chm., Defence and Aid Fund (UK), 1983–94. Pres., Cttee for Human Rights, Grenada, 1987–; Vice-Pres., Haldane Soc. of Socialist Lawyers, 1986–. Chairman: Broadwater Farm Inquiry, 1986; Liverpool 8 Inquiry, 1988–89. *Publications:* Where's the Justice?, 1986; The Passionate Advocate, 2007. *Heir: s* Hon. Thomas Adam Gifford, *b* 1 Dec. 1967. *Address:* 122–126 Tower Street, Kingston, Jamaica. *T:* 922 6056, *Fax:* 967 0225; 1 Mitre Court Buildings, Temple, EC4Y 7BS. *T:* (020) 7452 8900, *Fax:* (020) 7452 8999; *e-mail:* anthony.gifford@btinternet.com.

GIFFORD, Andrew Graham; Partner, Gifford & Partners, since 2002; adviser to British record industry, since 1982; *b* 3 Feb. 1953; *s* of Charles Henry Pearson Gifford, OBE and Laetitia Gifford (*née* Lyell), MBE; *m* 1990, Charlotte Montrésor; four *s*. *Educ:* Bedales; Edinburgh Univ. (BSc). Personal Assistant: to Rt Hon. David Steel, MP, 1975–76; office of Leader of Liberal Party, 1976–80; ran election tours for Leader of Liberal Party, 1979, and of Lib. Dem. Party, 1983 and 1987. Founder Partner and Chief Exec., GJW Govt Relns, 1980–2002; Founder Director: 4th Estate Publishing, 1983–2000; Heritage Oil & Gas, 1989–95; Director: Fleming Mid Cap Investment Trust, 1994–2005; Second London American Growth, 1997–; Moneyweek mag., 2000–02. Founder Chm., Assoc. of Professional Political Consultants, 1989–95. Hon. Treas., Green Alliance, 1990–2002. *Publication:* Handbook of World Development, 1985. *Recreations:* fishing, shooting. *Address:* 6 Hans Street, SW1X 0NJ. *Clubs:* Beefsteak; New (Edinburgh).

GIFFORD, Joshua Thomas, (Josh), MBE 1989; racehorse trainer, 1970–2003; *b* 3 Aug. 1941; *s* of late Thomas Gifford and Dinah Florence Gifford (*née* Newman); *m* 1969, Althea Meryl Roger-Smith; one *s* one *d*. Flat racing jockey, 1951–58; National Hunt jockey, 1958–70; rode 700 winners; champion jockey, 1962, 1963, 1967, 1968; National Hunt trainer, 1970–2003; trained 1586 winners, incl. Aldaniti, Grand National, 1981. *Recreations:* cricket, shooting, golf. *Address:* The Downs, Findon, Worthing, Sussex BN14 0RR. *T:* (01903) 872226, *Fax:* (01903) 8777232.

GIFFORD, Michael Brian; *b* 9 Jan. 1936; *s* of Kenneth Gifford and Maude Gifford (*née* Palmer); *m* Nancy Baytos-Fenton; two *s* two *d* by previous marrs. *Educ:* LSE (BSc Econ). Joined Leo Computers (later part of ICL), 1960; Man. Dir, ICL (Pacific), 1973–75; Chief Exec., Cadbury Schweppes Australia, 1975–78; Finance Dir, Cadbury Schweppes plc, 1978–83; Man. Dir and CE, Rank Orgn, 1983–96; Director: Fuji Xerox Ltd, 1984–96; English China Clays PLC, 1992–99; Gillette Co., 1993; Danka Business Systems plc, 1999–2005. *Address:* 1521 Alton Road, Suite 674, Miami Beach, FL 33139, USA.

GIFFORD, Michael John; HM Diplomatic Service; Counsellor, Foreign and Commonwealth Office, since 2007; *b* 2 April 1961; *s* of Henry Gifford and Gladys Mary Gifford (*née* Culverhouse); *m* 1986, Patricia Anne Owen; one *s* one *d*. *Educ:* Hastings Grammar Sch. Entered FCO, 1981; Arabic lang. trng, SOAS, 1982–83; Third Sec. (Commercial), Abu Dhabi, 1983–87; Second Sec. (Chancery), Oslo, 1988–90; on loan to Secretariat-Gen., EC, Brussels, 1990; Second, later First, Sec., FCO, 1991–93; First Secretary: (Econ.), Riyadh, 1993–97; FCO, 1997–2000; Counsellor and Dep. Hd of Mission, Cairo, 2001–04; Ambassador, Yemen, 2004–07. *Recreations:* reading, family. *Address:* c/o Foreign and Commonwealth Office, King Charles Street, SW1A 2AH.

GIFFORD, (Michael) Roger; UK Country Manager, SEB, since 2000; *b* St Andrews, 3 Aug. 1955; *s* of Douglas John and Hazel Mary Gifford; *m* 1st, 1983, Jane Lunzer (marr. diss. 2004); three *s* one *d* (and one *d* decd); 2nd, 2008, Clare Taylor. *Educ:* Sedbergh Sch.; Trinity Coll., Oxford (BA Hons). Internat. Banking, SG Warburg & Co. Ltd, 1978–82; SEB: Corp. Finance, then Primary Debt, later Equity Capital Markets, Enskilda Securities, 1982–90; Hd, Debt Capital Markets, 1990–93; Hd, London Br., 1992–94; Hd, Tokyo Br., 1994–99. Chairman: Swedish Chamber of Commerce UK, 2003–07; Assoc. of Foreign Banks UK, 2007–. Alderman, Cordwainer Ward, 2004–; Sheriff, City of London, 2008–Sept. 2009. Liveryman, Co. of Musicians, 2005–; Middle Warden, Co. of Internat. Bankers, 2007–; Sponsoring Alderman, Guild of PR Practitioners, 2007–. Mem., City of London Br., Royal Soc. of St George. Trustee: St Paul's Cath. Foundn, 2006–; St Paul's Cath. Choir Sch., 2006–; Governor: Summer Fields Sch., Oxford, 2001–07; King Edward's Sch., Witley, 2005–; Bridewell Hosp., 2005–. Chairman: English Chamber Orch. and Music Soc., 2001–; From Sweden Fest., 2004–06; Sibelius and Beyond Fest., 2007. Comdr, Order of Polar Star (Sweden), 2007. *Recreations:* chamber music, singing, gardens, walking, forestry. *Address:* 40 Inverness Street, NW1 7HB. *T:* (020) 7246 4000; *e-mail:* roger.gifford@seb.co.uk. *Clubs:* Cordwainer Ward, Bread Street Ward, City Livery; Royal Perth.

GIL-ROBLES GIL-DELGADO, José María; Member, European Parliament, 1989–2004 (President, 1997–99); *b* 17 June 1935; *m* 1963, Magdalena Casanueva (*d* 1999). *Educ:* Univ. of Deusto; Univ. of Salamanca. Legal Advr, Spanish Parlt, 1958; barrister, Madrid, Barcelona, Bilbao and Salamanca, 1959; Lectr in Law, Univ. of Complutense, 1959; Comité Director, Fedn of Christian Democrats, Spain, 1972. European Parliament: Pres., Institutional Affairs Cttee, 1991; Vice-Pres., 1994. Pres., European Movt Internat., 1999–. Freeman, City of Salamanca, 1998. Hon. Fellow, Catholic Univ. of Chile, 1998. Dr *hc* State Inst. for Internat. Relations, Moscow, 1998. Robert Schuman Medal; Gold Medal, City of Athens; Order of Francisco Morazán (Central American Parlt), 1997; Silver Medal of Galicia, 2000. Medalla del Mérito Agrícola (Spain); Grand Cross, Order of Isabel la Católica (Spain), 2000; Medal of the Republic (Uruguay), 1998; Grand Cross: Order of Merit (Chile), 1998; Order of Liberator San Martin (Argentina), 1998; Order Antonio José de Irizarri (Guatemala), 1999; Officer, Legion of Honour (France), 2000. *Publications:* Derecho de huelga, 1961; Commentarios a la ley de arrendamientos rústicos, 1981; Legislación agraria básica, 1986; Control y autonomías, 1986; Los derechos del europeo, 1993; Los Parlamentos de Europa y el Parlamento Europeo, 1997; Pasión por Europa, 2002. *Recreations:* reading, golf.

GILBART, Andrew James; QC 1991; **His Honour Judge Gilbart;** a Senior Circuit Judge, Hon. Recorder of Manchester and Resident Judge, Manchester Crown Court, since 2008 (a Circuit Judge, since 2004); *b* 13 Feb. 1950; *s* of Albert Thomas Gilbart and late Carol Christie Gilbart, Vinehall Sch., Robertsbridge, Sussex; *m* 1st, 1979, Morag Williamson (marr. diss. 2001); one *s* one *d*; 2nd, 2003, Paula Doone Whittell; two step *s* one step *d*. *Educ:* Westminster Sch. (Queen's Scholar); Trinity Hall, Cambridge (MA). Called to the Bar, Middle Temple, 1972, Bencher, 2000; elected to Northern Circuit,

1973; Hd of Chambers, Kings Chambers, Manchester and Leeds, 2001–04. An Asst Recorder, 1992–96; a Recorder, 1996–2004; a Dep. High Court Judge (Admin. Court), 2004–. Member: Restricted Patients Presidents Panel, Mental Health Review Tribunal, 2000–06; Lands Tribunal, 2006–. Member: Planning and Envmt Bar Assoc. (formerly Local Govt, Planning and Envmtl Bar Assoc.), 1986–2004 (Mem. Cttee, 1988–92); UK Envmtl Law Assoc., 1996–2004; Admin Law Bar Assoc., 1999–; Internat. Associate Mem., Amer. Bar Assoc., 1994–2004; Mem., Eur. Circuit of the Bar, 2002–04. *Publications:* articles in Jl of Planning and Environment Law and Local Govt Chronicle. *Recreations:* history, walking, theatre, computers, learning to sing. *Address:* Courts of Justice, Crown Square, Manchester M3 3FL.

GILBART-DENHAM, Lt-Col Sir Seymour (Vivian), KCVO 2002 (CVO 1994); Crown Equerry, 1987–2002, an Extra Equerry to the Queen, since 2002; *b* 10 Oct. 1939; *s* of Major Vivian Vandeleur Gilbart-Denham (killed in action, Narvik, 1940), Irish Guards and Diana Mary Beaumont; *m* 1976, Patricia Caroline, *e d* of Lt Col and Mrs Granville Brooking; two *d.* Commissioned, Life Guards, 1960; served UK, Germany, Cyprus and Far East; Adjutant, Life Guards, 1965–67; commanded Household Cavalry Regt, 1986–87. Vice-President: Royal Windsor Horse Show, 1988–; Royal Parks Equitation Trust, 1992–2002; Gtr London Region, Riding for the Disabled, 1994–2002; Pres., Coaching Club, 2001–02. Freeman, City of London, 1988. *Recreations:* carriage driving, shooting, ski-ing. *Address:* The Old Rectory, Temple Bar, Earsham, Bungay, Suffolk NR35 2TA. *Clubs:* White's, Royal Automobile.

GILBERD, Rt Rev. Bruce Carlyle, CNZM 2002; Bishop of Auckland, 1985–94; Chaplain, King's School, Remuera, 1997–2000; retired; *b* 22 April 1938; *s* of Carlyle Bond Gilberd and Dorothy Annie Gilberd; *m* 1963, Patricia Molly Tanton; two *s* one *d. Educ:* King's College, Auckland; Auckland Univ. (BSc); St John's Coll., Auckland (LTh Hons, STh). Deacon 1962, priest 1963, Auckland; Assistant Curate: Devonport, 1962–64; Ponsonby and Grey Lynn, 1965; Panmure, 1965–68; Vicar of Avondale, 1968–71; trainee Industrial Chaplain, Tees-side Industrial Mission, and Asst Curate of Egglescliffe, 1971–73; visited industrial missions in UK and Europe; Director, Interchurch Trade and Industrial Mission, Wellington, 1973–79; founding Mem., Wellington Industrial Relations Soc.; Hon. Asst Curate, Lower Hutt 1973–77, Waiwhetu 1977–79; Lectr, St John's Coll. Auckland, 1980–85; Priest-in-charge, Albany Greenhithe Mission Dist, 1995, St Thomas, Tamaki, 1996, dio. of Auckland. Pres., Christian Res. Assoc., Aotearoa, NZ, 1996–2000; Vice-Pres., Home and Family Soc., 1986–. Mem. Gen. Synod, NZ. Has travelled widely in UK, Europe, China, USA, S Africa and Pacific. NZ Commemorative Medal, 1990. *Publications:* (ed) Christian Ministry: a definition, 1984; (with Richard Whitfield) Taproots for Transformation, 2006; Future Focus, 2007. *Recreations:* fishing, surfing, sailing, travel, reading, writing, golf. *Address:* 81 Manaia Road, Tairua, 3508, New Zealand.

GILBERT; see Proesch, G.

GILBERT, family name of **Baron Gilbert**.

GILBERT, Baron *cr* 1997 (Life Peer), of Dudley, in the co. of West Midlands; **John William Gilbert;** PC 1978; PhD; *b* April 1927; *m* 1963, Jean Olive Ross Skinner; one *d* (and one *d* decd) of previous marriage. *Educ:* Merchant Taylors' Sch.; St John's Coll., Oxford; New York Univ. (PhD in Internat. Economics, Graduate Sch. of Business Administration). Chartered Accountant, Canada. Contested (Lab): Ludlow, 1966; Dudley, March 1968; MP (Lab) Dudley, 1970–74; Dudley E, Feb. 1974–1997. Opposition front-bench spokesman on Treasury affairs, 1972–74; Financial Secretary to the Treasury, 1974–75; Minister for Transport, DoE, 1975–76; Minister of State, MoD, 1976–79 and 1997–99. Member: Select Cttee on Expenditure, 1970–74; Select Cttee on Corporation Tax, 1973; Select Cttee on Defence, 1979–87; Select Cttee on Trade and Industry, 1987–92; Cttee on Intelligence and Security, 1994–97; Chm., PLP Defence Gp, 1981–83; Vice-Chm., Lab. Finance and Industry Group, 1983–92. Member: Fabian Soc.; RUSI; RIIA; IISS; GMB; WWF. FRGS 1993. Hon. LLD Wake Forest, S Carolina, 1983. *Address:* House of Lords, SW1A 0PW. *Club:* Reform.

See also N. Rogerson.

GILBERT, Prof. Alan David, AO 2008; DPhil; first President and Vice-Chancellor, University of Manchester, since 2004; *b* 11 Sept. 1944; *s* of Garnet E. Gilbert and Violet Gilbert (*née* Elsey); *m* 1967, Ingrid Sara Griffiths; two *d. Educ:* ANU (BA Hons 1965; MA 1967); Oxford Univ. (DPhil History 1973). Lectr, Univ. of Papua New Guinea, 1967–69; University of New South Wales: Lectr, 1973–77; Sen. Lectr, 1977–79; Associate Prof., 1979–81; Prof. of History, 1981–88; Pro-Vice-Chancellor, 1988–91; Vice-Chancellor: Univ. of Tasmania, 1991–95; Univ. of Melbourne, 1996–2004. Member: Australian Higher Educn Council, 1991–95; Council for Sci. and Technol., 2007–; UK Commn for Employment and Skills, 2007–. FASSA 1990. Hon. degrees: Tasmania; McGill; Melbourne; Edinburgh, 2004. *Publications:* Religion and Society in Industrial England, 1976; The Making of Post-Christian Britain, 1980; (with R. Currie and L. Horsley) Churches and Churchgoers, 1977; (Gen. Editor) Australians: a historical library, 11 Vols, 1987. *Recreation:* golf. *Address:* Office of the President and Vice-Chancellor, University of Manchester, Oxford Road, Manchester M13 9PL.

GILBERT, Francis Humphrey Shubrick; QC 1992; **His Honour Judge Gilbert;** a Circuit Judge, since 2001; Resident Judge, Plymouth Crown Court, since 2006; *b* 25 Jan. 1946; *s* of late Comdr Walter Raleigh Gilbert, RN, DL, Compton Castle, Devon and Joan Mary Boileau Gilbert; *m* 1975, Sarah Marian Kaye, *d* of late Col Douglas Kaye, DSO, DL, Brinkley Hall, Newmarket; one *s* two *d. Educ:* Stowe; Trinity Coll., Dublin (MA). Called to the Bar, Lincoln's Inn, 1970, Bencher, 2000. A Recorder, 1994–2001; Hd of Chambers, 1995–2001. Devon County Councillor, 1977–85. Pres., Pegasus Club, 2001. *Recreations:* sailing, shooting. *Address:* Plymouth Crown Court, The Law Courts, Armada Way, Plymouth PL1 2ER. *Club:* Royal Yacht Squadron.

GILBERT, Ian Grant; Under Secretary, International Relations Division, Department of Health and Social Security, 1979–85; retired; *b* Kikuyu, Kenya, 18 June 1925; *s* of Captain Alexander Grant Gilbert, DCM, indust. missionary, Lossiemouth and Kenya, and Marion Patrick Cruickshank; *m* 1st, 1960, Heather Margaret Donald, PhD (*d* 1999) (biographer of Lord Mount Stephen), *y d* of Rev. Francis Cantlie and Mary Donald, Lumphanan, Aberdeenshire; 2nd, 2001, Mrs Shirley Ann Parr. *Educ:* Fordyce Acad., Banffshire; Royal High Sch. of Edinburgh; Univ. of Edinburgh (MA 1950). Served HM Forces (Captain Indian Artillery), 1943–47. Entered Home Civil Service as Asst Principal and joined Min. of National Insurance, 1950; Private Sec. to Perm. Sec., 1953, and to Parly Sec., 1955; Principal, Min. of Pensions and Nat. Ins., 1956; seconded to HM Treasury, 1962–66; Asst Sec., Min. of Social Security (later DHSS), 1967; Head of War and Civilian Disabled Branches, DHSS, 1974–79. UK Member: Social Security, Health and Social Affairs Cttees, Council of Europe, Strasbourg, 1979–85; EEC Adv. Cttee on Social Security for Migrant Workers, Brussels, 1979–85; UK Delegate, Governing Body, Internat. Soc. Security Assoc., Geneva, 1979–85; Mem., UK Delegn to World Health Assembly, Geneva, 1979–84; Clerk/Advr to Select Cttee on European Legislation, House of Commons, 1987–90. Hon. Treasurer, Presbytery of England (Church of Scotland),

1965–77; Session Clerk, Crown Court Ch. of Scotland, Covent Garden, 1975–80. A Ch. of Scotland Mem., The Churches Main Cttee, 1986–2002. Chm., Caledonian Christian Club, 1984–86. Clerk to Govs, St Gregory's Sch., Marnhull, 1991–2002. *Recreations:* keeping half-an-acre in good heart, local and natural history, choral singing, France. *Address:* Wellpark, Moorside, Sturminster Newton, Dorset DT10 1HJ. *T:* (01258) 820306. *Club:* Royal Commonwealth Society.

GILBERT, Air Chief Marshal Sir Joseph (Alfred), KCB 1985 (CB 1983); CBE 1974; Deputy Commander-in-Chief, Allied Forces Central Europe, 1986–89; retired; *b* 15 June 1931; *s* of late Ernest and Mildred Gilbert; *m* 1955, Betty, *yr d* of late William and Eva Lishman; two *d. Educ:* William Hulme's Sch., Manchester; Univ. of Leeds (BA Hons, Econ. and Pol Science; Hon. LLD 1989). Commnd into RAF, 1952; Fighter Sqdns, 1953–61; Air Secretary's Dept, 1961–63; RAF Staff Coll., 1964; CO 92 (Lightning) Sqdn, 1965–67; jssc 1968; Sec., Defence Policy Staff, and Asst Dir of Defence Policy, 1968–71; CO, RAF Coltishall, 1971–73; RCDS, 1974; Dir of Forward Policy (RAF), 1975; ACAS (Policy), MoD, 1975–77; AOC 38 Group, 1977–80; ACDS (Policy), 1980–82; Asst Chief of Staff (Policy), SHAPE, 1983–84; Dep. C-in-C, RAF Strike Command, 1984–86. Vice Chm., Commonwealth War Graves Commn, 1993–98 (Comr, 1991–98); Trustee, Imperial War Mus., 1997–2002. Life Vice-Pres., RAFA, 1995. *Publications:* articles in defence jls. *Recreations:* grandchildren, Rugby, strategic affairs. *Address:* Brook House, Salisbury Road, Shrewton, Salisbury, Wiltshire SP3 4EQ. *T:* (01980) 620627. *Club:* Royal Air Force.

GILBERT, Martin James, CA; Chief Executive, Aberdeen Asset Management PLC, since 1991; *b* 13 July 1955; *m* Prof. Fiona Davidson; one *s* two *d. Educ:* Robert Gordon's Coll.; Aberdeen Univ. (MA, LLB). CA 1983. Deloitte Haskins & Sells, 1978–82; Brander & Cruickshank, 1982–83; Director: Aberdeen Develt Capital, 1986; Chaucer Hldgs, 1993– (non-exec. Chm., 1998–); Aberdeen Asian Smaller Co. Investment Trust, 1995–; FirstBus, subseq. FirstGroup, then First, 1995– (non-exec. Chm., 2000–); Aberdeen Global Income Fund, 1998; Aberdeen Asia Pacific Income Fund, 2000. Jun. Vice-Pres., ICAS, 2002–03. Dir, Aberdeen FC, 1997. *Recreations:* golf, ski-ing, sailing. *Address:* Aberdeen Asset Management PLC, 10 Queens Terrace, Aberdeen AB10 1YG. *Clubs:* Royal Thames Yacht; Royal Northern and University, Gordonians Hockey (Aberdeen); Leander; Royal & Ancient Golf (St Andrews); Royal Aberdeen Golf; Wimbledon Golf; Royal Selangor Golf; Deeside Golf.

GILBERT, Sir Martin (John), Kt 1995; CBE 1990; DLitt; FRSL; historian; Hon. Fellow of Merton College, Oxford, since 1994 (Fellow, 1962–94); Distinguished Fellow, Hillsdale College, Michigan, since 2002; Official Biographer of Sir Winston Churchill, since 1968; *b* 25 Oct. 1936; *s* of late Peter and Miriam Gilbert; *m* 1st, 1963, Helen Constance, *yr d* of late Joseph Robinson, CBE; one *d*; 2nd, Susan, *d* of late Michael Sacher; two *s*; 3rd, Esther Poznansky, *d* of late Ben Goldberg. *Educ:* Highgate Sch.; Magdalen Coll., Oxford (MA); DLitt Oxon 1999. Nat. Service (Army), 1955–57; Sen. Research Scholar, St Antony's Coll., Oxford, 1960–62; Vis. Lectr, Budapest Univ., 1961; Res. Asst (sometime Sen. Res. Asst) to Hon. Randolph S. Churchill, 1962–67; Vis. Prof., Univ. of S Carolina, 1965; Recent Hist. Correspt for Sunday Times, 1967; Res. Asst (Brit. Empire) for BBC, 1968; Historical Adviser (Palestine) for Thames Television, 1977–78. Visiting Professor: Tel-Aviv Univ., 1979; Hebrew Univ. of Jerusalem, 1980–82 (Vis. Lectr 1975); UCL, 1995–96; UCSD, 2002; Georgetown Univ., 2003; Visiting Lecturer: Univ. of Cape Town (Caplan Centre), 1984; MoD and Acad. of Sciences, Moscow, 1985; White House, Washington, 2002; India Internat. Centre, Delhi, 2002. Non-Govtl Rep., UN Commn on Human Rights (43rd Session), Geneva, 1987, (44th Session), Geneva, 1988. Mem., Prime Minister's delegn to Israel and Jordan, and to Washington, 1995. Script designer and co-author, Genocide (Acad. Award winner, best doc. feature film), 1981; Historical Consultant to Southern Pictures TV series, Winston Churchill: The Wilderness Years, 1980–81; Historical Adviser, BBC TV, for Auschwitz and the Allies, 1981–82; historical consultant, Yalta 1945, for BBC TV, 1982–83; writer and narrator, Churchill, BBC TV, 1989–91. Governor, Hebrew Univ. of Jerusalem, 1978–. Hon. Fellow, Univ. of Wales Lampeter, 1997. Hon. DLitt: Westminster Coll., Fulton, 1981; Buckingham, 1992; Gratz Coll., Penn, 2000; George Washington Univ., Washington, 2000; Western Ontario, 2003; Hebrew Univ. of Jerusalem, 2004. *Publications:* The Appeasers, 1963 (with Richard Gott), 3rd edn 2001 (trans. German, Polish, Romanian); Britain and Germany Between the Wars, 1964; The European Powers 1900–1945, 1965, 2nd edn 2002 (trans. Italian, Spanish); Plough My Own Furrow: The Life of Lord Allen of Hurtwood, 1965; Servant of India: A Study of Imperial Rule 1905–1910, 1966; The Roots of Appeasement, 1966; Recent History Atlas 1860–1960, 1966; Winston Churchill (Clarendon Biogs for young people), 1966; British History Atlas, 1968, 3rd edn 2002; American History Atlas, 1968, 4th edn 2002 (trans. Japanese); Jewish History Atlas, 1969, 6th edn 2002 (trans. Spanish, Dutch, Hebrew, Polish, Russian, Hungarian, Italian, Chinese); First World War Atlas, 1970, 2nd edn 1994 (trans. Spanish); Winston S. Churchill, vol. iii, 1914–1916, 1971, companion volume (in two parts) 1973; Russian History Atlas, 1972, 3rd edn 2002 (trans. Japanese); Sir Horace Rumbold: portrait of a diplomat, 1973; Churchill: a photographic portrait, 1974, 3rd edn 2000; The Arab-Israeli Conflict: its history in maps, 1974, 7th edn 2001 (trans. Spanish, Hebrew); Churchill and Zionism (pamphlet), 1974; Winston S. Churchill, vol. iv, 1917–1922, 1975, companion volume (in three parts), 1977; The Jews in Arab Lands: their history in maps, 1975, illustr. edn, 1976 (trans. Hebrew, Arabic, French, German); Winston S. Churchill, vol. v, 1922–1939, 1976, companion volume, part one, The Exchequer Years 1922–1929, 1980, part two, The Wilderness Years 1929–1935, 1981, part three, The Coming of War 1936–1939, 1982; The Jews of Russia: Illustrated History Atlas, 1976 (trans. Spanish); Jerusalem Illustrated History Atlas, 1977, 3rd edn 2008 (trans. Hebrew, Spanish); Exile and Return: The Emergence of Jewish Statehood, 1978; Children's Illustrated Bible Atlas, 1979; Final Journey, the Fate of the Jews of Nazi Europe, 1979 (trans. Dutch, Hebrew); Auschwitz and the Allies, 1981, 3rd edn 2001 (trans. German, Hebrew); Churchill's Political Philosophy, 1981; The Origin of the 'Iron Curtain' speech, 1981 (pamphlet); Atlas of the Holocaust, 1982, 3rd edn 2001 (trans. German, Hebrew, French, Polish, Japanese); Winston S. Churchill, vol. vi, Finest Hour, 1939–41, 1983 (Wolfson Award, 1983); The Jews of Hope: the plight of Soviet Jewry today, 1984 (trans. Hebrew, Japanese); Jerusalem: rebirth of a city, 1985; The Holocaust: the Jewish tragedy, 1986 (trans. Bulgarian, Macedonian); Winston S. Churchill, vol vii, Road to Victory, 1986; Shcharansky: hero of our time, 1986 (trans. Dutch, Hebrew); Winston S. Churchill, vol viii, 'Never Despair', 1945–65, 1988; Second World War, 1989, 3rd edn 2000 (trans. German, Italian, Portuguese, Japanese, Polish, Spanish, Czech); Churchill, A Life, 1991 (trans. Czech, Italian, Polish, Spanish, Danish); Atlas of British Charities, 1993; The Churchill War Papers, vol. 1, At the Admiralty, September 1939–May 1940, 1993, vol. 2, Never Surrender, May–December 1940, 1995, vol. 3, The Ever-Widening War, 1941, 2000; In Search of Churchill, 1994; First World War, a History, 1994 (trans. Polish, Italian, Spanish, Portuguese, Czech); The Day the War Ended: VE-Day 1945, 1995 (trans. Czech); Jerusalem in the Twentieth Century, 1996; The Boys: triumph over adversity, 1996 (trans. German); A History of the Twentieth Century, vol. 1, 1900–1933, 1997, vol. 2, 1933–1951, 1998, vol. 3, 1952–1999, 1999 (trans. German, Danish, Polish, Czech, Chinese); Holocaust Journey, Travelling in Search of the Past, 1997 (trans. Croatian); Israel: a history, 1998, 2nd edn 2008 (trans. Hungarian, Czech, Portuguese); Never Again: an illustrated history of the Holocaust, 2000 (trans. Italian, French, German, Polish, Dutch, Lithuanian); The Jews in the Twentieth Century: an illustrated history, 2001 (trans. Russian, Italian, Dutch, Danish, French, German, Czech); Letters to Auntie Fori: the 5000 year history of the Jewish people and their faith, 2002 (trans. Italian, German, Polish, Bulgarian, Portuguese, Chinese); The Righteous: the unsung heroes of the Holocaust, 2003 (trans. French, Italian, Bulgarian); D-Day, 2004; Winston Churchill's War Leadership, 2004 (trans. Portuguese, Greek, Czech); Churchill and America, 2005; Kristallnacht, Prelude to Destruction, 2006 (trans. Czech, Portuguese); Somme, the Heroism and the Horror of War, 2006 (trans. Dutch); The Will of the People, Churchill and Parliamentary Democracy, 2006; Churchill and the Jews, 2007 (trans. Hebrew); The Story of Israel, 2008 (trans. French); Atlas of the Second World War, 2008; Editor: A Century of Conflict: Essays Presented to A. J. P. Taylor, 1966; Churchill, 1967, and Lloyd George, 1968 (Spectrum Books); compiled Jackdaws: Winston Churchill, 1970; The Coming of War in 1939, 1973; contribs historical articles and reviews to jls (incl. Purnell's History of the Twentieth Century, Reader's Digest, New York Rev. of Books, History Today, The Listener). *Recreation:* drawing maps. *Address:* Merton College, Oxford OX1 4JD. *Club:* Athenæum.

GILBERT, Patrick Nigel Geoffrey; General Secretary of the Society for Promoting Christian Knowledge, 1971–92; *b* 12 May 1934; adopted *s* of late Geoffrey Gilbert and Evelyn (*née* Miller), Devon. *Educ:* Cranleigh Sch.; Merton Coll., Oxford. Lectr, S Berks Coll. of Further Educn, 1959–62; PA to Sir Edward Hulton, 1962–64; OUP, 1964–69; Linguaphone Group (Westinghouse), 1969–71 (Man. Dir in Group, 1970). World Assoc. for Christian Communication: Trustee, 1975–87; European Vice-Chm., 1975–82; representative to EEC, 1975–82, to Conf. of Eur. Churches, 1976–82, to Council of Europe, 1976–82, and to Central Cttee, 1979–84. Member: Bd for Mission and Unity of Gen. Synod, 1971–78 (Mem. Exec., 1971–76); Archbishops' Cttee on RC Relations, 1971–81; Church Inf. Cttee, 1978–81; Church Publishing Cttee, 1980–84; Council, Conf. of British Missionary Socs, 1971–78; Council, Christians Abroad, 1974–79; Exec., Anglican Centre, Rome, 1981–91 (Vice Chm. of Friends, 1984–91); British National Cttee, UNESCO World Book Congress, 1982. Greater London Arts Association: Mem. Exec., 1968–78; Hon. Life Mem., 1978; Chm., 1980–84 (Dep. Chm., 1979–80); Initiator, 1972 Festivals of London. Art Workers' Guild: Hon. Brother, 1971; Chm. Trustees and Hon. Treas., 1976–86 (Trustee, 1975). Chairman: Gp Eight Opera, 1962–72; Standing Conf. of London Arts Councils, 1975–78; Embroiderers' Guild, 1977–78 (Hon. Treas., 1974–77); Concord Multicultural Arts Trust, 1980–89; Harold Buxton Trust, 1983–92; Nikaean Club, 1984–92; Vice-President: Camden Arts Council, 1974–89 (Chm., 1970–74); Nat. Assoc. of Local Arts Councils, 1980–89 (Founder Chm., 1976–80); Mem., Arts Adv. Cttee, CRE, 1979; Steward, Artists' Gen. Benevolent Instn, 1971–93. Rep. of Archbishop of Canterbury to Inter-Church Travel, 1987–92; Consultant, Saga Travel, 1994–98. Trustee: Overseas Bishoprics Fund, 1971–92; All Saints Trust, 1978–92 (Chairman: F and GP and Investment Cttees); Schulze Trust, 1980–83 (Chm.); Dancers' Resettlement Fund, 1982–90 (Chm., Finance Cttee); Richards Trust, 1971–92; ACC Res. Fund, 1982–84; Vis. Trustee, Seabury Press, NY, 1978–80; Chm., Dancers' Resettlement Trust, 1987–90. Member, Executive: GBGSA, 1981–84, 1988–89; Assoc. of Vol. Colls, 1979–87; Member, Governing Body: SPCK India, 1971–92; SPCK Australia, 1977–92; SPCK (USA), 1984–92; SPCK NZ, 1989–92; Partners for World Mission, 1979–92; Governor: Contemp. Dance Trust, 1981–90; All Saints Coll., Tottenham, 1971–78; St Martin's Sch. for Girls, 1971–92 (Vice Chm., 1978–91; Rep. to Tertiary Educn Council, 1983–89); Ellesmere Coll., 1977–87 (Mem. ISCO Exec., 1984–86); St Michael's Sch., Petworth, 1978–88 (rep. to GBGSA); Roehampton Inst., 1978–92 (rep. to Assoc. of Vol. Colls, 1978–88; Chm., Audit Cttee, 1989–92); Pusey House, 1985–92; Patron, Pusey House Appeal, 1984–88; Fellow, Corp. of SS Mary and Nicholas (Woodard Schs), 1972–92 (Mem. Exec., 1981–92; Chm., S Div. Res. Cttee, 1972–84; Trustee, Endowment Fund; Dir, Corp. Trustee Co.). Member Development Cttee: SPAB, 1985–87; London Symphony Chorus, 1985–87; Nat. Sch. of Osteopathy, 1986–90; Bd Mem., Nat. Youth Dance Co., 1988–92; Mem. Council, Publishers Assoc., 1990–92. Cttee, London Europe Soc., 1985–93; Mem. Court, City Univ., 1986–92. Dir, Surrey Building Soc., 1988–93. Dep. Chm. and Chm., Exec. Cttee, Athenæum Club, 1985–89. Hon. Member: Assoc. for Develt in the Arts; Georgia Salzburger Soc., USA, 1986. JP Inner London, 1971–75. Freeman, City of London, 1966; Liveryman, Worshipful Co. of Woolmen (Master, 1985–86; Rep. to City and Guilds, 1986–92); Parish Clerk, All Hallows, Bread Street, 1981–93; Mem., Guild of Freemen (Court, 1991–93); Hon. Citizen, Savannah, Georgia, 1986. FRSA 1978; FCMI (FBIM 1982); FInstD 1982. Hon. DLitt Columbia Pacific, 1982. Order of St Vladimir, 1977. *Publications:* articles in various jls. *Recreations:* mountain walking, reading, travel, enjoying the Arts, golf. *Address:* 3 The Mount Square, NW3 6SU. *T:* (020) 7794 8893; PO Box 118, Udon Thani 41000, Thailand. *T:* (42) 347338.

GILBERT, Rev. Canon Roger Geoffrey; Rector of Falmouth, 1986–2002; Chaplain to the Queen, 1995–2002; *b* 18 June 1937; *s* of Geoffrey and Ruth Gilbert; *m* 1965, Marie-Pascale (*née* Berthelot); three *d. Educ:* Truro Secondary Modern Sch. for Boys; St Peter's Coll., Birmingham; King's Coll. London (BD; AKC); St Augustine's Coll., Canterbury. RAF, 1957–59. Asst Master, Hinchley Wood Sch., 1963–67; ordained deacon, 1970, priest, 1971; Asst Curate, Walton-on-Thames, 1970–74; Licensed to Officiate, Dio. of Europe, 1973–; Rector, St Mabyn with Helland, 1974–81; Priest-in-charge, Madron with Morvah, 1981–86. Hon. Canon of Truro Cathedral, 1994–2002, now Emeritus; Rural Dean of Carnmarth South, 1994–2000. Fellow, Woodard Corp., 1988–2002. *Recreations:* travel, Cornish-Breton history and culture, post-Impressionist painters, antiques, books. *Address:* 2 rue de Plouzon, 22690 Pleudihen-sur-Rance, Brittany, France. *T:* (2) 96882869.

GILBERT, Prof. Walter; Carl M. Loeb University Professor, Department of Molecular and Cellular Biology (formerly of Cellular and Developmental Biology), Harvard University, 1985–2005, now Carl M. Loeb Professor Emeritus; Vice Chairman, Myriad Genetics Inc., since 1992; Managing Director, BioVentures Investors; *b* Boston, 21 March 1932; *s* of Richard V. Gilbert and Emma (*née* Cohen); *m* 1953, Celia Stone; one *s* one *d. Educ:* Harvard Coll. (AB *summa cum laude* Chem. and Phys., 1953); Harvard Univ. (AM Phys., 1954); Cambridge Univ. (PhD Maths, 1957). National Science Foundn pre-doctoral Fellow, Harvard Univ. and Cambridge Univ., 1953–57, post-doctoral Fellow in Phys., Harvard, 1957–58; Harvard University: Asst Prof. in Phys., 1959–64; Associate Prof. of Biophys., 1964–68; Prof. of Biochem., 1968–72; Amer. Cancer Soc. Prof. of Molecular Biology, 1972–81; H. H. Timken Prof. of Science, 1986–87. Jt Founder, 1978, and Dir, 1978–84, Biogen NV (Chm. and Principal Exec. Officer, 1981–84). Guggenheim Fellow, Paris, 1968–69. Member: Amer. Acad. of Arts and Sciences, 1968; National Acad. of Sciences, 1976; Amer. Phys. Soc.; Amer. Soc. of Biol Chemists; Foreign Mem., Royal Soc., 1987–. Hon. DSc: Chicago, 1978; Columbia, 1978; Rochester, 1979; Yeshiva, 1981. Many prizes and awards, incl. (jtly) Nobel Prize for Chemistry, 1980. *Publications:* chapters, articles and papers on theoretical physics and molecular biology. *Address:* BioVentures Investors, 101 Main Street, Cambridge, MA 02142, USA; 15 Gray Gardens West, Cambridge, MA 02138, USA. *T:* (617) 8648778.

GILBERTSON, Barry Gordon, FRICS; Partner, PricewaterhouseCoopers, since 1996; President, Royal Institution of Chartered Surveyors, 2004–05; *b* 6 June 1951; *s* of Bertram David Gilbertson and Joan Marion Ivy Gilbertson (*née* Gordon); *m* 1974, Yvonne Gunning; one *s. Educ:* Westcliff High Sch. for Boys. FRICS 1974; ACIArb 1976; Registered Fixed Charge Receiver 1999; Counsellor of Real Estate 2000. Partner, Butler & Hatch Waterman, 1983–86; Man. Dir, Claridge Gp, 1988–91; Nat. Property Advr, Coopers & Lybrand, 1992–96. Vis. Prof. of Built Envmt, Univ. of Northumbria, 2003–. Mem., Bank of England Property Cttee, 2003–. Mem., UN Real Estate Adv. Gp, 2000–05. Fellow: Property Consultants Soc., 1987; Non-Administrative Receivers Assoc. (Founding Chm., 1995–96); Internat. Real Estate Fedn, 2003 (Mem., 2002–); Founding Dep. Chm., World Assoc. of Valuation Orgns, 2002–04. Internat. Associate Ed., Counselors of Real Estate, 2006–08. Trustee, Coll. of Estate Mgt, Univ. of Reading, 2006–. Gov., Westcliff High Sch. for Boys, 2007–. Mem., Nat. Scout Adv. Bd, Scout Assoc., 1983–87. Dir, Cranmer Court Tenants (Chelsea) Ltd, 2006–. FICPD 1998; MInstD 1983. Hon. Member: Assoc. of S African Quantity Surveyors, 2005; S African Council for Quantity Surveying Profession, 2005; Assoc. of Valuers in Romania, 2006. Mem., MENSA, 1976–. Pres., Rotary Club of Folkestone, 2003 (Mem., 1990–2004); Mem., Committee Club, 2002–. Freeman, City of London, 1996; Liveryman, Co. of Chartered Surveyors, 1996–. *Publications:* Vision for Valuation, 2004; travelogues and book reviews; contrib. articles to learned jls in UK and abroad. *Recreations:* family and friends, jogging, cricket, ski-ing, the arts and fun (not necessarily in that order), oh, and of course, the Archers! *Address:* 13 Newlands Court, Stow-on-the-Wold, Glos GL54 1HN. *T:* (office) (020) 7212 3511; *e-mail:* barry.gilbertson@uk.pwc.com.

GILBERTSON, Prof. David Dennis; Emeritus Professor, University of Wales, since 1998; *b* Stratford, London, 1 Sept. 1945; *s* of late Thomas Gilbertson and of Ivy Florence Joyce Gilbertson; *m* 1970, Barbara Mary Mitchell; one *s* two *d. Educ:* SW Ham Tech. Sch.; Univ. of Lancaster (BA Hons 1968); Univ. of Exeter (PGCE 1969); Univ. of Bristol (PhD 1974; DSc 1991). FGS 1983. Teacher, Pretoria Sch., London, 1964–65; Res. Asst in Geology, Univ. of Bristol, 1969–71; Lectr in Geography, Plymouth Poly., 1971–74, Univ. of Adelaide, 1974–77; Sheffield University: Lectr, 1977–85; Sen. Lectr, 1985–88; Reader, 1988–92; Prof., and Hd of Res. Sch. of Archaeology and Archaeol Scis, 1992–94; Prof. of Physical Geography, Inst. of Geography and Earth Scis, and Dir, Inst. of Earth Studies, 1994–97, Univ. of Wales, Aberystwyth, 1994–98; Prof. of Envmtl Science, Nene Centre for Res., UC Northampton, 1998–2000; Hd, Sch. of Conservation Scis, Bournemouth Univ., 2000–02. Vis. Prof. and Fulbright Schol., Univ. of Arizona, 1981–82; Munro Lectr, Edinburgh Univ., 1999; Dist. Vis. Schol., Adelaide Univ., 1999; Vis. Prof., Univ. of Plymouth, 2001–. Co-Director: UNESCO Libyan Valleys Archaeol Survey, 1988–96; Wadi Faynan Survey, Jordan, 1994–2007; Niah Caves Proj., Borneo, 1998–; Chm., Univ. of Wales Subject Panel for Envmtl Studies, 1996–98. Jt Founder and Associate Ed., Applied Geography, 1981–88; Sen. UK Ed., Jl of Archaeol Sci., 1992–98. J. R. Wiseman Prize, Archaeol Inst. of Amer., 2001. *Publications:* (jtly) The Pleistocene Succession at Kenn, Somerset, 1978; (jtly) In the Shadow of Extinction, 1984; Late Quaternary Environments and Man in Holderness, 1984; (jtly) Practical Ecology, 1985; (jtly) The Chronology and Environment of Early Man: a new framework, 1985; (jtly) Farming the Desert: the UNESCO Libyan Valley survey, 1996; (jtly) The Outer Hebrides: the last 14000 years, 1996; (ed jtly) The Archaeology of Drylands: living on the margins, 2000; The Human Use of Caves in Island and Peninsula South East Asia, 2005; Archaeology and Desertification, 2007; contribs to books, and papers in learned jls. *Recreations:* walking, railways—large and small, West Ham United, the Teign Estuary. *Address:* c/o School of Geography, University of Plymouth, Plymouth PL4 8AA; *e-mail:* dgilbertson@plymouth.ac.uk.

GILBERTSON, David Stuart; Chief Executive, EMAP plc, 2008; *b* 21 Sept. 1956; *s* of Donald Stuart Gilbertson and Jocelyn Mary Gilbertson (*née* Sim); *m* 1991, Danielle Donougher; one *s* one *d. Educ:* Trinity Hall, Cambridge (BA 1978). Editl and mgt posts with Metal Bulletin, Reuters and Reed Elsevier; joined LLP, 1987: Ed., Lloyd's List, 1987–94; Dir, 1992–96; Chief Exec., 1997–98; Chief Exec., 1998–2004, Man. Dir, 2004–07, Informa Gp plc; Chief Exec., Informa plc, 2007–08. Non-exec. Chm., John Brown Hldgs Ltd, 2005–. FRSA. *Recreation:* sport, especially football.

GILBEY, family name of **Baron Vaux of Harrowden**.

GILBEY, Sir (Walter) Gavin, 4th Bt *cr* 1893, of Elsenham Hall, Essex; *b* 14 April 1949; *s* of Sir (Walter) Derek Gilbey, 3rd Bt and of Elizabeth Mary, *d* of Col K. G. Campbell; *S* father, 1991; *m* 1st, 1980, Mary (marr. diss. 1984), *d* of late William E. E. Pacetti; 2nd, 1984, Anna (marr. diss. 1995), *d* of Edmund Prosser. *Educ:* Eton. *Clubs:* Army and Navy; Royal Dornoch Golf.

GILCHRIST, Andrew Charles; Project Manager, Unite, since 2008; *b* 5 Dec. 1960; *s* of Edward and Shirley Gilchrist; *m* 1985, Loretta Borman; one *s* one *d. Educ:* Bedford Modern Sch. Bedfordshire Fire Service, 1979–96; Mem., Exec. Council, 1993–2000, Nat. Officer, 1996–2000, Gen. Sec., 2000–05, Fire Bde Union; UK Co-ordinator, Service Employees Internat. Union/IB Teamsters, 2006–08. Mem., Gen. Council, TUC 2000–05 (Mem., Exec. Cttee, 2004–05). *Recreations:* cycling, walking, reading. *Address: e-mail:* painewon@msn.com.

GILCHRIST, Archibald, OBE 1996; Managing Director, 1971–79, and Chairman, 1978–79, Govan Shipbuilders; *b* 17 Dec. 1929; *m* 1958, Elizabeth Jean Greenlees; two *s* one *d. Educ:* Loretto; Pembroke Coll., Cambridge (MA). Barclay Curle & Co. Ltd, Glasgow, 1954–64, various managerial posts; ultimately Dir, Swan Hunter Group; Brown Bros & Co. Ltd, Edinburgh, 1964–72: Dep. Man. Dir, 1964; Man. Dir, 1969; Man. Dir, Vosper Private, Singapore, 1980–86; Dir, Management Search Internat. Ltd, 1986–89; Pt-time Bd Mem., Scottish Legal Aid Bd, 1986–96; non-executive Director: F. J. C. Lilley plc, 1987–93; RMJM Ltd, 1988–98; Scottish Friendly Assurance Soc. Ltd (formerly Glasgow Friendly Soc.), 1988–2000; Caledonian MacBrayne Ltd, 1990–97. Vice Chm., Royal Scottish National (formerly Royal Scottish) Orchestra, 1989–94 (Dir, 1987–94). Chm. Council, St Leonard's Sch., 1989–95; Gov., Glasgow Polytechnic, 1987–93. *Recreations:* golf, shooting, fishing, music. *Address:* Inchmaholm, 35 Barnton Avenue, Edinburgh EH4 6JJ. *Clubs:* New (Edinburgh); Hon. Company of Edinburgh Golfers.

GILCHRIST, Maj. Gen. Peter, CB 2004; Defence Attaché, Washington, and Head, British Defence Staff, United States of America, 2005–08; *b* 28 Feb. 1952; *s* of late Col David A. Gilchrist and of Rosemary Gilchrist (*née* Drewe); *m* 1981, Sarah-Jane Poyntz; one *s* one *d. Educ:* Marlborough Coll.; Sandhurst. Commnd Royal Tank Regiment, 1972; Troop Leader, 3RTR, Germany and NI, 1972–76; aic 1977; Schools Gunnery Instructor, Lulworth, 1978–80; Ops Officer and Adjutant, 3RTR, 1980–82; Div. II, Army Staff Course (psc†), 1983–84; COS, 20th Armd Bde, 1985–87; Comdr, Indep. Recce Sqn, Cyprus, 1986; Sqn Comdr (Challenger), 3RTR, 1988; Mil. Sec.'s Staff, 1989; Directing Staff, RMCS, 1990–93; CO, RTR, 1993–95; HCSC, 1996; Dep. DOR (Armour and

Combat Support Vehicles), 1996–98; Prog. Dir, Armd Systems, MoD PE, 1998–2000; Exec. Dir, 2000–04, Tech. Dir, 2004, Defence Procurement Agency, and Master Gen. of the Ordnance; Dep. Comdr Combined Forces Comd, Afghanistan, 2004–05. Col Comdt, RAC, 2000–04; Dep. Col Comdt, RTR, 2000–. Non-executive Director: DERA Facilities Bd, 2000–01; DSTL, 2001–04. Bronze Star Medal (USA), 2006. *Recreations:* sailing, ski-ing, field sports, gardening, DIY. *Address:* Chapel Cottage, Netherhope Lane, Tidenham, Chepstow, Mon NP16 7JD. *Club:* Army and Navy.

GILCHRIST, Prof. Roberta Lynn, DPhil; FSA; FBA 2008; Professor of Archaeology, University of Reading, since 1996; *b* 28 June 1965; *d* of John James Gilchrist and Gail Ann Foreman (*née* Campbell); *m* 2000, Dr John Miles Preston. *Educ:* Univ. of York (BA 1986; DPhil 1990). MIFA 1990. Lectr, UEA, 1990–95; Archaeologist, Norwich Cathedral, 1993–2005. Ed., World Archaeol., 1997–2006; Member, Editorial Board: Social Archaeol., 1999–; Church Archaeol., 2002–. Acad. Advr, Mus. of London Archaeol. Service, 1991–. TV presenter, Down to Earth, 1991–92. Member: Adv. Bd for Redundant Churches, 1998–2001; Ancient Monuments Adv. Cttee, English Heritage, 1998–2001. Member: Churches Cttee, Council for British Archaeol., 1989–95; Council: Soc. for Medieval Archaeol., 1990–93 (Pres., 2004–07); Inst. of Field Archaeol., 1992–98; British Archaeol Assoc., 1995–98; Soc. of Antiquaries of London, 2007–. FSA 2002. *Publications:* Gender and Material Culture: the archaeology of religious women, 1994; Contemplation and Action: the other monasticism, 1995; Gender and Archaeology: contesting the past, 1999; Norwich Cathedral Close: the evolution of the English cathedral landscape, 2005 (Outstanding Acad. Title Award, Choice); (with B. Sloane) Requiem: the medieval monastic cemetery in Britain, 2005 (Scholarly Pubn Award, British Archaeol Awards, 2006); contrib. articles to World Archaeol., Antiquity, Medieval Archaeol., Archaeol Jl, Jl British Archaeol Assoc. *Recreations:* singing, walking, gardening, cats, travel, food and wine. *Address:* Department of Archaeology, University of Reading, Whiteknights, Reading RG6 6AB. *T:* (0118) 931 6381, *Fax:* (0118) 931 6718; *e-mail:* r.l.gilchrist@reading.ac.uk.

GILCHRIST, William Alexander; Sheriff of Tayside, Central and Fife at Stirling, since 2006; *b* 15 Nov. 1951; *s* of William Gilchrist and Helen Lang Gilchrist (*née* Thomson). *Educ:* Stirling High Sch.; Edinburgh Univ. (LLB). Admitted solicitor, 1976; Crown Office and Procurator Fiscal Service, 1976–2006: Regl Procurator Fiscal, N Strathclyde, 1998–2002; Dep. Crown Agent, 2002–05; Area Procurator Fiscal, Lothian and Borders, 2005–06. Mem., Sentencing Commn, 2003–. *Recreations:* tennis, ski-ing. *Address:* Sheriff's Chambers, Sheriff Court House, Viewfield Place, Stirling FK8 1NH. *T:* (01786) 462191; *e-mail:* sheriffwagilchrist@scotcourts.gov.uk.

GILDEA, Prof. Robert Nigel, DPhil; FRHistS; Professor of Modern History, University of Oxford, and Fellow, Worcester College, Oxford, since 2006; *b* 12 Sept. 1952; *s* of Denis and Hazel Gildea; *m* 1987, Lucy Jean Lloyd; two *s* two *d*. *Educ:* Merton Coll., Oxford (BA, MA); St Antony's Coll., Oxford; St John's Coll., Oxford (DPhil 1978). FRHistS 1986. Jun. Res. Fellow, St John's Coll., Oxford, 1976–78; Lectr in Hist., KCL, 1978–79; University of Oxford: CUF Lectr in Modern Hist., 1979–96; Reader in Modern Hist., 1996–2002; Prof. of Modern French Hist., 2002–06; Fellow and Tutor in Modern Hist., Merton Coll., 1979–2006. Élie Halévy Vis. Prof., Inst. d'Etudes Politiques, Paris, 1999–2000. Chevalier, Ordre des Palmes Académiques (France), 1997. *Publications:* Education in Provincial France 1800–1914: a study of three departments, 1983; Barricades and Borders: Europe 1800–1914, 1987, 3rd edn 2002; The Third Republic from 1870 to 1914, 1988; The Past in French History, 1994; France since 1945, 1996, 2nd edn 2002 (Enid McLeod Prize, Franco-British Soc.); Marianne in Chains: in search of the German Occupation (Wolfson Hist. Prize), 2003; (ed jtly) Surviving Hitler and Mussolini: daily life in Occupied Europe, 2006; Children of the Revolution, 2008. *Recreations:* walking, swimming, music, cooking, Oxford United. *Address:* Worcester College, Oxford OX1 2HB. *T:* (01865) 278348, *Fax:* (01865) 278303.

GILDERNEW, Michelle; MP (SF) Fermanagh and South Tyrone, since 2001; Member (SF) Fermanagh and South Tyrone, Northern Ireland Assembly, since 1998; Minister for Agriculture and Rural Development, Northern Ireland, since 2007. *Educ:* Univ. of Ulster. Press Officer, Sinn Féin, 1997. Dep. Chm., Social Develt Cttee, 1999–2002, Mem., Centre Cttee, 2000–02, NI Assembly. *Address:* c/o House of Commons, SW1A 0AA; c/o Northern Ireland Assembly, Stormont Castle, Belfast BT4 3XX; (office) 82 Main Street, Lisnaskea, Co. Fermanagh BT92 0JD.

GILES, Alan James; Chairman, Fat Face, since 2006; *b* 4 June 1954; *s* of Ronald Arthur Giles and Christine Joyce Giles; *m* 1978, Gillian Margaret Rosser; two *d*. *Educ:* Merton Coll., Oxford (MA Physics); Graduate Sch. of Business, Stanford Univ. (MSc Mgt). Various buying roles, Boots the Chemists, 1975–82; Retail Develt Manager, 1982–84, Gen. Manager (Books), 1985–87, W.H. Smith; Ops and Develt Manager, Do It All, 1988–92; Managing Dir, Waterstone's, 1993–98; CEO, HMV Gp plc, 1998–2006. Non-executive Director: Somerfield plc, 1993–2004; Wilson Bowden plc, 2004–07; Rentokil Initial plc, 2006–; OFT, 2007–. *Recreations:* cycling, watching soccer.

GILES, Ann, (Mrs Keith Giles); see Howard, A.

GILES, Bill; see Giles, W. G.

GILES, Christopher Thomas; Economics Editor, Financial Times, since 2004; *b* 9 Nov. 1969; *s* of Gerald David Norman Giles and Rotraud Ursula Giles; *m* 2000, Katie Anne Roden; two *d*. *Educ:* Jesus Coll., Cambridge (BA 1991); Birkbeck Coll., London (MSc). Sen. Res. Economist, Inst. for Fiscal Studies, 1991–98; econs reporter, BBC, 1998–2000; Leader Writer, Financial Times, 2000–04. *Recreations:* family, cycling, marathon running, theatre. *Address:* Financial Times, One Southwark Bridge, SE1 9HL. *T:* (020) 7873 4315, *Fax:* (020) 7873 3083; *e-mail:* chris.giles@ft.com. *Club:* Tuesday.

GILES, Frank Thomas Robertson; Editor, The Sunday Times, 1981–83 (Deputy Editor, 1967–81); *b* 31 July 1919; *s* of late Col F. L. N. Giles, DSO, OBE, and Mrs Giles; *m* 1946, Lady Katharine Pamela Sackville, *o d* of 9th Earl De La Warr and Countess De La Warr; one *s* two *d*. *Educ:* Wellington Coll.; Brasenose Coll., Oxford (Open Scholarship in History; MA 1946). ADC to Governor of Bermuda, 1939–42; Directorate of Mil. Ops, WO, 1942–45; temp. mem. of HM Foreign Service, 1945–46 (Private Sec. to Ernest Bevin; Mem. of Sir Archibald Clark Kerr's mission to Java); joined editorial staff of The Times, 1946; Asst Correspondent, Paris, 1947; Chief Corresp., Rome, 1950–53, Paris, 1953–60; Foreign Editor, Sunday Times, 1961–77; Dir, Times Newspapers Ltd, 1981–85. Lectures: tours, USA, 1975, FRG, 1984; Gritti, Venice, 1985. Chm., Library Cttee, Britain-Russia Centre, 1993–99. Chm., Painshill Park Trust, 1985–96; Mem., Governing Body, British Inst. of Florence, 1986–2001; Governor: Wellington Coll., 1965–89; Sevenoaks Sch., 1967–92. *Publications:* A Prince of Journalists: the life and times of de Blowitz, 1962; Sundry Times (autobiog.), 1986; The Locust Years: the story of the Fourth French Republic 1946–1958, 1991 (Franco-British Soc. award); (ed) Corfu, the Garden Isle, 1994; Napoleon Bonaparte, England's Prisoner, 2001. *Recreations:* going to the opera; collecting, talking about, consuming the vintage wines of Bordeaux and Burgundy.

Address: 42 Blomfield Road, W9 2PF; Bunns Cottage, Lye Green, Crowborough, Ea Sussex TN6 1UY. *Clubs:* Brooks's, Beefsteak.

GILES, Hugh Peter; Head, Litigation and Employment Group, Treasury Solicitor' Department, since 2008; *b* 25 Jan. 1964; *s* of late Peter Giles and Mary Giles (*née* Cope) *m* 1997, Karen Duke; one *s* one *d*. *Educ:* Brentwood Sch.; Univ. of Nottingham (B. 1986). Admitted solicitor, 1991; Legal Adviser's Br., Home Office, 1991–99; Leg. Secretariat to the Law Officers, 1999–2001; team leader, Treasury Solicitor's Dep 2001–03; a legal dir, DTI, 2003–06; Dir, Legal Services Gp, DTI, subseq. BERR 2006–08. *Recreations:* family, cricket, Tottenham Hotspur. *Address:* Treasury Solicitor' Department, 1 Kemble Street, WC2B 4TS.

GILES, Rear-Adm. Sir Morgan Charles M.; see Morgan-Giles.

GILES, Roy Curtis, MA; Administrative Consultant, Busoga Trust, since 1991; Hea Master, Highgate School, 1974–89; *b* 6 Dec. 1932; *s* of Herbert Henry Giles and Doroth Alexandra Potter; *m* 1963, Christine von Alten; two *s* one *d*. *Educ:* Queen Elizabeth's Sch Barnet; Jesus Coll., Cambridge (Open Scholar). Asst Master, Dean Close Sch., 1956–6(Lektor, Hamburg Univ., 1960–63; Asst Master, Eton Coll., 1963–74, Head of Moder Languages, 1970–74. Educnl Selector, ABM (formerly ACCM), 1979–92; Mem., Hous of Bishops' Panel on Marriage Educn, 1983–89. Mem., Council of Management, Verno Educnl Trust (formerly Davies's Educn Services), 1975–2005; Governor: The Hall Hampstead, 1976–89; Channing Sch., 1977–89. *Recreations:* music, theatre, Centra Europe. *Address:* Chattan Court, Woodbury Lane, Axminster, Devon EX13 5TL. *T* (01297) 33720.

GILES, William George, (Bill Giles), OBE 1995; Chairman, The Weather People Ltd since 1998; *b* 18 Nov. 1939; *s* of Albert William George Giles and Florence Ellen Christin Giles; *m* 1st, 1961, Eileen Myrtle Lake (marr. diss. 1991); one *s* one *d*; 2nd, 1993, Patrici Maureen Stafford. *Educ:* Queen Elizabeth's Sch., Crediton; Bristol Coll. of Sci. and Tech Meteorological Office Coll. Meteorological Office, 1959; radio broadcaster, 1972 television broadcaster, 1975; Head, BBC Weather Centre, 1983–2000. Prix de Scientifiques, Fest. Internat. de Meteo, Paris, 1994. *Publications:* Weather Observations 1978; The Story of Weather, 1990. *Recreations:* gardening, golf, One Man Weather Show *Address:* 73 Lower Icknield Way, Chinnor, Oxon OX39 4EA.

GILHOOLY, John; Artistic and Executive Director, Wigmore Hall, since 200 (Executive Director, 2000–05); *b* 15 Aug. 1973; *s* of Owen Gilhooly and Helena (*né* Conway). *Educ:* University Coll., Dublin (BA Hons). Administrator, University Coll. Dublin, 1994–97; Manager, Harrogate Internat. Centre, 1997–2000. Chm., Koh Foundn Internat. Song Competition, 2006; Trustee, London Internat. String Quarte Competition, 2006–. Hon. Sec., Royal Philharmonic Soc., 2007–. Hon. FRAM 2006 *Address:* Wigmore Hall, 36 Wigmore Street, W1U 2BP; *e-mail:* jgilhooly@wigmore hall.org.uk.

GILHOOLY, John Francis, CB 2005; Chief Executive, Office of the Parliamentar Counsel, 2000–08; *b* 26 April 1945; *s* of Francis Gilhooly and Sarah Gilhooly (*né* Gavigan); *m* 1971, Gillian Marie (*née* Cunningham); two *s* two *d*. *Educ:* Clapham Coll. Grammar Sch. (RC); King's Coll., Cambridge (BA Econ 1970). Clerical Officer, the Exec. Officer, ODM, 1965–70; Econ. Asst, then Sen. Econ. Asst, ODA, 1970–74; Econ Adviser, Royal Commn on the Distribution of Income and Wealth, 1974–78; HM Treasury: Econ. Adviser, then Principal, 1978–84; Asst Sec. Pay Policy, Tax Policy, Ger Expenditure Policy, Training Review, 1984–92; Asst Dir (on loan), Capital Allowance Policy, Tax Law Rewrite, Inland Revenue, 1992–96; Mgt Advr, Office of Parly Counsel 1996–99. Guest Lectr, Inst. of Advanced Legal Studies, Univ. of London, 2005. FRS/ 2004. *Recreations:* reading, walking, family, friends. *Clubs:* Civil Service; St Andrews Ramblers.

GILL, Rt Hon. Lord; Brian Gill; PC 2002; a Senator of the College of Justice i Scotland, since 1994; Lord Justice Clerk and President of the Second Division of the Cou of Session, since 2001; *b* 25 Feb. 1942; *s* of Thomas and Mary Gill, Glasgow; *m* 1969 Catherine Fox; five *s* one *d*. *Educ:* St Aloysius' Coll., Glasgow; Glasgow Univ. (MA 1962 LLB 1964); Edinburgh Univ. (PhD 1975). Asst Lectr, 1964–65, Lectr, 1965–69 an 1972–77, Faculty of Law, Edinburgh Univ.; Advocate, 1967; Advocate Depute, 1977–79 Standing Junior Counsel: Foreign and Commonwealth Office (Scotland), 1974–77 Home Office (Scotland), 1979–81; Scottish Education Dept, 1979–81; QC (Scot.) 1981 Chm., Scottish Law Commn, 1996–2001. Called to the Bar, Lincoln's Inn, 1991, Hon Bencher, 2002. Keeper of the Advocates' Library, 1987–94. Dep. Chm., Copyrigh Tribunal, 1989–94. Chm., RSAMD, 1999–. FRSAMD 2002; FRSE 2004. Hon. LLD Glasgow, 1998; Strathclyde, 2003; St Andrews, 2006; Edinburgh, 2007; Hon. DAca RSAMD, 2006. *Publications:* The Law of Agricultural Holdings in Scotland, 1982, 3rd ed 1997; (ed) Scottish Planning Encyclopedia, 1996; articles in legal jls. *Recreation:* churc music. *Address:* Court of Session, Parliament House, Edinburgh EH1 1RQ. *T:* (0131) 24 6732. *Clubs:* Reform, MCC.

GILL, Adrian Anthony; journalist, Restaurant Critic, Television Critic and feature writer, Sunday Times; *b* 28 June 1954; *s* of George Michael Gill and Yvonne Gilan Gill *m* 1st, 1983, Cressida Connoly; 2nd, 1991, Amber Rudd; one *s* one *d*. *Educ:* S Christopher Sch., Letchworth; St Martin's Sch. of Art; Slade Sch. of Fine Art. Sometim illustrator, muralist, graphic designer, portrait painter, artist material salesman warehouseman, gents' outfitter, pizza chef, waiter, painter and decorator, gardene pornography salesman, maitre d', film lectr, moonshine runner, nanny, sugar cane cutte theatrical scene shifter, drawing master, plongeur, barman, male model, cookery teache writer and journalist. *Publications:* Sap Rising (fiction), 1996; The Ivy: the restaurant an its recipes, 1997; The Caprice, 1998; Starcrossed (fiction), 1999; A. A. Gill is Away, 2002 Table Talk, 2007. *Recreation:* journalism. *Address:* c/o Ed Victor, 6 Bayley Street, Bedfor Square, WC1B 3HB. *Clubs:* Chelsea Arts, Gerry's.

GILL, Sir Anthony (Keith), Kt 1991; FREng; Chairman, Docklands Light Railway 1994–99; *b* 1 April 1930; *s* of Frederick William and Ellen Gill; *m* 1953, Phyllis Cook; on *s* two *d*. *Educ:* High Sch., Colchester; Imperial Coll., London (BScEng Hons). Nationa Service officer, REME, 1954–56. Joined Bryce Berger Ltd, 1956, subseq. Director an Gen. Manager until 1972; Lucas CAV Ltd, 1972, subseq. Director and Gen. Manager unti 1978; Divisional Managing Director, Joseph Lucas Ltd, 1978; Lucas Industries: Jt Gp Man Dir, 1980–83; Gp Man. Dir, 1984–87 and Dep. Chm., 1986–87; Chm. and Chief Exec. 1987–94. Non-executive Director: Post Office Bd, 1989–91; National Power, 1990–98 Tarmac, 1992–2000. Chm., Teaching Co. Scheme Bd, 1991–96; Mem: Advr. Council on Science and Technology (formerly Adv. Council for Applied R&D), 1985–91; DT Technology Requirements Bd, 1986–88; Engineering Council, 1988–96 (Dep. Chm. 1994–95); Nat. Trng Task Force, 1991–93. Pres., IProdE, 1986–87; Mem., Council IMechE, 1986–92; Vice-Pres., Inst. of Management, 1993 (Chm. Council, 1996–99 Pres., 1998–99). Member Court: Univ. of Warwick, 1986–94; Cranfield Univ. (formerly Inst. of Technology), 1991– (Pro-Chancellor, 1991–2001). FREng (FEng 1983); FCG

1979; Fellow, City of Birmingham Polytechnic, 1989. Hon. FIET. Hon. DEng Birmingham, 1990; Hon. DSc: Cranfield, 1991; Southampton, 1992; Warwick, 1992; Hon. DTech Coventry, 1992; DUniv Sheffield Hallam, 1993. *Recreations:* boating, music. *Address:* The Point House, Astra Court, Hythe Marina Village, Hythe, Southampton SO45 6DZ. *T:* (023) 8084 0165. *Clubs:* Royal Thames Yacht; Royal Southampton Yacht.

GILL, Sir Arthur Benjamin Norman, (Sir Ben), Kt 2003; CBE 1996; Managing Director, Hawk Creative Business Park Ltd (Director, since 2007); Director, Hawkhills Consultancy Ltd, since 2004; President, Confederation of European Agriculture, 2000–04; *b* 1 Jan. 1950; *o s* of William Norman Gill and Annie (Nancy) Gill (*née* Almack); *m* 1973, Carolyn Davis; four *s*. *Educ:* Easingwold Primary Sch.; Barnard Castle Sch.; St John's Coll., Cambridge (MA Agric. 1971). Various posts at Namasagali Coll., Jinja, Uganda, 1972–75; i/c pig unit, Holderness, Humberside, 1975–77; running family farm, Vale of York, 1978–2007. National Farmers' Union: Mem. Council, 1985–2004; Vice-Chm., 1986–87, Chm., 1987–91, Livestock and Wool Cttee; Vice-Pres., 1991–92; Dep. Pres., 1992–98; Pres., 1998–2004. Chairman: Westbury Dairies Ltd, 2004–06; English Apples and Pears Ltd, 2007–; Director: Countrywide Farms plc, 2004–; Emissions Trading Worldwide Ltd (trading as One Planet), 2007–; non-exec. Dir, Eden Research plc, 2007–; Associate Dir, Sovereign Strategy, 2007–. Member: AFRC, 1991–94; BBSRC, 1994–97 (Chm., Agricl Systems Directorate, 1994–97; Mem., Biosci. for Industry Panel, 2007–); Mem. Panel, Agric., Natural Resources and Envmt, 1994–95, Agric., Horticulture and Forestry, 1995–99, Technology Foresight, OST. Chairman: Alternative Crops Technology Interaction Network, 1995–2004; Govt Biomass Task Force, 2004–05. Dir, FARM Africa, 1991–98. Mem. Council, Food from Britain, 1999–2005; Mem., Carnegie Commn on Rural Community Develt, 2004–07; Vice-Pres., COPA, 1999–2003; Mem., Governing Council, John Innes Centre, Norwich, 2002–; Mem., Governing Bd, Univ. of Lincoln, 2004–. Pres., Potato Growers Res. Assoc., Univ of Cambridge, 2004–. Vis. Prof., Leeds Univ., 1996–. Patron: Farmers Overseas Action Gp, 1998–; Rural Stress Inf. Network, 2000–07; St John Ambulance Bricks and Wheels Appeal, 2001; Pentalk, 2005–; Trustee, Plants & Us campaign, 2004–. FRAgS 1995; FIGD 1998. Hon. DSc: Leeds, 1997; Cranfield, 2000; UWE, 2002; Hon. DCL UEA, 2003. *Recreation:* rowing (Founder Mem., Guy Fawkes Boat Club, York). *Address:* Prospect Farm, Upper Dormington, Hereford HR1 4ED. *Club:* Farmers.

GILL, Brian; *see* Gill, Rt Hon. Lord.

GILL, Charan Singh, MBE 1998; Chairman, Harlequin Leisure Investments Ltd, since 2005; *b* 8 Dec. 1954; *s* of Mehar Singh Gill and Bhajan Kaur Gill; *m* 1974, Parminder Kaur Brar; one *s* four *d*. Engr, Yarrows Shipbuilder, 1969–79; restaurant manager, 1979–83; Asst Manager of insce co., 1983–86; insurance salesman, 1986–89; Man. Dir, Harlequin Leisure Gp, 1989–2005. Vice-Chm., Entrepreneurial Exchange, 2005–. Chm., Glasgow Restaurateurs Assoc., 2005–. Hon. Dr Paisley, 2004. *Recreations:* bhangra music, charity work. *Address:* Harlequin Leisure Investments Ltd, 1313 Argyle Street, Glasgow G3 8TL. *T:* (0141) 334 4633; *e-mail:* charangillmbe@yahoo.co.uk.

GILL, Prof. Christopher John, PhD; Professor of Ancient Thought, University of Exeter, since 1997; *b* 2 May 1946; *s* of Ross and Phyllis Gill; *m* 1981, Karen Ann Brown; four *s*. *Educ:* Cowbridge Grammar Sch., Glamorgan; St John's Coll., Cambridge (BA 1967, MA 1971); Yale Univ. (PhD 1970). Teaching asst, 1967–70, Instructor, 1970–71, Yale Univ.; Lectr, Univ. of Bristol, 1971–72; Lectr, 1972–83, Sen. Lectr, 1983–89, UCW, Aberystwyth; Sen. Lectr, 1989–94, Reader, 1994–97, Univ. of Exeter. Res. Fellow, Nat. Humanities Center, USA, 1981–82; Leverhulme Maj. Res. Fellow, 2003–06. *Publications:* Plato: the Atlantis story, 1980; (ed) The Person and the Human Mind: issues in ancient and modern philosophy, 1990; Greek Thought, 1995; Personality in Greek Epic, Tragedy and Philosophy: the self in dialogue, 1996; Plato: the symposium, 1999; (ed) Virtue, Norms, and Objectivity: issues in ancient and modern ethics, 2005; The Structured Self in Hellenistic and Roman Thought, 2006; co-ed vols of essays. *Recreations:* swimming, hill-walking, listening to 16th century choral music. *Address:* Department of Classics and Ancient History, University of Exeter, Exeter EX4 4RJ. *T:* (01392) 264270, *Fax:* (01392) 264377; *e-mail:* C.J.Gill@exeter.ac.uk.

GILL, Christopher John Fred, RD 1971; butcher and farmer; Hon. President, Freedom Association Ltd, since 2007 (Hon. Chairman, 2001–07); *b* 28 Oct. 1936; *m* 1960, Patricia M. (*née* Greenway); one *s* two *d*. *Educ:* Shrewsbury School. Chm., F. A. Gill Ltd, 1968–2006. Councillor, Wolverhampton BC, 1965–72. MP (C) Ludlow, 1987–2001. Member: Agriculture Select Cttee, 1989–95; Welsh Affairs Select Cttee, 1996–97. Vice Chairman: Cons. European Affairs Cttee, 1989–91 (Sec., 1988–89); Cons. Agric. Cttee, 1991–94 (Sec., 1990–91); Pres., Midlands W European Cons. Council, 1984–85. Member: Exec., 1922 Cttee, 1997–99; Council of Europe, 1997–99. *Address:* Billingsley Hall Farm, Bridgnorth, Shropshire WV16 6PJ.

GILL, Devinder Kaur; a Senior Immigration Judge, Asylum and Immigration Tribunal (formerly a Vice President, Immigration Appeal Tribunal), since 2003; a Recorder, since 2004; *b* 1958; *d* of I. S. G. Mahinder Gill. *Educ:* Wolfson Coll., Cambridge (LLM); Univ. of London (LLB ext.). Called to the Bar, Middle Temple, 1984; with various banks, including Singer & Friedlander, Samuel Montagu, HSBC and West LB; In-house Lawyer, Emerging Mkts, 1985–94; In-house Gp Lawyer, Finance, 1996–97; Legal Consultant, Emerging Mkts, 1997–2000. Adjudicator, Immigration Appellate Authy, 1998–2003. *Recreations:* gardening, music, reading, walking.

GILL, (Evelyn) Margaret, PhD; FRSE; Chief Scientific Advisor, Scottish Government (formerly Executive) Environment and Rural Affairs Department, since 2006; Professor of Integrated Land Use, University of Aberdeen, since 2006; *b* 10 Jan. 1951; *d* of William Alexander Morrison Gill and Eveline Elizabeth Gill (*née* Duthie). *Educ:* Univ. of Edinburgh (BSc Hons Agricl Sci.); Massey Univ., New Zealand (PhD); Open Univ. (BA Maths). Researcher, Grassland Res. Inst., AFRC, 1976–89; Researcher, 1989–94, Dir of Res., 1994–96, Natural Resources Inst., ODA; Chief Exec., Natural Resources Internat. Ltd, 1996–2000; Chief Exec. and Dir of Res., Macaulay Land Use Res. Inst., 2000–05. Hon. Prof., Univ. of Aberdeen, 2001. FRSE 2003. *Recreations:* hill-walking, ski-ing, classical music. *Address:* Scottish Government Environment and Rural Affairs Department, Pentland House, 47 Robb's Loan, Edinburgh EH14 1TY. *T:* (0131) 244 6042.

GILL, (George) Malcolm, FCIB; Head, Banking Department, Bank for International Settlements, 1995–99 (Deputy Head, 1991–95); *b* 23 May 1934; *s* of late Thomas Woodman Gill and Alice Muriel Gill (*née* Le Grice); *m* 1966, Monica Kennedy Brooks; one *s* one *d*. *Educ:* Cambridgeshire High Sch.; Sidney Sussex Coll., Cambridge (MA). Entered Bank of England, 1957: seconded to UK Treasury Delegation, Washington DC, 1966–68; Private Sec. to Governor, 1970–72; Asst Chief Cashier, 1975; seconded to HM Treasury, 1977–80; Chief Manager, Banking and Credit Markets, 1980–82; Head of Foreign Exchange Div., 1982–88; Asst Dir, 1987–88; Chief of the Banking Dept and Chief Cashier, 1988–91. *Recreations:* reading, gardening, music. *Address:* 3 Scotscraig, Radlett, Herts WD7 8LH.

GILL, Guy Serle G.; *see* Goodwin-Gill.

GILL, Jack, CB 1984; Chief Executive (formerly Secretary), Export Credits Guarantee Department, 1983–87; Executive Director (part-time), Government Relations, BICC plc, 1987–91; *b* 20 Feb. 1930; *s* of Jack and Elizabeth Gill; *m* 1954, Alma Dorothy; three *d*. *Educ:* Bolton Sch. Export Credits Guarantee Department: Clerical Officer, 1946; Principal, 1962; Asst Sec., 1970; Asst Sec., DTI, 1972–75; Export Credits Guarantee Department: Under Sec., 1975–79; Principal Finance Officer, 1978–79; Sec., Monopolies and Mergers Commn, 1979–81; Dep. Sec., and Dir of Industrial Devel Unit, DoI, 1981–83. Mem., BOTB, 1981–87. Consultant: NEI Power Projects Ltd, 1987–90; British Aerospace plc, 1987–89; CBI Council, 1988–91 (Chm., Public Procurement Contact Gp, 1990–91; Mem., Overseas Cttee, 1990–91). National Service, REME, 1948–50. *Recreations:* music (Bass, St Paul's Cath. Sunday Evening and Special Service Choirs, 1951–60), chess; occasional crossword setter for The Listener. *Address:* 9 Ridley Road, Warlingham, Surrey CR6 9LR. *T:* (01883) 622688.

GILL, Kenneth; General Secretary, Manufacturing, Science, Finance, 1989–92 (Joint General Secretary, 1988–89); Chairman, Morning Star, 1984–95; *b* 30 Aug. 1927; *s* of Ernest Frank Gill and Mary Ethel Gill; *m* 1st, 1953, Jacqueline Manley (marr. diss. 1964); 2nd, 1967, S. T. Paterson (marr. diss. 1990); two *s* one *d*; 3rd, 1997, Norma Bramley. *Educ:* Chippenham Secondary School. Engrg apprentice, 1943–48; Draughtsman Designer, Project Engr, Sales Engr in various cos, 1948–62; District Organiser, Liverpool and Ireland TASS, 1962–68; Editor, TASS Union Jl, 1968–72; Dep. Gen. Sec., 1972–74; Gen. Sec. AUEW (TASS), 1974–86, TASS—the Manufacturing Union, 1986–88. Pres., CSEU, 1988–89. Mem., Gen. Council, TUC, 1974–92 (Chm., 1985–86); Pres. of TUC, 1985–86. Mem., Commn for Racial Equality, 1981–87. Hon. Pres., Cuba Solidarity Campaign. *Recreations:* sketching, political caricaturing. *Address:* c/o Cuba Solidarity Campaign, Unite, Woodberry, 218 Green Lanes, N4 2HB. *T:* (020) 8800 0155.

GILL, Rt Rev. Kenneth Edward; Assistant Bishop of Newcastle (full time), 1980–98; *b* 22 May 1932; *s* of Fred and Elsie Gill; *m* 1957, Edna Hammond; one *s* two *d*. *Educ:* Harrogate Grammar School; Hartley Victoria Coll., Manchester. Ordained in Church of South India, deacon, 1958, presbyter, 1960; Mysore Diocese, 1958–72; Bishop of Karnataka Central Diocese, Church of S India, 1972–80. MA Lambeth, 2004; Hon. DD Serampore, 2006. *Publications:* Meditations on the Holy Spirit, 1979; Count us Equal, 1990; Roots to Fruits, 2001; Darkness to Light, 2004; A Multi-faceted Ministry, 2008. *Recreation:* gardening. *Address:* Kingfisher Lodge, 41 Long Cram, Haddington EH41 4NS. *T:* (01620) 822113; *e-mail:* k.gill@newcastle.anglican.org.

GILL, Malcolm; *see* Gill, G. M.

GILL, Margaret; *see* Gill, E. M.

GILL, Neena; Member (Lab), West Midlands Region, England, European Parliament, since July 1999; *b* 24 Dec. 1956; *d* of late Jasmer S. Gill and of Birjinder K. Gill; *m* 1992, Dr John Towner; one *s*. *Educ:* Watford High Sch.; Liverpool Poly. (Dep. Pres., Students' Union, 1979–80); London Business Sch. (BA Hons). Admin. Officer, Ealing LBC, 1981–83; Principal Housing Officer, UK Housing Trust, 1983–86; Chief Executive: ASRA Greater London Housing Assoc., 1986–90; New London Housing Gp, 1990–99. Former Director: Dalston City Partnership; Hackney Housing Partnership; former Mem., Macintyre Housing Assoc. Member: MSF; AEEU. FRSA; CIOH. *Recreations:* hill walking, football, antiques, minor bird watching, cinema, opera. *Address:* (office) Terry Duffy House, Thomas Street, West Bromwich B70 6NT. *T:* (0121) 569 1921, *Fax:* (0121) 569 1935.

GILL, Parmjit Singh; Member (Lib Dem), Leicester City Council, since 2003; *b* 20 Dec. 1966. Inf. Mgt and Security Consultant, Charnwood BC, until 2004. Contested (Lib Dem) Leicester S, 2001. MP (Lib Dem) Leicester S, July 2004–2005; contested (Lib Dem) same seat, 2005. *Address:* c/o Leicester City Council, New Walk Centre, Welford Place, Leicester LE1 6ZG.

GILL, Peter, OBE 1980; FRWCMD; dramatic author; Associate Director, Royal National Theatre, 1989–97; *b* Cardiff, 7 Sept. 1939; *s* of George John Gill and Margaret Mary Browne. *Educ:* St Illtyd's Coll., Cardiff. FRWCMD (FWCMD 1992). Associate Dir, Royal Court Theatre, 1970–72; Dir, 1976–80, Associate Dir, 1980, Riverside Studios, Hammersmith; Dir, Royal Nat. Theatre Studio, 1984–90. Productions include: *Royal Court:* A Collier's Friday Night, 1965; The Local Stigmatic, A Provincial Life, 1966; A Soldier's Fortune, The Daughter-in-law, Crimes of Passion, 1967; The Widowing of Mrs Holroyd, 1968; Life Price, Over Gardens Out, The Sleepers' Den, 1969; The Duchess of Malfi, 1971; Crete & Sergeant Pepper, 1972; The Merry-go-round, 1973; Small Change, The Fool, 1976; The York Realist, 2002; *Riverside Studios:* As You Like It, 1976; Small Change, 1977; The Cherry Orchard (own version), The Changeling, 1978; Measure for Measure, 1979; Julius Caesar, 1980; Scrape off the Black, 1980; *Royal National Theatre:* A Month in the Country, Don Juan, Scrape off the Black, Much Ado about Nothing, 1981; Danton's Death, Major Barbara, 1982; Kick for Touch, Tales from Hollywood, Antigone (co-dir), 1983; Venice Preserv'd, Fool for Love (transf. Lyric), 1984; The Murderers, As I Lay Dying (also adapted), A Twist of Lemon, In the Blue, Bouncing, Up for None, The Garden of England (co-dir), 1985; Mean Tears, 1987; Mrs Klein, 1988 (transf. Apollo, 1989); Juno and the Paycock, 1989; Cardiff East (also wrote), 1997; Friendly Fire, 1999; Luther, 2001; Scenes from the Big Picture, 2003; The Voysey Inheritance, 2006; *other London theatres:* O'Flaherty VC, Mermaid, 1966; The Way of the World, Lyric, Hammersmith, 1992; Uncle Vanya, Tricycle, 1995; Tongue of a Bird, Almeida, 1997; Certain Young Men, Almeida, 1999; Speed the Plow, New Ambassadors, 2000; Days of Wine and Roses, Donmar, 2005; George Dillon, Comedy Th., 2006; Gaslight, Old Vic, 2007; The Importance of Being Earnest, Vaudeville, 2008; *Royal Shakespeare Co.:* Twelfth Night, 1974; New England, 1994; A Patriot for Me, 1995; Romeo and Juliet, transf. Albery, 2004; has also produced plays by Shakespeare and modern writers at Nottingham, Edinburgh and in Canada, Germany, Switzerland and USA; *music theatre and opera* includes: Down By the Green Wood Side (co-dir), Bow Down (co-dir), Queen Elizabeth Hall, 1987; Marriage of Figaro, Opera North, 1987; *television* productions include: Grace, 1972; Girl, 1973; A Matter of Taste, Fugitive, 1974; Hitting Town, 1976; *radio* productions include: The Look Across the Eyes, 2001; Lovely Evening, 2001. *Publications:* plays: The Sleepers' Den, 1965; Over Gardens Out, 1969; Small Change, 1976; Small Change, Kick for Touch, 1985; In the Blue, Mean Tears, 1987; Cherry Orchard, 1996; The Look Across the Eyes, 1997; Cardiff East, 1997; Certain Young Men, 1999; The Seagull, 2000; The York Realist, 2001; Original Sin, 2002; The Look Across the Eyes, 2002; Lovely Evening, 2002. *Address:* c/o Casarotto Co. Ltd, 7–12 Noel Street, W1F 8GQ.

GILL, Robin Denys, CVO 1993; Founder and Chairman of Executive, since 1990 and Chairman, since 2002, Royal Anniversary Trust; Founder and Chairman, The Queen's Anniversary Prizes for Higher and Further Education, since 1993; *b* 7 Oct. 1927; *s* of Thomas Henry Gill and Marjorie Mary (*née* Butler); *m* 1st, 1951, Mary Hope Alexander (*d* 1986); three *s*; 2nd, 1991, Denise Spencer Waterhouse. *Educ:* Dulwich Coll.; Brasenose Coll., Oxford (MA; Hon. Fellow, 2005). Unilever plc, 1949–54; British Internat. Paper Ltd, 1954–59; Founder and Man. Dir, Border TV Ltd, 1960–64; Man. Dir, ATV Corp. Ltd, 1964–69; Chairman: ITCA, 1966–67; ITN, 1968–69; 1970 Trust Ltd, 1970–93; Ansvar Insce Co. Ltd, 1975–98; Standard Ind. Trust Ltd, 1970–81; various internat. private equity funds; Director: Reed Paper Gp Ltd, 1970–75; Hewlett Packard Ltd, 1975–92; Yarrow Plc, 1979–88; Baring Hambrecht Alpine Ltd, 1986–98; SD-Scicon plc, 1988–90. Member: Nat. Adv. Bd for Higher Educn; Oxford Univ. Appts Cttee; Vis. Cttee, RCA; Cttee, Royal Family Film, 1968–70. Pres., Brasenose Soc., 1995–96. *Recreations:* golf, sport, travel, art collecting, new projects. *Address:* PO Box 1, East Horsley, Surrey KT24 6RE. *T:* (01483) 285290. *Clubs:* Vincent's (Oxford); St George's Hill Golf; Free Foresters Cricket.

GILL, Rev. Prof. Robin Morton, PhD; Michael Ramsey Professor of Modern Theology, University of Kent (formerly University of Kent at Canterbury), since 1992; Non-Stipendiary Minister, Hollingbourne and Hucking, with Leeds and Broomfield, diocese of Canterbury, since 2003; *b* 18 July 1944; *s* of Alan Morton Gill and Mary Grace (*née* Hammond); *m* 1967, Jennifer Margaret Sheppard; one *s* one *d*. *Educ:* Westminster Sch.; King's Coll., London (BD 1966; PhD 1969); Birmingham Univ. (MSocSc 1972). Deacon, 1968; priest, 1969; Curate, Rugby St Andrews, 1968–71; Lectr, Newton Theol Coll., PNG, 1971–72; Edinburgh University: Lectr in Christian Ethics, 1972–86; Associate Dean, Faculty of Theol., 1985–88; Sen. Lectr, 1986–88; William Leech Res. Prof. in Applied Theol., Newcastle Univ., 1988–92. Priest-in-charge: St Philip, Edinburgh, 1972–75; Ford with Etal, Northumberland, 1975–87; St Mary, Coldstream, 1987–92; Area Dean, N Downs, dio. Canterbury, 2002–. Hon. Canon, Canterbury Cathedral, 1992–. *Publications:* The Social Context of Theology, 1975; Theology and Social Structure, 1977; Faith in Christ, 1978; Prophecy and Praxis, 1981; The Cross Against the Bomb, 1984; A Textbook of Christian Ethics, 1985, 3rd edn 2006; Theology and Sociology, 1987, 2nd edn 1995; Beyond Decline, 1988; Competing Convictions, 1989; Christian Ethics in Secular Worlds, 1991; Gifts of Love, 1991; Moral Communities, 1992; The Myth of the Empty Church, 1993; A Vision for Growth, 1994; Readings in Modern Theology, 1995; (with Lorna Kendall) Michael Ramsey as Theologian, 1995; (with Derek Burke) Strategic Church Leadership, 1996; Moral Leadership in a Postmodern Age, 1997; Euthanasia and the Churches, 1998; Churchgoing and Christian Ethics, 1999; (ed) The Cambridge Companion to Christian Ethics, 2000; (ed jtly) The New Dictionary of Pastoral Studies, 2002; A Sense of Grace, 2004; Health Care and Christian Ethics, 2006; (ed) Reflecting Theologically on AIDS, 2007. *Recreations:* running churches, playing the trumpet. *Address:* Cornwallis Buildings, The University, Canterbury, Kent CT2 7NF. *T:* (01227) 764000.

GILL, His Honour Stanley Sanderson; a Circuit Judge, 1972–87; *b* Wakefield, 3 Dec. 1923; *s* of Sanderson Henry Briggs Gill, OBE and Dorothy Margaret Gill (*née* Bennett); *m* 1954, Margaret Mary Patricia Grady; two *d* (one *s* decd). *Educ:* Queen Elizabeth Grammar Sch., Wakefield; Magdalene Coll., Cambridge (MA). Served in RAF, 1942–46: 514 and 7 (Pathfinder) Sqdns, Flt Lt 1945. Called to the Bar, Middle Temple, 1950; Asst Recorder of Bradford, 1966; Dep. Chm., WR Yorks QS, 1968; County Court Judge, 1971. Mem., County Court Rule Cttee, 1980–84. Chm., Rent Assessment Cttee, 1966–71. *Recreations:* walking, reading, painting. *Address:* 19 Hereford Court, Hereford Road, Harrogate HG1 2PX.

GILLAM, Sir Patrick (John), Kt 1998; Chairman, Asia House, 2003–05; Board Mentor, Career Management International; *b* 15 April 1933; *s* of late Cyril B. Gillam and Mary J. Gillam; *m* 1963, Diana Echlin; one *s* one *d*. *Educ:* London School of Economics (BA Hons History; Hon. Fellow, 1999). Foreign Office, 1956–57; British Petroleum Co. Ltd, 1957–91; Vice-Pres., BP North America Inc., 1971–74; General Manager, Supply Dept, 1974–78; Dir, BP International Ltd (formerly BP Trading Ltd), 1978–82; Man. Dir, BP, 1981–91; Chairman: BP Shipping Ltd, 1987–88; BP Minerals Internat. Ltd/Selection Trust Ltd, 1982–89; BP Coal Ltd, 1986–88; BP Coal Inc., 1988–90; BP America Inc., 1989–91; BP Nutrition, 1989–91; BP Oil International, 1990–91. Chairman: Booker Tate Ltd, 1991–93; Standard Chartered PLC, 1993–2003 (Dir, 1988–2003; Dep. Chm., 1991–93); Asda Gp, 1991–96; Royal & Sun Alliance Insurance Gp, 1997–2003. Chm., ICC UK, 1989–98; Mem. Exec. Bd, ICC Worldwide, 1991–98; Dir, Commercial Union, 1991–96. Mem., Court of Governors, LSE, 1989–; Trustee, Queen Elizabeth's Foundn for Disabled Develt Trust, 1984–2003. *Recreation:* gardening. *Address:* 3 St Leonard's Terrace, SW3 4QA.

GILLAN, Cheryl Elise Kendall, (Mrs J. C. Leeming); MP (C) Chesham and Amersham, since 1992; *b* 21 April 1952; *d* of Major Adam Mitchell Gillan and Mona Elsie Gillan (*née* Freeman); *m* 1985, John Coates Leeming, *qv*. *Educ:* Cheltenham Ladies' Coll.; Coll. of Law. FCIM DipM. International Management Group, 1976–84; British Film Year, 1984–86; Ernst & Young, 1986–91; Dir, Kidsons Impey, 1991–93. PPS to Lord Privy Seal, 1994–95; Parly Under-Sec. of State, DFEE, 1995–97; Opposition frontbench spokesman: on trade and industry, 1997–98; on foreign and commonwealth affairs and overseas develt, 1998–2001; on home affairs, 2003–05; an Opposition Whip, 2001–03; Shadow Sec. of State for Wales, 2005–. Chm., Bow Group, 1987. Freeman, City of London, 1991; Liveryman, Marketors' Co., 1991. *Recreations:* golf, music, gardening, animals. *Address:* House of Commons, SW1A 0AA. *T:* (020) 7219 3000. *Club:* Royal Automobile.

GILLAN, Prof. Michael John, DPhil; Professor of Physics, University College London, since 1998; *b* Birmingham, 3 Jan. 1944; *s* of Robert Urquhart Gillan and Margaret Jennings Gillan; *m* 1969, Mary Torrenza Paterson (*d* 1998); two *s* one *d*. *Educ:* Christ Church, Oxford (BA Physics 1965; DPhil Theoretical Physics 1968). SSO, Theoretical Physics Div., AERE Harwell, 1970–88; Prof. of Theoretical Physics, Univ. of Keele, 1988–98. *Publications:* approx. 250 articles in learned jls. *Recreations:* languages, music.

GILLEN, Hon. Sir John, Kt 1999; **Hon. Mr Justice Gillen;** a Judge of the High Court of Justice, Northern Ireland, since 1999; *b* 18 Nov. 1947; *s* of John Gillen and Susan Letitia Gillen; *m* 1976, Claire; two *d*. *Educ:* Methodist Coll., Belfast; The Queen's Coll., Oxford (BA 1969; BL). Called to the Bar, Gray's Inn, 1970; Barrister, 1970–83; QC (NI), 1983–99. *Recreations:* reading, music, sports. *Address:* Royal Courts of Justice, Chichester Street, Belfast BT1 3JF. *T:* (028) 9023 5111.

GILLES, Prof. Dennis Cyril; Professor of Computing Science, University of Glasgow, 1966–90; *b* 7 April 1925; *s* of George Cyril Gilles and Gladys Alice Gilles (*née* Batchelor); *m* 1955, Valerie Mary Gardiner; two *s* two *d*. *Educ:* Sidcup Gram. Sch.; Imperial Coll., University of London. Demonstrator, Asst Lectr, Imperial Coll., 1945–47; Asst Lectr, University of Liverpool, 1947–49; Mathematician, Scientific Computing Service, 1949–55; Research Asst, University of Manchester, 1955–57; Dir of Computing Lab., University of Glasgow, 1957–66. *Publications:* contribs to Proc. Royal Society and other scientific jls. *Address:* Elmtree, Lochard Road, Aberfoyle, Stirlingshire FK8 3SZ. *T:* (01877) 389070.

GILLES, Prof. Chevalier Herbert Michael Joseph, CMG 2005; MD; FRCP, FFPH Alfred Jones and Warrington Yorke Professor of Tropical Medicine, University Liverpool, 1972–86, now Emeritus; *b* 10 Sept. 1921; *s* of Joseph and Clementine Gille *m* 1955, Wilhelmina Caruana (*d* 1972); three *s* one *d*; *m* 1979, Dr Mejra Kačić-Dimiti *Educ:* St Edward's Coll., Malta; Royal Univ. of Malta (MD). Rhodes Schol. 1943. MS Oxon; FMCPH (Nig.), DTM&H. Served War of 1939–45 (1939–45 Star, Africa Sta VM). Mem., Scientific Staff, MRC Lab., Gambia, 1954–58; University of Ibadan: Lec Tropical Med., 1958–63; Prof. of Preventive and Social Med., 1963–65; Liverpo University: Sen. Lectr, Tropical Med., 1965–70; Prof. of Tropical Med. (Personal Chai 1970; Dean, Liverpool Sch. of Tropical Medicine, 1978–83. Vis. Prof., Tropic Medicine, Univ. of Lagos, 1965–68; Royal Society Overseas Vis. Prof., Univ. Khartoum, Sudan, 1979–80; Hon. Prof. of Tropical Medicine, Sun-Yat-Sen Med. Col Guangzhou, People's Republic of China, 1984; Visiting Professor: Public Health, Uni of Malta, 1989–; Internat. Health, Royal Colls of Surgeons, Ireland, 1994–; Tropic Medicine, Mahidol Univ., Bangkok, 1994–. Consultant Physician in Tropical Medicin Liverpool AHA(T) and Mersey RHA, 1965–86; Consultant in Malariology to the Arm 1974–86; Consultant in Tropical Medicine to the RAF, 1978–86, to the DHSS, 1980–8 Pres., RSTM&H, 1985–87; Vice President: Internat. Fedn of Tropical Medicin 1988–92; Liverpool Sch. of Tropical Medicine, 1991–; Hon. Pres., Malta Assoc. of Publ Health Physicians, 2001. Hon. MD Karolinska Inst., 1979; Hon. DSc Malta, 1984. Darlin Foundn Medal and Prize, WHO, 1990; Mary Kingsley Medal, Liverpool Sch. of Tropic Medicine, 1994; Manson Medal, RSTM&H, 2007. KJSJ 2006. Title of Chevalier award for medical work in the tropics. Officer, Nat. Order of Merit (Malta), 2003. *Publication* Tropical Medicine for Nurses, 1955, 4th edn 1975; Pathology in the Tropics, 1969, 2r edn 1976; Management and Treatment of Tropical Diseases, 1971; (jtly) A Sho Textbook of Preventive Medicine for the Tropics, 1973, 4th edn, as A Short Textbook Public Health Medicine for the Tropics, 2003; Atlas of Tropical Medicine ar Parasitology, 1976, 4th edn 1995 (BMA Book Prize, 1996); Recent Advances in Tropic Medicine, 1984; Human Antiparasitic Drugs, Pharmacology and Usage, 1985; Th Epidemiology and Control of Tropical Diseases, 1987; Management of Severe ar Complicated Malaria, 1991; Hookworm Infections, 1991; *edited:* Protozoal Disease 1999; Tropical Medicine—a clinical text, 4th edn 2006; Essential Malariology, 4th ec 2002. *Recreations:* swimming, music. *Address:* 3 Conyers Avenue, Birkdale, Southport PR 4SZ. *T:* (01704) 566664.

GILLESPIE, Dr Alan Raymond, CBE 2003; Chairman, Ulster Bank Group, since 200 *b* 31 July 1950; *s* of Charles Gillespie and Doreen Gillespie (*née* Murtagh); *m* 197 (Georgina) Ruth Milne; one *s* one *d*. *Educ:* Grosvenor High Sch., Belfast; Clare Coll Cambridge (BA 1972; MA 1973; PhD 1977; Hon. Fellow 2007). Citicorp Internation Bank Ltd, London and Geneva, 1976–86; Goldman Sachs & Co., NY, 1986–87; Goldma Sachs International, London, 1987–99 (Partner and Man. Dir, 1990–99); Chief Exec CDC Gp plc, 1999–2002. Non-exec. Dir, Elan Corp. plc, 1996–. Chm., Internat. Finan Facility for Immunization, 2005–. Chm., NI IDB, 1998–2002; Member: NI Eco Strategy Steering Gp, 1998–99; NI Econ. Council, 1999–2001. Pres., European Deve Finance Institns, 2001–02. Member: Adv. Bd, Judge Inst. of Mgt Studies, Univ. Cambridge, 1996–2003; Adv. Council, Prince's Trust, 1999–2002. Chm., Uni Challenge Fund, NI, 1999–. DUniv Ulster, 2001; Hon. LLD QUB, 2005. *Recreation* golf, tennis, ski-ing. *Address:* Ulster Bank Ltd, 11–16 Donegall Square East, Belfast BT 5UB. *Clubs:* Wisley Golf, St George's Hill Lawn Tennis, Kiawah Island.

GILLESPIE, Prof. Iain Erskine, MD, MSc, FRCS; Professor of Surgery, University Manchester, 1970–92 (Dean of Medical School, 1983–86); *b* 4 Sept. 1931; *s* of Jol Gillespie and Flora McQuarie; *m* 1957, Mary Muriel McIntyre; one *s* one *d*. *Edu* Hillhead High Sch., Glasgow; Univ. of Glasgow. MB ChB, 1953; MD (Hons) 1963; MS Manchester 1974; FRCSE 1959; FRCS 1963; FRCSGlas 1970. Series of progressiv surgical appts in Univs of Glasgow, Sheffield, Glasgow (again), 1953–70. Nat. servic RAMC, 1954–56; MRC grantee, 1956–58; US Postdoctoral Research Fellow, L Angeles, 1961–62; Titular Prof. of Surgery, Univ. of Glasgow, 1969. Vis. Prof. in US Canada, S America, Kenya, S Africa, Australia and New Zealand. Member: Cttee Surgical Res. Soc. of GB and Ireland, 1975–; Medical Sub-Cttee, UGC, 1975–86; Uni and Polytechnics Grants Cttee, Hong Kong, 1984–89. Non-exec. Mem., Centr Manchester HA, 1991–94. President: Manchester Med. Soc., 1994–95; Manchester L and Phil Soc., 1999–2001 (Mem. Council, 1995–98); Manchester Luncheon Clu 2005–07. *Publications:* jt editor and contributor to several surgical and gastroenterologic books; numerous articles in various med. jls of GB, USA, Europe. *Recreations:* non *Address:* 27 Athol Road, Bramhall, Cheshire SK7 1BR. *T:* (0161) 439 2811.

GILLESPIE, Ian; District Judge (Magistrates' Courts) (formerly Stipendiary Magistrate West Midlands Area, since 1991; *b* 8 Oct. 1945; *s* of James Alexander and Margaret Cice Gillespie; *m* 1974, Diana Mary Stevens. *Educ:* King Henry VIII Sch., Coventry. Admitte Solicitor of Supreme Court, 1973; Partner, Brindley Twist Tafft & James, Solicito Coventry, 1974–91; Actg Stipendiary Magistrate, Wolverhampton, 1989–91. *Recreation* walking, ski-ing, theatre, music, ballet, reading (especially British Naval history). *Addres* Coventry Magistrates' Court, Little Park Street, Coventry CV1 2SQ. *T:* (024) 7663 0666

GILLESPIE, Prof. John Spence; Head of Department of Pharmacology, Glasgo University, 1968–92; *b* 5 Sept. 1926; *s* of Matthew Forsyth Gillespie and Myrtle Mur Spence; *m* 1956, Jemima Simpson Ross; four *s* one *d*. *Educ:* Dumbarton Academ Glasgow Univ. MB ChB (Commendation), PhD. FRCP; FRSE. Hosp. Residen (Surgery), 1949–50; Nat. Service as RMO, 1950–52; hosp. appts, 1952–53; McCunn Re Schol. in Physiology, Glasgow Univ., 1953–55; Faulds Fellow then Sharpey Schol. Physiology Dept, University Coll. London, 1955–57; Glasgow University: Lectr Physiol., 1957–59; Sophie Fricke Res. Fellow, Royal Soc., in Rockefeller Inst., 1959–6 Sen. Lectr in Physiol., 1961–63; Henry Head Res. Fellow, Royal Soc., 1963–68; Vic Principal, 1983–87, 1988–91. *Publications:* articles in Jls of Physiol. and Pharmaco *Recreations:* gardening, painting. *Address:* 5 Boclair Road, Bearsden, Glasgow G61 2AE. (0141) 943 1395.

GILLESPIE, Jonathan William James, MA; Head Master, Lancing College, since 200 *b* 6 Dec. 1966; *s* of J. J. M. Gillespie and P. D. Gillespie; *m* 1992, Caroline Hotchkiss; tw *s*. *Educ:* Bedford Modern Sch.; Selwyn Coll., Cambridge (BA Hons 1989; PGCE 199 MA 1992). Asst Master, Highgate Sch., London, 1990–97; Hd of Modern Lang 1997–2001, Housemaster, Moredun House, 2001–06, Fettes Coll., Edinburg *Recreations:* Highland bagpipe, hockey, cricket, hillwalking. *Address:* Lancing Colleg Lancing, W Sussex BN15 0RW. *T:* (01273) 465802, *Fax:* (01273) 464720; *e-ma* hmsecretary@lancing.org.uk.

GILLESPIE, Robert Andrew Joseph; Vice Chairman, UBS Investment Bank, 2005–0 *b* Nottingham, 14 April 1955; *s* of John Robert Gillespie and Honora Margaret Littlefai *m* Carolyn Sarah Powell (separated); three *d*. *Educ:* Nottingham High Sch.; Univ. Durham (BA Hons Econs 1977). ACA. Price Waterhouse, 1977–81; S. G. Warbur subseq. SBC Warburg 1981–97: Dir, 1987–97; Hd, Eur. Investment Banking, 1995–9

UBS Investment Bank, 1997–2008: Jt Hd, Global Investment Banking, 1999–2005; Chief Exec., Europe, Middle East and Africa, 2004–06. Chm., Somerset House Trust, 2006–. Mem., Stop Organised Abuse Bd, NSPCC; Vice Pres., Save the Children. Mem. Council, Durham Univ., 2007–. *Recreations:* sailing, shooting, golf, rowing, reading. *Address:* 51 Lansdowne Road, W11 2LG. *T:* 07785 255542; *e-mail:* gillespieraj@msn.com. *Clubs:* Oriental; Leander.

GILLESPIE, Prof. Ronald James, CM 2007; PhD, DSc; FRS 1977; FRSC; FRSC (UK); FCIC; Professor of Chemistry, McMaster University, Hamilton, Ont, 1960–88, now Emeritus; *b* London, England, 21 Aug. 1924; Canadian citizen; *s* of James A. Gillespie and Miriam G. (*née* Kirk); *m* 1950, Madge Ena Garner; two *d*. *Educ:* London Univ. (BSc 1945, PhD 1949, DSc 1957). FRSC 1965; FCIC 1960; FRIC; Mem., Amer. Chem. Soc. Asst Lectr, Dept of Chemistry, 1948–50, Lectr, 1950–58, UCL; Commonwealth Fund Fellow, Brown Univ., RI, USA, 1953–54; McMaster University: Associate Prof., Dept of Chem., 1958–60; Prof., 1960–62; Chm., Dept of Chem., 1962–65. Professeur Associé, l'Univ. des Sciences et Techniques de Languedoc, Montpellier, 1972–73; Visiting Professor: Univ. of Geneva, 1976; Univ. of Göttingen, 1978. Nyholm Lectr, RSC, 1979. Faraday Soc. Hon. LLD: Dalhousie Univ., 1988; Concordia Univ., 1988; Dr *hc* Montpellier, 1991; Hon. DSc: McMaster, 1993; Lethbridge, 2007. Medals: Ramsay, UCL, 1949; Harrison Meml, Chem. Soc., 1954; Canadian Centennial, 1967; Chem. Inst. of Canada, 1977; Silver Jubilee, 1978; Henry Marshall Tory, Royal Soc. of Canada, 1983. Awards: Noranda, Chem. Inst. of Canada, 1966 (for inorganic chem.); Amer. Chem. Soc. N-Eastern Reg., 1971 (in phys. chem.); Manufg Chemists Assoc. Coll. Chem. Teacher, 1972; Amer. Chem. Soc., 1973 (for distinguished service in advancement of inorganic chem.), 1980 (for creative work in fluorine chem.); Chem. Inst. of Canada/Union Carbide, 1976 (for chemical educn); Izaak Walton Killam Meml, Canada Council (for outstanding contrib. to advancement of res. in chemistry), 1987. *Publications:* Molecular Geometry, 1972 (London; German and Russian trans, 1975); (jtly) Chemistry, 1986, 2nd edn, 1989; The VSEPR Model of Molecular Geometry, 1990 (trans. Russian, 1992; Italian, 1994); (jtly) Atoms, Molecules and Reactions: an introduction to chemistry, 1994; (jtly) The Chemical Bond and Molecular Geometry: from Lewis to electron densities, 2001; papers in Jl Amer. Chem. Soc., Canadian Jl of Chem., and Inorganic Chem. *Recreations:* ski-ing, sailing. *Address:* Department of Chemistry, McMaster University, Hamilton, ON L8S 4M1, Canada. *T:* (905) 6281502, *Fax:* (905) 5222509; *e-mail:* ronald.gillespie@sympatico.ca.

GILLESPIE, Simon Maxwell; Chief Executive, Multiple Sclerosis Society, since 2006; *b* Bromley, 17 Nov. 1959; *s* of Gordon Maxwell Gillespie and Margaret Cecilia Gillespie; *m* 1989, Dr Rosemary James. *Educ:* Corpus Christi Coll., Cambridge (BA 1981; MPhil 1994); Henley Mgt Coll. (MBA). Served RN, 1977–2000: CO, HMS Sheffield; Mil. Asst to Minister for the Armed Forces. Dir of Ops, Charity Commn, 2000–04; Hd of Ops, Healthcare Commn, 2004–06. *Recreations:* hill-walking, jogging, recreational golf. *Address:* Multiple Sclerosis Society, MS National Centre, 372 Edgware Road, NW2 6ND. *T:* (020) 8438 0700; *e-mail:* sgillespie@mssociety.org.uk.

GILLESPIE, Prof. Vincent Anthony, DPhil; FSA, FRHistS, FEA; J. R. R. Tolkien Professor of English Literature and Language (formerly J. R. R. Tolkien Professor of Medieval English Literature and Language), University of Oxford, and Fellow of Lady Margaret Hall, Oxford, since 2004; *b* 11 Feb. 1954; *s* of George Anthony Gillespie and Florence Doreen Gillespie (*née* Preston); *m* 1979, Margaret, (Peggy), Powell; two *s*. *Educ:* St Edward's Coll., Liverpool; Keble Coll., Oxford (BA, MA; DPhil 1981). Lectr in English, Univ. of Reading, 1977–80; University of Oxford: Lectr in English, 1980–98; Reader, 1998–2004; Fellow and Tutor in English, St Anne's Coll., 1980–2004 (Hon. Fellow, 2004). FRHistS 2003; FEA 2003; FSA 2004. *Publications:* (jtly) The English Medieval Book, 2001; Syon Abbey, 2002; Looking in Holy Books, 2008; articles in learned jls and collaborative books. *Recreations:* theatre, wine, music, retired double-bass player. *Address:* Lady Margaret Hall, Oxford OX2 6QA; *e-mail:* vincent.gillespie@ell.ox.ac.uk.

GILLETT, Rt Rev. David Keith; Bishop Suffragan of Bolton, 1999–2008; *b* 25 Jan. 1945; *s* of Norman and Kathleen Gillett; *m* 1988, Valerie Shannon. *Educ:* Leeds Univ. (BA Theol. 1st cl. 1965; MPhil 1968). Curate, St Luke's, Watford, 1968–71; Northern Sec., Pathfinders and Church Youth Fellowship's Assoc., 1971–74; Lectr, St John's Coll., Nottingham, 1974–79; Co-Leader, Christian Renewal Centre for Reconciliation, NI, 1979–82; Vicar of St Hugh's, Luton, 1982–88; Principal, Trinity Theol Coll., Bristol, 1988–99. Mem., Gen. Synod of C of E, 1985–88, 1990–99. Hon. Canon of Bristol Cathedral, 1991–99. *Publications:* Learning in the Local Congregation, 1979; The Darkness where God is, 1983; Trust and Obey, 1993; (ed jtly) Treasure in the Field: the Archbishops' Companion to the Decade of Evangelism, 1993; co-author and contributor to various books and reference works. *Recreations:* photography, gardening. *Address:* 10 Burton Close, Diss, Norfolk IP22 4YJ. *T:* (01379) 640309; *e-mail:* dkgillett@btinternet.com.

GILLETT, Sir Robin (Danvers Penrose), 2nd Bt *cr* 1959; GBE 1976; RD 1965; Underwriting Member of Lloyd's; Lord Mayor of London for 1976–77; *b* 9 Nov. 1925; *o s* of Sir (Sydney) Harold Gillett, 1st Bt, MC, and Audrey Isabel Penrose Wardlaw (*d* 1962); *S* father, 1976; *m* 1950, Elizabeth Marion Grace (*d* 1997), *e d* of late John Findlay, JP, Busby, Lanarks; two *s*; *m* 2000, Alwyne Winifred Cox (separated), JP, *widow* of His Honour Albert Edward Cox. *Educ:* Nautical Coll., Pangbourne. Served Canadian Pacific Steamships, 1943–60; Master Mariner 1951; Staff Comdr 1957; Hon. Comdr RNR 1971. Elder Brother of Trinity House; Fellow and Founder Mem., Nautical Inst. City of London (Ward of Bassishaw): Common Councilman 1965–69; Alderman 1969–96; Sheriff 1973; one of HM Lieuts for City of London, 1975; Chm. Civil Defence Cttee, 1967–68; Pres., City of London Civil Defence Instructors Assoc., 1967–78; Vice-Pres., City of London Centre, St John Ambulance Assoc.; Pres., Nat. Waterways Transport Assoc., 1979–83; Dep. Commonwealth Pres., Royal Life Saving Soc., 1981–96; Chm. Council, Maritime Volunteer Service, 1998–2000, Gov., 2000–. Vice-Chm., PLA, 1979–84. Master, Hon. Co. of Master Mariners, 1979–80. Trustee, Nat. Maritime Mus., 1982–92. Chm. of Governors, Pangbourne Coll., 1978–92. Chancellor, City Univ., 1976–77. FIAM (Pres., 1980–84; Gold Medal, 1982); FRCM 1991. Hon. DSc City, 1976. Gentleman Usher of the Purple Rod, Order of the British Empire, 1985–2000. KStJ 1977 (OStJ 1974). Gold Medal, Administrative Management Soc., USA, 1983. Officer, Order of Leopard, Zaire, 1973; Comdr, Order of Dannebrog, 1974; Order of Johan Sedia Mahkota (Malaysia), 1974; Grand Cross of Municipal Merit (Lima), 1977. *Publications:* A Fish out of Water (autobiog.), 2001; Dogwatch Doggerel, 2004. *Recreation:* sailing. *Heir: s* Nicholas Danvers Penrose Gillett, BSc, ARCS [*b* 24 Sept. 1955; *m* 1987, Haylie (marr. diss. 1998), *er d* of Dennis Brooks]. *Clubs:* City Livery, City Livery Yacht (Admiral), Guildhall, Royal Yacht Squadron, Royal London Yacht (Cdre, 1984–85), St Katharine's Yacht (Admiral).

GILLETT, Sarah, MVO, 1986; HM Diplomatic Service; Vice-Marshal of the Diplomatic Corps, and Director of Protocol, Foreign and Commonwealth Office, since 2006; *b* 21 July 1956; *d* of Sir Michael Cavenagh Gillett, KBE, CMG and Margaret Gillett. *Educ:* St Anthony's Leweston, Sherborne; Aberdeen Univ. (MA Hons). Joined HM Diplomatic Service, 1976: Third Sec., Washington, 1984–87; Third, later Second, Sec., Paris, 1987–90; on secondment to ODA, 1990–91; Central Eur. Dept, FCO, 1991–92; Vice-Consul (Inward Investment), Los Angeles, 1992–94; SE Asia Dept, FCO, 1994–97; First Sec., Brasilia, 1997–99; Counsellor and Dep. Head of Mission, Brasilia, 1999–2001; Consul-Gen., Montreal, 2002–05. *Recreation:* outdoor exercise. *Address:* Protocol Directorate, Foreign and Commonwealth Office, Old Admiralty Building, SW1A 2PA.

GILLFORD, Lord; Patrick James Meade; Founding Partner, 1995, Chairman, since 1996, The Policy Partnership; *b* 28 Dec. 1960; *s* and *heir* of Earl of Clanwilliam, *qv*; *m* 1st, 1989, Serena Emily (marr. diss. 1994), *d* of late Lt-Col B. J. Lockhart; one *d*; 2nd, 1995, Cara de la Peña; one *s* one *d*. *Educ:* Eton College. 1 Bn, Coldstream Guards, 1979–83. Exec., Hanson plc, 1983–90, attached Home Office as special advr to Home Sec., 1986–88; with Ian Greer & Associates, 1990–93; Man. Dir, Westminster Policy Partnership Ltd, 1993–95; Chm., Cleveland Bridge UK Ltd, 2001–04; Director: Polyus Gold, 2006–; Cedar Partners, 2006–. Councillor (C) Royal Bor. of Kensington and Chelsea, 1990–98 (Chm., Traffic and Highways Cttee). Mem. Bd of Trustees, British Sch. of Osteopathy, 1997–2000; Trustee, Benevolent Soc. of St Patrick, 1993–. Gov., Knightsbridge Sch., 2006–. *Recreations:* prison reform and prison sentencing policy, free fall parachuting, sub-aqua diving, Palladian architecture, golf, fishing, motorbiking. *Heir: s* Hon. John Maximillian Meade, *b* 28 Jan. 1998. *Address:* 51 Causton Street, SW1P 4AT. *T:* (020) 7976 5555; *e-mail:* pgillford@policypartnership.co.uk. *Clubs:* Turf, Chatham Dining; Mill Reef (Antigua, WI); New Zealand (Weybridge).

GILLHAM, Geoffrey Charles; Director, Estates (formerly Head, Estate Strategy Unit), Foreign and Commonwealth Office, 2004–07; *b* 1 June 1954; *s* of Peter George Gee Gillham and Alison Mary (*née* Jackman); *m* 1991, Nicola Mary Brewer, *qv*; one *s* one *d*. *Educ:* UWIST (BScEcon). Joined FCO, 1981: Second Sec., Caracas, 1983–85; on loan to Cabinet Office, 1986–88; FCO, 1988–89; First Secretary: Madrid, 1989–91; UK Delegn, OECD, Paris, 1991–95; First Sec., later Counsellor, FCO, 1995–98; Counsellor, New Delhi, 1998–2001; Hd, S European Dept, FCO, 2001–03; Asst Dir, EU (Mediterranean), FCO, 2003–04. *Recreations:* music, travel, sailing. *Address:* c/o Foreign and Commonwealth Office, King Charles Street, SW1A 2AH.

GILLHAM, Nicola Mary; *see* Brewer, N. M.

GILLIAM, Terry; animator, actor, writer; film director, since 1973; *b* Minneapolis, USA, 22 Nov. 1940; *s* of James H. and Beatrice Gilliam; *m* 1973, Maggie Weston; one *s* two *d*. *Educ:* Occidental Coll., LA, Calif. *Television:* resident cartoonist, We Have Ways of Making You Laugh, 1968; animator: Do Not Adjust Your Set, 1968–69; (also actor and co-writer), Monty Python's Flying Circus, 1969–74 and 1979; The Marty Feldman Comedy Machine, 1971–72; The Do-It-Yourself Film Animation, 1974; presenter, The Last Machine, 1995; *films:* co-writer, actor and animator: And Now For Something Completely Different, 1971; (also co-director) Monty Python and the Holy Grail, 1974; Monty Python's Life of Brian, 1979; Monty Python Live at the Hollywood Bowl, 1982; Monty Python's The Meaning of Life, 1983; (animator, writer) The Miracle of Flight, 1974; (writer, director) Jabberwocky, 1977; (co-writer, producer, director) Time Bandits, 1981; (co-writer, director) Brazil, 1985; (co-writer, director) The Adventures of Baron Münchhausen, 1989; (dir) The Fisher King, 1991; (dir) Twelve Monkeys, 1996; (co-writer, dir) Fear and Loathing in Las Vegas, 1998; Lost in La Mancha, 2002; (co-writer, dir) The Brothers Grimm, 2005; (co-writer, dir) Tideland, 2005. Public art installation, Past People of Potsdamer Platz, Potsdamer Platz, Berlin, 2006. Hon. DFA Occidental Coll., 1987; Hon. Dr RCA, 1989; Hon. DA Wimbledon Sch. of Arts, 2004. *Publications:* Animations of Mortality, 1978; Time Bandits, 1981; (jtly) The Adventures of Baron Münchhausen, 1989; Fear and Loathing in Las Vegas: not the screenplay, 1998; Gilliam on Gilliam, 1999; Dark Knights and Holy Fools, 1999; *contributed to:* Monty Python's Big Red Book, 1971; The Brand New Monty Python Book, 1973, Monty Python and the Holy Grail, 1977; Monty Python's Life of Brian, 1979; Monty Python's The Meaning of Life, 1983; The Pythons Autobiography by The Pythons, 2003. *Recreations:* too busy. *Address:* c/o The Casarotto Co., Waverley House, 7–12 Noel Street, W1F 8GQ.

GILLIBRAND, Philip Martin Mangnall; District Judge (Magistrates' Courts), Hampshire, since 2005 (Inner London, 2001–05); *b* 28 June 1951; *s* of late Frank Ivor Croft Gillibrand, Chorley, Lancs and Marjorie Joyce Gillibrand (*née* Golding); *m* 1979, Felicity Alexandra Augusta Priefert; one *s* one *d*. *Educ:* Reading Blue Coat Sch. (Aldsworth's Hosp.); Poly. of Central London (LLB Hons London (ext.) 1974). Called to the Bar, Gray's Inn, 1975; in practice at the Bar, London and on Western Circuit, 1975–2000: Bristol, 1982–93; Winchester, 1993–2000; Dep. Stipendiary Magistrate, Leicester, 1997–2000. Mem., Family Proceedings and Youth Court Panels, 2001–. Parish Councillor, Crawley, Hants, 1998–. *Recreations:* classic and historic motoring (Mem., Brooklands Soc.), motor racing (Mem., Mini Seven Racing Club), reading, music (Mem., Elgar Soc.), campanology, the countryside, family life. *Address:* c/o Westminster City Magistrates' Court, 70 Horseferry Road, SW1P 2AX.

GILLIBRAND, Sydney, CBE 1991; FREng; Chairman, AMEC plc, 1997–2004 (Director, 1995–2004); *b* 2 June 1934; *s* of Sydney and Maud Gillibrand; *m* 1960, Angela Ellen Williams; three *s* (and one *s* decd). *Educ:* Preston Grammar Sch.; Harris Coll., Preston; College of Aeronautics, Cranfield (MSc). FRAeS 1975 (Hon. FRAeS 1994); FREng (FEng 1987). English Electric: apprentice, Preston, 1950; Chief Stress Engr, 1966; Works Man., Preston, 1974; Special Dir, BAC (Preston) Ltd, 1974; Dir of Manufacturing, Mil. Aircraft Div., 1977; British Aerospace Aircraft Group: Div. Prodn Dir, Warton, 1978; Dep. Man. Dir, Warton Div., and Bd Mem., Aircraft Gp, 1981; Div. Man. Dir, Kingston/Brough Div., 1983, Weybridge Div., 1984; British Aerospace PLC: Man. Dir, Civil Aircraft Div., 1986; Dir, 1987–95; Vice-Chm., 1991–95; Sen. Corporate Advr, 1995–99; Chairman: British Aerospace (Commercial Aircraft) Ltd, 1988–89; Aerospace Companies, 1989–92. Director: ICL plc, 1996–2002; Messier-Dowty Internat. Ltd, 1998–; Powergen, 1999–2002; Chm., TAG Aviation (UK) Ltd, 1998–; Dir, TAG Aviation (Hldgs) SA, 2001–. Pres., SBAC, 1990–91. Hon. FIIE 2000. CCMI. Silver Medal, RAeS, 1981; James Watt Gold Medal, IMechE, 1997. *Recreation:* golf.

GILLIES, Prof. Malcolm George William, PhD, DMus; Vice-Chancellor and President, City University, since 2007; *b* 23 Dec. 1954; *s* of Frank Douglas Gillies and Beatrice Mary Belle Gillies (*née* Copeman); partner, 1980, Dr David Pear. *Educ:* Royal Coll. of Music; Australian National Univ. (BA 1978); Univ. of Queensland (DipEd 1978); Clare Coll., Cambridge (BA 1980); King's Coll. London (MMus 1981); Univ. of London (PhD 1987); Univ. of Melbourne (DMus 2004). Tutor, Lectr, then Sen. Lectr in Music, Univ. of Melbourne, 1981–92; Prof. of Music, 1992–99, Dean of Music, 1992–97, Univ. of Queensland; Exec. Dean and Pro-Vice-Chancellor, Univ. of Adelaide, 1999–2001; Australian National University: Dep. Vice-Chancellor (Educn), 2002–06; Vice-Pres. (Devlt), 2006–07. President: Australian Acad. of Humanities, 1998–2001; Nat. Acads Forum, 1998–2002; Australian Council for the Humanities, Arts and Soc. Scis, 2004–06; Chm., Nat. Scholarly Communications Forum, 2001–07. *Publications:* Bartók in Britain: a guided tour, 1989; Notation and Tonal Structure in Bartók's Later Works, 1989; Bartók

Remembered, 1990 (German edn, 1991; Spanish edn, 2004); (ed) Halsey Stevens, The Life and Music of Béla Bartók, 3rd edn 1993; (ed) The Bartók Companion, 1993; (ed with David Pear) The All-Round Man: selected letters of Percy Grainger 1914–1961, 1994; (ed) Northern Exposures, 1997; (ed jtly) Grainger On Music, 1999; (with David Pear) Portrait of Percy Grainger, 2002; (ed jtly) Self-Portrait of Percy Grainger, 2006. *Recreations:* swimming, arts, the 1890s. *Address:* Office of the Vice-Chancellor, City University, Northampton Square, EC1V 0HB. *T:* (020) 7040 8002; *e-mail:* malcolm.gillies@city.ac.uk.

GILLIES, Rt Rev. Robert Arthur; *see* Aberdeen and Orkney, Bishop of.

GILLIGAN, Prof. Christopher Aidan, DPhil, ScD; Professor of Mathematical Biology, University of Cambridge, since 1999; Fellow, King's College, Cambridge, since 1988; *b* 9 Jan. 1953; *s* of William Christopher Gilligan and Kathleen Mary Gilligan (*née* Doyle); *m* 1974, Joan Flood; one *s* three *d*. *Educ:* St Mary's Coll., Crosby; Keble Coll., Oxford (BA 1974; MA 1978); Wolfson Coll., Oxford (DPhil 1978); Univ. of Cambridge (ScD 1999). University of Cambridge: Univ. Demonstrator, 1977; Lectr, Dept of Applied Biol., 1982–89, Dept of Plant Scis, 1989–95; Reader in Mathematical Biol., 1995–99; Royal Soc. Leverhulme Trust Sen. Res. Fellow, 1998–99; BBSRC Professorial Fellow, Dept of Plant Scis, 2004–. King's College, Cambridge: Tutor, 1988–94; Mem. Coll. Council, 1988–91; Dir of Studies in Natural Sci., 1990–2004; Mem. Electors, 1995–98. Vis. Prof., Dept of Botany and Plant Pathol., Colorado State Univ., 1982. Member: Council, Nat. Inst. Agricl Botany, 1985–91; Governing Body, Silsoe Res. Inst., 1998–2006; Council, BBSRC, 2003– (Mem., Strategy Bd, 2005–); Adv. Cttee on Forest Res., Forestry Commn, 2006–; Chairman: BBSRC Crop Sci. Review, 2003–04; Commn of Evaluation on Plant Health and Envmt, Institut Nat. de la Recherche Agronomique, France, 2003; Adviser on agricl systems research: Scottish Exec. Envmt and Rural Affairs Dept, 1998–2003; Institut Nat. de la Recherche Agronomique, 2003–. Pres., British Soc. for Plant Pathol., 2001. Fellow, Royal Statistical Soc., 1995; Rothamsted Fellow, 1998–2006; Hon. Fellow, Amer. Phytopathol Soc., 2005. *Publications:* (ed) Mathematical Modelling of Crop Disease, 1985; numerous articles on botanical epidemiol. and modelling in biol. and mathematical biol. jls. *Recreations:* family, running, reading, travel. *Address:* Department of Plant Sciences, University of Cambridge, Downing Street, Cambridge CB2 3EA. *T:* (01223) 333900; *e-mail:* cag1@cam.ac.uk.

GILLILAND, David; *see* Gilliland, J. A. D.

GILLILAND, David Jervois Thetford; practising solicitor and farmer; *b* 14 July 1932; *s* of late Major W. H. Gilliland and of Mrs N. H. Gilliland; *m* 1st, 1958, Patricia, *o d* of late J. S. Wilson and Mrs Wilson (marr. diss. 1976); two *s* three *d*; 2nd, 1976, Jennifer Johnston, *qv*. *Educ:* Rockport Prep. Sch.; Wrekin Coll.; Trinity Coll., Dublin (BA 1954, LLB 1955). Qualified as solicitor, 1957, own practice. Mem. ITA, 1965–70; Chm., N Ireland Adv. Cttee of ITA, 1965–70. Chm., NI Heritage Gardens Cttee, 1991–; Mem. Council, Internat. Dendrology Soc., 1966–75, 2008– (Vice Pres., Ireland, 2008–); etc. *Recreations:* gardening, photography. *Address:* Brook Hall, 65 Culmore Road, Londonderry, Northern Ireland BT48 8JE. *T:* (028) 7135 1297.

GILLILAND, His Honour (James Andrew) David; QC 1984; a Circuit Judge, 1992–2007; a Judge, Technology and Construction Court, 2000–07; an Arbitrator, since 2007; *b* 29 Dec. 1937; *s* of James Albin Gilliland and Mary Gilliland (*née* Gray); *m* 1961, Elsie McCully; two *s*. *Educ:* Campbell College; Queen's University Belfast. LLB (1st Class Hons) 1960. Called to the Bar, Gray's Inn, 1964 (Holt Scholar, Atkin Scholar, Macaskie Scholar); Lectr in Law, Manchester University, 1960–72; a Recorder, 1989–92. *Recreations:* music, opera, stamp collecting, wind surfing, ski-ing. *Address:* Kings Chambers, 36 Young Street, Manchester M3 3FT. *T:* (0161) 832 9082. *Club:* Athenæum (Liverpool).

GILLILAND, Jennifer, (Mrs David Gilliland); *see* Johnston, J.

GILLINGHAM, (Francis) John, CBE 1982 (MBE mil. 1944); FRSE 1970; Professor of Neurological Surgery, University of Edinburgh, 1963–80, now Emeritus; at Royal Infirmary of Edinburgh and Western General Hospital, Edinburgh, 1963–80; Consultant Neuro-Surgeon to the Army in Scotland, 1966–80; *b* 15 March 1916; *s* of John H. Gillingham, Upwey, Dorset; *m* 1945, Irene Judy Jude; four *s*. *Educ:* Hardye's Sch., Dorset; St Bartholomew's Hosp. Medical Coll., London. Matthews Duncan Gold Medal, 1939, MRCS, LRCP Oct. 1939; MB BS (London) Nov. 1939; FRCS 1947; FRCSE 1955; FRCPE 1967. Prof. of Surgical Neurol., King Saud Univ., Saudi Arabia, 1983–85, now Emeritus. Advr in Neuro-Surgery, MoD, Kingdom of Saudi Arabia, 1980–83. Hon. Consultant in Neurosurgery, St Bartholomew's Hosp., London, 1981–. Hunterian Prof., RCS, 1957; Morison Lectr, RCP of Edinburgh, 1960; Colles Lectr, College of Surgeons of Ireland, 1962; Elsberg Lectr, College of Physicians and Surgeons, NY, 1967; Penfield Lectr, Middle East Med. Assembly, 1970; Syme Derby Lectr, Univ. of Hong Kong, 1982; Adlington Syme Oration, RACS, 1983. Hon. Mem., Soc. de Neurochirurgie de Langue Française, 1964; Hon. Mem., Soc. of Neurol. Surgeons (USA), 1965; Hon. Mem., Royal Academy of Medicine of Valencia, 1967; Hon. and Corresp. Mem. of a number of foreign neuro-surgical societies; Hon. Pres., World Fedn of Neurosurgical Socs. President: Medico-Chirurgical Soc. of Edinburgh, 1965–67; European Soc. of Stereostatic and Functional Neurosurgery, 1972–76; RCSE, 1979–82 (Vice-Pres., 1974–77; Mem., Court of Regents, 1990–2001). FRSA 1991. Hon. FRACS 1980; Hon. FCS Sri Lanka 1980; Hon. FRCSI 1981; Hon. FRCSGlas 1982. Hon. MD Thessaloniki, 1973. Jim Clark Foundn Award, 1979; Medal of City of Gdansk, Poland, 1980. *Publications:* Clinical Surgery: Neurological Surgery, 1969; Parkinson's Disease, 1969; Head Injuries, 1971; papers on surgical management of cerebral vascular disease, head and spinal injuries, Parkinsonism and the dyskinesias, epilepsy and other neurosurgical subjects. *Recreations:* sailing, travel, gardening (cactus). *Club:* Nautico (Javea, Alicante).

GILLINGHAM, Prof. John Bennett, FBA 2007; historian; Professor of History, London School of Economics and Political Science, 1995–98, now Emeritus; *b* 3 Aug. 1940; *s* of Arthur Gillingham and Irene Gillingham; *m* 1966, June Guy (marr. diss. 1978); two *d*. *Educ:* Rottingdean Primary Sch.; Brighton, Hove and Sussex Grammar Sch.; Queen's Coll., Oxford (BA Hons Modern Hist.; BPhil Medieval Hist.). Laming Travelling Fellow, Queen's Coll., Oxford, 1963–65; Lectr, then Sen. Lectr, LSE, 1965–95. Dir, Battle Conf. on Anglo-Norman Studies, 2000–04; Ed., Anglo-Norman Studies, 2000–04. *Publications:* Cromwell: portrait of a soldier, 1976; Richard the Lionheart, 1978, 2nd edn 1989 (trans. German, French; Prix Guillaume le Conquérant, 1997); The Wars of the Roses, 1981 (trans. Hungarian); (ed with Malcolm Falkus) Historical Atlas of Britain, 1981 (trans. Japanese); The Angevin Empire, 1984, 2nd edn 2001; (ed) Richard III: a medieval kingship, 1993; Richard Coeur de Lion: kingship, chivalry and war in the twelfth century, 1994; Richard I, 1999, 2nd edn 2001; The English in the Twelfth Century, 2000; (with Ralph Griffiths) Medieval Britain: a very short introduction, 2000 (trans. Chinese); Medieval Kingdoms, 2001; (with Danny Danziger) 1215 The Year of Magna Carta, 2003. *Recreation:* grandfather.

GILLINGS, Ven. Richard John; Archdeacon of Macclesfield, since 1994; *b* 17 Sep 1945; *s* of John Albert Gillings and Constance Ford Gillings; *m* 1972, Kathryn Mary Hil two *s* two *d*. *Educ:* Sale GS; St Chad's Coll., Durham (BA, Dip Biblical Studies); Lincol Theol Coll. Ordained deacon 1970, priest 1971; Curate, St George's, Altrinchan 1970–75; Priest i/c, then Rector, St Thomas', Stockport, 1975–83, and Priest i/c, Peter's, Stockport, 1978–83; Rector, Birkenhead Priory, 1983–93; Vicar, Bramhal 1993–2005. RD, Birkenhead, 1985–93; Hon. Canon, Chester Cathedral, 1992–9 Mem., Gen. Synod, 1980–. *Recreations:* music, cinema, theatre, railways, Rotary. *Addres* 5 Robin's Lane, Bramhall, Stockport, Cheshire SK7 2PE. *T:* (0161) 439 2254.

GILLINGWATER, Richard Dunnell, CBE 2008; Dean, Cass Business School, Cit University, since 2007; *b* 21 July 1956; *s* of Malcolm and Olive Gillingwater; *m* 198 Helen Margaret Leighton; one *s* three *d*. *Educ:* Chesterfield Grammar Sch.; St Edmun Hall, Oxford (MA Jurisprudence); Inst. for Mgt Develt, Lausanne (MBA). Articled Clerl Lovell, White and King, Solicitors, 1978–80; admitted solicitor, 1980; with Kleinwo Benson Ltd, 1980–90 (Dir, 1990); Barclays De Zoete Wedd: Dir, Corporate Financ 1990–92; Man. Dir, 1992; Jt Hd, Global Corporate Finance, 1995–98; Jt Dep. H 1998–2001, Chm., 2001–03, European Investment Banking, Credit Suisse First Bosto Chief Exec., 2003–06, Chm., 2006–07, Shareholder Exec., Cabinet Office. Chm., Fabe Music, 2002–07; non-executive Director: Kidde plc, 2004–05; Tomkins, 2005–; P&C 2005–06; Debenhams, 2006–; Scottish and Southern Energy, 2007–. Mem., Adv. Bd, Edmund Hall, Oxford, 2004–. *Recreations:* music, reading, walking, travelling. *Address:* Lichfield Road, Kew, Richmond, Surrey TW9 3JR.

GILLINSON, Sir Clive (Daniel), Kt 2005; CBE 1998; Executive and Artistic Directo Carnegie Hall, New York, since 2005; *b* 7 March 1946; *s* of Stanley Gillinson and Regin Schein; *m* 1979, Penelope Morsley; one *s* two *d*. *Educ:* Frensham Heights Sch.; Quee Mary Coll., London; Royal Acad. of Music (Recital Dip., May Mukle Prize). Mem Cello Section, LSO, 1970–84. Jt owner, Clive Daniel Antiques, 1978–86. Foundin Partner, Masterprize, 1997. Chm., Assoc. of British Orchestras, 1992–95; Gov. and Men Exec. Cttee, NYO of GB, 1995–2004; Man. Dir, LSO, 1984–2005. *Recreations:* tenni ski-ing, reading, theatre, cinema, carpentry. *Address:* Carnegie Hall, 881 7th Avenue, Nev York, NY 10019–3210, USA.

GILLMAN, Bernard Arthur, (Gerry Gillman); General Secretary, Society of Civil an Public Servants, 1973–85; *b* 14 April 1927; *s* of Elias Gillman and Gladys Gillman; *m* 195 Catherine Mary Antonia Harvey. *Educ:* Archbishop Tenison's Grammar Sch. Civ Service, 1946–53; Society of Civil Servants, 1953–85. Mem., Police Complaints Auth 1986–91. *Address:* 2 Burnham Street, Kingston-upon-Thames, Surrey KT2 6QR. *T* (020) 8546 6905. *Clubs:* Royal Over-Seas League, MCC.

GILLMAN, Derek Anthony; Executive Director and President, The Barnes Foundatio Merion, Pennsylvania, since 2006; *b* 7 Dec. 1952; *s* of Abraham Gillman and Esthe Gillman; *m* 1987, Yael Joanna Hirsch; one *s* two *d*. *Educ:* Clifton Coll., Bristol; Magdale Coll., Oxford (MA); Beijing Langs Inst.; Univ. of E Anglia (LLM). Chinese specialis Christie's Auctioneers, London, 1977–81; Curator, Dept of Oriental Antiquities, BM 1981–85; Keeper, Sainsbury Centre for Visual Arts, UEA, 1985–95; Dep. Dir, Interna Art and Collection Mgt, 1995–96, Curatorial and Educn Services, 1996–99, Nat. Gall. Victoria; Exec. Dir and Provost, 1999–2000, Pres. and Edna S. Tuttleman Dir, 2001–0 Pennsylvania Acad. of Fine Arts. Sen. Fellow, Melbourne Inst. of Asian Langs and Soc 1998–2003. *Publications:* The Idea of Cultural Heritage, 2006; contrib. to exhib catalogues; articles and reviews for Art, Antiquity and Law, SOAS Bull., Buddhist Forun Apollo, Orientations, Trans Oriental Ceramic Soc. *Recreations:* reading, painting. *Addres* The Barnes Foundation, 300 North Latch's Lane, Merion, PA 19066–1729, USA.

GILLMAN, Gerry; *see* Gillman, B. A.

GILLON, Karen Macdonald; Member (Lab) Clydesdale, Scottish Parliament, since 199 *b* 18 Aug. 1967; *d* of Edith Turnbull (*née* Macdonald); *m* 1999, James Gillon; two *s*. *Edu* Jedburgh Grammar Sch.; Birmingham Univ. (Cert. Youth and Community Work 1991 Project Worker, Terminal One youth project, Blantyre, 1991–94; Community Educ Worker, N Lanarkshire Council, 1994–97; PA to Rt Hon. Helen Liddell, MP, 1997–9 *Recreations:* sport, cooking, flower arranging, music. *Address:* Constituency Office, Wellgate, Lanark ML11 9DS. *T:* (01555) 660526.

GILLON, Prof. Raanan Evelyn Zvi, FRCP; Professor of Medical Ethics, School Medicine, Imperial College, London, 1995–99, now Emeritus (Visiting Professo 1989–94); part-time general practitioner; NHS Senior Partner, Imperial College Medic Partnership, 1991–2003; *b* Jerusalem, 15 April 1941; *s* of Diana Gillon and late Me Gillon; *m* 1966, Angela Spear; one *d*. *Educ:* Christ's Hospital; University College Londo (MB BS 1964); Christ Church, Oxford; Birkbeck College London (BA Phil 1st cl. Hon 1979; philosophy prize). MRCP 1974, FRCP 1988. Medical journalism, 1964–71 (Ed Medical Tribune); part-time GP, part-time philosophy student then teacher, 1974–200 Dir, Imperial Coll. Health Service, 1982–95; Dir of Teaching in Medical Ethics (for M course), KCL, 1986–89. Vis. Prof. in Med. Ethics, KCL, 1988–91. Chm., Imperial Col Ethics Cttee, 1984–93. Member: BMA, 1964 (Mem., 1998–, Vice-Chm., 2002–0 Ethics Cttee); Archbp of Canterbury's Adv. Gp on Med. Ethics, 1999–2006. Mem Governing Body, 1989–, Chm., 2000–, Inst. of Medical Ethics. Ed., Jl of Med. Ethic 1980–2001. FRSocMed 1966; Life Fellow, Hastings Center, USA, 2005. Hon. RC 1986. Hon. DSc Oxon, 2006. Henry Beecher Award, Hastings Center, USA, 199 Millennium Award, Norwegian Univ. of Sci and Tech., 2001. *Publications:* Philosophic Medical Ethics, 1986 (13 reprints); (Sen. Ed. and contrib.) Principles of Health Car Ethics, 1994; numerous papers on medical ethics. *Recreations:* enjoying the company o wife and daughter and sometimes the cats; reading moral philosophy and, intermittentl thrillers and novels, mostly recommended by Angela; playing (blowing?) own trumpet, o rather, Uncle Peter's trumpet, kindly lent in 1954; ski-ing, swimming, occasional activ walks on a golf course, cooking, winetasting, arguing and good company. *Address:* 4 Brynmaer Road, SW11 4EW. *T:* (020) 7622 1450.

GILMORE, Brian Terence, CB 1992; *b* 25 May 1937; *s* of late John Henry Gilmore an of Edith Alice Gilmore; *m* 1962, Rosalind Edith Jean Fraser (*see* R. E. J. Gilmore). *Edu* Wolverhampton Grammar Sch.; Christ Church, Oxford (Passmore-Edwards Prize, 195 BA Lit. Hum.; MA 1961). CRO and Diplomatic Service Admin Office, 1958–65: Privat Sec. to Perm. Sec., 1960–61, to Parly Under Sec., 1961–62; Asst Private Sec. to Sec. o State, 1962–64; British Embassy, Washington, 1965–68; Min. of Technology and DT 1968–72: Private Sec. to Minister of State, Industry, 1969–70, and to Lord Privy Seal an Leader of the House of Lords, 1971–72; CSD, 1972–81; Under Sec., 1979; Principal, C Coll., 1979–81; HM Treasury, 1981–88; Principal Estabt Officer and Principal Financ Officer, 1982–84; Dep. Sec., Office of Minister for CS, Cabinet Office, 1988–92; Dep Sec., DSS, 1992–94. Chairman: PYBT (E London), 1996–2000; Bart's and the Londo NHS Trust, 1999–2000. Vice-Pres., Soc. for Promotion of Hellenic Studies, 2000–. *Recreations:* reading, music, walking, Greece. *Address:* 3 Clarendon Mews, W2 2NR. *Club* Athenæum (Chm., 2000–03; Trustee).

GILMORE, Carol Jacqueline; *see* Ellis, C. J.

GILMORE, Prof. Ian Thomas, MD; PRCP; Consultant Physician, Royal Liverpool Hospital, since 1980; Professor of Medicine, University of Liverpool, since 1999; President, Royal College of Physicians, since 2006; *b* 25 Sept. 1946; *s* of James M. and Jean M. Gilmore; *m* 1975, Hilary Elizabeth Douglas; two *s* one *d*. *Educ:* Royal Grammar Sch., Newcastle upon Tyne; King's Coll., Cambridge (BA 1968; MB BChir 1971; MD 1979); St Thomas' Hosp., London. FRCP 1985. MRC Trng Fellow, St Thomas' Hosp., 1976–77; MRC Travelling Fellow, Univ. of Calif, San Diego, 1979–80. *Publications:* (ed) Gastrointestinal Emergencies, 1992; contrib. original articles, chapters and invited reviews on gastrointestinal and liver diseases. *Recreations:* golf, travel. *Address:* Royal College of Physicians, 11 St Andrews Place, NW1 4LE. *T:* (020) 7935 1174; *e-mail:* ian.gilmore@rcplondon.ac.uk. *Club:* Royal Liverpool Golf.

GILMORE, Margaret, (Mrs Eamonn Matthews); writer, broadcaster and analyst; *b* 9 Feb. 1956; *d* of late Rev. Canon Norman and of Barbara Gilmore; *m* 1993, Eamonn Matthews; one *s*. *Educ:* North London Collegiate Sch., Middlesex; Westfield Coll., London (BA Hons English). Reporter: Kensington Post, 1977–79; Independent Radio News, 1979–84; BBC N Ireland, 1984–85; Newsnight, BBC, 1986–89; This Week, ITV, 1989–92; Panorama, BBC, 1993–95; news corresp., 1995–97, envmt corresp., 1997–2000, home and legal affairs corresp., 2000–07, BBC. Mem. Bd, Food Standards Agency. Associate Fellow, RUSI, 2007–. *Recreations:* friends and family, playing the piano, supporting Reading Football Club. *Address:* c/o Knight Ayton Management, 114 St Martin's Lane, WC2N 4BE; *e-mail:* MargaretGilmore@btinternet.com; *web:* www.MargaretGilmore.com.

GILMORE, Rosalind Edith Jean, (Mrs B. T. Gilmore), CB 1995; Director, Zurich Financial Services AG, 1998–2007; *b* 23 March 1937; *o c* of Sir Robert Brown Fraser, OBE, and Betty Fraser; *m* 1962, Brian Terence Gilmore, *qv*. *Educ:* King Alfred Sch.; University Coll. London (BA; Fellow, 1989); Newnham Coll., Cambridge (BA, MA; Associate Fellow, 1986–95, Hon. Fellow, 1995). Asst Principal, HM Treasury, 1960–65; IBRD, 1966–67; Principal, HM Treasury, 1968–73; Prin. Pvte Sec. to Chancellor of Duchy of Lancaster, Cabinet Office, 1974; HM Treasury: Asst Sec., 1975–80; Press Sec. and Hd of Inf., 1980–82; Gen. Man., Corporate Planning, Dunlop Ltd, 1982–83; Dir of Marketing, Nat. Girobank, 1983–86; Directing Fellow, St George's House, Windsor Castle, 1986–89; re-instated, HM Treasury, and seconded to Bldg Socs Commn, 1989; Dep. Chm., 1989–91, Chm. (First Comr), 1991–94, Bldg Socs Commn; Chief Registrar of Friendly Socs, 1991–94; Industrial Assurance Comr, 1991–94; Dir of Regulation, Lloyd's of London, 1995. Chairman: Arrow Broadcasting, 1994–97; Homeowners Friendly Soc., 1996–98; Director: Mercantile Gp plc, 1986–89; London and Manchester Gp plc, 1988–89; BAT Industries, 1996–98; TU Fund Managers, 2000–06; Cons. Man., FI Gp plc, 1987–89. Mem., SIB, 1993–96; Comr, Nat. Lottery Commn, 2000–02. Director: Leadership Foundn, Washington, 1997– (Chm., 2005–07); Internat. Women's Forum, 2005– (Vice Pres., 1997–2001). Member: Board: Opera North, 1993–97; Moorfields Eye Hosp. NHS Trust, 1994–2000; Council, RCM, 1997–2007; Court, Cranfield Univ., 1992–. FRSA 1985; CCMI (CIMgt 1992). *Publication:* Mutuality for the Twenty-first Century, 1998. *Recreations:* swimming (Half Blue, Cambridge Univ.), music, house in Greece. *Address:* 3 Clarendon Mews, W2 2NR. *Club:* Athenæum.

GILMOUR, Alexander Clement, CVO 1990; Chairman, On Bourse Ltd, since 2001; *b* 23 Aug. 1931; *s* of Sir John Little Gilmour, 2nd Bt, and Lady Mary Gilmour; *m* 1954, Barbara M. L. Constance Berry; two *s* one *d*; *m* 1983, Susan Lady Chetwode. *Educ:* Eton. National Service, commn in Black Watch, 1950–52. With Joseph Sebag & Co. (subseq. Carr, Sebag), 1954–82; Director: Safeguard Industrial Investments, 1974–84; Tide (UK) Ltd, 1986–87; Exec. Dir, Equity Finance Trust Ltd, 1984–86. Dir, SW London, subseq. Thames, Community Foundn, 1995–2000. Consultant, Grieveson Grant, 1982. Chm., Nat. Playing Fields Assoc., 1976–88 (Past-Chm. Appeals Cttee, 10 yrs). Dir, Tate Gallery Foundn, 1986–88. Governor, LSE, 1969. *Recreations:* tennis, fishing, gardening. *Address:* c/o Drummonds Branch, Royal Bank of Scotland, 49 Charing Cross, SW1A 2DX. *Club:* Queen's.

GILMOUR, David Jon, CBE 2003; singer, guitarist and songwriter; *b* Cambridge, 6 March 1946; *s* of Douglas Gilmour and Sylvia Gilmour (*née* Wilson); *m* 1st, 1975, Virginia, (Ginger), Hasenbein (marr. diss.); one *s* three *d*; 2nd, 1994, Polly Samson; three *s* and one step *s*. *Educ:* Perse Sch. for Boys; Cambridgeshire Coll. of Arts and Technol. Joined Pink Floyd, 1968; albums include: A Saucerful of Secrets, 1968; Atom Heart Mother, 1970; Meddle, 1971; Obscured by Clouds, 1972; Dark Side of the Moon, 1973; Wish You Were Here, 1975; Animals, 1977; The Wall, 1979; The Final Cut, 1983; A Momentary Lapse of Reason, 1987; The Division Bell, 1994; solo albums: David Gilmour, 1978; About Face, 1984; On an Island, 2006. Ivor Novello Award for Lifetime Achievement, 2008. *Address:* c/o One Fifteen, 1 Globe House, Middle Lane Mews, N8 8PN.

GILMOUR, Sir David (Robert), 4th Bt *cr* 1926; writer; *b* 14 Nov. 1952; *er s* of Lord Gilmour of Craigmillar, PC (Life Peer) and of Lady Caroline Gilmour (*née* Montagu-Douglas-Scott); *S* to father's Btcy, 2007; *m* 1975, Sarah Anne, *d* of late M. H. G. Bradstock; one *s* three *d*. *Educ:* Eton; Balliol Coll., Oxford (BA Hons). FRSL 1990. Dep. Ed., Middle East International, 1979–81; Res. Fellow, St Antony's Coll., Oxford, 1996–97. *Publications:* Lebanon: the fractured country, 1983, 3rd edn 1987; The Transformation of Spain: from Franco to the constitutional monarchy, 1985; The Last Leopard: a life of Giuseppe di Lampedusa, 1988 (Marsh Biography Award, 1989), 5th edn 2007; The Hungry Generations, 1991; Cities of Spain, 1992; Curzon, 1994 (Duff Cooper Prize, 1995), 2nd edn 2003; The Long Recessional: the Imperial life of Rudyard Kipling, 2002 (Elizabeth Longford Prize for Historical Biography, 2003); The Ruling Caste: Imperial lives in the Victorian Raj, 2005; contrib. The Sunday Times, Spectator and The New York Review of Books. *Heir: s* Alexander Ian Michael Gilmour, *b* 19 Feb. 1980. *Address:* 27 Ann Street, Edinburgh EH4 1PL. *Club:* Brooks's.

GILMOUR, Sir John, 4th Bt *cr* 1897, of Lundin and Montrave, co. Fife; DL; farmer; *b* 15 July 1944; *er s* of Col Sir John (Edward) Gilmour, 3rd Bt, DSO, TD and Ursula Mabyn (*née* Wills); *S* father, 2007; *m* 1967, Valerie Jardine Russell; two *s* two *d*. *Educ:* Eton; Aberdeen Coll. of Agriculture. Director: Greenside Engineering Ltd, 1978–; Moredun Foundn, 1994–; Perth Race Course, 1999–; Pentland Science Parks Ltd, 2004–. DL Fife, 1988. *Recreations:* fishing, reading, horse racing. *Heir: s* John Nicholas Gilmour [*b* 15 Dec. 1970; *m* 1996, Airin Thamrin; two *s*]. *Address:* Balcormo Mains, Leven, Fife KY8 5QF. *T:* (01333) 360229.

GILMOUR, Nigel Benjamin Douglas; QC 1990; **His Honour Judge Gilmour;** a Circuit Judge, since 2000; *b* 21 Nov. 1947; *s* of late Benjamin Waterfall Gilmour and Barbara Mary Gilmour (subseq. Mrs E. Harborow); *m* 1972, Isobel Anne, *d* of E. Harborow; two *d*. *Educ:* Tettenhall Coll., Staffordshire; Liverpool Univ. (LLB Hons). Called to the Bar, Inner Temple, 1970; an Asst Recorder, 1984–90; a Recorder, 1990–2000. *Recreations:* wine, food. *Address:* Queen Elizabeth II Law Courts, Derby Square, Liverpool L2 1XA. *T:* (0151) 473 7373.

GILMOUR, Dr Roger Hugh, FIFST; Director, Centre for Emergency Preparedness and Response, Health Protection Agency, 2004–07; *b* 24 March 1942; *s* of late William Gilmour and of Elizabeth Gilmour; *m* 1968, Margaret Jean Chisholm; one *s* one *d*. *Educ:* Ross High Sch.; Edinburgh Univ. (BSc); Heriot-Watt Univ. (PhD 1969). FIFST 1989. Griffith Laboratories: Canada, 1969; UK/Internat., 1970–79; Pres., USA, 1979–83; CEO Agricl Genetics Co. Ltd, 1983–93; Business Develt Dir, Centre for Applied Microbiol. and Res., 1994–96; Chief Exec., Microbiol Res. Authy, and Centre for Applied Microbiol. and Res., 1996–2003; Dir, Business Div. and Porton Down site, HPA, 2003–04. Dir, MRC Collaborative Centre, 1992–99. Chm., NMT Gp plc, 1998–2004; Dir, Syntaxin Ltd, 2005–07. *Recreations:* walking, ski-ing, gardening, cycling. *Club:* Farmers.

GILPIN, Ven. Richard Thomas; Archdeacon of Totnes, 1996–2005, now Archdeacon Emeritus; *b* 25 July 1939; *s* of Thomas and Winifred Gilpin; *m* 1966, Marian Moeller; one *s* one *d*. *Educ:* Ashburton Coll.; Lichfield Theol Coll. Ordained deacon, 1963, priest, 1964; Assistant Curate: Whipton, 1963–66; Tavistock and Gulworthy, 1966–69; Vicar, Swimbridge, 1969–73; Priest-in-charge, W Buckland, 1970–73; Vicar, Tavistock and Gulworthy, 1973–91; Diocesan Dir of Ordinands, 1990–96, and Advr for Vocations, 1991–96, Exeter; Sub-Dean, Exeter Cathedral, 1992–96. Rural Dean, Tavistock, 1987–90. Prebendary, Exeter Cathedral, 1982–2001; Proctor in Convocation, 1995–2000, 2002–05. Ex-officio Mem., Coll. of Canons, Exeter Cathedral, 2001–05. *Recreations:* family, music, art, theatre, walking.

GILROY, Linda; MP (Lab and Co-op), Plymouth Sutton, since 1997; *b* 19 July 1949; *d* of late William Jarvie and Gwendoline Jarvie (*née* Grey); *m* 1987, Bernard Gilroy. *Educ:* Edinburgh Univ. (MA Hons History 1971); Strathclyde Univ. (Postgrad. Secl Dip. 1972), MITSA (Dip. in Consumer Affairs 1990). Dep. Dir, Age Concern Scotland, 1972–79; Regl Sec., subseq. Regl Manager, SW Office, Gas Consumers' Council, 1979–97. PPS to Minister of State for Local Govt, Dept of Transport, Local Govt and the Regions, 2000–05. Mem., Defence Select Cttee, 2005–. *Recreations:* swimming, walking, keep fit. *Address:* House of Commons, SW1A 0AA. *T:* (020) 7219 4746.

GILROY, Paul; QC 2006; barrister; *b* 1 May 1962; *s* of George Gilroy and Joan Gilroy (*née* McConnell); *m* 1996, Julie McKenzie Stephen; two *s* one *d*. *Educ:* Hutchesons' Grammar Sch., Glasgow; Univ. of Dundee (LLB Hons 1984). Called to the Bar, Gray's Inn, 1985; in practice as a barrister, 1985–, specialising in employment law, professional discipline and public inquiries. Attorney General's Provincial Panel, 2000–; an Employment Judge (pt-time) (formerly a Chm. (pt-time), Employment Tribunals), 2000–. Chairperson's list, Sports Dispute Resolution Panel, 2007–; Specialist Mem., Judicial Panel, FA, 2007–. *Recreations:* ski-ing, Manchester United FC, travel. *Address:* 9 St John Street, Manchester M3 4DN. *T:* (0161) 955 9000, *Fax:* (0161) 955 9001; *e-mail:* gilroyqc@9stjohnstreet.co.uk; Old Square Chambers, 10–11 Bedford Row, WC1R 4BU. *T:* (020) 7269 0300, *Fax:* (020) 7269 5281; *e-mail:* gilroyqc@oldsquare.co.uk.

GILSENAN, Prof. Michael Dermot Cole; David B. Kriser Professor of Middle Eastern Studies and Anthropology, New York University, since 1995; *b* 6 Feb. 1940; *s* of Michael Eugene Cole Gilsenan and Joyce Russell Horn. *Educ:* Eastbourne Grammar Sch.; Oxford Univ. BA (Oriental Studies), Dip. Anth., MA, DPhil (Soc. Anthropology). Research Fellow, Amer. Univ. in Cairo, 1964–66; Research studentship, St Antony's Coll., Oxford, 1966–67; Research Fellow, Harvard Middle East Center, 1967–68; Asst Prof., Dept of Anthropology, UCLA, 1968–70; Research Lectr, Univ. of Manchester, 1970–73; Associate Fellow, St Antony's Coll., Oxford, 1970–73; Lectr, 1973–78, Reader, 1978–83, Dept of Anthropology, University College London; Mem., Sch. of Social Sci., Inst. for Advanced Study, Princeton, 1979–80; Khalid bin Abdullah al Saud Prof. for study of contemp. Arab world, and Fellow of Magdalen Coll., Oxford Univ., 1984–95, Emeritus Fellow, 1995. Anthrop. field work, Egypt, 1964–66, Lebanon, 1971–72, Java and Singapore, 1999–2000, Singapore and Malaysia, 2001–02, 2003–05. Carnegie Corp. Scholar, 2003–05. Mem. Editl Bd, History and Anthropology and Ethnos, and formerly of Man, and Internat. Jl of Middle Eastern Studies, Past and Present; Series Editor, Society and Culture in the Modern Middle East, 1987–96. *Publications:* Saint and Sufi in Modern Egypt, 1973; Recognizing Islam, 1982; Lords of the Lebanese Marches, 1996. *Recreations:* music, theatre, being elsewhere. *Address:* Department of Middle Eastern and Islamic Studies, New York University, 50 Washington Square South, New York, NY 10012–1073, USA.

GILSON, Michael; Editor, The Scotsman, since 2006; *b* 1 March 1963; *s* of Kenneth and Janet Gilson; *m* 1988, Susan Hunt; two *s*. *Educ:* Temple Secondary Sch., Strood, Kent; Poly. of Wales (BA Hons Communication Stuidies). With local newspapers, Kent, 1985–88; travel in Peru, 1988–89; News Ed., Hull Daily Mail, 1989–94; Night Ed., Western Mail, 1994–96; Editor: Peterborough Evening Telegraph, 1996–2000; The News, Portsmouth, 2000–06. Mem., Code Cttee, Press Complaints Commn, 2004–. Mem., Johnston Press Editl Rev. Gp, 2003–. *Recreations:* football (player and sons' team coach), tennis, S American travel, trying to interest anyone in obscure 80's indie group, Orange Juice. *Address:* The Scotsman, 108 Holyrood Road, Edinburgh EH8 8AS. *T:* (0131) 620 8626; *e-mail:* mgilson@scotsman.com.

GILSON, Rev. Nigel Langley, DFC 1944; Methodist minister, retired; President of the Methodist Conference, 1986–87; *b* 11 April 1922; *s* of Clifford Edric and Cassandra Jeanette Gilson; *m* 1951, Mary Doreen (*née* Brown); four *d*. *Educ:* Holcombe Methodist Elementary; Midsomer Norton Co. Secondary; St Catherine's Soc., Oxford Univ. (MA Hons); Wesley House and Fitzwilliam House, Cambridge Univ. (BA Hons). Served RAF, 1941–45 (Navigator (Wireless) 107 Sqdn, 1944–45), Flying Officer. Methodist Minister: Tintagel, Cornwall, 1950–52; Newark-upon-Trent, 1952–58; Rhodesia Dist, 1958–67; Chaplain, Hunmanby Hall Sch., Filey, Yorks, 1967–71; Supt Minister of Oxford Methodist Circuit, 1971–75 and 1988–89; Chm., Wolverhampton and Shrewsbury Dist, 1975–88. *Recreations:* gardening, theatre, family, community and multi-cultural activities. *Address:* 30 Spencer Avenue, Yarnton, Kidlington, Oxon OX5 1NG. *T:* (01865) 378058.

GIMBLETT, (Catherine) Margaret (Alexandra Forbes); Sheriff of North Strathclyde at Dunoon, 1999–2005; part-time Sheriff, since 2005; *b* 24 Sept. 1939; *d* of Alexander Forbes Hendry and Margaret Hendry (*née* Whitehead); *m* 1965, Iain McNicol Gimblett; one *s* one *d*. *Educ:* St Leonard's Sch., St Andrews; Edinburgh Univ. (MA); Glasgow Univ. Sec. and PA, Humphreys & Glasgow Ltd, London, 1960–63; Staff Manager, John Lewis Partnership, London, 1963–67; Partner, Alexander Hendry & Son, subseq. Russel & Aitken, Denny, Solicitors, 1972–95; admitted solicitor, 1974; Temp. Sheriff, 1992–95; Sheriff, Glasgow and Strathkelvin, 1995–99. Churchill Fellowship, 1986. *Recreations:* gardening, walking, people, travelling.

GIMINGHAM, Prof. Charles Henry, OBE 1990; FRSE 1961; Regius Professor of Botany, University of Aberdeen, 1981–88 (Professor of Botany, since 1969); *b* 28 April 1923; *s* of late Conrad Theodore Gimingham and Muriel Elizabeth (*née* Blake), Harpenden; *m* 1948, Elizabeth Caroline, *o d* of late Rev. J. Wilson Baird, DD, Minister of St Machar's Cathedral, Aberdeen; three *d*. *Educ:* Gresham's Sch., Holt, Norfolk;

Emmanuel Coll., Cambridge (Open scholarship; BA 1944; ScD 1977); PhD Aberdeen 1948. FIBiol 1967. Research Asst, Imperial Coll., Univ. of London, 1944–45; University of Aberdeen: Asst, 1946–48, Lectr, 1948–61, Sen. Lectr, 1961–64, Reader, 1964–69, Dept of Botany. Vice Chm., NE Regl Bd, NCC for Scot., 1991–92; Member: Countryside Commn for Scotland, 1980–92; Sci Adv. Cttee, Scottish Natural Heritage, 1996–99 (Mem., NE Regl Bd, 1992–96); Bd of Management, Hill Farming Res. Organisation, 1981–87; Council of Management, Macaulay Inst. for Soil Research, 1983–87; Governing Body, Macaulay Land Use Res. Inst., 1987–90. Mem. Governing Body, Aberdeen Coll. of Educn, 1979–87. President: Botanical Soc. of Edinburgh, 1982–84 (Hon. British Fellow, Botanical Soc. of Scotland, 2004); British Ecological Soc., 1986–87 (Hon. Mem., 2004); Heather Trust, 2004–07. Founding Fellow, Inst. of Contemporary Scotland, 2000. Patron, Inst. of Ecology and Envmtl Mgt, 2000–. *Publications:* Ecology of Heathlands, 1972; An Introduction to Heathland Ecology, 1975; The Lowland Heathland Management Handbook, 1992; (ed) The Ecology, Land Use and Conservation of the Cairngorms, 2002; papers, mainly in botanical and ecological jls. *Recreations:* hill walking, photography, foreign travel, history and culture of Japan. *Address:* 4 Gowanbrae Road, Bieldside, Aberdeen AB15 9AQ.

GINGELL, Air Chief Marshal Sir John, GBE 1984 (CBE 1973; MBE 1962); KCB 1978; KCVO 1992; RAF, retired; Gentleman Usher of the Black Rod, Serjeant-at-Arms, House of Lords, and Secretary to the Lord Great Chamberlain, 1985–92; *b* 3 Feb. 1925; *e s* of late E. J. Gingell; *m* 1949, Prudence, *d* of late Brig. R. F. Johnson; two *s* one *d*. *Educ:* St Boniface Coll., Plymouth. Entered RAF, 1943; Fleet Air Arm, 1945–46 as Sub-Lt (A) RNVR; returned to RAF, 1951; served with Nos 58 and 542 Sqdns; CFS 1954; psc 1959; jssc 1965; comd No 27 Sqdn, 1963–65; Staff of Chief of Defence Staff, 1966; Dep. Dir Defence Ops Staff (Central Staff), 1966–67; Mil. Asst to Chm. NATO Mil. Cttee, Brussels, 1968–70; AOA, RAF Germany, 1971–72; AOC 23 Group, RAF Trng Comd, 1973–75; Asst Chief of Defence Staff (Policy), 1975–78; Air Member for Personnel, 1978–80; AOC-in-C, RAF Support Comd, 1980–81; Dep. C-in-C, Allied Forces Central Europe, 1981–84. Mem., Commonwealth War Graves Commn, 1986–91. Hon. Bencher, Inner Temple, 1990. *Recreations:* gardening, walking, music. *Club:* Royal Air Force.

GINGELL, Maj.-Gen. Laurie William Albert, CB 1980; OBE 1966 (MBE 1959); General Secretary, Officers' Pensions Society, 1979–90; *b* 29 Oct. 1925; *s* of late Major William George Gingell, MBE, MM, and of Elsie Grace Gingell; *m* 1949, Nancy Margaret Wadsworth; one *s* one *d*. *Educ:* Farnborough Grammar Sch.; Oriel Coll., Oxford. Commissioned into Royal Gloucestershire Hussars, 1945; transf. Royal Tank Regt, 1947; psc 1956; jssc 1961; Commanded: 1st Royal Tank Regt, 1966–67; 7th Armoured Bde, 1970–71; DQMG, HQ BAOR, 1973–76; Maj.-Gen. Admin, HQ UKLF, 1976–79. ADC to the Queen, 1974–76. Vice-Pres., Victory Services Club, 1997–2006 (Chm., 1989–97) FCMI (FBIM 1979). Freeman, City of London, 1979. *Recreations:* swimming, reading. *Address:* 49 Albion Crescent, Lincoln LN1 1EB. *T:* (01522) 875965.

GINGRICH, Newton Leroy, (Newt); Chief Executive Officer, Gingrich Group, since 1999; *b* 17 June 1943; *s* of late Robert Bruce Gingrich and of Kathleen (*née* Daugherty); *m* 1st, 1962, Jacqueline Battley (marr. diss. 1981); two *d*; 2nd, 1981, Marianne Ginther (marr. diss. 2000); 3rd, 2000, Callista Bisek. *Educ:* Emory Univ. (BA); Tulane Univ. (MA; PhD 1971). Taught history, W Georgia Coll., Carrollton, 1970–78; Mem. from 6th Dist of Georgia, US Congress, 1979–99 (Republican Whip, 1989–94); Speaker, US House of Representatives, 1995–99. Founder, Center for Health Transformation, 2003–. Gen. Chm., American Solutions for Winning the Future, 2007–. *Publications:* (jtly) Window of Opportunity: a blueprint for the future, 1984; (jtly) 1945, 1995; To Renew America, 1995; Lessons Learned the Hard Way, 1998; (jtly) Saving Lives and Saving Money, 2006; Winning the Future: a 21st contract with America, 2006; Rediscovering God in America, 2006; (with Nancy Desmond) The Art of Transformation, 2006; (with T. L. Maple) A Contract with the Earth, 2007; Real Change: from the world that fails to the world that works, 2008; *novels* (with William Forstchen): Grant Comes East, 2004; Gettysburg, 2004; Never Call Retreat, 2007; Pearl Harbor: a novel of December the 8th, 2007. *Address:* The Gingrich Group, 1425 K Street NW, Suite 350, Washington, DC 20005, USA.

GINNEVER, John Anthony; Director of Education, Leisure and Libraries, East Riding of Yorkshire, 1995–2002; *b* 24 June 1948; *s* of George Edward Ginnever and Olive Ginnever; *m* 1971, Wendy Marian Brown; one *s* one *d*. *Educ:* Hatfield Coll., Durham Univ. (BSc Hons 1970; PGCE 1971); Newcastle Univ. (MEd 1977). Teacher, 1971–77; Education Officer: Leeds MBC, 1978–82; Bucks CC, 1982–87; N Yorks CC, 1987–89; Dep. Dir of Educn, Newcastle MBC, 1989–95. Chm., Yorks and Humber Regl Adv. Cttee, Duke of Edinburgh's Award, 1998–. *Recreations:* birdwatching, hill walking, golf.

GINSBURG, Ruth Bader; Associate Justice of the Supreme Court of the United States, since 1993; *b* 15 March 1933; *d* of Nathan Bader and Celia Amster Bader; *m* 1954, Martin D. Ginsburg; one *s* one *d*. *Educ:* James Madison High Sch., Brooklyn; Cornell Univ. (BA Hons 1954); Harvard Law Sch.; Columbia Law Sch. (Kent Scholar; LLB, JD 1959). Clerk, Southern Dist, NY, 1959–61; Columbia Law Sch. Project on Internat. Procedure, 1961–63; Professor: Rutgers Univ. Sch. of Law, 1963–72; Columbia Law Sch., 1972–80; Circuit Judge, Court of Appeals for Dist of Columbia, 1980–93. American Civil Liberties Union: Gen. Counsel, 1973–80; Nat. Board, 1974–80; Counsel to Women's Rights Project, 1972–80. Fellow: Amer. Bar Foundn, 1978– (Exec. Cttee and Sec., 1979–89); Amer. Acad. of Arts and Scis, 1982– (Mem. Council, Foreign Relations, 1975–). *Publications:* (with A. Bruzelius) Civil Procedure in Sweden, 1965; (with A. Bruzelius) Swedish Code of Judicial Procedure, 1968; (jtly) Text, Cases and Materials on Sex-Based Discrimination, 1974, Supp. 1978; numerous contribs to learned jls. *Address:* Supreme Court, 1 First Street NE, Washington, DC 20543, USA.

GINZBURG, Prof. Vitaly Lazarevich, PhD, DSc; Professor, P. N. Lebedev Physical Institute, Russian Academy of Sciences; *b* 4 Oct. 1916; *s* of late Lazar Efimovich Ginzburg and Augusta Veniaminovna Vildauer-Ginzburg; *m* 1st, 1937, Olga Zamsha (marr. diss. 1946); one *d*; 2nd, 1946, Nina Ivanovna Ermakova. *Educ:* Moscow State Univ. (PhD 1940; DSc 1942). P. N. Lebedev Physical Inst., USSR, subseq. Russian, Acad. of Scis, 1940–: Hd, I. E. Tamm Theory Dept, 1971–88. Visiting Professor: Gorky State Univ., 1945–68; Moscow Inst. for Physics and Technol., 1968–. (Jtly) Nobel Prize for Physics, 2003. *Publications include:* Propagation of Electromagnetic Waves in Plasma, 1961; (jtly) Spatial Dispersion in Crystal Optics and the Theory of Exitons, 1966; (jtly) The Origin of Cosmic Rays, 1964; Theoretical Physics and Astrophysics, 1979; (jtly) High-Temperature Superconductivity, 1982; Waynflete Lectures on Physics, 1983; Physics and Astrophysics: a selection of key problems, 1985; (jtly) Astrophysics of Cosmic Rays, 1990; (jtly) Transition Radiation and Transition Scattering, 1990; (jtly) Superconductivity, 1994; The Physics of a Lifetime, 2001; articles in learned jls. *Address:* I. E. Tamm Theory Department, P. N. Lebedev Physical Institute, Russian Academy of Sciences, 53 Leninsky prospect, Moscow 119991, Russia.

GIOLITTI, Dr Antonio; Member, Commission of the European Communities, 1977–85; Senator, Italian Parliament, 1987–92; *b* 12 Feb. 1915; *s* of Giuseppe and Maria Giolitti; *m* 1939, Elena d'Amico; one *s* two *d*. *Educ:* Rome Univ. (Dr Law); Oxfor München. Dep., Italian Parlt, 1946–76; Minister of Budget and Economic Planning, 196 1970–72, 1973–74. Member: Italian Communist Party, 1943–57; Italian Socialist Part 1958–83; Exec., Italian Socialist Party, 1958–83; Sinistra Indipendente, 1987–9 *Publications:* Riforme e rivoluzione, 1957; Il comunismo in Europa, 1960; Un socialism possibile, 1967; Lettere a Marta, 1992. *Recreations:* music, walking. *Address:* Piazza Cairo 6, 00186 Rome, Italy.

GIORDANO, Sir Richard (Vincent), KBE 1989; Chairman, BG Group plc, 2000–((Chairman, BG (formerly British Gas) plc, 1994–2000); *b* March 1934; *s* of late Vincer Giordano and of Cynthia Giordano (*née* Cardetta); granted British citizenship, 2002; *m* 1s 1956 (marr. diss. 1993); one *s* two *d*; 2nd, 2000, Susan Ware (*d* 2001); 3rd, 200 Marguerite Rule Johnstone. *Educ:* Harvard Coll., Cambridge, Mass, USA (BA); Columb Univ. Law Sch. (LLB). Shearman & Sterling, 1959; Airco, Inc., 1963–78: Gp Vice Pres 1967; Gp Pres. and Chief Operating Officer, 1971; Chief Exec. Officer, Airco, Inc., 197 Chief Exec. Officer, BOC Gp, 1979–91; Chm., BOC, 1985–92, 1994–96; Gran Metropolitan plc: Bd Mem., 1985–97; Dep. Chm., 1991–97. Mem., CEGB, 1982–9 part-time Board Member: Rio Tinto plc (formerly RTZ Corp.), 1992–2005 (Dep. Chm 2000–05); Georgia Pacific Corp., Atlanta, Ga, 1984–; Reuters, 1991–94; non-executiv Director: Lucas Industries, 1993–94; Nat. Power. Hon. Fellow, London Business Sch 1994. Hon. Dr of Commercial Science, St John's Univ., 1975; Hon. LLD Bath, 199 *Recreations:* ocean sailing, tennis. *Address:* PO Box 1598, Lakeville, CT 06039, USA. (860) 4356617. *Clubs:* The Links, New York Yacht (New York).

GIPPS, Prof. Caroline Victoria, PhD; Vice Chancellor, University of Wolverhampto since 2005; *b* 2 Feb. 1948; *d* of John Stephen Davis and Adriaantje de Baat; *m* 1970, D Jonathan Henry William Gipps, *qv*; two *s*. *Educ:* St Winifred's Sch. for Gir Llanfairfechan; Univ. of Bristol (BSc Psychol 1968); Inst. of Education, London (MS 1973, PhD Psychol of Educn 1980). Primary sch. teacher, 1968–70; Researcher: Na Foundn for Educnl Res., 1970–74; Nat. Children's Bureau, London, 1975–77; Teachin Asst, Psychol. Dept, Univ. of British Columbia, 1977–79; Institute of Education, Londo Researcher, Lectr and Reader, 1980–94; Nuffield Res. Fellow, 1992; Hd, Curriculu Studies Dept, 1993–94; Prof. of Educn, 1994–2000; Dean of Res., 1994–99; Dep. Vic Chancellor, Kingston Univ., 2000–05. Pres., British Educnl Res. Assoc., 1992; Membe Panel for Educn, 1996 RAE; Steering Cttee, ESRC Teaching and Learning Res. Prog 1999–2004; Adv. Cttee, Staff and Educn Develt Assoc., 2002–05; Gen. Teaching Counc for England, 2003–05; Ext. Cttee on Examination Standards, QCA, 2003–05; Adv. Ctte Thomas Coram Res. Unit, Inst. of Educn, London, 2004–; ESRC Strategic Res. B 2005–; Advr, Wingate Foundn Scholarships, 1995–. AcSS 2001; FRSA. *Publications:* (jtly Language Proficiency in the Multiracial Junior School: a comparative study, 1975; (jtly Combined Nursery Centres, 1981; (jtly) Testing Children: standardised testing in Loc Education Authorities and schools, 1983; (jtly) Warnock's 18%: children with speci needs in the primary school, 1987; Beyond Testing: towards a theory of education assessment, 1994 (Japanese edn 2001); (with P. Murphy) A Fair Test?: assessmen achievement and equity, 1994 (Standing Council for Studies in Educn prize for be educnl book); Intuition or Evidence?: teachers and national assessment of seven year old 1995; (ed with P. Murphy) Equity in the Classroom: towards effective pedagogy for gir and boys, 1996; (with G. Stobart) Assessment: a teachers' guide to the issues, 3rd edn 199 (jtly) What Makes a Good Primary School Teacher?, 2000. *Recreations:* sailing, seabathin Handel opera, Mozart. *Address:* University of Wolverhampton, Wulfruna Stree Wolverhampton WV1 1SB. *T:* (01902) 322101; *e-mail:* c.gipps@wlv.ac.uk. *Club* Athenæum; Trearddur Bay Sailing.

See also Sir P. J. Davis.

GIPPS, Dr Jonathan Henry William, OBE 2000; Director, Bristol Zoo Gardens, an Bristol, Clifton and West of England Zoological Society Ltd, since 2001; *b* 7 July 1947; of late Capt. Louis H. F. P. Gipps, RN and Molly Joyce Gipps; *m* 1970, Caroline Victor Davis (*see* C. V. Gipps); two *s*. *Educ:* Imperial Coll., Univ. of London (BSc Zool. 1973 Royal Holloway Coll., Univ. of London (PhD 1977). RN, 1966–70. Post-doctor Research Fellow, Univ. of British Columbia, 1977–79; Lectr in Biology, Univ. of Bath 1980–81; Res. Fellow, RHBNC, 1981–84; Educn Officer, Computer Centre, Kingsto Poly., 1984–87; London Zoo: Curator of Mammals, 1987–91; General Curator, 1991–9 Dir, 1993–2001. Member, Council: UK Fedn of Zoos, subseq. British and Irish Assoc. c Zoos and Aquariums, 1995– (Hon. Treas., 1998–2001); European Assoc. of Zoos an Aquaria, 1999–2006 (Chm., Conservation Cttee, 1999–2002); World Assoc. of Zoos an Aquariums, 2005– (Chm., Conservation Cttee, 2002–). Trustee: Internat. Species In System, 2000–05; SS Great Britain Trust, 2007–. FRSA 1998. Hon. DSc Kingston, 199 *Publications:* (ed jtly) The Ecology of Woodland Rodents, 1981; (ed) Beyond Captiv Breeding: re-introducing endangered mammals to the wild, 1989. *Recreations:* fly-fishin making jewellery, sailing, baroque opera, ski-ing, cooking, travelling. *Address:* Bristol Zo Gardens, Guthrie Road, Bristol BS8 3HA.

GIRDWOOD, David Greenshields; Rector, St Columba's School, Kilmacolm, sinc 2002; *b* 14 Oct. 1957; *s* of Alexander and Margaret Girdwood; *m* 1985, Lisa Greig; two *d* *Educ:* St Andrews Univ. (BSc 1978); Jordanhill Coll. of Educn, Glasgow (PGCE 1979) Stirling Univ. (MEd 1985); Scottish Qualification for Headship, 2001. Teacher c Chemistry, 1979–85, Asst Hd of Science, 1985–87, Lornshill Acad., Alloa; Principa Teacher of Chemistry and Hd of Scis, 1987–96, Hd of Upper Sch., 1996–2002, Stewart Melville Coll., Edinburgh. Associate Assessor, HM Inspectorate of Educn, 1999–2002 *Recreations:* family activities, walking. *Address:* St Columba's School, Duchal Road Kilmacolm PA13 4AU. *Club:* East India.

GIRET, (Josephine) Jane; QC 2001; *b* 6 June 1944; *d* of late Bernard Leslie Barker an of Josephine Mamie Barker; *m* 1985, Joseph John Bela Leslie Giret. *Educ:* Queen Anne Sch., Caversham, Berks. Called to the Bar, Inner Temple, 1981; Mem. *ad eund*, Lincoln' Inn, 1992 (Bencher, 2004). *Recreations:* following the English Cricket Team, Barbado yoga. *Address:* 11 Stone Buildings, Lincoln's Inn, WC2A 3TG; 74 Alder Lodge, Rive Gardens, Stevenage Road, SW6 6NR. *T:* (020) 7831 6381.

GIRLING, (John) Anthony; Consultant, Girlings, Solicitors, 2000; President of the Lav Society, 1996–97; *b* 21 Aug. 1943; *s* of James William Girling, OBE and Annie Doris (*né* Reeves); *m* 1965, Lynne Margaret Davis; one *s* one *d*. *Educ:* Tonbridge Sch.; Guildfor Coll. of Law. Admitted Solicitor, 1966; Girlings, Solicitors: Partner, 1968; Man. Partne 1982–96; Chm., 1997–2000. Hon. Sec., 1974–80, Pres., 1980–81, Kent Law Soc.; Mem for Kent, Council of Law Soc., 1980–99. Hon. Sen. Mem., Darwin Coll., Univ. of Kent 1984. Fellow, Inst. of Advanced Legal Studies, Univ. of London, 1997–. Hon. LLD Kent 1998. *Publications:* contrib. to Law Soc. Gazette and other legal jls. *Recreations:* golf, ski ing, the countryside. *Address:* Penbourne, Mill View Court, Valley Road, Barham Canterbury, Kent CT4 6PL. *Clubs:* Ski of Great Britain; Canterbury Golf.

GIROLAMI, Sir Paul, Kt 1988; FCA; Chairman, Glaxo Holdings, 1985–94; *b* 25 Jan 1926; *m* 1952, Christabel Mary Gwynne Lewis; two *s* one *d*. *Educ:* London School c Economics (Hon. Fellow, 1989); FREconS; FIMC 1990. Chantrey & Button, Chartere

Accountants, 1950–54; Coopers & Lybrand, Chartered Accountants, 1954–65; Glaxo Holdings: Financial Controller, 1965; Finance Director, 1968; Chief Exec., 1980–86. Director: Inner London Board of National Westminster Bank, 1974–89; Credito Italiano Internat. UK, 1990–93; Forte plc, 1992–96; UIS France, 1994–. Member: Bd of Dirs, Amer. Chamber of Commerce (UK), 1983–; CBI Council, 1986–93; Appeal Cttee, ICA, 1987–; Stock Exchange Listed Cos Adv. Cttee, 1987–92. Chm., Senate for Chartered Accountants in Business, 1990–2000. Chm. Council, Goldsmiths' Coll., Univ. of London, 1994–2003; Mem. Open Univ. Vis. Cttee, 1987–89. Gov., NIESR, 1992–. Freeman, City of London; Liveryman, Goldsmiths' Co., 1980– (Mem., Ct of Assistants, 1986–; Prime Warden, 1995–96); Mem., Soc. of Apothecaries, 1993–. Hon. FCGI 1994; FCMI (FBIM 1986); FRSA 1986. Hon. DSc: Aston, 1990; Trieste, 1991; Sunderland, 1991; Bradford, 1993; Hon. LLD: Singapore, 1993; Warwick, 1996; Hon. DBA Strathclyde, 1993. Centenary Medal, UK SCI, 1992; Centenary Award, UK Founding Socs, 1992. Grand Cross, Order of the Holy Sepulchre, 1994. Grande Ufficiale, Ordine al Merito della Repubblica Italiana, 1987; Cavaliere al Merito del Lavoro, Italy, 1991; Insignia of the Order of the Rising Sun, Japan, 1991; Public Service Star, Singapore, 2000. *Recreations:* reading, music.

See also P. J. Girolami.

GIROLAMI, Paul Julian; QC 2002; barrister; *b* 5 Dec. 1959; *s* of Sir Paul Girolami, *qv*; *m* 1991, Deborah Bookman; one s two *d*. *Educ:* St Paul's Sch., London; Corpus Christi Coll., Cambridge. Called to the Bar, Middle Temple, 1983; Jun. Counsel to the Crown, Chancery, 1991–2000. *Address:* Maitland Chambers, 7 Stone Buildings, Lincoln's Inn, WC2A 3SZ. *T:* (020) 7406 1200, *Fax:* (020) 7406 1300; *e-mail:* clerks@maitlandchambers.com.

GIROUARD, Mark, PhD; writer and architectural historian; Slade Professor of Fine Art, University of Oxford, 1975–76; *b* 7 Oct. 1931; *s* of late Richard D. Girouard and Lady Blanche Girouard; *m* 1970, Dorothy N. Dorf; one *d*. *Educ:* Ampleforth; Christ Church, Oxford (MA); Courtauld Inst. of Art (PhD); Bartlett Sch., UCL (BSc, Dip. Arc). Staff of Country Life, 1958–66; studied architecture, Bartlett Sch., UCL, 1966–71; staff of Architectural Review, 1971–75. George Lurcy Vis. Prof., Columbia Univ., NY, 1987. Member: Council, Victorian Soc., 1979– (Founder Mem. 1958; Mem. Cttee, 1958–66); Royal Fine Art Commn, 1972–96; Royal Commn on Historical Monuments (England), 1976–81; Historic Buildings Council (England), 1978–84; Commn for Historic Buildings and Monuments, 1984–90 (Mem., Buildings Adv. Cttee, 1984–86; Mem., Historic Areas Adv. Cttee, 1985–89; Mem., Historic Bldgs Cttee, 1988–90); Council, Spitalfields Historic Buildings Trust, 1983– (Chm., 1977–83); Trustee, Architecture Foundn, 1992–99. Mem., Adv. Council, Paul Mellon Centre for Studies in British Art, 1990–96. FSA 1986; Hon. FRIBA, 1980. Hon. DLitt: Leicester, 1982; Buckingham, 1991. *Publications:* Robert Smythson and the Architecture of the Elizabethan Era, 1966, 2nd edn, Robert Smythson and the Elizabethan Country House, 1983; The Victorian Country House, 1971, 2nd edn 1979; Victorian Pubs, 1975, 2nd edn 1984; (jtly) Spirit of the Age, 1975 (based on BBC TV series); Sweetness and Light: the 'Queen Anne' movement 1860–1900, 1977; Life in the English Country House, 1978 (Duff Cooper Meml Prize; W. H. Smith Award, 1979); Historic Houses of Britain, 1979; Alfred Waterhouse and the Natural History Museum, 1981; The Return to Camelot: chivalry and the English gentleman, 1981; Cities and People, 1985; A Country House Companion, 1987; The English Town, 1990; Town and Country, 1992; Windsor: the most romantic castle, 1993; Big Jim: the life and work of James Stirling, 1998; Life in the French Country House, 2000; articles in Country Life, Architect. Rev., Listener. *Address:* 35 Colville Road, W11 2BT. *Club:* Beefsteak.

GIRVAN, Rt Hon. Sir (Frederick) Paul, Kt 1995; PC 2007; **Rt Hon. Lord Justice Girvan;** a Lord Justice of Appeal, Supreme Court of Judicature, Northern Ireland, since 2007; *b* 20 Oct. 1948; *s* of Robert Frederick Girvan and Martha Elizabeth (*née* Barron); *m* 1974, Karen Elizabeth Joyce; two *s* one *d*. *Educ:* Belfast Royal Acad.; Clare Coll., Cambridge (BA); Queen's Univ., Belfast; Gray's Inn. Called to the Bar: NI, 1971; Inner Bar (NI), 1982; Jun. Crown Counsel, NI, 1979–82; Justice of the High Court, NI, 1995–2007. Chancellor, Archdio. of Armagh, 1999–. Chairman: Council of Law Reporting for NI, 1994–2001; Law Reform Adv. Cttee for NI, 1997–2004 (Mem., 1994). Hon. Bencher, Gray's Inn, 1999. *Recreations:* badminton, walking, swimming, reading, modern languages, gardening, cooking, golf, painting. *Address:* Royal Courts of Justice, Chichester Street, Belfast, Northern Ireland BT1 3JF. *T:* (028) 9023 5111.

GISBOROUGH, 3rd Baron *cr* 1917; **Thomas Richard John Long Chaloner;** Lord-Lieutenant of Cleveland, 1981–96; Lieutenant of North Yorkshire, 1996–2001; *b* 1 July 1927; *s* of 2nd Baron and Esther Isabella Madeleine (*d* 1970), *yr d* of late Charles O. Hall, Eddlethorpe; *S* father, 1951; *m* 1960, Shane, *e d* of late Sidney Newton, London, and *g d* of Sir Louis Newton, 1st Bt; two *s*. *Educ:* Eton; Royal Agricultural Coll. 16th/5th Lancers, 1948–52; Captain Northumberland Hussars, 1955–61; Lt-Col Green Howards (Territorials), 1967–69. Mem., Rural Develt Commn, 1985–89. CC NR Yorks, 1964–74, Cleveland, 1974–77. Hon. Col, Cleveland County Army Cadet Force, 1981–92. President: British Ski Fedn, 1985–90; Assoc. of Professional Foresters, 1998–2001. DL N Riding of Yorks and Cleveland, 1973; JP Langbaurgh East, 1981–94. KStJ 1981. *Recreations:* field sports, ski-ing, tennis, bridge, piano. *Heir:* *s* Hon. Thomas Peregrine Long Chaloner [*b* 17 Jan. 1961; *m* 1992, Karen, *o d* of Alan Thomas]. *Address:* Gisborough House, Guisborough, Cleveland TS14 6PT. *T:* (01287) 630012, 07717 411110.

GISCARD d'ESTAING, Valéry; Grand Croix de la Légion d'Honneur; Croix de Guerre (1939–45); Member, Académie Française, 2003; President of the French Republic, 1974–81; President: Conseil Régional d'Auvergne, since 1986; Council of European Municipalities and Regions, since 1997; European Convention, since 2001; *b* Coblence, 2 Feb. 1926; *s* of late Edmond Giscard d'Estaing and May Bardoux; *m* 1952, Anne-Aymone de Brantes; two *s* two *d*. *Educ:* Lycée Janson-de-Sailly, Paris; Ecole Polytechnique; Ecole Nationale d'Administration. Inspection of Finances: Deputy, 1952; Inspector, 1954; Dep. Dir, Cabinet of Président du Conseil, June–Dec. 1954. Elected Deputy for Puy-de-Dôme, 1956; re-elected for Clermont N and SW, Nov. 1958, Nov.–Dec. 1962, March 1967, June 1968, March 1973, 1984, 1986 and 1988–89; Deputy for Puy-de-Dôme, 1993–2002; Sec. of State for Finance, 1959; Minister of Finance, Jan.–April 1962; Minister of Finance and Economic Affairs, April–Nov. 1962 and Dec. 1962–Jan. 1966; Minister of Economy and Finance, 1969–74. Pres., Nat. Fedn of Indep. Republicans, 1966–73 (also a Founder); Pres., comm. des finances de l'économie générale et du plan de l'Assemblée nationale, 1967–68; Chm., Commn of Foreign Affairs, Nat. Assembly, 1987–89, 1993–97. Mem., Eur. Parlt, 1989–93. Pres., Eur. Movt Internat., 1989–97. Mayor of Chamalières, 1967–74. Deleg. to Assembly of UN, 1956, 1957, 1958. Mem., Real Acad. de Ciencias Economicas y Financieras, Spain, 1995–. Nansen Medal, UNHCR, 1979; Gold Medal, Jean Monnet Foundn, 2001; Karl Prize, Aachen, 2003. *Publications:* Démocratie Française, 1976 (Towards a New Democracy, 1977); 2 Français sur 3, 1984; Le Pouvoir et la Vie (memoirs), 1988; L'Affrontement, 1991; Le Passage (novel), 1994; Dans 5 ans l'an 2000, 1995. *Address:* 11 rue Bénouville, 75116 Paris, France; (office) 199 Boulevard Saint-Germain, 75007 Paris, France. *Clubs:* Polo (Paris); Union Interalliée.

GISSING, Jason Mark Conrad; Co-Founder, Finance Director and Marketing Director, Ocado.com, since 2000; *b* UK, 25 Oct. 1970; *s* of Graham and Mikiko Gissing; *m* 2002, Katinka, *d* of late Arne Naess; one *s* one *d*. *Educ:* Oundle Sch., Northants; Worcester Coll., Oxford (BA Juris.). Investment banking analyst, then fixed income trader, Goldman Sachs, 1992–2000. *Recreations:* tennis, ski-ing, football, yoga, history, my wonderful family, trying to work out how to make the world a better place when Ocado stops demanding so much of my time. *Address:* c/o Ocado Ltd, Titan Court, Hatfield Business Park, Hatfield AL10 9NE; *e-mail:* jason@ocado.com. *Clubs:* Queen's, Campden Hill Lawn Tennis.

GITTINGS, (Harold) John; writer; *b* 3 Sept. 1947; *s* of Harold William Gittings and Doris Marjorie Gittings (*née* Whiting); *m* 1st, 1988, Andrea (*née* Fisher) (*d* 1995); two step *c*; 2nd, 2002, Barbara (*née* Lowenstein). *Educ:* Duke of York's Royal Military School, Dover. ACIS. Beecham Group, 1971–73; Peat Marwick Mitchell, Hong Kong, 1973–74; N. M. Rothschild & Sons, 1974–81; Continental Bank, 1981–82; Target Group, 1982–85; Man. Dir, Touche Remnant & Co. 1986–90; Chm., Greenfield Marketing, subseq. Greenfield Gp, 1992–96; Dir, Meltemi Entertainment Ltd, 1996–2000. *Recreations:* travel, collecting, film. *Address:* A Naurio, Aubiet 32270, France.

GITTUS, John Henry, DSc, DTech; FREng; Senior Technical Consultant: Chaucer plc, since 2002; NECSA (South Africa), since 2006; *b* 25 July 1930; *s* of Henry Gittus and Amy Gittus; *m* 1953, Rosemary Ann Geeves; one *s* two *d*. *Educ:* Alcester Grammar Sch.; BSc (1st Cl. Hons, Maths) London 1952; DSc Phys London 1976; DTech Metall Stockholm 1975. CEng, FREng (FEng 1989); FIMechE, FIS, FIMMM. British Cast Iron Res. Assoc., 1947–55; Mond Nickel Co., R&D Labs, Birmingham, 1955–60 (develt Nimonic series high temp. super alloys for aircraft gas turbine engines); United Kingdom Atomic Energy Authority, 1960–89: Research Manager, Springfields (develt nuclear fuel); Head, Water Reactor fuel develt; Head, Atomic Energy Tech. Br., Harwell; Director: Water Reactor Safety Research; Safety and Reliability Directorate, Culcheth; Communication and Information; Dir Gen., British Nuclear Forum, 1990–93; Senior Partner: SPA Consultants, 1993–; NUSYS Consultants, Paris, 1994–; AEA Technol., 1996–; Amersham, 1999–; Sumitomo Corp., 1999–; Senior Technical Consultant: Cox Power Hldgs, 1996–2002; Eskom, 1998–2002. Working Mem., Lloyd's Nuclear Syndicate, 1996–. Consultant: Argonne Nat. Lab., USA, 1968; Oak Ridge Nat. Lab., 1969. Visiting Professor: Ecole Polytechnique Fédérale, Lausanne, 1976; Univ. de Nancy, 1984; Regents' Prof., UCLA, 1990–91; Prof. of Risk Mgt, 1997–2006, Royal Acad. of Engrg Prof. of Integrated Business Develt, 2006–, Plymouth Univ.. Editor-in-Chief, Res Mechanica, 1980–91. *Publications:* Uranium, 1962; Creep, Viscoelasticity and Creep-fracture in Solids, 1979; Irradiation Effects in Crystalline Solids, 1979; (with W. Crosbie) Medical Response to Effects of Ionizing Radiation, 1989; numerous articles in learned jls. *Recreations:* old houses, old motor cars, old friends. *Address:* (office) 9 Devonshire Square, Cutlers Gardens, EC2M 4WL. *T:* (020) 7397 9700; (home) The Rectory, 19 Butter Street, Alcester, Stratford-upon-Avon B49 5AL; *e-mail:* john@gittus.com. *Club:* Royal Society of Medicine.

GIUDICE, Geoffrey Michael; Hon. Justice Giudice; Judge of the Federal Court, Australia, since 1997; President, Australian Industrial Relations Commission, since 1997; *b* 16 Dec. 1947; *s* of Rupert Emanuel Giudice and Emily Muriel Giudice; *m* 1970, Beth Hayden; three *s* one *d*. *Educ:* Xavier Coll., Melbourne; Univ. of Melbourne (BA 1970; LLB). Res. Officer, Hosp. Employees Union, 1971; IR Manager, Myer Emporium Ltd, 1972–78; Partner, Moule Hamilton and Derham, solicitors, 1979–84; Barrister, Victoria Bar, 1984–97. *Recreations:* tennis, bridge. *Address:* Australian Industrial Relations Commission, Level 4, 11 Exhibition Street, Melbourne, Vic 3000, Australia. *T:* (3) 86617829. *Clubs:* Athenæum (Melbourne); Melbourne Cricket, Victoria Racing.

GIULIANI, Rudolph William, Hon. KBE 2001; Mayor, City of New York, 1994–2001; founder, Chairman and Chief Executive, Giuliani Partners, since 2002; *b* 28 May 1944; *m* 1984; one *s* one *d*. *Educ:* Manhattan Coll. (AB); New York Univ. (JD). Legal Clerk to US Dist Court Judge, NYC, 1968–70; Asst Attorney, S Dist, NY, 1970–73; Exec. Asst Attorney, Dept of Justice, 1973–75; Associate Dep. Attorney Gen., 1975–77; with Patterson, Belknap, Webb and Tyler, 1977–81; Associate Attorney Gen., 1981–83; US Attorney, US Dist Court, S Dist, NY, 1983–89; with White & Case, 1989–90; with Anderson Kill Olick & Oshinsky PC, 1990–93. Republican Candidate for Mayor, NY, 1989. *Publication:* Leadership, 2002. *Address:* Giuliani Partners, 5 Times Square, New York, NY 10036, USA.

GLADDEN, Prof. Lynn Faith, OBE 2001; PhD; FRS 2004; FREng; Shell Professor of Chemical Engineering, since 2004, and Head of Department of Chemical Engineering, since 2006, University of Cambridge; Fellow, Trinity College, Cambridge, since 1999; *b* 30 July 1961; *d* of John Montague Gladden and Sheila Faith (*née* Deverell); partner, Dr Paul Alexander. *Educ:* Heathfield Sch., Harrow; Univ. of Bristol (BSc 1st cl. Hons (Chemical Physics) 1982); Keble Coll., Oxford (PGCE 1983); Trinity Coll., Cambridge (PhD 1987). FIChemE 1996; FRSC 2000; FInstP 2003. Pickering Res. Fellow, Royal Soc., 1986; University of Cambridge: Asst Lectr, 1987–91, Lectr, 1991–95; Reader in Process Engrg Sci., 1995–99; Prof. of Chem. Engrg Sci., 1999–2004. Miller Vis. Prof., Univ. of Calif., Berkeley, 1996. Member: Royal Soc./Royal Acad. of Engrg Adv. Gp to NPL, 2003–; EPSRC, 2006–; Council, Royal Soc., 2006–. FREng 2003. Beilby Medal, Inst. of Materials, Minerals and Mining, RSC, and Soc. of Chem. Industry, 1995; Tilden Lect. and Silver Medal, RSC, 2001. *Recreations:* reading, wine, modern art. *Address:* Jasmine Cottage, 79 Green End, Landbeach, Cambridge CB4 8ED. *T:* (01223) 334762, *Fax:* (01223) 334796; *e-mail:* Gladden@cheng.cam.ac.uk.

GLADSTONE, David Arthur Steuart, CMG 1988; HM Diplomatic Service, retired; *b* 1 April 1935; *s* of late Thomas Steuart Gladstone and Muriel Irene Heron Gladstone; *m* 1961, April (*née* Brunner); one *s* one *d*. *Educ:* Eton; Christ Church, Oxford (MA History). National Service, 1954–56; Oxford Univ., 1956–59. Annan, Dexter & Co. (Chartered Accountants), 1959–60; FO, 1960; MECAS, Lebanon, 1960–62; Bahrain, 1962–63; FO, 1963–65; Bonn, 1965–69; FCO, 1969–72; Cairo, 1972–75; British Mil. Govt, Berlin, 1976–79; Head of Western European Dept, FCO, 1979–82; Consul-Gen., Marseilles, 1983–87; High Comr, Colombo, 1987–91; Chargé d'Affaires *ai*, Kiev, 1992. Dir, SANE, 2002–. *Publication:* What shall we do with the Crown Prerogative?, 1998. *Recreations:* music, theatre, cinema, dreaming, landscape gardening. *Address:* 1 Mountfort Terrace, N1 1JJ.

GLADSTONE, Sir (Erskine) William, 7th Bt *cr* 1846; KG 1999; JP; Lord-Lieutenant of Clwyd, 1985–2000; *b* 29 Oct. 1925; *s* of Charles Andrew Gladstone, (6th Bt), and Isla Margaret (*d* 1987), *d* of late Sir Walter Erskine Crum; *S* father, 1968; *m* 1962, Rosamund Anne, *yr d* of late Major A. Hambro; two *s* one *d*. *Educ:* Eton; Christ Church, Oxford. Served RNVR, 1943–46. Asst Master at Shrewsbury, 1949–50, and at Eton, 1951–61; Head Master of Lancing Coll., 1961–69. Chief Scout of UK and Overseas Branches,

1972–82; Mem., World Scout Cttee, 1977–83 (Chm., 1979–81). DL Flintshire, 1969, Clwyd, 1974, Vice Lord-Lieut, 1984; Alderman, Flintshire CC, 1970–74. Chm., Rep. Body of Church in Wales 1977–92; Chairman: Council of Glenalmond Coll. (formerly Trinity Coll., Glenalmond), 1982–86; Govs, Ruthin Sch., 1987–92 (Patron, 1998–). JP Clwyd 1982. Hon. LLD Liverpool, 1998. *Publications:* various school textbooks. *Recreations:* reading history, watercolours, shooting, gardening. *Heir: s* Charles Angus Gladstone [*b* 11 April 1964; *m* 1988, Caroline, *o d* of Sir Derek Thomas, *qv*; two *s* four *d*]. *Address:* Hawarden Castle, Flintshire CH5 3PB. *T:* (01244) 520210.

GLADWIN, Rt Rev. John Warren; *see* Chelmsford, Bishop of.

GLADWYN, 2nd Baron *cr* 1960, of Bramfield, co. Suffolk; **Miles Alvery Gladwyn Jebb;** *b* 3 March 1930; *s* of 1st Baron Gladwyn, GCMG, GCVO, CB and Cynthia (*d* 1990), *d* of Sir Saxton Noble, 3rd Bt; *S* father, 1996. *Educ:* Eton; Magdalen Coll., Oxford (MA). Served as 2nd Lieut, Welsh Guards and Pilot Officer, RAFVR. Sen. management, BOAC, later British Airways, 1961–83. *Publications:* The Thames Valley Heritage Walk, 1980; A Guide to the South Downs Way, 1984; Walkers, 1986; A Guide to the Thames Path, 1988; East Anglia, 1990; The Colleges of Oxford, 1992; Suffolk, 1995; (ed) The Diaries of Cynthia Gladwyn, 1995; The Lord-Lieutenants and their Deputies, 2007. *Heir:* none. *Address:* E1 Albany, Piccadilly, W1J 0AR. *Clubs:* Brooks's, Beefsteak.

GLAIEL, Dr Sami; Ambassador of Syria to Tunisia, since 2002; *b* 2 Feb. 1941; *s* of George and Milia Glaiel; *m* 1975, Ghada Khoury; one *s* one *d*. *Educ:* Damascus Univ. (BA French Lit. 1965); Warsaw Univ. (Dip. Jlism 1969; PhD Political Scis 1973). Joined Min. of Foreign Affairs, Syria, 1974: First Sec., Perm. Mission to UN, NY, 1975–81; Dep. Dir, Dept of Internat. Orgns, then Dir, Dept of America, Min. of Foreign Affairs, 1981–84; Minister Counsellor, Perm. Mission to UN, 1984–87; Ambassador and Perm. Rep. to UN, Geneva and Vienna, 1987–90; Ambassador to Venezuela and Caribbean Is, 1990–94; Dir, Africa Dept, then Econ. Dept, Min. of Foreign Affairs, 1994–99; Ambassador to UK, 2000–02. *Address:* 119 Azouz Roubai, 2092 Almanar 3, PO Box 62 Almanar 2, Tunis, Tunisia.

GLAISTER, Lesley Gillian, FRSL; writer; *b* 4 Oct. 1956; *d* of Leonard Oliver Richard Glaister and Maureen Jillian Glaister (*née* Crowley); three *s*; *m* 2001, Andrew Greig. *Educ:* Open Univ. (BA 1st Cl. Hons Humanities); Univ. of Sheffield (MA Socio-Legal Studies). Adult Educn Tutor (pt-time), Sheffield, 1982–90; Lectr (pt-time), for MA in Writing, Sheffield Hallam Univ., 1993–. Writer-in-Residence, Cheltenham Fest. of Literature, and Univ. of Gloucester, 2002–03. FRSL 1994. Author of the Year, Yorkshire Post, 1994. *Play:* Bird Calls, Crucible Th., Sheffield, 2003. *Publications:* Honour Thy Father (Somerset Maugham Award, Betty Trask Award), 1990; Trick or Treat, 1991; Digging to Australia, 1992; Limestone and Clay, 1993; Partial Eclipse, 1994; The Private Parts of Women, 1996; Easy Peasy, 1997; Sheer Blue Bliss, 1999; Now You See Me, 2001; As Far As You Can Go, 2004; Nina Todd Has Gone, 2007. *Recreations:* walking, yoga, theatre, cinema. *Address:* 16 Kirkland Street, Peebles EH45 8EU; 1 Melvin Place, Stromness, Orkney KW16 3DD.

GLAISTER, Prof. Stephen, CBE 1998; PhD; Professor of Transport and Infrastructure, Department of Civil and Environmental Engineering, and Director, Railway Technology Strategy Centre, Imperial College, London, since 1998; *b* 21 June 1946; *s* of Kenneth Goodall Glaister and Mary Glaister (*née* Jones); *m* 1977, Alison Sarah Linning; one *s*. *Educ:* Univ. of Essex (BA 1967); LSE (MSc 1968; PhD 1976). Lectr in Econs, 1969–78, Cassel Reader, 1978–98, LSE. Member, Board: LRT, 1984–93; Transport for London, 2000–. Advisor: DfT (various dates); Rail Regulator, 1994–2001. Trustee, Rees Jeffreys Road Fund, 1979–. *Publications:* Mathematical Methods for Economists, 1972, 3rd edn 1984; Fundamentals of Transport Economics, 1981; Urban Public Transport Subsidies, 1982; (with C. M. Mulley) Public Control of the Bus and Coach Industry, 1983; (jtly) Application of Social Cost Benefit Analysis to London Transport Policies, 1983; (with Tony Travers) Meeting the Transport Needs of the City, 1993; (with Tony Travers) New Directions for British Railways?: the political economy of privatisation and regulation, 1993; (with R. Layard) Cost Benefit Analysis, 1994; (with Tony Travers) Tolls and Shadow Tolls, 1994; (with Tony Travers) An Infrastructure Fund for London, 1994; (jtly) London Bus Tendering, 1995; (jtly) London's Size and Diversity: the advantages in a competitive world, 1996; (with Dan Graham) Who Spends What on Motoring in the UK?, 1996; (jtly) Transport Policy in Britain, 1998; (jtly) Getting Partnerships Going: public private partnerships in transport, 2000; (with T. Grayling) A New Fares Contract for London, 2000; (jtly) Capital Asset: London's healthy contribution to jobs and services, 2000; (with Dan Graham) The Effect of Fuel Prices on Motorists, 2000; (jtly) A Reassessment of the Economic Case for CrossRail, 2001; (jtly) Streets Ahead: safe and liveable streets for children, 2002; (with T. Travers) Treasurehouse and Powerhouse, 2004; (with D. Graham) Pricing Our Roads: vision and reality, 2004; (with D. Graham) National Road Pricing: is it fair and practical?, 2006; (jtly) Roads and Reality, 2007; numerous articles in learned jls. *Recreation:* playing the oboe. *Address:* 39 Huntingdon Street, N1 1BP. *T:* (020) 7609 1401; *e-mail:* s.glaister@imperial.ac.uk.

GLAISYER, Ven. Hugh; Archdeacon of Lewes and Hastings, 1991–97, Archdeacon Emeritus, since 2007; *b* 20 Jan. 1930; *s* of Rev. Canon Hugh Glaisyer and Edith Glaisyer; *m* 1962, Alison Marion Heap; one *s* two *d*. *Educ:* Tonbridge Sch.; Oriel Coll., Oxford (MA 2nd cl. Hon. Mods, 2nd Cl. Theol.); St Stephen's House, Oxford. FO, RAF, 1954. Ordained, Manchester, 1956; Curate: St Augustine's, Tonge Moor, Bolton, 1956–62; Sidcup, 1962–64; Vicar, Christ Church, Milton-next-Gravesend, 1964–81; RD, Gravesend, 1974–81; Vicar, Hove, 1981–91; RD, Hove, 1982–91; Canon of Chichester Cathedral, 1982–91. *Recreations:* British shorthair cats, gardening. *Address:* Florence Villa, Hangleton Lane, Ferring, W Sussex BN12 6PP. *T:* (01903) 244688.

GLAMANN, Prof. Kristof, OBE 1985; Hon. FBA 1985; author; President, Carlsberg Foundation, 1976–93 (Director, since 1969); Chairman, Carlsberg Ltd, 1977–93 (Director, since 1969); *b* 26 Aug. 1923; *s* of Kai Kristof Glamann, bank manager, and Ebba Henriette Louise (*née* Madsen); *m* 1954, Kirsten Lise (*née* Jantzen), MA, lecturer; two *s*. *Educ:* Odense Katedral-skole; Univ. of Copenhagen (MA Hist. 1948, PhD Econ. Hist., 1958). University of Copenhagen: Research Fellow, 1948–56; Associated Prof., 1956–60; Prof. of History, 1960–80. Visiting Professor: Pennsylvania, 1960; Wisconsin, 1961; LSE 1964; Vis. Overseas Fellow, Churchill Coll., Cambridge, 1971–72, 1993; Toho Gakkai, Japan, 1977; Master, 4th May and Hassager Coll., Copenhagen, 1961–81. Chm., Scand. Inst. of Asian Studies, 1967–71; Hon. Pres., Internat. Econ. Hist. Assoc., 1974 (Pres., 1970–74; Vice-Pres., 1968–70). Director: Carlsberg Brewery Ltd, UK, 1977–93; Fredericia Brewery Ltd, 1975–93; Royal Copenhagen (Holmegaard) Ltd, 1975–93; Politiken Foundn, 1990. Chm., Danish State Research Council of Humanities, 1968–70; Mem. Bd, HM Queen Ingrid's Roman Foundn, 1980–2005; Vice-Pres., Scandinavia-Japan Sasakawa Foundn, 1985–2006; Member: Royal Danish Acad. of Science and Letters, 1969; Royal Danish Hist. Soc., 1961; Swedish Acad., Lund, 1963; Hist. Soc. of Calcutta, 1962; Corresp. FRHistS 1972; Founding Mem., Acad. Europaea, 1988; Fellow, Royal Belgian Acad., 1989. Editor, Scand. Econ. History Review, 1961–70. Hon. LittD Gothenburg, 1974. Erasmus Medal, Acad. Europaea, 2000. Comdr (I), Order of the Dannebrog, 1990 (Kt 1984); Comdr, Northern Star of Sweden, 1984; Order of Orang Nassau, Netherlands, 1984; Comdr, Falcon of Iceland, 1987; Das Grosse Verdienstkreu FRG, 1989; Order of Gorkha Dakshina Bahu, 3rd Cl., Nepal, 1989; Grand Comd Ordem do Mérito Agricola e Industrial, Portugal, 1992. *Publications:* History of Tobacc Industry in Denmark 1875–1950, 1950; Dutch-Asiatic Trade 1620–1740, 1958, 2nd ec 1981; (with Astrid Friis) A History of Prices and Wages in Denmark 1660–1800, vol. 1958; A History of Brewing in Denmark, 1962, rev. edn 2005; Studies in Mercantilisr 1966, 2nd edn 1984; European Trade 1500–1750, 1971; Carlsbergfondet, 197 Cambridge Econ. Hist. of Europe, vol. V, 1977; J. C. Jacobsen of Carlsberg, Brewer ar Philanthropist, 1991; The Carlsberg Foundation since 1970, 1993; Carl Jacobsen of Ne Carlsberg, 1995; The Carlsberg Group since 1970, 1997; Time Out: an essay, 1998; E Blandet Landhandel (memoirs), 2002; The Carlsberg Foundation: origin and first hundre years, 2003; (with Kirsten Glamann) The Scandinavian Pasteur: a biography of the scienti Emil Christian Hansen, 2004. *Recreations:* painting, walking. *Address:* Høeghsmindeparke 10, 2900 Hellerup, Denmark. *T:* 39403977.

GLAMIS, Lord; Simon Patrick Bowes Lyon; *b* 18 June 1986; *s* and *heir* of Earl Strathmore and Kinghorne, *qv*.

GLAMORGAN, Earl of; Robert Somerset; *b* 20 Jan. 1989; *s* and *heir* of Marquess Worcester, *qv*.

GLANCY, Robert Peter; QC 1997; a Recorder, since 1999; a President, Mental Healt Review Tribunal, since 1999; *b* 25 March 1950; *s* of Dr Cecil Jacob Glancy, JP and Ani Glancy; *m* 1976, Linda Simons; one *s* two *d*. *Educ:* Manchester Grammar Sch.; St John Coll., Cambridge (MA). Called to the Bar, Middle Temple, 1972, Bencher, 2007; practice at the Bar, 1973–; Asst Recorder, 1993–99. *Publication:* (jtly) The Personal Inju Handbook. *Recreations:* theatre, cinema, reading, watching Manchester United. *Address:* 2 Litchfield Way, Hampstead Garden Suburb, NW11 6NJ. *T:* (020) 8933 1938.

GLANUSK, 5th Baron *cr* 1899; **Christopher Russell Bailey,** TD 1977; Bt 185 consultant; *b* 18 March 1942; *o s* of 4th Baron Glanusk and Lorna Dorothy (*d* 1997), *o* of Capt. E. C. H. N. Andrews, MBE, RA; *S* father, 1997; *m* 1974, Frances Elizabeth, *o* of Air Chief Marshal Sir Douglas Lowe, *qv*; one *s* one *d*. *Educ:* Summerfields, Oxford; Etc Coll.; Clare Coll., Cambridge (BA 1964). Design Engr, English Electric Leo Lt 1964–66; Product Mkting Manager, Ferranti Ltd, 1966–78; Internat. Product Manage Bestobell Mobrey Ltd, 1978–83; Sales Engr, STC Telecommunication Ltd, 1984–8 General Manager: Autocar Equipment Ltd, 1986–97; Woolfram Research Europe Lt 1997–98. Territorial Army: Captain, Berks Yeo. Signal Sqdn, 1967–76, Cheshire Ye Signal Sqdn, 1976–79; Maj., HQ2 Signal Bde, 1979–83. *Heir: s* Hon. Charles Hen Bailey, *b* 12 Aug. 1976. *Address:* 51 Chertsey Road, Chobham, Surrey GU24 8PD.

GLANVILLE, Alec William; Assistant Under-Secretary of State, Home Office, 1975–8 retired; *b* 20 Jan. 1921; *y s* of Frank Foster and Alice Glanville; *m* 1941, Lilian Kathlee Hetherton; one *s* one *d*. *Educ:* Portsmouth Northern Secondary Sch.; Portsmou Municipal Coll. War service, RAMC, 1939–46. Exchequer and Audit Dept, 1939–4 General, Criminal, Police and Probation and After-care Depts, Home Office, 1947–8 (seconded to Cabinet Office, 1956–58); Private Sec. to Permanent Under Sec. of Stat 1949–50; Principal Private Sec. to Sec. of State, 1960–63; Sec., Interdepartmental Ctte on Mentally Abnormal Offenders, 1972–75.

GLANVILLE, Brian Lester; author and journalist since 1949; *b* 24 Sept. 1931; *s* of Jam Arthur Glanville and Florence Glanville (*née* Manches); *m* 1959, Elizabeth Pamela de Bo (*née* Manasse), *d* of Fritz Manasse and Grace Manasse (*née* Howden); two *s* two *d*. *Edi* Newlands Sch.; Charterhouse. Literary Advr, Bodley Head, 1958–62; Sunday Tim (football correspondent), 1958–92; The People (sports columnist), 1992–96; The Tim (football writer), 1996–98; Sunday Times, 1998–. *Publications:* The Reluctant Dictato 1952; Henry Sows the Wind, 1954; Soccer Nemesis, 1955; Along the Arno, 1956; Tl Bankrupts, 1958; After Rome, Africa, 1959; A Bad Streak, 1961; Diamond, 1962; (e The Footballer's Companion, 1962; The Director's Wife, 1963; The King of Hackne Marshes, 1965; A Second Home, 1965; A Roman Marriage, 1966; The Artist Type, 196 The Olympian, 1969; A Cry of Crickets, 1970; The Financiers, 1972; The History of th World Cup, 1973; The Thing He Loves, 1973; The Comic, 1974; The Dying of th Light, 1976; Never Look Back, 1980; (jtly) Underneath The Arches (musical), 1981; Visit to the Villa (play), 1981; Kissing America, 1985; Love is Not Love, 1985; (ed) Tl Joy of Football, 1986; The Catacomb, 1988; Champions of Europe, 1991; Story of th World Cup, 1993; Football Memories, 1999; Dictators, 2001; The Arsenal Stadiu History, 2006; England's Managers, 2007; *juvenile:* Goalkeepers are Different (nove 1971; Target Man (novel), 1978; The Puffin Book of Football, 1978; The Puffin Book Tennis, 1981. *Address:* 160 Holland Park Avenue, W11 4UH. *T:* (020) 7603 6908.

GLANVILLE, Philippa Jane, FSA; Academic Director (formerly Director), Waddesdo Manor, Buckinghamshire, 1999–2003; *b* 16 Aug. 1943; *d* of late Wilfred Henry Fo Robinson and of Jane Mary (*née* Home); *m* 1968, Dr Gordon Harris Glanville; two *s*. *Edu* Talbot Heath, Bournemouth; Girton Coll., Cambridge (MA Hist.); University Co London (Archives Admin). FSA 1968. Tudor and Stuart Curator, London Mus., 1966–7 Hd, Tudor and Stuart Dept, Mus. of London, 1972–80; Victoria and Albert Museum: As Keeper, Metalwork Dept, 1980–89; Curator, 1989–96, Chief Curator, 1996–9 Metalwork, Silver and Jewellery Dept. Consultant Curator, Gilbert Collection, 2001–0 Sen. Res. Fellow, 2004–07; Guest Curator, Nat. Archives, Drink: a History, 200 Member: Council for Care of Churches, 1997–2001; Westminster Abbey Fabric Comm 1998–; Arts Council, Nat. Museums of Wales, 2002–. Trustee: Bishopsland Educnl Trus 2003–; Geffrye Mus., 2005–. Mem. Cttee, Court Dining Res. Gp, 1989–; contributo Henry VIII inventory project, 1992–. Associate Fellow, Univ. of Warwick, 2003–0 Liveryman, Co. of Goldsmiths, 1991–. Mem., Editl Bd, Apollo, 2004–. *Publication* London in Maps, 1972; Silver in England, 1987; Silver in Tudor and Early Stuart Englan 1990; (with J. Goldsborough) Women Silversmiths 1685–1845, 1991; (ed and contrib Silver, 1996, 2nd edn 1999; (ed with Hilary Young and contrib.) Elegant Eating, 200 (contrib.) City Merchants and the Arts 1670–1720, 2004; (contrib.) East Anglian Silv 1550–1750, 2004; (contrib.) Britannia and Muscovy, 2006; (contrib.) Feeding Desir 2006; The Art of Drinking, 2007; (contrib.) Quand Versailles était meublé, 200 (contrib.) Treasures of the Church, 2008; contrib. articles in Antiquaries Jl, Burlingto Mag., Silver Society Jl, etc, and in exhibn catalogues. *Address:* 144 Kew Road, Richmor TW9 2AU.

GLANVILLE-JONES, Thomas; *see* Jones.

GLASBY, (Alfred) Ian; HM Diplomatic Service, retired; *b* 18 Sept. 1931; *s* of Frederic William Glasby and Harriet Maria Glasby; *m* 1970, Herma Fletcher; one *d*. *Edi* Doncaster Grammar Sch.; London School of Economics and Political Science (BSc Served HM Forces, 1950–52. Home Office, 1952–68; Second Sec., CO, later FCC 1968–71; Second, later First Sec. (Commercial and Energy), Washington, 1971–76; De High Comr, Hd of Chancery and Consul, Kampala, 1976; Hd, British Interests Sect

French Embassy, Kampala, 1976–77; First Sec., Hd of Chancery and Consul, Yaoundé, 1977–81, concurrently non-resident Chargé d'Affaires, Central Afr. Empire, Gabon, and Equatorial Guinea; Asst Hd, Consular Dept, FCO, 1981–84; Dep. Consul Gen., Sydney, 1984–88; Ambassador to People's Republic of the Congo, 1988–90. Director: Trust Co. of Australia (UK) Ltd, 1990–2004; Truco (Australia) Europe Ltd, 1990–2004. Hon. Chevalier, Ordre de Mérite (Republique Populaire du Congo). *Recreations:* Rugby, cricket, gardening. *Address:* Longridge, 3 Love Lane, Shaftesbury, Dorset SP7 8BG. *T:* (01747) 850389; 5 rue du Collet, Spéracèdes, near Grasse 06530, France. *T:* 493605311. *Clubs:* Royal Commonwealth Society, Lansdowne; Australasian Pioneers, NSW Rugby (Sydney).

GLASBY, John Hamilton; Treasurer, Devon and Cornwall Police Authority, since 1993; *b* 29 March 1950; *s* of James Ronald Glasby and Lucie Lillian Glasby (*née* Baxter); *m* 1st, 1971 (marr. diss. 1989); two *s* one *d*; 2nd, 2003, Vivienne Amanda Lloyd. *Educ:* Univ. of Sheffield (BA); Univ. of Birmingham (MSocSc); Liverpool Poly. Mem., CIPFA, 1982. Lectr in Econs, Univ. of E Anglia, 1972–73; Economist: Central Lancs New Town, 1973–76; Shropshire CC, 1976–82; Asst Dir of Finance, Dudley Metropolitan Borough, 1982–84; Devon County Council: Dep. Co. Treas., 1984–93; Co. Treas., 1993–96; Dir of Resources, 1996–2000. Treasurer: Dartmoor Nat. Park Authy, 1997–2000; Devon Fire Authy, 1998–2000. *Recreation:* amateur author, academic and fiction. *Address:* Devon and Cornwall Police Authority, Endeavour House, Woodwater Park, Pynes Hill, Exeter, Devon EX2 5WH.

GLASCOCK, Prof. John Leslie, PhD; Grosvenor Professor of Real Estate Finance, University of Cambridge, and Fellow of Pembroke College, Cambridge, since 2003; *b* 2 Jan. 1950; *s* of Leslie Albert Glascock and Clara Jean Glascock; *m* 1961, Linda Diane Brown; one *s* three *d*. *Educ:* Tennessee Technol Univ. (BSc (Business Admin (Econs)) 1971); Stetson Univ. (MBA 1974); Virginia Poly. Inst. and State Univ. (MEc 1978); Univ. of N Texas (PhD (Finance) 1984). Louisiana Real Estate Commn Endowed Chr of Real Estate and Prof. of Finance, 1988–96, Interim Dean, 1994–95, Orso Coll. of Business Admin, Louisiana State Univ.; Prof. of Finance and Real Estate and Hd, Dept of Finance, Sch. of Business Admin, Univ. of Connecticut, 1996–98; Oliver T. Carr Dist. Prof. of Real Estate Finance, Sch. of Business and Public Mgt, 1998–2003, Associate Dean for Res. and Doctoral Progs, 2001–03, George Washington Univ. Sec.-Treas., Amer. Real Estate and Urban Econs Assoc., 1993–; Pres., Southwest Finance Assoc., 1996–97; Bd Mem., Asian Real Estate Soc., 1999–. Member Editorial Board: Jl of Real Estate Finance and Econs, 1992– (Special Issue Ed., March 2000); Jl of Real Estate Practice and Educn, 1998–. *Publications:* over 50 refereed articles in jls and numerous reports and monographs. *Recreations:* travel, reading. *Address:* Department of Land Economy, University of Cambridge, 19 Silver Street, Cambridge CB3 9EP. *T:* (01223) 360394; *e-mail:* jlg43@cam.ac.uk.

GLASER, Dr Daniel Eduard; Head of Special Projects, Public Engagement, Wellcome Trust, since 2007 (Development Manager, 2006–07); *b* 1 April 1968; *s* of Denis Victor Glaser and Danya Ruth Glaser (*née* Samson); *m* 1996, Nathalie Claire Bloomberg; two *d*. *Educ:* George Eliot Jun. Sch.; Jews' Free Sch.; Westminster Sch.; Trinity Coll., Cambridge (BA Pt 1 Pure Maths, Pt 2 English Lit 1990); Sussex Univ. (MSc Knowledge Based Systems 1991); Weizmann Inst., Rehovot, Israel (PhD Neurobiol. 1999). University College London: Res. Fellow, Inst. of Ophthalmol., 1999–2000; Sen. Res. Fellow, Inst. of Cognitive Neurosci., 2000–06; Hon. Sen. Res. Fellow, 2006–. Scientist in Residence, ICA, 2001–02; Chair, London Café Scientifique, 2002–. Presenter, Under Laboratory Conditions, BBC TV, 2006. Mem., Camden Cycling Campaign, 2000–. NESTA Cultural Leadership Award, Nassau, Bahamas, 2005. *Publications:* Trust Me I'm a Scientist, 2004; contrib. scientific papers on visual cortex, brain imaging techniques and effect of experience on vision. *Recreations:* fatherhood, restaurants, berating motorists, egosurfing. *Address:* Wellcome Trust, Gibbs Building, 215 Euston Road, NW1 2BE. *T:* (020) 7611 8888, *Fax:* (020) 7611 8545; *e-mail:* d.glaser@wellcome.ac.uk.

GLASER, Prof. Donald Arthur; Professor of Physics and of Neurobiology (formerly of Molecular and Cell Biology), University of California, since 1960; *b* 21 Sept. 1926; *s* of William Joseph and Lena Glaser. *Educ:* Case Institute of Technology (BS 1946); California Inst. of Technology (PhD 1950). University of Michigan: Instr. of Physics, 1949–53; Asst Prof., 1953–55; Associate Prof., 1955–57; Prof. of Physics, 1957–59; University of California, Berkeley: Vis. Prof., 1959–60; Prof. of Physics, 1960–; Miller Res. Biophysicist, 1962–64; Prof. of Molecular Biol., 1964–89. National Science Foundation Fellow, 1961; Guggenheim Fellow, 1961–62. Grass Award Lectr, Soc. for Neurosci., 2002. Member: National Academy of Sciences (USA), 1962; NY Acad. of Science; Fellow Amer. Physical Soc.; FAAAS. Hon. ScD: Case Inst., 1959; Michigan, 2002. Henry Russel Award, 1955; Charles Vernon Boys Prize, 1958; Amer. Phys. Soc. Prize, 1959; Nobel Prize for Physics, 1960. *Publications:* chapters in: Topics in the Biology of Aging, 1965; Biology and the Exploration of Mars, 1966; Frontiers of Pattern Recognition, 1972; New Approaches to the Identification of Microorganisms, 1975; articles in Physical Review, Handbuch der Physik, Jl Molecular Biol., Pattern Recognition and Image Processing, Somatic Cell Genetics, Cell Tissue Kinetics, Computers and Biomed. Res., Proc. Nat. Acad. of Scis (USA), Suppl. to Investigative Ophthalmol & Visual Sci., Jl Opt. Soc. of Amer. A, Vision Res., Visual Neurosci., Cell Biophys, Perception, Computational Neuroscience, Neurocomputing, etc. *Address:* Glaser Laboratory, Department of Molecular and Cell Biology, University of California, 237 Hildebrand Hall, Berkeley, CA 94720–3206, USA; 41 Hill Road, Berkeley, CA 94708, USA.

GLASER, Milton; graphic designer; *b* 26 June 1929; *s* of Eugene and Eleanor Glaser; *m* 1957, Shirley Girton. *Educ:* High Sch. of Music and Art, NY; Cooper Union Art Sch., NY; Acad. of Fine Arts, Bologna (Fulbright Schol.). Joint Founder: Pushpin Studios, 1954; New York mag., 1968 (Pres. and Design Dir, 1968–77); WBMG, pubn design co., 1983; Milton Glaser Inc., 1974; *projects* include: 600 foot mural, New Federal Office Building, Indianapolis, 1974; Observation Deck and Perm. Exhibn, Twin Towers, World Trade Center, NY, 1975; Sesame Place, Pennsylvania, 1981–83; Grand Union Co. architecture, interiors and packaging; Internat. AIDS symbol and poster, WHO, 1987; Trattoria dell'Arte, NY, 1988; New York Unearthed mus., 1990; *solo exhibitions* include: MOMA, NY, 1975; Centre Georges Pompidou, Paris, 1977; Lincoln Center Gall., NY, 1981; Posters, Vicenza Mus., 1989; Art Inst. of Boston, 1995; *work in public collections* including: MOMA, NY; Israel Mus., Jerusalem; Nat. Archive, Smithsonian Instn, Washington; Cooper Hewitt Nat. Design Mus., NY. Member: Bd, Sch. of Visual Arts, NY, 1961–; Bd of Dirs, Cooper Union, NY. Amer. Inst. of Graphic Arts. Gold Medal, Soc. of Illustrators; St Gauden's Medal, Cooper Union; Prix Savignac, Urban Art Internat. and UNESCO, 1996; Honors Award, AIA, 1992; Lifetime Achievement Award, Cooper Hewitt Nat. Design Mus., 2004. *Address:* Milton Glaser Inc., 207 East 32nd Street, New York, NY 10016, USA. *T:* (212) 8893161, *Fax:* (212) 2134072; *e-mail:* studio@miltonglaser.com.

GLASGOW, 10th Earl of, *cr* 1703; **Patrick Robin Archibald Boyle;** DL; Lord Boyle, 1699; Viscount of Kelburn, 1703; Baron Fairlie (UK), 1897; television director/producer;

b 30 July 1939; *s* of 9th Earl of Glasgow, CB, DSC, and Dorothea, *o d* of Sir Archibald Lyle, 2nd Bt; *S* father, 1984; *m* 1975, Isabel Mary James; one *s* one *d*. *Educ:* Eton; Paris Univ. National Service in Navy; Sub-Lt, RNR, 1959–60. Worked in Associated Rediffusion Television, 1961; worked at various times for Woodfall Film Productions; Asst on Film Productions, 1962–64; Asst Dir in film industry, 1962–67; producer/director of documentary films, Yorkshire TV, 1968–70; freelance film producer, 1971–, making network television documentaries for BBC Yorkshire Television, ATV and Scottish Television. Formed Kelburn Country Centre, May 1977, opening Kelburn estate and gardens in Ayrshire to the public. Elected Mem. (Lib Dem), H of L, Jan. 2005. DL Ayrshire and Arran, 1995. *Recreations:* ski-ing, theatre. *Heir: s* David Michael Douglas Boyle, *b* 15 Oct. 1978. *Address:* Kelburn, Fairlie, Ayrshire KA29 0BE. *T:* (01475) 568204; (office) South Offices, Kelburn Estate, Fairlie, Ayrshire KA29 0BE. *T:* (01475) 568685.

GLASGOW, Archbishop of, (RC), since 2002; **Most Rev. Mario Joseph Conti;** *b* Elgin, Moray, 20 March 1934; *s* of Louis Joseph Conti and Josephine Quintilia Panicali. *Educ:* St Marie's Convent School and Springfield, Elgin; Blairs Coll., Aberdeen; Pontifical Gregorian Univ. (Scots College), Rome. PhL 1955, STL 1959. FRSE 1995. Ordained, Rome, 1958; Curate, St Mary's Cathedral, Aberdeen, 1959–62; Parish Priest, St Joachim's, Wick and St Anne's, Thurso (joint charge), 1962–77; Bishop of Aberdeen, 1977–2002. Chairman: Scottish Catholic Heritage Commn, 1980–; Commn for the Pastoral Care of Migrant Workers and Tourists (incl. Apostleship of the Sea, Scotland), 1978–85; Pres.-Treasurer, Scottish Catholic Internat. Aid Fund, 1978–85; Pres., National Liturgy Commn, 1981–85; Scottish Mem., Episcopal Bd, Internat. Commn for English in the Liturgy, 1978–87; Mem., Bishops' Jt Bio-ethics Cttee (formerly Cttee for Bio-ethical Issues), 1982–; Pres., Nat. Christian Doctrine and Unity Commn, 1985–; Vice-Pres., Catholic Bishops' Conf. of Scotland, 2002–; Consultor-Mem., Secretariat, later Council, for Promotion of Christian Unity (Rome), 1984–; Convener, Action of Churches Together in Scotland, 1990–93; Co-moderator, Jt Working Gp, WCC and RC Church, 1996–2006; Member: Pontifical Commn for Cultural Heritage of the Church, Rome, 1994–2004; Historic Bldgs Council of Scotland, 2000–03. Conventual Chaplain *ad honorem,* British Assoc., SMO Malta, 1991– (Principal Chaplain, 1995–2000, 2005–). Hon. DD Aberdeen, 1989. KCHS 1989. Commendatore, Order of Merit of the Italian Republic, 1981; Grande Ufficiale, Ordine della Stella della Solidarietà Italiana, 2007. *Publications:* Oh Help!: the making of an Archbishop, 2003; numerous articles in defence of the tradition of faith and Christian morality. *Recreations:* music, art, book browsing, TV, travel, swimming. *Address:* 40 Newlands Road, Glasgow G43 2JD. *T:* (office) (0141) 226 5898, *Fax:* (0141) 225 2600.

GLASGOW, (St Mary's Cathedral), Provost of; *see* Holdsworth, Very Rev. K.

GLASGOW, Edwin John, CBE 1998; QC 1987; *b* 3 Aug. 1945; *s* of late Richard Edwin, (Dick), Glasgow and Diana Geraldine Mary Glasgow (*née* Markby); *m* 1967, Janet Coleman; one *s* one *d*. *Educ:* St Joseph's Coll., Ipswich; University Coll. London (LLB; Fellow, 2004). Called to the Bar, Gray's Inn, 1969, Bencher, 1994. Mem., Internat. Court of Appeal, Fedn Internat. de l'Automobile, 2005–. Chm., Stafford Corporate Consulting, 2000–. Chairman: Financial Reporting Review Panel, 1992–97; Advocacy Teaching Council, 2005–08. Member: Adv. Council, Public Concern at Work, 2001– (Trustee, 1994–); Le Demi-Siècle de Londres, 2002–. Chm., Bentham Club, UCL, 2000–; Trustee: Mary Glasgow Language Trust, 1984– (Chm., 1984–); London Opera Players, 1985–. *Recreations:* family, friends, France, music. *Address:* 39 Essex Street, WC2R 3AT. *T:* (020) 7832 1111; Copper Hall, Watts Road, Thames Ditton, Surrey KT7 0BX; Entrechaux, Vaucluse, France. *Clubs:* Garrick, Royal Automobile (Chm. Stewards, 2005–); Harlequins FC (Chm. Trustees, 1995–2004); Thames Ditton Cricket (Vice-Pres., 2001–).

GLASGOW AND GALLOWAY, Bishop of, since 1998; **Most Rev. Dr Idris Jones;** Primus of the Episcopal Church in Scotland, since 2006; *b* 2 April 1943; *s* of Edward Eric Jones and Alice Gertrude (*née* Burgess); *m* 1973, Alison Margaret Williams; two *s*. *Educ:* St David's Coll., Lampeter, Univ. of Wales (BA; Hon. Fellow 2007); Univ. of Edinburgh (LTh); NY Theol Seminary (DMin 1987); Dip. Person Centred Therapy 1994. Curate, St Mary, Stafford, 1967–70; Precentor, Dundee Cathedral, 1970–73; Team Vicar, St Hugh, Gosforth, 1973–80; Chaplain, St Nicholas Hosp. (Teaching), 1975–80; Rector, Montrose with Inverbervie, 1980–89; Canon, St Paul's Cathedral, Dundee, 1984–92; Anglican Chaplain, Dundee Univ. and Priest-in-Charge, Invergowrie, 1989–92; Team Rector, Ayr, Girvan, Maybole, 1992–98; Dir, Pastoral Studies, Theol Inst., Edinburgh, 1995–98. Lay Psychotherapist: Dundee, 1990–92; Ayr, 1995–98. Gov., Hutcheson's Educnl Trust, 2002–. Patron, Hutcheson's Hosp., Glasgow, 2002–. Member: Glasgow XIII Club; Incorpn of Skinners & Glovers of Glasgow, 1999–. *Recreations:* walking, golf, music. *Address:* Bishop's Office, Diocesan Centre, 5 St Vincent Place, Glasgow G1 2DH.

GLASGOW AND GALLOWAY, Dean of; *see* Duncan, Very Rev. G. D.

GLASHOW, Prof. Sheldon Lee, PhD; Metcalf Professor of Mathematics and Science, Boston University, since 2000; Higgins Professor of Physics, Harvard University, 1979–2000, now Emeritus (Professor of Physics, 1966–84); *b* 5 Dec. 1932; *s* of Lewis and Bella Glashow; *m* 1972, Joan (*née* Alexander); three *s* one *d*. *Educ:* Cornell Univ. (AB); Harvard Univ. (AM, PhD). National Science Foundn Fellow, Copenhagen and Geneva, 1958–60; Res. Fellow, Calif Inst. of Technol., 1960–61; Asst Prof., Stanford Univ., 1961–62; Associate Prof., Univ. of Calif at Berkeley, 1962–66. Visiting Professor: CERN, 1968; Marseille, 1971; MIT, 1974 and 1980; Boston Univ., 1983; Univ. Schol., Texas A&M Univ., 1983–86. Consultant, Brookhaven Nat. Lab., 1966–80; Affiliated Senior Scientist, Univ. of Houston, 1983–96. Pres., Sakharov Internat. Cttee, Washington, 1980–85. Hon. DSc: Yeshiva, 1978; Aix-Marseille, 1982. Nobel Prize for Physics (jtly), 1979. *Publications:* (jtly) Interactions, 1988; The Charm of Physics, 1990; From Alchemy to Quarks, 1994; articles in learned jls. *Recreations:* scuba diving, tennis. *Address:* Department of Physics, 590 Commonwealth Avenue, Boston, MA 02215, USA; 30 Prescott Street, Brookline, MA 02446, USA.

GLASS, Anthony Trevor; QC 1986; a Recorder of the Crown Court, 1985–2005; *b* 6 June 1940. *Educ:* Royal Masonic School; Lincoln College, Oxford (MA). Called to the Bar, Inner Temple, 1965, Bencher, 1995. *Address:* Queen Elizabeth Building, Temple, EC4Y 9BS. *T:* (020) 7583 5766. *Club:* Garrick.

GLASS, Norman Jeffrey, CB 2000; Chief Executive, National Centre for Social Research, since 2001; *b* 31 May 1946; *s* of Philip Harris Glass and Anne (*née* Stein); *m* 1974, Marie-Anne Verger; one *s* one *d*. *Educ:* Trinity Coll., Dublin (BA); Univ. of Amsterdam (Post Grad. Dip). Shell Mex and BP, 1969–70; Economic Models Ltd, 1970–72; Lectr, Univ. of Newcastle upon Tyne, 1972–74; Res. Scholar, Internat. Inst. for Applied Systems Analysis, Vienna, 1974–75; Economic Adviser: DHSS, 1975–77; HM Treasury, 1977–79; Exchequer and Audit Dept, 1979–81; Sen. Econ. Advr, DHSS, 1981–86; Asst Sec., DoH, 1986–89; Dir, Analytical Services, DSS, 1989–92; Chief Economist, DoE, 1992–95; Dep. Dir (Micro-econs), HM Treasury, 1995–2001. Chm., Economic Policy Cttee, EU, 1999–2001 (Vice-Chm., 1997–99). Non-exec. Dir, Govt Offices for the Regions Bd, 2002–04. Board Member: Countryside Agency, 2003–06;

Skillforce, 2004–06; Commn for Rural Communities, 2006–. Chairman: High/Scope UK, 2001–06; Capacity, 2004–06. *Publications:* articles on social policy. *Recreations:* music, languages, gardening. *Address:* National Centre for Social Research, 35 Northampton Square, EC1V 0AX.

GLASS, Philip; American composer and performer; *b* 31 Jan. 1937; *s* of Benjamin Glass and Ida Glass (*née* Gouline); *m* 1st, JoAnne Akalaitis; one *s* one *d*; 2nd, Luba Burtyk; 3rd, Candy Jernigan; 4th, Holly Critchlow. *Educ:* Peabody Conservatory; Univ. of Chicago; Juilliard Sch. of Music. Has worked as a taxi-driver, plumber and furniture mover. Composer-in-Residence, Pittsburgh Public Schs, 1962–64; studied with Nadia Boulanger, Paris, 1964–66; Musical Dir, Mabou Mines Co., 1965–74; Founder: Philip Glass Ensemble, 1968; record companies: Chatham Square Productions, 1972; Point Music, 1991; music publishers: Dunvagen, Inc., 1982. *Compositions include: operas:* Einstein on the Beach, 1976; Satyagraha, 1980; The Photographer, 1982; The Civil Wars, 1984; Akhnaten, 1984; The Juniper Tree, 1986; The Making of the Representative for Planet 8, 1986; The Fall of the House of Usher, 1988; 1000 Airplanes on the Roof, 1988; The Hydrogen Jukebox, 1990; White Raven, 1991; The Voyage, 1992; Orphée, 1993; La Belle et la Bête, 1994; Les Enfants Terribles, 1996; Monsters of Grace, 1998; Galileo Galilei, 2002; Appomattox, 2007; *film scores:* Koyaanisqatsi, 1982; Mishima (Cannes Special Jury Prize), 1985; Powaqqatsi, 1987; The Thin Blue Line, 1989; Hamburger Hill, 1989; Mindwalk, 1990; A Brief History of Time, 1991; Anima Mundi, 1991; Candyman, 1992; Compassion in Exile, 1992; Candyman II, 1995; Jenipapo, 1995; Secret Agent, 1995; Bent, 1998; Kundun, 1998; The Truman Show (Golden Globe award for best score), 1998; Dracula, 1998; Naqoyqatsi, 2001; The Man in the Bath, 2001; Notes, 2001; Passage, 2001; Diaspora, 2001; The Hours, 2003; Taking Lives, 2004; Secret Windows, 2004; Notes on a Scandal, 2007; *theatre music:* Endgame, 1984; Cymbeline, 1989; (with Foday Musa Suso) The Screens, 1990; Henry IV, 1992; Woyzeck (Drama Desk Award), 1992; The Mysteries & What's So Funny?, 1992; In the Penal Colony, 2000; The Elephant Man, 2002; *dance music:* In the Upper Room, 1986; Witches of Venice, 1995; *instrumental works:* String Quartet no 1, 1966; Piece in the Shape of a Square, 1967; Strung Out, 1969; Music in Similar Motion, 1969; Music in Fifths, 1969; Music with Changing Parts, 1970; Music in Twelve Parts, 1974; Another Look at Harmony, 1974; North Star, 1977; Modern Love Waltz, 1979; Dance nos 1–5, 1979; Company, 1983; String Quartet no 2, 1983; String Quartet no 3, 1985; Songs from Liquid Days, 1986; Violin Concerto, 1987; The Light, 1987; Itaipu, 1988; Canyon, 1988; String Quartet no 4, 1989; Solo Piano, 1989; (with Ravi Shankar) Passages, 1990; String Quartet no 5, 1991; Low Symphony, 1992; Mato Grosso, 1992; Symphony no 2, 1994, no 3, 1995; Heroes Symphony, 1996; Symphony no 5, 1999; Concerto Fantasy, 2000; Concerto for Cello and Orchestra, 2001; Symphony no 6 (Plutonian Ode), 2001; Voices for Organ, Didgeridoo and Narrator, 2001; Dancissimo, 2001. Numerous awards and prizes, including: Benjamin Award, 1961; Fulbright Award, 1966–67. Officer, Order of Arts and Letters (France), 1995. *Publication:* Music by Philip Glass, ed R. T. Jones, 1987. *Address:* c/o Dunvagen Music Publishers, 632 Broadway, 9th Floor, New York, NY 10012, USA.

GLASSCOCK, John Lewis, FCIS; Director, British Aerospace PLC, 1982–87; *b* 12 July 1928; *s* of Edgar Henry and Maude Allison Glasscock; *m* 1959, Anne Doreen Baker; two *s*. *Educ:* Tiffin Sch.; University Coll. London (BA Hons). Served Royal Air Force, 1950–53. Joined Hawker Aircraft Ltd, 1953, Asst Sec., 1956, Commercial Man., 1961; Hawker Siddeley Aviation Ltd: Divl Commercial Man., 1964; Dir and Gen. Man. (Kingston), 1965–77; British Aerospace Aircraft Group: Admin. Dir, 1978; Commercial Dir, 1979; Man. Dir (Military), 1981; BAe PLC: Dep. Chief Exec., Aircraft Gp, and Man. Dir, Civil Aircraft Div., 1982–85; Commercial Dir, 1986–87. Mem. Supervisory Bd, Airbus Industrie, 1983–85. Mem. Council, SBAC, 1979–87. *Recreation:* golf. *Address:* West Meadow, The Wedges, Itchingfield, near Horsham, W Sussex RH13 0TA. *Clubs:* MCC, Royal Automobile.

GLASSER, Cyril, CMG 1999; Consultant, Sheridans, Solicitors, since 2001; *b* 31 Jan. 1942; *s* of late Phillip and Eva Glasser. *Educ:* Raine's Foundn Grammar Sch., London; London Sch. of Econs (LLB 1963; LLM 1966). Admitted solicitor, 1967; Sheridans, Solicitors: Partner, 1977–2001; Hd, Litigation Dept, 1977–99; Managing Partner, 1989–2001; Sen. Partner, 2001. Consultant on solicitors' costs to NBPI, 1967; Co-founder and Dir, Legal Action Gp, 1972–74; Legal Advr to ANC during Commn on Rhodesian Opinion, 1972; attached to Lord Chancellor's Dept as Special Consultant, Legal Aid Adv. Cttee, 1974–77. Vis. Prof. of Law, UCL, 1987–. Mem., Wkg Party to Review Legal Aid Legislation, 1974–77; Chm., Legal Aid Provisions Wkg Party, 1975–77; Mem., Social Scis and the Law Cttee, SSRC, 1979–83. Mem. Council, Law Soc., 1997–2001; Dir, Law Soc. Trustees Ltd, 1999–2005. Mem., Jt Tribunal on Barristers' Fees, 1998–2001. Advr, Experts' Cttee on Efficiency of Justice, Council of Europe, 1998–2000. Trustee, Legal Assistance Trust, 1985–2004. FRSA 1995; Fellow, Soc. Advanced Legal Studies, 1998. Member: Legal Practice Course Bd, 1999–2005 (Vice-Chm., 2000–01); Bar/Law Soc. Jt Academic Stage Bd, 2004–05; Common Professional Examination Bd, 2003–05 (Chm., 2004–06). Member: Mgt Cttee, Inst. Judicial Admin, Birmingham Univ., 1984–; Adv. Bd, Centre of Advanced Litigation, Nottingham Trent Univ., 1991–2002; Gov., 1996–, Mem. Council, 1999–2005, LSE. Member, Editorial Board: Modern Law Rev., 1992–; Internat. Jl Evidence and Proof, 1996–2002; Mem., Editl Adv. Bd, Litigator, 1994–98. Hon. LLD London Guildhall, 2002. *Publications:* contribs to legal jls, books, etc. *Address:* Sheridans, Whittington House, Alfred Place, WC1E 7EA. *T:* (020) 7079 0100.

GLASSER, Prof. Stanley; Head of Music, 1969–91, (first) Professor of Music, 1990–91, Goldsmiths' College, University of London, now Emeritus Professor; composer, ethnomusicologist and music consultant; *b* 28 Feb. 1926; *s* of Joe Glasser and Assia (*née* Kagan); *m* 1st 1951, Mona Vida Schwartz (marr. diss. 1965); one *s* one *d*; 2nd, 1971, Elizabeth Marianne Aylwin; two *s*. *Educ:* King Edward VII High Sch., Johannesburg; Univ. of the Witwatersrand (BComm (Econ) 1949); studied composition with Benjamin Frankel, 1950–52, Matyas Seiber, 1952–55; ethnomusicology res. under Dr Hugh Tracey, Internat. Liby of African Music, 1954–55; King's Coll., Cambridge (Music Tripos 1958; MA 1960). Music Dir, King Kong (African musical), 1958–60; Lectr and Asst Dir, Music Dept, Univ. of Cape Town, 1959–63; Music Critic, Cape Times, 1959–62; Goldsmiths' College, University of London: Music Tutor, Dept of Adult Studies, 1963–65; Lectr, 1966–69; established 1st UK electronic music teaching studio, 1971; Chm., Bd of Studies in Music, Univ. of London, 1981–83. Ext. examnr, univs and music colls, 1973–. Reader, CUP, 1981–83. Composer-in-residence, Standard Bank Nat. Arts Fest., 2001. Mem. and Treas., Internat. Cttee, ISCM, 1951–55; Chairman: Composers' Guild of GB, 1975; UK Br., Internat. Cttee for Traditional Music, 1979–84; and Trustee, Dagarti Arts, 1996–2005; Founder and Trustee, Rand Educn Fund, 1964–98; Trustee, Classic FM Charitable Trust, 1994–2002; Academic Governor, Richmond, American Internat. Univ. in London, 1980–; Music Consultant to Nat. Council for Culture, Arts & Letters, Kuwait, 1994–2004. Vis. Prof., Univ. of KwaZulu Natal, 2007. Hon. Fellow, Goldsmiths Coll., 2001. Hon. DMus Richmond, American Internat. Univ., 1997. Royal Philharmonic Soc. Prizeman, 1952; George Richards Prize, King's Coll., Cambridge, 1958; Kathleen Gurner Award, Goldsmiths' Coll., 1998. *Compositions include:* The Square (full-length ballet), 1961; Mr. Paljas (musical comedy, lyrics by Beryl Bloom), 1962; The Chameleon and Th Lizard (choral, Zulu text by Lewis Nkosi), 1973; The Gift (one-act comic chamber opera libretto by Ronald Duncan), 1976; Lalela Zulu (a cappella male sextet, Zulu poems b Lewis Nkosi), 1977; The Ward (song cycle, poems by Ronald Duncan), 198 Zonkizizwe (large choir, wind band and percussion, text by composer), 1991; Magnifica & Nunc Dimittis (chapel double choir a cappella), 1995; Ezra (sacred drama, text b Elisabeth Ingles), 1996; Noon (tone poem for orch.), 1997; A Greenwich Symphon (choir and orch., text by Elisabeth Ingles), 1999; Concerto for flugelhorn and chambe orch., 2001, revd 2004; The Planet of Love (text by Adolf Wood), 2002; Celebratio Dances (sinfonia and choir), 2002; Lewisham Hero (theatrical entertainment), 200 Crossroads (clarinet and piano), 2003; Insumansemane (a capella male sextet), 2005; Karo (for large orch.), 2008. *Publications:* (with Adolf Wood) 100 Songs of Southern Afric 1968; (contrib.) The New Grove Dictionary of Music and Musicians, 7th edn 1980; Th A-Z of Classical Music, 1994; various articles and reviews on music. *Recreations:* dinin with family and friends, Walt Kelly's Pogo Possum books, cowboy films. *Address:* c/ Woza Music, 46 Weigall Road, SE12 8HE. *T:* (020) 8852 1997. *Club:* Oxford an Cambridge.

GLASTONBURY, Virginia; Partner, Denton Wilde Sapte (formerly Denton Hall) LL Solicitors, since 1988; *b* 25 Feb. 1957; *d* of Rt Hon. Sir Frank Cooper, GCB, CMG, P and Lady Cooper (Peggie); *m* 1980, Richard Glastonbury; one step *s*. *Educ:* Bromley Hig Sch.; LMH, Oxford (BA (Modern Hist.) 1978). Admitted solicitor, 1982; Managin Partner, Denton Hall, 1999–2000; Man. Partner UK, 2000–02, Chief Exec., 2002–0 Denton Wilde Sapte. FRSA 2003; MInstD. *Recreations:* motor racing, cars, trave grandchildren. *Address:* Denton Wilde Sapte LLP, One Fleet Place, EC4M 7WS; *e-mai* virginia.glastonbury@dentonwildesapte.com.

GLAUBER, Prof. Roy Jay, PhD; Mallinckrodt Professor of Physics, Harvard Universit since 1976; *b* 1 Sept. 1925; *s* of Emanuel B. Glauber and Felicia Glauber (*née* Fox); *m* 196 Cynthia Marshall Rich (marr. diss. 1976); one *s* one *d*. *Educ:* Harvard University (B Physics 1946, MA 1947; PhD 1949). Staff mem., Theoretical Physics Div., Los Alamo New Mexico, 1944–46; Mem., Inst. for Advanced Study, Princeton, NJ, 1949–51; Re Fellow, Swiss Fed. Polytech. Dist., Zürich, 1950; Lectr, CIT, 1951–52; Harvar University: Lectr, 1952–53; Asst Prof., 1953–56; Associate Prof., 1956–62; Prof. Physics, 1962–76. Member: Amer. Acad. Arts and Scis; NAS; Royal Soc. NZ; Foreig Mem., Royal Soc., 1997. Member: Phi Beta Kappa; Sigma Xi. Max Born Award, Ame Optical Soc., 1985; (jtly) Nobel Prize in Physics, 2005. *Publications:* Quantum Theory Optical Coherence, 2006; numerous chapters in books, and articles in scientific jl *Recreation:* gardening. *Address:* Department of Physics, Lyman 331, Harvard University, 1 Oxford Street, Cambridge, MA 02138, USA. *T:* (617) 4952869, *Fax:* (617) 495041 *e-mail:* glauber@physics.harvard.edu. *Club:* Shop (Harvard Univ.).

GLAUERT, Audrey Marion, ScD; Fellow of Clare Hall, University of Cambridge, sinc 1966; Head of Electron Microscopy Department, Strangeways Research Laborator Cambridge, 1956–89 (Associate Director, 1979–85); *b* 21 Dec. 1925; *d* of late Herman Glauert, FRS and Muriel Glauert (*née* Barker); *m* 1959, David Franks (marr. diss. 1979 *Educ:* Perse Sch. for Girls, Cambridge; Bedford Coll., Univ. of London. BSc 1946, MS 1947, London; MA Cantab 1967, ScD Cantab 1970. Asst Lectr in Physics, Roya Holloway Coll., Univ. of London, 1947–50; Mem. Scientific Staff, Strangeways Re Lab., Cambridge, Sir Halley Stewart Research Fellow, 1950–89. Chairman: British Joi Cttee for Electron Microscopy, 1968–72; Fifth European Congress on Electro Microscopy, 1972; Pres., Royal Microscopical Soc., 1970–72, Hon. Fellow, 1973. Hon Member: French Soc. for Electron Microscopy, 1967; Microscopy (formerly Electro Microscopy) Soc. of America, 1990 (Dist. Scientist Award for Biol. Scis, 1990). J Cambridge, 1975–88. Editor: Practical Methods in Electron Microscopy, 1972–99; Jl Microscopy, Royal Microscopical Soc., 1986–88. *Publications:* Fixation Dehydration an Embedding of Biological Specimens, 1974; (ed) The Control of Tissue Damage, 198 Biological Specimen Preparation for Transmission Electron Microscopy, 1998; papers o cell and molecular biology in scientific jls. *Recreations:* sailing, gardening, working fo prison reform. *Address:* 29 Cow Lane, Fulbourn, Cambridge CB21 5HB. *T:* (0122 880463; Clare Hall, Herschel Road, Cambridge CB3 9AL; *e-mail:* amg44@cam.ac.uk.

GLAVES-SMITH, Frank William, CB 1975; Deputy Director-General of Fair Tradin 1973–79, retired; *b* 27 Sept. 1919; *m* 1st, 1941, Audrey Glaves (*d* 1989); one *s* one *d*; 2n 1990, Ursula Mary Murray. *Educ:* Malet Lambert High Sch., Hull. War Service, 1940–4 (Captain, Royal Signals). Called to the Bar, Middle Temple, 1947. Board of Trade, 194 Princ. Private Sec. to Pres. of Bd of Trade, 1952–57; Asst Secretary: HM Treasur 1957–60; Cabinet Office, 1960–62; Bd of Trade, 1962–65; Under-Sec., BoT, 1965–6 Dept of Employment and Productivity, 1969–70, DTI, 1970–73; Dep. Sec., 1975. Mem Export Guarantees Adv. Council, 1971–73. *Recreation:* fell-walking. *Address:* 8 Grang Park, Keswick, Cumbria CA12 4AY.

GLAVIN, William Francis; President, Babson College, Wellesley, Mass, 1989–96; *b* 2 March 1932; *m* 1955, Cecily McClatchy; three *s* four *d*. *Educ:* College of the Holy Cros Worcester, Mass (BS); Wharton Graduate Sch. (MBA). Vice-Pres., Operations, Servic Bureau Corp. (subsid. of IBM), 1968–70; Exec. Vice-Pres., Xerox Data Services, 197 Pres., Xerox Data Systems, 1970–72; Gp Vice-Pres., Xerox Corp., and Pres., Busine Development Gp, 1972–74; Rank Xerox Ltd: Man. Dir, 1974–80; Chief Operatin Officer, 1974–77; Chief Exec. Officer, 1977–80; Xerox Corp.: Exec. Vice-Pres. Chie Staff Officer, 1980–82; President: Reprographics and Ops, 1982–83; Business Equipme Gps, 1983–89 (Vice Chm., 1985–89). *Recreations:* golf, music, boating, tennis. *Address:* c/ Babson College, Babson Park, Wellesley, MA 02157, USA.

GLAZEBROOK, (Reginald) Mark; writer, curator, painter and lecturer on art; *b* 2 June 1936; *s* of late Reginald Field Glazebrook; *m* 1st, 1965, Elizabeth Lea Claridge (marr diss. 1969); one *d*; 2nd, 1974, Wanda Barbara O'Neill (*née* Osińska) (marr. diss. 2000); on *d*; 3rd, 2004, Cherry Moorsom (*née* Long Price). *Educ:* Eton; Pembroke Coll., Cambridg (MA); Slade School of Fine Art. Worked at Arts Council, 1961–64; Lectr at Maidston Coll. of Art, 1965–67; Art Critic, London Magazine, 1967–68; Dir, Whitechapel A Gall., 1969–71; Head of Modern English Paintings and Drawings, P. and D. Colnaghi & Co. Ltd, 1973–75; Gallery Director and Art History Lectr, San José State Univ., 1977–7 Dir, Albemarle Gall. Ltd, London, 1986–93. One-man exhibn, Mayor Gall., London 2000. FRSA 1971. *Publications:* (comp.) Artists and Architecture of Bedford Par 1875–1900 (catalogue), 1967; (comp.) David Hockney: paintings, prints and drawing 1960–1970 (catalogue), 1970; Edward Wadsworth 1889–1949: paintings, prints an drawings (catalogue), 1974; (introduction) John Armstrong 1893–1973 (catalogue), 197 (introduction) John Tunnard (catalogue), 1976; Sean Scully (catalogue), 1997; articles i London Magazine, Modern Painters, Royal Acad. Magazine, Spectator. *Recreations* cooking, cinema, swimming. *Address:* Flat 1, 28 Draycott Place, SW3 2SB. *Club* Beefsteak, Chelsea Arts, Lansdowne.

GLAZIER, John Francis, PhD; Principal, King Edward VI College, Stourbridg 2001–08; *b* 18 July 1950; *s* of Derrick Robert Glazier and Joan Agnes Glazier; *m* 1st, 1971

Marianne Frances Iszatt (marr. diss. 1992); three *d*; one *d*; 2nd, 1992, Janet Eileen Parnell (*née* Sykes); one step *s* one step *d*. *Educ:* Univ. of Leicester (BSc 1971); Nottingham Univ. (PhD 1978). Physics Lectr, Boston Coll., 1975–93; Hd of Dept, Telford Coll. of Arts and Technol., 1993–96; Rutland College: Vice Principal, 1996–97; Principal, 1997–2001. *Publication:* contrib. Qly Jl of RMetS. *Recreations:* hill walking, music, reading, foreign holidays, visiting art galleries, watching any sport on television, attending the local jazz club where I am one of the few not to pay a concessionary fee! *Address:* 27 Stourton Crescent, Stourbridge, West Midlands DY7 6RR. *T:* (01384) 878868; *e-mail:* jfglazier@yahoo.co.uk.

GLEDHILL, Anthony John, GC 1967; Divisional Auditor, NWS plc, 1993–97; *b* 10 March 1938; *s* of Harold Victor and Marjorie Edith Gledhill; *m* 1958, Marie Lilian Hughes; one *s* one *d*. *Educ:* Doncaster Technical High Sch., Yorks. Accounts Clerk, Officers' Mess, RAF Bruggen, Germany, 1953–56. Metropolitan Police: Cadet, 1956–57; Police Constable, 1957–75; Detective Sergeant, 1976–87; Investigator, PO Investigation Dept, 1987–88. Treas., Victoria Cross and George Cross Assoc. *Recreations:* golf, bowls, DIY, philately.

GLEDHILL, Rt Rev. Jonathan Michael; *see* Lichfield, Bishop of.

GLEDHILL, Keith Ainsworth, MBE 1994; Vice Lord-Lieutenant of Lancashire, 2002–05; President, Gledhill Water Storage Ltd, since 1998; *b* 28 Aug. 1932; *s* of Norman Gledhill and Louise (*née* Ainsworth); *m* 1956, Margaret Irene Burton; one *s*. *Educ:* Arnold Sch., Blackpool. Jun. Officer, MN, 1950–54; Nat. Service, RAF, 1954–56. Dir, Norman Gledhill & Co. Ltd, 1956–65; Sen. Exec., Delta Metal Gp, 1965–72; Founder, Gledhill Water Storage Ltd, 1972. Director: Nu-Rad Ltd, 1974–89; Thermalsense Ltd, 1978–82. Vice Chm., Blackpool Fylde & Wyre Soc. for the Blind, 1990–; Chm., Foxton Trust, 1992–. Mem. Council, Blackburn Cathedral, 2000–. Gov., Skelton Bounty, 1988–. FInstD 1968; MInstP 1970. DL 1986, High Sheriff, 1992–93, Lancs. Freeman, City of London, 1992; Liveryman, Co. of Plumbers, 1992–. KStJ 2002. *Recreations:* golf, travel. *Address:* c/o Gledhill Water Storage Ltd, Sycamore Estate, Squires Gate, Blackpool, Lancs FY4 3RL. *T:* (01253) 474431; *e-mail:* keithg@gledhill.net; 35 South Park Drive, Blackpool, Lancs FY3 9PZ. *T:* (01253) 764462. *Clubs:* Royal Lytham & St Anne's Golf; Fylde Rugby Union Football.

GLEDHILL, Michael Geoffrey James; QC 2001; **His Honour Judge Gledhill;** a Circuit Judge, since 2008; *b* 28 Dec. 1954; *s* of Geoffrey Gledhill and L. Barbara Gledhill (*née* Haigh); *m* 1988, Elizabeth Ann Miller Gordon. *Educ:* Christ Church, Oxford (MA Juris.). Called to the Bar, Middle Temple, 1976, Bencher, 2007; Asst Recorder, 1995–98; Recorder, 1998–2008; Hd of Chambers, 2 Dyers Buildings, 2002–08. Dep. Chancellor, Dio. of Salisbury, 2007. *Address:* Southwark Crown Court, 1 English Grounds, SE1 2HU.

GLEDHILL, Ruth; Religion Correspondent, The Times, since 1990; *b* 15 Dec. 1959; *d* of Rev. Peter Gledhill and Bridget Mary Gledhill (*née* Rathbone), Anglesey, N Wales; *m* 1st, 1989, John Edward Stammers (marr. diss. 1994); 2nd, 1996, Andrew Daniels (marr. diss. 2003); 3rd, 2006, Alan Lewis Duder Franks; one *s*. *Educ:* Thomas Alleyne's GS, Uttoxeter; London Coll. of Printing (HND); Birkbeck Coll., London (Cert. Religious Studies). With Uttoxeter Advertiser news service, 1980–81; Australasian Printer, Sydney, 1981–82; indentured, Birmingham Post & Mail, 1982–84; Industrial corresp., Birmingham Post, 1984; gen. news reporter and feature writer, Daily Mail, 1984–87; The Times: Home News Reporter, 1987–90; columnist, At Your Service, 1993–; also writer on dance sport for sports pages, 1997–; occasional corresp. on religion and new technology for Interface, 1998–2001. Guest presenter: Good Worship Guide, Yorks TV, 1996; ITV Sunday Worship, 1999. Member: IJA Commn on Rise of Neo-Fascism, 1993; BBC Governors' Independent Advice Panel: Religious Programmes, 1998. Mem., London Rotary, 1997–. *Publications:* (jtly) Birmingham is Not a Boring City, 1984; (ed and introd.) The Times Book of Best Sermons, annually 1995–2001; At A Service Near You, 1996; (ed) The Times Book of Prayers, 1997. *Recreations:* playing with my son, playing the guitar, reading and writing fiction. *Address:* The Times, 1 Pennington Street, E98 1TT. *T:* (020) 7782 5001, (home) (020) 8948 5871; *e-mail:* ruth.gledhill@thetimes.co.uk. *Club:* Reform.

GLEES, Ann Margaret; *see* Jefferson, A. M.

GLEESON, Hon. Anthony Murray, AC 1992 (AO 1986); Chief Justice of Australia, 1998–2008; *b* 30 Aug. 1938; *s* of Leo John Gleeson and Rachel Alice Gleeson; *m* 1965, Robyn Paterson; one *s* three *d*. *Educ:* St Joseph's Coll., Hunters Hill; Univ. of Sydney (BA, LLB). Called to the NSW Bar, 1963; QC 1974. Tutor in Law, St Paul's Coll., Sydney Univ., 1963–65; Part-time Lectr in Company Law, Sydney Univ., 1965–74. Chief Justice of NSW, 1988–98; Lt-Gov., NSW, 1989–98. Pres., Judicial Commn, NSW, 1988–98. Mem., Perm. Court of Arbitrators, 1999. Mem. Council, NSW Bar Assoc., 1979–85 (Pres., 1984 and 1985). Hon. Bencher, Middle Temple, 1989. Hon. LLD Sydney, 1999; DUniv: Griffith, 2001; Aust. Catholic Univ., 2005. *Recreations:* tennis, ski-ing. *Address:* c/o High Court of Australia, Parkes Place, Parkes, ACT 2600, Australia. *Club:* Australian (Sydney).

GLEESON, Dermot James; non-executive Chairman, M. J. Gleeson Group plc, since 2005 (Executive Chairman, 1998–2005); a Trustee, BBC Trust, since 2007 (a Governor, BBC, 2000–06); *b* 5 Sept. 1949; *s* of late Patrick Joseph Gleeson and Margaret Mary Gleeson (*née* Higgins); *m* 1980, Rosalind Mary Catherine Moorhead; one *s* one *d*. *Educ:* Downside; Fitzwilliam Coll., Cambridge (MA). Conservative Res. Dept, 1974–77; Mem., Cabinet of C. Tugendhat, EC, 1977–79; EEC Rep., Brussels, Midland Bank, 1979–81; Dep. Man. Dir, 1982–88, Chief Exec., 1988–98, M. J. Gleeson Gp plc. Chm., Major Contractors Gp, 2003–05. Mem. Bd, Housing Corp., 1986–92; Dir, CITB, 1996–2002. Trustee: Inst. of Cancer Res., 2006–; Fitzwilliam Mus. Develt Trust, 2006–. *Recreation:* family life, especially in the Outer Hebrides. *Address:* Hook Farm, White Hart Lane, Wood Street Village, Guildford, Surrey GU3 3EA. *Clubs:* Beefsteak (Chm., 2004–07), Royal Automobile.

GLEESON, Judith Amanda Jane Coomber; Senior Immigration Judge, Asylum and Immigration Tribunal (formerly a Vice President, Immigration Appeal Tribunal), since 2002; *b* 24 Aug. 1955; *d* of late Derek Young Coomber and Jennifer Isabel Coomber (*née* Strudwick); *m* 1980, Donald Frank Gleeson; one *s*. *Educ:* Lady Margaret Hall, Oxford (MA Jurisprudence 1977). Articled Linklaters & Paines, 1978–80; Solicitor, 1981; Hedleys Solicitors, 1981–95; an Employment Judge (formerly a Chm., Employment Tribunals), 1993–; Immigration Adjudicator, 1995–2002. *Recreations:* country walks, modern art, languages. *Address:* Asylum and Immigration Tribunal, Field House, 15 Bream's Buildings, EC4A 1DZ.

GLEITZMAN, Morris; author; *b* 9 Jan. 1953; *s* of Philip and Pamela Gleitzman; *m* 1974, Christine McCaul (marr. diss. 1994); one *s* one *d*. *Publications:* The Other Facts of Life, 1985; Two Weeks with the Queen, 1990; Second Childhood, 1990; Misery Guts, 1991; Worry Warts, 1991; Blabber Mouth, 1992; Sticky Beak, 1993; Puppy Fat, 1994; Belly Flop, 1996; Water Wings, 1996; (with P. Jennings) Wicked!, 1997; Bumface, 1998; Gift of the Gab, 1999; Toad Rage, 1999; (with P. Jennings) Deadly!, 2000; Adults Only, 2001; Toad Heaven, 2001; Boy Overboard, 2002; Teacher's Pet, 2003; Toad Away, 2003; Girl Underground, 2004; Worm Story, 2004; Once, 2005; Aristotle's Nostril, 2005; Doubting Thomas, 2006; Give Peas a Chance, 2007; Then, 2008; Toad Surprise, 2008. *Address:* c/o Penguin Books (Australia), 250 Camberwell Road, Camberwell, Vic 3124, Australia. *T:* (3) 98112400; *e-mail:* morris@morrisgleitzman.com.

GLEN, Ian Douglas; QC 1996; a Recorder, since 2000; *b* 2 April 1951; *s* of Douglas and Patricia Glen; *m* 1978, Helen O'Dowd; two *s*. *Educ:* Hutton Grammar Sch.; Wyggeston Grammar Sch.; King's Coll., London (LLB Hons). Called to the Bar, Gray's Inn, 1973, Bencher, 2003; Mem. *ad eundem*, Lincoln's Inn, 2005. Mem., Bar Council, 2003–. Hon. Res. Fellow, Bristol Univ., 1999. Mem. Court, Univ. of Bristol. FRSA. *Recreations:* seaside fairways, tranquil waters, after dinner speaking, dance music. *Address:* Guildhall Chambers, 23 Broad Street, Bristol BS1 2HG. *T:* (0117) 927 3366; 5 King's Bench Walk, Temple, EC4Y 7DN. *Clubs:* Soho House; India House (New York); Burnham and Berrow Golf, Royal Cinque Ports Golf.

GLEN, Marlyn Laing; Member (Lab) Scotland North East, Scottish Parliament, since 2003; *b* 30 Sept. 1951; *d* of Stewart and Rita Mitchell; *m* 1974, Neil Glen (*d* 2004); one *s* one *d*. *Educ:* Kirkton High Sch., Dundee; St Andrews Univ. (MA Hons); Dundee Univ. (DipEd; Dip Special Ed); Open Univ. (BA Hons; BSc Hons). Teacher, English, Stanley Park Comp. Sch., 1974–76, Belmont Acad., 1976–77; Asst Prin. Teacher of English, Ravenspark Acad., Irvine, 1977–82; Teacher of English and Learning Support (pt-time), Ravenspark Acad. and Auchenharvie Acad., Stevenston, 1982–90; Sen. Teacher, Craigie High Sch., Dundee, 1991–97; Principal Teacher, Support for Learning, Baldragon Acad., Dundee, 1997–2003. *Recreations:* music, theatre, literature, hill-walking. *Address:* Scottish Parliament, Holyrood, Edinburgh EH99 1SP; *e-mail:* marlyn.glen.msp@scottish.parliament.uk.

GLEN HAIG, Dame Mary (Alison), DBE 1993 (CBE 1977; MBE 1971); *b* 12 July 1918; *e d* of late Captain William James and Mary (*née* Bannochie); *m* 1943, Andrew Glen Haig (decd). *Educ:* Dame Alice Owen's Girls' School. Mem., Sports Council, 1966–82; Vice Pres., CCPR, 1982– (Chm., 1974–80); Mem., Internat. Olympic Cttee, 1982–93 (Hon. Mem., 1993–). Vice Pres., Sports Aid Foundn, 1987–; Life Pres., Disability Sport England (formerly British Sports Assoc. for the Disabled), 1991 (Pres., 1981–90); Hon. Pres., British Fencing Assoc. (formerly Amateur Fencing Assoc.), 1986– (Pres., 1974–86); Patron, Women's Sports Foundn, 1998–. British Ladies' Foil Champion, 1948–50; Olympic Games, 1948, 1952, 1956, 1960; Commonwealth Games Gold Medal, 1950, 1954, Bronze Medal, 1958; Captain, Ladies' Foil Team, 1950–57. Asst Dist Administrator, S Hammersmith Health District, 1975–82. Member: Adv. Council Women's Transport Service (FANY), 1980–2004 (Vice Pres., 2005–); Exec. Cttee, Arthritis and Rheumatism Council, 1992–. Chm. of Trustees, HRH The Princess Christian Hosp., Windsor, 1981–94; Trustee: Wishbone Trust, 1991–2003; Kennedy Inst., 1998–. *Recreations:* fencing, gardening. *Address:* 66 North End House, Fitzjames Avenue, W14 0RX. *T:* (020) 7602 2504; 3 Century Row, Middle Way, Oxford OX2 7LP. *T:* (01865) 554810. *Club:* Lansdowne.

GLENAMARA, Baron *cr* 1977 (Life Peer), of Glenridding, Cumbria; **Edward Watson Short;** PC 1964; CH 1976; Chairman, Cable and Wireless Ltd, 1976–80; *b* 17 Dec. 1912; *s* of Charles and Mary Short, Warcop, Westmorland; *m* 1941, Jennie, *d* of Thomas Sewell, Newcastle upon Tyne; one *s* one *d*. *Educ:* Bede College, Durham; LLB London. Served War of 1939–45 and became Capt. in DLI. Headmaster of Princess Louise County Secondary School, Blyth, Northumberland, 1947; Leader of Labour Group on Newcastle City Council, 1950; MP (Lab) Newcastle upon Tyne Central, 1951–76; Opposition Whip (Northern Area), 1955–62; Dep. Chief Opposition Whip, 1962–64; Parly Sec. to the Treasury and Govt Chief Whip, 1964–66; Postmaster General, 1966–68; Sec. of State for Educn and Science, 1968–70; Lord Pres. of the Council and Leader, House of Commons, 1974–76. Dep. Leader, Labour Party, 1972–76. Mem. Council, WWF, 1983–92. President: Finchale Abbey Training Coll. for the Disabled (Durham), 1985–; North East People to People, 1989–. Chancellor, Polytechnic of Newcastle upon Tyne, 1984–92, Univ. of Northumbria at Newcastle, 1992–. Freeman, City of Newcastle upon Tyne, 2001. Hon. FCP, 1965. Hon. DCL: Dunelm, 1989; Newcastle, 1998; DUniv Open, 1989; Hon. DLitt CNAA, 1990. *Publications:* The Story of The Durham Light Infantry, 1944; The Infantry Instructor, 1946; Education in a Changing World, 1971; Birth to Five, 1974; I Knew My Place, 1983; Whip to Wilson, 1989. *Recreation:* painting. *Address:* 21 Priory Gardens, Corbridge, Northumberland NE45 5HZ. *T:* (01434) 632880.

GLENAPP, Viscount; Fergus James Kenneth Mackay; *b* 9 July 1979; *s* and *heir* of 4th Earl of Inchcape, *qv*. *Educ:* Radley Coll.; Edinburgh Univ. (MA). *Address:* 9c Brechin Place, SW7 4QB.

GLENARTHUR, 4th Baron *cr* 1918; **Simon Mark Arthur;** DL; Bt 1903; *b* 7 Oct. 1944; *s* of 3rd Baron Glenarthur, OBE, and Margaret (*d* 1993), *d* of late Captain H. J. J. Howie; *S* father, 1976; *m* 1969, Susan, *yr d* of Comdr Hubert Wyndham Barry, RN; one *s* one *d*. *Educ:* Eton. Commissioned 10th Royal Hussars (PWO), 1963; ADC to High Comr, Aden, 1964–65; Captain 1970; Major 1973; retired 1975; Royal Hussars (PWO), TA, 1976–80. British Airways Helicopters Captain, 1976–82. A Lord in Waiting (Govt Whip), 1982–83; Parly Under Sec. of State, DHSS, 1983–85, Home Office, 1985–86; Minister of State: Scottish Office, 1986–87; FCO, 1987–89; elected Mem., H of L, 1999. Sen. Exec., 1989–96, Consultant, 1996–99, Hanson PLC; Dep. Chm., Hanson Pacific Ltd, 1994–96; Director: Aberdeen and Texas Corporate Finance Ltd, 1977–82; The Lewis Gp, 1993–95; Whirlybird Services Ltd, 1995–2004; Millennium Chemicals Inc., 1996–2004; Medical Defence Union Ltd, 2002–06; Audax Trading Ltd, subseq. Audax Global SARL, 2003– (Consultant, 2001–03); Consultant: BAe PLC, 1989–99; Chevron UK Ltd, 1994–97; Imperial Tobacco Gp, 1996–98. Chm., St Mary's Hosp., Paddington, NHS Trust, 1991–98 (Special Trustee, St Mary's Hosp., 1991–2000). Chm., Europ. Helicopter Assoc., 1996–2003; Dep. Chm., Internat. Fedn of Helicopter Assocs, 1996–97 and 2000–04 (Chm., 1997–2000); Pres., British Helicopter Adv. Bd, 2004– (Chm., 1992–2004). Pres., Nat. Council for Civil Protection, 1991–2003; Mem. Council, Air League, 1994–; Mem., Nat. Employers Liaison Cttee for Britain's Reserve Forces, 1996–2002; Chm., Nat. Employer Adv. Bd for Britain's Reserve Forces, 2002–. Scottish Patron, Butler Trust, 1994–; Gov., Nuffield Nursing Homes Trust, subseq. Nuffield Hosps, 2000–; Comr, Royal Hosp., Chelsea, 2001–07. Lieut, Queen's Body Guard for Scotland (Royal Co. of Archers). FCILT (FCIT 1999; MCIT 1979); FRAeS 1992. Liveryman, GAPAN, 1996. DL Aberdeenshire, 1988. *Recreations:* field sports, gardening, choral singing, organ-playing, barometers. *Heir:* *s* Hon. Edward Alexander Arthur, *b* 9 April 1973. *Address:* PO Box 11012, Banchory AB31 6ZJ. *Clubs:* Cavalry and Guards, Pratt's.

GLENCONNER, 3rd Baron *cr* 1911; **Colin Christopher Paget Tennant;** Bt 1885; Governing Director, Tennants Estate Ltd, 1967–91; Chairman, Mustique Co. Ltd, 1969–87; *b* 1 Dec. 1926; *s* of 2nd Baron Glenconner and Pamela Winefred (*d* 1989), 2nd *d* of Sir Richard Paget, 2nd Bt; *S* father, 1983; *m* 1956, Lady Anne Coke, LVO, *e d* of 5th

Earl of Leicester, MVO; one *s* twin *d* (and two *s* decd). *Educ:* Eton; New College, Oxford. Director, C. Tennant Sons & Co. Ltd, 1953; Deputy Chairman, 1960–67, resigned 1967. Goodwill Ambassador for St Lucia, 2006. *Heir:* *g s* Cody Charles Edward Tennant, *b* 2 Feb. 1994. *Address:* Beau Estate, PO Box 250, Soufrière, St Lucia, West Indies. *T:* and *Fax:* 4595057; *e-mail:* beauestate@candw.lc.

See also Lady Emma Tennant.

GLENDEVON, 2nd Baron *cr* 1964, of Midhope, Co. Linlithgow; **Julian John Somerset Hope;** opera producer; *b* 6 March 1950; *er s* of 1st Baron Glendevon and Elizabeth Mary (*d* 1998), *d* of (William) Somerset Maugham, CH; *S* father, 1996. *Educ:* Eton; Christ Church, Oxford. Resident Prod., WNO, 1973–75; Assoc. Prod., Glyndebourne Festival, 1974–81; other prodns for San Francisco Opera, Wexford and Edinburgh Festivals. *Heir:* *b* Hon. Jonathan Charles Hope, *b* 23 April 1952.

GLENDINNING, Hon. Victoria, (Hon. Mrs O'Sullivan), CBE 1998; FRSL; author and journalist, since 1969; *b* 23 April 1937; *d* of Baron Seebohm, TD and Evangeline, *d* of Sir Gerald Hurst, QC; *m* 1st, 1958, Prof. (Oliver) Nigel (Valentine) Glendinning (marr. diss. 1981); four *s*; 2nd, 1982, Terence de Vere White (*d* 1994); 3rd, 1996, Kevin (Patrick) O'Sullivan. *Educ:* St Mary's Sch., Wantage; Millfield Sch.; Somerville Coll., Oxford (MA Mod. Langs; Hon. Fellow, 2004); Southampton Univ. (Dip. in Social Admin). Part-time teaching, 1960–69; part-time psychiatric social work, 1970–73; Editorial Asst, TLS, 1974–78. FRSL 1982 (Vice-Pres., RSL, 2000–); Vice-Pres., English Centre, PEN, 2003 (Pres., 2001–03). Hon. DLitt: Southampton, 1994; Ulster, 1995; Dublin, 1995; York, 2000. *Publications:* A Suppressed Cry, 1969; Elizabeth Bowen: portrait of a writer, 1977; Edith Sitwell: a unicorn among lions, 1981; Vita: a biography of V. Sackville-West, 1983; Rebecca West: a life, 1987; The Grown-Ups (novel), 1989; Hertfordshire, 1989; Trollope, 1992; Electricity (novel), 1995; (ed with M. Glendinning) Sons and Mothers, 1996; Jonathan Swift, 1998; Flight (novel), 2002; Leonard Woolf: a life, 2006; (ed) Love's Civil War, 2008; reviews and articles in newspapers and magazines in Britain, Ireland and USA. *Address:* c/o David Higham Associates, 5–8 Lower John Street, Golden Square, W1F 9HA. *Club:* Athenæum.

GLENDYNE, 4th Baron *cr* 1922; **John Nivison;** Bt 1914; *b* 18 Aug. 1960; *o s* of 3rd Baron Glendyne and of Elizabeth, *y d* of Sir Cecil Armitage, CBE; *S* father, 2008.

GLENN, Sir Archibald; *see* Glenn, Sir J. R. A.

GLENN, John H(erschel), Jr; US Senator from Ohio (Democrat), 1975–98; *b* Cambridge, Ohio, 18 July 1921; *s* of John H. and Clara Glenn; *m* 1943, Anna Castor; one *s* one *d*. *Educ:* Muskingum Coll., New Concord, Ohio. Joined US Marine Corps, 1943; Served War (2 DFC's, 10 Air Medals); Pacific Theater, 1944; home-based, Capt., 1945–46; Far East, 1947–49; Major, 1952; served Korea (5 DFC's, Air Medal with 18 clusters), 1953. First non-stop supersonic flight, Los Angeles–New York (DFC), 1957; Lieut-Col, 1959. In Jan. 1964, declared candidacy for US Senate from Ohio, but withdrew owing to an injury; recovered and promoted Col USMC, Oct. 1964; retired from USMC, Dec. 1964. Became one of 7 volunteer Astronauts, man-in-space program, 1959; made 3-orbit flight in Mercury capsule, Friendship 7, 20 Feb. 1962 (boosted by rocket; time 4 hrs 56 mins; distance 81,000 miles; altitude 160 miles; recovered by destroyer off Puerto Rico in Atlantic). Vice-Pres. (corporate develt), Royal Crown Cola Co., 1966–68; Pres., Royal Crown Internat., 1967–69. Holds hon. doctorates, US and foreign. Awarded DSM (Nat. Aeronautics and Space Admin.), Astronaut Wings (Navy), Astronaut Medal (Marine Corps), etc, 1962; Galabert Internat. Astronautical Prize (jointly with Lieut-Col Yuri Gagarin), 1963; also many other awards and citations from various countries and organizations. *Address:* John Glenn School of Public Affairs, 110 Page Hall, 1810 College Road, Columbus, OH 43210, USA.

GLENN, Sir (Joseph Robert) Archibald, Kt 1966; OBE 1965; BCE; FIChemE, FIE (Aust.); Managing Director, 1953–73, Chairman, 1963–73, ICI Australia; *b* 24 May 1911; *s* of late J. R. Glenn, Sale, Vic., Aust.; *m* 1st, 1939, Elizabeth M. M. (*d* 1988), *d* of late J. S. Balderstone; one *s* three *d*; 2nd, 1992, Mrs Sue Debenham (*née* Hennesey). *Educ:* Scotch Coll. (Melbourne); University of Melbourne; Harvard (USA). Joined ICI Australia Ltd, 1935; Design and Construction Engr, 1935–44; Explosives Dept, ICI (UK), 1945–46; Chief Engineer, ICI Australia Ltd, 1947–48; Controller, Nobel Group, 1948–50; General Manager, 1950–52, ICI Australia Ltd; Director: Westpac Banking Corp. (formerly Bank of NSW), 1967–84; ICI, London, 1970–75; Hill Samuel Australia Ltd, 1973–83; Westralian Sands Ltd, 1977–85; Alcoa of Australia Ltd, 1973–86; Tioxide Australia Ltd, 1973–86; Newmont Pty Ltd, 1977–88; Chairman: Fibremakers Ltd, 1963–73; Rocky Dam Pty Ltd, 1968–; IMI Australia Ltd, 1970–78; Collins Wales Pty Ltd, 1973–84; I. C. Insurance Australia Ltd, 1973–85. Chancellor, La Trobe Univ., 1967–72 (Hon. DUniv 1981); Chairman: Council of Scotch Coll., 1960–81. Ormond Coll. Council, 1976–81; Member: Manufacturing Industry Advisory Council, 1960–77; Industrial Design Council, 1958–70; Australia/Japan Business Co-operation Cttee, 1965–75; Royal Melbourne Hospital Bd of Management, 1960–70; Melbourne Univ. Appointments Bd; Bd of Management, Melbourne Univ. Engrg Sch. Foundn, 1982–88; Council, Inst. of Pacific Affairs, 1976–; Governor, Atlantic Inst. of Internat. Affairs, 1970–88. Mem., Nat. Finance Cttee, Aust. Red Cross, 1982–98. J. N. Kirby Medal, 1970. *Recreations:* golf, tennis, collecting rare books. *Address:* 8 Freemans Road, Mount Eliza, Vic 3930, Australia. *T:* (3) 97875850. *Clubs:* Australian (Life Mem.), Melbourne (Life Mem.), Frankston Golf, Melbourne Univ. Boat (Melbourne).

GLENN, Paul Anthony; His Honour Judge Glenn; a Circuit Judge, since 2004; *b* 14 Sept. 1957; *m* 1985, Diane Burgess; two *s*. *Educ:* Liverpool Univ. (LLB Hons 1979). Called to the Bar, Gray's Inn, 1983; Magistrates' Court Service, 1980–85; County Prosecuting Solicitor's Office, Cheshire, 1985–86; CPS, 1986–90; in practice as a barrister, 1990–2004; a Recorder, 2000–04. *Recreations:* sport, avid supporter of Stoke City FC and enjoys watching Rugby and cricket. *Address:* Stoke-on-Trent Combined Court, Bethesda Street, Hanley, Stoke-on-Trent ST1 3BP. *T:* (01782) 854000.

GLENNERSTER, Prof. Howard, FBA 2002; AcSS; Co-Director, Centre for Analysis of Social Exclusion, 1997–2007, and Professor of Social Administration, 1984–2001, now Professor Emeritus, London School of Economics; *b* 4 Oct. 1936; *s* of John Howard Glennerster and Charlotte Nellie Glennerster; *m* 1962, Ann Dunbar Craine; one *s* one *d*. *Educ:* Letchworth Grammar Sch.; Wadham Coll., Oxford (BA PPE). Res. Asst, Labour Party Res. Dept, 1959–64; London School of Economics: Res. Officer, Higher Educn Res. Unit, 1964–68; Lectr in Social Admin, 1968–79; Reader, 1979–84; Chm., Suntory and Toyota Internat. Centres for Econs and Related Disciplines, 1994–2000; Hon. Fellow, 2005. Vis. Prof. or acad. visitor, Brookings Instn, 1972, 1996, 2000, Univs of Berkeley, Calif, 1982, Washington State, 1982 and Chicago, 1989. Mem., Sec. of State for Health's Adv. Cttee on Resource Allocation, 1997–. Director: Basic Skills Agency, 1997–2007; Mgt Cttee, King's Fund, 2002–07. AcSS 2000; FRSA 1995. *Publications:* Social Service Budgets and Social Policy, 1974; Planning for Priority Groups, 1983; Paying for Welfare, 1984, 3rd edn 1997; Implementing GP Fundholding, 1994; British Social Policy since 1945, 1995, 3rd edn 2007; The State of Welfare: the economics of social spending, 1998; Understanding the Finance of Welfare, 2003; contrib. numerous papers on econs of social policy to acad. jls. *Recreations:* walking, bird-watching, gardening, tending an allotment, watching cricket, enjoying grandchildren. *Address:* London School of Economics, Houghton Street, WC2A 2AE. *T:* (020) 7852 3560; *e-mail:* h.glennerster@lse.ac.uk. *Club:* Middlesex CC.

GLENNIE, Hon. Lord; Angus James Scott Glennie; a Senator of the College of Justice in Scotland, since 2005; farmer; *b* 3 Dec. 1950; *yr s* of Robert Nigel Forbes Glennie and Barbara Scott (*née* Nicoll); *m* 1981, Patricia Jean Phelan, *er d* of His Honour Judge Phelan, *qv*; three *s* one *d*. *Educ:* Sherborne Sch.; Trinity Hall, Cambridge (MA Hons). Called to the Bar, Lincoln's Inn, 1974, Bencher, 2007; QC 1991; admitted to Faculty of Advocates, 1992; QC (Scot.) 1998. *Recreations:* sailing, ski-ing, Real tennis. *Address:* Parliament House, Parliament Square, Edinburgh EH1 1RQ.

GLENNIE, Dame Evelyn (Elizabeth Ann), DBE 2007 (OBE 1993); FRAM, FRCM; percussionist; *b* 19 July 1965; *d* of Isobel and Arthur Glennie. *Educ:* Ellon Acad., Aberdeen; Royal Academy of Music (GRSM Hons, LRAM, ARAM; FRAM 1992; Queen's Commendation Prize); FRCM 1991. Shell Gold Medal, 1984; studied in Japan; Leonardo da Vinci Prize, 1987; début, Wigmore Hall, 1986; soloist in Zürich, Paris, Schwetzingen, Holland, Dublin, Norway, Australia; festivals of Aldeburgh, Bath, Edinburgh, Chichester, Salisbury; percussion and timpani concertos specially written; TV and radio presenting; numerous recordings and awards. Hon. DMus: Aberdeen, 1991; Bristol, 1995; Portsmouth, 1995; Leicester, Surrey, 1997; Belfast, Essex, Durham, 1998; Hon. DLitt: Warwick, 1993; Loughborough, 1995. Grammy Award, 1988. *Publication:* Good Vibrations (autobiog.), 1990. *Recreations:* reading, walking, cycling, art. *Address:* PO Box 6, Sawtry, Huntingdon, Cambs PE28 5WE. *T:* 0870 774 1492.

GLENNIE, Robert McDougall; Chairman and Chief Executive, New Galexy Partners Limited; *b* 4 April 1951. *Educ:* Jordanhill Coll. Sch., Glasgow; Univ. of Strathclyde (LLB). FCIS 2000 (MCIS). Admitted Solicitor, 1978. Joined McGrigor Donald, subseq. McGrigors, 1976; Partner, 1980–2002; Managing Partner of London Office, 1989; Sen. Partner, 2000–02; Chief Exec., KLegal Internat., 2002–04. Mem., Law Soc. of Scotland, 1977–. *Recreations:* hillwalking, cinema, tropical fruit farming. *Address:* 31 Hillgate Place, W8 7SL. *T:* (020) 7221 5726.

GLENNY, Misha; freelance journalist, writer and broadcaster, since 1993; *b* 25 April 1958; *s* of late Michael V. G. Glenny and of Juliet Sydenham (*née* Crum); *m* 1987, Snezana Curcic (marr. diss. 2001); one *s* one *d*; one *s* with Kirsty Lang. *Educ:* Bristol Univ. (BA Drama); Charles Univ., Prague. Rights editor, Verso publishing house, London, 1983–86; Central Europe Correspondent (based in Vienna): The Guardian, 1986–89; BBC World Service, 1989–93. Sony Special Award for Broadcasting, 1993; American Overseas Pressclub Award for Best Book on Foreign Affairs, 1993. *Publications:* The Rebirth of History: Eastern Europe in the age of democracy, 1990, 2nd edn 1993; The Fall of Yugoslavia, 1992, 2nd edn 1993; The Balkans 1804–1999: nationalism, war and the great powers, 1999; McMafia: crime without frontiers, 2008. *Address:* 138 Percy Road, W12 9QL.

GLENNY, Dr Robert Joseph Ervine, CEng, FIMMM; Consultant to UK Government, industry, and European Economic Community, 1983–2006; *b* 14 May 1923; *s* of late Robert and Elizabeth Rachel Glenny; *m* 1947, Joan Phillips Reid; one *s* one *d*. *Educ:* Methodist Coll., Belfast; QUB (BSc Chemistry); London Univ. (BSc Metallurgy, PhD). CEng, 1979; FIMMM (FIM 1958). Res. Metallurgist, English Electric Co. Ltd, Stafford, 1943–47; National Gas Turbine Establishment, 1947–70; Materials Dept, 1947–66; Head of Materials Dept, 1966–70; Supt, Div. of Materials Applications, National Physical Lab., 1970–73; Head of Materials Dept, RAE, 1973–79; Group Head of Aerodynamics, Structures and Materials Depts, RAE, 1979–83. *Publications:* research and review papers on materials science and technology, mainly related to gas turbines, in ARC (R&M series) and in Internat. Metallurgical Rev. *Recreations:* reading, gardening, walking. *Address:* 77 Gally Hill Road, Fleet, Hants GU52 6RU. *T:* (01252) 615877.

GLENTON, Anthony Arthur Edward, CBE 2000 (MBE mil. 1982); TD 1972 (bars 1980, 1986, 1992); DL; FCA; Senior Partner, Ryecroft Glenton, Chartered Accountants, Newcastle, since 1967; Director, 1988–2005, Chairman, 1994–2005, Port of Tyne Authority; *b* 21 March 1943; *s* of late Lt-Col Eric Cecil Glenton, Gosforth, Newcastle, and of Joan Lydia Glenton (*née* Taylor); *m* 1972, Caroline Ann, *d* of Maurice George Meade-King; one *s* one *d*. *Educ:* Merchiston Castle Sch., Edinburgh. FCA 1965. Chm., Charles W. Taylor & Son Ltd, Iron Founders, S Shields, 1995–2003; Dir, Newcastle Bldg Soc., 1987– (Chm., 1992–97). Joined Royal Artillery, Territorial Army, 1961: Lieut Col 1984; CO 101 (Northumbrian) Field Regt RA (V), 1984–86; Col 1986; Dep. Comdr, 15 Inf. Bde, 1986–89; ADC to the Queen, 1987–89; TA Advr to GOC Eastern Dist, 1989–94; Hon. Col, 101 (Northumbrian) Regt RA (V), 2005–. Chairman: N of England RFCA, 1999–2003 (Vice Chm., 1995–99); Northumberland Br., SSAFA Forces Help, 1989–. Freeman, City of London, 1981; Liveryman, Co. of Chartered Accountants of England and Wales, 1981. DL Northumberland, 1993. *Recreations:* shooting, sailing, contemporary art. *Address:* Whinbank, Rothbury, Northumberland NE65 7YJ. *T:* (01669) 620361; Palace Hill Cottage, St Cuthbert's Square, Holy Island of Lindisfarne, Northumberland TD15 2SP. *T:* (01289) 389312; Ryecroft Glenton, 32 Portland Terrace, Newcastle upon Tyne NE2 1QP. *T:* (0191) 281 1292. *Club:* Army and Navy.

GLENTORAN, 3rd Baron *cr* 1939, of Ballyalolly, Co. Down; **Thomas Robin Valerian Dixon,** CBE 1992 (MBE 1969); DL; Bt 1903; *b* 21 April 1935; *er s* of 2nd Baron Glentoran, KBE, PC; *S* father, 1995; *m* 1959, Rona, *d* of Captain G. C. Colville; three *s*; *m* 1990, Margaret Rainey. *Educ:* Eton. Man. Dir, Redland (NI) Ltd, 1971–92. Mem., Millennium Fund Commn, 1994–2005. Elected Mem., H of L, 1999; front bench opposition spokesman, H of L, on NI, 1998–, on sport, 2006–. Non-executive Director: NHBC, 2001–; BetonSports plc, 2004–. Comr, Irish Light House Service, 1996–. DL Antrim, 1995. *Recreations:* sailing, golf. *Heir:* *s* Hon. Daniel George Dixon [*b* 26 July 1959; *m* 1983, Leslie Hope Brooke; two *s*]. *Address:* Drumadarragh House, Ballyclare, Co. Antrim BT39 0TA; 16 Westgate Terrace, SW10 9BJ. *Clubs:* Royal Yacht Squadron, Royal Cruising.

GLESTER, John William; Chairman and Managing Director (formerly Principal), John Glester Consultancy Services, since 1996; Associate Director, Locum Consulting, since 2006; *b* 8 Sept. 1946; *o s* of late George Ernest Glester and Maude Emily Glester; *m* 1970, Ann Gleave Taylor (*d* 1998); two *s*. *Educ:* Plaistow Grammar Sch.; Reading Univ. (BA Hons). Joined Civil Service 1968; served DEA, DoE and Merseyside Task Force; Regl Controller, NW, DoE, 1985–88; Chief Exec., Central Manchester Develt Corp., 1988–96; Trust Fund Adminr, Lord Mayor of Manchester's Emergency Appeal Fund, 1996–98; Dir (Regl Strategy), NW Regl Develt Agency, 1999–2000. Chairman: Castlefield Management Co., 1992–2002; Castlefield Heritage Trust, 1996–2003; Hallogen Ltd (Bridgewater Hall), 1998–2004 (Dir, 1995–98); Ancoats Bldgs Preservation Trust, 2001–07 (Trustee, 2001–07); Commissions in the Environment, 2002–04; Urban Experience Ltd, 2002–04; Merseyside Housing Market Renewal, 2003–; Manchester

Salford Trafford NHS LIFT, 2003–07; Bolton, Rochdale and Heywood Middleton NHS LIFT, 2007–; Heritage Works, 2007–; Dir, Langtree Gp plc, 1999–2001; Consultant: Lloyds Metal Group plc, 1997–98; Dunlop Heywood, 1998–99; Valley and Vale Properties plc, 1998–2000. Chm., Network Space Consultative Cttee, 1999–2001. Director: Salford Phoenix, 1987–95; Manchester Arts Fest., 1989–93; Manchester Olympic Bid Cttee, 1990–93; Manchester 2000, 1992–94; Manchester City of Drama, 1992–94; Manchester Concert Hall Ltd, 1994–2004; Patterson Inst. for Cancer Res., 2001–03. Consultant, Commonwealth Games 2002, 2000–02. *Recreations:* cricket, football (West Ham United in particular), golf, music, theatre, cooking. *Address: e-mail:* john.glester@btinternet.com.

GLICK, Ian Bernard; QC 1987; a Recorder, 2000–06; *b* 18 July 1948; *s* of late Dr Louis Glick and Phyllis Esty Glick; *m* 1986, Roxane Eban; three *s. Educ:* Bradford Grammar School; Balliol College, Oxford (MA, BCL). President, Oxford Union Society, 1968. Called to the Bar, Inner Temple, 1970, Bencher, 1997. Junior Counsel to the Crown, Common Law, 1985–87; Standing Junior Counsel to DTI in Export Credit Cases, 1985–87. Chm., Commercial Bar Assoc., 1997–99. *Address:* 1 Essex Court, Temple, EC4Y 9AR.

GLICKSMAN, Brian Leslie, CB 2005; Treasury Officer of Accounts, HM Treasury, 2000–05; *b* 14 Dec. 1945; *s* of Henry and Kitty Glicksman; *m* 1971, Jackie Strachan; two *d. Educ:* Ealing Grammar Sch.; New Coll., Oxford (BA Maths); Warwick Univ. (MSc Mgt Sci. and OR). OR Scientist, CSD, 1969; Principal, DoE, 1976; Asst Dir, PSA, 1984; Sec. Royal Commn on Envmtl Pollution, 1987; Divl Manager, DoE, 1992. Mem., Audit Cttee, Office of Govt Commerce, 2001–07. Trustee, 2Care, 2004– (Vice-Chm., 2006–07; Chm., 2007–). Hon. Treas., CS Sports Council, 2006–. *Publication:* contrib. to Canadian Parly Rev. *Address:* 18 Worcester Road, Sutton, Surrey SM2 6PG.

GLIDEWELL, Rt Hon. Sir Iain (Derek Laing), Kt 1980; PC 1985; a Lord Justice of Appeal, 1985–95; a Justice of Appeal, 1998–2003, and President, 2003–04, Court of Appeal for Gibraltar; *b* 8 June 1924; *s* of late Charles Norman and Nora Glidewell; *m* 1950, Hilary, *d* of late Clinton D. Winant; one *s* two *d. Educ:* Bromsgrove Sch.; Worcester Coll., Oxford (Hon. Fellow 1986). Served RAFVR (pilot), 1942–46. Called to the Bar, Gray's Inn, 1949 (Bencher 1977, Treas. 1995). QC 1969; a Recorder of the Crown Court, 1976–80; Judge of Appeal, Isle of Man, 1979–80; a Judge of the High Court of Justice, Queen's Bench Division, 1980–85; Presiding Judge, NE Circuit, 1982–85. Chm., Judicial Studies Bd, 1989–92; Member: Senate of Inns of Court and the Bar, 1976–79; Supreme Court Rule Cttee, 1980–84. Chm., Panels for Examination of Structure Plans: Worcestershire, 1974; W Midlands, 1975; conducted: Heathrow Fourth Terminal Inquiry, 1978; Review of CPS, 1997–98. Hon. RICS, 1982. *Recreations:* vigorous gardening, walking, theatre. *Address:* Rough Heys Farm, Henbury, Macclesfield, Cheshire SK11 9PF. *Club:* Garrick.

GLIN, Knight of; *see* Fitz-Gerald, D. J. V.

GLOAG, Ann Heron, OBE 2004; Director, Stagecoach Holdings plc, since 1986 (Managing Director, 1986–94; Executive Director, 1986–2000); *b* 10 Dec. 1942; *d* of Iain and Catherine Souter; *m* 1st, 1965, Robin N. Gloag (*d* 2007); one *d* (one *s* decd); 2nd, 1990, David McCleary. *Educ:* Caledonian Road Primary School; Perth High School. Trainee Nurse, Bridge of Earn Hosp., Perth, 1960–65; Ward Sister, Devonshire Royal Hosp., Buxton, 1965–69; Theatre Sister, Bridge of Earn Hosp., 1969–80; Founding Partner, Gloagtrotter, re-named Stagecoach Express Services, 1980–83; Co-Director, Stagecoach Ltd, 1983–86 (acquired parts of National Bus Co., 1987 and 1989 and Scottish Bus Group, 1991). Scottish Marketing Woman of the Year, Scottish Univs, 1989; UK Businesswoman of the Year, Veuve Cliquot and Inst. of Dirs, 1989–90. *Recreations:* family, travel, charity support. *Address:* Stagecoach Group, 10 Dunkeld Road, Perth PH1 5TW.
See also B. Souter.

GLOAK, Graeme Frank, CB 1980; Solicitor for the Customs and Excise, 1978–82; *b* 9 Nov. 1921; *s* of late Frank and Lilian Gloak; *m* 1944, Mary, *d* of Stanley and Jane Thorne; one *s* one *d* (and one *s* decd). *Educ:* Brentwood School. Royal Navy, 1941–46; Solicitor, 1947; Customs and Excise: Legal Asst, 1947; Sen. Legal Asst, 1953; Asst Solicitor, 1967; Principal Asst Solicitor, 1971. Sec., Civil Service Legal Soc., 1954–62. Member: Dairy Produce Quota Tribunal, 1984–85; Agricl Wages Cttee for Essex and Herts, 1984–90 (Vice-Chm., 1987–90); Chm., Agricl Dwelling House Adv. Cttee, Essex and Herts, 1984–93. Member: Barking and Havering FPC, 1986–90; Barking and Havering FHSA, 1990–96; Barking and Havering HA, 1996–97. *Publication:* (with G. Krikorian and R. K. F. Hutchings) Customs and Excise, in Halsbury's Laws of England, 4th edn, 1973. *Recreations:* badminton, walking, watching cricket. *Address:* 31 Burses Way, Hutton, Brentwood, Essex CM13 2PL. *T:* (01277) 212748. *Clubs:* MCC; Essex County Cricket (Chelmsford).

GLOBE, Henry Brian; QC 1994; **His Honour Judge Globe;** a Senior Circuit Judge, since 2003; *b* 18 June 1949; *o s* of late Theodore Montague Globe and of Irene Rita Globe; *m* 1972, Estelle Levin; two *d. Educ:* Liverpool Coll.; Birmingham Univ. (LLB Hons). Called to the Bar, Middle Temple, 1972, Bencher, 2005; in practice on Northern Circuit, 1972–2003 (Junior, 1974; Treas., 2001–03); Standing Counsel to: DSS, 1985–94; HM Customs and Excise, 1992–94; Asst Recorder, 1987–90; a Recorder, 1991–2003; a Circuit Judge, 2003. Hon. Recorder, Liverpool, 2003–. Member: Bar Council, 2001–03; Criminal Cttee, Judicial Studies Bd, 2001–05; Criminal Justice Council, 2004–. Governor: King David Primary Sch., Liverpool, 1979–2001; King David High Sch., Liverpool, 1985–2000 (Chm., 1990–2000). Trustee, King David Foundn, 2001–. *Recreations:* tennis, bridge. *Address:* Queen Elizabeth II Law Courts, Derby Square, Liverpool L2 1XA. *T:* (0151) 473 7373; *e-mail:* hhjudge.globeqc@judiciary.gsi.gov.uk.

GLOCER, Thomas Henry; Chief Executive Officer, Reuters Group plc, since 2001; *b* NYC, 8 Oct. 1959; *s* of Walter Glocer and Ursula Glocer (*née* Goodman); *m* 1988, Maarit Leso; one *s* one *d. Educ:* Columbia Coll. (BA *summa cum laude* 1981); Yale Law Sch. (JD 1984). Mergers and acquisitions lawyer, Davis Polk and Wardwell, NY, Paris and Tokyo, 1985–93; joined Reuters, 1993: mem., Legal Dept, Gen. Counsel, Reuters America Inc., NYC, 1993–96; Exec. Vice-Pres., Reuters America Inc. and CEO, Reuters Latin America, 1996–98; Chief Executive Officer: Reuters business in the Americas, 1998–2001; Reuters Inf., 2000–01. Director: NYC Investment Fund, 1999–2003 (Mem., Exec. Cttee); Instinet Corp., 2000–05. Mem., Adv. Bd, Singapore Monetary Authy, 2001–05. Member: Corporate Council, Whitney Mus. of American Art, 2000–03; Corporate Adv. Gp, Tate Britain, 2005–. Author of computer software, incl. (jtly) Coney Island: a game of discovery, 1983. NY Hall of Sci. Award, 2000; John Jay Alumni Award, 2001. *Recreations:* tennis, windsurfing, ski-ing. *Address:* Reuters Group plc, 30 South Colonnade, Canary Wharf, E14 5EU.

GLOSTER, Hon. Dame Elizabeth, DBE 2004; **Hon. Mrs Justice Gloster;** a Judge of the High Court of Justice, Queen's Bench Division (Commercial Court), since 2004; *b* 5 June 1949; *d* of late Peter Gloster and Betty Gloster (*née* Read); *m* 1973, Stanley Eric Brodie, *qv* (marr. diss. 2005); one *s* one *d*; *m* 2008, Sir Oliver Popplewell, *qv. Educ:* Roedean Sch., Brighton; Girton Coll., Cambridge (BA Hons). Called to the Bar, Inner Temple, 1971, Bencher 1992; QC 1989; a Judge of the Courts of Appeal of Jersey and Guernsey, 1993–2004; a Recorder, 1995–2004. Mem., panel of Counsel who appear for DTI in company matters, 1982–89. Mem. Bd (non-exec.), CAA, 1992–93. *Address:* Royal Courts of Justice, Strand, WC2A 2LL.

GLOSTER, Prof. John, MD; Hon. Consulting Ophthalmologist, Moorfields Eye Hospital; Emeritus Professor of Experimental Opthalmology, University of London; *b* 23 March 1922; *m* 1947, Margery (*née* Williams); two *s. Educ:* Jesus Coll., Cambridge; St Bartholomew's Hosp. MB, BChir 1946; MRCS, LRCP 1946; DOMS 1950; MD Cantab 1953; PhD London 1959. Registrar, Research Dept, Birmingham and Midland Eye Hosp., 1950–54; Mem. Staff, Ophth. Research Unit, MRC, 1954–63; Prof. of Experimental Ophthalmology, Inst. of Ophth., Univ. of London, 1975–82; Dean of the Inst. of Ophthalmology, 1975–80. Mem. Ophth. Soc. UK; Hon. Mem., Assoc. for Eye Res. *Publications:* Tonometry and Tonography, 1966; (jtly) Physiology of the Eye, System of Ophthalmology IV, ed Duke-Elder, 1968; contribs to jls. *Address:* 14 Church Place, Ickenham, Middlesex UB10 8XB.

GLOUCESTER, Bishop of, since 2004; **Rt Rev. Michael Francis Perham;** *b* 8 Nov. 1947; *s* of Raymond Maxwell Perham and Marcelle Winifred Perham; *m* 1982, Alison Jane Grove; four *d. Educ:* Hardye's Sch., Dorchester; Keble Coll., Oxford (BA 1974; MA 1978); Cuddesdon Theol Coll. Curate, St Mary, Addington, 1976–81; Sec., C of E Doctrine Commn, 1979–84; Chaplain to Bp of Winchester, 1981–84; Team Rector, Oakdale Team Ministry, Poole, 1984–92; Canon Residentiary and Precentor, 1992–98, Vice Dean, 1995–98, Norwich Cathedral; Provost, subseq. Dean, of Derby, 1998–2004. Bishop Protector, Soc. of St Francis, 2005–. Member: Liturgical Commn of C of E, 1986–2001; Archbishops' Commn on Church Music, 1988–92; Gen. Synod of C of E, 1989–92 and 1993– (Chm., Business Cttee, 2001–04); Cathedrals' Fabric Commn for England, 1996–2001; Archbishops' Council, 1999–2004; Governing Body, SPCK, 2002– (Vice Chm., 2005–06; Chm., 2006–); Chairman: Praxis, 1990–97; Cathedrals' Liturgy Gp, 1994–2001; Hosp. Chaplaincies' Council, 2007–; Vice Chm., C of E Mission and Public Affairs Council, 2007–. Mem., Church Heritage Forum, 1999–2001. Pres., Retired Clergy Assoc., 2007–. Pro-Chancellor and Mem. Council, Univ. of Gloucestershire, 2007–. Fellow, Woodard Corp., 2000–04. FRSCM 2002. Hon. DPhil Gloucestershire, 2007. *Publications:* The Eucharist, 1978, 2nd edn 1981; The Communion of Saints, 1980; Liturgy Pastoral and Parochial, 1984; (with Kenneth Stevenson) Waiting for the Risen Christ, 1986; (ed) Towards Liturgy 2000, 1989; (ed) Liturgy for a New Century, 1991; (with Kenneth Stevenson) Welcoming the Light of Christ, 1991; Lively Sacrifice, 1992; (ed) The Renewal of Common Prayer, 1993; (ed) Model and Inspiration, 1993; (compiled) Enriching the Christian Year, 1993; Celebrate the Christian Story, 1997; The Sorrowful Way, 1998; A New Handbook of Pastoral Liturgy, 2000; Signs of Your Kingdom, 2002; Glory in our Midst, 2005. *Recreations:* reading, writing, creating liturgical texts, walking in the Yorkshire dales. *Address:* Bishopscourt, Pitt Street, Gloucester GL1 2BQ. *T:* (01452) 410022, 524598; *e-mail:* bshpglos@glosdioc.org.uk.

GLOUCESTER, Dean of; *see* Bury, Very Rev. N. A. S.

GLOUCESTER, Archdeacon of; *see* Sidaway, Ven. G. H.

GLOVER, Anne; *see* Glover, L. A.

GLOVER, Anne Margaret, CBE 2006; Co-Founder and Chief Executive Officer, Amadeus Capital Partners Ltd, since 1997; *b* 6 Feb. 1954; *d* of John and Mary Glover. *Educ:* Clare Coll., Cambridge (BA 1st Cl. Metallurgy and Materials Sci. 1976); Yale Sch. of Mgt (MPPM 1978). Sen. Tech. Associate, Bell Telephone Labs, Murray Hill, 1977; Cummins Engine Company: Asst to Vice Pres., Affiliated Enterprises, 1978–79; Rod Line Foreman, 1979–80; Engine Order Mgt Consultant, NY, 1980–81; Customer Services Team Advr, NY, 1981–83; Bain & Co., Boston: Consultant, 1983–85; Sen. Consultant, 1985–86; Manager, 1986–88; Asst Dir, Apax Partners & Co. Ventures, London, 1989–93; Chief Op. Officer, Virtuality Gp plc, Leicester, 1994–95; Founder and non-exec. Dir, Calderstone Capital, 1996–97. Member Board: Optos plc; Teraview Ltd; Glysure Ltd. Former Chm., British Venture Capital Assoc. Member: Technol. Strategy Bd; Women's Enterprise Task Force; Sir David Walker's Wkg Gp. *Address:* Amadeus Capital Partners Ltd, 16 St James's Street, SW1P 4HX. *T:* (020) 7024 6911, *Fax:* (020) 7024 6999; *e-mail:* aglover@amadeuscapital.com.

GLOVER, Dame Audrey (Frances), DBE 2004; CMG 1997; barrister; Leader, UK Delegation to UN Human Rights Commission, 1998–2003; *d* of Robert John Victor Lush and Frances Lucy de la Roche; *m* 1971, Edward Charles Glover, *qv*; two *s* two *d* (and one *s* decd). *Educ:* St Anne's Coll., Sanderstead, Surrey; King's Coll. London (LLB Hons). Called to the Bar, Gray's Inn, 1961; LCD, 1965–67; HM Diplomatic Service, 1967–97: joined Foreign Office, as Asst Legal Advr, 1967; Asst (Temp.), Attorney Gen's Dept, Australia, 1972–73; Advr on British Law, Liby of Congress, Washington, 1974–77; Legal Advr (Asst), FCO, 1978–85; Legal Advr, British Mil. Govt, Berlin, 1985–89; Legal Counsellor, FCO, and UK Agent to EC and Ct of Human Rights, 1990–94; Dir (with rank of Ambassador), OSCE Office of Democratic Instns and Human Rights, Warsaw, 1994–97. Sen. Advr to Coalition Provisional Authy, Iraq and to Iraqi Minister of Human Rights, 2004–06. Head, OSCE Election Observation Mission: Belarus, 2004; Kazakhstan, 2005; former Yugoslav Republic of Macedonia, 2006; Ukraine, 2007; Italy, 2008. Mem. Adv. Bd, British Inst. of Human Rights, 2004–; Chm., Internat. Adv. Council, LINKS, 1999–; Mem. Bd, Electoral Reform Internat. Services, 2005–. Trustee, Prison Reform Trust, 2006–. *Recreations:* collecting paintings, sailing, travelling, theatre. *Address:* Oak House, Thornham, Norfolk PE36 6LY. *Club:* Brancaster Staithe Sailing (Norfolk).

GLOVER, Prof. David Moore, PhD; FRSE; Arthur Balfour Professor of Genetics, University of Cambridge, since 1999 (Head, Department of Genetics, 1999–2004); Fellow, Fitzwilliam College, Cambridge, since 2004; Director, Cancer Research UK (formerly Cancer Research Campaign) Cell Cycle Genetics Group, since 1989; *b* 28 March 1948; *s* of Charles David Glover and Olivia Glover; *m* 2000, Magdalena Zernicka. *Educ:* Broadway Tech. Grammar Sch., Barnsley; Fitzwilliam Coll., Cambridge (BA 2nd Cl. Biochem.); ICRF and UCL (PhD 1972). FRSE 1992. Post-doctoral Res. Fellow, Stanford Univ., Calif, 1972–75; Imperial College, London: Lectr in Biochem., 1975–81; Sen. Lectr in Biochem., 1981–83; Reader in Molecular Genetics, 1983–86; Prof. of Molecular Genetics, 1986–89; Hd, Dept of Biochem., 1988–89; Prof. of Molecular Genetics, Dept of Biochem., 1989–92, Dept of Anatomy and Physiol., 1992–99, Univ. of Dundee. Jt Dir, 1979–86, Dir, 1986–89, CRC Eukaryotic Molecular Genetics Gp. Chief Scientist, Cambridge Div., Cyclacel Ltd, 1999–. Mem., EMBO, 1978. *Publications:* Genetic Engineering: cloning DNA, 1980; Gene Cloning: the mechanics of DNA manipulation, 1984; DNA Cloning: a practical approach (3 vols), 1985, 2nd edn (jtly with B. D. Hames) 1995; (with C. J. Hutchison) The Cell Cycle, 1995; (with S. Endow) Dynamics of Cell Division, 1998; contrib. numerous scientific papers. *Recreations:* music, reading, walking. *Address:* University of Cambridge, Department of Genetics, Downing Street, Cambridge CB2 3EH. *T:* (01223) 333999.

GLOVER, Edward Charles, CMG 2003; MVO 1976; HM Diplomatic Service, retired; Chairman, Board of Trustees, Iwokrama International Centre for Rainforest Conservation and Development, since 2005; *b* 4 March 1943; *s* of Edward and Mary Glover; *m* 1971, Audrey Frances Lush (*see* Dame A. F. Glover); two *s* two *d* (and one *s* decd). *Educ:* Goudhurst Sch. for Boys; Birkbeck Coll., London (BA Hons Hist., MPhil Hist.). Joined FO from BoT, 1967: Private Sec. to High Comr, Australia, 1971–73; Washington, 1973–77; Sec. to UK Delegn to UN Law of Sea Conf., 1978–80; on secondment to Guinness Peat Gp, 1981–83; Sect. Hd, Arms Control and Disarmament Dept, FCO, 1983–85; Senate Liaison Officer, BMG, Berlin, 1985–89; Dep. Hd, Near East and N Africa Dept, FCO, 1989–91; Hd, Mgt Rev. Staff, FCO, 1991–94; Dep. Hd of Mission and Consul-Gen., Brussels, 1994–98; High Comr to Guyana and Amb. to Suriname, 1998–2002; Quality and Efficiency Unit, FCO, 2002–03. Short term expert on Macedonia, Public Admin Internat., 2003–05; Adviser: on Foreign Affairs to Coalition Provisional Authy, Iraq, 2004; on Corporate Mgt Issues to Minister of Foreign Affairs, Iraq, 2004–05; on consular and visa matters to Foreign Minister, Bahamas, 2006; Associate Consultant, DFID Support: to Office of Prime Minister, Kosovo, 2006–07; to Min. of Foreign Affairs, Sierra Leone, 2008. Associate Fellow, Centre for Caribbean Studies, Univ. of Warwick, 2003–. Mem., RIIA, 1969–. Chm., NW Norfolk DFAS, 2003–06; Mem. Bd of Mgt, King's Lynn Preservation Trust, 2002–. Mem., Hakluyt Soc., 2003–. *Recreations:* tennis, reading, water-colour painting. *Address:* Oak House, Thornham, Norfolk PE36 6LY. *Club:* Brooks's.

GLOVER, Eric; Chairman, Intrabank Expert Witness, since 1998; Secretary-General, Chartered Institute of Bankers (formerly Institute of Bankers), 1982–94; *b* 28 June 1935; *s* of William and Margaret Glover; *m* 1960, Adele Diane Hilliard; three *s*. *Educ:* Liverpool Institute High Sch.; Oriel Coll., Oxford (MA). Shell International Petroleum (Borneo and Uganda), 1957–63; Institute of Bankers, later Chartered Institute of Bankers, 1963–; Asst Sec., 1964–69; Dir of Studies, 1969–82. Chm., Open and Distance Learning Quality Council (formerly Council for Accreditation of Correspondence Colls), 1993–98 (Mem., 1983–); Treas., British Accreditation Council for Indep. Further and Higher Educn, 1987– (Mem., 1985–); Pres., Teachers & Trainers of Financial Services, 1998–2007. Hon. Fellow, Sheffield Hallam Univ., 1992. Hon. FCIB 1994. Hon. MBA City of London Polytechnic, 1991. *Publications:* articles on banking education and expert witness work. *Recreations:* golf, swimming. *Address:* 12 Manor Park, Tunbridge Wells, Kent TN4 8XP. *T:* (01892) 531221.

GLOVER, Fiona Susannah Grace; Presenter, Saturday Live, Radio 4, since 2006; *b* 27 Feb. 1969; *d* of William and Priscilla Glover; partner, Rick Jones; one *s*. *Educ:* Prince's Mead Sch., Winchester; St Swithun's Sch., Winchester; Univ. of Kent (BA Hons Classical Hist. and Philosophy). Trainee reporter scheme, BBC, 1993; presenter: Gtr London Radio Breakfast Show, 1994–95; Travel Show, BBC 2, 1995–97; Five Live, BBC Radio, 1997–2003; Radio 4: Broadcasting House, 2004–06; Travellers' Tree, 2006–. *Publication:* Travels with My Radio, 2000. *Recreations:* cooking, domesticity, world wide radio. *Address:* c/o Vivienne Clore, The Richard Stone Partnership, 2 Henrietta Street, WC2E 8PS. *Club:* Groucho.

GLOVER, Jane Alison, CBE 2003; DPhil; FRCM; conductor; *b* 13 May 1949; *d* of late Robert Finlay Glover, TD, MA and of Jean Glover (*née* Muir), MBE. *Educ:* Monmouth School for Girls; St Hugh's Coll., Oxford (BA, MA, DPhil; Hon. Fellow, 1991). FRCM 1993. Oxford University: Junior Research Fellow, 1973–75, Sen. Res. Fellow, 1982–91, St Hugh's Coll.; Lecturer in Music: St Hugh's Coll., 1976–84; St Anne's Coll., 1976–80; Pembroke Coll., 1979–84; elected to OU Faculty of Music, 1979. Professional conducting début at Wexford Festival, 1975; thereafter, operas and concerts for: BBC; Glyndebourne (Musical Dir, Touring Opera, 1982–85); Royal Op. House, Covent Garden (début, 1988); ENO (début, 1989); Teatro la Fenice, Venice; Royal Danish Opera; Glimmerglass Opera, NY; Australian Opera; Chicago Opera; Berlin Staatsoper; London Symphony Orch.; London Philharmonic Orch.; Philharmonia Orch.; Royal Philharmonic Orch.; English Chamber Orch.; BBC Symphony Orch.; BBC Welsh Symphony Orch.; Scottish Nat. Orch.; Bournemouth Symphony Orch.; and many others in USA, Italy, Holland, Denmark, Canada, China, Hong Kong, Austria, Yugoslavia, Germany, France, Belgium, Australia, NZ, etc; Artistic Dir, London Mozart Players, 1984–91; Principal Conductor: London Choral Soc., 1983–99; Huddersfield Choral Soc., 1989–96; Music Dir, Music of the Baroque, Chicago, 2002–. A Gov., BBC, 1990–95. Radio and television documentaries and series, and presentation for BBC and LWT, esp. Orchestra, 1983, Mozart, 1985, Opera House, 1995, Musical Dynasties, 2000. Governor, RAM, 1985–90. Hon. DMus: Exeter, 1986; London, 1992; City, 1994; Glasgow, 1997; Hon. DLitt: Loughborough, 1988; Bradford, 1992; Brunel, 1996; DUniv Open, 1988; Hon. DMus CNAA, 1991. ABSA/Daily Telegraph Arts Award, 1990. *Publications:* Cavalli, 1978; Mozart's Women, 2005; contribs to: The New Monteverdi Companion, 1986; Monteverdi 'Orfeo' handbook, 1986; articles in Music and Letters, Proc. of Royal Musical Assoc., Musical Times, The Listener, TLS, Early Music, Opera, and others; many recordings. *Recreations:* theatre, ski-ing, walking. *Address:* c/o Askonas Holt Ltd, Lincoln House, 300 High Holborn, WC1V 7JH. *T:* (020) 7400 1700.

GLOVER, Julian Wyatt; actor; *b* 27 March 1935; *s* of late (Claude) Gordon Glover and Honor Ellen Morgan (*née* Wyatt); *m* 1st, 1957, Eileen Atkins (now Dame Eileen Atkins, *qv*) (marr. diss. 1966); 2nd, 1968, Isla Blair; one *s*. *Educ:* St Paul's Sch., Hammersmith; Alleyn's Sch., Dulwich. Full-time actor, 1957–; *theatre includes:* Royal Shakespeare Co.: Coriolanus, Henry VI, 1977; Henry IV, pts I and II, 1991–92 (best supporting actor, Olivier award, 1993); Julius Caesar, Romeo and Juliet, Stratford, transf. Barbican, 1995–96; All My Sons, Palace, Watford, 1992; Cyrano de Bergerac, Haymarket, 1992–93; An Inspector Calls, Aldwych, 1993–94; Chips With Everything, RNT, 1996–97; Prayers of Sherkin, Old Vic, 1997; Waiting for Godot, Piccadilly, 1998; Phèdre, Britannicus, Albery, 1998; A Penny for a Song, Whitehall, 1999; The Tempest, Nuffield, 2000; In Praise of Love, UK tour, 2001; King Lear, Shakespeare's Globe, 2001; Macbeth, Albery, 2003; Taking Sides, UK tour, 2003–04; Galileo's Daughter (Peter Hall Co.), 2004; The Dresser, UK tour, 2004, Duke of York's, 2005; Richard II, The Soldier's Tale, Old Vic, 2005; The Voysey Inheritance, NT, 2006; Shadowlands, Salisbury Playhouse, 2007; The President's Holiday, Hampstead, 2008; Dir, Hamlet, Norwich Playhouse, 1996; *films include:* Tom Jones, 1963; I Was Happy Here, 1965; The Empire Strikes Back, 1980; For Your Eyes Only, 1981; The Fourth Protocol, Cry Freedom, 1987; Indiana Jones and the Last Crusade, 1989; Treasure Island, 1990; King Ralph, 1991; Vatel, 2000; Two Men Went to War, The Book of Eve, Harry Potter and the Chamber of Secrets, 2002; Troy, 2004; *television includes:* Cover Her Face, 1985; The Chief, 1990; Born and Bred, 2002; In Search of Shakespeare, 2003; Waking the Dead, 2004; Trial and Retribution, 2005; The Impressionists, 2006. *Publication:* Beowulf, 1987. *Address:* c/o Conway Van Gelder Grant Ltd, 18–21 Jermyn Street, SW1Y 6HP.

GLOVER, Prof. Keith, FRS 1993; FREng, FIEEE, FInstMC; Professor of Engineerin since 1989, and Head of Department of Engineering, since 2002, University Cambridge; Fellow, Sidney Sussex College, Cambridge, since 1976; *b* 23 April 1946; *s* William Frank Glover and Helen Ruby Glover (*née* Higgs); *m* 1970, Jean Elizabe Priestley; one *s* one *d*. *Educ:* Dartford Grammar Sch., Kent; Imperial College Londo (BSc(Eng)); MIT (PhD). FIEEE 1993; FInstMC 1999. Development engineer, Marco Co., 1967–69; Kennedy Meml Fellow, MIT, 1969–71; Asst Prof. of Electric Engineering, Univ. of S California, 1973–76; Department of Engineering, University Cambridge: Lectr, 1976–87; Reader in Control Engineering, 1987–89; Head of In Engrg Div., 1993–2001. FREng 2000. Control Systems Award, IEEE, 2001. *Publicatior* (with D. C. McFarlane) Robust Controller Design using Normalized Coprime Fact Plant Descriptions, 1989; (with D. Mustafa) Minimum Entropy H-infinity Control, 199 (jtly) Robust and Optimal Control, 1996; contribs to control and systems jls. *Addres* Department of Engineering, Trumpington Street, Cambridge CB2 1PZ.

GLOVER, Kenneth Frank; Assistant Under-Secretary of State (Statistics), Ministry Defence, 1974–81, retired; *b* 16 Dec. 1920; *s* of Frank Glover and Mabel Glover; *m* 195 Iris Clare Holmes. *Educ:* Bideford Grammar Sch.; UC of South West, Exeter; LS (MScEcon). Joined Statistics Div., MoT, 1946; Statistician, 1950; Statistical adviser Cttee of Inquiry on Major Ports (Rochdale Cttee), 1961–62; Dir of Econs and Statisti at Nat. Ports Council, 1964–68; Chief Statistician, MoT and DoE, 1968–74. *Publicatior* various papers; articles in JRSS, Dock and Harbour Authority. *Recreations:* boatin idleness. *Address:* Little Hamletts, 26 Platway Lane, Shaldon, Teignmouth, South Devo TQ14 0AR. *T:* (01626) 872700.

GLOVER, Prof. L(esley) Anne, PhD; Professor of Molecular and Cell Biolog University of Aberdeen, since 2001; Chief Scientific Adviser for Scotland, since 2006; 19 April 1956; *d* of Wesley and Mary Johnstone Glover; *m* 1996, Ian George. *Edu* Dundee High Sch.; Edinburgh Univ. (BSc 1st Cl. Hons Biochem. 1978); King's Col Cambridge (MPhil 1979, PhD 1981). University of Aberdeen: Lectr in Biochem 1983–94; Sen. Lectr, 1994–98; Reader in Molecular and Cell Biol., 1998–2001. Ho Res. Fellow, Rowett Res. Inst., Aberdeen, 1992–; Res. Associate, Macaulay Land U Res. Inst., Aberdeen, 2002–. Mem., NERC, 2001–. Mem. Council, Soc. of Ge Microbiol., 1995–98. Mem., Bd of Trustees, Cl:aire, 2004–. Fellow, Amer. Acad. Microbiol., 1995; FRSE 2005. *Publications:* book chapters; numerous reviewed contribs learned jls; invited reviews and conf. abstracts. *Recreations:* sailing, reading. *Address:* Scho of Medical Sciences, University of Aberdeen, Institute of Medical Sciences, Foresterhi Aberdeen AB25 2ZD. *T:* (01224) 555799, *Fax:* (01224) 555844; *e-mail:* l.a.glover(abdn.ac.uk.

GLOVER, Myles Howard; Clerk, Worshipful Company of Skinners, 1959–90; *b* 18 De 1928; *yr s* of Cedric Howard Glover and Winifred Mary (*née* Crewdson); *m* 1969, Wenc Gillian, *er d* of C. M. Coleman; one *s* two *d*. *Educ:* Rugby; Balliol Coll., Oxford (MA Called to the Bar, Lincoln's Inn, 1954. Sec., CIFE, 1991–98. Chm., Cttee of Clerks Twelve Chief Livery Cos of City of London, 1975–81. Hon. Sec., GBA, 1967–9 Member: City & Guilds Art Sch. Cttee, 1960–71; Adv. Cttee, Gresham Coll., 1985–8 Governing Council: St Paul's Cathedral Choir Sch., 1986–90; Cambridge Tutors' Col 1993–94, 2000–04; Governing Body, St Leonards-Mayfield Sch., 1988–93; Hon. Add Mem., GBA Cttee, 1991–2003. Hon. Member: Old Tonbridgian Soc., 1986; O Skinners' Soc., 1990 (Leopard of the Year Trophy, 1990); CIFE, 1999. Liveryma Musicians' Co., 1954; Hon. Freeman: Fellmongers' Co., Richmond, N Yorks, 199 Skinners' Co., 1993. *Recreation:* music. *Address:* Wisteria Cottage, 31 The Gree Woodchurch, Ashford, Kent TN26 3PF. *T:* (01233) 860288.

GLOVER, Rt Rev. Patrick; *see* Free State, Bishop of the Diocese of the.

GLOVER, Maj.-Gen. Peter James, CB 1966; OBE 1948; *b* 16 Jan. 1913; *s* of late G. H Glover, CBE, Sheephatch House, Tilford, Surrey, and Mrs G. H. Glover; *m* 1946, Wenc Archer; one *s* two *d*. *Educ:* Uppingham; Cambridge (MA). 2nd Lieut RA, 1934; serve War of 1939–45, BEF France and Far East; Lieut-Col 1956; Brig. 1961; Comdt, Sch. Artillery, Larkhill, 1960–62; Maj.-Gen. 1962; GOC 49 Infantry Division TA and Nor Midland District, 1962–63; Head of British Defence Supplies Liaison Staff, Delh 1963–66; Director, Royal Artillery, 1966–69, retd. Col Comdt, RA, 1970–78. *Addres* Garden Cottage, Wallop House, Nether Wallop, Stockbridge, Hants SO20 8HE.

GLOVER, Stephen Charles Morton; journalist; *b* 13 Jan. 1952; *s* of Rev. Prebenda John Morton Glover and Helen Ruth Glover (*née* Jones); *m* 1982, Celia Elizabeth (*n* Montague); two *s*. *Educ:* Shrewsbury Sch.; Mansfield Coll., Oxford (MA). Dai Telegraph, 1978–85: leader writer and feature writer, 1978–85; parly sketch write 1979–81; Independent: Foreign Editor, 1986–89; Editor, The Independent on Sunda 1990–91; Associate Editor, Evening Standard, 1992–95; Columnist: Daily Telegrap 1996–98; Spectator, 1996–2005; Daily Mail, 1998–; Independent, 2005–. Dir, Newspape Publishing, 1986–92. Vis. Prof. of Journalism, St Andrews Univ., 1992. *Publications:* Pape Dreams, 1993; (ed) Secrets of the Press, 1999. *Address:* c/o Aitken Alexander Associate 18–21 Cavaye Place, SW10 9PT. *Club:* Beefsteak.

GLOVER, Hon. Sir Victor (Joseph Patrick), Kt 1989; GOSK 1992; legal consultan Chief Justice, Mauritius, 1988–94; *b* 5 Nov. 1932; *s* of Joseph George Harold Glover an Mary Catherine (*née* Reddy); *m* 1960, Marie Cecile Ginette Gauthier; two *s*. *Educ:* Collèg du St Esprit; Royal Coll., Mauritius; Jesus Coll., Oxford (BA (Hons) Jurisprudence Called to the Bar, Middle Temple, 1957. District Magistrate, 1962; Crown Counsel, 196 Sen. Crown Counsel, 1966; Prin. Crown Counsel, 1970; Parly Counsel, 1972; Puisn Judge, 1976; Sen. Puisne Judge, 1982. Actg Governor General, July 1988, May 1989, Jun 1990 and Feb. 1991; Actg Pres. of the Republic, 1992. Chm., Tertiary Educn Comm 1988–97; Pres., ESU, 1993–. Hon. Prof. of Civil Law, Univ. of Mauritius, 1986. Ho Bencher, Middle Temple, 1991. *Publications:* Abstract of Decisions of Supreme Court c Mauritius 1966–1981, 1982, Supplement 1982–1986, 1987; The Law of Seychell through the Cases, 1999; The New Mauritius Digest, 2000. *Recreations:* readin swimming, bridge. *Address:* 309 Chancery House, Port Louis, Mauritius. *Clubs:* Oxfo Union Society; Oxford University Boat.

GLOVER, Prof. Vivette Ann Susan, PhD, DSc; Professor of Perinatal Psychobiology Imperial College, London, since 2000; *b* 9 Oct. 1942; *d* of William Fownes Luttrell an Marguerite Luttrell; *m* 1966, Jonathan Glover; two *s* one *d* (and one *d* decd). *Educ:* St Paul Girls' Sch. (Foundn Schol.); Somerville Coll., Oxford (MA); University Coll. Londo (PhD 1970; DSc 1990). Res. Assistant, Chemistry Dept, UCL, 1971–76; Res. Biochemis 1976–81, Clinical Biochemist, 1981–98, Queen Charlotte's Hosp., London; Reader i Perinatal Psychobiol., ICSTM, 1998–2000. Adjunct Prof., Univ. of Rochester, USA 2004–. Hon. Sen. Lectr, Inst. of Psychiatry, London, 1994. Marcé Soc. Medal, 200 *Publications:* numerous contribs to jls incl. Nature, Lancet, BMJ. *Recreations:* cycling (t Soho and in English counties), reading novels, opera, football. *Address:* 3 Chalcot Squar NW1 8YB. *T:* (020) 7586 5312; *e-mail:* v.glover@imperial.ac.uk.

GLOVER, William James; QC 1969; a Recorder of the Crown Court, 1975–91; *b* 8 May 1924; *s* of late H. P. Glover, KC and Martha Glover; *m* 1956, Rosemary D. Long; two *s*. *Educ:* Harrow; Pembroke Coll., Cambridge. Served with Royal West African Frontier Force in West Africa and Burma, 1944–47. Called to the Bar, Inner Temple, 1950, Bencher, 1977. Second Junior Counsel to Inland Revenue (Rating Valuation), 1963–69. *Recreations:* photography, golf. *Address:* 6 Century House, Endless Street, Salisbury SP1 3UH.

GLUBE, Hon. Constance Rachelle, OC 2006; ONS 2005; Chief Justice, Court of Appeal, Nova Scotia, 1998–2004; *b* 23 Nov. 1931; *d* of Samuel Lepofsky, QC and Pearl Lepofsky (*née* Slonemsky); *m* 1952, Richard Glube (*d* 1997); three *s* one *d*. *Educ:* McGill Univ. (BA 1952); Dalhousie Univ. (LLB 1955). Called to the Canadian Bar, 1956. Barrister and Solicitor: Kitz Matheson, 1960–64; Fitzgerald & Glube, 1964–68; City of Halifax: Sen. Solicitor, 1969–74; City Manager, 1974–77; QC (Can.) 1974; Puisne Judge, 1977–82, Chief Justice, 1982–98, Supreme Court of NS. Hon. Mem., Canadian Bar Assoc., 2003. Hon. LLD: Dalhousie Law Sch., 1983; St Mary's, 2000; Hon. LHD Mt St Vincent Univ., 1998. Award of Merit, City of Halifax, 1977; Frances Fish Award (Women Lawyers), 1997; Justice Award, Canadian Inst. for Admin of Justice, 2003. Order of Nova Scotia, 2005. *Recreation:* gardening. *Address:* 5920 Inglewood Drive, Halifax, NS B3H 1B1, Canada. *T:* (902) 4246932.

GLUCKMAN, Prof. Peter David, DCNZM 2008 (CNZM 1997); DSc; FRACP; FRS 2001; FRSNZ; Director, Liggins Institute, University of Auckland, since 2001; *b* 8 Feb. 1949; *s* of Laurie Kalman Gluckman and Ann Jocelyn Gluckman (*née* Klippel); *m* 1970, Judith Lucy Nathan; one *s* one *d*. *Educ:* Univ. of Otago (MB ChB); Univ. of Auckland (MMedSci); Univ. of Calif, San Francisco (DSc). FRCPCH; FRSNZ 1988. Res. Fellow, Univ. of Auckland, 1973–76; Res. Fellow, 1976–78, Asst Prof., 1978–80, Dept of Paediatrics, Univ. of Calif, San Francisco; University of Auckland: Sen. Res. Fellow, 1980–88, Prof. and Chair, 1988–92, Dept of Paediatrics; Dean, Faculty of Med. and Health Scis, 1992–2001. FMedSci 2006. *Publications:* contrib. numerous papers to scientific jls relating to fetal physiology, neurosci., endocrinology of growth and evolutioning medicine. *Recreation:* travel. *Address:* Liggins Institute, University of Auckland, Private Bag 92019, Auckland, New Zealand. *T:* (9) 3737599. *Club:* Northern (Auckland).

GLUCKSMANN, Dame Margaret Myfanwy Wood; *see* Booth, Dame Margaret.

GLUCKSMANN, Prof. Miriam Anne, PhD; FBA 2005; Professor of Sociology, University of Essex, since 1996; *b* 8 April 1946; *d* of late Alfred Glucksmann, MD and Ilse Lasnitzki-Glucksmann, MD, PhD, DSc; partner, Prof. Mark Harvey. *Educ:* Perse Sch. for Girls, Cambridge; London Sch. of Econs and Political Sci. (BA, PhD 1972). Lecturer in Sociology: Brunel Univ., 1970–71; Univ. of Leicester, 1971–73; Sen. Lectr in Sociol., South Bank Poly., 1973–91; Sen. Lectr in Sociol., 1991–92, Reader in Sociol., 1992–96, Dept of Sociol., Univ. of Essex. *Publications:* Structuralist Analysis in Contemporary Social Thought, 1974; (as Ruth Cavendish) Women on the Line, 1982; Women Assemble: women workers and the new industries in inter-war Britain, 1990; Cotton and Casuals: the gendered organisation of labour in time and space, 2000; The New Sociology of Work, 2005. *Address:* Department of Sociology, Essex University, Wivenhoe Park, Colchester CO4 3SQ.

GLUE, George Thomas; Director-General of Supplies and Transport (Naval), Ministry of Defence, 1973–77; *b* 3 May 1917; *s* of Percy Albert Glue and Alice Harriet Glue (*née* Stoner); *m* 1947, Eileen Marion Hitchcock; one *d*. *Educ:* Portsmouth Southern Secondary School. Admiralty: Asst Naval Store Officer, 1937; Dep. Naval Store Officer, Mediterranean, 1940; Naval Store Officer, Mediterranean, 1943; Asst Dir of Stores, 1955; Suptg Naval Store Officer, Devonport, 1960; Dep. Dir of Stores, 1963; Dir of Stores, 1970; Dir, Supplies and Transport (Naval), 1971. *Recreation:* reading. *Address:* 18 Late Broads, Winsley, near Bradford-on-Avon, Wilts BA15 2NW. *T:* (01225) 722717.

GLYN, family name of **Baron Wolverton**.

GLYN, Sir Richard (Lindsay), 10th Bt *cr* 1759, and 6th Bt *cr* 1800; *b* 3 Aug. 1943; *s* of Sir Richard Hamilton Glyn, 9th and 5th Bt, OBE, TD, and Lyndsay Mary (*d* 1971), *d* of T. H. Baker; *S* father, 1980; *m* 1970, Carolyn Ann Williams (marr. diss. 1979); one *s* one *d*. *Educ:* Eton. Co-Founder: Ashton Farm, 1976; High Lea Sch., 1982; Founder: Gaunts House Centre, 1989; Richard Glyn Foundn, 1995; Honeybrook Victorian Farm & Country Park, 2002. *Recreation:* tennis. *Heir: s* Richard Rufus Francis Glyn, *b* 8 Jan. 1971. *Address:* Ashton Farmhouse, Wimborne, Dorset BH21 4JD. *T:* (01258) 840585.

GLYNN, Prof. Alan Anthony, MD; FRCP, FRCPath; Director, Central Public Health Laboratory, Colindale, London, 1980–88, retired; Visiting Professor of Bacteriology, London School of Hygiene and Tropical Medicine, 1983–88; *b* 29 May 1923; *s* of late Hyman and Charlotte Glynn; *m* 1962, Nicole Benhamou; two *d*. *Educ:* City of London Sch.; University Coll. London (Fellow, 1982) and UCH Med. Sch., London (MB, BS 1946, MD 1959). MRCP 1954, FRCP 1974; MRCPath 1963, FRCPath 1973. House Physician, UCH, 1946; Asst Lectr in Physiol., Sheffield Univ., 1947–49; National Service, RAMC, 1950–51; Registrar, Canadian Red Cross Meml Hosp., Taplow, 1955–57; St Mary's Hospital Medical School: Lectr in Bacteriology, 1958–61; Sen. Lectr, 1961–67; Reader, 1967–71; Prof., 1971–80; Hon. Consultant Bacteriologist, 1961–83; Visiting Prof. of Bacteriology, St. Mary's Hosp., 1980–83. Examr in Pathol., Univs of Edinburgh, 1974–76, 1983–85, Glasgow, 1975–78, and London, 1979–80. Member: DHSS Jt Cttee on Vaccination and Immunization, 1979–85; Adv. Gp, ARC Inst. for Res. in Animal Diseases. Almroth Wright Lectr, Wright-Fleming Inst., 1972; Erasmus Wilson Demonstrator, RCS, 1973. Mem. Editorial Board: Immunology, 1969–79; Parasite Immunity, 1979–87. *Publications:* papers on bacterial infection, genetics and immunity and hospital acquired infections. *Recreations:* theatre, walking. *Club:* Athenæum.

See also Prof. I. M. Glynn.

GLYNN, Prof. Ian Michael, MD, PhD, FRS 1970; FRCP; Professor of Physiology, University of Cambridge, 1986–95, now Emeritus; Fellow, Trinity College, since 1955 (Vice-Master, 1980–86); *b* 3 June 1928; 2nd *s* of late Hyman and Charlotte Glynn; *m* 1958, Jenifer Muriel, 2nd *d* of Ellis and Muriel Franklin; one *s* two *d*. *Educ:* City of London Sch.; Trinity Coll., Cambridge; University Coll. Hosp. 1st cl. in Pts I and II of Nat. Sci. Tripos; BA (Cantab) 1949; MB, BChir, 1952; MD 1970; FRCP 1987. House Phys., Central Middx Hosp., 1952–53; MRC Scholar at Physiol. Lab., Cambridge; PhD 1956. Nat. Service in RAF Med. Br., 1956–57. Cambridge University: Res. Fellow, 1955–59, Staff Fellow and Dir of Med. Studies, 1961–73, Trinity Coll.; Univ. Demonstrator in Physiology, 1958–63; Lecturer, 1963–70; Reader, 1970–75; Prof. Membrane Physiology, 1975–86. Vis. Prof., Yale Univ., 1969. Member: MRC, 1976–80 (Chm., Physiological Systems and Disorders Bd, 1976–78); Council, Royal Soc., 1979–81, 1991–92; AFRC (formerly ARC), 1981–86. Chm., Editorial Bd, Jl of Physiology, 1968–70. Hon. Foreign Mem., Amer. Acad. of Arts and Scis, 1984. Hon. MD Aarhus, 1988. *Publications:* (with J. C. Ellory) The Sodium Pump, 1985; An Anatomy of Thought: the origin and machinery of the mind, 1999; (with J. M. Glynn) The Life and Death of Smallpox, 2004; scientific papers dealing with transport of ions across living membranes, mostly in Jl of Physiology. *Address:* Trinity College, Cambridge CB2 1TQ. *T:* (01223) 338415; Daylesford, Conduit Head Road, Cambridge CB3 0EY. *T:* (01223) 353079.

See also Prof. A. A. Glynn.

GLYNN, Joanna Elizabeth; QC 2002; a Recorder, since 2000; *d* of Geraint David Vernet Glynn and Virginia Browell; *m* 1995, Christopher Tehrani; one *s*. Called to the Bar, Middle Temple, 1983; in practice, specialising in criminal and medical regulatory work. Asst Recorder, 1997–2000. Contrib. Ed., Archbold Criminal Pleading Evidence and Practice, annual edns, 1995–2006. *Publication:* (jtly) Fitness to Practise: health care regulatory law, principle and process, 2006. *Address:* 23 Essex Street, WC2R 3AA. *T:* (020) 7413 0353, *Fax:* (020) 7413 0374; *e-mail:* joannaglynn@23es.com.

GOAD, Sarah Jane Frances; JP; Lord-Lieutenant of Surrey, since 1997; *b* 23 Aug. 1940; *er d* of Uvedale Lambert and late Diana (*née* Grey) and step *d* of Melanie Grant Lambert, Denver, Colo; *m* 1961, Timothy Francis Goad, DL; two *s* one *d*. *Educ:* St Mary's, Wantage. Worked for Faber & Faber, 1959–70; Dir, Tilburstow Farms Co. Ltd, 1963–70; Partner, Lambert Farmers, 1970–94. JP Surrey, 1974; Dep. Chm., Family Panel, 1992–97; Mem., Surrey Magistrates' Soc., 1987–93. Trustee: St Mark's Foundn, 1971–; Love Walk (home for disabled), 1984–98 (Chm. Trustees, 1989–93); Surrey Care Trust, 1987–97 (Chm. Trustees, 1995–97); Chevening Estate, 2001–. Chm., Southwark Cathedral Council, 2000–; Lay Canon, Southwark Cathedral, 2004–. Pres., SE Reserve Forces' and Cadets' Assoc., 2006–. Governor: local C of E sch., 1970–90; Hazelwood Sch., 1979–84. Patron, Yvonne Arnaud Theatre, 2004–. DStJ 1997. *Recreations:* books, buildings, arts. *Address:* South Park, Bletchingley, Surrey RH1 4NE.

GOBBO, Hon. Sir James (Augustine), AC 1993; Kt 1982; CVO 2000; Chairman, National Library of Australia, since 2001; Commissioner for Italy, Victoria, 2001–06; *b* 22 March 1931; *s* of Antonio Gobbo and Regina Gobbo (*née* Tosetto); *m* 1957, Shirley Lewis; two *s* three *d*. *Educ:* Xavier Coll., Kew, Victoria; Melbourne Univ. (BA Hons); Magdalen Coll., Oxford Univ. (MA; Pres., OUBC, 1955; Mem., Boat Race Crew, 1954, 1955). Called to the Bar, Gray's Inn, London, 1956; Barrister and Solicitor, Victoria, Aust., 1956; signed Roll of Counsel, Victorian Bar, 1957; QC 1971; Supreme Court Judge, Victoria, 1978–94; Lt Gov., 1995–97, Governor, 1997–2000, of Victoria. Indep. Lectr in Evidence, Univ. of Melbourne, 1963–68. Comr, Victorian Law Reform Commn, 1985–88. Chairman: Aust. Refugee Council, 1977; Multicultural Taskforce for Aust. Bicentenary, 1982–84; Reference Gp into Public Liby Funding, 1987; Aust. Multicultural Affairs Council, 1987–91; Aust. Bicentennial Multicultural Foundn, 1988–97, 2001–; Palladio Foundn, 1989–97; Aust. Banking Industry Ombudsman Council, 1994–97; Electricity Industry Ombudsman Council, 1995–97; Council, Order of Australia, 2001– (Mem., 1982–92); Nat. Cttee of the Ageing, 2002–; Mercy Private Hosp., Melbourne, 1977–87 (Mem. Bd, Mercy Maternity Hosp., 1972–91); Caritas Christi Hospice, 1986–97; Order of Malta Hospice Home Care, 1986–97; Italian Historical Soc. of Vic, 1980–97. Member: Immigration Reform Gp, 1959–64; Aust. Inst. of Multicultural Affairs, 1979–86; Nat. Population Council, 1983–87; Victorian Health Promotion Foundn, 1989–97; Victorian Community Foundn, 1992–97; Nat. Adv. Cttee, Centenary of Fedn, 1994; Newman Coll. Council, 1970–85; Italo-Australian Educn Foundn, 1974–97; Palladio Trust, Univ. of Melbourne, 1989–; Cttee, Italian Services Inst., 1993–97, 2001–; Bd of Govs, Ian Potter Foundn, 2001–; Bd of Govs, CEDA, 2004–; Bd, Monash Inst. for Study of Global Movts, 2005–; Bd, St Vincent's Foundn, 2006; Pres., CO-AS-IT, 1979–84, 1986–94. Trustee: Victorian Opera Foundn, 1983–97; WWF, Australia, 1991–97. Vice-Pres., Aust. Assoc. of SMO Malta, 1984–87, Pres., 1987–97; Pres., Scout Assoc. of Victoria, 1987–97. Fellow, Rockefeller Foundn, Bellagio, 1994. Hon. Fellow Aust. Inst. of Valuers, 1985; Hon. Life Member: Aust. Inst. of Architects, 1997; Nat. Gall., Vic, 1999. Hon. LLD Monash, 1995; Hon. Dr Aust. Catholic Univ., 1996; Hon. Dr Jurisp. Bologna, 1998; Hon. LLD Melbourne, 2000. GCSG 2003. Commendatore, 1973, Grand Cross, 1998, Order of Merit, Republic of Italy; Kt Grand Cross, SMO Malta, 1982. *Publications:* (ed) Cross on Evidence (Australian edn), 1970–1978; various papers. *Address:* 8/25 Douglas Street, Toorak, Vic 3142, Australia. *T:* (3) 98266115.

GOBBY, Clive John; Director, South Africa and Regional Director, Southern Africa, British Council, 2000–03; *b* 2 June 1947; *m* 1978, Margaret Ann Edwards. *Educ:* Bective Secondary Mod. Sch., Northampton; Northampton GS; Leicester Univ. (BA 1968). Joined British Council, 1982; Dep. Manager, Enterprises, 1992–96; Network Manager, Grant in Aid Services, 1996; Dir, Turkey, 1997–2000. *Recreations:* walking, net surfing, dog training.

GOBLE, John Frederick; retired solicitor; *b* 1 April 1925; *o s* of John and Evileen Goble; *m* 1953, Moira Murphy O'Connor; one *s* three *d*. *Educ:* Finchley Catholic GS; Highgate Sch.; Brasenose Coll., Oxford (MA). Sub-Lieut, RNVR, 1944–46. Admitted solicitor, 1951; Herbert Smith: Partner, 1953–88; Hong Kong office, 1982–83; Sen. Partner, 1983–88. Crown Agents, 1974–82 (Dep. Chm., 1975–82); Director: British Telecommunications, 1983–91; Wren Underwriting Agencies, 1988–91. A Dep. Chm., City Panel on Takeovers and Mergers, 1989–97. Chm., St Barnabas Soc., 1992–95. Governor, Highgate Sch., 1976–96. Chm., The Friends of Highgate Sch. Soc., 1978–87; Pres., Old Cholmeleian Soc., 1983–84. KCSG 1994. *Recreations:* music, golf. *Address:* 114 Rivermead Court, Ranelagh Gardens, SW6 3SB; 3 Warren Court, Warren Road, Thurlestone, Kingsbridge, Devon TQ7 3NT. *Clubs:* Garrick, MCC, Hurlingham; New Zealand Golf (West Byfleet); Thurlestone Golf; Royal Mid-Surrey Golf; Honourable Company of Edinburgh Golfers (Muirfield).

GODARD, Jean-Luc; French film director; *b* 3 Dec. 1930; *s* of Paul Godard and Odile Godard (*née* Monad); *m* 1st, 1961, Anna Karina (marr. diss.); 2nd, 1967, Anne Wiazemsky. *Educ:* Collège de Nyon; Lycée Buffon; Faculté de Lettres, Paris. Former journalist and film critic: La Gazette du cinéma; Les Cahiers du cinéma. Mem., Conseil supérieur de la langue française, 1989. *Films include:* A bout de souffle, 1959 (prix Jean Vigo, 1960; Best Dir Award, Berlin Fest., 1960); Le Petit Soldat, 1960; Une femme est une femme, 1961 (Special Prize, Berlin Fest.); Les sept péchés capitaux, 1961; Vivre sa vie, 1962 (Special Prize, Venice Fest.); Les Carabiniers, 1963; Les plus belles escroqueries du Monde, 1963; Le Mépris, 1963; Paris vu par …, 1964; Une femme mariée, 1964; Alphaville, 1965; Pierrot le fou, 1965; Masculin-Féminin, 1966; Made in USA, 1966; Deux ou trois choses que je sais d'elle, 1966; La Chinoise, 1967 (Special Prize, Venice Fest.); Week-end, 1967; Loin du Vietnam, 1967; La Contestation, 1970; Ici et ailleurs, 1976; (jtly) Tout va bien, 1972; Moi je, 1974; Comment ça va?, 1975; Sauve qui peut, 1980; Passion, 1982; Prénom Carmen, 1983 (Golden Lion, Venice Fest.); Je vous salue Marie, 1985; Détective, 1985; Soigne ta droite, 1987; Le Roi Lear, 1987; Nouvelle vague, 1990; Hélas pour moi, 1993; JLG/JLG, 1995; For Ever Mozart, 1996; Eloge de l'amour, 2001; Notre Musique, 2005. Chevalier de l'ordre national du Mérite. *Publication:* Introduction à une véritable histoire du cinéma. *Address:* 15 rue du Nord, 1180 Rolle, Switzerland.

GODBER, Sir George (Edward), GCB 1971 (KCB 1962; CB 1958); Chief Medical Officer, Department of Health and Social Security, Department of Education and Science, and Home Office, 1960–73; *b* 4 Aug. 1908; *s* of late I. Godber, Willington Manor, Bedford; *m* 1935, Norma Hathorne Rainey (*d* 1999); two *s* one *d* (and two *s* two *d* decd). *Educ:* Bedford Sch.; New Coll., Oxford (Hon. Fellow, 1973); London Hospital; London Sch. of Hygiene. BA 1930, BM 1933, DM 1939, Oxon; MRCP 1935, FRCP 1947; DPH London 1936. Medical Officer, Min. of Health, 1939; Dep. Chief Medical Officer, Min. of Health, 1950–60. Chm., Health Educn Council, 1977–78 (Mem., 1976–78). QHP, 1953–56. Scholar in Residence, NIH Bethesda, 1975. Vice-Pres., RCN, 1973. Fellow: American Hospital Assoc., and American Public Health Assoc., 1961; British Orthopaedic Assoc.; Mem. Dietetic Assoc., 1961; Hon. Member: Faculty of Radiologists, 1958; British Pædiatric Assoc.; Royal Pharmaceut. Soc., 1973. FRCOG *ad eundem* 1966; FRCPsych 1973; FFCM 1974. Hon. FRCS 1973; Hon. FRCGP 1973; Hon. FRSocMed 1973. Hon. LLD: Manchester, 1964; Hull, 1970; Nottingham, 1973; Hon. DCL: Newcastle 1972; Oxford 1973; Hon. DSc Bath, 1979. Hon. Fellow, London Sch. of Hygiene and Tropical Medicine, 1976. Bisset Hawkins Medal, RCP, 1965; 150th Anniversary Medal, Swedish Med. Soc., 1966; Leon Bernard Foundn Medal, 1972; Ciba Foundn Gold Medal, 1970; Therapeutics Gold Medal, Soc. of Apothecaries, 1973. Lectures: Thomas and Edith Dixon Belfast, 1962; Bartholomew, Rotunda, Dublin, 1963; Woolmer, Bio-Engineering Soc., 1964; Monkton Copeman, Soc. of Apothecaries, 1968; Michael M. Davis, Chicago, 1969; Harold Diehl, Amer. Public Health Assoc., 1969; Rhys Williams, 1969; W. M. Fletcher Shaw, RCOG, 1970; Henry Floyd, Inst. of Orthopaedics, 1970; First Elizabeth Casson Meml, Assoc. of Occ. Therapists, 1973; Cavendish, W London Med.-Chir. Soc., 1973; Heath Clark, London Univ., 1973; Rock Carling, Nuffield Provincial Hosps Trust, 1975; Thom Bequest, RCSE, 1975; Maurice Bloch, Glasgow, 1975; Ira Hiscock, Yale, 1975; John Sullivan, St Louis, 1975; Fordham, Sheffield, 1976; Lloyd Hughes, Liverpool, 1977; Gale Meml, SW England Faculty RCGP, 1978; Gordon, Birmingham, 1979; Samson Gamgee, Birm. Med. Inst., 1979; W. H. Duncan, Liverpool, 1984; W. Pickles, RCGP, 1985; Green Coll., Oxford, 1988. *Publications:* (with Sir L. Parsons and Clayton Fryers) Survey of Hospitals in the Sheffield Region, 1944; The Health Service: past, present and future (Heath Clark Lectures), 1974; Change in Medicine (Rock Carling monograph), 1975; British National Health Service: Conversations, 1977; papers in Lancet, BMJ, Public Health. *Recreation:* gardening.

GODBER, John Harry; playwright, since 1981; *b* 18 May 1956; *s* of Harry Godber and Dorothy (*née* Deakin); *m* 1993, Jane Thornton; two *d*. *Educ:* Leeds Univ. (CertEd, BEd Hons, MA, MPhil). School teacher, 1979–83; writing for TV, 1981–; Artistic Dir, Hull Truck Theatre Co., 1984–. Prof. of Contemporary Theatre, Liverpool Hope Univ., 2004–. *Plays include:* Up 'N' Under, 1984 (filmed, 1997); Bouncers, 1986; Teechers, 1987; On the Piste, 1993; April in Paris, 1994; Passion Killers, 1994; Shakers: the musical, 1994; Lucky Sods, 1995; Weekend Breaks, 1997; Perfect Pitch, 1998; Unleashed, 1998; It started with a Kiss, 1998; Thick as a Brick, 1999 (filmed, 2004); On a Night Like This, 1999; Departures, 2001; Reunion, 2002; Screaming Blue Murder, 2003; Black Tie and Tails, 2003; Fly Me to the Moon, 2004; Beef and Yorkshire Pudding, 2004; Going Dutch, 2004; Wrestling Mad, 2005; Crown Prince, 2007; television series, Thunder Road (also filmed), 2002; television film, Oddsquad, 2005. Sunday Times Play-writing Award, 1981; Olivier Award for Comedy of Year, 1984. Hon. DLitt: Hull, 1988; Humberside, 1997. *Publications:* Up 'N' Under, 1985; Bouncers, 1986; John Godber: 5 plays, 1989; On the Piste, 1991; April in Paris, 1992; Blood Sweat and Tears, 1995; Lucky Sods, 1995; Passion Killers, 1995; Gym and Tonic, 1996; John Godber Plays: vols 1 and 2, 2001, vol. 3, 2003. *Recreations:* keep fit, reading, theatre, cinema, opera. *Address:* St Nicholas, Beech Hill Road, Swanland, North Ferriby HU14 3QY.

GODDARD, Andrew Stephen; QC 2003; *b* 5 Oct. 1959; *s* of Lt Col C. E. Goddard and Kathleen Goddard; one *s* two *d*. *Educ:* St John's Sch., Billericay; Chelmsford Coll. of Further Educn; Univ. of Sussex (BA 1st Cl. Hons Law); Inns of Court Sch. of Law. Called to the Bar, Inner Temple, 1985 (QE II Major Schol. 1984; Poland Prize 1985); barrister, specialising in internat. construction disputes, 1987–. *Recreations:* child rearing, peace and quiet. *Address:* 1 Atkin Building, Gray's Inn, WC1R 5AT. *T:* (020) 7404 0102, *Fax:* (020) 7405 7456; *e-mail:* agoddard@atkinchambers.law.co.uk.

GODDARD, Her Honour Ann Felicity; QC; a Circuit Judge, 1993–2008 (a Senior Circuit Judge, 1997–2008); *b* 22 Jan. 1936; *o c* of late Graham Elliott Goddard and Margaret Louise Hambrook Goddard (*née* Clark). *Educ:* Grey Coat Hosp., Westminster; Birmingham Univ. (LLB); Newnham Coll., Cambridge (LLM and Dip. in Comparative Legal Studies). Called to the Bar, Gray's Inn, 1960; Bencher, 1990; a Recorder, 1979–93. Member: Gen. Council of the Bar, 1988–93; Criminal Justice Consultative Council, 1992–93. Pres., British Acad. of Forensic Scis, 1995–96. Freeman, 1994, Liveryman, 1996–, Clockmakers' Co.; Liveryman, Gardeners' Co., 2003–. *Recreation:* travel. *Club:* Athenæum.

GODDARD, David Rodney, MBE 1985; Director, International Sailing Craft Association, 1966–96; *b* 16 March 1927; *s* of Air Marshal Sir Victor Goddard, KCB, CBE, and Mildred Catherine Jane, *d* of Alfred Markham Inglis; *m* 1951, Susan Ashton; three *s* one *d*. *Educ:* Bryanston School; Wanganui Collegiate Sch., New Zealand; Peterhouse, Cambridge. MA Hons Geography. Joined Royal Marines, 1944, hostilities only commn, 1946, demob. 1948. Whaling, United Whalers, 1949; Schoolmaster, 1950–52. Joined Somerset Light Infantry, 1952; active service, Malaya (mentioned in despatches, 1954); served: Germany, Kenya (King's African Rifles), Bahrein, N Ireland; retired at own request, as Major, 1968, to found and direct Internat. Sailing Craft Assoc. and Exeter Maritime Museum; Dir, Exeter Maritime Mus., 1968–88, 1991–96. *Recreations:* shooting, fishing, sailing, bird watching, photography. *Address:* The Mill, Lympstone, Exmouth, Devon EX8 5HD. *T:* (01395) 265575.

GODDARD, Harold Keith; QC 1979; barrister-at-law; a Recorder of the Crown Court, 1978–2001; a Deputy High Court Judge, 1993–2001; *b* 9 July 1936; *s* of late Harold Goddard and Edith Goddard, Stockport, Cheshire; *m* 1st, 1963, Susan Elizabeth (marr. diss.), *yr d* of late Ronald Stansfield and of Evelyn Stansfield, Wilmslow, Cheshire; two *s*; 2nd, 1983, Alicja Maria, *d* of late Czeslaw Lazuchiewicz and of Eleonora Lazuchiewicz, Lodz, Poland. *Educ:* Manchester Grammar Sch.; Corpus Christi Coll., Cambridge (Scholar; 1st Cl. Law Tripos 1957; MA, LLM). Bacon Scholar, Gray's Inn; called to the Bar, Gray's Inn, 1959. Practised on Northern Circuit, 1959–; Head of Chambers, 1983–2000. Member: CICB, 1993–2001; Mental Health Review Tribunal, 1998–. Chm., Disciplinary Appeals Cttee, 1974–80, Mem. Council, 1980–, Mem. Ct of Governors, 1981, UMIST. *Recreation:* golf. *Address:* Deans Court Chambers, 24 St John Street, Manchester M3 4DF. *T:* (0161) 214 6000. *Club:* Wilmslow Golf.

GODDARD, Prof. John Burgess, OBE 1986; Henry Daysh Professor of Regional Development Studies, since 1975 and Deputy Vice-Chancellor, 2001–08, University of Newcastle upon Tyne; *b* 5 Aug. 1943; *s* of Burgess Goddard and Molly Goddard (*née* Bridge); *m* 1966, Janet Patricia (*née* Peddle); one *s* two *d*. *Educ:* Latymer Upper Sch.; University Coll. London (BA); LSE (PhD). Lectr, LSE, 1968–75; Leverhulme Fellow, Univ. of Lund, 1974; University of Newcastle: Hon. Dir, Centre for Urban and Regional Develt Studies, 1978–; Dean, Faculty of Law, Envmt and Social Scis, 1994–98; Pro Vice-Chancellor, 1998–2001. Dir, ESRC Prog. on Inf. and Communications Technol. 1992–93. Advr, Trade and Industry Select Cttee, H of C, 1994–95. Chairman: Assoc. of Dirs of Res. Centres in Social Sciences, 1991–98; Assoc. of Res. Centres in the Social Scis 1998–99. Member: Northern Economic Planning Council, 1976–79; Human Geography Cttee, SSRC, 1976–80; Bd, Port of Tyne Authority, 1990–93; Bd, Tyne and Wear Sub-Regl Partnership, 2005–08. Chairman: NE Reg. Cttee, Community Fund, 2003–04 Voluntary and Community Sector Cttee, Big Lottery Fund, 2005–06. Governor University of Northumbria at Newcastle (formerly Newcastle upon Tyne Poly.) 1989–98. Editor, Regional Studies, 1980–85. AcSS 2003. FRSA 1992. Victoria Medal RGS, 1992. *Publications:* Office Linkages and Location, 1973; Office Location in Urban and Regional Development, 1975; The Urban and Regional Transformation of Britain 1983; Technological Change, Industrial Restructuring and Regional Development, 1986 Urban Regeneration in a Changing Economy, 1992; articles in professional jls.

GODDARD, Rt Rev. John William; *see* Burnley, Bishop Suffragan of.

GODDARD, Peter, CBE 2002; ScD; FRS 1989; Director, Institute for Advanced Study Princeton, since 2004; Fellow, St John's College, Cambridge, 1975–94 and since 2004 (Master, 1994–2004); *b* 3 Sept. 1945; *s* of Herbert Charles Goddard and Rosina Sarah Goddard (*née* Waite); *m* 1968, Helen Barbara Ross; one *s* one *d*. *Educ:* Emanuel Sch. London; Trinity Coll., Cambridge (BA 1966; MA, PhD 1971); ScD Cantab 1996. FInstP 1990. Res. Fellow, Trinity Coll., Cambridge, 1969–73; Vis. Scientist, CERN, Geneva 1970–72, 1978; Lectr in Applied Maths, Univ. of Durham, 1972–74; Mem., Inst. for Advanced Study, Princeton, NJ, 1974, 1988; Cambridge University: Asst Lectr 1975–76 Lectr 1976–89; Reader in Mathematical Physics, 1989–92; Prof. of Theoretical Physics 1992–2004; Dep. Dir, Isaac Newton Inst. for Mathematical Scis, 1991–94 (Sen. Fellow 1994–); Mem., Univ. Council, 2000–03; St John's College: Lectr in Maths 1975–91 Tutor 1980–87; Sen. Tutor 1983–87. Vis. Prof. of Maths and Physics, Univ. of Virginia 1983; SERC Vis. Fellow, Imperial Coll., 1987. Mem., Inst. for Theoretical Physics, Univ of California, Santa Barbara, 1986, 1990. Pres., LMS, 2002–03. Chm., Univ. of Cambridge Local Exams Syndicate, 1998–2003. Governor: Berkhamsted Schs, 1985–96 Emanuel Sch., 1992–2003; Shrewsbury Sch., 1994–2003; Hills Road Sixth Form Coll. Cambridge, 1999–2003 (Chm., 2001–03). Hon. Fellow, TCD, 1995. Dirac Medal and Prize, Internat. Centre for Theoretical Physics, Trieste, 1997. *Publications:* articles on elementary particle physics and mathematical physics in sci. jls. *Recreations:* informal flower arranging, mathematical physics, idle thought. *Address:* Institute for Advanced Study Einstein Drive, Princeton, NJ 08540, USA. *T:* (609) 7348200.

GODDARD, Air Vice-Marshal Peter John, CB 1998; AFC 1981; FRAeS; Senior Directing Staff (Air), Royal College of Defence Studies, 1996–98; *b* 17 Oct. 1943; *s* of John Bernard Goddard and Lily Goddard; *m* 1966, Valerie White; two *s*. *Educ* Nottingham High Sch. qwi, ndc, aws, rcds. FRAeS 1997. Joined RAF 1963; served 54 and 4 Hunter Sqns, 233 Harrier and 226 Jaguar OCUs; OC, 54 Jaguar Sqn, 1978–80 MoD, 1981–83; OC, Tri-nat. Tornado Trng Estabt, RAF Cottesmore, 1984–86; RCDS 1988; Dir, Air Armament, 1989–93; Dep. Comdr, Interim Combined Air Ops Centre 4 1993–96. Chm., Seckford Foundn, 2000–. *Recreations:* golf, gardening, walking. *Clubs* Royal Air Force; Felixstowe Ferry Golf.

GODDARD, Roy; independent business consultant, since 1988; Member, Independent Television Commission, 1991–97; *b* 21 Feb. 1939; *s* of Roy Benjamin Goddard and Emma Annie Coronation (*née* Beckett); *m* 1961, Sally Anne Pain; one *s* one *d*. *Educ:* Henry Thornton Grammar Sch.; Regent Street Polytechnic. Cummins Engine Co., 1964–68 Partner, Alexander Hughes & Associates, executive search consultants, 1968–70; Founder Goddard Kay Rogers & Associates, 1970–88. Chm., Network Gp of Cos, 1992–98; Mem Adv. Bd, Private Equity Div., Mercury Asset Mgt, 1997–2000; Director: Hg Capital (formerly Mercury Private Equity), 2001–; Hg Investment Mgt, 2002–07; Hg Pooled Mgt, 2002–. Member: IBA, 1990–91; GMC, 1994–99. Home Office selection panel appointee, Sussex Police Authy, 1994–2000; Ind. Assessor, Legal Aid Bd, 1996–98. Hon Vice Pres., Dyslexia Inst., 1997– (Chm., 1990–96). Freeman, City of London, 1981 Liveryman, Co. of Glaziers and Painters of Glass, 1981–. *Recreations:* water gardening, reading, eating, cinema, theatre. *Address:* Newells, Brighton Road, Lower Beeding, West Sussex RH13 6NQ. *T:* (01403) 891110. *Club:* Royal Automobile.

GODDEN, Charles Henry, CBE 1982; HM Diplomatic Service, retired; Governor (formerly HM Commissioner), Anguilla, 1978–83; *b* 19 Nov. 1922; *s* of late Charles Edward Godden and Catherine Alice Godden (*née* Roe); *m* 1943, Florence Louise Williams; two *d*. *Educ:* Tweeddale Sch., Carshalton; Morley Coll., Westminster. Served Army, 1941–46. Colonial Office, 1950–66 (seconded British Honduras, 1961–64: Perm Sec., External Affairs; Dep. Chief Sec.; Clerk of Executive Council); FCO, 1966–: First Sec., 1968; Asst Private Sec. to Sec. of State for Colonies; Private Secretary: to Minister of State, FCO, 1967–70; to Parly Under Sec. of State, 1970; First Sec. (Commercial) Helsinki, 1971–75; First Sec., Belize, 1975–76; Dep. High Comr and Head of Chancery Kingston, 1976–78. *Publication:* Trespassers Forgiven: memoirs of imperial service in the age of independence, 2008. *Recreations:* cricket, walking, reading. *Address:* Stoneleigh Blackboys, Sussex TN22 5JL. *T:* (01825) 890410. *Clubs:* MCC, Royal Commonwealth Society.

GODDEN, Prof. Malcolm Reginald, PhD; Rawlinson and Bosworth Professor of Anglo-Saxon, and Fellow of Pembroke College, Oxford, since 1991; *b* 9 Oct. 1945. *Educ* Devizes Grammar Sch.; Barton Peveril Sch., Eastleigh; Pembroke Coll., Cambridge (BA 1966; MA, PhD 1970). Res. Fellow, Pembroke Coll., Cambridge, 1969–72; Asst Prof. Cornell Univ., 1970–71; Lectr in English, Liverpool Univ., 1972–75; Univ. Lectr in English, and Fellow, Exeter Coll., Oxford, 1976–91. Exec. Editor, Anglo-Saxon England 1989–. *Publications:* Ælfric's Catholic Homilies, (ed) second series, 1979, (ed jtly) first series, 1997, introduction, commentary and glossary, 2000 (Gollancz Prize, British Acad., 2001); The Making of Piers Plowman, 1990; (ed jtly) The Cambridge Companion to Old English Literature, 1991; (ed jtly) Anglo-Saxon England, vol. 27, 1999; contribs to Anglia, English Studies, Anglo-Saxon England, Rev. of English Studies. *Address:* English Faculty, St Cross Building, Manor Road, Oxford OX1 3UQ; Pembroke College, Oxford OX1 1DW. *T:* (01865) 276444.

GODDEN, Tony Richard Hillier, CB 1975; Secretary, Scottish Development Department, 1980–87, retired; *b* 13 Nov. 1927; *o s* of late Richard Godden and Gladys Eleanor Godden; *m* 1953, Marjorie Florence Snell; one *s* two *d*. *Educ:* Barnstaple Grammar Sch.; London Sch. of Economics (BSc (Econ.) 1st cl.). Commissioned, RAF Education Branch, 1950. Entered Colonial Office as Asst Principal, 1951; Private Sec. to Parly Under-Sec. of State, 1954–55; Principal, 1956; Cabinet Office, 1957–59; transferred to Scottish Home Dept, 1961; Asst Sec., Scottish Development Dept, 1964; Under-Sec., 1969; Sec., Scottish Economic Planning Dept, 1973–80. Member: Council on Tribunals, 1988–94; Ancient Monuments Board for Scotland, 1990–95. Sec., Friends of Royal Scottish Acad., 1987–2000. *Address:* 9 Ross Road, Edinburgh EH16 5QN. *T:* (0131) 667 6556. *Club:* New (Edinburgh).

GODFRAY, Prof. (Hugh) Charles (Jonathan), PhD; FRS 2001; Hope Professor of Zoology (Entomology), and Fellow of Jesus College, University of Oxford, since 2006; *b* 27 Oct. 1958; *s* of Hugh and Annette Godfray; *m* 1992, Caroline Essil Margaret Elmslie. *Educ:* Millfield Sch., Som; St Peter's Coll., Oxford (MA; Hon. Fellow, 2001); Imperial Coll., London (PhD 1983). NERC Postdoctoral Fellow, Dept of Biol., Imperial Coll., London Univ., 1982–85; Demonstrator in Ecol., Dept of Zool., Univ. of Oxford, 1985–87; Imperial College, London University: Lectr, 1987–92, Reader, 1992–95, Dept of Biol Scis; Prof. of Evolutionary Biol., 1995–2006; Dir, NERC Centre for Population Biol., 1999–2006; Head, Div. of Biol., 2005–06. Mem., NERC, 2008–. Pres., British Ecol Soc., Sept. 2009–. Hon. Fellow, Nat. Hist. Mus., 2002–. Trustee, Royal Botanic Gdns, Kew, 2004–. Scientific Medal, Zool. Soc., 1994. *Publications:* Parasitoids, 1994; scientific papers in ecology and evolution. *Recreations:* natural history, gardening, opera, walking. *Address:* Department of Zoology, South Parks Road, Oxford OX1 3PS.

GODFREY, Daniel Charles; Director General, Association of Investment Companies (formerly Association of Investment Trust Companies), since 1998; Chairman, Personal Finance Education Group, 2000–03; *b* 30 June 1961; *s* of late Gerald Michael Godfrey, CBE; *m* 1994, Frederiki Androulla Perewiznyk; three *s* one *d*. *Educ:* Westminster Sch., Victoria Univ. of Manchester (BA Hons Econs). Life Inspr, UK Provident, 1982–85; Mktg Manager, Schroders, 1985–88; Project Manager, Mercury Asset Mgt, 1988–90; Mktg Manager, Laurentian Life, 1990–91; Proprietor, The Sharper Image, 1991–94; Mktg Dir, Flemings, 1994–98. Member: ICA, 1987–; IoD, 2001–. *Recreations:* football (watching), children (raising). *Address:* (office) 24 Chiswell Street, EC1Y 4YY. *T:* (020) 7282 5555. *Club:* London Capital.

GODFREY, Rt Rev. (Harold) William; *see* Peru, Bishop of.

GODFREY, Howard Anthony; QC 1991; a Recorder, since 1992; *b* 17 Aug. 1946; *s* of late Emanuel and of Amy Godfrey; *m* 1972, Barbara Ellinger; two *s*. *Educ:* William Ellis Sch.; LSE (LLB). Asst Lectr in Law, Univ. of Canterbury, NZ, 1969. Called to the Bar, Middle Temple, 1970 (Bencher, 2004), *ad eundem* Inner Temple, 1984; part-time Tutor, Law Dept, LSE, 1970–72; practising on SE Circuit, 1972–; called to the Bar, Turks and Caicos Is, 1996. Fellow, Soc. for Advanced Legal Studies, 1998. *Recreations:* wine and food, travel, humour. *Address:* 2 Bedford Row, WC1R 4BU. *T:* (020) 7440 8888, *Fax:* (020) 7242 1738.

GODFREY, Dr Malcolm Paul Weston, CBE 1986; Chairman, Public Health Laboratory Service Board, 1989–96; *b* 11 Aug. 1926; *s* of late Harry Godfrey and Rose Godfrey; *m* 1955, Barbara Goldstein; one *s* one *d* (and one *d* decd). *Educ:* Hertford Grammar Sch.; King's Coll., London Univ. (FKC 2000); KCH Med. Sch. (MB, BS (Hons and Univ. Medal) 1950); MRCP 1955, FRCP 1972. Hosp. posts at KCH, Nat. Heart and Brompton Hosps; RAF Med. Br., 1952–54; Fellow in Med. and Asst Physician (Fulbright Scholar), Johns Hopkins Hosp., USA, 1957–58; MRC Headquarters Staff, 1960–74: MO, 1960; Sen. MO, 1964; Principal MO, 1970; Sen. Principal MO, 1974; Dean, Royal Postgrad. Med. Sch., 1974–83 (Mem. Council, 1974–83, 1988–96; Chm., Audit Cttee, 1995–96; Hon. Fellow, 1985); Second Sec., MRC, 1983–88. University of London: Member: Senate, 1980–83; Court, 1981–83; Chm., Jt Med. Adv. Cttee, 1979–82. Mem., Faculty Bd of Clinical Medicine, Univ. of Cambridge, 1988–89. Chm., Brit. Council Med. Adv. Cttee, 1985–90; Member: Sci. Adv. Panel CIBA Foundn, 1974–91; Ealing, Hammersmith and Hounslow AHA(T), 1975–80; NW Thames RHA, 1980–83, 1985–88; Hammersmith SHA, 1982–83; Sec. of State's Adv. Gp on London Health Services, 1980–81; GMC, 1979–81. Lay Mem., Professional Standards Dept, Gen. Council of the Bar, 1990–95. Consultant Advr, WHO Human Reproduction Programme, 1979–90; Scientific Advr, Foulkes Foundn, 1983–89. Member, Council: Charing Cross Hosp. Med. Sch., 1975–80; St Mary's Hosp. Med. Sch., 1983–88; Royal Free Hosp. Sch. of Medicine, 1991–96; KCL, 1997–2001; Mem., Governing Body, BPMF, 1974–89; Chm., Council of Governors, UMDS of Guy's and St Thomas' Hosps, 1996–98 (Mem., 1990–96; Trustee, UMDS, 1998–); Mem., Special Trustees, Hammersmith Hosp., 1975–83. Pres., KCL Assoc., 2002–04 (Vice-Pres., 2000–02). Trustee, Florence Nightingale Fund, 1996–. Mem., Soc. of Scholars, Johns Hopkins Univ., USA, 2000. Gov., Quintin Kynaston Sch., 2000–03. Liveryman, Goldsmiths' Co., 1984– (Mem., Charity Cttee, 1998–2006); Mem. Court of Assts, Soc. of Apothecaries, 1979–94 (Master, 1989–90; Assistant Emeritus, 1995–). JP Wimbledon, 1972–92 (Chm. of the Bench and of Merton Magistrates' Courts Cttee, 1988–90 (Dep. Chm., 1987); Chm., Juvenile Panel, 1983–87). QHP, 1987–90. FRSA, 1989–92. Hon. Fellow, ICSM, 1999. *Publications:* contrib. med. jls on cardiac and respiratory disorders. *Recreations:* theatre, planning holidays (sometimes taking them), walking. *Address:* 17 Clifton Hill, St John's Wood, NW8 0QE. *T:* (020) 7624 6335, *Fax:* (020) 7328 9474.

GODFREY, Peter, FCA; Senior Partner, Ernst & Whinney, Chartered Accountants, 1980–86, retired; Chairman, Accounting Standards Committee, 1984–86 (Member, 1983–86); *b* 23 March 1924; *m* 1951, Heather Taplin; two *s* one *d*. *Educ:* West Kensington Central Sch. Served Army, 1942, until released, rank Captain, 1947. Qual. as an Incorporated Accountant, 1949; joined Whinney Smith & Whinney, 1949; admitted to partnership, 1959; Chm., Ernst & Whinney Internat., 1981–83, 1985–86. Appointed: BoT Inspector into Affairs of Pinnock Finance Co. (GB) Ltd, Aug. 1967; DTI Inspector into Affairs of Rolls-Royce Ltd, April 1971; Mem., ODM Cttee of Inquiry on Crown Agents, April 1975. Institute of Chartered Accountants: Mem., Inflation Accounting Sub-Cttee, 1982–84; Mem., Council, 1984–86. *Recreation:* family. *Address:* 2N Maple Lodge, Lythe Hill Park, Haslemere, Surrey GU27 3TE. *T:* (01428) 656729.

GODFREY, Sarah; *see* Radclyffe, S.

GODFREY, Rt Rev. William; *see* Godfrey, Rt Rev. H. W., Bishop of Peru.

GODLEY, family name of **Baron Kilbracken**.

GODLEY, Prof. Hon. Wynne Alexander Hugh; Professor of Applied Economics, University of Cambridge, 1980–93, now Emeritus (Director, 1970–85, Acting Director, 1985–87, Department of Applied Economics); Fellow of King's College, Cambridge, 1970–98, now Emeritus; *b* 2 Sept. 1926; *yr s* of Hugh John, 2nd Baron Kilbracken, CB, KC and Elizabeth Helen Monteith, *d* of Vereker Monteith Hamilton; *m* 1955, Kathleen Eleonora, *d* of Sir Jacob Epstein, KBE; one *d*. *Educ:* Rugby; New Coll., Oxford; Conservatoire de Musique, Paris. Professional oboist, 1950. Joined Economic Section, HM Treasury, 1956; Dep. Dir, Economic Sect., HM Treasury, 1967–70. Dir, Investing in Success Equities Ltd, 1970–85. Official Advr, Select Cttee on Public Expenditure, 1971–73; an Economic Consultant, HM Treasury, 1975; Mem., Panel of Indep. Forecasters, 1992–95. Visiting Professor: Aalborg Univ., 1987–88; Roskilde Univ., 1995; Distinguished Scholar, Jerome Levy Econs Inst., Annandale-on-Hudson, NY, 1991–92, 1993–95, 1996–2001; Vis. Sen. Res. Fellow, Cambridge Endowment for Res. and Finance, Univ. of Cambridge, 2001–04. Dir, Royal Opera House, Covent Garden, 1976–87. Excellence in Journalism Prize, Amer. Psychoanalytic Assoc., 2003. *Publications:* (with T. F. Cripps) Local Government Finance and its Reform, 1976; The Planning of Telecommunications in the United Kingdom, 1978; (with K. J. Coutts and W. D. Nordhaus) Pricing in the Trade Cycle, 1978; (with T. F. Cripps) Macroeconomics, 1983; (with M. Lavoie) Monetary Economics, 2007; articles, in National Institute Review, Economic Jl, London and Cambridge Economic Bulletin, Cambridge Economic Policy Review, Economica, Jl of Policy Modelling, Manchester School, Jl of Post Keynesian Econs, Banco Nazionale del Lavoro, Nationalokonomisk Tidsskrift, Political Qly, New Statesman and Society, Observer, Guardian, London Review of Books, Financial Times, Challenge, Cambridge Jl of Econs, Jl of Post Keynesian Econs. *Address:* Jasmine House, The Green, Cavendish, Suffolk CO10 8BB. *T:* (01787) 281166.

GODMAN, Norman Anthony, PhD; *b* 19 April 1938; *m* 1981, Patricia (*née* Leonard) (*see* Patricia Godman). *Educ:* Westbourne Street Boys' Sch., Hessle Road, Hull; Hull Univ. (BA); Heriot-Watt Univ. (PhD 1982). Nat. Service, Royal Mil. Police, 1958–60. Shipwright to trade teacher in Scottish further and higher educn; Contested (Lab) Aberdeen South, 1979. MP (Lab) Greenock and Port Glasgow, 1983–97, Greenock and Inverclyde, 1997–2001.

GODMAN, Patricia, (Trish); Member (Lab) West Renfrewshire, Scottish Parliament, since 1999; Deputy Presiding Officer, Scottish Parliament, since 2003; *d* of Martin Leonard and Cathie Craig; *m* 1981, Norman Anthony Godman, *qv*; three *s* from previous marriage. *Educ:* St Gerard's Secondary Sch.; Jordanhill Coll. (CQSW 1976). Social worker, Strathclyde Reg. Member (Lab): Strathclyde Regl Council, 1994–96; Glasgow City Council, 1996–99. *Recreations:* gardening, theatre, music, cinema, reading. *Address:* Scottish Parliament, Edinburgh EH99 1SP. *T:* (0131) 348 5837.

GODSAL, Lady Elizabeth Cameron, MBE 2002; Vice Lord-Lieutenant of Berkshire, since 2005; *b* 10 April 1939; *d* of 8th Earl of Courtown, OBE, TD and of Christina Margaret (*née* Cameron, now Mrs E. B. M. Tremlett); *m* 1962, Alan Anthony Colleton Godsal; one *s* two *d*. Comr, St John Ambulance, Berks, 1983–90; Chief Pres., St John Ambulance, 1990–96; Pres., St John Fellowship, 1996–2008. Mem., Indep. Monitoring Bd, HM YOI, Reading, 1993–2006 (Chm., 2000–03). High Sheriff, 1990–91, DL 1994, Berks. High Steward, Wokingham, 1992–. Patron and Pres., numerous orgns. GCStJ 2000. *Address:* Haines Hill, Twyford, Berks RG10 0NA. *T:* (0118) 934 5678.

GODSIFF, Roger Duncan; MP (Lab) Birmingham Sparkbrook and Small Heath, since 1997 (Birmingham, Small Heath, 1992–97); *b* 28 June 1946; *s* of late George and of Gladys Godsiff; *m* 1977, Julia Brenda Morris; one *s* one *d*. *Educ:* Catford Comprehensive Sch. Bank clerk, 1965–70; political officer, APEX, 1970–90; senior research officer, GMB, 1990–92. Mem. (Lab) Lewisham BC, 1971–90 (Mayor, 1977). Contested (Lab) Birmingham, Yardley, 1983. Chm., British-Japanese Parly Gp, 1994–. Chm., Charlton Athletic Charitable Trust, 2004–. *Recreations:* sport - particularly football and cricket, listening to music, spending time with family. *Address:* House of Commons, SW1A 0AA. *Clubs:* Rowley Regis Labour; Charlton Athletic Supporters.

GODSMARK, Nigel Graham; QC 2001; a Recorder, since 2000; *b* 8 Dec. 1954; *s* of Derek and Betty Godsmark; *m* 1982, Priscilla Howitt; one *s* two *d*. *Educ:* Queen Mary's Grammar Sch., Basingstoke; Univ. of Nottingham (LLB 1978). Called to the Bar, Gray's Inn, 1979; Asst Recorder, 1998–2000. *Recreations:* sport (Rugby, cricket), wine, family. *Address:* 7 Bedford Row, WC1R 4BU. *T:* (020) 7242 3555.

GODSON, Anthony; HM Diplomatic Service, retired; Executive Director, Prospect Burma, since 2007; *b* 1 Feb. 1948; *s* of late Percival Lawrence Godson and of Kathleen Elizabeth Godson (*née* Jennings); *m* 1977, Maryan Jane Margaret (*née* Hurst). Joined FCO, 1968; Attaché, Bucharest, 1970–72; Third Sec., Jakarta, 1972–76; Private Sec. to High Comr, Canberra, 1976–79; FCO, 1980–81; Second, later First, Sec., UKMIS to UN, NY, 1982–86; First Secretary: Kinshasa, 1987; FCO, 1988–89; Dep. Hd of Mission, Bucharest, 1990–92; UKMIS to UN, Geneva, 1992–95; FCO, 1996–97; Counsellor, later Dep. Hd of Mission and Consul Gen., Jakarta, 1998–2002; Counsellor, FCO, 2002–04; High Comr to Mauritius and Ambassador (non-res.) to Comoros, 2004–07. *Recreations:* ski-ing, tennis, music, photography. *Address:* Prospect Burma, Porters' Lodge, Rivermead Court, Ranelagh Gardens, SW6 3SF.

GODWIN, William Henry; *b* 29 Nov. 1923; *s* of George Godwin and Dorothy (*née* Purdon); *m* Lela Milosevic; one *s* one *d*. *Educ:* Colet Court; Lycée Français de Londres; St John's Coll., Cambridge. Called to the Bar, Middle Temple, 1948. Treasury Solicitor's Office, 1948–90; Under Sec., 1977; UK Agent before Europ. Ct of Justice, 1973–85; Legal Advr to Cabinet Office, European Secretariat, 1982–85. Consultant, 1985–98.

GODWIN-AUSTEN, Dr Richard Bertram, FRCP; Consultant Neurologist, Nottingham, Derby and South Lincolnshire Hospitals, 1970–97, Consultant Emeritus, since 1997; Secretary Treasurer-General, World Federation of Neurology, 1999–2006; *b* 4 Oct. 1935; *s* of late Annesley Godwin-Austen, CBE and Beryl Godwin-Austen; *m* 1st, 1961, Jennifer Jane (*d* 1996), *d* of Louis Himely; one *s* one *d*; 2nd, 1997, Deirdre, (Sally), *d* of FO Gerald Stark Toller. *Educ:* Charterhouse; St Thomas' Hosp., London (MB BS; MD 1968). FRCP 1976. Nat. Hosp. for Neurol., Queen Sq., 1964–70; clinical teacher in neurol., Faculty of Medicine, Univ. of Nottingham, 1970–97; Clinical Dir for Neuroservices, University Hosp., Nottingham, 1990–93. Chm., Sheffield Regl Adv. Cttee on Neurol. and Neurosurgery, 1990–93. Mem., Med. Adv. Panel, Parkinson's Disease Soc., 1970–97. Pres., Assoc. of British Neurologists, 1997–99; Vice-Pres., Eur. Fedn of Neurol Socs, 1996–2001; Mem., Eur. Bd of Neurol., 1996–2001. High Sheriff, Notts, 1994–95. *Publications:* The Neurology of the Elderly, 1990; The Parkinson's Disease Handbook, 1987, 2nd edn 1997; numerous contribs to peer-reviewed med. jls. *Recreations:* water-colour painting, sweet wines, Mexico. *Address:* 15 Westgate, Southwell, Notts NG25 0JN. *T:* (01636) 814126. *Clubs:* Garrick, Royal Society of Medicine.

GOEDERT, Michel, MD, PhD; FRS 2000; Member of Scientific Staff, since 1984, and Joint Head, Division of Neurobiology, since 2003, Medical Research Council Laboratory of Molecular Biology, Cambridge; *b* 22 May 1954; *s* of Pierre Goedert and Dr Marie-Antoinette Goedert (*née* Bové); one *s* with Dr Maria Grazia Spillantini. *Educ:* Athénée, Luxembourg; Univ. of Basel (MD 1980); Trinity Coll., Cambridge (PhD 1984). Mem., EMBO, 1997. FMedSci 2006. 1st Prize, Eur. Contest for Young Scientists and Inventors, 1973; Metropolitan Life Foundn Award for Med. Res., 1996; Potamkin Prize, Amer. Acad. Neurol., 1998; Prix Lions, Luxembourg, 2002. *Publications:* contrib. res. papers and reviews to scientific jls. *Address:* MRC Laboratory of Molecular Biology, Hills Road, Cambridge CB2 0QH. *T:* (01223) 402036.

GOEHR, Prof. Alexander; composer; Professor of Music, and Fellow of Trinity Hall, University of Cambridge, 1976–99, now Emeritus Professor and Fellow; *b* 10 Aug. 1932; *s* of Walter and Laelia Goehr. *Educ:* Berkhamsted; Royal Manchester Coll. of Music; Paris Conservatoire. Lectr, Morley Coll., 1955–57; Music Asst, BBC, 1960–67; Winston Churchill Trust Fellowship, 1968; Composer-in-residence, New England Conservatory, Boston, Mass, 1968–69; Associate Professor of Music, Yale University, 1969–70; West Riding Prof. of Music, Leeds Univ., 1971–76. Artistic Dir, Leeds Festival, 1975; Vis. Prof.,

Peking Conservatoire of Music, 1980. Reith Lectr, BBC, 1987. Mem., Bd of Dirs, Royal Opera House, 1982–84. Hon. Vice-Pres., SPNM, 1983–. Hon. Prof., Beijing Central Conservatory. Hon. Mem., Amer. Acad. and Inst. of Arts and Letters. Hon. FRMCM; Hon. FRAM 1975; Hon. FRNCM 1980; Hon. FRCM 1981. Hon. DMus: Southampton, 1973; Manchester, 1990; Nottingham, 1994; Siena, 1998; Cambridge, 2000. *Compositions include:* Songs of Babel, 1951; Fantasia Op. 4, 1954; String Quartet No. 1, 1957; La Belle Dame Sans Merci (ballet), 1958; Suite Op. 11, 1961; Hecuba's Lament, 1961; A Little Cantata of Proverbs, 1962; Concerto Op. 13, 1962; Little Symphony, 1963; Pastorals, 1965; Piano Trio, 1966; String Quartet No. 2, 1967; Romanza, 1968; Paraphrase, 1969; Symphony in One Movement, 1970; Concerto for Eleven, 1970; Concerto Op. 33, 1972; Chaconne for Wind, 1974; Lyric Pieces, 1974; Metamorphosis/Dance, 1974; String Quartet No. 3, 1976; Fugue on the notes of the Fourth Psalm, 1976; Romanza on the notes of the Fourth Psalm, 1977; Chaconne for Organ, 1979; Sinfonia, 1979; Kafka Fragments, 1979; Deux Etudes, 1981; Sonata, 1984; …a musical offering (JSB 1985), 1985; Symphony with Chaconne, 1986; …in real time, 1989; Still Lands, 1990; Bach Variations, 1990; Piano Quintet, 2000; …second musical offering (GFH 2001), 2001; Symmetry Disorders Reach, 2003; Marching to Carcassonne, 2003; *vocal:* The Deluge, 1958; Sutter's Gold, 1960; Virtutes, 1963; Arden Must Die (opera), 1966; Triptych (Naboth's Vineyard, 1968; Shadowplay, 1970; Sonata about Jerusalem, 1970); Psalm IV, 1976; Babylon the Great is Fallen, 1979; The Law of the Quadrille, 1979; Behold the Sun, 1981; Behold the Sun (opera), 1984; Eve Dreams in Paradise, 1988; Sing Ariel, 1990; The Death of Moses, 1992; Colossos or Panic, 1993; Arianna (opera), 1995; Schlussgesang, 1997; Kantan and Damask Drum (opera), 1999. *Address:* Trinity Hall, Cambridge CB2 1TJ; c/o Schott Music, 48 Great Marlborough Street, W1F 2BB.

GOERNE, Matthias; baritone; *b* Weimar, Germany, 31 March 1967. *Educ:* Studied under Prof. Beyer at Leipzig, Elizabeth Schwarzkopf and Dietrich Fischer-Dieskau. Début with Leipzig Radio SO; performances with Berlin Phil. Orch., Concentus Musicus, Concertgebouw; recitals in London, Amsterdam, Paris, Leipzig, Cologne and New York. Opera appearances include: Dresden Opera, and Komische Oper, Berlin, 1993; débuts, as Papageno, Salzburg Fest., 1997, Metropolitan Opera, NY, 1998; title rôle in Wozzek, Zürich, 1999. Numerous recordings. Gramophone Award; Diapason d'Or; Echo Prize, Germany; Cecilia Award, Belgium. *Address:* c/o Michael Kocyan Artists Management, Alt-Moabit 104A, 10559 Berlin, Germany.

GOFF, family name of **Baron Goff of Chieveley**.

GOFF OF CHIEVELEY, Baron *cr* 1986 (Life Peer), of Chieveley in the Royal County of Berkshire; **Robert Lionel Archibald Goff,** Kt 1975; PC 1982; DCL; FBA 1987; a Lord of Appeal in Ordinary, 1986–98; Senior Law Lord, 1996–98; *b* 12 Nov. 1926; *s* of Lt-Col L. T. Goff and Mrs Goff (*née* Denroche-Smith); *m* 1953, Sarah, *er d* of Capt. G. R. Cousins, DSC, RN; one *s* two *d* (and one *s* decd). *Educ:* Eton Coll.; New Coll., Oxford (MA 1953, DCL 1972; Hon. Fellow, 1986). Served in Scots Guards, 1945–48 (commnd 1945). 1st cl hons Jurisprudence, Oxon, 1950. Called to the Bar, Inner Temple, 1951; Bencher, 1975; QC 1967. Fellow and Tutor, Lincoln Coll., Oxford, 1951–55; in practice at the Bar, 1956–75; a Recorder, 1974–75; Judge of the High Ct, QBD, 1975–82; Judge i/c Commercial List, and Chm. Commercial Court Cttee, 1979–81; a Lord Justice of Appeal, 1982–86. Chm., Sub-Cttee E (Law and Instns), H of L Select Cttee on EC, 1986–88. Chairman: Council of Legal Educn, 1976–82 (Vice-Chm., 1972–76; Chm., Bd of Studies, 1970–76); Common Professional Examination Bd, 1976–78; Court, London Univ., 1986–91; Pegasus Scholarship Trust, 1987–2001. High Steward, Oxford Univ., 1991–2001. Hon. Prof. of Legal Ethics, Univ. of Birmingham, 1980–81; Lectures: Maccabean, British Acad., 1983; Lionel Cohen Meml, Hebrew Univ. of Jerusalem, 1987; Cassel, Stockholm Univ., 1993. Member: Gen. Council of the Bar, 1971–74; Senate of Inns of Court and Bar, 1974–82 (Chm., Law Reform and Procedure Cttee, 1974–76). Chm., British Inst. of Internat. and Comparative Law, 1986–2001 (Pres., 2001–). President: CIArb, 1986–91; Bentham Club, 1986; Holdsworth Club, 1986–87. Hon. Fellow: Lincoln Coll., Oxford, 1985; Wolfson Coll., Oxford, 2001; Amer. Coll. of Trial Lawyers, 1997. Hon. DLitt: City, 1977; Reading, 1990; Hon. LLD: Buckingham, 1990; London, 1990; Bristol, 1996. Grand Cross (First Class), Order of Merit (Germany), 1999. *Publication:* (with Prof. Gareth Jones) The Law of Restitution, 1966. *Address:* House of Lords, Westminster, SW1A 0PW.

GOFF, Martyn, CBE 2005 (OBE 1977); Hon. President, Henry Sotheran Ltd, since 2007 (Director and Executive Chairman, 1988–2007); *b* 7 June 1923; *s* of Jacob and Janey Goff. *Educ:* Clifton College. Served in Royal Air Force, 1941–46. Film business, 1946–48; bookseller, 1948–70; National Book League, then Book Trust: Dir, later Chief Exec., 1970–88; Dep. Chm., 1991–92 and 1996–97; Chm., 1992–96; Vice Pres., 2000–; Administrator, Booker, subseq. Man Booker, Prize, 1970–2006 (Chm., Adv. Cttee, 2002–06). Has lectured on: music; English fiction; teenager morality; the book trade, 1946–70; fiction reviewer, 1975–88, non-fiction, 1988–, Daily Telegraph. Founder and Chm., Bedford Square Bookbang, 1971. Member: Arts Council Literature Panel, 1970–78; Arts Council Trng Cttee, 1973–78; Greater London Arts Assoc. Literature Panel, 1973–81; British Nat. Bibliography Res. Fund, 1976–88; British Library Adv. Council, 1977–82; PEN Exec. Cttee, 1978–2003; Exec. Cttee, Gtr London Arts Council, 1982–88; Library and Information Services Council, 1984–86; Bd, British Theatre Assoc., 1983–85; Chairman: Paternosters '73 Library Adv. Council, 1972–74; New Fiction Soc., 1975–88; School Bookshop Assoc., 1977–; Soc. of Bookmen, 1982–84 (Pres., 1997–); 1890s Soc., 1990–99; Nat. Life Story Collections, 1996–2003; Poetry Book Soc., 1996–99 (Mem. Bd, 1992–99); Wingate Scholarships, H. H. Wingate Foundn, 1988–2003; Vice-Pres., Royal Over-Seas League, 1996–; Dir, Battersea Arts Centre, 1992–97 (Trustee, 1981–85); Trustee: Cadmean Trust, 1981–99; Nat. Literacy Trust, 1993–2003; Booker Prize Foundn, 2006–. Judge, Glenfiddich Awards, 1993. FIAL 1958, FRSA 1979. Hon. FRSL 2003. Hon. DLitt Oxford Brookes, 2003. *Publications: fiction:* The Plaster Fabric, 1957; A Season with Mammon, 1958; A Sort of Peace, 1960; The Youngest Director, 1961, new edn 1985; Red on the Door, 1962; The Flint Inheritance, 1965; Indecent Assault, 1967; The Liberation of Rupert Bannister, 1978; Tar and Cement, 1988; *non-fiction:* A Short Guide to Long Play, 1957; A Further Guide to Long Play, 1958; LP Collecting, 1960; Why Conform?, 1968; Victorian and Edwardian Surrey, 1972; Record Choice, 1974; Royal Pavilion, 1976; Organising Book Exhibitions, 1982; Publishing, 1988; Prize Writing, 1989. *Recreations:* travel, collecting paintings and sculptures, music. *Address:* 95 Sisters Avenue, SW11 5SW. *T:* (020) 7228 8164. *Clubs:* Athenæum, Savile, Groucho.

GOFF, Hon. Philip Bruce; MP (Lab) New Zealand, 1981–90 and since 1993, for Mount Roskill, since 1999; Minister of Defence and of Trade, since 2005; *b* 2 June 1953; *s* of Bruce Charles Goff and Elaine Loyola Goff; *m* 1979, Mary Ellen Moriarty; two *s* one *d*. *Educ:* Univ. of Auckland (MA 1st Cl. Hons); Nuffield Coll., Oxford. MP (Lab): Roskill, 1981–90 and 1993–96; New Lynn, 1996–99. Cabinet Minister: for Housing, Employment and Envmt, 1984–87; for Employment, Tourism, Youth Affairs and Associate Educn, 1987–89; for Educn, 1989–90; of Justice, and of For. Affairs and Trade, 1999–2005; of Pacific Is. Affairs, 2002–; for Disarmament and Arms Control, 2005–. *Recreations:* squash, travel, gardening. *Address:* Parliament Buildings, Wellington, New Zealand. *T:* (4) 4719370.

GOFF, Sir Robert (William Davis-), 4th Bt *cr* 1905; Director, O'Connor & Co., Art Dealers and Property Investment Co.; *b* 12 Sept. 1955; *s* of Sir Ernest William Davis-Goff, 3rd Bt, and of Alice Cynthia Davis-Goff (*née* Woodhouse); *S* father, 1980; *m* 1978, Nathalie Sheelagh, *d* of Terence Chadwick; three *s* one *d*. *Educ:* Cheltenham College, Glos. *Recreation:* shooting. *Heir: s* William Nathaniel Davis-Goff, *b* 20 April 1980. *Address:* Eairy Moar Farm, Glen Helen, Isle of Man.

GOFFE, Judith Ann, FCA; independent business consultant, since 1991; Member, Independent Television Commission, 1994–2003; *b* 6 March 1953; *d* of Albert Edward Goffe and Jennie Lucia Goffe (*née* Da Costa); *m* 1992, Peter Alexander Rose; one *s*. *Educ:* Immaculate Conception High Sch., Kingston, Jamaica; Reading Univ. (BSc 1976). Chartered Accountant, 1981; FCA 1991. Investment Dir, 3i Group plc, 1984–91. Director: Moorfields Eye Hosp. Trust, 1994–2004; Indep. Regulator of NHS Foundn Trusts, 1994–. Trustee, King's Fund. FRSA 1994. *Recreations:* collecting contemporary ceramics and jewellery, design, travel, family, food.

GOGGINS, Paul Gerard; MP (Lab) Wythenshawe and Sale East, since 1997; Minister of State, Northern Ireland Office, since 2007; *b* 16 June 1953; *s* of John Goggins and late Rita Goggins; *m* 1977, Wyn, *d* of Tom and Mary Bartley; two *s* one *d*. *Educ:* St Bede's Sch., Manchester; Birmingham Poly.; Manchester Poly. Child care worker, Liverpool Catholic Social Services, 1974–75; Officer-in-Charge, local authy children's home, Wigan, 1976–84; Project Dir, NCH Action for Children, Salford, 1984–89; Nat. Dir, Church Action on Poverty, 1989–97. Mem. (Lab) Salford MBC, 1990–98. PPS to Minister of State for Health, 1998–2000, to Sec. of State for Educn and Employment, 2000–01, to Home Sec., 2001–03; Parliamentary Under-Secretary of State: Home Office, 2003–06; NI Office, 2006–07. *Address:* House of Commons, SW1A 0AA. *T:* (constituency) (0161) 499 7900.

GOH CHOK TONG; Senior Minister, Prime Minister's Office, Singapore, since 2004; Chairman, Monetary Authority of Singapore, since 2004; *b* 20 May 1941; *m* Tan Choo Leng; one *s* one *d* (twins). *Educ:* Raffles Instn; Univ. of Singapore (1st cl. Hons Econs); Williams Coll., USA. Admin. Service, Singapore Govt, 1964–69; Neptune Orient Lines, 1969–77. MP for Marine Parade, 1976–; Sen. Minister of State for Finance, 1977–79; Minister: for Trade and Industry, 1979–81; for Health, 1981–85; for Defence, 1981–91; First Dep. Prime Minister, 1985–90; Prime Minister, 1990–2004. People's Action Party: Mem., Central Exec. Cttee, 1979–; First Organising Sec., 1979; Second Asst Sec. Gen., 1979–84; Asst Sec. Gen., 1984–89; First Asst Sec. Gen., 1989–92; Sec. Gen., 1992–. Formerly Chairman: Singapore Labour Foundn; NTUC Income, NTUC Fairprice. Medal of Honour, NTUC, 1987. *Recreations:* golf, tennis. *Address:* Prime Minister's Office, Orchard Road, Istana Annexe, Istana, Singapore 238823.

GOHEEN, Robert Francis; educator; President Emeritus, and Senior Fellow, Public and International Affairs, since 1981, Princeton University; *b* Venguria, India, 15 Aug. 1919; *s* of Dr Robert H. H. Goheen and Anne Ewing; *m* 1941, Margaret M. Skelly; two *s* four *d*. *Educ:* Princeton Univ. AB 1940; PhD 1948. Princeton University: Instructor, Dept of Classics, 1948–50; Asst Prof., 1950–57; Prof., 1957–72; President, 1957–72. Chm., Council on Foundns, 1972–77; US Ambassador to India, 1977–80; Dir, Mellon Fellowships in Humanities, 1982–92. Sen. Fellow in Classics, Amer. Academy in Rome, 1952–53; Dir Nat. Woodrow Wilson Fellowship Program, 1953–56. Member: Adv. Council, Centre for Advanced Study of India, Univ. of Pennsylvania; American Philosophical Soc.; American Academy of Arts and Sciences; Phi Beta Kappa; Trustee: Nat. Humanities Center; Bharatiya Vidya Bhavan (USA). Former Mem. Internat Adv. Bd, Chemical Bank; former Member of Board: Amer. Univ. in Beirut; Carnegie Foundn for Advancement of Teaching; Carnegie Endowment for Internat. Peace; United Bd of Christian Higher Educn in Asia; Rockefeller Foundn; Asia Soc.; Amer. Acad. in Rome; Inst. of Internat. Educn; Equitable Life; Thomson Newspapers Inc.; Dreyfus Third Century Fund; Midlantic Nat. Bank; Reza Shah Kabir Univ., Iran; Univ. Service Cttee, Hong Kong. Hon. degrees: Harvard, Rutgers, Yale, Temple, Brown, Columbia, New York, Madras, Pennsylvania, Hamilton, Middlebury, Saint Mary's (Calif), State of New York, Denver, Notre Dame, N Carolina, Hofstra, Nebraska, Dropsie, Princeton; Tusculum Coll.; Trinity Coll., USA; Coll. of Wooster; Jewish Theological Seminary of America; Ripon Coll.; Rider Coll. *Publications:* The Imagery of Sophocles' Antigone, 1951; The Human Nature of a University, 1969; articles. *Recreations:* books, golf. *Address:* 1 Orchard Circle, Princeton, NJ 08540, USA. *T:* (609) 9242751. *Clubs:* Princeton, Century Association (New York); Cosmos (Washington); Nassau, Pretty Brook (Princeton); Gymkhana, Delhi Golf (Delhi).

GOLD, David Laurence; Senior Partner, Herbert Smith, since 2005; *b* 1 March 1951; *s* of Michael Gold and Betty Gold; *m* 1978, Sharon Levy; two *s* one *d*. *Educ:* Westcliff High Sch. for Boys; London Sch. of Econs (LLB). Admitted Solicitor, 1975; Partner, 1983–, Head of Litigation, 2003–05, Herbert Smith. Pres., Southend and Westcliff Hebrew Congregation, 1997–2006. Freeman, Solicitors' Co., 1977. *Recreations:* theatre, cinema, bridge, travel, family. *Address:* Herbert Smith, Exchange House, Primrose Street, EC2A 2HS. *T:* (020) 7374 8000; *e-mail:* David.Gold@HerbertSmith.com.

GOLD, Jack; film director; *b* 28 June 1930; British; *m* 1957, Denyse (*née* Macpherson); two *s* one *d*. *Educ:* London Univ. (BSc (Econs), LLB). Asst Studio Manager, BBC radio, 1954–55; Editor, Film Dept, BBC, 1955–60; Dir, TV and film documentaries and fiction, 1960–. Desmond Davies Award for services to television, BAFTA, 1976. *TV films:* Tonight; Death in the Morning (BAFTA Award, 1964); Modern Millionairess; Famine; Dispute; 90 Days; Dowager in Hot Pants; World of Coppard (BAFTA Award, 1968); Mad Jack (Grand Prix, and Monte Carlo Catholic Award, 1971); Stocker's Copper (BAFTA Award, 1972); Arturo Ui; The Lump; Catholics (Peabody Award, 1974); The Naked Civil Servant (Italia Prize, 1976, Internat. Emmy, and Critics Award, 1976); Thank You Comrades; Marya; Charlie Muffin; A Walk in the Forest; Merchant of Venice; Bavarian Night; A Lot of Happiness (Kenneth Macmillan), 1981 (Internat. Emmy Award); Praying Mantis, Macbeth, L'Elegance, 1982; The Red Monarch, 1983; Good and Bad at Games, 1983; Sakharov, 1984 (Assoc. Cable Enterprises Award); Murrow, 1986 (Assoc. Cable Enterprises Award); Me and the Girls, 1985; Escape from Sobibor, 1987 (Golden Globe Award); Stones for Ibarra, 1988; The Tenth Man, 1989; Masterclass, 1989; Ball-trap on the Côte Sauvage, 1989; The Rose and the Jackal, 1990; She Stood Alone, 1991 (Christopher Award); The Last Romantics, 1992; Heavy Weather, 1995; Mute of Malice, 1997; Blood Money, 1997; Into the Blue, 1997; Kavanagh QC, 1998; Goodnight Mr Tom, 1998 (Silver Hugo Award, Chicago, 1998, BAFTA Award, 1999); The Remorseful Day, 2000 (BAFTA Award, 2001); End of Law, 2001; The John Thaw Story, 2002; The Brief, 2004; *cinema:* The Bofors Gun, 1968; The Reckoning, 1969; The National Health, 1973 (Evening News Best Comedy Award); Who?, 1974; Man Friday, 1974; Aces High, 1976 (Evening News Best Film Award); The Medusa Touch, 1977; The Sailor's Return, 1978 (jt winner, Martin Luther King Meml Prize, 1980; Monte Carlo Catholic Award, and Monte Carlo Critics Award, 1981; Karoly Vary Award, 1978), 1978; Little Lord

Fauntleroy, 1981 (Christopher Award); The Chain, 1985; The Lucona Affair, 1993; Return of the Native, 1994; Spring Awakening, 1994; *theatre:* The Devil's Disciple, Aldwych, 1976; This Story of Yours, 1987, Danger! Memory, 1988, Hampstead; Three Hotels, 1993, Crossing Jerusalem, 2003, Tricycle Th. *Recreations:* music, reading, tennis. *Address:* 24 Wood Vale, N10 3DP.

GOLD, Jacqueline; Chief Executive: Ann Summers, since 1993; Knickerbox, since 2000; *b* 16 July 1960; *d* of David Gold and late Beryl Gold; *m* 1980, Tony D'Silva (marr. diss. 1990). Royal Doulton, 1979; joined Gold Gp as wages clerk, 1979; launched Ann Summers Party Plan, 1981; acquired Knickerbox, 2000. Business Communicator of the Year, British Assoc. of Communications in Business, 2004. *Publications:* Good Vibrations (autobiog.), 1995; A Woman's Courage (autobiog.), 2007. *Recreations:* travelling, watching football, partying, shopping. *Address:* Gold Group House, Godstone Road, Whyteleafe, Surrey CR3 0GG. *T:* (01883) 629629; *e-mail:* Ghislain@annsummers.com.

GOLD, Jeremy Spencer; QC 2003; a Recorder, since 2000; *b* 15 July 1955; *s* of late Alfred Gold and Ruby Caroline Gold; *m* 1976, Joanne Driver. *Educ:* Brighton, Hove and Sussex Grammar Sch.; Univ. of Kent at Canterbury (BA Hons). Called to the Bar, Middle Temple, 1977; in practice as barrister specialising in criminal work, 1977–. *Recreations:* theatre, good food, good company. *Address:* Westgate Chambers, 64 High Street, Lewes, Sussex BN7 1XJ. *T:* (01273) 480510, *Fax:* (01273) 483179; *e-mail:* jeremy.gold@ntlworld.com.

GOLD, John (Joseph Manson); Public Relations Consultant, 1979–90, retired; Manager of Public Relations, Hong Kong Mass Transit Railway, 1975–79; *b* 2 Aug. 1925; *m* 1953, Berta Cordeiro; one *d. Educ:* Clayesmore Sch., Dorset. Yorkshire Evening News, 1944–47; London Evening News, 1947–52; Australian Associated Press (New York), 1952–55; New York Corresp., London Evening News, 1955–66; Editor, London Evening News, 1967–72; Dir, Harmsworth Publications Ltd, 1967–73. Free-lance writer and lectr, Far East, 1973–75.

GOLD, Nicholas Roger; Managing Director, ING Bank NV (formerly Baring Brothers and Co.), 1986–2008; *b* 11 Dec. 1951; *s* of Rev. (Guy) Alastair Whitmore Gold, TD, MA and Elizabeth Gold, JP; *m* 1983, Laura Arnold-Brown (marr. diss. 2005); one *s* two *d. Educ:* Felsted Sch.; Univ. of Kent; Coll. of Law. ACA 1977, FCA 1982. Chartered accountant, Touche Ross & Co., 1973–76; admitted solicitor, 1979; solicitor, Freshfields, 1977–86. Beach café proprietor, Winking Prawn brasserie, Salcombe, 1994–. Member: Council, RADA, 2003–; Bd, Prince's Foundn for Integrated Health, 2004–. *Recreations:* the arts, drawing, sailing, country pursuits, tennis, travel, especially in India. *Address:* 14 Northumberland Place, W2 5BS. *T:* (020) 7229 4773; *e-mail:* nicholasgold@aol.com. *Clubs:* Hurlingham; Orford Sailing.

GOLD, Stephen Charles, MA, MD, FRCP; Consulting Physician to: the Skin Department, St George's Hospital; St John's Hospital for Diseases of the Skin; King Edward VII Hospital for Officers; Former Hon. Consultant in Dermatology: to the Army; to Royal Hospital, Chelsea; *b* Bishops Stortford, Herts, 10 Aug. 1915; *yr s* of late Philip Gold, Stansted, Essex, and Amy Frances, *er d* of James and Mary Perry; *m* 1941, Betty Margaret, *o d* of late Dr T. P. Sheedy, OBE; three *s* one *d. Educ:* Radley Coll.; Gonville and Caius Coll., Cambridge; St George's Hosp. (Entrance Exhibnr); Zürich and Philadelphia. BA 1937; MRCS, LRCP 1940; MA, MB, BChir 1941; MRCP 1947; MD 1952; FRCP 1958. Served RAMC, 1941–46. Late Med. First Asst to Out-Patients, St George's Hosp., Senior Registrar, Skin Dept, St George's Hosp., Sen. Registrar, St John's Hosp. for Diseases of the Skin; Lectr in Dermatology, Royal Postgraduate Med. Sch., 1949–69. Sec., Brit. Assoc. of Dermatology, 1965–70 (Pres., 1979). FRSocMed (late Sec. Dermatological Section, Pres., 1972–73); Fellow St John's Hosp. Dermatological Soc. (Pres., 1965–66). *Publications:* St George's and Dermatology: evolution and progress, 1993; A Biographical History of British Dermatology, 1996.

GOLDBERG, David Gerard; QC 1987; *b* 12 Aug. 1947; *s* of late Arthur Goldberg and of Sylvia Goldberg; *m* 1981, Alison Ninette Lunzer (marr. diss. 2003); one *s* one *d. Educ:* Plymouth Coll.; London School of Economics (LLB, LLM). Called to the Bar, Lincoln's Inn, 1971, Bencher, 1997; practice at Revenue Bar, 1972–. Chm. Trustees, Surgical Workshop for Anatomical Prosection, 1994–. *Publications:* (jtly) Introduction to Company Law, 1971, 4th edn 1987; (jtly) The Law of Partnership Taxation, 1976, 2nd edn 1979; various articles and notes in legal periodicals mainly concerning taxation and company law. *Recreations:* reading, writing letters, thinking. *Address:* Gray's Inn Chambers, Gray's Inn, WC1R 5JA. *T:* (020) 7242 2642.

GOLDBERG, Rabbi David Julian, OBE 2004; Senior Rabbi, Liberal Jewish Synagogue, London, 1986–2004, now Emeritus Rabbi; *b* 25 Feb. 1939; *s* of Rabbi Dr Percy Selvin Goldberg and Frimette Goldberg; *m* 1969, Carole-Ann Marks; one *s* one *d. Educ:* Lincoln Coll., Oxford (MA); Leo Baeck Coll., London. Rabbinic ordination, 1971; Rabbi, Wembley and Dist Liberal Synagogue, 1971–75; Associate Rabbi, Liberal Jewish Synagogue, London, 1975–86. Hon. DD Manchester, 1999. *Publications:* (with John D. Rayner) The Jewish People: their history and their religion, 1987; To the Promised Land: a history of Zionist thought, 1996; The Divided Self: Israel and the Jewish psyche today, 2006. *Recreations:* music, opera, travel, walking, cricket, theatre. *Address:* c/o Liberal Jewish Synagogue, 28 St John's Wood Road, NW8 7HA; *e-mail:* djg@bartvillas.org.uk.
See also J. J. Goldberg.

GOLDBERG, Sir David (Paul Brandes), Kt 1996; DM; FRCP, FRCPsych; Professor of Psychiatry, 1993–99, and Director of Research and Development, 1993–99, Institute of Psychiatry, University of London, now Professor Emeritus; *b* 28 Jan. 1934; *s* of Paul Goldberg and Ruby Dora Goldberg; *m* 1966, Ilfra Joy Pink; one *s* three *d. Educ:* William Ellis Sch., London; Hertford Coll., Oxford (MA 1956; DM 1970; Hon. Fellow); St Thomas' Hosp.; Manchester Univ. (MSc 1974). FRCPsych 1974; FRCP 1976. Trained at Maudsley Hosp., 1962–69; Sen. Lectr, 1969–72, Prof., 1972–92, Univ. of Manchester. Visiting Professor: Medical Univ. of S Carolina, 1978–79; Univ. of WA, 1986. Non-exec. Chm., Psychiatry Res. Trust. Founder FMedSci 1998. FKC. *Publications:* Mental Illness in the Community: the pathway to psychiatric care, 1981; Common Mental Disorders: a biosocial model, 1991; Psychiatric Illness in Medical Practice, 1992; (with I. Goodyer) The Origins and Course of Common Mental Disorders, 2005. *Recreations:* walking, talking, travelling. *Address:* Institute of Psychiatry, King's College London, De Crespigny Park, SE5 8AF.

GOLDBERG, Jonathan Jacob; QC 1989; a Recorder, since 1993; *b* 13 Nov. 1947; *s* of late Rabbi Dr and Mrs P. Selvin Goldberg; *m* 1980, Alexis Jane (marr. diss. 1991), *e d* of Sir George Martin, *qv*; one *s* one *d. Educ:* Manchester Grammar Sch.; Trinity Hall, Cambridge (MA, LLM). Called to the Bar, Middle Temple, 1971; Member, NY State Bar, 1985. Mem. Presidency, Internat. Assoc. of Jewish Lawyers and Jurists, 1999–. *Recreations:* music, cinema, wine, travel. *Address:* 30 Ely Place, EC1N 6TD. *T:* (020) 7400 9600, *Fax:* (020) 7400 9630; *e-mail:* jgoldberg@elyplace.com.
See also D. J. Goldberg.

GOLDBERG, Pamela Jill; Chief Executive, Breast Cancer Campaign, since 1995; *b* 2 June 1945; *d* of late Jack and Norma Wolfowitz; *m* 1964, John Martin Goldberg; one *s* one *d. Educ:* Kingsmead Coll. for Girls, Johannesburg. Dir, Nordene Galls, S Africa, 1974–79; Talentmark Ltd, 1979–81; Res. Co-ordinator, Stephen Rose and Partners Ltd, 1981–88; London Partner, Lared Gp, 1988–95. Non-exec. Dir, Barnet FHSA, 1994–96. Mem. Council and Vice-Chm., AMRC, 1999–2004. Mem., Ct of Assistants, Needlemakers' Co., 2001–. FRSA. *Recreations:* food, family, friends. *Address:* Breast Cancer Campaign, Clifton Centre, 110 Clifton Street, EC2A 4HT. *T:* (020) 7749 3700, *Fax:* (020) 7749 3701; *e-mail:* pgoldberg@breastcancercampaign.org.

GOLDBERGER, Prof. Marvin Leonard, PhD; Professor of Physics, 1993–2000, now Emeritus, and Dean of Natural Sciences, 1994–99, University of California, San Diego; *b* 22 Oct. 1922; *s* of Joseph Goldberger and Mildred (*née* Sedwitz); *m* 1945, Mildred Ginsburg; two *s. Educ:* Carnegie Inst. of Technology (BS); Univ. of Chicago (PhD). Asst to Associate Prof., Univ. of Chicago, 1950–55; Prof., Univ. of Chicago, 1955–57; Princeton University: Higgins Prof. of Mathematical Physics, 1957–77; Chm., Dept of Physics, 1970–76; Joseph Henry Prof. of Physics, 1977–78; Pres., California Inst. of Technology, 1978–87; Dir, Inst. for Advanced Study, Princeton, NJ, 1987–91; Prof. of Physics, UCLA, 1991–93. Hon. ScD: Carnegie-Mellon, 1979; Notre Dame, Indiana, 1979; Brandeis, 1991; Hon. DHL: Hebrew Union Coll., 1980; Univ. of Judaism, 1982; Hon. LLD Occidental Coll., 1980. *Publications:* (jtly) Collision Theory, 1964; professional papers in Physical Rev. *Recreations:* jogging, cooking. *Address:* *e-mail:* mgoldberger@ucsd.edu.

GOLDBLATT, Prof. David, PhD; FRCP, FRCPCH; Consultant Paediatric Immunologist, since 1995, and Director, Clinical Research and Development, since 2004, Great Ormond Street Hospital for Children; Professor of Vaccinology, Institute of Child Health, University College London, since 2003; *b* 16 March 1960; *s* of Samuel Goldblatt and Betty (*née* Kramer); *m* 1994, Isobel Beatrice Pemberton; one *s* two *d. Educ:* Univ. of Cape Town (MB ChB); Univ. of London (PhD 1991). FRCPCH 2001; FRCP 2006. Trng as paediatrician and immunologist, Red Cross Children's Hosp., Cape Town, Queen Elizabeth Children's Hosp., Hackney, and Gt Ormond St Hosp for Sick Children, 1983–95. *Publications:* (contrib.) Oxford Textbook of Medicine, 4th edn 2003; (contrib.) Oxford Handbook of Tropical Medicine, 2nd edn 2005; contrib. numerous papers to learned jls incl. Lancet and BMJ. *Address:* Institute of Child Health, University College London, 30 Guilford Street, WC1N 1EH. *T:* (020) 7813 8491, *Fax:* (020) 7813 8494; *e-mail:* d.goldblatt@ich.ucl.ac.uk. *Club:* Arsenal Football.

GOLDBLATT, Simon; QC 1972. Called to the Bar, Gray's Inn, 1953 (Bencher, 1982). *Address:* 39 Essex Street, WC2R 3AT.

GOLDEN, Surgeon Rear-Adm. Francis St Clair, OBE 1981; Consultant in Applied Physiology, and Hon. Lecturer, Portsmouth University, since 1998; *b* 5 June 1936; *s* of Harry Golden and Nora Golden (*née* Murphy); *m* 1964, Jennifer (*née* Beard); two *s* one *d. Educ:* Presentation Coll., Cork; University Coll., Cork (MB BCh, BAO); London Univ. (Diploma in Aviation Medicine); Leeds Univ. (PhD Physiol). GP, Kingston on Thames, 1961–63; HMS Jaguar, 1963–64; RNAS Culdrose, 1964–67; RN Air Med. Sch., 1967–73; Inst. of Naval Medicine, 1973–85; MoD, 1985–86; Fleet MO, 1986–88; MO i/c Haslar, 1988–90; Surg. Rear-Adm., Support Med. Services, 1990–93, retd. QHP 1990–93. Consultant in Applied Physiol., Robens Inst., Surrey Univ., 1994–98. Chm., Med. and Survival Cttee, RNLI, 1994–2006. Hon. FNI 1982. OStJ. *Publications:* (with M. J. Tipton) Essentials of Sea Survival, 2002; papers in sci. jls and chapters in medical textbooks on immersion, drowning, hypothermia. *Recreations:* born again golfer, armchair Rugby. *Address:* 15 Beech Grove, Gosport, Hants PO12 2JE. *Clubs:* Royal Society of Medicine; Lee-on-the-Solent Golf (Capt., 1998–99).

GOLDHILL, Flora Taylor, CBE 2007; Director, Workforce Directorate, Department of Health, since 2007; *b* 13 Feb. 1953; *d* of Thomas Kissock and Flora (*née* McKenzie); *m* 1978, Jonathan Paul Goldhill. *Educ:* Morgan Academy, Dundee; Edinburgh Univ. (MA Hons). Civil Servant, DHSS and DoH, 1977–90; Chief Exec., HFEA, 1991–96; Head, Policy Mgt Unit, DoH, 1996–98; Dir of Personnel, DoH, 1999–2001; Prog. Dir, then Dir, Chief Nursing Officer's Directorate, DoH, 2001–07. Gov., Canonbury Primary Sch., 1994–2005 (Vice-Chm., 1996–2003). *Recreations:* family, friends, hill walking, horse riding. *Address:* Department of Health, Richmond House, 79 Whitehall, SW1A 2NS. *T:* (020) 7210 5749.

GOLDIE, Annabel MacNicoll; DL; Member (C) Scotland West, Scottish Parliament, since 1999; Leader, Scottish Conservative and Unionist Party, since 2005 (Deputy Leader, 1998–2005); *b* 27 Feb. 1950; *d* of Alexander MacIntosh Goldie and Margaret MacNicoll Goldie. *Educ:* Greenock Acad.; Strathclyde Univ. (LLB; Hon. Fellow 2004). Admitted Solicitor, 1974; Notary Public, 1978–2007. Apprentice Solicitor, McClure Naismith Brodie & Co., Glasgow, 1971–73; Asst Solicitor, Haddow & McLay, Glasgow, subseq. Dickson, Haddow & Co., 1973–77; Partner, Dickson, Haddow & Co., subseq. Donaldson, Alexander, Russell & Haddow, 1978–2006. Scottish Parliament: Dep. Convener, Enterprise and Lifelong Learning Cttee, 1999–2003; Convener, Justice 2 Cttee, 2003–06. Dir, Prince's Scottish Youth Business Trust, 1995–. Vice-Chm., 1992–95, Dep. Chm., 1995–97 and 1997–98, Chm., March–July 1997, Scottish Cons. and Unionist Party. Mem., Adv. Bd, W Scotland Salvation Army. Mem., Charing Cross Rotary Club, Glasgow. DL Renfrew, 1993. *Recreations:* gardening badly, walking happily, watching birds usually uncomprehendingly, listening to classical music enthusiastically, if not knowledgeably. *Address:* Scottish Parliament, Edinburgh EH99 1SP.

GOLDIE, Prof. Peter Lawrence, DPhil; Samuel Hall Professor of Philosophy, University of Manchester, since 2005; *b* 5 Nov. 1946; *s* of Kenneth and Norah Goldie; *m* 1990, Sophie Hamilton; two *s* by previous marriage. *Educ:* Felsted Sch., Essex; UCL (BA 1993); Balliol Coll., Oxford (BPhil 1995; DPhil 1997). Chief Executive: Abaco Investments PLC, 1983–86; British & Commonwealth Hldgs, 1987–89; Dir, Guinness Mahon, 1973–83. Lectr in Philosophy Magdalen Coll., Oxford, 1996–98; Lectr, 1998–2004, Reader in Philosophy, 2004–05, KCL. *Publications:* The Emotions, 2000; On Personality, 2004; articles in philosophical jls. *Recreation:* physical and mental exercise.

GOLDING, Baroness *cr* 2001 (Life Peer), of Newcastle-under-Lyme in the County of Staffordshire; **Llinos Golding;** *b* 21 March 1933; *d* of Rt Hon. Ness Edwards, MP and Elina Victoria Edwards; *m* 1st, 1957, Dr John Roland Lewis; one *s* two *d*; 2nd, 1980, John Golding (*d* 1999). *Educ:* Caerphilly Girls' Grammar Sch.; Cardiff Royal Infirmary Sch. of Radiography. Mem., Soc. of Radiographers. Worked as a radiographer at various times; Assistant to John Golding, MP, 1972–86. MP (Lab) Newcastle-under-Lyme, July 1986–2001. An Opposition Whip, 1987–92; opposition spokesman: on social security, 1992–95; on children and the family, 1993–95; on agric., fisheries and food, 1995–97. Mem., Select Cttee on Culture, Media and Sport, 1997–2001. Former Chm., All Party Parly Gp on Children; Joint Chairman: All Party Parly Gp on Homeless, 1989–99; All Party Parly Gp on Drugs Misuse, until 1998; All Party Parly Betting and Gaming Gp, 2006–; former Treas., All Party Parly Gp on Racing and Bloodstock. Admin. Steward,

BBB of C, 2004–. Member: BBC Gen. Adv. Council, 1988–91; Commonwealth War Graves Commn, 1992–2003. Chm., Angling Cttee, Countryside Alliance, 2004–. Chairman: Second Chance, children's charity, 2000–; Citizen Card, 2001–. Former Mem., Dist Manpower Services Cttee; Mem., N Staffs DHA, 1983–87. Sec., Newcastle (Dist) Trades Council, 1976–87. *Address:* House of Lords, SW1A 0PW. *Club:* Halmerend Working Men's (Audley).

GOLDING, Francis Nelson; architecture, planning and conservation consultant, since 2000; *b* 28 Jan. 1944; *s* of late Frank Edwards Golding and Ella Golding (*née* Morris); civil partnership 2006, Dr Satish Padiyar. *Educ:* King's Sch., Macclesfield; Clare Coll., Cambridge (Exhibnr; BA 1966; MA 2000). Min. of Public Building and Works, 1967; DoE, 1972; Royal Commn on the Press, 1975–77; Asst Sec., DoE, 1978; English Heritage: Head of Secretariat, 1984; Head of Properties, 1986–90; Sec., ICOMOS, 1992–94; Sec., Royal Fine Art Commn, 1995–99; Chief Exec., Commn for Architecture and the Built Envmt, 1999. Hon. FRIBA 2000. *Publication:* Building in Context, 2002. *Recreations:* Chinese pots and jade, going to India. *Address:* 3 Stonefield Street, N1 0HP. *T:* (020) 7278 1558.

GOLDING, (Harold) John, CBE 1992; PhD; FBA 1994; painter; Senior Tutor in the School of Painting, Royal College of Art, 1981–86 (Tutor, 1973); *b* 10 Sept. 1929; *s* of Harold S. Golding and Dorothy Hamer. *Educ:* Ridley Coll. (St Catherine's, Ontario); Univ. of Toronto (BA 1951); Courtauld Inst. of Art, Univ. of London (MA 1953; PhD 1957). Lectr, 1962–77, and Reader in History of Art, 1977–81, Courtauld Inst., Univ. of London; Slade Prof. of Fine Art, Cambridge Univ., 1976–77; Andrew W. Mellon Lectr in the Fine Arts, Nat. Gall. of Art, Washington, 1997. Co-Curator, Matisse Picasso exhibn, NY, London and Paris, 2002. Trustee, Tate Gallery, 1984–91. Hon. Fellow, RCA, 1987. *Publications:* Cubism 1907–14, 1959, 3rd edn 1988; (with Christopher Green) Leger & Purist Paris, 1970; Duchamp: The Bride Stripped Bare by her Bachelors, Even, 1972; (ed with Roland Penrose) Picasso 1881–1973, 1973; Visions of the Modern, 1994; (with Elizabeth Cowling) Picasso: sculptor/painter, 1994; Paths to the Absolute, 2000. *Address:* 24 Ashchurch Park Villas, W12 9SP. *T:* (020) 8749 5221.

GOLDING, John Anthony, CVO 1966; Queen's Messenger, 1967–80; *b* 25 July 1920; *s* of George Golding, Plaxtol, Kent; *m* 1950, Patricia May, *d* of Thomas Archibald Bickel; two *s*. *Educ:* Bedford Sch.; King's Coll., Auckland. Served with King's African Rifles and Military Administration, Somalia, 1939–46 (Captain). Entered Colonial Service, 1946; Dep. Provincial Comr, Tanganyika, 1961; Administrator, Turks and Caicos Is, 1965–67. *Publication:* Colonialism: the golden years, 1987. *Recreations:* gardening, fishing. *Address:* c/o Barclays Bank, 11 High Street, Hythe, Kent CT21 5AE.

GOLDING, Michael Redvers, OBE 2007; professional yachtsman, since 1992; Managing Director, Mike Golding Yacht Racing Ltd, since 2001; *b* 27 Aug. 1960; *s* of Jack and Margaret Golding; *m* 2002, Andrea Bacon; one *s*. *Educ:* Reading Blue Coats Sch., Sonning; Windsor and Eton Coll. Fire Officer, Royal Berks Fire and Rescue Service, 1979–92; professional yachtsman: competitor, British Steel Challenge (Gp 4) (2nd), 1992–93; world record for non-stop solo round the world from E to W in 125 days (Gp 4), 1993–94; skipper, British Admiral's Cup Team, 1995; competitor: BT Global Challenge (Gp 4) (1st), 1996–97; Around Alone solo round the world (Team Gp 4) (winner 1st leg, Charleston to Cape Town; retd 2nd leg), 1998–99; Transat Jacques Vabre: (Team Gp 4) (3rd), 1999; (Ecover) (2nd), 2001 and (3rd), 2003; Vendée Globe non-stop solo round the world W to E (Team Gp 4) (7th), 2000–01 (dismasted day 1, restarted 8 days after main fleet); first non-stop solo in both directions round the world, 2001; competitor: Route du Rhum solo transatlantic (Ecover) (2nd), 2002; Defi Atlantique solo transatlantic (Ecover) (1st), 2003; Transat solo transatlantic (Ecover) (1st), 2004; Vendée Globe solo circumnavigation (Ecover) (3rd), 2004–05; Imoca World Champion, 2004–05; Fico World Champion, 2005. *Publications:* No Law No God, 1993; Racing Skipper, 1999. *Recreations:* travel, cooking, mountain biking, cinema. *Address:* Mike Golding Yacht Racing Ltd, Enterprise House, Ocean Village, Southampton, Hants SO14 3XB. *T:* (023) 8063 4355, *Fax:* (023) 8057 4700; *e-mail:* info@mikegolding.com. *Clubs:* Royal Southampton Yacht (Hon. Mem.); Corinthian Yacht (Boston, Mass) (Hon. Mem.).

GOLDING, Prof. Raymund Marshall, AO 1994; FNZIC; FRACI; FInstP; FTSE; FRAS; Vice-Chancellor, James Cook University of North Queensland, 1986–96, now Emeritus Professor; *b* 17 June 1935; *s* of Austin E. Golding and Marion H. R. Golding; *m* 1962, Ingeborg Carl; two *d*. *Educ:* Auckland Univ., NZ (BSc 1957, MSc 1958); Cambridge Univ. (PhD 1963). FNZIC 1966; FInstP 1969; FRACI 1974; FTSE 1995; FRAS 2004. Res. and Sen. Res. Scientist, DSIR, NZ, 1957–68; University of New South Wales: Prof. of Theoretical and Physical Chemistry, 1968–86, then Emeritus Prof.; Mem., Bd of Sen. Sch. Studies, 1975–86; Pro-Vice-Chancellor, 1978–86. Dir, St George Hosp., 1982–86. Chm., Aust. Marine Sci. Consortium, 1984–2002; Dep. Chm., Consultative Gp on Marine Industries Sci. and Technol., 1990–94. Dir, PACON Internat., 1990–2002 (Hon. Chm., Australian Chapter, 1990–2002; Fellow, 2002); Chm., Nat. Unit for Multidisciplinary Studies of Spinal Pain, Townsville Gen. Hosp., 1996–2002; Member: Educn Cttee, NSW Chiropractic Registration Bd, 1983–2002; Chiropractors and Osteopaths Bd of Qld, 1991–2002. Mem. Council, PNG Univ. of Technol., 1986–93. Chm., Aust. Fest. of Chamber Music Pty, 1990–96; Director: Tropic Line Res. Theatre Ltd, 1992–94; Townsville Enterprise Ltd, 1990–96; Aust. Tourism Res. Inst., 1990–97. Mem., Crown-of-Thorns Res. Cttee, 1986–96. Trustee, WWF (Australia), 1988–94. FRSA 1977. Hon. Fellow, Korean Chem. Soc., 1985. Hon. DSc Univ. of NSW, 1986. *Publications:* Applied Wave Mechanics, 1969; The Goldings of Oakington, 1992; Quantum Mechanics in Chemical Physics—an exploration, 2008; contribs to books on chem. and med. subjects; numerous research papers and articles. *Recreations:* music, photography, astronomy, family history. *Address:* 5 Tolson Road, Mooloolah, Qld 4553, Australia. *T:* and *Fax:* (7) 54947689.

GOLDING, Ven. Simon Jefferies, CBE 2002; Hon. Priest, since 2003, and Adviser, Non-Stipendiary Ministry, since 2008 for the Diocese of Ripon and Leeds; *b* 30 March 1946; *s* of late George William Golding and Gladys Joyce Golding (*née* Henstridge); *m* 1968, Anne Reynolds; one *s* one *d*. *Educ:* HMS Conway Merchant Navy Cadet Sch.; Brasted Place Coll.; Lincoln Theol Coll. Navigating Officer, MN, and Lieut (X) RNR, 1963–69; ordained deacon 1974, priest 1975; Curate, St Cuthbert, Wilton, 1974–77; Chaplain, Royal Navy, 1977–2002; Chaplain of the Fleet, 1997–98; Archdeacon for RN and Principal Anglican Chaplain (Naval), 1998–2002; Dir Gen., Naval Chaplaincy Service and Chaplain of the Fleet, 2000–02. QHC 1997–2002; Hon. Canon, Gibraltar Cathedral, 1998–2002. Convenor, Ministerial Rev. Scheme, Dio. of Ripon and Leeds, 2003. Lay Advr, N Yorks Multi Agency Public Protection Arrangements, 2005–. Mem., Gen. Council, Royal Nat. Mission to Deep-Sea Fishermen, 2007–. *Address:* Arlanza, Hornby Road, Appleton Wiske, Northallerton DL6 2AF. *T:* (01609) 881185.

GOLDING, Terence Edward, OBE 1992; FCA; Director, Alexandra Palace Trading Ltd, since 2000; *b* 7 April 1932; *s* of Sydney Richard Golding and Elsie Golding; *m* 1955, Sheila Jean (*née* Francis); one *s* one *d*. *Educ:* Harrow County Grammar Sch. FCA 1967. Earls Court Ltd (Exhibition Hall Proprietors): Chief Accountant, 1960; Co. Sec., 1965; Financial Dir, 1972; Financial Dir, Olympia Ltd, and Earls Court & Olympia Ltd, 1973; Commercial Dir, Earls Court & Olympia Group of Cos, 1975; Chief Executive: Nat. Exhibn Centre, Birmingham, 1978–95; Internat. Convention Centre, Birmingham, 1990–95; Dep. Chm., Earls Court & Olympia Ltd, 1995–99; Chm., Expocentric plc, 2000–02. Member: Exhibition Liaison Cttee, 1979–97; Nat. Assoc. of Exhibn Hallowners, 1988–97. Director: British Exhibitions Promotion Council, 1981–83; Birmingham Convention and Visitor Bureau, 1981–93; Heart of England Tourist Bd, 1984–91; Central England, TEC, 1990–92; Birmingham Marketing Partnership, 1993–95; Chm., Exhibn Industry Fedn, 1995–97; Exhibition Venues Assoc., 1997–99. Hon. Mem. Council, Birmingham Chamber of Industry and Commerce, 1990–95. Midlander of the Year, 1990. *Recreation:* following sport. *Address:* Pinn Cottage, Pinner Hill, Pinner, Middx HA5 3XX. *T:* (020) 8866 2610.

GOLDINGAY, Rev. Prof. John Edgar, PhD; David Allan Hubbard Professor of Old Testament Studies, Fuller Theological Seminary, Pasadena, since 1997; *b* 20 June 1942; *s* of Edgar Charles and Ada Irene Goldingay; *m* 1967, Ann Elizabeth Wilson; two *s*. *Educ:* King Edward's School, Birmingham; Keble Coll., Oxford (BA); Nottingham University (PhD). Ordained deacon 1966, priest 1967; Asst Curate, Christ Church, Finchley, 1966–69; St John's College, Nottingham: Lectr, 1970–75; Dir of Acad. Studies, 1976–79; Registrar, 1979–85; Vice-Principal, 1985–88; Principal, 1988–97. DD Lambeth, 1997. *Publications:* Songs from a Strange Land, 1978; Approaches to Old Testament Interpretation, 1981; Theological Diversity and the Authority of the Old Testament, 1987; Daniel, 1989; (ed) Signs, Wonders and Healing, 1989; Models for Scripture, 1994; Models for the Interpretation of Scripture, 1995; (ed) Atonement Today, 1995; After Eating the Apricot, 1996; To The Usual Suspects, 1998; Men Behaving Badly, 2000; Isaiah, 2001; Walk On, 2002; Old Testament Theology, vol. 1, 2003, vol. 2, 2006; The Message of Isaiah 40–55, 2005; Isaiah 40–55, 2 vols, 2006; Psalms vol. 1, 2006, vol. 2, 2007, vol. 3, 2008; (ed) Uprooting and Planting, 2007. *Recreations:* family, Old Testament, rock music. *Address:* 111 South Orange Grove Boulevard, Apartment 108, Pasadena, CA 91105, USA. *T:* (626) 4050626, *Fax:* (626) 5845251; *e-mail:* johngold@fuller.edu.

GOLDMAN, Antony John, CB 1995; Director General, Civil Aviation, Department of the Environment, Transport and the Regions, 1996–99; *b* 28 Feb. 1940; *s* of Sir Samuel Goldman, KCB and step *s* of late Patricia Goldman (*née* Hodges); *m* 1964, Anne Rosemary Lane; three *s*. *Educ:* Marlborough College; Peterhouse, Cambridge (BA). International Computers Ltd, 1961–73; entered Civil Service, DoE, 1973; Private Sec. to Sec. of State for Transport, 1976–78; Asst Sec., 1977; seconded to HM Treasury, 1981–83; Under Sec., 1984. Non-exec. Dir, Hugh Baird & Sons, 1985–86. Chm., Eur. Air Traffic Control Harmonisation and Integration Prog., 1994–99; Vice-Pres., Eur. Civil Aviation Conf., 1997–99; Pres., Eurocontrol Council, 1998–99. Special Advr to H of L Select Cttee on Europe, 2001. Trustee, Watts Gall., 2004–. Hon. CRAeS 1997. Eur. Regl Airlines Award, 1993. *Recreations:* music, writing doggerel.

GOLDMAN, Prof. John Michael, DM; FRCP, FRCPath, FMedSci; Professor of Leukaemia Biology and Therapy, Imperial College School of Medicine, 1987–2004, now Emeritus; Chairman, Department of Haematology, Imperial College, London/Hammersmith Hospital, 1994–2004; Director, Leukaemia Research Fund Centre for Adult Leukaemia, 1992–2004; *b* 30 Nov. 1938; *s* of Carl Heinz Goldman and Berthe Goldman (*née* Brandt); *m* 1st, 1967, Jeannine Fuller (marr. diss.); one *d*; 2nd, 1972, Constance Wilson; one *s* one *d*. *Educ:* Westminster Sch. (Schol.); Magdalen Coll., Oxford (Ann Shaw Schol.; BM BCh 1963; DM 1981); St Bartholomew's Hosp., London. FRCP 1979; FRCPath 1986. Fellow in Hematology, Univ. of Miami, 1967–68; Fellow in Oncology, Massachusetts Gen. Hosp./Harvard Univ., 1968–70; mem. staff, MRC Leukaemia Unit, 1970–92, Cons. Haematologist, 1976–2004, Hammersmith Hosp. Ham-Wasserman Lectr, Amer. Soc. Hematology, 1997; McCredie Lectr, Leukemia Soc. Amer., 2000; Fogarty Schol., Hematology Br., Nat. Heart, Lung and Blood Inst., NIH, Bethesda, MD, 2005–06. Ed., Bone Marrow Transplantation, 1985–. Med. Dir, Anthony Nolan Bone Marrow Trust, 1987–; Scientific Advr, Kay Kendall Leukaemia Fund, 1991–2004; Chm. Adv. Cttee, Internat. Bone Marrow Transplant Registry, 1998–2001. President: Internat. Soc. for Exptl Hematology, 1984–85; Eur. Gp for Blood and Marrow Transplantation, 1990–94; Eur. Hematology Assoc., 1996–98. FMedSci 1999. Hon. MD: Louvain, 1993; Poitiers, 1995. *Publications:* contrib. scientific papers on haematology, leukaemia, lymphoma, stem cell transplantation and molecular biol. *Recreations:* reading, ski-ing, riding. *Address:* 33 Northumberland Place, W2 5AS. *T:* (020) 7727 6092.

GOLDMAN, Dr Lawrence Neil, FRHistS; Editor, Oxford Dictionary of National Biography, since 2004; Fellow and Tutor in Modern History, St Peter's College, Oxford, since 1990; *b* 17 June 1957; *s* of Basil Benjamin Goldman and Hilda Hannah Goldman (*née* Schmerkin); *m* 1985, Madeleine Jean McDonald; two *s* one *d*. *Educ:* Haberdashers' Aske's Sch., Elstree; Jesus Coll., Cambridge (BA 1979); Trinity Coll., Cambridge (PhD 2003); Yale Univ. FRHistS 2002. Harkness Fellow, Commonwealth Fund of NY, 1979–80; Res. Fellow, Trinity Coll., Cambridge, 1982–85; Lectr in Hist. and Politics, Dept for Continuing Educn, Univ. of Oxford, 1985–90. Vis. Prof., Univ. of S Carolina, 1994; Vis. Fellow, Humanities Res. Centre, ANU, 2006. Assessor, Univ. of Oxford, 2000–01. Pres., Thames and Solent Dist, WEA, 2002–04. Gov., NLCS, 2006–. *Publications:* (ed) The Blind Victorian: Henry Fawcett and British Liberalism, 1989; Dons and Workers: Oxford and adult education since 1850, 1995; Science, Reform and Politics in Victorian Britain: the Social Science Association 1857–1886, 2002; (ed with P. Ghosh) Politics and Culture in Victorian Britain: essays in memory of Colin Matthew, 2006; (ed) The Federalist, 2008; contribs to learned jls incl. English Histl Rev., Past and Present, Histl Jl. *Recreations:* walking, gardening, pottering. *Address:* Oxford DNB, Oxford University Press, Great Clarendon Street, Oxford OX2 6DP. *T:* (01865) 355010, *Fax:* (01865) 355035; *e-mail:* lawrence.goldman@oup.com; 4 Quarry Lane, Charlbury, Chipping Norton, Oxon OX7 3RN. *T:* (01608) 811439.

GOLDMARK, Peter Carl, Jr; Director, Climate and Air Program, Environmental Defense, since 2003; *b* 2 Dec. 1940; *m* 1964, Aliette Misson. *Educ:* Harvard Univ. (BA Govt *magna cum laude* with Highest Hons 1962; Phi Beta Kappa). History teacher, Putney Sch., Vermont, 1962–64; US Office of Econ. Opportunity, Washington, 1965–66; City of New York: Exec. Asst to Dir of Budget, 1966–68; Asst Budget Dir for Prog. Planning and Analysis, 1968–70; Exec. Asst to Mayor, 1970–71; Sec. of Human Services, Commonwealth of Massachusetts, 1971–74; Dir of Budget, State of NY, 1975–77; Exec. Dir, Port Authy of NY and NJ, 1977–85; Sen. Vice Pres., Times Mirror Co., 1985–88; Pres., Rockefeller Foundn, 1988–97; Chm. and CEO, Internat. Herald Tribune, 1998–2003. *Address:* Environmental Defense, 257 Park Avenue South, New York, NY 10010, USA.

GOLDREIN, Iain Saville; QC 1997; a Recorder, since 1999; *b* 10 Aug. 1952; *s* of Neville Clive Goldrein, *qv*; *m* 1980, Margaret de Haas, *qv*; one *s* one *d*. *Educ:* Merchant Taylors' Sch., Crosby; Hebrew Univ., Jerusalem; Pembroke Coll., Cambridge (exhibnr, Ziegler Prize for Law; Cambridge Squire Schol. for Law). Called to the Bar, Inner Temple, 1975; Dep. Head, No 7 Harrington Street Chambers, Liverpool, 2003– (Jt Hd, 1989–2003); Asst

Recorder, 1995–99. Mem., Mental Health Review Tribunal, 1999–2002. Vis. Prof., Nottingham Law Sch., 1991. Mediator, Acad. of Experts, 1992 (Companion, 1992). Fellow, Soc. of Advanced Legal Studies, 1998. FRSA 1992. Jt Ed.-in-Chief, Genetics Law Monitor, 2000–02; Consulting Ed., Practical Civil Court Precedents; Ed., In Brief, 2006–. *Publications:* Personal Injury Litigation: practice and precedents, 1985; Ship Sale and Purchase: law and technique, 1985, 4th edn (with C. Chance) 2003; (with K. H. P. Wilkinson) Commercial Litigation: pre-emptive remedies, 1987, 4th edn (with Sir Robin Jacob and P. M. Kershaw) 2003, internat. edn (with sub-editors) 2005; with Sir J. Jacob: Bullen and Leake and Jacob's Precedents of Pleadings, 13th edn 1990; Pleadings, Principles and Practice, 1990; (ed jtly) Insurance Disputes (loose-leaf), 1999–2003, hardback edn 2004; (ed jtly) Civil Court Practice, 1999–2008; (jtly) Human Rights and Judicial Review: case studies in context, 2001; with M. de Haas: Property Distribution on Divorce, 1983, 2nd edn 1985; Butterworths Personal Injury Litigation Service, 1988–; Structured Settlements, 1993, 2nd edn 1997; Medical Negligence: cost effective case management, 1997; (also ed jtly) Personal Injury Major Claims Handling: cost effective case management, 2000; (with J. Ryder) Child Case Management Practice, 2008. *Recreations:* Classical Hebrew, history, new ideas, anything aeronautical. *Address:* 7 Harrington Street, Liverpool L2 9YH. *T:* (0151) 242 0707; St John's Chambers, St John Street, Manchester M3 4DJ. *T:* (0161) 214 1500; 7 Bell Yard, WC2A 2JR. *Club:* Athenæum (Liverpool).

GOLDREIN, Margaret Ruth; *see* de Haas, M. R.

GOLDREIN, Neville Clive, CBE 1991; Senior Partner, Goldrein & Co., 1953–85; Consultant, Deacon Goldrein Green, Solicitors, 1985–92; *b* 28 Aug.; *s* of Saville and Nina Goldrein; *m* 1949, Dr Sonia Sumner, MB, BS Dunelm; one *s* one *d*. *Educ:* Hymers Coll., Hull; Pembroke Coll., Cambridge (MA). Served Army: commnd E Yorks Regt; served East Africa Comd (Captain). Admitted Solicitor of the Supreme Court, 1949; former Dep. Circuit Judge. Mem., Crosby Bor. Council, 1957–71; Mayor of Crosby, 1966–67, Dep. Mayor, 1967–68; Mem., Lancs CC, 1965–74; Merseyside County Council: Mem., 1973–86; Dep. Leader, Cons. Gp, 1974–77; Vice-Chm. of Council, 1977–80; Leader, 1980–81; Leader, Cons. Gp, 1981–86. Chm., Crosby Constituency Cons. Assoc., 1986–89. Area Vice-Pres., Sefton, St John Ambulance, 1980–87 (Chm., S Sefton Div., 1975–87); Member: NW Econ. Planning Council, 1966–72; Bd of Deputies of British Jews, 1966–85, 1992–2001; Council, Liverpool Univ., 1977–81; Council, Merseyside Chamber of Commerce, 1987– (Chairman: Envmt and Energy Cttee, 1993–2006; Rivers Cttee, 1990–93; Police Liaison Cttee, 1994–2003; Mem., Arts and Culture Cttee, 2006–); Regl Affairs Cttee, British Assoc. of Chambers of Commerce, 1993–97. Director: Merseyside Economic Develt Co. Ltd, 1981–87; Merseyside Waste Derived Fuels Ltd, 1983–86. Vice-Pres., Crosby Mencap, 1967–; Chm., Crosby Hall Residential Trust Appeal, 1989–91. Chm., Liverpool Royal Court Theatre Foundn, 1994–2005; Mem. Council, Liverpool Inst. for Performing Arts, 2005–. Governor, Merchant Taylors' Sch., Crosby, 1965–74. *Recreations:* videography, photography, music, freelance journalism. *Address:* Torreno, St Andrew's Road, Blundellsands, Merseyside L23 7UR. *T: and Fax:* (0151) 924 2065; *e-mail:* goldrein@aol.com. *Club:* Athenæum (Liverpool).

See also I. S. Goldrein.

GOLDRING, Rt Hon. Sir John (Bernard), Kt 1999; PC 2008; **Rt Hon. Lord Justice Goldring;** a Lord Justice of Appeal, since 2008; *b* 9 Nov. 1944; *s* of Joseph and Marianne Goldring; *m* 1970, Wendy Margaret Lancaster Bennett (*see* W. M. L. Goldring); two *s*. *Educ:* Wyggeston Grammar Sch.; Exeter Univ. (LLB). Called to the Bar, Lincoln's Inn, 1969, Bencher, 1996. Standing Prosecuting Counsel to Inland Revenue, Midland and Oxford Circuit, 1985–87; QC 1987; a Recorder, 1987–99; a Dep. Sen. Judge, Sovereign Base Areas, Cyprus, 1991–99; a Dep. High Court Judge, 1996–99; a Judge of the Courts of Appeal of Jersey and Guernsey, 1998–99; a Judge of the High Court of Justice, QBD, 1999–2008; a Presiding Judge, Midland Circuit, 2002–05. Comr, Judicial Appts Commn, 2006–. *Recreations:* gardening, ski-ing. *Address:* Royal Courts of Justice, Strand, WC2A 2LL.

GOLDRING, Mark Ian, CBE 2008; Chief Executive, Mencap, since 2008; *b* 8 March 1957; *s* of Stephen and Pamela Goldring; *m* 1989, Rachel Carnegie; one *s* one *d*. *Educ:* Keble Coll., Oxford (BA Law 1979); LSE (MSc Social Policy and Planning in Developing Countries 1989). VSO Volunteer Teacher, Sarawak, 1979–81; Legal Researcher, Linklaters & Paines, 1982; Field Officer, Caribbean, 1983–85, Field Dir, Bhutan, 1985–88, VSO; UNDP Asst Rep., 1990–91, Oxfam Country Rep., 1991–94, Bangladesh; DFID Social Develt Advr, Pacific, 1994–95; VSO Overseas Dir, 1995–99; Chief Exec., VSO, 1999–2008. Chm., Revolving Doors Agency, 2002–05; Trustee: Accenture Develt Partnership, 2002–; African Med. and Res. Foundn UK, 2008–. Volunteer: Sense, 2006–; Ham S.O.S., 2008–. *Recreations:* cycling, Rugby. *Address:* Mencap, 123 Golden Lane, EC1Y 0RT.

GOLDRING, Mary Sheila, OBE 1987; economist; presenter, Goldring Audit, Channel 4, 1992, 1993, 1994, 1995. *Educ:* Our Lady's Priory, Sussex; Lady Margaret Hall, Oxford (PPE). Air and Science correspondent, 1949–74, Business editor, 1966–74, Economist Newspaper; economist and broadcaster, 1974–; *television:* presenter, Analysis, BBC, 1977–87; Answering Back, Channel 4 interviews, 1989–91. Trustee, Science Museum, 1987–97. Fawley Foundn Lect., 1992. CRAeS 1995. Hon. DLitt UWE, 1994. Blue Circle Award for industrial journalism, 1979; Sony Radio Award for best current affairs programme (Analysis: Post-Recession Britain), 1985; Industrial Journalist Award, Industrial Soc., 1985; Outstanding Personal Contribution to Radio, Broadcasting Press Guild, 1986; Harold Wincott Award for Broadcasting, 1991; Industrial Journalist of the Year, Industrial Soc. and BP, 1991, 1995. *Publication:* Economics of Atomic Energy, 1957. *Recreation:* shopping.

GOLDRING, Wendy Margaret Lancaster, (Lady Goldring); Vice Lord-Lieutenant of Rutland, since 2006; *b* 10 July 1946; *d* of Ralph and Margaret Bennett; *m* 1970, John Bernard Goldring (*see* Rt Hon. Sir J. B. Goldring); two *s*. *Educ:* Farrington's Sch., Chislehurst; Univ. of Exeter (BA). Mem., Bd of Visitors, HMP Ashwell, 1984–92. Member: E Midlands Cttee, Nat. Lottery Charities Bd, 1995–99; County Bd, Prince's Trust, 2002–. Trustee, Uppingham Sch., 2000–. Pres., League of Friends, Rutland Meml Hosp., 2000–; Vice-Chm., Voluntary Action Rutland, 2001–. JP Rutland, 1984 (Chm. Bench, 1996–99); High Sheriff, 1999–2000, DL 2005, Rutland. *Recreations:* travel, gardening, history of art and architecture, reading. *Address:* c/o Lieutenancy Office, Catmose, Oakham, Rutland LE15 6HP.

GOLDSACK, Alan Raymond; QC 1990; **His Honour Judge Goldsack;** a Circuit Judge, since 1994; a Senior Circuit Judge, since 2002; *b* 13 June 1947; *s* of Raymond Frederick Goldsack, MBE and Mildred Agnes Goldsack (*née* Jones); *m* 1971, Christine Marion Clarke; three *s* one *d*. *Educ:* Hastings Grammar School; Leicester Univ. (LLB). Called to the Bar, Gray's Inn, 1970, Bencher, 2003; a Recorder, 1988–94. Hon. Recorder, Sheffield, 2002–. *Recreations:* gardening, walking. *Address:* Sheffield Crown Court, 50 West Bar, Sheffield S3 8PH.

GOLDSACK, John Redman, MBE 1971; consultant in tropical agriculture and development, since 1993; *b* 15 Aug. 1932; 2nd *s* of late Bernard Frank and Dorothy Goldsack; *m* 1962, Madeleine Amelia Rowena, *d* of late Stanley and Grace Kibbler; two *s* one *d*. *Educ:* Sutton Grammar Sch., Surrey; Wye Coll., London Univ. (BScAgric); Queens' Coll., Cambridge (DipAgric); Imperial Coll. of Tropical Agric., Trinidad (DTA). Agricl Officer, HMOCS, Kenya, 1956; Hd of Soil Conservation and Planning Officer, Min. of Lands and Settlement, Kenya, 1963–67; Hd of Land Develt Div., Min. of Agriculture, Kenya, 1967–70; Asst Agric. Advr, ODM, 1970–74; Agriculture Adviser: S African Develt Div., 1974–78; ME Develt Div., 1979–81; E African Develt Div., 1981–83; Sen. Agric. Advr, Asia Div., ODA, 1983–86; Dep. Chief Natural Resources Advr and Prin. Agriculture Advr, ODA, 1986–88; Minister and UK Perm. Rep. to UNFAO, Rome, 1988–93. Chm., Prog. Adv. Cttee, Natural Resources Systems Progs, ODA, 1995–99. *Recreations:* cricket, golf, natural history. *Address:* 47 Peverell Avenue East, Poundbury, Dorchester, Dorset DT1 3RH. *T: and Fax:* (01305) 266543. *Clubs:* Farmers, MCC.

GOLDSCHMIED, Marco Lorenzo Sinnott, RIBA; Chairman, Thames Wharf Studios Ltd, since 1984; Managing Director, Rogers Architects Ltd, 1984–2004; *b* 28 March 1944; *s* of Guido Rodolfo Goldschmied and Elinor Violet (*née* Sinnott); *m* 1969, Andrea Halvorsen; four *s* one *d*. *Educ:* Architectural Assoc. (AA Dip. 1969); Reading Univ. (MSc 1986). RIBA 1971. Associate Partner, Piano & Rogers, 1971–77; Founder Partner, Rogers Partnership, 1977–84; Vice-Pres., Richard Rogers Japan KK, 1988–2004. Teacher: AA, 1971; Glasgow Sch. of Art, 1999; Lectr, RIBA, 1981–99 (Pres., 1999–2001). Mem., Architects Registration Bd, 1997–2000 (Mem., European Adv. Gp, 1998–2000); Trustee, Architectural Assoc., 1991–93; Chm., European Awards, 1996–99, Educn Review, 1998–99, C4 Stirling Prize, 2001, RIBA. Royal Academy Summer Exhibitor, 2000. *Projects* include: Lloyd's HQ, City of London, 1978 (Civic Trust Award, 1987; RIBA Award, 1988); Fleetguard Manufg and Distribn Centre, Quimper, France, 1979–81; Inmos Microprocessor Factory, Newport, 1982 (British Steel Design Award, 1982; RIBA Award, 1983); PA Technology Res. Centre, Princeton, 1983; Linn-Sondek HQ, Glasgow, 1985 (RIBA Award); Billingsgate Mkt Restoration and Conversion, 1988 (Civic Trust Award, 1989); Reuters Computer Centre, London, 1988 (RIBA Award, 1990); Pumping Station, Victoria Docks, 1989; Terminal 5, Heathrow, 1990; Channel 4 HQ, 1994 (RIBA Award, and RFAC Award, 1995); European Court of Human Rights, Strasbourg, 1995; Learning Resource Centre, Thames Valley Univ., 1996 (RIBA Award, 1998); Europier Passenger Terminal, Heathrow, 1996 (RIBA Award, and British Steel Award, 1997); Bordeaux Law Courts, 1998; Lloyd's Register of Shipping HQ, 1999; Daiwa Europe Office, 1999; 88 Wood Street, London, 1999 (RIBA Award, 2000); Millennium Dome, Greenwich, 1999; Offices and Laboratories, Gifu, Japan, 1999; Lloyd's Register of Shipping HQ, 1999; Montevetro Apartments, London (RIBA Award, 2000); Nat. Assembly of Wales, Cardiff, 2001; 16 Ha Masterplan, News Internat., 2004; The Albany Th., Deptford. Chair: Appeal for Care of Victims of Torture, Med. Foundn, 1999–2001; Leadership Gp, Amnesty Internat., 2003–05; Marco Goldschmied Foundn, 2004–. Patron, Stephen Lawrence Trust, 2004–. TV and radio interviews. Hon. Mem., AIA. Hon. FRSA. *Publications:* (jtly) Architecture 98, 1998; articles in jls. *Recreations:* twentieth century European history, etymology, ski-ing, meditation, The Simpsons. *Address:* Thames Wharf Studios Ltd, Rainville Road, W6 9HA. *T:* (020) 7385 1235; *e-mail:* marco@thameswharf.net. *Club:* Reform.

GOLDSMITH, family name of **Baron Goldsmith.**

GOLDSMITH, Baron *cr* 1999 (Life Peer), of Allerton in the county of Merseyside; **Peter Henry Goldsmith;** PC 2001; QC 1987; European Chair of Litigation, Debevoise & Plimpton LLP, since 2007; *b* 5 Jan. 1950; *s* of late Sydney Elland Goldsmith, solicitor, and of Myra Nurick; *m* 1974, Joy; three *s* one *d*. *Educ:* Quarry Bank High Sch., Liverpool; Gonville and Caius Coll., Cambridge (Sen. Schol., Tapp Postgrad. Schol., Schuldham Plate, 1968–71; MA); UCL (LLM 1972; Fellow 2002). Called to the Bar, Gray's Inn (Birkenhead Schol.), 1972, Bencher, 1994; Avocat, Barreau de Paris, 1997; a Jun. Counsel to the Crown, Common Law, 1985–87; a Recorder, 1989–; Attorney Gen., 2001–07. Chairman: Bar Council, 1995 (Chairman: Legal Services Cttee, 1992–94; Internat. Relations Cttee, 1996); Bar Pro Bono Unit, 1996–2001 (Pres., 2001); Financial Reporting Review Panel, 1997–99 (Mem., 1995–97); Mem. Council, 1996–2001, Co-Chm., Human Rights Inst., 1998–2001, Internat. Bar Assoc. Personal Rep. of Prime Minister to Convention to draft EU Charter of Fundamental Rights, 1999–2000. Mem., Jt Human Rights Select Cttee, 2001. Member: Council, Public Concern at Work, 1995–2001; Exec. Cttee, GB–China Centre, 1997–2001; Adv. Bd, Cambridge Centre for Commercial and Corporate Law, 1998–. Fellow, American Law Inst., 1997. *Publications:* (contrib.) Common Law, Common Bond; articles in nat., internat. and legal press and jls. *Address:* House of Lords, SW1A 0PW; Debevoise & Plimpton LLP, Tower 42, Old Broad Street, EC2N 1HQ.

GOLDSMITH, Alexander Benedict Hayum; Director: Cavamont Holdings (formerly Cavamont Investment Advisers) Ltd, since 1998; Yetro Ltd, since 2001; *b* 10 Dec. 1960; *s* of Edward René David Goldsmith, *qv* and Gillian Marion (*née* Pretty); *m* 1990, Louisa Kate Slack; two *s* one *d*. *Educ:* Westminster Sch.; Jesus Coll., Cambridge (MA Social Anthropol. 1986). Researcher and fundraiser for Survival Internat., 1986; Publisher and Editor, Envmt Digest, 1987–90; Editor: Geographical Magazine, 1991–94; People and Places in Peril series, 1995; Green Futures mag., 1996–98; Dir, Book Runner Ltd, 1999–2003. Trustee: Ecology Trust, 2004–06; Cancer Prevention and Educn Soc. (formerly Cancer Prevention Soc.), 2000–05. FRGS 2002. *Recreations:* sailing, walking, ski-ing. *Clubs:* Groucho; Travellers (Paris).

GOLDSMITH, Alexander Kinglake, (Alick); HM Diplomatic Service, retired; *b* 16 Jan. 1938; *s* of Maj.-Gen. Robert Frederick Kinglake Goldsmith, CB, CBE and Brenda (*née* Bartlett); *m* 1971, Deirdre Stafford; one *s* one *d*. *Educ:* Sherborne; Trinity Coll., Oxford (MA Modern History). National Service, 1956–58 (DCLI and Queen's Own Nigeria Regt). Asst Principal, CRO, 1961; Hindi student, SOAS, 1962; Third Sec., New Delhi, 1963; FCO, 1967; First Sec. (Inf.), Wellington, NZ, 1971; FCO, 1975; Head of Chancery, E Berlin, 1978; FCO, 1980; Hd of Commonwealth Co-ordination Dept, FCO, 1982; seconded to Hong Kong Govt, 1984; Consul-Gen., Hamburg, 1986–90. Dir, Export Gp for the Constructional Industries, 1991–2001. *Recreations:* walking, swimming. *Address:* c/o Lloyds TSB, Butler Place, SW1H 0PR. *Club:* Royal Automobile.

GOLDSMITH, Edward René David; Founder, The Ecologist, 1969 (Editor, 1970–89, and 1997–98); *b* 8 Nov. 1928; *s* of late Frank B. H. Goldsmith, OBE, TD, MP (C) for Stowmarket, Suffolk, 1910–18, and Marcelle (*née* Mouiller); *m* 1st, 1953, Gillian Marion Pretty; one *s* two *d*; 2nd, 1981, Katherine Victoria James; two *s*. *Educ:* Magdalen Coll., Oxford (MA Hons). Adjunct Associate Prof., Univ. of Michigan, 1975; Vis. Prof., Sangamon State Univ., 1984. Contested (Ecology Party): Eye, Feb. 1974; Cornwall and Plymouth, European parly election, 1979. Hon. Right Livelihood Award, Stockholm, 1991; Internat. Forum on Globalization, First Annual Edward Goldsmith Lifetime Achievement Award, 2007. Chevalier, Légion d'Honneur, 1991. *Publications:* (ed) Can

Britain Survive?, 1971; (with R. Prescott-Allen) A Blueprint for Survival, 1972; The Stable Society, 1977; (ed with J. M. Brunetti) La Médecine à la Question, 1981; (with N. Hildyard) The Social and Environmental Effects of Large Dams, vol. I, 1984, (ed) vol. II, 1986, (ed) vol. III, 1992; (ed with N. Hildyard) Green Britain or Industrial Wasteland?, 1986; (ed with N. Hildyard) The Earth Report, 1988; The Great U-Turn, 1988; (with N. Hildyard and others) 5,000 Days to Save the Planet, 1990; The Way: an ecological world view, 1992; (ed with J. Mander) The Case against the Global Economy and for a Turn Towards the Local, 1996, UK edn as The Case against the Global Economy and for a Turn Towards Localisation, 2000. *Address:* 9 Montague Road, Richmond, Surrey TW10 6QW. *Clubs:* Brooks's; Travellers (Paris).

See also A. B. H. Goldsmith.

GOLDSMITH, Frank Zacharias Robin, (Zac); Director, The Ecologist magazine, since 2007 (Editor, 1997–2007); *b* Westminster, 20 Jan. 1975; *s* of late Sir James Michael Goldsmith and of Lady Annabel Goldsmith (formerly Lady Annabel Vane Tempest Stewart); *m* 1999, Sheherazade Ventura-Bentley; one *s* two *d*. *Educ:* Hawtreys; Eton Coll.; Internat. Honours Programme, Boston. Worked with Redefining Progress, San Francisco, 1994–95; joined Internat. Soc. for Ecology and Culture, 1995–97, based in Calif, Bristol and Ladakh, India (ran tourist educn prog. in Ladakh for part of time), now Assoc. Dir. Co-founder, FARM, 2002. Member Board: JMG Foundn; Fondation de Sauve; Association Goldsmith pour l'Environnement; L'Artisanat et le Monde Rural; Trustee, Royal Parks Foundn; Pres., Nat. Gardens Scheme, 2006–. Speeches at numerous venues incl. Schumacher Meml Lects, Oxford Union, colls, schs and Think Tanks in UK. (Jtly) Beacon Prize for Young Philanthropist of the Year, 2003; Internat. Envmtl Leadership Award, Global Green USA, 2004. *Publications:* contrib. newspapers incl. The Times, Sunday Times, Daily Mail, Mail on Sunday, Independent, Guardian, Observer, Standard, Express, Daily Telegraph, Tribune and many regl newspapers; over 50 articles for The Ecologist; articles for other magazines incl. Country Life (contrib. and ed special edn, Dec. 2002), Big Issue, New Statesman, Spectator, Week, Global Agenda 2003, Geographical, Tatler and Vanity Fair. *Address:* The Ecologist, Unit 102, Lana House Studios, 116–118 Commercial Street, E1 6NF. *T:* (020) 7422 8100, *Fax:* (020) 7422 8101; *e-mail:* Zeco@compuserve.com. *Club:* Travellers.

GOLDSMITH, Harvey Anthony, CBE 1996; Chief Executive, Artiste Management Productions Ltd, since 1973; *b* 4 March 1946; *s* of Sydney and Minnie Goldsmith; *m* 1971, Diana Gorman; one *s*. *Educ:* Christ's Coll.; Brighton Coll. of Tech. Partner, Big O Posters, 1966–67; organised first free open-air concert in Parliament Hill Fields, 1968; (with Michael Alfandary) opened Round House, Camden Town, 1968; Crystal Palace Gdn Party series of concerts, 1969–72; merged with John Smith Entertainments, 1970; formed Harvey Goldsmith Entertainments (rock tours promotions co.), 1976; acquired Allied Entertainments Gp (rock concert promotions co.), 1984; (with Mark McCormack) formed Classical Productions (to produce operas), 1986; Man. Dir, TBA Entertainment Corp. (Europe) Ltd, 2000–04. Promoter and producer of pop, rock and classical musical events, including: *concerts:* Bruce Springsteen; The Rolling Stones; Elton John; The Who; Pink Floyd; *opera:* Aida, 1988 and 1998, Carmen, 1989, Tosca, 1991, Earls Court; Pavarotti at Wembley, 1986; Pavarotti in the Park, 1991; The Three Tenors, 1996; Pavarotti World Tour, 2005. Producer: Live Aid, 1985; Net Aid, 2000; Live 8, 2005; Executive Producer: Nokia New Year's Eve, 2006; Live Earth - SOS, 2007. Chm., Ignition Internat., 2006–. Dir, British Red Cross Events Ltd, 2000–; Member: London Tourist Bd, 1994–2002 (Dir, 1993–2003); Prague Heritage Fund, 1994–; Mayor's Adv. Gp on Tourism, 2003–. Chairman: Nat. Music Fest., 1991; Concert Promoters' Bd, 1994–99; Co-Chm., President's Club, 1994–; Vice-Chm., Action Mgt Bd, Prince's Trust, 1993–2000; Trustee: Band Aid, 1985–; Live Aid, 1985–; Royal Opera House, 1995–2001; Vice-President: REACT, 1989–; Music Users' Council, 1994–; Mem., Communications Panel, BRCS, 1992–. Patron, Teenage Cancer Trust, 2006–. Chevalier des Arts et Lettres (France), 2006. *Recreation:* golf. *Address:* Artiste Management Productions Ltd, Level 3, 13–14 Margaret Street, W1W 8RN. *T:* (020) 7224 1992, *Fax:* (020) 7224 0111. *Clubs:* Royal Automobile, Home House; Century (NY); Vale de Lobo Golf.

GOLDSMITH, Jonathan; Secretary-General, Council of Bars and Law Societies of Europe, since 2002; *b* 22 Aug. 1953; *s* of Hans and Gisela Goldsmith; *m* 1978, Hermione St John Smith; two *d*. *Educ:* Trinity Coll., Oxford. Solicitor; Citizens Advice Bureaux: Advr, 1978–80; Community Lawyer, 1980–86; Law Society: Dep. Hd, Communications, 1986–95; Dir, Internat., 1995–2001. *Address:* Council of Bars and Law Societies of Europe, Avenue de la Joyeuse Entrée 1–5, 1040 Brussels, Belgium. *T:* (2) 2346510, *Fax:* (2) 2346511; *e-mail:* goldsmith@ccbe.eu.

GOLDSMITH, Philip; Director (observation of the Earth and its environment), European Space Agency, Paris, 1985–93; *b* 16 April 1930; *s* of late Stanley Thomas Goldsmith and Ida Goldsmith (*née* Rawlinson); *m* 1st, 1952, Daphne (*d* 1983), *d* of William Webb; two *s* two *d*; 2nd, 1990, Gail Lorraine. *Educ:* Almondbury Grammar Sch.; Pembroke Coll., Oxford (MA). Meteorologist with the Meteorological Office, 1947–54, incl. National Service, RAF, 1948–50; Research Scientist, AERE Harwell, 1957–67; Meteorological Office: Asst Director (Cloud Physics Research), 1967–76; Dep. Director (Physical Research), 1976–82; Dir (Res.), 1982–85. President: Royal Meteorological Society, 1980–82; Internat. Commn on Atmospheric Chem. and Global Pollution, 1979–83. *Publications:* articles in scientific jls mainly on atmospheric physics and chemistry and space research related to associated environmental concerns. *Recreations:* golf, gardening, antiques, old cars. *Address:* Hill House, Broad Lane, Bracknell, Berks RG12 9BY. *Clubs:* East Berks Golf, Woodsome Hall Golf.

GOLDSMITH, Walter Kenneth, FCA; Chairman, Estates & Management Ltd, since 2006; *b* 19 Jan. 1938; *s* of late Lionel and of Phoebe Goldsmith; *m* 1961, Rosemary Adele, *d* of Joseph and Hannah Salter; two *s* two *d*. *Educ:* Merchant Taylors' School. Admitted Inst. of Chartered Accountants, 1960; Manager, Mann Judd & Co., 1964; joined Black & Decker Ltd, 1966: Dir of Investment, Finance and Administration, Europe, 1967; Gen. Man., 1970; Man. Dir, 1974; Chief Executive and European Dir, 1975; Black & Decker USA, 1976–79: Corporate Vice-Pres. and Pres. Pacific Internat. Operations; Dir Gen., Inst. of Dirs, 1979–84; Chm., Korn/Ferry International Ltd, 1984–86; Gp Planning and Marketing Dir, Trusthouse Forte plc, 1985–87; Chm., Food from Britain, 1987–90; Chm., British Food & Farming Ltd (Dep. Chm., 1990). Chairman: Ansoll Estates Ltd, 1989–98; Trident, later Flying Flowers, Ltd, 1990–99; Ewart Parsons, 1992–97; Jumbo Internat. plc (formerly Self Sealing Systems Internat.), 1995–2002; Royal Stafford Tableware Ltd, 1997–2002; PremiSys Technologies plc (formerly WML, then PremiSys, Group plc), 1998–2001; ASAP Internat. Gp plc, 2000–01; NRC Gp plc, 2001–; Union Gp Ltd, 2003–04; Private Trading Systems Ltd, 2007–; AngelBourse Ltd, 2007–08; Energy Technique plc, 2007–; Deputy Chairman: MICE Gp, 1994–95; Asite plc, 2001–; Director: Bank Leumi (UK) plc, 1984– (Member: Audit-Remuneration Cttee, 1988– (Chm., 2005–); Credit Cttee, 1986–2008); Trusthouse Forte Inc., 1985–87; The Winning Streak Ltd, 1985–2000; Isys plc (Dep. Chm.), 1987–99; CLS Group, 1992–2000; Chambers & Newman, 1994–2000; Betterware, 1995–97 (Chm., 1990–97); Fitness First plc, 1997–2003; Beagle Hldgs, 1997–; Lifestyle Products Ltd, 1997–2000; Guiton Gp plc, 1998–2003; SCS Upholstery plc, 1998–2005; Visonic, 2004–; KBH Media Ltd, 2005–; Mercury Gp plc, 2006–; Mem. Adv. Bd, Kalchas, 1990–97; Advisor to: Rotch Property Gp, 1996–; Consensus Business Gp, 2006–. Member: English Tourist Board, 1982–84; BTA, 1984–86; Vice-Pres., British Overseas Trade Gp for Israel, 1992–2000 (Chm., 1987–91); Chairman: Governing Bd, Marketing Quality Assurance, 1990–; Assoc. of Small Self-Administered Pension Scheme and Self-Administered Personal Pension Scheme Proprietors, 2002–04. Mem., Internat. Adv. Bd, SOAS, 2007–. Treas., Leo Baeck Coll., 1987–89; Chm., Jewish Music Inst., 2003–08 (Vice Pres., 2008–); Mem., London Jewish Forum, 2007–. Council Member: Co-operation Ireland, 1985–90; RASE, 1988–95. Trustee, Israel Diaspora Trust, 1982–92; Chm., Grange Hospice Project, 1994–99. FRSA; CCMI. Liveryman, Worshipful Co. of Chartered Accountants in England and Wales, 1985. Free Enterprise Award, Aims for Industry, 1984. *Publications:* (with D. Clutterbuck): The Winning Streak, 1984; The Winning Streak Workout Book, 1985; The Winning Streak: Mark 2, 1997; (with Berry Ritchie) The New Elite, 1987. *Recreations:* boating, music, walking, travel. *Address:* 35 Park Lane, W1K 1RB.

GOLDSMITH, Zac; *see* Goldsmith, F. Z. R.

GOLDSTAUB, Anthony James; QC 1992; **His Honour Judge Goldstaub;** a Circuit Judge, since 2004; *b* 26 May 1949; *er s* of late Henry Goldstaub, engineer, and of Hilda (*née* Bendix); *m* 1st, 1982 (marr. diss. 1989); two *s*; 2nd, 1993, Moira Pooley; one *d*. *Educ:* Highgate Sch.; Nottingham Univ. (LLB 1971). Called to the Bar, Middle Temple, 1972; a Recorder, 1999–2004. A Pres., Mental Health Review Tribunals, 2002–. *Address:* Chelmsford Crown Court, New Street, Chelmsford CM1 1EL.

GOLDSTAUB, Jane Hilary, (Mrs T. C. Goldstaub); *see* Procter, J. H.

GOLDSTEIN, Alfred, CBE 1977; FREng; consulting engineer, 1951–93; Senior Partner, Travers Morgan & Partners, 1972–85; Chairman, Travers Morgan Group, 1985–87; *b* 9 Oct. 1926; *s* of late Sigmund and Regina Goldstein; *m* 1959, Anne Milford, *d* of late Col R. A. M. Tweedy and of Maureen Evans, and step *d* of Hubert Evans; two *s*. *Educ:* Rotherham Grammar Sch.; Imperial Coll., Univ. of London. BSc (Eng); ACGI 1946; DIC. FICE 1959; FIStructE 1959; FIHT (FIHE 1959); FREng (FEng 1979); FCGI 1984. Partner, R. Travers Morgan & Partners, 1951; early projects include: Oxford Univ. Parks Footbridge, 1949 (Grade II listed 1998); Bournemouth Bus Garage, 1950 (Grade II listed 1999); Winthorpe Bridge, Newark, 1962 (Grade II* listed 1998); responsible for planning, design and supervision of construction of major road and bridge projects and for planning and transport studies, incl. M23, Belfast Transportation Plan, Clifton Bridge, Nottingham, Elizabeth Bridge, Cambridge, Itchen Bridge, Southampton. Transport Consultant to Govt SE Jt Planning Team for SE Regional Plan; in charge London Docklands Redevelopment Study; Cost Benefit Study for 2nd Sydney Airport for Govt of Australia; Mem. Cttee on Review of Railway Finances, 1982; UK full mem., EC Article 83 Cttee (Transport), 1982–85; TRRL Visitor on Transport Res. and Safety, 1983–87. Member: Building Research Bd, subseq. Adv. Cttee on Building Research, 1963–66; Civil Engrg EDC on Contracting in Civil Engrg since Banwell, 1965–67; Baroness Sharp's Adv. Cttee on Urban Transport Manpower Study, 1967–69; Commn of Inquiry on Third London Airport, 1968–70; Urban Motorways Cttee, 1969–72; Genesys Bd, 1969–74; Chairman: DoE and Dept of Transport Planning and Transport Res. Adv. Council, 1973–79; DoE Environmental Bd, 1975–78; Mem., TRRL Adv. Cttee on Transport, 1974–80; Mem. Bd, Coll. of Estate Management, Reading Univ., 1979–92. *Publications:* papers and lectures, including: Criteria for the Siting of Major Airports, 4th World Airports Conf., 1973; Highways and Community Response, 9th Rees Jeffreys Triennial Lecture, RTPI, 1975; Environment and the Economic Use of Energy, (Plenary Paper, Hong Kong Transport Conf., 1982); Decision-taking under Uncertainty in the Roads Sector, PIARC Sydney, 1983; Investment in Transport (Keynote address, CIT Conf., 1983); Buses: social enterprise and business (main paper, 9th annual conf., Bus and Coach Council, 1983); Public Road Transport: a time for change (Keynote address, 6th Aust. passenger trans. conf., 1985); Private Enterprise and Highways (Nat. Res. Council conf., Baltimore, 1986); The Expert and the Public: local values and national choice (Florida Univ.), 1987; Travel in London: is chaos inevitable? (LRT), 1989. *Recreations:* carpentry, music, bridge. *Club:* Athenæum.

GOLDSTEIN, Prof. Harvey, FBA 1996; Professor of Social Statistics, University of Bristol, since 2005; *b* 30 Oct. 1939; *s* of Jack and Millicent Goldstein; *m* 1970, Barbara Collinge; one *s*. *Educ:* Oakthorpe Primary Sch., London; Hendon Grammar Sch.; Manchester Univ. (BSc Hons); University College London (Dip. Stats). Lectr in Statistics, Inst. of Child Health, 1964–71; Head of Statistics Section, Nat. Children's Bureau, 1971–76; Prof. of Statistical Methods, Inst. of Educn, Univ. of London, 1977–2005. *Publications:* (jtly) From Birth to Seven, 1972; (jtly) Assessment of Skeletal Maturity and Prediction of Adult Height, 1976; The Design and Analysis of Longitudinal Studies, 1979; (with C. Gipps) Monitoring Children, 1983; Multilevel Statistical Models, 1987, 3rd edn 2003; (with T. Lewis) Assessment, 1996; (with A. Leyland) Multilevel Modelling of Health Statistics, 2001. *Recreations:* playing the flute, walking, cycling, tennis. *Address:* Graduate School of Education, University of Bristol, Bristol BS8 1JA.

GOLDSTEIN, Prof. Joseph Leonard; physician, genetics educator; Paul J. Thomas Professor of Medicine, and Chairman, Department of Molecular Genetics, since 1977, Regental Professor, since 1985, University of Texas Southwestern Medical (formerly Health Science) Center at Dallas (Member of Faculty, since 1972); *b* 18 April 1940; *s* of Isadore E. and Fannie A. Goldstein. *Educ:* Washington and Lee University (BS); Univ. of Texas Health Science Center at Dallas (MD). Intern, then Resident in Medicine, Mass Gen. Hosp., Boston, 1966–88; clinical associate, NIH, 1968–70; Postdoctoral Fellow, Univ. of Washington, Seattle, 1970–72. Harvey Soc. Lecture, Rockefeller Univ., 1977. Member: Sci. Rev. Bd, Howard Hughes Med. Inst., 1978–84, Med. Adv. Bd, 1985–90 (Chm., 1995–2002; Trustee, 2002–); Bd of Dirs, Passano Foundn, 1985–; Sci. Adv. Bd, Welch Foundn, 1986–; Bd of Consultants, Meml Sloan-Kettering Cancer Center, 1992–; Bd of Trustees, Rockefeller Univ., 1994–; Bd of Govs, Scripps Res. Inst., 1996–; Bd of Sci. Advrs, Van Andel Res. Inst., 1996–; Sci. Adv. Cttee, Mass Gen. Hosp., 2005–; Bd of Dirs, Albert and Mary Lasker Foundn, 2007– (Chm., Awards Jury, 1996–). Fellow, Salk Inst., 1983–94. Member, editorial board: Jl Clin. Investigation, 1977–82; Annual Review of Genetics, 1980–85; Arteriosclerosis, 1981–87; Jl Biol Chemistry, 1981–85; Cell, 1983–; Science, 1985–98; Genomics, 1988–; Mol. Biol. of the Cell, 1992–97; Proc. Nat. Acad. Scis, 1992–. Member: Nat. Acad. of Scis (Lounsbery Award, 1979); Amer. Acad. of Arts and Scis, and other bodies; Foreign Mem., Royal Soc., 1991. Hon. DSc: Chicago, 1982; Rensselaer Polytechnic Inst., 1982; Washington and Lee, 1986; Paris-Sud, 1988; Buenos Aires, 1990; Southern Methodist, 1993; Miami, 1996; Rockefeller, 2001; Albany Med. Coll., 2004. Numerous awards from scientific instns, incl. Pfizer Award in Enzyme Chemistry, Amer. Chem. Soc., 1976; award in biol and med. scis, NY Acad. Scis, 1981; Albert Lasker Award in Basic Science (with Michael Brown), 1985; Nobel Prize (with Michael Brown) for Physiology or Medicine, 1985; Amer. Coll. of Physicians Award, 1986; US Nat. Medal of Science, 1988; Distinguished Alumni Award, NIH, 1991; Warren Alpert Foundn Prize, Harvard Med. Sch., 2000; Albany Med. Center Prize in

Med. and Biomed. Res., 2003; Distinguished Scientist Award, American Heart Assoc., 2003; Woodrow Wilson Award for Public Service, 2005; Builders of Sci. Award, Research!America, 2007. *Publications:* (jtly) The Metabolic Basis of Inherited Diseases, 5th edn 1983; papers on genetics educn and science subjects. *Address:* Department of Molecular Genetics, University of Texas Southwestern Medical Center at Dallas, 5323 Harry Hines Boulevard, Dallas, TX 75390–9046, USA; 3831 Turtle Creek Boulevard, Apt 22–B, TX 75219, USA.

GOLDSTEIN, Dr Michael, CBE 1997; FRSC; higher education consultant, since 2004; Vice-Chancellor, Coventry University, 1992–2004 (Director, Coventry Polytechnic, 1987–92); *b* 1 May 1939; *s* of Sarah and Jacob Goldstein; *m* 1962, Janet Sandra Skevington; one *s*. *Educ:* Hackney Downs Grammar School; Northern Polytechnic, London. BSc, PhD, DSc; CChem. Lectr, sen. lectr, principal lectr, Polytechnic of N London, 1963–73; Head of Dept of Chemistry, 1974–83 and Dean of Faculty of Science, 1979–83, Sheffield City Polytechnic; Dep. Dir, Coventry Lanchester Polytechnic, 1983–87. Mem., cttees and bds, CNAA, 1975–93, incl. Chm., CNAA Chem. Bd, 1978–84; Dep. Chm., Polys and Colls Admissions System, 1989–94; Member: UCAS, 1993–2001 (Dep. Chm., 1995–97; Chm., 1997–2001); Univs and Colls Employers Assoc., 1994–2001. Director: Coventry and Warwicks TEC, 1992–97; City Centre Co. (Coventry) Ltd, 1997–2002 (Vice-Chm., 1999–2002); Coventry and Warwicks Chamber of Commerce, Trng and Enterprise, 1997–2001; CV One Ltd, 2002– (Dep. Chm., 2004–); ContinYou Ltd, 2003–; Coventry and Warwicks NHS Partnership Trust, 2006–; Chairman: Creative Partnerships Coventry, 2004–; Heist Enterprises Ltd, 2004–06. Member: Adv. Cttee, Coventry Common Purpose, 1989–2004; Coventry is making it, 1992–95; Coventry and Warwicks LSC, 2001–07; Mgt Bd, Foundn Degree Forward, 2006–. Member: RSC Council, 1983–86, 1993–99; other RSC cttees, 1975–99 (Pres., Educn Div., 1993–95; Chm., Educn and Quals Bd, 1995–99); Chairman: Council for Registration of Forensic Practitioners, 2005–; Higher Educn Develt Gp, States of Jersey, 2005–. Trustee, Community Educn Develt Centre, 1996–2003. Hon. FCGI 1994. Hon. Fellow, Univ. of Worcester, 1998. Hon. DSc Warwick, 2003. *Publications:* contribs to sci. jls, chapters in review books. *Recreations:* Coventry City FC, exercise. *Address:* 33 Frythe Close, Kenilworth CV8 2SY. *T:* (01926) 854939.

GOLDSTEIN, Nathan Harold; a Senior Immigration Judge, Asylum and Immigration Tribunal (formerly a Vice President, Immigration Appeal Tribunal), since 2003; *b* 21 Sept. 1944; *s* of Joseph and Fay Goldstein; *m* 1988, Shelley Katrina Sofier; one *s* two *d*. *Educ:* Carmel Coll.; Hasmonean Grammar Sch.; Coll. of Law. Admitted solicitor, 1987; Equity Partner, Nelsons Solicitors, 1988–95. Immigration Adjudicator (pt-time), 1996–97; Special Adjudicator (pt-time), 1997–99; Immigration Adjudicator, 1999–2003; Legal Mem., Special Immigration Appeals Commn, 2005–; an Investigating Judge and Mem., Review Bodies, 2006–. Mem., Law Soc., 1987–. Mem., BFI, 1964–. Mem., Knightsbridge Speakers Club, 1983–2004. *Publications:* papers on immigration matters. *Recreations:* family, cinema, theatre, jazz, football (lifelong Arsenal supporter), my grandchildren, reading (incl. subscribing to endless magazines which I never throw away), taking or being taken by my dog Hitch for long walks on Hampstead Heath where I live. *Address:* Asylum and Immigration Tribunal, Field House, 15 Breams Buildings, EC4A 1DZ; *e-mail:* Nathan.Goldstein@judiciary.gsi.gov.uk.

GOLDSTEIN, His Honour Simon Alfred; a Circuit Judge, 1987–2003; *b* 6 June 1935; *s* of Harry and Constance Goldstein; *m* 1973, Zoë Philippa, *yr d* of late Basil Gerrard Smith, TD. *Educ:* East Ham Grammar Sch.; Fitzwilliam Coll., Cambridge (BA 1956). Educn Officer, RAF, 1957–60. Called to the Bar, Middle Temple, 1961; Dep. Circuit Judge, 1975; a Recorder, 1980–87. *Recreation:* bridge. *Address:* The Garden Flat, 15 Montagu Place, W1H 2ET.

GOLDSTEIN-JACKSON, Kevin Grierson; JP; writer; artist; company director; *b* 1946; *s* of H. G. and W. M. E. Jackson; *m* 1975, Jenny Mei Leng, *e d* of Ufong Ng, Malaysia; two *d*. *Educ:* Reading Univ. (BA Phil. and Sociol.); Southampton Univ. (MPhil Law). Staff Relations Dept, London Transport (Railways), 1966; Scottish Widows Pension & Life Assurance Soc., 1967; Prog. Organizer, Southern TV, 1970–73; Asst Prod., HK-TVB, Hong Kong, 1973; freelance writer/TV prod., 1973–75; Head of Film, Dhofar Region TV Service, Sultanate of Oman, 1975–76; Founder and Dir, Thames Valley Radio, 1974–77; Asst to Head of Drama, Anglia TV, 1977–81; Founder, TSW-Television South West: Programme Controller and Dir of Progs, 1981–85; Jt Man. Dir, 1981–82; Chief Exec., 1982–85. Writer of screenplays. Dir of private cos. Gov., Lilliput First Sch., Poole, 1988–93. FRSA 1978; FCMI (FBIM 1982); FInstD 1982; FFA 1988; FRGS 1989. Freeman, City of London, 1996. JP Poole, 1990. *Publications:* 18 books, including: The Right Joke for the Right Occasion, 1973; Encyclopaedia of Ridiculous Facts, 1975; Experiments with Everyday Objects, 1976; Things to make with Everyday Objects, 1978; Magic with Everyday Objects, 1979; Dictionary of Essential Quotations, 1983; Jokes for Telling, 1986; Share Millions, 1989; The Public Speaker's Joke Book, 1991; The Astute Private Investor, 1994; Quick Quips, 2002; contrib. financial and gen. pubns. *Recreations:* writing, TV, films, travel, music, walking, philosophical and sociological investigation.

GOLDSTONE, Prof. Anthony Howard, CBE 2008; FRCP, FRCPE; FRCPath; Professor, Department of Haematology, University College London, since 1999; Director, North London Cancer Network, since 2000; *b* 13 Sept. 1944; *s* of Norman Goldstone and Edith Goldstone; *m* 1970, Jennifer Anne Krantz; one *s* one *d*. *Educ:* Bolton Sch.; St John's Coll., Oxford (BM BCh 1968; MA); University Coll. Hosp. Med. Sch. (Fellow, UCL, 1993). FRCPE 1979; FRCP 1983; FRCPath 1987. Sen. House Officer, Gastrointestinal Unit, Western General Infirmary, Edinburgh, 1969–70; Sen. Registrar in Haematology, Addenbrooke's Hosp., Cambridge, 1973–76; University College Hospital, London: Consultant Haematologist, 1976–; Dir, Bone Marrow Transplantation, 1979–2000; Postgrad. Dean, UCH Med. Sch., 1984–87; Chm., UCH Med. Cttee, 1986–88; Med. Dir, 1992–2000, and Dir, Clinical Haematology and Cancer Services, 1997–2000, UCL Hosps NHS Trust. Chm., NE Thames Regl Haematologists, 1988–90. Mem. Bd, European Gp for Bone Marrow Transplantation, 1990–98; Nat. Co-ordinator, UK Adult Leukaemia Trials, 1987–. President: British Soc. for Blood and Bone Marrow Transplantation, 1999–2000; British Soc. for Haematology, 2000–01. *Publications:* (jtly) Leukaemias, Lymphomas and Allied Disorders, 1976; Examination Haematology, 1977; (jtly) Synopsis of Haematology, 1983; Low Grade Lymphoma, 2005; numerous papers on treatment of leukaemia, and bone marrow transplantation. *Recreations:* cuddling grandchildren, driving fast cars, hoping Manchester City won't be relegated. *Address:* Department of Haematology, University College London Hospitals, WC1E 6AU; 67 Loom Lane, Radlett, Herts WD7 8NX.

GOLDSTONE, David Joseph; Chairman and Chief Executive, Regalian Properties Plc, 1970–2001; *b* 21 Feb. 1929; *s* of Solomon Goldstone and Rebecca Goldstone (*née* Degotts); *m* 1957, Cynthia (*née* Easton); one *s* two *d*. *Educ:* Dynevor Secondary Sch., Swansea; London School of Economics and Political Science (LLB Hons; Hon. Fellow, 1995). Admitted Solicitor (Hons), 1955. Legal practice, 1955–66. Director: Swansea Sound Commercial Radio Ltd, 1974–96; Wales Millennium Centre Ltd, 1998–2006; Cardiff & Vale Hosp. Trust, 2006–. Mem., London First (formerly London Forum), 1993–97. Member Council: WNO, 1984–89; Royal Albert Hall, 1999–2006 (Hon. Vice Pres., 2007–). Mem., Court of Govs, LSE, 1985–; Dep. Chm., Council, London Univ., 2002–06 (Mem., 1994–2006). Mem. Court, 1999–2005, Chm., 2001–05, Coram Family. Special Adviser (Estates): Welsh Rugby Union, 2008–; NHS Wales, 2008–. Hon. Vice Pres., London Welsh Male Voice Choir, 2007–. *Recreations:* family, reading, sport. *Address:* Flat 4 Grosvenor Hill Court, 15 Bourdon Street, W1K 3PX. *Clubs:* Lansdowne, Bath & Racquets.

GOLDSTONE, David Julian; QC 2006; *b* 30 July 1962; *s* of Leslie and Barbara Goldstone; *m* 1991, Ruby Azhar; three *d*. *Educ:* Haberdashers' Aske's, Elstree; Emmanuel Coll., Cambridge (MA Law); New Coll., Oxford (BCL). Called to the Bar, Middle Temple, 1986; in practice at the Bar, 1989–: Queen Elizabeth Bldg, 1989–2002; Quadrant Chambers, 2002–. First Standing Counsel to the Admiralty, 1999–2006. Lectr (pt-time), LSE and KCL, 1985–88. *Recreations:* politics (Founding Mem., Soc. of liberal Lawyers, 2006), gardening, especially Mediterranean and sub-tropical plants, chess, Chelsea FC. *Address:* Quadrant Chambers, 10 Fleet Street, EC4Y 1AU. *T:* (020) 7583 4444, *Fax:* (020) 7583 4455; *e-mail:* david.goldstone@quadrantchambers.com.

GOLDSTONE, Prof. Jeffrey, PhD; FRS 1977; Professor of Physics, Massachusetts Institute of Technology, 1977–2004, now Emeritus (Cecil and Ida Green Professor in Physics, 1983–2004; Director, Center for Theoretical Physics, 1983–89); *b* 3 Sept. 1933; *s* of Hyman Goldstone and Sophia Goldstone; *m* 1980, Roberta Gordon; one *s*. *Educ:* Manchester Grammar Sch.; Trinity Coll., Cambridge (MA 1956, PhD 1958). Trinity Coll., Cambridge: Entrance Scholar, 1951; Res. Fellow, 1956; Staff Fellow, 1962; Hon. Fellow, 2000; Cambridge University: Lectr, 1961; Reader in Math. Physics, 1976. Vis. appointments: Institut for Teoretisk Fysik, Copenhagen; CERN, Geneva; Harvard Univ.; MIT; Inst. for Theoretical Physics, Santa Barbara; Stanford Linear Accelerator Center; Lab. de Physique Théorique, L'Ecole Normale Supérieure, Paris; Università di Roma I. Smith's Prize, Cambridge Univ., 1955; Dannie Heineman Prize, Amer. Phys. Soc., 1981; Guthrie Medal, Inst. of Physics, 1983; Dirac Medal, Internat. Centre for Theoretical Physics, 1991. *Publications:* articles in learned jls. *Address:* Department of Physics, (6–407) Massachusetts Institute of Technology, Cambridge, MA 02139, USA. *T:* (office) (617) 2536263; *e-mail:* goldston@mit.edu.

GOLDSTONE, Leonard Clement; QC 1993; **His Honour Judge Goldstone;** a Circuit Judge, since 2002; *b* 20 April 1949; *s* of Maurice and Maree Goldstone; *m* 1972, Vanessa, *yr d* of Donald Forster, *qv*; three *s*. *Educ:* Manchester Grammar Sch.; Churchill Coll., Cambridge (BA). Called to the Bar, Middle Temple, 1971, Bencher, 2004; a Recorder, 1992–2002. Pres., Mental Health Review Tribunal (Restricted Cases), 1999–2004. Treas., Northern Circuit, 1998–2001. *Recreations:* golf, bridge, music, theatre. *Address:* Courts of Justice, Crown Square, Manchester M60 9DJ. *Club:* Dunham Forest Golf and Country (Altrincham).

GOLDSTONE, His Honour Peter Walter; a Circuit Judge, 1978–97; *b* 1 Nov. 1926; *y s* of late Adolph Lionel Goldstone and Ivy Gwendoline Goldstone; *m* 1955, Patricia (*née* Alexander), JP; one *s* two *d*. *Educ:* Manchester Grammar Sch.; Manchester Univ. Solicitor, 1951. Fleet Air Arm, 1944–47. Partner in private practice with brother Julian S. Goldstone, 1951–71. Manchester City Councillor (L), 1962–65; Chm., Manchester Rent Assessment Panel, 1967–71; Reserve Chm., Manchester Rent Tribunal, 1969–71; Dep. Chm., Inner London QS, Nov. 1971; a Metropolitan Stipendiary Magistrate, 1971–78; a Recorder of the Crown Court, 1972–78. Designated Care Judge, Watford Care Centre, 1994–97. *Recreations:* walking, gardening, reading. *Address:* c/o Watford County Court, Cassiobury House, 11/19 Station Road, Watford WD1 1EZ. *T:* (01923) 249666. *Club:* MCC.

GOLDSWORTHY, Andrew Charles, (Andy), OBE 2000; artist and sculptor; *b* 25 July 1956; *s* of Frederick Goldsworthy and Muriel Goldsworthy (*née* Stangar); *m* 1982, Judith Gregson (marr. diss. 2006); two *s* two *d*. *Educ:* Harrogate Secondary Mod. Sch.; Harrogate High Sch.; Bradford Coll. of Art; Lancashire Poly. Has worked in Yorkshire, Cumbria and Dumfriesshire, 1978–. Hon. Fellow, Central Lancashire Univ., 1995. Hon. MA Bradford, 1993; Hon. DLit Glasgow, 2005. *Publications:* Touching North, 1989; Leaves, 1989; Hand to Earth, 1990; Andy Goldsworthy, 1990; Snow and Ice Drawings, 1992; Two Autumns, 1993; Stone, 1994; Black Stones—Red Pools, 1995; Wood, 1996; Cairns, 1997; Andy Goldsworthy (Arches), 1998; Arch, 1999; Wall, 2000; Time, 2000; Midsummer Snowballs, 2001; Refuges D'Art, 2002; Passage, 2004. *Address:* c/o Galerie Lelong, 528 West 26th Street, New York, NY 10001, USA.

GOLDSWORTHY, Rt Rev. (Arthur) Stanley; permission to officiate, diocese of The Murray, SA, since 1992; *b* 18 Feb. 1926; *s* of Arthur and Doris Irene Goldsworthy; *m* 1952, Gwen Elizabeth Reeves; one *s* one *d*. *Educ:* Dandenong High School, Vic; St Columb's Theological Coll., Wangaratta. Deacon 1951, priest 1952; Curate of Wodonga, in charge of Bethanga, 1951–52; Priest of Chiltern, 1952; Kensington, Melbourne, 1955; Yarrawonga, Wangaratta, 1959; Shepparton (and Archdeacon), 1972; Parish Priest of Wodonga, and Archdeacon of Diocese of Wangaratta, 1977; Bishop of Bunbury, 1977–83; an Assisting Bishop to Primate of Australia, 1983–84; Parish Priest: St John, Hendra, Brisbane, 1983–84; Gilgandra, Bathurst, 1986–89; Tailem Bend, Meningie, SA, 1989–92, retired. Chaplain, 1956–77, Visitor, 1977–84, Community of the Sisters of the Church. *Recreations:* music, gardening.

GOLDSWORTHY, Julia Anne; MP (Lib Dem) Falmouth and Camborne, since 2005; *b* 10 Sept. 1978; *d* of Edward Douglas Goldsworthy and Margaret Joan Goldsworthy. *Educ:* Fitzwilliam Coll., Cambridge (BA Hist. 2000); Daiichi Univ. of Econs, Japan (Japanese Exchange Schol.); Birkbeck Coll., London (Postgrad. Cert. Econs 2002). Res. asst to Matthew Taylor, MP, 2001; Sen. Educn/Econ. Advr to Lib Dems, 2003; Res. Advr, Truro Coll. Business Centre, 2004; Regeneration Officer, Carrick DC, 2004–05. *Recreations:* pilot gig rowing, music (piano and clarinet). *Address:* (office) 75 Trelowarren Street, Camborne, Cornwall TR14 8AL. *T:* and *Fax:* (01209) 716110; *e-mail:* info@juliagoldsworthy.org. *Clubs:* Falmouth Arts; Helford River Pilot Gig; Portreath Surf Lifesaving.

GOLDSWORTHY, Rt Rev. Stanley; *see* Goldsworthy, Rt Rev. A. S.

GOLDTHORPE, John Harry, CBE 2002; FBA 1984; Official Fellow, Nuffield College, Oxford, 1969–2002, now Emeritus; Visiting Professor of Sociology, Cornell University, 2003–06; *b* 27 May 1935; *s* of Harry Goldthorpe and Lilian Eliza Goldthorpe; *m* 1963, Rhiannon Esyllt (*née* Harry); one *s* one *d*. *Educ:* Wath-upon-Dearne Grammar School; University College London (BA Hons 1st Class Mod. Hist.); LSE. MA Cantab; MA Oxon. Asst Lectr, Dept of Sociology, Univ. of Leicester, 1957–60; Fellow of King's College, Cambridge, 1960–69; Asst Lectr and Lectr, Faculty of Economics and Politics, Cambridge, 1962–69. Lectures: Fuller, Univ. of Essex, 1979; Marshall, Univ. of Southampton, 1989; Aubert, Oslo Univ., 1993; Geary, Econ. and Social Res. Inst., Dublin, 1998; Cummings, McGill Univ., Montreal, 2001. MAE 1988. For. Mem., Royal

Swedish Acad. of Scis, 2001. Hon. FilDr Stockholm Univ., 1990. *Publications:* (with David Lockwood and others): The Affluent Worker: industrial attitudes and behaviour, 1968; The Affluent Worker: political attitudes and behaviour, 1968; The Affluent Worker in the Class Structure, 1969; (with Keith Hope) The Social Grading of Occupations, 1974; (with Fred Hirsch) The Political Economy of Inflation, 1978; Social Mobility and Class Structure in Modern Britain, 1980, 2nd edn 1987; Order and Conflict in Contemporary Capitalism, 1984; (with Hermann Strasser) Die Analyse Sozialer Ungleichheit, 1985; (contrib.) John H. Goldthorpe: consensus and controversy (ed Clark, Modgil and Modgil), 1990; (with Robert Erikson) The Constant Flux: a study of class mobility in industrial societies, 1992; (with Christopher Whelan) The Development of Industrial Society in Ireland, 1992; Causation, Statistics and Sociology, 1999; On Sociology, 2000, 2nd edn, 2 vols, 2007; (with Catherine Bunting and others) From Indifference to Enthusiasm: patterns of arts attendance in England, 2008; papers in Acta Sociologica, American Jl of Sociology, American Sociological Rev., British Jl of Sociology, Comparative Soc. Res., Cultural Trends, Sociological Review, Sociology, European Jl of Sociology, European Sociological Rev., Jl of Economic Perspectives, Proc. NAS, Poetics, Rationality and Society, Res. in Social Stratification and Mobility, Sociological Methods and Res., Sociologie du Travail, Rev. Française de Sociologie. *Recreations:* lawn tennis, bird watching, computer chess, cryptic crosswords. *Address:* 32 Leckford Road, Oxford OX2 6HX. *T:* (01865) 556602.

GOLLANCZ, Livia Ruth; Chairman, Victor Gollancz Ltd, 1983–89 (Governing Director, Joint Managing Director, 1965–85, Consultant, 1990–92); *b* 25 May 1920; *d* of Victor Gollancz and Ruth Lowy. *Educ:* St Paul's Girls' Sch.; Royal Coll. of Music (ARCM, solo horn). Horn player: LSO, 1940–43; Hallé Orch., 1943–45; Scottish Orch., 1945–46; BBC Scottish Orch., 1946–47; Covent Garden, 1947; Sadler's Wells, 1950–53. Joined Victor Gollancz Ltd as editorial asst and typographer, 1953; Dir, 1954. *Publication:* (ed and introd) Victor Gollancz, Reminiscences of Affection, 1968 (posthumous). *Recreations:* making music, gardening. *Address:* 26 Cholmeley Crescent, N6 5HA. *Club:* Alpine.

GOLOMBOK, Prof. Susan Esther, PhD; Professor of Family Research, and Director of Centre for Family Research, University of Cambridge, since 2006; Fellow, Newnham College, Cambridge, since 2006; *b* 11 Aug. 1954; *d* of Bennie and Kitty Golombok; *m* 1979, Prof. John Rust; one *s*. *Educ:* Hutchesons' Girls' Sch.; Univ. of Glasgow (BSc Hons 1976); Inst. of Educn, Univ. of London (MSc Child Develt 1977; PhD 1982). London University Institute of Psychiatry: Res. Psychologist, 1977–83; Lectr in Psychology, 1983–86; City University: Lectr, 1987–89; Sen. Lectr, 1989–90; Dir, Family and Child Psychology Res. Centre, 1989–2005; Reader, 1990–92; Prof. of Psychology, 1992–2005. Trustee: Laura Ashley Foundn, 1998–; One Plus One, 2005–; Brazelton Centre, 2006–. Freeman, City of London, 1986. *Publications:* (with Valerie Curran) Bottling It Up, 1985; (with John Rust) Modern Psychometrics, 1989, 2nd edn 1999; (with Robyn Fivush) Gender Development, 1994; (with Fiona Tasker) Growing Up in a Lesbian Family, 1997; Parenting: what really counts?, 2000; contribs to sci. jls. *Recreations:* reading, cinema, cooking, moving house. *Address:* Howe House, Huntingdon Road, Cambridge CB3 0LX. *T:* (01223) 277797.

GOMBRICH, Prof. Richard Francis, DPhil; Boden Professor of Sanskrit, Oxford University, 1976–2004; Fellow of Balliol College, Oxford, 1976–2004, now Emeritus Fellow; Academic Director, Oxford Centre for Buddhist Studies, since 2004; *b* 17 July 1937; *s* of Sir Ernst Hans Josef Gombrich, OM, CBE, FBA; *m* 1st, 1964, Dorothea Amanda Friedrich (marr. diss. 1984); one *s* one *d*; 2nd, 1985, Sanjukta Gupta. *Educ:* Magdalen Coll., Oxford (MA, DPhil); Harvard Univ. (AM). Univ. Lectr in Sanskrit and Pali, Oxford Univ., 1965–76; Fellow of Wolfson Coll., 1966–76, Emeritus Fellow, 1977. Stewart Fellow, Princeton Univ., 1986–87. Pres., Pali Text Soc., 1994–2002 (Hon. Sec., 1982–94). Ed., Clay Sanskrit Library, 2004–. Hon. DLitt Kalyani Univ., West Bengal, 1991; Hon. DEd De Montfort, 1996. Sri Lanka Ranjana (Sri Lanka), 1994; Vacaspati, Tirupati (India), 1997. *Publications:* Precept and Practice: traditional Buddhism in the rural highlands of Ceylon, 1971, 2nd edn, as Buddhist Precept and Practice, 1991; (with Margaret Cone) The Perfect Generosity of Prince Vessantara, 1977; On being Sanskritic, 1978; (ed with Heinz Bechert) The World of Buddhism, 1984; Theravada Buddhism: a social history from ancient Benares to modern Colombo, 1988, 2nd edn 2006; (with G. Obeyesekere) Buddhism Transformed, 1988; How Buddhism Began, 1996, 2nd edn 2006; contribs to oriental and anthropological journals. *Recreations:* singing, photography. *Address:* Balliol College, Oxford OX1 3BJ.

GOMERSALL, Sir Stephen (John), KCMG 2000 (CMG 1997); HM Diplomatic Service, retired; Chief Executive for Europe, Hitachi Ltd, since 2004; *b* 17 Jan. 1948; *s* of Harry Raymond Gomersall and Helen Gomersall; *m* 1975 (marr. diss. 2006); two *s* one *d*. *Educ:* Forest Sch., Snaresbrook; Queens' Coll., Cambridge (Mod. Langs, MA); Stanford Univ., Calif (MA 1970). Entered HM Diplomatic Service, 1970; Tokyo, 1972–77; Rhodesia Dept, FCO, 1977–79; Private Sec. to Lord Privy Seal, 1979–82; Washington, 1982–85; Econ. Counsellor, Tokyo, 1986–90; Head of Security Policy Dept, FCO, 1990–94; Dep. Perm. Rep., UK Mission to UN, 1994–98; Dir, Internat. Security, FCO, 1998–99; Ambassador to Japan, 1999–2004. *Recreations:* music, golf, composing silly songs. *Address:* Hitachi Europe Ltd, Whitebrook Park, Lower Cookham Road, Maidenhead SL6 8YA. *T:* (01628) 585000; *e-mail:* stephen.gomersall@hitachi-eu.com; 87 Highlands Heath, Portsmouth Road, Putney, SW15 3TY.

GOMEZ, Rt Rev. Drexel Wellington; *see* West Indies, Archbishop of.

GOMEZ, Jill; singer; *b* New Amsterdam, British Guiana; *d* of Albert Clyde Gomez and Denise Price Denham. *Educ:* Royal Academy of Music (FRAM 1986); Guildhall School of Music, London. Operatic début as Adina in L'Elisir d'Amore with Glyndebourne Touring Opera, 1968 (after winning John Christie Award), then Glyndebourne Fest. Opera, 1969, and has subseq. sung leading rôles, incl. Mélisande, Calisto, Anne Truelove in The Rake's Progress, Helena in A Midsummer Night's Dream; has appeared with The Royal Opera, English Opera Gp, ENO, WNO and Scottish Opera in rôles including Pamina, Ilia, Fiordiligi, The Countess in Figaro, Elizabeth in Elegy for Young Lovers, Tytania, Lauretta in Gianni Schicchi, the Governess in The Turn of the Screw, Jenifer in The Midsummer Marriage, Leila in Les Pêcheurs de Perles; with Kent Opera: Tatiana in Eugene Onegin, 1977; Violetta in La Traviata, 1979; Amyntas in Il Re Pastore, 1987; Donna Anna in Don Giovanni, 1988; created the rôle of Flora in Tippett's The Knot Garden, 1970, at Covent Garden, and of the Countess in Thea Musgrave's Voice of Ariadne, Aldeburgh, 1974; created title rôle in William Alwyn's Miss Julie for radio, 1977; title rôle BBC world première, Prokoviev's Maddalena, 1979; created rôle of Duchess, world première, Adès' Powder Her Face, 1995; other rôles include Donna Elvira, Cinna in Mozart's Lucio Silla, Cleopatra in Giulio Cesare, Teresa in Benvenuto Cellini, title rôle in Massenet's Thaïs, Blanche in Dialogues des Carmélites, Desdemona in Otello, Ludwigsburg, Zürich, Frankfurt, Lyons, Wexford, Amsterdam and London; première of Eighth Book of Madrigals, Monteverdi Fest., Zürich, 1979. Also recitalist, progs incl. A Spanish Songbook, Night and Day, and Fortunes of Love and War, perf. world-wide; concert repertoire includes Rameau, Bach, Handel (Messiah and cantatas), Haydn's Creation and Seasons, Mozart's Requiem and concert arias, Beethoven's Ninth, Berlioz's Nuits d'Eté, Brahms's Requiem, Fauré's Requiem, Ravel's Shéhérazade, Mahler's Second, Fourth and Eighth Symphonies, Strauss's Four Last Songs, Britten's Les Illuminations, Spring Symphony and War Requiem, Tippett's A Child of Our Time, Messiaen's Poèmes pour Mi, Webern op. 13 and 14 songs, and Schubert songs orch. Webern. Commissioned Cantiga—the song of Iñes de Castro (dramatic scena for soprano and orch.) from David Matthews (world première, BBC Prom., 1988). Regular engagements in France, Belgium, Holland, Germany, Scandinavia, Switzerland, Italy, Spain, Israel, America; masterclasses; festival appearances include Aix-en-Provence, Spoleto, Bergen, Versailles, Flanders, Holland, Prague, Edinburgh, Aldeburgh, Dartington, and BBC Prom. concerts. Recordings include three solo recitals (French, Spanish, and Mozart songs, with John Constable), Ravel's Poèmes de Mallarmé, Handel's Admeto, Acis and Galatea, Elvira in Don Giovanni, Fauré's Pelléas et Mélisande, Handel's Ode on St Cecilia's Day, Rameau's La Danse, Britten's Les Illuminations, Canteloube's Songs of the Auvergne, Villa Lobos' Bachianas Brasileiras no 5, Samuel Barber's Knoxville—Summer of 1915, Cabaret Classics (with John Constable), Britten's Blues, Cole Porter Songs, South of the Border, A Spanish Songbook (with John Constable), Tippett's A Child of Our Time; première recordings: David Matthew's Cantiga: the Song of Inés de Castro, Mahler's Seven Early Songs, Britten's Quatre Chansons Françaises, Tippett's The Knot Garden, Adès' Powder her Face.

GOMM, Richard Culling C.; *see* Carr-Gomm.

GOMME, Robert Anthony, CB 1990; Under Secretary, Department of the Environment, 1981–90, retired; *b* 19 Nov. 1930; *s* of Harold Kenelm Gomme and Alice Grace (*née* Jacques); *m* 1960, Helen Perris (*née* Moore); one *s* one *d*. *Educ:* Colfe's Grammar Sch., Lewisham; London School of Economics, Univ. of London (BScEcon 1955). National Service, Korean War, Corporal with Royal Norfolk Regt, 1951–52; Pirelli Ltd, 1955–66; NEDO, 1966–68; direct entrant Principal, Min. of Public Building and Works, 1968; Asst Sec., DoE, 1972–74, 1979–81; RCDS 1975; Cabinet Office, 1976–79; Department of the Environment: Dir of Defence Services, PSA, 1981–86; Prin. Finance Officer, 1987–90; Chief Exec., Crown Suppliers, 1990. Trustee: Friends of the National Libraries, 1991–97, 1999–2003; London Library, 1992–95, 1996–2000, 2001–05. Hon. Treas., Friends of Greenwich Park, 1992–95. *Publications:* George Herbert Perris: 1866–1920, the life and times of a radical, 2003; contrib. Oxford DNB and to learned jls. *Recreations:* historical research, music, theatre, travel. *Address:* 14 Vanbrugh Fields, Blackheath, SE3 7TZ. *T:* (020) 8858 5148.

GOMMIE, Marie-Claire Geneviève; *see* Alain, M.-C. G.

GOMPERTZ, (Arthur John) Jeremy; QC 1988; *b* 16 Oct. 1937; *s* of late Col Arthur William Bean Gompertz and Muriel Annie Gompertz (*née* Smith). *Educ:* Beaumont Coll.; Trinity Coll., Cambridge (MA). Called to the Bar, Gray's Inn, 1962, Bencher, 1997; in practice, South East Circuit; a Recorder, 1987–2002. Counsel for: Metropolitan Police, Stephen Lawrence Inquiry, 1998; Kelly family, Hutton Inquiry, 2003; Humberside Police, Bichard (Soham) Inquiry, 2004. Chm., Mental Health Review Tribunal, 1993. Mem., Jockey Club Security and Investigations Cttee, 2002–05. *Recreations:* racing and breeding, travel, ski-ing. *Address:* 5 Essex Court, Temple, EC4Y 9AH. *T:* (020) 7410 2000.

GÖNCZ, Árpád, Hon. GCB 1999; Hon. KCMG 1991; President, Republic of Hungary, 1990–2000; *b* 10 Feb. 1922; *s* of Lajos Göncz and Ilona Heimann; *m* 1947, Mária Zsuzsanna Gönter; two *s* two *d*. *Educ:* Pázmány Péter Univ. (DJ 1944); Univ. of Agric. Scis. Nat. Land Bank, 1942–45; Independent Smallholders' Party: Sec. to Gen. Sec.; Leader, Independent Youth; Editor in Chief, Generation (weekly), 1947–48; jobless from 1948, worked as welder and metalsmith; sentenced to life imprisonment for political activity, 1957; released under general amnesty, 1963; freelance writer and literary translator, esp. of English works, 1963–; Pres., Hungarian Writers' Union, 1989–90; founding mem., Free Initiatives Network, Free Democratic Fedn, Historic Justice Cttee; MP, regional list, 1990; Speaker of Parliament and President *ai*, Republic of Hungary, May–Aug. 1990. József Attila Literary Prize, 1983; Wheatland Prize, 1989; Premio Mediterraneo, 1991. *Publications:* Men of God (novel), 1974; Hungarian Medea (play), Iron Bars (play), 1979; Encounters (short stories), 1980; Balance (6 plays, incl. A Pessimistic Comedy, and Persephone), 1990; Homecoming (short stories), 1991; Shavings (essays), 1991. *Recreations:* reading, walking. *Address:* Kossuth tér 4, 1055 Budapest, Hungary. *T:* 4413550.

GONZÁLEZ MÁRQUEZ, Felipe; Member for Madrid, 1977–2000, for Seville, 2000–04, Congress of Deputies; Prime Minister of Spain and President, Council of Ministers, 1982–96; *b* 5 March 1942; *s* of Felipe González and Juana Márquez; *m* 1969, Carmen Romero Lopez; two *s* one *d*. *Educ:* Univ. of Seville (Law degree); Univ. of Louvaine. Opened first labour law office, Seville, 1966; Spanish Socialist Party (PSOE), 1964–: Mem., Seville Provincial Cttee, 1965–69; Mem., Nat. Cttee, 1969–70; Mem., Exec. Bd, 1970; First Sec., 1974–79, resigned; re-elected, 1979; Sec.-Gen., 1974–97. Former Chm., Socialist Parly Group. Chm., Global Progress Foundn (formerly Fundación Socialismo XXI), 1997–. Grand Cross: Order of Military Merit (Spain), 1984; Order of Isabel the Catholic (Spain), 1996. *Publications:* What is Socialism?, 1976; PSOE, 1977. *Address:* Gobelas 31, 28023 Madrid, Spain.

GONZÁLEZ-PÁRAMO, Dr José Manuel; Professor of Economics, Universidad Complutense, Madrid, since 1988; Member, Executive Board, European Central Bank, since 2004; *b* Madrid, 9 Aug. 1958. *Educ:* Univ. Complutense, Madrid (Econs degree 1980; PhD Econs 1985); Columbia Univ., New York (MA Econs 1983; MPhil Econs 1984; PhD Econs 1986). Universidad Complutense, Madrid: Res. Asst and Teaching Fellow, 1980–82; Associate Prof. of Econs, 1985–88; Hd, Public Finance Dept, 1986–94. Econ. Advr, Min. of Econ. and Finance, 1985–87; Banco de España: Sen. Econ. Advr, 1989–94; Gov., 1994–2004; Mem., Exec. Bd, 1998–2004. Advisory posts include: World Bank, Washington, 1984, 1989, 2000–02; Internat. Develt Bank, Argentina, 1998; EC, 1989, 1993; Spanish govt agencies, 1985–2004. Prof., World Bank Inst., 2001–02. Mem., Eur. Acad. Scis and Arts, 2000–. *Publications:* (jtly) Public Management, 1997; Costs and Benefits of Fiscal Discipline: the budget stability law in perspective, 2001; (with B. Moreno-Dodson) The Role of the State and Economic Consequences of Alternative Forms of Public Expenditures Financing, 2003; (jtly) Public Economics, 2004; (jtly) The Role of Government in Regional Development, 2006; numerous contribs to books and to jls on monetary and financial policy and fiscal and structural policies. *Address:* European Central Bank, Kaiserstrasse 29, 60311 Frankfurt am Main, Germany.

GONZI, Hon. Dr Lawrence, KUOM 2004; Prime Minister of Malta and Minister of Finance, since 2004; *b* 1 July 1953; *s* of Louis and Inez Gonzi; *m* 1977, Catherine Callus; two *s* one *d*. *Educ:* Univ. of Malta (LLD 1975). Practised law, 1975–88. Mem., Prisons Bd, 1987–88; Chairman: Pharmacy Board, 1987–88; Nat. Commn for Mental Health Reform, 1987–94 and 1994–96; Nat. Commn for Persons with Disabilities, 1987–94 (Pres., 1994–96); Electoral System (Revision) Commn, 1994–95. Chm., Bd of Dirs, Mizzi Orgn, 1989–97. Speaker, House of Reps, 1988–92 and 1992–96; elected to House of

Reps, from 2nd Dist, 1996; Opposition Party Whip, Sec. to Parly Gp and Shadow Minister for Social Policy, 1996–98; Minister for Social Policy and Leader, House of Reps, 1998–99, Dep. Prime Minister, 1999–2004. Sec.-Gen., 1997–98, Dep. Leader, 1999–2004, Nationalist Party. Gen. Pres., Malta Catholic Action Movement, 1976–86. *Address:* Office of the Prime Minister, Auberge de Castille, Valletta CMR 02, Malta. *T:* 22001400, *Fax:* 22001467; *e-mail:* lawrence.gonzi@gov.mt.

GOOCH, Anthony John; HM Diplomatic Service, retired; Deputy High Commissioner and Economic and Commercial Counsellor, Singapore, 1997–2000; *b* 28 Nov. 1941; *s* of John Edgar Gooch and Mary Elizabeth (*née* Bricknell); *m* 1966, Jennifer Jane Harrison (*d* 1984); one *d*; *m* 1988, Cynthia Lee Barlow. *Educ:* Latymer Upper Sch.; St Catharine's Coll., Cambridge (BA Hist.); Open Univ. (MA 2002). Pubns Editor, Europa Pubns, 1964–70; joined FCO, 1970: attachment to SEATO, Bangkok, 1972–74; Second, later First, Sec., FCO, 1974–80; First Secretary: (Economic), Stockholm, 1980–83; (Labour), Pretoria, 1984–88; FCO, 1988–92; (Commercial), Warsaw, 1992–96; Dir, Trade Promotion, and Consul-Gen., Warsaw, 1996–97. Inquiry Sec. (panellist), Competition Commn, 2002–. *Recreations:* tennis, gardening, cinema history. *Address:* 22 Trinity Place, Windsor, Berks SL4 3AT. *Clubs:* Windsor Lawn Tennis; Tanglin (Singapore).

GOOCH, Brig. Sir Arthur (Brian Sherlock Heywood), 14th Bt *cr* 1746, of Benacre Hall, Suffolk; DL; *b* 1 June 1937; *s* of late Col Brian Sherlock Gooch, DSO, TD and Monica Mary (*née* Heywood); *S* cousin, 2008; *m* 1963, Sarah Diana Rowena Perceval, JP; two *d*. *Educ:* Eton; RMA Sandhurst. Comdg The Life Guards, 1978–81. Hon. Col, Kent and Co. of London Yeomanry (Sharpshooters), 1992–99. DL Wilts 1998. *Recreation:* fishing. *Heir: b* Thomas Sherlock Heywood Gooch [*b* 12 Nov. 1943; *m* 1971, Elizabeth Clarice Joan Peyton; one *s* one *d*]. *Address:* Manor Farmhouse, Chitterne, Wilts BA12 0LG. *Club:* Army and Navy.

GOOCH, Graham Alan, OBE 1991; cricketer; Batting Coach, Essex County Cricket Club, since 2005 (Chief Coach, 2001–05); *b* 23 July 1953; *s* of late Alfred and of Rose Gooch; *m* 1976, Brenda Daniels; three *d* (incl. twins). *Educ:* Leytonstone. Batsman and bowler; first played for Essex CCC, 1973, Captain, 1986–94, retired, 1997; Member, England Test team, 1975–82 and 1986–Jan. 1995 (retired); played in S Africa, 1982; Captain of England, July 1988 and Sept. 1989–1993; 333 against India, highest score by a Test captain, 1990; 20 Test centuries; record no of runs (8900) in English Test cricket, 1995. England A team manager, Kenya and Sri Lanka tour, 1997–98; Manager, England Test tour, Australia, 1998–99. Mem., Selection Panel, ECB, 1997–99. *Publications:* Batting, 1980; (with Alan Lee) My Cricket Diary 1981, 1982; (with Alan Lee) Out of the Wilderness, 1985; Testing Times (autobiog.), 1991; (with Frank Keating) Gooch: My Autobiography, 1995. *Address:* c/o Essex County Cricket Club, County Ground, New Writtle Street, Chelmsford, Essex CM2 0PG. *T:* (01245) 252420.

GOOCH, Prof. John, PhD; FRHistS; Professor of International History, Leeds University, since 1992; *b* 25 Aug. 1945; *s* of George Gooch and Doris Evelyn (*née* Mottram); *m* 1967, Catherine Ann Staley; one *s* one *d*. *Educ:* Brockenhurst County High Sch.; King's Coll., Univ. of London (BA Hons History, class 1, 1966; PhD War Studies 1969). FRHistS 1975. Asst Lectr in History, 1966–67, Asst Lectr in War Studies, 1969, KCL; University of Lancaster: Lectr in History, 1969–81; Sen. Lectr, 1981–84; Reader in History, 1984–88; Prof. of History, 1988–92. Sec. of the Navy Sen. Res. Fellow, US Naval War Coll., 1985–86; Vis. Prof. of Military and Naval History, Yale Univ., 1988; Associate Fellow, Davenport Coll., Yale, 1988. Chm. of Council, Army Records Soc., 1983–2000; Vice-Pres., RHistS, 1990–94. Editor, Jl of Strategic Studies, 1978–; Gen. Editor, Internat. Relations of the Great Powers; Member of Editorial Board: European History Qly; Diplomacy and Statecraft; Terrorism and Small Wars; Security Studies; War in History. Premio Internazionale di Cultura, Città di Anghiari, 1983. Kt, Order of Vila Viçosa (Portugal), 1991. *Publications:* The Plans of War: the general staff and British military strategy *c.* 1900–1916, 1974; Armies in Europe, 1980; The Prospect of War: studies in British defence policy 1847–1942, 1981; Politicians and Defence: studies in the formulation of British defence policy 1847–1970, 1981; Strategy and the Social Sciences, 1981; Military Deception and Strategic Surprise, 1982; Soldati e Borghesi nell' Europa Moderna, 1982; Army, State and Society in Italy 1870–1915, 1989 (trans. Italian); Decisive Campaigns of the Second World War, 1989; (with Eliot A. Cohen) Military Misfortunes: the anatomy of failure in war, 1990; Airpower: theory and practice, 1995; The Boer War: direction, experience and image, 2000. *Recreations:* Italian food and wine. *Address:* Coverhill House, Coverhill Road, Oldham OL4 5RE. *T:* (0161) 678 8573. *Club:* Savile.

GOOCH, Sir Miles (Peter), 6th Bt *cr* 1866, of Clewer Park, Berkshire; *b* 3 Feb. 1963; *s* of Sir Trevor Sherlock Gooch, 5th Bt and Denys Anne (*née* Venables); *S* father, 2003; *m* 2000, Louise Alicia Spiret; two *d*. *Educ:* Victoria Coll., Jersey; Preston Poly. (BEng). *Heir: kinsman* John Daniel Gooch, VRD [*b* 9 Dec. 1935; *m* 1972, Ann Patricia Lubbock; two *d*].

GOOD, Anthony Bruton Meyrick, FCIPR; Founder Chairman, Good Consultancy Ltd, since 1988; Chairman: Cox & Kings Ltd, since 1975 (Director, since 1971); Flagship Group Ltd, since 1999; *b* 18 April 1933; *s* of Meyrick George Bruton Good and Amy Millicent Trussell; *m* (marr. diss.); two *d*. *Educ:* Felsted Sch. Mgt Trainee, Distillers Gp, 1950–52; Editorial Asst, Temple Press Ltd, 1952–55; PRO, Silver City Airways, 1955–60; Founder Chm., Good Relations Gp plc, 1961–88; Chairman: Tulip Star, 1984; Cox & Kings (India) Ltd, 1988– (Dir, 1980–); Good Relations (India) Ltd, 1988–; Flagship Gp Ltd, 1994; Sage Organic Ltd, 2001–; The Tranquil Moment, 2001–; Obento Ltd, 2004; Benney Watches plc, 2007; Director: IM Gp Ltd, 1977–; Q-Link International, 1999–; Neutrahealth plc, 2005–; UK India Business Council, 2005. FCIPR (FIPR 1975); FInstD 1994. *Recreations:* travel, reading, theatre. *Address:* Clench House, Wootton Rivers, Marlborough, Wilts SN8 4NT. *T:* (01672) 810126, *Fax:* (01672) 810869. *Club:* Royal Automobile.

GOOD, Diana Frances; Litigation Partner, Linklaters, since 1988; a Recorder, since 2001; *b* 16 July 1956; *d* of Michael and Valerie Hope; *m* 1981, Alexander Good; four *d*. *Educ:* Croydon High Sch., GPDST; St Anne's Coll., Oxford (BA Juris.); Chester Coll. of Law; Univ. of Aix-en-Provence (Dip. Etudes Supérieures). Admitted solicitor, 1981; joined Linklaters, 1979: Litigation Partner, Brussels, 1989–92; Finance and Policy Cttee, 1993–96; Diversity Cttee, 2000–; Internat. Bd, 2001–04. Adv. Bd, Advocates for Internat. Develt, 2007–. Trustee: British Inst. Internat. and Comparative Law, 2000–; Mary Ward Settlement and Legal Centre, 2008–. Mem. Bd, Red Shift Theatre Co., 2002–. *Recreations:* holidays/travelling, theatre and cinema, cycling, including 450 miles in NW Vietnam for Medical Foundation for Victims of Torture, reading and discussion with Book Club members. *Address:* Linklaters, One Silk Street, EC2Y 8HQ. *T:* (020) 7456 4328, *Fax:* (020) 7456 2222; *e-mail:* diana.good@linklaters.com. *Club:* City Law.

GOOD, Rt Rev. Kenneth Raymond; see Derry and Raphoe, Bishop of.

GOOD, Ven. Kenneth Roy; Archdeacon of Richmond, 1993–2006, now Emeritus; *b* 28 Sept. 1941; *s* of Isaac Edward Good and Florence Helen Good (*née* White); *m* 1970, Joan Thérèse Bennett; one *s* one *d*. *Educ:* Stamford Sch.; King's Coll., London (BD 1966;

AKC). Ordained deacon 1967, priest 1968; Asst Curate, St Peter, Stockton on Tees, 1967–70; Missions to Seamen: Port Chaplain, Antwerp, 1970–74, Kobe, 1974–79; Asst Gen. Sec., 1979–85; Vicar of Nunthorpe, 1985–93; RD of Stokesley, 1989–93. Hon. Canon, Kobe, 1985. *Recreations:* gardening, photography. *Address:* 18 Fox Howe, Coulby Newham, Middlesbrough TS8 0RU.

GOODACRE, Peter Eliot, RD 1979, with clasp 1991; Principal, College of Estate Management, Reading, 1992–2007, Hon. Fellow, 2007; President, Royal Institution of Chartered Surveyors, 2008–July 2009; *b* 4 Nov. 1945; *s* of Edward Leslie Goodacre and Cicely May (*née* Elliott); *m* 1971, Brita Christina Forsling; two *d*. *Educ:* Kingston Grammar Sch.; Coll. of Estate Management; Loughborough Univ. of Technology (MSc). FRICS 1980. Commnd RNR, 1965; Lt Comdr, 1979. In private practice, 1966–69; Lecturer: Coll. of Estate Mgt, 1970–73; Univ. of Reading, 1973–78, Sen. Lectr 1978–83; Vice-Principal, Coll. of Estate Mgt, 1984–92. Mem., Gen. Council, RICS, 1986– (Vice-Pres., 2005–08, Sen. Vice-Pres., 2007–08); Vice-Chm., 1997–98, Pres., 1998–99, Quantity Surveyors' Divl Council). Mem., Gtr London RFCA (Chm., Works and Bldgs Sub-Cttee, 1997–2003). Chm., James Butcher Housing Assoc., 2006–; Mem. Bd, Southern Housing Assoc., 2006–. Non-exec. Dir, Thames Valley Strategic Health Authy, 2004–06. Freeman, City of London, 1994; Liveryman, Chartered Surveyors' Co., 1995–. Trustee: Harold Samuel Educn Trusts, 1992–; Guy Bigwood Trust, 2007–. FCIOB 1999. *Publications:* Formula Method of Price Adjustment for Building Contracts, 1978, 2nd edn 1987; Cost Factors of Dimensional Co-ordination, 1981; Worked Examples in Quantity Surveying Measurement, 1982. *Recreations:* home and garden. *Address:* Kingsmead, West Drive, Sonning, Berks RG4 6GE. *T:* (0118) 969 2422. *Clubs:* Athenæum, MCC; Phyllis Court (Henley).

GOODALL, Sir (Arthur) David (Saunders), GCMG 1991 (KCMG 1987; CMG 1979); HM Diplomatic Service, retired; Chairman, Leonard Cheshire (the Leonard Cheshire Foundation), 1995–2000 (Chairman, International Committee, 1992–95); *b* 9 Oct. 1931; *o c* of late Arthur William and Maisie Josephine Goodall; *m* 1962, Morwenna, *y d* of late Percival George Beck Peecock; two *s* one *d*. *Educ:* Ampleforth; Trinity Coll., Oxford (1st Cl. Hons Lit. Hum., 1954; MA; Hon. Fellow, 1992). Served 1st Bn KOYLI (2nd Lieut), 1955–56. Entered HM Foreign (subseq. Diplomatic) Service, 1956; served at: Nicosia, 1956; FO, 1957–58; Djakarta, 1958–60; Bonn, 1961–63; FO, 1963–68; Nairobi, 1968–70; FCO, 1970–73; UK Delegn, MBFR, Vienna, 1973–75; Head of Western European Dept, FCO, 1975–79; Minister, Bonn, 1979–82; Dep. Sec., Cabinet Office, 1982–84; Dep. Under-Sec. of State, FCO, 1984–87; High Comr to India, 1987–91. Co-Chm., Anglo-Irish Encounter, 1992–97; Chm., British-Irish Assoc., 1997–2002. Vis. Prof., Inst. of Irish Studies, Univ. of Liverpool, 1996–2008. Vice-Chm., Council, Durham Univ., 1997–2000; Chairman: Governing Body, Heythrop Coll., Univ. of London, 2000–06; Abbot's Adv. Cttee, Ampleforth Coll., 2004–; Gov., Westminster Cathedral Choir Sch., 1994–2007. Pres., Irish Genealogical Res. Soc., 1992– (Fellow, 1978). Fellow, Heythrop Coll., Univ. of London, 2006. Hon. LLD Hull, 1994. Distinguished Friend of Oxford University, 2001. *Publications:* Remembering India, 1997; Ryedale Pilgrimage, 2000; contribs to: Ampleforth Jl; Tablet; Irish Genealogist; The Past. *Recreation:* painting in watercolours. *Address:* Greystones, Ampleforth, North Yorks YO62 4DU. *Clubs:* Garrick, Oxford and Cambridge.

GOODALL, David William, PhD (London); DSc (Melbourne); ARCS, DIC, FLS; FIBiol; Hon. Research Fellow, Centre for Ecosystem Management, Edith Cowan University, since 1998; *b* 4 April 1914; *s* of Henry William Goodall; *m* 1st, 1940, Audrey Veronica Kirwin (marr. diss. 1949); one *s*; 2nd, 1949, Muriel Grace King (marr. diss. 1974); two *s* one *d*; 3rd, 1976, Ivy Nelms (*née* Palmer). *Educ:* St Paul's Sch.; Imperial Coll. of Science and Technology (BSc). Research under Research Inst. of Plant Physiology, on secondment to Cheshunt and East Malling Research Stns, 1935–46; Plant Physiologist, W African Cacao Research Inst., 1946–48; Sen. Lectr in Botany, University of Melbourne, 1948–52; Reader in Botany, University Coll. of the Gold Coast, 1952–54; Prof. of Agricultural Botany, University of Reading, 1954–56; Dir, CSIRO Tobacco Research Institute, Mareeba, Qld, 1956–61; Senior Principal Research Officer, CSIRO Div. of Mathematical Statistics, Perth, Australia, 1961–67; Hon. Reader in Botany, Univ. of Western Australia, 1965–67; Prof. of Biological Science, Univ. of California Irvine, 1966–68; Dir, US/IBP Desert Biome, 1968–73; Prof. of Systems Ecology, Utah State Univ., 1969–74; Sen. Prin. Res. Scientist, 1974–79, Sen. Res. Fellow, 1979–83, Land Resources Management Div., CSIRO; Hon. Fellow, CSIRO Div. of Wildlife and Ecology, 1983–98. Hon. Dr in Natural Scis, Trieste Univ., 1990. *Publications:* Chemical Composition of Plants as an Index of their Nutritional Status (with F. G. Gregory), 1947; ed, Evolution of Desert Biota, 1976; editor-in-chief, Ecosystems of the World (series), 1977–; co-editor: Productivity of World Ecosystems, 1975; Simulation Modelling of Environmental Problems, 1977; Arid-land Ecosystems: Structure, Functioning and Management, vol. 1 1979, vol. 2 1981; Mediterranean-type Shrublands, 1981; Hot Deserts, 1985; numerous papers in scientific jls and symposium vols. *Recreations:* acting, reading, walking. *Address:* Centre for Ecosystem Management, Edith Cowan University, 100 Joondalup Drive, Joondalup, WA 6027, Australia.

GOODALL, Howard Lindsay; composer and broadcaster; National Ambassador for Singing, since 2007; *b* 26 May 1958; *s* of Geoffrey and Marion Goodall. *Educ:* New College Sch.; Stowe Sch.; Lord Williams' Sch., Thame; Christ Church, Oxford (MA 1979). ARCO 1975. Freelance composer, 1976–. *TV and film themes/scores* include: Blackadder; Red Dwarf; The Vicar of Dibley; The Thin Blue Line; 2.4 Children; Mr Bean; Rowan Atkinson in Revue; Q.I.; The Catherine Tate Show; *compositions* include: The Hired Man, 1984 (Ivor Novello Award for best musical, 1985); Girlfriends, 1987; Days of Hope, 1990; Silas Marner, 1993; Missa Aedis Christi, 1993; Marlborough Canticles, 1995; In Memoriam Anne Frank, 1995; The Kissing-Dance, 1998; We are the Burning Fire, 1998; The Dreaming, 2001; O Lord God of Time and Eternity, 2003; The Gathering Storm, 2003; Jason and the Argonauts, 2004; Mr Bean's Holiday, 2007; Eternal Light: a requiem, 2008. Presenter: BBC: Choir of the Year, 1990–; Channel Four: Howard Goodall's Organ Works (RTS Award for best original title music), 1997; Four Goes to Glyndebourne, 1997–98; Howard Goodall's Choir Works, 1998; Howard Goodall's Big Bangs, 2000 (BAFTA Award, Huw Weldon Award for Arts, Religion, Hist. and Sci., Peabody Award for Mass Journalism and Communication, IMZ TV Award for Best Documentary); Howard Goodall's Great Dates, 2002; Howard Goodall's Twentieth Century Greats, 2004; How Music Works, 2006. *Address:* c/o Caroline Chignell, PBJ Management, 7 Soho Street, W1D 3DQ. *T:* (020) 7287 1112, *Fax:* (020) 7287 1191; *e-mail:* general@pbjmgt.co.uk; *web:* www.howardgoodall.co.uk.

GOODALL, Dame Jane; see Goodall, Dame V. J.

GOODALL, Rt Rev. Lindsay; see Urwin, Rt Rev. L. G.

GOODALL, Rt Rev. Maurice John, MBE 1974; Bishop of Christchurch, 1984–90; *b* 31 March 1928; *s* of John and Alice Maud Goodall; *m* 1st, 1953, Nathalie Ruth Cummack; two *s* four *d*; 2nd, 1981, Beverley Doreen Moore. *Educ:* Christchurch Technical Coll.; College House, Univ. of NZ (BA 1950); Univ. of Canterbury (LTh 1964); Dip. Social

Work (Distinction) 1977; CQSW 1982. Asst Curate, St Albans, Dio. of Christchurch, 1951–54; Vicar of: Waikari, 1954–59; Shirley, 1959–67; Hon. Asst, Christchurch, St John's 1967–69; Chaplain, Kingslea Girls' Training Centre, 1967–69; City Missioner (dio. Christchurch), 1969–76; Nuffield Bursary, 1973; Dir, Community Mental Health Team, 1976–82; Dean of Christchurch Cathedral, 1982–84. *Publications:* (with Colin Clark) Worship for Today, 1967; (contrib.) Christian Responsibility in Society (ed Yule), 1977; contribs to journals. *Recreations:* walking, reading, NZ history. *Address:* Flat 1, 50 Crofton Road, Christchurch 5, New Zealand.

GOODALL, Air Marshal Sir Roderick Harvey, KBE 2001 (CBE 1990); CB 1999; AFC 1981, Bar 1987; FRAeS; Chief of Staff, Component Command Air North, NATO, 1999–2003; *b* 19 Jan. 1947; *s* of late Leonard George Harvey Goodall and Muriel Goodall (*née* Cooper); *m* 1973, Elizabeth Susan Haines; two *d. Educ:* Elizabeth Coll., Guernsey; RAF Coll., Cranwell. FRAeS 1997. Commissioned 1968; served Bahrain, UK and Germany, to 1981; RAF Staff Coll., 1981; PMC Barnwood, 1982; OC 16 Sqn, Laarbruch, 1983–85; MoD, 1986–87; Station Comdr, RAF Bruggen, 1987–89; RCDS 1990; Station Comdr, RAF Detachment, Bahrain, 1990; Dir, Air Offensive and Air Force Ops, MoD, 1991–93; AOC No 2 Gp, 1994–96; COS Perm. Jt HQ, 1996–98; Leader, RAF Officers Branch Structure Review Team, 1998–99. Pres., RAF Golf Assoc., 1995–2003. Trustee, Lloyds TSB Foundn for the Channel Isles, 2005–. *Recreations:* golf, photography, family. *Address:* c/o Lloyds TSB, 2 North Gate, Sleaford, Lincs NG34 7BL. *Club:* Royal Air Force.

GOODALL, Prof. Roger Morgan, PhD; FIET, FIMechE, FREng; Professor of Control Systems Engineering, Loughborough University, since 1994; *b* Finchley, 7 May 1946; *s* of Philip Morgan and Gwynedd Marie Goodall; *m* 1987, Lesley Allison Page; one *s* three *d. Educ:* Ashville Coll., Harrogate; Peterhouse, Cambridge (BA 1968); Loughborough Univ. (PhD 1989). FIET (FIEE 1992); FIMechE 1995; FREng 2007. Jun. Engr, GEC-AEI Electronics Ltd, 1968–70; PSO, British Rail Res., Derby, 1970–82; Lectr, 1982–87, Sen. Lectr, 1987–94, Electronic & Electrical Engrg Dept, Loughborough Univ. Chm., UK Automatic Control Council, 2005–08. Member: Rolls-Royce Electrical and Controls Adv. Bd, 2003–; Eur. Rail Res. Adv. Council, 2003–; Railway Tech. Strategy Adv. Gp, 2007–. Vice-Pres., IFAC, 2008–. Vice-Chm., Railway Div., IMechE, 2005–June 2009. *Publications:* Digital Control, 1991; contrib. learned jls incl. Proc. IEE, Proc. IMechE. *Recreations:* ski-ing, snowboarding, long walks with dogs, GPS gadgets. *Address:* Department of Electronic and Electrical Engineering, Loughborough University, Ashby Road, Loughborough, Leics LE11 3TU. *T:* (01509) 227009, *Fax:* (01509) 227108; *e-mail:* R.M.Goodall@lboro.ac.uk.

GOODALL, Dame (Valerie) Jane, DBE 2003 (CBE 1995); PhD; Scientific Director, Gombe Wildlife Research Institute, Tanzania, since 1967; *b* 3 April 1934; *er d* of Mortimer Herbert Morris-Goodall and Vanne Morris-Goodall (*née* Joseph); *m* 1st, 1964, Baron Hugo van Lawick (marr. diss. 1974); one *s*; 2nd, 1975, Hon. Derek Bryceson, Tanzanian MP (*d* 1980). *Educ:* Uplands Sch., Bournemouth; Cambridge Univ. (PhD 1965). Sec., Oxford Univ., 1952; worked as asst to Louis and Mary Leakey, Olduvai Gorge, 1957; engaged in res. into behaviour of chimpanzees, Gombe Stream Game Reserve, now Gombe Nat. Park, 1960–; res. in social behaviour of Spotted Hyena, Ngorongoro, 1968–69; dir. res. on behaviour of Olive Baboon, Gombe, 1972–82. Vis. Prof., Dept of Psychiatry and Program of Human Biology, Stanford Univ., 1971–75; Hon. Vis. Prof. in Zoology, Dar es Salaam Univ., 1973–; A. D. White Prof.-at-Large, Cornell Univ., 1996–. Vice-Pres., Animal Welfare Inst., BVA, 1987–; Mem. Adv. Bd, Albert Schweitzer Inst. for the Humanities, 1991–; Trustee, Jane Goodall Insts in UK, USA and Canada, and member of many other conservation and wildlife socs and foundns. Documentary films for television on research with chimpanzees incl. Fifi's Boys, BBC, 1995. Hon. FRAI 1991. UN Messenger for Peace, 2002–. Many hon. degrees. Numerous awards and prizes including: Franklin Burr Award for contrib. to Science, 1963, 1964, Centennial Award, 1988, Hubbard Medal, 1995, Nat. Geographic Soc.; Conservation Award, NY Zool Soc., 1974; Gold Medal, Soc. of Women Geographers, 1990; Kyoto Prize, 1990; Edinburgh Medal, 1991; Silver Medal, Zool Soc. of London, 1996; 60th Anniversary Medal, UNESCO, 2006. *Publications:* My Friends the Wild Chimpanzees, 1967; (with H. van Lawick) Innocent Killers, 1970; In the Shadow of Man, 1971; The Chimpanzees of Gombe: patterns of behaviour, 1986; Through A Window: 30 years observing the Gombe chimpanzees, 1990; (with Dale Peterson) Visions of Caliban, 1993; Jane Goodall: with love, 1994; Reason for Hope (autobiog.), 1999; contribs to learned jls; *for children:* (with H. van Lawick) Grub: the bush baby, 1972; My Life with the Chimpanzees, 1988; The Chimpanzee Family Book, 1989; Jane Goodall's Animal World: chimps, 1989; Animal Family Series, 1991; The Eagle and the Wren, 2000. *Address:* Jane Goodall Institute–UK, Orchard House, 51–67 Commercial Road, Southampton, Hants SO15 1GG; *e-mail:* info@janegoodall.org.uk. *Club:* Explorers' (New York).

GOODBODY, Clarissa Mary; *see* Farr, C. M.

GOODBOURN, Dr David Robin; General Secretary, Churches Together in Britain and Ireland, 1999–2006; President, Partnership for Theological Education, Manchester, since 2005; *b* 1 Aug. 1948; *s* of Albert Lewis Goodbourn and Olive Mary Goodbourn (*née* Pring); *m* 1972, Evlynn Ann Cassie; one *s* one *d. Educ:* Sir Roger Manwood's Sch., Sandwich; Univ. of Durham (BA 1969); Univ. of Manchester (MEd 1980; PhD 1989). Sec. for Student Work, Baptist Union of GB, 1969–71; Dir, Baptist World Poverty Educn Prog., 1971–73; Tutor, Northern Baptist Coll., and Lectr, Northern Coll. (URC and Congregational), 1973–85; Adult Educn Advr, Church of Scotland, 1985–94; Asst Dir, 1994–98, then Depute Dir, 1998–99, Ch of Scotland Bd of Parish Educn, and Dean, Scottish Churches Open Coll., 1996–99. Member: Bd and Exec., Christian Aid, 1999–2006; Central Cttee, WCC, 2006–; Governing Body, SPCK, 2006–; Chairman: Roots for Churches Ltd, 2002–05; Feed the Minds, 2006–. *Recreations:* walking, reading, and a moderately educated taste for malt whisky. *Address:* Luther King House, Brighton Grove, Manchester M14 5JP; 38 St Werburgh's Road, Chorlton cum Hardy, Manchester M21 0TJ.

GOODCHILD, David Hicks, CMG 1992; CBE 1973; Partner of Clifford Chance (formerly Clifford-Turner), Solicitors, 1962–91 (resident in Paris), retired; *b* 3 Sept. 1926; *s* of Harold Hicks Goodchild and Agnes Joyce Wharton Goodchild (*née* Mowbray); *m* 1954, Nicole Marie Jeanne (*née* Delamotte); one *s* one *d. Educ:* Felsted School. Lieut, Royal Artillery, 1944–48; articled clerk, Longmores, Hertford; qual. Solicitor, 1952; Mem., Paris Bar, 1992–2002. HAC, 1952–56. Chairman: Hertford British Hosp. Corp., 1976–2001; Victoria Home, 1982–2006. Hon. Pres., Franco-British Chamber of Commerce and Industry (formerly British Chamber of Commerce in France), 1982–2004 (Pres., British Chamber of Commerce in France, 1970–72). *Recreations:* golf, cricket. *Address:* 53 Avenue Montaigne, 75008 Paris, France. *T:* 42254927. *Clubs:* MCC, HAC.

GOODCHILD, David Lionel Napier, CMG 1986; a Director, Directorate-General of External Relations, Commission of the European Communities, 1985–86; *b* 20 July 1935; *s* of Hugh N. Goodchild and Beryl C. M. Goodchild. *Educ:* Eton College; King's College, Cambridge (MA). Joined Foreign Office, 1958; served Tehran, NATO (Paris), and FO, 1959–70; Dep. Political Adviser, British Mil. Govt, Berlin, 1970–72; transferred to EEC Brussels, 1973; Head of Division, 1973, Principal Counsellor then Director, 1979–86. *Address:* Linden, Hall Road, Lavenham, Sudbury, Suffolk CO10 9QU. *T:* (01787) 248339.

GOODCHILD, Marianne, (Mrs Trevor Goodchild); *see* Rigge, M.

GOODCHILD, Peter Robert Edward; writer and film producer; *b* 18 Aug. 1939; *s* of Douglas Richard Geoffrey Goodchild and Lottie May Goodchild; *m* 1968, Penelope Jane Pointon-Dick; two *d. Educ:* Aldenham Sch., Elstree; St John's College, Oxford (MA). CChem, FRSC 1979. General trainee, BBC, 1963; BBC TV: Director/Producer Horizon, 1965–69, Editor, 1969–76; Editor, Special Features, 1977–80; Head, Science Features Dept, 1980–84; Head, Plays Dept, 1984–89; Exec. Producer, BBC Films 1989–92. Director: Screen Partners, 1992–94; Stone City Films, 1995–98; Green Umbrella Films, 1998–2005. Pres., Dunchideock Treacle Mines, 2000–. Vice Pres. Exeter Rowing Club. Stage play: The Great Tennessee Monkey Trial, US tours, 2005 2007. SFTA Mullard Award, for Horizon, 1967, 1968, 1969; BAFTA Awards: best factual series, for Horizon, 1972, 1974; best drama series, Marie Curie, 1977, Oppenheimer 1980; Gold Award, Chicago Film Fest., for Black Easter, 1996. *Publications:* J. Robert Oppenheimer: shatterer of worlds, 1980; Edward Teller: the real Dr Strangelove, 2004 *plays:* Chicago Conspiracy Trial, 1993 (Gold Award, NY Radio Fest., 1995); Nuremberg 1995; In the Name of Security, 1998; Lockerbie on Trial, 2001; The Putney Debates 2002; The Real Dr Strangelove, 2006. *Recreations:* music, painting, rowing. *Address* Dunchideock House, Dunchideock, Exeter, Devon EX2 9TS. *Club:* Groucho.

GOODE, Cary; *see* Goode, P. C. A.

GOODE, Charles Barrington, AC 2001; Director, since 1991, Chairman, since 1995 Australia and New Zealand Banking Group Ltd; *b* 26 Aug. 1938; *s* of Charles Thomas Goode and Jean Florence (*née* Robertson); *m* 1987, Cornelia Masters (*née* Ladd; former wife of Baron Baillieu, *qv*); one step *s. Educ:* Univ. of Melbourne (BCom Hons) Columbia Univ., NY (MBA). Joined Potter Partners, 1961: Partner, 1969; Sen. Partner 1980–86; Chairman: Potter Partners Gp Ltd, 1987–89; Ian Potter Foundn Ltd, 1994–. Chairman: Australian United Investment Co. Ltd, 1990–; Diversified United Investment Ltd, 1991–; Woodside Petroleum Ltd, 1999–2006; Director: Pacific Dunlop Ltd 1987–99; Qld Investment Corp. Ltd, 1991–99; CSR Ltd, 1993–2000; Singapore Airlines Ltd, 1999–2006. Member: Melbourne Cttee, Ludwig Inst. for Cancer Res., 1981–92 Exec. Cttee, Anti-Cancer Council of Victoria, 1981–84; Cttee of Mgt, Royal Victorian Eye and Ear Hosp., 1982–86; Chm., Howard Florey Inst. Exptl Physiol. and Medicine 1997–2004. Pres., Inst. Public Affairs, 1984–93. Member of Council: Monash Univ. 1980–85 (Trustee, Monash Univ. Foundn, 1983–85); Australian Ballet Sch., 1980–86 Hon. LLD: Melbourne, 2001; Monash, 2002. Centenary Medal, 2003. *Recreations:* golf reading. *Address:* 801/6 Victoria Street, St Kilda, Vic 3182, Australia. *T:* (3) 95348585 *Fax:* (3) 95341019; Level 31, 100 Queen Street, Melbourne, Vic 3000, Australia. *T:* (3) 92734736, *Fax:* (3) 92736478. *Clubs:* Melbourne, Australian, Royal Melbourne Golf (Melbourne).

GOODE, Dr David Anthony, FLS; ecologist; Head of Environment, Greater London Authority, 2000–04; *b* 16 Jan. 1941; *s* of Rev. William Aubrey Goode and Vera Goode (*née* Parkinson); *m* 1966, Diana Lamble; one *s* one *d. Educ:* Queen's Sch., Möncher Gladbach, Germany; Malet Lambert High Sch., Hull; Univ. of Hull (BSc Sp. Hons Geol 1963; PhD Botany 1970); University Coll. London (Postgrad. Dip. Conservation) MIEEM 1991, FIEEM 2002 (Pres., 1994–97); CEnv 2005. Peatland Officer, 1967–69 Hd, Peatland Ecology, 1969–73, Nature Conservancy; PSO, 1973–76, Asst Chief Scientist, 1976–82, NCC; Sen. Ecologist, GLC, 1982–86; Dir, London Ecology Unit 1986–2000. Vis. Prof., UCL, 1994–; Hon. Prof., E China Normal Univ., Shanghai 1996–2000. Brian Walker Lect., Green Coll., Oxford, 2003. Member: Envmt Panel, C of E Bd for Social Responsibility, 1983–92; Terrestrial Life Scis Grants Panel, 1984–87 Expert Rev. Gp on Urban Envmtl Sci., 1993–94, NERC; Adv. Cttee, Envmtl Law Foundn, 1991–2000; RHS Sci. and Horticulture Cttee, 1994–2002; UK Biodiversity Action Plan Steering Gp, 1994–95 (Chm., Public Awareness Gp, 1994–95); UK Agenda 21 Steering Gp, 1995–2000; UK Biodiversity Gp, 1996–2001 (Chm., Local Issues Gp 1996–98); New Renaissance Gp, 1996–2002; Adv. Cttee, Darwin Initiative for Survival of the Species, 2000–06; UK Local Sustainability Gp, 2001–02; RHS Conservation and Envmt Cttee, 2001–; England Biodiversity Gp, 2003– (Chm., Urban Gp, 2003–); IUCN Task Force on Cities and Protected Areas, 2004–; Panel, UK Sustainable Devel, 2006–. Member Board: Field Studies Council Exec., 1979–85; London Ecology Centre Trust 1985–91; Think Green Campaign, 1985–91; Dir, Nat. Forest Co., 1998–2004; Chairman: Trust for Urban Ecology, 1987–91 (Pres., 1991–94); London Biodiversity Partnership 1997–2004; Vice-Chm., 1991–92, Chm., 1992–94, Vice-Pres., 2002–06, Tree Council Vice-Pres., British Assoc. Nature Conservationists, 1981–85; President: Reigate Soc. 1995–2000; Ecology and Conservation Studies Soc., 1999–2001; Biol Scis Section, BAAS 2000. Advr, Landscape and Arts Network, 2001–. Mem., British Ecol Soc., 1964– (Mem. Council, 1977–80 and 1988–92). FLS 1981 (Mem. Council, 1983–86); FRSA 1999 Heidelberg Award for Envmtl Excellence, 1999. *Publications:* Wild in London, 1986; (ed jtly) Ecology and Design in Landscape, 1986; contrib. numerous scientific papers and articles on envmtl topics. *Recreations:* photography, music, theatre, walking, ornithology, exploring the natural world. *Address:* 25 Vandon Court, Petty France, SW1H 9HE; *e-mail:* d.goode@ucl.ac.uk. *Club:* Athenæum.

GOODE, (Penelope) Cary (Anne); freelance garden designer, since 1992; proprietor Border Lines, garden tour company, since 2003; *b* 5 Dec. 1947; *d* of Ernest Edgar Spink and Rachel Atcherly Spink; *m* 1987, Richard Nicholas Goode. *Educ:* Westwing Sch. Royal Ascot Enclosure Office, 1971; MoD, 1973; Manager, retail business, 1978; Domestic and Social Sec., RCOG, 1980; Educn Administrator, British Heart Foundn. 1982; Dir, Asthma Res. Council, later Nat. Asthma Campaign, 1988–92. *Recreations:* gardening, vintage cars, dogs. *Address:* Rhodds Farm, Lyonshall, Hereford HR5 3LW. *T:* (01544) 340120.

GOODE, Sir Royston Miles, (Sir Roy), Kt 2000; CBE 1994 (OBE 1972); QC 1990; FBA 1988; barrister; Norton Rose Professor of English Law, Oxford University, 1990–98, now Emeritus Professor; Fellow, St John's College, Oxford, 1990–98, now Emeritus Fellow; *b* 6 April 1933; *s* of Samuel and Bloom Goode; *m* 1964, Catherine Anne Rueff; one *d. Educ:* Highgate School. LLB London, 1954; LLD London, 1976; DCL Oxon 2005. Admitted Solicitor, 1955. Partner, Victor Mishcon & Co., solicitors, 1966–71, Consultant 1971–88. Called to the Bar, Inner Temple, 1988; Hon. Bencher, 1992. Queen Mary College, University of London: Prof. of Law, 1971–73; Head of Dept and Dean of Faculty of Laws, 1976–80; Crowther Prof. of Credit and Commercial Law, 1973–89; Dir and Founder, Centre for Commercial Law Studies, 1980–89. Vis. Prof., Melbourne, 1975; Aust. Commonwealth Vis. Fellow, 1975. Chairman: Advertising Adv. Cttee, IBA, 1976–80; Pension Law Rev. Cttee, 1992–93; Member: Cttee on Consumer Credit, 1968–71; Monopolies and Mergers Commn, 1981–86; Deptl Cttee on Arbitration Law, DTI, 1986–; Council of the Banking Ombudsman, 1989–92. Justice: Mem. Council,

1975; Chm. Exec. Cttee, 1994–96 (Vice-Chm., 1988–94); Mem., Council of Mgt, British Inst. of Internat. and Comparative Law, 1982. Hon. President: Centre for Commercial Law Studies, 1990–; Oxford Inst. of Legal Practice, 1994–. Editor, Consumer Credit Law and Practice (looseleaf), 1999–. Hon. Fellow, QMW (Fellow, 1991). FRSA 1990. Hon. DSc (Econ) London, 1996; Hon. LLD UEA, 2003. *Publications:* Hire-Purchase Law and Practice, 1962, 2nd edn 1970, with Supplement 1975; The Hire-Purchase Act 1964, 1964; (with J. S. Ziegel) Hire-Purchase and Conditional Sale: a Comparative Survey of Commonwealth and American Law, 1965; Introduction to the Consumer Credit Act, 1974; (ed) Consumer Credit Legislation, 1977, reissued as Consumer Credit Law and Practice (looseleaf); Consumer Credit, 1978; Commercial Law, 1982, 3rd edn 2004; Legal Problems of Credit and Security, 1982, 3rd edn 2003; Payment Obligations in Commercial and Financial Transactions, 1983; Proprietary Rights and Insolvency in Sales Transactions, 1985, 2nd edn 1989; Principles of Corporate Insolvency Law, 1990, 3rd edn 2005; (jtly) Transnational Commercial Law, 2007. *Recreations:* chess, reading, walking, browsing in bookshops. *Address:* c/o St John's College, Oxford OX1 3JP; 42 St John Street, Oxford OX1 2LH. *Club:* Reform.

GOODENOUGH, Sir Anthony (Michael), KCMG 1997 (CMG 1990); HM Diplomatic Service, retired; Secretary-General, Order of St John, 2000–03; *b* 5 July 1941; *s* of Rear-Adm. Michael Grant Goodenough, CBE, DSO, and Nancy, *d* of Sir Ransford Slater, GCMG, CBE; *m* 1967, Veronica Mary, *d* of Col Peter Pender-Cudlip, LVO; two *s* one *d*. *Educ:* Wellington Coll.; New Coll., Oxford (MA 1980). Voluntary Service Overseas, Sarawak, 1963–64; Foreign Office, 1964; Athens, 1967; Private Secretary to Parliamentary Under Secretary, 1971, and Minister of State, FCO, 1972; Paris, 1974; FCO, 1977; Counsellor on secondment to Cabinet Office, 1980; Hd of Chancery, Islamabad, 1982; Hd, Personnel Policy Dept, FCO, 1986–89; High Comr, Ghana and Ambassador (non-resident), Togo, 1989–92; Asst Under-Sec. of State (Africa and Commonwealth), FCO, 1992–95; High Comr to Canada, 1996–2000. Governor: Goodenough Coll. for Overseas Graduates, 2000–; Wellington Coll., 2002– (Vice-Pres., 2004–). *Recreations:* reading, walking, gardening, bell-ringing. *Address:* The Old House, North Cheriton, Templecombe, Somerset BA8 0AE.

GOODENOUGH, Frederick Roger; DL; FCIB; Director: Barclays PLC, 1985–89; *b* 21 Dec. 1927; *s* of Sir William Macnamara Goodenough, 1st Bt, and late Lady (Dorothea Louisa) Goodenough; *m* 1954, Marguerite June Mackintosh; one *s* two *d*. *Educ:* Eton; Magdalene Coll., Cambridge (MA). MA Oxon; FCIB (FIB 1968). Joined Barclays Bank Ltd, 1950; Local Director: Birmingham, 1958; Reading, 1960; Oxford, 1969–87; Director: Barclays Bank UK Ltd, 1971–87; Barclays Internat. Ltd, 1977–87; Barclays Bank PLC, 1979–89; Adv. Dir, Barclays Bank Thames Valley Region, 1988–89; Mem., London Cttee, Barclays Bank DCO, 1966–71, Barclays Bank Internat. Ltd, 1971–80. Supernumerary Fellow, Wolfson Coll., Oxford, 1989–95 (Hon. Fellow, 1995). Sen. Partner, Broadwell Manor Farm, 1968–; Curator, Oxford Univ. Chest, 1974–93; Trustee: Nuffield Med. Benefaction, 1968–2002 (Chm., 1987–2002); Nuffield Dominions Trust, 1968–2002 (Chm., 1987–2002); Nuffield Orthopaedic Centre Trust, 1978–2003 (Chm., 1981–2003); Nuffield Oxford Hospitals Fund (formerly Oxford and Dist Hosps Improvement and Develt Fund), 1968–2003 (Chm., 1982–88); Radcliffe Med. Foundn, 1987–98; Oxford Preservation Trust, 1980–89; Pres., Oxfordshire Rural Community Council, 1993–98. Governor: Shiplake Coll., 1963–74 (Chm., 1966–70); Wellington Coll., 1968–74; Goodenough Coll. (formerly London Hse for Overseas Graduates), 1985–2006. Patron, Anglo-Ghanian Soc. (UK), 1991–. FLS (Mem., Council, 1968–75, Finance Cttee, 1968–2008; Treasurer, 1970–75); FRSA. High Sheriff, 1987–88, DL 1989, Oxfordshire. *Recreations:* shooting, fishing, photography, ornithology. *Address:* Broadwell Manor, Lechlade, Glos GL7 3QS. *T:* (01367) 860326. *Club:* Brooks's.

GOODENOUGH, Prof. John Bannister; Virginia H. Cockrell Centennial Professor of Engineering, University of Texas at Austin, since 1986; *b* 25 July 1922; *s* of Erwin Ramsdell Goodenough and Helen Lewis Goodenough; *m* 1951, Irene Johnston Wiseman. *Educ:* Yale Univ. (AB, Maths); Univ. of Chicago (MS, PhD, Physics). Meteorologist, US Army Air Force, 1942–48; Research Engr, Westinghouse Corp., 1951–52; Research Physicist (Leader, Electronic Materials Gp), Lincoln Laboratory, MIT, 1952–76; Prof. and Hd of Dept of Inorganic Chemistry, Oxford Univ., 1976–86. Raman Prof., Indian Acad. of Science, 1982–83 (Hon. Mem., 1980–). Member: Nat. Acad., of Engrg, 1976–; Presidential Commn on Superconductivity, 1989–90. Foreign Associate: Acad. of Scis, Institut de France, 1992; Acad. de Ciencias Exactas, Fisicas y Naturales, Spain, 2003. Dr *hc* Bordeaux, 1967; Santiago de Compostela, 2002. Von Hippel Award, Materials Res. Soc., 1989; Sen. Res. Award, Amer. Soc. of Engrg Educn, 1990; Univ. of Pennsylvania Medal for Dist. Achievement, 1996; John Bardeen Award, Minerals, Metals & Materials Soc., 1997; Olim Palladium Award, Electrochem. Soc., 1999–; Japan Prize, Sci. and Technol. Foundn of Japan, 2001. Associate Editor: Materials Research Bulletin, 1966–; Jl Solid State Chemistry, 1969–; Structure and Bonding, 1978–; Solid State Ionics, 1980–94; Superconductor Science and Technology, 1987–; Jl of Materials Chem., 1990–95; Chem. of Materials, 1990–; Co-editor, International Series of Monographs on Chemistry, 1979–86; Member Executive, Editorial Board: Jl of Applied Electrochem., 1983–88; European Jl of Solid State and Inorganic Chem., 1992–. *Publications:* Magnetism and the Chemical Bond, 1963; Les oxydes des métaux de transition, 1973; numerous research papers in learned jls. *Recreations:* walking, travel. *Address:* Texas Materials Institute, University of Texas at Austin, ETC 9.102, Austin, TX 78712, USA. *T:* (512) 4711646.

GOODENOUGH, Sir William (McLernon), 3rd Bt *cr* 1943, of Broadwell and Filkins, co. Oxford; Founder and Group Executive Chairman, Design Bridge Ltd, since 2002; *b* 5 Aug. 1954; *o s* of Sir Richard Edmund Goodenough, 2nd Bt and Jane Isobel Goodenough (*d* 1998); *S* father, 1996; *m* 1st, 1982, Louise Elizabeth Ortmans (marr. diss. 1998); one *s* two *d*; 2nd, 2002, Delia Mary, *d* of David Curzon-Price. *Educ:* Stanbridge Earls Sch.; Southampton Univ. Designer, Allied International Designers, 1980–83; Man. Dir, Allied International Designers (Singapore), 1983–86. *Recreations:* stalking, fishing, shooting, painting. *Heir: s* Samuel William Hector Goodenough, *b* 11 June 1992. *Address:* Beck Hall, Billingford, East Dereham, Norfolk NR20 4QZ. *Clubs:* Boodle's, Pratt's.

GOODERHAM, Peter Olaf, CMG 2007; PhD; HM Diplomatic Service; UK Permanent Representative to Office of the United Nations and other international organisations, Geneva, since 2008; *b* 29 July 1954; *s* of Leonard Eric Gooderham and Gerd Gooderham; *m* 1985, Carol Anne Ward. *Educ:* Univ. of Newcastle (BA Hons); Univ. of Bristol (PhD 1981). Res. Fellow, Centre for Russian and E European Studies, Univ. of Birmingham, 1981–83; joined FCO, 1983; Falkland Is Dept, FCO, 1983–85; Second, later First, Sec., UK Delegn to NATO, Brussels, 1985–87; First Secretary: W Africa Dept, FCO, 1987–90; Riyadh, 1990–93; Dep. Hd, Security Policy Dept, FCO, 1993–96; Counsellor (Econ. and Social), UK Mission to UN, NY, 1996–99; Counsellor (Pol and Mil.), Washington, 1999–2003; UK Rep. to Pol and Security Cttee, EU, and UK Perm. Rep. to WEU, Brussels (with rank of Ambassador), 2003–04; Dir, Middle E and N Africa, FCO, 2004–07. *Recreations:* travel, cinema, running. *Address:* UKMIS, 58 Avenue Louis Casaï, Case Postale 6, 1216 Cointrin, Geneva, Switzerland. *T:* (22) 9182358; *e-mail:* peter.gooderham@fco.gov.uk.

GOODEY, Felicity Margaret Sue, CBE 2001; DL; President, The Lowry, since 2004 (Chairman, 1994–2004); Chairman, University Hospital of South Manchester NHS Foundation Trust, since 2008; *b* 25 July 1949; *d* of Henry Ernest Arthur and Susan Elsie Goodey; *m* 1973, John R. Marsh; two *s*. *Educ:* St Austell Grammar Sch.; St Hugh's Coll., Oxford (BA Hons Hist. Oxon 1971). Graduate trainee and reporter, World at One, BBC Radio, 1971–85; Northern Corresp., 1974–75, Northern Industrial Corresp., 1975–85, BBC TV; Presenter, 1987–99: File on Four, Punters, Sunday Programme, R4; Northwest Tonight, Northwestminster, BBC TV; owner and manager, Felicity Goodey & Associates, 1989–98; Director, Precise Communications, 1998–2004; Interim Chief Exec., Mediacity:UK, 2006–07. Chairman: Lowry Operational & Develt Cos, 1994–2002; founder and non-exec. Dir, Excellence Northwest, 1993–; Bd Mem., Going for Green, 1994–98; Chairman: Cultural Consortium NW, 1999–2004; NW Tourism Forum, 2004–; Central Salford Urban Regeneration Co., 2005–; non-executive Director: Sustainability Northwest, 1994–98; Manchester Commonwealth Games Ltd, 1997–2002; Northwest Develt Agency, 1998–2002; Manchester Chamber of Commerce and Industry, 1999–2005 (Pres., 2001–02); Nord Anglia plc, 1999–2007; Gtr Manchester Chamber of Commerce and Industry, 2005–. Dir, Unique Communications Gp, 2004–07. Mem., AHRB, subseq. AHRC, 2003–07. Hon. Vice Pres., Northwest Riding for Disabled, 1978–; Trustee, Friends of Rosie (children's cancer res.), 1992–. Gov., Manchester Grammar Sch., 1994–. DL Greater Manchester, 1998. Hon. Fellow, Bolton Inst., 2002; Hon. FRIBA 2005. Hon. DLitt: Salford, 1996; Manchester Metropolitan, 2000; Hon. LLD Manchester, 2003. *Recreations:* the family, theatre, opera. *Address:* Central Salford URC Ltd, Digital World Centre, No. 1 Lowry Plaza, Salford Quays, M50 3UB; *e-mail:* felicitygoodey@centralsalford.com.

GOODFELLOW, Giles William Jeremy; QC 2003; *b* 14 Nov. 1960; *s* of late Keith Frank Goodfellow, QC and Rosalind Erica Goodfellow; *m* 1990, Dr Maha Rosa Saif; three *s*. *Educ:* Harrow Sch.; Trinity Coll., Cambridge (MA; Capt., Univ. Boxing Team); Univ. of Virginia Law Sch. (LLM). Called to the Bar, Middle Temple, 1983 (Harmsworth Schol.). Mem., Pump Court Tax Chambers, 1985–. *Publications:* (jtly) Inheritance Tax Planning, 1986; (jtly) Financial Provision and Taxation in Marriage Breakdown, 1989. *Recreations:* exercising and being exercised by children. *Address:* Pump Court Tax Chambers, 16 Bedford Row, WC1R 4EF. *T:* (020) 7414 8080, *Fax:* (020) 7414 8099; *e-mail:* clerks@pumptax.com. *Club:* Hawk's (Cambridge).

GOODFELLOW, Prof. Julia Mary, CBE 2001; PhD; FMedSci; FIBiol, FInstP; Vice-Chancellor, University of Kent, since 2007; *b* 1 July 1951; *d* of late Gerald Lansdall and Brenda Lansdall; *m* 1972, Peter Neville Goodfellow, *qv*; one *s* one *d*. *Educ:* Woking Co. Sch. for Girls; Reigate Co. Sch. for Girls; Univ. of Bristol (BSc Physics); Open Univ. (PhD Biophysics 1975). FIBiol 2000; FInstP 2002. NATO Res. Fellow, Stanford Univ., 1976–78; Birkbeck College, University of London: Res. Fellow, 1979–83; Lectr, then Sen. Lectr and Reader, 1983–95; Prof. of Biomolecular Scis, 1995–2001; Chm., Dept of Crystallography, 1996–2001; Vice-Master, 1998–2001; Hon. Fellow, 2005; Chief Exec. and Dep. Chm., BBSRC, 2002–07 (Mem., 1997–2007). Wellcome Trust Res. Leave Fellow, 1990–93. Chm., Wellcome Trust Molecular and Cell Panel, 1995–98. Member: CCLRC, 2000–04; RURAL Council, 2003–07; NESTA, 2005–. Member Governing Body: St Paul's Girls Sch., 2001–08; Acad. Med. Scis, 2002–05. FRSA; FMedSci 2001. Hon. DSc: Strathclyde, 2002; Bristol, 2002; Durham, 2005; DU Essex, 2004; Hon. DVSc Edinburgh, 2005. *Publications:* (ed) Molecular Dynamics: applications in molecular biology, 1990; (ed) Computer Modelling in Molecular Biology, 1992; (ed) Computer Simulation in Molecular Biology, 1995; numerous contribs to learned jls. *Recreations:* reading, family. *Address:* The Registry, University of Kent, Canterbury, Kent CT2 7NZ; *e-mail:* j.m.goodfellow@kent.ac.uk.

GOODFELLOW, Michael Robert, PhD; Director, Goodfellow Consulting Ltd, since 2007; Divisional Managing Director, QinetiQ plc (formerly Defence Evaluation and Research Agency, Ministry of Defence), 1998–2007; *b* 7 Aug. 1948; *s* of Henry Goodfellow, MBE and Eileen Goodfellow (*née* Muff); *m* 1972, Karon Elizabeth Taylor; one *s* one *d*. *Educ:* St Bartholomew's Grammar Sch., Newbury; Imperial Coll., London (BSc 1st Cl. Hons Theoretical Physics 1970; ARCS 1970; DIC 1974; PhD 1974). CEng, FIET (FIEE 1988); FInstP 1999. Student Asst, Rutherford High Energy Lab., 1967; Res. Student, UKAEA, 1970–73; Sen. Analyst, Scicon Ltd, BP Gp, 1973–76; PSO, Systems Analysis Res. Unit, Depts of the Envmt and Transport, 1976–79; project manager, then staff manager, subseq. business gp manager, Sema Gp plc, 1979–95 (on secondment as Commercial Dir, DRA, 1992); Commercial Dir, DRA, MoD, 1995–98. Director, 1987–91: Yard Ltd; Sema Scientific Ltd; Dowty-Sema Ltd; Stephen Howe Ltd; VSEL-CAP Ltd; CAP-DBE Ltd; non-executive Director: Army Base Repair Orgn, MoD, 1998–2005; Met Office, 2007–. Mem. Council, RUSI, 2006–. Chm., Mgt Cttee, Surrey and NE Hants Industrial Mission, 1998–2004. Gov., Holy Trinity Sch., Guildford, 1989–97 (Chm., Finance Cttee). Mem., IAM. FCMI (FIMgt 1998). *Recreations:* sailing, walking, gardening. *Address: e-mail:* Mike@Goodfellows.org.uk.

GOODFELLOW, Prof. Peter Neville, DPhil; FRS 1992; Senior Vice President, Discovery Research, GlaxoSmithKline, since 2001; *b* 4 Aug. 1951; *s* of Bernard Clifford Roy Goodfellow and Doreen Olga (*née* Berry); *m* 1972, Julia Mary Lansdall (*see* J. M. Goodfellow); one *s* one *d*. *Educ:* Bristol Univ. (BSc 1st Cl. Hons 1972); Oxford Univ. (DPhil 1975). MRC Postdoctoral Fellow, Oxford Univ., 1975–76; Stanford University: Jane Coffin Childs Postdoctoral Fellow, 1976–78; Amer. Cancer Soc. Sen. Fellow, 1978–79; Imperial Cancer Research Fund: Staff Scientist, 1979–83; Sen. Scientist, 1983–86; Principal Scientist, 1986–92; Arthur Balfour Prof. of Genetics, Cambridge Univ., 1992–96; Sen. Vice Pres., Biopharmaceuticals and Neuroscis, then Discovery, SmithKline Beecham Pharmaceuticals, 1996–2001. Founder FMedSci 1998. *Publications:* (ed) Genetic analysis of the cell surface in Receptors and Recognition, Vol. 16, 1984; (ed jtly) The Mammalian Y Chromosome: molecular search for the sex determining gene, 1987; (ed) Cystic Fibrosis, 1989; (ed jtly) Molecular genetics of muscle disease, 1989; (ed jtly) Sex determination and the Y chromosome, 1991; (ed jtly) Mammalian Genetics, 1992; numerous reviews and contribs to learned jls. *Recreations:* soccer, science, sex. *Address:* GlaxoSmithKline, Gunnels Wood Road, Stevenage, Herts SG1 2NY.

GOODHART, family name of **Baron Goodhart**.

GOODHART, Baron *cr* 1997 (Life Peer), of Youlbury in the co. of Oxfordshire; **William Howard Goodhart,** Kt 1989; QC 1979; *b* 18 Jan. 1933; *s* of late Prof. A. L. Goodhart, Hon. KBE, QC, FBA and Cecily (*née* Carter); *m* 1966, Hon. Celia McClare Herbert (*see* Lady Goodhart); one *s* two *d*. *Educ:* Eton; Trinity Coll., Cambridge (Scholar, MA); Harvard Law Sch. (Commonwealth Fund Fellow, LLM). Nat. Service, 1951–53 (2nd Lt, Oxford and Bucks Light Infantry). Called to the Bar, Lincoln's Inn, 1957, Bencher, 1986. Dir, Bar Mutual Indemnity Fund Ltd, 1988–97. Member: Council of Legal Educn, 1986–92; Conveyancing Standing Cttee, Law Commn, 1987–89; Tax Law Review Cttee, 1994–2003; Cttee on Standards in Public Life, 1997–2003; Select Cttee on EU, H of L, 1998–2001 and 2005–06; Select Cttee on Delegated Powers and Regulatory Reform, H of L, 1998–2002, 2006– (Chm., 2006–); Jt Cttee on Reform of H of L,

2002–03; Select Cttee on Econ. Affairs, H of L, 2003–05. Chm., Cambridge Univ. Court of Discipline, 1993–2000. Member: Internat. Commn of Jurists, 1993– (Exec. Cttee, 1995–2002; Vice-Pres., 2002–06); Council, Justice, 1972– (Vice Chm., 1978–88, Chm., 1988–94, Exec. Cttee; Chm., Council, 2006–); Council, RIIA, 1999–2002; leader of Human Rights Missions: to Hong Kong, 1991; Kashmir, 1993; to Israel, and The West Bank, 1994; Kenya, 1996; Sri Lanka, 1997. Contested: Kensington (SDP) 1983; (SDP/ Alliance) 1987; (Lib Dem) July 1988; (Lib Dem) Oxford West and Abingdon, 1992. Chairman: SDP Council Arrangements Cttee, 1982–88; Lib Dem Conf. Cttee, 1988–91; Lib Dem Lawyers Assoc., 1988–91; Mem., Lib Dem Policy Cttee, 1988–97 (Vice-Chm., 1995–97). Trustee: Campden Charities, 1975–90; Airey Neave Trust, 1999–2004; Fair Trials Abroad, 2002–. *Publications:* (with Prof. Gareth Jones) Specific Performance, 1986, 2nd edn 1996; reports of Human Rights Missions; contribs to Halsbury's Laws of England; articles in legal periodicals. *Recreations:* walking, ski-ing. *Address:* House of Lords, SW1A 0PW. *Clubs:* Brooks's; Century Association (New York).

See also C. A. E. Goodhart, Sir P. C. Goodhart.

GOODHART, Lady; Celia McClare Goodhart; Chairman, Family Planning Association, 1999–2005; Principal, Queen's College, Harley Street, London, 1991–99; *b* 25 July 1939; *er d* of 2nd Baron Hemingford and Elizabeth (*née* Clark) (*d* 1979); *m* 1966, William Howard Goodhart (*see* Baron Goodhart); one *s* two *d*. *Educ:* St Michael's, Limpsfield; St Hilda's Coll., Oxford (MA; Hon. Fellow 1989). HM Civil Service, MAFF, seconded to Treasury, 1960–66; Hist. Tutor, Queen's Coll., London and Westminster Tutors, 1966–81. Contested: (SDP) Kettering, 1983; (SDP Liberal Alliance) Kettering, 1987; (SDP) Northants (for European Parlt), 1984. Chairman: SDP Envmt Policy Gp, 1985–87; Women for Social Democracy, 1986–88; Member: SDP Nat. and Policy Cttees, 1984–88; Liberal Democrats Fed. Exec. Cttee, 1988–90; Pres., E Midlands Liberal Democrats, 1988–91. Member: Elizabeth Nuffield Educnl Fund, 1972–82; St Bartholomew's Hosp. Ethical Cttee, 1974–86; Lindop Cttee on Data Protection, 1976–78; Nat. Gas Consumer Councils, 1979–82 (also Chm., N Thames Gas Consumer Council); Women's Nat. Commn, 1986–89; Code Monitoring Cttee for Mkting of Infant Formulae in UK, 1986–90; Med. Audit Cttee, RCP, 1992; Council, GSA, 1997–99 (Sec., 1994–96, Chm., 1996–99, London Reg.); Council, Goldsmiths, Univ. of London, 2003–. President: Schoolmistresses and Governesses Benevolent Instn, 1991–; London Marriage Guidance Council, 1990–95; Chm., Youth Clubs, UK, 1988–91 (Vice-Pres., 1991–); Mem., First Forum (formerly Forum UK) (Chm., 2001–03). Gov., Compton Verney, 2006–. Chm. Bd Trustees, Oxford Univ. Soc. (formerly Oxford Soc.), 1996–2004; Trustee: CPRE, 1987–91; Oxford Univ. Nuffield Medical Benefaction, 1988–96; Childline, 1999–2004; Mem. Bd, Dignity in Dying. FRSA 1989. Hon. FCGI 2003. *Recreations:* sociability, bridge, tapestry. *Address:* 11 Clarence Terrace, NW1 4RD. *T:* (020) 7262 1319; Youlbury House, Boars Hill, Oxford OX1 5HH. *T:* (01865) 735477. *Clubs:* Reform; Cosmopolitan (New York).

See also H. T. Moggridge.

GOODHART, Prof. Charles Albert Eric, CBE 1997; PhD; FBA 1990; Norman Sosnow Professor of Banking and Finance, London School of Economics and Political Science, 1985–2002, now Emeritus; Joint Founder, 1987, Deputy Director, 1987–2005, and Member, since 2005, Financial Markets Group, London School of Economics; *b* 23 Oct. 1936; *s* of late Prof. Arthur Goodhart, Hon. KBE, QC, FBA, and Cecily (*née* Carter); *m* 1960, Margaret, (Miffy), Ann Smith; one *s* three *d*. *Educ:* Eton; Trinity Coll., Cambridge (scholar; 1st Cl. Hons Econs Tripos); Harvard Grad. Sch. of Arts and Sciences (PhD 1963). National Service, 1955–57 (2nd Lieut KRRC). Prize Fellowship in Econs, Trinity Coll., Cambridge, 1963; Asst Lectr in Econs, Cambridge Univ., 1963–64; Econ. Adviser, DEA, 1965–67; Lectr in Monetary Econs, LSE, 1967–69; Bank of England: Adviser with particular reference to monetary policy, 1969–80; a Chief Adviser, 1980–85; External Mem., Monetary Policy Cttee, 1997–2000. Mem., Adv. Cttee, Hong Kong Exchange Fund, 1990–97. Hon. Fellow, LSE, 2006. *Publications:* The New York Money Market and the Finance of Trade 1900–13, 1968; The Business of Banking 1891–1914, 1972; Money, Information and Uncertainty, 1975, 2nd edn 1989; Monetary Theory and Practice: the UK experience, 1984; The Evolution of Central Banks, 1985, rev. edn 1988; (ed jtly) The Operation and Regulation of Financial Markets, 1987; (ed) EMU and ESCB after Maastricht, 1992; (jtly) The Future of Central Banking, 1994; The Central Bank and the Financial System, 1995; (ed) The Emerging Framework of Financial Regulation, 1998; (jtly) Financial Regulation: why, how and where now?, 1998; (ed) Which Lender of Last Resort for Europe, 2000; (jtly) The Foreign Exchange Market, 2000; (ed jtly) Regulating Financial Services and Markets in the 21st Century, 2001; (ed jtly) Financial Crises, Contagion, and the Lender of Last Resort, 2002; (jtly) House Prices and the Macroeconomy, 2007; articles in econ. jls and papers contrib. to econ. books. *Recreation:* keeping sheep. *Address:* Financial Markets Group, London School of Economics and Political Science, Houghton Street, WC2A 2AE. *T:* (020) 7955 7555.

See also Baron Goodhart, Sir P. C. Goodhart.

GOODHART, David Forbes; Founder Editor, Prospect Magazine, since 1995; *b* 12 Sept. 1956; *s* of Sir Philip Carter Goodhart, *qv; m* 1990, Lucy Rosamond Kellaway; two *s* two *d*. *Educ:* Eton Coll.; York Univ. (BA 1st Cl. Hist./Politics 1979). Reporter, Yorkshire Evening Press, 1979–82; journalist, Financial Times, 1982–94 (incl. labour reporter, City reporter, Lex columnist, corresp. in Germany and employment ed.). FRSA. *Publications:* (with Patrick Wintour) Eddie Shah and the Newspaper Revolution, 1986; The Reshaping of the German Social Market, 1994; Progressive Nationalism: citizenship and the Left, 2006. *Recreations:* football, cricket, singing. *Address:* 52 Highbury Hill, N5 1AP. *T:* (020) 7255 1281, *Fax:* (020) 7255 1279; *e-mail:* david@prospect-magazine.co.uk. *Club:* Groucho.

GOODHART, Rear-Adm. (Hilary Charles) Nicholas, CB 1972; FRAeS; *b* 28 Sept. 1919; *s* of G. C. Goodhart; *m* 1975, Molly Copsey. *Educ:* RNC Dartmouth; RNEC Keyham. Joined RN, 1933; served in Mediterranean in HM Ships Formidable and Dido, 1941–43; trained as pilot, 1944; served as fighter pilot in Burma Campaign, 1945; trained as test pilot, 1946; served on British Naval Staff, Washington, 1953–55; idc 1965; Rear-Adm. 1970; Mil. Dep. to Head of Defence Sales, MoD, 1970–73, retired. World Gliding Champion, 2-seaters, 1956; British Gliding Champion, 1962, 1967 and 1971. Freedom of London, 1945; Mem. Ct of Grocers' Co., 1975, Master, 1981. US Legion of Merit, 1958. *Recreation:* computer programming. *Address:* Cable House, Lindridge Park, Teignmouth, Devon TQ14 9TF. *T:* (01626) 779790.

GOODHART, Sir Philip (Carter), Kt 1981; *b* 3 Nov. 1925; *s* of late Prof. Arthur Goodhart, Hon. KBE, QC, FBA, and Cecily (*née* Carter); *m* 1950, Valerie Winant; three *s* four *d*. *Educ:* Hotchkiss Sch., USA; Trinity Coll., Cambridge. Served KRRC and Parachute Regt (an Elder), 1943–47. Editorial staff, Daily Telegraph, 1950–54; Ed., Time and Tide, 1955; Editorial staff, Sunday Times, 1955–57. Mem., LCC Educn Cttee, 1956–57. Contested (C) Consett, Co. Durham, Gen. Election, 1950; MP (C) Beckenham, March 1957–1992. Parly Under-Sec. of State, Northern Ireland Office, and Minister responsible for Dept of the Environment (NI), 1979–81; Parly Under Sec. of State, MoD, 1981. Joint Hon. Sec., 1922 Cttee, 1960–79; Mem., Cons. Adv. Cttee on Policy,

1973–79; Chairman: Cons. Parly Defence Cttee, 1972–74 (Vice-Chm., 1974–79); Co Parly NI Cttee, 1976–79; Parly Select Cttee on Sound Broadcasting, 1983–87; Angl Taiwan Parly Gp, 1987–92. Member: British Delegation to Council of Europe and WE 1961–63; British Delegation to UN Gen. Assembly, 1963; North Atlantic Assemb 1964–79 and 1983–92; Leader, CPA Delegns to Australia, 1984, Sri Lanka, 198 Member: Council, Consumers' Assoc., 1959–68, 1970–79 (Vice-Pres., 1983–); Ad Council on Public Records, 1970–79; Exec. Cttee, British Council, 1974–79; Counc RUSI, 1973–76. Chairman: Bd of Sulgrave Manor, 1982–2002; Warship Preservati Trust, 1987–2006; Warrior Preservation Trust, 1993–97; Dir, Flagship Portsmou 1993–97. Chm. and Capt., Lords and Commons Ski Club, 1971–73. Order of the Brillia Star (China), 1992. *Publications:* (with Ian Henderson, GM) The Hunt for Kimathi, 19 Fifty Ships that Saved the World, 1965; (with Christopher Chataway) War witho Weapons, 1968; Referendum, 1970; The 1922: the history of the 1922 Committee, 197 Full-Hearted Consent, 1975; The Royal Americans, 2005; various pamphlets includin Stand on Your Own Four Feet: a study of work sharing and job splitting, 1982; Jo Ahead, 1984; Colonel George Washington: soldier of the King, 1993; The Roy Americans, 2005; A Stab in the Front: the Suez conflict, 2006. *Address:* 25 Abbotsbu Road, W14 8EJ. *T:* (020) 7602 8237. *Clubs:* Beefsteak, Carlton, Garrick.

See also Baron Goodhart, C. A. E. Goodhart, D. F. Goodhart.

GOODHART, Sir Robert (Anthony Gordon), 4th Bt *cr* 1911; Medical Practitione Beaminster, Dorset; *b* 15 Dec. 1948; *s* of Sir John Gordon Goodhart, 3rd Bt, FRCGP, a of Margaret Mary Eileen, *d* of late Morgan Morgan; *S* father, 1979; *m* 1972, Kathle Ellen, *d* of late Rev. A. D. MacRae; two *s* two *d*. *Educ:* Rugby; Guy's Hospital Medic School, London Univ. MB BS (Lond.), MRCS, LRCP, MRCGP, DObstRCO Qualification, 1972. *Recreation:* Real tennis. Heir: *s* Martin Andrew Goodhart, *b* 9 Se 1974.

GOODHEW, Duncan Alexander, MBE 1983; Director, LEA Events & Marketi Group, since 1997; *b* 27 May 1957; *s* of late Donald Frederick Goodhew and of Dolo Perle Goodhew (*née* Venn); *m* 1984, Anne Patterson; one *s* one *d*. *Educ:* Millfield Sch North Carolina State Univ. (BA Business Mgt 1979). International swimmer, 1976–8 Captain, England and GB squads, 1978–80; competitions: Montreal Olympic Game 1976; Commonwealth Games, 1978 (Silver Medal: 100m breast stroke; 200m brea stroke; 4×100 medley); World Championships, 1978 (Bronze Medal, 4×100 medl relay); Moscow Olympic Games, 1980 (Gold Medal, 100m breast stroke; Bronze Med 4×100 medley relay); Mem., 2-man and 4-man Bobsleigh teams, Europe Championships, 1981. Trustee: Teenage Cancer Trust, 1995–; City of London Sinfon Pres., Swimathon, 1987–; Vice President: Dyslexia Inst., 1994–; Youth Sport Tru 1995–. Patron: Disability Sport, England; The Aurora Charity; Hairline Internation Sparks; Cranial Facial Support Unit; James Powell Trust. Hon. Citizen, N Carolina. Ro Humane Soc. Award, 2001. *Publications:* Sink or Swim (with Victoria Hislop), 200 contrib. Financial Times. *Recreations:* sport (including squash, aerobics, cyclin photography, cooking. *Address:* Limelight Projects, 33–34 Rathbone Place, W1T 1JN. (020) 7299 4160.

GOODHEW, Most Rev. Richard Henry, (Harry), AO 2001; Archbishop of Sydn and Metropolitan of New South Wales, 1993–2001; *b* 19 March 1931; *s* of Baden Pow Richard Goodhew and Christina Delgarno Goodhew (*née* Fraser); *m* 1958, Pamela (n Coughlan); two *s* two *d*. *Educ:* Univ. of Wollongong (MA Hons; DLitt *hc* 1993); Moo Theol Coll. (ThL 2nd cl. Hons, Diploma 2nd cl. Hons). Ordained 1958; Curate, Matthew's, Bondi, NSW, 1958; Curate-in-charge, St Bede's, Beverly Hills, NSW 1959–63; with Bush Church Aid, Ceduna, SA, 1963–66; Rector: St Paul's, Carlingfor NSW, 1966–71; St Stephen's, Coorparoo, Qld, 1971–76; Rector and Senior Canon, Michael's Cathedral, Wollongong, 1976–79; Archdeacon of Wollongong and Camde 1979–82; Bishop of Wollongong, Asst Bishop in dio. of Sydney, 1982–93. *Recreatio* walking, reading, swimming. *Address:* 134A O'Briens Road, Figtree, NSW 252 Australia. *T:* (2) 42253332.

GOODIER, Gareth John; Chief Executive, Cambridge University Hospitals NI Foundation Trust, since 2006; *b* 5 Aug. 1951; *s* of Eric and Lilian Goodier; *m* 200 Lynette Katherine Isabella Morero (*d* 2004); one *s* one *d* by a previous marriage. *Ed* Sheffield University Med. Sch. (MB ChB 1974); Univ. of NSW (Masters Health Adm 1993). FAFPHM 1990; FRACMA 1995. Regional Director: Kimberley Health Reg 1989–91; Peninsula and Torres Strait Regl HA, 1991–93; Chief Executive Office Women's and Children's Health Service, WA, 1993–98; Royal Perth Hosp., 1998–200 Royal Brompton and Harefield NHS Trust, 2003–04; North West London Strategic H 2004–06. Consultant, World Bank projects in Lebanon and Kuwait, 2001–03. Berna Nicholson prize, Royal Aust. Coll. of Med. Administrators, 2005. *Recreations:* tenn chess, art, design, football, history, watching movies, current affairs, travel. *Addre* Cambridge University Hospitals NHS Foundation Trust, Box 146, Addenbrooke Hospital, Hills Road, Cambridge CB2 2QQ. *T:* (01223) 217510, *Fax:* (01223) 21620 *e-mail:* gareth.goodier@addenbrookes.nhs.uk.

GOODIN, David Nigel; His Honour Judge Goodin; a Circuit Judge, since 2003; *b* March 1953; *s* of Nigel Robin Fyson Goodin and Diana Goodin (*née* Luard); *m* 19 (marr. diss. 2003); two *s*. *Educ:* King's Sch., Ely; Coll. of Law. Admitted solicitor, 198 Higher Courts Advocate, 1995; articled to Norton, Rose, Botterell & Roche, London; practice as solicitor, Newmarket, Bury St Edmunds and Ipswich, 1980–2003; Founde Saunders Goodin Riddleston, 2000; Asst Recorder, 1996–2000; Recorder, 2000–0 Mem., Funding Rev. Cttee, Legal Services Commn, 1995–2003. Chm., Local Du Solicitor Cttee, 1987–95. *Recreation:* family and friends. *Address:* The Crown Court, Russell Road, Ipswich IP1 2AG.

GOODING, Anthony James Joseph S.; *see* Simonds-Gooding.

GOODING, Nigel Alexander; Chief Executive, Marine Fisheries Agency, since 2005 18 March 1956; *s* of Alexander Albert Gooding and Pearl Evelyn Gooding; *m* 1978, An Teresa Redwood; two *s* one *d*. *Educ:* Spencer Park Secondary Sch. Ministry Agriculture, Fisheries and Food, 1974–2001: Policy Advr on Vet. Medicines, 1985–89, o Animal Health, zoonoses, 1989–92; Co-ordination of UK Presidency of EU, 1992; He of Policy Br., UK Fisheries Enforcement, 1993; Chief Inspector of Fisheries, Eng. an Wales, DEFRA, 2003–05. *Recreations:* football, golf, reading, theatre, music, walkin *Address:* Marine Fisheries Agency, 3–8 Whitehall Place, SW1A 2HH. *T:* (020) 7270 831 *Fax:* (020) 7270 8345; *e-mail:* nigel.gooding@mfa.gsi.gov.uk.

GOODING, Stephen Leonard; Director, Road Pricing and Statistics (formerly Roa Performance and Strategy), Department for Transport, since 2004; *b* 20 Nov. 1960; *s* Leonard Armstrong Gooding and Margaret Jane Gooding (*née* Horan); *m* 1985, Bernadet Kearns; two *s*. *Educ:* Colfe's Sch., Lee; Univ. of Durham (BA Hons Politics 1982 Brebner, Allen & Trapp (chartered accountants), 1982; PSA, DoE, 1983; Dept Transport, 1987; Private Secretary: to Minister for Roads and Traffic, 1988; to Minister for Public Transport, 1989–91; Principal, 1991–97, Asst Sec., 1997–2000, Dept

Transport, subseq. DETR; Sec., CS Mgt Bd, Cabinet Office, 2000–01; Dir, Office of the Rail Regulator, 2001–04. *Recreations:* motorcycles, film, cookery, early, baroque and heavy rock music. *Address:* c/o Department for Transport, Great Minster House, 76 Marsham Street, SW1P 4DR. *T:* (020) 7944 4080; *e-mail:* steve.gooding@dft.gsi.gov.uk.

GOODING, Valerie Frances, CBE 2002; Chief Executive, British United Provident Association, 1998–2008; *b* 14 May 1950; *d* of Frank and Gladys Gooding; *m* 1986, Crawford Macdonald; two *s*. *Educ:* Leiston GS, Suffolk; Univ. of Warwick (BA Hons 1971); Kingston Univ. (Dip. Mgt Studies 1981). British Airways, 1973–96; Man. Dir, UK, BUPA, 1996–98. Director: BAA plc, 1998–2004; Standard Chartered plc, 2005–; LTA, 2005–; J. Sainsbury plc, 2007–; BBC, 2008–. Mem. Council, Univ. of Warwick, 2001–07. Trustee, British Mus., 2004–. Hon. DBA: Bournemouth, 1999; Middlesex. *Recreations:* tennis, theatre, travel, keeping fit, family life. *Address:* BUPA House, 15–19 Bloomsbury Way, WC1A 2BA. *Club:* Athenæum.

GOODISON, Sir Nicholas (Proctor), Kt 1982; Chairman: Stock Exchange, 1976–88; TSB Group, 1989–95; Courtauld Institute of Art, 1982–2002 (Governor, 2002–); National Art Collections Fund, 1986–2002; *b* 16 May 1934; *s* of Edmund Harold Goodison and Eileen Mary Carrington (*née* Proctor); *m* 1960, Judith Abel Smith; one *s* two *d*. *Educ:* Marlborough Coll.; King's Coll., Cambridge (Scholar; BA Classics 1958, MA; PhD Architecture and History of Art, 1981; Hon. Fellow, 2002). H. E. Goodison & Co., later Quilter Goodison, 1958–88: Partner, 1962; Chm., 1975–88; Chm., TSB Bank plc, 1989–2000; Dep. Chm., Lloyds TSB Gp plc, 1995–2000. Director: Ottoman Bank, 1986–92; Banque Paribas (Luxembourg) SA, 1986–88; Banque Paribas Capital Markets Ltd, 1986–88; Gen. Accident, 1987–95; British Steel, later Corus Gp plc, 1989–2002 (Dep. Chm., 1993–99). Mem. Council, Stock Exchange, 1968–88; President: Internat. Fedn of Stock Exchanges, 1985–86; British Bankers' Assoc., 1991–96; Vice Pres., Chartered Inst. of Bankers, 1989– (FCIB 1989); Member: Panel on Takeovers and Mergers, 1976–88; Council of Securities Industry, 1978–85; Securities Assoc., 1986–88. Mem. Council, Industrial Soc., 1976–2000; Chairman: Crafts Council, 1997–2005; Burlington Magazine Ltd, 2002–07 (Dir, 1975–2007); Burlington Magazine Foundn, 2002–; Dir, ENO, 1977–98 (Vice-Chm., 1980–98); Trustee, Nat. Heritage Meml Fund, 1988–97. Leader, Goodison Review, 2003 (report, Securing the Best for our Museums: Private Giving and Government Support, published 2004). Mem., Royal Commn on the Long Term Care of the Elderly, 1997–99; Trustee, 2002–, Chm., 2003–, Nat. Life Story Collection. Hon. Keeper of Furniture, Fitzwilliam Museum, Cambridge; President: Furniture History Soc., 1990– (Hon. Treas., 1970–90); Antiquarian Horological Soc., 1986–93; Walpole Soc., 2007–. Chm., Review Steering Gp, Nat. Record of Achievement, 1996–97; Pres., Heads, Teachers and Industry, 1999–2002; Member: Adv. Bd, Judge Inst. of Mgt Studies, 1999–2003; FEFCE, 2000–01. Governor, Marlborough Coll., 1981–97. CCMI; FSA, FRSA, Sen. FRCA; Hon. Fellow RA, 1987; Hon. FRIBA 1992; Hon. FBA 2004; Hon. FCGI, 2007. Hon. DLitt: City, 1985; London, 2003; Hon. LLD Exeter, 1989; Hon. DSc Aston, 1994; Hon. DArt De Montfort, 1998; Hon. DCL Northumbria, 1999. CINOA Prize for lifetime achievement in arts, 2004; Robinson Medal, V&A Mus., 2007. Chevalier, Légion d'Honneur, 1990. *Publications:* English Barometers 1680–1860, 1968, 2nd edn 1977; Ormolu: The Work of Matthew Boulton, 1974, rev. edn as Matthew Boulton: Ormolu, 2002; These Fragments, 2005; many papers and articles on history of furniture, clocks and barometers. *Recreations:* history of art, music, opera, walking. *Address:* PO Box 2512, W1A 5ZP. *Clubs:* Athenæum, Beefsteak, Arts.

GOODLAD, family name of **Baron Goodlad**.

GOODLAD, Baron *cr* 2005 (Life Peer), of Lincoln in the County of Lincolnshire; **Alastair Robertson Goodlad,** KCMG 1997; PC 1992; High Commissioner to Australia, 2000–05; *b* 4 July 1943; *y s* of late Dr John Goodlad and Isabel (*née* Sinclair); *m* 1968, Cecilia Barbara, 2nd *d* of late Col Richard Hurst and Lady Barbara Hurst; two *s*. *Educ:* Marlborough Coll.; King's Coll., Cambridge (MA, LLB). Contested (C) Crewe Div., 1970; MP (C) Northwich, Feb. 1974–1983, Eddisbury, 1983–99. An Asst Govt Whip, 1981–82; a Lord Commissioner of HM Treasury, 1982–84; Parly Under-Sec. of State, Dept of Energy, 1984–87; Comptroller of HM Household, 1989–90; Dep. Govt Chief Whip and Treasurer, HM Household, 1990–92; Minister of State, FCO, 1992–95; Parly Sec. to HM Treasury and Govt Chief Whip, 1995–97; Opposition frontbench spokesman on internat. develt, 1997–98. Chm., H of L Select Cttee on the Constitution, 2007–. *Address:* House of Lords, SW1A 0PW. *Clubs:* Brooks's, Beefsteak, Pratt's.

GOODLAND, Judith Mary; Head Mistress, Wycombe Abbey School, 1989–98; *b* 26 May 1938; *d* of Rolf Thornton Ferro and Joan (*née* O'Hanlon); *m* 1961, A. T. Goodland (marr. diss.); one *s* two *d*. *Educ:* Howell's Sch., Denbigh; Bristol Univ. (BA Hons); Charlotte Mason Coll., Ambleside (Cert Ed). Head, Modern Languages Dept, Cartmel Priory C of E Comprehensive Sch., 1968–72; Casterton Sch., Kirkby Lonsdale, 1980–83; Headmistress, St George's Sch., Ascot, 1983–88. FRSA 1994. *Recreations:* fell walking, bell ringing, bridge. *Address:* 10 Starnthwaite Ghyll, Crosthwaite, Kendal, Cumbria LA8 8JN.

GOODMAN, Dame Barbara; *see* Goodman, Dame P. B.

GOODMAN, Elinor Mary; freelance journalist; *b* 11 Oct. 1946; *d* of Edward Weston Goodman and Pamela Longbottom; *m* 1985, Derek John Scott, *qv* (marr. diss.). *Educ:* private schools, secretarial college. Financial Times: Consumer Affairs Corresp., 1971–78; Political Corresp., 1978–82; Channel Four News: Political Corresp., 1982–88; Political Ed., 1988–2005. Chm., Affordable Rural Housing Commn, 2005–06. Member Board: Countryside Agency, 2006; Commn for Rural Communities, 2006–. *Recreations:* riding, walking.

GOODMAN, Geoffrey George, CBE 1998; Founding Editor, British Journalism Review, 1989–2002, now Chairman Emeritus; broadcaster and commentator, BBC and commercial television and radio, since 1986; *b* 2 July 1921; *s* of Michael Goodman and Edythe (*née* Bowman); *m* 1947, Margit (*née* Freudenbergova); one *s* one *d*. *Educ:* elementary schs, Stockport and Manchester; grammar schs, London; LSE (BScEcon). RAF, 1940–46. Manchester Guardian, 1946–47; Daily Mirror, 1947–48; News Chronicle, 1949–59; Daily Herald, 1959–64; The Sun (IPC), 1964–69; Daily Mirror, 1969–86 (Industrial Editor, 1969–86; Asst Editor, 1976–86). Fellow, Nuffield Coll., Oxford, 1974–76. Broadcaster, BBC Current Affairs, and LBC/IRN, later London News Radio, 1986–97. Head of Govt's Counter-inflation Publicity Unit, 1975–76; Member: Labour Party Cttee on Industrial Democracy, 1966–67; Royal Commn on the Press, 1974–77; TGWU; NUJ. Chm., Hugh Cudlipp Trust, 2004–. Hon. MA Oxon. Descriptive Writer of the Year, Nat. Press Awards, 1971; Gerald Barry Award for Journalism, Granada TV Press Awards, 1984. *Publications:* General Strike of 1926, 1951; Brother Frank, 1969; The Awkward Warrior, 1979; The Miners' Strike, 1985; The State of the Nation, 1997; From Bevan to Blair, 2003; contrib. London Inst. of World Affairs, 1948. *Recreations:* pottering, poetry, supporting Tottenham Hotspur FC, and climbing—but not social. *Address:* 64 Flower Lane, Mill Hill, NW7 2JL. *Club:* Savile.

GOODMAN, Helen Catherine; MP (Lab) Bishop Auckland, since 2005; an Assistant Government Whip, since 2008; *b* 2 Jan. 1958; *d* of Alan Goodman and Hanne Goodman; *m* 1988, Charles; two *c*. *Educ:* Lady Manners Sch., Bakewell; Somerville Coll., Oxford (BA 1979). HM Treasury, 1980–97, latterly Hd of Strategy Unit; Advr to Prime Minister of Czechoslovakia, 1990; Dir, Commn on Future of Multi Ethnic Britain, 1998; Hd of Strategy, Children's Soc., 1998–2002; Chief Exec., Nat. Assoc. of Toy and Leisure Libraries, 2002–05. Parly Sec., Office of the Leader of the H of C, 2007–08. Mem., Public Accounts Cttee, 2005–07. *Address:* House of Commons, SW1A 0AA. *T:* (020) 7219 4346; *e-mail:* goodmanh@parliament.uk.

GOODMAN, Prof. John Francis Bradshaw, CBE 1995; PhD; CCIPD; Frank Thomas Professor of Industrial Relations, University of Manchester Institute of Science and Technology, 1975–2002 (Vice-Principal, 1979–81); *b* 2 Aug. 1940; *s* of Edwin and Amy Goodman; *m* 1967, Elizabeth Mary Towns; one *s* one *d*. *Educ:* Chesterfield Grammar Sch.; London Sch. of Economics (BSc Econ); MSc Manchester; PhD Nottingham. Personnel Officer, Ford Motor Co. Ltd, 1962–64; Lectr in Industrial Econs, Univ. of Nottingham, 1964–69; Industrial Relations Adviser, NBPI, 1969–70; Sen. Lectr in Industrial Relations, Univ. of Manchester, 1970–74; Chm., Manchester Sch. of Management, UMIST, 1977–79, 1986–94. Vis. Professor: Univ. of WA, 1981, 1984; McMaster Univ., 1985; Univ. of Auckland, 1996. Pres., British Univs Industrial Relations Assoc., 1983–86. Member: Council, ACAS, 1987–98; Training Bd, 1991–97, Council, 1993–97, ESRC. Dep. Chm., Central Arbitration Cttee, 1998–; Chairman: Professional Football Negotiating and Consultative Cttee, 2000–; Police Arbitration Tribunal, 2003–. *Publications:* Shop Stewards in British Industry, 1969; Shop Stewards, 1973; Rulemaking and Industrial Peace, 1977; Ideology and Shop-floor Industrial Relations, 1981; Employment Relations in Industrial Society, 1984; Unfair Dismissal Law and Employment Practice, 1985; New Developments in Employee Involvement, 1992; Industrial Tribunals and Workplace Disciplinary Procedures, 1998; contribs to British Jl of Industrial Relations, ILR, Industrial Relations Jl, Jl of Management Studies, Personnel Management, etc. *Recreations:* hill walking (compleat Munroist, 1997), football, ornithology, golf. *Address:* 2 Pott Hall, Pott Shrigley, Macclesfield, Cheshire SK10 5RT. *T:* (01625) 572480.

GOODMAN, Prof. Martin David, DPhil; FBA 1996; Professor of Jewish Studies, Oxford University, since 1996, and Fellow of Wolfson College, Oxford, since 1991; Fellow, Oxford Centre for Hebrew and Jewish Studies, since 1986; *b* 1 Aug. 1953; *s* of late Cyril Joshua Goodman and of Ruth (*née* Sabel); *m* 1976, Sarah Jane Lock; two *s* two *d*. *Educ:* Rugby; Trinity Coll., Oxford (MA; DPhil 1980). Kaye Jun. Res. Fellow, Oxford Centre for Postgrad. Hebrew Studies, 1976–77; Lectr in Ancient Hist., Birmingham Univ., 1977–86; Oxford University: Sen. Res. Fellow, St Cross Coll., 1986–91; Lectr in Roman Hist., Christ Church, Oxford, 1988–; Reader in Jewish Studies, 1991–96. Fellow, Inst. for Advanced Studies, Hebrew Univ. of Jerusalem, 1993. Pres., British Assoc. for Jewish Studies, 1995. Jt Ed., Jl of Jewish Studies, 1995–99; Ed., Jl of Roman Studies, 2000–03. *Publications:* State and Society in Roman Galilee, 1983, 2nd edn 2000; (trans. with Sarah Goodman) Johann Reuchlin, On the Art of the Kabbalah, 1983; (ed jtly) E. Schürer, The History of the Jewish People in the Age of Jesus Christ, vol. 3, pt 1 1986, pt 2 1987; The Ruling Class of Judaea, 1987; (with G. Vermes) The Essenes according to the Classical Sources, 1989; Mission and Conversion, 1994; The Roman World 44BC–AD180, 1997; (ed) Jews in a Graeco-Roman World, 1998; (ed jtly) Apologetics in the Roman Empire, 1999; (ed jtly) Representations of Empire: Rome and the Mediterranean world, 2002; (ed) The Oxford Handbook of Jewish Studies, 2002; Judaism in the Roman World: collected essays, 2007; Rome and Jerusalem: the clash of ancient civilizations, 2007. *Address:* Oriental Institute, Pusey Lane, Oxford OX1 2LE; 11 Carpenter Road, Edgbaston, Birmingham B15 2JW. *T:* (0121) 454 8609.

See also Prof. R. J. Goodman.

GOODMAN, His Honour Michael Bradley; a Circuit Judge, 1983–99; *b* 3 May 1930; *s* of Marcus Gordon Goodman and Eunice Irene May Goodman (*née* Bradley); *m* 1967, Patricia Mary Gorringe; two *d* (one *s* decd). *Educ:* Aldenham; Sidney Sussex Coll., Cambridge (MA). Called to the Bar, Middle Temple, 1953; Western Circuit; a Recorder of the Crown Court, 1972–83. Prosecuting Counsel to DHSS, 1975–83; Pres., Wireless Telegraphy Appeals Tribunal, 1977–88. Chancellor: Dio. Guildford, 1968–2002; Dio. Lincoln, 1970–98; Dio. Rochester, 1971–2005; Vicar-Gen., Province of Canterbury, 1977–83. Member: Commn on Deployment and Payment of the Clergy, 1965–67; C of E Legal Adv. Commn, 1973–2006 (Chm., 1986–96); Faculty Jurisdiction Commn, 1980–83; General Synod, Church of England, 1977–83; Lay Chm., Dulwich Deanery Synod, 1970–73. Chairman: William Temple Assoc., 1963–66; Ecclesiastical Judges Assoc., 1987–97. President: SE London Magistrates' Assoc., 1989–96; SE London Family Mediation Bureau, 1999–. Governor: Liddon Trust, London, 1964–2004; Pusey Hse, Oxford, 1965–88. *Address:* c/o Lloyds TSB, 9 Brompton Road, SW3 1DB.

GOODMAN, Michael Jack, MA, PhD; Social Security Commissioner (formerly National Insurance Commissioner), 1979–98, and Child Support Commissioner, 1993–98, Deputy Commissioner, 1999–2002; *b* 3 Oct. 1931; *s* of Vivian Roy Goodman and Muriel Olive Goodman; *m* 1958, Susan Kerkham Wherry; two *s* one *d*. *Educ:* Sudbury Grammar Sch., Suffolk; Corpus Christi Coll., Oxford (MA). PhD Manchester. Solicitor. Lectr, Gibson & Weldon, 1957; solicitor, Lincoln, 1958–60; Lectr, Law Society's Sch., 1961–63; Lectr, then Sen. Lectr in Law, Manchester Univ., 1964–70; Prof. of Law, Durham Univ., 1971–76; Perm. Chm. of Indust. Tribunals, Newcastle upon Tyne, 1976–79. Gen. Editor, Encyclopedia of Health and Safety at Work, 1974–. *Publications:* Industrial Tribunals' Procedure, 1976, 4th edn 1987; Health and Safety at Work: law and practice, 1988; contrib. Mod. Law Rev., and Conveyancer. *Recreations:* amateur radio (licence holder), church bell-ringing.

GOODMAN, Sir Patrick (Ledger), PCNZM 2002; Kt 1995; CBE 1990; Special Trade Ambassador of New Zealand, 1990; company director; President Emeritus, Goodman Fielder Ltd; *b* 6 April 1929; *s* of Athol Ledger Goodman and Delia Marion Goodman; *m* 1960, Hilary Gay Duncan; three *s*. *Educ:* St Patrick's Coll., Silverstream, NZ; Victoria University Coll., Wellington. Chairman: Heinz-Wattie, 1992–98; Quality Bakers of NZ, 1967–76; Goodman Group and subsidiaries, 1979–92; former Chm., Tourism Nelson. Founder Chm., NZ Business and Parlt Trust, 1991–92, now Patron; Trustee, Founders of Nelson; formerly Trustee: Massey Univ. Agric. Foundn; Bishop Suter Art Gall. (now Patron); Patron, Massey Univ. Food Foundn. Foundn Mem., NZ Rugby Foundn. Dist. Fellow, NZ Inst. of Dirs, 2003. Hon. DSc Massey. *Recreations:* golf, cricket, Rugby, boating, fishing. *Address:* 52 Tudor Street, Motueka, Nelson, New Zealand. *T:* (3) 5288314.

GOODMAN, Paul Alexander Cyril; MP (C) Wycombe, since 2001; *b* 17 Nov. 1959; *s* of Abel Goodman and Irene Goodman (*née* Rubens); *m* 1999, Fiona Gill; one *s*. *Educ:* Cranleigh Sch., Surrey; York Univ. (BA Hons Eng. Lit). Exec., Extel Consultancy, 1985–86; Res. Asst to Rt Hon. Tom King, MP, 1985–87; Mem., Policy Unit, Westminster CC, 1987–88; Novice, Quarr Abbey, 1988–90; Home Affairs Ed., Catholic

Herald, 1991–92; Leader Writer, Daily Telegraph, 1992; reporter, Sunday Telegraph, 1992–95; Comment Ed., Daily Telegraph, 1995–2001. Shadow Minister: for Work and Pensions, 2003–05; for Childcare, HM Treasury, 2005–; DCLG, 2007–. Member, Select Committee: on Work and Pensions, 2001–05; on Deregulation and Regulatory Reform, 2001–03. *Address:* House of Commons, SW1A 0AA.

GOODMAN, Dame (Pearl) Barbara, DBE 1989; QSO 1981; JP; Member, Auckland City Council, 1989–2001; *b* 5 Oct. 1932; *d* of late Horace Robinson and Lillie Robinson (*née* Shieff); *m* 1954, Harold Goodman (decd); two *s* one *d. Educ:* Parnell Sch.; St Cuthbert's Coll. Mayoress, City of Auckland, 1968–80; founding Trustee, HELP Foundn, 1980–85; Chm., Auckland Spastic Soc., 1980–84; Chm., Odyssey House Trust, 1981–92; former Mem. Exec. Cttee, NZ Fedn of Voluntary Welfare Organisations. Mem., NZ Internat. Trade Fair Cttee, 1985–89; Chm., Auckland 1990 Trust Board, 1989–91; Mem., Telethon Trust Bd, 1981. Guardian, NZ Women's Refuge Foundn; former Patron and Mem., Aotearoa NZ Peace Foundn; Patron: Child Safety Foundn; (Regional) Internat. Year of Disabled Persons, 1981. Member: Cttee, Shalom Court; Women's Internat. Zionist Orgn. Vice Patron, Auckland Cricket Assoc. *Publication:* For Flying Kiwis, 1990. *Recreations:* meeting people, travel, reading, cooking, embroidery. *Address:* 1/456 Remuera Road, Remuera, Auckland 1005, New Zealand. *T:* (9) 5201233, *Fax:* (9) 5200690; *e-mail:* barbara@goodman.co.nz.

GOODMAN, Perry; Director (Industry and Regions), The Engineering Council, 1990–92; *b* 26 Nov. 1932; *s* of Cyril Goodman and Anne (*née* Rosen); *m* 1958, Marcia Ann (*née* Morris); one *s* one *d. Educ:* Haberdashers' Aske's Hampstead Sch.; University Coll., London (BSc). MIMMM (MICeram 1964). 2nd Lieut, Royal Corps of Signals, 1955–57; Jt Head, Chemistry Res. Lab., then Project Leader, Morgan Crucible Co. Ltd, 1957–64; Sen. Scientific Officer, DSIR, 1964–65; Principal Scientific Officer, Process Plant Br., Min. of Technology, 1965–67; 1st Sec. (Scientific), 1968–70, Counsellor (Scientific), 1970–74, British Embassy, Paris; Research Gp, DoI, 1974–79; Hd, Policy and Perspectives Unit, DoI, 1980–81; Department of Trade and Industry: Hd, Design Policy/Technical Adv. Services for Industry, 1981–86; Hd, Electrical Engrg Br., 1986–90. Mem. Bd, Northern Engrg Centre, 1990–92. FRSA 1986. *Recreations:* travel, walking, conversation. *Address:* 118 Westbourne Terrace Mews, W2 6QG. *T:* (020) 7262 0925.

GOODMAN, Prof. Roger James, DPhil; Nissan Professor of Modern Japanese Studies, since 2003, and Head, Social Sciences Division, since 2008, University of Oxford; Fellow, St Antony's College, Oxford, since 1993 (Acting Warden, 2006–07); *b* 26 May 1960; *s* of late Cyril Joshua Goodman and of Ruth (*née* Sabel); partner, Carolyn Joy Dodd; two *s* one *d. Educ:* Rugby; King Edward VI Grammar Sch., Chelmsford; Univ. of Durham (BA 1981); St Antony's Coll., Oxford (DPhil 1987). Nissan Jun. Res. Fellow in Social Anthropol. of Japan, St Antony's Coll., Oxford, 1985–88; Lectr, Japan-Europe Ind. Res. Centre, Imperial Coll., Univ. of London, 1988–89; Reader in Japanese Studies, Dept of Sociol., Univ. of Essex, 1989–93; Lectr in Social Anthropol. of Japan, Univ. of Oxford, 1993–2003. Oxford University: Assessor, 1997–98; Chair, Japan Foundn Endowment Cttee, 1999–2006. *Publications:* Japan's International Youth: the emergence of a new class of schoolchildren, 1990; (ed jtly) Ideology and Practice in Modern Japan, 1992; (ed jtly) Case Studies on Human Rights in Japan, 1996; (ed jtly) The East Asian Welfare Model: welfare orientalism and the state, 1998; Children of the Japanese State: the changing role of child protection institutions in contemporary Japan, 2000; (ed) Family and Social Policy in Japan: anthropological approaches, 2002; (ed jtly) Can the Japanese Reform Their Education System?, 2003; (ed jtly) Global Japan: the experience of Japan's new minorities and overseas communities, 2003; (ed jtly) The Big Bang in Japanese Higher Education: the 2004 reforms and the dynamics of change, 2005; (ed jtly) Ageing in Asia, 2007. *Recreation:* hockey coach. *Address:* Nissan Institute of Japanese Studies, 27 Winchester Road, Oxford OX2 6NA. *T:* (01865) 274576; *e-mail:* roger.goodman@nissan.ox.ac.uk.

See also Prof. M. D. Goodman.

GOODMAN, Roy Peter, FRCO; conductor; violinist; Principal Guest Conductor, English Chamber Orchestra, since 2004; *b* 26 Jan. 1951; *s* of Peter and Mary Sheena Goodman; *m* 1st, 1970, Gillian Dey (marr. diss. 1992); two *s* one *d*; 2nd, 1992, Sally Jackson (marr. diss. 1999). *Educ:* King's Coll., Cambridge (chorister); Royal Coll. of Music; Berkshire Coll. of Educn. ARCO 1968, FRCO 1970; ARCM 1976. Head of Music: Alfred Sutton Boys' Sch., Reading, 1971–74; Bulmershe Comprehensive Sch., Reading, 1974–76; Sen. String Tutor, Berks, 1976–78; Dir of Music, Univ. of Kent, Canterbury, 1986–87; Dir, Early Music, RAM, 1987–89. Founder and Dir, Brandenburg Consort, 1975–2001; Co-Founder and Co-Dir, Parley of Instruments, 1979–86; Musical Dir, European Union Baroque Orch., 1988–2003; Principal Conductor: Hanover Band, 1986–94; Umeå Symphony Orchestra and Swedish Northern Opera, 1994–99; Manitoba Chamber Orch., Winnipeg, 1999–2005; Holland Symfonia, Amsterdam, 2003–06. Hon. FRCM 2005. Hon. DMus Hull, 2002. *Recreations:* squash, sailing, ski-ing. *Address:* 217 Birchanger Lane, Birchanger, Bishop's Stortford, Herts CM23 5QJ; *e-mail:* roy@roygoodman.com.

GOODSELL, (John) Andrew; Chief Executive, Acromas Holdings Ltd, and Chairman, Saga Group Ltd and AA Ltd, since 2007 (Joint Chief Executive: Saga Group Ltd, 2004–07; AA Ltd, 2007); *b* 4 Jan. 1959; *s* of John Leonard Goodsell and Pamela Doris Goodsell; *m* 1st, 1983, Claire Hornsby (marr. diss.); one *s* one *d*; 2nd, 1999, Virginia Hubert; one *s* two *d. Educ:* West Kent Coll. Norwich Winterthur Reinsurance Co. Ltd, 1978–87; Lloyds of London, 1987–92; Saga Group Ltd: Business Develt Manager, 1992–95; Business Develt Dir, 1995–99; Chief Exec., Saga Services and Saga Investment Direct, 1999–2001; Dep. Gp Chief Exec., 2001–04. Hon. Fellow, Harris Manchester Coll., Oxford, 2002. *Recreations:* cooking, ski-ing, sailing. *Address:* (office) Enbrook Park, Folkestone, Kent CT20 3SE. *T:* (01303) 771702, *Fax:* (01303) 771175.

GOODSHIP, Prof. Allen Edward, PhD; Professor of Orthopaedic Sciences, Royal Veterinary College, London, and the Institute of Orthopaedics, University College London, since 1996; Director, Institute of Orthopaedics and Musculoskeletal Science, University College London, since 2000; *b* 1 Feb. 1949; *m* 1975, Dawn Taylor; two *d. Educ:* Reigate Grammar Sch.; Sch. of Vet. Sci., Univ. of Bristol (BVSc 1972; PhD 1977). MRCVS 1972. Res. Asst, RCVS Trust Fund Scholar, 1972–74; University of Bristol: Temp. Lectr in Vet. Anatomy, 1974–76; Res. Asst, Horserace Betting Levy Bd, 1976–78, Lectr, 1978–88, Dept of Anatomy; Reader in Vet. Anatomy, 1988; Prof. of Comparative Biomed. Scis, 1988–96 (Vis. Prof., 1996–); Hd, Dept of Anatomy, 1992–96. Acad. Associate, QMW, 1996–; Convenor, Cell and Molecular Path. Res. Centre, Royal Nat. Orthopaedic Hosp. Trust, 1999–. Vis. Prof., Univ. of Guelph, 1989–; D. L. T. Smith Vis. Scientist, Univ. of Saskatoon, 1989–. Trustee, Silsoe Res. Inst., 2002–06; Director: Stanmore Implants Worldwide, 2000–08; Bristol Zoo Enterprises Ltd; Consultant: Orthopaedic Div., Johnson & Johnson (DePuy); Res. Centre, Smith & Nephew Gp; Co-inventor, VetCell. Vice Pres. and Univ. Rep. to Council, and Chm., Sci. Adv. Gp, Bristol & SW Zool Soc.; Member: Med. Adv. Bd, General Orthopaedics, Boston; Adv. Bd, MRC. Member: Orthopaedic Res. Soc., USA (Mem. Prog. Cttee, 1997–98); British Orthopaedic Res. Soc.; British Vet. Zool Soc.; Anatomical Soc. of GB and Ire.; Pres., Internat. Soc. for Fracture Repair, 1994–96 (Chm. Memship Cttee, 1994–). Scientific Ed Res. in Vet. Sci.; former Mem., Edtl Adv. Bd, Clinical Materials; Member Editori Board: Jl of Orthopaedic Trauma (Dep. Ed.); Equine & Comparative Exercise Physiolog Asst Ed., Equine Vet. Jl. Companion Fellow, British Orthopaedic Assoc. Hon. Mem Uruguay Orthopaedic Assoc., 1994–. Prof. W. M. Mitchell Meml Fund Award, RCV 1976; Gary Hampson Meml Prize for Orthopaedic Res., 1984; Edwin Walker Priz IMechE, 1988; Clinical Biomechanics Award, European Soc. of Biomechanics, 199 Prize for Spinal Res., AcroMed, 1992; Medal, Nat. Back Pain Assoc., 1994; Open Awar Equine Vet. Jl, 1995; Scheering Plough Animal Health Vet. Achievement Award, Anim Health Trust, 2001. *Publications:* (ed jtly) European Biomechanics: proceedings of the 6 meeting of the European Society of Biomechanics, 1988; book chapters and many articl in learned jls. *Recreations:* sailing, walking, gardening. *Address:* Institute of Orthopaedi and Musculoskeletal Science, University College London, Royal National Orthopaed Hospital Trust, Brockley Hill, Stanmore, Middx HA7 4LP. *T:* (020) 8909 5535, *Fa* (020) 8954 8560; Royal Veterinary College, Hawkshead Lane, North Mymms, Hatfiel Herts AL9 7TA. *T:* (01707) 666342, *Fax:* (01707) 666346.

GOODSMAN, James Melville, CBE 1993; Managing Director, 1995–97, Chairma 1997–2002, Michael Fraser Associates Ltd; Director, Michael Fraser & Co. Lt 1997–2002; *b* 6 Feb. 1947; *s* of late James K. Goodsman and Euphemia Goodsman, Elgi Moray; *m* 1990, Victoria, *y d* of late Col Philip Smitherman and Rosemary Smitherma CBE. *Educ:* Elgin Academy. Joined Cons. Party organisation, 1966; Agent: to Rt Ho Betty Harvie Anderson, 1970–74; to Rt Hon. Maurice Macmillan, 1974–8 Conservative Central Office: Dep. Agent, NW Area, 1980–84; Asst Dir (Communi Affairs), 1984–90; Head, Community and Legal Affairs, May–Sept. 1990; Dir, Cons. Par in Scotland, 1990–93. Director: ICP Ltd, 1997–2001; Capitalize Ltd, 2001–02. Hon. Sec One Nation Forum, 1986–90. Mem., Edinburgh Morayshire Club (Chm., 1996 *Publications:* contribs to Cons. party and community relations papers. *Recreation:* churc music. *Address:* Le Bourg, 61170 Coulognes-sur-Sarthe, France; *e-mail:* james.goodsman(orange.fr. *Club:* New (Edinburgh).

GOODSON, Rear-Adm. Frederick Brian, CB 1996; OBE 1982; Chairman: Sou Gloucestershire Primary Care Trust, since 2001; Trading Force Group, since 199 Explora Group plc, since 2003; *b* 21 May 1938; *m* 1965, Susan, (Sue), Mary Firmin; tw *s* two *d. Educ:* Campbell Coll. Coastal Forces, 1958–60; HMS Gambia and HMS Lio 1960–64; Aden, 1964–65; Supply Officer, HMS Diana, 1966–69; Staff, BRN Dartmouth, 1970–72; Exchange Service, USN, 1972–74; Comdr 1974; Exchang Service, Royal Naval Supply and Transport Service, 1975–78; Naval Sec's Dept, 1978–7 Supply Officer, HMS Invincible, 1980–81; Fleet Supply Officer, C-in-C Fleet, 1981–8 Capt. 1982; Sec., C-in-C Naval Home Comd, 1983–85; Dir, Naval Logistic Plannin 1985–87; Cdre comdg HMS Centurion, 1988–91; rcds 1992; Rear-Adm. 1993; ACD (Logistics), 1993–96. Chm., Bath and West Community NHS Trust, 1997–2001. Pre Calne Royal Naval Assoc., 2000–. MInstD 1996. CStJ 2002; Chm., Wilts, St Joh Ambulance, 1997–2005; Trustee, Orders of St John Care Trust, 2006–. *Recreation* offshore sailing, squash, country pursuits. *Address:* New Homestead Farm, Mountai Bower, North Wraxall, Chippenham, Wilts SN14 7AJ. *Clubs:* Bowood Golf an Country; Royal Naval Sailing Association.

GOODSON, Prof. Ivor Frederick, DPhil; Professor of Learning Theory, Educatio Research Centre, University of Brighton, since 2004; *b* 30 Sept. 1943; *s* of Frederick J. Goodson and Lily W. Goodson; *m* 1975, Mary L. Nuttall; one *s. Educ:* Forest Gramm Sch.; University Coll. London (BSc Econ); Inst. of Educn, Univ. of London; London Sc of Econs; DPhil Sussex 1979. University of Sussex: Res. Fellow, 1975–78; Dir, Eu Schools Unit, 1978–85; University of Western Ontario: Prof., Faculty of Educn, Facul of Grad. Studies and Centre for Theory and Criticism, 1986–96; Dir, Educnl Res. Uni 1989–96; Hon. Prof. of Sociol., 1993–98; Prof. of Educn, Sch. of Educn and Profession Develt, UEA, 1996–2004. Founding Ed. and Man. Ed., Jl Educn Policy, 1986–. Frederic Warner Schol., 1991–96, Susan B. Anthony Scholar in Residence and Prof., 1996–200 Margaret Warner Grad. Sch. of Educn and Professional Develt, Univ. of Rochester, N Vis. Internat. Guest Scientist, Max Planck Inst. of Human Develt and Educn, Berlin, 199 J. Woodrow Wilson Vis. Prof., Oppenheimer Foundn, Univ. of Witwatersrand, S 1996; Visiting Professor: Sch. of Educn, Univ. of Exeter, 2001–04; Centre for Educ Innovation, Univ. of Sussex, 2002–03; Stint Foundn Prof., Uppsala Univ., Swede 2003–08; Res. Associate, von Hugel Inst., St Edmund's Coll., Cambridge, 2004–; Catal Res. Prof., Univ. of Barcelona, 2005; Joss Owen Chair of Education, Univ. of Plymout 2007–. Dist. Vis. Professorial Award, Japanese Soc. for Promotion of Sci., Univ. of Toky 1993. *Publications:* School Subjects and Curriculum Change, 1983, 3rd edn 1993; Th Making of Curriculum: collected essays, 1988, 2nd edn 1995; Biography, Identity an Schooling, 1991; Through the Schoolhouse Door, 1993; Studying Curriculum: cases an methods, 1994; Curriculo: teoria e historia (Brazil), 1995, 3rd edn 1999; Historia d Coriculum (Spain), 1995; Att Starka Lararnas Roster: sex essaer om lararforskning o lararforskarsamarbete (Sweden), 1996; The Changing Curriculum: studies in soci construction, 1997; Studying School Subjects, 1997; Subject Knowledge: readings for th study of school subjects, 1998; Das Schulfach als Handlungsrahmen: vergleichen untersuchung zur geschichte und funktion der schulfächer (Germany), 1999; La Crisis d Cambio Curricular (Spain), 2000; (with P. Sikes) Life History Research in Education Settings: learning from lives, 2001; The Birth of Environmental Education (China), 200 (jtly) Cyber Spaces/Social Spaces: culture clash in computerised classrooms, 2002; Estudi del Curriculum: casos y métodos (Argentina), 2003; Professional Knowledge, Profession Lives: studies in education and change, 2003; Learning Curriculum and Life Politic selected works, 2005; Professional Knowledge, Professional Lives (China), 200 Professionel Viden. Professionelt Liv (Denmark), 2007; (ed jtly) Education, Globalisati and New Times, 2007. *Recreations:* tennis, walking and birdwatching, jazz and rhythm an blues, Norwich City FC supporter. *Address:* Education Research Centre, Mayfield Hous University of Brighton, Falmer, Brighton BN1 9PH. *T:* (01273) 644560.

GOODSON, Sir Mark (Weston Lassam), 3rd Bt *cr* 1922, of Waddeton Court, C Devon; *b* 12 Dec. 1925; *s* of Major Alan Richard Lassam Goodson (*d* 1941) (2nd *s* of 1 Bt) and Clarisse Muriel Weston (*d* 1982), *d* of John Weston Adamson; *S* uncle, 1986; 1949, Barbara Mary Constantine, *d* of Surg.-Capt. Reginald Joseph McAuliffe Andrew RN; one *s* three *d. Educ:* Radley; Jesus College, Cambridge. *Heir: s* Alan Regina Goodson [*b* 15 May 1960; *m* 1990, Melanie Lodder; one *s* one *d*]. *Address:* Bowmont Wa Yew Tree Road, Town Yetholm, Kelso, Roxburghshire TD5 8RY. *T:* (01573) 420322

GOODSON, Michael John; Assistant Auditor General, National Audit Office, 1984–9 *b* 4 Aug. 1937; *s* of late Herbert Edward William Goodson and Doris Maud Goodson; 1958, Susan Elizabeth (*née* Higley); one *s* one *d. Educ:* King Henry VIII Sch., Coventr Joined Exchequer and Audit Dept, 1955; Asst Auditor, 1955; Auditor, 1965; Private Se to Comptroller and Auditor Gen., 1967–70; Sen. Auditor, 1970; Health Servic Ombudsman (on secondment), 1973–76; Chief Auditor, Exchequer and Audit Dep 1976; Dep. Dir of Audit, 1978; Dir of Audit, 1981. *Recreations:* ornithology, mod engineering, caravanning. *Address:* 2 Bayley Mead, St John's Road, Boxmoor, Herts HP1 1US. *T:* (01442) 242611.

GOODSON-WICKES, Dr Charles; DL; consulting physician, company director, business consultant; Chief Executive, London Playing Fields Society, 1998–2007 (Chairman, 1997–98); *b* 7 Nov. 1945; *s* of late Ian Goodson Wickes, FRCP, Consultant Paediatrician and farmer, of Stock Harvard, Essex and of Monica Goodson-Wickes; *m* 1974, Judith Amanda Hopkinson, *d* of late Comdr John Hopkinson, RN, of Sutton Grange, near Stamford, Lincs; two *s*. *Educ:* Charterhouse; St Bartholomew's Hosp. (MB BS 1970). Called to the Bar, Inner Temple, 1972. Ho. Physician, Addenbrooke's Hosp., Cambridge, 1972; Surgeon-Capt., The Life Guards, 1973–77 (served BAOR, N Ireland, Cyprus); Silver Stick MO, Hsehold Cavalry, 1977; RARO, 1977–2000; re-enlisted as Lt-Col, 1991, for Gulf Campaign (served S Arabia, Iraq, Kuwait, with HQ 7 Armoured Bde). Clin. Asst, St Bart's Hosp., 1977–80; Consulting Phys., BUPA, 1977–86; Occupational Phys., 1980–94; formerly Med. advr to Barclays Bank, RTZ, McKinsey, Christie's, British Alcan, Collins, Meat & Livestock Commn etc; UK Advr, Norwegian Directorate of Health, 1983–94; Chm., Appeals Bd, Asbestos Licensing Regulations, 1982–87; Member: Med. Adv. Cttee, Industrial Soc., 1981–87; Fitness Adv. Panel, Inst. of Dirs, 1982–84. Director: Medarc Ltd, 1981–; Thomas Greg and Sons Ltd, 1992–; Nestor Healthcare Gp plc, 1993–99; Gyrus Gp plc, 1997–; and other internat. cos. Contested (C) Islington Central, 1979. MP (C) Wimbledon, 1987–97; contested (C) same seat, 1997. Vice-Pres., Islington South and Finsbury Cons. Assoc., 1982–97. PPS to Minister of State for Housing and Planning, DoE, 1992–94, to Financial Sec. to HM Treasury, 1994–95, to Sec. of State for Transport, 1995–96. Mem., Select Cttee on Members' Interests, 1992–94; Vice-Chm., Constitutional Affairs Cttee, 1990–91; Sec., Arts and Heritage Cttee, 1990–92; Vice Chm., Defence Cttee, 1991–92; Mem., Jt Cttee, Consolidation of Bills, 1987–92; Founder Chm., All Party, British-Colombian Gp, 1995–97; Vice Chm., All Party British-Russian Gp, 1993–97; Treas., All Party British Chinese Gp, 1992–97. Fellow, Industry and Parlt Trust, 1991; Patron, Hansard Soc., 2003–. Vice Chm., Cons. Foreign and Commonwealth Council, 1997–. Treas., Dr Ian Goodson Wickes Fund for Handicapped Children, 1979–88; Vice-Pres., Ex-Services Mental Welfare Soc., 1990–; Founder Chm., Countryside Alliance, 1997–99 (Patron, 2003–; Chm., 1994–98, Mem., Public Affairs Cttee, 1980–87, British Field Sports Soc.); Chm., Rural Trust, 1999–; Mem., London Sports Bd, 2000–03 (Chm., Envmt Cttee, 2001–03). Governor, Highbury Grove Sch., 1977–85. Pte, The Parachute Regt (TA), 1963–65. Founder Chm., Essex Kit Cat Club, 1965. DL Gtr London, 1999. *Publications:* The New Corruption, 1984; (contrib.) Another Country, 1999. *Recreations:* hunting, shooting, Real tennis, gardening, travel, history. *Address:* Watergate House, Bulford, Wilts SP4 9DY. *T:* (01980) 632344; 37 St James's Place, SW1A 1NS. *T:* (020) 7629 0981; *e-mail:* cgw@medarc-limited.co.uk. *Clubs:* Boodle's, Pratt's, MCC.

GOODWAY, Russell; Member (Lab), County Council of the City and County of Cardiff, since 1995; Business Development Director, Paramount Office Interiors Ltd, since 2008; *b* 23 Dec. 1955; *s* of Russell Donald Goodway and Barbara Mary Goodway (*née* Vizard); *m* 1979, Susan Yvonne Witchard; one *s*. *Educ:* Barry Boys' Comprehensive Sch.; University Coll., Swansea (BA Econs and Politics 1977). Partner, Keane Goodway & Co., Accountants, 1988–2000. Dep. Chm., Millennium Stadium plc, 1996–2004; Chief Exec., Cardiff Chamber of Commerce and Industry, 2005–07; Bd Mem., Cardiff Bay Develt Corp., 1993–2000. Member: Porthkerry Community Council, 1977–82 (Chm., 1980–81); Rhoose Community Council, 1982–87 (Chm., 1985–86); S Glamorgan County Council: Mem., 1985–96; Chm., Property Services Cttee, 1988–89; Chm., Finance Cttee, 1989–92; Leader, and Chm. Policy Cttee, 1992–96; Dep. Chm., 1992–93; County Council of City and County of Cardiff: first Leader of the Council, 1995–2004, Exec. Leader, 2002–04; Chairman: Policy Cttee, 1995–99; Council's Cabinet, 1999–2004; Lord Mayor of Cardiff, 1999–2003. Dep. Chm., Assembly of Welsh Counties, 1994–96. OStJ 2004. *Recreations:* sport, especially Rugby and tennis, reading political biographies, music. *Address:* County Hall, Atlantic Wharf, Cardiff CF10 4UW. *T:* (029) 2087 2020.

GOODWILL, Robert; MP (C) Scarborough and Whitby, since 2005; *b* 31 Dec. 1956; *s* of late Robert W. Goodwill and Joan Goodwill; *m* 1987, Maureen (*née* Short); two *s* one *d*. *Educ:* Bootham Sch., York; Univ. of Newcastle upon Tyne (BSc Hons Agriculture). Farmer, 1979–. Contested (C): Redcar, 1992; NW Leics, 1997; Cleveland and Richmond, 1994, Yorks S, May 1998, EP elecns. MEP (C) Yorks and the Humber Reg., 1999–2004; Dep. Cons. Leader, EP, 2003–04. *Recreations:* steam ploughing, travel, languages. *Address:* Southwood Farm, Terrington, York YO60 6QB. *T:* (01653) 648459; (constituency office) 21 Huntriss Row, Scarborough, N Yorks YO11 2ED.

GOODWIN, Christine, (Mrs Richard Goodwin); *see* Edzard, C.

GOODWIN, Daisy Georgia, (Mrs Marcus Wilford); television producer and writer; Founder, Silver River Productions, 2005; *b* London, 19 Dec. 1961; *d* of Richard Goodwin and Jocasta Innes; *m* 1988, Marcus Wilford; two *d*. *Educ:* Westminster Sch.; Trinity Coll., Cambridge (BA Hist. 1983); Columbia Univ. (Harkness Fellow). Producer, BBC, 1985–98; programmes include: Homefront, Bookworm; Editl Dir, Talkback Thames, 1998–2005; programmes include: Grand Designs, Property Ladder, The Apprentice, The Supersizers. Presenter, Essential Poems, BBC, 2003–. Chair, Poetry Book Soc., 2003–07. FRSA. *Publications:* Silver River: memoir, 2007; edited: The Nation's Favourite Love Poems, 1997; 101 Poems to Save Your Life, 1998; 101 Poems to Get You Through Day and Night, 1999; Essential Poems to Fall in Love With, 2003; Poems for Life, 2004. *Recreations:* collecting books with Daisy in the title, avoiding meetings, knitting, reading poetry and classic crime. *Address:* Silver River Productions, Brook House, 2–16 Torrington Place, WC1E 7HN. *T:* (020) 7307 2720, *Fax:* (020) 7907 3411; *e-mail:* daisy@silverriver.tv.

GOODWIN, Sir Fred(erick Anderson), Kt 2004; Chief Executive, Royal Bank of Scotland Group plc, since 2000 (Deputy Group Chief Executive, 1998–2000); *b* 17 Aug. 1958; *s* of Frederick Anderson Goodwin and Marylyn Marshall Goodwin (*née* Mackintosh). *Educ:* Paisley GS; Univ. of Glasgow (LLB). CA 1983; FCIBS 1996; FCIB 2002. Joined Touche Ross & Co., 1979, Partner, 1988–95; Dep. Chief Exec., 1995, Chief Exec., 1996–98, Clydesdale Bank PLC; Chief Exec., Yorkshire Bank, 1997–98. Director: Bank of China, 2006–; ABN AMRO, 2007–. Dir, Scottish Business Achievement Award Trust, 2001–03. Chairman: Prince's Trust, Scotland, 1999–2003; Prince's Trust, 2003–. DUniv: Paisley, 2001; Glasgow, 2002; Hon. LLD St Andrews, 2004. *Recreations:* restoring cars, golf. *Address:* Royal Bank of Scotland Group plc, Gogarburn, Edinburgh EH12 1HQ.

GOODWIN, Prof. Graham Clifford, PhD; FRS 2002; FIEEE, FAA, FTSE; Professor of Electrical Engineering, since 1983, and Assistant Director, Centre for Integrated Dynamics and Control, since 2002 (Director, 1997–2001), University of Newcastle, New South Wales; *b* NSW, 20 April 1945; *s* of C. H. R. F. Goodwin; *m* 1967, Rosslyn Mackintosh; one *s* one *d*. *Educ:* Broken Hill High Sch.; Univ. of NSW (BSc 1964; BE 1966; PhD 1970). Lectr, Imperial Coll., Univ. of London, 1971–74; University of Newcastle, New South Wales: Lectr, 1974–75, Sen. Lectr, 1976, Associate Prof., 1977–83, Dept of Electrical Engrg; Hd, Dept of Electrical and Computer Engrg, 1979–84; Dir, Centre for Industrial Control Sci., 1988–96; Dean, Faculty of Engrg, 1994–96; ARC Fedn Fellow, 2002–. *Publications:* (jtly) Control Theory, 1970; (jtly) Dynamic System Identification, 1977; (jtly) Adaptive Filtering, Prediction and Control, 1984; (jtly) Digital Estimation and Control, 1990; (ed jtly) Adaptive Control Filtering and Signal Processing, 1994; (jtly) Sampling in Digital Signal Processing and Control, 1996; (jtly) Fundamental Limitations in Filtering and Control, 1996; (jtly) Control System Design, 2000; (jtly) Constrained Control and Estimation, 2003; chapters in books and articles in learned jls. *Address:* School of Electrical Engineering and Computer Science, University of Newcastle, University Drive, Callaghan, NSW 2308, Australia.

GOODWIN, Prof. Guy Manning, DPhil; FRCPsych; W. A. Handley Professor of Psychiatry, and Fellow of Merton College, since 1996, and Head, Department of Psychiatry, University of Oxford; *b* 8 Nov. 1947; *s* of Kenneth M. Goodwin and Constance (*née* Hudson); *m* 1971, Philippa Catherine Georgeson; two *d*. *Educ:* Manchester GS; Exeter Coll., Oxford (open schol.; MA); Wolfson Coll., Oxford (Grad. Schol.; DPhil 1972); Magdalen Coll., Oxford (MB BCh 1978). FRCPE 1995–2000; FRCPsych 1995. Scholar, MRC, 1968–71; Fellow, Magdalen Coll., Oxford, 1971–76; House Physician, Nuffield Dept of Clin. Medicine, Oxford and House Surgeon, Horton Gen. Hosp., Banbury, 1978–79; Sen. House Officer, Nat. Hosp., Queen Sq., and Professorial Unit, Brompton Hosp., 1979–80; Registrar, Rotational Trng Scheme in Psychiatry, Oxford, 1980–83; MRC Clin. Trng Fellow, and Lectr, MRC Clin. Pharmacol. Unit, Oxford, 1983–86; MRC Clin. Scientist, Hon. Consultant Psychiatrist and Hon. Sen. Lectr, Edinburgh Univ., 1986–95; Prof. of Psychiatry, Edinburgh Univ., 1995–96. Res. Associate, Univ. of Washington, Seattle, 1972–74; Hobson Meml Schol., Oxford, 1975. Mem., Neuroscis and Mental Health Grants and Fellowships Cttee, Wellcome Trust, 1992–97. Pres., British Assoc. for Psychopharmacol., 2002–04 (Mem. Council, 1993–97). FMedSci 2006. *Publications:* contrib. learned jls on neurophysiol., psychopharmacol. and psychiatry. *Recreations:* football and opera passively, hillwalking actively. *Address:* Department of Psychiatry, Warneford Hospital, Oxford OX3 7JX.

GOODWIN, Leonard George, CMG 1977; FRCP; FRS 1976; Director, Nuffield Laboratories of Comparative Medicine, Institute of Zoology, The Zoological Society of London, 1964–80; Director of Science, Zoological Society of London, 1966–80; Consultant, Wellcome Trust, since 1984; *b* 11 July 1915; *s* of Harry George and Lois Goodwin; *m* 1940, Marie Evelyn Coates (*d* 2004); no *c*. *Educ:* William Ellis Sch., London; University Coll. London (Fellow, 1981); School of Pharmacy, London; University Coll. Hospital. BPharm 1935, BSc 1937, MB BS 1950 (London). MRCP 1966, FRCP 1972. Demonstrator, Sch. of Pharmacy, London, 1935–39; Head of Wellcome Labs of Tropical Medicine, 1958–63 (Protozoologist, 1939–63). Jt Hon. Sec., Royal Soc. of Tropical Medicine and Hygiene, 1968–74, Pres., 1979–81. Chairman: Trypanosomiasis Panel, ODM, 1974–77; Filariasis Steering Cttee, WHO Special Programme, 1978–82. Hon. Dir, Wellcome Museum for Med. Sci., 1984–85. Hon. FRPharmS (Hon. FPS 1977). Hon. DSc Brunel, 1986. Soc. of Apothecaries Gold Medal, 1975; Harrison Meml Medal, 1978; Schofield Medal, Guelph Univ., 1979; Silver Medal, Zoological Soc., 1980; Manson Medal, RSTM&H, 1992. Chm. Editorial Bd, Parasitology, 1980–. *Publications:* (pt author) Biological Standardization, 1950; (contrib.) Biochemistry and Physiology of Protozoa, 1955; (jointly) A New Tropical Hygiene, 1960, 2nd edn 1972; (contrib.) Recent Advances in Pharmacology, 1962; many contribs to scientific jls, mainly on pharmacology and chemotherapy of tropical diseases, especially malaria, trypanosomiasis and helminth infections. *Recreations:* dabbling in arts and crafts especially pottery (slipware), gardening and passive participation in music and opera. *Address:* Shepperlands Farm, Park Lane, Finchampstead, Berks RG40 4QF. *T:* (0118) 973 2153.

GOODWIN, Sir Matthew (Dean), Kt 1989; CBE 1981; CA; Chairman: CrestaCare plc, 1995–2000 (Director 1994–2000); Murray Enterprise plc, 1988–2001; *b* 12 June 1929; *s* of Matthew Dean Goodwin and Mary Gertrude Barrie; *m* 1st, 1955, Margaret Eileen Colvil (marr. diss. 1982); two *d*; 2nd, 1996, Margaret Adamson. *Educ:* Hamilton Acad.; Glasgow Acad. FO, RAF, 1952–54. Raeburn & Verel, Shipowners, 1954–56; Partner, Davidson Downe McGowan, CA, 1956–68; Exec. Dir, 1960–79, Chm., 1979–95, Hewden Stuart. Director: Irvine Develt Corp., 1980–90; F/S Assurance, 1980–89; Murray Ventures PLC, 1981–; Easpark Children's Home, 1989–2002; Chm., Scotcare Ltd, 1988–2000. Mem., Scottish Econ. Council, 1991–97. Jt Dep. Chm., Scottish Conservative Party, 1991– (Hon. Treas., 1982–90). DUniv Glasgow, 2001. *Recreations:* bridge, fishing, shooting, farming. *Address:* 87 Kelvin Court, Anniesland, Glasgow G12 0AH. *T:* (0141) 221 7331. *Club:* Western (Glasgow).

GOODWIN, Dr Neil, CBE 2007; CIHM; leadership academic and consultant, since 2006; *b* 1 March 1951; *s* of James and Dorothy Goodwin; *m* 1980, Sian Elizabeth Mary Holliday (marr. diss. 1992); two *s*; *m* 2006, Chris Hannah. *Educ:* North Salford County Secondary Sch.; London Business Sch. (MBA); Manchester Business Sch. (PhD). FIHM (FHSM 1990), CIHM 2006. NHS mgt posts, London, Manchester, Liverpool, Southport, Bromsgrove, Hertfordshire, 1969–85; General Manager, Central Middlesex Hosp., 1985–88; Chief Executive: St Mary's Hosp., subseq. St Mary's Hosp. NHS Trust, 1988–94; Manchester HA, 1994–2002; Chief Exec., Gtr Manchester Strategic HA, 2002–06. Vis. Prof. of Leadership Studies, Univ. of Manchester, 2004–, Durham Univ., 2006–. Dir, GoodwinHannah Ltd, 2006–. Interim Dir, Nuffield Trust, 2007–08. Advisor: E. C. Harris LLP, 2006–; Pinsent Masons, 2007–; CHKS, 2007–. Non-executive Director: UK Transplant Authy, 2000–05; Health Foundn, 2006–. Member: Orgnl Audit Council and Accreditation Cttee, King's Fund Coll., 1993–2000; Manchester TEC Investors in People accreditation panel, 1995–99; Cabinet Office review of public sector leadership, 2000; Scientific Cttee, 2000–05, Bd, 2005–, Eur. Health Mgt Assoc. Mem. Court, Manchester Univ., 2003–05. Editorial Adviser: British Jl of Health Care Mgt, 1998–; Jl of Mgt in Medicine, 1999–. MCMI (MBIM 1982); FRSA. *Publications:* Leadership in Healthcare: a European perspective, 2005; (contrib.) Perspectives in Public Health, 2006; (contrib.) Health Care Management, 2006; academic papers and articles on public sector leadership, customer care in hosps, leadership develt needs of chief execs and public health professionals, and internat. healthcare. *Recreations:* music, Coronation Street. *Address:* The Old School, Windmill Lane, Preston on the Hill, Cheshire WA4 4AZ; *e-mail:* neil@goodwinhannah.co.uk.

GOODWIN, Noël; *see* Goodwin, T. N.

GOODWIN, Paul; Associate Conductor, Academy of Ancient Music, since 1996; *b* 2 Sept. 1956; *s* of Norman and Audrey Goodwin; *m* 1995, Helen Gough; two *s* one *d*. *Educ:* City of London Sch.; Univ. of Nottingham (BMus); Hochschule für Music, Wien (Postgrad. Dip.); Guildhall Sch. of Music and Drama (Postgrad. Dip.). Chorister, Temple Ch Choir, London. Principal and solo oboist, English Consort, King's Consort, and London Classical Players, 1985–97; Prof. of Baroque Oboe, RCM, 1986–96; Musical Director: London Oboe band, 1985–97; Royal Coll. of Music baroque orch., 1993–99; Dartington Early Opera, 1995–2001; Principal Guest Conductor, English Chamber

Orch., 1997–2003; regular guest conductor in Europe and US, incl. Kammerorch. Basel, Sudwest Rundfunk Orch. Kaiserslautern, BBC Philharmonic, Hallé, CBSO, Nat. SO Washington; opera productions incl. Iphigenie en Tauride, Komische Oper Berlin; Idomeneo, Graz Opera; Orlando, Flanders Opera. *Recreations:* sailing, racquet sports. *Address:* c/o Melanie Moult, Askonas Holt, Lincoln House, 300 High Holborn, WC1V 7JH. *T:* (020) 7400 1751, *Fax:* (020) 7400 1799; *e-mail:* melanie.moult@askonasholt.co.uk.

GOODWIN, Dr Philip Paul; Regional Director, East and West Africa, British Council, since 2004; *b* 15 Feb. 1965; *s* of Dennis Paul Goodwin and Wendy Goodwin; *m* 1999, Annette Schwalbe; one *s* one *d*. *Educ:* Univ. of Reading (BSc Agricl Econs); Wye Coll., Univ. of London (MSc Rural Resource and Envmtl Policy; PhD Cultural Geog.). Professional musician and songwriter, 1989–93; volunteer, UNA Internat. Service, Mali, 1998; Res. Officer, ODI, 1999; British Council: Director: Develt Services, Pakistan, 1999–2002; Uganda, 2002–04. *Publications:* (with Tony Page) From Hippos to Gazelles: how leaders create leaders; contrib. refereed articles to Trans IBG, Society and Space: Envmt and Planning D, Jl Rural Studies. *Recreations:* songwriting and making records for an expanding public, avoiding using the telephone. *Address:* c/o British Council, 10 Spring Gardens, SW1A 2BN.

GOODWIN, Prof. Phillip Bramley, PhD; Professor of Transport Policy, University of the West of England, since 2005; *b* 6 March 1944; *s* of Dennis and Joan Goodwin; *m* 1966, Margaret Livesey (separated); one *d*. *Educ:* Henry Thornton Grammar Sch.; UCL (BSc Econs 1965; PhD Civil Engrg 1973). FCILT, FIHT. Res. Asst, LRD Ltd, 1965–66; Res., UCL, 1966–74; Transport Planner, GLC, 1974–79; Dep. Dir, 1979–81, Dir, and Reader, 1981–95, Transport Studies Unit, Univ. of Oxford; Prof. of Transport Policy and Dir, ESRC Transport Studies Unit, UCL, 1996–2004. Mem., Standing Adv. Cttee on Trunk Road Assessment, 1979–2000; Chm., Indep. Adv. Panel for Transport White Paper, 1997–98. Non-exec. Dir, Dover Harbour Bd, 1989–2005. Distinguished Contrib. Award, Instn of Highways and Transportation, 1998. Ed.-in-chief, Jl Transportation Res. (A) Policy & Practice, 2005–. *Publications:* Subsidised Public Transport and the Demand for Travel, 1983; Long Distance Transportation, 1983; (jtly) Transport and the Environment, 1991; (jtly) Trunk Roads and the Generation of Traffic, 1994; Car Dependence, 1995; (jtly) Transport and the Economy, 1999; approx. 200 articles in learned jls, conf. papers, and contribs to books on transport policy and travel behaviour. *Recreation:* Isla de el Hierro. *Address:* Centre for Transport and Society, University of the West of England, Bristol BS16 1QY.

GOODWIN, (Trevor) Noël; freelance critic, writer and broadcaster, specialising in music and dance; *b* 25 Dec. 1927; *s* of Arthur Daniel Goodwin and Blanche Goodwin (*née* Stephens); *m* 1st, 1954, Gladys Marshall Clapham (marr. diss. 1960); 2nd, Anne Myers (*née* Mason); one step *s*. *Educ:* mainly in France. BA (London). Assistant Music Critic: News Chronicle, 1952–54; Manchester Guardian, 1954–55; Music and Dance Critic, Daily Express, 1956–78; Exec. Editor, Music and Musicians, 1963–71; regular reviewer for: The Times, 1978–98; Internat. Herald Tribune, 1978–84; Opera News, 1975–90; Ballet News, 1979–86; Dance and Dancers, 1957– (Associate Editor, 1972–); Opera, 1984– (Overseas News Editor, 1985–91; Mem. Editl Bd, 1991–99). Member: Arts Council of GB, 1979–81 (Mem., 1973–81, Chm., 1979–81, Dance Adv. Panel; Mem., 1974–81, Dep. Chm., 1979–81, Music Adv. Panel; Council's rep. on Visiting Arts Unit of GB, 1979–81); Dance Adv. Panel, UK Branch, Calouste Gulbenkian Foundn, 1972–76; Nat. Enquiry into Dance Educn and Trng in Britain, 1975–80; Drama and Dance Adv. Cttee, British Council, 1973–88; HRH The Duke of Kent's UK Cttee for European Music Year 1985, 1982–84 (Chm., sub-cttee for Writers and Critics); Trustee-dir, Internat. Course for Professional Choreographers and Composers, 1975–2005. Pres., The Critics' Circle, 1977 (Jt Trustee, 1984–). Planned and presented numerous radio programmes of music and records for BBC Home and World Services, and contributed frequently to music and arts programmes on Radios 3 and 4. *Publications:* London Symphony: portrait of an orchestra, 1954; A Ballet for Scotland, 1979; (with Sir Geraint Evans) A Knight at the Opera, 1984; editor, Royal Opera and Royal Ballet Yearbooks, 1978, 1979, 1980; area editor and writer, New Grove Dictionary of Music and Musicians, 1981; (ed) A Portrait of the Royal Ballet, 1988; contribs to: Encyclopaedia Britannica, 15th edn, 1974; Encyclopaedia of Opera, 1976; Britannica Books of the Year, annually 1980–93; Cambridge Encyclopaedia of Russia and the Soviet Union, 1982, 2nd edn 1994; New Oxford Companion to Music, 1983; Pipers Enzyklopädie des Musiktheaters, 1986; New Grove Dictionary of Opera, 1992; Viking Opera Guide, 1993; International Dictionary of Ballet, 1993; Metropolitan Opera Guide to Recorded Opera, 1993; Penguin Opera Guide, 1995; International Encyclopedia of Dance, 1998; Larousse Dictionnaire de la danse, 2000; Oxford DNB. *Recreation:* philately. *Address:* 76 Skeena Hill, SW18 5PN. *T:* (020) 8788 8794.

GOODWIN, Prof. Trevor Walworth, CBE 1975; FRS 1968; Johnston Professor of Biochemistry, University of Liverpool, 1966–83; *b* 22 June 1916; British; *m* 1944, Kathleen Sarah Hill; three *d*. *Educ:* Birkenhead Inst.; Univ. of Liverpool. Lectr 1944, Sen. Lectr 1949, in Biochemistry, University of Liverpool; Prof. of Biochemistry and Agricultural Biochemistry, UCW, Aberystwyth, 1959. NSF Sen. Foreign Scientist, Univ. of Calif at Davis, 1964. Chairman: British Photobiol. Gp, 1964–66; Phytochemical Soc., 1968–70; MRC Biol Grants Cttee B, 1969–73; Cttee, Biochem. Soc., 1971–74 (Mem., 1953–57, 1962–64); Brit. Nat. Cttee for Biochem., 1976–82; Royal Soc. Internat. Exchange Cttee (Panel A), 1986–89, 1994–; Member: Council, Royal Society, 1972, 1974, 1985; UGC, 1974–81; SRC Science Bd, 1975–78; ARC Grants Bd, 1975–82; Wirral Educn Cttee, 1974–84; Lawes Agricl Trust Cttee, 1977–91; Exec. Cttee, FEBS, 1975–83 (Chm., Publication Cttee, 1975–83); Vice-Pres., Comité Internat. de Photobiologie, 1967–69. Mem. Court, UCW, Aberystwyth, 1965–; Rep. of Lord Pres. of Council on Court, Univ. of N Wales, Bangor, 1983–; Royal Soc. Rep., Court, Univ. of Liverpool, 1985–92. Governor: Birkenhead Inst., 1976–79; Wirral County Grammar Sch. for Girls, 1980–94 (Chm., 1990–94). Morton Lectr, Biochem. Soc., 1983. Corresp. Mem., Amer. Soc. Plant Physiologists, 1982; Hon. Member: Phytochemical Soc. of Europe, 1983; Biochem. Soc., 1985. Diplôme d'honneur, FEBS, 1984. Ciba Medallist, Biochemical Soc., 1970; Prix Roussel, Société Roussel Uclaf, 1982. Editor, Protoplasma, 1968–80; Mem., Editl Bd, Phytochemistry, 1966–96. *Publications:* Comparative Biochemistry of Carotenoids, 1952 (trans. Russian, 1956), 2nd edn, vol. 1 1980, vol. 2 1983; Recent Advances in Biochemistry, 1960; Biosynthesis of Vitamins, 1964 (trans. Japanese, 1966); (ed) Chemistry and Biochemistry of Plant Pigments, 1965, 3rd edn 1988; (with E. I. Mercer) Introduction to Plant Biochemistry, 1972, 2nd edn 1982 (trans. Russian, 1986); History of the Biochemical Society, 1987; (Subject Editor) Oxford Dictionary of Biochemistry and Molecular Biology, 1997; numerous articles in Biochem. Jl, Phytochemistry, etc. *Recreation:* gardening. *Address:* Monzar, 9 Woodlands Close, Parkgate, Neston CH64 6RU. *T:* (0151) 336 4494; *e-mail:* goodwinbiochemistry@bushinternet.com.

GOODWIN-GILL, Prof. Guy Serle, DPhil; Professor of International Refuge Law, University of Oxford, since 1998; Senior Research Fellow, All Souls College, Oxford, since 2002; *b* Ealing, 25 Dec. 1946; *s* of Walter Booth Goodwin and Josephine Esther Goodwin (*née* Brown) and step *s* of Ian Arthur Gill; *m* 1991, Sharon Anne Rusu. *Edu* Mill Hill Sch.; Wadham Coll., Oxford (BA Juris. 1968; DPhil 1974). Called to the Ba Inner Temple, 1971; Lectr, 1971–74, Sen. Lectr, 1974–76, Coll. of Law, London; Leg Advr, UNHCR, UK, Australia and Geneva, 1976–88; Vis. Prof., Osgoode Hall Law Sch 1988; Vis. Prof., 1988–89, Prof. of Law, 1989–97, Carleton Univ., Ottawa; Prof. c Asylum Law (pt-time), Univ. of Amsterdam, 1994–99; Rubin Dir of Res., Inst. of Eu Studies, Oxford Univ., 1997–2002; in practice at the Bar, Blackstone Chambers, 2000– Founding Ed. and Ed.-in-Chief, Internat. Jl Refugee Law, 1988–2001. Pres., Refuge Legal Centre, 1997–. Mem. Council, Overseas Develt Inst., 2007–. Pres., Media Appea Bd of Kosovo, 2000–03. Order of Independence (Jordan), 2007. *Publications:* Internation Law and the Movement of Persons Between States, 1978; The Refugee in Internation Law, 1983, 3rd edn with J. McAdam, 2007; Free and Fair Elections, 1994, 2nd edn 200 (with I. Cohn) Child Soldiers, 1994; (ed with S. Talmon and contrib.) The Reality c International Law: essays in honour of Ian Brownlie, 1997; Codes of Conduct fc Elections, 1998; (ed with I. Brownlie) Basic Documents on Human Rights, 4th edn 200 5th edn 2006. *Recreations:* music, cooking, gardening, cats. *Address:* All Souls College Oxford OX1 4AL. *T:* (01865) 279379; *e-mail:* guy.goodwin-gill@all-souls.ox.ac.uk.

GOODWYN, Charles Wyndham, LVO 2002; FRICS; FRPSL; Keeper, Roya Philatelic Collection, 1995–2002; *b* 11 March 1934; *s* of Charles Colin Goodwyn an Phylis Goodwyn; *m* 1962, Judith Elisabeth Ann Riley; two *s* two *d*. *Educ:* Wellingto Coll.; London Univ. (LLB Hons). FRICS 1964; FCIArb 1976. Joined Wilks Head & Ev Chartered Surveyors, 1956, Sen. Partner, 1990–95. Hon. FRICS. Royal Philateli Society: Mem., 1965–; Fellow, 1975, Hon. Fellow, 2000; Hon. Treas., 1981–82; Hor Sec., 1982–90; Vice Pres., 1990–92; Pres., 1992–94. Medal, Royal Philatelic Soc., 199 Signatory, Roll of Distinguished Philatelists, 1995; Award for Philatelic Achievemen Smithsonian Mus., 2003. *Publications:* The Crown Colony of Wei Hai Wei, 1985; Roya Reform, 1999; contrib. articles to London Philatelist, etc. *Recreations:* tennis, golf, crick *Address:* Hinton House, 132 High Street, Amersham, Bucks HP7 0EE. *T:* (01494) 72629 *Clubs:* Army and Navy, MCC.

GOODY, Sir John (Rankine), Kt 2005; FBA 1976; William Wyse Professor of Soci Anthropology, University of Cambridge, 1973–84, now Professor Emeritus; Fellow, S John's College, Cambridge, since 1960; *b* 27 July 1919; *m*; one *s* four *d*. *Educ:* St Alba Sch.; St John's Coll., Cambridge; Balliol Coll., Oxford. BA 1946, Dip. Anthrop. 194 PhD 1954, ScD 1969, Cantab; BLitt Oxon 1952. HM Forces, 1939–46. Educnl admi 1947–49; Cambridge Univ.: Asst Lectr, 1954–59; Lectr, 1959–71; Dir, African Studi Centre, 1966–73; Smuts Reader in Commonwealth Studies, 1972. Mem., Academ Europaea, 1991; Foreign Hon. Member: Amer. Acad. of Arts and Scis, 1980; NAS, 200 Hon. DLit Kent, 1996; Hon. LLD Toronto, 2002; Dhc Bordeaux, 2004; Hon. Dr: Pa Verlaine-Metz, 2006; Nanterre, Paris X, 2006. International Prize, Fondation Fysse 1991. Mem., Ordre des Palmes Académiques, 1993; Commandeur dans l'Ordre des Ar et des Lettres (France), 2006 (Chevalier, 1996; Officier, 2001). *Publications:* The Soci Organisation of the LoWiili, 1956; (ed) The Developmental Cycle in Domestic Group 1958; Death, Property and the Ancestors, 1962; (ed) Succession to High Office, 196 (with J. A. Braimah) Salaga: the struggle for power, 1967; (ed) Literacy in Traditiona Societies, 1968; Comparative Studies in Kinship, 1969; Technology, Tradition and th State in Africa, 1971; The Myth of the Bagre, 1972; (with S. J. Tambiah) Bridewealth an Dowry, 1973; (ed) The Character of Kinship, 1973; (ed) Changing Social Structure i Ghana, 1975; Production and Reproduction, 1977; The Domestication of the Savag Mind, 1977; (with S. W. D. K. Gandah) Une Recitation du Bagré, 1981; Cooking Cuisine and Class, 1982; The Development of the Family and Marriage in Europe, 198 The Logic of Writing and the Organization of Society, 1986; The Interface between th Oral and the Written, 1987; The Oriental, the Ancient and the Primitive, 1990; Th Culture of Flowers, 1993; The Expansive Moment, 1995; The East in the West, 199 Jack Goody: l'homme, l'écriture et la mort, 1996; Representations and Contradiction 1997; Oltre i Muri: la mia prigionia in Italia, 1997, French rev. edn 2004; Food and Love a cultural history of East and West, 1999; The European Family, 2000; The Power of th Written Tradition, 2000; (with S. W. D. K. Gandah) A Myth Revisited: the third Bagr 2003; Islam in Europe, 2003; Capitalism and Modernisation: the great debate, 2004; Th Theft of History, 2007; Ghana Revisited, 2008; Renaissances: the one or the many, 200 contrib. learned jls. *Address:* St John's College, Cambridge CB2 1TP. *T:* (01223) 338638

GOODYEAR, Charles Waterhouse, (Chip); Chief Executive Officer, BHP Billito 2003–07; *b* 18 Jan. 1958; *s* of Charles and Linda Goodyear; *m* 1992, Elizabeth Dabezie one *s* one *d*. *Educ:* Yale Univ. (BSc Geol., Geophys 1980); Wharton Sch. of Financ Univ. of Pennsylvania (MBA 1983). Kidder, Peabody & Co.: Associate, 1983–85; As Vice Pres., 1985–86; Vice Pres., 1986–89. Freeport-McMoRan, Inc.: Vice Pres Corporate Finance, 1989–93; Sen. Vice Pres. and Chief Investment Officer, 1993–9 Exec. Vice Pres. and Chief Financial Officer, 1995–97; Pres., Goodyear Capital Corp 1997–99; Chief Financial Officer, BHP Ltd, 1999–2001; Exec. Dir and Chief Deve Officer, BHP Billiton, 2001–03. *Recreations:* bicycling, ski-ing, fishing.

GOODYER, Prof. Ian Michael, MD; FRCPsych, FMedSci; Foundation Professor c Child and Adolescent Psychiatry, Cambridge University, since 1992; Fellow of Wolfso College, Cambridge, since 1993; *b* 2 Nov. 1949; *s* of Mark and Belle Goodyer; *m* 197 Jane Elizabeth Akister; one *s* one *d*. *Educ:* University College London; St George's Hosp Oxford Univ.; Newcastle Univ.; Brown Univ. MB BS, MD London; MRCPsych 197 FRCPsych 1990; DCH 1978. Sen. Lectr, Child/Adolescent Psych. and Consultant, Univ of Manchester and Salford HA, 1983–87; Cambridge University: Foundn Lectr in Chil Psych., 1987–92; Head, Developmental Psych. Section, 1992–. FMedSci 199 *Publications:* Life Experiences, Development and Child Psychopathology, 1991; Th Depressed Child and Adolescent: developmental and clinical perspectives, 1995, 2nd ed 2000; Unipolar Depression: a lifespan perspective, 2003; (with David Goldberg) Th Origins and Course of Common Mental Disorders, 2005; (jtly) Social Cognition an Developmental Psychopathology, 2008; contribs to learned jls. *Recreations:* keeping fi guitar. *Address:* Developmental Psychiatry Section, Douglas House, 18 Trumpingto Road, Cambridge CB2 2AH. *T:* (01223) 336098.

GOOLD, Sir George William, 8th Bt *cr* 1801, of Old Court, Cork; *b* 25 March 195 *o s* of Sir George Leonard Goold, 7th Bt and of Joy Cecelia Goold (now Joy, Lady Goold *S* father, 1997; *m* 1973, Julie Ann Crack; two *s*. *Heir: s* George Leonard Powell Goold, 1 Dec. 1975. *Address:* 180 Hargrave Street, Paddington, NSW 2021, Australia. *T:* (2 93621155.

GOOLEY, Michael David William, CBE 2007; FRGS; Founder and Chairma Trailfinders Ltd, since 1970; *b* 13 Oct. 1936; *s* of late Denis David Gooley and Lenni Frances May Gooley (*née* Woodward); *m* 1st, 1961, Veronica Georgina Broad (marr. diss 1970); two *d*; 2nd, 1971, Hilary Eila (marr. diss. 1981; she *d* 1993), *d* of Sir Paul Mallinso 3rd Bt; one *s* one *d*; 3rd, 1983, Bernadette Mary Woodward (marr. diss. 1997); 4th 200 Fiona Kathleen Leslie. *Educ:* St John's Beaumont Prep. Sch.; St George's, Weybridge RMA Sandhurst. Enlisted Regular Army, 1955: commnd 2nd Lieut, S Staffs Regt, 195 joined 22 SAS, 1958; served Malaya and Arabian Peninsula; Adjt, 21 SAS, 1961–63; 1st Bn Staffords, 1963; served Kenya; 2nd tour, 22 SAS, 1964; served Malay Peninsula, Borneo and S Arabia; retd 1965. Mil. Advr to Royalist Yemini Army, 1965–69. Leader, expedition Trans Africa, 1971. Founder Trustee, Mike Gooley Trailfinders Charity, 1995. FInstD 1978; FRGS 1996. Hon. Life FRSA 2005. Patron, Prostate Cancer Charity, 1998–. Trustee, Special Forces Club, 1996–2007. *Publication:* Trans Africa Route Report, 1972. *Recreations:* travel, aviation, pragmatic entrepreneuralism, wining and dining, supporting Ealing Trailfinders RFC. *Address:* (office) 9 Abingdon Road, W8 6AH. *Club:* Special Forces.

GOOSE, Julian Nicholas; QC 2002; a Recorder, since 1998; *b* 26 July 1961; *s* of Alan Charles Goose and Pauline Jean Goose; *m* 1987, Susan Frances Rose Bulmer; two *s* one *d. Educ:* Birkdale Sch.; Silverdale Sch.; Leeds Univ. (LLB Hons). Called to the Bar, Lincoln's Inn, 1984. Junior, NE Circuit, 1992. Hd of Zenith Chambers, 2004–. Mem., Advocacy Trng Council, 2004–. *Recreations:* squash, golf, friends, family. *Address:* Zenith Chambers, 10 Park Square, Leeds LS1 2LH; 9 Lincoln's Inn Fields, WC2A 3BP. *Clubs:* Alwoodley Golf; Chapel Allerton Lawn Tennis and Squash.

GOOSE, Margaret Elizabeth, OBE 2004; Vice President, Stroke Association, since 2006 (Chief Executive, 1997–2004); *b* 10 Oct. 1945; *d* of late Leonard Charles Goose and Gladys Muriel Goose (*née* Smith). *Educ:* Blyth Sch., Norwich; Newnham Coll., Cambridge (BA 1967; MA 1971). FHSM 1991. Gen. mgt in hosps and health authorities, 1967–82; Chief Exec., N Beds HA, 1982–92; Hd of Health and Mgt Develt Div., Nuffield Inst. for Health, Univ. of Leeds, 1993–97. Lay Mem., Council, RCP, 2004–08 (Chm., Patient and Carer Involvement Steering Gp, 2004–08; Trustee, 2008–). Gov., Health Foundn, 2007–. Pres., IHSM, 1989–90. Hon. MFPHM 1998. Hon. FRCP 2008. *Recreations:* walking, travel, theatre, music, friends.

GOPALAN, Coluthur, MD, DSc; FRCP, FRCPE; FRS 1987; President, Nutrition Foundation of India, New Delhi, since 1979; *b* 29 Nov. 1918; *s* of C. Doraiswami Iyengar and Mrs Pattammal; *m* 1940, Seetha Gopalan; one *s* one *d* (and one *s* decd). *Educ:* Univ. of Madras (MD); Univ. of London (PhD, DSc). Fellow, Acad. of Med. Scis, India, 1961; FIASc 1964; FNA 1966. Dir, Nat. Inst. of Nutrition, Hyderabad, 1960–74; Dir-Gen., Indian Council of Med. Res., New Delhi, 1975–79. Hon. DSc. Banares Hindu, 1982. *Publications:* Nutritive Value of Indian Foods, 1966; Nutrition and Health Care, 1984; Use of Growth Charts for Promoting Child Nutrition: a review of global experience, 1985; Combating Undernutrition: basic issues and practical approaches, 1987; Nutrition Problems and Programmes in South East Asia, 1987; Nutrition in Developmental Transition in South East Asia, 1992; Recent Trends in Nutrition, 1993; Towards Better Nutrition: problems and policies, 1993; Nutrition Research in South East Asia: the emerging agenda for the future, 1994; over 200 contribs to sci. jls; chapters on specific topics to several books on nutrition in internat. pubns on nutrition. *Recreation:* music. *Address:* Nutrition Foundation of India, C-13, Qutab Institutional Area, New Delhi 110016, India. *T:* (11) 6857814, 6965410. *Club:* India International Centre (New Delhi).

GORAI, Rt Rev. Dinesh Chandra; Bishop of Calcutta, 1982–1999; *b* 15 Jan. 1934; *m* Binapani; two *c. Educ:* Calcutta Univ. (BA 1956). Serampore Theological Coll. (BD 1959). Ordained, 1962; Methodist Minister in Calcutta/Barrackpore, 1968–70; first Bishop, Church of N India Diocese of Barrackpore, 1970–82; Dep. Moderator, 1980, Moderator, 1983–86, Church of N India. Hon. DD: Bethel Coll., 1985; Serampore Coll., 1991. *Publications:* Society at the Cross Road, 1968; (ed) Transfer of Vision: a leadership development programme for the Church of North India 1983–1986, 1984; New Horizons in Christian Ministry, 1993. *Address:* Binapani Villa, 28 Mahatma Ghandi Road, Keorapukur M., Calcutta 700 082, India.

GORARD, Anthony John; *b* 15 July 1927; *s* of William James and Rose Mary Gorard; *m* 1954, Barbara Kathleen Hampton; one *s* three *d. Educ:* Ealing Grammar School. Chartered Accountant, 1951; Manufacturing Industry, 1952–58; Anglia Television Ltd, 1959–67, Executive Director and Member of Management Cttee; Managing Director, HTV Ltd, 1967–78; Chief Exec., HTV Gp Ltd, 1976–78; Director: Independent Television Publications Ltd, 1967–78; Independent Television News Ltd, 1973–78; Chief Exec., Cardiff Broadcasting Co. Ltd, 1979–81; Consultant, Mitchell Beazley Television, 1982–83; hotel proprietor, 1983–87; restaurant owner, 1987–94. Chm., British Regional Television Association, 1970–71. *Recreations:* gardening, pottery, rambling. *Address:* 6 Shetland Close, Leigh Park, Westbury, Wilts BA13 2GN. *T:* (01373) 824261.

GORBACHEV, Mikhail Sergeyevich; President: International Foundation for Socio-Economic and Political Studies (Gorbachev Foundation), since 1992; Green Cross International, since 1993; Executive President of the Soviet Union, 1990–91; *b* 2 March 1931; *m* 1953, Raisa Gorbacheva (*d* 1999); one *d. Educ:* Moscow State Univ. (law graduate); Stavropol Agric. Inst. Machine operator, 1946; joined CPSU 1952; First Sec., Stavropol Komsomol City Cttee, 1956–58, later Dep. Head of Propaganda; 2nd, later 1st Sec., Komsomol Territorial Cttee, 1958–62; Party Organizer, Stavropol Territorial Production Bd of Collective and State Farms, 1962; Head, Dept of party bodies, CPSU Territorial Cttee, 1963–66; 1st Sec., Stavropol City Party Cttee, 1966–68; 2nd Sec., 1968–70, 1st Sec., 1970–78, Stavropol Territorial CPSU Cttee; Central Committee, Communist Party of Soviet Union: Mem., 1971–91; Sec., with responsibility for agric., 1978–85; Alternate Mem., 1979–80, then Mem., Political Bureau; Gen. Sec., 1985–91. Deputy, Supreme Soviet: USSR, 1970–89 (Chm., Foreign Affairs Commn of the Soviet of the Union, 1984–85; Mem., 1985–88, Chm., 1988–89, Presidium); RSFSR, 1980–90; Deputy, Congress of Peoples' Deps, USSR, 1989; Chm., Supreme Soviet, USSR, 1989–90. Freeman of Aberdeen, 1993. Hon. Citizen of Berlin, 1992. Nobel Peace Prize, 1990; Ronald Reagan Freedom Award, 1992. Orders of Lenin, of Red Banner of Labour, Badge of Honour. *Publications:* A Time for Peace, 1985; The Coming Century of Peace, 1986; Speeches and Writings (7 vols), 1986–90; Peace has no Alternative, 1986; Moratorium, 1986; Perestroika: new thinking for our country and the world, 1987; The August Coup, 1991; December, 1991; My Stand, 1992; The Years of Hard Decisions, 1993; Life and Reforms, 1995 (UK edn, Memoirs, 1996); Reflections on the Past and Future, 1998. *Address:* (office) 39 Leningradsky Prospekt bdg14, Moscow 125167, Russia. *T:* (095) 9439990, *Fax:* (095) 9439594.

GORDIEVSKY, Oleg Antonovich, CMG 2007; writer on political affairs; lecturer; *b* Moscow, 10 Oct. 1938; *s* of Anton Lavrentyevich Gordievsky and Olga Nikolayevna Gordievsky; *m* (marr. diss.); two *d. Educ:* Inst. of Internat. Relations, Moscow (Bachelor Internat. Relns). Dep. Hd of Station, Copenhagen, 1974–78; Actg Hd of Station, London, 1984–85, KGB; Secret Agent, SIS, 1974–85; arrested by KGB, evacuated to Moscow and subseq. escaped back to UK, 1985. Hon. DLitt Buckingham, 2005. *Publications:* (with C. Andrew) KGB: the inside story of its foreign operations from Lenin to Gorbachev, 1990; (with C. Andrew) Instructions from the Centre, 1991; (with C. Andrew) More Instructions from the Centre, 1992; Next Stop Execution, 1995; (with I. Rogatchi) Opaque Mirror, 1997; (with J. Andersen) De Rode Spioner, 2002; contrib. internat. and political magazines. *Recreations:* cycling, collection of dictionaries of Germanic languages.

Address: c/o A. M. Heath & Co. Ltd, 6 Warwick Court, WC1R 5DJ. *T:* and *Fax:* (01483) 417481; *e-mail:* navole1@aol.com.

GORDIMER, Nadine, FRSL; author; *b* 20 Nov. 1923; *d* of Isidore Gordimer and Nan Gordimer (*née* Myers); *m* Reinhold Cassirer; one *s* one *d. Educ:* Convent Sch.; Witwatersrand Univ. Neil Gunn Fellowship, Scottish Arts Council, 1981. Vice-Pres., PEN Internat. Goodwill Ambassador, UNDP. Hon. Member: Amer. Acad. of Art and Literature, 1979; Amer. Acad. of Arts and Sciences, 1980. DLit *hc* Leuven, Belgium, 1980; DLitt *hc* City Coll. of NY, 1985; Smith Coll., 1985; Harvard, 1986; Yale, 1986; Columbia, 1987; New Sch. for Social Res., 1987; York, 1987; Oxford, 1994. MLA Award, USA, 1981; Malaparte Prize, Italy, 1985; Nelly Sachs Prize, W Germany, 1985; Bennett Award, USA, 1986; Nobel Prize for Literature, 1991; Grinzane Cavour Prize, 2007. Comdr, Ordre des Arts et des Lettres (France); Order of the Southern Cross (S Africa); Order of Friendship (Cuba); Presidential Medal of Honour (Chile); Légion d'Honneur (France), 2007. *Publications: novels:* The Lying Days, 1953; A World of Strangers, 1958; Occasion for Loving, 1963; The Late Bourgeois World, 1966; A Guest of Honour, 1971 (James Tait Black Meml Prize, 1971); The Conservationist, 1974 (jtly, Booker Prize 1974; Grand Aigle d'Or, France, 1975); Burger's Daughter, 1979; July's People, 1981; A Sport of Nature, 1987; My Son's Story, 1990; None to Accompany Me, 1994; The House Gun, 1997; The Pickup, 2001; Get a Life, 2005; *stories:* The Soft Voice of the Serpent, 1953; Six Feet of the Country, 1956; Friday's Footprint, 1960 (W. H. Smith Lit. Award, 1961); Not for Publication, 1965; Livingstone's Companions, 1972; Selected Stories, 1975; Some Monday for Sure, 1976; A Soldier's Embrace, 1980; Something Out There, 1984; Jump, 1991; Loot, 2003; Beethoven was One-sixteenth Black, 2007; *non-fiction:* South African Writing Today (jt editor), 1967; The Essential Gesture: writing, politics and places, 1988; Writing and Being (Charles Eliot Norton Lectures), 1995; Living in Hope and History: notes from our century (essays), 1999; (ed and contrib.) Telling Tales, 2004. *Address:* c/o A. P. Watt, 20 John Street, WC1N 2DR.

GORDON, family name of **Marquess of Aberdeen and Temair, Marquess of Huntly** and of **Baron Gordon of Strathblane**.

GORDON OF STRATHBLANE, Baron *cr* 1997 (Life Peer), of Deil's Craig in Stirling; **James Stuart Gordon,** CBE 1984; Chairman, Scottish Radio Holdings, 1996–2005; *b* 17 May 1936; *s* of James Gordon and Elsie (*née* Riach); *m* 1971, Margaret Anne Stevenson; two *s* one *d. Educ:* St Aloysius' Coll., Glasgow; Glasgow Univ. (MA Hons). Political Editor, STV, 1965–73; Man. Dir, Radio Clyde, 1973–96; Chief Exec., Radio Clyde Hldgs, subseq. Scottish Radio Hldgs, 1991–96. Chairman: Scottish Exhibn Centre, 1983–89; Scottish Tourist Bd, 1998–2001 (Mem., 1997–98); Rajar, 2003–06; Vice-Chm., Melody Radio, 1991–97; Member: Scottish Develt Agency, 1981–90; Scottish Adv. Bd, BP, 1990–2003; Director: Clydeport Hldgs, 1992–98; Johnston Press plc, 1996–2007; Active Capital (formerly AIM) Trust plc, 1996–. Chm., Adv. Gp on Listed Sporting Events, 1997–98; Member: Cttee of Inquiry into Teachers' Pay and Conditions, 1986; Cttee to Review Funding of BBC, 1999. Trustee: John Smith Meml Trust, 1994–2007; Nat. Galls of Scotland, 1998–2002. Chm., Glasgow Common Purpose, 1995–97. Mem. Court, Univ. of Glasgow, 1984–97. Hon. DLitt Glasgow Caledonian, 1994; DUniv Glasgow, 1998. *Recreations:* ski-ing, walking, genealogy. *Address:* Deil's Craig, Strathblane, Glasgow G63 9ET. *T:* 07711 223149. *Clubs:* New (Edinburgh); Glasgow Art (Glasgow); Prestwick Golf.

GORDON, Very Rev. Alexander Ronald; Provost, St Andrew's Cathedral, Inverness, since 2005; *b* 16 Dec. 1949; *s* of Alexander Donald and Norah May Gordon; *m* 1979, Geraldine Worrall; one *s* two *d. Educ:* Nottingham Univ. (BPharm 1971); Leeds Univ. (DipTh 1976); Coll. of the Resurrection, Mirfield. MRPharmS 1972. Ordained deacon, 1977, priest, 1978; Asst Curate, St Michael and All Angels, Headingley, 1977–80; Asst Priest, St Peter and St Paul, Fareham, 1980–83; Vicar, St John Baptist, Cudworth, 1983–85; *locum tenens*, St Andrew, Tain, 1985–87; Priest-in-charge, Lairg, Dornoch and Brora, 1987–2001; Diocesan Dir of Ordinands, Dio. Moray, Ross and Caithness, 1990–2001; Canon, St Andrew's Cathedral, Inverness, 1995–2001 (Hon. Canon, 2001–); Chaplain, St Alban, Strasbourg, 2001–05; Asst Dir of Ordinands, Dio. Gibraltar in Europe, 2004–05. Associate Staff Mem., Church and Soc. Commn, Conf. of European Chs, 2004–. *Recreations:* music, travel, hill walking, reading detective and spy fiction, trying to get my computer to do what I want it to do. *Address:* St Andrew's Lodge, 15 Ardross Street, Inverness IV3 5NS. *T:* (01463) 233535; *e-mail:* canonalexgordon@ compuserve.com.

GORDON, Sir Andrew Cosmo Lewis D.; *see* Duff Gordon.

GORDON, Rt Rev. (Archibald) Ronald (McDonald); Canon and Sub-Dean of Christ Church, Oxford, 1991–96; an Assistant Bishop, diocese of Oxford, since 1991; *b* 19 March 1927; *s* of Sir Archibald Gordon, CMG, and Dorothy Katharine Gordon, Bridge House, Gerrards Cross, Bucks. *Educ:* Rugby Sch.; Balliol Coll., Oxford (Organ Schol., MA 1950); Cuddesdon Theol. Coll. Deacon 1952; priest 1953; Curate of Stepney, 1952–55; Chaplain, Cuddesdon Coll., 1955–59; Vicar of St Peter, Birmingham, 1959–67; Res. Canon, Birmingham Cathedral, 1967–71; Vicar of University Church of St Mary the Virgin with St Cross and St Peter in the East, Oxford, 1971–75; Bishop of Portsmouth, 1975–84; Bishop at Lambeth (Hd of Archbp's Staff), 1984–91; an Asst Bishop, Dio. of Southwark, 1984–91; Bishop to the Forces, 1985–90. Mem., H of L, 1981–84. Fellow of St Cross Coll., Oxford, 1975; Select Preacher, Univ. of Oxford, 1985, 1993, 1997. Mem., Church Assembly and General Synod and Proctor in Convocation, 1965–71; Chm., ACCM, 1976–83. Member: Court of Ecclesiastical Causes Reserved, 1991–2004; Archbishops' Commn on Cathedrals, 1992–94; Adv. Bd for Redundant Churches, 1992–98. Chm., Malaŵi Church Trust, 1993–95; Pres., Oxford Mission, 1992–2001. *Recreations:* piano playing, refraining from giving advice. *Address:* 16 East St Helen Street, Abingdon, Oxon OX14 5EA. *T:* (01235) 526956; *e-mail:* ronaldgordon.ab@ btinternet.com.

GORDON, Boyd; Fisheries Secretary, Department of Agriculture and Fisheries for Scotland, 1982–86; *b* 18 Sept. 1926; *er s* of David Gordon and Isabella (*née* Leishman); *m* 1951, Elizabeth Mabel (*née* Smith); two *d. Educ:* Musselburgh Grammar School. Following military service with the Royal Scots, joined the Civil Service, initially with Min. of Labour, then Inland Revenue; Department of Agriculture and Fisheries for Scotland: joined, 1953; Principal, Salmon and Freshwater Fisheries Administration and Fisheries R&D, 1962–73; Asst Secretary, Agriculture Economic Policy, EEC Co-ordination and Agriculture Marketing, 1973–82. *Recreations:* family and church affairs, gardening, sport of all kinds, though only golf as participant now, reading, playing and writing Scottish fiddle music. *Address:* 87 Duddingston Road, Edinburgh EH15 1SP. *Club:* Civil Service.

GORDON, Brian William, OBE 1974; HM Diplomatic Service, 1949–81, retired; Commercial Counsellor, Caracas, 1980–81; *b* 24 Oct. 1926; *s* of William and Doris Margaret Gordon; *m* 1951, Sheila Graham Young; two *s* one *d. Educ:* Tynemouth Grammar School. HM Forces (Lieut in IA), 1944–47; joined HM Foreign Service (now Diplomatic Service), 1949; served in: Saigon; Libya; Second Sec. in Ethiopia, 1954–58 and in Peru, 1959–61; HM Consul: Leopoldville, Congo, 1962–64; New York, 1965–67; Puerto Rico, 1967–69; Consul-General, Bilbao, 1969–73; Asst Head, Trade Relations and Export Dept, FCO, 1974–77; Dep. Consul-Gen., Los Angeles, 1977–80. *Recreations:* golf, walking. *Address:* 4 Cragside, Corbridge, Northumberland NE45 5EU.

See also I. W. Gordon.

GORDON, Charles; Member (Lab) Glasgow Cathcart, Scottish Parliament, since Sept. 2005; *b* 28 Oct. 1951; *m* 1st; two *s*; 2nd, Emma; one *s*. *Educ:* St Mungo's Acad., Glasgow. Member (Lab): Strathclyde Regl Council, 1987–96; Glasgow CC, 1995–2005 (Dep. Leader, 1997–99; Leader, 1999–2005). *Address:* (office) Somerville Drive, Mount Florida, Glasgow G42 9BA; Scottish Parliament, Edinburgh EH99 1SP.

GORDON, Sir Charles (Addison Somerville Snowden), KCB 1981 (CB 1970); Clerk of the House of Commons, 1979–83; *b* 25 July 1918; *s* of C. G. S. Gordon, TD, Liverpool, and Mrs E. A. Gordon, Emberton and Wimbledon; *m* 1943, Janet Margaret, (Jane), Beattie (*d* 1995); one *s* (one *d* decd). *Educ:* Winchester; Balliol Coll., Oxford. Served in Fleet Air Arm throughout War of 1939–45. Apptd Asst Clerk in House of Commons, 1946; Senior Clerk, 1947; Fourth Clerk at the Table, 1962; Principal Clerk of the Table Office, 1967; Second Clerk Assistant, 1974; Clerk Asst, 1976. Sec., Soc. of Clerks-at-the-Table in Commonwealth Parliaments, and co-Editor of its journal, The Table, 1952–62. *Publications:* Parliament as an Export (jointly), 1966; Editor, Erskine May's Parliamentary Practice, 20th edn, 1983 (Asst Editor, 19th edn); contribs to: The Table; The Parliamentarian. *Recreation:* dolce far niente. *Address:* 279 Lonsdale Road, Barnes, SW13 9QB. *T:* (020) 8748 6735.

GORDON, (Cosmo) Gerald (Maitland); His Honour Judge Gordon; a Circuit Judge, since 1990; a Senior Circuit Judge, Central Criminal Court, since 1994; *b* 26 March 1945; *s* of John Kenneth Maitland Gordon, CBE and Erica Martia Clayton-East; *m* 1973, Vanessa Maria Juliet Maxine Reilly-Morrison, LLB, AKC, barrister; two *s*. *Educ:* Eton. Called to the Bar, Middle Temple, 1966, Bencher, 2003. Asst Recorder, 1982–86; Recorder, 1986–90. Royal Borough of Kensington and Chelsea: Mem. Council, 1971–90; Chm., Works Cttee, 1978–80; Chm., Town Planning Cttee, 1988; Dep. Leader, 1982–88; Mayor, 1989–90. Chairman: Edwardes Square Scarsdale and Abingdon Assoc., 1990–2001; Westway Develt Trust (formerly N Kensington Amenity Trust), 1992–2002. Liveryman, Merchant Taylors' Co., 1995–. *Recreations:* food, wine, armchair sport. *Address:* Central Criminal Court, City of London, EC4M 7EH. *T:* (020) 7248 3277.

GORDON, Prof. David, FRCP, FMedSci; Visiting Professor, University of Copenhagen, since 2007; Vice-President, 2004–08, Professor of Medicine, 1999–2008, now Emeritus, University of Manchester; *b* 23 Feb. 1947; *s* of late Lawrence Gordon and of Pattie Gordon (*née* Wood); *m* Dr C. Louise Jones; three *s* one *d*. *Educ:* Whitgift Sch.; Magdalene Coll., Cambridge (BA 1967, MA 1971; MB BChir 1970); Westminster Med. Sch. MRCP 1972, FRCP 1989. Clin. appts, Leicester and Cambridge, 1970–72; St Mary's Hospital Medical School: Res. Fellow, 1972–74; Lectr in Medicine, 1974–80; Sen. Lectr in Medicine, 1980–83; Hon. Sen. Lectr in Medicine, 1983–94; Hon. Cons. Physician, St Mary's Hosp., London, 1980–94; Wellcome Trust: Asst Dir, 1983–89; Prog. Dir, 1989–98; Dir of Special Initiatives, 1998–99; Dean, Faculty of Medicine, Dentistry, Nursing and Pharmacy, Victoria Univ. of Manchester, then Faculty of Med. and Human Scis, Univ. of Manchester, 1999–2006. Hon. Consultant Physician, Manchester Royal Infirmary, Salford Royal Hosps and S Manchester Univ. Hosps, 1999–2006. Vis. Prof., QMUL. Director: Manchester Innovation Hldgs Ltd, 2002–04; UK Biobank Ltd, 2004–06. Member: Res. Sub-Gp, Task Force on Support of R&D in NHS, 1994; Academic Wkg Gp, HEFCE-CVCP-SCOP Cttee on Post Grad. Educn, 1995; Indep. Task Force on Clin. Academic Careers, CVCP, 1996–97; Res. Cttee, HEFCE, 1998–99; Chief Scientist Cttee, Scottish Office DoH, 1997–99; Pres., Assoc. of Med. Schs in Europe, 2004–; Chm., Council of Heads of Medical Schs, 2003–06; Dep. Chm., ORPHEUS, 2005–. FMedSci 1999. *Publications:* papers, reviews, etc on biomed. res., sci. policy and other subjects in learned jls. *Recreations:* music (cello), books, food, finding out what is going on. *Address:* Faculty of Health Sciences, University of Copenhagen, Blegdamsvej 3b, 2200 Copenhagen N, Denmark; *e-mail:* gordoncph@gmail.com.

GORDON, David Sorrell; Director, Milwaukee Art Museum, Wisconsin, USA, since 2002; *b* 11 Sept. 1941; *s* of late Sholom and Tania Gordon; *m* 1st, 1963, Enid Albagli (marr. diss. 1969); 2nd, 1974, Maggi McCormick; two *s*. *Educ:* Clifton College; Balliol College, Oxford (PPE, BA 1963); LSE; Advanced Management Program, Harvard Business Sch. FCA. Articles with Thomson McLintock, 1965–68; The Economist: editorial staff, 1968–78; Production and Develt Dir, 1978–81; Gp Chief Exec., Economist Newspaper Ltd, 1981–93; Chief Exec., ITN, 1993–95; Sec., Royal Acad. of Arts, 1996–2002. Director: Financial Times, 1983–93; eFinancial News, 1999– (Chm., 2001–); Profile Books, 1996–. Dir, South Bank Bd, 1986–96; a Governor, BFI, 1983–91. Chm., Contemporary Art Soc., 1991–98; Trustee: Tate Gall., 1993–98; Architecture Foundn, 1993–2002; Architecture Assoc. Foundn, 1995–98. Gov., LSE, 1990–2000. *Publication:* (with Fred Hirsch) Newspaper Money, 1975. *Recreation:* collecting stereoscopic photographs. *Address:* Milwaukee Art Museum, 700 North Art Museum Drive, Milwaukee, WI 53202, USA; *e-mail:* david.gordon@mam.org. *Clubs:* Garrick, Arts.

GORDON, Sir Donald, Kt 2005; Founder, Liberty International PLC (formerly TransAtlantic Holdings) (Chairman, 1981–2005; Life President, since 2005); *b* 24 June 1930; *s* of Nathan and Sheila Gordon; *m* 1958, Peggy Cowan; two *s* one *d*. *Educ:* King Edward VII Sch., Johannesburg. CA (SA). Partner, Kessel Feinstein, 1955–57; Founder, Chm. and CEO 1957–99, now Hon. Life Pres., Liberty Life Assoc. of Africa Ltd, subseq. Liberty Gp Ltd; Chairman: Liberty Hldgs, SA, 1968–99; Liberty InvestorsLtd, 1971–99; Guardian Nat. Insce Co. Ltd, 1980–99; Capital & Counties (UK), 1982–2005; Continental & Industrial Trust, 1986–93; Capital Shopping Centres plc, 1994–2005; Deputy Chairman: Standard Bank Investment Corp., 1979–99; Premier Gp Ltd, 1983–96; SAB Miller plc, 1989–99; Beverage & Consumer Industry Hldgs, 1989–99; Sun Life Corp., UK, 1992–95. Director: Guardbank Mgt Corp.Ltd, 1969–99; Guardian Royal Exchange Assurance (UK), 1971–94; Charter Life Insce Co. Ltd, 1985–99; GFSA Hldgs, 1990–94. Hon. DEconSc Witwatersrand, 1991; Hon. DCom Pretoria, 2005. Business Man of Year Award, Financial Mail (SA), 1965; Sunday Times (SA) Businessman of the Year, 1969; Special Award for Lifetime Achievement, Entrepreneur of the Year Awards, 2000; (UK) Top 100 Lifetime Achievement Award, Sunday Times (SA), 2004. *Recreations:* opera, ballet. *Address:* c/o Liberty International PLC, 40 Broadway, SW1H 0BT. *T:* (020) 7960 1200, *Fax:* (020) 7960 1333. *Clubs:* Rand, Johannesburg Country, Plettenburg Bay Country, Houghton Golf, (SA).

GORDON, Douglas; *see* Gordon, R. D.

GORDON, Douglas Lamont; artist; *b* 20 Sept. 1966; *s* of James Gordon and Mary Clements Gordon (*née* MacDougall). *Educ:* Glasgow Sch. of Art (BA Hons 1st cl.); Slade Sch. of Art (Postgrad. Res. Dip.). *Exhibitions* include: Lisson Gall., 1993, 1995 (solo), 1998, 2000; Hayward Gall., 1996, 1997, 2002; MOMA, Oxford, 1996; 10th Sydney Biennale, 1996; Venice Biennale (Premio 2000), 1997; Tate Liverpool, 2000; Superhumanatural, Nat. Galls of Scotland, 2006. Turner Prize, 1996. *Recreations:* eatin drinking, sleeping. *Address:* c/o Lisson Gallery, 52–54 Bell Street, NW1 5DA.

GORDON, Eileen; *b* 22 Oct. 1946; *d* of late Charles Leatt and Margaret Rose Leatt; Tony Gordon (decd); one *s* one *d*. *Educ:* Harold Hill Grammar Sch.; Shoreditch Com Sch.; Westminster Coll., Oxford (CertEd). Teacher; Asst to Tony Banks, MP, 1990–9 MP (Lab) Romford, 1997–2001. Contested (Lab) Romford, 1992 and 2001. Membe Broadcasting Select Cttee, 1998–2001; Health Select Cttee, 1999–2001.

GORDON, François; *see* Gordon, J. F.

GORDON, Gerald; *see* Gordon, C. G. M.

GORDON, Sir Gerald (Henry), Kt 2000; CBE 1995; QC (Scot.) 1972; LLD; Sheriff Glasgow and Strathkelvin, 1978–99; Temporary Judge of Court of Session and Hig Court of Justiciary, 1992–2004; Member, Scottish Criminal Cases Review Commissio since 1999; *b* 17 June 1929; *er s* of Simon Gordon and Rebecca Gordon (*née* Bulbin Glasgow; *m* 1957, Marjorie Joseph (*d* 1996), *yr d* of Isaac and Aimée Joseph (*née* Strump Glasgow; one *s* two *d*. *Educ:* Queen's Park Senior Secondary Sch., Glasgow; Univ. Glasgow (MA (1st cl. Hons Philosophy with English Literature) 1950; LLB (Distinctio 1953; PhD 1960); LLD Edinburgh 1968. National Service, RASC, 1953–55 (Staff-Sg Army Legal Aid, BAOR, 1955). Admitted Scottish Bar 1953; practice at Scottish Ba 1953, 1956–59; Faulds Fellow, Univ. of Glasgow, 1956–59. Procurator Fiscal Deput Edinburgh, 1960–65. University of Edinburgh: Sen. Lectr, 1965; Personal Prof. Criminal Law, 1969–72; Head of Dept of Criminal Law and Criminology, 1965–72; Pro of Scots Law, 1972–76; Dean of Faculty of Law, 1970–73; Vis. Prof., 2000–03. Sheriff S Strathclyde, Dumfries and Galloway at Hamilton, 1976–77. Commonwealth Vis. Fellov and Vis. Res. Fellow, Centre of Criminology, Univ. of Toronto, 1974–75. Tempora Sheriff, 1973–76. Member: Interdepartmental Cttee on Scottish Criminal Procedur 1970–77; Cttee on Appeals Criteria and Alleged Miscarriages of Justice Procedure 1995–96. Hon. FRSE 2002. Hon. LLD: Glasgow, 1993; Aberdeen, 2003. *Publication* The Criminal Law of Scotland, 1967, 2nd edn 1978; (ed) Renton and Brown's Crimin Procedure, 4th edn 1972, to 6th edn 1996; (ed) Scottish Criminal Case Reports, 1981– various articles. *Recreations:* Jewish studies, coffee conversation, crosswords.

GORDON, Hannah Campbell Grant; actress; *b* 9 April 1941; *d* of William Munr Gordon and Hannah Grant Gordon; *m* 1970, Norman Warwick; one *s*. *Educ:* St Den School for Girls, Edinburgh; Glasgow Univ. (Cert. Dramatic Studies); College Dramatic Art, Glasgow (Dip. in speech and drama). FRSAMD 1980. Hon. DLi Glasgow, 1993. Winner, James Bridie Gold Medal, Royal Coll. of Music and Dramati Art, Glasgow, 1962. *Stage:* Dundee Rep., Glasgow Citizens Theatre, Belgrade Theatr Coventry, Ipswich, Windsor; Can You Hear me at the Back, Piccadilly, 1979; The Killin Game, Apollo, 1980; The Jeweller's Shop, Westminster, 1982; The Country Girl, Apollo 1983; Light Up the Sky, Old Vic, 1985; Mary Stuart, Edinburgh Fest., 1987; Shirle Valentine, Duke of York's, 1989; Hidden Laughter, Vaudeville, 1991; An Ideal Husban Globe, 1992; The Aspern Papers, Wyndham's, 1996; My Fair Lady, Th. Royal, 2003, na tour, 2003–04; *television:* 1st TV appearance, Johnson Over Jordan, 1965; series: Grea Expectations, 1969; Middlemarch, 1969; My Wife Next Door, 1972; Upstair Downstairs, 1976; Telford's Change, 1979; Goodbye Mr Kent, 1983; Gardener Calendar, 1986; My Family and Other Animals, 1987; Joint Account, 1989; Midsome Murders, 1999; One Foot in the Grave (final episode), 2000; presenter, Watercolou Challenge, 1998–2001; *films:* Spring and Port Wine, 1970; The Elephant Man, 197 Made of Honour, 2008; numerous radio plays, recorded books and poetry and musi recitals. *Recreations:* gardening, cooking, walking, sailing. *Address:* c/o Conway Van Gelde Grant Ltd, 18–21 Jermyn Street, SW1Y 6HP.

GORDON, Ian William; Director, Service Policy and Planning, Scottish Executiv Health Department, 2003–06; *b* 27 Dec. 1952; *s* of Brian William Gordon, *qv*; *m* 197 Alison Margaret Bunting; two *s*. *Educ:* Strathallan Sch., Perth; Downing Coll., Cambridg (BA). Joined Civil Service, 1975: Dept of Energy, 1975–81; Scottish Office, 1981–9 Industry, 1981–85; Finance, 1985–86; Educn, 1986–90; Agriculture, 1990–93; Fisherie 1993–99 (Fisheries Sec., 1995–99); Head of Dept, Scotland Office, 1999–2002. Non exec. Dir, Cumbria PCT, 2007–.

GORDON, Isabel; *see* Allende, I.

GORDON, Maj.-Gen. James Charles Mellish, CBE 1992; General Secretary, Force Pension Society (formerly Officers' Pensions Society), 2000–07; Director, FPS Investme Co. Ltd, 2000–07; Managing Trustee, FPS Widows' Fund, 2000–07; *b* 3 Aug. 1941; *s* c Brig. Leonard Henry Gordon and Joyce Evelyn Mary Gordon (*née* Gurdon); *m* 196 Rosemary Stella Kincaid; two *s* one *d*. *Educ:* Tonbridge Sch.; RMA Sandhurs Commissioned RA 1961; served in UK, Germany, Singapore; RMCS, Shrivenha 1972; Staff Coll., Camberley, 1973; MoD, 1974–75; Comdr, D Batt., RHA, UK an BAOR, 1976–78; MA to MGO, MoD, 1978–80; CO 45 Field Regt RA, BAOR 1980–83; Col, ASD1, MoD, 1983–86; CRA 4th Armoured Div., BAOR, 1986–89; Di Mil. Ops, MoD, 1989–91; COS, HQ UKLF, 1991–94. Dir Gen., Assoc. of Trai Operating Cos, 1994–99 (Director: Rail Settlement Plan Ltd; Rail Staff Travel Ltd; Na Rail Enquiry Service). Corporate Fellow, Industry and Parlt Trust, 1998. Mem. Counc Officers' Assoc., 2000–. Trustee: Haig Homes, 2003–; Victory Services Assoc., 2005 (Chm., 2008–). *Recreations:* sailing, music, theatre, travel. *Club:* Army and Navy.

GORDON, Maj. Gen. James Henry, CBE 2006 (MBE 1991); Commander Britis Forces Cyprus and Administrator Sovereign Base Areas, since 2008; *b* London, 4 De 1957; *s* of Graeme and Kirsten Gordon; *m* 1996, Fiona Fairbairn; three *s*. *Educ:* Trinit Coll., Glenalmond; RMA Sandhurst; Staff Coll. CO 2nd Bn, RGJ, 1995–98; Dep. As COS Operational Support PJHQ, 1998–2001; Comdr, British Forces, Falkland Is 2002–03; COS, HQ NI, 2003–05; Dep. Comdr, Multinational Security Transitio Comd, Iraq, 2006; Dir Personal Services (Army), 2006–08. Queen's Body Guard fo Scotland (Royal Co. of Archers), 2001–. *Recreations:* field sports, ski-ing, sailing. *Club* Boodle's.

GORDON, (Jean) François, CMG 1999; CVO 2007; High Commissioner, Uganda 2005–08; *b* 16 April 1953; *s* of late Michael Colin Gordon and of Jeanine Marie Gordo (*née* Parizet); *m* 1977, Elaine Daniel; two *d*. *Educ:* Queen's Coll., Oxford (BA Hon Jurisprudence 1974); Université d'Aix et Marseille (Diplôme d'Etudes Supérieures 1975) Articled clerk, Ingledew Brown, 1975–78; admitted solicitor, 1979; joined HM Diplomatic Service, 1979: EU Dept, FCO, 1979–81; Second, later First Sec., Luanda 1981–83; First Secretary: UK Delegn to UN Conf. on Disarmament, Geneva, 1983–88 UN Dept, FCO, 1988–90; (Political), Nairobi, 1990–92; Africa Dept (Southern), FCO 1992–95; Dep. Hd, Drugs, Internat. Crime and Terrorism Dept, FCO, 1995–96; Hd Drugs and Internat. Crime Dept, FCO, 1996; Ambassador to Algeria, 1996–99; RCDS 2000; Ambassador to Côte d'Ivoire, and (non-resident) to Niger, Liberia and Burkin

Faso, 2001–04. *Recreations:* reading, mostly history and architecture, gardening, watching African wildlife, flying. *Clubs:* Travellers; Muthaiga Country (Nairobi).

GORDON, John Alexander, CB 1995; CEng; FRAeS; Partner, Gordon Consulting, since 1999; *b* 7 Nov. 1940; *s* of John and Eleanor Gordon; *m* 1962, Dyanne Calder; two *d.* *Educ:* RAF Colls, Henlow and Cranwell. CEng, MIMechE; FRAeS 1990. Engr Br., RAF, 1958–70; Ministry of Defence, Procurement Executive, 1970–95: mil. aircraft procurement, Dir Gen. Aircraft 1; projects incl. Harrier, Jaguar, Tornado and Eurofighter; Gen. Manager, NATO Eurofighter and Tornado Mgt Agency, 1996–99; Compliance Officer for Merger Undertakings, BAE Systems, 1999–2007. RAeS British Gold Medal, 1997. *Recreation:* carriage driving.

GORDON, John Keith; environmentalist; *b* 6 July 1940; *s* of late Prof. James Edward Gordon and of Theodora (*née* Sinker); *m* 1965, Elizabeth Shanks; two *s.* *Educ:* Marlborough Coll.; Cambridge Univ. (1st Cl. Hons History). Henry Fellow, Yale Univ., 1962–63; research in Russian history, LSE, 1963–66; entered FCO, 1966; Budapest, 1968–70; seconded to Civil Service Coll., 1970–72; FCO, 1972–73; UK Mission, Geneva, 1973–74; Head of Chancery and Consul, Yaoundé, 1975–77; FCO, 1977–80; Cultural Attaché, Moscow, 1980–81; Office of UK Rep. to European Community, Brussels, 1982–83; UK Perm. Deleg. to UNESCO, Paris, 1983–85; Head of Nuclear Energy Dept, FCO, 1986–88; Imperial College, London: Academic Visitor, Centre for Envmtl Technol., 1988–90; Dep. and Policy Dir, Global Envmt Res. Centre, 1990–94. Special Adviser: UK-UN Envmt and Develt Forum, 2000–04; Airportwatch (Alliance for Sustainable Aviation Policy), 2004–; Mem., UK Nat. Commn for UNESCO, 2004–07. Pres., Council for Educn in World Citizenship, 2004–. Contested (Lib Dem) Daventry, 1997. *Publications:* (with Caroline Fraser) Institutions and Sustainable Development, 1991; (with Tom Bigg) 2020 Vision, 1994; Canadian Round Tables, 1994; reports and articles on envmtl issues. *Recreations:* jogging, sailing, reading. *Address:* Well House, Bow Bridge, Reading Road, Wallingford, Oxon OX10 9HG.

GORDON, Kate; *see* Gordon, V. K.

GORDON, Sir Lionel Eldred Peter S.; *see* Smith-Gordon.

GORDON, Dr Lyndall Felicity, FRSL; writer; Senior Research Fellow, St Hilda's College, Oxford, since 1995; *b* 4 Nov. 1941; *d* of Harry Louis Getz and Rhoda Stella Getz (*née* Press); *m* 1963, Prof. Siamon Gordon, *qv*; two *d.* *Educ:* Univ. of Cape Town (BA Hons); Columbia Univ., NY (PhD 1973). Rhodes Vis. Fellow, St Hilda's Coll., Oxford, 1973–75; Asst Prof., Columbia Univ., NY, 1975–76; Lectr, Jesus Coll., Oxford, 1977–84; Fellow and Tutor, St Hilda's Coll., and CUF Lectr, Oxford Univ., 1984–95. FRSL 2003. *Publications:* Virginia Woolf: a writer's life, 1984, 4th edn 2006; Shared Lives, 1992, 2nd edn 2005; Charlotte Brontë: a passionate life, 1994, 2008; A Private Life of Henry James, 1998; T. S. Eliot: an imperfect life, 1998; Mary Wollstonecraft: a new genus, 2005 (US edn and UK pbk edn as Vindication: a life of Mary Wollstonecraft). *Recreation:* reading. *Address:* St Hilda's College, Oxford OX4 1DY.

GORDON, Prof. Michael John Caldwell, PhD; FRS 1994; Professor of Computer Assisted Reasoning, Computer Laboratory, University of Cambridge, since 1996; *b* 28 Feb. 1948; *m* 1979, Avra Jean Cohn; two *s.* *Educ:* Bedales Sch.; Gonville and Caius Coll., Cambridge (BA Maths); King's Coll., Cambridge (Dip. Linguistics); Edinburgh Univ. (PhD). Research Associate, Stanford Univ., 1974–75; University of Edinburgh: Res. Fellow, 1975–78; SRC Advanced Res. Fellow, 1978–81; University of Cambridge: Lectr, 1981–88; Reader in Formal Methods, 1988–96; Royal Soc./SERC Industrial Fellow, SRI International, 1987–89. *Publications:* The Denotational Description of Programming Languages, 1979; Programming Language Theory and its Implementation, 1988. *Recreation:* mushroom hunting. *Address:* Computer Laboratory, University of Cambridge, William Gates Building, J J Thompson Avenue, Cambridge CB3 0FD. *T:* (01223) 334627, *Fax:* (01223) 334678; *e-mail:* mjcg@cl.cam.ac.uk.

GORDON, Mildred; *b* 24 Aug. 1923; *d* of Dora and Judah Fellerman; *m* 1st, 1948, Sam Gordon (*d* 1982); one *s*; 2nd, 1985, Nils Kaare Dahl. *Educ:* Raines Foundation School; Pitman's College; Forest Teacher Training College. Teacher, 1945–85. Mem. Exec., London Labour Party, 1983–86; Jt Chm., Greater London Labour Policy Cttee, 1985–86. MP (Lab) Bow and Poplar, 1987–97. Mem., Select Cttee on Educn, Science and Arts, 1991–97; Chm., All-Party Parly Child Support Agency Monitoring Group, 1995–97; Vice Chm., PLP Educn Cttee and Social Services Cttee, 1990–92, 1997. Formerly, Advr, GLC Women's Cttee. Member: Bd, Tower Hamlets Business and Educn Partnership; Nat. Council, National Pensioner Convention (Mem. Exec. Cttee, London and SE Branch); EC Barnet 55+; Barnet Older Adults' Partnership Bd; Co-op Party; Gen. Cttee Finchley and Golders Green Labour Party. Patron: Gtr London Pensioners' Assoc. (also Delegate); Dockland Singers; Danesford Trust. Founder, Schs' Public Speaking Competition, Tower Hamlets. Freeman, London Bor. of Tower Hamlets, 1999. *Publications:* essays and articles on education. *Recreations:* pottery, designing and making costume jewellery, painting, writing poetry. *Address:* 28 Cumbrian Gardens, NW2 1EF.

GORDON, Nadia, (Mrs Charles Gordon); *see* Nerina, N.

GORDON, Pamela Joan; Chief Executive, City of Sheffield Metropolitan District, 1989–97; *b* 13 Feb. 1936; *d* of Frederick Edward Bantick and Violet Elizabeth Bantick; *m* 1st, 1959, Wallace Henry Gordon (*d* 1980); two *s*; 2nd, 1997, Peter Charles Hoad. *Educ:* Richmond (Surrey) Grammar School for Girls; St Hilda's Coll., Oxford (MA). Variety of posts with ILEA, GLC and LCC, 1957–81; Greater London Council: Asst Dir Gen., 1981–83; Dep. Dir of Industry and Employment, 1983–85; Chief Exec., London Bor. of Hackney, 1985–89. Member: Adv. Cttee, Constitution Unit, 1995–97; Local Govt Commn for England, 1998–2002; Indep. Panel of Assessors for Public Appts, 1999–2007; Electoral Commn, 2001–07 (Chm., Boundary Cttee for England, 2002–07). Pres., SOLACE, 1996–97. Gov., Sheffield Hallam Univ., 1995–2003. Hon. Fellow, Inst. of Local Govt Studies, Birmingham Univ., 1990. Columnist, Local Government Chronicle. *Publications:* articles on management, etc, in local govt jls. *Recreations:* opera, theatre, foreign travel. *Address:* 37 Monkswood, Gattonside, Melrose TD6 9NS. *T:* (01896) 823852.

GORDON, Richard, (Dr Gordon Ostlere), FRCA; author; *b* 15 Sept. 1921; *m* 1951, Mary Patten; two *s* two *d.* *Educ:* Selwyn Coll., Cambridge; St Bartholomew's Hosp. Med. Sch. Formerly: anaesthetist at St Bartholomew's Hospital, and Nuffield Dept of Anaesthetics, Oxford; assistant editor, British Medical Jl; ship's surgeon. Mem., Punch Table. *Publications:* Anaesthetics for Medical Students; Doctor in the House, and 16 sequels; 32 other novels and non-fiction (adapted for 8 films and 4 plays, radio and TV, and translated into 21 langs); (ed) The Literary Companion to Medicine; TV screenplay, The Good Dr Bodkin Adams; TV series, A Gentlemen's Club; contribs to Punch. *Recreations:* watching cricket and other sports. *Clubs:* Beefsteak, Garrick, MCC.

GORDON, Richard John Francis; QC 1994; a Recorder, since 2000; *b* 26 Nov. 1948; *s* of John Bernard Basil Gordon and Winifred Josephine (*née* Keenan); *m* 1975, Jane Belinda Lucey; two *s.* *Educ:* St Benedict's Sch., Ealing; Christ Church, Oxford (Open Schol.; MA); University Coll. London (LLM). Called to the Bar, Middle Temple, 1972, Bencher, 2003. Sen. Lectr in Admin. Law, KCL, 1991–93. Vis. Prof. of Law, UCL, 1994–. Editor-in-Chief, Administrative Court (formerly Crown Office) Digest, 1989–. Mem., Exec. Cttee, Admin. Law Bar Assoc., 1991–. *Publications:* The Law Relating to Mobile Homes and Caravans, 1978, 2nd edn 1985; Judicial Review: law and procedure, 1985, 2nd edn 1995; Crown Office Proceedings, 1990; Community Care Assessments, 1993, 2nd edn 1996; Human Rights in the United Kingdom, 1996; Judicial Review and Crown Office Practice, 2000; Judicial Review and the Human Rights Act, 2000; The Strasbourg Cases: leading cases from the European Human Rights Reports, 2001; (ed) Judicial Review in the New Millennium, 2003; EC Law in Judicial Review, 2006; contrib. to numerous legal jls on admin. law. *Recreations:* reading, writing. *Address:* Brick Court Chambers, 7–8 Essex Street, WC2R 3LD. *T:* (020) 7379 3550. *Club:* MCC.

GORDON, Robert Anthony Eagleson, CMG 1999; OBE 1983; HM Diplomatic Service, retired; Ambassador to the Socialist Republic of Vietnam, 2003–07; *b* 9 Feb. 1952; *s* of late Major Cyril Vivian Eagleson, MC, RE and of Clara Renata Romana Gordon (*née* Duse); *m* 1978, Pamela Jane Taylor; two *s* two *d.* *Educ:* King's Sch., Canterbury; Magdalen Coll., Oxford (MA Modern Langs). FCO 1973; Second Sec., Warsaw, 1975–77; First Sec., Santiago, 1978–83; FCO, 1983–87; First Sec., UK Deleg. to OECD, Paris, 1987–92; Counsellor and Dep. Head of Mission, Warsaw, 1992–95; Ambassador to Burma (Union of Myanmar), 1995–99; Head, SE Asia Dept, FCO, 1999–2003.

GORDON, (Robert) Douglas; HM Diplomatic Service, retired; Diplomatic Consultant, Royal Garden Hotel, Kensington, 1996–2006; *b* 31 July 1936; *s* of Robert Gordon and Helen (*née* MacTaggart); *m* 1st, 1960, Margaret Bruckshaw (marr. diss. 1990); one *s*; 2nd, 1990, Valerie Janet Brownlee, MVO. *Educ:* Greenock Acad.; Cardiff High Sch. for Boys. FO, 1954. National Service with RM, 1955–57; commnd 2 Lieut Wilts Regt, 1957. FO, 1958; Amman, 1958; MECAS, 1959; Abu Dhabi, 1961; Vienna, 1963; Second Sec. (Commercial), Kuwait, 1966; FCO, 1969; Second, later First Sec., Hd of Chancery and Consul, Doha, 1973; Asst to Dep. Gov., Gibraltar, 1976; FCO, 1979; HM Asst Marshal of the Diplomatic Corps, 1982; First Sec. (Commercial), Washington, 1984; Consul (Commercial), Cleveland, 1986; Ambassador, 1989–90, Consul-General, 1990, Aden; High Comr, Guyana, 1990–93, and Ambassador, Republic of Suriname, 1990–93; Ambassador, Republic of Yemen, 1993–95. Chm., British-Yemeni Soc., 1999–2005 (Hon. Vice Pres., 2005–). Freeman, City of London, 1984. Order of: Gorkha Dakshina Bahu, 5th Cl. (Nepal), 1980; King Abdul Aziz ibn Saud, 4th Cl. (Saudi Arabia), 1982; Officier, l'Ordre Nat. du Mérite (France), 1984. *Recreations:* photography, walking. *Address:* Melbrook, 73 North Road, Tollesbury, Essex CM9 8RQ.

GORDON, Maj. Gen. Robert Duncan Seaton, CMG 2005; CBE 1994; Managing Director, RGC Ltd, since 2006; *b* 23 Nov. 1950; *s* of Col Jack Gordon and Joan Gordon (*née* Seaton); *m* 1979, Virginia Brown, Toronto; two *s.* *Educ:* Wellington Coll.; St Catharine's Coll., Cambridge (MA Modern Hist.). Commnd 17th/21st Lancers, 1970; Staff Coll., 1982; COS, 4th Armoured Bde, 1983–84; MA (Lt-Col) to C-in-C BAOR/COMNORTHAG, 1987–90; CO 17th/21st Lancers, 1990–92; Sec. to Chiefs of Staff Cttee, MoD, 1992–94 (Col); Brig. 1993; HCSC 1994; Comdr, 19th Mechanized Bde, 1994–96; rcds 1996; DPR (Army), 1997–99; Maj.-Gen. 1999; GOC 2nd Div. in York, 1999–2000; GOC 2nd Div. in Edinburgh, and Gov. of Edinburgh Castle, 2000–02; Force Comdr, UN Mission in Ethiopia and Eritrea, 2002–04; retd 2005; Consultant to UN, 2005–07. Col Comdt, RAVC, 2001–07. *Recreations:* history, offshore sailing. *Address:* The Old Manor, Milton Road, Pewsey, Wilts SN9 5JJ. *Club:* Cavalry and Guards.

GORDON, Robert Ian Neilson; Member (C) Hertfordshire County Council, 1989–97 and since 2001 (Leader, since 2007; Deputy Leader, 2006–07; Executive Member for Performance and Resources, since 2006); *b* 29 March 1952; *s* of late Louis George Gordon (formerly Smith) and Patricia Dunella Mackay Gordon (*née* Neilson); *m* 1984, Susan Elizabeth Leigh; three *d.* *Educ:* Watford Grammar Sch.; Univ. of Sussex; Coll. of Law, Guildford and Lancaster Gate; City Univ. Joined Maffey & Brentnall, solicitors, Watford, 1974, as Articled Clerk; admitted Solicitor, 1978; Partner, Brentnall & Cox, subseq. Bryan & Gordon, then Bryan, Furby & Gordon, 1978–92, Consultant, 1992–93. Dir, Soc. of Genealogists, 1998–2001; Mem. Exec. Cttee, Fedn of Family Hist. Socs, 1998–2001; Sec., Soc. of Genealogists Enterprises Ltd, 1999–2001; non-exec. Dir, W Herts Community Health NHS Trust, 1998–2001. Mem. (C), Watford BC, 1982–90, 2002–06 (Leader of Opposition, 1984–86, 1988–90; Chm., Finance and Resources Scrutiny Cttee, 2002–03; Vice-Chm., 2003–04; Chm., 2004–05); Hertfordshire County Council: Dep. Leader, 1991–93; Leader of Opposition, 1993–96; Chm., Educn Cttee, 1992–93; Exec. Mem. for Children, Schs and Families, 2001–04, for Educn, 2004–06. Chairman: Herts Sch. Orgn Cttee, 2001–07; Herts Connexions Consortium Bd, 2002–05; E of England Strategic Authy Leaders, 2008–; Mem., 1995–97, 2001–05, 2007–, Chm., 1995–97, Herts Police Authy; Mem., Herts Learning and Skills Council, 2003–07; Member: Exec. Council, ACC, 1991–93; Gen. Assembly, LGA, 2006–. Mem., Gen. Teaching Council for England, 2006–. Contested (C): Torfaen, 1987; Watford, 1997; Eastern Reg., England, EP, 1999. Chairman: Watford Cons. Assoc., 1990–92, 1995–96; Herts County Cons. Fedn, 1997–; Mem., Cons. Nat. Local Govt Adv. Cttee, 1991–97. Chm., Nat. Employers Orgn for Sch. Teachers, 2003–07. Mem. Court, City Univ., 2001–06; Chm. Govs, Watford GS for Girls, 1998–2001; Clerk to Trustees, Watford Grammar Schs, 2001–. *Publication:* (ed) Posterity's Blessing: the journey of the Watford School of Music to the Clarendon Muse, 2008. *Recreations:* choral music, walking, photography. *Address:* 11 Grange Close, Watford, Herts WD17 4HQ. *T:* (01923) 236124.

GORDON, Sir Robert James, 10th Bt *cr* 1706, of Afton and Earlston, Kirkcudbrightshire; farmer, since 1958; *b* 17 Aug. 1932; *s* of Sir John Charles Gordon, 9th Bt and of Marion, *d* of late James B. Wright; *S* father, 1982; *m* 1976, Helen Julia Weston Perry. *Educ:* Barker College, Sydney; North Sydney Boys' High School; Wagga Agricultural Coll., Wagga Wagga, NSW (Wagga Dip. of Agric., Hons I and Dux). *Recreations:* tennis, ski-ing, swimming. *Heir:* none. *Address:* 126 Earlstoun Road, Guyra, NSW 2365, Australia. *T:* (2) 67791343.

GORDON, Prof. Robert Patterson, PhD, LittD; Regius Professor of Hebrew, Cambridge University, since 1995; Fellow, St Catharine's College, Cambridge, since 1995; *b* 9 Nov. 1945; *s* of Robert Gordon and Eveline (*née* Shilliday); *m* 1970, Helen Ruth Lyttle; two *s* one *d.* *Educ:* Methodist Coll., Belfast; St Catharine's Coll., Cambridge (BA 1st Cl. Hons Oriental Studies 1968; Tyrwhitt Scholarship and Mason Hebrew Prize, 1969; MA 1972; PhD 1973; LittD 2001). Asst Lectr in Hebrew and Semitic Langs, 1969–70, Lectr, 1970–79, Glasgow Univ.; Cambridge University: Lectr in Divinity, 1979–95; Fellow, St Edmund's Coll., 1985–89 (Tutor, 1986–89); Univ. Preacher, 1999. Macbride Sermon, Oxford Univ., 2000; Didsbury Lectures, Manchester, 2001; 11th Annual Biblical Studies Lectures, Samford Univ., Alabama, 2004. Sec., Internat. Orgn for Study of OT, 2001–04; Pres., SOTS, 2003. Review Ed., Vetus Testamentum, 1998–; Ed., Hebrew Bible and its Versions, monograph series, 2001–. *Publications:* 1 and 2 Samuel, 1984

(Chinese edn 2002); 1 and 2 Samuel: a commentary, 1986; (ed jtly) The Targum of the Minor Prophets, 1989; Studies in the Targum to the Twelve Prophets, 1994; (ed jtly) Wisdom in Ancient Israel, 1995; (ed) The Place is too Small for Us: the Israelite prophets in recent scholarship, 1995; (Consulting Ed.) New International Dictionary of Old Testament Theology and Exegesis, 1997; (ed) The Old Testament in Syriac: Chronicles, 1998; Hebrews: a new biblical commentary, 2000, 2nd edn, 2008; Holy Land, Holy City, 2004; (ed jtly) The Old Testament in its World, 2005; Hebrew Bible and Ancient Versions, 2006; (ed) The God of Israel, 2007; contrib. to learned jls incl. Jl Jewish Studies, Jewish Qly Rev., Jl Semitic Studies, Jl for Study of OT, Jl Theol Studies, Revue de Qumran, Vetus Testamentum, and to various composite vols. *Recreations:* jogging, otopianistics, local history (N Ireland). *Address:* 85 Barrons Way, Comberton, Cambridge CB3 7DR. *T:* (01223) 263153; Faculty of Asian and Middle Eastern Studies, Sidgwick Avenue, Cambridge CB3 9DA. *Club:* National.

GORDON, Robert Smith Benzie, CB 2000; Director-General of Justice (formerly Head of Justice Department), since 2004, and Head of Legal and Parliamentary Services, since 2002, Scottish Government (formerly Scottish Executive); *b* 7 Nov. 1950; *s* of William Gladstone Gordon and Helen Watt Gordon (*née* Benzie); *m* 1976, Joyce Ruth Cordiner; two *s* two *d.* *Educ:* Univ. of Aberdeen (MA Hons Italian Studies). Admin. trainee, Scottish Office, 1973–78; Principal, Scottish Develt Dept, 1979–85; Asst Sec., 1984; Principal Private Sec. to Sec. of State for Scotland, 1985–87; Dept of Agriculture and Fisheries for Scotland, 1987–90; Scottish Office, subseq. Scottish Executive: Mgt Orgn and Industrial Relns, 1990–91; Dir of Admin. Services, 1991–97; Under Sec., 1993; Head of Constitution Gp, 1997–98; Dep. Sec., 1998; Hd of Exec. Secretariat, 1999–2001; Hd of Finance and Central Services Dept, 2001–02; Chief Exec., Crown Office and Procurator Fiscal Service, 2002–04. *Address:* Scottish Government, St Andrew's House, Regent Road, Edinburgh EH1 3DG.

GORDON, Rt Rev. Ronald; *see* Gordon, Rt Rev. A. R. McD.

GORDON, Ronald Dingwall; Chairman, John Gordon & Son Ltd, since 2000; Vice Lord-Lieutenant of Nairnshire, since 1999; *b* 13 Nov. 1936; *s* of Ronald James Robertson Gordon and Mary Isabella Cardno Gordon; *m* 1961, Elizabeth Ancell Gordon; two *s* one *d.* *Educ:* Nairn Acad. Nat. Service, RAF, 1955–57. Joined John Gordon & Son, 1957; jt partner with father, 1961; sole trader, 1965–85; Man. Dir, 1985–2000. DL Nairnshire, 1991. *Recreations:* golf, fishing, gardening. *Address:* Achareidh House, Nairn IV12 4UD. *T:* and *Fax:* (01667) 452130; *e-mail:* rdgordon@tiscali.co.uk. *Clubs:* Royal and Ancient Golf, Royal Dornoch Golf, Nairn Golf (Capt., 1980–82; Vice Pres., 2000–05; Pres., 2006–).

GORDON, Prof. Siamon, PhD; FRS 2007; Glaxo-Wellcome Professor of Cellular Pathology, Oxford University, 1991–2008, now Emeritus (Professor of Cellular Pathology, 1989–91); Fellow, Exeter College, Oxford, 1976–2006, now Emeritus Fellow; *b* 29 April 1938; *s* of Jonah and Liebe Gordon; *m* 1963, Lyndall Felicity Getz (*see* L. F. Gordon); two *d.* *Educ:* South African Coll. Sch., Cape Town; Univ. of Cape Town (MB ChB 1961); Rockefeller Univ. (PhD 1971). Res. Asst, Wright-Fleming Inst., St Mary's, London, 1964–65; Rockefeller University, NY: Res. Associate, 1965–71; Asst Prof. of Cellular Immunology, 1971–76; Adjunct Associate Prof., 1976–; Reader in Exptl Pathology, Sir Wm Dunn Sch. of Pathology, Univ. of Oxford, 1976–89, Actg Hd of Dept, 1989–90, 2000–01. University of Oxford: Chairman: Physiol Scis Bd, 1984–86; Search Cttee, E. P. Abraham Bldg, 1999–2003; Member: General Bd, 1989–92; Med. Scis Div., 2000–03. Mem., Lister Scientific Adv. Cttee, 1987–92; Chm., Scientific Adv. Cttee, Inst. of Infection, Immunity and Molecular Medicine, Univ. of Cape Town, 2003–. Special Fellow and Scholar, Leukaemia Soc. of America, 1971–76; Vis. Scientist, Genetics, Oxford Univ., 1974–75. FMedSci 2003. Hon. Mem., Amer. Assoc. of Immunologists, 2004. Hon. DSc Cape Town, 2003. Marie T. Bonazinga Award, Soc. of Leukocyte Biol., 2003. *Publications:* contribs to jls of exptl medicine, immunology, cell biology, AIDS educn in Southern Africa. *Recreations:* reading biography, medical history. *Address:* c/o Sir William Dunn School of Pathology, South Parks Road, Oxford OX1 3RE.

GORDON, (Vera) Kate, (Mrs E. W. Gordon), CB 1999; Chair, Queen Elizabeth Hospital NHS Trust, King's Lynn; *b* 8 Oct. 1944; *d* of late Kenneth Timms and Elsie Timms (*née* Cussans); *m* 1977, Ernest William Gordon; one step *d.* *Educ:* Queen Anne Grammar School, York; St Hilda's College, Oxford (PPE Hons). Economic Asst, NEDO, 1966–70; Ministry of Agriculture, Fisheries and Food, 1970; Asst Private Sec. to Minister of Agric., 1974–75; seconded to European Secretariat of Cabinet Office, 1976–79; Principal Private Sec. to Minister of Agric. 1980–82; Asst Sec. responsible for marketing policy, MAFF, 1982–84; Counsellor, Paris, seconded to HM Diplomatic Service, 1984–88; Asst Sec. and Head of Sugar and Oilseeds Div., MAFF, 1988–89; Under Sec., Arable Crops Gp, MAFF, 1989–90; Minister (Agriculture), Office of the UK Perm. Rep., Brussels, 1990–95; Principal Finance Officer, MAFF, 1995–96; Dep. Sec., Agriculture, Crops and Commodities, later Agriculture and Food Industry, MAFF, 1996–2001; Policy Dir, Health and Safety Exec., 2001–04. Member: Basic Skills Agency, 2004–07; Peddars Way Housing Assoc., 2004–; Rail Passengers' Council, 2005–. Ordre du Mérite Agricole (France), 1988. *Address:* Holly House, 62A London Street, Swaffham, Norfolk PE37 7DJ. *T:* (01760) 723034; 42 The Foreshore, SE8 3AG. *T:* (020) 8691 0823.

GORDON, William John, FCIB; Chief Executive (formerly Managing Director), UK Banking Services, Barclays Bank plc, 1992–98; *b* 24 April 1939; *s* of Sidney Frank Gordon and Grace Louie Gordon; *m* 1963, Patricia Rollason; two *s.* *Educ:* King Edward VI Sch., Fiveways, Birmingham. FCIB 1979. Joined Barclays Bank, 1955: branch and regl appts, 1955–80; Asst Gen. Manager, Barclaycard, 1980–83; Regl Gen. Manager, Central UK, 1983–87; Dir, UK Corporate Services, 1987–90; Gp Personnel Dir, 1990–92; Dir, 1995–98. Chm., Barclays Pension Fund Trustees Ltd, 1996–2005; Ind. Dir, Britannia Bldg Soc., 1999– (Dep. Chm., 2004–). Mem., Herts Bridge Assoc. *Recreations:* bridge, golf, chess, music. *Address:* 9 High Elms, Harpenden AL5 2JU. *Club:* Mid Herts Golf (Wheathampstead).

GORDON BANKS, Matthew Richard William; Senior Advisor, Middle East and South East Asia, Advanced Research Assessment Group, Defence Academy, Ministry of Defence, since 2006; *b* 21 June 1961; *s* of Harry and Audrey Banks; *m* 1992, Jane, *d* of Michael Miller; one *s* one *d.* *Educ:* private; Sheffield City Polytechnic (BA Hons History and Econs); RMA Sandhurst; Donald Harrison Sch. of Business, SE Missouri State Univ., USA (MBA 2001). 1st Bn, 51st Highland Vols, 1979–81; Commnd, The Gordon Highlanders, 1981–83; War Disablement Pension, 1983. Barclays Bank, 1984–88; Private Sec. to Cecil Franks, MP, 1988–89. Dir, and Sen. Advr on ME Affairs, LBJ Ltd, 1989–. Mem., Wirral BC, 1984–90 (Chairman: Schs Cttee, 1985–86; Works Cttee, 1986–87). Contested (C) Manchester Central, 1987; MP (C) Southport, 1992–97; contested (C) same seat, 1997. PPS, DoE, 1996–97. Mem., Select Cttee on Transport, 1992–97; Chm., Anglo-Venezuela Parly Gp, 1993–97; Sec., Anglo-UAE Parly Gp, 1993–97. Advisor: Jt Security Industry Council, 2002–06; Internat. Inst. for Security Services, 2007–March 2009. Hon. Public Affairs Advr, Assoc. of Ophthalmologists, 2008–. Mem. (C) Cotswold DC, 2001–04 (Chm., Overview and Scrutiny Cttee). FRGS 1983. *Recreations:* walking, travel, reading, flying, fishing. *Address:* Gordon Castle, Fochabers, Morayshire IV32 7PQ. *Club:* Caledonian.

GORDON-BROWN, Alexander Douglas, CB 1984; Receiver for the Metropolita Police District, 1980–87; *b* 5 Dec. 1927; *s* of late Captain and Mrs D. S. Gordon-Brown *m* 1959, Mary Hilton; three *s.* *Educ:* Bryanston Sch.; New Coll., Oxford. MA; 1st cl. hon PPE. Entered Home Office, 1951; Sec., Franks Cttee on section 2 of Official Secrets Ac 1911, 1971; Asst Under-Sec. of State, Home Office, 1972–75, 1978–80; Under Sec Cabinet Office, 1975–78. Chm., Home Office Wkg Gp on Costs of Crime, 1988. Mem Nat. Council, 1991–97, Trustee, 1998–2000, Victim Support. *Recreations:* music, walking

GORDON CLARK, (Elizabeth) Jane; Trustee, Victoria and Albert Museum, sinc 2000; Founder/Designer: Davan Wetton Design, since 1977; Ornamenta Ltd, since 1987 *m* 1981, Sam Gordon Clark. *Educ:* Ruskin Sch. of Art, Oxford. Consultant, Fine A Develt plc, 1968–77. Solo exhibition, Hothouse Flowers: The Gallery at Oxo, 2003; Th Orangery, Holland Park, 2006. Chm., Friends of the V&A, 1994–2001. Mem. Bd, V&A Enterprises, 2005–. Mem., British Interior Design Assoc., 2003. *Publications:* Paper Magic 1991; Italian Style, 1999; Wallpaper in Decoration, 2001. *Club:* Chelsea Arts.

GORDON CUMMING, Sir Alexander Penrose, (Sir Alastair), 7th Bt *cr* 1804, o Altyre, Forres; *b* 15 April 1954; *s* of Sir William Gordon Cumming, 6th Bt and of Elisabet Gordon Cumming (*née* Hinde); *S* father, 2002; *m* 1991, Louisa Clifton-Brown; two *s* on *d.* *Educ:* Ludgrove; Harrow. Insurance broker, 1976–95; Penrose Forbes Ltd, 1995–200 R. K. Harrison, 2000–. *Recreations:* all country pursuits. *Heir:* *s* William Gordo Cumming, *b* 4 April 1993. *Address:* Altyre House, Forres, Morayshire IV36 2SH. *T* (01309) 673774, *Fax:* (01309) 672270. *Clubs:* Turf, Pratt's; Shikar.

GORDON-LENNOX, family name of **Duke of Richmond**.

GORDON LENNOX, Maj.-Gen. Bernard Charles, CB 1986; MBE 1968; *b* 19 Sept 1932; *s* of Lt-Gen. Sir George Gordon Lennox and Nancy Brenda Darell; *m* 1958, Sally Rose Warner; three *s.* *Educ:* Eton; Sandhurst. 2nd Lt, Grenadier Guards, 1953; Hon Kong, 1965; HQ Household Div., 1971; Commanding 1st Bn Grenadier Guards, 1974 Army Directing Staff, RAF Staff College, 1976–77; Command, Task Force H, 1978–79 RCDS, 1980; Dep. Commander and Chief of Staff, SE District, 1981–82; GOC Berli (British Sector), 1983–85; Sen. Army Mem., RCDS, 1986–88, retd. Regtl Lt-Co Grenadier Guards, 1989–95. Dir of Regions, Motor Agents Assoc., 1988–89. Chm. Guards' Polo Club, 1992–99. *Recreations:* field sports, cricket, squash, music. *Address:* c/ The Estate Office, Gordon Castle, Fochabers, Morayshire IV32 7PQ. *Clubs:* Army an Navy, MCC.

GORDON-MacLEOD, David Scott; HM Diplomatic Service; Manager, Foreign an Commonwealth Office Global Response Centre, since 2007; *b* 4 May 1948; *s* of Adan Denys Gordon-MacLeod and Margaret Rae Gordon-MacLeod (*née* Miller); *m* 1988 Adrienne Felicia Maria Atkins; two *s* two *d.* *Educ:* St Peter's Coll., Oxford (exhibitioner BA); Carleton Univ., Canada (MA). ODA, 1973–78; Mbabane, 1978–83; Second, late First Sec., Arms Control and Disarmament Dept, FCO, 1983–87; Dep. Hd of Missio Maputo, 1987–91; First Sec., Equatorial Africa Dept, FCO, 1991–92; Hd of Missil Technol., Defence Dept, FCO, 1992–94; Dep. Hd of Mission, Bogotá, 1995–97; Dir, EU and Econ. Affairs, Athens, 1998–2003; High Comr to Papua New Guinea, 2003–07 FRGS 1975. *Recreations:* family, travel, environmental issues, climbing, tennis, writing *Address:* c/o Foreign and Commonwealth Office, King Charles Street, SW1A 2AH.

GORDON-SAKER, Andrew Stephen; Master of the Supreme Court, Supreme Cour Costs Office, since 2003; *b* 4 Oct. 1958; *s* of Vincent Gordon-Saker and Gwendoline (*né* Remmers); *m* 1985, Liza Helen Marle; one *s* one *d.* *Educ:* Stonyhurst Coll.; Univ. of Anglia (LLB). Called to the Bar, Middle Temple, 1981; in practice, SE Circuit 1982–2003. Dep. Taxing Master of Supreme Court, 1994–2003. Mem., Cambridge Lega Aid Area Cttee, 1995–2003. Mem. (C) Camden LBC, 1982–86. Trustee, Jimmy's Nigh Shelter, Cambridge, 2000–03. *Recreations:* gardening, construction. *Address:* Suprem Court Costs Office, Clifford's Inn, Fetter Lane, EC4A 1DQ.

GORDON-SMITH, David Gerard, CMG 1971; Director-General in Legal Service Council of Ministers, European Communities, 1976–87; *b* 6 Oct. 1925; *s* of late Frederi Gordon-Smith, QC, and Elsie Gordon-Smith (*née* Foster); *m* 1952, Angela Kirkpatric Pile; one *d* (and one *s* decd). *Educ:* Rugby Sch.; Trinity Coll., Oxford. Served in RNVR 1944–46. BA (Oxford) 1948; called to the Bar, Inner Temple, 1949; Legal Asst, Coloni Office, 1950; Sen. Legal Asst, 1954; CRO, 1963–65; Asst Legal Adviser, CO, 1965–66 Legal Counsellor, CO, later FCO, 1966–72; Dep. Legal Advr, FCO, 1973–76. *Address* Kingscote, Westcott, Surrey RH4 3NX.

GORDON-SMITH, Prof. Edward Colin, FRCP, FRCPE, FRCPath, FMedSc Professor of Haematology, St George's, University of London (formerly St George' Hospital Medical School, London), 1987–2003, now Emeritus; *b* 26 June 1938; *s* of lat Gordon John Gordon-Smith and Valentine (*née* Waddington); *m* 1968, Moira Phelan; tw *s.* *Educ:* Oakham Sch.; Epsom Coll.; Exeter Coll., Oxford (MA, BSc, BM BCh) Westminster Med. Sch., London (MSc). FRCP 1978; FRCPath 1987; FRCPE 1999 House Officer, Westminster Hosp., 1964; Sen. House Officer, Nuffield Dept of Medicine Radcliffe Infirmary, Oxford, 1966; Lectr in Neurology, Churchill Hosp., Oxford 1966–67; Registrar in Haematology, Hammersmith Hosp., 1968–69; MRC Clinical Trn Fellow, RPMS Metabolic Unit, Oxford, 1970–71; Sen. Lectr 1972–83, Reader 1983–86 RPMS. Editor, Brit. Jl of Haematology, 1983–86. President: European Bone Marrow Transplant Gp, 1980; Internat. Soc. Explt Haematology, 1990–92; British Soc. fo Haematology, 1995; Vice-Pres., RCPath, 1996–99. Founder FMedSci 1998. Order o Prasidda Prabala Gorkha-Dakshin Bahu (2nd class), Nepal, 1984. *Publications:* papers o aplastic anaemia, bone marrow transplantation, inherited bone marrow disorders, cultur of human bone marrow and drug induced blood disorders. *Recreations:* golf, music gardening, arguing with the wireless. *Address:* 35 Park Road, Chiswick, W4 3EY. *T:* (020 8994 2112, *Fax:* (020) 8995 6631. *Club:* Royal Society of Medicine.

GORE; *see* Ormsby Gore.

GORE, family name of **Earl of Arran**.

GORE, Albert Arnold, Jr; Chairman, INdTV, since 2004; Founding Partner an Chairman, Generation Investment Management, since 2004; *b* 31 March 1948; *s* of lat Albert and Pauline Gore; *m* 1970, Mary Elizabeth, (Tipper), Aitcheson; one *s* three *d* *Educ:* Harvard and Vanderbilt Univs. Served US Army in Vietnam, 1969–71. Reporte and editorial writer, The Tennessean, 1971–76; livestock farmer, 1971–. Democrat Mem., US House of Representatives, 1977–85; Mem. for Tennessee, US Senate 1985–92; Chm., US Senate Delegn to Earth Summit, Rio de Janeiro, 1992; Vice-President of USA, 1993–2001; Presidential cand., US elections, 2000. Dir, Apple, 2003– Sen. Advr, Google, 2001–. Visiting Professor: Fisk Univ., 2001–; Middle Tenn Stat Univ., 2001–; UCLA, 2001–. (Jtly) Nobel Peace Prize, 2007. *Publications:* Earth in th

Balance: ecology and the human spirit, 1992; (with Tipper Gore): Joined at the Heart: the transformation of the American family, 2002; The Spirit of Family (photographs), 2002; An Inconvenient Truth: the crisis of global warming, 2007; The Assault on Reason, 2007. *Address:* 2100 West End Avenue, Nashville, TN 37205, USA.

GORE, Allan Peter; QC 2003; a Recorder, since 2000; *b* 25 Aug. 1951; *s* of Gerry and Hansi Gore; *m* 1981 (marr. diss.); three *d*; partner, Alison Taylor. *Educ:* Trinity Hall, Cambridge (MA 1973; LLB 1st class 1974). Called to the Bar, Middle Temple, 1977; in practice, specialising in personal injury (particularly asbestos and other industrial disease), clinical negligence and related legal negligence litigation. *Publications:* contributions to: Personal Injury Pleadings, ed by Patrick Curran, 2001; Personal Injury Handbook, 2001; Butterworths Personal Injury Litigation Service; Butterworths Civil Court Precedents. *Recreations:* travel, sport, music, cooking. *Address:* 12 King's Bench Walk, Temple, EC4Y 7EL. *T:* (020) 7583 0811, *Fax:* (020) 7583 7228; *e-mail:* gore@12kbw.co.uk.

GORE, (Francis) St John (Corbet), CBE 1986; FSA; *b* 8 April 1921; *s* of late Francis Gore and Kirsteen Corbet-Singleton; *m* 1st, 1951, Priscilla (marr. diss. 1975), *d* of Cecil Harmsworth King; one *s* one *d*; 2nd, 1981, Lady Mary Strachey (*d* 2000), *d* of 3rd Earl of Selborne, PC, CH. *Educ:* Wellington; Courtauld Inst. of Art. Served War, 1940–45, Captain, Royal Northumberland Fusiliers. Employed Sotheby's, 1950–55; National Trust: Adviser on pictures, 1956–86, Hon. Advr, 1986–; Historic Buildings Sec., 1973–81. Mem., Exec. Cttee, Nat. Art Collections Fund, 1964–97; Trustee: Wallace Collection, 1975–89; National Gall., 1986–94. *Publications:* Catalogue, Worcester Art Museum, Mass (British Pictures), 1974; various exhibn catalogues, incl. RA; contribs to Apollo, Country Life, etc. *Recreation:* sight-seeing. *Address:* Flat 5, 42 Sutherland Street, SW1V 4JZ. *Clubs:* Brooks's, Beefsteak.

See also Baron O'Hagan.

GORE, Frederick John Pym, CBE 1987; RA 1972 (ARA 1964); painter; Head of Painting Department, St Martin's School of Art, WC2, 1951–79, and Vice-Principal, 1961–79; *b* 8 Nov. 1913; *s* of Spencer Frederick Gore and Mary Johanna Kerr. *Educ:* Lancing Coll.; Trinity Coll., Oxford; studied art at Ruskin, Westminster and Slade Schs. Taught at: Westminster Sch. of Art, 1937; Chelsea and Epsom, 1947; St Martin's, 1946–79. Chm., RA exhibitions cttee, 1976–87. Trustee, Imperial War Mus., 1967–84 (Chm., Artistic Records Cttee, 1972–1986). *One-man exhibitions:* Gall. Borghèse, Paris, 1938; Redfern Gall., 1937, 1949, 1950, 1953, 1956, 1962; Mayor Gall., 1958, 1960; Juster Gall., NY, 1963; RA (retrospective), 1989. *Paintings in public collections include:* Contemporary Art Soc., Leicester County Council, GLC, Southampton, Plymouth, Rutherston Collection and New Brunswick. Served War of 1939–45: Mx Regt and RA (SO Camouflage). *Publications:* Abstract Art, 1956; Painting, Some Basic Principles, 1965; Piero della Francesca's 'The Baptism', 1969. *Recreation:* Russian folk dancing. *Address:* Flat 3, 35 Elm Park Gardens, SW10 9QF. *T:* (020) 7352 4940.

GORE, Prof. Martin Eric, PhD; FRCP; Consultant Cancer Physician, since 1989, and Medical Director, since 2006, Royal Marsden Hospital; Professor of Cancer Medicine, Institute of Cancer Research, London, since 2002; *b* 18 Feb. 1951; *s* of Bernard and Alexandra Gore; *m* 1979, Pauline Wren; three *s* one *d*. *Educ:* Summerfields, Oxford; Bradfield Coll., Berks; St Bartholomew's Med. Coll. (MB BS 1974; PhD 1985). FRCP 1994. Hon. Sen. Lectr, Inst. Cancer Res., London, 1998–2002. Chair, Gene Therapy Adv. Cttee, DoH, 2006–; Vice-Chair, Scientific Adv. Cttee on Genetically Modified Organisms, HSE, 2004–. *Publications:* joint editor: Biology of Gynaecological Cancer, 1995; Immunotherapy in Cancer, 1996; The Effective Management of Ovarian Cancer, 1999, 3rd edn 2004; Melanoma: critical debates, 2002; Cancer in Primary Care, 2003; Gynecologic Cancer: controversies in management, 2004; contrib. numerous articles on cancer. *Recreations:* walking with Barney (the dog), agonising over Fulham FC. *Address:* Royal Marsden Hospital, Fulham Road, SW3 6JJ. *T:* (020) 7808 2198, *Fax:* (020) 7808 2475; *e-mail:* martin.gore@rmh.nhs.uk.

GORE, Michael Edward John, CVO 1994; CBE 1991; HM Diplomatic Service, retired; Governor, Cayman Islands, 1992–95; *b* 20 Sept. 1935; *s* of late John Gore and Elsa Gore (*née* Dillon); *m* 1957, Monica Shellish; three *d*. *Educ:* Xaverian College, Brighton. Reporter, Portsmouth Evening News, 1952–55; Captain, Army Gen. List, 1955–59; Air Ministry, Dep. Comd. Inf. Officer, Cyprus and Aden, 1959–63; CRO, later FCO, 1963; served Jesselton, 1963–66, FCO, 1966–67, Seoul, 1967–71, Montevideo, 1971–74; First Sec., Banjul, 1974–78; FCO, 1978–81; Nairobi, 1981–84; Dep. High Comr, Lilongwe, 1984–87; Ambassador to Liberia, 1988–90; High Comr to the Bahamas, 1991–92. Mem., UK Dependent, then UK Overseas, Territories Conservation Forum, 1996–; Chm., Wider Caribbean Working Gp, 1997–2006. Member: Nature Photographers Portfolio, 1979– (Pres., 2001–); Zool Photographic Club, 1992–. Hon. Vice Pres., Birdlife Cyprus, 2003–. FRPS. *Publications:* The Birds of Korea (with Pyong-Oh Won), 1971; Las Aves del Uruguay (with A. R. M. Gepp), 1978; Birds of the Gambia, 1981, 2nd edn 1991; On Safari in Kenya: a pictorial guide to the national parks and reserves, 1984, 2nd edn, 2007; papers on birds and conservation; wild-life photographs in books and magazines. *Recreations:* ornithology, wildlife photography, fishing. *Address:* 5 St Mary's Close, Fetcham, Surrey KT22 9HE; *web:* www.wildlife-photography.net.

GORE, Sir Nigel (Hugh St George), 14th Bt *cr* 1621 (Ire.), of Magherabegg, Co. Donegal; grazier and farmer, since 1945; *b* 23 Dec. 1922; *yr s* of St George Richard Gore (*d* 1952, *great nephew* of Sir St George Ralph Gore, 9th Bt), and Loo Loo Ruth (*d* 1961), *d* of E. P. Amesbury; *S* nephew, 1993; *m* 1952, Beth Allison (*d* 1976), *d* of R. W. Hooper; one *d*. *Educ:* Church of England Grammar Sch., Brisbane; Gatton Agricl Coll. Served Army, 1940–45. *Heir: cousin* Hugh Frederick Corbet Gore [*b* 31 Dec. 1934; *m* 1963, Jennifer Mary Copp; one *s* two *d*]. *Clubs:* Toowoomba Range Probus, Returned Soldiers League (Toowoomba).

GORE, Paul Annesley, CMG 1964; CVO 1961; *b* 28 Feb. 1921; *o s* of late Charles Henry Gore, OBE and Hon. Violet Kathleen (*née* Annesley); *m* 1946, Gillian Mary, *d* of T. E. Allen-Stevens; two *s* (and one *s* decd). *Educ:* Winchester Coll.; Christ Church, Oxford. Military Service, 1941–46: 16/5 Lancers. Colonial Service, 1948–65; Dep. Governor, The Gambia, 1962–65. *Address:* 16 Brookside, Watlington, Oxon OX49 5AQ.

GORE, St John; *see* Gore, F. St J. C.

GORE, Prof. Van Jonathan; Vice-Chancellor, Southampton Solent University, since 2007; *b* Birmingham; *s* of John and Daisy Gore; *m* Jill Helen; two *d*. *Educ:* Univ. of Sheffield (BA Hons Hist. and Politics; MA Modern British Politics). Sheffield Polytechnic, subseq. Sheffield Hallam University, 1972–2001: Prof. of Quality Mgt; Hd of Communication Studies; Special Policy Advr to Vice-Chancellor; Sen. Vice-Principal, Southampton Inst., 2001–05; Dep. Vice-Chancellor, Southampton Solent Univ., 2005–07. *Recreations:* music, books, gardening, table tennis. *Address:* Southampton Solent University, East Park Terrace, Southampton SO14 0YN. *T:* (023) 8031 9216.

GORE-BOOTH, Sir Josslyn (Henry Robert), 9th Bt *cr* 1760 (Ire.), of Artarman, Sligo; *b* 5 Oct. 1950; *o s* of Sir Angus Gore-Booth, 8th Bt and Hon. Rosemary Myra Vane, *o d* of 10th Baron Barnard, CMG, OBE, MC, TD; *S* father, 1996; *m* 1980, Jane Mary, *o d* of Rt Hon. Sir Roualeyn Hovell-Thurlow-Cumming-Bruce; two *d*. *Educ:* Eton Coll.; Balliol Coll., Oxford (BA); Insead (MBA). Dir, Kiln Cotesworth Corporate Capital Fund plc, 1993–97. Chm., Herriot Hospice Homecare, 2007–. Patron, living of Sacred Trinity, Salford. *Recreations:* cooking, shooting. *Heir: cousin* (Paul Wyatt) Julian Gore-Booth [*b* 29 July 1968; *m* 1999, Amanda Marie McConnell; one *s* one *d*]. *Address:* Home Farm, Hartforth, Gilling West, Richmond, N Yorkshire DL10 5JS.

GORE-LANGTON; *see* Temple-Gore-Langton, family name of Earl Temple of Stowe.

GORE-RANDALL, Philip Allan, FCA; Chief Operating Officer and Director, HBOS plc and Bank of Scotland plc, since 2007; *b* 16 Dec. 1952; *s* of late Alec Albert Gore-Randall and of Joyce Margaret Gore-Randall; *m* 1984, Prof. Alison Elizabeth While; two *s*. *Educ:* Merchant Taylors' Sch., Northwood; University Coll., Oxford (MA 1975). FCA 1978. Arthur Andersen, subseq. Andersen, 1975–2002: Partner, 1986–2002; UK Man. Partner, Assurance and Business Advisory, 1995–97, Man. Partner, Assurance and Business Advisory, Europe, Africa, Middle East and India, 1996–97; UK Managing Partner, 1997–2001; Man. Partner, Global Ops, 2001–02; Chm. and CEO, Aon Risk Services, 2004–05; Dir, Aon Ltd, 2004–07; Chief Operating Officer, Aon UK, 2006–07. Non-exec. Dir, Compass Mgt Consulting Gp Hldgs Ltd, 2007–. *Recreations:* classical music/opera, good food, travel. *Address:* (office) The Mound, Edinburgh EH1 1YZ. *Club:* Vincent's (Oxford).

See also A. J. Randall.

GORELL, 5th Baron *cr* 1909, of Brampton, co. Derby; **John Picton Gorell Barnes;** Managing Director, Barnes Noble Edwards, chartered surveyors, Kettering, since 1993; Director of Property, Bee Bee Developments Ltd, since 2007; *b* 29 July 1959; *s* of Hon. Ronald Alexander Henry Barnes, *yr s* of 3rd Baron, and Gillian Picton Barnes; *S* uncle, 2007; *m* 1989, Rosanne Duncan; one *s* one *d*. *Educ:* Mount House Sch., Tavistock; N Staffordshire Poly. (BSc Est. Mgt 1983). Assoc. Dir, Lambert Smith Hampton, 1984–89. *Recreations:* sailing, gun dog training, Stoke City FC. *Heir: s* Hon. Oliver Gorell Barnes, *b* 4 April 1993.

GORHAM, Ven. Karen Marisa; Archdeacon of Buckingham, since 2007; *b* 24 June 1964. *Educ:* Mayflower Sch., Billericay; Trinity Coll., Bristol (BA 1995). Administrator: BTEC, 1982–86; RSA, 1986–88; ordained deacon, 1995, priest, 1996; Asst Curate, All Saints, Northallerton with Kirby Sigston, 1995–99; Priest-in-charge, St Paul's, Maidstone, 1999–2007; Area Dean, Maidstone, 2003–07; Asst Dir of Ordinands, Dio. of Canterbury, 2002–07. Hon. Canon, Canterbury Cathedral, 2006–07. Mem., Gen. Synod of C of E, 2003–07. *Recreations:* walking, travel, reading, theatre. *Address:* The Rectory, Stone, Aylesbury HP17 8RZ. *T:* (01865) 208264, *Fax:* (01296) 747424.

GORHAM, Martin Edwin, OBE 2005; Director: Gorham Partnership Ltd, since 2007; Douglas-Gorham Partnership Ltd, since 2008; *b* 18 June 1947; *s* of Clifford Edwin Gorham and Florence Ada Gorham; *m* 1st, 1968, Jean McNaughton Kerr (marr. diss. 1998); 2nd, 1998, Sally Ann Stevens (*née* Fletcher); one step *d*. *Educ:* Buckhurst Hill County High Sch.; Queen Mary Coll., Univ. of London (BA Hons History 1968). MHSM, DipHSM 1973. NHS Mgt Trainee, 1968; Deputy Hospital Secretary: Scarborough Gen. Hosp., 1970–72; Doncaster Royal Infirmary, 1972–75; Hosp. Manager, Northern Gen. Hosp., Sheffield, 1975–83; Dep. Dist Gen. Manager, Newcastle HA, 1983–86; Gen. Manager, Norfolk and Norwich Hosp., 1986–90; Dep. Regl Gen. Manager, SW Thames RHA, 1990–92; Chief Exec., London Ambulance Service, 1992–96; Dir of Projects, S Thames Regl Office, NHS Exec., DoH, 1996–98; Chief Executive: Nat. Blood Authy, 1998–2005; NHS Blood and Transplant, 2005–07. Pres., European Blood Alliance, 2001–07. Trustee, Princess Royal Trust for Carers, 2001–06. *Recreations:* travel, music, books, art, ski-ing, food and wine, gardening. *Address:* 20 Grange Road, Bishop's Stortford, Herts CM23 5NQ. *T:* (01279) 501876. *Clubs:* Commonwealth Trust, Royal Society of Medicine.

GORHAM, Robin Stuart; HM Diplomatic Service, retired; Lecturer, Diplomatic Academy of London, Westminster University; Consultant, Commonwealth Secretariat; *b* 15 Feb. 1939; *s* of Stuart Gorham and Dorothy Gorham (*née* Stevens); *m* 1st, 1966, Barbara Fechner (marr. diss. 1991); three *d*; 2nd, 1992, Joanna Bradbury (marr. diss. 2004). *Educ:* Sutton Manor High Sch.; Oriel Coll., Oxford (MA). CRO, 1961–62; Ottawa, 1962–64; Centre for Econ. Studies, 1964–65; Bonn, 1965–66; Central European Dept, FCO, 1967–69; First Secretary: (External Affairs and Defence) and Dep. Hd of Chancery, Tokyo, 1970–74; (Commercial and Develt), Accra, 1974–77; ME Dept, FCO, 1977–79; Hd of Chancery, Helsinki, 1980–83; Counsellor and Dep. High Comr, Lusaka, 1983–86; rcds, 1987; Hd, W Indian and Atlantic Dept, FCO, 1988–91; Dep. Hd of Mission, Lagos, 1991–94; Head of Protocol Dept and Asst Marshal of Diplomatic Corps, FCO, 1994–98. *Recreations:* fox-hunting, tall ship sailing, Himalayan trekking. *Address:* The Arch, Thornham Hall Stables, Thornham Magna, Eye, Suffolk IP23 8HA. *T:* (01379) 783938; L'Oreneta, Barri d'Amunt, 66150 Corsavy, France. *T:* (4) 68834094.

GORING, Sir William (Burton Nigel), 13th Bt *cr* 1627; Member of London Stock Exchange since 1963; *b* 21 June 1933; *s* of Major Frederick Yelverton Goring (*d* 1938) (6th *s* of 11th Bt) and Freda Margaret (*d* 1993), *o d* of N. V. Ainsworth; *S* uncle, Sir Forster Gurney Goring, 12th Bt, 1956; *m* 1st, 1960, Hon. Caroline Thellusson (marr. diss. 1993), *d* of 8th Baron Rendlesham and of Mrs Patrick Barthropp; 2nd, 1993, Mrs Judith Rachel Walton Morison (*d* 1995), *d* of Rev. R. J. W. Morris, OBE; 3rd, 1998, Mrs Stephanie Bullock, *d* of George Carter, DFC. *Educ:* Wellington; RMA Sandhurst. Lieut, The Royal Sussex Regt. Master, Co. of Woolmen, 2000–01. *Recreation:* bridge. *Heir: kinsman* Richard Harry Goring [*b* 10 Sept. 1949; *m* 1972, Penelope Ann, *d* of J. K. Broadbent; three *s* three *d*]. *Address:* c/o Citigroup Quilter, St Helen's, 1 Undershaft, EC3A 8BB. *Club:* Hurlingham.

GORMALLY, Michael Anthony Peter Thomas; Headmaster, The Cardinal Vaughan Memorial School, Kensington, since 1997; *b* 30 Jan. 1956; *s* of Charles Gormally and Frances Edna Gormally. *Educ:* Inst. of Education, Univ. of London (BA Hons French). ACP 1986. Cardinal Vaughan Memorial School, 1981–: Asst Master, 1981–84; Hd, Modern Langs, 1984–90; Sen. Master, 1990–95; Dep. Headmaster, 1995–97. FRSA 1998. *Recreations:* reading, playing the piano, cooking. *Address:* Cardinal Vaughan Memorial School, 89 Addison Road, W14 8BZ. *T:* (020) 7603 8478.

GORMAN, Christopher Nicoll; Partner, Linklaters & Paines, Solicitors, 1972–97 (Managing Partner, 1991–95); *b* 29 Aug. 1939; *s* of late James Gorman and Louise Barbara (*née* Rackham); *m* 1967, Anne Beech (*d* 1996); one *s* one *d*. *Educ:* Royal Liberty Sch., Romford; St Catharine's Coll., Cambridge (MA, LLM). Admitted Solicitor, 1965. *Publications:* (ed) Nelson's Tables of Company Procedure, 6th edn 1975 to 8th edn 1983; (ed) Westby Nunn's Company Secretarial Handbook, 7th edn 1977 to 11th edn 1992. *Recreations:* books and bookshops, outdoor activity, unfinished business. *Address:* 4

Windhill, Bishop's Stortford, Herts CM23 2NG. *T:* (01279) 656028. *Clubs:* Athenæum, Royal Automobile.

GORMAN, Sir John Reginald, Kt 1998; CVO 1961; CBE 1974 (MBE 1959); MC 1944; DL; Member (UU) Down North, 1998–2003, and Deputy Speaker, 1999–2002, Northern Ireland Assembly; *b* 1 Feb. 1923; *s* of Major J. K. Gorman, MC; *m* 1948, Heather, *d* of George Caruth, solicitor, Ballymena; two *s* two *d*. *Educ:* Rockport, Haileybury and ISC; Portora; Glasgow Univ.; Harvard Business Sch. FCIT, FIPM; MIH. Irish Guards, 1941–46, Normandy, France, Belgium, Holland, Germany (Captain, 1944–46). Royal Ulster Constabulary, 1946–60; Chief of Security, BOAC, 1960–63 (incl. Royal Tour of India, 1961); Personnel Dir and Mem. Bd of Management, BOAC, 1964–69; British Airways: Regional Man., Canada, 1969–75; Regional Man., India, Bangladesh, Sri Lanka, 1975–79; Vice-Chm. and Chief Exec., NI Housing Exec., 1979–85; Dir, Inst. of Dirs, NI, 1986–95. Dir, NI Airports Bd, 1985–92. Pres., British Canadian Trade Assoc., 1972–74; Vice-Chm., Federated Appeal of Montreal, 1973–74. Chm., Bd of Airline Representatives, India, 1977–79; Chm., Inst. of Housing (NI), 1984. Chm., NI Forum for Political Dialogue, 1996–98. DL, 1982, High Sheriff, 1987–88, Co. Down. Kt Hospitaller, SMO of St John of Malta, NI, 1997. Chevalier, Légion d'Honneur, 2005. *Publication:* The Times of My Life: an autobiography, 2002. *Recreations:* gardening, bee keeping, country pursuits. *Address:* 10 Strangford Avenue, Killyleagh, Co. Down BT30 9UJ. *T:* (028) 4482 8400. *Clubs:* Cavalry and Guards; Ulster Reform (Belfast).

GORMAN, Prof. Neil Thomson, PhD; FRCVS; DL; Vice-Chancellor, Nottingham Trent University, since 2003; *b* 10 Sept. 1950; *s* of George Stewart Gorman and Madge Isobella Gorman; *m* 1975, Susan Mary (*née* Smith); one *s* one *d*. *Educ:* Univ. of Liverpool (BVSc 1974); Wolfson Coll., Cambridge (PhD 1977; Hon. Fellow, 2006). MRCVS 1974, FRCVS 1980. Asst Prof., Univ. of Florida, 1980–84; Lectr in Clinical Vet. Medicine, Univ. of Cambridge, 1984–87; Prof. of Vet. Surgery, Univ. of Glasgow, 1987–93; Hd of Res., Waltham, 1993–97; Vice-Pres., Masterfoods Europe, 1997–2002. President: British Small Animal Vet. Assoc., 1992–93; RCVS, 1997–98. Diplomate: American Coll. of Vet. Internal Medicine, 1988; Eur. Coll. of Vet. Internal Medicine, 2005. DL Notts, 2007. Hon. DVMS Glasgow, 2004; Hon. DVSc Liverpool, 2006. *Publications:* Advances in Veterinary Immunology, vol. 1 1983, vol. 2 1985; Contemporary Issues in Small Animal Medicine, 1986; Clinical Veterinary Immunology, 1988, 2nd edn 1990; Basic and Applied Chemotherapy, 1992; Canine Medicine and Therapeutics, 1998; 150 scientific articles. *Recreations:* sport, golf, opera, ballet. *Address:* Nottingham Trent University, Burton Street, Nottingham NG1 4BU. *T:* (0115) 848 6561, *Fax:* (0115) 848 6158; *e-mail:* neil.gorman@ntu.ac.uk.

GORMAN, Teresa Ellen; *b* Sept. 1931; *m*. *Educ:* Fulham Co. Sch.; London Univ. (BSc 1st cl. Hons). Founder and manager of own company. Mem., Westminster City Council, 1982–86. MP (C) Billericay, 1987–2001. Contested (Ind.) Streatham, Oct. 1974. Founder and Chairman: Alliance of Small Firms & Self Employed People Ltd, 1974; Amarant Trust, 1986. Mem., Cons. Women's Nat. Cttee, 1983. *Publications:* The Bastards: dirty tricks and the challenge to Europe, 1993; The Amarant Book of HRT, 1989; No, Prime Minister!, 2001; research papers for IEA, Adam Smith Inst., CPS.

GORMANSTON, 17th Viscount *cr* 1478; **Jenico Nicholas Dudley Preston;** Baron Gormanston (Ire.), 1365; Baron Gormanston (UK), 1868; Premier Viscount of Ireland; *b* 19 Nov. 1939; *s* of 16th Viscount and Pamela (who *m* 2nd, 1943, M. B. O'Connor, Irish Guards; he *d* 1961, she *d* 1975), *o d* of late Capt. Dudley Hanly, and Lady Marjorie Heath (by her 1st marriage); *S* father, who was officially presumed killed in action, France, 9 June 1940; *m* 1st, 1974, Eva Antoine Landzianowska (*d* 1984); two *s*; 2nd, 1997, Lucy Arabella, former wife of David Grenfell and *d* of Edward Fox, *qv* and of Tracy Reed. *Educ:* Downside. *Heir: s* Hon. Jenico Francis Tara Preston, *b* 30 April 1974. *Address:* 27A Ifield Road, SW10 9AZ.

GORMLEY, Antony Mark David, OBE 1998; RA 2003; sculptor; *b* London, 30 Aug. 1950; *s* of Arthur John Constantine Gormley and Elspeth Gormley (*née* Brauninger); *m* 1980, Vicken Parsons; two *s* one *d*. *Educ:* Trinity Coll., Cambridge (BA Hist. of Art; Hon. Fellow 2003); Central Sch. of Art, London; Goldsmiths' Sch. of Art, London (BA Fine Art; Hon. Fellow, Goldsmiths Coll., 1998); Slade Sch. of Fine Art (Boise travelling scholar, 1979). Mem., Arts Council England (formerly Arts Council of England), 1998–. Trustee: Baltic Centre for Contemp. Art, 2004–07; British Mus., 2007–. Numerous *solo exhibitions* in Europe, America, Japan and Australia, 1980–, including: Whitechapel Art Gall., 1981; Louisiana Mus. of Modern Art, Denmark, 1989; American Field, US touring exhibn, 1991; Recent Iron Works, LA, 1992; Tate Gall., Liverpool, 1993; European Field, touring exhibn, 1993–95; Irish Mus. of Modern Art, Dublin, 1994; Lost Subject, White Cube, London, 1994; Escultura, Portugal, 1994; Field for the British Isles, GB tour, 1994–95, Hayward Gall., 1996, Gt Court Gall., BM, 2002 and Yorks Sculpture Park, 2005; Kohji Ogura Gall., Nagoya, 1995; Drawings, San Antonio, USA, 1995; Critical Mass, Vienna, 1995, RA, 1998; New Work, Sarajevo, 1996; Inside the Inside, Brussels, 1996; Arts 04, St Remy de Provence, France, 1996; Still Moving, retrospective tour, Japan, 1996–97; Drawings 1990–94, Ind. Art Space, London, 1996; Cuxhaven, and Total Strangers, Cologne, 1997; Neue Skulpturen, Cologne, 1998; Critical Mass, RA, 1998; Insiders, Brussels, 1999; Intimate Relations, Ontario and Cologne, 1999; European Field, Malmö, 1999; Quantum Clouds, Paris, 2000; Asian Field, China tour, 2003, ICA Singapore, Sydney Biennial, 2006; Baltic Centre, Gateshead, 2003; Clearing, White Cube, London, 2004; Display, Tate Britain, 2004; New Works, Sean Kelly Gall., NY, 2005; Another Place, Crosby Beach, Merseyside, 2005; Certain Made Places, Tokyo, 2005; Inside Australia, Melbourne, 2005; Altered States, Naples, 2006; Breathing Room, Paris, 2006; Blind Light, Hayward Gallery, Sean Kelly Gall., NY, 2007; Bodies in Space, Berlin, 2007; Feeling Material, Berlin, 2007; Ataxia, Melbourne, 2007; Firmament, White Cube, London, 2008; *group exhibitions* include: British Sculpture in the 20th Century, Whitechapel Art Gall., 1981; Biennale de Venezia, Venice, 1982 and 1986; An Internat. Survey of Recent Painting and Sculpture, Mus. of Modern Art, NY, 1984; Documenta 8, Kassel, 1987; Avant-garde in the Eighties, LA Co. Mus. of Art, 1987; Starlit Waters, Tate Gall., Liverpool, 1988; GB–USSR, Kiev, Moscow, 1990; British Art Now, touring Japan, 1990; Arte Amazonas, Rio de Janeiro, 1992, Berlin, 1993, Dresden, 1993, Aachen, 1993; From Beyond the Pale, Irish Mus. of Modern Art, Dublin, 1994; Un Siècle de Sculpture anglaise, Jeu de Paume, Paris, 1996; Malmö, Sweden, 1996; Sydney, Lisbon and Knislinge, Sweden, 1998; Presence, Liverpool, 1999; Trialogo, Rome, 2000; Tate Liverpool, 2004; Millennium Galls, Sheffield, 2005; Figure/Sculpture, Vienna, 2005; Henry Moore - Epoch und Echo, Künzelsau, Germany, 2005; Zero Degrees, Sadler's Wells, 2005; Space: Now & Then, Fundament Foundn, Tilburg, 2005; To the Human Future, Mito Contemporary Art Center, Japan, 2006; Asian Field, Sydney Biennale, 2006; 60 Years of Sculpture, Arts Council Collection, Yorks Sculpture Park, 2006; Turner Prize: a retrospective, Tate Britain, 2007; Reflection, Pinchuk Art Centre, Kiev, 2007; Fourth Plinth Proposals, Nat. Gall., 2008; work in private and public collections worldwide, including: Tate Gall., London; Scottish Gall. of Modern Art, Edinburgh; Jesus Coll., Cambridge; Art Gall. of NSW, Sydney; Louisiana Mus., Denmark; Israel Mus., Jerusalem; Sapporo Sculpture Park, Hokkaido, Japan; Mus. of Contemporary Art, LA; sculpture in public places: Out of the Dark, Kassel, Germany, 1987; Open Space, Rennes, France, 1993; Iron Man, Birmingham, 1994; Havmann, Mo I Rana, Norway, 1995; Angel of the North, Gateshead, 1998 (Civic Trust Award, 2000); Quantum Cloud, Greenwich, 2000; Sound II, Winchester Cathedral, 2001; Planets, British Library, 2002; Inside Australia, Lake Ballard, Australia, 2003; Broken Column, Stavanger, Norway, 2003; Another Place, Crosby, 2003; Fai Spazio, Poggibonsi, Italy, 2004; You, Roundhouse, London, 2006; Resolution, Shoe Lane, London, 2007. FRSA 2000. Hon. FRIBA 2001. Hon. doctorates incl. Sunderland, 1998; UCE, 1998; Open, 2001; Cambridge, 2003; Newcastle upon Tyne, 2004; Teesside, 2004; Liverpool, 2006; UCL, 2006. Turner Prize, 1994; South Bank Award, 1999.

See also P. B. Gormley.

GORMLEY, (Paul) Brendan, MBE 2001; Chief Executive, Disasters Emergency Committee, since 2000; *b* 2 Sept. 1947; *s* of Arthur John Constantine Gormley and Elspeth Gormley; *m* 1974, Sally Henderson; two *s* one *d*. *Educ:* Strasbourg Univ. (Bacc. en Théologie); Trinity Coll., Cambridge (BA Social and Pol Scis 1973). OXFAM: Country Dir, Niger, 1976–78; Regl Dir, W Africa, 1978–83; Country Dir, Egypt, 1983–85; Asst to Overseas Dir, Evaluation Officer, Area Co-ordinator for Africa (N), HQ based, 1985–91; Africa Dir, 1991–2000. Trustee: Noel Buxton Trust, 2002–; One World Broadcasting Trust, 2004–. *Publication:* (contrib.) Indigenous Knowledge System and Development, ed David Brokenshaw, 1980. *Recreations:* sailing, golf. *Address:* Foxburrow Barn, Hailey, Witney, Oxon OX29 9UH. *T:* (01993) 773592; *e-mail:* bgormley@dec.org.uk.

See also A. M. D. Gormley.

GORMLY, Allan Graham, CMG 2005; CBE 1991; Chairman, BPB plc (formerly BPB Industries), 1997–2004 (Deputy Chairman, 1996–97; Director, 1995–2004); *b* 18 Dec. 1937; *s* of William Gormly and Christina Swinton Flockhart Arnot; *m* 1962, Vera Margaret Grant; one *s* one *d*. *Educ:* Paisley Grammar School. CA. Peat Marwick Mitchell & Co., 1955–61; Rootes Group, 1961–65; John Brown PLC, 1965–68; Brownlee & Co. Ltd, 1968–70; John Brown PLC, 1970: Finance Director, John Brown Engineering Ltd, 1970–77; Director, Planning and Control, John Brown PLC, 1977–80; Dep. Chairman, John Brown Engineers and Constructors Ltd, 1980–83; Gp Man. Dir, John Brown PLC, 1983–92; Chief Exec., Trafalgar House, 1992–94 (Dir, 1986–95); Dir, 1990–96, Dep. Chm., 1992–94, Chm., 1994–96, Royal Insce Hldgs; Dir and Dep. Chm., Royal & Sun Alliance, 1996–98. Chm., Q-One Biotech Ltd, 1999–2003; Director: Brixton Estates, subseq. Brixton plc, 1994–2003 (Chm., 2000–03); European Capital Co., 1996–2000; Bank of Scotland, 1997–2001. Chm., Overseas Projects Bd, 1988–91; Dep. Chm., Export Guarantees Adv. Council, 1990–92; Member: BOTB, 1988–92; Review Body on Top Salaries, 1990–92; FCO Bd of Mgt, 2000–04. *Recreations:* golf, music. *Address:* 56 North Park, Gerrards Cross, Bucks SL9 8JR.

GORRIE, Donald Cameron Easterbrook, OBE 1984; DL; Member (Lib Dem) Central Scotland, Scottish Parliament, 1999–2007; *b* 2 April 1933; *s* of Robert Maclagan Gorrie and Sydney Grace Gorrie (*née* Easterbrook); *m* 1957, Astrid Margaret Salvesen; two *s*. *Educ:* Hurst Grange Sch., Stirling; Oundle Sch.; Corpus Christi Coll., Oxford (MA Classical Mods and Modern History). Schoolmaster, Gordonstoun Sch., 1957–60; School Master and Dir of Phys. Educn, Marlborough Coll., 1960–66; Researcher and Adult Educn Lectr in Scottish History, 1966–68; Dir of Res., 1968–71, Dir of Admin, 1971–75, Scottish Liberal Party; Founder, Edinburgh Translations Ltd, 1976 (Dir, 1976–); Jt Founder, Scoted Ltd, 1978 (Dir, 1978–84). Member (L, subseq. Lib Dem): Edinburgh Town Council, 1971–75; also Group Leader: Lothian Regl Council, 1974–96; City of Edinburgh DC, 1980–96, City of Edinburgh Council, 1995–97. MP (Lib Dem) Edinburgh West, 1997–2001. Scottish Parliament: Committee Member: Procedures, 1999–2003 (Convener, 2005–07); Local Govt, 1999–2001; Transport and Envmt, 2000–01; Finance, 2001–02; Justice, 2001–03; Communities, 2003–05; Standards, 2003–07; Lib Dem spokesman on culture, sport, voluntary sector, older people. Member of Board/Committee: Edinburgh Fest., 1975–80, 1988–97; Royal Lyceum Theatre, 1975–97; Scottish Chamber Orch., 1988–96; Lothian Assoc. of Youth Clubs, 1975–97; Castle Rock Housing Assoc., 1973–97; Queen's Hall, Edinburgh, 1980–; Corstorphine Dementia Project, 2007– (Chm., 2007–), and other local orgns; Chm., Edinburgh Youth Orch., 2000–03; Convener: Diverse Attractions, 1984–99; Edinburgh City Youth Café, 1990–97 (Hon. Pres., 1997–); Sec., Friends of Corstorphine Hill, 2007–. Hon. President, Lothian Assoc. Youth Clubs; Edinburgh Athletic Club; Corstorphine AAC; Vice Pres., Achilles Club. DL City of Edinburgh, 1996. *Recreations:* former Scottish native record holder for 880 yards, reading, music, opera, drama, visiting ruins. *Address:* 9 Garscube Terrace, Edinburgh EH12 6BW. *Club:* Achilles (Vice Pres., 2006–).

GORRINGE, Christopher John, CBE 1999; Chief Executive, All England Lawn Tennis and Croquet Club, Wimbledon, 1983–2005; *b* 13 Dec. 1945; *s* of Maurice Sydney William Gorringe and Hilda Joyce Gorringe; *m* 1976, Jennifer Mary Chamberlain; two *d*. *Educ:* Bradfield Coll., Berks; Royal Agricl Coll., Cirencester. MRICS. Asst Land Agent, Iveagh Trustees Ltd (Guinness family), 1968–73; Asst Sec., 1973–79, Sec., 1979–83, All England Lawn Tennis and Croquet Club. Hon. Fellow, Roehampton Univ. (formerly Univ. of Surrey, Roehampton), 1998. *Recreations:* lawn tennis, squash, soccer. *Clubs:* East India, Devonshire, Sports and Public Schools; All England Lawn Tennis and Croquet, International Lawn Tennis of GB, Queen's, St George's Hill Lawn Tennis, Rye Lawn Tennis (Pres.), Jesters.

GORRINGE, Rev. Prof. Timothy Jervis; St Luke's Professor of Theological Studies, University of Exeter, since 1998; *b* 12 Aug. 1946; *s* of R. C. and M. V. Gorringe; *m* 1972, Carol (*née* James) (*d* 2004); one *s* two *d*; *m* 2008, Gill (*née* Westcott). *Educ:* St Edmund Hall, Oxford (BA 1969); Univ. of Leeds (MPhil 1975). Ordained deacon, 1972, priest, 1973; Curate, St Matthew's, Chapel Allerton, 1972–75; Chaplain, Wadham Coll., Oxford, 1975–78; Lectr, Tamil Nadu Theol Seminary, India, 1979–86; Chaplain, Fellow and Tutor in Theol., St John's Coll., Oxford, 1986–95; Reader in Contextual Theol., Univ. of St Andrews, 1995–98. *Publications:* Redeeming Time, 1986; Discerning Spirit, 1990; God's Theatre: a theology of Providence, 1991; Capital and the Kingdom: theological ethics and economic order, 1994; Alan Ecclestone: priest as revolutionary, 1994; God's Just Vengeance: crime, violence and the rhetoric of salvation, 1996; The Sign of Love: reflections on the Eucharist, 1997; Karl Barth: against hegemony, 1999; The Education of Desire, 2001; A Theology of the Built Environment, 2002; Furthering Humanity: a theology of culture, 2004; Crime, 2004; Harvest: food, farming and the churches, 2006. *Recreations:* bee keeping, wine-making, vegetable gardening, folk music, climbing. *Address:* Venbridge House, Cheriton Bishop, Devon EX6 6HD. *T:* (01392) 264242; *e-mail:* T.J.Gorringe@exeter.ac.uk.

GORROD, Prof. John William, FRCPath; CChem, FRSC; FIBiol; Professor of Biopharmacy, King's College London, 1984–97, now Emeritus; Research Professor, Chelsea Department of Pharmacy, 1990–97; Visiting Professor of Toxicology, University of Essex, 1997–2008; *b* 11 Oct. 1931; *s* of Ernest Lionel and Carrie Rebecca Gorrod; *m* 1954, Doreen Mary Collins; two *s* one *d*. *Educ:* Brunel Coll. of Advanced Technology

Chelsea Coll. (DCC, PhD, DSc). FRSC 1980; FRCPath 1984; FIBiol 1998. Biochem. Asst, Inst. of Cancer Res., 1954–64; Res. Fellow, Univ. of Bari, Italy, 1964; Sen. Student, Royal Commn for Exhibn of 1851, 1965–68; University of London: Lectr 1968–80, then Reader 1980–84, in Biopharmacy, Chelsea Coll.; Hd, Chelsea Dept of Pharmacy, King's Coll., 1984–90; Chm., Univ. Bd of Studies in Pharmacy, 1986–88; Hd of Div. of Health Science, KCL, 1988–89; FKC 1996. Dir, Drug Control and Teaching Centre, Sports Council, 1985–91. Member: Council, Internat. Soc. for Study of Xenobiotics (Pres., 2000–01); Educn Cttee, Pharmaceutical Soc. of GB, 1986–91; Assoc. for Res. in Indoor Air, 1989–95; Council, Indoor Air Internat., 1990–97; Associates for Res. in Substances of Enjoyment, 1990–92; Air Transport Users Cttee, CAA, 1990–93; Scientific Bd, Inst. of Drug and Pharmacokinetics Res., Develt and Applications, Ege Univ., Turkey, 1994–; Council, Tobacco Sci. and Health Policy, Inst. for Sci. and Health, St Louis, USA, 2004–; Scientific Adv. Bd, Philip Morris Internat., Neuchâtel, 2006–. Vis. Prof., Univs of Bologna, Bari, and Kebangsaan, Malaysia; Canadian MRC Vis. Prof., Univs of Manitoba and Saskatchewan, 1988; Vis. Prof., Chinese Acad. of Preventive Medicine, 1991. Mem., Polstead Parish Council, 1999–2003. Hon. MPS, 1982; Corresp. Mem., German Pharm. Soc., 1985. Hon. Fellow: Greek Pharmaceutical Soc., 1987; Turkish Assoc. of Pharmacists, 1988; Sch. of Pharmacy, Univ. of London, 2002. Gold Medal, Comenius Univ., Bratislava, 1991. Editorial Board: Xenobiotica; Europ. Jl of Metabolism and Pharmacokinetics; Toxicology Letters; Anti-Cancer Res. *Publications:* Drug Metabolism in Man (ed jtly), 1978; Biological Oxidation of Nitrogen, 1978; Drug Toxicity, 1979; Testing for Toxicity, 1981; (ed jtly) Biological Oxidation of Nitrogen in Organic Molecules, 1985; (ed jtly) Development of Drugs and Modern Medicines, 1986; (ed jtly) Metabolism of Xenobiotics, 1987; (ed jtly) Molecular Aspects of Human Disease, 1989; (ed jtly) Molecular Basis of Neurological Disorders and their Treatment, 1991; (ed jtly) Nicotine and Related Alkaloids, 1993; Analytical Determination of Nicotine and Related Compounds and their Metabolites, 1999; contribs to Xenobiotica, Europ. Jl Drug Metabolism, Jl Pharm. Pharmacol, Mutation Res., Anti-Cancer Res., Jl Nat. Cancer Inst., Drug Metabolism Revs, Med. Sci. Res., Drug Metabolism & Drug Interact., Jl of Chromatography. *Recreations:* trying to understand government policies on tertiary education, travel, books, running (slowly!). *Address:* (home) The Rest Orchard, Polstead Heath, Suffolk CO6 5BG. *Fax:* (01787) 211753; *e-mail:* jgorr@essex.ac.uk. *Clubs:* Athenæum; Hillingdon Athletic (Middx).

GORST, Sir John (Michael), Kt 1994; *b* 28 June 1928; *s* of late Derek Charles Gorst and Tatiana (*née* Kolotinsky); *m* 1954, Noël Harington Walker; five *s*. *Educ:* Ardingly Coll.; Corpus Christi Coll., Cambridge (MA). Advertising and Public Relations Manager, Pye Ltd, 1953–63; Trade Union and Public Affairs Consultant, John Gorst & Associates, 1964–95. Public relations adviser to: British Lion Films, 1964–65; Fedn of British Film Makers, 1964–67; Film Production Assoc. of GB, 1967–68; BALPA, 1967–69; Guy's Hosp., 1968–74. Founder: Telephone Users' Assoc., 1964–80 (Sec. 1964–70); Local Radio Assoc. 1964 (Sec., 1964–71). Contested (C) Chester-le-Street, 1964; Bodmin, 1966; MP (C) Hendon North, 1970–97; contested (C) Hendon, 1997. Sec., Cons. Consumer Protection Cttee, 1973–74; Member: Employment Select Cttee, 1979–87; Nat. Heritage Select Cttee, 1992–97; Vice-Chm., All Party War Crimes Cttee, 1987–97; Chairman: Cons. Media Cttee, 1987–90; British Mexican Gp, 1992–97. *Recreations:* woodwork, chess. *Address:* Holway Mill Barn, Sandford Orcas, Sherborne, Dorset DT9 4RZ. *T:* (01963) 220395; *e-mail:* sirjohng@hotmail.com.

GORT, 9th Viscount *cr* 1816 (Ire.); **Foley Robert Standish Prendergast Vereker;** Baron Kiltarton 1810; photographer; *b* 24 Oct. 1951; *er s* of 8th Viscount Gort and of Bettine Mary Mackenzie, *d* of Godfrey Greene; *S* father, 1995; *m* 1st, 1979, Julie Denise Jones (marr. diss. 1984); 2nd, 1991, Sharon Quayle; one *s* one *d*. *Educ:* Harrow. *Recreation:* golf. *Heir: s* Robert Foley Prendergast Vereker, *b* 5 April 1993. *Address:* The Coach House, Arbory Street, Castletown, Isle of Man IM9 1LJ. *T:* (01624) 822295.

GOSCHEN, family name of **Viscount Goschen**.

GOSCHEN, 4th Viscount *cr* 1900; **Giles John Harry Goschen;** a Director, Barchester Advisory, 2000–02; *b* 16 Nov. 1965; *s* of 3rd Viscount Goschen, KBE, and of Alvin Moyana Lesley, *yr d* of late Harry England, Durban, Natal; *S* father, 1977; *m* 1991, Sarah Penelope, *d* of late Alan Horsnail; one *s* two *d*. *Educ:* Eton. A Lord in Waiting (Govt Whip), 1992–94; Parly Under-Sec. of State, Dept of Transport, 1994–97; elected Mem., H of L, 1999. With Deutsche Bank, 1997–2000; Korn/Ferry International. *Heir: s* Hon. Alexander John Edward Goschen, *b* 5 Oct. 2001.

GOSCHEN, Sir Edward (Alexander), 4th Bt *cr* 1916 of Beacon Lodge, Highcliffe, co. Southampton; *b* 13 March 1949; *s* of Sir Edward Goschen, 3rd Bt, DSO and of Cynthia, *d* of Rt Hon. Sir Alexander Cadogan, OM, GCMG, KCB, PC; *S* father, 2001; *m* 1976, Louise Annette (*d* 2006), *d* of Lt-Col R. F. L. Chance, MC and Lady Ava Chance; one *d*. *Educ:* Eton. *Heir: cousin* Sebastian Bernard Goschen, *b* 1 Jan. 1959.

GOSDEN, Prof. Christine Margaret, PhD; FRCPath; Professor of Medical Genetics, University of Liverpool, since 1993; *b* 25 April 1945; *d* of George G. H. Ford and Helena P. S. Ford; *m* 1971, Dr John Gosden. *Educ:* Univ. of Edinburgh (BSc Hons; PhD 1971). MRCPath, FRCPath. Res. Fellow, Univ. of Edinburgh, 1971–73; Mem., MRC Sen. Scientific Staff, MRC Human Genetics Unit, Western Gen. Hosp., Edinburgh, 1973–93; Vis. Prof. in Human Genetics, Harris Birthright Centre for Fetal Medicine, and Dept of Obstetrics and Gynaecology, King's Coll. Hosp. Sch. of Medicine and Dentistry, 1987–93; Hon. Consultant, Liverpool Women's Hosp., 1993. Mem., HFEA, 1996. Researcher, scriptwriter, co-presenter, etc of films (incl. contrib. to TV series Dispatches (Saddam's Secret Time Bomb) and 60 Minutes, 1998) and author of articles on med. effects of chemical and biological weapons use. *Publications:* (jtly) Is My Baby All Right?, 1994; numerous scientific papers, articles and contribs to books on human genetics, fetal medicine, mental illness, childhood and adult cancers and med. effects of chemical and biological weapons. *Recreations:* campaigner for human rights, whalewatching, alpine gardening, organ and harpsichord music, modern poetry. *Address:* University Department of Pathology, Royal Liverpool University Hospital, School of Cancer Studies, Duncan Building, Daulby Street, Liverpool L69 3GA.

GOSDEN, Prof. Christopher Hugh, PhD; FBA 2005; Professor of European Archaeology, University of Oxford, since 2007; Fellow, Keble College, Oxford, since 2006; *b* 6 Sept. 1955; *s* of Hugh and Margaret Gosden; *m* 1992, Jane Kaye; one *s* one *d*. *Educ:* Univ. of Sheffield (BA 1977; PhD 1983). Vis. Fellow, ANU, 1984–85; Lectr, then Sen. Lectr, Dept of Archaeol., La Trobe Univ., Melbourne, 1986–93; Oxford University: Lectr, 1994–2004, Prof. of Archaeology, 2004–06, Hd, 2004–07, Sch. of Archaeol.; Curator, Pitt Rivers Museum, 1994–2006; Fellow, St Cross Coll., 1994–2006. *Publications:* Social Being and Time: an archaeological perspective, 1994; Archaeology and Anthropology: a changing relationship, 1999; (with J. Hather) The Prehistory of Food, 1999; (with C. Knowles) Collecting Colonialism: material culture and colonial change in Papua New Guinea, 2001; Prehistory: a very short introduction, 2003; Archaeology and Colonialism, 2004; papers and monographs. *Recreations:* reading, running and resting. *Address:* School of Archaeology, 34 Beaumont Street, Oxford OX1 2PG. *T:* (01865) 284651, *Fax:* (01865) 284657; *e-mail:* chris.gosden@prm.ox.ac.uk.

GOSDEN, John Harry Martin; racehorse trainer; *b* 30 March 1951; *s* of late John Montague Gosden and Peggie Gosden; *m* 1982, Rachel Dene Serena Hood; two *s* two *d*. *Educ:* Eastbourne Coll.; Emmanuel Coll., Cambridge (MA; athletics blue, 1970–73). Sussex Martletts schoolboy cricketer, 1967–68; Mem., Blackheath Rugby Club, 1969–70; Mem., British Under-23 Rowing Squad, 1973. Assistant trainer to: Noel Murless, 1974–76; Vincent O'Brien, 1976–77; trainer, USA, 1979–88: trained 8 State champions, Calif, 3 Eclipse Award winners; in top 10 US trainers throughout 1980s; England, 1989–: by 2007, over 1600 UK winners (fastest 1000 winners trained in UK); over 125 Group Stakes winners, incl. Derby, St Leger, English and French 1000 Guineas. *Recreations:* opera, polo, ski-ing, environmental issues. *Address:* Clarehaven Stables, Newmarket, Suffolk CB8 7BY.

GOSDEN, Prof. Roger Gordon; Professor, and Director of Research in Reproductive Biology, Weill Medical College, Cornell University, since 2004; *b* 23 Sept. 1948; *s* of Gordon Conrad Jason Gosden and Peggy (*née* Butcher); *m* 1st, 1971, Carole Ann Walsh (marr. diss. 2003); two *s*; 2nd, 2004, Lucinda Leigh Veeck. *Educ:* Bristol Univ. (BSc); Darwin Coll., Cambridge (PhD 1974); Edinburgh Univ. (DSc 1989). CBiol, FIBiol 1987. MRC Fellow, Physiological Lab., Cambridge, 1973–74, 1975–76; Population Council Fellow, Duke Univ., N Carolina, 1974–75; Lectr and Sen. Lectr and Dep. Head, Dept of Physiol., Edinburgh Univ. Med. Sch., 1976–94; Prof. of Reproductive Biol., Leeds Univ., 1994–99; Hon. Consultant, Leeds Gen. Infirmary and St James's Univ. Hosp., Leeds, 1994–99; Res. Dir, Dept of Obstetrics and Gynecology, McGill Univ., Montreal, 1999–2001; The Howard and Georgeanna Jones Prof. of Reproductive Med., and Scientific Dir, Jones Inst. for Reproductive Med., Eastern Virginia Med. Sch., 2001–04. Guest Scientist: Univ. of Southern California, 1979, 1980, 1981, 1987; Univ. of Naples, 1989; Visiting Professor: Univ. of Washington, Seattle, 1999; Univ. of Leeds, 1999–2003; Univ. of Guangzhou, China; Adjunct Prof., McGill Univ., 2001–. Scientific conf. organiser. Mem., Bd of Prison Visitors, Wetherby, 1996–99. Elder, Church of Scotland, 1982–. FRSA 1996. Occasional broadcasts. *Publications:* Biology of Menopause, 1985; Cheating Time, 1996; Transplantation of Ovarian and Testicular Tissues, 1996; Designer Babies, 1999; (ed jtly) Biology and Pathology of the Oocyte, 2003; (ed jtly) Preservation of Fertility, 2004; technical articles and contribs to popular press. *Recreations:* natural history, writing. *Address:* Center for Reproductive Medicine and Infertility, Weill Medical College, Cornell University, 1305 York Avenue, New York, NY 10021, USA.

GOSFORD, 7th Earl of, *cr* 1806; **Charles David Nicholas Alexander John Sparrow Acheson;** Bt (NS) 1628; Baron Gosford 1776; Viscount Gosford 1785; Baron Worlingham (UK) 1835; Baron Acheson (UK) 1847; *b* 13 July 1942; *o s* of 6th Earl of Gosford, OBE, and Francesca Augusta, *er d* of Francesco Cagiati, New York; *S* father, 1966; *m* 1983, Lynnette Redmond. *Educ:* Harrow; Byam Shaw Sch. of drawing and painting; Royal Academy Schs. Chm., Artists Union, 1976–80; Mem. Visual Arts Panel, Greater London Arts Assoc., 1976–77; Council Member, British Copyright Council, 1977–80. Represented by: Barry Stern Gall., Sydney; Phillip Bacon Galls, Brisbane; Solander Gall., Canberra; Von Bertouch Gall., Newcastle, NSW. *Heir: u* Hon. Patrick Bernard Victor Montagu Acheson [*b* 4 Feb. 1915; *m* 1946, Judith, *d* of Mrs F. B. Bate, Virginia, USA; three *s* two *d*].

GOSKIRK, (William) Ian (Macdonald), CBE 1986; Partner, Coopers & Lybrand Deloitte, 1990–92; *b* 2 March 1932; *s* of William Goskirk and Flora Macdonald; *m* 1969, Hope Ann Knaizuk; one *d*. *Educ:* Carlisle Grammar Sch.; Queen's Coll., Oxford (MA). Served REME, 1950–52. Shell Internat. Petroleum, 1956–74; Anschutz Corp., 1974–76; BNOC, 1976–85; Man. Dir, BNOC Trading, 1980–82; Chief Exec., BNOC, 1982–85; Dir, Coopers & Lybrand Associates, 1986–90. *Recreation:* gardening.

GOSLING, Allan Gladstone; Sales Director, PSA Projects, Property Services Agency, Department of the Environment, 1991–92, retired (Operational Director, 1990–91); Consultant to TBV Consult, 1992–95; *b* 4 July 1933; *s* of late Gladstone Gosling and of Elizabeth Gosling (*née* Ward); *m* 1961, Janet Pamela (*née* Gosling); one *s* one *d*. *Educ:* Kirkham Grammar Sch.; Birmingham Sch. of Architecture. DipArch; RIBA 1961; FRIAS 1988 (RIAS 1984); FFB 1991. Asst Architect, Lancs County Council, 1950–54; Birmingham Sch. of Architecture, 1954–57; Surman Kelly Surman, Architects, 1957–59; Royal Artillery, 1959–61; Army Works Organisation, 1961–63; Min. of Housing R&D Group, 1963–68; Suptg Architect, Birmingham Regional Office, Min. of Housing, 1968–72; Regional Works Officer, NW Region, PSA, 1972–76; Midland Regional Dir, PSA, 1976–83; Dir, Scottish Services, PSA, 1983–90. *Recreations:* walking, gardening, watercolour painting, DIY. *Address:* 11 The Moorlands, Four Oaks Park, Sutton Coldfield, West Midlands B74 2RF.

GOSLING, Sir Donald, KCVO 2004; Kt 1976; Joint Chairman, National Car Parks Ltd (formerly Central Car Parks), 1950–98; Chairman, Palmer & Harvey Ltd, since 1967; *b* 2 March 1929; *s* of Maisie Jordan; *m* 1959, Elizabeth Shauna (marr. diss. 1988), *d* of Dr Peter Ingram and Lecky Ingram; three *s*. Joined RN, 1944; served Mediterranean, HMS Leander. Mem., Council of Management, White Ensign Assoc. Ltd, 1970– (Chm., 1978–83; Vice Pres., 1983–93; Pres., 1993–); Mem., Exec. Cttee, Imperial Soc. of Kts Bachelor, 1977– (Hon. Dep. Kt Principal). Chm., Berkeley Square Ball Trust, 1982–; Trustee: Fleet Air Arm Museum, Yeovilton, 1974–2000 (Chm., Mountbatten Meml Hall Appeals Cttee, 1980); RYA Seamanship Foundn, 1981–; Vice Pres., King George's Fund for Sailors, 1993–; Patron: Submarine Meml Appeal, 1978–; HMS Ark Royal Welfare Trust, 1986–. Hon. Capt., 1993, Hon. Cdre, 2005, RNR. Younger Brother, Trinity House, 1998. Pres., TS Saumarez Sea Cadets. Hon. Freeman, Shipwrights' Co. Mem., Grand Order of Water Rats, 1999. *Recreations:* swimming, sailing, shooting. *Address:* (office) 21 Bryanston Street, Marble Arch, W1H 7PR. *T:* (020) 7499 7050. *Clubs:* Royal Thames Yacht, Royal London Yacht, Royal Naval Sailing Association, Thames Sailing, Royal Yacht Squadron; Saints and Sinners.

GOSLING, Justin Cyril Bertrand; Principal, St Edmund Hall, Oxford, 1982–96; *b* 26 April 1930; *s* of Vincent and Dorothy Gosling; *m* 1958, Margaret Clayton; two *s* two *d*. *Educ:* Ampleforth Coll.; Wadham Coll., Oxford (BPhil, MA). Univ. of Oxford: Fereday Fellow, St John's Coll., 1955–58; Lectr in Philosophy, Pembroke Coll. and Wadham Coll., 1958–60; Fellow in Philosophy, St Edmund Hall, 1960–82; Sen. Proctor, 1977–78. Barclay Acheson Prof., Macalester Coll., Minnesota, 1964; Vis. Res. Fellow, ANU, Canberra, 1970 (Pro-Vice-Chancellor, 1989–95). *Publications:* Pleasure and Desire, 1969; Plato, 1973; (ed) Plato, Philebus, 1975; (with C. C. W. Taylor) The Greeks on Pleasure, 1982; Weakness of the Will, 1990; articles in Mind, Phil Rev. and Proc. Aristotelian Soc. *Recreations:* gardening, intaglio printing, recorder music. *Address:* 124 Caldecott Road, Abingdon, Oxon OX14 5EP.

GOSLING, Prof. Leonard Morris, PhD; CBiol, FIBiol; Professor of Animal Behaviour, University of Newcastle, 1999–2008; *b* 22 Jan. 1943; *s* of William Richard Gosling and Marian (*née* Morris); *m* 1977, Dr Marion Petrie; two *d*. *Educ:* Wymondham Coll.,

Norfolk; Queen Mary Coll., London (BSc Zool. 1965); University Coll., Nairobi (PhD 1975). CBiol, FIBiol 1989. Ministry of Agriculture, Fisheries and Food: SSO, Coypu Res. Lab., 1970–73; PSO, Mammal Ecology Gp, 1974–85; SPSO, Central Science Lab., 1986–93; Dir of Sci., Zool Soc. of London and Dir, Inst. of Zool., 1993–99. Hon. Lectr, UEA, 1978–81; Vis. Prof., UCL, 1994–. Leader, Mt Zebra Project, Namibia Nature Foundn, 2005–. Member, Council: Mammal Soc., 1982–85; Assoc. for Study of Animal Behaviour, 1988–90 (Sec., Ethical Cttee, 1991–94); Royal Vet. Coll., 1994–99; Mem., Mgt Cttee, UCL Centre for Ecology and Evolution, 1995–99. *Publications*: (ed with M. Dawkins) Ethics in Research on Animal Behaviour, 1992; (ed with W. J. Sutherland) Behaviour and Conservation, 2000; numerous articles in learned jls and books on population biol. and behavioural ecology. *Recreations*: drawing, ditching, formerly Rugby. *Address*: c/o School of Clinical Medical Sciences, University of Newcastle, Newcastle upon Tyne NE2 4HH. *T*: (0191) 222 5232; *e-mail*: l.m.gosling@ncl.ac.uk.

GOSS, James Richard William; QC 1997; a Recorder, since 1994; *b* 12 May 1953; *s* of His Honour Judge William Alan Belcher Goss and of Yvonne Goss; *m* 1982, Dawna Elizabeth Davies; two *s* three *d*. *Educ*: Charterhouse; University Coll., Durham (BA). Called to the Bar, Inner Temple, 1975, Bencher, 2002. *Address*: 6 Park Square East, Leeds LS1 2LW. *T*: (0113) 2459763. *Club*: Colonsay Golf.

GOSS, Prof. Richard Oliver, PhD; Professor Emeritus, Cardiff University; *b* 4 Oct. 1929; *s* of late Leonard Arthur Goss and Hilda Nellie Goss (*née* Casson); *m* 1st, Lesley Elizabeth Thurbon (marr. diss. 1983); two *s* one *d*. 2nd, 1994, Gillian Mary (*née* Page). *Educ*: Christ's Coll., Finchley; HMS Worcester; King's Coll., Cambridge. Master Mariner 1956; BA 1958; MA 1961; PhD 1979. FCIT 1970; MNI (Founder) 1972; FNI 1977; FRINA 1998; FRSA 1993. Merchant Navy (apprentice and executive officer), 1947–55; NZ Shipping Co. Ltd, 1958–63; Economic Consultant (Shipping, Shipbuilding and Ports), MoT, 1963–64; Econ. Adviser, BoT (Shipping), 1964–67; Sen. Econ. Adviser (Shipping, Civil Aviation, etc), 1967–74; Econ. Adviser to Cttee of Inquiry into Shipping (Rochdale Cttee), 1967–70; Under-Sec., Depts of Industry and Trade, 1974–80; Prof., Dept of Maritime Studies, 1980–95, Dist. Res. Prof., 1995–96, UWIST, subseq. Univ. of Wales Coll. of Cardiff, Prof. Emeritus, Univ. of Wales, Cardiff, 1996. Nuffield/ Leverhulme Travelling Fellow, 1977–78. Governor, Plymouth Polytechnic, 1973–84; Mem. Council: RINA, 1969–2002; Nautical Inst. (from foundn until 1976); Member: CNAA Nautical Studies Bd, 1971–81; CNAA Transport Bd, 1976–78. Pres. (first), Internat. Assoc. of Maritime Economists, 1992–94. Editor and Editor-in-Chief, Maritime Policy and Management, 1985–93. Hon. PhD Piraeus, 1999. Premio Internazionale delle Comunicazioni Cristoforo Colombo, Genoa, 1991. *Publications*: Studies in Maritime Economics, 1968; (with C. D. Jones) The Economies of Size in Dry Bulk Carriers, 1971; (with M. C. Mann, et al) The Cost of Ships' Time, 1974; Advances in Maritime Economics, 1977; A Comparative Study of Seaport Management and Administration, 1979; Policies for Canadian Seaports, 1984; Port Authorities in Australia, 1987; Collected Papers, 1990; numerous papers in various jls, transactions and to conferences. *Recreations*: local history, travel. *Address*: 1 Weir Gardens, Pershore, Worcs WR10 1DX. *T*: (01386) 561140.

GOSS, Hon. Wayne Keith; Chair, Deloitte Touche Tohmatsu, Australia, since 2005 (Managing Partner, 1999–2003); Member, National Board, Deloitte Touche Tohmatsu, since 2003; *b* 26 Feb. 1951; *s* of Allan James Goss and Norma Josephine Goss; *m* 1981, Roisin Anne Hirschfeld; one *s* one *d*. *Educ*: Univ. of Queensland (LLB 1975; MBA 1997). Admitted solicitor, 1973; Partner, Goss and Downey, 1977–83. MLA (ALP) Salisbury, 1983–86 and Logan, Queensland, 1986–98; Opposition Minister for Lands, Forestry and Police, 1983–86, for Justice, 1986–88; Leader of Opposition, 1988–89; Premier of Queensland, 1989–96; Minister for the Arts, 1989–92, for Economic and Trade Develt, 1989–96. Chairman: Lincolne Scott Pty Ltd, 2000–05; Ausenco Ltd, 2003–; Director: Peplin Ltd, 2000–05; Ingeus Ltd, 2003–07. Chairman: Qld Art Gall. 2001–2008; Goodwill Games Brisbane Ltd, 1998–2002; Adv. Council, Graduate Sch. of Govt, Univ. of Sydney, 2003–06. FAICD 2000. Hon. Dr: Queensland Univ. of Technol., 2001; Griffith, 2003; Univ. of Queensland, 2007. *Address*: 315 Indooroopilly Road, Indooroopilly, Qld 4068, Australia.

GOSSCHALK, His Honour Joseph Bernard; a Circuit Judge, 1991–2007; *b* 27 Aug. 1936; *s* of late Lionel Samuel Gosschalk and of Johanna (*née* Lion); *m* 1973, Ruth Sandra Jarvis; two *d*. *Educ*: East Ham Grammar Sch.; Magdalen Coll., Oxford (MA Jurisprudence). Called to the Bar, Gray's Inn, 1961; Asst Recorder, 1983–87; Head of Chambers, Francis Taylor Bldg, Temple, EC4, 1983–91; a Recorder, SE Circuit, 1987–91. *Recreations*: theatre, reading, foreign travel, golf.

GOSTIN, Larry, DJur; Associate Dean and Linda D. and Timothy J. O'Neill Professor of Global Health Law, Georgetown University Law Center, since 1994; Professor of Health Policy, Johns Hopkins School of Public Health (formerly Hygiene and Public Health), since 1994; Director, Center for Law and the Public's Health (WHO Collaborating Center); *b* 19 Oct. 1949; *s* of Joseph and Sylvia Gostin; *m* 1977, Jean Catherine Allison; two *s*. *Educ*: State Univ. of New York, Brockport (BA Psychology); Duke Univ. (DJur 1974). Dir of Forensics and Debate, Duke Univ., 1973–74; Fulbright Fellow, Social Res. Unit, Univ. of London, 1974–75; Legal Dir, MIND (Nat. Assoc. for Mental Health), 1975–83; Gen. Sec., NCCL, 1983–85; Harvard University: Sen. Fellow of Health Law, 1985–86; Lectr, 1986–87; Adjunct Prof. in Health Law, Sch. of Public Health, 1988–94; Exec. Dir, Amer. Soc. of Law and Medicine, 1986–94. Legal Counsel in series of cases before Eur. Commn and Eur. Court of Human Rights, 1974–. Vis. Prof., Sch. of Social Policy, McMaster Univ., 1978–79; Vis. Fellow in Law and Psychiatry, Centre for Criminological Res., Oxford Univ., 1982–83. Chm., Advocacy Alliance, 1981–83; Member: National Cttee, UN Internat. Year for Disabled People, 1981; Legal Affairs Cttee, Internat. League of Socs for Mentally Handicapped People, 1980–; Cttee of Experts, Internat. Commn of Jurists to draft UN Human Rights Declarations, 1982–; Adv. Council, Interights, 1984–; AE Trust, 1984–85; WHO Expert Cttee on Guidelines on the Treatment of Drug and Alcohol Dependent Persons, 1985; WHO Steering Cttee, Internat. Ethical Guidelines for Human Population Res., 1990–; Nat. Bd of Dirs, Amer. Civil Liberties Union, 1986– (Mem. Exec. Cttee, 1988–). Western European and UK Editor, Internat. Jl of Law and Psychiatry, 1978–81; Exec. Ed., Amer. Jl of Law and Medicine, 1986–; Ed.-in-chief, Jl of Law, Medicine and Health Care, 1986–. Hon. LLD SUNY, 1994. Rosemary Delbridge Meml Award for most outstanding contribution to social policy, 1983. *Publications*: A Human Condition: vol. 1, 1975; vol. 2, 1977; A Practical Guide to Mental Health Law, 1983; The Court of Protection, 1983; (ed) Secure Provision: a review of special services for mentally ill and handicapped people in England and Wales, 1985; Mental Health Services: law and practice, 1986; Human Rights in Mental Health: an international report for the World Federation for Mental Health, 1988; Civil Liberties in Conflict, 1988; Surrogate Motherhood: politics and privacy, 1990; AIDS and the Health Care System, 1990; Implementing the Americans with Disabilities Act: rights and responsibilities of all Americans, 1993; Rights of Persons who are HIV Positive, 1996; Human Rights and Public Health in the AIDS Pandemic, 1997; Public Health Law: power, duty, restraint, 2000; Public Health Law and Ethics: a reader, 2002; The Human

Rights of Persons with Intellectual Disabilities: different but equal, 2003; The AID[S] Pandemic: complacency, injustice and unfulfilled expectations, 2004; articles in learned j[ls]. *Recreations*: family outings, walking on the mountains and fells of the Lake District. *Address*: Georgetown University Law Center, 600 New Jersey Avenue NW, Washington, D[C] 20001–2022, USA. *T*: (202) 6629373.

GOSWAMI, Prof. Usha Claire, DPhil; Professor of Education, University of Cambridge since 2003; Fellow, St John's College, Cambridge, 1990–97 and since 2003; *b* 21 Fe[b]. 1960; *d* of late Roshan Lal Goswami and of Elisabeth Irene Goswami (*née* Zenner); [*m*] 1995, Mark Thomson (marr. diss. 2004); one *d*. *Educ*: St John's Coll., Oxford (BA Ho[n] Exptl Psychol.; DPhil Psychol.); Univ. of London Inst. of Educn (PGCE Primary Educ[n] Res. Fellow, Merton Coll., Oxford, 1986–87 and 1988–89; Harkness Fellow, Univ. [of] Illinois, 1987–88; Lectr in Exptl Psychol., Univ. of Cambridge, 1990–97; Prof. [of] Cognitive Develtl Psychol., UCL, 1997–2002. AcSS 2004; FRSA. *Publications*: (with [P] Bryant) Phonological Skills and Learning to Read, 1990; Analogical Reasoning i[n] Children, 1992; Cognition in Children, 1997; (ed) Blackwell Handbook of Childhoo[d] Cognitive Development, 2002; (ed) Cognitive Development, 2007; Cognitiv[e] Development: the learning brain, 2008; contrib. papers to scientific jls. *Recreation[s]*: enjoying my daughter, travel, reading. *Address*: St John's College, Cambridge CB2 1T[P] *T*: (01223) 338600, *Fax*: (01223) 337720; *e-mail*: ucg1@cam.ac.uk.

GOSWELL, Sir Brian (Lawrence), Kt 1991; FRICS; Chairman: ISS Group Lt[d] 2000–07; ISS Safe Havens Ltd, 2002–07; Intelligence and Security Solutions Lt[d] 2002–07; *b* 26 Nov. 1935; *s* of late Albert George Goswell and Florence Emily (*n*[ée] Barnett); *m* 1961, Deirdre Gillian Stones; two *s*. FRICS 2000 (FSVA 1968). Mil. servic[e] Oxford and Bucks Light Infantry, 1954–57. Joined Healey & Baker, Surveyors, 195[7] Partner, 1969; Managing Partner, 1977; Dep. Sen. Partner, 1988–97; Dep. Chm 1997–2000; Consultant, 2000–02. Chairman: Roux Restaurants Ltd, 1988–96; Avon Ci[ty] Ltd, 1989–98; Sunley Secure II PLC, 1993–99; Brent Walker Gp PLC, 1993–97; Willia[m] Hill Gp Ltd, 1994–97; Pubmaster Ltd, 1994–96; Internat. Security Mgt Gp Lt[d] 1998–2002. Member: Adv. Bd, Sir Alexander Gibb & Partners Ltd, 1990–96; Adv. Pane[l] AAIM Gp Plc (formerly AAIM Property Fund Ltd), 2005–07. Pres., 1993–94, and Mem[b] Bd of Mgt, British Council for Offices; Pres., Amer. Chamber of Commerce (UK) 1994–98; Member: Adv. Bd, Fulbright Commn, 1997–; Duke of Edinburgh's Awar[d] Internat. Fellowship, 1997–. President: ISVA, 1986–87; Land Inst., 1997–. Trustee Conservative and Unionist Agents' Superannuation Fund. FRSA 1993. *Recreation[s]*: cricket, horse-racing, shooting, fishing. *Address*: Pipers, Camley Park Drive, Pinkney[s] Green, Maidenhead, Berks SL6 6QF. *T*: (01628) 630768. *Clubs*: Carlton (Vice-Pres[,] Political Cttee, 1998–), United & Cecil, City Livery, Rifles London Officers, MCC Leander (Henley-on-Thames).

GOTO, Mi Dori, (Midori); violinist; *b* Osaka, Japan, 25 Oct. 1971; *d* of Setsu Goto. *Educ* Professional Children's Sch., New York; Juilliard Sch. of Music, New York; New Yor[k] Univ. (BA). Début with New York Philharmonic Orch., 1982; concert and recit[al] appearances worldwide. Founder and Pres., Midori Foundn, 1992. Numerous recording[s] *Address*: c/o ICM, 40 West 57th Street, New York, NY 10019, USA.

GOTT, Haydn; a District Judge (Magistrates' Courts) (formerly Metropolitan Stipendiar[y] Magistrate), since 1992; *b* 29 April 1946; *s* of Alan Gott and Delia Mary Gott (*née* Pugh[);] *m* 1975, Brigid Mary Kane (marr. diss. 2002); one *s* one *d*; *m* 2004, Susan Valerie Gree[n] *qv*. *Educ*: Manchester Grammar Sch.; Oxford Univ. (MA). Admitted solicitor, 197[2] Partner, Alexander & Partners, solicitors, 1975–92. Legal Mem., Mental Health Revie[w] Tribunal, 1986–. *Recreations*: sport, music. *Address*: Stratford Magistrates' Court, E15 4S[B] *T*: (020) 8437 6000. *Club*: Ronnie Scott's.

GOTT, Richard Willoughby; journalist; Literary Editor, The Guardian, 1992–94; *b* 2[8] Oct. 1938; *s* of Arthur Gott and Mary Moon; *m* 1st, 1966, Ann Zammit (marr. diss. 1981[)] one adopted *s* one adopted *d*; 2nd, 1985, Vivien Ashley. *Educ*: Winchester Coll.; Corpu[s] Christi Coll., Oxford (MA). Res. Asst, RIIA, 1962–65; Leader Writer, Guardia[n] 1964–66; Res. Fellow, Inst. de Estudios Internacionales, Univ. of Chile, 1966–69; Foreig[n] Editor, Tanzanian Standard, Dar es Salaam, 1970–71; Third World corresp., Ne[w] Statesman, 1971–72; The Guardian: Latin American corresp., 1972–76; Foreign New[s] Editor, 1977–78; Features Editor, 1978–89; Asst Editor, 1988–94. Editor, Pelican Lati[n] American Library, 1969–78; Dir, Latin American Newsletters, 1973–79. Contested (Ind[)] North Hull, by-election 1966. Order of Francisco Miranda, 1st cl. (Venezuela), 200[2]. *Publications*: The Appeasers (with Martin Gilbert), 1963; Guerrilla Movements in Lati[n] America, 1970; Land Without Evil: Utopian journeys across the South Americ[an] watershed, 1993; In the Shadow of the Liberator: Hugo Chavez and the transformation o[f] Venezuela, 2000; Cuba: a new history, 2004. *Recreation*: travelling. *Address*: 88 Ledbur[y] Road, W11 2AH. *T*: (020) 7229 5467.

GOTT, Susan Valerie; *see* Green, S. V.

GOTTLIEB, Anthony John; author and journalist; *b* 26 May 1956; *s* of Felix Gottlie[b] and Jutta Gottlieb; *m* 1989, Miranda Seymour (marr. diss. 2005). *Educ*: John Lyon Sch[,] Harrow-on-the-Hill; Gonville and Caius Coll., Cambridge (MA Philos. 1979); Universit[y] Coll. London. The Economist, 1984–89: Science Ed., 1988–91; Surveys Ed., 1991–9[4] Exec. Ed., 1997–2006. Ivan Boesky Fellow, Harvard Univ., 1986. *Publications*: Socrate[s] 1997; The Dream of Reason: a history of Western philosophy, 2000. *Recreations*: musi[c] writing comedy, reading. *Address*: 60 West 57th Street, New York, NY 10019, USA.

GOTTLIEB, Bernard, CB 1970; retired; *b* 1913; *s* of late James Gottlieb and Pauline (*née* Littaur); *m* 1955, Sybil N. Epstein; one *s* one *d*. *Educ*: Haberdashers' Hampstead Sch[;] Queen Mary Coll., London Univ. BSc First Class Maths, 1932. Entered Civil Service a[s] an Executive Officer in Customs and Excise, 1932. Air Ministry, 1938; Asst Private Sec 1941, and Private Sec., 1944, to Permanent Under-Sec. of State (late Sir Arthur Street[)] Control Office for Germany and Austria, 1945; Asst Sec., 1946. Seconded to Nationa[l] Coal Board, 1946; Min. of Power, 1950; Under-Sec., 1961, Dir of Establishmen[t] 1965–69; Under-Sec., Min. of Posts and Telecommunications, 1969–73; Secretariat, Pa[y] Board, 1973–74, Royal Commn for Distribution of Income and Wealth, 1974–78 research with Incomes Data Services, 1978–90. Gwilym Gibbon Research Fellow Nuffield Coll., Oxford, 1952–53. *Club*: Reform.

GOTTLIEB, Robert Adams; dance and book critic; Editor-in-Chief, The New Yorke[r] 1987–92; *b* 29 April 1931; *s* of Charles and Martha Gottlieb; *m* 1st, 1952, Muriel Higgin[s] (marr. diss. 1965); one *s*; 2nd, 1969, Maria Tucci; one *s* one *d*. *Educ*: Columbia Coll., NY[;] Cambridge Univ. Simon & Schuster, publishers, 1955–68 (final positions, Editor-in-Chi[ef] and Vice-Pres.); Pres. and Editor-in-Chief, Alfred A. Knopf, publishers, 1968–87. Pres Louis B. Mayes Foundn. *Publications*: Reading Jazz, 1996; (jtly) Reading Lyrics, 200[0] *Recreations*: ballet, classic film, shopping.

GOUDIE, family name of **Baroness Goudie**.

GOUDIE, Baroness *cr* 1998 (Life Peer), of Roundwood in the London Borough of Brent; **Mary Teresa Goudie;** strategic and management consultant, since 1998; *b* 2 Sept. 1946; *d* of Martin Brick and Hannah Brick (*née* Foley); *m* 1969, Thomas James Cooper Goudie, *qv*; two *s*. *Educ:* Our Lady of the Visitation; Our Lady of St Anselm. Asst Dir, Brent Peoples' Housing Assoc., 1977–80; Sec. and Organiser, Labour Solidarity Campaign, 1980–84; Director: The Hansard Soc., 1985–89; The House Magazine, 1989–90; Public Affairs Dir, WWF, 1990–95; public affairs consultant, 1995–98. Mem. (Lab) Brent LBC, 1971–78. Vice Chm., Labour Peers, 2001–03. Hon. LLD Napier, 2000. *Publications:* various articles. *Recreations:* the Labour Party, family, gardening, travelling, art, food and wine, reading. *Address:* (office) 11 Groom Place, SW1X 7BA. *T:* (020) 7245 9181, *Fax:* (020) 7235 9879. *Club:* Reform.

GOUDIE, Prof. Andrew Shaw; Master, St Cross College, Oxford, since 2003; *b* 21 Aug. 1945; *s* of late William and Mary Goudie; *m* 1987, Heather (*née* Viles); two *d*. *Educ:* Dean Close Sch., Cheltenham; Trinity Hall, Cambridge. BA, PhD Cantab; MA, DSc 2002, Oxon. Oxford University: Departmental Demonstrator, 1970–76; Univ. Lectr, 1976–84; Prof. of Geography, 1984–2003; Head: Dept of Geography, 1984–94; Sch. of Geography and the Envmt, 2002–03; Fellow, Hertford Coll., 1976–2003 (Hon. Fellow, 2003); Pro-Vice-Chancellor, 1995–97; Head of Develt Prog., 1995–97. Hon. Secretary: British Geomorphological Res. Gp. 1977–80 (Chm., 1988–89); RGS, 1981–88; Member: Council, Inst. of British Geographers, 1980–83; British Nat. Cttee for Geography, 1982–87. Dep. Leader: Internat. Karakoram Project, 1980; Kora Project, 1983. President: Geographical Assoc., 1993–94; Section E, BAAS, 1995–96; Internat. Assoc. of Geomorphologists, 2005– (Vice-Pres., 2002–05). Cuthbert Peek award, RGS, 1975; Geographic Soc. of Chicago Publication award, 1982; Founder's Medal, RGS, 1991; Mungo Park Medal, RSGS, 1991; Medal, Royal Belgian Acad., 2002; Farouk El-Baz Prize for Desert Res., Geol Soc. of America, 2007. *Publications:* Duricrusts of Tropical and Sub-tropical Landscapes, 1973; Environmental Change, 1976, 3rd edn 1992; The Warm Desert Environment, 1977; The Prehistory and Palaeogeography of the Great Indian Desert, 1978; Desert Geomorphology, 1980; The Human Impact, 1981, 5th edn 1999; Geomorphological Techniques, 1981, 3rd edn 1990; The Atlas of Swaziland, 1983; Chemical Sediments and Geomorphology, 1983; The Nature of the Environment, 1984, 4th edn 2001; (jtly) Discovering Landscape in England and Wales, 1985; The Encyclopædic Dictionary of Physical Geography, 1985, 3rd edn 2000; (jtly) Landshapes, 1989; The Geomorphology of England and Wales, 1990; Techniques for Desert Reclamation, 1990; Climate, 1997; Great Warm Deserts of the World, 2002; Encyclopedia of Geomorphology, 2004; Desert Dust in the Global System, 2006; Global Environments through the Quaternary, 2007; contribs to learned jls. *Recreations:* bush life, old records, old books. *Address:* St Cross College, Oxford OX1 3LZ. *T:* (01865) 278490. *Clubs:* Geographical; Gilbert (Oxford).
See also T. J. C. Goudie.

GOUDIE, Andrew William, PhD; FRSE; Chief Economic Adviser, since 1999, and Director-General of Economy (formerly Head, Finance and Central Services Department), since 2003, Scottish Government (formerly Scottish Office, then Scottish Executive); *b* 3 March 1955; *s* of Britton Goudie and Joan Goudie; *m* 1978, Christine Lynne Hurley; two *s* two *d*. *Educ:* Queens' Coll., Cambridge (Wrenbury Schol.; BA Econs, MA; PhD 1992); Open Univ. (BA Maths and Stats). University of Cambridge: Research Officer, Dept of Applied Econs, 1978–85; Res. Fellow, Queens' Coll., 1981–83; Fellow and Dir of Studies, Robinson Coll., 1983–85; Sen. Economist, World Bank, Washington, 1985–90; Sen. Economic Advr, Scottish Office, 1990–95; Principal Economist, OECD Develt Centre, Paris, 1995–96; Chief Economist, DFID (formerly ODA), 1996–99. Hon. DLitt Strathclyde, 2003. *Publications:* articles in learned jls, incl. Econ. Jl, Jl Royal Statistical Soc., Economica, Scottish Jl Political Economy. *Address:* Scottish Government, St Andrew's House, Edinburgh EH1 3DG. *T:* (0131) 244 3430.

GOUDIE, James; *see* Goudie, T. J. C.

GOUDIE, Rev. John Carrick, CBE 1972; Assistant Minister at St John's United Reformed Church, Northwood, 1985–88, retired; *b* 25 Dec. 1919; *s* of late Rev. John Goudie, MA and Mrs Janet Goudie, step *s* of late Mrs Evelyn Goudie; unmarried. *Educ:* Glasgow Academy; Glasgow Univ. (MA); Trinity Coll., Glasgow. Served in RN: Hostilities Only Ordinary Seaman and later Lieut RNVR, 1941–45; returned to Trinity Coll., Glasgow to complete studies for the Ministry, 1945; Asst Minister at Crown Court Church of Scotland, London and ordained, 1947–50; Minister, The Union Church, Greenock, 1950–53; entered RN as Chaplain, 1953; Principal Chaplain, Church of Scotland and Free Churches (Naval), 1970–73; on staff of St Columba's Church of Scotland, Pont Street, 1973–77; Minister of Christ Church URC, Wallington, 1977–80; on staff of Royal Scottish Corp., London, 1980–84. QHC 1970–73. *Recreations:* tennis, the theatre. *Address:* 309 Howard House, Dolphin Square, SW1V 3PF. *T:* (020) 7798 8537. *Club:* Army and Navy.

GOUDIE, (Thomas) James (Cooper); QC 1984; a Recorder, since 1986; a Deputy High Court Judge (Queen's Bench Division), since 1995; *b* 2 June 1942; *s* of late William Cooper Goudie and Mary Isobel Goudie; *m* 1969, Mary Teresa Brick (*see* Baroness Goudie); two *s*. *Educ:* Dean Close Sch.; London School of Economics (LLB Hons). FCIArb 1991. Solicitor, 1966–70; called to the Bar, Inner Temple, 1970 (Bencher, 1991). A Dep. Chm., 2000–, Pres., 2007–, Information Tribunal (for nat. security appeals). Chairman: Law Reform Cttee, Gen. Council of the Bar, 1995–96; Administrative Law Bar Assoc., 1994–96; Soc. of Labour Lawyers, 1994–99; Bar European Gp, 2001–03. Contested (Lab) Brent North, Feb. and Oct. 1974; Leader of Brent Council, 1977–78. Gov., LSE, 2001–. *Publications:* (ed jtly and contrib.) Judicial Review, 1992, 3rd edn 2005; (ed with P. Elias, and contrib.) Butterworths Local Government Law, 1998; (ed jtly and contrib.) Local Authorities and the Human Rights Act 1998, 1999. *Address:* 11 King's Bench Walk, Temple, EC4Y 7EQ. *T:* (020) 7583 0610.
See also A. S. Goudie.

GOUGH, family name of **Viscount Gough**.

GOUGH, 5th Viscount *cr* 1849, of Goojerat, of the Punjaub, and Limerick; **Shane Hugh Maryon Gough;** Bt 1842; Baron Gough 1846; Irish Guards, 1961–67; *b* 26 Aug. 1941; *o s* of 4th Viscount Gough and Margaretta Elizabeth (*d* 1977), *o d* of Sir Spencer Maryon-Wilson, 11th Bt; *S* father, 1951. *Educ:* Abberley Hall, Worcs; Winchester Coll. Mem. Queen's Bodyguard for Scotland, Royal Company of Archers. Member: Exec. Council, RNIB; Scottish Lifeboat Council, RNLI. FRGS. *Heir:* none. *Address:* Keppoch Estate Office, Strathpeffer, Ross-shire IV14 9AD. *T:* (01997) 421224; 17 Stanhope Gardens, SW7 5RQ. *Clubs:* Pratt's, White's, MCC.

GOUGH, Rear-Adm. Andrew Bankes, CB 2000; Secretary-General, Order of St John, since 2003; *b* 22 June 1947; *s* of late Gilbert Bankes Gough and Pauline Gough; *m* 1971, Susanne Jensen, Copenhagen; two *s*. *Educ:* Bridgnorth Grammar Sch.; Britannia Royal Naval Coll. Joined RN, 1965; flying tours, 1970–76; i/c, HMS Bronington, 1976–78; 824 Naval Air Sqdn, 1978–80; i/c, 737 Naval Air Sqdn, 1980–81; SS Uganda, Falklands Task Force, 1982; HMS Glamorgan, 1982–84; JSDC, 1985; MoD, 1985–87; in command HM Ships: Broadsword, 1987–88; Beaver, 1988; Brave, 1988–89; RCDS, 1990; MoD, 1991–93; Dep. UK Mil. Rep. to NATO, 1993–96; Comdr, Standing Naval Force, Atlantic, 1996–97; ACOS (Policy/Requirements), Supreme HQ Allied Powers in Europe, 1997–2000. Dep. Chief Exec., 2000–02, Man. Dir, 2003, Affinitas Ltd; Man. Dir, AFFAS Ltd, 2003. MNI; FCMI. KStJ 2004. *Recreations:* military history, house restoration, Bordeaux wine. *Club:* Army and Navy.

GOUGH, Sir (Charles) Brandon, Kt 2002; DL; FCA; Chancellor, University of East Anglia, since 2003; *b* 8 Oct. 1937; *s* of late Charles Richard Gough and Mary Evaline (*née* Goff); *m* 1961, Sarah Smith; one *s* two *d*. *Educ:* Douai Sch.; Jesus Coll., Cambridge (MA); BA Open Univ., 2005. FCA 1974. Joined Cooper Brothers & Co. subseq. Coopers & Lybrand, 1964, Partner 1968; Chm., 1983–94; Mem., Exec. Cttee, Coopers & Lybrand (Internat.), 1982–94 (Chm., 1985 and 1991–92); Chm., Coopers & Lybrand Europe, 1989, and 1992–94. Chairman: Yorkshire Water, then Kelda Gp, 1996–2000; De La Rue plc, 1997–2004 (Dir, 1994–2004); Locate in Kent Ltd, 2006–; Govt Dir, BAe plc, 1987–88; Director: British Invisibles, 1990–94; S. G. Warburg Gp, 1994–95 (Dep. Chm., 1995); National Power, 1995–2000; George Wimpey, 1995–99; Montanaro UK Smaller Cos Investment Trust plc, 1998–2005 (Chm., 1999–); Singer & Friedlander Gp, 1999–2005; Innogy Hldgs, 2000–02; Partnership Council, Freshfields, 1996–2000; Chm., Montanaro European Smaller Cos, 2000–04. Mem. Council, Inst. of Chartered Accountants in England and Wales, 1981–84; Chm., CCAB Auditing Practices Cttee, 1981–84 (Mem., 1976–84); Member: Accounting Standards Review (Dearing) Cttee, 1987–88; Financial Reporting Council, 1990–96. City University Business School: Chm., City Adv. Panel, 1986–91 (Mem., 1980–91); Mem. Council, 1986–93 (Chm., 1992–93); Chm., Finance Cttee, 1988–91; Member: Council of Lloyd's, 1983–86; Cambridge Univ. Careers Service Syndicate, 1983–86; Governing Council, 1984–88, Council, 1988–94, President's Cttee, 1992–94, Business in the Community; Council for Industry and Higher Educn, 1985–93; Management Council, GB-Sasakawa Foundn, 1985–96; UK Nat. Cttee, Japan-European Community Assoc., 1989–94; CBI Task Force, Vocational Educn and Trng, 1989; CBI Educn & Trng Affairs Cttee, 1990–94; Council, Foundn for Educn Business Partnerships, 1990–91; Council, City Univ., 1991–93; Council, Prince of Wales Business Leaders Forum of Internat. Business in the Community, 1992–94. Chairman: Common Purpose Trust, 1991–97 (Trustee, 1989–97); Nat. Trng Task Force working gp on role of TECs in local econ. develt, 1991–92; Doctors' and Dentists' Pay Review Body, 1993–2001; HEFCE, 1993–97. Mem., Council of Management, Royal Shakespeare Theatre Trust, 1991–97; Trustee: GSMD Foundn, 1989–95; Hospice in the Weald, 2003–; Canterbury Cathedral Trust Fund, 2006–; Leeds Castle Foundn, 2006– (Chm., 2007–). DL Kent, 2005. Hon. DSc City, 1994; Hon. DCL UEA, 2003. Lloyd's Silver Medal, 1986. *Recreations:* music, gardening. *Address:* University of East Anglia, Norwich NR4 7TJ.

GOUGH, Prof. Douglas Owen, PhD; FRS 1997; Professor of Theoretical Astrophysics, University of Cambridge, since 1993 (Director, Institute of Astronomy, 1999–2004); Fellow, Churchill College, Cambridge, since 1972; *b* 8 Feb. 1941; *s* of Owen Albert John Gough and Doris May Gough (*née* Camera); *m* 1965, Rosanne Penelope Shaw; two *s* two *d*. *Educ:* Hackney Downs Sch.; St John's Coll., Cambridge (BA 1962; MA 1966; PhD 1966). Res. Associate, Jt Inst. for Lab. Astrophysics, Univ. of Colo, 1966–67; Nat. Acad. of Scis Sen. Postdoctoral Resident Res. Associate, Inst. for Space Studies, NY, 1967–69; Vis. Mem., Courant Inst. of Mathematical Scis, NYU, 1967–69; University of Cambridge: Mem., Grad. Staff, Inst. of Theoretical Astronomy, 1969–73; Lectr in Astronomy and Applied Maths, 1973–85; Reader in Astrophysics, 1985–93; Dep. Dir, Inst. of Astronomy, 1993–99. Astronome Titulaire Associé des Observatoires de France, 1977; SRC Sen. Fellow, 1978–83; Prof. Associé, Univ. of Toulouse, 1984–85; Hon. Prof. of Astronomy, QMW, Univ. of London, 1986–; Fellow Adjoint, Jt Inst. for Lab. Astrophysics, Boulder, Colo, 1986–; Scientific Co-ordinator, Inst. for Theoretical Physics, Univ. of Calif, Santa Barbara, 1990; Vis. Prof., Stanford Univ., 1996–. Lectures: James Arthur, Harvard, 1982; Sir Joseph Larmor, Cambridge Philosophical Soc., 1988; Wernher von Braun, Marshall Space Flight Center, 1991; Morris Loeb, Harvard, 1993; Halley, Oxford Univ., 1996; Bishop, Columbia Univ., 1996; R. J. Tayler Meml, RAS, 2000. Member, Editorial Board: Solar Physics, 1983–2004; Fundamentals of Cosmic Physics, 1985–93; Inverse Problems, 1997–2003; Advr, Encyclopedia of Astronomy and Astrophysics, Inst. of Physics, 1997–2000. FInstP 1997. For. Mem., Royal Danish Acad. of Scis and Letters, 1998. William Hopkins Prize, Cambridge Philosophical Soc., 1984; George Ellery Hale Prize, Amer. Astronomical Soc., 1994; Eddington Medal, RAS, 2000. Mousquetaire d'Armagnac, 2001. *Publications:* mainly res. papers and reviews in scientific jls. *Recreations:* cooking, listening to music. *Address:* Institute of Astronomy, Madingley Road, Cambridge CB3 0HA. *T:* (01223) 337548.

GOUGH, Rev. Canon Flora Jane Louise; *see* Winfield, Rev. Canon F. J. L.

GOUGH, Janet, MA; Director of Cathedrals and Church Buildings, Archbishop's Council, since 2008; *b* 1 Aug. 1940; *d* of Clifford Gough and Sarah (*née* Allen). *Educ:* Ludlow High Sch.; Newnham Coll., Cambridge (BA Hons, MA). St Paul's Girls' Sch., 1964–71; Manchester Grammar Sch., 1972; Worcester High Sch. for Girls, 1973; St Paul's Girls' Sch., 1973–98, High Mistress, 1993–98. Governor: Dulwich Coll., 1999–; Oundle Sch., 2002–. *Recreations:* book collecting, architecture, music. *Address:* 58 Corve Street, Ludlow, Shropshire SY8 1DU.

GOUGH, Rev. Canon Jonathan Robin Blanning; Royal Army Chaplains' Department, since 2005; *b* 11 May 1962; *s* of Alec Robin Blanning Gough and Margaret Gough (*née* Elliston); *m* 1985, Rev. Canon Flora Jane Louise Winfield, *qv*. *Educ:* Exeter Sch.; St David's UC, Lampeter (BA Hons 1983); St Stephen's House, Oxford; Westminster Coll., Oxford (MTh 1996). Ordained deacon, 1985, priest, 1986; Assistant Curate: Braunton, 1985–86; Matson, 1986–89; Royal Army Chaplains' Department, 1989–2001: served: NI, 1990–92 and 2000–01; Bosnia (UN Protection Force), 1993–94 and 1995, (NATO Stabilisation Force), 1997; Kosovo (NATO Kosovo Force), 1999–2000; Archbishop of Canterbury's Sec. for Ecumenism, 2001–05. Hon. Canon: Holy Trinity Cathedral, Gibraltar, 2002–05; St Paul's Cathedral, Nicosia, 2006–. FRSA 2003. *Recreations:* music, history, country pursuits. *Address:* c/o Ministry of Defence Chaplains (Army), Trenchard Lines, Upavon, Wilts SN9 6BE.

GOUGH, Michael Charles, CEng, FIET, FBCS; Chief Executive, National Computing Centre, since 2000; *b* 21 May 1960; *s* of Cyril John Gough and Evelyn Rose Gough; *m* 1982, Lesley Irene Baglee; three *s*. *Educ:* Univ. of Liverpool (BSc Hons Computational and Statistical Sci. 1981); MSc Computer Sci. 1987). CITP 2002; CEng 2006; FIET 2006; FBCS 2006. Computer software engr, Fraser Williams, 1981–87; Project Manager, CAP Gp Plc, 1987–89; IT Dir, CERT Plc, 1989–91; Dir, Technol. Strategy, SEMA Gp Plc, 1991–2000. Director: Dynamic Systems Develt Method Consortium, 1997–2003; AIRTO, 2000–03. MInstD 1996. *Recreations:* music: teaching, playing and composing, photography, the Methodist Church. *Address:* c/o National Computing Centre, Oxford

House, Oxford Road, Manchester M1 7ED. *T:* (0161) 242 2235, *Fax:* (0161) 242 2499; *e-mail:* michael.gough@ncc.co.uk.

GOUGH, Piers William, CBE 1998; RA 2001; RIBA; architect; Partner, CZWG Architects, since 1975; *b* 24 April 1946; *s* of late Peter Gough and Daphne Mary Unwin Banks; *m* 1991, Rosemary Elaine Fosbrooke Bates. *Educ:* Uppingham Sch., Rutland; Architectural Assoc. Sch. of Architecture. Principal works: Phillips West 2, Bayswater, 1976; Lutyens Exhibn, Hayward Gall., 1982; Cochrane Sq., Glasgow, 1987–; China Wharf, 1988, The Circle, 1990, Bermondsey; Craft, Design and Technol. Bldg, 1988, two boarding houses, 1994, Bryanston Sch.; Street-Porter House, 1988, 1–10 Summers St, 1994, Clerkenwell; Crown St Regeneration Proj., Gorbals, 1991–2004; Westbourne Grove Public Lavatories, 1993; Brindleyplace Café, Birmingham, 1994–97; Bankside Lofts, Southwark, 1994–99; 19th and 20th century galls, 1995–96, Regency galls, 2003, Nat. Portrait Gall.; Soho Lofts, Wardour Street, 1995; Leonardo Centre, Uppingham Sch., 1995; The Glass Building, Camden, 1996–99; Camden Wharf, Camden Lock, 1996–2002; Green Bridge, Mile End Park, 1997–2000; Westferry Studios, Isle of Dogs, 1999–2000; Bankside Central, 2000–02; Allen Jones' Studio, Ledwell, 2000–01; Samworths' Boarding House, Uppingham Sch., 2000–01; Site A, Edinburgh Park, 2000–01; Tunnel Wharf, Rotherhithe, 2001; Fulham Island Site, 2001–02; Ladbroke Green, 2002–; Queen Elizabeth Square and Crown Street Corner, Gorbals, 2003–04; Saved Exhibn, Hayward Gall., 2003–04; Steedman St, SE17, 2006; Bling Bling Building, Liverpool, 2006. Commissioner: English Heritage, 2000–07 (Mem., London Adv. Cttee, 1995–2003; Mem., Urban Panel, 1999–2003); CABE, 2007–. Pres., AA, 1995–97 (Mem. Council, 1970–72, 1991–99; Trustee, 1999–2007). Trustee, Artangel, 1994–2004; a Design Champion for Kent, 2004–. Television: (co-writer and presenter) The Shock of the Old (series), Channel 4, 2000. Hon. Fellow, Queen Mary, Univ. of London, 2001. DUniv Middlesex, 1999. *Publication:* English Extremists, 1988. *Recreation:* swimming. *Address:* CZWG Architects LLP, 17 Bowling Green Lane, EC1R 0QB. *T:* (020) 7253 2523, *Fax:* (020) 7250 0594; *e-mail:* piersgough@czwgarchitects.co.uk.

GOUGH, Rachel Mary; *see* Sandby-Thomas, R. M.

GOULBORN, Caroline Barbara; a District Judge (Magistrates' Courts), since 2004; *b* 9 Sept. 1949; *d* of Sydney Aubrey Goulborn and Peggy Goulborn (*née* Millhouse). *Educ:* Wycombe High Sch.; Trent Polytech. (BA Hons (Law) 1978). Admitted solicitor, 1981; Assistant Solicitor: Huntsmans, Nottingham, 1981–84; Nelsons, Nottingham, 1985–88; Sen. Partner, Fletcher's Solicitors, 1989–2004. *Recreations:* long-distance Wycombe Wanderers supporter, Sutton Bonington Cricket Club (Vice Pres.), reading. *Address:* Derby Magistrates' Court, St Mary's Gate, Derby DE1 3JR. *T:* (01332) 362000; *e-mail:* DistrictJudge.Goulborn@judiciary.gsi.gov.uk.

GOULD, family name of **Baron Gould of Brookwood** and **Baroness Gould of Potternewton**.

GOULD OF BROOKWOOD, Baron *cr* 2004 (Life Peer), of Brookwood in the County of Surrey; **Philip Gould;** Founder, Philip Gould Associates, polling and political strategy, 1985; *b* 30 March 1950; *s* of Wilfred Caleb Gould and Fennigien Anna Gould (*née* de-Jager); *m* 1985, Gail Ruth Rebuck, *qv*; two *d*. *Educ:* Knaphill Secondary Modern Sch., Woking; E London Coll.; Univ. of Sussex (BA Politics); LSE (MA with Dist. Hist. of Political Thought); London Business Sch. (Sloan Fellow (Dist.)). Account Dir, Wasey, Campbell-Ewald, 1975–79; Dir, Tinker and Partners, 1979–81; Founder, Brignull LeBas Gould, 1981–83; Mgt Dir, Doyle Dane Bernbach, 1984–85. Vis. Prof., LSE. Trustee, Policy Network. *Publication:* The Unfinished Revolution, 1998. *Recreations:* friends, family, QPR, tennis, reading, travel. *Address:* House of Lords, SW1A 0PW. *T:* (home) (020) 7486 5255.

GOULD OF BROOKWOOD, Lady; *see* Rebuck, G. R.

GOULD OF POTTERNEWTON, Baroness *cr* 1993 (Life Peer), of Leeds in the Metropolitan County of West Yorkshire; **Joyce Brenda Gould;** a Deputy Speaker, House of Lords, since 2002; *b* 29 Oct. 1932; *d* of Sydney and Fanny Manson; *m* 1952, Kevin Gould (separated); one *d*. *Educ:* Cowper Street Primary Sch.; Roundhay High Sch. for Girls; Bradford Technical Coll. Dispenser, 1952–65; Labour Party: Mem., 1951–; Asst Regional Organiser, 1969–75; Asst Nat. Agent and Chief Women's Officer, 1975–85; Dir of Organisation, 1985–93. Opposition spokesperson on women's affairs, 1995–97; a Baroness in Waiting (Govt Whip), 1997–98. Chm., All Party Parly Gp on Pro-Choice, 1995–. Member: Council of Europe, 1993–96 (Ldr, Delegn to UN Conf. on Women, Beijing, 1995); WEU, 1993–96; CPA, 1998–; IPU, 1998–; Fellow, Parlt and Industry Trust. Mem., Ind. Commn on Voting Systems, 1998–; Vice-Chm., Hansard Soc., 2002–06. Chairman:, Ind. Adv. Cttee for Sexual Health, 2003–; Women's Nat. Commn, 2008– (Interim Chm., 2007–08). Sec., Nat. Jt Cttee of Working Women's Orgns, 1975–85; Vice-Pres., Socialist Internat. Women, 1978–86. President: BEA, 1998–2007; FPA, 1999–; Brighton and Hove Fabian Soc., 2001–; Straight Talking, 2007–. Chm., Mary MacArthur Holiday Trust, 1994–2007. Patron: FORWARD, 1996–; Brighton and Hove Women's Centre, 2000–; Yorks MESMAC, 2008–; Vice Patron, Impact's 30th Anniv. Appeal, 2008. Hon. FFSRH (Hon. FFPRHC 2006); Hon. Fellow, British Assoc. for Sexual Health and HIV, 2007. Health Champion, Charity Champion Awards, 2007. *Publications:* (ed) Women and Health, 1979; pamphlets on feminism, socialism and sexism, women's right to work, and on violence in society; articles and reports on women's rights and welfare. *Recreations:* relaxing, sport as a spectator, theatre, cinema, reading. *Address:* 12 Warenne Street, Hove, E Sussex BN3 8EG; House of Lords, SW1A 0PW.

GOULD, Bryan Charles, CNZM 2005; Vice-Chancellor, Waikato University, New Zealand, 1994–2004; *b* 11 Feb. 1939; *s* of Charles Terence Gould and Elsie May Driller; *m* 1967, Gillian Anne Harrigan; one *s* one *d*. *Educ:* Auckland Univ. (BA, LLM); Balliol Coll., Oxford (MA, BCL). HM Diplomatic Service: FO, 1964–66; HM Embassy, Brussels, 1966–68; Fellow and Tutor in Law, Worcester Coll., Oxford, 1968–74. MP (Lab): Southampton Test, Oct. 1974–1979; Dagenham, 1983–94; an opposition spokesman on trade, 1983–86, on economy and party campaigns, 1986–87, on Trade and Industry, 1987–89, on the environment, 1989–92, on national heritage, 1992 (Mem. of Shadow Cabinet, 1986–92). Presenter/Reporter, TV Eye, Thames Television, 1979–83. Chm., Foundn for Res., Sci. and Technol., 2008–. Hon. Dr Waikato, 2006. *Publications:* Monetarism or Prosperity?, 1981; Socialism and Freedom, 1985; A Future for Socialism, 1989; Goodbye to All That (memoirs), 1995; The Democracy Sham, 2006. *Recreations:* gardening, food, wine. *Address:* 239 Ohiwa Beach Road, Opotiki, New Zealand.

GOULD, David John, CB 2004; Chief Operating Officer, Defence Equipment and Support, Ministry of Defence, since 2007; *b* 9 April 1949; *s* of James McIntosh Gould and Joan Vivienne Gould; *m* 1st, 1973; two *s* one *d*; 2nd, 2001, Christine Lake. *Educ:* West Buckland Sch., Barnstaple; Univ. of Sussex (Hons, French and European Studies). Joined MoD Naval Weapons Dept, 1973; Materiel Finance (Air), 1978; NATO Defence College, 1980; MoD (Air), 1981; UK Delegn to NATO, 1983; Asst Sec., Materiel Finance (Air), 1987; Head of Resources and Programmes (Air), 1990; Assistant Under-Secretary of State: (Supply and Orgn) (Air), 1992; Policy, 1993; seconded to Cabin Office, 1993–95; Asst Under-Sec. of State, Fleet Support, 1995–99; Dir Gen., Finance an Business Plans, Defence Logistics Orgn, MoD, 1999–2000; Dep. Chief Exec., Defenc Procurement Agency, 2000–07. Silver Jubilee Medal, 1977. *Recreations:* fitness, Ba Rugby, fly fishing (Avon and tributaries), music, especially opera and lieder. *Addres* Defence Equipment and Support, MoD Abbey Wood, Bristol BS34 8JH. *T:* (0117) 91 0009; *e-mail:* des-c_o_o-ps@mod.uk.

GOULD, Edward John Humphrey, MA; FRGS; Master, Marlborough Colleg 1993–2004; *b* Lewes, Sussex, 31 Oct. 1943; *s* of Roland and Ruth Gould; *m* 1970, Jennif Jane, *d* of I. H. Lamb; two *d*. *Educ:* St Edward's Sch., Oxford; St Edmund Hall, Oxfor (BA 1966, MA 1970, DipEd 1967). FRGS 1974. Harrow School, 1967–83: Asst Maste 1967–83; Head, Geography Dept, 1974–79; Housemaster, 1979–83; Headmaster, Felste Sch., 1983–93. Chm., ISC, 2006–07 (Mem., Council, and Policy Cttee (Chm., 2000 2000–02); Member: Indep. Schs Curriculum Cttee, 1985–92 (Chm., 1990–92); B QCA, 2002–07; Bd, United Learning Trust, 2004– (Dep, Chm., 2008–); Bd, ESU, 2004 (Dep. Chm., 2005–); Nat. Council for Educnl Excellence, 2007–. Chairman: ISIS Eas 1989–93; HMC, 2002. Governor: St Edward's Sch., Oxford, 2003–; Harrow Sch., 2004 Norwich Sch., 2004–. JP Essex, 1989–93. FRSA 1993. *Recreations:* Rugby (Oxford Blu 1963–66), swimming (Half Blue, 1965), rowing (rep. GB, 1967), music. *Address:* Bret Cottage, Cross Lane, Brancaster, Norfolk PE31 8AE. *Clubs:* East India, Devonshire, Spor and Public Schools; Vincent's (Oxford).

GOULD, Matthew Steven, MBE 1998; HM Diplomatic Service; Principal Privat Secretary to the Secretary of State for Foreign and Commonwealth Affairs, since 2007; 20 Aug. 1971; *s* of Sidney and Jean Gould. *Educ:* Orley Farm Sch., Harrow; St Paul's Sch Barnes; Peterhouse, Cambridge (BA Theol. 1993). Teacher, Nyarukunda Secondary Sch Zimbabwe, 1989–90; entered FCO, 1993; Manila, 1994–97; Speech Writer to Foreig Sec., 1997–99; Dep. Hd, Consular Div., FCO, 1999–2001; Political Counsello Islamabad, 2002–03; Dep. Hd of Mission, Tehran, 2003–05; Counsellor (Foreign an Security Policy), Washington, 2005–07; Pvte Sec. for For. Affairs to Prime Minister (o secondment), 2007. *Recreations:* horse-riding, ski-ing, movies, curry. *Address:* c/o Foreig and Commonwealth Office, King Charles Street, SW1A 2AH.

GOULD, Patricia, CBE 1978; RRC 1972; Matron-in-Chief, Queen Alexandra's Roy Naval Nursing Service, 1976–80; *b* 27 May 1924; *d* of Arthur Wellesley Gould. *Edu* Marist Convent, Paignton. Lewisham Gen. Hosp., SRN, 1945; Hackney Hosp., CMB I, 1946; entered QARNNS, as Nursing Sister, 1948; accepted for permanent servic 1954; Matron, 1966; Principal Matron, 1970; Principal Matron Naval Hosps, 197 QHNS 1976–80. OStJ (Comdr Sister), 1977. *Recreations:* gardening, photography.

GOULD, Peter John Walter; Director, Gould Advisory Services Ltd; Chief Executiv Northamptonshire County Council, 2000–07; Clerk to Lord-Lieutenant Northamptonshire, 2000–07; *b* 10 Feb. 1953; *s* of Morris Edwin Gould and Hilda Annet Gould; *m* 1977, June Lesley Sutton; one *s*. *Educ:* Yeovil Sch., Som; NE London Pol (BScSoc, London Univ.). Res. Fellow, Sch. for Independent Study, NE London Poly 1976; London Borough of Lambeth, 1977–98: Hd of Strategy, 1995; Dir of Personne 1996–98; Corporate Dir, Middlesbrough Unitary Council, 1998–2000. *Recreations:* musi opera, flute, cooking, literature, social history. *Address:* Brome Park Farm, Brome Avenu Eye, Suffolk IP23 7HW.

GOULD, Robert; JP; DL; Member, Glasgow City Council, 1994–2003 (Leade 1994–97); *b* 8 Feb. 1935; *s* of James and Elizabeth Gould; *m* 1953, Helen Wire; two *s* tw *d*. *Educ:* Albert Secondary Sch. Formerly with BR. Entered local government, 197 Glasgow Corp., 1970–74; Mem., Strathclyde Regl Council, 1974–96 (Leader, 1992–96 JP Glasgow; DL Glasgow, 1997. *Recreations:* all sports (spectator), hill-walking. *Addres* Flat 6D, 15 Eccles Street, Springburn, Glasgow G22 6BJ. *T:* (0141) 558 9586.

GOULD, Prof. Warwick Leslie; Professor of English Literature, University of Londo since 1995; Director, Institute of English Studies, School of Advanced Study, Universit of London, since 1999; *b* 7 April 1947; *s* of Leslie William Gould and Fedora Gould (*n* Green). *Educ:* Brisbane Grammar Sch.; Univ. of Queensland (BA 1st Cl. Hons Englis Language and Lit. 1969). Royal Holloway College, then Royal Holloway and Bedfor New College, University of London: Lectr in English Language and Lit., 1973–86; Se Lectr, 1986–91; Reader in English Lit., 1991–95; British Acad. Res. Reader, 1992–9 Prof., 1995–; Dep. Prog. Dir, 1994–97, Prog. Dir, 1997–99, Centre for English Studie Sch. of Advanced Study, Univ. of London; Dep. Dean, Sch. of Advanced Study, 2000–0 University of London: Member: Senate, 1990–94; Academic Council, 1990–9 Academic Cttee, 1994–2000; Council, 1995–2000 and 2002–. FRSL 1997; FRSA 199 FEA 1999. Cecil Oldman Meml Medal for Bibliography and Textual Criticism, Leed Univ., 1993. Editor, Yeats Annual, 1983–. *Publications:* (jtly) Joachim of Fiore and th Myth of the Eternal Evangel, 1987, 2nd edn, as Joachim of Fiore and the Myth of th Eternal Evangel in the Nineteenth and Twentieth Centuries, 2001; (ed jtly) The Secr Rose: stories by W. B. Yeats, 1981, 2nd edn 1992; (ed jtly) The Collected Letters of W B. Yeats, Vol. II 1896–1990, 1997; (jtly) Gioacchino da Fiore e il mito dell'Evangel eterno nella cultura europea, 2000; (ed jtly) Mythologies by W. B. Yeats, 2005. *Recreatio* book collecting. *Address:* Institute of English Studies, Room 308, Senate House, Mal Street, WC1E 7HU. *T:* (020) 7862 8673, *Fax:* (020) 7862 8720; *e-mail:* warwick.gould@ sas.ac.uk.

GOULDBOURNE, Rev. Dr Ruth Mary Boyd; Joint Minister, Bloomsbury Centra Baptist Church, since 2006; *b* 5 July 1961; *d* of Derek Boyd Murray and Giles Watso Murray; *m* 1984, Ian Duncan Gouldbourne. *Educ:* Drummond High Sch., Edinburgh; S Andrews Univ. (MA 1983); King's Coll. London (BD 1986); Royal Holloway an Bedford New Coll., Univ. of London (PhD 2000); Bristol Univ. (Postgrad. Dip Counselling 2004). Baptist Minister, Bunyan Meeting Free Ch, 1988–95; Tutor, Bristo Baptist Coll., 1995–2006. *Publication:* Reinventing the Wheel: women and ministry i English Baptist history, 1997; The Flesh and the Feminine: gender and theology in th writings of Caspar Schwenckfeld, 2007; (jtly) On Being the Church, 2008. *Recreation* reading, live theatre, watching Rugby, wine, being bemused at being in Who's Wh cross-stitch. *Address:* Bloomsbury Central Baptist Church, 235 Shaftesbury Avenu WC2H 8EP. *T:* (020) 7240 0544, *Fax:* (020) 7836 6843.

GOULDEN, Sir (Peter) John, GCMG 2001 (KCMG 1996; CMG 1989); HM Diplomatic Service, retired; consultant; *b* 21 Feb. 1941; *s* of George Herbert Goulden an Doris Goulden; *m* 1962, Diana Margaret Elizabeth Waite; one *s* one *d*. *Educ:* King Edwar VII Sch., Sheffield; Queen's Coll., Oxford (BA 1st Cl. Hons History, 1962). HM Diplomatic Service, 1962–2001: Ankara, 1963–67; Manila, 1969–70; Dublin, 1976–7 Head of Personnel Services Dept, 1980–82; Head of News Dept, FCO, 1982–8 Counsellor and Hd of Chancery, Office of the UK Permt Rep. to EEC, Brussel 1984–87; Asst Under-Sec. of State, FCO, 1988–92; Ambassador to Turkey, 1992–9 Ambassador and UK Perm. Rep. to N Atlantic Council and to Perm. Council of WEU

1995–2001. Chm., Victoria Interchange Gp, 2007–. Trustee, Greenwich Foundn, 2003–. *Recreations:* music, theatre, opera, family.

GOULDER, Catharine Anne O.; *see* Otton-Goulder.

GOULDING, Jeremy Wynne Ruthven, MA; Headmaster, Shrewsbury School, since 2001; *b* 29 Aug. 1950; *s* of Denis Arthur and Doreen Daphne Goulding; *m* 1974, Isobel Mary Fisher; two *s* two *d*. *Educ:* Becket Sch., Nottingham; Magdalen Coll., Oxford (MA, PGCE). Asst Master and Head of Divinity, Abingdon Sch., 1974–78; Head of Divinity, 1978–83, and Housemaster, Oldham's Hall, 1983–89, Shrewsbury Sch.; Headmaster: Prior Park Coll., 1989–96; Haberdashers' Aske's Sch., 1996–2001. Freeman, Haberdashers' Co., 2001. *Recreations:* music-making, hill-walking. *Address:* Headmaster's House, Shrewsbury School, Shropshire SY3 7BA. *T:* (01743) 280525.

GOULDING, Very Rev. June; *see* Osborne, Very Rev. J.

GOULDING, Sir Lingard; *see* Goulding, Sir W. L. W.

GOULDING, Sir Marrack (Irvine), KCMG 1997 (CMG 1983); Warden of St Antony's College, Oxford, 1997–2006; *b* 2 Sept. 1936; *s* of Sir Irvine Goulding; *m* 1st, 1961, Susan Rhoda D'Albiac (marr. diss. 1996), *d* of Air Marshal Sir John D'Albiac, KCVO, KBE, CB, DSO, and of Lady D'Albiac; two *s* one *d*; 2nd, 1996, Catherine Pawlow (marr. diss. 2004), *d* of Alexandre Pawlow and Alla Sobkevitch de Vicens. *Educ:* St Paul's Sch.; Magdalen Coll., Oxford (1st cl. hons. Lit. Hum. 1959). Joined HM Foreign (later Diplomatic) Service, 1959; MECAS, 1959–61; Kuwait, 1961–64; Foreign Office, 1964–68; Tripoli (Libya), 1968–70; Cairo, 1970–72; Private Sec., Minister of State for Foreign and Commonwealth Affairs, 1972–75; seconded to Cabinet Office (CPRS), 1975–77; Counsellor, Lisbon, 1977–79; Counsellor and Head of Chancery, UK Mission to UN, NY, 1979–83; Ambassador to Angola, and concurrently to São Tomé e Principe, 1983–85; United Nations, New York: Under Sec.-Gen., Special Political Affairs, later Peace-Keeping Ops, 1986–93; Under Sec.-Gen., Political Affairs, 1993–97. *Publication:* Peacemonger, 2002. *Recreations:* travel, birdwatching. *Address:* 11 St Gabriel's Manor, 25 Cormont Road, SE5 9RH. *T:* (020) 7820 0284. *Club:* Oxford and Cambridge.

GOULDING, Paul Anthony; QC 2000; *b* 24 May 1960; second *s* of Byron and Audrey Goulding; *m* 1984, June Osborne (see Very Rev. J. Osborne); one *s* one *d*. *Educ:* Latymer Sch.; St Edmund Hall, Oxford (BA 1st Cl. Jurisprudence 1981; BCL 1982; MA). Tutor in Law, St Edmund Hall, Oxford, 1982–84; called to the Bar, Middle Temple, 1984; practising barrister, 1985–. Chm., 1998–2000, Vice-Pres., 2000–04, Employment Lawyers Assoc.; Member: Mgt Cttee, Bar Pro Bono Unit, 2000–03; Mgt Bd, European Employment Lawyers Assoc., 2001–05. *Publications:* European Employment Law and the UK, 2001; Employee Competition: covenants, confidentiality, and garden leave, 2007. *Recreations:* football (FA coach), tennis, opera, ballet. *Address:* Blackstone Chambers, Blackstone House, Temple, EC4Y 9BW. *T:* (020) 7583 1770. *Club:* Reform.

GOULDING, Sir (William) Lingard (Walter), 4th Bt *cr* 1904; Headmaster of Headfort Preparatory School, 1977–2000; *b* 11 July 1940; *s* of Sir (William) Basil Goulding, 3rd Bt, and Valerie Hamilton (Senator, Seanad Éireann), *o d* of 1st Viscount Monckton of Brenchley, PC, GCVO, KCMG, MC, QC; *S* father, 1982, but his name does not appear on the Official Roll of the Baronetage. *Educ:* Ludgrove; Winchester College; Trinity College, Dublin (BA, HDipEd). Computer studies for Zinc Corporation and Sulphide Corporation, Conzinc Rio Tinto of Australia, 1963–66; Systems Analyst, Goulding Fertilisers Ltd, 1966–67; Manager and European Sales Officer for Rionore, modern Irish jewellery company, 1968–69; Racing Driver, formulae 5000, 3 and 2, 1967–71; Assistant Master: Brook House School, 1970–74; Headfort School (IAPS prep. school), 1974–76. *Recreations:* squash, cricket, running, bicycling, tennis, music, reading, computers. *Heir:* *b* Timothy Adam Goulding [*b* 15 May 1945; *m* 1971, Patricia Mohan]. *Address:* The Habitaunce, Headfort Estate, Kells, Co. Meath, Ireland. *T:* (46) 49952.

GOULDSBROUGH, Catherine Mary; *see* Newman, C. M.

GOULSTONE, Very Rev. (Thomas Richard) Kerry; Dean of St Asaph Cathedral, 1993–2001; *b* 5 June 1936; *s* of Thomas Louis and Elizabeth Goulstone; *m* 1963, Lyneth Ann Harris; one *s* one *d*. *Educ:* Llanelli Boys' Grammar Sch.; St David's University Coll., Lampeter (BA); St Michael's Theol Coll., Llandaff. Deacon 1959, priest 1960, St David's; Curate: Llanbadarn Fawr, 1959–61; St Peter's, Carmarthen, 1961–64; Vicar: Whitchurch with Solva, 1964–67; Gorslas, 1967–76; Burry Port with Pwll, 1976–84; St Peter's, Carmarthen, 1984–93; Canon, St David's Cathedral, 1986–91; RD of Carmarthen, 1988–91; Archdeacon of Carmarthen, 1991–93. Chaplain, West Wales Hosp., 1984–93. *Recreations:* music, sport, collecting porcelain. *Address:* 25 Parc Tyisha, Burry Port SA16 0RR. *T:* (01554) 832090.

GOULTY, Alan Fletcher, CMG 1998; HM Diplomatic Service, retired; Ambassador to Tunisia, 2004–08; *b* 2 July 1947; *s* of late Anthony Edmund Rivers Goulty and of Maisie Oliphant Goulty (*née* Stein); *m* 1983, Lillian Craig Harris, OBE; one *s* by former marr. *Educ:* Bootham School, York; Corpus Christi College, Oxford (MA 1972). FCO 1968; MECAS, 1969–71; Beirut, 1971–72; Khartoum, 1972–75; FCO, 1975–77; Cabinet Office, 1977–80; Washington, 1981–85; FCO, 1985–90; Counsellor, 1987; Head of Near East and N Africa Dept, 1987–90; Dep. Head of Mission, Cairo, 1990–95; Ambassador to Sudan, 1995–99; Fellow, Weatherhead Center for Internat. Affairs, Harvard Univ., 1999–2000; Dir, Middle East and N Africa, FCO, 2000–02; UK Special Rep. for Sudan, 2002–04, for Darfur, 2005–06. Cross of St Augustine, Lambeth, 2002. Grand Cordon du Wissam Alaouite (Morocco), 1987. *Recreations:* Real tennis, lawn tennis, chess, bird-watching, gardening. *Clubs:* Travellers, Royal Over-Seas League, MCC.

GOUNARIS, Elias; Ambassador; Permanent Representative of Greece to the United Nations, New York, 1999–2002; *b* 7 Sept. 1941; *s* of Panayotis and Christine Gounaris; *m* 1970, Irene Hadjilias. *Educ:* Univ. of Athens (LLM). Military Service, 1964–66; Attaché, Min. of Foreign Affairs, Athens, 1966–67; 3rd Sec., 1967; Consul, New York, 1969–73; Head, Section for Cyprus Affairs, Min. of Foreign Affairs, 1973–75; Sec., Perm. Mission of Greece to Internat. Orgns, Geneva, 1975–79; Counsellor, 1976; Dep. Chief of Mission, Belgrade, 1979–83; Head, American Desk, Min. of Foreign Affairs, 1983–87; Minister Counsellor, then Minister, Bonn, 1987–89; Minister Plenipotentiary, 1988; Ambassador to Moscow with parallel accreditation to Mongolia, 1989–93; Ambassador to UK, 1993–96; Dir Gen. for Pol Affairs, Min. of For. Affairs, Greece, 1996–99. Grand Cross: Order of the Phoenix (Greece); Order of the Lion (Finland), 1996; of Civil Merit (Spain); Commander: Order of Merit (Germany); Order of Merit (Italy), 1997; Grand Silver Badge of Honour with star (Austria). *Recreations:* jogging, classical music, reading, antique hunting. *Address:* Akadimias Street 1, 10671 Athens, Greece. *Clubs:* Brooks's; Athenean (Athens).

GOURDAULT-MONTAGNE, Maurice, Hon. CMG 2004; Hon. LVO 1992; Ambassador of France to the Court of St James's, since 2007; *b* Paris, 16 Nov. 1953; *s* of Col Jean Gourdault-Montagne and Colette Nelly Bastide; *m* 1980, Soline de Courrèges d'Agnos; two *s* three *d*. *Educ:* Institut d'Études Politiques, Paris (MA 1975); Faculté de Droit, Paris II (MA 1976); Institut Nat. des Langues et Civilisations Orientales (MA 1977; Dip. Hindi and Urdu 1977). Joined Min. of Foreign Affairs, 1978; Indian Desk, 1978–81; First Sec., New Delhi, 1981–83; Pvte Sec. to Sec. Gen., 1983–86; Advr to Foreign Minister for Parlt and Press, 1986–88; Counsellor, Bonn, 1988–91; Dep., then Actg Spokesman, Min. of Foreign Affairs, 1991–93; Dep. Principal Sec. to the Foreign Minister, 1993–95; Principal Sec., Head of Prime Minister's Office, 1995–97; Ambassador to Japan, 1998–2002; Sen. Diplomatic Advr to President of France and G8 Sherpa, 2002–07. Chevalier: de l'Ordre national du Mérite, 1998; de la Légion d'Honneur, 2001. *Recreations:* music (opera), history, linguistics, hiking and mountaineering. *Address:* 11 Kensington Palace Gardens, W8 4QP. *T:* (020) 7073 1000.

GOURGEON, Pierre-Henri; President and Chief Operating Officer, Air France, since 1998; Deputy Chief Executive Officer, Air France-KLM, since 2004; *b* 28 April 1946; *s* of Henri Gourgeon and Hélène (*née* Deiziani); *m* 1969, Mireille Blanc; one *s* one *d*. *Educ:* Lycée Gautier à Alger, Algeria; Lycée Louis-le-Grand, Paris; Ecole polytechnique, Paris; Ecole nationale supérieure de l'aeronautique; California Inst. of Technol. (MSc). Fighter pilot, French Air Force; engrg posts in aeronautical tech. and prodn depts, MoD, 1971–81; Mem., Prime Minister's staff, 1981–83; Special Tech. Advr to Minister of Labour and Vocational Trng, 1984; Vice-Pres. i/c mil. progs, Soc. nationale d'études et de constructions de moteurs d'avions, 1985–88; Special Advr to Minister of Transport, Equipt and Housing, 1988–90; Dir Gen., Civil Aviation Authorities, 1990–93; Pres., Eur. Civil Aviation Conf., 1993; Air France Group, 1993–: Chairman: and CEO, Servair Gp, 1993–96; and CEO, Esterel, 1996–97; Amadeus Internat., 1997–2002; Exec. Vice-Pres. for Corporate Develt and Internat. Affairs, 1997–98. Officier, Ordre national du Mérite; Chevalier de la Légion d'honneur. *Recreations:* flying, ski-ing. *Address:* Air France, 45 rue de Paris, 95747 Roissy cedex, France.

GOURGEY, Alan; QC 2003; *b* 27 Oct. 1961; *s* of Zaki and Vilma Gourgey; *m* 1987, Rosalynd Samuels; two *s* one *d*. *Educ:* Epsom Coll.; Bristol Univ. (LLB Hons); Inns of Court Sch. of Law. Called to the Bar, Lincoln's Inn, 1984; in practice, specialising in commercial litigation. *Recreations:* 5-a-side football, golf, Daf Yomi, my family. *Address:* 11 Stone Buildings, Lincoln's Inn, WC2A 3TG. *T:* (020) 7831 6381, *Fax:* (020) 7831 2575; *e-mail:* gourgey@11stonebuildings.com.

GOURIET, Gerald William; QC 2006; *b* 31 March 1947; *s* of Geoffrey George Gouriet, CBE and Annie Wallace (*née* Campbell). *Educ:* Royal Coll. of Music (BMus). Called to the Bar, Inner Temple, 1974; in practice at the Bar, 1974–; writing film music, Hollywood, 1991–99. *Recreation:* music, film, theatre. *Address:* Francis Taylor Building, Inner Temple, EC4Y 7BY. *T:* (020) 7735 6123; *e-mail:* geraldgouriet@btinternet.com. *Club:* Garrick.

GOURLAY, Gen. Sir (Basil) Ian (Spencer), KCB 1973; CVO 1990; OBE 1956 (MBE 1948); MC 1944; Vice President, United World Colleges, since 1990 (Director General, 1975–90); *b* 13 Nov. 1920; *er s* of late Brig. K. I. Gourlay, DSO, OBE, MC and Victoria May Gourlay (*née* Oldrini); *m* 1948, Natasha, *d* of Col Dimitri Zinovieff and Princess Elisaveta Galitzine; one *s* one *d*. *Educ:* Eastbourne Coll. Commissioned RM, 1940; HMS Formidable, Arctic, Indian Ocean, Mediterranean, 1941–44; 43 Commando, Yugoslavia, Italy, 1944–45; 45 Commando, Hong Kong, 1946–48; Instructor, RNC Greenwich, 1948–50; Adjt RMFVR, City of London, 1950–52; Instructor, RM Officers' Sch., 1952–54; psc 1954; Bde Major, 3rd Commando Bde, Malta, Cyprus, Suez landings, 1955–57 (despatches); OC RM Officers' Trng Wing, Infantry Training Centre RM, 1957–59; 2nd in Comd, 42 Commando, Singapore, 1959–61; GSO1, HQ Plymouth Gp, 1961–63; CO 42 Commando, Singapore, Borneo, 1963–65; Col GS, Dept of CGRM, Min. of Defence, 1965–66; Col 1965; Comdr, 3rd Commando Bde, Singapore, 1966–68; Maj.-Gen. Royal Marines, Portsmouth, 1968–71; Commandant-General, Royal Marines, 1971–75; Lt-Gen., 1971; Gen., 1973. Vice Patron, RM Museum. *Clubs:* Army and Navy, MCC; Royal Navy Cricket (Vice-Pres.).

GOURLAY, Gen. Sir Ian; *see* Gourlay, Gen. Sir B. I. S.

GOURLAY, Robert Martin, (Robin); Chairman, awg (formerly Anglian Water) plc, 1994–2003; *b* 21 April 1939; *s* of late Cleland Gourlay and Janice (*née* Martin); *m* 1971, Rosemary Puckle Cooper; one *s* two *d*. *Educ:* Sedbergh Sch.; St Andrews Univ. (BSc). Joined BP, 1958: Gen. Manager, BP of Greece, 1970–74; European Finance and Planning Co-ordinator, 1975–77; Asst Gen. Manager, Corporate Planning, 1978–79; Gen. Manager, Public Affairs, 1979–83; BP Australia: Dir, Refining and Marketing, 1983–86; Chief Exec., 1986–90; Chm., BP PNG, 1986–90; Dir, BP NZ, 1988–90; Chief Exec., BP Nutrition, 1990–94. Chairman: Rugby Gp plc, 1994–2000 (non-exec. Dir, 1994–96); Fundamental Data, 2000–; Director: Beazer Gp (formerly Beazer Homes) plc, 1995–2001; Astec (BSR) plc, 1996–99. Bd Mem., Australia Staff Coll., Mt Eliza, 1986–90; Chm., BITC, Victoria, 1988–90. Mem. Council, WaterAid, 1995–2002; Chm., Meath Epilepsy Trust, 2004–. Chm., Sedbergh Sch., 2002–. *Recreations:* music, gardening, tennis. *Club:* Boodle's.

GOURLAY, Sir Simon (Alexander), Kt 1989; President, National Farmers' Union, 1986–91; *b* 15 July 1934; *s* of David and Helga Gourlay; *m* 1st, 1956, Sally Garman; one *s*; 2nd, 1967, Caroline Mary Clegg; three *s*. *Educ:* Winchester; Royal Agricultural College. National Service, Commission 16th/5th Lancers, 1954–55. Farm manager, Cheshire, 1956–58; started farming on own account at Knighton, 1958; Man. Dir, Maryvale Farm Construction Ltd, 1977–85; Dir, Agricl Mortgage Corp., 1991–2002; Vice Chm., Hereford HA, 1996–2000. Chm., BFREM Ltd, 2000–01; Dir, Britannica Fare Ltd, 2000–03. Chm., Guild of Conservation Grade Producers, 1992–2004. Gov., Harper Adams Agricl Coll., 1992–99. *Recreations:* gardening, music, hill walking. *Address:* Hill House Farm, Knighton, Powys LD7 1NA. *T:* (01547) 528542.

GOURLEY, Prof. Brenda Mary; Vice-Chancellor, Open University, since 2002; *b* 1 Dec. 1943; *d* of William and Irene Elliott; *m* 1966, James Ednie Gourley; three *s* one *d*. *Educ:* Univ. of Witwatersrand (Cert. Theory of Accountancy); Univ. of S Africa (MBL). Professional Accountant; Dep. Vice-Chancellor and Principal, 1988–93, Vice-Chancellor and Principal, 1994–2001, Univ. of Natal. Member, Board: ACU, 1997– (Chm., 2007–); Internat. Assoc. of Univs, 2000–; Unesco Bd of Educn, 2005–06. Hon. LLD Nottingham, 1997; Hon. DHL Richmond, Amer. Internat. Univ. in London, 2004; Hon. DEd Abertay, 2004; Hon. DPhil Allama Iqbal, 2007. *Publications:* (contrib.) Universities and Business: partnering for the knowledge society, 2006; contrib. The Independent, THES etc. *Recreations:* reading, gardening, walking. *Address:* Vice-Chancellor's Office, Open University, Walton Hall, Milton Keynes MK7 6AA. *T:* (01908) 653214, *Fax:* (01908) 655093. *Club:* Athenæum.

GOVE, Michael Andrew; MP (C) Surrey Heath, since 2005; *b* 26 Aug. 1967; *s* of Ernest and Christine Gove; *m* 2001, Sarah Vine; one *s* one *d*. *Educ:* Robert Gordon's Coll., Aberdeen; Lady Margaret Hall, Oxford (BA). Reporter, Aberdeen Press and Jl, 1989; researcher/reporter, Scottish TV, 1990–91; reporter, BBC News and Current Affairs,

1991–95; editor, 1995–2005, writer, 1995–, The Times. *Publications:* Michael Portillo, 1995; The Price of Peace: a study of the Northern Ireland peace process, 2000; Celsius 7/7, 2005. *Address:* c/o House of Commons, SW1A 0AA. *T:* (020) 7219 3000.

GOVENDER, Very Rev. Rogers Morgan; Dean of Manchester, since 2006; *b* 29 June 1960; *s* of Joseph and Sheila Govender; *m* 1985, Celia; one *s* one *d*. *Educ:* St Paul's Coll., Grahamstown, RSA (DipTh 1985); Univ. of Natal (BTh 1997). Ordained deacon, 1985, priest, 1986; Curate, Christ Church, Overport, S Africa, 1985–87; Rector: St Mary's, Greyville, Durban, SA, 1988–93; St Matthew's, Hayfields, Pietermaritzburg, 1993–97; Archdeacon, Pietermaritzburg, 1997–99; Rector, St Thomas, Berea, Durban, 1999–2000; Priest-in-charge, Christ Church, Didsbury, Manchester, 2000–06; Area Dean, Withington, 2003–06. *Recreations:* fishing, walking, reading, listening to music (esp. rock, classical and folk). *Address:* 1 Booth-Clibborn Court, Park Lane, Salford M7 4PJ. *T:* (0161) 833 2220; *e-mail:* dean@manchestercathedral.org.

GOVENDIR, Ian John; Head of Development (formerly of Big Gifts and Legacies), National Deaf Children's Society and Deaf Child Worldwide, since 2007; *b* 5 April 1960; *s* of Philip Govendir and Eve Karis Govendir (*née* Cohen). *Educ:* City of London Poly. (HND (Dist.) Business and Finance); Univ. of Lancaster (MA Mktg). MCIM 1990; MInstF 1992. Asst Product Manager, then Showroom Manager, Sony UK Ltd, 1979–83; Direct Marketing Manager, Bull Computers, 1988–92; Head of Direct Marketing/Fundraising, BRCS, 1992–94; Chief Exec., British Lung Foundn, 1994–96; marketing and fundraising consultant, Ian Govendir Marketing, 1997–2000; Marketing Manager, Jewish Care, 2000–02; Chief Exec., Complementary Health Trust, 2002–03; Head of Fundraising, Carers UK, 2003–04; on sabbatical, travelling the world, Sri Lanka tsunami relief, 2004–05; life coach, 2006–. Part-time Lectr in Marketing, London Guildhall Univ., 1992–95. Sec., UK Coalition Trust, 1996–97; Trustee, Jewish AIDS Trust, 1998–2003. FRSA 1996. *Recreations:* swimming, travel, cooking, gardening, preservation of national heritage, such as National Trust, architecture old and new, effect of religions on society, Middle Eastern politics, digital photography. *Address:* *e-mail:* Ian@Iancoach.com.

GOVETT, William John Romaine; *b* 11 Aug. 1937; *s* of John Romaine Govett and Angela Mostyn (*née* Pritchard); *m* 1st, Mary Hays; two *s* one *d*; 2nd, Penelope Irwin; one *d*; 3rd, 1994, Jacqueline de Brabant. *Educ:* Sandroyd; Gordonstoun. National Service, commnd Royal Scots Greys, 1956–58. Joined John Govett & Co. Ltd, 1961; Chm., 1974–86; Dep. Chm., 1986–90. Director: Legal & General Gp, 1972–96; Govett Oriental Investment Trust, 1972–98; Govett Strategic Investment Trust, 1975–98; Scottish Eastern Investment Trust, 1977–98; Govett Amer. Smaller Cos Trust (formerly Govett Atlantic Investment Trust), 1979–98; Union Jack Oil Co., 1981–94; 3i (formerly Investors in Industry), 1984–98; Coal Investment Nominees NCB Pension Fund, 1985–96; Ranger Oil (UK), 1988–95; Ranger Oil (N Sea), 1995–97; Halifax Financial Services (Hldgs), 1998–2002; Halifax Life, 1998–2002; Halifax Unit Trust Mgt, 1998–2002; Halifax Fund Mgt, 1998–2002; Insight Investment Mgt (formerly Clerical and Medical Investment Mgt) Ltd, 2002–. Chairman: Hungarian Investment Co., 1990–98; 3i Smaller Quoted Cos Trust, 1996–2006; Govett Mexican Horizons Investment Co. Ltd, 1991–96. Advr, Mineworkers' Pension Scheme, 1996–2003. Trustee: NACF, 1985–; Tate Gall., 1988–93. *Recreations:* modern art, fishing.

GOW, Gen. Sir (James) Michael, GCB 1983 (KCB 1979); DL; Commandant, Royal College of Defence Studies, 1984–86; *b* 3 June 1924; *s* of late J. C. Gow and Mrs Alastair Sanderson; *m* 1946, Jane Emily Scott, *e d* of late Capt. and Hon. Mrs Mason Scott; one *s* four *d*. *Educ:* Winchester College. Enlisted Scots Guards, 1942; commnd 1943; served NW Europe, 1944–45; Mil. Div., Quadripartite Control Commn, Berlin, 1945–46; Malayan Emergency, 1949; Equerry to HRH the Duke of Gloucester, 1952–53; psc 1954; Bde Major 1955–57; Regimental Adjt Scots Guards, 1957–60; Instructor Army Staff Coll., 1962–64; comd 2nd Bn Scots Guards, Kenya and England, 1964–66; GSO1, HQ London District, 1966–67; comd 4th Guards Bde, 1968–69; idc 1970; BGS (Int) HQ BAOR and ACOS G2 HQ Northag, 1971–73; GOC 4th Div. BAOR, 1973–75; Dir of Army Training, 1975–78; GOC Scotland and Governor of Edinburgh Castle, 1979–80; C-in-C BAOR and Comdr, Northern Army Gp, 1980–83 (awarded die Plakette des deutschen Heeres); ADC Gen. to the Queen, 1981–84. Colonel Commandant: Intelligence Corps, 1973–86; Scottish Division, 1979–80. Mem., Queen's Body Guard for Scotland, Royal Company of Archers, 1963– (Capt., 2003; non active list, 2005). UK Mem., Eurogroup US Tour, 1983. UK Kermit Roosevelt Lectr, USA, 1984. President: Royal British Legion, Scotland, 1986–96; Earl Haig Fund Scotland, 1986–96 (Vice Pres., 1996–); Nat. Assoc. of Supported Employment, 1993–96; Officers' Assoc. Scotland, 1995–96 (Vice Pres., 1996–); Chairman: Scottish Ex-Services' Charitable Orgn, 1989–96; Scots at War Trust, 1992–; Patron, Disablement Income Group Scotland, 1993–. Vice-President: Royal Patriotic Fund Corp., 1983–88; Scottish Nat. Instn for War Blinded, 1995–; Mem. Council, Erskine Hosp., 1990– (Hon. Pres., 1979–80); Mem., Thistle Foundn, 2000–. Chm., Queen Victoria Sch., Dunblane, 1979–80; Vice-President: Royal Caledonian Schs, Bushey, 1980–96; Royal Caledonian Schs Educnl Trust, 1996–. Trustee Emeritus, Ludus Baroque (Chm., 1999–2005). County Comr, British Scouts W Europe, 1980–83 (Silver Acorn). Freeman: City of London, 1980; State of Kansas, USA, 1984; Freeman and Liveryman, Painters' and Stainers' Co., 1980. Elder of Church of Scotland, Canongate Kirk, 1988–. FSAScot 1991–2002. DL Edinburgh, 1994. *Publications:* Trooping the Colour: a history of the Sovereign's Birthday Parade by the Household troops, 1989; Jottings in a General's Notebook, 1989; General Reflections: a military man at large, 1991; articles in mil. and hist. jls. *Recreations:* sailing, music, travel, reading. *Address:* 18 Ann Street, Edinburgh EH4 1PJ. *T:* (0131) 332 4752. *Clubs:* Pratt's, Highland Society of London, Third Guards, Blue Seal.

See also J. M. Drake, R. C. Gow, Lt-Col Sir W. H. M. Ross.

GOW, Dame Jane; *see* Whiteley, Dame J. E.

GOW, John Stobie, PhD; CChem, FRSC; FRSE 1978; Secretary-General, Royal Society of Chemistry, 1986–93; *b* 12 April 1933; *s* of David Gow and Anne Scott; *m* 1955, Elizabeth Henderson; three *s*. *Educ:* Alloa Acad.; Univ. of St Andrews (BSc, PhD). Res. Chemist, ICI, Billingham, 1958; Prodn Man., Chem. Co. of Malaysia, 1966–68; ICI: Res. Man., Agric. Div., 1968–72; Gen. Man. (Catalysts), Agric. Div., 1972–74; Res. Dir, Organics, 1974–79; Dep. Chm., Organics, 1979–84; Man. Dir, Speciality Chemicals, 1984–86. Assessor, SERC, 1988–94; Sec., CSTI, 1995–2001; Dir, Sci., Engrg and Manufacturing Technol. Assoc., 2002–05. FRSA 1980. *Publications:* papers and patents in Fertilizer Technology and Biotechnology. *Recreations:* choral music, golf. *Address:* 19 Longcroft Avenue, Harpenden, Herts AL5 2RD. *T:* (01582) 764889.

GOW, Gen. Sir Michael; *see* Gow, Gen. Sir J. M.

GOW, Neil; QC (Scot.) 1970; Sheriff of South Strathclyde, at Ayr, 1976–2005; *b* 24 April 1932; *s* of Donald Gow, oil merchant, Glasgow; *m* 1959, Joanna, *d* of Comdr S. D. Sutherland, Edinburgh; one *s*. *Educ:* Merchiston Castle Sch., Edinburgh; Glasgow and Edinburgh Univs. MA, LLB. Formerly Captain, Intelligence Corps (BAOR). Carnegie Scholar in History of Scots Law, 1956. Advocate, 1957–76. Standing Counsel to Min. of Social Security (Scot.), 1964–70. Contested (C): Kirkcaldy Burghs, Gen. Elections of 196 and 1966; Edinburgh East, 1970; Mem. Regional Council, Scottish Conservative Assoc An Hon. Sheriff of Lanarkshire, 1971. Pres., Auchinleck Boswell Soc. Jt editor, Crime an Prejudice, Channel 4, 1993; writer, Tests of Evidence, Radio Scotland, 1995 (Gol Medal, NY Radio City Awards, 1998). FSA (Scot.). *Publications:* A History of Scottis Statutes, 1959; Jt Editor, An Outline of Estate Duty in Scotland, 1970; A History o Belmont House School, 1979; numerous articles and broadcasts on legal topics an Scottish affairs. *Recreations:* golf, shooting, classic cars. *Address:* Old Auchenfail Hall, b Mauchline, Ayrshire KA5 5TA. *T:* (01290) 550822. *Clubs:* Western (Glasgow); Prestwic Golf.

GOW, Roderick Charles, OBE 2002; Founder and Chairman, Gow & Partners Grou since 2002; *b* 9 Sept. 1947; *s* of Gen. Sir (James) Michael Gow, *qv*; *m* 1st, 1977, Ann Bayart (*d* 2000); two *s*; 2nd, 2001, April Riddle. *Educ:* Winchester Coll.; Trinity Coll Cambridge (BA 1970, MA 1972). ACIB 1982. Capt., Scots Guards, NW Germany, N and Belgium, 1966–78; ADC to Chm., Mil. Cttee, NATO, Brussels, 1975–77; Instructo RMA, Sandhurst, 1977–78. Barclays Bank, London and NY, 1978–83 (Vice-Pres., t 1983); Russell Reynolds Associates, London, 1983–91 (Man. Dir, UK, then Man. Di Internat., 1986–91); Chief Exec., GKR Gp, London, 1991–93, NY, 1993–95; Exec. Vic Pres. and Co-Hd, Global Financial Services Practice, NY, LAI Worldwide, later TMP 1995–2000; Chm., Americas, later Dep. Chm., Worldwide, Amrop Internat., 1995–9 Odgers, Ray & Berndtson: London Dir, 2000–02; Chm. Bd, Practice and Financia Services Practice, 2000–02. Chm., Adv. Bd, Moore Clayton & Co., 2002–03. Chm Action Resource Centre, 1991–93. Chm., British American Chamber of Commerce o NY and London, 1999–2001; Chm., Pres. and Vice-Pres., British American Busine Council, 2001–03. Mem., Adv. Council, Prince of Wales Business Trust, 2002–03. Mem Adv. Council, LSO (Co-Chm., Amer. Foundn), 2001–. Mem., Guild of Interna Bankers, 2001–. FIPD; FRSA. Mem., Royal Co. of Archers, Queen's Bodyguard fo Scotland, 1982–. *Recreations:* shooting, sailing, music. *Address:* Gow & Partners, 4 Berkeley Square, W1J 5AW; *e-mail:* roddy.gow@gowpartners.com. *Clubs:* Brooks's Pratt's, Cavalry and Guards; Indian Harbor Yacht (Greenwich, CT); Fairfield Hun (Fairfield, CT); Leash (NYC).

GOWAN, David John, CMG 2005; HM Diplomatic Service, retired; *b* 11 Feb. 1949; of Prof. Ivor Lyn Gowan and Gwendoline Alice Gowan (*née* Pearce); *m* 1975, Marna Iren Williams; two *s*. *Educ:* Nottingham High Sch.; Ardwyn Grammar Sch., Aberystwyth Balliol Coll., Oxford (MA Eng. Lang. and Lit.). Asst Principal, MoD, 1970–73; Home CS 1973–75; joined HM Diplomatic Service, 1975: Second Sec., FCO, 1975–76; Russia lang. trng, 1976–77; Second, then First Sec., Moscow, 1977–80; First Sec., FCO 1981–85; Hd of Chancery and Consul, Brasilia, 1985–88; on secondment to Cabine Office, 1988–89; Asst Hd, Soviet Dept, FCO, 1989–90; on secondment, as Counsello Cabinet Office, 1990–91; Counsellor (Commercial and Know How Fund), Moscow 1992–95; Counsellor and Dep. Hd of Mission, Helsinki, 1995–99; Counsellor, FCO 1999; Sen. Associate Mem., St Antony's Coll., Oxford, 1999–2000; Minister, Moscow 2000–03; Ambassador to Serbia and Montenegro, 2003–06. Guest Mem., St Antony Coll., Oxford, 2007–; Hon. Sen. Res. Fellow, Univ. of Birmingham, 2008–. Mem. Bishop's Council, 2007–, Synod, 2008–, Dio. in Europe. *Publication:* How the EU Ca Help Russia, 2000. *Recreations:* reading, walking, travel, music, theatre. *Address:* Blackmore Road, Malvern, Worcs WR14 1QX. *T:* (01684) 565707. *Club:* Athenæum.

GOWANS, Sir James (Learmonth), Kt 1982; CBE 1971; FRCP 1975; FRS 1963 Secretary General, Human Frontier Science Programme, Strasbourg, 1989–93; Secretary Medical Research Council, 1977–87; *b* 7 May 1924; *s* of John Gowans and Selma Josefin Ljung; *m* 1956, Moyra Leatham; one *s* two *d*. *Educ:* Whitgift Middle Sch., Croydon King's Coll. Hosp. Med. Sch. (MB BS (Hons) 1947; Fellow, 1979); Lincoln Coll., Oxfor (BA (1st cl. Hons Physiology) 1948; MA; DPhil 1953; Hon. Fellow, 1984). MR Exchange Scholar, Pasteur Institute, Paris, 1952–53; Research Fellow, Exeter Coll. Oxford, 1955–60 (Hon. Fellow, 1983–); Fellow, St Catherine's Coll., Oxford, 1961–8 (Hon. Fellow, 1987); Henry Dale Res. Prof. of Royal Society, 1962–77; Hon. Dir, MR Cellular Immunology Unit, 1963–77; Dir, 1980–86, Sen. Sci. Advr, 1988–90, Celltec Ltd. Consultant: WHO Global Prog. on AIDS, 1987–88; 3i plc, 1988–92. Member MRC, 1965–69; Adv. Bd for Res. Councils, 1977–87; Director: Charing Cross Sunle Res. Centre, 1989–91; European Initiative for Communicators of Science, Munich 1995–99. Royal Society: Mem. Council and a Vice-Pres., 1973–75; Assessor to MRC 1973–75. Member: Governing Council, Internat. Agency for Res. on Cancer, Lyon 1980–87; Sci. Cttee, Fondation Louis Jeantet de Médicine, Geneva, 1984–87; Council, S Christopher's Hospice, 1987–98; Res. Progs Adv. Cttee, Nat. MS Soc., NY, 1988–90 Awards Assembly, Gen. Motors Cancer Res. Foundn, NY, 1988–90; Chm., Scientifi Adv. Cttee, Lister Inst. of Preventive Medicine, 1994–97. Non-exec. Dir, Tavistock an Portman NHS Trust, 1994–97. Delegate, OUP, 1971–77. FRSA 1994. Founder FMedSc 1998. Vis. Prof., NY Univ. Sch. of Med., 1967; Lectures: Harvey, NY, 1968; Willian Withering, Birmingham, 1970; Foundation, RCPath, 1970; Dunham, Harvard, 1971 Bayne-Jones, Johns Hopkins, 1973; Langdon Brown, RCP, 1980; Harveian Orator RCP, 1987. Foreign Associate, Nat. Acad. of Scis, USA, 1985. Mem., Academi Europaea, 1991. Hon. Member: Amer. Assoc. of Immunologists; Amer. Soc. o Anatomists. Hon. ScD Yale, 1966; Hon. DSc: Chicago, 1971; Birmingham, 1978 Rochester, NY, 1987; Hon. MD: Edinburgh, 1979; Sheffield, 2000; Hon. DM Southampton, 1987; Hon. LLD Glasgow, 1988. Gairdner Foundn Award, Toronto, 1968 Paul Ehrlich Ludwig-Darmstaedter Prize, Frankfurt, 1974; Royal Medal, Royal Society 1976; Feldberg Foundn Award, 1979; Wolf Prize in Medicine, Wolf Foundn, Israel, 1980 Medawar Prize, 1990; Galen Medal, Soc. of Apothecaries, 1991. *Publications:* articles ir scientific journals. *Address:* 75 Cumnor Hill, Oxford OX2 9HX. *T:* (01865) 862304.

GOWANS, James Palmer; JP; DL; Lord Provost of Dundee and Lord-Lieutenant of the City of Dundee, 1980–84; *b* 15 Sept. 1930; *s* of Charles Gowans and Sarah Gowans (*né* Palmer); *m* 1950, Davina Barnett (*d* 2000); one *s* three *d* (and one *s* one *d* decd). *Educ* Rockwell Secondary School, Dundee. With National Cash Register Co., Dundee 1956–94. Elected to Dundee DC, May 1974; Mem., Dundee City Council, 1975–92. JI 1977; DL Dundee 1984. *Recreations:* golf, motoring. *Address:* 41 Dalmahoy Drive, Dunde DD2 3UT. *T:* (01382) 84918.

GOWANS, Gen. John; General of The Salvation Army, 1999–2002; *b* 13 Nov. 1934; of John and Elizabeth Gowans; *m* 1957, Gisèle Marie Bonhotal; two *s*. *Educ:* Halesowe Grammar Sch.; William Booth Meml Trng Coll. Served with Salvation Army 1955–2002; commnd officer, in Liverpool, N Wales, London, Manchester, Yorkshire Nottingham, 1955–77; Chief Sec., Paris, 1977–81; Leader for Southern California, LA 1981–86; Territorial Commander in: France, 1986–93; Australia E and PNG, 1993–97 UK and Republic of Ireland, 1997–99. Freeman, City of London, 2000. *Publications:* C Lord!, 1977, 3rd edn 1996; There's a boy here… (autobiog.); libretto for ten Salvatio Army musicals. *Recreations:* reading, gardening, English literature, drama. *Address:* c/o The Salvation Army, 101 Queen Victoria Street, EC4P 4EP. *T:* (020) 7332 0101.

GOWAR, Prof. Norman William; Chairman, Office of the Independent Adjudicator for Higher Education, since 2003; Principal, Royal Holloway (Royal Holloway and Bedford New College), University of London, 1990–2000; Professor Emeritus, University of London, since 2000; *b* 7 Dec. 1940; *s* of Harold James and Constance Dawson-Gowar; *m* 1st, 1963, Diane May Parker (marr. diss.); one *s* one *d*; 2nd, 1981, Prof. Judith Margaret Greene, *d* of Lord Gordon-Walker, PC, CH. *Educ:* Sir George Monoux Grammar Sch.; City Univ. (BSc, MPhil). FIMA. English Electric Co., 1963; Lectr in Maths, City Univ., 1963; Open University: Lectr and Sen. Lectr, 1969; Prof. of Mathematics, 1983; Dir, Centre for Maths Educn, 1983; Pro-Vice-Chancellor, 1977–81; Dep. Vice-Chancellor, 1985–90; Dir, Open Coll., 1986. Vis. Fellow, Keble Coll., Oxford, 1972. Member, Council: CNAA, 1979–83; NCET, 1986–91 (Chm., Trng Cttee); Mem. Bd, CVCP, 1998–2000; Mem., Fulbright Commn, 2001–05. Chm. and Dir, Open Univ. Educational Enterprises Ltd, 1988–90. Dir, Surrey TEC, 1991–93. Mem., London Math. Soc. Governor: South Bank Univ. (formerly Polytechnic), 1992–95; UCS, 1993–2000; Rugby Sch., 1994–2004; Middlesex Univ., 2000–04; Sussex Univ., 2004–. Mem. Council, IMA, 1993–96. FRSA. Hon. Fellow, Royal Holloway, Univ. of London, 2002. Hon. DSc City, 1994; DUniv Open, 2001. *Publications:* Mathematics for Technology: a new approach, 1968; Basic Mathematical Structures, vol. 1, 1973, vol. 2, 1974; Fourier Series, 1974; Invitation to Mathematics, 1980; articles and TV series. *Address:* Luckhurst, Stone-cum-Ebony, Tenterden, Kent TN30 7JJ.

GOWDY, David Clive, CB 2001; Permanent Secretary, Department of Health, Social Services and Public Safety, Northern Ireland, 1997–2005; *b* 27 Nov. 1946; *s* of Samuel David Gowdy and Eileen Gowdy (*née* Porter); *m* 1973, Linda Doreen Traub; two *d*. *Educ:* Royal Belfast Academical Instn; Queen's Univ. Belfast (BA, MSc). Min. of Finance, NI, 1970; N Ireland Office, 1976; Exec. Dir, Industrial Develt Bd for NI 1985; Under Sec., Dept of Econ. Develt, NI, 1987; Under Sec., Dept of Health and Social Services, NI, 1990; Dir of Personnel, NICS, 1994. Vis. Prof., Univ. of Ulster, 2006–. Mem. Bd, Belfast Charitable Soc., 2006–. *Recreations:* exercise and relaxation. *Address:* Bangor, Co. Down.

GOWENLOCK, Prof. Brian Glover, CBE 1986; PhD, DSc; FRSE; FRSC; Professor of Chemistry, 1966–90, Leverhulme Emeritus Fellow, 1990–92, Heriot-Watt University; *b* 9 Feb. 1926; *s* of Harry Hadfield Gowenlock and Hilda (*née* Glover); *m* 1953, Margaret L. Davies; one *s* two *d*. *Educ:* Hulme Grammar Sch., Oldham; Univ. of Manchester (BSc, MSc, PhD). DSc Birmingham. FRIC 1966; FRSE 1968. Asst Lectr in Chemistry 1948, Lectr 1951, University Coll. of Swansea; Lectr 1955, Sen. Lectr 1964, Univ. of Birmingham; Dean, Faculty of Science, Heriot-Watt Univ., 1969–72, 1987–90. Vis. Scientist, National Res. Council, Ottawa, 1963; Erskine Vis. Fellow, Univ. of Canterbury, NZ, 1976; Hon. Res. Fellow, 1992–2002, Hon. Vis. Prof., 2002–05, Exeter Univ. Mem., UGC, 1976–85, Vice-Chm., 1983–85. Methodist local preacher, 1946–. *Publications:* (with Sir Harry Melville) Experimental Methods in Gas Reactions, 1964; (with James C. Blackie) First Year at the University, 1964; (with Alex Anderson) Chemistry in Heriot-Watt 1821–1991, 1998; contribs to scientific jls. *Recreation:* genealogy. *Address:* Riccarton, 5 Roselands, Sidmouth, Devon EX10 8PB. *T:* (01395) 516864.

GOWER; see Leveson Gower.

GOWER, David Ivon, OBE 1992; broadcaster and journalist; *b* 1 April 1957; *s* of Richard Hallam Gower and Sylvia Mary Gower (*née* Ford); *m* 1992, Thorunn Ruth Nash; two *d*. *Educ:* King's Sch., Canterbury; University Coll., London. Professional cricketer, 1975–93; Leicestershire, 1975–89; Hampshire, 1990–93; 117 Test matches for England, 1978–92; 8,231 Test runs (3rd highest for England), incl. 18 centuries; captained England 32 times, 1984–86, 1989; retired from 1st class cricket, Nov. 1993. PR consultant (cricket sponsorship), Nat. Westminster Bank, 1993–2000. BBC Cricket Commentator, 1994–99; Presenter: Gower's Cricket Monthly, BBC TV, 1995–98; David Gower's Cricket Weekly, BBC Radio 5, 1995–98; Internat. Cricket, Sky Sports, 1999–; panel mem., They Think It's All Over, BBC TV, 1996–2003. Columnist, Sunday Times, 2002–. Hon. MA: Southampton Inst. (Nottingham Trent Univ.), 1993; Loughborough, 1994. Hon. Blue, Heriot-Watt Univ. *Publications:* With Time to Spare, 1979; Heroes and Contemporaries, 1983; A Right Ambition, 1986; On the Rack, 1990; Gower, The Autobiography, 1992. *Recreations:* ski-ing, safari, Cresta Run, tennis. *Address:* c/o Jon Holmes Media Ltd, 5th Floor, Holborn Gate, 26 Southampton Buildings, WC2A 1PQ. *Clubs:* East India, MCC (Mem. Cttee, 2000–03), Home House; St Moritz Tobogganing.

GOWER, His Honour John Hugh; QC 1967; a Circuit Judge, 1972–96; a Deputy Circuit Judge, 1996–99; *b* 6 Nov. 1925; *s* of Henry John Gower, JP and Edith (*née* Brooks); *m* 1960, Shirley Mameena Darbourne; one *s* one *d*. *Educ:* Skinners' Sch., Tunbridge Wells. RASC, 1945–48 (Staff Sgt). Called to the Bar, Inner Temple, 1948, Bencher, 1995; Dep. Chm., Kent QS, 1968–71; Resident and Liaison Judge of Crown Courts in E Sussex, 1986–96. Mem., Lord Chancellor's Adv. Cttee on Legal Educn and Conduct, 1991–96 (Vice-Chm., 1994–96). Chm., Kent and Sussex Area Criminal Justice Liaison Cttee, 1992–96; Pres., E Sussex Magistrates' Assoc., 1997–99 (Vice-Pres., 1986–97). Indep. Assessor, UK Govt Review of NI Criminal Justice System, 1998–2000; reviewed and reported on prosecutions conducted by Solicitor's Office of HM Customs and Excise, 2000–01. Pres., Tunbridge Wells Council of Voluntary Service, 1974–88. Hon. Vice-Pres., Kent Council of Voluntary Service, 1971–86. Pres., Kent Assoc. of Parish Councils, 1963–71. Chm., Southdown and Eridge Hunt, 1985–91. Churchwarden, St Michael and All Angels, Withyham, 2005–07. Freeman, City of London (by purchase), 1960. *Recreations:* fishing, riding, gardening, tapestry, painting. *Address:* The Coppice, Lye Green, Crowborough, E Sussex TN6 1UY.

See also P. J. de P. Gower.

GOWER, Peter John de Peauly; QC 2006; a Recorder, since 2002; *b* 30 Nov. 1960; *s* of His Honour John Hugh Gower, *qv*; *m* 1993, Emma Clout; two *s*. *Educ:* Lancing Coll.; Christ Church, Oxford (Classics Schol.; MA Juris.). Called to the Bar, Lincoln's Inn, 1985; in practice specialising in criminal law; Standing Counsel to DTI, 1991–. Chm., Kent Bar Mess, 2007–. *Recreations:* spending time with the family, reading, walking, gardening, horses, fishing. *Address:* 6 Pump Court, Temple, EC4Y 7AR. *T:* (020) 7797 8400, *Fax:* (020) 7797 8401; *e-mail:* petergower@6PumpCourt.co.uk.

GOWER ISAAC, Anthony John; see Isaac.

GOWERS, Andrew; Global Co-Head of Communications, Marketing and Brand Management, Lehman Brothers, 2006–08; *b* 19 Oct. 1957; *s* of Michael and Anne Gowers; *m* 1982, Finola Clarke; one *s* one *d*. *Educ:* Trinity Sch., Croydon; Gonville and Caius Coll., Cambridge (MA 1980). Reuters, London, Brussels and Zurich, 1980–83; Financial Times, 1983–2005: on foreign staff, 1983–84; Agric. Corresp., 1984–85; Commodities Ed., 1985–87; ME Ed., 1987–90; Features Ed., 1990–92; Foreign Ed., 1992–94; Dep. Ed., 1994–97; Actg Ed., 1997–98; Ed.-in-Chief, FT Deutschland, 1998–2001; Editor, 2001–05. *Publication:* Arafat: the biography, 1990. *Recreations:* food, wine, tennis, film, music.

GOWERS, Prof. (William) Timothy, PhD; FRS 1999; Rouse Ball Professor of Mathematics, University of Cambridge, since 1998; Fellow of Trinity College, Cambridge, since 1995; *b* 20 Nov. 1963; *s* of William Patrick Gowers and Caroline Molesworth Gowers; *m* 1988, Emily Joanna (marr. diss. 2007), *d* of Sir Keith (Vivian) Thomas, *qv*; two *s* one *d*; *m* 2008, Julie, *d* of Alain and Sylvie Barreau; one *s*. *Educ:* Eton Coll.; Trinity Coll., Cambridge (BA; PhD 1990). Res. Fellow, Trinity Coll., Cambridge, 1989–93; Lectr, 1991–94, Reader, 1994–95, UCL; Lectr, Univ. of Cambridge, 1995–98. Hon. Fellow, UCL, 1999. European Mathematical Soc. Prize, 1996; Fields Medal, 1998. *Publications:* Mathematics: a very short introduction, 2002; (ed) The Princeton Companion to Mathematics, 2008; contrib. papers in mathematical jls. *Recreation:* jazz piano. *Address:* Department of Pure Mathematics and Mathematical Statistics, Centre for Mathematical Sciences, Wilberforce Road, Cambridge CB3 0WB. *T:* (01223) 337999.

GOWING, Nicholas Keith, (Nik); Main Presenter, BBC World TV, BBC News, since 2000 (Presenter, 1996–2000); *b* 13 Jan. 1951; *s* of Donald James Graham Gowing and Margaret Mary Gowing (*née* Elliott); *m* 1982, Judith Wastall Venables; one *s* one *d*. *Educ:* Latymer Upper Sch.; Simon Langton Grammar Sch., Canterbury; Bristol Univ. Reporter, Evening Chronicle, Newcastle upon Tyne, 1973–74; Presenter and Reporter, Granada TV, 1974–78; joined ITN, 1978; Rome Corresp., 1979; Eastern Europe Corresp., Warsaw, 1980–83; Foreign Affairs Corresp., 1983–87, Diplomatic Corresp., 1987–89, Diplomatic Editor, 1989–96, Channel 4 News. Fellow, Shorenstein Center, J. F. Kennedy Sch., Harvard Univ., 1994; Vis. Fellow, Keele Univ., 1998–. Consultant: Carnegie Commn on Preventing Deadly Conflict, 1996–97; on Wars and Information Mgt, EC Humanitarian Office, 1997–98. Vice Chair and Gov., Westminster Foundn for Democracy, 1996–2005; Governor: British Assoc. for Central and Eastern Europe, 1996–2008; Ditchley Foundn, 2000–; Member: IISS 1990; Council, 1998–2004, Exec. Council, 2000–02, RIIA; Adv. Council, Wilton Park, 1998–; Adv. Bd, Birmingham Univ. Centre for Studies in Security and Diplomacy, 1999–; Cttee, Project on Justice in Times of Transition, 1999–; Steering Cttee, Konigswinter Conf., 1999–; Exec. Cttee and Council, RUSI, 2005–; Council, ODI, 2007–; Cttee, Rory Peck Trust, 1996–; Trustee, Liddell Hart Archive, KCL, 2004–. *Publications:* The Wire, 1988; The Loop, 1993. *Recreations:* cycling, ski-ing, authorship, lecturing, chairing conferences. *Address:* BBC TV Centre, W12 7RJ. *T:* (020) 8225 8137; *e-mail:* nik.gowing@bbc.co.uk.

GOWON, Gen. Dr Yakubu, PhD; jssc, psc; founder President and Chairman, Yakubu Gowon Center for National Unity and International Co-operation; *b* Garam, Pankshin Div., Plateau State, Nigeria, 19 Oct. 1934; *s* of Yohanna Gowon (an Angas, a Christian evangelist of CMS) and Saraya Gowon; *m* 1969, Victoria Hansatu Zakari; one *s* two *d*. *Educ:* St Bartholomew's Schs (CMS), Wusasa, and Govt Coll., Zaria, Nigeria; Warwick Univ. (BA Hons 1978; PhD). Regular Officer's Special Trng Sch., Teshie, Ghana; Eaton Hall Officer Cadet Sch., Chester, RMA, Sandhurst, Staff Coll., Camberley and Joint Services Staff Coll., Latimer (all in England). Enlisted, 1954; commissioned, 1956; served in Cameroon, 1960; Adjt, 4th Bn Nigerian Army, 1960 (Independence Oct. 1960); UN Peace-Keeping Forces, Congo, Nov. 1960–June 1961 and Jan.–June 1963 (Bde Major). Lt-Col and Adjt-Gen., Nigerian Army, 1963; Comd, 2nd Bn, Nigerian Army, Ikeja, 1966; Chief of Staff, 1966; Head of Fed. Mil. Govt, and C-in-C, Armed Forces of Fed. Republic of Nigeria, July 1966–1975; Maj.-Gen. 1967; maintained territorial integrity of his country by fighting, 1967–70, to preserve unity of Nigeria (after failure of peaceful measures) following on Ojukwu rebellion, and declared secession of the Eastern region of Nigeria, July 1967; created 12 equal and autonomous states in Nigeria, 1967; Biafran surrender, 1970; promoted Gen., 1971. Chairman: Base Development (Nigeria) Ltd (formerly Kanawa Industries (Nigeria) Ltd), Kano, 1987; National Oil and Chemical Marketing Co., Lagos, 1996; Industrial and General Insurance Co. Ltd. Chm. Trustees, Commonwealth Human Ecology Foundn, 1986–. Is a Christian; works for internat. peace and security within the framework of OAU and UNO; Chm., Nigeria Prays. Vis. Prof., Jos Univ., 1987–. Hon. LLD Cambridge, 1975; also hon. doctorates from Univs of Ibadan, Lagos, ABU-Zaria, Nigeria at Nsukka, Benin, Ife, and Shaw Univ., USA, 1973. Holds Grand Cross, etc, of several foreign orders. *Publication:* Faith in Unity, 1970. *Recreations:* squash, lawn tennis, pen-drawing, photography, cinephotography. *Address:* (office) POB 3995, Garki, Abuja, Nigeria. *Clubs:* Army and Navy, Les Ambassadeurs.

GOWRIE, 2nd Earl of, *cr* 1945; **Alexander Patrick Greysteil Hore-Ruthven;** PC 1984; Baron Ruthven of Gowrie, 1919; Baron Gowrie, 1935; Viscount Ruthven of Canberra, 1945; Chairman, The Magdi Yacoub Institute (formerly Harefield Research Foundation), since 2003; Director, Sotheby's Holdings Inc., 1985–98 (Chairman, Sotheby's Europe, 1987–94); *b* Dublin, 26 Nov. 1939; *er s* of late Capt. Hon. Alexander Hardinge Patrick Hore-Ruthven, Rifle Bde, and Pamela Margaret (as Viscountess Ruthven of Canberra, she *m* 1952, Major Derek Cooper, MC, The Life Guards), 2nd *d* of late Rev. A. H. Fletcher; *S* grandfather, 1955; *m* 1st, 1962, Xandra (marr. diss. 1973), *yr d* of Col R. A. G. Bingley, CVO, DSO, OBE; one *s*; 2nd, 1974, Adelheid Gräfin von der Schulenburg, *y d* of late Fritz-Dietlof, Graf von der Schulenburg. *Educ:* Eton; Balliol Coll., Oxford. Visiting Lectr, State Univ. of New York at Buffalo, 1963–64; Tutor, Harvard Univ., 1965–68; Lectr in English and American Literature, UCL, 1969–72. Fine Art consultant, 1974–79. Provost, RCA, 1986–95. Chm., Arts Council of England, 1994–98. Chairman: The Really Useful Gp, 1985–90; Development Securities, 1995–99; Fine Art Fund, 2002–. A Conservative Whip, 1971–72; Parly Rep. to UN, 1971; a Lord in Waiting (Govt Whip), 1972–74; Opposition Spokesman on Economic Affairs, 1974–79; Minister of State: Dept of Employment, 1979–81; NI Office, 1981–83 (Dep. to Sec. of State); Privy Council Office (Management and Personnel), 1983–84; Minister for the Arts, 1983–85; Chancellor, Duchy of Lancaster, 1984–85. FRSL 2003. Freeman, City of London, 1976. Picasso Medal, UNESCO, 1996. *Publications:* A Postcard from Don Giovanni, 1972; (jt) The Genius of British Painting, 1975; (jt) The Conservative Opportunity, 1976; Derek Hill: an appreciation, 1987; The Domino Hymn: poems from Harefield, 2005; Third Day: new and selected poems, 2008. *Recreation:* book reviewing. *Heir: s* Viscount Ruthven of Canberra, *qv*. *Address:* The Magdi Yacoub Institute, Heart Science Centre, Harefield, Middlesex UB9 6JH.

See also Hon. M. W. M. K. H. Ruthven.

GOY, David John Lister; QC 1991; *b* 11 May 1949; *s* of late Rev. Leslie Goy and Joan Goy; *m* 1970; Jennifer Anne Symington; three *s*. *Educ:* Haberdashers' Aske's School, Elstree; King's College London. Called to the Bar, Middle Temple, 1973, Bencher, 2007. Chm., Revenue Bar Assoc., 2005–08. *Publication:* VAT on Property, 1989, 2nd edn 1993. *Recreations:* running and other sports. *Address:* Gray's Inn Chambers, Gray's Inn, WC1R 5JA. *T:* (020) 7242 2642.

GOYMER, Andrew Alfred; His Honour Judge Goymer; a Circuit Judge, since 1999; *b* 28 July 1947; *s* of late Richard Kirby Goymer and of Betty Eileen Goymer (*née* Thompson); *m* 1972, Diana Mary, *d* of late Robert Harry Shipway, MBE and of Sheila Mary Shipway; one *s* one *d*. *Educ:* Dulwich Coll.; Pembroke Coll., Oxford (Hull Schol.; MA). Called to the Bar, Gray's Inn, 1970 (Gerald Moody Entrance Schol., Holker Sen. Exhibnr, Arden Atkin and Mould Prizeman); practised, S Eastern Circuit, 1972–99; admitted to NSW Bar, 1988; Asst Recorder, 1987–91; Recorder, 1991–99. Mem.,

Forensic Sci. Adv. Council, 2007–. *Address:* Southwark Crown Court, 1 English Grounds, SE1 2HU. *T:* (020) 7522 7200.

GOZNEY, Sir Richard Hugh Turton, KCMG 2006 (CMG 1993); HM Diplomatic Service; Governor and Commander-in-Chief of Bermuda, since 2007; *b* 21 July 1951; *s* of Thomas Leonard Gozney and Elizabeth Margaret Lilian Gozney (*née* Gardiner); *m* 1982, Diana Edwina Baird; two *s*. *Educ:* Magdalen Coll. Sch., Oxford; St Edmund Hall, Oxford (BA Hons Geol. 1973). Teacher, Tom Mboya Rusinga Secondary Sch., Kenya, 1970; joined FO, 1973; Jakarta, 1974–78; Buenos Aires, 1978–81; FCO, 1981–84; Hd of Chancery, Madrid, 1984–88; Asst Private Sec., later Private Sec., to Foreign Sec., FCO, 1989–93; High Comr, Swaziland, 1993–96; Head of Security Policy Dept, FCO, 1996–97; Chief of Assessments Staff, Jt Intelligence Orgn, Cabinet Office, 1998–2000; Ambassador, Indonesia, 2000–04; High Comr, Nigeria, 2004–07, and Ambassador (non-resident) to Benin, 2005–07, and to Equatorial Guinea, 2006–07. *Publications:* Gibraltar and the EC, 1993; Birds on the Abuja Golf Course, 2007. *Recreations:* bird-watching, walking. *Address:* Government House, Hamilton, Bermuda; c/o Foreign and Commonwealth Office, King Charles Street, SW1A 2AH.

GRAAFF, Sir David (de Villiers), 3rd Bt *cr* 1911, of Cape Town; farmer, since 1964; wine farmer and producer of De Grendel wines, since 2000; *b* 3 May 1940; *er s* of Sir de Villiers Graaff, 2nd Bt and of Helena Le Roux Graaff (*née* Voigt); *S* father, 1999; *m* 1969, Sally Williams; three *s* one *d*. *Educ:* Diocesan Coll.; Stellenbosch Univ. (BSc Agric.); Grenoble Univ. (Premier Degré); Magdalen Coll., Oxford (BA Hons; MA). MP (Nat. Party), Wynberg, 1987–98; Dep. Minister, Trade and Industry, 1991–94. Mem., Audit Commn, 1992–94. Dir, Deciduous Fruit Bd, 1983–87. Director: Graaff's Trust, 1969–; Milnerton Estates, 1969–. Hon. Col, Cape Garrison Artillery, 2000–. *Recreation:* golf. *Heir: s* de Villiers Graaff [*b* 16 July 1970; *m* 2000, Gaedry Kriel]. *Address:* De Grendel, PO Box 15192, Panorama 7506, Cape Town, South Africa. *T:* (21) 5587030. *Clubs:* Cape Town, Royal Cape Golf.

GRABHAM, Sir Anthony (Herbert), Kt 1988; FRCS; Chairman, British Medical Journal Group, 1995–2005; *b* 19 July 1930; *s* of John and Lily Grabham; *m* 1960, Eileen Pamela Rudd; two *s* two *d*. *Educ:* St Cuthbert's Grammar School, Newcastle upon Tyne. MB BS Durham. RSO, Royal Victoria Infirmary, Newcastle upon Tyne; Consultant Surgeon, Kettering and District Gen. Hosp., 1965–95. Chm., BMA Services, 1982–2002; Dir, PPP, 1984–96, Vice-Chm., PPP Healthcare Gp plc, 1996–99. British Medical Association: Chairman: Central Cttee for Hosp. Med. Services, 1975–79; Council, 1979–84; Pres., 2002–03. Chairman: Jt Consultants Cttee, 1984–90; Cttee, BMJ, 1993–; Member: GMC, 1979–99; Council, World Med. Assoc., 1979–84; Hon. Sec. and Treasurer, Commonwealth Med. Assoc., 1982–86 (Vice-Pres., 1980–84). *Address:* Rothesay House, 56 Headlands, Kettering, Northants NN15 6DG. *T:* (01536) 513299. *Club:* Army and Navy.

GRABINER, family name of **Baron Grabiner**.

GRABINER, Baron *cr* 1999 (Life Peer), of Aldwych in the City of Westminster; **Anthony Stephen Grabiner;** QC 1981; a Recorder, 1990–99; a Deputy High Court Judge, since 1994; *b* 21 March 1945; *e s* of late Ralph Grabiner and Freda Grabiner (*née* Cohen); *m* 1983, Jane, *er d* of Dr Benjamin Portnoy, TD, JP, MD, PhD, FRCP, Hale, Cheshire; three *s* one *d*. *Educ:* Central Foundn Boys' Grammar Sch., London, EC2; LSE, Univ. of London (LLB 1st Cl. Hons 1966, LLM with Distinction 1967). Lincoln's Inn: Hardwicke Scholar, 1966; called to the Bar, 1968; Droop Scholar, 1968; Bencher, 1989. Standing Jun. Counsel to Dept of Trade, Export Credits Guarantee Dept, 1976–81; Jun. Counsel to the Crown, 1978–81. Mem., Financial Markets Law Cttee, Bank of England, 2002–06. Non-executive Director: Next plc, 2002; Wentworth Ltd, 2005–; non-exec. Chm., Arcadia Gp, 2002–. Chm., Ct of Govs, LSE, 1998– (Mem., 1991–; Vice-Chm., 1993–98). *Publications:* (ed jtly) Sutton and Shannon on Contracts, 7th edn 1970; contrib. Banking Documents, to Encyclopedia of Forms and Precedents, 5th edn, 1986. *Recreations:* theatre, golf. *Address:* 1 Essex Court, Temple, EC4Y 9AR. *T:* (020) 7583 2000; *e-mail:* agrabiner@oeclaw.co.uk. *Clubs:* Garrick, MCC; Wentworth Golf.

GRABINER, Michael; Partner, Apax Partners, since 2002; Chairman, Partnerships for Schools, since 2005; *b* 21 Aug. 1950; *s* of Henry Grabiner and Renée (*née* Geller); *m* 1976, Jane Olivia Harris; three *s* one *d*. *Educ:* St Alban's Sch.; King's Coll., Cambridge (MA Econ; Pres., Students' Union, 1972–73). Joined Post Office, 1973: Personal Asst to Man. Dir, Telecommunications, 1976–78; London Business Sch. (Sloan Prog.), 1980–81; British Telecommunications: Controller, Commercial Finance Divl HQ, 1982–84; Dep. Dir, Mktg, 1984–85; General Manager: Northern London Dist, 1985–88; City of London Dist, 1988–90; Director: Quality and Orgn, 1990–92; Global Customer Service, Business Communications Div., 1992–94; BT Europe, 1994–95; Chief Executive: Energis Communications Ltd, then Energis plc, 1996–2001. Director: BT Telecommunications SA Spain, 1994–95; VIAG InterKom Germany, 1994–95; Telenordia Sweden, 1994–95; Albacom Italy, 1994–95; Chairman: Planet Online, 1998–2000; Spectrum Strategy Consultants, 2003–07; non-executive Director: Littlewoods plc, 1998–2002; Emblaze Systems, 2000–05; Chelsfield plc, 2002–04; Synetrix Hldgs Ltd, 2004–; Telewest Global Inc., 2004–06; Tim Hellas Telecommunications SA, 2005–06; Bezeq, 2006–. Mem. (Lab) Brent BC, 1978–82 (Chm., Develt Cttee, 1980–82). Dir, E London Partnership, 1994–95. Treas., Reform Synagogues of GB, 2002–05. Chairman: UK Jewish Film Fest., 2004–06; UK Movt for Reform Judaism, 2005–08. Freeman, City of London, 1995; Mem., Co. of Inf. Technologists, 1995. ACMA 1979. *Fax:* (020) 8959 5020; *e-mail:* mikegrabiner@hotmail.com.

See also S. Grabiner.

GRABINER, Stephen; Partner and Head of Media, Apax Partners, since 1999; *b* 30 Sept. 1958; *s* of Henry and Renée Grabiner (*née* Geller); *m* 1984, Miriam Lœbl; two *s* one *d*. *Educ:* Univ. of Sheffield (BA 1981); Manchester Business Sch. (MBA 1983). Mgt Consultant, Coopers and Lybrand, 1983–86; Telegraph plc: Mktg Dir, 1986–93; Dep. Man. Dir, 1993–94; Man. Dir, 1994–96; Exec. Dir, UK Consumer Publishing, United News and Media plc, 1996–98; Chief Exec., ONdigital, 1998–99. *Recreations:* family, tennis. *Address:* (office) 15 Portland Place, W1B 1PT. *T:* (020) 7872 6353, *Fax:* (020) 7872 6444.

See also M. Grabiner.

GRACE, Clive Lester, DPhil; Chairman, Local Better Regulation Office, since 2007; *b* 5 Aug. 1950; *s* of Henri Hyams Grace and Mary Madeline Grace; *m* 1982, Vivienne Robins (now V. Robins-Grace); one *s* two *d*. *Educ:* Univ. of Birmingham (BSocSc 1971); Univ. of Calif (MA Govt 1972); Wolfson Coll., Oxford (DPhil Law and Sociol. 1984); Open Univ. (Professional Dip. in Mgt). Solicitor of the Supreme Court, 1981. Hd of Legal Br., ILEA, 1987–89; Dir of Law and Admin, London Bor. of Southwark, 1989–95; Chief Exec., Torfaen CBC, 1995–2003; Dir-Gen., Audit Commn in Wales, 2003–05; Dep. Auditor Gen. for Wales, 2004–05. Mem., Wales Adv. Forum, BT, 2000–; Observer Mem., Financial Reporting Council, 2004–07; Chairman: Internat. Panel, CIPFA, 2006–; Res. Councils UK Shared Services Ltd, 2007–. Non-exec. Chm., Supporta plc, 2007–. Hon. Secretary: SOLACE, 1998–2002; SOLACE Foundn, 1998– (Chm., SOLACE Foundn Imprint, 2005–). Hon. Res. Fellow, Cardiff Business Sch., 2005–. *Publications:* Sociological Inquiry and Legal Phenomena, 1979; Social Workers, Children and the Law, 1986. *Recreations:* ski-ing, walking, golf. *Address:* The Old Rectory, Llanellen Road, Llanfoist, Abergavenny, Monmouthshire NP7 9NF. *T:* (01873) 851289; *e-mail:* clivegrace@hotmail.com. *Club:* Reform.

GRACE, John Oliver Bowman; QC 1994; *b* 13 June 1948; *s* of late Oliver Grace, MBE, TD and Marjorie (*née* Bowman); *m* 1973, Carol S. Roundhill; two *s* one *d*. *Educ:* Marlborough; Southampton Univ. (LLB Hons). Called to the Bar, Middle Temple, 1973, Bencher, 2001. *Recreations:* gardening, modern art, reading, music, cricket, church, brick-laying, sailing. *Address:* 3 Serjeants' Inn, EC4Y 1BQ. *T:* (020) 7427 5000. *Clubs:* 4W's (Wandsworth); Whitstable Yacht.

GRACEY, Howard, OBE 1998; FIA, FIAA, FPMI; consulting actuary; Senior Partner, R. Watson and Sons, 1993–95 (Partner, 1970–95); *b* 21 Feb. 1935; *s* of late Charles Douglas Gracey and Margaret Gertrude (*née* Heggie); *m* 1960, Pamela Jean Bradshaw; one *s* two *d*. *Educ:* Birkenhead Sch. FIA 1959; FIAA 1982; FPMI 1977; ASA 1978. National Service, 1960–61 (2nd Lieut). Royal Insurance Co., 1953–69. Church Comr, 1978–95; Member: Gen. Synod of C of E, 1970–97; C of E Pensions Bd, 1970–97 (Chm., 1980–97); Archbishops' Commn on orgn of C of E; Treasurer, S Amer. Missionary Soc., 1975–93 (Chm., 1994–2004); Pres., Pensions Management Inst., 1983–85; Chm., Assoc. of Consulting Actuaries, 1991–93. Mem. Council, St John's Coll., Nottingham, 1998–2003. *Recreations:* fell-walking, photography. *Address:* Cowdry Barn, Birdham Road, Chichester, W Sussex PO20 7BX.

GRACEY, John Halliday, CB 1984; Director General (Deputy Secretary), Board of Inland Revenue, 1981–85; Commissioner of Inland Revenue, 1973–85; *b* 20 May 1925; *s* of Halliday Gracey and Florence Jane (*née* Cudlipp); *m* 1950, Margaret Procter; three *s*. *Educ:* City of London Sch.; Brasenose Coll., Oxford (MA). Army, 1943–47. Entered Inland Revenue, 1950; HM Treasury, 1970–73. Hon. Treas., NACRO, 1987–98. *Recreations:* walking, reading, music. *Address:* 3 Woodberry Down, Epping, Essex CM16 6RJ. *T:* (01992) 572167. *Club:* Reform.

GRACIAS, His Eminence Cardinal Oswald; *see* Bombay, Archbishop of, (RC).

GRADE, Michael Ian, CBE 1998; Chairman: Pinewood-Shepperton (formerly Pinewood Studios) Ltd, since 2000; Ocado, since 2006; Executive Chairman and Chief Executive, ITV, since 2007; *b* 8 March 1943; *s* of Leslie Grade and *g s* of Olga Winogradski; *m* 1st, 1967, Penelope Jane (*née* Levinson) (marr. diss. 1981); one *s* one *d*; 2nd, 1982, Hon. Sarah Lawson (marr. diss. 1991), *y d* of 5th Baron Burnham; 3rd, 1998, Francesca Mary (*née* Leahy); one *s*. *Educ:* St Dunstan's Coll., London. Daily Mirror: Trainee Journalist, 1960; Sports Columnist, 1964–66; Theatrical Agent, Grade Organisation, 1966; joined London Management and Representation, 1969, Jt Man. Dir until 1973; London Weekend Television: Dep. Controller of Programmes (Entertainment), 1973; Dir of Programmes and Mem. Bd, 1977–81; Pres., Embassy Television, 1981–84; Controller, BBC1, 1984–86; Dir of Programmes, BBC TV, 1986–87; Chief Exec., Channel Four, 1988–97; First Leisure Corporation: Dir, 1991–2000; non-exec. Chm., 1995–97; Chm., 1997–98; Chief Exec., 1997–2000. Chairman: VCI plc, 1995–98; Octopus Publishing Gp, 2000–01; Bd of Govs, BBC, 2004–06; Hemscott plc, 2000–06; Director: ITN, 1989–93; Delfont Macintosh Theatres Ltd, 1994–99; Charlton Athletic FC, 1997–; New Millennium Experience Co., 1997–2001; Camelot Gp, 2000–04 (Chm., 2002–04); Reel Enterprises Ltd, 2002–04; SMG, 2003–04; Television Corp., 2003–04. Chm. Develt Council, RNT, 1997–2004; Member: Council, LAMDA, 1981–93; Council, RADA, 1996–2004; Council, BAFTA, 1981–82, 1986–88 (Vice-Pres., 2004–); 300 Group; Milton Cttee; British Screen Adv. Council, 1986–97; Council, Cinema and Television Benevolent Fund, 1993–2004; Council, Royal Albert Hall, 1997–2004. Chm., Wkg Gp, Fear of Crime, 1989; Mem., Nat. Commn of Inquiry into Prevention of Child Abuse, 1994–96; Chm., Index on Censorship, 2000–04. President: TV and Radio Industries Club, 1987–88; Newspaper Press Fund, 1988–89; Entertainment Charities Fund, 1994–; Vice-Pres., Children's Film Unit, 1993–97; Director: Open Coll., 1989–97; Cities in Schools, 1991–96; Gate Theatre, Dublin, 1990–2004; Internat. Council, Nat. Acad. of Television Arts and Scis, 1991–97; Jewish Film Foundn, 1997–99. Trustee, Band Aid; Dep. Chm., Soc. of Stars, 1995–; Hon. Treas., Stars Organisation for Spastics, 1986–92. FRTS 1991 (Pres., 1995–97); Fellow, BAFTA, 1994. Hon. Prof., Thames Valley Univ., 1994. Hon. LLD Nottingham, 1997. *Publication:* It Seemed Like a Good Idea at the Time (autobiog.), 1999. *Recreation:* entertainment. *Address:* ITV, 200 Gray's Inn Road, WC1X 8HF. *Club:* Royal Thames Yacht.

GRADIN, Anita Ingegerd; Chairperson, Swedish Council for Working Life and Social Research, 2000–06; *b* 12 Aug. 1933; *d* of Ossian Gradin and Alfhild Gradin; *m* Bertil Kersfelt; one *d*. *Educ:* Grad. Fr. Sch. of Social Work and Public Admin, Stockholm. Journalist in various newspapers, 1950–63; Mem., Social Welfare Planning Cttee, Stockholm, 1963–67; MP, 1968–92; posts include: Chairperson: Council, Cttee on Educn and Financial Affairs; Cttee on Migration, Refugees and Democracy, Council of Europe; Cabinet Minister for Migration and Equality between Women and Men, 1982–86; Minister for Foreign Trade and Eur. Affairs, 1986–91; Swedish Ambassador to Austria, Slovenia and UN, 1992–95; Mem., Commn of EC, 1995–99. Vice-Chairperson, Nat. Fedn of Social Democratic Women, 1975–92; Vice-Pres., Socialist Internat., 1983–92; Pres., Socialist Internat. Women, 1986–92. Member: Bd, Stockholm Sch. of Econs, 2001–; Bd, Center for Gender Medicine, Karolinska Inst., 2002–. FD *hc* Umeå, 2002. Pro Merito Medal, Council of Europe, 1982; Wizo Woman of the Year Award, 1986; Marisa Bellizario European Prize, Italy, 1998; King's Medal, Royal Order of Seraphim, Sweden, 1998. Cavalieri di Gran Croce (Italy), 1991; Order of Merit (Austria) 1995; European of the Year, 2007. *Recreations:* swimming, walking in the woods, stamps, fishing. *Address:* Fleminggatan 85, 11245 Stockholm, Sweden; *e-mail:* gradin.kersfelt@lelia.com.

GRADY, Prof. Monica Mary, (Mrs I. Wright), PhD; Professor of Planetary and Space Sciences, Open University, since 2005; *b* 15 July 1958; *d* of James and Mary Grady; *m* 1986, Prof. Ian Wright; one *s*. *Educ:* Notre Dame Grammar Sch., Leeds; Durham Univ. (BSc); Cambridge Univ. (PhD). Natural History Museum: researcher in meteorites, 1991–97; Hd, Div. of Petrology and Meteoritics, 1997–2005. Hon. Reader in Meteoritics, 2000–04, Hon. Prof., 2004, UCL. Christmas Lectures, Royal Instn, 2003. *Publications:* (ed jtly) Meteorites: their flux with time and impact effects, 1998; The Catalogue of Meteorites, 5th edn 2000; Search for Life, 2001; (with S. S. Russell) Meteorites, 2002; A Voyage in Space and Time, 2003; contrib. numerous papers to peer-reviewed jls. *Recreations:* reading, gardening, crossword puzzles. *Address:* Planetary Space Sciences Research Institute, Open University, Walton Hall, Milton Keynes MK7 6AA. *T:* (01908) 659251, *Fax:* (01908) 858022; *e-mail:* m.m.grady@open.ac.uk.

GRADY, Terence, MBE 1967; HM Diplomatic Service, retired; Ambassador at Libreville, 1980–82; *b* 23 March 1924; *s* of Patrick Grady and Catherine (*née* Fowles); *m*

1960, Jean Fischer; one *s* four *d*. *Educ:* St Michael's Coll., Leeds. HM Forces, 1942–47; Foreign Office, 1949; HM Embassy: Baghdad, 1950; Paris, 1951; Asst Private Secretary to Secretary of State for Foreign Affairs, 1952–55; HM Legation, Budapest, 1955–58; HM Embassy, Kabul, 1958–60; FO, 1960–63; Vice Consul, Elisabethville, 1963; Consul, Philadelphia, 1964–69; UK High Commission, Sydney, 1969–72; FCO, 1972–75; Head of Chancery, Dakar, 1975–77; Consul, Istanbul, 1977–80. *Recreations:* tennis, walking. *Address:* 58 The Close, Norwich NR1 4EH. *Club:* Norfolk (Norwich).

GRAEF, Roger Arthur, OBE 2006; writer, director and producer of films; criminologist; *b* NYC, 18 April 1936; UK citizen, 1995; *m* 1st, 1971, Karen Bergemann (marr. diss. 1983); one *s* one *d*; 2nd, 1986, Susan Mary Richards. *Educ:* Horace Mann Sch., NYC; Putney Sch., Vermont; Harvard Univ. (BA Hons). Directed, USA, 26 plays and operas; also directed CBS drama; Observer/Dir, Actors Studio, NYC, 1958–62; resident in England, 1962–; Director, London: Period of Adjustment (Royal Court, Wyndham's); Afternoon Men (Arts); has written, produced and directed more than 100 films; *films for television include:* The Life and Times of John Huston, Esq., 1965; (Exec. Producer) 13-part Who Is series, 1966–67 (wrote/dir. films on Pierre Boulez, Jacques Lipchitz, Walter Gropius, Maurice Béjart); Günter Grass' Berlin, 1965; Why Save Florence?, 1968; In the Name of Allah, 1970; The Space between Words, 1971–72; A Law in the Making, 1973; Inside the Brussels HQ, 1975; Is This the Way to Save our Cities?, 1975; Decision series: British Steel, etc, 1976–77, British Communism, 1978 (Royal Television Soc. Award); Pleasure at Her Majesty's, The Secret Policeman's Ball, 1977–78; Inside Europe, 1977–78; Police series, 1980–82 (BAFTA Award); Police: Operation Carter, 1981–82; Nagging Doubt, 1984; The Fifty-Minute Hour, 1984; Maybe Baby, 1985; Comic Relief, 1986; Closing Ranks, 1987; The Secret Life of the Soviet Union, 1990; Turning the Screws, 1993; Look at the State We're In, 1995; In Search of Law and Order (UK), 1995; Breaking the Cycle, 1996; In Search of Law and Order (USA), 1998; Keeping it in the Family, 1998; The Siege of Scotland Yard, 1999; Race Against Crime, 1999; Masters of the Universe, 1999; Looks That Kill, 2000; executive producer: Who's Your Father, 2000; Not Black and White, 2001; September Mourning, Feltham Sings, 2002; Rail Cops, Welcome to Potters Bar, 2003; Who Cares for Granny?, 2003; The Protectors, 2004; Who am I Now?, 2004; Rail Cops 2, 2004; producer/director, Police 2001, 2001; Series Editor: Inside Europe, 1977–78; Signals, 1988–89; *radio*: The Illusion of Information, 2000. Mem., Devclt Control Review (Dobry Cttee), Chm., Study Gp on Public Participation in Planning, and Mem., Cttee on Control of Demolition, DoE, 1974–76; Member: Commn on Child and Adolescent Mental Health, 1997–98; Prince's Trust Wkg Party on surviving damage in childhood, 1997–98; Fulbright Commn, 2000– (Chm., Police Scholarships Cttee, 1999–); Advr, Oxford Probation Studies Unit, 1997–; Social Affairs Advr, Paul Hamlyn Foundn, 1999–. Chm., AIP, 1988–89; Member: Council, ICA, 1970–82; Council, BAFTA, 1976–77; Bd, Channel Four, 1980–85; Governor, BFI, 1974–78. Adviser on broadcasting to Brandt Commn, 1979–80; Media Advisor: Collins Publishing, 1983–88; London Transport (Mem. Bd, LTE, 1976–79; co-designer, new London Bus Map). Pres., Signals Internat. Trust, 1990–; Trustee: Koestler Trust for Prisoners' Art, 1995–; Butler Trust, 1997–2001; Divert Trust, 1999–2000. Chm., Youth Advocate Prog. UK, 2002–. Chairman: Book Aid, 1991; Théâtre de Complicité, 1991–; Bd Mem., Photographers' Gall., 2003. Member: Collège Analytique de Securité Urbaine, 1993–98; British Soc. of Criminology; Vis. Fellow, Mannheim Centre for the Study of Criminology and Criminal Justice, LSE, 1993–. Visiting Professor: Broadcast Media, Oxford Univ., 1999–2000; Univ. of London, 2001–02. FRTS 1996; Fellow, BAFTA, 2004. *Publications:* Talking Blues, 1989; Living Dangerously, 1992; Why Restorative Justice?, 2000; contrib. Daily Telegraph, The Times (media columnist, 1992–94), Sunday Telegraph, Observer, Daily Mail, Mail on Sunday, Evening Standard, Police Review, The Independent, Guardian, Sunday Times, Independent on Sunday. *Recreations:* tennis, flute, photography, Dorset. *Address:* 72 Westbourne Park Villas, W2 5EB. *T:* (020) 7727 7868. *Clubs:* Beefsteak, Groucho, Pilgrims.

GRAF, (Charles) Philip, CBE 2003; Deputy Chairman, Ofcom, since 2006 (Chairman, Content Board, since 2006); *b* 18 Oct. 1946; *s* of Charles Henry Graf and Florence (*née* Mulholland); *m* 1st, 1970, Freda Mary Bain (marr. diss. 2003); three *d*; 2nd, 2004, Kirstan Anne Marnane. *Educ:* Methodist Coll., Belfast; Carlmont High Sch., Calif; Clare Coll., Cambridge (MA). Circulation Mktg Controller, Thomson Regl Newspapers, 1978–83; Asst Man. Dir, Liverpool Daily Post and Echo, 1983–85; Chief Exec., Trinity Paper and Packaging, 1986–90; Corporate Develt Dir, 1990–93, Chief Exec., 1993–99, Trinity plc; Chief Exec., Trinity Mirror plc, 1999–2002. Dir, TDG plc, 2003–07; Partner, Praesta Partners LLP, 2005–. Chairman: Press Standards Bd of Finance, 2004–05; Broadband Stakeholders Gp, 2005. Dir, Archant Ltd, 2006–. Trustee, Crisis, 2004–. *Recreations:* reading, opera, watching Rugby, soccer and cricket, theatre.

GRAF, Prof. Hans-Friedrich, PhD; Professor of Environmental Systems Analysis, University of Cambridge, since 2003; *b* 6 Jan. 1950; *s* of Dr Hans and Ilse Graf; *m* 1997, Dr Marie-Luise Waguer-Kuschfeldt; two *d*. *Educ:* Humboldt Univ., Berlin (MSc Met. 1974; PhD Met. 1979; Habilitation Dr *scientiae naturalis*, 1989). Scientific Asst, Humboldt Univ., Berlin, 1974–78; Industrial Meteorologist, Kombinat Kraftwerksanlagenbau, Berlin, 1978–79; Scientific Asst, Meteorol Inst., Humboldt Univ., Berlin, 1979–90; Sen. Scientist, Max-Planck-Inst. for Meteorol., Hamburg, 1991–2003. Suehring Medal, Deutsche Meteorologische Gesellschaft, 1989. *Publications:* more than 100 book chapters and papers in jls. *Address:* Department of Geography, University of Cambridge, Cambridge CB2 3EN. *T:* (01223) 330242; *e-mail:* hfg21@cam.ac.uk.

GRAF, Stefanie; German tennis player, 1982–99; Founder, and Chairman, Children for Tomorrow, since 1998; *b* 14 June 1969; *d* of Peter and Heidi Graf; *m* 2001, André Agassi, *qv*; one *s* one *d*. Has won 107 singles titles, including 22 Grand Slam titles: French Open, 1987–88, 1993, 1995–96, 1999; Australian Open, 1988–90, 1994; Wimbledon, 1988–89, 1991–93, 1995–96; US Open, 1988–89, 1993, 1995–96. Olympic Gold Medal, Seoul, 1988; Olympic Silver Medal, Barcelona, 1992; Olympic Order, 1999. *Publication:* (jtly) Wege zum Erfolg, 1999. *Address:* Stefanie Graf Marketing, Gartenstrasse 1, 68723 Schwetzingen, Germany.

GRAFTON, 11th Duke of, *cr* 1675; **Hugh Denis Charles FitzRoy,** KG 1976; DL; Earl of Euston, Viscount Ipswich; Captain Grenadier Guards; *b* 3 April 1919; *e s* of 10th Duke of Grafton, and Lady Doreen Maria Josepha Sydney Buxton (*d* 1923), *d* of 1st Earl Buxton; *S* father, 1970; *m* 1946, Fortune (*see* Duchess of Grafton); two *s* three *d*. *Educ:* Eton; Magdalene Coll., Cambridge. ADC to the Viceroy of India, 1943–46. Vice-Chm. of Trustees, Nat. Portrait Gall., 1967–92; Mem., Royal Fine Art Commn, 1971–94. Chairman: Architectural Heritage Fund, 1976–94; Cathedrals Adv. Commn, 1981–91; Member: Hist. Bldgs Council for England, 1953–84; Hist. Bldgs Adv. Cttee, 1984–2001, Cathedrals and Churches Adv. Cttee, 1984–2001, English Heritage; Properties Cttee, Nat. Trust, 1981–94; President: Suffolk Preservation Soc., 1957–; SPAB, 1989–; Trustee: Sir John Soane's Mus. (Chm., 1975–97); Hist. Churches Preservation Trust (Chm., 1980–97); Tradescant Trust, 1976–99; Buildings at Risk Trust, 1986–2000; Patron, Historic Houses Assoc. President: Internat. Students House, 1972–; East Anglia Tourist Bd, 1973–93; British Soc. of Master Glass Painters. Patron, Hereford Herd Book Soc. DL Suffolk, 1973. Hon. DCL East Anglia, 1990. *Heir:* *s* Earl of Euston, *qv*. *Address:* Euston Hall, Thetford, Norfolk IP24 2QW. *T:* (01842) 753282. *Club:* Boodle's.

GRAFTON, Duchess of; (Ann) Fortune FitzRoy, GCVO 1980 (DCVO 1970; CVO 1965); Mistress of The Robes to The Queen, since 1967; *o d* of Captain Eric Smith, MC, LLD, Lower Ashfold, Slaugham; *m* 1946, Duke of Grafton, *qv*; two *s* three *d*. Lady of the Bedchamber to the Queen, 1953–66. SRCN Great Ormond Street, 1945; Mem. Bd of Governors, The Hospital for Sick Children, Great Ormond Street, 1952–66; Patron, Nurses' League. President: W Suffolk Mission to the Deaf; W Suffolk Decorative and Fine Arts Soc.; Bury St Edmunds Br., BHF; Vice-President: Suffolk Br., Royal British Legion Women's Section; Trinity Hospice, Clapham Common, 1951–. Governor: Felixstowe Coll.; Riddlesworth Hall. Patron: Relate, W Suffolk; Guildhall String Ensemble; Clarence River Historical Soc., Grafton, NSW. JP County of London, 1949, W Suffolk, 1972–90. *Address:* Euston Hall, Thetford, Norfolk IP24 2QW. *T:* (01842) 753282.

See also Jeremy F. E. Smith.

GRAFTON, NSW, Bishop of, since 2003; **Rt Rev. Keith Francis Slater;** *b* 13 Dec. 1949; *s* of George Richard Slater and Edna May Slater (*née* Eriksen); *m* 1969, Lorraine Margaret Halvorson; two *s*. *Educ:* Univ. of Qld (BA); St Francis Theol Coll., Brisbane (ThL); Kelvin Grove Teachers' Coll., Brisbane (Dip. Teaching); Brisbane Coll. of Theology (MMin 2007). Ordained deacon and priest, 1975; Asst Curate, St Saviour's, Gladstone, 1975–78; Priest i/c, 1978–80, Rector, 1980–82, St Peter's, Springsure; Rector: St Luke's, Ekibin, Brisbane, 1982–87; St Saviour's, Gladstone, 1987–94; St Clement's-on-the-Hill, Stafford, Brisbane, 1994–2003; Archdeacon of Lilley, Brisbane, 1996–2003. *Address:* PO Box 4, Grafton, NSW 2460, Australia. *T:* (2) 66424122, *Fax:* (2) 66431814; *e-mail:* bishopgrafton@nor.com.au.

GRAFTON, Peter Witheridge, CBE 1972; Senior Partner, G. D. Walford & Partners, Chartered Quantity Surveyors, 1978–82 (Partner 1949–78), retired; *b* 19 May 1916; *s* of James Hawkins Grafton and Ethel Marion (*née* Brannan); *m* 1st, 1939, Joan Bleackley (*d* 1969); two *d* (and one *s* one *d* decd); 2nd, 1971, Margaret Ruth Ward; two *s*. *Educ:* Westminster City Sch.; Sutton Valence Sch.; Coll. of Estate Management. FRICS. Served War of 1939–45, Queen's Westminster Rifles, Dorsetshire Regt and RE, UK and Far East (Captain). Pres., RICS, 1978–79 (Vice-Pres., 1974–78); Mem. and Past Chm., Quantity Surveyors Council; Mem. Council, Construction Industries Research and Information Assoc., 1963–69; Member: Research Adv. Council to Minister of Housing and Construction, 1967–71; Nat. Cons. Council for Building and Civil Engrg Industries, 1968–76; British Bd of Agrément, 1973–88; Chm., Nat. Jt Consultative Cttee for Building Industry, 1974–75 (Mem., 1970–77). Master, Worshipful Co. of Chartered Surveyors, 1983–84. Trustee, United Westminster Schs; Governor, Sutton Valence Sch., 1971–96 (Chm., 1976–91); Chm., Old Suttonians Assoc., 1971–75 (Pres., 1996–2005). Contested (L) Bromley, 1950. *Publications:* numerous articles on techn. and other professional subjects. *Recreations:* golf (founder, Chm., 1962–94, Pres., 1994–, Public Schs Old Boys Golf Assoc., Co-donor Grafton Morrish Trophy; past Captain and past Pres. of Chartered Surveyors Golfing Soc.); writing. *Address:* 57 Padbrook, Limpsfield, Oxted, Surrey RH8 0DZ. *T:* (01883) 716685. *Clubs:* Reform; Tandridge Golf.

GRAFTON-GREEN, Patrick; Senior Partner, Michael Simkins LLP, since 2006; *b* 30 March 1943; *s* of George Grafton-Green and Brigid Anna Grafton-Green (*née* Maxwell); *m* 1982, Deborah Susan Goodchild; two *s* two *d*. *Educ:* Ampleforth Coll., York; Wadham Coll., Oxford (MA 1965). Joined Theodore Goddard, later Addleshaw Goddard, solicitors, 1966; qualif. as solicitor, 1969; Partner, 1973–2006; Head, Media and Communications Dept, 1993–2006; Sen. Partner, 1997–2003; Chm., 2003–06. *Recreations:* cricket, music, theatre. *Address:* Michael Simkins LLP, 45–51 Whitfield Street, W1T 4HB. *T:* (020) 7907 3034. *Club:* MCC.

GRAHAM, family name of **Duke of Montrose** and **Baron Graham of Edmonton**.

GRAHAM, Marquis of; James Alexander Norman Graham; *b* 16 Aug. 1973; *s* and *heir* of Duke of Montrose, *qv*; *m* 2004, Cecilia, *d* of late Francesco Manfredi. *Educ:* Eton; Univ. of Edinburgh (BSc); Univ. of Cape Town (MSc). *Address:* Auchmar, Drymen, Glasgow G63 0AG.

GRAHAM OF EDMONTON, Baron *cr* 1983 (Life Peer), of Edmonton in Greater London; **Thomas Edward Graham;** PC 1998; *b* 26 March 1925; *m* 1950, Margaret (*d* 2005), *d* of Frederick Golding; two *s*. *Educ:* elementary sch.; WEA Co-operative College. BA Open Univ., 1976. Newcastle-on-Tyne Co-operative Soc., 1939–52; Organiser, British Fedn of Young Co-operators, 1952–53; Educn Sec., Enfield Highway Co-operative Soc., 1953–62; Sec., Co-operative Union Southern Section, 1962–67; Nat. Sec., Co-operative Party, 1967–74. Mem. and Leader, Enfield Council, 1961–68. MP (Lab and Co-op) Enfield, Edmonton, Feb. 1974–1983; contested (Lab) Edmonton, 1983. PPS to Minister of State, Dept of Prices and Consumer Protection, 1974–76; a Lord Comr of HM Treasury, 1976–79; Opposition spokesman on the environment, 1980–83; Opposition Chief Whip, H of L, 1990–97. Chm., Labour Peers' Gp, 1997–2000. FCMI. *Address:* 2 Clerks Piece, Loughton, Essex IG10 1NR.

GRAHAM, Alastair Carew; Head Master, Mill Hill School, 1979–92; *b* 23 July 1932; *s* of Col J. A. Graham and Mrs Graham (*née* Carew-Hunt); *m* 1969, Penelope Rachel Beaumont; two *d*. *Educ:* Winchester Coll.; Gonville and Caius Coll., Cambridge (1st Cl. Mod. and Med. Langs). Served 1st Bn Argyll and Sutherland Highlanders, 1951–53. Foy, Morgan & Co. (City), 1956–58; Asst Master, Eton, 1958; House Master, 1970–79. *Recreations:* European travel, DFAS, walking, theatre and opera, music listening, gardening, educn.

See also Maj.-Gen. J. D. C. Graham.

GRAHAM, Sir (Albert) Cecil, Kt 2008; FRCP, FRCPCH; Consultant Paediatrician, Queen Elizabeth Hospital, St Michael, Barbados, 1964–95, now Emeritus; Consultant Paediatrician, Children's Development Centre, St Michael, Barbados, 1981–95, now Emeritus; *b* Bridgetown, Barbados, 22 Jan. 1928; *s* of George Washington Graham and Cecil Graham; *m* 1975, Margaret Letitia McCurdy; one *s* three *d* by a previous marriage. *Educ:* Harrison Coll.; McGill Univ.; Guy's Hosp., London (MB BS 1954; DCH 1955). MRCP 1962, FRCP 1974; FRCPCH 1985, Hon. FRCPCH 2002. Commonwealth Scholar, 1961–62, House Officer, Neonatal Unit, 1962, Hammersmith Hosp. Founder Mem., Parent Educn for the Develt of Barbados, 1972–; Advr, Caribbean Assoc. for Mental Retardation and Develtl Disabilities. Mem., Imperial Soc. of Knights Batchelor. Gold Cross of Merit (Barbados), 1982. *Recreations:* music, gardening. *Address:* Cap Rock, 39 Prior Park, 7th Avenue, St James, BB23006, Barbados. *T:* 4246444, *Fax:* 4217287; *e-mail:* m.b@caribsurf.com. *Club:* Rotary (Barbados).

GRAHAM, Alexander; television producer; Chief Executive, Wall to Wall Media, since 1997; *b* 28 Oct. 1953; *s* of Alexander and Jean Graham; *m* 2000, Maeve Haran; one *s* two *d*. *Educ:* West Coats Primary Sch., Cambuslang; Hamilton Acad.; Glasgow Univ. (MA Hons English Lit. and Sociol.); City Univ. (Dip. Journalism). Reporter, Bradford

Telegraph and Argus, 1978–79; researcher and producer, LWT, 1979–83; Editor, Diverse Reports, 1983–86, Media Show, 1987–91, Channel 4; Jt Man. Dir, Wall to Wall Media, 1991–97; Executive Producer: Baby It's You, 1993; Our Boy, 1997; A Rather English Marriage, 1998; The 1900 House, 1999; The 1940s House, 2001; Edwardian Country House, 2003; New Tricks, 2002–; Who Do You Think You Are?, 2004–. Vis. Fellow, Bournemouth Media Sch., 2004–. Producers Association for Cinema and Television: Mem. Council, 1991–; Vice Chm., 1995–96 and 1999–2000; Chm., 2006–07. FRSA 2004; FRTS 2006. *Recreations:* cooking, singing, walking, Arsenal FC, single malt whisky. *Address:* 8 Spring Place, Kentish Town, NW5 3ER. *T:* (020) 7241 9214; *e-mail:* alex.graham@walltowall.co.uk. *Club:* Century.

GRAHAM, Sir Alexander (Michael), GBE 1990; JP; Chairman, Employment Conditions Abroad International Ltd, 1993–2005 (Director, 1992–2005); Lord Mayor of London, 1990–91; *b* 27 Sept. 1938; *s* of Dr Walter Graham and Suzanne Graham (*née* Simon); *m* 1964, Carolyn, *d* of Lt-Col Alan Wolryche Stansfeld, MBE; three *d*. *Educ:* Fyvie Village Sch.; Hall Sch., Hampstead; St Paul's Sch. National Service, 1957–59; commnd Gordon Highlanders; TA 1959–67; Chm., Nat. Employers Liaison Cttee for TA and Reserve Forces, 1992–97. Joined Norman Frizzell & Partners Ltd, 1957: Dir, 1967–93; Man. Dir, 1973–90; Dep. Chm., 1990–93; Underwriting Member of Lloyd's, 1978–2000; Director: Folgate Insce Co. Ltd, 1975–2001, 2004–05 (Chm., 1995–2001); Folgate Partnership Ltd, 2002–05; Chairman: FirstCity Insce Brokers, 1993–98; Euclidian plc, 1994–2001. Mercers' Co.: Liveryman, 1971–; Mem., Ct of Assistants, 1980; Master, 1983–84; Mem., Ct of Common Council, City of London, 1978–79; Alderman for Ward of Queenhithe, 1979–2004; Pres., Queenhithe Ward Club, 1979–2004. Sheriff, City of London, 1986–87; HM Lieut, City of London, 1989–2004. Hon. Liveryman, Co. of Chartered Secretaries and Administrators, 1992; Hon. Freeman: Insurers' Co., 1992; Merchant Adventurers of York, 1983. President: CS Motoring Assoc., 1993–2006; British Insurance Law Assoc., 1994–96; Vice-Pres., Insurance Inst. of London, 1978–. Governor: Hall Sch., Hampstead, 1975–93; Christ's Hosp. Sch., 1979–2004; King Edward's Sch., Whitley, 1979–2004; St Paul's Sch., 1980–93, 2003– (Chm., 2004–; Vice Pres., 1988–2000, Dep. Pres., 2000–01, Pres., 2001–03, Old Pauline Club; Chm., Gen. Charitable Trust, 1997–2004); St Paul's Girls' Sch., 1980–93, 2004–; City of London Boys' Sch., 1983–85; City of London Girls' Sch., 1992–95; Mem. Council, Gresham Coll., 1983–93; Trustee, Morden College, 1988– (Chm., 1995–); Chancellor, City Univ., 1990–91. Trustee: United Response, 1988–2002 (Chm., 1993–2002); Lord Mayor's 800th Anniversary Trust, 1989–2000; Temple Bar Trust, 1992–2004; Vice Pres., 1992–, and Hon. Life Mem., 1993, Macmillan Cancer Relief (formerly Cancer Relief Macmillan Fund); Vice Pres., Garden House Hospice, 1992–; Hon. Mem., Ct, HAC, 1979–2004; Mem., Exec. Cttee, Army Benevolent Fund, 1991–98; Chm. Council, Order of St John, Herts, 1993–2001; Mem., Royal Soc. of St George, 1981–; Vice Pres., Royal Soc. of St George, Herts Br., 1999–. Vice Pres., Herts Agricl Show, 1996–. Gentlemen Usher of the Purple Rod, Order of the British Empire, 2000–. FCII 1964; FBIIBA 1967; FCIS 1990; FInstD 1975; CCMI (CBIM 1991); FRSA 1980. JP City of London, 1979. Hon. Keeper of the Quaich, 1992; Commandeur de l'Ordre du Tastevin, 1985; Vigneron d'Honneur et Bourgeois de St Emilion, 1999. Hon. DCL City, 1990. KStJ 1990. Silver Medal, City of Helsinki, 1990; Medal, City of Santiago, 1991. Order of Wissam Alouite (Morocco), 1987; Grand Cross Order of Merit (Chile), 1991. *Recreations:* wine, calligraphy, genealogy, music, reading, silver, bridge, golf, swimming, tennis, shooting, ski-ing, avoiding gardening. *Address:* Walden Abbotts, Whitwell, Hitchin, Herts SG4 8AJ. *T:* and *Fax:* (01438) 871223. *Clubs:* Garrick, City Livery; Royal Worlington and Newmarket Golf, Mid Herts Golf, Lloyd's Golf (Capt. 1994, Pres., 1996).

See also Lt-Gen. Sir P. W. Graham.

GRAHAM, Sir Alistair; *see* Graham, Sir J. A.

GRAHAM, Rt Rev. Andrew Alexander Kenny; Hon. Assistant Bishop, diocese of Carlisle, since 1997; *b* 7 Aug. 1929; *o s* of late Andrew Harrison and Magdalene Graham; unmarried. *Educ:* Tonbridge Sch.; St John's Coll., Oxford (Hon. Fellow, 1986); Ely Theological College. Curate of Hove Parish Church, 1955–58; Chaplain and Lectr in Theology, Worcester Coll., Oxford, 1958–70; Fellow and Tutor, 1960–70, Hon. Fellow, 1981; Warden of Lincoln Theological Coll., 1970–77; Canon and Prebendary of Lincoln Cathedral, 1970–77; Bishop Suffragan of Bedford, 1977–81; Bishop of Newcastle, 1981–97. Chairman: ACCM, 1984–87; Doctrine Commn, 1987–95. DD Lambeth, 1995; Hon. DCL Northumbria, 1997. *Recreation:* hill walking. *Address:* Fell End, Butterwick, Penrith, Cumbria CA10 2QQ. *T:* (01931) 713147. *Clubs:* Oxford and Cambridge; Northern Counties (Newcastle).

GRAHAM, Lt Gen. Andrew John Noble, CBE 2002 (MBE 1993); Director, Defence Academy of the UK, since 2008; *b* 21 Oct. 1956; *er s* and heir of Sir John (Alexander Noble) Graham, Bt, *qv*; *m* 1984, Susie Mary Bridget, *er d* of Rear Adm. John Patrick Bruce O'Riordan, *qv*; one *s* three *d*. *Educ:* Trinity Coll., Cambridge (BA Hons). Commnd Argyll and Sutherland Highlanders, 1979; served in UK, NI, Hong Kong, Cyprus, S Georgia, MoD, 1979–88; acsc 1988; 1 Argyll and Sutherland Highlanders, Germany, 1989–90; MoD, 1990–92; Directing Staff, Army Staff Coll., 1992–95; CO, 1st Bn, Argyll and Sutherland Highlanders (Princess Louise's), 1995–97; Comdr, 3rd Inf. Bde, 1999–2001; Dir, Army Resources and Plans, MoD, 2001–03; Dep. Comdg Gen., Multinat. Corps, Iraq, 2004; Dir Gen., Army Trng and Recruiting, subseq. Army Recruiting and Trng Div., 2004–07. Colonel: Argyll and Sutherland Highlanders (Princess Louise's), 2000–06; Royal Regt of Scotland, 2007–. Mem., Queen's Body Guard for Scotland (Royal Company of Archers), 1998– (Mem. Council, 2003). Officer, Legion of Merit (USA), 2006. *Recreations:* piping, outdoor sports, destructive gardening, travel/history reading, hobby smallholding. *Address:* Home Headquarters, Argyll and Sutherland Highlanders (Princess Louise's), The Castle, Stirling FK8 1EH. *T:* (01786) 475165, *Fax:* (01786) 446038. *Clubs:* Caledonian, MCC; Royal Scots (Edinburgh).

GRAHAM, Andrew Winston Mawdsley; Master, Balliol College, Oxford, since 2001; *b* 20 June 1942; *s* of late Winston Mawdsley Graham, OBE, FRSL; *m* 1970, Peggotty Fawssett. *Educ:* Charterhouse; St Edmund Hall, Oxford (MA (PPE); Hon. Fellow, 2002). Economic Assistant: NEDO, 1964; Dept of Economic Affairs, 1964–66; Asst to Economic Adviser to the Cabinet, 1966–68; Economic Adviser to Prime Minister, 1968–69; Balliol College, Oxford: Fellow, 1969–2001; Tutor in Econs, 1969; Estates Bursar, 1978; Investment Bursar, 1979–83; Vice Master, 1988 and 1992–94; Acting Master, 1997–2001; Policy Adviser to Prime Minister (on leave of absence from Balliol), 1974–75; Economic Advr to Shadow Chancellor of Exchequer, 1988–92, to Leader of the Opposition, 1992–94. Tutor, Oxford Univ. Business Summer Sch., 1971, 1972, 1973 and 1976; Acting Dir, Oxford Internet Inst., 2002 (Chm., Adv. Bd, 2001–). Vis. Researcher, SE Asian Central Banks Res. and Trng Centre, Malaysia, 1984; Vis. Fellow, Griffith Univ., Brisbane, 1984; Vis. Scholar, MIT, and Vis. Fellow, Center for Eur. Studies, Harvard, 1994; Sen. Fellow, Gorbachev Foundn of N America, 1999–. Founder Mem., Editl Bd, Liby of Political Economy, 1982–. Member: Council of Mgt, Templeton Coll., Oxford, 1990–95; Council, Oxford Univ., 2005–. Member: Wilson Cttee to Review the Functioning of Financial Institutions, 1977–80; Economics Cttee, SSRC, 1978–80; British Transport Docks Bd, 1979–82; Chm., St James Gp (Economic Forecasting), 1982–84, 1985–92. Mem., ILO/Jobs and Skills Prog. for Africa (JASPA) Mission to Ethiopia, 1982; Hd, Queen Elizabeth House/Food Studies Gp team assisting Govt of Republic of Zambia, 1984; Consultant, BBC, 1989–92; Mem. Bd, Channel Four Television Ltd, 1998–2005. Mem., Media Adv. Cttee, IPPR, 1994–97; Trustee: Foundn for Information Policy Res., 1998–2000; Esmée Fairbairn Foundn, 2003–05; Scott Trust 2005–. Hon. DCL Oxford, 2003. *Publications:* (ed) Government and Economies in the Postwar Period, 1990; (jtly) Broadcasting, Society and Policy in the Multimedia Age, 1997. *Recreation:* windsurfing on every possible occasion. *Address:* Balliol College, Oxford OX1 3BJ. *T:* (01865) 277710.

GRAHAM, Anne Silvia, (Lady Graham); Chairman, South Cumbria Health Authority 1988–94; *b* 1 Aug. 1934; *o d* of late Benjamin Arthur Garcia and Constance Rosa (*née* Journeaux). *Educ:* Francis Holland Sch., SW1; LSE (LLB). Called to the Bar, Inner Temple, 1958; Yarborough-Anderson Scholar, 1959. Joined Min. of Housing and Local Govt, 1960; Dep. Legal Advr, DoE, 1978–86. Mem. Court, Lancaster Univ., 1993–2006. *Recreations:* gardening, arts, music.

GRAHAM, Antony Richard Malise; management consultant, retired; Director, Clive & Stokes International, 1985–95; *b* 15 Oct. 1928; *s* of late Col Patrick Ludovic Graham, MC, and Barbara Mary Graham (*née* Jury); *m* 1st, 1958, Gillian Margaret Cook (marr. diss. 1996); two *s* one *d*; 2nd, 2006, Mrs Alny Mary Younger (*née* Burton). *Educ:* Abberley Hall; Nautical Coll., Pangbourne. Merchant Navy, 1945–55 (Master Mariner). Stewarts and Lloyds Ltd, 1955–60; PE Consulting Group Ltd, management consultants, 1960–72 (Regional Dir, 1970–72); Regional Industrial Dir (Under-Sec.), DTI, 1972–76; Dir, Barrow Hepburn Gp, and Maroquinerie Le Tanneur et Tanneries du Bugey SA, 1976–81, Chm., Paton & Sons (Tillicoultry) Ltd, 1981–82; Dir, DTI, 1983–85. Contested (C) Leeds East, 1966. *Recreations:* sailing, oil painting. *Address:* Old Bank House, Haddington, E Lothian EH41 3JS.

GRAHAM, (Arthur) William; JP; Member (C) South Wales East, National Assembly for Wales, since 1999; *b* 18 Nov. 1949; *s* of late William Douglas Graham and of Eleanor Mary Scott (*née* Searle); *m* 1981, Elizabeth Hannah, *d* of late Joshua Griffiths; one *s* two *d*. *Educ:* Blackfriars; Coll. of Estate Mgt, London. FRICS 1974. Principal, Graham & Co., Chartered Surveyors, 1970–. Newport Harbour Comr, 1990–2005 (Chm., 2001). Member: Gwent CC, 1985–89; Newport County BC, subseq. CC, 1988–2004 (Leader, Conservative Gp, 1992–2004). National Assembly for Wales: Chm., Educn Cttee, 1999–2001; Chief Whip, Cons. Gp, 2001–; opposition spokesman on local govt and housing, 2001–03; on social justice, 2003–07; Shadow Leader of the House, 2007–; First Assembly Comr for Resources, 2007–. Gov., Rougemont Sch. Trust, 1991–2005 (Chm., 2002–05). JP Newport, 1979. *Recreations:* breeder of pedigree Suffolk sheep, foreign travel. *Address:* The Volland, Lower Machen, Newport NP10 8GY. *T:* (01633) 440419. *Club:* Carlton.

GRAHAM, Billy; *see* Graham, William F.

GRAHAM, Sir Cecil; *see* Graham, Sir A. C.

GRAHAM, Charles Robert Stephen; QC 2003; *b* 1 April 1961; *s* of Major (Cosmo) Stephen Graham and Mary Graham; *m* 1991, Jane Lindsay; three *s*. *Educ:* Ludgrove Sch., Wokingham; Wellington Coll., Crowthorne; University Coll., Oxford (1st cl. Greats (Lit. Hum.) 1984); City Univ. (Dip Law 1985). Called to the Bar, Middle Temple, 1986; in practice, specialising in commercial law; Mem., SE Circuit. *Address:* One Essex Court, Temple, EC4Y 9AR. *T:* (020) 7583 2000, *Fax:* (020) 7583 0118; *e-mail:* cgraham@oeclaw.co.uk.

GRAHAM, Prof. Christopher Forbes, DPhil; FRS 1981; Professor of Animal Development, and Professorial Fellow, St Catherine's College, University of Oxford, 1985–2007, now Professor Emeritus; *b* 23 Sept. 1940. *Educ:* St Edmund Hall, Oxford (BA 1963); DPhil Oxon 1966. Formerly Junior Beit Memorial Fellow in Med. Research, Sir William Dunn Sch. of Pathology. Lectr, Zoology Dept, Oxford Univ., 1970–85. Member: Brit. Soc. Cell Biology; Brit. Soc. for Developmental Biology; Soc. for Experimental Biology; Genetical Soc. *Publication:* The Developmental Biology of Plants and Animals, 1976, new edn as Developmental Control in Plants and Animals, 1984. *Address:* Department of Zoology, University of Oxford, South Parks Road, Oxford OX1 3PS.

GRAHAM, Christopher Sidney Matthew; Director General, Advertising Standards Authority, since 2000; *b* 21 Sept. 1950; *s* of late David Maurice Graham and Rosemary West Graham (*née* Harris); *m* 1985, Christine Harland (*née* McLean). *Educ:* Canterbury Cathedral Choir Sch.; St Edward's Sch., Oxford; Univ. of Liverpool (Pres., Guild of Undergrads, 1971–72; BA Hons Hist. 1973). BBC News Trainee, 1973–75; Producer: General Talks, Radio, BBC Manchester, 1976–78; Television Current Affairs, BBC, Lime Grove, 1979–87; A Week in Politics, Channel 4, 1987–88; Dep. Editor, The Money Prog., BBC, 1988–89; Asst Editor, 1989–90, Man. Editor, 1990–93, BBC Television News; Man. Editor, BBC News Progs, 1994–95; Sec., BBC, 1996–99. Chm., European Advertising Standards Alliance, 2003–05. Non-exec. Dir, Electoral Reform Services Ltd, 2001–. Lay Mem., Bar Standards Bd, 2006–. Mem. (L), Liverpool City Council, 1971–74. Contested (L) Wilts N, 1983, 1987. *Recreations:* media, music, history. *Address:* Advertising Standards Authority, Mid City Place, 71 High Holborn, WC1V 6QT. *T:* (020) 7492 2244.

GRAHAM, David; *see* Graham, S. D.

GRAHAM, Douglas; *see* Graham, M. G. D.

GRAHAM, Rt Hon. Sir Douglas (Arthur Montrose), KNZM 1999; PC 1998; Minister of Justice, 1990–97, Minister in charge of Treaty of Waitangi Negotiations, 1991–99, and Attorney General, 1997–99, New Zealand; *b* 12 Jan. 1942; *s* of late Robert James Alister Graham and Patricia Kennedy Graham; *m* 1966, Beverley Virginia Cordell; two *s* one *d*. *Educ:* Southwell Preparatory Sch.; Auckland GS; Auckland Univ. (BL 1965). Barrister and solicitor, 1968–84; Sen. Partner, Graham & Co., Solicitors, 1972–84. MP (N) New Zealand, 1984–99, for Remuera, 1984–96; Minister of Cultural Affairs, and of Disarmament and Arms Control, 1990–96. Hon. Dr Waikato, 1998. *Publication:* Trick or Treaty?, 1997. *Recreations:* music, gardening. *Address:* 3A Martin Avenue, Remuera, Auckland, New Zealand. *T:* (9) 5242921; *e-mail:* douglas.graham@xtra.co.nz.

GRAHAM, Duncan Gilmour, CBE 1987; Senior Partner, Duncan Graham Consultants, 1991–2001; *b* 20 Aug. 1936; *s* of Robert Gilmour Graham and Lilias Turnbull Graham (*née* Watson); *m* 1st, 1962, Margaret Gray Graham (*née* Cairns) (marr. diss. 1991); two *s* one *d*; 2nd, 1991, Wendy Margaret Wallace. *Educ:* Hutcheson's, Glasgow; Univ. of Glasgow (MA (Hons) History); Jordanhill Coll. of Education (Teachers' Secondary Cert.). Teacher of History: Whitehill Sec. Sch., Glasgow, 1959–62; Hutcheson's, Glasgow, 1962–65; Lectr in Social Studies, Craigie Coll. of Educn, Ayr, 1965–68; Asst Dir of

Educn, Renfrewshire, 1968–70; Sen. Depute Dir of Educn, Renfrewshire, 1970–74, Strathclyde Regl Council, 1974–79; Advr to COSLA and Scottish Teachers' Salaries Cttee, 1974–79; County Educn Officer, Suffolk, 1979–87; Chief Exec., Humberside CC, 1987–88; Chm. and Chief Exec., Nat. Curriculum Council, 1988–91. Advr to ACC, 1982–88; Mem., Burnham Cttee, 1983–87 and of ACAS Indep. Panel, 1986. Sec., Co. Educn Officers Soc., 1985–87; Chm., Assoc. of Educn Officers, 1985; Project Dir, DES Teacher Appraisal Study, 1985–86; Chm., Nat. Steering Gp on Teacher Appraisal, 1987–90. Member: BBC North Adv. Council, 1988–91; Lincs and Humberside Arts Council, 1988–91; Yorks and Humberside Arts, 1991–94; Council of Nat. Foundn for Educnl Res., 1984, and 1989–90; Exec. Council, Industrial Soc., 1988–90; Chm., Nat. Mathematics Wkg Gp, 1988. Mem. Exec., Caravan Club, 1997–2000. Chairman: Eden Rivers Trust, 2000–03; Cumbria Local Access Forum, 2003–; Fellrunner Village Bus, 2004–08; Youth Work in Cumbria Partnership, 2005–08. FRSA 1981. *Publications:* Those Having Torches, 1985; In the Light of Torches, 1986; Sense, Nonsense and the National Curriculum, 1992; A Lesson For Us All, 1992; Sunset on the Clyde, 1993, 3rd edn 2005; The Education Racket, 1996; Visiting Distilleries, 2001, 2nd edn 2003; many articles in nat. press and educn and local govt jls. *Recreations:* garden railways, walking, fly-fishing. *Address:* Parkburn, Colby, Appleby, Cumbria CA16 6BD. *T:* (01768) 352920.

GRAHAM, Elizabeth; Director of Education, London Borough of Enfield, 1994–2003; *b* 25 Jan. 1951. *Educ:* Knightswood Secondary Sch., Glasgow; Edinburgh Univ. (MA History); Moray House Coll. of Educn, Edinburgh (PGCE). Teacher, Stirlingshire CC, 1971–73; Head of Dept, Waltham Forest LBC, 1973–81; Professional Asst, Haringey LBC, 1982–84; Asst Educn Officer, Enfield LBC, 1984–89; Asst Dir of Educn, Redbridge LBC, 1989–94. *Recreations:* cats, the crusades. *Address:* c/o London Borough of Enfield, PO Box 56, Civic Centre, Silver Street, Enfield EN1 3XQ.

GRAHAM, George; Manager, Tottenham Hotspur Football Club, 1998–2001; *b* Scotland, 30 Nov. 1944; *m* 1998, Sue Schmidt. Professional football player, 1962–77: Aston Villa, 1962–64; Chelsea, 1964–66 (League Cup, 1965); Arsenal, 1966–72 (League and FA Cups, 1971); Manchester United, 1972–74; Portsmouth, 1974–76; Crystal Palace, 1976–77; twelve Scotland caps; coach: Queen's Park Rangers, 1977; Crystal Palace, 1977–82; Manager: Millwall, 1982–86; Arsenal, 1986–95 (League Cup, 1987, 1993; League Champions, 1989, 1991; FA Cup, 1993; European Cup Winners' Cup, 1994); Leeds, 1996–98; Tottenham Hotspur, 1998–2001 (League Cup, 1999).

GRAHAM, (George) Ronald (Gibson), CBE 1986; Partner, 1968–2000, Senior Partner, Maclay, Murray & Spens, Solicitors, Glasgow, Edinburgh and London; *b* 15 Oct. 1939; *o s* of James Gibson Graham, MD, and Elizabeth Waddell; *m* 1965, Mirren Elizabeth Carnegie; three *s*. *Educ:* Glasgow Academy; Loretto Sch., Musselburgh; Oriel Coll., Oxford (MA); Glasgow Univ. (LLB). Director: Scottish Widows' Fund and Life Assce Soc., 1984–2000; Scottish Widows Bank PLC, 1995–2002; Second Scottish National Trust plc, 2002–04. Co-ordinator of Diploma in Legal Practice, 1979–83; Clerk to Gen. Council, Glasgow Univ., 1990–96, Mem. Ct, 1996–2004. Mem. Council, 1977–89, Pres., 1984–85, Law Soc. of Scotland. Gov., Jordanhill Coll. of Educn, Glasgow, 1991–93; Chm. of Govs, Loretto Sch., 2004–07. *Recreations:* fishing, golf, swimming, walking. *Address:* Carse of South Coldoch, Gargunnock, by Stirling FK8 3DF. *T:* (01786) 860397. *Club:* Western Baths (Glasgow).

GRAHAM, Gordon; *see* Graham, L. G.

GRAHAM, Gordon; *see* Graham, W. G.

GRAHAM, Ian James Alastair, OBE 1999; FSA; Director, Maya Corpus Program, Peabody Museum of Archaeology, Harvard University, since 1993; *b* 12 Nov. 1923; *s* of Captain Lord Alastair Graham, RN, *y s* of 5th Duke of Montrose, and Lady Meriel Olivia Bathurst (*d* 1936), *d* of 7th Earl Bathurst; unmarried. *Educ:* Winchester Coll.; Trinity Coll., Dublin. RNVR (A), 1942–47; TCD 1947–51; Nuffield Foundn Research Scholar at The National Gallery, 1951–54; independent archaeological explorer in Central America, 1959–68; Res. Fellow, 1968–75, Asst Curator, 1975–93, Peabody Mus. of Archaeol., Harvard Univ. Occasional photographer of architecture. Hon. LHD Tulane, 1998; Hon. DLitt Dublin, 2000. MacArthur Foundn Prize Fellowship, 1981; Lifetime Achievement Award, Soc. for Amer. Archaeology, 2004. *Publications:* Splendours of the East, 1965; Great Houses of the Western World, 1968; Archaeological Explorations in El Peten, Guatemala, 1967; Corpus of Maya Hieroglyphic Inscriptions, 20 parts, 1975–; Alfred Maudslay, a Biography, 2002. *Address:* Chantry Farm, Campsey Ash, Suffolk IP13 0PZ; c/o Peabody Museum, Harvard University, Cambridge, MA 02138, USA.

GRAHAM, Sir James Bellingham, 11th Bt *cr* 1662; researcher in history and art history; *b* 8 Oct. 1940; *e s* of Sir Richard Bellingham Graham, 10th Bt, OBE, and Beatrice, OBE (*d* 1992), *d* of late Michael Hamilton-Spencer-Smith, DSO, MC; *S* father, 1982; *m* 1986, Halina, *d* of Major Wiktor Grubert, soldier and diplomat and Eleonora Grubert. *Educ:* Eton College; Christ Church, Oxford (MA). Researcher in fine and decorative arts, Cecil Higgins Mus. and Art Gall., Bedford, 1980–96; Curator (with Halina Graham), Norton Conyers and its collections, 1996–. *Publications:* Guide to Norton Conyers, 1976, revised 2004; (with Halina Graham) Cecil Higgins, Collector Extraordinary, 1983; (with Halina Graham) A Guide to the Cecil Higgins Museum and Art Gallery, 1987; reviews of art exhibitions. *Recreations:* travel, visiting historic houses and museums, early science fiction. *Address:* Norton Conyers, Wath, near Ripon, N Yorks HG4 5EQ. *T:* (01765) 640333.

GRAHAM, Sir James (Fergus Surtees), 7th Bt *cr* 1783, of Netherby, Cumberland; farmer; *b* 29 July 1946; *s* of Sir Charles Graham, 6th Bt and of Isabel Susan Anne, *d* of Major R. L. Surtees, OBE; *S* father, 1997; *m* 1975, Serena Jane, *yr d* of Ronald Frank Kershaw; one *s* two *d*. *Educ:* Milton Abbey; Royal Agricl Coll., Cirencester. Lloyd's Reinsurance Broker, 1969–90. *Heir:* *s* Robert Charles Thomas Graham, *b* 19 July 1985. *Address:* The Kennels, Netherby, Longtown, Cumbria CA5 5PD. *T:* (01228) 791262.

GRAHAM, James Lowery, OBE 1991; DL; Deputy Chairman, Border Television Ltd, Carlisle, 2001–06; *b* 29 Oct. 1932; *s* of William and Elizabeth Graham; *m* 1984, Ann Routledge; two *d* by previous marr. *Educ:* Whitehaven Grammar School. Journalist, North West Evening Mail, Barrow, 1955–62; News Editor, Border Television, 1962–67; Producer, BBC, Leeds, 1967–70; BBC: Regional News Editor, North, 1970–75; Regional Television Manager, North East, 1975–80; Head of Secretariat, Broadcasting House, 1980–82; Border Television plc: Man. Dir, 1982–96; Dep. Chm., 1990–96; CEO and Chm., 1996–98; non-exec. Chm., 1999–2001. Sec., BBC Central Music Adv. Council, 1981–82; Jt Sec., Broadcasters' Audience Res. Bd, 1980–82. Dir, Indep. Television Publications, 1982–89. Chairman: Independent Television Facilities Centre Ltd, 1987–2007; Beat 106 FM, Glasgow, 2001–05; Director: Oracle Teletext, 1988–93; Radio Borders, 1989–93; Radio SW Scotland, 1989–93 (Chm., 1990–93); Bay Radio Ltd, 1992–94; Central Scotland Radio, 1993–95; Century (formerly North East) Radio, 1993–2000; Border Radio Holdings, 1997–2000; Century Radio 105, 1998–2000; Sunderland City Radio, 1998; Reliance Security Gp plc, 1999–2002. Pres., Prix Italia, 1998–2002, now Hon. Life Pres. (ITVA rep., 1987–). Dir, Educnl Broadcasting Services Trust, 1992–2008. Member: BAFTA; Internat. Council, Nat. Acad. of Television Arts and Scis, NY, 1999–; European Movement; Co-operative Internationale de Recherche et d'Action en Matière de Communication (European Producers). Governor: Newcastle Polytechnic, 1975–80; Cumbria Inst. of Art (formerly Coll. of Art and Design), 1995–2007; Mem. Court, Univ. of Central Lancs, 2006–. DL Cumbria 2000. FRSA 1987. FRTS 1994. Hon. Fellow, Central Lancashire, 2001. Hon. DCL Northumbria, 1999. News Film Award, RTS, 1975; Beffroi d'Or, Lille (European regional broadcasting award), 1983; RTS Regl Broadcasting Award, 1989. *Recreations:* hill walking, ski-ing, cycling. *Address:* Carlisle, Cumbria; Whistler, BC, Canada. *Club:* Groucho.

GRAHAM, Sir James (Thompson), Kt 1990; CMG 1986; farmer, since 1946; Director, 1979–89, Chairman, 1982–89, New Zealand Dairy Board, retired; *b* 6 May 1929; *s* of Harold Graham and Florence Cecily Graham; *m* 1955, Ina Isabelle Low; one *s* two *d*. *Educ:* New Plymouth Boys' High Sch. Dir, NZ Co-op Dairy Co., 1974–89 (Chm., 1979–82). *Recreations:* golf, tennis, bowls. *Address:* 131c Oceanbeach Road, Mount Maunganui, New Zealand. *T:* (75) 754043.

GRAHAM, Sir John (Alexander Noble), 4th Bt *cr* 1906, of Larbert; GCMG 1986 (KCMG 1979 CMG 1972); HM Diplomatic Service, retired; Registrar, Order of Saint Michael and Saint George, 1987–2001; Director, Ditchley Foundation, 1987–92; *b* 15 July 1926; *s* of Sir John Reginald Noble Graham, 3rd Bt, VC, OBE and Rachel Septima (*d* 1984), *d* of Col Sir Alexander Sprot, 1st and last Bt; *S* father, 1980; *m* 1st, 1956, Marygold Ellinor Gabrielle Austin (*d* 1991); two *s* one *d*; 2nd, 1992, Jane, *widow* of Christopher Howells. *Educ:* Eton Coll.; Trinity Coll., Cambridge. Army, 1944–47; Cambridge, 1948–50; HM Foreign Service, 1950; Middle East Centre for Arab Studies, 1951; Third Secretary, Bahrain 1951, Kuwait 1952, Amman 1953; Asst Private Sec. to Sec. of State for Foreign Affairs, 1954–57; First Sec., Belgrade, 1957–60, Benghazi, 1960–61; FO 1961–66; Counsellor and Head of Chancery, Kuwait, 1966–69; Principal Private Sec. to Foreign and Commonwealth Sec., 1969–72; Cllr (later Minister) and Head of Chancery, Washington, 1972–74; Ambassador to Iraq, 1974–77; Dep. Under-Sec. of State, FCO, 1977–79; Ambassador to Iran, 1979–80; Deputy Under-Sec. of State, FCO, 1980–82; Ambassador and UK Permanent Representative to NATO, Brussels, 1982–86. *Heir:* *s* Lt Gen. Andrew John Noble Graham, *qv*. *Address:* Salisbury Place, Church Street, Shipton under Wychwood, Oxon OX7 6BP. *Club:* Army and Navy.

GRAHAM, Sir (John) Alistair, Kt 2000; Chairman: British Transport Police Authority, since 2004; PhonepayPlus (formerly ICSTIS) the Premium Rate Services Regulator, since 2006; *b* 6 Aug. 1942; *s* of late Robert Graham and Dorothy Graham; *m* 1967, Dorothy Jean Wallace; one *s* one *d*. *Educ:* Royal Grammar Sch., Newcastle upon Tyne. FCIPD (FITD 1989; FIPM 1989). Clerical Asst, St George's Hosp., Morpeth, 1961; Admin Trainee, Northern Regional Hosp. Bd, 1963; Higher Clerical Officer, Royal Sussex County Hosp., Brighton, 1964; Legal Dept, TGWU, 1965; The Civil and Public Services Association: Asst Sec., 1966; Asst Gen. Sec., 1975; Dep. Gen. Sec., 1976; Gen. Sec., 1982–86; Chief Executive: Industrial Soc., 1986–91; Calderdale & Kirklees TEC, 1991–96; Leeds TEC, 1996–2000; Chairman: Police Complaints Authy, 2000–04; W Yorks Strategic HA, 2002–03; Northern and Yorks Regl Comr, NHS Appts Commn, 2003–04; Mem., British Transport Police Cttee, 2004; Mem., 2003–07, Chm., 2004–07, Cttee on Standards in Public Life. Chm., Shareholders' Trust FI Group, 1991–97. Vis. Fellow, Nuffield Coll., Oxford, 1984–92; Vis. Prof., Mgt Sch., Imperial Coll., London Univ., 1989–91. External assessor, teacher trng courses, Univ. of Huddersfield, 1993–96. Chairman: BBC S and E Regl Adv. Council, 1987–90; Training and Develt Lead Body, 1989–94; Member: Personnel Lead Body, 1991–94; BBC Educn Broadcasting Council, 1991–97; Restrictive Practices Court, 1993–99; Bd, Univ. of Huddersfield Trng and Quality Services Certification Div., 1993–96; Overview Gp on producing standards for Teachers, Teacher Trng Agency, 1996–97; Employment Appeal Tribunal, 2003–; (non-exec.) Mgt Bd, Inf. Comr's Office, 2004–. Fitness to Practise Cttee, General Optical Council, 2004–. Non-exec. Dir, Mgt Bd, Information Commn, 2004–. Mem., TUC Gen. Council, 1982–84, 1985–86. Mem., 1988–97, Chm., Staff Cttee, 1991–97, OU Council. Trustee, Duke of Edinburgh Study Conf., 1989–92. Mem., Work, Income and Social Policy Cttee, Joseph Rowntree Foundn, 1997–2000. Vice-Pres., Opera North, 2002– (Bd Mem., 1989–2002, Chm. Finance Cttee, 1996–97); Mem. Mgt Cttee, Huddersfield Contemp. Music Fest., 1992–97; Chm., Yorks Youth and Music, 1995–97. Assessor, Guildford and Woolwich Inquiry, 1990–94; Chm., Parades Commn for NI, 1997–2000. Contested (Lab) Brighton Pavilion, 1966. DUniv: Open, 1999; Bradford, 2006. *Recreations:* music, theatre. *Address:* PhonepayPlus, 1st Floor, Clove Building, 4 Maguire Street, SE1 2NQ.

GRAHAM, Maj.-Gen. John David Carew, CB 1978; CBE 1973 (OBE 1966); Secretary to the Administrative Trustees of the Chevening Estate, 1978–86; *b* 18 Jan. 1923; *s* of late Col J. A. Graham, late RE, and Constance Mary Graham (*née* Carew-Hunt); *m* 1956, Rosemary Elaine Adamson; one *s* one *d*. *Educ:* Cheltenham Coll. psc 1955; jssc 1962. Commissioned into Argyll and Sutherland Highlanders, 1942 (despatches, 1945); served with 5th (Scottish) Bn, The Parachute Regt, 1946–49; British Embassy, Prague, 1949–50; HQ Scottish Comd, 1956–58; Mil. Asst to CINCENT, Fontainebleau, 1960–62; comd 1st Bn, The Parachute Regt, 1964–66; Instr at Staff Coll., Camberley, 1967; Regtl Col, The Parachute Regt, 1968–69; Comdr, Sultan's Armed Forces, Oman, 1970–72; Indian Nat. Defence Coll., New Delhi, 1973; Asst Chief of Staff, HQ AFCENT, 1974–76; GOC Wales, 1976–78. Hon. Col, Kent ACF, 1981–88 (Chm., Kent ACF Cttee, 1979–86); Hon. Col, 203 (Welsh) Gen. Hosp., RAMC, TA, 1983–88. Freeman, City of London, 1992. OStJ 1978, and Chm., St John Council for Kent, 1978–86; CStJ 1983. Order of Oman, 1972. *Publications:* Ponder Anew: reflections on the twentieth century, 1999; (with Humphrey Metzgen) Caribbean Wars Untold: a salute to the British West Indies, 2007. *Address:* Montrose, 58 Rendez-Vous Ridge East, Christ Church, Barbados, WI.

See also A. C. Graham.

GRAHAM, Rev. John Galbraith, MBE 2005; crossword setter as Araucaria, since 1958; *b* 16 Feb. 1921; *s* of Rt Rev. Eric and Phyllis Norton Graham; *m* 1st, 1952, Ernesta Mary Davies; 2nd, 1983, Margaret Crawshaw Entwistle. *Educ:* St Edward's Sch., Oxford; King's Coll., Cambridge (Schol.; MA); Ely Theol Coll. Served RAF, 1942–45, navigator/bomb-aimer (mentioned in dispatches, 1945). Ordained deacon, 1948, priest, 1949; Curate, St John, E Dulwich, 1948–49; Chaplain, St Chad's Coll., Durham, 1949–52; Curate: Aldershot, 1952–55; Beaconsfield, 1955–62; Chaplain, Reading Univ., 1962–72; Curate, St Peter, Eaton Sq., London, 1972–74; Rector, Houghton with Wyton, Dio. Ely, 1974–78. *Publications:* Monkey Puzzles, Vol. 1, 2002, Vol. 2, 2004; Chambers Book of Araucaria Crosswords, 2003; Chambers 2nd Book of Araucaria Crosswords, 2005; Chambers 3rd Book of Araucaria Crosswords, 2006. *Recreations:* quizzes, bridge, friends. *Address:* 31 Rectory Lane, Somersham, Huntingdon PE28 3EL.

GRAHAM, Prof. (John) Michael (Russell), PhD; FREng; Professor of Unsteady Aerodynamics, Imperial College, University of London, since 1990; *b* 26 April 1942; *s* of George Desmond Graham and Evelyn Ann Graham (*née* Russell); *m* 1966, Philippa Gabrielle Freeman; one *s* one *d*. *Educ:* Epsom Coll., Surrey; Clare Coll., Cambridge (BA

Maths, MA); Imperial Coll., Univ. of London (PhD Aeronautical Engrg). Lectr, 1970–90, Head of Dept of Aeronautics, 1999–2003, Imperial Coll., Univ. of London. FRAeS 1999; FCGI 2000; FREng 2006; FRINA 2007. *Recreations:* walking, climbing, squash. *Address:* Department of Aeronautics, Imperial College, SW7 2AZ; *e-mail:* m.graham@imperial.ac.uk.

GRAHAM, Sir John (Moodie), 2nd Bt *cr* 1964; Director, Kinnegar Inns Ltd, since 1981; Chairman, John Graham (Dromore) Ltd, 1966–83; *b* 3 April 1938; *s* of Sir Clarence Graham, 1st Bt, MICE, and Margaret Christina Moodie (*d* 1954); *S* father, 1966; *m* 1970, Valerie Rosemary (marr. diss. 1983), *d* of late Frank Gill, Belfast; three *d*; civil partnership 2006, David Galway. *Educ:* Trinity Coll., Glenalmond; Queen's Univ., Belfast. BSc, Civil Engineering, 1961. Joined family firm of John Graham (Dromore) Ltd, Building and Civil Engineering Contractors, on graduating from University. Director: Electrical Supplies Ltd, 1967–83; Concrete (NI) Ltd, 1967–83; Ulster Quarries Ltd; Graham (Contracts) Ltd, 1971–83; Fieldhouse Plant (NI) Ltd, 1976–83. Chm., Concrete Soc., NI, 1972–74; Senior Vice-Pres., Concrete Soc., 1980; Pres., Northern Ireland Leukaemia Research Fund, 1967. Mem., Lloyd's, 1977–2004. *Recreations:* sailing, photography.

GRAHAM, John Strathie; Chief Executive, Historic Scotland, since 2004; *b* 27 May 1950; *s* of Sir Norman Graham, *qv*; *m* 1979, Anne Janet Stenhouse; two *s* one *d*. *Educ:* Edinburgh Academy; Corpus Christi College, Oxford (BA Lit. Hum.). Joined Scottish Office, 1972; Private Sec. to Minister of State, 1975–76; Industrial Develt and Electricity Divs, 1976–82; Private Sec. to Sec. of State, 1983–85; Asst Sec., Planning and Finance Divs, 1985–91; Under Sec. (Local Govt), Envmt Dept, 1991–96; Prin. Finance Officer, 1996–98; Sec. and Head, Scottish Office Agric., Envmt and Fisheries Dept, then Scottish Exec. Rural Affairs Dept, subseq. Scottish Exec. Envmt and Rural Affairs Dept, 1998–2004. *Recreations:* music, hillwalking. *Address:* Longmore House, Salisbury Place, Edinburgh EH9 1SH.

GRAHAM, Rev. Prof. (Lawrence) Gordon, PhD; FRSE; Henry Luce Professor of Philosophy and the Arts, Princeton Theological Seminary, since 2006; Director, Princeton Center for the Study of Scottish Philosophy, since 2007; *b* 15 July 1949; *s* of William Moore Graham and Hyacinth Elizabeth (*née* Donald); *m* 1971; two *s* two *d*. *Educ:* Univ. of St Andrews (MA); Univ. of Durham (MA; PhD 1975). FRSE 1999. University of St Andrews: Lectr in Moral Philosophy, 1975–88; Reader, 1988–95; Dir of Music, 1991–95; Regius Prof. of Moral Philosophy, Univ. of Aberdeen, 1996–2005; Stanton Lectr, Univ. of Cambridge, 2005. Ordained deacon, 2005, priest, 2006, Scottish Episcopal Church. Sec., Scots Philosophical Club, 1987–2001. *Publications:* Historical Explanation Reconsidered, 1983; Politics in its Place, 1986; Contemporary Social Philosophy, 1988, 4th edn 1995; The Idea of Christian Charity, 1990; Living the Good Life, 1990, 2nd edn 1994; The Shape of the Past, 1997; Ethics and International Relations, 1997, 2nd edn 2008; Philosophy of the Arts, 1997, 3rd edn 2005; The Internet: a philosophical inquiry, 1999; Evil and Christian Ethics, 2000; Genes: a philosophical inquiry, 2002; Universities: the recovery of an idea, 2002; Eight Theories of Ethics, 2004; The Re-enchantment of the World, 2007. *Recreations:* music, walking, cookery. *Address:* Princeton Theological Seminary, 64 Mercer Street, Princeton, NJ 08542–0803, USA.

GRAHAM, (Malcolm Gray) Douglas; DL; Chairman: The Midland News Association Ltd, since 1984 (Deputy Chairman, 1978–84); Claverley Co., since 1993; Deputy Chairman, Guiton Group Ltd, since 2003; *b* 18 Feb. 1930; *s* of late Malcolm Graham and Annie Jeanette Robinson; *m* 1980, Sara Anne Elwell (*née* Anderson). *Educ:* Shrewsbury Sch. National Service, RM, 1948–50. Newspaper trng, UK and Australia, 1950–53; Dir, Express & Star (Wolverhampton) Ltd, 1957. President: Young Newspapermen's Assoc., 1969; W Midlands Newspaper Soc., 1973–74; Chm., Evening Newspaper Advertising Bureau, 1978–79. DL Shropshire, 1997. *Recreation:* shooting. *Address:* Roughton Manor, Bridgnorth, Shropshire WV15 5HE. *T:* (01746) 716209.

GRAHAM, His Honour Martin; QC 1976; a Circuit Judge, 1986–2000; *b* 10 Feb. 1929; *m* 1962, Jane Filby; one *d*. *Educ:* Emanuel School; Trinity College, Oxford (Scholar; MA, PPE). Called to the Bar, Middle Temple, 1952; a Recorder, 1986. Nat. Service, Officer BAOR, 1953–55. *Recreations:* swimming, tennis. *Address:* 7 Oakeshott Avenue, Highgate, N6 6NT. *Clubs:* Reform, Royal Automobile, Hurlingham.

GRAHAM, Michael; *see* Graham, J. M. R.

GRAHAM, Sir Norman (William), Kt 1971; CB 1961; FRSE; Secretary, Scottish Education Department, 1964–73, retired; *b* 11 Oct. 1913; *s* of William and Margaret Graham; *m* 1949, Catherine Mary Strathie; two *s* one *d*. *Educ:* High Sch. of Glasgow; Glasgow Univ. Dept of Health for Scotland, 1936; Private Sec. to Permanent Under-Sec. of State, 1939–40; Ministry of Aircraft Production, 1940; Principal Private Sec. to Minister, 1944–45; Asst Sec., Dept of Health for Scotland, 1945; Under-Sec., Scottish Home and Health Dept, 1956–63. Hon. DLitt Heriot-Watt, 1971; DUniv Stirling, 1974. *Recreations:* golf, gardening. *Address:* 42 Charteris Road, Longniddry, East Lothian EH32 0NT. *T:* (01875) 852130. *Club:* New (Edinburgh).

See also J. S. Graham.

GRAHAM, Sir Peter, KCB 1993 (CB 1982); QC 1990; First Parliamentary Counsel, 1991–94; *b* 7 Jan. 1934; *o s* of late Alderman Douglas Graham, CBE, Huddersfield, and Ena May (*née* Jackson); *m* 1st, Judith Mary Dunbar; two *s*; 2nd, Anne Silvia Garcia; 3rd, Janet, *o d* of late Capt. William Eric Walker, TD, Mayfield, Sussex. *Educ:* St Bees Sch., Cumberland (scholar); St John's Coll., Cambridge (scholar, 1st cl. Law Tripos, MA, LLM, McMahon Law Studentship). Served as pilot in Fleet Air Arm, 1952–55, Lieut, RNR. Called to the Bar, Gray's Inn, 1958 (Holker Exhbn; H. C. Richards Prize, Ecclesiastical Law; Bencher, 1992), Lincoln's Inn, 1982; joined Parliamentary Counsel Office, 1959; Parly Counsel, 1972–86; with Law Commn, 1979–81; Second Parly Counsel, 1987–91. External Examr (Legislation), Univ. of Edinburgh, 1977–81; Consultant: in Legislative Drafting, Office of Attorney-Gen., Dublin, 1994–96; to Hassans (formerly J. A. Hassan & Partners), Gibraltar, 1997–. Mem., Tax Law Review Cttee, Inst. of Fiscal Studies, 1994–2006. Mem., Council, Huddersfield Univ., 1992–96. Hon. Legal Adviser, Historic Vehicle Clubs Cttee, 1967–86. *Recreations:* restoring and enjoying vintage and classic cars, la bonne cuisine. *Address:* Le Petit Château, La Vallette, 87190 Magnac Laval, France. *Club:* Sette of Odd Volumes.

GRAHAM, Sir Peter (Alfred), Kt 1987; OBE 1969; FCIB; Chairman, Crown Agents for Oversea Governments and Administrations, 1983–90; *b* 25 May 1922; *s* of Alfred Graham and Margaret (*née* Winder); *m* 1953, Luned Mary (*née* Kenealy-Jones); two *s* two *d*. *Educ:* St Joseph's Coll., Beulah Hill. FCIB (FIB 1975). Served War, RNVR: Pilot, FAA. Joined The Chartered Bank of India, Australia and China, 1947; 24 yrs overseas banking career, incl. appts in Japan, India and Hong Kong; i/c The Chartered Bank, Hong Kong, 1962–70; Chm. (1st), Hong Kong Export Credit Insurance Corp., 1965–70; General Manager, 1970, Dep. Man. Dir, 1975, Gp Man. Dir, 1977–83, Sen. Dep. Chm., 1983–87, Chm., 1987–88, Standard Chartered Bank, London. Director: Standard Chartered Finance Ltd, Sydney (formerly Mutual Acceptance Corp.), 1974–87; First Bank Nigeria, Lagos, 1976–87; Union Bank Inc., Los Angeles, 1979–88; Singapore Land Ltd 1988–89; Employment Conditions Abroad Ltd, 1988–94; Dolphin Hldgs Ltd, Bermuda 1995–99; Chairman: Standard Chartered Merchant Bank Ltd, 1977–83; Mocatta Commercial Ltd, 1983–87; Mocatta & Goldsmid Ltd, 1983–87; Equatorial Bank 1989–93; Deputy Chairman: Chartered Trust plc, 1983–85; Governing Body, ICC UK 1985–92; Mem., Bd of Banking Supervision, 1986–87; Pres., Inst. of Bankers, 1981–83 City University: Chm., Adv. Cttee, 1981–86, Council, 1986–92, Business Sch.; Chm. Council, 1986–92; Mem., Court, 1997–2000. Formerly Chm., Exchange Banks' Assoc. Hong Kong; Mem., Govt cttees connected with trade and industry, Hong Kong. CCM (CBIM 1981); FRSA 1983. Freeman, City of London, 1982. Hon. DSc City Univ., 1985 *Recreations:* golf, tennis. *Clubs:* Naval, Royal Automobile, Oriental; Hong Kong (Hong Kong); Rye Golf.

GRAHAM, Peter Donald, CMG 1997; Senior Partner, 1950–2003, Consultant Counsel since 2003, Graham, Thompson & Co; *b* 11 Oct. 1928; *m* 1951, Jolanta Maria Poplawska (*d* 1995); one *s* one *d*. *Educ:* Queen's Coll., Nassau, Bahamas; Bishop's Coll. Sch. Lennoxville, Canada; Univ. of London (LLB). Called to the Bar, Lincoln's Inn, 1949 Mem., Bahamas House of Assembly, 1956–72; Minister of Labour and Minister of Housing, 1964–67; Dir, Central Bank of the Bahamas, 1992–99. Mem., Bahamas Bar Assoc. *Recreations:* golf, tennis. *Address:* PO Box N272, Nassau, Bahamas. *Clubs:* Lyford Cay (Nassau); Nassau Lawn Tennis.

GRAHAM, Dr Peter John; Director, Change Programme, Health and Safety Executive 2002–03 (Board Member, 1994–2003); *b* 16 Sept. 1943; *s* of John Graham and late Judy Graham; *m* 1968, Janice Head; three *s*. *Educ:* St Joseph's Coll., Stoke-on-Trent; Liverpool Univ. (BSc; PhD Maths 1968). DTI, 1969–79; 1st Sec., UK Perm. Repn, Brussels 1979–82; DTI, 1982–84; Dept of Employment, 1984–88; Health and Safety Executive Hazardous Substances Div., 1988–91; General Policy Br., 1991–93; Offshore Safety Div. 1993–94; Dir, Health, 1994–99; Dir, Strategy and Analytical Support, 1999–2002. Lay Mem. Bd, Faculty of Occupational Medicine, 2005. Chm., Centre 33, St Albans, 2003–.

GRAHAM, Lt-Gen. Sir Peter (Walter), KCB 1991; CBE 1981 (OBE 1978; MBE 1972); GOC Scotland and Governor of Edinburgh Castle, 1991–93, retired; *b* 14 March 1937; *s* of Dr Walter Graham and Suzanne Graham (*née* Simon); *m* 1963, Alison Mary MB ChB, MRCGP, *d* of D. B. Morren, TD; three *s*. *Educ:* Fyvie Village School Aberdeenshire; Hall Sch., Hampstead; St Paul's Sch.; RMA Sandhurst; psc (Aust), ocds (Can). Commissioned, The Gordon Highlanders, 1956; regtl appts, Dover, BAOR Scotland, Kenya, 1957–62; HQ Highland Bde, 1962–63; Adjt, 1 Gordons, Kenya Scotland, Borneo (despatches), 1963–66; Staff Capt., HQ (1 Br) Corps, 1966–67; Aust Staff Coll., 1968; Co. Comdr, 1 Gordons, BAOR, 1969–70; Bde Maj., 39 Inf. Bde Ulster, 1970–72; 2nd i/c 1 Gordons, Scotland, Ulster, Singapore, 1972–74; MA to Adjt-Gen., MoD, 1974–75; CO 1 Gordons, Scotland, Ulster, 1976–78; COS HQ 3rd Armd Div., BAOR, 1978–82; Comdr UDR, 1982–84 (despatches); Nat. Defence Coll. Canada, 1984–85; Dep. Mil. Sec., MoD, 1985–87; GOC Eastern Dist, 1987–89; Comdt RMA Sandhurst, 1989–91. Col, The Gordon Highlanders, 1986–94; Col Comdt, The Scottish Div., 1991–93. Mem., Royal Company of Archers, Queen's Body Guard for Scotland, 1986–. Chm., Gordon Highlanders Regtl Trust Fund, 1986–2004; Vice Patron The Gordon Highlanders Mus., 2003– (Chm., Mgt Cttee, 1994–2003). Burgess of Guild City of Aberdeen, 1994. Hon. DLitt Robert Gordon Univ., Aberdeen, 1996. *Publications* (with Pipe Major B. MacRae) The Gordon Highlanders Pipe Music Collection, Vol. 1 1983, 3rd edn 1986, Vol. 2, 1985; (contrib.) John Baynes, Soldiers of Scotland, 1988 contrib. to Jl of RUSI. *Recreations:* stalking, hill walking, reading, pipe music, amusing grandchildren, gardening under wife's directions. *Address:* c/o Home HQ The Highlanders, Viewfield Road, Aberdeen AB15 7XH.

See also Sir A. M. Graham.

GRAHAM, Prof. Philip Jeremy; Chairman, Association of Child Psychology and Psychiatry, 2002–04; *b* 3 Sept. 1932; *s* of Jacob Rackham Graham and Pauline Graham; *m* 1960, Nori (*née* Burawoy); two *s* one *d*. *Educ:* Perse Sch., Cambridge; Cambridge Univ (MA); University Coll. Hosp., London. FRCP 1973; FRCPsych 1972. Consultant Psychiatrist: Maudsley Hosp., London, 1966–68; Hosp. for Sick Children, Great Ormond Street, London, 1968–74; Prof. of Child Psychiatry, 1975–94 and Dean, 1985–90, Inst. of Child Health, London Univ.; Prof. of Child Psychiatry, Univ. of Oslo, 1994–2000; Lectr, Dept of Develtl Psychiatry, Univ. of Cambridge, 1994–2000; Sen. Mem., Wolfson Coll. Cambridge, 1994–2002. Chm., Nat. Children's Bureau, 1994–2000 (Chm., Child Policy Rev. Gp, 1987–89). President: European Soc. for Child and Adolescent Psychiatry 1987–91; Psychiatry Section, RSM, 1994–95; Vice-Pres., RCPsych, 1996–98. Hon. FRCPCH 1993; Hon. FRCPsych 2004. *Publications:* A Neuropsychiatric Study in Childhood (jtly), 1970; (ed) Epidemiological Approaches to Child Psychiatry, 1977; (jtly) Child Psychiatry: a developmental approach, 1986, 4th edn 2007; (ed) Cognitive Behaviour Therapy for Children and Families, 1998, 2nd edn 2004; The End of Adolescence, 2004; Susan Isaacs: freeing the minds of children, 2008; various publications on child and adolescent psychiatry. *Recreations:* walking, chess. *Address:* 27 St Alban's Road, NW5 1RG.

GRAHAM, Sir Ralph Stuart, 14th Bt *cr* 1629 (NS), of Esk, Cumberland; *b* 5 Nov. 1950; *s* of Sir Ralph Wolfe Graham, 13th Bt and of Geraldine, *d* of Austin Velour; *S* father, 1988, but his name does not appear on the Official Roll of the Baronetage; *m* 1st, 1972, Roxanne (*d* 1978), *d* of Mrs Lovette Gurzan; 2nd, 1979, Deena Vandergrift; one adopted *s*. *Heir:* *b* Robert Bruce Graham [*b* 14 Nov. 1953; *m* 1974, Denise, *d* of T. Juranich; two *s*].

GRAHAM, Robert Martin; Chief Executive, British United Provident Association, 1984–91; *b* 20 Sept. 1930; *s* of Francis P. Graham and Margaret M. Graham (*née* Broderick); *m* 1959, Eileen (*née* Hoey); two *s* two *d*. *Educ:* Dublin; ACII. Hibernian Fire and General Insurance Co. Ltd, 1948–57; Voluntary Health Insurance Board, 1957–82 (to Chief Exec.); Dep. Chief Exec., BUPA 1982–84. Chm., Board of Management, Meath Hosp., 1972–82; Pres., Internat. Fedn of Voluntary Health Service Funds, 1988–90 (Dep. Pres., 1986–88); Vice-Pres., Assoc. Internationale de la Mutualité, 1990– (Mem. Bd of Govs, 1978–91); Mem., Central Council, Federated Voluntary Hosps, Ireland, 1978–82. *Address:* 39 Garratts Lane, Banstead, Surrey SM7 2ED. *Clubs:* Royal Automobile, Rotary Club of London.

GRAHAM, Ronald; *see* Graham, G. R. G.

GRAHAM, Dr Ronald Cairns, CBE 1992; General Manager, Tayside Health Board, 1985–93 (Chief Administrative Medical Officer, 1973–85); *b* 8 Oct. 1931; *s* of Thomas Graham and Helen Cairns; *m* 1959, Christine Fraser Osborne; two *s* one *d*. *Educ:* Airdrie Acad.; Glasgow Univ. MB, ChB Glasgow 1956; DipSocMed Edin. 1968; FFCM 1973; FRCPE 1983. West of Scotland; house jobs, gen. practice and geriatric med., 1956–62; Dep. Med. Supt, Edin. Royal Infirmary, 1962–65; Asst Sen. Admin. MO, SE Regional Hosp. Bd, 1965–69; Dep. and then Sen. Admin. MO, Eastern Regional Hosp. Bd, 1969–73. Mem. Court, Univ. of Dundee, 1994–2003. *Recreations:* fishing, bowling. *Address:* 34 Dalgleish Road, Dundee DD4 7JT. *T:* (01382) 455426.

GRAHAM, (Stewart) David; QC 1977; Partner, Cork Gully, 1985–92; *b* 27 Feb. 1934; *s* of late Lewis Graham and of Gertrude Graham; *m* 1959, Corinne Carmona; two *d. Educ:* Leeds Grammar Sch.; St Edmund Hall, Oxford (MA, BCL). Called to the Bar, Middle Temple, 1957; Harmsworth Law Scholar, 1958. Mem. Council, Justice, 1976–96 (Chm., Cttee on Protection of Small Investor, 1989–92; Chm., Cttee on Insolvency, 1993–94); Mem., Insolvency Rules Adv. Cttee, 1984–86; Chm., Law, Parly and Gen. Purposes Cttee, Bd of Deputies of British Jews, 1983–88. Indep. Mem. Council, The Insurance Ombudsman Bureau, 1993–2001; Associate Mem., British and Irish (formerly UK) Ombudsman Assoc., 1994–. Vis. Fellow, Centre for Commercial Law, QMW, London, 1992–; Vis. Prof., Faculty of Business, Centre for Insolvency Law and Policy, Kingston Univ., 2004–. Member Committee: Stanmore Soc., 2001–; Harrow Heritage Trust, 2002–. Chm. Editorial Bd, Insolvency Intelligence, 1988–94. FRSA 1995. *Publications:* (ed jtly) Williams and Muir Hunter on Bankruptcy, 18th edn 1968, 19th edn 1979; (contrib.) Longman's Insolvency, 1986; (contrib.) Muir Hunter on Personal Insolvency, 2002; (contrib.) Oxford DNB, 2005; (ed) legal textbooks; contrib. Internat. Insolvency Review. *Recreations:* biography, music, drama, travel, history of insolvency. *Address:* 6 Grosvenor Lodge, Dennis Lane, Stanmore, Middx HA7 4JE. *T:* (020) 8954 3783.

GRAHAM, Stuart Twentyman, CBE 1981; DFC 1943; FCIS, FCIB; Chairman, Aitken Hume Bank (formerly Aitken Hume) Ltd, 1985–93; *b* 26 Aug. 1921; *s* of late Twentyman Graham; *m* 1948, Betty June Cox (*d* 1999); one *s. Educ:* Kilburn Grammar Sch. Served War, 1940–46: commissioned, RAF, 1942. Entered Midland Bank, 1938; Jt Gen. Manager, 1966–70; Asst Chief Gen. Manager, 1970–74; Chief Gen. Manager, 1974–81; Gp Chief Exec., 1981–82; Dir, 1974–85. Chairman: Northern Bank Ltd, 1982–85; International Commodities Clearing House Ltd, 1982–86; Director: Allied Lyons plc, 1981–92; Sheffield Forgemasters Holdings, 1983–85; Aitken Hume International, 1985–93; Scotia (formerly Efamol) Hldgs, 1985–95. *Recreations:* music, reading. *Club:* Royal Air Force.

GRAHAM, Susan Alesta; mezzo soprano; *b* 23 July 1960; *d* of Floyd Ben Graham and Betty Fort. *Educ:* Midland Lee High Sch.; Texas Technical Univ.; Manhattan Sch. of Music. Opera début in Vanessa, St Louis, 1988. Regular performances with NY Metropolitan Opera, 1991–, and at Salzburg Fest.; other appearances include: Royal Opera, 1994–; WNO, 1994–; Glyndebourne; Vienna State Opera; La Scala; Paris Opéra, etc. Rôles include: title rôle, Chérubin; Octavian in Der Rosenkavalier; Dorabella in Così fan tutte; Cherubino in Le Nozze di Figaro; title rôle, Arianna; title rôle, Iphigénie en Tauride; Charlotte in Werther; title rôle, Béatrice et Bénédict; Marguerite in La damnation de Faust; title rôle in world première of Monteverdi's Arianna. Numerous recitals and recordings. Metropolitan Opera Nat. Council Award, 1988.

GRAHAM, Teresa Colomba, CBE 2008 (OBE 1998); business and government advisor, since 2003; *b* Newcastle upon Tyne, 8 March 1956; *d* of Albert Rea and Anna Rea (*née* Mastroianni). *Educ:* Univ. of Newcastle upon Tyne (BA Eng. Linguistics 1977). FCA 1982. Price Waterhouse, 1977–90; Baker Tilly, 1990–2003. Chm., Salix Finance, 2004–; non-exec. dir of various cos. Seconded to Enterprise and Deregulation Unit, 1986–87; Mem., Deregulation Adv. Panel, 1988–90; Dep. Chm., Better Regulation Task Force, subseq. Better Regulation Commn, 1997–2007 (Chm. gp on report Better Routes to Redress, 2004; Chm. Subgp on report Regulation—Less is More, 2005); leader, independent review of Small Firms Loan Guarantee, 2003–04 (Graham Review of Small Firms Loan Guarantee, 2004); Chm., Admin. Burdens Adv. Bd, HMRC, 2006–. Ind. Regulator, RICS, 2007–. *Recreations:* walking, travelling, reading, cinema, art. *Address:* 9 Eccleston Square, SW1V 1NP. *T:* 07767 486486, *Fax:* (020) 7630 6264; *e-mail:* teresa@ teresagraham.co.uk.

GRAHAM, Thomas; *b* 5 Dec. 1943; *m* Joan Bagley; two *s.* Engineer with Rolls-Royce, 1965–78; Office Manager, Robertson and Ross, solicitors, 1982–87. Mem., Strathclyde Reg. Council, 1978–87. MP Renfrew and Inverclyde, 1987–97, Renfrewshire, 1997–2001 (Lab 1987–98, Ind. 1998–2001). *Address:* 265 Gilmartin Road, Linwood, Paisley PA3 3SU.

GRAHAM, Rear-Adm. Wilfred Jackson, CB 1979; *b* 17 June 1925; *s* of late William Bryce Graham and Jean Hill Graham (*née* Jackson); *m* 1951, Gillian Mary Finlayson (*d* 2004); three *s* one *d. Educ:* Rossall Sch., Fleetwood, Lancs. Served War of 1939–45, Royal Navy: Cadet, 1943; specialised in gunnery, 1951; Comdr 1960; Captain 1967; IDC, 1970; Captain, HMS Ark Royal, 1975–76; Flag Officer, Portsmouth, 1976–79, retired. Dir and Sec., RNLI, 1979–87. Mem. Council, Rossall Sch., 1988–95. Gov., E. Hayes Dashwood Foundn, 1994–2004. FNI 1987. *Recreation:* walking. *Address:* Yarnfield Cottage, Maiden Bradley, Warminster, Wilts BA12 7HY. *Clubs:* Royal Naval Sailing Association, Royal Yacht Squadron.

GRAHAM, William; *see* Graham, A. W.

GRAHAM, Hon. William Carvel; PC (Can) 2002; QC (Can.); MP (Liberal) Toronto Centre (formerly Rosedale, then Toronto Centre-Rosedale), Canada, 1993–2007; *b* 17 March 1939; *s* of Francis Ronald Graham and Helen Payne Graham (*née* White); *m* 1962, Catherine Elizabeth Curry; one *s* one *d. Educ:* Univ. of Toronto (BA 1961; LLB 1964); Univ. of Paris (DJur). Barrister and solicitor, Fasken and Calvin, 1967–80, Partner, 1983; Prof. of Law, 1980–94, and Dir, Centre for Internat. Studies, 1986–88, Univ. of Toronto. Minister of Foreign Affairs, 2002–04, of Nat. Defence, 2004–06. Chancellor, Trinity Coll., Univ. of Toronto, 2007–. Chevalier, Legion of Honour (France), 1984; Chevalier, Order of the Pléiade (France), 1999. *Publications:* contrib. to books and jls on internat. trade law and public internat. law. *Address:* c/o Trinity College, 6 Hoskin Avenue, Toronto, ON M5S 1H8, Canada.

GRAHAM, William Franklin, (Billy Graham), Hon. KBE 2001; evangelist; *b* Charlotte, NC, 7 Nov. 1918; *s* of late William Franklin Graham and Morrow (*née* Coffey); *m* 1943, Ruth McCue Bell (*d* 2007); two *s* three *d. Educ:* Florida Bible Institute, Tampa (ThB); Wheaton Coll., Ill (AB). Ordained to Baptist ministry, 1939; first Vice-Pres., Youth for Christ Internat., 1945–50; Pres., Northwestern Coll., Minneapolis, 1947–52; Evangelistic campaigns, 1946–; world-wide weekly broadcast, 1950–; many evangelistic tours of Great Britain, Europe, the Far East, South America, Australia and Russia. Chairman, Board of World Wide Pictures Inc. Holds numerous honorary degrees in Divinity, Laws, Literature and the Humanities, from American universities and colleges; also varied awards from organisations, 1954–, inc. Templeton Foundn Prize, 1982; President's Medal of Freedom Award, 1983; Congressional Gold Medal, 1996. *Publications include:* Peace with God, 1953; World Aflame, 1965; Jesus Generation, 1971; Angels— God's Secret Agents, 1975; How to be Born Again, 1977; The Holy Spirit, 1978; Till Armageddon, 1981; Approaching Hoofbeats: the four horsemen of the Apocalypse, 1983; A Biblical Standard for Evangelists, 1984; Unto the Hills, 1986; Facing Death and the Life After, 1987; Answers to Life's Problems, 1988; Hope for the Troubled Heart, 1991; Storm Warning, 1992; Just As I Am, 1997; Hope for Each Day, 2002; The Journey, 2006. *Recreations:* swimming, walking. *Address:* (office) 1 Billy Graham Parkway, Charlotte, NC 28210, USA. *T:* (704) 4012432.

GRAHAM, (William) Gordon, MC 1944 (Bar 1945); Editor, LOGOS, 1990–2005, Editor Emeritus, since 2006; Group Chairman, Butterworth Publishers, 1975–90 (Chief Executive, 1974–87); *b* 17 July 1920; *s* of Thomas Graham and Marion Hutcheson; US citizen, 1963; *m* 1st, 1943, Margaret Milne, Bombay (*d* 1946); one *d*; 2nd, 1948, Friedel Gramm, Zürich (*d* 1992); one *d*; 3rd, 1994, Betty Cottrell, USA. *Educ:* Hutchesons' Grammar Sch.; Glasgow Univ. (MA 1940). Commissioned, Queen's Own Cameron Highlanders, 1941; served in India and Burma, 1942–46: Captain 1944, Major 1945; GSO II India Office, 1946. Newspaper correspondent and publishers' representative in India, 1946–55; Internat. Sales Manager, 1956–63, Vice-Pres., 1961–63, McGraw-Hill Book Co., New York; Man. Dir, McGraw-Hill Publishing Co., UK, 1963–74; Director: W & R Chambers, Edinburgh, 1974–83; International Publishing Corp., 1975–82; Reed Publishing Gp, 1982–90; Chairman: Internat. Electronic Publishing Res. Centre Ltd, 1981–84; Publishers Database Ltd, 1982–84; Bd, R. R. Bowker Co., 1986–90; Mem. Bd, Polish Scientific Publishers, 1994–99. Chm., Soc. of Bookmen, 1972–75; Publishers Association: Mem. Council, 1972–87; Chm., Electronic Publishing Panel, 1980–83; Vice Pres., 1984–85, 1987–88; Pres., 1985–87. Member Board: British Liby, 1980–86; Eur. Foundn for Liby Co-operation, 1991–95. Trustee: Kraszna-Krausz Foundn, 1987–97 (Chm. Trustees, 1990–95); Kohima Educnl Trust, 2002–. Correspondent, Christian Science Monitor, 1946–56. FRSA 1978. DUniv Stirling, 1993. *Publications:* As I Was Saying: essays on the international book business, 1994; Butterworths: history of a publishing house, 1997; The Trees are all Young on Garrison Hill, 2005; From Trust to Takeover: an intimate history of Butterworths 1943–67, 2006; articles in US and British trade press. *Recreations:* writing, fostering transatlantic understanding, landscape gardening, singing sentimental songs. *Address:* White Lodge, Beechwood Drive, Marlow, Bucks SL7 2DH. *T:* (01628) 483371; Juniper Acres, 1039 Hurricane Road, Keene, NY 12942, USA.

GRAHAM, Yvonne Georgette; Headmistress, Clifton High School, Bristol, 1996–97; *b* 31 Aug. 1943; *d* of J. van Gorkom and M. E. van Gorkom-Pas; *m* 1967, Lt-Col I. G. Graham, RE (retd); two *s. Educ:* Alexander Hegius-Gymnasium-Deventer; Amsterdam Univ. (MA); London Univ. Various teaching posts in England, Germany and Holland, 1965–90; Headmistress, Lavant House Sch., Chichester, 1990–95. *Recreations:* reading, travel, theatre, music. *Address:* 20 Stanton Drive, Chichester, West Sussex PO19 5QN. *T:* (01243) 528111.

GRAHAM-BRYCE, Ian James, CBE 2001; DPhil; Principal and Vice-Chancellor, University of Dundee, 1994–2000, now Principal Emeritus; *b* 20 March 1937; *s* of late Alexander Graham-Bryce, FRCS, and Dame Isabel Graham-Bryce, DBE; *m* 1959, Anne Elisabeth Metcalf; one *s* three *d. Educ:* William Hulme's Grammar Sch., Manchester; University Coll., Oxford (Exhibnr). BA, MA, BSc, DPhil (Oxon); FRSC, CChem 1981; FRSE 1996. Research Asst, Univ. of Oxford, 1958–61; Lectr, Dept of Biochemistry and Soil Sci., UCNW, Bangor, 1961–64; Sen. Scientific Officer, Rothamsted Experimental Station, 1964–70; Sen. Res. Officer, ICI Plant Protection Div., Jealott's Hill Res. Station, Bracknell, Berks, 1970–72; Special Lectr in Pesticide Chemistry, Dept of Zoology and Applied Entomology, Imperial Coll. of Science and Technology, 1970–72 (Vis. Prof., 1976–79); Rothamsted Experimental Station: Head, Dept of Insecticides and Fungicides, 1972–79; Dep. Director, 1975–79; Dir, East Malling Res. Stn, Maidstone, Kent, 1979–86 (Trustee, 1986–, Chm., 2001–, Develt and Endowment Fund, subseq. E Malling Trust for Horticl Res.); Cons. Dir, Commonwealth Bureau of Horticulture and Plantation Crops, 1979–86; Hon. Lectr, Dept of Biology, Univ. of Strathclyde, 1977–80; Hd of Envmtl Affairs Div., Shell Internat. Petroleum Maatschappij BV, 1986–94. Pres., British Crop Protection Council, 1996–2000 (Hon. Vice-Pres., 2000–02). Society of Chemical Industry, London: Pres., 1982–84; Mem. Council, 1969–72 and 1974–89; Hon. Sec., Home Affairs, 1977–80; Chm., Pesticides Gp, 1978–80; Sec., Physico-Chemical and Biophysical Panel, 1968–70, Chm., 1973–75; Mem., British Nat. Cttee for Chemistry, 1982–84. President: Assoc. of Applied Biologists, 1988 (Vice-Pres., 1985–87); Scottish Assoc. for Marine Sci., 2000–04. Chm., Agrochemical Planning Gp, IOCD, 1985–88; Mem., Scientific Cttee, Eur. Chemical Industry Ecol. and Toxicol. Centre, 1988–94; Vice-Chm., Environmental Res. Wkg Gp, Industrial R&D Adv. Cttee to EC, 1988–91; Member: NERC, 1989–96 (Chm., Polar Sci. and Technol. Bd, 1995–96); Royal Commn on Envmtl Pollution, 2000–. Member, Board of Directors: British Council Educnl Counselling Service, 1996–98; Quality Assurance Agency for Higher Educn, 1997–98; Rothamsted Experimental Station, 2000–04; Convener, Cttee of Scottish Higher Educn Principals, 1998–2000; Vice Pres., CVCP, 1999–2000. Governor: Long Ashton Res. Stn, 1979–85; Wye Coll., 1979–86, Imperial Coll., 1985–2001, Univ. of London; Hon. Advr, Zhejiang Wanli Univ., China, 1999–. Member, Editorial Board: Chemico-Biological Interactions, 1973–77; Pesticide Science, 1978–80; Agriculture, Ecosystems and Environment, 1978–87. Mem., Old Members' Trust, University Coll., Oxford, 2004–. FRSA 1996. Hon. LLD Dundee, 2001. British Crop Protection Council Medal, 2000. *Publications:* Physical Principles of Pesticide Behaviour, 1980; papers on soil science, plant nutrition, crop protection, and envmtl matters in sci. jls. *Recreations:* music (espec. opera), ski-ing and other sports. *Club:* Athenæum.

GRAHAM-CAMPBELL, Prof. James Alastair, FBA 2001; FSA, FSAScot; FRHistS; Professor of Medieval Archaeology, University of London, at University College, 1991–2002, now Emeritus; *b* 7 Feb. 1947; *s* of David John Graham-Campbell and Joan Sybil Graham-Campbell (*née* Maclean). *Educ:* Eton Coll.; Trinity Coll., Cambridge (MA, PhD); Bergen Univ.; Oslo Univ.; UCL. FSA 1977. Asst Lectr in Archaeology, UC Dublin, 1971–73; University College London: Lectr, 1973–82; Reader in Medieval Archaeology, 1982–91; Fellow, 2003. Vis. Prof., Univ. of Minnesota, 1981; British Acad. Res. Reader, 1988–90; O'Donnell Lectr, Univ. of Wales, 1989; Crabtree Orator, UCL, 1990; Rhind Lectr, Soc. of Antiquaries of Scotland, 1996; Special Prof. of Viking Studies, Nottingham Univ., 2003–Sept. 2009; Hon. Prof., Aarhus Univ., 2004–08. Mem., Ancient Monuments Adv. Cttee, English Heritage, 1992–97. Sec., Soc. for Medieval Archaeology, 1976–82 (Hon. Vice-Pres., 2001–). *Publications:* Viking Artefacts, 1980; The Viking World, 1980, 3rd edn 2001; (jtly) The Vikings, 1980; (ed) Cultural Atlas of the Viking World, 1994; The Viking-Age Gold and Silver of Scotland, 1995; (jtly) Vikings in Scotland: an archaeological survey, 1998; (ed with G. Williams) Silver Economy in the Viking Age, 2007; (ed with M. Valor) The Archaeology of Medieval Europe, Vol. 1, 2007; numerous articles in learned jls. *Recreations:* cooking, gardening, opera, ballet. *Address:* Institute of Archaeology (UCL), 31–34 Gordon Square, WC1H 0PY. *Club:* Athenæum.

GRAHAM-DIXON, Andrew Michael; writer and presenter, BBC Television, since 1992; Chief Art Critic, Sunday Telegraph, since 2004; *b* 26 Dec. 1960; *s* of Anthony Philip Graham-Dixon, *qv*, and Suzanne Graham-Dixon (*née* Villar); *m* 1985, Sabine Marie-Pascale Tilly; one *s* two *d. Educ:* Westminster Sch.; Christ Church, Oxford (MA 1st Cl. English); Courtauld Inst. Chief Art Critic, 1986–97, Chief Arts Feature Writer, 1997–99, The Independent; Chief Arts Feature Writer, Sunday Telegraph Mag., 1999–2004. Television series include: A History of British Art, 1996; Renaissance, 1999; The Secret of Drawing, 2006; Art of Eternity, 2007; Art of Spain, 2008. BP Arts Journalist of Year, 1988, 1989, 1990; Hawthornden Prize for Art Criticism, 1991; 1st Prize, Reportage Section, Montreal Internat. Fest. of Films, 1994. *Publications:* Howard Hodgkin: paintings,

1994; A History of British Art, 1996; Paper Museum: writings about paintings, mostly, 1996; Renaissance, 1999; In the Picture: the year through art, 2003; Michelangelo and the Sistine Chapel, 2008. *Recreations:* golf, horse-racing. *Address:* Sunday Telegraph Magazine, 111 Buckingham Palace Road, SW1W 0DT. *Clubs:* Royal Society of Arts; Muswell Hill Golf.

GRAHAM-DIXON, Anthony Philip; QC 1973; *b* 5 Nov. 1929; *s* of late Leslie Charles Graham-Dixon, QC; *m* 1956, Margaret Suzanne Villar; one *s* one *d.* *Educ:* Westminster Sch.; Christ Church, Oxford. MA (1st Cl. Hon. Mods, 1st Cl. Lit. Hum.). RNVR, 1953–55, Lieut (SP). Called to the Bar, Inner Temple, 1956, Bencher 1982; Member of Gray's Inn, 1965–. Mem. Council, Charing Cross Hosp. Medical School, 1976–83. Chm., London Concertino Ltd, 1982–. Dep. Chm., PHLS, 1988–96 (Mem. Bd, 1987–96). Gov., Bedales Sch., 1988–96. Trustee, SPNM, 1988–97 (Chm. Trustees, 1994–97). Chm., London Jupiter Orch. Trust Ltd, 2001–. Liveryman, Goldsmiths' Co., 1980–. *Publication:* (mem. adv. bd) Competition Law in Western Europe and the USA, 1976. *Recreations:* music (especially opera), gardening. *Address:* 46A Courtfield Gardens, SW5 0NA. *T:* (020) 7373 1461; Masketts Manor, Nutley, Uckfield, East Sussex TN22 3HD. *T:* (01825) 712010.

See also A. M. Graham-Dixon.

GRAHAM-HARRISON, Robert Montagu, CMG 2003; Senior Clerk, House of Lords, 2003–08; *b* 16 Feb. 1943; *s* of Francis Laurence Theodore Graham-Harrison, CB and Carol Mary St John, *d* of Sir Francis Stewart, CIE; *m* 1977, Kathleen Patricia, *d* of John and Mary Gladys Maher; two *d.* *Educ:* Eton Coll.; Magdalen Coll., Oxford. VSO India, 1965; GLC, 1966; Min. of Overseas Development, later Overseas Development Administration, then Dept for Internat. Develt, 1967–2003; World Bank, Washington, 1971–73; Private Sec. to Minister for Overseas Development, 1978; Asst Sec., ODA, 1979; Hd, British Develt Div. in E Africa, Nairobi, 1982–86; Hd, E Asia Dept, ODA, 1986–89; Alternate Exec. Dir, World Bank, Washington, 1989–92; UK Exec. Dir, EBRD, 1992–97; Dir, British Develt Co-op Office, New Delhi, 1997–2003. *Recreations:* hill walking, travel, tennis. *Address:* 122 St George's Avenue, N7 0AH.

GRAHAM-MOON, Sir Peter Wilfred Giles; *see* Moon.

GRAHAM-SMITH, Sir Francis; *see* Smith.

GRAHAM-TOLER, family name of **Earl of Norbury**.

GRAHAME, Christine; Member (SNP) South Scotland, Scottish Parliament, since 1999; *b* 9 Sept. 1944; *d* of Christie and Margaret Grahame; *m* (marr. diss.); two *s.* *Educ:* Edinburgh Univ. (MA 1966; DipEd 1967; LLB 1984; DipLP 1985). Schoolteacher, secondary schs, 1967–80; solicitor, 1986–99. Shadow Minister for Social Justice, Scottish Exec., 2004–07. Scottish Parliament: Convenor: Cross Party Gp, Borders Rail; Justice Cttee I, 2001–03; Health Cttee, 2003–04; Health and Sport Cttee, 2007–. *Recreations:* cats, trad jazz, gardening and drinking malt at the same time. *Address:* Scottish Parliament, Edinburgh EH99 1SP. *T:* (0131) 348 5729.

GRAHAME-SMITH, Prof. David Grahame, CBE 1993; Rhodes Professor of Clinical Pharmacology, University of Oxford, 1972–2000; Hon. Director, Smith Kline Beecham Centre of Applied Neuropsychobiology, Oxford University, 1990–99; Fellow of Corpus Christi College, Oxford, 1972–2000, now Emeritus (Vice-President, 1998–99); *b* 10 May 1933; *s* of George E. and C. A. Smith; *m* 1957, Kathryn Frances, *d* of Dr F. R. Beetham; two *s.* *Educ:* Wyggeston Grammar Sch., Leicester; St Mary's Hosp. Medical Sch., Univ. of London. MB BS (London) 1956; MRCS, LRCP 1956; MRCP 1958; PhD (London) 1966; FRCP 1972. House Phys., Paddington Gen. Hosp., London, 1956; House Surg., Battle Hosp., Reading, 1956–57. Captain, RAMC, 1957–60. Registrar and Sen. Registrar in Medicine, St Mary's Hosp., Paddington, 1960–61; H. A. M. Thompson Research Scholar, RCP, 1961–62; Saltwell Research Scholar, RCP, 1962–65; Wellcome Trust Research Fellow, 1965–66; Hon. Med. Registrar to Med. Unit, St Mary's Hosp., 1961–66; MRC Travelling Fellow, Dept of Endocrinology, Vanderbilt Univ., Nashville, Tennessee, USA, 1966–67; Sen. Lectr in Clinical Pharmacology and Therapeutics, St Mary's Hosp. Med. Sch., Univ. of London, 1967–71; Hon. Cons. Physician, St Mary's Hosp., Paddington, 1967–71; Hon. Dir, MRC Unit of Clin. Pharm., Radcliffe Infirmary, Oxford, 1972–93. Vis. Prof., Peking Union Medical Coll., Beijing, China, 1985–. Non-exec. Mem., Oxfordshire HA, 1992–98. Member: Cttee on Safety of Medicines, 1975–86; Jt Cttee on Vaccination and Immunisation, 1987–89; Chairman: Adv. Gp on Hepatitis, 1987–89; Adv. Council on Misuse of Drugs, 1988–98. Lilly Prize, Clinical Sect., British Pharmacol Soc., 1995 (Hon. Fellow, 2007); Lifetime Achievement Award, British Assoc. of Psychopharmacology, 2002. *Publications:* (with J. K. Aronson) Oxford Textbook of Clinical Pharmacology and Drug Therapy, 1984, 3rd edn 2002; papers on biochemical, therapeutic and med. matters in scientific jls. *Recreation:* jazz. *Address:* Romney, Lincombe Lane, Boars Hill, Oxford OX1 5DY.

GRAINGE, Lucian Charles; Chairman and Chief Executive, Universal Music Group International, since 2005; *b* London, 29 Feb. 1960; *s* of Cecil and Marion Grainge; *m* 2002, Caroline Lewis; one *s* one *d* and one step *d.* *Educ:* Queen Elizabeth Grammar Sch., Barnet, London. Hd, Creative Dept, April Music/CBS UK, 1979–82; Dir and Gen. Manager, RCA Music UK, 1982–85; A&R Dir, MCA UK, 1985–86; Man. Dir, PolyGram Music Publishing UK, 1986–93; Gen. Manager, A&R and Business Affairs, 1993–97, Man. Dir, 1997–99, Polydor Records UK; Dep. Chm., 1999–2001, Chm. and Chief Exec., 2001–05, Universal Music UK. Mem. Bd, Internat. Fedn of Phonographic Industry, 2005–. *Recreations:* soccer, automobiles. *Address:* Universal Music Group International, 364–366 Kensington High Street, W14 8NS. *T:* (020) 7471 5006, *Fax:* (020) 7471 5391; *e-mail:* lucian.grainge@umusic.com.

GRAINGER, Ian Richard Peregrine L.; *see* Liddell-Grainger.

GRAINGER, John Andrew, CMG 2005; HM Diplomatic Service; Deputy Legal Adviser, Foreign and Commonwealth Office, since 2003; *b* 27 Aug. 1957; *m* 1998, Katherine Veronica Bregou; one *s.* Called to the Bar, Lincoln's Inn, 1981. Joined HM Diplomatic Service, 1984; Asst Legal Advr, FCO, 1984–89; First Sec. (Legal Advr), BMG Berlin, 1989–91; Asst Legal Advr, FCO, 1991–94; Legal Counsellor: FCO, 1994–97; UK Mission to UN, NY, 1997–2001; FCO, 2001–03. *Address:* Foreign and Commonwealth Office, King Charles Street, SW1A 2AH.

GRAMMENOS, Prof. Constantinos Theophilos, Hon. OBE 1994; DSc; Pro Vice-Chancellor, City University, London, since 1998; Professor of Shipping, since 1986, Deputy Dean, since 2001, Sir John Cass Business School, City of London (formerly City University Business School); *b* 23 Feb. 1944; *s* of late Commander Theophilos C. Grammenos and Argyro (*née* Spanakos); *m* 1972, Anna C. Papadimitriou; one *s.* *Educ:* Third State Sch. of Athens; Pantion Univ. (BA); Univ. of Wales (MSc); City University (DSc). National Service, Greek Navy, 1968–70. Nat. Bank of Greece, 1962–74 (shipping finance expert, head office, 1972–74); independent researcher and advr, 1977–82; Vis. Prof., 1982–86, Founder and Hd of Centre for Shipping, Trade and Finance, 1984–2002, Actg Dean, 2000, City Univ. Business Sch. Visiting Professor: World Maritime Univ. Malmö, 1990–95; Univ. of Antwerp, 2000–. Chm., Man. Cttee, Internat. Hellenic Univ. Thessaloniki. Founder, 1999, and Chm., 1999–, City of London Biennial Meeting; Pres. Internat. Assoc. of Maritime Economists, 1998–2002; Member: Bd of Dirs, Alexander S Onassis Public Benefit Foundn, 1995–; American Bureau of Shipping, 1996–; Balti Exchange, 1997–. Mem., Bd of Trustees, Inst. of Marine Engineers Meml Trust, 2000– Freeman, City of London, 2000; Liveryman, Shipwrights' Co., 2002–. Archon o Ecumenical Patriarchate of Constantinople, 1994. FRSA 1996; FCIB 2004. Seatrade Personality of the Year, 1998. *Publications:* Bank Finance for Ship Purchase, 1979; (ed) Th Handbook of Maritime Economics and Business, 2002; various papers and studies i shipping finance. *Recreations:* music, theatre, walking. *Address:* Sir John Cass Busines School, 106 Bunhill Row, EC1Y 8TZ. *T:* (020) 7040 8670. *Club:* Travellers.

GRAN, Maurice Bernard; scriptwriter, since 1978; *b* 26 Oct. 1949; *s* of Mark an Deborah Gran; *m* 1994, Carol James; one *s* one *d.* *Educ:* William Ellis Sch., London University Coll. London (BSc Internat. Relations 1971). Mgt trainee, Dept o Employment, 1971; Manager, Tottenham Employment Exchange, 1974–76; marketin develt advr, 1976–78, Manager, London Employment Intelligence Unit, 1978–80, Dep of Employment. Co-Founder and Company Dir, Alomo Productions, 1988–2001. Wit Laurence Marks, scriptwriter, 1980–: main *television* credits: Shine on Harvey Moon 1982–85, 1995; The New Statesman, 1987–91 (BAFTA Award, Best Comedy, 1990) Birds of a Feather, 1989–98; Love Hurts, 1991–93; Goodnight Sweetheart, 1993–99 Mosley, 1997; *radio:* My Blue Heaven, 2006; Dr Freud Will See You Now, Mr Hitle 2007; My Blue Wedding, 2007; *stage:* Playing God, Stephen Joseph Th., Scarborough 2005; The New Statesman - Episode 2006, nat. tour, 2006. BAFTA Councillor, 1994–95 BAFTA Writers Award, 1992. *Publications:* with Laurence Marks: Holding the Fort, 1981 The New Statesman Scripts, 1992; Dorien's Diary, 1993; Shine on Harvey Moon, 1995 *Recreations:* watching football, theatre, film. *Address:* 61 Gratton Road, Cheltenham GL5 2BZ. *Club:* Groucho.

GRANARD, 10th Earl of, *cr* 1684 (Ire.); **Peter Arthur Edward Hastings Forbes;** B (NS) 1628; Viscount Granard, Baron Clanehugh (Ire.), 1675; Baron Granard (UK), 1806 *b* 15 March 1957; *s* of Hon. John Forbes (*d* 1982), *yr s* of 8th Earl, and of Joan, *d* of A Edward Smith; *S* uncle, 1992; *m* 1980, Noreen Mitchell; three *s* one *d.* *Heir: s* Viscoun Forbes, *qv.* *Address:* Strathallan Cliff House, Strathallan Road, Onchan, Isle of Man.

GRANATT, Michael Stephen Dreese, CB 2001; Partner, Luther Pendragon, sinc 2004; *b* 27 April 1950; *s* of Arthur Maurice Granatt and Denise Sylvia Granatt (*née* Dreese) *m* 1974, Jane Veronica Bray; one *s* three *d.* *Educ:* Westminster City Sch.; Queen Mar Coll., London. Sub-ed., subseq. Dep. Chief Sub-ed., Kent & Sussex Courier, 1973–77 Prodn Ed., Industrial Relns Services, 1977–79; Asst Ed., Dept of Employment, 1979–81 Press Officer, Home Office, 1981–83; Sen. Press Officer, 1983–85, Chief Press Office 1985–86, Hd of Inf., 1986–89, Dept of Energy; Dir, Public Affairs and Interna Communication, Metropolitan Police Service, 1989–92; Director of Communicatio DoE, 1992–94; Home Office, 1995–98; Hd of Profession, Govt Inf. Service, subseq. Gov Inf. and Communication Service, 1997–2003 (Dir-Gen., 2002–03); also Hd of Civi Contingencies Secretariat, Cabinet Office, 2001–02. Vis. Prof., Univ. of Westminste 2003–. Chairman: London Emergency Press Officers' Gp, 1989–92; Nat. Industries Pres Officers' Gp, 1992–94; Media Emergency Forum, 1996–2003; UK Press Card Authy 2004–; Bd Mem., Sci. Media Centre, Royal Instn, 2004–. Co-ordinator, Club of Venice 2003–04. Gov., Mary Hare Schs, 2004–. FRSA 1993; FCIPR (FIPR 2000). Master, Cit of London Guild of Public Relns Practitioners, 2005–06. *Publication:* (contrib.) Disaster and the Media, 1999. *Recreations:* photography, reading science fiction, gadgets. *Addres* c/o Luther Pendragon, Priory Court, Pilgrim Street, EC4V 6DR. *T:* (020) 7618 9100 *Club:* Savage.

GRANBY, Marquis of; Charles John Montague Manners; *b* 3 July 1999; *s* and *heir* o Duke of Rutland, *qv.*

GRAND, Stephen Lewis, OBE 2000; independent scientist and writer, since 1999; *b* 1 Feb. 1958; *s* of Dennis and Jean Grand; *m* 1979, Ann Nicholson (marr. diss. 2007); one *s* *Educ:* self-taught. Sen. Programmer, Millennium Ltd, 1993–96; Dir of Technology Cyberlife Technology Ltd, 1996–99; Dir, Cyberlife Research Ltd, 1999–. NESTA Fellow, 2002–03. Hon. Fellow: Cognitive Sci., Univ. of Sussex, 1997–99; Psychology Univ. of Cardiff, 2001–; Biomimetics, Univ. of Bath, 2002–. DUniv Open, 2008 *Publications:* Creation: life and how to make it, 2000; Growing Up With Lucy: how t build an android in twenty easy steps, 2003. *Recreation:* work! *Address:* *e-mail:* steve@ cyberlife-research.net.

GRANDAGE, Michael; Artistic Director, Donmar Warehouse, London, since 2002; *b* 2 May 1962. *Educ:* Humphry Davy Grammar Sch., Cornwall; Central Sch. of Speech an Drama, London. Theatre director, 1995–; Associate Dir, Crucible Th., Sheffield 2000–05. *Productions* include: Crucible Theatre, Sheffield: What the Butler Saw, 1997 Twelfth Night, 1998; The Country Wife, As You Like It, transf. Lyric, Hammersmit (Best Director award, Evening Standard, Critics' Circle; award for theatre, South Ban Show), 2000; Edward II, Don Juan, 2001; Richard III, The Tempest, transf. Old Vic 2002; A Midsummer Night's Dream, 2003; Suddenly Last Summer, 2004; Don Carlos 2004, transf. Gielgud Th., 2005 (Best Director award, Evening Standard, 2005); Donma Warehouse: Good, 1999; Passion Play, transf. Comedy Th. (Best Director award, Evenin Standard, Critics' Circle), Merrily We Roll Along (Best Director award, Critics' Circle Olivier Award for Best New Musical), 2000; Privates on Parade, 2001; The Vortex, 2002 Caligula (Olivier Award for Best Dir, 2004), After Miss Julie, 2003; Henry IV, Granc Hotel (Olivier Award for Outstanding Musical; Best Director award, Evening Standard 2005), 2004; Guys and Dolls (at Piccadilly Th.), The Wild Duck, 2005 (Best Directo award, Critics' Circle, 2005); The Cut, 2006; Frost/Nixon, 2006, transf. Gielgud, 2006 NY, 2007; John Gabriel Borkman, 2007; Othello, 2007; The Chalk Garden, Ivanov (a Wyndham's Th.), 2008; Almeida Theatre: The Doctor's Dilemma, 1998; The Jew o Malta, 1999; Evita, Adelphi Th., 2006. Hon. Fellow, Central Sch. of Speech and Drama DUniv: Sheffield Hallam, 2002; Sheffield, 2004. *Address:* Donmar Warehouse, 41 Earlhan Street, WC2H 9LX. *T:* (020) 7845 5800, *Fax:* (020) 7240 4878; *e-mail:* mgrandage@ donmarwarehouse.com.

GRANGE, Kenneth Henry, CBE 1984; RDI, FCSD; product designer; in privat practice, since 1958; *b* 17 July 1929; *s* of Harry Alfred Grange and Hilda Gladys (*née* Long) *Educ:* London. Technical Illustrator, RE, 1948–50; Design Asst, Arcon Chartered Architects, 1948; Bronek Katz & Vaughn, 1950–51; Gordon Bowyer & Partners 1951–54; Jack Howe & Partners, 1954–58; Founding Partner, Pentagram Design 1972–91. Pres., CSD, 1987–88; Master of Faculty, RDI, 1985–87. RDI 1969; FCSD (FSIAD 1959). Hon. Prof., Heriot-Watt, 1987. Hon. Dr RCA, 1985; DUniv: Heriot-Watt, 1986; De Montfort, 1998; Staffs, 1998; Open, 2003. 10 Design Council Awards Duke of Edinburgh Award for Elegant Design, 1963; Prince Philip Designers Prize, 2001 *Recreations:* memories of tennis, ski-ing. *Address:* 53 Christchurch Hill, NW3 1LG.

GRANGER, Sir Clive (William John), Kt 2005; PhD; Research Professor, Department of Economics, University of California, San Diego, 1974–2003; *b* 4 Sept. 1934; *s* of Edward John Granger and Evelyn Agnes Granger; *m* 1960, Patricia Anne Loveland; one *s* one *d*. *Educ:* Univ. of Nottingham (BA 1st cl. (Maths); PhD (Stats) 1959). Lectr, then Reader, then Prof., Dept of Maths and Econs, Univ. of Nottingham, 1956–74. Hon. DSc: Nottingham, 1992; Carlos III, Madrid, 1996; Stockholm Sch. of Econs, 1998; Loughborough, 2002; Aarhus, 2003. Nobel Prize in Econs, 2003. *Publications:* Spectral Analysis of Economic Time Series, 1964, trans. French 1969; (jtly) Predictability of Stock Market Prices, 1970; (jtly) Speculation, Hedging and Forecasts of Commodity Prices, 1970, trans. Japanese 1976; (jtly) Forecasting Economic Time Series, 1977, 2nd edn 1986; (jtly) Introduction to Bilinear Time Series Models, 1978; Forecasting in Business and Economics, 1980, 2nd edn 1989, trans. Chinese 1993, Japanese, 1994; Modeling Economics Series: readings in econometric methodology, 1990; (ed jtly) Long Run Economic Relationships: readings in cointegration, 1991; (jtly) Modeling Nonlinear Dynamic Relationships, 1993; Empirical Modeling in Economics: specification and evaluation, 1999; (jtly) The Dynamics of Deforestation and Economic Growth in the Brazilian Amazon, 2003; Festschrift: Cointegration, Causality, and Forecasting, ed. Robert F. Engle and Halbert White, 1999; Essays in Econometrics: collected papers of Clive W. J. Granger, ed E. Ghysels *et al*, 2 vols, 2001; numerous contribs to jls. *Recreations:* body surfing in summer, walking all the year round, reading, art appreciation. *Address:* Department of Economics, University of California, San Diego, La Jolla, CA 92093–0508, USA. *T:* (858) 5343856, *Fax:* (858) 5347040; *e-mail:* cgranger@ucsd.edu.

GRANGER, John; Headmaster, Bournemouth School, since 1996; *b* Heston, Middx, 5 Aug. 1949; *s* of Raymond and Mary Jane, (Jenny), Granger; *m* 1974, Heather Pyatt; two *d*. *Educ:* Spring Grove Grammar Sch.; Atlantic Coll.; Univ. of Hull (BSc Hons Applied Physics; PGCE). Sci. teacher, Plymstock Sch., 1973–74; Hd of Physics, 1977–87, Hd of Sci., 1987–96, Dep. Headmaster, 1991–96, Torquay Boys' GS, 1974–96. FRSA. *Recreations:* keeping fit, being with the family, music. *Address:* Bournemouth School, East Way, Bournemouth BH8 9PY. *T:* (01202) 512609; *e-mail:* office@bournemouth-school.org.

GRANGER, Richard; Director General, NHS Information Technology, and Chief Executive Officer, NHS Connecting for Health, Department of Health, 2002–08; *b* 21 April 1965; *m* 1998, Gabrielle Virag; one *s* two *d*. *Educ:* Univ. of Bristol (BSc Hons (Geol.) 1987). Geologist, Geoservices SA, Singapore and Australia, 1987–89; Andersen Consulting, 1989–96 (Manager, 1993–96); Prog. Dir, Electronic Data Systems, 1996–98; Partner, Deloitte & Touche, 1998–2002. *Publications:* articles on electronic govt and electronic health. *Recreations:* family, cycling, walking, books. *Clubs:* Reform, Ronnie Scott's; Cycle Touring.

GRANT; *see* Lyall Grant.

GRANT, family name of **Countess of Dysart** and **Baron Strathspey**.

GRANT, Alexander (Marshall), CBE 1965; Artistic Director, National Ballet of Canada, 1976–83; *b* Wellington, New Zealand, 22 Feb. 1925; *s* of Alexander and Eleather Grant. *Educ:* Wellington Coll., NZ. Arrived in London, Feb. 1946, to study with Sadler's Wells School on Scholarship given in New Zealand by Royal Academy of Dancing, London; Sadler's Wells Ballet (later Royal Ballet Company), Aug. 1946–76. Dir, Ballet for All (touring ballet company), 1971–76 (Co-director, 1970–71). Senior Principal, London Fest. Ballet, later English National Ballet, 1985–91; Guest Artist: Royal Ballet, 1985–89; Joffrey Ballet, USA, 1987–89. Frequent judge at internat. ballet competitions, notably Varna (Bulgaria), Paris, Budapest, Jackson, Mississippi and Moscow. Danced leading rôles in following: Mam'zelle Angot, Clock Symphony, Boutique Fantasque, Donald of the Burthens, Rake's Progress, Job, Three Cornered Hat, Ballabile, Cinderella, Sylvia, Madame Chrysanthème, Façade, Daphnis and Chloé, Coppélia, Petrushka, Ondine, La Fille Mal Gardée, Jabez and the Devil, Perséphone, The Dream, Jazz Calendar, Enigma Variations, Sleeping Beauty (Carabosse), A Month in the Country, La Sylphide, The Nutcracker, Napoli, Shéhérazade, Variations on a Theme of Purcell, Don Quixote; *films:* Tales of Beatrix Potter (Peter Rabbit and Pigling Bland); Steps of the Ballet. Icon Award, NZ Arts Foundn, 2005; Queen Elizabeth II Coronation Award, RAD, 2007. *Recreations:* gardening, cinema and theatre going, cuisine.

GRANT, Andrew Robert; Headmaster, St Albans School, since 1993; *b* Rochford, 29 April 1953; *s* of Walter Frank Grant and Joan Grant (*née* Bartram); *m* 1977, Hilary Sheena Kerr (*née* Charlton); two *s*. *Educ:* Southend High Sch.; Corpus Christi Coll., Cambridge (Open Exhibn; BA Hons English 1975; PGCE 1976). Asst Master, Merchant Taylors' Sch., Northwood, 1976–83; Hd of English, Whitgift Sch., Croydon, 1983–90; Second Master, Royal Grammar Sch., Guildford, 1990–93. Chairman: HMC/GSA Educn and Academic Policy Cttee, 2002–05 (Mem., 2000–06); London Div., HMC, 2006–07; Member: Jt Assocs Curriculum Gp, 2000–06; Tomlinson 14–19 Rev. Assessment Gp, 2003–05; QCA 14–19 Adv. Gp, 2004–06; HMC/GSA Univs Cttee, 2005–; Ind. State Schs Partnership Forum, DCSF, 2006–. Mem. Court, Univ. of Hertfordshire, 2006–; Governor: Lochinver House Sch., 1993–; Moorlands Sch., 1994–; Abbots Hill Sch., 1994–; Beechwood Park Sch., 2005–. FRSA. *Recreations:* theatre, literature, music, cycling, squash, sailing. *Address:* St Albans School, Abbey Gateway, St Albans, Herts AL3 4HB. *T:* (01727) 855521, *Fax:* (01727) 843447; *e-mail:* hm@st-albans-school.org.uk. *Clubs:* East India; Hawks (Cambridge).

GRANT, Andrew Young; Chief Operating Officer: (formerly Principal), Grant Leisure Group, 1982–2005; Chief Operating Officer, Grant Leisure Inc., since 2005; Chairman, Real Live Leisure Co. Ltd, since 1999; *b* 8 April 1946; *s* of Marshall Grant and Marilyn Greene (*née* Phillips); *m* 1st, 1969, Dietra (marr. diss.); one *d*; 2nd, 1973, Lindy Lang (marr. diss.); one *d*; *m* 2005, Debra Gould. *Educ:* Univ. of Oregon (BSc). Personnel Manager, Universal Studios Tour, Universal City, Calif, 1967–69; Dir of Personnel, Busch Gardens, LA, 1969–71, Ops Dir, 1971–73; Gen. Manager, Squaw Valley Ski Resort, 1973–74; Gen. Manager, Busch Gardens, 1974–76; Dir, Economic Research Associates, LA, 1976–79; Dep. Dir, Zoological Soc., San Diego, 1979–83; Dir, Leeds Castle Enterprises, 1983–88; Director: Granada Studios Tour, 1987–90; Grant Leisure Developments, 1987–; Real Live Leisure, 1998–; Blackpool Zoo, 2003–; Man. Dir, Zoo Operations Ltd, Zoological Soc., 1988–91; Principal, Internat. Spirit Develt Corp. Ltd (formerly Internat. Spirit Management Co.), 1995–. Member: Internat. Assoc. of Amusement Parks and Attractions, 1975–; Tourism Soc., 1988–; Tourism and Leisure Industries Sector Gp, NEDC, 1990–; Urban Land Inst., 1998–. Mem. Bd, YMCA, 2006–. *Publication:* Nearly Human: the gorilla's guide to good living, 2007. *Recreations:* running, fishing, golf, tennis. *Address:* Grant Leisure Inc., 830 Norman Lane, Montecito, CA 93108, USA. *T:* (805) 4035873; *e-mail:* aygrant@cox.net.

GRANT, Ann; Vice Chairman, Standard Chartered Capital Markets Ltd, since 2005; *b* 13 Aug. 1948. *Educ:* Univ. of Sussex; SOAS, Univ. of London (MSc 1971). Joined FCO, 1971; Calcutta, 1973–75; Dept of Energy, 1976–79; Head of Chancery and Consul, Maputo, 1981–84; First Sec. (Energy), Office of UK Perm. Rep. to EU, Brussels, 1987–89, resigned; Communications Dir, Oxfam, 1989–91; rejoined FCO, 1991; Counsellor (Econ. and Social Affairs), UK Mission to UN, NY, 1992–96; Counsellor, FCO, 1996–98; Dir, African Dept, FCO, 1998–2000; High Comr, South Africa, 2000–05. *Address:* c/o Standard Chartered Bank, 1 Aldermanbury Square, EC2V 7SB.

GRANT, Sir Anthony, Kt 1983; solicitor and company director; *b* May 1925; *m* Sonia Isobel; one *s* one *d*. *Educ:* St Paul's Sch.; Brasenose Coll., Oxford. Army 1943–48, Third Dragoon Guards (Capt.). Admitted a solicitor, 1952. MP (C): Harrow Central, 1964–83; Cambs SW, 1983–97. Opposition Whip, 1966–70; Parly Sec., Board of Trade, June-Oct. 1970; Parliamentary Under-Secretary of State: Trade, DTI, 1970–72; Industrial Develt, DTI, 1972–74. Chm., Cons. back bench Trade Cttee, 1979–83; Mem., Foreign Affairs Select Cttee, 1980–83. A Vice-Chm., Conservative Party Organisation, 1974–76; Mem. Exec., 1922 Cttee, 1978–97. Formerly Member: Council of Europe (Chm., Econ. Cttee, 1980–87); WEU. Pres., Guild of Experienced Motorists. Trustee, Howard Foundn, 2000–. Dir, British Human Assoc., 2002–. Freeman, City of London; Master, Guild of Freemen, 1979–80, 1997–98; Liveryman, Co. of Solicitors. *Recreations:* watching Rugby and cricket, playing golf; Napoleonic history. *Address:* Whiteacre, The Chase, Oxshott, Surrey KT22 0HR. *Clubs:* Carlton; Walton Heath Golf, Meridien Golf.

GRANT of Monymusk, Sir Archibald, 13th Bt *cr* 1705; *b* 2 Sept. 1954; *e s* of Captain Sir Francis Cullen Grant, 12th Bt, and of Lady Grant (Jean Margherita, *d* of Captain Humphrey Douglas Tollemache, RN), who *m* 2nd, 2nd Baron Tweedsmuir, CBE, CD; *S* father, 1966; *m* 1982, Barbara Elizabeth, *e d* of A. G. D. Forbes, Drumminnor Castle, Rhynie, Aberdeenshire; two *d*. *Address:* House of Monymusk, Aberdeenshire AB51 7HL. *T:* (01467) 651220.

GRANT, Charles Peter; Co-founder, 1995, and Director, since 1998, Centre for European Reform; *b* 9 Oct. 1958; *s* of Peter Forbes Grant and Elizabeth Ann Grant (*née* Shirreff). *Educ:* Selwyn Coll., Cambridge (BA Hons Hist. 1980); Grenoble Univ. (Dip. French). Journalist, Euromoney, 1981–86; joined The Economist, 1986; financial journalist, 1986–89; Brussels corresp., 1989–93; home news, 1993–94; Defence Ed., 1994–98. Dir and Trustee, British Council, 2002–. Member: Bd, Moscow Sch. of Pol Studies, 2002–; Cttee for Russia in a United Europe, 2002–. Chevalier, Ordre Nat. du Mérite (France), 2004. *Publications:* Delors: inside the house that Jacques built, 1994; Can Britain Lead in Europe?, 1998; EU 2010: an optimistic vision of the future, 2000; Transatlantic Rift: how to bring the two sides together, 2003; What Happens if Britain Votes No?, 2005; Europe's Blurred Boundaries: rethinking enlargement and neighbourhood policy, 2006; European Choices for Gordon Brown, 2007; Preparing for the Multipolar World: European foreign and security policy in 2020, 2007. *Recreations:* classical music, hill-walking. *Address:* Centre for European Reform, 14 Great College Street, SW1P 3RX. *T:* (020) 7233 1199, *Fax:* (020) 7233 1117; *e-mail:* charles@cer.org.uk. *Club:* Reform.

GRANT, Sir Clifford (Harry), Kt 1977; Chief Stipendiary Magistrate, Western Australia, 1982–90; *b* England, 12 April 1929; *m* 1962, Karen Ann Ferguson. *Educ:* Montclair, NJ, USA; Harrison Coll., Barbados; Liverpool Coll.; Liverpool Univ. (LLB (Hons) 1949). Solicitor, Supreme Court of Judicature, 1951; Comr for Oaths, 1958; in private practice, London; apptd to HM Overseas Judiciary, 1958; Magistrate, Kenya, 1958, Sen. Magistrate, 1962; transf. to Hong Kong, Crown Solicitor, 1963, Principal Magistrate, 1965; transf. to Fiji, Sen. Magistrate, 1967; admitted Barrister and Solicitor, Supreme Court of Fiji, 1969; Chief Magistrate, 1971; Judge of Supreme Court, 1972; Chief Justice of Fiji, 1974–80. Pres., Fiji Court of Appeal, and Chm., Judicial and Legal Services Commn, 1974–80; sole Comr, Royal Commn on Crime, 1975 (report published 1976). Sometime Actg Governor-General, 1973–79. Fellow, Flinders Univ. Foundn, 1992. Fiji Independence Medal, 1970. *Publications:* articles for legal jls. *Recreations:* evolutionary biology and psychology, mythology, literature, music. *Address:* c/o 121 Hamilton Street, Stirling, WA 6021, Australia.

GRANT, Dr David, CBE 1997; FREng, FIET; Vice-Chancellor, Cardiff University, since 2001; *b* 12 Sept. 1947; *s* of Edmund Grant and Isobel Scorer Grant (*née* Rutherford); *m* 1974, Helen Joyce Rutter; one *s* one *d*. *Educ:* Univ. of Durham (PhD 1974). FIET (FIEE 1984); FREng (FEng 1997). Reyrolle Parsons Gp, 1966–77; United Technologies Corp., 1977–84; Gp Technical Dir, Dowty Gp, 1984–91; Technical Dir, GEC, then Marconi plc, 1991–2001. Member: EPSRC, 2001–06; UK Technol. Strategy Bd, 2007–. Vice-Pres., RAEng, 2007–. Mensforth Internat. Gold Medal, IEE, 1996. *Recreation:* classic cars. *Address:* Cardiff University, Main Building, Park Place, Cardiff CF10 3AT.

GRANT, Donald Blane, CBE 1989; TD 1964; Partner, KMG Thomson McLintock, CA (formerly Moody Stuart & Robertson, then Thomson McLintock & Co.), 1950–86; *b* 8 Oct. 1921; *s* of Quintin Blane Grant and Euphemia Phyllis Grant; *m* 1944, Lavinia Margaret Ruth Ritchie; three *d*. *Educ:* High Sch. of Dundee. CA 1948. Served War, RA, 1939–46: TA Officer, retd as Major. Director: Dundee & London Investment Trust PLC, 1969–93; HAT Group PLC, 1969–86; Don Brothers Buist PLC, 1984–87. Inst. of Chartered Accountants of Scotland: Mem. Council, 1971–76; Vice Pres., 1977–79, Pres., 1979–80. Chairman: Tayside Health Bd, 1984–91; Scottish Legal Aid Bd, 1986–91. Mem. Court, Univ. of Dundee, 1992–2002. Hon. LLD Dundee, 1989. *Recreations:* shooting, fishing, golf, bridge, gardening. *Clubs:* Institute of Directors; New (Edinburgh); Royal and Ancient Golf (St Andrews); Panmure Golf (Carnoustie); Blairgowrie Golf (Rosemount).

GRANT, Donald David, CB 1985; Director General, Central Office of Information, 1982–85; *b* 1 Aug. 1924; *s* of Donald Herbert Grant and Florence Emily Grant; *m* 1954, Beatrice Mary Varney; two *d*. *Educ:* Wandsworth Sch. Served War, RNVR, Sub-Lt (A), 1942–46. Journalist, Evening Standard, Reuters, 1946–51; Dir, Sidney Barton Ltd, PR Consultants, 1951–61; Chief Information Officer, Min. of Aviation and Technology, 1961–67; Dir, Public Relations, STC Ltd, 1967–70; Director of Information: GLC, 1971–72; DTI, 1972–74; Home Office, 1974–82. Vis. Prof., Graduate Centre for Journalism, City Univ., 1986–90. *Recreation:* sailing. *Address:* Bayards House, Bayards Cove, Dartmouth, Devon TQ6 9AT. *T:* (01803) 833095. *Club:* Dartmouth Yacht.

GRANT, Hugh John Mungo; actor; *b* 9 Sept. 1960; *s* of James Murray Grant and late Fynvola Susan Grant (*née* Maclean). *Educ:* Latymer Upper Sch., Hammersmith; New Coll., Oxford (BA). Began career in theatre performing in Jockeys of Norfolk (written with Chris Lang and Andy Taylor); actor in theatre, TV and films; co-founder, 1994, and producer for Simian Films. *Films include*: White Mischief, Maurice (Best Actor, jtly with James Wilby, Venice Film Fest.), 1987; Lair of the White Worm, La Nuit Bengali, 1988; Impromptu, 1989; Bitter Moon, 1992; Remains of the Day, 1993; Four Weddings and a Funeral (Golden Globe Award, BAFTA Award, Evening Standard Peter Sellers Award for Comedy, 1995), Sirens, 1994; The Englishman Who Went Up a Hill but Came Down a Mountain, Nine Months, An Awfully Big Adventure, Sense and Sensibility, 1995; Restoration, 1996; Notting Hill, 1999 (Evening Standard Peter Sellers Award for Comedy, Empire Film Awards Best British Actor, 2000); Small Time Crooks, 2000; Bridget Jones's Diary, 2001 (Evening Standard Peter Sellers Award for Comedy, 2002); About A Boy, 2002 (Empire Film Awards Best British Actor, London Critics' Circle Film

Awards Best British Actor, 2003); Two Weeks Notice, Love Actually, 2003; Bridget Jones: The Edge of Reason, 2004; American Dreamz, 2006; Music and Lyrics, 2007; Simian Films productions: Extreme Measures, 1996; Mickey Blue Eyes, 1998.

GRANT, Ian David, CBE 1988; Chairman, The Crown Estate (formerly First Crown Estate Commissioner), since 2002; Crown Estate Commissioner for Scotland, since 1996; *b* Dundee, 28 July 1943; *s* of late Alan H. B. Grant and of Florence O. Grant; *m* 1968, Eileen May Louisa Yule; three *d. Educ:* Strathallan Sch.; East of Scotland College of Agriculture (Dip.). Vice Pres. 1981–84, Pres. 1984–90, National Farmers' Union of Scotland; Mem., Scottish Council, CBI, 1984–96. Mem. Bd, 1988–90, Chm., 1990–98, Scottish Tourist Bd; Mem. Bd, BTA, 1990–98. Director: East of Scotland Farmers Ltd, 1978–2002; Clydesdale Bank PLC, 1989–97; NFU Mutual Insce Soc. Ltd, 1990–2008 (Dep. Chm., 2003–08); Scottish and Southern Energy plc (formerly Scottish Hydro Electric PLC), 1992–2003 (Dep. Chm., 2000–03); Scottish Exhibition Centre Ltd, 1998– (Dep. Chm., 2001–02; Chm., 2002–); Chm., Cairngorms Partnership, 1998–2003. Vice Pres., Royal Smithfield Club, 1996. FRAgS 1987. Hon. DBA Napier, 1999. *Recreations:* travel, gardening, reading, music. *Address:* Leal House, Loyal Road, Alyth PH11 8JQ.

GRANT, (Ian) Nicholas; Chairman, Mediatrack Research Ltd, since 2007 (Managing Director, 1992–2002, Chairman, 2002, Mediatrack); *b* 24 March 1948; *s* of late Hugo and of Cara Grant; *m* 1977, Rosalind Louise Pipe; one *s* one *d. Educ:* Univ. of London (LLB); Univ. of Warwick (MA, Industrial Relns). Confederation of Health Service Employees: Research Officer, 1972–74; Head of Research and Public Relations, 1974–82; Dir of Communications, Labour Party, 1982–85; Public Affairs Advr, Mirror Group Newspapers and Maxwell Communication Corp., 1985–89. Chm., Internat. Assoc. for the Measurement and Evaluation of Communication (formerly Assoc. of Media Evaluation Cos, then Assoc. for Measurement and Evaluation of Communication), 2005– (Dep. Chm., 1997–2005). Member: Council, London Borough of Lambeth, 1978–84; Lambeth, Southwark and Lewisham AHA, 1978–82; W Lambeth DHA, 1982–83. Contested (Lab) Reigate, 1979. *Publications:* contrib. to: Economics of Prosperity, ed D. Blake and P. Ormerod, 1980; Political Communications: the general election campaign of 1983, ed I. Crewe and M. Harrop, 1985. *Recreations:* walking, reading, photography. *Address:* Mediatrack Research Ltd, 1 Northumberland Avenue, Trafalgar Square, WC2N 5BW. *T:* (020) 7430 0699; *e-mail:* ngrant@mediatrack.com. *Club:* Reform.

GRANT, Prof. Ian Philip, DPhil; FRS 1992; CMath; Professor of Mathematical Physics, University of Oxford, 1992–98, now Emeritus Professor; Tutorial Fellow in Mathematics, Pembroke College, Oxford, 1969–98, now Emeritus Fellow; *b* 15 Dec. 1930; *er s* of Harold Hyman Grant and Isabella Henrietta Ornstien; *m* 1958, Beryl Cohen; two *s. Educ:* St Albans Sch., Herts; Wadham Coll., Oxford (Open Scholar; MA; DPhil 1954). CMath 1992. SSO, 1957–61, PSO, 1961–64, UKAEA, Aldermaston; Res. Fellow, Atlas Computer Lab., SRC, 1964–69; Lectr in Maths, 1969–90, Reader in Mathematical Physics, 1990–92, Oxford Univ.; Res. Fellow in Maths, 1964–69, Actg Master, 1984–85, Pembroke Coll., Oxford. Visiting Professor: McGill Univ., 1976; Abo Akademi, Finland, 1977; Inst. de Fisica, Univ. Nacional Autónoma de México, 1981; Imperial Coll., London, 2001–. Governor: Royal Grammar Sch., High Wycombe, 1981–99; St Paul's Schs, 1993–2001. *Publications:* Relativistic Quantum Theory of Atoms and Molecules, 2006; papers in learned jls on relativistic quantum theory in atomic and molecular physics, and on radiative transfer theory in astrophysics and atmospheric science. *Recreations:* walking, music, theatre-going, gardening, travel. *Address:* Mathematical Institute, 24–29 St Giles', Oxford OX1 3LB. *T:* (01865) 273525; 6 Woodlands Close, Headington, Oxford OX3 7RY. *T:* (01865) 762156.

GRANT, Rt Rev. James Alexander, AM 1994; Assistant Bishop, Diocese of Melbourne, 1985–99; Dean of St Paul's Cathedral, Melbourne, 1985–99; *b* 30 Aug. 1931; *s* of late V. G. Grant, Geelong; *m* 1983, Rowena Margaret Armstrong. *Educ:* Trinity College, Univ. of Melbourne (BA Hons); Melbourne College of Divinity (BD). Deacon 1959 (Curate, St Peter's, Murrumbeena), priest 1960; Curate, West Heidelberg 1960, Broadmeadows 1961; Leader Diocesan Task Force, Broadmeadows, 1962; Domestic and Examining Chaplain to Archbishop of Melbourne, 1966–70; Chaplain, Trinity Coll., Univ. of Melbourne, 1970–75, Fellow, 1975; Bishop Coadjutor, dio. of Melbourne, 1970–85; Chairman, Brotherhood of St Laurence, 1971–87 (Director, 1969); Pres., Diocesan Mission to Streets and Lanes, 1987–97. Jubilee Medal, 1977; Centenary Medal, Australia, 2003. *Publications:* (with Geoffrey Serle) The Melbourne Scene, 1957; Perspective of a Century—Trinity College 1872–1972, 1972. *Recreation:* historical research. *Address:* 151 Park Drive, Parkville, Vic 3052, Australia. *Club:* Melbourne (Melbourne).

GRANT, Janet; *see* Thompson, J.

GRANT, Sir (John) Anthony; *see* Grant, Sir A.

GRANT, John Donald; Consultant, Grant & Fairgrieve, 1988–1996; *b* 31 Oct. 1926; *s* of Ian and Eleanor Grant; *m* 1951, Helen Bain Fairgrieve Wilson (*d* 2003), *d* of late James Wilson and Clara Wilson; two *s. Educ:* various schs; King's Coll., Cambridge (Exhibnr; MA Natural Scis). National Service, REME, 1947–49; TA, London Rifle Bde, 1949–56. N Thames Gas Bd, 1949–60; Imperial Chemical Industries: Plastics Div., 1960–71; Head Office, 1971–82; Chief Exec., FIMBRA (formerly NASDIM), 1983–88. Dir, Cadogan Management Ltd, 1991–95. Chairman: Strategic Planning Soc., 1989–91; Fedn of Software Systems, 1989–91. Mem., Money Management Council, 1989–2001. Chm., Henley Alumni Assoc., 1996–98; Mem. Ct of Govs, Henley Mgt Coll., 1996–99. *Recreations:* opera, music, travel (particularly to islands). *Club:* Oxford and Cambridge.

GRANT, Sir John Douglas Kelso, KCMG 2005 (CMG 1999); HM Diplomatic Service, retired; President, BHP Billiton Europe, since 2007; *b* 17 Oct. 1954; *s* of Douglas Marr Kelso Grant and Audrey Stevenson Grant (*née* Law); *m* 1983, Anna Maria Lindvall; one *s* two *d. Educ:* Edinburgh Acad.; St Catharine's Coll., Cambridge (BA 1976). HM Diplomatic Service: W African Dept, FCO, 1976; Stockholm, 1977–80; Russian lang. trng, 1980–81; Moscow, 1982–84; Morgan Grenfell and Co. Ltd, 1985–86; Press Office, FCO, 1986–89; UK Permt Repn to EU, 1989–93 (Press Spokesman, later External Relns) and 1994–97 (Counsellor, External Relns); European Secretariat, Cabinet Office, 1993–94; Principal Private Sec. to Sec. of State for Foreign and Commonwealth Affairs, 1997–99; Ambassador to Sweden, 1999–2003; UK Permanent Rep. to EU, Brussels, 2003–07. *Recreations:* cross-country ski-ing, walking. *Address:* BHP Billiton, Neathouse Place, SW1V 1BH.

GRANT, John Stephen; author; business consultant, since 1999; *b* Hythe, Kent, 8 Nov. 1964; *s* of Paul and Ursula Grant; *m* 1998, Yong Cho; one *s. Educ:* Emmanuel Coll., Cambridge (BA Hons Natural Scis 1987); Birkbeck Coll., London (MSc Psychodynamics of Infant Develt 2002). Trainee, J. Walter Thomson, 1987–89; Account Planning, BMP DDB Needham, 1989–94; Planning Dir, Chiat Day, 1994–95; Co-founder, St Luke's Communications, 1995–99. Associate: Demos, 2007–; Forum for the Future, 2008–. Non-exec. Dir, Onzo Ltd, 2007–. Creative Dir, Ministry of Sound, 2005–06. *Publications:* The New Marketing Manifesto, 1999; After Image, 2002; The Brand Innovation

Manifesto, 2006; The Green Marketing Manifesto, 2007. *Recreation:* electronic music composition. *Address: e-mail:* thejohngrant@btinternet.com.

GRANT, Keith Wallace; Dean, Faculty of Design, Kingston University (formerly Polytechnic), 1988–99; *b* 30 June 1934; *s* of Randolph and Sylvia Grant; *m* 1968, Deanna (*née* Bergsma); one *s* one *d. Educ:* Trinity Coll., Glenalmond; Clare Coll., Cambridge (MA). Account Exec., W. S. Crawford Ltd, 1958–62; General Manager: Covent Garden Opera Co., later Royal Opera, 1962–73; English Opera Group, 1962–73; Sec., Royal Soc. of Arts, 1973–77; Dir, Design Council, 1977–88. Called to the Bar, Middle Temple 2001. Member: Adv. Council, V&A Mus., 1977–83; PO Stamp Adv. Cttee, 1978–87; Exec. Bd, Internat. Council of Socs of Industrial Design, 1983–87; Chm., Nat. Lead Body for Design, 1995–98. Chm., English Music Theatre Co., 1979–92; Mem., Management Cttee, Park Lane Gp, 1988–95; Sec., Peter Pears Award for Singers, 1988–95. Governor: Central Sch. of Art and Design, 1974–77; Birmingham Polytechnic, 1981–86; Edinburgh Coll. of Art, 1982–86; Mem. Ct, Brunel Univ., 1985–89. Hon. Prof., Heriot-Watt Univ. 1987. Hon. Fellow, Birmingham City Univ. (formerly Birmingham Poly., later Univ. of Central England), 1988. Hon. FCSD (Hon. FSIAD, 1983). *Address:* 43 St Dunstan's Road, W6 8RE. *Club:* Garrick.

GRANT, Kenneth Isaac; a District Judge (Magistrates' Courts) (formerly Metropolitan Stipendiary Magistrate), since 1999; *b* 14 Nov. 1951; *s* of late Samuel Grant and of Merci Grant; *m* 1980, Irene Whilton; one *s* one *d. Educ:* Haberdashers' Aske's Sch., Elstree; Univ. of Sussex (BA); Coll. of Law. Admitted Solicitor, 1977; Solicitor, Darlington & Parkinson 1977–99, Sen. Partner, 1990–99. Chm., Area Cttee, Legal Aid Bd, 1994–99 (Chm., Area 14 Regional Cttee, 1997–99). *Recreations:* theatre, opera. *Address:* South Western Magistrates' Court, 176A Lavender Hill, Battersea, SW11 1JU. *T:* 0845 601 3600. *Club:* Hurlingham.

GRANT, Rev. Canon Malcolm Etheridge; Vicar of Eaton Bray with Edlesborough, diocese of St Albans, since 2002; *b* 6 Aug. 1944; *s* of Donald Etheridge Grant and Nelli Florence May Grant (*née* Tuffey); *m* 1984, Katrina Russell Nuttall (*née* Dunnett); one *s* one *d. Educ:* Dunfermline High School; Univ. of Edinburgh (Bruce of Grangehill Bursar 1962; BSc (Hons Chemistry); BD (Hons New Testament); Divinity Fellowship, 1969, Edinburgh Theological College. Deacon 1969, priest 1970; Assistant Curate: St Mary's Cathedral, Glasgow, 1969–72; St Wulfram's, Grantham (in charge of Church of the Epiphany, Earlesfield), 1972; Team Vicar of Earlesfield, Grantham, 1972–78; Priest-in-charge, St Ninian's, Invergordon, 1978–81; Examining Chaplain to Bishop of Moray, Ross and Caithness, 1979–81; Provost and Rector: St Mary's Cathedral, Glasgow, 1981–91; St Andrew's Cathedral, Inverness, 1991–2002 (Hon. Canon, 2002–); Rector, St Paul's, Strathnairn, and Priest i/c, St Mary's-in-the-Fields, Culloden, 1991–97. RD of Dunstable, 2004–. Member, Highland Regional Council Education Cttee, 1979–81. *Address:* The Vicarage, 11 High Street, Eaton Bray, Dunstable, Beds LU6 2DN. *T:* (01525) 220261.

GRANT, Prof. Malcolm John, CBE 2003; LLD; AcSS; Provost and President, University College London, since 2003; *b* 29 Nov. 1947; *s* of Francis William Grant and Vera Jessica Grant; *m* 1974, Christine (*née* Endersbee); two *s* one *d. Educ:* Waitaki Boys' High Sch., NZ; Univ. of Otago (LLB 1970; LLM 1973; LLD 1986). AcSS 2000. Called to the Bar, Middle Temple, 1998, Bencher, 2004. Lectr, subseq. Sen. Lectr in Law, Southampton Univ., 1972–86; University College London: Sen. Lectr in Law, 1986–88, Prof. of Law, and Vice-Dean, Faculty of Laws, 1988–91; Cambridge University: Prof. of Land Economy, 1991–2003; Pro-Vice-Chancellor, 2002–03; Fellow of Clare Coll. 1991–2003. Chairman: Local Govt Commn for England, 1996–2002 (Mem., 1992–; Dep. Chm., 1995–96); Ind. Panel on Remuneration of Councillors in London, 1999–2004; Agric. and Envmt Biotechnol. Commn, 2000–05; Steering Bd for Nat. Public Debate on Genetic Modification, 2002–03; Mem., ESRC, 2008–. Mem., 2000–, Chm., 2004–08, Standards Cttee, GLA. Mem. Bd, Catalyst, 2005–. Chm., Russell Gp, 2006–; Governor Ditchley Foundn, 2002– (Mem., Council of Mgt, 2003–); London Business Sch., 2003–. Royal Instn, 2006–; Mem., Internat. Council, Free Univ. of Berlin, 2006–. Mem. Council, British-Malaysian Soc., 2005–. Patron, New London Orch., 2005–. Hon. MRTPI 1993; Hon. MRICS (Hon. ARICS 1995). Hon. LLD Otago, 2006. Gen. Editor, Encyclopedia of Planning Law and Practice, 1981–2005 (Consultant Editor, 2005–); Consultant Editor, Encyclopedia of Environmental Law, 1993–. Officier, Ordre National du Mérite (France), 2004. *Publications:* Planning Law Handbook, 1981; Urban Planning Law, 1982, 2nd Suppl. 1990; Rate Capping and the Law, 1985, 2nd edn 1986; Permitted Development, 1989, 2nd edn 1996; (ed jtly) Concise Lexicon of Environmental Terms 1995; Singapore Planning Law, 1999. Environmental Court Report, 2000. *Recreations:* electronic gadgets, opera, woodlands. *Address:* Provost's Office, University College, London, Gower Street, WC1E 6BT. *T:* (020) 7679 7234.

GRANT, Margaret; *see* Exley, M.

GRANT, (Martin Alistair) Piers; His Honour Judge Grant; a County Court Judge (peripatetic), Northern Ireland, since 2005; *b* 1 April 1950; *s* of Ranald and Maureen Grant; *m* 1977, Siobhan Bell; three *d. Educ:* Queen's Univ., Belfast (LLB Hons 1974). Called to the Bar, 1975; Dep. County Court Judge, 1992–2005. *Recreations:* travel, reading, family, tennis, golf. *Address:* c/o Royal Courts of Justice, Chichester Street, Belfast BT1 3JF. *Clubs:* Army and Navy; Royal Belfast Golf.

GRANT, Martin James; Chief Executive Officer, RoadChef Motorways Holdings, since 2004; *b* 29 June 1949; *s* of James and Barbara Grant; *m* 1979, Helena Kay; two *s. Educ:* King Henry VIII, Coventry; Nottingham Univ. (BSc). Marks and Spencer, 1971–74; Grand Metropolitan, 1974–79; Holt Lloyd, 1979–82; Imperial Foods, 1982–83; Whitbread & Co. plc, 1983–90; Allied Lyons, subseq. Allied Domecq, 1990–98, Managing Director: Ansells Ltd, 1990–95; Allied Domecq Leisure, 1995–98; Chief Executive: Vaux Gp, 1998–99; Inn Partnerships, 1999–2002. Fellow, Mktg Soc., 1995. Treas., BII, 2000– (CBII 2003). *Recreations:* military music, military history. *Address:* RoadChef Motorways Holdings, RoadChef House, Betty's Lane, Norton Canes, Cannock, Staffs WS11 9UX.

GRANT, Dame Mavis, DBE 1999; Headteacher, Canning Street Primary School, Newcastle upon Tyne, since 1999; *b* 1 Feb. 1948; *d* of Joseph S. Edgar and Edna M. Edgar (*née* Hewson); *m* 1970, Roger M. Grant. *Educ:* Northumberland Coll. of Educn (CertEd and Cert. Advanced Educn Studies). Teaching in primary schools, Herts, Northumberland and Newcastle upon Tyne, 1969–: Dep. Headteacher, Cowgate Primary Sch., Newcastle upon Tyne, 1978–84; Headteacher, Mary Trevelyan Primary Sch., Newcastle upon Tyne 1984–99. *Recreations:* reading, theatre, travel, dining out, watching Newcastle United Football Club.

GRANT, Michael John, CEng, FICE, FCT; Managing Director, Aaronite Partners Ltd, since 2006; *b* 3 Aug. 1953; *s* of Michael George Grant and Zena Grant (*née* Vernem); *m* 1979, Maureen Hampson; one *s* two *d. Educ:* North East London Poly. (BSc Hons Civil Engrg); City Univ. Business Sch., London (MBA Finance); Harvard Business Sch. (AMP)

Trainee engr, Sir Alexander Gibb & Partners Consulting Engrs, 1971–72; Civil Engineer: DoE, 1972–78; BRB, 1978–84; Financial Analyst, Laing & Cruikshank (Stock Brokers), 1985–86; Dir of Corporate Finance and Gp Treas., Eurotunnel plc, 1987–98; Property Dir, Railtrack, 1998–99; Chief Exec., Strategic Rail Authy, 1999–2001; Franchising Dir, OPRAF, 1999–2001; Dir, Cable & Wireless, 2003–06; Chm., Cable & Wireless USA, 2003–06; Chief Restructuring Officer, Deutsche Woolworth, 2007–. Director: Eurotunnel Finance & Services, 1987–98; Broadgate Plaza, 1998–99; Railtrack Develts, 1999; BRB, 1999; non-executive Director: Liverpool Vision, 1999–; Great Eastern Telecommunications, Cayman Islands, 2004–06; Monaco Telecom, 2004–05; Mobile One, Singapore, 2004–06; Torexretail plc, 2007. Strategic Advr, UK Parliamentary Estate, 2007. *Recreations:* travel, live music, sport. *Club:* Reform.

GRANT, Nicholas; see Grant, I. N.

GRANT of Dalvey, Sir Patrick Alexander Benedict, 14th Bt *cr* 1688 (NS); Chieftain of Clan Donnachy, (Donnachaidh); Managing Director, Grants of Dalvey Ltd, since 1988; *b* 5 Feb. 1953; *e s* of Sir Duncan Alexander Grant, 13th Bt, and Joan Penelope (*d* 1991), *o d* of Captain Sir Denzil Cope, 14th Bt; *S* father, 1961; *m* 1981, Dr Carolyn Elizabeth Highet, MB ChB, DRCOG, MRCGP (marr. diss. 2005), *d* of Dr John Highet, Glasgow; two *s. Educ:* St Conleth's Coll., Dublin; The Abbey Sch., Fort Angustus; Univ. of Glasgow (LLB 1981). Former deer-stalker, inshore fisherman. *Recreations:* professional competing piper, deerstalking, shooting. *Heir: s* Duncan Archibald Ludovic Grant, *b* 19 April 1982. *Address:* Tomintoul House, Flichity, Inverness-shire IV1 2XD. *Club:* New (Edinburgh).

GRANT, Prof. Patrick Spencer, DPhil; Cookson Professor of Materials, Oxford University, since 2004; Fellow, St Catherine's College, Oxford, since 2004; *b* 24 Feb. 1966; *s* of Richard Arthur Grant and Ann Dorothy Grant (*née* Reynolds); *m* 1999, Dr Zena Louise Forster; two *s* one *d. Educ:* Univ. of Nottingham (BEng Metallurgy and Materials Sci. 1987); St Edmund Hall, Oxford (DPhil Materials 1991). University of Oxford: Department of Materials: Res. Asst, 1990–92; SERC Postdoctoral Fellow, 1992–94; Royal Soc. Res. Fellow, 1994–2002; Lectr, 2002–04; Dir, Oxford Centre for Advanced Materials and Composites, 1999–2004; Jun. Res. Fellow, Jesus Coll., 1993–95; Sen. Res. Fellow, Linacre Coll., 1995–2004. Dir, Faraday Advance, 2000–07. *Publications:* papers on process-microstructure relationships and modelling of materials processing. *Recreations:* running, classical guitar. *Address:* Department of Materials, Oxford University, Parks Road, Oxford OX1 3PH. *T:* (01865) 283703, *Fax:* (01865) 848785; *e-mail:* patrick.grant@materials.ox.ac.uk.

GRANT, Peter David; International Director, Tearfund, since 2005; *b* 31 May 1958; *s* of late Desmond John Noel Grant and of Judith Mary Grant; *m* 1985, Stella Elizabeth Lucy Flower; one *s* one *d. Educ:* King Edward VI Sch., Birmingham; St John's Coll., Cambridge (BA (Econs) 1980; MA); LSE (MSc Econs). Economist, Govt of Malaŵi (ODI Fellow), 1980–82; Consultant, Coopers & Lybrand Associates, 1983–86; Pricing Strategy Manager, British Telecom Internat., 1986–90; Overseas Development Administration, later Department for International Development: Economist ATP, India, 1990–92; First Sec. (Econ.), Dhaka, 1992–96; Head: Internat. Econs Dept, 1996–98; Econ. Policy and Res. Dept, 1998–2000; Asia Policy Dept, and Dep. Dir, Asia, 2000–02; Dir, Internat., 2002–05. Co-Chm., OECD/DAC Poverty Reduction Network, 1999–2001. *Publication:* Poor No More, 2008. *Recreations:* theology, travel, tennis. *Address:* Tearfund, 100 Church Road, Teddington, Middx TW11 8QE. *T:* (020) 8977 9144; *e-mail:* peter.grant@tearfund.org.

GRANT, Peter James, CBE 1997; Deputy Chairman, London Merchant Securities, 1994–2007 (Director, 1985–2007); *b* 5 Dec. 1929; 2nd *s* of late Lt-Col P. C. H. Grant, Scots Guards, and Mrs Grant (*née* Gooch); *m* 1st, Ann, *d* of late Christopher Pleydell-Bouverie; one *s* one *d*; 2nd, Paula, *d* of late E. J. P. Eugster; one *s* two *d. Educ:* Winchester; Magdalen Coll., Oxford. Lieut, Queen's Own Cameron Highlanders. Edward de Stein & Co., 1952, merged with Lazard Brothers & Co. Ltd, 1960; Vice-Chm., 1983–85; Dep. Chm., 1985–88, Lazard Bros & Co.; Dir, 1973–95, Vice-Chm., 1976, Chm., 1983–95, Sun Life Assurance Soc. Chairman: Highlands and Islands Airports, 1993–2001; Egypt Investment Co., 1996–; CDP-Concord Egyptian Direct Investment Fund Ltd, subseq. Egyptian Direct Investment Fund Ltd, 2000–; Concord Coral Fund Ltd, 2006–; Director: Walter Runciman plc, 1973–90; Standard Industrial Gp, 1966–72; Charrington, Gardner, Lockett & Co. Ltd, 1970–74; Scottish Hydro, 1990–94; Union des Assurances de Paris International, 1989–91 (Internat. Adv. Bd, 1991–95); BNP (UK) plc, subseq. BNP Paribas UK Hldgs Ltd, 1991–2005; Transatlantic Hldgs, 1992–95. Member: Industrial Develt Adv. Bd, 1985–92; CAA, 1993–95; Cromarty Firth Port Authority, 1994–2000 (Chm., 2000). Mem. Council and Chm., Finance Cttee, British Red Cross Soc., 1972–85; Mem. Council, Inst. of Dirs, 1989–99. *Recreations:* shooting, golf, gardening. *Address:* Mountgerald, near Dingwall, Ross-shire IV15 9TT. *T:* (01349) 62244; 2 Windsor Court, Jubilee Place, SW3 3TB. *T:* (020) 7349 9099. *Clubs:* Boodle's, Caledonian.

GRANT, Prof. Peter Mitchell, PhD; FRSE; FREng, FIET, FIEEE; Regius Professor of Engineering, since 2007, and Head of School of Engineering and Electronics, since 2002, University of Edinburgh; *b* 20 June 1944; *s* of George Mitchell Grant and late Isobel Margaret (*née* Wilkinson); *m* 1974, Marjory Renz; two *d. Educ:* Heriot-Watt Univ. (BSc 1966); Univ. of Edinburgh (PhD 1975). FIET (FIEE 1988); FIEEE 1996; FRSE 1997; FREng 1997. Develt Engr, Plessey Co., 1966–70; Sen. Applications Engr, Hughes Microelectronics Ltd, 1970–71; University of Edinburgh: Res. Fellow, 1971–76; Lectr, 1976–82; Reader, 1982–87; Prof. of Electronic Signal Processing, 1987–2007; Hd, Dept of Electronics and Electrical Engrg, 1999–2002. Vis. Prof., Stanford Univ., 1977–78; Vis. Staff Mem., MIT Lincoln Laboratory, 1985–86. Pres., European Assoc. for Signal Speech and Image Processing, 2000–02. Hon. DEng: Heriot-Watt, 2006; Napier, 2007. Faraday Medal, IEE, 2004. *Publications:* Digital Communications, 1998, 2nd edn 2002; Digital Signal Processing, 1999, 2nd edn 2003. *Address:* School of Engineering and Electronics, University of Edinburgh, The King's Buildings, Mayfield Road, Edinburgh EH9 3JL. *T:* (0131) 650 5569, *Fax:* (0131) 650 6554; *e-mail:* Peter.Grant@ed.ac.uk.

GRANT, Prof. Peter Raymond, FRS 1987; FRSCan 2003; Class of 1877 Professor of Zoology, Princeton University, since 1989; *b* 26 Oct. 1936; *s* of late Frederick Thomas Charles and Mavis Irene Grant (later Reading); *m* 1962, Barbara Rosemary Matchett; two *d. Educ:* Whitgift Sch.; Cambridge Univ. (BA Hons); Univ. of British Columbia (PhD). Seessel-Anonymous Postdoctoral Fellow in Biology Dept of Yale Univ., 1964–65; Asst Prof. 1965–68, Associate Prof. 1968–73, Prof. 1973–78, McGill Univ.; Prof., Univ. of Michigan, 1977–85; Prof. of Biology, Princeton Univ., 1985–89. FLS 1986. Hon. PhD Uppsala, 1986; Hon. DSc: McGill, 2000; San Francisco, Quito, 2005. *Publications:* Ecology and Evolution of Darwin's Finches, 1986, 2nd ed 1999; (with B. R. Grant) Evolutionary Dynamics of a Natural Population, 1989 (Wildlife Soc. Publication Award, 1991); (with B. R. Grant) How and Why Species Multiply, 2008; contribs to Science, Nature, Proc. Royal Society, Proc. Nat. Acad. of Scis (USA), etc. *Recreations:* walking, tennis, music. *Address:* Department of Ecology and Evolutionary Biology, Princeton University, Princeton, NJ 08544–1003, USA. *T:* (609) 2585156.

GRANT, Piers; see Grant, M. A. P.

GRANT, Rhoda; Member (Lab) Highlands and Islands, Scottish Parliament, 1999–2003 and since 2007; Founder, Positive Politics, political advice consultancy, 2003; *b* 26 June 1963; *d* of Donald and Morag MacCuish; *m* 1989, (Christopher) Mark Grant. *Educ:* Open Univ. (BSc Hons Social Sci.). Administrator: Highland Regl Council, 1987–93; UNISON, 1993–99. Contested (Lab) Inverness E, Nairn and Lochaber, Scottish Parly elecns, 2003. *Address:* 26 Tomnahurich Street, Inverness IV3 5DS.

GRANT, Richard E.; actor and writer; *b* 5 May 1957; *né* Richard Grant Esterhuysen; *m* 1986, Joan Washington; one *d. Educ:* Waterford-Kamhlaba, Swaziland; Univ. of Cape Town (BA English). *Films:* Withnail and I, 1986; How to Get Ahead in Advertising, 1988; Warlock, Killing Dad, Henry and June, 1989; LA Story, The Player, Hudson Hawk, 1990; Dracula, The Age of Innocence, 1991; Jack and Sarah, 1993; Prêt-à-Porter, 1994; Twelfth Night, Portrait of a Lady, 1995; Serpent's Kiss, 1996; Keep the Aspidistra Flying, 1997; Cold Light of Day, All for Love, The Match, 1998; Little Vampire, 1999; Gosford Park, 2002; Monsieur Napoleon, Bright Young Things, 2003; Tooth, Colour Me Kubrick, 2004; (writer and dir) Wah-Wah, Penelope, 2006; Filth and Wisdom, 2008; *television:* Trial and Retribution, Scarlet Pimpernel, 1999; Young Sherlock Holmes, Hildegarde, 2000; Hound of the Baskervilles, 2002; Above and Beyond, 2005; Miss Marple: Nemesis, Dalziel and Pascoe, 2006; *theatre:* The Play What I Wrote, Wyndhams, 2002; Otherwise Engaged, Criterion, 2005. *Publications:* With-Nails: film diaries, 1996; By Design: Hollywood novel, 1998; Wah-Wah: film diaries, 2006. *Recreation:* scuba diving. *Address:* c/o Independent Talent Group Ltd, Oxford House, 76 Oxford Street, W1D 1BS. *T:* (020) 7636 6565.

GRANT, Dr Richard Sturge; Executive Director, Asia New Zealand Foundation, since 2008; *b* 3 Nov. 1945; *s* of Sydney Wallace Grant and Eva Grant; *m* 1973, Cherrilyn Gaye Turnbull; two *d. Educ:* Victoria Univ. of Wellington (MA Hons); Univ. de Clermont-Ferrand (Dr d'Univ.). Department of External Affairs, Wellington, 1968; French Govt Scholar, 1968–70; NZ Embassy, Paris, 1971–75; Min. of Foreign Affairs, 1976–78; Counsellor and Dep. Head of Mission, Vienna, 1978–81; Consul-Gen., Noumea, 1982–85; Head, European Div., Min. of Foreign Affairs, 1985–86; Consul-Gen., Sydney, 1987–90; Ambassador, Bonn, 1990–94; Dir, Australia Div., Min. of Foreign Affairs, 1994–97; High Comr for NZ in the UK, 1997–99; Ambassador for NZ in France, 1999–2002; Dep. Sec., Min. of Foreign Affairs and Trade, NZ, 2002–04; High Comr for NZ in Singapore, 2004–08. Visiting Scholar: John F. Kennedy Sch. of Govt, Harvard Univ., 1999; Oxford Internet Inst., Oxford Univ., 2004. *Recreations:* tennis, cricket, reading. *Address:* (office) Asia New Zealand Foundation, 36 Customhouse Quay, PO Box 10 144, Wellington 6143, New Zealand. *Clubs:* Royal Automobile; Royal Wellington Golf (NZ).

GRANT, Rodney Arandall; His Honour Judge Grant; a Circuit Judge, since 1995; *b* 8 May 1944; *s* of Thomas and Olive Grant; *m* 2007, Catherine Jane Grimshaw. *Educ:* Leeds Grammar Sch.; Trinity Coll., Oxford (Minor Scholar; MA Mod. Langs). Called to the Bar, Inner Temple, 1970; NE Circuit, 1970–95; Head of Chambers, 1992–95; a Recorder, 1993–95. Mem., Adv. Panel, Rugby Football League, 2005. *Recreations:* cookery, travel, jazz, reading, music. *Address:* c/o Circuit Administrator, 17th Floor, West Riding House, Albion Street, Leeds LS1 5AA.

GRANT, Lt-Gen. Sir Scott (Carnegie), KCB 1999 (CB 1995); Chief Royal Engineer, 1999–2004; *b* 28 Sept. 1944; *s* of Maurice and Margaret Wotherspoon Gibb Grant; *m* 1973, Catharine Susan Pawsey; one *s* one *d. Educ:* King's Sch., Pontefract; RMA Sandhurst; Clare Coll., Cambridge (MA). Commissioned Royal Engineers, 1965; Regtl duty Aden, Sharjah, BAOR and UK, 1965–73; Instructor, RMA, 1973–74; student, Staff Coll., 1975–76; MoD, 1977–78; Sqn Comdr, BAOR, 1979–80; Instructor, Staff Coll., 1981–82; CO 26 Engineer Regt, 1982–84; MoD, 1985; SHAPE, 1986–87; Comdr, 33 Armoured Brigade, 1988–89; RCDS 1990; Army Member, Prospect Team, 1991; Dir Gen. of Army Trng, 1991–93; Team Leader, Army Command Structure Review, 1993; GOC, UK Support Comd (Germany), 1994–95; Comdt, RCDS, 1996–98; QMG, 1998–2000. Col, The Queen's Lancashire Regt, 1993–99; Colonel Commandant: King's Div., 1997–2001; RE, 1997–2004. Dir, Customer Support, 2001–04, Vice-Pres., Ops, 2004–07, Thales UK; non-exec. Dir, NAAFI, 2001–07 (Dep. Chm., 2006–07). *Recreations:* 20th Century art and literature. *Clubs:* Army and Navy; Hawks (Cambridge).

GRANT, Sharon Margaret; Chairman, Commission for Patient and Public Involvement in Health, since 2003; *b* 28 Oct. 1952; *d* of Philip Arthur Lawrence and Margaret Theresa Lawrence; *m* 1998, Bernard Alexander Montgomery Grant, MP (*d* 2000). *Educ:* Tonbridge Girls' Grammar Sch.; Univ. of Birmingham (BSocSci Social Admin 1974, MSocSci Comparative Social Policy 1984). Campaigner on social equality issues, 1975–; Sen Lectr in Social Policy, Hatfield Polytechnic, 1977–87; Tutor and Examiner, Open Univ., 1984–87; Parly Sec. to late Bernie Grant, MP, 1987–2000. Councillor, London Bor. of Haringey, 1984–90. Founder and Sec., Bernie Grant Trust, 2000–; Dir, Bernie Grant Centre Partnership Ltd. *Recreations:* gardening, gym, travel. *Address:* Commission for Patient and Public Involvement in Health, 7th Floor, 120 Edmund Street, Birmingham B3 2ES. *T:* (0121) 222 4500. *Club:* Royal Commonwealth Society.

GRANT PETERKIN, Maj. Gen. (Anthony) Peter, CB 2003; OBE 1990; Serjeant at Arms, House of Commons, 2005–07; *b* 6 July 1947; *s* of late Brig. James Grant Peterkin, DSO and of Dorothea Grant Peterkin; *m* 1974, Joanna, *d* of Sir Brian Young, *qv*; one *s* one *d. Educ:* Ampleforth; RMA Sandhurst; Durham Univ. (BA 1971; MSc 1980). Commnd Queen's Own Highlanders; ADC to CGS, 1973–74; Indian Staff Coll., 1980; Australian JSSC, 1986; CO, 1st Bn, 1987–89; MA to Mil. Sec., 1989–91; MA, UN Observer Mission, Iraq and Kuwait, 1991; Comdr, 24 Airmobile Bde, 1993–94; rcds, 1995; Dep. Mil. Sec., 1996–98; Sen. Directing Staff, RCDS, 1999; Man. Dir, OSCE Mission, Kosovo, April–Sept. 1999; GOC 5th Div., 2000; Mil. Sec., 2000–03. Chm., ACF, 2005–08. Chm., Saigon Children's Charity, 2000–07. *Recreations:* travelling in Indochina, football, cleaning ditches. *Address:* Grange Hall, Forres, Moray IV36 2TR. *Club:* Army and Navy.

GRANT-SUTTIE, Sir James (Edward); see Suttie.

GRANTCHESTER, 3rd Baron *cr* 1953; **Christopher John Suenson-Taylor;** *b* 8 April 1951; *e s* (twin) of 2nd Baron Grantchester, CBE, QC and of Betty, *er d* of Sir John Moores, CBE; *S* father, 1995; *m* 1st, 1973, Jacqueline (marr. diss.), *d* of Dr Leo Jaffé; two *s* two *d*; 2nd, 2001, Jillian Margaret, *d* of Adrian Wood. *Educ:* Winchester; LSE (BSc Econ). Elected Mem., H of L, 2003. *Heir: s* Hon. Jesse David Suenson-Taylor, *b* 6 June 1977. *Address:* Lower House Farm, Back Coole Lane, Audlem, Crewe, Cheshire CW3 0ER.

GRANTHAM, Bishop Suffragan of, since 2006; **Rt Rev. Timothy William Ellis,** DPhil; *b* 26 Aug. 1953; *s* of Albert and Betty Ellis; *m* 1976, Susan Weston; two *s* one *d. Educ:* King's Coll., London (AKC 1975); York Univ. (DPhil 1998). Ordained deacon,

1976, priest, 1977; Asst Curate, St John, Old Trafford, 1976–80; Vicar, St Thomas, Pendleton and Chaplain to Salford Coll. of Technol., 1980–87; Vicar, St Leonard, Norwood, 1987–2001; Priest i/c, St Hilda, Shiregreen, 1994–97; RD Ecclesfield, 1994–99; Archdeacon of Stow and Lindsey, 2001–06. Sec., 1988–94, Chm., 1999–2001, Sheffield DAC; Member, Fabric Advisory Committee: York Minster, 2000–; Sheffield Cathedral, 2000–; Lincoln Minster, 2005–. Hon. Canon, Sheffield Cathedral, 2000–01. *Recreations:* Sheffield Wednesday FC, wine, foreign travel, golf. *Address:* Saxonwell Vicarage, Church Street, Long Bennington, Newark NG23 5ES. *T:* (01522) 529241.

GRANTHAM, Roy Aubrey, CBE 1990; National Secretary, APEX Partnership (white collar section of GMB), 1989–91; *b* 12 Dec. 1926; *m* 1964, Maura Teresa (marr. diss. 1988; remarried 2005); two *d*. *Educ:* King Edward Grammar Sch., Aston, Birmingham. Association of Professional, Executive, Clerical & Computer Staff: Midland area Organiser, 1949; Midland area Sec., 1959; Asst Sec., 1963; Gen. Sec., 1970–89, when APEX merged with GMB. Mem., TUC Gen. Council, 1983–92. Exec. Mem., Labour Cttee for Europe. Member: Royal Commn on Environmental Pollution, 1976–79; CNAA, 1976–79; IBA, 1984–90; former Mem., MSC, subseq. Training Commn. Director: Chrysler UK Ltd, 1977–79, Talbot UK Ltd, 1979–81; Ansvar Insce Co. Ltd, 1990–97. Governor, Henley Management Coll., 1979–91; Mem., Ditchley Foundn, 1982–97. Chm., UK Temperance Alliance, 1989–2001. Councillor (Lab), London Bor. of Croydon, 1994–2002. *Publication:* Guide to Grading of Clerical and Administrative Work, 1968. *Recreations:* walking, reading, chess. *Address:* 3 Guild Road, Aston Cantlow, Warwicks B95 6JA.

GRANTLEY, 8th Baron *cr* 1782; **Richard William Brinsley Norton;** Baron of Markenfield 1782; a Director, Project and Export Finance, HSBC Bank plc (formerly HSBC Investment Bank), 1997–2005; *b* 30 Jan. 1956; *er s* of 7th Baron Grantley, MC and of Lady Deirdre Freda Mary Hare (who *m* 2001, Ian Bayley Curteis, *qv*), *e d* of Earl of Listowel, GCMG, PC; *S* father, 1995. *Educ:* Ampleforth Coll.; New Coll., Oxford (Open Schol. in Maths; BA (Law), MA). Pres., Oxford Union Soc., 1976. Cons. Res. Dept, 1977–81; Morgan Grenfell & Co. Ltd, 1981–97; Dir, Morgan Grenfell Internat., 1994–97. Contested (C) Wentworth, 1983. Councillor, RBK&C, 1982–86. Leader, UKIP, H of L, 1997. Kt SMO Malta, 1981. *Recreations:* bridge, smoking. *Heir: b* Hon. Francis John Hilary Norton [*b* 30 Sept. 1960; *m* 2004, Eva, *d* of Mr and Mrs Elemér Figder, Budapest]. *Address:* 8 Halsey Street, SW3 2QH. *T:* (home) (020) 7589 7531. *Club:* Pratt's.

GRANVILLE, 6th Earl *cr* 1833; **Granville George Fergus Leveson Gower;** Viscount Granville 1815; Baron Leveson 1833; *b* 10 Sept. 1959; *s* of 5th Earl Granville, MC and of Doon Aileen (*née* Plunket); *S* father, 1996; *m* 1997, Anne, *o d* of Bernard Topping; one *s* two *d*. *Heir: s* Lord Leveson, *qv*. *Address:* Callernish, Lochmaddy, Isle of N Uist, Western Isles HS6 5BZ.

GRANVILLE-CHAPMAN, Gen. Sir Timothy (John), GBE 2007 (CBE 1991); KCB 2001; Vice Chief of the Defence Staff, 2005–May 2009; Aide-de-Camp General to the Queen, since 2003; *b* 5 Jan. 1947; *s* of Guy Granville-Chapman and Elsa Granville-Chapman (*née* Campbell); *m* 1971, Elizabeth Stevens; one *s* one *d*. *Educ:* Charterhouse; Christ's Coll., Cambridge (BA Law 1968; MA 1972). VSO, Tanzania, 1965. Commissioned RA, 1968; regtl duties, 1968–77; Staff Coll., 1978–79; MA to Comdr, 1st BR Corps, 1980–82; CO 1st Regt RHA, 1985–88; Higher Command and Staff Course, 1988; Mil. Doctrine Author, 1988; Policy Staff, MoD, 1989–90; Comdr 12th Armd Bde, 1990–93; Dir, Army Staff Duties, MoD, 1994; ACGS, MoD, 1994–96; Comdt, Jt Services Comd and Staff Coll., 1997–99; Adjutant Gen., 2000–03; C-in-C Land Comd, 2003–05. Col, Dorset Yeomanry, 1997–; Pres. and Col Comdt, HAC, 2003–. Master Gunner, St James's Park, 2008–. Gov., Harrow Sch., 1997–. *Recreations:* sailing, some country pursuits, architecture, clocks. *Address:* Artillery House, Artillery Centre, Larkhill, Salisbury, Wilts SP4 8QT.

GRANZIOL, Dr Markus Johannes; non-executive Chairman, Eurex, since 2002 (non-executive Director, since 1997); *b* 21 Jan. 1952; *m* Manuela Fornera; one *s* three *d*. *Educ:* Univ. of Zurich (MA Econs; PhD Econs 1980). University of Zurich: res. analyst, Inst. for Empirical Res. in Econs, 1976–85; Lectr in Macroecons and Financial Theory, Dept of Juris. and Pol Sci., 1978–90; COS, Dept III, Swiss Nat. Bank, Zurich, 1985–87; Swiss Bank Corporation, 1987–98: Man. Dir and Hd, Securities Dept, 1987–94; Man. Dir, Hong Kong and Global Hd, Equities Business, 1994–95; Jt Global Hd, Equities Business, SBC Warburg, 1995–96 (also Mem. Exec. Bd and Investment Banking Bd); Gen. Manager and Mem., Gp Exec. Bd, 1996–98; Global Hd, Equities and Fixed Income, Warburg Dillon Read, 1998–99; CEO, 1999–2001, Chm., 2000–02, UBS Warburg; Mem., Gp Exec. Bd, UBS AG, 1999–2002. Non-exec. Mem. Bd, Zurich Financial Services, 2002–04; Incentive Asset Mgt, 2005–. Vis. Schol., Grad. Sch. of Business Admin, Univ. of Chicago, 1981–82. *Publications:* contribs to scientific jls. *Recreations:* sports, piano. *Address:* Virt-x, 34th Floor, One Canada Square, Canary Wharf, E14 5AA.

GRASS, Günter Wilhelm; German writer and artist; *b* Danzig, 16 Oct. 1927; *m* 1st, 1954, Anna Schwarz; three *s* (inc. twin *s*) one *d*; 2nd, 1979, Ute Grunert. *Educ:* Volksschule and Gymnasium, Danzig; Düsseldorf Kunstakademie; Hochschule für Bildende Künste, Berlin. Lecture Tour of US, 1964, and many other foreign tours. Member: Deutscher PEN, Zentrum der Bundesrepublik; Verband Deutscher Schriftsteller; Amer. Academy of Arts and Sciences. Prizes: Lyric, Süddeutscher Rundfunk, 1955; Gruppe 47, 1958; Bremen Literary, 1959 (prize money withheld); Literary, Assoc. of German Critics, 1960; Meilleur livre étranger, 1962; Georg-Büchner, 1965; Fontane, Berlin, 1968; Theodor-Heuss, 1969; Internat., Mondello, 1978; Antonio-Feltrinelli, 1982; Grinzane Cavour, 1992; Chodowiecki, 1992; Hidalgo, 1993; Bayerischen Akad. der Schönen Künste, 1994; (with Philip Roth) Karel Capek, 1994; Hans Fallada, 1995; Sonning, 1995; Thomas Mann, 1996; Asturias, 1999; Nobel Prize for Literature, 1999; medals: Ossietzky, 1968; Hermann Kesten, 1995. *Publications: novels:* Die Blechtrommel, 1959 (The Tin Drum, 1962; filmed 1979); Katz und Maus, 1961 (Cat and Mouse, 1963); Hundejahre, 1963 (Dog Years, 1965); Örtlich betäubt, 1969 (Local Anaesthetic, 1970); Aus dem Tagebuch einer Schnecke, 1972 (From the Diary of a Snail, 1974); Der Butt, 1977 (The Flounder, 1978); Das Treffen in Telgte, 1979 (The Meeting at Telgte, 1981); Kopfgeburten, 1980 (Headbirths, 1982); Die Rättin, 1986 (The Rat, 1987); Unkenrufe (The Call of the Toad), 1992; Ein weites Feld (A Wide Field), 1995; Im Krebsgang (Crabwalk), 2002; *poetry:* (also drawings) Die Vorzüge der Windhühner, 1956; (also drawings) Gleisdreieck, 1960; Ausgefragt, 1967; Ach Butt, dein Märchen geht böse aus, 1983; Novemberland, 1994; (also paintings) Fundsachen für Nichtleser, 1997; Letzte Tänze, 2003; Lyrische Beute, 2004; *poetry in translation:* Selected Poems, 1966; Poems of Günter Grass, 1969; In the Egg and other poems, 1978; Novemberland: selected poems 1956–1993, 1996; *drama:* Hochwasser, 1957 (Flood, 1968); Noch zehn Minuten bis Buffalo, 1958 (Only Ten Minutes to Buffalo, 1968); Onkel, Onkel, 1958 (Onkel, Onkel, 1968); Die bösen Köche, 1961 (The Wicked Cooks, 1968); Die Plebejer proben den Aufstand, 1966 (The Plebeians rehearse the Uprising, 1967); Davor, 1969; *prose:* Über das Selbstverständlische, 1968 (Speak Out!, 1969); Dokumente zur politischen Wirkung, 1971; Der Bürger und seine Stimme, 1974; Denkzettel, 1978; Aufsätze zur Literatur, 1980; Zeichnen und Schreiben, Band I, 1982, Band II, 1984; Widerstand lernen, 1984; On Writing and Politics 1967–83, 1985; Zunge Zeigen, 1988 (Show Your Tongue, 1989); Two States - One Nation?, 1990; Schreiben nach Auschwitz, 1990; Deutscher Lastenausgleich, 1990; Ein Schnäppchen namens DDR, 1990; Deutschland, einig Vaterland, 1990; Alptraum und Hoffnung, 1990; Gegen die verstreichende Zeit, 1991; Rede vom Verlust, 1992; Angestiftet, Partei zu ergreifen, 1994; Die Deutschen und ihre Dichter, 1995; Gestern, vor 50 Jahren (correspondence with Kenzaburo Öe), 1995; Beim Häuten der Zwiebel (memoir), 2006 (Peeling the Onion, 2007); *graphic work:* Mit Sophie in die Pilze gegangen, 1987; Totes Holz, 1990; Brief aus Altdöbern, 1991; Vier Jahrzehnte, 1991; In Kupfer, auf Stein, 1994; Der Schatten: Hans Christian Andersens Märchen gesehen von Günter Grass (The Shadow: Hans Christian Andersen's stories, seen by Günter Grass), 2004. *Address:* Glockengiesserstrasse 21, 23552 Lübeck, Germany.

GRATTAN, Donald Henry, CBE 1989; Chairman: Adult Continuing Education Development Unit, 1984–91; National Council for Educational Technology (formerly Council for Educational Technology), 1985–91 (Member, 1973–84); *b* St Osyth, Essex, 7 Aug. 1926; *s* of Arthur Henry Grattan and Edith Caroline Saltmarsh; *m* 1950, Valma Dorothy Morgan; one *s* one *d*. *Educ:* Harrow Boys Grammar Sch.; King's Coll., Univ. of London. BSc 1st Cl. Hons, Mathematics Dip. in Radio-Physics. Jun. Scientific Officer, TRE, Gt Malvern, 1945–46; Mathematics Teacher, Chiswick Grammar Sch., 1946–50; Sen. Master, Downer Grammar Sch., Middx, 1950–56. BBC: Sch. Television Producer, 1956–60; Asst Head, Sch. Television, 1960–64; Head of Further Educn, Television, 1964–70; Asst Controller, Educnl Broadcasting, 1970–72, Controller, 1972–84. Member: Open Univ. Council, 1972–84 and Univ. Delegacy for Continuing Educn, 1978–84; Vis. Cttee, Open Univ., 1987–92; Adv. Council for Adult and Continuing Educn, 1978–83; European Broadcasting Union Working Party on Educn, 1972–84; Venables' Cttee on Continuing Educn, 1976–78. Chm., Adult Literacy Support Services Fund, 1975–80. Mem., Royal TV Soc., 1982–. Chm., 1993–96, Vice-Pres., 2001–, Marlow Soc. FRSA 1988. DUniv Open, 1985. Burnham Medal of BIM for services to Management Educn, 1969. *Publications:* Science and the Builder, 1963; Mathematics Miscellany (jt, BBC), 1966; numerous articles. *Recreations:* education (formal and informal), planning and organizing people. *Address:* Delabole, 3 Gossmore Close, Marlow, Bucks SL7 1QG. *T:* (01628) 473571.

GRATTAN-BELLEW, Sir Henry Charles, 5th Bt *cr* 1838; *b* 12 May 1933; *s* of Lt-Col Sir Charles Christopher Grattan-Bellew, 4th Bt, MC, KRRC and Maureen Peyton, *niece* and adopted *d* of late Sir Thomas Segrave, Shenfield, Essex; *S* father, 1948; *m* 1st, 1956, Naomi Ellis (marr. diss. 1966); 2nd, 1967, Gillian Hulley (marr. diss. 1973); one *s* one *d*; 3rd, 1978, Elzabé Amy (*née* Body) (marr. diss. 1993), *widow* of John Westerveld, Pretoria, Tvl, SA. *Educ:* St Gerard's, Bray, Co. Wicklow; Ampleforth Coll., York. Publisher: Horse and Hound, SA, and Sustagen Supersport, 1977. Sports administrator, leading radio and TV commentator, hotelier, thoroughbred breeder and owner, author. *Heir: s* Patrick Charles Grattan-Bellew [*b* 7 Dec. 1971; *m* 2000, Liezel Wallis]. *Address:* Rozel, 8 Foxrock Mount, Dublin 18, Ireland; Little Saltee Island, Kilmore Quay, Wexford, Ireland.

GRATTON, Paul; Director, Direct Valuations Ltd, since 1989; *b* 10 Nov. 1959; *s* of Robert and Audrey Gratton; *m* 1997, Elizabeth; three *s*. *Educ:* Nottingham High Sch. Various posts incl. mgt posts, Midland Bank plc, 1978–89; Financial Services Dir, First Direct, 1989–96; Ops Dir, Prudential Banking, 1996–98; Chief Operating Officer, Prudential Banking plc/Egg plc, 1998–2000; Dep. Chief Exec., 2000–01, CEO, 2001–06, Egg plc; Exec. Chm., Artilium (formerly Future Internet Technologies) plc, 2006–07 (non-exec. Dir, 2007–). Non-exec. Chm., EvoCell.

GRATWICK, Stephen; QC 1968; *b* 19 Aug. 1924; *s* of late Percival John Gratwick, Fawkham, Kent; *m* 1954, Jocelyn Chaplin, Horton Kirby, Kent; four *d*. *Educ:* Charterhouse; Balliol Coll., Oxford. Oxford 1942–44; Signals Research and Devel. Estabt, 1944–47. BA (Physics) 1946; MA 1950. Called to the Bar, Lincoln's Inn, 1949; Bencher, 1976. *Recreations:* swimming, making and mending things. *Address:* Haymist, 14a Kippington Road, Sevenoaks TN13 2LH.

GRATWICKE, Charles James Phillip; His Honour Judge Gratwicke; a Circuit Judge, since 2003; *b* 25 July 1951; *s* of Phillip and Maeve Gratwicke; *m* 1981, Jane Vivien Meyer; two *s* one *d*. *Educ:* Franciscan Coll., Buckingham; Leeds Univ. (LLB Hons). Called to the Bar, Middle Temple, 1974; in practice as barrister, 1974–2003; a Recorder, 1998–2003. Part-time Chairman, Disciplinary Committee: Potato Mktg Bd, 1990–2003; MMB, 1991–96. *Recreations:* long distance walking, sailing, mercantile matters, marine painting, London in all its forms and history. *Address:* The Crown Court, New Street, Chelmsford, Essex CM1 1EL. *Clubs:* National Liberal; Seven Seas.

GRAVENEY, David Anthony, OBE 2006; Vice President, Professional Cricketers' Association, since 2003 (General Secretary, subseq. Chief Executive, 1994–2003); *b* 2 Jan. 1953; *s* of Ken Graveney and late Jeanne Graveney; *m* 1978, Julie Anne Smith Marriott; one *s* one *d*. *Educ:* Millfield Sch., Somerset. Gloucestershire CCC, 1972–90, Captain 1981–88; Somerset CCC, 1991; Durham CCC, 1992–94, Captain 1992–93. Treasurer, Professional Cricketers' Assoc., 1979–94. Manager: England cricket team, South Africa tour, 1990; England A team, Australia tour, 1996; England cricket team, One-Day series, Australia, 1998–99, and World Cup, 1999; Selector, England cricket team, 1995–96; Chm. of Selectors, 1997–2008; Performance Manager, ECB, 2008–. *Recreations:* golf, watching Rugby. *Address:* 6 Southover Close, Westbury-on-Trym, Bristol BS9 3NG.

GRAVES, family name of **Baron Graves**.

GRAVES, 10th Baron *cr* 1794 (Ire.); **Timothy Evelyn Graves;** *b* 27 March 1960; *s* of 9th Baron Graves and Marjorie Ann (*née* Holder), OAM; *S* father, 2002. *Heir:* none.

GRAVES, Christopher James Mitchell; Director, Tudor Trust, since 1986 (Project Officer, 1985–86); *b* 6 April 1956; *s* of Desmond James Turner Graves and Mary Kathleen Graves (*née* Mitchell); *m* 1986, Amanda Patricia Mayhew; one *s* two *d*. *Educ:* Westminster Sch.; Queens' Coll., Cambridge (BA 1978, MA 1981, DipArch 1981). RIBA 1983. Architect, Trehearne, Norman, Preston & Partners, 1981–85. *Recreations:* watercolours, opera, singing, watching a failing football team. *Address:* Tudor Trust, 7 Ladbroke Grove, W11 3BD. *T:* (020) 7727 8522.

GRAVES, Rev. Dr Peter Charles; Minister, Wesley Methodist Church, Cambridge, and Methodist Chaplain to the Universities in Cambridge, 2000–08; *b* 23 March 1943; *s* of Walter and Eileen Graves; *m* 1976, Patricia Mary Campbell; two *s* one *d*. *Educ:* Handsworth Theol Coll., Birmingham; Union Theol Seminary, Virginia (ThM, DMin); London Univ. (Cert Ed). Minister: Enfield Circuit (St John's, Goffs Oak), 1968–69; Highgate Circuit (Holly Park), 1969–72; Chaplain and Associate Lectr, Enfield Coll. of Technol., 1969–72; Chaplain and Sen. Lectr, 1972–77, Sen. Chaplain and Hd of Student Welfare, 1977–79, Middlesex Poly.; Minister: Epsom, 1979–89; Cullercoats, 1989–95; Superintendent Minister, Methodist Central Hall, Westminster, 1995–2000. Methodist Tutor, North East Ordination Course, 1990–95; Tutor, Wesley Study Centre, Cranmer

Hall, Durham, 1992–95; Chaplain to Methodist MPs and Leader, Methodist Parly Fellowship, 1995–2000. Finch Lectr, High Point Univ., NC, USA, 1997. Vice Pres., Bible Soc., 1998–. Chm. Judges, Times Preacher of the Year Award, 1998–2000. Broadcaster, Premier Radio, London, 1997–. *Publications:* Living and Praying the Lord's Prayer, 2002; contrib. New Daylight, 1997–2005. *Recreations:* travel, theatre, family life. *Address:* 84 Pierce Lane, Fulbourn, Cambs CB1 5DL.

GRAVES, Rupert; actor; *b* Weston-super-Mare, 30 June 1963; *m* 2001, Susie Lewis; two *s* one *d*. *Educ:* Wyvern Comp. Sch. Early career in a circus; London theatrical début, King's Head, Islington; film actor, 1986–. *Theatre includes:* Torch Song Trilogy, Albery, 1985; The Importance of Being Earnest; Candida, 1988; 'Tis Pity She's a Whore, NT, 1988; A Madhouse in Goa, Lyric, Hammersmith, 1989; Les Enfants du Paradis, Barbican, 1996; Hurlyburly, Old Vic, transf. Queen's, 1997; The Iceman Cometh, Almeida, 1998; Closer, NY, 1999; The Caretaker, Comedy, 2000; The Elephant Man, NY, 2002; Dumb Show, Royal Court, 2004; The Exonerated, Riverside Studios, 2006. *Films include:* A Room with a View, 1986; Maurice, 1987; A Handful of Dust, 1988; Where Angels Fear to Tread, 1991; Damage, 1992; The Madness of King George, 1994; Different for Girls, 1996; Intimate Relations, Mrs Dalloway, 1997; All My Loved Ones, 1999; Extreme Ops, 2003; Rag Tale, 2005; V for Vendetta, 2005; Intervention, 2006; Death at a Funeral, 2006; The Waiting Room, 2008. *Television includes:* Fortunes of War, 1987; Open Fire, 1994; The Tenant of Wildfell Hall, 1996; Blonde Bombshell, 1999; The Forsyte Saga, 2002; Charles II: The Power and the Passion, 2003; Clapham Junction, The Dinner Party, 2007; God on Trial, 2008. *Address:* c/o PFD, Drury House, 34–43 Russell Street, WC2B 5HA.

GRAY; *see* Pereira Gray.

GRAY, 23rd Lord *cr* 1445; **Andrew Godfrey Diarmid Stuart Campbell-Gray;** *b* 3 Sept. 1964; *s* of 22nd Lord Gray and Patricia Margaret (*née* Alexander); *S* father 2003; *m* 1993, Hon. Lucy, *y d* of 2nd Baron Elton, *qv*; one *s* one *d*. *Heir: s* Master of Gray, *qv*.

GRAY, Master of; Hon. Alexander Godfrey Edward Diarmid Campbell-Gray; *b* 7 Oct. 1996; *s* and *heir* of Lord Gray, *qv*.

GRAY, Alasdair James; self-employed verbal and pictorial artist; *b* 28 Dec. 1934; *s* of Alexander Gray and Amy (*née* Fleming); *m* 1st, 1961, Inge Sørensen (marr. diss.); one *s*; 2nd, 1991, Morag McAlpine. *Educ:* Glasgow Sch. of Art (Scottish Educn Dept Dip. in mural painting and design); Jordanhill Teachers' Trng Coll. (CertEd). Part-time teacher and painter, 1958–62; theatrical scene painter, 1962–63; social security scrounger, 1963–64; painter and playwright, 1965–76 (8 one-man exhibns, two retrospective; 17 TV and radio plays broadcast; 4 plays staged); Glasgow's official artist-recorder for People's Palace local history mus., 1977; Writer-in-Residence, 1977–79, Consulting Prof. of Creative Writing, 2001–03, Glasgow Univ.; mural decorator, Oran Mor Leisure Centre, Glasgow, 2003–. Collections of paintings owned by: Collins Gall., Strathclyde Univ.; People's Palace local history mus., Glasgow Green; Hunterian Gall., Glasgow Univ.; personal archives lodged with Nat. Liby of Scotland, Edinburgh. *Publications: novels:* Lanark, 1981; 1982 Janine, 1984; The Fall of Kelvin Walker, 1985; Something Leather, 1990; McGrotty and Ludmilla, 1990; Poor Things, 1992; A History Maker, 1994; Old Men in Love, 2007; *short story collections:* Unlikely Stories Mostly, 1983; (with J. Kelman and A. Owens) Lean Tales, 1985; Ten Tales Tall and True, 1993; Mavis Belfrage, 1996; The Ends of Our Tethers: thirteen sorry stories, 2003; *poetry:* Old Negatives, 1989; Sixteen Occasional Poems, 2000; *play:* Working Legs (a play for people without them), 1997; *non-fiction:* Saltire Self-Portrait no 4 (autobiog.), 1989; (ed) The Book of Prefaces, 2000; A Short Survey of Classic Scots Writing, 2001; *polemics:* Why Scots Should Rule Scotland, 1992; Why Scots Should Rule Scotland, 1997; (with A. Tomkins) How We Should Rule Ourselves, 2005.

GRAY, Anthony James; *b* 12 Feb. 1936; *o s* of Prof. Sir James Gray, CBE, MC, FRS; *m* 1st, 1963, Lady Lana Mary Gabrielle Baring (*d* 1974), *d* of 3rd Earl of Cromer, KG, GCMG, MBE, PC; one *s* one *d*; 2nd, 1980, Mrs Maxine Redmayne (*d* 2007), *er d* of Captain and Mrs George Brodrick. *Educ:* Marlborough Coll.; New Coll., Oxford (MA). C. T. Bowring & Co. (Insurance) Ltd, 1960–64; Sen. Investment Analyst, de Zoete & Gorton, 1965–67; Head of Equity Research and Partner, James Capel & Co., 1967–73. Member, London Stock Exchange, 1971–73. Dep. Dir, Industrial Development Unit and Dir, Industry Studies, Dept of Trade and Industry, 1973–75; Special Industrial Advr, Dept of Industry, 1975–76; Assoc., PA Management Consultants Ltd, 1977–81; Chief Exec., Cogent Gp (technol. transfer collaboration with Assoc. of Indep. Contract Res. Orgns), 1982–88; Chm., various advanced technol. cos, 1982–96; Assoc., HSBC Bank plc (Regl Advr), 2000–03. Member: Foundries EDC (NEDO), 1973–75; Hammersmith and Fulham DHA, 1982–85; Research and Manufacturing Cttee, CBI, 1988–90; Science and Industry Cttee, BAAS, 1989–91. Member Council: Charing Cross Hosp. Med. Sch., 1982–84; ERA Technology Ltd (formerly Electrical Res. Assoc.), 1986–89. Governor: Cobham Hall Sch., Kent, 1966–70; British American Drama Acad., 1996–99. Director: Apollo Soc., 1966–73; Nat. Trust Concert Soc., 1966–73. FRSA. *Recreations:* fishing, music. *Address:* The Old Coach House, Reepham, Norfolk. *Clubs:* Beefsteak, Garrick.

GRAY, Bryan Mark, MBE 2001; DL; Chairman: North West Development Agency, 2002–08; Baxi Technologies, 2001–08; Pro Chancellor, Lancaster University, since 2003; *b* 23 June 1953; *s* of late Clifford Benjamin Gray and June Mary Gray; *m* 1976, Lydia Ann Wallbridge; three *s*. *Educ:* Wath-upon-Dearne Grammar Sch.; Univ. of York (BA (Chemistry) 1974). Joined ICI, 1974; commercial appointments: Sales Office, Birmingham; ICI Petrochemicals and Plastics Div., Wilton; ICI Films and ICI Advanced Materials, Welwyn Garden City; Man. Dir, EVC Compounds Ltd, 1989–93; Commercial Dir, 1993, Chief Exec., 1994–2000, Baxi Partnership; Dep. Chm., Baxi Gp Ltd, 2000–04. Chairman: Westmorland Ltd, 2005–; Urban Splash Hotels, 2006–; non-exec. Dir, United Utilities Water plc, 2008–. Chairman: NW Reg., CBI, 2000–02; Central Heating Inf. Council, 2000–03; Mem., LSC, 2004–08. Pres., Soc. of British Gas Industries, 2000–01; Vice President: European Heating Industries Assoc., 2002–04; Micropower Council, 2005–. Founder Chm., Nat. Football Mus., 1995–2001; Board Member: NW Cultural Consortium, 2003– (Chm., 2007–); Liverpool Culture Co. Ltd, 2003–; Trustee, Nat. Mus. Liverpool, 2004–; Mem., Lake Dist Nat. Park Authy, 2006–. Chairman: Churches Trust in Cumbria, 2008–; Lowther Castle and Gardens Trust, 2008–. Chm., Preston Post Grad. Med. Centre, 1996–2004; Gov., Univ. of Central Lancashire, 1999–2002. Hon. Prof., Dept of Built Envmt, Univ. of Nottingham, 2003–. Vice Patron, Deafway, 2002–. Reader, Liverpool Dio., C of E, 1981–. FRSA. DL 2002, High Sheriff, 2003–04, Lancs. *Recreations:* heritage, Midland Railway, scrapbooks, Preston North End. *Address:* c/o North West Development Agency, Renaissance House, PO Box 37, Centre Park, Warrington WA1 1XB. *T:* (01925) 400183, *Fax:* (01925) 400404; *e-mail:* bryan.gray@nwda.co.uk. *Club:* Preston North End Football (Chm., 1994–2001, Vice Pres., 2001–).

GRAY, Charles; *see* Gray, J. C. R.

GRAY, Hon. Sir Charles (Antony St John), Kt 1998; a Judge of the High Court, Queen's Bench Division, 1998–2008; *b* 6 July 1942; *s* of late Charles Herbert Gray and Catherine Margaret Gray; *m* 1st, 1968, Rosalind Macleod Whinney (marr. diss. 1990); one *s* one *d*; 2nd, 1995, Susan (*née* Eveleigh) (*d* 1997), former wife of Hon. Sir John Astor, MBE, ERD; 3rd, 2001, Cynthia Elizabeth Selby. *Educ:* Winchester; Trinity College, Oxford (scholar; Hon. Fellow 2003). Called to the Bar, Lincoln's Inn, 1966, Bencher, 1991; QC 1984; a Recorder, 1990–98. *Recreations:* travel, music, tennis, ski-ing. *Address:* The Old Rectory, Puncknowle, Dorchester, Dorset DT2 9BW. *Club:* Brooks's.

GRAY, Sir Charles (Ireland), Kt 2007; CBE 1994; JP; Member, North Lanarkshire Council, 1995–2007 (Chairman, Education Committee, 1995–2007); *b* 25 Jan. 1929; *s* of Timothy Gray and Janet (*née* Brown); *m* 1952, Catherine Creighton Gray; three *s* two *d*. *Educ:* Coatbridge. Dept of Public Affairs, Scotrail, 1946; Mem. (later Chm.), Lanark DC, 1958–64; Mem., Lanark CC, 1964–75; founder Mem., 1975–96, first Vice-Convener, and Leader 1986–92, Strathclyde Regl Council. Leader, UK delegn to Euro Cttee of the Regions, 1994–98. Pres., Convention of Scottish Local Authorities, 1992–94. Member: Scottish Exhibn and Conf. Centre, 1986–91; Scottish Enterprise Bd, 1990–93. FRSA 1991; FEIS 2005. JP Strathclyde, 1970. *Recreations:* music, reading, politics. *Address:* 9 Moray Place, Chryston G69 9LZ. *T:* (0141) 779 2962.

GRAY, Christopher Mark, FRCO; Director of Music, Truro Cathedral, since 2008; *b* Bangor, NI, 2 June 1978; *s* of Denis and Anne Gray. *Educ:* Pembroke Coll., Univ. of Cambridge (BA 1999); Royal Coll. of Music (Dip. 2000). FRCO 2005. Organ Scholar, Guildford Cathedral, 1999–2000; Asst Dir of Music, Truro Cathedral, 2000–08. *Recreation:* surfing. *Address:* Truro Cathedral, 14 St Mary's Street, Truro, Cornwall TR1 2AF. *T:* (01872) 276782; *e-mail:* christophergray@trurocathedral.org.uk.

GRAY, (Clemency Anne) Rose; chef and owner, The River Cafe London, since 1987; *b* 28 Jan. 1939; *d* of Clement Nelson Swann and Elizabeth Anne Lawrence; *m* 1961, Michael Selby Gray (marr. diss.); one *s* two *d*; *m* 2004, David Robin MacIlwaine; one *s*. *Educ:* Guildford Sch. of Art (BA Fine Art). Teacher of fine art, London, 1960–63; designer and manufacturer of paper lights and furniture, 1963–68; importer of French stoves and cookers, 1969–80; chef, Nell's Nightclub, NY, 1985–86. Founder, Cooks in Schs, 2005. *Publications:* with Ruth Rogers: River Cafe Cook Book, 1995; River Cafe Cook Book Two, 1997; The Italian Kitchen, 1998; River Cafe Cook Book Green, 2000; River Cafe Cook Book Easy, 2003; River Cafe Two Easy, 2005; River Cafe Pocket Books, 2006. *Recreations:* gardening, wine, travelling, eating. *T:* (020) 7386 4250, *Fax:* (020) 7386 4201; *e-mail:* info@rivercafe.co.uk.

GRAY, David; *see* Gray, J. N. D.

GRAY, David John; Chief Executive Officer (formerly Managing Partner), Eversheds, since 2003; *b* 9 Jan. 1955; *s* of Allan and Vena Gray; *m* 1984, Julie Sergeant. *Educ:* Magdalene Coll., Cambridge (BA (Law) 1976). Admitted solicitor, 1979; Equity Partner, Hepworth and Chadwick, 1982; Eversheds: Hd of Corporate, Leeds and Manchester, 1995–98; Dep. Managing Partner, Leeds and Manchester, and Head of Corporate, 1998–2000; Managing Partner, Leeds and Manchester, 2000–03. *Recreations:* golf, National Hunt racing, football. *Address:* Eversheds, Senator House, 85 Queen Victoria Street, EC4V 4JL. *Club:* Alwoodley Golf.

GRAY, Dr Denis Everett, CBE 1983 (MBE 1972); JP; Resident Staff Tutor, since 1957, and Senior Lecturer, 1967–84, Department of Extramural Studies, University of Birmingham; *b* 25 June 1926; *s* of Charles Norman Gray and Kathleen Alexandra (*née* Roberts); *m* 1949, Barbara Joyce, *d* of Edgar Kesterton. *Educ:* Bablake Sch., Coventry; Univ. of Birmingham (BA); Univ. of London; Univ. of Manchester (PhD). Tutor-organiser, WEA, S Staffs, 1953–57. Chairman: Jt Negotiating Cttees for Justices' Clerks and Justices' Clerks' Assts, 1978–86; Central Council of Magistrates' Courts Cttees, 1980–86 (Dep. Chm., 1978–80); Member: Magistrates' Courts Rule Cttee, 1982–86; Lord Chancellor's Adv. Cttee on Trng of Magistrates, 1974–84. JP Solihull, 1962; Dep. Chm., 1968–71 and 1978–82, Chm., 1971–75, Solihull Magistrates; Chm., Licensing Cttee, 1972–76. *Publication:* Spencer Perceval: the evangelical Prime Minister, 1963. *Recreations:* travel, church architecture, reading. *Address:* 11 Brueton Avenue, Solihull, West Midlands B91 3EN. *T:* (0121) 705 2935.

GRAY, Rev. Canon Dr Donald Clifford, CBE 1998; TD 1970; Canon of Westminster and Rector of St Margaret's, Westminster Abbey, 1987–98, Canon Emeritus, since 1998; Chaplain to HM The Queen, 1982–2000; Chaplain to the Speaker, House of Commons, 1987–98; *b* 21 July 1930; *s* of Henry Hackett Gray and Constance Muriel Gray; *m* 1955, Joyce (*née* Jackson); one *s* two *d*. *Educ:* Newton Heath Technical High Sch.; King's Coll., London and Warminster (AKC); Univ. of Liverpool (MPhil); Univ. of Manchester (PhD). Curate, Leigh Parish Church, 1956–60; Vicar: St Peter's, Westleigh, 1960–67; All Saints', Elton, Bury, 1967–74; Rector of Liverpool, 1974–87; RD of Liverpool, 1975–81; Canon Diocesan of Liverpool, 1982–87. Proctor-in-Convocation for Manchester, 1964–74; Mem., Gen. Synod, 1980–87. President: Soc. for Liturgical Study, 1998– (Chm., 1978–84); Societas Liturgica, 1987–89 (Treas. 1981–87); Mem., Liturgical Commn, 1968–86; Chm., Jt Liturgical Gp, 1989–94 (Mem., 1969–96; Sec., 1980–89); Mem., Cathedrals Fabric Commn, 1991–96. Chairman: Liverpool Luncheon Club, 1981–82; Alcuin Club, 1987–. CF (TA), 1958–67; CF (T&AVR), 1967–77; QHC, 1974–77. FRHistS 1988; FSA 2007. KStJ 2003. *Publications:* (contrib.) Worship and the Child, 1975; (contrib.) Getting the Liturgy Right, 1982; (contrib.) Liturgy Reshaped, 1982; (ed) Holy Week Services, 1983; Earth and Altar, 1986; (ed) The Word in Season, 1988; (contrib.) Towards Liturgy 2000, 1989; (contrib.) Liturgy for a New Century, 1990; Chaplain to Mr Speaker, 1991; Ronald Jasper: his life, his work and the ASB, 1997; (contrib.) They Shaped Our Worship, 1998; All Majesty and Power: royal prayers, 2000; Percy Dearmer, 2000; Memorial Services, 2002; (contrib.) Liturgy in a Postmodern World, 2003; (contrib.) St Paul's: the Cathedral Church of London, 2004; (contrib.) Oxford DNB, 2004; (contrib.) Strengthen For Service, 2005; (contrib.) Liturgical Renewal as a Way to Christian Unity, 2005; The 1927–28 Prayer Book Crisis, part i, 2005, part ii, 2006; (contrib.) The Oxford Handbook of English Literature & Theology, 2007. *Recreations:* watching cricket, reading modern poetry. *Address:* 3 Barn Hill Mews, Stamford, Lincs PE9 2GN. *T:* (01780) 765024, *Fax:* (01780) 756183. *Clubs:* Army and Navy; Athenæum (Pres., 1983–84), Artists' (Liverpool).

GRAY, Prof. Douglas, FBA 1989; J. R. R. Tolkien Professor of English Literature and Language, University of Oxford, 1980–97, now Emeritus; Professorial Fellow of Lady Margaret Hall, Oxford, 1980–97, now Hon. Fellow; *b* 17 Feb. 1930; *s* of Emmerson and Daisy Gray; *m* 1959, Judith Claire Campbell; one *s*. *Educ:* Wellington College, NZ; Victoria Univ. of Wellington (MA 1952); Merton Coll., Oxford (BA 1954, MA 1960). Asst Lecturer, Victoria Univ. of Wellington, 1952–54; Oxford University: Lectr, Pembroke and Lincoln Colls, 1956–61; Fellow, Pembroke Coll., 1961–80, now Emeritus; University Lectr in English Language, 1976–80. Mem. Council, EETS, 1981–2005; Pres., Soc. for Study of Mediæval Langs and Lit., 1982–86. De Carle Lectr, Univ. of Otago, 1989; M. M. Bhattacharya Lectr, Calcutta Univ., 1991. Hon. LitD Victoria Univ. of Wellington, 1995. *Publications:* (ed) Spenser, The Faerie Queene, Book 1, 1969; Themes and Images in the Medieval English Religious Lyric, 1972; (ed) A Selection of Religious

Lyrics, 1975; (part of) A Chaucer Glossary, 1979; Robert Henryson, 1979; (ed with E. G. Stanley): Middle English Studies presented to Norman Davis, 1983; Five Hundred Years of Words and Sounds for E. J. Dobson, 1983; (ed) The Oxford Book of Late Medieval Verse and Prose, 1985; (ed) J. A. W. Bennett, Middle English Literature, 1986; (ed jtly) From Anglo-Saxon to Early Middle English: studies presented to E. G. Stanley, 1994; Selected Poems of Robert Henryson and William Dunbar, 1998; (ed) The Oxford Companion to Chaucer, 2003; Later Medieval English Literature, 2008; articles on medieval literature. *Address:* Lady Margaret Hall, Oxford OX2 6QA; 31 Nethercote Road, Tackley, Oxon OX5 3AW.

GRAY, Dulcie; *see* Denison, D. W. C.

GRAY, (Edna) Eileen (Mary), CBE 1997 (OBE 1978); Chairman, 1990–2007, President, 2008, London Youth Games; *b* 25 April 1920; *d* of late William Thomas Greenaway and Alice Evelyn Mary (*née* Jenkins); *m* 1946, Walter Herbert Gray (*d* 2001); one *s*. *Educ:* St Saviour's and St Olave's Grammar Sch. for Girls, London. Inspectorate for Fighting Vehicles, 1940–45. Invited to ride for women's cycling team, in Copenhagen, 1946; campaigner for internat. recognition of women in cycling; Team Manager, GB team, inaugural World Championship for Women, Paris, 1958. Mem., Exec. Cttee, British Cycling Fedn, 1958–87 (Pres., 1973–86); Pres., Women's Cycle Racing Assoc., 1963–76; Mem., British Cycling Nat. Council. Vice-Pres., British Olympic Assoc., 1992– (Vice-Chm., 1988–92). Internat. Official, Commonwealth Games, Edmonton, 1978, and Brisbane, 1982. Mem., Kingston upon Thames BC, 1982–98 (Mayor of Kingston, 1990–91). Trustee, London Marathon Trust. Freeman, City of London, 1987. Olympic Order, IOC, 1993. *Address:* 129 Grand Avenue, Surbiton, Surrey KT5 9HY. *T:* (020) 8399 0068.

GRAY, Dr George Gowans, CBE 2000; FIMechE; Chairman, National Physical Laboratory, 1995–2002; *b* 21 Jan. 1938; *s* of Alexander Newlands Gray and Elizabeth Hunter Gray (*née* Gowans); *m* 1959, Grace Alicia Edmondson; one *s* two *d* (and one *s* decd). *Educ:* Linlithgow Acad.; Edinburgh Univ. (BSc Hons 1958); Corpus Christi Coll., Cambridge (PhD 1972). MIMechE 1972, FIMechE 1990. Engineer: Pratt & Whitney (Canada), 1960–63; RCA Ltd (Canada), 1963–69; Researcher, Univ. of Cambridge, 1969–71; Manager, 1972–74, Dir, 1974–87, RCA Ltd (UK); Chm., Serco Gp plc, 1987–99; Director: Misys plc, 1996–2002; Regus Business Centres plc, 1999–2002 (Chm., 2000–02). Member: Security Vetting Appeals Panel, 1997–; PPARC, 2003–05. Mem. Court and Council, Imperial Coll. London, 2004– (Dep. Chm., 2006–). *Publications:* papers in engrg jls. *Recreations:* walking, reading, golf, theatre. *Clubs:* Oxford and Cambridge; Wentworth Golf.

GRAY, George Thomas Alexander; First Legislative Counsel for Northern Ireland, since 1996; *b* 20 Jan. 1949; *s* of George Gray and Eveline Gray; *m* 1985, Mary Louise Gray; two *s*. *Educ:* Annadale Grammar Sch., Belfast; The Queen's University of Belfast (LLB 1st Cl. Hons). Called to the Bar of N Ireland; Draftsman, 1971–88, Second Legislative Counsel, 1988–96, Office of the Legislative Counsel for NI. *Recreation:* cricket. *Address:* Office of the Legislative Counsel, Parliament Buildings, Stormont, Belfast BT4 3SW. *T:* (028) 9052 1304.

GRAY, Prof. George William, CBE 1991; PhD; FRS 1983; FRSE; CChem, FRSC; Research Consultant; Emeritus Professor, University of Hull, since 1992; *b* 4 Sept. 1926; *s* of John William Gray and Jessie Colville (*née* Hunter); *m* 1953, Marjorie Mary (*née* Canavan); three *d*. *Educ:* Univ. of Glasgow (BSc); Univ. of London (PhD). CChem, FRSC 1972; FRSE 1989. Joined staff of Chem. Dept, Univ. of Hull, 1946; Sen. Lectr, 1960; Reader, 1964; Prof. of Organic Chem., 1978; G. F. Grant Prof. of Chem., 1984–90. Res. Co-ordinator, Merck Ltd (formerly BDH Ltd), 1990–93. Vis. Prof., Univ. of Southampton, 1990–2002; Vis. Sen. Fellow, DERA, 1999. For. Associate, Engrg Acad. of Japan, 1995; Hon. Mem., Internat. Liquid Crystal Soc., 1998. Hon. MRIA 2001. Hon. DSc: Hull, 1991; Nottingham Trent, 1994; Southampton, 1996; East Anglia, 1997; Aberdeen, 2001; Exeter, 2002. Clifford Paterson Prize Lectr, Royal Soc., 1985. Queen's Award for Technol Achievement, 1979; Rank Prize for Optoelectronics, 1980; Leverhulme Medal, Royal Soc., 1987; SCI Medallist, 1993; Kyoto Laureate, Inamori Foundn, 1995; Karl Ferdinand Braun Medal, Soc. for Inf. Display, 1996; Fréedericksz Medal, Russian Liquid Crystal Soc., 1997. Editor, Liquid Crystals, 1992–2002. *Publications:* Molecular Structure and the Properties of Liquid Crystals, 1962; (ed and jtly with P. A. Winsor) Liquid Crystals and Plastic Crystals, 1974; (ed jtly with G. R. Luckhurst) The Molecular Physics of Liquid Crystals, 1979; (with J. W. Goodby) Smectic Liquid Crystals – textures and structures, 1984; (ed) Thermotropic Liquid Crystals, 1987; (ed jtly) Handbook of Liquid Crystals, Vols 1–3, 1998; 360 pubns on liquid crystals in Jl Chem. Soc., Trans Faraday Soc., Phys. Rev., Molecular Cryst. and Liquid Cryst., Jl Chem. Phys., and Proc. IEEE. *Recreations:* gardening, philately. *Address:* Juniper House, Furzehill, Wimborne, Dorset BH21 4HD. *T:* (01202) 880164, *Fax:* (01202) 840702; *e-mail:* ggray83828@aol.com.

GRAY, Gilbert; QC 1971; a Recorder of the Crown Court, 1972–98; *b* 25 April 1928; *s* of late Robert Gray, JP, Scarborough, and of Mrs Elizabeth Gray; *m* 1954, Olga Dilys Gray (*née* Thomas), BA, JP; two *s* two *d*. *Educ:* Scarborough Boys' High Sch.; Leeds Univ. (LLB). Pres., Leeds Univ. Union. Called to the Bar, Gray's Inn, 1953; Bencher, 1979. Leader of NE Circuit, 1984–87. *Recreation:* sailing. *Address:* 3 Raymond Buildings, Gray's Inn, WC1R 5BH; Park Court Chambers, 16 Park Place, Leeds LS1 1SJ; Treasurer's House, York.

GRAY, (Hamish) Martin (Vincent); Chairman, The Evolution Group plc, since 2005; Director: Miller Insurance Services Ltd, 2001–07; Miller Investments Ltd, 2004–07; *b* 8 June 1946; *s* of Kenneth Dunwell Gray and Helen McGeorge Gray; *m*; two *s*; *m* 2nd, 1992, Alison Margaret Wells. *Educ:* Cockburn High Sch., Leeds. FCIB. Appts with National Westminster Bank, 1963–99; Head of Group Planning, Business Develt Div., 1986–88; Asst Gen. Manager, Group Develt, 1988–89; Gen. Manager, UK Branch Business, 1990–92; Chief Exec., UK Br. Business, later NatWest UK, 1992–98; Exec. Dir, Retail and Commercial Businesses and Main Bd Dir, 1993–99. Dir, Nat. Savings & Investments, 2005–. Chm., Mktg Adv. Cttee, England and Wales Cricket Bd, 2000–03. *Recreations:* walking, gardening, cricket. *Address:* The Evolution Group plc, 100 Wood Street, EC2V 7AN.

GRAY, Prof. Hanna Holborn, PhD; Harry Pratt Judson Distinguished Service Professor of History, University of Chicago, since 1993 (President, 1978–93, now President Emeritus); *b* 25 Oct. 1930; *d* of Hajo and Annemarie Holborn; *m* 1954, Charles Montgomery Gray. *Educ:* Bryn Mawr Coll., Pa (BA); Univ. of Oxford (Fulbright Schol.); Univ. of Harvard (PhD). Instructor, Bryn Mawr Coll., 1953–54; Harvard University: Teaching Fellow, 1955–57, Instr, 1957–59, Asst Prof., 1959–60, Vis. Lectr, 1963–64; Asst Prof., Univ. of Chicago, 1961–64, Associate Prof., 1964–72; Dean and Prof., Northwestern, Evanston, Ill, 1972–74; Provost, and Prof. of History, Yale Univ., 1974–78, Acting Pres., 1977–78. Hon. degrees include: LHD: Duke, 1982; Brandeis, 1983; Amer. Coll. of Greece, 1986; Univ. of Chicago, 1996; LLD: Dartmouth Coll., Yale, 1978; Brown, 1979; Rochester, Notre Dame, 1980; Michigan, 1981; Princeton, 1982; Georgetown, 1983; Columbia, 1987; Toronto, 1991; Harvard, 1995; DLitt: Oxford, 1979; Washington, 1985. Charles Frankel Prize, 1993; Centennial Medal, Harvard Univ. 1994; Dist. Service Award in Educn, Inst. of Internat. Educn, 1994; Fritz Redlich Dist. Alumni Award, Internat. Inst. of Educn, 2004; DL, Pontifical Inst. of Mediaeval Studies, Toronto, 2005. *Publications:* ed (with Charles M. Gray) Jl Modern History, 1965–70; articles in professional jls. *Address:* (office) 1126 E 59th Street, Chicago, IL 60637, USA. *T:* (773) 7027799. *Clubs:* Quadrangle (Chicago); Cosmopolitan (New York City).

GRAY, Rt Hon. Herb(ert Eser), CC 2003; PC 1969; Chairman, Canadian Section, International Joint Commission, since 2002; *b* 25 May 1931; *s* of Harry and Fannie Gray; *m* 1967, Sharon Sholzberg; one *s* one *d*. *Educ:* McGill Univ., Montreal; Osgoode Hall Law Sch., Toronto. Mem., Ontario Bar. MP (L) Windsor West, Canada, 1962–2002; Minister without Portfolio (Finance), 1969–70; of Nat. Revenue, 1970–72; of Consumer and Corporate Affairs, 1972–74; of Industry, Trade and Commerce, 1980–82; of Regl Econ. Expansion, 1982; Pres., Treasury Bd, 1982–84; Opposition House Leader, 1984–90; Dep. Leader of the Opposition, 1989–90, Leader, 1990–91; Finance Critic for Official Opposition, 1991–93; Solicitor Gen. and Leader of the Govt in H of C, 1993–97; Dep. Prime Minister of Canada, 1997–2002. *Address:* (office) 22nd Floor, 234 Laurier Avenue W, Ottawa, ON K1P 6K6, Canada.

GRAY, Iain Cumming; Member (Lab) East Lothian, Scottish Parliament, since 2007; *b* Edinburgh, 7 June 1957; *s* of Robert and Catherina Gray; *m* 1997, Gillianne (*née* McCormack); one *d*, and two step *d*. *Educ:* Inverness Royal Acad.; Edinburgh Univ. (BSc Hons). Physics teacher: Gracemount High Sch., Edin., 1978–82; Escola Agrária, Chokwe, Mozambique, 1982–83; Inveralmond High Sch., Livingston, 1983–86; Campaign Manager, OXFAM, Scotland, 1986–99. MSP (Lab) Edinburgh Pentlands, 1999–2003; contested same seat, 2003; Scottish Executive: Deputy Minister: for Community Care, 1999–2000; for Justice, 2000–01; Minister: for Social Justice, 2001–02; for Enterprise, Transport and Lifelong Learning, 2002–03. Special Advr to Sec. of State for Scotland, 2003–07. *Recreations:* football (season ticket, Hibernian FC), reading, hill-walking. *Address:* Scottish Parliament, Edinburgh EH99 1SP.

GRAY, (James Northey) David; Principal, Daniel Stewart's and Melville College, and Mary Erskine School, Edinburgh, since 2000; *b* 30 April 1955; *s* of Baron Gray of Contin, PC; *m* 1978, Lynda Harlow; one *s* two *d*. *Educ:* Fettes Coll.; Univ. of Bristol (BA Hons, PGCE). English teacher, Henbury Sch., Bristol, 1978–80; Partner, Key Lang. Sch., Athens, 1980–85; teacher, English and Modern Greek, Dulwich Coll., 1985–88; Hd of English, Leeds GS, 1988–92; Headmaster, Pocklington Sch., E Yorks, 1992–2000. *Recreations:* cricket, golf, cross-country running, music, Anglo-Saxon literature, Balkan current affairs. *Address:* Daniel Stewart's and Melville College, Queensferry Road, Edinburgh EH4 3EZ. *T:* (0131) 311 1000, *Fax:* (0131) 311 1099; *e-mail:* principal@esmgc.com.

GRAY, James Whiteside; MP (C) Wiltshire North, since 1997; *b* 7 Nov. 1954; *s* of Very Rev. John Rodger Gray, VRD, sometime Moderator, Gen. Assembly of C of S, and of Dr Sheila Gray; *m* 1980, Sarah Ann Beale (marr. diss. 2007); two *s* one *d*. *Educ:* Hillhead Primary Sch., Glasgow; Glasgow High Sch.; Glasgow Univ. (MA Hons); Christ Church, Oxford. Grad. mgt trainee, P&O, 1977–78; Shipbroker, Anderson Hughes & Co., 1978–84; Mem., Baltic Exchange, 1978–91, 1997–; Dir, Baltic Futures Exchange, 1989–91; Man. Dir, GNI Freight Futures, 1985–92; Special Advr to Sec. of State, DoE, 1992–95; Dir, Westminster Strategy Ltd, 1995–97. Dep. Chm., Wandsworth Tooting Cons. Assoc., 1994–96. Contested (C) Ross, Cromarty and Skye, 1992. An Opposition Whip, 2000–01; Opposition front bench spokesman on defence, 2001–02, on countryside, 2002–05; Shadow Sec. of State for Scotland, 2005. Member, Select Committee: on Envmtl Affairs, 1997–2000; on DEFRA, 2007–; Jt Chm., All-Party Minerals Gp, 1998–2000; Chairman: All-Party Multiple Sclerosis Gp, 2004–; All-Party Parly Gp for the Army, 2004–; Vice-Chm., All-Party Parly Gp on Deafness, 2004–07. Chm., Cons. Rural Action Gp, 2003–05; Cons. Defence and Foreign Affairs Policy Gp, 2006–07. Mem., UK Delegn, Council of Europe and WEU, 2007–. Chm., Horse and Pony Taxation Cttee, 1999–2002. Graduate, Armed Forces Parly Scheme, 1997–98, Post-grad. Scheme, 2001; rcds, 2003; Vis. Parly Fellow, St Antony's Coll., Oxford, 2005–06. Served HAC (TA), 1977–84 (Mem., Court of Assts, 2002–07); Vice-Pres., HAC Saddle Club. Vice-Chm., Charitable Properties Assoc., 2002–; President: Chippenham Br. Multiple Sclerosis Soc., 2000–06 (Patron, Devizes Br., 2007–); Assoc. of British Riding Schs, 2001–; Consultant, British Horse Industry Confedn, 1999–2002. Patron, Mutual Support, 2006–. Freeman, City of London, 1982. *Publications:* Financial Risk Management in the Shipping Industry, 1985; Futures and Options for Shipping, 1987 (Lloyds of London Book Prize); Shipping Futures, 1990; Crown vs Parliament: who decides on going to war (thesis), 2003. *Recreations:* countryside, riding horses. *Address:* House of Commons, SW1A 0AA. *T:* (020) 7219 6237. *Clubs:* Pratt's; Chippenham Constitutional (Pres., 1999–); Wootton Bassett Conservative.

See also *J. C. R. Gray.*

GRAY, Sir John (Archibald Browne), Kt 1973; MA, MB, ScD; FRS 1972; Member External Scientific Staff, MRC, 1977–83: working at Marine Biological Association Laboratory, Plymouth, 1977–93; *b* 30 March 1918; *s* of late Sir Archibald Gray, KCVO, CBE; *m* 1946, Vera Kathleen Mares; one *s* one *d*. *Educ:* Cheltenham Coll.; Clare Coll. Cambridge (Hon. Fellow, 1976); University Coll. Hospital. BA 1939; MA 1942; MB, BChir 1942; ScD 1962. Service Research for MRC, 1943–45; Surg. Lieut, RNVR, 1945–46; Scientific Staff of MRC at Nat. Inst. for Med. Research, 1946–52; Reader in Physiology, University Coll., London, 1952–58; Prof. of Physiology, University Coll. London, 1959–66; Medical Research Council: Second Sec., 1966–68; Sec., 1968–77. Dep. Chm., 1975–77. Chm., EC Cttee for Medical Res., 1972–76; Member of Council, Marine Biol Assoc., 1969–88 (Vice-Pres., 1988–); Freshwater Biol Assoc., 1981–88 (Pres. 1983–88; Chm. of Council, 1985–88; Vice-Pres., 1988–). QHP 1968–71. FIBiol; FRCP 1974. Hon. DSc Exeter, 1985. *Publications:* papers, mostly on sensory receptors and sensory nervous system, in Jl of Physiology, Procs of Royal Soc. series B, Jl of Marine Biol Assoc. etc. *Recreation:* painting. *Address:* Seaways, Kingsway, Kingsand, near Plymouth PL10 1NG. *T:* (01752) 822745.

GRAY, Sir (John Armstrong) Muir, Kt 2005; CBE 1998; MD; FRCP, FRCPSGlas, FFPH; Programmes Director, UK National Screening Committee, since 1995, and Director of Clinical Knowledge, Process and Safety, Department of Health, since 2004; *b* 21 June 1944; *yr s* of late John Gray and Nancie Gray (*née* Armstrong); *m* 1974, Jacqueline Elizabeth Rosenthal; two *d*. *Educ:* Jordanhill Coll. Sch.; Univ. of Glasgow (MB, ChB 1969; MD 1981); Univ. of Bristol (DPH 1973). FFPH (FFPHM 1984); MRCGP 1985; FRCPSGlas 1989; FRCP 1993. House surgeon, Western Infirmary, Glasgow, 1966–70; Sen. House Officer, Aberdeen, 1970–71; SMO, City of Oxford, 1972–74; Public Health Specialist, Oxfordshire HA, 1974–91; Dir, Health Policy and Public Health, Oxford RHA, 1991–94; Dir of R&D, Anglia and Oxford RHA, then Anglia and Oxford Reg. Office, NHS Exec., DoH, 1994–98; Dir, Inst. of Health Scis, Univ. of Oxford

1999–2002. Fellow, Green Coll., Oxford, 1984–94, Fellow Emeritus, 1994. Co-ordinator: Nat. Breast Cancer Screening Prog., 1988–91; Nat. Cervical Screening Prog., 1988–94. Advr, WHO, 1984–91. Hon. DSc UEA 1998. *Publications:* Man Against Disease, 1979; Take Care of Your Elderly Relative, 1980; Football Injuries, 1981; Prevention of Diseases in the Elderly, 1985; Evidence Based Healthcare, 1996; The Resourceful Patient, 2002; articles in med., epidemiology and public health jls. *Recreations:* reading, ornithology, linguistics, combating the effects of biological ageing. *Address:* 59 Lakeside, Oxford OX2 8JQ. *T:* (01865) 554066.

GRAY, (John) Charles (Rodger), CMG 2003; HM Diplomatic Service; HM Marshal of the Diplomatic Corps, since 2008; *b* 12 March 1953; *s* of Very Rev. John Rodger Gray, VRD, sometime Moderator, Gen. Assembly of C of S, and of Dr Sheila M. Gray (*née* Whiteside); *m* 1988, Anne-Marie Lucienne Suzanne, *d* of Marquis and Marquise de Dax d'Axat, Paris; three *s*. *Educ:* High Sch. of Glasgow; Glasgow Univ. (MA). Entered HM Diplomatic Service, 1974; W Africa Dept, FCO, 1974; Polish lang. trng, 1975; Third, later Second, Sec., Warsaw, 1976–79; Eastern European and Soviet Dept, FCO, 1979–83; First Sec., UK Delegn, OECD, Paris, 1983–87; Seconded Assessments Staff, Cabinet Office, 1987–89; Foreign and Commonwealth Office: Deputy Head: Central African Dept, 1989; Central European Dept, 1989–92; Hd, Eastern Adriatic Dept, 1992–93; Counsellor and Hd of Chancery, Jakarta, 1993–96; Fellow, Centre for Internat. Affairs, Harvard Univ., 1996–97; Counsellor, Washington, 1997–2002; Hd, ME Dept, FCO, 2002–04; Iran Coordinator, FCO, 2004–05; Ambassador to Morocco, 2005–08. *Recreation:* history. *Address:* Ambassadors' Court, St James's Palace, SW1A 1BL; *e-mail:* charles.gray@royal.gsx.gov.uk. *Club:* New (Edinburgh).
See also J. W. Gray.

GRAY, Prof. John Clinton, PhD; Professor of Plant Molecular Biology, since 1996, and Head, Department of Plant Sciences, since 2003, University of Cambridge; Fellow, Robinson College, Cambridge, since 1977; *b* 9 April 1946; *s* of William John Gray and Edith Grace Gray (*née* Tooke); *m* 1971, Julia Hodgetts; one *s* one *d*. *Educ:* Sir Joseph Williamson's Mathematical Sch., Rochester; Simon Langton Grammar Sch., Canterbury; Univ. of Birmingham (BSc 1967; PhD 1970); MA Cantab 1977. Res. Fellow, Univ. of Birmingham, 1970–73; Res. Biochemist, UCLA, 1973–75; University of Cambridge: SRC Res. Fellow, 1975–76; Demonstrator, 1976–80; Lectr, 1980–90; Reader in Plant Molecular Biol., 1990–96. Nuffield Foundn Sci. Res. Fellow, 1983–84; Royal Soc. Leverhulme Trust Res. Fellow, 1991–92. Non-exec. Dir, Horticulture Res. Internat., 1997–2003. Member: SERC Biol Scis Cttee, 1990–93; EMBO, 1994–; Council, Sainsbury Lab., 1999–. Plant Sci. Advr, Gatsby Charitable Foundn, 1996–. Trustee, Sci. and Plants for Schs, 1991–. Mem., Midlands Assoc. of Mountaineers, 1967–. *Publications:* (ed with R. J. Ellis) Ribulose Bisphosphate Carboxylase-Oxygenase, 1986; (ed with D. L. Hallahan) Plant Trichomes, 2000; papers in scientific jls. *Recreations:* growing plants, mountains. *Address:* Department of Plant Sciences, University of Cambridge, Downing Street, Cambridge CB2 3EA. *T:* (01223) 333925; Robinson College, Grange Road, Cambridge CB3 9AN; 47 Barrons Way, Comberton, Cambridge CB3 7EQ. *T:* (01223) 263325.

GRAY, John Malcolm, CBE 1996; Chairman, Hongkong and Shanghai Banking Corporation Ltd, 1993–96; *b* 28 July 1934; *s* of Samuel Gray and Christina (*née* Mackay-Sim); *m* 1984, Ursula Siong Koon; three *d*. *Educ:* Strathallan Sch., Scotland. With Hongkong and Shanghai Banking Corp. Ltd, 1952–96; Dep. Chm., Harvey Nichols Gp, 1996–2002. Dir, World Maritime Ltd, Bermuda, 1984–2004. Chm., Hong Kong Port Develt Bd, 1990–96. MEC, Hong Kong, 1993–95; Mem., Governor's Business Council, Hong Kong, 1993–96. *Recreations:* reading, golf. *Clubs:* Hong Kong (Hong Kong); Penang (Malaysia).

GRAY, Prof. John Michael, DPhil; FBA 2000; Professor of Education, University of Cambridge, since 2001; *b* 25 March 1948; *s* of Ronald Gray and Patricia Gray (*née* Martin); *m* 1st, 1977, Susan Lendrum (marr. diss. 1985); one *d*; 2nd, 2005, Prof. Jean Rudduck (*d* 2007). *Educ:* Exeter Coll., Oxford (BA); Harvard Univ. (EdM); Sussex Univ. (PGCE, DPhil 1976). Asst to Dir, Shelter, 1966–67; Res. Asst, Harvard Univ., 1970–72; teacher, ILEA, 1974–75; Res. Fellow, Edinburgh Univ., 1975–79; Sheffield University: Lectr, 1979–84; Reader, 1984–86; Prof., 1987–93; Jt Dir, Qualitative and Quantative Studies, Educn Res. Gp, 1988–93; Res. Co-ordinator Social Scis, 1989–93; Dir of Res., Homerton Coll., Cambridge, 1994–2001. Vis. Prof., Inst. of Educn, Univ. of London, 1996–2000. Mem., Res. Adv. Cttee, DfES, 2002–06. Mem. Cttees, 1985–96, Chm., Wkg Party on Future of Educnl Res., 1992, ESRC. Mem. Bd and Chm., Res. Cttee, TTA, 1997–2000; Chairman: Standards Cttee, Oxford, Cambridge and RSA Exams Bd, 2001–; Syndic of Cambridge Assessment, 2001–. *Publications:* jointly: Reconstructions of Secondary Education, 1983; Elton Enquiry into School Discipline, 1989; National Youth Cohort Study of England and Wales (1988–94), Good School, Bad School, 1995; Merging Traditions, 1996; Inspecting Schools, 1996; Gender and Educational Performance, 1998; Improving Schools, 1999; Quality and Equity in European Education, 2004; Schools on the Edge, 2006. *Address:* Homerton College, Cambridge CB2 2PH. *T:* (01223) 767649.

GRAY, Prof. John Nicholas, DPhil; Professor of European Thought, London School of Economics and Political Science, 1998–2007; Emeritus Professor, University of London, since 2008; *b* 17 April 1948; *s* of Nicholas Chatt Wardle Gray and Joan Gray (*née* Bushby); *m* 1988, Mieko Kawai. *Educ:* South Shields Grammar-Technical Sch. for Boys; Exeter Coll., Oxford (BA Hons 1971; MA 1976; DPhil 1978). Lectr in Political Theory, Univ. of Essex, 1973–76; Fellow and Tutor in Politics, Jesus Coll., Oxford, 1976–98; Prof. of Politics, Univ. of Oxford, 1996–98. Vis Prof. in Govt, Harvard Univ., 1986; Olmsted Vis. Prof. in Social Philosophy, Yale Univ., 1994. DUniv Open, 2006. *Publications:* Mill on Liberty: a defence, 1983, 2nd edn 1996; Hayek on Liberty, 1984, 3rd edn 1998; Liberalism, 1986, 2nd edn 1995; Liberalisms: essays in political philosophy, 1989; Post-liberalism: studies in political thought, 1993; Beyond the New Right: markets, government and the common culture, 1993; Enlightenment's Wake: politics and culture at the close of the modern age, 1995; Isaiah Berlin, 1995; Endgames: questions in late modern political thought, 1997; Voltaire and Enlightenment, 1998; False Dawn: the delusions of global capitalism, 1998, 3rd edn 2002; Two Faces of Liberalism, 2000; Straw Dogs: thoughts on humans and other animals, 2002; Al Qaeda and What It Means To Be Modern, 2003, 2nd edn 2007; Heresies: against progress and other illusions, 2004; (contrib.) The Political Theory of John Gray, 2007; Black Mass: apocalyptic religion and the death of Utopia, 2007. *Recreations:* reading, films, music. *Address:* c/o Tracy Bohan, The Wylie Agency, 17 Bedford Square, WC1B 3JA; *e-mail:* tbohan@wylieagency.co.uk. *Club:* Beefsteak.

GRAY, Kenneth Walter, CBE 1992; PhD; FREng; FInstP, FIET; Chairman, Ocean Blue Software, since 2006; *b* 20 March 1939; *s* of late Robert W. Gray and Ruby M. Gray; *m* 1962, Jill Henderson (marr. diss. 2006); two *s* one *d*. *Educ:* Blue Coat Sch.; Univ. of Wales (BSc, PhD). FInstP 1991; FIET (FIEE 1992); FREng (FEng 1996). Research on magnetic resonance, as Nat. Res. Council of Canada post-doctoral Fellow, Univ. of British Columbia, Vancouver, 1963–65; research on semiconductor devices and on radiometry, N American Rockwell Science Center, Thousand Oaks, Calif, 1965–70; research on devices and systems at Royal Signals and Radar Estabt, 1971; Supt Solid State Physics and Devices Div., 1976; Head of Physics Group, 1979; RCDS 1981; Royal Signals and Radar Establishment: CSO, MoD, Dep. Dir (Applied Physics), 1982–84; Under Sec., Dep. Dir (Information Systems), 1984; Dir of Res., 1984–86, Technical Dir, 1986–96, THORN EMI plc; Technical Dir, EMI Group plc, Aug.–Dec. 1996; Exec. Chm., Thorn Software, 1987–89; Technical Dir, Thorn Security and Electronics, 1991–93; Man. Dir, Thorn Transaction, 1993–96. Chairman: Scipher plc, 1996–2004; London Biofuels, 2006–08; non-exec. Dir, British Steel, 1995–99. Visiting Research Fellow: Univ. of Newcastle, 1972–74; Univ. of Leeds, 1976–; Vis. Prof., Univ. of Nottingham, 1986–. Member: DTI Innovation Adv. Bd, 1988–93; SERC, 1991–94; Technology Foresight Steering Cttee, OST, 1993–97; HEFCW, 1996–2002. Hon. DSc Nottingham Trent, 1998. *Publications:* over 30 scientific and technical papers in various learned jls. *Recreations:* tennis, bridge.

GRAY, Kevin Adrian; a District Judge (Magistrates' Courts) (formerly Stipendiary Magistrate), Essex, since 1995; *b* 12 Oct. 1947; *s* of Kenneth Thomas Gray and Gladys Gray; *m* 1st, 1971 (marr. diss.); one *s* one *d*; 2nd, 2005, Anita Poole. *Educ:* Portsmouth Southern Grammar Sch.; Kingston Poly. (LLB Hons). Police Officer, Portsmouth City Police, later Hampshire Constabulary, 1964–71; admitted Solicitor, 1976; Sen. Partner, Gray Purdue & Co., 1977–90; sole practitioner, 1990–92; Partner, Gregsons, 1993–94; Acting Metropolitan Stipendiary Magistrate, 1993–95. *Recreations:* clay shooting, walking, cookery, fishing. *Address:* c/o Southend Magistrates' Court, 80 Victoria Avenue, Southend-on-Sea, Essex SS2 6EU. *T:* (office) (01245) 313300.

GRAY, Prof. Kevin John, PhD, LLD, DCL; FBA 1999; Professor of Law, University of Cambridge, since 1993; Fellow, 1981–90 and since 1993, and Dean, 2004–05 and since 2006, Trinity College, Cambridge; *b* 23 July 1951; *s* of late Bryce Holmes Gray, Belfast, and Priscilla Margaret Gray (*née* McCullough), Lisburn; *m* 1996, Susan, *d* of late Arthur Walter David Francis and Helen Francis (*née* Waggott). *Educ:* Trinity Hall, Cambridge (BA 1972 (1st Cl. Law Tripos Parts I and II); MA, PhD 1976; Yorke Prize, 1977; LLD 1991); DCL Oxford, 1994. Called to the Bar, Middle Temple, 1993. University of Cambridge: Jt Coll. Lectr, Queens' and Trinity Colls, 1975–77; Fellow, Queens' Coll., 1975–81; Asst Lectr and Lectr in Law, 1978–90; Univ. Advocate, 1986–88; Res. Fellow, ANU, 1990; Drapers' Prof. of Law, QMW, Univ. of London, 1991–93. Vis. Fellow, ANU, 1979, 1989, 1998, 2005–06; Sen. Vis. Res. Fellow, St John's Coll., Oxford, 1993–94; Leverhulme Trust Major Res. Fellow, 2008–; Visiting Professor: Grad. Sch. of Law, Univ. of Osaka, 2001; Univ. of NSW, 2003; Univ. of Stellenbosch, 2005 and 2008; Univ. of Tasmania, 2006; Nat. Univ. of Singapore, 2006, 2007, 2008. Associate Mem., Acad. Internat. de Droit Comparé, 1995; Overseas Res. Fellow, Nat. Res. Foundn of SA, 2005. Member: Access, Conservation and Envmt Gp (formerly Access and Conservation Cttee), British Mountaineering Council, 2002–; AHRC (formerly AHRB) Peer Rev. Coll., 2004–07. Jun. and sen. internat. athlete, 1968–69. *Publications:* Reallocation of Property on Divorce, 1977; Elements of Land Law, 1987, 5th edn (with S. F. Gray) 2008; (with S. F. Gray) Land Law, 1999, 5th edn 2007; other books and articles on law, legal theory, human rights, and the envmt. *Recreations:* mountaineering, rock climbing. *Address:* Trinity College, Cambridge CB2 1TQ. *T:* (01223) 314520.

GRAY, Linda Esther, (Mrs Peter McCrorie); retired as opera singer, now teaching; *b* 29 May 1948; *d* of James and Esther Gray; *m* 1971, Peter McCrorie; one *d*. *Educ:* Greenock Academy; Royal Scottish Academy of Music and Drama. Cinzano Scholarship, 1969; Goldsmith Schol., 1970; James Caird Schol., 1971; Kathleen Ferrier Award, 1972; Christie Award, 1972. London Opera Centre, 1969–71; Glyndebourne Festival Opera, 1972–75; Scottish Opera, 1974–79; Welsh Opera, 1980; English National Opera, 1979; American début, 1981; Royal Opera House: Sieglinde, 1982; Fidelio, 1983. Records: Tristan und Isolde, 1981; Wagner's Die Feen, 1983. Principal rôles: Isolde, Sieglinde, Kundry (Wagner); Tosca (Puccini); Fidelio (Beethoven). *Publication:* A Life Behind Curtains (autobiog.), 2007. *Recreations:* cooking, swimming. *Address:* 35 Green Lane, New Malden, Surrey KT3 5BX.

GRAY, Margaret Caroline, MA Cantab; Headmistress, Godolphin and Latymer School, 1963–73; *b* 25 June 1913; *d* of Rev. A. Herbert Gray, DD, and Mrs Gray (Mary C. Dods, *d* of Principal Marcus Dods of New Coll., Edinburgh). *Educ:* St Mary's Hall, Brighton; Newnham Coll., Cambridge. Post graduate fellowship to Smith Coll., Mass, USA, 1935–36. Asst History mistress, Westcliff High Sch. for Girls, 1937–38; Head of History Dept, Mary Datchelor Girls' Sch., Camberwell, 1939–52; Headmistress, Skinners' Company's Sch., Stamford Hill, 1952–63. Chm., Nat. Advisory Centre on Careers for Women, 1970–91. Governor: Francis Holland Schs, 1974–99; Hampton Sch., 1976–88; West Heath Sch., Sevenoaks, 1974–89; Unicorn Sch., Kew, 1974–89; Chm. of Trustees, Godolphin and Latymer Bursary Fund, 1976–. Hon. Sec., IndependentAge (formerly RUKBA), Kingston-upon-Thames, 1973–. Elder, St John's Wood URC, 1960–. *Recreations:* gardening, motoring, walking. *Address:* 1 Ennerdale Road, Kew, Richmond TW9 3PG. *T:* (020) 8940 4439.

GRAY, Martin; *see* Gray, H. M. V.

GRAY, Ven. Martin Clifford; Archdeacon of Lynn, since 1999; *b* 19 Jan. 1944; *s* of John Oscar Gray and Lilian Annie Bertha Gray; *m* 1966, Pauline Jean Loader; three *s*. *Educ:* West Ham Coll. of Technology (DipChemEng; AWHCT 1967); Westcott House, Cambridge. Process Engineer, May & Baker, Norwich, 1968–70; Process Engr, Plant Supt, Project Manager, 1970–78, Dow Chemical, Kings Lynn, Norfolk and Bilbao, Spain. Deacon 1980, priest 1981; Asst Curate, St Faith's, Gaywood, Kings Lynn, 1980–84; Vicar, St Peter's, Sheringham, 1984–94; Rector, Lowestoft St Margaret Team Ministry, Suffolk, 1994–99. *Recreations:* golf, hill-walking. *Address:* Holly Tree House, Whitwell Road, Sparham, Norfolk NR9 5PN.

GRAY, Lt-Gen. Sir Michael Stuart, KCB 1986; OBE 1970; DL; Lieutenant of the Tower of London, 1995–98; Chairman, MS&P (Rosedale) Ltd, incorporating Milburn Arms Hotel, Rosedale Abbey, N Yorkshire, 2003–08; *b* Beverley, E Yorkshire, 3 May 1932; *e s* of Lieut Frank Gray, RNVR (killed in action 1940), and Joan Gray (*née* Gibson); *m* 1958, Juliette Antonia Noon, Northampton; two *s* one *d*. *Educ:* Beverley Grammar Sch.; Christ's Hosp., Horsham; RMA Sandhurst. FCMI; FInstD; FICFM. Enlisted RA, 1950; commissioned E Yorkshire Regt, 1952; served Malaya; transf. to Parachute Regt, 1955; served Cyprus, Suez, Jordan, Greece, Bahrain, Aden, N Ireland; sc Camberley, 1963; BM HQ 44 Para Bde Gp TA, 1964–65; Co. Comd 2 Para, 1965–66; MoD (MOI), 1967–69; commanded 1st Bn Parachute Regt, 1969–71; DS Staff Coll., Camberley, 1971–73; Col GS 1 Div. BAOR, 1973–75; RCDS 1976; last Comdr 16 Para Bde, 1977; Comdr 6 Field Force and COMUKMF, 1977–79; Comdr British Army Staff and Mil. Attaché, Washington, 1979–81 (Mil. Advr to Gov. of Bermuda; Mem., UN Mil. Cttee, NY), and Head of British Def. Staff and Def. Attaché, Washington, 1981; GOC SW Dist, and Maj.-Gen., UKMF(L), 1981–83; COS, HQ BAOR, 1984–85; GOC SE Dist and Comdr Jt Force HQ, 1985–88, retd. Dep. Col Comdt, Parachute Regt, 1986–90, Col Comdt, 1990–93. Hon. Colonel: 10 Para (V), 1984–88; 250 (Hull) Field Amb. RAMC

(V), 1991–99. Consultant, Brittany Ferries (wrote Battlefield Tours audio tapes of Pegasus Trail, 1989 and British D-Day Trail, 1994), 1988–96; Defence Industries Advr, Airborne Systems, IRVIN-GQ Ltd (formerly Wardle Storeys plc), 1989–2007; Chm., IRVIN-GQ Parachute Museum Ltd, 2007–. Dir and Co. Sec., Chesterford Wealth Mgt Gp, 2000–. Chm., Airborne Assault Normandy Trust (AAN), to preserve the history of 6 AB Division in Normandy, 1972–; Pres. d'Honneur, Assoc. Franco Britannique de gestion de la Batterie de Merville, 1986–; Citoyen d'honneur, Merville-Franceville Plage, 2007; Trustee: AB Forces Security Fund, 1986–2007; AB Forces Charities (formerly AB Forces Charities Develt Trust), 1990–2000 (Chm., 1990–94); Pres., York Br., 1991–, Vice Pres., NI Br. and Tyneside Br., 2000–, Parachute Regt Assoc.; Vice Pres., Army Parachute Assoc. (Free Fall), 1987– (Pres., 1981–87); Normandy Veterans Association: Vice-Pres., Goole Br., 1988–; Pres., Leeds Br., 1991–; Pres., Grimsby Br., 1995–; Pres., E Yorks Cttee, King George's Fund for Sailors, 2000– (Chm., 1988–2000); Mem., Amicable Soc. of Blues, 1989– (Pres., 2007); Patron: Combined Ex-Service Assoc., Bridlington, 1988–; Yorks Air Mus., Elvington, 1999–; Normandy MN Meml Fund, 2002–05; Pres., Dover & Dist MN Meml Fund, 2007–. Mem. Council, 2001–04, Dep. Patron, 2004–05, BESO. Chairman: Thelma Turner Homes Ltd, 1996–2001; Thelma Turner Charitable Trust, 1998–2002. Hon. Brother, Trinity House, Hull, 2000–. Freeman, City of London, 1983. DL ER of Yorks, 1997. Officier, Légion d'Honneur (France), 1994. *Recreations:* military history, gardening, DIY, photography, painting. *Address:* The Old Forge, Canal Head, Pocklington, York YO42 1NW. *Club:* Army and Navy.

GRAY, Morag Graham, MBE 2005; Independent Director, British Horseracing Authority, since 2007; Director, Black and White Communication (Scotland) Ltd, since 2004; *b* 12 Oct. 1962; *d* of Bill and Mary Chalmers; *m* 1993, Nigel Gray (marr. diss. 1998); partner, Angus Crichton-Miller. *Educ:* Lanark Grammar Sch.; Univ. of Strathclyde (BA 1983). Product Manager, British Telecom, 1983–88; Clerk of the Course, Scottish Racing, 1988–90; Planning Exec., 1990–97, Racing Dir, 1997–2000, Racecourse Assoc.; Chief Exec., Hamilton Park Racecourse, 2000–04; Dir, Racecourse Assoc., 2002–04. Mem. Council, Strathclyde Business Sch., 2004–. *Recreations:* horseracing, Scottish Rugby, fitness, food. *Address:* c/o British Horseracing Authority, 151 Shaftesbury Avenue, WC2H 8AL; *e-mail:* morag@blackandwhite.uk.com.

GRAY, Sir Muir; *see* Gray, Sir J. A. M.

GRAY, Muriel Janet, (Mrs H. Barbour); presenter and broadcaster; *b* 30 Aug. 1958; *d* of Adam and Elizabeth Gray; *m* 1991, Hamish Barbour; two *s* one *d. Educ:* Glasgow Sch. of Art (BA Hons Graphic Design). Asst Hd of Design, Mus. of Antiquities, Edinburgh, 1980–83; presenter and broadcaster, 1982–: *television* includes: The Tube, The Media Show, Design Awards, Art is Dead, The Munro Show, The Snow Show; *radio* includes: Start the Week, Whatever Gets You Through, various progs for Radio Scotland; newspaper and magazine columnist, including: Time Out, Sunday Mirror, Sunday Correspondent, Scotland on Sunday, Sunday Herald. Rector, Edinburgh Univ., 1988–91. *Publications:* The First Fifty, 1991; The Trickster, 1994; Furnace, 1997; The Ancient, 2001; Kelvingrove: portal to the world, 2006. *Recreations:* growing trees, mountaineering, chess, snow boarding, horror cinema. *Address:* IWC Media, St George's Studios, 93–97 St George's Road, Glasgow G3 6JA. *T:* (0141) 353 3222, *Fax:* (0141) 353 3221.

GRAY, Paul Edward, ScD; Chairman of the Corporation, 1990–97, Hon. Chairman and President Emeritus, 1997–2003, Massachusetts Institute of Technology; *b* 7 Feb. 1932; *s* of Kenneth Frank Gray and Florence (*née* Gilleo); *m* 1955, Priscilla Wilson King; one *s* three *d. Educ:* Massachusetts Inst. of Technol. (SB 1954, SM 1955, ScD 1960). Served Army, 1955–57 (1st Lieut). Massachusetts Institute of Technology: Mem., Faculty of Engrg, 1960–71, 1990–2007; Class of 1922 Prof. of Electrical Engrg, 1968–71; Dean, Sch. of Engrg, 1970–71; Chancellor, 1971–80; Pres., 1980–90; Mem., 1971–2007 (now Life Mem. Emeritus) of Corp. Emeritus Trustee, Museum of Science, Boston; Life Trustee, Wheaton Coll., Mass. Fellow, Amer. Acad. of Arts and Sciences; Member: National Acad. of Engrg (Treas., 1994–2001); Mexican National Acad. of Engrg; Life Fellow, IEEE. *Address:* c/o Massachusetts Institute of Technology, 77 Massachusetts Avenue, Cambridge, MA 02139, USA; 100 Memorial Drive, Apt 11–4A, Cambridge, MA 02142, USA.

GRAY, Paul Lucas, DPhil; Managing Director, Public Service Solutions Ltd; *b* 20 Jan. 1957; *s* of Alfred N. Gray and Doris J. Gray (*née* Hutchens); *m* 1982, Patricia Ann Wright (marr. diss. 2005). *Educ:* Univ. of Durham (BA Hons); Univ. of Birmingham (DPhil). Lectr, 1980–84, Sen. Lectr and Asst Principal, 1984–86, Merseyside; Sen. Educn Officer, Cambs CC, 1986–90; Dep. Chief Educn Officer, Devon CC, 1990–96; Dir of Educn, Surrey CC, 1996–2006. Chm., QCA Curriculum and Assessment Cttee, 1999–. Mem. Bd, Nat. Youth Agency, 1999–. Freeman, City of London, 2004. FRSA 1997. *Recreations:* sport, music, literature, sailing. *Address:* 22 Falconhurst, The Crescent, Surbiton, Surrey KT6 4BP. *T:* (020) 8390 3839.

GRAY, Paul Richard Charles, CB 2000; Chairman, HM Revenue and Customs, 2006–07 (Deputy Chairman, 2004–06); *b* 2 Aug. 1948; *s* of Rev. Sidney Gray and Ina (*née* Maxey); *m* 1972, Lynda Elsie Braby; two *s. Educ:* Wyggeston Boys' Sch., Leicester; LSE (BSc Econ 1969). Dept of Econ. Affairs, 1969; HM Treasury, 1969–77; with Booker McConnell Ltd, 1977–79; HM Treasury: Principal, 1979–83; Asst Sec., 1984–87; Econ. Affairs Private Sec. to Prime Minister, 1988–90; Under Sec., Monetary Gp, 1990–93; Dir, Personnel and Support Services, 1994–95; Dir, Budget and Public Finances, 1995–98; Hd of Policy Gp, DSS, 1998–99; Gp Dir, Children, Pensioners and Disabled, DSS, subseq. DWP, 1999–2001; Man. Dir, Pensions and Disability, 2001–04, Second Permanent Sec., 2002, DWP. Dir (non-exec.), Laing Management Ltd, 1993–95. *Recreations:* family, walking, Wensleydale sheep.

GRAY, Paul Shapter, FRSC; Director, Environment and Climate and Marine Science and Technology Programme, European Commission, 1992–97; *b* 18 Sept. 1932; *s* of Frederick Archibald and Vera Emma Gray; *m* 1958, Diane Lillian Platt; one *s* one *d* (and one *s* decd). *Educ:* St Chad's Coll., Wolverhampton; Birmingham Univ. (BSc Hons; MSc). FRSC (FRIC 1967). Chief Chemist, Midland Tar Distillers, 1954–57; Sen. Research Fellow, Ministry of Power, 1957–59; Head of Div., Reactor Chemistry, UKAEA, Winfrith, 1959–63; Ops Controller, OECD DRAGON (high temp. gas cooled reactor expt), 1963–73; European Commission, 1973–97: Dep. Head of Div., Elimination of Technical Barriers to Trade, 1977–81; Head of Service, Wood, Paper and Construction Industries, 1981–83; Head of Div., Food Law and Food Trade, 1983–91; Advr for industrial aspects of biotechnology, 1991–92. Sci. Advr, European Assoc. for Global Ocean Observing System, 1996–2001; Mem., Sci. Cttee, Royal Inst. for sustainable mgt of natural resources and promotion of clean technols, Belgium, 1997–; Royal Society of Chemistry: Member: Council, 2004–05; Prof. Affairs Bd, 2005–07; Pres., Belgium Section, 2005–. Hon. DSc Birmingham, 1999. *Publications:* jointly: Radionuclides in the Food Chain, 1988; Chernobyl, 1991; EU Committees as Influential Policymakers, 1998; Food Safety Regulation, 1999; numerous pubns in scientific and economic jls. *Recreations:* music, singing, sailing, playwriting, gardening.

GRAY, Prof. Peter, MA, PhD, ScD (Cantab); FRS 1977; CChem, FRSC; Master 1988–96, now Life Fellow, Gonville and Caius College, Cambridge; *b* Newport, 25 Aug. 1926; *er s* of late Ivor Hicks Gray and Rose Ethel Gray; *m* 1st, 1952, Barbara Joan Hume PhD (*d* 1992), 2nd *d* of J. B. Hume, London; two *s* two *d*; 2nd, 1996, Rachel Katharine *d* of late P. A. Buxton, FRS, and *widow* of C. Herzig, CBE. *Educ:* Newport High Sch. Gonville and Caius Coll., Cambridge (Major Schol., 1943; Prizeman, 1944, 1945 and 1946; BA 1st cl. hons Nat. Sci. Tripos, 1946; Dunlop Res. Student, 1946; PhD 1949; ScD 1963). Ramsay Meml Fellow, 1949–51; Fellow, Gonville and Caius Coll., 1949–53; ICI Fellow, 1951; University Demonstrator in Chem. Engrg, University of Cambridge 1951–55; Physical Chemistry Dept, University of Leeds: Lectr, 1955; Reader, 1959; Prof 1962; Head of Dept, 1965–88; Chm., Bd of Combined Faculties of Science and Applied Science, 1972–74; Hon. Vis. Prof., 1988–2001; University of Cambridge: Chm., Faculty of Engrg, 1989–94; Mem., Council of Senate, 1990–96; Mem., Financial Bd, 1991–94 Gauss Prof., Univ. of Göttingen, 1979, 1986; Visiting Professor: Univ. of BC, 1958–59 Univ. of W Ont., 1969; Macquarie Univ., 1980; Beijing Univ. of Technol., 1984; Univ of Paris, 1986; Calabria Univ., 1988; Lectures: H. C. Hottel, Orléans, 1990; Pierre Bruylants, Louvain, 1994; Larmor, Cambridge, 1995; Visitor, Fire Res. Orgn, 1984–90 (G. R. Nice Lectr, 1989). Mem. Council: Faraday Soc., 1965 (Vice-Pres., 1970–83 1985–95; Treasurer, 1973; Pres., 1983–85); Chemical Soc., 1969. Pres., Cambridge Phil Soc., 1992–93. Chairman: Schiff Foundn, 1989–95; Oppenheimer Fund, 1988–95 Trustee, Edward Boyle Meml Trust, 1989–98; Mem. Adv. Council, Ramsay Meml Fellowship Trust, 1982–2002. Hon. DSc Leeds, 1997. Meldola Medal, Royal Inst. Chem. 1956; Marlow Medal, Faraday Soc., 1959; B. Lewis Gold Medal, Combustion Inst., 1978 Award for Combustion, Royal Soc. of Chemistry, 1986; Italgas Prize for Chemistry, 1988 Associate Editor, Royal Society, 1983–97; Member, Editorial Board: Combustion and Flame, 1976–82; Dynamics and Stability of Systems, 1986–; Jl of Non equilibrium Thermodynamics, 1990–95; Discrete Dynamics in Nature & Soc., 1995–; Internat. Jl of Discrete Chaotic Dynamics, 1995–. *Publications:* (with S. K. Scott) Chemical Oscillations and Instabilities, 1990; (ed with S. K. Scott and G. Nicolis) Spatial Inhomogeneities and Transient Behaviour in Chemical Kinetics, 1990; (with J. M. T Thompson) Chaos and Dynamical Complexity, 1990; (with J. E. Field) Energetic Materials, 1992; numerous papers on phys. chem. subjects in scientific jls. *Recreation:* hill walking. *Address:* Gonville and Caius College, Cambridge CB2 1TA. *T:* (01223) 332478, *Fax:* (01223) 332456; 2 Fendon Close, Cambridge CB1 7RU. *T:* (01223) 212660.

GRAY, Peter Francis; Chairman, Gray & Co., since 1987; *b* 7 Jan. 1937; *s* of Rev. George Francis Selby Gray; *m* 1978, Fiona Bristol; two *s. Educ:* Marlborough; Trinity College Cambridge. MA; FCA. Served Royal Fusiliers, attached 4th Kings African Rifles, Uganda 1956–58. HM Foreign Service, 1963–64; SG Warburg & Co., 1964–66; Cooper Brothers & Co., 1966–69; Samuel Montagu & Co., 1970–77; Head of Investment Div., Crown Agents for Oversea Govts & Admins, 1977–83; Man. Dir, Touche Remnant & Co 1983–87; Chairman: Dynastic Mgt Ltd, 2006–; New Europe Property Investments 2007–; Anglo Japanese Investment Co., 2007–; Director: Graphite Enterprise Trust plc 2002–; VTI India Pharma Fund, 2005–. Member, Advisory Board: Mellenthin Corporate Finance, 2004–; Al Farida Investments, 2007–. Dep. Chm., Assoc. of Investment Trust Cos, 1985–87. *Recreations:* literature, music. *Address:* 1 Bradbourne Street, SW6 3TF *Club:* Brooks's.

GRAY, Phillip; Chief Executive, Chartered Society of Physiotherapy, since 1998; *b* 3 April 1949; *s* of Paul and Sally Gray; *m* 1979, Pauline Tierney; two *s* three *d. Educ:* Liverpool Poly. (grad. IPM 1970); UC, Cardiff (BSc Econs 1st Cl. Hons 1976; Pres. Students' Union, 1976–77); LSE (MSc Industrial Relations 1978). Personnel Officer Plessey Electronics, Liverpool, 1968–73; Dir of Industrial Relations, Chartered Soc. of Physiotherapy, 1978–90; Dir of Labour Relations, RCN, 1990–98. Member: NHS Workforce Develt Bd; NHS Older People's Services Taskforce; Primary Care Alliance Exec.; Allied Health Professions Fedn. Hon. FCSP. *Recreations:* squash, walking, football poetry, collecting books, family and five children. *Address:* Chartered Society of Physiotherapy, 14 Bedford Row, WC1R 4ED. *T:* (020) 7306 6641, *Fax:* (020) 7306 6643; *e-mail:* grayp@csphysio.org.uk.

GRAY, Richard Dennis; Director of Development and Consultant, North East Institute Newcastle upon Tyne, since 2005; *b* 19 Sept. 1951; *s* of John Dennis and Betty Gray; *m* 1976, Cherry Elizabeth Allen; two *s. Educ:* Carre's Grammar Sch.; Bristol Univ. (BA History and History of Art); Manchester Univ. AMA. Asst Keeper and Keeper Manchester City Art Galls, 1974–89; Director: Manchester City Art Galls, 1989–98 Compton Verney, 1998–2005. Member: English Ceramic Circle, 1976–; Glass Circle 1981–; Cttee, Glass Assoc., 1983–87; Cttee, Northern Ceramic Soc., 1986–89; NW Museums Service Adv. Panel, 1988–98 (Mem., Bd of Management, 1994–98); W Midlands Mus. Policy Forum, 2004–. Indep. Assessor, Reviewing Cttee on Export of Works of Art; Ext. Examnr, Manchester Polytechnic, 1989–92. Trustee: Spode Mus 1989–; Rekonstruktsiya Trust, 1991–93. *Publications:* The History of Porcelain, Chapter 1, 1982; catalogues and inventories, Manchester City Art Galleries; articles and book reviews for arts jls. *Recreations:* music, fishing, walking. *Address:* c/o The Literary and Philosophical Society, 23 Westgate Road, Newcastle upon Tyne NE1 1SE.

GRAY, Prof. Richard John, PhD; FBA 1993; Professor of Literature, University of Essex, since 1990; *b* 5 Jan. 1944; *s* of George Ernest Gray and Helen Gray; *m* 1st, 1965 Joyce Mary Gray (marr. diss. 1991); one *s* one *d*; 2nd, 1991, Sheona Catherine Binnie; one *s* one *d. Educ:* St Catharine's Coll., Cambridge (BA, MA, PhD). Sen. Res. Schol., St Catharine's Coll., Cambridge, 1966–67; Harkness Fellow, for res. in US Univs, 1967–69 Lectr, Sen. Lectr and Reader in Literature, Univ. of Essex, 1969–90. Robert E. McNair Vis. Prof. in Southern Studies, Univ. of South Carolina, 1993. Lectures: Ecclar Centre BL, 2004; Sarah Toyphena Phillips, British Acad., 2005; Lamar, USA, 2006; Fullbrook Bristol, 2008. Editor, Jl of Amer. Studies, 1997–2001. Research awards of: Amer. Philos Soc., 1979; Internat. Communications Agency, 1981; Humanities Res. Bd, 1995, 1998 AHRB, 1997, 2000; British Acad., 2006. *Publications:* American Verse of the Nineteenth Century, 1973; American Poetry of the Twentieth Century, 1976; The Literature of Memory: modern writers of the American South, 1977; Robert Penn Warren: essays 1980; American Fiction: new readings, 1983; Writing the South: ideas of an American region (C. Hugh Holman Award, Soc. for Study of Southern Lit.), 1986, 2nd edn 1997 American Poetry of the Twentieth Century, 1990; (ed) The Complete Poems of Edgar Allan Poe, 1993; The Life of William Faulkner: a critical biography, 1994; (ed) Selected Poems of Edgar Allan Poe, 1996; Southern Aberrations: writers of the American South and the problems of regionalism, 2000; Companion to the Literature and Culture of the American South, 2004; A History of American Literature, 2004; A Web of Words: the great dialogue of Southern literature, 2007; Transatlantic Exchanges: the South in Europe - Europe in the American South, 2007. *Recreations:* running, tennis, wine tasting, cycling cinema, travel. *Address:* Department of Literature, University of Essex, Wivenhoe Park Colchester, Essex CO4 3SQ. *T:* (01206) 872590.

GRAY, Richard Paul; QC 1993; *b* 1 Nov. 1945; *s* of John Montgomery Gray and Margaret Elizabeth Gray (*née* Welsh); *m* 1977, Emma Serena Halpin; one *s. Educ*

Tonbridge Sch.; St Andrew's Univ. (LLB). MCIArb 2004. Called to the Bar, Inner Temple, 1970. *Recreations:* family, gardens, games.

GRAY, Hon. Sir Robert McDowall, (Sir Robin), Kt 1994; *b* 2 July 1931; *s* of Adam Gray and Elsie McDowall; *m* 1957, Mary Thomson (*d* 1981); one *s* two *d*. *Educ:* George Watson's Boys' Coll., Edinburgh. Served 4th/7th Royal Dragoon Guards, 1949–51; immigrated to NZ, as farm labourer, 1952; purchased farm, 1956; entered politics, 1978; MP (Nat.) Clutha, 1978–96; Whip, 1985, Sen. Whip, 1987; Speaker, NZ House of Reps, 1990–93; Minister of State, Associate Minister of For. Affairs and Trade, 1993–96. Chm., Parly Service Commn, 1990–93.

GRAY, Hon. Sir Robin; *see* Gray, Hon. Sir Robert McD.

GRAY, Robin; Member, Parliamentary Boundary Commission for England, since 1999; Deputy Electoral Commissioner and Member, Boundary Committee for England, since 2002; *b* 16 April 1944; *s* of Robert George and Jeannie Gray; *m* 1971, Kathleen Rosemary Kuhn; two *d*. *Educ:* Woking County Grammar Sch. for Boys; London Univ. (BA Hons). UKAEA, 1962–64; HM Treasury, 1964–70; Asst Sec. to Crowther Cttee on Consumer Credit, 1968–70; Min. of Housing and Local Govt, subseq. DoE, 1970–92; seconded to Water Resources Bd, 1973–75, to W Sussex CC, 1982–83; Sec., London and Metropolitan Govt Staff Commn, 1984–86; PSA, 1986–92; Under Sec., 1988–92; Dir of Civil Projects, 1988–89; Dir, Marketing and Planning, 1990–92; Internat. Dir, 1991–92; Business Develt Dir, PSA Projects Ltd, 1992–93. Mem., Local Govt Commn for England, 1996–2002. Management consultant, 1993–. *Recreations:* cricket, walking and other outdoor activities, talking. *Address:* c/o Boundary Commission for England, PO Box 31060, 1 Drummond Gate, SW1V 2FF.

GRAY, Hon. Robin (Trevor), BAgrSc; Chairman, Botanical Resources Australia Pty Ltd, since 1996; Partner, Evers Gray Consultants, since 1996; *b* 1 March 1940; *s* of late Rev. W. J. Gray; *m* 1965, Judith, *d* of late A. G. Boyd; two *s* one *d*. *Educ:* Box Hill High Sch.; Dookie Agricl Coll., Melbourne Univ. Teacher, 1961–65 (in UK, 1964); agricl consultant, Colac, Vic, 1965, Launceston, Tas, 1965–76; pt-time Lectr in Agricl Econs, Univ. of Tasmania, 1970–76. MHA (L) for Wilmot, Tas, 1976–85, for Lyons, 1985–95; Dep. Leader of the Opposition, Tasmania, 1979–81; Leader of the Opposition, 1981–82 and 1989–91; Premier of Tasmania and Treasurer, 1982–89; Minister: for Racing and Gaming, 1982–84; for Energy, 1982–88; for Forests, 1984–86; for State Develt, 1984–89; for Small Business, 1986–89; for Status of Women, 1989; for Antarctic Affairs, 1989; for Science and Technology, 1989; for Primary Industry, Fisheries and Energy, 1992–95; for the TT-Line, 1993–95. Director: Gunns Ltd, 1996–; Fujii Tasmania Pty Ltd, 1996–2000; AMC Search Ltd, 1996–; Agribusiness Project Mgt Pty Ltd, 1999–; Evergreen Olive Oil Pty Ltd, 2000–. Trustee: Tasmanian Wool Museum, 1996–; Norfolk Trust, 2000–. *Recreations:* gardening, golf. *Address:* 11 Beech Road, Launceston, Tas 7250, Australia.

GRAY, Rose; *see* Gray, C. A. R.

GRAY, Victor William; Director, Rothschild Archive, 1993–2004; *b* 27 Oct. 1946; *s* of William Albert Gray and Eva Thirza (*née* Bint); *m* 1967, Jennifer Anne Whittle; one *s* one *d*. *Educ:* King's Coll., Cambridge (BA Hons Eng., MA). County Archivist, Essex, 1978–93. Chm., Nat. Council on Archives, 1996–2001; Member: Lord Chancellor's Adv. Council on Public Records, 1992–98; Royal Commn on Historical Manuscripts, 2000–03; Bd, MLA (formerly Resource: Council for Museums, Archives and Libraries), 2000–04. Pres., Soc. of Archivists, 2005–08 (Chm., 1989–91). FSA 2007. DU Essex, 1993. Ellis Prize for dist. contribs to archival theory and practice, Soc. of Archivists, 2002. *Publications:* numerous articles on archives for prof. jls, esp. Jl of Soc. of Archivists. *Recreations:* reading, walking, collecting dictionaries. *Address:* 3 Butlers Cottages, Hatfield Peverel, Essex CM3 2NG. *T:* (01245) 380835; *e-mail:* grayvw@globalnet.co.uk.

GRAY, Sir William (Hume), 3rd Bt *cr* 1917; Director: Eggleston Hall Ltd; William Gray Associates; *b* 26 July 1955; *s* of William Talbot Gray (*d* 1971) (*er s* of 2nd Bt), and of Rosemarie Hume Gray, *d* of Air Cdre Charles Hume Elliott-Smith; *S* grandfather, 1978; *m* 1984, Catherine Victoria Willoughby (marr. diss. 1998), *y d* of late John Naylor and of Mrs Jerram, Wadebridge, Cornwall; one *s* two *d*; *m* 2001, Juliet Rachel, *d* of Mr and Mrs D. J. Jackson, Headlam, Co. Durham; one *s*. *Educ:* Aysgarth School, Bedale, Yorks; Eton College; Polytechnic of Central London BA (Hons) Architecture; DipArch; RIBA. High Sheriff, Durham, 1998–99. *Recreation:* sport. *Heir: s* William John Cresswell Gray, *b* 24 Aug. 1986. *Address:* Eggleston Hall, Barnard Castle, Co. Durham DL12 0AG. *T:* (01833) 650553.

GRAY DEBROS, Winifred Marjorie, (Mrs E. Gray Debros); *see* Fox, W. M.

GRAYDON, Air Chief Marshal Sir Michael (James), GCB 1993 (KCB 1989); CBE 1984; FRAeS; non-executive Director, Thales plc, since 1999; Military Adviser, Airtanker, since 2001; Chairman, Symbiotics Ltd, since 2005; *b* 24 Oct. 1938; *s* of James Julian Graydon and Rita Mary Alkan; *m* 1963, Margaret Elizabeth Clark. *Educ:* Wycliffe Coll.; RAF Coll., Cranwell. Qualified Flying Instructor No 1 FTS, Linton-on-Ouse, 1960–62; No 56 Sqn, 1962–64; No 226 OCU, 1965–67 (Queen's Commendation); Flight Comd, No 56 Sqn, 1967–69; RAF Staff Coll., Bracknell, 1970; PSO to Dep. C-in-C Allied Forces Central Region, Brunssum, 1971–73; Operations, Joint Warfare, MoD, 1973–75; NDC, Latimer, 1976; OC No 11 Sqn, Binbrook, 1977–79; MA to CDS, MoD, 1979–81; OC RAF Leuchars, 1981–83; OC RAF Stanley, Falkland Is, 1983; RCDS, 1984; SASO 11 Gp, Bentley Priory, 1985–86; ACOS Policy, SHAPE, 1986–89; AOC-in-C, RAF Support Comd, 1989–91; AOC-in-C, RAF Strike Comd, and C-in-C, UK Air Forces, 1991–92; CAS, and Air ADC to the Queen, 1992–97. Member: Cttee of Mgt, RNLI, 1998–; Council, Air League, 2007–; Vice-Patron, Air Cadet Council, 1999–; President: Battle of Britain Meml Trust, 1999–; The Officers' Assoc., 2000–. Chm., Air Sqdn, 2005–. Mem. Council, Church Schs Co., 1997– (Dep. Chm., 2003–); Governor: Wycliffe Coll., 1986– (Vice-Chm., 1992–); Sutton's Hosp. in Charterhouse, 1998– (Chm., 2006–). Chm., Lincs Br., ESU, 2003–. FRAeS 1993. Freeman, City of London, 1995; Liveryman, GAPAN, 1996–. *Publications:* contrib. to professional jls. *Recreations:* golf, flying, reading. *Address:* c/o Lloyds TSB, Cox and King's Branch, PO Box 1190, 7 Pall Mall, SW1Y 5NA. *Clubs:* Royal Air Force; Royal & Ancient Golf (St Andrews).

GRAYLING, Prof. Anthony Clifford, DPhil; FRSL; Professor of Philosophy, Birkbeck College, University of London, since 2005; *b* 3 April 1949; *s* of Henry Clifford Grayling and Ursula Adelaide Burns; *m* 1970, Gabrielle Yvonne Smyth (marr. diss. 1979); one *s* one *d*; partner, 1999, Katie Hickman; one *d*. *Educ:* Sussex Univ. (BA Hons 1971, MA 1976); London Univ. (BA Hons ext. 1975); Magdalen Coll., Oxford (DPhil 1981). Lectr in Philosophy, St Anne's Coll., Oxford, 1983–91; Lectr in Philosophy, 1991–99, Reader, 1999–2005, Birkbeck Coll., Univ. of London. Supernumerary Fellow, St Anne's Coll., Oxford, 1991–; Vis. Prof., Univ. of Tokyo, 1998. FRSA 2004; FRSL 2007. *Publications:* An Introduction to Philosophical Logic, 1982, 3rd edn 1997; The Refutation of Scepticism, 1985; Berkeley: the central arguments, 1986; Wittgenstein, 1988; (jtly, as Li Xiao Jun) The Long March to the Fourth of June, 1990; (with S. Whitfield) A Literary Companion to China, 1994; (ed) Philosophy, vol. 1, A Guide Through the Subject, 1995, vol. 2, Further Through the Subject, 1998; Russell, 1996; Moral Values, 1997; The Quarrel of the Age: the life and times of William Hazlitt, 2000; The Meaning of Things, 2001; The Reason of Things, 2002; What is Good?, 2003; The Mystery of Things, 2003; (ed) Robert Herrick: lyrics of love and desire, 2003; The Heart of Things, 2005; Descartes, 2005; Among the Dead Cities, 2006; Against All Gods, 2007; Truth, Meaning and Reality, 2007; Towards the Light, 2007; The Choice of Hercules, 2007; Scepticism and the Possibility of Knowledge, 2008. *Address:* Birkbeck College, 14 Gower Street, WC1E 6DP. *T:* (020) 7631 6383, *Fax:* (020) 7631 6564; *e-mail:* a.grayling@bbk.ac.uk. *Clubs:* Athenæum, Beefsteak, Groucho.

GRAYLING, Christopher Stephen; MP (C) Epsom and Ewell, since 2001; *b* 1 April 1962; *s* of John Terence Grayling and Elizabeth Grayling; *m* 1987, Susan Dillistone; one *s* one *d*. *Educ:* Royal Grammar Sch., High Wycombe; Sidney Sussex Coll., Cambridge (MA Hist.). BBC News producer, 1985–88; producer and editor, Business Daily, Channel 4, 1988–91; Commissioning Editor, BBC Select, 1991–93; Dir, Charterhouse Prodns, 1993; Div. Dir, Workhouse Ltd, 1993–95; Dir, SSVC Gp, 1995–97; Change Consultant and Eur. Mktg Dir, Burson-Marsteller, 1997–2001. An Opposition Whip, 2002; Opposition front bench spokesman on health, 2002–03, on higher and further educn, 2003–05; Shadow Leader, H of C, 2005; Shadow Secretary of State: for Transport, 2005–07; for Work and Pensions, 2007–. *Publications:* The Bridgewater Heritage, 1984; A Land Fit for Heroes, 1985; (jtly) Just Another Star, 1988; The Story of Joseph Holt, 1985, 2nd edn 1999. *Recreations:* football, cricket. *Address:* House of Commons, SW1A 0AA. *T:* (020) 7219 8194.

GRAYSON, David Roger, CBE 1999 (OBE 1994); Chair of Corporate Responsibility and Director, Doughty Centre for Corporate Responsibility, Cranfield School of Management, since 2007; a Director, Business in the Community, since 1995; *b* 26 May 1955; *s* of Henry Eric Fitton Grayson and Patricia Grayson (*née* Clayton). *Educ:* Mount St Mary's Coll.; Downing Coll., Cambridge (MA Law); Free Univ. of Brussels (Wiener Anspach Schol.; MA 1978); Newcastle Univ. (MBA 1985). Brand Mgt, Procter and Gamble, 1978–80; Co-Founder and Dir, Project NE, 1980–86; Jt Man. Dir, Prince's Youth Business Trust, 1986–87; Business in the Community, 1987–: Jt Man. Dir, resp. for ops and staff, 1989–92; Man. Dir, Business Strategy Gp., 1992–95. Visiting Fellow: Sch. of Mgt, Imperial Coll., 1998–2007; Teesside Business Sch., 2004–07; Vis. Prof., London Guildhall Univ., 2000–03; Vis. Sen. Fellow, Kennedy Sch. of Govt, Harvard, 2006–. Chairman: Business Link Nat. Assessment Panel, DTI, 1993–97; Business Link Nat. Accreditation Bd, 1996–2000; Nat. Disability Council, 1996–2000; UK Small Business Consortium, 2002–; Mem. Bd, Strategic Rail Authority (formerly BRB), 2000–05. Principal, BLU, 2001–06. Internat. lectures on MBA and exec. mgt progs. Chm. Judges, UK Capital Enterprise, 2005–06. Ambassador, Nat. AIDS Trust, 2000–; Trustee: Prince of Wales Innovation Trust, 1989–; AbilityNet, 2000–02; Responsibility in Gambling Trust, 2004–; Chm., Housing 21, 2006–. Gov., Lilian Baylis Sch., Lambeth, 2000–05. Patron, SCOPE, 2003–. FRSA 1991. Hon. LLD London South Bank, 2005. *Publications:* (contrib.) Mastering Enterprise, 1996; (contrib.) What If..., 2000; (jtly) Everybody's Business: managing risks and opportunities in today's global society, 2001; Corporate Social Opportunity, 2004; (contrib.) Entrepreneurship: a catalyst for urban regeneration, 2004; (contrib.) Sustainable Enterprise, 2004; (contrib.) The Accountable Corporation, 2005. *Recreations:* scuba diving, travel; happiest in, on or underwater, preferably in warm climates. *Address:* Cranfield School of Management, Cranfield, Bedford MK43 0AL; *e-mail:* david.grayson@cranfield.ac.uk; *web:* www.davidgrayson.net. *Club:* Royal Automobile.

GRAYSON, Sir Jeremy (Brian Vincent), 5th Bt *cr* 1922, of Ravenspoint, Co. Anglesey; photographer; *b* 30 Jan. 1933; *s* of Brian Harrington Grayson (*d* 1989), 3rd *s* of 1st Bt and of Sofia Maria (*née* Buchanan); *S* uncle, 1991; *m* 1958, Sara Mary, *d* of C. F. Upton; three *s* three *d* (and one *d* decd). *Educ:* Downside. *Heir: s* Simon Jeremy Grayson, *b* 12 July 1959.

GREATOREX, Barbara; Headteacher, Wallington High School for Girls, since 2002; *b* 11 March 1951; *d* of Benjamin John Jackson and Millicent Claire Jackson; two *s* one *d*. *Educ:* Warwick Univ. (BSc Hons); York Univ. (PGCE); Open Univ. (MA). Sen. Teacher, Joseph Rowntree Sch., 1995–97; Dep. Headteacher, Wolverhampton Girls' High Sch., 1997–2002. *Recreations:* birdwatching, reading, travelling. *Address:* Wallington High School for Girls, Woodcote Road, Wallington, Surrey SM6 0PH. *T:* (020) 8647 2380, *Fax:* (020) 8647 2270; *e-mail:* bgreatorex@suttonlea.org.

GREATOREX, Raymond Edward, FCA; Executive Chairman, Baker Tilly, 2002–06; *b* 28 May 1940; *s* of late Percy Edward and Lilian Alice Greatorex; *m* 1982, Barbara Anne (*née* Booth); one *d*. *Educ:* Westcliff High Sch.; Lewes Co. Grammar Sch. FCA 1975. Joined Sydenham, Snowden Nicholson & Co., chartered accountants, subseq. Sydenham & Co., 1959; Partner, 1970; firm merged into Hodgson Harris, 1980, Hodgson Impey, 1985, then Kidsons Impey, 1990, and merged with Baker Tilly, 2002; Mem., Nat. Exec. and Regl Man. Partner, Southern England, 1990–94; Chm., HLB Internat., 1994–99; Nat. Managing Partner, HLB Kidsons, 2000–02. Liveryman and Freeman, City of London; Master, Co. of Farriers, 2002–03. Mem., RSA 2003. *Recreations:* horse-racing, cricket (watching!), gardening, travelling, reading autobiographies. *Address:* Beeches Brook, Strood Green, Wisborough Green, Billingshurst, W Sussex RH14 0HP. *T:* (01403) 700796. *Clubs:* East India, MCC.

GREATREX, Neil; National President and General Secretary, Union of Democratic Mineworkers, since 1993; *b* 1 April 1951; *s* of late John Edward and Joyce Irene Greatrex; *m* 1972, Sheila Waterhouse; two *d*. *Educ:* Greenwood Drive Jun. Sch.; Mowlands Intermediate Sch.; Ashfield Comprehensive Sch. Bentinck Colliery, 1965–85. National Union of Mineworkers: Cttee Mem., 1970–74; Branch Treas., 1974–80; Branch Pres., 1980–85; full-time Area Official, 1985–86; Union of Democratic Mineworkers: Area Pres., 1986–88; Nat. Vice-Pres., 1988–93. *Recreations:* Do It Yourself, shooting. *Address:* Miners' Offices, Berry Hill Lane, Mansfield, Notts NG18 4JU. *T:* (01623) 626094; 2 Chestnut Avenue, Kirkby in Ashfield, Notts NG17 8BB. *T:* (01623) 758346.

GREAVES, family name of **Baron Greaves**.

GREAVES, Baron *cr* 2000 (Life Peer), of Pendle in the county of Lancashire; **Anthony Robert Greaves;** *b* 27 July 1942; *s* of Geoffrey Greaves and Moyra Greaves (*née* Brookes); *m* 1968, Heather Ann (*née* Baxter); two *d*. *Educ:* Queen Elizabeth GS, Wakefield; Hertford Coll., Oxford (BA Hons Geog.). Teacher/Lectr, 1968–74; Organising Sec., Assoc. of Liberal Councillors, 1977–85; Man. Dir, Hebden Royd Publications Ltd, (Lib Dem publications), 1985–90; second-hand book dealer, Liber Books, 1992–. Member: (L) Colne BC, 1971–74; (L then Lib Dem): Pendle BC, 1973–92, 1994–98, 2004–; Lancs CC, 1973–97. *Publication:* (with Rachael Pitchford) Merger: the inside story, 1988. *Recreations:* climbing, mountain/hill walking, wild flowers, cycling, politics. *Address:* 3 Hartington Street, Winewall, Colne, Lancashire BB8 8DB. *T:* (01282) 864346, *T:* (office) (020) 7219 8620.

GREAVES, Graham Charles; aviation consultant, since 2005; *b* 5 July 1945; *s* of Joseph Clarence Greaves and Jane Isabella Greaves; *m* 1975, Pamela Ann Ellson; two *d*. *Educ:* Loughborough Univ. (BSc Hons Transport Mgt and Planning). FCILT (FCIT 1995; FILT 2000). Civil Engr, City of Birmingham, 1964–71; Professional and Technol. Officer, Civil Engr, W Midlands Regl Office, Depts of Transport and the Envmt, 1971–79; various mgt posts, HQ London, Heathrow and Gatwick, BAA, 1979–85; Ops Manager, Manchester Airport, 1985–87; Ops Dir/Man. Dir, Cardiff Airport, 1987–95; Mgt Cons., BAe and independent, 1995–98; Dir Gen. and Chief Exec., CIT, 1998–99; independent aviation consultant, 2000–02; Airport Develt Dir, Newquay Cornwall Internat. Airport, 2002–04; Man. Dir, Gloucestershire Airport Ltd, 2004. Visiting Lecturer: in aviation studies, Loughborough Univ., 1995–; in business mgt in transport studies, UWE, 2001–06. MCMI (MIMgt 1984). *Publication:* ACI Marketing Handbook, 1995. *Recreations:* British history, military and civil aviation, photography, cricket. *Address:* Grove House, Lyonshall, Herefordshire HR5 3JP.

GREAVES, James Peter, (Jimmy); TV broadcaster, since 1983; football correspondent, The Sun; *b* 20 Feb. 1940; *s* of James and Mary Greaves; *m* Irene Barden; two *s* two *d* (and one *s* decd). *Educ:* Kingswood Sch., Hainault. Professional footballer (inside forward), 1957; played for: Chelsea, 1957–61; AC Milan, 1961; Tottenham Hotspur, 1961–70 (FA Cup wins, 1962, 1967); West Ham, 1970–71; scored record 357 goals in First Division, 55 goals in FA Cup ties; played 57 times for England (scored 44 goals). *Publications* include: Greavsie (autobiog.), 2003; (with N. Giller): This one's on me, 1981; It's a funny old life, 1990; The Heart of the Game, 2005. *Address:* c/o Sports Department, The Sun, 1 Virginia Street, E98 1SN.

GREAVES, Jeffrey; HM Diplomatic Service, retired; Consul General, Alexandria, 1978–81; *b* 10 Dec. 1926; *s* of Willie and Emily Greaves; *m* 1949, Joyce Mary Farrer; one *s* one *d*. *Educ:* Pudsey Grammar Sch. Served RN, 1945–48. Joined HM Foreign Service, 1948; FO, 1948; Benghazi, 1951; Vice Consul, Tehran, 1953; ME Centre for Arab Studies, 1955; Second Sec. and Vice Consul, Paris, 1960; Vice Consul, Muscat, 1962; Second Sec. and Consul, Athens, 1965; Second Sec. (Commercial), Cairo, 1968; First Sec. and Consul, Muscat, 1970; First Sec. (Com.), Bangkok, 1972; FCO, 1976. *Address:* 7 Pitchstone Court, Leeds LS12 5SZ. *T:* (0113) 257 7238.

GREAVES, John Western, CMG 1998; Vice President, Canning House, since 2005 (Chairman, 2001–05); Chairman, Lattitude Global Volunteering (formerly GAP Activity Projects), since 2007; *b* 6 Sept. 1939; *s* of Sir Western Greaves, KBE and Marjorie Nahir (*née* Wright); *m* 1965, Margaret Anne Berg; one *s* three *d*. *Educ:* Uppingham Sch.; Leeds Univ. (BSc Hons Chem. Engrg). Business Manager: ICI Argentina, Buenos Aires, 1965–73; ICI Europa, Brussels, 1973–79; ICI Plastics, 1979–81; Corporate Planning, ICI, 1981–85; Regl Exec., Latin America, Zeneca, 1992–97; Business Dir, Zeneca Agrochemicals, 1997–2000. Chairman: Latin American Crop Protection Assoc., 1993–96; Latin American Trade Adv. Gp, 1995–98. Dir, Bd, Inst. of Latin American Studies, London Univ., 1996–99. *Recreations:* family, home, travel, reading, sailing. *Address:* Bramshott Thatch, Rectory Lane, Bramshott, Hants GU30 7QZ. *T:* (01428) 722243; Las Terrazas, Portals, Mallorca. *Clubs:* Liphook Golf; Tortugas Country (Buenos Aires), Santa Ponsa Yacht (Mallorca).

GREAVES, Prof. Malcolm Watson, MD, PhD; FRCP; Senior Consultant Dermatologist, Singapore National Skin Centre, since 2005; Clinical Professor, Faculty of Medicine, National University of Singapore, since 2006; *b* 11 Nov. 1933; *s* of Donald Watson Greaves and Kathleen Evelyn Greaves; *m* 1964, Evelyn Yeo; one *s* one *d*. *Educ:* Epsom College; Charing Cross Med. Sch. MD, PhD London. MRC Clinical Res. Fellow, UCL, 1963–66; Reader in Dermatology, Univ. of Newcastle upon Tyne, 1966–75; Prof. of Dermatology, Univ. of London, 1975–99, now Emeritus; Dean, St John's Inst. of Dermatology, UMDS of Guy's and St Thomas' Hosps, 1989–95. Prof. of Dermatology, Nat. Univ. of Malaysia, 2001–02. Sen. Consultant in Dermatology, Singapore Gen. Hosp., 2003–05. Chm., Scientific Cttee and Trustee, Skin Disease Res. Fund, 1980–96; Mem., Cttee on Safety of Medicines, DHSS, 1982–89. President: European Soc. for Dermatol Research, 1984; Sect. of Dermatol., RSM, 1996; Chm., Therapy and Audit Cttee, British Assoc. of Dermatologists, 1994–96. Prog. Dir, American Acad. of Dermatol., 1998–2001. Internat. Hon. Mem., Amer. Dermatol. Assoc., 1987; Hon. Member: Amer. Soc. for Investigative Dermatol., 1989; Malaysian Dermatol Assoc., 1995; British Assoc. of Dermatologists, 2000; Austrian Dermatological Soc., 2000; Eur. Soc. for Dermatol Res., 2000; Lithuanian Dermatol Assoc., 2000. Mem. Management Bd Exec., UMDS, 1990–95; Mem. Governing Body, Sch. of Pharmacy, Univ. of London, 1990–95. FAMS 2005. Sir Archibald Gray Gold Medal, British Assoc. of Dermatologists, 1998; Leo Von Zumbusch Gold Medal, Univ. München, 1998; Cert. of Appreciation, Internat. Cttee of Dermatol., 2001; Dist. Res. Award, Eur. Acad. of Dermatol. and Venereol., 2005. *Publications:* Pharmacology of the Skin, Vol. I, Pharmacology of Skin Systems and Autocoids in Normal and Inflamed Skin, 1989; Vol. II, Methods, Absorption, Metabolism, Toxicity, Drugs and Diseases, 1989; (ed) Urticaria and Angioedema, 2004; Itch: basic mechanisms and therapy, 2004. *Recreation:* swimming. *Address:* City Towers #01–323, 317 Bukit Timah Road, Singapore 259711. *Clubs:* Athenæum; Tanglin (Singapore).

GREAVES, Mary; *see* Bownes, M.

GREAVES, Prof. Melvyn Francis, FRS 2003; Chairman, Section of Haemato-Oncology, Institute of Cancer Research, since 2006; *b* 12 Sept. 1941; *s* of Edward and Violet Greaves; *m* 1966, Josephine Pank; one *s* one *d*. *Educ:* City of Norwich Grammar Sch.; University Coll. London; Middlesex Hosp. Med. Sch. BSc, PhD London. FRCPath 1997. Vis Scientist, Karolinska Inst., Stockholm, 1968–69; Res. Fellow, Nat. Inst. for Med. Res., London, 1969–72; Res. Scientist, Dept of Zoology, UCL, 1972–76; Hd, Membrane Immunology Dept, Imperial Cancer Res. Fund, 1976–84; Dir, Leukaemia Res. Fund Centre, Inst. of Cancer Res., London, 1984–2005. Hon. MRCP 1987. FMedSci 1999. Paul Martini Prize (Germany), 1977; Peter Debye Prize (Holland), 1981; King Faisal Internat. Prize for Medicine, 1988; José Carreras Prize (Europe), 2001. *Publications:* T and B Lymphocytes, 1973; Cellular Recognition, 1975; Atlas of Blood Cells, 1981, 2nd edn 1988; Monoclonal Antibodies to Receptors, 1984; Cancer: the evolutionary legacy, 2000; contribs to bio-med. jls. *Recreations:* music, cooking, photography, natural history, being grandad. *Address:* Institute of Cancer Research, Sutton, Surrey SM2 5NG.

GREEN, Sir Albert A.; *see* Aynsley-Green.

GREEN, Sir Allan (David), KCB 1991; QC 1987; *b* 1 March 1935; *s* of late Lionel and Irene Green; *m* 1st, 1967, Eva (*d* 1993), *yr d* of Prof. Artur Attman and Elsa Attman, Gothenburg, Sweden; one *s* one *d*; 2nd, 2004, Anna, *er d* of late Lemuel Harries and of Muriel Harries, Kilvrough, Gower. *Educ:* Charterhouse; St Catharine's Coll., Cambridge (Open Exhibnr, MA). Served RN, 1953–55. Called to the Bar, Inner Temple, 1959, Bencher, 1985; Jun. Prosecuting Counsel to the Crown, Central Criminal Court, 1977, Sen. Prosecuting Counsel, 1979, First Senior Prosecuting Counsel, 1985; a Recorder, 1979–87; DPP and Hd of Crown Prosecution Service, 1987–91. Mem., Gen. Council of the Bar, 1992. *Recreation:* music, especially opera. *Address:* 2 Hare Court, Temple, EC4 7BH. *Clubs:* Athenæum, Garrick.

GREEN, Andrew Curtis; farmer and horticulturist, since 1960; *b* 28 March 1936; *s* of Christopher Green and Marjorie (*née* Bennett); *m* 1966, Julia Margaret (*née* Davidson); tw *s*. *Educ:* Charterhouse; Magdalene Coll., Cambridge. MA (Nat. Scis), Dip. of Agricultur Commnd RNVR, 1954–56. Farm management, 1960–67; founded Greens of Soha farming and horticultural business, 1967; Director: Elsoms Spalding Seed Co., 1982– Spearhead Internat. Ltd, 1999–; Chm., Hassy Ltd, 1983–89. Mem., AFRC, 1984–8 Mem., E England Regl Cttee, NT. Founder, Kingfishers Bridge Wetland Creatio Project, 1995. FLS 1978; Hon. FIHort 1986 (Industrial Mem. Council, 1988–94); FRAg 1995. Extra Mem., Court of Skinners' Co., 1994–96. *Recreations:* sailing, fishing, shootin ski-ing, wildlife conservation. *Address:* Kingfishers Bridge, Wicken, Ely, Cambs CB7 5X *Clubs:* Army and Navy, Farmers; Hawks (Cambridge).

GREEN, Sir Andrew (Fleming), KCMG 1998 (CMG 1991); HM Diplomatic Servic retired; Founder Chairman, Migrationwatch UK, since 2001; *b* 6 Aug. 1941; *s* of late C Captain J. H. Green, RAF, and Beatrice Mary (*née* Bowditch); *m* 1968, C. Jane Churchi one *s* one *d*. *Educ:* Haileybury and ISC; Magdalene Coll., Cambridge (MA). Served as 2n Lieut, RGJ, 1962–65; joined HM Diplomatic Service, 1965; Middle East Centre for Ar Studies, 1966–68; Aden, 1968–69; Asst Political Agent, Abu Dhabi, 1970–71; Fir Secretary, FCO, 1972–74; Private Sec. to Minister of State, FCO, 1975, and t Parliamentary Under Sec. of State, 1976; First Secretary, UK Delegn to OECD, Pari 1977–79; First Sec., FCO, 1980–81; Counsellor, Washington, 1982–85; Counsellor, H of Chancery and Consul Gen., Riyadh, 1985–88; Counsellor, FCO, 1988–9 Ambassador to Syria, 1991–94; Asst Under-Sec. of State (Middle East), FCO, 1994–9 Ambassador to Saudi Arabia, 1996–2000. Chm., Med. Aid for Palestinians, 2002–0 *Recreations:* tennis, sailing, bridge. *Address:* 89 St George's Square, SW1V 3QW.

GREEN, Andrew Michael Walter; Librarian, National Library of Wales, since 1998; 30 Sept. 1952; *s* of Harry Green and Ellen Martha Kennedy Green (*née* Allan); *m* 198 Carys Evans; two *d*. *Educ:* Hoylandswaine Primary Sch.; Queen Elizabeth Grammar Sch Wakefield; Gonville and Caius Coll., Cambridge (BA 1973; MA 1975; Wace Medal fo Classical Archaeology 1973); Coll. of Librarianship, Wales (Dip. Librarianship 1975 MCLIP (ALA 1977). Asst Librarian, UC, Cardiff, 1975–88; Arts and Social Studi Librarian, UWCC, 1988–89; Sub-Librarian (Services and Collection Develt), Univ. Sheffield, 1989–92; Librarian, 1992–95, Dir of Library and Information Services, 1996–9 UC, Swansea. Vice-Chm., 2000–02, Chm., 2002–04, SCONUL. Hon. Fellow: Univ. Wales, Swansea, 2001; NE Wales Inst. of Higher Educn, 2003; Univ. of Wales, Lampete 2006. *Publications:* numerous articles on library and information studies. *Recreation* running, cycling, walking, music, looking out of windows. *Address:* 30 Caswell Driv Caswell, Swansea SA3 4RJ. *T:* (01792) 361260.

GREEN, Anthony Eric Sandall, RA 1977 (ARA 1971); NEAC 2002; Member, Londo Group, 1964; artist (painter); *b* 30 Sept. 1939; *s* of late Frederick Sandall Green and Mar Madeleine (*née* Dupont); *m* 1961, Mary Louise Cozens-Walker; two *d*. *Educ:* Highga Sch., London; Slade Sch. of Fine Art, University Coll. London (Fellow, UCL, 1991 Henry Tonks Prize for drawing, Slade Sch., 1960; French Govt Schol., Paris, 196 Gulbenkian Purchase Award, 1963; Harkness Fellowship, in USA, 1967–69. Trustee, R 2000–08. Has exhibited in: London, New York, Haarlem, Rotterdam, Stuttga Hanover, Helsingborg, Malmö, Tokyo, Brussels, W Berlin, Chicago and Sydne Paintings in various public collections, including: Tate Gallery; Metropolitan Mus. of Ar N York; Olinda Museum, Brazil; Baltimore Mus. of Art, USA; Mus. of Fine Art, Bosto USA; Nat. Mus. of Wales; Gulbenkian Foundn; Arts Council of GB; British Counc Victoria and Albert Mus.; Contemporary Art Soc.; Frans Hals Mus., Holland; Boyman van Bevningen Mus., Holland; Ulster Mus., Belfast; Ikeda and Niigata Mus., Setagaya A Mus., Metropolitan, Tokyo; Hiroshima; Fukuoka. Featured Artist, RA Summer Exhib 2003. Hon. RBA 1998; Hon. ROI 2004. Exhibit of the Year award, RA, 197 *Publication:* A Green Part of the World, 1984. *Recreations:* travelling, family life. *Addres* Mole End, 40 High Street, Little Eversden, Cambridge CB23 1HE. *T:* (01223) 26229 *Fax:* (01223) 265656.

GREEN, Prof. Anthony Richard, PhD; FRCP, FRCPath, FMedSci; Professor Haemato-Oncology, University of Cambridge and Addenbrooke's Hospital, since 199 *b* 13 Oct. 1955; *s* of John Richard Green and Jeanne Dorothy Green; *m* 1984, Sar Frances Rann; one *s* two *d*. *Educ:* Highgate Sch.; Queens' Coll., Cambridge; Universi Coll. Hosp., London (PhD 1987). FRCP 1995; FRCPath 1997. Jun. hosp. posts, Londo 1980–84; Clinical Res. Fellow, ICRF, 1984–87; Lectr in Haematology, Univ. Hosp. Wales, Cardiff, 1987–89; CRC Hamilton Fairley Travelling Fellow, Walter & Eliza H Inst., Melbourne, 1989–91; Wellcome Trust Sen. Clinical Fellow, Dept of Haematolog Cambridge Univ., 1991–99. FMedSci 2001. *Recreations:* family, friends, hill walking, scul diving. *Address:* Department of Haematology, Cambridge Institute for Medical Researc Hills Road, Cambridge CB2 2XY.

GREEN, Arthur; Senior Partner, Grant Thornton, 1986–88, retired; President, Institu of Chartered Accountants in England and Wales, 1987–88; *b* 15 June 1928; *s* of Arth Henry and Elizabeth Burns Green; *m* 1952, Sylvia Myatt; one *s* one *d*. *Educ:* Liverpo Collegiate. FCA. Qualified Chartered Accountant, 1950; Partner, Bryce Hanmer & C Liverpool, 1954 (merged Thornton Baker; later Grant Thornton); Nat. Managing Partne Thornton Baker, 1975–84; Chm. and Man. Dir, Grant Thornton International, 1984–8 Vice-Pres., 1985–86, Dep. Pres., 1986–87, ICA. *Recreations:* golf, theatre. *Address:* U Yonder, Herbert Road, Salcombe, Devon TQ8 8HP. *T:* (01548) 842075.

GREEN, Prof. Ben Joseph, PhD; Herchel Smith Professor of Pure Mathemati University of Cambridge, since 2006; Fellow, Trinity College, Cambridge, since 2006; 27 Feb. 1977; *s* of late Robert Norman Green and of Judith Mary Green; partner, Lu Jane Colwell. *Educ:* Trinity Coll., Cambridge (BA Hons Maths 1998, MA 2001; Ph 2003). Res. Fellow, Trinity Coll., Cambridge, 2001–05; Prof. of Pure Maths, Univ. Bristol, 2005–06. *Publications:* contrib. learned jls. *Recreations:* cycling, hill-walkin cricket, jazz. *Address:* Trinity College, Cambridge CB2 1TQ; *e-mail:* b.j.green(dpmms.cam.ac.uk.

GREEN, Rev. Bernard; General Secretary, Baptist Union of Great Britain, 1982–9 Moderator of the Free Church Federal Council, 1988–89; *b* 11 Nov. 1925; *s* of Geor Samuel Green and Laura Annie Agnes (*née* Holliday); *m* 1952, Joan Viccars; two *s* one *Educ:* Wellingborough Sch.; Bristol Baptist Coll.; Bristol Univ. (BA); Regent's Park Col Oxford, and St Catherine's Coll., Oxford (MA); London Univ. BD taken externall Served War as coal-miner, 1944–47. Ordained as Baptist Minister, 1952; pastorates Yardley, Birmingham, 1952–61; Mansfield Road, Nottingham, 1961–76; Horfiel Bristol, 1976–82. Dir, Baptist Insce Co., 1982–93. Vice Pres., Churches' Council f Health and Healing, 1988–99. Regular broadcaster on BBC Radio Nottingham un 1976 and on BBC Radio Bristol until 1982. *Publications:* (jtly) Patterns and Prayers f

Christian Worship, 1991; (ed jtly) Baptist Praise and Worship, 1991; Tomorrow's Man: a biography of James Henry Rushbrooke, 1997; Crossing the Boundaries: a history of the European Baptist Federation 1949–1999, 1999. *Recreations:* reading, music (listening), gardening.

GREEN, Brian Russell; QC 1997; *b* 25 July 1956; *s* of late Bertram Green and Dora Green (*née* Rinsler); *m* 1994, Yvonne Mammon; one *s* one *d*, and two step *d*. *Educ:* Ilford County High Sch. for Boys; St Edmund Hall, Oxford (BA, BCL). Called to the Bar, Middle Temple, 1980; Mem., Lincoln's Inn, 1991. *Recreations:* travel, hill-walking, ski-ing, the arts. *Address:* Wilberforce Chambers, 8 New Square, Lincoln's Inn, WC2A 3QP. *T:* (020) 7306 0102.

GREEN, Prof. Brynmor Hugh, OBE 1995; Sir Cyril Kleinwort Professor of Countryside Management, University of London, Wye College, 1987–96, now Professor Emeritus; *b* 14 Jan. 1941; *s* of Albert Walter Green and Margaret Afona Green (*née* Griffiths); *m* 1965, Jean Armstrong; two *s*. *Educ:* Dartford Grammar Sch.; Univ. of Nottingham (BSc 1st Cl. Hons Botany, PhD Plant Ecol.). Lectr in Plant Ecology, Dept of Botany, Univ. of Manchester, 1965–68; Dep. Regl Officer (SE) 1968–69, Regl Officer (SE) 1969–75, Nature Conservancy Council; Lectr and Sen. Lectr, Wye Coll., 1975–87. A Countryside Comr, 1984–93. Vice-Pres., Kent Wildlife Trust, 2002–. Churchill Fellow, 1999. *Publications:* Countryside Conservation: landscape ecology, planning and management, 1981, 3rd edn 1996; (jtly) The Diversion of Land: conservation in a period of farming contraction, 1990; (jtly) The Changing Role of the Common Agricultural Policy: the future of farming in Europe, 1991; (jtly) Threatened Landscapes: conserving cultural environments, 2001; numerous chapters in books, conf. reports, sci. jls. *Recreations:* golf, watercolour sketching, bird-watching. *Address:* Heatherbank, 49 Brockhill Road, Saltwood, Hythe, Kent CT21 4AF. *T:* (01303) 261093.

GREEN, Candida L.; *see* Lycett Green.

GREEN, Charles Frederick; Director, 1982–89, and Deputy Group Chief Executive, 1986–89, National Westminster Bank; *b* 20 Oct. 1930; *m* 1956, Rev. Pauline (*née* Jackson); two *s* one *d*. *Educ:* Harrow County School. FCIB (FIB 1971). Nat. Service, RAF, 1949–51 (Flying Officer). Joined National Provincial Bank, 1946, Secretary, 1967–70; Head of Planning, National Westminster Bank, 1970; Manager, Lombard Street, 1972; Managing Dir, Centre-file, 1974; General Manager: Business Develt Div., 1977; Financial Control Div., 1982. Chairman: CBI/ICC Multinational Affairs Panel, 1982–87; Overseas Cttee, CBI, 1987–89; Dir, Business in the Community, 1981–91 (Vice-Chm., 1985–89); Mem. Council, PSI, 1984–98 (Treas., 1984–93). Mem., General Synod, 1980–90; Vice-Chm., C of E Bd for Social Responsibility, 1983–91; Chm., Industrial and Econ. Affairs Cttee, 1986–93; Mem., Central Stewardship Cttee, Central Bd of Finance, 1991–99 (Chm., 1993–99); Trustee, Church Urban Fund, 1987–89. Chm., Co. of Glos Community Foundn, 1991–2000 (Trustee, 1990–2005; Vice Pres., 2005–); Vice-Chm., Dio. of Gloucester Bd of Finance, 1991–2000; Mem., Council for Charitable Support, 1989–93; Chm., Glenfall House Trust, 1996–2002; Trustee: Small Business Res. Trust, 1986–96; Monteverdi Choir, 1986–2001; Charities Aid Foundn, 1989–98; Church Housing Trust, 1992–2005. Governor: Westonbirt Sch., 1990–2003; Monkton Combe Sch., 1990–96; Mem. Council, Cheltenham & Gloucester Coll. of Higher Educn, subseq. Univ. of Gloucestershire, 1993–2002 (Vice-Chm. Council, 1994–2002; Fellow, 1990). FCMI (FBIM 1982); FRSA 1994. Hon. FLCM 1988. Freeman, City of London, 1990. *Recreations:* opera, concert music, drama. *Address:* The Old House, Parks Farm, Old Sodbury, Bristol BS37 6PX. *Clubs:* Athenæum, Langbourn Ward.

GREEN, Charlotte Rosamund; newsreader, BBC Radio 4, since 1985; *b* 4 May 1956; *y d* of Geoffrey Hugh Green, CB and of Ruth Hazel (*née* Mercy). *Educ:* Haberdashers' Aske's Sch. for Girls; Univ. of Kent at Canterbury (BA Hons Eng. and American Lit.). Joined BBC as studio manager, 1978; continuity announcer and newsreader, 1985; newsreader, Today, BBC Radio 4, 1986–; regular participant in The News Quiz, 1987–; producer and presenter, Morning has Broken, BBC Radio 4, 1986–91; presenter, News Speak, BBC World Service, 1999; narrator, Music in Camera, BBC TV, 1989. Trustee, Univ. of Kent Develt Trust, 2003–. Judge, BBC Frank Gillard Annual Local Radio Awards, 2000–02. Most Attractive Female Voice on the Radio award, Radio Times, 2002. *Recreations:* theatre, books, art, music, laughing with friends, supporting Tottenham Hotspur FC. *Address:* BBC Television Centre, Wood Lane, W12 7RJ.

GREEN, Christopher Edward Wastie, MA; FCILT; non-executive Director, Network Rail, since 2005; *b* 7 Sept. 1943; *s* of James Wastie Green and Margarita Mensing; *m* 1966, Waltraud Mitzie Petzold; one *s* one *d*. *Educ:* St Paul's School, London; Oriel College, Oxford. MA Mod. Hist. British Rail: Management Trainee, 1965–67; served Birmingham, Nottingham, Hull, Wimbledon; Passenger Operating Manager, HQ, 1979–80; Chief Operating Manager, Scotland, 1980–83; Dep. Gen. Manager, Scotland, 1983–84; Gen. Manager, Scottish Region, 1984–86; Dir, Network SouthEast, 1986–91; Managing Director: InterCity, 1992–94; ScotRail, 1994–95; Chief Exec. and Comr, English Heritage, 1995–96; Director: Gibb Rail Ltd, 1996–99; Gibb Ltd, 1996–99; Chief Exec., Virgin Trains, 1999–2004; Dir, 1999–2004, Chm., 2004–05, Virgin Rail Gp. Director: Eurotunnel, 1995–2004; Connex Rail, 1998–99. Chm., Rail Forum, 2004–07. Mem., Regl Council, CBI, 1986. President: Railway Study Assoc., 1989–90, 1997–98; Railway Convalescent Homes, 2002–; Vice Pres., CIT, 1988; Mem., Railway Heritage Trust Adv. Panel, 2003–. Mem. Adv. Bd, Cranfield Univ. Logistics and Transportation Centre, 1996–; Trustee, Royal Liverpool Phil. Orch., 2004–. Hon. DBA IMCB, 2002; DUniv UCE, 2002. *Recreations:* music, reading, walking, canals, architecture. *Address:* 14 Meadway, Berkhamsted, Herts HP4 2PN. *T:* (01442) 862978, *Fax:* (01442) 878543; *e-mail:* chris@artgreen.co.uk.

GREEN, Prof. Christopher Kenneth, PhD; FBA 1999; Emeritus Professor of History of Art, Courtauld Institute of Art, 2008; *b* 1943; *m* Charlotte Sebag-Montefiore; one *s* one *d*. *Educ:* Christ's Coll., Cambridge (BA 1966); London Univ. (MA); PhD. Courtauld Institute of Art: successively Asst Lectr, Lectr, Reader in and Prof. of History of Art; Curator, Roger Fry exhibn, 1999; Co-curator, Henri Rousseau exhibn, 2005. Leverhulme Res. Fellow, 1997–98. Trustee, Nat. Museums Liverpool, 2001–. *Publications:* Léger and the Avant-Garde, 1976; Cubism and its Enemies, 1987; (jtly) Juan Gris, 1992; European Avant-Gardes, 1995; One Man Show (novel), 1995; (ed) Art Made Modern: Roger Fry's vision of art, 1999; Art in France 1900–1940, 2000; Picasso: architecture and vertigo, 2005; exhibn catalogues. *Recreation:* finding calm. *Address:* Courtauld Institute of Art, Somerset House, Strand, WC2R 0RN.

GREEN, Colin Raymond; Chairman, Hermes Group Pension Scheme, since 2002; *b* 16 April 1949; *s* of Gerald and Maisie Green; *m* 1975, Hazel Ruth Lateman; one *s* one *d*. *Educ:* Hampton Grammar Sch.; LSE (LLB Hons); Coll. of Law; WUJS Post-grad. Inst., Israel. Solicitor, 1973; Paisner & Co., 1971–74; Partner, Clintons, 1975–77; Solicitor's Office, Post Office, 1977; British Telecommunications: Solicitor's Office, 1981; Head, Privatisation Div., 1982–84; Head, M&A Div., 1984–85; Dir, Commercial Dept, 1985–89; Solicitor, 1989–94; Chief Legal Adviser, 1989–99; Secretary, 1994–2002; Mem. Exec. Cttee, 1996–2002; Gp Commercial Dir, 1999–2002. Trustee, BT Pension Scheme, 1994–2002. Chm., BT Telecomunicaciones SA, 2001–02; Director: Vio (Worldwide) Ltd, 1998–2001; Airtel SA, 1999–2001; Sen. non-exec. Dir, ECI Telecom Inc., 2002–07. Chm., Shalom Nursery Ltd, 2007–. Dir, Centre for Dispute Resolution, 1995–2000. Chm., Green Aid, 2004–. Chm., Kingston Israel Cttee, 2002–; Mem. Bd, Kingston/Surbiton Synagogue, 2002–. Trustee, Nightingale House, 2003–. *Recreations:* music (playing and composing), walking, reading, theatre, football. *Address:* Hermes, Lloyds Chambers, 1 Portsoken Street, E1 8HZ. *T:* (020) 7702 0888.

GREEN, Damian Howard; MP (C) Ashford, since 1997; *b* 17 Jan. 1956; *s* of Howard and late Audrey Green; *m* 1988, Alicia Collinson; two *d*. *Educ:* Reading Sch.; Balliol Coll., Oxford (MA 1st cl. Hons. PPE). Producer, BBC Financial Unit, 1980–82; Business Producer, Channel 4 News, 1982–84; Business News Ed., The Times, 1984–85; Business Ed., Channel 4 News, 1985–87; Presenter and City Ed., Business Daily prog., Channel 4, 1987–92; Prime Minister's Policy Unit, 1992–94; Public Affairs Advr, 1994–97. Opposition spokesman: on employment and higher educn; 1998–99; on the envmt, 1999–2001; Shadow Educn Sec., 2001–03; Shadow Transport Sec., 2003–04; Shadow Minister for Immigration, 2005–. Contested (C) Brent E, 1992. Trustee, Communities Develt Foundn, 1997–2001; Vice-Chm., John Smith Meml Trust, 2004–. *Publications:* ITN Budget Factbook, annually 1984–86; A Better BBC, 1990; Communities in the Countryside, 1995; The Four Failures of the New Deal, 1998; Better Learning, 2002; More Than Markets, 2003; (with David Davis) Controlling Economic Migration, 2006. *Recreations:* cricket, football, opera, cinema. *Address:* House of Commons, SW1A 0AA. *T:* (020) 7219 3000.

GREEN, Sir David; *see* Green, Sir G. D.

GREEN, David Charles, CBE 2001; *b* 3 June 1943; *s* of Phillip and Eileen Green; *m* 1969, Anne Patricia Ward; one *s* one *d*. *Educ:* Latymer Upper Sch. Exec. Officer, Traders Road Transport Assoc., 1966–71; Freight Transport Association: Regl Controller, 1971–87; Exec. Dir, 1987–93; Dir-Gen., 1993–2000; Exec. Vice-Pres., 2001–03. Pres., Internat. Road Transport Union, 1995–2001. *Publications:* numerous articles and reports on freight transport and logistics. *Recreations:* golf, cricket, modern political history.

GREEN, David George, PhD; Director, Civitas: Institute for the Study of Civil Society, since 2000; *b* 24 Jan. 1951; *s* of George Green and Kathleen Mary (*née* Ellis); *m* 1980, Catherine Walker; one *s* one *d*. *Educ:* Newcastle upon Tyne Univ. (BA Hons 1973; PhD 1980). Pt-time Lectr, Newcastle upon Tyne Poly., 1974–81; Res. Fellow, ANU, 1981–83; Res. Fellow, 1984–86, Dir, Health and Welfare Unit, 1986–2000, Inst. of Economic Affairs. Mem. (Lab), Newcastle upon Tyne CC, 1975–81. *Publications:* Power and Party in an English City, 1981; Mutual Aid or Welfare State, 1984; Working Class Patients and the Medical Establishment, 1985; Challenge to the NHS, 1986; The New Right, 1987; Everyone a Private Patient, 1988; Reinventing Civil Society, 1993; Community without Politics, 1996; From Welfare State to Civil Society, 1996; Benefit Dependency, 1998; An End to Welfare Rights, 1999; Delay, Denial and Dilution, 2000; Stakeholder Health Insurance, 2000; Health Care in France and Germany, 2001; Crime and Civil Society, 2005; We're (Nearly) All Victims Now!, 2007. *Recreation:* walking. *Address:* Civitas, 77 Great Peter Street, SW1P 2EZ.

GREEN, Prof. David Headley, AM 2006; FRS 1991; FAA; Director, Research School of Earth Sciences, Australian National University, 1994–2001, now Professor Emeritus (Deputy Vice-Chancellor, 1998); *b* 29 Feb. 1936; *s* of Ronald Horace Green and Josephine May Headley; *m* 1959, Helen Mary McIntyre; three *s* three *d*. *Educ:* Univ. of Tasmania (BSc Hons 1957; MSc 1959; DSc 1988); Univ. of Cambridge (PhD 1962). FAA 1974; Fellow, Aust. Inst. of Mining and Metallurgy, 1987. Geologist, Bureau of Mineral Resources, Geology and Geophysics, Canberra, 1957–59; Postgrad. Scholarship, Royal Commn for Exhibn of 1851, 1959–62; Research School of Earth Sciences, Australian National University: Res. Fellow, 1962–65; Fellow, 1965–68; Sen. Fellow, 1968–74; Professorial Fellow, 1974–76; Prof. of Geology, Univ. of Tasmania, 1977–93. Chief Science Advr, Dept of Arts, Sport, Envmt, Tourism and Territories, 1991–93. Hallimond Lect., Mineralogical Soc., 1996. For. Mem., Russian Acad. of Scis, 2003. Fellow: Amer. Geophysical Union, 2004; Mineralogical Soc., 2004. Hon. Fellow: Eur. Union of Geoscis, 1985; Geol Soc. of America, 1986. Hon. DLitt Tasmania, 1994. Edgeworth David Medal, Royal Soc., NSW, 1968; Stillwell Medal, Geol Soc. of Australia, 1977; Mawson Medal, 1982, Jaeger Medal, 1990, Aust. Acad. of Sci.; A. G. Werner Medaille, Deutsche Mineralogische Ges., 1998; Murchison Medal, Geol Soc., 2000; Humboldt Research Prize, 2001; Centenary Medal (Australia), 2002. *Publications:* numerous articles in fields of experimental petrology and geochemistry, in learned jls. *Recreations:* tennis, music. *Address:* Research School of Earth Sciences, Australian National University, Canberra, ACT 0200, Australia. *T:* (2) 61252488, *Fax:* (2) 61250756.

GREEN, David John Mark; QC 2000; a Recorder, since 2000; Director, HM Revenue and Customs (formerly HM Customs and Excise) Prosecutions Office, since 2004; *b* 8 March 1954; *s* of John Geoffrey Green and Margaret Rowena Green (*née* Millican); *m* 1980, Kate Sharkey; one *s* two *d*. *Educ:* Christ's Hosp., Horsham; St Catharine's Coll., Cambridge (MA Hons). Defence Intelligence Staff, MoD, 1975–78; called to the Bar, Inner Temple, 1979; practising barrister, 1979–; an Asst Recorder, 1995–2000. Liveryman, Co. of Gardeners, 2000– (Mem., Ct of Assts, 2007–). *Recreations:* walking, gardening. *Address:* HM Revenue and Customs Prosecutions Office, New King's Beam House, 22 Upper Ground, SE1 9BT. *T:* 0870 785 8348. *Club:* Garrick.

See also G. S. Green.

GREEN, Prof. David Mino Allen; Vice Chancellor and Chief Executive, and Professor of Economics, University of Worcester (formerly University College Worcester), since 2003; *b* 12 Aug. 1952; *s* of Prof. Mino Green, *qv*; *m* 1999, Catherine Nicole Mortimore; two *d*. *Educ:* Westminster Sch.; St John's Coll., Cambridge (MA, BA Econs 1973). Res./Campaigns Officer, Shelter (Scotland), 1973–74; Founder, Welfare Rights Service, Harlow DC, Essex, 1975–77; Economist, Imres Ltd, 1977–79; South Bank Polytechnic, then South Bank University: Lectr, 1979–84; Sen. Lectr, 1984–89; Principal Lectr and Hd of Econs, 1989–94; Jt Hd of Sch., Business Sch., 1994–98; Prof. of Econs, and Dean of Leeds Business Sch., Leeds Metropolitan Univ., 1998–2001; Pro Vice Chancellor, Thames Valley Univ., 2001–02. Board Member: W Midlands Regl Sports Bd, 2005–; Teaching and Develt Agency for Schs, 2006–. *Publications:* Banking and Financial Stability in Central Europe, 2002; contrib. numerous articles to econ. and socio-econ. learned jls. *Recreations:* family life, cooking, cricket, tennis, reading, travelling, ski-ing, sailing. *Address:* Vice Chancellor's Office, University of Worcester, St John's Campus, Henwick Grove, Worcester WR2 6AJ. *T:* (01905) 855123, *Fax:* (01905) 424638; *e-mail:* vc@worc.ac.uk. *Clubs:* Hurlingham; Worcestershire County Cricket.

GREEN, Prof. Dennis Howard, FBA 1992; Schröder Professor of German, University of Cambridge, 1979–89; Fellow of Trinity College, Cambridge, since 1949; *b* 26 June 1922; *s* of Herbert Maurice Green and Agnes Edith Green (*née* Fleming); *m* 1st, 1947, Dorothy Warren (marr. diss. 1972; she *d* 2006); one *d*; 2nd, 1972, Margaret Parry (*d* 1997);

3rd, 2001, Sarah Redpath. *Educ:* Latymer Upper Sch., London; Trinity Coll., Cambridge; Univ. of Basle. Univ. of Cambridge, 1940–41 and 1945–47; Univ. of Basle (Dr Phil.), 1947–49; Military service (RAC), 1941–45; Univ. Lectr in German, St Andrews, 1949–50; Research Fellowship, Trinity Coll., Cambridge (first year held *in absentia*), 1949–52; Univ. Lectr in German, Cambridge, 1950–66; Teaching Fellowship, Trinity Coll., Cambridge, 1952–66; Head of Dept of Other Languages, 1956–79, and Prof. of Modern Languages, Cambridge, 1966–79; Visiting Professor: Cornell Univ., 1965–66; Auckland Univ., 1966; Yale Univ., 1969; ANU, Canberra, 1971; UCLA, 1975; Univ. of Pennsylvania, 1975; Univ. of WA, 1976; Univ. of Freiburg, 1990; Vis. Fellow, Humanities Res. Centre, Canberra, 1978. Fellow, Netherlands Inst. for Advanced Study, Wassenaar, 1998. Pres., MHRA, 1997. *Publications:* The Carolingian Lord, 1965; The Millstätter Exodus: a crusading epic, 1966; (with Dr L. P. Johnson) Approaches to Wolfram von Eschenbach, 1978; Irony in the Medieval Romance, 1979; The Art of Recognition in Wolfram's Parzival, 1982; Medieval Listening and Reading, 1994; Language and History in the early Germanic World, 1998; The Beginnings of Medieval Romance: fact and fiction 1150–1220, 2002; Women Readers in the Middle Ages, 2007; reviews and articles in learned journals. *Recreations:* walking and foreign travel. *Address:* Trinity College, Cambridge CB2 1TQ. *T:* (01223) 339517.

GREEN, Prof. Diana Margaret, CBE 2007; PhD; DL; consultant; Founder and Director, Diana Green Consultancy Ltd, since 2008; Key Associate: Leadership Foundation for Higher Education, since 2008 (Member, 2003–07); Active Human Capital Ltd, since 2008; *b* 10 April 1943; *d* of Charles Edward Harris and Joan Harris (*née* Beresford); *m* 1967, Neville A. Green (marr. diss. 1979). *Educ:* South Park High Sch. for Girls, Lincoln; Reading Univ.; Queen Mary Coll., London (BSc Econ.); London Sch. of Econs (PhD Econ. 1976). HM CS, 1969–76; Lectr, Sen. Lectr and Actg Hd, Dept of Politics and Govt, City of London Poly., 1976–83; University of Central England: Hd of Dept, 1984–87; Asst Dir, 1987–92; Pro Vice-Chancellor, 1992–98; Vice-Chancellor, Sheffield Hallam Univ., 1998–2007. Consultant (part-time), DTI, 1976–81. Member: Quality Assessment Cttee, HEFCE, 1992–96; Higher Educn Innovation Fund Expert Gp, HEFCE/DTI, 2001–; Better Regulation Stakeholder Gp, DfES, 2003–; Chm., SRHE, 1998–99. Member: Black Country Develt Corp., 1992–94; Alexandra NHS Healthcare Trust, 1996–98. Member: W Midlands Regl Council, CBI, 1994–98; W Midlands IoD, 2008–; Birmingham Chamber of Commerce and Industry, 2008–. Founder Dir, Midlands Excellence, 1996–99; Director: Phoenix Sports UK, 1997–2000; Sheffield TEC, 1998–2001; Sheffield Industrial Mus. Trust, 1998–2002; Sheffield First for Investment, 1999–2002; Sheffield Galls and Museums Trust, 2000–08; Sheffield One, 2000–07; UUK, 2001–07; Creative Sheffield, 2006–07; Centre for Cities, 2006–. Former Mem. Council, All Party Parly Univ. Gp (now Hon. Mem.). Trustee: AGORA, Forum for Culture and Educn, 2007–; Air Safety Trust, Guild of Air Pilots and Navigators, 2006–; Flying Scholarships for the Disabled Trust, 2007–. FRSA. Freeman, City of London, 1998; Freeman, 2005, Liveryman, 2008, Guild of Air Pilots and Air Navigators; Freeman, Guild of Educators, 2008. DL W Midlands, 2008. *Publications:* articles, chapters, books and reports on industrial change and quality in higher education; contrib. to THES. *Recreations:* flying light aircraft, music, art, theatre.

GREEN, Rev. Canon (Edward) Michael (Bankes); Senior Research Fellow, Wycliffe Hall, Oxford, since 1997; Co-Rector, Holy Trinity Church, Raleigh, North Carolina, since 2005; *b* 20 Aug. 1930; British; *m* 1957, Rosemary Wake (*née* Storr); two *s* two *d*. *Educ:* Clifton Coll.; Oxford and Cambridge Univs. BD Cantab 1966. Exeter Coll., Oxford, 1949–53 (1st cl. Lit. Hum.); Royal Artillery (Lieut, A/Adjt), 1953–55; Queens' Coll., Cambridge, 1955–57 (1st cl. Theol. Tripos Pt III; Carus Greek Testament Prize; Fencing Blue), and Ridley Hall Theol Coll., 1955–57; Curate, Holy Trinity, Eastbourne, 1957–60; Lectr, London Coll. of Divinity, 1960–69; Principal, St John's Coll., Nottingham (until July 1970, London Coll. of Divinity), 1969–75; Canon Theologian of Coventry, 1970–76, Canon Theologian Emeritus, 1978–; Rector of St Aldate's, Oxford, 1975–87 (with Holy Trinity, Oxford, 1975–82 and with St Matthew, 1982–87); Prof. of Evangelism at Regent Coll., Vancouver, Univ. of BC, 1987–92. Member: Doctrine Commission of the Church, 1968–77; Church Unity Commn, 1974–. Archbishops' Advr in Evangelism, 1992–2001; leader of missions, overseas and in UK. Hon. DD Toronto, 1992; DD Lambeth, 1996. *Publications:* Called to Serve, 1964; Choose Freedom, 1965; The Meaning of Salvation, 1965; Man Alive, 1967; Runaway World, 1968; Commentary on 2 Peter and Jude, 1968; Evangelism in the Early Church, 1970; Jesus Spells Freedom, 1972; New Life, New Lifestyle, 1973; I Believe in the Holy Spirit, 1975, new edn 1985; You Must Be Joking, 1976; (ed) The Truth of God Incarnate, 1977; Why Bother With Jesus?, 1979; Evangelism—Now and Then, 1979; What is Christianity?, 1981; I Believe in Satan's Downfall, 1981; The Day Death Died, 1982; To Corinth with Love, 1982; World on the Run, 1983; Freed to Serve, 1983; The Empty Cross of Jesus, 1984; Come Follow Me, 1984; Lift Off to Faith, 1985; Baptism, 1987; Matthew for Today, 1988; Ten Myths about Christianity, 1988; Evangelism Through the Local Church, 1990; Reflections from the Lions Den, 1990; Who is this Jesus?, 1991; My God, 1992; On Your Knees, 1992; Good News and How to Share It, 1993; Acts for Today, 1993; (with Alister McGrath) Springboard for Faith, 1993; (with Paul Stevens) New Testament Spirituality, 1994; How Can I Lead a Friend to Christ?, 1995; Critical Choices, 1995; Strange Intelligence, 1997; Evangelism for Amateurs, 1998; After Alpha, 1998; Bible Reading for Amateurs, 1999; Churchgoing for Amateurs, 2000; The Message of Matthew, 2000; Asian Tigers for Christ, 2001; Adventure of Faith (autobiog.), 2001; But don't all religions lead to God?, 2002; Sharing your faith with a friend, 2002; Thirty Years that changed the world, 2002; The Books the Church Suppressed, 2005; contribs to various jls. *Recreations:* family, countryside pursuits, squash, fly fishing. *Address:* 7 Little Acreage, Old Marston, Oxford OX3 0PS. *T:* (01865) 248387, *Fax:* (01865) 792083; 2731 Anderson Drive, Raleigh, NC 27609, USA; *e-mail:* embgreen@gmail.com.

GREEN, Sir Edward (Patrick) Lycett, 6th Bt *cr* 1886, of Wakefield, Yorkshire and Ken Hill, Norfolk; *b* 14 Oct. 1950; *s* of late Richard David Rafe Lycett Green and (Marie) Patricia (*née* Maguire); *S* cousin, 2003; *m* 1st, 1971, Cordelia Sarah (marr. diss. 1975), *d* of C. B. Stretton Wilson; 2nd, 1977, Annette Patricia Josephine, *d* of O. P. J. Rochfort; two *d*. *Educ:* Stowe. *Heir: uncle* Rupert William Lycett Green [*b* 24 Oct. 1938; *m* 1963, Candida Betjeman (*see* Candida Lycett Green); two *s* three *d*].

GREEN, Dr Frank Alan, CEng, FIMMM; Principal, Charing Green Associates, since 1983; non-executive Director: 2 GC Active Management Ltd, since 2000; Somerset Health Authority, 2001–02; *b* 29 Oct. 1931; *s* of Frank Green and Winifred Hilda (*née* Payne); *m* 1957, Pauline Eleanor Tayler; one *s* two *d*. *Educ:* Mercers Sch., London; Univ. of London (BSc, PhD); Univ. of Exeter (MA 2002). CEng 1980; FIMMM (FIM 1978). UKAEA, 1956–57; various appts, Glacier Metal Co. Ltd (Associated Engrg Gp), 1957–65; Technical Dir, Alta Friccion SA, Mexico City, 1965–68; Manufg Dir, Stewart Warner Corp., 1968–72; Marketing Develt Manager, Calor Gp, 1972–74; Manufg Dir, 1974–77, Man. Dir, 1977–81, British Twin Disc Ltd; Industrial Advr (Under-Sec.), DTI, 1981–84. Director: Gen. Technology Systems (Scandinavia), 1989–91; Gen. Technology Systems (Portuguesa), 1989–91; Principal Consultant, General Technology Systems Ltd, 1984–90. Dir, Anglo-Mexican Chamber of Commerce, Mexico City, 1966–68. Member of Council: Inst. of Metals, 1990–91; Inst. of Materials, 1992–94; Chm., W of Englan Metals and Materials Assoc., 1999–2000. *Publications:* contrib. technical, medical ethical historical and managerial books and jls in UK and Mexico. *Recreations:* photography military history, rough walking. *Address:* Fernlea House, 49 Ditton Street, Ilminster, Som TA19 0BW.

GREEN, Prof. Gary George Reginald, DPhil; Director, York Neuroimaging Centre and Professor of Neuroimaging, University of York, since 2004; *b* 27 May 1951; *s* of Harry Clifford Green and Iris Ellen Green (*née* Asser); *m* 1981, Rose Hilton; one *s* one *d*. *Educ* Burnt Mill Comp. Sch., Harlow; Hertford Coll., Oxford (MA 1979; DPhil 1976; BM BCh 1979). E. P. Abrahams Fellow, Hertford Coll., Oxford, 1978–80; University o Newcastle upon Tyne: Lectr, 1980–95; Reader, 1995–2004; Dir, Inst. of Neuroscience 2003–04. Chm., Am Systems Ltd, 1987–95; Dir, YNI Ltd, 2004–. Mem. Court, RCS 1994–2000. Vice-Chm., Wellcome Trust Neurosci. and Mental Health Cttee, 200 (Mem., 2000–04). Trustee, Jesmond Swimming Pool, 2002–04. FRSocMed; FRSA *Publications:* articles on neurosci., non-linear dynamics, child language and neurologica problems in learned jls. *Recreations:* making my wife laugh, gardening, swimming. *Address* Wanwood House, Front Street, Benton, Newcastle upon Tyne NE7 7XE. *T:* (01904 435346, *Fax:* (01904) 435356; *e-mail:* gary.green@ynic.york.ac.uk. *Club:* Royal Society of Medicine.

GREEN, Geoffrey Stephen; Senior Partner, Ashurst (formerly Ashurst Morris Crisp) since 1998; *b* 3 Sept. 1949; *s* of John Geoffrey Green and Margaret Rowena Green (*né* Millican); *m* 1982, Sarah Charlton Chesshire; three *s*. *Educ:* Forest Sch.; St Catharine' Coll., Cambridge (MA). Admitted Solicitor, 1975. Solicitor, 1975–, Partner, 1983– Ashurst (formerly Ashurst Morris Crisp). *Recreations:* golf, tennis, riding. *Address:* (office Broadwalk House, 5 Appold Street, EC2A 2HA. *T:* (020) 7638 1111.

See also D. J. M. Green.

GREEN, Gerard Nicholas Valentine; Chief Executive, Health Care Projects Ltd, sinc 1999 (Executive Director, 1997); *b* 6 Aug. 1950; *s* of James Arnold Green and Margarath Ella Green; *m* 1977, Maralyn Ann Ranger; one *s* one *d*. *Educ:* Highgate Sch.; Universit Coll., London (BA); Univ. of Warwick (MA); Birkbeck Coll., London (MA). AHSM Nat. admin. trainee, 1974–75; Dep. Hosp. Sec., St George's Hosp., SW17, 1975–77; As Sector Administrator, Cane Hill Hosp., Surrey, 1977–79; Sector Administrato Farnborough Hosp., Kent, 1979–82; Administrator, KCH, 1982–84; Chief Exec. Office Tabuk Military Hosp., Saudi Arabia, 1984–87; Dist Gen. Man., Bromley HA, 1987–89 Regl Gen. Man., SE Thames RHA, 1989–94; Chief Exec., Royal Hosps NHS Trus 1994–97. Dir, HCP (Defence Projects) Ltd, 2001–. Non-exec. Dir, Meridian Hosp. Co 2000–05; Chairman: Derby Healthcare plc, 2003–06; Central Nottinghamshire Hosps plc 2005–07; HCP (Canada) Ltd, 2006–. Mem., UKCC, 1993–98. FRSA 1989. *Recreations* travel, reading. *Address:* Health Care Projects Ltd, 3 White Oak Square, London Road Swanley, Kent BR8 7AG. *Club:* Reform.

GREEN, Sir (Gregory) David, KCMG 2004 (CMG 1999); Director-General, Britis Council, 1999–2007; *b* 2 Dec. 1948; *s* of Thomas Dixon Green and Mary Mabella Gree (*née* Walley); *m* 1977, Corinne Butler; three *d*. *Educ:* Leys Sch., Cambridge; Keswick Ha Coll. of Educn, Norwich (Cert Ed); Trinity Hall, Cambridge (BEd). Volunteer, VSO Pakistan, 1967–68; teaching, Conisborough and Rotherham, 1972–76; Dir, Children' Relief Internat., 1976–79; Save the Children Fund: Staff Develt and Trng Officer, 197 Dep. Dir of Personnel, 1982; Dir of Personnel, 1983; Dir of Personnel and Admin 1988–90; Dir, VSO, 1990–99. Dir and Council Mem., Council for Colony Holidays fo School-children, 1970–80; Mem. Council, VSO, 2000–. Member: Laurence Olivie Awards Panel, 1984–85; Council, English Stage Co., 2005–. Chm., Prince's Sch. o Traditional Arts, 2008–. Gov., Univ. of the Arts London, 2007–. Chm., Roya Commonwealth Soc., 2008–. Chair, Dartington Hall Trust, 2008–. FRGS 1991; FRS 1990. Freeman, City of London, 2006. Freeman, City of Freetown, Sierra Leone, 2004 Hon. FCT 2006. *Publication:* Chorus, 1977. *Recreations:* theatre, music, painting.

GREEN, Hon. Sir Guy (Stephen Montague), AC 1994; KBE 1982; CVO 200 Governor of Tasmania, 1995–2003; *b* 26 July 1937; *s* of Clement Francis Montague Gree and Beryl Margaret Jenour Green; *m* 1963, Rosslyn Mary Marshall; two *s* two *d*. *Edu* Launceston Church Grammar Sch.; Univ. of Tasmania. Alfred Houston Schol (Philosophy) 1958; LLB (Hons) 1960. Admitted to Bar of Tasmania, 1960; Partne Ritchie & Parker Alfred Green & Co. (Launceston), 1963–71; Magistrate 1971–73; Chie Justice of Tasmania, 1973–95; University of Tasmania: Mem., Faculty of Law, 1974–85 Chancellor, 1985–95. Lieut-Gov., Tasmania, 1982–95; Adminr, Commonwealth o Australia, May–Aug. 2003. Pres., Tasmanian Bar Assoc., 1968–70; Chm., Council of Lav Reporting, 1978–85; Dep. Chm., Australian Inst. of Judicial Admin, 1986–88. Chm Tasmanian Cttee, Duke of Edinburgh's Award Scheme in Australia, 1975–80; Di Winston Churchill Meml Trust, 1975–85 (Dep. Nat. Chm., 1980–85; Chm. Tasmania Regional Cttee, 1975–80); Chairman: Bd, Ten Days on the Island, 2003–; Trustee Tasmanian Mus. and Art Gall., 2004–. Chm. Cttee, Internat. Antarctic Inst., 2004– Member: Bd, Menzies Foundn, 2005–; Menzies Res. Inst., 2005–; Trustee and Mem Foundn Council, Constitution Educn Fund Australia. Nat. Pres., Order of Australi Assoc., 2004–07. St John Ambulance, Australia: Pres., Tasmanian Council, 1984–92 Priory Exec. Officer, 1984–91; Chancellor, 1991–95; Dep. Prior, 1995–2003. Hon Antarctic Ambassador for Tasmania, 2005–. Hon. Prof., Antarctic Climate and Ecosystem Co-operative Res. Centre, Univ. of Tasmania, 2005–. Hon. LLD Tasmania, 1996. KS 1985. *Address:* 13 Marine Terrace, Battery Point, Hobart, Tas 7004, Australia. *Clul* Tasmanian (Hobart).

GREEN, Harriet; Chief Executive Officer, Premier Farnell plc, since 2006; *b* 12 Dec 1961; *d* of late Dermot Green and of Nerys Allen; *m* 2004, Graham Clarkson; two step *Educ:* Univ. of London (BA Hons Medieval Hist. 1983); London Sch. of Econs (Busine Psychol. 1985); Harvard Business Sch.; Aspen Inst.; Ashridge Mgt Coll. Man. Dir, Macr Gp, 1985–94; Arrow Electronics Inc.: Vice Pres., Europ. Mktg, 1994–96; Pres., Arrow N Europe and Africa, and Corp. Vice Pres., 1996–2000; Pres., Arrow CMS, N Americ 2000–01; Hd, Global Strategy and New Business Develt, 2002; Pres., Asia Pacifi 2002–06. Former Mem., Young Presidents Assoc. *Recreations:* yoga, reading, theatre hiking, horse-riding, cycling. *Address:* Premier Farnell plc, 25–28 Old Burlington Street W1S 3AN. *T:* (020) 7851 4102, *Fax:* (020) 7851 4110; *e-mail:* harrietkgreen@ premierfarnell.com.

GREEN, Henrietta-Jane; food writer, since 1977; broadcaster; company director, sinc 1987; food consultant, since 1989; *b* 27 Oct. 1948; *d* of Aubrey and Valerie Green. *Edu* Sarum Hall Prep. Sch.; Queen's Coll., Harley St; Royal Acad. of Dramatic Art (Dip. Stag Mgt). Free-lance journalist and consultant; Founder, FoodLoversBritain.com, an organiser of FoodLovers' Fairs. Mem., London Food Bd; Trustee, Jane Grigson Trus *Publications:* Fine Flavoured Food, 1978; The Marinade Cookbook, 1978; RAC Foo Routes, 1988; 10 Minute Cuisine, 1991; The Festive Food of England, 1991; Henriett Green's New Country Kitchen, 1992; A Glorious Harvest, 1994; Fresh From the Garden 1994; Henrietta Green's Food Lovers' Guide to Britain, 1994, 1996; British Food Find

1997; The Food Lovers' Christmas, 1997; Henrietta's Home Cooking, 1997; Recipes from an English Country Garden, 1998; Henrietta Green's Farmers' Market Cookbook, 2001. *Recreations:* walking, talking, shopping, playing with my dog, eating, movies, looking at gardens, gardening, looking at buildings. *Address:* FoodLovers (Britain) Ltd, Unit 106, Buspace Studios, Conlan Street, W10 5AP. *T:* (020) 8206 6111, *Fax:* (020) 8206 6112; *e-mail:* office@foodloversbritain.com. *Club:* Groucho.

GREEN, Ven. John, QHC 2006; Director General, Naval Chaplaincy Service, Chaplain of the Fleet and Archdeacon for the Royal Navy, since 2006; *b* 14 Aug. 1953; *s* of Albert Frederick and Lilian Green; *m* 1977, Janette Silvester; two *s. Educ:* S W Ham Co. Tech. Sch.; NE London Poly. (Grad. Inst. Physics); Lincoln Theol Coll. (BCS 1983). Project engr, Thorn Lighting Ltd, 1974–80 (Sen. Engr, 1977–80); ordained deacon 1983, priest 1984; Curate: St Michael and All Angels, W Watford, 1983–86; St Stephen's, St Albans, 1986–91; Chaplain, RN, 1991–: HMS Sultan, 1991–92; 3rd Destroyer Sqdn, 1992–93; HM Naval Base, Portsmouth, 1993–94; HMS Excellent, 1994–95; Minor Warfare Vessel Flotilla, 1996–98; Staff Chaplain to Chaplain of the Fleet, 1998–2001; HMS Ark Royal, 2001–03; HMS Collingwood, 2003–06. *Recreations:* music, inland waterways and boating, photography. *Address:* Leach Building, Mail Point 1.2, Whale Island, Portsmouth PO2 8DX. *T:* (023) 9262 5208; *e-mail:* john.green107@mod.uk.

GREEN, John Edward, PhD; FREng, FRAeS, FAIAA; Consultant and Chief Scientist to Aircraft Research Association Ltd, since 1995 (Chief Executive, 1988–95); *b* 26 Aug. 1937; *s* of John Green and Ellen Green (*née* O'Dowd); *m* 1959, Gillian (*née* Jackson); one *s* one *d. Educ:* Birkenhead Inst. Grammar Sch.; St John's Coll., Cambridge (Scholar; BA 1959; MA 1963; PhD 1966). CEng 1972; FRAeS 1978. Student Apprentice, Bristol Aircraft Ltd, 1956; De Havilland Engine Co., 1959–61; Royal Aircraft Establishment, 1964–81: Head of Transonic/Supersonic Wind Tunnel Div., 1971; Head of Propulsion Div., 1973; Head of Noise Div., 1974; Head of Aerodynamics Dept., 1978–81; Dir, Project Time and Cost Analysis, MoD (PE), 1981–84; Minister-Counsellor Defence Equipment, and Dep. Head of British Defence Staff, Washington, 1984–85; Dep. Dir (Aircraft), RAE, 1985–87. Vis. Prof., Cranfield Univ., 1996–2004. President: Internat. Council of the Aeronautical Scis, 1996–98 (Mem. Council, 1986–2000; Chm., Prog. Cttee, 1992–96; Life Mem., 2002); RAeS, 1996–97 (Mem. Council, 1986–2000; Vice Pres., 1992–95; Hon. Treas., 1992–96); Mem. Council, AIRTO, 1988–95. Mem. Court, Cranfield Univ. (formerly Cranfield Inst. of Technol.), 1988– (Mem. Council, 1995–2005). Royal Aeronautical Society: Goldstein Lectr, 1991; Busk Prize, 1992; de Havilland Lectr, 2000; Westland Prize, 2002; Templer Lectr, 2004; Lanchester Lectr, 2005; Wilbur and Orville Wright Lectr, 2006; Hodgson Prize, 2005; Gold Award, 2005; J. D. North Lectr, 2008; R. K. Pierson Lectr, 2008. FREng (FEng 1994); FAIAA 1999. Maurice Roy Medal, Internat. Council of Aeronautical Scis, 2006. *Publications:* contribs to books and learned jls, chiefly on fluid mechanics, aerodynamics and envmtl impact of aviation. *Recreations:* music, mountain walking (Munroist, 1994). *Address:* 1 Leighton Street, Woburn, Beds MK17 9PJ. *T:* (01525) 290631.

GREEN, John Louis, FCA; Chairman: Principal Investment Management, since 2000; Principal Investment Management Holdings, since 2001; *b* 2 March 1945; *s* of Stanley and Rose Green; *m* 1972, Kathleen Whelan; three *s* one *d. Educ:* Merchant Taylors' Sch., Northwood; Oriel Coll., Oxford (MA). FCA 1970. Price Waterhouse & Co., 1966–69; Kleinwort Benson, 1969–70; McAnally Montgomery & Co., 1970–79; James Capel, 1979–92; HSBC Investment Bank, 1992–96, Man. Dir, HSBC-Capel UK, 1995–96; Chief Exec., James Capel Investment Mgt, 1996–98. Chairman: Inventive Leisure plc, 2000–06; Merchant Security, 2006–. Dir various cos. *Recreations:* golf, opera, reading. *Address:* Hursley House, The Warren, East Horsley, Surrey KT24 5RH. *T:* (01483) 282600. *Clubs:* Royal Automobile; Wisley Golf.

GREEN, John Michael, CB 1976; Commissioner, 1971–85, Deputy Chairman, 1973–85, Board of Inland Revenue; *b* 5 Dec. 1924; *s* of late George and Faith Green; *m* 1951, Sylvia (*née* Crabb) (*d* 1999); one *s* one *d. Educ:* Merchant Taylors' Sch., Rickmansworth; Jesus Coll., Oxford (MA (Hons)). Served War, Army, RAC, 1943–46. Entered Inland Revenue as Asst Principal, 1948; served in HM Treasury, as Principal, 1956–57; Asst Sec., 1962; Under Sec., Bd of Inland Revenue, 1971. Mem., NW Surrey HA, 1989–95. *Recreation:* gardening. *Address:* 36 Copper Beech House, Heathside Crescent, Woking, Surrey GU22 7BB. *T:* (01483) 772599. *Club:* Reform.

GREEN, Dr John Timothy; Chief Co-ordinating Officer, Imperial College London, since 2004; *b* 1 Jan. 1944; *s* of Thomas Albert Green and Joan (*née* Chamberlain); *m* 1985, Susan Mary Shattock; one *s. Educ:* King Edward's Five Ways Sch., Birmingham; Queens' Coll., Cambridge (BA 1966; MA 1970; PhD Maths 1970). Queens' College, Cambridge: Bye Fellow, 1970–72; Fellow, 1972–93; Lectr in Maths, 1972–93; Dean of Coll., 1972–77; Tutor, 1977–80; Sen. Tutor, 1980–93; Life Fellow, 1993; Chief Exec., RSocMed, 1993–96; Dir, Historic Properties (London), English Heritage, 1997–98; Sec., Faculty of Medicine, Imperial Coll., London, 1998–2004. Director: S Leics Garages Ltd, 1985–95; Pennant Hotels Ltd, 1987–95; RSM Press Ltd, 1993–96; Chadwyck-Healey Ltd, 1997–99; Kennedy Inst. of Rheumatology, 1999–; NW London Hosps Trust, 2001–; Imperial Coll. Bioincubator Ltd, 2004–; Ind. Dir, 3i plc, 1996–. Member: CBI Professions Wkg Gp, 1995–96; London First Medicine, 1995–96. Recruitment Advr, FCO, 1992–99. Trustee: Harpur Trust, Bedford, 1984–87; Project Hope, 1995–2001 (Vice-Chm., 1998–2001). Governor: Hills Rd Sixth Form Coll., Cambridge, 1993–98; Perse Sch., Cambridge, 2001–. *Publications:* contrib. Jl Fluid Mechanics and others. *Recreations:* opera, music, fell-walking. *Address:* 40 Newton Road, Cambridge CB2 8AL. *T:* (01223) 353756.

GREEN, Katherine Anne, (Kate), OBE 2005; JP; Chief Executive, Child Poverty Action Group, since 2004; *b* 2 May 1960; *d* of Maurice Green and Jessie Craig Green (*née* Bruce); *m* 1985, Richard Duncan Mabb (marr. diss. 2006). *Educ:* Currie High Sch., Midlothian; Univ. of Edinburgh (LLB Hons 1982). Barclays Bank, 1982–97; Whitehall and Industry Gp Secondee to Home Office, 1997–99; Dir, NCOPF, 2000–04. Member: Lord Chancellor's Adv. Cttee, City of London, 2001–; Nat. Employment Panel, 2001–07; London Child Poverty Commn, 2006–. Dir, Project Fresh Start, 2001–03. Treas., 2000–07, Trustee, 2006–07, Family and Parenting (formerly Nat. Family and Parenting) Inst. Trustee: Avenues Youth Project, 2000–05; Inst. for Fiscal Studies, 2004–; Friends Provident Foundn, 2007–. JP City of London, 1993. *Recreations:* theatre, books, swimming, food. *Address:* (office) 94 White Lion Street, N1 9PF. *T:* (020) 7837 7979, *Fax:* (020) 7837 6414; *e-mail:* kgreen@cpag.org.uk.

GREEN, Sir Kenneth, Kt 1988; MA; Vice-Chancellor (formerly Director), Manchester Metropolitan University (formerly Manchester Polytechnic), 1981–97; *b* 7 March 1934; *s* of James William and Elsie May Green; *m* 1961, Glenda (*née* Williams); one *d. Educ:* Helsby Grammar Sch.; Univ. of Wales, Bangor (BA 1st Cl. Hons); Univ. of London (MA). 2nd Lieut, S Wales Borderers, 1955–57. Management Trainee, Dunlop Rubber Co., 1957–58; Teacher, Liverpool, 1958–60; Lecturer: Widnes Technical Coll., 1961–62; Stockport College of Technology, 1962–64; Sen. Lectr, Bolton College of Education, 1964–68; Head of Educn, City of Birmingham College of Education, 1968–72; Dean of Faculty, Manchester Polytechnic, 1973–81. Vice-Chm., Manchester TEC, 1989–93 (Mem. Bd, 1989–93); Member: Council, CNAA, 1985–93; UFC, 1989–93. Non-exec. Dir, Halton PCT, 2002–06. Chm., Council of Mgt, Rathbone Soc., 1993–95; Jt Chm., Rathbone Community Industry Ltd, 1995–97. Member, Governing Body: The Heath Comprehensive Sch., Runcorn, 1988–92; Victoria Rd Co. Primary Sch., Runcorn, 1990– (Chm., 1993–2003). Chm., Halton Duke of Edinburgh Award Cttee, 1998–. CCMI (CIMgt 1996). Hon. Mem., Manchester Literary & Philosophical Soc.; Hon. MRNCM; Hon. Fellow, Bolton Inst. of Higher Educn, 1997. Hon. LLD Manchester, 1992; Hon. DLitt: Salford, 1997; Manchester Metropolitan, 1998. *Recreations:* Rugby football, beer tasting. *Address:* 40 Royden Avenue, Runcorn, Cheshire WA7 4SP. *T:* (01928) 575201.

GREEN, Rt Rev. Laurence Alexander; *see* Bradwell, Area Bishop of.

GREEN, Prof. Leslie, DPhil; Professor of the Philosophy of Law, University of Oxford, since 2007; Fellow of Balliol College, Oxford, since 2007; *b* Bridge of Weir, Scotland, 27 Nov. 1956; *s* of Robert Frederick Green and Elizabeth Laird Mackie; *m* 1980, Prof. Denise Réaume. *Educ:* Queen's Univ., Kingston, Ont (BA 1978); Nuffield Coll., Oxford (MPhil 1980; DPhil 1984). Darby Fellow and Tutor in Pol Theory, Lincoln Coll., Oxford, 1983–85; Prof. of Law and Philos., 1986–2006, Prof., 2007–, Osgoode Hall Law Sch., York Univ., Toronto. Visiting Professor: Boalt Hall Sch. of Law, Univ. of Calif, Berkeley, 1995; Sch. of Law, Univ. of Texas, Austin, 2002–06; Hauser Global Law Sch. Prog., NY Univ. Sch. of Law, 2007; Vis. Fellow, Centre for Law and Philos., Columbia Law Sch., NY, 2003. *Publications:* The Authority of the State, 1988; Law and the Community, 1989; articles in jls incl. Oxford Jl of Legal Studies, Legal Theory, Michigan Law Rev., NYU Law Rev., Philos. Qly, Jl of Pol Philos., Canadian Jl of Law and Jurisprudence, Osgoode Hall Law Jl, etc. *Recreation:* music. *Address:* Balliol College, Oxford OX1 3BJ. *T:* (01865) 277777; *e-mail:* leslie.green@law.ox.ac.uk.

GREEN, Prof. Leslie Leonard, CBE 1989; PhD; FInstP; Professor of Experimental Physics, University of Liverpool, 1964–86, now Emeritus; Director, Daresbury Laboratory, 1981–88; *b* 30 March 1925; *s* of Leonard and Victoria Green; *m* 1952, Dr Helen Therese Morgan; one *s* one *d. Educ:* Alderman Newton's Sch., Leicester; King's Coll., Cambridge (MA, PhD). FInstP 1966. British Atomic Energy Proj., 1944–46; University of Liverpool: Lectr, 1948–57; Sen. Lectr, 1957–62; Reader, 1962–64; Dean, Faculty of Sciences, 1969–72; Pro-Vice-Chancellor, 1978–81. Mem., SRC Nuclear Physics Bd, 1972–75 and 1979–82. *Publications:* articles on nuclear physics in scientific jls. *Address:* Oakwood House, Eastbury, Hungerford, Berks RG17 7JP.

GREEN, Lucinda Jane, MBE 1978; three-day event rider; *b* 7 Nov. 1953; *d* of Maj.-Gen. George Erroll Prior-Palmer, CB, DSO and Lady Doreen Hersey Winifred Prior-Palmer; *m* 1981, David (marr. diss. 1992), *s* of Burrington Green, Brisbane; one *s* one *d. Educ:* St Mary's, Wantage; Idbury Manor, Oxon. Member of winning Junior European Team, 1971; Winner, 3 Day Events: Badminton Horse Trials Championships, 1973, 1976, 1977, 1979, 1983, 1984; Burghley, 1977, 1981; Individual European Championships, 1975, 1977; World Championship, 1982; Member: Olympic Team, Montreal, 1976, Los Angeles, 1984; European Championship Team: Luhmühlen, W Germany, 1975 (team Silver Medallist and individual Gold Medallist); Burghley, 1977 (team Gold Medallist), 1985 (team Gold Medallist), 1987 (team Gold Medallist); European Team, 1979, 1983 (team and individual Silver Medallist); Alternative Olympic Team, 1980; World Championship Team: Kentucky, 1978; Luhmühlen, W Germany, 1982 (team and individual Gold Medallist). Co-presenter, Horses, Channel 4, 1987; Commentator: BBC, Badminton, 1987–2005; BBC, Olympic Games, 1988; Channel 7, Australia, Olympic Games, 1992, 1996, 2000 and 2004; Presenter, Rural Rides, Meridian TV, 1997 and 1998. Editorial Consultant, Eventing, 1989–92. *Publications:* Up, Up and Away, 1978; Four Square, 1980; Regal Realm, 1983; Cross-Country Riding, 1986, 2nd edn 1995; The Young Rider, 1993. *Recreations:* driving, ski-ing, scuba diving, travelling abroad. *Address:* The Tree House, Appleshaw, Andover SP11 9BS.

GREEN, Prof. Sir Malcolm, Kt 2007; DM; FRCP; Vice Principal, Faculty of Medicine, 1997–2006, and Head of National Heart and Lung Institute, 2001–06, Imperial College of Science, Technology and Medicine; Professor of Respiratory Medicine, Imperial College, 1998–2006, now Professor Emeritus; Consultant Physician, Royal Brompton Hospital (formerly Brompton Hospital), 1975–2006; *b* 25 Jan. 1942; *s* of late James Bisdee Malcolm Green and Frances Marjorie Lois Green; *m* 1971, Julieta Caroline Preston; two *s* two *d* (and one *d* decd). *Educ:* Charterhouse Sch. (Foundn Scholar); Trinity Coll., Oxford (Exhibnr; BA 1963; BSc 1965; MA, BM, BCh 1967; DM 1978); St Thomas's Hosp. Med. Sch. (Scholar). FRCP 1980 (MRCP 1970). Jun. appts, St Thomas' and Brompton Hosps, 1968–71; Lectr, Dept of Medicine, St Thomas' Hosp., 1971–74; Radcliffe Travelling Fellow, Harvard University Med. Sch., 1971–73; Sen. Registrar, Westminster and Brompton Hosps, 1974–75; Consultant Physician and Physician i/c Chest Dept, St Bartholomew's Hosp., 1975–86; Dean, Nat. Heart and Lung Inst., 1988–90 (Mem., Cttee of Management, 1988–95); Dir, BPMF, 1991–96; Campus Dean, St Mary's Hosp., 1997–2001. Member: Supraregl Services Adv. Cttee, 1991–96; NHS Taskforce on Res. (Culyer Cttee), 1993–94; Health of the Nation Wider Health Wkg Gp, 1991–97; NHS Central R&D Cttee, 1995–2002 (Chm., 1999); NHS Exec. Bd, 1999; Chm., NHS R&D Bd, 1999; acting Dir, R&D for NHS, 1999. Chm., Exec. Cttee and Nat. Council, British Lung Foundn, 1984–94 (Pres. and Chm., Council, 1994–2001); Chm. Acad. Steering Gp, BPMF, 1989–90; Member, Committees of Management, Institutes of Child Health, Psychiatry, Neurology, Ophthalmology, Cancer Research, Dental Surgery, and RPMS, 1991–96. Member: Bd of Govs, Nat. Heart and Chest Hosps, 1988–90; Senate, 1998–2004, Council, 1997–2005, Imperial Coll., London. Chm., London Medicine, 1996–2000; Bd Mem., London First Centre, 1996–99, London First, 2000–02; Adv. Bd, Medtel, 2006–; Adv. Bd, Brompton Cross Clinic, 2006–. Non-executive Director: St Mary's NHS Trust, 1997–2001; Royal Brompton and Harefield Hosps, 2001–06. Trustee: Heart Disease and Diabetes Res. Trust, 1988–2003; Fledgeling Charity Funds, 1993–98; Nat. Heart and Lung Foundn, 2000–. Treasurer, 1977–85, Pres., 1992–2001, United Hosps Sailing Club. FMedSci 2000. *Publications:* chapters and articles in med. books and jls on gen. medicine, respiratory medicine and respiratory physiology. *Recreations:* sailing, ski-ing. *Address:* 38 Lansdowne Gardens, SW8 2EF. *T:* (020) 7622 8286. *Clubs:* Royal Thames Yacht; Itchenor Sailing (Commodore); Royal Yacht Squadron; Imperial Poona Yacht (Hon. Sec.).

GREEN, Prof. Malcolm Leslie Hodder, PhD; FRS 1985; CChem, FRSC; Professor of Inorganic Chemistry, 1989–2003, now Emeritus, and Head of Department, Inorganic Chemistry Laboratory, 1988–2003, University of Oxford; Fellow of St Catherine's College, Oxford, 1988–2003; *b* 16 April 1936; *s* of late Leslie Ernest Green, MD and Sheila Ethel (*née* Hodder); *m* 1965, Jennifer Clare Bilham; two *s* one *d. Educ:* Denstone Coll.; Acton Technical Coll. (BSc); Imperial Coll. of Science and Technol., London Univ. (DIC, PhD 1958); MA Cantab. CChem, FRSC 1981. Asst Lectr in Inorganic Chem., Univ. of Cambridge, 1960–63; Fellow of Corpus Christi Coll., Cambridge, 1961–63; University of Oxford: Septcentenary Fellow and Tutor in Inorganic Chem., Balliol Coll., 1963–88; Deptl Demonstrator, 1963; Lectr, 1965–88; British Gas Royal Soc.

Sen. Res. Fellow, 1979–86. A. P. Sloan Vis. Prof., Harvard Univ., 1973; Sherman Fairchild Vis. Scholar, CIT, 1981. Tilden Lectr and Prize, RSC, 1982; Debye Lectr, Cornell Univ., 1985; Sir Edward Frankland Prize Lectr, 1988; Ernest H. Swift Lectr, CIT, 1998. A Founder and Dir, Oxford Catalysts Gp Plc. Dr *hc* Universidade Técnica de Lisboa, 1996. Corday-Morgan Medal and Prize in Inorganic Chem., Chemical Soc., 1974; Medal for Transition Metal Chem., Chemical Soc., 1978; Award for Inorganic Chem., ACS, 1984; RSC Award for Organometallic Chem., 1986; Karl-Ziegler Prize, Ges. Deutscher Chemiker, 1992; Davy Medal, Royal Soc., 1995; Award for Organometallic Chem., ACS, 1997; Sir Geoffrey Wilkinson Medal, RSC, 1999. *Publications:* Organometallic Compounds: Vol. II, The Transition Elements, 1968; (with G. E. Coates, P. Powell and K. Wade) Principles of Organometallic Chemistry, 1968. *Address:* St Catherine's College, Oxford OX1 3UJ.

GREEN, Malcolm Robert, DPhil; Member, City of Glasgow Council, 1995–2007; Lecturer in Roman History, University of Glasgow, 1967–98; *b* 4 Jan. 1943; *m* 1971; one *s* two *d*. *Educ:* Wyggeston Boys' School, Leicester; Magdalen College, Oxford. MA, DPhil. Member: Glasgow Corp., 1973–75; Strathclyde Regional Council, 1975–96 (Chairman: Educn Cttee, 1982–90; Envmt Sub-Cttee, 1990–94; Racial Equality Sub-Cttee, 1994–96); Chm., Educn Cttee, 1996–99, Chief Whip, subseq. Business Manager, 1999–2005, City of Glasgow Council. Chairman: Educn Cttee, Convention of Scottish Local Authorities, 1978–90; Management Side, Scottish Jt Negotiating Cttees for Teaching Staff in Sch. and Further Educn, 1977–90; Nat. Cttee for In-Service Training of Teachers, 1977–86; Scottish Cttee for Staff Develt in Educn, 1987–91. Commissioner, Manpower Services Commn, 1983–85. *Recreation:* talking politics. *Address:* 46 Victoria Crescent Road, Glasgow G12 9DE. *T:* (0141) 339 2007.

GREEN, Margaret Beryl; *see* Clunies Ross, M. B.

GREEN, Rt Rev. Mark, MC 1945; an Assistant Bishop, Diocese of Chichester, 1982–2006; *b* 28 March 1917; *s* of late Rev. Ernest William Green, OBE, and Miranda Mary Green; unmarried. *Educ:* Rossall Sch.; Lincoln Coll., Oxford (MA). Curate, St Catharine's, Gloucester, 1940; Royal Army Chaplains' Dept, 1943–46 (despatches, 1945); Dir of Service Ordination Candidates, 1947–48; Vicar of St John, Newland, Hull, 1948–53; Short Service Commn, Royal Army Chaplains' Dept, 1953–56; Vicar of South Bank, Teesside, 1956–58; Rector of Cottingham, Yorks, 1958–64; Vicar of Bishopthorpe and Acaster Malbis, York, 1964–72; Hon. Chaplain to Archbp of York, 1964–72; Rural Dean of Ainsty, 1964–68; Canon and Prebendary of York Minster, 1963–72; Bishop Suffragan of Aston, 1972–82; Hon. Assistant: Christ Church, St Leonards-on-Sea, 1982–94; St Mary, Eastbourne, 1994–2006. Chm. of Governing Body, Aston Training Scheme, 1977–83; Provost, Woodard Schs Southern Div., 1982–89. Hon. DSc Aston, 1980. *Publication:* Diary of Doubt and Faith, 1974. *Address:* The College of St Barnabas, Blackberry Lane, Lingfield RH7 6NJ. *T:* (01342) 872824.

GREEN, Matthew Roger; Senior Partner, and Planning Consultant since 2005, Green Planning Solutions LLP; *b* 12 April 1970; *s* of Roger Hector Green and Pamela Gillian Green; *m* 1999, Sarah Louise Henthorn. *Educ:* Birmingham Univ. (BA (Hons) Medieval Studies). Sales and Marketing Manager, Plaskit Ltd, 1991–96; self employed, working in timber products and PR sectors, 1996–2003. Director: Shropshire Affordable Homes Ltd, 2005–; Noah Ltd, 2007–. Contested (Lib Dem) Wolverhampton SW, 1997; MP (Lib Dem) Ludlow, 2001–05; contested (Lib Dem) same seat, 2005. *Recreations:* cricket, mountaineering. *Address:* (office) 3A High Street, Much Wenlock, Shropshire TF13 6AA; *e-mail:* mghome@btconnect.com. *Club:* Liberal.

GREEN, Michael; *see* Green, N. M.

GREEN, Rev. Canon Michael; *see* Green, Rev. Canon E. M. B.

GREEN, Prof. Michael Boris, FRS 1989; John Humphrey Plummer Professor of Theoretical Physics and Fellow of Clare Hall, University of Cambridge, since 1993; *b* 22 May 1946; *s* of late Absalom and Genia Green; *m* 2005, Prof. Joanna Chataway; one *d*. *Educ:* Churchill Coll., Cambridge (BA, PhD; Rayleigh Prize 1969). Res. Fellow, Inst. for Advanced Study, Princeton, NJ, 1970–72; Fellowships in Cambridge, 1972–77; SERC Advanced Fellow, Oxford, 1977–79; Lectr, Queen Mary Coll., London Univ., 1979–85; Prof. of Physics, QMC, later QMW, 1985–93. Vis. Associate, Caltech, Pasadena, for periods during 1981–85; Nuffield Science Fellowship, 1984–86; SERC Sen. Fellowship, 1986–91. Maxwell Medal and Prize, 1987, Dirac Medal and Prize, 2004, Inst. of Physics; Hopkins Prize, Cambridge Philosophical Soc., 1987; Dirac Medal, Internat. Centre for Theoretical Physics, Trieste, 1989; Dannie Heinemann Prize, APS, 2002; Naylor Prize, London Math. Soc., 2008. *Publications:* Superstring Theory, vols I and II (with J. H. Schwarz and E. Witten), 1987; many contribs to physics and mathematics jls. *Address:* Department of Applied Mathematics and Theoretical Physics, University of Cambridge, Cambridge CB3 0WA.

GREEN, Dr Michael Frederick; Consultant Physician, Department of Geriatric Medicine, Board of Health, Guernsey, 1984; *b* 29 Aug. 1939; *s* of Frederick and Kathleen Green; *m* 1977, Janet Mary; seven *s* one *d*. *Educ:* Dulwich Coll.; Jesus Coll., Cambridge (MA); St Thomas' Hosp. (MB BChir). FRCP 1980. Consultant, N Middlesex and St Ann's Hosps, 1969–71; Consultant, Dept of Geriatric Medicine, Royal Free Hospital, 1972–84. Mem., GMC, 1973–79. Medical Adviser, Royal Life Saving Soc., 1970–84; Post Grad. Tutor/Clinical Sec., Princess Elizabeth Hosp., St Martin, Guernsey, 1990. Member various bodies mainly involved with the elderly, including: British Geriatrics Soc.; Cruse (Nat. Assoc. for Widows); British Soc. for Research on Ageing. Governor: Queen Elizabeth Schs, Barnet, 1973–79; Christchurch Sch., Hampstead, 1980–83. Founder Chm., Friends of Elizabeth Coll., Guernsey, 1989–90. Mem. Bd, Jl of Medical Ethics, 1980–84; Chm., Editl Bd, Geriatric Medicine, 1984 (Medical Editor, 1971–84). *Publications:* Health in Middle Age, 1978; co-author books and articles on medical admin, geriatric medicine, hypothermia, neurology, endocrinology, rehabilitation, pressure sores, psychiatry of old age. *Recreations:* family, gardening, swimming and lifesaving, magic, writing, broadcasting, lecturing and teaching.

GREEN, Michael John; Controller, BBC Radio 4, 1986–96; Deputy Managing Director, BBC Network Radio, 1993–96; *b* 28 May 1941; *s* of David Green and Kathleen (*née* Swann); *m* 1965, Christine Margaret Constance Gibson; one *s* one *d*. *Educ:* Repton Sch.; Barnsley Grammar Sch.; New Coll., Oxford (BA Modern Langs). Swiss Broadcasting Corp., 1964–65; Sheffield Star, 1965–67; Producer, BBC Radio Sheffield, 1967–70; Documentary Producer, BBC Manchester, 1970–77; Editor, File on Four, 1977; Head of Network Radio, Manchester, 1978–86. Chm., Radio Acad., 1990–95. Mem., NCC, 1997–2001. *Recreations:* France, cinema, collecting glass.

GREEN, Michael Philip; Director and Co-Founder, Tangent Industries Ltd, since 1968; *b* 2 Dec. 1947; *s* of Cyril and Irene Green; *m* 1st, 1972, Hon. Janet Frances Wolfson (*see* Hon. J. F. W. de Botton) (marr. diss. 1989); two *d*; 2nd, 1990, Theresa Mary Buckmaster (*see* T. M. Green); three *s* one *d*. *Educ:* Haberdashers' Aske's School. Chairman: Carlton Communications Plc, 1983–2004 (Chief Exec., 1983–91); Carlton Television Ltd 1991–94; Director: GMTV Ltd, 1992–2004; Reuters Holdings PLC, 1992–99; ITN 1993–2004 (Chm., 1993–95); Getty Communications plc, 1997–98; Thomson SA 2001–04. Founder, Tangent Charitable Trust, 1984; Chm., The Media Trust, 1997–. Trustee, Sainsbury Centre for Mental Health, 2001–. Hon. DLitt City, 1999. *Recreations* reading, bridge, television. *Address:* Tangent Industries Ltd, 21 South Street, W1K 2XB *T:* (020) 7663 6464. *Club:* Portland.

GREEN, Prof. Mino, FIET; Professor of Electrical Device Science, Electrica Engineering, 1983–92, now Emeritus, Senior Research Fellow, since 1992, Imperia College of Science and Technology; *b* 10 March 1927; *s* of Alexander and Elizabet Green; *m* 1951, Diana Mary Allen; one *s* one *d*. *Educ:* Dulwich Coll.; University Coll. Durham Univ. (BSc, PhD, DSc). Group Leader: Solid State Res., Lincoln Laboratory MIT, 1951–55; Res., Zenith Radio Corp., USA, 1956–60; Associate Dir Electrochemistry Lab., Univ. of Pennsylvania, 1960–62; Man. Dir, Zenith Radio Research Corp. (UK) Ltd, 1962–72; Lectr, then Reader, Elec. Engrg Dept, Imperial Coll of Science and Technology, 1972–83. *Publications:* Solid State Surface Science, vols I, I and III (ed), 1969–73; many pubns (and some patents) on various aspects of semiconducto and optical device science and of nano-science and technol. *Recreations:* walking, ar appreciation. *Address:* 55 Gerard Road, SW13 9QH. *T:* (020) 8748 8689. *Club* Hurlingham.

See also D. M. A. Green.

GREEN, Miranda Jane A.; *see* Aldhouse-Green.

GREEN, (Nevill) Philip; Chief Executive, United Utilities plc, since 2006; *b* 12 Ma 1953; *s* of Harry Green and Sheila Saviker (*née* Emery); *m* 1977, Judy Rippon; two *d*. *Educ* UC of Swansea, Wales (BA Hons); London Business Sch. (MBA). DHL: Regl Dir Northern Europe and Anglophone Africa, 1990–94; Chief Operating Officer, Europe an Africa, Worldwide Network, 1994–99; CEO, Trading Solutions Div., 1999–2001, Chie Operating Officer, 2001–03, Reuters Gp Plc; Chief Exec., Royal P&O Nedlloyd 2003–06. *Recreations:* walking, cricket, Africa, wine, music. *Address:* United Utilities plc Haweswater House, Lingley Mere Business Park, Great Sankey, Warrington, Cheshire WA5 3LP. *T:* (01925) 237005, *Fax:* (01925) 237020; *e-mail:* philip.green@uuplc.co.uk *Clubs:* Royal Automobile, MCC.

GREEN, Nicholas Nigel, PhD; QC 1998; a Recorder, since 2004; *b* 15 Oct. 1958; *s* c John Reginald Green and Pauline Barbara Green; *m* 1990, Fiona Clare Cramb; one *s* on *d*. *Educ:* King Edward's VI Sch., Camp Hill, Birmingham; Univ. of Leicester (LLB 1980) Univ. of Toronto (LLM 1981); Univ. of Southampton (PhD 1985). Lectr in Law, Univ of Southampton, 1981–85; pt-time Lectr in Law, UCL, 1985–87; called to the Bar, Inne Temple, 1986 (Bencher, 2002; Exec. Cttee, 2003–); in practice at the Bar, 1986–. Chm Bar European Gp, 1999–2001; Bar Council of England and Wales: Vice Chm., Internat Relns Cttee, 2000–02; Chm., European Cttee, 2003–05; Chm., Legal Services Cttee 2006–; Mem., Gen. Mgt Cttee, 2002–. UK Perm. Rep. of CCBE to European Court c Justice, Court of First Instance and EFTA Court, 2000–02. Vis. Prof. of Law, Univ. c Durham, 2000–; Hon. Prof. of Law, Univ. of Leicester, 2005–. *Publications:* Commercia Agreements and Competition Law: practice and procedure in the UK and EEC, 1986, 2n edn (jtly) 1997; (jtly) The Legal Foundations of the Single European Market, 1991; ove 50 articles in legal jls worldwide. *Recreations:* family, swimming (former internationa 1976–77), collecting Victorian watercolours. *Address:* Brick Court Chambers, 7–8 Esse Street, WC2R 3LD.

GREEN, Dr (Norman) Michael, FRS 1981; affiliated to Department of Mathematica Biology, National Institute for Medical Research, since 1992; *b* 6 April 1926; *s* of Ernes Green and Hilda Margaret Carter; *m* 1953, Iro Paulina Moschouti; two *s* one *d*. *Edu* Dragon Sch., Oxford; Clifton Coll., Bristol; Magdalen Coll., Oxford (BA; Athletics Blue Cross Country Blue); UCH Med. Sch., London (PhD). Res. Student, Univ. c Washington, Seattle, 1951–53; Lectr in Biochemistry, Univ. of Sheffield, 1953–55; Res Fellow and Lectr in Chem. Pathol., St Mary's Hosp. Med. Sch., London, 1956–62; Vis Scientist, NIH, Maryland, 1962–64; Res. Staff, Divs of Biochem. and Protein Structure NIMR, 1964–91. *Publications:* research papers on the structure of proteins and c membranes, in scientific jls. *Recreations:* mountain climbing, geometry. *Address:* 57 Hal Lane, Mill Hill, NW7 3PS.

GREEN, Sir Owen (Whitley), Kt 1984; Chairman, BTR plc, 1984–93 (Managin Director, 1967–86); *b* Stockton-on-Tees, 14 May 1925; *m* 1948, Doreen Margaret Spar (*d* 2006); one *s* two *d*. FCA 1950. Served RNVR, 1942–46. BTR, 1956–93. Dir, Th Spectator, 1988–93. Trustee, Natural History Mus., 1986–95. Businessman of the Yea 1982; BIM Gold Medal, 1984; Founding Societies' Centenary Award, ICA, 1985 *Recreation:* golf. *Address:* Edgehill, Succombs Hill, Warlingham, Surrey CR6 9JG.

GREEN, Patrick G.; *see* Grafton-Green.

GREEN, Dame Pauline, DBE 2003; Chief Executive, Co-operatives UK (formerly Co-operative Union Ltd), since 2000; *b* 8 Dec. 1948; *d* of late Bertram Wiltshire and of Luc Wiltshire; *m* 1971, Paul Adam Green (marr. diss. 2003); one *s* one *d*. *Educ:* John Kell Secondary Modern Sch. for Girls, Brent; Kilburn Poly.; Open Univ. (BA); London Schoo of Economics (MSc). Sec., 1981, Chair, 1983, Chipping Barnet Labour Party. MEP (Lab London N, 1989–99; London Reg., 1999; Leader: European PLP, 1993–94; Gp of Pty c Eur. Socialists, 1994–99. Contested (Lab) Arkley ward, Barnet Council elecns, 1986. Parl Asst, Co-operative Movement, 1986–89. Pres., Co-operative Congress, 1997; Vice Pres. Socialist International, 1994–. Mem., NEC, Labour Party, 1998–99. Mem., USDAW *Recreations:* music, swimming. *Address:* (office) Holyoake House, Hanover Street Manchester M60 0AS.

GREEN, Prof. Peter James, PhD; FRS 2003; Professor of Statistics, since 1989, an Henry Overton Wills Professor of Mathematics, since 2003, University of Bristol; *b* 2 April 1950; *s* of late Frank Green and Joyce (*née* Walder); *m* 1984, Elizabeth Jane Bennett two *d*. *Educ:* Solihull Sch.; Pembroke Coll., Oxford (BA 1971, MA); Univ. of Sheffiel (MSc; PhD 1976). CStat 2000. Lectr in Stats, Univ. of Bath, 1974–78; Lectr, then Sen Lectr in Stats, Univ. of Durham, 1978–89. Various vis. appts at foreign univs, 1979–. Pres Royal Statistical Soc., 2001–03. FIMS 1991. Guy Medals, Bronze, 1987 and Silver, 1999 Royal Statistical Soc; Royal Soc. Wolfson Res. Merit Award, 2006. *Publications:* (with B Silverman) Nonparametric Regression and Generalized Linear Models, 1994; (ed with S Richardson and N. L. Hjort) Highly Structured Stochastic Systems, 2003; contrib numerous papers to learned jls. *Recreations:* learning to fly, biking, running, mountains *Address:* School of Mathematics, University of Bristol, Bristol BS8 1TW. *T:* (0117) 92 7967; *e-mail:* P.J.Green@bristol.ac.uk.

GREEN, Prof. Peter Morris; author and translator, since 1953; Professor of Classics University of Texas at Austin, 1972–97 (James R. Dougherty Jr Centennial Professor c Classics, 1982–84, 1985–97), now Emeritus; Adjunct Professor of Classics, University c

Iowa, since 1998; *b* 22 Dec. 1924; *o c* of late Arthur Green, CBE, MC, LLB, and Olive Slaughter; *m* 1st, 1951, Lalage Isobel Pulvertaft (marr. diss.); two *s* one *d*; 2nd, 1975, Carin Margreta, *y d* of late G. N. Christensen, Saratoga, USA. *Educ:* Charterhouse; Trinity Coll., Cambridge. Served in RAFVR, 1943–47: overseas tour in Burma Comd, 1944–46. 1st Cl. Hons, Pts I and II, Classical Tripos, 1949–50; MA and PhD Cantab 1954; Craven Schol. and Student, 1950; Dir of Studies in Classics, 1951–52; Fiction Critic, London Daily Telegraph, 1953–63; Literary Adviser, The Bodley Head, 1957–58; Cons. Editor, Hodder and Stoughton, 1960–63; Television Critic, The Listener, 1961–63; Film Critic, John o'London's, 1961–63; Mem. Book Soc. Cttee, 1959–63. Former Mem. of selection cttees for literary prizes: Heinemann Award, John Llewellyn Rhys, W. H. Smith £1000 Award for Literature. Translator of numerous works from French and Italian, including books by Simone de Beauvoir, Fosco Maraini, Joseph Kessel. FRSL 1956; Mem. Council, Royal Society of Literature, 1958–63 (resigned on emigration). In 1963 resigned all positions and emigrated to Greece as full-time writer (1963–71). Visiting Professor of Classics: Univ. of Texas, 1971–72; UCLA, 1976; Mellon Prof. of Humanities, Tulane Univ., 1986; Vis. Prof. of History, Univ. of Iowa, 1997–98; Sen. Fellow for independent study and res., National Endowment for the Humanities, 1983–84; Vis. Res. Fellow and Writer-in-Residence, Princeton Univ., 2001; King Charles II Dist. Vis. Prof. in Classics and Ancient Hist., 2004, Whichard Dist. Vis. Prof. in the Humanities, 2006, E Carolina Univ. Editor, Syllecta Classica, 1999–. *Publications:* The Expanding Eye, 1953; Achilles His Armour, 1955; Cat in Gloves (pseud. Denis Delaney), 1956; The Sword of Pleasure (W. H. Heinemann Award for Literature), 1957; Kenneth Grahame 1859–1932: A Study of his Life, Work and Times, 1959; Essays in Antiquity, 1960; Habeas Corpus and other stories, 1962; Look at the Romans, 1963; The Laughter of Aphrodite, 1965, repr. 1993; Juvenal: The Sixteen Satires (trans.), 1967, 3rd edn 1998; Armada from Athens: The Failure of the Sicilian Expedition 415–413 BC, 1970; Alexander the Great: a biography, 1970; The Year of Salamis 480–479 BC, 1971, rev. as The Greco-Persian Wars, 1996; The Shadow of the Parthenon, 1972; The Parthenon, 1973; A Concise History of Ancient Greece, 1973; Alexander of Macedon 356–323 BC: a historical biography, 1974, repr. 1991; Ovid: The Erotic Poems (trans.), 1982; Beyond the Wild Wood: the world of Kenneth Grahame, 1982; Medium and Message Reconsidered: the changing functions of classical translation, 1986; Classical Bearings: interpreting ancient history and culture, 1989; Alexander to Actium: the historical evolution of the Hellenistic Age, 1990, rev. edn 1993; (ed) Hellenistic History and Culture, 1993; Yannis Ritsos: The Fourth Dimension (trans.), 1993; Ovid: The Poems of Exile (trans.), 1994, rev. edn 2005; Apollonios Rhodios: The Argonautika (trans. and commentary), 1997; From Ikaria to the Stars, 2004; The Poems of Catullus (trans.), 2005; Diodorus Siculus Bks 11–12.37.1: Greek History 480–431 BCE the alternative version, 2006; Alexander the Great and the Hellenistic Age: a short history, 2007. *Recreations:* travel, swimming, walking, avoiding urban life. *Address:* c/o Department of Classics, University of Iowa, 404 Jefferson Building, Iowa City, IA 52242, USA. *T:* (319) 3419805/6573; *e-mail:* peter-green-1@uiowa.edu. *Club:* Savile.

GREEN, Sir Philip, Kt 2006; retail executive; *b* 15 March 1952; *m* 1990, Cristina; one *s* one *d*. Took over family property company, 1973; bought: Jean Jeanie, 1985 (sold to Lee Cooper, 1986); Owen Owen, 1994; Olympus Sports, 1995 (merged with Sports Division, 1996; sold to JJB Sports, 1998); Mark One, 1996; Shoe Express, 1997 (sold, 1998); Sears (incl. Miss Selfridge, Wallis, Warehouse, Freemans), 1999; Bhs, 2000; Arcadia (incl. Top Shop, Dorothy Perkins, Evans, Burton), 2002; Chm. and Chief Exec., Amber Day, 1988–92. *Address:* Bhs Ltd, Marylebone House, 129–137 Marylebone Road, NW1 5QD.

GREEN, Philip; *see* Green, N. P.

GREEN, Robert James; Member (Lib Dem), Reading Borough Council, 1995–2008; Mayor of Reading, 2000–01; *b* 27 Jan. 1937; *er s* of Ronald Percy Green and Doris Rose (*née* Warman); *m* 1960, Jill Marianne Small; one *d* (one *s* decd). *Educ:* Kent College, Canterbury. Executive Officer, Board of Trade, 1957; Asst Principal, 1963, Principal, 1967, Min. of Housing and Local Govt; Secretary, Water Resources Board, 1972–74; Asst Secretary: Dept of the Environment, 1974; Dept of Transport, 1980; Under Sec., 1982; Regl Dir, Northern Reg., 1982–83, and Yorks and Humberside Reg., 1982–86; Dir of Rural Affairs, DoE, 1988–91; Dir, Local Govt, 1991–92; Prin. Estabt and Finance Officer, Office of the Rail Regulator, 1993–94. Non-exec. Dir, Butterley Bricks Ltd, 1988–90. Mem. (Lib Dem), Berks CC, 1995–98. Hon. Freeman, Bor. of Reading, 2008. *Recreation:* theatre, including amateur dramatics. *Address:* Runge's Cottage, 11 St Andrews Road, Caversham, Reading RG4 7PH.

GREEN, Maj.-Gen. Robert Leslie Stuart; *b* 1 July 1925; *s* of Leslie Stuart Green and Eliza Dorothea Andrew; *m* 1952, Nancy Isobel Collier; two *d*. *Educ:* Chorlton Sch. 2nd Bn Black Watch, India, 1944–46; 6 Airborne Div., Palestine, 1946; 2 Parachute Bde, UK and Germany, 1946–47; 1st Bn HLI, UK, ME and Cyprus, 1947–56; ptsc 1959; jssc 1962; 1st Bn Royal Highland Fusiliers, UK, Aden, Germany and Gibraltar, 1959–69, Comd 1967–69; staff appt 1970; Military Dir of Studies, RMCS, 1970–72; Sen. Military Officer, Royal Armament Res. and Develt Estabt, 1973–75; Vice-Pres., Ordnance Bd, 1976–78, Pres., March–June 1978. Col, The Royal Highland Fusiliers, 1979–91. Hon. Vice Pres., CARE, 1995– (Exec. Gov., 1980–90; Chm., 1991–95). Freeman, City of London, 1983. FCMI. *Recreations:* fishing, music. *Address:* Royal Bank of Scotland, 43 Curzon Street, Mayfair, W1Y 7RF.

GREEN, Rodney Alan Rupert; Chief Executive, Leicester City Council, 1996–2008; *b* 7 Feb. 1953; *s* of Timothy Green and Mercy Green (*née* Mathison); *m* 1975, Helen Frances Benjamin; two *s*. *Educ:* Christ's Hosp., Horsham; Emmanuel Coll., Cambridge (MA 1974). Greater London Council: cttee clerk, Dir-Gen.'s Dept, 1974–76; Scientific Br. Staffing Officer, 1976–78; Surrey County Council: Head, Teaching Personnel Section 1978–82; Principal: Schools, 1982–84; Special Needs, 1984–87; Asst Co. Educn Officer, 1987–91; Asst Chief Exec., W Glamorgan CC, 1991–96. Director: Leics TEC, 1998–2001; Nat. Space Centre, 1998–2006); Leicester Regeneration Co., 2001–06; Leicestershire Cares, 2001–08; Member: Adv. Panel on Beacon Scheme, 2005–; Inst. of Community Cohesion, 2006–08; Migration Impacts Forum, 2007–08. Hon. LLD De Montfort, 2003. *Publication:* 90,000 Hours: managing the world of work, 2002. *Recreations:* films, theatre, travel, Leicester Tigers Rugby, swimming, Biblical studies, feasting.

GREEN, Prof. Roger, FRCP; Professor of Physiology, University of Manchester, 1981–2005, now Professor Emeritus; *b* 9 Feb. 1942; *s* of Donald Victor and Joyce Green; *m* 1965, Rita Mavis; one *s* two *d*. *Educ:* Univ. of Sheffield (MB ChB 1965); Univ. of Manchester (MSc 1981). FRCP 2002. House Officer posts, Sheffield Royal Hosp., 1965–66; University of Manchester: Asst Lectr, Lectr, Sen. Lectr, then Reader in Physiol., 1966–81; Dean: Undergrad. Med. Studies, 1993–97; Medical Sch., 1997–2003. Hon. DSc: St Andrews, 2004; Keele, 2004. *Publications:* contribs to physiological jls. *Recreation:* brass bands. *Address:* 105 Heaton Park Road, Manchester M9 0QQ. *T:* (0161) 795 9983.

GREEN, Stephen Keith; Group Chairman, HSBC Holdings plc, since 2006 (Group Chief Executive, 2003–06); *b* 7 Nov. 1948; *s* of late Dudley Keith Green and of Dorothy Rosamund Mary Green; *m* 1971, Janian Joy; two *d*. *Educ:* Lancing Coll.; Exeter Coll., Oxford (BA PPE); MIT (MSc Pol Sci.). ODA, FCO, 1971–77; McKinsey & Co. Inc., 1977–82; Hong Kong & Shanghai Banking Corp. Ltd, 1982–92; HSBC Hldgs plc, 1993– (Exec. Dir, Investment Banking and Markets, 1998–2003). Member, Supervisory Bd: HSBC Trinkaus & Burkhardt KGaA, Germany, 1993–; Crédit Commercial de France, 2001–; Director: HSBC Bank plc, 1995– (Chm., 2005–); PEC Concerts Ltd, 1999–2001. Dir, Poplar Housing and Regeneration Community Assoc., 2000–. Ordained deacon 1987; priest 1988; NSM, dio. of London. *Publication:* Serving God? Serving Mammon?, 1996. *Recreations:* opera, art, European literature, walking. *Address:* HSBC Holdings plc, 8 Canada Square, E14 5HQ. *T:* (020) 7992 3601. *Club:* Athenæum.

GREEN, Susan Valerie; District Judge (Magistrates' Courts), Inner London, since 2001; *b* 1 Nov. 1954; *d* of Nat Green and Ettie Green (*née* Blacker); *m* 2004, Haydn Gott, *qv*. *Educ:* Birmingham Univ. (LLB); Coll. of Law, Guildford. Admitted solicitor, 1981; J. P. Malnick and Co., subsequently Malnick & Rance: articled clerk, 1979–81; Asst Solicitor, 1981–82; Partner, 1982–98; Consultant, Traymans, 1998–2000. Formerly Sec. and Pres., NE London Law Soc.; Pres., London Criminal Courts Solicitors' Assoc., 1998–99. *Recreations:* sports, cookery, travel, all things Australasian. *Address:* c/o Camberwell Green Magistrates' Court, D'Eynsford Street, SE5 7UP. *T:* (020) 7805 9802.

GREEN, Terence Anthony; Chief Executive, Clothing, Tesco, since 2005; *b* 9 Oct. 1951; *s* of Henry Green and Nora Green (*née* Sayers); *m* 1981, Geraldine A. Daniels (marr. diss. 1996); one *s* two *d*; one *d* by Vanessa Field. *Educ:* Liverpool Univ. (BSc Maths; BSc (Hons) Maths, Computer Sci. and Stats). Exec. Dir, Burton Gp plc, 1992–98; Chief Executive: Debenhams, 1992–98; Topshop and Top Man, 1995–98; Debenhams plc, 1998–2000 (Debenhams demerged from Burton Gp, 1998); Bhs Ltd, 2000–02; Allders, 2003–05. Non-exec. Dir, First Choice Holidays plc, 1997. FRSA 1997. *Recreations:* food, opera, reading, collecting art and fine wines.

GREEN, Theresa Mary, CBE 2008; Chairman, Royal Marsden NHS Foundation Trust (formerly NHS Trust), since 1998; *b* 29 July 1964; *d* of Richard Buckmaster and Jacqueline Buckmaster (*née* Leche); *m* 1990, Michael Philip Green, *qv*; three *s* one *d*. *Educ:* Putney High Sch.; Lady Margaret Hall, Oxford (MA); City Univ. (LLB 1993). Called to the Bar, Middle Temple, 1994. Head of Corporate Communications, Carlton Communications Plc, 1986–90. Non-exec. Dir, Royal Berkshire and Battle Hosps NHS Trust, 1994–98. Member: Res. Ethics Cttee, Royal Marsden Hosp., 1994–98 (Chm., 1996); Bd of Trustees, Inst. of Cancer Res., 1998–. Trustee, Nat. Portrait Gall., 1999–2002. *Address:* Royal Marsden NHS Foundation Trust, Fulham Road, SW3 6JJ.

GREEN-ARMYTAGE, John McDonald; non-executive Chairman, AMEC plc, since 2004 (non-executive Director, since 1996); Chairman, JZ International Ltd, since 1996; *b* 6 June 1945; *s* of John Whitla Green-Armytage and Elizabeth McDonald Green-Armytage; *m* 1977, Susan Rosemary Le Messurier; one *s* three *d*. *Educ:* McGill Univ., Montreal (BA (Econs) 1966); Columbia Univ., NY (MBA 1970). Joined N. M. Rothschild & Sons Ltd, 1970, exec. Dir, 1977–82, non-exec. Dir, 1988–97; Man. Dir, Guthrie Corp. plc, 1982–88; Jt Chm. and CEO, Kelt Energy plc, 1990–91; William Baird plc: non-exec. Dir, 1992–94; CEO, 1995–96; Dep. Chm., 1996. *Recreations:* country pursuits, polo, sailing. *Address:* c/o AMEC plc, 76–78 Old Street, EC1V 9RU. *Clubs:* Brooks's, Turf; Guards Polo.

GREEN-PRICE, Sir Robert (John), 5th Bt *cr* 1874; landowner; Assistant Professor of English, Chiba University of Commerce, 1982–97; *b* 22 Oct. 1940; *o s* of Sir John Green-Price, 4th Bt, and Irene Marion (*d* 1954), *d* of Major Sir (Ernest) Guy Lloyd, 1st Bt, DSO; *S* father, 1964. *Educ:* Shrewsbury. Army Officer, 1961–69; Captain, RCT, retd. ADC to Governor of Bermuda, 1969–72. Lectr in English, Teikyo Univ., 1975–82. Part-time Lecturer: Keio Univ., 1977–97; Waseda Univ., 1986–97; Guest Lectr, NHK Radio, 1978–83. *Heir: uncle* Powell Norman Dansey Green-Price [*b* 22 July 1926; *m* 1963, Ann Stella, *d* of late Brig. Harold George Howson, CBE, MC, TD; one *s* one *d*].

GREENALL, family name of **Baron Daresbury**.

GREENAWAY, Prof. David; Professor of Economics, since 1987, Vice Chancellor, since 2008, University of Nottingham; *b* 20 March 1952; *s* of David and Agnes Greenaway; *m* 1975, Susan Elizabeth Hallam; two *s*. *Educ:* Henry Mellish Grammar Sch.; London Univ. (BSc ext. 1974); Liverpool Univ. (MCom 1975); DLitt Nottingham 1997. Lectr in Econs, Leicester Poly., 1975–78; University of Buckingham: Lectr, 1978–83; Sen. Lectr, 1983–85; Reader, 1985–86; Prof. of Econs, 1986–87; Pro-Vice-Chancellor, Univ. of Nottingham, 1994–2001, 2004–08. Non-executive Director: Nottingham HA, 1994–98; Queen's Med. Centre, Nottingham Univ. Hosp. NHS Trust, 2001–. Member: Council, 1990–97, Exec., 1991–97, REconS; Acad. Adv. Council, IEA, 1991–2004; Technology Foresight Steering Gp, 1994–95; Council, ESRC, 1997–2001; Armed Forces Pay Review Body, 1997– (Chm., 2004–); Sen. Salaries Rev. Body, 2004–; Chair, Panel for Econs and Econometrics, RAE, HEFCE, 2001 and 2008 (Vice Chair, 1996). Adviser: UNIDO, 1983; World Bank, 1986, 1988; GATT, 1986; DTI, 1994; UNECE, 1994; Commonwealth Secretariat, 1997; Asian Develt Bank, 1997; Caribbean Regl Negotiating Machinery, 2000; Dept for Transport, 2003–04. Gov., NIESR, 1995–. FRSA 1994; AcSS 2000. *Publications:* International Trade Policy, 1983; (jtly) Economics of Intra-Industry Trade, 1986; (jtly) Imperfect Competition and International Trade, 1986; Companion to Contemporary Economic Thought, 1991; (jtly) Evaluating Trade Policy in Developing Countries, 1993; (jtly) Economics of Commodity Markets, 1999; Globalisation and Labour Markets, 2000; Adjusting to Globalisation, 2005; papers in learned jls. *Recreations:* golf, tennis, football, wine, reading. *Address:* School of Economics, University of Nottingham, University Park, Nottingham NG7 2RD. *T:* (0115) 951 5469; 1 Dormy Close, Bramcote, Nottingham NG9 3DE.

GREENAWAY, Frank, PhD; CChem, FRSC, FSA, FMA; Research Fellow, The Science Museum, 1980–91 (Hon. Fellow, 1992); Reader in the History of Science, Davy-Faraday Research Laboratory of the Royal Institution, 1970–85; *b* 9 July 1917; 3rd *s* of late Henry James Greenaway; *m* 1942, Margaret (Miranda), 2nd *d* of late R. G. Heegaard Warner and *widow* of John Raymond Brumfit; three *d* (one *s* and one step *s* decd). *Educ:* Cardiff High Sch.; Jesus Coll., Oxford (Meyricke Exhibitioner; MA); University Coll. London (PhD). Served War of 1939–45, RAOC, as Inspecting Ordnance Officer, 1940–41 (invalided). Science Master: Bournemouth Sch., 1941–42; Epsom Gram. Sch., 1942–43; Passport Control, 1943–44; Research Labs, Kodak Ltd, 1944–49; Asst Keeper, Science Museum, 1949; Dep. Keeper, 1959; Keeper, Dept of Chemistry, 1967–80. Regents' Fellow, Smithsonian Instn, Washington, DC, 1985. Member Council: Brit. Soc. for the Hist. of Science, 1958–68, 1974–78 (Vice-Pres. 1962–65); Museums Assoc., 1961–70, 1973–76 (Hon. Editor, 1965–70); Mem. Brit. Nat. Cttee, ICOM, 1956–58, 1962–71, 1977–83; Royal Institution: Mem., 1990–93, Vice-Pres., 1992–93, Council; Chm., Cttee of Visitors, 1964–65. Membre Correspondant de l'Académie Internationale d'Histoire des Sciences, 1963; Member: Council, Soc. for History of Alchemy and Chemistry, 1967–74 (Sec., 1967–74); History of Medicine Adv. Panel, The Wellcome Trust, 1968–74; Higher Educn Adv. Cttee, The Open Univ., 1970–73; British Nat. Cttee for Hist. of Sci., 1972–81; British Nat. Cttee, ICSU, 1972–77; Council, Internat. Union of the Hist. and Philos. of Science, 1972–81 (Sec., 1972–77); Council of Management,

Royal Philharmonic Soc., 1980–84, 1986–89; President: Commonwealth Assoc. of Museums, 1979–83; Nonsuch Antiquarian Soc., 1990–97. Boerhaave Medal, Leyden Univ., 1968. *Publications:* Science Museums in Developing Countries, 1962; John Dalton and the Atom, 1966; (ed) Lavoisier's Essays Physical and Chemical, 1971; (ed with Roger French) Science in the Early Roman Empire, 1986; Science International: the history of the International Council of Scientific Unions, 1996; Chymica Acta (autobiog.), 2007; Editor, Royal Institution Archives, 1971; Official Publications of the Science Museum; Papers on history of chemistry and on museology. *Recreations:* music, travel. *Address:* St Luke's Residential Home, Marshland Square, Emmer Green, Reading RG4 8RP. *T:* (0118) 947 9952. *Club:* Athenæum.

GREENAWAY, Sir John (Michael Burdick), 3rd Bt *cr* 1933, of Coombe, Surrey; DL; farmer, since 1980; *b* 9 Aug. 1944; *o s* of Sir Derek Burdick Greenaway, 2nd Bt, CBE, and Sheila Beatrice Greenaway (*née* Lockett); *S* father, 1994; *m* 1982, Susan Margaret (*née* Birch); one *s* one *d*. *Educ:* Harrow Sch.; Grenoble Univ. The Life Guards, 1965–70. Dir, Daniel Greenaway & Sons Ltd, 1970–79. DL Northants, 2005. *Recreations:* ski-ing, tennis, riding. *Heir: s* Thomas Edward Burdick Greenaway, *b* 3 April 1985. *Address:* Lois Weedon House, Weedon Lois, Towcester, Northants NN12 8PJ. *T:* (01327) 860472.

GREENAWAY, Peter, CBE 2007; film director, painter and writer; Professor of Cinema Studies, European Graduate School, Saas-Fee, Switzerland; *b* 5 April 1942; *m*; two *d*. *Educ:* Forest Sch.; Walthamstow Coll. of Art. Film Editor, Central Office of Information, 1965–76. Maker of short films, 1966–, of feature length films, 1978–. *Exhibitions:* Lord's Gall., 1964; The Physical Self, Rotterdam, 1991; 100 Objects to Represent the World, Acad. of Fine Arts, Vienna, 1992; Flying Out of this World, Louvre, 1992; Watching Water, Venice, 1993; Some Organising Principles, Swansea, 1993; The Audience of Macon, Cardiff, 1993; The Stairs, Geneva, 1994, Munich, 1995; Spellbound, London, 1996; Flying Over Water, Barcelona, 1997; *one-man shows:* Canterbury, 1989; Carcassone, Paris, 1989; NY, Melbourne, Liège, Tokyo, Fukoa, Munich, Copenhagen, Oddense, Brussels, 1990; Brentford, Dublin, 1991; Bremen, NY, 1992; Tempe, Ariz, and Salzburg, 1994; Biel-Bienne, Switzerland, New York, and Munich, 1995; Milan, Ghent, and Thessaloniki, 1996; Manchester, 1998; Edinburgh, 1999; *group shows* include: Freezeframe, Lamont Gall., 1996; The Director's Eye, Mus. of Modern Art, Oxford, 1996. *Films:* (writer and director): Train, 1966; Tree, 1966; Five Postcards from Capital Cities, 1967; Revolution, 1967; Intervals, 1969; Erosion, 1971; H is for House, 1973; Windows, 1975; Water Wrackets, 1975; Goole by Numbers, 1976; Dear Phone, 1977; 1–1Co, 1978; A Walk Through H, 1978; Vertical Features Remake, 1978; The Falls, 1980 (Special Award, BFI); Act of God, 1981 (Best short film, Melbourne Film Fest.); Zandra Rhodes, 1981; The Draughtsman's Contract, 1982; Four American Composers, 1983; Making a Splash, 1984; (jtly) A TV Dante-Canto V, 1984; Inside Rooms—The Bathroom, 1985; A Zed and Two Noughts, 1985; The Belly of an Architect, 1986; Fear of Drowning, 1988; Drowning by Numbers, 1988 (Prize for Best Artistic Contribution, Cannes Film Fest.); The Cook, the Thief, his Wife and her Lover, 1989; Prospero's Books, 1990; M is for Man, Music, Mozart, 1991; Rosa, 1992; Darwin, 1992; The Baby of Macon, 1993; The Stairs, Geneva, 1994; The Pillow Book, 1996; The Bridge, 1996; 8½ Women, 1999; *operas:* Rosa: a Horse Drama, 1994; Writing to Vermeer, 1999. Officier de l'Ordre des Arts et des Lettres (France), 1998. *Publications:* The Falls, 1993; filmscripts and exhibn catalogues.

GREENBERG, Daniel Isaac; Parliamentary Counsel, since 2003; *b* 5 Sept. 1965; *s* of Dr Morris Greenberg and Dr Gillian Greenberg (*née* Freeman); *m* 1988, Julia Sharon Becker; two *s* two *d*. *Educ:* Trinity Coll., Cambridge (BA); Inns of Court Sch. of Law. Legal Advr, Lord Chancellor's Dept, 1988–91; Asst Parly Counsel, 1991–95; Sen. Asst Parly Counsel, 1995–99; Dep. Parly Counsel, 1999–2003. *Publications:* (ed) Stroud's Judicial Dictionary, 6th edn 2000, 7th edn 2006; (ed) Craies on Legislation, 9th edn 2008; contrib. articles on Jewish law and philosophy to Jewish Chronicle. *Recreations:* teaching Jewish law and philosophy, reading. *Address:* Office of the Parliamentary Counsel, 36 Whitehall, SW1A 2AY. *T:* (020) 7210 6604; *e-mail:* dgreenberg@hotmail.co.uk.

GREENBERG, Joanna Elishever Gabrielle; QC 1994; a Recorder, since 1995; *b* 28 Nov. 1950; *d* of Ivan Marion Greenberg and Doris Rosalie Greenberg (*née* Sandground). *Educ:* Brondesbury and Kilburn High Sch. for Girls; King's Coll. London (LLB, AKC). Called to the Bar, Gray's Inn, 1972, Bencher, 2002; an Asst Recorder, 1992–95. Chm., Police Appeals Tribunals, 1997–. *Address:* 4 Breams Buildings, EC4A 1HP. *T:* (020) 7092 1900.

GREENBURGH, Matthew Steven; Vice Chairman and Senior Vice President, Merrill Lynch & Co., Inc., since 2008; *b* London, 6 March 1961; *s* of Raymond Greenburgh and Virginia Greenburgh (*née* Rothman); *m* 1990, Helen Elisabeth Payne; one *s* one *d*. *Educ:* Westminster Sch.; Worcester Coll., Oxford (BA Hons Philos. and Econs). Barclays Merchant Bank/BZW, 1983–87; Enskilda Securities, 1987–91; Baring Brothers, 1991–98, Dir, 1995–98; Merrill Lynch, 1998–: Co-Head, Global Financial Instns Gp, 2001–06; Vice Chm., Global Investment Banking, 2006–08. *Recreations:* arboriculture, puericulture, culture. *Address:* c/o Merrill Lynch, 2 King Edward Street, EC1A 1HQ.

GREENBURY, Sir Richard, Kt 1992; Chairman, 1991–99, and Chief Executive, 1988–99, Marks & Spencer plc; *b* 31 July 1936; *s* of Richard Oswald Greenbury and Dorothy (*née* Lewis); *m* 1st, 1959, Sian Eames Hughes (marr. diss.); two *s* two *d*; 2nd, 1985, Gabrielle Mary McManus (marr. diss. 1996); 3rd, 1996, Sian Eames (*née* Hughes). *Educ:* Ealing County Grammar Sch. Joined Marks & Spencer Ltd as Jun. Management Trainee, 1952; Alternate Dir, 1970; Full Dir, 1972; Jt Man. Dir, 1978–85; Chief Operating Officer, 1986–88. Non-executive Director: British Gas, 1976–87; MB Group (formerly Metal Box), 1985–89; ICI, 1992–93; Lloyds Bank, 1992–97; Zeneca, 1993–99; Electronics Boutique, 2000–03; Mem. Supervisory Bd, Philips Electronics NV, 1998–. Trustee, Royal Acad., 1992–97. Patron, Samaritans, 1992–2000. *Recreations:* tennis, reading, music. *Address:* Ambarrow Wood, Ambarrow Lane, Sandhurst, Berks GU47 8JE. *Clubs:* All England Lawn Tennis and Croquet, International Tennis Club of GB.

GREENE, Anthony Hamilton Millard K.; *see* Kirk-Greene.

GREENE, Graham Carleton, CBE 1986; publisher; Chairman, London Merchant Securities plc, 2000–07 (Director, 1996–2007); Chairman of Trustees, British Museum, 1996–2002 (Trustee, 1978–2002); *b* 10 June 1936; *s* of Sir Hugh Carleton Greene, KCMG, OBE and Helga Mary Connolly; *m* 1957, Judith Margaret (marr. diss. 1976), *d* of Rt Hon. Lord Gordon-Walker, CH, PC; *m* 1976, Sally Georgina Horton (marr. diss. 1984), *d* of Sidney Wilfred Eaton; one *s*, and one step *s* one step *d*. *Educ:* Eton; University Coll., Oxford (MA). Merchant Banking, Dublin, New York and London, 1957–58; Secker & Warburg Ltd, 1958–62; Jonathan Cape, 1962–90 (Man. Dir, 1966–88). Director: Chatto & Jonathan Cape, subseq. Chatto, Virago, Bodley Head & Jonathan Cape Ltd, 1969–88 (Chm., 1970–88); Jackdaw Publications Ltd (Chm., 1964–88); Cape Goliard Press Ltd, 1967–88; Guinness Mahon Holdings Ltd, 1968–79; Australasian Publishing Co. Pty Ltd, 1969–88 (Chm., 1978–88); Sprint Productions Ltd, 1971–80; Book Reps (New Zealand) Ltd, 1971–88 (Chm., 1984–88); CVBC Services Ltd (Chm., 1972–88); Guinness Peat Group PLC, 1973–87; Grantham Book Storage Ltd (Chm., 1974–88); Triad Paperbacks Ltd, 1975–88; Chatto, Virago, Bodley Head & Jonathan Cape Australia Pty Ltd (Chm., 1977–88); Greene, King PLC, 1979–2004; Statesman & Nation Publishing Co. Ltd, 1980–85 (Chm., 1981–85); Statesman Publishing Co. Ltd, 1980–85 (Chm., 1981–85); Nation Pty Co. Ltd (Chm., 1981–87); New Society Ltd (Chm., 1984–87); Random House Inc., 1987–88; Random House UK Ltd, 1988–90; British Museum Co. (formerly British Museum Publications) Ltd, 1988–2002 (Chm., 1988–96); Merlin Internat. Green, subseq. Jupiter Internat. Green Investment Trust plc, 1989–2001; Henry Sotheran Ltd, 1990–; Ed Victor Ltd, 1991–; Rosemary Sandberg Ltd, 1991–2002; Libra KFT (Budapest), 1991–; Chm., Frontline Club, 2003–. Pres., Publishers Assoc., 1977–79 (Mem. Council, 1969–88; Trustee, 1995–97); Member: Book Develt Council, 1970–79 (Dep. Chm., 1972–73); Internat. Cttee, Internat. Publishers Assoc., 1977–88 (Exec. Cttee, 1981–88); Groupe des Editeurs de Livres de la CEE, (Fedn of European Publishers), 1977–86 (Pres., 1984–86); Arts Council Working Party Sub-Cttee on Public Lending Right, 1970; Paymaster General's Working Party on Public Lending Right, 1970–72; Bd, British Council, 1977–88; Chairman: Nat. Book League, 1974–76 (Dep. Chm., 1971–74); Nat. Book Cttee, 1994–95; Museums and Galls Commn, 1991–96; Mem. Gen. Cttee, Royal Literary Fund, 1975. Chairman: Friends of Musica nel Chiostro, 1993–2004; Garsington Opera Ltd, 2006– (Mem. Adv. Cttee, 1990–96; Dir, 1996–); Mem., Adv. Bd, Mus. of Modern Art, Oxford, 1992–96. Trustee: George Bernard Shaw Estate, 1986–; Trollope Soc., 1989–2004; Han Suyin Trust (formerly Han Suyin Fund for Scientific Exchange), 1989–; Open Coll. of the Arts, 1990–97; Chm., BM Develt Trust, 1986–93 (Vice Chm., 1993–2004); Pres., BM Foundn Inc., 1989–90; Dir, American Friends of BM, 1990–2002. Vice-Pres., GB-China Centre, 1997– (Chm., 1986–97); Gov., Compton Verney House Trust, 1995– (Chm., 2005–); Member: Bd, Sainsbury Inst. for Study of Japanese Arts and Culture, 1999–; Stiftung Hans Arp und Sophie Tauber Arp, 1999–; Stiftung Temple Gift, 2000–. Freeman, City of London, 1960; Liveryman, Fishmongers' Co., 1960–. Hon. DLitt: Keele, 2002; Buckingham, 2004; Hon. DCL UEA, 2002. Chevalier de l'Ordre des Arts et des Lettres, France, 1985. *Address:* D2 Albany, Piccadilly, W1J 0AP. *T:* (020) 7734 0270, *Fax:* (020) 7437 5251; *e-mail:* grahamc.greene@virgin.net.

GREENE, Jenny, (Mrs Michael Boys-Greene); Editor, Country Life, 1986–93, retired; *b* 9 Feb. 1937; *d* of Captain James Wilson Greene and Mary Emily Greene; *m* 1971, John Gilbert (marr. diss. 1987); *m* 1994, Michael Boys-Greene. *Educ:* Rochelle Sch., Cork; Trinity Coll., Dublin; Univ. of Montpellier, France. Researcher, Campbell-Johnson Ltd, 1963–64; Account-Exec., Central News, 1964–65; Account-Exec., Pemberton Advertising, 1965–66; Publicity Exec., Revlon, 1966–71; Beauty Editor, Woman's Own, 1971–75; Features Writer and Theatre Critic, Manchester Evening News, 1975–77; Asst Editor, Woman's Own, 1977–78; Editor: Homes and Gardens, 1978–86; A La Carte, 1984–85; columnist, Today, 1985–87. Contrib., Country Life and Gardens Illustrated, 1998–. *Recreations:* gardening, cooking. *Address:* 14 rue l'Epi de Saint Sauveur, 17740 St Martin de Re, France.

GREENE, Peter Livesey; a District Judge, Principal Registry of Family Division, since 2004; *b* 21 June 1947; *s* of late George Greene, MBE and of Nell Greene; *m* 1986, Linda Rowell; three *d*. *Educ:* Manchester Coll. of Commerce (LLB); Guildford Coll. of Law. Admitted solicitor, 1972; Sen. Partner, Greene D'sa, 1977–94, Greene Deavin, 1994–2001, Solicitors, Leicester; Dep. Dist Judge, 1999–2004. *Recreations:* hill walking, music, cycling, theatre. *Address:* Principal Registry of the Family Division, First Avenue House, 42–49 High Holborn, WC1V 6NP. *T:* (020) 7947 6000.

GREENE, Rt Rev. Samuel Rolland, CMG 2004; President, Bahamas Christian Council, 2001; *b* 3 Dec. 1938; *s* of Herbert and Petrel Greene; *m* 1964, Shirley; one *s* one *d* (and two *s* decd). *Educ:* Bahamas Teachers' Coll.; Univ. of Birmingham; Univ. of Manchester; Univ. of Miami; Templeton Theol Seminary. Asst teacher, 1961–63; Head Master, 1963–75; First Asst Sec., 1975–81; Dep. PS, 1981–83; Under Sec., 1983–88; Actg PS, 1988–89; Asst GM, 1989–92. Associate Minister, 1980–86; Pastor, 1986–95; Bishop, 1995. *Publication:* A More Excellent Way, 2001. *Recreation:* swimming. *Address:* Nassau, Bahamas.

GREENER, Sir Anthony (Armitage), Kt 1999; Chairman, Qualifications and Curriculum Authority, since 2002; Deputy Chairman, British Telecommunications plc, 2001–06; *b* 26 May 1940; *s* of William and Diana Marianne Greener; *m* 1974, Min Ogilvie; one *s* one *d*. *Educ:* Marlborough Coll. FCMA. Marketing Manager, Thames Board Mills, 1969; Retail Controller 1972, Dir 1974, Alfred Dunhill Ltd; Man. Dir, Alfred Dunhill Ltd, subseq. Dunhill Holdings plc, 1975; Man. Dir, United Distillers, 1987–92, Chm., 1996–97; Guinness PLC: Dir, 1986–97; Jt Man. Dir, 1989–91; Chief Exec., 1992–97; Chm., 1993–97; Jt Chm., 1997–98, Chm., 1998–2000, Diageo plc; Chm., University for Industry Ltd, 2000–04. Director: Louis Vuitton Moet Hennessy, 1989–97; Reed International, 1990–98; Reed Elsevier, 1993–98. Board Member: United Learning Trust, 2005–; Williams Sonoma, 2007–; WNS Global Services, 2007–. *Recreations:* ski-ing, sailing. *Address:* Qualifications and Curriculum Authority, 83 Piccadilly, W1J 8QA. *Clubs:* Royal Ocean Racing; Royal Yacht Squadron (Cowes).

GREENER, George Pallister, CBE 2005; PhD; FCIWEM; Chairman: British Waterways, 1999–2005; Big Food (formerly Iceland) Group plc, 2001–05; Strategic Health Authority for London, 2006–08; *b* 14 July 1945; *m* 1969, Rosemary Orchard; one *s*. *Educ:* Newcastle upon Tyne Univ. (BSc Hons 1966); PhD Southampton 1969. Joined Mars Gp, 1971; Man. Dir, Mars UK, 1986–91; Dir, BAT Industries, 1991–96; Chief Exec., BAT UK Financial Services, 1993–96; Chm. and Chief Exec., Allied Dunbar Assurance, 1991–96; Chairman: Eagle Star Hldgs, 1993–96; Threadneedle Asset Mgt, 1994–96; Chief Exec., Hillsdown Hldgs, 1996–98; Chm., Swallow Gp, 1999–2000. Non-executive Director: Reckitt & Coleman, subseq. Reckitt Benckiser, 1996–2006; J. P. Morgan Fleming American Investment Trust, 1999–. Mem. Ct, Univ. of Newcastle upon Tyne, 2005–07. FRSA. *Recreations:* piano playing, horse riding. *Address:* 5 Horbury Mews, W11 3NL.

GREENER, Very Rev. Jonathan Desmond Francis; Dean of Wakefield, since 2007; *b* 9 March 1961; *s* of Desmond Walter Kingsley Greener and Maureen Frances (*née* Murden); *m* 2006, Pamela Green. *Educ:* Reigate Grammar Sch.; Trinity Coll., Cambridge (BA 1983, MA 1987); Coll. of the Resurrection, Mirfield. Sales and Export Manager, A & M Hearing Ltd, 1984–89. Ordained deacon, 1991, priest, 1992; Asst Curate, Holy Trinity with St Matthew, Southwark, 1991–94; Bp of Truro's Domestic Chaplain, 1994–96; Vicar, Ch of the Good Shepherd, Brighton, 1996–2003; Archdeacon of Pontefract, 2003–07. Co-ordinator, Archbp of Canterbury's Romania Liaison Gp, 1993–2006; Chm., Nat. Archdeacons' Forum, 2007. *Publication:* (contrib.) The Fire and the Clay, 1993. *Recreations:* France, icons, ski-ing. *Address:* The Deanery, Cathedral Close, Margaret Street, Wakefield WF1 2DP. *T:* (01924) 210005.

GREENFIELD, Baroness *cr* 2001 (Life Peer), of Ot Moor in the County of Oxfordshire; **Susan Adele Greenfield,** CBE 2000; DPhil; Professor of Pharmacology, Oxford University, since 1996; Fellow, since 1985, and Senior Research Fellow, since 1999,

Lincoln College, Oxford; Hon. Research Fellow, St Hilda's College, Oxford, since 1999; Director, Royal Institution, since 1998; *b* 1 Oct. 1950; *d* of Reginald Myer Greenfield and Doris Margaret Winifred Greenfield; *m* 1991, Peter William Atkins, *qv* (marr. diss. 2005). *Educ:* Godolphin and Latymer Sch. for Girls; St Hilda's Coll., Oxford (BA Hons Exp. Psychol. 1973; MA 1978; DPhil 1977; Hon. Fellow, 1999). Dame Catherine Fulford Sen. Scholarship, St Hugh's Coll., Oxford, 1974; MRC Training Fellow, Univ. Lab. of Physiol., Oxford, 1977–81; Collège de France, Paris; Royal Soc. Study Visit Award, 1978; MRC-INSERM French Exchange Fellow, 1979–80; Oxford University: Jun. Res. Fellow, Green Coll., 1981–84; Lectr in Synaptic Pharmacol., 1985–96. Co-founder: Synaptica Ltd, 1997; BrainBoost Ltd, 2002. Gresham Prof. of Physic, Gresham Coll., 1995–99; Vis. Fellow, Inst. of Neuroscience, La Jolla, USA, 1995; Vis. Dist. Scholar, Queen's Univ., Belfast, 1996. Adelaide Thinker in Residence, 2004–06; Chancellor, Heriot-Watt Univ., 2006–. Mem., Nat. Adv. Cttee on Cultural and Creative Educn, 1998–; Pres., ASE, 2000; Vice-Pres., Assoc. of Women in Sci. and Engrg, 2001. Trustee, Science Mus., 1998–2003. Non-executive Director: Britech Foundn Ltd, 2002–06; Oxford Inspires Ltd, 2002–05; Israel Britain Business Council, 2002; Young Foresight Ltd, 2003; Bank Leumi (UK), 2003–06; Cherwell Capital plc, 2004–06; Enkephala Ltd, 2005–. Presenter, Brain Story, BBC 2, 2000. Dimbleby Lectr, 1999. FRSE 2007. Hon. Fellow, Cardiff Univ., 2000. Hon. FRCP 2000. Numerous hon. degrees. Michael Faraday Award, Royal Soc., 1998; Woman of Distinction, Jewish Care, 1998; Hon. Australian of Year, 2006. Chevalier, Légion d'Honneur (France), 2003. *Publications:* (ed with C. B. Blakemore) Mindwaves, 1987; (with G. Ferry) Journey to the Centers of the Brain, 1994; Journey to the Centers of the Mind, 1995; (ed) The Human Mind Explained, 1996; The Human Brain: a guided tour, 1997; (ed) Brain Power, 2000; Private Life of the Brain, 2000; Brain Story, 2000; Tomorrow's People, 2003; ID: the quest for identity in the 21st Century, 2008; contribs to learned jls, press and media. *Recreations:* squash, dance. *Address:* Department of Pharmacology, University of Oxford, Mansfield Road, Oxford OX1 3QT. *T:* (01865) 271852. *Club:* Athenæum.

GREENFIELD, Edward Harry, OBE 1994; Chief Music Critic, The Guardian, 1977–93; *b* 30 July 1928; *s* of Percy Greenfield and Mabel (*née* Hall). *Educ:* Westcliff High Sch.; Trinity Hall, Univ. of Cambridge (MA). Joined staff of Manchester Guardian, 1953: Record Critic, 1955; Music Critic, 1964; succeeded Sir Neville Cardus as Chief Music Critic, 1977. Broadcaster on music and records for BBC radio. Mem., critics' panel, Gramophone, 1960–. Pres., Fedn of Recorded Music Socs, 1997–. Master, Art Workers Guild, 2002. Hon. GSM 1991. Goldener Verdienstzeichen, Salzburg, 1981. *Publications:* Puccini: keeper of the seal, 1958; monographs on Joan Sutherland, 1972, and André Previn, 1973; (with Robert Layton, Ivan March and initially Denis Stevens) Stereo Record Guide, 9 vols, 1960–74; Penguin Stereo Record Guide, 5th edn 1986; (jtly) Penguin Guide to Compact Discs, Cassettes and LPs, 1986, 4th edn as Penguin Guide to Compact Discs, 1992, 19th edn 2008; Penguin Guide to Opera on Compact Discs, 1993. *Recreations:* work, living in Spitalfields. *Address:* 16 Folgate Street, E1 6BX. *T:* (020) 7377 7555. *Club:* Critics' Circle.

GREENFIELD, Howard; *see* Greenfield, R. H.

GREENFIELD, Dr Peter Rex; Senior Principal Medical Officer, Department of Health (formerly of Health and Social Security), 1983–91, retired; *b* 1 Dec. 1931; *s* of late Rex Youhill Greenfield and Elsie Mary Greenfield (*née* Douthwaite); *m* 1954, Faith Stella, *d* of George and Stella Gigg; eight *s* two *d*. *Educ:* Cheltenham College; Pembroke College, Cambridge (BA 1954; MB BChir 1957; MA 1985); St George's Hosp. Med. Sch., London. DObst RCOG 1960. 2nd Lieut, R Signals, 1950–51; House appts, St George's Hosp., 1958; Gen. Med. Pract., Robertsbridge, Sussex, 1959–69; MO, Vinehall Sch., Robertsbridge, 1964–69; MO, Battle Hosp., 1964–69; joined DHSS, 1969; Chief Med. Advr (Social Security), 1983–86. Mem., Jt Formulary Cttee, British Nat. Formulary, 1978–82; Chm., Informal Working Gp on Effective Prescribing, 1981–82. Medical Mem., The Appeals Service, 1996–2001. Chm. of Trustees, Chaseley Home for Disabled Ex-Servicemen, Eastbourne, 1995–2001 (Trustee, 1983–2003). QHP 1987–90. Hon. Mem., BPA, 1991–96; Hon. FRCPCH 1996. Mem., Salehurst PCC, 1995–. *Publications:* contribs to med. jls on geriatric day care, hypothermia and DHSS Regional Med. Service. *Recreations:* golf, swimming, walking, music, pinball. *Address:* Lorne House, Bellhurst Road, Robertsbridge, East Sussex TN32 5DW. *T:* (01580) 880209.

GREENFIELD, (Robert) Howard, FCA; CIGEM; Project Director, British Gas plc, 1990, retired; *b* 4 Feb. 1927; *s* of James Oswald Greenfield and Doris Burt Greenfield; *m* 1951, Joyce Hedley Wells; one *s* one *d*. *Educ:* Rutherford Coll., Newcastle upon Tyne. FCA 1953; CIGEM (CIGasE 1982). Northern Gas Board, 1956–74, Regional Service Manager, 1968–74; Northern Gas: Dir of Customer Service, 1974; Dir of Marketing, 1976; Dep. Chm., 1977; Chm., N Eastern Reg., 1982–85; Regl Chm., British Gas, N Western, 1985–89. OStJ 1988. *Recreations:* salmon fishing, photography.

GREENGARD, Prof. Paul, PhD; Vincent Astor Professor and Head, Laboratory of Molecular and Cellular Neuroscience, Rockefeller University, New York, since 1983; *b* 11 Dec. 1925; *m* 1986, Ursula von Rydingsvard; two *s* one *d*. *Educ:* Hamilton Coll., NY (AB 1948); Univ. of Pennsylvania; Johns Hopkins Univ. (PhD Neurophysiol. 1953). Served USNR, 1943–46. Research posts at: Inst. of Psychiatry, Univ. of London, 1953–54; Molteno Inst., Univ. of Cambridge, 1954–55; NIMR, London, 1955–58; Lab. of Clinical Biochem., NIH, 1958–59; Dir, Dept of Biochem., Geigy Res. Labs, NY, 1959–67; Prof. of Pharmacol. and Psychiatry, Yale Univ. Sch. of Medicine, 1968–83. Visiting Professor: Albert Einstein Coll. of Medicine, NY, 1968–70; Depts of Pharmacol. and Microbiol., Vanderbilt Univ. Sch. of Medicine, Nashville, 1968; Henry Bronson Prof. of Pharmacol., Yale Univ. Sch. of Medicine, 1981; Wellcome Vis. Prof. in Basic Med. Scis, Univ. of Iowa, 1986. Founder and Series Editor: Advances in Biochemical Psychopharmacol., 1968–; Advances in Cyclic Nucleotide and Protein Phosphorylation Res., 1971–; mem., numerous editl bds and editl adv. bds. Hon. MD Karolinska Inst., 1987. Holds numerous awards including: Award in the Neuroscis, NAS, 1991; Ralph W. Gerard Prize in Neurosci., Soc. For Neurosci., 1994; Charles A. Dana Award for Pioneering Achievements in Health, 1997; Nobel Prize in Physiol. or Medicine, 2000. *Publications:* Cyclic Nucleotides, Phosphorylated Proteins and Neuronal Function, 1978; (with E. J. Nestler) Protein Phosphorylation in the Nervous System, 1984; contrib. numerous chapters and reviews. *Address:* Laboratory of Molecular and Cellular Neuroscience, Rockefeller University, 1230 York Avenue, New York, NY 10021, USA. *T:* (212) 3278780.

GREENGROSS, family name of **Baroness Greengross**.

GREENGROSS, Baroness *cr* 2000 (Life Peer), of Notting Hill in the Royal Borough of Kensington and Chelsea; **Sally Greengross,** OBE 1993; Chief Executive, International Longevity Centre UK, since 2004 (Chairman, 2000–04); Vice-President, Age Concern England, since 2002 (Director, then Director General 1987–2000); *b* 29 June 1935; *m* 1959, Sir Alan Greengross, *qv*; one *s* three *d*. *Educ:* Brighton and Hove High Sch.; LSE. Formerly linguist, executive in industry, lectr and researcher; Asst Dir, 1977–82, Dep. Dir, 1982–87, Age Concern England. Secretary General: Internat. Fedn on Ageing, 1982–87 (Vice-Pres. (Europe), 1987–2001); Eurolink Age, 1989–2001. Jt Chm. Bd, Age Concern Inst. of Gerontology, KCL, 1987–2000. Member: Bd, Britain in Europe, 1999–2006; Sub-Cttee F, Select Cttee on EU, H of L, 2000–03; Sub-Cttee G, H of L, 2004–07. Chm., Experience Corps, 2001–05. Vice-Pres., LGA, 2001–. Independent Member: UN Network on Ageing, 1983–2000; WHO Network on Ageing, 1983–2000; Mem., OFCOM Adv. Gp on Older and Disabled People, 2004–06. Member: HelpAge Internat., 2000–07; Adv. Council, Internat. Assoc. of Homes and Services for the Ageing, 2002–. Mem., Commn for Equality and Human Rights, 2006–. Former Member: Inner London Juvenile Court Panel; Management Bd, Hanover Housing Gp. Gov., Pensions Policy Inst., 2002– (Pres., 2004–); Adviser: Internat. Centre for Health and Soc., UCL, 2000–; Good Corp., 2000–; Merck Inst. of Ageing and Health, 2001–05; Chm. Adv. Cttee, English Longitudinal Study on Ageing, UCL, 2000–; Co-Chair, Alliance for Health and the Future, 2003–. Patron: Action on Elder Abuse, 1999–; Groundwork Foundn, 1999–; Pennell Initiative, 1999–; Sheffield Inst. for Studies on Ageing, 1999–; Care and Repair England, 1999–; Ransackers, 2006–; Hon Ambassador, Help Age Internat; Trustee, Help Age Internat. Sri Lanka. Hon. Pres., Women for Europe, 1999–. FRSH 1994; FRSA 1994. Hon. FIA 2001. Hon. DLitt: Ulster, 1994; Brunel, 2002; Keele, 2004; DUniv: Kingston, 1996; Open, 2002; Leeds Metropolitan, 2002; Hon. LLD Exeter, 2000. UK Woman of Europe Award, EC, 1990. *Publications:* (ed) Ageing: an adventure in living, 1985; (ed) The Law and Vulnerable Elderly People, 1986; (jtly) Living, Loving and Ageing, 1989; and others on ageing issues and social policy. *Recreations:* countryside, music. *Address:* House of Lords, SW1A 0PW. *T:* (020) 7219 5494. *Clubs:* Reform, Hurlingham, Royal Society of Medicine.

GREENGROSS, Sir Alan (David), Kt 1986; DL; Chairman and Managing Director, Indusmond (Diamond Tools) Ltd; Director: Blazy & Clement Ltd and associated companies; South West Trains, since 2001; *b* 1929; *m* 1959, Sally (*see* Baroness Greengross); one *s* three *d*. *Educ:* University Coll. Sch.; Trinity Coll., Cambridge (Sen. Schol.; MA). Formerly Member Council, London Borough of Camden (past Alderman). Dep. Traffic Comr, 1968–70. GLC: Member (C), 1977–84; Leader, Planning and Communications Policy, 1979–81; Leader of the Opposition, 1983–84. Director: Port of London Authority, 1979–83; London First Centre, 1994–; Chm., London Regl Passengers Cttee, 1996–2000; Mem., Central Rail Users Consultative Cttee, 1996–2000 (Dep. Chm., 1999–2000). Chm., Bloomsbury and Islington HA, 1990–93. Vis. Prof., City of London Polytechnic, 1988–. Dir, The Roundhouse Black Arts Centre, 1988–89. Chairman: Steering Gp, Inst. for Metropolitan Studies, 1989–; Policy Gp, Bartlett Sch. of the Built Envmt, UCL, 1993–2005; Director: Built Envmt Res. Foundn, 1996–; STEP Foundn, 2005–. Member, Governing Council: UCS, 1987–2005; UCL, 1991–2005 (Vice Chm., 2003–05). DL Greater London, 1986. Hon. Fellow, UCL, 1999. *Clubs:* Hurlingham, Royal Society of Medicine.

GREENHALGH, Colin Ayton, CBE 2003 (OBE 1997); DL; MA; Principal, Hills Road Sixth Form College, Cambridge, 1984–2002; Vice Chairman, since 2002, and Senior Independent Director, since 2006, Cambridge University Hospitals NHS Foundation Trust (formerly Addenbrooke's NHS Trust) (non-executive Director, 2001–02); *b* 11 Aug. 1941; *s* of Robert Ayton Greenhalgh and Ethel Mary Henderson (*née* Cattermole); *m* 1966, Vivienne Christine Grocock, PhD; one *s* two *d*. *Educ:* Gateway Sch., Leicester; St John's Coll., Cambridge (MA); Univ. of Nottingham (PGCE). Teacher of Hist., Bradford Grammar Sch., 1964–70; Hd of Hist., Hd of Upper Sch. and Dep. Hd, Bulmershe Sch., Reading, 1970–76; Dep. Hd and Second Master, St Bartholomew's Sch., Newbury, 1976–84. Non-exec. Dir, Cambs HA, 2000–01. Mem., Cambs LEA Inspectorate, 1991–92; Further Education Funding Council: Mem., Eastern Regl Cttee, 1993–98, Quality Assessment Cttee, 1997–2001; Registered Inspector, 1998–2001; Board Member: Learning and Skills Develt Agency (formerly Further Educn Develt Agency), 1999–2003; Further Educn Cttee, SHA, 1998–2002; Mem., Appeals Panel, 2000–, Malpractice Panel for Internat. Exams, 2004–, Oxford, Cambridge and RSA Exams Bd. Registered OFSTED Inspector, 2001–; educnl consultant, 2002–. Cambridgeshire Association of Secondary Heads: Sec., 1988–89; Chm., 1989–90. Mem., Univ. of Cambridge Sports Centre Appeal Cttee, 2003–05. Trustee, Cambridge Centre for Sixth Form Studies, 2002–; Chm. of Trustees, Addenbrooke's Recreational and Develt Trust, 2004–. Governor: Stapleford Primary Sch., 1992–2007; Grammar Sch. at Leeds, 2005–. Hon. Sen. Mem., Wolfson Coll., Cambridge, 1990–. Hon. Fellow, Anglia Poly. Univ., 2002. Chm., Johnian Soc., St John's Coll., Cambridge, 1999– (Sec., 1992–99); Mem., Rotary Club, Cambridge, 1988–. Mem., Stapleford Parish Council, 1996–2002. DL Cambs, 1998. *Recreations:* churches and country houses, cinema, collecting books, sport, travel, Venice. *Address:* Cambridge University Hospitals NHS Foundation Trust, Hills Road, Cambridge CB2 2QQ. *Clubs:* MCC; Hawks; Cambridge University Cricket; Leicestershire County Cricket.

GREENHALGH, Jack; Vice-Chairman, Cavenham Ltd, 1974–81; retired; *b* 25 July 1926; *s* of Herbert Greenhalgh and Alice May (*née* Clayton); *m* 1951, Kathleen Mary Hammond (*d* 1983); two *s* two *d*. *Educ:* Manchester Grammar Sch.; Trinity Coll., Cambridge (MA Hons). Marketing Dept, Procter & Gamble Ltd, Newcastle upon Tyne, 1950–59; Marketing Dir, Eskimo Foods Ltd, Cleethorpes, 1959–64; Dir of Continental Ops, Compton Advertising Inc., NY, 1964–65; Cavenham Ltd, 1965–81: Man. Dir, 1968–79. FCMI. *Recreations:* golf, sailing.

GREENHALGH, Paul; Director and President, Corcoran Gallery of Art and College of Art and Design, Washington; *b* 21 Oct. 1955; *s* of William Greenhalgh and Marie Joan Greenhalgh; *m* 1981 (marr. diss.); two *s*. *Educ:* Bolton Smithills Grammar Sch.; Univ. of Reading (BA); Courtauld Inst., Univ. of London (MA). Lectr, Cardiff Inst., 1980–87; Dep. Curator of Ceramics and Glass, V&A Mus., 1988–92; Tutor in Art History, RCA, 1990–92; Hd of Art History, Camberwell Coll. of Arts, 1992–94; Hd of Res., V&A Mus., 1994–2000; Curator, Art Nouveau 1890–1914 exhibn, V&A and Nat. Gall. of Art, Washington, 2000, Metropolitan Mus., Tokyo, 2001; Pres., NSCAD Univ. (formerly Nova Scotia Coll. of Art and Design), 2001–06. Academic Editor, Manchester Univ. Press, 1989–. Mem., Crafts Council Educn Cttee, 1992–. Hon. Fellow, Res. Dept, V&A Mus., 2001. Hon. PhD Brighton, 2007. *Publications:* Ephemeral Vistas: great exhibitions, expositions universelles and world's fairs 1850–1939, 1988; (ed) Modernism in Design, 1990; Quotations and Sources on Design and the Decorative Arts 1800–1990, 1993; (ed) Art Nouveau 1890–1914, 2000; The Essential Art Nouveau, 2000; The Persistence of Craft, 2002; The Modern Ideal: the rise and collapse of idealism in the visual arts from the enlightenment to postmodernism, 2005. *Recreations:* running, soccer, hockey. *Address:* Corcoran Gallery of Art and College of Art and Design, 500 Seventeenth Street, NW, Washington, DC 20006–4804, USA. *T:* (902) 4948114.

GREENHALGH, Prof. Roger Malcolm, FRCS; Emeritus Professor of Surgery and Head of Imperial College of Science, Technology and Medicine Vascular Research Group at Charing Cross Hospital, since 2006; Hon. Consultant Surgeon, Charing Cross Hospital, since 1976; *b* 6 Feb. 1941; *s* of John Greenhalgh and Phyllis Poynton; *m* 1964, Karin Maria Gross; one *s* one *d*. *Educ:* Clare Coll., Cambridge; St Thomas' Hosp., London. BA 1963, BChir 1966, MB, MA 1967, MChir 1974, MD 1983 (Cantab); FRCS 1971. Ho. Surg.,

1967, Casualty Officer, 1968, St Thomas' Hosp.; Sen. Ho. Officer, Hammersmith Hosp., 1969; Registrar in Surgery, Essex County Hosp., Colchester, 1970–72; Lectr and Sen. Registrar in Surgery, St Bartholomew's Hosp., 1972–76; Sen. Lectr in Surgery, Charing Cross Hosp., 1976–81; Head of Dept of Surgery, 1981, Prof. of Surgery, 1982–2006, Chm. of Dept of Surgery, 1989–2006, Dean, 1993–97, Charing Cross Hosp. Med. Sch., later Charing Cross and Westminster Med. Sch.; Chm., Directorate of Surgery, 1994–98, Chief of Vascular Surgical Service, 1998–2002, Hammersmith Hosps NHS Trust. Chm., Eur. Examining Bd, Surgery Qualification, 1995–2002; President: Surgery sect., EU of Medical Specialities, 1998–2002; Eur. Bd of Surgery, 2002–06; Eur. Fedn of Surgical Specialties, UEMS, 2004–. Sometime examiner, Univs of Cambridge, London, Edinburgh, Bristol, Leicester, UCD, Southampton, Birmingham, Hong Kong. Chairman: Liaison Cttee, Bioengrg Centre, Roehampton, London, 1985–88; Riverside Med. Council, 1992–93; Member: Scientific Cttee on Tobacco and Health (formerly Ind. Scientific Enquiry into Smoking and Health), 1979–; Working Party Nat. Screening Prog. for Abdominal Aortic Aneurysm, 2004–. Vice-President: Section of Surgery, RSM, 1986–89; BRCS, 1992–; Sec. Gen. and Chm. Exec. Cttee, Assoc. of Internat. Vascular Surgeons, 1982–2005; Chm. Dirs and Trustees, European Soc. for Vascular Surgery, 1987– (Mem. Council, 1987–93); Mem. Council, Assoc. of Surgeons of GB and Ireland, 1993–; Pres., Vascular Soc. of GB and Ire., 1999–2000. Hon. FRCSE 1998; Hon. FRCSI 2007; Hon. Member: S African Vascular Surgical Soc., 1989; Canadian Vascular Soc., 1991; Polish Surgical Soc., 1991; German Vascular Soc., 1992; Hellenic Surgical Soc., 1992; Eur. Soc. for Vascular Surgery, 1993; Brazilian Angiology Soc., 1994; Hellenic Vascular Surg. Soc., 1995; Mediterranean League of Vascular Surgeons, 1996; Soc. for Vascular Surgery, 2001 (Corresp. Mem., 1991); Austrian Vascular Soc., 2002; Swiss Vascular Soc., 2003. Moynihan Fellow of Assoc. of Surgeons, 1974; Hunterian Prof., RCS, 1980; Protem Prof., Brigham Hosp., Harvard Med. Sch., 1984; Boone Powell Prof., Baylor Dallas Med. Sch., 1984; Hunter Sweeney Prof., Duke Univ., 1991; Mannick Vis. Prof., Harvard Univ., 1996. Sir Peter Freyer Lect., Univ. of Galway, 1995; Scott Heron Lect., QUB, 1999; Michael van Vloten Lect., Eindhoven, 2003. Hon. Dr: Warsaw Med. Acad., 2002; Athens Univ., 2005. Chm. Editl Bd, European Jl of Vascular Surgery, 1987–93; Mem. Editl Bd, Annals of Surgery, 1991–; Ed., Vascular News, 1998–. *Publications:* Progress in Stroke Research, 1, 1979; Smoking and Arterial Disease, 1981; Hormones and Vascular Disease, 1981; Femoro-distal bypass, 1981; Extra-Anatomic and Secondary Arterial Reconstruction, 1982; Progress in Stroke Research, 2, 1983; Vascular Surgical Techniques, 1984, 2nd edn 1989, 3rd edn as Vascular and Endovascular Surgical Techniques, 1994, 4th edn 2001; Diagnostic Techniques and Assessment Procedures in Vascular Surgery, 1985; Vascular Surgery: issues in current practice, 1986; Indications in Vascular Surgery, 1988; Limb Salvage and Amputations for Vascular Disease, 1988; The Cause and Management of Aneurysms, 1990; The Maintenance of Arterial Reconstruction, 1991; Vascular Surgical Emergencies, 1992; Surgery for Stroke, 1993; Vascular Imaging for Surgeons, 1995; Trials and Tribulations of Vascular Surgery, 1996; Clinical Surgery, 1996; Inflammatory and thrombotic problems in vascular surgery, 1997; Indications in Vascular and Endovascular Surgery, 1998; The Durability of Vascular and Endovascular Surgery, 1999; Vascular and Endovascular Opportunities, 2000; The evidence for vascular and endovascular reconstruction, 2002; Vascular and Endovascular Controversies, 2003; Vascular and Endovascular Challenges, 2004; Towards Vascular and Endovascular Consensus, 2005; More Vascular and Endovascular Controversies, 2006; More Vascular and Endovascular Challenges, 2007. *Recreations:* tennis, ski-ing, swimming, music. *Address:* 271 Sheen Lane, East Sheen, SW14 8RN. *T:* (020) 8878 1110. *Clubs:* Athenæum, Garrick.

GREENHILL, family name of **Baron Greenhill.**

GREENHILL, 3rd Baron *cr* 1950, of Townhead; **Malcolm Greenhill;** retired from Ministry of Defence; *b* 5 May 1924; *s* of 1st Baron Greenhill, OBE and Ida, *d* of late Mark Goodman; *S* brother, 1989. *Educ:* Kelvinside Acad., Glasgow; Glasgow Univ. (BSc). CPA. Ministries of Aircraft Production and Supply, 1944–54; UK Scientific Mission, Washington DC, USA, 1950–51; UKAEA, 1954–73; MoD, 1973–89. *Recreation:* gardening. *Address:* 28 Gorselands, Newbury, Berks RG14 6PX. *T:* (01635) 45651. *Club:* Civil Service.

GREENING, Justine; MP (C) Putney, since 2005; *b* 30 April 1969. *Educ:* Oakwood Comprehensive Sch., Rotherham; Thomas Rotherham Coll.; Univ. of Southampton (BSc 1990); London Business Sch. (MBA 2000). ACA 1995. Audit Asst, PriceWaterhouse, 1991–94; Audit Asst Manager, Revisuisse PriceWaterhouse, 1995–96; Finance Manager, SmithKline Beecham, 1996–2001; Business Strategy Manager, GlaxoSmithKline, 2001–02; Sales and Mktg Finance Manager, Centrica, 2002–05. Mem. (C), Epping Town Council, 1999. Contested (C) Ealing, Acton and Shepherd's Bush, 2001. *Address:* (office) 3 Summerstown Road, SW17 0BQ; House of Commons, SW1A 0AA.

GREENING, Rear-Adm. Sir Paul (Woollven), GCVO 1992 (KCVO 1985); Master of HM's Household, 1986–92; an Extra Equerry to the Queen, since 1983; *b* 4 June 1928; *s* of late Captain Charles W. Greening, DSO, DSC, RN, and Mrs Molly K. Greening (*née* Flowers); *m* 1951, Monica (*d* 2008), *d* of late Mr and Mrs W. E. West, East Farndon, Market Harborough; one *s* one *d*. *Educ:* Mowden Sch., Brighton; Nautical Coll., Pangbourne. Entered RN, 1946; Midshipman, HMS Theseus, 1947–48; Sub-Lt and Lieut, HM Ships Zodiac, Neptune, Rifleman, Asheldham (CO), and Gamecock, 1950–58; Lt-Comdr, HM Ships Messina (CO), Loch Killisport, Urchin, and Collingwood, 1958–63; Comdr 1963; CO HMS Lewiston, and SO 2nd Minesweeping Sqdn, 1963–64; jssc 1964; Naval Plans, MoD (Navy), 1965–67; CO HMS Jaguar, 1967–68; Fleet Plans Officer, Far East Fleet, 1969–70; Captain 1969; CO HMS Aurora, 1970–71; Captain Naval Drafting, 1971–74; Sen. Officers War Course, 1974; Dir of Officers Appts (Seamen), MoD (Navy), 1974–76; Captain BRNC Dartmouth, 1976–78; Naval Secretary, 1978–80; Flag Officer, Royal Yachts, 1981–85; retired 1985. ADC to the Queen, 1978. Mem. Council, Mission to Seafarers (formerly Missions to Seamen), 1994–2007. Younger Brother of Trinity House, 1984–. Vice Pres., Assoc. of Royal Yachtsmen, 1999–. *Recreations:* golf, gardening, following cricket. *Clubs:* Army and Navy; Corhampton Golf.

GREENISH, Rear Adm. Philip Duncan, CBE 2003; CEng, FIET; Chief Executive, Royal Academy of Engineering, since 2003; *b* Sept. 1951; *s* of Comdr Geoffrey Greenish, OBE, RN and late Alice Greenish; *m* 1972, Wendy Midmer; two *s* one *d*. *Educ:* Cheltenham Coll.; Durham Univ. (BSc Hons Engrg Sci.). CEng 1989; FIET (FIEE 2001). Captain Weapon Trials and Acceptance, 1992–94; MA to Chief of Defence Procurement, 1994–96; rcds 1997; Director: Operational Requirements (Sea Systems), 1997–99; Equipment Capability (Above Water Battlespace), 1999–2000; COS (Corporate Develt) to C-in-C Fleet, 2000–02; COS (Support) to C-in-C Fleet, 2002–03. ADC to the Queen, 1997–2000. Member: CCLRC, 2005–07; STFC, 2007–; Engrg and Technology Bd, 2007–. Trustee, Daphne Jackson Trust, 2004–. *Recreations:* tennis, golf, ski-ing, music, gardening. *Address:* Royal Academy of Engineering, 3 Carlton House Terrace, SW1Y 5DG.

See also S. Greenish.

GREENISH, Simon; Director, Bletchley Park Trust, since 2006; *b* 11 Oct. 1949; *s* of Geoffrey Harrold Greenish and Alice Thierens; *m* 1986, Gillian (*née* Wilkinson); two *d*. *Educ:* Durham Univ. (BSc Hons Eng. Sci. 1971). CEng, MICE 1975. Engr, N Beds BC, 1971–80; Prin. Engr, CAA, 1980–95; Develt Manager, 1995–2004, Dir of Collections, 2004–06, RAF Mus. *Recreation:* music. *Address:* Cartref, Grange Road, Felmersham, Beds MK43 7EU. *T:* (office) (01908) 272682, (home) (01234) 782559; *e-mail:* simongreenish@btinternet.com.

See also Rear Adm. P. D. Greenish.

GREENLAND, Dennis James, DPhil; FRS 1994; FIBiol; Scientific Dir, CAB International, 1987–92; *b* 13 June 1930; *s* of James John and Lily Florence Greenland; *m* 1955, Edith Mary Johnston; one *s* two *d*. *Educ:* Portsmouth Grammar Sch.; Christ Church, Oxford (MA, DPhil). Lecturer: Univ. of Ghana, 1955–59; Waite Agricl Res. Inst. Adelaide, 1959–63; Reader and Head of Soil Science, Waite Agricl Res. Inst., 1963–70; Professor and Head of Dept of Soil Science, Univ. of Reading, 1970–79; Director of Research, Internat. Inst. of Tropical Agriculture, Nigeria, 1974–76 (on secondment from Univ. of Reading); Dep. Dir Gen., Internat. Rice Res. Inst., Los Baños, Philippines, 1979–87. Vis. Prof., Univ. of Reading, 1987–2007. Chm., Scientific Adv. Panel, Commonwealth Develt Corp., 1992–96. FIBiol 1974; FWA 1987. Hon. Member: Amer. Soc. of Soil Science, 1993; Amer. Soc. of Agronomy, 1993. Hon. DrAgSci Ghent, 1982; Hon. DSc Ohio State, 2003. *Publications:* contributions: (jtly) The Soil Under Shifting Cultivation, 1960; (ed jtly) Soil Conservation and Management in the Humid Tropics, 1977; (ed jtly) Chemistry of Soil Constituents, 1978; (ed jtly) Soil Physical Properties and Crop Production in the Tropics, 1979; (ed) Characterisation of Soils in Relation to Their Classification and Management for Crop Production: some examples from the humid tropics, 1981; (ed jtly) The Chemistry of Soil Processes, 1981; (ed jtly) Soil Resilience and Sustainable Land Use, 1994; The Sustainability of Rice Farming, 1997; (ed jtly) Land Resources: on the edge of the Malthusian precipice, 1997; numerous scientific articles in learned jls. *Recreations:* walking, watching cricket. *Address:* Berrylands, Riverside Gardens Romsey SO51 8HN.

GREENOAK, Francesca; writer; Alexander Teacher, Arts Educational School, Tring Park, since 2000; *b* 6 Sept. 1946; *d* of Francis Buchanan Greenoak and Alice Lavinia (*née* Marston); *m* 1981, John Kilpatrick; one *s* one *d*. *Educ:* St Mary's Convent Grammar Sch., Woodford Green; Univ. of Essex (BA Hons); Alexander Re-Educn Centre. Book Club Associates, 1968; Editor: George Harrap, 1970; Penguin Educn, Penguin Books, 1972; Chameleon Publishing Co-operative, 1974; Gardening Correspondent: She mag. 1978–80; The Times, 1986–94; Gardens Ed., Good Housekeeping, 1993–96; Express Saturday, 1997–99. Mem. Council, Garden History Soc., 1999–2002 (Ed., Garden History Soc. News, 1999–; Chm., Educn and Publns Cttee, 2000–); Mem., 1999–, Dir, 2005–, Soc. of Teachers of the Alexander Technique (Mem. Council, 2000–05). Ed., Alexander Jl, 2001–. Leverhulme Res. Award, to study cultural and natural history of churchyards, 1995. *Publications:* Guide to Wildflowers, 1977; All The Birds of the Air, 1979, 2nd edn as British Birds: their folklore, names and literature, 1997; Forgotten Fruit, 1983; (with R. Mabey) Back to the Roots, 1983; God's Acre, 1985, 2nd edn as Wildlife in Churchyards, 1993; (ed) Journals of Gilbert White, 3 vols, 1989; Glorious Gardens, 1989; Fruit and Vegetable Gardens, 1990; Water in Small Gardens, 1996, 2nd edn as Water Features for Small Gardens, 2002; Natural Style for Gardens, 1998, 2nd edn as The Natural Garden, 2001; Gardens of the National Trust for Scotland, 2005. *Recreations:* literature, gardening, botany, music, education and science. *Address:* 4 Wood Row, Wigginton, Tring, Herts HP23 6HS.

GREENOCK, Lord; Alan George Cathcart; *b* 16 March 1986; *s* and *heir* of Earl Cathcart, *qv*. *Educ:* Stowe. *Address:* Gateley Hall, North Elmham, Dereham, Norfolk NR20 5EF.

GREENSHIELDS, Robert McLaren; HM Diplomatic Service, retired; Counsellor, Foreign and Commonwealth Office, 1985–88; *b* 27 July 1933; *s* of late Brig. James Greenshields, MC, TD, and of Mrs J. J. Greenshields; *m* 1960, Jean Alison Anderson; one *s* two *d*. *Educ:* Edinburgh Academy; Lincoln Coll., Oxford (MA Hons). National Service, 2nd Lieut Highland Light Infantry, 1952–54. District Officer, Tanganyika, HMOCS, 1958–61; Asst Master and Housemaster, Gordonstoun Sch., 1962–68; HM Diplomatic Service, 1969–88. *Recreations:* ornithology, conservation, farming.

GREENSLADE, Roy; freelance journalist, broadcaster and author, since 1992; Professor of Journalism, City University, since 2003; *b* 31 Dec. 1946; *s* of Ernest Frederick William Greenslade and Joan Olive (*née* Stocking); *m* 1984, Noreen Anna Taylor (*née* McElhone); one step *s* one step *d*. *Educ:* Dagenham County High Sch.; Sussex Univ. (BA (Hons) Politics, 1979). Trainee journalist, Barking Advertiser, 1962–66; Sub-Editor: Lancashire Evening Telegraph, 1966–67; Daily Mail, 1967–69; The Sun, 1969–71; researching and writing book, 1973–75; Daily Star, 1979–80; Daily Express, 1980–81; Daily Star, 1981; Asst Editor, The Sun, 1981–87; Man. Editor, Sunday Times, 1987–90; Editor, Daily Mirror, 1990–91; Consultant Editor, Today and Sunday Times, 1991. Columnist: Observer, 1996; Guardian, 1996–2005; Daily Telegraph, 2005–06; Evening Standard, 2006–. Dir, Impact Books, 1993–98. Presenter: Mediumwave, Radio 4, 1995–96; Britain Talks Back, TV, 1996–97. Mem. Bd, British Journalism Review, 1994–. FRSA 2004. Hon. DLitt Brighton, 1999. *Publications:* Goodbye to the Working Class, 1975; Maxwell's Fall, 1992; Press Gang, 2003. *Recreations:* reading, tennis. *Address:* Brighton BN2 1GA.

GREENSPAN, Alan, Hon. KBE 2002; President, Greenspan Associates LLC, since 2006; Chairman, Board of Governors of the Federal Reserve System, USA, 1987–2006; *b* 6 March 1926; *o s* of late Herbert Greenspan and Rose (*née* Goldsmith); *m* 1997, Andrea Mitchell. *Educ:* New York Univ. (BS 1948; MA 1950; PhD 1977). Pres., 1954–74 and 1977–87, Townsend-Greenspan & Co., NY. Director: Trans World Financial Co., 1962–74; Dreyfus Fund, 1970–74; Gen. Cable Corp., 1973–74, 1977–78; Sun Chemical Corp., 1973–74; Gen. Foods Corp., 1977–85; J. P. Morgan & Co., 1977–87; Mobil Corp., 1977–87; ALCOA, 1978–87. Consultant to Council of Economic Advisers, 1970–74, to US Treasury, 1971–74, to Fed. Reserve Board, 1971–74; Chairman: Council of Economic Advisers, 1974–77; Nat. Commn on Social Security Reform, 1981–83; Dir, Council on Foreign Relations; Presidential Commn on Financial Structure and Regulation, 1971, on an All-Volunteer Armed Force, 1971; Member: President's Econ Policy Adv. Board, 1981–87; President's Foreign Intell. Adv. Board, 1983–85. Hon degrees from Edinburgh, Harvard, Leuven, Pennsylvania and Yale univs. Jefferson Award, 1976; William Butler Meml Award, 1977; US Presidential Medal of Freedom, 2005; Commander, French Legion of Honour, 2003. *Publication:* The Age of Turbulence, 2007. *Address:* (office) 1133 Connecticut Avenue NW, Suite 810, Washington, DC 20036, USA.

GREENSTOCK, Sir Jeremy (Quentin), GCMG 2003 (KCMG 1998; CMG 1991); HM Diplomatic Service, retired; Director, Ditchley Foundation, since 2004; King of Arms, Most Distinguished Order of St Michael and St George, since 2007; *b* 27 July 1943; *s* of late John Wilfrid Greenstock and Ruth Margaret Logan; *m* 1969, Anne Derryn Ashford Hodges; one *s* two *d*. *Educ:* Harrow Sch.; Worcester Coll., Oxford (MA Lit

Hum.; Hon. Fellow, 2006). Asst Master, Eton Coll., 1966–69; entered HM Diplomatic Service, 1969; MECAS, 1970–72; Dubai, 1972–74; Private Sec. to the Ambassador, Washington, 1974–78; FCO, 1978–83 (Planning Staff, Personnel Ops Dept, N East and N African Dept); Counsellor (Commercial), Jedda, 1983–85, Riyadh, 1985–86; Hd of Chancery, Paris, 1987–90; Asst Under-Sec. of State, FCO, 1990–93; Minister, Washington, 1994–95; Dep. Under Sec. of State, FCO, 1995; Pol Dir, FCO, 1996–98; UK Perm. Rep. to UN, 1998–2003; UK Special Rep. for Iraq, 2003–04. Special Advr, BP Gp, 2004–; non-exec. Dir, De La Rue plc, 2005–. Member: Adv. Gp, UN Develt Fund for Women, 2005–; Internat. Adv. Gp, Brookings Instn, 2007–; Nat. Security Commn, IPPR, 2007–. Trustee, Internat. Rescue Cttee (UK), 2006–. Mem. Adv. Council, Oxford Philomusica Orchestra, 2007–. Gov., London Business Sch., 2005–07. Hon. FKC 2006. *Recreations:* travel, music, golf, ski-ing. *Address:* Ditchley Park, Enstone, Chipping Norton, Oxon OX7 4ER. *Club:* Oxford and Cambridge.

GREENTREE, (William Wayne) Chris; Chief Executive, LASMO Group, 1982–93; *b* 6 April 1935; *s* of J. Murray and Grace M. Greentree; *m* 1st, 1956, Patricia Ann Hugo (marr. diss. 1990); four *d* (and one *d* decd); 2nd, 1990, Hilary J. Wilson; one *d*. *Educ:* Moose Jaw Technical High Sch., Saskatoon; Univ. of Alberta (BSc Hons, PEng). Joined Shell Canada, 1957: technical and managerial appts, onshore and offshore exploration; Ranger Oil London, 1972–79: Man. Dir, 1976; Mapco Inc. USA: Sen. Vice Pres. Exploration and Production, 1979–82. Ordre National du Mérite (Gabon), 1987. *Recreations:* golf, ski-ing.

GREENWAY, family name of **Baron Greenway**.

GREENWAY, 4th Baron *cr* 1927; **Ambrose Charles Drexel Greenway;** Bt 1919; photographer and author; *b* 21 May 1941; *s* of 3rd Baron Greenway and of Cordelia Mary, *d* of late Major Humfrey Campbell Stephen; *S* father, 1975; *m* 1985, Mrs Rosalynne Schenk. *Educ:* Winchester. Chairman: Marine Soc., 1994–2000; Sail Trng Assoc., subseq. Tall Ships Youth Trust, 2001–03; World Ship Trust, 2003–. Elected Mem., H of L, 1999. *Publications:* Soviet Merchant Ships, 1976; Comecon Merchant Ships, 1978; A Century of Cross Channel Passenger Ferries, 1980; A Century of North Sea Passenger Steamers, 1986. *Recreations:* ocean racing and cruising, swimming. *Heir:* *b* Hon. Nigel Paul Greenway [*b* 12 Jan. 1944; *m* 1979, Gabrielle, *e d* of Walter Jean Duchardt; two *s*]. *Address:* c/o House of Lords, SW1A 0PW. *Club:* House of Lords Yacht.

GREENWAY, Prof. Diana Eleanor, PhD; FBA 2001; Professor of Medieval History, University of London, 1998–2003; Hon. Fellow, Institute of Historical Research, University of London, since 2004; *b* 1937; *d* of Charles and Winifred Greenway. *Educ:* Aylesbury Grammar Sch.; Girton Coll., Cambridge (BA Hist. 1959; MA 1963; PhD 1967). Asst Archivist, Lambeth Palace Liby, 1963–64; University of London: Ed., Fasti Ecclesiae Anglicanae 1066–1300 (10 vols, 1968–2005), at Inst. of Historical Res., 1964–2003; teaching hist. and palaeography, 1966–97; Reader in Medieval Hist., 1993–98. Founder and Chair, Univ. of London Palaeography and Diplomatic Teachers' Gp, 1993–98. Gen. Ed., Oxford Medieval Texts, 1974–97. Literary Dir, RHistS, 1982–87. Dir, Summer Insts in Palaeography, Newberry Liby, Chicago, 1985, 1990 and 1994. British Rep., Assembly of Repertorium Fontium Historiae Medii Aevi, 1993–2003. *Publications:* Charters of the Honour of Mowbray 1107–91, 1972; (ed jtly) Early Yorkshire Families, 1973; (ed jtly) Richard fitzNigel: Dialogus de Scaccario, 1983; (ed jtly) Tradition and Change: essays in honour of Marjorie Chibnall, 1985; (ed jtly) Handbook of British Chronology, 1986; (jtly) The Chronicle of Jocelin of Brakelond, 1989; Henry, Archdeacon of Huntingdon: Historia Anglorum, 1996; (ed jtly) The Book of the Foundation of Walden Monastery, 1999; Saint Osmund, Bishop of Salisbury 1078 to 1099, 1999; Henry of Huntingdon: The History of the English People 1000–1154, 2002; contrib. articles to learned jls. *Recreations:* birdwatching, dragonflies. *Address:* Institute of Historical Research, University of London, Senate House, WC1E 7HU.

GREENWAY, Harry; *b* 4 Oct. 1934; *s* of John Kenneth Greenway and Violet Adelaide (*née* Bell); *m* 1969, Carol Elizabeth Helena, *e d* of late Major John Robert Thomas Hooper, barrister at law and Metropolitan Stipendiary Magistrate, and Dorinda Hooper (*née* de Courcy Ireland); one *s* two *d*. *Educ:* Warwick Sch.; College of St Mark and St John, London; Univ. of Caen, Normandy. Assistant Master, Millbank Sch., 1957–60; successively, Head of English Dept, Sen. Housemaster, Sen. Master, Acting Dep. Head, Sir William Collins Sch., 1960–72; Dep. Headmaster, Sedgehill Sch. (Comprehensive for 2,000 plus pupils), 1972–79. Contested (C) Stepney, 1970, Stepney and Poplar, Feb. and Oct. 1974; MP (C) Ealing North, 1979–97; contested (C) same seat, 1997. Vice-Chm., Greater London Cons. Members, 1981–97; Chairman: All Party Adult Educn Cttee, 1979–97; All Party Parly Friends of Cycling, 1987–95; Member: Parly Select Cttee on Educn, Science and the Arts, 1979–92; Parly Select Cttee on Employment, 1992–95, on Educn and Employment, 1995–97; Vice-Chairman: Cons. Parly Educn Cttee, 1983–87 (Sec., 1981); Cons. Parly Sports Cttee, 1990–97 (Sec., 1986–90); Parly Sec., Cons. National Adv. Cttee on Educn, 1981–94; Sec., Cons. Parly Arts and Heritage Cttee, 1986–87. Parly Sec., Cons. Nat. Educn Soc., 1995–97 (Dep. Pres., 1998–); Chm., Mauritius Parly Gp, 1983–97. Led All Party Parly Delegn to Sri Lanka, 1985, to Gibraltar, 1989, to Zaire, 1990. Pres., Cons. Trade Unionist Teachers, 1982–83; Chm., Educn Cttee, British-Atlantic Cttee, 1971–85; Open University: Mem. Council, 1981–99; Audit Cttee, 1997–99; Grievance Cttee, 1998–99; Mem., Educn Cttee, NACRO, 1985–88. President: Age Concern, Greenford, Northolt and Perivale, 1980–; Ealing Youth Choir, 1985–; Nat. Equine Welfare Council, 1990–; Assoc. of British Riding Schs, 1993–2003; Spencer Hockey Club, 2000–03; Mem. Council, British Horse Soc., 1973–97 (Trustee, 1998–2006); Mem. Bd of Govs, Horse Rangers Assoc., 2000–02; Founder Trustee, The Greater London Equestrian Centres Trust Ltd; Trustee, Teenage Cancer Trust, 1991–2007. Vice-Pres., Greenford Br., RBL, 1977–. Chm., National Prayer Breakfast, 1995. Freeman: City of London, 1986; London Bor. of Ealing, 2008; Liveryman, Farriers' Co., 1986–2006. DUniv Open, 2001. Award of Merit, 1980, President's Award, 2006, Sefton Award, 2007, British Horse Soc. Kt Comdr's Cross, Order of Merit (Poland), 1998. *Publications:* Adventure in the Saddle, 1971; (ed and compiled) Electing to Bat: tales of glory and disaster from the Palace of Westminster, 1996; regular contributor to educnl and equestrian jls. *Recreations:* riding (Asst Instructor, BHS, 1966), ski-ing, choral music, hockey (Vice-Pres., England Schoolboys' Hockey Assoc.; Founder, Lords and Commons Hockey Club), tennis, cricket, parliamentary parachutist. *Address:* 64 Cambridge Street, Westminster, SW1V 4QQ. *Clubs:* St Stephen's, National, MCC, Middlesex CC, Lord's Taverners, Ski Club of Gt Britain; Worcs CC.

GREENWAY, John Robert; MP (C) Ryedale, since 1987; *b* 15 Feb. 1946; *s* of Thomas William and Kathleen Greenway; *m* 1974, Sylvia Ann Gant; two *s* one *d*. *Educ:* Sir John Deane's Grammar School, Northwich; London College of Law. Midland Bank, 1964; Metropolitan Police, 1965–69; Equitable Life Assurance Soc., 1970–71; National Provident Instn, 1971–72; own firm of insurance brokers, J. R. Greenway, subseq. Greenway Middleton, & Co. Ltd, York, then Greenway Smart and Cook Ltd, now Smart and Cook Ltd, 1972–. Treasurer, Ryedale Cons. Assoc., 1984–86; Mem., North Yorks CC, 1985–87; Vice-Chm., N Yorks Police Authy, 1986–87. PPS to Minister of State, MAFF, 1991–92; Opposition front bench spokesman on home affairs, 1997–2000, on sport and tourism, 2000–03. Mem., Home Affairs Select Cttee, 1987–97. Chm., Jt Scrutiny Cttee, Draft Gambling Bill, 2003–05; Sec., Cons. backbench Health Cttee, 1988–91; Vice-Chairman: Cons. backbench Agricl Cttee, 1989–97; All Party Football Cttee, 1989–; Chairman: All Party Racing and Bloodstock Cttee, 1993–97; All Party Insce and Financial Services Gp, 1992– (Sec., 1991–92); Jt Chm., All Party Opera Gp, 1994–. Elected rep. to Council of Europe, 2005–. Dir, Responsibility in Gambling Trust, 2006–. Pres., Inst. of Insce Brokers, 1987–; Chm., Fedn of Insce and Investment Intermediary Assocs, 1998–2001; Mem., Insce Brokers Registration Council, 1991–2001. *Recreations:* opera, football (Pres., York City FC), wine, travel, gardening. *Address:* House of Commons, SW1A 0AA.

GREENWELL, (Arthur) Jeffrey, CBE 1991; DL; Chief Executive, Northamptonshire County Council, 1973–96; Independent Adjudicator, Department for Communities and Local Government (formerly Department of the Environment, Transport and the Regions, later Department for Transport, Local Government and the Regions, then Office of the Deputy Prime Minister), since 1998; *b* 1 Aug. 1931; *s* of late George Greenwell and of Kate Mary Greenwell (*née* Fleming), Durham; *m* 1958, Margaret Rosemary, *d* of late Sidney David Barnard; one *s* two *d*. *Educ:* Durham Sch.; University Coll., Oxford (MA). FCIS. Solicitor (Hons). Nat. Service, RHA, 1950–51. Articled to Town Clerk, Newcastle upon Tyne, 1955–58; law tutor, Gibson & Weldon, 1958–59; Asst Solicitor, Birmingham Corp., 1959–61; Hants County Council: Asst Solicitor, 1961–64; Asst Clerk, 1964–67; Dep. Clerk of Council, Dep. Clerk of the Peace and Dep. Clerk, Hants River Authy, 1967–73; Clerk of Northants Lieutenancy, 1977–96. Chm., Assoc. of Co. Chief Execs, 1993–94 (Hon. Sec., 1980–84); Hon. Sec., SOLACE, 1984–88 (Pres., 1991–92); President: CIS, 1989; Northants Assoc. of Local Councils, 1974–96. Chm., Home Office Gp on Juvenile Crime, 1987. Vice-Pres., Internat. City Management Assoc., 1990–92; Chm., Northants ACRE, 1998–2002; Vice-Chm., Northants CPRE, 2002–. Trustee, Central Festival Opera. Gov., UC, Northampton, 1998–2002. Freeman, City of London, 1989 (Pres., Aldgate Ward Club, 2008–Feb. 2009); Liveryman, Chartered Secretaries' and Administrators' Co. (Master, 2005–06). DL Northants, 1996. Freeman, City of Durham, 1992. *Recreations:* bridge, travel, local history, going to meetings. *Address:* 2 Hillside Way, Northampton NN3 3AW. *T:* (01604) 401858.

GREENWELL, Sir Edward (Bernard), 4th Bt *cr* 1906; DL; farmer, since 1975; *b* 10 June 1948; *s* of Sir Peter McClintock Greenwell, 3rd Bt, TD, and of Henrietta (who *m* 1985, Hugh Kenneth Haig), 2nd *d* of late Peter and Lady Alexandra Haig-Thomas; *S* father, 1978; *m* 1974, Sarah Louise Gore-Anley; one *s* three *d*. *Educ:* Eton; Nottingham University (BSc); Cranfield Institute of Technology (MBA). Pres., CLA, 2001–03. DL Suffolk, 1988. *Heir:* *s* Alexander Bernard Peter Greenwell, *b* 11 May 1987. *Address:* Gedgrave Hall, Woodbridge, Suffolk IP12 2BX. *T:* (01394) 450440. *Club:* Turf.

GREENWELL, Jeffrey; *see* Greenwell, A. J.

GREENWOOD, Alan Eliezer; His Honour Judge Greenwood; a Circuit Judge, since 2000; *b* 5 June 1947; *s* of Rabbi Hans Isaac Grunewald and Martha Grunewald; *m* 1975, Naomi (*née* Ohayon); two *s* one *d*. *Educ:* University Coll., London (LLB Hons). Called to the Bar, Middle Temple, 1970; in practice at the Bar, 1971–2000. *Recreations:* travel, film, theatre, football, tennis, ski-ing, swimming, cycling. *Address:* Harrow Crown Court, Hailsham Drive, Harrow HA1 4TU.

GREENWOOD, Allen Harold Claude, CBE 1974; FRAeS; JP; Deputy Chairman, British Aerospace, 1977–83 (Member, Organizing Committee, 1976–77); Chairman, British Aircraft Corporation, 1976 (Deputy Chairman, 1972–75); *b* 4 June 1917; *s* of Lt-Col Thomas Claude Greenwood and Hilda Letitia Greenwood (*née* Knight). *Educ:* Cheltenham Coll.; Coll. of Aeronautical Engineering. Pilot's Licence, 1939. Joined Vickers-Armstrongs Ltd, 1940; served RNVR (Fleet Air Arm), 1942–52 (Lt-Cmdr); rejoined Vickers-Armstrongs Ltd, 1946, Dir, 1960; British Aircraft Corp., 1962, Dep. Man. Dir, 1969; Director: British Aircraft Corp. (Holdings), 1972; BAe Australia Ltd, 1977–83; Chm., BAe Inc., 1977–80. Director: SEPECAT SA, 1964; Europlane Ltd, 1974–83; Chairman: Panavia GmbH, 1969–72; Remploy Ltd, 1976–79 (Vice-Chm., 1973). Pres., Assoc. Européenne des Constructeurs de Materiel Aerospatial, 1974–76; Pres., 1970–72, Dep. Pres., 1981–82, SBAC; Vice-Pres., Engineering Employers' Fedn, 1982–83; Mem., National Def. Industry Council, 1970–72. Pres., Cheltenham Coll. Council, 1980–85; Member: Council, Cranfield Inst. of Technology, 1970–79; Council, CBI, 1970–77; Assoc. of Governing Bodies of Public Schools, 1982–85; Council, St John's Sch., Leatherhead, 1970–85 (Chm., 1979–85). JP Surrey 1962, Hampshire, 1975. Freeman, City of London. Liveryman, Company of Coachmakers, Guild of Air Pilots. General Comr for Income Tax, 1970–74. *Address:* Belmoir Lodge, Milford Road, Lymington, Hants SO41 8DJ. *T:* (01590) 671515. *Clubs:* White's, Royal Automobile; Royal Lymington Yacht.

GREENWOOD, Prof. Christopher John, CMG 2002; QC 1999; Professor of International Law, London School of Economics, since 1996; *b* 12 May 1955; *o s* of Murray Guy Greenwood and Diana Maureen (*née* Barron); *m* 1978, Susan Anthea, *d* of late Geoffrey and Patricia Longbotham; two *d*. *Educ:* Wellingborough Sch.; Magdalene Coll., Cambridge (MA, LLB; Whewell Schol. in Internat. Law 1977). Pres., Cambridge Union Soc., 1976. Called to the Bar, Middle Temple, 1978, Bencher, 2003; Fellow, Magdalene Coll., Cambridge, 1978–96; Asst Lectr in Law, 1981–84, Lectr, 1984–96, Univ. of Cambridge. Mem., Panel of Arbitrators: Law of the Sea Convention, 1998–; ICSID, 2004–. Gov., Ditchley Foundn, 2001–. Jt Editor, International Law Reports, 1990–. *Publications:* Essays on War in International Law, 2006; contrib. articles in Brit. Year Book of Internat. Law, Internat. and Comparative Law Qly, Modern Law Rev. and other legal jls. *Recreations:* politics, walking. *Address:* Essex Court Chambers, 24 Lincoln's Inn Fields, WC2A 3EG. *T:* (020) 7813 8000; Law Department, London School of Economics, Houghton Street, WC2A 2AE. *T:* (020) 7955 7250. *Clubs:* Athenæum, Oxford and Cambridge.

GREENWOOD, David Ernest; Research Director, Centre for European Security Studies, Groningen, since 1997; *b* 6 Feb. 1937; *s* of Ernest Greenwood and Doris (*née* Cowsill); *m* 1st, 1960, Helen Ramshaw (marr. diss.); two *s*; 2nd, 1986, Margaret McRobb (*née* Cruickshank). *Educ:* Manchester Grammar Sch.; Liverpool Univ. (BA, MA). Educn Officer, RAF, 1959–66; Economic Advr, MoD, 1966–67; University of Aberdeen: Lectr 1967, Sen. Lectr 1970, Reader 1975, in Higher Defence Studies; Dir, Centre for Defence Studies, 1976–97. Vis. Fellow, IISS, 1974–75; Visiting Professor: Nat. Defense Acad., Yokosuka, 1981–82; Univ. of Nat. and World Econ., Sofia, 1994–; Czech Mil. Acad., Brno, 1996–; Olin Prof., USAF Acad., Colorado Springs, 1991–92. Member: FCO Adv. Panel on Arms Control and Disarmament, 1974–; Honeywell Adv. Council, 1981–85; ACOST Study Gp on Defence R&D, 1987–88. *Publications:* Budgeting for Defence, 1972; (jtly) British Security Policy and the Atlantic Alliance: prospects for the 1990s, 1987; The European Defence Market, 1991; Resource Allocation and Resources Management in Defence, 1996; (jtly) Towards Shared Security: seven-nation perspectives, 2001; (jtly) Organising National Defences for NATO Membership, 2001; numerous monographs, res.

reports, contribs to symposia, jl and newspaper articles. *Recreations:* cooking, golf, racing. *Address:* 7 Westhill Grange, Westhill AB32 6QJ. *T:* (01224) 741508; 31a Lutkenieuwstraat, 9712 AW Groningen, Netherlands. *T:* (50) 3132520. *Club:* Royal Air Force.

GREENWOOD, Duncan Joseph, CBE 1993; PhD, DSc; FRS 1985; CChem, FRSC; FIHort; Head of Soils and Crop Nutrition, 1966–92, Associate Fellow, Warwick University, since 2004, Warwick Horticulture Research International (formerly National Vegetable Research Station, later AFRC Institute of Horticultural Research, then Horticulture Research International), Wellesbourne, Warwick (Emeritus Fellow, 1992–2004); *b* 16 Oct. 1932; *s* of Herbert James Greenwood and Alison Fairgrieve Greenwood. *Educ:* Hutton Grammar Sch., near Preston; Liverpool Univ. (BSc 1954); Aberdeen Univ. (PhD 1957; DSc 1972). CChem, FRSC 1977; FIHort 1986. Res. Fellow, Aberdeen Univ., 1957–59; Res. Leader, National Vegetable Res. Station, 1959–66. Vis. Prof. of Plant Scis, Leeds Univ., 1985–93; Hon. Prof. of Agricl Chem., Birmingham Univ., 1986–93. Chm., Agriculture Gp, Soc. of Chemical Industry, 1975–77; President: Internat. Cttee of Plant Nutrition, 1978–82; British Soc. of Soil Science, 1990–92. Lectures: Blackman, Univ. of Oxford, 1982; Distinguished Scholars, QUB, 1982; Hannaford, Univ. of Adelaide, 1985; Shell, Univ. of Kent, 1988; Amos, Wye Coll., 1989. Hon. Lifetime Mem., Assoc. of Applied Biologists, 2004. Sir Gilbert Morgan Medal, Soc. of Chemical Industry, 1962; Res. Medal, RASE, 1979; inaugural Grower of the Year Award for Lifetime Achievement, 2000; President's Medal, Inst. of Horticulture, 2004. *Publications:* over 180 scientific papers on soil science, crop nutrition and fertilizers. *Address:* 23 Shelley Road, Stratford-upon-Avon, Warwicks CV37 7JR. *T:* (01789) 204735.

GREENWOOD, Prof. Geoffrey Wilson, PhD, DMet; FRS 1992; FInstP; FIMMM; FREng; Professor of Metallurgy, University of Sheffield, 1966–94, now Emeritus; *b* 3 Feb. 1929; *s* of Richard Albert Greenwood and Martha Alice (*née* Wilson); *m* 1954, Nancy Cole; two *s* one *d*. *Educ:* Grange Grammar Sch., Bradford; Univ. of Sheffield (BSc, PhD, DMet). FInstP 1966; FIMMM (FIM 1966); FREng (FEng 1990). SO and SSO, UKAEA, Harwell, 1953–60; Head, Fuel Materials Section, Berkeley Nuclear Labs, CEGB, 1960–65; Res. Manager, Scis Div., Electricity Council Res. Centre, 1965–66. Pro-Vice-Chancellor, Univ. of Sheffield, 1979–83. L. B. Pfeil Prize, Inst. Metals and Iron and Steel Inst., 1972; Rosenhain Medal, Metals Soc., 1975; Griffith Medal, Inst. of Materials, 1995. *Publications:* contribs to Metallurgy, Materials Science, Physics and Engrg. *Recreations:* music (oboe and piano playing), travel, variety of outdoor activities. *Address:* Department of Engineering Materials, University of Sheffield, Sir Robert Hadfield Building, Mappin Street, Sheffield S1 3JD. *T:* (0114) 222 5517; 26 Stumperlowe Hall Road, Sheffield S10 3QS. *T:* (0114) 230 3565. *Club:* Hallam Rotary (Sheffield).

GREENWOOD, Jeffrey Michael; Senior Partner, Nabarro Nathanson, 1987–95; *b* 21 April 1935; *s* of Arthur Greenwood and Ada Greenwood (*née* Gordon); *m* 1964, Naomi Grahame; three *s* one *d*. *Educ:* Raine's Foundation Sch.; LSE; Downing Coll., Cambridge (MA, LLM). Admitted solicitor 1960; Partner, Nabarro Nathanson, 1963–95, Consultant, 1995–2001. Dir, Bank Leumi (UK), 1990–2005; Chairman: Wigmore Property Investment Trust, 1996–2004; Stow Securities, 1997–2007; Dep. Chm., Jewish Chronicle, 1994–2005. Chm., CCETSW, 1993–98. Chairman: Jewish Welfare Bd, 1986–90; Jewish Care, 1990; Council Member: Jewish Historical Soc. of England, 1993–; Hampstead Garden Suburb Trust (Law Soc. Appointee), 1984–87; Trustee, Policy Res. Inst. for Ageing and Ethnicity, 2000–. Founder Mem., Campaign Cttee, ProHelp. Liveryman, Glovers' Co. *Publications:* articles in learned jls. *Recreations:* conversing with grandchildren, swimming, literature, travel. *Address:* (office) 5 Spencer Walk, Hampstead High Street, NW3 1QZ. *T:* (020) 7794 5281, *Fax:* (020) 7794 0094; *e-mail:* jeff@thegreenwoods.org.

GREENWOOD, Dr Jeremy John Denis, CBE 2008; Director, British Trust for Ornithology, 1988–2007 (Hon. Research Fellow, 2007); *b* 7 Sept. 1942; *s* of Denis Greenwood and Phyllis Marjorie Greenwood (*née* Leat); *m* 1971, Cynthia Anne Jones; two *d*. *Educ:* Royal Grammar Sch., Worcester; St Catherine's Coll., Oxford (BA 1964); Univ. of Manchester (PhD 1972). MIBiol 1990. Dundee University: Asst Lectr in Zoology, 1967–70; Lectr in Biol Scis, 1970–87; University of East Anglia: Hon. Lectr, 1994–98; Hon. Reader, 1998–2002; Hon. Prof., 2002–; Hon. Professor: Univ. of Birmingham, 2003–; Univ. of St Andrews, 2007–. Vis. Prof. in Animal Ecology, Univ. of Khartoum, 1976. Natural Environment Research Council: Workshop on Grey Seal Population Biol., 1979–84; Special Cttee on Seals, 1986–96; Terrestrial Life Scis Cttee, 1988–91; Data Adv. Gp, 2000–01. Chairman: Exec. Cttee, European Bird Census Council, 1992–98; Scientific and Tech. Adv. Gp, Langholm Demonstration Project, 2007–; Member: Council, RSPB, 1983–88; Adv. Cttee on Birds, NCC, 1988–91; Envtl Res. Cttee, British Agrochem. Assoc., 1988–93; Grants Cttee, Internat. Council for Bird Preservation, British Section, 1988–92; Council, British Ornith. Union, 1989–93; Sci. Adv. Cttee, Wildfowl & Wetlands Trust, 1989–92; Professional Affairs Cttee, Inst. of Ecology and Envmtl Management, 1991–93; Scottish Wildlife Trust Conservation Cttee, 2007–; Nature Conservation Panel, NT, 2007–; Vice Pres., 2003–05, Pres., 2005–, Europ. Ornithologists' Union. Director: West Palaearctic Birds Ltd, 1990–2000; BB 2000 Ltd, 2001–. Pres., Scottish Ornithologists' Club, 1987. Hon. DSc Birmingham, 2007. Trustee, British Birds Charitable Trust, 2001–. Editor, Bird Study, 1984–87; Member, Editorial Board: Heredity, 1988–92; Biol Conservation, 2001–. *Publications:* (ed jtly) Joint Biological Expedition to North East Greenland 1974, 1978; (ed jtly) Birds as Monitors of Environmental Change, 1993; papers in learned jls; chapters in books. *Recreations:* birdwatching, walking, gardening. *Address:* Centre for Research into Ecological and Environmental Modelling, University of St Andrews, Fife KY16 9LZ.

GREENWOOD, Prof. Norman Neill, DSc Melbourne; PhD, ScD Cambridge; FRS 1987; CChem, FRSC; Professor of Inorganic and Structural Chemistry, University of Leeds, 1971–90, now Emeritus; *b* Melbourne, Vic, 19 Jan. 1925; *er s* of Prof. J. Neill Greenwood, DSc and Gladys, *d* of late Moritz and Bertha Uhland; *m* 1951, Kirsten Marie Rydland, Bergen, Norway; three *d*. *Educ:* University High School, Melbourne; University of Melbourne; Sidney Sussex Coll., Cambridge. Laboratory Cadet, CSIRO Div. of Tribophysics, Melbourne, 1942–44; BSc Melbourne 1945, MSc Melbourne 1948; DSc Melbourne 1966. Masson Memorial Medal, Royal Australian Chem. Institute, 1945. Resident Tutor and Lecturer in Chemistry, Trinity Coll., Melbourne, 1946–48. Exhibn of 1851, Overseas Student, 1948–51; PhD Cambridge 1951; ScD Cambridge 1961. Senior Harwell Research Fellow, 1951–53; Lectr, 1953–60, Senior Lectr, 1960–61, in Inorganic Chemistry, Univ. of Nottingham; Prof. of Inorganic Chemistry, Univ. of Newcastle upon Tyne, 1961–71. Visiting Professor: Univ. of Melbourne, 1966; Univ. of Western Australia, 1969; Univ. of Western Ontario, 1973; Univ. of Copenhagen, 1979; La Trobe Univ., Melbourne, 1985; Wuhan Univ., People's Republic of China, 1985; Toho Univ., Tokyo, 1991–93; National Science Foundation Distinguished Vis. Prof., Michigan State Univ., USA, 1967. International Union of Pure and Applied Chemistry: Mem., 1963–83; Vice-Pres., 1975–77, Pres., 1977–81, Inorganic Chemistry Div.; Chm., Internat. Commn on Atomic Weights, 1969–75. Chemical Society: Vice Pres., 1979–80; Pres., Dalton Div., 1979–81; Award in Main Group Chemistry, 1975. Vice-Pres., 1989–90, Pres., 1990–91, Section B, Chemistry, BAAS. Lectures: Tilden, Chemical Soc., 1966–67; Hofmann, Ge Deutscher Chemiker, 1983; Liversidge, RSC, 1983; first Egon Wiberg, Munich Univ 1989; Ludwig Mond, RSC, 1991; Humphry Davy, Royal Soc., 2000. MRI 1998. Fo Associate, Académie des Sciences, Institut de France, 1992. Dr *hc* de l'Université de Nanc I, 1977; DSc *hc* Toho Univ., Tokyo, 2000. *Publications:* Principles of Atomic Orbital 1964 (rev. edns 1968, 1973, 1980); Ionic Crystals, Lattice Defects, and Nonstoichiometr 1968; (jointly) Spectroscopic Properties of Inorganic and Organometallic Compound vols I–IX, 1968–76; (with W. A. Campbell) Contemporary British Chemists, 1971; (wit T. C. Gibb) Mössbauer Spectroscopy, 1971; Periodicity and Atomic Structure, 197 (with B. P. Straughan and E. J. F. Ross) Index of Vibrational Spectra, vol. I, 1972, (wit E. J. F. Ross) vol. II, 1975, vol. III, 1977; The Chemistry of Boron, 1973, rev. edn 197 (with A. Earnshaw) Chemistry of the Elements, 1984, rev. edn 1997; numerous origin papers and reviews in chemical jls and chapters in scientific monographs. *Recreation* music, travel. *Address:* Department of Chemistry, University of Leeds, Leeds LS2 9J *e-mail:* n.n.greenwood@chem.leeds.ac.uk.

GREENWOOD, Peter Gerard, CBE 1997; Member (Lab) Blackburn Unitary (former Borough) Council, 1982–2000 (Mayor, 1997–98); Chairman, Association of Distri Councils, 1995–97; *b* 20 Dec. 1939; *s* of James Greenwood and Mary Quinn; *m* 196 Dorothy Edmundson; three *s*. *Educ:* Blackburn Coll. (Dip Mgt Services 1979); Ruski Coll., Oxford (Dip Lab. Studies 1981). Apprentice Engineer, 1955–61; Enginee 1961–79; Ruskin Coll., Oxford, 1979–81; various posts, 1981–86. Blackburn Boroug Council: Chairman: Finance and Performance Wkg Gp, 1986–87; Mgt and Finance Sub Cttee, 1987–89; Policy & Resources Cttee, 1989–94; Leader, 1989–94. Vice Chm Blackburn Coll., 1982–92. Chairman: Chapterhouse (ADC) Ltd, 1993; ADC (Propertie Ltd, 1996 (Dir, 1995); Dir, ADC (Trustees) Ltd, 1994. Vice Chm., Central Bodies Adv Gp, 1996–97 (Mem., 1993–97). *Publications:* articles in local govt press. *Recreation* politics, current affairs, reading. *Address:* 44 Rosewood Avenue, Blackburn, Lancs BB 9SZ. *T:* (01254) 696039. *Club:* Queens Park Working Men's.

GREER, Adrian, CMG 2004; Director of Learning, Creativity and Society, Britis Council, since 2004; *b* 26 April 1957; *s* of David Smith Greer and Christine Greer (*n* Dawson); *m* 1985, (Mary) Diana Cuddy; one *s* three *d*. *Educ:* Queen Mary's Gramma Sch., Walsall; St Andrews Univ. (MA Eng. Lang. and Lit.). CPFA 1984. Auditor, Na Audit Office, 1979–84; joined British Council, 1984; Finance Develt Office, 1984–8 Finance Manager, Japan, 1985–88; Finance Project Manager, 1988–89, Chief Accountan 1989–91, London; Director: Lesotho and Swaziland, 1991–93; Zambia, 1993–96; Europ (Develt and Trng Services), 1996–98; Asia and Americas (Develt and Trng Services 1998–2000; Cultural Counsellor and Dir, Russia, 2000–04. FRSA. *Recreations:* trave sport, running. *Address:* c/o British Council, 10 Spring Gardens, SW1A 2BN.
See also K. Greer.

GREER, Bonnie; writer; *b* Chicago, 16 Nov. 1948; *d* of late Ben Greer and of Willie Ma Greer; naturalised British citizen, 1997; *m* 1993, David Hutchins, solicitor. *Educ:* De Pa Univ., Chicago (BA Hist. 1974). Studied playwriting: with David Mamet, St Nichol Th., Chicago, 1975–76; with Elia Kazan, Actors Studio, NYC, 1982–86; Arts Counc Playwright in Residence: Soho Th., 1990; Black Th. Co-op., 1992. Plays include: 191 1977; Diary of a Slave Girl, 1984; Roadhouse, 1985; Zebra Days, 1989; Dancing on Blac Water, 1996; Ella, Meet Marilyn, 2006; Equiano, Esclave, Maitre, Survivant, 2006; radi plays include Marilyn and Ella Backstage at the Mocambo, 2005, and various adaptatio and translations; television: White Men Are Cracking Up, 1996; Reflecting Skin (also c producer), 2004. Critic, Late Review and Newsnight Review, BBC2, 1998–200 Trustee, BM, 2005–. Mem., Acad. Bd, RADA. Judge: Orange Prize, 2000; Samu Johnson Prize, 2003; Whitbread First Novel Prize, 2003. FRSA 2003. DuNouy Prize f Playwriting, Phoenix Th., NYC, 1979; Verity Bargate Award, 1992. *Publications:* So Ve English (short stories), 1989; Hanging By Her Teeth (novel), 1994; How Maxine Learne To Like Her Legs (short stories), 1995; Entropy (novel), 2007; Black Plays Thre *Recreations:* reading popular books on theoretical maths esp. Prime Number Theory an the Riemann Hypothesis, collecting studio jewellery, listening and dancing to jazz, so and funk music, the gym. *Address:* c/o Serpents Tail, 4 Blackstone Mews, N4 1BT. (020) 7354 1949, *Fax:* (020) 7704 6467; *e-mail:* dhutch3693@aol.com. *Clubs:* Union, 4 South Molton Street.

GREER, Prof. David Clive; Professor of Music, University of Durham, 1986–2001, no Emeritus (Chairman, Music Department, 1986–94); *b* 8 May 1937; *s* of William Macka Greer and Barbara (*née* Avery); *m* 1st, 1961, Patricia Margaret Regan (*d* 1999); two *s* o *d*; 2nd, 2002, Harriet, *d* of Lt-Col Sir John Marling, 4th Bt, OBE. *Educ:* Dulwich Col Queen's Coll., Oxford (BA 1960; MA 1964); MusD TCD, 1991. Lectr in Musi Birmingham Univ., 1963–72; Hamilton Harty Prof. of Music, QUB, 1972–84; Prof. Music, Univ. of Newcastle upon Tyne, 1984–86. Mellon Vis. Fellow, 1989, Maye Foundn Fellow, 1991 and 2007, Huntington Liby, Calif; Folger Vis. Fellow, Folg Shakespeare Liby, Washington, 1994 and 1998. Mem. Bd, Arts Council of NI, 1972–8 Chm., Mgt Cttee, and Guest Conductor, Ulster Orch., 1972–84; Mem. Council, Roy Musical Assoc., 1977–90. FRSA 1986. Editor, Proceedings, subseq. Jl, of Royal Music Assoc., 1977–90. *Publications:* (ed) English Madrigal Verse, 1967; Hamilton Harty: his li and music, 1979, 2nd edn 1980; Hamilton Harty: early memories, 1979; (ed) Collect English Lutenist Partsongs, 2 vols, 1987–89, and other editions of 16th and 17th centu music; A Numerous and Fashionable Audience: the story of Elsie Swinton, 1997; (e John Dowland, Ayres for four voices, 2000; Musicology and Sister Disciplines: pas present, future, 2000; (contrib.) New Grove Dictionary of Music and Musicians, D Musik in Geschichte und Gegenwart; articles in Music and Letters, Music Review Musical Times, Shakespeare Qly, English Studies, Notes & Queries, Lute Soc. *Recreations:* reading, cinema, walking. *Address:* The Music School, Palace Green, Durha DH1 3RL. *T:* (0191) 334 3150; *e-mail:* d.c.greer@durham.ac.uk. *Club:* Athenæum.

GREER, Prof. Germaine, PhD; writer and broadcaster; Professor of English an Comparative Studies, Warwick University, 1998–2003; *b* Melbourne, 29 Jan. 1939. *Edu* Melbourne Univ. (BA 1959); Sydney Univ. (MA 1962); Commonwealth Scholarsh 1964; Cambridge Univ. (PhD 1967). Sen. Tutor in English, Sydney Univ., 1963–64; As Lectr, then Lectr in English, Warwick Univ., 1967–72; Lectr, American Program Burea 1973–78; Prof. of Modern Letters, Univ. of Tulsa, 1980–83; Founder Dir, Tulsa Cent for Studies in Women's Literature, 1981; Special Lectr and Unofficial Fellow, Newnha Coll., Cambridge, 1989–98. Vis. Prof., Univ. of Tulsa, 1979. Proprietor, Stump Cro Books, 1988–. *Publications:* The Female Eunuch, 1970; The Obstacle Race: the fortun of women painters and their work, 1979; Sex and Destiny: the politics of human fertil 1984; Shakespeare, 1986; The Madwoman's Underclothes: selected journalism, 1986; (jtly) Kissing the Rod: an anthology of 17th century women's verse, 1988; Daddy, W Hardly Knew You, 1989 (J. R. Ackerly Prize; Premio Internazionale Mondello); (ed) T Uncollected Verse of Aphra Behn, 1989; The Change: women, ageing and t menopause, 1991; Slip-shod Sibyls: recognition, rejection and the woman poet, 1995; (jtly) The Surviving Works of Anne Wharton, 1997; The Whole Woman, 1999; (ed) 10 Poems by 101 Women, 2001; The Boy, 2003; (ed) Poems for Gardeners, 2003; Whitefe

Jump Up: the shortest way to nationhood, 2004; Shakespeare's Wife, 2007; contribs to Journalist. *Address:* c/o Aitken Alexander Associates Ltd, 18–21 Cavaye Place, SW10 9PT.

GREER, Prof. Ian Andrew, MD; FRCP, FRCPE, FRCPGlas, FRCPI, FRCOG, FFSRH; FMedSci; Dean, Hull York Medical School, since 2007. *Educ:* Univ. of Glasgow (MB ChB 1980; MD 1986). MRCP 1984, FRCP 2001; MRCOG 1987, FRCOG 1999; FRCPGlas 1994; FRCPE 1999; FRCPI 2006; MFFP 1994, FFSRH (FFFP 2008). Registrar in Medicine, Glasgow Royal Infirmary, 1983–85; Lectr in Obstetrics and Gynaecol., Univ. of Edinburgh, 1987–90; Clinical Res. Scientist, MRC Reproductive Biol. Unit, Edinburgh, 1990–91; Glasgow University: Muirhead Prof., 1991–2000; Regius Prof., 2000–06; Head, Dept of Obstetrics and Gynaecology, 1991–2006; Depute Dean, 2003–06. FMedSci 2006. *Publications:* (jtly) Haemostasis and Thrombosis in Obstetrics and Gynaecology, 1992; Venous Thromboembolism in Obstetrics and Gynaecology, in Bailliere's Clinical Obstetrics and Gynaecology, 1997; (jtly) Mosby's Colour Atlas and Text of Obstetrics and Gynaecology, 2000; (with A. J. Thomson) Antenatal Disorders for the MRCOG, 2000; Pregnancy: the inside guide, 2003; Venous Thrombosis in Women, 2003; (jtly) Problem-based Obstetrics and Gynaecology, 2003; (jtly) The Menopause in Practice, 2003; (jtly) Practical Obstetric Haematology, 2005; (jtly) Preterm Labour, 2005; Fertility and Conception, 2007; (jtly) Women's Vascular Health, 2007; (jtly) Maternal Medicine, 2007; contrib. numerous res. papers and rev. articles on haemostasis and thrombosis, medical disorders in pregnancy and labour and preterm labour. *Address:* Hull York Medical School, University of York, Heslington, York YO10 5DD.

GREER, Ian Bramwell; Chairman, Corporate and Government Relations International Ltd, since 1998; *b* 5 June 1933; *s* of Bramwell and Janet Greer. *Educ:* Cranbrook Coll., Essex; Victoria Sch., Glasgow. Conservative Central Office and Party Agent, 1956–67; Nat. Dir, Mental Health Trust, 1967–70; Man. Dir, Russell Greer & Associates, 1970–82; Chairman: Ian Greer Associates, 1982–96; Internat. Govt Relations, 1997–2004. *Publications:* Right to be Heard, 1985; One Man's Word, 1997. *Recreations:* antiques, walking, gardening, dogs. *Address:* The Long House, PO Box 213, Stellenbosch, Western Cape 7599, South Africa. *Club:* Royal Automobile.

GREER, Kenneth; Executive Director of Education, Fife Council, since 2005; *b* 21 Nov. 1953; *s* of David Smith Greer and Christine Greer (*née* Dawson); *m* 1977, Lorna Murray (*d* 2001); two *s. Educ:* St Edmund's Coll., Ware; Univ. of St Andrews (MA Hons English Lang. and Lit.); Moray House Coll. (PGCE); Open Univ. (MA Educn). Teacher: Lanark GS, 1976–78; Whitburn Acad., 1978–80; Buckhaven High Sch., 1980–84; Dunfermline High Sch., 1984–90; Advr in English, Grampian Reg., 1990–94; HM Inspector of Schs, 1994–2003; Sen. Educn Manager, Fife Council, 2003–05. Trustee, Link Community Develt, Scotland, 2007–. *Recreations:* running, ski-ing, reading. *Address:* Education Service, Fife Council, Rothesay House, Rothesay Place, Glenrothes, Fife KY7 5PQ. *T:* (01592) 583372; *e-mail:* kenneth.greer@fife.gov.uk.

See also A. Greer.

GREET, Rev. Dr Kenneth Gerald; Secretary of the Methodist Conference, 1971–84; President of the Methodist Conference, 1980–81; Moderator, Free Church Federal Council, 1982–83; Vice-President, World Disarmament Campaign, since 1994; *b* 17 Nov. 1918; *e s* of Walter and Renée Greet, Bristol; *m* 1947, Mary Eileen Edbrooke; one *s* two *d. Educ:* Cotham Grammar Sch., Bristol; Handsworth Coll., Birmingham. Minister: Cwm and Kingstone Methodist Church, 1940–42; Ogmore Vale Methodist Church, 1942–45; Tonypandy Central Hall, 1947–54; Sec., Dept of Christian Citizenship of Methodist Church, 1954–71; Member: BCC, 1955–84 (Chm. of Exec., 1977–81); World Methodist Council, 1957–2001 (Chm., Exec. Cttee, 1976–81); Chairman: Exec., Temperance Council of Christian Churches, 1961–71; World Christian Temperance Fedn, 1962–72. Pres., Methodist Peace Fellowship, 1999–. Rep. to Central Cttee, WCC, Addis Ababa, 1971, Nairobi, 1975. Beckly Lectr, 1962; Willson Lectr, Kansas City, 1966; Cato Lectr, Sydney, 1975. Chm. Govs, Southlands Coll., Wimbledon, 1987–97. Hon. DD Ohio, USA, 1968; DUniv Surrey, 1998. *Publications:* The Mutual Society, 1962; Man and Wife Together, 1962; Large Petitions, 1964; Guide to Loving, 1965; The Debate about Drink, 1969; The Sunday Question, 1970; The Art of Moral Judgement, 1970; When the Spirit Moves, 1975; A Lion from a Thicket, 1978; The Big Sin: Christianity and the arms race, 1983; What Shall I Cry?, 1986; Life of Jabez Bunting, 1995; Fully Connected (autobiog.), 1997. *Recreations:* reading, photography. *Address:* 89 Broadmark Lane, Rustington, Sussex BN16 2JA. *T:* (01903) 773326; *e-mail:* greet@surefish.co.uk.

GREETHAM, (George) Colin; Headmaster, Bishop's Stortford College, 1971–84; *b* 22 April 1929; *s* of late George Cecil Greetham and of Gertrude Greetham (*née* Heavyside); *m* 1963, Rosemary (*née* Gardner); two *s* one *d. Educ:* York Minster Song Sch.; St Peter's Sch., York; (Choral Scholar) King's Coll., Cambridge. BA (Hons) History Tripos Cantab, Class II, Div. I, 1952; Certif. of Educn (Cantab), 1953. *Recreations:* music, choral training, horticulture, bowls. *Address:* Chapelhead Farm, Crossroads, Keith, Banffshire AB55 6LQ.

GREGG, Prof. Paul James, MD; FRCS; Professor of Orthopaedic Surgical Science, University of Durham, since 2000; Consultant Orthopaedic Surgeon, South Tees Acute Hospitals NHS Trust, since 2000; *b* 26 Nov. 1945; *s* of George Ernest Gregg and Hebe Elizabeth Gregg; *m* 1977, Jennifer Hall; one *d. Educ:* St Peter's Sch., York; Med. Sch., Univ. of Newcastle upon Tyne (MB BS 1969; MD 1977). FRCS 1974; FRCSE *ad hominem* 1998. House Physician and House Surgeon, Royal Victoria Infirmary, Newcastle upon Tyne, 1969–70; surgical trng, Newcastle upon Tyne hosps, 1971–74; University of Newcastle upon Tyne: Demonstrator in Anatomy, 1970–71; Sen. Res. Associate, MRC Decompression Sickness Res. Team, 1976–77; Lectr in Orthopaedic Surgery, 1979–83; Sen. Registrar in Orthopaedic Surgery, N Reg. Trng Prog., 1977–79; Clin. Res. Fellow, Massachusetts Gen. Hosp., 1982–83; Sen. Lectr in Orthopaedic Surgery, Univ. of Edinburgh, 1983–85; Foundation Prof. of Orthopaedic Surgery, Univ. of Leicester, 1985–97; Prof. of Trauma and Orthopaedic Surgery, Univ. of Newcastle upon Tyne, 1997–2000. Pres., British Orthopaedic Assoc., 2002–03. *Publications:* Fractures and Dislocations: principles of management, 1995; contribs to books; more than 100 scientific papers. *Recreations:* walking, golf. *Address:* The Old Vicarage, Grinton, Richmond, N Yorks DL11 6HR.

GREGG, Paul Richard; Chairman, Apollo Cinemas, since 2003; *b* 2 Oct. 1941; *m* 1970, Anita Kim, (Nita), Grehan; two *s* one *d. Educ:* Hull Nautical Coll. ABC Cinema Gp, 1961–65; Star Gp of Cinemas, 1965–67; Pressed Steel Fisher Ltd, 1967–70; Entertainment Dir, Rover Motor Co., 1968–70; Entertainment and Tourist Manager, Southport DC, 1970–77; Chm., Apollo Leisure Gp plc, 1978–2001. Mem., Variety Club of GB (former Pres.; Chief Barker, 1991). *Recreation:* theatre.

GREGORIADIS, Prof. Gregory, PhD, DSc; Founder, Director of Research and Board Member, Lipoxen plc, since 1998; Professor and Head, Centre for Drug Delivery Research, School of Pharmacy, University of London, 1990–2001, now Professor Emeritus; *b* 27 Feb. 1934; *s* of late Christos Gregoriadis and Athina Sakellariou; *m* 1968, Susan Byron-Brown; one *s* one *d. Educ:* Univ. of Athens (BSc 1958); McGill Univ. (MSc 1966; PhD 1968); DSc London 2002. Research Fellow: Albert Einstein Coll. of Medicine, 1968–70; Royal Free Hosp. Sch. of Medicine, 1970–72; Sen. Scientist, MRC, 1972–93. Pres., Internat. Liposome Soc., 2003–. Fellow, Amer. Assoc. of Pharmaceutical Scientists, 1998. 15 NATO Scientific Affairs Div. awards, 1980–98; Founder's Award, Controlled Release Soc., 1994; Bangham Award, Liposome Res. Days Inc., 1995; Lifetime Achievement Award, Jl of Drug Targeting, 2008. *Publications:* (ed) Drug Carriers in Biology and Medicine, 1979; (ed jtly) Liposomes in Biology and Medicine, 1980; (ed jtly) Targeting of Drugs, 1982, 10th edn 2000; (ed) Liposome Technology, 1984, 3rd edn 2007; (ed) Liposomes as Drug Carriers: recent trends and progress, 1988; (ed jtly) Vaccines, 1989, 5th edn 1997; over 300 papers on drug and vaccine targeting. *Recreations:* creative writing, history and philosophy of Ancient Athens, politics. *Address:* Lipoxen plc, London Bioscience Innovation Centre, 2 Royal College Street, NW1 0NH.

GREGORIOS, His Eminence The Most Rev. the Archbishop of Thyateira and Great Britain; *see* Theocharous, Archbishop Gregorios.

GREGOROWSKI, Rt Rev. Christopher John; an Assistant Bishop of Cape Town (Bishop of Table Bay), 1998–2005; *b* 19 Feb. 1940; *s* of William Victor Gregorowski and Doris Alice Gregorowski (*née* Skinner); *m* 1964, Margaret Merle Perold; two *d* (and one *d* decd). *Educ:* Diocesan Coll., Rondebosch, S Africa; Univ. of Cape Town (BA, MA); Birmingham Univ. (DPS); Cuddesdon Coll., Oxford. Deacon 1963, priest 1964, Anglican Church of Southern Africa (formerly Church of Province of S Africa); Rector: St Cuthbert's, Tsolo, 1968–74; St Thomas, Rondebosch, 1974–86; All Saints, Somerset West, 1986–98. *Publications:* Why a Donkey was Chosen, 1975; The Bible for Little Children, 1982; Fly, Eagle, Fly!, 1982, 2nd edn 2000; Angelo at the Waterfront, 2008. *Recreations:* marathon running, reading, walking, ornithology. *Address:* 15 Starke Road, Bergvliet, 7945, South Africa. *T:* (21) 7125136. *Clubs:* Cape Town, Western Province Cricket, Spartan Harriers Athletic (Cape Town).

GREGORY, Alan Thomas, CBE 1984; Director, Willis Corroon (formerly Willis Faber) plc, 1987–97; *b* 13 Oct. 1925; *s* of Lloyd Thomas Gregory and Florence Abbott; *m* 1st, 1952, Pamela Douglas Scott (*d* 1986); one *s* two *d*; 2nd, 1988, Mrs Marion Newth (*née* Nash), JP (*d* 2007). *Educ:* Dulwich Coll.; St John's Coll., Cambridge (Classics). Directed into coal mining, coal face worker, 1944; Min. of Power, 1948; JSSC 1957; Chm., NATO Petroleum Planning Cttee, 1967–70; joined British Petroleum, 1971; Gen. Manager, BP Italiana, 1972–73; Dir, Govt and Public Affairs, 1975–85, and Dir, UK and Ireland Region, 1980–85, British Petroleum Co.; Chm., BP Oil Ltd, 1981–85; Director: BP Chemicals International Ltd, 1981–85; National Home Loans Corp., 1985–91. Governor, Queen Mary Coll., London Univ., 1981–87. President, Inst. of Petroleum, 1982–84. Univ. Comr, 1988–95. Churchwarden, St Mary's, Stoke D'Abernon, 1990–92. *Recreations:* books, gardening, theatre. *Address:* 10 Summerhays, Cobham, Surrey KT11 2HQ. *T:* (01932) 864457. *Club:* Travellers.

GREGORY, Rear-Adm. Alexander Michael, OBE 1987; Chief Executive, Energy Industries Council, 2004–07; *b* 15 Dec. 1945; *s* of Vice-Adm. Sir (George) David (Archibald) Gregory, KBE, CB, DSO and Florence Eve Patricia Gregory (*née* Hill); *m* 1970, Jean Charlotte Muir; four *d. Educ:* Marlborough; BRNC Dartmouth. Served HM Ships Albion, Aisne, Narwhale, Otter, Warspite, Courageous, Odin (Australia), Finwhale (i/c), Repulse 1965–80; Staff, US 3rd Fleet, Hawaii, 1980–82; HMS Renown (i/c), 1982–85; Comdr 10th SM Sqdn and HMS Resolution (i/c), 1985–86; Jt Services Defence Coll., 1987; Naval Warfare, MoD, 1987–88; HMS Cumberland (i/c), 1988–91; Captain, 10th Submarine Sqdn, 1991–93; Naval Staff Duties, MoD, 1993–94; Naval Attaché, Washington, 1994–97; Flag Officer, Scotland, Northern England and NI, 1997–2000. Chief Exec., Mechanical and Metal Trades Confedn, 2001–04. Mem., Queen's Body Guard for Scotland, Royal Company of Archers. *Recreations:* fishing, ski-ing, gardening.

GREGORY, Maj. Gen. Andrew Richard; Director General Personnel and Director General Service Conditions (Army), Ministry of Defence, since 2008; *b* 19 Nov. 1957; *s* of Lt Col Richard B. Gregory and Alison Gregory (*née* Egerton); *m* 1986, Sally Ann Sheard; two *s. Educ:* Malsis Sch.; Sedbergh Sch.; St John's Coll., Cambridge (BA Eng 1979; MA 1982). Graduate trainee/shift foreman, Metal Box Co. Ltd, 1975–81; Army: jun. officer appts, UK, NI and Germany, 1982–97; CO, 1st Regt RHA, UK and Bosnia, 1997–2000; Dir, Army Jun. Div., JSCSC, 2000–02; Comdr, RA and Dep. Comdr, 1st (UK) Armoured Div., Germany and Iraq, 2002–04; ACOS Comd and Battlespace Mgt, HQ Land Comd, 2004–06; Team Leader, HQ Land Comd and HQ Adjt Gen. Co-location Study, 2006–08. *Recreations:* golf, ski-ing, tennis, the brute force part of gardening. *Address:* HQ Land Forces, Trenchard Lines, Upavon, Pewsey, Wilts SN9 6BE.

GREGORY, Rt Rev. Clive Malcolm; *see* Wolverhampton, Bishop Suffragan of.

GREGORY, Conal Robert; company director, wine consultant and financial journalist; *b* 11 March 1947; *s* of Patrick George Murray Gregory and Marjorie Rose Gregory; *m* 1971, Helen Jennifer Craggs; one *s* one *d. Educ:* King's College Sch., Wimbledon; Univ. of Sheffield (BA Hons Mod. Hist. and Pol Theory and Instns, 1968). Master of Wine by examination, Vintners' Co., 1979. Manager, Saccone & Speed Vintage Cellar Club, 1971–73; Wine Buyer, Reckitt & Colman, 1973–77; Editor, Internat. Wine and Food Soc.'s Jl, 1980–83; Dir, Standard Fireworks Ltd, 1987–92; Chm., Internat. Wine and Spirit Competition Ltd, 1997–98; Dir, Jackson Prentice Ltd, 1999–2004. Contested Lakenham, Norwich City election, 1976; Norfolk County Councillor, Thorpe Div., 1977–81; Vice-Pres., Norwich Jun. Chamber of Commerce, 1975–76; Mem., E Anglia Tourist Bd, 1979–81. Chairman: Norwich N Cons. Assoc., 1980–82; Norwich CPC, 1978–81; Vice-Chm., Eastern Area CPC, 1980–83; Member: Cons. Eastern Area Agric. Cttee, 1975–79; Cons. Provincial Council, Eastern Area, 1978–83; Chm. and Founder, Bow Gp of E Anglia, 1975–82; Nat. Vice-Chm., Bow Gp, 1976–77. MP (C) York, 1983–92. Hon. Treas., British/Cyprus CPA Gp, 1987–92; Sec., UK-Manx Parly Gp, 1987–92; Chm., Cons. Parly Food and Drinks Industries Cttee, 1989–92 (Vice-Chm., 1985–89); Vice-Chairman: Cons. Parly Tourism Cttee, 1985–92; Cons. Parly Transport Cttee, 1987–89 and 1990–92 (Sec., 1983–87); All Party Parly Hospice Gp, 1990–92; All Party Parly Tourism Cttee, 1991–92 (Sec., 1983–91); Mem. Cttee, British Atlantic Gp of Young Politicians, 1983–92 (Chm., 1988–89; Pres., 1989–92); Pres., York Young Conservatives, 1982–93; Vice-President: Nat. Soc. of Cons. and Unionist Agents, Yorks Br., 1983–92; York Br., UNA, 1983–92. Parliamentary Consultant: The Market Res. Soc., 1984–91; Consort Hotels Ltd, 1984–91; Consultant: Andry Montgomery Ltd, 1979–97; Smith & Taylor Ltd, 1992–2000; CC&C Research, 1993–96; Cash Centres Ltd, 1995–2002; Emphasis Research and Marketing, 1997–2003; Jackson Nugent Vintners Ltd, 1997–. Fellow, Industry and Parlt Trust, 1984–87. Private Member's Bills on consumer safety, 1985, on smoke alarms, 1991, on cheque fraud, 1992. Patron, Nat. Trust for Welfare of the Elderly, 1983–92; Founder Mem., Wymondham Br., CEMS, 1979; Member: Wymondham Abbey PCC, 1982–83; Humbleyard Deanery Synod, 1982–83; High Steward's Cttee, York Minster Fund, 1983–89; York Archaeol Trust, 1983–; York Georgian Soc., 1982–92, 2002–; York Civic Trust, 1982–92, 2007–; 20th/21st Century British Art Fair Council, 1992–; ESU, 1994–. Governor, Heartsease Sch., Norwich, 1977–83; Member, Court of Governors: Univ. of Sheffield, 1977–; Univ. of York,

1983–92; Univ. of Hull, 1983–92. Sen. Judge, Internat. Wine Challenge, 2003–. Wine Corresp., Catering Times, 1979–83. Personal Finance Regional Journalist of the Year: Bradford & Bingley, 2007; BIBA, 2007. *Publications:* (with W. Knock) Beers of Britain, 1975; (with R. A. Adley) A Policy for Tourism?, 1977; A Caterer's Guide to Drinks, 1979; (with M. Shersby and A. McCurley) Food for a Healthy Britain, 1987; The Cognac Companion, 1997; contribs to The Times, Scotsman, Yorkshire Post, etc. *Address:* c/o Jackson Nugent Vintners Ltd, 30 Homefield Road, Wimbledon Village, SW19 4QF.

GREGORY, Janice; Member (Lab) Ogmore, National Assembly for Wales, since 1999; *b* 10 Jan. 1955; *d* of Sir Raymond Powell, MP and of Marion Grace (*née* Evans); *m* 1977, Michael Gregory; two *d.* Parly Asst to Sir Raymond Powell, MP, 1991–99. Member: Fabian Soc., 1980; Co-op. Party, 1980; USDAW, 1982; TGWU, 1997; Unite the Union (formerly Amicus), 2002. *Address:* National Assembly for Wales, Cardiff Bay, Cardiff CF99 1NA; (constituency office) 44a Penybont Road, Pencoed, Bridgend CF35 5RA.

GREGORY, (John) Peter; JP; CEng, FIMechE; Director, ASL Ltd, 1986–91; *b* 5 June 1925; *s* of Mr and Mrs P. Gregory; *m* 1949, Lilian Mary (*née* Jarvis); one *s* one *d.* *Educ:* Ernest Bailey Sch., Matlock; Trinity Hall, Cambridge (Scholar, MA). CEng, FIMechE 1970. Served War, RAF Pilot, 1943–47. Joined Cadbury Bros Ltd, 1949, Dir 1962; Vice Chm., Cadbury Ltd, 1969–70, Dir, Cadbury Schweppes, 1971–82 (Chm., Overseas Gp and Internat. Tech. Dir, 1973–80); Director: National Vulcan Engrg Ins. Group Ltd, 1970–79; Amalgamated Power Engrg Ltd, 1973–81; Chm., Data Recording Instruments Ltd, 1982–84. Gen. Comr of Income Tax, 1978–82. Chm. Trustees, Middlemore Homes, 1970–82. Liveryman, Needlemakers' Co. JP Birmingham, 1979. *Recreations:* music, bridge, country pursuits, sailing. *Address:* 5 Place Stables, Place Road, Fowey, Cornwall PL23 1DR. *Clubs:* Carlton; Royal Fowey Yacht.

GREGORY, Prof. Kenneth John, CBE 2007; PhD, DSc; CGeog; Warden, Goldsmiths' College, University of London, 1992–98, now Professor Emeritus and Hon. Fellow; *b* 23 March 1938; *s* of Frederick Arthur Gregory and Marion Gregory; *m* Margaret Christine Wilmot; one *s* two *d.* *Educ:* University College London (BSc Special 1959; PhD 1962; DSc 1982; Fellow 1999). University of Exeter: Lectr in Geography, 1962–72; Reader in Physical Geography, 1972–76; University of Southampton: Prof. of Geography, 1976–92; Head of Geography Dept, 1978–83; Dean of Science, 1984–87; Dep. Vice-Chancellor, 1988–92; Vis. Prof., 1998–. Hon. Res. Fellow, UCL, 1993–; Hon. Prof., Univ. of Birmingham, 1997–2008; Leverhulme Emeritus Fellow, 1998–2001. Vis. Lectr, Univ. of New England, NSW, 1975; Distinguished Visiting Professor, 1987: Univ. Kebangsaan; Arizona State Univ.; Snyder Lectr, Univ. of Toronto, 1990. Pres., Commn on Global Continental Palaeohydrology, Internat. Assoc. on Union for Quaternary Res., 1999–2004 (Vice-Pres., 1992). Trustee, Horniman Mus. and Gardens, 1997–2003. Gov., Southampton Solent Univ. (formerly Southampton Inst.), 1998–2007 (Vice Chm., Bd of Govs, 1999–2007). For. Mem., Polish Acad. of Arts and Scis, 1995. Freeman, City of London, 1997; Liveryman, Goldsmiths' Co., 1998– (Freeman, 1997; Mem., Educn Cttee, 1999–2006). Hon. Fellow, Goldsmiths' Coll., 1998. Hon. DSc: Southampton, 1997; Greenwich, 1997; DUniv Southampton Solent, 2008. Back Award, 1980, Founder's Medal, 1993, RGS; Linton Award, British Geomorphological Res. Gp, 1999; Scottish Geographical Medal, RSGS, 2000. *Publications:* (with A. H. Shorter and W. L. D. Ravenhill) Southwest England, 1969; (with D. E. Walling) Drainage Basin Form and Process, 1973; (jtly) An Advanced Geography of the British Isles, 1974; (with E. Derbyshire and J. R. Hails) Geomorphological Processes, 1979; The Yellow River, 1980; The Nature of Physical Geography, 1985 (trans. Russian and Portuguese); (ed jtly) The Encyclopedic Dictionary of Physical Geography, 1985; (ed) Energetics of Physical Environment, 1987; (ed jtly) Human Activity and Environmental Processes, 1987; (ed jtly) Palaeohydrology in Practice, 1987; (ed jtly) Horizons in Physical Geography, 1988; (ed) The Earth's Natural Forces, 1990; (ed) The Guinness Guide to the Restless Earth, 1991; (ed jtly) Temperate Palaeohydrology, 1991; (ed jtly) Global Continental Palaeohydrology, 1995; (ed jtly) Global Continental Changes: the context of palaeohydrology, 1996; (ed jtly) Evaluating Teacher Quality in High Education, 1996; (ed) Geological Conservation Review Fluvial Geomorphology of Great Britain, 1997; (ed jtly) Palaeohydrology and Environmental Change, 1998; The Changing Nature of Physical Geography, 2000; (ed jtly) Palaeohydrology: understanding global change, 2003; (with P. W. Downs) River Channel Management, 2004; (ed) Physical Geography, 4 vols, 2005; (jtly) Environmental Sciences: a companion primer, 2008. *Recreations:* travel, gardening, reading. *Address:* 9 Poltimore Road, Guildford, Surrey GU2 7PT; *e-mail:* k.j.gregory@ntlworld.com.

GREGORY, Peter; *see* Gregory, J. P.

GREGORY, Prof. Peter John, PhD; FIBiol, FRASE; Director, Scottish Crop Research Institute, since 2005; *b* 19 July 1951; *s* of Joseph Henry Gregory and June Rosamond Gregory; *m* 1973, Jane Sandra Crump; two *s.* *Educ:* Chatham House Grammar Sch.; Univ. of Reading (BSc Soil Sci.); Univ. of Nottingham (PhD Soil Sci. 1977). FIBiol 1994. Lectr, Univ. of Reading, 1980–89; Principal Res. Scientist, CSIRO Div. of Plant Industry, Australia, 1990–93; University of Reading: Prof. of Soil Sci., 1994–2005; Pro-Vice-Chancellor, 1998–2003, 2004–05; Vis. Prof. of Soil Sci., 2005–. Chair, Global Envmtl Change and Food Systems, 2001–06. Vis. Prof., Univ. of Abertay, 2005–. Hon. Professor: Univ. of Dundee, 2005–; Univ. of Glasgow, 2006–. FRASE 2004. *Publications:* Root Development and Function, 1987; Soils in the Urban Environment, 1991; Crop Production on Duplex Soils, 1992; Land Resources: on the edge of the Malthusian precipice?, 1997; Science in the Garden, 2002; Plant Roots: growth, activity and interactions with soil, 2006; numerous scientific papers on soil/plant interactions in learned jls and books. *Recreations:* gardening, folk dancing. *Address:* Scottish Crop Research Institute, Invergowrie, Dundee DD2 5DA.

GREGORY, Peter Roland; JP; Director, Personnel, Management and Business Services, subsequently Personnel and Accommodation, National Assembly for Wales, 2000–03; *b* 7 Oct. 1946; *s* of Tom and Ruby Gregory; *m* 1978, Frances Margaret Hogan. *Educ:* Sexeys Grammar Sch., Blackford, Som; University College Swansea (BA Hons 1968); Manchester Univ. (PhD 1972). Joined Welsh Office, 1971; Private Sec. to Perm. Sec., 1974–75; Principal, 1976; Asst Sec., 1982; Under Sec., Transport, Planning and Envmt Gp, 1990–94; Dir, Health Dept, 1994–99; Dir, NHS Wales, 1999–2000. JP Somerset, 2006. *Recreations:* walking, theatre, music. *Address:* Littlemoor House, Littlemoor Road, Mark, Somerset TA9 4NG.

GREGORY, Philip John; His Honour Judge Gregory; a Circuit Judge, since 2004; *b* 13 Jan. 1953; *s* of John Godfrey Gregory and late Winifred Gregory; *m* 1979, Deborah Ann (*née* Lane); one *s* two *d.* *Educ:* Moseley Grammar Sch., Birmingham; Pembroke Coll., Oxford (MA). Called to the Bar, Middle Temple, 1975; in practice as barrister, specialising in personal injury, 1975–2004; Asst Recorder, 1998–2000, Recorder, 2000–04. *Recreations:* Rugby, tennis, reading. *Address:* Birmingham Crown Court, Queen Elizabeth II Law Courts, 1 Newton Street, Birmingham B4 7NA. *T:* (0121) 681 3300.

GREGORY, Philip William, MBE 2008; Chairman, United Bristol Healthcare NHS Trust, 1998–2006; *b* 30 Sept. 1947; *s* of late Thomas Douglas Gregory and Winifred (*née* Brooks); partner, Rosemary Clarke. *Educ:* Beaminster Comprehensive Sch., Dorse Southampton Coll. of Technology (Dip. Municipal Admin). Regl Official, NALGC 1974–82; SW Regl Sec., TUC, 1982–93. Member: Dorset AHA, 1974–79; Somers AHA, 1979–91. Member Board: South West Electricity, 1985–89; Bristol Develt Corp 1988–96; DTI Develt Bd for SW, 1988–97; SW Regl Chm., Nat. Training Award 1993–97; Chm., Community Foundn Network, 1995–2000; Member: Employmer Tribunal, 1975–; Bristol Initiative, 1989–2006. Mem. (Lab Co-op), Lockleaze Ward Bristol CC, 1992–99. Treas., Lockleaze Neighbourhood Trust, 1996–2006. *Recreation* golf, gardening, walking, watching cricket (Somerset). *Address:* 2 Oxford Lane, Brixhan Devon TQ5 8PP.

GREGORY, Dr Philippa; author; *b* 9 Jan. 1954; *d* of Arthur Gregory and Elaine Grego (*née* Wedd); *m* Anthony Mason; one *s* one *d.* *Educ:* Univ. of Sussex (BA 1979); Univ. Edinburgh (MLitt; PhD 1984). Newspaper journalist, 1971–75; BBC Radio journalis 1975–; book reviewer, TV presenter, broadcaster and playwright, 1986–. Founde Gardens for The Gambia, 1993. *Publications:* Wideacre, 1986; The Favoured Child, 198 Meridon, 1990; Mrs Hartley and the Growth Centre, 1991; The Wise Woman, 199 Fallen Skies, 1994; The Little House, 1995; A Respectable Trade, 1997 (televised); Earthl Joys, 1999; Virgin Earth, 2000; The Other Boleyn Girl, 2001 (televised 2003, filme 2008); The Queen's Fool, 2003; The Virgin's Lover, 2004; The Constant Princess, 200 The Boleyn Inheritance, 2006; The Other Queen, 2008. *Recreations:* child-raising (children, 5 step-children), riding, gardening, ski-ing, hiking, loafing. *Address:* c/o Roge Coleridge & White, 20 Powis Mews, W11 1JN.

GREGORY, Richard John, OBE 2004; Yorkshire Bank Chair, National Australia Grou Europe Ltd, since 2005; *b* 18 Aug. 1954; *s* of John and Joan Gregory. Trainee, Doncast Gazette, 1972–75; gen. reporter, Doncaster Evening Post, 1976; labour corresp. an industrial corresp., Sheffield Morning Telegraph, 1977–79; News Ed., Granada T 1979–81; Yorkshire Television: News Ed., 1981–82; Producer, 1982–84; Ed., Calenda 1984–89; Hd of News, 1989–92; Controller, 1992–93; Dir, Regl Progs, 1993–95; Dir Broadcasting, 1995; Man. Dir, Broadcasting, Yorkshire Tyne Tees, 1996–97; Man. Di 1997–2002. Non-executive Director: Yorkshire Bank, 2000–; Clydesdale Bank, 2000- Imagesound plc, 2002– (Chm., 2002–05; Sen. Ind. non-exec. Dir, 2005–); Sheffie University Enterprises Ltd, 2005–07. Member: Bd, BITC, 2001–08 (Chm., Yorks an Humber Regl Leadership Team, 2001–08); Yorkshire Forward (formerly Yorks an Humber Regl Develt Agency), 1998–2004 (Dep. Chm., 1999–2004); Chairman: Yor Initiative, 1997–2001; Yorkshire Science, 2006–. Chm., Chesterfield Royal Hosp. NH Foundn Trust, 2006–. Mem., Yorkshire Culture (formerly Yorks Regl Cultur Consortium), 2000–04. Mem. Council, Inst. for Employment Studies, 2003–05. Chm Sheffield Hallam Univ., 1999–2003 (Gov., 1992–2003). Trustee Dir, Sheffield Galls an Mus Trust, 2002–08. Hon. DLit: Bradford, 1999; Sheffield Hallam, 2003. *Recreation:* Pea District. *Address:* (office) Studio 5, Eccles House Business Centre, Eccles Lane, Hop Valley, Derbys S33 6RW.

GREGORY, Prof. Richard Langton, CBE 1989; DSc; FRS 1992; FRSE 196 Professor of Neuropsychology and Director of Brain and Perception Laborator University of Bristol, 1970–88, now Professor Emeritus and Senior Research Fellow; *b* 2 July 1923; *s* of C. C. L. Gregory, astronomer, and Patricia (*née* Gibson); *m* 1st, 195 Margaret Hope Pattison Muir (marr. diss. 1966); one *s* one *d*; 2nd, 1967, Freja Ma Balchin (marr. diss. 1976). *Educ:* King Alfred Sch., Hampstead; Downing Coll Cambridge, 1947–50 (Hon. Fellow, 1999); DSc Bristol, 1983. Served in RAF (Signals 1941–46; Research, MRC Applied Psychology Research Unit, Cambridge, 1950–5 Univ. Demonstrator, then Lecturer, Dept of Psychology, Cambridge, 1953–67; Fellow Corpus Christi Coll., Cambridge, 1962–67 (Hon. Fellow, 1997); Professor of Bionic Dept of Machine Intelligence and Perception, Univ. of Edinburgh, 1967–70 (Chm. Dept, 1968–70). Founder and Chm. Trustees, 1983–91, Pres., 1991–99, The Explorato Hands-on Science Centre. President: Section J, British Assoc. for Advancement Science, 1975, Section X, 1986, and Section Q, 1989 and 1990; Experimental Psycho Soc., 1981–82. Member: Royal Soc. Cttee for Public Understanding of Sci., 1986–9 BBC Sci. Consultative Gp, 1988–93. Royal Institution: Manager, 1971–74; Men Council and Vice-Pres., 1991–94; Christmas Lectr, 1967–68. Medawar Lectr, Royal Soc 2001. Hon. FInstP 1999; Hon. FBAASc 2006. DUniv: Open, 1990; Stirling, 1990; Hor LLD Bristol, 1993; Hon. DSc: E Anglia, 1996; Exeter, 1996; York, 1998; UMIST, 199 Keele, 1999; Edinburgh, 2000; Wolverhampton 2004. Craik Prize for Physiologic Psychology, St John's Coll., Cambridge, 1958; CIBA Foundn Research Prize, 195 Waverley Gold Medal, 1960; Capire Internat. Prize, Internat. Cttee for Promotion Advanced Educnl Res., Italy; Primo Rovis Prize, Trieste Internat. Foundn for Scientifi Progress and Freedom, Italy; Michael Faraday Medal, Royal Soc., 1993; Lord Croo Medal, Spectacle Makers' Co., 1996; Hughlings Jackson Medal, RSocMed, 200 Founder Editor, Perception, 1972. *Publications:* Recovery from Early Blindness (with Jea Wallace), 1963; Eye and Brain, 1966, 5th edn 1998; The Intelligent Eye, 1970; Concep and Mechanisms of Perception, 1974; (ed jtly) Illusion in Nature and Art, 1973; Mind i Science, 1981; Odd Perceptions (essays), 1986; (ed) Oxford Companion to the Minc 1987, 2nd edn 2004; Evolution of the Eye and Visual System, vol. 2 of Vision and Visu Dysfunction, 1991; Even Odder Perceptions (essays), 1994; The Artful Eye, 1995; Mirro in Mind, 1996; articles in various scientific jls and patents for optical and recordin instruments and a hearing aid; radio and television appearances. *Recreations:* punning an pondering. *Address:* 23 Royal York Crescent, Clifton, Bristol BS8 4JX. *Clubs:* Athenæum Chelsea Arts.

GREGORY, Roger Michael; Deputy Receiver for the Metropolitan Police, 1989–9 retired; *b* 1 June 1939; *s* of Walter James Gregory and Catherine Emma Gregory (*n* Regan); *m* 1961, Johanna Margaret O'Rourke; five *s* two *d.* *Educ:* Gillingham (Ken Grammar Sch.; Univ. of Herts (BA Hons 2006). Joined Metropolitan Police Civil Staf 1957; Hd of Operations, Police National Computer Unit, 1976; Dep. Dir of Financ Metropolitan Police, 1981; Dir of Computing, Metropolitan Police, 1983. *Recreation* cricket, bridge, gentle gardening. *Address:* 29 Milton Road, Harpenden, Herts AL5 5LA.

GREGORY, Ronald, CBE 1980; QPM 1971; DL; Chief Constable of West Yorkshir Metropolitan Police, 1974–83, retired; *b* 23 Oct. 1921; *s* of Charles Henry Gregory an Mary Gregory; *m* 1942, Grace Miller Ellison; two *s.* *Educ:* Harris College. Joined Polic Service, Preston, 1941. RAFVR, 1942–44; RNVR(A), 1944–46. Dep. Chief Constabl Blackpool, 1962–65; Chief Constable, Plymouth, 1965–68; Dep. Chief Constable, Devo and Cornwall, 1968–69; Chief Constable, West Yorkshire Constabulary, 1969–74. D West Yorks, 1977. *Recreations:* golf, sailing, ski-ing.

GREGORY-HOOD, Peter Charles Freeman; HM Diplomatic Service, retired; *b* 1 Dec. 1943; *s* of late Col A. M. H. Gregory-Hood, OBE, MC and Diana, *d* of Sir Joh Gilmour, 2nd Bt (she *m* 2nd, Sir John Beith, KCMG); *m* 1966, Camilla Bethell (*d* 2006) three *d.* *Educ:* Summerfields, St Leonard's; Eton Coll.; Aix-en-Provence Univ., Trinit Coll., Cambridge (BA Econs and Sociol.); Univ. of Buckingham (MA Biography 2003) Joined FCO, 1965: Third Sec., Dakar, 1967–69; Third, later Second Sec., Tel Aviv

1969–71; First Secretary: FCO, 1972–76; (Commercial), Paris, 1976–80; FCO, 1980–86; (Inf.), New Delhi, 1986–90; Counsellor and Consul-Gen., Casablanca, 1990–95; Dep. High Comr, Colombo, 1995–98. *Recreations:* tennis, golf, swimming, theatre. *Address:* Loxley Hall, Loxley, Warwick CV35 9JP. *Clubs:* White's, Royal Over-Seas League; Rotary (Stratford-upon-Avon); Tadmarton Heath Golf.

GREGSON, family name of **Baron Gregson**.

GREGSON, Baron *cr* 1975 (Life Peer), of Stockport in Greater Manchester; **John Gregson,** AMCT, CIMgt; DL; non-Executive Director, Fairey Group plc (formerly Fairey Holdings Ltd), 1989–94; with British Steel plc (formerly British Steel Corporation), 1976–94; *b* 29 Jan. 1924. Joined Stockport Base Subsidiary, 1939; Fairey R&D team working on science of nuclear power, 1946; appointed to Board, 1966. Non-executive Dir, Innvotec Ltd (formerly Electra Corporate Ventures Ltd), 1989–99; non-exec. Dir, OSC Process Engineering Ltd, 1995. Mem., NRA, 1992–95. Member: H of L Select Cttee on Sci. & Technol., 1980–99; H of L Select Cttee on Sustainable Develt, 1994–96; President: Parly and Scientific Cttee, 1986–89; Finance and Industry Gp of Labour Party. Vice Pres., Assoc. of Metropolitan Authorities, 1984. President: Defence Manufacturers Assoc., 1984–2000; Envmtl Industries Commn, 1994–96. Chairman: Waste Mgt Industry Trng and Adv. Bd, 1985–2000; Onyx Envmtl Trust, 1997–2003. Chm. Adv. Council, RMCS Shrivenham, 1985–99; Member Court: UMIST, 1976–99; Univ. of Manchester, 1995–97. Hon. Fellow, Manchester Polytechnic, 1983; Hon. FIProdE 1982; Hon. FREng (Hon. FEng 1986); Hon. FICE 1987; Hon. FIET. DUniv Open, 1986; Hon. DSc: Aston, 1987; Cranfield; Hon. DTech Brunel, 1989; Hon. DSc RMCS, 1990. DL Greater Manchester, 1979. *Recreations:* mountaineering, ski-ing, sailing, gardening. *Address:* 12 Rosemont Road, Richmond-upon-Thames, Surrey TW10 6QL. *T:* and *Fax:* (020) 8948 2244; The Spinney, Cragg Vale, Mytholmroyd, Hebden Bridge, West Yorks HX7 5SR; 407 Hawkins House, Dolphin Square, SW1V 3XL.

GREGSON, Charles Henry; Chief Executive Officer, PR Newswire, since 2005; *b* 7 June 1947; *s* of Geoffrey and Anne Gregson; *m* 1972, Caroline Blake; two *s*. *Educ:* Harrow; Trinity Hall, Cambridge (MA). Solicitor; Clifford-Turner & Co., 1970–74; Gp Solicitor and Company Sec., Mills & Allen Internat. plc, later MAI plc, subseq. United Business Media, 1974–77, Dir, 1984–2007; Chief Executive: Shepperton Studios Ltd, 1975–79; Harlow Butler/Garban Gp, 1980–98; exec. Chm., 1998–2001, non-exec. Chm., 2001–, ICAP plc (formerly Garban plc, then Garban-Intercapital plc); non-exec. Dir, International Personal Finance plc. *Recreations:* deerstalking, gardening, National Hunt racing. *Address:* Hope Farm, The Haven, Billingshurst RH14 9DN. *T:* (01403) 822066; *e-mail:* charles.gregson@prnewswire.com. *Club:* Turf.

GREGSON, Prof. Edward; composer; Principal, Royal Northern College of Music, Manchester, 1996–2008; *b* 23 July 1945; *s* of Edward Gregson and May Elizabeth (*née* Eaves); *m* 1967, Susan Carole Smith; two *s*. *Educ:* Manchester Central Grammar Sch.; Royal Academy of Music (GRSM, LRAM); Goldsmiths' Coll., Univ. of London (BMus Hons). Lectr in Music, Rachel McMillan Coll., London, 1970–76; Sen. Lectr, 1976–89, Reader, 1989–94, and Prof. of Music, 1994–96, Goldsmiths' Coll., Univ. of London. Hon. Prof. of Music, Univ. of Manchester, 1996. Mem., Music Industry Forum, DCMS, 1998–2001; Bd Mem., Cultural Consortium Northwest, 2003–04; Chm., Conservatoires UK, 2004–08. Vice-Chm., Composers' Guild, 1976–78; Chm., Assoc. of Professional Composers, 1989–91; Director: PRS, 1995–; Associated Bd of Royal Schs of Music, 1996–2008; Hallé Orch., 1998–2006. Gov. and Feoffee, Chetham's Sch. of Music, 1996–. Trustee, Nat. Foundn for Youth Music, 1999–2003. Fellow, Dartington Coll. of Arts, 1997. FRAM 1990; Hon. FLCM 1999; FRCM 2000. Hon. DMus: Sunderland, 1996; Lancaster, 2006; Hon. DArts Manchester Metropolitan, 2003; DUniv UCE, 2007. *Compositions include:* Oboe Sonata, 1965; Brass Quintet, 1967; Music for Chamber Orchestra, 1968; Horn Concerto, 1971; Essay for Brass Band, 1971; Tuba Concerto, 1976; Music for the York Cycle of Mystery Plays, 1976 and 1980; Connotations for Brass Band, 1977; Metamorphoses, 1979; Trombone Concerto, 1979; Trumpet Concerto, 1983; Piano Sonata in one movement, 1983; Contrasts for orchestra, 1983, revised 2001 as Contrasts—a concerto for orch.; Dances and Arias, 1984; Festivo, 1985; Missa Brevis Pacem, 1988; RSC History Play Cycles: Plantagenets Trilogy, 1988–89; Henry IV Parts 1 and 2, 1990–91; Celebration, 1991; Of Men and Mountains, 1991; The Sword and the Crown, 1991; Blazon, 1992; Clarinet Concerto, 1994; Concerto for Piano and Wind, 1995; The Kings Go Forth, 1996; Stepping Out, 1996; A Welcome Ode, 1997; …And the Seven Trumpets, 1998; Three Matisse Impressions, 1998; The Dance, forever the Dance, 1999; Violin Concerto, 2000; The Trumpets of the Angels, 2000; An Age of Kings, 2004; Shadow of Paradise, for Oboe and Percussion, 2005; Saxophone Concerto, 2006; A Song for Chris - concerto for cello and chamber orchestra, 2007; Rococo Variations, 2008. *Publications:* music articles in professional jls. *Recreations:* walking, wine, watching sport. *Address:* Rose Cottage, Shrigley Road, Pott Shrigley, Macclesfield, Cheshire SK10 5SA. *Clubs:* Savile, Royal Over-Seas League.

GREGSON, Prof. Peter John, FREng, FIAE; DL; President and Vice-Chancellor, Queen's University, Belfast, since 2004; *b* 3 Nov. 1957; *s* of Howard Davenport Gregson and Susan Katharine Gregson (*née* Lunn); *m* 1983, Rachael Kathleen McClaughry; three *d*. *Educ:* Imperial Coll., London (BSc Eng 1980 (Bessemer Medal); PhD 1983 (Matthey Prize, 2000)). CEng 1983, FREng 2000; FIMMM (FIM 1998); FIEI 2005; MRIA 2007; FIAE 2007; CMMI 2007. University of Southampton: Lectr in Engrg Materials, 1983–90; Sen. Lectr, 1990–92; Reader, 1992–95; Prof. of Aerospace Materials, 1995–2004; Hd, Engrg Materials, 1995–99; Dir of Res., Faculty of Engrg and Applied Sci., 1993–99; Dep. Hd, Sch. of Engrg Scis, 1999–2000; Dep. Vice-Chancellor, 2000–04. Academic Director: Luxfer Advanced Technol. Centre, 1999–2001; Defence and Aerospace Res. Partnership in Advanced Metallic Airframes, 1999–2004; DePuy Internat. Univ. Technol. Partnership, 2000–04. Director: Southampton Innovations Ltd, 2000–04; Southampton Asset Mgt Ltd, 2000–04; Photonic Innovations Ltd, 2000–04; Univ. of Southampton Hldgs Ltd, 2000–04; SULIS Innovations, 2002–04; NI Sci. Park, 2004–; QUBIS Ltd, 2004–; QUB Bookshop, 2004–; Rolls Royce Gp plc, 2007–; Chm., SETsquared, 2002–04. Sen. Res. Fellow, DERA, 1997–2001; Consultant: Johnson & Johnson/DePuy Internat., 1986–2004; Alcan Internat., 1989–93. Mem., DTI/OST Materials Foresight Panel, 1997–99. Mem. Council, CCLRC, 2003–07. Institute of Materials: Chairman: Alloy Design Cttee, 1991–92; Metals Sci. Cttee, 1992–93; Materials Strategy Commn, 1997–99; Mem. Council, Royal Acad. Engrg, 2005–. EPSRC: Member: Structural Materials Coll., 1994–2005; Engrg Rev. Panel, 1999; User Panel, 2005–07; Chm., Postgrad. Trng Prog. Panel, 2000. Trustee: Southampton Univ. Develt Trust, 2000–04; Wessex Med. Trust, 2001–04; Windsor Leadership Trust, 2002–. Associate Ed., Jl Materials Letters, 1990–2004. FCGI 2006. DL Belfast. Donald Julius Groen Prize, IMechE, 1994; Rosenhain Medal and Prize, Inst. Materials, 1996. *Publications:* numerous scientific papers in learned jls, on engrg performance of aerospace materials and computational and experimental modelling of load bearing med. devices. *Recreations:* opera, gardening, tennis, sailing. *Address:* Queen's University, Belfast, Belfast BT7 1NN. *T:* (028) 9097 5134. *Club:* Athenæum.

GREGSON, Sir Peter (Lewis), GCB 1996 (KCB 1988; CB 1983); Permanent Secretary, Department of Trade and Industry, 1989–96; *b* 28 June 1936; *s* of late Walter Henry Gregson and Lillian Margaret Gregson. *Educ:* Nottingham High Sch.; Balliol Coll., Oxford. Classical Hon. Mods, class I; Lit. Hum. class I; BA 1959; MA 1962. Nat Service, 1959–61; 2nd Lieut RAEC, attached to Sherwood Foresters. Board of Trade: Asst Principal, 1961; Private Sec. to Minister of State, 1963–65; Principal, 1965; Resident Observer, CS Selection Bd, 1966; London Business Sch., 1967; Private Sec. to the Prime Minister, 1968–72 (Parly Affairs, 1968–70; Econ. and Home Affairs, 1970–72); Asst Sec., DTI, and Sec., Industrial Development Adv. Bd, 1972–74; Under Sec., DoI, and Sec., NEB, 1975–77; Under Sec., Dept of Trade, 1977–80, Dep. Sec. (Civil Aviation and Shipping), 1980–81; Dep. Sec., Cabinet Office, 1981–85; Perm. Under-Sec. of State, Dept of Energy, 1985–89. Sen. Ind. Dir, Scottish Power plc, 1996–2004; Dir, Woolwich plc, 1998–2000; Chm., Woolwich Pension Fund Trust Co. Ltd, 1999–2000. Chm., Beckenham and Bromley NT Centre, 2003–06. CCMI (CBIM 1988; Mem., Bd of Companions, 1996–2002 (Dep. Chm., 1999–2002)); FRSA 1999. *Recreations:* gardening, listening to music. *Address:* 36A Elwill Way, Beckenham, Kent BR3 6RZ. *T:* (020) 8650 5925.

GREIG, Geordie Carron; Editor, Tatler, since 1999; *b* 16 Dec. 1960; *s* of Sir (Henry Louis) Carron Greig, *qv*; *m* 1995, Kathryn Elizabeth Terry; one *s* twin *d*. *Educ:* Eton Coll.; St Peter's Coll., Oxford (MA English Lit. and Lang.). Reporter: South East London and Kentish Mercury, 1981–83; Daily Mail, 1984–85; Today, 1985–87; Sunday Times: Reporter, 1987–89; Arts Corresp., 1989–91; NY Corresp., 1991–95; Literary Editor, 1995–99. FRSA 2005. *Publication:* Louis and the Prince, 1999. *Address:* Vogue House, Hanover Square, W1R 0AD. *T:* (020) 7499 9080. *Clubs:* White's, Colony Rooms.

GREIG, Sir (Henry Louis) Carron, KCVO 1995 (CVO 1973); CBE 1986; DL; Chairman, Horace Clarkson PLC (formerly H. Clarkson (Holdings) plc), 1976–93; Director, James Purdey & Sons Ltd, 1972–2000; an Extra Gentleman Usher to the Queen, since 1995 (Gentleman Usher, 1961–95); *b* 21 Feb. 1925; *s* of late Group Captain Sir Louis Greig, KBE, CVO, DL; *m* 1955, Monica Kathleen, *d* of late Hon. J. J. Stourton, TD; three *s* one *d*. *Educ:* Eton. Scots Guards, 1943–47, Captain. Joined H. Clarkson & Co. Ltd, 1948; Dir, 1954; Man. Dir, 1962; Chairman: H. Clarkson & Co. Ltd, 1973–85; Baltic Exchange (formerly Baltic Mercantile and Shipping Exchange), 1983–85 (Dir, 1978–85); Director: Williams & Glyn's Bank, 1983–85; Royal Bank of Scotland, 1985–95; Charterhouse, 1990–93. Vice-Chm., Not Forgotten Assoc., 1979–96. Chm., Schoolmistresses and Governesses Benevolent Instn, 1992–2003 (Dep. Chm., 1966–92). Governor, United World Coll. of the Atlantic, 1985–96. DL Hants, 1992. *Address:* Brook House, Fleet, Hants GU51 2RF; Binsness, Forres, Moray. *Clubs:* White's; Royal Findhorn Yacht.
See also G. C. Greig.

GREIG, Kenneth Muir, PhD; Rector, Hutchesons' Grammar School, Glasgow, since 2005; *b* 30 March 1960; *s* of Walter and Margaret Greig; *m* 1987, Josephine Claire Berenice Taylor; one *s* one *d*. *Educ:* George Heriot's Sch., Edinburgh; Worcester Coll., Oxford (BA 1981, MA); Univ. of Edinburgh (PhD 1984). Exploration geologist, BP, 1984–87; Maths Teacher and Housemaster, Christ's Hosp., 1987–93; Hd of Maths and Dir of Studies, Dollar Acad., 1993–2000; Headmaster, Pangbourne Coll., 2000–05. *Recreations:* watching Rugby, rowing, beachcombing, bagpipes. *Address:* Hutchesons' Grammar School, Beaton Road, Glasgow G41 4NW. *T:* (0141) 423 2933, *Fax:* (0141) 424 0251; *e-mail:* rector@hutchesons.org.

GREIG, Lesley Gillian; *see* Glaister, L. G.

GREIG-SMITH, Peter William, DPhil; Director, Swift Impact Ltd, since 2007; *b* 17 May 1953; *s* of late Peter Greig-Smith and of Edna (*née* Gonzalez); *m* 1st, 1978, June Ann Fettes (marr. diss. 2000); one *s* one *d*; 2nd, 2001, Lindsay Ann Murray. *Educ:* Aberdeen Univ. (BSc Hons Zoology 1975); Sussex Univ. (DPhil Behavioural Ecology 1980). Joined MAFF, 1980; Res. Scientist, Agricl Sci. Service, 1980–86; Head of Envmtl Res., 1986–90, of Conservation and Envmt Protection, 1990–92, Central Sci. Lab.; Head of Aquatic Envmt Protection, 1992–94, Dir, 1994–97, Directorate of Fisheries Res.; Chief Exec., Centre for Envmt, Fisheries and Aquaculture Sci., 1997–2004; Asst Dir, Special Projects, Envmt and Transport Dept, 2004–05, Actg Dir, Envmt and Regulation, 2005, Cambs CC. *Publications:* edited jointly: Field Margins, 1987; Field Methods for the Study of Environmental Effects of Pesticides, 1988; Pesticides, Cereal Farming and the Environment: the Boxworth project, 1992; Ecotoxicology of Earthworms, 1992; ECOtoxicology: ecological dimensions, 1996; numerous articles in sci. jls. *Recreations:* mountains, golf, DIY. *Address:* Street Farmhouse, Stanway, Colchester, Essex.

GREINER, Hon. Nicholas Frank, (Nick), AC 1994; *b* 27 April 1947; *s* of Nicholas and Clare Greiner; *m* 1970, Kathryn Callaghan (AO 2001); one *s* one *d*. *Educ:* St Ignatius Coll., Riverview; Sydney Univ. (BEc Hons); Harvard Univ. (MBA High Dist.). Asst Vice-Pres., Boise Cascade Corp., USA, 1970–71; NSW Dir and Chief Exec., White River Corp., 1972–80; Chm., Harper & Row (Australasia), 1977–83. Chairman: Baulderstone Hornibrook, 1993–2004; United Utilities Australia Pty Ltd (formerly North West Water), 1993–; Natwest Markets, 1993–97 (Dir, 1992–98); IAMA (formerly SBS-IAMA) Ltd, 1994–2000; W. D. & H. O. Wills, 1996–99 (Dir, 1995–99); British American Tobacco Australasia, 1999–2004; BMC Media, 1999–2002; Nuance Australia, 2001–; Bilfinger Berger Australia Pty Ltd, 2003–; Bradken Resources Pty Ltd, 2004– (Dir, 2002–04); Healthcare Australia Ltd, 2006–; BlueStar Print Gp, 2007–; PMI, 2008– (Dir, 2007–); Co-Chair, Ausflag Ltd, 1996–2000; Deputy Chairman: Stockland Trust Property Gp, 1992–; Coles Myer, 1995–96 (Dir, 1992–2000); Castle Harlan Australian Mezzanine Pty Ltd, 2000–. Director: Australian Vintage Pty Ltd (formerly Brian McGuigan Wines, subseq. McGuigan Simeon Wines), 1992–; QBE Insce Gp, 1992–2007; Blue Freeway, 2006–; Consultant: Clayton Utz, 1992–2004; Citigroup, 1997–; Deloitte Touche Tohmatsu, 1999–2004. Prof., Macquarie Grad. Sch. of Management, 1992–2004. Dir, Harvard Business Sch. Alumni Assoc. Bd. Chm., Australian Subscription Television and Radio Assoc., 2003–. MP (L) Ku-ring-gai, NSW, 1980–92; Shadow Minister for Urban Affairs, June 1981; Shadow Treasurer, and Shadow Minister for Housing and Co-operatives, Oct. 1981; Leader of State Opposition, 1983–88; Shadow Treasurer, and Shadow Minister for Ethnic Affairs, 1983; Premier, Treasurer, and Minister for Ethnic and Aboriginal Affairs, NSW Coalition Govt, 1988–92. Gov., CEDA, 2005–. Director: Sydney Organising Cttee for Olympic Games, 1993–2000; S Sydney Rugby League Club, 2003–06. President: Squash Australia, 1996–2000; Soccer Australia, 2001–02. *Recreations:* walking, ski-ing, theatre, opera, spectator sports. *Address:* Level 10, 139 Macquarie Street, Sydney, NSW 2000, Australia.

GRENFELL, family name of **Baron Grenfell**.

GRENFELL, 3rd Baron *cr* 1902; **Julian Pascoe Francis St Leger Grenfell;** Baron Grenfell of Kilvey (Life Peer) 2000; a Deputy Speaker, House of Lords, since 2002; *b* 23 May 1935; *o s* of 2nd Baron Grenfell, CBE, TD, and of Elizabeth Sarah Polk, *o d* of late Captain Hon. Alfred Shaughnessy, Montreal, Canada; *S* father, 1976; *m* 1st, 1961, Loretta Maria Reali (marr. diss. 1970), Florence; one *d*; 2nd, 1970, Gabrielle Raab (marr. diss.

1987), Berlin; two *d*; 3rd, 1987, Mrs Elisabeth Porter (marr. diss. 1992), Washington, DC; 4th, 1993, Mrs Dagmar Langbehn Debreil, *yr d* of late Dr Carl Langbehn, Berlin. *Educ:* Eton; King's Coll., Cambridge. BA (Hons), President of the Union, Cambridge, 1959. 2 Lieut, KRRC (60th Rifles), 1954–56; Captain, Queen's Royal Rifles, TA, 1963; Programme Asst, ATV Ltd, 1960–61; frequent appearances and occasional scripts, for ATV religious broadcasting and current affairs series, 1960–64. Joined World Bank, Washington, DC, 1965; Chief of Information and Public Affairs for World Bank Group in Europe, 1970; Dep. Dir, European Office, 1973; Special rep. of World Bank to UN, 1974–81; Special Advr, 1983–87, Sen. Advr, 1987–90; Head of Ext. Affairs, European Office, 1990–95; Sen. Advr, European Office, 1995, retired. UK Delegn to Parly Assemblies of Council of Europe and WEU, 1997–99. Chm., Econ. and Financial Subcttee, H of L Select Cttee on EU, 1999 and 2001–02; Principal Dep. Chm. of Cttees and Chm., Select Cttee on EU, 2002–08. Chevalier de la Légion d'Honneur (France), 2005. *Publications:* Margot (novel), 1984; The Gazelle (novel), 2004. *Recreations:* walking, European history. *Heir: cousin* Francis Pascoe John Grenfell [*b* 28 Feb. 1938; *m* 1977, Elizabeth Katharine, *d* of Hugh Kenyon]. *Address:* c/o House of Lords, SW1A 0PW. *Club:* Royal Green Jackets.

GRENFELL, Andrée, (Mrs David Milman); Director, Milman International Australia, since 1990; *b* 14 Jan. 1940; *d* of Stephen Grenfell (writer) and Sybil Grenfell; *m* 1st, 1972, Roy Warden; two step *s*; 2nd, 1984, David Milman; two step *s*. *Educ:* privately. Graduate Diploma in Agric., Hawkesbury Agricl Coll., 1989. Man. Dir, Elizabeth Arden Ltd, UK, 1974–76; Pres., Glemby Internat., UK and Europe, 1976–80; Sen. Vice Pres., Glemby Internat., USA, 1976–80. Chm., Kelly Burrell & Jones, 1988–91; Director: Harvey Nichols Knightsbridge, 1972–74; Peter Robinson Ltd, 1968–72; Non-executive Director: NAAFI, 1981–83; Prince of Wales Res. Inst., Sydney, 1994–2004. Mem. Council, Inst. of Dirs, 1976; FCMI (FBIM 1977). Mem., Cercle des Amis de la Veuve. Business Woman of the Year, FT, 1979. *Recreations:* riding, dressage, swimming, yoga. *Address:* 3/1 Rosemont Avenue, Woollahra, NSW 2025, Australia. *T:* (2) 93275964, *Fax:* (2) 93275964.

GRENFELL, Prof. Bryan Thomas, OBE 2002; DPhil; FRS 2004; Alumni Professor, Pennsylvania State University, since 2004; *b* 7 Dec. 1954; *s* of Bryan and Gwenda Grenfell; *m* 1996, Catherine Williams. *Educ:* Imperial Coll., London (BSc; ARCS); Univ. of York (MSc; DPhil 1981). Res. Fellow, Dept of Biol., Imperial Coll., London, 1981–86; Lectr, Dept of Animal and Plant Scis, Univ. of Sheffield, 1986–90; Department of Zoology, University of Cambridge: Lectr, 1990–98; Reader, 1998–2002; Prof. of Population Biol., 2002–04; Fellow, Girton Coll., Cambridge, 2001–04. *Publications:* (ed with A. P. Dobson) Ecology of Infectious Diseases in Natural Populations, 1995; numerous papers in learned jls. *Recreations:* cooking, reading, hiking. *Address:* Mueller Laboratory, Pennsylvania State University, University Park, PA 16802–5301, USA. *T:* (814) 8630278, *Fax:* (814) 8659131.

GRENFELL, (Jeremy) Gibson; QC 1994; a Recorder, since 1992; *b* 13 Dec. 1945; *s* of Edward Gerald James Grenfell and June (*née* Hunkin). *Educ:* Falmouth Grammar Sch.; Fitzwilliam Coll., Cambridge (Open Exhibnr, MA). Called to the Bar, Middle Temple, 1969 (Harmsworth Schol.; Bencher, 2003). *Address:* 6 King's Bench Walk, Temple, EC4Y 7DR. *T:* (020) 7583 0410.

GRENFELL, Simon Pascoe; His Honour Judge Grenfell; a Circuit Judge, since 1992; Senior Circuit Judge, since 2002; *b* 10 July 1942; *s* of late Osborne Pascoe Grenfell and Margaret Grenfell; *m* 1974, Ruth De Jersey Harvard; one *s* three *d*. *Educ:* Fettes College; Emmanuel College, Cambridge (MA). Called to the Bar, Gray's Inn, 1965; practice on NE Circuit; a Recorder, 1985–92; Designated Civil Judge: Bradford Group of Courts, 1998–2000; Leeds Group of Courts, 2000–. Chancellor, dio. of Ripon, 1992–. *Recreations:* music, sailing, coarse gardening, internet information.

GRENIER, Rear-Adm. Peter Francis, (Frank), CB 1989; self-employed glass engraver; *b* 27 Aug. 1934; *s* of late Dr F. W. H. Grenier and Mrs M. Grenier; *m* 1957, Jane Susan Bradshaw; two *s* one *d* (and one *s* decd). *Educ:* Montpelier School, Paignton; Blundell's School, Tiverton. Entered RN (Special Entry), 1952; Midshipman, Mediterranean Fleet, 1953; commissioned, 1955; joined Submarine service, 1956; 1st command (HMS Ambush), 1965; final command (HMS Liverpool), 1982; Chief of Staff to C-in-C Naval Home Command, 1985–87; FO Submarines, and Comdr Submarine Forces E Atlantic, 1987–89. Defence Advr, H of C Defence Cttee, 1991–98. Vice-Pres., Royal Naval FA, 1988–. Liveryman: Painter-Stainers' Co., 1984; Glass Sellers' Co., 1987. Chm. of Govs, Blundell's Sch., 1991–96 (Gov., 1986–96). AFGE 1998. *Recreations:* family, sketching and painting, golf. *Address:* 2 Grange Cottages, North Cadbury, Yeovil, Somerset BA22 7BY. *T:* (01963) 440176, *Fax:* (01963) 440389. *Club:* Army and Navy.

GRENVILLE; *see* Freeman-Grenville, family name of Lady Kinloss.

GRENVILLE, Dr Jane Clare, FSA; Pro-Vice-Chancellor for Students, University of York, since 2007; Commissioner, English Heritage, 2001–08; *b* 17 June 1958; *d* of Henry William Grenville and Helen Caroline Grenville (*née* Westmacott). *Educ:* Girton Coll., Cambridge (BA Hons Archaeol. and Anthropol., MA 1983); Univ. of York (PhD 2005). MIFA 1993; IHBC 1996; FSA 2002. Caseworker, Listed Buildings Resurvey for Yorkshire and Humberside, 1984–87; Res. Officer, Chester Rows Res. Project, 1987–88; Historic Buildings Officer, Council for British Archaeol., 1988–91; University of York: Lectr, 1991–2000; Sen. Lectr in Archaeol., 2000–; Hd, Dept of Archaeology, 2001–06. Trustee: York Civic Trust, 2006–; York Museums Trust, 2008–. *Publications:* Medieval Housing, 1997; Managing the Historic Rural Landscape, 1999. *Recreations:* dogs, academic Russian roulette. *Address:* University of York, Heslington, York YO10 5DD. *T:* (01904) 433481, *Fax:* (01904) 433490; *e-mail:* jcg2@york.ac.uk.

GRENVILLE, Prof. John Ashley Soames; Professor of Modern History, University of Birmingham, 1969–94, now Emeritus; *b* Berlin, 11 Jan. 1928; *m* 1st, 1960, Betty Anne Rosenberg (*d* 1974), New York; three *s*; 2nd, 1975, Patricia Carnie; one *d* one step *d*. *Educ:* Mistley Place and Orwell Park Prep. Sch.; Cambridge Techn. Sch.; corresp. courses; Birkbeck Coll.; LSE; Yale Univ. BA, PhD London; FRHistS. Postgrad. Schol., London Univ., 1951–53; Asst Lectr, subseq. Lectr, Nottingham Univ., 1953–64; Commonwealth Fund Fellow, 1958–59; Postdoctoral Fellow, Yale Univ., 1960–63; Reader in Modern History, Nottingham Univ., 1964–65; Prof. of Internat. History, Leeds Univ., 1965–69. Vis. Prof., Queen's Coll., NY City Univ., 1964, etc; Guest Professor, Univ. of Hamburg, 1980, 1994. Chm., British Univs History Film Consortium, 1968–71; Mem. Council: RHistS, 1971–73; List and Index Soc., 1966–71; Baeck Inst., London, 1981–. Consultant, American and European Bibliographical Centre, Oxford and California and Clio Press, 1960–88; Dir of Film for the Historical Assoc., 1975–78; Historical Adviser, World History, ZDF, German Television, 1982–98. Editor: Fontana History of War and Society, 1969–78; Leo Baeck Year Book, 1992–. *Publications:* (with J. G. Fuller) The Coming of the Europeans, 1962; Lord Salisbury and Foreign Policy, 1964, 2nd edn 1970; (with G. B. Young) Politics, Strategy and American Diplomacy: studies in foreign policy 1873–1917, 1966, 2nd edn 1971; Documentary Films (with N. Pronay), The Munich Crisis, 1968; The End of Illusions: from Munich to Dunkirk, 1970; The Major International Treatie 1914–1973: a history and guide, 1974, 3rd edn (jtly) 1900–1999, 2000; Europe Reshape 1848–78, 1975, enlarged edn, 2000; Nazi Germany, 1976; World History of th Twentieth Century I, 1900–1945, 1980; Collins World History of the Twentiet Century, 1994, 2nd edn 1998 (trans. Russian and Chinese), rev. edn as World Histor from the Twentieth to the Twenty-first Century, 2004; contrib. various learned jls *Recreations:* listening to music, travel, tutoring students. *Address:* University o Birmingham, School of History, Birmingham B15 2TT. *Club:* Athenæum.

GRENVILLE-GREY, Wilfrid Ernest; Civil Society advocate at United Nations, Nev York, 1991–2006; *b* 27 May 1930; *s* of late Col Cecil Grenville-Grey, CBE and Monic Grenville-Grey (*née* Morrison-Bell); *m* 1st, 1963, Edith Sibongile Dlamini (marr. diss 1989), *d* of Rev. Jonathan Dlamini, Johannesburg; two *s* one *d*; 2nd, 2006, Cynthi Elizabeth, *d* of Stanley Goddard, Barbados and NYC. *Educ:* Eton; Worcester College Oxford (scholar; MA); Yale University (Henry Fellow, 1953–54). 2nd Lieut, KRRC 1949–50. Overseas Civil Service, Nyasaland, 1956–59; Booker McConnell Ltd, 1960–63 Mindolo Ecumenical Foundn, Zambia, 1963–71 (Dir, 1966–71); Sec., Univ. Stud Project on Foreign Investments in S Africa, 1971–72; Dir, Centre for Internat. Briefing Farnham Castle, 1973–77; Internat. Defence and Aid Fund for Southern Africa, Londo and UN, 1978–83; Sec. for Public Affairs to Archbishop of Canterbury, 1984–87; Britis Dir, Global Forum of Spiritual and Parly Leaders on Human Survival, 1987–88; Interna Develt Dir, Icewalk, 1988–89. DHL Ignatius Univ., Ohio, 2005. *Publications:* All in a African Lifetime, 1969; UN Jigsaw, 2000; anthologies of aphorisms: Sixty Marker Buoy and Anchors, 1960, 1965, 1970 and 1975. *Recreations:* gardening, apophthegms. *Address* Park Lodge, Goodwood, Chichester, West Sussex PO18 0QA. *Club:* Travellers.

GRESHAM, Prof. (Geoffrey) Austin, TD 1966; FRCPath, FRCPE; Professor o Morbid Anatomy and Histopathology, Cambridge, 1973–92; Fellow, 1964–92, nov Emeritus, and President, 1976–79, Jesus College, Cambridge; Home Office Pathologis 1968–92; *b* 1 Nov. 1924; *s* of Thomas Michael and Harriet Anne Gresham; *m* 195(Gweneth Margery Leigh; three *s* two *d*. *Educ:* Grove Park Sch., Wrexham; Gonville an Caius Coll., Cambridge (Tancred Student and Schol.; Schuldham Plate; MA; ScD; Hon Fellow, 2001); King's Coll. Hosp., London (Burney Yeo Schol., Todd and Jelf Medallis MB BChir, MD). FRCPath 1973; FRCPE 1994. Served RAMC, 1950–52, Lt-Co RAMC V, 1961. Cambridge University: Demonstrator and Lectr in Pathology, 1953–62 Univ. Morbid Anatomist, 1962–73; Sec., Faculty Bd of Medicine, 1956–61; Chm., MI Cttee, 1991–2003; Dep. to Regius Prof. of Physic, 1991–2003; Dep. to Vice Chancello 1993–95. Consultant Mem., Cambridge Dist Management Team, 1974–84; Chairmar Cambridge Dist Medical Cttee, 1974–84; Medical Staff Leave Cttee, 1974–84; Cambridg Dist Ethical Cttee, 1974–84; Member: European Atherosclerosis Soc., 1959–; Britis Atherosclerosis Discussion Gp, 1965–. Roy Cameron Meml Lectr, RCPath, 1983. Mem Bd of Governors, United Cambridge Hosps, 1972–74. Hon. Fellow, British Assoc. o Forensic Medicine, 1996. Scientific Medal, Univ. of Tokyo, 1985. *Publications* Introduction to Comparative Pathology, 1962; Biological Aspects of Occlusive Vascul Disease, 1964; Colour Atlas of General Pathology, 1971, 2nd edn 1993; Primat Atherosclerosis, 1976; Colour Atlas of Forensic Pathology, 1977; Post Morter Procedures, 1979; Reversing Atherosclerosis, 1980; Arterial Pollution, 1981; Wounds an Wounding, 1987; contrib. chapters, and papers in many jls, about pathology. *Recreation* gardening, playing organ, wine, silver, talking. *Address:* 18 Rutherford Road, Cambridg CB2 2HH. *T:* (01223) 841326.

GRETTON, family name of **Baron Gretton**.

GRETTON, 4th Baron *cr* 1944, of Stapleford; **John Lysander Gretton;** *b* 17 April 197 *s* of 3rd Baron Gretton and of Jennifer Ann (*see* Jennifer, Lady Gretton); *S* father, 1989; 2006, Sarah Elizabeth Anne, *er d* of Alfred Attard; one *s*. *Educ:* Shrewsbury; RA Cirencester. *Heir: s* Hon. John Frederick Bruce Gretton, *b* 9 June 2008.

GRETTON, Jennifer, Lady; Jennifer Ann Gretton; Lord-Lieutenant of Leicestershir since 2003; owner, Stapleford Estate; *b* 14 June 1943; *o d* of Edmund Sandford Moore an Emily Joan Moore; *m* 1970, Hon. John Henrik Gretton (later 3rd Baron Gretton; he 1989); one *s* one *d*. *Educ:* York Coll. for Girls. Member: Leics and Rutland CLA Ctte 1989–; Envmt and Water Cttee, CLA, 1994–98. President: Melton Mowbray & Distri Model Engrg Soc., 1989–; Rural Community Council (Leics and Rutland), 1994–; Lei Orgn for the Relief of Suffering, 1999–; St John Council, Leics, 2003–; Leics and Rutlan Cttee, Army Benevolent Fund, 2003–; Vice-President: Scout Council, Leics, 2003– E Midlands RFCA, 2003– (Pres., Leics and Rutland County Cttee, 2003–); Leics an Rutland Branch, Magistrates' Assoc., 2004–. Member: Cttee, Somerby PCC, 1991–; Lei Cathedral Council, 2003–. Patron: Royal Leics Regt Mus. Appeal, 2003–; Sir Fran Whittle Commem. Gp, 2003–; Heart of the Nat. Forest Foundn, 2003–; Change Ashb Now, 2003–; Leics and Rutland Wildlife Trusts, 2004–. DL 2001, JP 2003, Leic *Recreations:* sport, music, all aspects of steam. *T:* (01664) 454607.
See also Baron Gretton.

GRETTON, Prof. George Lidderdale, WS; Lord President Reid Professor of Lav University of Edinburgh, since 1994; a Scottish Law Commissioner, since 2006; *b* 10 Nov 1950; *s* of David Foster Gretton and Patience Mary Gretton (*née* Lidderdale); *m* 197 Helen Jessica Morgan; two *s* one *d*. *Educ:* King Edward's Sch., Birmingham; Univ. o Durham (BA); Univ. of Edinburgh (LLB). WS 1980. Lectr, Sen. Lectr, and Reader, Univ of Edinburgh, 1981–94. FRSE 2002. *Publications:* The Law of Inhibition an Adjudication, 1996; (with K. Reid) Conveyancing (2005), 2005; contribs to books, an jls incl. Edinburgh Law Rev., Scots Law Times, Jl Business Law, Eur. Rev. of Private Law *Address:* University of Edinburgh, School of Law, Old College, South Bridge, Edinburg EH8 9YL; *e-mail:* G.Gretton@ed.ac.uk.

GRETTON, Vice Adm. Michael Peter, CB 1998; CVO 2005; Chairman, Wincheste and Eastleigh Healthcare NHS Trust, since 2007; Director, Ninety plc; *b* 14 March 194 *s* of Vice Adm. Sir Peter Gretton, KCB, DSO, OBE, DSC, MA and late Dorothy (*née* D Vivier); *m* 1973, Stephanie O'Neill; one *s* three *d*. *Educ:* Ampleforth Coll.; BRN Dartmouth; Trinity Coll., Oxford (BA PPE; MA). Joined RN, 1963; served HM Torquay, Tiger, Rothesay, Ark Royal and Bacchante; commanded: HMS Bossingto 1972–73; HMS Ambuscade, 1977–80; RCDS, 1987; commanded: HMS Invincibl 1988–90; NATO Standing Naval Force Atlantic, 1990–91; Dir of Naval Staff Dutie MoD, 1991–93; comd UK Task Force and NATO Anti-Submarine Warfare Strikin Force, 1993–94; Rep. of SACLANT in Europe, 1994–98. Dir, Duke of Edinburgh Award, 1998–2005; World Challenge Ltd, 2005–07. Chm., Hants and IoW Yout Options, 2007–. Governor: St Edward's Sch., Oxford, 1985–2008; Farleigh Sch., Re Rice, 1992–2004; St Mary's Sch., Shaftesbury, 1998–2008. Pres., RN RFU, 1993–9 Mem. Council, Tall Ships Youth Trust (formerly Sail Training Assoc.), 1999–. Chm HMS Whimbrell (1942–49) Battle of the Atlantic Meml, 2004–. FNI 1994. *Recreation* sport, sightseeing, listening to music. *Clubs:* Naval (Pres., 2005–); I Zingari.

GREVE, Prof. John; Professor of Social Policy and Administration, University of Leeds, 1974–87, now Emeritus; *b* 23 Nov. 1927; *s* of Steffen A. and Ellen C. Greve; *m* (marr. diss. 1986); one *s* one *d*. *Educ:* elementary and secondary Schs in Cardiff; London Sch. of Economics (BSc(Econ)). Various jobs, incl. Merchant Navy, Youth Employment Service, and insurance, 1946–55; student, 1955–58; research work, then Univ. teaching, 1958–. Has worked in Norway at research institutes. Community Programmes Dept, Home Office, 1969–74; Prof. of Social Admin, Univ. of Southampton, 1969–74. Hon. Vis. Prof., 1987–88, Hon. Sen. Res. Fellow, 1988–2002, Univ. of York. Chm., Care and Support Services Ltd, 1995–97. Mem., Royal Commn on Distribution of Income and Wealth, 1974–79; directed GLC Enquiry into Homelessness in London, 1985–86; Member: Bd, East Thames Housing Group (formerly Mem. Management Cttee, E London Housing Assoc.), 1988–98; York CHC, 1997–2002; Cardiff CHC, 2004–. *Publications:* The Housing Problem, 1961 (and 1969); London's Homeless, 1964; Private Landlords in England, 1965; (with others) Comparative Social Administration, 1969, 2nd edn 1972; Housing, Planning and Change in Norway, 1970; Voluntary Housing in Scandinavia, 1971; (with others) Homelessness in London, 1971; Low Incomes in Sweden, 1978; (jtly) Sheltered Housing for the Elderly, 1983; Homelessness in Britain, 1990, rev. edn 1991; Poland—the reform of housing, 1994; various articles and papers, mainly on social problems, policies and administration, a few short stories. *Recreations:* walking, painting, listening to music, writing, good company. *Address:* 39 Beulah Road, Rhiwbina, Cardiff CF14 6LU.

GREVILLE, family name of **Earl of Warwick**.

GREVILLE, Brig. Phillip Jamieson, CBE 1972; freelance writer on defence, foreign affairs and Australian history; Australian Director, International Institute for Prisoners of War, since 1992; *b* 12 Sept. 1925; *s* of Col S. J. Greville, OBE and Mrs D. M. Greville; *m* 1948, June Patricia Anne Martin; two *s* one *d* (and one *s* one *d* decd). *Educ:* RMC Duntroon; Sydney Univ. (BEng). 2/8 Field Co., 2nd AIF, New Guinea, 1945; 1 RAR Korea (POW), 1951–53; Senior Instructor SME Casula, 1953–55; CRE, RMC Duntroon, 1955–58; Staff Coll., Camberley and Transportation Trng UK, 1959–61; Dir of Transportation AHQ, 1962–65; GSO1 1st Div., 1966; CE Eastern Comd, 1969–71; Comdr 1st Australian Logistic Support Group, Vietnam, 1971; Actg Comdr 1st Australian Task Force, Vietnam, 1971–72 (CBE); Dir of Transport, 1973–74; Dir Gen., Logistics, 1975–76; Comdr, Fourth Mil. District, 1977–80, retired. Adelaide Advertiser: Defence Writer, 1980–86; Pacific Defence Reporter, 1987–92. Dir, Dominant Australia Pty, 1982–86. Nat. Pres., RUSI of Aust., 1983–84. FIE(Aust), FCILT. *Publications:* A Short History of Victoria Barracks Paddington, 1969; The Central Organisation for War and its Application to Movements, 1975, Sapper series (RE Officers in Australia); The Army Portion of the National Estate, 1977; Why Australia Should Not Ratify the New Law of War, 1989; vol. 4, History of the Royal Australian Engineers, 1999. *Recreation:* golf. *Address:* 3 River Downs Crescent, River Downs, Qld 4212, Australia. *Club:* United Services (Brisbane).

GREWAL, Harnam Singh, CBE 1990; ED 1976; Secretary for the Civil Service, Government Secretariat, Hong Kong, 1987–90, retired; *b* 5 Dec. 1937; *s* of late Joginder Singh Grewal and Ajaib Kaur; *m* 1973, Shiv Pal Kaur Chima; one *s* one *d*. *Educ:* Sir Ellis Kadoorie Sch.; King's Coll., Univ. of Hong Kong (BA Hons 1959; DipEd 1960); Pembroke Coll., Cambridge Univ. (BA 1962; MA 1974). Asst Educn Officer, Hong Kong, 1962; Admin Officer, 1964; Dist Officer, Tai Po, 1970; Dep. Dir of Urban Services, New Territories, 1976; Dep. Sec. for CS, 1980; Comr of Customs and Excise, 1984; Sec. for Transport, 1986. Royal Hong Kong Regt (The Volunteers), 1963–84, Major (retd); Hon. Col, 1987–90. *Recreation:* lawn bowls. *Address:* 3495 Cadboro Bay Road, Victoria, BC V8R 5K7, Canada.

GREY; *see* De Grey.

GREY, family name of **Earl Grey**.

GREY, 6th Earl *cr* 1806; **Richard Fleming George Charles Grey;** Bt 1746; Baron Grey, 1801; Viscount Howick, 1806; *b* 5 March 1939; *s* of late Albert Harry George Campbell Grey (Trooper, Canadian Army Tanks, who *d* on active service, 1942) and Vera Helen Louise Harding; *S* cousin, 1963; *m* 1st, 1966, Margaret Ann (marr. diss. 1974), *e d* of Henry Bradford, Ashburton; 2nd, 1974, Stephanie Caroline, *o d* of Donald Gaskell-Brown and formerly wife of Surg.-Comdr Neil Leicester Denham, RN. *Educ:* Hounslow Coll.; Hammersmith Coll. of Bldg (Quantity Surveying). Public relations consultant. Chm., London Cremation Co., 1992–; Dir, Covent Garden Quality, 1993–. President: Assoc. of Cost and Executive Accountants, 1978; Cremation Soc. of GB, 1992–. Mem., Liberal Party. *Recreations:* golf, sailing. *Heir:* *b* Philip Kent Grey [*b* 11 May 1940; *m* 1968, Ann Catherine, *y d* of Cecil Applegate, Kingsbridge, Devon; one *s* one *d*].

GREY de WILTON, Viscount; Julian Francis Martin Grosvenor; *b* 8 June 1959; *s* of Earl of Wilton, *qv*; *m* 1987, Danielle (marr. diss. 1989), sixth *d* of Theo Rossi, Sydney, Australia; one *s* (*b* 2006).

GREY OF CODNOR, 6th Baron *cr* 1397 (in abeyance 1496–1989); **Richard Henry Cornwall-Legh;** *b* 14 May 1936; *s* of 5th Baron Grey of Codnor, CBE and Dorothy (*d* 1993), *er d* of J. W. Scott; *S* father, 1996; *m* 1974, Joanna Storm, 7th *d* of Sir Kenelm Cayley, 10th Bt; three *s* one *d*. *Educ:* Stowe. High Sheriff, 1993, DL 1995, Cheshire. *Heir:* *s* Hon. Richard Stephen Cayley Cornwall-Legh [*b* 24 March 1976; *m* 2005, Annie Helen, *y d* of Frederick Riches; one *s*]. *Address:* High Legh House, Knutsford, Cheshire WA16 0QR. *Clubs:* Boodle's, MCC.

GREY, Alan Hartley, OBE 1999; HM Diplomatic Service, retired; Judge, Council of Europe Administrative Tribunal (formerly Member, Council of Europe Appeals Board), 1993–96; *b* 26 June 1925; *s* of William Hartley Grey and Gladys Grey; *m* 1950, Joan Robinson (*d* 1985); one *s* one *d*. *Educ:* Bootle Secondary Sch. for Boys. RAF, 1943–48; Foreign Service (Br. B), 1948; Tel Aviv, 1949; Tabriz and Khorramshahr, 1950–52; 3rd Sec., Belgrade, 1952–54; Vice-Consul, Dakar, 1954–57; Second Sec. (Commercial), Helsinki, 1958–61; FO, 1961–64; Second Sec. (Econ.), Paris, 1964–66; FO (later FCO), 1966–70; Consul (Commercial), Lille, 1970–74; FCO, 1974–82; Ambassador at Libreville, 1982–84; re-employed in FCO (as Staff Assessor), 1985–90. Vice Chm., Lambeth Horticl Soc., 1998–. *Recreation:* gardening.

GREY, Sir Anthony (Dysart), 7th Bt *cr* 1814; former Inspector, Department of Industrial Affairs, Government of Western Australia; *b* 19 Oct. 1949; *s* of Edward Elton Grey (*d* 1962) (*o s* of 6th Bt) and of Nancy, *d* of late Francis John Meagher, Perth, WA; *S* grandfather, 1974; *m* 1970 (marr. diss.); *m* 1993, Alison Turner; one *s* three *d*. *Educ:* Guildford Grammar School, WA. *Recreations:* fishing, painting. *Heir:* *s* Thomas Jasper Grey, *b* 30 April 1998. *Address:* 86 Kingsway Gardens, 38 Kings Park Road, W Perth, WA 6005, Australia.

GREY, Dame Beryl (Elizabeth), DBE 1988 (CBE 1973); a Director, Royal Opera House, 1999–2003; Prima Ballerina, Sadler's Wells Ballet, now Royal Ballet, 1941–57; Artistic Director, London Festival Ballet, 1968–79; *b* London, 11 June 1927; *d* of late Arthur Ernest Groom; *m* 1950, Dr Sven Gustav Svenson (*d* 2008); one *s*. *Educ:* Dame Alice Owens Girls' Sch., London. Professional training: Madeline Sharp Sch., Sadler's Wells Sch. (Schol.), de Vos Sch. Début Sadler's Wells Co., 1941, with leading Ballerina rôles following same year in Les Sylphides, The Gods Go A'Begging, Le Lac des Cygnes, Act II, Comus. First full-length ballet, Le Lac des Cygnes on 15th birthday, 1942. Has appeared since in leading rôles of many ballets including: Sleeping Beauty, Giselle, Sylvia, Checkmate, Ballet Imperial, Donald of the Burthens, Homage, Birthday Offering, The Lady and the Fool. Film: The Black Swan (3 Dimensional Ballet Film), 1952. Left Royal Ballet, Covent Garden, Spring 1957, to become free-lance ballerina. Regular guest appearances with Royal Ballet at Covent Garden and on European, African, American and Far Eastern Tours. Guest Artist, London's Festival Ballet in London and abroad, 1958–64. First Western ballerina to appear with Bolshoi Ballet: Moscow, Leningrad, Kiev, Tiflis, 1957–58; First Western ballerina to dance with Chinese Ballet Co. in Peking and Shanghai, 1964. Engagements and tours abroad include: Central and S America, Mexico, Rhodesia and S Africa, Canada, NZ, Lebanon, Germany, Norway, Sweden, Denmark, Finland, Belgium, Holland, France, Switzerland, Italy, Portugal, Austria, Czechoslovakia, Poland, Rumania; Producer: Sleeping Beauty, 1967; Swan Lake, 1972, London Fest. Ballet; Giselle, Western Australia Ballet, 1984, 1986; Sleeping Beauty, Royal Swedish Ballet, Stockholm, 1985, 2002. Regular television and broadcasts in England and abroad; concert narrator. Dir-Gen., Arts Educational Trust and Teacher Trng Coll., 1966–68. Vice-Pres., Royal Acad. of Dancing, 1980– (Exec. Mem., 1982–89); Pres., Dance Council of Wales, 1981–2004; Life Pres., ISTD, 2002– (FISTD 1960; Mem. Council, 1966–91; Chm., 1984–91; Pres., 1991–2001; ISTD Imperial Award for Outstanding Service, 1987, Lifetime Achievement Award, 2004); Mem. Bd, BRB, 1995–99; Mem. Council, 1984–96, Mem. Exec., 1995–96, Council for Dance Educn and Training. Trustee: London City Ballet, 1978–92; Adeline Genée Theatre, 1982–90; Royal Ballet Benevolent Fund, 1982– (Chm. Trustees, 1992–); Dance Critics Circle, 2005– (Patron, 2005–); Vice Chm., Dance Teachers Benevolent Fund, 1984–2004 (Trustee, 1981–); President: Keep Fit Assoc., 1992–93; E Grinstead Operatic Soc., 1986–; English Nat. Ballet, 2005–; Vice-President: Music Therapy Charity, 1980–; British Fedn of Music Festivals, 1985–; London Ballet Circle, 2001–. Governor: Dame Alice Owens Girls' Sch., London, 1960–77; Frances Mary Buss Foundn, 1963–72; Royal Ballet Cos, 1993–2002 (Vice Chm. Govs, 1995–2002). Patron: British Sch. of Osteopathy, 1987–; Benesh Inst. of Choreology, 1988–; Dancers' Career Develt (formerly Dancers' Resettlement Trust), 1988–; Nature Cure Clinic, 1988–2005; Tanya Bayona Princess Poutiatine Acad. of Ballet, Malta, 1988–2005; Language of Dance Centre, 1990–; Friends of Sadler's Wells Theatre, 1991–; Pro-Dogs, 1991–2005; Osteopathic Centre for Children, 1992–; Furlong Research Foundn, 1993– (Trustee, 2005–); AMBER Trust, 1995–; Theatre Design Trust, 1995–; Legat Foundn, 1998–; Sussex Opera and Ballet Soc., 2001–; Discs, 2005– (Trustee, 1993–2005); Early Dance Circle, 2007–; Vice-Patron, BASE, 2007–. Hon. DMus: Leicester, 1970; Univ. of London, 1996; Hon. DLitt: City, 1974; Buckingham, 1993; Hon. DEd CNAA, 1989. Queen Elizabeth II Coronation Award, Royal Acad. of Dancing, 1995; Critics' Circle Award for Service to Dance, 2002. *Publications:* Red Curtain Up, 1958; Through the Bamboo Curtain, 1965; My Favourite Ballet Stories, 1981; *relevant publications:* biographical studies (by Gordon Anthony), 1952, (by Pigeon Crowle), 1952; Beryl Grey, Dancers of Today (by Hugh Fisher), 1955; Beryl Grey, a biography (by David Gillard), 1977. *Recreations:* music, opera, reading, swimming. *Address:* Fernhill, Priory Road, Forest Row, Sussex RH18 5JE. *T:* (01342) 822539.

GREY, John Egerton, CB 1980; Clerk Assistant and Clerk of Public Bills, House of Lords, 1974–88; *b* 8 Feb. 1929; *s* of late John and Nancy Grey; *m* 1961, Patricia Hanna (*d* 2007); two adopted *s*. *Educ:* Dragon Sch., Oxford; Blundell's; Brasenose Coll., Oxford. MA, BCL. Called to the Bar, Inner Temple, 1954; practised at Chancery Bar, 1954–59. Clerk in Parliament Office, House of Lords, 1959–88. Adviser, Colchester CAB, 1989–99. *Recreations:* gardening, boating. *Address:* 51 St Peters Road, West Mersea, Colchester, Essex CO5 8LL. *T:* (01206) 383007. *Clubs:* Arts; West Mersea Yacht.

GREY, Maj.-Gen. John St John, CB 1987; *b* 6 June 1934; *s* of late Major Donald John Grey, RM and Doris Mary Grey (*née* Beavan); *m* 1958, Elisabeth Ann (*née* Langley); one *s* one *d*. *Educ:* Christ's Hospital. rcds, ndc, psc(M), osc(US). Commissioned 2/Lt 1952; Commando service, Malta, Egypt, Cyprus, 1955–64; Cruiser HMS Lion as OC RM, 1964–65; Instructor, Army Sch. of Infantry, 1967–69; US Marine Corps, 1970–71; Commanded 45 Cdo Gp (incl. tours in N Ireland and Arctic Norway), 1976–78; Mil. Sec. and Col Ops/Plans, MoD, 1979–84; Maj.-Gen. RM Commando Forces, 1984–87; RM COS, 1987–88, retired. Clerk, Pewterers' Co., 1988–96. Col Comdt RM, 1995–98. Pres., SSAFA, Devon, 1993–2007. Mem. Council, Exeter and Dist, ESU, 2000–. Trustee, Northcott Devon Foundn. *Recreations:* sailing, walking. *Address:* c/o Lloyds TSB, 19–20 Wellington Street, Teignmouth, S Devon TQ14 8HW. *Clubs:* Army and Navy; Royal Naval Sailing Association (Portsmouth); Royal Marines Sailing.

GREY, Robin Douglas; QC 1979; a Recorder of the Crown Court, 1979–99; *b* 23 May 1931; *s* of Dr Francis Temple Grey, MA, MB, and Eglantine Grey; *m* 1st, 1972, Berenice Anna Wheatley (marr. diss.); one *s* one *d*; 2nd, 1993, Mrs Annick Regnault. *Educ:* Summer Fields Prep. Sch., Oxford; Eastbourne Coll.; London Univ. (LLB Hons). Called to the Bar, Gray's Inn, 1957. Crown Counsel, Colonial Legal Service, Aden, 1959–63 (Actg Registrar Gen. and Actg Attorney Gen. for short periods); practising barrister, 1963–; Dep. Circuit Judge, 1977. FCO Consultant to Govt of Russian Fedn, 1993–; led FCO team to Moscow on Jury Trials, 1993. Chm., Home Office Police Appeals Tribunals, 1990–2006; Legal Assessor to GMC, 1995–2008. Member: Internat. Bar Assoc., 1994; Cttee, Criminal Bar Assoc., 1990–93 (Chm., Internat. Sub-Cttee, 1993); Cttee, European Criminal Bar Assoc., 1998–; British Acad. of Forensic Sciences. *Recreations:* tennis, golf, fishing. *Address:* Queen Elizabeth Building, Temple, EC4Y 9BS. *T:* (020) 7583 5766; 184 Bromyard House, Bromyard Avenue, W3 7BN. *Clubs:* Hurlingham, New Cavendish.

GREY, Wilfrid Ernest G.; *see* Grenville-Grey.

GREY-THOMPSON, Dame Tanni (Carys Davina), DBE 2005 (OBE 2000; MBE 1993); wheelchair athlete; *b* 26 July 1969; *d* of Peter Alexander Harvey Grey and Sulwen Davina Grey (*née* Jones); *m* 1999, Dr (Robert) Ian George Thompson; one *d*. *Educ:* Loughborough Univ. (BA Hons Politics & Admin 1991). Develt Officer, UK Athletics, 1996–2000. Member Council: Sports Council for Wales, 1996–2002; UK Sport, 1998–2003; Dep. Chm., UK Lottery Sports Fund; Member Board: Winston Churchill Meml Trust, 2006–; V, 2006–. Has represented GB at 100m–800m distances, 1987–: competitor: Paralympics, 1988, 1992, 1996, 2000 and 2004 (winner 16 medals, incl. 11 Gold Medals); Olympics, 1992 and 1996 (in exhibn 800m), 2000, 2004; World Championships (winner 11 medals, incl. 5 Gold Medals); has broken over 30 world records; winner, London Marathon, 1992, 1994, 1996, 1998, 2001, 2002. Pro-Vice-Chancellor, Staffordshire Univ., 2004–. Hon. Fellow: UWCC, 1997; UWIC, Swansea Univ., Coll. of Ripon and York St John, 2001; John Moores Univ., Liverpool, 2004. Hon. MA Loughborough, 1994; Hon. Dr Sport Staffordshire, 1998; Hon. DBA Southampton, 1998; Hon. MSc Manchester Metropolitan, 1998; DUniv: Surrey, 2000;

Open, 2004; Hon. Master Teesside, 2001; Hon. Dr: Leeds Metropolitan, 2001; Wales, Loughborough, 2002; Newcastle, Oxford Brookes, Sheffield Hallam, 2005; Hull, 2006; Hon. LLD: Exeter, 2003; Heriot-Watt, 2004; Leicester, 2005. *Publications:* Seize the Day (autobiog.), 2001; Aim High, 2007. *Address:* c/o Creating Excellence, Equity House, 1 Knight Street, South Woodham Ferrers, Chelmsford, Essex CM3 5SE. *T:* and *Fax:* (01245) 328303.

GREY-WILSON, Christopher, PhD; VMH; Editor, Alpine Garden Society, since 1990; *b* 28 Sept. 1944; *s* of late Vyvyan William Grey-Wilson and Jean Grey-Wilson (*née* Parsley); *m* 1978, Christine Mary Dent; one *d. Educ:* Churston Ferrers Grammar Sch.; Wye Coll., Univ. of London (BSc Hort. 1967); Reading Univ. (PhD 1976). Botanist (PSO), Royal Botanic Gardens, Kew, 1968–90. Editor: Curtis's Botanical Magazine, incl. Kew Magazine, 1983–89; The New Plantsman, subseq. The Plantsman, 2001–05. Botanical Scientific expeditions: Iran and Afghanistan, 1971; Nepal, 1973, 1978, 1989; Kenya and Tanzania, 1976, 1979; Sri Lanka, 1978; W China, 1987, 1994. *Publications:* The Alpine Flowers of Britain and Europe, 1979, 2nd edn 1995; Impatiens of Africa, 1980; (jtly) Bulbs, 1981; (jtly) Gardening on Walls, 1983; The Genus Cyclamen, 1988; The Genus Dionysia, 1989; The Illustrated Flora of Britain and Northern Europe, 1989; Poppies, 1993, 2nd edn 2000; Mediterranean Wild Flowers, 1993; The Alpine Garden, 1994; (jtly) Gardening with Climbers, 1997; Cyclamen, 1997, 2nd edn 2002; Clematis: the genus, 2000; How to Identify Wild Flowers, 2000; Wildflowers of Britain and Northern Europe, 2003; numerous scientific papers in Kew Bulletin, gen. papers in The Garden, Bull. of Alpine Garden Soc., The Alpine Gardener, Gardens News and The New Plantsman. *Recreations:* gardening, walking, drawing, photography, listening to classical music. *Address:* Red Lion Barn, East Church Street, Kenninghall, Norfolk NR16 2EP.

GRIBBIN, John Richard, PhD; writer; Visiting Fellow in Astronomy, University of Sussex, since 1993; *b* 19 March 1946; *s* of William James Gribbin and Lilla (*née* Reed); *m* 1966, Mary Murray; two *s. Educ:* Univ. of Sussex (BSc Physics 1966; MSc Astronomy 1967); University Coll., Cambridge (PhD Astrophysics 1971). Asst Editor, Nature, 1970–75; Vis. Fellow, Sci. Policy Res. Unit, 1975–78; Physics Consultant, New Scientist, 1978–98. FRAS 1972; FRMetS 1985; FRSL 1999. *Publications:* (jtly) The Jupiter Effect, 1974; Our Changing Climate, 1975; Forecasts, Famines and Freezes, 1976; Galaxy Formation, 1976; Astronomy for the Amateur, 1976; Our Changing Universe, 1976; Our Changing Planet, 1977; White Holes, 1977; (ed and contrib.) Climatic Change, 1978; The Climatic Threat, 1978 (US edn as What's Wrong with our Weather?); This Shaking Earth, 1978; Timewarps, 1979; Climate and Mankind, 1979; Weather Force, 1979; (jtly) The Sixth Winter (novel), 1979; Future Worlds, 1979; The Strangest Star, 1980 (US edn as The Death of the Sun); Carbon Dioxide, Climate and Man, 1981; Genesis, 1981; (jtly) The Jupiter Effect Reconsidered, 1982; (ed and contrib.) Cosmology Today, 1982; (jtly) The Weather Book, 1982; (jtly) The Monkey Puzzle, 1982; Brother Esau (novel), 1982; Future Weather, 1982; Beyond the Jupiter Effect, 1983; Spacewarps, 1983; (jtly) The Redundant Male, 1984; In Search of Schrödinger's Cat, 1984; In Search of the Double Helix, 1985; (ed and contrib.) The Breathing Planet, 1986; In Search of the Big Bang, 1986, rev. edn 1998; The Omega Point, 1987; The Hole in the Sky, 1988; (jtly) Double Planet (novel), 1991; Father to the Man (novel), 1989; (jtly) Cosmic Coincidences, 1989; (jtly) Winds of Change, 1989; Hothouse Earth, 1990; (jtly) The Cartoon History of Time, 1990; Blinded by the Light, 1991; (jtly) Reunion (novel), 1991; (jtly) Ragnarok (novel), 1991; (jtly) The Matter Myth, 1991; (jtly) Stephen Hawking, 1992; In Search of the Edge of Time, 1992 (US edn as Unveiling the Edge of Time); Innervisions, 1993; In the Beginning, 1993; (jtly) Albert Einstein, 1993; Schrödinger's Kittens and the Search for Reality, 1995; (jtly) Darwin, 1995; (jtly) Origins, 1997; Cosmology, 1998; Watching the Universe, 1998 (US edn as The Case of the Missing Neutrinos); In Search of SUSY, 1998 (US edn as The Search for the Superstrings); (jtly) Empire of the Sun, 1998; (ed and contrib.) A Brief History of Science, 1998; The Birth of Time, 1999; The Little Book of Science, 1999; Dalla scimmia all'universo, 1999; Get a Grip on the New Physics, 1999; (jtly) Deep Space, 1999; (jtly) The First Chimpanzee, 2001; Space, 2001; (jtly) XTL, 2001; (jtly) The Mating Game, 2001; Science: a history, 2002; Quantum Physics, 2002; Deep Simplicity, 2004; The Fellowship, 2005; The Origins of the Future, 2006; The Universe: a biography, 2007; *with Mary Gribbin:* Weather, 1985; The One Per Cent Advantage, 1988; Children of the Ice, 1990; Too Hot to Handle?: the greenhouse effect, 1992; Being Human, 1993; Time and Space, 1994; Companion to the Cosmos, 1996; Fire on Earth, 1996; Watching the Weather, 1996; Richard Feynman, 1997; Time and the Universe, 1997; Curie, Halley, Newton, Darwin, Faraday, Galileo, and Einstein, all in In 90 Minutes series, 1997; Q is for Quantum, 1998; Almost Everyone's Guide to Science, 1998; Chaos and Uncertainty, 1999; Stardust, 2000; Ice Age, 2001; Big Numbers, 2003; How Far is Up?, 2003; FitzRoy, 2003; The Science of Philip Pullman's His Dark Materials, 2003; Deep Simplicity, 2004; Inventing the Future, 2004; Annus Mirabilis: Einstein in 1905, 2005; Flower Hunters, 2008. *Recreations:* watching Kent CCC, collecting vinyl 45 rpm records, travel. *Address:* Astronomy Group, University of Sussex, Falmer, Brighton BN1 9RH; *e-mail:* j.r.gribbin@sussex.ac.uk.

GRIBBON, Deborah, PhD; Director, J. Paul Getty Museum, 2000–04; Vice President, J. Paul Getty Trust, 2000–04; *b* 11 June 1948; *d* of Daniel M. and Jane Gribbon; *m* 1976, Dr Winston Alt; two *d. Educ:* Wellesley Coll., Mass (BA Art Hist. 1970); Harvard Univ. (MA Fine Arts 1972; PhD 1982). Teaching Fellow, Dept of Fine Arts, Harvard Univ., 1972–74; Curator, Isabella Stewart Gardner Mus., 1976–84; Instructor, Extension Sch., Harvard Univ., 1982–84; J. Paul Getty Museum: Asst Dir, 1984–87; Associate Dir for Curatorial Affairs, 1987–91; Associate Dir and Chief Curator, 1991–98; Dep. Dir and Chief Curator, 1998–2000. Mem. Bd, Courtauld Inst., 2001; Mem., Internat. Women's Forum, 2003–. Phi Beta Kappa, 1970. *Publications:* Sculpture in the Isabella Stewart Gardner Museum, 1978; (with J. Walsh) The J. Paul Getty Museum and its Collections: a museum for a new century, 1997; contrib. articles to Burlington Mag. and Connoisseur.

GRIBBON, Edward John; JP; Under Secretary, Board of Inland Revenue, 1991–2000; Director, Compliance Division, 1996–2000; *b* 10 July 1943; *s* of late Henry Derwent Gribbon and Dorothy Gribbon (*née* Boyd); *m* 1968, Margaret Nanette Flanagan; one *s* two *d. Educ:* Coleraine Academical Instn; Univ. of London (LLB). FCA. Qualified as Chartered Accountant, 1965; joined Inland Revenue as HM Inspector of Taxes, 1966; HM Principal Inspector of Taxes, 1981; Dep. Dir of Operations, 1989; Dir, Business Profits Div., 1991–96. JP N Herts, 2002. Gov., N Herts Coll., 2004–. *Recreations:* family, photography, local church, ornithology, philately.

GRIBBON, Maj.-Gen. Nigel St George, OBE 1960; Assistant Chief of Staff, (Intelligence), Supreme Headquarters Allied Powers Europe, 1970–72; *b* Feb. 1917; *s* of late Brig. W. H. Gribbon, CMG, CBE; *m* 1943, Rowan Mary MacLiesh; two *s* one *d. Educ:* Rugby Sch.; RMC Sandhurst. King's Own Royal Regt, 1937–42; Aldershot, 1937; Madras, 1938–39; Karachi, 1940; active service, Iraq, 1941–42 (Habbaniya-Felujah, 1942) (wounded); GSO3 10th Indian Div., 1942; Staff Coll. Quetta, 1943; G2 HQ 55 Inf. Div., 1944; Army Airborne Transport Develt Centre, 1945; Bde Major, 1st Parachute Bde, 1946; served Palestine, 1946, Trieste, 1947–48, GSO2 Jt Intelligence Cttee (Far E), 1948–50; RAF Staff Coll., 1947; DAAG WO, 1953–55; HK, 1954–55; OC 5 King's Own, 1958–60; AMS WO, 1960–62; Comdr 161 Bde, 1963–65; Canadian Nat. Defen Coll., 1965–66; DMC MoD, 1966–67; BGS (I) BAOR and ACOS Northern Army G 1967–69. Man. Dir, Partnerplan Public Affairs Ltd, 1973–75; BAC Delegate, Cong Atlantique, Paris, 1975; Man. Dir, Sallingbury Ltd, 1977–85 (Chm., 1975–77 a 1984–85); Sallingbury Casey Ltd, 1986–87; Dir, Gatewood Engineers Ltd, 1976–83; no exec. Dir, Chancellor Insurance Co. Ltd, 1986–92; Operational Planning Consulta Venice-Simplon Orient Express, 1980–84. Chm., 1982–97, Vice-Pres., 1997–2001, U Falkland Is Trust. Canada-UK Chamber of Commerce: Mem. Council, 1979–99; Chr Trade Cttee, 1980; Pres., 1981; Chm., Jt Cttee, Canada-UK and Canadian Chambers Commerce, 1982–91. Hd of Secretariat, European Channel Tunnel Gp and Public Affa Cttee, 1980–85; Chairman: Forces Financial Services, 1983–85; SHAPE Assoc. (U Chapter), 1984–; Member: Eur. Atlantic Gp, 1974–87; Council, British Atlantic Ctte 1975–93 (Mem. Exec. Cttee, 1983–88); Council, Mouvement Européen Franç (Londres), 1979–87; Council, Wyndham Place Trust, 1979–82; Cttee, Amer. Europe Atlantic Cttee, 1985–92; Adv. Cttee, Shackleton Meml Fund, 1995–97; Mil. Mem Canadian War Meml Foundn, 1988–94. Vice-Pres., King's Own Affairs, 1974–8 Founder and Vice-Pres., Lancaster Mil. Heritage Group, 2000–04. Associate, Arm Forces Art Soc., 2005–. Member: Woodland Trust; Exec. Council, Rugbeian Sc Commentator, BBC Radio 4, 1979–80; lectr on public affairs; organiser of chamber mus concerts, 1991–. Freeman, City of London; Liveryman, Worshipful Co. of Shipwrigh 1982–. *Recreation:* watercolour sketching. *Address:* Danny House, Hurstpierpoint, Sussex BN6 9BB. *Clubs:* Army and Navy (Mem., Gen. and Finance Cttees, 1989–92 Little Ship (Rear Commodore Training, 1978–80; Hon. Life Mem.).

GRICE, Ian Michael; Group Chief Executive, Alfred McAlpine plc, since 2003; *b* 2 Ma 1953; *s* of James Frederick and late Joan Grice; *m* Patricia; two *d. Educ:* Royal Gramm Sch., High Wycombe; Loughborough Univ. (BSc Hons Civil Engrg). MICE. Enginee John Laing plc, 1974–76; Mowlem plc, 1976–79; Kier plc, 1979–81; Mowlem pl 1981–95; Alfred McAlpine plc, 1995–. *Recreations:* golf, shooting, watching footbal walking. *Address:* Alfred McAlpine plc, Kinnaird House, 1 Pall Mall East, SW1Y 5AZ. (020) 7930 6255, *Fax:* (020) 7930 9860.

GRICE, Paul Edward; Clerk and Chief Executive, Scottish Parliament, since 1999; *b* Oct. 1961; *s* of Kenneth William Grice and Maureen (*née* Power); *m* 1987, Elaine Rosi two *d. Educ:* Archbishop Holgate's Sch., York; York Coll. of Arts and Technol.; Univ. Stirling (BSc Econs and Envmtl Sci.). Dept of Transport, 1985–87; DoE, 1987–9 Scottish Office, Edinburgh, 1992–99: Head of Housing and Urban Regeneration Br 1992–95; Head of Mgt and Change Unit, 1995–97; Head of Division, Constitutio Group: Referendum, Scotland Bill, 1997–98; Dir of Implementation, 1998–99. Mem. C Univ. of Stirling, 2005–. Hon. FRIAS 2006. *Recreations:* squash, cycling, reading, theatr ballet. *Address:* Scottish Parliament, Holyrood, Edinburgh EH99 1SP. *T:* (0131) 348 5255

GRIDLEY, family name of **Baron Gridley**.

GRIDLEY, 3rd Baron *cr* 1955; **Richard David Arnold Gridley;** Senior Lecturer i Leisure and Tourism and Information Technology, South Downs College of Furthe Education, since 1995; *b* 22 Aug. 1956; *o s* of 2nd Baron Gridley and Edna Lesley, *e d* o Richard Wheen; *S* father, 1996; *m* 1st, 1979, Amanda Mackenzie (marr. diss.); 2nd, 198 Suzanne Elizabeth Hughes; one *s* one *d. Educ:* Monckton Combe; Portsmouth Polytech Univ. of Brighton (BA). Project manager, construction industry, 1980–92. Patron, Car for the Wild Internat., 1996. *Address:* 68 Freshfield Gardens, Waterlooville, Hants PO 7TL; *e-mail:* lordgrid@hotmail.com.

GRIERSON, Prof. Donald, OBE 2000; PhD, DSc; FRS 2000; FIBiol; Professor of Plan Physiology, Nottingham University, since 1986; *b* 1 Oct. 1945; *s* of John Harvey Grierso and Margaret (*née* Head); *m* 1965, Elizabeth Carole Judson; two *s* two *d. Educ:* Univ. of Anglia (BSc 1967); Univ. of Edinburgh (Ellis Prize in Physiol. 1970; PhD 1971); DS Nottingham 1999. FIBiol 1985. Plant Physiologist, British Sugar Corp. Res. Lab. Norwich, 1967–68; University of Nottingham: Asst Lectr in Plant Physiol., 1971–74 Lectr, 1974–82; Nuffield Foundn Sci. Res. Fellow, 1981–82; Reader, 1982–86; Head Dept of Physiol. and Envmtl Sci., 1988–91 and 1992–94; Plant Sci. Section, 1988–97 Plant Sci. Div., 1997–2002; Sch. of Bioscis, 2000–02; Pro-Vice-Chancellor for Res. an Industry, 2003–07. EMBO Res. Fellow, Genetics Dept, Univ. of Tubingen, 1975–76 Chm., Sainsbury Lab. Council, 2000–04. Hon. DSc l'Institut Nat. Polytechnique d Toulouse, 2000. Res. Medal, RASE, 1990. *Publications:* (with S. N. Covey) Plan Molecular Biology, 1984, 2nd edn 1988 (English, Mandarin Chinese and Spanish edns) edited: (with H. Smith) The Molecular Biology of Plant Development, 1982; (with H Thomas) Developmental Mutants in Higher Plants, 1987; (with G. W. Lycett) Geneti Engineering of Crop Plants, 1990; (with G. W. Lycett and G. A. Tucker) Mechanisms and Applications of Gene Silencing, 1996; Plant Biotechnology, vol. I, 1991, vol. II, 1991, vol III, 1993; contrib. numerous refereed scientific papers and articles. *Recreations:* walking boating, gardening. *Address:* Plant Sciences Division, School of Biosciences, University o Nottingham, Sutton Bonington Campus, Loughborough LE12 5RD. *T:* (0115) 951 6333.

GRIERSON, Sir Ronald (Hugh), Kt 1990; Vice-Chairman, General Electric Co., 1968–91; Chairman: GEC International, 1991–95; Advisory Board, Blackstone Group, since 1989; Bain & Co. International, since 1988; *b* Nürnberg, Bavaria, 1921; *s* of Mr and Mrs E. J. Griessmann (name changed by Deed Poll in 1943); *m* 1966, (Elizabeth) Heather, Viscountess Bearsted (*d* 1993), *er d* of Mr and Mrs G. Firmston-Williams; one *s*, and one step *d. Educ:* Realgymnasium, Nürnberg; Lycée Pasteur, Paris; Highgate Sch., London; Balliol Coll., Oxford. Served HM Forces 1940–47 (despatches); TA, 1948–54. Staff Mem., The Economist, 1947–48; S. G. Warburg & Co., 1948–86 (Dir, 1958–68 and 1980–86); Dep. Chm. and Man. Dir, IRC, 1966–67; Chm., Orion Bank, 1971–73; Dir-Gen., Industrial and Technological Affairs, EEC, 1973–74; Sen. Partner, Panmure Gordon & Co., 1974–76. Board Member: BAC, 1970–71; Internat. Computers, 1974–76; Davy Internat., 1969–73; Nat. Bus Co., 1984–86; RJR Nabisco Inc. (formerly R. J. Reynolds), 1977–89; Chrysler Corp., 1983–91; W. R. Grace & Co., 1987–94; Daily Mail & Gen. Trust, 1994–2001; Chime Communications, 1998–2003. Chairman: European Orgn for Cancer Treatment Res., 1976–2000; South Bank Bd, 1984–90. Mem., Bd of Trustees, Phillips Collection, Washington, 1980–98. Member: Atlantic Coll. Council, 1960–70; Harvard Coll. Faculty, 1964–65; CNAA, 1978–84; Arts Council of GB, 1984–88; Ernst von Siemens Foundn, 1977–98; Bd of Visitors, N Carolina Sch. of the Arts, 1984–90; European Arts Foundn, 1987–88; Trustee: Prince of Liechtenstein Foundn, 1991–; European Studies Foundn, Oxford Univ., 1991–; Royal Acad., 2003–. Hon. Dr of Law, Grove City Coll., USA, 1986. Commander: Order of Merit (Italy), 1980; Légion d'honneur (France), 1994; Order of Merit (Austria), 2002; SMO (Malta), 2006; Comdr's Cross, Order of Merit (Germany), 1993. *Address:* 40 Berkeley Square, W1J 5AL. *Clubs:* White's, Pratt's, Beefsteak; Brook (New York).

GRIESE, Sister Carol, CHN; Religious Sister since 1970; *b* 26 Sept. 1945; *d* of Gwendoline and Donald Griese. *Educ:* Merrywood Grammar School, Bristol; King's College London (BA Hons English 1968); Clare Hall, Cambridge (Cert. Theol. 1970). Member, Community of the Holy Name, 1970–; Lay Rep. of Religious in General

Synod, 1980–95. Mem., Crown Appointments Commn, 1990–92. *Recreations:* reading, walking. *Address:* Convent of the Holy Name, Morley Road, Oakwood, Derby DE21 4QZ. *T:* (01332) 671716.

GRIEVE, Alan Thomas, CBE 2003; Chairman, Jerwood Foundation, since 1991; *b* 22 Jan. 1928; *s* of late Lewis Miller Grieve and Doris Lilian (*née* Amner); *m* 1st, 1957, Anne, *d* of Dr Lawrence Dulake (marr. diss. 1971); two *s* one *d*; 2nd, 1971, Karen Louise, *d* of late Michael de Sivrac Dunn; one *s* one *d*. *Educ:* Aldenham; Trinity Hall, Cambridge (MA, LLM). Nat. Service, 2nd Lieut, 14/20 King's Hussars; Capt., City of London Yeo., TA. Admitted solicitor, 1953; Senior Partner: Taylor & Humbert, 1979–82; Taylor Garrett, 1982–88; Consultant: Taylor Joynson Garrett, 1988–2002; Taylor Wessing, 2002–. Director: Baggeridge Brick plc, 1964–2003; Wilson Bowden plc, 1993–96, and other cos; Chm., Reliance Resources Ltd, 1978–97. Mem., Educnl Assets Bd, 1988–90. Chm., Racehorse Owners Award, 1978–99. Mem. Council, Royal Court Th., 2000–. Trustee: Med. Insce Agency Charity, 1992–98; Hereford Mappa Mundi Trustee Co. Ltd, 1998–; RCP, 2007– (Mem., F and GP Bd, 1986–92). Pres., Trinity Hall Assoc., Cambridge, 2001–03. Vice Cdre, Sea Cadets Assoc., 2001–. Patron, Brendoncare for the Elderly, 1993–; Ambassador, Samaritans, 1999–. Hon. FTCL 2002; Hon. FRCP 2002. *Publication:* Purchase Tax, 1958. *Recreations:* performing and visual arts, country life, collecting. *Address:* (office) 22 Fitzroy Square, W1T 6EN. *T:* (020) 7388 6287, *Fax:* (020) 7388 6289; Stoke Lodge, Clee Downton, Ludlow, Salop SY8 3EG. *T:* (01584) 823413, *Fax:* (01584) 823419. *Clubs:* Boodle's; Hawks (Cambridge); Baur au Lac (Zurich).

See also Baron Harlech.

GRIEVE, Dominic Charles Roberts; QC 2008; MP (C) Beaconsfield, since 1997; barrister; *b* 24 May 1956; *s* of William Percival Grieve, QC; *m* 1990, Caroline Hutton; two *s* (and one *s* decd). *Educ:* Westminster Sch.; Magdalen Coll., Oxford (MA Modern History). Called to the Bar, Middle Temple, 1980, Bencher, 2004. Mem., Hammersmith and Fulham LBC, 1982–86. Contested (C) Norwood, 1987. Opposition front bench spokesman: for Scotland and on constitutional affairs, 1999–2001; on home affairs, 2001–03; Shadow Attorney-Gen. and spokesman on community cohesion, 2003–08; Shadow Home Sec., 2008–. Member: Jt Select Cttee on Statutory Instruments, 1997–2001; Select Cttee on Envmtl Audit, 1997–2001. Chm. Res. Cttee, 1992–95, Chm. Exec. Cttee, 2006–, Soc. of Cons. Lawyers. Member: Council, Justice, 1997–; Franco-British Soc., 1997–; Luxembourg Soc., 1997–. Mem., London Dio. Synod, C of E, 1995–2001. *Recreations:* mountaineering, ski-ing, scuba diving, fell walking, travel, architecture. *Address:* House of Commons, SW1A 0AA. *T:* (020) 7219 3000; 1 Temple Gardens, EC4Y 9BB. *T:* (020) 7353 0407. *Club:* Carlton.

GRIEVE, Michael Robertson Crichton; QC 1998; a Recorder, since 2000; *b* 12 Aug. 1951; *s* of Hon. Lord Grieve, VRD and Lorna St John Grieve, *y d* of late Engineer Rear-Adm. E. P. St J. Benn, CB; *m* 1983, Nadine Hilary Dyer; one *s*. *Educ:* Edinburgh Acad.; Sedbergh Sch.; New Coll., Oxford (BA PPE 1st cl. Hons 1972). Called to the Bar, Middle Temple, 1975; in practice at the Bar, 1975–; an Asst Recorder, 1998–2000. *Recreations:* playing and watching football, tennis, music. *Address:* Doughty Street Chambers, 11 Doughty Street, WC1N 2PL. *T:* (020) 7404 1313. *Clubs:* Riverside Racquet, Queen's Park Rangers Football.

GRIEVES, David, CBE 1988; Vice Chairman, British Steel plc, 1991–94; Chairman, BSC Industry plc, 1995–98 (Deputy Chairman, 1980–95); *b* 10 Jan. 1933; *s* of Joseph and Isabel Grieves; *m* 1960, Evelyn Muriel Attwater; two *s*. *Educ:* Durham Univ. BSc. PhD. Graduate apprentice, United Steel cos, 1957; Labour Manager, Appleby Frodingham Steel Co., 1962; British Steel Corporation: Manager, Industrial Relations, S Wales Group, 1967; Gen. Man., Stocksbridge and Tinsley Park Works, 1971; Personnel Dir, Special Steels Div., 1973; Dir, Indust. Relations, 1975; Man. Dir, Personnel and Social Policy, 1977; Dir, BSC, later British Steel plc, 1983. Chairman: Avesta Sheffield, 1992–94; Xansa plc pension funds, 1995–2004. Mem. (non-exec.), Post Office, 1990–98. Mem., Employment Appeal Tribunal, 1983–2003. *Address:* 4 Oak Way, West Common, Harpenden, Herts AL5 2NT. *T:* (01582) 767425.

GRIEVES, John Kerr; Senior Partner, Freshfields, 1990–96; *b* 7 Nov. 1935; *s* of Thomas and Nancy Grieves; *m* 1961, Ann Gorrell (*née* Harris); one *s* one *d*. *Educ:* King's Sch., Worcester; Keble Coll., Oxford (MA Law); Harvard Business Sch. (AMP). Articled clerk and asst solicitor, Pinsent & Co., Birmingham, 1958–61; joined Freshfields, 1963; Partner, 1964–96; Deptl Man. Partner, Company Dept, 1974–78; Man. Partner, 1979–85; Head, Corporate Finance Group, 1985–89. Director: British Invisibles, 1992–96; Northern Electric plc, 1996–97; Enterprise Oil plc, 1996–2002; Barclays Private Bank Ltd, 1997–2006; Hillsdown Holdings plc, 1997–98; New Look Group plc, 1998–2004 (Chm., 2001–04); Chairman: First Leisure Corp. plc, 1998–2000; Esporta plc, 2000–02; Advr, Apax Partners, 1996–99. Mem., Reporting Financial Review Panel, 1998–. Officer, Order of the Crown (Belgium), 1993. *Recreations:* the arts (especially music), sport. *Address:* 7 Putney Park Avenue, SW15 5QN. *T:* (020) 8876 1207. *Club:* Athenæum.

GRIEW, Prof. Stephen, PhD; Emeritus Professor and Senior Scholar, Atkinson College, York University, Toronto, since 1993; Adjunct Professor of Gerontology, St Thomas University, Fredericton, 2001–08 (Visiting Professor, 1998–99); *b* 13 Sept. 1928; *e s* of late Harry and Sylvia Griew, London, England; *m* 1st, 1955, Jane le Geyt Johnson (marr. diss.); one *s* two *d* (and one *s* decd); 2nd, 1977, Eva Margareta Ursula, *d* of late Dr and Fru Johannes Ramberg, Stockholm, Sweden; one *d* and one step *s*. *Educ:* Univ. of London (BSc, Dip Psych); Univ. of Bristol (PhD). Vocational Officer, Min. of Labour, 1951–55; Univ. of Bristol: Research Worker, 1955–59; Lectr, 1959–63; Kenneth Craik Research Award, St John's Coll., Cambridge, 1960; Prof. of Psychology: Univ. of Otago, Dunedin, NZ, 1964–68 (Dean, Faculty of Science, 1967–68); Univ. of Dundee, 1968–72; Vice-Chancellor, Murdoch Univ., Perth, WA, 1972–77; Chm., Dept of Behavioural Science, Faculty of Medicine, Univ. of Toronto, 1977–80; Pres., 1980–85, University Prof., 1986–87, Athabasca Univ.; Dean, 1987–90, Prof. of Admin. Studies, 1990–93, Atkinson Coll., York Univ., Toronto; Pres., Senior Univ., Toronto, 1993–95; Adjunct Prof. of Psychol., 1993–, Dir, Inst. for Behavioural Res. in Health, 1996–97, Curtin Univ. of Technol., Perth, WA. Consultant, OECD, Paris, 1963–64; Expert, ILO, Geneva, 1966–67; Mem., Social Commn of Rehabilitation Internat., 1967–75; Consultant, Dept of Employment, 1970–72; Vis. Prof., Univ. of Western Ont., London, Canada, 1970 and 1971; Vis. Fellow, Wolfson Coll., Cambridge, 1985–86; Vis. Professorial Fellow, Curtin Univ. of Technol., Perth, 1993. Vice-Pres., Australian Council on the Ageing, 1975–76. FBPsS 1960; Fellow, Gerontological Soc. (USA), 1969. *Publications:* Beyond Permissiveness, 1992; handbooks and monographs on ageing and vocational rehabilitation, and articles in Jl of Gerontology and various psychological jls. *Recreations:* music, travel, writing. *Address:* Department of Gerontology, St Thomas University, Fredericton, NB E3B 5G3, Canada.

GRIFFEE, Andrew John; Controller, BBC English Regions, since 1999; *b* 25 Aug. 1961; *s* of John William Griffee and Kathleen Sandra Griffee; *m* 1988, Helen Caroline Emery; one *s* one *d*. *Educ:* Duke of York's Military Sch., Dover; Highbury Coll. of Technol. (NCTJ Proficiency 1981); Univ. of Manchester (BA 1st cl. Hons 1986); Stanford Univ. (Exec. Develt Prog. 2001). Reporter: Poole and Dorset Herald, 1982–86; Northern Echo, 1986–87; Bath Evening Chronicle, 1987–89; Asst News Editor, BBC Bristol, 1989–92; Editor, News and Current Affairs, 1992–96, Head of Regl and Local Progs, 1996–99, BBC South. Member: RTS (W Mids; former Patron); Radio Acad. *Address:* BBC English Regions, Level 10, The Mailbox, Royal Mail Street, Birmingham B1 1XL.

GRIFFIN, Major Sir (Arthur) John (Stewart), KCVO 1990 (CVO 1974; MVO 1967); Press Secretary to HM Queen Elizabeth the Queen Mother, 1956–91; *b* 1924; *s* of Arthur Wilfrid Michael Stewart Griffin and Florence May Griffin; *m* 1962, Henrietta Montagu Douglas Scott (*d* 2008); two *s*. *Educ:* Harrow School. Regular Army Officer, The Queen's Bays, later The Queen's Dragoon Guards, 1942–58. *Recreations:* cricket, fishing, shooting. *Address:* Barton's Cottage, Bushy Park, Teddington, Middx TW11 0EA. *Club:* MCC.

GRIFFIN, Avril; *see* MacRory, A.

GRIFFIN, Prof. George Edward, PhD; FRCP, FMedSci; Professor of Infectious Diseases and Medicine, since 1992, Chairman, Department of Cellular and Molecular Medicine, since 2003, and Vice Principal for Research, since 2004, St George's, University of London (formerly St George's Hospital Medical School); *b* 27 Feb. 1947; *s* of Herbert Griffin and Enid Mary Griffin (*née* Borril); *m* 1972, Daphne Joan Haylor (*d* 1998), Romford; two *s* one *d*. *Educ:* Malet Lambert Grammar Sch., Kingston upon Hull; King's Coll., London (BSc); St George's Hosp. Med. Sch. (MB BS); Univ. of Hull (PhD 1974); Harvard Univ. (Harkness Fellow). MRCP 1979, FRCP 1988. Registrar and Tutor in Medicine, RPMS, 1977–78; St George's Hospital Medical School: Lectr in Medicine, 1978–82; Wellcome Trust Sen. Lectr, 1982–90; Dir, Wellcome Trust Clinical Tropical Unit, 1994–; Chm., Dept of Internal Medicine, 1994–; Hon. Cons. Physician, St George's Hosp., 1988–. Vis. Prof. of Medicine, Univ. of Michigan, 1992–. Chm., Adv. Cttee on Dangerous Pathogens, DoH, 2005– (Mem., 1994–98); Expert Advr, H of L Select Cttee on Fighting Infection, 2002–03. Wellcome Trust: Member: Infection and Immunity Panel, 1989–94; Tropical Interest Gp, 1991–94; Internat. Interest Gp, 1991–; Medical Research Council: Chm., Cttee for Develt and Implementation of Vaccines, 1994–; Member: Physiological Medicine and Infection Bd, 1994–; AIDS Vaccine Cttee, 1995–; HIV Virucidal Cttee, 1995–; Bd, PHLS, 1995–2002. Founder FMedSci 1998. *Publications:* scientific and clinical papers relating to pathogenesis of infection, vaccines. *Recreations:* walking, gardening, music. *Address:* 8 Buxton Drive, New Malden, Surrey KT3 3UZ. *T:* (020) 8949 4953. *Club:* Royal Automobile.

GRIFFIN, Prof. James Patrick, DPhil; White's Professor of Moral Philosophy, University of Oxford, 1996–2000; Fellow, Corpus Christi College, Oxford, 1996–2000, now Emeritus Fellow; *b* 8 July 1933; *s* of Gerald Joseph Griffin and Catherine Griffin (*née* Noonan); *m* 1966, Catherine Maulde von Halban (*d* 1993); one *s* one *d*. *Educ:* Choate Sch., Wallingford, Conn; Yale Univ. (BA 1955); Oxford Univ. (DPhil 1960; MA 1963). University of Oxford: Rhodes Schol., Corpus Christi Coll., 1955–58; Sen. Schol., St Antony's Coll., 1958–60; Lectr, Christ Church, 1960–66; Fellow and Tutor in Philosophy, Keble Coll., 1966–96 (Hon. Fellow, 1996); Lectr in Philosophy, 1964–90; Radcliffe Fellow, 1982–84; Reader, 1990–96. Visiting Professor: Univ. of Wisconsin, 1970, 1978; Univ. of Santiago de Compostela, 1988, 1995; Gtr Philadelphia Philosophy Consortium, 1989; ITAM, Mexico, 1994; UNAM, Mexico, 1995, etc; Adjunct Prof., Centre for Applied Philosophy and Public Ethics, Canberra, 2002–; Dist. Vis. Prof., Rutgers Univ., 2002–. Medal, Nat. Educn Commn, Poland, 1992. Hon. DFil Santiago de Compostela, 2003. Order of Diego de Lusada (Venezuela), 1999. *Publications:* Wittgenstein's Logical Atomism, 1964, repr. 1997; Well-Being: its meaning, measurement and moral importance, 1986; (jtly) Values, Conflict and the Environment, 1989, 2nd edn 1996; Value Judgement: improving our ethical beliefs, 1996; On Human Rights, 2008; articles in philosophical jls. *Recreations:* eating, drinking. *Address:* 10 Northmoor Road, Oxford OX2 6UP. *T:* (01865) 554130. *Clubs:* Brooks's, Oxford and Cambridge.

GRIFFIN, Janet Mary, (Mrs Paul Griffin); *see* Turner, J. M.

GRIFFIN, Prof. Jasper, FBA 1986; Professor of Classical Literature, and Public Orator, Oxford University, 1992–2004; Fellow and Tutor in Classics, Balliol College, Oxford, 1963–2004; *b* 29 May 1937; *s* of Frederick William Griffin and Constance Irene Griffin (*née* Cordwell); *m* 1960, Miriam Tamara Dressler; three *d*. *Educ:* Christ's Hospital; Balliol College, Oxford (1st Cl. Hon. Mods 1958; 1st Cl. Lit. Hum. 1960; Hertford Scholar 1958; Ireland Scholar 1958). Jackson Fellow, Harvard Univ., 1960–61; Oxford University: Dyson Research Fellow, Balliol Coll., 1961–63; Reader in Classical Lit., 1990–92. T. S. Eliot Meml Lectr, Univ. of Kent at Canterbury, 1984. *Publications:* Homer on Life and Death, 1980; Homer, 1980; Snobs, 1982; Latin Poets and Roman Life, 1985; The Mirror of Myth, 1986; (ed with J. Boardman and O. Murray) The Oxford History of the Classical World, 1986; Virgil, 1986; Homer, The Odyssey, 1987; Homer, Iliad ix, 1995. *Address:* Balliol College, Oxford OX1 3BJ. *T:* (01865) 77782.

GRIFFIN, Sir John; *see* Griffin, Sir A. J. S.

GRIFFIN, Dr John Parry, BSc, PhD, MB, BS; FRCP, FRCPath, FFPM; Director, Askelepieion (formerly John Griffin Associates) Ltd, since 1994; Hon. Consultant, Lister Hospital, Stevenage; *b* 21 May 1938; *o s* of late David J. Griffin and Phyllis M. Griffin; *m* 1962, Margaret, *o d* of late Frank Cooper and Catherine Cooper; one *s* two *d*. *Educ:* Howardian High Sch., Cardiff; London Hosp. Medical Coll. Lethby and Buxton Prizes, 1958; BSc (1st Cl. Hons) 1959; PhD 1961; George Riddoch Prize in Neurology, 1962; MB BS 1964; LRCP, MRCS 1964; MRCP 1980, FRCP 1990; FRCPath 1986 (MRCPath 1982); FFPM 1989. Ho. Phys., London Hosp. Med. Unit, and Ho. Surg., London Hosp. Accident and Orthopaedic Dept, 1964–65; Lectr in Physiology, King's Coll., London, 1965–67; Head of Clinical Research, Riker Laboratories, 1967–71; SMO, Medicines Div., 1971–76; PMO, Medicines Div., and Medical Assessor, Cttee on Safety of Medicines, 1976–77; SPMO and Professional Head of Medicines Div., DHSS, 1977–84; Med. Assessor, Medicines Commn, 1977–84; Dir, Assoc. of the British Pharmaceutical Industry, 1984–94. Faculty Mem., Scripps Med. Res. Center, San Diego, 1997–98; Vis. Prof., Univ. of Surrey, 2000–05. Mem., Jt Formulary Cttee for British Nat. Formulary, 1978–84; UK Rep., EEC Cttee on Proprietary Med. Products; Chairman: Cttee on Prop. Med. Products Working Party on Safety Requirements, 1977–84; ICH Working Party on Safety Requirements, 1987–94. Mem. Bd, Faculty of Pharmaceutical Med., RCP, 1993–2005 (Chm., Bd of Examiners, 1997–2003; Mem., Fellowship Cttee, 1998–2005; Acad. Registrar, 2003–). Ed. in Chief, Adverse Reactions and Toxicology Reviews, 1990–2003. FRSocMed. Thomas Young Lectr and Gold Medallist, St George's Hosp. Med. Sch., 1992. Commemorative Medal, Faculty of Pharm. Med., 2005. *Publications:* (jtly) Iatrogenic Diseases, 1972, 3rd edn 1985; (jtly) Manual of Adverse Drug Interactions, 1975, 5th edn 1997; (jtly) Drug Induced Emergencies, 1980; Medicines: research, regulation and risk, 1989, 2nd edn 1992; International Medicines Regulations, 1989; (jtly) Textbook of Pharmaceutical Medicine, 1993, 5th edn 2006; Regulation of Medicinal Products, 2003; numerous articles in sci. and med. jls, mainly on aspects of neurophysiology, clinical pharmacology, toxicology and pharmacoeconomics. *Recreations:* gardening, local history. *Address:* Quartermans, Digswell Lane, Digswell, Herts AL6 0SP.

GRIFFIN, Keith Broadwell, DPhil; Distinguished Professor of Economics, University of California, Riverside, 1988–2004 (Chairman, Department of Economics, 1988–93); *b* 6 Nov. 1938; *s* of Marcus Samuel Griffin and Elaine Ann Broadwell; *m* 1956, Dixie Beth Griffin; two *d. Educ:* Williams Coll., Williamstown, Mass (BA; Hon DLitt, 1980); Balliol Coll., Oxford (BPhil, DPhil). Fellow and Tutor in Econs, Magdalen Coll., Oxford, 1965–76, Fellow by special election, 1977–79; Warden, Queen Elizabeth House, Oxford, 1978–79 (Actg Warden, 1973 and 1977–78); Dir, Inst. of Commonwealth Studies, Oxford, 1978–79 (Actg Dir, 1973 and 1977–78); Pres., Magdalen Coll., Oxford, 1979–88. Chief, Rural and Urban Employment Policies Br., ILO, 1975–76; Vis. Prof., Inst. of Econs and Planning, Univ. of Chile, 1962–63 and 1964–65; Dist. Vis. Prof., Amer. Univ. in Cairo, 2001; Vis. Fellow, Oxford Centre for Islamic Studies, 1998. Consultant: ILO, 1974, 1982, 1994, 1996, 1997; Internat. Bank for Reconstruction and Develt, 1973; UN Res. Inst. for Social Develt, 1971–72; FAO, 1963–64, 1967, 1978; Inter-Amer. Cttee for Alliance for Progress, 1968; US Agency for Internat. Develt, 1966; UNDP, 1989, 1991–98, 2001–02, 2004. Res. Advr, Pakistan Inst. of Develt Econs, 1965, 1970; Sen. Advr, OECD Develt Centre, Paris, 1986–88; Economic Advr, Govt of Bolivia, 1989–91. Member: Council, UN Univ., 1986–92; UN Cttee for Develt Planning, 1987–94; Chm., UN Res. Inst. for Social Develt, 1988–95. Mem., World Commn on Culture and Develt, 1994–95. Pres., Develt Studies Assoc., 1978–80. FAAAS 1997. *Publications:* (with Ricardo ffrench-Davis) Comercio Internacional y Politicas de Desarrollo Economico, 1967; Underdevelopment in Spanish America, 1969; (with John Enos) Planning Development, 1970; (ed) Financing Development in Latin America, 1971; (ed with Azizur Rahman Khan) Growth and Inequality in Pakistan, 1972; The Political Economy of Agrarian Change, 1974, 2nd edn 1979; (ed with E. A. G. Robinson) The Economic Development of Bangladesh, 1974; Land Concentration and Rural Poverty, 1976, 2nd edn 1981; International Inequality and National Poverty, 1978; (with Ashwani Saith) Growth and Equality in Rural China, 1981; (with Jeffrey James) The Transition to Egalitarian Development, 1981; (ed) Institutional Reform and Economic Development in the Chinese Countryside, 1984; World Hunger and the World Economy, 1987; Alternative Strategies for Economic Development, 1989; (ed with John Knight) Human Development and the International Development Strategy for the 1990s, 1990; (ed) The Economy of Ethiopia, 1992; (ed with Zhao Renwei) The Distribution of Income in China, 1993; (with Terry McKinley) Implementing a Human Development Strategy, 1994; (ed) Poverty and the Transition to a Market Economy in Mongolia, 1995; Studies in Globalization and Economic Transitions, 1996; (ed) Social Policy and Economic Transformation in Uzbekistan, 1996; (ed) Economic Reform in Vietnam, 1998; Studies in Development Strategy and Systemic Transformation, 2000; (ed) Poverty Reduction in Mongolia, 2003. *Recreation:* travel. *Address:* 24870 SW Mountain Road, West Linn, OR 97068, USA.

GRIFFIN, Kenneth James, OBE 1970; Deputy Chairman, Ugland International, 1993–97; *b* 1 Aug. 1928; *s* of late Albert Griffin and Catherine (*née* Sullivan); *m* 1951, Doreen Cicely Simon (*d* 1992); one *s* one *d* (and one *s* decd). *Educ:* Dynevor Grammar Sch., Swansea; Swansea Technical College. Area Sec., ETU, 1960; Dist Sec., Confedn of Ship Building Engrg Unions, 1961; Sec., Craftsmen Cttee (Steel), 1961; Mem., Welsh Council, 1968; Mem., Crowther Commn on Constitution (Wales), 1969; Joint Sec., No 8 Joint Industrial Council Electrical Supply Industry, 1969; Industrial Adviser, DTI, 1971–72; Co-ordinator of Industrial Advisers, DTI, 1972–74; Special Adviser, Sec. of State for Industry, 1974; part-time Mem., NCB, 1973–82; a Dep. Chm., British Shipbuilders, 1977–83; Chm., Blackwall Engrg, 1983–85; Member: Suppl. Benefits Commn, 1968–80; Solicitors Disciplinary Tribunal, 1982–2002; Tribunal, Inst. of Legal Execs, 1992–. Chm., Network Housing Assoc., 1991–97; Vice-Chm., UK Housing Trust, 1989–; Mem. Bd, Housing Corp., 1995–2002; Exec. Advr, Mobile Training, 1989–90. *Recreations:* golf, music, reading. *Address:* 214 Cyncoed Road, Cyncoed, Cardiff CF23 6RS. *T:* (029) 2075 2184. *Club:* Reform.

GRIFFIN, Paul, MBE 1961; MA Cantab; writer; *b* 2 March 1922; *s* of late John Edwin Herman Griffin; *m* 1946, Felicity Grace, *d* of late Canon Howard Dobson; one *s* one *d. Educ:* Framlingham Coll.; St Catharine's Coll., Cambridge. Served War in Gurkhas, India, Burma, Malaya, 1940–46; North-West Frontier, 1941–43; Chindits, 1943–44. Asst Master and Senior English Master, Uppingham Sch., 1949–55; Principal, English Sch. in Cyprus, 1956–60; Headmaster, Aldenham Sch., 1962–74; Principal, Anglo-World Language Centre, Cambridge, 1976–82; Treasurer, Corp. of Sons of the Clergy, 1978–86. Cambridge University Seatonian Prize, 2001 and 2007. *Publications:* Sing Jubilee, 1996; Nearly Funny Poems, 1996; Songs About Suffolk, 1997; Going Away, 1999; Lighthearted Lines, 2000; The Sound of Violins, 2003; Diamonds for Aphrodite, 2006; collaborated in: How to Become Ridiculously Well-Read in One Evening, 1985; How to Become Absurdly Well-Informed about the Famous and Infamous, 1987; The Dogsbody Papers, 1988; How to Be Tremendously Tuned-in to Opera, 1989; How to Be Well-Versed in Poetry, 1990; How to Be European, 1991; poems, humour, articles, broadcasts. *Recreation:* literary competitions. *Address:* 1 Crombie House, The Common, Southwold, Suffolk IP18 6AL. *T:* (01502) 723709.

GRIFFIN, Robert; Headmaster, Exeter School, since 2003; *b* 17 June 1962; *s* of Paschal and Patricia Griffin; *m* 1989, Allison White; one *s* one *d. Educ:* Wallington High Sch. for Boys; Christ Church, Oxford (MA Mod. Langs 1985; Arteaga prize); Univ. of York (PGCE Mod. Langs 1989). Asst Master, Markham Coll., Lima, 1986–88; Asst Master and Hd of Mod. Langs, Haileybury, Hertford, 1989–98; Second Master, Royal Grammar Sch., Guildford, 1998–2003. *Recreations:* cycling, walking on Dartmoor, the works of García Márquez and Neruda, United Ushers, visiting National Trust properties. *Address:* Exeter School, Victoria Park Road, Exeter, Devon EX2 4NS. *T:* (01392) 273679; *e-mail:* headmaster@exeterschool.org.uk. *Club:* East India.

GRIFFIN, Very Rev. Victor Gilbert Benjamin; Dean of St Patrick's Cathedral, Dublin, 1969–91; *b* 24 May 1924; *s* of Gilbert B. and Violet M. Griffin, Carnew, Co. Wicklow; *m* 1958, Daphne E. Mitchell; two *s. Educ:* Kilkenny Coll.; Mountjoy Sch., and Trinity Coll., Dublin (MA, 1st class Hons in Philosophy). Ordained, 1947; Curacy: St Augustine's, Londonderry, 1947–51; Christ Church, Londonderry, 1951–57; Rector of Christ Church, Londonderry, 1957–69. Lecturer in Philosophy, Magee Univ. Coll., Londonderry, 1950–69. Hon. MRIAI 1992. Hon. DD TCD, 1992. *Publications:* Trends in Theology 1870–1970, 1970; Anglican and Irish, 1976; Pluralism and Ecumenism, 1983; The Mark of Protest: experience of a Southern Protestant in Northern Ireland and the Republic, 1993; The Churches and Sectarianism in Ireland, 1995; Swift and His Hospital, 1995; Swift's Message to Ireland Today, 1996; Enough Religion to Make us Hate: reflections on religion and politics in Ireland, 2002; Holding the Centre: Anglicanism in Ireland, 2007; Basic Christianity: a catechism, 2008; contrib. to New Divinity. *Recreations:* music, golf. *Address:* 7 Tyler Road, Limavady, N Ireland BT49 0DW. *Clubs:* Friendly Brothers of St Patrick, Kildare Street and University (Dublin).

GRIFFINS, Roy Jason, CB 2003; Head, UK Delegation to Channel Tunnel Intergovernmental Commission, since 2006; Chairman, London City Airport, since 2007; *b* 8 May 1946; *s* of Manuel Griffins and Betty Griffins; *m* 1984, Margaret Alison Redfern; one *d. Educ:* Blackpool Grammar Sch.; Bristol Univ. (BA). Barclays Bank Foreign Branches, 1967–68; Systems Analyst, Internat. Computers Ltd, 1968–70; Sen. Systems Analyst, with BBC, 1970–74; Copywriter, Krohn Advertising, Montreal, 1975–76; Principal, Wildlife Conservation, DoE, 1976–77; First Sec. (Envmt), UK Representation to EC, Brussels (on secondment), 1978–80; Sec. to Third London Airport Inquiry, DoE, 1981–83; Department of Transport: Principal (Aviation), then Head, Airports Policy, 1984–87; Principal Private Sec. to Sec. of State for Transport, 1987–89; Counsellor, Washington (on secondment), 1990–93; Asst Sec., Channel Tunnel Rail Link, Dept of Transport, 1993–96; Dir, Railways, DETR, 1996–99; Dir-Gen., Civil Aviation, DETR, subseq. DTLR, then DfT, 1999–2004; UK Public Affairs Dir, Eurotunnel, 2004; Dir-Gen., Airports Council Internat. for Europe, 2004–06. Mem., Franco-British Council, 2006–. Non-exec. Dir, London Ambulance Service, 2006–. *Recreations:* tennis, France, films, food. *Address:* 55 Brookfield, Highgate West Hill, N6 6AT. *Club:* Reform.

GRIFFITH, Rev. (Arthur) Leonard; Lecturer in Homiletics, Wycliffe College, Toronto, 1977–87, retired; *b* 20 March 1920; *s* of Thomas Griffiths and Sarah Jane Taylor; *m* 1947, Anne Merelie Cayford; two *d. Educ:* Public and High Schs, Brockville, Ont; McGill Univ., Montreal (BA, McGill, 1942); United Theological Coll., Montreal (BD 1945; Hon. DD 1962); Mansfield Coll., Oxford, England, 1957–58. Ordained in The United Church of Canada, 1945; Minister: United Church, Arden, Ont, 1945–47; Trinity United Church, Grimsby, Ont, 1947–50; Chalmers United Church, Ottawa, Ont, 1950–60; The City Temple, London, 1960–66; Deer Park United Church, Toronto, 1966–75; ordained in Anglican Church 1976; Minister, St Paul's Church, Bloor St, Toronto, 1975–85 (Hon. Asst, 1995–). Hon. DD Wycliffe Coll., Toronto, 1985. *Publications:* The Roman Letter Today, 1959; God and His People, 1960; Beneath The Cross of Jesus, 1961; What is a Christian?, 1962; Barriers to Christian Belief, 1962; A Pilgrimage to the Holy Land, 1962; The Eternal Legacy, 1963; Pathways to Happiness, 1964; God's Time and Ours, 1964; The Crucial Encounter, 1965; This is Living!, 1966; God in Man's Experience, 1968; Illusions of our Culture, 1969; The Need to Preach, 1971; Hang on to the Lord's Prayer, 1973; We Have This Ministry, 1973; Ephesians: a positive affirmation, 1975; Gospel Characters, 1976; Reactions to God, 1979; Take Hold of the Treasure, 1980; From Sunday to Sunday, 1987. *Recreations:* music, drama, travelling, adult education, bridge.

GRIFFITH, (Edward) Michael (Wynne), CBE 1986; Vice Lord-Lieutenant for the County of Clwyd, since 1986; *b* 29 Aug. 1933; *e s* of Major H. W. Griffith, MBE; *m* Jill Grange, *d* of Major D. P. G. Moseley, Dorfold Cottage, Nantwich; one *s* (and two *s* decd). *Educ:* Eton; Royal Agricultural College. Regional Dir, National Westminster Bank Ltd, 1974–92; Mem. Welsh Bd, Nationwide Anglia Bldg Soc., 1986–89. High Sheriff of Denbighshire, 1969. Chairman: Clwyd HA, 1980–90; National Trust Cttee for Wales, 1984–91 (Mem., National Trust Exec. and Council, 1989–2000); Countryside Council for Wales, 1991–2000; Glan Clwyd Hosp. Trust, 1993–2001; Denbighshire and Conwy Hosp. Trust, 1993–2001; Council, Univ. of Wales Coll. of Medicine, 1997–2004; Univ. of Wales Audit Cttee, 2002–; Higher Educn Wales Chairs, 2002–04; Dir, Land Authority Wales, 1989–90. Member: Countryside Commn Cttee for Wales, 1972–78; Min. of Agriculture Regional Panel, 1972–77; ARC, 1973–82; UFC (Wales), 1989–92; HEFCW, 1992–95; British Library Bd, 1992–95. Pres., CPRW, 2003–06. Mem. Council, Cardiff Univ., 2004–. FRSA 1993; FLS 1995. DL Clwyd, 1985. *Address:* Greenfield, Trefnant, Clwyd LL16 5UE. *T:* (01745) 730633. *Club:* Boodle's.

GRIFFITH, Prof. John Aneurin Grey, LLB London, LLM London; Hon. LLD Edinburgh 1982, York, Toronto, 1982, Manchester 1987; FBA 1977; Barrister-at-law; Chancellor of Manchester University, 1986–93; Emeritus Professor of Public Law, University of London; *b* 14 Oct. 1918; *s* of Rev. B. Grey Griffith and Bertha Griffith; *m* 1941, Barbara Eirene Garnet, *d* of W. Garnet Williams; two *s* one *d. Educ:* Taunton Sch.; LSE. British and Indian armies, 1940–46. Lectr in Law, UCW, Aberystwyth, 1946–48; Lectr in Law and Reader, LSE, 1948–59, Prof. of English Law, 1959–70, Prof. of Public Law, 1970–84. Vis. Professor of Law: Univ. of California at Berkeley, 1966; York Univ., 1985. Mem., Marlow UDC, 1950–55, and Bucks CC, 1955–61. Editor, Public Law, 1956–81. *Publications:* (with H. Street) A Casebook of Administrative Law, 1964; Central Departments and Local Authorities, 1966; (with H. Street) Principles of Administrative Law, 5th edn, 1973; Parliamentary Scrutiny of Government Bills, 1974; (with T. C. Hartley) Government and Law, 1975, 2nd edn 1981; (ed) From Policy to Administration, 1976; The Politics of the Judiciary, 1977, 5th edn 1997; Public Rights and Private Interests, 1981; (with M. T. Ryle) Parliament, 1989; Judicial Politics, since 1920: a chronicle, 1993; articles in English, Commonwealth and American jls of law, public administration and politics. *Recreations:* drinking beer, writing bad verse. *Address:* 2 The Close, Spinfield Lane, Marlow, Bucks SL7 2LA.

GRIFFITH, Rev. Leonard; *see* Griffith, Rev. A. L.

GRIFFITH, Martin Peter W.; *see* Wyn Griffith.

GRIFFITH, Michael; *see* Griffith, E. M. W.

GRIFFITH, Nia Rhiannon; MP (Lab) Llanelli, since 2005; *b* 4 Dec. 1956; *d* of Prof. T. Gwynfor Griffith and Dr Rhiannon Griffith (*née* Howell); *m* (marr. diss.). *Educ:* Univ. of Oxford (BA 1st cl. Hons Mod. Foreign Langs 1979); UCNW, Bangor (PGCE 1980). Language teacher: Oldham, 1981–83; Queen Elizabeth Cambria Sch., Carmarthen, 1983–85; Hd of Langs Faculty, Gowerton Comp. Sch., Swansea, 1986–92; Advr and Schs Inspector, Estyn, 1992–97; Hd of Langs, Morriston Comp. Sch., Swansea, 1997–2005. Mem. (Lab), Carmarthen Town Council, 1987–99 (Sheriff, 1998; Dep. Mayor, 1998). *Publications:* Ciao! Book 2: a textbook for teaching Italian, 1990; 100 Ideas for Teaching Languages, 2005. *Address:* (office) 6 Queen Victoria Road, Llanelli SA15 2TL; House of Commons, SW1A 0AA.

GRIFFITH EDWARDS, James; *see* Edwards.

GRIFFITH-JONES, David Eric; QC 2000; **His Honour Judge David Griffith-Jones;** a Circuit Judge, since 2007; *b* Nairobi, 7 March 1953; *s* of Sir Eric Newton Griffith-Jones, KBE, CMG, QC and Mary Patricia Griffith-Jones; *m* 1st, 1978, Deborah Judith Laidlaw Mockeridge (marr. diss. 1983); 2nd, 1984, Virginia Ann Meredith Brown; two *s* one *d. Educ:* Marlborough Coll.; Bristol Univ. (LLB 1974). FCIArb 1991. Called to the Bar, Middle Temple, 1975; Asst Recorder, 1992–97; Recorder, 1997–2007. Asst Boundary Comr, 2000–. Part-time Pres., Mental Health Review Tribunal, 2002–. Member: Sports Disputes Resolution Panel, 2000–; Panel of Sports Arbitrators, CIArb, 2002–; Chairman: Drugs Appeal Tribunal, ICC Champions Trophy, 2004, ICC Johnny Walker Series, 2005, ICC Under-19 World Cup, 2006, World Cup, 2007; Appeals Cttee, LTA, 2004–06. CIArb accredited mediator, 2003. *Publications:* Law and the Business of Sport, 1997; (contrib.) Sport: law and practice, 2003. *Recreations:* sport, country pursuits. *Address:* Maidstone Combined Court Centre, The Law Courts, Barker Road, Maidstone, Kent ME16 8EQ. *Clubs:* Sevenoaks Rugby Football, Falconhurst Cricket, Royal Cinque Ports Golf (Kent).

GRIFFITH-JONES, John Guthrie; Chairman and Senior Partner, KPMG UK, since 2006 (Chief Executive, 2002–06); *b* 11 May 1954; *s* of Mervyn Griffith-Jones and Joan (*née* Baker); *m* 1990, Cathryn Mary Stone; one *s* one *d*. *Educ:* Eton; Trinity Hall, Cambridge (BA 1975). Peat Marwick Mitchell, subseq. KPMG: joined 1975; Partner, Corporate Finance, 1987–2002. Served TA, Royal Green Jackets, 1975–90. Liveryman, Co. of Skinners, 1997–. *Recreations:* tennis, sailing, bridge. *Address:* KPMG, 8 Salisbury Square, EC4Y 8BB. *T:* (020) 7311 8059, *Fax:* (020) 7311 8499; *e-mail:* john.griffith-jones@kpmg.co.uk.

GRIFFITH-JONES, Richard Haydn; His Honour Judge Griffith-Jones; a Circuit Judge, since 1999; *b* 29 June 1951; *s* of Wyn and Mary Griffith-Jones; *m* 1974, Susan Hale; three *s* one *d*. *Educ:* Solihull Sch.; Leeds Univ. (LLB Hons). Called to the Bar, Middle Temple, 1974; a Recorder, 1994–99. Liaison Judge to Birmingham Magistrates and Sutton Coldfield Magistrates, 2006–. *Publication:* contrib. to Law Qly Rev. *Recreations:* poultry keeping, watching Association football. *Address:* Queen Elizabeth II Building, Newton Street, Birmingham B4 7NA.

GRIFFITH-JONES, Rev. Robin Guthrie; Master of The Temple, Temple Church, since 1999; *b* 29 May 1956; *s* of Mervyn and Joan Griffith-Jones. *Educ:* Westminster; New Coll., Oxford (MA); Westcott House; Christ's Coll., Cambridge (MA). Christie's (English Drawings and Watercolours), 1978–84; ordained deacon, 1989, priest, 1990; Curate, St Jude, Cantril Farm and Stockbridge Village, Liverpool, 1989–92; Chaplain: Lincoln Coll., Oxford, 1992–99; to Lord Mayor of London, 2002–03. Vis. Lectr, KCL, 2008–. *Publications:* The Four Witnesses, 2000; The Gospel according to St Paul, 2004; The Da Vinci Code and the Secrets of the Temple, 2006; Mary Magdalene, 2008. *Address:* Master's House, Temple, EC4Y 7BB. *T:* (020) 7353 8559. *Clubs:* Athenæum, Pratt's.

GRIFFITH WILLIAMS, Hon. Sir John, Kt 2007; **Hon. Mr Justice Griffith Williams;** a Judge of the High Court of Justice, Queen's Bench Division, since 2007; *b* 20 Dec. 1944; *s* of Griffith John Williams, TD and Alison Williams; *m* 1971, Mair Tasker Watkins, *d* of Rt Hon. Sir Tasker Watkins, VC, GBE, PC; two *d*. *Educ:* King's School, Bruton; The Queen's College, Oxford (BA). Served 4th Bn, RWF (TA), 1965–68; Welsh Volunteers (TAVR), 1968–71 (Lieut). Called to the Bar, Gray's Inn, 1968, Bencher, 1994; a Recorder, 1984–2000; QC 1985; a Dep. High Court Judge, 1993–2000; a Circuit Judge, 2000–01; a Sen. Circuit Judge and Hon. Recorder of Cardiff, 2001–07. Mem., Criminal Injuries Compensation Bd, 1999–2000. Mem., Bar Council, 1990–93; Leader, Wales and Chester Circuit, 1996–98 (Treas., 1993–95). Asst Comr, Boundary Commn for Wales, 1994–2000. Chancellor, dio. of Llandaff, 1999– (Dep. Chancellor, 1996–99). Hon. Fellow, Cardiff Univ., 2008. *Recreation:* golf. *Address:* Royal Courts of Justice, Strand, WC2A 2LL. *Clubs:* Cardiff and County (Cardiff); Royal Porthcawl Golf.

GRIFFITHS, family name of **Barons Griffiths**, **Griffiths of Burry Port** and **Griffiths of Fforestfach**.

GRIFFITHS, Baron *cr* 1985 (Life Peer), of Govilon in the County of Gwent; **William Hugh Griffiths,** Kt 1971; MC 1944; PC 1980; a Lord of Appeal in Ordinary, 1985–93; *b* 26 Sept. 1923; *s* of late Sir Hugh Griffiths, CBE, MS, FRCS; *m* 1949, Evelyn (*d* 1998), *d* of Col K. A. Krefting; one *s* three *d*; *m* 2000, Baroness Brigstocke, CBE (*d* 2004). *Educ:* Charterhouse; St John's Coll., Cambridge (Hon. Fellow, 1985). Commissioned in Welsh Guards, 1942; demobilised after war service, 1946. Cambridge, 1946–48. BA 1948. Called to the Bar, Inner Temple, 1949, Bencher, 1971; QC 1964; Treasurer of the Bar Council, 1968–69. Recorder of Margate, 1962–64, of Cambridge, 1964–70; a Judge of the High Court of Justice, Queen's Bench Division, 1971–80; a Lord Justice of Appeal, 1980–85. A Judge, National Industrial Relations Court, 1973–74. Chm., Security Commn, 1985–92; Mem., Adv. Council on Penal Reform, 1967–70; Chm., Tribunal of Inquiry on Ronan Point, 1968; Vice-Chm., Parole Bd, 1976–77; Mem., Chancellor's Law Reform Cttee, 1976–93; Pres., Senate of the Inns of Court and the Bar, 1982–84; Chm., Lord Chancellor's Adv. Cttee on Legal Educn and Conduct, 1991–93. Hon. Mem., Canadian Bar Assoc., 1981; Hon. Fellow: Amer. Inst. of Judicial Admin, 1985; Amer. Coll. of Trial Lawyers, 1988. Hon. LLD: Wales, 1987; De Montfort, 1993. *Recreations:* cricket, golf, fishing. *Address:* c/o House of Lords, SW1A 0PW. *Clubs:* Garrick, MCC (Pres., 1990–91); Hawks (Cambridge); Royal and Ancient (St Andrews) (Captain, 1993–94); Sunningdale Golf.

See also D. C. P. McDougall, D. H. R. Matthews.

GRIFFITHS OF BURRY PORT, Baron *cr* 2004 (Life Peer), of Pembrey and Burry Port in the County of Dyfed; **Rev. Dr Leslie John Griffiths;** Superintendent Minister, Wesley's Chapel, since 1996; President of the Methodist Conference, 1994–95; *b* 15 Feb. 1942; *s* of late Sidney and Olwen Griffiths; *m* 1969, Margaret, *d* of Alfred and Kathleen Rhodes; two *s* one *d*. *Educ:* Llanelli Grammar Sch.; Univ. of Wales (BA); Univ. of Cambridge (MA); Univ. of London (PhD). Junior Res. Fellow, University Coll. of S Wales and Monmouthshire, Cardiff, 1963; Asst Lectr in English, St David's Coll., Lampeter, 1964–67; trained for Methodist Ministry, Wesley Ho., Cambridge, 1967–70; Asst Minister, Wesley Church, Cambridge, 1969–70; Petit Goâve Circuit, Haïti, 1970–71; Port-au-Prince Circuit and Asst Headmaster, Nouveau Collège Bird, 1971–74; Minister, Reading Circuit, 1974–77; Superintendent Minister: Cap Haïtien Circuit, Haïti, 1977–80; Wanstead and Woodford Circuit, 1980–86; W London Mission, 1986–91; Finchley and Hendon Circuit, 1991–96. Hon. Canon, St Paul's Cathedral, 2000– (Mem. Council). Trustee: Addiction Recovery Foundn, 1989–2004; Sir Halley Stewart Trust, 1999–; Art and Christianity Enquiry, 1999–. Dir, Birnbeck Housing Assoc., 1992–96. Gov., Bd of Christian Aid, 1990–98 (Chm., Africa and ME Cttee, 1991–95); Chm., Bd of Govs, Southlands Coll., 1997–2003; Mem. Council, Univ. of Surrey Roehampton (formerly Roehampton Inst.), 1997–2003; Gov. and Trustee, Central Foundn Schs of London, 2000–; Trustee, Wesley House, Cambridge, 2002–04 (Chm., F and GP Cttee, 2002–04). Chairman: Methodist Church's European Reference Gp, 1996–99; Churches Adv. Council on Local Broadcasting, 1996–2000; Coll. of Preachers, 2004–. Hon. Fellow: Sarum Coll., 2001; Sion Coll., 2002; Cardiff Univ., 2005; St David's Coll., Lampeter, 2006. *Publications:* A History of Haïtian Methodism, 1991; Letters Home, 1995; The Aristide Factor, 1997; Touching the Pulse: worship and our diverse world, 1998; Voices from the Desert, 2002; (with J. Potter) World Without End?, 2007. *Recreations:* fun and fellowship spiced with occasional moments of solitude. *Address:* Wesley's Chapel, 49 City Road, EC1Y 1AU. *T:* (020) 7253 2262. *Club:* Graduate Centre (Cambridge).

GRIFFITHS OF FFORESTFACH, Baron *cr* 1991 (Life Peer), of Fforestfach in the county of West Glamorgan; **Brian Griffiths;** Vice Chairman, Goldman Sachs (Europe), since 1991; *b* 27 Dec. 1941; *s* of Ivor Winston Griffiths and Phyllis Mary Griffiths (*née* Morgan); *m* 1965, Rachel Jane Jones; one *s* two *d*. *Educ:* Dynevor Grammar School; London School of Economics, Univ. of London. (BSc (Econ), MSc (Econ)). Assistant Lecturer in Economics, LSE, 1965–68, Lecturer in Economics, 1968–76; City University: Prof. of Banking and Internat. Finance, 1977–85; Dir, Centre for Banking and Internat. Finance, 1977–82; Dean, Business Sch., 1982–85; Head of Prime Minister's Policy Unit, 1985–90. Vis. Prof., Univ. of Rochester, USA, 1972–73; Prof. of Ethics, Gresham Coll., 1984–87; Dir, Bank of England, 1984–86 (Mem., Panel of Academic Consultants, 1977–86). Director: Herman Miller, 1991–; Times Newspapers, 1991–; HTV (Wales), 1991–93; Servicemaster, 1992–2007; Telewest, 1994–98; English, Welsh and Scottish Railway, 1996–; Chairman: Trillium, 1998–; Westminster Health Care, 1999–2002. Chairman: Centre for Policy Studies, 1991–2000; Sch. Exams and Assessment Council, 1991–93; Trustees, Lambeth Fund, 1997–. Fellow: Trinity Coll., Carmarthen, 1997; Swansea Inst. of HE, 2003; Sarum Coll., 2006; Univ. of Wales, Swansea, 2006. Hon. DSc City, 1999; Hon. DSc(Econ) Wales, 2004. *Publications:* Is Revolution Change? (ed and contrib.), 1972; Mexican Monetary Policy and Economic Development, 1972; Invisible Barriers to Invisible Trade, 1975; Inflation: The Price of Prosperity, 1976; (ed with G. E. Wood) Monetary Targets, 1980; The Creation of Wealth, 1984; (ed with G. E. Wood) Monetarism in the United Kingdom, 1984; Morality and the Market Place, 1989. *Address:* c/o House of Lords, SW1A 0PW. *Club:* Garrick.

GRIFFITHS, (Albert) John; Member (Lab) Newport East, National Assembly for Wales, since 1999; *b* 19 Dec. 1956; *s* of Albert John Griffiths and Hannah Griffiths (*née* O'Connor); *m* 1978, Alison Kim Hopkins; two *s*. *Educ:* UC, Cardiff (LLB Hons Law); Dip. in Social Studies, 1996. Lectr in Further Educn and Higher Educn, 1988–89; Production Exec., 1989–90; solicitor, 1990–99. Dep. Minister for Health and Social Care, 2003–07, for Educn, Lifelong Learning and Skills (formerly for Skills), 2007–, Nat. Assembly for Wales. Chm., All Party Gp on Internat. Devel t, 2004–, on Sport, 2004–. *Recreations:* cricket, tennis, running, circuit training, reading, travel. *Address:* National Assembly for Wales, Cardiff Bay, Cardiff CF99 1NA. *T:* (029) 2089 8307.

GRIFFITHS, Prof. Allen Phillips; Professor of Philosophy, University of Warwick, 1964–92, now Emeritus; Director, Royal Institute of Philosophy, 1979–94; *b* 11 June 1927; *s* of John Phillips Griffiths and Elsie Maud (*née* Jones); *m* 1st, 1948, Margaret Lock (*d* 1974); one *s* one *d*; 2nd, 1984, Vera Clare (marr. diss. 1990). *Educ:* University Coll., Cardiff (BA; Hon. Fellow 1984); University Coll., Oxford (BPhil). Sgt, Intell. Corps, 1945–48 (despatches). Asst Lectr, Univ. of Wales, 1955–57; Lectr, Birkbeck Coll., Univ. of London, 1957–64. Pro-Vice-Chancellor, Univ. of Warwick, 1970–77. Vis. Professor: Swarthmore Coll., Pa, 1963; Univ. of Calif, 1967; Univ. of Wisconsin, 1965 and 1970; Carleton Coll., Minnesota, 1985. Silver Jubilee Medal, 1977. *Publications:* (ed) Knowledge & Belief, 1967; (ed) Of Liberty, 1983; (ed) Philosophy and Literature, 1984; Philosophy and Practice, 1985; (ed) Contemporary French Philosophy, 1988; (ed) Key Themes in Philosophy, 1989; (ed) Wittgenstein Centenary Essays, 1990; (ed) A. J. Ayer Memorial Essays, 1992; (ed) The Impulse to Philosophise, 1993; articles in learned philosophical jls. *Address:* 6 Brockley Road, West Bridgford, Nottingham NG2 5JY. *T:* (0115) 878 1059; *e-mail:* cyfaill@ntlworld.com. *Club:* West Bridgford Conservative.

GRIFFITHS, Alun Brynmor, MW; Wine Director, Berry Bros & Rudd Ltd, Wine Merchants, since 1996; *b* 29 Dec. 1953; *s* of Islwyn ap Ifan Griffiths and Olwen Enid Griffiths; *m* 1981, Helen Mary Hayes; two *s*. *Educ:* Glyn Grammar Sch., Epsom; University Coll. of Wales, Aberystwyth (BA Hons French). MW 1991. Manager: Stones of Belgravia, wine merchants, 1976–81; Butlers Wine Bar, London, 1981–83; Sales Exec., Enotria Wines, London, 1983–85; Admin Manager, Fields Wine Merchants, London, 1985–87; Wine buyer: Fortnum & Mason, 1987–92; Harrods, 1992–94; Gen. Manager Heathrow, Berry Bros & Rudd Ltd, 1994–96. Hospitalier de Pomerol, 1989; Jurade de St Emilion, 1990; Comdr de Bontemps du Medoc et du Graves, 1992; Chevalier du Tastevin, 2001. *Recreations:* squash, horse-racing, food and wine, walking, tennis. *Address:* *e-mail:* alun.griffiths@bbr.com.

GRIFFITHS, Rt Rev. Ambrose; *see* Griffiths, Rt Rev. M. A.

GRIFFITHS, Dame Anne; *see* Griffiths, Dame E. A.

GRIFFITHS, Antony Vaughan, FBA 2000; Keeper, Department of Prints and Drawings, British Museum, since 1991; *b* 28 July 1951; *s* of late Richard Cerdin Griffiths and Pamela de Grave Griffiths (*née* Hetherington). *Educ:* Highgate Sch.; Christ Church, Oxford (BA); Courtauld Inst. of Art, London Univ. (MA). Joined Dept of Prints and Drawings, BM, 1976, as Asst Keeper; Dep. Keeper, 1981–91. *Publications:* Prints and Printmaking, 1980, 2nd edn 1996; (with Reginald Williams) The Department of Prints and Drawings in the British Museum: a user's guide, 1987; Prints for Books: book illustration in France 1760–1800, 2004; British Museum exhibn catalogues; contribs to learned jls, esp. Print Qly. *Address:* 1 Highbury Hill, N5 1SU.

GRIFFITHS, Prof. Christopher Ernest Maitland, MD; FRCP, FRCPath; Professor of Dermatology, since 1994, and Head, School of Translational Medicine, since 2007, University of Manchester; *b* Dudley, 14 June 1954; *s* of Sir (Ernest) Roy Griffiths and of Winifred Griffiths; *m* 1992, Dr Tamara Wang; two *d*. *Educ:* Dulwich Coll.; St Thomas' Hosp. Med. Sch., Univ. of London (BSc 1st Cl. Hons 1976; MB BS 1979; MD1991). FRCP 1995; FRCPath 2002. Jun. hosp. doctor posts, London, 1979–85; Wellcome Trust Clin. Res. Trng Fellow, St Mary's Hosp. Med. Sch., London, 1985–87; Sen. Res. Fellow, then Asst Prof. of Dermatol., Univ. of Michigan, 1987–93; Hon. Consultant Dermatologist, Salford Royal NHS Foundn Trust, and Hd, Gtr Manchester Dermatol. Centre, 1994–. Non-exec. Dir, University Hosp. of S Manchester NHS Foundn Trust, 2008–. Pres., British Assoc. of Dermatologists, 2004–05. Co-founder and Hon. Sec., Internat. Psoriasis Council, 2004–. *Publications:* (ed jtly) Rook's Textbook of Dermatology, 7th edn 2004; contrib. Lancet, New England Jl Medicine, BMJ and specialist dermatology jls on psoriasis, ageing skin and brain-skin interaction. *Recreations:* cricket, ornithology, exploring Welsh hillsides. *Address:* Dermatology Centre, Irving Building, Salford Royal Hospital, Manchester M6 8HD. *T:* (0161) 206 4392, *Fax:* (0161) 206 1095; *e-mail:* Christopher.Griffiths@manchester.ac.uk. *Club:* Royal Automobile.

GRIFFITHS, Hon. Clive Edward, AO 1997; JP; consultant and company director, since 2001; Agent-General for Western Australia, 1997–2001; *b* Perth, WA, 20 Nov. 1928; *s* of T. E. Griffiths and D. M. Beattie; *m* 1st, 1949, Myrtle Holtham (marr. diss. 1995; she *d* 1996); one *d*; 2nd, 1995, Norma Marie Paonessa. *Educ:* Fremantle Boys' High Sch.; Kalgoorlie Sch. of Mines. Electrical Engineer and Contractor, 1953–66. City Councillor, S Perth, 1962–66; MLC (L), WA, 1965–97 (Pres., 1977–97); Parly Sec., Lib Party and Jt Govt Parties, 1974–77; Regl Rep. for Australia and Pacific Region, 1988–90, Chm., Exec. Cttee, 1990–93, Commonwealth Parly Assoc. JP W Australia, 1983. *Recreations:* sailing, football, cricket. *Address:* PO Box 412, Melville, WA 6956, Australia. *T:* (8) 932 99039; *e-mail:* haigroad@iinet.net.au. *Clubs:* Royal Over-Seas League, East India; Shelley Sailing.

GRIFFITHS, Courtenay Delsdue McVay; QC 1998; a Recorder, since 2000; *b* 10 Oct. 1955; *s* of Wrenford Dacosta Griffiths and Adelaide Tamonda Griffiths; *m* 1985, Angela Maria Hill; three *s*. *Educ:* Bablake Sch., Coventry; LSE, London Univ. (LLB Hons 1979). Called to the Bar, Gray's Inn, 1980, Bencher, 2002; Legal Asst, GLC Police Cttee, 1980–84; Revson Fellow, Urban Legal Studies Prog., City Coll., CUNY, 1984–85; in practice at the Bar, 1985–; an Asst Recorder, 1999–2000; Head of Chambers, 2002–. Hon. Lectr in Law, KCL, 1987–. Hon. PhD: Leeds Metropolitan, 2005; Coventry, 2005. *Recreations:* swimming, squash, music (reggae and soul), play piano, drawing and painting.

GRIFFITHS, David Hubert; Clerk/Adviser, House of Commons European Scrutiny Committee (formerly Select Committee on European Legislation), since 1998; *b* 24 Dec. 1940; *s* of late Hubert Griffiths and Margaret Joan Waldron; *m* Mary Abbott; one *s* one *d.* *Educ:* Kingswood School, Bath; St Catharine's College, Cambridge (MA). Joined Ministry of Agriculture, Fisheries and Food as Asst Principal, 1963; Principal, 1968; Asst Secretary, 1975; Under Secretary, 1982–97; Hd, European Communities Gp, 1982–83; Fisheries Sec., 1983–87; Hd, Food, Drink and Marketing Policy Gp, 1987–90; Dir of Establishments, 1990–94; Hd, Arable Crops and Horticulture Gp, 1995–97. Non-exec. Dir, ICI (Paints Div.), 1985–87. *Recreations:* cooking, music. *Address:* (office) 7 Millbank, SW1P 3JA.

GRIFFITHS, David Laurence; His Honour Judge Griffiths; a Circuit Judge, since 1989; *b* 3 Aug. 1944; *s* of late Edward Laurence Griffiths and of Mary Middleton Pudge; *m* 1971, Sally Hollis; four *d.* *Educ:* Christ's Hospital; Jesus College, Oxford (MA). Called to the Bar, Lincoln's Inn, 1967; Asst Recorder, 1981; Recorder, 1985. *Recreations:* walking, cycling, watching Rugby and cricket, opera, history, classical music. *Address:* Winchester Combined Court, The Law Courts, Winchester SO23 9EL.

GRIFFITHS, Ven. Dr David Nigel, FSA; Archdeacon of Berkshire, 1987–92, now Emeritus; Chaplain to The Queen, 1977–97; *b* 29 Oct. 1927; *o s* of late William Cross Griffiths, LDS, and Doris May (*née* Rhodes); *m* 1953, Joan Fillingham; two *s* one *d.* *Educ:* King Edward's Sch., Bath; Cranbrook; Worcester Coll., Oxford (MA; Gladstone Meml Prize, Arnold Historical Essay Prize); Lincoln Theol Coll.; PhD Reading, 1991. An economist before ordination; Consultant at FAO, Rome, 1952–53. Curate, St Matthew, Northampton, 1958–61; Headquarters Staff, SPCK, 1961–67; Rector of Minster Parishes, Lincoln, 1967–73; Vice-Chancellor and Librarian, Lincoln Cathedral, 1967–73; Rector of Windsor, 1973–87; Rural Dean of Maidenhead, 1977–82 and 1985–87; Hon. Canon of Christ Church, Oxford, 1983–88, now Emeritus. Warden, St Anne's Bede Houses, Lincoln, 1993–98. Trustee: Lincolnshire Old Churches Trust, 1995–; Jews' Court, Lincoln and Bardney Abbey, 1999–. Served TARO and RMFVR, 1946–50; Chaplain, RNR, 1963–77 (Reserve Decoration, 1977); OCF, Household Cavalry, 1973–87, 1st Bn Irish Guards, 1977–80. FSA 1973. Fredson Bowers Award, Bibliographical Soc. of America, 1996; Bibliographical Soc. Award (UK), 1997. *Publications:* The Bibliography of the Book of Common Prayer, 2002; articles on bibliography and church history. *Recreations:* walking, bibliomania. *Address:* 2 Middleton's Field, Lincoln LN2 1QP. *T:* (01522) 525753; *e-mail:* david27.g@mac.com.

GRIFFITHS, Elaine Mary, (Mrs P. Doyle), FRCS, FRCSE; Consultant Cardiac Surgeon, Cardiothoracic Centre Liverpool NHS Trust, since 1993; *b* 15 Jan. 1955; *d* of Hedley and Kathleen Griffiths; *m* 2000, Dr Peter Doyle; two step *d.* *Educ:* Bullerswood Sch., Chislehurst; King's College Med. Sch., London (MB BS 1979; AKC 1979). FRCS 1985; FRCSE 1985. Surgical trng, principally at Southampton, Royal Brompton, Harefield and St George's Hosps; Hon. Dir, Cardiothoracic Studies, Univ. of Liverpool Med. Sch., 1994–. Member: DoH Ext. Ref. Gp for Nat. Service Framework for Coronary Heart Disease, 1998–2000; Welsh NHS Ext. Ref. Gp, Welsh Nat. Framework for Coronary Heart Disease, 1999–2002; Doctors' Forum, DoH, 2002–; Med. Devices Adv. Gp, H of C, 2005–. Royal College of Surgeons of England: Consultant Appts Assessor, 1998–; Regl Rep., Women in Surgical Trng Scheme, 2005–; Mem. Council, RCSE, 2006–. Member: Exec., Soc. of Cardiothoracic Surgeons of GB and Ire., 1997–2000; Amer. Soc. of Women in Cardiothoracic Surgery, 1996–. Member: BMA; British Assoc. of Med. Managers. Founder Mem., Heart of Mersey Charity, 2001–. *Recreations:* foreign travel, ski-ing, gardening, collecting horse sculptures, ancient coins and netsuke, looking after pets: Koi carp, tropical fish, dog and two cats. *Address:* Cardiothoracic Centre Liverpool NHS Trust, Thomas Drive, Liverpool L14 3PE. *T:* (0151) 293 2393; *e-mail:* elaine.griffiths@ctc.nhs.uk.

GRIFFITHS, Sir Eldon (Wylie), Kt 1985; Patron, World Affairs Councils of America, since 2004 (National Chairman, 2001, then Chairman Emeritus); *b* 25 May 1925; *s* of Thomas H. W. Griffiths and Edith May; *m*; one *s* one *d.* *Educ:* Ashton Grammar Sch.; Emmanuel Coll., Cambridge (MA); MA Yale. Fellow, Saybrook Coll., Yale, 1948–49; Correspondent, Time and Life magazines, 1949–55; Foreign Editor, Newsweek, 1956–63; Columnist, Washington Post, 1962–63; Conservative Research Department, 1963–64. MP (C) Bury St Edmunds, May 1964–1992; Parly Sec., Min. of Housing and Local Govt, June–Oct. 1970; Parly Under-Sec. of State, DoE, and Minister for Sport, 1970–74; opposition spokesman on trade and industry, and Europe, 1974–76. Former Chairman: Anglo-Iranian Parly Gp; Anglo-Polish Parly Gp. Pres., Special Olympics (UK). Consultant/Adviser, Nat. Police Federation, to 1988; President: Assoc. of Public Health Inspectors, 1969–70; Friends of Gibraltar; World Affairs Council, Orange County, California. Regents' Prof., Univ. of California, Irvine. Dir, Center for Internat. Business, Chapman Univ., Orange, Calif. Dir, US and UK cos. Hon. Freeman, City of London; Hon. Citizen, Orange County, California. Medal of Honour, Republic of China, Taiwan. *Recreations:* reading, swimming, cricket. *Address:* World Affairs Councils of America, 29091 Ridgeview, Laguna Niguel, CA 92677, USA. *Club:* Carlton.

GRIFFITHS, Dame (Elizabeth) Anne, DCVO 2005 (CVO 1995; LVO 1988; MVO 1960); Librarian and Archivist to The Duke of Edinburgh, since 1983; *b* 2 Nov. 1932; *d* of William Hugh Stevenson and Elizabeth Margaret Stevenson (*née* Wallace); *m* 1960, David Latimer Griffiths (*d* 1982), Dir, McKinsey & Co.; three *s* one *d* (and one *d* decd). *Educ:* St Leonard's Sch., St Andrews. Lady Clerk in the Office of The Duke of Edinburgh, 1952–60. *Recreation:* watching sport, particularly football, cricket, golf and Rugby.
See also R. W. Ellis, H. A. Stevenson.

GRIFFITHS, Harold Morris; Assistant Secretary, HM Treasury, 1978–86; *b* 17 March 1926; *s* of Rt Hon. James Griffiths, CH; *m* 1st, 1951, Gwyneth Lethby (*d* 1966); three *s* one *d*; 2nd, 1966, Elaine Burge (*née* Walsh); two *s.* *Educ:* Llanelly Grammar Sch.; London Sch. of Economics. Editorial Staff: Glasgow Herald, 1949–55; Guardian, 1955–67; Information Division, HM Treasury: Deputy Head, 1967–68, Head, 1968–72; Asst Sec., HM Treasury, 1972–75; Counsellor (Economic), Washington, 1975–78. *Address:* The Old Coach House, Park Road, Hampton Hill, Middx TW12 1HR. *T:* (020) 8979 1214.

GRIFFITHS, Howard; Command Secretary, RAF Logistics Command, 1994–98; *b* 20 Sept. 1938; *s* of Bernard and Olive Griffiths; *m* 1963, Dorothy Foster (*née* Todd); one *s* one *d.* *Educ:* London School of Economics (BScEcon, MScEcon). Ministry of Defence: Research Officer, 1963–69; Principal, Army Dept, 1970–72; Central Staffs, 1972–76; Asst Secretary, Head of Civilian Faculty, National Defence Coll., 1976–78; Procurement Executive, 1978–80; Deputy and Counsellor (Defence), UK Delegn, Mutual and Balanced Force Reductions (Negotiations), Vienna, 1980–84; Asst Sec., Office of Management and Budget, 1984–86; Asst Sec. and Head of Defence Arms Control Unit, 1986–88; Asst Under Sec. of State (Policy), 1988–91; Fellow, Center for Internat. Affairs, Harvard Univ., 1991–92; Assistant Under Secretary of State: (Ordnance), 1992; (Supply and Orgn) (Air), 1993–94. *Address:* 95 Brands Hill Avenue, High Wycombe HP13 5PX.
See also L. Griffiths.

GRIFFITHS, Howard; Editor-in-Chief, Pulse, 2003–05 (Editor, 1979–2003); Group Editor, The Practitioner, 1994–2005 (Editor, 1988–94); *b* 6 Aug. 1947; *m* 1977, Lynda Smith; three *d.* *Educ:* Cowbridge Grammar School; Merton College, Oxford (BA). Feature writer, Pulse, 1973. *Recreation:* family.

GRIFFITHS, Jane Patricia; Editor, European Court of Human Rights, Strasbourg, since 2007; *b* 17 April 1954; *d* of late John Griffiths and of Patricia Griffiths (*née* Thomas); *m* 1st, 1975, Ralph Spearpoint (marr. diss. 1994); one *s* one *d*; 2nd, 1999, Andrew Tattersall. *Educ:* Univ. of Durham (BA Hons Russian). GCHQ linguist, 1977–84; Editor, BBC Monitoring, 1984–97. Mem. (Lab), Reading BC, 1989–99. MP (Lab) Reading E, 1997–2005. Languages teacher, Riga, Latvia and E London, 2006–07. *Publication:* (with John Newman) Bushido, 1988. *Recreations:* urban living, fancy rats. *Address:* 18 rue de Molsheim, Strasbourg 67000, France.

GRIFFITHS, John; *see* Griffiths, A. J.

GRIFFITHS, John Calvert, CMG 1983; QC 1972; SC (Hong Kong) 1997; *b* 16 Jan. 1931; *s* of Oswald Hardy Griffiths and Christina Flora Griffiths; *m* 1958, Jessamy, *er d* of Prof. G. P. Crowden and Jean Crowden; three *d*; *m* 1999, Marie Charlotte Biddulph. *Educ:* St Peter's Sch., York (scholar); Emmanuel Coll., Cambridge (sen. exhibnr) (BA 1st Cl. Hons 1955; MA 1960). Called to the Bar, Middle Temple, 1956 (Bencher, 1983); Hong Kong, 1979; a Recorder, 1972–90. Attorney-General of Hong Kong, 1979–83. Mem. Exec. and Legislative Councils, and Chm. Hong Kong Law Reform Commn, 1979–83. Chm., Telecommns (Competition Provisions) Appeal Bd, HK, 2000–; Mem. Competition Policy Rev. Cttee, 2005–. Member: Exec. Cttee, General Council of the Bar, 1967–71, 1983–89 (Treas., 1987); Senate of Inns of Court and the Bar, 1984–86 (Mem., Exec. Cttee, 1973–77); Council of Legal Educn, 1983–; Nat. Council of Social Service, 1974–79; Greater London CAB Exec. Cttee, 1978–79; (co-opted) Develt and Special Projects Cttee, 1977–79; Court, Hong Kong Univ., 1980–84; Exec. Cttee, Prince Philip Cambridge Scholarships, 1980–84. Chm., Middle Temple Soc. (Hong Kong), 2000–. Lieutenant, RE, 1949–50 (Nat. Service). *Recreations:* fishing, reading, gardening. *Address:* Des Voeux Chambers, 10F Bank of East Asia Building, 10 Des Voeux Road Central, Hong Kong. *T:* 25263071; Brick Court Chambers, 7–8 Essex Street, WC2R 3LD. *T:* (020) 7379 3550. *Clubs:* Flyfishers', Hurlingham; Hong Kong, Hong Kong Jockey (Hong Kong).

GRIFFITHS, John Charles; JP; Chairman: Minerva Arts Channel, since 1989; Minerva Vision, since 1989; *b* 19 April 1934; *s* of Sir Percival Griffiths, KBE, CIE; *m* 1st, 1956, Ann Timms (marr. diss.); four *s*; 2nd, 1983, Carole Jane Mellor (marr. diss.); one *d.* *Educ:* Uppingham; Peterhouse, Cambridge (MA). Dep. General Manager, Press Association, 1968–70; PR adviser, British Gas, 1970–74; Chm., MSG Public Relations, 1974–78; Chm. and founder, The Arts Channel, 1983–89. Chairman: National League of Young Liberals, 1962–64 (Mem., Nat. Exec., 1964–66); Assoc. of Liberals in Small Business and Self Employed, 1980; Pres., Liberal Party, 1982–83. Contested (L): Ludlow, 1964; Wanstead and Woodford, 1966; Bedford, Feb. 1974, Oct. 1974. Develt Dir, Bardsey Island Trust, 1992–96. Chm. Govs, Llangynidr Sch., 1993–95. Trustee, Nat. Asthma Campaign, subseq. Asthma UK, 2002–. JP Cardiff, 1960. *Publications:* The Survivors, 1964; Afghanistan, 1967; Modern Iceland, 1969; Three Tomorrows, 1980; The Science of Winning Squash, 1981; Afghanistan: key to a continent, 1981; The Queen of Spades, 1983; Flashpoint Afghanistan, 1986; The Third Man: the life and times of William Murdoch, 1992; Nimbus, 1994; Fathercare, 1997; Imperial Call, 1997; Afghanistan: a history of conflict, 2001; Hostage, 2003; Tea, 2006. *Recreations:* conversation, reading, music, walking. *Address:* Greenbank, Savage Hill, Newland, Glos GL16 8NH.

GRIFFITHS, Sir John N.; *see* Norton-Griffiths.

GRIFFITHS, John Pankhurst, RIBA; Clerk to the Worshipful Company: of Chartered Architects, 1995–2000; of Tylers and Bricklayers, 1996–97; *b* 27 Sept. 1930; *s* of late William Bramwell Griffiths and Ethel Doris Griffiths (*née* Pankhurst); *m* 1959, Helen Elizabeth (*née* Tasker); two *s* one *d.* *Educ:* Torquay Grammar School; King George V School, Southport; School of Architecture, Manchester Univ. Dip Arch. Resident architect, Northern Nigeria, for Maxwell Fry, 1956–58; staff architect, Granada Television, 1959; Founder and first Dir, Manchester Building Centre, 1959–65; Head of Tech. Inf., Min. of Public Buildings and Works, later DoE, 1965–77; formed Building Conservation Assoc. later Building Conservation Trust, 1977, Dir, 1979–93. Mem. Bd of Mgt, Surrey Historic Bldgs Trust, 1996–2000; Trustee, Tylers and Bricklayers Craft Trust, 1993–96. *Publications:* articles in tech. and prof. jls. *Recreations:* looking at buildings, writing, speaking, cooking. *Address:* 19 Watchbell Street, Rye, E Sussex TN31 7HB.

GRIFFITHS, (John) Peter (Gwynne); QC 1995; a Recorder, since 1991; *b* 9 Dec. 1945; *m* 1st (marr. diss.); four *c*; *m* 2nd; two *c.* *Educ:* Bristol Univ. (Civil Engrg); UWIST (LLB Hons). Work in oil exploration industry, 1968–70; called to the Bar, Gray's Inn, 1970; Asst Recorder, 1987–91. Mem., Welsh Arts Council, then Arts Council of Wales, 1992; Chm., Visual Arts Bd for Wales; Vice-Pres., Cywaith Cymru (formerly Welsh Sculpture Trust). *Publication:* (ed jtly) Injuries at Work, 1996. *Recreations:* angling, sailing, ski-ing, the arts. *Address:* 2 Bedford Row, WC1R 4BU. *T:* (020) 7440 8888.

GRIFFITHS, Lawrence; a Recorder of the Crown Court, 1972–93; *b* 16 Aug. 1933; *s* of Bernard Griffiths, CBE and Olive Emily Griffiths (*née* Stokes); *m* 1959, Josephine Ann (*née* Cook), JP; one *s* two *d.* *Educ:* Gowerton Grammar Sch.; Christ's Coll., Cambridge (MA). Called to the Bar, Inner Temple, 1957; practised Swansea, 1958–99; Mem. Wales and Chester Circuit; Prosecuting Counsel to Inland Revenue for Wales and Chester Circuit, 1969–93; Standing Counsel to HM Customs and Excise for Wales and Chester Circuit, 1989–93. Mem., Mental Health Review Tribunal for Wales, 1970–91. *Recreations:* wine, walking, travel by sea, snooker. *Address:* 26 Hillside Crescent, Uplands, Swansea SA2 0RD. *T:* (01792) 473513; (chambers) Iscoed Chambers, 86 St Helens Road, Swansea SA1 4BQ. *T:* (01792) 652988. *Club:* Bristol Channel Yacht (Swansea).
See also H. Griffiths.

GRIFFITHS, Martin Alexander; QC 2006; *b* 27 April 1962; *s* of Roy Arnold Griffiths and Susan Reay Gail Griffiths (*née* Landon); *m* 1995, Susan Jane Burden, barrister, only *d* of Kenneth John Burden; two *s* one *d.* *Educ:* City of London Sch. (Temple Chorister; John Carpenter Schol.); New Coll., Oxford (Open Schol.; BA 1st Cl. Hons Modern Hist. and Modern Langs 1984; MA 1988); City Univ. (Dip. Law 1985); Inns of Court Sch. of Law. Called to the Bar, Inner Temple, 1986 (Duke of Edinburgh Schol., Horace Avory Schol., Inner Temple Award); in practice at the Bar, 1986–. Volunteer, Waterloo Legal Advice Service, 1988–93; Mem., Mgt Cttee, N Kensington Law Centre, 2007–; Chm., Professional Conduct Sub-Cttee, London Maritime Arbitrators Assoc., 2007–. Trustee, Westbourne Trust, 1989–. Sponsor: New Coll., Oxford Burden Griffiths Awards, 2001–; Brenda Landon Pye Portrait Prize, Chelsea Coll. of Art, 2006–. Accompanist, Bayswater Suzuki Gp, 2004–06. *Recreations:* the piano, the library, the gym, Chelsea FC. *Address:* Essex Court Chambers, 24 Lincoln's Inn Fields, WC2A 3EG. *T:* (020) 7813 8000, *Fax:* (020) 7813 8080. *Club:* Travellers.

GRIFFITHS, Rt Rev. (Michael) Ambrose, OSB; Bishop of Hexham and Newcastle, (RC), 1992–2004, now Emeritus; Assistant Priest, St Mary's, Leyland, since 2004; *b* 4 Dec. 1928; *s* of Henry and Hilda Griffiths. *Educ:* Ampleforth Coll.; Balliol Coll., Oxford (MA, BSc Chemistry). Entered monastery at Ampleforth, 1950; theological studies at S Anselmo, Rome, 1953–56; ordained priest, 1957; Prof. of Theology at Ampleforth, 1963; Sen. Science Master, Ampleforth Coll., 1967; Inspector of Accounts for English Benedictine Congregation, 1971 and 1985–92; Procurator (Bursar) at Ampleforth, 1972; Abbot of Ampleforth, 1976–84; Parish Priest, St Mary's, Leyland, Preston, 1984–92. Mem. Public School Bursars' Assoc. Cttee, 1975. *Recreation:* walking. *Address:* St Mary's, Broadfield Walk, Leyland, Preston PR25 1PD.

GRIFFITHS, Nigel; MP (Lab) Edinburgh South, since 1987; Parliamentary Secretary, Privy Council Office, and Deputy Leader, House of Commons, 2005–07; *b* 20 May 1955; *s* of late Lionel and Elizabeth Griffiths; *m* 1979, Sally, *d* of Hugh and Sally McLaughlin. *Educ:* Hawick High Sch.; Edinburgh Univ. (MA 1977); Moray House Coll. of Education. Joined Labour Party, 1970; Pres., EU Labour Club, 1976–77; Sec., Lothian Devolution Campaign, 1978; Rights Adviser to Mental Handicap Pressure Group, 1979–87. City of Edinburgh: District Councillor, 1980–87 (Chm., 1986–87; Chm., Housing Cttee; Chm., Decentralisation Cttee); Member: Edinburgh Festival Council, 1984–87; Edinburgh Health Council, 1982–87; Exec., Edinburgh Council of Social Service, 1984–87; Wester Hailes Sch. Council, 1981. Opposition Whip, 1987–89; Opposition front bench spokesman on consumer affairs, 1989–97; Parly Under-Sec. of State, 1997–98, Parly Under-Sec. of State (Minister for Small Business), 2001–05, DTI. Exec. Mem. and Convenor, Finance Cttee, Scottish Constitutional Convention. Vice Pres., Inst. of Trading Standards Admin, 1994–. Member: War on Want, SEAD, Amnesty Internat., Anti-apartheid, Friends of the Earth, Nat. Trust, Ramblers' Assoc. *Publications:* Guide to Council Housing in Edinburgh, 1981; Council Housing on the Point of Collapse, 1982; Welfare Rights Survey, 1981; various welfare rights guides. *Recreations:* squash, travel, live entertainment, badminton, hill walking and rock climbing, architecture, reading, politics. *Address:* 30 McLaren Road, Edinburgh EH9 2BN. *T:* (0131) 667 1947; (office) 31 Minto Street, Edinburgh EH9 2BT. *T:* (0131) 662 4520; House of Commons, SW1A 0AA. *T:* (020) 7219 3442.

GRIFFITHS, Paul Anthony; writer; Music Critic of The New Yorker, 1992–96; *b* 24 Nov. 1947; *s* of Fred Griffiths and Jeanne Veronica (*née* George); *m* 1st, 1977; two *s*; 2nd, 1998, Anne Kathryn West. *Educ:* King Edward's Sch., Birmingham; Lincoln Coll., Oxford (BA, MSc). Area Editor for Grove's Dictionary of Music and Musicians, 6th edn, 1973–76; Asst Music Critic, 1979–82, Music Critic, 1982–92, The Times. Chevalier, Ordre des Arts et des Lettres (France), 2002. *Publications:* A Concise History of Modern Music, 1978; Boulez, 1978; A Guide to Electronic Music, 1979; Modern Music, 1980; Cage, 1981; Igor Stravinsky: The Rake's Progress, 1982; Peter Maxwell Davies, 1982; The String Quartet, 1983; György Ligeti, 1983, 2nd edn 1997; Bartók, 1984; Olivier Messiaen, 1985; New Sounds, New Personalities, 1985; The Thames & Hudson Encyclopaedia of 20th-Century Music, 1986; Stravinsky, 1992; Modern Music and After, 1995; The Sea on Fire: Jean Barraqué, 2003; The Penguin Companion to Classical Music, 2004 (repr. as The New Penguin Dictionary of Music, 2006); The Substance of Things Heard: writings about music, 2005; A Concise History of Western Music, 2006; *novels*: Myself and Marco Polo, 1989; The Lay of Sir Tristram, 1991; let me tell you, 2008; *libretti*: The Jewel Box, 1991; Marco Polo, 1996; What Next?, 1999; The General, 2007. *Recreation:* swimming. *Address:* Disgwylfa 2, Manorbier, SA70 7TE.

GRIFFITHS, Prof. Paul David, MD; Professor of Virology, Royal Free and University College Medical School (formerly Royal Free Hospital School of Medicine), since 1989; *b* 30 Jan. 1953; *s* of George Griffiths and Jean Beckett (formerly Griffiths, *née* Pring); *m* 1979, Brenda Louise Attenborough; three *s*. *Educ:* St Bartholomew's Hosp. Med. Coll., Univ. of London (BSc 1974; MB BS Hons 1977; MD 1982); DSc (Med) London, 1995. FRCPath 1996. Lawrence Postgrad. Res. Schol., 1979; Lectr, Bart's Med. Coll., 1979–82; Fogarty Internat. Scholar, NIH, USA, 1980–81; Royal Free Hospital School of Medicine, London University: Sen. Lectr in Virology, 1982–86; Reader, 1986–87; Chm., Univ. Div. of Pathology and Communicable Diseases, 1991–95. William Julius Mickle Fellow, London Univ., 1991. Member: UK med. socs; Internat. AIDS Soc.; Fellow, Amer. Soc. for Microbiol., 2003. Editor, Reviews in Medical Virology, 1990–. Ian Howat Prize in Med. Microbiol., 1975, Wheelwright Prize for Paediatrics, 1977, St Bartholomew's Hosp. Med. Coll.; Wellcome Award, European Gp for Rapid Viral Diagnosis, 1988. *Publications:* papers on viruses, HIV/AIDS, herpes viruses and cytomegalovirus. *Recreations:* family, music, viruses, bridge. *Address:* Royal Free and University College Medical School, Royal Free Campus, Department of Virology, Rowland Hill Street, Hampstead NW3 2PF. *T:* (020) 7794 0500.

GRIFFITHS, Paula Whitmore Llewellyn; ordinand, Westcott House, Cambridge, since 2008; Head, Cathedral and Church Buildings Division (Secretary: Council for the Care of Churches; Cathedrals Fabric Commission for England), Archbishops' Council, 2002–07; *b* 30 June 1949; *d* of Rev. John Whitmore Griffiths and Evelyn Doreen Griffiths (*née* Pearson); *m* 1st, 1971 (marr. diss. 1978); two *d*; 2nd, 2006, Roger John Mance. *Educ:* S Hampstead High Sch. (GPDST); Lady Margaret Hall, Oxford (BA (Mod. Hist.) 1971; MA 1975). Departments of the Environment and Transport, 1972 and 1976–92: Principal, 1982; posts incl. Hd, branches in Planning Land Use Policy Directorate, 1983–87, and Heritage Sponsorship Div., 1987–92; English Heritage, 1992–2002: Head: SE Team, 1993–94; Anglia Team, 1994–99; Asst Regl Dir, E of England Region, 1999–2002. FRSA 1985. *Publications:* articles in conservation and church jls. *Recreations:* travel, walking, poetry, travel writing, watching sunlight on fields.

GRIFFITHS, Peter; *see* Griffiths, J. P. G.

GRIFFITHS, Peter Anthony; Chairman, Queen Victoria Hospital NHS Foundation Trust, since 2005; *b* 19 May 1945; *m* 1966, Margaret Harris; two *s*. *Educ:* Swansea Technical Coll. Regl admin. trainee, Welsh Hosp. Bd, Cardiff Royal Inf., 1963–66; nat. admin. trainee, Birmingham Reg./Nuffield Centre, Leeds, 1966–69; Dep. Hosp. Sec., E Birmingham HMC, 1969–71; Dep. Dist Administrator, Hosp. Sec., Southampton and SW Hampshire Health Dist (Teaching), 1971–76; Dist Administrator, Medway Health Dist, 1976–81; Actg Area Administrator, Kent AHA, 1981–82; Dist Administrator 1982–84, Dist Gen. Man. 1984–88, Lewisham and N Southwark HA; Regl Gen. Manager, SE Thames RHA, 1988–89; Dep. Chief Exec., NHS Management Exec., 1990–91; Chief Exec., Guy's and Lewisham NHS Trust, 1991–94; Dep. Chief Exec., King's Fund, 1994–97; Chief Exec., The Health Quality Service, 1997–2004. Non-exec. Dir, Sussex Downs and Weald PCT, 2002–05. Chm., NHS Pensioners' Trust, 2005– (Trustee, 2002–). *Recreation:* golf. *Address:* Queen Victoria Hospital NHS Foundation Trust, Holtye Road, East Grinstead, West Sussex RH19 3DZ.

GRIFFITHS, Prof. Peter Denham, CBE 1990; MD, FRCPath, FRCPE; Professor of Biochemical Medicine 1968–89, and Dean, Faculty of Medicine and Dentistry, 1985–89, University of Dundee (Vice-Principal, 1979–85); Hon. Consultant Clinical Chemist, Tayside Health Board, 1966–89; *b* 16 June 1927; *s* of Bernard Millar Griffiths and Florence Marion Fletcher; *m* 1949, Joy Burgess; three *s* one *d*. *Educ:* King Edward VI Sch., Southampton; Guy's Hosp. Med. Sch., Univ. of London (BSc 1st Cl. Hons, MD). LRCP, MRCS; FRCPath 1978; FRCPE 1998. Served RN, 1946–49. Jun. Lectr in Physiol., Guy's Hosp. Med. Sch., 1957–58; Registrar, then Sen. Registrar in Clin. Path., Guy's and Lewisham Hosps, London, 1958–64; Consultant Pathologist, Harlow Gp of Hosps, Essex, 1964–66; Sen. Lectr in Clin. Chemistry, Univ. of St Andrews and subseq. Univ. of Dundee, 1966–68. Pres., Assoc. of Clin. Biochemists, UK, 1987–89 (Chm. Council, 1973–76); Member: Tayside Health Bd, 1977–85; GMC, 1986–93; various cttees of SHHD and DHSS, 1969–98. Dir, Drug Development (Scotland), 1982–89. Dir, Dundee Rep. Theatre, 1977–90. FCMI; FRSA. Consulting Editor, Clinica Chimica Acta, 1986–96 (Mem. Editl Bd, 1976; Jt Editor-in-Chief, 1979–85). *Publications:* contrib. scientific and med. jls (pathology, clin. chemistry, computing). *Recreations:* music, gardening, walking. *Address:* 52 Albany Road, West Ferry, Dundee DD5 1NW. *T:* (01382) 776772.

GRIFFITHS, Peter Harry Steve; *b* 24 May 1928; *s* of W. L. Griffiths, West Bromwich; *m* 1962, Jeannette Christine (*née* Rubery); one *s* one *d*. *Educ:* City of Leeds Training Coll. BSc (Econ.) Hons London, 1956; MEd Birmingham, 1963. Headmaster, Hall Green Road Sch., West Bromwich, 1962–64. Senior Lectr in Economic Hist., The Polytechnic, Portsmouth (formerly Portsmouth Coll. of Technology), 1967–79. Fulbright Exchange Prof. of Economics, Pierce Coll., Los Angeles, Calif, 1968–69. Councillor, Smethwick, 1955–64 (Chm., Education Cttee; Leader, Conservative Group of Councillors, 1960–64). MP (C): Smethwick, 1964–66; Portsmouth N, 1979–97; contested (C) Portsmouth N, Feb. 1974, and 1997. *Publication:* A Question of Colour?, 1966. *Recreations:* motoring, writing, computing. *Club:* Sloane.

GRIFFITHS, Peter John; higher education management consultant, since 2000; *b* 19 April 1944; *s* of Ronald Hugh Griffiths and Emily Vera (*née* Cockshutt); *m* 1968, Lesley Florence (*née* Palmer) (marr. diss. 1993); two *d*. *Educ:* Battersea Grammar Sch.; Univ. of Leicester (BA Classics); McMaster Univ. (MA Classics). University of London: Asst to Principal, 1968–70; Asst Sec. to Cttee of Enquiry into governance of the university, 1970–72; Special Duties Officer, Vice-Chancellor's and Principal's Office, 1972–78; Dep. Head, Legal and Gen. Div., Court Dept, 1978–82; Asst Clerk of the Court, 1982–85; Dep. Clerk of the Court, 1985–87; Clerk of the Court, 1987–91; Dir of Resources and Planning, 1991–93; Sec. and Chief Admin. Officer, Charing Cross and Westminster Med. Sch., 1993–97; Dep. Sec., Imperial Coll. Sch. of Medicine, 1997–2000. *Recreation:* choral singing. *Address:* Upland House, Upland Road, Sutton, Surrey SM2 5HW. *T:* (020) 8643 3599.

GRIFFITHS, Phillip A., PhD; Faculty Member, School of Mathematics, and Chairman, Science Institutes Group, Institute for Advanced Study, Princeton, since 2004; *b* 18 Oct. 1938; *s* of Phillip Griffiths and Jeanette (*née* Field); *m* 1st, 1958, Ann Lane Crittenden-Witt (marr. diss.); one *s* one *d*; 2nd, 1968, Marian Folsom Jones; two *d*. *Educ:* Wake Forest Univ. (BS 1959); Princeton Univ. (PhD 1962). University of California, Berkeley: Miller Fellow, 1962–64, 1975–76; Faculty Mem., 1964–67; Princeton University: Vis. Prof., 1967–68; Prof., 1968–72; Mem., Inst. for Advanced Study, 1968–70; Harvard University: Prof., 1972–83; Dwight Parker Robinson Prof. of Maths, 1983; Provost and James B. Duke Prof. of Maths, Duke Univ., 1983–91; Dir, IAS, Princeton, 1991–2003. Member: US Nat. Sci. Bd, 1991–96; Council on Foreign Relations, 2002–. Sen. Advr, Mellon Foundn, 2001–. Member, Board of Directors: Bankers Trust New York Corp., 1994–99; Oppenheimer Funds, 1999–; GSI Lumonics, 2001–. Sec., Internat. Mathematical Union, 1999–2006; Chm., Sci. Insts Gp, NGO, 1999–. Mem., US Nat. Acad. of Scis, 1979. Hon. DSc Wake Forest, 1973; Dr *hc* Angers, France, 1979; Hon. degree Peking, 1983. Leroy P. Steele Prize, Amer. Math. Soc., 1971; Dannie Heineman Prize, Acad. of Scis, Göttingen, 1979. *Publications:* (with J. Adams) Topics in Algebraic and Analytic Geometry, 1974; Entire Holomorphic Mappings in One and Several Complex Variables, 1976; (with J. Harris) Principles of Algebraic Geometry, 1978; An Introduction to the Theory of Special Divisors on Algebraic Curves, 1980; (jtly) Exterior Differential Systems, 1980; (jtly) Geometry of Algebraic Curves, Vol. I, 1985; Algebraic Curves, 1985; (with G. R. Jensen) Differential Systems and Isometric Embeddings, 1987; contrib. Annals of Math. Studies, Progress in Maths. *Recreation:* sailing. *Address:* School of Mathematics, Institute for Advanced Study, Einstein Drive, Princeton, NJ 08540, USA. *T:* (609) 7348000.

GRIFFITHS, Prof. Ralph Alan, OBE 2005; PhD; DLitt; FRHistS; Professor of Medieval History, University of Wales, Swansea, 1982–2002, now Emeritus; Emeritus Leverhulme Fellow, 2003–05; *b* 4 Nov. 1937; *er s* of Thomas Rowland Griffiths and Marion Lovin Griffiths (*née* Jones). *Educ:* Lewis Sch., Pengam, Gwent; Univ. of Bristol (BA 1959; PhD 1963; DLitt 1983). FRHistS 1966. Research Asst, Bd of Celtic Studies, Univ. of Wales, 1961–64; University of Wales, Swansea: Asst Lectr, 1964–66; Lectr, 1966–71; Sen. Lectr, 1971–78; Reader, 1978–82; Dean of Admissions, 1990–2002; Pro-Vice-Chancellor, 1998–2002. Visiting Professor: Dalhousie Univ., Canada, 1964; Ohio Univ., 1977, 1981; Haverford Coll., USA, 1977, 1981; Lectures: James Ford in English Hist., Univ. of Oxford, 1993; Sir John Rhys, British Acad., 2001; Stenton, Reading Univ., 2001; Virgoe, UEA, 2003; Bond, St George's Chapel, Windsor, 2006. Member: Royal Commn on Ancient and Historical Monuments (Wales), 1990– (Chm., 1999–2009); Hist. and Archaeol Panel, Humanities Res. Bd, 1994–96; Adv. Council on Public Records, 1996–2001; Adv. Council, Inst. of Histl Res., 1996–2003 (Hon. Fellow, 2005). Member, Council: RHistS, 1987–91 (Vice-Pres., 1992–96; Hon. Vice-Pres., 2003–); Royal Instn, S Wales, 2004–. Hon. Sec., Glamorgan Co. History Trust, 1974–2002; Trustee, Glamorgan-Gwent Archaeol Trust, 1985–98; Pres., S Wales Record Soc., 1994–97, 2004–07. Gen. Ed., Gwent County History, 2004–. *Publications:* The Principality of Wales in the Later Middle Ages, I: South Wales 1277–1536, 1972; The Reign of King Henry VI, 1981, 2nd edn 1998; (with R. S. Thomas) The Making of the Tudor Dynasty, 1985, 3rd edn 2005; (with J. Cannon) The Oxford Illustrated History of the British Monarchy, 1988, 2nd edn 1998; King and Country: England and Wales in the Fifteenth Century, 1990; Sir Rhys ap Thomas and his Family, 1993; Conquerors and Conquered in Medieval Wales, 1994; (with J. Gillingham) Medieval Britain: a very short history, 2000; (ed) The Fourteenth and Fifteenth Centuries, 2003; The Household Book of Sir Edward Don, 2004; (with J. E. Law) Rawdon Brown and the Anglo-Venetian Relationship, 2005; (ed jtly) Gwent County History II: age of the Marcher lords, 2008; In Conversation with Napoleon Bonaparte: J. H. Vivian's visit to the island of Elba, 2008; contrib. to books and learned jls. *Recreations:* music, travel, American writing, Shakespeare. *Address:* Department of History, Swansea University, Swansea SA2 8PP.

GRIFFITHS, Richard, OBE 2008; actor; *b* Thornaby-on-Tees, 31 July 1947; *s* of Thomas Griffiths, steelworker, and Jane Griffiths (*née* Denmark); *m* Heather. *Educ:* St Bede's RC Boys' Secondary Modern Sch.; Stockton/Billingham Tech. Coll.; Northern Sch. of Music (Drama Dept); RCA, Manchester; Sch. of Theatre, Manchester Poly. (Dip. Speech and Drama (Hons); Dip. Associateship). *Stage* includes: Royal Shakespeare Company: Henry VIII, 1983; Once in a Lifetime; Volpone, 1983; Red Star, 1984; After Aida, 1988, Verdi's Messiah, Old Vic; Rules of the Game, 1992, The Life of Galileo, 1994, Almeida; Art, 1997, 2001, Heroes, 2005, Wyndham's; Katherine Howard, 1998, The

Man Who Came to Dinner, 1999, Chichester Fest. Th.; Luther, NT, 2001; The History Boys, NT, 2004, NY, 2006 (Evening Standard and Critics' Circle Awards, 2004, Olivier Award, 2005, Tony Award, 2006, for best actor); Equus, Gielgud, 2007; *films* include: Gandhi, 1982; Gorky Park, 1983; A Private Function, 1984; Greystoke, 1984; Whoops Apocalypse, 1986; Withnail and I, 1988; King Ralph, 1991; Naked Gun 2½, 1991; Funny Bones, 1995; Sleepy Hollow, 2000; Vatel, 2000; Harry Potter and the Philosopher's Stone, 2001; Harry Potter and the Chamber of Secrets, 2002; Harry Potter and the Prisoner of Azkaban, 2004; The History Boys, 2006; *television* includes: Bird of Prey, 1982; The Cleopatras, 1983; Merry Wives of Windsor, 1983; The Marksman, 1987; Ffizz, 1987; A Kind of Living, 1988; Pie in the Sky, 1994; In the Red, 1998; Gormenghast, 2000; Hope and Glory, 2000; tlc, 2002; Ballet Shoes, 2007; numerous radio appearances. Awards include: Carleton Hobbs, BBC, 1970; Best Supporting Actor, Clarence Derwent, 1979; Best Newcomer, and Best Supporting Actor, Plays and Players, 1979; Gold (Best Actor), 1994, Silver, 1996, Sony Radio Awards; Gold, Assoc. of Colls, 2000. Hon. DLitt: Durham, 1998; Teesside, 2006. *Address:* c/o Dalzell & Beresford, 26 Astwood Mews, SW7 4DE.

GRIFFITHS, Richard Anthony; Senior Partner, Farrer & Co., 1993–2000; *b* 30 Oct. 1936; *s* of Howel Harris Griffiths and Rena Kelford Griffiths; *m* 1970, Sheila Mary Wallace; two *d*. *Educ:* Denstone Coll.; Trinity Coll., Cambridge (MA). Admitted Solicitor, 1963; Partner, Farrer & Co., 1966–2000. Dir, London Cremation Co. plc, 2000–. Life Trustee, Sir John Soane's Mus., 1994– (Chm., 1997–2008). Mem. Council, ICRF, 1997–2002. FRSA. *Recreations:* golf, theatre, travel. *Address:* Wyndham House, Wickham Market, Suffolk IP13 0QU. *Clubs:* Oxford and Cambridge; Aldeburgh Golf.

GRIFFITHS, Richard Perronet, RIBA; Founding Partner, Richard Griffiths Architects, 1993; *b* 21 Feb. 1954; *s* of Richard Cerdin Griffiths and Pamela Griffiths (*née* Hetherington); *m* 1985, Penelope Roskell; one *s* one *d*. *Educ:* Highgate Sch.; Trinity Hall, Cambridge (BA 1976, DipArch); Architectural Assoc. (Grad. Dip. Conservation). RIBA 1983; AABC. Worked with Frederick Burn, Christophe Grillet and Julian Harrap before setting up Richard Griffith Architects, 1993. Major projects include: Sutton House (NT); St Pancras Chambers; Freston Tower (Landmark Trust); Lambeth Palace; Burghley House; Kenilworth Castle (English Heritage). Cathedral Architect, Southwark Cathedral, St Albans Abbey and Russian Orthodox Cathedral, London. Member: Cttee, SPAB, 1993–99; Awards Panel, RIBA, 2004–. Trustee, Churches Conservation Trust, 2000–06. *Publications:* articles in ASCHB Trans, SPAB News, Architects' Jl. *Recreation:* music (bassoon). *Address:* c/o Richard Griffiths Architects, 5 Maidstone Mews, 72/76 Borough High Street, SE1 1GN. *T:* (020) 7357 8788, *Fax:* (020) 7403 7887; *e-mail:* richard@rgarchitects.com.

GRIFFITHS, Robert; *see* Griffiths, W. R.

GRIFFITHS, Prof. Roderic Keith, CBE 2000; Professor of Public Health Practice, University of Birmingham, since 1990; President, Faculty of Public Health Medicine, Royal Colleges of Physicians of the UK, 2004–07; *b* 12 April 1945; *s* of Tom and Olwen Griffiths; *m* 1st, 1967, Margaret Ash (marr. diss. 1993); one *s* two *d*; 2nd, 1995, Lois Parker. *Educ:* Birmingham Univ. (BSc, MB ChB 1969). Lectr in Anatomy, 1970, in Social Medicine, 1978, Birmingham Univ.; GP in Birmingham, 1975; Dir of Public Health, Central Birmingham HA, 1982; Regl Dir of Public Health, W Midlands, DoH (formerly W Midlands RHA), 1993–2004. Chm., Assoc. of CHCs England and Wales, 1979–81. Mem., Birmingham Lunar Soc., 1992–. *Publications:* articles on stress in bones, and public health in UK. *Recreations:* ski-ing, pottery, sailing very occasionally, creative writing. *Address: e-mail:* rod.griff@gmail.com.

GRIFFITHS, Roger Noel Price, MA Cantab; Membership Secretary, The Headmasters' Conference, 1990–97 (Deputy Secretary, The Headmasters' Conference and Secondary Heads' Association, 1986–89); *b* 25 Dec. 1931; *er s* of late William Thomas and of Annie Evelyn Griffiths; *m* 1966, Diana, *y d* of late Capt. J. F. B. Brown, RN; three *d*. *Educ:* Lancing Coll.; King's Coll., Cambridge. Asst Master at Charterhouse, 1956–64; Headmaster, Hurstpierpoint Coll., 1964–86. Governor: Mill Hill Sch., 1987–92; Tormead Sch., 1987–94; Prebendal Sch., Chichester, 1987–; Worth Sch., 1990–99. Mem., Management Cttee, Pallant House Trust, Chichester, 1987–92. Asst to Court of Worshipful Co. of Wax Chandlers, 1985, Master, 1990. MA Oxon, by incorporation, 1960. JP Mid Sussex, 1976–86. *Recreations:* music, theatre, bowls. *Address:* Hanbury Cottage, Cocking, near Midhurst, West Sussex GU29 0HF. *T:* (01730) 813503. *Clubs:* East India, Devonshire, Sports and Public Schools; Sussex (Sussex).

GRIFFITHS, Siân Meryl, (Mrs Ian Wylie), OBE 2000; FFPH, FRCP; Professor of Public Health, and Director, School of Public Health, Chinese University of Hong Kong, since 2005; *b* 20 March 1952; *d* of late John Daniel Griffiths, FRCS and of Rosemary Marjorie Griffiths (*née* Quick); *m* 1st, 1978, Anthony Chu (marr. diss. 1986); two *d*; 2nd, 1987, Ian Martin Wylie, *qv*; one *s*. *Educ:* Felixstowe College; N London Collegiate Sch.; New Hall, Cambridge (MB BChir 1977; MA). MSc London, 1981. DRCOG 1979; FFPH (FFPHM 1991); FRCP 1998. Clinical MO, KCH, 1979–80; Res. Fellow, NY, 1981; Dist. MO, City and Hackney HA, 1985–87; Consultant in Public Health Medicine, Oxford RHA, 1988–90; Dir of Public Health and Health Policy, SW Thames RHA, 1990–93, Oxfordshire HA, 1994–2002; Consultant in Public Health Medicine, Oxford Radcliffe Hosps NHS Trust, 2002–05; Sen. Fellow, Oxford Inst. for Ethics and Communication in Health Care Practice, Oxford Univ., 2002–05. Hon. Sen. Clin. Lectr, Oxford Univ., 1997–; Vis. Prof., Oxford Brookes Univ., 1999–2005. Mem., Health Policy Forum, IPPR, 1998–2000; Advr, Democratic Health Network, 1999–2001. Co-Chair, Assoc. of Public Health, 1995–99; Chairman: Pharmacy Healthlink, 2003–04; NHS Alliance Health Network, 2004–05; Member Board: NAHAT, 1995–98; FPH (formerly FPHM), 1999–2005 (Treas., 1995–99; Vice-Pres., 2000–01; Pres., 2001–04; Chm., Internat. Cttee, 2004–05); New Opportunities Fund, 1998–2004; Postgrad. Med. Educn Trng Bd, 2003–05; HPA, 2003–05; Mem., Nat. Cancer Task Force, 2001–05; Co-Chm., Hong Kong Govt SARS Expert Review, 2003. Trustee, Thames Valley Partnership, 1999–2001. Member: Adv. Cttee, Common Purpose, 1999–2003; Nat. Workforce Develt Bd, 2002–04; Nat. Cycling Strategy Bd, 2002–04; Adv. Gp on Physical Activity, 2002–04. *Publications:* Indicators for Mental Health, 1990; Creating a Common Profile, 1990; (ed jtly) Prevention of Suicide, 1993; (ed) Perspectives in Public Health, 1999; Health of Rough Sleepers, 2002; Change and Development of Specialist Public Health Practice, 2005; New Perspectives on Public Health, 2006; Public Health and Primary Care, 2006; contribs to med. jls. *Recreations:* spending time with family, films, theatre. *Address:* School of Public Health, Chinese University of Hong Kong, Prince of Wales Hospital, Shatin New Territory, Hong Kong.

GRIFFITHS, Tania Veronica; QC 2006; a Recorder, since 2000; *b* 7 Dec. 1959; *d* of Robert and Vera Griffiths; one *s* two *d*. *Educ:* Our Lady of Lourdes RC Primary Sch., Southport; Christ the King RC Comp. Sch., Southport; Liverpool Poly. (BA Hons Law 1981). Called to the Bar, Gray's Inn, 1982; Treasury Counsel, 2002–. *Recreations:* I love my football (Liverpool FC), my dogs and my kids (not necessarily in that order!). *Address:* Exchange Chambers, Pearl Assurance House, Derby Square, Liverpool L2 9XX. *T:* (0151 236 7747, *Fax:* (0151) 236 3433; *e-mail:* griffithsqc@exchangechambers.co.uk.

GRIFFITHS, Trevor; playwright; *b* 4 April 1935; *s* of Ernest Griffiths and Anne Conno *Educ:* Manchester Univ. BA (Hons) Eng. Lang. and Lit. Teaching, 1957–65; Educ Officer, BBC, 1965–72. Writer's Award, BAFTA, 1981. *Publications:* Occupations, 1972 3rd edn 1980; Sam Sam, 1972; The Party, 1974, 2nd edn 1978; Comedians, 1976, 2n edn 1979; All Good Men, and Absolute Beginners, 1977; Through the Night, and Suc Impossibilities, 1977; Thermidor and Apricots, 1977; (jtly) Deeds, 1978; (trans.) Th Cherry Orchard, 1978; Country, 1981; Oi for England, 1982; Sons and Lovers (televisio version), 1982; Judgement Over the Dead (television screenplays of The Last Place o Earth), 1986; Fatherland (screenplay), and Real Dreams, 1987; Collected Plays fo Television, 1988; Piano, 1990; The Gulf Between Us, 1992; Hope in the Year Tw 1994; Thatcher's Children, 1994; Who Shall Be Happy…?, 1996; Collected Stage Play Vol. 1, 1996; Food for Ravens, 1998; Camel Station, 2001; These are the Times: a life o Thomas Paine, 2005; Trevor Griffiths: theatre plays one, 2007; Trevor Griffiths: theatr plays two, 2007. *Address:* c/o United Agents, 12–26 Lexington Street, W1F 0LE.

GRIFFITHS, William Arthur; Director, Acklea Homes Ltd, since 2004; *b* 25 May 194 *s* of Glyndwr and Alice Rose Griffiths; *m* 1963, Margaret Joan Dodd (marr. diss. 1988 two *s* one *d*. *Educ:* Owen's Sch., London; Queens' Coll., Cambridge; Univ. o Manchester. VSO, 1959–60. Probation Officer, Southampton, 1965–71; Home Office 1971–76; Chief Probation Officer, N Ireland, 1977–84; Dir, NCVO, 1985–86; mg consultant, 1986–95; Principal Inspector, Social Services, Bucks CC, 1995–2002; Asst Di Nat. Soc. for Epilepsy, 2002–04. Official Visitor, Ministry of Community Devel Singapore, 1982 and 1985. Mem., Westminster CC, 1990–94. *Recreations:* literature travel, horseracing. *Address:* Mavis Bank, Church Road, Greatworth, Banbury OX1 2DU. *T:* (01295) 711983.

GRIFFITHS, (William) Robert; QC 1993; SC (NSW) 1999; *b* 24 Sept. 1948; *s* of lat (William) John Griffiths and of Megan Marjorie Griffiths (*née* Green); *m* 1984, Angela Ma Crawford; one *s* two *d*. *Educ:* Haverfordwest Grammar Sch.; St Edmund Hall, Oxfor (Open Schol.; BCL, MA). Called to the Bar, Middle Temple, 1974, Bencher, 2004; Jur Counsel to the Crown (Common Law), 1989–93; admitted as Legal Practitioner, NSW 1998, Sen. Counsel, 1999; Special Advocate, 2004. Chairman: Test Match Ground Consortium, 1998–2002; First Class Forum Internet Working Party, 2000–0 Marylebone Cricket Club: Member: Cttee, 2000–01, 2001–03 (resigned re. Zimbabwe 2006–; Estates Sub-Cttee, 1996–2004; Cricket Cttee, 2000–04; Indoor Sch. and Coachin Sub-Cttee, 2000–. Freeman, City of London, 1997. *Recreations:* reading, collectin modern first editions, British paintings, 18th and 19th century furniture; crick (Schoolboy Cricket Internat., Wales, 1966–68; rep. Glamorgan CCC (non first-class 1967–68, OUCC and OUCC (Authentics), 1968–72), Rugby (Schoolboy Internat Wales, 1965–66), travel. *Address:* 4/5 Gray's Inn Square, Gray's Inn, WC1R 5AY. *T* (020) 7404 5252; Selborne Wentworth Chambers, 174 Phillip Street, Sydney, NSW 200 Australia. *T:* (2) 92334081; Lascelles Great House, Holetown, Barbados, WI. *T:* 432126 *Club:* MCC (Mem. Cttee).

GRIFFITHS, Winston James; Chairman: Abertawe Bro Morgannwg University NH Trust, since 2008; Bro Morgannwg NHS Trust, 2005–08; Wales Council for Voluntar Action, since 2006; *b* 11 Feb. 1943; *s* of (Rachel) Elizabeth Griffiths and (Evan) Georg Griffiths; *m* 1966, (Elizabeth) Ceri Griffiths; one *s* one *d*. *Educ:* State schools in Brecor University College of South Wales and Monmouthshire, Cardiff. BA, DipEd. Taught i Tanzania, Birmingham, Barry, Cowbridge. Non-exec. Dir, Welsh Biofuels, 2005–0 Mem., Ct of Govs, Nat. Mus. and Galls of Wales, 1998–2005. European Parliament: ME (Lab) Wales South, 1979–89; Hon. Life Mem., 1989; a Vice Pres., 1984–87; former Chm Parliamentarians for World Order, then Parliamentarians Global Action for Disarmamen Develt and World Reform; former Mem., delegn to S Asia. MP (Lab) Bridgend 1987–2005. Opposition front bench spokesman on: envmtl protection, 1990–92, o education, 1992–94; on Welsh affairs, 1994–97; Parly Under-Sec. of State, Welsh Office 1997–98. Mem., Speaker's Panel of Chairmen, 2001–05; All-Party Parliamentary Groups Chairman: British Indonesia, 2001–05; Sierra Leone, 2004–05; Co-Chm., Stree Children, 2001–05; Vice-Chm., Botswana, 2003–05; Sec., Southern Africa, 2001–0 Co-Sec., Children in Wales, 2001–05. H of C Rep., EU Convention on Charter o Fundamental Rights, 1999–2000. Member: Labour Movt for Europe (Sec., 2002); Labou Campaign for Electoral Reform. Member: Christian Socialist Movement; Amnest International; Fabian Society; Anti-Apartheid Movement; Socialist Educn Assoc.; Sociali Health Assoc.; Exec. Bd, Internat. Islamic Christian Council for Reconciliation an Reconstruction, 2003–; Vice-Chm., British Cttee for Iran Freedom, 2003–. Presiden Kenfig Hill and Dist Male Voice Choir, 1986–; Porthcawl Choral Soc., 1993–; Cef Cribwr Boys' and Girls' (formerly Boys') Club, 1987–2007. Methodist local preache 1966–. *Address:* Tŷ Llon, John Street, Y Graig, Cefn Cribwr, Mid Glamorgan CF32 0AB *T:* (01656) 740526.

GRIGG, family name of **Baron Altrincham**.

GRIGG, Prof. Ronald Ernest, PhD; FRS 1999; Professor of Medicinal Chemistry, sinc 2000 (Professor of Organic Chemistry, 1989–2000), and Director, Molecular Innovatio Diversity and Automated Synthesis (Midas) Centre, since 1994, University of Leeds; 1935. *Educ:* Univ. of Nottingham (PhD). Lectr, Dept of Chemistry, Univ. of Nottingham 1965–74; Prof. of Organic Chemistry, QUB, 1974–89. Co-ordinator, Eur. Network o Cascade Combinatorial Chem., 1998. Royal Society of Chemistry: Chm., Heterocycli Gp, 1985–87; Heterocyclic Chemistry Medal, 1985; Tilden Medal and Lectr, 1986; Pedle Medal and Lectr, 1998. *Publications:* contribs to sci. jls. *Address:* School of Chemistry University of Leeds, Leeds LS2 9JT.

GRIGGS, Prof. David John, PhD; FRMetS; Professor of Mathematical Sciences an Director, Monash Sustainability Institute, Monash University, Australia, since 2007; *b* 1 April 1958; *s* of Robert William Griggs and Barbara Griggs (*née* Musgrave); *m* 1982 Hillarie Jean Paston; one *s* one *d*. *Educ:* Helsby Grammar Sch. for Boys; UMIST (BS Hons (Physics) 1979; PhD (Atmospheric Physics) 1982). Post Doctoral Fellow: Univ. o Toronto, 1982–84; UMIST, 1984–86; joined Meteorological Office, 1986: Hd, Senso Develt, 1987–91; Internat. Manager, 1991–96; Hd, Wkg Gp I, Tech. Support Unit Intergovtl Panel on Climate Change, 1996–2001; Dir, Hadley Centre for Climat Prediction and Res., 2001–06 and Dep. Chief Scientist, 2005–06; Dir, Govt Business, Me Office, 2006–07. Gen. Sec., RMetS, 1993–96. Vilho Vaisala Award, WMO, 1992 *Publications:* co-ed and contrib., Reports of Intergovtl Panel on Climate Change, 1997 1999, 2001; scientific papers on glaciation processes in clouds. *Recreations:* trying to kee fit, sports, music. *Address:* Monash Science Centre, Building 74, Monash University Clayton Campus, Wellington Road, Vic 3800, Australia; *e-mail:* dave.griggs@ msi.monash.edu.au.

GRIGGS, Rt Rev. Ian Macdonald; Bishop Suffragan of Ludlow, 1987–94; Hon Assistant Bishop, Diocese of Carlisle, since 1994; *b* 17 May 1928; *s* of late Donal

Nicholson Griggs and Agnes Elizabeth Griggs; *m* 1953, Patricia Margaret Vernon-Browne; two *s* three *d* (and one *s* decd). *Educ:* Brentwood School; Trinity Hall, Cambridge (MA); Westcott House, Cambridge. Curate, St Cuthbert, Copnor, dio. Portsmouth, 1954–59; Domestic Chaplain to Bishop of Sheffield, 1959–64; Diocesan Youth Chaplain (part-time), 1959–64; Vicar of St Cuthbert, Fir Vale, dio. Sheffield, 1964–71; Vicar of Kidderminster, 1971–83; Hon. Canon of Worcester Cathedral, 1977–83; Archdeacon of Ludlow, 1984–87; Priest-in-Charge, St Michael, Tenbury, 1984–88. Mem., Gen. Synod of C of E, 1984–87. Chm., Churches' Council for Health and Healing, 1990–99. Governor: Bedstone Coll., 1987–93; Atlantic Coll., 1988–2002; Chm., Coll. of the Ascension, Selly Oak, 1992–94. *Recreations:* hill-walking, dinghy sailing. *Address:* Rookings, Patterdale, Penrith, Cumbria CA11 0NP. *T:* (017684) 82064.

GRIGGS, Jeremy David; His Honour Judge Griggs; a Circuit Judge, since 1995; Designated Civil Judge for Devon and Cornwall, since 2006; *b* 5 Feb. 1945; *s* of Celadon Augustine Griggs and Ethel Mary Griggs (*née* Anderson); *m* 1st, 1971, Wendy Anne Russell (*née* Culham) (marr. diss. 1982); two *s* one *d*; 2nd, 1985, Patricia Maynard; two step *d*. *Educ:* St Edward's Sch., Oxford; Magdalene Coll., Cambridge (MA). Called to the Bar, Inner Temple, 1968; Mem., Western Circuit, 1968–; a Recorder, 1990–95. Bar Rep., CCBE, 1990–94. Chm., London Choral Soc., 1986–90. *Publication:* A South African Childhood, 2006. *Recreations:* playing the piano, keeping honey bees. *Address:* Exeter Combined Court Centre, The Castle, Exeter EX4 3TH. *Club:* Victory Services.

GRIGGS, Norman Edward, CBE 1976; Vice-President, The Building Societies Association, since 1981 (Secretary-General, 1963–81); *b* 27 May 1916; *s* of late Archibald Griggs and late Maud Griggs (*née* Hewing); *m* 1947, Livia Lavinia Jandolo; one *s* one step *s*. *Educ:* Newport Grammar Sch.; London Sch. of Econs and Polit. Science (BScEcon). FCIS. Accountancy Dept, County of London Electric Supply Co. Ltd, 1933–40; service in RE and RAPC, Middle East, 1940–46; Asst Sec., Glass Manufrs' Fedn, 1946–52; Sec., Plastics Inst., 1952–56; Asst Sec., Building Socs Assoc., 1956–61, Dep. Sec. 1961–63. Sec.-Gen., Internat. Union of Building Socs and Savings Assocs, 1972–77; Vice-Pres., Metropolitan Assoc. of Building Socs, 1981–89. *Publications:* poetry: Life in the Withered Shell, 1990; Sharp-Eyed and Wary, 1991; The Solitary Watcher, 1995; Life on the Brink, 1999. *Recreation:* print addict. *Address:* 5 Gledhow Gardens, SW5 0BL. *T:* (020) 7373 5128.

GRIGOR, (William Alexander) Murray; independent film maker and exhibition designer; Director: Viz Ltd, since 1972; Channel Four Television, 1995–99; *b* 20 June 1939; *s* of James McIntosh Grigor and Katharine Grigor (*née* Murray); *m* 1968, (Joan) Barbara Sternschein (*d* 1994); two *d*. *Educ:* Loretto Sch.; St Andrews Univ. (BSc). Film Editor, BBC, 1963–67; Dir, Edinburgh Internat. Film Fest., 1967–72 (Hon. Chm., 1991–94). Mem. Production Bd, BFI, 1968–72. *Films include:* Mackintosh, 1968; Big Banana Feet, 1975; The Architecture of Frank Lloyd Wright, 1981; Eduardo Paolozzi—Sculptor, 1986 (Rodin Prize, Paris Biennale, 1992); Carlo Scarpa, 1996; Nineveh on the Clyde (Prix Desjardins, Montreal), 2000; The Work of Angels, 2001; (jtly) Is Mise an Teanga (I am the Tongue), 2003; Sir John Soane—British Architect—American Legacy, 2005; television series, Face of Russia, 1998. *Exhibitions:* Scotch Myths, Edinburgh Fest., 1981; Scotland Creates, McLellan, Glasgow, 1990; Seeds of Change, Royal Mus. of Scotland, 1992; The Sixties, Barbican, 1992; The Unknown Genius: Alexander Greek Thomson, Glasgow 1999; John Byrne at 60, Paisley Mus. and Art Galls, 2000. UK/US Bicentennial Fellow in the Arts, 1976; Hon. FRIAS 1994; Hon. FRIBA 1999. Reith Award, RTS, 1990. *Publication:* (with Richard Murphy) The Architects' Architect, 1993; (with Sir Sean Connery) Being a Scot, 2008. *Recreations:* architectural and landscape forays, home and abroad. *Address:* (office) 4 Bank Street, Inverkeithing, Fife KY11 1LR. *T:* (01383) 412811. *Clubs:* Chelsea Arts; Scottish Arts (Edinburgh).

GRIGSON, Hon. Sir Geoffrey (Douglas), Kt 2000; **Hon. Mr Justice Grigson;** a Judge of the High Court of Justice, Queen's Bench Division, since 2000; Presiding Judge, North Eastern Circuit, 2004–05; *b* 28 Oct. 1944; *s* of Frederic Walter Grigson and Nora Marion Grigson; *m* 1967, Jay Sibbring (marr. diss. 1998); two *s* one *d*. *Educ:* Denstone Coll.; Selwyn Coll., Cambridge (MA). Called to the Bar, Gray's Inn, 1968; Midland and Oxford Circuit; a Recorder, 1985–89; a Circuit Judge, 1989–2000; a Permanent Judge, CCC, 1993–2000. A Dep. Sen. Judge, Sovereign Base Area, Cyprus, 1997–2000. *Recreations:* reading newspapers, walking. *Address:* Royal Courts of Justice, Strand, WC2A 2LL. *Clubs:* Athenæum, Achilles.

GRIGSON, Sophie; freelance food writer and broadcaster, since 1983; *b* 19 June 1959; *d* of late Geoffrey Edward Harvey Grigson and Jane Grigson; *m* 1992, William Black (marr. diss. 2005); one *s* one *d*. *Educ:* UMIST (BSc Hons Maths). Cookery Correspondent: Evening Standard, 1986–93; Independent, 1993–94; Sunday Times Magazine, 1994–96; Restaurant Reviewer, Independent on Sunday, 1997–98. Presenter: television: Grow Your Greens, and, Eat Your Greens, 1993; Travels à la Carte, 1994; Sophie's Meat Course, 1995; Taste of The Times, 1997; Sophie Grigson's Herbs, 1999; Feasts for a Fiver, 1999; Sophie's Sunshine Food, 2000; Sophie's Weekends, 2003; radio: Curious Cooks, 1994, 1995. Trustee, Jane Grigson Trust, 1991– (Chairperson, 1993–96, 2007–). Food Writer of the Year, Restaurateurs' Assoc. of GB, 1992; Magazine Writer of the Year, 1998, Cookery Journalist of 2001, Guild of Food Writers. *Publications:* Food For Friends, 1987; (with J. Molyneux) The Carved Angel Cookbook, 1990; Sophie's Table, 1990; Sophie Grigson's Ingredients Book, 1991; The Students' Cookbook, 1992; Eat Your Greens, 1993; (with William Black) Travels à la Carte, 1994; Sophie's Meat Course, 1995; Sophie Grigson's Taste of The Times, 1997; (with William Black) Fish, 1998; Sophie Grigson's Herbs, 1999; Feasts for a Fiver, 1999; Sunshine Food, 2000; The Complete Sophie Grigson Cookbook, 2001; My Favourite Family Recipes, 2003; Sophie's Country Kitchen, 2003; The First-Time Cook, 2004; Vegetables, 2006. *Recreations:* travel, reading, eating. *Address:* c/o Borra Garson, Deborah McKenna Ltd, 10 Tideway Yard, 125 Mortlake High Street, SW14 8SN. *T:* (020) 8876 0051.

GRILLS, Michael Geoffrey; a Recorder of the Crown Court, 1982–2000; a District Judge, 1991–2000; *b* 23 Feb. 1937; *s* of Frank and Bessie Grills; *m* 1969, Ann Margaret Irene (*née* Pyle); two *d*. *Educ:* Lancaster Royal Grammar Sch.; Merton Coll., Oxford (MA). Admitted Solicitor, 1961; Partner with Crombie Wilkinson & Robinson, York, 1965; County Court and District Registrar, York and Harrogate District Registries, 1973–90. *Recreations:* music, tennis, golf. *Address:* Cobblestones, Skelton, York YO30 1XX. *T:* (01904) 470246.

GRIME, Prof. (John) Philip, PhD; FRS 1998; Director, Buxton Climate Change Impacts Laboratory, Unit of Comparative Plant Ecology, since 1989, and Professor, 1983–98, now Emeritus, University of Sheffield; *b* 30 April 1935; *s* of Robert and Gertrude Grime; *m* 1st, 1966, Jean Carol Sorensen (marr. diss. 1982); one *s*; 2nd, 2000, Sarah Margaret Buckland. *Educ:* Middleton Grammar Sch., Lancs; Sheffield Univ. (BSc; PhD 1960). Postgrad. researcher, Univ. of Sheffield, 1960–63; Ecologist, Connecticut Agricl Expt Stn, 1963–65; University of Sheffield: Res. Ecologist, Nature Conservancy Grassland Res. Unit, 1965–71; Dep. Dir, NERC Unit of Comparative Ecol., 1971–89. Vice Pres., British Ecological Soc., 1989–91. Foreign Mem., Royal Netherlands Acad.

Arts and Sci., 1991; Hon. Member: Lund Ecological Soc., 1992; Ecol Soc. of America, 1998. Hon. Dr Univ. of Nijmegen, Netherlands, 1998. Marsh Award for Ecol., British Ecol Soc., 1997. *Publications:* Ecological Atlas of Grassland Plants (with P. S. Lloyd), 1973; Plant Strategies and Ecological Processes, 1979; (jtly) Comparative Plant Ecology: a functional approach to common British species, 1988; Plant Strategies, Vegetation Processes and Ecosystem Properties, 2001; numerous contribs to scientific jls. *Recreation:* league and friendly cricket. *Address:* Unit of Comparative Plant Ecology, University of Sheffield, Sheffield S10 2TN; 24 Delph House Road, Crosspool, Sheffield S10 5NR. *T:* (0114) 267 1214.

GRIME, Mark Stephen Eastburn; QC 1987; *b* 16 March 1948; *s* of R. T. Grime, ChM, FRCS, and late M. D. Grime; *m* 1973, Christine Emck; two *d*. *Educ:* Wrekin College; Trinity College, Oxford (Scholar; MA). FCIArb 1997. Called to the Bar, Middle Temple, 1970, Bencher, 1997; practising Northern Circuit, 1970–; Asst Recorder, 1988–90; Recorder, 1990–2003; Technol. and Construction Recorder, 1998–2003. Chairman: Disciplinary Appeal Tribunal, UMIST, 1980–2003; Northern Arbitration Assoc., 1994–98 (Mem. Council, 1990–94); Northern Circuit Med. Law Assoc., 1999–2002. *Recreations:* antiquarian horology, sailing. *Address:* Homestead Farm, Jackson's Edge, Disley, Cheshire SK12 2JR. *T:* (01663) 766976; Deans Court Chambers, 24 St John Street, Manchester M3 4DF. *T:* (0161) 214 6000.

GRIME, Philip; see Grime, J. P.

GRIMES, Hon. Roger (Dale); MHA (L) Exploits, 1989–2005; Leader of the Opposition, Newfoundland and Labrador, Canada, 2003–05; *b* 2 May 1950; *s* of late Fred and Winnie Grimes; *m* 1996, Mary Ann Lewis; one *d*. *Educ:* Meml Univ. of Newfoundland (BSc.; BEd 1972; MEd 1988). High Sch. teacher, 1972–89. Pres., Newfoundland and Labrador Teachers' Assoc., 1985–87; Dir, Canadian Teachers' Fedn 1985–87. Parly Asst to Premier of Newfoundland and Labrador, 1989–91; Minister: of Employment and Labour Relns, 1991–93; of Tourism, Culture and Recreation, 1993–96; of Educn, 1996–98; of Mines and Energy, 1998–99; of Health and Community Services, 2000–01; Premier of Newfoundland and Labrador, 2001–03. *Recreations:* recreational hockey, jogging, golf, softball, reading.

GRIMLEY, Very Rev. Robert William; Dean of Bristol, since 1997; *b* 26 Sept. 1943; *s* of William Bracebridge Grimley and Gladys Mary (*née* Draper); *m* 1968, Joan Elizabeth Platt; two *s* one *d*. *Educ:* Derby Sch.; Christ's Coll., Cambridge (BA 1966; MA 1970); Wadham Coll., Oxford (BA 1968; Ellerton Theol Essay Prize, 1974; MA 1976); Ripon Hall, Oxford. Ordained deacon 1968, priest 1969; Asst Curate of Radlett, 1968–72; Chaplain, King Edward's Sch., Birmingham and Hon. Curate, St Mary, Moseley, 1972–84; Vicar, St George's, Edgbaston, 1984–97. Examining Chaplain to the Bishop of Birmingham, 1988–97; Bishops' Inspector of Theol Colls, 1998–. Chaplain to the High Sheriff of W Midlands, 1988–89. A Church Comr for England, 2007– (Mem., Bishoprics and Cathedrals Cttee, 2005–). Trustee, Bishop's Palace, Wells, 2005–06. Governor: The Queen's Coll., Birmingham, 1974–97; The Foundn of the Schs of King Edward VI in Birmingham, 1991–97; Bristol Cathedral Sch., 1997–; Kingswood Sch., 1998–. Hon. DLitt UWE, 2004. *Recreations:* reading, Europe, languages, bread-making. *Address:* The Deanery, 20 Charlotte Street, Bristol BS1 5PZ. *T:* (0117) 926 2443, (Cathedral) (0117) 926 4879; *e-mail:* dean@bristol.anglican.org.

GRIMLEY EVANS, Sir John, Kt 1997; FRCP; Professor of Clinical Geratology (formerly Geriatric Medicine), University of Oxford, 1985–2002; Fellow of Green Templeton College (formerly Green College), Oxford, since 1985; *b* 17 Sept. 1936; *s* of Harry Walter Grimley Evans and Violet Prenter Walker; *m* 1966, Corinne Jane Cavender; two *s* one *d*. *Educ:* King Edward's Sch., Birmingham (Foundn Scholar); St John's Coll., Cambridge (Rolleston Scholar; MA, MD); Balliol Coll., Oxford (DM); FFPH. Res. Asst, Nuffield Dept of Clin. Med., Oxford, 1963–65; Vis. Scientist, Sch. of Public Health, Univ. of Michigan, 1966; Res. Fellow, Med. Unit, Wellington Hosp., NZ, 1966–69; Lectr in Epidemiology, LSHTM, 1970–71; Consultant Physician, Newcastle Gen. Hosp., 1971–73; Prof. of Medicine (Geriatrics), Univ. of Newcastle upon Tyne, 1973–84. Chairman: Specialist Adv. Cttee on Geriatric Medicine, Jt Cttee for Higher Med. Trng, 1979–86; Cttee on Ethical Issues in Medicine, 2000–; Member: WHO Expert Panel on Care of Elderly, 1984– (Rapporteur, 1987); MRC, 1992–95 (Chm., Health Services Res. Cttee, 1989–92; Chm., Health Service and Public Health Res. Bd, 1992–94); Cttee on Med. Aspects of Food Policy, DoH, 1992–2000 (Chm., 1999–2000); GMC, 1994–99; Central R & D Cttee, DoH, 1997–2003; Royal College of Physicians: Chairman: Examining Bd, Dip. in Geriatric Medicine, 1985–90; Geriatric Medicine Cttee, 1989–94; Pro-censor, 1990–91; Censor, 1991–92; Vice-Pres., 1993–95; Harveian Orator, 1997. Founder FMedSci 1998. Editor, Age and Ageing, 1988–95. *Publications:* Care of the Elderly, 1977; (jtly) Advanced Geriatric Medicine (series), 1981–88; (jtly) Improving the Health of Older People: a world view, 1990; (jtly) The Oxford Textbook of Geriatric Medicine, 1992, 2nd edn 2000; papers on geriatric medicine and epidemiology of chronic disease. *Recreations:* fly-fishing, literature. *Address:* Donnington Farmhouse, Meadow Lane, Iffley, Oxford OX4 4ED. *Club:* Royal Society of Medicine.

GRIMMETT, Prof. Geoffrey Richard, DPhil; Professor of Mathematical Statistics, Cambridge University, since 1992; Professorial Fellow of Churchill College, Cambridge, since 1999; *b* 20 Dec. 1950; *s* of Benjamin and Patricia Grimmett; *m* 1986, Rosine Bonay; one *s*. *Educ:* King Edward's Sch., Birmingham; Merton Coll., Oxford (BA 1971; MSc 1972; MA, DPhil 1974). Jun. Res. Fellow, New Coll., and IBM Res. Fellow, Oxford Univ., 1974–76; Bristol University: Lectr, 1976–85; Reader, 1985–89; Prof. of Maths, 1989–92; Cambridge University: Dir, Statistical Lab., 1994–2000; Mem. Council, Churchill Coll., 2000–02; Hd, Dept of Pure Maths and Math. Stats, 2002–07. Vis. appts at Cornell Univ., Univ. of Arizona, Univ. of Rome II, Univ. of Utah, UCLA, UBC, Univ. of Paris, etc. Man. Ed., Probability Theory and Related Fields, 2000–05. Public Schs Foil Champion, 1968; GB Under 20 Foil Champion, 1970; Member: GB Fencing Team, 1973–77; Olympic Foil Team, 1976. Hon. FIA 1999. *Publications:* (with D. R. Stirzaker) Probability and Random Processes, 1982, 3rd edn 2001; (with D. J. A. Welsh) Probability: an introduction, 1986; Percolation, 1989, 2nd edn 1999; (with D. R. Stirzaker) One Thousand Exercises in Probability, 2001; The Random-Cluster Model, 2006; contrib. to learned jls. *Recreations:* mountaineering, music. *Address:* Statistical Laboratory, University of Cambridge, Wilberforce Road, Cambridge CB3 0WB. *T:* (01223) 337957. *Clubs:* Alpine; Climbers'.

GRIMSBY, Bishop Suffragan of, since 2000; **Rt Rev. David Douglas James Rossdale;** *b* 22 May 1953; *m* 1982, Karen; two *s*. *Educ:* King's Coll., London; Westminster Coll., Oxford (MA 1990); Roehampton Inst. (MSc 2000). Ordained deacon 1981, priest, 1982; Curate, Upminster, 1981–86; Vicar: St Luke, Moulsham, 1986–90; Cookham, 1990–2000; Area Dean of Maidenhead, 1994–2000. Hon. Canon, Christ Church, Oxford, 1999–2000; Canon and Preb., Lincoln Cathedral, 2000–. Gov., Wellington Coll., 2004–. *Recreations:* travel, cookery. *Address:* Bishop's House, Church Lane, Irby-upon-Humber, Grimsby DN37 7JR. *T:* (01472) 371715.

GRIMSEY, Elizabeth Jon, CBE 2002; LVO 1977; Director of Judicial Services (formerly of Policy), 2003–07, and of Corporate Diversity, 2006–07, Legal and Judicial Services Group, Ministry of Justice (formerly Department for Constitutional Affairs); *b* 31 May 1947; *d* of Archibald Charles Sermon and Betty Elaine Sermon (*née* Swanborough); *m* 1976, Colin Robert Grimsey (*d* 2002); one *s* one *d*. *Educ:* Old Palace Sch., Croydon; Univ. of Durham (BA Hons 1968). Home Office: Asst Principal, 1968–73; Principal, 1973–77 and 1983–86; Head of Division: Personnel and Immigration Depts, 1986–90; Prison Service, 1990–96; Dir, Corporate Services, 1996–99, Judicial Gp, 1999–2003, LCD. Trustee, International Social Service (UK), 2005–. *Recreations:* family, reading, music, theatre going, supporting Crystal Palace FC.

GRIMSEY, Inga Margaret Amy, (Mrs G. R. Dunn); Director General, Royal Horticultural Society, since 2006; *b* 20 Oct. 1952; *d* of Robert Jessup Grimsey and Annelise Grimsey (*née* Albeck); *m* 2002, Geoffrey Richard Dunn. *Educ:* Gravesend Grammar Sch.; Regent Street Poly. (BA Hons (Finance) Business Studies). Man. Dir, Anonymous (fashion chain), Storehouse plc, 1983–91; Chief Exec., Ski Club of GB, 1991–96; National Trust: Man. Dir, National Trust (Enterprises), 1996–2001; Territory Dir, 2001–05; Hd, Trading, NPG, 2005–06. *Recreations:* ski-ing, opera, gardening. *Address:* Royal Horticultural Society, 80 Vincent Square, SW1P 2PE.

GRIMSHAW, John Roland, CBE 2008 (MBE 1996); Engineer and Director, since 1981, Chief Executive, 1984–2008, Sustrans; *b* 12 July 1945; partner, Sue Learner; two *s* one *d*. *Educ:* Gonville and Caius Coll., Cambridge (BA Engrg 1966). Engr, Taylor Woodrow, 1963–68; VSO, Uganda, 1969–70; engr, MRM (Bristol), 1971–80. Asst Hon. Engr, Cyclbag, 1977–83. Board Member: Railway Paths Ltd, 1997–; Cycling England, 2005–. *Recreation:* sculpture. *Address:* Sustrans, National Cycle Network Centre, 2 Cathedral Square, College Green, Bristol BS1 5DD. *T:* (0117) 915 0232, *Fax:* (0117) 915 0225; *e-mail:* john.grimshaw@sustrans.org.uk.

GRIMSHAW, Sir Nicholas (Thomas), Kt 2002; CBE 1993; PRA (RA 1994); Chairman, Nicholas Grimshaw & Partners Ltd, architects, planners and industrial designers, since 1980; President, Royal Academy of Arts, since 2004; *b* 9 Oct. 1939; *s* of Thomas Cecil Grimshaw and Hannah Joan Dearsley; *m* 1972, Lavinia, *d* of late John Russell, CBE; two *d*. *Educ:* Wellington College; Edinburgh College of Art; Architectural Assoc. Sch. AA Dip. Hons 1965; RIBA 1967; FCSD (FSIAD 1969); numerous prizes and scholarships. Major projects include: Channel Tunnel terminal, Waterloo (Mies van der Rohe Pavilion Award, 1994, RIBA Building of the Year Award, 1994); British Pavilion for Expo '92, Seville, Spain; Financial Times Printing Plant (Royal Fine Art Commn/Sunday Times Building of the Year Award, 1989); Pusan Internat. Rly Terminus, Korea, 1996; Zurich Airport Expansion, 1996; Regl HQ for Orange Telephones, Darlington, 1996; restoration of Paddington Stn, 1996; restoration of existing Spa and new building, Bath, 1997; Caixa Galicia Art Foundn, La Coruña, Spain, 1997; Berlin Stock Exchange and Communications Centre; British Airways Combined Operations Centre, Heathrow; HQ for Igus GmbH, Cologne; RAC Rescue Services HQ; Satellite and Piers, Heathrow Airport; Research Centre for Rank Xerox; BMW HQ, Bracknell; Herman Miller Factory, Bath; Oxford Ice Rink; Gillingham Business Park; J. Sainsbury Superstore, Camden; Head Office and Printing Press for Western Morning News; redevelopment of Terminal One, Manchester Airport, for MA plc; teaching and res. bldg, Univ. of Surrey; head office for Mabeg GmbH, Soest (RIBA Internat. Award), 1999; Eden Project, St Austell, 2000; Exhibn Hall, Frankfurt Fair, 2000; HQ and factory for Pfeiffer Vacuum, Dortmund, 2000; high-speed rly stn, Biljmer, Amsterdam, 2000; Plant Sci. Centre, St Louis, USA, 2001; Nat. Space Sci. Centre, Leicester, 2001; Ijburg Bridge, Amsterdam, 2001; HQ and assembly plant for Rolls Royce, Goodwood, Sussex, 2001; NE Wing, RCA, 2001; Minerva Bldg, St Botolph's, City of London, 2001; Millennium Point, Birmingham, 2001; Inst. of Cancer Studies, UCL, 2001; New Engrg Bldg, UCL, 2001; HQ for Lloyds TSB, London, 2002; Spine House, Cologne, 2002; London Stock Exchange, 2003; KPMG Berlin HQ, 2003; Southern Cross Stn, Melbourne, 2006; Newport City Footbridge, Wales, 2007; Experimental Media and Perf. Arts Centre for Rensselaer Poly. Inst., Albany, NY, 2007; Steel Mus., Monterrey, Mexico, 2007; New Academic Bldg for LSE, 2008; London Southbank Univ. new bldg, 2008. Pres. Council, AA, 1999–2001. Assessor for: British Construction Industry Awards; DoE; British Gas; Scottish Devolt Agency. Hon. Mem., Bund Deutscher Architekten, 1997. Hon. FAIA 1995; Hon. FRIAS 2002. Hon. DLitt South Bank, 1993. Awards and Commendations include: RIBA, 1975, 1978, 1980, 1983, 1986, 1989, 1990, 1991, 1994, 1995, 1999, 2001, 2002, 2003, 2004; Financial Times (for Industrial Architecture), 1977, 1980, 1995; Structural Steel Design, 1969, 1977, 1980, 1989, 1993, 1994, 1995, 1999, 2000, 2001, 2002, 2003; Civic Trust, 1978, 1982, 1989, 1990, 1991, 1996; British Construction Industry Awards, 1988, 1989, 1992, 1993, 1995; Royal Fine Art Commn/Sunday Times Bldg of the Year Award, 1989, 1993, 1994, 1999, 2001, 2004; Constructa Preis for Industrial Architecture in Europe, 1990; Quaternario Foundn Internat. Award for Innovative Technol. in Architecture, 1993; AIA/London UK Chapter Design Excellence Award, 1995, 2001, 2005; Nat. Heritage Arts Sponsorship Scheme Award, 1995; Design Innovation Award, 1996; British Council for Offices Award, 1996; Internat. Brunel Award, 1996; Leisure Property Award for best regeneration scheme, 2001; European Award for Aluminium in Architecture, 2001. *Publications:* Nicholas Grimshaw & Partners: product and process, 1988; (jtly) Architecture, Industry and Innovation: the work of Nicholas Grimshaw & Partners 1966–88, 1995; (jtly) Structure, Space & Skin: the work of Nicholas Grimshaw & Partners 1988–93, 1993; Equilibrium: the work of Nicholas Grimshaw & Partners 1993–99, 2000; articles for RSA Jl. *Recreations:* sailing, tennis. *Address:* 57 Clerkenwell Road, EC1M 5NG. *T:* (020) 7291 4141.

See also T. Traeger.

GRIMSTON, family name of **Baron Grimston of Westbury** and of **Earl of Verulam**.

GRIMSTON, Viscount; James Walter Grimston; *b* 6 Jan. 1978; *s* and *heir* of Earl of Verulam, *qv*; *m* 2008, Lady Rosanagh Innes-Ker, *d* of Duke of Roxburghe, *qv* and Lady Jane Dawnay, *qv*. *Educ:* Eton; St Edmund Hall, Oxford (MSc).

See also Countess of Verulam.

GRIMSTON OF WESTBURY, 3rd Baron *cr* 1964; **Robert John Sylvester Grimston;** Bt 1952; *b* 30 April 1951; *er s* of 2nd Baron Grimston of Westbury and of Hon. June Mary, *d* of 5th Baron de Mauley; *S* father, 2003; *m* 1984, Emily Margaret, *d* of Major John Shirley; two *d*. *Educ:* Eton; Reading Univ. (BSc). ACA 1985. Commnd, The Royal Hussars (PWO), 1970–81 (Captain 1976). *Heir:* *b* Hon. Gerald Charles Walter Grimston [*b* 4 Sept. 1953; *m* 1980, Katherine Evelyn (*née* Kettle); two *s* one *d*].

GRIMSTONE, Gerald Edgar; Chairman: Candover Investments plc, since 2006; Standard Life plc, since 2007; *b* 27 Aug. 1949; *s* of Edgar Wilfred Grimstone and Dorothy Yvonne Grimstone; *m* 1973, Hon. Janet Suenson-Taylor (marr. diss. 1995); one *s* two *d*. *Educ:* Winterbourne Primary Sch.; Whitgift Sch.; Merton Coll., Oxford (MA, MSc). NATO-CCMS Fellow, Wolfson Coll., Oxford. Civil Service, 1972–86, Asst Sec., HM Treasury, 1984–86; J. Henry Schroder Wagg, 1986–99: Head: Internat. Finance Adv. Dept, 1992–94; Investment Banking, Asia Pacific, 1994–97; Investment Banking, N America, 1997–98; Global Vice-Chm., Investment Banking, 1998–99; Mem., Horserac Totalisator Bd, 1999–2006. Member: RAF Strike Comd Bd, 2000–07; RAF Air Com Bd, 2007. *Publications:* contribs on pollution to learned jls. *Recreations:* travelling, tidyin my office, my friends and family, our house in Thailand. *Address:* c/o Candove Investments, 20 Old Bailey, EC4M 7LN. *Clubs:* Athenæum, Royal Air Force; Hon Kong, China (Hong Kong).

GRIMTHORPE, 5th Baron *cr* 1886; **Edward John Beckett;** Bt 1813; *b* 20 Nov. 195 *er s* of 4th Baron Grimthorpe, OBE and of Lady Grimthorpe (*see* Elizabeth, Lad Grimthorpe); *S* father, 2003; *m* 1992, Mrs Carey Elisabeth McEwen, *yr d* of Robi Graham; one *s*. *Heir:* *s* Hon. Harry Maximillian Beckett, *b* 28 April 1993. *Address:* Hur Croft, Market Street, Fordham, Ely CB7 5LQ.

GRIMTHORPE, Elizabeth, Lady; Elizabeth Beckett, DCVO 1995 (CVO 1983 Lady of the Bedchamber to HM Queen Elizabeth The Queen Mother, 1973–2002; *b* 2 July 1925; 2nd *d* of 11th Earl of Scarbrough, KG, GCSI, GCIE, GCVO, PC and Katharin Isabel, Countess of Scarbrough, DCVO, K-i-H Gold Medal; *m* 1954, Hon. Christophe John Beckett, later 4th Baron Grimthorpe, OBE (*d* 2003); two *s* one *d*. *Address:* Westov Hall, York YO60 7NE. *T:* (01653) 618225.

GRIMWADE, Sir Andrew (Sheppard), Kt 1980; CBE 1977; Australian industrialis cattle breeder and arts patron; *b* 26 Nov. 1930; *s* of late Frederick and Gwendole Grimwade; *m* 1st, 1959, Barbara (*d* 1990), *d* of J. B. D. Kater; one *s*; 2nd, 1994, Marsh *d* of Hon. Dr Reginald John David Turnbull. *Educ:* Melbourne Grammar Sch.; Trinit Coll., Melbourne Univ. (Exhib. Eng.; BSc); Oriel Coll., Oxford (swimming blue; MA FRACI, FAIM. Principal, Green Valley Cattle Co., 1959–; Man. Dir, Carba Ind. Lt 1960–70; Chairman: Kemtron Ltd, 1964–88; Australian Cons. Ind. Ltd, 1975–82; Beoli Village Ltd; Vice-Chm., Nat. Mutual Life Assoc., 1988–92 (Dir, 1970–92); Dep. Chm Turoa Ski Resort Ltd, 1986–2001; Director: Commonwealth Ind. Gases Ltd, 1960–9 (Dep. Chm., 1987–90)); Nat. Aust. Bank, 1965–85; IBM (Aust.) Ltd, 1971–92; Son (Aust.) Pty Ltd, 1974–92. Member: Bd, Melbourne UP, 1996–2002; Adv. Bd, Deutsche Menzies Pty Ltd, 1998–; Dep. Chm., Cert. Aust. Angus Beef Pty, 1996–2003. Mem., fir Aust. Govt Trade Mission to China, 1973. Member: Australian Govt Remuneratio Tribunal, 1974–82; Bd, Rev. of Victorian Govt Salaries and Allowances, 1980. Pres Walter and Eliza Hall Inst. of Med. Research, 1978–92 (Mem. Bd, 1963–92; Laureat 2007); Founding and Life Mem., Miegunyah Fund, Melbourne Univ., 1987–; Patron Miegunyah Press. Chairman: Australian Art Exhibn Corp. (Chinese Exhibn), 1976–7 Australian Govt Official Estabts Trust, 1976–82; Trustee, Victorian Arts Centre, 1980–9 Emeritus Trustee, Nat. Gallery of Vic, 1990– (Trustee, 1964–90; Pres., 1976–90); De Chm., Art Foundn of Victoria, 1976–90; Dep. Pres., Australiana Fund, 1978–82; Chm Royal Soc. of Victoria Foundn, 2007–08. Member: Council for Order of Australi 1975–82; Felton Bequests' Cttee, 1973– (Chm., 2004–). Hon. Life Mem., RACI; Hor Mem., Royal Soc. of Victoria. *Publications:* Involvement: The Portraits of Clifton Pug and Mark Strizic, 1968; (with Dr G. Vaughan) Great Philanthropists on Trial, 200 *Recreations:* ski-ing, Australian art. *Address:* PO Box 607, Mansfield, Vic 3724, Australia.

GRIMWADE, Rev. Canon John Girling; Chaplain to the Queen, 1980–90; permissio to officiate, dioceses of Gloucester and Oxford, since 1989; *b* 13 March 1920; *s* of Herbe Alfred and Edith Grimwade; *m* 1951, Adini Anne Carus-Wilson; one *s* one *d*. *Educ:* Col Court; St Paul's Sch.; Keble Coll., Oxford; Cuddesdon Coll. MA Oxon. Friend Ambulance Unit, 1940–45. Curate of Kingston-upon-Thames, 1950–53; Curat University Church of St Mary-the-Virgin, Oxford, and Secretary of Oxford Univ Student Christian Movement, 1953–56; Vicar of St Mark's, Smethwick, 1956–62; Recto of Caversham, 1962–81, and Priest-in-Charge of Mapledurham, 1968–81; Rector c Caversham and Mapledurham, 1981–83; Priest-in-Charge, Stonesfield, Oxford, 1983–8 Chm., House of Clergy, Oxford Diocesan Synod, 1976–82; Agenda Sec., Oxford Di Synod, 1983–88; Diocesan Press Officer, Oxford, 1983–89. Hon. Canon of Chri Church, Oxford, 1974–90, Hon. Canon Emeritus, 1990–. *Recreation:* gardening. *Addres* 88 Alexander Drive, Cirencester, Glos GL7 1UJ.

GRIMWOOD, Sam Jayne; *see* Baker, S. J.

GRINDLEY, Prof. Nigel David Forster, PhD; FRS 2006; Professor of Molecul Biophysics and Biochemistry, Yale University, since 1986; *b* 24 Nov. 1945; *s* of Er Edward Grindley and Evelyn Marion Grindley; partner, Catherine Mary Joyce; one *s* on *d*. *Educ:* Gonville and Caius Coll., Cambridge (BA 1967); Univ. of London (PhD 1974 Mem., Scientific Staff, Central Public Health Lab., London, 1967–73; Postdocto Fellow: Biol Scis, Carnegie-Mellon Univ., 1973–75; Molecular Biophysics and Biochem Yale Univ., 1975–78; Asst Prof. of Biol Scis, Univ. of Pittsburgh, 1978–80; Yal University: Asst Prof. of Molecular Biophysics and Biochem., 1980–83, Associate Prof 1983–86; Chm., Dept of Molecular Biophysics and Biochem., 2003–06. NAT Postdoctoral Fellow, SRC, 1974–76; Guggenheim Fellow, 1987–88. Ed., Molecular an Gen. Genetics, 1985–91; Member, Editorial Board: Jl Bacteriol., 1988–93; Molecul Microbiol., 1990–2003 (Mem., Editl Adv. Bd, 2005–). World Health Organisatio Mem., Immunol. of Leprosy Molecular Biol. Subcttee, Geneva, 1987–90 (Mem., Steerin Cttee, 1990–92); Immunol. of Mycobacterial Disease Steering Cttee, 1992–96; Mem NIH Study Section, Microbial Physiol. and Genetics, 1988–92. Merit Award, NIH 1991–2001. *Publications:* contrib. to learned jls. *Address:* Department of Molecul Biophysics and Biochemistry, Yale University, 266 Whitney Avenue, New Haven, C 06520–8114, USA. *T:* (203) 4328991; *e-mail:* nigel.grindley@yale.edu.

GRINDROD, Most Rev. John Basil Rowland, KBE 1983; Archbishop of Brisbane an Metropolitan of Queensland, 1980–89; Primate of Australia, 1982–89; *b* 14 Dec. 1919; of Edward Basil and Dorothy Gladys Grindrod; *m* 1949, Ailsa W. (*d* 1981), *d* of G Newman; two *d*; *m* 1983, Mrs Dell Cornish, *d* of S. J. Caswell. *Educ:* Repton School Queen's College, Oxford (BA 1949; MA 1954); Lincoln Theological College. Deaco 1951, priest, 1952, Manchester; Curate: St Michael's, Hulme, 1951–54; Bundaberg, Qld 1954–56; Rector: All Souls, Ancoats, Manchester, 1956–60; Emerald, Qld, 1960–61; S Barnabas, N Rockhampton, Qld, 1961–65; Archdeacon of Rockhampton, Qld, 1960–6 Vicar, Christ Church, S Yarra, Vic, 1965–66; Bishop of Riverina, NSW, 1966–71; Bisho of Rockhampton, 1971–80. Hon. ThD 1985. *Address:* Unit 7152, 101 Lindfield Roa Helensvale, Qld 4212, Australia.

GRINDROD, Prof. Peter, CBE 2005; Technical Director, and Co-founde Numbercraft Ltd, Oxford, since 1998; *b* Oxford, 22 Nov. 1959; *s* of Alan and Alm Grindrod; *m* 1985, Dora Louise Bennett; three *s* one *d*. *Educ:* Bristol Univ. (BSc Hon Maths 1981); Dundee Univ. (PhD Maths 1984). Res. Fellow in Maths, Dundee Univ 1983–85; Oxford University: Jun. Lectr, 1985–88, SRC Advanced Fellow in Math 1988–89, Mathematical Inst.; Jun. Res. Fellow, Brasenose Coll., 1985–88; Dynamic Systems Gp Leader, Intera Inf. Technologies, later QuantSci, Henley-on-Thame 1989–98. Visiting Professor: in Applied Maths, Univ. of Bath, 2001–; in Applied Industri Maths, Oxford Univ., 2005–08. Mem., User Panel, 1999– (Chm., 2000–04), Mem Council, 2000–04, EPSRC. Mem. Council, Inst. of Maths and its Applications, 1996–

(Pres., 2006–08). Mem., Bioinformatics Cttee, Wellcome Trust, 1999–2002. *Publications:* Patterns and Waves: theory and applications of reaction-diffusion equations, 1990, 2nd edn 1995; contrib. numerous papers to learned jls. *Recreations:* published poet, guitarist, football fan (Manchester United). *Address:* Numbercraft Ltd, Magdalen Centre, The Oxford Science Park, Oxford OX4 4GA. *T:* (01865) 784264; *e-mail:* peter_grindrod@hotmail.com.

GRINLING, Jasper Gibbons, CBE 1978; Chairman, London Jazz Radio plc, 1989–91, retired; *b* 29 Jan. 1924; *s* of late Lt-Col Antony Gibbons Grinling, MBE, MC, and Jean Dorothy Turing Grinling; *m* 1950, Jane Moulsdale; one *s* two *d. Educ:* Harrow (Scholar); King's Coll., Cambridge (Exhibnr, BA). Served War, 12th Lancers, 1942–46 (Captain). Joined W. & A. Gilbey Ltd, 1947, Dir 1952; Man. Dir, Gilbeys Ltd, 1964; Man. Dir, International Distillers & Vintners Ltd, 1967; Dir, North British Distillery Co. Ltd, 1968–86; Dir of Corporate Affairs, Grand Metropolitan, 1981–85, Dir of Trade Relations, 1985–86; Chm., The Apple & Pear Develt Council, 1986–89. Pres., EEC Confedn des Industries Agricoles et Alimentaires, 1976–80; Mem. Council, Scotch Whisky Assoc., 1968–86. CCMI (FBIM 1969). Chevalier, Ordre National du Mérite, France, 1983. *Publication:* The Annual Report, 1986. *Recreations:* gardening, jazz drumming, painting. *Address:* The Old Vicarage, Helions Bumpstead, near Haverhill, Suffolk CB9 7AS. *T:* (01440) 730316.

GRINSTEAD, Sir Stanley (Gordon), Kt 1986; FCA; Chairman and Director, Harmony Leisure Group, 1989–92; *b* 17 June 1924; *s* of Ephraim Grinstead and Lucy Grinstead (*née* Taylor); *m* 1955, Joyce Preston; two *d. Educ:* Strodes, Egham. Served Royal Navy, 1943–46 (Pilot, FAA). Franklin, Wild & Co., Chartered Accountants, 1946–56; Hotel York Ltd, 1957; Grand Metropolitan Ltd, 1957–62; Union Properties (London) Ltd, 1958–66; Grand Metropolitan Ltd, 1964–87: Dep. Chm. and Group Man. Dir, 1980–82; Gp Chief Exec., 1982–86; Chm., 1982–87; Chm., Reed Internat., 1988–89 (Dir, 1981–90). Trustee, FAA Museum. Vice-Pres., CGLI, 1986–90. CCMI. Master, Brewers' Co., 1983–84. *Recreations:* gardening, cricket, racing, breeding of thoroughbred horses. *Clubs:* Army and Navy, MCC; Surrey County Cricket (Hon. Treas., 1987–94).

GRINYER, Prof. Peter Hugh; Emeritus Professor, University of St Andrews, since 1993; *b* 3 March 1935; *s* of Sidney George and Grace Elizabeth Grinyer; *m* 1958, Sylvia Joyce Boraston; two *s. Educ:* E Ham Grammar Sch.; Balliol Coll., Oxford (BA, subseq. MA, PPE); LSE (PhD in Applied Economics). Unilever Sen. Managerial Trainee, 1957–59; PA to Man. Dir, E. R. Holloway Ltd, 1959–61; Lectr and Sen. Lectr, Hendon Coll. of Tech., 1961–64; Lectr, 1965–69, Sen. Lectr, 1969–72, City Univ.; Reader, 1972–74, Prof. of Business Strategy, 1974–79, City Univ. Business School; Esmée Fairbairn Prof. of Econs (Finance and Investment), Univ. of St Andrews, 1979–93 (Vice-Principal, 1985–87, Actg Principal). Chairman: St Andrews Management Inst., 1989–96; St Andrews Strategic Management Ltd, 1989–96. Visiting Professor: Stern Sch. of Business, New York Univ., 1992, 1996–98; Imperial Coll., London, 2002–; Erskine Fellow, Univ. of Canterbury, NZ, 1994. Member: Business and Management Studies Sub-Cttee, UGC, 1979–85; Scottish Legal Aid Bd, 1992–2000; Appeal Tribunals Panel, Competition Commn, 2000–03; Competition Appeal Tribunals, 2003–. Founding Dir, Glenrothes Enterprise Trust, 1983–86; Director: John Brown PLC, 1984–86; Don and Low (Hldgs) Ltd (formerly Don Bros Buist), 1985–91; Ellis and Goldstein (Hldgs) PLC, 1987–88; Chm., McIlroy Coates, 1991–95. *Publications:* (with J. Wooller) Corporate Models Today, 1975, 2nd edn 1979; (with G. D. Vaughan and S. Birley) From Private to Public, 1977; (with J.-C. Spender) Turnaround: the fall and rise of Newton Chambers, 1979; (with D. G. Mayes and P. McKiernan) Sharpbenders, 1988; (with Dr Foo Check Teck) Organizing Strategy: Sun Tzu business warcraft, 1994; some 55 papers in academic jls. *Recreations:* hill walking, golf. *Address:* 60 Buchanan Gardens, St Andrews, Fife KY16 9LX. *Club:* Royal & Ancient Golf (St Andrews).

GRISHAM, John; author; *b* 8 Feb. 1955; *m* Renée Jones; one *s* one *d. Educ:* Mississippi State Univ. (BS Accounting); Univ. of Mississippi (JD 1981). Mem., Miss. Bar, 1981; Law practice, Southaven, 1981–91; Mem. (Democrat), Miss. House of Reps, 1984–90. *Publications:* The Firm, 1991; The Pelican Brief, 1992; A Time to Kill, 1992; The Client, 1993; The Chamber, 1994; The Rainmaker, 1995; The Runaway Jury, 1996; The Partner, 1997; The Street Lawyer, 1998; The Testament, 1999; The Brethren, 2000; A Painted House, 2001; The Summons, 2002; The King of Torts, 2003; Bleachers, 2003; The Last Juror, 2004; The Broker, 2005; Playing for Pizza, 2007; The Appeal, 2008; *non-fiction:* The Innocent Man, 2006. *Recreations:* reading, coaching baseball. *Address:* c/o Doubleday & Co. Inc., 1540 Broadway, New York, NY 10036, USA.

GRIST, John Frank; broadcasting consultant; Supervisor of Parliamentary Broadcasting, 1991–93 (Supervisor of Broadcasting, House of Commons, 1989–91); *b* 10 May 1924; *s* of Austin Grist, OBE, MC, and Ada Mary Grist (*née* Ball); *m* Gilian, *d* of Roger Cranage and Helen Marjorie Rollett; one *s* one *d* (and one *d* decd). *Educ:* Ryde Sch., IoW; London Sch. of Economics and Political Science (BSc Econ); Univ. of Chicago. RAF Pilot, 1942–46. BBC External Services, 1951–53; seconded to Nigerian Broadcasting Service, 1953–56; BBC TV Talks and Current Affairs at Lime Grove, 1957–72, producer of political programmes and Editor of Gallery and of Panorama; Hd of Current Affairs Gp, 1967–72; Controller, English Regions BBC, 1972–77; US Rep., BBC, 1978–81; Man. Dir, Services Sound and Vision Corp., 1982–88. Specialist Advr to Select Cttee on Televising of Proceedings of H of C, 1988–89. Observer, Russian Election, 1993; Advr, Indep. Media Commn, S African Elections, 1994. BP Press Fellow, Wolfson Coll., Cambridge, 1988. Gov., Royal Star and Garter Home, 1986–94. FRTS 1986 (Mem. Council, 1984–88). *Publication:* Grace Wyndham Goldie, First Lady of Television, 2006. *Address:* 4 Burlington House, Kings Road, Richmond, Surrey TW10 6NW. *T:* (020) 8940 6351. *Club:* Reform.

GRIST, Prof. Norman Roy, FRCPE; Professor of Infectious Diseases, University of Glasgow, 1965–83, now Emeritus; *b* 9 March 1918; *s* of Walter Reginald Grist and Florence Goodwin Grist (*née* Nadin); *m* 1943, Mary Stewart McAlister. *Educ:* Shawlands Acad., Glasgow; University of Glasgow (BSc 1939; MB ChB (Commendation), 1942). MRCPE 1950, FRCPE 1958; Founder Mem., 1963, FRCPath 1967; MRCPGlas 1980, FRCPGlas 1983. Ho. Phys. Gartloch Hosp., 1942–43; RAMC, GDO 223 Fd Amb. and RMO 2/KSLI, 1943–46; Ho. Surg. Victoria Inf., Glasgow, 1946–47; Res. Phys., Ruchill Hosp., Glasgow, 1947–48; Research Asst, Glasgow Univ. Dept of Infectious Diseases, 1948–52; Lectr in Virus Disease, Glasgow Univ., 1952–62, and Regional Adviser in Virology to Scottish Western Reg. Hosp. Bd, 1960–74; Reader in Viral Epidemiology, Glasgow Univ., 1962–65. Mem., Expert Adv. Panel on Virus Diseases to WHO, 1967–2001. Pres., Glasgow Natural History Soc., 1993–96. Hon. Mem., Assoc. of Clin. Pathology, 1989. Bronze Medal, Helsinki Univ., 1973; Orden Civil de Sanidad, cat. Encomienda, Spain, 1974. *Publications:* Diagnostic Methods in Clinical Virology, 1966, 3rd edn, 1979; (with D. Reid and I. W. Pinkerton) Infections in Current Medical Practice, 1986; (with D. O. Ho-Yen, E. Walker and G. R. Williams) Diseases of Infection, 1987, 2nd edn 1993; numerous contribs to British and international med. jls. *Recreations:* gardener's mate, natural history. *Address:* 5A Hyndland Court, 6A Sydenham Road, Glasgow G12 9NR. *T:* (0141) 339 5242.

GRIST, Maj.-Gen. Robin Digby, CB 1994; OBE 1979; Director, Gloucestershire Enterprise Ltd, since 2001; Chairman, Quality South West Ltd, since 2003 (Director, since 2001); *b* 21 Oct. 1940; *s* of late Lt-Col and Mrs Digby Grist; *m* 1971, Louise Littlejohn; one *s* two *d. Educ:* Radley Coll.; Royal Military Acad., Sandhurst. Commnd, Gloucestershire Regt, 1960; seconded to Army Air Corps, 1965–69 (despatches, 1968); CO 1st Bn Gloucestershire Regt, 1979–82; Comdr 6 Airmobile Bde, 1985–86; rcds 1987; Mil. Attaché and Comdr Brit. Army Staff, Washington, USA, 1988–89; Dir, AAC, 1989–92; Dir Gen., AGC, 1992–94. Col, The Gloucestershire Regt, 1990–94, The Royal Gloucestershire, Berkshire and Wiltshire Regt, 1994–2001. Chm., Glos Community Foundn, 2000–05. DL Gloucestershire, 1995–2002. *Publication:* Their Laurels are Green: a short history of The Royal Gloucestershire, Berkshire and Wiltshire Regiment, 1997. *Recreations:* fishing, gardening. *Address:* Regimental Headquarters, Royal Gloucestershire, Berkshire and Wiltshire Regiment, Custom House, Gloucester GL1 2HE. *Club:* Army and Navy.

GRISWOLD, Rt Rev. Frank Tracy, III; Presiding Bishop, Episcopal Church in the United States of America, 1998–2006; *b* 18 Sept. 1937; *s* of Frank Tracy Griswold Jr and Luisa Johnson (*née* Whitney); *m* 1965, Phoebe Wetzel; two *d. Educ:* Harvard Univ. (BA 1959); Gen. Theol Seminary (Cert. 1960); Oriel Coll., Oxford (BA 1962; MA 1966). Ordained deacon 1962, priest 1963; Curate, Church of the Redeemer, Bryn Mawr, Penn, 1963–67; Rector: St Andrew's, Yardley, Penn, 1967–74; St Martin-in-the-Fields, Philadelphia, 1974–85; Bishop Coadjutor of Chicago, 1985–87; Bishop of Chicago, 1987–97. Hon. DD: Gen. Theol Seminary, 1985; Seabury-Western Theol Seminary, 1985; Nashotah House, Wisconsin, 2000; Univ. of the South, 2001; Berkeley Divinity Sch., 2002.

GRITTON, Susan; soprano; Principal with English National Opera, 2000–02; *b* 31 Aug. 1965; *m*; two *c. Educ:* Univ. of Oxford; Univ. of London. Major rôles include: title rôle, Theodora, Glyndebourne; Governess in Turn of the Screw, Snape Maltings; Marenka in The Bartered Bride, Liù in Turandot and Micaëla in Carmen, Royal Opera, Covent Gdn; Fiordiligi in Così fan Tutte, Konstanze in Die Entführung aus den Serail, Vitellia in La Clemenza di Tito, Romilda in Xerxes, Cleopatra in Giulio Cesare and title rôle of Rodelinda, Bayerische Staatsoper, Munich; Pamina in Magic Flute, Countess in Le Nozze di Figaro, Fiordiligi in Così fan Tutte and title rôle of Cunning Little Vixen, ENO; Donna Anne in Don Giovanni, Opera de Montréal; Ellen Orford in Peter Grimes, Opera Australia; has performed with Rome Opera, Teatro la Fenice, Venice, Th. des Champs Elysées, Paris and Mostly Mozart Fest., NY. Recitalist at Wigmore Hall (solo début, 1994) and Lincoln Centre, NY; has performed in concert with orchestras including LSO, Orch. of the Age of Enlightenment, Berlin Philharmonic and NY Philharmonic. Has made numerous recordings. Kathleen Ferrier Meml Prize, 1994. *Address:* c/o Askonas Holt Ltd, Lincoln House, 300 High Holborn, WC1V 7JH.

GROBEL, Peter Denis Alan Christian Joseph; His Honour Judge Grobel; a Circuit Judge, since 2001; *b* 11 Aug. 1944; *s* of Cyril Peter Grobel and Kathleen (*née* Donaghy); *m* 1975, Susan Twemlow, LRAM; three *s* one *d. Educ:* Mt St Mary's Coll.; University Coll. London (LLB Hons). Called to the Bar, Lincoln's Inn, 1967; in practice at common law bar, 1971–2001; a Recorder, SE Circuit, 1991–2001. Chm., Special Educnl Needs Tribunal, 1994–2001. Chm. of Govs, St Teresa's Sch., Effingham, 2002–. *Address:* c/o Inner London Crown Court, SE1 6AZ.

GROCOCK, Dr (Catherine) Anne; Assistant Registrar, University of Oxford, since 2006; *b* 7 March 1947; *d* of late Arthur Raymond Grocock and Alice Grace Grocock. *Educ:* Westonbirt Sch.; St Anne's Coll., Oxford (BA Zool. 1968; MA, DPhil 1973). University of Oxford: Deptl Demonstrator in Human Anatomy, 1973–79; Deptl Res. Asst, 1979–80 and 1982–85, and ICRF Res. Fellow, 1985–89, Dept of Human Anatomy; Lectr in Anatomy, Merton Coll., Oxford, 1977–80 and 1985–89; Bursar and Official Fellow, St Antony's Coll., Oxford, 1990–97; Exec. Dir, Royal Soc. of Medicine, 1997–2006. Chm., Reproduction Res. Inf. Services Ltd, 1988–93. Member: Defence Estates Audit Cttee, 2006–; Veterinary Labs Agency Owners' Adv. Bd, 2007–. Non-exec. Dir, Oxfordshire and Bucks Mental Health Trust, 2008–. Trustee: Nat. Mus. Sci. and Industry, 1996–2006 (Chm. Audit Cttee, 1997–2006; Dep. Chm. of Trustees, 2002–06); Royal Med. Benevolent Fund, 1998–2004; Nuffield Oxford Hosp. Fund, 2001– (Chm., 2005–). Member: Court, ICSTM, 2001–06; Council, Taunton Sch., 1990–2001; Gov., Westonbirt Sch., 1991–97. Trustee, Oxford Soc., 1995–2003; Pres., ASM, St Anne's Coll., Oxford, 1997–2000. FRSA 2000. *Publications:* contribs to learned jls in reproductive physiology. *Recreations:* opera, sculpture.

GROCOTT, family name of **Baron Grocott.**

GROCOTT, Baron *cr* 2001 (Life Peer), of Telford in the County of Shropshire; **Bruce Joseph Grocott;** PC 2002; Captain of the Hon. Corps of Gentleman at Arms (Government Chief Whip in the House of Lords), 2002–08; *b* 1 Nov. 1940; *s* of Reginald Grocott and Helen Grocott (*née* Stewart); *m* 1965, Sally Barbara Kay Ridgway; two *s. Educ:* Hemel Hempstead Grammar Sch.; Leicester and Manchester Univs. BA (Pol), MA (Econ). Admin. Officer, LCC, 1963–64; Lectr in Politics, Manchester Univ., Birmingham Polytechnic, and N Staffs Polytechnic, 1964–74. Television presenter and producer, 1979–87. Chm., Finance Cttee, Bromsgrove UDC, 1972–74. Contested (Lab): SW Herts, 1970; Lichfield and Tamworth, Feb. 1974, 1979; The Wrekin, 1983. MP (Lab): Lichfield and Tamworth, Oct. 1974–1979; The Wrekin, 1987–97; Telford, 1997–2001. Parliamentary Private Secretary: to Minister for Local Govt and Planning, 1975–76; to Minister of Agriculture, 1976–78; Dep. Shadow Leader, H of C, 1987–92; Opposition front bench spokesman on foreign affairs, 1992–93; PPS to Leader of the Opposition, 1994–97, to Prime Minister, 1997–2001; a Lord in Waiting (Govt Whip), 2001–02. Mem., Select Cttee on Nat. Heritage, 1994–95. *Recreations:* sport, steam railways. *Address:* House of Lords, SW1A 0PW. *Club:* Trench Labour.

GROCOTT, Susan; QC 2008; a Recorder, since 2003; *b* Rochdale, 30 March 1963; *d* of late Peter and Joan Grocott. *Educ:* Oulder Hill Community Sch., Rochdale; Exeter Coll., Oxford (BA). Called to the Bar, Middle Temple, 1986. *Recreations:* literature, shopping, fine dining. *Address:* Deans Court Chambers, 24 St John Street, Manchester M3 4DF. *T:* (0161) 214 6000, *Fax:* (0161) 214 6001; *e-mail:* grocott@deanscourt.co.uk.

GROENING, Matthew Abram; cartoonist; *b* Portland, Oregon, 15 Feb. 1954; *s* of Homer Philip Groening and Margaret Ruth Groening (*née* Wiggum); *m* 1987, Deborah Lee Caplan (marr. diss. 1999); two *s. Educ:* Lincoln High Sch., Portland, Oregon; Evergreen State Coll. (BA 1977). Worked at LA Reader, 1979–85; cartoonist, weekly comic strip, Life in Hell, 1980–; creator: The Simpsons, interludes on The Tracey Ullman Show, 1987–89; TV series, The Simpsons, 1990– (also Exec. Prod.); TV series, Futurama (also Co-developer), 1999–2003; Exec. Prod., TV film, Olive the Other Reindeer, 1999; The Simpsons Movie, 2007. Co-founder, Life in Hell, Inc., 1985; President: Matt

Groening Prodns, Inc., 1988–; Bongo Entertainment, Inc., 1993–; Founder and Publisher: Bongo Comics Gp, 1993–; Zongo Comics, 1995–. *Publications:* Love is Hell, 1985; Work is Hell, 1986; School is Hell, 1987; Childhood is Hell, 1988; Greetings from Hell, 1989; Akbar and Jeff's Guide to Life, 1989; The Postcards That Ate My Brain, 1990; The Big Book of Hell, 1990; The Simpsons Xmas Book, 1990; Greetings from the Simpsons, 1990; With Love from Hell, 1991; The Simpsons Rainy Day Fun Book, 1991; The Simpsons Uncensored Family Album, 1991; The Simpsons Student Diary, 1991; How to Go to Hell, 1991; Maggie Simpson's Alphabet Book, 1991; Maggie Simpson's Counting Book, 1991; Maggie Simpson's Book of Colors and Shapes, 1991; Maggie Simpson's Book of Animals, 1991; The Road to Hell, 1992; The Simpsons Fun in the Sun Book, 1992; Making Faces with the Simpsons, 1992; Bart Simpson's Guide to Life, 1993; The Simpsons Ultra-Jumbo Rain-Or-Shine Fun Book, 1993; Cartooning with the Simpsons, 1993; Bongo Comics Group Spectacular, 1993; Binky's Guide to Love, 1994; Simpsons Comics Extravaganza, 1994; Simpsons Comics Spectacular, 1994; Bartman: the best of the best, 1994; Simpsons Comics Simps-O-Rama, 1995; Simpsons Comics Strike Back, 1995; Simpsons Comics Wing Ding, 1997; The Huge Book of Hell, 1997. *Address:* c/o Fox Broadcasting Company, PO Box 900, Beverly Hills, CA 90213, USA.

GROGAN, John Timothy; MP (Lab) Selby, since 1997; *b* 24 Feb. 1961; *s* of late John Martin Grogan and Maureen Grogan (*née* Jennings). *Educ:* St Michael's Coll., Leeds; St John's Coll., Oxford (BA Hons 1982; Pres., Student Union, 1982). Asst to Leader, Wolverhampton Council, 1985–87; Communications Dir, Leeds CC, 1987–94; Press Officer, Eur. Parly Lab. Party, 1994–95; Conf. Organiser, Yorks, 1995–97. Contested (Lab): Selby, 1987, 1992; York, EP elecn, 1989. *Recreations:* running, football, keen supporter of Bradford City FC and Yorks CCC. *Address:* House of Commons, SW1A 0AA; (office) 58 Gowthorpe, Selby, North Yorks YO8 4ET. *T:* (01757) 291152. *Club:* Yorks CC.

GRONN, Prof. Peter Christian, PhD; Professor of Education, University of Cambridge, since 2008; *b* Melbourne, 15 Nov. 1946; *s* of Lorenz Christian Gronn and Ena Winifred Gronn; *m* 1972, Barbara Jean Reith; one *d* (and one *d* decd). *Educ:* Canterbury State Sch.; Camberwell Central Sch.; Camberwell High Sch.; Univ. of Melbourne (BA Hons 1968; DipEd 1969); Monash Univ. (BEd 1973; PhD 1979). Teacher, Educn Dept of Vic, Australia, 1970–73; Lectr in Politics, State Coll. of Vic, Burwood, 1974–79; Faculty of Education, Monash University: Lectr, 1980–84; Sen. Lectr, 1985–94; Associate Prof., 1995–2003; Prof. of Educn, 2003–07; Prof. of Public Service, Educnl Leadership and Mgt, Dept of Educnl Studies, Univ. of Glasgow, 2007–08. Fellow, Australian Council of Educnl Leaders, 1997. FRSA 2004. *Publications:* The Making of Educational Leaders, 1999; The New Work of Educational Leaders, 2003; contrib. articles to jls, incl. Leadership Qly, Jl Educnl Admin, Australian Jl Educn, Australian Historical Studies. *Recreations:* reading, music, travel, walking, sport, gardening, house renovating. *Address:* Faculty of Education, University of Cambridge, 184 Hills Road, Cambridge CB2 8PQ. *T:* (01223) 767600.

GRONOW, David Gwilym Colin, MSc, PhD; Central Member, Engineering, Marketing and Research, Electricity Council, 1985–90, retired; *b* Leigh-on-Sea, 13 Jan. 1929; *s* of David Morgan Gronow and Harriet Hannah Gronow; *m* 1st, 1953, Joan Andrew Bowen Jones (marr. diss. 1970); one *s* one *d*; 2nd, 1970, Rosemary Freda Iris Keys. *Educ:* North Street Elem. Sch., Leigh-on-Sea; Grammar Sch., Swansea; University Coll. London (MSc, PhD). Institute of Aviation Medicine, RAF Farnborough, Hants: Jun. Technician, 1951–53; Sci. Officer, then Sen. Sci. Officer, 1953–57; Sen. Sci. Officer, UKAEA, Capenhurst, Cheshire, 1957; Second Asst Engr, then Sen. Asst Engr, CEGB, HQ Operations Dept, London, 1957–64; Asst Commercial Officer/Asst Chief Commercial Officer/Chief Commercial Officer, SSEB, Glasgow, 1964–78; Marketing Advr, 1978–80, Commercial Advr, 1980–85, Electricity Council, London. *Recreations:* travel, bird watching, theatre, horse racing, the stock market. *Address:* 8 Arundel Way, Highcliffe, Christchurch, Dorset BH23 5DX.

GROOM, Brian William Alfred; Editor, Comment and Analysis, Financial Times, since 2005; *b* 26 April 1955; *s* of Fred and Muriel Groom; *m* 1980, Carola May Withington; one *s* one *d*. *Educ:* Manchester Grammar Sch.; Balliol Coll., Oxford (BA Hons). Journalist: Goole Times, 1976–78; Financial Times, 1978–88; Dep. Editor, 1988–94, Editor, 1994–97, Scotland on Sunday; Financial Times: British and Regl Affairs Ed., 1997–2000; Political Ed., 2000–02; Ed., European Edn, 2002–05. *Recreations:* reading, cinema, cricket, walking. *Address:* Financial Times, 1 Southwark Bridge, SE1 9HL. *T:* (020) 7873 3000.

GROOM, Maj.-Gen. John Patrick, CB 1984; CBE 1975 (MBE 1963); Director General, Guide Dogs for the Blind Association, 1983–89; *b* Hagley, Worcs, 9 March 1929; *s* of Samuel Douglas Groom and Gertrude Groom (*née* Clinton); *m* 1951, Jane Mary Miskelly; three *d*. *Educ:* King Charles I Sch., Kidderminster; Royal Military Academy, Sandhurst. Enlisted as Sapper, Dec. 1946; commnd into RE, 1949; regimental service, N Africa, Egypt, Singapore, Malaya, UK, 1949–59; sc Camberley, 1960; War Office, 1961–63; regimental service, UK, Aden, 1963–65 (despatches); Directing Staff, Staff Coll., 1965–68; Regimental Comdr, BAOR, 1968–70; MoD, Military Operations, 1970–71; Dep. Sec., Chiefs of Staff Cttee, 1971–73; HQ Near East Land Forces, Cyprus, 1973–75; RCDS 1976; Comdr, Corps of Royal Engineers, BAOR (Brig.), 1976–79; Chief Engineer, HQ BAOR, 1979–82; Head of Army Trng Rev. Team, MoD (Army), 1982–83. Col Comdt, 1983–91, Rep. Col Comdt, 1986, RE. Chairman: GDBA (Trading Co.) Ltd, 1984–89; GDBA (Recreational Services) Co. Ltd, 1986–89; (non-exec.) BKP Environmental Services Ltd, 1992–99; Dir, GDBA (Pension Fund Trustees) Ltd, 1985–89; Hon. Vice-Pres., Internat. Fedn of Guide Dog Schs, 1989–. Chm., Reach Foundn, 1993–96; Member: Adv. Bd, Talking Newspapers, 1988; Council, Oakhaven Hospice, 1992–96. Governor: Gordon's Sch., Woking, 1982–88; Sandle Manor Sch., Fordingbridge, 1984–88. Vice-Chm., Solent Protection Soc., 1994–99; Chm., Adv. Bd, Yarmouth Harbour Comrs, 1997–2002. Member: RYA, 1982–; ASA, 1982–. FCMI (FBIM 1979); FIPlantE 1976; Fellow, RSPB 1975. Freeman, City of London, 1978; Liveryman, Worshipful Co. of Plumbers, 1978–92. *Recreations:* ocean sailing, country pursuits, the environment. *Address:* Medlar House, 6 Grove Pastures, Lymington, Hants SO41 3RG. *T:* (01590) 675710. *Clubs:* Royal Ocean Racing; Royal Engineer Yacht; Royal Lymington Yacht; British Kiel Yacht (Germany) (Life Mem.); Kieler Yacht (Germany) (Hon. Mem.).

GROOM, Michael John, FCA; President, Institute of Chartered Accountants in England and Wales, 2001–02; *b* 18 July 1942; *s* of Thomas Rowland Groom and Eliza Groom; *m* 1966, Sheila Mary Cartwright; two *d*. *Educ:* St Chad's Grammar Sch., Wolverhampton; Cotton Coll., N Staffs. FCA 1964. Articled, Plevey & Co., Chartered Accountants, 1958–63; Sen. Clerk, Dixon Hopkinson, Chartered Accountants, 1963–65; Sec. and Dir, Thorneville Properties Ltd/Aldridge Builders Ltd, 1965–67; Manager/Partner, Camp Ravenscroft & Co., Chartered Accountants, 1967–71; in practice as chartered accountant, 1971–76, 1981–89; Partner, Tansley Witt/Binder Hamlyn, Chartered Accountants, 1976–81. Mem. Council, ICAEW, 1975–2004. Dep. Chm., Financial Reporting Council, 2001–02; Chm., CCAB, 2001–02; Mem., Takeover Panel, 2001–02. Non-exec. dir of cos; lectr and consultant on strategy formulation in the medium-sized business, th rôle of the non-exec. director, mgt and financial advice, professional practice mg Freeman, City of London, 1977; Liveryman, Chartered Accountants' Co., 1977 (Mem. Ct of Assts, 1994–2006); Trustee, Chartered Accountants' Livery Charity, 2004–06. Hon DBA Wolverhampton, 2003. *Publications:* The Chartac Administration Manual, 1975 Financial Management in the Professional Office, 1977; (jtly) Cash Control in the Smalle Business, 1978; (jtly) Current Cost Accounting the Easy Way, 1980; (jtly) Budgeting an Cash Management, 1981; joint author and series editor, 1975–81: The Charta Accounting Manual; The Chartac Auditing Manual; The Chartac Taxation Manual; Th Chartac Accounting and Auditing Model File. *Recreations:* ballet, theatre, music photography, travel, food and wine. *Address:* 14 High Meadows, Compton Wolverhampton WV6 8PH. *T:* and *Fax:* (01902) 753816. *Club:* Albert Lawn Tenni (Wolverhampton).

GROOM, Hon. Raymond John; MHA (L) for Denison, Tasmania, 1986–2001 Chairman, Southern Cross Care (Tasmania) Inc.; *b* 3 Sept. 1944; *s* of Raymond Jame Groom and Eileen Margaret (*née* Waters); *m* 1967, Gillian M. Crisp; four *s* two *d*. *Edu* Burnie High Sch., Tasmania; Univ. of Melbourne (LLB 1967). Barrister and Solicitor Supreme Court, Victoria, 1968, Tasmania, 1970; practised: Melbourne, 1968–69; Burnie 1969–76; Partner, Hudson and Mann, Tasmania, 1969–76. Sec., Law Liby Cttee, NW Tasmania Law Soc., 1969–75; Mem. Council, Bar Assoc., Tasmania, 1974–75. MHR Braddon, Tasmania, 1975–84; Federal Minister for: Envmt, Housing, Community Devel 1977–78; Housing and Construction, 1978–80; Mem., Parly Delegn to Bangladesh, India Sri Lanka, 1978; Leader, Australian Delegn to ESCAP UN Meeting, Manila (Chm., Firs Session), 1979; Chm., S Pacific Commonwealth and State Housing Ministers Conf., NZ 1980; Tasmania: Minister for Forests, Sea Fisheries and Mines, and Minister Assisting th Premier, 1986–89; Dep. Premier, 1988; Dep. Leader, Liberal Party, 1986–91; Shadow Attorney-General and Shadow Minister for Deregulation, 1989–91; Leader c Opposition, Shadow Treas. and Shadow Minister for Commonwealth and State Relns 1991–92; Premier of Tasmania, 1992–96; Treas. and Minister for Economic Develt 1992–93; Minister for State Develt and Resources, for Forests, and for Mines, 1993–96 Attorney-General, Minister for Justice, Minister for Tourism and for Workplac Standards, 1996–98; Shadow Minister: for Justice and for Tourism, 1998–99; for Industri Relns and for Workplace Standards, 1998–2001; for Educn and Trng and for Public Secto Mgt, 1999–2001; for Consumer Affairs, for Justice and Shadow Attorney-Gen., 2001 Chm., Australian Construction Industry Council, 1979–80. Dep. Pres., Administrativ Appeals Tribunal (Australia). Stolen Generations Assessor, Tasmania. *Recreations:* family painting, golf, football. *Address:* 25 Cromwell Street, Battery Point, Tas 7004, Australi *T:* (3) 62248181. *Clubs:* Melbourne Cricket; Royal Hobart Golf; Royal Yacht (Tasmania).

GROOMBRIDGE, Jeremy Carl, CB 2008; Director of Transformation and Produc Management, Jobcentre Plus, since 2006; *b* Derby, 10 Oct. 1955; *s* of late Deni Groombridge and of Betty Groombridge; *m* 1983, Sandra Young; three *s*. *Educ:* Spondo Park Grammar Sch.; Wilmorton Coll. Joined DHSS, 1974; Private Sec. to Sec. of Stat for Health and Social Security, 1988–90; Hd, Policy Develt Unit, Benefits Agency, Leeds 1990–92; Hd, Unemployment Benefit Policy, 1992–94, Policy Manager, Jobseekers an Incentives, 1994–2001, DSS; Dir, Implementation Prog., Jobcentre Plus, 2002–06. Mem. Scotch Malt Whisky Soc. *Recreations:* family, lay preacher, photography, travel, whisk (quality malts only). *Address:* Jobcentre Plus, Caxton House, Tothill Street, SW1H 9NA *T:* (020) 7829 3375.

GROOTENHUIS, Prof. Peter, FREng, FIMechE; Professor of Mechanical Engineerin Science, Imperial College of Science, Technology and Medicine, 1972–89, now Emeritu Professor and Senior Research Fellow; *b* 31 July 1924; *yr s* of Johannes C. Grootenhui and Anna C. (*née* van den Bergh); *m* 1954, Sara J. Winchester, *o c* of late Major Charles C Winchester, MC, The Royal Scots (The Royal Regt), and Margaret I. (*née* de Havilland) one *d* one *s*. *Educ:* Nederlands Lyceum, The Hague; City and Guilds College. BS MechEng 1944, PhD, DIC, DSc London Univ.; Apprenticeship and Design Office Bristol Aero Engine Co., 1944–46; Lectr 1949, Reader 1959, Mech. Eng. Dept, Imperia College, research in heat transfer and in dynamics; Dir, Derritron Electronics, 1969–82 Partner, Grootenhuis Allaway Associates, consultants in noise and vibration, 1970–93 Associate Mem., Ordnance Board, 1965–70. Mem. Governing Body, Imperial College 1974–79. Freeman, City of London, 1984; Liveryman, Engineers' Co., 1985–. FCG 1976; Mem., Inst. of Acoustics; Fellow, Soc. of Environmental Engineers (Pres. 1964–67); FREng (FEng 1982). *Publications:* technical papers to learned jls, and patents *Recreations:* sailing, gardening. *Club:* Athenæum.

GROSBERG, Prof. Percy, PhD; CEng, MIMechE, FTI; Research Professor of Textil Engineering, 1961–90, and Head of Department of Textile Industries, 1975–83 an 1987–89, University of Leeds, now Emeritus Professor; Marcus Sieff Professor of Textil Technology, Shenkar College of Engineering and Design (formerly of Textil Technology and Fashion), Ramat Gan, Israel, since 1991; *b* 5 April 1925; *s* of late Rev and Mrs Gershon Grosberg, Tel-Aviv; *m* 1951, Queenie Fisch; one *s* one *d* (and one decd). *Educ:* Parktown Boys' High Sch., Johannesburg; Univ. of the Witwatersrand University of Leeds. BScEng, MScEng, PhD Witwatersrand; CEng, MIMechE 1965; FT 1966 (Hon. FTI 1988). Sen. Res. Officer S African Wool Textile Res. Inst., 1949–55 University of Leeds: ICI Res. Fellow, 1955; Lectr in Textile Engrg, 1955–61. Hon Fellow, Shenkar Coll. of Textile Technology and Fashion, Israel, 1993. Warner Memoria Medal, 1968; Textile Inst. Medal, 1972; Distinguished Service Award, Indian Inst. o Technol., Delhi, 1985. *Publications:* An Introduction to Textile Mechanisms, 1968 Structural Mechanics of Fibres, Yarns and Fabrics, 1969; Yarn Production: theoretica aspects, 1999; papers on rheology of fibrous assemblies, mechan. processing of fibres, an other res. topics in Jl of Textile Inst., Textile Res. Jl, and other sci. jls. *Recreations:* music travel. *Address:* Apartment 25, 55 Shlomo Hamelech Street, Netanya 42267, Israel.

GROSE, Vice-Adm. Sir Alan, KBE 1989; Group Executive, Security, De Beer Consolidated Mines Ltd, 1993–2000; *b* 24 Sept. 1937; *s* of George William Stanley Gros and Ann May Grose (*née* Stanford); *m* 1961, Gillian Ann (*née* Dryden Dymond); two *s* on *d*. *Educ:* Strodes School; Britannia Royal Naval College, Dartmouth. Served Mediterranean and S Atlantic, 1957–63; sub-specialised in Navigation, 1964; RAN 1964–66; Home, W Indies, Med., 1966–72; Comd, HMS Eskimo, 1973–75; Staff of C in-C, Naval Home Command, 1975–77; MoD, 1977–79; RCDS 1980; Comd, HMS Bristol, 1981–82; RN Presentation Team, 1983–84; Comd, HMS Illustrious, 1984–86 Flag Officer, Sept. 1986; ACDS, Operational Requirements (Sea Systems), MoD 1986–88; Flag Officer Flotilla Three and Comdr, Anti-Submarine Warfare Striking Force 1988–90; Flag Officer Plymouth, Naval Base Comdr Devonport, Comdr Central Su Area Eastern Atlantic, and Comdr Plymouth Sub Area Channel, 1990–92, retired. Hon Fellow, Liverpool John Moores Univ., 1993. *Recreations:* genealogy, opera, hom computers. *Address:* c/o Barclays Bank, Princess Street, Plymouth PL1 2HA; *e-mail* sagrose@mweb.co.za. *Club:* Cape Town.

GROSS, Prof. David Jonathan, PhD; Director, Kavli Institute for Theoretical Physics, since 1997, and Frederick W. Gluck Professor of Theoretical Physics, since 2002, University of California, Santa Barbara; *b* 19 Feb. 1941; *s* of Bertram Meyer Gross and Nora Gross (*née* Faine); *m* 1st, 1962, Shulamith Toaff; two *d*; 2nd, 2001, Jacquelyn Savani. *Educ:* Hebrew Univ., Jerusalem (BSc 1962); Univ. of Calif, Berkeley (PhD 1966). Princeton University: Asst Prof., 1969–71; Associate Prof., 1971–73; Prof., 1973–86; Eugene Higgins Prof. of Physics, 1986–95; Thomas Jones Prof. of Math. Physics, 1995–97, now Emeritus; Prof., Univ of Calif, Santa Barbara, 1997–. (Jtly) Nobel Prize in Physics, 2004. *Address:* Kavli Institute for Theoretical Physics, Kohn Hall, University of California, Santa Barbara, CA 93106, USA.

GROSS, John Jacob; writer and editor; *b* 12 March 1935; *s* of late Abraham Gross and Muriel Gross; *m* 1965, Miriam May (*see* M. M. Gross) (marr. diss. 1988); one *s* one *d*. *Educ:* City of London Sch.; Wadham Coll., Oxford. Editor, Victor Gollancz Ltd, 1956–58; Asst Lectr, Queen Mary Coll., Univ. of London, 1959–62; Fellow, King's Coll., Cambridge, 1962–65; Literary Editor, New Statesman, 1973; Editor, TLS, 1974–81; editorial consultant, Weidenfeld (Publishers) Ltd, 1982; on staff of New York Times, 1983–88; Dir, Times Newspapers Holdings, 1982; theatre critic, Sunday Telegraph, 1989–2005. A Trustee, National Portrait Gall., 1977–84. Hon. DHL Adelphi Univ., 1995. *Publications:* The Rise and Fall of the Man of Letters (1969 Duff Cooper Memorial Prize), 1969; Joyce, 1971; (ed) The Oxford Book of Aphorisms, 1983; (ed) The Oxford Book of Essays, 1991; Shylock, 1992; (ed) The Modern Movement, 1992; (ed) The Oxford Book of Comic Verse, 1994; (ed) The New Oxford Book of English Prose, 1998; A Double Thread (memoir), 2001; (ed) After Shakespeare: an anthology, 2002; (ed) The New Oxford Book of Literary Anecdotes, 2006. *Address:* Flat 16, 2 Porchester Gardens, W2 6JL. *Club:* Beefsteak.

See also S. Gross.

GROSS, Miriam Marianna, (Lady Owen); Senior Editor, Standpoint magazine, since 2008; *b* 12 May 1939; *d* of late Kurt May and of Wera May; *m* 1st, 1965, John Jacob Gross, *qv* (marr. diss. 1988); one *s* one *d*; 2nd, 1993, Sir Geoffrey Owen, *qv*. *Educ:* Dartington Hall Sch.; St Anne's Coll., Oxford (MA). Observer: Dep. Lit. Editor, 1969–81; Woman's Editor, 1981–84; Arts Editor, Daily Telegraph, 1986–91; Literary Editor, Sunday Telegraph, 1991–2005. Editor, Book Choice, Channel Four TV, 1986–91. *Publications:* (ed) The World of George Orwell, 1971; (ed) The World of Raymond Chandler, 1976. *Recreations:* painting, tennis. *Address:* 24A St Petersburgh Place, W2 4LB. *T:* (020) 7538 7191.

See also S. Gross.

GROSS, Hon. Sir Peter (Henry), Kt 2001; **Hon. Mr Justice Gross;** a Judge of the High Court, Queen's Bench Division, since 2001; Presiding Judge, South Eastern Circuit, 2004–08; *b* 13 Feb. 1952; *s* of late Sam Lewis Gross and Fanny Alice Gross; *m* 1985, Ruth Mary Cullen; two *s*. *Educ:* Herzlia Sch., Cape Town; Univ. of Cape Town (BBusSc, MBusSc); Oriel Coll., Oxford (Rhodes Scholar, MA, BCL, Eldon Scholar). Called to the Bar, Gray's Inn, 1977, Bencher, 2000; admitted to the Bar of NSW, 1986; QC 1992; a Recorder, 1995–2001. Chairman: London Common Law and Commercial Bar Assoc., 1995–97; Bar Educn and Trng Cttee, 1998–2000; Bar Internat. Relations Cttee, 2001. Chm., Adv. Bd, Inst. of Law, City Univ., 2003–05. *Publication:* Legal Aid and its Management, 1976. *Recreations:* jogging, cricket, sailing, cross-country ski-ing. *Address:* Royal Courts of Justice, Strand, WC2A 2LL. *Club:* Oxford and Cambridge.

GROSS, Solomon Joseph, CMG 1966; *b* 3 Sept. 1920; *s* of late Abraham Gross; *m* 1948, Doris Evelyn Barker (*d* 2000); two *d*. *Educ:* Hackney Downs Sch.; University Coll., London. RAF, Burma, India. Ministry of Supply, 1947; OEEC, Paris, 1948–51; British Embassy, Washington, 1951–53; Board of Trade, 1954–57; British Trade Commr, Pretoria, SA, 1958–62; Principal British Trade Commr, Ghana, 1963–66; British Deputy High Commr, Ghana, 1966–67; Board of Trade, 1967–69; Minister, British Embassy, Pretoria, 1969–73; Chargé d'Affaires at various times in Ghana and S Africa; Under-Sec., Dept of Industry, 1974–80; Dir for Regional Affairs, British Technology Gp, 1983–84. Bd Mem., BSC, later British Steel plc, 1978–90; Dir, Technical Audit Group Ltd, 1986–90. Mem., Overseas Cttee, CBI, 1987–90; Mem., External Relations Cttee and Chm., USA Wkg Pty, UNICE, Brussels, 1987–90. *Recreations:* gardening, history, do-it-yourself. *Address:* 38 Barnes Court, Station Road, New Barnet, Herts EN5 1QY. *T:* (020) 8449 2710.

GROSS, Susanna, (Mrs John Preston); Literary Editor, Mail on Sunday, since 1999; *b* 31 July 1968; *d* of John Jacob Gross, *qv* and Miriam Marianna Gross, *qv*; *m* 2005, John Preston; one *s* one *d*. *Educ:* Godolphin and Latymer Sch., Hammersmith; Univ. of York (BA Philosophy). Obituaries Ed., Daily Mail, 1993–96; Features Ed., Harpers & Queen, 1996–97; Dep. Ed., The Week, 1997–2000; bridge columnist, Spectator, 2000–. *Recreations:* bridge, blackjack, hiking. *Address:* 11 Luxemburg Gardens, W6 7EA; Mail on Sunday, Northcliffe House, 2 Derry Street, W8 5TS. *T:* (020) 7938 7059.

GROSSART, Sir Angus (McFarlane McLeod), Kt 1997; CBE 1990; DL; Managing Director, since 1969, and Chairman, Noble Grossart Ltd, Merchant Bankers, Edinburgh, since 1990; merchant banker; *b* 6 April 1937; 3rd *s* of William John White Grossart and Mary Hay Gardiner; *m* 1978, Mrs Gay Thomson; one *d*. *Educ:* Glasgow Acad.; Glasgow Univ. (MA 1958, LLB 1960). CA 1962; Mem., Faculty of Advocates, 1963. Practised at Scottish Bar, 1963–69. Chm., Scottish Investment Trust PLC, 1975–2003; major directorships include: Edinburgh US Tracker Trust (formerly American Trust), 1973–2007; Royal Bank of Scotland plc, 1982–2005 (Vice Chm., 1996–2005); Alexander & Alexander, 1985–97; Scottish Financial Enterprise, 1987–2001; British Petroleum Scottish Bd, 1990–2005; Trinity Mirror (formerly Mirror Gp) PLC, 1998–2007; Scottish & Newcastle plc, 1998–2008; Chairman: Scotland Internat., 1997–; Edinburgh Partners, 2006–; Lyon and Turnbull, 2004–; Dep. Chm., Edinburgh Fund Managers PLC, 1991–2002 (Chm., 1983–91). Mem., Scottish Develt Agency, 1974–78; Dir, St Andrews Management Inst., 1990–97 (Chm. Adv. Council, 1994–97). Chairman, Board of Trustees: National Galleries of Scotland, 1988–97 (Trustee, 1986–97); Nat. Museums Scotland, 2006–; Trustee and Dep. Chm., Nat. Heritage Meml Fund, 1999–2005; Trustee: Culture and Sport Glasgow, 2007–; High Steward of Scotland's Dumfries House Trust, 2007–. Vice Pres., Scottish Opera, 1986–93; Director: Edinburgh Internat. Film Festival, 1994–96; Friends of Royal Scottish Acad., 1989–97; Chm., Fine Art Soc., 1998–. Formerly: Trustee, Scottish Civic Trust; Dir, Scottish Nat. Orch.; Mem., Scottish Industrial Develt Adv. Bd. FRSE 1998. DL Edinburgh, 1996. Livingstone Captain of Industry Award, 1990. Hon. FCIBS 1999. Hon. LLD: Glasgow, 1985; Aberdeen, 2006; Hon. DBA Strathclyde, 1998; Hon. DLitt St Andrews, 2004. Lord Provost of Glasgow Award for public service, 1994; Walpole Medal of Excellence, 2003. Formerly, Scottish Editor, British Tax Encyc., and British Tax Rev. *Recreations:* golfing (runner-up, British Youths' Golf Championship, 1957; Captain, Scottish Youths' Internat., 1956 and 1957), the applied and decorative arts, Scottish painting, Scottish castle restoration. *Address:* 48 Queen Street, Edinburgh EH2 3NR. *T:* (0131) 226 7011. *Clubs:* New, Honourable Company of Edinburgh Golfers (Edinburgh); Royal and Ancient (St Andrews).

GROSSMAN, Loyd Daniel Gilman, OBE 2003; FSA; broadcaster, writer; *b* Boston, Mass, 16 Sept. 1950; *s* of late David K. Grossman and Helen Katherine Grossman (*née* Gilman); *m* 1985, Hon. Deborah Jane (marr. diss. 2005), *d* of Baron Puttnam, *qv*; two *d*. *Educ:* Marblehead High Sch.; Boston Univ. (BA *cum laude*); London School of Economics (MSc Econ.). Design Editor, Harpers and Queen, 1981–84; Contributing Editor: Sunday Times, 1984–86; Condé Nast Traveller, 2006–. *Television* includes: deviser or writer or presenter: Through the Keyhole, 1983–2003; Behind the Headlines; MasterChef, 1990–2000 (Glenfiddich Award, 1996); The Dog's Tale, 1993; Junior MasterChef, 1995–99; Off Your Trolley, 1995; Conspicuous Consumption, 1996; The World on a Plate, 1997; Loyd on Location, 1999–2001; History of British Sculpture, 2003; Build Britain, 2007; Step Up to the Plate, 2008. Presenter, Composers at Home, BBC Radio 3, 2004–. Member: Bd, mda (formerly Museum Documentation Assoc.), 1998–2001; MLA (formerly Museums, Libraries and Archives Council, subseq. Resource: Council for Mus, Archives and Libraries), 1999–2006 (Chm., Designation Challenge Fund, 2001–03); Commissioner: Museums and Galleries Commn, 1996–2000; English Heritage, 1997–2003 (Chairman: Mus. and Collections Adv. Cttee, 1997–2001; Nat. Blue Plaques Panel, 2003–06; Mus and Archives Panel, 2001–03); Royal Commn on Histl Monuments of England, 1999–2003; Chm., 2000, Co-Chm., 2001–, Museums and Galleries Month; Chairman: Campaign for Mus, 1995–; The 24 Hour Mus., 2000–05; Public Monuments and Sculpture Assoc., 2001–07; Nat. Mus Liverpool, 2005–08; Churches Conservation Trust, 2007–; Dep. Chm., Liverpool Culture Co., 2005–07; Vice-Chm., NW Regl Cultural Consortium, 2000–02; Mem. Bd, Culture Northwest: Cultural Consortium for England's Northwest, 2002– (Chm., 2004–); Pres., British Assoc. of Friends of Mus, 2005–. Trustee: Mus. of Sci. and Industry in Manchester, 1999–2002; St Deiniol's Liby, 2003–08 (Fellow, 2008). Mem., Court of Govs, LSE, 1996– (Mem. Council, 2003–08); Chm., Univ. for the Creative Arts, 2008–. Chm., Conservation Awards, 1998–2003; Chm. of Judges, Gulbenkian Prize for Mus, 2004. Vice-President: Sick Children's Trust; Merseyside Civic Soc., 2007–; Chm., Better Hosp. Food Panel, NHS, 2001–06; Patron: Assoc. for Heritage Interpretation, Shark Trust; Liver Sketching Club, 2005–; Hon. Patron, Hosp. Caterers Assoc. Hon. Life Mem., Dogs Trust (formerly Nat. Canine Defence League). FRSA; FSAScot; FRSocMed 2004. Hon. DLitt Chester, 2007. *Publications:* The Social History of Rock Music, 1975; Harpers and Queen Guide to London's 100 Best Restaurants, 1987; The Dog's Tale, 1993; Loyd Grossman's Italian Journey, 1994; (ed) Courvoisier's Book of the Best, 1994–96; The World on a Plate, 1997; The 125 Best Recipes Ever, 1998; Foodstuff, 2002; articles on architecture, design and food in newspapers and magazines. *Recreations:* fishing, scuba diving (PADI Divemaster), looking at buildings, tennis, chess, the Boston Red Sox, playing Gibson guitars. *Clubs:* Brooks's, Flyfishers', Hurlingham, Chelsea Arts, Lansdowne; Artists (Liverpool).

GROSVELD, Prof. Franklin Gerardus, (Frank), PhD; FRS 1991; Professor and Head of Department of Cell Biology and Genetics, Erasmus University, Rotterdam, since 1993; *b* 18 Aug. 1948; *m*; two *s*. *Educ:* Univ. of Amsterdam (MSc); McGill Univ. (PhD). Sen. Scientist, NIMR, 1982–93. *Publications:* papers on human globin genes. *Address:* Department of Cell Biology, Erasmus MC, Dr Molewaterplein 50, 3015 GE Rotterdam, PO Box 2040, 3000 CA Rotterdam, The Netherlands.

GROSVENOR, family name of **Earl of Wilton** and of **Duke of Westminster**.

GROSVENOR, Earl; Hugh Richard Louis Grosvenor; *b* 29 Jan. 1991; *o s* and *heir* of Duke of Westminster, *qv*.

GROSZ, Stephen Ernest; Partner, Bindman & Partners, solicitors, since 1981; *b* 14 April 1953; *s* of Emil, (Joe), Grosz and Therese Grosz (*née* Baer); *m* 1981, Judith Beale (marr. diss. 1995). *Educ:* William Ellis Sch.; Clare Coll., Cambridge (BA 1974); Université Libre de Bruxelles (licencié special en droit européen 1976). Joined Bindman & Partners, 1976. Significant cases include: Marshall *v* Southampton & SW Hants AHA, instrumental in changing UK law on equal rights for retirement age and for compensation for discrimination; R *v* Sec. of State for Foreign & Commonwealth Affairs ex parte World Develt Movt, in which the High Court declared unlawful aid for construction of the Pergau Dam in Malaysia; R *v* Lord Chancellor ex parte Witham, quashing changes to court fees as contrary to constitutional rights of access to the courts; R *v* MoD ex parte Lustig-Prean and Lustig-Prean & others *v* UK, concerning the rights of homosexuals & lesbians to serve in the armed forces; Abdulaziz & others *v* UK, instrumental in removing sex discrimination from the immigration rules; Silver & others *v* UK, instrumental in removing restrictions on prisoners' rights to respect for correspondence; Sutherland *v* UK, in which the European Commission of Human Rights ruled unlawful discrimination in the age of consent for gay men; R *v* Sec. of State for Home Dept, ex parte Amnesty Internat. & others, concerning disclosure of med. reports relating to extradition of Augusto Pinochet; Sahin *v* Turkey, concerning ban on headscarves in Turkish univs; Goodwin *v* UK, concerning recognition of transexuals; Ghaidan *v* Ghodin, concerning succession rights for same-sex partners. Gov., 1992–2004, Mem. Adv. Bd, 2004–, British Inst. of Human Rights; Chm., Domestic Human Rights Reference Gp, Law Soc., 2004–; Member: Mgt Cttee, Public Law Project, 1991–2001; Council, Justice, 1997–; Council, Liberty, 2001–03; Member Advisory Board: Judicial Review Qly, 1996–; Educn, Public Law and the Individual, 1996–. Mem., Editl Bd, Civil Procedure, 2000–. *Publications:* (jtly) Human Rights: the 1998 Act and the European Convention, 2000; *contributions to:* Public Interest Law, 1986; Atkin's Court Forms, 1987; Public Interest Perspectives in Environmental Law, 1995; Judicial Rev. in the New Millennium, 2003; articles and reviews in newspapers and legal jls. *Recreations:* cycling, walking, choral singing, eating and drinking, trying to make people laugh. *Address:* (office) 275 Gray's Inn Road, WC1X 8QB. *T:* (020) 7833 4433.

GROTE, Dr John David, OBE 1991; Director, British Council, Egypt, 2001–05; *b* 5 Sept. 1945; *s* of Roy and Dorothy Grote; *m* 1st, 1970, Pauline Bolton (marr. diss. 1979); one *s* one *d*; 2nd, 1979, Barbara Elzbieta Orzechowska (*née* Smigielska). *Educ:* Rydens Co. Secondary Sch.; Southampton Univ. (BSc 1st Cl. Hons Maths 1967; PhD 1971). Temp. Lectr, Maths Dept, Univ. of Southampton, 1970–71; Res. Fellow, Control Theory Centre, Warwick Univ., 1971–74; British Council, 1974–2005: Sci. Advr, 1974–75; Sci. Officer, Poland, 1975–79; Staff Inspector, 1979–82; Dep. Dir, Computer Systems, 1982–83; Science Officer: Germany, 1983–86; Japan, 1987–91; Director: Hungary, 1991–96; Singapore, 1996–2000. *Recreations:* reading, thinking, wine, walking with my wife. *Address:* Bridgeford House, 68 Belle Vue Road, Wivenhoe, Essex CO7 9LD; *e-mail:* johngrote_99@yahoo.com.

GROTRIAN, Sir Philip Christian Brent, 3rd Bt *cr* 1934; *b* 26 March 1935; *s* of Robert Philip Brent Grotrian (*d* on active service, 1945) (*y s* of 1st Bt), and Elizabeth Mary, *d* of Major Herbert Hardy-Wrigley; *S* uncle, 1984; *m* 1st, 1960, Anne Isabel, *d* of Robert Sieger Whyte, Toronto; one *s*; 2nd, 1979, Sarah Frances, *d* of Reginald Harry Gale, Montreal; one *s* one *d*. *Educ:* Eton; Trinity Coll., Toronto. *Heir: s* Philip Timothy Adam Brent Grotrian, *b* 9 April 1962. *Address:* RR3, Mansfield, ON L0N 1M0, Canada; Calle Ample 2, Regencós, Gerona, Spain.

GROUND, (Reginald) Patrick; QC 1981; *b* 9 Aug. 1932; *s* of late Reginald Ground and Ivy Elizabeth Grace Ground (*née* Irving); *m* 1964, Caroline Dugdale; three *s* one *d*. *Educ:* Beckenham and Penge County Grammar Sch.; Lycée Gay Lussac, Limoges, France; Selwyn Coll., Cambridge (Open Exhibnr; MA Mod. Langs, French and Spanish); Magdalen Coll., Oxford (MLitt, Mod. History). Inner Temple Studentship and Foster Boulton Prize, 1958; called to the Bar, Inner Temple, 1960, Bencher, 1987. National Service, RN, 1954–56: Sub-Lt RNVR; served in Mediterranean Fleet and on staff of C-in-C Mediterranean; rep. RN at hockey and lawn tennis; Lt-Comdr RNR. Worked for FO on staff of Wilton Park European Conf. Centre, 1958–60. Councillor, London Bor. of Hammersmith, 1968–71 (Chm., Cttees responsible for health and social services, 1969–71). Contested (C): Hounslow, Feltham and Heston, Feb. and Oct. 1974, and 1979; Feltham and Heston, 1992 and 1997. MP (C) Feltham and Heston, 1983–92. PPS to the Solicitor General, 1987–92. Treasurer and Pres., Oxford Univ. Cons. Assoc., 1958; Chm., Fulham Soc., 1975–96. *Publications:* articles on housing, security of tenure and paying for justice. *Recreations:* lawn tennis, theatre, sailing, travel, forestry. *Address:* 13 Ranelagh Avenue, SW6 3PJ. *T:* (020) 7736 0131. *Clubs:* Brooks's, Carlton.

GROVE, Dr Andrew Steven; Senior Advisor to Executive Management, Intel Corporation, since 2005 (President, 1979–97; Chief Executive Officer, 1987–98; Chairman, 1997–2005); *b* Budapest, 2 Sept. 1936; *m* 1958, Eva; two *d*. *Educ:* City Coll. of NY (BSc Chem. Engrg); Univ. of Calif, Berkeley (PhD Chem. Engrg). FIEEE. Asst Dir of R&D, Fairchild Semiconductor, 1967–68; joined Intel, 1968. Mem., Nat. Acad. of Engrg. Fellow, Amer. Acad. of Arts & Scis, 1994. Hon. DEng Worcester. Engrg Leadership Recognition Award, 1987; Heinz Foundn Award for Technol. and the Econ., 1995; Time Man of the Year, 1997; IEEE 2000, Medal of Honour, 1998. *Publications:* Physics and Technology of Semiconductor Devices, 1967; High Output Management, 1983; One-on-One With Andy Grove, 1987; Only the Paranoid Survive, 1996. *Address:* Intel Corporation, 2200 Mission College Boulevard, Santa Clara, CA 95052–8119, USA.

GROVE, Sir Charles Gerald, 5th Bt *cr* 1874; *b* 10 Dec. 1929; *s* of Walter Peel Grove (*d* 1944) (3rd *s* of 2nd Bt) and Elena Rebecca, *d* of late Felipe Crosthwaite; *S* brother, 1974, but his name does not appear on the Official Roll of the Baronetage. *Heir:* *b* Harold Thomas Grove, *b* 6 Dec. 1930.

GROVE, Sir Edmund (Frank), KCVO 1982 (CVO 1974; LVO 1963; MVO 1953); Chief Accountant of the Privy Purse, 1967–82, and Serjeant-at-Arms, 1975–82, retired; *b* 20 July 1920; *s* of Edmund Grove and Sarah Caroline (*née* Hunt); *m* 1945, Grete Elisabet (*d* 2007), *d* of Martinus Skou, Denmark; two *d*. Served War, RASC, ME, 1940–46 (C-in-C's Commendation). Entered the Household of King George VI, 1946 and of Queen Elizabeth II, 1952. Chevalier: Order of the Dannebrog, Denmark, 1974; Légion d'Honneur, France, 1976; Officer, Order of the Polar Star, Sweden, 1975. *Recreation:* gardening. *Address:* Chapel Cottage, West Newton, King's Lynn, Norfolk PE31 6AU.

GROVE, Rear-Adm. John Scott, CB 1984; OBE 1964; RN retired, 1985; nuclear engineering consultant to Ministry of Defence, 1985–99; *b* 7 July 1927; *s* of late William George Grove and Frances Margaret Scott Grove; *m* 1950, Betty Anne (*née* Robinson); one *s* (one *d* decd). *Educ:* Dundee High Sch.; St Andrews Univ. University Coll., 1944–47 (BScEng 1st Cl. Hons). National Service, Royal Engineers, 1947–48; Instructor Br., Royal Navy, 1948–50; Electrical Engrg Br., RN, 1950, qualified in Submarines, 1953; post graduate trng in Nuclear Engrg, Imperial Coll., London, 1958–59; sea service in HMS Forth and HM Submarines Tally-Ho, Turpin (FO Subs' Commendation, special op., 1955), Porpoise, Dreadnought (1st Sen. Engrg Officer, RN first nuclear sub., 1960–64); service in Ship Dept, 1964–67; staff of Flag Officer Submarines, 1967–70; Naval Asst to Controller of the Navy, 1970–73; staff of Flag Officer Submarines, 1975–77; commanded HMS Fisgard, 1977–79; Chief Strategic Systems Exec. (formerly Chief Polaris Exec.), 1980–85; Chief Naval Engr Officer, 1983–85. Comdr 1963; Captain 1970; Rear-Adm. 1980. Dir, Devonport Mgt Ltd, Devonport Royal Dockyard, 1987–91; engrg consultant 1991–98. Gov., British Maritime Technol. (Quality Assurance), 1990–94. Chm., Friends of RN Mus. and HMS Victory, 1995–99. Master, Engineers' Co., 1994–95 (Sen. Warden, 1993–94). *Recreations:* walking, gardening. *Address:* Maryfield, South Close, Wade Court, Havant, Hants PO9 2TD. *T:* (023) 9247 5116.

GROVE, Trevor Charles; JP; journalist; *b* 1 Jan. 1945; *s* of Ronald and Lesley Grove; *m* 1975, Valerie Jenkins (*see* V. Grove); one *s* three *d*. *Educ:* St George's, Buenos Aires; Radley; St Edmund Hall, Oxford. Editorial Staff, Spectator, 1967–70; Leader Writer, then Features Editor, Evening Standard, 1970–78; Asst Editor, Sunday Telegraph, 1978–80; Sen. Asst Editor, Observer, 1980–83; Editor, Observer Magazine, 1983–86; Asst Editor, Daily Telegraph, 1986–89; Editor, Sunday Telegraph, 1989–92; Gp Exec. Ed. and Dep. Ed., Daily Telegraph, 1992–94; Launch Editor, El Periódico de Tucumán, Argentina, 1994; Chm., Inside Time: The Prisoners' Newspaper, 2004–. JP Haringey, 1999. Trustee, Butler Trust, 2006–. *Publications:* (co-ed) Singlehanded, 1984; (ed) The Queen Observed, 1986; The Juryman's Tale, 1998; The Magistrate's Tale, 2002; One Dog and His Man, 2003. *Recreations:* playing tennis, messing about in a boat, learning the tango, walking the dog. *Address:* 14 Avenue Road, Highgate, N6 5DW. *T:* (020) 8348 2621.

GROVE, Valerie; feature writer, The Times, since 1992; *b* 11 May 1946; *d* of Doug Smith, cartoonist; *m* 1st, 1968, David Brynmor Jenkins (marr. diss. 1975); 2nd, 1975, Trevor Charles Grove, *qv*; one *s* three *d*. *Educ:* South Shields Grammar Sch.; Kingsbury County Grammar Sch.; Girton Coll., Cambridge (MA 1969). Evening Standard, 1968–87; Sunday Times, 1987–92. *Publications:* (as Valerie Jenkins) Where I Was Young, 1976; (as Valerie Grove): The Compleat Woman, 1987; Dear Dodie: the life of Dodie Smith, 1996; Laurie Lee: the well-loved stranger, 1999; A Voyage Round John Mortimer, 2007. *Recreations:* tennis, archives, tango, walking Dalmatian. *Address:* 14 Avenue Road, Highgate, N6 5DW. *T:* (020) 8348 2621; *e-mail:* vgrove@dircon.co.uk.

GROVE-WHITE, Prof. Robin Bernard; Professor of Environment and Society, Institute for Environment, Philosophy and Public Policy, Lancaster University, 2000–05, now Emeritus; *b* 17 Feb. 1941; *s* of Charles William Grove-White and Cecile Mary Rabbidge; *m* 1st, 1970, Virginia Harriet Ironside (marr. diss.); one *s*; 2nd, 1979, Helen Elizabeth Smith; two *s* one *d*. *Educ:* Uppingham Sch.; Worcester Coll., Oxford (BA). Freelance writer for TV, radio, press and advertising in UK, Canada and US, 1963–70; McCann-Erickson Ltd, London, 1970; Asst Secretary, 1972–80, Dir, 1981–87, CPRE; Res. Fellow, Centre for Envmtl Technol., Imperial Coll., London, 1987–89; Lancaster University: Sen. Res. Fellow, 1989–91; Dir, Centre for Study of Envmtl Change, 1991–2001. Member: Forestry Commn, 1991–98; Agric. and Envmt Biotechnology Commn, 2000–05. Chm., Greenpeace UK, 1997–2003. *Publications:* (contrib.) Politics of Physical Resources, 1975; (contrib.) Future Landscapes, 1976; (with Michael Flood) Nuclear Prospects, 1976; contribs to New Scientist, Nature, Times, Independent, and numerous academic jls. *Recreations:* walking, cricket. *Address:* Brynddu, Llanfechell, Ynys Mon LL68 0RT. *T:* (01407) 710245.

GROVENOR, Prof. Christopher Richard Munro, DPhil; FInstP; Professor of Materials, since 2004, and Head, Department of Materials, since 2005, University of Oxford; Fellow, St Anne's College, Oxford, since 1990; *b* 21 Oct. 1955; *s* of John an Christine Grovenor; *m* 1987, Susan Ruth Ortner; two *d*. *Educ:* Marlborough Coll.; S Catherine's Coll., Oxford (MA, DPhil). FInstP 2004. Lectr in Materials, Univ. of Oxforc 1986–. *Publications:* contribs on relationship between microstructure and properties c functional materials. *Recreations:* cricket, bassoonist. *Address:* Department of Material University of Oxford, Parks Road, Oxford OX1 3PH. *T:* (01865) 273737; *e-mai* chris.grovenor@materials.ox.ac.uk.

GROVER, Derek James Langlands, CB 1999; consultant, since 2005; Group Directc of Distributed Learning, NHSU, Department of Health, 2004–05; *b* 26 Jan. 1949; *s* c Donald James Grover and late Mary Barbara Grover; *m* 1972, Mary Katherine Morgar one *s*. *Educ:* Hove County Grammar Sch. for Boys; Clare Coll., Cambridge (Found Schol. 1970; BA Eng. Lit. 1971, MA 1975; Grene Prize 1971). Various positions, Dept c Employment, 1971–78; Cabinet Office, 1978–80; MSC, 1980–87; Training Agency Head of Personnel, 1987–89; Dir of Youth Training, 1989; Dir of Systems and Strategy 1989; Dir of Trng Strategy and Standards, later of Trng Strategy and Infrastructure 1990–94; Dep. Chief Exec. and Sen. Dir of Operations, Employment Service, 1994–97 Dir of Employment and Adult Trng, DFEE, 1997–98; Dir, Skills and Lifelong Learning then Adult Learning Gp, DfEE, then DfES, 1998–2002; Dir of Develt, NHSU, 2002–0 Chair: NIACE Enquiry on ESOL, 2005–06; Nat. ESOL Adv. Forum, 2007–. FRS 1991. MCIPD (MIPM 1993). *Recreations:* music, reading, walking, watching cricke *Address:* 8 Oakbrook Road, Sheffield S11 7EA.

GROVES, His Honour Richard Bebb, TD 1966; RD 1979; a Circuit Judge 1985–2000; *b* 4 Oct. 1933; *s* of George Thomas Groves and Margaret Anne (*née* Bebb); *r* 1958, Eileen Patricia (*née* Farley); one *s* one *d*. *Educ:* Bancroft's Sch., Woodford Greer Essex; DipFrench Open, 2003. Admitted Solicitor of the Supreme Court, 1960. Partner H. J. Smith & Co. and Richard Groves & Co., 1962–85. Dep. Circuit Judge, 1978–80; Recorder, 1980–85. Nijmegen Medal, Royal Netherlands League for Physical Culture 1965 and 1966. *Recreations:* Royal Naval Reserve, tennis, philately, walking, reading *Club:* Royal Automobile.

GRUBB, Prof. Andrew, LLD; Senior Immigration Judge and Training Judge, Asylur and Immigration Tribunal, since 2005; *b* 24 March 1958; *s* of late Graham Grubb and c Valerie Grubb; *m* 1988, Helga Anne Moore; two *s* one *d*. *Educ:* Brynmaw Comprehensive Sch.; Selwyn Coll., Cambridge (BA 1st Cl. Hons 1979; MA 1983); LLI London 1998. Called to the Bar, Inner Temple, 1980 (Scarman Schol., 1980; Certificat of Honour 1980). Cambridge University: Law Fellow, Fitzwilliam Coll., 1981–90; As Univ. Lectr, 1984–89, Univ. Lectr, 1989–90, in Law; King's College, London: Sen. Lec in Law, 1990–92; Reader in Med. Law, 1992–94; Prof. of Health Care Law, 1994–98 acting Dir, 1992–93, Dir, 1993–97, Centre of Med. Law and Ethics; Prof. of Med. Law 1998–2004, Hd of Sch., 1999–2004, Vis. Prof., 2004–, Cardiff Law Sch., Cardiff Univ Trng Immigration Adjudicator, Immigration Appellate Authy, 2004–05. Visitin Professor of Law: Boston Univ. Sch. of Law, 1989; Univ. of New Mexico Sch. of Law 1989. Member: Ethical Cttee, RCP, 1994–2004; HFEA, 1997–2003; U Xenotransplantn Regulatory Authy, 2003–04; Nuffield Council on Bioethics, 2003–04 pt-time Immigration Adjudicator, 1996–2004; Chm., Indep. Review Panel (NH Complaints), Wales, 1998–99. Vice Pres., Wales Medico-Legal Soc., 2000–. Founde FMedSci 1998. Editor, Medical Law Review, 1993–2004. Ver Heyden de Lance Medico-Legal Prize, Cambridge Univ., 1991. *Publications:* (with I. Kennedy) Medica Law: cases and materials, 1989, rev. edn, Medical Law: text with materials, 1994, 3rd ed 2000; (with D. Pearl) Blood Testing, AIDS and DNA Profiling: law and policy, 199 (jtly) Doctors' Views on the Management and Care of Patients in Persistent Vegetativ State: a UK study, 1997; (ed) Principles of Medical Law, (with I. Kennedy) 1998, 2nd ed 2004. *Recreations:* music and music trivia, appreciating electric guitars, the Wels countryside, Welsh Rugby. *Address:* Asylum and Immigration Tribunal, Columbu House, Langstone Business Park, Chepstow Road, Langstone, Newport NP18 2LX. *T* (01633) 416749.

GRUBB, Deborah Mary Hinton; Chair: Gardner Arts Centre, since 2001; South Ea Regional Arts Council, since 2002; *b* 21 Feb. 1946; *d* of Joe Grubb and Winifred Grub (*née* Axtell); *m* 2000, Peter Guttridge. *Educ:* Haberdashers' Aske's Sch. for Girls; UC Cardiff (BA Hons). Various posts in local govt, theatre and PR; Dir, Arts, Recreation an Tourism, Brighton and Hove CC, 1991–2000. Mem., Arts Council England (formerl Arts Council of England), 2002–05. *Recreations:* theatre, gardening, travel. *Address:* Ban Cottage, Streat Lane, Streat, Hassocks, W Sussex BN6 8RT. *T:* (01273) 890573; *e-mai* deborahgrubb@btinternet.com.

GRUBB, George Darlington Wilson; Lord Lieutenant and Lord Provost of Edinburgh since 2007; *b* 5 Dec. 1935; *s* of Robert Birnie Grubb and Georgina Wilson Grubb (*n* Pratt); *m* 1960, Elizabeth Grant; one *s* one *d*. *Educ:* James Gillespie's Boys' Sch.; Roya High Sch.; Open Univ. (MA 1974; BPhil 1983); Univ. of Edinburgh (BD 1978); Sa Francisco Theol Seminary (DMin 1993). Ordained, C of S, 1962; Sqdn Leader Chaplair RAF, 1962–70; Parish Minister, Craigsbank Ch, Edinburgh, 1971–2001. Mem. (Li Dem) Edinburgh CC, 1999– (Chm., Lib Dem Gp, 2000–07). Pres., Edinburgh Interna Sci. Fest.; Director and Chairperson: Edinburgh Internat. Fest. Soc.; Edinburgh Mi Tattoo Ltd; Edinburgh Mil. Tattoo (Charities) Ltd. Dir, Dynamic Earth Charitable Trus *Recreations:* running, reading, being with grandchildren. *Address:* City Chambers, Hig Street, Edinburgh EH1 1YJ. *T:* (0131) 529 4000, *Fax:* (0131) 529 4010; *e-mai* lord.provost@edinburgh.gov.uk.

GRUBB, Prof. Michael John, PhD; Chief Economist, Carbon Trust, since 2005; Senic Research Associate, Faculty of Economics, Cambridge University, since 2005; *b* Southall Middx, 29 Feb. 1960; *s* of Martyn Patrick and Anne Isobel Grubb; *m* 2005, Joann Depledge; one *s* two *d*. *Educ:* King's Coll., Cambridge (BA 1982; PhD 1987). Res. Fellow Electrical Engrg, Imperial Coll., London, 1986–88; Res. Fellow, 1988–92, Hd, Energ and Envmt Prog., 1993–98, RIIA; Prof. of Climate Change and Energy Policy, Imperia Coll., London, 1999–2001; Associate Dir of Policy, Carbon Trust, 2002–04. Mem., UI Climate Change Cttee; Chm., Climate Strategies. Lead Author, Intergovtl Panel o Climate Change: Assessment Reports II 1996, III 2001 and IV 2007. *Publications:* Energ Policies and the Greenhouse Effect, vol. 1 1990, vol. 2 (ed) 1991; (ed) Emerging Energ Technologies: impacts and policy implications, 1992; The Earth Summit Agreements: guide and assessment, 1993; Renewable Energy Strategies for Europe: vol. 1 1995, vol. 1997; The Kyoto Protocol: a guide and assessment, 1999; (ed jtly) A Low Carbo Electricity System for the UK: technology, economics and policy, 2008; Planetar Economics, 2009. *Recreations:* time with family; music: Whitehall choir, guitar. *Address:* Clements Inn, SW1Y 4LE. *T:* (020) 7170 7039; *e-mail:* michael.grubb@ carbontrust.co.uk.

GRUBB, Prof. Peter John, PhD, ScD; Professor of Investigative Plant Ecology Cambridge University, 2000–01, now Emeritus; Fellow, Magdalene College, Cambridge 1960–2002, now Emeritus (President, 1991–96); *b* 9 Aug. 1935; *s* of Harold Amos Grub and Phyllis Gertrude (*née* Hook); *m* 1965, Elizabeth Adelaide Anne, *d* of Charles Edwar and Adelaide Gertrude Hall; one *s* one *d.* *Educ:* Royal Liberty Sch.; Magdalene Coll., Cambridge (Schol.; BA 1957; PhD 1962; ScD 1995). Magdalene College, Cambridge: John Stothert Bye Fellow, 1958–60; Res. Fellow, 1960; Tutor, 1963–74; Jt Dir of Studies in Natural Scis, 1980–96; Cambridge University: Demonstrator in Botany, 1961–64; Lectr, 1964–92; Reader, 1992–2000. Nuffield-Royal Soc. Bursar, Univ. of Adelaide, 1963; Hon. Res. Fellow, ANU, 1970–71; Vis. Prof., Cornell Univ., 1982, 1987; Sen. Vis. Researcher, CSIRO Tropical Forest Res. Centre, Atherton, 1992–2000; Vis. Prof., ICSTM, 1999–2007. Editor: Jl of Ecology, 1972–77; Biol Flora of British Isles, 1978–87. Jt Leader, Cambridge Expedn to Colombian Cordillera Oriental, 1957; Leader, Oxford Univ. Expedn to Ecuador, 1960. President: Brit. Ecol Soc., 1990–91 (Hon. Mem., 2001; first Award for outstanding service to the Soc., 2003); Cambridge Philosophical Soc., 1990–91. Frank Smart Prize in Botany, Cambridge Univ., 1956; Rolleston Meml Essay Prize, Oxford Univ., 1963. *Publications:* (with P. F. Stevens) Forests of Mt Kerigomna, Papua New Guinea, 1985; (ed with J. B. Whittaker) Toward a More Exact Ecology, 1989; papers in ecol and botanical jls. *Recreations:* history of buildings and landscape, biographies. *Address:* Magdalene College, Cambridge CB3 0AG. *T:* (01223) 332109.

GRUBBS, Prof. Robert Howard, PhD; Victor and Elizabeth Atkins Professor of Chemistry, California Institute of Technology, Pasadena, since 1990 (Professor of Chemistry, 1978–90); *b* 27 Feb. 1942; *s* of Henry Howard Grubbs and Evelyn Faye Grubbs; *m* 1967, Helen M. O'Kane; two *s* one *d.* *Educ:* Univ. of Florida, Gainesville (BS Chem 1963, MS Chem 1965); Columbia Univ., NY (PhD Chem 1968). NIH Postdoctoral Fellow, Stanford Univ., Calif, 1968–69; Asst Prof., 1969–73, Associate Prof., 1973–78, Michigan State Univ., E Lansing. MACS 1964; MNAS 1989; Fellow, Amer. Acad. of Arts and Scis, 1994; FRCS 2004. Hon. MRIA 1999; Hon. FRSC 2006. Hon. Prof., Shanghai Inst. of Organic Chemistry, Chinese Acad. of Scis, 2001. Camille and Henry Dreyfus Teacher-Scholar Award, 1975; American Chemical Society Awards: Nat. Award in Organometallic Chem., 1988; Arthur C. Cope Scholar, 1990; Polymer Chemistry, 1995; Herman F. Mark Polymer Chemistry, 2000; Herbert C. Brown for Creative Res. in Synthetic Methods, 2001; Arthur C. Cope, 2002; for Creative Res. in Homogenous or Heterogeneous Catalysis, 2003; Richard C. Tolman Medal, 2003; Pauling Award Medal, 2003; Kirkwood Medal, 2005; Nagoya Univ. Medal of Organic Chemistry, 1997; Fluka Prize, Reagent of the Yr, 1998; Benjamin Franklin Medal in Chemistry, Franklin Inst., 2000; Bristol-Myers Squibb Dist. Achievement Award in Organic Synthesis, 2004; August Wilhelm von Hofmann Denkmünze, German Chem. Soc., 2005; (jtly) Nobel Prize in Chemistry, 2005; Havinga Medal, Leiden Univ., 2006. *Publications:* 420 research pubns and 83 patents issued. *Recreations:* rock climbing, walking. *Address:* Chemistry & Chemical Engineering, MC 164–30, California Institute of Technology, Pasadena, CA 91125, USA. *T:* (626) 3956003, *Fax:* (626) 5649297; *e-mail:* rhg@caltech.edu.

GRUBEN, Baron Thierry de; *see* de Gruben.

GRUDER, Jeffrey Nigel; QC 1997; *b* 18 Sept. 1954; *s* of late Bernard Gruder and of Lily Gruder; *m* 1979, Gillian Vera Hyman; one *s* two *d.* *Educ:* City of London Sch.; Trinity Hall, Cambridge (MA). Called to the Bar, Middle Temple, 1977; in practice at the Bar, 1978–. *Recreations:* reading, theatre, collecting art. *Address:* Essex Court Chambers, 24 Lincoln's Inn Fields, WC2A 3EG. *T:* (020) 7813 8000.

GRUFFYDD, Prof. (Robert) Geraint, FBA 1991; Director, University of Wales Centre for Advanced Welsh and Celtic Studies, Aberystwyth, 1985–93; *b* 9 June 1928; *s* of Moses and Ceridwen Griffith; *m* 1953, Elizabeth Eluned Roberts; two *s* one *d.* *Educ:* University Coll. of N Wales, Bangor (BA; Hon. Fellow, 1993); Jesus Coll., Oxford (DPhil; Hon. Fellow, 1992). Asst Editor, Geiriadur Prifysgol Cymru, 1953–55; Lectr, Dept of Welsh, UCNW, 1955–70; Prof. of Welsh Language and Literature, UCW, Aberystwyth, 1970–79; Librarian, Nat. Library of Wales, 1980–85. Vice-Pres., Univ. of Wales, Aberystwyth, 1996–2001. Chairman: Welsh Books Council, 1980–85; Welsh Language Section, Welsh Acad., 1986–90; Bd of Celtic Studies, Univ. of Wales, 1991–93. President: Cambrian Archæol Assoc., 1991–92; Internat. Congress of Celtic Studies, 1995–2003. Consulting Ed., Geiriadur Prifysgol Cymru (A Dictionary of the Welsh Language), 1999–. Hon. Fellow, Univ. of Wales, Aberystwyth, 2004. Hon. DLitt Wales, 1997. *Publications:* (ed) Meistri'r Canrifoedd, 1973; (ed) Cerddi '73, 1973; (ed) Bardos, 1982; (ed) Cerddi Saunders Lewis, 1986; Dafydd ap Gwilym, 1987; (ed) Y Gair ar Waith, 1988; Llenyddiaeth y Cymry, ii, 1989; (gen. editor) Cyfres Beirdd y Tywysogion (Poets of the Princes series), 7 vols, 1991–96; (consulting ed.) Cyfres Beirdd yr Uchelwyr (Poets of the Nobility series), 36 vols, 1994–; (co-ed) Hispano-Gallo-Brittonica, 1995; (ed) A Guide to Welsh Literature, Vol. 3, 1997; (co-ed) Gwaith Einion Offeiriad a Dafydd Ddu o Hiraddug, 1997; articles, etc, on Welsh literary and religious history in various collaborative vols and learned jls. *Recreations:* reading, walking, travel. *Address:* Eirianfa, Caradog Road, Aberystwyth, Ceredigion SY23 2JY. *T:* (01970) 623396.

GRUGEON, Sir John (Drury), Kt 1980; DL; Chairman, Kent Police Authority, 1992–98; *b* 20 Sept. 1928; *s* of Drury Grugeon and Sophie (*née* Pratt); *m* 1st, 1955, Mary Patricia (*née* Rickards) (marr. diss. 1986); one *s* one *d*; 2nd, 1989, Pauline Lois (*d* 2006), *widow* of Dr Roland Phillips. *Educ:* Epsom Grammar Sch.; RMA Sandhurst. Commissioned, The Buffs, Dec. 1948; served 1st Bn in Middle and Far East and Germany; Regimental Adjt, 1953–55; Adjt 5th Bn, 1956–58; left Army, 1960. Joined Save and Prosper Group, 1960. Kent County Council: Mem., 1967–2001; Leader, 1973–82; Vice-Chm., 1987–89; Chm., 1989–91, 1997–99; Chairman: Superannuation Fund, 1982–87; Fire and Public Protection Cttee, 1984–87. Chm., Policy Cttee, Assoc. of County Councils, 1978–81 (Chm., Finance Cttee, 1976–79); Vice Chm., Assoc. of Police Authorities, 1997–98 (Chm., Finance Gp, 1997–98). Dir, Internat. Garden Fest. '84, Liverpool, 1982–83. Chm., Tunbridge Wells HA, 1984–92. Member: SE Economic Planning Council, 1971–74; Medway Ports Authority, 1977–93; Dep. Chm., Medway (Chatham) Dock Co., 1983–92. Jt Vice-Chm., Cons. Nat. Adv. Cttee for Local Govt, 1975–82. Chm., Brett Envmt Trust, 2001–07. Liveryman, Ironmongers' Co., 1977–. DL Kent, 1986. Hon. Fellow, Canterbury Christ Church UC, 2002. *Recreations:* cricket, shooting, local govt. *Address:* 3 Eastgate Road, Tenterden, Kent TN30 7AH. *T:* (01580) 763494. *Clubs:* Carlton, MCC; Kent County CC.

GRÜNBERG, Prof. Peter Andreas; Helmholtz Professor, Forschungszentrum Jülich, Germany, since 2007; *b* Pilsen, 18 May 1939; s of Feodor A. Grünberg and Anna Grünberg; *m* 1966, Helma Prausa; one *s* two *d.* *Educ:* Johann Wolfgang Goethe Univ., Frankfurt (Intermediate Dip. Physics 1962); Darmstadt Univ. of Technol. (Dip. 1966; Dr 1969); Univ. of Cologne (Privatdozent 1984). Postdoctoral Fellow, NRCC, Carleton Univ., Ottawa, 1969–72; Res. Scientist, Inst. Solid State Res., Forschungszentrum Jülich, 1972–2004. Res. at Argonne Nat. Lab., Ill, 1984–85; Adjunct Prof., Univ. of Cologne, 1992–; res. at Univ. of Sendai and Tsukuba Res. Centre, Japan, 1998. Member: Max Planck Soc.; Acad. of Sci. in N Rhine-Westfalia; Gerhard Herzberg Gesellschaft, Darmstadt. Hon. Dr: Ruhr Univ., Bochum, 2002; RWTH Aachen, 2007; Cologne, 2008; Saarland, 2008. German Future Prize, Pres. of FRG, 1998; Manfred von Ardenne Prize for Applied Physics, Eur. Soc. of Thin Films, 2004; Eur. Inventor of Year, EC and Eur. Patent Office, 2006; Stern Gerlach Medal, German Physics Soc., 2007; jointly: APS Internat. Prize for New Materials, 1994; Magnetism Award, IUPAP, 1994; Hewlett-Packard Europhysics Prize, 1997; Japan Prize, Sci. and Technol. Foundn of Japan, 2007; Wolf Foundn Prize in Physics, Israel, 2007; Nobel Prize in Physics, 2007. *Publications:* contrib. jls incl. Physics Rev., Jl Materials Sci. and Engrg, Jl IMMM, Applied Physics, Vacuum. *Recreations:* golf, table tennis, tennis. *Address:* Forschungszentrum Jülich, Institut für Festköperforschung, 52425 Jülich, Germany.

GRUNDY, David Stanley, CB 1997; Commissioner for Policy and Resources, Forestry Commission, 1992–97; *b* 10 April 1943; *s* of Walter Grundy and Anne Grundy (*née* Pomfret); *m* 1965, Elizabeth Jenny Schadla Hall; one *s.* *Educ:* De La Salle Coll., Manchester; Jesus Coll., Cambridge (MA); Jesus Coll., Oxford (MPhil). Asst Principal, MOP, 1967–70; Asst Private Sec. to Minister, Min. of Technology, 1970–71; Principal, DTI, 1971–73; Economic Adviser: FCO, 1976–78; DoE, 1978–79; Chief Economic Advr, Govt of Vanuatu, 1979–81; Forestry Commission: Chief Economist, 1982–90; Comr for Finance and Admin, 1990–92. Member: Scottish Ornithological Club; Scottish Wildlife Trust. *Publication:* (ed) The Birds of Scotland, 2007. *Recreations:* angling, bird watching, gardening, tennis. *Address:* 9 Ann Street, Edinburgh EH4 1PL. *Club:* Dean Tennis (Edinburgh).

GRUNDY, Prof. Emily Marjata Dorothea, PhD; Professor of Demographic Gerontology, London School of Hygiene and Tropical Medicine, since 2003; *b* 24 July 1955; *d* of late John Grundy and of Dorothea Grundy (now Sheppard); partner, M. S. Murphy; one *s* one *d* (twins). *Educ:* King's Coll., Cambridge (BA (Hist.) 1976); LSHTM (MSc (Med. Demography) 1979); Univ. of London (PhD Medicine 1989). Res. Officer, Dept of Health Care of Elderly, Univ. of Nottingham, 1981–83; Res. Fellow, Social Stats Res. Unit, City Univ., London, 1983–86; Lectr, then Reader, in Social Gerontology, KCL, 1986–98; Reader in Social Gerontology, LSHTM, 1998–2003. *Publications:* Women's Migration, Marriage, Fertility and Divorce, 1989; (jtly) Living Well into Old Age, 1997; approx. 100 papers in learned jls and book chapters. *Recreations:* family and friends, cycling. *Address:* Centre for Population Studies, London School of Hygiene and Tropical Medicine, 49–51 Bedford Square, WC1B 3DP. *T:* (020) 7299 4668; *e-mail:* emily.grundy@lshtm.ac.uk.

GRUNDY, (James) Milton; Founder and Chairman, The Milton Grundy Foundation (formerly Warwick Arts Trust), since 1978; *b* 13 June 1926. *Educ:* Cowley Sch.; Sedbergh Sch.; Gonville and Caius Coll., Cambridge (MA). Called to the Bar, Inner Temple, 1954. Founder and Chm., Gemini Trust for the Arts, 1959–66; Founder Mem. and Pres., Internat. Tax Planning Assoc., 1975–; Charter Mem., Peggy Guggenheim Collection, 1980–89; Chm., Internat. Management Trust, 1986–96; Trustee: Nat. Museums and Galls of Merseyside, 1987–96; New End Theatre, Hampstead, 1994–96. *Publications:* Tax and the Family Company, 1956, 3rd edn 1966; Tax Havens, 1968, 8th edn (with Aparna Nathan, as Offshore Business Centres) 2008; Venice, 1971, 6th edn 2007; The World of International Tax Planning, 1984; (jtly) Asset Protection Trusts, 1990, 3rd edn 1997; (with V. I. Atroshenko) Mediterranean Vernacular, 1991; Essays in International Tax Planning, 2001; More Essays in International Tax Planning, 2007. *Recreation:* conversation. *Address:* Gray's Inn Tax Chambers, Gray's Inn, WC1R 5JA. *T:* (020) 7242 2642.

GRUNDY, Jennifer Anne; JP; Vice Lord-Lieutenant of Merseyside, since 2004; *b* 29 Sept. 1935; *d* of Edward and Marjorie Denton; *m* 1956, Martin Anthony Wilson Grundy (*d* 2007); one *s* four *d.* *Educ:* Huyton Coll. Co. Dir, Res. into Ageing, 1980–90; Chm., Warrington Community Trust, 1993–95. Trustee, Age Concern Liverpool, 1999–2005. JP Knowsley, 1975 (Chm. Bench, 2000–03); DL Merseyside, 1989. *Recreations:* calligraphy, narrow-boating, gardening, traditional canal painting. *Address:* Stanley Cottage, 60 Roby Road, Roby, Liverpool L36 4HF. *T:* (0151) 489 1159; *e-mail:* grundy500@tiscali.co.uk.

GRUNDY, Rev. Canon Malcolm Leslie; Director, Foundation for Church Leadership, since 2005; *b* 22 March 1944; *s* of Arthur James Grundy and Gertrude Alice Grundy; *m* 1972, Wendy Elizabeth Gibson; one *s.* *Educ:* Sandye Place Sch., Beds; Mander Coll., Bedford; King's Coll., London (AKC 1968); Open Univ. (BA 1976). Ordained deacon 1969, priest 1970; Curate, St George's, Doncaster, 1969–72; Chaplain and Sen. Chaplain, Sheffield Industrial Mission, 1972–80; Dir of Educn, dio. of London, 1980–86; Team Rector of Huntingdon, 1986–91; Dir, Avec, 1991–94; Archdeacon of Craven, 1994–2005; Actg Dean, Bradford Cathedral, 2004–05. Hon. Canon of Ely, 1988–94; Canon Emeritus, Bradford, 2005. *Publications:* Light in the City, 1990; An Unholy Conspiracy, 1992; Community Work, 1995; (ed) The Parchmore Partnership, 1995; Management and Ministry, 1996; Understanding Congregations, 1998; (contrib.) Managing, Leading, Ministering, 1999; (jtly) Faith on the Way, 2000; What They Don't Teach You at Theological College, 2003; What's New in Church Leadership, 2007. *Recreations:* classic cars, gardening, writing. *Address:* 4 Portal Road, York YO26 6BQ.

GRUNDY, Sir Mark, Kt 2006; Executive Principal, Collegiate Academy Trust comprising Shireland Collegiate Academy and George Salter Collegiate Academy, since 2007; *b* 19 July 1959; *s* of James and Gloria Grundy; *m* 1985, Denise Long; two *s.* *Educ:* Hawtonville Jun. Sch., Newark; Magnus Grammar Sch., Newark; Loughborough Univ. (MSc Human Biol. 1983). Teacher, Darlaston Comp. Sch., Walsall, 1984–87; Sen. Teacher, Thorns Community Coll., Dudley, 1987–92; Dep. Headteacher, Wodensborough Community Technology Coll., Wednesbury, 1992–97; Headteacher, Shireland Lang. Coll., Smethwick, 1997–2007. Exec. Dir, George Salter High Sch., West Bromwich, 2003–07. Consultant Headteacher, DfES, 2001–03. FRSA 2007. *Recreations:* hockey, tennis, watching sport, ICT. *Address:* Shireland Collegiate Academy, Waterloo Road, Smethwick B66 4ND. *T:* (0121) 558 8086, *Fax:* (0121) 558 8377; *e-mail:* m.grundy@shireland.sandwell.sch.uk.

GRUNDY, Stephanie Christine; legal consultant, legislative drafting and financial services; *b* 11 Dec. 1958; *d* of Harry Grundy and June (*née* Hazell). *Educ:* Grange Sch., Oldham; Hertford Coll., Oxford (Schol.; Gibbs Prize; MA, BCL). Called to the Bar, Middle Temple, 1983. Research Asst, Law Commn, 1985; Asst Parly Counsel, 1985–92; on secondment to Law Commn, 1988–90; Legal Advr, Treasury Solicitor's Dept, 1992–2000; Lawyer, FSA, 2000–05; consultancy services to govt depts, IMF, Shearman and Stirling, Bindman and Partners, Lord Lester of Herne Hill, MPs, and others, 2000–. *Recreations:* yoga, mountaineering, architecture. *Address:* 1 Friend Street, EC1V 7NS.

GRUNENBERG, Dr Christoph; Director, Tate Liverpool, since 2001; *b* 28 Oct. 1962; *s* of Johannes and Marlis Grunenberg; *m* 1994, Gina. *Educ:* Johann Wolfgang Goethe Gymnasium, Frankfurt am Main; Courtauld Inst. of Art, Univ. of London (MA 1988; PhD 1993). Res. Asst, Nat. Gall. of Art, Washington, 1990–91; Asst Curator, Kunsthalle Basel, 1993–95; Curator, 1995–99, Actg Dir, 1997–98, Inst. of Contemporary Art, Boston; Curator, Contemporary Art, Collections Div., Tate Gall., London, 1999–2001. *Publications:* Mark Rothko, 1991; (ed) Gothic: transmutations of horror in late twentieth century art, 1997; (ed) Enterprise: venture and process in contemporary art, 1997; (ed) FRIEZE: wall paintings by Franz Ackerman, John Armleder, Margaret Kilgallen, Sarah

Morris and Alexander Scott, 1999; (ed with Victoria Pomery) Marc Quinn, 2002; (ed) Summer of Love: art of the psychedelic era, 2005; (ed with J. Harris) Summer of Love: psychedelic art, social crisis and counterculture in the 1960s, 2005. *Recreations:* books, reading, music, travel. *Address:* Tate Liverpool, Albert Dock, Liverpool L3 4BB. *T:* (0151) 702 7500, *Fax:* (0151) 709 4166; *e-mail:* christoph.grunenberg@tate.org.uk.

GRUNWALD, Henry Cyril; QC 1999; *b* 15 Aug. 1949; *s* of Eugen Grunwald and Hetty Grunwald (*née* Steppel); *m* 1976, Alison Appleton; two *s* two *d*. *Educ:* City of London Sch.; University Coll. London (LLB Hons; Fellow, 2006). Called to the Bar, Gray's Inn, 1972, Bencher, 2002. Pres., Bd of Deputies of British Jews, 2003– (Vice-Pres., 1997–2000, Sen. Vice-Pres., 2000–03); Warden, Hampstead Synagogue, 1997–2008; Chm., Jewish Leadership Council, 2004–. Pres., Relate N London, 2007– (Trustee, 1996–); Vice-Chm., Holocaust Meml Day Trust, 2005–; Patron, Interfaith Youth Trust, 2007–. *Recreations:* family, friends, theatre, reading, travel. *Address:* Charter Chambers, 33 John Street, WC1N 2AT. *T:* (020) 7832 0300. *Club:* Royal Automobile.

GRYBAUSKAITĖ, Dalia, PhD; Member, European Commission, since 2004; *b* Vilnius, 1 March 1956. *Educ:* Leningrad Univ. (degree in Econs 1983); Moscow Acad. of Public Scis (PhD 1988); Foreign Service Sch., Georgetown Univ., Washington. Hd, Dept of Sci., Inst. of Econs, 1990–91; Prog. Dir, Prime Minister's Office, Lithuania, 1991; Director: European Dept, Min. of Internat. Econ. Relns, 1991–93; Econ. Relns Dept, Min. of Foreign Affairs, 1993–94; Envoy and Minister, Lithuanian Mission to EU, Brussels, 1994–95; Minister, Lithuanian Embassy, USA, 1996–99; Deputy Minister: of Finance, 1999–2000; of Foreign Affairs, 2000–01; Minister of Finance, 2001–04. *Address:* European Commission, Rue de la Loi 200, 1049 Brussels, Belgium.

GUAY, Richard; Canadian barrister and arbitrator; *b* Montreal, 15 Nov. 1943; *s* of late Maurice Guay and Irène (*née* Brassard); *m* 1980, Marie-France Fortier; one *s* one *d*. *Educ:* Coll. Jean de Brébeuf, Montreal; Univ. of Montreal (law degree). Radio Canada: journalist, Montreal, 1966–69; Corresp., UN and NY, 1969–71; Lectr, Sch. of Journalism, Dakar Univ., 1971–73; Co-ordinator of Intergovtl Relns, Min. of Communications, Quebec, 1973–75; Counsellor to Dep. Minister, Min. of Culture, 1975–76. National Assembly, Quebec: Mem. for Taschereau, 1976–85; Parly Asst, Min. of Communications, 1976–79, Min. of Housing, 1979–82; Dep. Leader of Govt, 1982–83; Speaker, 1983–85. Mem. Bd, Internat. Assoc. of French-speaking Parliamentarians, 1983–85 (Grand Officier, Ordre de la Pléiade, 1991); Canadian Rep., Internat. Exec., CPA, 1983–85; Lawyer, specialising in arbitration, Montreal, 1986–95; Agent Gen., then Deleg. Gen., for Quebec in London, 1995–99; Deleg. Gen. for Quebec in Brussels, 1999–2002; Lawyer, Montreal, 2002–. *Recreations:* music, reading, ski-ing.

GUBBAY, Hon. Anthony Roy; Chief Justice of Zimbabwe, 1990–2001; *b* 26 April 1932; *s* of Henry and Gracia Gubbay; *m* 1962, Alice Wilma Sanger; two *s*. *Educ:* Univ. of Witwatersrand, SA (BA); Jesus Coll., Cambridge Univ. (MA, LLM; Hon. Fellow, 1992). Admitted to practice, 1957; emigrated to S Rhodesia, 1958; in private practice as advocate, Bulawayo; SC 1974; Judge: of the High Court, 1977–83; of the Supreme Court, 1983–90. Pres., Valuations Bd, 1974–77; National President: Special Court for Income Tax Appeals, 1974–77; Fiscal Court, 1974–77; Patents Tribunal, 1974–77. Chairman: Legal Practitioners' Disciplinary Tribunal, 1981–87; Law Develt Commn, 1990–2001; Judicial Service Commn, 1990–2001. Mem., Perm. Court of Arbitration, 1993–. Mem., Commonwealth Reference Gp on the promotion of human rights of women and the girl child through the Judiciary, 1996–. Patron, Commonwealth Magistrates' and Judges' Assoc., 1994–2001. Pres., Oxford and Cambridge Soc. of Zimbabwe. Hon. Bencher, Lincoln's Inn, 1997. Hon. Mem., Soc. of Legal Scholars, 2004. DU Essex, 1994; Hon. LLD: London, 2002; Witwatersrand, 2005. Peter Gruber Foundn's Annual Justice Award, 2001. Great Cross, Order of Rio Branco (Brazil), 1999. *Recreations:* classical music, philately, tennis. *Address:* 26 Dacomb Drive, Chisipite, Harare, Zimbabwe. *T:* (4) 496882; *e-mail:* gubbay@zol.co.zw. *Club:* Harare.

GUBBAY, Raymond Jonathan, CBE 2001; Managing Director, Raymond Gubbay Ltd, since 1966; *b* 2 April 1946; *s* of late David and Ida Gubbay; *m* 1972, Johanna Quirke (marr. diss. 1988); two *d*. *Educ:* University Coll. Sch., Hampstead. Concert promoter, 1966–: regular series of concerts at major London concert halls, including: Royal Festival Hall; Royal Albert Hall; The Barbican (*c* 1,200 concerts, 1982–); also major regl arenas and concert venues; has presented many of the world's greatest artists in concert; The Ratepayers Iolanthe, South Bank and Phoenix Theatre, 1984; The Metropolitan Mikado, South Bank, 1985; also Royal Opera prodn of Turandot, Wembley Arena, 1991; Royal Albert Hall: Centenary prodn of La Bohème, 1996; Carmen, 1997; Swan Lake, 1997; Madam Butterfly, 1998; Romeo and Juliet, 1998; Tosca, 1999; Sleeping Beauty, 2000; Aida, 2001; Cavalleria Rusticana and Pagliacci, 2003; Strictly Gershwin, 2008; Royal Festival Hall: D'Oyly Carte Opera Co., 1998 and 1999 (also Queen's Th., 1998–99, and Savoy Th., 2000, 2001, 2002, 2003); Follies, 2002; On Your Toes, 2003; Carmen Jones, 2007; Bolshoi Ballet, Th. Royal, 2001; Ute Lemper, Queen's Th., 1999, Savoy Th., 2001; Pirates of Penzance, Savoy Th., 2004; Barber of Seville, Marriage of Figaro, Savoy Opera, Savoy Th., 2004; tours and seasons by various visiting ballet cos, incl. Stanislavsky Ballet, RFH, 2001, 2003, 2004; Carl Rosa Gilbert and Sullivan season, Gielgud Th., 2008. Founder, City of London Antiques and Fine Art Fair, Barbican Exhibn Halls, 1987–92. Mem. Council, Corps of Army Music, 2001–. Hon. FRAM 1988; Hon FTCL 2000. FRSA 2001. *Recreations:* living in Paris and Provence, having six grandchildren. *Address:* Dickens House, 15 Tooks Court, EC4A 1QH. *T:* (020) 7025 3750, *Fax:* (020) 7025 3751; *e-mail:* info@raymondgubbay.co.uk.

GUBBAY, Dr Susan, (Mrs A. R. Davis), FRICS; independent marine consultant working on projects for public sector, private sector, and non-governmental organisations on marine ecology, marine conservation and integrated coastal management, since 1994; *b* 8 Sept. 1957; *d* of Eldred Gubbay and Flora Gubbay; *m* 1986, Alan Ramsay Davis. *Educ:* Lancaster Univ. (BSc Hons Ecol.); York Univ. (DPhil Marine Ecol.). FRICS. Conservation Officer, 1984–88, Sen. Conservation Officer, 1988–94, Marine Conservation Soc. Buckland Prof. (Marine Protected Areas and Fisheries), Buckland Foundn, 1993. Specialist Advr to H of C Envmt Select Cttee inquiry into Coastal Zone Protection and Planning, 1991–94; Mem., Ministerial Gp reviewing EU Commn Fisheries Policy, 1995–96. Wildlife and Countryside Link: Chair: Jt Marine Wkg Gp, 1993–94; Marine Gp, 1993–96; Member: Action Plan Steering Gp, UK Biodiversity, 1994–95; Cttee, UK Marine Biodiversity, 1997–99; Council, English Nature, 1998–2004; Council, Countryside Council for Wales, 2008–. Marine and Coastal Biol Diversity expert on Roster of Experts for Convention on Biol Diversity, 1998–. Pres., Eur. Coastal Assoc. of Sci. and Technol. (EUROCOAST), 1994–96. External Examiner: MSc Coastal and Marine Resource Mgt, Univ. of Portsmouth, 1999–2004; Marine Resource Mgt, Univ. of Aberdeen, 2001–05. FRSA 1995. *Publications:* (ed) Marine Protected Areas: principles and techniques for management, 1995; numerous contribs on marine conservation to jls, reports and popular articles. *Recreations:* the great outdoors (above and below sea level), scuba diving, natural history, clarinet, gardening, photography, travel.

GUBBINS, Prof. David, PhD; FRS 1996; CPhys, FInstP; Professor of Geophysics, University of Leeds, since 1989; *b* 31 May 1947; *s* of late Albert Edmund Gubbins and of Joyce Lucy Gubbins; *m* 1972, (Margaret) Stella McCloy; one *s* two *d*. *Educ:* King Edward VI Grammar Sch., Southampton; Trinity Coll., Cambridge (BA, PhD). CPhys, FInst 1996. Vis. Res. Fellow, Univ. of Colorado, 1972–73; Instructor in Applied Maths, MIT 1973–74; Asst Prof., Inst. of Geophysics and Planetary Physics, UCLA, 1974–76 Cambridge University: Res. Assistant and Sen. Assistant in Res., Dept of Geodesy an Geophysics, 1976–81; Asst Dir of Res., Dept of Earth Scis, 1981–89; Fellow of Churchi Coll., 1978–90. Fellow, Amer. Geophys. Union, 1985; Foreign Mem., Norwegian Acad of Arts and Sci., 2005. Murchison Medal, Geol Soc., 1999; Gold Medal, RAS, 2003; Joh Adam Fleming Medal, Amer. Geophys. Union, 2004; Chree Medal, Inst. of Physics, 2005 Love Medal, Eur. Geoscis Union, 2007. *Publications:* Seismology and Plate Tectonics 1990; Time Series Analysis and Inverse Theory for Geophysicists, 2004; (ed) Encyclopedi of Geomagnetism and Paleomagnetism, 2007; scientific papers. *Recreations:* sailing swimming. *Address:* School of Earth and Environment, University of Leeds, Leeds LS 9JT. *T:* (0113) 343 5255. *Club:* Wigtown Bay Sailing.

GUBERT, Walter Alexander; Vice Chairman, since 1988, Chairman, Europe, Middl East and Africa, since 2004, and Member, Executive Committee, since 2005, J. P. Morga Chase & Co. (formerly J. P. Morgan); *b* Merano, Italy, 15 June 1947; *m* 1974, Carolin Espagno; two *d*. *Educ:* Univ. of Florence (Dr in Law 1970); INSEAD (MBA 1973). Joine J. P. Morgan, Paris, 1973; Hd, Capital Mkts, USA, 1981–87; Leader, J. P. Morga Securities, EMEA and Asia, 1987–88; Dir, 1988–; Hd, Global Investment Banking 1988–2000; Sen. Exec. in London, 1989–; Chm., JP Morgan Investment Bank, 2000– *Recreations:* golf, piano, history, books. *Address:* J. P. Morgan Chase & Co., 1 Aldermanbury, EC2V 7RF. *T:* (020) 7325 5087; *e-mail:* walter.gubert@jpmorgan.com *Clubs:* Queenswood Golf; Wisley Golf.

GUCKIAN, Dr Noel Joseph, OBE 2001; HM Diplomatic Service; Ambassador t Oman, since 2005; *b* 6 March 1955; *s* of William Joseph Guckian and late Mary Patrici Joan Guckian (*née* Kelly); *m* 1990, Lorna Ruth Warren; one *s* three *d*. *Educ:* Notre Dam Internat. Sch., Rome; New Univ. of Ulster (BA Hons History 1976); UCW, Aberystwyt (MSc Econ, Internat. Politics 1977; PhD Internat. Politics 1985). FCO 1980; Arabic a SOAS, 1983–84; Jedda, 1984–87; 1st Sec., Financial, Paris, 1988; Head, British Interes Section, Tripoli, 1990; Head, Political Section, Kuwait, 1991–92; Counsellor and Dep Head of Mission, Muscat, 1994–97; Dep. Hd of Mission and Consul-Gen., Tripol 1998–2002 (Hd, British Interests Sect., 1998–99, then Chargé d'Affaires *ai* on restoratio of diplomatic relns, 1999); Dep. Hd of Mission, Damascus, 2002–04; Consul Gen. Northern Iraq, 2004–05. *Recreations:* fly-fishing, diving, sailing. *Address:* c/o Foreign an Commonwealth Office, SW1A 2AH. *Clubs:* Royal Commonwealth Society, Roya Over-Seas League; Salisbury and District Angling.

GUÉGUINOU, Jean, Hon. GCVO 1996; Officier de la Légion d'Honneur, 200 (Chevalier 1991); Officier de l'Ordre du Mérite, 1995 (Chevalier, 1979); Commandeu Ordre des Arts et des Lettres, 2007; Ambassadeur de France, 2000; Chairman, Frenc Section, Franco British Council, since 2007; *b* 17 Oct. 1941. *Educ:* Ecole National d'Administration. Press and Inf. Dept, Min. of Foreign Affairs, Paris, 1967–69; Secon Sec., London, 1969–71; Chargé de Mission, Private Office of Ministre d'Etat, Minister c Nat. Defence, 1971–73; Asst Private Sec., then Special Advr to Minister of Foreign Affairs 1973–76; Principal Private Sec. to Minister of State resp. to Prime Minister, 1976–77 Head of Southern Africa and Indian Ocean Dept, Min. of Foreign Affairs, 1977–82 Consul Gen., Jerusalem, 1982–86; Dir of Press and Inf. Dept, Min. of Foreign Affairs, an Ministry Spokesman, 1986–90; French Ambassador: in Prague, 1990–93 (Czechoslovakia 1990–92; Czech Republic, 1993); to UK, 1993–98; to the Holy See, 1998–2001 Ambassador and Perm. Deleg. of France to UNESCO, 2002–07. Mem. Governing Body Agence France Presse, 1986–90. KSG 1976. *Address:* 5 avenue Montespan, 75116 Paris France; Conseil Franco Britannique, 66 rue de Bellechasse, 75007 Paris, France.

GUERIN, Orla, Hon. MBE 2005; Africa Correspondent, BBC TV, since 2006; *b* Dublin 15 May 1966; *d* of late Patrick James Guerin and of Monica Guerin; *m* 2003, Michae Georgy. *Educ:* Coll. of Commerce, Dublin (Journalism Cert. 1985); University Coll. Dublin (MA Film Studies 1999). Joined RTE, 1987, E Europe Correspondent, 1990–94 BBC: joined as news correspondent, 1995; S Europe Correspondent, 1996–2000; ME Correspondent, 2001–05. DU Essex, 2002; Hon. Dr Dublin Inst. of Technology, 2005 Hon. degree Open, 2007. *Address:* BBC Television Centre, Wood Lane, W12 7RJ.

GUERITZ, Rear-Adm. Edward Findlay, CB 1971; OBE 1957; DSC 1942, and Bar 1944; *b* 8 Sept. 1919; *s* of Elton and Valentine Gueritz; *m* 1947, Pamela Amand Bernhardina Britton, *d* of Commander L. H. Jeans, and *widow* of Lt-Comdr E. M. Britton RN; one *s* one *d*. *Educ:* Cheltenham Coll. Entered Navy, 1937; Midshipman, 1938; serve War of 1939–45 (wounded; DSC and Bar): HMS Jersey, 5th Flotilla, 1940–41; Combine Ops (Indian Ocean, Normandy), 1941–44; HMS Saumarez (Corfu Channel incident) 1946; HMS Troubridge, 1947; Army Staff Coll., Camberley, 1948; Staff of C-in-C Atlantic and Junior Naval Liaison Officer to UK High Comr, S Africa, 1954–56; Near Eas Operations, 1956 (OBE); Staff of FO Sea Training, 1957–58; Dep. Dir, RN Staff Coll. 1959–61; Naval Staff, Admty, 1961–63; idc 1964; Captain of Fleet, Far East Fleet 1965–66; Dir of Defence Plans (Navy), 1967; Dir, Jt Warfare Staff, MoD, 1968; Admiral President, Royal Naval Coll., 1968–70 (concurrently first Pres., RN Staff Coll.); Comdt Jt Warfare Estabt, 1970–72. Lt-Comdr 1949; Comdr 1953; Captain 1959; Rear-Adm 1969; retd 1973. Dep. Dir and Editor, 1976–79, Dir and Editor-in-Chief, 1979–81 RUSI. Specialist Adviser, House of Commons Select Cttee on Defence, 1975–95. Chie Hon. Steward, Westminster Abbey, 1975–85. President: Soc. for Nautical Res., 1974–9 (Hon. Vice Pres., 1990); J and K Class Destroyer Assoc., 1990–99; Vice-Pres., RN Commando Assoc., 1993–2004; Vice Chairman: Council for Christian Approaches t Defence and Disarmament, 1974–80; Victoria League, 1985–88; Marine Soc., 1988–9 (Vice Pres., 1991); Member Council: Fairbridge-Drake Soc., 1981–90; British Atlanti Cttee, 1977–89; HOST (Hosting for Overseas Students Trust), 1987–90 (founding Governor). Mem., Bd of War Studies, Univ. of London, 1969–85. *Publications:* (jtly) Th Third World War, 1978; (ed jtly) Ten Years of Terrorism, 1979; (ed jtly) Will the Well Run Dry, 1979; (ed jtly) Nuclear Attack: Civil Defence, 1982; editor, RUSI Brassey' Defence Year Book, 1977–78, 1978–79, 1980, 1981. *Recreations:* history, gardening *Address:* Hemyngsby, 56 The Close, Salisbury, Wilts SP1 2EL. *Club:* Army and Navy.

GUERNSEY, Lord; Heneage James Daniel Finch-Knightley; *b* 29 April 1985; *s* and *heir* of Earl of Aylesford, *qv*. *Educ:* Stowe Sch.; Univ. of Newcastle upon Tyne. *Recreations* ski-ing, archery, field sports. *Address:* c/o Packington Hall, Meriden, Warwickshire CV7 7HF.

GUERNSEY, Dean of; *see* Mellor, Very Rev. K. P.

GUEST; *see* Haden-Guest.

GUEST, family name of **Viscount Wimborne**.

GUEST, Prof. Anthony Gordon, CBE 1989; QC 1987; FBA 1993; FCIArb; Barrister-at-Law; Professor of English Law, King's College, University of London, 1966–97; *b* 8 Feb. 1930; *o s* of late Gordon Walter Leslie Guest and Marjorie (*née* Hooper), Maidencombe, Devon; unmarried. *Educ:* Colston's Sch., Bristol; St John's Coll., Oxford (MA). Exhibr and Casberd Schol., Oxford, 1950–54; 1st cl. Final Hon. Sch. of Jurisprudence, 1954. Bacon Schol., Gray's Inn, 1955; Barstow Law Schol., 1955; called to the Bar, Gray's Inn, 1956, Bencher, 1978. University Coll., Oxford: Lectr, 1954–55; Fellow and Prælector in Jurisprudence, 1955–65; Dean, 1963–64; Reader in Common Law to Council of Legal Educn (Inns of Court), 1967–80. Travelling Fellowship to S Africa, 1957; Mem., Lord Chancellor's Law Reform Cttee, 1963–84; Mem., Adv. Cttee on establishment of Law Faculty in University of Hong Kong, 1965; UK Deleg. to UN Commn on Internat. Trade Law, NY, Geneva and Vienna, 1968–84 and 1986–87, to UN Conf. on Limitation of Actions, 1974. Vis. Prof., Univ. of Leuven, 2004–05. Mem., Board of Athlone Press, 1968–73; Mem. Governing Body, Rugby Sch., 1968–88. FKC 1982; FCIArb 1984; FRSA 2004. Served Army and TA, 1948–50 (Lieut RA). *Publications:* (ed) Anson's Principles of the Law of Contract, 21st to 26th edns, 1959–84; Chitty on Contracts: (Asst Editor) 22nd edn 1961, 28th edn to 30th edns, 1999–2008, (Gen. Editor) 23rd to 27th edns, 1968–94; (ed) Oxford Essays in Jurisprudence, 1961; The Law of Hire-Purchase, 1966; (Gen. Editor) Benjamin's Sale of Goods, 1st to 7th edns, 1974–2006; (ed jtly) Encyclopedia of Consumer Credit, 1975; (jtly) Introduction to the Law of Credit and Security, 1978; (ed) Chalmers and Guest on Bills of Exchange, 14th edn to 16th edns, 1991–2005; Only Remember Me (anthology), 1993; articles in legal jls. *Address:* 17 Ranelagh Grove, SW1W 8PA. *T:* (020) 7730 2799. *Club:* Garrick.

GUEST, Christopher; *see* Haden-Guest, 5th Baron.

GUEST, Ivor Forbes, FRAD 1982; Chairman, 1969–93, Member, 1965–93, Executive Committee, a Vice-President, since 1993, Royal Academy of Dancing; Solicitor; *b* 14 April 1920; *s* of Cecil Marmaduke Guest and Christian Forbes Guest (*née* Tweedie); *m* 1962, Ann Hutchinson; no *c. Educ:* Lancing Coll.; Trinity Coll., Cambridge (MA). Admitted a Solicitor, 1949; Partner, A. F. & R. W. Tweedie, 1951–83, Tweedie & Prideaux, 1983–85. Organised National Book League exhibn of books on ballet, 1957–58; Mem. Cttee, Soc. for Theatre Research, 1955–72; Chm., Exec. Cttee, Soc. for Dance Research, 1982–97 (Pres., 1998–); Jt Pres., Dolmetsch Early Dance Soc., 1990–; Member: Exec. Cttee, British Theatre Museum, 1957–77 (Vice-Chm., 1966–77); Cttee, The Theatre Museum, 1984–89 (Mem., Adv. Council, 1974–83). Editorial Adviser to the Dancing Times, 1963–; Trustee: Calvert Trust, 1976–; Cecchetti Soc. Trust, 1978–2006; Radcliffe Trust, 1997– (Sec., 1966–96). DUniv Surrey, 1997. Queen Elizabeth II Coronation Award for services to ballet, 1992; Lifetime Achievement Award, Congress on Res. in Dance, 2000. Chevalier, Ordre des Arts et des Lettres (France), 1998. *Publications:* Napoleon III in England, 1952; The Ballet of the Second Empire, 1953–55; The Romantic Ballet in England, 1954; Fanny Cerrito, 1956; Victorian Ballet Girl, 1957; Adeline Genée, 1958; The Alhambra Ballet, 1959; La Fille mal gardée, 1960; The Dancer's Heritage, 1960; The Empire Ballet, 1962; A Gallery of Romantic Ballet, 1963; The Romantic Ballet in Paris, 1966; Carlotta Zambelli, 1969; Dandies and Dancers, 1969; Two Coppélias, 1970; Fanny Elssler, 1970; The Pas de Quatre, 1970; Le Ballet de l'Opéra de Paris, 1976, 2nd edn 2001, English edn 2006; The Divine Virginia, 1977; Adeline Genée: a pictorial record, 1978; Lettres d'un Maître de ballet, 1978; contrib. Costume and the 19th Century Dancer, in Designing for the Dancer, 1981; Adventures of a Ballet Historian, 1982; Jules Perrot, 1984; Gautier on Dance, 1986; Gautier on Spanish Dancing, 1987; Dr John Radcliffe and his Trust, 1991; Ballet in Leicester Square, 1992; (contrib.) Musica in Scena, 1995; The Ballet of the Enlightenment, 1996; Ballet Under Napoleon, 2002. *Address:* 17 Holland Park, W11 3TD. *T:* (020) 7229 3780; *e-mail:* ivorguest@lodc.org. *Club:* Garrick.

GUEST, Prof. John Rodney, FRS 1986; Professor of Microbiology, Sheffield University, 1981–2000, now Emeritus; *b* 27 Dec. 1935; *s* of Sidney Ramsey Guest and Dorothy Kathleen Guest (*née* Walker); *m* 1962, Barbara Margaret (*née* Dearsley); one *s* two *d. Educ:* Campbell College, Belfast; Leeds Univ. (BSc); Trinity Coll., Oxford Univ. (DPhil). Guinness Fellow, Oxford, 1960–62, 1965; Fulbright Scholar and Research Associate, Stanford, 1963, 1964; Sheffield University: Lectr, Sen. Lectr, Reader in Microbiology, 1965–81. SERC Special Res. Fellow, 1981–86. Marjory Stephenson Prize Lectr, Soc. Gen. Microbiol., 1992; Leeuwenhoek Lectr, Royal Soc., 1995. *Publications:* contribs to Jl of Gen. Microbiol., Biochem. Jl, Microbiol., Molec. Microbiol. *Recreations:* walking in the Peak District, beekeeping. *Address:* Department of Molecular Biology and Biotechnology, Sheffield University, Western Bank, Sheffield S10 2TN. *T:* (0114) 222 4406.

GUEST, Melville Richard John, OBE 2007; Chief Executive, Asia House, 1996–2002; *b* 18 Nov. 1943; *s* of late Ernest Melville Charles Guest and Katherine Mary Guest; *m* 1970, Beatriz Eugenia, (Jenny), Lopez Colombres de Velasco; four *s. Educ:* Rugby Sch.; Magdalen Coll., Oxford (MA Jurisprudence). HM Diplomatic Service, 1966–96: Third, later Second, Sec., Tokyo, 1967–72; Pvte Sec. to Parly Under-Sec. of State, FCO, 1973–75; First Sec., Paris, 1975–79; FCO, 1979–80; Prés.-Dir Gén., Soc. Française des Industries Lucas, 1980–85; Dir, Thomson-Lucas SA, 1980–85; Director: Franco-British Chamber of Commerce, 1980–85; Channel Tunnel Gp, 1985–86; Counsellor (Commercial), Tokyo, 1986–89; Counsellor (Political) and Consul General, Stockholm, 1990–93; Head, S Pacific Dept, 1993–94, SE Asian Dept, 1994–96, FCO. Executive Director: UK-Korea Forum for the Future, 1998–2007; UK-Japan 21st Century Gp, 2001–; Rapporteur, UK-India Round Table, 2000–. Sen. Adviser, Imperial Coll. London, 2005–. Mem., Bd of Govs, Ampleforth Coll., 1989–96. *Address: e-mail:* melvilleguest@hotmail.com. *Club:* Hurlingham.

GUETERBOCK, family name of **Baron Berkeley**.

GUGGENHEIM, Anna Maeve; Her Honour Judge Guggenheim; QC 2001; a Circuit Judge, since 2006; *b* 2 Sept. 1959; *d* of Peter Francis Guggenheim and Maura Teresa Guggenheim (*née* McCarthy); *m* 1987, Mark Eban; one *s* one *d. Educ:* King Edward VI High Sch. for Girls, Edgbaston; Somerville Coll., Oxford (BA Juris. 1981). Called to the Bar, Gray's Inn, 1982; barrister, 1982–2005; a Recorder, 2002–05. *Recreation:* sailing. *Address:* Wood Green Crown Court, Woodall House, Lordship Lane, Wood Green, N22 5LF.

GUILD, Ivor Reginald, CBE 1985; FRSE; Partner in Shepherd and Wedderburn, WS, 1951–94; *b* 2 April 1924; 2nd *s* of Col Arthur Marjoribanks Guild, DSO, TD, DL, and Phyllis Eliza Cox. *Educ:* Cargilfield; Rugby; New Coll., Oxford (MA); Edinburgh Univ. (LLB). FRSE 1990. WS 1950. Procurator Fiscal of the Lyon Court, 1960–94; Bailie of Holyrood House, 1980–95; Registrar, Episcopal Synod of Episc. Church in Scotland, 1967–2007; Chancellor, diocese of: Edinburgh, 1985–95; St Andrews, 1985–98. Chairman: Edinburgh Investment Trust Ltd, 1974–94 (Dir, 1972–94); Dunedin Income Growth Investment Trust plc (formerly First Scottish American Investment Trust plc), 1973–94 (Dir, 1964–94); Dunedin Worldwide Investment Trust plc (formerly Northern American Investment Trust plc), 1973–94 (Dir, 1964–94); Scottish Oriental Smaller Companies Trust PLC, 1995–2004; Dir, New Fulcrum Investment Trust, 1986–2005. Member: Council on Tribunals, 1976–85; Interception of Communications Tribunal, 1985–96; Immigration Appeal Adjudicator, 1988–95. Chm., Nat. Mus. of Antiquities of Scotland, 1981–85. Editor, Scottish Genealogist, 1959–94. *Recreations:* genealogy, golf. *Club:* New (Edinburgh).

GUILD, Rear-Adm. Nigel Charles Forbes, CB 2003; PhD; FIET, FIMarEST; Senior Responsible Owner (Carrier Strike), Ministry of Defence, since 2003; *b* 9 Feb. 1949; *s* of Surg. Capt. William John Forbes Guild and Joan Elizabeth Guild (*née* Innes); *m* 1971, Felicity Jean Wilson; two *s. Educ:* Fernden Sch.; Bryanston Sch.; BRNC Dartmouth; Trinity Coll., Cambridge (BA); Univ. of Bristol (PhD 1979; Hon. DEng 2006). MIEE 1980; MIMA 1980; FIMarEST 2001; FIET (FIEE 2002); FREng 2007. Joined Royal Navy, 1966; HMS Hermes, 1972–75; Weapons Trials, 1976–78; British Underwater Test and Evaluation Centre Project, 1979–82; HMS Euryalus, 1982–84 and 1986–87; Future Projects (Naval), 1984–85; HMS Beaver, 1987–88; Staff Weapons Engr Officer to FO Sea Trng, 1988–90; MA to Chief of Defence Procurement, 1991–92; CSO (E) Surface Flotilla, 1993–95; Project Dir, PE, MoD, 1996–99; Controller of the Navy, and Exec. Dir 4, Defence Procurement Agency, MoD, 2000–03; Chief Naval Engr Officer, 2003–08. *Publications:* contrib. papers on Fuzzy Logic. *Recreations:* rowing, village pantomime, steam boating. *Address:* Ministry of Defence, Main Building, Whitehall, SW1A 2HB. *Club:* Leander (Henley on Thames).

GUILDFORD, Bishop of, since 2004; **Rt Rev. Christopher John Hill;** Clerk of the Closet to the Queen, since 2005; *b* 10 Oct. 1945; *s* of Leonard and Frances V. Hill; *m* 1976, Hilary Ann Whitehouse; three *s* one *d. Educ:* Sebright Sch., Worcs; King's Coll., London (BD Hons; Relton Prize for Theology, 1967; MTh 1968; AKC 1967). Deacon 1969, priest 1970. Asst Curate, Dio. of Lichfield: St Michael's, Tividale, 1969–73; St Nicholas, Codsall, 1973–74; Asst Chaplain to Archbp of Canterbury for Foreign Relations, 1974–81; Archbp's Sec. for Ecumenical Affairs, 1982–89; Hon. Canon of Canterbury Cathedral, 1982–89; Chaplain to the Queen, 1987–96; Canon Residentiary, 1989–96, Precentor, 1990–96, St Paul's Cathedral; Bishop Suffragan of Stafford, 1996–2004. Anglican Secretary: Anglican-RC Internat. Commn (I), 1974–81, Internat. Commn (II), 1983–90 (Mem., 1990–91); Anglican-Lutheran Eur. Commn, 1981–82; Consultant: C of E—German Churches Commn, 1987–90; C of E—Nordic-Baltic Churches Commn, 1989–92; Co-Chairman: C of E—French Lutheran and Reformed Conversations, 1994–98; Meissen Theol Conf., 1998–; Chm., C of E Council for Christian Unity, 2008– (Mem., 1989–96; Mem., 1996–2007, Vice-Chm., 1998–2007, Faith and Order Adv. Gp). Member: Legal Adv. Commn, Gen. Synod of C of E, 1991–; House of Bishops, Gen. Synod of C of E, 1999– (Chm., Women Bishops' Gp, 2005–06; Mem., Theol Gp, 2006–); Wkg Pty on Women in the Episcopate, 2001–04 (Vice-Chm., 2003–04); Wkg Party on Bishops' Legal Costs, Fees Adv. Commn, 2003; Liturgical Commn, 2003–; Discipline Commn, 2004–. Guestmaster, Nikaean Club, 1982–89. Co-Chm., London Soc. of Jews and Christians, 1991–96; Vice-Chm., 1993–2002, Chm., 2002–, Ecclesiastical Law Soc. *Publications:* (ed jtly) Anglicans and Roman Catholics: the search for unity, 1995; (ed jtly) Documents in the Debate: papers on Anglican orders, 1997; miscellaneous ecumenical, ecclesiological and legal articles. *Recreations:* Radio 3, mountain walking, detective stories, Italian food, GWR, unaffordable wine. *Address:* Willow Grange, Woking Road, Guildford, Surrey GU4 7QS. *T:* (01483) 590500. *Club:* Athenæum.

GUILDFORD, Dean of; *see* Stock, Very Rev. V. A.

GUILFORD, 10th Earl of, *cr* 1752; **Piers Edward Brownlow North;** Baron Guilford 1683; *b* 9 March 1971; *s* of 9th Earl of Guilford and Osyth Vere Napier, *d* of Cyril Napier Leeston Smith; *S* father, 1999; *m* 1994, Michèle Desvaux de Marigny; one *s* one *d. Heir:* Lord North, *qv. Address:* Waldershare Park, Dover, Kent CT15 5BA. *T:* (01304) 820245.

GUILFOYLE, Hon. Dame Margaret (Georgina Constance), AC 2005; DBE 1980; Chair, Judicial Remuneration Tribunal, 1995–2001; Deputy Chair, Infertility Authority, 1995–2001; *b* 15 May 1926; *d* of William and Elizabeth McCartney; *m* 1952, Stanley M. L. Guilfoyle; one *s* two *d. Educ:* ANU (LLB 1990). FCIS; FCPA. Senator for Victoria, 1971–87; Minister: for Education, Commonwealth of Australia, 1975; for Social Security, 1975–80; for Finance, 1980–83. Dep. Chm., Mental Health Res. Inst., 1988–2001; Dir, Aust. Children's TV Foundn, 1989–2002 (Dep. Chm., 1989–2002). Mem., Infertility Treatment Authy, 1996–2003. *Recreations:* reading, gardening. *Address:* 21 Howard Street, Kew, Vic 3101, Australia. *Club:* Lyceum (Melbourne).

GUILLAUME, Gilbert Pierre; Judge, International Court of Justice, 1987–2005 (President, 2000–03), now Judge *ad hoc*; *b* 4 Dec. 1930; *s* of Pierre Guillaume and Berthe (*née* Brun); *m* 1961, Marie-Anne Hidden; one *s* two *d. Educ:* Univ. of Paris (LLM Law and Econ.); Inst. of Political Scis, Paris (Dip.); Ecole Nat. d'Admin. Mem., Council of State, France, 1957–96; Legal Advr, Secretariat for Civil Aviation, France, 1968–79; Director of Legal Affairs: OECD, 1978–79; Ministry of Foreign Affairs, France, 1979–87. Pres. or Mem., ICSID and other arbitration tribunals. Grand Officier de la Légion d'Honneur (France) 2005. *Publications:* Terrorisme et Droit International, 1989; Les grandes crises internationales et le droit, 1994; La Cour Internationale de Justice à l'Aube du XXIe Siècle, 2003. *Address:* 36 rue Perronet, 92200 Neuilly-sur-Seine, France. *Fax:* (1) 47456784; *e-mail:* g.ma.guillaume@orange.fr.

GUILLE, Very Rev. John Arthur; Dean of Southwell, since 2007; *b* 21 May 1949; *s* of Arthur Leonard Guille and Winifred Maud Guille (*née* Lane); *m* 1976, Susan Stallard; one *s* two *d. Educ:* Guernsey GS for Boys; Christ Church Coll., Canterbury (CertEd London 1970); Salisbury and Wells Theol Coll.; BTh Southampton 1979. Teacher of Religious Studies: Stockbridge Co. Secondary Sch., 1970–72; St Sampson's Secondary Sch., 1972–73; ordained deacon 1976, priest 1977; Curate, Chandler's Ford, 1976–80; Priest i/c, St John, Surrey Road, Bournemouth, 1980–84, Vicar, St John with St Michael, 1984–89; Rector, St André de la Pommeraye, Guernsey, 1989–99; Vice Dean, Guernsey, 1996–99; Archdeacon of Basingstoke, 1999–2000; Canon Residentiary, Winchester Cathedral, 1999–2007; Archdeacon of Winchester, 2000–07. *Publication:* A Millennium of Archdeacons, 2003. *Recreations:* walking, gardening, family history. *Address:* The Residence, Vicar's Court, Southwell NG25 0HP.

GUILLEBAUD, Rev. (Jette) Margaret; Curate, Salisbury Cathedral, since 2005; *b* 24 March 1948; *d* of Justin Brooke and Kirsten (*née* Møller-Larsen); *m* 1st, 1971, Robin Simon, *qv* (marr. diss. 1978); one *s* one *d*; 2nd, 1984, Hugh Guillebaud. *Educ:* Wycombe Abbey Sch. (Head Girl); Exeter Univ. (BA Hons Eng.); Ripon Coll., Cuddesdon. Tutor, Oxford Sch. of English, Verona, Italy, 1971–72; Examr, Oxford Exams Bd, 1972–75; Tutor, Open Univ., 1973–75; Man. Dir, Jobline Employment Agency, 1989–91; Chairman: SW Arts, 1991–97; English Regl Arts Bds, 1993–94; Mem., Arts Council of England, 1994–97. Ordained deacon, 2005, priest, 2006. Chm., Glos Ambulance NHS Trust, 1991–93. Director: Cheltenham Festivals Ltd, 1991–96; at Bristol (formerly Bristol 2000), 1995–2001; Harbourside Centre, Bristol, 1995–2000; South West Film Commn, 1997–2002. Mem. Bd, Salisbury Internat. Arts Festival, 2006–. Trustee, Holburne Mus., Bath, 1997–2002. Governor: Bath Spa UC (formerly Bath Coll. of Higher Educn),

1996–98; Wyvern Coll., 2007–. Mem., Univ. of Gloucestershire Develt Adv. Bd, 2001–03. JP S Glos, 1988–98. FRSA 1992. Hon. MA UWE, 1998. *Recreations:* opera, theatre, visual arts, fishing, travel. *Address:* The Dovecote, Mount Sorrel, Broad Chalke, Salisbury, Wilts SP5 5HQ.

GUILLEM, Sylvie, Hon. CBE 2003; ballet dancer; *b* Paris, 23 Feb. 1965. *Educ:* Ecole de Danse, Paris Opera. With Paris Opera, 1981–89, Etoile, 1984; with Royal Ballet Co., 1989–; guest artist with other cos, 1989–. Lead roles in: Giselle; Swan Lake; La Bayadère; Cinderella; Sleeping Beauty; Romeo and Juliet; Raymonda; Manon; Don Quixote; Marguerite and Armand; Lilac Garden; Carmen; Winter Dreams. Title role created for her in Sissi, Rudra Béjart Co.; other created roles in: In the Middle, somewhat Elevated; Le Martyre de Saint-Sebastien; Firstext. Prod Giselle for Nat. Ballet of Finland, 1999, for La Scala, Milan, 2001. Comdr des Arts et des Lettres (France), 1988; Chevalier de la Légion d'Honneur (France), 1994; Officier de l'Ordre du Mérite (France), 1999. *Address:* c/o Royal Ballet Company, Royal Opera House, Covent Garden, WC2E 9DD.

GUILLEMIN, Prof. Roger Charles Louis, MD, PhD; Distinguished Professor, Salk Institute, La Jolla, since 1997; *b* Dijon, France, 11 Jan. 1924 (naturalized US Citizen, 1963); *s* of Raymond Guillemin and Blanche (*née* Rigollot); *m* 1951, Lucienne Jeanne Billard; one *s* five *d*. *Educ:* Univ. of Dijon (BA 1941, BSc 1942); Faculty of Medicine, Lyons (MD 1949); Univ. of Montreal (PhD 1953). Resident Intern, univ. hosps, Dijon, 1949–51; Associate Dir, then Asst Prof., Inst. of Exper. Medicine and Surgery, Univ. of Montreal, 1951–53; Prof. of Physiol. and Dir, Labs for Neuroendocrinology, Baylor Coll. of Med., Houston, 1953–70; Associate Dir, Dept of Exper. Endocrinol., Coll. de France, Paris, 1960–63; Resident Fellow and Res. Prof., and Chm., Labs for Neuroendocrinology, Salk Inst. for Biol Studies, 1970–89; Dist. Prof., Whittier Inst. for Diabetes and Endocrinology, La Jolla, 1989–94 (Dir, 1993–94). Adjunct Professor: of Physiol., Baylor Coll. of Med., 1970–; of Medicine, UCSD, 1970–94. Member: Nat. Acad. of Sciences, USA, 1974; Amer. Acad. Arts and Scis, 1976; Amer. Physiol Soc.; Endocrine Soc. (Pres., 1986); Soc. of Exptl Biol. and Medicine; Internat. Brain Res. Orgn; Internat. Soc. Res. Biol Reprodn. Foreign Associate: Acad. des Sciences, France; Acad. Nat. de Médecine, Paris; Hon. Mem., Swedish Soc. of Med. Scis; Foreign Mem., Acad. Royale de Médecine de Belgique. Mem. Club of Rome. Hon. DSc: Rochester, NY, 1976; Chicago, 1977; Manitoba, 1984; Kyung Hee Univ., Seoul, Korea, 1986; Univ. de Paris VII, 1986; Madrid, 1988; Univ. Claude Bernard, Lyon, 1989; Laval Univ., Quebec, 1990; Sherbrooke Univ., Quebec, 1997; Hon. MD: Ulm, 1978; Montreal, 1979; Univ. Libre de Bruxelles, Belgium, 1979; Turin, 1985; Barcelona, 1988; Univ. Claude Bernard, Lyon I, 1989; Laval Univ., Quebec, 1996; Hon. LMed Baylor Coll. of Med., 1978. Gairdner Internat. Award, 1974; Lasker Award, USA, 1975; Dickson Prize in Medicine, Univ. of Pittsburgh, 1976; Passano Award in Med. Sci., Passano Foundn, Inc., 1976; Schmitt Medal in Neuroscience, Neurosciences Res. Prog., MIT, 1977; National Medal of Science, USA, 1977; (jtly) Nobel Prize in Physiology or Medicine, 1977; Barren Gold Medal, USA, 1979; Dale Medal (Soc. for Endocrinology), UK, 1980; Ellen Browning Scripps Soc. Medal, Scripps Meml Hosps Foundn, San Diego, 1988; Dist. Scientist Award, Nat. Diabetes Res. Coalition, 1996. Légion d'Honneur, France, 1974. *Publications:* scientific pubns in learned jls. *Recreation:* computer art (one-man shows, Milan, 1991, Houston, 1996, Paris, 1999). *Address:* The Salk Institute, 10010 N Torrey Pines Road, La Jolla, CA 92037–1099, USA.

GUILLERY, Prof. Rainer Walter, PhD; FRS 1983; Professor of Anatomy, University of Marmara, since 2007; Visiting Professor, Department of Anatomy, University of Wisconsin, 1996–2002, now Professor Emeritus; *b* 28 Aug. 1929; *s* of Hermann Guillery and Eva (*née* Hackel); *m* 1954, Margot Cunningham Pepper (marr. diss. 2000); three *s* one *d*. *Educ:* University Coll. London (BSc, PhD; Fellow, 1987). Asst Lectr, subseq. Reader, Anatomy Dept, UCL, 1953–64; Associate Prof., subseq. Prof., Anatomy Dept, Univ. of Wisconsin, Madison, USA, 1964–77; Prof., Dept of Pharmacol and Physiol Sciences, Univ. of Chicago, 1977–84; Dr Lee's Prof. of Anatomy and Fellow of Hertford Coll., Univ. of Oxford, 1984–96. Pres., Anatomical Soc. of GB&I, 1994–96. Editor-in-chief, European Jl of Neuroscience, 1988–92. *Publications:* (jtly) Exploring the Thalamus, 2001, 2nd edn 2006; contrib. Jl of Anat., Jl of Comp. Neurol., Jl of Neuroscience, and Brain Res. *Address:* Department of Anatomy, Medical Faculty, Marmara University, Haydar Pasa, Tibbiye Cd, Istanbul 34668, Turkey; Altunizade, Erzurum Sitesi, Dadslar SK 10/4, Istanbul 34662, Turkey. *T:* 216 340 8667.

GUILLOU, Prof. Pierre John, MD; FRCS, FMedSci; Professor of Surgery, St James's University Hospital, Leeds, since 1993; Dean of the School of Medicine, University of Leeds, 1998–2002; *b* 30 Oct. 1945; *s* of Sarah Anne Guillou (*née* Greenfield) and Yves Guillou; *m* 1998, Patricia Katherine Ollerenshawe; one *s* one *d* from previous marriage. *Educ:* Normanton Grammar Sch.; Univ. of Leeds (BSc; MB ChB 1970; MD 1975). Leeds Gen. Infirmary and St James's Univ. Hosp., 1970–73; S Manchester Univ. Hosp., 1973–74; Surgical Registrar, Leeds Gen. Infirmary, 1974–76; Lectr in Surgery, Univ. of Leeds, 1976–79; MRC Fellow in Immunology, Hôpital Necker, Paris, 1979–80; Sen. Lectr in Surgery, Univ. of Leeds, 1980–88; Prof. of Surgery, Imperial Coll. of Sci., Technology and Medicine and Dir, Academic Surgical Unit, St Mary's Hosp., London, 1988–93. Visiting Professor: Aust. Surgical Res. Soc., 1989, 1992; Univ. of Richmond, Va, 1992; S African Surgical Res. Soc., 1993; Ethicon, Malaysia, 1995; Sir Arthur Sims Commonwealth Prof., 1996; Lectures: Crookshank, Royal Soc. of Radiologists, 1990; Smith, Univ. of WA, 1991; A. B. Mitchell, QUB, 1991; jt meeting of Royal Colls of Surgeons of India and Glasgow, Madras, 1992; G. B. Ong, also Wilson T. S. Wang Internat. Surgical Symposium on Surgical Oncology, Chinese Univ. of Hong Kong, 1992, 1994; Annual Scientific Meeting of the Royal Coll. of Surgeons of Thailand, 1993; Stanford Cade, RCS, 1994; Marjorie Budd, Univ. of Bristol, 1995; 12th Asia Pacific Cancer Conf., Singapore, 1995. Member: James IV Assoc. of Surgeons, 1992–; Eur. Surgical Assoc., 1994–. Founder FMedSci 1998. Ed., British Jl of Surgery, 1994–2003; Ed.-in-Chief, Internat. Jl of Med. Robotics and Computer-Assisted Surgery, 2003–. *Publications:* (ed) Surgical Oncology, 1991; Clinical Surgery, 1992; numerous papers on immunology, cell biology and surgery in treatment of cancer. *Recreations:* work, golf, fishing, work. *Address:* Academic Surgical Unit, Clinical Sciences Building, St James's University Hospital, Beckett Street, Leeds LS9 7TF. *T:* and *Fax:* (0113) 244 9618. *Club:* Royal Society of Medicine.

GUINERY, Paul Trevor; broadcaster; *b* 19 Jan. 1957; *s* of Dennis William Prickett and Eileen Grace Guinery. *Educ:* St Paul's Sch.; Royal Coll. of Music (ARCM 1975); Queen's Coll., Oxford (BA 1979). Joined BBC, 1980: studio manager, 1980–85; announcer and newsreader: World Service, 1985–89; Radio 3, 1989–2002; Presenter: Your Concert Choice, 1990–92; Concert Hall, 1992–98; Sacred and Profane, 1993–98; Choral Voices, 1998; Sounding the Millennium, 1999; Choirworks, 1999–2003. Vice-Chm., Delius Soc., 2001–03. *Publications:* Delius and Fenby (with Lyndon Jenkins), 2004; articles in Delius Soc. Jl. *Recreations:* playing the piano, theatre, collecting sheet music. *Address:* 68 Cambridge Street, SW1V 4QQ.

GUINNESS, family name of **Earl of Iveagh** and **Baron Moyne**.

GUINNESS, Hon. Desmond (Walter); writer; *b* 8 Sept. 1931; *yr s* of 2nd Baron Moyne and of Hon. Diana Mitford (now Hon. Lady Mosley); *m* 1st, 1954, Marie-Gabrielle von Urach (marr. diss. 1981; she *d* 1989); one *s* one *d*; 2nd, Penelope, *d* of Graham and Teresa Cuthbertson. *Educ:* Gordonstoun; Christ Church, Oxford (MA). Founder, 1958, and Chm., 1958–91, Irish Georgian Society to work for the study of, and protection of buildings of architectural merit in Ireland, particularly of the Georgian period. Hon. LLD TCD, 1980. *Publications:* Portrait of Dublin, 1967; Irish Houses and Castles, 1971; Mr Jefferson, Architect, 1973; Palladio, 1976; Georgian Dublin, 1980; The White House: an architectural history, 1981; Newport Preserv'd, 1982; (with Jacqueline O'Brien) Great Irish Houses and Castles, 1992; (with Jacqueline O'Brien) Dublin: a Grand Tour, 1994. *Clubs:* Chelsea Arts; Kildare Street and University, Royal Irish Automobile, Friendly Brothers of St Patrick (Dublin).

GUINNESS, Sir Howard (Christian Sheldon), Kt 1981; VRD 1953; *b* 3 June 1932; *s* of late Edward Douglas Guinness, CBE and Martha Letière (*née* Sheldon); *m* 1958, Evadne Jane Gibbs; two *s* one *d*. *Educ:* King's Mead, Seaford, Sussex; Eton Coll. National Service RN (midshipman); Lt-Comdr RNR. Union Discount Co. of London Ltd, 1953; Guinness Mahon & Co. Ltd, 1953–55; S. G. Warburg & Co. Ltd, 1955–85 (Exec. Dir 1970–85). Dir, Harris & Sheldon Gp Ltd, 1960–81; Dir and Dep. Chm., Youghal Carpets (Holdings) Ltd, 1972–80. Director: Quality Milk Producers Ltd, 1988–2000; Riyad Bank Europe, 1993–99. Chm., N Hampshire Conservative Assoc., 1971–74; Vice-Chm. 1974, Chm. 1975–78, and Treasurer 1978–81, Wessex Area, Cons. Assoc. Mem. Council English Guernsey Cattle Soc., 1963–72, 1996–99. *Recreations:* ski-ing, tennis. *Address:* The Manor House, Glanvilles Wootton, Sherborne, Dorset DT9 5QF. *T:* (01963) 210217. *Club:* White's.

See also Sir J. R. S. Guinness.

GUINNESS, Sir John (Ralph Sidney), Kt 1999; CB 1985; FSA; Chairman, Trinity Group Finance Ltd, 1999–2003; *b* 23 Dec. 1935; *s* of late Edward Douglas Guinness and Martha Letière (*née* Sheldon); *m* 1967, Valerie Susan North; one *s* one *d* (and one *s* decd). *Educ:* Rugby Sch.; Trinity Hall, Cambridge (BA Hons History, MA Hons). Union Discount Co. Ltd, 1960–61; Overseas Develt Inst., 1961–62; joined FO, 1962; Econ. Relations Dept, 1962–63; Third Sec., UK Mission to UN, New York, 1963–64; seconded to UN Secretariat as Special Asst to Dep. Under-Sec. and later Under-Sec. for Econ. and Social Affairs, 1964–66; FCO, 1967–69; First Sec. (Econ.), Brit. High Commn Ottawa, 1969–72; seconded to Central Policy Rev. Staff, Cabinet Office, 1972–75; Counsellor, 1974; Alternate UK Rep. to Law of the Sea Conf., 1975–77; seconded to CPRS, 1977–79; transferred to Home Civil Service, 1980; Under-Sec., 1980–83, Dep. Sec., 1983–91, Permanent Sec., 1991–92, Dept of Energy. Chm., British Nuclear Fuels 1992–99; Director: Guinness Mahon Hldgs, 1993–99; Ocean Gp, 1993–2000; Mithras Investment Trust, 1994–2006. Governor, Oxford Energy Inst., 1984–92. Chairman Reviewing Cttee on Export of Works of Art, 1995–2004; Expert Panel, Heritage Lottery Fund, 2005; Expert Panel, NHMF, 2006–. Member: E Anglia Regl Cttee, NT, 1989–94; Develt Cttee, Nat. Portrait Gall., 1994–99; Council, BITC, 1992–99; Pres. Cttee, CBI 1997–99 (Mem. Council, 1993–97); Dir, UK-Japan 2000 Gp, 1995–99. Mem., Adv. Council, Business Div., Prince's Trust, 1999–; Trustee: Prince's Youth Business Trust 1992–99; Royal Collection Trust, 2001–07; Nat. Maritime Mus., 2005–; Heritage Conservation Trust, 2006–. Gov., Compton Verney House Trust, 2000–03. Hon. Freeman, Co. of Fuellers, 1999. FSA 2005. Hon. Fellow: Mgt Sch., Lancaster Univ. 1997; Univ. of Central Lancashire, 1998. *Recreation:* iconography. *Clubs:* Brooks's; Beefsteak.

See also Sir H. C. S. Guinness.

GUINNESS, Sir Kenelm (Ernest Lee), 4th Bt *cr* 1867; formerly independent engineering consultant; *b* 13 Dec. 1928; *s* of late Kenelm Edward Lee Guinness and Mrs Josephine Lee Guinness; *S* uncle, 1954; *m* 1961, Mrs Jane Nevin Dickson; two *s*. *Educ:* Eton Coll.; Massachusetts Institute of Technology, USA. Late Lieut, Royal Horse Guards. With IBRD, Washington, 1954–75. *Heir:* *s* Kenelm Edward Lee Guinness, *b* 30 Jan. 1962. *Address:* (home) Rich Neck, Claiborne, MD 21624, USA. *T:* (410) 7455079. *Club:* Cruising of America.

GUINNESS, William Loel Seymour; Chairman, Sibir Energy Plc, since 1999; *b* 28 Dec. 1939; *s* of Thomas Loel Evelyn Guinness, OBE and Lady Isabel Guinness (*née* Manners, later Throckmorton), *d* of 9th Duke of Rutland; *m* 1st, 1971, Elizabeth Lynn Day (marr. diss. 1994); two *s* one *d*; 2nd, 2003, Lucia Gomez de Parada. *Educ:* Ludgrove; Eton. Commnd Irish Guards, 1959–61. Non-exec. Dir, Henry Ansbacher, 1983–93, and other cos. Mem. (C), Daventry DC, 1976–83 (Leader, 1977–83). *Recreations:* golf, photography, gardening, travelling. *Address:* Zanroc, Chemin de Ballegue 58, 1066 Epalinges, Switzerland. *T:* (21) 7843427, *Fax:* (21) 7843565; *e-mail:* bguinness@gmail.com. *Clubs:* White's, Pratt's; Swinley Forest Golf; Royal West Norfolk Golf (Brancaster); Golf de Lausanne; Corviglia (St Moritz).

GUISE, Sir (Christopher) James, 8th Bt *cr* 1783, of Highnam Court, Glos; *b* 10 July 1930; *s* of Sir Anselm William Edward Guise, 6th Bt and Nina Margaret Sophie, *d* of Sir James Augustus Grant, 1st Bt; *S* brother, 2007; *m* 1969, Mrs Carole Hoskins Benson (*née* Master); one *s* one *d*. *Educ:* Wellesley House; Stowe. Business and banking career in London and S Africa; now retired company Dir. *Recreations:* fishing, shooting, gardening. *Heir:* *s* Anselm Mark Guise [*b* 7 Feb. 1971; *m* (marr. diss.)]. *Address:* Weir Farm, Elmore, Glos GL2 3NS; *e-mail:* jamie.guise@virgin.net. *Clubs:* Turf, Beefsteak, MCC.

GUIVER, Rev. Fr George Paul Alfred, CR; Superior, Community of the Resurrection, since 2003; *b* 18 Dec. 1945; *s* of Alfred and Doris Guiver. *Educ:* St Chad's Coll., Durham (BA 1968); Cuddesdon Coll., Oxford (Cert. in Theology 1973). Ordained deacon 1973, priest 1974; Curate, Mill End and Heronsgate with West Hyde, St Albans, 1973–76; Priest-in-charge, Bishop's Frome, Castle Frome, Acton Beauchamp and Evesbatch, Hereford, 1976–82; Community of the Resurrection, 1983–; Vice-Principal, Coll. of the Resurrection, 1990–2002. Hon. Lectr, Leeds Univ., 1990–. *Publications:* Company of Voices: daily prayer and the people of God, 1988; Faith in Momentum: the distinctiveness of the church, 1990; (ed) The Fire and the Clay: the priest in today's church, 1993; Everyday God, 1994; Pursuing the Mystery: worship and daily life as presences of God, 1996; (ed) Priests in a People's Church, 2001. *Recreations:* cycling and recycling. *Address:* Community of the Resurrection, Mirfield, W Yorks WF14 0BN. *T:* (01924) 483301, *Fax:* (01924) 490489; *e-mail:* GGuiver@mirfield.org.uk.

GULL, Prof. Keith, CBE 2004; PhD; FRS 2003; Wellcome Trust Principal Research Fellow, and Senior Research Fellow, Lincoln College, since 2002, and Professor of Molecular Biology, since 2004, University of Oxford; *b* 29 May 1948; *s* of David Gull and Doris Gull (*née* Manging); *m* 1972, Dianne Hilary Leonora Elgar; one *s* one *d*. *Educ:* Queen Elizabeth Coll., Univ. of London (BSc Hons 1969, PhD 1972, Microbiology). University of Kent: Lectr, 1972–82; Sen. Lectr, 1982–84; Reader, 1984–86; Prof. of Cell Biology, 1986–89; Prof. of Molecular Biology, Univ. of Manchester, 1989–2002. Vis. Sen. Scientist, Sandoz Inst., Vienna, 1978; Vis. Prof., McArdle Lab. for Cancer Res., Univ. of Wisconsin, 1982. Darwin Lectr, BAAS, 1983; Marjory Stephenson Lectr, Soc. for Gen.

Microbiology, 1996. FMedSci 1999. *Publications:* numerous contribs to books and scientific jls. *Recreations:* fly fishing, painting. *Address:* Sir William Dunn School of Pathology, University of Oxford, South Parks Road, Oxford OX1 3RE. *T:* (01865) 285455; *e-mail:* keith.gull@path.ox.ac.uk.

GULL, Sir Rupert (William Cameron), 5th Bt *cr* 1872, of Brook Street; company director; *b* 14 July 1954; *s* of Sir Michael Swinnerton Cameron Gull, 4th Bt and Yvonne (*d* 1975), *o d* of Dr Albert Oliver Macarius Heslop, Cape Town; *S* father, 1989; *m* 1980, Gillian Lee, *d* of Robert MacFarlaine; three *d. Educ:* Diocesan Coll., Cape Town; Cape Town Univ. *Heir: cousin* Angus William John Gull [*b* 24 Dec. 1963; *m* 1988, Jacqueline Mary, *d* of Gerald Edgar Ford]. *Address:* 2 Harcourt Road, Claremont, Cape Town, South Africa.

GULLAND, Robert Rainsford M.; *see* Milner-Gulland.

GULLICK, Stephen John; His Honour Judge Gullick; a Circuit Judge, since 1998; Resident Judge, Bradford Crown Court, since 2001; *b* 22 Feb. 1948; *s* of late David and Evelyn Gullick; *m* 1973, Lesley Steadman; two *s. Educ:* Taunton Sch.; Birmingham Univ. (LLB 1970). Called to the Bar, Gray's Inn, 1971; in practice at the Bar, 1971–98; a Recorder, 1990–98; Standing Counsel, NE Circuit, HM Customs and Excise, 1991–98. Hon. Recorder, Bradford, 2002. *Recreations:* campanology, watching sport. *Address:* Bradford Combined Court Centre, Exchange Square, Bradford BD1 1JA.

GULLIFORD, Rev. William Douglas FitzGerald; Vicar, Guild Church of St Dunstan-in-the-West, since 2000; *b* 23 Sept. 1969; *s* of Maurice Nicholas Gulliford and Caroline Mary Louise Gulliford; *m* 1993, Béatrice Priscilla Marie Rambaud; one *s* two *d. Educ:* Taunton Sch.; Richard Huish Coll., Taunton; Selwyn Coll., Cambridge (BA 1991; MA 1995); Westcott House, Cambridge. Ordained deacon, 1994, priest, 1995; Asst Curate, All Saints', Banstead, 1994–97; Asst Priest, St Paul's, Knightsbridge, 1997–2000; Rector, St Mary le Strand with St Clement Danes, 2002–08. Dir of Ordinands, Dio. of Europe, 2003–. Chaplain: GSMD, 1997–2001; to Bishop of London, 2000–02; Courtauld Inst. of Art, 2003–. Gen. Sec., Anglican & Eastern Churches Assoc., 2000–04. Hon. Chaplain to: Aldermanic Sheriff of London, 2005–06; Lord Mayor of London, 2006–07. *Recreations:* domestic ecumenism, theatre, other people's gardening. *Address:* Hen & Chicken Court, 184a Fleet Street, EC4A 2HD. *T:* and *Fax:* (020) 7405 1929; *e-mail:* william.gulliford@london.anglican.org. *Club:* Sion College.

GULLY, family name of **Viscount Selby**.

GUMBEL, Elizabeth-Anne, (Mrs Michael Wainwright); QC 1999; *d* of Walter and Muriel Gumbel; *m* 1984, Michael Wainwright; one *s* one *d. Educ:* St Paul's Girls' Sch.; Wycombe Abbey Sch.; Lady Margaret Hall, Oxford (MA). Called to the Bar, Inner Temple, 1974, Bencher, 2002. *Address:* 1 Crown Office Row, EC4Y 7HH.

See also Rev. N. G. P. Gumbel.

GUMBEL, Rev. Nicholas Glyn Paul; Vicar, Holy Trinity, Brompton, since 2005; *b* 28 April 1955; *s* of Walter and Muriel Gumbel; *m* 1978, Philippa Hislop; two *s* one *d. Educ:* Trinity Coll., Cambridge (BA Law 1976); Wycliffe Hall, Oxford (MA Theol. 1986). Called to the Bar, Middle Temple, 1977; in practice as barrister, 1977–83; ordained deacon, 1986, priest, 1987; Curate, Holy Trinity, Brompton, 1986–2005. Pioneer of Alpha Course (a practical introduction to Christian faith, running in over 35,000 churches in 163 countries); Alpha Chaplain, 1996–2005. Vice Pres., Tear Fund, 2008. Hon. DPhil Glos, 2007. *Publications:* Alpha: questions of life, 1993, 4th edn 2003; Searching Issues, 1994, 5th edn 2004; How to Run the Alpha Course: telling others, 1994, 4th edn 2004; A Life Worth Living, 1994, 3rd edn 2001; Challenging Lifestyle, 1996, 3rd edn 2001; The Heart of Revival, 1997; 30 Days, 1999, 2nd edn 2001; The Da Vinci Code: a response, 2005, 2nd edn 2006; Wilberforce: the challenge for today, 2007; Is God a Delusion?, 2008. *Address:* Holy Trinity Brompton, Brompton Road, SW7 1JA.

See also E.-A. Gumbel.

GUMBS, Hon. Sir Emile (Rudolph), Kt 1994; Chief Minister, Anguilla, 1977–80 and 1984–94; *b* 18 March 1928; *s* of Johnson Emile Gumbs and Inez Beatrice Gumbs (*née* Carty); *m* 1st, 1964, Janice Anne Bradley; one *s* one *d*; 2nd, 1993, Louisa Josephine DeRoche (MBE 2006). *Educ:* St Kitts/Nevis Grammar Sch. Captain, Schooner Warspite, 1955–64; Manager, Anguilla Road Salt Co., 1964–77 and 1980–84. Elected Rep., Road N Anguilla, 1968–94; Minister of Govt, 1976–80 and 1984–94. *Recreations:* sailing, fishing, bird watching. *Address:* Sandy Ground, PO Box 70, Anguilla, British West Indies. *T:* 4972711, *Fax:* 4973292.

GUMLEY-MASON, Frances Jane, MA; broadcaster and journalist; Headmistress, St Augustine's Priory, Ealing, since 1995; *b* 28 Jan. 1955; *o d* of late Franc Stewart Gumley and Helen Teresa (*née* McNicholas); name changed to Gumley-Mason by statutory declaration, 1995; *m* 1988, Andrew Samuel Mason (now Gumley-Mason); one *s* one *d. Educ:* St Augustine's Priory, Ealing; Newnham Coll., Cambridge (MA). Parly research, 1974; Braille transcriber, 1975; Catholic Herald: Editorial Assistant and Assistant Literary Editor, Dec. 1975; Literary Editor and Staff Reporter, 1976–79; Editor, 1979–81; RC Asst to Head of Religious Broadcasting, and sen. producer, religious progs, radio, and producer, religious television, 1981–88; Series Editor, Religious Programmes, C4, 1988–89; guest producer, scriptwriter and presenter, BBC World Service and Radio 4, 1989–94. Mistress of The Keys, Guild of Catholic Writers, 1983–88. *Publications:* (as F. J. Gumley, with Brian Redhead): The Good Book, 1987; The Christian Centuries, 1989; The Pillars of Islam, 1990; Protestors for Paradise, 1993; (jtly) Discovering Turkey, 1995. *Recreation:* playing with children's toys. *Address:* St Augustine's Priory, Hillcrest Road, Ealing, W5 2JL.

GUMMER, family name of **Baron Chadlington**.

GUMMER, Rt Hon. John Selwyn; PC 1985; MP (C) Suffolk Coastal, since 1983 (Eye, Suffolk, 1979–83); *b* 26 Nov. 1939; *s* of late Canon Selwyn Gummer and Sybille (*née* Mason); *m* 1977, Penelope Jane, *yr d* of John P. Gardner; two *s* two *d. Educ:* King's Sch., Rochester; Selwyn Coll., Cambridge (Exhibr). BA Hons History 1961; MA 1971; Chm., Cambridge Univ. Conservative Assoc., 1961; Pres., Cambridge Union, 1962; Chm., Fedn of Conservative Students, 1962. Editor, Business Publications, 1962–64; Editor-in-Chief, Max Parrish & Oldbourne Press, 1964–66; BPC Publishing: Special Asst to Chm., 1967; Publisher, Special Projects, 1967–69; Editorial Coordinator, 1969–70. Mem., ILEA Educn Cttee, 1967–70; Dir, Shandwick Publishing Co., 1966–81; Man. Dir, EP Gp of Cos, 1975–81; Chairman: Selwyn Shandwick Internat., 1976–81, Siemssen Hunter Ltd, 1979–80 (Dir, 1973–80). Contested (C) Greenwich, 1964 and 1966; MP (C) Lewisham W, 1970–Feb. 1974; PPS to Minister of Agriculture, 1972; an additional Vice-Chm., Conservative Party, 1972–74; an Asst Govt Whip, 1981; a Lord Comr of HM Treasury, 1981–83; Parly Under-Sec. of State for Employment, Jan.–Oct. 1983; Minister of State, Dept of Employment, 1983–84; Paymaster-Gen., 1984–85; Chm., Cons. Party, 1983–85; Minister of State: MAFF, 1985–88; DoE, 1988–89; Minister of Agric., Fisheries and Food, 1989–93; Sec. of State for the Envmt, 1993–97. Chairman: Cons. Gp for Europe, 1997–2000; Marine Stewardship Council, 1998–2005. Chairman: Sancroft Internat. Ltd, 1997–; Valpak Ltd, 1998–; Veolia Water UK (formerly General Utilities Ltd), 2004– (Dir, 1997–). Mem., Gen. Synod of the Church of England, 1979–92; joined Roman Catholic Church, 1993. *Publications:* (jtly) When the Coloured People Come, 1966; The Permissive Society, 1971; (with L. W. Cowie) The Christian Calendar, 1974; (contrib.) To Church with Enthusiasm, 1969; (contrib.) Faith In Politics, 1987; Christianity and Conservatism, 1990. *Address:* House of Commons, SW1A 0AA.

See also Baron Chadlington.

GUMMETT, Prof. Philip John, PhD; Chief Executive, Higher Education Funding Council for Wales, since 2004; *b* 26 Oct. 1947; *s* of Rev. Philip Charles Gummett and Morfydd Ioli Gummett (*née* Brown); *m* 1969, Karen Hope Thurgood; one *s* one *d. Educ:* Univ. of Birmingham (BSc); Univ. of Manchester (MSc; PhD). University of Manchester: Lectr in Sci. and Technol. Policy, 1974–81; Sen. Lectr, 1981–94; Prof. of Govt and Technol. Policy, 1994–2000; Pro-Vice-Chancellor, 1997–2000; Dir, PREST (Prog. of Policy Res. in Engrg, Sci. and Technol.), Manchester, 1997–2000; Dir of Higher Educn, HEFCW, 2000–04. Advr to UK and European Parlts and EC. *Publications:* Scientists in Whitehall, 1980; (ed with J. Reppy) The Relations Between Defence and Civil Technologies, 1988; (with W. Walker) Nationalism, Internationalism and the European Defence Market, 1993; (ed) Globalisation and Public Policy, 1996; (ed with R. Bud) Cold War Hot Science: applied research in Britain's defence laboratories 1945–1990, 1999. *Recreations:* reading, walking, cycling, music. *Address:* Higher Education Funding Council for Wales, Linden Court, Ty Glas Avenue, Cardiff CF14 5DZ. *T:* (029) 2068 2251, *Fax:* (029) 2076 3163; *e-mail:* philip.gummett@hefcw.ac.uk.

GUMMOW, Hon. William Montague Charles, AC 1997; **Hon. Justice Gummow;** Justice, High Court of Australia, since 1995; *b* 9 Oct. 1942; *s* of W. C. R. Gummow and A. C. Gummow (*née* Benson). *Educ:* Sydney Grammar Sch.; Univ. of Sydney (BA 1962; LLB 1965; LLM 1970). Admitted Solicitor, Supreme Court of NSW, 1966; Partner, Allen, Allen & Hemsley, 1969–76; admitted to NSW Bar, 1976; in practice at the Bar, 1976–86; QC (NSW) 1986; Judge, Federal Court of Australia, 1986–95. Clarendon Law Lectr, Oxford Univ., 1999; WA Lee Equity Lectr, Qld Univ. of Technol., 2002; Sir Maurice Byers Lectr, NSW Bar Assoc., 2005. Mem., Amer. Law Inst., 1997. Hon. LLD Sydney, 1992. *Publications:* Jacobs' Law of Trusts in Australia, 3rd edn 1971 to 6th edn (jtly) 1997; Equity: doctrines and remedies, 1975, 3rd edn (jtly) 1992; Cases and Materials on Equity and Trusts, 1975, 4th edn 1993. *Address:* Judges' Chambers, High Court of Australia, PO Box 6309, Kingston, ACT 2604, Australia. *T:* (2) 62706955. *Club:* Australian (Sydney).

GUNAWARDENA, Jeremy Harin Charles, PhD; Director, Virtual Cell Program, Department of Systems Biology, Harvard Medical School, since 2004; *b* 12 Nov. 1955; *s* of late Charles Gunawardena and of Yvonne Gunawardena (*née* Weerakoon). *Educ:* Imperial Coll., London (BSc); Trinity Coll., Cambridge (MA; PhD 1983). L. E. Dickson Instr, Dept of Mathematics, Univ. of Chicago, 1981–83; Res. Fellow in Mathematics, Trinity Coll., Cambridge, 1983–87; Hewlett-Packard Laboratories: Mem., Technical Staff, 1987–2001; Dir, Basic Res. Inst. in the Mathematical Scis, 1994–2001; Vis. Scientist and Hd of Systems Biol., Bauer Center for Genomics Res., Harvard Univ., 2002–04. Vis. Schol., Dept of Computer Sci., Stanford Univ., 1992–94; Vis. Res. Fellow, Trinity Coll., Cambridge, 1995; Prof. Invitée, Ecole Normale Supérieure, Paris, 2000. Mem., EPSRC, 1999–2002. *Publication:* (ed) Idempotency, 1998. *Recreations:* tennis, cricket, classical music, flying aeroplanes. *Address:* Department of Systems Biology, Harvard Medical School, 200 Longwood Avenue, Boston, MA 02115, USA. *T:* (617) 4324839.

GUNN, John Angus Livingston; Head of Heritage and Tourism Group, Department of National Heritage, 1992; *b* 20 Nov. 1934; *s* of late Alistair L. Gunn, FRCOG, and Mrs Sybil Gunn, JP; *m* 1959, Jane, *d* of Robert Cameron; one *s* one *d. Educ:* Fettes Coll., Edinburgh (Foundationer); Christ Church, Oxford (Scholar; BA 1st Cl. Hons in Classical Hon. Mod., 1955, and in final sch. of Psychology, Philosophy and Physiology, 1957; Passmore-Edwards Prizeman, 1956; MA). National Service, commnd in S Wales Borderers (24th Regt), 1957–59. Entered Min. of Transport, 1959; Principal Private Sec. to Ministers of Transport, 1967–68; Asst Sec., MoT, DoE and Civil Service Dept, 1969–75; Under-Sec., DoE, 1976–92; Greater London Housing and Planning Directorate, 1976; Water Directorate, 1981; Water Privatisation Directorate, 1987; Heritage and Royal Estate Directorate, 1990.

GUNN, Prof. John Charles, CBE 1994; MD; FMedSci, FRCPsych; Professor of Forensic Psychiatry, Institute of Psychiatry, 1978–2002, now Emeritus; *b* 6 June 1937; *s* of late Albert Charles Gunn and Lily Hilda Edwards; *m* 1st, 1959, Celia Willis (marr. diss. 1986, she *d* 1989); one *s* one *d*; 2nd, 1989, Pamela Jane Taylor, *qv. Educ:* Brighton, Hove and Sussex Grammar Sch.; Reigate Grammar Sch.; Birmingham Univ. (MB ChB 1961; Acad. DPM 1966; MD 1969). MRCPsych 1971, FRCPsych 1980. Queen Elizabeth Hosp., Birmingham, 1961–63; Maudsley Hosp., 1963–67; Institute of Psychiatry: Res. Worker, 1967–69; Lectr, 1969–71; Sen. Lectr, 1971–75; Dir, Special Hosps Res. Unit, 1975–78. H. B. Williams Vis. Prof. to Aust. and NZ, 1985. Advisor, H of C Select Cttees on Violence in Marriage, 1975, on Prison Med. Service, 1986; Member: Home Sec's Adv. Bd on Restricted Patients, 1982–91; Royal Commn on Criminal Justice, 1991–93; Parole Bd for England and Wales, 2006–. WHO Specialist Advisor in Forensic Psychiatry to China, 1987; Consultant, Eur. Cttee for Prevention of Torture, 1993–. Royal College of Psychiatrists: Chm., Res. Cttee, 1976–80; Dep. Chief Examr, 1993–95; Mem., Council, 1977–83, 1997–2004; Mem., Exec. Cttee, 1998–2004; Chm., Faculty of Forensic Psychiatry, 2000–04; Mem., Ct of Electors, 2003–. Founder FMedSci 1998. Editor, Criminal Behaviour and Mental Health, 1991–. *Publications:* Epileptics in Prison, 1977; Psychiatric Aspects of Imprisonment, 1978; Current Research in Forensic Psychiatry and Psychology, vols 1–3, 1982–85; Violence in Human Society, 1983; (ed with P. J. Taylor) Forensic Psychiatry: clinical, legal and ethical issues, 1993. *Recreations:* theatre, opera, cinema, photography, walking, living with Pamela. *Address:* PO Box 725, Bromley BR2 7WF; *e-mail:* j.gunn@iop.kcl.ac.uk. *Clubs:* Athenæum, Royal Society of Medicine.

GUNN, John Humphrey; company director and venture capitalist; Deputy Chairman, Ludgate Investments Ltd; *b* 15 Jan. 1942; *s* of Francis (Bob) Gunn and Doris Gunn; *m* 1965, Renate Sigrid (*née* Boehme); three *d. Educ:* Sir John Deane's Grammar School, Northwich; Univ. of Nottingham (BA Hons 1964). Barclays Bank, 1964–68; Astley & Pearce, 1968–85; Chief Executive: Exco International, 1979–85; British & Commonwealth Holdings, 1986–87 and 1990 (Chm., 1987–90). Dir, John Duncan & Co., 1992–2001. Hon. LLD Nottingham, 1989. *Recreations:* golf, ski-ing, mountain walking, classical music, opera. *Address:* 6th Floor, 80 Cannon Street, EC4N 6HL. *T:* (020) 7621 5770. *Clubs:* MCC; Downhill Only (Wengen).

GUNN, Marion Ballantyne; Head of Fire Service and Emergency Planning Division, Scottish Executive Justice Department (formerly Scottish Office Home and Health, then Home, Department), 1992–2001; *b* 31 Oct. 1947; *d* of Dr Allan Christie Tait and Jean Ballantyne Hay; *m* 1985, Donald Hugh Gunn (*d* 2007); one step *s. Educ:* Jordanhill College School; Dumfries Academy; Univ. of Edinburgh (MA Hons 1969); Open Univ. (BA

1975). Management trainee, Lewis's, Bristol, 1969–70; joined Scottish Office, 1970; posts in Scottish Educn Dept and Scottish Develt Dept, 1970–90; Asst Sec., 1984; Head of Roads Policy and Programme Div., 1987; Head of Water Policy Div., 1990. Research Fellow, Univ. of Glasgow, 1983–84. *Recreations:* gardening, badminton. *Address:* 32 Warriston Avenue, Edinburgh EH3 5NB. *T:* (0131) 552 4476.

GUNN, Pamela Jane; *see* Taylor, P. J.

GUNN, Sir Robert (Norman), Kt 1995; DL; Chairman, Further Education Funding Council for England, 1992–97; Chairman, 1985–90, Chief Executive, 1983–87 and Director, 1976–90, The Boots Company PLC; *b* 16 Dec. 1925; *s* of late Donald Macfie Gunn and Margaret (*née* Pallister); *m* 1956, Joan Parry, JP (*d* 2008); one *d*. *Educ:* Royal High Sch., Edinburgh; Worcester Coll., Oxford (MA). Served RAC, 1944–47 (Lieut). Joined Boots, 1951; Merchandise Buyer, 1962–70; Head of Warehousing and Distribn, 1971–73; Dir of Property, 1973–78; Dir, Industrial Div., 1979–83 (Man. Dir 1980–83); Vice-Chm., 1983–85. Director: Foseco plc (formerly Foseco Minsep), 1984–91; East Midlands Electricity, 1990–95; Nottingham Building Soc., 1990–97. Member: Bd of Management, Assoc. of British Pharmaceutical Industry, 1981–84 (Vice-Pres., 1983–84); Council, CBI, 1985–90; PCFC, 1989–93; HEFCE, 1992–94. CCMI (CBIM 1983); FInstD 1985; FRSA. DL Notts, 1995. Hon. LLD Nottingham, 1993. *Recreations:* gardening, travel. *Address:* Tor House, Pinfold Lane, Elston, near Newark, Notts NG23 5PD.

GUNN-JOHNSON, Ven. David Allan; Archdeacon of Barnstaple, since 2003; *b* 2 May 1949; *s* of Sidney and Violet Winifred Johnson; *m* 1979, Susan Wells; two *d*. *Educ:* St Stephen's House, Oxford. Ordained deacon 1981, priest 1982; Assistant Curate: Oxhey, 1981–84; Cheshunt, 1984–88; Team Rector, Colyton, 1988–2003; RD, Honiton, 1990–96; Preb., Exeter Cathedral, 1999–2003. STh (Archbp's Schol. of Theol.) 1985, MA 1995, Lambeth. *Recreations:* historical research, theatre (writing, directing and performing), motorcycling. *Address:* Stage Cross, Sanders Lane, Bishops Tawton, Barnstaple EX32 0BE. *T:* (01271) 375475, *Fax:* (01271) 377934; *e-mail:* archdeacon.of.barnstaple@exeter.anglican.org.

GUNNELL, Sally Jane Janet, OBE 1998 (MBE 1993); athlete, retired 1997; television presenter and motivational speaker; *b* 29 July 1966; *m* 1992, Jonathan Bigg; three *s*. *Educ:* Chigwell High School. Life Member, Essex Ladies' Club, 1978; GB Team Captain, 1992–97; 400 m hurdles wins include: Olympic Champion, 1992; World Champion, 1993; World Record Holder, 1993; European Champion, 1994; Commonwealth Champion, 1994; also Commonwealth Champion, 100 m hurdles, 1986, 1990. *Publications:* Running Tall, 1994; Be Your Best, 2001. *Address:* Old School Cottage, School Lane, Pyecombe, W Sussex BN45 7FQ.

GUNNING, Prof. Brian Edgar Scourse, FRS 1980; FAA 1979; Professor of Plant Cell Biology, Australian National University, 1974–97, now Emeritus; *b* 29 Nov. 1934; *s* of William Gunning and Margaret Gunning (*née* Scourse); *m* 1964, Marion Sylvia Forsyth; two *s*. *Educ:* Methodist Coll., Belfast; Queen's Univ., Belfast (BSc (Hons), MSc, PhD); DSc ANU. Lecturer in Botany, 1957–65, Reader in Botany, 1965–74, Queen's Univ., Belfast. Hon. MRIA 1999. *Publications:* Ultrastructure and the Biology of Plant Cells (with Dr M. Steer), 1975; Intercellular Communication in Plants: studies on plasmodesmata (with Dr A. Robards), 1976; (with M. Steer) Plant Cell Biology, 1996; contribs to research jls. *Recreations:* hill walking, photography. *Address:* 29 Millen Street, Hughes, ACT 2605, Australia. *T:* (2) 62812879.

GUNNING, Sir Charles Theodore, 9th Bt *cr* 1778, of Eltham, Kent; CD 1964; RCN retired; engineering consultant, Promaxis Systems Inc., Ottawa; *b* 19 June 1935; *s* of Sir Robert Gunning, 8th Bt and of Helen Nancy, *d* of Vice-Adm. Sir Theodore John Hallett, KBE, CB; *S* father, 1989; *m* 1st, 1969, Sarah (marr. diss. 1982), *d* of Col Patrick Arthur Easton; one *d*; 2nd, 1989, Linda Martin (*née* Kachmar). *Educ:* Canadian Mil. Coll.; RNEC Plymouth; Tech. Univ. of NS. PEng. Chm., Nat. Council in Canada, Royal Commonwealth Soc., 1990–93 (Pres., Ottawa Br.; a Nat. Vice-Chm.). Silver Jubilee Medal, 1977; Golden Jubilee Medal, 2002. *Heir:* *b* John Robert Gunning [*b* 17 Sept. 1944; *m* 1st, 1969, Alina Tylicki (marr. diss. 1995); two *s* one *d*; 2nd, 1999, Diane Grosschmidt]. *Address:* 2940 McCarthy Road, Ottawa, ON K1V 8K6, Canada.

GUNNYEON, William James, FRCP, FFOM, FRCGP; Chief Medical Adviser and Chief Scientist, Department for Work and Pensions, since 2005; *b* 10 June 1953; *s* of late William Campbell Gunnyeon and Muriel Gunnyeon (*née* Dunn, latterly Shearer); *m* 1975, Joan Elizabeth Moorcroft; two *s*. *Educ:* Dundee Univ. (MB ChB 1977). DIH 1984. FFOM 1994; FRCP 1999; FRCGP 2003. House Officer, Stirling Royal Infirmary, 1977–78; MO, RAF, 1978–83; Med. Advr, then Sen. Med. Advr, OMS Ltd, 1983–92; Principal Med. Advr, Grampian Regl Council, 1992–96; Dir, Grampian Occupational Health Service, 1996–97; Liberty Occupational Health: Dir, Occupational Health, 1997–99; Chief Exec., 1999–2000; Med. Dir, Aon, subseq. Capita, Health Solutions, 2000–05. Faculty of Occupational Medicine: Registrar, 1999–2001; Pres., 2002–05; Mem. Council, RCP, 2002–05; Member: Acad. of Med. Royal Colls, 2002–05; Specialist Trng Authy, 2002–05. Chm., Assoc. of Local Authy Med. Advrs, 1995–97. *Publication:* (jtly) Fitness to Teach, 2000. *Recreations:* gardening, hill-walking, travel, reading, classical music. *Address:* *e-mail:* bill.gunnyeon@btopenworld.com.

GUNSTON, Sir John (Wellesley), 3rd Bt *cr* 1938, of Wickwar, Co. Gloucester; company director; *b* 25 July 1962; *s* of Sir Richard Gunston, 2nd Bt and of Mrs Joan Elizabeth Marie Gunston; *S* father, 1991; *m* 1990, Rosalind (marr. diss. 1998), *y d* of Edward Gordon Eliott; one *s*. *Educ:* Harrow; RMA Sandhurst. BSAP Reserve, Rhodesia, 1979–80. Commnd 1st Bn Irish Guards, 1981. Since 1983 has covered wars, revolutions and foreign travel assignments in: Afghanistan, Albania, Brazil, Burma, Colombia, Egypt, Eritrea, Israel (West Bank and Gaza), Lebanon, Liberia, South Africa, Sudan, Uganda, Ulster (esp. Derry) and also in North America, Eastern Europe and South East Asia. Dir, North-West Frontier Productions, 1995–; Man. Dir, Hard News Ltd, 1998–. Chm., Rory Peck Trust and Award, 1995–97. Fellow: Soc. of Authors, 1994; RSAA, 1995; FRGS 1988; FRAS 1998. *Recreations:* books, biking and ballistics. *Heir:* *s* Richard St George Gunston, *b* 3 July 1992. *Address:* c/o 127 Piccadilly, W1E 6YZ. *Clubs:* Cavalry and Guards, Special Forces.

GUNTER, John Forsyth; freelance theatre and opera designer; Associate Designer, Royal National Theatre, since 1991 (Head of Design, 1989–91); *b* 31 Oct. 1938; *s* of late Herbert and Charlotte Gunter; *m* 1969, Micheline McKnight; two *d*. *Educ:* Bryanston Public Sch.; Central Sch. of Art and Design (Dip. with distinction). Started career in rep. theatre in GB; Resident Designer: English Stage Co., 1965–66 (subseq. designed 28 prodns for co.); Zürich Schauspielhaus, 1970–73; freelance design work, 1973–, for West End, NT, RSC, Old Vic, Chichester, New York, Sydney, Los Angeles; also for Peter Hall Co. seasons, 1997, 1998 and 2003; designer of operas: for cos in GB, Italy, Germany, Austria, Holland, Australia, USA and Russia; Glyndebourne Fest. Op., 1985–; Royal Opera House, Covent Gdn, 1997–; ENO; La Scala, Milan, 1988; Salzburg, 2005; Los Angeles, 2005; Baden-Baden, 2008; St Petersburg, 2008. Head, Theatre Dept, Central Sch. of Art and Desi 1974–82. FRSA 1982. Many awards for design of Guys and Dolls, NT, 1982, incl. SW Award for Best Design 1982, Drama Magazine Best Design Award 1982, Plays and Play Award for Best Design 1983; Plays and Players and Olivier Awards for Best Design 19 for design of Wild Honey, NT, 1984; Emmy Award, 1994, for set design of Porgy a Bess. *Recreations:* getting out into the countryside, tennis. *Address:* c/o Richard Hai Performing Arts, 6 Windmill Street, W1T 2JB.

GUPTA, Atul; Chief Executive Officer, Burren Energy plc, since 2006 (Chief Operati Officer, 1999–2006); *b* 15 Dec. 1959; *s* of Satya Pal Gupta and Sarmishta Gupta; *m* 19 Anjali Garg, MSc; two *d*. *Educ:* Sidney Sussex Coll., Cambridge (BA Hons 1981; ME Chem. Eng. 1993); Heriot-Watt Univ., Edinburgh (MEng Pet. Eng.). Charterho Petroleum plc, 1983–86; Petrofina SA, 1986–90; Monument Oil plc, 1990–99, Gen. Turkmenistan, 1996–99. *Recreations:* football, cricket, art, reading. *Address:* Burren Ene plc, 11 Strand, WC2N 5HR. *T:* (020) 7984 1900, *Fax:* (020) 7484 1510.

GUPTA, Prof. Sunetra, PhD; novelist; Professor of Theoretical Epidemiolo Department of Zoology, University of Oxford, since 2006; *b* Calcutta, 15 March 1965 of Dhruba and Minati Gupta; *m* 1994, Adrian Vivian Sinton Hill, *qv*; two *d*. *Ed* Princeton Univ. (AB 1987); Univ. of London (PhD 1992). University of Oxford: Ju Res. Fellow, Merton Coll., 1993–96; Department of Zoology: Wellcome Trust Sen. R Fellow, 1995–99; Reader, 1999–2006. *Publications:* novels: Memories of Rain, 1992; T Glassblower's Breath, 1993; Moonlight into Marzipan, 1995; A Sin of Colour, 19 contrib. scientific articles to Science, Nature, Lancet. *Recreations:* cinema, art, gardeni architecture. *Address:* Department of Zoology, University of Oxford, South Parks Ro Oxford OX1 3PS. *T:* (01865) 281225; *e-mail:* sunetra.gupta@zoo.ox.ac.uk.

GURDON, family name of **Baron Cranworth**.

GURDON, Sir John (Bertrand), Kt 1995; DPhil; FRS 1971; Chairman, Company Biologists, Cambridge, since 2001; Master, Magdalene College, Cambridge, 1995–20 (Hon. Fellow, 2002); *b* 2 Oct. 1933; *s* of late W. N. Gurdon, DCM, formerly Assington, Suffolk, and Elsie Marjorie (*née* Byass); *m* 1964, Jean Elizabeth Margaret Cur one *s* one *d*. *Educ:* Edgeborough; Eton (Fellow, 1978–93); Christ Church, Oxford (I 1956; DPhil 1960). Beit Memorial Fellow, 1958–61; Gosney Research Fellow, Calif. In Technol., 1962; Departmental Demonstrator, Dept of Zool., Oxford, 1963–64; V Research Fellow, Carnegie Instn, Baltimore, 1965; Lectr, Dept of Zoology, Oxfo 1965–72; Research Student, Christ Church, 1962–72; Mem. Staff, MRC Lab. Molecular Biology, Cambridge, 1972–83 (Hd, Cell Biology Div., 1979–83); Fello Churchill Coll., Cambridge, 1973–94; John Humphrey Plummer Prof. of Cell Biolog Univ. of Cambridge, 1983–2001; Chm., Wellcome Cancer Res. Campaign Ins Cambridge, 1991–2001. Fullerian Prof. of Physiology and Comparative Anatomy, Ro Instn, 1985–91. Lectures: Harvey Soc., NY, 1973; Dunham, Harvard, 1974; Croonia Royal Soc., 1976; Carter-Wallace, Princeton, 1978; Woodhull, Royal Instn, 198 Florey, Aust., 1988; Fischberg Meml, Geneva, 1989; Rutherford, Royal Soc., 199 Rodney Porter Meml, Oxford, 1999; Hitchcock, Berkeley, USA, 2006. Pres., Intern Soc. Develt Biol., 1989–93. Gov., The Wellcome Trust, 1995–2000. Chm., Co. Biologists, 2001–. Hon. Foreign Member: Amer. Acad. of Arts and Scis, 1978; Forei Associate: Nat. Acad. of Sciences, USA, 1980; Belgian Royal Acad. of Scis, Letters a Fine Arts, 1984; Foreign Member: Amer. Philos. Soc., 1983; Lombardy Acad. Sci., Ita 1989; Acad. Les Sciences, France, 1990; Inst. of Medicine, USA, 2004. Hon. Stude Christ Church, Oxford, 1985; Hon. Fellow, Churchill Coll., Cambridge, 2007. Ho DSc: Chicago, 1978; René Descartes, Paris, 1982; Oxford, 1988; Hull, 1998; Glasgo 2000; Cambridge, 2007. Albert Brachet Prize (Belgian Royal Academy), 1968; Scienti Medal of Zoological Soc., 1968; Feldberg Foundn Award, 1975; Paul Ehrlich Awar 1977; Nessim Habif Prize, Univ. of Geneva, 1979; CIBA Medal, Biochem. Soc., 198 Comfort Crookshank Award for Cancer Research, 1983; William Bate Hardy Pri Cambridge Philos. Soc., 1984; Prix Charles Léopold Mayer, Acad. des Scis, France, 198 Ross Harrison Prize, Internat. Soc. Develt Biol., 1985; Royal Medal, Royal Soc., 198 Emperor Hirohito Internat. Prize for Biology, Japan Acad., 1987; Wolf Prize in Medici Israel, 1989; Jan Waldenstram Medal, Swedish Oncol. Soc., 1991; Dist. Service Awar Miami, 1992; Edridge Green Medal, RCOphth, 1997; Jean Brachet Meml Prize, Intern Soc. Differentiation, 2000; Conklin Medal, Soc. Develt. Biol., 2001; Copley Med Royal Soc., 2003. *Publications:* Control of Gene Expression in Animal Developme 1974; articles in scientific jls, especially on nuclear transplantation. *Recreations:* ski-in tennis, horticulture, Lepidoptera. *Address:* Whittlesford Grove, Whittlesford, Cambrid CB22 4NZ. *Club:* Eagle Ski.

GURNEY, Nicholas Bruce Jonathan; Chairman, North Bristol NHS Trust, since 200 *b* 20 Jan. 1945; *s* of Comdr Bruce William George Gurney and Cynthia Joan Watki Gurney (*née* Winn, later Mason); *m* 1st, 1970, Patricia Wendy Tulip (marr. diss. 1987 two *s* one *d*; 2nd, 1989, Caroline Mary (*née* Bentley). *Educ:* Wimbledon College; Christ College, Cambridge. BA 1966, MA 1969. Lectr in English, Belize Teachers' Traini College, Belize, as part of British Volunteer Programme, 1966–67; MoD 1967; A Private Sec., Minister of State for Defence, 1970–72; Civil Service Dept, 1972–74; Priva Sec. to Lord Privy Seal and Leader of House of Lords, 1974–77; Civil Service Dept a Management Personnel Office, 1978–83; Grade 3, Cabinet Office, and CS Com 1983–88; Dept of Health, 1988–90; Chief Exec., Wokingham DC, 1990–93; City Mg subseq. Chief Exec., Portsmouth CC, 1994–2003; Chief Exec., Bristol CC, 2003–0 *Address:* North Bristol NHS Trust, Trust Headquarters, Beckspool Road, Frencha Bristol BS16 1JE.

GURNEY, Prof. Robert James, OBE 2001; PhD; Professor of Environmental Scienc (formerly of Physical Geography), and Director of NERC Environmental Systems Scienc Centre, University of Reading, since 1990; *b* 31 March 1951; *s* of James William Stratto Gurney and Jeanne Mary Gurney; *m* 1977, Charlotte Mary (*née* Carr); one *s* one *d*. *Edu* King's Coll. London (BSc Hons); Univ. of Bristol (PhD). Res. Fellow, Inst. of Hydrolog 1975–80; Research Associate: NASA Goddard Space Flight Center, Maryland, 1981–8 Dept of Civil Engrg, Univ. of Maryland, 1983–84; Hd, Hydrological Scis Branch, NAS Goddard Space Flight Center, Maryland, 1984–90. Chm., ReadiBus, 1993–200 FRMetS 1970. *Publications:* (with E. T. Engman) Remote Sensing in Hydrology, 199 (ed jtly) Atlas of Satellite Observations Related to Global Climate Change, 1993; (with K A. Browning) Global Energy and Water Cycles, 1999. *Recreation:* charitable work. *Addres* Environmental Systems Science Centre, University of Reading, Harry Pitt Building, P Box 238, 3 Earley Gate, Reading RG6 6AL. *T:* (0118) 378 8741, *Fax:* (0118) 378 641 *e-mail:* rjg@mail.nerc-essc.ac.uk.

GURNEY, Tim, OBE 2006; HM Diplomatic Service, retired; Deputy Hig Commissioner, Canberra, 2006–08; *b* 28 April 1955; *s* of Brian and Joy Gurney; *m* 197 Denise Elizabeth Harker; one *s* one *d*. Joined FCO, 1973; Istanbul, 1976–79; Karach 1979–82; Montreal, 1982–85; Second Secretary: FCO, 1985–88; (Chancery/Inf.), Accr 1988–90; Dep. Dir, British Inf. Services, NY, 1991–96; First Sec., FCO, 1996–98; Dep

Governor, Bermuda, 1998–2003; Dep. Hd of Mission, Kabul, 2003–05. *Recreations:* scuba diving instructor, soccer referee, photography.

GURR, Dr Michael Ian; Maypole Scientific Services, private nutrition consultancy, 1990–99; Partner, Isles of Scilly Specialist Crops, 1999–2006; Chairman, Isles of Scilly Wildlife Trust, 2001–2005; *b* 10 April 1939; *s* of Henry Ormonde Gurr and Hilda Ruth Gurr; *m* 1963, Elizabeth Anne Mayers; two *s* one *d*. *Educ:* Dunstable Grammar Sch.; Univ. of Birmingham (BSc, PhD). Postdoctoral Fellowship, Harvard Univ., 1964–66; Unilever European Fellowship of Biochem. Soc., State Univ. of Utrecht, 1966–67; Res. Scientist, Unilever Res. Lab., Sharnbrook, Bedford, 1967–78; Hd, Department of Nutrition, Nat. Inst. for Res. in Dairying, Shinfield, Reading, 1978–85; Dir, Reading Lab. of AFRC Inst. of Food Res., 1985–86; Nutrition Consultant and Hd of Nutrition Dept, MMB, 1986–90. Visiting Professor: Univ. of Reading, 1986–99; Oxford Poly., later Oxford Brookes Univ., 1990–99. Chairman: Editl Bd, British Jl of Nutrition, 1988–90; Editl Adv. Bd, British Nutrition Foundn, 1994–99; Man. Ed., Nutrition Research Reviews, 1991–99. *Publications:* Lipid Biochemistry: an introduction (jtly), 1971, 5th edn 2002; Role of Fats in Food and Nutrition, 1984, 2nd edn 1992; numerous original pubns and reviews. *Recreations:* sailing, walking, gardening, piano playing, choral singing. *Address:* Vale View Cottage, Maypole, St Mary's, Isles of Scilly TR21 0NU. *T:* (01720) 422224.

GURRÍA TREVIÑO, (José) Angel; Secretary-General, Organisation for Economic Co-operation and Development, since 2006; *b* Tampico, Mexico, 8 May 1950; *s* of Francisco José Gurría Lacroix and Carmen Treviño Humana; *m* 1973, Lulu Ululani Quintana Pali; one *s* two *d*. *Educ:* Univ. Nacional Autónoma de México (BA Econs); Univ. of Leeds (MA Econs). Financial analyst, Federal Power Commn, 1968–70; COS to Dep. Mayor of City of Mexico, 1970; COS to Dep. CEO, then CEO, Nafinsa (Mexico's Develt Bank); Hd, Dept of Negotiations of Foreign Loans, Nafinsa; Dep. Financial Manager, Rural Develt Fund, 1975–76; Perm. Rep. to Internat. Coffee Orgn, London, 1976–78; Treasury posts, 1978–92: Dep. Dir, Public Debt; Dir, Foreign Debt; Gen. Dir, Public Credit; Dep. Sec. for Internat. Affairs; Pres. and CEO, Bancomext (Mexico's Export/Import Bank), 1992–93, Nafinsa, 1993–94; Sec. for Internat. Affairs, Institnl Revolutionary Party (PRI), 1993–94; Minister: of Foreign Affairs Mexico, 1994–97; of Finance and Public Credit, 1998–2000. Holds numerous foreign decorations. *Publications:* contribs on econs, debt develt and governance. *Address:* Organisation for Economic Co-operation and Development, 2 rue André Pascal, 75775 Paris Cedex 16, France; *e-mail:* secretary.general@oecd.org.

GURU-MURTHY, Krishnan; presenter, Channel 4 News, since 1998; *b* 5 April 1970; *s* of Krishnan and Indrani Guru-Murthy; *m* 2005, Lisa Jane Colles; one *s* one *d*. *Educ:* Queen Elizabeth's Grammar Sch., Blackburn; Hertford Coll., Oxford (BA Hons PPE). BBC: presenter: Open to Question, 1988–89; East, 1989–90; presenter/reporter, Newsround, 1991–94; reporter, Newsnight, 1994–97; presenter, News 24, 1997–98. Columnist: Eastern Eye, 2001–03; Metro, 2002–06. Vis. Prof., London Metropolitan Univ., 2008–. *Recreations:* music, food, golf. *Address:* Channel 4 News, ITN, 200 Gray's Inn Road, WC1X 8XZ. *T:* (020) 7833 3000; *e-mail:* krishnan.guru-murthy@itn.co.uk. *Clubs:* Groucho, Soho House, Cobden.

GUSTERSON, Prof. Barry Austin, PhD; FRCPath; Professor of Pathology, since 2000, and Chairman, Division of Cancer Sciences and Molecular Pathology, 2002–07, University of Glasgow; *b* Colchester, 24 Oct. 1946; *s* of Joseph Austin Gusterson and Doris Edith (*née* Fairweather); *m* 1972, Ann Josephine Davies; one *s* two *d*. *Educ:* St Bartholomew's Hosp., London (BSc Physiol. 1967; MB BS 1976); Royal Dental Hosp. (BDS 1972); Inst. Cancer Res. (PhD 1980). FRCPath 1995. Sen. Clinical Scientist and Cons., Ludwig Inst. Cancer Res., London, 1983–86; Cons. in Histopathol., Royal Marsden Hosp., 1984–; Prof. of Histopathol., and Chm., Sect. of Cell Biol and Exptl Pathol., Inst. of Cancer Res., London Univ., 1986–2000. Founding Dir, Toby Robins Breast Cancer Res. Centre, London, 1998–. Dir, Pathology, Internat. Breast Cancer Study Gp, Berne, 1995–. Oakley Lectr, Pathological Soc. of GB and Ire., 1986. Chm., Pathology Gp, Orgn Eur. Cancer Insts, Geneva, 1992–96 (Mem., Faculty Bd, 1992–96); Mem., Faculty Bd, Eur. Soc. Mastology, Milan, 1994–. Mem., Brit. Soc. Cell Biol. *Publications:* contrib. chapters in books and numerous articles to professional jls. *Recreations:* antique English glass and furniture, gardening, walking, reading. *Address:* Division of Cancer Sciences and Molecular Pathology, Department of Pathology, Western Infirmary, Glasgow G11 6NT. *T:* (0141) 211 2233.

GUTCH, Richard Evelyn; Chief Executive, Futurebuilders England, 2004–08; *b* 17 Nov. 1946; *s* of Sir John Gutch, KCMG, OBE, and of Diana Mary Gutch (*née* Worsley); *m* 1971, Rosemary Anne Capel Pike; two *s*. *Educ:* Winchester Coll.; Gonville and Caius Coll., Cambridge (BA); University Coll. London (MPhil). Town planning posts in Camden and S Yorks, 1970–76; Sen. Lectr, Planning Unit, PCL, 1976–80; Asst to Chief Exec., Brent LBC, 1980–85; Asst Dir, NCVO, 1985–92; Chief Exec., Arthritis Care, 1992–2001; Dir for England and Strategic Progs, Community Fund, 2001–04. FRSA 1992. *Publications:* reports and booklets. *Recreations:* the arts, Venice, the Isle of Wight, walking, carpentry, gardening. *Address:* 2 Whitehall Gardens, Chiswick, W4 3LT. *T:* (020) 8995 7292.

GUTERRES, António Manuel de Oliveira; United Nations High Commissioner for Refugees, since 2005; *b* 30 April 1949; *m* (wife decd); one *s* one *d*. *Educ:* Technical Univ. of Lisbon. Electrical engr; Asst Prof., Technical Univ. of Lisbon, 1973–75; Chief of Staff to Sec. of State for Industry, 1974–75. Deputy (Socialist), Portuguese Parlt, 1976–83 and 1985–93; Prime Minister of Portugal, 1995–2002. Mem., Commn for European Integration, 1976–79; Pres., Parly Commn for Economy and Finance, 1977–79, for Territory Admin, Local Power and Envmt, 1985–88; Strategic Develt Dir, State Investment and Participation Agency, 1984–85. Mem., Parly Assembly, Council of Europe, 1981–83. Mem., Municipal Assembly of Fundão, 1979–95 (Pres.). Portuguese Socialist Party: joined 1974; Mem., Nat. Secretariat, 1986–88; Pres., Parly Gp, 1988–91; Sec.-Gen., 1992–2001; Vice Pres., 1992–99, Pres., 1999–2005, Socialist Internat. Founder and Vice Pres., Portuguese Assoc. for Consumer Protection, 1973–74; Mem., Assoc. for Economic and Social Develt, 1970–96. *Publications:* articles in jls. *Address:* (office) 94 Rue de Montbrillant, CP 2500, 1211 Geneva 2, Switzerland.

GUTFREUND, Prof. Herbert, FRS 1981; Professor of Physical Biochemistry, University of Bristol, 1972–86, now Emeritus; Scientific Member (external), Max-Planck-Institut für medizinische Forschung, Heidelberg, since 1987; Hon. Scientist, Rutherford Appleton Laboratory, Oxfordshire, since 2001; *b* 21 Oct. 1921; *s* of late Paul Peter Gutfreund and Clara Angela Gutfreund; *m* 1958, Mary Kathelen, *er d* of late Mr and Mrs L. J. Davies, Rugby; two *s* one *d*. *Educ:* Vienna; Univ. of Cambridge (PhD). Research appts at Cambridge Univ., 1947–57; Rockefeller Fellow, Yale Univ., 1951–52; part-time Research Associate, Yale Univ., 1953–58; Principal Scientific Officer, National Inst. for Research in Dairying, Univ. of Reading, 1957–65; Visiting Professor: Univ. of California, 1965; Max Planck Inst., Göttingen, 1966–67; Reader in Biochemistry and Director of Molecular Enzymology Laboratory, Univ. of Bristol, 1967–72. Visiting appointments: Univ. of Leuven, 1972; Univ. of Adelaide, 1979; Univ. of Alberta, 1983. Part-time Scholar in Residence, NIH, Bethesda, 1986–89. Hon. Member: British Biophysical Soc., 1990; Amer. Soc. for Biochem. and Molecular Biol., 1993; Biochemical Soc., 1996. *Publications:* An Introduction to the Study of Enzymes, 1966; Enzymes: physical principles, 1972; (ed) Chemistry of Macromolecules, 1974; (ed) Biochemical Evolution, 1981; Biothermodynamics, 1983; Kinetics for the Life Sciences, 1995; papers and reviews on many aspects of physical biochemistry. *Recreations:* mountain walking in Austria, cooking, reading general literature and philosophy of science, listening to music and all other good things in life. *Address:* Somerset House, Chilton Road, Upton, Oxon OX11 9JL. *T:* (01235) 851468; *e-mail:* h.gutfreund@bristol.ac.uk. *Club:* Oxford and Cambridge.

GUTFREUND, John Halle; President, Gutfreund & Co. Inc., since 1993; Senior Adviser, Collins Stewart LLC (formerly C. E. Unterberg, Towbin), since 2002; *b* 14 Sept. 1929; *s* of B. Manuel Gutfreund and Mary Halle Gutfreund; *m* 1st, 1958, Joyce L. Gutfreund; three *s*; 2nd, 1981, Susan K. Gutfreund; one *s*. *Educ:* Oberlin College, Ohio (BA 1951). Served in Army, Korea, 1951–53; Salomon Brothers, 1953–91: Exec. Partner, 1966; Managing Partner, 1978; Chm. and Chief Exec., 1981–91; Chm., Pres. and Chief Exec., Salomon Inc., 1986–91. Vice-Chm., NY Stock Exchange, 1985–87; formerly: Mem., Bd of Dirs, Securities Industry Assoc.; Mem., Bd of Govs and Pres., Bond Club of NY; Chm., Downtown-Lower Manhattan Assoc.; Chm., Wall Street Cttee for Lincoln Center's 1986–87 Corporate Fund Campaign. Member: Council on Foreign Relations; Brookings Instn; past Mem., Tri-Lateral Commn. Director: AXES LLC; Nutrition 21 Inc. (formerly Ambi Inc.); Evercel Inc.; LCA-Vision Inc.; Advr, Universal Bond Fund. Dir, Montefiore Medical Center Corp. (Mem. Exec. Cttee, Bd of Trustees; Mem., Financial and Real Estate Cttees); Lifetime Mem., NY Public Library (Vice-Chm., Corporate Congress). Trustee, Aperture Foundn (Chm. Emeritus); Hon. Trustee, Oberlin Coll. Hon. DH Oberlin Coll., 1987. *Address:* Collins Stewart LLC, 350 Madison Avenue, 11th Floor, New York, NY 10017, USA. *T:* (212) 3898287.

GUTHARDT, Rev. Dame Phyllis (Myra), DBE 1993; PhD; retired Methodist minister; *b* 1 Aug. 1929; *d* of Johan Detlef Guthardt and Amelia Guthardt. *Educ:* University of New Zealand: Auckland (BA 1957); Canterbury (MA 1959); Newnham Coll., Cambridge (PhD 1963). Primary school teacher, 1950–53; Methodist theol trng, 1954–56; ordained, 1959 (first woman ordained in NZ); active ministry in Methodist and Presbyterian parishes, incl. hosp. and univ. chaplaincy, 1957–90. Pres., Methodist Ch of NZ, 1985–86; Mem. Praesidium, World Methodist Council, 1986–91. Chancellor, Univ. of Canterbury, 1999–2002 (Mem. Council, 1981–2002; Pro-Chancellor, 1992–99). Hon. Dr Waikato, 1986; Hon. LLD Canterbury, 2003. *Publications:* contrib. theol jls. *Recreations:* music, reading, restoring house, gardening. *Address:* 5 Cholmondeley Lane, Governors Bay, RD1 Lyttelton, New Zealand. *T:* (3) 3299675.

GUTHRIE, family name of **Baron Guthrie of Craigiebank.**

GUTHRIE OF CRAIGIEBANK, Baron *cr* 2001 (Life Peer), of Craigiebank in the City of Dundee; **Gen. Charles Ronald Llewelyn Guthrie,** GCB 1994 (KCB 1990); LVO 1977; OBE 1980; DL; Chief of the Defence Staff, 1997–2001; Aide-de-Camp General to the Queen, 1993–2001; *b* 17 Nov. 1938; *s* of late Ronald Guthrie and Nina (*née* Llewelyn); *m* 1971, Catherine, *er d* of late Lt Col Claude Worrall, MVO, OBE, Coldstream Guards; two *s*. *Educ:* Harrow; RMA Sandhurst. Commnd Welsh Guards, 1959; served: BAOR, Aden; 22 SAS Regt, 1965–69; psc 1972; MA (GSO2) to CGS, MoD, 1973–74; Brigade Major, Household Div., 1976–77; Comdg 1st Bn Welsh Guards, Berlin and N Ireland, 1977–80; Col GS Military Ops, MoD, 1980–82; Commander: British Forces New Hebrides, 1980; 4th Armoured Brigade, 1982–84; Chief of Staff 1st (BR) Corps, 1984–86; GOC NE Dist and Comdr 2nd Infantry Div., 1986–87; ACGS, MoD, 1987–89; Comdr 1 (BR) Corps, 1989–91; Comdr Northern Army Gp, 1992–93; C-in-C BAOR, 1992–94; CGS, 1994–97. Director: N. M. Rothschild & Sons, 2001–; Peter Hambro Mining. Vis. Prof., Dept of War Studies, KCL, 2002–. Col Comdt, Intelligence Corps, 1986–95; Col, The Life Guards, 1999–; Gold Stick to the Queen, 1999–; Col Comdt, SAS Regt, 2000–. President: Army Saddle Club, 1991–96; Army LTA, 1991–99; Fedn of London Youth Clubs, 2001–; Action Research, subseq. Action Medical Research, 2001–; Army Benevolent Fund, 2002–; Weston Spirit, 2003–07. Chm., Liddle Hart Archives, 2002–; Mem. Council, IISS, 2002–07. Freeman, City of London, 1988; Liveryman, Painter Stainers' Co., 1989. DL Dorset, 2007. Hon. FKC 2002. Kt, SMO Malta, 1999. Comdr, Legion of Merit (USA), 2001. *Publication:* (with Sir Michael Quinlan) Just War: the just war tradition: ethics in modern warfare, 2007. *Recreations:* tennis, opera, travel. *Address:* PO Box 25439, SW1P 1AG. *Clubs:* White's, Beefsteak, All England Lawn Tennis and Croquet.

See also J. D. Guthrie.

GUTHRIE, Rev. Donald Angus; Rector, Holy Spirit Episcopal Church, Missoula, Montana, 1979–93; *b* 18 Jan. 1931; *s* of Frederick Charles and Alison Guthrie; *m* 1st, 1959, Joyce Adeline Blunsden (*d* 1976); two *s* one *d*; 2nd, 1977, Lesley Josephine Boardman (marr. diss. 1983); 3rd, 1984, Carolyn Wallop Alderson. *Educ:* Marlborough Coll.; Trinity Coll., Oxford (MA). Rector, St John's Church, Selkirk, 1963–69; Vice-Principal, Episcopal Theological Coll., Edinburgh, 1969–74; Priest-in-Charge, Whitburn Parish Church, Tyne and Wear, 1974–76; Provost, St Paul's Cathedral, Dundee, 1976–77; Episcopal Chaplain to Univ. of Montana, 1977–79. *Recreations:* walking, reading. *Address:* 5115 Clearview Way, Missoula, MT 59803, USA.

GUTHRIE, (Garth) Michael, OBE 2007; Deputy Chairman, Welcome Break Holdings Ltd, since 2002 (Director, since 1997; Chairman, 2000–02); *b* 30 April 1941; *s* of Harry and Ann Guthrie; *m* 1963, Joyce Fox; one *s* two *d*. *Educ:* Blackpool Catering Coll. (FHCIMA). Joined Mecca Leisure, 1961; Man. Dir, 1980; Chm., 1981–90; Chief Exec., 1985–90; Founder Dir, 1990, Chm. and Chief Exec., 1991–96, BrightReasons Gp; Chm. and CEO, Pavilion Services Gp, 1991–94; Jt Dep. Chm., Queensborough Hldgs, 1997–2000. Non-exec. Dir, Mission Capital plc, 2005–. Chm., 1996–98, Dep. Chm., 1998–2000, Tomorrow's People Trust. Hon. Fellow, Oxford Brookes Univ. 1995. *Recreations:* ski-ing, swimming, gardening. *Address:* Hyde Heath Farm, Bullbaiters Lane, Hyde Heath, Amersham, Bucks HP6 5RW.

GUTHRIE, James Dalglish; QC 1993; a Recorder, since 1999; *b* 21 Feb. 1950; *s* of late Ronald Guthrie and Nina Guthrie (*née* Llewelyn); *m* 1981, Lucille Gay Page-Roberts; one *s* one *d*. *Educ:* Harrow; Worcester Coll., Oxford (BA Modern History). Called to the Bar, Inner Temple, 1975, Bencher, 2000; admitted as barrister: Turks and Caicos Is, 1995; St Lucia, 1997; St Vincent and The Grenadines, 1998; Trinidad and Tobago, 2000; St Kitts and Nevis, 2005; Grenada, 2006; Bermuda, 2007; Belize, 2008. *Recreations:* bonefishing, travel. *Address:* 3 Hare Court, Temple, EC4Y 7BJ. *T:* (020) 7415 7800. *Club:* Turf.

See also Baron Guthrie of Craigiebank.

GUTHRIE, Sir Malcolm (Connop), 3rd Bt *cr* 1936; *b* 16 Dec. 1942; *s* of Sir Giles Connop McEacharn Guthrie, 2nd Bt, OBE, DSC, and of Rhona, *d* of late Frederic Stileman; *S* father, 1979; *m* 1967, Victoria, *o d* of late Brian Willcock; one *s* one *d*. *Educ:* Millfield. *Heir: s* Giles Malcolm Welcome Guthrie [*b* 16 Oct. 1972; *m* 2000, Susan, *e d* of

Bill and Sheila Thompson]. *Address:* Brent Eleigh, Belbroughton, Stourbridge, Worcestershire DY9 0DW.

GUTHRIE, Michael; *see* Guthrie, G. M.

GUTHRIE, Robert Bruce, PhD; Principal, Hockerill Anglo-European College, 1996–2008; *b* 16 Jan. 1949; *s* of Robert Guthrie and Edith Guthrie (*née* Wilcock); *m* 1970, Christine Haswell; one *s* one *d*. *Educ:* Sale County Grammar Sch. for Boys; Univ. of Leeds (BSc Hons Phys 1969; PhD Ceramics 1975); Univ. of Durham (MBA Distn 1995). Teacher and House Tutor: Bedstone Coll., 1973–74; Stonyhurst Coll., 1974–79; Housemaster and Hd of Sci., Dover Coll., 1979–90; Hd, St George's Sch., Rome, 1991–94. Chm., State Boarding Schs Assoc., 2000–02. Trustee, Hockerill Sports Trust, 2006–. *Publications:* ceramics patent and papers, 1972; contrib. to educnl books and papers. *Recreations:* Rugby (England Schools, British Universities and Yorkshire), keeping fit, photography, reading short poems. *Address:* 4 Catmose Park Road, Oakham, Rutland LE15 6HN. *Club:* Bishop's Stortford Hockey (Vice Pres.).

GUTHRIE, Robert Isles Loftus, (Robin); Director of Social and Economic Affairs, Council of Europe, 1992–98; *b* 27 June 1937; *s* of late Prof. W. K. C. Guthrie, FBA and of Adele Marion Ogilvy, MA; *m* 1963, Sarah Julia Weltman; two *s* one *d*. *Educ:* Clifton Coll.; Trinity Coll., Cambridge (MA); Liverpool Univ. (CertEd); LSE (MScEcon). Head of Cambridge House (Univ. settlement in S London), 1962–69; teacher, ILEA, 1964–66; Social Develt Officer, Peterborough Develt Corp., 1969–75; Asst Dir, Social Work Service, DHSS, 1975–79; Dir, Joseph Rowntree Meml Trust, 1979–88; Chief Charity Comr for England and Wales, 1988–92. Mem., expedns in Anatolia, British Inst. of Archaeol. at Ankara, 1958–62. Member: Arts Council of GB, 1979–81 and 1987–88 (Regional Cttee, 1976–81); Council, Policy Studies Institute, 1979–88; Council, York Univ., 1982–94; UK Cttee, Eur. Cultural Foundn, 2004–; Council, Leeds Univ., 2004–05; Chairman: Yorkshire Arts Assoc., 1984–88; Council of Regional Arts Assocs, 1985–88; Jessie's Fund, 1998–; Yorkshire Regl Arts Bd, 2000–02; Rodolfus Choir, 2001– (Trustee, 1998–); York Mus and Gall. Trust, 2002–; York St John Coll., 2003–; Trustee: York Early Music Foundn, 1995–2003 (Chm., 1995–2001); Thalidomide Trust, 1999–. FRSA. Hon. DLitt Bradford, 1991. *Publications:* (ed) Outlook, 1963; (ed) Outlook Two, 1965; The Good European's Dilemma, 2000; various articles, speeches and lectures. *Recreations:* music, mountains, travel, sheep. *Address:* Braeside House, Acomb Road, York YO24 4EZ.

GUTHRIE, Roy David, (Gus), AM 1996; PhD, DSc; FTSE, FRSC, FRACI; Director, Gus Guthrie Consulting Pty Ltd, since 1996; *b* 29 March 1934; *s* of David Ephraim Guthrie and Ethel (*née* Kimmins); *m* 1st, 1956, Ann Hoad (marr. diss. 1981); three *s*; 2nd, 1982, Lyn Fielding. *Educ:* Dorking Grammar Sch.; King's Coll., Univ. of London (BSc, PhD, DSc). Shirley Inst., Manchester, 1958–60; Asst Lectr, then Lectr, Univ. of Leicester, 1960–63; Lectr, then Reader, Univ. of Sussex, 1963–73; Griffith University, Brisbane: Foundation Prof. of Chemistry, 1973–81; Inaugural Chm., School of Science, 1973–78; Pro-Vice-Chancellor, 1980–81; Professor Emeritus, 1982; Sec. Gen., Royal Soc. of Chemistry, 1982–85; Pres., NSW Inst. of Technol., 1986–87, Vice-Chancellor and Pres., Univ. of Technol., Sydney, 1988–96. Chm., Qld Innovation Council, 1999–2002. Mem. Council, Univ. of Sunshine Coast, 1999–2005. Chm., Buderim Foundn, 2003–04. DUniv: Griffith, 1981; UTS, 1996; Hon. LLD Humberside, 1995. *Publications:* An Introduction to the Chemistry of Carbohydrates (with J. Honeyman), 2nd edn 1964, 3rd edn 1968, 4th edn 1974; over 130 scientific papers. *Recreations:* theatre, music, tai chi, croquet, caring clowning. *Address:* PO Box 369, Buderim, Qld 4556, Australia.

GUTTERIDGE, Charles Norman, FRCP, FRCPath; Medical Director, Barts and the London NHS Trust, since 2002; *b* 15 March 1952; *s* of Frank and Mary Gutteridge; *m* 1976, Charlotte Lorimer; two *s*. *Educ:* Rugby Sch.; Trinity Hall, Cambridge (BA, MB BChir 1976); London Hosp. Med. Coll. FRCP 1995; FRCPath 1997. Dist MO, Soufrière Dist, St Lucia, WI, 1977–79; training posts in gen. medicine and haematology, 1980–88; Wellcome Res. Training Fellow in Haematology, 1985–88; Sen. Lectr in Haematol., and Hon. Consultant Haematologist, Newham Gen. Hosp., 1988–2002, Actg Chief Exec., 1996–97, Med. Dir, 1997–2001, Newham Healthcare NHS Trust. *Address:* Barts and the London NHS Trust, Royal London Hospital, Whitechapel Road, E1 1BB; *e-mail:* charles.gutteridge@bartsandthelondon.nhs.uk.

GUTTRIDGE, Deborah Mary Hinton; *see* Grubb, D. M. H.

GUY, Alan James, DPhil; FRHistS, FRAS, FSA; Director, National Army Museum, since 2004; *b* 13 July 1950; *s* of late James Alfred Guy and Florence Elizabeth Guy (*née* Farr); *m* 1975, Vivien Ruth Wilson; one *s*. *Educ:* Keble Coll., Oxford (MA 1976; DPhil 1983). National Army Museum: Curator, Dept of Weapons, 1977–86; Special Asst to Dir, 1986–88; Asst Dir (Collections), 1988–2000; Asst Dir (Admin), 2000–04. FRHistS 1989; FRAS 1999; FSA 2001. *Publications:* Oeconomy and Discipline: officership and administration in the British Army 1714–1763, 1985; Colonel Samuel Bagshawe and the Army of George II, 1990; (with P. B. Boyden) Soldiers of the Raj: the Indian Army 1660–1947, 1997; (with P. B. Boyden and M. Harding) Ashes and Blood: the British Army in South Africa 1795–1914, 1999. *Recreation:* baroque opera and its substitutes. *Address:* c/o National Army Museum, Royal Hospital Road, SW3 4HT. *T:* (020) 7730 0717, *Fax:* (020) 7823 6573; *e-mail:* aguy@national-army-museum.ac.uk.

GUY, Diana; a Deputy Chairman, Competition Commission, since 2004 (Member, 2001–04); *b* 27 March 1943; *d* of late Charles Stanley Eade and Vera Dorothy Eade (*née* Manwaring); *m* 1968, John Robert Clare Guy; two *s*. *Educ:* Lady Margaret Hall, Oxford (MA Juris.). Admitted solicitor; Partner, 1973–95, Consultant, 1995–2001, Theodore Goddard. *Publication:* (with G. I. F. Leigh) The EEC and Intellectual Property, 1981. *Recreations:* reading, walking, spending time at our house in France. *Address:* Competition Commission, Victoria House, Southampton Row, WC1B 4AD. *T:* (020) 7271 0108, *Fax:* (020) 7271 0203; *e-mail:* diana.guy@cc.gsi.gov.uk.

GUY, Frances Mary; HM Diplomatic Service; Ambassador to Lebanon, since 2006; *b* 1 Feb. 1959; *d* of David Guy and Elizabeth Guy (*née* Hendry); *m* 1989, Guy Raybaudo; one *s* two *d*. *Educ:* Aberdeen Univ. (MA Hons); Johns Hopkins Univ., Bologna (Dip.); Carleton Univ., Ottawa (MA Internat. Relns). Entered FCO, 1985: lang. trng, 1987; Second Sec. (Chancery), Khartoum, 1988–91; First Secretary: FCO, 1991–95; and Hd, Pol Section, Bangkok, 1995–96; Dep. Hd of Mission, Addis Ababa, 1997–2001; Ambassador to the Yemen, 2001–04; Hd, Engaging the Islamic World Gp, FCO, 2004–06. *Recreations:* swimming, tennis. *Address:* c/o Foreign and Commonwealth Office, King Charles Street, SW1A 2AH. *Club:* Royal Commonwealth Society.

GUY, Geoffrey William; Founder, and Executive Chairman, GW Pharmaceuticals plc, since 1998; *b* 30 Sept. 1954; *m* 1986, Katherine Mary Husk. *Educ:* St Bartholomew's Hosp. Med. Coll., Univ. of London (BSc Pharmacol. 1976; MB BS 1979). MRCS, LRCP 1979; LMSSA 1979; Dip. Pharmaceutical Medicine, RCP, 1984. Various hosp. appts, incl. St Bartholomew's, Southampton Gen. Hosp. and New Addenbrooke's Hosp., Cambridge, 1979–81; Internat. Clin. Res. Co-ordinator, Pierre Fabre Labs, France, 1981–83; D Clin. Develt, Napp Labs, 1983–85; Founder, 1985, Chief Exec., 1985–97, Ethical Hld Plc; Founder, 1989, Chm., 1989–97, Phytopharm Plc (floated on NASDAQ; listed London Stock Exchange, 1996). Chm. Bd, Weldmar Hospice Care Trust; Patron, Mji Neema, Kenya Orphanage Charity. Liveryman, Soc. of Apothecaries. Venturer of Ye Award, 3i, 1997. *Publications:* (ed jtly) The Medicinal Uses of Cannabis and Cannabinoi 2004; contrib. various scientific papers on drug develt, drug delivery, pharmacokineti narcotics, cannabis and cannabinoids. *Recreations:* Real tennis, boating. *Address:* c/o G Pharmaceuticals Plc, Porton Down Science Park, Salisbury, Wilts SP4 0JQ. *T:* (0198 557000, *Fax:* (01980) 557111.

GUY, John Westgarth, OBE 1986; HM Diplomatic Service, retired; Consul General, Petersburg, 1996–2000; *b* 17 July 1941; *s* of late John Westgarth Guy and Stella (*n* Sanderson); *m* 1st, 1961, Sylvia Kathleen Stokes (*d* 2002); one *s* one *d*; 2nd, 2005, Theln Georgina Barbieri (*née* Larter). *Educ:* Queen Mary's Sch. for Boys, Basingstoke. CRO 1960; Karachi, 1961–63; Calcutta, 1964–67; Vice Consul, New York, 1968–70; FCO 1970–72; Third Secretary: Moscow, 1972–73; Jakarta, 1974; Second Sec., São Paul 1975–77; FCO, 1977–79; DTI, 1979–80; First Secretary: Yaoundé, 1981–84; Mapu 1984–87; FCO, 1987–91; High Comr, PNG, 1991–94; RCDS, 1995. *Recreation:* sailir *Address:* Hill Cottage, Church Street, Upton Grey, Basingstoke, Hants RG25 2RA.

GUY, Captain Robert Lincoln, LVO 1980; RN; Executive Director: Japan Socie 1997–2007; Hong Kong Association and Hong Kong Society, since 2002; *b* 4 Sept. 194 *s* of late John Guy and Susan Guy; *m* 1981, Rosemary Ann Walker; two *d*. *Educ:* Radl Coll. Entered BRNC Dartmouth, 1966; ADC to Governor and Commander-in-Chi Gibraltar, 1973; commanded: HMS Ashton, 1974; HMS Kedleston, 1975; HMS Siriu 1984–85. Equerry to the Queen, 1977–80; First Lieut, HMS Antelope (sunk in acti 1982), 1981–82. Lieut 1971; Lt-Comdr 1979; Comdr 1983; Captain 1991. *Recreation* polo, ski-ing, shooting. *Address:* The Barn House, Lees Hill, South Warnborough, Hoo Hants RG29 1RQ. *Club:* White's.

GUYTON, Marjorie A.; *see* Allthorpe-Guyton.

GUZ, Prof. Abraham, MD; FRCP; Professor of Medicine, Charing Cross a Westminster Medical School, University of London, 1981–94; Emeritus Professo Imperial College School of Medicine, since 1998; *b* 12 Aug. 1929; *s* of Akiwa Guz a Esther Guz; *m* 1957, Nita (*née* Florenz); three *d*. *Educ:* Grocers' Co. Sch.; Charing Cro Hosp. Med. Sch., Univ. of London (MB BS 1952; MD 1967). MRCP 1954, FRCP 196 Hosp. appts, Charing Cross Hosp., 1952–53; Asst Lectr in Pharmacol., Charing Cro Hosp. Med. Sch., 1953–54; RAMC 1954–56; Hosp. appts, RPMS, Hammersmith Hosp 1956–57; Research Fellow: Harvard Med. Sch., 1957–59; Cardiovascular Res. Ins Univ. of California, 1959–61; Lectr in Medicine, 1961, later Sen. Lectr and Reade Charing Cross Hosp. Med. Sch. Pro-Censor and Censor, RCP, 1979–87. Visiti Scientist, Univ. Lab. of Physiology, Oxford, 1994–. Treas., Med. Res. Soc., 200 Fellow, Imperial Coll. Sch. of Medicine, 2000–. *Publications:* Dyspnoea, 1984; articles mechanisms underlying breathlessness, mechanisms resp. for ventilatory response exercise, measurement of performance of left ventricle. *Recreations:* family, violin quartet, Jewish culture study. *Address:* 3 Littleton Road, Harrow, Middx HA1 3SY. (020) 8422 2786; (office) Charing Cross Hospital, Fulham Palace Road, W6 8RF. *T:* (02 8846 7337, *Fax:* (020) 8846 7326; *e-mail:* a.guz@imperial.ac.uk.

GWILLIAM, John Albert, MA Cantab; Headmaster of Birkenhead School, 1963–88; 28 Feb. 1923; *s* of Thomas Albert and Adela Audrey Gwilliam; *m* 1949, Pegi Llo George; three *s* two *d*. *Educ:* Monmouth Sch.; Trinity Coll., Cambridge. Assistant Mast Trinity Coll., Glenalmond, 1949–52; Bromsgrove Sch., 1952–56; Head of Lower Sc Dulwich Coll., 1956–63. *Address:* Araulfan, 13 The Close, Llanfairfechan, Gwyne LL33 0AG.

GWILLIAM, Kenneth Mason; Visiting Professor of Transport Economics, Institute f Transport Studies, University of Leeds; *b* 27 June 1937; *s* of John and Marjorie Gwillia *m* 1987, Sandra Wilson; two *s* by former *m*. *Educ:* Magdalen Coll., Oxford (BA 1st C Hons PPE). Res. Asst, Fisons Ltd, 1960–61; Lecturer: Univ. of Nottingham, 1961–6 Univ. of E Anglia, 1965–67; Prof. of Transport Economics, Univ. of Leeds, 1967–8 Prof. of Econs of Transport and Logistics, Erasmus Univ., Rotterdam, 1989–93; Pri Transport Economist, then Econ. Advr, Transport, World Bank, Washingto 1993–2002. Director: Nat. Bus Co., 1978–82; Yorkshire Rider, 1986–88. Editor, Jl Transport Economics and Policy, 1977–87. *Publications:* Transport and Public Polic 1964; Economics and Transport Policy, 1975; (jtly) Deregulating the Bus Industry, 198 Cities on the Move, 2002. *Recreations:* walking, golf. *Address:* 12, 720 Grand Traver Drive, Dade City, FL 33525, USA.

GWILLIAM, Michael Colin; Planning and Transport Director, South East Englar Regional Assembly, 2001–06; *b* 4 Jan. 1948; *s* of late Alfred and Grace Gwilliam; *m* 1s 1970, Mary (marr. diss. 1995); two *d*; 2nd, 1996, Janice; two step *d*. *Educ:* Keble Col Oxford (MA Hist.); University Coll. London (DipTP); De Montfort Univ., Leicest (DMS). Chief Planner, Leics CC, 1985–88; Co. Planning Officer, Bedfordshire C 1988–96; Dir, The Civic Trust, 1996–2000. Vice-Pres., County Planning Officers' So 1995–96. FRSA 1989. Hon. RICS 1999. *Publications:* Sustainable Renewal of Suburba Areas, 1999; Small Town Vitality, 2000. *Recreations:* hill-walking, gardening, bonsa music.

GWILLIAM, Robert John; Senior Associate Solicitor, British Telecommunications PL 1990–96; *b* 6 Jan. 1943; *s* of Benjamin Harold Gwilliam and Dora Gwilliam; *m* 1966, Lin Mary Ellway; two *s*. *Educ:* Lydney Grammar Sch.; Nottingham Univ. (BA Hons Law Cambridge Univ. (Dip. Criminology); College of Law. Admitted Solicitor, 196 practised in Local Govt Prosecuting Depts, 1969–83; Chief Prosecuting Solicitor f Hampshire, 1983–86; Chief Crown Prosecutor, Crown Prosecution Service: Lond South/Surrey Area, 1986; Inner London Area, 1987; London and SE Regl Dir, Grade 1987–89. *Recreations:* supporting Rugby, dog walking in Purbeck, the internet. *Address:* The Downs, Seymer Road, Swanage, Dorset BH19 2AL.

GWILT, George David, FFA; General Manager, 1979–84, Managing Director a Actuary, 1984–88, Standard Life Assurance Company; *b* 11 Nov. 1927; *s* of Richard Llo Gwilt and Marjory Gwilt (*née* Mair); *m* 1956, Ann Dalton Sylvester; three *s*. *Edu* Sedbergh Sch.; St John's Coll., Cambridge (MA). FFA 1952; FBCS. Joined Standard Li Assurance Co., 1949: Asst Official, 1956; Asst Actuary, 1957; Statistician, 196 Mechanisation Manager, 1964; Systems Manager, 1969; Dep. Pensions Manager, 197 Pensions Actuary, 1973; Asst General Manager and Pensions Manager, 1977; Asst Ge Man. (Finance), 1978. Dep. Chm., Associated Scottish Life Offices, 1986–88. Speci Advr in Scotland, Citicorp, 1989–91; Director: Hammerson Property Investment a Develt Corp., 1979–94; Scottish Mortgage and Trust, 1983–98; European Assets Tr NV, 1979–2000; Hodgson Martin, 1989–2000. Trustee, TSB of South of Scotla 1966–83. Member: Younger Cttee on Privacy, 1970–72; Monopolies and Merge

Commn, 1983–87. Pres., Faculty of Actuaries, 1981–83. Convener, Scottish Poetry Library, 1988–2001. *Recreation:* flute playing. *Address:* 39 Oxgangs Road, Edinburgh EH10 7BE. *T:* (0131) 445 1266. *Clubs:* Royal Air Force; New (Edinburgh).

GWILT, Michael Peter; Managing Director, Drive Cam Inc., since 2006; *b* 29 April 1957; *s* of Geoffrey and Joy Gwilt; *m* 1984, Cheryl Harrison; one *s. Educ:* Bishop Perowne C of E Sch., Worcester; King's Sch., Worcester. Family business, R. & G. Gwilt Engineering, 1975–82; Uniweld Ltd, 1983–84; joined Interleasing (UK) Ltd, 1984: Sales and Mktg Dir, 1988–94; Managing Director: Interleasing North, 1994–97; Cowie Interleasing, 1997; Gp Man. Dir, Arriva plc, 1998; Gp Man. Dir, Onlyfair Denmark ApS, subseq. CEO, Fleet Logistics Internat. NV, 1999–2006. *Recreations:* swimming, travelling, theatre, ballet, reading, cycling.

GWYER, Ven. Judith; *see* Rose, Ven. K. J.

GWYN, Alison Frances M.; *see* Moore-Gwyn.

GWYNEDD, Viscount; David Richard Owen Lloyd George; *b* 22 Jan. 1951; *s* and heir of 3rd Earl Lloyd George of Dwyfor, *qv; m* 1985, Pamela, *o d* of late Alexander Kleyff; two *s. Educ:* Eton. *Heir: s* Hon. William Alexander Lloyd George, *b* 16 May 1986.

GWYNN, Dominic Leigh Denys; Partner, Martin Goetze and Dominic Gwynn, Organ Builders, since 1979; *b* 18 Aug. 1953; *s* of Kenneth Leigh Maxwell Gwynn and Elisabeth (*née* Molenaar); *m* 1976, Antonia Rosamund Cordy; two *d. Educ:* Christ's Hosp.; St John's Coll., Oxford (BA Hons; MA). Major projects include: reconstructions: 1716 Handel organ, St Lawrence Whitchurch, Little Stanmore, 1994; 1743 organ, St Helen Bishopsgate, London, 1995; new organs: Handel House Mus., 1998; Magdalene Coll., Cambridge, 2000; reconstruction, two early Tudor organs, Early English Organ Project, 2000–01; restoration, 1829 organ, St James Bermondsey, London, 2002. *Publications:* (contrib.) Performing Purcell's Music, 1995; Historic Organ Conservation, 2001; contribs to Jl British Inst. of Organ Studies, Organ Yearbook and Organists Review. *Recreations:* choral singing, early modern church, social and cultural history. *Address:* 12 Burcott Road, Wells, Somerset BA5 2EQ. *T:* (01749) 675955, *T:* (office) (01909) 485635.

GWYNN-JONES, Peter Llewellyn, CVO 1998 (LVO 1994); Garter Principal King of Arms, since 1995; Genealogist, Order of the Bath, Order of St Michael and St George, and Order of St John, since 1995; *b* 12 March 1940; *s* of late Major Jack Llewellyn Gwynn-Jones, Cape Town, and Mary Muriel Daphne, *d* of Col Arthur Patrick Bird Harrison, and step *s* of late Lt-Col Gavin David Young, Long Burton, Dorset. *Educ:* Wellington Coll.; Trinity Coll., Cambridge (MA). Assistant to Garter King of Arms, 1970; Bluemantle Pursuivant of Arms, 1973; Secretary, Harleian Society, 1981–94; House Comptroller of College of Arms, 1982–95; Lancaster Herald of Arms, 1982–95. Inspector of Regtl Colours, 1995–, of RAF Badges, 1996–. Freeman and Liveryman: Painter Stainers' Co., 1997; Scriveners' Co., 1997. Hon. Citizen, State of Tennessee, 1991. FSA 1997. KStJ 1995. *Publications:* Heraldry, 1993; The Art of Heraldry, 1998. *Recreations:* tropical forests, wildlife conservation, fishing. *Address:* College of Arms, Queen Victoria Street, EC4V 4BT. *T:* (020) 7248 0911; 79 Harcourt Terrace, SW10. *T:* (020) 7373 5859.

GWYNNE, Andrew John; MP (Lab) Denton and Reddish, since 2005; *b* 4 June 1974; *s* of Richard John Gwynne and Margaret Elisabeth Gwynne (*née* Ridgway); *m* 2003, Allison Louise Dennis; two *s* one *d. Educ:* Univ. of Salford (BA Hons Politics and Contemp. Hist.); NE Wales Inst. of Higher Educn (HND Business and Finance). Asst to EDS Prog. Manager, ICL, Manchester, 1990–92; Mem., Year 2000 Team, Nat. Computing Centre, 1999–2000; European Co-ordinator, office of Arlene McCarthy, MEP, 2000–01; researcher, office of Andrew Bennett, MP, 2000–05. PPS to Minister of State, Home Office, 2005–07, to Home Sec., 2007–. Mem. (Lab) Tameside MBC, 1996–2008. *Recreations:* history, reading, computing, spending time with family. *Address:* House of Commons, SW1A 0AA. *T:* (020) 7219 4708; *e-mail:* gwynnea@parliament.uk; (constituency office) Town Hall, Market Street, Denton M34 2AP. *T:* (0161) 320 1504, *Fax:* (0161) 320 1503.

GWYNNE, Emily; *see* Maitlis, E.

GWYNNE JONES, family name of **Baron Chalfont**.

GWYTHER, Christine; Member (Lab) Carmarthen West and South Pembrokeshire, National Assembly for Wales, 1999–2007; Member, Pembrokeshire Coast National Park Authority, since 2007; *b* 9 Aug. 1959; *d* of Ivor George Gwyther and Marjorie Gwyther (*née* Doidge). *Educ:* Pembroke Sch.; UC, Cardiff. Milford Haven Waterway Enterprise Zone, 1986; local govt officer, S Pembrokeshire DC, 1987–96, Pembrokeshire CC, 1996–99. National Assembly for Wales: Sec. for Agric. and Rural Devel, 1999–2000; Chm., Econ. Devel and Transport Cttee, 2003–07. Contested (Lab) Carmarthen W and S Pembs, Nat. Assembly for Wales, 2007. Welsh Chair, Interreg III Prog. Monitoring Cttee, 2002. Mem., Pembrokeshire Business Club. Mem., RSPB.

GYLLENHAMMAR, Dr Pehr Gustaf; Chairman: Majid Al Futtaim Holding LLC, since 2004; Reuters Founders Share Co. Ltd, since 1999; Vice Chairman, Europe, Rothschild, since 2003; *b* 28 April 1935; *s* of Pehr Gustaf Victor Gyllenhammar and Aina Dagny Kaplan; *m* 1959, Eva Christina, *d* of Gunnar Ludvig Engellau; one *s* three *d. Educ:* University of Lund. LLB. Mannheimer & Zetterlöf, solicitors, 1959; Haight, Gardner, Poor & Havens, NY, 1960; Amphion Insurance Co., Gothenburg, 1961–64; Skandia Insurance Co., 1965, Exec. Vice-Pres., 1968, Pres. and Chief Exec. Officer, 1970; AB Volvo, Gothenburg, 1970, Man. Dir and Chief Exec. Officer, 1971; Chm. and Chief Exec. Officer, 1983–90, Exec. Chm. Bd of Dirs, 1990–93, Volvo; Dep. Chm., Commercial Union plc, 1997–98; Chm., CGU, subseq. CGNU, then Aviva, plc, 1998–2005. Chairman: MC European Capital (Holdings), SA, 1994–96; Lazard AB, 1999–2003; Investment AB Kinnevik, 2004–07; Sen. Advr, Lazard Frères & Co., 1996–2003; Dir of companies in Sweden, Netherlands, UK and USA. Member: Internat. Adv. Cttee, Chase Manhattan Bank, NA, NY, 1972–95; Bd, Cttee of Common Market Automobile Constructors, 1977–91; Bd, Assoc. des Constructeurs Européens d'Automobiles, 1991–93; Bd, Fedn of Swedish Industries, 1979–93; Roundtable of European Industrialists, 1982–93; Chm., European Financial Services Round Table, 2001–06. Mem. Bd Trustees, Rockefeller Univ., NY, 1991–96; Chm. Bd Trustees, LPO, 2006–. Lethaby Prof., Royal Coll. of Art, London, 1977; Mem., Royal Swedish Acad. of Engineering Scis, 1974. Hon. DM Gothenburg Univ., 1981; Hon. DTech Brunel, 1987; Hon. DEng Technical Univ., NS, 1988; Hon. DSocSc Helsinki, 1990; Hon. DEc Gothenburg, 2003. Golden Award, City of Gothenburg, 1981. Officer, Royal Order of Vasa, 1973; King's Medal, with Ribbon of Order of Seraphim, 1981; Commander: Order of Lion of Finland, 1977 (Comdr 1st Class 1986); Ordre National du Mérite, France, 1980; St Olav's Order, Norway, 1984; Légion d'honneur, France, 1987; Order of Leopold, Belgium, 1989; Kt Grand Officer, Order of Merit, Italy, 1987. *Publications:* Mot sekelskiftet på måfå (Toward the Turn of the Century, at Random), 1970; Jag tror på Sverige (I Believe in Sweden), 1973; People at Work (US), 1977; En industripolitik för människan (Industrial policy for human beings), 1979; Fortsättning följer… (To Be Continued…), 2000. *Recreations:* tennis, sailing, ski-ing, riding. *Address:* 18B Charles Street, Mayfair, W1J 5DU.

GYPPS, Godfrey Howard; His Honour Judge Gypps; a Circuit Judge, since 2003; Designated Family Judge for the County of Essex, and Chairman, Essex Family Justice Council, since 2005; *b* 24 March 1947; *s* of Jack and Hilda Gypps; *m* 1974, Judith Wendy Falkner; two *d. Educ:* Colchester Royal Grammar Sch.; Queen Mary Coll., Univ. of London (LLB Hons 1969). Admitted solicitor, 1972; on teaching staff, Coll. of Law, 1972–90; Dist Judge, 1991–2003; on secondment to staff of Hd of Civil Justice, 1998 and 2000. Vis. Fellow, Dept of Law, Univ. of Essex, 1998–. Member: Civil Procedure Rule Cttee, 1997–2001; Civil Justice Council, 2002–03. *Publications:* contribs to various legal pubns and periodicals. *Recreations:* the countryside, dogs, radio. *Address:* Chelmsford County Court, Priory Place, New London Road, Chelmsford, Essex CM2 0PP. *Club:* Army and Navy.

H

HAAVISTO, Heikki Johannes; Chairman Board of Directors, Raisio Group, 1997–2001 (Chairman, Administrative Council, 1977–96); *b* Turku, Finland, 20 Aug. 1935; *s* of Urho and Alli Haavisto; *m* 1964, Maija Rihko; three *s. Educ:* Univ. of Helsinki (MSc, LLM). Hd of Dept, Oy Vehnä Ab, 1963–66; Sec.-Gen., Central Union of Agricl Producers and Forest Owners, 1966–75 (Pres., 1976–94); Member, Administrative Council: Osuuskunta Metsäliitto, Helsinki, 1976–93 (Vice-Chm. and Pres., 1976–93); Central Union Co-op. Banks, Helsinki, 1985–93; Minister of For. Affairs, Finland, 1993–95. Chm., Delegn, Finnish Co-operative Pellervo, Helsinki, 1979–2001. Mem., Internat. Policy Council on Agric. and Trade, Washington, 1988–2000. Mem., Centre Party, Finland. Hon. PhD Turku; Hon. Dr Agr. & For., Hon. DVM Helsinki, 1995. *Address:* Hintsantie 2, 21200 Raisio, Finland.

HABERFELD, Dame Gwyneth; *see* Jones, Dame G.

HABGOOD, family name of **Baron Habgood**.

HABGOOD, Baron *cr* 1995 (Life Peer), of Calverton in the county of Buckinghamshire; **Rt Rev. and Rt Hon. John Stapylton Habgood;** PC 1983; MA, PhD; Archbishop of York, 1983–95; *b* 23 June 1927; *s* of Arthur Henry Habgood, DSO, MB, BCh, and Vera (*née* Chetwynd-Stapylton); *m* 1961, Rosalie Mary Anne Boston; two *s* two *d. Educ:* Eton; King's Coll., Cambridge (Hon. Fellow, 1986); Cuddesdon Coll., Oxford. Univ. Demonstrator in Pharmacology, Cambridge, 1950–53; Fellow of King's Coll., Cambridge, 1952–55; Curate of St Mary Abbots, Kensington, 1954–56; Vice-Principal of Westcott House, Cambridge, 1956–62; Rector of St John's Church, Jedburgh, 1962–67; Principal of Queen's College, Birmingham, 1967–73; Bishop of Durham, 1973–83. Hulsean Preacher, Cambridge Univ., 1987–88; first Athenæum Lectr, 1998; Bampton Lectr, Oxford Univ., 1999; Gifford Lectr, Aberdeen Univ., 2000. Moderator, Church and Society Sub-Unit, WCC, 1983–91. Pro-Chancellor, Univ. of York, 1985–90. Chm., UK Xenotransplantation Interim Regulatory Authy, 1997–2003. Hon. Bencher, Inner Temple, 2000. Hon. DD: Durham, 1975; Cambridge, 1984; Aberdeen, 1988; Huron, 1990; Hull, 1991; Oxford, Manchester, and York, 1996; London, 2005; Hon. DHL York Coll., Pa, 1995. *Publications:* Religion and Science, 1964; A Working Faith, 1980; Church and Nation in a Secular Age, 1983; Confessions of a Conservative Liberal, 1988; Making Sense, 1993; Faith and Uncertainty, 1997; Being a Person, 1998; Varieties of Unbelief, 2000; The Concept of Nature, 2002; (ed jtly) Glory Descending: Michael Ramsey and his writings, 2005. *Recreations:* painting, mending things. *Address:* 18 The Mount, Malton, N Yorks YO17 7ND. *Club:* Athenæum.

HABGOOD, Anthony John; Chairman: Whitbread Group plc, since 2005; Bunzl plc, since 1996 (Chief Executive, 1991–96); *b* 8 Nov. 1946; *s* of John Michael Habgood and Margaret Diana Middleton Habgood (*née* Dalby); *m* 1974, Nancy Atkinson; two *s* one *d. Educ:* Gonville and Caius Coll., Cambridge (MA Econ 1972); Carnegie Mellon Univ., Pittsburgh (MS Indust. Admin 1970). Boston Consulting Gp, 1970–86: Director, 1976; Management Cttee, 1979; Exec. Cttee, 1981; Tootal Group, 1986–91: Director, 1986; Chief Exec., 1991. Director: Geest, 1988–93; Power Gen, 1993–2001; SVG Capital (formerly Schroder Ventures Internat. Investment Trust), 1995–; NatWest Gp, 1998–2000; Marks and Spencer, 2004–05; Chm., Mölnlycke Health Care, 2006–07. *Recreations:* country pursuits. *Address:* Whitbread Group plc, 130 Jermyn Street, SW1Y 4UR. *Club:* Royal Norfolk and Suffolk Yacht.

HACKER, Alan Ray, OBE 1988; clarinettist and conductor; *b* 30 Sept. 1938; *s* of Kenneth and Sybil Hacker; *m* 1st, 1959, Anna Maria Sroka; two *d*; 2nd, 1977, Karen Evans (marr. diss. 1994); one *s*; 3rd, 1995, Margaret Lee. *Educ:* Dulwich Coll.; Royal Academy of Music. FRAM. Joined LPO, 1958; Prof., RAM, 1960–76; Lectr, 1976–84, Sen. Lectr in Music, 1984–87, Univ. of York. Founded: Pierrot Players (with S. Pruslin and H. Birtwistle), 1965; Matrix, 1971; Music Party for authentic performance of classical music, 1972; Classical Orch., 1977; Guest Cond., Orchestra la Fenice, Venice, 1981–; operatic cond. début, Den Bergtagna, Sweden, 1986, York Fest., 1988; conducted 1st major British prodn of Mozart's La Finta Giardiniera, 1989; German operatic début, Don Giovanni, Così fan Tutte, Stuttgart, 1991, Julius Caesar, Halle, Ulisse, Stuttgart, 1992; La Cenerentola, Barcelona, 1993; King Arthur, Stuttgart, 1995; Xerxes, Cologne, 1996; Alcina, Stuttgart, 1998; Saul, Berlin, 1999. Orchestral work with: Südwestfunk and Berlin Radio Orch., 1992; Orchestre Nat. de Lille, 1996; Gürzenich Orchester, Cologne, 1996. First modern "authentic" perfs, 1977–, incl: Mozart's Symphonies 39, 40; Beethoven's Symphonies 2, 3, 7, 9 and Egmont; Haydn's Harmonie and Creation Masses, Symphony 104 and Trumpet Concerto. Revived basset clarinet and restored orig. text, Mozart's concerto and quintet, 1967; revived baroque clarinet (hitherto unplayed), 1975. Solo clarinettist, premieres of music by Birtwistle, Boulez, Morton Feldman, Goehr, Maxwell Davies, Stockhausen, Blake, Mellers and Salvatore Sciarrino; conductor, premiere of opera by Judith Weir; cond 5 staged perfs of Bach's St John Passion for European Music Year, 1984; basset clarinettist and saxophonist, Birtwistle's The Bacchai, 2002; conductor and basset clarinettist, Birtwistle's The Io Passion, 2004. Sir Robert Mayer Lectr, Leeds Univ., 1972–73. Mem. Fires of London, 1970–76; Dir, York Early Music Festival. Teacher, lectr and conductor, Banff Centre, Canada, 1986–. Many recordings. *Publications:* Scores of Mozart Concerto and Quintet, 1972; 1st edn of reconstructed Mozart Concerto, 1973; Schumann's Soiréestucke, 1985. *Recreation:* cookery. *Address:* Hindlea, Broughton, Malton, N Yorks YO17 6QJ.

HACKER, Rt Rev. George Lanyon; Hon. Assistant Bishop, diocese of Carlisle, since 1994; Bishop Suffragan of Penrith, 1979–94; *b* 27 Dec. 1928; *s* of Edward Sidney Hacker and Carla Lanyon; *m* 1969, June Margaret Erica Smart; one *s* one *d. Educ:* Kelly College, Tavistock; Exeter College, Oxford (BA 1952, MA 1956); Cuddesdon College, Oxford. Deacon 1954, priest 1955, Bristol; Curate of St Mary Redcliffe, Bristol, 1954–59;

Chaplain, King's College London at St Boniface Coll., Warminster, 1959–64; Perpetua Curate, Church of the Good Shepherd, Bishopwearmouth, 1964–71; Rector of Tilehurst Reading, 1971–79. Pres., Rural Theol. Assoc., 1989–94; Pres., Age Concern Cumbria 1991–2007 (Chm., 1987–91); Chm., Age Concern Eden, 1994–2000; Episcopal Adv Anglican Young People's Assoc., 1987–94. Editor, Chrism, 1996–2008. *Publication:* Th Healing Stream: Catholic insights into the ministry of healing, 1998. *Recreations* gardening, book binding, writing poetry. *Address:* Keld House, Milburn, Penrith Cumbria CA10 1TW. *T:* (01768) 361506; *e-mail:* bishhack@btopenworld.com.

HACKER, Peter Michael Stephen, DPhil; Fellow and Tutor in Philosophy, 1966–2006 now Emeritus Research Fellow, and Librarian, 1986–2006, St John's College, Oxford; *b* 15 July 1939; *s* of Emeric Hacker and Thea Hacker (*née* Mendel); *m* 1963, Sylvia Dolore Imhoff; two *s* one *d. Educ:* Queen's Coll., Oxford (MA); St Antony's Coll., Oxfor (DPhil). Jun. Res. Fellow, Balliol Coll., Oxford, 1965–66; British Acad. Res. Reade 1985–87; Leverhulme Res. Fellow, 1991–94. Visiting Professor: Swarthmore Coll., Pa 1973, 1986; Univ. of Michigan, Ann Arbor, 1974; Queen's Univ., Ont, 1985. *Publications* Insight and Illusion, 1972, 2nd edn 1986; Appearance and Reality, 1987; (ed) Th Renaissance of Gravure: the art of S. W. Hayter, 1988; Wittgenstein: meaning and mind 1990; (ed) Gravure and Grace: the engravings of Roger Vieillard, 1993; Wittgenstein mind and will, 1996; Wittgenstein's Place in Twentieth Century Analytic Philosophy 1996; Wittgenstein: connections and controversies, 2001; (with M. R. Bennett Philosophical Foundations of Neuroscience, 2003; (jtly) Neuroscience and Philosophy 2007; Human Nature: the categorial framework, 2007; (with M. R. Bennett) A Histor of Cognitive Neuroscience, 2008; with G. P. Baker: Wittgenstein: understanding an meaning, 1980, 2nd edn 2004; Frege: logical excavations, 1984; Language, Sense an Nonsense, 1984; Scepticism, Rules and Language, 1984; Wittgenstein: rules, grammar an necessity, 1985. *Recreations:* art history, music. *Address:* St John's College, Oxford OX 3JP.

HACKER, Richard Daniel; QC 1998; *b* 1954; *s* of Samuel Hacker and Lilli Hacker; *n* 1988, Sarah Anne, *d* of R. J. Millar, Bath; one *d. Educ:* Haberdashers' Aske's Sch. Downing Coll., Cambridge (Wiener Anspach Schol., 1976; BA Law 1976; MA 1979) Univ. Libre de Bruxelles (Licence Spéciale en Droit Européen (Distinction) 1978). Calle to the Bar: Lincoln's Inn, 1977 (Hardwicke Schol.; Student of the Year Prize); *ad eunden* Gray's Inn, 1989; British Virgin Islands, 2003; in practice at the Bar, 1979–. Asst Parl Boundary Comr, 2000–; Chm., Inquiry into Herts Parly Constituency Boundaries, 2000 *Recreations:* travel, food, family life. *Address:* 3–4 South Square, Gray's Inn, WC1R 5HP *T:* (020) 7696 9900, *Fax:* (020) 7696 9911; *e-mail:* contact@hacker.plus.com.

HACKETT, Dennis William; journalist; publishing and communications consultant Director, Media Search & Selection Ltd, 1988–98; *b* 5 Feb. 1929; *s* of James Josep Hackett and Sarah Ellen Hackett (*née* Bedford); *m* 1st, 1953, Agnes Mary Collins; two one *d*; 2nd, 1974, Jacqueline Margaret Totterdell; one *d. Educ:* De La Salle College Sheffield. Served with RN, 1947–49. Sheffield Telegraph, 1945–47 and 1949–54; Dail Herald, 1954; Odhams Press, 1954; Deputy Editor, Illustrated, 1955–58; Daily Express 1958–60; Daily Mail, 1960; Art Editor, Observer, 1961–62; Deputy Editor, 1962, Editor 1964–65, Queen; Editor, Nova, 1965–69; Publisher, Twentieth Century Magazine 1965–72; Editorial Dir, George Newnes Ltd, 1966–69; Dir, IPC Newspapers, 1969–71 Associate Editor, Daily Express, 1973–74; TV critic: The Times, 1981–85; Tablet 1984–92; Editorial Consultant, You, The Mail on Sunday magazine, 1982–86; Exec Editor, 1986–87, Editor-in-chief, 1987, Today; Editor-in-Chief, M, The Observe Magazine, 1987–88; Editor, Management Today, 1992–94. Chm., Design and A Directors' Assoc., 1967–68. *Publications:* The History of the Future: Bemrose Corporatio 1826–1976, 1976; The Big Idea: the story of Ford in Europe, 1978. *Recreations:* reading walking. *Address:* 7 Foster Drive, Broadway Grange, Leamington Road, Broadway WR12 7EA. *Club:* Royal Automobile.

HACKETT, John Wilkings, CMG 1989; Director, Financial, Fiscal and Enterpris Affairs, Organisation for Economic Co-operation and Development, Paris, 1979–89; *b* 2 Jan. 1924; *s* of Albert and Bertha Hackett; *m* 1952, Anne-Marie Le Brun. *Educ:* LSI (BSc(Econ) 1950); Institut d'Etudes Politiques, Paris (Diplôme 1952); Univ. of Paris (D d'état ès sciences economiques 1957). Served RN, 1942–46. Economic research 1952–57; OECD, 1958–89. FRSA 1986. *Publications:* Economic Planning in France (wit A.-M. Hackett), 1963; L'Economie Britannique—problèmes et perspectives, 1966; (wit A.-M. Hackett) The British Economy, 1967; articles on economic subjects in British an French economic jls. *Recreations:* music, painting, reading. *Address:* 48 rue de la Bienfaisance, 75008 Paris, France. *Club:* Cercle de l'Union Interalliée (Paris).

HACKETT, Peter, OBE 1990; DL; PhD; FREng; Director, 1993–94, and Principal 1970–94, Camborne School of Mines (first Fellow, 1990); Adviser on Cornwall, Exete University, 1994–98; *b* 1 Nov. 1933; *s* of Christopher and Evelyn Hackett; *m* 1958, Esmé Doreen (*née* Lloyd); one *s* one *d. Educ:* Mundella Grammar Sch.; Nottingham Univ. (BS 1st Cl. Hons Mining Engrg; PhD). FIMM 1971, Hon. FIMMM (Hon. FIMM 1993) FREng (FEng 1983). Lecturer, Nottingham Univ., 1958–70; Vis. Lectr, Univ. o Minnesota, 1969; Vis. Professor, Univ. of California at Berkeley, 1979. Pres., IMM 1989–90. Chm., Port of Falmouth Sailing Assoc., 1997–2002. DL Cornwall, 1993 *Publications:* contribs to learned jls on geotechnical subjects and mining engrg educn *Recreations:* sailing, classic vehicles. *Club:* Royal Cornwall Yacht (Falmouth).

HACKING, family name of **Baron Hacking**.

HACKING, 3rd Baron *cr* 1945, of Chorley; **Douglas David Hacking;** Bt 1938 International Arbitrator; Solicitor of Supreme Court of England and Wales, since 1977

Attorney and Counselor-at-Law of State of New York, since 1975; Barrister-at-law, 1963–76 and since 1999; Chartered Arbitrator, since 1999; *b* 17 April 1938; *er s* of 2nd Baron Hacking, and Daphne Violet (*d* 1998), *e d* of late R. L. Finnis; *S* father, 1971; *m* 1st, 1965, Rosemary Anne, *e d* of late Francis P. Forrest, FRCSE; two *s* one *d*; 2nd, 1982, Dr Tessa M. Hunt, MB, MRCP, FRCA, *er d* of late Roland C. C. Hunt, CMG; three *s*. *Educ:* Aldro School, Shackleford; Charterhouse School; Clare College, Cambridge (BA 1961, MA 1968). Served in RN, 1956–58; Ordinary Seaman, 1956; Midshipman, 1957; served in HMS Ark Royal (N Atlantic), 1957; HMS Hardy (Portland) and HMS Brocklesby (Portland and Gibraltar), 1958; transferred RNR as Sub-Lt, 1958, on completion of National Service; transf. List 3 RNR, HMS President, 1961; Lieut 1962; retired RNR, 1964. Called to the Bar, Middle Temple, Nov. 1963 (Astbury and Harmsworth Scholarships). With Simpson, Thacher and Bartlett, NYC, 1975–76; with Lovell, White and King, 1976–79; Partner: Lane & Partners, 1979–81; Richards Butler, 1981–94; Sonnenscheins, 1994–99; Mem., Littleton Chambers, 2000–. Mem., H of L Select Cttee on the European Community, 1989–93, 1995–99. Chm. Steering Cttee, London Internat. Arbitration Trust, 1980–81. Trustee, Carthusian Trust, 1971–2001. Gov., Charlotte Sharman Sch., Southwark, 1996–97. Member: Amer. Bar Assoc.; Bar Assoc. of City of New York; Indian Council of Arbitration, 1997–; Swiss Arbitration Assoc., 2000–. FCIArb; Fellow: Singapore Inst. of Arbitration; Malaysian Inst. of Arbitration. Pres., Assoc. of Lancastrians in London, 1971–72, 1998. Apprenticed to Merchant Taylors' Co., 1955, admitted to Freedom, 1962; Freedom, City of London, 1962. FCIArb 1979. *Recreations:* cycling, mountain walking. *Heir: s* Hon. Douglas Francis Hacking, *b* 8 Aug. 1968. *Address:* 27 West Square, Kennington, SE11 4SP. *T:* (020) 7735 4400; *e-mail:* ddh@london-arbitration.com; Littleton Chambers, 3 King's Bench Walk, Temple, EC4Y 7HR. *T:* (020) 7797 8600, *Fax:* (020) 7797 8699; *e-mail:* david.hacking@littletonchambers.co.uk. *Clubs:* Reform, MCC.

HACKING, Anthony Stephen; QC 1983; *b* 12 Jan. 1941; *s* of late John and Joan Hacking, Warwick; *m* 1969, Carin, *d* of late Dr Svante and of Brita Holmdahl, Gothenburg; one *d* three *s*. *Educ:* Warwick Sch.; Lincoln Coll., Oxford (MA Jurisprudence). Called to the Bar, Inner Temple, 1965, Bencher, 1993; a Recorder, 1985–2006; a Dep. High Ct Judge (QBD), 1993–2001. Hd of Chambers, 1999–2005. Legal Assessor, GMC, 1999–; accredited Mediator, Family Mediators' Assoc., 2007–. *Address:* 1 King's Bench Walk, Temple, EC4Y 7DB. *T:* (020) 7936 1500, *Fax:* (020) 7936 1590.

HACKING, Prof. Ian MacDougall, CC 2004; PhD; FRSC; University Professor, University of Toronto, 1991–2003, now University Professor Emeritus (Professor, Department of Philosophy, 1981–2003); Chair, philosophie et histoire des concepts scientifiques, Collège de France, 2000–06, now Professeur honoraire; *b* 18 Feb. 1936; *s* of Harold Eldridge Hacking and Margaret Elinore Hacking (née MacDougall); *m* 1983, Judith Baker; one *s* two *d*. *Educ:* Univ. of British Columbia (BA 1956); Trinity Coll., Cambridge (BA 1958, MA 1962; PhD 1962; Hon. Fellow, 2000). Res. Fellow, Peterhouse, Cambridge, 1962–64; Asst Prof., then Associate Prof. of Philos., Univ. of British Columbia, 1964–69, seconded to Makerere UC, by External Aid, Canada, 1967–69; Univ. Lectr in Philos., Univ. of Cambridge and Fellow, Peterhouse, Cambridge, 1969–74 (Hon. Fellow, 2005); Stanford University: Fellow, Center for Advanced Study in the Behavioral Scis, 1974–75; Prof., 1975–82; Henry Waldegrave Stuart Prof. of Philos., 1981–82. FRSC 1986; Fellow Amer. Acad. of Arts and Scis, 1991; Corresp. FBA, 1995. *Publications:* Logic of Statistical Inference, 1965; A Concise Introduction to Logic, 1972; Why Does Language Matter to Philosophy?, 1975; The Emergence of Probability, 1975, 2nd edn 2006; Representing and Intervening, 1983; The Taming of Chance, 1990; Le Plus pur nominalisme: L'énigme de Goodman: 'vleu' et usages de 'vleu', 1993; Rewriting the Soul: multiple personality and the sciences of memory, 1995; Mad Travelers: reflections on the reality of transient mental illnesses, 1998; The Social Construction of What?, 1999; Probability and Inductive Logic, 2001; Historical Ontology, 2002. *Recreations:* canoeing, mountain hiking. *Address: e-mail:* ihack@chass.utoronto.ca.

HACKITT, Judith Elizabeth, (Mrs D. J. Lea), CBE 2006; FIChemE; Chair, Health and Safety Executive (formerly Health and Safety Commission), since 2007 (Member, 2002–06); *b* 1 Dec. 1954; *d* of Kenneth G. Hackitt and Kathleen Rhoda Hackitt (*née* Jeffcott); *m* 1977, David John Lea; two *d*. *Educ:* Queen Elizabeth Grammar Sch., Atherstone, Warwicks; Imperial Coll., London (BSc (Eng) 1975). ACGI 1972; FIChemE 2001. Eur. Pigments Ops Dir, 1990–96, Gp Risk Manager, 1996–98, Elementis plc; Dir, Business and Envmt, 1998–2002, Dir Gen., 2002–06, CIA; Dir of Implementation, CEFIC, Brussels, 2006–07. Non-exec. Dir, Oxon HA, 1995–98. Co-Chair, EU Chemicals Policy Strategy Gp, 2002–05. Member: Chemistry Leadership Council, 2003–05; Bd and Steering Gp, Internat. Council of Chem. Assocs, 2001–05. *Recreations:* music (ageing rock stars), walking, ski-ing, good food and wine. *Address:* Health and Safety Executive, Rose Court, 2 Southwark Bridge, SE1 9HS. *T:* (020) 7717 6612, *Fax:* (020) 7717 6616; *e-mail:* chair@hse.gsi.gov.uk.

HACKLAND, Brian Anthony; Regional Director, Government Office for the East of England, since 2005; *b* 3 March 1951; *s* of Alan Keith Hackland and Catherine Mary Hackland; *m* 1978, Sarah Ann Spencer, *qv*; two *s*. *Educ:* Univ. of Natal (BSc Hons Botany and Entomology 1974); Balliol Coll., Oxford (Rhodes Schol.; BA Hons Pol, Philos. and Econs 1977); DPhil Pol Sci. Oxon 1984. Parly Asst to Shadow Sec. of State for NI, 1985–88; Investigator with Local Govt Ombudsman, 1988–90; on secondment as Ombudsman, Bedfordshire CC, 1990; Department of the Environment: Team Leader, Housing Action Trusts Prog., 1991–93, Central Finance, 1993–95; Private Sec. to Minister for Local Govt, Housing and Regeneration, 1995–97; Hd, Air and Envmt Quality Div., 1997–99; Sen. Policy Advr (Envmt and Transport), Prime Minister's Policy Directorate, 1999–2001; Dir, Town and Country Planning, ODPM, 2002–05. *Publication:* (with Gwyneth Williams) Dictionary of Contemporary Southern African Politics, 1985. *Recreations:* gardening, walking, cycling. *Address:* Government Office for the East of England, Eastbrook, Shaftesbury Road, Cambridge CB2 2DF.

HACKLAND, Sarah Ann; *see* Spencer, S. A.

HACKNEY, Archdeacon of; *see* Dennen, Ven. Lyle.

HACKNEY, Arthur, RWS 1957 (VPRWS 1974–77); RE 1960 (Hon. RE 1982); ARCA 1949; artist; Principal Lecturer (formerly Deputy Head), Fine Art Department, West Surrey College of Art and Design (Farnham Centre) (formerly Farnham School of Art), 1979–85, retired; *b* 13 March 1925; *s* of late J. T. Hackney; *m* 1955, Mary Baker, ARCA; two *d*. *Educ:* Burslem Sch. of Art; Royal Coll. of Art, London. Served in Royal Navy, Western Approaches, 1942–46. Travelling scholarship, Royal College of Art, 1949; part-time Painting Instructor, Farnham Sch. of Art, 1950, Lecturer, 1962; Head of Dept: Graphic, 1963–68; Printmaking, 1968–79. Work represented in Public Collections, including Bradford City Art Gallery, Victoria and Albert Museum, Guildhall Art Gall., Ashmolean Museum, Wellington Art Gallery (NZ), Nottingham Art Gallery, Keighley Art Gallery (Yorks), Wakefield City Art Gallery, Graves Art Gallery, Sheffield, Preston Art Gallery, City of Stoke-on-Trent Art Gall., Kent Educn Cttee, Staffordshire Educn Cttee, RCA. Mem., Fine Art Bd, CNAA, 1975–78. Work reproduced in 20th Century Painters and Sculptors, by Francis Spalding, 1990. *Address:* Woodhatches, Spoil Lane, Tongham, Farnham, Surrey GU10 1BP. *T:* (01252) 323919. *Club:* Chelsea Arts.

HACKNEY, Roderick Peter, PhD; PPRIBA; Managing Director, Rod Hackney & Associates, since 1972; *b* 3 March 1942; *s* of William Hackney and Rose (*née* Morris); *m* 1964, Christine Thornton; one *s*. *Educ:* John Bright's Grammar School, Llandudno; Sch. of Architecture, Manchester Univ. (BAArch 1966, MA 1969, PhD 1979). ARIBA 1969; FCIArb 1977; ASAI; FFB 1987; MCIOB 1987. Job Architect, EXPO '67, Montreal, for Monorail Stations; Housing Architect, Libyan Govt, Tripoli, 1967–68; Asst to Arne Jacobsen, Copenhagen, working on Kuwait Central Bank, 1968–71. Established Castward Ltd, building and develt firm, 1983 (Sec., 1983–92). Royal Institute of British Architects: Pres., 1987–89; Mem. Council, 1978–84 (Vice-Pres., Public Affairs, and Overseas Affairs, 1981–83), and 1991–99 (Vice-Pres., Internat. Affairs, 1992–94); Hon. Librarian, 1998–99; Chairman: Discipline Hearings Cttee, 2001–03; Discipline Cttee, 2003–07; Dir, RIBAC Cos, 1996–2001. Mem. Council, Internat. Union of Architects, 1981–85, and 1991–, First Vice-Pres., 1985–87, Pres., 1987–90. Vis. Prof., Paris, 1984; Special Prof., Nottingham Univ., 1987–90; Vis. Prof., Xian Univ., China, 1999; has lectured in Europe, N and S America, Asia, Middle East, Australia and Africa. Chm., Times/RIBA Community Enterprise Scheme, 1985–89; Mem. Council, Nat. Historical Bldg Crafts Inst., 1989–; Advr on regeneration and inner city problems in Sweden, Italy, Brazil, USA, Russia, Dubai, China and Germany, 1990–; Internat. Advr, Centre for Internat. Archl Studies, Univ. of Manchester Sch. of Architecture, 1992–; Jury Mem., overseas housing develts; Juror for internat. competitions in Netherlands and China, 1992–; Mem., Adv. Gp, UN World Habitat Awards, 2003–; deleg., UK and overseas confs. Chairman: Trustees, Inner City Trust, 1986–97; British Architectl Liby Trust, 1999–2001. President: Snowdonia (formerly Snowdonia Nat. Park) Soc., 1987–2005; N Wales Centre, NT, 1990–2008. Patron: Llandudno Mus. and Art Gall., 1988–2007; Dome Project, Buxton, 2000–07. Hon. FAIA 1988; Hon. FRAIC 1990; Hon. Fellow: United Architects of Philippines, 1988; Fedn of Colls of Architects, Mexico, 1988; Indian Inst. of Architecture, 1990; Hon. Member: Superior Council of Colls of Architects of Spain, 1987; Architectural Soc. of China, 2003. Hon. DLitt Keele, 1989. Awards and prizes include: DoE Award for Good Design in Housing (1st Prize), 1975; 1st Prize, St Ann's Hospice Arch. Comp., 1976; RICS Conservation Award, 1980; Sir Robert Matthew Prize, IUA, 1981; PA Consulting Gp Award for Innovation in Bldg Design and Construction (for Colquhoun St, Stirling), 1988; Award for work and leader of Community Arch. Movt, Charleston, USA, 1989; The Times, BITC, and Housing and Homeless Award, 1993. *Television:* Build Yourself a House, 1974; Community Architecture, 1977; BBC Omnibus, 1987; consultant, Europe by Design, BBC, 1991; *radio:* The Listener, 1986; Third Ear, 1990; Call to Account, 1992; Woman's Hour, 1992; Common Ground, 1996. Consultant, World Architecture Review Agency, China, 1992; Advr, Habitat Center News Jl, India, 1992–. *Publications:* Highfield Hall: a community project, 1982; The Good the Bad and the Ugly, 1990; Good Golly Miss Molly (music play), 1991; articles in UK and foreign architectural jls. *Recreations:* outdoor pursuits, walking, photography, travelling, looking at buildings, speaking at conferences. *Address:* St Peter's House, Windmill Street, Macclesfield, Cheshire SK11 7HS. *Club:* Royal Commonwealth Society.

HACKSTON, Fiona C.; *see* Clarke-Hackston.

HACKWOOD, Ven. Paul Colin; Archdeacon of Loughborough, since 2005; *b* 1961; *m* Josie; two *s*. *Educ:* Bradford Coll. of Educn (DipHE 1982); Huddersfield Polytech. (BSc 1984); Birmingham Univ. (DipTh 1988); Queen's Coll., Birmingham; Bradford Business Sch. (MBA 2005). Ordained deacon, 1989, priest, 1990; Curate, Horton, 1989–93; Social Responsibility Advr, Dio. St Albans, 1993–97; Vicar, Thornbury, 1997–2005. *Address:* The Archdeaconry, 21 Church Road, Glenfield, Leicester LE3 8DP.

HADAWAY, Lisa; *see* Armstrong, L.

HADDACKS, Vice-Adm. Sir Paul (Kenneth), KCB 2000; Lieutenant-Governor, Isle of Man, since 2005; *b* 27 Oct. 1946; *s* of late Kenneth Alexander Haddacks and of Edith Lillian Haddacks (*née* Peardon); *m* 1970, Penny Anne Robertson; one *s*. *Educ:* Plymouth Coll.; Kingswood Sch., Bath; BRNC; RN Staff Coll., RCDS. Joined RN 1964; commanded HM Ships: Scimitar, 1971–72; Cleopatra, 1981–82; Naiad, 1982–83; Intrepid, 1986–88; US Naval Acad., 1979–80; Asst Dir, Navy Plans, 1984–86; Dep. Dir, Naval Warfare, 1988–89; Comdr, RN Task Force, Gulf, 1990; Captain of the Fleet, 1991–94; Asst CoS (Policy) to SACEUR, 1994–97; UK Mil. Rep., HQ NATO, 1997–2000; Dir, NATO Internat. Mil. Staff, 2001–04. CStJ 2006. *Recreations:* family, travel. *Address:* Government House, Onchan, Isle of Man IM3 1RR. *Clubs:* Army and Navy; Royal Naval Sailing Association.

HADDAOUI, Khalil; Moroccan Ambassador to the Court of St James's, 1991–99; *b* 21 April 1937; *m*; three *c*. *Educ:* School of Higher Business Studies, Paris; Inst. of Internat. Relations, Paris. Joined Ministry of Foreign Affairs, 1966; served Rome, London, Algiers, Madrid; Adviser to Moroccan Minister for Foreign Affairs, 1976; Ambassador to Liberia and Sierra Leone, 1982, to UN, 1985; Dir of Internat. Orgn, 1986, of European and American Affairs, 1990, Min. for Foreign Affairs. *Address:* c/o Moroccan Embassy, 49 Queen's Gate Garden, SW7 5NE.

HADDINGTON, 13th Earl of, *cr* 1619; **John George Baillie-Hamilton;** Lord Binning, 1613; Lord Binning and Byres, 1619; *b* 21 Dec. 1941; *o s* of 12th Earl of Haddington, KT, MC, TD, and Sarah (*d* 1995), *y d* of G. W. Cook, Montreal; *S* father, 1986; *m* 1st, 1975, Prudence Elizabeth (marr. diss. 1981), *d* of A. Rutherford Hayles; 2nd, 1984, Susan Jane Antonia, 2nd *d* of John Heyworth; one *s* two *d*. *Educ:* Ampleforth. *Heir: s* Lord Binning, *qv*. *Address:* Mellerstain, Gordon, Berwickshire TD3 6LG. *Clubs:* Turf, Chelsea Arts; New (Edinburgh).

HADDO, Earl of; George Ian Alastair Gordon; *b* 4 May 1983; *s* and *heir* of Marquess of Aberdeen and Temair, *qv*. *Educ:* Harrow; Oxford Brookes Univ. (BSc Hons Real Est. Mgt 2005). With Knight Frank LLP, 2005–06; Rutley Capital Partners LLP, 2007–.

HADDON, Kenneth William, FCA; Chairman, Axa Reinsurance UK plc, 1994–99 (Chief Executive Officer, 1987–98); *b* 30 April 1938; *s* of William Percy Haddon and Constance Margaret Haddon; *m* 1966, Jarmaine (*née* Cook); one *s* one *d*. *Educ:* Minchenden Grammar Sch. FCA 1960. Nat. Service, RAF, 1960–62. Chartered Accountant, Thomson McLintock, 1962–64; London Reinsurance Co., later Netherlands Reinsurance Gp, then NRG London Reinsurance Co.: Sec. and Accountant, 1964; various posts, 1964–82; Gen. Manager, 1983–87. Chairman: London Underwriting Centre, 1995–98, and 1999–2001; London Processing Centre, 1997–99; London Internat. Insce and Reinsce Mkt Assoc., 1997–98. FRSA. *Recreations:* golf, gardening. *Clubs:* City of London, Langbourn Ward; Brookmans Park Golf.

HADDON-CAVE, Charles Anthony; QC 1999; a Recorder, since 2000; *b* 20 March 1956; *s* of Sir (Charles) Philip Haddon-Cave, KBE, CMG; *m* 1980, Amanda Charlotte Law; two *d*. *Educ:* King's Sch., Canterbury; Pembroke Coll., Cambridge (MA). Called to the Bar, Gray's Inn, 1978, Bencher, 2003; in practice as barrister, London and Hong Kong, 1980–. *Recreations:* art, music, triathlon. *Address:* Quadrant Chambers, Quadrant House, 10 Fleet Street, EC4Y 1AU. *T:* (020) 7583 4444. *Club:* Garrick.

HADDRILL, Stephen Howard; Director General, Association of British Insurers, since 2005; *b* 12 Jan. 1956; *s* of Albert George and Pauline Haddrill; *m* 1983, Joanne Foakes; two *s*. *Educ:* Trinity Sch., Croydon; New Coll., Oxford (BA Modern Hist. and Econs). Joined Department of Energy, 1978: Private Sec. to Sec. of State, 1987–89; Asst Sec., Nuclear Power Policy, 1989–90; Mem., Governor's Central Policy Unit, Hong Kong Govt, 1991–94; Department of Trade and Industry, 1994–2005: Dep. Dir, Competitiveness Unit, 1994–98; Dir, Consumer Affairs, 1998–2000; Dir, Employment Relns, 2000–02; Dir Gen., Fair Markets, 2002–05. *Recreations:* gardening, sailing. *Address:* Association of British Insurers, 51 Gresham Street, EC2V 7HQ. *T:* (020) 7216 7301.

HADEN-GUEST, family name of **Baron Haden-Guest**.

HADEN-GUEST, 5th Baron *cr* 1950, of Saling, Essex; **Christopher Haden-Guest;** film director, writer, actor and musician (as Christopher Guest); *b* 5 Feb. 1948; *s* of 4th Baron Haden-Guest and of Jean Haden-Guest (*née* Hindes); *S* father, 1996; *m* 1984, Jamie Lee Curtis; one *s* one *d* (both adopted). *Educ:* The Stockbridge Sch.; New York Univ. *Films:* (writer, director and actor): Waiting for Guffman, 1997; Best in Show, 2000; For Your Consideration, 2006; (writer and director): The Big Picture, 1989; Mighty Wind, 2004; (writer and actor) This is Spinal Tap, 1984; (dir) Almost Heroes, 1998. Scriptwriter for TV and radio progs. *Recreations:* fly-fishing, ski-ing. *Heir:* *b* Hon. Nicholas Haden-Guest [*b* 5 May 1951; *m* 1st, 1980, Jill Denby (marr. diss. 1988); one *d*; 2nd, 1989, Pamela Rack; one *d*]. *Address:* 212 26th Street #300, Santa Monica, CA 90402, USA.

HADFIELD, Antony; Senior Partner, Hadfield Associates, 1997–2005; *b* 9 Sept. 1936; *s* of Thomas Henry Hadfield and Edna (*née* Cooke); *m* 1959, Dorothy Fay Osman; one *s*. *Educ:* Sheffield; Brighton; Middx Poly. (BA). CEng 1966; FIET (FIEE 1975). Design engr, Plessey, 1958–62; design and project engr, Metal Industries Gp, 1962–65; design engr, CEGB, 1965–67; Sen. Engr and Manager, Eastern Electricity, 1967–77; Area Manager, Yorks Electricity, 1977–79; Dir of Engrg, Midlands Electricity, 1979–85; Chief Exec. and Dep. Chm., NI Electricity (formerly NI Electricity Service), 1985–91; Man. Dir, 1991–94, Chief Exec., 1994–97, Northern Electric plc; Chief Exec., Teesside Power Ltd, 1998–2000 (Dir, 1991–97). Chairman: Northern Inf. Systems Ltd, 1994–97; NEDL Ltd, 1994–97; Northern Utility Services Ltd, 1994–97; Sovereign Exploration Ltd, 1996–97; Dep. Chm., BCN Data Systems Ltd, 1998–2000. Associate, PB Power Ltd, 1997–2004. Mem., Competition (formerly Monopolies and Mergers) Commn, 1998–2005. Chm., Power Div., IEE, 1992–93. Chm., BITC, Tyneside, 1993–97. CCMI (CIMgt 1987); FRSA 1993. *Recreations:* mountaineering, sailing.

HADFIELD, Mark; a District Judge (Magistrates' Courts), since 2005; *b* 6 July 1960; *s* of late William Hadfield and Marie Helen Hadfield; *m* 1993, Denise Ferns; one *d*. *Educ:* St Augustine's Grammar Sch., Manchester; Liverpool Poly. (BA Hons Law). Admitted solicitor, 1985; in private practice with Colin Watson Solicitors, Warrington, 1985–2005; Solicitor Advocate, 1995. *Recreations:* golf, supporting Manchester City FC. *Address:* Sheffield Magistrates' Court, Castle Street, Sheffield S3 8LU. *T:* (0114) 252 1805, *Fax:* (0114) 272 0129.

HADFIELD, Sir Ronald, Kt 1995; QPM 1989; DL; Police Advisor to North Wales Tribunal into Child Abuse, 1996–98; Chief Constable, West Midlands, 1990–96; *b* 15 July 1939; *s* of George and Phyllis Marjorie Hadfield; *m* 1961, Anne Phyllisia Worrall; one *s* one *d*. *Educ:* Chadderton Grammar School. Joined Oldham Borough Police Force, 1958; served in Lancashire and Greater Manchester Police Forces; Asst Chief Constable, Derbyshire Constabulary, 1981; Dep. Chief Constable, 1986, Chief Constable, 1987, Nottinghamshire Constabulary. Advr in communications and law to cos in Midlands. DL W Midlands, 1994. *Recreations:* golf, fishing.

HADID, Zaha Mohammad, CBE 2002; RA 2005; architectural designer; *b* Baghdad, 31 Oct. 1950. *Educ:* Sch. of Architecture, Architectural Assoc., London (Diploma Prize). Lectr, AA, 1977, 1980; Vis. Design Critic, Harvard Grad. Sch. of Design, 1986; Vis. Prof., 1987, Kenzo Tange Prof., 1994, Columbia Univ., NY; Sullivan Prof., Univ. of Illinois, 1997; Guest Prof., Hochschule für Bildende Kunst, Hamburg, 1997. *Projects* include: 59 Eaton Place, SW1, 1980 (RIBA, Gold Medal, 1982); Hamburg Docklands Bauforum 1, 1985, Bauforum 2, 1989; Tomigaya and Azabu-Jyuban, Tokyo, 1987; Monsoon Restaurant, Sapporo, Japan, 1989 (completed 1990); Bordeaux Docklands, 1989; Osaka Folly, 1989 (completed 1990); Vitra Fire Station, Weil am Rhein, 1990 (completed 1993); Hotel Billie Strauss, Stuttgart, 1992–95; Kunst und Medienzentrum Rheinhafen, Düsseldorf, 1993; Cardiff Bay Opera House, 1994–96 (Opera House Trust First Prize, 1994; Special Award, Royal Acad. Summer Exhibn, 1995); Spittelau Viaduct Mixed Use Project, Vienna, 1994–97; Contemporary Arts Center, Cincinnati, 1998; Contemporary Arts Centre, Rome; Science Centre, Wolfsburg; Bridge Structure, Abu Dhabi; Tram station, Strasbourg; Maggie's Centre, Victoria Hosp., Fife, 2006. Has exhibited in Europe, Japan, and USA; has lectured in Europe, USA, Australia, Brazil, Canada, China, Hong Kong, Jordan, Lebanon, Mexico, Taiwan, Thailand, and UAE. Pritzker Architecture Prize, 2004. *Publications:* articles in newspapers, magazines and architectl and design jls. *Address:* (office) Studio 9, 10 Bowling Green Lane, EC1R 0BQ. *T:* (020) 7253 5147, *Fax:* (020) 7251 8322.

HADLEE, Sir Richard (John), Kt 1990; MBE 1980; New Zealand cricketer, retired; *b* 3 July 1951; *s* of late Walter Hadlee, CBE; *m* 1973, Karen Ann Marsh; two *s*; *m* 1999, Dianne Taylor. *Educ:* Christchurch Boys' High Sch. Played for: Canterbury, 1972–89; Nottinghamshire (UK), 1978–87 (made 1000 runs and took 100 wickets in English season, 1984); Tasmania, 1979–80; Test début for NZ, 1973; toured: Australia, 1972–73, 1973–74, 1980–81, 1985–86; England, 1973, 1978, 1983, 1986, 1990; India, 1976, 1988; Pakistan, 1976; Sri Lanka, 1983–84, 1987; West Indies, 1984–85. Holder of world record of 431 Test wickets, 1990 (passed previous record of 373 in 1988). *Publication:* Rhythm and Swing (autobiog.), 1989. *Club:* MCC (Hon. Life Mem.).

HADLEY, David Allen, CB 1991; Deputy Secretary (Agricultural Commodities, Trade and Food Production), Ministry of Agriculture, Fisheries and Food, 1993–96; *b* 18 Feb. 1936; *s* of Sydney and Gwendoline Hadley; *m* 1965, Veronica Ann Hopkins; one *s*. *Educ:* Wyggeston Grammar Sch., Leicester; Merton Coll., Oxford. MA. Joined MAFF, 1959; Asst Sec., 1971; HM Treas., 1975–78; Under Sec., 1981–87, Dep. Sec., 1987–89, MAFF; Dep. Sec., Cabinet Office, 1989–93. *Recreations:* gardening, music. *Address:* Old Mousers, Dormansland, Lingfield, Surrey RH7 6PP.

HADLEY, Gareth Morgan; Commissioner responsible for East of England and East Midlands regions, Appointments Commission, since 2007; *b* 22 April 1951; *s* of Ronald Hadley and Gweneth Doreen Hadley (*née* Morgan). *Educ:* Harrow Weald Grammar Sch University Coll. London (BSc); Henley Mgt Coll. (MA). FCIPD. Greater Londo Council, 1972–86: Asst to Hd of Industrial Relns, 1980–81; Head: Central Recruitmen 1981–83; craft, operative manual and fire service employee relns, 1983–86; Asst Dir c Personnel, ILEA, 1986–89; British Railways Board, 1989–97: Gp Employee Rel Manager, 1989–94; Director: Employee Relns, 1994–97; Human Resources, N and W Passenger Ops, 1994–97; Principal, Gareth Hadley Associates, 1997–99; Dir of Personne HM Prison Service, 1999–2006. Chairman: British Transport Police Pension Fund 1992–97; ScotRail Railways Ltd, 1996–97. Human Resources Advr, Nat. Offender Mg Service, 2004–05. Dir, Skills for Justice (Justice Sector Skills Council), 2004–06. Mem Inf. and Consultation Taskforce, 2002–04, Employee Relations Panel, 2003–08, CIPD Mem. Adv. Bd, SW London Academic Network, Inst. of Mgt and Leadership in Health 2008–. Vis. Fellow, Kingston Univ., 2005–. MInstD 1997. *Recreations:* opera, food an drink. *Address:* Appointments Commission, Blenheim House, West One, Duncomb Street, Leeds LS1 4PL. *T:* (0113) 394 6745; *e-mail:* gareth.hadley@appointments.org.uk 29 Bemish Road, Putney, SW15 1DG; *e-mail:* gareth.hadley@lowerputney.demon.co.uk *Club:* Savile.

HADLEY, Graham Hunter; economic and business management consultant; Senio Adviser, National Economic Research Associates, 1996–2007; *b* 12 April 1944; *s* of lat Dr A. L. Hadley and Mrs L. E. Hadley; *m* 1971, Lesley Ann Smith; one *s*. *Educ:* Eltha Coll., London; Jesus Coll., Cambridge (BA Hons Mod. Hist.); Harvard Business Sch (AMP 1991). Entered Civil Service (Min. of Aviation), 1966; Dept of Energy, 1974 seconded to: Civil Service Commn, 1976–77; British Aerospace, 1980–81; Under-Sec Dept of Energy, 1983; Sec., CEGB, 1983–90; Exec. Dir, 1990–95, and Man. Di Internat. Business Develt, 1992–95, National Power. Mem., Competition (former Monopolies and Mergers) Commn, 1998–2007. Dir, de Havilland Aircraft Heritag Centre (formerly Mus. Trust), 1990–; Trustee and Dir, Cirencester Brewery Arts, 2006– *Recreations:* include cricket, long-distance walking, theatre, architecture, aviation. *Address* Sundance House, Cold Aston, Cheltenham GL54 3BN.

HADRILL, Andrew Frederic W.; *see* Wallace-Hadrill.

HAENDEL, Ida, CBE 1991; violinist; *b* Poland, 15 Dec. 1928; Polish parentage. Bega to play at age of 3½; amazing gift discovered when she picked up her sister's violin an started to play. Her father, a great connoisseur of music, recognised her unusual talent an abandoned his own career as an artist (painter) to devote himself to his daughter; studie at Warsaw Conservatoire and gained gold medal at age of seven; also studied with suc masters as Carl Flesch and Georges Enesco. British début, Queen's Hall, with Sir Henr Wood, playing Brahms' Violin Concerto. Gave concerts for British and US troops and i factories, War of 1939–45; after War, career developed to take in North and Sout America, USSR and Far East, as well as Europe; has accompanied British orchestras suc as London Philharmonic, BBC Symphony and English Chamber on foreign tour including Hong Kong, China, Australia and Mexico; performs with major orchestra worldwide, incl. Berlin Philharmonic, Boston Symphony, and Concertgebouw. Ha performed with conductors such as Beecham, Klemperer, Szell, Celibidache, Mata Pritchard, Rattle, Haitink, Ashkenazy; performances include appearances at BBC Prom A major interpreter of Sibelius, Brahms and Beethoven. Concerts, Edinburgh Fest. masterclasses. Huberman Prize; Sibelius Medal, Sibelius Soc. of Finland, 1982. *Publication* Woman with Violin (autobiog.), 1970. *Address:* c/o Ernest Gilbert Association, 10 Wheeler Avenue, Pleasantville, NY 10570, USA.

HAFFENDEN, Prof. John Charles Robert, DPhil; FBA 2007; FRSL; Researc Professor of English Literature, University of Sheffield, since 2005; *b* 19 Aug. 1945; *s* o Donald Haffenden and Sheila McCulloch Haffenden; *m* 1973, Susan Bellville (marr. diss 1977). *Educ:* Trinity Coll., Dublin (MA 1970); St Peter's Coll., Oxford (DPhil 1977) Educn Officer, Oxford Prison, 1970–73; Lectr in English, Univ. of Exeter, 1973–74 Lectr, 1975, Sen. Lectr, 1985; Reader, 1988, Prof. of English Literature, 1994–2004 Univ. of Sheffield. *Publications:* Viewpoints: poets in conversation, 1981; The Life of John Berryman, 1982; Novelists in Interview, 1985; (ed) The Complete Poems of Willian Empson, 2000; William Empson: among the Mandarins, 2005; William Empson: agains the Christians, 2006; (ed) Selected Letters of William Empson, 2006; contrib. t periodicals incl. London Rev. of Books, Essays in Criticism and PN Rev. *Recreations* country walking, travel, art and architecture, filleting research libraries, consuming min chocolates. *Address:* 104 Ashdell Road, Sheffield S10 3DB. *T:* (0114) 222 8464. *Club* Royal Over-Seas League.

HAGARD, Dr Spencer; international consultant in health promotion and public health since 1989; *b* 25 Oct. 1942; *s* of Maurice (Bozzie) Markham (killed in action, 11 June 1944) and Eva Markham (*née* Mearns, subseq. Hagard) and, by adoption, of late Noe Hagard; *m* 1968, Michele Dominique, *d* of late Stanislas and Madeleine Aquarone; two one *d*. *Educ:* Varndean Grammar Sch., Brighton; Univ. of St Andrews (MB ChB 1968) Univ. of Glasgow (PhD 1977); MA Cantab 1977. DPH 1972; FFPH (FFCM 1981). Jun med. appts, Arbroath, London and Dorking; MO and Med. Supt, Kawolo Hosp., Lugazi Uganda, 1971–72; MO, Health Dept, Glasgow, 1972–74; Trainee in Community Med. Greater Glasgow Health Bd, 1974–77; Specialist in Comm. Med., Cambs AHA, 1977–82 Dist MO, Cambridge HA, 1982–87; Chief Exec., HEA, 1987–94; Sen. Lectr, 1999–2005 Course Organiser, MSc (Health Promotion Scis), 2001–03, Hd, Health Promotion Res Unit, 2002–04, and Distance Learning Tutor, 2007–, LSHTM. Associate Lectr, Univ. o Cambridge Sch. of Clinical Med., 1977–87; Vis. Prof., Univ. of Bergen, 2001–02. Hon Consultant, Camden PCT (formerly Camden and Islington Community Health Service Trust), 1996–2005; Consultant: WHO, 1991–; DFID, 1999–2004; World Bank 2000–05; Health Policy Advr, Hungarian Govt, 1996–2000. National Association for the Education of Sick Children: Mem. Council, 1995–2002; Trustee, 1997–2005; Chm. o Trustees, 2000–05. Sec., Eur. Cttee for Health Promotion Develt, 1995–2004; Mem., EC Health Policy Forum, 2006–; Mem., Bd of Trustees, Internat. Union for Health Promotion and Educn, 1991–2007 (Pres., 1996–2001; Mem., Regl Cttee for Europe 2007–). FRSA 1997. *Publications:* Health, Society and Medicine (with Roy Acheson) 1984; papers in BMJ and other learned jls. *Recreations:* marriage, family, studying human beings, politics, gardening, reading, photography, appreciation of art, music, sporting new dawns (Brighton & Hove Albion, Sussex CCC). *Address:* 396 Milton Road, Cambridge CB4 1SU. *T:* (01223) 563774, *Fax:* (01223) 423970; *e-mail:* spencer@hagard.net.

HAGART-ALEXANDER, Sir Claud; *see* Alexander.

HAGEN, Martin John, FCA; Consultant, Deloitte, since 2007; Deputy President, Institute of Chartered Accountants in England and Wales, 2008–June 2009, President, from July 2009; *b* Leeds, 20 Sept. 1951; *s* of Christopher and Nancy Hagen; *m* 1978, Hilary Channell; three *s*. *Educ:* Herringthorpe Primary Sch., Rotherham; Rotherham Gramma Sch.; Thomas Rotherham Coll.; Sheffield Poly. FCA 1973. With Knox Franklin & Co. Sheffield, 1969–73; with Spicer and Pegler, London, 1974–81, Bristol, 1981–89; Touche Ross, Bristol, 1989–93; Deloitte & Touche, Bristol, 1993–2005. Mem., Regulatory Decisions Cttee, FSA, 2005–. Non-exec. Dir, Oxonica plc, 2006–08. *Recreations:* playing acoustic guitar, Bristol City Football Club, wine, all things French, travel. *Address:* Institute of Chartered Accountants in England and Wales, Chartered Accountants Hall, PO Box 433, EC2P 2BJ. *T:* (020) 7920 8473, *Fax:* (020) 7628 1874; *e-mail:* martin.hagen@icaew.com.

HAGERTY, William John Gell, (Bill); writer and broadcaster; Editor, British Journalism Review, since 2002; *b* 23 April 1939; *s* of William (Steve) Hagerty and Doris Hagerty (*née* Gell); *m* 1st, 1965, Lynda Beresford (marr. diss. 1990); one *s* one *d* (and one *d* decd); 2nd, 1991, Elizabeth Vercoe (*née* Latta); one *s*. *Educ:* Beal Grammar Sch., Ilford. Local newspapers, East London, 1955–58; RAF Nat. Service, 1958–60; local newspapers, Sunday Citizen, Daily Sketch, 1960–67; Daily Mirror, 1967–81; Sunday Mirror and Sunday People, 1981–85; Managing Editor (Features), Today, 1986; Editor, Sunday Today, 1987; Deputy Editor: Sunday Mirror, 1988–90; Daily Mirror, 1990–91; Editor, The People, 1991–92; Theatre Critic, 1993–95, Film Critic, 1994–95, Today; Theatre Critic: various pubns, 1996–2003; The Sun, 2004–. Consultant, Tribune, 1993–2004, 2007–. Mem., BAFTA. Mem. Council, 2002–, Vice-Chm., 2007–, Journalists' Charity (formerly Newspaper Press Fund); Dir, London Press Club, 2008–. *Publications:* Flash, Bang, Wallop! (with Kent Gavin), 1978; Read All About It, 2003. *Recreations:* jazz, watching cricket, lunch with Keith Waterhouse. *Address:* Bull Cottage, 10/11 Strand-on-the-Green, Chiswick, W4 3PQ. *Club:* Gerry's.

HAGESTADT, John Valentine; adviser on foreign direct investment, since 1998; *b* 11 Oct. 1938; *s* of late Leonard and Constance Hagestadt; *m* 1963, Betty Tebbs; three *d*. *Educ:* Dulwich Coll.; Worcester Coll., Oxford (BA). Asst Principal, Min. of Aviation, 1963; Principal, BoT, 1967; Nuffield Travelling Fellow, 1973–74; Asst Sec., Vehicles Div., Dept of Industry, 1976; Asst Sec., Overseas Trade Div. (Middle East and Latin America), Dept of Trade, 1980; Dir, British Trade Develt Office, NY 1982; Dir, Invest in Britain Bureau, NY, 1984–87; Head, N Amer. Br., DTI, 1987–93; Dir, Govt Office for London, 1994; Dir, Invest in Britain Bureau, DTI, 1995–96; Advr, Internat. Investment, OECD, 1997–98. *Address:* 14 Carlisle Mansions, Carlisle Place, SW1P 1HX. *T:* and *Fax:* (020) 7828 0042.

HAGGAN, Nicholas Somerset; QC 2003; a Recorder, since 2000; *b* 25 Aug. 1955; *s* of David Anthony Haggan and Hope Haggan; *m* 1993, Julie Carolyn Owen. *Educ:* Monkton Combe Sch., Bath; Coll. of Law, London. Called to the Bar: Middle Temple, 1977; NI, 1986; in practice, specialising in crime and regulatory offences, particularly in relation to compliance issues in the field of consumer law and health and safety at work; Asst Recorder, 1997–2000. *Recreations:* running, food and wine, cooking, gardening, travel. *Address:* 12 College Place, Fauvelle Buildings, Southampton, Hants SO15 2FE. *T:* (023) 8032 0320, *Fax:* (023) 8032 0321.

HAGGARD, Prof. Mark Peregrine, CBE 2001; PhD; FMedSci; Medical Research Council External Staff, Cambridge, since 2002; founder Director, Medical Research Council Institute of Hearing Research, 1977–2002; *b* 26 Dec. 1942; *m* 1962, Liz (*née* Houston); two *s*. *Educ:* Edinburgh Univ. (MA Psych, 1st cl. hons); Corpus Christi Coll., Cambridge (PhD Psych 1967). Univ. Demonstrator in Experimental Psychology, Univ. of Cambridge, 1967–71; Prof. of Psychology and Head of Dept, QUB, 1971–76; sabbatical, 1975–76; Special Prof. in Audiological Scis, Nottingham Univ., 1980. Founder FMedSci 1998. Hon. FRCSE 2001. *Publications:* Screening Children's Hearing, 1991; Research in the Development of Effective Services for Hearing-impaired People, 1993; contribs to learned jls. *Recreations:* ski-ing, choral music. *Address:* MRC Cognition and Brain Sciences Unit, 15 Chaucer Road, Cambridge CB2 7EF. *Club:* Royal Society of Medicine.

HAGGART, Mary Elizabeth; *see* Scholes, M. E.

HAGGETT, Prof. Peter, CBE 1993; FBA 1992; Professor of Urban and Regional Geography, 1966–98, now Emeritus Professor, and Acting Vice-Chancellor, 1984–85, University of Bristol; *b* 24 Jan. 1933; *s* of Charles and Elizabeth Haggett, Pawlett, Somerset; *m* 1956, Brenda Woodley; two *s* two *d*. *Educ:* Dr Morgan's Sch., Bridgwater; St Catharine's Coll., Cambridge (Exhib. and Scholar; MA 1958; PhD 1970; ScD 1985). Asst Lectr, University Coll. London, 1955–57; Demonstrator and University Lectr, Cambridge, 1957–66, and Fellow, Fitzwilliam Coll., 1963–66 (Hon. Fellow, 1994). Leverhulme Research Fellow (Brazil), 1959; Canada Council Fellow, 1977; Erskine Fellow (NZ), 1979; Res. Fellow, Res. Sch. of Pacific Studies, ANU, 1983. Visiting Professor: Berkeley; Monash; Pennsylvania State; Toronto; Western Ontario; Wisconsin; Hill Prof., Minnesota, 1994. Provost, Inst. for Advanced Studies, Bristol Univ., 1996–99. Member, SW Economic Planning Council, 1967–72. Governor, Centre for Environmental Studies, 1975–78; Member: Council, RGS, 1972–73, 1977–80; UGC, 1985–89; Nat. Radiological Protection Bd, 1986–93; Chm., Hist. of Med. Grants Panel, Wellcome Trust, 1994–2000. Vice-Pres., British Acad., 1995–97. Hon. Fellow, Bristol Univ., 1998. Hon. Foreign Mem., Amer. Acad. of Arts and Sci., 2006. Hon. DSc: York, Canada, 1983; Durham, 1989; Copenhagen, 1999; UWE, 2004; UCL, 2008; Hon. LLD Bristol, 1986; Hon. FilDr Helsinki, 2003. Cullum Medal of American Geographical Soc., 1969; Meritorious Contribution Award, Assoc. of American Geographers, 1973; Patron's Medal, RGS, 1986; Prix Internationale de Géographie, 1991; Lauréat d'Honneur, IGU, 1992; Scottish Medal, RSGS, 1993; Anders Retzius Gold Medal, Sweden, 1994. *Publications:* Locational Analysis in Human Geography, 1965; Geography: a modern synthesis, 1972, 4th edn, 1983; The Geographer's Art, 1990; Geographical Structure of Epidemics, 2000; Geography: a global synthesis, 2001; *jointly:* (with R. J. Chorley): Models in Geography, 1967; Network Analysis in Geography, 1969; (with M. D. I. Chisholm) Regional Forecasting, 1971; (with A. D. Cliff and others): Elements of Spatial Structure, 1975; Spatial Diffusion, 1981; Spatial Aspects of Influenza Epidemics, 1986; Atlas of Disease Distributions, 1988; Atlas of AIDS, 1992; Measles: an historical geography, 1993; Deciphering Global Epidemics, 1998; Island Epidemics, 2000; World Atlas of Epidemic Diseases, 2004; research papers on related geographical topics. *Recreations:* Somerset history, cricket. *Address:* 5 Tun Bridge Close, Chew Magna, Somerset BS40 8SU. *Club:* Oxford and Cambridge.

HAGGETT, Stuart John, MA; Headmaster, English School, Nicosia, since 2003; *b* 11 April 1947; *s* of William Francis and Doreen Ada Haggett; *m* 1971, Hilary Joy Hammond; two *d*. *Educ:* Dauntsey's Sch., West Lavington, Wilts; Downing Coll., Cambridge (MA 1972); PGCE London (ext.), 1970. Canford Sch., Wimborne, Dorset, 1970–83: Head of Modern Languages, 1973–83; Housemaster, 1975–83; Second Master, King's Sch., Rochester, 1983–88; Headmaster, Birkenhead Sch., 1988–2003. *Recreations:* France (travel and culture), sport, theatre, architecture, cooking. *Address:* English School, PO Box 23575, 1684 Nicosia, Cyprus.

HAGGIE, Dr Paul; HM Diplomatic Service, retired; Deputy Director (Africa), Foreign and Commonwealth Office, 2001–04; *b* 30 Aug. 1949; *s* of George Henry Haggie and Eva Haggie (*née* Hawke); *m* 1979, Rev. Deborah (marr. diss. 2000), *d* of Douglas Graham Frazer, CBE; one *s* one *d*. *Educ:* Royal Grammar Sch., Newcastle upon Tyne; Manchester Univ. (BA; PhD 1974). Joined HM Diplomatic Service, 1974: Second, later First Sec., Bangkok, 1976–80; First Secretary: FCO, 1980–82; Islamabad, 1982–86; FCO, 1986–89; Pretoria, 1989–93; Counsellor, FCO, 1993–94; on secondment to Cabinet Office as Sec., Requirements and Resources, 1994–96; FCO, 1996–98; Counsellor and UK Perm. Rep. to ESCAP, Bangkok, 1998–2001. *Publications:* Britannia at Bay: the defence of the British Empire against Japan 1931–1941, 1981; contrib. various articles to historical jls. *Recreations:* sailing, scuba, music, history (esp. maritime). *Address:* 2 Marc Brunel Way, Historic Dockyard, Chatham, Kent ME4 4BH. *Clubs:* Royal Automobile; Royal Bangkok Sports (Thailand).

HAGUE, Prof. Clifford Bertram; freelance consultant; Professor, School of the Built Environment, Heriot-Watt University, 2002–06, now Emeritus (Professor, School of Planning and Housing, Edinburgh College of Art, Heriot-Watt University, 1995–2002); *b* 22 Aug. 1944; *s* of Bertram Hague and Kathleen Mary Hague; *m* 1966, Irene Williamson; one *s* three *d*. *Educ:* Magdalene Coll., Cambridge (MA); Univ. of Manchester (DipTP). MRTPI 1973. Planning Asst, Glasgow Corp., 1968–69; Edinburgh College of Art, Heriot-Watt University: Lectr, 1969–73; Sen. Lectr, 1973–90; Head, Sch. of Planning and Housing, 1990–95. Mem., Permanent Internat. Wkg Party, European Biennial of Towns and Town Planning, 1996–; UK Nat. Contact, European Spatial Planning Observation Network, 2001–06 and 2008–. Member: Jury, Internat. Urban Planning and Design Competition for the banks of Huangpu River, 2001; Internat. Jury, Detailed Construction Plan, Qingdao Olympic Sailing, 2003; Jury, planning of Olympic Central Green and Forest Park, Beijing, 2003. Pres., RTPI, 1996–97; Pres. and CEO, 2000–06, Sec. Gen., 2006–, Commonwealth Assoc. of Planners. AcSS; FRSA; Fellow, Higher Educn Acad., 2004. Series Ed., RTPI Library Series, 2000–08. Centenary Medal, Technical Univ. of Brno, 2000. *Publications:* The Development of Planning Thought: a critical perspective, 1984; (ed with P. Jenkins) Place Identity, Participation and Planning, 2005; (jtly) Making Planning Work: a guide to approaches and skills, 2006; articles in Town Planning Rev., Town and Country Planning, Planning, etc. *Recreations:* Manchester United, cricket, theatre. *Address:* School of the Built Environment, Heriot-Watt University, Edinburgh EH14 4AS.

HAGUE, Prof. Sir Douglas (Chalmers), Kt 1982; CBE 1978; Hon. Fellow, Green Templeton College (formerly Templeton College), Oxford, since 2005 (Associate Fellow, 1983–2005); Emeritus Fellow, Saïd Business School, Oxford, since 2008; *b* Leeds, 20 Oct. 1926; *s* of Laurence and Marion Hague; *m* 1947, Brenda Elizabeth Fereday (marr. diss. 1986); two *d*; *m* 1986, Janet Mary Leach. *Educ:* Moseley Grammar Sch.; King Edward VI High Sch., Birmingham; University of Birmingham. Assistant Tutor, Faculty of Commerce, Birmingham Univ., 1946; Assistant Lecturer, University College, London, 1947–50, Lecturer, 1950–57; Reader in Political Economy in University of London, 1957; Newton Chambers Professor of Economics, University of Sheffield, 1957–63. Visiting Professor of Economics, Duke Univ., USA, 1960–61; Head of Department of Business Studies, University of Sheffield, 1962–63; Professor of Applied Economics, University of Manchester, 1963–65; Prof. of Managerial Economics, Manchester Business Sch., 1965–81, Dep. Dir, 1978–81, Vis. Prof., 1981–; Vis. Prof., Imperial Coll. of Science and Technol., London, 1988–92. Chairman: Metapraxis Ltd, 1984–90; Doctus Consulting Europe, 1991–94; Wire Ltd, 1999–2000; Oxford Strategy Network, 1984–2000. Director: Economic Models Ltd, 1970–78; The Laird Gp, 1976–79; CRT Gp, 1990–96 (Chm., 1992–93). Rapporteur to International Economic Association, 1953–78, Editor General, 1981–86; Chm., ESRC, 1983–87; Member Working Party of National Advisory Council on Education for Industry and Commerce, 1962–63; Consultant to Secretariat of NEDC, 1962–63; Member: Treasury Working Party on Management Training in the Civil Service, 1965–67; EDC for Paper and Board, 1967–70; (part-time) N Western Gas Board, 1966–72; Working Party, Local Govt Training Bd, 1969–70; Price Commn, 1973–78 (Dep. Chm., 1977); Director: Manchester School of Management and Administration, 1964–65; Centre for Business Research, Manchester, 1964–66. Member Council, Manchester Business School, 1964–81; Chairman, Manchester Industrial Relations Society, 1964–66; President, NW Operational Research Group, 1967–69; British Chm., Carnegie Project on Accountability, 1968–72; Jt Chm., Conf. of Univ. Management Schools, 1971–73; Chairman: DoI Working Party, Kirkby Manufacturing and Engineering Co., 1978; Professional Develt Cttee, Inst. of Dirs, 1993–96; Planning Cttee, Oxford Risk Inst., 1998–99. Trustee, Demos, 1996–. Economic adviser to Mrs Thatcher, Gen. Election campaign, 1979; Adviser to PM's Policy Unit, 10 Downing St, 1979–83. Industrial Consultant. Hon. LittD Sheffield, 1987. *Publications:* Costs in Alternative Locations: The Clothing Industry (with P. K. Newman), 1952; (with A. W. Stonier) A Textbook of Economic Theory, 1953, 4th edn 1973; (with A. W. Stonier) The Essentials of Economics, 1955; The Economics of Man-Made Fibres, 1957; (ed) Stability and Progress in the World Economy, 1958; (ed) The Theory of Capital, 1961; (ed) Inflation, 1962; (ed with Sir Roy Harrod) International Trade Theory in a Developing World, 1965; (ed) Price Formation in Various Economies, 1967; Managerial Economics, 1969; (ed with Bruce L. R. Smith) The Dilemma of Accountability in Modern Government, 1970; Pricing in Business, 1971; (with M. E. Beesley) Britain in the Common Market: a new business opportunity, 1973; (with W. E. F. Oakeshott and A. A. Strain) Devaluation and Pricing Decisions: a case study approach, 1974; (with W. J. M. Mackenzie and A. Barker) Public Policy and Private Interests: the institutions of compromise, 1975; (with Geoffrey Wilkinson) The IRC: an experiment in industrial intervention, 1983; (with Peter Hennessy) How Adolf Hitler reformed Whitehall, 1985; (ed) The Management of Science, 1991; Beyond Universities: a new republic of the intellect, 1991; Transforming the Dinosaurs, 1993; (with Kate Oakley) Spin-offs and Start-ups in UK Universities, 2000; (with Christine Holmes) Oxford Entrepreneurs, 2006; articles in economic, financial and management journals. *Recreations:* church organs, watching Manchester United. *Address:* Green Templeton College, Oxford OX2 6HG. *T:* (01865) 274775. *Club:* Athenæum.

HAGUE, Ffion Llywelyn; Member, Advisory Committee, Barclays Wealth Private Bank, since 2007; *b* 21 Feb. 1968; *d* of (John) Emyr Jenkins, *qv*, and Myra (*née* Samuel); *m* 1997, William Jefferson Hague, *qv*. *Educ:* Jesus Coll., Oxford (BA English Lit. 1989); UCW, Aberystwyth (MPhil Welsh Lit. 1993). Joined CS, 1991; Private Sec. to Sec. of State for Wales, 1994–97; Dir of Policy and Planning, Arts & Business (formerly Dir of Ops, ABSA), 1997–2000; Director: Leonard Hull Internat., 2000–02; Hanson Green, 2003–08. Mem. Bd, British Council, 1999–2002. Mem. Adv. Council, LSO, 1998–; Trustee: Voices Foundn, 1998–2005; Action on Addiction, 2001–04; Outward Bound Trust, 2002–. *Publication:* The Pain and the Privilege: the women in Lloyd George's life, 2008. *Address:* Advisory Committee, Barclays Bank plc, 43 Brook Street, W1Y 2PB.

HAGUE, Rt Hon. William (Jefferson); PC 1995; MP (C) Richmond, Yorks, since Feb. 1989; *b* 26 March 1961; *s* of Timothy Nigel Hague and Stella Hague; *m* 1997, Ffion Llywelyn Jenkins (*see* F. L. Hague). *Educ:* Wath-upon-Dearne Comprehensive School; Magdalen College, Oxford (MA); Insead (MBA). Pres., Oxford Union, 1981; Pres., Oxford Univ. Cons. Assoc., 1981. Management Consultant, McKinsey & Co., 1983–88. Political Adviser, HM Treasury, 1983. Contested (C) Wentworth, S Yorks, 1987. PPS to Chancellor of the Exchequer, 1990–93; Parly Under-Sec. of State, DSS, 1993–94; Minister for Social Security and Disabled People, DSS, 1994–95; Sec. of State for Wales,

1995–97; Leader, Cons. Party and Leader of the Opposition, 1997–2001; Shadow Foreign Sec., 2005–. *Publications:* William Pitt the Younger, 2004 (History Book of the Year, British Book Awards, 2005); William Wilberforce, 2007. *Address:* House of Commons, SW1A 0AA. *T:* (020) 7219 3000. *Clubs:* Beefsteak, Carlton, Buck's, Pratt's, Budokwai.

HAHN, Carl Horst, Dr rer. pol.; German business executive; *b* 1 July 1926; *m* 1960, Marisa Traina; three *s* one *d*. Chm. Bd, Continental Gummi-Werke AG, 1973–81; Chm. Mgt Bd, Volkswagen AG, 1981–92. Member, Supervisory Board: Hanseatisches Wein- und Sekt-Kontor, Hamburg; Perot Systems, Dallas; Member, International Advisory Board: Instituto de Empresa, Madrid; Textron Inc., Providence; Indesit Co. (formerly Merloni Electrodomestic), Fabriano. Board Member: Mayo Clinic Stiftung, Frankfurt; Global Consumer Acquisition Corp., NY; Lauder Inst., Wharton Sch., Philadelphia; Mem. Internat. Adv. Cttee, Salk Inst., La Jolla, Calif. *Address:* Hollerplatz 1, 38440 Wolfsburg, Germany. *T:* (5361) 26680, *Fax:* (5361) 266815.

HAHN, Prof. Frank Horace, FBA 1975; Professor of Economics, University of Cambridge, 1972–92, now Emeritus; Fellow of Churchill College, Cambridge, since 1960; *b* 26 April 1925; *s* of Dr Arnold Hahn and Maria Hahn; *m* 1946, Dorothy Salter; no *c*. *Educ:* Bournemouth Grammar School; London School of Economics (Hon. Fellow, 1989). PhD London, MA Cantab. Univ. of Birmingham, 1948–60, Reader in Mathematical Economics, 1958–60; Univ. Lectr in Econs, Cambridge, 1960–67; Prof. of Economics, LSE, 1967–72; Frank W. Taussig Res. Prof., Harvard, 1974–75. Visiting Professor: MIT, 1956–57; Univ. of California, Berkeley, 1959–60; Schumpeter Prof., Vienna Univ. of Econs and Business Admin, 1984; Prof. Ordinario, Univ. of Siena, 1992–2000. Fellow, Inst. of Advanced Studies in Behavioural Sciences, Stanford, 1966–67. Mem. Council for Scientific Policy, later Adv. Bd of Res. Councils, 1972–75. Fellow, Econometric Soc., 1962; Vice-Pres., 1967–68; Pres., 1968–69; Pres., Royal Economic Soc., 1986–89. Managing Editor, Review of Economic Studies, 1965–68. Foreign Hon. Mem., Amer. Acad. of Arts and Sciences, 1971; Hon. Mem., Amer. Economic Assoc., 1986; For. Associate, US Nat. Acad. of Scis, 1988; Mem., Academia Europaea, 1989. Hon. DSocSci Birmingham, 1981; Hon. DLitt: East Anglia, 1984; Leicester, 1993; Dr Econ *hc* Strasbourg, 1984; Hon. DSc(Econ) London, 1985; DUniv York, 1991; Hon. PhD Athens, 1993; Dr *hc* Paris X (Nanterre), 1999. Palacky Gold Medal, Czechoslovak Acad. of Scis, 1991. *Publications:* (with K. J. Arrow) General Competitive Analysis, 1971; The Share of Wages in the National Income, 1972; Money and Inflation, 1982; Equilibrium and Macro-Economics, 1984; Money, Growth and Stability, 1985; (ed and contrib.) The Economics of Missing Markets, Information and Games, 1989; (with Robert Solow) A Critical Essay on Modern Macroeconomic Theory, 1995; (ed jtly and contrib.) General Equilibrium: problems and prospects, 2003; articles in learned journals. *Address:* 16 Adams Road, Cambridge CB3 9AD. *T:* (01223) 352560.

HAIDAR, Salman; High Commissioner for India in the United Kingdom, 1998; *b* 17 June 1938; *s* of Mohammed Haidar and Mumtaz Abdullah; *m* Kusum; one *s* one *d*. *Educ:* St Stephen's Coll.; Delhi Univ. (Hons English); Magdalene Coll., Cambridge (BA Hons English). Joined Indian Foreign Service, 1960; Cairo, 1961–63; UK, 1963–66; First Sec., Kabul, 1970–72; Counsellor and Minister, and Dep. Permt Rep., Permt Mission of India, NY, 1977–80; Ambassador to Bhutan, 1980–83; Dep. and acting High Comr, UK, 1987–91; Ambassador to China, 1991–92; Sec. (East), responsible for Africa, Asia, Latin America, ME and Central Asia, 1992; Foreign Sec., 1995–97. *Publication:* (ed) The Afghan War and its Geopolitical Implications for India, 2004. *Recreation:* tennis. *Clubs:* Delhi Gymkhana, Delhi Golf.

HAIG, family name of **Earl Haig**.

HAIG, 2nd Earl *cr* 1919; **George Alexander Eugene Douglas Haig,** OBE 1966; RSA 2006 (ARSA 1988); Viscount Dawick, *cr* 1919; Baron Haig and 30th Laird of Bemersyde; is a painter; Member, Queen's Body Guard for Scotland; *b* March 1918; *o s* of 1st Earl and Hon. Dorothy Vivian (*d* 1939) (Author of A Scottish Tour, 1935), *d* of 3rd Lord Vivian; *S* father, 1928; *m* 1st, 1956, Adrienne Thérèse, *d* of Derrick Morley; one *s* two *d*; 2nd, 1981, Donna Geroloma Lopez y Royo di Taurisano. *Educ:* Stowe; Christ Church, Oxford. MA Oxon. 2nd Lieut Royal Scots Greys, 1938; retired on account of disability, 1951, rank of Captain; Hon. Major on disbandment of HG 1958; studied painting Camberwell School of Art; paintings in collections of Arts Council and Scottish Nat. Gallery of Modern Art. War of 1939–45 (prisoner). Member: Royal Fine Art Commission for Scotland, 1958–61; Council and Executive Cttee, Earl Haig Fund, Scotland, 1950–65 and 1966– (Pres., 1980–86); Scottish Arts Council, 1969–75; President, Scottish Craft Centre, 1950–75. Member Council, Commonwealth Ex-Services League, 1960–96; President: Officers' Association (Scottish Branch), 1987–95 (Chm., 1977–87); Nat. Ex-Prisoner of War Assoc., 1998–2005; Vice-President: Friends of St George's Meml Church, Ypres, 1955–; Scottish National Institution for War Blinded; Royal Blind Asylum and School; President Border Area British Legion, 1955–61; Chairman SE Scotland Disablement Advisory Cttee, 1960–73; Vice-Chairman, British Legion, Scotland, 1960, Chairman, 1962–65, Pres., 1980–86; Chm., Bd of Trustees, Scottish National War Memorial, 1983–95 (Trustee, 1961–95); Trustee, National Gallery of Scotland, 1962–72; Chairman: Berwickshire Civic Soc., 1971–73; Friends of DeMarco Gall., 1968–71. Berwickshire: DL 1953; Vice-Lieutenant, 1967–70; DL Ettrick and Lauderdale (and Roxburghshire), 1977–93. KStJ 1977. FRSA 1951. *Publication:* My Father's Son (autobiog.), 2000. *Heir:* *s* Viscount Dawick, *qv*. *Address:* Bemersyde, Melrose, Scotland TD6 9DP. *T:* (01835) 822762. *Clubs:* Cavalry and Guards; New (Edinburgh).
See also Baron Astor of Hever.

HAIG, General Alexander Meigs, Jr; Chairman and President, Worldwide Associates, Inc., since 1984; Strategic Adviser, SaVi Media Group, since 2005; *b* 2 Dec. 1924; *m* 1950, Patricia Fox; two *s* one *d*. *Educ:* schs in Pennsylvania; Univ. of Notre Dame; US Mil. Acad., West Point (BS); Univs of Columbia and Georgetown (MA); Ground Gen. Sch., Fort Riley; Armor Sch., Fort Knox; Naval and Army War Colls. 2nd Lieut 1947; Far East and Korea, 1948–51; Europe, 1956–59; Vietnam, 1966–67; CO 3rd Regt, subseq. Dep. Comdt, West Point, 1967–69; Sen. Mil. Adviser to Asst to Pres. for Nat. Security Affairs, 1969–70; Dep. Asst to Pres. for Nat. Security Affairs, 1970–73; Vice-Chief of Staff, US Army, Jan.–July 1973, retd; Chief of White House Staff, 1973–74 when recalled to active duty; Supreme Allied Commander Europe, 1974–79, and Commander-in-Chief, US European Command, 1974–79. President and Chief Operating Officer, United Technologies, 1979–81. Secretary of State, USA, 1981–82. Sen. Fellow, Hudson Inst. for Policy Research, 1982–84. Director: MGM Mirage Inc.; Metro-Goldwyn-Mayer Inc.; Interneuron Pharmaceuticals, Inc.; SDC International, Inc.; CompuServe Interactive Services Inc. Member: Presidential Cttee on Strategic Forces, 1983–; Presidential Commn on Chemical Warfare Review, 1985; Bd of Special Advisers, President's Commn on Physical Fitness and Sports, 1984. Host of own weekly television progs, World Business Review, then 21st Century Business. Hon. LLD: Niagara; Utah; hon. degrees: Syracuse, Fairfield, Hillsdale Coll., 1981. Awarded numerous US medals, badges and decorations; also Vietnamese orders and Cross of Gallantry; Medal of King Abd el-Aziz (Saudi Arabia). *Publications:* Caveat: realism, Reagan and foreign policy, 1984; Inner Circles, 199 *Recreations:* tennis, golf. *Address:* *e-mail:* ahaig@aol.com.

HAIG, David; actor and writer; *m* Jane Galloway; five *c*. *Theatre includes:* seasons with RS 1983, 1986; Tom and Viv, Royal Court, 1984, NY, 1985; Our Country's Good (Olivi Award for best actor in a new play), Royal Court, 1988; Berenice, RNT, 1990; De Funny, Vaudeville, 1994; Fair Ladies at a Game of Poem Cards, RNT, 1996; A Wyndham's, 1997, NY, 1998; My Boy Jack (also writer), Hampstead, 1997; House a Garden, RNT, 2000; Gasping (tour), 2000; Life x 3, Savoy, 2002; Hitchcock Blond Royal Court, transf. Lyric, 2003; Journey's End, Comedy, 2004; Mary Poppins, Prin Edward, 2004; Donkey's Years, Comedy, 2006; The Country Wife, Haymarket, 200 The Sea, Haymarket, 2007; writer, The Good Samaritan, Hampstead, 2000. *Films inclu* The Moon Stallion, 1978; Dark Enemy, 1984; Morons from Outer Space, 1985; Fo Weddings and a Funeral, 1994; Two Weeks Notice, 2002; *television includes:* Portrait of Marriage, 1990; Soldier, Soldier, 1991; Love on a Branch Line, 1993; Nice Day at t Office, 1994; The Thin Blue Line (series), 1995; Keeping Mum, 1997; Talking Heads 1998; Station Jim, 2001; Crime and Punishment, 2002; Hustle, 2004; My Boy Jack (al writer), 2007. *Address:* c/o United Agents, 12–26 Lexington Street, W1F 0LE.

HAIG, Ian Maurice, AM 1988; Senior Counsel, Global Agenda, since 1996; *b* 13 De 1936; *s* of P. K. Haig; *m* 1959, Beverley, *d* of J. A. Dunning, OBE; two *s* one *d*. *Ed* Pulteney Grammar School, Adelaide; University of Adelaide. Private Sec. to Pres. Senate, Canberra, 1958–59; Asst Sec., Commonwealth Parly Conf., London, 1960; Pub Relations Officer, Shell Co. of Australia, 1962; British Foreign Office School of Mid East Studies, 1963; Asst Trade Comr and Trade Comr, Los Angeles, 1966–68; Tra Comr, Beirut, 1969–73; Ambassador at large, Middle East, 1973; Ambassador to Sau Arabia, Kuwait and United Arab Emirates, 1974–76; Australian Comr, Hong Ko 1976–79; Dir of Administration, A.C.I. Ltd, 1979–81; Man. Dir, A.C.I. Fibreglass (Aust 1982; Agent Gen. for Victoria in London, 1983–85 and 1988–90; Chm., Immigratio Panel, 1987; Dir, Aust. Wheat Bd, 1985–88; Chief Exec., Monash-ANZ Centre f Internat. Briefing, 1990–96. *Publications:* Arab Oil Politics, 1978; Oil and Alternati Sources of Energy, 1978; Australia and the Middle East, 1983. *Recreations:* cricket, go *Address:* 11/546 Toorak Road, Toorak, Vic 3142, Australia. *Clubs:* MCC; Australi (Melbourne); Royal Melbourne Golf.

HAIG, Dame Mary Alison G.; *see* Glen Haig.

HAIGH, Brian Roger; Lecturer for Hawksmere plc, 1993–2001; *b* 19 Feb. 1931; *s* Herbert Haigh and Ruth Haigh (*née* Lockwood); *m* 1953, Sheila Carter; one *d* (one decd). *Educ:* Hillhouse Central School, Huddersfield. Min. of Supply, 1949; Nation Service, RAF, 1949–51. Min. of Supply/Min. of Aviation, 1951–62; NATO Bullp Production Orgn, 1962–67 (Head of Contracts, Finance and Admin, 1965–67); Min. Technology, Aviation Supply, Defence (Defence Sales Orgn), 1968–73 (Asst Dir, Sal 1971–73); Nat. Defence Coll., 1973–74; Ministry of Defence: Asst Dir, Contracts, 197 Dir of Contracts (Weapons), Dec. 1974; Principal Dir of Navy Contracts, 1978; Und Secretary, 1980; Dir-Gen., Defence Contracts, 1980–86. Dir of Professional Educn a Trng, Lion Worldwide Div., Keiser Enterprises Inc., 1986–91. *Recreations:* family, musi opera, bridge. *Address:* c/o Barclays Bank plc, Kingston Business Centre, 9 Clarence Roa Kingston-upon-Thames KT1 1NY.

HAIGH, (Christopher) Nigel (Austin), OBE 1992; Member, Management Boar European Environment Agency (nominated by European Parliament), 2000; *b* 23 Fe 1938; *s* of Anthony Haigh, CMG and Gertrude, (Pippa), Haigh (*née* Dodd); *m* 197 Carola Pickering; two *d*. *Educ:* Eton; King's Coll., Cambridge (MA Mech. Scis). N Service, 2nd Lieut, RB, 1956–58. Tech Assistant, F. B. Dehn and Co., Chartered Pate Agents, 1962–68; Co. Patent Agent, Tracked Hovercraft Ltd, 1968–70; Sen. Pate Agent, BSC, 1970–72; Asst Sec., Anti-Concorde Project, 1972–73; Civic Trust, 1973–8 Institute for European Environmental Policy, London: Hd of London Office, 1980–8 Dir, 1990–98. Non-exec. Dir, Merlin, subseq. Jupiter, Internat. Green Investment Tru 1989–94. Mem., Envmt Agency, 1995–2000; Vice-Pres., European Envmtl Burea 1975–79; Chm., Green Alliance, 1989–97. Specialist Advr, H of L Select Cttee on E 1982–93. Hon. Res. Fellow, Faculty of Laws, UCL, 1990–; Vis. Res. Fellow, Imperi Coll. Centre for Envmtl Tech., 1991–. Member, Editorial Board: Jl of Envmtl La 1989–; Internat. Envmtl Affairs, 1989–99. *Publications:* EEC Environmental Policy a Britain, 1984, 2nd edn 1987; (ed) Manual of Environmental Policy: the EU and Brita (looseleaf), 1992. *Recreations:* painting, looking at paintings, looking at towns. *Address:* Grove Lane, Camberwell, SE5 8ST. *T:* (020) 7703 2719.

HAIGH, Edward; Assistant General Secretary, Transport and General Workers' Unio 1985–91; *b* 7 Nov. 1935; *s* of Edward and Sarah Ellen Haigh; *m* 1st, 1958, Patricia (ma diss. 1982); one *s* two *d*; 2nd, 1982, Margaret; two step *d*. *Educ:* St Patrick's RC Sc Birstall; St Mary's RC Sch., Batley, W Yorks. Carpet weaver, 1956–69; shop stewa 1960–69; National Union of Dyers, Bleachers and Textile Workers: Dist Organis 1969–73; Dist Sec., 1973–77; Nat. Organiser/Negotiator, 1977–79; Asst Gen. Se 1979–82; Nat. Sec., Textile Gp, TGWU, 1982–85. Mem., Labour Party NEC, 1982–9 JP Batley, W Yorks, 1971–85. *Recreations:* politics (Labour Party), Rugby League footba cricket. *Club:* Birstall Irish Democratic League (W Yorks).

HAIGH, Maurice Francis; a Recorder of the Crown Court, 1981–96; a Chairman Tribunals, 1984–2001; *b* 6 Sept. 1929; *s* of William and Ceridwen Francis Haigh. *Ed* Repton. Asst cameraman in film production; worked for Leslie Laurence Productions L London, Manchester Film Studios, and finally for Anglo-Scottish Pictures Ltd at Lond Film Studios, Shepperton, 1946–49; in commerce, 1950–52. Called to the Bar, Gray's In 1955. *Recreations:* reading, cycling, walking.

HAIGH, Nigel; *see* Haigh, C. N. A.

HAILSHAM, 3rd Viscount *cr* 1929, of Hailsham, co. Sussex; **Douglas Martin Hogg;** P 1992; QC 1990; Baron 1928; MP (C) Sleaford and North Hykeham, since 19 (Grantham, 1979–97); *b* 5 Feb. 1945; *er s* of Baron Hailsham of Saint Marylebone (L Peer), PC, KG, CH, FRS (who disclaimed his hereditary peerages for life, 1963); *S* fath 2001; *m* 1968, Sarah Boyd-Carpenter (*see* Baroness Hogg); one *s* one *d*. *Educ:* Et (Oppidan Schol.); Christ Church, Oxford (Schol.; Pres., Oxford Union). Called to t Bar, Lincoln's Inn, 1968 (Kennedy Law Schol.). Mem., Agric. Select Cttees, 1979–8 PPS to Chief Sec., HM Treasury, 1982–83; an Asst Govt Whip, 1983–84; Parly Und Sec. of State, Home Office, 1986–89; Minister of State (Minister for Industry a Enterprise), DTI, 1989–90; Minister of State, FCO, 1990–95; Minister of Agricultu Fisheries and Food, 1995–97. *Heir:* *s* Hon. Quintin John Neil Martin Hogg, *b* 12 O 1973. *Address:* House of Commons, SW1A 0AA.
See also Hon. Dame M. Hogg.

HAILSHAM, Viscountess; *see* Hogg, Baroness.

HAIN, Rt Hon. Peter (Gerald); PC 2001; MP (Lab) Neath, since April 1991; *b* 16 Feb. 1950; *s* of Walter and Adelaine Hain; *m* 1st, 1975, Patricia Western (marr. diss. 2002); two *s*; 2nd, 2003, Dr Elizabeth Haywood. *Educ:* Queen Mary College, London (BSc Econ 1st cl. hons); Univ. of Sussex (MPhil). Brought up in S Africa, until family forced to leave in 1966, due to anti-apartheid activity, since when lived in UK. Union of Communication Workers: Asst Research Officer, 1976–87; Head of Research, 1987–91. Chm., Stop the Seventy Tour campaign, 1969–70; Nat. Chm., Young Liberals, 1971–73; Press Officer, Anti-Nazi League, 1977–80. Contested (Lab) Putney, 1983, 1987. An Opposition Whip, 1995–96; an Opposition Spokesman on employment, 1996–97; Parly Under-Sec. of State, Welsh Office, 1997–99; Minister of State, FCO, 1999–2000 and 2001–02; Minister of State, DTI, Jan.–June 2001; Sec. of State for Wales, 2002–08; Leader, H of C, 2003–05; Sec. of State for NI, 2005–07; Sec. of State for Work and Pensions, 2007–08. *Publications:* Don't Play with Apartheid, 1971; Community Politics, 1976; Mistaken Identity, 1976; (ed) Policing the Police, vol. I, 1978, vol. II, 1980; Neighbourhood Participation, 1980; Crisis and Future of the Left, 1980; Political Trials in Britain, 1984; Political Strikes, 1986; A Putney Plot?, 1987; The Peking Connection (novel), 1995; Ayes to the Left, 1995; Sing the Beloved Country, 1996. *Recreations:* soccer, cricket, Rugby, motor racing, fan of Chelsea FC and Neath RFC, rock and folk music fan. *Address:* House of Commons, SW1A 0AA. *T:* (020) 7219 3000; 39 Windsor Road, Neath SA11 1NB. *T:* (01639) 630152; *e-mail:* neathoffice@peterhain.org. *Clubs:* Neath Workingmen's; Neath Rugby; Resolven Rugby; Resolven Royal British Legion Institute.

HAINER, Herbert; Chief Executive Officer and Chairman, Executive Board, adidas AG (formerly adidas-Salomon AG), since 2001; *b* Dingolfing, Germany, 3 June 1954; *m* Angela; two *d. Educ:* Univ. of Landshut (degree in Business Studies 1979). Div. Manager, Sales and Mktg Germany, Procter & Gamble GmbH, 1979–87; adidas Germany: Sales Dir Hardware (Bags, Rackets, Balls), 1987–89; Sales Dir Field (Footwear, Textiles, Hardware), 1989–91; Nat. Sales Dir, 1991–93; Man. Dir (Sales and Logistics), 1993–95; adidas AG, then adidas-Salomon AG: Sen. Vice Pres. (Sales and Logistics), Europe, Africa, Middle East Reg., 1996–97; Mem., 1997–, Dep. Chm., 2001, Exec. Bd. Member Supervisory Board: Bayerische Versicherungsbank AG, Munich; Engelhorn KGaA, Mannheim; Dep. Chm. Supervisory Bd, FC Bayern München AG, Munich. *Address:* adidas AG, Adi-Dassler-Str. 1, 91074 Herzogenaurach, Germany.

HAINES, Sir Andrew (Paul), Kt 2005; MD; FRCP, FRCGP, FFPH; FMedSci; Director (formerly Dean), and Professor of Public Health and Primary Care, London School of Hygiene and Tropical Medicine, University of London, since 2001; *b* 26 Feb. 1947; *s* of Charles George Thomas Haines and Lilian Emily Haines; *m* 1st, 1982, June Marie Power (marr. diss. 1987); 2nd, 1998, Dr Anita Berlin; two *s. Educ:* King's Coll., London (MB BS 1969; MD Epidemiology 1985). MRCP 1971, FRCP 1993; MRCGP 1976, FRCGP 1993; MFCM 1987, FFPH (FFPHM 1992). Mem. Scientific Staff, MRC Epidemiology and Med. Care Unit, 1974–87; part-time Sen. Lectr in General Practice, Middlesex Hosp. Med. Sch., 1980–84, St Mary's Hosp. Med. Sch., 1984–87; on secondment as Dir, R&D, NE Thames RHA, subseq. N Thames Reg., NHS Exec., 1993–96; Prof. of Primary Health Care, UCL, 1987–2000; Head, Dept of Primary Care and Population Scis, Royal Free and UC Med. Sch., 1998–2000. Mem., MRC, 1996–98; Chairman: Health Services and Public Health Bd, 1996–98; Health and Social Care Policy Cttee, Univs UK, 2007–; Mem., Scientific Adv. Cttee, AMRC, 1998–2004. Mem., UN Intergovernmental Panel on Climate Change, 1993–96, 1998–2001; Consultant, 1998, Mem., Adv. Cttee on Health Res., 2004–, WHO. Founder FMedSci 1998. Hon. Fellow, UCL, 2006. For. Associate Mem., Inst. of Medicine, USA. *Publications:* (ed jtly) Climate Change and Human Health, 1996; (ed jtly) Evidence Based Practice in Primary Care, 1998; (ed jtly) Getting Research Findings into Practice, 1998; numerous articles in medical and scientific jls. *Recreations:* travel, environmental issues. *Address:* London School of Hygiene and Tropical Medicine, Keppel Street, WC1E 7HT. *T:* (020) 7927 2278.

HAINES, Christopher John Minton; Chairman, Harlequin Football Club, 1998–2004; *b* 14 April 1939; *m* 1967, Christine Cobbold; two *s* two *d. Educ:* Stowe. The Rifle Brigade, 1957–68; sugar trade, 1968–89; Chm., James Budgett & Son, 1984–89. Non-executive Director: Devonshire Arms (Bolton Abbey), 1995–; SPG Media (formerly Sterling Publg Gp) plc, 1996– (Chm., 1996–2001). Chief Exec., The Jockey Club, 1989–93. *Recreations:* music, gardening, racing. *Club:* Turf.
See also M. Haines.

HAINES, Joseph Thomas William; Assistant Editor, The Daily Mirror, 1984–90; Group Political Editor, Mirror Group Newspapers, 1984–90; *b* 29 Jan. 1928; *s* of Joseph and Elizabeth Haines; *m* 1955, Irene Betty Lambert; no *c. Educ:* Elementary Schools, Rotherhithe, SE16. Parly Correspondent, The Bulletin (Glasgow) 1954–58, Political Correspondent, 1958–60; Political Correspondent: Scottish Daily Mail, 1960–64; The Sun, 1964–68; Dep. Press Sec. to Prime Minister, Jan.–June 1969; Chief Press Sec. to Prime Minister, 1969–70 and 1974–76, and to Leader of the Opposition, 1970–74; Feature Writer, 1977–78, Chief Leader Writer, 1978–90, The Daily Mirror. Political Columnist, Today, 1994–95. Director: Mirror Gp Newspapers (1986) Ltd, 1986–92; Scottish Daily Record & Sunday Mail Ltd, 1986–92. Mem. Tonbridge UDC, 1963–69, 1971–74. Mem., Royal Commn on Legal Services, 1976–79. *Publications:* The Politics of Power, 1977; (co-editor) Malice In Wonderland, 1986; Maxwell, 1988; Glimmers of Twilight (memoir), 2003. *Recreations:* heresy and watching football. *Address:* 1 South Frith, London Road, Southborough, Tunbridge Wells, Kent TN4 0UQ. *T:* (01732) 365919.

HAINES, Margaret Patricia Joyce, FCLIP; University Librarian, Carleton University, Ottawa, since 2006; *b* Ottawa, 28 May 1950; *d* of Ernest and Mary Haines; *m* 1st, Roderick Stewart Taylor (marr. diss. 1989); 2nd, 1991, Ian Cordery (marr. diss. 2007); one step *d. Educ:* Carleton Univ. (BA Psychol. 1970); Univ. of Toronto (MLS 1975). Librarian, Health Scis Educn Centre, Mohawk Coll., Hamilton, Canada, 1975–78; Dir, Liby Services, Children's Hosp. of Eastern Ontario, Ottawa, 1978–88; Associate Instructor (Inf. Sci.), Univ. of Toronto, 1988–89; Dir, Inf. Resources, Kings' Fund, London, 1989–94; NHS Liby Advr, DoH, 1995–96; Chief Exec., Liby and Inf. Commn, 1996–2000; Dir, Res. and Knowledge Mgt, NHS SE London, 2000–02; Actg Dir, Knowledge Mgt, NHS Modernisation Agency, 2002–03; Dir, Inf. Services and Systems, KCL, 2003–06. Pres., CLIP, 2004–05. Pres., Ontario Hosp. Libraries Assoc., 1987. Hon. FCLIP 2006 (FCLIP 2004). Barnard Prize, LA, 1996. *Publications:* contrib. numerous articles to liby and information jls and chapters in books, including: Health Care Librarianship and Information Work, 2nd edn 1995; (jtly) Getting Research Findings into Practice, 1998; (jtly) Challenge and Change in the Information Society, 2003. *Recreations:* gardening, travelling, reading. *Address:* Maxwell MacOdrum Library, Carleton University, 1125 Colonel By Drive, Ottawa, ON K1S 5B6, Canada. *T:* (613) 5202725, *Fax:* (613) 5202750; *e-mail:* margaret_haines@carleton.ca.

HAINES, Miranda, (Mrs Luke Taylor); writer; Consultant Editor, Geographical magazine, 2002–05 (Editor, 1999–2002); *b* 15 Oct. 1968; *d* of Christopher Haines, *qv; m* 1998, Luke Taylor. *Educ:* Manchester Coll., Oxford (BA Hons English Lit.). International Herald Tribune, 1993–96; freelance writer, London, 1996–97; Editor, Traveller magazine, 1997–98. *Publications:* (ed jtly) The Traveller's Handbook, 1998; (ed jtly) The Traveller's Health Book, 1998; (contrib.) A Pilgrimage to Mecca, 2008. *Recreation:* travelling. *Address:* 2 Souldern Road, W14 0JE.

HAINES, Patricia, (Trish); Chief Executive, Worcestershire County Council, since 2008; *d* of David and Roberta Calvert; *m* 1991, Terence Haines; two *s*, and one step *s* three step *d. Educ:* Belfast Royal Acad.; Univ. of Bradford (BA Hons, CQSW 1979); Henley Mgt Coll. (MBA 1994). Case worker, Manchester Law Centre, 1979–80; Intake Social Worker, Bradford MBC, 1980–83; Fostering and Adoption Social Worker, Kirklees MBC, 1983–86; Sen. Social Worker, Bradford MBC, 1986–87; Prin. Social Worker, Social Services, Berks CC, 1987–92; Prin. Staff Officer, Suffolk Social Services, 1992–96; Asst Dir, Social Services, Hereford and Worcs CC, 1996–97; Dir of Social Services, Warwicks CC, 1997–2002; Chief Exec., Reading BC, 2002–08. Vice-Pres., 2006–July 2008, Pres., 2008–July 2009, SOLACE. *Recreations:* enjoying family life, going to the races. *Address:* Worcestershire County Council, County Hall, Spetchley Road, Worcester WR5 2NP. *T:* (01905) 766100; *e-mail:* chiefexec@worcestershire.gov.uk.

HAINES, Ronald William Terence, FICE, FIStructE; Director of Construction Services, HM Prison Service, 1993–96; *b* 19 Dec. 1937; *s* of John William Haines and Mary Agnes Power; *m* 1957, Linda, *d* of Sidney and Lilian Hampton; one *s* two *d. Educ:* South East London Tech. Coll.; Regent Street Poly.; City Univ. MCIWEM. Design Engineer: William Harbrow & Co., 1954–56; Liverpool Reinforced Concrete Co., 1956–58; Civil and Structl Engr, Min. of Works and MPBW, 1958–67; Chief Civil and Structl Engr, Home Office, 1967–87; Dep. Dir of Works, HM Prison Service, Home Office, 1987–93. *Recreations:* organic farming, walking, theatre. *Address:* Barklye Farm, Swife Lane, Broad Oak, Heathfield, E Sussex TN21 8UR.

HAINES, Timothy Michael; Creative Director and Founder, Impossible Pictures Ltd, since 2002; *b* 14 Oct. 1960; *s* of Douglas and Ann Haines; *m* 1989, Clare Worgan; three *s* two *d. Educ:* Tonbridge Sch., Kent; University Coll. of N Wales, Bangor (BSc Hons Zool.; Hon. Fellow 2004). Medical journalist, Doctor newspaper, 1981–85; Producer: BBC Radio, 1986–88; BBC TV Sci. and Features, 1989–2001; progs include Tomorrow's World, Horizon, QED; Creator and Producer, Walking with Dinosaurs, 1999; Exec. Producer, Walking with Beasts, Lost World, Ballad of Big Al; Exec. Producer, Space Odyssey, Ocean Odyssey, Walking with Monsters; Co-creator and Exec. Producer, Primeval, 2007, Primeval 2, 2008. *Publications:* Walking with Dinosaurs, 1999; Walking with Beasts, 2001; Space Odyssey, 2004; Complete Guide to Prehistoric Life, 2005. *Recreations:* watching film and TV, gardening, walking. *Address:* Impossible Pictures, 12 Great Portland Street, W1W 8QN. *T:* (020) 7636 4401.

HAIRD, Susan Margaret, CB 2007; Deputy Chief Executive, UK Trade & Investment, since 2004; *b* 10 Oct. 1952; *d* of Douglas Haird and late Myrah Haird; *m* 1979, David Lee Simpson; one *s* one *d. Educ:* Dollar Acad.; St Andrews Univ. (MA Hons Hist. and Econs); Coll. of Europe, Bruges (Cert. and Dip. in Advanced Eur. Studies). Stage at EC, 1976; joined Department of Trade and Industry, 1976: Private Secretary: to Perm. Sec., 1978; to Parly Under-Sec., 1979; Commercial Relns and Exports Div., 1980–84; Personnel Div. 1985–89; Industrial Materials Div., 1989; Equal Opportunities Div., Cabinet Office (on loan), 1989–92; Atomic Energy Div., 1992–96; Office of Manpower Econs, 1996–99; Director: Export Control, 1999–2000; Export Control and Non-Proliferation, 2000–02; UK Gov., IAEA and UK Mem., Exec. Council, Orgn for Prohibition of Chemical Weapons, 2000–02; Dir, Human Resources and Change Mgt, DTI, 2002–04. *Recreations:* family, travel, swimming. *Address:* UK Trade & Investment, Kingsgate House, 66–74 Victoria Street, SW1E 6SW.

HAIRE, William David Adams; Permanent Secretary, Department of Education, Northern Ireland, since 2006; *b* 14 April 1956; *s* of Prof. James Haire and Dr Margaret Haire; *m* 1984, Bronwen Jess; two *d. Educ:* Queens' Coll., Cambridge (BA 1979); Univ. of Ulster (MSc). Joined Dept of Manpower Services, NI, 1980; on secondment, UKRep, Brussels, 1990–93; Director: Equality and Industrial Relns, Dept of Econ. Develt, 1993–97; Internat. Mktg, Industrial Develt Bd for NI, 1997–2000; Dir, Econ. Policy Unit, 2000–02, Second Perm. Sec., 2002–04, Office of First and Dep. First Minister; Perm. Sec., Dept for Employment and Learning, 2004–06. *Recreations:* gardening, walking, reading. *Address:* Department of Education, Rathgael House, 43 Balloo Road, Bangor, Northern Ireland BT19 7PR. *T:* (028) 9127 9309; *e-mail:* will.haire@deni.gov.uk.

HAITES, Prof. Neva Elizabeth, OBE 2006; PhD; FRCPE; FRCPath; Professor of Medical Genetics, since 1996, and Vice-Principal and Head of College of Life Sciences and Medicine, since 2004, University of Aberdeen; *b* 4 June 1947; *d* of Jack Kingsbury and Neva (née Gartside); *m* 1971, (Binnert) Roy Haites; two *d. Educ:* Somerville House, Brisbane; Univ. of Queensland (BSc; PhD 1974); Univ. of Aberdeen (MB ChB 1980). MRCPath 1996; FRCPE 1997. Lectr in Med. Genetics, Univ. of Aberdeen, 1986–96; Hon. Consultant Clinical Geneticist, 1991–, and Hd of Service in Med. Genetics, 1992–2006, Aberdeen Royal Hosps NHS Trust. Mem., HFEA, 2003–07. FMedSci 2000. *Publication:* (ed jtly) Familial Breast and Ovarian Cancer: genetics, screening and management, 2002. *Address:* Department of Medicine and Therapeutics, University of Aberdeen, Polwarth Building, Foresterhill, Aberdeen AB25 2ZD; 32 Cairn Road, Bieldside, Aberdeen AB15 9AL.

HAITINK, Bernard, Hon. CH 2002; Hon. KBE 1977; Commander, Order of Orange Nassau, 1988; Principal Conductor, Chicago Symphony Orchestra, since 2006; Music Director: Royal Opera House, Covent Garden, 1987–2002; Dresden Staatskapelle, 2002–04; *b* Amsterdam, 4 March 1929. *Educ:* Amsterdam Conservatory. Studied conducting under Felix Hupke, but started his career as a violinist with the Netherlands Radio Philharmonic; in 1954 and 1955 attended annual conductors' course (org. by Netherlands Radio Union) under Ferdinand Leitner; became 2nd Conductor with Radio Union at Hilversum with co-responsibility for 4 radio orchs and conducted the Radio Philharmonic in public during the Holland Fest., in The Hague, 1956; conducted the Concertgebouw Orch., Oct. 1956; then followed guest engagements with this and other orchs in the Netherlands and elsewhere. Debut in USA, with Los Angeles Symph. Orch., 1958; 5 week season with Concertgebouw Orch., 1958–59, and toured Britain with it, 1959; apptd (with Eugen Jochum) as the Orchestra's permanent conductor, Sept. 1961; sole artistic dir and permanent conductor of the orch., 1964–88; toured Japan, USSR, USA and Europe; 1974; début at Royal Opera House, Covent Garden, 1977. London Philharmonic Orchestra: Principal Conductor, Artistic Dir, 1967–79; toured: Japan, 1969; USA, 1970, 1971, 1976; Berlin, 1972; Holland, Germany, Austria, 1973; USSR, 1975. Musical Dir, Glyndebourne Opera, 1978–88; conducted Figaro for rebuilt opera house of Glyndebourne (60th anniversary), 1994; Music Dir, EU Youth Orch., 1994–99; Principal Guest Conductor, Boston Symph. Orch., 1995–2004, now Conductor Emeritus. Appearances at BBC Promenade Concerts and at Tanglewood, Salzburg, Edinburgh and Lucerne Festivals. Hon. RAM 1973. Hon. DMus: Oxford, 1988; Leeds, 1988; RCM, 2004. Bruckner Medal of Honour, 1970; Gold Medal, Internat. Gustav Mahler Soc., 1971; Erasmus Prize, Netherlands, 1991. Chevalier de L'Ordre des Arts et des Lettres,

1972; Officer, Order of the Crown (Belgium), 1977. *Address:* c/o Askonas Holt Ltd, Lincoln House, 300 High Holborn, WC1V 7JH.

HAJDUCKI, Andrew Michael; QC (Scot.) 1994; FSAScot; *b* London, 12 Nov. 1952; *s* of Henryk Hajducki, civil engineer, and Catherine Maxwell Moore, teacher; *m* 1st, 1980, Gayle Shepherd (marr. diss. 1998); two *s* one *d* (and one *s* decd); 2nd, 2002, Katharine Lilli Dodd. *Educ:* Dulwich Coll.; Downing Coll., Cambridge (BA 1975; MA 1979). FSAScot 1990. Called to the Bar, Gray's Inn, 1976; Advocate at Scots Bar, 1979–; Tutor, Edinburgh Univ., 1979–81; reporter, Session Cases, 1980; temp. Sheriff, 1987–99. Safeguarder: Lothian Reg. Children's Panel, 1987–96; Edinburgh and E Lothian Children's Panels, 1996–98; Reporter, Scottish Legal Aid Bd, 1999–; Arbitrator, Motor Insurers' Bureau (Untraced Drivers) scheme, 2000–03. Contested (Scottish L), local govt elections, 1979–84. *Publications:* The North Berwick & Gullane Branch Lines, 1992; Scottish Civic Government Licensing Law, 1994, 2nd edn 2003; The Haddington, Macmerry & Gifford Branch Lines, 1994; The Lauder Light Railway, 1996; Civil Jury Trials, 1998, 2nd edn 2005; (contrib.) Scottish Licensing Handbook, 1999; (contrib.) Renton & Brown's Statutory Offences, 1999; articles in Scots Law Times and other legal, local history and railway jls. *Recreations:* reading, travel, local history and topography, marathon running. *Address:* Advocates' Library, Parliament House, Edinburgh EH1 1RF. *T:* (0131) 226 2881.

HAJI-IOANNOU, Sir Stelios, Kt 2006; Founder, and Chairman, easyGroup, since 1998; *b* 14 Feb. 1967; *s* of Loucas Haji-Ioannou. *Educ:* LSE; City of London Business Sch. (Masters). Joined Troodos Maritime, 1988; Founder: Stelmar Tankers, based in Athens and London, 1992; easyJet Airline Co. Ltd, 1995 (Chm., 1995–2002; non-exec. Dir, 2005–); easyInternetcafé (formerly easyEverything), 1999; easyCar, 2000; easyValue.com, 2000; easyMoney, 2001; easyCinema, 2003; easyBus, 2004; easy4men, 2004; easyPizza, 2004; easyMusic, 2004; easyHotel, 2005; easyMobile, 2005; easyCruise, 2005; easyWatch, 2005; easyVan, 2006, easyOffice, 2007. Founder, Cyprus Marine Envmt Protection Assoc., 1992. *Recreation:* yachting. *Address:* easyGroup, The Rotunda, 42/43 Gloucester Crescent, NW1 7DL. *T:* (020) 7241 9000.

HAJNAL, John, FBA 1966; Professor of Statistics, London School of Economics, 1975–86 (Reader, 1966–75); *b* 26 Nov. 1924; *s* of late Kálmán and Eva Hajnal-Kónyi; *m* 1950, Nina Lande; one *s* three *d*. *Educ:* University Coll. Sch., London; Balliol Coll., Oxford. Employed by: Royal Commission on Population, 1944–48; UN, New York, 1948–51; Office of Population Research, Princeton Univ., 1951–53; Manchester Univ., 1953–57; London Sch. of Economics, 1957–. Vis. Fellow Commoner, Trinity Coll., Cambridge, 1974–75; Vis. Prof., Rockefeller Univ., NY, 1981. Mem. Internat. Statistical Institute. *Publications:* The Student Trap, 1972; papers on demography, statistics, mathematics, etc. *Address:* 95 Hodford Road, NW11 8EH. *T:* (020) 8455 7044.

HAKESLEY-BROWN, Roswyn Ann, CBE 2007; author; consultant in healthcare education, since 1996; *b* 2 Aug. 1945; *d* of Hector Redvers Hakesley; *m* 1968, Alan Graham Brown; one *s* one *d*. *Educ:* SE Staffs Co. Commercial Secondary Sch., Wednesbury; Univ. of Birmingham (Cert Ed); Open Univ. (BA Social Studies); Univ. of Warwick (MPhil Sociol.); Royal Hosp., Wolverhampton (RGN 1966); New Cross Hosp., Wolverhampton (RM 1967); London Univ. (DipN 1970). Nurse Tutor, Queen Elizabeth Hosp., Birmingham, 1973–84; Principal Lectr, Birmingham Poly., later UCE, Birmingham, 1984–96. Florence Nightingale Schol., 1995. Pres., RCN, 2000–02. Mem., Refugee Healthcare Professionals' Steering Gp, DoH, 2002–06; Chm., Refugee Nurses' Task Force, 2003–04. Trustee: ExtraCare Charitable Trust for Older People, 1997–2006; Patients' Assoc., 2007–. FRSH 1990. Member: Soc. of Authors, 1992; Sigma Theta Tau Internat., 1996; Honor Sch. of Nursing. Commng Ed., reviewer and mem., editl bds. *Publications:* Individualised Care: the role of the ward sister, 1989; Portfolios and Profiling for Nurses, 1992, 2nd edn 1995; (with B. Hawkesley) Learning Skills, Studying Styles and Profiling, 1996; chapters, reviews, prefaces and articles. *Recreations:* antique collecting, the National Trust, partying, picnics, having fun, reading, watching films, ballet, plays, listening to classical music. *Address:* c/o Royal College of Nursing, 20 Cavendish Square, W1G 0RN. *Club:* New Cavendish.

HAKIM, Prof. Nadey, MD, PhD; FRCS, FRCSI; Consultant Surgeon, and Surgical Director, Transplant Unit, Hammersmith Hospital, London, since 2005; Max Thorek Professor of Surgery, University of Chicago, since 2008; *b* 9 April 1958; *s* of Subhy Elias A. Hakim and Katy Hakim (*née* Namur); *m* 1992, Nicole Abounader; one *s* three *d*. *Educ:* René Descartes Univ., Paris (MD 1983); University Coll. London (PhD 1991). Fellow in Surgery: Mayo Clinic, Rochester, Minn, 1987–89; Univ. of Minnesota, 1993–95; Consultant Surgeon, 1995–2005 and Surgical Dir, Transplant Unit, 1996–2005, St Mary's Hosp., London. Hon. Consultant Paediatric Transplant Surgeon, Gt Ormond St Hosp., 1996–2001; Hon. Consultant Transplant Surgeon: Royal Free Hosp., 1996–2001; Hammersmith Hosp., 1998–2005; Harefield Hosp., 2000–. Hon. Professor of Surgery: Univ. of São Paulo, 1999; Baskent Univ., Ankara, 2006–; Lima Univ., Peru, 2006–; Lyon Univ., 2007. Ed.-in-Chief, Internat. Surgery, 2001–. First Vice-Pres., 2000–02, Pres., 2004–06, Internat. Coll. Surgeons; Pres., Transplant Sect., RSM, 2001–03. Non-exec. Dir, Medicsight, 2003–. FACS; FICS. Fellow, Internat. Napoleonic Soc., 2008. KStJ 1998; KCJSJ 2007. Hon. Dr: Charles Univ., Prague, 1998; Aden, 2003; Lima, 2007. Laureate, Faculty of Medicine, Paris, 1994; Prize of Excellence in Medicine, Makhzoum Foundn, 1998; J. Wesley Alexander Award for outstanding res. in transplantation, 2007. *Publications:* (jtly) Enteric Physiology of Transplanted Intestine, 1994; (ed) Introduction to Organ Transplantation, 1997; British Symposium Pancreas Transplantation, 1998; Access Surgery, 2001; joint editor: Transplantation Surgery, 2001; Pancreas and Islet Transplantation, 2002; History of Organ and Cell Transplantation, 2003; Complications in Surgery, 2005; Hernias Update, 2005; Composite Tissue Allograft, 2005; Atlas of Transplantation, 2005; Haemostasis in Surgery, 2005; Living Related Transplants, 2005; Morbid Obesity, 2006. *Recreations:* sculpture, clarinet, languages. *Address:* 34 Hocroft Road, NW2 2BL.

See also N. S. Hakim.

HAKIM, Naji Subhy; organist and composer; Professor of Musical Analysis, Conservatoire National de Boulogne-Billancourt, since 1988; Organist, Eglise de la Trinité, Paris, since 1993; *b* Beirut, 31 Oct. 1955; *s* of Subhy Elias A. Hakim and Katy Hakim; *m* 1980, Marie-Bernadette Dufourcet; one *s* one *d*. *Educ:* Ecole Nationale Supérieure des Télécommunications, Paris (Ingénieur); Conservatoire National Supérieur de Musique, Paris. Organist, Basilique du Sacré-Coeur, Paris, 1985–93. Vis. Prof., RAM, 1993–. Mem., Consociatio Internat. Musicae Sacrae, Rome. Dr *hc* Saint-Esprit, Lebanon, 2002. Prix André Caplet, Académie des Beaux-Arts, 1991; first prizes at internat. organ, improvisation and composition competitions. Papal honour, Augustae crucis insigne pro Ecclesia et Pontifice, 2007. *Compositions* include: works for organ, violin, flute, guitar, trumpet, Fantasy for Piano and Orchestra, Concerto for Violin and String Orchestra, four concertos for organ, an oratorio, symphony, Les Noces de l'Agneau, and a symphonic poem, Hymne de l'Univers; three Masses. *Publications:* Guide Pratique d'Analyse Musicale, 1991, 5th edn 1999; Anthologie Musicale pour l'Analyse de la Forme, 1995; The Improvisation Companion, 2000. *Address:* Conservatoire de Boulogne-Billancourt, 2 Rue de la Belle Feuille, 92100 Boulogne-Billancourt, France; *e-mail:* mail@najihakim.com.

See also N. Hakim.

HAKKINEN, Mika; racing driver; *b* Helsinki, 28 Sept. 1968; *m* Erja Honkanen; one *s* one *d*. Driver in: Go-karts, 1974–86 (five times Finnish champion); Formula Ford 1600, 198 (Finnish, Swedish and Nordic champion); Opel Lotus Euroseries Championship, 198 Formula 3, 1989–90 (British champion, 1990) and 2005–; Formula 1: Lotus team 1991–93; McLaren team, 1993–2001. Grand Prix wins: European, 1997; Australia, 199 Brazil, 1998, 1999; Spain, 1998, 1999, 2000; Monaco, 1998; Austria, 1998, 200 Germany, 1998; Luxembourg, 1998; Japan, 1998, 1999; Hungary, 1999, 2000; Canad 1999; Belgium, 2000; USA, 2001; Britain, 2001; Drivers' World Champion, 1998, 1999

HAKTANIR, Korkmaz; Ambassador of Turkey to Egypt, since 2003; *b* 24 Jan. 1943; Handan; one *s* one *d*. *Educ:* Ankara Univ. Joined Ministry of Foreign Affairs, Turke 1965; Dep. Hd of Mission, Perm. Delegn to UN, 1984–88; Dep. and Directorate Ge for Bilateral Political Affairs, 1988–91; Ambassador: to Iran, 1991–94; to Poland, 1994–9 Dep. and Under-Sec., Min. of Foreign Affairs, 1996–2000; Ambassador to UK, 2000–0 *Address:* Turkish Embassy, 25 Sharia Felaki, Cairo, Egypt. *Clubs:* Cavalry and Guard Travellers.

HALBERG, Sir Murray (Gordon), ONZ 2008; Kt 1988; MBE 1961; *b* 7 July 1933; of Raymond Halberg; *m* 1959, Phyllis, *d* of Alex Korff; two *s* one *d*. *Educ:* Avonda College. Started internat. distance running, Commonwealth Games, 195 Commonwealth Gold Medals, 3 miles, 1958, 1962; Olympic Gold Medal, 5,000 metre Rome, 1960; world records at 2 miles and 3 miles, 1961, participant in 4x1 mile record Founder, Halberg Trust (to honour sporting excellence and to support children wi disabilities).

HALBERT, Derek Rowland; His Honour Judge Halbert; a Circuit Judge, since 199 *b* 25 March 1948; *s* of Ronald Halbert and Freda Mabel Halbert (*née* Impett); *m* 197 Heather Rose Ashe; two *d*. *Educ:* King's Sch., Chester; Selwyn Coll., Cambridge (M Law 1974); Open Univ. (BA Technol. 1984). Called to the Bar, Inner Temple, 197 Mem., Wales and Chester Circuit, 1971–; a Recorder, 1991–95; Designated Civil Judg Chester and N Wales, 2003–07; Cheshire, 2007–. *Recreations:* walking, tennis. *Addres* Chester Civil Justice Centre, Trident House, Little St John Street, Chester CH1 1S *Club:* Leander (Henley).

HALDANE, Prof. (Frederick) Duncan (Michael), PhD; FRS 1996; Eugene Higgi Professor of Physics, Princeton University, since 1999 (Professor of Physics, 1990–99); 14 Sept. 1951; *s* of Frederick Paterson Haldane and Ljudmila Haldane (*née* Renko); 1981, Odile Marie Elisabeth Belmont; one *s* one *d*. *Educ:* St Paul's Sch.; Christ's Coll Cambridge (BA 1973; MA; PhD 1978). FInstP. Physicist, Inst. Laue-Langevin, Grenobl 1977–81; Asst Prof., Univ. of Southern California, 1981–85; Mem. Technical Sta AT&T Bell Labs, 1985–87; Prof. of Physics, Univ. of California, San Diego, 1987–9 Fellow: Amer. Phys. Soc. (Oliver E. Buckley Prize in Condensed-Matter Physics, 1993 Amer. Acad. of Arts and Scis; FAAAS 2001. *Publications:* contribs to Jl of Physics, Physic Review and other learned jls. *Address:* 74 Maclean Circle, Princeton, NJ 08540, USA. (609) 9211531.

HALE OF RICHMOND, Baroness *cr* 2004 (Life Peer), of Easby in the County of Nort Yorkshire; **Brenda Marjorie Hale,** DBE 1994; PC 1999; a Lord of Appeal in Ordinar since 2004; *b* 31 Jan. 1945; *d* of Cecil Frederick Hale and Marjorie Hale (*née* Godfrey); 1st, 1968, Anthony John Christopher Hoggett, *qv* (marr. diss. 1992); one *d*; 2nd, 199 Julian Thomas Farrand, *qv*. *Educ:* Richmond High School for Girls, Yorks; Girto College, Cambridge (MA; Hon. Fellow, 1996). University of Manchester: Asst Lectr i Law, 1966; Lectr, 1968; Sen. Lectr, 1976; Reader, 1981; Prof., 1986–89. Vis. Prof., KCI 1990–; Vis. Fellow, Nuffield Coll., Oxford, 1997–2005. Called to the Bar, Gray's In 1969; Barrister, Northern Circuit, 1969–72; Law Comr, 1984–93; QC 1989; a Recorde 1989–94; a Judge of the High Court, Family Div., 1994–99; Family Div. Liaison Judge fo London, 1997–99; a Lord Justice of Appeal, 1999–2004. Legal Mem., Mental Healt Review Tribunal for NW Region, 1979–80; Member: Council on Tribunals, 1980–8 Civil and Family Cttee, Judicial Studies Bd, 1990–94; Human Fertilisation an Embryology Authy, 1990–93. Chm., Mgt Cttee, Royal Courts of Justice Advice Burea 2002–03. Man. Trustee, Nuffield Foundn, 1987–2002; Governor, Centre for Policy o Ageing, 1990–93. President: Nat. Family Mediation, 1994– (Chm., Nat. Famil Conciliation Council, then Nat. Assoc. of Family Mediation and Conciliation Service 1989–93); Assoc. of Women Barristers, 1998–2005; UK Assoc. of Women Judges, 2004– Chancellor, Bristol Univ., 2004–; Visitor, Girton Coll., Cambridge, 2004–. Editor, Jl o Social Welfare Law, 1978–84. Hon. FBA 2004; Hon. FRCPsych 2007. Hon. LL Sheffield, 1989; London Guildhall, 1996; Manchester, 1997; Bristol, 2002; Cambridg 2005; Hull, 2006; KCL, 2007; Oxford, 2007; City, 2007; Reading, 2007; DUniv Esse 2005. *Publications:* Mental Health Law, 1976, 4th edn 1996; Parents and Children, 197 4th edn 1993; (jtly) The Family Law and Society: Cases and Materials, 1983, 6th edn 200 (with S. Atkins) Women and the Law, 1984; Mental Health Law, in Halsbury's Laws England, 4th edn 1992; From the Test Tube to the Coffin: choice and regulation in privat life (Hamlyn Lectures), 1996; many contribs to legal periodicals and other text *Recreations:* domesticity, drama, duplicate bridge. *Address:* House of Lords, SW1A 0PW *Club:* Athenæum.

HALE, David John; His Honour Judge Hale; a Circuit Judge, since 1994; *b* 18 Ju 1948; *s* of John and Kathleen Hale; *m* 1st, 1974, Lynn Thomas (*d* 1998); 2nd, 1999, M Eileen Rafferty (*née* Hawthornthwaite). *Educ:* Calday Grange GS, West Kirby; Liverpo Univ. (LLB (Hons)). Called to the Bar, Gray's Inn, 1970; in practice, 1970–94; Wales an Chester Circuit. *Address:* Warrington Crown Court, Legh Street, Warrington WA1 1UR *T:* (01925) 256700.

HALE, Prof. Geoffrey, PhD; Chief Executive Officer, BioAnalab Ltd, since 200 Visiting Professor, Sir William Dunn School of Pathology, University of Oxford; *b* 2 Sep 1953; *s* of Harold and Christine Hale; *m* 1977, Gillian Hutson; one *s* two *d*. *Edu* Fitzwilliam Coll., Cambridge (MA; PhD 1977). University of Cambridge: Research Ass Dept of Biochem., 1977–80; Sen. Res. Associate, Dept of Pathology, 1980–95; Universit of Oxford: Res. Dir, Therapeutic Antibody Centre, 1995–2007; Reader in Therapeut Immunol., 1998–2000; Prof. of Therapeutic Immunol., 2000–07. *Publications:* numerou contribs on protein chemistry and therapeutic uses of monoclonal antibodies in various jl *Recreations:* playing the piano, watching the garden grow.

HALE, Norman Morgan, CB 1992; Under Secretary, Department of Health (former of Health and Social Security), 1975–93; *b* 28 June 1933; *s* of late Thomas Norman Ha and Ada Emily Hale, Evesham, Worcs; *m* 1965, Sybil Jean (*née* Maton); one *s* one *d*. *Edu* Prince Henry's Grammar Sch., Evesham; St John's Coll., Oxford (MA). Min. of Pension and National Insurance, 1955; Asst Sec., Nat. Assistance Bd, 1966; Min. of Social Security

1966; CSD, 1970–72. Consultant: MoD, 1994; Medicines Control Agency, 1994–2003; National Trust, 1995–97. Churchwarden Emeritus, St Mary the Virgin, Ewell (Churchwarden, 1993–97). Chm. of Govs, Ewell Grove Infant Sch., 1998–2005. *Recreations:* gardening, historical geography. *Address:* 64 Castle Avenue, Ewell, Epsom, Surrey KT17 2PH. *T:* (020) 8393 3507. *Club:* Oxford and Cambridge.

HALE, Raymond, CPFA; County Treasurer, Leicestershire County Council, 1977–97; *b* 4 July 1936; *s* of Tom Raymond Hale and Mary Jane (*née* Higgin); *m* 1959, Ann Elvidge; one *s*. *Educ:* Baines Grammar Sch., Poulton-le-Fylde. Lancashire CC, 1952–54; served Royal Air Force, 1954–56; Lancashire CC, 1956–61; Nottinghamshire CC, 1961–65; Leicestershire CC, 1965–97. Treasurer: Leics Police Authy, 1977–97; Leicester Univ. Med. Sch. and Associated Leics Teaching Hosps Jt Trust (Medisearch), 1988–; Access Cttee for England, 1997–99; Chm., Hind Sisters Homes Charity, 1993–; Treas. and Co. Sec., Leics Guild of Disabled, 1999– (Vice-Chm., 1990–97). *Recreations:* Rugby, cricket, gardening. *Address:* The Stables, Main Street, Nailstone, Nuneaton, Warwicks CV13 0QB. *T:* (01530) 264174.

HALE, Rt Rev. Stephen John; an Assistant Bishop, Diocese of Melbourne (Bishop of the Eastern Region), since 2001; *b* Sydney, 26 June 1955; *s* of William James and Patricia Edna Hale; *m* 1986, Karen (*née* Ellis); one *s* one *d*. *Educ:* Univ. of Sydney (BA 1975; DipEd 1976); Moore Theol Coll., Sydney (BTh 1983; DipArts (Theol.) 1984). Secondary teacher, NSW Dept of Educn, 1977–80; ordained deacon 1985, priest 1985, Sydney; Curate, St Paul's, Castle Hill, NSW, 1985–88; Youth Dir, dio. Melbourne, 1988–96; Vicar, St John's, Diamond Creek, Vic, 1996–2001. Chm. Council, ACCESS ministries (formerly Christian Educn in Schs), 2006– (Mem. Council, 2002); Chm., Anglican Diocesan Schs Commn, Vic, 2002–. Chm., Arrow Leadership Aust. Inc., 1994–; Mem. Bd, Benetas Vic, 2004. Pres., Council, Diamond Creek Primary Sch., 1998–2001. *Recreations:* swimming, surfing, theatre, golf, travel, tennis. *Address:* 8 Stanley Grove, Canterbury, Vic 3126, Australia; Anglican Diocese of Melbourne, 209 Flinders Lane, Melbourne, Vic 3000, Australia. *T:* (3) 96534220, *Fax:* (3) 96534266.

HALES, Antony John, CBE 2008; Chairman: Navy, Army, Air Force Institutes Ltd, since 2001; Workspace Group plc, since 2002; British Waterways, since 2005; *b* 25 May 1948; *s* of Sidney Alfred Hales and Margaret Joan (*née* Wood); *m* 1975, Linda Churchlow; three *s* one *d*. *Educ:* Repton; Bristol Univ. (BSc Chem). With Cadbury Schweppes, 1969–79; Mkting Dir, Joshua Tetley & Son, 1979–83; Managing Director: Halls Oxford & West Brewery Co., 1983–85; Ind Coope-Taylor Walker, 1985–87; Retail Dir, Allied Breweries, 1987; Man. Dir, Ansells, 1987–89; Chief Exec., J. Lyons & Co., 1989–91; Dir, 1989–99, Chief Exec., 1991–99, Allied Lyons, then Allied Domecq; Chairman: Allied Domecq Spirits & Wine Ltd (formerly Hiram Walker Gp), 1992–99; Allied Domecq (formerly Allied Lyons) Retail, 1992–99. Director: Hyder PLC (formerly Welsh Water), 1993–97; Aston Villa plc, 1997–2006; non-executive Director: HSBC (formerly Midland) Bank, 1994–2001; David Halsall Internat., 2000–05; Tempo Hldgs, 2000–01; Reliance Security Gp, 2001–05; SIS Hldgs, 2002–; IPF Gp plc (formerly Provident Financial plc), 2006–. Chm., Nat. Manufg Council, CBI, 1993–95. Hon. Governor, RSC, 2000–.

HALES, Prof. Frederick David, FREng, FIMechE, FIMA; Professor of Surface Transport, Loughborough University of Technology, 1968–93, now Professor Emeritus; *b* 19 Dec. 1930; *s* of Christina Frances and Frederick David Hales; *m* 1955, Pamela Hilary Warner; one *s* one *d* (and one *d* decd). *Educ:* Kingswood Grammar Sch.; Bristol Univ. (BSc Hons Maths, PhD). Sigma Xi. Asst Chief Aerodynamicist, Bristol Aircraft, 1953–60; Group Research Head, MIRA, 1960–67; Vis. Scientist, Stevens Inst., Hoboken, 1967–68; Loughborough University: Hd of Dept of Transport Technology, 1982–89; Pro-Vice-Chancellor, 1984–85, Sen. Pro-Vice-Chancellor, 1985–87; acting Vice-Chancellor, 1987–88; Dean of Engrg, 1989–92. Mem., Tech. Adv. Council to Ford Motor Co., 1985–93; Scientific Visitor to Dept of Transport, 1986–90. FREng (FEng 1990). Hon. DSc Loughborough, 2000. *Publications:* papers on dynamics and vehicle control and stability. *Recreations:* sailing, photography, wine, wood carving, painting. *Address:* 14 Kenilworth Avenue, Loughborough, Leics LE11 4SL. *T:* (01509) 261767. *Clubs:* Rutland Sailing, Clyde Cruising.

HALEY, Prof. Keith Brian, PhD; CMath, FIMA; Professor of Operational Research, Birmingham University, 1968–99, now Emeritus; *b* 17 Nov. 1933; *s* of Arthur Leslie Haley and Gladys Mary Haley; *m* 1960, Diana Elizabeth Mason; one *s*. *Educ:* King Edward VI, Five Ways, Birmingham; Birmingham Univ. (BSc, PhD). FIMA 1970; CompOR 1997. OR Scientist, NCB, 1957–59; Birmingham University: Lectr, 1959–63; Sen. Lectr, 1963–68; Head, Dept of Engrg Prodn, 1981–89; Head, Centre for Ergonomics and OR, 1990–91; Dir, Centre of Applied Gerontology, 1991–95; Hd, Sch. of Manufg and Mech. Engrg, 1994–96. President: ORS, 1982–83 (Mem. Council, 2007–; Chm., Pubns Cttee); IFORS, 1992–94 (Vice-Pres., 1983–86); Editor, Jl of ORS, 1972–80. Governor, Bromsgrove Sch., 1968–. *Publications:* Mathematical Programming for Business and Industry, 1966; Operational Research '75, 1976; Operational Research '78, 1979; Search Theory and Applications, 1980; Applied Operations Research in Fishing, 1981; many articles. *Recreations:* squash, bridge. *Address:* 22 Eymore Close, Selly Oak, Birmingham B29 4LB. *T:* (0121) 475 3331.

HALFORD, Alison Monica; Member (Lab) Delyn, National Assembly for Wales, 1999–2003; *b* 8 May 1940; *d* of William Charles Halford and Yvonne (*née* Bastien). *Educ:* Notre Dame Grammar Sch., Norwich. Metropolitan Police, 1962–83; Asst Chief Constable (most senior post for woman in UK), Merseyside Police, 1983–92. Mem. (Lab) Flintshire CC, 1995–99. Mem., Cons. Party, 2006–; Advr on policing matters to Shadow Sec. of State for Wales, 2006–. Police Long Service and Good Conduct Medal, 1984. Following police tapping her telephone in sex discrimination case, brought action in which Court of Human Rights ruled, 1997, that statutory warning required; resulted in introduction of Regulation of Statutory Powers Act 2000. *Publication:* No Way up the Greasy Pole (autobiog.), 1993; Leaks from the Back Benches (autobiog.), 2007. *Recreations:* birdwatching, serving the community, theatre, painting, bridge, music, charity work.

HALFORD, Prof. Stephen Edgar, PhD; FRS 2004; Professor of Biochemistry, University of Bristol, since 1995; *b* 22 Sept. 1945; *s* of Walter R. Halford and Jessie M. Halford (*née* Edgar). *Educ:* Univ. of Bristol (BSc 1967; PhD 1970). Department of Biochemistry, University of Bristol: Lectr, 1976–89; Reader, 1989–95. *Publications:* numerous scientific papers. *Recreation:* turf. *Address:* Department of Biochemistry, School of Medical Sciences, University of Bristol, University Walk, Bristol BS8 1TD; *e-mail:* s.halford@bristol.ac.uk.

HALFPENNY, Ven. Brian Norman, CB 1990; Team Rector of the Parish of the Ridge, Redditch, 1991–2001; Hon. Assistant Priest, St Lawrence, Bourton-on-the-Water, since 2001; *b* 7 June 1936; *s* of Alfred Ernest Halfpenny and Fanny Doris Halfpenny (*née* Harman); *m* 1961, Hazel Beatrice Cross; three *d*. *Educ:* George Dixon Grammar Sch., Birmingham; St John's Coll., Oxford (BA 1960; MA 1964); Wells Theol Coll. Curate, Melksham, 1962–65; Chaplain, RAF, 1965–91; served RAF Stations Cosford, Wildenrath, Leeming, Hong Kong, Brize Norton, Halton, Akrotiri; RAF Coll., Cranwell, 1982–83; Asst Chaplain-in-Chief, Support Comd, 1983–85, Strike Comd, 1985–88; QHC 1985–91; Chaplain-in-Chief and Archdeacon, RAF, 1988–91; Priest i/c St Clement Danes, 1988–91; Canon and Prebendary, Lincoln Cathedral, 1989–91; permission to officiate, dio. Gloucester, 2001–. Co. Chaplain, RBL, Worcs, 1994–2001. Mem., Gen. Synod of C of E, 1988–91. Vice-Pres., Clergy Orphan Corp., 1988–91. Mem. Council, RAF Benevolent Fund, 1988–91; Visitor, Soldiers' and Airmen's Scripture Readers Assoc., 1988–91. *Recreations:* music, theatre, running. *Address:* 80 Roman Way, Bourton-on-the-Water, Cheltenham, Glos GL54 2EW. *T:* (01451) 821589. *Clubs:* Royal Air Force; Oxford Union Society.

HALIFAX, 3rd Earl of, *cr* 1944; **Charles Edward Peter Neil Wood;** JP; DL; Bt 1784; Viscount Halifax, 1866; Baron Irwin, 1925; Vice Lord-Lieutenant, East Riding of Yorkshire, 1996–2006; *b* 14 March 1944; *s* of 2nd Earl of Halifax and Ruth (*d* 1989), *d* of late Captain Rt Hon. Neil James Archibald Primrose, MC, sometime MP; *S* father, 1980; *m* 1976, Camilla, *d* of late C. F. J. Younger, DSO, TD; one *s* one *d*. *Educ:* Eton; Christ Church, Oxford. Contested (C) Dearne Valley, Feb. and Oct. 1974. High Steward of York Minster, 1988–. JP Wilton Beacon, 1986, Bridlington, 2001; DL Humberside, 1983–96, 2005. *Heir:* *s* Lord Irwin, *qv*. *Address:* Garrowby, York YO41 1QD. *Clubs:* White's, Pratt's.

HALIFAX, Archdeacon of; *see* Freeman, Ven. R. J.

HALL, Prof. Alan, PhD; FRS 1999; Alfred P. Sloan Professor and Chairman, Cell Biology Program, Sloan-Kettering Institute, since 2006; *b* 19 May 1952. *Educ:* Wadham Coll., Oxford (BA 1974); Harvard Univ. (PhD 1977). Post-doctoral Fellow, Univ. of Edinburgh, 1977–79, Zürich Univ., 1979–80; Senior Scientist: Inst. for Cancer Res., 1980–92; UCL, 1992–93; Prof. of Cell and Molecular Biol., Dept of Biochem. and Molecular Biol., 1993–2006, and Dir, MRC Cell Biol. Unit and Lab. for Molecular Cell Biol., 2001–06, UCL. FMedSci 2004. Gairdner Internat. Award, Gairdner Foundn, 2006. *Publications:* contribs to jls. *Address:* Cell Biology Program, Memorial Sloan-Kettering Cancer Center, 1275 York Avenue, New York, NY 10021, USA.

HALL, Rt Rev. (Albert) Peter; Bishop Suffragan, then Area Bishop, of Woolwich, 1984–96; Hon. Assistant Bishop, diocese of Birmingham, since 1997; *b* 2 Sept. 1930; *s* of William Conrad Hall and Bertha Gladys Hall; *m* 1957, Valerie Jill Page; two *s*. *Educ:* Queen Elizabeth Grammar School, Blackburn; St John's Coll., Cambridge (MA Mod. Langs); Ridley College, Cambridge. Deacon 1955, priest 1956; Curate: St Martin, Birmingham, 1955–60; St Mary Magdalene, Avondale, Zimbabwe, 1960; Rector of Avondale, Zimbabwe, 1963–70; Rector of Birmingham, 1970–84. *Recreation:* mountain walking. *Address:* 27 Jacey Road, Birmingham B16 0LL.

HALL, Alexandra Mary H.; *see* Hall Hall.

HALL, Prof. Alfred Rupert, LittD; FBA 1978; Professor of the History of Science and Technology, Imperial College of Science and Technology, University of London, 1963–80; *b* 26 July 1920; *s* of Alfred Dawson Hall and Margaret Ritchie; *m* 1st, 1942, Annie Shore Hughes; two *d*; 2nd, 1959, Marie Boas (*see* M. B. Hall). *Educ:* Alderman Newton's Boy's Sch., Leicester; Christ's Coll., Cambridge (scholar). LittD Cantab 1975. Served in Royal Corps of Signals, 1940–45. 1st cl. Historical Tripos Part II, 1946; Allen Scholar, 1948; Fellow, Christ's Coll., 1949–59, Steward, 1955–59; Curator, Whipple Science Mus., Cambridge and University Lectr, 1950–59. Medical Research Historian, University of Calif, Los Angeles, 1959–60, Prof. of Philosophy, 1960–61; Prof. of History and Logic of Science, Indiana Univ., 1961–63. Royal Society Lectures: Wilkins, 1973; Leeuwenhoek, 1988. FRHistS. Pres., British Soc. for History of Science, 1966–68; Pres., Internat. Acad. of the History of Science, 1977–81; Wellcome Trust: Chm., Adv. Panel on History of Medicine, 1974–80; Co-ordinator, History of Medicine, 1981–85. Co-editor, A History of Technology, 1951–58. Corresp. Mem., Soc. for the History of Technology, 1970. Hon. Laureate, Univ. of Bologna, 1999. Silver Medal, RSA, 1974; (jtly) Sarton Medal, History of Science Soc., 1981. *Publications:* Ballistics in the Seventeenth Century, 1952; The Scientific Revolution, 1954; From Galileo to Newton, 1963; The Cambridge Philosophical Society: a history 1819–1969, 1969; Philosophers at War, 1980; Short History of the Imperial College, 1982; The Revolution in Science 1500–1750, 1983; Henry More: Magic, Religion and Experiment, 1990; with Marie Boas Hall: Unpublished Scientific Papers of Isaac Newton, 1962; Correspondence of Henry Oldenburg, 1965–86; (with Laura Tilling) Correspondence of Isaac Newton, vols 5–7, 1974–77; (ed with Norman Smith) History of Technology, 1976–83; (with B. A. Bembridge) Physic and Philanthropy: a history of the Wellcome Trust, 1986; Isaac Newton: Adventurer in Thought, 1992; Newton, his Friends and his Foes, 1993; All was Light, 1993; Essays on the History of Science and Technology, 1994; Isaac Newton: Eighteenth Century perspectives, 1998; contributor to Isis, Annals of Science, etc. *Address:* 14 Ball Lane, Tackley, Oxford OX5 3AG. *T:* (01869) 331257.

HALL, Prof. Andrew James, PhD; FRCP; Professor of Epidemiology, London School of Hygiene and Tropical Medicine, University of London, since 2000; *b* 9 Feb. 1951. *Educ:* Guy's Hosp. Med. Sch., London Univ. (MB BS 1973); London Sch. of Hygiene and Tropical Medicine (MSc 1982); Southampton Univ. (PhD 1986). MRCP 1976, FRCP 1994; MFPHM 1990; FFPH 1996. Epidemiologist, Internat. Agency for Res. on Cancer, WHO, 1986–90; Sen. Lectr in Epidemiol., 1990–96, Reader in Epidemiol., 1996–2000, LSHTM. Mem., cttees of WHO, MRC and DoH. Member: Bd, PHLS, 1997–2004; Bd, HPA, 2003–; Chm., Jt Cttee on Vaccines and Immunisation, 2006– (Mem., 2002–06). FMedSci 2007. *Publications:* (with D. J. P. Barker) Practical Epidemiology, 2nd edn 1991; numerous contribs to scientific literature. *Recreations:* listening to live music, Asian cooking, running, photography. *Address:* London School of Hygiene and Tropical Medicine, Keppel Street, WC1E 7HT. *T:* (020) 7927 2272; *e-mail:* andy.hall@lshtm.ac.uk.

HALL, Andrew Joseph; QC 2002; *b* 17 Feb. 1953; *s* of James Clement Hall and Jane Hall. *Educ:* Marist Coll.; Univ. of Birmingham (LLB); Inst. of Criminol., Univ. of Sheffield (MA). Admitted solicitor, 1980; in practice as solicitor, 1980–90, Partner, Hodge, Jones & Allen, London, 1982–90; called to the Bar, Gray's Inn, 1991, Bencher, 2005; in practice as barrister, 1991–. Member: Gen. Council of the Bar, 1998–; Criminal Bar Assoc., 1998– (Chm., 2006–07); Bar Human Rights Cttee, 1999–. Mem., Editl Bd, Internat. Jl Evidence and Proof, 1998–. *Publications:* Emergency Procedures Handbook, 1986; Criminal Justice in Crisis, 1993; Confidentiality and Mental Health, 2001; Guide to the Proceeds of Crime Act, 2002. *Recreations:* African skies, Spanish mountains. *Address:* Doughty Street Chambers, 11 Doughty Street, WC1N 2PL. *T:* (020) 7404 1313, *Fax:* (020) 7404 2283; *e-mail:* hallaj@aol.com.

HALL, Andrew Rotely, OBE 1994; HM Diplomatic Service; Ambassador to Nepal, since 2006; *b* 3 May 1950; *s* of David and Sheila Hall; *m* 1973, Kathie Wright; two *d*. *Educ:* Univ. of Keele (BA Hons); Sch. of Oriental and African Studies, Univ. of London (PhD 1982). Joined HM Diplomatic Service, 1980; First Secretary: New Delhi, 1984–87; FCO, 1987–91; Dep. Hd of Mission and Consul, Kathmandu, 1991–95; FCO, 1995–2003; Dep.

High Comr in Eastern India, Kolkata, 2003–06. *Address:* c/o Foreign and Commonwealth Office, King Charles Street, SW1A 2AH. *Club:* Tollygunge (Kolkata).

HALL, Anthony Stewart, (Tony); Director, Central Council for Education and Training in Social Work, 1986–97; *b* 26 Oct. 1945; *s* of Dora Rose Ellen Hall (*née* Rundle) and Albert Hall; *m* 1968, Phoebe Katharine Souster; one *s* one *d*. *Educ:* Gillingham Grammar School; London Sch. of Economics (BScSoc). Research Student, LSE, 1968–71; Lectr in Management and Organisation Studies, Nat. Inst. for Social Work, 1971–73; Lectr in Social Admin, Univ. of Bristol, 1973–78; Dir, Assoc. of British Adoption and Fostering Agencies, 1978–80; Dir and Sec., British Agencies for Adoption and Fostering, 1980–86; Dep. Man. Dir, Retirement Security Ltd, 1997. *Publications:* A Management Game for the Social Service (with J. Algie), 1974; The Point of Entry: a study of client reception in the social services, 1975; (ed) Access to Birth Records: the impact of S.26 of the Children Act 1975, 1980; (with Phoebe Hall) Part-time Social Work, 1980; (series editor) Child Care Policy and Practice, 1982–86; chapters in books and articles in professional and learned jls. *Recreations:* photography, genealogy, watching sport and old films, music, stamps, computers, World of Warcraft. *Address:* 115 Babington Road, Streatham, SW16 6AN. *T:* (020) 8480 9045; *e-mail:* tony_hall@dsl.pipex.com.

HALL, Anthony William, (Tony), CBE 2006; Chief Executive (formerly Executive Director), Royal Opera House, since 2001; *b* 3 March 1951; *s* of late Donald William Hall and of Mary Joyce Hall; *m* 1977, Cynthia Lesley Hall (*née* Davis); one *s* one *d*. *Educ:* King Edward's Sch., Birmingham; Birkenhead Sch., Merseyside; Keble Coll., Oxford (Exhibnr; MA). Joined BBC as News trainee, 1973; Producer: World Tonight, 1976; New York (Radio), 1977; Sen. Producer, World at One, 1978; Output Editor, Newsnight, 1980; Sen. Producer, Six O'Clock News, 1984; Asst Editor, Nine O'Clock News, 1985; Editor: News and Election '87, 1987; News and Current Affairs, BBC TV, 1988–90; Dir, 1990–93, Man. Dir, 1993–96, News and Current Affairs, BBC; Chief Exec., BBC News, 1996–2001. Non-executive Director: HM Customs and Excise, 2002–05; Channel 4, 2005–. Mem., King's Healthcare Expert Reference Gp, 1995–96. Mem., Steering Cttee, Regeneration through Heritage, BITC, 1999–2000; Chairman: Strategic Skills Council, Creative and Cultural Industries, 2004–; Music and Dance Adv. Gp, DFES, 2004–; Mem., Olympics Cultural Adv. Bd, DCMS, 2006–. Chm., Theatre Royal, Stratford, 2001– (Dir, 1999–). Mem., Mgt Cttee, Clore Leadership Prog., 2005–. Non-exec. Dir, Univ. for Industry, 2003–06. Hon. Vis. Fellow, City Univ., 1999–2000. Mem. Council, Brunel Univ., 1999–2003. Patron, Newsworld, 1999; Gov. for Media, World Econ. Forum, 2000. Mem. Cttee, Race for Opportunity, 1999–2001 (as Race Champion led BBC's campaign on diversity and race issues). Liveryman, Painter Stainers' Co., 1989–. FRTS 1994 (Chm., 1998–2000); FRSA 1997. *Publications:* King Coal: a history of the miners, 1981; Nuclear Politics, 1984; articles in various periodicals. *Recreations:* architecture, opera, ballet, walking, gardening, my family. *Address:* c/o Royal Opera House, Covent Garden, WC2E 9DD. *T:* (020) 7212 9112.

HALL, Sir Basil (Brodribb), KCB 1977 (CB 1974); MC 1945; TD 1952; Member, European Commission of Human Rights, 1985–93; Legal Adviser, Broadcasting Complaints Commission, 1981–93; *b* 2 Jan. 1918; *s* of late Alfred Brodribb Hall and of Elsie Hilda Hall, Woking, Surrey; *m* 1955, Jean Stafford Gowland; two *s* one *d*. *Educ:* Merchant Taylors' Sch. Articled Clerk with Gibson & Weldon, Solicitors, 1935–39; admitted Solicitor, 1942. Served War of 1939–45: Trooper, Inns of Court Regt, 1939; 2nd Lieut, 12th Royal Lancers, 1940; Captain, 27th Lancers, 1941; Major, 27th Lancers, 1942. Legal Asst, Treasury Solicitor's Dept, 1946; Sen. Legal Asst, 1951; Asst Treasury Solicitor, 1958; Principal Asst Solicitor, 1968; Dep. Treasury Solicitor, 1972; HM Procurator Gen. and Treasury Solicitor, 1975–80. Chm., Civil Service Appeal Bd, 1981–84 (Dep. Chm., 1980–81). Mem. Council, Nat. Army Museum, 1981–92. *Recreations:* military history, travel. *Address:* Woodlands, 16 Danes Way, Oxshott, Surrey KT22 0LX. *T:* (01372) 842032. *Clubs:* Athenæum, Cavalry and Guards.

HALL, Rev. Bernard, SJ; Spiritual Director, Infirmary of the Roman Delegation, Society of Jesus (Director, 2001); *b* 17 Oct. 1921. *Educ:* St Michael's Coll., Leeds; Heythrop Coll., Oxford. LicPhil, STL. Captain RA, 1941–46. Entered Society of Jesus, 1946; ordained priest, 1955; Provincial of the English Province, Society of Jesus, 1970–76; Rector, Collegio San Roberto Bellarmino, Rome, 1976–82 and 1989–94; English Asst to Father General, SJ, Rome, 1982–88; Superior, Jesuit Hse of Writers, Rome, 1994–2001. *Address:* Residenza di San Pietro Canisio, via dei Penitenzieri 20, 00193 Rome, Italy.

HALL, Betty, CBE 1977; Regional Nursing Officer, West Midlands Regional Health Authority, 1974–81; *b* 6 June 1921; *d* of John Hall and Jane (*née* Massey), Eagley, Lancs. *Educ:* Bolton Sch.; Royal Infirm., Edinburgh (RGN); Radcliffe Infirm., Oxford and St Mary's Hosp., Manchester (SCM); Royal Coll. of Nursing (RNT). Nursed tuberculous patients from concentration camps, Rollier Clinic, Leysin, 1948–49; Ward Sister, Salford Royal Hosp., 1949–51; Sister Tutor, Royal Masonic Hosp., London, 1952–54; Principal Tutor, St Luke's Hosp., Bradford, 1954–61 (Mem. Leeds Area Nurse Trng Cttee); King Edward's Hosp. Fund Admin. Staff Coll., 1961–62; Work Study Officer to United Bristol Hosps, 1961–64; Asst Nursing Officer to Birmingham Regional Hosp. Bd, 1964–65, Regional Nursing Officer, 1966–81. Mem., Exec. Cttee, Grange-over-Sands Abbeyfield Soc., 1982–93. Hon. Sec., Grange-over-Sands RUKBA, 1987–2001. *Recreations:* reading, tapestry making, cricket. *Address:* Chailey, Ash Mount Road, Grange-over-Sands, Cumbria LA11 6BX. *Club:* Naval and Military.

HALL, Brian; *see* Hall, F. B.

HALL, Prof. Bronwyn Hughes, PhD; Professor of Economics, University of California at Berkeley, since 1999; Professor of Economics of Technology, University of Maastricht, since 2005; *b* 1 March 1945; *d* of Richard Roberts Hughes and Elizabeth Flandreau Hughes; *m* 1966, Robert Ernest Hall (marr. diss. 1983); one *s* one *d*. *Educ:* Wellesley Coll., Mass (BA 1966); Stanford Univ. (PhD 1988); MA Oxon 1997. Programmer: Lawrence Berkeley Lab., Berkeley, Calif, 1963–66; Lyman Lab. of Physics, Harvard Univ., 1966–67; Lawrence Berkeley Lab., 1967–70; Sen. Programmer, Harvard Inst. of Econ. Res., 1971–77; National Bureau of Economic Research, Cambridge, Massachusetts: Research Economist, 1977–88; Res. Associate, 1988–; Asst. Prof., 1987–94, Assoc. Prof., 1994–99, Univ. of Calif, Berkeley; Internat. Res. Associate, Inst. for Fiscal Studies, London, 1995–; Prof. of Econs, and Fellow of Nuffield Coll., Oxford Univ., 1996–2001. Sloan Dissertation Fellow, 1985–86; Hoover Instn Nat. Fellow, 1992–93; Professorial Res. Fellow, UNU-MERIT, Netherlands, 2005–. Mem., Sci. Technol. and Econ. Policy Bd, Nat. Res. Council, Washington, 1999–2005. Owner and Chief Exec. Officer, TSP Internat., Palo Alto, Calif, 1977–. Mem., Sigma Xi Soc., 1966. Associate Editor: Econs of Innovation and New Technol., 1994– (Mem. Edtl Bd, 1989–94); Jl of Economic Behavior and Organization, 2001–07; Mem. Adv. Bd, Internat. Finance jl, 1997–2005; Mem., Editl Bd, Res. Policy, 2006–. Mem. Internat. Adv. Bd, New Econ. Sch., Moscow, 1997–. *Publications:* TSP 4.3 User's Manual, 1977, rev. edn, version 5.0, 2005; TSP 4.3 Reference Manual, 1977, rev. edn, version 5.0, 2005; contrib. articles to Amer. Econ. Rev., Econometrica, Jl Industrial Econs, Jl Econometrics, Brookings Papers on Econ. Activity, Econs of Innovation and New Technol., Rand Jl of Econs, Industrial and Corp. Change. *Recreations:* travel, walking, opera, painting. *Address:* Department of Economics University of California at Berkeley, Berkeley, CA 94720, USA. *T:* (510) 6423878.

HALL, Christopher Myles; Editor of The Countryman, 1981–96; *b* 21 July 1932; *s* of Gilbert and Muriel Hall; *m* 1957, Jennifer Bevan Keech (marr. diss. 1980); one *s* one *d* lives with Kate Ashbrook, *qv*. *Educ:* Berkhamsted Sch.; New Coll., Oxford (2nd cl. Hons PPE); Kellogg Coll., Oxford (MSt English Local History, with distinction, 1996) Reporter and Feature-writer, Daily Express, 1955–58; Sub-editor and Leader-writer Daily Mirror, 1958–61; Feature-writer and Leader-writer, Daily Herald/Sun, 1961–65 Special Asst (Information): to Minister of Overseas Develt, 1965–66; to Minister of Transport, 1966–68; Chief Information Officer, MoT, 1968; Ramblers' Association: Sec. 1969–74; Mem. Exec. Cttee, 1982–84; Vice-Chm., 1984–87; Chm., 1987–90; Pres. 1990–93; Vice-Pres., 1993–; Chm., Oxfordshire Area, 1984–87, 1994–97, 2002–07 Footpaths and Publicity Sec., 1997–98; Dir, Council for Protection of Rural England 1974–80. Pres., The Holiday Fellowship, 1974–77; Vice-Chm., S Reg. Council of Sport and Recreation, 1976–82; Member: DoT Cttee of Inquiry into Operators' Licensing 1977–79; Common Land Forum, 1984–86; Countryside Access Forum, Oxon CC 2003–06; Hon. Sec., Chiltern Soc., 1965–68; Chm., Oxfordshire Local Hist. Assoc. 2001–. Columnist, Rambling Today, 1993–96; Editor, Oxfordshire Local History, 1997– *Publications:* How to Run a Pressure Group, 1974; (jtly) The Countryside We Want, 1988 The Countryman's Yesterday, 1989; Scenes from The Countryman, 1992; contributions to: Motorways in London, 1969; No Through Road, 1975; The Countryman's Britain 1976; Book of British Villages, 1980; Sunday Times Book of the Countryside, 1981 Walker's Britain, 1982; Britain on Backroads, 1985; Making Tracks, 1985; (with John Tookey) The Cotswolds, 1990; pamphlets; contrib. to Oxford DNB, Vole, The Countryman, New Statesman, New Scientist, The Geographical Magazine, Country Living, The Guardian and various jls. *Recreations:* local history, walking in the countryside *Address:* Telfer's Cottage, Turville, Henley-on-Thames RG9 6QL. *T:* (01491) 638396. *Club:* Oxford and Cambridge.

HALL, David, CBE 1983; QPM 1977; consultant in security and personnel management Chief Constable of Humberside Police, 1976–91; *b* 29 Dec. 1930; *s* of Arthur Thomas Hall and Dorothy May Charman; *m* 1952, Molly Patricia Knight; two *s*. *Educ:* Richmond and East Sheen Grammar School for Boys. Joined Metropolitan Police and rose through ranks from PC to Chief Supt, 1950–68; Staff Officer to Chief Inspector of Constabulary Col Sir Eric St Johnson, 1968; Asst Chief Constable, 1970, Dep. Chief Constable, 1976 Staffordshire Police. Vice-Pres., Assoc. of Chief Police Officers of England, Wales and NI 1982–83, Pres. 1983–84. CCMI (CBIM 1988). Freeman, City of London, 1987. OStJ 1980. *Recreations:* gardening, walking, playing the piano. *Address:* Fairlands, 1 Copper Beech Close, West Leys Park, Kemp Road, Swanland, North Ferriby HU14 3LR.

HALL, David John, CMG 2001; Deputy Chief Executive and Director, Central Services Group, British Trade International, 1999–2001; *b* 15 July 1942; *s* of late Alexander G. Hall and Molly Hall, Aberdeen; *m* 1965, Elizabeth Adams; one *s* two *d*. *Educ:* Trinity Coll. Glenalmond; Pembroke Coll., Oxford (BA Mod. Langs). FO, 1964–67; Bahrain 1967–69; Dubai, 1969–70; FCO, 1970–74; Bonn, 1974–76; joined Dept of Trade, later DTI, 1976; Asst Sec., 1982; Counsellor (Trade and Envmt), Washington, 1988; Under-Sec., 1991; Dir, Projects Export Promotion, 1991–97; Dep. Dir-Gen., Export Promotion, DTI, and Dir, Overseas Trade, FCO, 1997–99. *Recreations:* music, gardening, dogs.

HALL, Prof. Sir David (Michael Baldock), Kt 2003; FRCP, FRCPCH; Hon. Professor of Community Paediatrics, University of Cape Town, since 2007; Professor of Community Paediatrics, University of Sheffield, 1993–2005, now Emeritus; President, Royal College of Paediatrics and Child Health, 2000–03; *b* 4 Aug. 1945; *s* of Ronald Hall and Ethel Gwen Hall (*née* Baldock); *m* 1966, Susan M. Luck; two *d*. *Educ:* Reigate Grammar Sch.; St George's Hosp., London Univ. (MB BS; BSc; Univ. Gold Medal). FRCP 1986; FRCPCH 1996. SMO, Baragwanath Hosp., Johannesburg, 1973–76; Sen Registrar, Charing Cross Hosp., 1976–78; Consultant Paediatrician, St George's Hosp., 1978–93. Hon. FRCPE 2003. *Publications:* Health for All Children, 1989, 4th edn 2002; Child with a Disability, 1996; contrib. numerous papers to jls, etc. *Recreations:* horses, travel. *Address:* Storrs House Farm, Storrs Lane, Stannington, Sheffield S6 6GY; *e-mail:* d.hall@sheffield.ac.uk.

HALL, Col David Stevenson, CBE 1993; TD 1971 (and bars 1977, 1983, 1989); Chairman: Meadowcroft Management Ltd, since 1985; NHS Logistics Agency, 2000–02; *b* 29 March 1938; *s* of late Robert Hall and Maude Hall; *m* 1962, Marion Esmé Blundstone; one *s* one *d*. *Educ:* Scarborough Coll. Nat. Service, RAOC, 1956–58. Man. Dir, UDS Tailoring Ltd, 1979–81; Chm. and Man. Dir, Collier Holdings plc, 1982–85. Non-executive Director: Sharp and Law plc, 1989–90; Toye plc, 1994–95. Chairman: United Leeds Teaching Hosps NHS Trust, 1995–98; NHS Supplies, 1998–2000. Trustee, RAOC Charitable Trust, 1993–2000. RAOC (TA), 1958–93; Col, 1985–89; ADC, 1986–91; TA Col Logistics MoD/UKLF, 1989–93; Hon. Col, RAOC Specialist Units, 1991–93; Combat Services Support Group, RLC(V), 1995–2000. Freeman, City of London, 1993. *Recreations:* cricket, reading. *Address:* Courtways, Potterton Court, Barwick in Elmet, Leeds LS15 4HP. *T:* (0113) 281 3587. *Clubs:* Army and Navy (Vice-Chm., 2003–05), MCC.

HALL, Duncan; Managing Director, Duncan Hall Associates Ltd, since 1998; *b* 2 Sept. 1947; *s* of Leslie and Joan Elizabeth Hall; *m* 1970, Jane Elizabeth Menzies (marr. diss. 2003); two *s* one *d*. *Educ:* Acklam Hall Grammar Sch.; LLB Hons. Articled Clerk and Senior Legal Assistant, Wellingborough UDC, 1970–74; Corby District Council: PA to Chief Exec., 1974–75; Asst Chief Exec., 1975–78; Housing and Property Controller, 1978–79; Chief Exec., 1980–87; Chief Exec., Teesside Develt Corp., 1987–98. CCMI; FRSA. *Recreations:* reading, travel, music, theatre, shooting. *Address:* Duncan Hall Associates Ltd, Number One, South Green, Staindrop, Darlington, Co. Durham DL2 3LD. *T:* (01833) 660077, *Fax:* (01833) 660088.

HALL, Edward Peter; theatre director; *b* 27 Nov. 1966; *s* of Sir Peter Reginald Frederick Hall, *qv* and Jacqueline Hall; *m* 2000, Issy van Randwyck; one *d*. *Educ:* Bedales Sch.; Univ. of Leeds; Mountview Theatre Sch. Associate, NT, 2004–; Associate Director: Watermill Th. Co., 2006–; Old Vic, 2006–; Founder and Artistic Dir, Propeller Th. Co., 1997–. Watermill Theatre productions: Othello, 1995; Propeller Theatre Co. productions include: Henry V, 1997; The Comedy of Errors, 1998; Twelfth Night, 1999; Rose Rage (adaptation of Shakespeare's Henry VI trilogy), 2001, transf. Th. Royal, Haymarket, 2002; A Midsummer Night's Dream, transf. Comedy Th., 2003; The Winter's Tale, 2005; The Taming of the Shrew, and Twelfth Night, 2006, transf. Old Vic, 2007; For Services Rendered, 2007; other productions include: Two Gentlemen of Verona, Henry V, 2000; Julius Caesar, RSC, 2001; Edmond, 2003, A Funny Thing Happened on the Way to the Forum, 2004, Once in a Lifetime, 2005, NT; A Streetcar Named Desire, Roundabout Th., NY, 2005; The Deep Blue Sea, Vaudeville, 2008; (co-dir) Tantalus, Denver, 2000, UK tour and Barbican, 2001; The Constant Wife, Apollo, 2002; Macbeth, Albery, 2002; Calico, Duke of York's, 2004. Director: Into Exile, Dear Exile, Radio 4; episodes of TV series, Miss Marple, Trial and Retribution, and Kingdom. *Publication:* Rose Rage, 2001;

(ed) A Midsummer Night's Dream, 2003. *Address:* c/o Rebecca Blond Associates, 69A Kings Road, SW3 4NX.

HALL, Sir Ernest, Kt 1993; OBE 1986; DL; pianist and composer, since 1954; property developer, since 1971; Chairman, Dean Clough Business, Arts and Education Centre, since 1983; *b* 19 March 1930; *s* of Ernest and Mary Elizabeth Hall; *m* 1st, 1951, June (*née* Annable) (*d* 1994); two *s* two *d*; 2nd, 1975, Sarah (*née* Wellby); one *s*. *Educ:* Bolton County Grammar Sch.; Royal Manchester Coll. of Music (ARMCM (teacher and performer) 1950–51; Royal Patron's Fund Prize for Composition, 1951). Textile manufr, 1961–71. Dep. Chm., Eureka! Children's Museum, 1989–2000; Mem., Arts Council of England (formerly of GB), 1990–97; Chm., Yorks and Humberside Arts Bd, 1991–97; Pres., Yorks Business in the Arts, 1990–; Vice-Pres., RSA, 1994–99. Trustee: Yorkshire Sculpture Park, 1989–2003; Henry Moore Foundn, 1999–2002. Chancellor, Univ. of Huddersfield, 1996–2003. DL W Yorks, 1991. Hon. Fellow: Huddersfield Polytechnic, 1989; Leeds Polytechnic, 1991; Bolton Inst., 1994. DUniv: York, 1986; Leeds Metropolitan, 1996; Hon. DLitt Bradford, 1990; Hon. DArt Bristol Poly., 1991; Hon. LLD Leeds, 1996. Envmt Award, Business and Industry Panel, RSA, 1988; Guildhall Helping Hand, Nat. Fedn of Self-Employed and Small Businesses, 1989; Special Free Enterprise Award, Aims of Industry, 1989; Best Practice Award, BURA, 1992; Lifetime Achievement Award, Inst. for Social Inventions, 1992; Albert Medal, RSA, 1994; Montblanc de la Culture UK Award, Fondation d'Enterprise, France, 1996; Goodman Award, ABSA, 1997. *Recreations:* gardening, art collecting, theatre, languages. *Address:* Dean Clough, Halifax HX3 5AX. *T:* (01422) 250250, *Fax:* (01422) 255250.

HALL, Fiona Jane; Member (Lib Dem) North East Region, European Parliament, since 2004; *b* 15 July 1955; *d* of Edward and Dorothy Cutts; *m* 1975, Michael Hall; two *d*. *Educ:* St Hugh's Coll., Oxford (MA Mod. Langs 1976); Oxford Poly. (PGCE). Teacher in self-help sch., Naledi, Gaborone, Botswana, 1977–79; pt-time, supply teacher, tutor, 1986–95; Asst to Newcastle City Councillors, 1994–97; Press Officer to Lembit Öpik, MP and Richard Livsey, MP, 1997–99; Researcher and Organiser to Rt Hon. Alan Beith, MP, 1999–2004. *Address:* The School House, Whittingham, Alnwick, Northumberland NE66 4UP. *T:* (01665) 574383; *e-mail:* fionahall@europarl.europa.eu.

HALL, (Frederick) Brian; Master (Care and Protection), Supreme Court of Judicature of Northern Ireland, 1986–2006; *b* 2 Oct. 1934; *s* of Frederick Hall and late Mary Hall (*née* Kernahan); *m* 1965, Isobel Frances Deirdre Boyce; two *d*. *Educ:* Coleraine Academical Inst.; Queen's Univ. Belfast (LLB). Admitted Solicitor, NI, 1958; Legal Adviser, Min. of Home Affairs, 1972; Asst Solicitor, NI Office, 1973; Dep. Dir, NI Court Service, 1979; Official Solicitor to Supreme Court, NI, 1982. Mem., Sec. of State's Cttee on County Courts and Magistrates' Courts, 1974. *Recreations:* golf, travel, reading. *Address:* c/o Royal Courts of Justice, PO Box 410, Chichester Street, Belfast BT1 3JF. *T:* (028) 9023 5111. *Club:* Royal Belfast Golf.

HALL, Sir (Frederick) John (Frank), 3rd Bt *cr* 1923; *b* 14 Aug. 1931; *er s* of Sir Frederick Henry Hall, 2nd Bt, and Olwen Irene (*d* 1993), *yr d* of late Alderman Frank Collis, Stokeville, Stoke-on-Trent, and Deganwy, Llandudno; *S* father, 1949; *m* 1st, 1956, Felicity Anne (marr. diss. 1960), *d* of late Edward Rivers-Fletcher, Norwich, and of Mrs L. R. Galloway; 2nd, 1961, Patricia Ann Atkinson (marr. diss. 1967); two *d*; re-married, 1967, 1st wife, Felicity Anne Hall; two *d*. *Educ:* Bryanston Sch. Personnel Manager, Universal Pattern & Precision Engineering Co. Ltd, 1955–59; Personnel Officer, The Nestlé Co. Ltd, 1959–63; Personnel Man., SC Johnson & Sons Ltd, 1963–65; UK Head Office Trng and Mgt Develt Man., The Nestlé Co. Ltd, 1965–67; Gp Personnel Man., Findus Ltd, 1967–69; Sen. Man., McLintock Mann & Whinney Murray, 1969–76; Dir, Thomson McLintock Associates, 1976–87; founder Chm., KPMG Career Consultancy Services, 1983–93; Partner, KPMG Peat Marwick, 1987–93, retd. Dir, Roffey Park Inst., 1978–90 (Vice Chm., 1983–85; Chm., 1985–87). *Recreations:* music, collecting antique gramophone records, magic (Mem., The Magic Circle). *Heir: b* David Christopher Hall [*b* 30 Dec. 1937; *m* 1st, 1962, Irene (marr. diss. 1987), *d* of William Duncan, Aberdeen; one *s* one *d*; 2nd, 1991, Annie Madelaine Renée Olivier, adopted *d* of late Bottemanne Raould]. *Address:* Carradale, 29 Embercourt Road, Thames Ditton, Surrey KT7 0LH. *T:* (020) 8398 2801.

HALL, Gareth John; Director, Department for the Economy and Transport (formerly Enterprise, Innovation and Networks), Welsh Assembly Government, since 2006; *b* 26 June 1956; *s* of late Trevor John Carenville Hall and Margaret Gwendoline Hall (*née* Jones); *m* 1986, Moira Llewellyn. *Educ:* Brecon Boys' Grammar Sch.; Bristol Poly. (BSc 1977); Univ. of Reading (MSc 1981); Cardiff Univ. (MBA 1989); JSDC. MRICS 1980. Valuation Office, SE London, 1977–80; Defence Land Agent, Wales, MoD, 1981–91; Welsh Development Agency: Sen. Manager on land reclamation, property and regeneration projects, 1991–97; Regl Dir, SW Wales, Strategy Develt, 1997–2004; Chief Exec., 2004–06. Vis. Lectr, Sch. of City and Regl Planning, Cardiff Univ., 1995–. *Recreations:* exploring Sustrans cycle routes, ride-on lawn mowing. *Address:* Department for the Economy and Transport, Welsh Assembly Government, Cathays Park, Cardiff CF10 3NQ. *T:* (029) 2082 6646; *e-mail:* gareth.hall@wales.gsi.gov.uk. *Club:* Cameo (Cardiff).

HALL, Prof. George Martin, PhD, DSc; FRCA; Foundation Professor of Anaesthesia, St George's Hospital Medical School, since 1992; *b* 14 May 1944; *s* of George Vincent Hall and Dora Hortensia Hall; *m* 1964, Marion Edith Burgin; one *d*. *Educ:* University Coll. Hosp. Med. Sch. (MB BS 1967; PhD 1976); DSc London, 1999. FRCA 1971. Royal Postgraduate Medical School: Sen. Lectr in Anaesthesia, 1977–85; Reader, 1985–89; Prof. of Clinical Anaesthesia, 1989–92. Hunterian Prof., RCS, 1983–84. *Publications:* How to Write a Paper, 1994, 2nd edn 1998; How to Survive in Anaesthesia, 1997; Short Practice of Anaesthesia, 1997; Diabetes: emergency and hospital management, 1999; Perioperative Care of the Eye Patient, 2000; How to Present at Meetings, 2001; res. papers on anaesthesia and physiology. *Recreations:* running, cycling, supporting Staffordshire. *Address:* Department of Anaesthesia and Intensive Care Medicine, St George's Hospital Medical School, SW17 0RE. *T:* (020) 8725 2615. *Club:* Farmers'.

HALL, Rev. Canon George Rumney, CVO 2003 (LVO 1999); Rector of the Sandringham Group of Parishes, and Domestic Chaplain to the Queen, 1987–2003; Chaplain to the Queen, 1989–2007; *b* 7 Nov. 1937; *s* of John Hall; *m* 1965, Diana Lesley Brunning; one *s* one *d*. *Educ:* Brasted Place, Kent; Westcott House, Cambridge. Deacon 1962, priest 1963; Assistant Curate: St Philip's, Camberwell, 1962–65; Holy Trinity, Waltham Cross, 1965–67; Rector of Buckenham, Hassingham, Strumpshaw, dio. Norwich, 1967–74; Chaplain: St Andrew's Psychiatric Hosp., Norwich, 1967–72; HM Prison, Norwich, 1972–74; Vicar of Wymondham, 1974–87; RD of Humbleyard, 1986–87; Hon. Canon, Norwich Cathedral, 1987–2003, now Canon Emeritus; RD of Heacham and Rising, 1989–2001. Founder Mem., Wymondham Branch of Mind Day Centre; Mem. Bd, Cotman Housing Assoc., Norwich. *Recreations:* walking, reading, theatre, music. *Address:* Town Farm Cottage, Lynn Road, Bircham, King's Lynn, Norfolk PE31 6RJ. *T:* (01485) 576134.

HALL, Sir Graham (Joseph), Kt 2003; CEng, FIET; Chairman, Leeds Bradford International Airport, since 2007; *b* 12 Oct. 1943; *s* of Herbert and Phyllis Hall; *m* 1963, Pamela Wilmot; one *s* one *d*. *Educ:* Doncaster Technical Coll.; Rotherham Coll. of Tech. (DipEE 1967); Blackburn Coll. of Tech. CEng 1977; FIET (FIEE 1988). Commercial Dir, 1984–89, Divl Dir, Energy Supply, 1989–91, Yorkshire Electricity Bd; Gp Exec. Dir, 1991–97, Gp Ops Dir, 1997, Chief Exec., 1998–2001, Yorkshire Electricity Gp plc. Chm., Regl Develt Agency for Yorkshire and the Humber (Yorkshire Forward), 1998–2003. Mem. Ct Dirs, Bank of England, 2001–07. Chm., Yorks and the Humber Regl Council, CBI, 1997–99. CCMI 2002 (FIMgt 1987). Hon. DEng Bradford, 1999. *Recreations:* gardening, golf.

HALL, Prof. Henry Edgar, FRS 1982; Emeritus Professor of Physics, University of Manchester, since 1995; *b* 1928; *s* of John Ainger Hall; *m* 1962, Patricia Anne Broadbent; two *s* one *d*. *Educ:* Latymer Upper Sch., Hammersmith; Emmanuel Coll., Cambridge. BA 1952; PhD 1956. At Royal Society Mond Laboratory, Cambridge, 1952–58; Senior Student, Royal Commission for the Exhibition of 1851, 1955–57; Research Fellow of Emmanuel Coll., 1955–58; Lecturer in Physics, 1958–61, Prof. of Physics, 1961–95, Univ. of Manchester. Visiting Professor: Univ. of Western Australia, 1964; Univ. of Oregon, 1967–68; Cornell Univ., 1974, 1982–83; Univ. of Tokyo, 1985. Simon Memorial Prize (with W. F. Vinen), 1963; Guthrie Medal and Prize, 2004. *Publications:* Solid State Physics, 1974; papers in scientific journals. *Recreation:* mountain walking. *Address:* The Schuster Laboratory, The University, Manchester M13 9PL.

HALL, Air Vice-Marshal Hubert Desmond, CB 1979; CMG 2003; CBE 1972; AFC 1963; FRAeS; RAF retd; *b* 3 June 1925; *s* of Charles William and Violet Victoria Kate Hall; *m* 1951, Mavis Dorothea (*née* Hopkins). *Educ:* Portsmouth Municipal Coll. Commissioned RAF, 1945; RAF Coll., Cranwell QFI, 1951–55; Flt Comdr, 9 Sqdn, 1955–56; 232 OCU Gaydon, Sqdn Ldr, Medium Bomber Force; Instructor, Wing Comdr 1962; 3 Group Headquarters (Training), 1963–65; Air Warfare Coll., 1965; commanded No 57 Sqdn (Victors), 1966–68; Gp Captain Nuclear Operations SHAPE HQ, 1968–71; comd RAF Waddington, 1971–73; Overseas Coll. of Defence Studies India, 1974; MoD: Director (Air Cdre) of Establishments, RAF, 1975–77; Air Comdr Malta, 1977–79; Air Vice-Marshal 1979; Defence Advr, Canberra, 1980–82. Pres., ACT, Australian-Britain Soc., 1993–. Mem., Lord's Taverners, ACT, 1989– (Foundg Chm., 1985–88). Mem., St John Council, ACT, 1983–. KStJ 1992. Queen's Commendation, 1957. *Recreations:* gardening, reading. *Clubs:* Royal Air Force; Commonwealth (Canberra).

HALL, Sir Iain (Robert), Kt 2002; education consultant; Headteacher, Parrs Wood Technology College, Manchester, 1991–2003; *b* 13 Feb. 1943; *s* of Edward and Annie Hall; three *s* from former *m*. *Educ:* Liverpool Collegiate Sch.; Liverpool Univ. (BSc). Physics teacher, Liverpool Inst., 1965–72; Hd of Sci., Brookfield Sch., Kirkby, 1972–78; Dep. Headteacher, Glenburn High Sch., Lancs, 1978–82; Headteacher, Breckfield Sch., Liverpool, 1982–91. Mem., Gov. Council, Nat. Coll. of Sch. Leadership, 2002; Associate Dir, Specialist Schs and Academies Trust, 2002–; Dir of Leadership, Future Leaders, 2006–. *Publications:* Nuffield Physics, 1985; contribs to various educnl mags. *Recreations:* cooking, supporter of Liverpool FC. *Address: e-mail:* IainRHall@btconnect.com.

HALL, James Douglas Ellis; Chief Executive, Identity and Passport Service, since 2006; Registrar General for England and Wales, since 2008; *b* 9 Oct. 1954; *s* of (William) Douglas Hall and (Helen) Elizabeth Hall; *m* 1980, Carol; two *d*. *Educ:* Edinburgh Acad.; Univ. of Edinburgh (MA Hons Pol Studies). Accenture, 1976–2006: UK Man. Partner, 1994–2000; Global Man. Partner, Technol. and Systems Integration, 2001–05. Commn on Public Policy and British Business, 1996–97. Trustee, Save Britain's Heritage. *Recreations:* rod and gun. *Address:* Identity and Passport Service, Globe House, 89 Eccleston Square, SW1V 1PH. *T:* (020) 7901 2747, *Fax:* (020) 7901 2425.

HALL, Prof. James Snowdon, CBE 1976; Professor of Agriculture, Glasgow University, and Principal, West of Scotland Agricultural College, 1966–80; *b* 28 Jan. 1919; *s* of Thomas Blackburn Hall and Mary Milburn Hall; *m* 1942, Mary Smith; one *s* one *d*. *Educ:* Univ. of Durham (BSc Hons). FRAgS, FIBiol. Asst Technical Adviser, Northumberland War Agric. Exec. Commn, 1941–44; Lectr in Agriculture, Univ. of Newcastle upon Tyne, 1944–54; Principal, Cumbria Coll. of Agriculture and Forestry, 1954–66. *Address:* 26 Earls Way, Doonfoot, Ayr KA7 4HE. *T:* (01292) 441162.

HALL, Janice Elizabeth, (Jan), OBE 1996; Partner, JCA Group, since 2005; *b* 1 June 1957; *d* of John Brian Hall and Jean Hall; *m* 1996, Dr David Costain; one *s*. *Educ:* St Anne's Coll., Oxford (MA Hons). Mktg Manager, ICI, 1979–83; Chm. and Chief Exec., Coley Porter Bell, 1983–93; Eur. Chief Exec., GGT Gp, 1994–97; Partner, Spencer Stuart, 1997–2005. Sen. non-exec. Dir, First Choice Holidays, 1994–2003. Advr on CS Appointments. Hon. Prof., Warwick Business Sch., 1995– (Mem., Bd, 1993–). Mem. Council, IoD, 1991–2005. *Address:* 37 St John's Wood Road, NW8 8RA. *T:* (020) 7286 5740.

HALL, Jean Morag; *see* Rankine, J. M.

HALL, Joan Valerie, CBE 1990; Member, Central Transport Consultative Committee, 1981–86; *b* 31 Aug. 1935; *d* of late Robert Percy Hall and Winifred Emily Umbers. *Educ:* Queen Margaret's Sch., Escrick, York; Ashridge House of Citizenship. Contested (C) Barnsley, 1964 and 1966. MP (C) Keighley, 1970–Feb. 1974; PPS to Minister of State for Agriculture, Fisheries and Food, 1972–74. Vice-Chm., Greater London Young Conservatives, 1964. Chm., Sudan Studies Soc. of UK, 1989–92. Mem. Council, Univ. of Buckingham (formerly University Coll. Buckingham), 1977–. *Address:* 7 Greenland, High Hoyland, Barnsley, South Yorks S75 4AZ. *T:* (01226) 380117.

HALL, Sir John; *see* Hall, Sir F. J. F.

HALL, John; *see* Hall, W. J.

HALL, Sir John, Kt 1991; DL; Chairman: Cameron Hall Developments Ltd, 1973–93; Newcastle United Football Club, 1992–97; a Director, Bank of England, 1996–98; *b* 21 March 1933; *m* Mae; one *s* one *d*. *Educ:* Bedlington Grammar Sch. Chartered surveyor. Developed MetroCentre (shopping and leisure complex), Gateshead, 1985. Mem., Millennium Commn, 1994–2000. Gordon Grand Fellow, Yale Univ., 1991. DL Co. Durham, 2007. Hon. DCL: Newcastle upon Tyne, 1988; Durham, 1995. NE Business Man of the Year, 1987. *Address:* Wynyard Hall, Billingham, Cleveland TS22 5NF.

HALL, Ven. John Barrie; Archdeacon of Salop, since 1998; *b* 27 May 1941; *s* of Arthur Cyril Hall and Beatrice Hall (*née* Clark); *m* 1963, Kay Deakin; three *s*. *Educ:* Salisbury and Wells Theol Coll. Self-employed in garage and caravan sales until 1982; ordained deacon 1984, priest 1985; Curate, St Edward, Cheddleton, 1984–88; Vicar, Rocester, then Rocester and Croxden with Hollington, 1988–98. Mem., Gen. Synod of C of E, 2002–. Hon. Canon of Lichfield Cathedral, 1999. Lichfield Diocese: Chairman: Redundant Church Users' Cttee, 2001–; Child Protection Cttee, 2002–; Pastoral Cttee, 2006–; Vice Chm., Bd of Finance, 2007–. Mem., C of E Inter-Diocesan Finance Forum, 2007–. Pres.,

Adv. Cttee, Telford Christian Council, 2007–. Chm., Shropshire Historical Churches Trust, 1998–. *Recreations:* reading, a little walking, most sports (now watching only), cooking. *Address:* Tong Vicarage, Shifnal, Shropshire TF11 8PW. *T:* (01902) 372622.

HALL, Sir John (Bernard), 3rd Bt *cr* 1919; Chairman, The Nikko Bank (UK) plc, 1992–95 (Managing Director, 1990–92); *b* 20 March 1932; *s* of Lieut-Col Sir Douglas Montgomery Bernard Hall, DSO, 2nd Bt, and Ina Nancie Walton (Nancie Lady Hall), *d* of late Col John Edward Mellor, CB (she *m* 2nd, 1962, Col Peter J. Bradford, DSO, MC, TD, who *d* 1990; she *d* 1998); *S* father, 1962; *m* 1957, Delia Mary (*d* 1997), *d* of late Lieut-Col J. A. Innes, DSO; one *s* two *d*; *m* 1998, Diana Joan Tower, *d* of late Surg.-Comdr E. R. Sorley and *widow* of Peter Ravenshear. *Educ:* Eton; Trinity Coll., Oxford (MA). FCIB 1976. Lieut, Royal Fusiliers (RARO). J. Henry Schroder Wagg & Co. Ltd, formerly J. Henry Schröder & Co., 1955–73 (Dir, 1967–73); Director: The Antofagasta (Chili) and Bolivia Rly Co. Ltd, 1967–73; Bank of America International, 1974–82; Man. Dir, European Brazilian Bank, subseq. Eurobraz, 1983–89 (Dir, 1976–89); a Vice-Pres., Bank of America NT & SA, 1982–90; Chm., Assoc. of British Consortium Banks, 1985–86. Chm., Anglo-Colombian Soc., 1978–81. Mem., St Alban's Diocesan Synod and Bd of Finance, 1992–2000. Pres., Metropolitan Soc. for the Blind, 2004–. FRGS 1988; FRSA 1989. Mem., Lord Mayor of London's No 1 Cttee, 1993–95; Liveryman: Clothworkers' Co., 1957 (Mem., Court of Assts, 1987–97, Asst Emeritus, 1997; Master, 1999–2000); Guild of Internat. Bankers, 1997. Mem. Court, Univ. of Leeds, 1994–2000. *Recreations:* travel, fishing. *Heir: s* David Bernard Hall, *b* 12 May 1961. *Address:* Deanery Lodge, Church Walk, Hadleigh, Ipswich, Suffolk IP7 5ED. *T:* (01473) 828966. *Clubs:* Boodle's, Lansdowne.

HALL, Sir John Douglas Hoste, 15th Bt *cr* 1687 (NS), of Dunglass, Haddingtonshire; *b* 7 Jan. 1945; *s* of Sir Douglas Basil Hall, 14th Bt, KCMG and Rachel Marion Gartside-Tippinge; *S* father, 2004; *m* 1972, Angela Margaret, *d* of George Keys; two *s*. *Educ:* Dover Coll.; Gonville and Caius Coll., Cambridge (BA); Southampton Univ. (Cert Ed). Vice-Principal (Academic), Dartington Coll. of Art, 1990–2002. *Publications: (poems):* Between the Cities, 1968; Days, 1972; Meaning Insomnia, 1978; Malo-lactic Ferment, 1978; Couch Grass, 1978; Else Here: selected poems, 1999; Couldn't You?, 2007; The Week's Bad Groan, 2008; (*novel*) Apricot Pages, 2005. *Heir: s* Thomas James Hall, *b* 10 Dec. 1975.

HALL, Dr John Lewis; Senior Fellow, National Institute of Standards and Technology, USA, Emeritus since 2004; *b* Aug. 1934; *s* of John Ernest Hall and Elizabeth Rae Hall (*née* Long); *m* 1958, Marilyn Charlene Robinson; two *s* one *d*. *Educ:* Carnegie-Mellon Univ., Pittsburgh (BS 1956, MS 1958; PhD Physics 1961). National Bureau of Standards, later National Institute of Standards and Technology, USA: Postdoctoral Res. Associate, Washington, 1961–62; Physicist, Boulder, Colo, 1962–75; Sen. Scientist, 1975–2004; Lectr, Dept of Physics, Univ. of Colorado, 1977–. Adv. Prof., E China Normal Univ., Shanghai, 1995. Mem., NAS. (Jtly) Nobel Prize for Physics, 2005. Légion d'Honneur (France), 2004. *Publications:* (ed) Laser Spectroscopy III, 1977; papers in jls; 11 US patents. *Recreations:* music, electronic hobbies, reading, travel. *Address:* JILA, University of Colorado, Boulder, CO 80309–0440, USA. *T:* (303) 4927843, *Fax:* (303) 4925235; *e-mail:* jhall@jila.colorado.edu.

HALL, John Peirs; Chief Executive (formerly Managing Director), Brewin Dolphin Holdings plc, 1987–2007; *b* 26 June 1940; *s* of Robert Noel Hall and Doreen Cecelia Hall (*née* Russell); *m* 1965, Sarah Gillian Page; three *s* (and one *s* decd). *Educ:* Stowe. Reid Hurst-Brown, Stockbrokers, 1959–65; joined Wontner Renwick & Francis, 1965, which became Wontner Dolphin & Francis, 1970, then Brewin Dolphin, 1974; Partner, 1967; Chm., Mgt Cttee, 1980. Chm., Assoc. of Private Client Investment Managers and Stockbrokers, 2006–. Freeman, City of London, 1970; Mem., Ct of Assts, Co. of Merchant Taylors, 1993– (Master, 2005–06). *Recreations:* sailing, golf, breeding British White cattle, parrot fancying, Suffolk horse ploughing. *Address:* Chalkhouse Green Farm, Kidmore End, near Reading RG4 9AZ. *T:* (0118) 972 3631. *Clubs:* City of London; Royal Yacht Squadron, Island Sailing; Huntercombe Golf.

HALL, Very Rev. John Robert; Dean of Westminster, since 2006; Dean of the Order of the Bath, since 2006; *b* 13 March 1949; *e s* of late Ronald John Hall, FCIB, FCIS and Katie Margaret Brock Hall (*née* Walker). *Educ:* St Dunstan's Coll.; St Chad's Coll., Durham (BA Hons Theol.); Cuddesdon Theol Coll. Head of RE, Malet Lambert High Sch., Hull, 1971–73; ordained deacon 1975, priest 1976; Curate, St John the Divine, Kennington, 1975–78; Priest-in-charge, All Saints', S Wimbledon, 1978–84; Vicar, St Peter's, Streatham, 1984–92; Dir of Educn, Dio. Blackburn, 1992–98; Residentiary Canon, Blackburn Cathedral, 1994–98, Canon Emeritus, 2000 (Hon. Canon, 1992–94, 1998–2000); Gen. Sec., C of E Bd of Educn, subseq. Chief Educn Officer, C of E, and Gen. Sec., Nat. Soc. for Promoting Religious Educn, 1998–2006; Hon. Curate, St Alban's, S Norwood, 2003–06. Examng Chaplain to Bp of Southwark, 1988–92. Member: Gen. Synod of C of E, 1984–92; C of E Bd of Educn, 1991–92; Lancs Educn Cttee, 1992–98; Council, National Soc., 1997–98; Gen. Teaching Council, 2000–04. Chm., Fedn of Catholic Priests, 1991–94. Mem. Council, Sch. of St Mary and St Anne, Abbots Bromley, 1992–2002; Governor: St Martin's Coll., Lancaster, 1992–98; St Dunstan's Coll., 2002–; Chm. Govs, Westminster Sch., 2006–; Member, Governing Body: Urban Learning Foundn, 1998–2002; Canterbury Christ Church Univ. (formerly University Coll.), 1999–2006 (Hon. Fellow, 2007). Trustee: St Gabriel's Trust, 1998–2006; 2011 Trust. Fellow, Woodard Corp., 1992–. FRSA 2002. Hon. DD Roehampton, 2007; Hon. DTheol Chester, 2008. *Publications:* (contrib.) Distinctiveness in Church Schools, 1998; (jtly) Governing and Managing Church Schools, 2nd edn 2003; contrib. Church Times, TES, Parly Brief, Guardian, C of E Newspaper, Tablet, etc. *Recreations:* music, British political history. *Address:* The Deanery, Westminster Abbey, SW1P 3PA. *Club:* Athenæum.

HALL, Dr John Tristan Dalton; University Librarian, University of Durham, since 1989; *b* 28 Oct. 1945; *m* 1970, Inge Lise Lindqvist; one *s* two *d*. *Educ:* Lady Lumley's Sch., Pickering; Univ. of Manchester (BA 1968; PhD 1977); MA Cantab 1989. Asst Librarian, John Rylands Univ. Library of Manchester, 1971–78; Sub-Librarian (Special Collections), Edinburgh Univ. Library, 1978–86; Dep. Librarian, Cambridge Univ. Library, 1986–89; Fellow, Darwin Coll., Cambridge, 1987–89. *Publications:* Manuscript Treasures in Edinburgh University Library: an album of illustrations, 1980; The Tounis College: an anthology of Edinburgh University student journals 1823–1923, 1985; articles and reviews in learned jls. *Recreations:* music, pottery, gardening.

HALL, Jonathan David D.; *see* Durham Hall.

HALL, Maj.-Gen. Jonathan Michael Francis Cooper, CB 1998; OBE 1987; Lieutenant Governor, Royal Hospital, Chelsea, 1997–2005; *b* 10 Aug. 1944; *s* of Charles Richard Hall and Rosemary Hall (*née* Beckwith); *m* 1968, Sarah Linda Hudson; two *d*. *Educ:* Taunton Sch.; RMA Sandhurst. Commissioned 3rd Carabiniers, 1965; Staff Coll., 1977; commanded Royal Scots Dragoon Guards, 1984–86 and 12th Armd Bde, 1988–90; Higher Command and Staff Course, 1988; Mem., RCDS, 1991; Dep. Mil. Sec., MoD(A), 1992–93; DRAC, 1994; GOC Scotland, and Gov., Edinburgh Castle, 1995–97. Colonel Commandant: RAVC, 1995–2001; Scottish Div., 1995–97; Col, Royal Scots Drago Guards, 1998–2003. Mem., HM Body Guard of Hon. Corps of Gentlemen-at-Ar 1999–. Trustee: RACWM Benevolent Fund, 1998–; VC and GC Assoc., 2004–; Ar Mus Ogilby Trust, 2004–. Mem., Ethical Review Process, Imperial Coll., London, 200 Designated Mem., Ethics and Welfare Gp, BVA, 2007–. Managing Consultant, Comp Fundraising Ltd, 2006–; Consultant, Third Millennium Information Ltd, 2006–. Me Sherborne Abbey PCC and Deanery Synod, 2006–. Chm. and Mem. Council, Order St John, Dorset, 2008–. Gov., Taunton Sch., 2007–. FCMI (FIMgt 1997). Hon. Associ Mem., BVA, 1996. Freeman, City of London, 2006; Liveryman, Farriers' Co., 200 OStJ 1998. *Recreations:* country, music, travel. *Address:* Orchard House, Nether Compt Sherborne, Dorset DT9 4QA. *Clubs:* Cavalry and Guards (Mem. Adv. Council; Trust 2007–), MCC, Pratt's; Woodroffe's.

HALL, Judith Myfanwy Sarah, (Mrs A. Becker); Editor, BBC Homes & Antiq magazine, 1994–2002; Editor-in-Chief, BBC Good Homes magazine, 1997–2002; *b* July 1947; *d* of late Norman Alfred Hall and of Vera May Hall; *m* 1984, Andrew Beck one *s*. *Educ:* Eltham Hill Grammar Sch. for Girls; Warwick Univ. Editl Asst, Everyma Liby, 1968–71; Asst Fiction Ed., Woman's Weekly, 1971–74; Fiction Ed., 1974– Features Ed., 1976–80, Woman's Jl; Deputy Ed., Woman's World, 1980–82; Dep. E 1982–84, Ed., 1984–87, Woman's Realm; Editor, Woman's Weekly, 1987–92; freelan journalist and TV script editor, 1992–94. Editor of Year, Specialist Interest Magazin BSME, 1995. *Recreations:* local history, modern fiction, theatre, cinema, gardening.

HALL, Julian; His Honour Judge Julian Hall; a Circuit Judge, since 1986; Reside Judge, Oxford Combined Court Centre, since 2002; authorised to sit in the Court Appeal (Criminal Division), since 2007; *b* 13 Jan. 1939; *s* of late Dr Stephen Hall, FR and Dr Mary Hall, Boarstall Tower, Bucks; *m* 1st, 1968, M. Rosalind Perry (marr. d 1988); one *s* one *d*; 2nd, 1989, Ingrid Cecilia, *er d* of late Rev. Canon Ronald Lunt, M *Educ:* Eton (Scholar); Christ Church, Oxford (Scholar; MA); Trinity Coll., Dublin (LL ARCM (flute). Industrial Chemist, Shell Internat. Chemical Co., 1961–63. Called to t Bar, Gray's Inn, 1966, Bencher, 2002; in practice in Common Law Chambers Northern Circuit, Manchester, 1966–86; Standing Prosecuting Counsel to Inla Revenue, Northern Circuit, 1985–86; a Recorder, 1982–86; Resident Judg Northampton Combined Court Centre, 2000–02; Hon. Recorder of Oxford, 200 Tutor judge, Judicial Studies Bd, 1989–93. Chm., Northants Family Mediation Servic 1995–2000; Pres., Mental Health Rev. Tribunals, 1997–. *Recreation:* making music, orchestras, choirs and at home. *Address:* c/o Oxford Crown Court, St Aldate's, Oxfo OX1 1TL. *T:* (01865) 264200.

See also C. E. Henderson.

HALL, Sir Kenneth Octavius, ON 2006; GCMG 2007; OJ 2004; PhD; Governo General of Jamaica, since 2006; *b* Lucea, Hanover, Jamaica; *m* Rheima Holding. *Ed* Univ. of W Indies, Mona (BA 1966); Univ. of W Indies, Trinidad (Dip. Internat. Rel 1967); Queen's Univ., Ontario (MA Hist. 1967; PhD 1971). Teacher, Rusea's High Sc Jamaica, 1961–63; Admin. Officer, Min. of Agric., Govt of Jamaica, 1966; teaching as Div. of Social Scis, Univ. of WI, St Augustine, Trinidad and Tobago, 1966–67; Instructo Hist. Dept, Queen's Univ., Ontario, 1969–71; Asst Prof. of Hist., SUNY, 1971–73; Lec Hist. Dept, Univ. of WI, Mona, Jamaica, 1972–73; Faculty Res. Associate, Foreign ar Comparative Studies, Syracuse Univ., NY, 1973–84; State University of New Yor Oswego: Associate Prof. of Hist., 1973–84; Asst Provost, 1982–84; Prof. of His 1984–86; Central Administration, Albany: Asst Vice-Chancellor for Acad. Prog 1984–88; Asst Provost for Acad. Progs, 1988–89; Vice Pres. for Acad. Affairs and Dean Faculty, SUNY at Old Westbury, 1990–94; Principal, Univ. of WI, Mona, Jamaic 1996–2006. Caribbean Community Secretariat, Guyana: Chief, Res. and Conf. Sectio 1975–76; Dir, Gen. Services and Admin, 1976–77; Dep. Sec.-Gen., 1994–96. *Publication* (ed) Education and the Black Experience, 1979; The Group of 77: strengthening negotiating capacity, 1979; Imperial Proconsul: Sir Hercules Robinson and South Afric 1881 to 1889, 1980; (ed) Makers of the Twentieth Century, 1982; (with D. Ben Globalisation: a calculus of inequality, perspectives from the South, 2000; (with D. Ben Contending with Destiny: the Caribbean in the 21st Century, 2000; CARICOM: uni in adversity, 2000; The Caribbean Community: beyond survival, 2001; Reinventi CARICOM: the road to a new integration, 2002; Integrate or Perish!: perspectives leaders of the integration movement 1963–1999, 1999, 2nd edn 2003; (with D. Ben Caribbean Imperatives: regional governance and integrated development, 2005; Rex N Rex Nettleford, selected speeches, 2006; (with D. Benn) Production Integration i CARICOM: from theory to action, 2006; (with Rheima Holding) Tourism: the driver change in the Jamaican economy?, 2006; (with Myrtle Chuck-A-Sang): Integratio CARICOM's key to prosperity, 2006; CARICOM Single Market and Economy: genes and prognosis, 2007; CARICOM Single Market and Economy: challenges, benefi prospects, 2007; Confronting Challenges, Maximising Opportunities: a new diploma for market access, 2007; Intervention Border and Maritime Issues in CARICOM, 200 The Caribbean Integration Process: a people-centred approach, 2007; contrib. chapters i books and articles in jls and papers on history and current issues in the Caribbean. *Addres* Office of the Governor-General, King's House, Hope Road, Kingston 10, Jamaica, We Indies. *T:* 9276424, *Fax:* 9786025; *e-mail:* kingshouse@kingshouse.gov.jm.

HALL, Prof. Laurance David, PhD; FRS(Can) 1982; CChem, FRSC, FCIC; (first Herchel Smith Professor of Medicinal Chemistry, University of Cambridge, 1984–200 and Fellow, Emmanuel College, since 1987; *b* 18 March 1938; *s* of Daniel William Ha and Elsie Ivy Hall; *m* 1962, Winifred Margaret (*née* Golding); twin *s* two *d*. *Educ:* Leyto County High Sch.; Bristol Univ. (BSc 1959; PhD 1962); MA Cantab 1990. FCIC 197 FRSC 1985. Post-doctoral Fellow, Ottawa Univ., 1962–63; Dept of Chemistry, Univ. British Columbia: Instr II, 1963–64; Asst Prof., 1964–69; Associate Prof., 1969–73; Prof 1973–84. Alfred P. Sloan Foundn Res. Fellow, 1971–73; Canada Council Killam Res Fellow, 1982–84. Lederle Prof., RSM, 1984; Vis. Professor: Univ. of NSW, 1967; Univ of Cape Town, 1974; Northwestern Univ., Evanston, Ill, 1982. Lectures include: Va Cleave, Univ. of Saskatchewan, Regina, 1983; Cecil Green, Galveston Univ., Texas 1983; Brotherton, Leeds Univ., 1985; Philip Morris, Richmond Univ., Va, 1985; Scott Cambridge Univ., 1986; Larmor, Cambridge Philosophical Soc., 1986; C. B. Purves McGill Univ., 1987; Eduard Faber Med. Physics, Univ. of Chicago, 1990; Friday Evening Discourse, Royal Instn, London, 1991, 1997; Merck Frosst, Montreal, 1994; public, 1995 Henderson Trust, 1996, RSChem; Horizon, Cleveland Clinic Foundn, Ohio, 1995 Harry Hallam Meml, Swansea, 1998. Fellow, Cambridge Philosophical Soc. Hon. DS Bristol, 2000. Jacob Bielly Faculty Res. Prize, Univ. of BC, 1974; Tate and Lyle Awar for Carbohydrate Chemistry, Chemical Soc., 1974; Merck, Sharpe and Dohme Lectur Award, Chemical Inst. of Canada, 1975; Corday Morgan Medal and Prize, Chemical Soc. 1976; Barringer Award, Spectroscopy Soc. of Canada, 1981; Interdisciplinary Award RSC, 1988; Chemical Analysis and Instrumentation Award, RSC, 1990. *Publications:* ove 530 research pubns. *Recreations:* music, travel, research. *Address:* Emmanuel College, S Andrew's Street, Cambridge CB2 3AP; *e-mail:* ldh11@cam.ac.uk.

HALL, Sir Laurence Charles B.; *see* Brodie-Hall.

HALL, Lee; dramatist; *b* 20 Sept. 1966; *s* of Peter and Sylvia Hall; *m* 2003, Beeban Kidron. *Educ:* Benfield Comprehensive Sch., Newcastle; Fitzwilliam Coll., Cambridge (BA English Lit.). Writer in Residence: Live Th., Newcastle upon Tyne, 1997–98; RSC, 1998–99. *Plays:* I Luv You Jimmy Spud (radio), 1995 (Sony Award); Spoonface Steinberg (radio), 1996; The Student Prince (TV), 1996; Mr Puntila and his Man Matti (trans.), Almeida, 1997; Cooking with Elvis, Live Th., transf. Whitehall, 2000; A Servant to Two Masters, RSC at Young Vic, 2000; The Good Hope, NT, 2001; Two's Company/Child of the Snow, Bristol Old Vic, 2005; Billy Elliot—the Musical, Victoria Palace, 2005; *films:* Billy Elliot, 2000; Gabriel and Me, 2001. *Publications:* Spoonface Steinberg and other plays, 1996; Cooking with Elvis, 1999; A Servant to Two Masters (new adaptation), 2000; Pinocchio (new adaptation), 2000; Billy Elliot (screenplay), 2001; The Good Hope (new adaptation), 2001; Plays 1, 2002; Plays 2, 2003. *Recreations:* cooking, reading, sleeping. *Address:* c/o Judy Daish Associates, 2 St Charles Place, W10 6EG.

HALL, Margaret Dorothy, OBE 1973; RDI 1974; Head of Design, British Museum, 1964–2001; *b* 22 Jan. 1936; *d* of Thomas Robson Hall and Millicent (*née* Britton). *Educ:* Bromley County Grammar Sch.; Bromley College of Art; Royal College of Art (DesRCA). Design Assistant: Casson, Condor & Partners, 1960–61; Westwood Piet & Partners, 1961–63; Dennis Lennon & Partners, 1963–64; British Museum, 1964–2001: exhibitions designed include: Masterpieces of Glass, 1968; Museum of Mankind, 1970; Treasures of Tutankhamun, 1972; Nomad and City, 1976; Captain Cook in the South Seas, 1979. Designer, Manuscripts and Men, National Portrait Gallery, 1969. Chm., Gp of Designers/Interpreters in Museums, 1978–81; Mem. Council, RSA, 1984–89. FCSD (FSIAD 1975–90; MSIAD 1968) (Chm., SIAD Salaried Designers Cttee, 1979–81). Chm., Wynkyn de Worde Soc., 1982. Governor, Ravensbourne College of Art, 1973–78. FRSA 1974; FMA 1983. *Publication:* On Display: a grammar of museum exhibition design, 1987. *Club:* Double Crown (Pres., 1998).

HALL, Dr Marie Boas, FBA 1994; Reader in History of Science and Technology, University of London, 1964–80, Reader Emeritus, since 1980; *b* 18 Oct. 1919; *d* of Ralph Philip Boas and Louise (*née* Schutz); *m* 1959, Alfred Rupert Hall, *qv. Educ:* Radcliffe Coll. (AB 1940; MA 1942); Cornell Univ. (PhD 1949). Assistant Professor of History: Univ. of Mass, 1949–52; Brandeis Univ., 1952–57; Associate Prof., UCLA, 1957–61; Prof. of Hist. and Logic of Sci., Indiana Univ., 1961–63; Sen. Lectr, Imperial Coll., Univ. of London, 1963–64. Guggenheim Fellow, 1955–56. Mem., Liby Cttee, Royal Soc., 1983–93. Fellow, Amer. Acad. of Arts and Scis, 1955–63. Mem., Académie internat. d'histoire des sciences, 1960; Sec., Hist. of Science Soc., 1953–57. Pfizer Award, 1959, (jtly) Sarton Medal, 1981, Hist. of Science Soc. *Publications:* The Establishment of the Mechanical Philosophy, 1952, 2nd edn 1981; Robert Boyle and Seventeenth Century Chemistry, 1958; The Scientific Renaissance 1450–1630, 1962, repr. 1994; Robert Boyle on Natural Philosophy, 1965; All Scientists Now: the Royal Society in the Nineteenth Century, 1984; Promoting Experimental Learning: experiment and the Royal Society 1660–1727, 1991; The Library and Archives of the Royal Society, 1992; Henry Oldenburg: shaping the Royal Society, 2002; with A. R. Hall: Unpublished Scientific Papers of Isaac Newton, 1962; A Brief History of Science, 1962, 2nd edn 1988; The Correspondence of Henry Oldenburg, 13 vols, 1965–86; contribs to major history of science jls. *Address:* 14 Ball Lane, Tackley, via Kidlington, Oxon OX5 3AG. *T:* (01869) 331257.

HALL, Melanie Ruth; QC 2002; *b* 29 Dec. 1959; adopted *d* of George and Ruth Payne; *m* 1991, Martin Harold Hall; one *s* two *d. Educ:* Durham Univ. (BA). Called to the Bar, Inner Temple, 1982. Non-exec. Dir, Home Housing Ltd, 1995–99. *Address:* Monckton Chambers, Gray's Inn, WC1R 5NR. *T:* (020) 7405 7211, *Fax:* (020) 7405 2084.

HALL, Dr Michael George, FRS 1993; scientific consultant, since 1991; *b* 16 Oct. 1931; *s* of George Albert Victor Hall and Mabel Hall (*née* Gittins); *m* 1964, Merete Blatz; one *s* one *d. Educ:* Sydney Grammar Sch.; Univ. of Sydney (BSc, BE, MEngSc, PhD). Research in Fluid Dynamics at Aerodynamics Dept, RAE, 1958–91, retired 1991; sabbatical at Dept of Mechanics, Johns Hopkins Univ., 1966–67. Founder-Director, Hall C. F. D. Ltd, 1991–2003. *Publications:* contribs on fluid dynamics to sci. and tech. jls. *Recreations:* ski-ing, walking, do-it-yourself. *Address:* 8 Dene Lane, Farnham, Surrey GU10 3PW. *T:* (01252) 793283.

HALL, Michael Harold Webster, FSA; Editor, Apollo, since 2004; *b* 6 July 1957; *s* of Dr L. W. Hall and late Barbara Hall. *Educ:* Cambridgeshire High Sch. for Boys; Trinity Hall, Cambridge (BA 1980); Birkbeck Coll., London (MA). Ed., Thames and Hudson, 1982–89; Country Life: architectural writer, 1989–94; architectural ed., 1994–98; Dep. Ed., 1998–2004. FSA 2003. Trustee: Emery Walker Trust, 1999–; Victorian Soc., 2000–06; Marc Fitch Fund, 2007–. *Publications:* The English Country House: from the archives of Country Life, 1994, repr. 2001; Waddesdon Manor, 2002; (ed) Gothic Architecture and its Meanings 1550–1830, 2002; contrib. articles to Country Life, Architectural Hist., Jl Soc. of Architectural Historians, Furniture Hist., Jl British Inst. of Organ Studies, etc. *Address:* c/o Apollo, 22 Old Queen Street, SW1H 9HP. *T:* (020) 7961 0106, *Fax:* (020) 7961 0115; *e-mail:* michael.hall@apollomag.com.

HALL, Prof. Michael Robert Pritchard, FRCP, FRCPE; Professor of Geriatric Medicine, University of Southampton, 1970–87, now Emeritus; Hon. Consultant Physician, Southampton University Hospitals, 1970–87; *b* 13 May 1922; *s* of Augustus Henry Hall, MC and Elizabeth Jane Lord; *m* 1947, Joan Jardine, (Eileen), *d* of Dr John McCartney; two *d. Educ:* Shrewsbury Sch.; Worcester Coll., Oxford (MA, BM, BCh). FRCP 1970; FRCPE 1971. Served War, Indian Army, 1941–46 (Temp. Captain). Consultant Physician, Newcastle upon Tyne Gen. Hosp., 1962–70; Hon. Lecturer in Medicine: Univ. of Durham, 1962–63; Univ. of Newcastle upon Tyne, 1963–70. Auckland Savings Bank Vis. Prof., Univ. of Auckland, NZ, 1974; Vis. Lecturer: Dalhousie Univ., NS, 1979; (Tayside Health Bd), Univ. of Dundee, 1981; Examr, Dip. of Geriatric Medicine, RCP, 1985–91. Chairman: British Soc. for Res. on Ageing, 1976–79; Assoc. of Professors of Geriatric Medicine, 1985–86; European Cttee, Sandoz Foundn of Gerontological Research, 1986–90 (Mem., 1990–92); Member: DHSS Cttee for Review of Medicines, 1976–82; Fitness and Health Adv. Gp to Sports Council, 1977–90; Southampton and SW Hants CHC, 1997–2001 (Chm., 1999–2001); Governing Body and Exec. Cttee, Age Concern (England), 1975–77 and 1980–83; Council, Internat. Assoc. of Gerontology, 1981–85; President: Tissue Viability Soc., 1983–84; Bath Res. Inst. for Care of the Elderly, 1987–94; Chm., Age Concern (Hants), 1992–95; Life Vice-Pres., Northumberland Cheshire Home, 1970; Vice-Pres., Research into Ageing (formerly British Foundn for Age Res.), 1998– (Trustee and Gov., 1979–97); Member: NEC, Abbeyfield Soc., 1989–93 (Chm., Extra Care Cttee, 1989–90; Chm., Care and Develt Cttee, 1990–93); Council, RSAS, 1989–96; BMA, 1953–; British Geriatrics Soc., 1963– (President's Medal, 1992); Trustee: Brendoncare Foundn, 1984–2006 (Vice-Chm., 1986–99); McCarthy Foundn, 1987–96. FRSocMed 1991. *Publications:* Medical Care of the Elderly, 1978, 3rd edn 1993; chapters and contribs to various books on aspects of ageing and geriatric medicine; articles and papers in med. jls. *Recreations:* fly-fishing, golf, gardening. *Address:* Peartree Cottage, Emery Down, Lyndhurst, Hants SO43 7FH. *T:* (023) 8028 2541. *Club:* MCC.

HALL, Michael Thomas; MP (Lab) Weaver Vale, since 1997 (Warrington South, 1992–97); *b* 20 Sept. 1952; *s* of late Thomas and Veronica Hall; *m* 1975, Lesley Evelyn Gosling; one *s. Educ:* Padgate Coll. of Higher Educn (Teachers' Cert. 1977); N Cheshire Coll., Victoria Univ., Manchester (BEd Hons 1987). Scientific Asst, ICI Ltd, 1969–73; teaching history and physical educn, Bolton, 1977–85; support teacher, Halton Community Assessment Team, 1985–92. Councillor, Warrington Borough Council, 1979–93: Chairman: Envmtl Health Cttee, 1981–84; Finance Sub-Cttee, 1984–85; Policy and Resources Cttee, 1985–92; Dep. Leader of Council, 1984–85, Leader 1985–92. Member, Parish Council: Great Sankey, 1979–83; Birchwood and Croft, 1983–87; Poulton with Fearnhead, 1987–93. PPS to Ldr of the House of Commons and Pres. of the Council, 1997–98; an Asst Govt Whip, 1998–2001; PPS to Sec. of State for Health, 2001–05. Member: Modernisation Select Cttee, 1997–98; Culture, Media and Sports Select Cttee, 2005–. Mem., Public Accounts Cttee, 1992–97; Chm., Labour Party Back Bench Educn Cttee, 1996–97. *Recreations:* tennis, reading, cooking. *Address:* House of Commons, SW1A 0AA.

HALL, Nigel John, RA 2003; sculptor; *b* 30 Aug. 1943; *s* of Herbert John Hall and Gwendoline Mary Hall (*née* Olsen); *m* 1986, Manijeh Yadegar. *Educ:* Bristol Grammar Sch.; West of England Coll. of Art; Royal Coll. of Art (MA). Harkness Fellow, USA, 1967–69; Tutor, RCA, 1971–74; Principal Lectr, Chelsea Sch. of Art, 1974–81. Ext. Examr, RCA, Goldsmiths Coll., Brighton Univ., Reading Univ., Middlesex Univ., Central Sch. of Art, W Surrey Coll. of Art. Mem. Faculty, British Sch. at Rome, 1979–83. Member: CNAA, 1975–76; Bursaries Cttee, 1975, Exhibns Cttee, 1983, Arts Council. First solo exhibn, Galerie Givaudan, Paris, 1967. *Solo exhibitions include:* Robert Elkon, NY, 1974, 1977, 1979, 1983; Annely Juda Fine Art, London, 1978, 1981, 1985, 1987, 1991, 1996, 2000, 2003; Galerie Maeght, Paris, 1981, 1983; Staatliche Kunsthalle, Baden-Baden, 1982; Nishimura Gall., Tokyo, 1980, 1984, 1988; Garry Anderson Gall., Sydney, 1987, 1990; Hans Mayer Gall., Düsseldorf, 1989, 1999; Fondation Veranneman, Kruishoutem, Belgium, 1987, 1995, 1997; Galerie Ziegler, Zurich, 1986, 1988, 1995; Park Gall., Seoul, 1997, 2000; Galerie Konstruktiv Tendens, Stockholm, 2000; Schoenthal Monastery, Switzerland, 2001; Galerie Scheffel, Bad Homburg, 2004, 2007; Kunsthalle, Mannheim, 2004; Galleri C. Hjärne, Helsingborg, 2004; Park Gall., Seoul, 2005; Annely Juda Fine Art, London, 2005; Centre Cultural Contemporani Pelaires, Palma de Mallorca, 2007; Yorks Sculpture Park, 2008; Park Gall., Seoul, 2008; *group exhibitions include:* Kassel, 1977; Whitechapel Gall., 1981; Tokyo Metropolitan Mus., 1982; Le Havre Mus. of Fine Art, 1988; MOMA, NY, 1993; Fogg Art Mus., Harvard Univ., 1994; Schloss Ambras, Innsbruck, 1998; British Council touring exhibn, Pakistan, S Africa, Zimbabwe, 1997–99; York City Art Gall. and tour, 2001–02; Bad Homburg, Germany, 2003; Beaufort Triennial, Ostend, 2006. *Commissions:* Australian Nat. Gall., Canberra, 1982; IBM, London, 1983; Airbus Industrie, Toulouse, 1984; Mus. of Contemp. Art, Hiroshima, 1985; Olympic Park, Seoul, 1988; Clifford Chance, London, 1992; Glaxo Wellcome Res., Stevenage, 1994; NTT, Tokyo, 1996; Bank of America, London, 2003; Saïd Business Sch., Univ. of Oxford, 2005; Bank for Internat. Settlements, Basel, 2007. *Work in collections including:* Tate Gall.; Musée Nat. d'Art Moderne, Paris; Nat. Gall., Berlin; MOMA, NY; Australian Nat. Gall., Canberra; Art Inst. of Chicago; Kunsthaus, Zurich; Tokyo Metropolitan Mus.; Musée d'Art Moderne, Brussels; Louisiana Mus., Denmark; Nat. Mus. of Art, Osaka; Mus. of Contemp. Art, Sydney; Dallas Mus. of Fine Art; Tel Aviv Mus.; Los Angeles Co. Mus.; Nat. Mus. of Contemp. Art, Seoul. *Relevant publication:* Nigel Hall: sculpture and works on paper, by A. Lambirth, 2008. *Address:* 11 Kensington Park Gardens, W11 3HD. *T:* (020) 7727 3162, *Fax:* (020) 7229 1852.

HALL, Patrick; MP (Lab) Bedford, since 1997; *b* 20 Oct. 1951. *Educ:* Bedford Modern Sch.; Birmingham Univ.; Oxford Poly. Local Govt Planning Officer; Bedford Town Centre Co-ordinator. Mem., Bedfordshire CC, 1989–97. Contested (Lab) Bedfordshire N, 1992. *Address:* House of Commons, SW1A 0AA; Broadway House, 4/6 The Broadway, Bedford MK40 2TE.

HALL, Rt Rev. Peter; *see* Hall, Rt Rev. A. P.

HALL, Peter Dalton, CB 1986; Under Secretary, Solicitor's Office, Board of Inland Revenue, 1979–86; *b* 1 Aug. 1924; *s* of Edward and Kathleen Hall; *m* 1952, Stella Iris Breen (*d* 2007); four *s* two *d. Educ:* Rishworth Sch.; St Catharine's Coll., Cambridge (exhibnr; MA, LLB). Served War of 1939–45, Intelligence Corps; seconded to AIF and served with US Forces in New Guinea and Philippines; SEALF, 1946–47 (GOC-in-C Commendation); Major. Called to the Bar, Middle Temple, 1951; Inland Revenue Solicitor's Office, 1952–88. Mem., Bar Council 1967–70; Clerk to City of London Comrs, 1988–99. Parish Councillor, 1967–. Non-exec. Dir, Milton Keynes HA, 1992–93. Freeman, City of London, 1993. *Publications:* contrib. legal works. *Recreations:* grandchildren (15), gardening, music, conservation. *Address:* Apple Tree Cottage, Woughton-on-the-Green, Bucks MK6 3BE. *T:* and *Fax:* (01908) 679504.

HALL, Sir Peter (Edward), KBE 1993; CMG 1987; HM Diplomatic Service, retired; *b* 26 July 1938; *s* of late Bernard Hall and Monica Hall (*née* Blackbourn); *m* 1972, Marnie Kay; one *s* one *d. Educ:* Portsmouth Grammar Sch.; HM Services (Jt Services Sch. for Linguists); Pembroke Coll., Cambridge (Scholar; 1st Cl. parts I and II, Mediaeval and Modern Langs Tripos). Foreign Office, 1961–63; 3rd Sec., Warsaw, 1963–66; 2nd Sec., New Delhi, 1966–69; FCO (European Integration Dept), 1969–72; 1st Sec., UK Permanent Representation to EEC, 1972–76; Asst Head, Financial Relations Dept, FCO, 1976–77; Counsellor, Caracas, 1977–78; Hd of British Information Services, NY, 1978–83 and Counsellor, British Embassy, Washington, 1981–83; Dir of Res., FCO, 1983–86; Under Sec., Cabinet Office, 1986–88; Vis. Schol., Stanford Univ., 1988–89; Ambassador to Yugoslavia, 1989–92; Advr to Lord Carrington, 1992, Lord Owen, 1992–93, Peace Conf. on Yugoslavia; Ambassador to Argentina, 1993–97. *Recreations:* reading (A. Powell, Byron), music (Rolling Stones, Mozart). *Address:* 13 Raby Place, Bathwick, Bath BA2 4EH. *Club:* Garrick.

HALL, Prof. Peter Gavin, DPhil; FRS 2000; Professor of Statistics and Australian Research Council Federation Fellow, University of Melbourne, since 2006; *b* 20 Nov. 1951; *s* of William Holman Hall and Ruby Violet (*née* Payne-Scott); *m* 1977, Jeannie Jean Chien Loh. *Educ:* Univ. of Sydney (BSc 1st Cl. Hons); Australian Nat. Univ. (MSc 1976); Brasenose Coll., Oxford (DPhil 1976). Lectr in Stats, Univ. of Melbourne, 1976–78; Australian National University: Lectr in Stats, 1978–82; Sen. Lectr, 1983–85; Reader, 1986–88; Prof. of Stats, 1988–2006. FIMS 1984; FAA 1987; Fellow, Amer. Statistical Assoc., 1996; Corresp. FRSE, 2002. Dr *hc* Univ. Catholique de Louvain, 1997. Medal, Australian Mathematical Soc., 1986; Rollo Davison Prize, Cambridge Univ., 1986; Lyle Medal, 1989, Hannan Medal, 1995, Australian Acad. of Sci.; Pitman Medal, Statistical Soc. of Australia, 1990. *Publications:* (with C. C. Heyde) Martingale Limit Theory and its Applications, 1980; Rates of Convergence in the Central Limit Theorem, 1982; Introduction to the Theory of Coverage Processes, 1988; The Bootstrap and Edgeworth Expansion, 1992; contrib. numerous papers. *Recreations:* photography, interests in railway and aviation. *Address:* Department of Mathematics and Statistics, University of Melbourne, Melbourne, Vic 3010, Australia.

HALL, Sir Peter (Geoffrey), Kt 1998; FBA 1983; Professor of Planning, University College London, since 1992; Director, Institute of Community Studies, 2001–04; *b* 19 March 1932; *s* of Arthur Vickers Hall and Bertha Hall (*née* Keefe); *m* 1st, 1962, Carla Maria Wartenberg (marr. diss. 1966); 2nd, 1967, Magdalena Mróz; no *c*. *Educ:* Blackpool Grammar Sch.; St Catharine's Coll., Cambridge Univ. (MA, PhD; Hon. Fellow, 1988). Asst Lectr, 1957, Lectr, 1960, Birkbeck Coll., Univ. of London; Reader in Geography with ref. to Regional Planning, London Sch. of Economics and Political Science, 1966; University of Reading: Prof. of Geography, 1968–89, now Prof. Emeritus; Head, Dept of Geog., 1968–80; Chm., Sch. of Planning Studies, 1971–77 and 1983–86; Dean of Urban and Regional Studies, 1975–78; Prof. of City and Regl Planning, 1980–92, and Dir, Inst. of Urban and Regl Develt, 1989–92, Univ. of Calif, Berkeley, now Prof. Emeritus; Dir, Sch. of Public Policy, UCL, 1995–99. Member: SE Regional Planning Council, 1966–79; Nature Conservancy, 1968–72; Transport and Road Research Laboratory Adv. Cttee on Transport, 1973–78; Environmental Bd, 1975–79; SSRC, 1975–80 (Chm., Planning Cttee); EEC Expert Gp on New Tendencies of Social and Economic Develt, 1975–77; Standing Adv. Cttee on Trunk Road Assessment, 1978–80; DETR Urban Task Force, 1998–99; Exec. Cttee, Regional Studies Assoc., 1967–78 (Hon. Jl Editor, 1967–78); Exec. Cttee, Fabian Soc., 1964–80 (Chm. 1971–72). Pres., TCPA, 2004– (Chm., 1995–99). Special Advr, Sec. of State for Environment, 1991–94. Chm., Blackpool Urban Regeneration Co., 2005–08. Editor, Built Environment, 1977–. Governor, Centre for Environmental Studies, 1975–80. Chm., Tawney Soc., 1983–85 (Vice-Chm., 1982–83). FRGS; Hon. RTPI 1975; Hon. RIBA 2000. Hon. DSS: Birmingham, 1989; London, 2004; Hon. PhD Lund Univ., Sweden, 1992; Hon. LittD: Sheffield, 1995; Newcastle, 1995; London Guildhall, 2002; Hon. DEng Technical Univ. of Nova Scotia, 1996; Hon. DArts Oxford Brookes, 1997; Hon. LLD: Reading, 1999; Manchester, 2001; Hon. DSc West of England, 2000; Hon. DTech Greenwich, 2004. Ebenezer Howard Meml Medal, TCPA, 1999; Prix Vautrin Lud, Internat. Fest. of Geography, 2001; Gold Medal, RTPI, 2003; Dep. Prime Minister's Lifetime Achievement Award, 2004; Balzan Prize, Internat. Balzan Foundn, 2005. *Publications:* The Industries of London, 1962; London 2000, 1963 (reprint, 1969); Labour's New Frontiers, 1964; (ed) Land Values, 1965; The World Cities, 1966, 3rd edn 1984; Containment of Urban England, 1973; Urban and Regional Planning, 1974, 2nd edn 1982; Europe 2000, 1977; Great Planning Disasters, 1980; Growth Centres in the European Urban System, 1980; The Inner City in Context, 1981; Silicon Landscapes, 1985; Can Rail Save the City?, 1985; High Tech America, 1986; Cities of Tomorrow, 1988; London 2001, 1989; The Rise of the Gunbelt, 1991; Technoples of the World, 1994; Sociable Cities, 1998; Cities in Civilization, 1998; Urban Future 21, 2000; Working Capital, 2002; To-morrow: a peaceful path to real reform, 2003; The Polycentric Metropolis, 2006; London Voices London Lives, 2007. *Recreations:* writing, reading, talking. *Address:* Bartlett School, University College London, Wates House, 22 Gordon Street, WC1H 0QB; 12 Queens Road, W5 2SA. *Club:* Athenæum.

HALL, Peter George; (part-time) Chairman, Snamprogetti Ltd, 1988–97; *b* 10 Dec. 1924; *s* of Charles and Rosina Hall; *m* 1949, Margaret Gladys (*née* Adams); two *s* two *d*. *Educ:* Sandown, IoW, Grammar Sch.; Southampton Univ. (BScEng). Anglo-Iranian Oil Co., 1946–51; Esso Petroleum Co. Ltd: various positions at Fawley Refinery, 1951–63; Manager, Milford Haven Refinery, 1963–66; Employee Relations Manager, 1966–70; Vice-Pres., General Sekiyu Seisei, Tokyo, 1971–74; Asst Gen. Man., Refining, Imperial Oil Ltd, Toronto, 1974–76; Refining Man., Exxon Corp., New York, 1976–77; Director, Esso Petroleum Co. Ltd, London, 1977–78; Vice-Pres., Esso Europe Inc. London, 1979–81; Man. Dir, Esso Petroleum Co., 1982–84; Pres., Esso Norge, 1984–87. *Recreations:* opera, classical music, walking, gardening. *Address:* Oakley, Mill Lane, Burley, Ringwood, Hants BH24 4HP.

HALL, Sir Peter (Reginald Frederick), Kt 1977; CBE 1963; director of plays, films and operas; own producing company, Peter Hall Co., formed 1988; Artistic Director, Old Vic, 1997; *b* Bury St Edmunds, Suffolk, 22 Nov. 1930; *s* of late Reginald Edward Arthur Hall and Grace Pamment; *m* 1956, Leslie Caron (marr. diss. 1965); one *s* one *d*; *m* 1965, Jacqueline Taylor (marr. diss. 1981); one *s* one *d*; *m* 1982, Maria Louise Ewing, *qv* (marr. diss. 1990); one *d*; *m* 1990, Nicola Frei; one *d*. *Educ:* Perse Sch., Cambridge; St Catharine's Coll., Cambridge (MA Hons; Hon. Fellow, 1964). Professional début directing The Letter, Th. Royal, Windsor, 1953; Director: Oxford Playhouse, 1954–55; Arts Theatre, London, 1955–57 (directed several plays incl. first productions of Waiting for Godot (new prodn, Old Vic, 1997), South, Waltz of the Toreadors); formed own producing company, International Playwrights' Theatre, 1957, and directed their first production, Camino Real; at Sadler's Wells, directed his first opera, The Moon and Sixpence, 1957. First productions at Stratford: Love's Labour's Lost, 1956; Cymbeline, 1957; first prod. on Broadway, The Rope Dancers, Nov. 1957. Plays in London, 1956–58: Summertime, Gigi, Cat on a Hot Tin Roof, Brouhaha, Shadow of Heroes; Madame de..., Traveller Without Luggage, A Midsummer Night's Dream and Coriolanus (Stratford), The Wrong Side of the Park, 1959; apptd Dir of Shakespeare Fest., Stratford upon Avon, Jan. 1960, founded RSC as a permanent ensemble, and responsible for its move to Aldwych Theatre, 1960; Man. Dir at Stratford-on-Avon and Aldwych Theatre, London, 1960–68; Associate Dir, RSC, 1968–73; Dir, Nat. Theatre, 1973–88; Artistic Dir, Glyndebourne Fest., 1984–90; Founder Dir, Rose Th., Kingston, 2003–08, now Dir Emeritus. Plays produced/directed for *Royal Shakespeare Company:* Two Gentlemen of Verona, Twelfth Night, Troilus and Cressida, 1960; Ondine, Becket, Romeo and Juliet, 1961; The Collection, Troilus and Cressida, A Midsummer Night's Dream, 1962; The Wars of the Roses (adaptation of Henry VI Parts 1, 2 and 3, and Richard III), 1963 (televised for BBC, 1965); Sequence of Shakespeare's histories for Shakespeare's 400th anniversary at Stratford: Richard II, Henry IV Parts 1 & 2, Henry V, Henry VI, Edward IV, Richard III, 1964; The Homecoming, Hamlet, 1965; The Government Inspector, Staircase, 1966; The Homecoming (NY) (Tony Award for Best Dir), 1966; Macbeth, 1967; A Delicate Balance, Silence, Landscape, 1969; The Battle of the Shrivings, 1970; Old Times, 1971 (NY, 1971, Vienna, 1972; Th. Royal, Bath and tour, 2007); All Over, Via Galactica (NY), 1972; Julius Caesar, 1995; plays produced/directed for *National Theatre:* The Tempest, 1973; John Gabriel Borkman, Happy Days, 1974; No Man's Land, Hamlet, 1975; Tamburlaine the Great, 1976; No Man's Land (NY), Volpone, Bedroom Farce, The Country Wife, 1977; The Cherry Orchard, Macbeth, Betrayal, 1978; Amadeus, 1979, NY 1981 (Tony Award for Best Director); Othello, 1980; Family Voices, The Oresteia, 1981, 1986 (Evening Standard Award for Best Director, 1981); Importance of Being Earnest, 1982; Other Places, 1982; Jean Seberg, 1983; Animal Farm, Coriolanus, 1984; Martine, Yonadab, 1985; The Petition, Coming into Land, 1986; Antony and Cleopatra (Evening Standard Award for Best Director), Entertaining Strangers, 1987; The Tempest, Cymbeline, Winter's Tale, 1988; The Oedipus Plays, 1996; The Bacchai, 2002; plays produced/directed for *Peter Hall Company:* Orpheus Descending, NY, 1988; Merchant of Venice, 1989; The Wild Duck, Phoenix, 1990; The Homecoming, Comedy, 1990; Twelfth Night, The Rose Tattoo, Tartuffe, Playhouse, 1991; Four Baboons Adoring the Sun, NY, 1992; Sienna Red, 1992; All's Well That Ends Well, RSC, 1992; An Ideal Husband, Globe, 1992, Haymarket, Old Vic, 1996; The Gift of the Gorgon, Wyndham's, 1993; Separate Tables, Albery, 1993; Lysistrata, Old Vic and Wyndhams, 1993; She Stoops to Conquer, Queen's, 1993; Piaf, Piccadilly, 1993; An Absolute Turkey, Globe, 1994; On Approval, Playhouse, 1994; Hamlet, Gielgud, 1994; The Master Builder, 1995, Mind Millie for Me, 1996, A Streetcar Named Desire, 1997, Haymarket; Waste, The Seagull, King Lear, Waiting for Godot, Old Vic, 1997; The Misanthrope, Major Barbara, Filumena, Kafka's Dick, Piccadilly, 1998; Mrs Warren's Profession, Strand, 2002; Betrayal, Design for Living, As You Like It, Where There's a Will, Th. Royal, Bath, 2003; Galileo's Daughter, Man and Superman, Th. Royal, Bath, 2004; The Dresser, Duke of York's, 2005; Much Ado About Nothing, Private Lives, You Never Can Tell, Waiting for Godot, Th. Royal, Bath, 2005, transf. New Ambassadors, 2006; Measure for Measure, Habeas Corpus, Th. Royal, Bath, 2006; Pygmalion, Th. Royal, Bath, 2007, transf. Old Vic, 2008; Little Nell, Animal Farm, Th. Royal, Bath, 2007; The Portrait of a Lady, A Doll's House, Born in the Gardens, Th. Royal, Bath, 2008; *other productions:* Amadeus, Old Vic, 1998; Lenny, Queen's, 1999; Cuckoos, Gate, Notting Hill, 2000; Tantalus, Denver, 2000, UK tour and Barbican, 2001; Japes, The Royal Family, 2001, Lady Windermere's Fan, 2002, Th. Royal, Haymarket; Betrayal, Duchess, 2003; Happy Days, Arts, 2003; As You Like It, Rose Th., Kingston, 2004, US tour 2005; Whose Life Is It Anyway?, Comedy, 2005; Hay Fever, Th. Royal, Haymarket, 2006; Amy's View, Garrick, 2006; Uncle Vanya, Rose Th., Kingston, 2008; The Vortex, Apollo, 2008. *Films:* Work is a Four Letter Word, 1968; A Midsummer Night's Dream, Three into Two Won't Go, 1969; Perfect Friday, 1971; The Homecoming, 1973; Akenfield, 1974; She's Been Away, 1989; Orpheus Descending, 1991; Final Passage, 1996. *Opera:* at Covent Garden: Moses and Aaron, 1965; The Magic Flute, 1966; The Knot Garden, 1970; Eugene Onegin, Tristan and Isolde, 1971; Salome, 1988; Albert Herring, 1989; at Glyndebourne: La Calisto, 1970; Il Ritorno d'Ulisse in Patria, 1972; The Marriage of Figaro, 1973, 1989; Don Giovanni, 1977; Così Fan Tutte, 1978, 1988; Fidelio, 1979; A Midsummer Night's Dream, 1981, 2001; Orfeo ed Euridice, 1982; L'Incoronazione di Poppea, 1984, 1986; Carmen, 1985; Albert Herring, 1985, 1986, 2002, 2008; Simon Boccanegra, 1986, 1998; La Traviata, 1987; Falstaff, 1988; Otello, 2001; La Cenerentola, 2005, 2007; at Metropolitan Opera, NY: Macbeth, 1982; Carmen, 1986; at Bayreuth: The Ring, 1983; at Geneva: Figaro, 1983; at Los Angeles: Salome, 1986; Così Fan Tutte, 1988; The Magic Flute, 1992; at Chicago: Figaro, 1987, Salome, 1988; Otello, 2001; The Midsummer Marriage, 2005; at Houston: New Year (world première), 1989. *Television:* Presenter, Aquarius (LWT), 1975–77; Carmen, 1985; Oresteia (C4), L'Incoronazione di Poppea, Albert Herring, 1986; La Traviata, 1987; The Marriage of Figaro, 1989; (series) The Camomile Lawn (C4), 1992. Associate Prof. of Drama, Warwick Univ., 1964–67. Mem., Arts Council, 1969–73; Founder Mem., Theatre Dirs' Guild of GB, 1983–. Wortham Prof. of Performing Arts, Houston Univ., 1999–2004; Chancellor, Kingston Univ., 2000–. DUniv York, 1966; Hon. DLitt Reading, 1973; Essex, 1993; Hon. LittD: Liverpool, 1974; Leicester, 1977; Cambridge, 2003; Bath, 2005; London, 2007. Hamburg Univ. Shakespeare Prize, 1967; Standard Special Award, 1979; Standard Award for outstanding achievement in Opera, 1981; Lifetime Achievement Award, South Bank Show, 1998; Olivier Special Award for Lifetime Achievement, 1999; Lifetime Achievement Award, NY Theater Hall of Fame, 2006. Chevalier de l'Ordre des Arts et des Lettres, 1965. *Publications:* (with John Barton) The Wars of the Roses, 1970; (with Inga-Stina Ewbank) John Gabriel Borkman, an English version, 1975; Peter Hall's Diaries (ed John Goodwin), 1983; Animal Farm, a stage adaptation, 1986; (with Inga-Stina Ewbank) The Wild Duck, an English adaptation, 1990; Making an Exhibition of Myself (autobiog.), 1993; (with Nicki Frei) trans. Feydeau, An Absolute Turkey, 1994; (with Inga-Stina Ewbank) The Master Builder, an English version, 1995; The Necessary Theatre, 1999; Exposed by the Mask, 2000; Shakespeare's Advice to the Players, 2003. *Recreation:* music. *Club:* Garrick.

See also E. P. Hall.

HALL, Prof. Philip, PhD; Professor of Applied Mathematics, since 1996, and Director, Mathematical Sciences Research Institute, Imperial College London; *b* 21 Feb. 1950; *s* of John Thomas Hall and Pamela Hall; *m* 1973, Eileen Haig; two *d*. *Educ:* Goole Grammar Sch.; Imperial Coll., London (BSc 1971; PhD 1973). Reader in Maths, Imperial Coll. London, 1984–85; Prof. of Maths, Exeter Univ., 1985–90; Beyer Prof. of Maths, Manchester Univ., 1990–96; Hd, Dept of Maths, ICSTM, 1996. Sen. Fellow, EPSRC, 1990–95. *Publications:* about 120 articles on fluid dynamics, mostly with relevance to aerodynamics and transition to turbulence. *Recreations:* golf, reading, theatre, travelling. *Address:* Department of Mathematics, 180 Queen's Gate, S Kensington Campus, Imperial College London, SW7 2AZ. *T:* (020) 7594 8480, *Fax:* (020) 7594 8517; *e-mail:* phil.hall@ic.ac.uk.

HALL, Philip David; Chairman, Phil Hall Associates, since 2005; *b* 8 Jan. 1955; *s* of Norman Philip Hall and Olive Jean Hall; *m* 1997, Marina Thomson, patent attorney; one *s* one *d*. *Educ:* Beal Grammar Sch., Ilford. Reporter: Dagenham Post, 1974–77; Ilford Recorder, 1977–80; Sub-editor: Newham Recorder, 1980–84; Weekend Magazine, 1984–85; The People: Reporter, 1985–86; Chief Reporter, 1986–89; News Editor, 1989–92; News Editor, Sunday Express, 1992–93; News of the World: Asst Editor (Features), 1993–94; Dep. Editor, 1994–95; Editor, 1995–2000; with Max Clifford Associates, 2000; Ed.-in-chief, Hello! magazine, 2001–02; Man. Dir, Contract Publg Div., Press Assoc., 2002–03; Dir of Editorial Develt, Trinity Mirror, 2003–05. Mem., Press Complaints Commn, 1998–2000, 2002–03. Member: Guild of Editors; PPA, 2001–02. *Recreations:* golf, cinema, theatre. *Address:* Phil Hall Associates, 19 Cato Street, W1H 5HR. *T:* (020) 7535 3350. *Club:* Brough Golf.

HALL, Raymond Walter, CBE 1993; FREng; Chief Executive, Magnox Electric plc, 1996–98; *b* 24 Sept. 1933; *s* of Alfred Henry Hall and Elsie Frieda Hall; *m* 1955, Diane Batten; one *s* three *d*. *Educ:* Portsmouth, Grays Thurrock, and Gravesend Colls of Technology. FIMechE 1981; FIET (FIEE 1983); FINucE 1983; FREng (FEng 1993). Engineering and managerial positions, CEGB, 1975–89: Station Manager: Trawsfynydd Nuclear Power Station, 1975–77; Hinkley Point A & B Nuclear Power Stations, 1978–82; Corporate Trng Manager, 1983–85; Corporate Dir of Personnel, 1986–87; Divl Dir of Generation, 1988–89; Exec. Dir, Operations, Nuclear Electric plc, 1990–95. World Association of Nuclear Operators: Gov., Main Bd, 1993–97; Chm., Paris Centre, 1993–97; Chairman: Orgn Producteurs d'Energie Nucléaire, 1994–97; British Nuclear Industry Forum, 1997–2002 (Mem. Bd, 1996–2002). Trustee, Bristol Exploratory, 1992–2000. FRSA 1980; FCMI (FIMgt 1980); FIPD 1988. Freeman: City of London, 1996; Worshipful Co. of Engrs, 1996 (Liveryman, 1997–). *Publications:* contribs to learned jls on nuclear engrg matters. *Recreations:* music, gardening, walking, golf, travel. *Address:* Kingsthorn, Staplehay, Taunton, Somerset TA3 7HA. *T:* and *Fax:* (01823) 252325.

HALL, Rev. Roger John, MBE 1999; QHC 2006; Chaplain of the Chapel Royal of St Peter ad Vincula, HM Tower of London, since 2007; a Deputy Priest in Ordinary to the Queen, since 2007; *b* 1 Dec. 1953; *s* of Sydney and Patricia Hall; *m* 1979, Barbara Mary Hutchinson; one *s* two *d*. *Educ:* Wolsingham Sch., Co. Durham; Lincoln Theological Coll. Ordained deacon, 1984, priest, 1985; Asst Curate, St Giles, Shrewsbury with St Eata's, Atcham, 1984–87; Regtl Chaplain, 1987–90; Brigade Sen. Chaplain, 1990–95; Amport House: Asst Warden, 1996–98; Warden, 1998–2000; Dep. Asst Chaplain Gen.,

Germany, 2000–01; Sen. Chaplain, Guard's Chapel, 2001–03; Asst Chaplain Gen., 2003–07. Mem., Forces Synod, 1993–; Dir of Ordinands, 1996–2001; Warden of Readers, 1998–. Nat. Chaplain, BLESMA, 2001–; Hon. Chaplain: Co. of City of London Solicitors, 2007–; Co. of Builders Merchants, 2007–; Guild of Arts Scholars, Dealers and Collectors, 2007–; Co. of Security Professionals, 2007–. Member: Family Support Working Pty, SSAFA, 1998–; Scottish Veterans Housing Assoc., 2003–. Mem., Stone Masons' Co., 2007–; Mem., Anglo-German Soc. QCVS 1995. *Recreations:* music, art, reading, travel, ski-ing, shooting, café culture. *Address:* Chaplain's House, 1 The Green, HM Tower of London, EC3N 4AB. *T:* (020) 3166 6796; *e-mail:* revrjhall@aol.com. *Club:* Army and Navy.

HALL, Ruth, CB 2004; FRCP, FRCPCH, FFPH; Director, Health Protection Agency South West, since 2006; *b* 8 Feb. 1948; *d* of Robert and Molly Dobson; *m* 1971, William Hall; two *s* two *d. Educ:* Sch. of St Helen and St Katherine, Abingdon; King's Coll. Hosp. Med. Sch., London (MB BS 1970). LRCP, MRCS 1970; FFPH (FFPHM 1994); FRCPCH 1997; FRCP 2000. Posts in London, 1970–71, Chester, 1971–73, and N Wales, 1973–97; Dir of Public Health, N Wales HA, 1995–97; CMO, Welsh Office, then Welsh Assembly Govt, 1997–2005; Dir of Public Health, Avon, Glos and Wilts Strategic HA, 2005–06. Member: MRC, 1997–2005; Envmt Agency, 2005–. Vis. Prof., Faculty of Health and Social Care, UWE, 2006–. *Address:* (office) The Wheelhouse, Bond's Mill, Stonehouse, Gloucester GL10 3RF.

HALL, Sasha; *see* Wass, S.

HALL, Simon Robert Dawson, MA; Warden of Glenalmond College, 1987–91; *b* 24 April 1938; *s* of late Wilfrid Dawson Hall and Elizabeth Helen Hall (*née* Wheeler); *m* 1961, Jennifer Harverson; two *s. Educ:* Tonbridge School; University College, Oxford. 2nd Lieut, 7th Royal Tank Regt, 1956–58. Asst Master, Gordonstoun School, 1961–65; Joint Headmaster, Dunrobin School, 1965–68; Haileybury: Asst Master, 1969–79; Senior Modern Languages Master, 1970–76; Housemaster, Lawrence, 1972–79; Second Master, 1976–79; Headmaster, Milton Abbey School, 1979–87. 21st SAS Regt (TA), 1958–61; Intelligence Corps (V), 1968–71. *Recreations:* reading, music, motoring, sailing, hill-walking. *Address:* 2 Stone Hill, Bloxham, Banbury, Oxon OX15 4PT.

HALL, Prof. the Rev. Stuart George; Priest-in-Charge, St Michael's, Elie, and St John's, Pittenweem, 1990–98; Professor of Ecclesiastical History, King's College, University of London, 1978–90; *b* 7 June 1928; *s* of George Edward Hall and May Catherine Hall; *m* 1953, Brenda Mary Henderson; two *s* two *d. Educ:* University Coll. Sch., Hampstead; New Coll., and Ripon Hall, Oxford (BA 1952, MA 1955, BD 1973). National Service, Army, 1947–48. Deacon 1954, priest 1955; Asst Curate, Newark-on-Trent Parish Church, 1954–58; Tutor, Queen's Coll., Birmingham, 1958–62; Lectr in Theology, Univ. of Nottingham, 1962–73, Sen. Lectr, 1973–78. Pres., Acad. Internat. des Scis Religieuses, 2006–09. Editor for early church material, Theologische Realenzyklopädie. *Publications:* Melito of Sardis On Pascha and fragments: (ed) texts and translations, 1979; Doctrine and Practice in the Early Church, 1991, 2nd edn 2005; (ed) Gregory of Nyssa, Homilies on Ecclesiastes, 1993; (ed with Averil Cameron) Eusebius, Life of Constantine, 1999; Heritage and Hope: the Episcopal churches in the East Neuk of Fife 1805–2005, 2004; (ed jtly) Decoding Early Christianity: truth and legend in the Early Church, 2007; contrib. to Cambridge History of Christianity, Cambridge Ancient History, Expository Times, Heythrop Jl, Jl of Eccles. History, Jl of Theol Studies, Religious Studies, Studia Evangelica, Studia Patristica, Theology and Theologische Realenzyklopädie. *Recreations:* gardening, choral music. *Address:* 15 High Street, Elie, Leven, Fife KY9 1BY. *T:* (01333) 330216.

HALL, Prof. Stuart McPhail, FBA 2005; Professor of Sociology, The Open University, 1979–98, now Emeritus; Visiting Professor, Goldsmiths College, London University; *b* 3 Feb. 1932; *s* of Herman and Jessie Hall; *m* 1964, Catherine Mary Barrett; one *s* one *d. Educ:* Jamaica Coll.; Merton Coll., Oxford (MA; Rhodes Scholar, 1951; Hon. Fellow, 2001). Editor, New Left Review, 1957–61; Lectr, Film and Mass Media Studies, Chelsea Coll., London Univ., 1961–64; Centre for Cultural Studies, Univ. of Birmingham: Res. Fellow, 1964–68; Actg Dir, 1968–72; Dir, 1972–79. Vis. Prof., Tavistock Inst., 2001. Hon. Fellow, Portsmouth Polytechnic, 1988; Centenary Fellow, Thames Polytechnic, 1990. Hon. DLitt: Massachusetts, 1989; City, Kingston, Oxford Brookes, 1993; Sussex, 1994; Leeds, Middlesex, Keele, 1995; East London, London, 1998; W Indies, 1999; Birmingham, Tampere, Teesside, 2000; RCA, 2003; Hon. DCL Durham, 2001. *Publications:* (jtly) The Popular Arts, 1964; (ed jtly) Resistance Through Rituals, 1974; (jtly) Policing The Crisis, 1978; Culture, Media, Language, 1980; (ed jtly) The Politics of Thatcherism, 1983; State and Society in Contemporary Britain, 1984; Politics and Ideology, 1986; The Hard Road to Renewal, 1988; (jtly) Questions of Cultural Identity, 1996; Critical Dialogues in Cultural Studies, 1996; Representations, 1997; *festschrift:* Without Guarantees, 2000. *Address:* 21 Ulysses Road, NW6 1ED.

HALL, Susan Margaret; *see* Standring, S. M.

HALL, Suzanne; Headmistress, Rugby High School, 1998–2006; *b* 5 Jan. 1946; *d* of John and Louise Keats; *m* 1971, Eric Lonsdale Hall; two *s. Educ:* Braintree Grammar Sch.; Univ. of Wales (BSc Hons Chem. 1969); Univ. of Southampton (PhD research). Cancer res., ICRF, 1966; Information Scientist, 1970; teacher, 1975; Dep. Hd, Chelmsford Co. High Sch., 1993–98. *Publications:* papers on x-ray crystallography in Jl of Chemical Soc. *Recreations:* reading, crosswords, Scrabble, gardening. *Address:* The Old Vicarage, Church Lane, Dunton Bassett, S Leics LE17 5JX. *T:* (01455) 202036.

HALL, Col Thomas Armitage, CVO 1998; OBE 1966; Lieutenant, HM Body Guard of Honourable Corps of Gentlemen at Arms, 1994–98; *b* 13 April 1928; *s* of Athelstan Argyle Hall and Nancy Armitage Hall (*née* Dyson); *m* 1954, Mariette Hornby; two *s* four *d. Educ:* Heatherdown Sch.; Eton Coll. Commissioned, 11th Hussars, 1947, Berlin; ADC to CIGS, 1952–53; Adjutant, 11 H Malayan Emergency, 1953–56 (despatches); Army Staff Coll., 1960–61; Sqdn Leader 11 H, Aden, Gulf, Kenya, Kuwait, 1961–62; Instr, RN Staff Coll., Greenwich, 1962–64; CO 11 H, Germany, 1965–66; Equerry to King of Thailand, 1966; Regtl Col, Royal Hussars, 1974–83; Advr to Crown Prince of Japan, 1983–85. Regl Dir, Lloyds Bank, 1983–85. Chm., Internat. Lang. Centres, 1971–88. High Sheriff, Oxon, 1981–82. FRSA. *Recreations:* ski-ing, shooting, travel, architecture. *Address:* Marylands Farm, Chiselhampton, Oxford OX44 7XD. *T:* (01865) 890350. *Club:* Cavalry and Guards (Chm., 1990–96; Vice Pres., 2007–).

HALL, Thomas William; Under-Secretary, Department of Transport, 1976–79 and 1981–87; retired; *b* 8 April 1931; *s* of Thomas William and Euphemia Jane Hall; *m* 1961, Anne Rosemary Hellier Davis; two *d. Educ:* Hitchin Grammar Sch.; St John's Coll., Oxford (MA); King's Coll., London (MA). Asst Principal, Min. of Supply, 1954; Principal: War Office, Min. of Public Building and Works, Cabinet Office, 1958–68; Asst Sec., Min. of Public Building and Works, later DoE, 1968–76; Under Sec., Depts of Environment and Transport, 1979–81. Member: Road Traffic Law Review, 1985–88; Transport Tribunal, 1990–99. *Recreations:* literature, gardening, walking. *Address:* 43 Bridge Road, Epsom, Surrey KT17 4AN. *T:* (01372) 725900.

HALL, Victor Edwin; His Honour Judge Victor Hall; a Circuit Judge, since 1994; *b* 2 March 1948; *s* of Robert Arthur Victor James Hall and Gwladys (*née* Fukes); *m* 1974, Rosemarie Berdina Jenkinson; two *s. Educ:* Univ. of Hull (LLB 1969). Lectr in Law, Kettering Tech. Coll., 1969–71; called to the Bar, Inner Temple, 1971; an Asst Recorder, 1983–88; a Recorder, 1988–94. Asst Parly Boundary Comr, 1991–93; Mem./Pres., Mental Health Review Tribunals, 1997–2003. Member: Cttee, Council of Circuit Judges, 1997–2002 (Treas., 1999–2001); Family Rules Cttee, 2001–04; Jt Course Dir, Family Seminars, 2002–03, Dir of Studies, 2004–06, Judicial Studies Bd. Mem. Bd, Internat. Orgn for Judicial Trng, 2004–06; Mem. Adv. Cttee, Commonwealth Judicial Educn Inst., 2004–06; Sec.-Gen., European Judicial Trng Network, Brussels, 2008–. Adjunct Prof. of Law, City Univ., Hong Kong, 2005–08. *Recreations:* sailing (and dreaming about being on the water!), cookery, fell walking, gardening, cricket.

HALL, (Wallace) John; Regional Director, DTI East (Cambridge), Department of Trade and Industry, 1989–94; *b* 5 Oct. 1934; *s* of Claude Corbett Hall and Dulcie Hall (*née* Brinkworth); *m* 1962, Janet Bowen; three *d. Educ:* Crypt Sch., Gloucester; Hertford Grammar Sch.; Downing Coll., Cambridge (MA Classics). National Service, RAF, 1953–55. Pirelli-General Cable Works Ltd, 1958–62; Sales Manager, D. Meredew Ltd, 1962–67; Principal, Min. of Technology, 1967–70; Dept of Trade and Industry, Civil Aviation Policy, 1970–72; Consul (Commercial), São Paulo, Brazil, 1972–76; Asst Secretary, Dept of Trade, Shipping Policy, 1976–79; Counsellor (Economic), Brasilia, 1979–81; Consul-Gen., São Paulo, 1981–83; Assistant Secretary, DTI: Internat. Trade Policy, 1983–85; Overseas Trade (E Asia), 1985–89. *Recreations:* bridge, croquet, walking. *Address:* 27 Wilbury Road, Letchworth, Herts SG6 4JW.

HALL, Prof. Wendy, (Mrs Peter Chandler), CBE 2000; PhD; FREng; Professor of Computer Science, since 1994, and Head, School of Electronics and Computer Science, since 2002, University of Southampton; *b* 25 Oct. 1952; *d* of Kenneth D. Hall and Elizabeth Hall; *m* 1980, Dr Peter E. Chandler. *Educ:* Ealing Grammar Sch. for Girls; Univ. of Southampton (BSc Maths 1974; PhD 1977); City Univ. (MSc Computer Sci. 1986). CEng 1990; FIET (FIEE 1998). Lecturer: in Engrg, Oxford Poly., 1977–78; La Sainte Union Coll. of Higher Educn, 1978–84; Lectr, 1984–90, Sen. Lectr, 1990–94, Dept of Electronics and Computer Sci., Univ. of Southampton. Mem., EPSRC, 1997–2002 (Sen. Fellow, 1996–2001). Member: Prime Minister's Council for Sci. and Technol., 2004–; Scientific Council, European Res. Council, 2005–. FBCS 1996 (Pres., 2003–04); FREng 2000 (Sen. Vice Pres., 2005–); FCGI 2002. Hon. Fellow, Cardiff Univ., 2004. Hon. DSc Oxford Brookes, 2002; Hon. PhD Pretoria, 2007. *Publications:* (jtly) Rethinking Hypermedia: the microcosm approach, 1996; (jtly) Hypermedia and the Web: an engineering approach, 1999; articles in jls, conf. proceedings. *Recreations:* rapidly becoming a keep-fit fanatic, spending many hours in the local gym and swimming pool; walking with my husband, particularly in the New Forest; fine wines and dining, travelling, theatre; favourite form of relaxation is reading a good book on a sunny beach or shopping! *Address:* School of Electronics and Computer Science, University of Southampton, Southampton SO17 1BJ. *T:* (023) 8059 2388.

HALL, William, CBE 1991; DFC 1944; FRICS; Member of the Lands Tribunal for Scotland, 1971–91, and for England and Wales, 1979–91; *b* 25 July 1919; *s* of Archibald and Helen Hall; *m* 1945, Margaret Semple (*née* Gibson); one *s* three *d. Educ:* Paisley Grammar Sch. FRICS 1948. Served War, RAF (pilot) 1939–45 (despatches, 1945). Sen. Partner, R. & W. Hall, Chartered Surveyors, 1949–79. Chm., Scottish Br., RICS, 1971; Member: Valuation Adv. Council, 1970–80; Erskine Hosp. Exec., 1976–99. Hon. Sheriff, Paisley, 1974–. *Recreation:* golf. *Address:* Windyridge, Brediland Road, Paisley, Renfrewshire PA2 9HF. *T:* (01505) 813614.

HALL, William Joseph; JP; Lord-Lieutenant of Co. Down, since 1996; *b* 1 Aug. 1934; *s* of late Capt. Roger Hall and Marie Hall; *m* 1964, Jennifer Mary Corbett; one *s* one *d. Educ:* Ampleforth Coll., York. SSC, Irish Guards, 1952–56. With W. C. Pitfield & Hugh McKay, investment mgt co., then with Shell Oil, Canada, 1956–62; dir of own wine wholesale business, also sheep farmer and commercial narcissus bulb grower, 1962–90, retired. Mem., Lord Chancellor's Adv. Cttee on JPs, 1975– (Chm., Ards Div., 1996–). County Down: JP 1973; DL 1975–93; High Sheriff, 1983; Vice Lord Lieutenant, 1993–96. NI ACF, 1967–79 (Hon. Major, 1980; Pres., NI ACFA, 1999–2002); Pres., RFCA NI, 2000–05; Chm., Ulster Br., Irish Guards Assoc., 1979–. Hon. Col, 1st Bn (NI), ACF, 2003–05. Vice Pres., RBL, NI, 2005–. CStJ 1997. *Recreations:* field sports in general, bridge, travel abroad when time allows! *Address:* The Mill House, Narrow Water, Warrenpoint, Co. Down, Northern Ireland BT34 3LW. *T:* (028) 4175 4904, *Fax:* (028) 4175 4990. *Clubs:* Army and Navy; Down Hunt (Downpatrick).

HALL HALL, Alexandra Mary, (Mrs D. C. Twining); HM Diplomatic Service; Political Counsellor, New Delhi, since 2006; *b* 1 Feb. 1964; *d* of late Francis Alleyne Hall Hall and Mary Hall Hall (*née* Whittaker); *m* 2002, Daniel Charles Twining; one *s. Educ:* Durham Univ. (BA Jt Hons Politics and Econs 1986); Sch. of Oriental and African Studies, Univ. of London (Advanced Thai); FCO Advanced Thai Dip. 1999. Entered FCO, 1986; Desk Officer, SE Asian Dept, FCO, 1987–88; Second Sec., Political and Inf. Officer, Bangkok, 1989–93; Hd, Humanitarian Section, UN Dept, FCO, 1993–95; European Secretariat, Cabinet Office (on secondment), 1995–97; Hd, ME Peace Process Section, FCO, 1997–98; First Sec. (Political), Washington, 1999–2001; Counsellor, on secondment to US State Dept, Washington, 2002–04; Hd of Human Rights, Democracy and Good Governance Gp, FCO, 2004–06. *Recreations:* travel, tennis, ski-ing, archery, dogs, hard labour to convert a scrap of wilderness in W Virginia, USA into the American answer to Sissinghurst, Kent. *Address:* c/o Foreign and Commonwealth Office, King Charles Street, SW1A 2AH. *T:* (India) (11) 24192207/8.

HALL-MATTHEWS, Rt Rev. Anthony Francis Berners, PhD; Provincial Chaplain, Third Order of Society of St Francis, since 2003; *b* 14 Nov. 1940; *s* of Rev. Cecil Berners Hall and Barbara (who *m* 1944, Rt Rev. Seering John Matthews); *m* 1966, Valerie Joan Cecil; two *s* three *d. Educ:* Sanctuary School, Walsingham, Norfolk; Southport School, Queensland; St Francis Theol Coll., Milton, Brisbane; James Cook Univ., Qld (Graduate Dip. of Arts, 1997; PhD 2005). ThL Aust. Coll. of Theology, 1962. Asst Curate at Darwin, 1963–66; Chaplain, Carpentaria Aerial Mission, 1966–84, and Rector of Normanton, 1966–76; Hon. Canon of Carpentaria, 1970–76; Archdeacon of Cape York Peninsula, 1976–84; Priest-in-charge of Cooktown, Dio. Carpentaria, 1976–84; Bishop of Carpentaria, 1984–96; Bishop Resident in Mareeba, Dio. N Qld, 1999–2000. Principal, Carpentaria Consulting Services, 1997–2006. *Publication:* A Remarkable Venture of Faith, 2007. *Recreations:* flying, reading, composting. *Address:* 5 Wattle Close, Yungaburra, Queensland 4884, Australia. *T:* (7) 40953188.

HALL-SMITH, Vanessa Frances; Director, British Institute of Florence, since 2004; *b* 30 April 1951; *d* of late Patrick Hall-Smith and Angela Hall-Smith; *m* 1981, Alper Ali Riza, *qv*; two *d. Educ:* Roedean Sch., Brighton; Univ. of Exeter (LLB); Johannes

Gutenberg Univ. Mainz; Univ. d'Aix-Marseilles. Called to the Bar, Inner Temple, 1976; Sec., Internat. Law Assoc., 1976–79; admitted solicitor, 1993; Partner: Simkins Partnership, Solicitors, 1996–2000; Harrison Curtis Solicitors, 2001–03. *Publication:* (contrib. ed) Butterworths Encyclopaedia of Forms and Precedents, Advertising vol., 5th edn 1993. *Recreations:* cooking, books, music, armchair sport. *Address:* British Institute of Florence, Palazzo Lanfredini, Lungarno Guicciardini 9, 50125 Florence, Italy. *T:* (055) 26778200, *Fax:* (055) 26778253; *e-mail:* director@britishinstitute.it.

HALL WILLIAMS, Richard; *see* Williams.

HALLAM, Bishop of, (RC), since 1997; **Rt Rev. John Rawsthorne;** *b* Crosby, Merseyside, 12 Nov. 1936. Priest, 1962; Titular Bishop of Rotdon and an Auxiliary Bishop of Liverpool, 1981–97. Pres., St Joseph's Coll., 1982–90. *Address:* Bishop's House, 75 Norfolk Road, Sheffield S2 2SZ. *T:* (0114) 278 7988.

HALLAM, David John Alfred; writer, journalist and blogger; Managing Director, Horizon Glen Ltd, since 2003; *b* 13 June 1948; *s* of Arthur Ernest Hallam and Marjorie Ethel Hallam (*née* Gibbs); *m* 1988, Claire Vanstone; two *s* one *d. Educ:* Upton House Secondary Modern Sch., London; Univ. of Sussex (BA). Res. Asst, Sussex CC, 1971–73; Information Officer, Birmingham Social Services Dept, 1973–80; Public Relations Officer, Nat. Children's Home, 1984–89; Dir of Communications, Birmingham Heartlands and Solihull NHS Trust, 2000–02. Mem., Sandwell BC, W Midlands, 1976–79. MEP (Lab) Hereford and Shropshire, 1994–99; contested (Lab) W Midlands Reg., 1999. Mem., Agricl Cttee, 1994–99, Substitute Mem., Budget Cttee, 1997–99, Europ. Parlt; Mem., Slovak Delegn, 1995–99; Substitute Mem. of Israel Delegn and to EU African, Caribbean and Pacific Parly Assembly, 1994–99. Contested (Lab): Shropshire and Staffordshire, European parly elections, 1984, 1989; Hereford, 2001. MCIM; MCIPR. Methodist local preacher. Editor, The Potter, newspaper, 1982–94. *Publication:* Eliza Asbury: her cottage and her son, 2003. *T:* (0121) 429 4207; *e-mail:* davidhallam5@aol.com; *web:* www.methodistpreacher.com.

HALLAM SMITH, Elizabeth, PhD; FSA, FRHistS; Director of Information Services and Librarian, House of Lords, since 2006; *b* 5 Nov. 1950; *d* of Edwin William Lewis Hallam and Barbara Mary Hallam; *m* 1975, Terence Stephen Smith (marr. diss. 2004); one *s* one *d. Educ:* Bath High Sch. for Girls; Westfield Coll., London (BA Hons Hist.; PhD Hist.). FRHistS 1980; FSA 1982. Tutorial Fellow, Univ. of Reading, 1975–76; Public Record Office: Asst Keeper, 1976–88; Hd, Publishing and Publicity, 1988–94; Dir, Public Services, 1994–2003; Dir, Nat. Adv. and Public Services, National Archives, 2003–06. Chm., Nat. Council on Archives, 2005–06. Vice Pres., Soc. of Antiquaries of London, 1998–2002; Hon. Vice Pres., Soc. of Genealogists, 1999–. FRSA 1999. *Publications:* Capetian France 987–1328, 1980, 2nd edn 2001 (with Judith Everard); Domesday Book through Nine Centuries, 1986; (ed) The Plantagenet Chronicles, 1986; (ed) Chronicles of the Crusades, 1989; (ed with Andrew Prescott) The British Inheritance: a treasury of historic documents, 1999; articles on inf. sci. in learned jls. *Recreations:* travel, walking, music, gardens, historical research, websurfing. *Address:* House of Lords, SW1A 0PW. *T:* (020) 7219 3240; *e-mail:* hallamsmithe@parliament.uk.

HALLATT, Rt Rev. David Marrison; an Assistant Bishop, Diocese of Sheffield, since 2001; *b* 15 July 1937; *s* of John Vincent Hallatt and Edith Elliott Hallatt; *m* 1967, Margaret Smitton; two *s. Educ:* Birkenhead School; Southampton Univ. (BA Hons Geography 1959); St Catherine's Coll., Oxford (BA Theology 1962; MA 1966). Curate, St Andrew's, Maghull, Liverpool, 1963–67; Vicar, All Saints, Totley, dio. Sheffield, 1967–75; Team Rector, St James & Emmanuel, Didsbury, Manchester, 1975–89; Archdeacon of Halifax, 1989–94; Bishop Suffragan of Shrewsbury, 1994–2001. *Recreations:* walking, birdwatching, music, crosswords. *Address:* 1 Merbeck Grove, High Green, Sheffield S35 4HE. *T:* (0114) 284 4440; *e-mail:* david.hallatt@btopenworld.com.

HALLCHURCH, David Thomas, TD 1965; Chief Justice, Turks and Caicos Islands, West Indies, 1996–98; *b* 4 April 1929; *s* of Walter William Hallchurch and Marjorie Pretoria Mary Hallchurch (*née* Cooper); *m* 1st, 1954, Gillian Mary Jagger (marr. diss. 1972); three *s;* 2nd, 1972, Susan Kathryn Mather Brennan; one step *s* one step *d. Educ:* Bromsgrove Sch.; Trinity Coll., Oxford (MA Hons). Called to the Bar, Gray's Inn, 1953; Whitehead Travelling Scholarship, Canada and USA, 1953–54; practised as barrister-at-law on Midland and Oxford Circuit, 1954–60 and 1964–96; a Recorder, 1980–97. Puisne Judge, Botswana, 1986–88; Actg Chief Justice, Turks and Caicos Is, 1993. Pt-time Immigration Adjudicator, 1990–96; Asst Comr, Parly Boundary Commn for England, 1992. Legal Mem., Mental Health Review Tribunal for the West Midlands, 1979–86. Major, Staffs Yeomanry (Queen's Own Royal Regiment), TA, 1953–66. *Recreations:* cricket, drawing (cartoons). *Address:* Neachley House, Tong, Shifnal, Shropshire TF11 8PH. *Club:* Vincent's (Oxford).

HALLETT; *see* Hughes-Hallett.

HALLETT, Anthony Philip; Chairman: Cafe Monet Ltd, since 2000; Cleanevent UK Ltd, since 2002; *b* 11 Feb. 1945; *s* of late Maurice George Hallett and Ann Halliwell Bailey; *m* 1972, Faith Mary Holland-Martin; three *s. Educ:* Ipswich Sch.; Britannia RN Coll. Joined RN 1963; served in HM Ships Victorious and Hermes; Flag Lieut, Hong Kong; HMS Eskimo; RNC Greenwich; BRNC, 1975–77; MoD, 1978–79; HMS Invincible, 1979–81; served C-in-C Fleet, 1982–83; HMS Illustrious, 1983–85; MoD, 1986–90; RNSC Greenwich, 1990–91; Sec. to Chief of Fleet Support, 1992–94; Captain, RN, retd 1995. Rugby Football: Navy Captain, 1969; 11 caps; played for US Portsmouth, Banbury, Blackheath, Richmond, Oxfordshire, S Counties, Combined Services, Hong Kong *v* England 1971. Rugby Football Union: Mem., 1979–97; Privilege Mem., 1997–; Chm., Ground Cttee, 1979–95; Chm., Twickenham Stadium Redevelt, 1991–95; Sec., 1995–97; Chief Exec., 1997; Selector and Chm., RN RU, 1985–94. Richmond Football Club: Chm., 1991–95 and 1999–2004; Chief Exec., 1998–99; Pres., 2004–07. *Recreations:* gardening (Mem., Nat. Gardens Scheme), paintings, all sports. *Address:* Whitcombe, Overbury, Tewkesbury GL20 7NZ. *T:* (01386) 725206. *Clubs:* Turf, MCC (Assoc. Mem.), Lord's Taverners; Royal Mid-Surrey Golf; Wooden Spoon (Whitstable).

HALLETT, Prof. Christine Margaret, PhD; FRSE; Professor of Social Policy, since 1995, and Principal and Vice-Chancellor, since 2004, University of Stirling; *b* 4 May 1949; *d* of Richard William Hallett and Gwendoline Hallett (*née* Owen). *Educ:* Newnham Coll., Cambridge (BA 1970); Loughborough Univ. (PhD Social Policy 1994). Civil servant, DHSS, 1970–74; research and teaching posts: Oxford Univ., 1974–76; Keele Univ., 1976–83; Univ. of WA, 1983–84; Univ. of Leicester, 1984–89; University of Stirling: Reader in Social Policy, 1989–95; Sen. Dep. Principal, 2001–03. FRSE 2002. *Publications:* (with O. Stevenson) Child Abuse: aspects of interprofessional co-operation, 1979; The Personal Social Services in Local Government, 1982; (ed) Women and Social Services Department, 1989; (with E. Birchall) Co-ordination and Child Protection, 1992; Interagency Co-ordination in Child Protection, 1995; (with E. Birchall) Working Together in Child Protection, 1995; (ed) Women and Social Policy: an introduction, 1996; (ed jtly) Social Exclusion and Social Work, 1998; (ed jtly) Hearing the Voices of

Children: social policy for a new century, 2003; monographs; contrib. learned jls. *Recreations:* golf, walking, tennis, music. *Address:* The Principal's Office, University of Stirling, Stirling FK9 4LA. *T:* (01786) 467011, *Fax:* (01786) 462087; *e-mail:* principal@stir.ac.uk.

HALLETT, Rt Hon. Dame Heather (Carol), DBE 1999; PC 2005; **Rt Hon. Lady Justice Hallett;** a Lord Justice of Appeal, since 2005; *b* 16 Dec. 1949; *d* of late Hugh Hallett, QPM and of Doris Hallett; *m* 1974, Nigel Wilkinson, *qv;* two *s. Educ:* St Hugh's Coll., Oxford (MA; Hon. Fellow, 1999). Called to the Bar, Inner Temple, 1972, Bencher, 1993; QC 1989; a Recorder, 1989–99; a Dep. High Court Judge, 1995–99; a Judge of the High Court of Justice, Queen's Bench Div., 1999–2005. Leader, S Eastern Circuit, 1995–97; Presiding Judge, Western Circuit, 2001–04. Member: Judicial Studies Bd., 2000–04; Judicial Appts Commn, 2006– (Vice-Chm., 2007). Chm., Gen. Council of the Bar, 1998 (Vice Chm., 1997). Hon. LLD Derby, 2000; DUniv Open, 2004. *Recreations:* theatre, music, games. *Address:* Royal Courts of Justice, Strand, WC2A 2LL.

HALLETT, Rob Leonard; President, International AEG Live, since 2007 (Senior Vice President, 2004–07); *b* London, 9 March 1958; *s* of Vernon Harold Leonard Hallett and Alma Victoria Hallett (*née* Braham); *m* Yvette Isha Allen; one *s. Educ:* Holy Cross Primary Sch., Uckfield; Uckfield Sch.; Lewes Tertiary Coll. Dir, DBA Artist Agency, 1980–84; Man. Dir, Performance and Trident Studios, 1984–90; Director: Marshall Arts Ltd, 1990–2000; Mean Fiddler plc, 2000–04. *Recreations:* watching Chelsea FC, food, wine, not accepting universal alibi. *Address:* AEG Live, 25 Canada Square, E14 5LQ. *T:* (020) 7536 2645, *Fax:* (020) 7536 2603; *e-mail:* rob@aeglive.co.uk.

HALLETT, Victor George Henry; Deputy Social Security Commissioner and Deputy Child Support Commissioner, 1993–95; *b* 11 Feb. 1921; *s* of Dr Denys Bouhier Imbert Hallett; *m* 1947, Margaret Hamlyn (*d* 2003). *Educ:* Westminster; Queen's Coll., Oxford (exhibitioner; MA). Served War, 1939–45 (wounded 1945, despatches 1946). Called to the Bar, Inner Temple, 1949. Mem., Land Registration Rules Cttee, 1971–76; Conveyancing Counsel of the Court, 1971–76; Nat. Insce, subseq. Social Security, Comr, 1976–93. *Publications:* Key and Elphinstone's Conveyancing Precedents (ed jtly), 15th edn, 1952; Prideaux's Precedents in Conveyancing (ed jtly), 25th edn, 1953; Hallett's Conveyancing Precedents, 1965; (with Nicholas Warren) Settlements, Wills and Capital Transfer Tax, 1979. *Address:* 20 Ashley Court, Ashley Road, Epsom, Surrey KT18 5AJ. *Club:* Travellers.

HALLGARTEN, His Honour Anthony Bernard Richard; QC 1978; a Circuit Judge, 1993–2004; Mercantile List Judge, Central London County Court, 1996–2004; arbitrator, since 2004; *b* 16 June 1937; *s* of late Fritz and Friedel Hallgarten; *m* 1962, Katherine Borchard (marr. diss. 1996); one *s* three *d; m* 1998, Theresa Carlson (*née* Tower). *Educ:* Merchant Taylors' Sch., Northwood; Downing Coll., Cambridge (BA). Called to the Bar, Middle Temple, 1961 (Barstow Scholar, Inns of Court, 1961); Bencher, 1987 (Reader, Lent 2006); a Recorder, 1990–93. Chm., Bar/Inns' Councils Jt Regulations Cttee, 1990–93. Mem., London Maritime Arbitrators' Assoc., 2008. Chair, Management Cttee, Camden Victim Support, 1989–93. *Recreations:* ski-ing, SW France, cycling. *Address:* 20 Essex Street, WC2R 3AL. *Clubs:* Garrick, MCC.

HALLIDAY, Prof. Alexander Norman, PhD; FRS 2000; Professor of Geochemistry, University of Oxford, since 2004; Fellow of St Hugh's College, Oxford, since 2004; *b* 11 Aug. 1952; *s* of Ronald James Rivers Halliday and Kathleen Elizabeth Halliday; *m* 1986, Christine Craig Young; two *s. Educ:* Univ. of Newcastle upon Tyne (BSc Hons Geol.; PhD Physics). Postdoctoral Fellow, 1976–81, Lectr, 1981–86, Scottish Univs Res. and Reactor Centre, E Kilbride; Department of Geological Sciences, University of Michigan: Associate Prof., 1986–91; Prof., 1991–98; Adjunct Prof., 1998–2000; Prof., ETH, Zürich, 1998–2004. Mem., NERC, 2004–. Pres., Geochemical Soc., 1995–97. Fellow, Amer. Geophysical Union, 2000 (Bowen Award, 1998). *Publications:* over 200 articles in sci. jls. *Recreation:* cycling. *Address:* St Hugh's College, Oxford OX2 6LE.

HALLIDAY, Charlotte Mary Irvine, NEAC 1961; RWS 1976 (ARWS 1971); topographical artist; Keeper, New English Art Club, since 1989; *b* 5 Sept. 1935; *d* of late Edward Halliday, CBE, RP, RBA and Dorothy Halliday. *Educ:* Francis Holland Sch.; Royal Academy Sch. *Commissions* include: construction of the Shell Centre, 1957–59; head offices of many City banks and insurance cos, incl. Willis Faber, Nat West Tower; clubs, colleges, major ecclesiastical buildings, incl. St Paul's and Salisbury Cathedrals; numerous stately and private homes. *Publications:* (illus.) A. Stuart Gray, Edwardian Architecture, 1985; (with A. Stuart Gray) Fanlights, a visual architectural history, 1990. *Recreations:* London Orpheus Choir, walking in the Downs, cats. *Address:* 36A Abercorn Place, St John's Wood, NW8 9XP. *T:* (020) 7289 1924; St Magnus Cottage, Houghton, near Arundel, W Sussex.

HALLIDAY, Prof. Fred, FBA 2002; ICREA Research Professor, Institut Barcelona d'Estudis Internacionals, since 2008; *b* 22 Feb. 1946; *s* of Arthur Halliday and Rita (*née* Finigan); *m* Prof. Maxine Molyneux; one *s. Educ:* Ampleforth Coll.; Univ. of Oxford (BA 1st Cl.); School of Oriental and African Studies (MSc); London School of Economics (PhD 1985). London School of Economics and Political Science: Dept of Internat. Relations, 1983–2008; Prof. of Internat. Relations, 1985–2008; Montague Burton Prof. of Internat. Relations, 2005–08; Dir Designate, Middle East Centre, 2006–08. Visiting Professor: Fundació CIDOB, 2004–05; Institut Barcelona d'Estudis Internacionals, 2005–08; Internat. Advr, Barcelona Centre for Contemporary Culture, 2005–. Associate Fellow, Inst. for Policy Studies, Washington, 1990–; Fellow, Transnational Inst., Amsterdam and Washington, 1973–85. Sen. Fellow, 21st Century Trust; Mem., Adv. Council, The Foreign Policy Centre, 1999–2004; Gov., LSE, 1994–98. AcSS 1999–2006. Contributing Ed., Middle East Reports, 1978–; Mem. Editl Bd, New Left Rev., 1969–83; columnist: Opendemocracy, 2004–; La Vanguardia, 2004–. *Publications:* Arabia without Sultans, 1974; Iran: dictatorship and development, 1978; (with Maxine Molyneux) The Ethiopian Revolution, 1981; Threat from the East?, 1982; The Making of the Second Cold War, 1983, 2nd edn 1986; Cold War, Third World, 1989; Revolution and Foreign Policy: the case of South Yemen 1967–1987, 1990; Arabs in Exile: the Yemen communities in Britain, 1992; Rethinking International Relations, 1994; Islam and the Myth of Confrontation, 1996; Revolution and World Politics: the rise and fall of the sixth great power, 1999; Nation and Religion in the Middle East, 2000; The World at 2000, 2000; Two Hours That Shook the World, 2001; The Middle East in International Relations, 2005; 100 Myths About the Middle East, 2005. *Recreations:* translation, travel, lunch, photography. *Address:* Institut Barcelona d'Estudis Internacionals, 12 Caller Elisabets, 08006 Barcelona, Spain.

HALLIDAY, Prof. Ian Gibson, PhD; FInstP; FRSE; Chief Executive, Scottish Universities Physics Alliance, since 2005; Professor, University of Edinburgh, since 2005; President, European Science Foundation, since 2006; *b* 5 Feb. 1940; *s* of John Alexander Halliday and Gladys (*née* Taylor); *m* 1965, Ellenor Gardiner Hervey Wilson; one *s* one *d. Educ:* Kelso High Sch.; Perth Acad.; Edinburgh Univ. (MA 1961; MSc 1962); Clare Coll., Cambridge (PhD 1964). Instructor, Princeton Univ., 1964–66; Fellow, Christ's Coll.,

Cambridge, 1966–67; Imperial College, University of London: Lectr, 1967–75; Reader, 1975–90; Prof., 1990–92; University of Wales, Swansea: Prof. of Physics and Hd of Dept, 1992–98; Dean of Graduate Sch., 1993–96; Hon. Prof., 2002–; Hon. Fellow, 2005; Chief Exec., PPARC, 1998–2005. Chm., Prior Options Review of Royal Observatories, 1995. Member: PPARC, 1994–98; European Res. Adv. Bd, 2001–07; Reconfiguration and Collaboration Panel, 1998–, Res. Libraries Review, 2001–02, HEFCE. Member: Bd, World Premier Inst., MEXT, Japan, 1998–; Governing Bd, Fermi Res. Alliance, Fermi Nat. Accelerator Lab., Chicago, 2007–. Hon. DSc: Edinburgh, 2005; Wales, 2006; Glasgow, 2006. *Publications:* numerous papers on theoretical particle physics in Nuclear Physics, Physics Letters. *Recreations:* sewin fishing, golf, tennis. *Address:* Derwent House, Walkley Hill, Rodborough, Stroud GL5 3TX; *e-mail:* Ian.Halliday@e-halliday.org.

HALLIDAY, John Frederick, CB 1994; Deputy Under Secretary of State, Home Office, 1990–2001; *b* 19 Sept. 1942; *s* of E. Halliday; *m* 1970, Alison Burgess; four *s. Educ:* Whitgift School, Croydon; St John's College, Cambridge (MA). Teacher, under VSO, Aitchison College, Lahore, 1964–66; Home Office, 1966; Principal Private Sec. to Home Sec., 1980; Asst Under-Sec. of State, Home Office, 1983–87; Under Sec., DHSS, then Dept of Health, 1987–90, on secondment. *Publication:* Making Punishments Work (Govt report), 2001. *Recreations:* music, gardening, theatre.

HALLIDAY, Prof. Michael Alexander Kirkwood; Professor of Linguistics in the University of Sydney, 1976–87, Emeritus Professor, since 1988; *b* 13 April 1925; *s* of late Wilfrid J. Halliday and Winifred Halliday (*née* Kirkwood). *Educ:* Rugby School; SOAS, University of London (BA); MA, PhD, Cambridge. Served Army, 1944–47. Asst Lectr in Chinese, Cambridge Univ., 1954–58; Lectr in General Linguistics, Edinburgh Univ., 1958–60; Reader in General Linguistics, Edinburgh Univ., 1960–63; Dir, Communication Res. Centre, UCL, 1963–65; Linguistic Soc. of America Prof., Indiana Univ., 1964; Prof. of General Linguistics, UCL, 1965–71; Fellow, Center for Advanced Study in the Behavioral Sciences, Stanford, Calif., 1972–73; Prof. of Linguistics, Univ. of Illinois, 1973–74; Prof. of Language and Linguistics, Essex Univ., 1974–75. Visiting Professor of Linguistics: Yale, 1967; Brown, 1971; Nairobi, 1972; Nat. Univ. of Singapore, 1990–91; Internat. Christian Univ., Tokyo, 1992; Lee Kuan Yew Distinguished Visitor, Nat. Univ. of Singapore, 1986; Hon. Sen. Res. Fellow, Birmingham Univ., 1991; Dist. Vis. Prof., Univ. of HK, 2003–04. FAHA 1979. Corresp. FBA 1989; For. Mem., Academia Europaea, 1994. Guest Prof., Peking Univ., 1995. Hon. Fellow: Univ. of Wales, Cardiff, 1998; Central Inst. of English and For. Langs, Hyderabad, India, 1999. Dr *hc* Nancy, 1968; Hon. DLitt: Birmingham, 1987; York (Canada), 1988; Athens, 1995; Macquarie, 1996; Lingnan, Hong Kong, 1999; DUniv Open, 2002; Hon. LLD British Columbia, 2007. *Publications:* The Language of the Chinese 'Secret History of the Mongols', 1959; (with A. McIntosh and P. Strevens) The Linguistic Sciences and Language Teaching, 1964; (with A. McIntosh) Patterns of Language, 1966; Intonation and Grammar in British English, 1967; A Course in Spoken English: Intonation, 1970; Explorations in the Functions of Language, 1973; Learning How To Mean, 1975; (with R. Hasan) Cohesion in English, 1976; System and Function in Language, ed G. Kress, 1976; Language as Social Semiotic, 1978; An Introduction to Functional Grammar, 1985; Spoken and Written Language, 1985; (with J. Martin) Writing Science, 1993; (with C. Matthiessen) Construing Experience through Meaning, 1999; (with W. Greaves) Intonation in the Grammar of English, 2008; Complementarities in Language, 2008; Collected Papers, vols 1 and 2, 2002, vol. 3, 2003, vols 4 and 5, 2004, vols 6 and 7, 2005, vol. 8, 2006, vols 9 and 10, 2007; articles in Jl of Linguistics, Word, Trans of Philological Soc., Functions of Lang., etc. *Address:* PO Box 42, Urunga, NSW 2455, Australia.

HALLIDAY, Norman Pryde; Consultant Adviser to Minister of Health, Saudi Arabia, since 1996; *b* 28 March 1932; *s* of late James and Jessie Thomson Hunter Halliday; *m* 1953, Eleanor Smith; three *s* one *d. Educ:* Woodside, Glasgow; King's Coll., London; King's Coll. Hosp. Med. Sch. SRN 1955; MB BS, MRCS, LRCP 1964; DCH RCPGlas 1969; MBA: Warwick, 1991; Open Univ., 1992. Various posts in clinical medicine, incl. Registrar (Paediatrics), KCH, London; SMO, DHSS, 1972; SPMO (Under Sec.), DHSS, later DoH, 1977–92. Gen. Man., Eur. Dialysis and Transplant Assoc., 1994–95. Tutor: Open Univ., 1992–; Warwick Univ., 1992–. QHP 1990–93. *Publications:* articles on medical subjects in professional journals. *Recreations:* photography, sub aqua diving, fashion, DIY, cross-bow shooting. *Address:* Gurrs Farm, Crowborough Hill, Crowborough, E Sussex TN6 2SD. *T:* (01892) 669132.

HALLIDAY, Rt Rev. Robert Taylor; Bishop of Brechin, 1990–96; *b* 7 May 1932; *s* of James Halliday and Agnes Logan Halliday (*née* Scott); *m* 1960, Georgina Mabel, (Gena) (*née* Chadwin); one *d. Educ:* High Sch. of Glasgow; Univ. of Glasgow (MA, BD); Episcopal Theol Coll., Edinburgh. Deacon 1957; priest 1958. Assistant Curate: St Andrew's, St Andrews, 1957–60; St Margaret's, Newlands, Glasgow, 1960–63; Rector, Church of the Holy Cross, Davidson's Mains, Edinburgh, 1963–83; External Lectr in New Testament, Episcopal Theol Coll., Edin., 1963–74; Canon of St Mary's Cathedral, Edinburgh, 1973–83; Rector of St Andrew's, St Andrews, 1983–90; Tutor in Biblical Studies, Univ. of St Andrews, 1984–90; warrant, dio. of Edinburgh, 1997–. Hon. Canon, Trinity Cathedral, Davenport, Iowa, 1990. *Recreations:* walking, reading, visiting gardens, shredding appeals from Uganda. *Address:* 28 Forbes Road, Edinburgh EH10 4ED. *T:* (0131) 221 1490.

HALLIDAY, S. F. P.; *see* Halliday, F.

HALLIDAY, Sandra Pauline, CEng; Founder and Principal, Gaia Research, since 1996. *Educ:* Warwick Univ. (BSc Hons Engrg Design and Appropriate Technology); Reading Univ. (MPhil 1999). MCIBSE 1994. Research at Univs of Bath and Reading, 1986–91; Founder, then Head of Centre for Construction Ecology, BSRIA, 1990–95. Current research projects incl. solar design, innovative building membranes, daylighting, low allergy housing, teaching, research and guidance in sustainable building design, model briefs for sustainable devel of schs, communities. Royal Acad. of Engrg Vis. Prof. in Sustainable Engrg Design, Univ. of Strathclyde, 2003–. FRSA. *Publications:* Green Guide to the Architects' Job Book, 2000, 2nd edn 2007; Anarchi: animal architecture, 2003; Sustainable Construction, 2008; papers, articles, technical reports and conf. proceedings. *Recreations:* squash, Go, walking, cycling, ecology.

HALLIDAY, Prof. Timothy Richard, DPhil; Professor in Biology, The Open University, since 1991; *b* 11 Sept. 1945; *s* of Jack and Edna Halliday; *m* 1970, Carolyn Bridget Wheeler; one *s* two *d. Educ:* Marlborough Coll.; New Coll., Oxford (MA, DPhil); King's Coll., Cambridge (CertEd). Lectr, Sen. Lectr and Reader, 1977–91, Open Univ. Internat. Dir, IUCN/SSC Declining Amphibian Populations Task Force, 1994–2006. Chm., Conservation and Consultancy Bd, Zool Soc. of London, 1993–96. *Publications:* Vanishing Birds, 1978; Sexual Strategy, 1980; (with K. Adler) The Encyclopedia of Reptiles and Amphibians, 1986 (numerous foreign language edns); (with K. Adler) The New Encyclopedia of Reptiles and Amphibians, 2002. *Recreations:* biological illustration, gardening, travel. *Address:* 21 Farndon Road, Oxford OX2 6RT. *T:* (01865) 512163; Department of Biological Sciences, The Open University, Milton Keynes MK7 6AA. *T:* (01908) 653831.

HALLIGAN, Prof. Aidan William Francis, MD; FRCP, FRCOG; Director of Education, University College London Hospital, since 2007; *b* Dublin, 17 Sept. 1957; *s* of Michael and Maureen Halligan; *m* 1985, Dr Carol Mary Sarah Furlong; three *d. Educ:* Templeogue Coll., Dublin; Trinity Coll., Dublin (MB BCh BAO, MA); MD. MRCOG 1991, FRCOG 2004; MRCPI 1996; FFPH (FFPHM 2003); FRCP 2004. SHO, Royal City of Dublin Hosp., St James's and Rotunda Hosps, Dublin, 1986–88; Registrar, Rotunda Hosp., then Mater Misericordiae Hosp., Dublin, 1989–90; Res. Registrar, Rotunda Hosp., Dublin, 1991–93; Lectr, 1993–94, Sen. Lectr, 1994–97, in Obstetrics and Gynaecology, Leicester Univ.; Consultant Obstetrician and Gynaecol., Leicester Royal Infirmary, 1994–97; Prof. of Fetal Maternal Medicine, Leicester Univ. and Univ. Hosps of Leicester NHS Trust, 1997–99; Postgrad. Dir, Training, Obstetrics and Gynaecol., 1995–99, Hd, Obstetric Service, 1998–99, Univ. Hosps of Leicester NHS Trust; Prog. Trng Dir, Obstetrics and Gynaecol., S Trent, 1995–99; Hd, NHS Clinical Governance Support Team, 1999–2002; Dep. CMO, DoH, 2003–05; Dir of Clinical Governance for NHS, 1999–2006; Chief Exec., Elision Health Ltd, 2006–08. Visiting Professor: Dept of Surgical Oncology and Technol., Imperial Coll. London, 2005–; Postgrad. Med. Sch., Univ. of Surrey, 2007–Aug. 2009. *Publications:* articles in Br. Jl of Obstetrics and Gynaecol., BMJ, Lancet, Jl of Hypertension, Obstetrics and Gynecol., Hypertension in Pregnancy, Amer. Jl of Obstetrics and Gynecol., Br. Jl of Clinical Governance, and other learned jls. *Recreations:* reading, walking. *Address:* University College London Hospital, 250 Euston Road, NW1 2PG. *T:* 0845 1555000, ext. 8822; *e-mail:* Aidan.halligan@uclh.nhs.uk.

HALLIGAN, Liam James; Chief Economist, Prosperity Capital Management, since 2008; Financial Columnist, GQ Magazine, since 2007; *b* 29 April 1969; *s* of Martin Thomas Halligan and Evelyn Halligan (*née* Thorp); partner, Lucy Ward; one *s* two *d. Educ:* John Lyon Sch., Harrow (entrance schol., head boy); Univ. of Warwick (BSc 1st Cl. Hons Econs 1991); St Antony's Coll., Oxford (MPhil Econs 1994). Economics Intern: Internat. Food Policy Res. Inst., 1991; IMF, 1992; Hd of Res., Social Mkt Foundn, 1993; Res. Economist, and author, Russian Econ. Trends, LSE, 1994–95; Moscow Reporter, The Economist, 1995–96; columnist, Moscow Times, 1995–96; Political Corresp., FT, 1996–98; Econs Corresp., Channel 4 News, 1998–2006; columnist: Sunday Business, 2000–01; Business Section, Sunday Telegraph, 2001– (Econs Ed., 2005–07). Wincott Business Broadcaster of Year, Harold Wincott Foundn, 1999; Business Journalist of Year (Broadcast), World Leadership Forum, 2004, 2005; Business and Finance Journalist of Year, British Press Awards, 2007; Columnist of Year, Workworld, 2007. *Publications:* (with Frank Field) Europe Isn't Working, 1994; contrib. numerous articles for Economist Intelligence Unit and Wall St Jl. *Recreations:* family, sailing, rowing, guitar, double bass, football, roller-skating. *Address:* c/o Knight Ayton Management, 114 St Martin's Lane, WC2N 4BE. *T:* (020) 7836 5333; *e-mail:* info@knightayton.co.uk.

HALLINAN, Mary Alethea; *see* Parry Evans, M. A.

HALLIWELL, Prof. Richard Edward Winter; William Dick Professor of Veterinary Clinical Studies, Royal (Dick) School of Veterinary Studies, University of Edinburgh, 1988–2002, now Emeritus (Dean, Faculty of Veterinary Medicine, 1990–94 and 2000–02); *b* 16 June 1937; *s* of Arthur Clare Halliwell and Winifred Dorothea Goode; *m* 1963, Jenifer Helen Roper; two *d. Educ:* St Edward's Sch., Oxford; Gonville and Caius Coll., Cambridge (MA, VetMB, PhD); MRCVS. Jun. Fellow in Vet. Surgery, Univ. of Bristol, 1961–63; private vet. practice, London, 1963–68; Vis. Fellow in Dermatology, Univ. of Pennsylvania Sch. of Vet. Med., 1968–70; Wellcome Vet. Fellowship Univ. of Cambridge, 1970–73; Asst Prof. of Dermatology, Univ. of Pennsylvania Sch. of Vet. Med., 1973–77; Prof. and Chm., Dept of Med. Scis, Univ. of Florida Coll. of Vet. Med., 1977–88; Prof., Dept of Med. Microbiol., Univ. of Florida Coll. of Med., 1977–88. UK Rep., EC Adv. Cttee on Vet. Trng, 1994–98. President: Amer. Acad. of Veterinary Allergy, 1978–80; Amer. Assoc. of Veterinary Immunologists, 1984; Amer. Coll. of Veterinary Dermatology, 1984–86; Eur. Assoc. of Estabs for Vet. Educn, 1994–98 (Hon. Life Pres., 2002); Eur. Coll. of Vet. Dermatology, 1996–98; World Congress of Vet. Dermatology Assoc., 1999–; Royal College of Veterinary Surgeons: Treas., 2001–02; Jun. Vice-Pres., 2002–03; Pres., 2003–04; Sen. Vice-Pres., 2004–05. FMedSci 1999. Dr *hc* Warsaw Agricl Univ., 2003. *Publications:* (with N. T. Gorman) Veterinary Clinical Immunology, 1989; (with C. von Tscharner) Advances in Veterinary Dermatology, 1990; numerous pubns in area of clin. immunology and vet. dermatology. *Recreations:* wine, music, travelling. *Address:* 2A Ainslie Place, Edinburgh EH3 6AR. *T:* (0131) 225 8765.

HALLON, Gayle, (Mrs J. A. Hodgson); Her Honour Judge Hallon; a Circuit Judge, South Eastern Circuit, since 1992; *b* 10 Aug. 1946; *d* of late Douglas Hallon, VRD, FRCS and Enid (*née* Bailey); *m* 1971, John Arnold Hodgson. *Educ:* Cheltenham Ladies' Coll.; St Hugh's Coll., Oxford (MA). Called to the Bar, Inner Temple, 1968; practised at the Bar, 1969–92; Recorder, 1987–92. *Recreations:* gardening, acting. *Address:* The Court House, College Road, Bromley, Kent BR1 3PX. *T:* (020) 8290 9620.

HALLS, Andrew David, MA; Head Master, King's College School, Wimbledon, since 2008; *b* 29 Jan. 1959; *s* of Gerald and Barbara Halls; *m* 1987, Véronique Le Droff; two *d. Educ:* Shenley Court Sch., Birmingham; Gonville and Caius Coll., Cambridge (Schol.; BA Double 1st Cl. Hons English 1981; MA). English teacher: Chigwell Sch., 1981–84; Whitgift Sch., 1984–89; Hd of English, Bristol GS, 1989–95; Dep. Headmaster, Trinity Sch., 1995–98; Master, Magdalen Coll. Sch., 1998–2007. *Recreations:* family, reading, theatre, running. *Address:* King's College School, Wimbledon, SW19 4TT.

HALLS, David John; Director of Music, Salisbury Cathedral, since 2005; *b* 14 Jan. 1963; *s* of William and Sally Halls; *m* 1986, Nicola Holman; three *s* two *d. Educ:* Worcester Coll., Oxford (BA Hons Music 1984, MA); Winchester (PGCE 1985). FRCO 1985. Organ Scholar, Winchester Cath., 1984; Salisbury Cathedral: Asst Organist, 1985–2000; Asst Dir of Music, 2000–05. *Recreations:* reading, wine, football, cricket. *Address:* Ladywell, 33 The Close, Salisbury SP1 2EJ. *T:* (01722) 555125, *Fax:* (01722) 555117; *e-mail:* d.halls@salcath.co.uk.

HALNAN, His Honour Patrick John; a Circuit Judge, 1986–97; *b* 7 March 1925; *s* of E. T. and A. B. Halnan; *m* 1955, Judith Mary (*née* Humberstone) (*d* 2003); four *c. Educ:* Perse Sch., Cambridge; Trinity Coll., Cambridge (MA). Army, 1943–47 (incl. RA in Burma); TA, 1951–58 (incl. 23 SAS). Solicitor. Asst Solicitor, Hants CC, 1954–58; Clerk to the Justices, Cambs, 1958–78; Metropolitan Stipendiary Magistrate, 1978–86; a Recorder, 1983–86; SE Circuit. Sec., Justices' Clerks' Soc., 1972–76, Pres., 1978. Chm., Road Traffic Cttee, Magistrates' Assoc., 1981–87. *Publications:* (ed with Prof. R. M. Jackson) Leo Page, Justice of the Peace, 3rd edn 1967; (ed) Wilkinson's Road Traffic Offences, 7th edn 1973 to 14th edn 1989; (with David Latham) Drink/Driving Offences, 1979; Road Traffic, 1981; Drink/Drive: the new law, 1984. *Recreations:* Freemasonry, travelling, bridge, postal history. *Address:* Gretton Court, Girton, Cambridge CB3 0QN. *Club:* Oxford and Cambridge.

HALONEN, Tarja Kaarina; President of Finland, since 2000; *b* Helsinki, 24 Dec. 1943; *m* (marr. diss.); one *d*; *m* 2000, Pentti Arajarvi. *Educ:* Univ. of Helsinki (ML). Lawyer,

Lainvalvonta Oy, 1967–68; Social Welfare Officer and Organizing Sec., Nat. Union of Finnish Students, 1969–70; Lawyer, Cultural Orgn of Finnish Trade Unions, 1970–74; lawyer, 1975–79. Parly Sec. to Prime Minister, 1974–75; Mem., Helsinki CC, 1977–96. MP (SDP), Finland, 1979–2000; Chm., Parly Social Affairs Cttee, 1984–87; Minister, Min. of Social Affairs and Health, 1987–90; Minister: for Nordic Co-operation, 1989–91; of Justice, 1990–91; for Foreign Affairs, 1995–2000. *Address:* Office of the President, Mariankatu 2, 00170 Helsinki, Finland.

HALPERN, David Anthony; QC 2006; *b* 23 May 1956; *s* of Cecil and Audrey Halpern; *m* 1981, Dr Helen Kahn; two *s* one *d*. *Educ:* St Paul's Sch., London; Magdalen Coll., Oxford (Exhibnr; MA Juris). Called to the Bar, Gray's Inn, 1978; in practice as barrister, 1979–, specialising in commercial chancery work and professional negligence. *Publication:* (contrib.) Jackson & Powell on Professional Liability, 6th edn 2006. *Recreations:* piano, cycling, travel, cold-water swimming. *Address:* (chambers) 4 New Square, Lincoln's Inn, WC2A 3RJ. *T:* (020) 7822 2000; *e-mail:* d.halpern@4newsquare.com.

HALPERN, Prof. Jack, FRS 1974; FRS(Can) 2005; Louis Block Distinguished Service Professor of Chemistry, University of Chicago, since 1984; *b* Poland, 19 Jan. 1925 (moved to Canada, 1929; USA 1962); *s* of Philip Halpern and Anna Sass; *m* 1949, Helen Peritz; two *d*. *Educ:* McGill Univ., Montreal. BSc 1946, PhD 1949. NRC Postdoc. Fellow, Univ. of Manchester, 1949–50; Prof. of Chem., Univ. of Brit. Columbia, 1950–62 (Nuffield Foundn Travelling Fellow, Cambridge Univ., 1959–60); Prof. of Chem., Univ. of Chicago, 1962–71, Louis Block Prof., 1971–84. Visiting Professor: Univ. of Minnesota, 1962; Harvard Univ., 1966–67; CIT, 1969; Princeton Univ., 1970–71; Copenhagen Univ., 1978; Firth Vis. Prof., Sheffield, 1982; Sherman Fairchild Dist. Scholar, CIT, 1979; Guest Scholar, Kyoto Univ., 1981; Phi Beta Kappa Vis. Scholar, 1990; R. B. Woodward Vis. Prof., Harvard Univ., 1991; External Sci. Mem., Max Planck Institut für Kohlenforschung, Mulheim, 1983–; Lectureships: 3M, Univ. of Minnesota, 1968; FMC, Princeton Univ., 1969; Du Pont, Univ. of Calif., Berkeley, 1970; Frontier of Chemistry, Case Western Reserve Univ., 1971, 1989; Venable, Univ. of N Carolina, 1973; Ritter Meml, Miami Univ., 1980; University, Univ. of Western Ontario, F. J. Toole, Univ. of New Brunswick, 1981; Werner, Univ. of Kansas, Lansdowne, Univ. of Victoria, 1982; Welch, Univ. of Texas, 1983; Kilpatrick, Illinois Inst. of Tech., 1984; Dow, Univ. of Ottawa, Boomer, Univ. of Alberta, 1985; Bailar, Univ. of Illinois, 1986; Priestley, Penn State Univ., 1987; Taube, Stanford Univ., 1988; Res. Schol., Drew Univ., Liebig. Univ. of Colorado, 1989; Kennedy, Washington Univ., Karcher, Univ. of Oklahoma, Nieuland, Notre Dame, Swift, CIT, Hutchison, Univ. of Rochester, 1992; Rhone-Poulenc, Scripps Res. Inst., Basolo, Northwestern Univ., 1993; Patrick, Kansas State Univ., Jonassen, Tulane Univ., 1995. Associate Editor: Jl of Amer. Chem. Soc.; Inorganica Chimica Acta; Procs of Nat. Acad. of Scis; Mem. Editorial Bds: Accounts of Chemical Research; Jl of Catalysis; Catalysis Reviews; Jl of Coordination Chem.; Inorganic Syntheses; Jl of Molecular Catalysis; Jl of Organometallic Chemistry; Amer. Chem. Soc. Advances in Chemistry series; Gazzetta Chimica Italiana; Organometallics; Catalysis Letters; Reaction Kinetics and Catalysis Letters; Co-editor, OUP International Series of Monographs in Chemistry. Member: Nat. Sci. Foundn Chemistry Adv. Panel, 1967–70; MIT Chemistry Vis. Cttee, 1968–70; Argonne Nat. Lab. Chemistry Vis. Cttee, 1970–73; Amer. Chem. Soc. Petroleum Res. Fund Adv. Bd, 1972–74; NIH Medicinal Chem. Study Sect., 1975–78 (Chm., 1976–78); Princeton Univ. Chem. Adv. Council, 1982–85; Chemistry Adv. Cttee, CIT, 1991–95; Trans-Atlantic Sci. and Humanities Prog. Adv. Bd, Humboldt Foundn, 2001–; Encyclopaedia Britannica Univ. Adv. Cttee, 1985–. Mem., Bd of Trustees and Council, Gordon Research Confs, 1968–70; Chm., Gordon Conf. on Inorganic Chem., 1969; Chm., Amer. Chemical Soc. Div. of Inorganic Chem., 1971; Mem., 1985–, Mem., Council, 1990–, Chm., Chem. Sect., Vice-Pres., 1993–2001, Nat. Acad. of Scis (For. Mem., 1984–85). Chm., German-Amer. Acad. Council, 1993–96, Chm. Bd of Trustees, 1996–99. Member: Bd of Dirs, Renaissance Soc., 1984–87; Bd of Govs, Smart Mus., Univ. of Chicago, 1988–; Adv. Bd, Court Theatre, Univ. of Chicago, 1989–; Dir, Amer. Friends of Royal Soc., 2000–. Fellow, Amer. Acad. of Arts and Sciences, 1967; Sci. Mem., Max Planck Soc., 1983. Hon. FRSC 1987. Hon. DSc: Univ. of British Columbia, 1986; McGill Univ., 1997. Holds numerous honours and awards, including: Amer. Chem. Soc. Award in Inorganic Chem., 1968; Chem. Soc. Award, 1976; Humboldt Award, 1977; Kokes Award, Johns Hopkins Univ., 1978; Amer. Chem. Soc. Award for Distinguished Service in the Advancement of Inorganic Chemistry, 1985; Willard Gibbs Medal, 1986; Bailar Medal, Univ. of Illinois, 1986; Hoffman Medal, German Chem. Soc., 1988; Chemical Pioneer Award, Amer. Inst. of Chemists, 1991; Paracelsus Prize, Swiss Chem. Soc., 1992; Basolo Medal, Northwestern Univ., 1993; Robert A. Welch Award in Chemistry, 1994; Amer. Chem. Soc. Award in Organometallic Chemistry, 1995; Henry Alberts Award, Internat. Precious Metals Inst., 1995. Cross of Merit (Germany), 1996. *Publications:* Editor (with F. Basolo and J. Bunnett) Collected Accounts of Transition Metal Chemistry, vol. I, 1973, vol. II, 1977; contrib. articles on Catalysis and on Coordination Compounds to Encyclopaedia Britannica; numerous articles to Jl of Amer. Chemical Soc. and other scientific jls. *Recreations:* art, music, theatre. *Address:* Department of Chemistry, University of Chicago, 929 East 57th Street, Chicago, IL 60637, USA. *T:* (773) 7027095. *Club:* Quadrangle (Chicago).

HALPERN, Sir Ralph (Mark), Kt 1986; Chairman, Halpern Associates, since 1994; Chairman, 1981–90, and Chief Executive, 1978–90, Burton Group plc (Managing Director, 1978); *b* 24 Oct. 1938; *m* (marr. diss.); one *d*; *m* 2003, Laura; one *s*. *Educ:* St Christopher School, Letchworth. Started career as trainee, Selfridges; joined Burton Group, 1961; founder, Top Shop, 1970. Member: President's Cttee, CBI, 1984–90; President's Cttee, Business in the Community, 1991–92; Adv. Council, Prince's Youth Business Trust, 1991–. Chm., British Fashion Council, 1990–94. Local Councillor, Surrey; Chm., E Surrey Rural Police and Community Partnership Gp. FInstD; CCMI.

HALSALL, Hazel Anne; *see* Blears, H. A.

HALSBURY, 4th Earl of; *see* Giffard, A. E.

HALSEY, Prof. Albert Henry, FBA 1995; Professor of Social and Administrative Studies, University of Oxford, 1978–90, now Emeritus; Professorial Fellow of Nuffield College, Oxford, 1962–90, now Emeritus; *b* 13 April 1923; *m* 1949, Gertrude Margaret Littler; three *s* two *d*. *Educ:* Kettering Grammar Sch.; London Sch. of Econs (BSc (Econ); PhD; Hon. Fellow, 1993); MA Oxon. RAF, 1942–47; student LSE, 1947–52; Research Worker, Liverpool Univ., 1952–54; Lectr in Sociology, Birmingham Univ., 1954–62; Dir, Dept of Social and Admin. Studies, Oxford Univ., 1962–78. Fellow, Center for Advanced Study of Behavioral Sciences, Palo Alto, Calif, 1956–57; Vis. Prof. of Sociology, Univ. of Chicago, 1959–60. Adviser to Sec. of State for Educn, 1965–68; Chm. of CERI at OECD, Paris, 1968–70. Reith Lectr, 1977. MAE 1992; Foreign Associate, Amer. Acad. of Educn.; Foreign Mem., Amer. Acad. of Arts and Scis, 1988. Hon. Fellow: Goldsmiths' Coll., 1992; Westminster Coll., 1996; Royal Statistical Soc., 1999. Hon. DSocSc Birmingham, 1987; DUniv Open, 1990; Hon. DLitt: Glamorgan, 1994; Leicester, 1995; Warwick, 1995. *Publications:* (jtly) Social Class and Educational Opportunity, 1956; (jtly) Technical Change and Industrial Relations, 1956; (with J. E. Floud) The Sociology of Education, Current Sociology VII, 1958; (jtly) Education, Economy and Society, 196 Ability and Educational Opportunity, 1962; (with G. N. Ostergaard) Power in Co operatives, 1965; (with Ivor Crewe) Social Survey of the Civil Service, 1969; (with Marti Trow) The British Academics, 1971; (ed) Trends in British Society since 1900, 1972; (e Educational Priority, 1972; Traditions of Social Policy, 1976; Heredity and Environmen 1977; Change in British Society, 1978, 4th edn 1995; (jtly) Origins and Destination 1980; (with Norman Dennis) English Ethical Socialism, 1988; Decline of Donnis Dominion, 1992, 2nd edn 1995; No Discouragement, 1996; (jtly) Education, Cultur Economy, Society, 1997; (ed) British Social Trends: the twentieth century, 2000; History of Sociology in Britain, 2004; (with R. G. Runciman) British Sociology fro Within and Without, 2005; Democracy in Crisis?, 2007; numerous articles and review *Address:* 28 Upland Park Road, Oxford OX2 7RU. *T:* (01865) 558625.

HALSEY, Rt Rev. (Henry) David; Bishop of Carlisle, 1972–89; *b* 27 Jan. 1919; *s* George Halsey, MBE and Gladys W. Halsey, DSc; *m* 1947, Rachel Margaret Neil Smit four *d*. *Educ:* King's Coll. Sch., Wimbledon; King's Coll., London (BA); Wells Theo College. Curate, Petersfield, 1942–45; Chaplain, RNVR, 1946–47; Curate, St Andrew Plymouth, 1947–50; Vicar of: Netheravon, 1950–53; St Stephen, Chatham, 1953–6 Bromley, and Chaplain, Bromley Hosp., 1962–68; Rural Dean of Bromley, 1965–6 Archdeacon of Bromley, 1966–68; Bishop Suffragan of Tonbridge, 1968–72. Entere House of Lords, 1976. *Recreations:* cricket, sailing, reading, gardening, walking. *Addres* Bramblecross, Gully Road, Seaview, Isle of Wight PO34 5BY.

See also D. French.

HALSEY, Rev. John Walter Brooke, 4th Bt *cr* 1920 (but uses designation Brother Joh Halsey); *b* 26 Dec. 1933; *s* of Sir Thomas Edgar Halsey, 3rd Bt, DSO, and of Jean Margar Palmer, *d* of late Bertram Willes Dayrell Brooke; *S* father, 1970. *Educ:* Eton; Magdalen College, Cambridge (BA 1957). Deacon 1961, priest 1962, Diocese of York; Curate o Stocksbridge, 1961–65; Brother in Community of the Transfiguration, 1965–. *Heir: cous* Nicholas Guy Halsey, TD [*b* 14 June 1948; *m* 1976, Viola Georgina Juliet, *d* of Ma George Thorne, MC, DL; one *s*]. *Address:* The Hermitage, 23 Manse Road, Rosli Midlothian EH25 9LF.

HALSEY, Philip Hugh, CB 1986; LVO 1972; Deputy Secretary, Department o Education and Science, 1982–88; *b* 9 May 1928; *s* of Sidney Robert Halsey and Edit Mary Halsey; *m* 1956, Hilda Mary Biggerstaff; two *s*. *Educ:* University Coll. London (BSc Fellow, 1992). Headmaster, Hampstead Sch., 1961; Principal, DES, 1966; Under-Sec 1977. Chm. and Chief Exec., Sch. Exams and Assessment Council, 1988–91; Mem., Sch Teachers' Review Body, 1991–96.

HALSEY, Simon Patrick; Chorus Director, City of Birmingham Symphony Orchestr since 1983; Chief Conductor, Berlin Rundfunk Chor, since 2001; Principal Conducto Choral Programme, Northern Sinfonia, since 2004; *b* 8 March 1958; *s* of Louis Arthu Owen Halsey and Evelyn Elisabeth (*née* Calder); *m* 1986, Lucy Jane Lunt; one *s* one *Educ:* chorister, New Coll., Oxford; Winchester Coll.; King's Coll., Cambridge (Chor. Schol.; BA 1979; MA 1983); Royal Coll. Music (Schol.). Conductor, Scottish Oper (Opera-Go-Round), 1979; Dir of Music, Univ. of Warwick, 1980–88; Princip Conductor, City of Birmingham Touring Opera, 1987–2000; Chorus Dir, De Vlaams Opera, Antwerp, 1991–94; Artistic Dir, BBC Nat. Chorus of Wales, 1995–200 Founding Conductor, European Voices, 1999–; Chief Conductor, Netherlands Radi Choir, 2002–08 (Chief Guest Conductor, 1995–2002). Chief Guest Conductor, Sydne Philharmonia Choirs, 1997–2001; frequent Guest Conductor of choruses, Châtelet Th Paris, 1996–, and Salzburg Fest., 1998–; Chorus Dir, Sydney Olympic Games, 200 Consultant Ed., Faber Music, 1994–. Hon. Dr UCE, 2000; Hon. MA Warwick, 2007 Recording awards include: Gramophone Record of Year, Gramophone Magazin (many); Deutsche Schallplatten Kritiek Preis (many); Grammy, 2008. *Publications:* Ed., 3 vols of choral music, 1995–. *Recreations:* reading, walking. *Address:* Granby House, 27 High Street, Henley-in-Arden, Warwickshire B95 5BG. *T:* (01564) 794873.

HALSTEAD, Sir Ronald, Kt 1985; CBE 1976; Deputy Chairman, British Steel pl (formerly British Steel Corporation), 1986–94; *b* 17 May 1927; *s* of Richard and Bessi Harrison Halstead; *m* 1968, Yvonne Cecile de Monchaux (*d* 1978); two *s*. *Educ:* Lancaste Royal Grammar Sch.; Queens' Coll., Cambridge (Hon. Fellow, 1985). MA, FRSC Research Chemist, H. P. Bulmer & Co., 1948–53; Manufg Manager, Macleans Ltd 1954–55; Factory Manager, Beecham Products Inc. (USA), 1955–60; Asst Managing Di Beecham Research Labs, 1960–62; Vice-Pres. (Marketing), Beecham Products Inc (USA), 1962–64; Pres., Beecham Research Labs Inc. (USA), 1962–64; Chairman: Foo and Drink Div., Beecham Group Ltd, 1964–67; Beecham Products, 1967–84; Man. Di (Consumer Products) Beecham Gp, 1973–84; Chm. and Chief Exec., Beecham Gp 1984–85. Dir, Otis Elevator Co. Ltd (UK), 1978–83; non-executive Director: BSC, late British Steel, 1979–94; The Burmah Oil PLC, 1983–89; Amer. Cyanamid Co. (USA) 1986–94; Davy Corp. plc, 1986–91; Gestetner Holdings PLC, 1986–95; Laurentia Financial Gp, 1991–95. Mem. Egg Re-organisation Commn, 1967–68; Pres., Incorp. Soc of Brit. Advertisers, 1971–73; Chairman: British Nutrition Foundn, 1970–73; Knittin Sector Gp (formerly Knitting Sector Working Party), NEDO, 1978–90; Bd for Foo Studies, Reading Univ., 1983–86; Garment and Textile Sector Gp, NEDO, 1991–93 CAB Internat., 1995–98; Cons. Foreign and Commonwealth Council, 1995–. Vice Chairman: Proprietary Assoc. of GB, 1968–77; Advertising Assoc., 1973–81; Food an Drink Industries Council, 1973–76; Member: Council and Exec. Cttee, Food Manufr Fedn Inc., 1966–85 (Pres., 1974–76); Council, British Nutrition Foundn, 1967–79 Cambridge Univ. Appts Bd, 1969–73; Council, CBI, 1970–86; Council, BIM, 1972–77 Council, Univ. of Buckingham (formerly University Coll. at Buckingham), 1973–95 Council, Nat. Coll. of Food Technol., 1977–78 (Chm. Bd, 1978–83); Council, Univ. o Reading, 1978–98; AFRC, 1978–84; Council, Trade Policy Res. Centre, 1985–89 Monopolies and Mergers Commn, 1993–99 (Mem., Newspaper Panel, 1980–92) Industrial Develt Adv. Bd, 1984–93 (Chm., 1985–93); Council and Exec. Cttee, Imperia Soc. of Knights Bachelor, 1986–2002; Pres., EIA, 1991. Dir and Hon. Treas., Centre fo Policy Studies, 1984–93. Trustee, Inst. of Economic Affairs, 1980–93. Governor, Ashridg Management Coll., 1970–2006 (Vice-Chm., 1977–2006); President: Nat. Advertisin Benevolent Soc., 1978–80; Inst. of Packaging, 1981–82 (a Vice-Pres., 1979–81). Fellow Marketing Soc., 1981; FCMI; FInstM; FRSA; FRSC. Hon. Fellow, Inst. of Food Sci. an Technol., 1983–84. Hon. DSc: Reading, 1982; Lancaster, 1987. *Recreations:* sailing, squas racquets, ski-ing. *Address:* 37 Edwardes Square, W8 6HH. *T:* (020) 7603 9010. *Clubs* Athenæum, Brooks's, Hurlingham, Carlton, Royal Thames Yacht.

HALTON, Prof. David John, EdD; Vice Chancellor, University of Glamorgan, sinc 2005; *b* 23 June 1949; *s* of late Kenneth Robert Depledge Halton and Margaret Alice (*né* Searle); *m* 1973, Yvonne Geneste Ambrose; three *d*. *Educ:* Beckenham and Peng Grammar Sch. for Boys; Thames Poly. (BA 1972); Roehampton Inst. (PGCE 1973) Aston Univ. (MSc 1976); Univ. of Leicester (EdD 1998). Teacher, Hurlinghan Comprehensive Sch., 1973–76; Lectr, N Tyneside Coll. of Further Educn, 1977–80; He of Dept of Business and Marketing, Coll. for Distributive Trade, 1980–86; Dean, Busines

Sch., N London Poly., 1987–90; Dep. Rector, Nene Coll., Northampton, 1990–99; Dep. Vice-Chancellor, Dep. Chief Exec., and Prof. of Higher Educn, UWE, Bristol, 1999–2004, Prof. Emeritus, 2004–. *Publications:* Theories of Education Management in Practice, 1998; Pricing Toolkit for Higher Education, 2001. *Recreations:* playing blues piano, running, ornithology. *Address:* University of Glamorgan, Pontypridd CF37 1DL. *T:* (01443) 482001, *Fax:* (01443) 482390; *e-mail:* djhalton@glam.ac.uk.

HALVERSON, Hon. Robert George, OBE 1978; Ambassador for Australia to Ireland and the Holy See, 1999–2002; *b* 22 Oct. 1937; *m* 1958, Margaret Charlton; three *s* one *d*. *Educ:* Swinburne Tech. Coll.; Canberra Coll. of Advanced Education. Joined RAAF, 1956; commnd, 1957; retired in rank of Gp Capt., 1981; with Robertson Thompson Partners, 1981–84. MP (L) Casey, Victoria, 1984–98; Chief Opposition Whip, 1994–96; Speaker, House of Reps, Australia, 1996–98. *Address:* PO Box 19, Holbrook, NSW 2644, Australia.

HAM, Prof. Christopher John, CBE 2004; PhD; Professor of Health Policy and Management, University of Birmingham, since 1992; *b* 15 May 1951; *s* of Raymond Percival Thomas Ham and Agnes Anne Ham (*née* Evans); *m* 1980, Ioanna Burnell; two *s* one *d*. *Educ:* Cardiff High Sch.; Univ. of Kent (BA MPhil); Univ. of Bristol (PhD 1983). Research Asst, Univ. of Leeds, 1975–77; Lectr in Health Policy, Univ. of Bristol, 1977–86; Fellow, King's Fund Coll. and King's Fund Inst., 1986–92; Dir, Health Services Mgt Centre, Univ. of Birmingham, 1992–2000; Policy Analyst, 2000–01, Dir, Strategy Unit, 2001–04, DoH (on secondment). Non-exec. Dir, Heart of England NHS Foundn Trust, 2007– (Gov., 2005); Gov., Health Foundn, 2006–; Trustee, Canadian Health Services Res. Foundn, 2006–. Advr to World Bank, WHO, Audit Commn, NAO, BMA, RCP, etc. FRSocMed; Founder FMedSci 1998. Hon. FRCP 2004. *Publications:* Policy Making in the NHS, 1981; Health Policy in Britain, 1982, 5th edn 2004; (with M. J. Hill) The Policy Process in the Modern Capitalist State, 1984; Managing Health Services, 1986; (jtly) Health Check: health care reforms in an international context, 1990; The New NHS: organisation and management, 1991; (jtly) Priority Setting Processes for Healthcare, 1995; Public, Private or Community: what next for the NHS?, 1996; Management and Competition in the NHS, 1994, 2nd edn 1997; (ed) Health Care Reform, 1997; (with S. Pickard) Tragic Choices in Health Care: the case of Child B, 1998; (with A. Coulter) The Global Challenge of Health Care Rationing, 2000; The Politics of NHS Reform 1988–1997, 2000; (with S. McIver) Contested Decisions, 2000; (with G. Robert) Reasonable Rationing, 2003. *Recreations:* sport, music, theatre, reading, travel. *Address:* Health Services Management Centre, University of Birmingham, Birmingham B15 2RT. *T:* (0121) 414 6214.

HAM, Sir David Kenneth R.; *see* Rowe-Ham.

HÄMÄLÄINEN-LINDFORS, Sirkka Aune-Marjatta, DSc; Director: Investor AB, since 2004 (Vice Chairman); KONE Corporation, since 2004; SanomaWSOY, since 2004; Docent and Adjunct Professor in Economics, Helsinki School of Economics and Business Administration, since 1991; *b* 8 May 1939; *m* Bo Lindfors; two *c*. *Educ:* Helsinki Sch. of Econs and Business Admin (BSc Econs 1961; MSc Econs 1964; Licentiate of Sci. (Econs) 1979; DSc 1981). Economics Department, Bank of Finland: Economist, 1961–72; Head of Office, 1972–79; acting Head of Econs Dept, 1979–81; Dir, Econs Dept, Finnish Min. of Finance, 1981–82; Bank of Finland: Dir resp. for macroeconomic analysis and monetary and exchange rate policy, 1982–91; Mem. of Bd, 1991–92; Gov. and Chm. of Bd, 1992–98; Mem., Exec. Bd, European Central Bank, 1998–2003. Member: Council, European Monetary Inst., 1992–98; Economic Council of Finland, 1992–98; Nat. Bd of Economic Defence, 1992–98; Internat. Adv. Council, CEPS, 1993–98; Bd, Foundn for Economic Educn, 1996–2007; Develt Prog. of Nat. Strategy, 1996–98; Chm., Bd of Financial Supervision Authy, 1996–97. Member: Bd, Finnish Nat. Theatre, 1992–98; Supervisory Bd, Finnish Cultural Foundn, 1996–2005; Chairman: The Raging Roses, theatre gp, 1997–99; Bd, Finnish Nat. Opera, 2007–. Hon. Dr Turku Sch. of Econs and Business Admin, 1995. Comdr, 1st Cl., Order of White Rose (Finland); Merit Medal, 1st Cl., Order of White Star (Estonia). *Publications:* numerous articles on economics and monetary policy.

HAMANN, Paul; Managing Director and Creative Director, Wild Pictures Ltd, since 2005; Chairman, Reprieve, since 2000; *b* 9 Nov. 1948; *s* of Leonard Hamann and Anita Davies; *m* 1st, 1971, Kay Allen (marr. diss. 1981); (one *d* decd); 2nd, 1981, Marilyn Wheatcroft (marr. diss. 1999); one *s* one *d*. Dir and Prod., over 50 documentaries for BBC TV, 1976–88: incl. Your Life in Their Files, Sister Genevieve, Pushers, I Call It Murder, The Survivalists, At the Edge of the Union, A Company, Transmit and be Damned, Africa's Last Colony, Phantom, Lest We Forget, The Duty Men (Best Factual Series Award, BAFTA, 1987), Fourteen Days in May (Grierson Award, BFI, 1988); Editor, BBC 1 Documentaries, 1989–93: series incl. Inside Story, Rough Justice, Children's Hospital; Head of Documentaries, 1994–97, Chair, Factual Bd, 1996–99, Head of Documentaries and Hist. and of Community Prog. Unit, 1997–2000, BBC TV; Creative Director, Factual Progs, Shine Ltd, 2000–05: progs incl. Macintyre's Millions, Warrior School, Snatched, The Day I'll Never Forget, The Death Belt, My Shakespeare with Baz Luhrmann. Executive Producer: feature film, Bullet Boy, 2005; Putin's Palace, Execution of a Teenage Girl, Romanov: King of Hearts, World's Tallest Man, 2006. Mem. Council, BAFTA, 1993–96. *Publications:* (with Peter Gillman) The Duty Men, 1987; contrib. professional jls. *Recreations:* my children, popular culture, opera, ski-ing, Brazil, The Pineapple.

HAMBIDGE, Most Rev. Douglas Walter, DD; Principal, St Mark's Theological College, and Assistant Bishop, Dar es Salaam, 1993–95; *b* London, England, 6 March 1927; *s* of Douglas Hambidge and Florence (*née* Driscoll); *m* 1956, Denise Colvill Lown; two *s* one *d*. *Educ:* London Univ.; London Coll. of Divinity. BD, ALCD; DD, Anglican Theol. Coll. of BC, 1970. Asst Curate, St Mark's, Dalston, 1953–56; Rector: All Saints, Cassiar, BC, 1956–58; St James, Smithers, BC, 1958–64; Vicar, St Martin, Fort St John, BC, 1964–69; Canon, St Andrew's Cathedral, Caledonia, 1965–69; Bishop of Caledonia, 1969–80; Bishop of New Westminster, 1980; Archbishop of New Westminster and Metropolitan of Province of BC, 1981–93. Mem., ACC, 1987–93 (Mem., Standing Cttee, 1990–93). Pres., Missions to Seamen, 1980–93. Chancellor, Vancouver Sch. of Theology, 1999–2007 (Mem. Bd of Governors, 1980–85). *Address:* 1621 Golf Club Drive, Delta, BC V4M 4E6, Canada; *e-mail:* douglashambidge@dccnet.com.

HAMBLEDEN, 4th Viscount *cr* 1891; **William Herbert Smith;** *b* 2 April 1930; *e s* of 3rd Viscount and Patricia, GCVO (*d* 1994), *d* of 15th Earl of Pembroke, MVO; *S* father, 1948; *m* 1st, 1955, Donna Maria Carmela Attolico di Adelfia (marr. diss. 1988), *d* of late Count Bernardo Attolico and of Contessa Eleonora Attolico di Adelfia, Via Porta Latina, Rome; five *s*; 2nd, 1988, Mrs Lesley Watson. *Educ:* Eton. *Heir: s* Hon. William Henry Bernard Smith [*b* 18 Nov. 1955; *m* 1983, Sarah Suzanne, *d* of Joseph F. Anlauf and Mrs Suzanne K. Anlauf; two *d*]. *Address:* The Estate Office, Hambleden, Henley-on-Thames, Oxon RG9 6SG. *T:* (01491) 571252.

HAMBLEN, Prof. David Lawrence, CBE 2001; FRCSE, FRCS, FRCSGlas; Professor of Orthopaedic Surgery, University of Glasgow, 1972–99, now Emeritus; Hon. Consultant Orthopaedic Surgeon, 1972–2002, and Chairman, 1997–2002, Greater Glasgow Health Board; *b* 31 Aug. 1934; *s* of Reginald John Hamblen and Bessie Hamblen (*née* Williams); *m* 1968, Gillian Frances Bradley; one *s* two *d*. *Educ:* Roan Sch., Greenwich; Univ. of London (MB BS 1957); PhD Edinburgh 1975. FRCSE 1962; FRCS 1963; FRCSGlas 1976. Fulbright Fellow, Harvard; Fellow, Massachusetts Gen. Hosp., 1966–67; Lectr in Orthopaedics, Nuffield Orthopaedic Centre, Univ. of Oxford, 1967–68; Sen. Lectr in Orthopaedic Surgery, Univ. of Edinburgh and Hon. Consultant Orthopaedic Surgeon to SE Regl Hosp. Bd, Scotland, 1968–72. Hon. Consultant in Orthopaedic Surgery to the Army in Scotland, 1976–99. Vis. Prof., Univ. of Strathclyde (Nat. Centre for Trng and Educn in Prosthetics and Orthotics), 1981–. Non-exec. Dir, W Glasgow Hosps Univ. NHS Trust, 1994–97. Chm. Council, Jl of Bone and Joint Surgery, 1995–2001. Pres., British Orthopaedic Assoc., 1990–91 (Hon. Fellow, 2002); Member: British Hip Soc. (Pres., 2001–02); European Hip Soc. Hon. DSc: Strathclyde, 2003; Glasgow, 2003. *Publications:* (ed with J. C. Adams): Outline of Fractures, 10th edn 1992 to 12th edn 2007; Outline of Orthopaedics, 11th edn 1990 to 13th edn 2001. *Recreations:* golf, music, reading. *Address:* 3 Russell Drive, Bearsden, Glasgow G61 3BB. *T:* (0141) 942 1823. *Club:* Royal Society of Medicine.

HAMBLEN, Derek Ivens Archibald, CB 1978; OBE 1956; *b* 28 Oct. 1917; *s* of late Leonard Tom Hamblen and Ruth Mary Hamblen, *d* of Sir William Frederick Alphonse Archibald; *m* 1950, Pauline Alison (*d* 2002), *d* of late Gen. Sir William Morgan, GCB, DSO, MC; one *s* one *d*. *Educ:* St Lawrence Coll., Ramsgate; St John's Coll., Oxford (Casberd Exhibn); Portuguese Essay Prize, 1938; BA Hons (Mod. Langs) 1940, MA 1949. Served War, 1940–46: 1st Army, N Africa, 1942–43; Major, GS, AFHQ, N Africa and Italy, and Adv. Mission to British Mil. HQ, Greece, 1944–45; GSO1, Allied Commn for Austria, 1945–46; Lt-Col, 1946. War Office, later Ministry of Defence, 1946–77: seconded HQ British Troops, Egypt, 1946–47; Asst Sec., Office of UK High Commn in Australia, 1951–55; seconded Foreign Office, 1957–60; Asst Sec., 1964–68; a Special Advr to NATO and SHAPE, 1968–74; Under Sec., 1974–77, retired. Mem. Bd of Governors, St Lawrence Coll., 1977–91 (Vice-Pres., 1991–2004). FRSA 1987. Medal of Merit, 1st cl. (Czechoslovakia), 1946. *Recreations:* cricket, hockey (represented Oxford *v* Cambridge, 1940), golf, music, reading. *Address:* c/o Lloyds TSB, East Grinstead, West Sussex RH19 1AH. *Clubs:* MCC; Vincent's (Oxford).

See also N. A. Hamblen.

HAMBLEN, Nicholas Archibald; QC 1997; a Recorder, since 2000; *b* 23 Sept. 1957; *s* of Derek Ivens Archibald Hamblen, *qv*; *m* 1985, Kate Hayden; one *s* one *d*. *Educ:* Westminster Sch.; St John's Coll., Oxford (MA); Harvard Law Sch. (LLM). Called to the Bar, Lincoln's Inn, 1981; specialist in commercial law; an Asst Recorder, 1999–2000. *Address:* 20 Essex Street, WC2R 3AL. *Clubs:* MCC, Hurlingham; Vincent's (Oxford).

HAMBLETON, Prof. Kenneth George, FREng; Professor of Defence Engineering, University College London, 1991–2001, now Emeritus; *b* 15 Jan. 1937; *s* of George William Hambleton and Gertrude Nellie Hambleton (*née* Brighouse); *m* 1959, Glenys Patricia Smith; one *s* one *d*. *Educ:* Chesterfield Grammar Sch.; Queens' Coll., Cambridge (MA). CEng, FIET; FRAeS; FREng (FEng 1994). Services Electronics Res. Lab., Baldock, 1958–73; ASWE, Portsdown, 1973–81; a Dep. Dir, ASWE, 1981–82; Dir, Strategic Electronics-Radar, MoD PE, 1982–85; Asst Chief Scientific Advr (Projects and Res.), MoD, 1985–86; Dir Gen., Air Weapons and Electronic Systems, 1986–90, Air 3, 1990–91, MoD. *Publications:* numerous articles and letters in nat. and internat. physics and electronic jls. *Recreations:* chess, bridge, golf, music—especially jazz.

HAMBLIN, Jeffrey John, OBE 1999; Chief Executive, British Tourist Authority, 1999–2002; *b* 11 April 1945; *s* of late John Birkbeck Hamblin and Florence Hamblin; *m* 1968, Valerie Whitehead. *Educ:* Northern Counties Coll.; Univ. of Newcastle upon Tyne. Geography teacher, Newcastle, 1966–72; Develt Officer, Northumbria Tourist Bd, 1972–78; Dir, E Midlands Tourist Bd, 1978–85; British Tourist Authority: Manager, Canada, 1985–88; General Manager: Northern Europe, 1988–91; Europe, 1991–93; The Americas, 1993–98. Member Board: Hamilton Community Care Access Centre, Ont, 2005–06; Hamilton, Niagara, Haldimand, Brant Community Care Access Centre, Ont, 2006–. *Recreations:* golf, philately, gardening, reading. *Address:* 1460 Limeridge Road East, Hamilton, ON L8W 3J9, Canada.

HAMBLING, Sir (Herbert) Hugh, 3rd Bt *cr* 1924; *b* 3 Aug. 1919; *s* of Sir (Herbert) Guy (Musgrave) Hambling, 2nd Bt; *S* father, 1966; *m* 1st, 1950, Anne Page Oswald (*d* 1990), Spokane, Washington, USA; one *s*; 2nd, 1991, Helen (*d* 2004), *widow* of David Gavin. *Educ:* Wixenford Preparatory Sch.; Eton Coll. British Airways Ltd, 1937–39. RAF Training and Atlantic Ferry Command, 1939–46. British Overseas Airways: Montreal, 1948; Seattle, 1950; Manager, Sir Guy Hambling & Son, 1956; BOAC Representative, Douglas, Los Angeles, and Boeing Co., Seattle, 1957–75; Royal Brunei Airlines Rep., Boeing Co., Seattle, 1975–96. *Heir: s* (Herbert) Peter Hugh Hambling [*b* 6 Sept. 1953; *m* 1991, Lorayn Louise, *d* of late Frank Koson; three *s*]. *Address:* 1219 Evergreen Point Road, Medina, WA 98039, USA. *T:* (425) 4540905, *Fax:* (425) 4542048; Rookery Park, Yoxford, Suffolk IP17 3HQ. *T:* (01728) 668310.

HAMBLING, Maggi, OBE 1995; artist; *b* 23 Oct. 1945; *d* of late Harry Hambling and Marjorie Hambling (*née* Harris). *Educ:* Hadleigh Hall Sch., Suffolk; Amberfield Sch., Suffolk; Ipswich Sch. of Art; Camberwell Sch. of Art (DipAD 1967); Slade Sch. of Fine Art (HDFA 1969). Boise Travel Award, NY, 1969; first Artist in Residence, Nat. Gall., London, 1980–81; Tutor in Painting and Drawing, Morley Coll. *One-man exhibitions include:* Paintings and Drawings, Morley Gall., London, 1973; New Oil Paintings, Warehouse Gall., London, 1977; Drawings and Paintings on View, Nat. Gall., 1981; Pictures of Max Wall, Nat. Portrait Gall., 1983 (and tour); Maggi Hambling, Serpentine Gall., 1987 (and tour); An Eye Through a Decade, Yale Center for British Art, Newhaven, Conn, 1991; Towards Laughter, Northern Centre for Contemporary Art, 1993–94 (and tour); Maggi Hambling, Marlborough Fine Art, London, 1996; A Matter of Life and Death, Yorkshire Sculpture Park, 1997; also exhibn, A Statue for Oscar Wilde, Nat. Portrait Gall., and Hugh Lane Gall. of Modern Art, Dublin, 1997; statue, A Conversation with Oscar Wilde, bronze and granite, Adelaide Street, London, 1998; Good Friday paintings, drawings and sculpture, Gainsborough's House, Sudbury, Suffolk, 2000, LMH, Oxford, 2001; Henrietta Moraes, Marlborough Fine Art, London, 2001; Father, Morley Gall., London, 2001; The Very Special Brew Series, Sotheby's, 2003; North Sea Painting, Aldeburgh Fest., 2003; Scallop, Aldeburgh beach, 2003; Portraits of People and the Sea, Marlborough Fine Art, 2006; No Straight Lines, Fitzwilliam Mus., Cambridge and tour, 2007; Waves Breaking, Marlborough Fine Art, 2007; Waves and Waterfalls, Abbot Hall Art Gall., Kendal, Marlborough Fine Art, London, 2008; *public collections include:* Arts Council; Ashmolean Mus., Oxford; Australian Nat. Gall.; Birmingham City Art Gall.; British Council; BM; Contemporary Art Soc.; Fitzwilliam Mus., Cambridge; Gulbenkian Foundn, Lisbon; Harris Mus. and Art Gall., Preston; Imperial War Mus.; Nat. Gall.; Nat. Portrait Gall.; Rugby Collection; Scottish Nat. Gall. of Modern Art, Edinburgh; Scottish

Nat. Portrait Gall., Edinburgh; Southampton Art Gall.; Swindon Art Gall.; Tate Gall.; V&A Mus.; Wakefield Art Gall.; Whitworth Art Gall.; Yale Center for British Art. Hon. Fellow: New Hall, Cambridge, 2004; Univ. of the Arts, London, 2004. *Publications:* (with John Berger) Maggi & Henrietta, 2001; (with Andrew Lambirth) Maggi Hambling: the works, 2006. *Recreation:* tennis. *Address:* Morley College, Westminster Bridge Road, SE1 7HT. *Club:* Chelsea Arts.

HAMBLY, Christl Ann; *see* Donnelly, C. A.

HAMBRO, James Daryl; Chairman, J. O. Hambro Capital Management Ltd, since 1994; *b* 22 March 1949; *s* of late Jocelyn Hambro, MC and Ann Silvia Hambro (*née* Muir); *m* 1981, Diana Cherry; three *d. Educ:* Eton College; Harvard Business Sch. Hambros Bank, 1970–85 (Exec. Dir, 1982–85); J. O. Hambro & Co., subseq. J. O. Hambro Ltd, 1986–99. Chairman: Ashtenne Hldgs, 1997–2005; Singer & Friedlander AIM VCT, 2000–; Hansteen Holdings, 2005–. Director: Wilton's (St James's) Ltd, 1992–; Primary Health Properties, 1996–; Capital Opportunities Trust, 1997–2003; Enterprise Capital Trust, 1997–2004; Biocompatibles Internat., 2002–03. Dep. Chm., Peabody Trust, 1998–2005; Chairman: Internat. Students' Trust, 1988–; Henry Smith's Charity, 2007–. *Recreations:* shooting, golf, farming. *Address:* J. O. Hambro Capital Management Ltd, Ryder Court, 14 Ryder Street, SW1Y 6QB; 15 Elm Park Road, SW3 6BP; Manor Farm, Kimberley, Wymondham, Norfolk NR9 4DT. *T:* (01603) 759329. *Clubs:* White's; Royal West Norfolk.

    See also R. A. Hambro, R. N. Hambro.

HAMBRO, Peter Charles Percival; Executive Chairman, Peter Hambro Mining Plc, since 1994; *b* 18 Jan. 1945; *s* of late Lt Col Everard Hambro and of Mary Hambro; *m* 1968, Karen Brodrick; three *s. Educ:* Eton Coll. Founder, Peter Hambro Ltd, 1990. Chm., Sundeala Ltd; Dir, Hambros Bank & Trust Ltd; Non-exec. Dep. Chm., Aricom Plc; non-exec. Dir, Russian Timber Gp Ltd. *Recreation:* painting. *Clubs:* White's, Pratt's.

HAMBRO, Richard Alexander; Chairman, J. O. Hambro Investment Management Ltd, since 1986; *b* 1 Oct. 1946; 2nd *s* of late Jocelyn Olaf Hambro, MC; *m* 1st, 1973, Hon. Charlotte Soames (marr. diss. 1982); one *d*; 2nd, 1984, Juliet Mary Elizabeth Grana (*née* Harvey) (marr. diss. 1992); 3rd, 1993, Mary James (*née* Briggs). *Educ:* Eton; Univ. of Munich. Joined Hambros Bank, 1966, Director, 1979; Pres., Hambro America Inc., 1977–82; Chairman: I. Hennig & Co., 1987–; The Money Portal plc, 2003–; Wilton's (St James's), 2003– (Dir, 1968–); Smith's Hldgs Ltd, 2003–; Newmarket Racecourses Trust, 2004–; Franco's, 2005–. Chm., SA Business Initiative, 1995–. Dep. Pres., Macmillan Cancer Support (formerly Cancer Relief Macmillan Fund, then Macmillan Cancer Relief), 2001– (Chm., 1991–2001); Pres., Bowel Cancer UK (formerly Colon Cancer Concern), 2004– (Chm., 1995–2004); Chairman: Jt British Cancer Charities, 1995–; Develt Bd, Inst. of Cancer Res., 2003–. Trustee, Burdett Trust for Nursing, 2005–. Gov., London Clinic, 2000–. *Recreations:* golf, horse racing. *Address:* Waverton House, Sezincote, Moreton-in-Marsh, Glos GL56 9TB. *T:* (01386) 700700; 4 Egerton Place, SW3 2EF. *T:* (020) 7589 7483. *Clubs:* White's, Royal Automobile, Jockey; The Brook (New York) (Gov.).

    See also J. D. Hambro, R. N. Hambro.

HAMBRO, Rupert Nicholas; Chairman, J. O. Hambro Ltd, since 1986 (Group Managing Director, 1986–94); *b* 27 June 1943; *s* of late Jocelyn Olaf Hambro, MC and Ann Silvia (*née* Muir); *m* 1970, Mary Robinson Boyer; one *s* one *d. Educ:* Eton; Aix-en-Provence. Peat Marwick Mitchell & Co., 1962–64; joined Hambros Bank, 1964, Director, 1969, Dep. Chm., 1980, Chm., 1983–86; Chairman: Rupert Hambro & Partners Ltd, 1986–; J. O. Hambro Magan Ltd, 1988–96; J. O. Hambro Mansford Ltd, 1998–. Director: Anglo American Corporation of South Africa, 1981–97; Chatsworth House Trust Ltd, 1982–2004; Racecourse Hldgs Trust Ltd, 1985–94; Telegraph Group Ltd (formerly Daily Telegraph PLC, then The Telegraph plc), 1986–2003; Sedgwick Group plc, 1987–92; Triton Europe plc, 1987–90; Pioneer Concrete Hldgs PLC, 1989–99; Hamleys plc, 1988–96 (Chm., 1989–94); KBC Peel Hunt Ltd (formerly Peel Hunt plc), 2000–03; Business for Sterling, 2002–07; Open Europe Ltd, 2006–07; Mem. Supervisory Bd, Bank Gutmann AG, 2000–; Chairman: Wilton's (St James's) Ltd, 1987–2003; Mayflower Corp. Plc, 1988–2004; Internat. Adv. Bd, Montana AG, Vienna, 1988–2000; Fenchurch plc, 1993–97; CTR Group plc, 1990–97; Longshot plc, 1996–2007; Woburn Golf & Country Club Ltd, 1998–2003; Longshot Health & Fitness Ltd, 1999–2007; Third Space Gp Ltd, 1999–2007; Jermyn Street Assoc. Ltd, 2000–03; Roland Berger & Partners Ltd, 2000–02; Walpole Cttee Ltd, 2000–05; Longshot Hotels Ltd, 2001–04; Kapital Ventures PLC, 2001–06; Cazenove & Loyd Ltd, 2004–. Chairman: Assoc. of International Bond Dealers, 1979–82; Soc. of Merchants Trading to the Continent, 1995–. Member: SE Econ. Planning Council, 1971–74; Internat. Council, US Information Agency, 1988–2005. Treas., NACF, 1991–2003; Chm. Govs, Mus. of London, 1998–2005; Co. Chm., Mus. in Docklands, 2003–05; Patron, RBS, 1997–. Chm. Council, Univ. of Bath in Swindon, 2000–07; Mem. Council, Univ. of Bath, 2004–. Vice-Chm., 1991–96, Dep. Pres., 2001–, NABC; Chairman: Trustees, Boys' Club Trust, 1991–2000; Partners of the World, 1990–97; Chiswick House & Gardens Trust, 2005–; Trustee, Silver Trust, 1987–; Patron, 2005–08, Pres., 2008–, British Assoc. of Adoption and Fostering; Patron, Assoc. of British Designer Silversmiths, 2006–. Dep. Pres., Anglo-Danish Soc., 1987–. Freeman, Fishmongers' Co., 1969–; Liveryman, Goldsmiths' Co., 1994– (Mem. Ct of Assts 1998–). Hon. Fellow, Univ. of Bath, 1998. Walpole Award of British excellence, 2005. Knight of the Falcon (Iceland), 1986. *Recreations:* country pursuits. *Address:* J. O. Hambro Ltd, 118 New Bond Street, W1S 1EW. *T:* (020) 7493 7820. *Clubs:* White's, Pratt's, Groucho, Walbrook; Jupiter Island (Florida).

    See also J. D. Hambro, R. A. Hambro.

HAMEED, Baron *cr* 2007 (Life Peer), of Hampstead in the London Borough of Camden; **Khalid Hameed,** CBE 2004; DL; Chairman, Alpha Hospital Group, since 2003; Chairman and Chief Executive, London International Hospital, since 2006; *s* of Prof. M. Abdul Hameed and Rashida Abdul Hameed; *m* 1989, Dr Ghazala Hameed; two *s* two *d* and one step *s* one step *d. Educ:* Lucknow Univ., India (BSc; DPA; MB BS; DSc); London Univ. (DTM&H). FRCP 2006. CEO, Cromwell Hosp., London, 1990–2005. Chairman: Commonwealth Youth Exchange Council, 1999–; Internat. Students Hall, 2007–; Trustee: British Muslim Res. Council, 2005–; Ethnic Minorities Foundn, 2005–; Political Council for Co-existence, 2006–; Woolfe Inst. of Abrahamic Faiths, 2007–. Chm., Friends of BL, 2008–. Pres., Little Foundn, 2007–. Patron, Three Faiths Forum, 2006–. High Sheriff, 2006–07, DL 2007, Greater London. Sternberg Award for Interfaith Work, 2006; Ambassador of Peace Award, Universal Peace Fedn, 2007. *Recreations:* chess, cricket, poetry, polo, bridge. *Address:* House of Lords, SW1A 0PW; *e-mail:* hameedlondon@aol.com. *Clubs:* Athenæum, Mosimann's, MCC; Guards Polo.

HAMER, Christopher John; Ombudsman for Estate Agents, since 2006; *b* 26 Dec. 1952; *s* of late Ronald and Olive Hamer; *m* 1975, Sarah Anne Preston; three *s. Educ:* Thornbury Grammar Sch., Glos; Dorset Inst. of Higher Educn (HNC Business Studies). HM Customs & Excise, Dover, Southampton and London, 1974–84; Private Sec. to Parly Comr for Admin., 1984–85; Mem., Mgt and Efficiency Unit, Cabinet Office, 1985–88; Dir Services, Insurance Ombudsman Bureau, 1988–96; Gen. Manager, Personal Investme Authy Ombudsman Bureau, 1996–2000; Hd, Product Risk, HSBC Insce, 2000–0 *Recreations:* motoring, First and Second World Wars, disasters. *Address:* Ombudsman f Estate Agents, Beckett House, 4 Bridge Street, Salisbury, Wilts SP1 2LX. *T:* (0172 333306, *Fax:* (01722) 332296; *e-mail:* christopher.hamer@oea.co.uk.

HAMID, Rt Rev. David; *see* Gibraltar in Europe, Suffragan Bishop of.

HAMID, David; Chairman: MFI, since 2006; Nationwide Autocentres, since 200 Operating Partner, Merchant Equity Partners, since 2006; *b* 11 Dec. 1951; *s* of Osman an Doreen Hamid; *m* 1984, Gillian Joy; three *s* one *d. Educ:* Alleyne's Grammar Sch Stevenage; Univ. of Bradford (BSc Hons Industrial Technol. and Mgt). Marketi Director: Jewellery Div., Alfred Dunhill, 1985–86; Supasnaps, 1987; Managing Directo Dixons Financial Services, 1988–90; Mastercare Ltd, 1990–95; Commercial Service Di Dixons Gp plc, 1995–98; Gp Man. Dir, PC World, 1998–2001; Chief Operating Office Dixons Gp plc, 2001–03; CEO, Halfords Gp plc, 2003–05. Chm., Music for Yout 2008–. *Recreations:* field hockey, playing in a rock band, golf. *Address:* Merchant Equi Partners, 10 Bruton Street, W1J 6PX. *Club:* Royal Automobile.

HAMILL, Keith, FCA; Chairman, Tullett Prebon (formerly Collins Stewart, then Collin Stewart Tullett) plc, since 2000; *b* 7 Dec. 1952; *s* of Gerard Hamill and Edith Hamill; 1975, Angela Sylvia Green; three *s. Educ:* Cambridge Grammar Sch. for Boys; Univ. Nottingham (BA Politics). FCA 1989. Price Waterhouse, 1975–98 (Partner, 1987–88 Dir, Financial Control, Guinness PLC, 1988–91; Finance Director: United Distillers pl 1991–93; Forte plc, 1993–96; W H Smith plc, 1996–2000; Chm., W H Smith N Americ 1996–2000. Chairman: Alterian plc, 2000–; Go Ltd, 2001–02; Luminar plc, 2001–0 Moss Bros Gp PLC, 2001–; Bertram Books Ltd, 2001–07; Travelodge, 2003–; Heat Lambert Gp Ltd, 2005–; Dep. Chm., Collins Stewart plc, 2006–; Dir, Newmark Racecourse Ltd, 2002–; non-executive Director: Electrocomponents plc, 1999–; Willia Hill PLC, 2000–01; Tempus Gp PLC, 2000–01; TDG plc, 2001–05; Cadm Communications Corp., 2002–07. Mem., Urgent Issues Task Force, Accountir Standards Bd, 1992–98; Chm., Financial Reporting Cttee, CBI, 1993–97. Treas 1997–2003, Pro-Chancellor, 2003–, Univ. of Nottingham. Dir, Greenwich and Bexle Hospice, 1999–. *Recreations:* opera, horse racing, soccer, golf. *Address:* Tullett Prebon pl Cable House, 54 New Broad Street, EC2M 1ST. *T:* (020) 7523 8443. *Clubs:* Roy Automobile; Chislehurst Golf.

HAMILTON; *see* Baillie-Hamilton, family name of Earl of Haddington.

HAMILTON; *see* Dalrymple Hamilton and Dalrymple-Hamilton.

HAMILTON; *see* Douglas-Hamilton.

HAMILTON, family name of **Duke of Abercorn,** of **Lord Belhaven,** and of **Baron Hamilton of Dalzell, Hamilton of Epsom** and **HolmPatrick.**

HAMILTON, 15th Duke of, *cr* 1643, Scotland, **AND BRANDON,** 12th Duke of, 1711, Great Britain; **Angus Alan Douglas Douglas-Hamilton;** Premier Peer Scotland; Hereditary Keeper of Palace of Holyroodhouse; *b* 13 Sept. 1938; *e s* of 14 Duke of Hamilton and Brandon, PC, KT, GCVO, AFC, and Lady Elizabeth Percy, OB DL, *er d* of 8th Duke of Northumberland, KG; *S* father, 1973; *m* 1972, Sarah (*d* 1994), of Sir Walter Scott, 4th Bt; two *s* two *d*; *m* 1998, Kay Carmichael, *d* of Norman Dutcl *Educ:* Eton; Balliol Coll., Oxford (BA (Engrg) 1960; MA 1982). CEng, MIMechE; FBI Flt Lieut RAF; invalided, 1967. Flying Instructor, 1965; Sen. Commercial Pilot, 196 Test Pilot, Scottish Aviation, 1970–72; Authorised Display Pilot, 1998. Mem. Counc Cancer Res. UK (formerly CRC), 1978–. Mem., Queen's Body Guard for Scotlan 1975–. Mem., Royal Scottish Pipers Soc., 1977; Mem., Piobaireachd Soc., 1979; Patro British Airways Pipe Band, 1977–. Hon. Air Cdre, No 2 (City of Edinburgh) Maritim HQ Unit, RAuxAF, 1982–93. KStJ 1974 (Prior, Order of St John in Scotland, 1975–82 *Publication:* Maria R, 1991. *Heir:* *s* Marquess of Douglas and Clydesdale, *qv.* *Addres* Lennoxlove, Haddington, E Lothian EH41 4NZ. *T:* (01620) 823720. *Club:* Royal A Force.

    See also Baron Selkirk of Douglas.

HAMILTON, Marquess of; James Harold Charles Hamilton; *b* 19 Aug. 1969; *s* an *heir* of Duke of Abercorn, *qv*; *m* 2004, Tanya, *d* of late Douglas Nation; two *s.* A Page Honour to the Queen, 1982–84. *Heir:* *s* Viscount Strabane, *qv.* *Address:* Barons Cour Omagh, Co. Tyrone BT78 4EZ.

HAMILTON OF DALZELL, 5th Baron *cr* 1886; **Gavin Goulburn Hamilton;** *b* 8 Oc 1968; *s* of 4th Baron Hamilton of Dalzell and (Ann Anastasia) Corinna (Helena) Hamilt (*née* Dixon); *S* father, 2006; *m* 1997, Harriet Louise, *yr d* of Thomas Roskill; three *d* (inc twins). *Educ:* Eton Coll.; Buckingham Univ. (BSc). ACA 1994. Smith & Williamso chartered accountants, 1990–95; DHL International (UK) Ltd, 1995–2007. *Recreation* shooting, gardening. *Heir:* *b* Hon. Robert Pierson Hamilton [*b* 29 July 1971; *m* 200 Joanna Maria van der Hem; three *d*]. *Address:* Harrington Hall, Shifnal, Shropshire TF1 9DR. *T:* (01952) 730870; *e-mail:* gavin.hamilton@ukgateway.net. *Club:* Boodle's.

HAMILTON OF EPSOM, Baron *cr* 2005 (Life Peer), of West Anstey in the county Devon; **Archibald Gavin Hamilton,** Kt 1994; PC 1991; *b* 30 Dec. 1941; *yr s* of 3r Baron Hamilton of Dalzell, GCVO, MC; *m* 1968, Anne Catharine Napier; three *d. Edu* Eton Coll. Borough Councillor, Kensington and Chelsea, 1968–71. Contested (C Dagenham, Feb. and Oct., 1974. MP (C) Epsom and Ewell, April 1978–2001; PPS to Se of State for Energy, 1979–81, to Sec. of State for Transport, 1981–82; an Asst Govt Whi 1982–84; a Lord Comr of HM Treasury (Govt Whip), 1984–86; Parly Under-Sec. of Stat for Defence Procurement, MoD, 1986–87; PPS to Prime Minister, 1987–88; Minister State, MoD, 1988–93. Member: Intelligence and Security Cttee, 1994–97; Select Ctte on Standards in Public Life, 1995; Select Cttee on Members' Interests, 1995. Chm., 192 Cttee, 1997–2001 (Exec. Mem., 1995–97). Gov., Westminster Foundn for Democrac 1993–99. *Address:* House of Lords, SW1A 0PW. *Clubs:* White's, Pratts.

HAMILTON, Rt Hon. Lord; Arthur Campbell Hamilton; PC 2002; Lord Justic General of Scotland and Lord President of the Court of Session, since 2005; *b* 10 Jun 1942; *s* of James Whitehead Hamilton and Isobel Walker Hamilton (*née* McConnell); 1970, Christine Ann Croll; one *d. Educ:* The High School of Glasgow; Glasgow Univ Worcester Coll., Oxford (BA; Hon. Fellow, 2003); Edinburgh Univ. (LLB). Admitt member, Faculty of Advocates, 1968; QC (Scot.) 1982; Standing Junior Counsel: t Scottish Development Dept, 1975–78; to Board of Inland Revenue (Scotland), 1978–8 Advocate Depute, 1982–85; Judge, Courts of Appeal, Jersey and Guernsey, 1988–9 Pres., Pensions Appeal Tribunals for Scotland, 1992–95; a Senator of the Coll. of Justic in Scotland, 1995–2005. *Recreations:* hill walking, music, history. *Address:* Court of Sessio Parliament House, Edinburgh EH1 1RQ. *T:* (0131) 240 6701. *Club:* New (Edinburgh)

HAMILTON (NZ), Bishop of, (RC), since 1994; **Most Rev. Denis George Browne,** CNZM 2001; *b* 21 Sept. 1937; *s* of Neville John Browne and Catherine Anne Browne (*née* Moroney). *Educ:* Holy Name Seminary, Christchurch, NZ; Holy Cross College, Mosgiel, NZ. Assistant Priest: Gisborne, 1963–67; Papatoetoe, 1968–71; Remuera, 1972–74; Missionary in Tonga, 1975–77; Bishop of Rarotonga, 1977–83; Bishop of Auckland, 1983–94. Hon. DD. *Recreation:* golf. *Address:* Chanel Centre, PO Box 4353, Hamilton East 2032, New Zealand.

HAMILTON, Adrian Walter; QC 1973; commercial arbitrator and mediator, retired; a Recorder of the Crown Court, 1974–95; *b* 11 March 1923; *er s* of late W. G. M. Hamilton, banker, Fletching, Sussex and of late Mrs S. E. Hamilton; *m* 1966, Jill, *d* of S. R. Brimblecombe, Eastbourne; two *d. Educ:* Highgate Sch.; Balliol Coll., Oxford (BA 1st cl. Jurisprudence 1948; MA 1954; Jenkyns Law Prize; Paton Meml Student, 1948–49). Served with RN, 1942–46: Ord. Seaman, 1942; Sub-Lt RNVR, 1943, Lieut 1946. Cassel Scholar, Lincoln's Inn, 1949; called to Bar, Lincoln's Inn, 1949 (Bencher 1979), Middle Temple and Inner Temple; Dep. High Court Judge, 1982–95. Mem., Senate of Inns of Court and the Bar, 1976–82, Treas., 1979–82; Mem. Council, Inns of Court, 1987–91. Mem., Council of Legal Educn, 1977–87. Chairman: Appellate Cttee for Exam. Irregularities, London Univ., 1985–; Mental Health Review Tribunals, 1986–95; Lautro Disciplinary Cttees, 1991–94. Inspector, Peek Foods Ltd, 1977. *Recreations:* family, golf, sailing, gardening. *Address:* 7 King's Bench Walk, Temple, EC4Y 7DS. *T:* (020) 7583 0404. *Clubs:* Garrick; Piltdown Golf.

HAMILTON, Alexander Macdonald, CBE 1979; Senior Partner, 1977–90, Consultant, 1990–94, McGrigor Donald, Solicitors, Glasgow; *b* 11 May 1925; *s* of John Archibald Hamilton and Thomasina Macdonald or Hamilton; *m* 1953, Catherine Gray; two *s* one *d. Educ:* Hamilton Acad. (Dux, 1943); Glasgow Univ. (MA 1948, LLB 1951). Solicitor. Served War, RNVR, 1943–46. Dir, Royal Bank of Scotland, 1978–96 (Vice Chm., 1990–96). Law Soc. of Scotland: Mem. Council, 1970–82; Vice-Pres., 1975–76; Pres., 1977–78. Pres., Glasgow Juridical Soc., 1955–56. Vice-Pres. and Chm., 1978–85, Pres., 2002–08, Greater Glasgow Scout Council; Pres., Clyde Regl Scout Council, 2008–; Cttee Chm., Scottish Council, Scout Assoc., 1986–92. Sec., Cambuslang Old Parish Church, 1991– (Session Clerk, 1969–91); Vice-Chm., Cambuslang Community Council, 1978–94. *Recreations:* golf, sailing. *Address:* 30 Wellshot Drive, Cambuslang, Glasgow G72 8BT. *T:* (0141) 641 1445. *Clubs:* Western (Glasgow); Royal Northern & Clyde Yacht.

HAMILTON, Alfred William, (Wilfred); Deputy Secretary, Department of Enterprise, Trade and Investment, Northern Ireland, 2001–08; *b* 13 June 1948; *s* of Albert George Hamilton and Anna Hamilton (*née* Christie); *m* 1972, Sandra Magill; one *s* one *d. Educ:* Boys' Model Sch., Belfast. Dip. Admin and Mgt. Northern Ireland Civil Service: posts in mgt services, Rayner Scrutinies, NI Econ. Council and Eur. Div., Dept of Health and Social Services, 1967–91; Asst Sec., 1991; Head of Finance Div., 1991–95, Head of Finance, EU and Efficiency Div., 1995–2001, Dept of Econ. Develt. *Recreations:* golf, sport in general, reading. *Address:* c/o Department of Enterprise, Trade and Investment, Netherleigh, Massey Avenue, Belfast BT4 2JP.

HAMILTON, Sir Andrew Caradoc, 10th Bt *cr* 1646, of Silverton Hill, Lanarkshire; *b* 23 Sept. 1953; *s* of Sir Richard Hamilton, 9th Bt and Elizabeth Vidal Barton; *S* father, 2001; *m* 1984, Anthea Jane Huntingford; three *d. Educ:* Charterhouse; St Peter's Coll., Oxford (BA). *Heir: cousin* Paul Howden Hamilton [*b* 24 Dec. 1951; *m* 1980, Elizabeth Anne Harrison; two *d*].

HAMILTON, Prof. Andrew David, PhD; FRS 2004; Benjamin Silliman Professor of Chemistry and Provost, Yale University, 2004–09; Vice-Chancellor, University of Oxford, from Oct. 2009; *b* 3 Nov. 1952; *m* 1981, Jennifer Letton; two *s* one *d. Educ:* Univ. of Exeter (BSc 1974); Univ. of British Columbia (MSc 1976); Univ. of Cambridge (PhD 1980). Asst Prof. of Chem., Princeton Univ., 1981–88; University of Pittsburgh: Associate Prof., 1988–92; Prof. of Chem., 1992–97; Hd, Dept. of Chem., 1994–97; Yale University: Irénée duPont Prof. of Chem., 1997–2004; Prof. of Molecular Biophysics and Biochem., 1998–2009; Hd, Dept of Chemistry, 1999–2003; Dep. Provost for Sci. and Technol., 2003–04. *Publications:* articles in learned jls. *Address:* Department of Chemistry, Yale University, 225 Prospect Street, PO Box 208107, New Haven, CT 06520–8107, USA; (from Oct. 2009) University of Oxford, Wellington Square, Oxford OX1 2JD.

HAMILTON, Andrew Ninian Roberts; His Honour Judge Andrew Hamilton; a Circuit Judge, Midland Circuit, since 2001; *b* 7 Jan. 1947; *s* of Robert Bousfield Hamilton and Margery Wensley Iowerth Hamilton (*née* Roberts); *m* 1982, Isobel Louise Goode; one *s* one *d. Educ:* Cheltenham Coll.; Birmingham Univ. (LLB). Called to the Bar, Gray's Inn, 1970; in practice, Midland and Oxford Circuit; Asst Recorder, 1993–99; a Recorder, 1999–2001. Mem. (C) Nottingham CC, 1973–91 (Chairman: Transport Cttee, 1976; Archaeology Cttee, 1987–91; Vice-Chm., Leisure Services Cttee, 1987–88; Hon. Alderman, 1991). Chairman: Nottingham Civic Soc., 1978–83 (Vice-Pres., 1983–); Nottingham Civic Soc. Sales Ltd, 1988–2001; Nottingham Park Conservation Trust, 1992–; Dir, Nottingham and Notts United Services Club, 1994–2001. Chm., Nottingham Bar Mess, 1995–2001. External examiner, BVC, Nottingham Trent Univ., 1997–2000. Contested (C) Ilkeston, Oct. 1974. *Publications:* Nottingham's Royal Castle and Ducal Palace, 1976, 5th edn 1999; Nottingham, City of Caves, 1978, 3rd edn 2004; Historic Walks in Nottingham, 1978, 2nd edn 1985. *Recreations:* tennis, ski-ing, golf, walking, local history. *Address:* Derby Crown Court, Morledge, Derby DE1 2XE. *Club:* Nottingham and Notts United Services.

HAMILTON, Angus Warnock; a District Judge (Magistrates' Courts), since 2005; *b* 1 June 1957; *s* of Sir James Arnot Hamilton, *qv. Educ:* Univ. of Leicester (LLB 1979); Univ. of Sheffield (MA Socio-Legal Studies 1980); Guildford Coll. of Law. Trainee solicitor, 1981–83; admitted solicitor, 1983; solicitor in private practice, 1983–97; solicitor/sole Principal, Hamiltons Solicitors, 1997–2005; a Dep. Dist Judge, 1998–2005. Mem., Gambling Appeals Tribunal, 2007–. *Publications:* (with Rosemary Jay) Data Protection Law and Practice: a guide to the Data Protection Act 1998, 1999, 2nd edn 2003; *contributions to:* Liberating Cyberspace, 1998; Staying Legal, 1999; Advising HIV+ Clients: a guide for lawyers, 1999; Advising Gay and Lesbian Clients: a guide for lawyers, 1999. *Recreations:* travel, photography, cinema, live music, weight training, scuba-diving, charity management. *Address: e-mail:* Angus.hamilton@btinternet.com. *Clubs:* Athenæum, The Hospital.

HAMILTON, Arthur Campbell; *see* Hamilton, Rt Hon. Lord.

HAMILTON, Arthur Richard C.; *see* Cole-Hamilton.

HAMILTON, David; MP (Lab) Midlothian, since 2001; *b* 24 Oct. 1950; *s* of Agnes and David Hamilton; *m* 1969, Jean Macrae; two *d. Educ:* Dalkeith High Sch. Coalminer, 1965–84; Landscape Supervisor, Midlothian DC, 1987–89; Training Officer and Placement Officer, Craigmillar Fest. Soc., 1989–92; Chief Exec., Craigmillar Opportunities Trust, 1992–2000. Mem., Midlothian Council, 1995–2001. Hon. Pres., Midlothian Community Artists, 1995. *Recreations:* films, current affairs. *Address:* (constituency office) 95 High Street, Dalkeith, Midlothian EH22 1AX.

HAMILTON, David Stewart, MBE 2006; Director of Legal Services for Metropolitan Police Service (formerly Solicitor to Commissioner of Police of the Metropolis), 1995–2006; *b* 1 April 1946; *s* of late Ralph James Hamilton and of Jean Isabel Hamilton; *m* 1975, Maureen Underwood; two *d. Educ:* Highgate Sch.; Coll. of Law, Lancaster Gate. Articled Clerk, 1965–70, Asst Solicitor, 1970–71, Partner, 1971–78, D. Miles Griffiths Piercy & Co.; Asst Solicitor, 1978–79, Partner, 1979–80, Gaitskell Dodgson & Bleasdale; joined Solicitor's Dept, Metropolitan Police, 1980: Sen. Legal Asst, 1981–85; Asst Solicitor, 1985–95. Member: Law Soc., 1970–; Commonwealth Lawyers Assoc., 1996–; Life Member: Assoc. of Police Lawyers, 2006; ACPO, 2006. *Recreations:* walking the dog, steam railways, narrowboating with beer drinking friends. *Address:* c/o Directorate of Legal Services, Metropolitan Police, New Scotland Yard, Broadway, Victoria, SW1H 0BG. *T:* (020) 7230 7353.

HAMILTON, Donald Rankin Douglas; His Honour Judge Donald Hamilton; a Circuit Judge, since 1994; *b* 15 June 1946; *s* of Allister McNicoll Hamilton and Mary Glen Hamilton (*née* Rankin); *m* 1974, (Margaret) Ruth Perrens; one *s* one *d. Educ:* Rugby Sch.; Balliol Coll., Oxford (BA). Called to the Bar, Gray's Inn, 1969 (Atkin Schol. 1970); pupillage in Birmingham, 1970–71; practised in Birmingham, 1971–94; Designated Family Judge, Birmingham, 1996–2008. Mem., Council of Mgt, CBSO, 1974–80; Dir, CBSO Soc. Ltd, 1984–99; Trustee, City of Birmingham Orchestral Endowment Fund. *Recreation:* music. *Address:* Birmingham Family Courts, The Priory Courts, 33 Bull Street, Birmingham B4 6DS.

HAMILTON, Douglas Owens; Senior Partner, Norton Rose (formerly Norton, Rose, Botterell & Roche), 1982–94; *b* 20 April 1931; *s* of Oswald Hamilton and Edith Hamilton; *m* 1962, Judith Mary Wood; three *s. Educ:* John Fisher Sch., Purley, Surrey; Univ. of London (LLB). Admitted Solicitor, 1953; joined Botterell & Roche, 1955, Partner, 1959; Exec. Partner, Norton, Rose, Botterell & Roche, 1976–82. Mem., Chancellor's Court of Benefactors, Oxford Univ., 1990–94. Chm., Thames Nautical Trng Trust Ltd, 1995–98; Vice-Chm., Marine Soc., 1993–99; Hon. Treasurer: British Maritime Charitable Foundn, 1987–97; British Polish Legal Assoc., 1989–93. *Recreation:* travelling. *Address:* Boarsney, Salehurst, East Sussex TN32 5SR.

HAMILTON, Duncan Graeme; Advocate at Scottish Bar; political adviser to First Minister, Scottish Government (formerly Scottish Executive), since 2007; *b* 3 Oct. 1973; *s* of Rev. David Gentles Hamilton and Elsa Catherine Hamilton (*née* Nicolson). *Educ:* Glasgow Univ. (MA 1st Cl. Hons Hist.); Edinburgh Univ. (LLB Scots Law); Kennedy Sch. of Govt, Harvard Univ. (Kennedy Schol.). Asst Brand Manager, Proctor & Gamble, 1995; Aide and advr to Alex Salmond, MP, 1997–99. MSP (SNP) Highlands and Is, 1999–2003; Mem., Health and Community Care Cttee, 1999–2000, Enterprise and Life Long Learning Cttee, 2000–03, Justice Cttee, 2001–03, Scottish Parlt. Mem., SNP, 1994–; Asst to SNP Chief Exec., 1998–99. Mem. Council, London Information Network on Conflict and State-building, 2003–; spokesman for Caucasus Caspian Commn, 2007. *Recreations:* football, reading, friends. *Address:* c/o Faculty of Advocates, Parliament House, Edinburgh EH1 1RF.

HAMILTON, Dundas; *see* Hamilton, J. D.

HAMILTON, Eben William; QC 1981; *b* 12 June 1937; *s* of late Rev. John Edmund Hamilton, MC and Hon. Lilias Hamilton (*née* Maclay); *m* 1st, 1973, Catherine Harvey (marr. diss. 1977); 2nd, 1985, Themy Rusi Bilimoria, *y d* of late Brig. Rusi Bilimoria. *Educ:* Winchester; Trinity Coll., Cambridge. Nat. Service: 4/7 Royal Dragoon Guards, 1955–57; Fife and Forfar Yeomanry/Scottish Horse, TA, 1958–66. Called to the Bar, Inner Temple, 1962, Bencher, 1985; admitted (*ad hoc*): Hong Kong Bar, 1978; Singapore Bar, 1982; Cayman Bar, 2001. Dep. High Court Judge, Chancery Div., 1990–. Jt DTI Inspector, Atlantic Computers plc, 1990–94. FRSA 1988. *Address:* 3rd Floor South, 6 Stone Buildings, Lincoln's Inn, WC2A 3XT. *T:* (020) 7242 7650. *Club:* Garrick.
See also Martha Hamilton.

HAMILTON, Sir Edward (Sydney), 7th and 5th Bt, *cr* 1776 and 1819; *b* 14 April 1925; *s* of Sir (Thomas) Sydney (Percival) Hamilton, 6th and 4th Bt, and Bertha Muriel, *d* of James Russell King, Singleton Park, Kendal; *S* father, 1966. *Educ:* Canford Sch. Served Royal Engineers, 1943–47; 1st Royal Sussex Home Guard, 1953–56. *Recreations:* Spiritual matters, music. *Heir:* none. *Address:* The Cottage, Fordwater Road, East Lavant, Chichester, West Sussex PO18 0AL. *T:* (01243) 527414.

HAMILTON, Hon. Dame Eleanor (Warwick); *see* King, Hon. Dame E. W.

HAMILTON, Fabian; MP (Lab) Leeds North East, since 1997; *b* 12 April 1955; *s* of late Mario Uziell-Hamilton and Her Honour Adrianne Uziell-Hamilton; *m* 1980, Rosemary Ratcliffe; one *s* two *d. Educ:* Brentwood Sch., Essex; Univ. of York (BA Hons). Graphic designer (own company), 1979–94; computer systems consultant, 1994–97. Leeds City Council: Mem. (Lab), 1987–97; Chm., Employment and Econ. Develt Cttee, 1994–96; Chm., Educn Cttee, 1996–98. Mem., Select Cttee on Foreign Affairs, 2001–. Contested (Lab) Leeds NE, 1992. Trustee, Nat. Heart Res. Fund, 1999–. Gov., Northern Sch. of Contemporary Dance. *Recreations:* film, theatre, opera, photography, cycling. *Address:* House of Commons, SW1A 0AA. *T:* (020) 7219 3493.

HAMILTON, Prof. George, MD; FRCS; Professor of Vascular Surgery, Royal Free and University College School of Medicine, University of London, since 2003; Consultant in Vascular and General Surgery, Royal Free Hampstead NHS Trust, since 1987; Consultant Vascular Surgeon, Great Ormond Street Hospital for Sick Children NHS Trust, since 1998; Surgeon to the Queen, since 2007; *b* 2 Sept. 1947; *s* of George Hamilton and Ginetta Luccacini Hamilton; *m* 1980, Margaret Handyside; one *s* two *d. Educ:* St Modan's High Sch., Stirling; Univ. of Glasgow Sch. of Medicine (MB ChB; MD 2002). DObstRCOG 1974; FRCS 1977; FRCSGlas *ad eundem* 2007. Charing Cross Hosp., London; Surg. Registrar, Basildon Hosp.; Royal Free Hospital, subseq. Royal Free and University College, School of Medicine: Surg. Res. Fellow, 1980; Lectr in Surgery, 1981–87; Hon. Sen. Lectr, 1987–2003; Clin. Sub-Dean, 1997–2005; Faculty (formerly Site) Tutor, Royal Free Campus, 2000–05. Clin. Res. Fellow, Mass Gen. Hosp. and Harvard Sch. of Medicine, 1985–86. Surgeon to the Royal Household, 2001–07. Pres., Vascular Soc. of GB and Ireland, 2006–07. Mem., British Fulbright Scholars' Assoc. *Publications:* (ed jtly) Renal Vascular Disease, 1995; contribs to learned jls of surgery and vascular surgery and disease. *Recreations:* family, good food and wine, travel, cinema, theatre, water sports, walking, ski-ing. *Address:* University Department of Surgery, Royal Free Hospital, Pond Street, NW3 2QG. *T:* (020) 7830 2163; 34 Circus Road, NW8 9SG. *T:* (020) 7586 9180, *Fax:* (020) 7586 9458.

HAMILTON, Iain McCormick; His Honour Judge Iain Hamilton; a Circuit Judge, since 2000; Designated Family Judge for Greater Manchester, since 2005; *b* 11 Nov. 1948; *s* of James Hamilton and Mary Isabella Hamilton; *m* 1975, Marilyn Tomlinson; one *s* two *d. Educ:* Heversham Grammar Sch.; Manchester Poly. (BA Hons Law). Admitted solicitor, 1974; Walls, Johnston & Co., Stockport, 1974–94; Jones Maidment Wilson, Manchester, 1994–2000; Asst Recorder, 1992–96; Recorder, 1996–2000. Pres., Stockport Law Soc., 1990–91. Chm., 1992–93 and 1996–99, Patron, 2001–, Child Concern. *Recreations:* music, reading, cooking. *Address:* Manchester County Court, Manchester Civil Justice Centre, 1 Bridge Street, Manchester M60 9DJ. *T:* (0161) 240 5000.

HAMILTON, Ian Lethame; Chief Executive, St George's Healthcare NHS Trust, 1999–2003; *b* 24 July 1951; *s* of Robert Hamilton and Margaret Henderson (*née* McKay). *Educ:* Larkhall Acad.; Glasgow Coll. of Technol. CIPFA 1974. Supervisory accountant, 1975–78, Asst Chief Accountant, 1978–81, Strathclyde Regl Council; Regl Finance Officer, Housing Corp., 1981–83; Dep. Dir of Finance, Wandsworth HA, 1983–88; Project Manager, King's Fund Centre for Health Services Develt, 1988–89 (on secondment); Resource Mgt Project Manager, Wandsworth HA, 1989–91; Dir of Service Develt, 1991–98, Dep. Chief Exec., 1998–99, St George's Healthcare NHS Trust. *Recreations:* gardening, reading, country walks. *Address:* 20 Artesian Road, W2 5AR.

HAMILTON, Ian Robertson; QC (Scot.) 1980; *b* Paisley, Scotland, 13 Sept. 1925; *s* of John Harris Hamilton and Martha Robertson; *m* 1974, Jeannette Patricia Mari Stewart, Connel, Argyll; one *s*, and one *s* two *d* by former marriage. *Educ:* John Neilson Sch., Paisley; Allan Glens Sch., Glasgow; Glasgow and Edinburgh Univs (BL). Served RAFVR, 1943–48. Called to the Scottish Bar, 1954 and to the Albertan Bar, 1982. Advocate Depute, 1962; Dir of Civil Litigation, Republic of Zambia, 1964–66; Hon. Sheriff of Lanarks, 1967; retd from practice to work for National Trust for Scotland and later to farm in Argyll, 1969; returned to practice, 1974; Sheriff of Glasgow and Strathkelvin, May–Dec. 1984; resigned commn Dec. 1984; returned to practice. Founder, Castle Wynd Printers, Edinburgh, 1955 (published four paper-back vols of Hugh MacDiarmid's poetry, 1955–56). Founder and first Chm., The Whichway Trust, to provide adventure training for young offenders, 1988. Chief Pilot, Scottish Parachute Club, 1978–80. Student Pres., Heriot-Watt Univ., 1990–96; Rector, Aberdeen Univ., 1994–96. Hon. Research Fellow, 1997, Hon. LLD 1997, Aberdeen. Hon. Brother, Sir William Wallace Free Colliers, 1997. *Publications:* No Stone Unturned, 1952 (also New York); The Tinkers of the World, 1957 (Foyle award-winning play); The Taking of the Stone of Destiny, 1991; *autobiography:* A Touch of Treason, 1990; A Touch More Treason, 1994; contrib. various jls. *Recreations:* motor biking, neophobia. *Address:* Lochnabeithe, North Connel, Oban, Argyll PA37 1QX. *T:* (01631) 710427.

HAMILTON, Sir James (Arnot), KCB 1978 (CB 1972); MBE 1952; FRSE; FREng; Permanent Under-Secretary of State, Department of Education and Science, 1976–83; *b* 2 May 1923; *m* 1947, Christine Mary McKean (marr. diss.); three *s*. *Educ:* University of Edinburgh (BSc). Marine Aircraft Experimental Estab., 1943: Head of Flight Research, 1948; Royal Aircraft Estab., 1952; Head of Projects Div., 1964; Dir, Anglo-French Combat Aircraft, Min. of Aviation, 1965; Dir-Gen. Concorde, Min. of Technology, 1966–70; Deputy Secretary: (Aerospace), DTI, 1971–73; Cabinet Office, 1973–76. Dir, Hawker Siddeley Gp, 1983–91; Mem. Adv. Bd, Brown & Root (UK) Ltd, 1983–97; Chm., Brown & Root (UK) Ltd (later Brown & Root Ltd), 1998–2000; Director: Smiths Industries plc, 1984–93; Devonport Royal Dockyard, 1987–97. Trustee, British Museum (Natural Hist.), 1984–88. President: Assoc. for Science Educn, 1984–85; NFER in England and Wales, 1984–98. Vice-Pres., Council, Reading Univ., 1983–95; Vice-Chm. Council, UCL, 1985–98. FREng (FEng 1981); FRAeS 1983. Hon. FIMechE 1980. DUniv Heriot-Watt, 1983; Hon. LLD CNAA, 1983. *Publications:* papers in Reports and Memoranda series of Aeronautical Research Council, Jl RAeS, and technical press. *Address:* 32 Alison Way, Winchester, Hants SO22 5BT. *T:* (01962) 942001. *Club:* Athenæum.

See also A. W. Hamilton.

HAMILTON, (James) Dundas, CBE 1985; Chairman: Wates City of London Properties plc, 1984–94; LWT Pension Trustees Ltd, 1992–94; *b* 11 June 1919; *o s* of late Arthur Douglas Hamilton and Jean Scott Hamilton; *m* 1954, Linda Jean (*d* 2008), *d* of late Sinclair Frank Ditcham and Helen Fraser Ditcham; two *d*. *Educ:* Rugby; Clare Coll., Cambridge. Served War, Army (Lt-Col RA), 1939–46. Member, Stock Exchange, 1948, Mem. Council, 1972–78 (Dep. Chm., 1973–76). Partner, 1951–86, Sen. Partner, 1977–85, Fielding, Newson-Smith & Co. Chairman: TSB Commercial Holdings (formerly UDT Holdings), 1985–90 (Dir, 1983–90); United Dominions Trust Ltd, 1985–89; Director: Richard Clay plc, 1971–84 (Vice-Chm., 1981–84); LWT (Holdings) plc, 1981–91; Datastream Hldgs Ltd, 1982–86; TSB Gp plc, 1985–90; TSB Investment Management Ltd, 1986–88; Archival Facsimiles Ltd, 1986–89; WIB Publications Ltd, 1987–98 (Chm., 1990–98); Camp Hopson & Co., 1991–2002 (Chm., 2002). Dep. Chm., British Invisible Exports Council, 1976–86; Member: Exec. Cttee, City Communications Centre, 1976–88; City and Industrial Liaison Council, 1987–98 (Chm., 1970–73 and 1991–95). Governor, Pasold Res. Fund, 1976–90 (Chm., 1978–86). Member: Council of Industrial Soc., 1959–78 (Exec. Cttee, 1963–68; Life Mem., 1978); Adv. Bd, RCDS, 1980–87. Contested (C) East Ham North, 1951. FRSA 1988. *Publications:* The Erl King (radio play), 1949; Lorenzo Smiles on Fortune (novel), 1953; Three on a Honeymoon (TV series), 1956; Six Months Grace (play, jointly with Robert Morley), 1957; Stockbroking Today, 1968, 2nd edn 1979; Stockbroking Tomorrow, 1986; 21 Years to Christmas (short stories and verse), 1994. *Recreations:* writing, swimming, golf, watching tennis. *Address:* 45 Melbury Court, W8 6NH. *T:* (020) 7602 3157. *Clubs:* City of London, Hurlingham, All England Lawn Tennis and Croquet; Royal and Ancient Golf (St Andrews); Hankley Common; Worplesdon; Kandahar Ski.

HAMILTON, His Honour John; a Circuit Judge, 1987–2006; *b* 27 Jan. 1941; *s* of late John Ian Hamilton and Mrs Margaret Walker; *m* 1965, Patricia Ann Hamilton (*née* Henman); two *s* one *d*. *Educ:* Durlston Court Prep. Sch., New Milton, Hants; Harrow (schol.); Hertford Coll., Oxford (schol.; MA Jurisp.). Called to the Bar, Gray's Inn, 1965; a Recorder, 1985. KStJ 1982. *Recreations:* golf, bridge, gardening. *Address:* Red Stack, Anstey, near Buntingford, Herts SG9 0BN. *T:* (01763) 848536.

HAMILTON, Kirstie Louise, (Mrs Charles Stewart-Smith); Partner, Tulchan Communications, 2002–07; *b* 5 April 1963; *d* of Elizabeth Kate Marie Hamilton and Mark Robert Hamilton; *m* 1998, Charles Stewart-Smith; two *s*. *Educ:* Hillcrest High Sch., Hamilton, NZ. Columnist, National Business Review, NZ, 1988–89; Business Correspondent, Evening Standard, 1989–92; Business Correspondent, 1992–95, Dep. City Editor, 1995–96, Sunday Times; City Editor, The Express and Sunday Express, 1996–97; City Editor, Sunday Times, 1997–2002. *Recreations:* riding, ski-ing. *Address:* 37 Stockwell Park Crescent, SW9 0DQ.

HAMILTON, Sir Malcolm William Bruce S.; *see* Stirling-Hamilton.

HAMILTON, Martha, (Mrs R. R. Steedman), OBE 1988; Headmistress, St Leonards School, St Andrews, 1970–88; *d* of Rev. John Edmund Hamilton and Hon. Lilias Maclay; *m* 1977, Robert Russell Steedman, *qv*. *Educ:* Roedean Sch.; St Andrews Univ. (MA Hons Hist.); Cambridge Univ. (DipEd); Edinburgh Univ. (Dip. Adult Educn). Principal, Paljor Namgyal Girls' High School, Gangtok, Sikkim, 1959–66. Mem., Task Force to examine under-achievement in schs in Scotland, 1996. Member: Assoc. for Protection of Rural Scotland Award Panel, 1989–92; Fife Health Bd, 1991–98 (Vice Chm., 1994–98); Court of Dirs, Edinburgh Acad., 1992–2000. Convenor, Assoc. for Applied Arts, 1992–98. Gov., New Sch., Butterstone, 1997–2003. Awarded Pema Dorji (for services to education), Sikkim, 1966. *Recreations:* travel, bird-watching. *Address:* Muir of Blebo, Blebo Craigs, by Cupar, Fife KY15 5UG.

See also E. W. Hamilton.

HAMILTON, (Mostyn) Neil; Chairman, Sheila Childs Recruitment Ltd, since 2004; broadcaster, writer, entertainer, actor; *b* 9 March 1949; *s* of Ronald and Norma Hamilton; *m* 1983, (Mary) Christine Holman. *Educ:* Amman Valley Grammar School; University College of Wales, Aberystwyth (BSc Econ, MSc Econ); Corpus Christi College, Cambridge (LLB). Called to the Bar, Middle Temple, 1979. MP (C) Tatton, 1983–97; contested (C) same seat, 1997. PPS to Minister of State for Transport, 1986–87; an Asst Govt Whip, 1990–92; Parly Under-Sec. of State, DTI, 1992–94. Mem., Select Cttee on Treasury and Civil Service, 1987–90; Vice-Chm., Conservative backbench Trade and Industry Cttee, 1984–90 (Sec., 1983 and 1994–97); Secretary: Cons. backbench Finance Cttee, 1987–90 and 1995–97; UK–ANZAC Parly Gp, 1984–97; Chm., All Party Anglo-Togo Parly Gp, 1988–97. Columnist, Sunday Express, 2007–. Vice-Pres., Small Business Bureau, 1985–97. Vice-Pres., Cheshire Agricl Soc., 1986–. Actor, Jack and the Beanstalk, Yvonne Arnaud Th., Guildford, 2002–03; narrator, Rocky Horror Show, 30th anniversary tour, 2002–03; actor/performer, Lunch with the Hamiltons, Edinburgh Fest. 2006, 2007, 2008. *Publications:* UK/US Double Taxation, 1980; The European Community—a Policy for Reform, 1983; (ed) Land Development Encyclopaedia, 1981–; (jtly) No Turning Back, 1985; Great Political Eccentrics, 1999; pamphlets on state industry, schools and the NHS. *Recreations:* gardening, opera, the arts, architecture and conservation, country pursuits, silence. *Address:* Bradfield Manor, Hullavington, Wilts SN14 6EU.

HAMILTON, Myer Alan Barry K.; *see* King-Hamilton.

HAMILTON, Neil; *see* Hamilton, M. N.

HAMILTON, Sir Nigel, KCB 2008; Head of Northern Ireland Civil Service, since 2002; *b* 19 March 1948; *s* of James and Jean Hamilton; *m* 1974, Lorna Woods; two *s*. *Educ:* Queen's Univ., Belfast (BSc Hons); Henley Mgt Coll.; Federal Exec. Inst., Virginia; Univ. of Ulster. Joined NICS, 1970; posts in phys. develt areas, incl. roads, water and housing; Asst Sec., Housing and Local Govt Div., 1975; Under Sec., Central Community Relns, Urban Regeneration, 1990–98; Perm. Sec., Dept of Educn, 1998–2001; Perm. Sec., Dept for Regl Develt, 2001–02. *Recreations:* Rugby (Pres., Ulster Referees Soc., 1996–97), golf.

HAMILTON, Nigel John Mawdesley; QC 1981; *b* 13 Jan. 1938; *s* of late Archibald Dearman Hamilton and Joan Worsley Hamilton (*née* Mawdesley); *m* 1963, Leone Morag Elizabeth Gordon (*d* 2006); two *s*. *Educ:* St Edward's Sch., Oxford; Queens' Coll., Cambridge. Nat. Service, 2nd Lieut, RE, Survey Dept, 1956–58. Assistant Master: St Edward's Sch., Oxford, 1962–63; King's Sch., Canterbury, 1963–65. Called to the Bar, Inner Temple, 1965, Bencher, 1989. Mem., Gen. Council of the Bar, 1989–94. Mem. (C) for Chew Valley, Avon CC, 1989–93. *Recreation:* fishing. *Address:* New Bailey Chambers, Ground Floor, Marshall House, Ringway, Preston PR1 2QD. *Club:* Flyfishers'.

HAMILTON, Peter Bryan, MA; Head Master of Haberdashers' Aske's School, since 2002; *b* 28 Aug. 1956; *s* of Brian George Hamilton and Clara Hamilton (*née* Marchi); *m* 1st, 1981, Danièle Lahaye (marr. diss. 1987); one *d*; 2nd, 1993, Sylvie (*née* Vulliet); one *d*. *Educ:* King Edward VI Grammar Sch., Southampton; Christ Church, Oxford (1st Cl Hons Modern Languages 1979; MA). Head of French, Radley Coll., 1981–89; Head of Modern Langs and Housemaster of Wren's, Westminster Sch., 1989–96; Head Master, King Edward VI Sch., Southampton, 1996–2002. Examnr in French, Oxford and Cambridge Schs Exam. Bd, 1992–97. Governor: Stroud Sch., 1997–2002; Princes' Mead, 1997–2002; Durlston Court Sch., 1999–2002; Reddiford Sch., 2003–; Lochinver House, 2004–. *Recreations:* canoeing, hill walking, karate, sailing, ski-ing, squash, wind surfing, comparative literature, French and German cinema, opera, classical music. *Address:* Haberdashers' Aske's School, Butterfly Lane, Elstree, Borehamwood, Herts WD6 3AF.

HAMILTON, Reeta; *see* Chakrabarti, R.

HAMILTON, Richard, CH 2000; painter; *b* 24 Feb. 1922; *s* of Peter and Constance Hamilton; *m* 1st, 1947, Terry O'Reilly (*d* 1962); one *s* one *d*; 2nd, 1991, Rita Donagh. *Educ:* elementary; Royal Academy Schs; Slade Sch. of Art. Jig and Tool draughtsman, 1940–45. Lectr, Fine Art Dept, King's Coll., Univ. of Durham (later Univ. of Newcastle upon Tyne), 1953–66. *Devised exhibitions:* Growth and Form, 1951; Man, Machine and Motion, 1955. *Collaborated on:* This is Tomorrow, 1956; 'an Exhibit', 1957; exhibn with D. Roth, ICA New Gall., 1977. *One man art exhibitions:* Gimpel Fils, 1951; Hanover Gall., 1955, 1964; Robert Fraser Gall., 1966, 1967, 1969; Whitworth Gall., 1972; Nigel Greenwood Inc., 1972; Serpentine Gall., 1975; Stedelijk Mus., Amsterdam, 1976; Waddington Gall., 1980, 1982, 1984; Anthony d'Offay Gall., 1980, 1991, 1995; Charles Cowles Gall., NY, 1980; Galérie Maeght, Paris, 1981; Tate Gall., 1983–84; Thorden and Wetterling, Stockholm, 1984; DAAD Gall., Berlin, 1985; Fruitmarket Gall., Edinburgh, 1988; Moderna Museet, Stockholm, 1989; Venice Biennale, 1993; San Francisco Mus. of Modern Art, 1996; other exhibitions abroad include: Kassel, 1967, 1997 (Arnold Bode Prize); New York, 1967; Milan, 1967, 1968, 1969, 1971, 1972, 1974, 1990; Hamburg, 1969; Berlin, 1970, 1971, 1973; Bremen, 1998; Imaging James Joyce's Ulysses, British Mus., 2002; A Host of Angels, Venice Biennale, 2007; *retrospective exhibitions:* Tate Gallery, 1970 (also shown in Eindhoven and Bern), 1992; Guggenheim Museum, New York, 1973 (also shown in Cincinnati, Munich, Tübingen, Berlin); Musée Grenoble, 1977; Kunsthalle Bielefeld, 1978; Kunstmus., Winterthur, 1990 (also shown in Hannover and Valencia); Tate Gall., 1992; Irish Mus. of Modern Art, Dublin, 1992; MACBA, Barcelona, 2003. William and Noma Copley award, 1960; John Moores prize, 1969; Talens Prize International, 1970; Golden Lion of Venice, 1993; Gold Medal, Ljubljana Print Trianalle, 1999; Beckman Prize, Frankfurt, 2007. *Publication:* Collected Words 1953–1982, 1982. *Address:* c/o Tate Gallery, Millbank, SW1P 4RG.

HAMILTON, His Honour Richard Graham; a Circuit Judge, 1986–97; Chancellor, Diocese of Liverpool, 1976–2002; *b* 26 Aug. 1932; *s* of late Henry Augustus Rupert Hamilton and Frances Mary Graham Hamilton; *m* 1960, Patricia Craghill Hamilton (*née* Ashburner); one *s* one *d*. *Educ:* Charterhouse; University Coll., Oxford (MA); MA Screenwriting, Liverpool John Moores Univ., 1999. Called to the Bar, Middle Temple, 1956; a Recorder, 1974–86. Regular broadcasting work for Radio Merseyside, inc. scripts: Van Gogh in England, 1981; Voices from Babylon, 1983; A Longing for Dynamite, 1984; Dark Night, 1988 (winner of first prize for a short religious play, RADIUS); Murder Court productions (dramatised trials), Liverpool: The Maybrick Case, 1989; The Veronica Mutiny, 1990; Threatening Behaviour, 2006. *Publications:* Foul Bills and Dagger Money,

1979; All Jangle and Riot, 1986; A Good Wigging, 1988. *Recreations:* reading, walking, films. *Club:* Athenæum (Liverpool).

HAMILTON, Dr Russell Douglas, FFPH; Director of Research and Development, Department of Health; *b* 6 Sept. 1955; *s* of Ronald Adrian Hamilton and June Grace Hamilton; *m* 1993, Angela Carole Shore; two *d*. *Educ:* Pimlico High Sch.; James Cook Univ. (BSc Hons 1976); Univ. of London (PhD Physiol. 1990); Brunel Univ./Henley Mgt Coll. (MBA 1993). DipM 1993; FFPH 2003. Tutor, James Cook Univ., 1976; SO in Respiratory Medicine, Flinders Med. Centre, Adelaide, 1977–79; SO, then Principal Clinical Scientist, Acad. Dept of Medicine, Charing Cross Hosp., 1980–93; Regl R&D Manager, SW RHA and NHS Exec. S and W, 1993–98; Department of Health: Regl Dir, R&D, then Hd of R&D Div. S, 1998–2003; Hd, Res. Policy and Strategy, then Dep. Dir of R&D, 2003. Director, National NHS R&D Programmes: in Asthma, 1998–2003; in Complex Disability, 1998–2003; in Cancer, 1998–2007. Mem., Govt Chief Scientific Advr's Cttee, 2004–. Member: various sci. and professional adv. cttees, 1991–; Consumers in NHS Res., 1999–2004; Res. for Patient Benefits Wkg Party, 2003–04. Member, Board: NCRI (formerly Nat. Cancer Res. Funders Forum), 2000–; UK Clinical Res. Collaboration, 2004–; Office for Strategic Coordination of Health Res., 2007–. *Publications:* contrib. papers esp. on respiratory physiology in health and disease. *Recreations:* family, sailing, hill walking, music. *Address:* Department of Health, Richmond House, 79 Whitehall, SW1A 2NS. *T:* (020) 7210 5786.

HAMILTON, Simon Terence; Member (DemU) Strangford, Northern Ireland Assembly, since 2007; *b* Newtownards, Co. Down, 17 March 1977; *s* of Frank and Muriel Hamilton; *m* Nicola Karen McAvoy; one *s*. *Educ:* Comber Primary Sch.; Regent Hse Sch., Newtownards; Queen's Univ. Belfast (BA Hons Modern Hist. and Politics 1999; BLegS Hons Law 2001). Auditor, PricewaterhouseCoopers, 2001–03; Press Officer, DUP, 2003–07. Mem. (DemU) Ards BC, 2005–. Member: Orange Order; Royal Black Instn. *Recreations:* reading, walking, travelling. *Address:* 4 Bridge Street Link, Comber, Co. Down BT23 5YH. *T:* (028) 9187 0900, *Fax:* (028) 9187 0949; *e-mail:* simonhamilton@dup.org.uk.

HAMILTON, Her Honour Susan, (Mrs Eric Kelly); QC 1993; a Circuit Judge, 1998–2007; *m* 1977, Dr Eric Peter Kelly; two *s*. *Educ:* Hove Grammar Sch. for Girls. Called to the Bar, Middle Temple, 1975; a Recorder, 1996–98. *Publications:* The Modern Law of Highways, 1981; (contrib.) Halsbury's Laws of England, vol. 21, 4th edn, 1995, vol. 39(1), 4th edn, 1998; (contrib.) Encyclopaedia of Forms and Precedents, 5th edn, 1986. *Recreations:* sailing, gardening, tapestry, travelling. *Address:* c/o Bromley County Court, Court House, College Road, Bromley, Kent BR1 3PX. *Club:* Royal Southern Yacht.

HAMILTON, Wilfred; *see* Hamilton, A. W.

HAMILTON, William Francis Forbes, CA; Chairman, Macrae & Dick Ltd, since 1994; Vice Lord-Lieutenant, Inverness, since 2002; *b* 19 April 1940; *s* of late Col William Hamilton, OBE, CA and of Amy Constance Hamilton (*née* Forbes); *m* 1971, Anne Davison, MB BS; one *s*. *Educ:* Inverness Royal Acad.; Edinburgh Univ. (BCom 1961). CA 1967. Macrae & Dick Ltd: Co. Sec., 1968–80; Finance Dir, 1971–80; Man. Dir, 1980–2003. Dir, Highlands & Islands Airports Ltd, 1995–2001; Chm., Menzies BMW, 1998–. Mem., Distributor Council, BL Cars, 1977–78. Member, Highland Committee: Scottish Council Develt and Ind., 1971–2007; Police Dependants' Trust, 1998–. Director: Highland Hospice, 1992–95; Highland Hospice Trading Co., 1995–2008. Trustee, Fresson Trust, 1991–. DL Inverness, 2000. *Recreations:* sailing, travel. *Address:* Craigrory, North Kessock, Inverness IV1 3XH. *T:* (01463) 230430, *Fax:* (01463) 668990; *e-mail:* wffhamilton@macraeanddick.co.uk. *Club:* Royal Highland Yacht.

HAMILTON-DALRYMPLE, Sir Hew; *see* Dalrymple.

HAMILTON FRASER, Donald; *see* Fraser.

HAMILTON-RUSSELL, family name of **Viscount Boyne**.

HAMILTON-SMITH, family name of **Baron Colwyn**.

HAMLEY, Donald Alfred, CBE 1985; HM Diplomatic Service, retired; *b* 19 Aug. 1931; *s* of Alfred Hamley and Amy (*née* Brimacombe); *m* 1958, Daphne Griffith; two *d*. *Educ:* Devonport High Sch., Plymouth. Joined HM Foreign (subseq. Diplomatic) Service, 1949; Nat. Service, 1950–52; returned to FO; served in: Kuwait, 1955–57; Libya, 1958–61; FO, 1961–63; Jedda, 1963–65 and 1969–72; Rome, 1965–69; seconded to DTI, 1972–73; Commercial Counsellor, Caracas, 1973–77; seconded to Dept of Trade, 1977–80; Consul-Gen., Jerusalem, 1980–84; retired, 1984. *Address:* 1 Forge Close, Hayes, Bromley BR2 7LP. *T:* (020) 8462 6696. *Club:* Royal Automobile.

HAMLIN, Prof. Michael John, CBE 1994; FICE, FREng; FRSE; consulting water engineer, since 1984; Principal and Vice Chancellor of the University of Dundee, 1987–94; *b* 11 May 1930; *s* of late Dr Ernest John Hamlin and Dorothy Janet Hamlin; *m* 1951, Augusta Louise, *d* of late William Thomas Tippins and Rose Louise Tippins; three *s*. *Educ:* St John's Coll., Johannesburg; Dauntsey's Sch.; Bristol Univ. (BSc); Imperial Coll. of Science and Technol., London (DIC). FIWEM (FIWES 1973); FICE 1981; FREng (FEng 1985); FRSE 1990. Asst Engineer, Lemon & Blizard, Southampton, 1951–53; Engineer: Anglo-American Corp., Johannesburg, 1954–55; Stewart, Sviridov & Oliver, Johannesburg, 1955; Partner, Rowe & Hamlin, Johannesburg, 1956–58; Univ. of Witwatersrand, 1959–60; University of Birmingham, 1961–87: Prof. of Water Engrg, 1970–87; Hd of Dept of Civil Engrg, 1980–87; Pro Vice-Chancellor, 1985–86; Vice-Principal, 1986–87. Chm., Aquatic and Atmospheric Phys. Scis Grants Cttee, NERC, 1975–79; Member: Severn Trent Water Authority, 1974–79; British National Cttee for Geodesy and Geophysics, 1979–84 (Chm., Hydrology Sub-Cttee, 1979–84); Scottish Econ. Council, 1989–93; Internat. Relns Cttee, 1992–95, Scientific Unions Cttee, 1995–99, Royal Soc. President: Internat. Commn on Water Resource Systems of the Internat. Assoc. of Hydrological Scis (IAHS), 1983–87; British Hydrological Soc., 1995–97. International Union of Geodesy and Geophysics: Mem., Council, 1992–2000; Mem., 1991–2007, Chm., 2003–07, Finance Cttee. Chm., Scottish Centre for Children with Motor Impairment, 1991–94. Hon. Life Mem., Guild of Students, Birmingham Univ., 1980; Hon. Mem., Students' Assoc., Dundee Univ., 1994–. FRCPS (Glas) 1992; Hon. FRCGP 1993. Dist. Fellow, Internat. Med. Univ., Kuala Lumpur, 1999. Hon. LLD: St Andrews, 1989; Dundee, 1996; Hon. DEng: Birmingham, 1995; Bristol, 2000; Hon. DLitt Southern Queensland, 2003. President's Premium, IWES, 1972. OStJ 1991. *Publications:* contribs on public health engrg and water resources engrg in learned jls. *Recreations:* walking, gardening. *Address:* The Coombes, Hope Bagot, Ludlow, Shropshire SY8 3AQ.

HAMLISCH, Marvin; composer, conductor, pianist, entertainer; *b* 2 June 1944; *s* of Max and Lilly Hamlisch; *m* 1989, Terre Blair. *Educ:* Professional Children's Sch.; Queen's Coll., NY; Juilliard Sch., NY. Début as a pianist, Minnesota Orch., 1975; solo concert tours; conductor of various orchestras throughout USA; Musical Dir and Conductor, Barbra Streisand tour, 1994 (Emmy Awards for Outstanding Individual Achievement in Music and Lyrics and in Music Direction, 1995); Principal Pops Conductor: Pittsburgh SO, 1995–; Baltimore SO, 1996–2000; National SO, Washington, 2000–; Milwaukee SO; San Diego Symphony. Mem., ASCAP. *Compositions* include: *film scores:* The Swimmer, 1968; Bananas, 1971; The Way We Were (Acad. and Grammy Awards for Best Original Score, and for Best Song of the Year for title song), 1974; Starting Over, 1979; Ordinary People, 1980; Sophie's Choice, 1982; *film themes:* Three Men and a Baby, 1987; January Man, 1988; The Experts, 1989; *songs:* Sunshine Lollipops and Rainbows; Good Morning America; Nobody Does it Better; One Song (for Barcelona Olympics), 1992; *musicals:* A Chorus Line, 1975 (Pulitzer Prize); They're Playing Our Song, 1979; The Goodbye Girl, 1993; Sweet Smell of Success, 2000; *symphony in one movement*, Anatomy of Peace, 1991. Acad. Award for best adaptation, for The Sting, 1974; Grammy Awards: Best New Artist, 1974; Best Pop Instrumental, for The Entertainer, 1974. *Publication:* The Way I Was (autobiog.), 1992. *Recreation:* loves to travel.

HAMLYN, Prof. David Walter; Professor of Philosophy and Head of Philosophy Department, Birkbeck College, University of London, 1964–88, now Professor Emeritus (Head of Classics Department, 1981–86); Vice-Master, Birkbeck College, 1983–88, Fellow, 1988; *b* 1 Oct. 1924; *s* of late Hugh Parker Hamlyn and Gertrude Isabel Hamlyn; *m* 1949, Eileen Carlyle Litt; one *s* one *d*. *Educ:* Plymouth Coll.; Exeter Coll., Oxford. BA (Oxon) 1948, MA 1949 (1st cl. Lit. Hum., 1st cl. Philosophy and Psychology, 1950). War Service, RAC and IAC, Hodson's Horse (Lieutenant), 1943–46. Research Fellow, Corpus Christi Coll., Oxford, 1950–53; Lecturer: Jesus Coll., Oxford, 1953–54; Birkbeck Coll., London, 1954–63, Reader, 1963–64. Pres., Aristotelian Soc., 1977–78. Member: Council, Royal Inst. of Philosophy, 1968– (Vice-Chm., 1991–95; Mem. Exec., 1971–97); Nat. Cttee for Philosophy, 1986–92 (Hon. Vice-Pres., 1992–2003). Mem., London Univ. Senate, 1981–87 (Mem. several cttees; Chm., Academic Council Standing Sub-cttee in Theology, Arts and Music, 1984–87); Governor: Birkbeck Coll., 1965–69; City Lit., 1982–86 (Vice-Chm., 1985–86); Central London Adult Educn Inst., 1987–90; Chm. Governors, Heythrop Coll., 1971–78, Mem., 1984–95, Fellow, 1978. Mem., Wissenschaftliche Leitung der Schopenhauerges., 1992–. Editor of Mind, 1972–84; Consulting Editor, Jl of Medical Ethics, 1981–90. *Publications:* The Psychology of Perception, 1957 (repr. with additional material, 1969); Sensation and Perception, 1961; Aristotle's *De Anima*, Books II and III, 1968; The Theory of Knowledge, 1970 (USA), 1971 (GB); Experience and the Growth of Understanding, 1978 (Spanish trans., 1981; Korean trans., 1990); Schopenhauer, 1980; Perception, Learning and the Self, 1983; Metaphysics, 1984 (Korean trans., 2000); History of Western Philosophy, 1987 (Dutch trans., 1988; Portuguese trans., 1990; Swedish trans., 1995); In and Out of the Black Box, 1990; Being a Philosopher, 1992; Understanding Perception, 1996; contrib. to several other books and to many philosophical, psychological and classical jls. *Recreations:* playing and listening to music, reading, gardening. *Address:* 38 Smithy Knoll Road, Calver, Hope Valley, Derbyshire S32 3XW. *T:* (01433) 631326.

HAMLYN, Peter John, MD; FRCS; Consultant Neurological and Spinal Surgeon: St Bartholomew's Hospital, since 1990; The Royal London Hospital, since 1996; *b* 10 Aug. 1957; *s* of David William Hamlyn and Paula Anne Hamlyn (*née* Bowker); *m* 1994, Geraldine Marie Frances Shepherd; three *s*. *Educ:* N Cestrian Grammar Sch.; Solihull Sixth Form Coll.; University Coll. London (BSc 1st Cl. Hons Neurosci. 1979; MB BS 1982; MD 1994 (Rogers Prize)). FRCS 1986; FInstLM (FISM 1995). Dir, Sport and Exercise Medicine, Queen Mary, Univ. of London, 2003–07. Chm., Ministerial Wkg Gp on Safety and Medicine in Sport, DCMS, 2001. Corresp. in sports medicine, Daily Telegraph, 1993–. Founder, 1992, and Vice-Chm., 1997–, British Brain and Spine Foundn. Med. Advr, London 2012 Olympic Bid; Mem., London Specialist Trng Cttee in Sport and Exercise Medicine. *Publication:* Neurovascular Compression of the Cranial Nerves in Neurological and Systematic Disease, 1999. *Recreation:* sculpture.

HAMM, John (Frederick), MD; Chairman, Assisted Human Reproduction Canada, since 2006; Premier of Nova Scotia, Canada, 1999–2006; *b* 8 April 1938; *m* 1964, Genesta Hartling; two *s* one *d*. *Educ:* Univ. of King's Coll., Halifax (BSc 1958); Dalhousie Med. Sch. (MD 1963). Family physician, 1963–93. MLA (PC) Pictou Centre, Nova Scotia, 1993–2006; Leader of Opposition, NS, 1995–98. Leader, PC Party of NS, 1995–2006. Mem., Provincial Med. Bd, NS, 1963–96. President: Coll. of Family Physicians, NS; Pictou Co. Med. Soc., 1971–73; Med. Soc. of NS, 1977. Pres., Aberdeen Hosp. Med. Staff, 1986–88; Chm., Aberdeen Hosp. Foundn, 1990–92. Former Warden, St George's Ch. *Recreations:* hockey, running, wood working.

HAMMARBERG, Thomas; Commissioner for Human Rights, Council of Europe, since 2006; *b* 2 Jan. 1942; *s* of Harald and Naima Hammarberg; *m* 1997, Alfhild Petren; one *s*. *Educ:* Stockholm Sch. of Econs (BS). Foreign Editor, daily Expressen, then Swedish broadcasting, 1970–80; Secretary General: Amnesty Internat., 1980–86; Save the Children-Sweden, 1986–92; Ambassador and Special Advr to the Foreign Minister, 1994–2002; Sec. Gen., Olof Palme Internat. Center, Stockholm, 2002–06. Vice Chm., UN Cttee on the Rights of the Child, 1991–96; Special Rep. of the UN Sec. Gen. in Cambodia, 1996–2000. King of Sweden Hon. Medal, 2005. *Publications:* books in Swedish on media reporting and human rights matters. *Recreation:* ski-ing. *Address:* Office of the Commissioner for Human Rights, Council of Europe, 67075 Strasbourg, France. *T:* (3) 90215063; *e-mail:* thomas.hammarberg@coe.int.

HAMMARSKJÖLD, Knut (Olof Hjalmar Åkesson); Director, since 1948, and Chairman, 1987–94, now Emeritus Chairman, Sydsvenska Dagbladet AB, Newspaper Group, Malmö; Minister Plenipotentiary, since 1966; *b* Geneva, 16 Jan. 1922; Swedish; *m*; four *s*. *Educ:* Stockholm Univ. Entered Swedish Foreign Service, 1946; served in Paris, Vienna, Moscow, Bucharest, Kabul, Sofia, 1947–55; 1st Sec., Foreign Office, 1955–57; Head of Foreign Relations Dept, Royal Bd of Civil Aviation, Stockholm, 1957–59; Dep. Head of Swedish Delegn to OEEC, Paris, 1959–60; Dep. Sec.-Gen., EFTA, Geneva, 1960–66; International Air Transport Association (IATA): Dir Gen., 1966–84; Chm. Exec. Cttee, 1981–84; Internat. Affairs Counsel, 1985–86; Mem., Inst. of Transport, London; Dir, Inst. of Air Transport, Paris, 1974–; Dir-Gen., Atwater Inst. Inf./Communications, Montreal, 1985–98; Mem., Internat. Aviation Management Training Inst., Montreal; Director: Prisma Transport Consultants Ltd, Geneva/Brussels, 1987–; Blenheim Aviation Services Ltd, 1992–. Chm., I-L Consult Baltic, Suders/Hamra, Gotland, 1994–. Chm., Ind. Commn for Reform of UNESCO, 1989–93; Sen. Special Advr to Dir Gen. of UNESCO, 1993–; Hon. Ambassador, UNESCO, 1991. Hon. Fellow, Canadian Aeronautics and Space Inst., Ottawa; Hon. Academician, Mexican Acad. of Internat. Law; Hon. FCIT (London). Edward Warner Award, ICAO, 1983. Comdr (1st cl.), Order of North Star (Sweden); NOR (Sweden); Légion d'Honneur (France); Grand Cross Order of Civil Merit (Spain); Grand Officer, Order of Al-Istiqlal (Jordan); Commander: Order of Lion (Finland); Oranje Nassau (Netherlands); Order of Falcon (1st cl.) (Iceland); Order of Black Star (Benin). *Publications:* articles on political, economic and aviation topics. *Recreations:* music, painting, ski-ing.

HAMMER, James Dominic George, CB 1983; Chairman, Certification Management Council, Zurich (formerly Eagle Star) Certification Ltd, 1996–2001; *b* 21 April 1929; *s* of E. A. G. and E. L. G. Hammer; *m* 1955, Margaret Eileen Halse; two *s* one *d. Educ:* Dulwich Coll.; Corpus Christi Coll., Cambridge. BA Hons Mod. Langs. Joined HM Factory Inspectorate, 1953; Chief Inspector of Factories, 1975–84; Dep. Dir Gen., HSE, 1985–89. Dir, UK SKILLS, 1990–2000. Pres., Internat. Assoc. of Labour Inspection, 1984–93; Chairman: Nat. Certification Scheme for In-Service Inspection Bodies, 1990–92; Nat. Steering Cttee, Eur. Year of Safety, Health and Hygiene at Work 1992, 1991–93; NACCB, 1992–95; Nat. Exam. Bd in Occupational Safety and Health, 1992–95. Vice Chm., Camberwell HA, 1982–91; Associate Mem., King's Healthcare, 1992–97. FIOSH 1992. *Address:* 10 Allison Grove, Dulwich, SE21 7ER. *T:* (020) 8693 2977.

HAMMERBECK, Brig. Christopher John Anthony, CB 1991; CBE 2007; Executive Director, British Chamber of Commerce in Hong Kong, since 1994; *b* 14 March 1943; *s* of Sqn Leader O. R. W. Hammerbeck and I. M. Hammerbeck; *m* 1974, Alison Mary Felice (marr. diss. 1996); one *s* two *d. Educ:* Mayfield Coll., Sussex. Commnd, 1965; 2nd RTR, 1965–70; Air Adjt, Parachute Sqn, RAC, 1970–72; GSO3 (Ops), HQ 20 Armoured Bde, 1972–74; psc, 1975; DAA&QMG, HQ 12 Mechanised Bde, 1976–78; Sqn Comdr, 4th RTR, 1978–80; DAAG(O), MoD, 1980–82; Directing Staff, Army Staff Coll., 1982–84; CO, 2nd RTR, 1984–87; Col, Tactical Doctrine/Op. Requirement 1 (BR) Corps, 1987–88; RCDS, 1989; Comdr, 4th Armoured Brigade, 1990–92; Dep. Comdr, British Forces Hong Kong, 1992–94. Pres., Inst. of Export (HK), 2004–. President: Hong Kong Br., RBL, 1995–; HK Ex-Servicemen's Assoc., 1995–. Member: Hong Kong Inst. of Dirs, 2001–; Hong Kong Sea Cadets Council, 2004–. MCMI. Hon. Citizen, Xiamen City, China, 2006. *Recreations:* sailing, golf, ski-ing, bobsleigh, reading, travel. *Address:* British Chamber of Commerce in Hong Kong, Emperor Group Centre, 288 Hennessy Road, Wanchai, Hong Kong. *Clubs:* Army and Navy, Royal Over-Seas League; Shek O, Hong Kong (Hong Kong).

HAMMERSLEY, (Constance) Ann; *see* Cryer, C. A.

HAMMERSLEY, Rear-Adm. Peter Gerald, CB 1982; OBE 1965; *b* 18 May 1928; *s* of late Robert Stevens Hammersley and Norah Hammersley (*née* Kirkham); *m* 1959, Audrey Cynthia Henderson Bolton; one *s* one *d. Educ:* Denstone Coll.; RNEC Manadon; Imperial Coll., London (DIC). Served RN, 1946–82; Long Engrg Course, RNEC Manadon, 1946–50; HMS Liverpool, 1950–51; Advanced Marine Engrg Course, RNC Greenwich, 1951–53; HMS Ocean, 1953–54; joined Submarine Service, 1954; HMS Alaric, HMS Tiptoe, 1954–58; Nuclear Engrg Course, Imperial Coll., 1958–59; First Marine Engineer Officer, first RN Nuclear Submarine, HMS Dreadnought, 1960–64; DG Ships Staff, 1965–68; Base Engineer Officer, Clyde Submarine Base, 1968–70; Naval Staff, 1970–72; Asst Director, S/M Project Team, DG Ships, 1973–76; CO, HMS Defiance, 1976–78; Captain, RNEC Manadon, 1978–80; CSO (engrg) to C-in-C Fleet, 1980–82. Comdr 1964; Captain 1971; Rear-Adm. 1980; Chief Exec., British Internal Combustion Engine Manufacturers' Assoc., 1982–85; Dir, British Marine Equipment Council, 1985–92. Fellow, Woodard Schs Corp., 1992–98. Gov., Denstone Coll., 1986–98 (Chm., 1994–98). Master, Engineers' Co., 1988–89. *Recreations:* walking, gardening, golf. *Address:* Wistaria Cottage, Linersh Wood, Bramley, near Guildford GU5 0EE. *Club:* Army and Navy.

HAMMERSLEY, Philip Tom, CBE 2000 (OBE 1989); CEng; Chairman, University Hospitals of Leicester NHS Trust, 2000–06; *b* 10 Feb. 1931; *s* of Tom Andrew Hammersley and Winifred Hammersley (*née* Moyns); *m* 1954, Lesley Ann Millage; two *s* one *d. Educ:* Bancroft's Sch.; Imperial Coll., Univ. of London (BSc Eng.). CEng 1965; MIMechE 1965. Tech. Officer, ICI Plastics Div., 1954–65; Clarks Ltd: Chief Engr, 1965–68; Prodn Services Manager, 1968–71; Dir, Children's Div., 1971–79; Pres., Striderite Footwear, Boston, Mass, 1979–81; British Shoe Corporation, Leicester: Factories Dir, 1981–87; Man. Dir, Freeman, Hardy & Willis, 1987–89; Commercial Dir, 1989–90; non-exec. Dir, BSS Gp PLC, 1991–99 (Dep. Chm., 1995; Chm., 1995–99). Vice-Chm., Leics HA, 1990–92; Chm., Leicester Royal Infirmary NHS Trust, 1992–97; Regl Chm., Trent, NHS Exec., DoH, 1997–99. Chm. Council, Shoe & Allied Trades Res. Assoc., 1983–86; Pres., Brit. Footwear Manufacturers Fedn, 1986–87; Chm., E Midlands Regl Council, CBI, 1988–90. Chm., Nat. Space Sci. Centre (Ops) Ltd, 2001–; Trustee, Nat. Space Sci. Centre, 1997–2001, 2006–. Freeman, City of London, 1983; Mem., Patten Makers' Co., 1983–. Hon. DBA De Montfort, 1999; Hon. LLD Leicester, 2008. *Recreations:* golf, theatre, music. *Address:* The Hollies, Wibtoft, near Lutterworth, Leics LE17 5BB. *T:* (01455) 220363. *Clubs:* East India, MCC; Leicestershire Golf.

HAMMERTON, His Honour Rolf Eric; a Circuit Judge, 1972–94; *b* 18 June 1926; *s* of Eric Maurice Hammerton and Dora Alice Hammerton (*née* Zander); *m* 1953, Thelma Celestine Hammerton (*née* Appleyard); one *s* three *d. Educ:* Brighton, Hove and Sussex Grammar Sch.; Peterhouse, Cambridge (MA, LLB). Philip Teichman Prize, 1952; called to the Bar, Inner Temple, 1952; Sussex County Courts: Designated Judge, Children's Cases, 1990–94; Principal Judge, Civil Matters, 1992–94. Contributing Editor, Butterworth's County Court Precedents and Pleadings, 1985–2000. Liveryman, Cooks' Co., 1979– (Master, 2002–03). *Recreation:* cooking.
  See also V. L. Hammerton.

HAMMERTON, Veronica Lesley; Her Honour Judge Hammerton; a Circuit Judge, since 2005; *b* 1 Oct. 1954; *d* of His Honour Rolf Eric Hammerton, *qv;* *m* 1981, David John Knight; one *s* one *d. Educ:* Cheltenham Ladies' Coll.; Girton Coll., Cambridge (BA 1976). Called to the Bar, Inner Temple, 1977; Asst Recorder, 1996–2000; a Recorder, 2000–05. Legal Mem., Mental Health Rev. Tribunal, 2003–. *Recreations:* embroidery, sailing, tennis, theatre-going. *Address:* Tunbridge Wells County Court, Merevale House, 42–46 London Road, Tunbridge Wells, Kent TN1 1DP.

HAMMETT, Ven. Barry Keith, CB 2006; Chaplain of the Fleet, Archdeacon for the Royal Navy and Director General, Naval Chaplaincy Service, 2002–06; *b* 9 Oct. 1947; *s* of George and Irene Hammett. *Educ:* Eltham Coll.; Magdalen Coll., Oxford (BA 1971, MA 1974); St Stephen's House, Oxford; Ven. English Coll., Rome (exchange student). Ordained deacon 1974, priest 1975; Asst Curate, St Peter's, Plymouth, 1974–77; Chaplain, RN, 1977–2006: Staff Chaplain, MoD, 1986–90; Principal, Armed Forces' Chaplaincy Centre, 1996–2000. QHC 1999–2006. Hon. Canon: Portsmouth Cathedral, 2002–06, Hon. Canon Emeritus, 2006; Cathedral Chapter, Dio. in Europe (Gibraltar), 2003–06. *Recreations:* travel, historic houses, gardening, motoring, photography, genealogy. *Address:* 1 de Port Heights, Corhampton, Hants SO32 3DA.

HAMMICK, Sir Stephen (George), 5th Bt *cr* 1834; OBE 2004; DL; *b* 27 Dec. 1926; *s* of Sir George Hammick, 4th Bt; *S* father, 1964; *m* 1953, Gillian Elizabeth Inchbald; two *s* one *d. Educ:* Stowe. Royal Navy as Rating (hostilities only), 1944–48; RAC Coll., Cirencester, 1949–50; MFH Cattistock Hunt, 1961 and 1962. Mem. (C), Dorset CC, 1958– (Vice-Chm., 1985–88; Chm., 1988–93). High Sheriff, Dorset, 1981–82, DL Dorset, 1989. Farmer, with 450 acres. *Recreations:* hunting, fishing, sailing. *Heir:* *s* Paul St

Vincent Hammick [*b* 1 Jan. 1955; *m* 1984, Judith Mary, *d* of Ralph Ernest Reynolds. *Address:* Badgers, Wraxall, Dorchester DT2 0HN. *T:* (01935) 83343.

HAMMOND, Sir Anthony (Hilgrove), KCB 2000 (CB 1992); Standing Counsel t General Synod of the Church of England, since 2000; *b* 27 July 1940; *s* of late Colone Charles William Hilgrove Hammond and Jessie Eugenia Hammond (*née* Francis); *m* 1988 Avril Collinson. *Educ:* Malvern Coll.; Emmanuel Coll., Cambridge (BA, MA, LLM Admitted Solicitor of Supreme Court, 1965. Articled with LCC, 1962; Solicitor, GLC 1965–68; Home Office: Legal Assistant, 1968; Sen. Legal Assistant, 1970; Asst Legal Adv 1974; Principal Asst Legal Advr, 1980–88, Legal Advr, 1988–92, Home Office and N Office; Solicitor and Dep. Sec., then Dir Gen. Legal Services, DTI, 1992–97; HM Procurator Gen., Treasury Solicitor and Queen's Proctor, 1997–2000; Legal Counsel t Hakluyt & Co. Ltd, 2001–05. Mem. Bd, Inst. of Advanced Legal Studies, 1997–. Fellow Soc. of Advanced Legal Studies, 1997. Freeman, City of London, 1991; Liveryman, Glas Sellers' Co., 1991– (Master, 2007). Hon. QC 1997. *Recreations:* bridge, music, opera walking, birdwatching. *Address:* General Synod, Church House, Great Smith Stree SW1P 3NZ.

HAMMOND, Eric Albert Barratt, OBE 1977; General Secretary, Electrical, Electroni Telecommunication and Plumbing Union, 1984–92; *b* 17 July 1929; *s* of Arthur Edga Hammond and Gertrude May Hammond; *m* 1953, Brenda Mary Edgeler; two *s. Educ* Corner Brook Public Sch. Shop Steward, 1953–63; Branch Sec., 1958–63, Exec Councillor, 1963–84, EETPU. Borough and Urban District Councillor, 1958–63. Mem TUC Gen. Council, 1983–88. Member: Electronics EDC, 1967–92; Industria Development Adv. Bd, 1977–87; Adv. Council on Energy Conservation, 1974–77; (part time) Monopolies and Mergers Commn, 1978–84; Engrg Council, 1984–90; ACARD 1985–87; NEDC, 1989–92; Lord Chancellor's Adv. Cttee on Legal Educn and Conduc 1991–98; Employment Appeal Tribunal, 1992–2000; Chm., Electronic Components an Technology Sector Gp (formerly Electronic Components Sector Working Party, 1975–92. Mem. Bd, Kent Thame-side, Groundwork, 1991–95. Gov., Gravesen Grammar Sch. for Boys, 1987– (Vice-Chm., 1989–94, Chm., 1994–2006); Chm Support Kent Schools, 1998–. *Publication:* Maverick: the life of a union rebel, 1992 *Recreations:* gardening, photography. *Address:* 9 Dene Holm Road, Northfleet, Kent DA1 8LF. *Club:* Gravesend Rugby.

HAMMOND, Prof. Gerald, PhD; FBA 1998; John Edward Taylor Professor of Englis Literature, University of Manchester, 1993–2006; *b* 3 Nov. 1945; *s* of Frank Georg Hammond and Ruth Hammond (*née* Wallen); *m* 1971, Patsy Talat Naheed Khaliq; one one *d. Educ:* University Coll. London (BA 1968; PhD 1974). University of Mancheste Lectr, 1971–83, Sen. Lectr, 1983–90, Reader, 1990–93, in English; Dean: Faculty of Arts 1999–2002; Internat. and Grad. Educn, 2002–03; Faculty of Engrg and Physical Sci 2003–04; Associate Vice Pres., Grad. Educn, 2005–06. Res. Posts Co-ordinator, Britis Acad., 2002–05. Distinguished Vis. Humanities Prof., Auburn Univ., Alabama, 1987; Na Sci. Council of Taiwan Res. Fellow, 1997–98. Chatterton Lecture, 1985, Warto Lecture, 1995, British Acad. *Publications:* (ed) The Metaphysical Poets, 1974; (ed) Joh Skelton: poems, 1980; The Reader and Shakespeare's Young Man Sonnets, 1981; Th Making of the English Bible, 1984; (ed) Sir Walter Ralegh, 1984; (ed) Elizabethan Poetry Lyrical and Narrative, 1984; (ed) Richard Lovelace: poems, 1987; Fleeting Things: Englis poets and poems 1616–1660, 1990; Horseracing: a book of words, 1992; articles in learne jls, reviews. *Recreation:* horseracing. *Address:* 29 Belfield Road, Manchester M20 6BJ. T (0161) 445 2399; *e-mail:* gerald.hammond@man.ac.uk.

HAMMOND, His Honour James Anthony; a Circuit Judge, 1986–2008; *b* 25 July 1936; *s* of James Hammond and Phyllis Eileen Hammond; *m* 1963, Sheila Mar Hammond, JP (*née* Stafford); three *d. Educ:* Wigan Grammar Sch.; St Catherine's Coll. Oxford (MA). Called to the Bar, Lincoln's Inn, 1959; National Service, 1959–61; Recorder, 1980–86. Councillor: Up Holland UDC, 1962–66; Skelmersdale and Hollan UDC, 1970–72. Chairman: NW Branch, Society of Labour Lawyers, 1975–86; W Lanc CAB, 1982–86; Pres., NW Branch, Inst. for Study and Treatment of Delinquency, 1987– *Recreations:* hockey, walking, sailing. *Clubs:* Wigan Hockey (Vice Pres., 1983–); Orre Rugby Union Football.

HAMMOND, (John) Martin; Headmaster, Tonbridge School, 1990–2005; *b* 15 Nov 1944; *s* of late Thomas Chatterton Hammond and Joan Cruse; *m* 1974, Meredith Jan Shier; one *s* one *d. Educ:* Winchester Coll. (Scholar); Balliol Coll., Oxford (Domu Scholar; Hertford Scholar and (1st) de Paravicini Scholar, (2nd) Craven Scholar, 1st Cl Hons Mods, 1963; Chancellor's Latin Prose Prize, Chancellor's Latin Verse Prize, Irelan Scholar, 1964; Gaisford Greek Prose Prize, Gaisford Greek Verse Prize (jtly), 1965; 2n Cl. Lit. Hum. 1966). Asst Master, St Paul's Sch., 1966–71; Teacher, Anargyrios Sch. Spetsai, Greece, 1972–73; Asst Master, Harrow Sch., 1973–74; Head of Classics, 1974–80 and Master in College, 1980–84, Eton Coll.; Headmaster, City of London Sch., 1984–90 Mem., Gen. Adv. Council of BBC, 1987–91. *Publications:* Homer, The Iliad (trans.), 1987 Homer, The Odyssey (trans.), 2000; Marcus Aurelius (trans. and notes), 2006. *Address* Shepherds' Hey, Hundon Road, Barnardiston, Haverhill, Suffolk CB9 7TJ. *T:* (01440 786441.

HAMMOND, (Jonathan) Mark; Chief Executive, West Sussex County Council, sinc 2004; *b* 8 Aug. 1961; *s* of Rev. Leslie Hammond and Sherry Hammond; *m* 1993, Susa Margaret Postle; one *s. Educ:* Kingswood Sch., Bath; Magdalene Coll., Cambridge (B Hons Hist. 1983). Department of the Environment, 1985–93: Private Sec. to Sir Gordon Manzie, 1987–89; Global Atmosphere Div., 1989–93; First Sec., Washington, 1993–97 Hd of Econ. and Envmt Policy, Surrey CC, 1997–2000; Dir, Envmt and Develt, W Sussex CC, 2000–04. Dir, W Sussex Econ. Partnership, 2004–. *Recreations:* golf, reading crosswords. *Address:* West Sussex County Council, County Hall, West Street, Chichester West Sussex PO19 1RQ. *T:* (01243) 777950; *e-mail:* markhammond@westsussex.gov.uk *Club:* Goodwood Golf.

HAMMOND, Julia Jessica; *see* Eccleshare, J. J.

HAMMOND, Mark; *see* Hammond, J. M.

HAMMOND, Martin; *see* Hammond, J. M.

HAMMOND, Michael Harry Frank, CBE 1990; DL; Chief Executive and Town Clerk Nottingham City Council, 1974–90; *b* 5 June 1933; *s* of late Edward Cecil Hammond and Kate Hammond; *m* 1965, Jenny Campbell; two *s* one *d. Educ:* Leatherhead; Law Society Sch. of Law; Nottingham Univ. (LLM Internat. Law 1996). Admitted solicitor, 1958; Ass Sol. in Town Clerk's office, Nottingham, 1961–63; Prosecuting Sol., 1963–66; Asst Town Clerk, 1966–69; Dep. Town Clerk, Newport, Mon, 1969–71; Dep. Town Clerk Nottingham, 1971–74. Hon. Secretary: Major City Councils Gp, 1977–88; Notts County Br., Assoc. of District Councils, 1974–88; Chairman: Assoc. of Local Authority Chie Execs, 1984–85; E Midlands Br., Soc. of Local Authority Chief Execs, 1988–90; Pres. Notts Law Soc., 1989–90 (Vice-Pres., 1988–89). Mem., Nat. Forest Adv. Bd, 1991–95

Ambassador, Nat. Forest, 2005–. Member: Midlands Regl Cttee, N British Housing Assoc., 1992–97; Develt Steering Gp, St John's Coll., Nottingham, 1995–2000; URC E Midlands Province Listed Bldgs Adv. Cttee, 1995–2000; Notts Valuation Tribunal, 1998–2005 (Chm., 2001–05). Trustee, Hillsborough Disaster Appeal Fund, 1989–96; Chm., E Midlands Chair in Stroke Medicine Appeal, 1991–92. British Red Cross Society: Pres., 1995–2002, Notts Br. (Trustee, 1992–97; Dep. Pres., 1994); Nat. Trustee, 1998–2000; Mem., Midlands Reg. Council, 1998–2002; Trustee, Nottingham Almshouse and Nottingham Annuity Charities, 1994–. Governor, Nottingham High Sch., 1990–2003. An Elections Supervisor, Rhodesia/Zimbabwe Independence Elections, 1980. Mem., Magdala Debating Soc., 1990–94. Mem., RAI, 1993. DL Notts, 1990. Rhodesia Medal, 1980; Zimbabwe Independence Medal, 1980. *Recreations:* bowls, gardening, travel. *Address:* 15 Crow Park Drive, Burton Joyce, Nottingham NG14 5AS. *T:* (0115) 931 4180. *Clubs:* Nottingham and Notts United Services (Nottingham); Queen Anne's Bowling Green (Pres., 1999–2000); Nottingham Rugby (Mem. Cttee, 1994–97); Notts CC.

HAMMOND, Prof. Norman David Curle, FSA, FBA; Archaeology Correspondent, The Times, since 1967; Professor of Archaeology, Boston University, and Associate in Maya Archaeology, Peabody Museum, Harvard University, since 1988; *b* 10 July 1944; *er s* of late William Hammond and Kathleen Jessie Hammond (*née* Howes); *m* 1972, Jean, *er d* of late A. H. Wilson and Beryl Wilson; one *s* one *d. Educ:* Varndean GS; Peterhouse, Cambridge (Trevelyan Schol.; BA 1966; Dip. Classical Archaeol. 1967; MA 1970; PhD 1972; ScD 1987). FSA 1974 (Mem. Council, 1996–99). Centre of Latin American Studies, Cambridge: Res. Fellow, 1967–71; Leverhulme Res. Fellow, 1972–75; Res. Fellow, Fitzwilliam Coll., Cambridge, 1973–75; Sen. Lectr, Univ. of Bradford, 1975–77; Rutgers University: Vis. Prof., 1977–78; Associate Prof., 1978–84; Prof. of Archaeol., 1984–88; Chm., Dept of Archaeol., Boston Univ., 2005–07. Irvine Chair of Anthropol., Calif. Acad. of Scis, 1984–85; Fellow in Pre-Columbian Studies, Dumbarton Oaks, Washington, 1988; Rockefeller Foundn Scholar, Bellagio, 1997. Visiting Professor: Univ. of California, Berkeley, 1977; Jilin Univ., Changchun, 1981; Univ. of Paris, Sorbonne, 1987; Univ. of Bonn, 1994; Visiting Fellow: Worcester Coll., Oxford, 1989; Peterhouse, Cambridge, 1991, 1996–97; McDonald Inst., Cambridge Univ., 1997, 2004; All Souls Coll., Oxford, 2004; Clare Hall, Cambridge, 2004. Lectures: Curl, RAI, 1985; Bushnell, Cambridge Univ., 1997; Willey, Harvard Univ., 2000; Brunswick Distinguished, MMA, 2001; Taft, Univ. of Cincinnati, 2006; Holleyman, Sussex Univ., 2006. Acad. Trustee, Archaeol. Inst. of America, 1990–93 (Stone Lect., 1998; Brush Lect., 2001; Anawalt Lect., 2006). Hon. Mem., Phi Beta Kappa, 1989. Corresp. FBA 1998 (Reckitt Lect., 2006). Mem. editl bds, archaeol. jls, USA, UK, 1984–; editor, Afghan Studies, 1976–79; Consulting Editor, Liby of Congress, 1977–89; archaeol. consultant, Scientific American, 1979–95. Excavations and surveys: Libya and Tunisia, 1964; Afghanistan, 1966; Belize, 1970–2002 (Lubaantun, Nohmul, Cuello, La Milpa); Ecuador, 1972–84. Hon. DSc Bradford, 1999. Press Award, British Archaeol Awards, 1994, (jtly) 1998; Soc. of Antiquaries Medal, 2001, Silver Medal, 2007. *Publications:* (ed) South Asian Archaeology, 1973; (ed) Mesoamerican Archaeology, 1974; Lubaantun: a Classic Maya realm, 1975; (ed) Social Process in Maya Prehistory, 1977; (ed with F. R. Allchin) The Archaeology of Afghanistan, 1978; (ed with G. R. Willey) Maya Archaeology and Ethnohistory, 1979; Ancient Maya Civilisation, 1982, 5th edn 1994, numerous foreign edns; (gen. editor) Archaeology Procs, 44th Congress of Americanists, 1982–84; (ed) Nohmul: excavations 1973–83, 1985; (ed) Cuello: an early Maya community in Belize, 1991; The Maya, 2000; contribs to learned and unlearned jls. *Recreations:* heraldry, genealogy, serendipity. *Address:* Wholeway, Harlton, Cambridge CB23 1ET. *T:* (01223) 262376; Department of Archaeology, Boston University, 675 Commonwealth Avenue, Boston, MA 02215–1406, USA. *T:* (617) 3581651. *Clubs:* Athenæum; Tavern (Boston).

HAMMOND, Prof. Paul Francis, FBA 2002; Professor of Seventeenth-Century English Literature, University of Leeds, since 1996; *b* 8 Oct. 1953; *s* of Ronald Francis Hammond and Maureen Margaret Hammond (*née* Butler). *Educ:* Peter Symonds' Sch., Winchester; Trinity Coll., Cambridge (BA, MA; PhD 1979; LittD 1996). Fellow, Trinity Coll., Cambridge, 1978–82; University of Leeds: Lectr in English, 1978–89; Sen. Lectr, 1989–95; Reader in Seventeenth-Century Literature, 1995–96. Vis. Fellow Commoner, Trinity Coll., Cambridge, 2007; Leverhulme Trust Res. Fellow, 2007–08. An Associate Ed., New, later Oxford, DNB, 1998–2002. *Publications:* John Oldham and the Renewal of Classical Culture, 1983; (ed) Selected Prose of Alexander Pope, 1987; John Dryden: a literary life, 1991; (ed jtly) The Poems of John Dryden, 5 vols, 1995–2005; Love Between Men in English Literature, 1996; Dryden and the Traces of Classical Rome, 1999; (ed jtly) John Dryden: Tercentenary Essays, 2000; (ed) Restoration Literature: an anthology, 2002; Figuring Sex between Men from Shakespeare to Rochester, 2002; (ed jtly) Shakespeare and Renaissance Europe, 2004; The Making of Restoration Poetry, 2006; articles on seventeenth century English literature in scholarly jls. *Recreations:* Paris and Berlin. *Address:* School of English, University of Leeds, Leeds LS2 9JT. *T:* (0113) 343 4739.

HAMMOND, Philip; MP (C) Runnymede and Weybridge, since 1997; *b* 4 Dec. 1955; *s* of Bernard Lawrence Hammond and Doris Rose Hammond; *m* 1991, Susan Carolyn, *d* of E. Williams-Walker; one *s* two *d. Educ:* Shenfield Sch., Brentwood; University Coll., Oxford (Open Scholar, 1st cl. PPE, MA). Various posts, Speywood Labs Ltd, 1977–81; Dir, Speywood Medical Ltd, 1981–83; established and ran medical equipment distribution co., and dir, medical equipment manufg cos, 1983–94; Partner, CMA Consultants, 1993–95; Director: Castlemead Ltd, 1984–; Castlemead Homes Ltd, 1994–; Consort Resources Ltd, 2000–03. Consultant, Govt of Malawi, 1995–97. Contested (C) Newham NE, June 1994. Opposition spokesman on health and social services, 1998–2001, on trade and industry, 2001–02; on local and devolved govt, 2002–05; Shadow Chief Sec. to HM Treasury, 2005 and 2007–; Shadow Sec. of State for Work and Pensions, 2005–07. Mem., Select Cttee on Envmt, Transport and the Regions, 1997–98, on Trade and Industry, 2002. Sec., Cons. Parly Health Cttee, 1997–98. *Recreations:* reading, cinema, walking. *Address:* House of Commons, SW1A 0AA. *T:* (020) 7219 4055. *Club:* Carlton.

HAMMOND, Richard Mark; television presenter and journalist, since 1990; *b* 19 Dec. 1969; *s* of Alan and Eileen Hammond; *m* 2002, Amanda Etheridge; two *d. Educ:* Solihull Boys' Sch.; Ripon Grammar Sch.; Harrogate Coll. of Art and Technol. Presenter and producer: BBC Radio York, 1989–92; BBC Radio Stations: Leeds, Newcastle, Cleveland, Cumbria and Lancs; presenter: Men and Motors; Livetime; Top Gear, 2002–; Brainiac: Science Abuse, 2003–06; Should I Worry About?, 2003–05; columnist, Daily Mirror, 2005–. *Publications:* What Not to Drive, 2005; Richard Hammond's Car Confidential, 2006; Can You Feel the Force?, 2006; On the Edge: my story, 2007; As You Do...: adventures with Evel, Oliver and the Vice-president of Botswana, 2008. *Recreations:* motorcycling, writing, painting, photography, horse-riding, cycling, running.

HAMMOND, Roy John William; Director, City of Birmingham Polytechnic, 1979–85; *b* 3 Oct. 1928; *s* of John James Hammond and Edith May Hammond; *m* 1st, 1949, Audrey Cecilia Dagmar Avello (*d* 1988); three *d*; 2nd, 1990, Dorothy Forder. *Educ:* East Ham Grammar Sch.; University College of the South West, Exeter; Sorbonne, Paris. BA Hons, 1st Cl. French and Latin, London. Royal Air Force Education Branch, 1952–56; Asst Lectr, Blackburn Municipal Technical Coll. and School of Art, 1956–59; Hd of Dept, Herefordshire Technical Coll., 1960–66; Hd, Dept of Professional and Gen. Studies, Leeds Poly., 1966–71; Asst Dir, City of Birmingham Poly., 1971–79. Hon. Fellow, Birmingham City Univ. (formerly City of Birmingham Poly., later Univ. of Central England), 1985. FRSA. *Recreations:* cricket, theatre, music, walking, golf. *Club:* Aston Wood Golf (Pres., 2001–05).

HAMMOND, Simon Tristram; His Honour Judge Simon Hammond; a Circuit Judge, since 1993; *b* 5 Jan. 1944; *s* of Philip J. Hammond and Sylvia D. (*née* Sillem); *m* 1976, Louise (*née* Weir); one *s* two *d. Educ:* Eastbourne Coll.; Coll. of Law. Articled to Philip J. Hammond, Leicester; admitted Solicitor, 1967; Solicitor, later Partner, Victor J. Lissack, London, 1968–76; Partner, Philip J. Hammond & Sons, Leicester, 1977–93. An Asst Recorder, 1985–90; a Recorder, 1990–93. Asst Comr to Parly Boundary Commn for England, 1992. Member: Law Soc's Standing Cttee on Criminal Law, 1982–91; Crown Court Rules Cttee, 1988–93; Enforcement Sub-cttee, Home Office Rev. of Magistrates Court Procedure, 1989–90. Churchwarden, 1990–. *Recreations:* horses, ski-ing, vegetable gardening. *Address:* c/o Circuit Administrator's Office, Midland Circuit, The Priory Courts, 33 Bull Street, Birmingham B4 6DW.

HAMMOND, Stephen William; MP (C) Wimbledon, since 2005; *b* 4 Feb. 1962; *s* of Bryan Norman Walter and Janice Eve Hammond; *m* 1991, Sally Patricia Brodie; one *d. Educ:* King Edward VI Sch., Southampton; Queen Mary Coll., London (BSc Econ Hons). Reed Stenhouse Investment Services, 1983–85; Canada Life, 1985–87; UBS Phillips & Drew, 1987–91; Dir, Kleinwort Benson Securities, 1991–98; Commerzbank, 1998–2003, Dir of Res., 1999–2001. Mem., Merton BC, 2002–06. Contested (C): Warwickshire North, 1997; Wimbledon, 2001. Shadow Minister for Transport, 2005–. *Address:* House of Commons, SW1A 0AA. *T:* (020) 7219 1029; *e-mail:* hammonds@parliament.uk, stephen.hammond@wimbledonconservatives.org.uk. *Clubs:* Royal Wimbledon Golf, Royal Wimbledon Hockey, Wimbledon Civic Forum (Pres.), Wimbledon Society.

HAMMOND-CHAMBERS, (Robert) Alexander; Chairman, Ivory & Sime, 1985–91; Chairman, Dobbies Garden Centres plc, 1994–2007; *b* 20 Oct. 1942; *s* of late Robert Rupert Hammond-Chambers and of Leonie Elise Noble (*née* Andrews); *m* 1968, Sarah Louisa Madeline (*née* Fanshawe); two *s* one *d. Educ:* Wellington College; Magdalene College, Cambridge (Hons Economics). Ivory & Sime: joined 1964; Partner, 1969; Director, 1975, upon incorporation; Dep. Chm., 1982. Chairman: Fidelity Special Values plc, 1994–; Aurora Investment Trust plc, 2002–; Hunter Property Fund Management, 2003–; Hansa Trust, 2004– (Dir, 2002–); Director: Internat. Biotechnology Trust plc, 2001–; Montanaro European Smaller Companies plc, 2004–, and other cos. Chm., Assoc. of Investment Trust Cos, 2003–05 (Dep. Chm., 2002–03); Overseas Governor, Nat. Assoc. of Securities Dealers Inc., 1984–87. Chm., Edinburgh Green Belt Trust, 1991–2001. *Recreations:* tennis, photography, golf, writing. *Address:* The Old White House, 3 Liberton Tower Lane, Edinburgh EH16 6TQ. *T:* (0131) 672 1697. *Clubs:* Pilgrims; New, Hon. Co. of Edinburgh Golfers (Edinburgh).

HAMMOND-STROUD, Derek, OBE 1987; concert and opera baritone; Professor of Singing, Royal Academy of Music, 1974–90; *b* 10 Jan. 1926; *s* of Herbert William Stroud and Ethel Louise Elliott. *Educ:* Salvatorian Coll., Harrow, Middx; Trinity Coll. of Music, London; in Vienna and Munich with Elena Gerhardt and Gerhard Hüsch. Glyndebourne Festival Opera, 1959; Sadler's Wells Opera (later ENO), 1961; Royal Opera, Covent Garden, 1971; Houston Grand Opera, USA, 1975; Netherlands Opera, 1976; Metropolitan Opera, NY, 1977; Teatro Colón, Buenos Aires, 1981; Munich State Opera, 1983. Concerts and Lieder recitals at Edinburgh, Aldeburgh, Munich and Vienna Festivals, and in Spain, Iceland and Denmark. BBC Promenade Concerts, 1968–. Pres., Univ. of London Opera Gp, 1971. Freeman, City of London, 1952; Hon. RAM 1976; Hon. FTCL, 1982. Sir Charles Santley Meml Gift, Worshipful Co. of Musicians, 1988. Recordings include: The Ring (Goodall); Der Rosenkavalier (de Waart). *Recreations:* chess, study of philosophy. *Address:* 18 Sutton Road, Muswell Hill, N10 1HE. *T:* (020) 8883 2120.

HAMNETT, Prof. Andrew, DL; DPhil; CChem, FRSC; FRSE; Principal and Vice-Chancellor, University of Strathclyde, 2001–09; *b* 12 Nov. 1947; *s* of Albert Edward Hamnett and Dorothy Grace Hamnett (*née* Stewart); *m* 1976, Suzanne Marie Parkin; three *d. Educ:* William Hulme's Grammar Sch., Manchester; University Coll., Oxford (Open Schol.; BA Hons Chem. 1970); St John's Coll., Oxford (Sen. Schol.; DPhil 1973). CChem, FRSC 1991; FRSE 2002. Jun. Res. Fellow in Chemistry, Queen's Coll., Oxford, 1972–77; Deptl Res. Asst, then Lectr in Inorganic Chemistry, Oxford Univ., 1977–89; Fellow by Special Election, then Tutorial Fellow, St Catherine's Coll., Oxford, 1980–89; University of Newcastle upon Tyne: Prof. of Physical Chemistry, 1989–2000; Pro-Vice-Chancellor, 1993–2000. Killam Fellow, Univ. of BC, 1974–76. DL Glasgow City, 2004. Hon. DSc Technical Univ. Lodz, Poland, 2005. *Publications:* (with P. A. Christensen) Techniques and Mechanism in Electrochemistry, 1994; (ed with R. G. Compton) Novel Methods of Studying the Electrode-Electrolyte Interface, 1989; (jtly) Electrochemistry, 1998; numerous papers and review articles on physical and inorganic chemistry. *Recreations:* music, languages, philately. *Address:* University of Strathclyde, 16 Richmond Street, Glasgow G1 1XQ. *T:* (0141) 548 2000. *Clubs:* Athenæum, Caledonian.

HAMNETT, Katharine; fashion designer; *b* 16 Aug. 1947; *d* of Gp Capt. James Appleton. *Educ:* Cheltenham Ladies' Coll.; St Martin's Sch. of Art. Set up Tuttabankem (with Anne Buck), 1969–75; freelance designer in London, Paris, Milan, New York and Hong Kong, 1975–79; established Katharine Hamnett Ltd, 1979, and subseq. launched men's and women's collections, Asia, Europe, USA; transf. production to Italy, 1989, moving from manufacturing to licensing base. Vis. Prof., London Inst., 1997–. Numerous awards include British Fashion Designer of the Year, 1984. *Publications:* contribs to fashion magazines and newspapers. *Recreations:* gardening, agriculture, photography, archaeology, travel. *Address: e-mail:* info@katharinehamnett.com.

HAMNETT, Thomas Orlando; Chairman, Greater Manchester Council, 1975–76, Vice-Chairman, 1976; *b* 28 Sept. 1930; *s* of John and Elizabeth Hamnett; *m* 1954, Kathleen Ridgway; one *s* five *d. Educ:* Stockport Jun. Techn. Sch. Sheetmetal craftsman, 1946. Member, Manchester City Council, 1963 until re-organisation (Vice-Chm., Health Cttee, Chm. sub cttee on Staff on Cleansing Cttee, Mem. Policy and Finance Cttees), and 1978–92 (Member: Direct works, Markets, and Personnel Cttees; Transportation, Education, and Recreation and Arts Cttees, Greater Manchester Council; Chm., Environmental Services Cttee, City Council, Manchester, 1982). *Recreations:* football, cricket, table tennis. *Address:* 22 Harris Avenue, Denton, Manchester M34 2PX. *T:* (0161) 320 1069. *Club:* Gorton Trades and Labour (Chm.).

HAMON, Francis Charles, OBE 2000; Deputy Bailiff, Jersey, 1995–2000; Chairman, Channel Television, 2000–05; *b* 30 July 1939; *s* of Clifford Charles Hamon and Lily Kathleen (*née* Le Gentil); *m* 1963, Sonia Muriel Parslow; one *s* one *d. Educ:* Victoria Coll., Jersey. First staff announcer, Channel TV, 1962–64; Asst Land Officer, States of Jersey, 1964–66; called to the Bar: Middle Temple, 1966; Jersey, 1968; in private practice in

Jersey, 1968–87; Sen. Partner, Crill, Cubitt-Sowden & Tomes, 1985–87; Comr (Judge), Royal Court, Jersey, 1988–95, 2001–. Director: Royal Bank of Scotland (Jersey) Ltd, 1982–95 (Dep. Chm., 1986–95); Media Hldgs Ltd, 2000–01; Channel Television (Hldgs) Ltd, 2001–06. Comr, Jersey Financial Services Commn, 2000–03. Chm., Jersey Arts Trust, 1992–95. Founder Member: Good Theatre Co.; Jersey Fencing Club; Jersey Rugby Fives Assoc. Gov., Victoria Coll., 1987–97. *Publication:* The Phoenix Too Frequent: the story of Jersey's Opera House, 2004. *Recreations:* theatre, bird-watching, travel, Rugby fives, reading. *Address:* La Maison du Sud, Rue de la Pièce Mauger, Trinity, Jersey JE3 5HW. *T:* (01534) 863199.

HAMPDEN; *see* Hobart-Hampden.

HAMPDEN, 7th Viscount *cr* 1884, of Glynde, co. Sussex; **Francis Anthony Brand;** *b* London, 17 Sept. 1970; *s* of 6th Viscount Hampden and of Cara Brand (*née* Proby); *S* father, 2008; *m* 2004, Dr Caroline Pryor, *d* of His Honour Robert Charles Pryor, *qv*; one *s* one *d*. *Educ:* Windlesham House Sch.; Millfield Sch.; Edinburgh Univ.; Cranfield Sch. of Mgt. *Heir: s* Hon. Lucian Anthony Brand, *b* 3 Nov. 2005. *Address:* Glynde Place, Glynde, East Sussex BN8 6SX. *T:* (01273) 858224.

HAMPEL, Sir Ronald (Claus), Kt 1995; Chairman: ICI plc, 1995–99; United Business Media (formerly United News & Media), 1999–2002; *b* 31 May 1932; *s* of Karl Victor Hugo Hampel and Rutgard Emil Klothilde Hauck; *m* 1957, Jane Bristed Hewson; three *s* one *d*. *Educ:* Canford Sch., Wimborne; Corpus Christi Coll., Cambridge (MA Mod. Lang. and Law; Hon. Fellow, 1996). Nat. service, 2nd Lt, 3rd RHA, 1951–52. Joined ICI, 1955; Vice-Pres., ICI US, 1973–77; Gen. Manager, Commercial, 1977–80; Chairman: ICI Paints, 1980–83; ICI Agrochemicals, 1983–85; Dir, ICI, 1985–99; Chief Operating Officer, 1991–93, Dep. Chm. and Chief Exec., 1993–95, ICI plc. Non-executive Director: Powell Duffryn, 1984–88; Commercial Union, 1988–95; BAE Systems (formerly British Aerospace), 1989–2002; ALCOA, USA, 1995–2005; Templeton Emerging Markets Investment Trust, 2003– (Chm., 2004–07); Adv. Dir, Teijin, Japan, 2000–04. Dir, Amer. Chamber of Commerce, 1986–91; Chm., Cttee on Corporate Governance, 1995–98; Member: Listed Cos Adv. Cttee, Stock Exchange, 1996–99; Nomination Cttee, NY Stock Exchange, 1996–98; Adv. Cttee, Karlpreis Aachen, 1997–2001. Mem. Exec. Cttee, British North America Cttee, 1989–95. Mem., European Round Table, 1995–99. Chm. Trustees, Eden Project, 2000–07. CCMI (CBIM 1985). *Recreations:* tennis, golf, ski-ing, music. *Clubs:* MCC, All England Lawn Tennis; Royal & Ancient.

HAMPSHER-MONK, Dame Susan Catherine; *see* Leather, Dame S. C.

HAMPSHIRE, Prof. Michael John, CBE 1987; Research Professor of Electronic Information Technology, University of Salford, 1990–2004; *b* 13 Oct. 1939; *s* of Jack and Hilda May Hampshire; *m* 1962, Mavis (*née* Oakes); one *d*. *Educ:* Heckmondwike Grammar Sch.; Univ. of Birmingham (BSc Physics, PhD Elec. Engrg). University of Salford: Lectr, 1964; Sen. Lectr, 1972; Prof. of Solid State Electronics, 1978–85, of Electronic IT, 1985–90; Chm., Dept of Electronic and Electrical Engrg, 1981–89; Asst Man. Dir, 1989–95, Dir, 1989–98, Salford Univ. Business Services Ltd. Consultant: Ferranti, 1970–74; Volex Gp, 1977–99 (Chm., R&D Cttee, 1987–92); Thorn EMI Flow Measurement, 1980–88. Founder and Chm., Vertec (Electronics), 1982–92 (Dir, 1992–98). Commendation EPIC Award, 1982; Academic Enterprise Award, 1982; Techmart Technology Transfer Trophy, 1984. Hon. FIED 2001 (Hon. MIED 1982). *Publications:* Electron Physics and Devices, 1969; 80 pubns and patents on solid state electronics and electronic systems, vehicle multiplexing, innovation. *Recreations:* music, golf. *Address:* 3 Brookfield, Upper Hopton, Mirfield, West Yorks WF14 8HL.

HAMPSHIRE, Nancy Lynn Delaney, (Lady Hampshire); *see* Cartwright, N. L. D.

HAMPSHIRE, Susan, OBE 1995; actress; *b* 12 May; *d* of George Kenneth Hampshire and June Hampshire; *m* 1st, 1967, Pierre Granier-Deferre (marr. diss. 1974); one *s* (one *d* decd); 2nd, 1981, Sir Eddie Kulukundis, *qv*. *Educ:* Hampshire Sch., Knightsbridge. *Stage:* Expresso Bongo, Saville, tour, 1959; 'that girl' in Follow That Girl, Vaudeville, 1960; Fairy Tales of New York, Comedy, 1961; Marion Dangerfield in Ginger Man, Royal Court, 1963; Past Imperfect, St Martin's and Savoy, 1964; Kate Hardcastle in She Stoops to Conquer, tour, 1966; On Approval, tour, 1966; Mary in The Sleeping Prince, St Martin's, tour, 1968; Nora in A Doll's House, Greenwich, 1972; Katharina in The Taming of the Shrew, Shaw, 1974; Peter in Peter Pan, Coliseum, 1974; Jeannette in Romeo and Jeannette, tour, 1975; Rosalind in As You Like It, Shaw, 1975; title rôle in Miss Julie, Greenwich, 1975; Elizabeth in The Circle, Haymarket, 1976; Ann Whitefield in Man and Superman, Savoy, 1978; Siri Von Essen in Tribades, Hampstead, 1978; Victorine in An Audience Called Edouard, Greenwich, 1978; Irene in The Crucifer of Blood, Haymarket, 1979; Ruth Carson in Night and Day, Phoenix, 1979; Elizabeth in The Revolt, New End, 1980; Stella Drury in House Guest, Savoy, 1981; Elvira in Blithe Spirit, Vaudeville, 1986; Marie Stopes in Married Love, Wyndhams, 1988; Countess in A Little Night Music, Piccadilly, 1989; Mrs Anna in The King and I, Sadler's Wells, 1990; Gertrude Lawrence in Noel and Gertie, Duke of York's, 1991; Felicity, Countess of Marshwood in Relative Values, Savoy, 1993; Suzanna in Suzanna Andler, Battersea, 1995; Alicia in Black Chiffon (tour), 1996; Sheila in Relatively Speaking (tour), 2000; Felicity, Countess of Marshwood in Relative Values (tour), 2002; Miss Shepherd in The Lady in the Van (tour), 2004–05; Fairy Godmother in Cinderella, Wimbledon, 2005, Woking, 2006; The Bargain (tour), 2007; Kitty in The Circle, Chichester, 2008; *TV Serials:* Katy in What Katy Did; Andromeda (title rôle), Fleur Forsyte in The Forsyte Saga (Emmy Award for Best Actress, 1970), Becky Sharp in Vanity Fair (Emmy Award for Best Actress, 1973), Sarah Churchill, Duchess of Marlborough, in The First Churchills (Emmy Award for Best Actress, 1971), Glencora Palliser in The Pallisers; Lady Melfont in Dick Turpin; Signora Neroni in The Barchester Chronicles; Martha in Leaving, 2 series; Going to Pot, 3 series; Don't tell Father; Esme Harkness in The Grand, 2 series; Coming Home; Monarch of the Glen, 7 series; Sparkling Cyanide. *Films include:* During One Night, The Three Lives of Thomasina, Night Must Fall, Wonderful Life, Paris in August, The Fighting Prince of Donegal, Monte Carlo or Bust, Rogan, David Copperfield, Living Free, A Time for Loving, Malpertius (E. Poe Prizes du Film Fantastique, Best Actress, 1972), Neither the Sea Nor the Sand, Roses and Green Peppers, Bang. Dir, Conservation Foundn, 1995–; Mem. Exec. Cttee, Population Concern; Pres., Dyslexia Inst.; Vice-Pres., Internat. Tree Foundn. Hon. DLitt: London, 1981; City, 1984; St Andrews, 1986; Exeter, 2001; Hon. DEd Kingston, 1994; Hon. DArts Pine Manor Coll., Boston, USA, 1994. *Publications:* Susan's Story, 1981; The Maternal Instinct, 1984; Lucy Jane at the Ballet, 1989; Lucy Jane on Television, 1989; Trouble Free Gardening, 1989; Every Letter Counts, 1990; Lucy Jane and the Dancing Competition, 1991; Easy Gardening, 1991; Lucy Jane and the Russian Ballet, 1993; Rosie's First Ballet Lesson, 1996. *Recreations:* gardening, music, the study of antique furniture. *Address:* c/o Dallas Smith, United Agents, 12–26 Lexington Street, W1F 0LE. *T:* (020) 7166 5248.

HAMPSON, Christopher, CBE 1994; Chairman: RMC Group, 1996–2002; British Biotech plc, 1998–2002; *b* 6 Sept. 1931; *s* of Harold Ralph Hampson and Geraldine Mary Hampson; *m* 1954, Joan Margaret Cassils Evans; two *s* three *d*. *Educ:* McGill Univ. (BE Chem 1952). Vice-Pres., 1956–78 and Sen. Vice-Pres., 1982–84, Canadian Industri Canada; Imperial Chemical Industries: Gen. Manager, Planning, 1978–82; Man. Dir a Chief Exec. Officer, ICI Australia, 1984–87; Exec. Dir, ICI, 1987–94; Chm., Yorksh Electricity Gp, 1994–97. Non-executive Director: SNC-Lavalin Group, 1992–20(TransAlta Corp., 1993–2003; BG plc, 1997–2000; Lattice Gp plc, 2000–02. Mem. E 1996–99, Dep. Chm., 1999–2000, Environment Agency. *Recreations:* tennis, ski-ir *Address:* 77 Kensington Court, W8 5DT. *Clubs:* Boodle's, Hurlingham; York (Toronto

HAMPSON, Christopher; choreographer; *b* 31 March 1973; *s* of Geoffrey and Jani Hampson. *Educ:* Royal Ballet Schs, White Lodge and Upper Sch. Soloist with Engli Nat. Ballet, 1992–99; rôles include: principal role in Square Dance; Drosselmeyer Nutcracker; Headmistress in Graduation Ball; Dancing Master in Cinderella; also creat soloist role in Symphonic Dances, and Caterpillar in Alice in Wonderland; Ballet Mast London City Ballet and Royal NZ Ballet, 1999–2000; guest teacher/coach: English N Ballet; Royal Swedish Ballet; Royal NZ Ballet; Atlanta Ballet; National Th., Pragu Royal Acad. of Dance; English Nat. Ballet Sch. Created ballets: for English Natio Ballet: Perpetuum Mobile, 1997; Country Garden, 1998; Concerto Grosso, 1999; Doul Concerto, 2000; Nutcracker, 2002; Trapeze, 2003; for London City Ballet: Dinaresa Canciones, 1999; for Royal New Zealand Ballet: Saltarello, 2001; Romeo and Juli 2002; Esquisses, 2005; for National Theatre, Prague: Giselle, 2004; for Atlanta Ball USA: Sinfonietta Giocosa, 2005; for Royal Festival Hall: A Christmas Carol, 2000; Royal Academy of Dance: La Vision, Caprice, 2003. Award for Best Classical Choreo Critics' Circle, 2002; Award for Outstanding Achievement in Dance, Barclays Th., 20(*Recreations:* music, theatre, wine. *Address:* *e-mail:* chris@christopherhampson.com.

HAMPSON, Dr Keith; *b* 14 Aug. 1943; *s* of Bertie Hampson and Mary Elizabeth Nob *m* 1st, 1975, Frances Pauline (*d* 1975), *d* of late Mathieu Donald Einhorn and of Elle Ruth Einhorn; 2nd, 1979, Susan, *d* of Mr and Mrs John Wilkie Cameron. *Educ:* Ki James I Grammar Sch., Bishop Auckland, Co. Durham; Univ. of Bristol; Harvard Un BA, CertEd, PhD. Personal Asst to Edward Heath, 1966 and 1970 Gen. Elections and his House of Commons office, 1968; Lectr in American History, Edinburgh Uni 1968–74. Mem., Gen. Adv. Council, IBA, 1980–88. MP (C) Ripon, Feb. 1974–198 Leeds North West, 1983–97; contested (C) Leeds North West, 1997. PPS: to Minister f Local Govt, 1979–83; to Sec. of State for Environment, 1983; to Sec. of State for Defenc 1983–84. Member: Select Cttee on Trade and Industry, 1987–97; Public Accou Commn, 1992–97; Vice Chairman: Cons. Parly Educn Cttee, 1975–79; Cons. Pa Defence Cttee, 1988–89 (Sec., 1984–88). Mem., Educn Adv. Cttee of UK Commn f UNESCO, 1980–84. Vice President: WEA, 1978–97; Assoc. of Business Executiv 1979–; Vice-Chm., Youthaid, 1979–83. UK Project Manager, DFID and FCO funds f democracy progs in Russia, 1998–; Sec., Internat. Adv. Bd, Moscow Sch. of Pol Studi 2003–. *Recreations:* DIY, music. *Club:* Carlton.

HAMPSON, Prof. Norman, FBA 1980; Professor of History, University of Yo 1974–89; *b* 8 April 1922; *s* of Frank Hampson and Elizabeth Jane Fazackerley; *m* 194 Jacqueline Gardin; two *d*. *Educ:* Manchester Grammar Sch.; University Coll., Oxfo (MA); Dr de l'Univ. Paris. Service in Royal Navy, 1941–45. Manchester Univ., 1948–6 Lectr and Sen. Lectr; Prof. of Modern History, Univ. of Newcastle, 1967–74. Hon. DL Edinburgh, 1989. *Publications:* La Marine de l'an II, 1959; A Social History of the Fren Revolution, 1963; The Enlightenment, 1968; The First European Revolution, 1969; T Life and Opinions of Maximilien Robespierre, 1974; A Concise History of the Fren Revolution, 1975; Danton, 1978; Will and Circumstance: Montesquieu, Rousseau a the French Revolution, 1983; Prelude to Terror, 1988; Saint-Just, 1991; The Perfidy Albion, 1998; Not Really What You'd Call a War, 2001. *Address:* 305 Hull Road, Yo YO10 3LU. *T:* (01904) 412661.

HAMPSON, Peter, CBE 2003; QPM 1998; Director General, National Crimin Intelligence Service, 2003–06; *b* 8 Jan. 1947; *s* of Maj. Ronald Hampson, MBE and Edi Hampson; *m* 1971, Pamela Mary Cotes; one *s* two *d*. *Educ:* Sandford Orleigh Sc Newton Abbot; King's Coll. London (LLB 1982; AKC). Joined Metropolitan Poli Service, 1967: Constable, 1967–71; Chief Superintendent, 1991–94; Asst Ch Constable, Surrey Police, 1994–96; Asst Inspector of Constabulary, Home Offic 1996–99; Chief Constable, W Mercia Constabulary, 1999–2003. Trustee: Surr Community Foundn; Police Rehabilitation Trust. Gov., Treloar Coll., Alton. FRS 1992. OStJ 1998. *Recreations:* family and friends, reading, theatre, cycling, music, St Jo Ambulance, National Trust, Surrey Community Foundn, Police Rehabilitation Trust.

HAMPSON, Stephen Fazackerley; Under Secretary, Scottish Executive (forme Scottish Office), 1993–2002; *b* 27 Oct. 1945; *s* of Frank Hampson and Helen (*née* Elli *m* 1970, Gunilla Brunk; one *s* one *d*. *Educ:* University Coll., Oxford (BPhil; MA). Lec Aberdeen Univ., 1969–71; Economist, NEDO, 1971–75; various posts, Scottish Offic 1975–78, and at Scottish Office, then Scottish Executive, 1981–2002 (Head: Envmt G 1993–2000; Enterprise and Industrial Affairs Gp, 2000–02); First Sec., FCO, New Dell 1978–81. Mem. Bd, British Trade Internat., 2000–02. Mem., Council, WWF Scotlan 2002–. Hon. FCIWEM 1998. *Address:* Glenelg, Park Road, Kilmacolm PA13 4EE. (01505) 872615.

HAMPSON, Sir Stuart, Kt 1998; Chairman, John Lewis Partnership, 1993–2007; *b* 7 Ja 1947; *s* of Kenneth and Mary Hampson; *m* 1973, Angela McLaren; one *s* one *d*. *Edi* Royal Masonic Sch., Bushey; St John's Coll., Oxford (BA Mod. Langs, MA; Hon. Fello 2001). Board of Trade, 1969–72; FCO UKMIS to UN, Geneva, 1972–74; Dept of Pric and Consumer Protection, 1974–79; Dept of Trade, 1979–82; John Lewis Partnershi 1982–2007: Dir of Research and Expansion, 1986; Dep. Chm., 1989. Dep. Chn London First, 1992–97; Chm., Centre for Tomorrow's Company, 1998–99. Chm., RS 1999–2001 (Treas., 1997–98; Dep. Chm., 1998–99, 2001–02). President: Royal Agri Soc. of England, 2005–06; Job Ownership Ltd, 2005–. Hon. FCGI 2002. Hon. DB Kingston, 1998; Southampton Inst., 2001; Middlesex 2007.

HAMPSON, (Walter) Thomas; singer; *b* Elkhart, Indiana, 28 June 1955; *s* of Walt Hampson and Ruthye Hampson; one *d*. *Educ:* Eastern Washington Univ. (BA Govt); Fo Wright Coll.; Music Acad. of West. Début in Hansel and Gretel, 1974; with Düsseldo Ensemble, 1981–84; title rôle in Der Prinz von Homburg, Darmstadt, 1982; débu Cologne, Munich, Santa Fé, 1982–84; Metropolitan Opera, NY, Vienna Staatsope Covent Garden, 1986; La Scala Milan, Deutsche Oper, Berlin, 1989; Carnegie Hall, Sa Francisco Opera, 1990; rôles include: Marcello in La Bohème; Guglielmo in Così fa tutte; Figaro in Il Barbiere di Siviglia; Count in Le Nozze di Figaro; Ulisse in Il Ritorn d'Ulisse in Patria; Lescaut in Manon; Count in La Traviata; Vicomte de Valmont Dangerous Liaisons (world première, 1996); Marquis de Posa in Don Carlos; Riccardo I Puritani; Wolfram in Tannhäuser; Oreste in Iphigénie en Tauride; Amfortas in Parsifa Mandryka in Arabella; Renato in Un Ballo in Maschera; Athanael in Thais; title rôles: Do Giovanni; Der Prinz von Homburg; Billy Budd; Hamlet; Eugene Onegin; William Te Werther (seldom-performed baritone version); Doktor Faust; Der Riese vom Steinfe (world première, 2002); Macbeth. Has performed with Wiener Philharmoniker, N

Philharmonic, LPO and Chicago Symphony orchs. Recital repertoire includes Schumann, Mahler and American Art Song. Has made numerous recordings. Hon. RAM 1996; Hon. Mem., Wiener Konzerthaus, 2004. Hon. Dr: San Francisco Conservatory of Music; Whitworth Coll., USA. Awards include: Gold Medal, Internat. Mahler Soc.; Lotte Lehman Medal, Music Acad. of West, 1979; Edison Prize, Netherlands, 1990 and 1992; Grand Prix du Disque, 1990, 1996, Echo Klassik, 1995, Deutsche Schallplattenpreis; Cannes Classical Award, 1994; Citation of Merit, Nat. Arts Club, 1997; Vienna Kammersänger, 1999; Austrian Medal of Honour in Arts and Scis, 2004; Edison Life Achievement Award, 2005. Chevalier de l'Ordre des Arts et des Lettres (France), 2002. *Publications:* (ed jtly) Mahler Songs: critical edition, 1993; (ed jtly) Schumann/Heine 20 Lieder und Gesänge: critical edition. *Address:* Wallfischgasse 11/17, 1010 Vienna, Austria; c/o Universal Music Classical Artists Management and Productions, Bond House, 247–353 Chiswick High Road, W4 4HS.

HAMPSTEAD, Archdeacon of; *see* Lawson, Ven. M. C.

HAMPTON, 7th Baron *cr* 1874; **John Humphrey Arnott Pakington;** Bt 1846; Creative Director, Band & Brown Communications, London, since 2000; *b* 24 Dec. 1964; *s* of 6th Baron Hampton and of Jane Elizabeth Farquharson Pakington (*née* Arnott); *S* father, 2003; *m* 1996, Siena, *yr d* of Remo Caldato; one *s*. *Educ:* Exeter Coll. of Art and Design (BA Hons). *Recreations:* gardening, sport, photography. *Heir: s* Hon. Charles Richard Caldato Pakington, *b* 2 May 2005.

HAMPTON, Alison Wendy; Her Honour Judge Hampton; a Circuit Judge, since 2002; Designated Civil Judge, Leicester and Northampton; *b* 14 March 1955; *d* of Wing Comdr Gordon Hampton, OBE, DFC and Eve Hampton; *m* 1977, Nigel Haynes. *Educ:* Abbeydale Girls' Grammar Sch., Sheffield; Leicester Univ. (LLB Hons). Called to the Bar, Gray's Inn, 1977; Circuit Jun., Midland and Oxford Circuit, 1987–88. Mem., WI, 1995–. *Recreations:* fine arts, fine food, cycling, walking, scuba diving, ski-ing, cats. *Address:* Leicester County Court, Wellington Street, Leicester LE1 6HG.

HAMPTON, Bryan; Head of Exports to the Americas, Department of Trade and Industry, 1992–95; *b* 4 Dec. 1938; *s* of William Douglas Hampton and Elizabeth Cardwell; *m* 1964, Marilyn Joseph; five *d*. *Educ:* Harrow County Grammar Sch. for Boys. Board of Trade: Exec. Officer, 1957; Asst Private Sec. to Parly Sec., 1961; Private Sec. to Minister of State (Lords), 1963; Asst Principal, 1965; Second Sec., UK Delegn to EFTA/GATT, Geneva, 1966; Principal, DTI, 1969; Asst Sec., Dept of Energy, 1974; Counsellor (Energy), Washington, 1981–86; Head, Br. 1, Atomic Energy Div., 1986–89, Dir, Personnel, 1989–92, Dept of Energy. Gov., Chenies Sch., 1996–2000. *Recreations:* music, golf. *Address:* Byfields, 15 Greenbury Close, Chorleywood, Herts WD3 5QT. *T:* (01923) 282311. *Club:* Northwood Golf.

HAMPTON, Christopher James, CBE 1999; FRSL; playwright; *b* 26 Jan. 1946; *s* of Bernard Patrick Hampton and Dorothy Patience Hampton (*née* Herrington); *m* 1971, Laura Margaret de Holesch; two *d*. *Educ:* Lancing Coll.; New Coll., Oxford (MA; Hon. Fellow, 1997). First play: When Did You Last See My Mother?, 1964 (perf. Royal Court Theatre, 1966; transf. Comedy Theatre; prod. at Sheridan Square Playhouse, New York, 1967). Resident Dramatist, Royal Court Theatre, Aug. 1968–70. FRSL 1976 (Mem. Council, 1984–90). Officier, l'Ordre des Arts et des Lettres (France), 1997. *Plays:* Total Eclipse, prod. Royal Court, 1968; The Philanthropist, Royal Court and Mayfair, 1970 (Evening Standard Best Comedy Award, 1970; Plays & Players London Theatre Critics Best Play, 1970), NY, 1971, Chichester, 1985; Savages, Royal Court, 1973, Comedy, 1973, LA, 1974 (Plays & Players London Theatre Critics Best Play, Jt Winner, 1973; Los Angeles Drama Critics Circle Award for Distinguished Playwriting, 1974); Treats, Royal Court, 1976, Mayfair, 1976, Garrick, 2007; Able's Will, BBC TV, 1977; After Mercer, NT, 1980; The History Man (from Malcolm Bradbury) BBC TV, 1981; Total Eclipse (rev. version) Lyric, Hammersmith, 1981; The Portage to San Cristobal of A. H. (from George Steiner), Mermaid, 1982; Tales from Hollywood, LA, 1982, NT 1983 (Standard Best Comedy Award, 1983), Donmar, 2001; Les Liaisons Dangereuses (from Laclos), RSC, 1985, transf. Ambassadors Th., 1986, NY, 1987 (Plays & Players London Theatre Critics Best Play, Jt Winner, 1985; Time Out Best Production Award, 1986; London Standard Best Play Award, 1986; Laurence Olivier Best Play Award, 1986; NY Drama Critics' Circle Best For. Play Award, 1987); Hotel du Lac (from Anita Brookner), BBC TV, 1986 (BAFTA Best TV Film Award, 1987); The Ginger Tree (from Oswald Wynd), BBC TV, 1989; White Chameleon, NT, 1991; Alice's Adventures Under Ground, NT, 1994; The Talking Cure, NT, 2002; *musicals:* Sunset Boulevard (book and lyrics with Don Black), LA, 1993, NY, 1994 (Tony Award: Best Original Score, 1995; Best Book of a Musical, 1995); Dracula (book and lyrics with Don Black), La Jolla, 2001, NY, 2004; *opera:* Waiting for the Barbarians (libretto, based on novel by J. M. Coetzee; music by Philip Glass), Erfurt, 2005, Austin, Texas, 2007; Appomattox (libretto; music by Philip Glass), San Francisco, 2007; *translations:* Marya, by Isaac Babel, Royal Court, 1967; Uncle Vanya, by Chekhov, Royal Court, 1970; Hedda Gabler, by Ibsen, Fest. Theatre, Stratford, Ont, 1970, Almeida, Islington, 1984, rev. version, NT, 1989; A Doll's House, by Ibsen, NY, 1971, Criterion, 1973, NY, 1975, W Yorks Playhouse, 2005; Don Juan, by Molière, Bristol Old Vic, 1972; Tales from the Vienna Woods, by Horváth, NT, 1977; Don Juan Comes Back from the War, by Horváth, NT, 1978; Ghosts, by Ibsen, Actors' Co., 1978; The Wild Duck, by Ibsen, NT, 1979; The Prague Trial, by Chereau and Mnouchkine, Paris Studio, 1980; Tartuffe, by Molière, RSC, 1983; Faith, Hope and Charity, by Horváth, Lyric, Hammersmith, 1989; Art, by Yasmina Reza, Wyndhams, 1996 (Standard Best Comedy Award and Laurence Olivier Best Comedy Award, 1997), NY (Tony Award, Best Play), 1998; An Enemy of the People, by Ibsen, RNT, 1997; The Unexpected Man, by Yasmina Reza, RSC, 1998, NY, 2000; Conversations After a Burial, by Yasmina Reza, Almeida, 2000; Life x 3, by Yasmina Reza, RNT, transf. Old Vic, 2000, NY 2003; Three Sisters, by Chekhov, Playhouse, 2003; The Seagull, by Chekhov, Royal Court, 2007; *screenplays:* A Doll's House, 1973; Tales From the Vienna Woods, 1979; The Honorary Consul, 1983; The Good Father, 1986 (Prix Italia 1988); Wolf at the Door, 1986; Dangerous Liaisons, 1988 (Academy Award, and Writers Guild of America Award, for best adapted screenplay; Critics' Circle Award for best screenplay, 1989; BAFTA best screenplay award, 1990); Total Eclipse, 1995; Mary Reilly, 1996; The Quiet American, 2002; Atonement, 2007; (*also directed*): Carrington, 1995 (Special Jury Prize, Cannes Fest., 1995); The Secret Agent, 1996; Imagining Argentina, 2003. *Publications:* When Did You Last See My Mother?, 1967; Total Eclipse, 1969, rev. version, 1981; The Philanthropist, 1970, 2nd edn 1985, The Philanthropist and other plays, 1991; Savages, 1974; Treats, 1976, rev. version, 2007; Able's Will, 1979; Tales from Hollywood, 1983, 2nd edn 2001; The Portage to San Cristobal of A. H. (George Steiner), 1983; Les Liaisons Dangereuses, 1985; Dangerous Liaisons: the film, 1989; The Ginger Tree, 1989; White Chameleon, 1991; (with Don Black) Sunset Boulevard, 1993; Alice's Adventures Under Ground, 1995; Carrington, 1995; Total Eclipse: the film, 1996; Plays One, 1997; The Secret Agent and Nostromo (Conrad), 1997; Collected Screenplays, 2002; The Talking Cure, 2002; Hampton on Hampton, ed Alastair Owen, 2005; *translations:* Isaac Babel, Marya, 1969; Chekhov, Uncle Vanya, 1971; Ibsen, Hedda Gabler, 1972, rev. version 1989; Ibsen, A Doll's House, 1972, 2nd edn 1989; Molière, Don Juan, 1972; Horváth, Tales from the Vienna Woods, 1977, 2nd edn 2000; Horváth, Don Juan Comes Back from the War, 1978; Ibsen, The Wild Duck, 1980; Ibsen, Ghosts, 1983; Molière, Tartuffe, 1984, 2nd edn 1991; Horváth, Faith, Hope and Charity, 1989; Yasmina Reza, Art (Scott Moncrieff Trans. Prize, Translators' Assoc.), 1997; Ibsen, An Enemy of the People, 1997; Yasmina Reza, The Unexpected Man, 1998; Yasmina Reza, Conversations After a Burial, 2000; Yasmina Reza, Life x 3, 2000; Chekhov, Three Sisters, 2004; Chekhov, The Seagull, 2007. *Recreations:* travel, cinema. *Address:* 2 Kensington Park Gardens, W11 3HB. *Club:* Dramatists'.

HAMPTON, Sir Geoffrey; *see* Hampton, Sir L. G.

HAMPTON, John; a Recorder of the Crown Court, 1983–98; *b* 13 Nov. 1926; *e s* of late Thomas Victor Hampton and Alice Maud (*née* Sturgeon), Oulton Broad; *m* 1954, Laura Jessie, *d* of Ronald Mylne Ford and Margaret Jessie Ford (*née* Coghill), Newcastle-under-Lyme; three *d*. *Educ:* Bradford Grammar School; University College London (LLB). Served Royal Navy, 1945–47. Called to the Bar, Inner Temple, 1952; NE Circuit; Solicitor General and Attorney General; Dep. Circuit Judge, 1975–82. Dep. Chm., Agricultural Land Tribunal, Yorks and Lancs Area, 1980–82, Yorks and Humberside Area, 1982–99; Dep. Traffic Comr, NE Traffic Area, 1988–94. *Recreations:* mountaineering, sailing. *Address:* c/o 37 Park Square, Leeds LS1 2NY. *T:* (0113) 243 9422.

HAMPTON, Kay; Lecturer in Sociology, School of Law and Social Sciences, Glasgow Caledonian University, since 2000; Lead Commissioner, 2002–07, and Chairman, 2006–07, Commission for Racial Equality (Deputy Chairman, 2003–06); *b* 25 Dec. 1957; *m* Russell Hampton; two *d*. *Educ:* Univ. of Durban-Westville, SA (BA Hons 1985; MA (Sociol.) *cum laude* 1987). Res. Asst, 1978–79, Researcher, 1980–89, Inst. for Social and Econ. Res., Univ. of Durban-Westville, SA; Researcher, Strategic Planning Dept, City of Durban Municipality, 1990–93; Res. Fellow, 1994–96, Res. Dir, 1996–2000, Scottish Ethnic Minorities Res. Unit, Glasgow Caledonian Univ. Observer, Exec. Cttee, West of Scotland Community Relns Council, 1994–98; Mem. Adv. Cttee, Scottish Poverty Information Unit, 1996–99; Member Committee: SCVO Race Equality Adv. Gp, 1996–2002; Apna Ghar (Scotland's first black-led housing assoc.), 1997–99; Board Member: Nat. Lottery Charities Bd, subseq. Community Fund, 1998–2004 (Chm. Scotland Cttee, 1998–2004); Meridian, Black and Ethnic Minority Women's Information and Resource Centre, 2000–01; Res. Advr, Black and Ethnic Minority Infrastructure in Scotland (BEMIS), 1998–99; non-executive Director: Positive Action in Housing, 1999–2002; Scottish Refugee Council, 2003–; Chm., Saheliya, Women's Mental Health Project, 1999–2000. Mem. Editl Bd, Scottish Youth Issues Jl, 2000–04. ILTM. Mem. AUT. Bronze Medal for Scientific Achievement, SA Assoc. for Advancement in Scis, 1988. *Publications:* (contrib. chapter) Ageing in South Africa, 1989; articles in Scottish Youth Issues Jl, Internat. Jl of Health Promotion and Educn, SA Jl of Sociol., Jl of Scottish Anti-racist Fedn in Community Develt and Social Work, Scottish Ethnic Minorities Res. Unit occasional papers series. *Recreation:* attempting to make a difference by promoting fairness and justice! *Address:* *e-mail:* k.Hampton@gcal.ac.uk, Kay.Hampton@virgin.net.

HAMPTON, Sir (Leslie) Geoffrey, Kt 1998; Director, Midlands Leadership Centre, since 1999, KPMG Professor of Education Leadership, since 2005, and Pro Vice Chancellor, since 2006, University of Wolverhampton (Dean of Education, 2000–06); *b* 2 Aug. 1952; *s* of Leslie and Irene Hampton; *m* 1975, Christine Joyce Bickley; two *s*. *Educ:* King Alfred's Coll., Winchester (Cert Ed); Southampton Univ. (BEd); Birmingham Univ. (MEd). Teacher of Technology, Pensnett Sch., Dudley, W Midlands, 1973–86 (Dep. Head, 1985–86); Dep. Head, Buckpool Sch., Dudley, 1986–93; Headteacher, Northicote Sch., Wolverhampton, 1993–99. Co-Dir, Nat. ICT Res. Centre, 2001–03. Chief Advr to Minister for Sch. Standards, Black Country Challenge Prog., 2007–. Member: Nat. Adv. Gp, Basic Skills Agency, 2002–07; Bd, Black Country Partnership for Learning, 2006–; Adv. Bd, Nat. Educn Business Partnerships, 2007–08. Associate Dir, Specialist Schs and Academies Trust, 2005–; Leader, Educn and Skills, Black Country Consortium, 2006–. Chm., Walsall Educn Bd, 2003–. Hon. DEd King Alfred's Coll., Winchester, 2003. *Publications:* (contrib.) Developing Quality Systems in Education, ed G. Doherty, 1994; (jtly) Transforming Northicote, 2000; (jtly) A Guide to Teacher Professional Development, 2004. *Recreations:* DIY, cycling, gardening. *Address:* University of Wolverhampton, Walsall Campus, Gorway Road, Walsall WS1 3BD.

HAMPTON, Sir Philip (Roy), Kt 2007; Chairman, J. Sainsbury plc, since 2004; *b* 5 Oct. 1953; *m* 1983, Amanda Lowe; two *s*. *Educ:* Lincoln Coll., Oxford (MA English 1975); INSEAD, Fontainebleau (MBA 1980). ACA 1978. Lazard Brothers, 1981–89: corporate finance rôles, 1981–86; Exec. Dir, 1987–89; Group Finance Director: British Steel, 1990–96; British Gas, then BG, 1996–2000; BT Gp, 2000–02; Gp Finance Dir, Lloyds TSB Gp plc, 2002–04. Non-exec. Dir, Belgacom, 2004–. *Recreations:* history, sailing, ski-ing. *Address:* J. Sainsbury plc, 33 Holborn, EC1N 2HT. *Club:* Royal Thames Yacht.

HAMPTON, Surgeon Rear-Adm. Trevor Richard Walker, CB 1988; FRCPE; Surgeon Rear-Admiral (Operational Medical Services), 1987–89; *b* 6 June 1930; *s* of Violet and Percy Hampton; *m* 1st, 1952, Rosemary (*née* Day); three *d*; 2nd, 1976, Jennifer (*née* Bootle) (*d* 2002); 3rd, 2004, Kate Wilson. *Educ:* King Edward VII Grammar School, King's Lynn; Edinburgh University. MB ChB 1954; MRCPE 1964. Resident House Officer, Edinburgh Royal Infirmary, 1954–55; joined RN as Surgeon Lieut, 1955; served in HM Ships Ganges, Harrier and Victorious, 1955–62; Clinical Asst, Dept of Medicine, Edinburgh Univ., 1964; RN Hosp., Gibraltar, 1965–68; Consultant Physician, RN Hospitals, Plymouth, 1969–74, Haslar, 1975–79; MO i/c, RN Hosp., Gibraltar, 1980–82, RN Hosp., Plymouth, 1982–84; Surgeon Rear-Adm., Support Medical Services, 1984–87. QHP 1983–89. OStJ 1983. *Publications:* contribs to Jl of RN Med. Service. *Recreations:* reading, writing, resting.

HAMWEE, Baroness *cr* 1991 (Life Peer), of Richmond upon Thames; **Sally Rachel Hamwee;** Member (Lib Dem), 2000–08 and Chairman, 2001–02, 2003–04, 2005–06 and 2007–08, London Assembly, Greater London Authority (Deputy Chairman, 2000–01, 2002–03, 2004–05 and 2006–07); Consultant (formerly Partner), Clintons, solicitors; *b* 12 Jan. 1947; *d* of late Alec Hamwee and Dorothy (*née* Saunders). *Educ:* Manchester High Sch. for Girls; Girton Coll., Cambridge (MA). Admitted as solicitor, 1972. Councillor, London Borough of Richmond upon Thames, 1978–98 (Chm., Planning Cttee, 1983–87; Vice Chm., Policy and Resources Cttee, 1987–92); Chair, London Planning Adv. Cttee, 1986–94; Chm., Members' Policy Gp, London and SE Regl Planning Conf., 1989–91. Vice Chm., Assoc. of Liberal Democrat Councillors, 1988–99; Member: Nat. Exec., Liberal Party, 1987–88; Federal Exec., Liberal Democrats, 1989–91; Lib Dem spokesman on planning and housing, 1993–98, on local govt, 1991–, also transport and the regions, 1997–2001, and on ODPM, subseq. DCLG, 2001–, H of L. Chm., Budget Cttee, GLA, 2000–08. Member: Adv. Council, London First, 1996–98 (Dir, 1993–96); Council, Parents for Children, 1977–86; Council of Mgt, Refuge (formerly Chiswick Family Rescue), 1991–2005; Joseph Rowntree Foundn Inquiry, Planning for Housing, 1992–94; Council, Family Policies Study Centre, 1994–2000. Legal Advr, Simon Community, 1980–2000; Dir, In Harmony, 1994–98; Chm., Xfm Ltd, 1996–98. Mem. Bd, Arts Council London, 2006–. Vice-Pres., TCPA, 2002– (Pres.,

1995–2002); Jt Pres., London Councils, 2005–. *Address:* 101A Mortlake High Street, SW14 8HQ. *T:* (020) 8878 1380.

HAN Suyin, (Dr Elizabeth Comber); doctor and author; (*née* Elizabeth Kuanghu Chow); *b* 12 Sept. 1917; *d* of Y. T. Chow (Zhou) (Chinese) and M. Denis (Belgian); *m* 1st, 1938, General P. H. Tang (*d* 1947); one *d*; 2nd, 1952, L. F. Comber (marr. diss. 1968); 3rd, 1971, Vincent Ruthnaswamy. *Educ:* Yenching Univ., Peking, China; Brussels Univ., Brussels, Belgium; London Univ., London, England. Graduated MB BS, London (Hons) in 1948, a practising doctor until 1964. *Publications: as Han Suyin:* Destination Chungking, 1942; A Many Splendoured Thing, 1952; And the Rain My Drink, 1956; The Mountain Is Young, 1958; Cast but One Shadow and Winter Love, 1962; The Four Faces, 1963; China in the Year 2001, 1967; The Morning Deluge, 1972; Wind in the Tower, 1976; Lhasa, the Open City, 1977; Les Cent Fleurs: La Peinture Chinoise, 1978; La Chine aux Mille Visages, 1980; Chine: Terre Eau et Hommes, 1981; Till Morning Comes, 1982; The Enchantress, 1985; A Share of Loving, 1987; Han Suyin's China, 1988; Fleur de Soleil, 1988; Tigers and Butterflies, 1990; Les Yeux de Demain, 1992; Eldest Son: Zhou Enlai and the making of modern China (1898–1976), 1994; *autobiography:* China: autobiography, biography, history (6 vols): The Crippled Tree, 1965; A Mortal Flower, 1966; Birdless Summer, 1968; My House Has Two Doors, 1980; Phoenix Harvest, 1980; Wind in my Sleeve, 1992. *Recreations:* economics studies, lecturing, founding exchanges in science. *Address:* 37 Montoie, Lausanne 1007, Switzerland.

HANAN, Dame Elizabeth (Ann), DNZM 1998; Deputy Mayor, Dunedin City, 1998–2004 (City Councillor, 1986–2004); *b* 21 Aug. 1937; *d* of Sir John Patrick Walsh, KBE; *m* 1966, John Murray Hanan; one *s* two *d*. *Educ:* Columba Coll.; Otago Girls' High Sch.; Otago Univ. (BSc 1961; Dip. Recreation and Sport 1983). Secondary School Teacher, Christchurch, London and Dunedin, 1960–66, 1984–88; Supervisor and Demonstrator, Chemistry, Univ. of Otago, 1975–86; Tutor, Otago Poly., 1982–85. Member: NZ Council, 1986–88, Bd, 1989–98, Consumers' Inst. of NZ; Electrical Workers' Registration Bd, 1993–98 (Presiding Mem., 1993–97). Member: Otago Br., Fedn of Univ. Women, 1961– (Pres., 1990–92); Nat. Exec., Plunket Soc., 1972–74; Bd, Otago Mus. Trust, 1986–2001 (Chair, 1987–99); Otago Theatre Trust, 1986–2001; Bd of Mgt, Fortune Theatre, 1995–2006 (Pres., 2003–06); Discovery World, 1989–98; Mgt Cttee, Theomin Gall., 2001–07; Chair, Assoc. of Science and Technology Centres, 1994–96; Pres., NZ Internat. Science Fest., Dunedin, 1996–2004 (Mem. Cttee, 2004–). Commemoration Medal, 1990, Suffrage Centennial Medal, 1993, NZ. *Publication:* Playgrounds and Play, 1981 (trans. Japanese 1993). *Recreations:* walking, reading, computers, genealogy, theatre, gardening. *Address:* 159 Highgate, Dunedin, New Zealand. *T:* and *Fax:* (3) 4774388. *Club:* University (Dunedin).

HANBURY-TENISON, (Airling) Robin, OBE 1981; DL; MA, FLS, FRGS; farmer; President, Survival International (Chairman, since 1969); *b* 7 May 1936; *s* of late Major Gerald Evan Farquhar Tenison, Lough Bawn, Co. Monaghan, Ireland, and Ruth, *o surv. c* of late John Capel Hanbury, JP, DL, Pontypool Park, Monmouthshire; *m* 1st, 1959, Marika Hopkinson (*d* 1982); one *s* one *d*; 2nd, 1983, Mrs Louella Edwards (High Sheriff of Cornwall, 2006–07), *d* of Lt Col G. T. G. Williams, DL, and late Mrs Williams, Menkee, St Mabyn, Cornwall; one *s*. *Educ:* Eton; Magdalen Coll., Oxford (MA). Made first land crossing of South America at its widest point, 1958 (Mrs Patrick Ness Award, RGS, 1961); explored Tassili N'Ajjer, Tibesti and Aïr mountains in Southern Sahara, 1962–66; crossed S America in a small boat from the Orinoco to Buenos Aires, 1964–65; Geographical Magazine Amazonas Expedn, by Hovercraft, 1968; Trans-African Hovercraft Expedn (Dep. Leader), 1969; visited 33 Indian tribes as guest of Brazilian Govt, 1971; Winston Churchill Memorial Fellow, 1971; British Trans Americas Expedn, 1972; explored Outer Islands of Indonesia, 1973; Eastern Sulawesi, 1974; Sabah, Brunei, Sarawak, 1976; RGS Mulu (Sarawak) Expedn (Leader), 1977–78; expedns to Ecuador, Brazil and Venezuela, 1980–81; rode across France, 1984; rode along Great Wall of China, 1986; rode through New Zealand, 1988; led mission for IUCN, Friends of the Earth and Survival Internat. to Malaysia to investigate imprisonment of envmtl protesters, 1988; rode as pilgrim to Santiago de Compostela, 1989; rode across Spain driving 300 cattle on Trans Humance, 1991; visited tribal peoples of E Siberia for Survival Internat., 1992 and 1994; rode route of proposed Pennine Bridleway, 1994; visited: tribal people of Arunachal Pradesh, NE India, 1995; Innu of Labrador, 1997; Tuareg of Ténére desert, S Sahara, 1999, 2002, 2003; Bushmen of the Kalahari, 2005; Kimberley, Australia rock art, 2006; rode through Albania, 2007; climbed Mt Roraima, Venezuela, 2008; Mulu (film for C4), 1999. Chief Executive: BFSS, 1995–97; Countryside Alliance (BFSS, Countryside Business Gp and Countryside Movt), 1997–98 (Patron, 2003); organised Countryside Rally, 1997, Countryside March, 1998. Comr of Income Tax, 1965–95; Mem., SW Regl Panel, MAFF, 1993–96; Mem. of Lloyd's, 1976–95. Mem., Invest in Britain (formerly Think British) Campaign, 1987–; Trustee, Ecological Foundn, 1988–2004; President: Cornwall Wildlife Trust, 1988–95; Rain Forest Club, 2001–05; Patron: Cornwall Heritage Trust, 1994–; Countryside Alliance, 2003–. DL Cornwall, 2003. Mem. Council, RGS, 1968–70, 1971–76, 1979–82 (Vice-Pres., 1982–86); Patron's Medal, RGS, 1979; Krug Award of Excellence, 1980; Farmers Club Cup, 1998; Personality of the Year, Internat. Council for Game and Wildlife Conservation, 1998; Contribution to Countryside Award, CLA, 2000; Medal of Italian Chamber of Deputies, Pio Manzù Centre, 2000; Mungo Park Medal, RSGS, 2001. Dr *hc* Mons-Hainaut, 1992. *Publications:* The Rough and the Smooth, 1969, 2nd edn 2005; Report of a Visit to the Indians of Brazil, 1971; A Question of Survival, 1973, 2nd edn 2005; A Pattern of Peoples, 1975, 2nd edn 2005; Mulu: the rain forest, 1980, 3rd edn 2005; Aborigines of the Amazon Rain Forest: the Yanomami, 1982; Worlds Apart (autobiog.), 1984, 3rd edn 2005; White Horses Over France, 1985, 2nd edn 2005; A Ride along the Great Wall, 1987, 2nd edn 2005; Fragile Eden: a ride through New Zealand, 1989, 2nd edn 2005; Spanish Pilgrimage: a canter to St James, 1990, 2nd edn 2005; (ed) The Oxford Book of Exploration, 1993, 2nd edn 2005; Worlds Within, 2005; (ed) The Seventy Great Journeys in History, 2006; *for children:* Jake's Escape, 1996; Jake's Treasure, 1998; Jake's Safari, 1998; articles in: The Times, Telegraph, Spectator, Daily Mail, Sunday Express, etc; articles and reviews in Geographical Magazine (numerous), Geographical Jl, Ecologist, Literary Review, TLS, New Scientist, Traveller, Country Life, Field, etc. *Recreations:* travelling, riding across countries. *Address:* Cabilla Manor, Bodmin, Cornwall PL30 4DW. *T:* (01208) 821224; *e-mail:* robin@cabilla.co.uk; *web:* www.robinsbooks.co.uk. *Clubs:* Travellers, Pratt's, Geographical.

See also Sir R. Hanbury-Tenison.

HANBURY-TENISON, Sir Richard, KCVO 1995; JP; Lord-Lieutenant of Gwent, 1979–2000; *b* 3 Jan. 1925; *e s* of late Major G. E. F. Tenison, Lough Bawn, Co. Monaghan, Ireland, and Ruth, *o c* of late J. C. Hanbury, JP, DL, Pontypool Park, Monmouthshire; *m* 1955, Euphan Mary, *er d* of late Major A. B. Wardlaw-Ramsay, 21st of Whitehill, Midlothian; three *s* two *d*. *Educ:* Eton; Magdalen Coll., Oxford. Served Irish Guards, 1943–47 (Captain, wounded). Entered HM Foreign Service, 1949: 1st Sec., Vienna, 1956–58; 1st Sec. (and sometime Chargé d'Affaires), Phnom Penh, 1961–63, and Bucharest, 1966–68; Counsellor, Bonn, 1968–70; Head of Aviation and Telecommunications Dept, FCO, 1970–71; Counsellor, Brussels, 1971–75; retired from Diplomatic Service, 1975. South Wales Regional Dir, Lloyds Bank, 1980–91 (Chm. 1987–91). Dir, Gwent TEC, 1991–99. Mem. Court and Council, Nat. Museum of Wales 1980–2002 (Chm., Art Cttee, 1986–90). President: Gwent Assoc. of Vol. Orgns (formerly Monmouthshire Rural Community Council), 1959–; Internat. Tree Foundn, Wales; S David's Assoc. Hospice Care, 1998–; Gwent Local Hist. Council, 1979–; Gwent County History Assoc., 1998–; Gwent County Scout Council, 1979–2000. President: TA&VRA for Wales, 1985–90; S Wales Regl Cttee, TA&VRA, 1990–2000. Hon. Col, 3rd (V) Bn The Royal Regt of Wales, 1982–90. DL 1973, High Sheriff 1977, JP 1979, Gwent. Hon Fellow, UCW, Newport, 1997. KStJ 1990 (CStJ 1980). Dulverton Flagon, Timber Growers (UK), 1990. Foundn Mem., Order of St Woolos, 2006 (for service to dio. of Monmouth). *Publications:* The Hanburys of Monmouthshire, 1995; The Sheriffs of Monmouthshire and Gwent, 2008. *Recreations:* reading history, forestry. *Address:* Clytha Park, Abergavenny NP7 9BW; Lough Bawn, Co. Monaghan, Eire. *Clubs:* Boodle's; Kildare Street and University (Dublin).

See also A. R. Hanbury-Tenison.

HANBURY-TENISON, Robin; *see* Hanbury-Tenison, A. R.

HANBURY-TRACY, family name of **Baron Sudeley**.

HANCOCK, Prof. Barry William, MD; FRCP, FRCPE, FRCR; Yorkshire Cancer Research Professor of Clinical Oncology, University of Sheffield, since 1988; *b* 25 Jan. 1946; *s* of George Llewellyn Hancock and Sarah Hancock; *m* 1969, (Christine Diana) Helen Spray; one *s* one *d*. *Educ:* Univ. of Sheffield Med. Sch. (MB ChB 1969; MD 1977); Univ. of London (DCH 1971). FRCP 1985; FRCPE 1995; FRCR 1995. Lectr, 1974–78, Sen. Lectr, 1978–86, Reader, 1986–88, in Medicine, Univ. of Sheffield; Dir of Supraregional Gestational Trophoblastic Tumour Service (N of England and Wales), 1991–; Yorks Cancer Res. Dir of Cancer Res., 2000–. Chm., Renal Clinical Studies Gp, NCRI, 2001–. Pres., Internat. Soc. for Study of Trophoblastic Diseases, 2007–. New Year Hons Award, Lord Mayor of Sheffield, 1999; Sheffield Community Hero Award (Health), 2002; Centenary Achievement Medal, Sheffield Univ., 2005. *Publications:* (ed) Assessment of Tumour Response, 1982; (ed jtly) Immunological Aspects of Cancer, 1985; (ed jtly) Lymphoreticular Disease, 1985; (jtly) Lecture Notes in Clinical Oncology, 1986; (ed) Cancer Care in the Community, 1996; (ed) Cancer Care in the Hospital, 1996; (ed jtly) Gestational Trophoblastic Disease, 1997, 2nd edn 2003; (ed jtly) Malignant Lymphoma, 2000; over 250 articles in med. jls. *Recreations:* railways, ornithology, philately, tennis. *Address:* (home) Treetops, 253 Dobcroft Road, Ecclesall, Sheffield S11 9LG. *T:* (0114) 23 1433; Academic Unit of Clinical Oncology, Weston Park Hospital, Whitham Road, Sheffield S10 2SJ. *T:* (0114) 226 5007; *e-mail:* b.w.hancock@sheffield.ac.uk.

HANCOCK, Brian John; Director, PRIME Partners Ltd, since 2003; Employment Liaison Officer, Dash Training Ltd, since 2007; *b* 8 Aug. 1950; *s* of John and Joan Hancock; *m*; one *s* one *d*. *Educ:* Poly. of Wales (BSc Chem. Engrg 1974); Aston Univ. (Post Grad. Dip. Occupnl Safety and Health, 1986); Cardiff Univ. Business Sch. (Post Grad. Cert. in Sustainable Profitable Growth and Leadership, 2007). Registered Safety Practitioner, 1994; MIOSH 1992; AMIChemE. Chemical Project Engr, Monsanto Ltd, 1974–76; Shift Prodn Supervisor, 1976–80, Asst Plant Manager, 1980–85, ReChem International Ltd; Chemical Specialist Inspector of Factories, Health and Safety Inspectorate, 1985–88; Health, Safety and Envmt Supt, BP Chemicals, 1988–92; health, safety and envmt consultant and advr, and Dir of own consultancy, 1992–2000. National Assembly for Wales: Mem., (Plaid Cymru) Islwyn, 1999–2003; contested (Plaid Cymru) Islwyn, 2003; Newport West, 2007. Gov., primary and secondary schs, 1985–2000. Chair, Alexis Enterprises Ltd, 2003–05; Gen. Manager, Phoenix Community Transport, 2003–06. Chair, Plaid Cymru Cangen De Islwyn South Br., 2005–. Chm., Pontywaun Boat Club. Mem., CAMRA. *Recreations:* running and athletics (Chair, Newport Harriers AC), Rugby, DIY. *T:* (01633) 601934. *Clubs:* Newport Harriers Athletic; Risca Rugby Football (Mem. Cttee).

HANCOCK, Christine; European Director, Oxford Health Alliance, since 2006. *Educ:* London School of Economics (BScEcons). RGN. Formerly: Chief Nursing Officer, Bloomsbury Health Authority; General Manager, Waltham Forest Health Authority; Gen. Sec., RCN, 1989–2001; Pres., Internat. Council of Nurses, 2001–05. *Address:* Oxford Health Alliance, 1st Floor, 28 Margaret Street, W1W 8RZ.

HANCOCK, Very Rev. Christopher David, PhD; Director, Centre for the Study of Christianity in China, King's College London (formerly at Oxford), since 2005; *b* 18 Feb. 1954; *s* of late Rev. Dr Ronald and of Vera Hancock; *m* 1975, Suzie Nichols; one *s* one *d*. *Educ:* Highgate Sch.; Queen's Coll., Oxford (BA 1975, MA 1980); Cranmer Hall, Durham (BA 1978); St John's Coll., Durham (PhD 1984). Ordained deacon 1982, priest 1983; Curate, Holy Trinity with St John, Leicester, 1982–85; Chaplain, Magdalene Coll. Cambridge, 1985–88; Asst, 1988–91, Associate Prof., 1991–94, Virginia Theol Seminary, USA; Vicar, Holy Trinity, Cambridge, 1994–2002; Dean of Bradford, 2002–04. *Recreations:* music, sport, woodwork, walking, fishing, bird-watching, films, family. *Address:* 3 College Farm Cottages, Garford, Abingdon, Oxon OX13 5PF. *Club:* Oxford and Cambridge.

HANCOCK, Christopher Patrick; QC 2000; a Recorder, since 2004; *b* 7 June 1960; *s* of Alan Hancock and Dr (Rosemary) Ann Turner; *m* 1985, Diane Galloway; two *s*. *Educ:* Perse Sch. for Boys, Cambridge; Trinity Coll., Cambridge (MA Hons); Harvard Law Sch. (LLM). Called to the Bar, Middle Temple, 1983; in practice at the Bar, 1985–. *Recreations:* golf, music, watching football, family, Cub Scout leader. *Address:* 20 Essex Street, WC2R 3AL. *T:* (020) 7583 9294.

HANCOCK, Sir David (John Stowell), KCB 1985; retired civil servant and investment banker; *b* 27 March 1934; *s* of late Alfred George Hancock and Florence Hancock (*née* Barrow); *m* 1966, Sheila Gillian Finlay; one *s* one *d*. *Educ:* Whitgift Sch.; Balliol Coll. Oxford. 2nd Lieut, RTR, 1953–54. Asst Principal, Bd of Trade, 1957; transf. to HM Treasury, 1959; Principal, 1962; Harkness Fellow, 1965–66; Private Sec. to Chancellor of the Exchequer, 1968–70; Asst Sec., 1970; Financial and Economic Counsellor, Office of UK Permanent Rep. to European Communities, 1972–74; Under Sec., 1975–80; Dep. Sec., 1980–82; Dep. Sec., Cabinet Office, 1982–83; Perm. Sec., DES, 1983–89; Exec. Dir, Hambros Bank Ltd, 1989–98; Dir, Hambros PLC, 1989–98; Sen. Advr, S. G. Hambros, 1998–99. Dir, European Investment Bank, 1980–82. Chairman: Dyvell (Hldgs) Ltd, 1990–94; MRC Pension Trust Ltd, 1991–2004; Combined Landfill Projects Ltd, 1993–2001; Director: AXA Equity & Law plc, 1992–95; Royal National Theatre Enterprises Ltd, 2003–05. Sen. Advr, Newcourt, subseq. Tyco, Capital, 1999–2002. Chm., NFHA Inquiry into Governance of Housing Assocs, 1994–95. Chairman: British Selection Cttee of Harkness Fellowships, 1988–92 (Mem., 1984–92); Foundn for Young Musicians, 1990–99; Member: E London Partnership, 1991–98; Royal Nat. Theatre Bd, 1996–2002; South Bank Bd, 2000–02; Court, Luton Univ., 1998–2001; British American Drama Acad. Bd, 2003–08; Governor: City Lit. Inst., 2000–01; Whitgift Sch., 2000–08. Trustee: St Catharine's Foundn, Cumberland Lodge, 1989–2008; Société Gén. UK Defined Benefit Pension Scheme, 2003–07; Chm., St Katharine and Shadwell Trust,

1990–99. Pres., Old Whitgiftian Assoc., 2000–01. Freeman, City of London, 1989. FRSA 1986; CCMI (CBIM 1987). Hon. LLD Poly. of E London, 1990. *Recreations:* reading, gardening, theatre, opera. *Clubs:* Athenæum, Civil Service.

HANCOCK, Elisabeth Joy; Head, Old Palace School, Croydon, 2000–04; *b* 2 Dec. 1947; *d* of Reginald Arthur Lord and Evelyn Maud Mary Lord; *m* 1970, Barry Steuart Hancock; one *d. Educ:* Queen's Coll., Harley Street; Nottingham Univ. (BA Hons); Univ. of Sussex (PGCE). GB East Europe Centre, 1969; Nevill Sch., Hove, 1969–72; Brighton and Hove High Sch. (GPDST), 1972–89, Dep. Hd, 1986–89; Head, Bromley High Sch. (GDST), 1989–2000. FRSA 1988. *Publication:* Teaching History, 1970. *Recreations:* theatre, opera, watching cricket. *Address:* c/o Old Palace School, Old Palace Road, Croydon CR0 1AX.

HANCOCK, Group Captain Ethnea Mary, RRC 1990; Director and Matron-in-Chief, Princess Mary's Royal Air Force Nursing Service, and Deputy Director, Defence Nursing Services (Organisation), 1991–94; *b* 5 April 1937; *d* of late Sydney Ludwig Hancock and Catherine Teresa Hancock (*née* O'Dea). *Educ:* Convent of the Cross, Boscombe; University Coll. Hosp., London; RGN 1958; Southlands Hosp., Shoreham; Whittington Hosp., London; RM 1960; BA Hons Open Univ. 2003. Joined PMRAFNS, 1961–65; Columbia Presbyterian Medical Center, NY, 1966–67; rejoined PMRAFNS, 1967; served RAF Hosps and Units, UK, N Africa, Cyprus, Singapore, Germany; appts include Sen. Matron, RAF Hosp., Ely, 1985–87; MoD, 1987–88; Principal Nursing Officer, PMRAFNS, 1988–91. QHNS, 1991–94. *Recreations:* home and garden, music, travelling, ski-ing, golf. *Address:* Nationwide Building Society, PO Box 8888, Swindon SN3 1TS. *Club:* Royal Air Force.

HANCOCK, Frances Winifred; *see* Done, F. W.

HANCOCK, Geoffrey Francis, CMG 1977; HM Diplomatic Service, retired; Foreign and Commonwealth Office, 1979–82; *b* 20 June 1926; *s* of Lt-Col Sir Cyril Hancock, KCIE, OBE, MC; *m* 1960, Amelia Juana Aragon; one *s* one *d. Educ:* Wellington; Trinity Coll., Oxford. MA 1951. Third Sec., Mexico City, 1953; Second Sec., Montevideo, 1956; Foreign Office, 1958; Madrid, 1958; FO, 1960; MECAS, 1962; First Sec., Baghdad, 1964–67 and 1968–69; FCO, 1969–73; Counsellor, Beirut, 1973–78. Founder, Middle East Consultants, 1983. *Recreations:* music, sailing. *Address:* c/o Lloyds TSB, 8/10 Waterloo Place, SW1Y 4BE. *Clubs:* Athenæum, Royal Air Force.

HANCOCK, Prof. Gus, PhD; Professor of Chemistry, since 1996, and Head, Physical and Theoretical Chemistry Laboratory, since 2005, University of Oxford; Fellow, Trinity College, Oxford, since 1976; *b* Chell, 17 Nov. 1944; *s* of Reginald and Mary Hancock; *m* 1971, Rosemary Margaret Norfolk Brown; one *s* one *d. Educ:* Bangor Grammar Sch., Co. Down; Trinity Coll., Dublin (Louis Claude Purser Schol. and Foundn Schol.; BA Hons Natural Scis; MA); Peterhouse, Cambridge (PhD Physical Chem. 1971). Res. Asst, Univ. of Calif, San Diego, 1971–73; Wissenschaftlicher Angestellte, Univ. Bielefeld, 1973–76; Lectr in Physical Chem., Oxford Univ., 1976–96. Vis. Prof. of Chem., Stanford Univ., 1989. Corday Morgan Medal and Prize, 1982, Reaction Kinetics Award, 1995, Polanyi Medal, Gas Kinetics Gp, 2002, RSC; Italgas Prize for Sci. and Technol. for the Envmt, 2000. *Publications:* contrib. jls and books. *Address:* 124 Divinity Road, Oxford, OX4 1LW. *T:* (01865) 275439; *e-mail:* gus.hancock@chem.ox.ac.uk.

HANCOCK, Herbert Jeffrey, (Herbie); jazz pianist and composer; *b* Chicago, 12 April 1940; *s* of Wayman Edward Hancock and Winnie Hancock (*née* Griffin); *m* 1968, Gudrun Meixner; one *d. Educ:* Grinnell Coll., Iowa; Roosevelt Univ., Chicago; Manhattan Sch. of Music; New Sch. for Social Res. Owner and publisher, Hancock Music Co., 1962–; founder, Hancock and Joe Prodns, 1989–. Pres., Harlem Jazz Music Center Inc. Performances with: Chicago SO, 1952; Coleman Hawkins, Chicago, 1960; Donald Byrd, 1960–63; Miles Davis Quintet, 1963–68. Composer of music for films: Blow Up, 1966; The Spook Who Sat by the Door, 1973; Death Wish, 1974; A Soldier's Story, 1984; Jo Jo Dancer, Your Life is Calling, 1986; Action Jackson, 1988; Colors, 1988; Harlem Nights, 1989; Livin' Large, 1991; writer of score and actor in film, 'Round Midnight, 1986 (Acad. Award for best original score, 1986). Numerous awards. *Albums include:* Takin' Off, 1963; Succotash, 1964; Speak Like a Child, 1968; Fat Albert Rotunda, 1969; Mwandishi, 1971; Crossings, 1972; Sextant, 1972; Headhunters, 1973; Thrust, 1974; Man-Child, 1975; The Quintet, 1977; V. S. O. P., 1977; Sunlight, 1978; An Evening with Herbie Hancock and Chick Corea in Concert, 1979; Feets Don't Fail Me Now, 1979; Monster, 1980; Lite Me Up, 1982; Future Shock, 1983; Sound System, 1984; (with Foday Musa Suso) Village Life, 1985; (with Dexter Gordon) The Other Side of 'Round Midnight, 1987; Perfect Machine, 1988; Jamming, 1992; Cantaloupe Island, 1994; Tribute to Miles, 1994; Dis Is Da Drum, 1995; The New Standard, 1996; (with Wayne Shorter) 1 + 1, 1997; Gershwin's World, 1998; Return of the Headhunters, 1998; future 2 future, 2001; Possibilities, 2005; River: the Joni letters, 2007 (Grammy Award, 2008). *Address:* Hancock Music Co., Suite 1600, 1880 Century Park East, Los Angeles, CA 90067, USA.

HANCOCK, Janet Catherine, LVO 2005; FRGS; HM Diplomatic Service; Deputy High Commissioner, Malta, since 2005; *b* 5 Jan. 1949; *d* of Joseph Paul Knox and Alice Cecælia (*née* Ouzman); *m* 1973, Roger Arnold Hancock (marr. diss. 1976); *m* 2007, David Kemp. *Educ:* Convent of Jesus and Mary, Felixstowe and Ipswich; St Anne's Coll., Oxford (MA); Birkbeck Coll., London (MA). Entered FCO, 1971: res. analyst, 1971–94; Beirut, 1985, 1986, 1987; Hd, ME and N Africa Res. Gp, 1994–2000; Actg Dep. Head of Mission, Jerusalem, 1998; Dep. Hd of Mission, Tunis, 2000–04. FRGS 1998. *Publications:* contrib. articles to Mediterranean Politics, Jl Royal Soc. for Asian Affairs, etc. *Recreations:* riding, natural history, dalmatians. *Address:* c/o Foreign and Commonwealth Office, King Charles Street, SW1A 2AH.

HANCOCK, Prof. Keith Jackson, AO 1987; Vice-Chancellor, The Flinders University of South Australia, 1980–87; Senior Deputy President, Australian Industrial Relations Commission (formerly Australian Conciliation and Arbitration Commission), 1992–97 (Deputy President, 1987–92); *b* 4 Jan. 1935; *s* of late A. S. Hancock and Mrs R. D. Hancock; three *s* one *d. Educ:* Univ. of Melbourne (BA); Univ. of London (PhD). Tutor in Economic History, Univ. of Melbourne, 1956–57; Lectr in Economics, Univ. of Adelaide, 1959–63; Professor of Economics, 1964–87, now Emeritus, and Pro-Vice-Chancellor, 1975–79, Flinders Univ. of SA. Hon. Vis. Fellow, Univ. of Adelaide, 1998–; Professorial Fellow, Nat. Inst. of Labour Studies, 1998–. Chairman: Cttee of Inquiry into S Australian Racing Industry, 1972–74; Nat. Superannuation Cttee of Inquiry, 1973–77; Cttee of Review of Aust. Industrial Relns Law and Systems, 1983–85; Mem., Review Gp on Aust. Financial Instns, 1983. Chm., Energy Industry Ombudsman (SA) Ltd, 2000–09. Pres., Acad. of Social Sciences in Australia, 1981–84. FASSA 1968. Hon. Fellow, LSE, 1982. Hon. DLitt Flinders, 1987. *Publications:* The National Income and Social Welfare, 1965; (with P. A. Samuelson and R. H. Wallace) Economics (Australian edn), 1969, 2nd edn 1975; (ed jtly) Applied Economics: readings for Australian students, 1975; Incomes Policy in Australia, 1981; (ed jtly) Japanese and Australian Labour Markets: a comparative study, 1983; (ed) Australian Society, 1989; contrib. to various racing industry, superannuation, and financial and industrial law systems reports in Australia; articles in Economic Jl, Economica, Amer. Econ. Rev. and other jls. *Recreations:* bridge, sailing, music. *Address:* 6 Maturin Road, Glenelg, SA 5045, Australia. *T:* (8) 82948667. *Clubs:* Adelaide (Adelaide); Royal South Australian Yacht Squadron.

HANCOCK, Michael Thomas, CBE 1992; MP (Lib Dem) Portsmouth South, since 1997; *b* 9 April 1946; *m* 1967, Jacqueline, *d* of Sidney and Gwen Elliott; one *s* one *d. Educ:* well. Member: Portsmouth City Council, 1971– (for Fratton Ward, 1973–; Leader, Lib Dem Gp, 1989–97; Chm., Planning and Econ. Develt Cttee, 1991–94; Exec. Mem., Planning, Econ. Develt, Tourism and Property, 2003–); Hampshire County Council, 1973–97 (Leader of the Opposition, 1977–81, 1989–93; Leader, Lib Dem Gp, 1989–97; Leader of Council, 1993–97). Joined SDP, 1981 (Mem., Nat. Cttee, 1984); contested Portsmouth S (SDP) 1983, (SDP/Alliance) 1987. MP (SDP) Portsmouth S, June 1984–87. Lib Dem parly spokesman on defence, 1997–2001. Member: Public Admin Cttee, 1997–99; Select Cttee on Defence, 1998–; Panel of Chairmen, 2000–; UK Parly Delegn to Council of Europe, 1997– (Mem. Bd, Lib Dems; Chm., Youth and Support Cttee); WEU Parly Assembly (Leader, Liberal Gp); NATO Parly Assembly (Dep. Leader, Liberal Gp). Contested (Lib Dem) Wight and Hampshire South, Eur. Parly elecns, 1994. Dist Officer for Hants, IoW and CI, Mencap, 1989–97. Vice Chairman: Portsmouth Operating Co., 1992–; Portsmouth Docks, 1992–. Dir, Daytime Club, BBC, 1987–90. Bd of Dirs, Drug Rehabilitation Unit, Alpha Drug Clinic, Alpha House, Droxford, 1971–; Chm., Southern Br., NSPCC, 1989–. Trustee, Royal Marine Museum, 1993. Hon. Alderman, Hants, 1997. Hon. award for contrib. to Anglo-German relations, Homborn, W Germany, 1981. *Publications:* contribs to various jls. *Recreations:* people, living life to the full. *Address:* (office) 1A Albert Road, Southsea PO5 2SE. *T:* (office) (023) 9286 1055; House of Commons, SW1A 0AA. *Clubs:* too many to mention.

HANCOCK, Ven. Peter; Archdeacon of The Meon, since 1999; *b* 26 July 1955; *s* of Kenneth and Jean Hancock; *m* 1979, Elizabeth Jane Sindall; two *s* two *d. Educ:* Price's Sch., Fareham; Selwyn Coll., Cambridge (BA 1976; MA 1979); Oak Hill Theol Coll. (BA 1980). Ordained deacon 1980, priest 1981; Curate: Christ Church, Portsdown, 1980–83; Radipole and Melcombe Regis Team Ministry, 1983–87; Vicar, St Wilfrid, Cowplain, 1987–99; RD of Havant, 1993–98; Diocesan Dir of Mission, Portsmouth, 2003–07. Hon. Canon, Portsmouth Cathedral, 1997–99. *Recreations:* walking, reading, third world issues, swimming, contemporary music, ski-ing, golf. *Address:* Victoria Lodge, 36 Osborn Road, Fareham, Hants PO16 7DS. *T:* (01329) 280101.

HANCOCK, Ronald John; business consultant; Director: Insituform Ltd, 1987–94; Travelines, 1991–94; Permaline, 1991–94; *b* 11 Feb. 1934; *s* of George and Elsie Hancock; *m* 1970, Valerie Hancock; two *d. Educ:* Dudley Grammar Sch., Dudley. FCMA. Served HM Forces, 1952–61. Schweppes Ltd, 1962–63; Mullard Ltd, 1963–66; Valor Group, 1966–68; BL Ltd, 1968–85. Chairman: Leyland Vehicles, 1981–85; Leyland Vehicles Exports Ltd, 1981–85; Bus Manufacturers Limited, 1981–85; Bus Manufacturers (Holdings) Ltd, 1981–85; Eastern Coachworks Ltd, 1981–85; Bristol Commercial Vehicles Ltd, 1981–85; Self-Changing Gears Ltd, 1981–85; Bedfordshire Chamber of Training Ltd, 1990–92; Director: BL Staff Trustees Ltd, 1981–85; Leyland Nigeria Ltd, 1981–85; BL International Ltd, 1981–85; Land Rover-Leyland International Holdings Ltd (formerly BLIH), 1982–85; Land Rover-Leyland Ltd, 1983–85; Chloride Gp plc, 1985–87; Man. Dir, AWD Ltd, 1987–90. *Recreations:* travel, reading. *Address:* Bath Hill Court, Bath Road, Bournemouth BH1 2HS.

HANCOCK, Sheila, OBE 1974; actress and director; *d* of late Enrico Hancock and Ivy Woodward; *m* 1st, 1955, Alexander Ross (*d* 1971); one *d*; 2nd, 1973, John Thaw, CBE (*d* 2002); one *d. Educ:* Dartford County Grammar Sch.; Royal Academy of Dramatic Art. Acted in Repertory, Theatre Workshop, Stratford East, for 8 years. Associate Dir, Cambridge Theatre Co., 1980–82; Artistic Dir, RSC Regional Tour, 1983–84; acted and directed, NT, 1985–86. Dir, The Actors Centre, 1978–. West End starring roles in: Rattle of a Simple Man, 1962; The Anniversary, 1966, 2005; A Delicate Balance (RSC), 1969; So What About Love?, 1969; Absurd Person Singular, 1973; Déjà Revue, 1974; The Bed Before Yesterday, 1976; Annie, 1978; Sweeney Todd, 1980; The Winter's Tale, RSC, Stratford 1981, Barbican 1982; Peter Pan, Barbican, 1982–83; The Cherry Orchard, The Duchess of Malfi, National, 1985–86; Greenland, Royal Court, 1988; Prin, Lyric, Hammersmith, 1989, Lyric, Shaftesbury Avenue, 1990; A Judgement in Stone, The Way of the World, Lyric, Hammersmith, 1992; Harry and Me, Royal Court, 1996; Lock Up Your Daughters, Chichester, 1996; Then Again…, Lyric, Hammersmith, 1997; Vassa, Albery, 1999; Under the Blue Sky, Royal Court, 2000; In Extremis, RNT, 2000; Arab-Israeli Cookbook, Gate, 2004; The Anniversary, Garrick, 2005; Cabaret, Lyric, 2006; The Birthday Party, Lyric, Hammersmith, 2008. Has starred in several successful revues; appeared on Broadway in Entertaining Mr Sloane. Directed: The Soldier's Fortune, Lyric, Hammersmith, 1981; A Midsummer Night's Dream, RSC, 1983; The Critic, National, 1986. *Films:* The Love Child, 1987; Making Waves, 1987; Hawks, 1988; Buster, 1988; Three Men and a Little Lady, 1990; Hold Back the Night, 1999; Love and Death on Long Island, 2000; Yes, 2005. *Television:* many successes, including The Rag Trade, Jumping the Queue, The Rivals, and several comedy series, incl. Gone to the Dogs, 1991, Gone to Seed, 1992, Brighton Belles, 1993; other appearances include: The Buccaneers, 1994; Dangerous Lady, 1994; Close Relations, 1998; Eastenders, Love or Money, The Russian Bride, 2001; Bedtime, 2001, 2002, 2003; Bait, 2002; 40 Something, 2003; Grumpy Old Women, 2003, 2004, 2005; Feather Boy, 2004; Bleak House, 2005; After Thomas, 2006; wrote and acted in Royal Enclosure, 1990. Awards: Variety Club, London Critics, Whitbread Trophy (for best Actress on Broadway). *Publications:* Ramblings of an Actress, 1987; The Two of Us, 2004; Just Me, 2008. *Recreations:* reading, music. *Address:* c/o Independent Talent Group Ltd, Oxford House, 76 Oxford Street, W1D 1BS.

HAND, Prof. David John, PhD; FBA 2003; Professor of Statistics, Imperial College London, since 1999; *b* 30 June 1950; *s* of Peter Hand and Margaret Hand; *m* 1993, Dr Shelley Channon; two *d. Educ:* Christ Church, Oxford (BA Maths 1972); Southampton Univ. (MSc Stats 1974; PhD Pattern Recognition 1977). CStat 1993. Statistician, Inst. of Psychiatry, 1977–88; Prof. of Statistics, Open Univ., 1988–99. Pres., Royal Statistical Soc., 2008. Hon. FIA 1999. Guy Medal in Silver, Royal Statistical Soc., 2002. *Publications:* Discrimination and Classification, 1981; Finite Mixture Distributions, 1981; Kernel Discriminant Analysis, 1982; Artificial Intelligence and Psychiatry, 1985; Multivariate Analysis of Variance and Repeated Measures, 1987; (ed) The Statistical Consultant in Action, 1987; Analysis of Repeated Measures, 1990; (ed) Artificial Intelligence Frontiers in Statistics, 1993; (ed) AI and Computer Power: the impact on statistics, 1994; (ed) A Handbook of Small Data Sets, 1994; Elements of Statistics, 1995; Biplots, 1996; Practical Longitudinal Data Analysis, 1996; Construction and Assessment of Classification Rules, 1997; (ed) Statistics in Finance, 1998; Intelligent Data Analysis, 1999; Advances in Intelligent Data Analysis, IDA–99, 1999; Principles of Data Mining, 2001; (ed) Advances in Intelligent Data Analysis, IDA 2001, 2001; Pattern Detection and Discovery, 2002; Methods and Models in Statistics, 2004; Measurement Theory and Practice, 2004; (ed) Selected Papers of Sir David Cox, 2005; Information Generation, 2006; over 200 scientific articles. *Address:* Department of Mathematics, Imperial College London, 180 Queen's

Gate, SW7 2AZ. *T:* (020) 7594 8521, *Fax:* (020) 7594 1191; *e-mail:* d.j.hand@imperial.ac.uk.

HAND, Prof. Geoffrey Joseph Philip, DPhil; Barber Professor of Jurisprudence in the University of Birmingham, 1980–92, now Professor Emeritus; *b* 25 June 1931; *s* of Joseph and Mary Macaulay Hand. *Educ:* Blackrock Coll.; University Coll., Dublin (MA); New Coll., Oxford (DPhil); King's Inns, Dublin. Called to Irish Bar, 1961. Lecturer: Univ. of Edinburgh, 1960; Univ. of Southampton, 1961; University Coll., Dublin, 1965; Professor: University Coll., Dublin, 1972–76; European University Inst., Fiesole, 1976–80; Dean of Faculty of Law, University Coll., Dublin, 1970–75. Chairman: Arts Council of Ireland, 1974–75; Irish Manuscripts Commn, 1998. Mem. Council, RIA, 1994–98 (Vice Pres., 1996–97). *Publications:* English Law in Ireland 1290–1324, 1967; Report of the Irish Boundary Commission 1925, 1969; (with Lord Cross of Chelsea) Radcliffe and Cross's English Legal System, 5th edn 1971, 6th edn 1977; (with J. Georgel, C. Sasse) European Election Systems Handbook, 1979; Towards a Uniform System of Direct Elections, 1981; (ed with J. McBride) Droit sans Frontières, 1991; numerous periodicals. *Recreations:* listening to classical music, playing chess. *Address:* 72 Granitefield, Dun Laoghaire, Republic of Ireland. *Clubs:* Oxford and Cambridge; Royal Irish Yacht (Dun Laoghaire); Kildare Street and University (Dublin); Casino Maltese (Valletta).

HAND, Graham Stewart; Chief Executive, British Expertise (formerly British Consultants & Construction Bureau), since 2004; *b* 3 Nov. 1948; *s* of Ronald Charles Hand and Mary Fraser Hand (*née* Stewart); *m* 1973, Anne Mary Seton Campbell; one *s* one *d* (and one *s* decd). *Educ:* RMA Sandhurst; St John's Coll., Cambridge (MA 1979). Regular Army, 1969–80; FCO, 1980–2004: served UN Dept, 1980–82; Dakar, 1982–84; News Dept, FCO, 1984–87; Head of Chancery, Helsinki, 1987–90; Aid Policy Dept, ODA, 1991–92; Head of Human Rights Policy Dept, FCO, 1992–94; Dep. High Comr, Nigeria, 1994–96; RCDS, 1997; Ambassador to Bosnia and Herzegovina, 1998–2001; Chargé d'Affaires, Tajikistan, 2002; Ambassador to Algeria, 2002–04. *Recreations:* opera, choral singing, sailing, golf, cooking. *Address:* British Expertise, One Westminster Palace Gardens, Artillery Row, SW1P 1RJ.

HAND, Jessica Mary; HM Diplomatic Service; Director, Operations and Business Change (formerly Counsellor (Management)) and Consul-General, Moscow, since 2004; *b* 1 Sept. 1957; *d* of William Evan Pearce and Mary Elizabeth Pearce (*née* Pimm); *m* 1999, Lt Col Robert Wayne Hand, US Army (retd). *Educ:* Aberdeen Univ. (MA Jt Hons, French and Internat. Relations). PA to Dir, NERC Research Vessel Base, Barry, 1976–78; sales co-ordinator for wine co., Cardiff, 1983–85; joined FCO, 1985; Second Sec., FCO, 1985–87; Dakar, Senegal, 1987–90; First Sec., UN Dept, 1990–92, African Dept (Southern), 1992–94, FCO; lang. trng, 1994–95; Ambassador to Belarus, 1996–99; Dep. Hd, Non-Proliferation Dept, FCO, 1999–2001; Asst Pol Advr, Allied Forces North, 2002–04. *Recreations:* campanology, walking, reading, cooking, music (classical, jazz and anything to dance to). *Address:* c/o Foreign and Commonwealth Office, King Charles Street, SW1A 2AH.

HAND, John Lester; QC 1988; **His Honour Judge Hand;** a Circuit Judge, since 2008; *b* 16 June 1947; *s* of John James and Violet Hand; *m* 1st, 1972, Helen Andrea McWatt (marr. diss.); 2nd, 1990, Lynda Ray Ferrigno; one *d*. *Educ:* Huddersfield New College; Univ. of Nottingham (LLB 1969). Called to the Bar, Gray's Inn, 1972, Bencher, 1996; Northern Circuit, 1972; Recorder, 1991–2008. Mem., Employment Appeal Tribunal, 2002–04. *Recreations:* computers, travel. *Address:* Snaresbrook Crown Court, 75 Hollybush Hill, E11 1QW; *e-mail:* jlh@johnhandqc.co.uk.

HANDCOCK, family name of **Baron Castlemaine**.

HANDFORD, Rt Rev. (George) Clive, CMG 2007; Bishop in Cyprus and the Gulf, 1996–2007; President Bishop, Episcopal Church in Jerusalem and the Middle East, 2002–07; an Assistant Bishop, diocese of Ripon and Leeds; *b* 17 April 1937; *s* of Cyril Percy Dawson Handford and Alice Ethel Handford; *m* 1962, Anne Elizabeth Jane Atherley; one *d*. *Educ:* Hatfield Coll., Durham (BA); Queen's Coll., Birmingham and Univ. of Birmingham (DipTh). Curate, Mansfield Parish Church, 1963–66; Chaplain: Baghdad, 1967; Beirut, 1967–73; Dean, St George's Cathedral, Jerusalem, 1974–78; Archdeacon in the Gulf and Chaplain in Abu Dhabi and Qatar, 1978–83; Vicar of Kneesall with Laxton, and Wellow and Rufford, 1983–84; RD of Tuxford and Norwell, 1983–84; Archdeacon of Nottingham, 1984–90; Suffragan Bishop of Warwick, 1990–96. ChStJ 1976. *Address:* Wayside, 1 The Terrace, Kirby Hill, Boroughbridge, York YO51 9DQ. *T:* (01423) 325406.

HANDLEY, Ven. (Anthony) Michael; Archdeacon of Norfolk, 1993–2002, now Emeritus; *b* 3 June 1936; *s* of Eric Harvey Handley and Janet Handley; *m* 1962, Christine May Adlington; two *s* one *d*. *Educ:* Spalding Grammar School; Selwyn Coll., Cambridge (MA Hons); Chichester Theological Coll. Asst Curate, Thorpe St Andrew, 1962–66; Anglican Priest on Fairstead Estate, 1966–72; Vicar of Hellesdon, 1972–81; RD of Norwich North, 1979–81; Archdeacon of Norwich, 1981–93. Proctor in Convocation, 1980–85; Mem., General Synod, 1990–95. Research Project, The Use of Colour, Shape, and Line Drawings as Experiential Training Resources, 1976. *Publication:* A Parish Prayer Card, 1980. *Recreations:* climbing mountains, painting, bird watching. *Address:* 25 New Street, Sheringham, Norfolk NR26 8EE. *T:* (01263) 820928.

HANDLEY, Mrs Carol Margaret; Headmistress, Camden School for Girls, 1971–85; *b* 17 Oct. 1929; *d* of Claude Hilary Taylor and Margaret Eleanor Taylor (*née* Peebles); *m* 1952, Eric Walter Handley, *qv*. *Educ:* St Paul's Girls' Sch.; University Coll. London (BA; Fellow 1977). Asst Classics Mistress: North Foreland Lodge Sch., 1952; Queen's Gate Sch., 1952; Head of Classics Dept, Camden Sch. for Girls, 1956; Deputy Headmistress, Camden Sch. for Girls, 1964. Sen. Mem., Wolfson Coll., Cambridge, 1989–. Member Council: RHC, then RHBNC, 1977–95; Middx Hosp. Med. Sch., 1980–84; Mem. Governors and Council, Bedford Coll., 1981–85; Partnership Gov., Comberton Village Coll., 2004– (Chm., 2006). Pres., Classical Assoc., 1996–97. *Publications:* (jtly) A Greek Anthology, 2002; coursebooks for students of classics; articles and book reviews for classical jls. *Recreation:* gardening. *Address:* Colt House, 44 High Street, Little Eversden, Cambs CB3 7HE.

HANDLEY, Sir David John D.; *see* Davenport-Handley.

HANDLEY, David Thomas, CMG 2000; HM Diplomatic Service, retired; Director, Group Strategic Analysis, BAE SYSTEMS, since 2000; *b* 31 Aug. 1945; *s* of late Leslie Thomas Handley and Frances Handley (*née* Harrison); *m* 1st, 1967, Lilian Duff (marr. diss. 1977); one *s* one *d*; 2nd, 1978, Susan Elizabeth Beal; two *s* one *d* (and one *d* decd). *Educ:* Univ. of Newcastle upon Tyne (BA Jt Hons Politics and Econs). British Leyland Motor Corp., 1967–72; joined FCO, 1972: language studies, MECAS, Lebanon, 1974–76; First Sec., Budapest, 1978–81; Hd of British Interests Sect. and Chargé d'Affaires, Guatemala City, 1984–87; Counsellor: Cairo, 1990–93; FCO, 1993–2000. Co-Chair, Bd of Govs, Bedales Sch., 2005–. *Recreations:* family, friends, fitness, fun. *Address:* The Red Hous Froxfield, Hants GU23 1BB. *T:* (01730) 827039.

HANDLEY, Prof. Eric Walter, CBE 1983; FBA 1969; Professor of Ancient Literatur Royal Academy, since 1990; Fellow, Trinity College, Cambridge, since 1984; *b* 12 No 1926; *s* of late Alfred W. Handley and A. Doris Cox; *m* 1952, Carol Margaret Taylor (*s* C. M. Handley). *Educ:* King Edward's Sch., Birmingham; Trinity Coll., Cambridg Stewart of Rannoch Schol. and Browne Medal, 1945. University College London: As Lectr in Latin and Greek, 1946; Lectr, 1949; Reader, 1961; Prof. of Latin and Gree 1967–68; Prof. and Head of Dept of Greek, 1968–84; Hon. Fellow, 1989; Dir, 1967–8 Sen. Res. Fellow, 1995–, Inst. of Classical Studies, Univ. of London; Regius Prof. Greek, Cambridge Univ., 1984–94. Vis. Lectr on the Classics, Harvard, 1966; Vis. Mem Inst. for Advanced Study, Princeton, 1971; Visiting Professor: Stanford Univ., 197 Melbourne Univ., 1978; Vis. Senior Fellow, Council of the Humanities, Princeton, 198 Sec. Council Univ. Classical Depts, 1969–70, Chm., 1975–78. President: Classical Assoc 1984–85; Hellenic Soc., 1993–96; Foreign Sec., British Academy, 1979–88. Unic Académique Internationale: Mem., Commn des Affaires Internes, 1984–91; Mem. Bureau, 1991–2000; Vice-Pres., 1995–97, 1999–2000; Mem., Comité Scientifiqu Fondation Hardt, Geneva, 1978–99 (Conseil, 1995–99). Member: Academia Europae 1988; Norwegian Acad. of Science and Letters, 1996. Foreign Mem., Societas Scientiaru Fennica, 1984; Hon. Mem., Hungarian Acad. of Scis, 1993; Corresp. Mem., Acad. Athens, 1995. Chm., Gilbert Murray Trust, 1988–2006 (Hon. Pres., 2006–). Hon. R 1990. Dr *hc* Athens, 1995. (Jtly) Cromer Greek Prize, 1958. *Publications:* (with John Re The Telephus of Euripides, 1957; The Dyskolos of Menander, 1965; (contrib.) Cambrid History of Classical Literature, 1985; (with André Hurst) Relire Ménandre, 1990; (jtl The Oxyrhynchus Papyri LIX, 1992; (with J.-M. Bremer) Aristophane, 1993; (with J. I Green) Images of the Greek Theatre, 1995; (jtly) The Oxyrhynchus Papyri LXIV, 199 papers in class. jls, etc. *Recreations:* walking, travel. *Address:* Trinity College, Cambrid CB2 1TQ. *Club:* Oxford and Cambridge.

HANDLEY, Ven. Michael; *see* Handley, Ven. A. M.

HANDLEY, Paul; Editor, Church Times, since 1995; *b* 29 May 1958; *s* of Arnold Terenc Handley and Margaret Hardy; *m* 1980, Terence MacMath; two *s* two *d*. *Educ:* Colcheste Royal Grammar Sch.; Goldsmiths' Coll., Univ. of London (BA English 1980). New Editor, Church of England Newspaper, 1981–85; freelance publisher, writer, 1986–8 Reporter, Church Times, 1988–90; Press Sec. to Archbishop of Canterbury, 1990–9 freelance writer, 1992–94; News Editor, Church Times, 1994. *Address:* c/o Churc Times, 13–17 Long Lane, EC1A 9PN. *T:* (020) 7776 1060; *e-mail:* editor(churchtimes.co.uk.

HANDLIN, Prof. Oscar; Carl M. Loeb University Professor, Harvard University, sinc 1984; Director, Harvard University Library, 1979–84; *b* 29 Sept. 1915; *m* 1st, 1937, Ma Flug; one *s* two *d*; 2nd, 1977, Lilian Bombach. *Educ:* Brooklyn Coll. (AB); Harvard (MA PhD). Instructor, Brooklyn Coll., 1938–39; Harvard Univ.: Instructor, 1939–44; As Prof., 1944–48; Associate Prof., 1948–54; Prof. of History, 1954–65; Charles Warre Prof. of Amer. Hist., and Dir, Charles Warren Center for Studies in Amer. Hist., 1965–7 Carl H. Pforzheimer Univ. Prof., 1972–84; Harmsworth Prof. of Amer. History, Oxfo Univ., 1972–73. Dir, Center for Study of History of Liberty in America, 1958–67; Chm US Bd of Foreign Scholarships, 1965–66 (Vice-Chm. 1962–65). Hon. Fellow, Brande Univ., 1965. Hon. LLD: Colby Coll., 1962; Harvard, 1993; Hon. LHD: Hebrew Unic Coll., 1967; Northern Michigan, 1969; Seton Hall Univ., 1972; Hon. HumD Oaklan 1968; Hon. LittD Brooklyn Coll., 1972; Hon. DHL: Boston Coll., 1975; Lowell, 198 Cincinnati, 1981; Massachusetts, 1982; Clark Univ., Mass, 1989. *Publications:* Boston Immigrants 1790–1865, 1941; (with M. F. Handlin) Commonwealth, 1947; Danger i Discord, 1948; (ed) This Was America, 1949; Uprooted, 1951, 2nd edn 1972; Adventur in Freedom, 1954; American People in the Twentieth Century, 1954 (rev. edn 1963); (jtly) Harvard Guide to American History, 1954; Chance or Destiny, 1955; (ed) Reading in American History, 1957; Race and Nationality in American Life, 1957; Al Smith an his America, 1958; (ed) Immigration as a Factor in American History, 1959; John Dewey Challenge to Education, 1959; (ed) G. M. Capers, Stephen A. Douglas, Defender of th Union, 1959; Newcomers, 1960; (ed jtly) G. Mittleberger, Journey to Pennsylvania, 196 (ed) American Principles and Issues, 1961; (with M. F. Handlin) The Dimensions Liberty, 1961; The Americans, 1963; (with J. E. Burchard) The Historian and the Cit 1963; Firebell in the Night, 1964; A Continuing Task, 1964; (ed) Children of th Uprooted, 1966; The History of the United States, vol. 1, 1967, vol. 2, 1968; America: History, 1968; (with M. F. Handlin) The Popular Sources of Political Authority, 196 The American College and American Culture, 1970; Facing Life: Youth and the Famil in American History, 1971; A Pictorial History of Immigration, 1972; (with M. Handlin) The Wealth of the American People, 1975; Truth in History, 1979, 2nd ed 1997; The Distortion of America, 1981, 2nd edn 1997; with L. Handlin: Abraham Linco and the Union, 1980; A Restless People, 1982; Liberty and Power, 1986; Liberty i Expansion, 1989; Liberty in Peril, 1992; Liberty and Equality, 1994; From the Oute World, 1997. *Address:* 18 Agassiz Street, Cambridge, MA 02140, USA. *Club:* Facult (Cambridge, Mass).

HANDOVER, Richard Gordon, CBE 2008; Chairman, Alexon Group plc, since 200 *b* 13 April 1946; *s* of Gordon Handover and Hilda Handover (*née* Dyke); *m* 1972, Veronic Joan Woodhead; one *s* two *d*. *Educ:* Blundell's Sch. W H Smith, 1964–2005: various jur managerial appts, 1964–74; sen. mgt appts, 1974–89; Man. Dir, Our Price Music 1989–95; joined main co. bd, 1995; Man. Dir, W H Smith News, 1995–97; Gp Chie Exec., W H Smith Gp plc, subseq. W H Smith PLC, 1997–2003; Chm., 2003–05. Non executive Director: Nationwide Bldg Soc., 2000–; Royal Mail, 2002–. Chm., Adu Learning Inspectorate, 2002–07. Chm., Age Concern Enterprises Ltd, 1992–99; Di BITC, 1999–2005; Vice Chm., Kids Company, 2005–. Chm. Govs, Dauntsey's Sch 2005. Chm., Wilts and Swindon Community Foundn, 2005. *Recreations:* tennis, gol horses, painting. *Address:* Alexon Group plc, 40–48 Guildford Street, Luton LU1 2PB.

HANDS, Gregory William; MP (C) Hammersmith and Fulham, since 2005; *b* 14 Nov 1965; *s* of Edward and Mavis Hands; *m* 2005, Irina Hundt; one *s* one *d*. *Educ:* D Challoner's Grammar Sch.; Robinson Coll., Cambridge (BA 1989). Banker, 1989–9 Mem. (C), Hammersmith and Fulham BC, 1998–2006. *Address:* (office) 4 Greyhoun Road, W6 8NX; House of Commons, SW1A 0AA.

HANDS, Guy; Chief Executive Officer, Terra Firma Capital Partners, since 2002; *b* 2 Aug. 1959; *s* of Christopher and Sally Hands; *m* 1984, Julia Caroline Ablethorpe; two two *d*. *Educ:* Judd Sch., Tonbridge; Mansfield Coll., Oxford (BA Hons PPE, MA). Hd o Eurobond Trading, Goldman Sachs, 1982–94 (Trading, 1986; Hd, Global Asse Structuring Gp, 1990); Founder and Man. Dir, Principal Finance Gp, Nomura Interna plc, 1994–2001. *Recreations:* films, wine, fine art. *Address:* Terra Firma Capital Partners Lt 2 More London Riverside, SE1 2AP. *T:* (020) 7015 9500.

HANDS, Terence David, (Terry), CBE 2007; theatre and opera director; Director, Clwyd Theatr Cymru (formerly Theatr Clwyd), since 1997 (Artistic Consultant, 1996–97); *b* 9 Jan. 1941; *s* of Joseph Ronald Hands and Luise Berthe Kohler; *m* 1st, 1964, Josephine Barstow (marr. diss. 1967); 2nd, 1974, Ludmila Mikael (marr. diss. 1980); one *d*; partner, 1988–96, Julia Lintott; two *s*; 3rd, 2002, Emma (*née* Lucia). *Educ:* Woking Grammar Sch.; Birmingham Univ. (BA Hons Eng. Lang. and Lit.); RADA (Hons Dip.). Founder-Artistic Dir, Liverpool Everyman Theatre, 1964–66 (Hon. Dir, 1996); Artistic Dir, RSC Theatregoround, 1966–67; Associate Dir, 1967–77, Jt Artistic Dir, 1978–86, Chief Exec. and Artistic Dir, 1986–91, Director Emeritus, 1991–, RSC; Consultant Dir, Comédie Française, 1975–80. Vis. Prof., ATRiuM, Univ. of Glamorgan, 2007–. Associate Mem., RADA; Hon. Fellow, Shakespeare Inst. Jt Pres., Arvon Foundn, 1990–; Hon. FRWCMD (Hon. FWCMD 2002); Hon. Fellow, NE Wales Inst. of HE, 2002. Hon. DLitt: Birmingham, 1988; Liverpool, 2006; Hon. Dr Middlesex, 1997. Chevalier des Arts et des Lettres, 1973. *Director* (for Liverpool Everyman Theatre, 1964–66): The Importance of Being Earnest; Look Back in Anger; Richard III; The Four Seasons; Fando and Lis; *Artistic Director* (for RSC Theatregoround): The Proposal, 1966; The Second Shepherds' Play, 1966; The Dumb Waiter, 1967; Under Milk Wood, 1967; *directed for RSC:* The Criminals, 1967; Pleasure and Repentance, 1967; The Latent Heterosexual, 1968; The Merry Wives of Windsor, 1968, Japan tour, 1970; Bartholomew Fair, 1969; Pericles, 1969; Women Beware Women, 1969; Richard III, 1970, 1980; Balcony, 1971, 1987; Man of Mode, 1971; The Merchant of Venice, 1971; Murder in the Cathedral, 1972; Cries from Casement, 1973; Romeo and Juliet, 1973, 1989; The Bewitched, 1974; The Actor, 1974; Henry IV, Parts 1 and 2, 1975; Henry V, 1975, USA and European Tour, 1976; Old World, 1976; Henry VI parts 1, 2 and 3 (SWET Award, Dir of the Year, Plays and Players, Best Production, 1978), Coriolanus, 1977, European tour, 1979; The Changeling, 1978; Twelfth Night, The Children of the Sun, 1979; As You Like It, Richard II, 1980; Troilus and Cressida, 1981; Arden of Faversham, Much Ado About Nothing, 1982 (European tour and Broadway, 1984), Poppy, 1982; Cyrano de Bergerac, 1983 (SWET Best Dir award), Broadway, 1984 (televised, 1984); Red Noses, 1985; Othello, 1985; The Winter's Tale, 1986; Scenes from a Marriage, 1986; Julius Caesar, 1987; Carrie (Stratford and Broadway), 1988; (with John Barton) Coriolanus, 1989; Romeo and Juliet, 1989; Singer, 1989; Love's Labours Lost, 1990; The Seagull, 1990; Tamburlaine the Great, 1992 (Evening Standard Award, London Drama Critics Award, 1993); *directed for Royal National Theatre:* The Merry Wives of Windsor, 1995; *directed for Chichester Festival Theatre:* Hadrian VII, 1995; The Visit, 1995; *directed for Birmingham Rep.:* The Importance of Being Earnest, 1995 (transf. Old Vic, 1995); *directed for Theatr Clwyd/Clwyd Theatr Cymru:* The Importance of Being Earnest, (also Birmingham and Toronto), Equus, A Christmas Carol, 1997; The Journey of Mary Kelly, The Norman Conquests, 1998; Twelfth Night, Macbeth, Under Milk Wood, 1999; Private Lives, 2000; King Lear, Bedroom Farce, The Rabbit, 2001; Rosencrantz and Guildenstern are Dead, Betrayal, Romeo and Juliet, The Four Seasons, 2002; Blithe Spirit, The Crucible, Pleasure and Repentance, 2003; One Flew Over the Cuckoo's Nest, 2004; Troilus and Cressida, Night Must Fall, 2005; A Chorus of Disapproval, Memory, 2006; Arcadia, 2007; Cherry Orchard, 2007; *directed for Comédie Française:* Richard III, 1972 (Meilleur Spectacle de l'Année award); Pericles, 1974; Twelfth Night, 1976 (Meilleur Spectacle de l'Année award); Le Cid, 1977; Murder in the Cathedral, 1978; *directed for Paris Opéra:* Verdi's Otello, 1976 (televised 1978); *directed for Burg Theatre, Vienna:* Troilus and Cressida, 1977; As You Like It, 1979; *directed for Royal Opera:* Parsifal, 1979; *directed for Teatro Stabile di Genova, Italy:* Women Beware Women, 1981; *directed for Schauspielhaus, Zürich:* Arden of Faversham, 1992; *directed for Recklinghausen:* Buffalo Bill, 1992; *directed for Bremen:* Simon Boccanegra, 1992; *directed for National Theatre, Oslo:* Merry Wives of Windsor, 1995; The Pretenders, 1996; The Seagull, 1998; Sag Mir Wo Die Blumen Sind, Berlin, 1993; Hamlet, Marigny Theatre, Paris, 1994; Royal Hunt of the Sun, Tokyo, 1996; *recording:* Murder in the Cathedral, 1976; *television:* Cyrano de Bergerac, 1984. *Publications:* trans. (with Barbara Wright) Genet, The Balcony, 1971; Pleasure and Repentance, 1976; (ed Sally Beauman) Henry V, 1976; Hamlet (French trans.), 1994; contribs to Theatre 72, Playback. *Address:* c/o Clwyd Theatr Cymru, Mold, Flintshire CH7 1YA.

HANDS, Dr Timothy Roderick; Master, Magdalen College School, Oxford, since 2008; *b* 30 March 1956; *s* of Rory Hands and late Catherine Hands (*née* Walker); *m* 1988, Jane, *er d* of Ian and Ann Smart; two *s*. *Educ:* Emanuel Sch., Battersea; Guildhall Sch. of Music and Drama; King's Coll. London (BA 1st Cl. English Lang. and Lit.; William Stebbing Prize, 1976, J. S. Brewer Prize, 1977, EETS and L. M. Faithfull Prizes, 1978; AKC with Credit; 1st Leathes Prizeman, 1978; Coll. Jelf Medallist); St Catherine's Coll., Oxford (Sen. Schol.); Oriel Coll., Oxford (R. W. B. Burton Sen. Schol.; DPhil 1984). Stipendiary Lectr, Oriel Coll., Oxford, 1985–86; Asst Master, King's Sch., Canterbury, 1986–94 (Housemaster, Galpin's, 1990–94); Second Master, Whitgift Sch., 1994–97; Headmaster, Portsmouth Grammar Sch., 1997–2007. Conductor, Schola Cantorum of Oxford, 1982–85. Mem., Editl Bd, Conf. and Common Room, 2000–. Member: Admiralty Interview Bd, 1998–2004; Indep. State Sch. Partnership Forum, DFES, 2002–04. Mem., ISC Wkg Gp on Access to Indep. Educn, 2000–03. Mem., Ext. Adv. Bd, Oxford Univ. Faculty of English, 2006–. Headmasters' and Headmistresses' Conference: Sec., 2003–04, Chm., 2004–05, S Central Div.; Mem. Cttee, 2003–; Mem., 2003–, Co-Chair, 2005–, HMC/GSA Univs Cttee. Bishop's Rep., Portsmouth Cathedral Council, 2001–05. Founding Chm., Portsmouth Festivities, 2000–07 (Chm., Trustees and Bd of Dirs, 2006–07; Patron, 2007–). Trustee: Portsmouth Cathedral, 1999–2005; HMS Warrior 1860, 2003–. Gov., Alleyn's Sch., 2005–. *Publications:* A George Eliot Chronology, 1989; Thomas Hardy: distracted preacher, 1989; A Hardy Chronology, 1992; (contrib.) New Perspectives on Thomas Hardy, 1994; Thomas Hardy: writers in their time, 1995; (contrib.) The Achievement of Thomas Hardy, 2000; (contrib.) Oxford Reader's Companion to Hardy, 2000; Ideas to Assemble, 2006; Heads: expert advice for changing times, 2007; literary and musical articles, editions and reviews. *Recreations:* classical music, sport, especially Rugby and cricket, writing. *Address:* Magdalen College School, Oxford OX4 1BH. *T:* (01865) 242191. *Club:* East India.

HANDY, Charles Brian, CBE 2000; author; *b* 25 July 1932; *s* of Archdeacon Brian Leslie Handy and Joan Kathleen Herbert Handy (*née* Scott); *m* 1962, Elizabeth Ann Hill; one *s* one *d*. *Educ:* Oriel Coll., Oxford (BA 1956; MA 1966; Hon. Fellow, 1998); MIT (SM 1967). Shell Internat. Petroleum Co., 1956–65; Charter Consolidated Ltd, 1965–66; Sloan Sch. of Management, MIT (Internat. Faculty Fellow), 1967–68; London Business School, 1968–94; Prof., 1972–77; Vis. Prof., 1977–94; Fellow, 1994; Warden, St George's House, Windsor Castle, 1977–81. Chm., Royal Soc. for Encouragement of Arts, Manufactures and Commerce, 1987–89. FCGI 2000. Hon. Fellow: Inst. of Educn, London Univ., 1999; St Mary's Coll., Twickenham, 1999. Hon. DLitt: Bristol Poly., 1988; Open Univ., 1989; UEA, 1993; QUB, 1998; Middlesex, 1998; Exeter, 1999; Essex, Hull, Durham, 2000; Hon. LLD Dublin, 2006. *Publications:* Understanding Organizations, 1976, 4th edn 1999; Gods of Management, 1978, 2nd edn 1991; Future of Work, 1982; Understanding Schools as Organizations, 1986; Understanding Voluntary Organizations, 1988; The Age of Unreason, 1989; Inside Organizations, 1990; Waiting for the Mountain to Move, 1991; The Empty Raincoat, 1994; Beyond Certainty (essays), 1995; The Hungry Spirit, 1997; The New Alchemists, 1999; Thoughts for the Day, 1999; The Elephant and the Flea, 2001; Reinvented Lives, 2002; Myself and Other More Important Matters, 2006; The New Philanthropists, 2006. *Address:* 1A Fairhaven, 73 Putney Hill, SW15 3NT. *T:* (020) 8788 1610; Old Hall Cottages, Bressingham, Diss, Norfolk IP22 2AG. *T:* (01379) 687546; *e-mail:* candehandy@aol.com.

HANDY, Prof. Nicholas Charles, ScD; FRS 1990; Professor of Quantum Chemistry, Cambridge University, 1991–2004, now Professor Emeritus; Fellow, St Catharine's College, Cambridge, 1965–2004, now Fellow Emeritus; *b* 17 June 1941; *s* of late Kenneth George Edwards Handy and of Ada Mary Handy (*née* Rumming); *m* 1967, Elizabeth Carole Gates; two *s*. *Educ:* Clayesmore Sch., Dorset; St Catharine's College, Cambridge (MA, PhD); ScD Cantab 1996. Cambridge University: Salters' Fellow, 1967–68; Demonstrator, 1972–77; Lectr, 1977–89; Reader in Quantum Chemistry, 1989–91; Steward, 1971–88, Pres., 1994–97, St Catharine's Coll. Harkness Fellow, Johns Hopkins Univ., 1968–69; Vis. Prof., Berkeley, Bologna, Sydney, Georgia. Lennard-Jones Lectr, 1983, Boys-Rahman Lectr, 2004, RSC. Mem., Internat. Acad. of Quantum Molecular Science, 1988–. Dr *hc* Univ. de Marne-la-Vallée, France, 2000. Prize in Theoretical Chem., RSC, 1987; Schrodinger Medal, World Assoc. of Theoretically Oriented Chemists, 1997; Leverhulme Medal, Royal Soc., 2002. *Publications:* papers in learned jls of chem. phys. *Recreations:* gardening, bridge, philately, travel. *Address:* Department of Chemistry, Lensfield Road, Cambridge CB2 1EW. *T:* (01223) 336373.

HANGARTNER, John Robert Wilfred; Principal Director, Brett Cook Consulting Ltd, since 2000; Consultant Pathologist, Guy's and St Thomas' Hospitals, since 2002; *b* 5 Feb. 1955; *s* of John Hangartner and Ita Patricia (*née* Brett); *m* 1980, Jillian Mary Ansell; one *s* one *d*. *Educ:* Merchant Taylors' Sch., Northwood; Guy's Hosp. Med. Sch., Univ. of London (BSc Hons 1976; MB BS 1979); Open Univ. (MBA 1995). MRCS, LRCP 1979; MRCPath 1988, FRCPath 1997. Clin. Lectr in Histopathology, St George's Hosp. Med. Sch., 1983–88; Department of Health: SMO, 1988–91; Temp. PMO, 1991–93; PMO, 1993; Under Sec., and SPMO, 1993–97; CMO, Guardian Health Ltd, 1997–2000; Sen. Med. Advr, PPP healthcare, 1999–2000; Gp Med. Advr, Capio Healthcare (UK), 2001–03; Med. Advr, CS Healthcare, 2004–; Clin. Dir, Diagnostic and Therapeutic Services Directorate, 2004–05, Divisional Dir, Core Clinical Services Div., 2004–06, Guy's and St Thomas' NHS Foundn Trust. Chm., Hosp. Jun. Staff Cttee, BMA, 1984–85. FRSA 1994. *Recreations:* photography, singing. *Address:* Brett Cook Consulting Ltd, 11 Annesley Road, Blackheath, SE3 0JX. *T:* (020) 8319 3164, 07773 335608, *Fax:* (020) 8319 8775.

HANHAM, family name of **Baroness Hanham**.

HANHAM, Baroness *cr* 1999 (Life Peer), of Kensington in the Royal Borough of Kensington and Chelsea; **Joan Brownlow Hanham,** CBE 1997; JP; Chairman, St Mary's Hospital NHS Trust, 2000–07; *b* 23 Sept. 1939; *d* of Alfred Spark and Mary (*née* Mitchell); *m* 1964, Dr Iain William Ferguson Hanham; one *s* one *d*. *Educ:* Hillcourt Sch., Dublin. Royal Borough of Kensington and Chelsea: Mem. (C), 1970–; Mayor, 1983–84; Leader of Council, 1989–2000; Chairman: Town Planning Cttee, 1984–86; Social Services Cttee, 1987–89; Policy and Resources Cttee, 1989–2000. Chm., Policy Cttee, London Boroughs Assoc., 1991–95. An Opposition Whip, H of L, 2000–; Opposition spokesman for local govt, housing, planning and the regions, 2002–. Mem., Mental Health Act Commn, 1983–90; non-exec. Mem., NW Thames RHA, 1983–94; non-exec. Dir, Chelsea and Westminster Health Care NHS Trust, 1994–2000. Vice-Pres., Commonwealth Inst., 1998–2000. JP City of London Commn 1984, and Inner London Family Proceedings Court, 1992. Freeman, City of London, 1984. *Recreations:* music, travel. *Address:* c/o The Town Hall, Hornton Street, W8 7NX. *Club:* Hurlingham.

HANHAM, Prof. Harold John; Vice-Chancellor, University of Lancaster, 1985–95; *b* Auckland, New Zealand, 16 June 1928; *s* of John Newman Hanham and Ellie Malone; *m* 1973, Ruth Soulé Arnon, *d* of Prof. Daniel I. Arnon, Univ. of Calif, Berkeley. *Educ:* Mount Albert Grammar Sch.; Auckland UC (now Univ. of Auckland); Univ. of New Zealand (BA 1948, MA 1950); Selwyn Coll., Cambridge (PhD 1954). FRHistS 1960; FAAAS 1974. Asst Lectr to Sen. Lectr, in Govt, Univ. of Manchester, 1954–63; Prof. and Head of Dept of Politics, Univ. of Edinburgh, 1963–68; Prof. of History, 1968–73 and Fellow of Lowell House, 1970–73, Harvard Univ.; Prof. of History and Political Science, 1972–85 and Dean, Sch. of Humanities and Social Sci., 1973–84, MIT; Hon. Prof. of History, Univ. of Lancaster, 1985–. Mem., ESRC, 1986. Guggenheim Fellow, 1972–73. Hon. AM Harvard, 1968. John H. Jenkins Prize for Bibliography, Union Coll., 1978. *Publications:* Elections and Party Management, 1969, 2nd edn 1978; The Nineteenth-Century Constitution, 1969; Scottish Nationalism, 1969; Bibliography of British History 1851–1914, 1976. *Recreations:* discovering Canada, squash. *Clubs:* Oxford and Cambridge, Royal Commonwealth Society; St Botolph (Boston).

HANHAM, Sir Michael (William), 12th Bt *cr* 1667; DFC 1945; RAFVR; *b* 31 Oct. 1922; *s* of Patrick John Hanham (*d* 1965) and Dulcie (*d* 1979), *yr d* of William George Daffarn and *widow* of Lynn Hartley; *S* kinsman, Sir Henry Phelips Hanham, 11th Bt, 1973; *m* 1954, Margaret Jane (*d* 2007), *d* of W/Cdr Harold Thomas, RAF retd, and Joy (*née* MacGeorge); one *s* one *d*. *Educ:* Winchester. Joined RAF 1942, as Aircrew Cadet; served No 8 (Pathfinder) Gp, Bomber Command, 1944–45; FO 1945. At end of war, retrained as Flying Control Officer; served UK and India, 1945–46; demobilised, 1946. Joined BOAC, 1947, Traffic Branch; qualified as Flight Operations Officer, 1954; served in Africa until 1961; resigned, 1961. Settled at Trillinghurst Farmhouse, Kent and started garden and cottage furniture making business, 1963; moved to Wimborne, 1974; now engaged with upkeep of family house and estate. Governor, Wimborne Minster, 1977–. *Recreations:* conservation (Vice-Chm. Weald of Kent Preservation Soc., 1972–74, 1976–2000; Mem. Cttee, Wimborne Civic Soc., 1977–), preservation of steam railways, painting. *Heir:* *s* William John Edward Hanham [*b* 4 Sept. 1957; *m* 1st, 1982, Elizabeth Anne Keyworth (marr. diss. 1988), *yr d* of Paul Keyworth, Farnham and Mrs Keith Thomas, Petersfield; 2nd, 1996, Jennifer, *o d* of Harold Sebag-Montefiore, *qv*]. *Club:* Royal Air Force.

HANKES, Sir Claude, KCVO 2006; strategist and financial adviser; *b* 8 March 1949; name changed from Claude Dunbar Hankes-Drielsma by Deed Poll, 2006. *Educ:* Grey. With Manufacturers Hanover, 1968–72; Robert Fleming & Co. Ltd, 1972–77, Director 1974–77; Chm., Management Cttee, Price Waterhouse and Partners, 1983–89. Advr to Bd, (Corange) Boehringer Mannheim, 1988–94; Dep. Chm., Leutwiler and Partners Ltd, 1992–96; Chm., Shaw & Bradley Ltd, 1993–; Interim Chm., Roland Berger Strategy Consultants Ltd, 2003–05. Masterminded resolution to S African debt crisis, 1985–86; Chm., Adv. Cttee to Kingdom of Jordan on Strategic Economic Policy Issues, 1993–94; Advisor: to Iraq, 2003, to Iraq Governing Council, 2003–04, to Iraq on macro strategic issues, 2005–06; Trade Bank of Iraq, 2007–. Testified to US Congress on UN Oil for Food scandal, 2004. Trustee: Windsor Leadership Trust, 1998– (Chm., 2000–07); Hawthornden Internat. Retreat for Writers, 2008–. Hon. Fellow and Life Mem. Council, St George's House, Windsor Castle, 2006 (Trustee and Advr, 2000–06); Hon. Mem., Coll. of St George, Windsor Castle, 2006 (Hon. Fellow and Advr, 2002–06). Hon. Fellow, Corpus Christi Coll., Oxford. *Publication:* Nobel Industrier indep. report,

Stockholm, 1991. *Recreations:* hiking, photography, surfing. *Address:* 1 Berkeley Street W1J 8DJ; *e-mail:* sirclaude@officeofsirclaudehankes.co.uk. *Club:* Turf.

HANKES-DRIELSMA, Sir Claude Dunbar; *see* Hankes, Sir Claude.

HANKEY, family name of **Baron Hankey**.

HANKEY, 3rd Baron *cr* 1939, of The Chart, Surrey; **Donald Robin Alers Hankey;** *b* 12 June 1938; *s* of 2nd Baron Hankey, KCMG, KCVO and Frances Bevyl Stuart-Monteth (*d* 1957); *S* father, 1996; *m* 1st, 1963, Margaretha Thorndahl (marr. diss. 1974); 2nd, 1974, Eileen Désirée (marr. diss. 1994), *yr d* of Maj.-Gen. Stuart Battye, CB; two *d*; 3rd, 1994, June, *d* of late Dr Leonard Taboroff. *Educ:* Rugby; University Coll. London (DipArch). RIBA. Founder, 1973, Chm., 1973–2006, Consultant 2006–, Gilmore Hankey Kirke Ltd, architects, planners and conservation specialists (part of the GHK Group of cos incl. engrg, econs and mgt). Vice-Pres., ICOMOS (UK), 2002– (Vice-Chm., 1997–2002); Vice-Chm., Historic Bldgs Adv. Gp, MoD, 1999–2004. Founder and former Chm., All Party Gp on Architecture and Planning. Consultant to: World Bank; ODA; UN Develt Prog.; Council of Europe; British govt depts; owners of historic and private houses. FRSA. *Recreations:* piano, the arts, cultural anthropology, tennis, ski-ing. *Heir:* *b* Hon. Alexander Maurice Alers Hankey, PhD [*b* 18 Aug. 1947; *m* 1970, Deborah Benson (marr. diss. 1990)]. *Address:* 8 Sunset Road, SE5 8EA.

HANKINS, (Frederick) Geoffrey; Chairman, Fitch Lovell plc, 1983–90 (Chief Executive, 1982–89); Director, Booker plc, 1990–97; *b* 9 Dec. 1926; *s* of Frederick Aubrey Hankins and Elizabeth (*née* Stockton); *m* 1951, Iris Esther Perkins; two *d*. *Educ:* St Dunstan's College. Commissioned Army, 1946–48; J. Sainsbury management trainee, 1949–51, manufacturing management, 1951–55; Production/Gen. Manager, Allied Suppliers, 1955–62; Production Dir, Brains Food Products, 1962–69; Kraft Foods, 1966–69; Gen. Man., Millers, Poole, 1970–72, Man. Dir, 1972–82, Chm., 1975–86; Fitch Lovell: Dir, 1975–90; Chm., Manufacturing Div., 1975–84; Chairman: Robirch, 1975–84; Jus Rol, 1976–85; Blue Cap Frozen Food Services, 1975–84; Newforge Foods, 1979–84; Bells Bacon (Evesham), 1980–83; L. Noel, 1982–84; Dir, Salaison Le Vexin, 1980–90. Liveryman, Poulters' Co., 1982–. *Recreations:* genealogy, antiques, practical pursuits. *Address:* 15 Little Fosters, Chaddesley Glen, Canford Cliffs, Poole, Dorset BH13 7PB.

HANKINS, Prof. Harold Charles Arthur, CBE 1996; PhD; FREng, FIET; Principal, 1984–95, Vice-Chancellor, 1994–95, University of Manchester Institute of Science and Technology; *b* 18 Oct. 1930; *s* of Harold Arthur Hankins and Hilda Hankins; *m* 1955, Kathleen Higginbottom; three *s* one *d*. *Educ:* Crewe Grammar Sch.; Univ. of Manchester Inst. of Science and Technol. (BSc Tech, 1st Cl. Hons Elec. Engrg, 1955; PhD 1971). CEng, FREng (FEng 1993); FIET (FIEE 1975); AMCT 1952. Engrg Apprentice, British Rail, 1947–52; Electronic Engr, subseq. Asst Chief Engr, Metropolitan Vickers Electrical Co. Ltd, 1955–68; Univ. of Manchester Inst. of Science and Technology: Lectr in Elec. Engrg, 1968–71; Sen. Lectr in Elec. Engrg, 1971–74; Prof. of Communication Engrg, and Dir of Med. Engrg Unit, 1974–84; Vice Principal, 1979–81; Dep. Principal, 1981–82; Actg Principal, 1982–84. Non-executive Director: THORN EMI Lighting Ltd, 1979–85; Bodycote International, 1992–97; Dir, Inward, 1992–95; Mem. Bd, Trafford Park Develt Corp., 1996–98; Chairman: Trafford Park Manufacturing Inst., 1997–2002 (Hon. Pres., 2002–); Elliott Absorbant Products, 1999–. Instn of Electrical Engineers: Mem., NW Centre Cttee, 1969–77, Chm. 1977–78; Chm., M2 Exec. Cttee, 1979–82; Mem., Management and Design Div. Bd, 1980–82. Chm., Chemical Engrg, Instrumentation, Systems Engrg Bd, CNAA, 1975–81; Member: Cttee for Science and Technol., CNAA, 1975–81; Cttee of Vice-Chancellors and Principals, 1984–95; Parly Scientific Cttee, 1985–95; Engrg Council, 1993–95; Bd of Govs, Manchester Polytechnic, 1989–2001 (Hon. Fellow, 1984); Bd of Govs, South Cheshire Coll., 1990–96; Pres., Cheadle Hulme Sch., 1996–; Chm., Mil. Educn Cttee, Gtr Manchester Univs, 2002–07. Hon. DSc Manchester, 1995; DUniv Open, 1996; Hon. DEng UMIST, 1996. Reginald Mitchell Gold Medal, Assoc. of Engrs, 1990. *Publications:* 75 papers in learned jls; 10 patents for research into computer visual display systems. *Recreations:* military history, hill walking, music, choral work. *Address:* Rosebank, Kidd Road, Glossop, Derbyshire SK13 7PN. *T:* (01457) 853895.

HANKS, Patrick Wyndham, PhD; lexicographer; Associate Professor, Natural Language Processing Department, Masaryk University, Brno, since 2006; *b* 24 March 1940; *s* of Wyndham George Hanks and Elizabeth Mary (*née* Rudd); *m* 1st, 1961, Helga Gertrud Ingeborg Lietz (marr. diss. 1968); one *s* one *d*; 2nd, 1979, Julie Eyre (marr. diss. 1996); two *d*. *Educ:* Ardingly Coll., Sussex; University Coll., Oxford (BA, MA); Masaryk Univ., Brno (PhD). Editor, Dictionaries and Reference Books, Hamlyn Group, 1964–70; Man. Dir, Laurence Urdang Associates, 1970–79; Dir, Surnames Res. Project, Univ. of Essex, 1980–83; Project Manager, Cobuild, Univ. of Birmingham, 1983–87; Chief Editor, Collins English Dictionaries, 1987–90; Manager, then Chief Editor, Current English Dictionaries, OUP, 1990–2000; Adjunct Prof., Dept of Computer Sci., Brandeis Univ., 2002–06; Consultant, Electronic Dictionary of the German Lang., Berlin-Brandenburg Acad. of Scis, 2003–06. Vis. Scientist (corpus lexicography), AT&T Bell Labs, 1988–90; Chief Investigator, Hector project in corpus analysis, Systems Res. Centre, Digital Equipment Corp., Palo Alto, 1992–93; Vis. Prof., Masaryk Univ., Brno, Czech Repub., 2003. *Publications:* (ed) Hamlyn World Dictionary, 1971; (ed) Collins English Dictionary, 1979, 2nd edn 1986; (with J. Corbett) Business Listening Tasks, 1986; (managing editor) Collins Cobuild English Language Dictionary, 1987; (with F. Hodges) Dictionary of Surnames, 1988; (with F. Hodges) Dictionary of First Names, 1990; (ed jtly) Oxford Concise Dictionary of First Names, 1992, 2nd edn 1997; (ed jtly) New Oxford Dictionary of English, 1998; (ed) New Oxford Thesaurus of English, 2000; Dictionary of American Family Names, 2003; articles in Computational Linguistics, Corpus Linguistics, Computing and the Humanities, Internat. Jl of Lexicography, Onoma, Names, and other jls. *Recreations:* onomastics, bridge, hiking, punting.

HANKS, Tom; actor; *b* 9 July 1956; *s* of Amos Hanks and Janet; *m* 1st, 1978, Samantha Lewes (marr. diss. 1985); one *s* one *d*; 2nd, 1988, Rita Wilson; two *s*. *Educ:* Calif State Univ. *Films* include: Splash, 1984; Bachelor Party, 1984; The Money Pit, 1986; Dragnet, 1987; Big, 1988; Punchline, 1988; Turner and Hooch, 1989; The Bonfire of the Vanities, 1990; A League of their Own, 1992; Sleepless in Seattle, 1993; Philadelphia, 1994 (Best Actor Award, Berlin Film Fest.; Acad. Award for Best Actor); Forrest Gump, 1995 (Acad. Award for Best Actor); Apollo 13, 1995; (also writer and dir) That Thing You Do!, 1997; Saving Private Ryan, 1998; You've Got Mail, 1999; The Green Mile, 2000; Cast Away, 2001; Road to Perdition, 2002; Catch Me If You Can, 2003; The Ladykillers, The Terminal, 2004; The Da Vinci Code, 2006; Charlie Wilson's War, 2007; *television* includes: Bosom Buddies, 1980–82; co-prod., Band of Brothers, 2001. *Address:* c/o Creative Artists Agency, 2000 Avenue of the Stars, Los Angeles, CA 90067, USA.

HANLEY, Rt Hon. Sir Jeremy (James), KCMG 1997; PC 1994; chartered accountant, company director, lecturer and broadcaster; *b* 17 Nov. 1945; *s* of late Jimmy Hanley and of Dinah Sheridan; *m* 1973, Verna, Viscountess Villiers (*née* Stott); one *s*, one step *d*, and one *s* by previous marriage. *Educ:* Rugby. FCA 1969; FCCA 1980; FCIS 1980. Pe Marwick Mitchell & Co., 1963–66; Lectr in law, taxation and accountancy, Andersc Thomas Frankel, 1969, Dir 1969; Man. Dir, ATF (Jersey and Ireland), 1970–73; De Chm., The Financial Training Co. Ltd, 1973–90; Sec., Park Place PLC, 1977–83; Chm Fraser Green Ltd, 1986–90. Non-executive Director: ITE Gp, 1997–; Brass Tac Publishing, 1997–2000; GTECH Hldgs Corp., 2001–; Eur. Adv. Bd, Credit Lyonna 2000–05; NYMEX Europe, 2005–07; Willis Hldgs Inc., 2006–; Langbar Internat., 2006 CSS Stellar plc; Blue Hackle Ltd; Chairman: Internat. Trade and Investment Missior 1997–2002; AdVal Gp plc, 1998–2003; Braingames Network plc, 2000–02; Falcon Fur Mgt Ltd, 2000–03; Onslow Suffolk Ltd. Sen. Consultant, Kroll Associates, 2003–0 Mem. Adv. Bd, Talal Abu-Ghazaleh Internat., 2004–05. Dir, Arab-British Chamber Commerce, 1998–. Parly Advr to ICA, 1986–90. Contested (C) Lambeth Central, Ap 1978, 1979. MP (C) Richmond and Barnes, 1983–97; contested (C) Richmond Par 1997. PPS to Minister of State, Privy Council Office (Minister for CS and the Arts 1987–90, to Sec. of State for Envmt, 1990; Parly Under-Sec. of State, NI Office, 1990–9 (Minister for Health, Social Security and Agric., 1990–92, for Pol Develt, Communi Relns and Educn, 1992–93); Minister of State for the Armed Forces, MoD, 1993–9 Chm. of Cons. Party and Minister without Portfolio, 1994–95; Minister of State, FCC 1995–97. Mem., H of C Select Cttee on Home Affairs, 1983–87 (Mem., Subcttee c Race Relns and Immigration, 1983–87); Jt Vice-Chm., Cons. Back-bench Trade an Industry Cttee, 1983–87. Member: British-American Parly Gp, 1983–97; Anglo-Frenc Parly Gp, 1983–97; British-Irish Interparly Body, 1990; Life Member: CPA, 1983; IPU 1983; Chm., Cons Candidates Assoc., 1982–83. Member: Bow Gp, 1974– (Chm., Hom Affairs Cttee); European Movt, 1974–97; Mensa, 1968–. Vice-Pres., British-Irania Chamber of Commerce, 2002–06 (Chm., 2000–02). Freeman, City of London, 198 Liveryman, Chartered Accountants' Co., 1993– (Mem., Ct of Assts, 1996–; Maste 2005–06). *Recreations:* cookery, chess, cricket, languages, theatre, cinema, music, gol *Address:* 6 Buttsmead, Northwood, Middlesex HA6 2TL. *T:* (01923) 826675; Berry Hea House, Victoria Road, Brixham, Devon TQ5 9AR. *Clubs:* Garrick, Pilgrims, Lord Taverners, St Stephen's; Brixham Rotary, Brixham Yacht.

HANMER, Sir John (Wyndham Edward), 8th Bt *cr* 1774; JP; DL; *b* 27 Sept. 1928; *s* Sir (Griffin Wyndham) Edward Hanmer, 7th Bt, and Aileen Mary (*d* 1967), *er d* of Captai J. E. Rogerson; *S* father, 1977; *m* 1954, Audrey Melissa, *d* of Major A. C. J. Congrev two *s*. *Educ:* Eton. Captain (retired), The Royal Dragoons. Director: Chester Race Co 1978–2004; Ludlow Race Club, 1980–2004; Bangor-on-Dee Races, 1980–2003. Lord the Manor, Bettisfield, Co. of Wrexham. JP Flintshire, 1971; High Sheriff of Clwyd, 197 DL Clwyd, 1978. *Recreations:* horseracing, shooting. *Heir:* *s* (Wyndham Richard) Gu Hanmer [*b* 27 Nov. 1955; *m* 1986, Elizabeth A., *yr d* of Neil Taylor; two *s* one *d*]. *Addres* The Mere House, Hanmer, Whitchurch, Shropshire SY13 3DG. *T:* (01948) 83038 *Club:* Army and Navy.

See also Sir James Wilson, Bt.

HANN, Air Vice-Marshal Derek William; Director-General RAF Personal Service Ministry of Defence, 1987–89, retired; *b* 22 Aug. 1935; *s* of Claude and Ernestine Hanr *m* 1st, 1958, Jill Symonds (marr. diss. 1987); one *s* one *d*; 2nd, 1987, Sylvia Jean Holde *Educ:* Dauntsey's Sch., Devizes. Joined RAF, 1954; served in Fighter (65 Sqdn) an Coastal (201 and 203 Sqdns) Commands and at HQ Far East Air Force, 1956–68; MoD 1969–72 and 1975–77; Comd No 42 Sqdn, RAF St Mawgan, 1972–74; Comd RAF S Mawgan, 1977–79; RCDS 1980; Dir of Operational Requirements 2, MoD, 1981–84; of S, HQ No 18 Gp, 1984–87. *Recreations:* theatre, music, horology, campanology *Address:* 12 Westbourne Gardens, Hove BN3 5PP. *T:* (01273) 719362; *e-mai* hannderek@yahoo.co.uk.

HANNA, Brian Petrie, CBE 2000; Chairman: Northern Ireland Advisory Committee British Council, since 2004; Northern Ireland Local Government Staff Commission, sinc 2005; Member, Northern Ireland Public Service Commission, since 2006; *b* 15 Dec. 194 *m* 1968, Sylvia Campbell; one *d*. *Educ:* Royal Belfast Academical Instn; Belfast Coll. c Technol.; Ulster Coll., NI Poly. (DMS). FCIEH. Belfast Corporation: Clerical Asst, Cit Treasurer's Dept, 1959; Health Department: Clerical Officer, 1960–61; Pupil Publi Health Inspector, 1961–65; Public Health Inspector, 1965–73; Sen. Trng Advr, Food an Drink ITB, 1974–75; Principal Public Health Inspector, Eastern Gp Public Health Cttee Castlereagh BC, 1975–77; Belfast City Council: Dep. Dir, 1978–84, Dir, 1984–92 Envmtl Health Services; Dir, Health and Envmtl Services, 1992–94; Chief Exec 1994–2002. Royal Acad. of Engrg Vis. Prof. on Sustainable Develt, Ulster Univ 2003–05. Mem., UK Sustainable Develt Commn, 2000–04. Non-exec. Dir, Ivy Woo Properties Ltd, 2005–. Gov., Royal Belfast Academical Instn, 2001–; Mem. Senate, QUB 2002–. CCMI (CIMgt 2001). Hon. DSc (Econ) QUB, 2001. *Recreations:* apart from m family, the sport of hockey (Past Pres., Irish Hockey Union).

HANNA, Carmel; Member (SDLP) South Belfast, Northern Ireland Assembly, sinc 1998; *b* 26 April 1946; *d* of John and Mary McAleenan; *m* 1973, Eamon Hanna; one *s* thre *d*. *Educ:* Our Lady's Grammar Sch., Newry; Belfast City Hosp. (SRN); Royal Maternit Hosp. (SCM). Staff nurse in hosps in Belfast (Accident and Emergency), Guernsey, an Dublin, 1967–73; Staff Nurse, Musgrave Park Hosp., 1984–93; Social Services, South an East Belfast HSS Trust, 1993–98. Mem. (SDLP) Belfast CC, 1997–. Northern Irelan Assembly: Minister for Employment and Learning, 2001–02; SDLP health spokesperso Chair, Cttee on Standards and Privileges, 2007–; Member: Health Cttee, 1998–; Assembl and Exec. Review Cttee. Chm., All-Party Gp on Internat. Develt, 2000. *Recreations* gardening, travel, Irish history, cooking. *Address:* 12 Bawnmore Road, Belfast BT9 6LA *T:* (028) 9066 7577, 9068 3535.

HANNA, Prof. David Colin, PhD; FRS 1998; Professor of Physics, since 1988, an Deputy Director, Optoelectronics Research Centre, since 1989, University o Southampton; *b* 10 April 1941; *s* of James Morgan Hanna and Vera Elizabeth Hanna (*né* Hopkins); *m* 1968, Sarah Veronica Jane Heigham; two *s*. *Educ:* Nottingham High Sch. Jesus Coll., Cambridge (BA 1962); Southampton Univ. (PhD 1967). University o Southampton: Lectr, Dept of Electronics, 1967–78; Sen. Lectr, 1978–84; Reader, Dept o Physics, 1984–88. Consiglio Nazionale della Ricerca Vis. Fellow, Politecnico di Milano 1971; Alexander von Humboldt Fellow, Univ. of Munich, 1978–79. Dir-at-Large, 1996 Fellow, 1998, Optical Soc. of America. Max Born Medal and Prize, German Physical Soc. 1993; Quantum Electronics and Optics Prize, Eur. Physical Soc., 2000; Alexander vo Humboldt Res. Award, Alexander von Humboldt Foundn, 2000; Charles Hard Towne Award, Optical Soc. of Amer., 2003. *Publications:* Nonlinear Optics of Free Atoms an Molecules, 1979; more than 250 papers in learned jls on lasers and nonlinear optics *Recreations:* walking, climbing, gardening, cooking, sailing, music, theatre, travel. *Address* Optoelectronics Research Centre, University of Southampton, Southampton SO17 1BJ *T:* (023) 8059 2150.

HANNAH, Prof. Leslie; Visiting Professor, London School of Economics, since 2007; *b* 15 June 1947; *s* of Arthur Hannah and Marie (*née* Lancashire); *m* 1984, Nuala Barbara Zahedieh (*née* Hockton) (marr. diss. 1998), *e d* of Thomas and Deirdre Hockton; one *s* and two step *d. Educ:* Manchester Grammar Sch.; St John's and Nuffield Colleges, Oxford. MA, PhD, DPhil. Research Fellow, St John's Coll., Oxford, 1969–73; Lectr in economics, Univ. of Essex, 1973–75; Lectr in recent British economic and social history, Univ. of Cambridge, and Fellow and Financial Tutor, Emmanuel Coll., Cambridge, 1976–78; London School of Economics: Dir, Business History Unit, 1978–88; Prof. of Business Hist., 1982–97; Pro-Dir, 1995–97; Acting Dir, 1996–97; Dean, City Univ. Business Sch., subseq. Sir John Cass Business Sch., City of London, 1997–2000, Vis. Prof., 2000–03; Chief Exec., Ashridge Mgt Coll., 2000–03; Prof. of Economics, Univ. of Tokyo, 2004–07; Dir d'Etudes Associé, Ecole des Hautes Etudes en Scis Sociales, Paris, 2007. Vis. Prof., Harvard Univ., 1984–85. Director: NRG London Reinsurance, 1986–93; London Econs Ltd, 1991–2000. *Publications:* Rise of the Corporate Economy, 1976, 2nd edn 1983; (ed) Management Strategy and Business Development, 1976; (with J. A. Kay) Concentration in Modern Industry, 1977; Electricity before Nationalisation, 1979; Engineers, Managers and Politicians, 1982; Entrepreneurs and the Social Sciences, 1983; Inventing Retirement, 1986; (with M. Ackrill) Barclays, 2001; (with K. Wada) Invisible Hand Strikes Back, 2001; contribs to jls. *Recreation:* England. *Address:* 332 Lauderdale Tower, Barbican, EC2Y 8NA. *Club:* Institute of Directors.

HANNAH, His Honour William; a Circuit Judge, 1988–95; *b* 31 March 1929; *s* of William Bond Hannah and Elizabeth Alexandra Hannah; *m* 1950, Alma June Marshall; one *s* one *d. Educ:* Everton School, Notts. RAF 1947–52; Police Officer, 1952–77. Called to the Bar, Gray's Inn, 1970; in practise, NE Circuit, 1977–88; a Recorder, 1987–88; Resident Judge, Teesside, 1993–96; Dep. Chief Justice, Supreme Ct of St Helena, S Atlantic, 1996–2001. *Recreations:* golf, swimming, walking, theatre. *Address:* c/o New Court Chambers, 3 Broad Chare, Newcastle upon Tyne NE1 3DQ. *Club:* South Shields Golf.

HANNAM, Sir John (Gordon), Kt 1992; *b* 2 Aug. 1929; *s* of Thomas William and Selina Hannam; *m* 1st, 1956, Wendy Macartney; two *d*; 2nd, 1983, Mrs Vanessa Wauchope (*née* Anson). *Educ:* Yeovil Grammar Sch. Studied Agriculture, 1945–46. Served in: Royal Tank Regt (commissioned), 1947–48; Somerset LI (TA), 1949–51. Studied Hotel industry, 1950–52; Managing Dir, Hotels and Restaurant Co., 1952–61; Developed Motels, 1961–70; Chm., British Motels Fedn, 1967–74, Pres. 1974–80; Mem. Council, BTA, 1968–69; Mem. Economic Research Council, 1967–85. MP (C) Exeter, 1970–97. PPS to: Minister for Industry, 1972–74; Chief Sec., Treasury, 1974. Mem., Select Cttee on Procedure, 1993–97; Secretary: Cons. Parly Trade Cttee, 1971–72; All-Party Disablement Gp, 1974–92 (Co-Chm., 1992–97); 1922 Cttee, 1987–97; Mem., Govt Adv. Cttee on Transport for Disabled, 1983–97; Chairman: Anglo-Swiss Parly Gp, 1987–97; West Country Cons. Cttee, 1973–74, 1979–81; Cons. Party Energy Cttee, 1979–92; Arts and Leisure Standing Cttee, Bow Group, 1975–84; Vice-Chairman: Arts and Heritage Cttee, 1974–79; British Cttee of Internat. Rehabilitation, 1979–92. Captain: Lords and Commons Tennis Club, 1975–97; Lords and Commons Ski Club, 1977–82; Cdre, House of Commons Yacht Club, 1975. Mem., Snowdon Working Party on the Disabled, 1975–76; Chm. Trustees, Snowdon Awards Scheme, 1997–. Vice-President: Disablement Income Gp; Alzheimers Soc.; Council, Action Medical Research (formerly Action Research for Crippling Diseases); Disabled Motorists Gp; Disabled Drivers Assoc.; Rehabilitation UK, 2005– (Bd Mem., 1995–2005). Member: Bd, Nat. Theatre, 1979–92; Glyndebourne Festival Soc.; Council, British Youth Opera, 1989– (Chm., 1997–). Hon. MA Open, 1986. *Recreations:* music (opera), theatre, sailing (anything), ski-ing (fast), Cresta tobogganing (foolish), gardening; county tennis and hockey (Somerset tennis champion, 1953). *Address:* 85 Bromfelde Road, SW4 6PP. *Clubs:* Royal Yacht Squadron, All England Lawn Tennis, International Lawn Tennis.

HANNAN, Daniel John; Member (C) South East Region, England, European Parliament, since 1999; *b* 1 Sept. 1971; *s* of late Hugh R. Hannan and of Lavinia M. Hannan (*née* Moffat); *m* 2000, Sara Maynard; two *d. Educ:* Marlborough; Oriel Coll., Oxford (MA). Leader writer, Daily Telegraph, 1996–. Dir, European Res. Gp, 1994–99. *Publications:* Time for a Fresh Start in Europe, 1993; Britain in a Multi-Speed Europe, 1994; The Challenge of the East, 1996; A Guide to the Amsterdam Treaty, 1997; What if we vote No?, 2004; The Case for EFTA, 2005; Direct Democracy, 2006. *Recreation:* Shakespeare. *Address:* (office) The Coach House, Worthy Park, Winchester, Hants SO21 1AN. *Clubs:* Garrick, Pratt's.

HANNAN, Menna; *see* Richards, M.

HANNAY, family name of **Baron Hannay of Chiswick**.

HANNAY OF CHISWICK, Baron *cr* 2001 (Life Peer), of Bedford Park in the London Borough of Ealing; **David Hugh Alexander Hannay,** GCMG 1995 (KCMG 1986; CMG 1981); CH 2003; *b* 28 Sept. 1935; *s* of late Julian Hannay; *m* 1961, Gillian Rex; four *s. Educ:* Winchester; New Coll., Oxford (Hon. Fellow 2001). Foreign Office, 1959–60; Tehran, 1960–61; 3rd Sec., Kabul, 1961–63; 2nd Sec., FO, 1963–65; 2nd, later 1st Sec., UK Delegn to European Communities, Brussels, 1965–70; 1st Sec., UK Negotiating Team with European Communities, 1970–72; Chef de Cabinet to Sir Christopher Soames, Vice President of EEC, 1973–77; Head of Energy, Science and Space Dept, FCO, 1977–79; Head of Middle East Dept, FCO, 1979; Asst Under-Sec. of State (European Community), FCO, 1979–84; Minister, Washington, 1984–85; Ambassador and UK Permanent Rep. to Eur. Communities, Brussels, 1985–90; British Perm. Rep. to UN, 1990–95; retd from Diplomatic Service, 1995. British Govt Special Rep. for Cyprus, 1996–2003; Prime Minister's Personal Envoy to Turkey, 1998; EU Presidency Special Rep. for Cyprus, 1998. Mem., EU Select Cttee, 2002–06, Intergovtl Orgns Cttee, 2007, H of L; Vice-Chairman: All Party Parly Gp on UN, 2005–; All Party Parly Gp on EU, 2006–. Mem., UN Sec.-General's High Level Panel on Threats, Challenges and Change, 2003–04. Chm., UNA of UK, 2006–. Non-executive Director: Chime Communications, 1996–2006; Aegis, 2000–03; Mem., Bd, Salzburg Seminar, 2002–05. Mem., Bd, Centre for European Reform, 1997–; Mem., Council of Britain in Europe, 1999–2005. Chm., Internat. Adv. Bd, EDHEC Business Sch., 2003–; Mem., Internat. Adv. Bd, Judge Business Sch., Univ. of Cambridge, 2004–. Gov., Ditchley Foundn, 2005–. Mem. Court and Council, 1998–, Pro-Chancellor, 2001–06, Birmingham Univ. Hon. DLitt Birmingham, 2003. *Publications:* Cyprus: the search for a solution, 2004; New World Disorder: the UN after the Cold War – an insider's view, 2008. *Recreations:* travel, gardening, photography. *Address:* 3 The Orchard, W4 1JZ. *Club:* Travellers.

HANNAY, Elizabeth Anne Scott; *see* Prescott-Decie, E. A. S.

HANNEN, Rt Rev. John Edward; Bishop of Caledonia, 1981–2001; Rector of St Barnabas, Victoria, since 2001; *b* 19 Nov. 1937; *s* of Charles Scott Hannen and Mary Bowman Hannen (*née* Lynds); *m* 1977, Alana Susan Long; two *d. Educ:* McGill Univ. (BA); College of the Resurrection, Mirfield (GOE). Asst Curate, St Alphege's, Solihull, Warwicks, 1961–64; Priest in Charge, Mission to the Hart Highway, Diocese of Caledonia, BC, 1965–67; Priest, St Andrew's, Greenville, BC, 1967–68; Priest in Charge, Church of Christ the King, Port Edward, BC, 1969–71; Rector, Christ Church, Kincolith, BC, 1971–81; Regional Dean of Metlakatla, 1972–78; Acting Metropolitan, Ecclesiastical Province of BC and Yukon, 1993–94. Chm., Council of the North, Gen. Synod, Anglican Ch of Canada, 1993–95. Hon. DD Manitoba, 1997. *Recreation:* music. *Address:* Church of St Barnabas, PO Box 5252, Victoria, BC V8R 6N4, Canada.

HANNETT, John; General Secretary, Union of Shop, Distributive and Allied Workers, since 2004; *b* 23 June 1953; *s* of John and Mary Hannett; *m* 1979, Linda Sargeant; one *s* one *d. Educ:* St George's RC High Sch., Liverpool. Union of Shop, Distributive and Allied Workers: Area Organiser, 1985–90; Nat. Officer, 1990–97; Dep. Gen. Sec., 1997–2004. *Recreation:* football. *Address:* USDAW, 188 Wilmslow Road, Manchester M14 6LJ. *T:* (0161) 224 2804, *Fax:* (0161) 257 2566.

HANNIGAN, James Edgar, CB 1981; Deputy Secretary, Department of Transport, 1980–88; *b* 12 March 1928; *s* of late James Henry and Kathleen Hannigan; *m* 1955, Shirley Jean Bell (*d* 2001); two *d. Educ:* Eastbourne Grammar Sch.; Sidney Sussex Coll., Cambridge (BA). Civil Service, 1951; Asst Sec., Housing Div., Min. of Housing and Local Govt, 1966–70; Asst Sec., Local Govt Div., DoE, 1970–72. Under Sec. 1972; Regional Dir for West Midlands, DoE, 1972–75; Chm., West Midlands Economic Planning Bd, 1972–75; Dir of Housing 'B', DoE, 1975–78; Dep. Sec., 1978; NI Office, 1978–80. Mem., Internat. Exec. Cttee, PIARC, 1985–90. Trustee, Clapham Junction Disaster Fund, 1989–90.

HANNIGAN, Robert Peter; Security Adviser to the Prime Minister, and Head of Security, Intelligence and Resilience, Cabinet Office, since 2007; *b* 23 Feb. 1965; *s* of Peter Hannigan and Pamela Christine Hannigan (*née* Atkinson); *m* 2000, Celia Geraldine Hayes; one *s* one *d. Educ:* Wadham Coll., Oxford (MA 1987); Heythrop Coll., London (BD 1994); Inst. of Educn, London (PGCE 1998). Northern Ireland Office: Dep. Dir of Communications, 2000–01; Dir of Communications, 2001–04; Associate Pol Dir, 2004–05; Dir Gen., Political, 2005–07. *Address:* Cabinet Office, 70 Whitehall, SW1A 2AS; *e-mail:* ps.roberthannigan@cabinet-office.x.gsi.gov.uk.

HANNINGFIELD, Baron *cr* 1998 (Life Peer), of Chelmsford in the co. of Essex; **Paul Edward Winston White;** DL; farmer; Member (C), since 1970, and Leader, 1998–99 and since 2001, Essex County Council; *b* 16 Sept. 1940; *s* of Edward Ernest William White and Irene Joyce Gertrude White (*née* Williamson). *Educ:* King Edward VI Grammar Sch., Chelmsford (Nuffield Scholarship). Chm., 1989–92, Leader, Cons. Gp, 2001–, Essex CC. Chairman: Council, Local Educn Authorities, 1990–92; Eastern Area, FEFC, 1992–97. Dep. Chm., LGA, 1997–2001. Mem., EU Cttee of the Regions (Vice Pres., European People's Party, 1998–; Vice Pres., Transport and Information Soc. Commn, 1998–2000). Mem. Ct, Essex Univ., 1980–. DL Essex, 1991. *Publications:* many contribs to local govt jls. *Recreations:* gardening, wine and food, travel, walking the dog. *Address:* Pippins Place, Helmons Lane, West Hanningfield, Chelmsford, Essex CM2 8UW. *T:* (01245) 400229.

HANNON, Rt Rev. Brian Desmond Anthony; Bishop of Clogher, 1986–2001; *b* 5 Oct. 1936; *s* of late Ven. Arthur Gordon Hannon and of Hilda Catherine Stewart-Moore Hannon (*née* Denny); *m* 1964, Maeve Geraldine Audley (*née* Butler); three *s. Educ:* Mourne Grange Prep. School, Co. Down; St Columba's Coll., Co. Dublin; Trinity Coll., Dublin (BA Hons 1959, 1st Class Divinity Testimonium 1961). Deacon 1961, priest 1962; Diocese of Derry: Curate-Assistant, All Saints, Clooney, Londonderry, 1961–64; Rector of Desertmartin, 1964–69; Rector of Christ Church, Londonderry, 1969–82; RD of Londonderry, 1977–82; Diocese of Clogher: Rector of St Macartin's Cathedral, Enniskillen, 1982–86; Canon of Cathedral Chapter, 1983; Dean of Clogher, 1985. Chm., Council for Mission in Ireland, C of I, 1987–99. Pres., CMS (Ireland), 1990–96; Chm., Irish Council of Churches, 1992–94; Co-Chm., Irish Inter-Church Meeting, 1992–94; Mem., WCC Central Cttee, 1983–92. Chm. of Western (NI) Education and Library Bd, 1985–87 and 1989–91 (Vice-Chm., 1987–89 and 1991–93). Hon. MA TCD, 1962. *Publication:* (editor/author) Christ Church, Londonderry—1830 to 1980—Milestones, Ministers, Memories, 1980. *Recreations:* walking, music, travel, sport. *Address:* Drumconnis Top, 202 Mullaghmeen Road, Ballinamallard, Co. Fermanagh, N Ireland BT94 2DZ. *T:* (028) 6638 8557; *e-mail:* bdah@btinternet.com.

HANNON, Richard Michael; racehorse trainer; *b* 30 May 1945; *m* 1966, Josephine Ann McCarthy; two *s* four *d* (of whom two *s* one *d* are triplets). First trainer's licence, 1970; wins include: 2000 Guineas, 1973 (Mon Fils), 1987 (Don't Forget Me), 1990 (Tirol); Irish 2000 Guineas, 1987 (Don't Forget Me), 1990 (Tirol); leading trainer, 1992; trained record number of winners (182), 1993 season. *Address:* East Everleigh Stables, Marlborough, Wilts SN8 3EY.

HANON, Bernard; Officier, Ordre National du Mérite, 1980; Managing Director, Hanon Associés, since 1986; *b* 7 Jan. 1932; *s* of Max Hanon and Anne Smulevicz; *m* 1965, Ghislaine de Bragelongne; two *s. Educ:* HEC 1955; Columbia Univ. (MBA 1956; PhD 1962). Dir of Marketing, Renault Inc., USA, 1959–63; Asst Prof. of Management Sci., Grad. Sch. of Business, NY Univ., 1963–66; Head, Dept of Economic Studies and Programming, 1966–69, Dir of Corporate Planning and Inf. Systems, 1970–75, Régie Nat. des Usines Renault; Dir, Renault Automotive Ops, 1976; Executive Vice President: i/c Automobile Div., 1976–81; Renault Gp, 1981; Chm. and Pres., Régie Nationale des Usines Renault, 1981–85. *Address:* Hanon Associés, 31 rue François 1er, 75008 Paris, France. *Clubs:* Racing Club de France, Automobile Club de France (Paris); Golf de St Germain.

HANRAHAN, Brian; Diplomatic Editor, BBC Television, since 1997; *b* 22 March 1949; *s* of Thomas Hanrahan; *m* 1986; one *d. Educ:* Essex University (BA). BBC, 1971–: Far East correspondent, 1983–85; Moscow correspondent, 1986–89; Diplomatic correspondent, 1989–97. DU Essex, 1990. *Publication:* (with Robert Fox) I Counted Them All Out and I Counted Them All Back, 1982. *Address:* c/o World Affairs Unit, BBC TV Centre, Wood Lane, W12 7RJ.

HANRATTY, James Robert Anthony, RD 1987; Immigration Judge (formerly Adjudicator), since 1997; *b* 6 Feb. 1946; *s* of Dr J. F. Hanratty, OBE, KSG, and Irene Hanratty (*née* Belton); *m* 1975, Pamela Hoare; one *s* two *d. Educ:* Stonyhurst Coll.; Coll. of Law. Admitted solicitor, UK 1970, Hong Kong 1982. Criminal Appeal Office, Royal Courts of Justice, 1971–74; Lawyer, LCD, H of L, 1974–81; Sen. Crown Counsel, Attorney Gen.'s Chambers, Hong Kong, 1981–85; Asst Sec., Hd, Judicial Appts Div., LCD, 1985–88; Administrator and Chief Exec., Royal Courts of Justice, 1988–91; Dep. Legal Advr, then Legal Advr, to British Side of Sino-British Liaison Gp on Handover of Hong Kong to China, Hong Kong, 1991–97. Marking Examr in Criminal Law, Law Soc., 1971–81. Pres., Council of Immigration Judges for Eng., Wales and Scotland, 2001–03. Joined RNR as ordinary seaman, 1971; Lieut Comdr, 1994, retd. Member: RYA, 1990–; RNSA, 2002–. *Publications:* contrib. various articles to legal jls on internat. law aspects of the Hong Kong Handover and Immigration Law. *Recreations:* sailing, tennis, watching cricket, club life, family. *Address:* Immigration Appellate Authority, Taylor House, 88 Rosebery Avenue, EC1R 4QU. *Clubs:* Athenæum, Hurlingham (Cttee 2000–03);

RNVR Yacht (Cdre, 2002–04); Royal Southampton Yacht; Royal Hong Kong Yacht; Deauville Yacht.

HANRATTY, Mary Bridget, CBE 2003; Director of Nursing and Midwifery Education, Beeches Management Centre, Dungannon, Northern Ireland, 1997; *b* 15 Nov. 1943; *d* of Edward Holland and late Rose Anne Holland; *m* 1967, (Malachy) Oliver Hanratty; two *s*. *Educ:* BA, MSc. RGN; RMN; RNT. Dir, Nurse Educn, 1991–97; involved in professional regulation of nurses, midwives and health visitors. Mem., 1989–2002, Vice-Pres., 1998–2002, UKCC; Mem., NMC, 2001 (Vice-Pres., 2001–05). *Recreations:* foreign travel, crosswords, entertaining.

HANRETTY, Gerald Francis; QC (Scot.) 2002; *b* 13 April 1958; *s* of Peter Hanretty and Margaret Hanretty (*née* Soutar); *m* 1979, Moira Walker; two *s* one *d*. *Educ:* St Mirin's Acad., Paisley; Univ. of Glasgow (LLB). Solicitor, 1980–89; admitted Advocate, 1990; Advocate Depute, 2001–03; Chm. (pt-time), Mental Health Tribunal for Scotland, 2005–. *Recreations:* family interests, reading, Formula One racing. *Address:* c/o Advocates' Library, Parliament House, Edinburgh EH1 1RF.

HANROTT, Francis George Vivian, CBE 1981; Chief Officer, Technician Education Council, 1973–82; *b* 1 July 1921; *s* of late Howard Granville Hanrott and Phyllis Sarah Hanrott; *m* 1953, Eileen Winifred Appleton; three *d*. *Educ:* Westminster Sch.; King's Coll., Univ. of London (BA Hons). Served War, RN (Air Br.), 1940–45; Lieut (A) RNVR. Asst Master, St Marylebone Grammar Sch., 1948–50; Lectr, E Berks Coll. of Further Educn, 1950–53; Asst Educn Officer, Wilts, 1953–56; Staff Manager, GEC Applied Electronics Labs, 1956–59; Asst Educn Officer, Herts, 1959–66; Registrar and Sec., CNAA, 1966–73. Hon. MA Open Univ., 1977. *Address:* Coombe Down House, Salcombe Road, Malborough, Kingsbridge, Devon TQ7 3BX. *T:* (01548) 842721.

HÄNSCH, Dr Klaus; Member (SPD), European Parliament, since 1979 (President, 1994–97); *b* Sprottau, Silesia, 15 Dec. 1938; *s* of Willi Hänsch and Erna (*née* Sander); *m* 1969, Ilse Hoof. *Educ:* Univ. of Cologne (degree in Pol Sci. 1965); Univ. of Paris; Univ. of Berlin (PhD 1969). Escaped from Silesia to Schleswig-Holstein, 1945. Mil. Service, 1959–60. Res. Asst, Otto Suhr Inst., Free Univ. of Berlin, 1966–68; Ed., Dokumente, 1968–69; Advr to Rep. of FRG under Franco-German Treaty, 1969–70; Press Officer, 1970–79 and expert advr, 1977–79, to Minister for Sci. and Res., N Rhine/Westphalia; Lectr, Duisburg Univ., 1976– (Hon. Prof., 1994). European Parliament: Member: Foreign Affairs and Security and other cttees, 1979–94; For. Affairs, Human Rights, Common Security and Defence Policy Cttee, 1997–; Vice-Chm., Party of Eur. Socialists Gp, 1997–; Adv. Mem., Bundestag Cttee on EC issues, 1985–95; Chm., Delgn for relns with US, 1987–89. Member: SPD, 1964–; ÖTV (Union of Tspt and Public Service Workers). *Publications:* pamphlets, contribs to books, and many articles on politics and society in France and on issues relating to unification of Europe and European security policy. *Address:* European Parliament, Rue Wiertz, 1047 Brussels, Belgium; Europabüro, Kavelleriestrasse 16, 40213 Düsseldorf, Germany. *T:* (211) 13622254.

HÄNSCH, Dr Theodor Wolfgang; Director, Department of Laserspectroscopy, Max Planck Institute for Quantum Optics, since 1986; Professor of Physics, Ludwig Maximilians University, Munich, since 1986; *b* Heidelberg, 30 Oct. 1941. *Educ:* Helmholtz Gymnasium, Heidelberg; Univ. of Heidelberg (Physics Dip. 1966; PhD 1969). Asst Prof., Inst. of Applied Physics, Univ. of Heidelberg, 1969–70; Stanford University: NATO Postdoctoral Fellow, 1970–72; Associate Prof. of Physics, 1972–75; Prof. of Physics, 1975–86; Consulting Prof., 1988–; Exec. Dir, Max Planck Inst. for Quantum Optics, 1993–96 and 2003–04; Chm., Physics Dept, Ludwig Maximilians Univ., 2001–02. Visiting Professor: Coll. de France, 1978; Univ. of Kyoto, 1979; Univ. of Florence, 1979, 1995–; Fudan Univ., Shanghai, 1982; Ecole Normale Supérieure, Paris, 1992; Gordon Moore Dist. Schol., CIT, Pasadena, 2001. Member, Editorial Board: Applied Physics B, 1983–; Physics in Perspective, 1997–; Springer Series in Optical Scis, 1998–; Laser Physics Rev., 2004–. Fellow: APS, 1973; Optical Soc. of America, 1973. Member: Amer. Acad. Arts and Scis, 1983; Bavarian Acad. Arts and Scis, 1991; Berlin-Brandenberg Acad. Scis, 2005. Awards include: Alexander von Humboldt Sen. US Scientist Award, 1977; Michelson Medal, Franklin Inst., Philadelphia, 1986; Einstein Medal for Laser Sci., 1995; Arthur L. Schawlow Prize for Laser Sci., APS, 1996; Arthur L. Schawlow Award, Laser Inst. of America, 2000; Quantum Electronics and Optics Prize, Eur. Physical Soc., 2001; Alfried Krupp Prize for Sci., 2002; I. I. Rabi Award, IEEE, 2005; Frederic Ives Medal, Optical Soc. of America, 2005; Otto-Hahn Prize for Chemistry and Physics, 2005; (jtly) Nobel Prize in Physics, 2005. Order of Merit: Germany, 2003; Bavaria, 2003. *Publications:* numerous articles. *Address:* Faculty of Physics, Ludwig Maximilians University, Schellingstrasse 4/111, 80799 Munich, Germany. *T:* (89) 21803212, *Fax:* (89) 285192; *e-mail:* t.w.haensch@physik.uni.muenchen.de, t.w.haensch@lmu.de.

HANSEN, Alan David; football commentator, BBC, since 1992; *b* 13 June 1955; *s* of John and Anne Hansen; *m* 1980, Janette Rhymes; one *s* one *d*. *Educ:* Lornshill Acad. Professional footballer, Liverpool FC, 1977–91: League Champions, 1979, 1980, 1982, 1983, 1984, 1986, 1988, 1990; Capt., FA Cup winning team, 1986, 1988; winners: European Cup, 1978, 1981, 1984; League Cup, 1981, 1982, 1983, 1984. Presenter: Football's Dream Factory, BBC, 2001; Club or Country, BBC, 2003; Life After Football, BBC, 2005. *Publications:* Tall, Dark and Hansen, 1988; Matter of Opinion, 1999. *Clubs:* Hillside Golf; Southport and Birkdale Cricket.

HANSEN, Diana Jill; Director, Somerset House Trust, 2002–05; *b* 24 March 1948. *Educ:* Univ. of Sussex. HM Treasury, 1969–89; Dir, VAT Control, and a Comr, HM Customs and Excise, 1989–91; Asst Under-Sec. of State, Air, 1992, Finance, 1993, MoD (PE), Programmes, 1994, MoD; Comd Sec., HQ Land Comd, 1998–2002.

HANSEN, Prof. Jean-Pierre, DèS; FRS 2002; Professor of Theoretical Chemistry, 1997–2007, now Emeritus, and Fellow of Corpus Christi College, since 1997, University of Cambridge; *b* 10 May 1942; *s* of late Georges Hansen and Simone Flohr; *m* 1971, Martine Bechet; one *d*. *Educ:* Athénée Grand-Ducal de Luxembourg; Univ. de Liège (Licence en Sciences Physiques, 1964); Univ. de Paris (DèS 1969). CChem, FRSC 1998. Chargé de recherche, CNRS, France, 1967–73; Prof. of Physics, Univ. Pierre et Marie Curie, Paris, 1973–87; Directeur Adjoint, 1987–93, Prof. and Hd of Dept of Physics, 1987–97, Ecole Normale Supérieure, Lyons. Miller Prof., Univ. of Calif at Berkeley, 1992. Mem., Inst. Universitaire de France, 1992–97. Hon. Dr Liège, 2008. Grand Prix de l'Etat, Académie des Sciences, Paris, 1990; Prix Spécial, Soc. Française de Physique, 1998; Liquid Matter Prize, Eur. Physical Soc., 2005; Rumford Medal, Royal Soc., 2006. Chevalier de l'Ordre de la Couronne de Chêne (Luxembourg), 1997. *Publications:* (jtly) Theory of Simple Liquids, 1976, 3rd edn 2006; (ed jtly) Liquids, Freezing and the Glass Transition, 1991; (jtly) Basic Concepts for Simple and Complex Liquids, 2003; papers in internat. jls. *Recreations:* history of art, classical music, hill walking. *Address:* Department of Chemistry, Lensfield Road, Cambridge CB2 1EW. *T:* (01223) 336376.

HANSEN, Hon. John William, DCNZM 2008; a Judge, High Court of New Zealan 1995–2008; Executive Judge, South Island, 1997–2008; Senior Puisne Judge, 2005–08; Fairlie, NZ, 11 May 1944; *s* of William John and Jane Hansen; *m* 1966, Ann; one *s* one *Educ:* Wakari Prim. Sch., Dunedin; Dunedin North Intermediate Sch., Dunedin; Otag Boys' High Sch., Dunedin; Univ. of Otago (LLB 1968). Admitted solicitor, 1966, calle to the Bar, 1967, Supreme Court of NZ, admitted solicitor and called to the Bar, Suprem Court of WA, 1985; Clerk, Collier & Taylor, Dunedin, 1966; Solicitor, Aspinall, Joel Co., Dunedin, 1967; Barrister and Solicitor, John E. Farry, Dunedin, 1969; Partner, Joh E. Farry & Hansen, Dunedin, 1969–79; Hong Kong Judiciary, 1979–88: various Magistrate, Coroner, Dist Court Judge, Family Court Judge, Master of the Suprem Court; High Court of New Zealand: Master, 1988; Temp. Judge, 1993–95. Membe Rules Cttee and Rules Sub-Cttee, Hong Kong Supreme Court; Law Reform Comm Hong Kong; Rules Cttee of NZ, 1988–98; Dept for Courts Change Bd, 1997–200 Chm., NZ Case Mgt Cttee, 1996–2004; Mediator, Singapore Court Dispute Resolutio Centre, 1997–. Inns of Court Fellow, Lincoln's Inn and Inst. of Advanced Legal Studie London, 1998. Foundn Pres., Otago Br., NZ Legal Assoc. Manager: Hong Kong Crick XI to Malaysia and Singapore, 1983, to ICC Associate Mems Trophy, UK, 1986; N Team, Hong Kong Internat. Cricket Sixes Tournament, 2003; Mem., Code of Condu Commn, ICC, 2007–; Chm., Final Appeals Cttee, Rugby World Cup, 2007. Chm Kaikorai Rugby Football Club Inc., Dunedin; Capt. of Cricket, Kowloon Cricket Clu Hong Kong; Pres., Willows Cricket Club, Christchurch, 2003–. F. W. Guest Meml Lect Univ. of Otago, 2006. Former music reviewer, South China Morning Post, Hong Kon book reviewer, Christchurch Press. NZ Medal, 1990. *Publications:* contribs to various leg jls. *Recreations:* Rugby, cricket, hiking, reading, book reviewing, music, poetry, la reform, cooking, wine. *Address:* Totara, Wolffs Road, RD6, Rangiora 7476, Ne Zealand. *T:* (3) 3125843; *e-mail:* totaraa@xtra.co.nz.

HANSEN, Peter Allen Olsen; Senior Consultant, DRAKE Australia; Directo PALTECH Pty Ltd, since 1993; City West Water, Melbourne, since 2005; Souther Health Region, Victoria, since 2005; Chiropractors Registration Board of Victoria, sinc 2006; *b* 26 Feb. 1946; *s* of Allen and Bobbie Hansen; *m* 1989, Patricia, *d* of Raymond an Bridget Pegler; two *s* one *d*. *Educ:* Haileybury Coll., Melbourne; Monash Univ. (BEcons With Australian Consolidated Industries Ltd, 1973–2000: various posts, incl. Ge Manager, Corporate Affairs and Envmt, 1995–2000; Agent-General for Victoria i London, 2000–04. Mem., Australian Commn for the Future, 1991–94; Victorian Reli Cttee, 1986–93. Member: Australian Plastics Industry Assoc., 1987–90; Envmt Ctte Business Council of Australia, 1992–97. Keep Australia Beautiful Council, Vic, 1983–8 Life Mem., Nat. Gall. of Victoria. FAICD. Hon. Mem., Royal Over-Seas Leagu (Councillor, Vic). *Recreations:* pétanque, painting, visual and performing arts. *Address:* P Box 516, North Melbourne, Vic 3051, Australia.

HANSENNE, Michel; Member (Christian Social Party), European Parliamen 1999–2004; *b* 23 March 1940; *s* of Henri and Charlier Georgette Hansenne; *m* 1978, Mm Gabrielle Vanlandschoot; one *s* one *d*. *Educ:* Liège Univ. (Dr Law 1962; degree in Eco and Finance, 1967). Research work, Univ. of Liège, 1962–72. Mem. Belgian Parliamen 1974–89; Minister: for French Culture, 1979–81; for Employment and Labour, 1981–8 for Civil Service, 1988–89; Dir-Gen., ILO, 1989–99. Mem., EPP Gp, EP, 1999–200 *Publications:* Emploi, les scénarios du possible, 1985; Un garde-fou pour la mondialisatio le BIT dans l'après-guerre froide, 1999; articles in national and international jls. *Addres* 28 rue des Deux Eglises, 4120 Neupre, Belgium.

HANSFORD, John Edgar, CB 1982; Under-Secretary, Defence Policy and Matéri Group, HM Treasury, 1976–82, retired; *b* 1 May 1922; *s* of Samuel George Hansfor ISO, MBE, and Winifred Louise Hansford; *m* 1947, Evelyn Agnes Whitehorn (*d* 2005 one *s*. *Educ:* Whitgift Middle Sch., Croydon. Clerical Officer, Treasury, 1939. Served Wa of 1939–45: Private, Royal Sussex Regt, 1940; Lieutenant, Royal Fusiliers, 1943; serv in: Africa, Mauritius, Ceylon, India, Burma, on secondment to King's African Rifle demobilised, 1946. Exec. Officer, Treasury, 1946–50; Higher Exec. Officer, Regional B for Industry, Leeds, 1950–52; Exchange Control, Treasury, 1952–54; Agricultural Polic Treasury, 1954–57; Sen. Exec. Officer, and Principal, Defence Div., Treasury, 1957–6 Principal, Social Security Div., Treasury, 1961–66; Public Enterprises Div., 1966–6 Overseas Develt Div., 1967–70; Asst Sec., Defence Policy and Matériel Div., Treasur 1970–76; Under-Sec. in charge of Gp, 1976. *Recreations:* gardening, motoring.

HANSON, Brian John Taylor, CBE 1996; Joint Secretary, Panel of Reference of th Anglican Communion, 2005–08; Registrar and Legal Adviser to General Synod o Church of England, 1975–2001; Joint Principal Registrar, Provinces of Canterbury an York, 1980–2001; Registrar, Convocation of Canterbury, 1982–2001; *b* 23 Jan. 1939; *o* of Benjamin John Hanson and Gwendoline Ada Hanson (*née* Taylor); *m* 1972, Debora Mary Hazel, *yr d* of Lt-Col R. S. P. Dawson, OBE; two *s* three *d*. *Educ:* Hounslow Coll. Law Society's Coll. of Law; Univ. of Wales (LLM 1994). Solicitor (admitted 1963) an ecclesiastical notary; in private practice, Wilson Houlder & Co., 1963–65; Solicitor wit Church Comrs, 1965–99; Asst Legal Advr to General Synod, 1970–75; Dir of Lega Services, Archbishops' Council, 1999–2001. Reviewer, Commn for Healt Improvement, 2001–04; Mem., Healthcare Commn Appeals Panel, 2005–. Mem. Notaries Public Disciplinary Tribunal, 2001–. Member: Legal Adv. Commn of Gener Synod, 1980–2001 (Sec., 1970–86); Gen. Council, Ecclesiastical Law Soc., 1987–200 Chm., Chichester Dio. Bd of Patronage, 1998–; Vice-Pres., Chichester Diocesan Synod 2001–. Lay Canon, Gibraltar Cathedral, Dio. in Europe, 2003–. Pres., Soc. fo Maintenance of the Faith, 1999–. Guardian, Nat. Shrine of Our Lady of Walsingham 1984–; Fellow, Corp. of SS Mary and Nicholas (Woodard Schools), 1987–; Membe Council: St Luke's Hosp. for the Clergy, 1985–2001 (Archbishop's Nominee, St Luke' Res. Foundn, 1998–); Chichester Cath., 2000–. Governor: St Michael's Sch., Burto Park, 1987–94; Pusey House, Oxford, 1993–2005 (Vice-Pres., 2005–); Quainton Ha Sch., 1994–2005. Warden of the Lower Liberty, St Andrew, Holborn, 2002–. Freeman City of London, 1991; Liveryman, Co. of Glaziers and Painters of Glass, 1992–. FRS 1996; FInstD 1998. DCL Lambeth, 2001. *Publications:* (ed) The Canons of the Church o England, 2nd edn 1975, 5th edn 1993; (ed) The Opinions of the Legal Advisor Commission, 6th edn 1985; (ed) Atkin's Court Forms, ecclesiastical vol., 1992, 2nd ed 1996; (jtly) Moore's Introduction to English Canon Law, 3rd edn 1992. *Recreations:* th family, gardening, genealogy. *Address:* Quarry House, Horsham Road, Steyning, W Sussex BN44 3AA. *T:* (01903) 812214.

HANSON, Sir (Charles) Rupert (Patrick), 4th Bt *cr* 1918, of Fowey, Cornwall Revenue Assistant, HM Inspector of Taxes, since 1993; *b* 25 June 1945; *s* of Sir Charle John Hanson, 3rd Bt and late Patricia Helen (*née* Brind; subseq. Mrs Miéville); *S* father 1996; *m* 1977, Wanda Julia, *d* of Don Arturo Larrain, Santiago, Chile; one *s*. *Educ:* Eton Coll.; Polytech. of Central London. BA (CNAA) Modern Langs; Dip. in Technical and Specialised Trans. Technical, legal and commercial translator, 1977–83; TEFL (part-time) 1981–83; voluntary charity worker, 1984–85; Inland Revenue, 1986–. *Recreations:* classical music, writing poetry, tennis, walking. *Heir:* *s* Alexis Charles Hanson, *b* 25 March 1978.

HANSON, Rt Hon. David George; PC 2007; MP (Lab) Delyn, since 1992; Minister of State, Ministry of Justice, since 2007; *b* 5 July 1957; *s* of late Brian George Hanson and of Glenda Doreen (*née* Jones); *m* 1986, Margaret Rose Mitchell; two *s* two *d*. *Educ:* Verdin Comprehensive, Winsford, Ches.; Hull Univ. (BA Hons, PGCE). Vice-Pres., Hull Univ. Students' Union, 1978–79. Management trainee, Co-op. Union/Plymouth Co-op. Soc., 1980–82; with Spastics Soc., 1982–89; Dir, RE-SOLV (Soc. for Prevention of Solvent Abuse), 1989–92. Councillor: Vale Royal BC, 1983–91 (Leader, Lab Gp and Council, 1989–91); Northwich Town Council, 1987–91. Contested (Lab): Eddisbury, 1983; Delyn, 1987; Cheshire W (European Parlt), 1984. PPS to Chief Sec. to HM Treasury, 1997–98; an Asst Govt Whip, 1998–99; Parly Under-Sec. of State, Wales Office, 1999–2001; PPS to the Prime Minister, 2001–05; Minister of State, NI Office, 2005–07. *Recreations:* football, family, cinema. *Address:* House of Commons, SW1A 0AA. *T:* (020) 7219 5064; (constituency office) 64 Chester Street, Flint, Flintshire CH6 5DH. *T:* (01352) 763159.

HANSON, Derrick George; financial consultant; writer, director of companies; Chairman: Moneyguide Ltd, since 1978; Albany Investment Trust plc, 2000–04 (Director, 1980–2004); barrister; *b* 9 Feb. 1927; *s* of late John Henry Hanson and of Frances Elsie Hanson; *m* 1st, 1951, Daphne Elizabeth (*née* Marks) (*d* 1971); one *s* two *d*; 2nd, 1974, Hazel Mary (*née* Buckley) (*d* 1984); 3rd, 1986, Patricia (*née* Skillicorn). *Educ:* Waterloo Grammar Sch.; London Univ. (LLB (Hons)); Liverpool Univ. (LLM); Lancaster Univ. (MPhil). Called to the Bar, Lincoln's Inn, 1952. Joined Martins Bank Ltd, 1943; Chief Trustee Manager, Martins Bank Ltd, 1963; Dir and Gen. Manager, Martins Bank Trust Co. Ltd, 1968; Dir and Gen. Manager, Barclays Bank Trust Co. Ltd, 1969–76; Chairman: Barclays Unicorn Ltd, 1972–76; Barclays Life Assce Co. Ltd, 1972–76; City of London & European Property Co. Ltd, 1980–86; Key Fund Managers Ltd, 1984–87; Birmingham Midshires Bldg Soc., 1988–90 (Dir, 1982–90); British Leather Co. Ltd, 1993–94 (Dir, 1983–94); A. C. Morrell Employees' Trust, 1983–95; Director: Barclaytrust Property Management Ltd, 1971–76; Barclays Bank plc, Manchester Bd, 1976–77; Toye & Co. plc, 1981–92; James Beattie PLC, 1984–97; Sen. Adviser (UK), Manufacturers Hanover Trust Co., 1977–79; Adviser, Phillips Gp, Fine Art Auctioneers, 1977–82. Assessor, Cameron Tribunal, 1962; Dir, Oxford Univ. Business Summer Sch., 1971. Chm., Southport and Formby DHA, 1986–89; Member: NW Industrialists' Council, 1977–83; South Sefton Health Authority, 1979–82; Mersey RHA, 1982–86. Pres., Assoc. of Banking Teachers, 1979–88. Mem. Council, Liverpool Univ., 1980–84; Chm., Christian Arts Trust, 1980–86, 1996–2004. Mem., NW Regl Cttee, NT, 1990–96. Hon. FCIB 1987. Hon. Fellow, City Univ., 1977–86. *Publications:* Within These Walls: a century of Methodism in Formby, 1974; Service Banking, 1979; Moneyguide: The Handbook of Personal Finance, 1981; Dictionary of Banking and Finance, 1985; God and the Profits, 1998; Favourite Hymns: their stories and their meaning, vols I–X, 2003–08. *Recreations:* golf, gardening, hill-walking. *Address:* Fell Dale, Deepdale, Patterdale, Penrith, Cumbria CA11 0NR. *Clubs:* Royal Automobile; Formby Golf (Formby, Lancs).

HANSON, James Donald; Chairman, Georgica plc, since 2000; *b* 4 Jan. 1935; *s* of late Mary and Leslie Hanson; *m* 1st, 1959, Patricia Margaret Talent (marr. diss. 1977); two *s*; 2nd, 1978, Anne Barbara Asquith. *Educ:* Heath Grammar School, Halifax. ACA 1956, FCA 1966. Joined Arthur Andersen & Co., Chartered Accountants, 1958; established north west practice, 1966, Managing Partner, North West, 1968–82; Sen. Partner, UK, 1982–89; Man. Partner, Strategic Affairs and Communications, Andersen Worldwide, 1989–97. Chm., Northern Leisure plc, 1999–2000. Member: Internat. Operating Cttee, 1982–97; Internat. Board of Partners, 1985–97; Manchester Soc. of Chartered Accountants, 1967–81 (Pres., 1979); Council, CBI, 1982–97. Mem., Council and Court, Manchester Univ., 1982–; Chm., Manchester Univ. Superannuation Scheme. *Recreations:* ski-ing, tennis. *Address:* 4 Lowndes Street, SW1X 9ET.

HANSON, Sir John (Gilbert), KCMG 1995; CBE 1979; Warden, Green College, Oxford, 1998–2006; *b* 16 Nov. 1938; *s* of Gilbert Fretwell Hanson and Gladys Margaret (*née* Kay); *m* 1962, Margaret Clark (*d* 2003); three *s*. *Educ:* Manchester Grammar Sch.; Wadham Coll., Oxford (BA Lit. Hum. 1961, MA 1964; Hon. Fellow, 1997). Asst Principal, WO, 1961–63; British Council: Madras, India, 1963–66; ME Centre for Arab Studies, Lebanon, 1966–68; Rep., Bahrain, 1968–72; Dep. Controller, Educn and Science Div., 1972–75; Representative, Iran, and Counsellor (Cultural) British Embassy, Tehran, 1975–79; Controller, Finance Div., 1979–82; RCDS, 1983; Head, British Council Div. and Minister (Cultural Affairs), British High Commn, New Delhi, 1984–88; Dep. Dir-Gen., 1988–92; Dir-Gen., 1992–98. Patron, GAP, 1989–98. Member: Franco-British Council, 1992–98; UK-Japan 2000 Gp, 1993–98; Council, VSO, 1993–98; Chm., Bahrain-British Foundn, 1997–2005. Pres., British Skin Foundn, 1997–2002. Member Governing Council: Soc. for S Asian Studies, 1989–93; SOAS, 1991–99; Univ. of London, 1996–99. Trustee: Charles Wallace (India) Trust, 1998–2000; Research in Specialist and Elderly Care, 2008. FRSA 1993; CCMI (CIMgt 1993). Hon. Fellow: St Edmund's Coll., Cambridge, 1998; Green Coll., Oxford, 2006. Hon. DLitt Oxford Brookes, 1995; Hon. Dr: Humberside, 1996; Greenwich, 1996. *Recreations:* books, music, sport, travel. *Address:* c/o Green Templeton College, Oxford OX2 6HG. *Clubs:* Royal Over-Seas League, MCC; Gymkhana (Madras).

HANSON, Neil; Under Secretary, and Controller, Newcastle upon Tyne Central Office, Department of Health and Social Security, 1981–83; *b* 21 March 1923; *s* of late Reginald William Hanson and Lillian Hanson (*née* Benson); *m* 1st, 1950, Eileen Ashworth (*d* 1976); two *s*; 2nd, 1977, Margaret Brown-Smelt. *Educ:* City of Leeds Sch. Served War, 1942–46, N Africa, Sicily, Italy. Jun. Clerk, Leeds Social Welfare Cttee, 1939; Clerical Officer, 1948–50, Exec. Officer, 1950–56, Nat. Assistance Bd; Manager, Suez and Hungarian Refugee Hostels, 1956–59; Higher Exec. Officer, 1959–62, Sen. Exec. Officer, 1963–66, Nat. Assistance Bd; Principal, Min. of Social Security, 1967–73; Sen. Principal, 1973–76, Asst Sec., 1976–80, DHSS. *Recreations:* bowls, bridge, music, walking. *Address:* 7 Woodville Court, Leeds LS8 1JA. *T:* (0113) 266 7870.

HANSON, Richard Peter; Joint Founder and Chief Executive Officer, Doughty Hanson & Co., since 1989; *b* 21 Feb. 1956; *s* of Henry and Harriet Hanson; *m* 1993, Birgid Klein (marr. diss. 2007); one *s* one *d*. *Educ:* Univ. of Southampton (BSc Econ 1977). With Nat. Westminster Bank, 1977–83; County Bank, 1983–85; Standard Chartered Bank, 1985–89; Chairman: London Clubs Internat. Ltd, 1989–91; TAG Heuer SA, 1995–97; Impress Metal Packaging BV, 1997–; FL Selenia Sarl, 2000–04; Rank Hovis McDougall Ltd, 2000–05 (Dir, 2005–06); Balta Industries NV, 2004–; LM Glasfiber Hldg A/S, 2005–. *Recreations:* golf, fly fishing. *Address:* Doughty Hanson & Co., 45 Pall Mall, SW1Y 5JG. *T:* (020) 7663 9300.

HANSON, Sir Rupert; *see* Hanson, Sir C. R. P.

HANSON, Samantha; *see* Bond, S.

HANWORTH, 3rd Viscount *cr* 1936, of Hanworth, co. Middlesex; **David Stephen Geoffrey Pollock;** Bt 1922; Baron Hanworth 1926; Professor of Economics, University of Leicester; *b* 16 Feb. 1946; *er s* of 2nd Viscount Hanworth and of Isolda Rosamond, *yr d* of Geoffrey Parker; *S* father, 1996; *m* 1968, Elizabeth Liberty, *e d* of Lawrence Vambe, MBE; two *d*. *Educ:* Wellington Coll.; Guildford Tech. Coll.; Sussex Univ. (BA); Univ. of Southampton (MSc); Univ. of Amsterdam (DEcon). Lectr, Dept of Economics, 1971–92, Reader in Econometrics, 1992, QMC, then QMW, later QMUL. *Heir: nephew* Harold William Charles Pollock, *b* 30 April 1988.

HAPGOOD, Mark Bernard; QC 1994; *b* 2 April 1951; *m* 1978, Linda Fieldsend; two *d*. *Educ:* Nottingham Univ. (LLB). Called to the Bar, Gray's Inn, 1979, Bencher, 2003. *Publications:* (ed) Paget's Law of Banking, 10th edn 1989 to 13th edn 2007; (contrib.) Halsbury's Laws of England, vol. 3 (1): Banking, reissue, 2005; Bills of Exchange, vol. 4 (1), reissue, 2002. *Recreations:* running, 16th/17th century financial documents. *Address:* Brick Court Chambers, 7–8 Essex Street, WC2R 3LD. *Club:* St Enedoc Golf.

HARBAGE, William John Hirons; QC 2003; a Recorder, since 2000; *b* 7 Feb. 1960; *s* of late Thomas William (John) Harbage, solicitor, and of Patricia Margaret Harbage (*née* Amis); *m* 1986, Julia Mary Herschel Dunkerley; one *s* two *d*. *Educ:* Haileybury Coll.; St John's Coll., Cambridge (BA Hons Law 1982, MA 1986). Short Service Limited Commn, 7th Duke of Edinburgh's Own Gurkha Rifles, 1979. Called to the Bar, Middle Temple, 1983; in practice as barrister, specialising in criminal law, 1983–; Asst Recorder, 1999–2000. Chm. Appeal Bd, Prescription Medicines Code of Practice Authy, 2006–. *Recreations:* family, sport, food and wine. *Address:* 36 Bedford Row, WC1R 4JH. *T:* (020) 7421 8000; *e-mail:* wharbage@36bedfordrow.co.uk. *Club:* Luffenham Heath Golf.

HARBERD, Prof. Nicholas Paul, PhD; Sibthorpian Professor of Plant Science, University of Oxford, since 2008; Fellow, St John's College, Oxford, since 2008; *b* 15 July 1956; *s* of David and Muriel Harberd; *m* 1993, Jessica Ruth Harris; one *s* one *d*. *Educ:* Christ's Coll., Cambridge (MA; PhD 1981). Res. Project Leader, John Innes Centre, Norwich, 1990–2007. Hon. Prof., UEA, 2004–07. *Publications:* Seed to Seed, 2006; papers in learned jls incl. Nature, Science, Proc. NAS, Genes and Develt, Current Biol., Plant Cell. *Recreations:* music (playing piano, organ and Javanese gamelan music), walking. *Address:* Department of Plant Sciences, University of Oxford, South Parks Road, Oxford OX1 3RB.

HARBERTON, 11th Viscount *cr* 1791 (Ire.); **Henry Robert Pomeroy;** Baron Harberton 1783; *b* 23 April 1958; *s* of late Major Hon. Robert William Pomeroy and (Winifred) Anne (*née* Colegate); *S* uncle, 2004; *m* 1990, Caroline Mary, *d* of Jeremy Grindle; two *s*. *Heir: s* Hon. Patrick Christopher Pomeroy, *b* 10 May 1995.

HARBIDGE, Ven. Adrian Guy; Archdeacon of Bournemouth, since 2000; *b* 10 Nov. 1948; *s* of John and Pat Harbidge; *m* 1975, Bridget West-Watson; one *s* one *d*. *Educ:* Marling Sch., Stroud; St John's Coll., Durham (BA); Cuddesdon Coll., Oxford. Purser, Mercantile Marine, 1970–73. Deacon 1975, priest 1976; Curate, Romsey Abbey, 1975–80; Vicar: St Andrew's, Bennett Road, Bournemouth, 1980–86; Chandler's Ford, 1986–99; RD of Eastleigh, 1993–99; Archdeacon of Winchester, 1999–2000. Hon. Canon, St Peter's Cathedral, Tororo, Uganda, 2000. *Publication:* Those whom DDO hath joined together…, 1996. *Recreations:* landscape gardening, walking, cycling. *Address:* Glebe House, 22 Bellflower Way, Chandler's Ford, Hants SO53 4HN. *T:* (023) 8026 0955.

HARBISON, Dame Joan (Irene), DBE 2004 (CBE 1992); Member: Northern Ireland Judicial Appointments Commission, since 2005; Regulation and Quality Improvement Authority, since 2005; a Civil Service Commissioner, since 2006; *b* 21 Jan. 1938; *d* of Tom and Jane McAllister; *m* 1966, Jeremy Harbison; one *d*. *Educ:* Victoria Coll., Belfast; QUB (BA 1960; MSc (Educnl Psychol.) 1972). Sen. Lectr, Stranmillis Coll., Belfast, 1972–97. Deputy Chm., Eastern Health and Social Services Bd, NI, 1984–89; Chair, CRE (NI), 1997–99; Chief Comr, Equality Commn for NI, 1999–2005. Member: GDC, 1990–99; HFEA, 1990–96; Standing Adv. Commn on Human Rights, 1989–96. Chair, Age Concern NI. *Publications:* (with Jeremy Harbison) A Society Under Stress: children and young people in NI, 1980; (ed) Children of the Troubles, 1983; (ed) Growing Up in Northern Ireland, 1989. *Recreations:* travel, food and wine.

See also J. B. McAllister.

HARBISON, Dr Samuel Alexander, CB 1998; international health and safety consultant; HM Chief Inspector of Nuclear Installations, Health and Safety Executive, 1991–98; *b* 9 May 1941; *s* of Adam Harbison and Maude Harbison (*née* Adams); *m* 1st, 1964, Joyce Margaret Buick (marr. diss. 1991); three *d*; 2nd, 1991, Margaret Gail (*née* Vale) (*d* 2005). *Educ:* Queen's Univ., Belfast (Hons BSc); Univ. of California, Los Angeles (MSc); Univ. of London (PhD). Reactor Physicist, UKAEA, Windscale, 1962–64; Research and Teaching Asst, UCLA, 1964–66; Research at Rutherford High Energy Lab., Harwell, 1966–69; Sen. Lectr, Royal Naval Coll., Greenwich, 1969–74; Nuclear Installations Inspectorate, HSE, 1974–98. Chm., Defence Nuclear Safety Cttee, 2001–06. *Publications:* An Introduction to Radiation Protection (with A. Martin), 1972, 5th edn 2006; numerous sci. and tech. papers in learned jls. *Recreations:* gardening, music, walking. *Address:* Winnats, Whitehill Road, Meopham, Kent DA13 0NS.

HARBISON, Air Vice-Marshal William, CB 1977; CBE 1965; AFC 1956; RAF, retired; Vice-President, British Aerospace Inc., Washington, DC, 1979–92; *b* 11 April 1922; *s* of W. Harbison; *m* 1950, Helen, *d* of late William B. Geneva, Bloomington, Illinois; two *s*. *Educ:* Ballymena Academy, N Ireland. Joined RAF, 1941; 118 Sqdn Fighter Comd, 1943–46; 263, 257 and 64 Sqdns, 1946–48; Exchange Officer with 1st Fighter Group USAF, 1948–50; Central Fighter Estabt, 1950–51; 4th Fighter Group USAF, Korea, 1952; 2nd ATAF Germany: comd No 67 Sqdn, 1952–55; HQ No 2 Group, 1955; psc 1956; Air Min. and All Weather OCU, 1957; comd No 29 All Weather Sqdn Fighter Comd, Acklington and Leuchars, 1958–59; British Defence Staffs, Washington, 1959–62; jssc 1962; comd RAF Leuchars Fighter Comd, 1963–65; ndc 1965–66; Gp Capt. Ops: HQ Fighter Comd, 1967–68; No 11 Group Strike Comd, 1968; Dir of Control (Ops), NATCS, 1968–72; Comdr RAF Staff, and Air Attaché, Washington, 1972–75; AOC 11 Group, RAF, 1975–77. *Recreations:* flying, motoring. *Address:* 3292 Annandale Road, Falls Church, VA 22042, USA.

HARBORD, Clare Mary Petre; Director of Communications, Ministry of Justice, since 2007; *b* London, 25 Jan. 1957; *d* of late Captain Thomas Hornsby and of Hon. Patricia Mary Hornsby (*née* Dent, now Bence); *m* 1984, Robert Harbord (marr. diss. 2005); two *s* one *d*. *Educ:* Woldingham Sch., Surrey; Southampton Univ. (BA Hons Archaeol.). Journalist, IPC Mags, 1980–85; Sen. Account Manager, Valin Pollen, 1986–88; PR Manager, Corporate Communications, Eagle Star, 1988–99; Dir, Countrywide, Porter Novelli, 1999–2003; Hd of Communications, E.ON UK, 2004–07. FCIPR 2007. *Recreations:* archaeology, travelling, theatre, films, swimming. *Address:* Ministry of Justice, Selborne House, 54 Victoria Street, SW1E 6QW; *e-mail:* clare.harbord@justice.gsi.gov.uk.

HARBORD-HAMOND, family name of **Baron Suffield**.

HARBORNE, Peter Gale; HM Diplomatic Service, retired; Clerk Adviser to the European Scrutiny Committee, House of Commons, since 2004; *b* 29 June 1945; *s* of late

Leslie Herbert and Marie Mildred Edith Harborne; *m* 1976, Tessa Elizabeth Henri; two *s*. *Educ:* King Edward's Sch., Birmingham; Birmingham Univ. (BCom). Dept of Health, 1966–72; FCO, 1972–74; First Sec., Ottawa, 1974–75; First Sec., Commercial, Mexico City, 1975–78; Lloyd's Bank Internat., 1979–81; FCO, 1981–83; Head of Chancery, Helsinki, 1983–87; Dep. Head of Mission, Budapest, 1988–91; Counsellor, FCO, 1991–95; Ambassador, Slovak Republic, 1995–98; High Comr, Trinidad and Tobago, 1999–2004. *Recreations:* watching cricket, playing tennis, the arts, cross-country ski-ing. *Address:* House of Commons, 7 Millbank, SW1P 3JA. *Club:* MCC.

HARBOTTLE, Rev. Anthony Hall Harrison, LVO 1979; Priest-in-charge of East Dean with Friston and Jevington, 1995–96 (Rector, 1981–95); Chaplain to the Queen, 1968–95; *b* 3 Sept. 1925; *y s* of Alfred Charles Harbottle, ARIBA, and Ellen Muriel, *o d* of William Popham Harrison; *m* 1955, Gillian Mary, *o d* of Hugh Goodenough; three *s* one *d*. *Educ:* Sherborne Sch.; Christ's Coll., Cambridge (MA); Wycliffe Hall, Oxford. Served War in Royal Marines, 1944–46. Deacon 1952, priest 1953; Asst Curacies: Boxley, 1952–54; St Peter-in-Thanet, 1954–60; Rector of Sandhurst with Newenden, 1960–68; Chaplain of the Royal Chapel, Windsor Great Park, 1968–81. Founder Mem., Kent Trust for Nature Conservation, 1954; Mem., Green Alliance, 1984. County Chaplain, Royal British Legion (Sussex), 1982–2002. Special Life Mem., British Entomol and Natural Hist. Soc., 1998. FRES 1971. *Publications:* contribs to entomological jls, on lepidoptera. *Recreations:* butterflies and moths, nature conservancy, entomology, ornithology, philately, coins, Treasury and bank notes, painting, cooking, lobstering. *Address:* 44 Summerdown Road, Eastbourne BN20 8DQ.

HARBOTTLE, (George) Laurence; Consultant, Harbottle & Lewis, Solicitors (Senior Partner, 1955–95); *b* 11 April 1924; *s* of George Harbottle and Winifred Ellen Benson Harbottle. *Educ:* The Leys Sch., Cambridge; Emmanuel Coll., Cambridge (MA). Solicitor 1952. Served War: commnd RA, 1942; Burma and India; Temp. Captain; Adjt 9th Fd Regt, 1945–47. Theatre Companies: Chairman: Theatre Centre, 1959–88; Prospect, 1966–77; Royal Exchange (69), 1968–83; Cambridge, 1969–92; Director: The Watermill, 1970–75; The Bush (Alternative), 1975–77. Arts Council: Mem., 1976–77–78; Mem., Drama Panel, 1974–78; Chairman: Housing the Arts, 1977–78; Trng Cttee, 1977–78; Chm. of Govs, Central Sch. of Speech and Drama, 1982–99 (Vice Chm., 1977–82); Chm., ICA, 1986–90 (Dep. Chm., 1977–86). Hon. Solicitor: Soc. for Theatre Res.; Nat. Council for Drama Trng. Pres., Theatrical Management Assoc., 1979–85 (Hon. Vice-Pres., 1992–); Vice-President: Music Users Council, 1985–; Theatres Adv. Council, 1986–88; Theatres Nat. Cttee, 1986–91. Member: Justice Cttee on Privacy, 1970; Theatres Trust, 1980–99 (Chm., 1992–99); Equity Trust Fund, 2006– (Trustee, 1989–94). Gov., City Literary Inst., 1990–94; Trustee: Olivier Foundn, 1990–; Peggy Ramsay Foundn, 1992–. Hon. Fellow, Birkbeck Coll., Univ. of London, 2006. Award for theatrical achievement, TMA, 1996; award for services to drama trng, Conf. of Drama Schs, 2004. *Recreations:* works of art, gardening. *Address:* c/o Harbottle & Lewis, Hanover House, 14 Hanover Square, W1S 1HP.

HARBOUR, Malcolm; Member (C) West Midlands, European Parliament, since 1999; *b* 19 Feb. 1947; *s* of John and Bobby Harbour; *m* 1969, Penny Johnson; two *d*. *Educ:* Bedford Sch.; Trinity Coll., Cambridge (MA Mech Eng); Aston Univ. Business Sch. (Dip. Mgt Studies). CEng, MIMechE, 1975; FIMI 1984. Engr Apprentice, BMC Longbridge, 1967–69; Design and Develt Engr, BMC, 1969–72; Product Planning Manager, Rover-Triumph, 1972–76; Project Manager, Medium Cars, BL Cars, 1976–80; Austin-Rover: Director: Business Planning, 1980–82; Mkting, 1982–84; Sales, UK and Ireland, 1984–86; Overseas Sales, 1986–89; Founder Partner, Harbour Wade Brown, motor industry consultants, 1989–99; Founder Dir, Internat. Car Distrib. Prog., 1993–2006; Project Dir, 3 Day Car Prog., 1998–99. European Parliament: Cons. spokesman on internal market, 1999–2004; Member: Cttee for Legal Affairs and Internal Market, 1999–; Cttee for Industry, External Trade, Res. and Energy, 1999–2004; Cons. Delegn Bureau, 1999–2003; Delegn to Japan, 1999; Cttee for Internal Mkt and Consumer Protection, 2004–; Cttee for Industry, Technol., Res. and Energy, 2004–; Cttee Co-ordinator, EPP-ED Gp, 2004–; Vice-Pres., Sci. and Technol. Panel, 2002–; Co-Chm., Eur. Forum for the Automobile and Soc., 2000–; Chairman: Ceramics Industry Forum, 2000–; Cons. Technol. Forum, 2004–; Rapporteur: Eur. Commn Reform, 2000; Universal Service in Electronic Communications, 2001; Internal Market Strategy, 2003; Motor Vehicle Type Approval, 2007. Mem., Internat. Policy Cttee, Royal Soc., 2003–. Guardian, Birmingham Assay Office, 2007–. Gov., Eur. Internet Foundn, 2003–. *Publications:* reports on the car industry for DTI, OECD, etc. *Recreations:* choral singing, motor sport, travel, cooking. *Address:* Manor Cottage, Manor Road, Solihull, W Midlands B91 2BL. *T:* (0121) 711 3158; European Parliament, Rue Wiertz, 1047 Brussels, Belgium. *T:* (2) 2845132; *e-mail:* Malcolm.Harbour@europarl.europa.eu.

HARCOURT; *see* Vernon-Harcourt, family name of Baron Vernon.

HARCOURT, Prof. Geoffrey Colin, AO 1994; PhD, LittD; FASSA; AcSS; Fellow and College Lecturer in Economics, Jesus College, Cambridge, 1982–98, now Emeritus Fellow (President, 1988–89 and 1990–92); Reader (*ad hominem*) in the History of Economic Theory, Cambridge University, 1990–98, now Emeritus; *b* 27 June 1931; *s* of Kenneth Kopel Harcourt and Marjorie Rahel (*née* Gans); *m* 1955, Joan Margaret Bartrop; two *s* two *d*. *Educ:* Malvern Grammar Sch.; Wesley Coll., Melbourne; Queen's Coll., Univ. of Melbourne (BCom (Hons) 1954; MCom 1956; Hon. Fellow, 1998); King's Coll., Cambridge. PhD 1960, LittD 1988, Cantab. University of Adelaide: Lectr in Econs, 1958–62; Sen. Lectr, 1963–65; Reader, 1965–67; Prof. of Econs (Personal Chair), 1967–85, Prof. Emeritus 1988; Cambridge University: Lectr in Econs and Politics, 1964–66, 1982–90; Fellow and Dir of Studies in Econs, Trinity Hall, 1964–66. Leverhulme Exchange Fellow, Keio Univ., Tokyo, 1969–70; Visiting Fellow: Clare Hall, Cambridge, 1972–73; ANU, 1997; Sugden Fellow, Queen's Coll., Univ. of Melbourne, 2002; Visiting Professor: Scarborough Coll., Univ. of Toronto, 1977, 1980; Univ. of Melbourne, 2002; Hon. Prof., Univ. of NSW, 1997, 1999. Howard League for Penal Reform, SA Branch: Sec., 1959–63; Vice-Pres., 1967–74; Pres., 1974–80. Mem., Exec. Cttee, Campaign for Peace in Vietnam, 1967–75 (Chm., 1970–72). Mem., Aust. Labor Party Nat. Cttee of Enquiry, 1978–79. Pres., Econ. Soc. of Aust. and NZ, 1974–77; Mem. Council, Roy. Econ. Soc., 1990–95. FASSA 1971 (Exec. Cttee Mem., 1974–77). Lectures: Wellington-Burnham, Tufts Univ., USA, 1975; Edward Shann Meml, Univ. of WA, 1975; Newcastle, in Pol Economy, Univ. of Newcastle, NSW, 1977; Academy, Acad. of Social Scis in Aust., 1978; G. L. Wood Meml, Univ. of Melbourne, 1982; John Curtin Meml, ANU, 1982; Special Lectr in Econs, Manchester Univ., 1983–84; Nobel Conf., Minnesota, USA, 1986; Laws, Univ. of Tennessee at Knoxville, USA, 1991; Second Donald Horne Address, Melbourne, 1992; Sir Halford Cook, Queen's Coll., Melbourne, 1995; Kingsley Martin Meml, Cambridge, 1996; Annual Colin Clark, Univ. of Qld, 1997. AcSS 2003. Hon. Mem., European Soc. for Hist. of Economic Thought, 2004. Distinguished Fellow: Economic Soc. of Australia, 1996; Hist. of Econs Soc., 2004. Hon. LittD De Montfort, 1997; Hon. DCom Melbourne, 2003; Hon Dr rer. pol Fribourg, 2003. *Publications:* (with P. H. Karmel and R. H. Wallace) Economic Activity, 1967 (trans. Italian, 1969); (ed jtly) Readings in the Concept and Measurement of Income, 1969, 2nd edn 1986; (ed with N. F. Laing) Capital and Growth: Selected Readings, 197 (trans. Spanish, 1977); Some Cambridge Controversies in the Theory of Capital, 197 (trans. Italian, 1973, Polish and Spanish, 1975, Japanese 1980); Theoretical Controvers and Social Significance: an evaluation of the Cambridge controversies (Edward Shan Meml Lecture), 1975; (ed) The Microeconomic Foundations of Macroeconomics, 197 The Social Science Imperialists: selected essays (ed Prue Kerr), 1982; (ed) Keynes and h Contemporaries, 1985; (ed with Jon Cohen) International Monetary Problems an Supply-Side Economics: Essays in Honour of Lorie Tarshis, 1986; Controversies i Political Economy (selected essays, ed O. F. Hamouda), 1986; On Political Economis and Modern Political Economy (selected essays, ed C. Sardoni), 1992; Markets, Madne and a Middle Way (Second Annual Donald Horne Address), 1992; Post-Keynesian Essay in Biography: portraits of Twentieth Century political economists, 1993; (ed jtly) Th Dynamics of the Wealth of Nations, Growth, Distribution and Structural Change: essay in honour of Luigi Pasinetti, 1993; (ed jtly) Income and Employment in Theory an Practice: essays in memory of Athanasios Asimakopulos, 1994; Capitalism, Socialism an Post-Keynesianism: selected essays, 1995; (ed with P. A. Riach) A 'Second Edition' of Th General Theory, 2 vols, 1997; 50 Years a Keynesian and other essays, 2001; Selected Essay on Economic Policy, 2001; (ed) L'Économie Rebelle de Joan Robinson, 2001; (ed jtly Editing Economics: essays in honour of Mark Perlman, 2002; (with Prue Kerr) Joa Robinson: critical assessments of leading economists, 5 vols, 2002; (ed jtly) Capit Theory, 3 vols, 2005; The Structure of Post-Keynesian Economics: the core contribution of the pioneers, 2006; many articles in learned jls and chapters in edited books. *Recreations:* cricket, Australian rules football, running (not jogging), bike riding, reading, politic *Address:* Jesus College, Cambridge CB5 8BL; 43 New Square, Cambridge CB1 1EZ. *T* (01223) 360833. *Clubs:* Melbourne Cricket, South Australian Cricket Association.

HARCOURT, Geoffrey David, RDI 1978; DesRCA; freelance consultant designe since 1962; *b* 9 Aug. 1935; *s* of William and Barbara Harcourt; *m* 1965, Jean Mar Vaughan Pryce-Jones; one *s* one *d*. *Educ:* High Wycombe Sch. of Art; Royal Coll. of Ar DesRCA, Silver Medal 1960. FSIAD 1968. Designer: Latham, Tyler, Jensen, Chicag 1960–61; Jacob Jensen, Copenhagen, 1961; Andrew Pegram Ltd, London, 1961–6 consultant, Artifort, Holland, 1962–95 (domestic and business furniture designer; man models still in prodn including RCA Silver Medal chair of 1960 in Italy). Visiting Lecture High Wycombe Coll. of Art and Design, 1963–74; Leicester Polytechnic, 1982–93; Ex Assessor for BA Hons degrees, Kingston Polytechnic, 1974–77, Loughborough Coll. o Art and Design, 1978–81, Belfast Polytechnic, 1977–81 and Buckinghamshire Coll. o Higher Educn, 1982–85; Ext. Examnr, RCA, 1996–98. Chair design for Artifort awarde first prize for creativity, Brussels, 1978; Member: Design Awards Cttee, Design Counci 1979–80; Furniture Design Wkg Party, EDC, 1986–87; Chm., RSA Bursaries Ctte (Furniture Design Section, 1982–86, Ceramics Section, 1989–91, Woven Textile 1992–94, Footwear, 1996–97); approved consultant, Design Council 'Support for Desig initiative. Work exhibited: permanent collection, Stedelijk Mus., Amsterdam, 1967 Prague Mus. of Decorative Arts, 1972; Science Mus., London, 1972; Design Counci London and Glasgow, 1976 and 1981; Eye for Industry Exhibn, V&A, 1987; Nederland Textielmuseum, 1988; Manchester Prize exhibn, City Art Gall., 1988; St George's Hall Windsor Exhibn, Architecture Foundn, London, 1993; RCA Centennial Exhibn, 1996 Master, Faculty of RDI, 2003–05. Chm., Adv. Panel to Lord Lieutenant of Oxfordshire 1998–2000. FRSA 1979. Freeman, City of London; Liveryman, Worshipful Co. o Furniture Makers (Chm., Design Awards Cttee, 1994–97). JP Thame and Henley 1981–2000 (Chm., Youth Court Panel, 1993–95; Chm. Bench, 1996–98). *Recreations* painting, cooking, golf. *Address:* The Old Vicarage, Benson, Oxfordshire OX10 6SF *Clubs:* Leander (Assoc. Mem.); Goring and Streatley Golf.

HARCOURT, Michael Franklin; Senior Associate, Sustainable Development Researc Initiative (formerly Sustainable Development Research Institute), University of Britis Columbia, since 1996; Premier of British Columbia, 1991–96; Special Adviser to Premie of British Columbia, since 2003; *b* Edmonton, Alta, 6 Jan. 1943; *e s* of Frank and Stell Louise Harcourt; *m* 1971, Beckie Salo; one *s*. *Educ:* Sir Winston Churchill High Sch. Vancouver; University of British Columbia (LLB 1968). Lawyer, Vancouver, 1968–72 Alderman, 1972–80, Mayor, 1980–86, City of Vancouver. MLA (NDP) Vancouve Centre, 1986–91, Vancouver-Mt Pleasant, 1991–96; Leader of the Opposition, BC 1987–92. Director: Vancouver Port Authy, 1998–; Vancouver Airport Authy, 1998– Exec. Mem., Nat. Roundtable on Envmt and Economy, 1996–. *Publications:* (with Joh Lekich) Plan B: one man's journey from tragedy to triumph (autobiog.), 2004; City Making in Paradise, 2007. *Recreations:* tennis, golf, ski-ing, watching basketball an football. *Address:* 4707 Trafalgar Street, Vancouver, BC V6L 2M8, Canada.

HARCOURT-SMITH, Air Chief Marshal Sir David, GBE 1989; KCB 1984; DFC 1957; aviation consultant; Chairman, Chelworth Defence Ltd, since 1991; Controlle Aircraft, Ministry of Defence, Procurement Executive, 1986–89, retired; *b* 14 Oct. 1931 *s* of late Air Vice-Marshal G. Harcourt-Smith, CB, CBE, MVO, and of M. Harcourt-Smith; *m* 1957, Mary (*née* Entwistle); two *s* one *d*. *Educ:* Felsted Sch.; RAF College Commnd 1952; flying appts with Nos 11, 8 and 54 Squadrons; Staff Coll., 1962; OC No 54 Squadron, 1963–65; PSO to AOC-in-C, Tech. Training Comd, 1965–67; Defence Planning Staff, 1967–68; OC No 6 Squadron, 1969–70; Central Tactics and Trials Organisation, 1970–72; OC RAF Brüggen, 1972–74; Dir of Op. Requirements 1974–76; RCDS, 1977; Comdt, RAF Coll., Cranwell, 1978–80; Asst Chief of Air Staf (Op. Reqs), 1980–84; AOC-in-C, RAF Support Command, 1984–85. Dir, DESC 1991–. Gov., Downe House, 1993. *Recreations:* walking, golf. *Address:* c/o Barclays Bank 13 High Street, Shaftesbury, Dorset SP7 8JD. *Club:* Royal Air Force.

HARDAKER, Rev. Canon Ian Alexander; Clergy Appointments Adviser, 1985–98 Chaplain to the Queen, 1994–2002; *b* 14 May 1932; *s* of Joseph Alexander Hardaker and Edna Mary (*née* Theede); *m* 1963, Susan Mary Wade Bottom; two *s* two *d*. *Educ:* Kingston Grammar Sch.; Royal Military Acad., Sandhurst; King's Coll., London (BD, AKC). Commnd East Surrey Regt, 1952. Curate, Beckenham Parish Ch., 1960–65; Vicar of Eynsford and Rector of Lullingstone, 1965–70; Vicar of St Stephen's, Chatham, 1970–85 Rural Dean of Rochester, 1978–85. St Augustine's Medal, 1998. *Recreations:* walking, photography, family, gardening. *Address:* The Old Post Office, Huish Champflower, Wiveliscombe, Taunton, Somerset TA4 2EY.

HARDAKER, Paul James, PhD; FRMetS, CMet, CEnv; Chief Executive, Royal Meteorological Society, since 2006; *b* 14 Sept. 1966; *s* of Jack Hardaker and late Judith Mary Bolton (*née* James); *m* 2001, Lynwen Davies. *Educ:* Univ. of Essex (BSc 1st Cl. Hons 1988; PhD Maths 1992); Univ. of Portsmouth (Dip Mgt Studies 1998). FRMetS 1993; CMet 2001; CEnv 2005. Sen. Res. Fellow, Dept of Maths, Essex Univ., 1989–93; Meteorological Office, subseq. Met Office, 1993–2006; Sen. Scientist, then Hd of Internat. Business Unit, 1993–96; Weather Radar Prog. Manager and UK Hydrology Advr, 1996–99; Hd, Remote Sensing and Observations Develt, 1999–2002; Gp Hd, New Products and Services, 2002–04; Chief Govt Advr, 2004–06. Visiting Professor: Envmt Scis, Salford Univ., 1999–; Univ. of Reading, 2006–. Chm., Flood Risk from Extreme Events prog., NERC, 2005–. Ed., Atmospheric Sci. Letters, 1998–2006. Non-executive

Director: Reading PCT, 2005–07; Berks West PCT, 2007–. Interim Man. Dir, EcoConnect Ltd, 2004; non-exec. Dir, WeatherXchange, 2002–05. Trustee, RMetS, 1996–2006. *Publications:* contibutor to: Hydrometeorology and Climatology, 1997; Weather Radar Technology for Water Resources Management, 1997; Weather Radar: principle advances and applications, 2004; Known Risk, 2005; numerous contribs to learned jls. *Recreations:* tennis, gardening, dancing, music, golf. *Address:* Royal Meteorological Society, 104 Oxford Road, Reading RG1 7LS. *T:* (0118) 956 8500; *e-mail:* chiefexec@rmets.org.

HARDCASTLE, Prof. Jack Donald, CBE 1998; MChir (Cantab); FRCP, FRCS; Lead Clinician, Mid Trent Cancer Network, 1998–2005; Professor of Surgery, University of Nottingham, 1970–98, then Emeritus; *b* 3 April 1933; *s* of Albert Hardcastle and Bertha (*née* Ellison); *m* 1965, Rosemary Hay-Shunker; one *s* one *d*. *Educ:* St Bartholomew's Grammar Sch., Newbury; Emmanuel Coll., Cambridge (Senior Scholar 1954; BA, MA; Windsor Postgrad. Schol.); London Hospital (Open Scholarship 1955; MB, BChir, MChir (Distinction)). MRCP 1961; FRCS 1962; FRCP 1984. House Phys./Surg., Resident Accoucheur, London Hosp., 1959–60; Ho. Surg. to Prof. Aird, Hammersmith Postgraduate Hosp., 1961–62; London Hospital: Research Asst, 1962; Lectr in Surgery, 1963; Registrar in Surgery, 1964; Registrar in Surgery, Thoracic Unit, 1965; Sen. Registrar in Surgery, 1965; Sen. Registrar, St Mark's Hosp., London, 1968; Sen. Lectr in Surgery, London Hosp., 1968. Sir Arthur Sims Commonwealth Travelling Prof., RCS, 1985; Mayne Vis. Prof., Univ. of Brisbane, 1987. Member Council: RCS, 1987–99 (Dir, Raven Dept of Educn, 1994–99; Vice-Pres., 1995–97); Med. Protection Soc., 1995–2003 (Dir). Founder FMedSci 1998. Hon. FRCSGlas. Gold Medal, RCS, 2000. *Publications:* Isolated Organ Perfusion (with H. D. Ritchie), 1973; various scientific papers. *Recreations:* ski-ing, walking. *Address:* Field House, 32 Marlock Close, Fiskerton, Notts NG25 0UB.

HARDCASTLE, (Jesse) Leslie, OBE 1974; exhibition and museum consultant, since 1996; *b* 8 Dec. 1926; *s* of Francis Ernest Hardcastle and Dorothy Schofield; *m* 1968, Vivienne Mansel Richards; two *s*. *Educ:* St Joseph's College, Croydon. British Lion Film Productions, 1943–44; Royal Navy, 1944–47. British Film Inst., 1947–94; Telekinema Festival of Britain, 1951; London Film Fest. admin, 1958–91; Controller, NFT, 1968–91; Museum of the Moving Image: originator, 1981–88; Curator, 1988–94. A Governor, BFI, 2004–. Sec., Projected Picture Trust, 1994–. Pres., The Soho Soc.; Founder Mem., Soho Housing Assoc. *Recreations:* community work, theatre, music, cinema. *Address:* 37c Great Pulteney Street, W1R 3DE.

HARDCASTLE, Prof. William John, PhD; FBA 2004; FRSE; Research Professor and Director, Speech Science Research Centre (formerly Scottish Centre for Speech and Communication Science Research), Queen Margaret University (formerly Queen Margaret University College), Edinburgh, since 2003; *b* 28 Sept. 1943; *s* of late Gilbert William Hardcastle and Gwendolen Rose Hardcastle (*née* Barber); *m* 1969, Francesca MacDonald; two *s* one *d*. *Educ:* Brisbane Grammar Sch.; Univ. of Queensland (BA 1966; MA 1967); Univ. of Edinburgh (Dip. Phonetics 1968; PhD 1971). Lectr, Inst. für Phonetik, Univ. Kiel, 1972–74; University of Reading: Lectr, Dept of Linguistic Sci., 1974–81; Reader, 1981–89; Prof. of Speech Scis, 1989–93; Queen Margaret University College, Edinburgh: Hd, Dept of Speech and Lang. Scis, 1993–99; Dean: Health Scis, 1999–2002; Res., 2002–03. Vis. Lectr, Sch. of English and Linguistics, Macquarie Univ., Sydney, 1978–79. Member: Acad. Accreditation Panel, Royal Coll. of Speech and Lang. Therapists, 1988; Res. and Commercialisation Cttee, Univs Scotland, 1996–2007; Res. Policy and Adv. Cttee, SHEFC, 1999–2004; Linguistics Panel (sub-panel Phonetics), RAE 2001, 2001; Linguistics Panel, RAE 2008, 2005–. Member Editorial Board: Speech Communication, 1982–92; Clinical Linguistics and Phonetics, 1992–; Internat. Jl Lang. and Communication Disorders, 2001–. Consultant, Lawrence Erlbaum publishers, 2000–. Pres., Internat. Clinical Phonetics and Linguistics Assoc., 1991–2001. Fellow, Inst. Acoustics, 1996–2002; FRSA 1997; FRSE 2007. Mem., Norwegian Acad. of Sci. and Letters, 2007. Hon. FRCSLT 2003. Hon. DSc Napier, 2007. *Publications:* Physiology of Speech Production, 1976; (with P. Dalton) Disorders of Fluency and their Effects on Communication, 1977, 2nd edn 1989; (ed with A. Marchal) Speech Production and Speech Modelling, 1990; (ed with J. Laver) Handbook of Phonetic Sciences, 1997; (ed with N. Hewlett) Coarticulation: theory, data and techniques, 1999; contribs to conf. procs and vols of studies, res. papers in phonetic, linguistic and speech therapy jls. *Recreations:* walking the Scottish hills, badminton, golf, gardening. *Address:* Queen Margaret University, Musselburgh EH21 6UU. *T:* (0131) 474 0000; *e-mail:* whardcastle@qmu.ac.uk.

HARDEN, Peter William Mason; Publisher, Harden's, since 1991; *b* 1 June 1966; *s* of John and Susan Harden; *m* 1996, Francesca Elizabeth Freeman; two *s* one *d*. *Educ:* King's Sch., Chester; Trinity Coll., Cambridge (BA 1987). Saudi International Bank, 1987–90; publishing, mkt res. and restaurant reviewing, 1991–. *Publications:* Harden's London Restaurants, annually, 1992–; Harden's UK Restaurants, annually, 1999–; compiler and editor of 7 other Harden's Guides, incl. Harden's London Party, Conference and Event Guide, 1993– (now annually), and Harden's London Bars and Pubs, 1995, 3rd edn 2005; (ed) Harden's London Baby Guide, 2002, 2nd edn 2004. *Recreations:* gym, tennis. *Address:* Harden's Ltd, 14 Buckingham Street, WC2N 6DF. *T:* (020) 7839 4763, *Fax:* (020) 7839 7561; *e-mail:* ph@hardens.com. *Clubs:* Hawks (Cambridge); Leander.

See also R. J. M. Harden.

HARDEN, Richard John Mason; Publisher, Harden's, since 1991; *b* 26 July 1959; *s* of John and Susan Harden; *m* 2000, Jeanette Elizabeth Holland; two *d*. *Educ:* King's Sch., Chester; Christ's Coll., Cambridge (BA 1981). Called to the Bar, Middle Temple, 1982; Baring Brothers, 1983–84; Samuel Montagu, 1984–91; publishing, mkt res. and restaurant reviewing, 1991–. *Publications:* Harden's London Restaurants, annually, 1992–; Harden's UK Restaurants, annually, 1999–; London Party, Conference and Event Guide, 1993– (now annually). *Recreation:* wandering around cities. *Address:* Harden's Ltd, 14 Buckingham Street, WC2N 6DF. *T:* (020) 7839 4763, *Fax:* (020) 7839 7561; *e-mail:* mail@hardens.com.

See also P. W. M. Harden.

HARDENBERGER, (Ulf) Håkan; musician; international trumpet soloist; *b* 27 Oct. 1961; *s* of Åke and Mona Hardenberger; *m* 1986, Heidi Thomassen; two *s*. *Educ:* Paris Conservatory. Concerts as soloist with orchestras including LA Philharmonic, Chicago Symphony, Vienna Phil., London Phil., London Symphony, Philharmonia, Orch. des Bayerische Rundfunk, Accademia Nazionale di Santa Cecilia, NHK Symphony; festivals include Lucerne, Salzburg, BBC Proms. Hon. RAM 1992. *Address:* c/o KDS UK Ltd, 40 St Martin's Lane, WC2N 4ER.

HARDIE, family name of **Baron Hardie**.

HARDIE, Baron *cr* 1997 (Life Peer), of Blackford in the City of Edinburgh; **Andrew Rutherford Hardie;** PC 1997; a Senator of the College of Justice in Scotland and Lord of Session, since 2000; *b* 8 Jan. 1946; *s* of late Andrew Rutherford Hardie and of Elizabeth Currie Lowe; *m* 1971, Catherine Storrar Elgin; two *s* one *d*. *Educ:* St Mungo's Primary Sch., Alloa; St Modan's High Sch., Stirling; Edinburgh Univ. (MA, LLB Hons). Enrolled Solicitor, 1971; Mem., Faculty of Advocates, 1973; Advocate Depute, 1979–83; QC (Scot.) 1985; Lord Advocate, UK, 1997–99, Scotland, 1999–2000. Treasurer, 1989–94, Dean, 1994–97, Faculty of Advocates. Hon. Bencher, Lincoln's Inn, 1998. *Address:* 4 Oswald Road, Edinburgh EH9 2HF. *T:* (0131) 667 7542.

HARDIE, Dr Alexander, OBE 1990; consultant in security sector reform; *b* 5 March 1947; *s* of Alexander Merrie Hardie and Phyllis A. I. Hardie; *m* 1971, Jillian Hester Rowlands (marr. diss. 2004); one *s* two *d*. *Educ:* Aberdeen Grammar Sch.; Bristol Grammar Sch.; Univ. of Edinburgh (MA); Corpus Christi Coll., Oxford (DPhil). Jun. Research Fellow, Univ. of Bristol, 1972–73; HM Diplomatic Service, 1973–2001: FCO, 1973–77; First Secretary: Budapest, 1977–78; Bucharest, 1979–81; FCO, 1981–86; Lusaka, 1986–90; FCO, 1990–93; Counsellor, Pretoria, 1993–97; FCO, 1997–2001. Hon. Res. Associate in Classics, Royal Holloway, London Univ., 1998–2001; Fellow and Bursar, Oriel Coll., Oxford, 2001–04. *Publication:* Statius and the Silvae, 1983. *Recreations:* classical studies, golf. *Address:* The Old School House, Clava, Culloden, Inverness-shire IV2 5EL.

HARDIE, (Charles) Jeremy (Mawdesley), CBE 1983; Research Associate, Centre for Philosophy of Natural and Social Sciences, London School of Economics, since 2000; Chairman: Open Foundation, since 2004; Blanc Brasseries plc, since 2006; China Dialogue, since 2008; *b* 9 June 1938; *s* of Sir Charles Hardie, CBE; *m* 1st, 1962, Susan Chamberlain (marr. diss. 1976); two *d* two *s*; 2nd, 1978, Xandra, Countess of Gowrie (marr. diss. 1994), *d* of late Col R. A. G. Bingley, CVO, DSO, OBE; one *d*; 3rd, 1994, Kirsteen Margaret Tait. *Educ:* Winchester Coll.; New Coll., Oxford (2nd Cl. Hon. Mods, 1st Cl. Lit. Hum.); Nuffield Coll., Oxford (BPhil Econs). ACA 1965, Peat, Marwick, Mitchell & Co.; Nuffield Coll., Oxford, 1966–67; Jun. Res. Fellow, Trinity Coll., Oxford, 1967–68; Fellow and Tutor in Econs, Keble Coll., Oxford, 1968–75 (Hon. Fellow, 1998). Partner, Dixon Wilson & Co., 1975–82. Chairman: Nat. Provident Instn, 1980–89 (Dir, 1972–89, Dep. Chm., 1977); Alexander Syndicate Management Ltd, 1982–95; Radio Broadland Ltd, 1983–85 (Dir, 1983–90); D. P. Mann Underwriting Agency Ltd, 1983–99; W. H. Smith Gp, 1994–99 (Dir, 1988–99; Dep. Chm., 1992–94); Touch Clarity Ltd, 2001–04; Loch Fyne Restaurants Ltd, 2002–05. Director: Alexanders Discount Co. Ltd, 1978–87 (Dep. Chm., 1981–84; Chm., 1984–86); John Swire & Sons Ltd, 1982–98; Amdahl (UK) Ltd, 1983–86; Mercantile House Holdings Ltd, 1984–87; Additional Underwriting Agencies (No 3) Ltd, 1985–2007; Alexanders Laing & Cruickshank Gilts Ltd, 1986–87 (Chm., 1986); Northdoor Hldgs, 1989–93. Chm., Centre for Economic Policy Res., 1984–89; Treas., REconS, 1987–93; Dep. Chm., NAAFI, 1986–92 (Dir, 1981–). Member: Monopolies and Mergers Commn, 1976–83 (Dep. Chm., 1980–83); Council, Oxford Centre for Management Studies, 1978–85; Hammersmith Health Authority, 1982–83; Arts Council of GB, 1984–86; Peacock Cttee on Financing of BBC, 1985–86. Mem. Council, KCL, 1992–2004 (Dep. Chm., 1997–2004; FKC 2004). Contested Norwich South, (SDP) 1983, (SDP/Alliance) 1987. Trustee: Esmée Fairbairn Foundn, 1972– (Chm., 2003–07); Butler Trust, 1985–87; IPPR, 2000–; Somerset Hse Trust, 2001–; Internat. Hse, 2007–. *Recreations:* sailing, ski-ing, tennis, walking. *Address:* 23 Arlington Road, NW1 7ER. *T:* (020) 7387 1697.

HARDIE, Prof. (David) Grahame, PhD; FRS 2007; FRSE; FMedSci; Professor of Cellular Signalling, University of Dundee, since 1994; *b* 25 April 1940; *s* of Grahame McLean Hardie and Bertha Tyson Hardie; *m* 1977, Linda Margaret; four *s*. *Educ:* Downing Coll., Cambridge (BA 1971); Heriot-Watt Univ. (PhD). University of Dundee: Lectr, 1977–87; Sen. Lectr, 1987–90; Reader, 1990–94. Member: Physiol Medicine and Infections Bd, MRC, 1997–2001; Molecular and Cell Panel, Wellcome Trust, 2001–04; Internat. Conf. Grant and Short Visits Panel, Royal Soc., 2008–; Chairs and Prog. Grants Cttee, BHF, 2008–. FRSE 1998; FMedSci 2002. *Publications:* Biochemical Messengers, 1991; over 260 reviews, chapters and scientific papers. *Recreations:* sailing, hill walking. *Address:* Division of Molecular Physiology, College of Life Sciences, University of Dundee, Dundee DD1 5EH. *T:* (01382) 384253; *e-mail:* d.g.hardie@dundee.ac.uk.

HARDIE, Brig. Donald David Graeme, CVO 2008; TD 1968; JP; FIMMM; Lord-Lieutenant, Dunbartonshire (formerly Strathclyde Region, Districts of Dumbarton, Clydebank, Bearsden and Milngavie, Strathkelvin, Cumbernauld and Kilsyth), 1990–2007; Keeper of Dumbarton Castle, since 1996; *b* 23 Jan. 1936; *m* 1st, 1961, Rosalind Allan Ker (marr. diss. 1998); two *s*; 2nd, 1999, Sheena Roome. *Educ:* Larchfield, Blairmore and Merchiston Castle Schools. U.T.R. Management Trainee, 1956–59; F. W. Allen & Ker, 1960–61; with J. & G. Hardie & Co., 1961–2001, Dir, 1966–2001, Chm., 1990–2001; Man. Dir, 2001–05, Chm., 2005–, Preston Stretchform Ltd (formerly Hardie Mgt Consultants, then Hardie Internat. Sales); Director: Gilbert Plastics, 1973–76; Hardie Polymers, 1976–2001; Hardie Polymers (England), 1989–2001; Ronaash, 1988–2000; Tullochan Trust Ltd (Trustee, 1996). Commissioned 41st Field Regt RA, 1955; Battery Comdr, 277 (Argyll & Sutherland Highlanders) Regt, RA TA, 1966; CO GSV OTC, 1973; TA Colonel: Lowlands, 1976; DES, 1980; Scotland, 1985; Hon. Colonel: Glasgow and Lanarks Bn, ACF, 1990–2000; 105 Air Defence Regt, RA(V), 1992–99; ACF Brig. Scotland, 1983–87; Chm., RA Council for Scotland, 1996–2001. President: SSAFA, 1992–2007; Dunbartonshire Scout Council, and Girl Guides, 1994–2007; Boys Bde, Argyll and Lennox, 1999–2007; Highland RFCA, 2005–; Vice-Pres., Nat. Artillery Assoc., 2002–. Hon. Col Comdt, RA, 2003–07. Patron: Cornerstone, 1999–; Craighalbert Centre, 1999–. Chieftain, Loch Lomond Games, 1996–. JP Dumbarton, 1990. FIMMM (FPRI 1984). KStJ 1997. *Recreations:* ski-ing, sailing, shooting, fishing. *Address:* Boturich, by Alexandria, Dunbartonshire G83 8LX. *T:* (01389) 721818. *Clubs:* Royal Scots (Edinburgh); Royal Northern and Clyde Yacht.

HARDIE, Grahame; *see* Hardie, D. G.

HARDIE, Jeremy; *see* Hardie, C. J. M.

HARDIE, Michael John, OBE 1989; HM Diplomatic Service, retired; *b* 14 July 1938; *s* of John Thomas Hardie and Annie Smethurst; *m* 1st, 1967, Patricia Louisa Hulme (marr. diss. 1986); two *s* one *d*; 2nd, 1990, Jean Fish; one step *s* one step *d*. *Educ:* St Ambrose Coll., Hale Barns, Cheshire; De La Salle Coll., Salford. HM Forces (Intelligence Corps), 1957–59; FO 1959; served Bahrain, Elisabethville, Bathurst, Sofia, Vienna, Munich and Cape Town, to 1979; First Secretary, 1979; BMG Berlin, 1979–81; Malta, 1981–83; FCO, 1983–86; Lagos, 1986–89; Counsellor, 1988; New Delhi, 1990–93; High Comr, Gambia, 1994–95. *Recreations:* golf, music. *Address:* 4 Came Court, Woodhall Spa, Lincs LN10 6DA.

HARDIE, Philip Russell, PhD; FBA 2000; Hon. Professor of Latin Literature, Cambridge University and Senior Research Fellow, Trinity College, Cambridge, since 2006; *b* 13 July 1952; *s* of late Miles Clayton Hardie, OBE and Pauline Le Gros (*née* Clark); partner, Susan Elizabeth Griffith; two *s*. *Educ:* St Paul's Sch., London; Corpus Christi Coll., Oxford (MA); MPhil London; PhD Cantab 1990. Editl Asst, Oxford Dictionaries, 1977–80; P. S. Allen Jun. Res. Fellow, Corpus Christi Coll., Oxford, 1980–84; Guest Faculty appt in Classical Hist., Sarah Lawrence Coll., NY, 1984–85; Cambridge

University: Fellow and Coll. Lectr in Classics, Magdalene Coll., 1986–90; Fellow, 1990–2002, Emeritus Fellow, 2005, New Hall; Reader in Latin Lit., 1998–2002; Corpus Christi Prof. of Latin Lang. and Lit., and Fellow of Corpus Christi Coll., Oxford, 2002–06. *Publications:* Virgil's Aeneid: cosmos and imperium, 1986; The Epic Successors of Virgil, 1993; (ed) Virgil Aeneid 9, 1994; Virgil, 1998; Ovid's Poetics of Illusion, 2002; (ed) The Cambridge Companion to Ovid, 2002; (ed) The Cambridge Companion to Lucretius, 2007. *Recreations:* walking, music. *Address:* Trinity College, Cambridge CB2 1TQ. *T:* (01223) 338400.

HARDIE BOYS, Rt Hon. Sir Michael, GNZM 1996; GCMG 1996; QSO 2001; PC 1989; Governor General of New Zealand, 1996–2001; *b* Wellington, 6 Oct. 1931; *s* of Hon. Mr Justice Reginald Hardie Boys and Edith May (*née* Bennett); *m* 1957, Edith Mary Zohrab; two *s* two *d*. *Educ:* Wellington Coll.; Victoria Univ. (BA, LLB). Admitted Barrister and Solicitor, 1954; Partner, Scott Hardie Boys & Morrison, 1955–80; Chm., Legal Aid Bd, 1978–80; Judge of NZ High Court, 1980–89; Judge of the Court of Appeal, NZ, 1989–96. Pres., Wellington Dist Law Soc., 1979; Treas., NZ Law Soc., 1980. Hon. Bencher, Gray's Inn, 1994. Hon. Fellow, Wolfson Coll., Cambridge, 1995. Hon. LLD Victoria Univ. of Wellington, 1997.

HARDING, family name of **Baron Harding of Petherton**.

HARDING OF PETHERTON, 2nd Baron *cr* 1958, of Nether Compton; **John Charles Harding;** farmer, 1968–90; *b* 12 Feb. 1928; *s* of Field Marshal 1st Baron Harding of Petherton, GCB, CBE, DSO, MC, and Mary Gertrude Mabel (*d* 1983), *er d* of late Joseph Wilson Rooke, JP; *S* father, 1989; *m* 1966, Harriet, *d* of Maj.-Gen. James Francis Hare, CB, DSO; two *s* one *d*. *Educ:* Marlborough College; Worcester Coll., Oxford (BA). National Service, 1945–48; 2nd Lieut, 11th Hussars (PAO), 1947; demobilised, 1948; Oxford Univ., 1948–51; Regular Commn, 11th Hussars (PAO), 1953; retired from Army, 1968. *Recreations:* hunting, racing. *Heir:* *s* Hon. William Allan John Harding [*b* 5 July 1969; *m* 2000, Susannah, *o d* of Richard Ratcliff; two *s* one *d*]. *Address:* Myrtle Cottage, Lamyatt, near Shepton Mallet, Somerset BA4 6NP. *T:* (01749) 812292.

See also J. D. Penrose.

HARDING, Prof. Alan Paul, DPhil; Professor of Urban and Regional Governance and Director, Institute for Political and Economic Governance, University of Manchester, since 2007; *b* 14 Sept. 1958; *s* of late Alan Harding and of Ada Harding; *m* 2006, Karen Kauffman; one *s* one *d* (twins). *Educ:* Andrew Marvell Sen. High Sch., Hull; Middx Univ. (BA Humanities); LSE (MSc Econ); Nuffield Coll., Oxford (DPhil Politics). Res. Associate, Centre for Urban Studies, Univ. of Liverpool, 1988–92; Sen. Res. Fellow, 1992–94, Prof. of Urban Policy and Politics, 1994–99, European Inst. for Urban Affairs, Liverpool John Moores Univ.; Prof. of Urban and Regl Governance and Co-Dir, Centre for Sustainable Urban and Regl Futures, Univ. of Salford, 1999–2007. *Publications:* European Cities Towards 2000, 1994; Regional Government in Britain: an economic solution?, 1996; Is There a 'Missing Middle' in English Governance?, 2000; Changing Cities, 2005; Bright Satanic Mills, 2007; articles in Internat. Jl of Urban and Regl Res., Urban Studies, Urban Affairs Rev., British Jl of Political Sci., W European Politics, Govt and Policy, etc. *Recreations:* family driving holidays, flying alone, Thai food, pre-post-modern music, traipsing around lower division England watching Hull City. *Address:* Institute for Political and Economic Governance, Bridgeford Building, Oxford Road, Manchester M13 9PL. *T:* (0161) 275 0796, *Fax:* (0161) 275 0793; *e-mail:* alan.harding@manchester.ac.uk.

HARDING, Prof. Anthony Filmer, PhD; FBA 2001; FSA; Anniversary Professor of Archaeology, University of Exeter, since 2004; *b* 20 Nov. 1946; *s* of Edward Filmer Harding and Enid (*née* Price); *m* 1976, Lesley Eleanor Forbes; two *s*. *Educ:* Corpus Christi Coll., Cambridge (MA, PhD 1973). FSA 1983. Durham University: Lectr in Archaeol., 1973–88; Sen. Lectr, 1988–90; Prof. of Archaeol., 1990–2004. Pres., European Assoc. of Archaeologists, 2003–. *Publications:* (with J. M. Coles) The Bronze Age in Europe, 1979; The Mycenaeans and Europe, 1984; Henge Monuments and Related Sites of Great Britain, 1987; Die Schwerter im ehemaligen Jugoslawien, 1995; European Societies in the Bronze Age, 2000; (with J. Ostoja-Zagórski and others) Sobiejuchy: a fortified site of the Early Iron Age in Poland, 2004; (with R. Sumberová and others) Velim: violence and death in Bronze Age Bohemia, 2007; Warriors and Weapons in Bronze Age Europe, 2007. *Recreations:* music, gardening, walking. *Address:* Department of Archaeology, University of Exeter, North Park Road, Exeter EX4 4QE. *T:* (01392) 264520.

HARDING, Brian John; Director, Food and Farming Group, Department for Environment, Food and Rural Affairs, since 2007; *b* 24 Sept. 1952; *s* of Edwin Ernest Harding and Hilda Mary Harding; *m* 1975, Pamela Bliss; one *s* one *d*. *Educ:* Queen Elizabeth's Sch., Crediton; UCL (BA Geog.). Ministry of Agriculture, Fisheries and Food, subseq. Department for Environment, Food and Rural Affairs: admin trainee, 1974–78; Private Sec. to Minister of State, 1978–80; Sec. to Zuckerman Rev. of Badgers and Bovine TB, 1980–81; Hd of Branch, Food Standards Div., 1981–84; Desk Officer (Agric.), European Secretariat, Cabinet Office, 1984–85 (on secondment); First Sec. (Agric. and Commercial), Washington, 1985–89 (on secondment); Head: Regl Mgt Div., 1990–92; Milk Div., 1992–96; Financial Policy Div., 1996–2000; Director: Policy and Corporate Strategy Unit, 2000–03; Wildlife, Countryside and Land Use, 2003–06; Sustainable Food Chain, 2006–07. *Recreations:* walking, reading, gardening, painting in water colours. *Address:* Department for Environment, Food and Rural Affairs, Nobel House, 17 Smith Square, SW1P 3JR; *e-mail:* brian.harding@defra.gsi.gov.uk.

HARDING, Daniel John; conductor; Music Director, Mahler Chamber Orchestra, since 2003; *b* 31 Aug. 1975; *s* of Dr John Harding and Caroline Harding (*née* Cameron); *m* 2000, Beatrice Muthelet; one *s* one *d*. *Educ:* Chetham's Sch. of Music, Manchester; Trinity Hall, Cambridge. Assistant to Music Director: CBSO, 1993–94; Berlin Philharmonic Orch., 1995–96; Principal Conductor, Trondheim SO, 1997–2000; Music Director: die Deutsche Kammerphilharmonie, Bremen, 1999–2003; Swedish Radio SO, 2007–; Principal Guest Conductor, LSO, 2006–. Débuts: BBC Proms, 1996; Berlin Philharmonic Orch., 1996; Royal Opera Hse, Covent Garden, 2002. Has made numerous recordings. Chevalier, Ordre des Arts et des Lettres (France), 2002. *Recreations:* match-going Manchester United supporter, playing Championship Manager. *Address:* c/o Askonas Holt Ltd, Lincoln House, 300 High Holborn, WC1V 7JH. *T:* (020) 7400 1700, *Fax:* (020) 7400 1799.

HARDING, Prof. Dennis William, MA, DPhil; FRSE; Abercromby Professor of Archaeology, University of Edinburgh, 1977–2007; *b* 11 April 1940; *s* of Charles Royston Harding and Marjorie Doris Harding. *Educ:* Keble Coll., Oxford (BA, MA, DPhil). Assistant Keeper, Dept of Antiquities, Ashmolean Museum, Oxford, 1965–66; Lecturer in Celtic Archaeology, 1966, Sen. Lectr, 1975–77, Univ. of Durham; University of Edinburgh: Dean, Faculty of Arts, 1983–86; Vice-Principal, 1988–91. Member: Board of Trustees, National Museum of Antiquities of Scotland, 1977–85; Ancient Monuments Board for Scotland, 1979–83; Scottish Postgrad. Studentships Awards Cttee, 1981–2001 (Chm., 1997–2001). FRSE 1986. *Publications:* The Iron Age in the Upper Thames Basin, 1972; The Iron Age in Lowland Britain, 1974; (with A. J. Challis) Later Prehistory fro the Trent to the Tyne, 1975; ed and contrib., Archaeology in the North: Report of th Northern Archaeological Survey, 1976; ed and contrib., Hillforts: later prehistor earthworks in Britain and Ireland, 1976; Prehistoric Europe, 1978; (with I. M. Blake an P. J. Reynolds) An Iron Age Settlement in Dorset: excavation and reconstruction, 199 (with T. N. Dixon) Dun Bharabhat, Cnip: an Iron Age settlement in West Lewis, 200 (with S. M. D. Gilmour) The Iron Age Settlement at Beirgh, Riof, Isle of Lewis, 200 The Iron Age in Northern Britain, 2004; The Archaeology of Celtic Art, 2007.

HARDING, Derek William; Executive Secretary, Royal Statistical Society, 1986–92; 16 Dec. 1930; *o s* of late William Arthur Harding; *m* 1954, Daphne Sheila, *yr d* of la Reginald Ernest Cooke; one *s* one *d*. *Educ:* Glendale Grammar Sch., London; Univ. Bristol (BSc). FInstP, CPhys, CEng. Develt Engr, Pye Ltd, 1954–56; Sen. Physics Maste Thornbury Grammar Sch., Bristol, 1956–60; Sen. Lectr in Physical Science, St Paul Coll., Cheltenham, 1960–64; Asst Organiser, Nuffield Foundn Science Teaching Projec 1964–67; joined staff of Instn Metallurgists, 1967, Registrar-Sec., 1969–76; Sec.-Gen British Computer Soc., 1976–86. Pres., Rotary Club of Enfield, 2000–01. *Recreation:* of shore sailing. *Address:* 29 The Mansions, Compton Street, Eastbourne, E Sussex BN2 4AP. *T:* (01323) 411942.

HARDING, Sir (George) William, KCMG 1983 (CMG 1977); CVO 1972; HM Diplomatic Service, retired; *b* 18 Jan. 1927; *s* of late Lt Col G. R. Harding, DSO, MB and Grace Henley (*née* Darby); *m* 1955, Sheila Margaret Ormond Riddel (*d* 2002); four *Educ:* Aldenham; St John's College, Cambridge. Royal Marines, 1945–48. Entered HM Foreign Service, 1950; served (other than in London) in Singapore, 1951–52; Burm 1952–55; Paris, 1956–59; Santo Domingo, 1960–63; Mexico City, 1967–70; Pari 1970–74; Ambassador to Peru, 1977–79; Asst Under-Sec. of State, FCO, 1979–8 Ambassador to Brazil, 1981–84; Dep. Under-Sec. of State, FCO, 1984–86. Mem Trilateral Commn, 1988–93. Vis. Fellow, Harvard Centre for Internat. Affairs, 198 Chairman: First Spanish Investment Trust, 1987–96; Thai-Euro Fund, 1988–97; Britis Thai Business Gp, 1995–97; Dir, Lloyds Bank Plc, 1988–93. Chairman: Margaret Me Amazon Trust, 1988–94; Anglo-Peruvian Soc., 1987–89; Brazilian Chamber Commerce in Britain, 1988–91. Vice-Pres., RGS, 1991–93; Mem. Council, RIIA 1988–94. *Address:* La Dreyrie, 24510 Pezuls, France.

HARDING, Hazel, CBE 2006; Leader, Lancashire County Council, since 2001; *b* 1 Dec. 1946; *d* of Trevlyn William Sanderson and Florence Ward Sanderson; *m* 197 Steven Harding (marr. diss. 2002); four *d*. Member (Lab): Lancashire CC, 1985– (Chm 1997–98; Chm., Lancs Educn Authy, 1998–2001); Rossendale BC, 1990–94, 1995–9 Board Member: Burnley Healthcare Trust, 1997–2002; Lancs LSC, 2000–06. Loc Government Association: Member: Educn Exec., 1998–2005; Children's Bd, 2005– Founder Mem., Gen. Teaching Council of England, 2000. *Recreations:* avoiding the gym playing with grandchildren. *Address:* 21 Hawthorne Meadows, Crawshawbooth Rossendale, Lancs BB4 8BF. *T:* (01706) 215767; *e-mail:* hazel.harding@cc.lancscc.gov.uk

HARDING, Rev. James Owen Glyn; Director and Chief Executive, National Societ for the Prevention of Cruelty to Children, 1995–2000, now Vice-President; *b* 18 Oc 1942; *s* of Walter James Harding and Elizabeth May Harding; *m* 1965, Sally Goldie; one two *d*. *Educ:* Pinner Grammar Sch.; Univ. of Sussex (BA); Univ. of Exeter (Home Offic Letter of Recognition in Child Care); NE Oecumenical Course. Royal Borough of Kensington and Chelsea: Child Care Officer and Sen. Child Care Officer, Children Dept, 1968–71; Area Officer and Asst Dir, Social Services Dept, 1971–85; Nationa Society for the Prevention of Cruelty to Children: Dir, Child Care, 1986–89; Dep. Chie Exec. and Dir of Children's Services, 1989–95. Mem., Commn of Inquiry on death of Kimberley Carlisle, 1987. Ordained deacon, 2006, priest, 2007; non-stipendiary Ass Curate, Holy Redeemer, Acomb and York Workplace Chaplaincy, 2006–. *Publication* (jtly) A Child in Mind, 1987; The Parentalk Guide to Being a Grandparent, 2001; contrib to various jls on social work and children's issues. *Recreations:* writing, literature, walking sport, the theatre. *Address:* c/o NSPCC, 42 Curtain Road, EC2A 3NH.

HARDING, Keith; Member (C) Mid Scotland and Fife, Scottish Parliament, 1999–2003 *b* 21 Nov. 1938; *s* of late Cyril Dennis Harding and Ella Evelyn Harding; *m* 1974, Elizabet Anne Fowler; one *s* one *d*. *Educ:* Chipping Norton GS; Oxford Coll. of Further Educn Newsagent and banker. Mem (C) Stirling DC, then Stirling Council, 1986–99 (Leade 1993–96; Opposition Leader, 1996–99). Contested (Scottish People's Alliance) Stirling Scottish Parly elecns, 2003.

HARDING, Rt Rev. Malcolm Alfred Warden; Bishop Suffragan, Anglican Networ in Canada, since 2007; *b* 28 June 1936; *s* of Henry Warden Harding and Grace (*né* Walker); *m* 1962, Marylou (*née* Richards); one *s* two *d*. *Educ:* Univ. of Western Ontari (BA 1959); Huron Coll. (LTh 1962); Univ. of Manitoba (BSW 1965, MSW 1966 Ordained deacon, 1962; i/c of five rural parishes, dio. of Fredericton, 1962–63; Chil Welfare Worker, Children's Aid Soc., Ont., 1963–64; Social Worker, 1966–68 Supervisor, 1968–73, Manitoba Dept of Health and Social Develt; ordained priest, 1973 Priest-in-charge, Birtle, Solsgirth, 1973–78; Rector, St George's, Brandon, 1978–92 Archdeacon of Brandon, 1986–92; Diocesan Administrator, Brandon, 1992; Bishop o Brandon, 1992–2001. Ambassador for Anglican Renewal Ministries, Canada, 2001–06 Hon. DD Huron, 1993. *Recreations:* model railroad, fishing, reading, railway enthusias *Address:* 17 Durum Drive, Brandon, MB R7B 3M3, Canada.

HARDING, Air Vice-Marshal Peter John, CB 1993; CVO 1998; CBE 1985; AFC 1974; FRAeS; Defence Services Secretary to the Queen, Director General of Reserv Forces and Cadets, and Assistant Chief of Defence Staff (Personnel), 1994–98; *b* 1 Jun 1940; *s* of John Fitz Harding and Marjorie Clare; *m* 1966, Morwenna Jacquiline St John Grey; two *s*. *Educ:* Solihull School. Joined RAF, 1960; Pilot, 249 Sqn, Cyprus, 1962–65 RAF Coll., 1965–70; Cyprus, 1971–72; Waddington, 1972–74; RNC, 1974; RAF Germany, 1974–76; OC Pilot Buccaneers Sqns, 1977–80; Directing Staff, RAF Sta Coll., 1981; Station Comdr, Honington, 1982–84; RCDS 1985; Dir Nuclear Systems MoD, 1986–88; Dep. C-in-C, RAF Germany, 1989–91; Dep. COS (Ops), HQ AAFCE 1991–94. ADC to the Queen, 1982–84. Dep. Chm. Govs, Taunton Sch., 2001– (Gov 2000–). Legion of Merit (USA), 1998. *Recreations:* cricket, golf, gardening, family philately, hobby farming, classic cars. *Clubs:* Royal Air Force, Innominate, Pilgrims.

HARDING, Marshal of the Royal Air Force Sir Peter (Robin), GCB 1988 (KCB 1983; CB 1980); FRAeS; Chairman and Chief Executive, Merlyn Internationa Associates, 1997–2006; *b* 2 Dec. 1933; *s* of late Peter Harding and Elizabeth Clear; *m* 1955 Sheila Rosemary May; three *s* one *d*. *Educ:* Chingford High Sch. Joined RAF, 1952; Pilot 12 Sqdn, 1954–57; QFI and Flt Comdr, RAF Coll., Cranwell, 1957–60; Pilot, 1 Sqdn RAAF, 1960–62; sc 1963; Air Secretary's Dept, MoD, 1964–66; OC, 18 Sqdn, Gutersl and Acklington, 1966–69; jssc, Latimer, 1969–70; Defence Policy Staff, MoD, 1970–71 Director, Air Staff, Briefing, MoD, 1971–74; Station Comdr, RAF Brüggen, 1974–76 ADC to the Queen, 1975; Dir of Defence Policy, MoD, 1976–78; Asst Chief of Sta (Plans and Policy), SHAPE, 1978–80; AOC No 11 Group, 1981–82; VCAS, 1982–84

VCDS, 1985; AOC-in-C, RAF Strike Comd, and C-in-C, UK Air Forces, 1985–88; Chief of Air Staff, 1988–92; Chief of the Defence Staff, 1992–94. Dep. Chm., GEC Marconi Ltd, 1995–98; Chm., Thorlock Internat. Ltd, 1999–2000. Member: Partnership Korea, 1995–99; Anglo Korean Forum, 1995–99. FRAeS 1983, Hon. CRAeS 1989; FRSA 1988. Liveryman, GAPAN, 1989. Member: Council, Winston Churchill Meml Trust, 1990–; Leonard Cheshire Conflict Recovery Centre, 1998–2005. Vice Pres., Guild of Aviation Artists, 1994–. Hon. DSc Cranfield, 1990. Comdr, Legion of Merit (USA), 1992. *Publications:* articles for professional jls, magazines and books. *Recreations:* pianoforte, bridge, birdwatching, shooting, fishing. *Clubs:* Beefsteak, Garrick.

HARDING, Sir Roy (Pollard), Kt 1985; CBE 1978; *b* 3 Jan. 1924; *s* of W. F. N. Harding, BEM and P. E. Harding; *m* 1948, Audrey Beryl Larkin, JP; two *s* one *d*. *Educ:* Liskeard Grammar Sch.; King's Coll., Univ. of London (BSc, AKC, DPA). CMath, FIMA; FZS. Ballistics research, schools and college teaching, to 1950; Educn Admin, Wilts, Bucks, Herts, Leics, to 1960; Dep. Chief Educn Officer, 1960–66, Chief Educn Officer, 1966–84, Bucks. Adviser: County Councils Assoc., 1972–74; Assoc. of County Councils, 1973–84 (incl. Finance, 1978–81, Policy, 1981–84); Council of Local Educn Authorities, 1975–84. Member: Printing and Publishing Ind. Trng Bd, 1970–72; BBC Further Educn Adv. Council, 1970–75; Burnham Cttee, 1972–77; Sec. of State's Vis. Cttee, Cranfield Inst. of Technology, 1976–81; DES/Local Authority Expenditure Steering Gp, Educn, 1976–84; Councils and Educnl Press (Longmans) Editorial Adv. Panel, 1977–86; Teaching of Mathematics in Schools (Cockcroft) Cttee, 1978–82; Educn Management Inf. Exchange, 1981–89; Board, Nat. Adv. Body for Higher Educn, 1982–84; A Level (Higginson) Cttee, 1987–88; Assoc. of Educn Cttees Trust, 1989–; CBI Educn Foundn, 1990–94; Educn Cttee, Royal Soc., 1991–96 (Vice-Chm., 1995–96); various univ. cttees, incl. Open Univ. Council, 1985–96; Chairman: County Educn Officers' Soc., 1978–79 (Sec., 1973–76); Educn Policy Interchange Cttee, 1979–89; Open Univ. INSET Sector Programme Bd, 1983–87; Governing Body, Staff Coll. (formerly Further Educn Staff Coll.), 1986–95; EMIS Ltd, 1988–91; FEFCE Tariff Adv. Cttee, 1993–98; Vice-Chm., Secondary Exams Council, 1983–86. President: Soc. of Educn Officers, 1977–78 (Mem. Exec., 1974–79; Chm. Internat. Cttee, 1980–83; Gen. Sec., 1984–89); British Educnl Equipment Assoc., 1980–83; Educn Sect., BAAS, 1986–87; Nat. Inst. Adult Continuing Educn, 1988–94; IMA, 1990, 1991 (Council, 1983–88, 1990–97). Centenary Fellow, Thames Polytechnic, 1990. DUniv Open, 1985; Hon. LLD Leicester, 1995. Wappenteller, Rheinland/Pfalz, Germany, 1978. Gold Cross of Merit, Polish Govt in Exile, 1984. *Recreations:* travel, music. *Address:* 27 King Edward Avenue, Aylesbury, Bucks HP21 7JE. *T:* (01296) 423006.

HARDING, Wilfrid Gerald, CBE 1978; FRCP, FFCM, DPH; Area Medical Officer, Camden and Islington Area Health Authority (Teaching), 1974–79; Hon. Consultant in Community Medicine, University College Hospital, London, 1971–79; *b* 17 March 1915; *s* of late Dr *hc* Ludwig Ernst Emil Hoffmann and Marie Minna Eugenie (*née* Weisbach); *m* 1st, 1938, Britta Charlotta Haraldsdotter, Malmberg (marr. diss. 1970); three *s*; 2nd, 1973, Hilary Maxwell. *Educ:* Französisches Gymnasium, Berlin; Süddeutsches Landerziehungsheim, Schondorf, Bavaria; Woodbrooke Coll., Selly Oak, Birmingham; University Coll. London; University Coll. Hosp. Med. Sch. MRCS, LRCP 1941; DPH London 1949; MRCP 1968; FFCM 1972; Hon. FFCM 1986; FRCP 1972. Interned twice, in 1939 and 1940. Ho. Phys. and Ho. Surg., UCH, 1941–42; Asst MOH, City of Oxford, 1942–43; RAMC, 1943–47, Field Units in NW Europe, 1 Corps Staff and Mil. Govt, Lt-Col (Hygiene Specialist). In charge of health services, Ruhr Dist of Germany, CCG, 1947–48; LSHTM, 1948–49; career posts in London public health service, 1949–64; MOH, London Bor. of Camden, and Principal Sch. MO, ILEA, 1965–74. Hon. Lectr, Dept of Sociol., Bedford Coll., London Univ., 1969–77; Civil Consultant in Community Medicine to RAF, 1974–78. Chm. of Council, Soc. of MOH, 1966–71 (Pres. 1971–72); Chm., Prov. Bd of FCM, Royal Colls of Physicians of UK, 1971–72 (Vice-Pres., 1972–75, Pres., 1975–78). Member: Central Health Services Council and Standing Med. Adv. Cttee, 1966–71 and 1975–78; Standing Mental Health Adv. Cttee, 1966–71; Bd of Studies in Preventive Med. and Public Health, Univ. of London, 1963–79; Council, UCH Med. Sch., 1965–78; Bd of Management, LSHTM, 1968–82; Council for Educn and Trng of Health Visitors, 1965–77; Council, ASH, 1970–73 and 1978–82; Public Health Laboratory Service Bd, 1972–83. Armed Services Med. Adv. Bd, 1975–78; GMC, 1979–84; Vice-Chm., Dartford and Gravesham CHC, 1984–89. Chm., DHSS Working Gp on Primary Health Team, 1978–80 (reported 1981). Hon. Advr, Office of Health Econs. Councillor, Sevenoaks DC, 1979–99 (Vice-Chm., 1996–97; Chm., 1997–98); Chm., Farningham Parish Council, 1983–89. Chm., Farningham Woods Nature Reserve, 1983–2001. Broadcasts on public health and community medicine. *Publications:* papers on public health and community med. in medical books and jls; Parkes Centenary Meml Lecture (Community, Health and Service), 1976. *Recreations:* watching river birds, music, wine. *Address:* Bridge Cottage, High Street, Farningham, Dartford DA4 0DW. *T:* (01322) 862733. *Club:* Athenæum.

HARDING, Sir William; *see* Harding, Sir G. W.

HARDINGE, family name of **Viscount Hardinge** and **Baron Hardinge of Penshurst**.

HARDINGE, 7th Viscount *cr* 1846, of Lahore and of King's Newton, Derbyshire; **Andrew Hartland Hardinge;** Bt 1801; *b* 7 Jan. 1960; *s* of 5th Viscount Hardinge and of Zoë Anne, *d* of Hon. Hartland de Montarville Molson, OBE, Montreal; *S* brother, 2004; *m* 1990, Sophia Mary (*née* Bagnell); two *s* one *d*. *Educ:* The Gow Sch.; Trinity Coll. Sch. Gallery owner. *Recreations:* shooting, fishing. *Heir: s* Hon. Thomas Henry de Montarville Hardinge, *b* 19 June 1993. *Address:* 20 Niton Street, SW6 6NJ. *T:* (020) 7385 8678. *Club:* White's.

HARDINGE OF PENSHURST, 4th Baron *cr* 1910; **Julian Alexander Hardinge;** Chairman, Mallory International, since 2002; Director: Hardinge Simpole Publishing, since 2001; ESQN Ltd, since 2002; *b* 23 Aug. 1945; *s* of 3rd Baron Hardinge of Penshurst and Janet Christine Goschen (*d* 1970), *d* of late Lt-Col Francis Cecil Campbell Balfour, CIE, CVO, CBE, MC; *S* father, 1997. *Educ:* Eton; Trinity Coll., Cambridge. A Page of Honour to HM the Queen, 1959–62. Booksellers' Association: Dir, Book Tokens Ltd, 1984–2004; Chairman: Coll. and Univ. Booksellers Gp, 1985–87; Export Booksellers Gp, 1993–95; Batch.co.uk, 2002–06 (Dir, 1998–2006). Dir, John Smith & Son, Booksellers, 1998–2001. Chm., Mind Sports Olympiad, 1998–2002. *Heir: b* Hon. Hugh Francis Hardinge, *b* 9 April 1948. *Address:* Upper Yewdale, 7 Links Road, Budleigh Salterton, Devon EX9 6DF.

HARDMAN, Ven. Christine Elizabeth; Archdeacon of Lewisham, since 2001; *b* 27 Aug. 1951; *d* of Wynford Atkins and Margaret Elizabeth Atkins; *m* 1971, Roger John Hardman; two *d*. *Educ:* Queen Elizabeth's Girls' Grammar Sch., Barnet; Univ. of London (BScEcon (ext.) 1973); Westminster Coll., Oxford (MTh 1994). Ordained deaconess 1984, deacon 1987, priest 1994; Deaconess, Markyate Street, 1984–88; Course Dir, St Albans MTS, later St Albans and Oxford Ministry Course, 1988–96; Vicar, Holy Trinity, Stevenage, 1996–2001; RD Stevenage, 1999–2001. *Recreations:* cycling, running, cinema, theatre. *Address:* Trinity House, 4 Chapel Court, Borough High Street, SE1 1HW.

HARDMAN, John Nimrod, FCA; Chairman: ASDA Group PLC (formerly ASDA-MFI), 1988–91 (Deputy Chairman, 1986–87; Director, 1984–91); Dewhurst Butchers, 1996–2006; *b* 8 Oct. 1939; *s* of late Harry John Hardman and of Florence Gladys Sybil Anne Hardman (*née* Dolby); *m* 1966, Joan McHugh; one *s* one *d*. *Educ:* Quarry Bank High Sch., Liverpool; Liverpool Univ. (BComm Hons). FIGD. Duncan Watson & Short, Chartered Accts, 1962–66; RCA Corp., 1967–69; Finance Dir, Thorn Colour Tubes Ltd, 1969–75; Dir, Europe, Africa and Far East, RCA Corp. Picture Tube Div., 1976–80; Finance Director: Oriel Foods, 1981; ASDA Stores, 1981–84 (Man. Dir, 1984–89); Director: Maples Stores plc, 1995–98; Adderley Featherstone plc, 1991–2007. Director: Leeds Develt Corp., 1988–92; Yorks Electricity Bd, 1989–97. CCMI; FRSA. *Recreations:* golf, tennis, shooting, cricket. *Address:* Hillside, Spofforth Hill, Wetherby, Yorks LS22 4SF. *Clubs:* Lord's Taverners'; Liverpool Artists, Royal Liverpool Golf, Liverpool Racquets (Liverpool); Pannal Golf (Harrogate).

HARDMAN, Richard Frederick Paynter, CBE 1998; CGeol, FGS; consultant explorationist, since 2002; Director, Atlantic Petroleum Ltd, since 1994; Director and Technical Adviser, FX Energy Inc., since 2003; *b* 2 May 1936; *s* of late Dr Charles Ramsay Hardman and of Mary Hardman (*née* Barnsley); *m* 1st, 1960, Janet Quintrell Treloar (marr. diss.); two *s* two *d*; 2nd, 1982, Marilyn Merryweather (marr. diss.); one *d*; 3rd, 1995, Elizabeth Jane Atkinson (*d* 2008). *Educ:* Arnold Sch., Blackpool; Corpus Christi Coll., Oxford (MA). FGS 1959; CGeol 1991. Nat. Service, RN, 1954–56. Geologist with BP, in UK, Libya, Kuwait, Colombia, 1959–69; Exploration Manager with Amoco, Superior Oil and Amerada Hess, based in London and Norway, 1969–88; Exploration Dir, Amerada Hess Ltd, 1989–98; Amerada Hess International Ltd: Vice-Pres., NW Europe, 1996–98; Dir and Vice-Pres., Exploration, 1998–2001; Exploration Dir, Regal Petroleum, 2005–06. Dir, DENERCO OIL A/S, 1997–2001. Mem., Programme Bd, Brit. Geol Survey, 1993–95. Mem., NERC, 1998–2003 (Chm., Sci and Innovation Strategy Bd, 2001–03). Geological Society: Chm., Petroleum Gp, 1987–90; Pres., 1996–98. Chm., Petroleum Exploration Soc. of GB, 1985–86; Pres., Earth Sci. Teachers Assoc., 1993–95. Chm., Artsline, 2001–03. Chair, Friends of Southwark Cathedral, 2002–06. Petroleum Gp Silver Medal, 2002, William Smith Medal, 2003, Geol Soc. *Publications:* (ed jtly) Tectonic Events Responsible for Britain's Oil and Gas Reserves, 1990; (ed) Exploration Britain: geological insights for the next decade, 1992; papers on chalk as an oil and gas reservoir. *Recreations:* geology, jam making, theatre, music, ski-ing, wide open spaces. *Address:* The Long Barn, Treen, St Levan, Penzance TR19 6LG. *T:* (01736) 810991. *Club:* Athenæum.

HARDMAN MOORE, John Halstead; *see* Moore, J. H. H.

HARDSTAFF, Veronica Mary; Member (Lab), Sheffield City Council; *b* 23 Oct. 1941; *d* of Rev. Ernest Tutt and Mary Tutt; *m* 1964 (marr. diss. 1977); one *s* one *d*. *Educ:* Manchester Univ. (BA Hons German); Cologne Univ. Teacher of German and French: High Storrs Girls' GS, Sheffield, 1963–66; St Peter's Sec. Mod. Sch., Sheffield, 1969–70; Knottingley High Sch., 1977–79; Frecheville Sch., Sheffield, 1979–86; Birley Sch., Sheffield, 1986–94. Mem. (Lab), Sheffield CC, 1971–78. MEP (Lab) Lincs and Humberside S, 1994–99; contested (Lab) Yorks and Humber Reg., 1999. Vice-Chm., Jt Parly Cttee, EP-Poland, 1995–99. *Recreations:* reading, walking, classical music, playing flute. *Address:* 43 Northfield Court, Sheffield S10 1QR. *T:* (0114) 267 6549. *Club:* Sheffield Trades and Labour.

HARDWICK, Very Rev. Christopher George, PhD; Dean of Truro, since 2005; *b* 7 Oct. 1957; *s* of Keith Hardwick and Vera Elizabeth Hardwick; *m* 1982, Linda Dorothy Hicks; one *s* one *d*. *Educ:* King Edward VI Sch., Lichfield; Ripon Coll., Cuddesdon; Open Univ. (BA 1994); Birmingham Univ. (MA 1996; PhD 2000). ACIB 1979. Ordained deacon, 1992, priest, 1993; Asst Curate, Worcester SE Team, 1992–95; Chaplain (part-time): St Richard's Hospice, Worcester, 1992–95; RNIB (New Coll.) Worcester, 1992–95; Rector: Ripple, Earls Croome with Hill Croome and Strensham, 1995–2005; Upton upon Severn and Ch of the Good Shepherd, Hook Common, 2000–05. RD Upton, 1997–2005; Hon. Canon, Worcester Cathedral, 2003–05. Chm., Worcester Diocesan House of Clergy, 2002–05; Proctor in Convocation, Gen. Synod, 2004–05. A Church Comr, 2007–. *Recreations:* choral music, current affairs, reading, cooking, entertaining. *Address:* The Deanery, The Avenue, Truro TR1 1HR. *T:* (01872) 245006, *Fax:* (01872) 277788. *Club:* National Liberal.

HARDWICK, Nicholas Lionel; Chairman, Independent Police Complaints Commission, since 2004 (Shadow Chairman, 2003–04); *b* 19 July 1957; *s* of Lionel and Nancy Hardwick; one *d*; *m* 1985, Susan Heaven; one *s*. *Educ:* Epsom Coll.; Hull Univ. (BA Hons English Lit. 1979). Youth Training Manager, NACRO, 1980–85; Dep. Chief Exec., Soc. Voluntary Associates, 1986; Chief Executive: Centrepoint, 1986–95; British Refugee Council, subseq. Refugee Council, 1995–2003. Special Advr, Rough Sleeping, DoE, 1991. Chm., European Council for Refugees and Exiles, 1999–2003. Chm., Gtr London Radio Adv. Council, 1993–95; Mem., BBC SE Regl Adv. Cttee, 1993–95. Mem., Social Security Adv. Cttee, 1994–99; Mem., Holocaust Meml Day Steering Gp, 2001–05. Bd Mem., Stonebridge HAT, 1994–97. FRSA 1995. Hon. DSSc Wolverhampton, 2002. *Recreations:* walking, Spain. *Address:* (office) 90 High Holborn, WC1 6BH.

HARDWICKE, 10th Earl of, *cr* 1754; **Joseph Philip Sebastian Yorke;** Baron Hardwicke 1733; Viscount Royston 1754; *b* 3 Feb. 1971; *s* of Philip Simon Prospero Rupert Lindley, Viscount Royston (*d* 1973) and Virginia Anne (*d* 1988), *d* of Geoffrey Lyon; *S* grandfather, 1974. *Heir: cousin* Charles Edward Yorke, *b* 18 March 1951.

HARDY; *see* Gathorne-Hardy, family name of Earl of Cranbrook.

HARDY, Alan; Member (C) for Brent North, Greater London Council, 1967–86 (Chairman, Finance and Establishment Committee, 1977–81); *b* 24 March 1932; *s* of late John Robert Hardy and Emily Hardy; *m* 1972, Betty Howe, *d* of late Walter and Hilda Howe. *Educ:* Hookergate Grammar Sch.; Univ. of Manchester; Inst. of Historical Res., Univ. of London (MA). Res. Asst to Sir Lewis Namier, History of Parliament Trust, 1955–56; Res. Officer and Dep. Dir, London Municipal Soc., 1956–63; Mem. British Secretariat, Council of European Municipalities, 1963–64. Member: Local Authorities' Conditions of Service Adv. Bd, 1977–81; Nat. Jt Council for Local Authorities' Services (Manual Workers), 1977–81. Mem. Bd, Harlow Develt Corp., 1968–80. Hon. Life Pres., Brent North Conservative Assoc., 1986. Contested (C) Islington SW, 1966. *Publications:* Queen Victoria Was Amused, 1976; The Kings' Mistresses, 1980. *Recreation:* admiring old things. *Address:* The Old Garden, 20 Ledger Lane, Outwood, Wakefield WF1 2PH. *T:* (01924) 823771. *Club:* Naval.

HARDY, Anna Gwenllian; *see* Somers Cocks, A. G.

HARDY, Prof. Barbara Gladys, FBA 2006; Professor of English Literature, Birkbeck College, University of London, 1970–89, now Emeritus; teacher and author; *b* 27 June 1924; *d* of Maurice and Gladys Nathan; *m* Ernest Dawson Hardy (decd); two *d*. *Educ:*

Swansea High Sch. for Girls; University Coll. London (BA, MA). FRSL 1997. Subsequently on staff of English Dept of Birkbeck Coll., London; Prof. of English, Royal Holloway Coll., Univ. of London, 1965–70. Dir, Yeats Summer School, 1990–91. Pres., Dickens Soc., 1987–88; Vice-Pres., Thomas Hardy Soc., 1991–. Hon. Prof. of English, UC Swansea, 1991. Fellow, Welsh Acad., 1982. Hon. Mem., MLA. Hon. Fellow: Birkbeck Coll., London, 1991; RHBNC, 1992; Univ. of Wales, Swansea, 1998. DUniv Open, 1981. *Publications:* The Novels of George Eliot, 1959 (Rose Mary Crawshay Prize); The Appropriate Form, 1964; (ed) George Eliot: Daniel Deronda, 1967; (ed) Middlemarch: Critical Approaches to the Novel, 1967; The Moral Art of Dickens, 1970; (ed) Critical Essays on George Eliot, 1970; The Exposure of Luxury: radical themes in Thackeray, 1972; (ed) Thomas Hardy: The Trumpet-Major, 1974; Tellers and Listeners: the narrative imagination, 1975; (ed) Thomas Hardy: A Laodicean, 1975; A Reading of Jane Austen, 1975; The Advantage of Lyric, 1977; Particularities: readings in George Eliot, 1982; Forms of Feeling in Victorian Fiction, 1985; Narrators and Novelists: collected essays, 1987; Swansea Girl, 1993; London Lovers (novel), 1996 (Sagittarius Prize, 1997); Henry James: the later writing, 1996; Shakespeare's Storytellers, 1997; Thomas Hardy: imagining imagination, 2000; Dylan Thomas: an original language, 2000; Severn Bridge: new and selected poems, 2001; George Eliot: a critic's biography, 2006; The Yellow Carpet: new and selected poems, 2006; Dickens and Creativity, 2008. *Address:* c/o Birkbeck College, Malet Street, WC1E 7HX.

HARDY, Rev. Canon Brian Albert; Rector, All Saints, St Andrews, 1991–96; *b* 3 July 1931; *s* of Albert Charles Hardy and Edith Maude Sarah Mabe. *Educ:* City Boys' School, Leicester; St John's Coll., Oxford (MA, DipTheol); Westcott House, Cambridge. Curate, Rugeley, Staffs, 1957–62; Chaplain, Downing Coll., Cambridge, 1962–66; Livingston (West Lothian) Ecumenical Team Ministry, 1966–74; Churches' Planning Officer for Telford, Salop, 1974–78; Chaplain, Coates Hall Theological Coll., Edinburgh, 1978–82; Rector, St Columba's by the Castle Episcopal Church, Edinburgh, 1982–91; Episcopalian Chaplain, Royal Infirmary of Edinburgh and Royal Edinburgh Hosp., 1982–86; Dean of the dio. of Edinburgh, 1986–91. Hon. Canon, Edinburgh Cathedral, 1991. *Recreations:* music, especially choral and piano; cycling. *Address:* 3/3 Starbank Road, Newhaven, Edinburgh EH5 3BN. *T:* (0131) 551 6783.

HARDY, David Ian Brooker; Director, Distance Education International, since 2007; *b* 28 Sept. 1950; *s* of Leslie Hardy and Ruth Eveline Hardy (*née* Brooker); *m* 1979, Christine Mary Wilson; two *d*. *Educ:* Bradford Grammar Sch.; Univ. of London (BSc Hons); Univ. of Leeds (Grad. Cert Ed). Chartered FCIPD. Dept of Educn, Leeds City Council, 1979–85; Department of Education and Science: Yorks and Humberside, 1985–86; Nat. Manager, Post Experience Vocational Educn, 1986–90; Asst Sec., 1990; Chief Exec., 1990–2000, Hon. Pres., 2000–01, Open Poly., then Open Learning Foundn; Chief Exec., Open Learning Internat., 2002–07. Moderator, BTEC, 1982–85; Member, CNAA, 1991–92; Pres., Eur. Assoc. Distance Teaching Univs, 1999–2001; Vice Pres. (Europe), Internat. Council for Open and Distance Educn, 1999–2002; Mem., Eur. Open and Distance Learning Liaison Cttee, 1999–2002. Hon. Mem., Central Asian Business Women's Assoc., 2007–. Mem. Council, Bradford Chamber of Commerce, 1982–86. *Publications:* (jtly) Onchocerciasis in Zaire, 1977; articles in learned jls. *Recreations:* Central Asia, swimming, fell walking, travel. *Address:* The Farmhouse, Lycrome Road, Lye Green, Chesham, Bucks HP5 3LD. *T:* (01494) 786043.

HARDY, David Malcolm; Head, Strategic Market Development, MF Global, since 2007; *b* 16 July 1955; *s* of Roy Hardy and late Mary (*née* Ebsworth); *m* 1981 (marr. diss. 1995); one *s* one *d*; *m* 1995, Marion Dorothy Brazier. *Educ:* Westcliff High Sch. ACIB; FCT. Barclays Bank, 1973–81; Barclays Merchant Bank, 1981–85; LCH.Clearnet (formerly London Clearing House), 1985–2006, Gp Chief Exec., 1987–2006. Director: London Commodity Exchange (1986) Ltd, 1991–96; Internat. Petroleum Exchange of London Ltd, 1993–99; Futures and Options Assoc., 1993–2006; Inst. of Financial Markets, US, 2000–. Mem., FSA Practitioner Panel, 2001–06. FRSA. Freeman, City of London, 1994; Liveryman, Co. of World Traders, 1993; Mem., Guild of Internat. Bankers, 2005–. *Recreations:* golf, photography. *Address:* (office) Sugar Quay, Lower Thames Street, EC3R 6DU; *e-mail:* oak.park@mac.com. *Club:* Royal Automobile.

HARDY, Sir David (William), Kt 1992; Chairman, Transport Research Laboratory, 1996–2007; Chairman of Trustees, National Maritime Museum, 1995–2005 (Trustee, since 1992); *b* 14 July 1930; 3rd *s* of late Brig. John H. Hardy, CBE, MC; *m* 1957, Rosemary, *d* of late Sir Godfrey F. S. Collins, KCIE, CSI, OBE; one *s* one *d*. *Educ:* Wellington Coll.; Harvard Business School (AMP). Chartered Accountant. Served 2nd RHA, 2/Lt, 1953–54. Funch Edye & Co. Inc., NY, New Orleans and Norfolk, Va, 1954–64 (Dir, 1960); Vice Pres. Finance and Admin, Imperial Tobacco, USA, 1964–70; HM Govt Co-ordinator of Industrial Advrs, 1970–72; Gp Finance Dir, Tate & Lyle Ltd, 1972–77; Dir, Ocean Transport & Trading PLC, 1977–83; Chairman: Ocean Inchcape, 1980–83; London Park Hotels, 1983–87; Globe Investment Trust, 1983–90 (Dir, 1976–90); Docklands Light Railway, 1984–87; Swan Hunter, 1986–88; MGM Assurance, 1986–2000 (Dep. Chm., 1985–86; Dir, 1985–2000); Europa Minerals, 1991–94; Bankers Trust Investment Management, 1992–94; Burmine Ltd, 1992–96; Y. J. Lovell, 1994–99; Colliers Capital UK, 2004–07; Committed Capital UK, 2004–; 100 Group Chartered Accountants, 1986–88; LDDC, 1988–92 (Dep. Chm., 1988); Deputy Chairman: LRT, 1984–87; Agricultural Mortgage Corp., 1985–92 (Dir, 1973–); Director: Sturge Holdings PLC, 1985–95; Waterford Wedgwood plc (formerly Waterford Glass), 1984–90; Paragon Group, 1985–88; Aberfoyle Holdings, 1986–91; Chelsea Harbour Ltd, 1986–90; Electra Kingsway Managers Hldgs Ltd, 1990–91; Tootal Gp, 1990–91; CIBA-GEIGY, 1991–96; Hanson, 1991–2001; J. A. Devenish, 1991–93; Stirling-Lloyd Holdings, 1992–; James Fisher & Sons, 1993– (Chm., 1993–94); Milner Estates (formerly Conrad Ritblat) plc, 1996–99; Imperial Tobacco Gp, 1996–2001; Sons of Gwalia, 1996–99; Milner Consultancies, 2000–01; Fitzhardinge, 2001–04; Colliers CRE, 2004–07; Adv. Dir, HSBC Investment Banking, 1995–97. Chm., Engrg Marketing Adv. Cttee, DTI, 1989–90; Member: NEDC Cttee for Agriculture, 1970–72; Export Credit Guarantees Adv. Council, 1973–78; Industrial Develt Adv. Bd, DTI, 1992–96; Co-opted Council of Inst. of Chartered Accountants, 1974–78; Economic and Fiscal Policy Cttee, CBI, 1981–88; Council, BIM, 1974–78 (CCMI (CBIM 1975)). Mem., Develt Cttee, NACF, 1988–98; Vice Chm., St Katherine and Shadwell Trust, 2000 (Mem., 1990–); Founder Mem., Royal Albert Dock Trust, 1992–; Dir, Greenwich Millennium Trust, 1996–2001; Trustee, Mary Rose Trust, 2000–. Pres., Poplar, Blackwall and Dist Rowing Club, 1992–; Patron, Pitlochry Angling Club, 1994–. Gov., Chelsea Open Air Nursery Sch., 1992–2004 (Dep. Chm., 1994–2004). Hon. British Consul, Norfolk, Va, 1960–62. Member: Co. of Chartered Accountants, 1976; Co. of Shipwrights, 1990. Younger Brother, Trinity House, 1996. FCILT (FCIT 1988). Hon. LLD Greenwich, 2003. *Address: e-mail:* seahardy@aol.com. *Clubs:* Brooks's, Beefsteak, MCC, Flyfishers', HAC.

HARDY, Sir James (Gilbert), Kt 1981; OBE 1975; Consultant, Hardy Wine Company, since 2003; Director/Trustee, HM Bark Endeavour Foundation, since 1996; Chairman, Advisory Committee, Natural Heritage Trust, since 1998; *b* 20 Nov. 1932; *s* of Tom Mayfield Hardy and Eileen C. Hardy; *m* 1st, 1956, Anne Christine Jackson (marr. diss. 1991); two *s*; 2nd, 1991, Joan Margaret McInnes. *Educ:* St Peter's Coll., Adelaide, SA; Australian Sch. of Mines; S Australian Inst. of Technol. (Dip. in Accountancy). FCPA FAICD. National Service, 13th Field Artillery Regt, Adelaide, 1951. Elder Smith & Co Ltd, 1951; J. C. Correll & Co., 1952; Thomas Hardy & Sons Pty Ltd, Winemakers Adelaide, 1953–92: Shipping Clerk, Sales Rep., Sales Supervisor and Lab. Asst, 1953–62 Dir and Manager, Sydney Br., 1962–77; Regional Dir, Eastern Australia, 1977–81; Chm of Dirs, 1981–92; Chm. of Dirs, Houghton Wines Pty Ltd, 1981–92; Dir, BRL Hardy Ltd, 1992–2002. Director: S Australian Film Corp., 1981–87; America's Cup Challenge 1983 Ltd, 1981–85; Advertiser Newspapers Ltd, 1983–88; Lorna Hodgkinson Sunshine Home Ltd, 1993–2003. Dep. Chm., Racing Rules Cttee, Yachting Fedn, 1969–81; Dir of Sailing/Captain, S Australian Challenge for the Defence of America's Cup 1984–87 Vice Pres., Internat. 12 Metre Assoc., 1986–92. Treasurer, Liquor Trade Supervisor Council of NSW, 1965–70; Fellow, Catering Inst. of Australia, 1972; Pres., Wine and Brandy Assoc. of NSW, 1980–83. NSW Chm., Aust. National Travel Assoc., 1976; Vice Pres., Royal Blind Soc. of NSW, 1980–88 (Mem. Council, 1967–91); Pres., NSW Aust Football League and Sydney Football League, 1982–83; Pres., "One and All" Sailing Ship Assoc. of SA Inc., 1981–90; Chm., Adelaide 1998 Commonwealth Games Bid, 1990–92 Mem., Bd of Advice, Rothmans Nat. Sport Foundn, 1985–87; Trustee: Rothmans Foundn, 1987–93; Sydney Cricket and Sports Ground Trust, 1990–95; Mem., Council Australian Nat. Maritime Mus., 1992–97. Chairman: Adv. Cttee, Life Educn Centre of SA, 1988–91; Landcare Australia Ltd Foundn, 1994–98. Member: Exec. Cttee Neurosurgical Res. Foundn of SA, 1988–2004; Adv. Bd, John Curtin Sch. of Medical Res., ANU, Canberra, 1982–87. Dep. Grand Master, United Grand Lodge of NSW 1977–80. Australian Yachtsman of the Year, 1981. *Recreation:* yachting (skipper or helmsman in America's Cup and Admiral's Cup races). *Address:* Hardy Wine Co., PO Box 96, Botany, NSW 1455, Australia. *T:* (2) 96665855, *Fax:* (2) 93169738. *Clubs:* Royal Ocean Racing; Australian, Tattersalls, Royal Sydney Yacht Squadron (Sydney); Cruising Yacht of Australia (NSW); Royal Perth Yacht; Royal Queensland Yacht; Fort Worth Boat (Texas, USA).

HARDY, Maj.-Gen. John Campbell, CB 1985; LVO 1978; Administrator, Sion College, 1993–2000; *b* 13 Oct. 1933; *s* of late General Sir Campbell Hardy, KCB, CBE DSO; *m* 1961, Jennifer Mary Kempton; one *s* one *d*. *Educ:* Sherborne Sch. Joined Royal Marines, 1952; 45 Commando, 1954; HMS Superb, 1956; Instructor, NCOs' School Plymouth, 1957; 42 Commando, 1959; 43 Commando, 1962; Adjt, Jt Service Amphibious Warfare Centre, 1964; Company Comdr, 45 Commando, 1965; sc Bracknell, 1966; Instr, RNC Greenwich, 1967; Extra Equerry to Prince Philip, 1968–69 SO, Dept of CGRM, 1969; Rifle Company Comdr, 41 Commando, 1971; ndc Latimer 1972; Staff of Chief of Defence Staff, 1973; Staff Officer HQ Commando Forces, 1975 CO RM Poole, 1977; COS and Asst Defence Attaché, British Defence Staff Washington 1979; ADC to the Queen, 1981–82; Chief of Staff to Comdt Gen. RM, 1982–84; DCS (Support) to C-in-C Allied Forces N Europe, 1984–87. Col Comdt, RM, 1990–94. Dir British Digestive Foundn, 1987–92. Gen. Comr of Taxes, 1989–. Gov., Dashwood Foundn, 1998–. *Address:* c/o National Westminster Bank plc, 31 High Street, Deal, Kent CT14 6EW. *Club:* Army and Navy.

HARDY, John Sydney; QC 2008; a Recorder, since 2002; *b* London, 12 Dec. 1953; *s* of Sydney and Margaret Hardy; *m* 1990, Claire McCririck; one *s* one *d*. *Educ:* Christ's Hosp. Magdalen Coll., Oxford (BA Hons Modern Hist.). Teacher, Priory Sch., Banstead Surrey, 1977–86. Called to the Bar, Gray's Inn, 1988; in practice as barrister specialising in extradition and serious fraud. *Recreations:* music and opera, Rugby Union, cricket, golf food and wine, travel. *Address:* 3 Raymond Buildings, Gray's Inn, WC1R 5BH.

HARDY, Prof. Michael Christopher, OBE 2001; Programme Leader, Intercultural Dialogue, British Council, since 2008; *b* 24 April 1949; *s* of Wilfred Alexander Hardy and Barbara Linington Hardy; *m* 1973, Dorothy Marjorie Skinner; one *s* one *d*. *Educ:* London Univ. (BSc Hons Econs ext. 1971); Univ. of London Inst. of Educn (Cert. Further and Higher Educn 1972); Brunel Univ. (MA Econs 1976). Lectr in Econs, Orpington Coll. 1973–77; Sen. Lectr in Econs, Leeds Metropolitan Univ., 1977–87; Hd, Sch. of Econs 1987–95, Prof. of Internat. Business, 1990–95, Lancs Polytechnic, subseq. Univ. of Central Lancs, now Prof. Emeritus; British Council: Dir, Private Sector Develt, 1995–97 Regl Dir for Develt Services, ME, 1997–2001; Mem., Sen. Mgt Team and Dir, Develt Services, 2001–04; Dir, Indonesia, 2004–08. *Publication:* (jtly) Controversies in Applied Economics, 1987. *Recreations:* cooking, family, gadgets. *Address:* British Council, 10 Spring Gardens, SW1A 2BN. *T:* (020) 7389 4222, *Fax:* (020) 7389 4758; *e-mail:* mike.hardy@britishcouncil.org.

HARDY, Michael James Langley; Director for Telecommunications Policy and Postal Services, Directorate-General for Information Technologies and Industries, and Telecommunications, Commission of the European Communities, 1992–93; *b* 30 Jan. 1933; *s* of James Hardy and Rosina (*née* Langley); *m* 1959, Dr Swana Metger; one *s* two *d*. *Educ:* Beckenham Grammar Sch.; Magdalen Coll., Oxford (Exhibnr; BA 1956; MA 1959); Magdalene Coll., Cambridge (LLB 1957; LLM 1963); Exeter Sch. of Art and Design, Univ. of Plymouth (BA (Fine Art) 1996, MA 2002). Called to the Bar, Gray's Inn, 1957. Asst Lecturer, Law Faculty: Manchester Univ., 1958–59; KCL, 1959–60; Legal Officer, later Sen. Legal Officer, Legal Service, UN, 1960–73; Legal Adviser, Govt of Nepal, 1968–69 (on leave of absence from UN); Commn of the European Communities, 1973–93: Legal Adviser, Legal Service, 1973–77; Head of Div., Japan, Australia and NZ, Directorate-General for External Relations, 1978–82; Head of Commn Delegn, New York, 1982–87; Dir for Gen. Affairs, Directorate-Gen. for Telecommunications, Information Industries and Innovation, 1987–92. *Publications:* Blood Feuds and the Payment of Blood Money in the Middle East, 1963; Modern Diplomatic Law, 1968; (with T. Grumley-Grennan) Gidleigh: a Dartmoor village past and present, 2000; articles in legal and political science jls. *Recreations:* walking, talking. *Address:* Castle House, Gidleigh, Devon TQ13 8HR. *T:* (01647) 433567.

HARDY, Sir Richard (Charles Chandos), 5th Bt *cr* 1876, of Dunstall Hall, co. Stafford; *b* 6 Feb. 1945; *o s* of Sir Rupert Hardy, 4th Bt and of Hon. Diana Joan Allsopp, *er d* of 3rd Baron Hindlip; *S* father, 1997; *m* 1972, Venetia, *d* of late Simon Wingfield Digby, TD; four *d*. *Educ:* Eton. *Heir: cousin* Gerald Alan Hardy [*b* 4 April 1926; *m* 1953, Carolyn, *d* of Maj.-Gen. Arthur Charles Tarver Evanson, CB, MC; two *d*]. *Address:* Springfield House, Gillingham, Dorset SP8 5RD.

HARDY, Robert; *see* Hardy, T. S. R.

HARDY, His Honour Robert James; a Circuit Judge, 1979–94; *b* 12 July 1924; *s* of James Frederick and Ann Hardy; *m* 1951, Maureen Scott; one *s* one *d*. *Educ:* Mostyn House Sch.; Wrekin Coll.; University Coll., London (LLB). Served, 1942–46, Royal Navy, as Pilot, Fleet Air Arm. Called to the Bar, 1950; a Recorder of the Crown Court, 1972–79. *Recreation:* sailing. *Address:* 12 Bollin Mews, Prestbury, Cheshire SK10 4DP. *T:* (01625) 820026; Betlem, Mallorca.

HARDY, Rt Rev. Robert Maynard, CBE 2001; Hon. Assistant Bishop, Diocese of Carlisle, since 2002; *b* 5 Oct. 1936; *s* of Harold and Monica Mavie Hardy; *m* 1970, Isobel Mary, *d* of Charles and Ella Burch; two *s* one *d*. *Educ:* Queen Elizabeth Grammar School, Wakefield; Clare College, Cambridge (MA). Deacon 1962, priest 1963; Assistant Curate, All Saints and Martyrs, Langley, Manchester, 1962; Fellow and Chaplain, Selwyn College, Cambridge, 1965 (Hon. Fellow, 1986); Vicar of All Saints, Borehamwood, 1972; Priest-in-charge, Aspley Guise, 1975; Course Director, St Albans Diocese Ministerial Training Scheme, 1975; Incumbent of United Benefice of Aspley Guise with Husborne Crawley and Ridgmont, 1980; Bishop Suffragan of Maidstone, 1980–86; Bishop of Lincoln, 1986–2001; Bishop to HM Prisons, 1985–2001. Hon. DD Hull, 1992; Hon. DLitt Lincoln, 2002. *Recreations:* walking, gardening, reading. *Address:* Carleton House, Back Lane, Langwathby, Penrith, Cumbria CA10 1NB. *T:* (01768) 881210.

HARDY, (Timothy Sydney) Robert, CBE 1981; FSA; actor and writer; *b* 29 Oct. 1925; *s* of late Major Henry Harrison Hardy, CBE, and Edith Jocelyn Dugdale; *m* 1st, 1952, Elizabeth (marr. diss.), *d* of late Sir Lionel Fox and Lady Fox; one *s*; 2nd, 1961, Sally (marr. diss. 1986), *d* of Sir Neville Pearson, 2nd Bt, and Dame Gladys Cooper, DBE; two *d*. *Educ:* Rugby Sch.; Magdalen Coll., Oxford (Hons degree, Eng. Lit.). *Stage:* Shakespeare Meml Theatre, 1949–51; London, West End, 1951–53; Old Vic Theatre, 1953–54; USA, 1954 and 1956–58 (plays incl. Hamlet and Henry V); Shakespeare Meml 1959 Centenary Season; Rosmersholm, Comedy, 1960; The Rehearsal, Globe, 1961; A Severed Head, Criterion, 1963; The Constant Couple, New, 1967; I've Seen You Cut Lemons, Fortune, 1969; Habeas Corpus, Lyric, 1974; Dear Liar, Mermaid, 1982; Winnie, Victoria Palace, 1988; Body and Soul, Albery, 1992; Churchill, in Celui qui a dit non, Paris, 1999; *films include:* The Far Pavilions, 1983; The Shooting Party, 1985; Jenny's War, 1985; Paris by Night, 1988; War and Remembrance, 1988; Mary Shelley's Frankenstein, 1994; A Feast at Midnight, 1995; Sense and Sensibility, 1996; Mrs Dalloway, 1997; The Tichborne Claimant, 1998; The Barber of Siberia, 1998; My Life So Far, 1998; An Ideal Husband, 1999; Harry Potter and the Chamber of Secrets, 2002; Harry Potter and the Prisoner of Azkaban, 2004; Harry Potter and the Goblet of Fire, 2005; Harry Potter and the Order of the Phoenix, 2007; *television:* David Copperfield; Age of Kings, 1960; Trouble-shooters, 1966–67; Elizabeth R, 1970; Manhunt, 1970; Edward VII, 1973; All Creatures Great and Small, 1978–80, 1983, 1985, 1987–90; Speed King; Fothergill; Winston Churchill—The Wilderness Years, 1981; Paying Guests, 1986; Make and Break, 1986; Churchill in the USA, 1986; Hot Metal, 1987, 1988; Northanger Abbey, 1987; Marcus Welby in Paris (film), 1988; Sherlock Holmes, 1991; Inspector Morse, 1992; Middlemarch, 1993; Castle Ghosts, 1995, 1996 and 1997; Gulliver's Travels (film), Bramwell, 1996; Nancherro, 1998; Midsomer Murders, Tenth Kingdom, 1999; Justice in Wonderland, 2000; Bertie and Elizabeth, 2002; Lucky Jim, Death in Holy Orders, 2003. Author of TV documentaries: Picardy Affair, 1962; The Longbow, 1972; Horses in our Blood, 1977; Gordon of Khartoum, 1982. Consultant, Mary Rose Trust, 1979– (Trustee, 1991–); Trustee, WWF (UK), 1983–89; Mem., Bd of Trustees of the Royal Armouries, 1984–95; Chm., Berkshire, Buckinghamshire and Oxfordshire Naturalists' Trust Appeal, 1984–90. FSA 1996. Master, Court of Worshipful Co. of Bowyers, 1988–90; Mem., Co. of Woodmen of Arden, 1981–. Hon. DLitt: Reading, 1990; Durham, 1997; Portsmouth, 2007. *Publications:* Longbow, 1976, 3rd edn 2006; The Great War-Bow, 2004. *Recreations:* archery, bowyery. *Address:* c/o Chatto & Linnit, 123A King's Road, SW3 4PL. *Clubs:* Buck's, Royal Toxophilite, British Longbow.

HARDYMAN, Norman Trenchard, CB 1984; Secretary, Universities Funding Council, 1988–90 (University Grants Committee, 1982–89); *b* 5 Jan. 1930; *s* of late Rev. Arnold Victor Hardyman and Laura Hardyman; *m* 1961, Carol Rebecca Turner; one *s* one *d*. *Educ:* Clifton Coll.; Christ Church, Oxford. Asst Principal, Min. of Educn, 1955; Principal 1960; Private Sec. to Sec. of State for Educn and Science, 1966–68; Asst Sec. 1968–75, Under-Sec., 1975–79, DES; Under-Sec., DHSS, 1979–81. Mem., UGC for Univ. of S Pacific, 1990–2001. Treasurer, Univ. of Exeter, 1991–2001. Hon. LLD Exeter, 2002. *Recreations:* walking, gardening, reading, photography. *Address:* 3 Hill View Road, Hanbury Park, Worcester WR2 4PN. *T:* (01905) 339368.

HARE, family name of **Viscount Blakenham** and **Earl of Listowel**.

HARE, Sir David, Kt 1998; FRSL 1985; playwright; *b* 5 June 1947; *s* of Clifford Theodore Rippon Hare and Agnes Cockburn Hare; *m* 1st, 1970, Margaret Matheson (marr. diss. 1980); two *s* one *d*; 2nd, 1992, Nicole Farhi, *qv*. *Educ:* Lancing Coll.; Jesus Coll., Cambridge (MA Hons; Hon. Fellow, 2001). Founded Portable Theatre, 1968; Literary Manager and Resident Dramatist, Royal Court, 1969–71; Resident Dramatist, Nottingham Playhouse, 1973; founded Joint Stock Theatre Group, 1975; US/UK Bicentennial Fellowship, 1997; founded Greenpoint Films, 1982; Associate Dir, Nat. Theatre, 1984–88, 1989–97. Hon. DLit Cambridge, 2005. Officier, l'Ordre des Arts et des Lettres (France), 1997. *Author of plays:* Slag, Hampstead, 1970, Royal Court, then NY, 1971; The Great Exhibition, Hampstead, 1972; Knuckle (televised, 1989), Comedy, 1974; Fanshen, Joint Stock, 1975, NT 1992; The Secret Rapture, NT, 1988, NY, 1989 (dir, NY only), Lyric, 2003; Racing Demon, NT, 1990, NY, 1995; Murmuring Judges, NT, 1991; The Absence of War, NT, 1993 (televised, 1996); Skylight, RNT, 1995, NY and Wyndhams, 1996, Vaudeville, 1997; Amy's View, RNT, transf. Aldwych, 1997, NY 1999, Garrick, 2006; The Judas Kiss, Playhouse, then NY, 1998; Via Dolorosa, Royal Court, 1998 (also actor), NY, 1999, Duchess Th., 2002; The Breath of Life, Haymarket, 2002; The Permanent Way, Out of Joint Th. Co., NT, 2004; Stuff Happens, NT, 2004, NY 2006; The Vertical Hour, NY, 2006, Royal Court, 2008; Gethsemane, NT 2009; *author and director of plays:* Brassneck (with Howard Brenton), Nottingham Playhouse, 1973; Teeth 'n' Smiles, Royal Court, 1975, Wyndhams, 1976; Plenty, NT, 1978, NY, 1983, Albery (dir. J. Kent), 1999; A Map of the World, Adelaide Fest., 1982, NT, 1983, NY, 1985; (with Howard Brenton) Pravda, NT, 1985; The Bay at Nice, and Wrecked Eggs, NT, 1986; My Zinc Bed, Royal Court, 2000; *opera libretto:* The Knife, NY Shakespeare Fest., 1987 (also directed); *TV films:* Man Above Men, 1973; Licking Hitler, 1978 (also directed); Dreams of Leaving, 1980 (also directed); Saigon—Year of the Cat, 1983; Heading Home, 1991; My Zinc Bed, 2008. *Directed:* The Party, NT, 1974; Weapons of Happiness, NT, 1976; Total Eclipse, Lyric, Hammersmith, 1981; King Lear, NT, 1986; The Designated Mourner, RNT, 1996; Heartbreak House, Almeida, 1997; The Year of Magical Thinking, NY, 2007, NT, 2008. *Adapted:* Pirandello, The Rules of the Game, NT, 1971, Almeida, 1992; Brecht, Life of Galileo, Almeida, 1994, NT, 2006; Brecht, Mother Courage and her Children, RNT, 1995; Chekhov, Ivanov, Almeida, 1997; Schnitzler (La Ronde), The Blue Room, Donmar Warehouse, 1998, NY 1999, Th. Royal, Haymarket, 2000; Chekhov, Platonov, Almeida, 2001; Lorca, The House of Bernarda Alba, NT, 2005; Gorky, Enemies, Almeida, 2006; The Life of Galileo, NT, 2006. *Films:* wrote and directed: Wetherby, 1985; Paris by Night, 1988; Strapless, 1989; (screenplay) Plenty, 1985; Damage (adapted from novel by Josephine Hart), 1992; The Secret Rapture, 1994; dir., The Designated Mourner, 1997; wrote and acted, Via Dolorosa, 2000; (screenplay) The Hours (adapted from novel by Michael Cunningham), 2002; (screenplay) The Reader (adapted from novel by Bernard Schlink), 2008. *Publications:* Slag, 1970; The Great Exhibition, 1972; Knuckle, 1974; Brassneck, 1974; Fanshen, 1976; Teeth 'n' Smiles, 1976; Plenty, 1978; Licking Hitler, 1978; Dreams of Leaving, 1980; A Map of the World, 1982; Saigon, 1983; Pravda, 1985; Wetherby, 1985; The Bay at Nice and Wrecked Eggs, 1986; The Secret Rapture, 1988; Paris By Night, 1989; Strapless, 1990; Racing Demon, 1990; Writing Lefthanded, 1991; Heading Home, 1991; Murmuring Judges, 1991; The Absence of War, 1993; Asking Around, 1993; Rules of the Game, 1994; Skylight, 1995; Mother Courage, 1995; Plays One, 1996; Plays Two, 1996; Amy's View, 1997; Ivanov, 1997; The Judas Kiss, 1998; The Blue Room, 1998; Via Dolorosa, 1998; Acting Up, 1999; My Zinc Bed, 2000; Platonov, 2001; The Hours, 2002; The Breath of Life, 2002; Collected Screenplays, 2002; The Permanent Way, 2003; Stuff Happens, 2004; The House of Bernarda Alba, 2005; Obedience, Struggle and Revolt, 2005; Enemies, 2006; The Vertical Hour, 2006; Plays Three, 2008.

HARE, Ewan Nigel Christian, (Nick); Chairman, Canadian Hunger Foundation-Partners in Rural Development, 2002; Chair, International Committee, Canadian Comprehensive Auditing Foundation, since 2004; Deputy Secretary-General (Development Co-operation) of the Commonwealth, 1993–99; *b* 11 May 1939; *m* 1985, Raina Ho; one *s* two *d*. *Educ:* Earlham Coll. (BA); Carleton Univ. (DPA). First Sec., Canadian High Commn, Accra, 1969–72; Canadian International Development Agency: Regl Dir, Asia SE, 1972–76; Regl Dir, Central and S Africa, 1976–78; Dir-Gen., Resources Br., 1978–80; Dir-Gen., UN Progs, 1980–84; Ambassador of Canada to Zaire, Rwanda, Burundi and Congo, 1984–87; Dir, Africa Trade Div., Dept of Foreign Affairs, Ottawa, 1987–88; Dir-Gen., Industrial Co-operation Prog., Canadian Internat. Develt Agency, 1988–91; Canadian High Comr to Nigeria and Ambassador to Benin, 1991–93. Board Member: Retired Hds of Mission Assoc., 2003–; Pearson Peacekeeping Centre, 2004–. *Recreations:* ski-ing, canoeing, jogging, sailing. *Clubs:* Royal Commonwealth Society; Canadian Kennel; Leonberger (Ontario).

HARE, Prof. Lisa Anne; *see* Jardine, L. A.

HARE, Margaret Flora, (Mrs David Hare); *see* Spittle, M. F.

HARE, Sir Nicholas (Patrick), 7th Bt *cr* 1818, of Stow Hall, Norfolk; *b* 27 Aug. 1955; *o s* of Sir Philip Hare, 6th Bt and Anne Lisle Hare (*née* Nicholson); *S* father, 2000; *m* 1982, Caroline Keith, *d* of T. P. K. Allan; two *s*. *Educ:* Bryanston. *Heir:* *s* Thomas Hare, *b* 7 Aug. 1986. *Address:* Tavern House, Sopworth, Chippenham, Wilts SN14 6PR.

HARE, Nick; *see* Hare, E. N. C.

HARE, Nicole, (Lady Hare); *see* Farhi, N.

HARE, Paul Webster, LVO 1985; HM Diplomatic Service; Project Director, Shanghai World EXPO 2010, UK Trade and Investment, since 2005; *b* 20 July 1951; *s* of Maurice Leslie Hare and Anne Dorothy Hare (*née* Webster); *m* 1978, Lynda Carol Henderson, *d* of Ian Stuart McWalter Henderson, CBE, GM, KPM and Marie Beatrice Henderson (*née* Green); three *s* three *d*. *Educ:* Leeds Grammar Sch. (Foundn Schol.); Trinity Coll., Oxford (Open Schol., MA 1st Cl. Hons PPE 1972). Qualified as solicitor, with Herbert Smith & Co., London, 1973–75; TEFL, Biella and Genoa, Italy, 1976; Corporate Finance Dept, J. Henry Schroder Wagg & Co., London, 1976–78; entered HM Diplomatic Service, 1978: Private Sec. to Ambassador to EC, Brussels, 1979–80; First Sec. and Hd of Chancery, Lisbon, 1981–85; FCO, 1985–88; Consul and Dep. Dir, Investment, USA, NY, 1988–94; Dep. Hd of Mission and Counsellor (Commercial and Economic), Caracas, 1994–97; Hd, Non-Proliferation Dept, FCO, 1997–2001; Ambassador to Republic of Cuba, 2001–04; Vis. Fellow, Weatherhead Center for Internat. Relations, Harvard Univ., 2004–05. Pres., Baseball Softball UK, 2000–. Order of Prince Henry the Navigator (Portugal), 1985; Order of 5 May 1810, Barinas (Venezuela), 1995. *Recreations:* family, music (piano, lieder), sport (squash, baseball, tennis), writing novels. *Address:* c/o Foreign and Commonwealth Office, King Charles Street, SW1A 2AH.

HARE, Rt Rev. Richard; *see* Hare, Rt Rev. Thomas Richard.

HARE, Rt Rev. (Thomas) Richard; Suffragan Bishop of Pontefract, 1971–92; *b* 29 Aug. 1922; *m* 1963, Sara (*d* 1999), *d* of Lt-Col J. E. Spedding, OBE; one *s* two *d*. *Educ:* Marlborough; Trinity Coll., Oxford; Westcott House, Cambridge. RAF, 1942–45. Curate of Haltwhistle, 1950–52; Domestic Chaplain to Bishop of Manchester, 1952–59; Canon Residentiary of Carlisle Cathedral, 1959–65; Archdeacon of Westmorland and Furness, 1965–71; Vicar of St George with St Luke, Barrow-in-Furness, 1965–69; Vicar of Winster, 1969–71. *Address:* Wood Cottage, Mirehouse, Keswick, Cumbria CA12 4QE. *T:* (017687) 72996.

HARE DUKE, Rt Rev. Michael Geoffrey; Bishop of St Andrews, Dunkeld and Dunblane, 1969–94; *b* 28 Nov. 1925; *s* of late A. R. A. Hare Duke, Civil Engineer; *m* 1949, Grace Lydia Frances McKean Dodd; one *s* three *d*. *Educ:* Bradfield Coll.; Trinity Coll., Oxford. BA 1949, MA 1951. Sub-Lt, RNVR, 1944–46. Deacon 1952, priest 1953; Curate, St John's Wood Church, 1952–56; Vicar, St Mark's, Bury, 1956–62; Pastoral Dir, Clin. Theol. Assoc., 1962–64; Vicar, St Paul's, Daybrook, and Pastoral Consultant to Clin. Theol. Assoc., 1964–69; OCF, E Midland Dist HQ, 1968–69. Chairman: Scottish Pastoral Assoc., 1970–74; Scottish Assoc. for Mental Health, 1978–85; Age Concern Scotland, 1994–2000; Nat. Forum on Older Volunteering, 2001–04. Mem. Editorial Bd, Contact Magazine, 1962–79. Hon. DD St Andrews, 1994. *Publications:* (jtly) The Caring Church, 1963; (jtly) First Aid in Counselling, 1968; Understanding the Adolescent, 1969; The Break of Glory, 1970; Freud, 1972; Good News, 1976; Stories, Signs and Sacraments in the Emerging Church, 1982; (ed) Praying for Peace, 1991; Hearing the Stranger, 1994; One Foot in Heaven, 2001; contributor to: Expository Times, Blackfriars, New Christian, Church Quarterly Review, Church Times, Contact. *Address:* 2 Balhousie Avenue, Perth PH1 5HN. *T:* and *Fax:* (01738) 622642; *e-mail:* bishmick@blueyonder.co.uk.

HAREN, Sir Patrick (Hugh), Kt 2008; PhD; FREng, FIET; Deputy Chairman, Viridian Group PLC, since 2007 (Group Chief Executive, 1998–2007); *b* 4 Aug. 1950; *s* of James Joseph Haren and Sarah Haren; *m* 1971, Anne Elizabeth McNally; two *s*. *Educ:* Queen's Univ. Belfast (BSc 1971; PhD 1976); University Coll., Dublin (MBA 1986). FIET (FIEE 1990); FREng (FEng 1998). Power Systems Engrg, Electricity Supply Bd, Dublin, 1971–73; Engr, Superconducting Magnet Prog., CERN, Geneva, 1976–78; Electricity Supply Board, Dublin: engrg appts, 1978–84; Divl Manager, Strategic Planning, 1985–87; Regl Accountant, 1987–88; Manager, Business Ventures, 1988–89; Dir, 1989–92; Dir, Hoermann Electronics Ltd, 1990–91; Chief Exec., NI Electricity, 1992–98; Chm., NI Electricity plc, 1999–2008. Mem. Study Cttee, Power System Operation and Control, CIGRE, 1982–86. *Publications:* technical papers in power system operation and computer control. *Recreations:* ski-ing, walking, languages. *Address:* Viridian Group PLC, 120 Malone Road, Belfast BT9 5HT. *T:* (028) 9066 8416.

HAREWOOD, 7th Earl of, *cr* 1812; **George Henry Hubert Lascelles,** KBE 1986; Baron Harewood, 1796; Viscount Lascelles, 1812; President, British Board of Film Classification, 1985–97; *b* 7 Feb. 1923; *er s* of 6th Earl of Harewood, KG, GCVO, DSO, and HRH Princess Mary (Princess Royal; who *d* 28 March 1965); *S* father, 1947; *m* 1st, 1949, Maria Donata (marr. diss. 1967; she *m* 1973, Rt Hon. (John) Jeremy Thorpe), *d* of late Erwin Stein; three *s*; 2nd, 1967, Patricia Elizabeth, *d* of Charles Tuckwell, Australia; one *s* and one step *s*. *Educ:* Eton; King's Coll., Cambridge (MA; Hon. Fellow, 1984). Served War of 1939–45, Capt. Grenadier Guards (wounded and prisoner, 1944, released May 1945); ADC to Earl of Athlone, 1945–46, Canada. Editor of magazine "Opera" 1950–53; Royal Opera House, Covent Garden: a Dir, 1951–53; on staff, 1953–60; a Dir, 1969–72; Chm. Bd, ENO (formerly Sadler's Wells Opera), 1986–95 (Man. Dir, 1972–85); Artistic Director: Edinburgh Internat. Festival, 1961–65; Leeds Festival, 1958–74; Adelaide Festival 1988; Artistic Adviser: New Philharmonia Orch., London, 1966–76; Buxton Fest., 1993–98; Man. Dir, English Nat. Opera North, 1978–81. Governor of BBC, 1985–87. Chm., Music Advisory Cttee of British Council, 1956–66; Chancellor of the Univ. of York, 1963–67; Member: Arts Council, 1966–72; Gen. Adv. Council of BBC, 1969–77. President: English Football Assoc., 1963–72; Leeds United Football Club, 1962–. Hon. RAM, 1983; Hon. LLD: Leeds, 1959; Aberdeen, 1966; Hon. DMus Hull, 1962; DUniv York, 1982. Janáček Medal, 1978. *Publications:* (ed) Kobbé's Complete Opera Book, 1953, 4th edn 1997; The Tongs and the Bones (autobiog.), 1981; Kobbé's Illustrated Opera Book, 1989; Pocket Kobbé, 1994. *Heir:* *s* Viscount Lascelles, *qv*. *Address:* Harewood House, Leeds LS17 9LG.

See also Barry Tuckwell.

HARFORD, Sir (John) Timothy, 3rd Bt *cr* 1934; Vice-Chairman, 1985–87, Deputy Chairman, 1987–93, Chairman, 1993–99, Wesleyan and General, then Wesleyan Assurance Society; *b* 6 July 1932; *s* of Sir George Arthur Harford, 2nd Bt and Anstice Marion (*d* 1993), *d* of Sir Alfred Tritton, 2nd Bt; *S* father, 1967; *m* 1962, Carolyn Jane Mullens; two *s* one *d*. *Educ:* Harrow Sch.; Worcester Coll., Oxford (BA); Harvard Business Sch. Philip Hill Higginson Erlangers Ltd, 1960–63; Director: Birmingham Industrial Trust Ltd, 1963–67; Singer & Friedlander Ltd, 1970–88 (Local Dir, 1967–69); Dep. Chm., Wolseley-Hughes Gp, then Wolseley Gp, 1983–97; Chm., 1990–94, Dep. Chm., 1994–97, Kwik Save Gp; Dep. Chm., Wagon Industrial Holdings, 1991–98. *Recreations:* wine and food, travel. *Heir:* *s* Mark John Harford [*b* 6 Aug. 1964; *m* 1999, Louise, *d* of Robert Langford]. *Address:* South House, South Littleton, Evesham, Worcs WR11 8TJ. *T:* (01386) 832827. *Club:* Boodle's.

HARGREAVES, Andrew Raikes; Senior Adviser and Group Director, Government Affairs, European Aeronautic Defence and Space Company UK Ltd (UK Chairman, 2000–05); *b* 15 May 1955; *s* of Col and Mrs D. W. Hargreaves; *m* 1978, Fiona Susan, *o d* of G. W. Dottridge; two *s*. *Educ:* Eton; St Edmund Hall, Oxford (MA Hons). Auctioneer and valuation expert, Christies, 1977–81; executive, Hill Samuel & Co. Ltd, 1981–83; Asst Dir, Sanwa Internat. Ltd, 1983–85; Asst Dir J. Henry Schroder Wagg & Co. Ltd, 1985–87; Consultant: Schroders plc, 1987–92; Midlands Electricity plc, 1989–97; UK Man. Dir, Daimler-Benz, subseq. DaimlerChrysler, Aerospace AG, 1997–2000. Contested (C) Blyth Valley, 1983. MP (C) Birmingham, Hall Green, 1987–97; contested (C) same seat, 1997. PPS to Ministers of State, FCO, 1992–97. Member: Select Cttee on Information, 1992–97; Select Cttee for Parly Comr for Admin, 1993–97; Secretary: back bench Urban and Inner Cities Cttee, 1987–91 (Chm., 1992–94); back bench Defence Cttee, 1992–94 (Vice-Chm., 1994–97). Mem., Bow Gp. *Recreations:* fishing, gardening, walking, antiques, art. *Address:* EADS (UK) Ltd, 111 Strand, WC2R 0AG. *Club:* Boodle's.

HARGREAVES, David Harold, PhD; Fellow, Wolfson College, Cambridge, 1988–2006, now Emeritus; *b* 31 Aug. 1939; *s* of Clifford and Marion Hargreaves. *Educ:* Bolton School; Christ's College, Cambridge (MA, PhD). Asst Master, Hull Grammar Sch., 1961–64; Research Associate, Dept of Sociology and Social Anthropology, Univ. of Manchester, 1964–65; Lectr, Senior Lectr then Reader, Dept of Education, Univ. of Manchester, 1965–79; Reader in Education and Fellow of Jesus College, Oxford, 1979–84; Chief Inspector, ILEA, 1984–88; University of Cambridge: Prof. of Educn, 1988–2000; Member: Gen. Bd of the Faculties, 1989–92; Local Exams Syndicate, 1990–92; Bd of Grad. Studies, 1990–92; Chairman: Council, Sch. of Humanities and Soc. Scis, 1990–92; Cttee on the Training and Develt of Univ. Teachers, 1990–92; Needs Cttee, 1991–92. Chief Executive, QCA, 2000–01. Vis. Prof., Univ. of Manchester, 2003–. Member: Educn Res. Bd, SSRC, 1979–82; Educn Adv. Council, Royal Opera House, Covent Garden, 1985–90; Educn Adv. Council, IBA, 1988–90; ESRC, 1991–95; Res. Cttee, Teacher Trng Agency, 1995–97; Educn Cttee, NESTA, 1999; Nat. Educnl Res. Forum, 1999; Jt Vice-Chm., Sec. of State for Educn and Employment's Standards Task Force, 1997–2000; Policy Advr to Sec. of State for Educn and Skills, 2001–02; Bd Mem., 1999–2000, Chm., 2002–05, British Educnl Communications and Technol. Agency. Chairman: Eastern Arts Bd, 1991–94; Res. Centres Bd, 1992–94; Internat. Adv. Council on Quality of Educn, NSW, 1993–95. Non-exec. Dir, W Suffolk Hosps NHS Trust, 1998–2000. Sen. Associate, Demos, 2003. Consultant: Lifelong Learning Foundn, 2002–04; Paul Hamlyn Foundn, 2002–07; Specialist Schs Trust, 2003 (Associate Dir, Develt and Res.); Trustee, Villiers Park Educnl Trust, 2004–07. Mem., Educn Cttee, LSO, 2002–05. FRSA 1984; Founding AcSS, 1999. Hon. FCT 2001. Hon. EdD Wolverhampton, 2002. *Publications:* Social Relations in a Secondary School, 1967; Interpersonal Relations and Education, 1972; (jtly) Deviance in Classrooms, 1975; The Challenge for the Comprehensive School, 1982; (jtly) Planning for School Development, 1990; (jtly) The Empowered School, 1991; The Mosaic of Learning, 1994; (jtly) On-the-Job Training for Surgeons, 1997; (jtly) On-the-Job Training for Physicians, 1997; Creative Professionalism, 1998; Education Epidemic, 2003; Learning for Life, 2004. *Recreation:* the arts. *Club:* Athenæum.

HARGREAVES, Prof. Ian Richard; Strategic Communications Director, Foreign and Commonwealth Office, since 2008 (on secondment); Professor of Journalism, University of Wales, Cardiff, since 1998; *b* 18 June 1951; *s* of Ronald and Edna Hargreaves; *m* 1st, 1972, Elizabeth Anne Crago (marr. diss. 1991); one *s* one *d*; 2nd, 1993, Adele Esther Blakebrough, *d* of Rev. E. and M. Blakebrough; two *d*. *Educ:* Burnley Grammar Sch.; Altrincham Grammar Sch.; Queens' Coll., Cambridge (MA). Community worker, Kaleidoscope Project, 1972–73; Reporter, Keighley News, 1973–74; Journalist, Bradford Telegraph & Argus, 1974–76; Financial Times, 1976–87: Industrial Corresp.; Transport Corresp.; New York Corresp.; Social Affairs Ed.; Resources Ed.; Features Ed.; Man. Ed., 1987–88, Controller, 1988–89, Dir, 1989–90, News and Current Affairs, BBC; Dep. Editor, The Financial Times, 1990–94; Editor: Independent, 1994–96; New Statesman & Soc., then New Statesman, 1996–98; Gp Dir, Corporate and Public Affairs, BAA plc, 2003–06; Sen. Partner, OFCOM, 2007–08. Mem. Bd, S London and Maudsley NHS Trust, 2000–03. Chm., Demos, 1997–2002. Member Board: New Statesman, 1996–2003; Greenpeace UK, 1997–2002; Presentable, 2001–03; OFCOM, 2002–. *Publications:* Sharper Vision: the BBC and the communications revolution, 1993; (with Ian Christie) Tomorrow's Politics: the third way and beyond, 1998; Who's Misunderstanding Whom?: science and the media, 2000; Journalism: truth or dare?, 2003; A Very Short Intro to Journalism, 2005. *Recreations:* football, fell-walking, tennis. *Address:* c/o Foreign and Commonwealth Office, King Charles Street, SW1A 2AH. *T:* (020) 7008 6197.

HARGREAVES, Prof. John Desmond; Professor of History, University of Aberdeen, 1962–85; *b* 25 Jan. 1924; *s* of Arthur Swire Hargreaves and Margaret Hilda (*née* Duckworth); *m* 1950, Sheila Elizabeth (*née* Wilks); one *s* two *d*. *Educ:* Skipton Grammar Sch.; Bootham; Manchester Univ. War service, 1943–46. Asst Principal, War Office 1948; Lectr in History: Manchester Univ., 1948–52; Fourah Bay Coll., Sierra Leone 1952–54; Aberdeen Univ., 1954–62. Vis. Prof., Union Coll. Schenectady, New York 1960–61; Univ. of Ibadan, 1970–71. Mem., Kidd Cttee on Sheriff Court Records, 1966 Pres., African Studies Assoc. (UK), 1972–73. Hon. DLitt Sierra Leone, 1984. *Publications* Life of Sir Samuel Lewis, 1958; Prelude to the Partition of West Africa, 1963; West Africa the Former French States, 1967; France and West Africa, 1969; West Africa Partitioned Vol. I, The Loaded Pause, 1974, Vol. II, The Elephants and the Grass, 1985; The End o Colonial Rule in West Africa, 1979; Aberdeenshire to Africa, 1981; Decolonization ir Africa, 1988, 2nd edn 1996; (ed) Aberdeen University 1945–81, 1989; Academe anc Empire, 1994; Adrian Adams in Kounghani, 2005. *Recreations:* theatre, community arts *Address:* Balcluain, Raemoir Road, Banchory, Kincardine AB31 5UJ. *T:* (01330) 825588.

HARGREAVES, Dr Jonathan Watson, CBE 2008; Board Member, British Waterways since 2008; Chief Executive Officer, Scottish Water, 2002–07; *b* 10 March 1950; *m* 1974 Hilary; two *d*. *Educ:* Hatfield Poly. (BSc); Durham Univ. (PhD). MIBiol; FICE 2005. Business Develt Manager, Northumbrian Water Gp, 1990–91; Managing Director: Entec Europe Ltd, 1991–93; Northumbrian Water Ltd, and Dir, Northumbrian Water Gp plc 1993–96; Northumbrian Lyonnaise Internat. Div., Suez Lyonnaise, 1996–2000; CEO, E of Scotland Water, 2000–02. Trustee, Baltic Centre for Contemporary Art, Gateshead *Recreations:* gardening, theatre, DIY. *Address:* British Waterways, Willow Grange, Church Road, Watford, Herts WD17 4QA.

HARGREAVES, (Joseph) Kenneth, MBE 2007; Secretary, Association of Conservative Clubs, 1995–99; *b* 1 March 1939; *s* of James and Mary Hargreaves. *Educ:* St Mary's Coll., Blackburn; Manchester Coll. of Commerce. ACIS. Standard Cost/Wages Clerk, NCB 1957–61; Audit Asst, Treasurer's Dept, Lancs CC, 1961–63; Office Manager, Shopfitters (Lancashire) Ltd, Oswaldtwistle, 1963–83. MP (C) Hyndburn, 1983–92; contested (C) Hyndburn, 1992. Nat. Chm., Right to Life, 2000–; Pres., Accrington and Dist Blind Soc., 1999–. ACIS, 1962; FFA, 1989. Fellow, Inst. of Financial Accountants. *Recreations:* Gilbert and Sullivan, classical music, travel. *Address:* 9 Hippings Vale, Oswaldtwistle, Accrington, Lancs BB5 3LH. *T:* (01254) 230401.

HARINGTON, Michael Kenneth; His Honour Judge Harington; a Circuit Judge, since 2000; *b* 9 Aug. 1951; *s* of late Kenneth Douglas Evelyn Herbert Harington, and Maureen Helen (*née* McCalmont); *m* 1984, Deirdre Christine Kehoe; one *s* two *d*. *Educ:* Eton Coll.; Christ Church, Oxford (MA). Called to the Bar, Inner Temple, 1974; a Recorder, 1998. *Recreations:* golf, shooting. *Address:* Gloucester County Court, Kimbrose Way, Gloucester GL1 2DE. *Club:* MCC.

HARINGTON, Sir Nicholas (John), 14th Bt *cr* 1611; Legal Adviser, Export Credits Guarantee Department, 1988–2002; *b* 14 May 1942; *s* of His Honour John Charles Dundas Harington, QC (*d* 1980) (*yr s* of 12th Bt) and Lavender Cecilia Harington (*d* 1982), *d* of late Major E. W. Denny, Garboldisham Manor, Diss; *S* uncle, 1981. *Educ:* Eton; Christ Church, Oxford (MA Jurisprudence). Called to the Bar, 1969. Employed in Persian Gulf, 1971–72. Joined Civil Service, 1972. *Recreations:* numerous. *Heir:* *b* David Richard Harington [*b* 27 June 1944; *m* 1983, Deborah (*née* Catesby); two *s*]. *Address:* The Ring o'Bells, Whitbourne, Worcester WR6 5RT. *T:* (01886) 821819.

HARKER, (Ronald) David, OBE 2003; Chief Executive, Citizens Advice (formerly National Association of Citizens Advice Bureaux), since 1997; *b* 2 March 1951; *s* of Stanley Harker and Mary Harker (*née* Macaulay); *m* 1980, Diane Summers; one *s*. *Educ:* Queen Elizabeth Grammar Sch., Darlington; Univ. of E Anglia (BA Social Studies 1972); Univ. of Essex (MA Sociol. 1973); Univ. of South Bank (Dip Finance 1982); London Business Sch. (MBA 1986). Dep. Gen. Sec., Voluntary Action Lewisham, 1974–78; Res. and Press Asst, COHSE, 1978–79; Policy Analyst, London Borough of Camden, 1979–80; Dir, Lady Margaret Hall Settlement, 1980–84; Director: CAG Consultants, 1985–89; Nat. Deafblind and Rubella Assoc. (Sense), 1989–97. Mem., Lewisham LBC, 1982–86. Non-exec. Dir, PIRC Ltd, 1985–2002. Member: NHS Modernisation Bd, 2000–04; UK Standing Cttee on Euro Preparations, 2003–; Council, Advertising Standards Authority, 2007–. Trustee, Alcohol Recovery Project, 1994–97. *Recreations:* sailing, cycling, ski-ing, walking. *Address:* Citizens Advice, Myddelton House, 115/123 Pentonville Road, N1 9LZ. *T:* (020) 7833 7038, *Fax:* (020) 7833 4371; *e-mail:* david.harker@citizensadvice.org.uk. *Club:* Southwold Sailing.

HARKNESS, Very Rev. James, KCVO 2005; CB 1993; OBE 1978; Moderator of the General Assembly of The Church of Scotland, 1995–96; a Chaplain to the Queen in Scotland, 1996–2006 (an Extra Chaplain, 1995–96 and since 2006); Dean of the Chapel Royal in Scotland, 1996–2006; *b* 20 Oct. 1935; *s* of James and Jane Harkness; *m* 1960, Elizabeth Anne Tolmie; one *s* one *d*. *Educ:* Univ. of Edinburgh (MA). Asst Minister, North Morningside Parish Church, Edinburgh, 1959–61; joined RAChD, 1961: Chaplain: 1 KOSB, 1961–65; 1 Queen's Own Highlanders, 1965–69; Singapore, 1969–70; Dep. Warden, RAChD Centre, 1970–74; Senior Chaplain: N Ireland, 1974–75; 4th Div., 1975–78; Asst Chaplain Gen., Scotland, 1980–81; Senior Chaplain: 1st British Corps, 1981–82; BAOR, 1982–84; Dep. Chaplain Gen. to the Forces, 1985–86, Chaplain Gen., 1987–95. QHC 1982–95. Chaplain, BLESMA, 1995–2002; Nat. Chaplain, 1995–2002, Pres., 2001–06, RBL, Scotland. Chm., Bd of Dirs, Carberry, 1998–2001. Mem., Pensions Appeal Tribunals, Scotland, 1999–2005. Chm., Veterans Scotland, 2003–06. Member: Scot. Adv. Cttee, ICRF, 1995–2000; Bd, Mercy Corps, Scotland, 2001–; Pres., Soc. of Friends, St Andrew's, Jerusalem, 1998–2005. President: ACFA, Scotland, 1996–2004; Earl Haig Fund Scotland, 2001–06; Officers' Assoc. Scotland, 2001–06. Trustee: Nat. Prayer Breakfast for Scotland, 1996–; Liberating Scots Trust, 1998–2001; Anglo Israel Assoc., 2001– (Mem., Exec. Cttee, 1995–2001); Scottish Nat. War Meml, 2003–; Gen. Trustee, Church of Scotland, 1996–. Gov., Fettes Coll., 1999–. Patron, St Mary's Music Sch., Edinburgh, 1995–2000. FRSA 1992. DD Aberdeen, 2000. ChStJ 1999 (OStJ 1988; Dean, Order of St John, Scotland, 2005–). *Recreations:* general pursuits. *Address:* 13 Saxe Coburg Place, Edinburgh EH3 5BR. *Clubs:* New, Royal Scots (Edinburgh).

HARKNESS, Rear-Adm. James Percy Knowles, CB 1971; *b* 28 Nov. 1916; *s* of Captain P. Y. Harkness, West Yorkshire Regt, and Gladys Dundas Harkness (*née* Knowles); *m* 1949, Joan, *d* of late Vice-Adm. N. A. Sulivan, CVO; two *d*. Dir-Gen., Naval Manpower, 1970; retired 1972.

HARKNESS, John Diamond; First Scottish Parliamentary Counsel to the United Kingdom, 2000–02; *b* 14 July 1944; *s* of Jack Harkness and Isabel Harkness. *Educ:* High Sch. of Glasgow; Univ. of Glasgow (MA, LLB). Legal Asst, then Sen. Legal Asst, Office of Solicitor to Sec. of State for Scotland, 1971–79; Asst, then Depute Scottish Parliamentary Counsel, 1979–2000; Asst Legal Sec. to Lord Advocate, 1979–99. *Recreations:* reading, music, travel. *Address:* 10 The Limes, Linden Gardens, W2 4ET.

HARLAND, Rt Rev. Ian; an Hon. Assistant Bishop: Diocese in Europe, since 2000; Diocese of Bradford, since 2002; *b* 19 Dec. 1932; *s* of late Canon Samuel James Harland

and of Brenda Gwendolyn Harland; *m* 1967, Susan Hinman; one *s* three *d*. *Educ*: Dragon School, Oxford; Haileybury; Peterhouse, Cambridge (MA); Wycliffe Hall, Oxford. Teaching at Sunningdale School, 1956–58; Curate, Melton Mowbray, 1960–63; Vicar, Oughtibridge, Sheffield, 1963–72; Member, Wortley RDC, 1969–73; Vicar, St Cuthbert, Fir Vale, Sheffield, 1972–75; Priest-in-charge, All Saints, Brightside, 1973–75; RD of Ecclesfield, 1973–75; Vicar of Rotherham, 1975–79; RD of Rotherham, 1976–79; Archdeacon of Doncaster, 1979–85; Bishop Suffragan of Lancaster, 1985–89; Bishop of Carlisle, 1989–2000. Proctor in Convocation, 1975–85. Hon. Treas., The Middle Way, 1998–2000. Pres., Abbotsholme Sch., 1999–2002. Entered H of L, 1996. *Recreations*: politics, sport. *Address*: White House, 11 South Street, Gargrave, Skipton BD23 3RT. *T*: (01756) 748623.

HARLAND, Air Marshal Sir Reginald (Edward Wynyard), KBE 1974; CB 1972; AE 1945; engineering and management consultant; *b* 30 May 1920; *s* of Charles Cecil Harland and Ida Maud (*née* Bellhouse); *m* 1942, Doreen Rosalind, *d* of late W. H. C. Romanis; two *s* two *d* (and one *s* decd). *Educ*: Summer Fields, Oxford; Stowe; Trinity Coll., Cambridge (MA). Served War of 1939–45: RAE Farnborough, 1941–42; N Africa, Italy and S France, 1942–45. Techn. trng, techn. plans and manning depts, Air Min., 1946–49; pilot trng, 1949–50; Chief Engrg Instructor, RAF Coll., Cranwell, 1950–52; Guided Weapon trng, RMCS Shrivenham, 1952–53; Thunderbird Project Officer: RAE Farnborough, 1953–55; Min. of Supply, 1955–56; psa 1957; Ballistic Missile Liaison Officer, (BJSM) Los Angeles, 1958–60; CO, Central Servicing Develt Estab., Swanton Morley, 1960–62; STSO, HQ No 3 (Bomber) Gp, Mildenhall, 1962–64; AO i/c Engrg, HQ Far East Air Force, Singapore, 1964–66; Harrier Project Dir, HQ Min. of Technology, 1967–68; idc 1969; AOC No 24 Group, RAF, 1970–72; AO Engineering, Air Support Command, 1972; AOC-in-C, RAF Support Command, 1973–77. Technical Dir, W. S. Atkins & Partners, 1977–82; Consultant to Short Brothers Ltd, 1983–88. Mem. Council, IMgt (formerly BIM), 1973–78, 1980–86, 1987–90, 1992–98; President: Soc. Environmental Engrs, 1974–78 (Fellow, 1977); IIExE, 1997–99 (Fellow, 1997); Vice-Chm., CEI, 1983–84. Chairman: Suffolk Preservation Soc., 1988–91; Suffolk Professional Engrs, 1991–97; Suffolk Br., Cambridge Soc., 1998–2005; Gov., ESU, 1993–2000; President: East Reg., ESU, 1992–; Old Stoic Soc., 1999–2000; Bury St Edmunds Soc., 2004– (Chm., 1993–94). Contested Bury St Edmunds, (SDP) 1983, (SDP/Alliance) 1987. Sen. Academic Fellow, Leicester Poly. (now De Montfort Univ.), 1989. CEng 1966; FIMechE 1967; FIET (FIEE 1964); FRAeS 1967; CCMI (FBIM 1974; Verulam Medal, 1991); Hon. FAPM 2003 (FAPM 1988). FRSA 1993. *Publications*: occasional articles in engrg and management jls. *Recreations*: better management, better government. *Address*: 49 Crown Street, Bury St Edmunds, Suffolk IP33 1QX. *T*: (01284) 763078; *e-mail*: rewharland@aol.com. *Club*: Royal Air Force.

HARLE, John Crofton, FGSM; saxophonist, composer, conductor; Founder and Managing Director, Harle Records, since 2005; *b* 20 Sept. 1956; *s* of Jack Harle and Joyce Harle (*née* Crofton); *m* 1985, Julia Jane Eisner (marr. diss. 2004); two *s*. *Educ*: Newcastle Royal Grammar Sch.; Royal Coll. of Music (Foundn Schol.; ARCM (Hons) 1978); private study in Paris, 1981–82. FGSM 1990. Leader of Myrha Saxophone Quartet, 1977–82; formed duo with pianist John Lenehan, 1979; saxophone soloist, 1980–, with major internat. orchs, incl. LSO, English Chamber Orch., LPO, Amsterdam Concertgebouw, New World Symphony; Principal Saxophone, London Sinfonietta, 1987–97; Prof. of Saxophone, Performance and Music History, GSMD, 1988–. Formed: Berliner Band, 1983; John Harle Band, 1988. Compositions for several ensembles, 1983–, incl. London Brass and LSO. Frequent composer and soloist on TV (incl. BBC series, Silent Witness, and History of Britain) and feature films; regular broadcaster on BBC Radio; featured in One Man and his Sax, BBC2 TV, 1988. Has made many recordings. Major works written for him by Dominic Muldowney, Ned Rorem, Richard Rodney Bennett, Luciano Berio, Michael Nyman, Gavin Bryars, Mike Westbrook, Stanley Myers, Harrison Birtwistle, Michael Torke, John Tavener, Sally Beamish. Founder, Sospiro Leadership Masterclasses, 2007–; speaker and lectr on leadership, music and well-being, 2007–. Dannreuther Concerto Prize, Royal Coll. of Music, 1980; GLAA Young Musician, 1979, 1980. *Publication*: John Harle's Saxophone Album, 1986. *Recreation*: work. *Address*: The Old Malthouse, Cave Lane, Goodnestone, Kent CT3 1PB. *T*: (01304) 842822; *e-mail*: john@sospiro.com. *Clubs*: East India, Royal Over-Seas League.

HARLECH, 6th Baron *cr* 1876; **Francis David Ormsby Gore;** *b* 13 March 1954; *s* of 5th Baron Harlech, KCMG, PC, and Sylvia (*d* 1967), *d* of Hugh Lloyd Thomas, CMG, CVO; *S* father, 1985; *m* 1986, Amanda Jane (marr. diss. 1998), *d* of Alan T. Grieve, *qv*; one *s* one *d*. *Educ*: Worth. Heir: *s* Hon. Jasset David Cody Ormsby Gore, *b* 1 July 1986. *Address*: Glyn Hall, Talsarnau, Harlech, Gwynedd LL47 6TE. *Club*: Brooks's.

HARLECH, Pamela, Lady; journalist and producer; *b* 18 Dec. 1934; *d* of Ralph Frederick Colin and Georgia Talmey; *m* 1969, 5th Baron Harlech, KCMG, PC (*d* 1985); one *d*. *Educ*: Smith Coll., Northampton, Mass; Finch Coll. (BA). London Editor, (American) Vogue, 1964–69; Food Editor, (British) Vogue, 1971–82; freelance journalist, 1972–; prodn work for special events, 1986–87; Commissioning Editor, Thames and Hudson, Publishers, 1987–89. Chairman: Women's Playhouse Trust, 1984–94; V&A Enterprises, 1987–94; English Nat. Ballet, 1990–2000; Council, British Amer. Arts Assoc., 1990–92; Bath Shakespeare Festival, 2004–; Trustee, V&A Mus., 1986–94; Member: Welsh Arts Council, 1981–85; Arts Council of GB, 1986–90; South Bank Bd, 1986–94; Council, Managing Bd, Cruisaid, 1987–96; Council, ABSA, 1988–95 (Chm., Judging Panel for Awards, 1989–90); Bd, Th. Royal, Bath, 2001–; Bd, Wales Millennium Centre, 2002–07. Pres., Bath Cancer Support, 1998–. *Publications*: Feast without Fuss, 1976; Pamela Harlech's Complete Guide to Cooking, Entertainment and Household Management, 1981; Vogue Book of Menus, 1985. *Recreations*: music, cooking, laughing.

HARLEN, Prof. Wynne, OBE 1991; PhD; Director, Scottish Council for Research in Education, 1990–99; *b* 12 Jan. 1937; *d* of Arthur Mitchell and Edith (*née* Radcliffe); *m* 1958, Frank Harlen (*d* 1987); one *s* one *d*. *Educ*: St Hilda's Coll., Oxford (BA 1958; MA 1961); Univ. of Bristol (PhD 1974). Asst teacher, Cheltenham Ladies' Coll., 1959–60; Lectr, St Mary's Coll. of Educn and Glos Coll. of Art, 1960–66; Research Fellow: Univ. of Bristol, 1966–73; Univ. of Reading, 1973–77; Sen. Res. Fellow, KCL, 1977–84; Sidney Jones Prof. of Science Educn, Univ. of Liverpool, 1985–90. Visiting Professor: Univ. of Liverpool, 1990–2001; Bristol Univ., 2000–; Project Dir, Univ. of Cambridge, 2003–. Bernard Osher Fellow, Exploratorium, San Francisco, 1995. Chair, Sci. Expert Gp, OECD Student Assessment Project, 1998–2003. President: British Educnl Res. Assoc., 1993–94; Educn Sect., BAAS, 2001–02. FEIS 1999. Editor, Primary Sci. Rev., 1999–2004. *Publications include*: Science 5/13: a formative evaluation, 1977; Guides to Assessment: Science, 1983; New Trends in Primary Science Education, 1983; Teaching and Learning Primary Science, 1985, 2nd edn 1994; Primary Science: taking the plunge, 1985, 2nd edn 2001; The Teaching of Science, 1992, 4th edn 2004; Enhancing Quality in Assessment, 1994; Developing Primary Science, 1997; Effective Teaching of Science: a review of research, 1999; Teaching, Learning and Assessing Science: 5–12, 2000, 4th edn 2006; Assessment of Learning, 2007; Student Assessment and Testing, 2008; numerous articles in jls incl. Internat. Jl Sci. Educn, Studies in Educnl Evaluation, Cambridge Jl

Educn, Curriculum Jl, Brit. Educnl Res. Jl, Res. Papers in Educn, Jl Curriculum Studies, Assessment in Educn, Studies in Sci. Educn. *Recreations*: opera, orchestral music, hill-walking, gardening. *Address*: Haymount Coach House, Bridgend, Duns, Berwickshire TD11 3DJ.

HARLEY, Gen. Sir Alexander (George Hamilton), KBE 1996 (OBE 1981); CB 1991; Master Gunner, St James's Park, 2001–08; Senior Military Adviser, Thales Air Systems, since 2003; *b* India, 3 May 1941; *s* of late Lt-Col William Hamilton Coughtrie Harley, 1st Punjab Regt and later Royal Indian Engineers, and of Eleanor Blanche (*née* Jarvis); *m* 1967, Christina Valentine, *d* of late Edmund Noel Butler-Cole and Kathleen Mary (*née* Thompson); two *s*. *Educ*: Caterham Sch.; RMA Sandhurst. Commissioned RA 1962; 1962–73: 7 Para Regt RHA; Staff Capt. MoD; Adjutant; Canadian Staff Coll.; Mil. Asst to Chief of Jt Intelligence, MoD, 1974–75; Battery Comdr, 1975–78 (despatches); Directing Staff, Staff Coll., 1978–79; CO 19 Field Regt RA, 1979–82; Col Defence Staff, and Operations Centre, Falklands War, MoD, 1983–85; Comdr 33 Armd Brigade, 1985–87; Chief of Ops, Northern Army Group, 1988–90; Asst Chief Jt Ops, Overseas and Gulf War, MoD, 1990–93; Administrator, Sovereign Base Areas, and Comdr British Forces Cyprus, 1993–95; DCDS Commitments, and Dir Jt Ops, MoD, 1995–97. Adjt Gen., 1997–2000; ADC Gen. to the Queen, 1998–2000. Col Comdt, HAC, RHA, 1998–2003. Chm., Purple International, 2001–07. Pres., Combined Services Hockey, 1995–2000 (Hon. Vice-Pres., 2001–); Patron: The Nordics Hockey Club, 1992–; Army Hockey Assoc., 2005–. Hon. Vice Pres., Raleigh Internat. Gov., King's Sch., Bruton, 2001–. FCMI (FBIM 1982). Freeman: City of London, 2002; Wheelwrights' Co., 2002. *Recreations*: country pursuits, dry stone walls. *Address*: Artillery House, Artillery Centre, Larkhill, Salisbury, Wilts SP4 8QT. *Club*: Naval and Military.

HARLEY, Ian, FCA, FCIB; Chief Executive, Abbey National plc, 1998–2002; *b* 30 April 1950; *s* of Michael Harley and Mary Harley (*née* Looker); *m* 1975, Rosalind Caroline Smith; three *s*. *Educ*: Falkirk High Sch.; Edinburgh Univ. (MA 1972). FCA 1982; FCIB 1998. Articled Clerk, Touche Ross, 1972–76; Corporate Planning Team, Morgan Crucible, 1976; joined Abbey National, 1977. Dir, Dah Sing Financial Hldgs, Hong Kong, 1998–2002; non-executive Director: Rentokil Initial plc, 1999–2007; British Energy plc, 2002–; Remploy Ltd, 2004–; Chm., Rentokil Initial Pension Trustee Ltd, 2007–. Pres., CIB, 2001–02. Chm., Ct of Govs, Whitgift Foundn, 2007– (Gov., 2002–). *Recreations*: reading, walking, cycling. *Club*: Oriental.

HARLING, Christopher Charles, (Kit), FRCP, FFOM, FFPH; Consultant Occupational Physician, Derriford Hospital, Plymouth, since 2006; Director (part-time), NHS Plus, since 2002; *b* 12 Jan. 1951; *s* of Robert and Dorothy Harling; *m* 1976, Philippa Ann Capper; two *s*. *Educ*: Leeds GS; Manchester GS; Keble Coll., Oxford (MA); University Coll. Hosp. Med. Sch. (MB BS). DAvMed 1988; FFOM 1991; FRCP 1995; FFPH (FFPHM 1999). Res. Fellow and Hon. Registrar, Inst. Envmtl and Offshore Medicine, Univ. of Aberdeen, 1979–80; Area MO, NCB, 1981–84; Consultant Occupational Physician: Sheffield HA, 1984–88; Bristol Royal Infirmary, 1988–2005; Sen. Lectr in Occupl Medicine, Univ. of Bristol, 1988–2005. Civilian Consultant Advr in Occupational Medicine to RN, 1993–; Hon. Advr in Occupational Medicine to RNLI, 2005– (Mem., Med. and Survival Sub-cttee, 2005–). MO, RNR, 1988–96 (PMO, HMS Flying Fox, 1995–96). Hon. Sec., Specialist Trng Authy of Med. Royal Colls, 1999–2008 (Mem., 1996–98; Vice-Chm., 1998–99); Sec., 1987–90, Chm., 1990–93, Assoc. NHS Occupational Physicians; Mem. Council, 1982–84, Mem., NHS Work Gp, 1985–87, SOM; Faculty of Occupational Medicine, Royal College of Physicians: Examr, 1990–99, Dep. Chief Examr, 1993–94; Vice-Dean, 1994–96; Dean, later Pres., 1996–99; Chm., Ethics Cttee, 1999–2007. Vice Chm., Salcombe Harbour Bd, 2006–. *Publications*: papers on ethics, occupational medicine and health care workers. *Recreations*: sailing, flying, polar bears. *Club*: Naval.

HARLOE, Prof. Michael Howard, PhD; Vice-Chancellor, University of Salford, since 1997; *b* 11 Oct. 1943; *s* of Maurice Edward and May Cecilia Harloe; *m* 1976, Judy Rosilyn Philip; one *s* two *d*. *Educ*: Watford Boys' GS; Worcester Coll., Oxford (MA 1970); PhD Essex 1984. Res. Asst, Borough of Swindon, 1967–69; Res. Officer, LSE, 1969–72; PSO, Centre for Envmtl Studies, London, 1972–80; University of Essex: Lectr, 1980–84, Sen. Lectr, 1984–87, Reader, 1987–90, Prof., 1990–97, Dept of Sociology; Dean of Social Scis, 1988–91; Pro-Vice-Chancellor, 1992–97. AcSS 2000. *Publications*: (jtly) The Organisation of Housing: public and private enterprise in London, 1974; Swindon, A Town in Transition: a study in urban development and overspill policy, 1975; (ed) Captive Cities: studies in the political economy of cities and regions, 1977; (ed) New Perspectives in Urban Change and Conflict, 1981; (ed with E. Lebas) City, Class and Capital, 1981 (US edn 1982); Private Rented Housing in the United States and Europe, 1985; (jtly) Housing and Social Change in Europe and the USA, 1988; (ed and contrib.) Place, Policy and Politics, 1990; (with M. Martens) New Ideas for Housing: the experience of three countries, 1990; (ed jtly) Divided Cities: New York and London in the contemporary world, 1992; The People's Home: social rented housing in Europe and America, 1995; (ed) Sociology of Urban Communities, Vols I–III, 1996; (ed jtly) Cities After Socialism: urban and regional change and conflict in post-Socialist societies, 1996; (jtly) Working Capital: life and labour in contemporary London, 2002. *Recreations*: gardening, travel, reading, sociology. *Address*: University of Salford, Salford M5 4WT. *T*: (0161) 295 5050. *Club*: Oxford and Cambridge.

HARLOW, Archdeacon of; see Taylor, Ven. P. F.

HARLOW, Prof. Carol R., PhD; FBA 1999; Professor of Public Law, London School of Economics, University of London, 1989–2002, now Emeritus; *b* 28 Aug. 1935; *d* of late Prof. Charles Harold Williams and Clare Williams (*née* Pollak); *m*; one *s* one *d*. *Educ*: King's Coll., London (LLB 1956; LLM 1970); LSE (PhD 1980). Lectr, Kingston Poly., 1972–76; Lectr, 1976–86, Reader, 1986–89, LSE. Jean Monnet Prof., European Univ. Inst., 1995, 1996. Hon. QC 1996. *Publications*: Compensation and Government Torts, 1982; (jtly) Law and Administration, 1984, 2nd edn 1997; Understanding Tort Law, 1986, 3rd edn 2005; (jtly) Pressure Through Law, 1992; Accountability in the European Union, 2002; Tort Law and Beyond (Clarendon Lectures), 2004. *Recreations*: theatre, gardening, walking, painting. *Address*: Law Department, London School of Economics, Houghton Street, WC2A 2AE. *T*: (020) 7955 7266.

HARMAN, Rt Hon. Harriet; PC 1997; QC 2001; MP (Lab) Camberwell and Peckham, since 1997 (Peckham, Oct. 1982–1997); Lord Privy Seal and Leader of the House of Commons, and Minister for Women and for Equality, since 2007; Deputy Leader and Chair of Labour Party, since 2007; *b* 30 July 1950; *d* of late John Bishop Harman, FRCS, FRCP, and of Anna Charlotte Harman; *m* 1982, Jack Dromey; two *s* one *d*. *Educ*: St Paul's Girls' Sch.; York Univ. Brent Community Law Centre, 1975–78; Legal Officer, NCCL, 1978–82. Opposition Chief Sec. to the Treasury, 1992–94; opposition front bench spokesman: on employment, 1994–95; on health, 1995–96; on social security, 1996–97; Sec. of State for Social Security, 1997–98; Solicitor-Gen., 2001–05; Minister of State, DCA, subseq. MoJ, 2005–07. Mem., NEC, Labour Party, 1993–. *Publications*: Sex

Discrimination in Schools, 1977; Justice Deserted: the subversion of the jury, 1979; The Century Gap, 1993. *Address:* House of Commons, SW1A 0AA.

HARMAN, Gen. Sir Jack (Wentworth), GCB 1978 (KCB 1974); OBE 1962; MC 1943; Deputy Supreme Allied Commander, Europe, 1978–81, retired; *b* 20 July 1920; *s* of late Lt-Gen. Sir Wentworth Harman, KCB, DSO, and late Dorothy Harman; *m* 1st, 1947, Gwladys May Murphy (*d* 1996), *d* of Sir Idwal Lloyd and *widow* of Lt-Col R. J. Murphy; one *d*, and two step *d*; 2nd, 2001, Sheila Florence Perkins (*née* Gurdon), *widow* of Maj. Christopher Perkins, Hampshire Regt. *Educ:* Wellington Coll.; RMC Sandhurst. Commissioned into The Queen's Bays, 1940, Bt Lt-Col, 1958; Commanding Officer, 1st The Queen's Dragoon Guards, 1960–62; commanded 11 Infantry Bde, 1965–66; attended IDC, 1967; BGS, HQ Army Strategic Command, 1968–69; GOC, 1st Div., 1970–72; Commandant, RMA Sandhurst, 1972–73; GOC 1 (British) Corps, 1974–76; Adjutant-General, 1976–78. ADC Gen. to the Queen, 1977–80. Col, 1st The Queen's Dragoon Guards, 1975–80; Col Comdt, RAC, 1977–80. Dir, Wilsons Hogg Robinson (formerly Wilsons (Insurance Brokers)), 1982–88. Vice-Chairman: Nat. Army Museum, 1980–87; AA, 1984–90 (Mem. Cttee, 1981–85). *Address:* Sandhills House, Dinton, near Salisbury, Wilts SP3 5ER. *T:* (01722) 716288. *Club:* Cavalry and Guards.

HARMAN, Sir Jeremiah (LeRoy), Kt 1982; a Justice of the High Court, Chancery Division, 1982–98; *b* 13 April 1930; *er s* of late Rt Hon. Sir Charles Eustace Harman, PC; *m* 1960, Erica Jane (marr. diss. 1986), *e d* of late Hon. Sir Maurice Richard Bridgeman, KBE; two *s* one *d*; *m* 1987, Katharine Frances Goddard Pulay (*d* 2002), *d* of late Rt Hon. Sir Eric Sachs and *widow* of George Pulay. *Educ:* Horris Hill Sch.; Eton Coll. Served Coldstream Guards and Parachute Regt, 1948–51; Parachute Regt (TA), 1951–55. Called to the Bar, Lincoln's Inn, 1954, Bencher, 1977, Treas., 2000; QC 1968; called to Hong Kong Bar, 1978, Singapore Bar, 1980; Mem., Bar Council, 1963–67. Dir, Dunford & Elliott Ltd, 1972–79. *Recreations:* fishing, watching birds, reading, listening to music. *Address:* c/o Treasury Office, Lincoln's Inn, WC2A 3TL.

HARMAN, Sir John (Andrew), Kt 1997; Chairman, Environment Agency, 2000–08 (Member of Board, 1995–2008); *b* 30 July 1950; *s* of John E. Harman and Patricia J. Harman (*née* Mullins); *m* 1971, Susan Elizabeth Crowther; one *s* three *d*. *Educ:* St George's Coll., Weybridge; Manchester Univ. (BSc Hons Maths); Huddersfield Coll. of Educn (Technical) (PGCE). Maths teacher, Greenhead Coll., Huddersfield, 1973–79; Head of Maths, Barnsley 6th Form Coll., 1979–90; Sen. Lectr in Maths, Barnsley Coll., 1990–97. Joined Labour Party, 1977: various posts, incl. Br. Sec., Co-ordinating Cttee Chm. and Constituency Vice-Chm.; Mem., Policy Commns on Envmt, 1995–96, and Local Govt, 1995–. Member (Lab): W Yorks CC, 1981–86 (Vice-Chm. 1982–85, Chm. 1985–86, Finance Cttee); Kirklees MDC, 1986–2000 (Leader, Council, and Labour Gp, 1986–99). Dep. Chm. 1988–92, Vice-Chm. 1992–97, AMA; Local Government Association: Dep. Leader, Labour Gp, 1997–2000; Chm., Urban Commn, 1997–2000. Mem., Sec. of State's New Deal Task Force, 1997–2001; Member, UK Delegation to: Earth Summit, Rio de Janeiro, 1992; UN Commn on Sustainable Develt. Chm., Kirklees Stadium Develt Ltd, 1993–. Dir, Energy Saving Trust, 1997–. Trustee: Nat. Coal Mining Mus., 2004–; Forum for the Future, 2007–. Contested (Lab) Colne Valley, 1987, 1992. FRSA 1994. Hon. FICE 2000; Hon. FIWM 2002; Hon. FIWEM 2002; Hon. FSE 2005. Hon. DCL Huddersfield, 2000. *Recreations:* music, reading, gardening, Huddersfield Town AFC. *Address:* 82A New North Road, Huddersfield HD1 5NE.

HARMAN, Richard Stuart; Headmaster, Uppingham School, since 2006; *b* 11 March 1959; *s* of late Donald George Harman and of Jean Patricia Harman (*née* Harrison); *m* 1989, Dr Karin Voth; one *d*. *Educ:* Trinity Coll., Cambridge (BA English Lit. 1981); Exeter Univ. (PGCE). Sales Exec., Acad. Press/Harcourt Brace Internat. (Publishers), 1981–83; teacher of English and Drama, Marlborough Coll., 1984–88; Eastbourne College: Hd of English, 1988–91; Housemaster, 1991–95; Co-educn Co-ordinator, 1995–97; Registrar and Dir of Drama, 1997–2000; Headmaster, Aldenham Sch., Elstree, 2000–06. *Recreations:* sports, theatre, music, travel. *Address:* Uppingham School, Rutland LE15 9QE. *Clubs:* East India, Lansdowne.

HARMAN, Robert Donald; QC 1974; a Recorder of the Crown Court, 1972–97; a Judge of the Courts of Appeal of Jersey, 1986–98, and of Guernsey, 1986–99; *b* 26 Sept. 1928; *o s* of late Herbert Donald Harman, MC and Dorothy (*née* Fleming); *m* 1st, 1960, Sarah Elizabeth (*d* 1965), *o d* of late G. C. Cleverly; two *s*; 2nd, 1968, Rosamond Geraldine, 2nd *d* of late Comdr G. T. A. Scott, RN; two *d*. *Educ:* privately; St Paul's Sch.; Magdalen Coll., Oxford. Called to the Bar, Gray's Inn, 1954, Bencher, 1984; South-Eastern Circuit; a Junior Prosecuting Counsel to the Crown at Central Criminal Court, 1967–72; a Senior Treasury Counsel, 1972–74. Mem., Senate of the Inns of Court and the Bar, 1985–87. Appeal Steward, BBB of C, 1981–98. Liveryman, Goldsmiths' Co. *Address:* 2 Harcourt Buildings, Temple, EC4Y 9DA. *T:* (020) 7353 2112; The Clock House, near Sparsholt, Winchester, Hants SO21 2LX. *T:* (01962) 776461. *Clubs:* Garrick, Beefsteak, Pratt's; Swinley Forest Golf.

HARMER, David John; Vice Chairman, Grooms-Shaftesbury Board, since 2007 (Chairman, Shaftesbury Society, 2005–07); Chief Executive, John Grooms Housing Association, 1988–2005; *b* 14 May 1940; *s* of Stanley James Arthur Harmer and Eileen Joan (*née* Callaghan); *m* 1971, Janet Arnott Dodds; one *s* one *d*; one *s* one *d* from previous *m*. *Educ:* Dulwich Coll.; Spurgeon's Coll. Surveyor, Portman Family Settled Estates, 1957–61; Ministerial Assistant, W Ham Central Mission, 1961–62; Church Pastor, Shaftesbury Soc., 1964–71; Founder, 1971, Dep. Dir, 1971–88, Shaftesbury Soc. Housing Assoc. Member: Exec., Christian Alliance Housing Assoc., 1987–90; Regl Exec., Nat. Housing Fedn, 1987–95 (Chm., 1990–93); Chm., Nat. Wheelchair Housing Assoc. Gp, 1992–95. Shaftesbury Society, then Grooms-Shaftesbury: Member: Council, 1995–; Urban Action Cttee, 1995– (Chm., 1997–99); Audit Cttee, 2001–; Pay Review Panel, 2002; Chief Exec.'s Appts Panel, 2002; Chm., Grooms-Shaftesbury Merger Project Gp, 2006–07. Mem., West Ham Central Mission Wkg Gp, 2000–01. Link Trustee, Nash Coll., Bromley, 2003– (Mem., Resources Cttee; Chm. Govs, 2005–). Mem., John Grooms Disability Enquiry, 2003. Freeman, City of London, 2002. *Recreations:* housing and disability issues, Church and Christian activities, exhibition budgerigars (Sec., 2000–, Pres., 2008, Croydon Budgerigar Soc.), fuchsias. *Address:* Remrah, 21 Lackford Road, Chipstead, Surrey CR5 3TB.

HARMSWORTH, family name of **Viscount Rothermere** and **Baron Harmsworth.**

HARMSWORTH, 3rd Baron *cr* 1939, of Egham; **Thomas Harold Raymond Harmsworth;** publisher; *b* 20 July 1939; *s* of Hon. Eric Beauchamp Northcliffe Harmsworth (*d* 1988) and Hélène Marie (*d* 1962), *d* of Col Jules Raymond Dehove; *S* uncle, 1990; *m* 1971, Patricia Palmer, *d* of late M. P. Horsley; two *s* three *d*. *Educ:* Eton; Christ Church, Oxford (MA). Nat. Service, Royal Horse Guards (The Blues), 1957–59 (2nd Lieut). Stockbroker, 1962–74; DHSS, 1974–88. Chm., Dr Johnson's House Trust. *Publications:* Gastronomic Dictionary: French-English, 2003; Gastronomic Dictionary: Spanish-English, 2004; Gastronomic Dictionary: Italian-English, 2005; Gastronomic Dictionary: Portuguese–English, 2008. *Recreations:* sundry, including music. *Heir: s* Hon. Dominic Michael Eric Harmsworth [*b* 18 Sept. 1973; *m* 1999, Veronica Patricia, *d* of L and Veronica Ausset, San Fernando, Chile; two *s* two *d*]. *Address:* The Old Rectory, Sto Abbott, Beaminster, Dorset DT8 3JT. *T:* (01308) 868139. *Clubs:* Carlton, Brooks's.

HARMSWORTH, Sir Hildebrand Harold, 3rd Bt *cr* 1922; gardening writer; *b* 5 Ju 1931; *s* of Sir Hildebrand Alfred Beresford Harmsworth, 2nd Bt, and Elen, *d* of Nic Billenstein, Randers, Denmark; *S* father, 1977, but his name does not appear on t Official Roll of the Baronetage; *m* 1960, Gillian Andrea (*d* 2005), *o d* of William Jo Lewis; one *s* two *d*. *Educ:* Harrow; Trinity College, Dublin. *Heir: s* Hildebrand Esmo Miles Harmsworth [*b* 1 Sept. 1964; *m* 1988, Ruth Denise, *d* of Dennis Miles; one *s* tv *d*]. *Address:* Ewlyn Villa, 42 Leckhampton Road, Cheltenham GL53 0BB.

HARNDEN, Prof. David Gilbert, PhD; FRCPath; FRSE 1982; FIBiol; Chairma South Manchester University Hospitals NHS Trust, 1997–2002; *b* 22 June 1932; *s* William Alfred Harnden and Anne McKenzie Wilson; *m* 1955, Thora Margaret Seatt three *s*. *Educ:* George Heriot's School, Edinburgh; University of Edinburgh. BSc. Lec Univ. of Edinburgh, 1956–57; Sci. Mem., Radiobiology Unit, MRC, Harwell, 1957–5 Sci. Mem., Clinical and Population Cytogenetics Unit, MRC, Edinburgh, 1959–69; Pr of Cancer Studies, Univ. of Birmingham, 1969–83; Dir, Paterson Labs, later Paterson In for Cancer Res., Christie Hosp. and Holt Radium Inst., later Christie Hosp. NHS Tru 1983–97; Hon. Prof. of Experimental Oncology, 1983–97, Prof. Emeritus, 1998–, Un of Manchester; Emeritus Fellow, CRC, 1997. Chairman: Educn Cttee, Cancer R Campaign, 1987–92; NW Regl Adv. Cttee on Oncology Services, 1991–95. Dir, Chris Hosp. (NHS) Trust, 1991–97. Trustee: New Heart/New Start, Wythenshawe Ho Transplant Fund, 1998–2002; Gray Lab. Cancer Res. Trust, 2000–06; Chm., Truste Friends of Rosie, Children's Cancer Res. Fund, 1999–. Hon. MRCP 1987. Chn Editorial Bd, British Jl of Cancer, 1983–98. Mem., NRPB, 1995–99. *Publications:* pape on cancer research and human genetics in learned jls. *Recreation:* sketching people a places. *Address:* Tanglewood, Ladybrook Road, Bramhall, Stockport SK7 3NE. *T:* (016 485 3214; *e-mail:* dgharnden@btinternet.com.

HARNEY, Mary; TD (Prog. Dem.) Dublin Mid West; Minister for Health and Childre since 2004; Leader, Progressive Democrats, 1993–2006 and since 2007; *b* March 1953; 2001, Brian Geoghegan. *Educ:* Convent of Mercy, Inchicore, Dublin; Presentati Convent, Clondalkin, Co. Dublin; Trinity Coll., Dublin (BA). Contested (FF) Dublin S 1977. Mem. Dublin CC, 1979–91. Senator, 1977–81; TD Dublin SW, then Dublin M West: FF, 1981–85; Prog. Dem., 1985–; Minister: of Envmtl Protection, 1989–92; f Enterprise, Trade and Employment, 1997–2004; Tánaiste, 1997–2006. Progressiv Democrats: Co-Founder, 1985; Dep. Leader, and Spokesperson on Justice, Equality ar Law Reform, 1993. *Address:* Department of Health, Hawkins House, Dublin 2, Ireland

HARPER, Most Rev. Alan Edwin Thomas; *see* Armagh, Archbishop of, and Prima of All Ireland.

HARPER, Dr Caroline Anne, OBE 2000; Chief Executive, Sightsavers Internationa since 2005; *b* 4 May 1960; *d* of Douglas and Barbara Harper. *Educ:* Bristol Univ. (BSc Churchill Coll., Cambridge (PhD 1986). British Gas, 1985–91; Amerada Hess, 1991–200 (Man. Dir, Amerada Hess Gas); CEO, Harper & Associates, 2002–05. *Recreations:* ski-in travel. *Address:* 4A Wellington Close, W11 2AN. *T:* (020) 7467 0515; *e-mail:* harper_ca(hotmail.com.

HARPER, Air Vice-Marshal Christopher Nigel, CBE 2002; Air Officer Commandin No 1 Group, since 2007; *b* 25 March 1957; *s* of late Denis Alan Harper and of Cynthi Nancy Harper; *m* 1980, Janet Elizabeth Edwards; one *s* (and one *s* decd). *Educ:* Alleyn Sch., Dulwich; King's Coll., London (MA Defence Studies). Joined RAF, 1976; office trng, RAF Henlow, 1976 (Sword of Honour); with 41 (Fighter) Sqdn, 1979–81; with No 31 and 14 Sqdns, 1982–85; Jaguar Qualified Weapons Instructor, 1984; Exchange tou Canadian Air Force flying CF-18 Hornet with 421 Sqdn, 1986–89; Eurofighter Projec Officer, MoD, 1989–92; RAF Staff Coll., Bracknell, 1992; MA to Minister (Arme Forces), MoD, 1992–94; OC No 41 (F) Sqdn, 1994–97; Exec. Officer to Comdr AAFCE 1997–99; Stn Comdr, RAF Coltishall, 1999–2001 (dispatches, Iraq, 2002); Air Cdr Typhoon, HQ 1 Gp, 2002–04; Dir, Jt Commitments, MoD, 2004–05; COS Ops, HC Strike Comd, 2005–07. Staff Pilot, No 5 Air Experience Flight, RAF Wyton, 2001– Pres., RAF Flying Clubs' Assoc., 2005–; Hon. Pres., No 1475 Sqdn ATC, 2003–. FCM (FIMgt 1997). *Recreations:* flying, shooting, running, golf, cooking. *Address:* No 1 Group RAF High Wycombe, Bucks HP14 4UE. *Clubs:* Royal Air Force; Strangers' (Norwich).

HARPER, David Ross, CBE 2002; FFPH; CBiol, FIBiol; Chief Scientist and Head o Profession for Scientists, since 1996, and Director General of Health Improvement an Protection, since 2008, Department of Health; *b* 6 June 1955; *s* of Frank Harper an Louise Harper (*née* Mason); *m* 1978, Lorraine Chadwick; two *s* one *d*. *Educ:* Univ. o Dundee (BSc Hons Microbiol. 1977); Univ. of Birmingham (PhD Microbial Biochem 1982). CBiol, FIBiol 1995; FFPH 2006. Hd, Microbiol. Unit, Metropolitan Police Forensic Sci. Lab., 1981–89; Department of Health: Head: Microbiol. Pathology Services 1989–91; Food Microbiol. Sci. Unit, 1991–94; Dangerous Pathogens, Biotechnol. an Envmtl Microbiol. Unit, 1994–2000; Envmt Br., 2000–03; Dir Gen. for Health Protection, Internat. Health and Scientific Develt, 2003–08. *Publications:* articles in jls *Recreations:* music, sport, motorcycles. *Address:* Department of Health, Richmond House, 79 Whitehall, SW1A 2NS. *T:* (020) 7210 5522, *Fax:* (020) 7210 5908; *e-mail:* david.harper@dh.gsi.gov.uk.

HARPER, Donald John; Chief Scientist, Royal Air Force, 1980–83; *b* 6 Aug. 1923; *s* of Harry Tonkin and Caroline Irene Harper; *m* 1947, Joyce Beryl Kite-Powell; two *d*. *Educ:* Purley County Grammar Sch. for Boys; Queen Mary Coll., London (1st cl. BSc (Eng) 1943). CEng, FRAeS. Joined Aero Dept, RAE Farnborough, 1943; Scientific Officer, Spinning Tunnel, 1947–49; High Speed and Transonic Tunnel, 1950–59; Sen. Scientific Officer; Principal Scientific Officer, 1955; Dep. Head of Tunnel, 1958–59; Space Dept RAE, Satellite Launching Vehicles, 1960–62; Senior Principal Scientific Officer, MoD, Central Staff, 1963–65; Head of Assessment Div., Weapons Dept, RAE, 1966–68; Dir of Project Time and Cost Analysis, MoD (PE), 1968–71; Dir-Gen., Performance and Cost Analysis, MoD (PE), 1972–77; Dir-Gen. Research C, MoD (PE), 1978–83. Mem. Council, RAeS, 1990–92. *Publications:* contrib. Aeronautical Res. Council reports and memoranda and techn. press. *Recreations:* music, especially choral singing; gardening, home improvement, family history research, fell-walking.

HARPER, Dame Elizabeth (Margaret Way), DBE 1995; farmer, retired; *b* 20 June 1937; *d* of Jack Horsford Horrell and Margaret Faith Horrell (*née* Rickard); *m* 1956, Charles John Harper; two *s* (one *d* decd). *Educ:* Lagmhor Sch., Mid-Canterbury, NZ; Ashburton High Sch.; Craighead Diocesan Sch., Timaru. Save the Children: Br. Sec., 1970–84; Pres., Ashburton Br., 1984–87; S Island Vice-Pres., 1987–89; NZ Pres., 1990–93. Red Cross volunteer, Dist Nursing Service, 1984–; night sitter volunteer for terminally ill, 1987–. Mem. Bd, Ashburton Benevolent Trust, 1998–. Save the Children Award for Dist. and Meritorious Service, 1994. *Recreations:* golf, sewing, knitting.

HARPER, Sir Ewan William, Kt 2003; CBE 1997; JP; Chief Executive: United Church Schools Trust (formerly The Church Schools Company), since 1990; United Learning Trust, since 2002 (Governor, since 2002); *b* 21 June 1939; *s* of Leonard Robert Harper and Enid Harper (*née* Redman); *m* 1965, Jennifer Margaret Hoare-Scott; one *s* three *d*. *Educ:* Marlborough Coll.; Trinity Hall, Cambridge (Open Exhibnr; MA Hist). Man. Dir, 1972–87, Chm., 1985–87, Harper and Tunstall Ltd; Dir, Restoration of Lambeth Palace Chapel, 1987–88; Sec., Archbishops' Commn on Rural Areas, 1988–90. Mem., Hurd Commn on Office of Archbishop of Canterbury, 2000. Chm., Northants Industry Year, 1986; Vice Chm., Bd of Visitors, Wellingborough Borstal, 1970–82. Lay Mem., Chapter of Peterborough Cath., 2002–07. Governor: Benenden Sch., 1983–92 (Chm., Benenden Sch. Trust); Oundle Sch., 1992–2003; Maidwell Hall, 1993–2000; UC Northampton, 1997–2002. Trustee: Lambeth Fund, 1983–; Academy Sponsors Trust, 2004–06. JP Northants, 1973. *Recreations:* gardening, golf, tennis, watercolours, history. *Address:* United Church Schools Trust, Titchmarsh, Northants NN14 3DA. *T:* (01832) 735105, *Fax:* (01832) 734760; *e-mail:* ewh@church-schools.com. *Clubs:* Athenæum, MCC.
See also M. C. Harper.

HARPER, Prof. Fred, PhD; educational consultant, Central and Eastern Europe, since 1997; Dean, Seale-Hayne Faculty of Agriculture, Food and Land Use, University of Plymouth (formerly Plymouth Polytechnic), 1989–97, now Emeritus Professor of Agriculture; *b* 7 June 1947; *s* of Frederick and Queenie Elizabeth Harper; *m* 1971, Moyna Carole Hunter (marr. diss. 1996); one *d*. *Educ:* Univ. of Nottingham (BSc Hons Agric., PhD). Lecturer: Writtle Agricl Coll., Chelmsford, 1971–75; and Dir of Studies, Univ. of Edinburgh, 1975–82; Vice-Principal and Dir of Studies, Harper Adams Agricl Coll., Shropshire, 1983–88; Principal, Seale-Hayne Coll., Devon, 1988–89. ARAgS, 1993. *Publications:* The Principles of Arable Crop Production, 1983; numerous pubns on crop physiology and production, agricl educn and overseas agriculture. *Recreations:* walking, travel, observing wildlife, watching sport. *Address:* 11 The Village, Shobrooke, Crediton, Exeter EX17 1AU. *T:* (01363) 776105.

HARPER, Heather Mary, (Mrs E. J. Benarroch), CBE 1965; soprano; Professor of Singing and Consultant, Royal College of Music, 1985–93; Director of Singing Studies, Britten-Pears School, Aldeburgh, since 1986; *b* 8 May 1930; *d* of late Hugh Harper, Belfast; *m* 1973, Eduardo J. Benarroch. *Educ:* Trinity Coll. of Music, London. Has sung many principal roles incl. Arabella, Ariadne, Marschallin, Chrysothemis, Elsa and Kaiserin, at Covent Garden, Glyndebourne, Sadler's Wells, Bayreuth, Teatro Colon (Buenos Aires), Edinburgh Fest., La Scala, NY Met, San Francisco, Deutsche Oper (Berlin), Frankfurt, Netherlands Opera, Canadian Opera Co., Toronto, and sang at every Promenade Concert season, 1957–90; created the soprano role in Benjamin Britten's War Requiem in Coventry Cathedral in 1962; soloist at opening concerts: Maltings, Snape, 1967; Queen Elizabeth Hall, 1967. Toured USA, 1965, and USSR, 1967, with BBC SO; toured USA annually, 1967–91, and appeared regularly at European music fests; toured: Japan and S Korea as Principal Soloist Soprano with Royal Opera Co., 1979; Australia and Hong Kong with BBC Symph. Orch., 1982; has also sung in Asia, Middle East, Australia and S America; Principal Soloist Soprano with Royal Opera House Co., visit to Los Angeles Olympic Games, 1984; Principal Soloist with BBC Philharmonic Orch.'s first South American tour, 1989. Has made many recordings, incl. works of Britten, Beethoven, Berg, Mahler, Mozart, Strauss and Verdi; broadcasts frequently throughout the world, and appears frequently on TV; Masterclasses for advanced students and young professionals, Britten-Pears Sch.; retired from operatic stage, 1984, from concert stage, 1991. Member: BBC Music Panel, 1989; RSA Music Panel, 1989. FTCL; FRCM 1988; Hon. RAM, 1972. Hon. DMus Queen's Univ., Belfast, 1966; Hon. DLitt Ulster, 1992. Edison Award, 1971; Grammy Nomination, 1973; Grammy Award, 1979, 1984, 1991; Best vocal performance for Ravel's Shéhérazade; Grand Prix du Disque, 1979. *Recreations:* gardening, cooking.

HARPER, James Norman; barrister; a Recorder of the Crown Court, 1980–84; *b* 30 Dec. 1932; *s* of late His Honour Judge Norman Harper and Iris Irene Harper; *m* 1956, Blanka Miroslava Eva Sigmund (*d* 1999); one *s* one *d*. *Educ:* Marlborough Coll.; Magdalen Coll., Oxford (BA Hons). Called to the Bar, Gray's Inn, 1957; Attorney Gen. of NE Circuit, 1992–96. Pres., Northumberland County Hockey Assoc., 1982–2002. *Recreations:* cricket, hockey, painting. *Address:* (chambers) 33 Broad Chare, Newcastle upon Tyne NE1 3DQ. *T:* (0191) 232 0541. *Club:* MCC.

HARPER, Prof. John Lander, CBE 1989; DPhil; FRS 1978; Emeritus Professor of Botany, University of Wales, since 1982: Head, Unit of Plant Population Biology, School of Plant Biology, Bangor, 1982–90; *b* 27 May 1925; *s* of John Hindley Harper and Harriett Mary (*née* Archer); *m* 1954, Borgny Lerø; one *s* two *d*. *Educ:* Lawrence Sheriff Sch., Rugby; Magdalen Coll., Oxford (BA, MA, DPhil). Demonstr, Dept of Agriculture, Univ. of Oxford, 1951, Lectr 1953; Rockefeller Foundn Fellow, Univ. of Calif., 1960–61; Prof. of Agricultural Botany, 1960, Prof. of Botany, 1977–82 and Head of Sch. of Plant Biology, 1967–82, University Coll. of North Wales, Bangor. Vis. Prof., Univ. of Exeter, 1999–. Member: NERC, 1971–81; AFRC, 1980–90; Jt Nature Conservation Cttee, 1991–94. Trustee, Natural Hist. Mus., 1993–97. For. Assoc., US Nat. Acad. of Sciences, 1984. Hon. DSc Sussex, 1984; Dr (*hc*) Univ. Nacional Autónoma de México, 1997. *Publications:* Biology of Weeds, 1960; Population Biology of Plants, 1977; (with M. Begon and C. Townsend) Ecology: organisms, populations and communities, 1985, 4th edn 2006; Fundamentals of Ecology, 2000, 3rd edn 2008; papers in Jl of Ecol., New Phytologist, Annals of Applied Biol., Evolution, and Proc. Royal Soc. (Editor, Series B, 1993–98). *Recreation:* gardening. *Address:* The Lodge, Chapel Road, Brampford Speke, Exeter EX5 5HG. *T:* (01392) 841929. *Club:* Farmers'.

HARPER, Prof. John Martin, PhD; FRCO(CHM); Director, International Centre for Sacred Music Studies, Bangor University, since 2008; *b* 11 July 1947; *s* of Geoffrey Martin and Kathleen Harper; *m* 1970, Cynthia Margaret Dean (marr. diss.); three *s*; *m* 1991, Sally Elizabeth Roper. *Educ:* King's Coll. Sch., Cambridge; Clifton Coll., Bristol; Selwyn Coll., Cambridge (Organ Scholar; MA); Birmingham Univ. (PhD); MA Oxon. Dir, Edington Music Fest., 1971–78; Dir of Music, St Chad's Cathedral, Birmingham, 1972–78; Lectr in Music, Birmingham Univ., 1974–75, 1976–81; Asst Dir of Music, King Edward's Sch., Birmingham, 1975–76; Fellow, Organist, Informator Choristarum and Tutor in Music, Magdalen Coll., and Univ. Lectr in Music, Oxford, 1981–90; University College of North Wales, then University of Wales, Bangor: Prof. of Music, 1991–98; Res. Prof., 1998–; Dir Gen., RSCM, 1998–2007. Leverhulme Fellow, 1997–98; Vis. Scholar, Sarum Coll., 2005–. Founder Dir, Centre for Advanced Welsh Music Studies, 1994–2003. Founder Editor, Welsh Music History, 1996–99. Mem. Council, Plainsong and Medieval Music Soc., 1994– (Chm., 1998–2006); Trustee, Early English Organ Project, 1999–2005 (Chm., 2000–05). Recordings, 1974–, incl. The English Anthem (5 vols 1990), The English Carol (1984), The Victorian Carol (1990), all with Magdalen Coll. Choir. FRSCM 2007. Hon. FGCM 1996. Benemerenti Papal award, 1978. *Publications:* choral compositions, 1974–; (ed) Orlando Gibbons: consort music, 1982; The Forms and Orders of Western Liturgy, 1991; (ed) Hymns for Prayer and Praise, 1996; (ed) Music for Common Worship (7 vols), 2000–; (ed) The Light of Life, 2002; The Spirit of the Lord, 2004; (ed jtly) Psallam, 2006; contribs to: New Grove Dictionary of Music and Musicians, 1980, 2000; Frescobaldi Studies, 1987; Die Musik in Geschichte und Gegenwart, 1994; Blackwell History of Music in Britain, Vol. 2, 1995; Oxford DNB; articles and reviews in music jls and papers. *Address:* Bethania, Llangoed, Beaumaris, Anglesey LL58 8PH.

HARPER, (John) Michael; Chairman: Vitec plc, since 2004; BBA Aviation plc, since 2007; *b* 2 Jan. 1945; *s* of Mark and Kathleen Harper; *m* 1st, 1968, Julia Carey (marr. diss. 1979); one *s* one *d*; 2nd, 1979, Judith Soesan; two *s* one *d*. *Educ:* King's Coll., London (BSc Eng, AKC, 1966); Imperial Coll., London (MSc 1967). Managing Director: Vickers S. Marston, 1975–80; BAJ Vickers, 1980–84; Graviner Ltd, 1984–88; Divl Man. Dir, 1988–99, Dir, 1999–2000, Williams plc; Chief Exec., Kidde plc, 2000–05. Non-executive Director: Umeco plc, 2002–07; Ricardo plc, 2003–; Catlin Gp plc, 2005–. *Recreations:* sport generally, particularly cricket, football, Rugby; ballet, theatre. *Address:* Barley End, Stocks Road, Aldbury, Herts HP23 5RZ. *T:* (01442) 851055, *Fax:* (01442) 851571. *Clubs:* Travellers, MCC.

HARPER, Prof. (John) Ross, CBE 1986; Founder, 1961, and Senior Partner, 1961–2001, Ross Harper & Murphy, Solicitors; Consultant, Harper Macleod, since 2001 (Senior Partner, 1991–2001); Professor of Law, Strathclyde University, 1986–2002, now Emeritus; *b* 20 March 1935; *s* of late Rev. Thomas Harper, BD, STM, PhD and Margaret Simpson Harper (later Clarkson); *m* 1963, Ursula Helga Renate Gathman; two *s* one *d*. *Educ:* Hutchesons' Boys' Grammar School; Glasgow Univ. (MA, LLB). Pres., Students Rep. Council, 1955. Pres., Scottish Union of Students, 1956–58; Chm., Internat. Students' Conf., 1958. Asst Solicitor, McGettigan & Co., Glasgow, 1959; founded Ross Harper & Murphy, 1961. Temp. Sheriff, 1979–89; a Parly Comr, 1992–. Pres., Law Soc. of Scotland, 1988–89 (Vice-Pres., 1987–88). Pres., Glasgow Bar Assoc., 1975–78; International Bar Association: Chm., Criminal Law Div., 1983–87; Chm., Gen. Practice Section, 1990–92 (Sec. and Treas., 1988–90); Vice-Pres., 1992–94; Pres., 1994–96. Chairman: Mining (Scotland), 1997–2007 (Jt Chm., 1993–95); Scottish Coal, 1997–2007; Alarm Protection Ltd, 2000–; Scottish Biopower Ltd, 2004–; Eur. Scanning Clinic Ltd, 2004–07; Admiralty Resources NL (Australia), 2005–. Chm., Finance Cttee, Greater Glasgow Health Board, 1984–87; Non-exec. Dir, Scottish Prison Service, 1993–96. Consultant, Makanyane Safari Lodge, SA, 2001–. Trustee, Nat. Galls of Scotland, 1996–99. Contested (C): Hamilton, 1970; W Renfrewshire, Feb. and Oct. 1974. Founder Chm., Soc. of Scottish Cons. Lawyers, 1982–86; Pres., Scottish Cons. & Unionist Assoc., 1989 (Hon. Sec., 1986–89). *Publications:* A Practitioner's Guide to the Criminal Courts, 1985; Glasgow Rape Case, 1985; Fingertip Criminal Law, 1986; Global Law in Practice, 1997; pamphlets on devolution, referendums, etc. *Recreations:* bridge, angling. *Address:* 67 Cadogan Square, SW1X 0DY. *Club:* Caledonian.

HARPER, Joseph Charles; QC 1992; *b* 21 March 1939; *e s* of Frederick Charles Harper and Kitty (*née* Judah); *m* 1984, Sylvia Helen Turner (marr. diss. 1994); two *d*. *Educ:* Charterhouse; LSE (BA, LLB, LLM). ARCM 1960. Lectr, later Hd, Dept of Law, Kingston Poly., 1965–70; called to the Bar: Gray's Inn, 1970 (Bencher, 2000); Antigua, 1985. Mem. Council, Justice, 1979–91. *Publications:* (Specialist Editor) Hill and Redman, Law of Landlord and Tenant (looseleaf), 17th edn 1982, 18th edn 1988–; (ed and contrib.) Halsbury's Laws of England, vol. 8(I) Compulsory Acquisition of Land, vol. 46 Town and Country Planning; (ed) Planning Encyclopedia, 2006–. *Recreations:* music (especially playing the French horn), bibliomania. *Address:* Landmark Chambers, 180 Fleet Street, EC4A 2HG. *T:* (020) 7430 1221. *Club:* Garrick.

HARPER, Malcolm Charles, CMG 2000; international consultant, since 2004; Joint President, United Nations Association, since 2004 (Director, 1982–2004); *b* 21 June 1939; *s* of Leonard Robert Harper and Enid Harper (*née* Redman); *m* 1966, Ann Patricia Broad; one *s* two *d*. *Educ:* Marlborough Coll.; Trinity Hall, Cambridge (MA Hons Hist. and Theol.). Lay Personal Asst to Anglican Archbp of Cape Town, 1961–62; with OXFAM, 1963–81: served in E Africa, 1968–71; Emergencies Officer, 1972–75; Communications Dir, 1975–81; in Cambodia, 1979–80. Mem. Exec. Cttee, World Fedn of UNAs, Geneva, 1981–2004 (Chm., 1995–2000). Mem. Bd, Internat. Broadcasting Trust, 1978–. Gov., Burford Sch., Oxon, 1987– (Chm., 1993–2008); Mem. Bd of Govs, Internat. Students House, 1994–. Trustee: Afghanaid, 2005–; Commonwealth Soc. for the Deaf, 2005–; Landmine Action Trust, 2007–. Sec., Friends of N Uganda, 2004–. Mem., RIIA, 1999–. Albert Einstein Gold Medal, UNESCO, 1995; Soka Gakkai Internat. Medal (Japan), 1999. *Publications:* contrib. chapters to several UN-orientated books. *Recreations:* cricket, long-distance walking, jogging, photography, theatre. *Address:* The Cottages, Church Lane, Charlbury, Oxon OX7 3PX. *T:* and *Fax:* (01608) 810464. *Clubs:* Royal Commonwealth Society, MCC, Cricketers'; Charlbury Cricket (Oxon), Nonnunquam Cricket.
See also Sir E. W. Harper.

HARPER, Mark; MP (C) Forest of Dean, since 2005; *b* 26 Feb. 1970; *m* 1999, Margaret Whelan. *Educ:* Headlands Sch., Swindon; Swindon Coll.; Brasenose Coll., Oxford (BA 1991). Auditor, KPMG, 1991–95; Intel Corporation (UK) Ltd: Sen. Finance Analyst, 1995–97; Finance Manager, 1997–2000; Ops Manager, 2000–02; own accountancy practice, Forest of Dean, 2002–06. Contested (C) Forest of Dean, 2001. Shadow Minister: for Defence, 2005–07; for Disabled People, 2007–. *Address:* (office) 53 High Street, Cinderford, Glos GL14 2SU; House of Commons, SW1A 0AA.

HARPER, Michael; see Harper, J. M.

HARPER, Monica Celia, CMG 2004; HM Diplomatic Service, retired; Head of International Relations, Shakespeare's Globe, 2005–06; *b* 18 Aug. 1944; *d* of late Frank Ernest Harper and Renee Alice Harper. *Educ:* Reading Univ. and Sorbonne (BA Hons); City of London Coll. (Dip. Business Studies). Entered HM Diplomatic Service, 1967; FCO, 1967–69; on secondment to internat. staff of SEATO, Bangkok, 1969–72; attached to Ecole Nat. d'Admin, Paris, 1973–74; Third Sec., BMG, Berlin, 1974–77; Second Secretary: Bonn, 1977–79; Personnel Ops Dept, FCO, 1979–82; Mexico City, 1982–84; Press and Inf. Officer, UK Delegn to NATO, 1984–88; First Sec., Western European Dept (Germany), 1989–94; Dep. Hd of Mission, Luxembourg, 1994–98; Consul Gen., Lille, 1998–2004; Counsellor, FCO, 2004. *Recreations:* music, theatre, cinema, food. *Address:* 51 Tudor Way, Church Crookham, Hants GU52 6LX.

HARPER, Prof. Peter Stanley, Kt 2004; CBE 1995; DM; FRCP; University Research Professor in Human Genetics, Cardiff University, since 2004; *b* 28 April 1939; *m*; two *s* three *d*. *Educ:* Exeter Coll., Oxford (BA 1964; MA, DM 1972). With Sir Cyril Clarke, Nuffield Inst. for Med. Genetics, Liverpool, 1967–69; with Dr Victor McKusick, Div. of Med. Genetics, Johns Hopkins Hosp., Baltimore, 1969–71; UWCM, Cardiff, 1971–2004, Prof. of Med. Genetics, 1981–2004. *Publications:* Myotonic Dystrophy, 1979, 3rd edn 2001; Practical Genetic Counselling, 1981, 6th edn 2004; (ed) Huntington's Disease, 1991, 3rd edn 2002; Landmarks in Medical Genetics, 2004. *Recreations:* natural history, music. *Address:* Institute of Medical Genetics, Cardiff University, Heath Park, Cardiff CF14 4XN. *T:* (029) 2074 4057; *e-mail:* HarperPS@cf.ac.uk.

HARPER, Richard Saul; District Judge, Principal Registry of the Family Division, since 1994; *b* 19 June 1953; *s* of Alfred and Netta Harper; *m* 1988, Amanda Louise Price; two *s* one *d*. *Educ:* Magdalen Coll., Oxford (MA). Called to the Bar, Gray's Inn, 1975; practising barrister, 1976–94. *Publications:* Child Care Law: a basic guide for practitioners, 1991; Medical Treatment and the Law: the protection of adults and minors in the Family Division, 1999. *Recreations:* international affairs, reading, sport. music. *Address:* Principal Registry of the Family Division, First Avenue House, 42–49 High Holborn, WC1V 6NP. *T:* (020) 7947 6943.

HARPER, Robin Charles Moreton; Member (Green) Lothians, Scottish Parliament, since 1999; *b* 4 Aug. 1940; *s* of late Comdr C. H. A. Harper, OBE, RN and Jessicca Harper; *m* 1994, Jennifer Helen Carter (*née* Brown); one step *s*. *Educ:* Aberdeen Univ. (MA); Edinburgh Univ. (Dip. Guidance & Curriculum). Teacher: Braehead Sch., Fife, 1964–68, 1970–71; Kolanya Sch., Kenya, 1968; Amukura Sch., Kenya, 1969; teacher: English, Newbattle High Sch., 1971–72; Modern Studies, Boroughmuir High Sch., 1972–99. Rector: Edinburgh Univ., 2000–03; Aberdeen Univ., 2005–08. Co-convener, Scottish Green Party, 1999–. FEIS; FRSA. *Recreations:* hill walking, music, photography. *Address:* Scottish Parliament, Edinburgh EH99 1SP. *T:* (0131) 348 5000.

HARPER, Ross; *see* Harper, J. R.

HARPER, Stephen Joseph; PC (Can.) 2004; MP (Alliance, then C) Calgary Southwest, since 2002; Prime Minister of Canada, since 2006; *b* 30 April 1959; *s* of late Joseph Harper and Margaret Johnstone; *m* 1993, Laureen Teskey; one *s* one *d*. *Educ:* Richview Collegiate Inst.; Univ. of Calgary. Chief Aide to Jim Hawkes, MP, 1985; Exec. Asst, then Chief Advr and Speech Writer to Deborah Grey, MP, 1989–93. Vice-Pres., 1997, Pres., 1997–2001, Nat. Citizens' Coalition. Contested (Reform) Calgary W, 1988. MP (Reform), Calgary W, 1993–97; Leader of the Opposition, 2002–04, 2004–06. Founding Mem., Reform Party, 1993; Leader, Canadian Alliance, 2002–03; Co-founder, 2003, Leader, 2004–, Cons. Party of Canada. *Address:* (office) 80 Wellington Street, Ottawa, ON K1A 0A2, Canada.

HARPER, William Ronald; a Director, Thames Water, 1982–97; *b* 5 June 1944; *s* of William and Dorothy Harper; *m* 1969, Susan Penelope (*née* Rider); two *s* two *d*. *Educ:* Barton Peveril Grammar Sch., Eastleigh, Hants. IPFA 1965. Hampshire CC, 1960–64; Eastbourne CBC, 1964–68; Chartered Inst. of Public Finance and Accountancy, 1968–70; Greenwich London BC, 1970–74; Thames Water Authority: joined 1974; Dir of Finance, 1982; Dir of Corporate Strategy, 1984; Man. Dir, 1986; Dep. Chm., Thames Water Utilities, 1989; Thames Water PLC: Bd Mem., 1989–97; Gp Dir, Corporate Activities, 1992; Divl Dir, Products, 1994; Strategy Dir, 1996–97. Chm., Foundn for Water Res., 1989–94. Member: Council, Water Services Assoc., 1990–94; Bd of Management, Water Training, 1991–99 (Chm., 1993–99). CEN Rapporteur-Water, 1998–. *Address:* 37 Kidmore End Road, Reading, Berks RG4 8SN. *T:* (0118) 947 4476.

HARPIN, Richard David; Chief Executive, Homeserve plc, since 1999; *b* Huddersfield, 10 Sept. 1964; *s* of David and Phillipa Harpin; *m* 1997, Kate; two *s* one *d*. *Educ:* Royal Grammar Sch., Newcastle upon Tyne; York Univ. (BA Hons Econs). Brand Manager, Procter and Gamble, 1986–90; Harpin Ltd, 1988–; Sen. Consultant, Deloitte, 1990–91; Franchisee, Mortgage Advice Shop, Middlesbrough, 1991–92; Man. Dir, Homeserve GB Ltd, 1993–99. Non-executive Chairman: Heating Components and Equipt Ltd, 1998–2004; Amsys Rapid Prototype and Tooling Ltd, 1999–2001; non-executive Director: Professional Properties Ltd, 1990–99; Baker Tilly Consulting, 1992–97; Mortgage Advice Bureau, 1997–2000. *Recreations:* off piste and heliski-ing, swimming, mountain biking. *Address:* Homeserve plc, Cable Drive, off Green Lane, Walsall WS2 7BN. *T:* (01922) 659701; *e-mail:* richard.harpin@homeserve.com.

HARPUM, Charles, LLD; barrister; Fellow, Downing College, Cambridge, 1977–2001, now Emeritus; *b* 29 March 1953; *s* of Dr John Richard Harpum and Beatrice Doreen Harpum (*née* Harper). *Educ:* Queen Elizabeth Grammar Sch., Penrith; Cheltenham Grammar Sch.; Downing Coll., Cambridge (BA 1st Cl. Hons with Dist. 1975; LLB 1st Cl. Hons with Dist. 1977; Chancellor's Medal; MA 1979; LLD 2003). Called to the Bar, Lincoln's Inn, 1976, Bencher, 2001. Asst Lectr in Law, 1979–84, Lectr, 1984–98, Cambridge Univ.; a Law Comr, 1994–2001. Vis. Schol., Sch. of Law, Univ. of Va, Charlottesville, USA, 1991. *Publications:* (contrib.) Megarry and Wade's Law of Real Property, 7th edn 2008; (jtly) Registered Land, 2002; (jtly) Registered Land: law and practice under the Land Registration Act 2002, 2004; numerous articles on property law in learned jls. *Recreations:* travelling, listening to classical music, drinking single island malts. *Address:* Falcon Chambers, Falcon Court, EC4Y 1AA. *T:* (020) 7353 2484.

HARRAP, Prof. Kenneth Reginald, CBE 1998; PhD, DSc; CChem, FRSC; Partner, Weston & Harrap Consulting, since 1997; Professor of Biochemical Pharmacology, Institute of Cancer Research, 1984–97, now Emeritus; *b* 20 Nov. 1931; *s* of George Ernest Harrap and Lilian Florence Olive Harrap (*née* Critchley); *m* 1st, 1954, Kathleen Ann Gotts (marr. diss. 1980); two *d*; 2nd, 1983, Beverley Jane Weston. *Educ:* George Green Sch.; London Univ. (BSc 1955; PhD 1961; DCC 1963; DSc 1977). CChem 1975; FRSC 1980. Institute of Cancer Research, Royal Marsden Hospital: Lectr, subseq. Sen. Lectr, in Chemistry, 1954–64; Head, Leukaemia Biochemistry Gp, 1964–70; Head of Department: Applied Biochemistry, 1970–77; Biochemical Pharmacology, 1977–82; Chm., Drug Develt Section, 1982–94; Dir, CRC Centre for Cancer Therapeutics, 1994–97; Fellow and Vis. Scientist, 1997–; Emeritus Fellow, and Award of Distinction, CRC, 1998. Bruce F. Cain Meml Award, Amer. Assoc. of Cancer Res., 1995, NZ Cancer Soc., 1996; Barnett Rosenberg Award, Internat. Symposium on Platinum Compounds in Cancer Chemotherapy, 1995. *Publications:* 400 papers in learned jls, contribs to books, reviews etc. *Recreations:* yachting and off-shore cruising, wildlife, concert music, opera. *Address:* Little Orchard, Wonham Way, Peaslake, Surrey GU5 9PA. *Club:* Sussex Yacht.

HARREL, David Terence Digby; Partner, S. J. Berwin, Solicitors, since 1982 (Senior Partner, 1992–2006); *b* 23 June 1948; *s* of Capt. H. T. Harrel; *m* 1974, Julia Mary Reeves; two *s* one *d*. *Educ:* Marlborough Coll.; Bristol Univ. (LLB). William Charles Crocker: articled clerk, 1971–74; Asst Solicitor, 1974–77; Partner, 1977–79; Partner, Burton & Ramsden, 1979–81. *Recreations:* golf, tennis, fishing, shooting, walking, reading. *Address:* 10 Moreton Terrace Mews North, SW1V 2NT. *Club:* Royal St George's Golf (Sandwich).

HARRELL, Lynn Morris; 'cellist; *b* 30 Jan. 1944; *s* of Mack Harrell, Metropolitan Opera baritone and Marjorie Harrell (*née* Fulton), violinist. *Educ:* Julliard Sch. of Music; Curtis Inst. of Music. Principal 'Cellist, Cleveland Orch., 1963–71; Professor: College Conservatory of Music, Cincinatti, 1971–77; Juilliard Sch. of Music, 1977–86; Internat. Chair of 'Cello Studies, RAM, 1987–95; Piatigorsky Chair, Sch. of Music, USC, 1987–93; Artistic Dir, Los Angeles Philharmonic Inst., 1988–92; Principal, RAM, 1993–95; prof. of 'cello, Shepherd Sch. of Music, Rice Univ., Houston, 2002–; Prof., Musikhochschule Lübeck, 2002–. Numerous awards and Grammys. *Recreations:* fishing, golf, chess. *Address:* c/o Independent Artists (London) Ltd, 4–6 Soho Square, W1D 3PZ.

HARRHY, Eiddwen Mair; soprano; Professor of Vocal Studies, Royal College of Music, since 2001; *b* 14 April 1949; *d* of David and Emily Harrhy; *m* Greg Strange, journalist and broadcaster; one *d*. *Educ:* St Winefride's Convent, Swansea; Royal Manchester College of Music (Gold Medal Opera Prize); Paris (Miriam Licette Prize). Welsh Nat. Opera Chorus, 1970–71; Glyndebourne Festival Opera Chorus, 1971–73; début at Royal Opera House, Covent Garden, Wagner Ring Cycle, 1974; début, ENO, 1975; performances: Welsh Nat. Opera; La Scala Milan; Teatro Colon Buenos Aires; ENO; Glyndebourne; Opera North; Scottish Opera; UK and overseas orchestras; BBC promenade concerts; Australia, NZ, Hong Kong, S America, Europe, Scandinavia, USA; numerous recordings. Vis. Prof. at Conservatoires in Vienna, Stockholm, Prague, Utrecht, Vilnius. FRWCMD (FWCMD 2002); FRSA 2003. *Recreations:* chamber music, ski-ing, golf.

HARRIES, family name of **Baron Harries of Pentregarth.**

HARRIES OF PENTREGARTH, Baron *cr* 2006 (Life Peer), of Ceinewydd in the County of Dyfed; **Rt Rev. Richard Douglas Harries;** Bishop of Oxford, 1987–2006; an Hon. Assistant Bishop, Diocese of Southwark, since 2006; *b* 2 June 1936; *s* of late Brig. W. D. J. Harries, CBE and Mrs G. M. B. Harries; *m* 1963, Josephine Bottomley, MA, MB, BChir, DCH; one *s* and *d*. *Educ:* Wellington Coll,; RMA, Sandhurst; Selwyn Coll., Cambridge (MA 1965; Hon. Fellow, 1998); Cuddesdon Coll., Oxford. Lieut, Royal Corps of Signals, 1955–58. Curate, Hampstead Parish Church, 1963–69; Chaplain, Westfield Coll., 1966–69; Lectr, Wells Theol Coll., 1969–72; Warden of Wells, Salisbury and Wells Theol Coll., 1971–72; Vicar, All Saints, Fulham, 1972–81; Dean, King's Coll., London, 1981–87. GOE examnr in Christian Ethics, 1972–76; Dir, Post Ordination Trng for Kensington Jurisdiction, 1973–79. Chm., C of E Bd for Social Responsibility, 1996–2001; Vice-Chairman: Council of Christian Action, 1979–87; Council for Arms Control, 1982–87; Member: Home Office Adv. Cttee for reform of law on sexual offences, 1981–85; ACC, 1994–2003; Bd, Christian Aid, 1994–2002; Royal Commn on H of L reform, 1999; Nuffield Council on Bioethics, 2002–; HFEA, 2002–07. Chairman: Southwark Ordination Course, 1982–87; Shalom; ELTSA (End Loans to Southern Africa), 1982–87; CCJ, 1992–2001; H of L Select Cttee on Stem Cell Res., 2001–02. Pres., Johnson Soc., 1988–89. Consultant to Archbishops of Canterbury and York on Interfaith Relns, with special resp. for Jewish Christian relns, 1986–92 (Sir Sigmund Sternberg Award, 1989). Founder, Oxford Abrahamic Gp, 1992. Radio and TV work. Vis. Prof., Liverpool Hope UC, 2002; Hon. Prof. of Theol., KCL, 2006–. Lectures: Hockerill, and Drawbridge, London, 1982; Stockton, London Business Sch., 1992; Pall Mall, Inst. of Dirs, 1993; Theological, QUB, 1993; Heslington, York, 1994; Drummond, Stirling, 2007. FKC 1983; FRSL 1996; Hon. FMedSci 2004. Hon. Fellow, St Anne's Coll., Oxford, 2006. Hon. DD London, 1994; DUniv: Oxford Brookes, 2001; Open, 2006. *Publications:* Prayers of Hope, 1975; Turning to Prayer, 1978; Prayers of Grief and Glory, 1979; Being a Christian, 1981; Should Christians Support Guerillas?, 1982; The Authority of Divine Love, 1983; Praying Round the Clock, 1983; Prayer and the Pursuit of Happiness, 1985; Morning has Broken, 1985; Christianity and War in a Nuclear Age, 1986; C. S. Lewis: the man and his God, 1987; Christ is Risen, 1988; Is There a Gospel for the Rich?, 1992; Art and the Beauty of God, 1993; The Real God, 1994; Questioning Belief, 1995; A Gallery of Reflections: the Nativity of Christ, 1995; In the Gladness of Today, 1999; God Outside the Box: why spiritual people object to Christianity, 2002; After the evil: Christianity and Judaism in the shadow of the holocaust, 2003; The Passion in Art, 2004; Praying the Eucharist, 2004; The Re-enchantment of Morality: wisdom for a troubled world, 2008; *edited:* (jtly) Seasons of the Spirit, 1984; The One Genius; Through the Year with Austin Farrer, 1987; (jtly) Two Cheers for Secularism, 1998; (jtly) Christianity: two thousand years, 2001; (jtly) Abraham's Children: Jews, Christians and Muslims in conversation, 2006; *edited and contributed:* What Hope in an Armed World?, 1982; Reinhold Niebuhr and the Issues of Our Time, 1986; *contributed to:* Stewards of the Mysteries of God, 1979; Unholy Warfare, 1983; The Cross and the Bomb, 1983; Dropping the Bomb, 1985; Julian, Woman of our Time, 1985; If Christ be not raised, 1986; The Reality of God, 1986; A Necessary End, 1991; The Straits of War: Gallipoli remembered, 2000; That Second Bottle: essays on John Wilmot, Earl of Rochester, 2000; A Companion to English Renaissance Literature and Culture, 2000; Runcie: on reflection, 2002; Comparative Theology: essays for Keith Ward, 2003; Jesus in History, Thought and Culture, 2003; The Ethics of War, 2006; Britain's Next Bomb: what next?, 2006; The Price of Peace: just war in the twenty-first century, 2007; What makes us Human?, 2007; Does God Believe in Human Rights?, 2007; articles in Theology, The Times, The Observer and various other periodicals. *Recreations:* theatre, literature, walking, lecturing on cruises. *Address:* House of Lords, SW1A 0PW.

HARRIES, Prof. John Edward, PhD; CPhys, FInstP; FRMetS; Professor of Earth Observation, Imperial College of Science, Technology and Medicine, since 1994; *b* 26 March 1946; *s* of Brynmor and Marion Harries; *m* 1968, Sheila Margaret Basford; two *s* one *d*. *Educ:* Univ. of Birmingham (BSc Hons Physics 1967); King's Coll., London (PhD Physics 1971). Nat. Physical Lab., 1967–80; SO, later SSO, then PSO; Hd, Envmtl Standards Gp, 1976–80; Rutherford Appleton Laboratory, 1980–93; SPSO and Hd, Geophysics and Radio Div., 1980–84; DCSO, 1984; Associate Dir and Hd of Space Science Dept, 1984–93. Mem., NERC, 1995–97. President: Internat. Radiation Commn, 1992–96; RMetS, 1994–96. *Publications:* Earthwatch: the climate from space, 1991; more than 100 articles in books, jls and magazines. *Recreations:* walking, reading, music, supporting Welsh Rugby. *Address:* Blackett Laboratory, Imperial College, Prince Consort Road, SW7 2AZ. *T:* (020) 7594 7670; *e-mail:* j.harries@imperial.ac.uk.

HARRINGTON, 11th Earl of, *cr* 1742; **William Henry Leicester Stanhope;** Viscount Stanhope of Mahon and Baron Stanhope of Elvaston, Co. Derby, 1717; Baron Harrington, 1729; Viscount Petersham, 1742; late Captain 15th/19th Hussars; *b* 24 Aug. 1922; *o s* of 10th Earl and Margaret Trelawney (Susan) (*d* 1952), *d* of Major H. H. D. Seaton; *S* father, 1929; *m* 1st, 1942, Eileen (from whom he obtained a divorce, 1946; she *d* 1999), *o d* of late Sir John Grey, Enville Hall, Stourbridge; one *s* one *d* (and one *d* decd); 2nd, 1947, Anne Theodora (from whom he obtained a divorce, 1962), *o d* of late Major Richard Arenbourg Blennerhassett Chute; one *s* two *d*; 3rd, 1964, Priscilla Margaret, *d* of Hon. A. E. Cubitt and Mrs Ronald Dawnay; one *s* one *d*. *Educ:* Eton; RMC Sandhurst. Served War of 1939–45, demobilised 1946. Owns about 700 acres. Became Irish Citizen, 1965. *Heir: s* Viscount Petersham, *qv*. *Address:* The Glen, Ballingarry, Co. Limerick, Eire.
See also Baron Ashcombe, Earl Cawdor.

HARRINGTON, Dr Albert Blair, CB 1979; Head of Civil Service Department Medical Advisory Service, 1976–79; *b* 26 April 1914; *s* of late Albert Timothy Harrington and Lily Harrington; *m* 1939, Valerie White (*d* 1996); one *d*. *Educ:* Brisbane Grammar Sch., Qld; Aberdeen Univ. MB, ChB 1938, MD 1944. House Phys., Woodend Hosp., Aberdeen, 1938–39; service in RAMC (Field Amb., Blood Transfusion Phys., Neurologist), 1940–45; MO (Head Injuries) and Dep. Supt, Stoke Mandeville Hosp., 1946–48; Med. Supt, Dunston Hill Hosp., Gateshead, 1948–50; SMO (Pensions), Cleveleys, 1950–53; Med. Supt, Queen Mary's Hosp., Roehampton, 1954–56; SMO, Dept of Health (Hosp. Bldg and later Regional Liaison Duties), 1956–68; PMO (Hosp. Bldg), 1968–73; SPMO (Under-Sec.), DHSS, 1973–76. Chm., CS Med. Appts Bds, 1979–86. FFCM (Foundn

Fellow) 1972. *Publications:* articles on Sjögren's Disease, paralytic poliomyelitis, and hospital planning, medical care and the work of the Medical Advisory Service. *Recreations:* gardening, country life; formerly tennis. *Address:* 59 Lauderdale Drive, Petersham, Richmond, Surrey TW10 7BS. *T:* (020) 8940 1345. *Club:* Athenæum.

HARRINGTON, Illtyd; JP; DL; *b* 14 July 1931; *s* of Timothy Harrington and Sarah (*née* Burchell); unmarried. *Educ:* St Illtyd's RC Sch., Dowlais; Merthyr County Sch.; Trinity Coll., Caermarthen. Member: Paddington Borough Council, 1959–64; Westminster City Council, 1964–68 and 1971–78, Leader, Lab. Gp, 1972–74; GLC, 1964–67 and for Brent S, 1973–86: Alderman, 1970–73; Chairman, Policy and Resources Cttee, 1973–77, Special Cttee, 1985–86; Dep. Leader, 1973–77, 1981–84; Dep. Leader of the Opposition, 1977–81; Chm. of the Council, 1984–85. Special Advr to Chm. and Leader of ILEA, 1988–90; Waterways Advr to Mayor of London, 2001–. JP Willesden 1968. First Chairman, Inland Waterways Amenity Adv. Council, 1968–71; Chm., London Canals Consultative Cttee, 1965–67, 1981–; Vice Pres., IWA, 1990–; Member: British Waterways Bd, 1974–82; BTA, 1976–80. Member: Bd, Theatre Royal, Stratford E, 1978–; Bd, Wiltons Music Hall, 1979–; Nat. Theatre Bd, 1975–77; Bd, National Youth Theatre, 1976–; Globe Theatre Trust, 1986–2001; Chm., Half Moon Theatre, 1978–90; Director: Soho Poly Theatre, 1981–2001; The Young Vic, 1981–2001. Chm., Nat. Millennium Maritime Fest., 1997–2000; Mem., London Dockland Mgt Adv. Gp, 1997–. President: Grand Union Canal Soc., 1974–; Islington Boat Club, 1985–; SE Region, IWA, 1986–; Immunity (Legal aid facility for AIDS victims), 1986–; Chairman: Kilburn Skills, 1977–2001; Battersea Park Peace Pagoda, 1984–; Limehouse Basin Users Gp, 1986–; Vice Pres., Coventry Canal Soc., 1970–. Gov., London Marathon, 1980–91. Trustee: Kew Bridge Pumping Mus., 1976–; Queen's Jubilee Walkway, 1977–; Chiswick Family Rescue, 1978–2001; Arthur Koestler Awards for Prisoners, 1987–; CARE, 1987–; Dominica Overseas Student Fund, 1987–; Mem., Montgomery Canal Trust, 1988–; Managing Trustee, Mutual Municipal Insurance Co., 1985–96. Governor, Brunel Univ., 1981–87. Patron: Westminster Cathedral Appeal, 1977–; Abandoned and Destitute Children Appeal (India), 2006–. DL Greater London, 1986. Contributor, The Guardian, 1982–; Books Ed., Camden Jl gp of papers, 1995–. *Recreations:* defender of local government; laughing, singing and incredulity. *Address:* 44 Belbourne Court, Bread Street, Brighton, BN1 1TT. *T:* (01273) 732693. *Club:* Savile.

HARRINGTON, Prof. (John) Malcolm, CBE 1992; MD; FRCP, FFOM, FFOMI, FMedSci; Foundation Professor of Occupational Health, now Emeritus, and Director, Institute of Occupational Health, University of Birmingham, 1981–2000; *b* 6 April 1942; *s* of John Roy Harrington and Veda Naomi Harrington; *m* 1967, Madeline Mary Davies; one *d. Educ:* King's Coll., London (BSc, MSc); Westminster Hosp. Med. Sch. MD 1976; FFOM 1981; FRCP 1982; FFOMI 1994; MFPHM 1996, FFPH 2006. Hospital appointments, 1966–69; Lectr in Occupational Medicine, LSHTM, 1969–75; Vis. Scientist, Centers for Disease Control, Atlanta, US Public Health Service, 1975–77; Sen. Lectr in Occupational Medicine, LSHTM, 1977–80. Chm., Ind. Injuries Adv. Council, 1982–96. Gov., Royal Devon and Exeter NHS Foundn Trust, 2007–. Founder FMedSci 1998; Hon. FRSocMed 2004. *Publications:* (ed jtly) Occupational Hygiene, 1980, 3rd edn 2005; (with F. S. Gill) Occupational Health, 1983, 5th edn 2007; (ed) Recent Advances in Occupational Health, Vol. 2 1984, Vol. 3 1987; (ed jtly) Hunter's Diseases of Occupation, 10th edn 2009; papers in scientific professional jls. *Recreations:* music, gardening, cricket, reading biographies, theatre. *Address:* 1 The Cliff, Budleigh Salterton, Devon EX9 6JU. *Clubs:* Athenæum, Royal Society of Medicine.

HARRINGTON, Patrick John; QC 1993; a Recorder, since 1991; *b* 23 June 1949; *s* of late Murtagh Joseph Harrington and Eileen Mary Harrington (*née* Kelly); *m* 1975, Susan Jane, BSc, *o c* of Captain K. W. Bradley, RN; one *s* one *d. Educ:* Ebbw Vale Grammar Sch.; Birmingham Coll. of Commerce (LLB Hons (London) 1972); Univ. of Wales (MA Eng. Lit. 2007). Called to the Bar, Gray's Inn, 1973, Bencher, 2001; Leader, Wales and Chester Circuit, 2000–03; Hd of Chambers, 2005–. Chm., Gwent Health Research Ethics Cttee, 1993–97. Protector: Millennium Awards Trust, 2003–; Legacy Trust, 2006–. *Publication:* (with Bobby Graham) The Session Man, 2004. *Recreations:* playing and listening to music, tennis, ski-ing, classic motoring, horse racing, collecting books. *Address:* Farrar's Building, Temple, EC4Y 7BD; Broom House, Raglan, Monmouthshire NP15 2HW. *Clubs:* Cardiff and County; Ebbw Vale Rugby Football; Glamorgan CC.

HARRIS, family name of **Barons Harris, Harris of Haringey, Harris of Peckham** and of **Earl of Malmesbury**.

HARRIS, 8th Baron *cr* 1815, of Seringapatam and Mysore and of Belmont, Kent; **Anthony Harris;** *b* 8 March 1942; *s* of 7th Baron Harris and of Laura Cecilia (*née* McCausland); *S* father, 1996; *m* 1966, Anstice, *d* of Alfred Winter; two *d. Heir: cousin* Rear-Adm. Michael George Temple Harris, *qv.*

HARRIS OF HARINGEY, Baron *cr* 1998 (Life Peer), of Hornsey in the London Borough of Haringey; **(Jonathan) Toby Harris;** *b* 11 Oct. 1953; *s* of Prof. Harry Harris, FRS and of Muriel Hargest; *m* 1979, Ann Sarah Herbert; two *s* one *d. Educ:* Haberdashers' Aske's Sch., Elstree; Trinity Coll., Cambridge (BA Hons NatScis and Econ). Chair, Cambridge Univ. Labour Club, 1973; Pres., Cambridge Union Soc., 1974. Economics Div., Bank of England, 1975–79; Electricity Consumers' Council, 1979–86, Dep. Dir, 1983; Dir, Assoc. of CHCs for England and Wales, 1987–98. Chm., Toby Harris Associates, 1998–. Non-exec. Dir, London Ambulance Service NHS Trust, 1998–2005. Consultant Advr, KPMG, 1999–; Trng Advr, Infolog Ltd, 1998–2005; Sen. Associate, King's Fund, 1999–2004; Special Advr to the Bd, Transport for London, 2004–; Mem., Public Sector Adv. Council, Anite, 2005–06. Mem., Haringey BC, 1978–2002 (Chair, Social Services Cttee, 1982–87; Leader, 1987–99). Mem. (Lab) Brent and Harrow, London Assembly, GLA, 2000–04 (Leader, Labour Gp, 2000–04); Member: Adv. Cabinet, Mayor of London, 2000–04; Metropolitan Police Authy, 2004– (Chm., 2000–04). Dep. Chair, AMA, 1991–96 (Chair, Social Services Cttee, 1986–93); Chair: Assoc. of London Authorities, 1993–95 (Dep. Chair, 1990–93; Chair, Social Services Cttee, 1984–88); Assoc. of London Govt, 1995–2000; LBTC-Training for Care, 1986–94; Local Govt Anti-Poverty Unit, 1994–97; Local Government Association: Chairman: Labour Gp, 1996–2004; Community Safety Panel, 1997–98; Mem., Exec., 1999–2003; Vice-Pres., 2005–. Nat. Chair, Young Fabian Gp, 1976–77; Chair, Hornsey Labour Party, 1978, 1979, 1980; Mem., Labour Party Nat. Policy Forum, 1992–2004; Co-opted Mem., Lab. Party Local Govt Cttee, 1993–2004. Chm., All-Party Parly Gp on Policing, 2005–; Treas., Parly IT Cttee, 2005–; Mem., H of L Select Cttee Inquiry on Personal Internet Security, 2006–07. Dep. Chair, Nat. Fuel Poverty Forum, 1981–86; Member: London Drug Policy Forum, 1990–98; Jt London Adv. Panel, 1996–97. Jt Chair: London Pride Partnership, 1995–98; London Waste Action, 1997–2000; Founding Chair, Inst. of Commissioning Professionals, 2007–; Member: King's Fund Orgnl Audit Adv. Council, 1991–98; Exec. Cttee, RADAR, 1991–93; Nat. Nursery Exam. Bd, 1992–94; Home Office Adv. Council on Race Relations, 1992–97; Bd, London First, 1993–2002; Exec. Council, RNIB, 1993–94; Cttee of Regns of EU, 1994–2002; NHS Charter Advisor's Gp, 1997–98; London Pension Funds Authority, 1998–2000; Metropolitan Police Cttee, 1998–2000; Bd, London Develt Partnership, 1998–2000; Police Counter-Terrorism Bd, 2007–; Police Counter-Terrorism Ministerial Adv. Gp, 2007–. Chair, Wembley Nat. Stadium Trust, 1997–. Trustee: Evening Standard Blitz Meml Appeal, 1995–99; Help for Health Trust, 1995–97; The Learning Agency, 1996–98; Safer London Foundn, 2005–; Bilimankwhe Arts, 2008–. London Ambassador, CSV, 2005–. Mem. Adv. Bd, Three Faiths Forum, 2003–. Patron, The Larches, 2002–. Mem. Court, Middx Univ., 1995–. Governor: Nat. Inst. for Social Work, 1986–94; Sch. of St David and St Katherine, 1978–96; St Mary's Schs, Hornsey, 1978–96. FRSA 1993. Freeman, City of London, 1998. DUniv Middx, 1999. *Publications:* (with Nick Butler and Neil Kinnock) Why Vote Labour?, 1979; (contrib.) Economics of Prosperity, 1980; (ed with Jonathan Bradshaw) Energy and Social Policy, 1983; (contrib.) Rationing in Action, 1993; (contrib.) Whistleblowing in the Health Service: accountability, law, and professional practice, 1994. *Recreations:* reading, walking, theatre, classical music, opera. *Address:* House of Lords, SW1A 0PW.

HARRIS OF PECKHAM, Baron *cr* 1995 (Life Peer), of Peckham in the London Borough of Southwark; **Philip Charles Harris,** Kt 1985; Chairman: Harris Ventures Ltd, since 1988; Carpetright plc, since 1993; *b* 15 Sept. 1942; *s* of Charles William Harris, MC and Ruth Ellen (*née* Ward); *m* 1960, Pauline Norma Chumley (*see* Dame P. N. Harris); three *s* one *d. Educ:* Streatham Grammar School. Chm., 1964–88, Chief Exec., 1987–88, Harris Queensway Plc; Chm., C. W. Harris Properties Ltd, 1988–97. Dir, Harveys Hldgs, 1986–2000; non-executive Director: Great Universal Stores, 1986–2004; Fisons Plc, 1986–94; Molyneux Estates, 1990–95; Matalan plc, 2004–06; Arsenal FC, 2005–. Mem., British Show Jumping Assoc., 1974–. Chm., Guy's and Lewisham NHS Trust, 1991–93; Vice-Chm., Lewisham Hospital NHS Trust, 1993–97; Member: Council of Governors, UMDS of Guy's and St Thomas' Hosps, 1984–98 (Hon. Fellow, 1992); Court of Patrons, RCOG, 1984–98; Chm., Generation Trust, 1984–; Dir, Outward Bound Trust, 2001–03; Lead Sponsor, Harris Fedn of S London Schools. Dep. Chm., Cons. Party Bd of Treasurers, 1993–97. Dep. Chm., Nat. Appeal Bd, NSPCC, 1998–2007. Trustee, RA, 1998–2005. Freeman, City of London, 1992. Hon. Fellow, Oriel Coll., Oxford, 1989; FGCL 1995; Hon. FRCR 1993. Hon. DEc Richmond Coll., London, 1996; Hon. LLD South Bank, 1998. Hambro Business Man of the Year, 1983; Ernst & Young UK Entrepreneur of the Year, 2007. *Recreations:* football, cricket, show jumping, tennis. *Address:* Carpetright plc, Harris House, Purfleet By Pass, Purfleet, Essex RM19 1TT.

HARRIS OF RICHMOND, Baroness *cr* 1999 (Life Peer), of Richmond in the county of North Yorkshire; **Angela Felicity Harris;** DL; *b* 4 Jan. 1944; *d* of late Rev. George Henry Hamilton Richards and Eva Richards; *m* 1st, 1965, Philip Martin Bowles (marr. diss. 1975); one *s*; 2nd, 1976, John Philip Roger Harris. *Educ:* Canon Slade Grammar Sch., Bolton, Lancs. Air Stewardess, 1963–65; Careers Advr and Employment Asst, 1974–76. Member (L, then Lib Dem): Richmond Town Council, 1978–81 and 1991–99; Richmondshire DC, 1978–89; N Yorks CC, 1981–2001. Chm., N Yorks Police Authy, 1995–2001. Dep. Chm., Assoc. of Police Authorities, 1997–2001. Chm., EU Select Sub-Cttee F, H of L, 2000–04; Spokesperson, Police, 2003–; Dep. spokesperson, NI, 2003–. Dep. Chm., Industry and Parliament Trust; Pres., Nat. Assoc. of Chaplains to the Police; Trustee, Police Rehabilitation Centre. DL N Yorks, 1994. *Address:* House of Lords, SW1A 0PW.

HARRIS, Prof. Adrian Llewellyn, FRCP; Cancer Research UK (formerly ICRF) Professor of Clinical Oncology, Oxford University, since 1988; Fellow of St Hugh's College, Oxford; *b* 10 Aug. 1950; *s* of Luke and Julia Harris; *m* 1975, Margaret Susan Denman; one *s* one *d. Educ:* Univ. of Liverpool (BSc Hons Biochem. 1970; MB ChB Hons 1973); DPhil Oxon 1978. MRCP 1975, FRCP 1985. Hosp. appts, Liverpool, 1973–74; Clinical Scientist, MRC Clinical Pharmacology Unit, Radcliffe Infirmary, Oxford and Nuffield Dept of Medicine, 1975–78; Registrar in Academic Unit, Royal Free Hosp., 1978–80; Lectr and Sen. Registrar, Inst. for Cancer Res., Royal Marsden Hosp., 1980–82; Vis. Researcher, Imp. Cancer Res. Fund Mutagenesis Lab., London, 1982–83; Prof. of Clinical Oncology, Newcastle upon Tyne Univ., 1983–88. *Publications:* papers on growth factors in cancer, mechanisms by which cancers become resistant to treatment, hormone and drug treatment of cancer. *Recreations:* swimming, modern dance, science fiction. *Address:* Cancer Research UK Laboratories, Weatherall Institute of Molecular Medicine, John Radcliffe Hospital, Oxford OX3 9DS.

HARRIS, Hon. Dame Anna Evelyn Hamilton; *see* Pauffley, Hon. Dame A. E. H.

HARRIS, Anthony David, CMG 1995; LVO 1979; HM Diplomatic Service, retired; Managing Partner, Gemini Consultants, Dubai, since 2001; *b* 13 Oct. 1941; *s* of Reginald William Harris and Kathleen Mary Harris (*née* Daw); *m* 1st, 1970, Patricia Ann Over (marr. diss. 1988); one *s*; 2nd, 1988, Sophie Kisling; two *s* one *d. Educ:* Plymouth College; Exeter College, Oxford (BA, 2nd cl. Hons Lit. Hum.). Third Sec., Commonwealth Relations Office, 1964; Middle East Centre for Arab Studies, Lebanon, 1965; Third, later Second Sec., and Vice-Consul, Jedda, 1967; Second Sec. (Inf.), Khartoum, 1969; First Sec., FCO, 1972; First Sec., Head of Chancery and Consul, Abu Dhabi, 1975; First Sec., UK Mission to UN, Geneva, 1979; Counsellor, FCO, 1982; seconded to MoD as Regl Marketing Dir 1 (Arabian Peninsula and Pakistan), 1983; Dep. Head of Mission, Cairo, 1986; Head of Information Dept, FCO, 1990–93; Scrutiny of Security in FCO, 1993–94; Ambassador to UAE, 1994–98. Director: Robert Fleming and Co. Ltd, 1999–2000; Technocraft Motor Corp., Iran, 2001–; 0700-Skyships GmbH, Munich, 2001–; estabd Gemini Consultants, Dubai, 2001, in association with Jefferson Waterman Internat., Washington. Mem. Council, RSAA, 1999–2001. Dep. Chm. (Gulf Affairs), Next Century Foundn, 1999–. *Recreations:* shooting (HM the Queen's Prize, Bisley, 1964; British team to Canada, 1974), ski-ing, climbing, diving, aviation, motor-racing. *Address:* PO Box 504914, Dubai, UAE. *Clubs:* Reform; Commonwealth Rifle (Bisley).

HARRIS, Anthony Geoffrey S.; *see* Stoughton-Harris.

HARRIS, Anthony George, CBE 2005 (OBE 1991); Principal, Harper Adams Agricultural College, 1977–94, retired; *b* 29 July 1929; *s* of John and Emily Kate Harris; *m* 1955, Sylvia Pyle; one *s* one *d* (and two *s* decd). *Educ:* Seale-Hayne Agricl Coll. (NDA, CDA Hons). FIBiol, FRAgS. Lectr in Agric., Dorset Coll. of Agric., 1953–55; Lectr in Crop Production, Harper Adams Agricl Coll., 1955–58; Vice-Principal, Walford Coll. of Agric., 1958–66; Principal, Merrist Wood Agric. Coll., 1967–77. Chm., W Midlands Rural Affairs Forum, 2002–05. Hon. FRASE 1999. DUniv Open 1996. BCPC Medal, 1998. *Publications:* Crop Husbandry, 1961; Farm Machinery, 1965, 2nd edn 1974. *Recreations:* walking, reading. *Club:* Farmers'.

HARRIS, Rt Rev. Mgr Anthony John, SCA; priest, Our Lady of the Visitation, Greenford, 1994–2004; *b* 6 May 1940; *s* of Philip John Harris and Eileen (*née* Kelly). *Educ:* St Patrick's Seminary, Thurles, Co. Tipperary (graduated in Phil. and Theol.). Ordained as Pallottine Priest, 1965; Dean of Discipline, 1965; Assistant Priest: Clerkenwell, 1965–68; Hastings, 1968–73; joined Chaplains' Br., RAF, 1973; served in UK, Germany, Cyprus and Ascension Island; Asst Principal Chaplain, 1986–92; Prin. RC Chaplain to RAF, 1992–94; VG, RAF, 1992–94. Prelate of Honour, 1992. *Recreations:* walking, swimming. *Address:* 514 Longbridge Road, Barking, Essex IG11 9BY. *Clubs:* Royal Air Force; Essex.

HARRIS, Prof. Anthony Leonard, CGeol; FRSE, FGS; Professor of Geology, University of Liverpool, 1987–2001, now Emeritus; Distinguished Visiting Fellow, Cardiff University, since 2002; *b* 11 May 1935; *s* of Thomas Haydn Harris and Dora Harris (*née* Wilkinson); *m* 1959, Noreen Jones; one *s* one *d. Educ:* Cardiff High Sch.; University College of Wales, Aberystwyth (BSc, PhD). Geologist and Principal Geologist, British Geol Survey, 1959–71; Liverpool University: Lectr, Sen. Lectr, then Reader, 1971–87; Head, Dept of Earth Scis, 1983–94; Dean, Faculty of Science, 1994–2000. Hon. Res. Assoc., Nat. Mus. of Wales, 2004–. Pres., Geol Soc., 1990–92. Fellow, Geol Soc. of Amer., 1978. Sometime Captain Men's Hockey: UCW; Univ. of Wales; Edinburgh Civil Service. Major John Coke Medal, Geol Soc., 1985; C. T. Clough Meml Medal, Geol Soc. of Edinburgh, 1989; Silver Medal, Liverpool Geol Soc., 2003. *Publications:* (ed and contrib.) Caledonides of the British Isles, 1979; The Caledonian-Appalachian Orogen, 1988; papers in learned jls. *Recreations:* music, ornithology. *Address:* Department of Earth Sciences, Cardiff University, Cathays Park, Cardiff CF10 3YE; Pentwyn, St Andrews Major, Vale of Glamorgan CF64 4HD. *Clubs:* Geological Society; Rotary (Dinas Powys).

HARRIS, Basil Vivian, CEng, MIET; Chief Engineer, Communications Division, Foreign and Commonwealth Office, 1979–81, retired; *b* 11 July 1921; *s* of late Henry William and Sarah May Harris; *m* 1943, Myra Winifred Mildred Newport (*d* 1997). *Educ:* Watford Grammar School. GPO Engineering Dept (Research), 1939; served RAF, 1943–46; GPO Engineering Dept (Radio Branch), 1946; Diplomatic Wireless Service, FCO, 1963; Dep. Chief Engineer, Communications Division, FCO, 1971. *Publications:* contribs to technical jls on communications. *Recreations:* golf, photography, travel. *Address:* 13 Decoy Drive, Eastbourne, Sussex BN22 0AB. *T:* (01323) 505819. *Club:* Royal Eastbourne Golf.

HARRIS, Ven. Brian; *see* Harris, Ven. R. B.

HARRIS, Brian Nicholas, FRICS; Consultant, CB Richard Ellis (formerly Richard Ellis, then Richard Ellis St Quintin), Chartered Surveyors and International Property Consultants, since 1996 (Chairman of Partnership, 1984–93; Partner, 1961–96); *b* 12 Dec. 1931; *s* of Claude Harris and Dorothy (*née* Harris); *m* 1961, Rosalyn Marion Caines; two *d. Educ:* King Alfred's Sch., Wantage; College of Estate Management. Chartered Surveyor. Chm., City of London Br. of RICS, 1984–85; Member of Council: London Chamber of Commerce, 1985– (Dep. Chm., 1990–92; Pres., 1992–94; Bd Mem., 1989–96); ABCC, 1992–98 (Mem. Bd, 1994–98; Chm., Southern Reg., 1994–96); Australian British Chamber of Commerce (UK), 1988–2000; Mem., Aust. and NZ Trade Adv. Cttee, 1991–98. Chairman: Heathrow Airport Support Gp, 1993–99; Priority Sites Ltd, 2001–03; Educn Develt Internat. plc, 2003–05; Bann System Ltd, 2005–; Bd Mem., London First, 1993–94. Hon. Property Advr, Order of St John, 1996–2001. Chairman: London Chamber of Commerce Educnl Trust, 2000–05; Britain Australia Soc., 2002–03. Gov., Woldingham Sch., 1986–93 (Dep. Chm., 1991–93). FRSA 1987. Mem., Court of Common Council, City of London, 1996–; Sheriff, City of London, 1998–99; Mem. Ct of Assts, Co. of Glaziers and Painters of Glass, 1990– (Master, 2003); Liveryman, Co. of World Traders, 1989–. *Recreations:* flyfishing, gardening, golf. *Address:* Grants Paddock, Grants Lane, Limpsfield, Surrey RH8 0RQ. *T:* (01883) 723215. *Clubs:* Carlton, City of London, Flyfishers'; Tandridge Golf.

HARRIS, Brian Thomas, OBE 1983; QC 1982; *b* 14 Aug. 1932; *s* of Thomas and Eleanor Harris; *m* 1957, Janet Rosina Harris (*née* Hodgson); one *s* one *d. Educ:* Henry Thornton Grammar Sch.; King's Coll., Univ. of London. LLB (Hons). Called to the Bar, Gray's Inn, 1960; joined London Magistrates' Courts, 1963; Clerk to the Justices, Poole, 1967–85; Dir, Professional Conduct Dept, 1985–94, Sec., Exec. Cttee, Jt Disciplinary Scheme, 1986–94, ICAEW. Member: Juvenile Courts Committee, Magistrates' Assoc., 1973–85; NACRO Juvenile Crime Adv. Cttee, 1982–85; former member: CCETSW working party on legal trng of social workers (report, 1974); NACRO cttee on diversion (Zander report, 1975); HO/DHSS working party on operation of Children and Young Persons' Act 1969 (report, 1978); ABAFA working party on care proceedings (report, 1979). Chairman: Membership and Disciplinary Tribunal, PIA, 1994–2002; Disciplinary Tribunal, SFA, 1994–2002; Appeals Tribunal, Assoc. of Accounting Technicians, 1996–2002. Reviewer of Complaints: ICAS, 2001–; Assoc. of Accounting Technicians, 2002–. Pres., Justices' Clerks Soc., 1981–82. Editor: Justice of the Peace Review, 1982–85 (Legal Editor, 1973; Jt Editor, 1978); The Regulator and Professional Conduct Qly, 1994–98. *Publications:* Criminal Jurisdiction of Magistrates, 1969, 11th edn 1988; Warrants of Search and Entry, 1973; The Courts, the Press and the Public, 1976; The Rehabilitation of Offenders, 1976, 3rd edn 1999; New Law of Family Proceedings in Magistrates' Courts, 1979; (ed jtly) Clarke Hall and Morrison on Children, 1985; The Law and Practice of Disciplinary and Regulatory Proceedings, 1995, 4th edn 2006; The Tribunal Member, 1995; The Literature of the Law, 1998; Injustice, 2006; Intolerance, 2008; (ed) entry on Magistrates in Halsbury's Laws of England, 4th edn 1979. *Recreation:* the contemplation of verse. *Address:* Church Barn, High Street, Yardley Hastings, Northants NN7 1ER. *T:* (01604) 696071; *e-mail:* brian@bthydly.demon.co.uk.

HARRIS, Cecil Rhodes, FCIS, FSCA; Deputy Chairman, Trade Indemnity PLC, 1986–93; Chief Executive, Commercial Union Assurance Company Ltd, 1982–85; *b* 4 May 1923; *s* of Frederick William Harris and Dorothy Violet Plum; *m* 1946, Gwenyth Evans; one *s* two *d. Educ:* private schools. FCIS 1950; FSCA 1951. Joined Employers Liability Assurance, 1949, Asst Sec., 1961–64, Overseas Manager, Northern & Employers, 1965–68; Commercial Union Assurance Co. Ltd: Asst Gen. Man., 1969–73; Dep. Gen. Man., 1974; Dir and Sec., 1975–78; Exec. Dir, 1979; Dep. Chief Gen. Man., 1980–82. *Recreations:* tennis, study of the Scriptures. *Address:* Ashley, 35a Plough Lane, Purley, Surrey CR8 3QJ. *T:* (020) 8668 2820.

HARRIS, Charles; *see* Harris, G. C. W.

HARRIS, Christopher H.; *see* Heaton-Harris.

HARRIS, Prof. Christopher John, DPhil; Professor of Mathematical Economics, University of Cambridge and Fellow, King's College, Cambridge, since 1995; *b* 22 Sept. 1960; *s* of Colin Christopher Harris and Barbara Kay (*née* Hall); *m* 1993, Qun Li. *Educ:* Oundle Sch.; Corpus Christi Coll., Oxford (BA Maths 1981); Nuffield Coll., Oxford (MPhil Econ 1983; DPhil Econ 1984). Prize Research Fellow, Nuffield Coll., Oxford, 1983–84; Univ. Lectr in Econs, Univ. of Oxford and Fellow of Nuffield Coll., 1984–94. Vis. Prof., MIT, 1990–91; Vis. Fellow, Princeton Univ., 2000–01; British Acad. Res. Prof., 2000–03. Richard B. Fisher Mem., IAS, 2001–02. *Publications:* articles on dynamic games and theory of industrial organisation in Econometrica, Rev. of Econ. Studies, Jl of Econ. Theory, etc. *Recreations:* walking, running, swimming. *Address:* Faculty of Economics and Politics, Austin Robinson Building, Sidgwick Avenue, Cambridge CB3 9DD.

HARRIS, Prof. Christopher John, PhD, DSc; FIMA, FREng, FIET; Lucas Professor of Aerospace Systems Engineering, 1987–96, Professor of Computational Intelligence, 1996–2003, now Professor Emeritus, and Head, Department of Electronic and Computer Science, 1999–2002, University of Southampton; *b* 23 Dec. 1945; *s* of George Harris and Hilda Harris; *m* 1965, Ruth Joy Harris; one *s* two *d. Educ:* Univ. of Leicester (BSc); MA Oxon; Univ. of Southampton (PhD 1972; DSc 2002). FIMA 1979; CEng 1979; FIET (FIEE 1991); FREng (FEng 1996). Lecturer: Hull Univ., 1967–72; UMIST, 1972–76; Oxford Univ., 1976–80; Fellow, St Edmund Hall, Oxford, 1976–80; Dep. Chief Scientist, MoD, 1980–84; Prof., Cranfield Inst. of Technol., 1984–86; Dir, Nat. Defence Technol. Centre in Data and Information Fusion, MoD, 2002–04. Hon. Professor: Univ. Hong Kong, 1991; Huazhong Univ., China, 1991; Sen. Res. Fellow, Imperial Coll. London, 2004–. Achievement Medal, 1998, Faraday Medal, 2001, IEE. *Publications:* (with J. F. Miles) Stability of Linear Systems, 1980, 2nd edn 1985; (with J. M. Valenca) Stability of Input-output Dynamic Systems, 1983, 2nd edn 1987; (ed) Applications of Artificial Intelligence to C^2 Systems, 1988; (jtly) Intelligent Control: aspects of fuzzy logic and neural nets, 1993; (with M. Brown) Neurofuzzy Adaptive Modelling and Control, 1994; (jtly) Advanced Adaptive Control, 1995; Adaptive Neural Network Control of Robotic Manipulators, 1998; Data Based Modelling, Estimation and Control, 2002. *Recreations:* scuba diving, gardening, fly fishing. *Address:* 14 Beechwood Rise, West End, Southampton, Hants SO18 3PW. *T:* (023) 8047 2363.

HARRIS, Colleen Lorraine, MVO 2004; Director, Dignity Management Consultancy, since 2007; *b* 24 Sept. 1955; *d* of late Gladstone Meertins and Sheila Meertins; *m* 1976, Wayne Harris; two *s.* Press Officer to Prime Minister, 1987–88; various Govt PR roles, 1988–97; Hd, Media Planning for Dep. Prime Minister, 1997–98; Dep. Press Sec., 1998–2000, Press Sec., 2000–03, to Prince of Wales; Strategy and Communications Dir, CRE, 2003–06; Interim Dir of Communications, Equality and Human Rights Commn, 2007. Chm., Caribbean Bd, 2002–08. Member: CRUK, 2003–; Press Complaints Commn, 2006–. FRSA 2006; MCIPR 2008. Member: Council, Royal Albert Hall, 2004–; Bd, Hackney Empire, 2008–. *Recreations:* music, cooking, listening to the radio. *Address:* (office) 100 Seymour Place, W1H 1NE. *Clubs:* Soho House, Arts.

HARRIS, David Anthony; *b* 1 Nov. 1937; *s* of late E. C. Harris and Betty Harris; *m* 1st, 1962, Diana Joan Hansford (*d* 1996); one *s* one *d*; 2nd, 1998, Mrs Alison Bunker. *Educ:* Mount Radford Sch., Exeter. Jun. Reporter, Express and Echo, Exeter, 1954–58. Nat. Service, commnd Devonshire and Dorset Regt, 1958; Staff Captain (Public Relns) GHQ, MELF, 1959. Reporter, Western Morning News, 1960–61; joined Daily Telegraph, Westminster Staff, 1961; Political Correspondent, Daily Telegraph, 1976–79; MEP (C) Cornwall and Plymouth, 1979–84. Chm., Parly Lobby Journalists, 1977–78. Mem. (C) Bromley, and Bromley, Ravensbourne, GLC, 1968–77; Chm. Thamesmead Cttee, 1971–73. Contested (C) Mitcham and Morden, Feb. 1974. MP (C) St Ives, 1983–97. PPS to Minister of State for Foreign and Commonwealth Affairs, 1987–88, to Sec. of State for Foreign and Commonwealth Affairs, 1988–89, to Dep. Prime Minister and Leader of Commons, 1989–90. Member, Select Committee: on Agriculture, 1983–87; on Broadcasting, 1988–97; on Foreign Affairs, 1991–97; on Social Security, 1991–92. Chairman: Cons. Fisheries Cttee, 1987–97; W Country Cons. MPs, 1991–92. Leading Cons. spokesman for Cornwall, 1997–2001. Chm., Seafood Cornwall, 2004–. Mem. Council, Royal Nat. Mission to Deep Sea Fishermen, 1993–, Dep. Chm., 2007–. Vice Chm., Duchy Health Charity, 2005–. Churchwarden, St Piran's, Perran-ar-Worthal, 2001–05. *Recreations:* gardening, reading obituaries. *Address:* Trewedna Farm, Perranwell Station, near Truro, Cornwall TR3 7PQ.

HARRIS, David John, CMG 1999; PhD; Professor of Public International Law, 1981–2003, now Emeritus, and Co-Director, Human Rights Law Centre, since 1993, University of Nottingham; *b* 3 July 1938; *s* of Sidney and May Harris; *m* 1963, Sandra Jean Nelson; two *s. Educ:* Sutton High Sch., Plymouth; KCL (LLB 1959); LSE (LLM 1961). Asst Lectr, QUB, 1962–63; University of Nottingham: Asst Lectr, 1963–64; Lectr, 1964–73; Sen. Lectr in Law, 1973–81; Head, Law Dept, 1987–90. Mem., Cttee of Indep. Experts, European Social Charter, 1990–96. *Publications:* (ed) Garner's Environmental Law, 5 vols, 1973–2005; Cases and Materials on Public International Law, 1973, 6th edn 2004; (with S. Bailey and B. Jones) Civil Liberties: cases and materials, 1980, 5th edn 2001; The European Social Charter, 1984, 2nd edn (with J. Darcy) 2001; (with M. O'Boyle and C. Warbrick) The Law of the European Convention on Human Rights, 1995. *Recreations:* travelling, walking. *Address:* School of Law, The University, Nottingham NG7 2RD. *T:* (0115) 951 5701.

HARRIS, David Michael; QC 1989; **His Honour Judge Harris;** a Circuit Judge, since 2001; *b* 7 Feb. 1943; *s* of Maurice and Doris Harris; *m* 1970, Emma Lucia Calma; two *s* one *d. Educ:* Liverpool Institute High School for Boys; Lincoln Coll., Oxford (BA 1964; MA 1967); Trinity Hall, Cambridge (PhD 1969). Asst Lectr in Law, Manchester Univ., 1967–69. Called to the Bar, Middle Temple, 1969; Bencher, 1997; Asst Recorder, 1984–88; a Recorder, 1988–2001; a Dep. High Ct Judge, 1993–. *Publications:* (ed jtly) Winfield and Jolowicz on Tort, 9th edn, 1971; (ed jtly) Supplement to Bingham's Modern Cases on Negligence, 3rd edn, 1985. *Recreations:* the Arts, travel, sport. *Address:* c/o Courts of Justice, Crown Square, Manchester M60 9DJ. *T:* (0151) 243 6000.

HARRIS, Prof. David Russell, FBA 2004; FSA; Professor of Human Environment, Institute of Archaeology, University College London, 1979–98, now Professor Emeritus (Director, 1989–96); *b* 14 Dec. 1930; *s* of Dr Herbert Melville Harris and Norah Mary Harris; *m* 1957, Helen Margaret Wilson; four *d. Educ:* St Christopher Sch., Letchworth; Oxford Univ. (MA, BLitt); Univ. of California, Berkeley (PhD). Nat. Service, RAF, 1949–50. Teaching Asst and Instructor, Univ. of California, 1956–58; Lectr, QMC, London, 1958–64; Lectr and Reader, UCL, 1964–79. Member: Mus. of London Archaeol. Cttee, 1984–91; English Heritage Sci. and Conservation Panel, 1985–99; Chm., Sci.-based Archaeol. Cttee, SERC, 1989–92. President: Prehistoric Soc., 1990–94; UK Chapter, Soc. for Economic Botany, 1995–97; Anthropol. and Archaeol. Sect., BAAS, 2000. Hon. Fellow, UCL, 2000. *Publications:* Plants, Animals and Man in the Outer Leeward Islands, 1965; (with B. W. Hodder) Africa in Transition, 1967; Human Ecology in Savanna Environments, 1980; (with G. C. Hillman) Foraging and Farming, 1989; Settling Down and Breaking Ground: rethinking the neolithic revolution, 1990; (with K. D. Thomas) Modelling Ecological Change, 1991; The Archaeology of V. Gordon Childe, 1994; The Origins and Spread of Agriculture and Pastoralism in Eurasia, 1996; (jtly) Plants for Food and Medicine, 1998. *Recreations:* mountain walking, archaeological-ecological travel. *Address:* Institute of Archaeology, University College London, 31–34 Gordon Square, WC1H 0PY. *T:* (020) 7679 7495. *Club:* Athenæum.

HARRIS, Evan; MP (Lib Dem) Oxford West and Abingdon, since 1997; *b* 21 Oct. 1965; *s* of Prof. Frank Harris, *qv. Educ:* Blue Coat Sch., Liverpool; Wadham Coll., Oxford (BA Hons Physiol.); Oxford Univ. Med. Sch. (BM BCh 1991). House Officer, John Radcliffe Hosp. and Royal Liverpool Univ. Hosp., 1991–92; Sen. House Officer (Medicine), Central Oxford Hosps, 1992–94; Hon. Registrar in Public Health, and Regl Task Force MO, Oxford Regl Postgrad. Dept of Med. Educn and Oxfordshire HA, 1994–97. Mem.

Council, BMA, 1994–97 (Mem., Med. Ethics Cttee, 1999–). Parly Lib Dem spokesman on: NHS, 1997–99; higher educn and women's issues, 1999–2001; health, 2001–03; science, 2005–. Chm., All Party Kidney Gp, 1999–; Officer, All Party Gps on Refugees, and on AIDS, 1997–; Member: Sci. and Technol. Select Cttee, 2003–; Jt Select Cttee on Human Rights, 2005–. *Publications:* contribs to med. jls. *Recreations:* chess, bridge, squash, television. *Address:* 32A North Hinksey Village, Oxford OX2 0NA. *T:* (01865) 250424; House of Commons, SW1A 0AA. *T:* (020) 7219 5128. *Club:* Oxford Rotary.

HARRIS, Frank; *see* Harris, W. F.

HARRIS, Prof. Frank, CBE 1996; FMedSci; Dean, Faculty of Medicine and Biological Sciences (formerly of Medicine) and Professor of Paediatrics, University of Leicester, 1990–2000, now Professor Emeritus; Hon. Consultant Paediatrician, Leicester Royal Infirmary, 1990–2000; *b* 6 Oct. 1934; *s* of David and Miriam Harris; *m* 1963, Brenda van Embden; two *s*. *Educ:* Univ. of Cape Town (MB ChB 1957; MMed (Paed), 1963; MD 1964); CertHE Oxon 2006. FRCPE 1975; FRCP 1982; FRCPCH 1997 (Hon. FRCPCH 2000). Groote Schuur and Red Cross War Memorial Children's Hosp., Cape Town; CSIR Res. Fellow, Dept of Medicine, Univ. of Cape Town; Lectr and Sen. Lectr in Child Health, Univ. of Sheffield, 1965–74; University of Liverpool: Prof. of Child Health and Dir, Inst. of Child Health, 1974–89; Pro-Vice-Chancellor, 1981–84; Dean, Faculty of Medicine, 1985–89; Hon. Cons. Paediatrician to Royal Liverpool Children's Hosps at Myrtle Street and Alderhey. Exec. Sec., Council of Deans of UK Med. Schs and Faculties, 1992–96. Member: Liverpool AHA and DHA, 1977–84; Mersey RHA, 1983–89; Trent RHA, 1990; Vice-Chm., Leics HA, 1993–97, 1998–2000 (non-exec. Dir, 1990–). Member: Cttee on Review of Medicines, 1981–90; Cttee on Safety of Medicines, 1990–92; Joint Planning Adv. Cttee, DoH, 1990–94; GMC, 1990–99 (Overseas Review Bd, 1992–96; Educn Cttee, 1994–99; Preliminary Proceedings Cttee, 1994–99; Registration Cttee, 1997–99; Overseas Cttee, 1997–98); NAHAT Wkg Gp on Teaching, Res. and Audit, 1992–93; Scientific Cttee, EU Alban Prog., 2003–. Member: Exec., Univ. Hosps Assoc., 1991–98; Exec. Cttee, Assoc. of Med. Schs in Europe, 1993–99; Adv. Cttee on Med. Trng, EC, 1994–2001 (Chm., 1999–2001). Examr for RCP and Univs, UK and overseas. Founder FMedSci 1998. *Publications:* Paediatric Fluid Therapy, 1973; chapters in med. books; contribs to med. jls. *Recreations:* bridge, history. *Address:* 39 Frenchay Road, Oxford OX2 6TG.

See also E. Harris.

HARRIS, (Geoffrey) Charles (Wesson); QC 1989; **His Honour Judge Charles Harris;** a Circuit Judge, since 1993; *b* 17 Jan. 1945; *s* of late G. Hardy Harris and M. J. P. Harris (*née* Wesson); *m* 1970, Carol Ann Alston; two *s* one *d*. *Educ:* Repton; Univ. of Birmingham (LLB). Called to the Bar, Inner Temple, 1967; practice on Midland and Oxford Circuit and in London, 1967–93; a Recorder, 1990–93; Designated Civil Judge: Oxford and Northampton, 1998–2001; Oxford/Thames Valley, 2001–. Member: Parole Bd, 1995–2000; Crown Court Rule Cttee, 1997–2005; Cttee, Council of Circuit Judges, 2002–. Contested (C) Penistone, Yorks, Oct. 1974. *Publications:* contrib. to Halsbury's Laws of England, 4th edn 1976, and other legal publications; magazine articles on stalking and ballooning. *Recreations:* history, architecture, fireworks, stalking, ski-ing. *Address:* c/o Oxford Combined Court, St Aldates, Oxford. *Clubs:* Travellers, Kandahar.

HARRIS, Sir Henry, Kt 1993; FRCP; FRCPath; FRS 1968; Regius Professor of Medicine, University of Oxford, 1979–92; Head of the Sir William Dunn School of Pathology, 1963–94; Hon. Director, Cancer Research Campaign, Cell Biology Unit, 1963–92; Fellow of Lincoln College, Oxford, 1963–79, Hon. Fellow 1980; Student of Christ Church, Oxford, 1979–92, Emeritus Student, 1992, Hon. Student, 2007; *b* 28 Jan. 1925; *s* of late Sam and Ann Harris; *m* 1950, Alexandra Fanny Brodsky; one *s* two *d*. *Educ:* Sydney Boys' High Sch. and University of Sydney, Australia; Lincoln Coll., Oxford. Public Exhibnr, University of Sydney, 1942; BA Mod. Langs, 1944; MB BS 1950; Travelling Schol. of Austr. Nat. Univ. at Univ. of Oxford, 1952; MA; DPhil (Oxon), 1954, DM 1979. Dir of Research, Brit. Empire Cancer Campaign, at Sir William Dunn Sch. of Pathology, Oxford, 1954–59; Visiting Scientist, Nat. Institutes of Health, USA, 1959–60; Head of Dept of Cell Biology, John Innes Inst., 1960–63; Prof. of Pathology, Univ. of Oxford, 1963–79. Vis. Prof., Vanderbilt Univ., 1968; Walker-Ames Prof., University of Washington, 1968; Foreign Prof., Collège de France, 1974. Non-exec. Mem., Oxford RHA, 1990–92; Hon. Consulting Pathologist, Oxford HA, 1992. Member: ARC, 1968–78 (Chm., Animals Res. Bd, 1976–78); Council, European Molecular Biology Organization, 1974–76; Council, Royal Society, 1971–72; Scientific Adv. Cttee, CRC, 1961–85; Governor, European Cell Biology Organization, 1973–75. Lectures: Almroth Wright, 1968; Harvey, Harvey Soc. NY, 1969; Dunham, Harvard, 1969; Jenner Meml, 1970; Croonian, Royal Soc., 1971; Nat. Insts of Health, USA, 1971; Foundation, RCPath, 1973; Woodhull, Royal Instn, 1975; Rotherham, Lincoln Coll., Oxford, 1979; Herbert Spencer, Oxford Univ., 1979, 1992; Opening Plenary, Internat. Congress of Cell Biology, 1980; First Distinguished, in Experimental Pathology, Pittsburgh Univ., 1982; Louis Gross Meml, NY, 1983; Claude Bernard, Acad. des Sciences, Paris, 1984; Jean Brachet Meml, Vancouver, 1990; Kettle, RCPath, 1991; Romanes, Oxford Univ., 1993. Foreign Hon. Mem., Amer. Acad. Arts and Sciences; Foreign Mem., Max-Planck Soc.; Hon. Member: Amer. Assoc. of Pathologists; German Soc. of Cell Biology; Corresp. Member: Amer. Assoc. for Cancer Res.; Aust. Acad. of Science. Foreign Correspondent, Waterford Striped Bass Derby Assoc.; Hon. Fellow, Cambridge Philosophical Soc. Hon. FRCPA. Hon. DSc Edinburgh, 1976; Hon. MD: Geneva, 1982; Sydney, 1983. Feldberg Foundn Award, Ivison Macadam Meml Prize, RCSE; Prix de la Fondation Isabelle Decazes de Noüe for cancer research; Madonnina Prize for medical scis (City of Milan), 1979; Royal Medal, Royal Soc., 1980; Osler Medal, RCP, 1984; Katherine Berkan Judd Award, Sloan-Kettering Inst., NY, 1991. *Publications:* Nucleus and Cytoplasm, 1968, 3rd edn, 1974; Cell Fusion, 1970; La Fusion cellulaire, 1974; The Balance of Improbabilities, 1987; The Cells of the Body: a history of somatic cell genetics, 1995; The Birth of the Cell, 1999; Things Come to Life, 2002; Remnants of a Quiet Life, 2006; Boveri Concerning the Origin of Malignant Tumours, 2008; papers on cellular physiology and biochemistry, in scientific books and jls, and some fiction. *Recreation:* history. *Address:* c/o Sir William Dunn School of Pathology, South Parks Road, Oxford OX1 3RE. *T:* (01865) 275500.

HARRIS, Hugh Christopher Emlyn; Director, Global Network, London First, since 1999 (Director of Operations, 1995–99); *b* 25 March 1936; *s* of Thomas Emlyn Harris and Martha Anne (*née* Davies); *m* 1968, Pamela Susan Woollard; one *s* one *d*. *Educ:* The Leys Sch., Cambridge; Trinity Coll., Cambridge (BA 1959; MA). ACIB 1963; FCIPD (FIPM 1990, FIPD). Bank of England, 1959–94: Chief of Corporate Services, 1984–88; Associate Dir, 1988–94; Comr, CRE, 1995–2000 (Dep. Chm., 1996–2000). Director: BE Services Ltd, 1984–94; BE Museum Ltd, 1989–94; BE Property Holdings Ltd, 1989–94; Securities Management Trust Ltd, 1987–94; Solefield School Educational Trust Ltd, Sevenoaks, 1986–2001. Dir, London Film Commn, 1996–2000. Member: Business Leaders Team, BITC Race for Opportunity Campaign, 1994–98; Windsor Fellowship Adv. Council, 1988–94; Council, London Civic Forum, 2001–. Vice Pres., Bankers Benevolent Fund, 1990–. Gov., Newham Coll. of Further Educn, 2005–. Chm., Broad St Ward Club, 2002–03; Liveryman, Turners' Co., 1993–. Hon. Treas., Kemsing Br., RBL, 1971–. FRSA. *Recreations:* tennis, watching Rugby, films, opera, ballet. *Address:* London First, 3 Whitcomb Street, WC2H 7HA. *T:* (020) 7665 1570; *e-mail:* hharris@londonfirst.co.uk.

HARRIS, Air Cdre Irene Joyce, (Joy), CB 1984; RRC 1976; SRN, SCM; Director, Nursing Services (RAF), and Matron-in-Chief, Princess Mary's Royal Air Force Nursing Service, 1981–84; *b* 26 Sept. 1926; *d* of late Robert John Harris and Annie Martha Harris (*née* Breed). *Educ:* Southgate County Sch.; Charing Cross Hosp.; The London Hosp.; Queen Mary's Maternity Home, Hampstead. SRN 1947, SCM 1950. Joined Princess Mary's RAF Nursing Service, 1950; gen. nursing and midwifery duties in UK, Singapore, Germany and Cyprus; Dep. Matron, 1970; Sen. Matron, 1975; Principal Matron, 1978; Dep. Dir, Nursing Services (RAF), 1981. QHNS 1981–84. *Recreations:* travel, ornithology, music, archaeology, gardening. *Address:* 51 Station Road, Haddenham, Ely, Cambs CB6 3XD. *Club:* Royal Air Force.

HARRIS, Sir Jack Wolfred Ashford, 2nd Bt *cr* 1932; Chairman, Bing Harris & Co. Ltd, Wellington, NZ, 1935–78 (Director until 1982), retired; *b* 23 July 1906; *er s* of Rt Hon. Sir Percy Harris, 1st Bt, PC, and Frieda Bloxam (*d* 1962); *S* father, 1952; *m* 1933, Patricia (*d* 2002), *o d* of A. P. Penman, Wahroonga, Sydney, NSW; two *s* one *d*. *Educ:* Shrewsbury Sch.; Trinity Hall, Cambridge. BA (Cantab) History; then one year's study in Europe. Joined family business in New Zealand, 1929, and became director shortly afterwards. Past Pres. Wellington Chamber of Commerce. Served during War of 1939–45, for three years in NZ Home Forces. *Publication:* Memoirs of a Century (autobiog.), 2007. *Recreations:* gardening, fishing, swimming. *Heir:* *s* Christopher John Ashford Harris [*b* 26 Aug. 1934; *m* 1957, Anna, *d* of F. de Malmanche, Auckland, NZ; one *s* two *d*]. *Address:* Parkwood, Warbler Grove, Belvedere Road, Waikanae, Wellington, New Zealand. *Clubs:* Union (Sydney); Wellington (Wellington, NZ).

HARRIS, Jeffery Francis, FCA; Chairman, Filtrona, since 2005; *b* 8 April 1948; *s* of Ernest and Kathleen Veronica Harris; *m* 1976, Elizabeth Helen Hancock; two *s*. *Educ:* Rendcomb Coll., Cirencester; Southampton Univ. (BSc Hons 1970). FCA 1979. Trainee chartered accountant, 1970; with Barton Mayhew & Co., later Ernst & Young, 1980–85; UniChem, subseq. Alliance UniChem, 1985–2005: Gp Chief Accountant, 1985–86; Finance Dir, 1986–91; Dep. Chief Exec., 1991–92; Chief Exec., 1992–2001; Chm., 2001–05. Board Member: Bunzl plc, 2000–; Associated British Foods plc, 2003–; ANZAG AG (Germany), 2004–. Chm., British Assoc. of Pharmaceutical Wholesalers, 1996–98; Pres., GIRP-European Assoc. of Pharmaceutical Wholesalers, 2003–. Hon. DBA Kingston Univ., 2003. *Recreations:* walking, ski-ing, cycling, gardening, opera. *Address:* Filtrona, Avebury House, 201–249 Avebury Boulevard, Milton Keynes MK9 1AU. *T:* (01908) 359100.

HARRIS, Jeremy Michael; Director of Public Affairs, University of Oxford, since 2005; Fellow of New College, Oxford, since 2006; *b* 31 Oct. 1950; *s* of late David Arnold Harris and of Beryl May Harris (*née* Howe); *m* 1983, Susan Lynn Roberts; one *s* one *d*. *Educ:* Sevenoaks Sch., Kent; Clare Coll., Cambridge (MA Hons); Nottingham Univ. (PGCE 1972). BBC News: Reporter, BBC Radio News, 1978–82; Madrid Corresp., 1982–86; Moscow Corresp., 1986–89; Foreign Affairs Corresp., 1989–90; Washington Corresp., 1990–95; Radio Presenter, BBC Current Affairs Progs incl. World Tonight, and Today, 1995–99; Archbishop of Canterbury's Sec. for Public Affairs, and Dep. Chief of Staff, Lambeth Palace, 1999–2005. *Recreations:* theatre, maps, walking. *Address:* University of Oxford, Wellington Square, OX1 2JD. *Club:* Arts.

HARRIS, Joanne Michèle Sylvie; author; *b* 3 July 1964; *d* of Robert Ian Short and Jeannette Payen-Short; *m* 1988, Kevin Steven Harris; one *d*. *Educ:* St Catharine's Coll., Cambridge (BA Mod. and Mediaeval Langs; MA 1985); Sheffield Univ. (PGCE 1987). Hon. DLit: Huddersfield, 2003; Sheffield, 2004. *Publications:* The Evil Seed, 1992; Sleep, Pale Sister, 1994; Chocolat, 1999; Blackberry Wine, 2000; Five Quarters of the Orange, 2001; Coastliners, 2002; (with F. Warde) The French Kitchen, 2002; Holy Fools, 2003; Jigs and Reels, 2004; Gentlemen and Players, 2005; (with F. Warde) The French Market, 2005; The Lollipop Shoes, 2007; Runemarks, 2007. *Recreations:* mooching, lounging, strutting, strumming, priest-baiting and quiet subversion of the system. *Address:* c/o Eldon House, Sharp Lane, Almondbury, Huddersfield, HD5 8XL. *Club:* Arts.

HARRIS, Joanne Olga Charlotte; Her Honour Judge Harris; a Circuit Judge, since 2007; *b* London, 13 July 1958; *d* of Dennis Harris and Marguerite, (Peggy), Harris; partner, Michael O'Donnell (decd); two *s*. *Educ:* Liverpool Univ. (BA Hons); London Sch. of Econs and Pol Sci. (MSc); Inns of Court Sch. of Law. Called to the Bar, Gray's Inn, 1991; Dep. Dist Judge, 2002; Recorder, 2004–07. *Recreation:* ski-ing and other holidays. *Address:* Watford County Court, Cassiobury House, 11–19 Station Road, Watford, Herts WD17 1EZ. *T:* (01923) 699400, *Fax:* (01923) 699404.

HARRIS, Very Rev. John; Dean of Brecon, and Vicar of Brecon St Mary with Battle and Llanddew, 1993–98; *b* 12 March 1932; *s* of Richard and Ivy Harris; *m* 1956, Beryl June Roberts; two *s* one *d*. *Educ:* St David's Coll., Lampeter (BA 1955); Salisbury Theol Coll. Ordained deacon 1957, priest 1958; Curate: Pontnewynydd, 1957–60; Bassaleg, 1960–63; Vicar: Penmaen, 1963–69; St Paul, Newport, 1969–84; Maindee, 1984–93; RD of Newport, 1977–93. Canon, St Woolos Cath., 1984–93. *Recreations:* classical archæology, music, ballet, natural history. *Address:* 40 Mounton Drive, Chepstow, Monmouthshire NP16 5EH.

HARRIS, Prof. John Buchanan, PhD; CBiol, FIBiol; Professor of Experimental Neurology, Faculty of Medical Sciences, Newcastle University, 1980–2007, now Emeritus (Director of International Postgraduate Studies, 2002–05); Head of Neurotoxicology, Chemicals Division, Health Protection Agency, Newcastle upon Tyne, 2004–07; *b* 18 Jan. 1940; *s* of John Benjamin Sargent Harris and Mary Isobel Harris; *m* 1965, Christine Margaret Holt; one *s* one *d* (and one *s* decd). *Educ:* Tiffin Sch.; Bradford Inst. of Technol.; Univ. of Bradford (PhD 1967); BPharm (London ext. 1963). MRPharmS 1964; FIBiol 1981; CBiol 1990. Research Asst, Univ. of Bradford, 1963–67; Newcastle upon Tyne University: Sen. Res. Associate, 1967–72; Principal Res. Associate, 1972–74; Sen. Lectr, 1974–80. Wellcome Fellow, Univ. of Lund, Sweden, 1970–71; MRC/NIH Fellow, UCLA, 1977–78; Wellcome/Ramaciotti Fellow, Monash Univ., Melbourne, 1980. *Publications:* (ed) Muscular Dystrophy and Other Inherited Diseases of Skeletal Muscle in Animals, 1979; (ed jtly) Natural Toxins: animal, plant and microbial, 1986; (ed jtly) Muscle Metabolism, Vol. 4 (3) of Baillière's Endocrinology and Metabolism, 1990; (ed jtly) Medical Neurotoxicology, 1999. *Address:* Institute of Neuroscience, Faculty of Medical Sciences, Newcastle University, Framlington Place, Newcastle upon Tyne NE2 4HH. *T:* (0191) 222 6977, *Fax:* (0191) 222 5772; *e-mail:* j.b.harris@ncl.ac.uk.

HARRIS, John Charles, CBE 2007; solicitor; International Management and Legal Consultant, John Harris Consultancy, since 1986; Board Member: Northern Counties Housing Association Ltd, since 1990 (Chairman, 1994–2000; Vice Chairman, 1994, 2002–03)); Guinness Trust Group, since 2007; *b* 25 April 1936; *s* of Sir Charles Joseph

William Harris, KBE and Lady Harris (Emily (*née* Thompson)); *m* 1961, Alison Beryl Sturley; one *s* one *d*. *Educ:* Dulwich College (LCC scholarship); Clare College, Cambridge. MA, LLM. 2nd Lieut, Intelligence Corps, 1954–56. UKAEA (seconded to OECD), 1959–63; articled to Town Clerk, Poole, 1963–66; Asst Sol., then Senior Asst Sol., Poole BC, 1966–67; Asst Sol., then Principal Asst to Chief Exec. and Town Clerk, 1967–71, Dep. Town Clerk, 1972–73, County Borough of Bournemouth; County Sec., 1973–83, Chief Exec. and County Clerk, 1983–86, S Yorks CC; Dir, S Yorks Passenger Transport Exec., 1984–86; Sec. to Yorkshire and Humberside County Councils Assoc., 1984–86; Dir, S Yorks Residuary Body, 1985–86; Clerk to Lord Lieutenant of S Yorks, 1984–86; Public Sector Adviser/Associate Consultant: PA Consulting Gp, 1986–91; Daniel Bates Partnership, 1991–95. Chair: Coal Authy, 1999–2007; Coal Forum, 2007–. Adviser to AMA Police and Fire Cttee, 1976–86; Member: Home Office Tripartite Working Party on Police Act 1964, 1983–86; Rampton SHSA Cttee, 1989–96; Arts Council Touring Bd, 1989–92; Pontefract HA, 1990–93; Council, Local Govt Internat. Bureau, 1993–96. Mem., Exec. Council, Solace, 1984–86; Executive Director: Solace Internat. (1992) Ltd, 1992–2000; Solace Internat. Southern Africa Pty Ltd, 1993–2001; Dir, Trustee, and Mem. Bd, Homeless Internat. Ltd, 1998–2000; Dir, South Africa Housing Network Trust Ltd, 1998–2001; Jt Chm., Ivory Park/Wakefield Educn Partnership, 2002–; Chairman: Northern Counties Specialised Housing Assoc. Ltd, 1994–2007; Mid Yorks Hospitals NHS Trust, 2008– (non-exec. Dir, 2007); Rossington Eco-Town Partnership, 2008–. Chm., Soc. of County Secretaries, 1983–84; Mem., Law Society. Independent Member: W Yorks Police Authy, 1994–99; Police Cttee, AMA, 1995; MoD Police Cttee, 2003–07; Chm., Audit Cttee, 2004–, Mem., Owner's Adv. Bd, 2007–, MoD Police and Guarding Agency. Hon. PR Officer, S Yorks and Humberside Region, Riding for Disabled Assoc., 1983–92 (Mem., Publications Cttee, 1987–90); Trustee: S Yorks Charity Inf. Service, 1977–87; Housing Assocs Charitable Trust, 1994–96; Founder Mem./Sec., Barnsley Rockley Rotary Club, 1976–79 (Hon. Sec.); Vice-Chm. and Sec., Friends of Opera North, 1979–86; Member: Council/Co., and Develt Cttee, Opera North, 1980–95; Guild of Freemen, City of London, 1967; Justice; European Movement; Actsa. Governor, Wakefield Dist Community Sch. (formerly Ackworth Moor Top, then Felkirk Community Special Sch.), 1996– (Chm., 1998–). DL S Yorks, 1986. FRSA 1984. *Recreations:* being with family and friends, opera, foreign travel, visiting South Africa, supporting community development in Ivory Park Township, Midrand. *Address:* Long Lane Close, High Ackworth, Pontefract, Yorks WF7 7EY. *T:* (01977) 795450, *Fax:* (01977) 795470; *e-mail:* jcharris@lineone.net.

HARRIS, Dr John Edwin, MBE 1981; FRS 1988; FREng; nuclear scientist; *b* 2 June 1932; *s* of late John Frederick Harris and Emily Margaret (*née* Prosser); *m* 1956, Ann Foote; two *s* two *d*. *Educ:* Larkfield Grammar Sch., Chepstow; Dept of Metallurgy, Univ. of Birmingham (BSc 1953, PhD 1956, DSc 1973). FIMMM (FIM 1974); FREng (FEng 1987); FInstP 1992. Joined Associated Electrical Industries, 1956; CEGB, 1959–89; seconded to Sheffield Univ., 1959–61; Berkeley Nuclear Labs, 1961–89, Sect. Head, 1966–89; Univ. Liaison Manager, Nuclear Electric plc, 1989–90. Visiting Professor: Nuclear Engrg, Manchester Univ., 1991–; Corrosion Sci., UMIST, 1992–2004; Materials and Manufacture, Univ. of Plymouth (formerly Plymouth Poly.), 1992–; Visiting Lecturer: Bristol Univ., 1992–; Oxford Univ., 1992–. Member: Bd, British Nuclear Energy Soc., 1974–88; Watt Cttee Wkg Party on Atmospheric Attack on Inorganic Materials, 1987; Hon. Advisor on materials: repairs to St Paul's Cathedral, 1979; restoration of Albert Meml, 1988; roofing of BM, 1999. Mem., Home Office Wkg Party on Adjudications in HM Prisons, 1974; Chm., Leyhill Prison Bd of Visitors, 1973–74. Mem., Assoc. of British Science Writers. Vice Chm., British Pugwash, 2002–. Public Lectr, Tate Gall., 1984; Molecule Club Lectr, 1985 and 1987; Friday Evening Discourse, Royal Instn, 1998. Member, Editorial Board: Material Science and Technology, 1985–; Euro Materials, 1994–; Ed., Interdisciplinary Sci. Reviews, 1996–2002, subseq. Ed. Emeritus. FRSA 1989. Internat. Metallographic Soc. Award, 1976; Esso Gold Medal, Royal Soc., 1979; Interdisciplinary Award, RSC, 1987; Andrew Bryan Award, IMMM, 2006. *Publications:* (ed) Physical Metallurgy of Reactor Fuel Elements, 1975; Vacancies '76, 1977; (jtly) Metals and the Royal Society, 1999; scientific papers on nuclear metallurgy, deformation and corrosion; articles in New Scientist and The Guardian. *Recreations:* writing popular science articles, studying decay of buildings. *Address:* Church Farm House, 28 Hopton Road, Upper Cam, Dursley, Glos GL11 5PB. *T:* (01453) 543165; *e-mail:* j.harris106@btinternet.com. *Club:* Cam Bowling (non-playing member).

HARRIS, John Frederick, OBE 1986; FSA; Curator, British Architectural Library's Drawing Collection and Heinz Gallery, 1960–86; Consultant: to Collection, Canadian Centre for Architecture, 1986–88 (Member Advisory Board, 1983–88); Heinz Architectural Center, Carnegie, 1991–94; Victoria and Albert Museum Primary Galleries Project, 1996–2001; *b* 13 Aug. 1931; *s* of Frederick Harris and Maud (*née* Sellwood); *m* 1960, Eileen Spiegel, New York; one *s* one *d*. *Educ:* Cowley C of E School. Itinerant before 1956; Library of Royal Inst. of Architects, 1956. Mem., Mr Paul Mellon's Adv. Bd, 1966–78; Trustee, Amer. Mus. in Britain, 1974–88; Chm., Colnaghi & Co., 1982–92. President: Internat. Confedn on Architectural Museums, 1981–84 (Chm., 1979–81; Hon. Life Pres., 1984); Marylebone Soc., 1978–80; Twentieth Century Soc. (formerly Thirties Soc.), 1986– (Mem. Cttee, 1979–); Member: Council, Drawing Soc. of America, 1962–68; Council, Victorian Soc., 1974–; Nat. Council, Internat. Council of Monuments and Sites, 1976–83; Soc. of Dilettanti, 1977–; Member Committee: Soc. of Architectural Historians of GB, 1958–66; Georgian Gp, 1970–74, 1986–89; Save Britain's Heritage, 1970–; Stowe Landscape, 1980–2001 (Patron, Stowe Gardens Buildings Trust, 1986–92); Bldg Museum Proj., 1980–86; Garden History, 1980–84; Jl of Garden History, 1980–89. Member: Adv. Council, Drawings Center, NY, 1983–89; Management Cttee, Courtauld Inst. of Art, 1983–87; Somerset House Building Cttee, 1986–89; Council, Royal Archaeol. Inst., 1984–86; Adv. Cttees, Historic Bldgs and Monuments Commn, 1984–88; Ashton Meml Steering Gp, 1984–86; GLC Historic Buildings Panel, 1984–86; Ambrose Congreve Award, 1980–82; Ashmole Archive Cttee, 1985–87; Adv. Bd, Irish Architectural Archive, 1988–91; Appeal Cttee, Painshill Park Trust, 1988–89; Spencer House Restoration Cttee, 1986–95; Nat. Trust Arts Panel, 1996–; Trustee: Architecture Foundn, 1991–94; Save Europe's Heritage, 1996–; Holburne Mus., Bath, 2000–06; Council, Georgian Gp, 2007–. Andrew W. Mellon Lectr in Fine Arts, Nat. Gall., Washington, 1981; Slade Prof. of Fine Art, Univ. of Oxford, 1982–83. Exhibitions Organizer: The King's Arcadia, 1973; The Destruction of the Country House (with Marcus Binney), 1974; The Garden, 1979; Dir, British Country House Exhibn, Nat. Gall., Washington, 1982–83; many exhibns in Heinz Gall.; travelling exhibns and catalogues: Italian Architectural Drawings, 1966; Sir Christopher Wren, 1970; Designs of the British Country House, 1985. FSA 1968; FRSA 1975; Hon. FRIBA 1972; Hon. MA Oxon, 1982; Hon. Brother Art Workers' Guild, 1972. Harris Testimonial Medal, 1999. Editor, Studies in Architecture, 1976–99. *Publications:* English Decorative Ironwork, 1960; Regency Furniture Designs, 1961; (ed), The Prideaux Collection of Topographical Drawings, 1963; (jtly) Lincolnshire, 1964; (contrib.) The Making of Stamford, 1965; (jtly) Illustrated Glossary of Architecture, 1966, 2nd edn 1969; (jtly) Buckingham Palace, 1968; Georgian Country Houses, 1968; (contrib.) Concerning Architecture, 1968; Sir William Chambers, Knight of the Polar Star, 1970 (Hitchcock Medallion 1971); (ed) The Rise and Progress of the Present State of Planting, 1970; (ed jtly) The Country Seat, 1970; Catalogue of British Drawings for Architecture, Decoration, Sculpture and Landscape Gardening in American Collections, 1971; A Country House Index, 1971, 2nd edn 1979; Catalogue of the Drawings Collection RIBA: Inigo Jones and John Webb, 1972; (contrib.) Guide to Vitruvius Britannicus, 1972; (jtly) The King's Arcadia: Inigo Jones and The Stuart Court, 1973; Catalogue of the Drawings Collection RIBA: Colin Campbell, 1973; Headfort House and Robert Adam, 1973; (jtly) The Destruction of the Country House, 1974; Gardens of Delight, The Art of Thomas Robins, 1976; Gardens of Delight, The Rococo English Landscape of Thomas Robins, 1978; (jtly) Catalogue of Drawings by Inigo Jones, John Webb and Isaac de Caus in Worcester College, Oxford, 1979; A Garden Alphabet, 1979; (ed) The Garden Show, 1979; The Artist and the Country House, 1979 (Sir Banister Fletcher prize, 1979), 2nd edn 1986; (contrib.) Village England, 1980; (contrib.) Lost Houses of Scotland, 1980; The English Garden 1530–1840: a contemporary view, 1981; (contrib.), John Claudius Loudon and the Early Nineteenth Century in Great Britain, Washington, 1980; (jtly) Interiors, 1981; The Palladians, 1981; Die Hauser der Lords und Gentlemen, 1982; William Talman, Maverick Architect, 1982; (contrib.) SAVE Gibraltar's Heritage, 1982; Architectural Drawings in the Cooper Hewitt Museum, New York, 1982; (contrib.) Vanishing Houses of England, 1982; (contrib.) Macmillan Encyclopedia of Architecture, 1982; (contrib.) Great Drawings from the Collection of Royal Institute of British Architects, 1983; (jtly) Britannia Illustrata Knyff & Kip, 1984; The Design of the British Country House, 1985; (jtly) Inigo Jones—Complete Architectural Drawings, 1989; (contrib.) In Honor of Paul Mellon, Collector and Benefactor, 1986; (contrib.) Canadian Centre for Architecture Building and Gardens, 1989; (contrib.) The Fashioning and Functioning of the British Country House, 1989; (jtly) Jamaica's Heritage: an untapped resource, 1991; (contrib.) Writers and their Houses, 1993; The Palladian Revival: Lord Burlington, his villa and garden at Chiswick, 1994; The Artist and the Country House, 1995; (ed jtly and contrib.) Sir William Chambers: architect to George III, 1996; (contrib.) Chambers and Adelcranz, 1997; No Voice from the Hall: early memories of a country house snooper, 1998; (contrib.) Summerson and Hitchcock, 2002; Echoing Voices: more memories of a country house snooper, 2002; (contrib.) Kinaslott, 2002; (contrib.) Description of the Idea and General-Plan for an English Park, 2004; Moving Rooms: the trade in architectural salvages, 2007; The Duke of Beaufort his House, 2007; A Passion for Building: the amateur architect in England 1650–1850, 2007; articles in Apollo, and other jls. *Recreation:* flinting.

HARRIS, John Frederick, CEng, FIET; Chairman, Telefax Holdings Ltd, since 1995; *b* 9 Dec. 1938; *s* of Jack Harris and Lily Harris; *m* 1960, Diana Joyce Brown; one *s* two *d*. *Educ:* Central Grammar School, Birmingham. Technical posts, Midlands Electricity, 1955–70; managerial posts, Southern Electricity, 1970–78; Chief Engineer, NW Electricity Board, 1978–79, Dep. Chm., 1979–82; Chm., E Midlands Electricity Bd, then E Midlands Electricity plc, 1982–94. Dir, Nottingham Develt Enterprise, 1992–95. Gov., Nottingham Trent Univ., 1993–95; Trustee, Djanogly City Tech. Coll., 1990–. Pres., Nottingham VSO, 1984–. CCMI. Hon. DTech. *Recreation:* golf. *Club:* Reform.

HARRIS, John Howard; Director, Children, Schools and Families, Hertfordshire County Council, since 2003; *b* 27 Sept. 1956; *s* of James Edward Harris and Mary Mildred Harris; *m* 1982, Pauline Donnelly; one *d*. *Educ:* St Catharine's Coll., Cambridge (BA Hons Hist. 1979); Univ. of London Inst. of Educn (PGCE (Dist.); Storey Miller Prize); Essex Inst. of Higher Educn (Dip. Professional Studies in Educn (Dist.) 1986). London Borough of Newham: teacher: Langdon Sch., 1980–82; Forest Gate Community Sch., 1982–87; Advr for Tech. and Vocational Educn Initiative, 1987–90; Essex County Council: Sen. Co. Inspector, 14–19 Curriculum, 1990–91; Principal Co. Inspector, 1991–92; Service Manager, Community Educn and Post-16 Liaison, 1992–95; Sen. Educn Officer, 1995–96; Asst Dir, Educn, 1996–99, Dir of Educn, 1999–2003, Westminster CC; Sen. Educn Exec., CAPITA Strategic Educn Services, 2003. *Recreations:* reading, film, travel, cycling, running (ran Paris Marathon), football (supporting Leyton Orient FC). *Address:* Havering-atte-Bower, Romford RM4 7PP. *T:* (office) (01992) 555700; *e-mail:* john.harris@hertscc.gov.uk.

HARRIS, Air Marshal Sir John (Hulme), (Win), KCB 1992 (CB 1991); CBE 1982; Air Officer Commanding No 18 Group (RAF Strike Command) and Commander Maritime Air Eastern Atlantic and Allied Forces Northwestern Europe (formerly Channel), 1992–96; *b* 3 June 1938; *s* of late George W. H. Harris and Dorothy Harris (*née* Hulme); *m* 1962, Williamina (*née* Murray); two *s*. *Educ:* English Sch., Cairo; King Edward VII Sch., King's Lynn. No 224 Sqn, RAF, 1960–62; RAF Leeming, Flying Instructor, 1963–67; Exchange Officer, US Navy Air Test and Evaluation Sqn, Florida, 1968–70; Central Tactics and Trials Organisation, 1970–73; OC No 201 Sqn, 1973–75; Nat. Defence Coll., 1975–76; OPCON (CCIS) Project Team, Northwood, 1976–78; SASO, RAF Pitreavie Castle, 1979; OC RAF Kinloss, 1979–81; MA to Dir, Internat. Mil. Staff, Brussels, 1982–83; RCDS, 1984; Dir Training (Flying), RAF, 1985–87; Comdt Gen. RAF Regiment and Dir Gen. of Security (RAF), 1987–89; ACDS (Logistics), 1990–91; COS, HQ No 18 Gp (RAF Strike Comd), 1991–92. ADC to the Queen, 1979–81. *Recreations:* fly fishing for salmon, trout and navigators, gardening, travel. *Address:* c/o Lloyds TSB, Cox's and King's Branch, 7 Pall Mall, SW1Y 5NA. *Club:* Royal Air Force.

HARRIS, Prof. John Morley, DPhil; FMedSci; Sir David Alliance Professor of Bioethics, University of Manchester, since 1997; *b* 21 Aug. 1945; *s* of Albert Harris and Ruth Harris; *m* 1978, Sita Williams; one *s*. *Educ:* University of Kent at Canterbury (BA 1966); Balliol Coll., Oxford (DPhil 1976). Lectr in Philosophy, 1974–77, Sen. Lectr, 1977–79, City of Birmingham Poly.; Associate Lectr in Philosophy, Brunel Univ., 1977–79; University of Manchester: Lectr in Philosophy, 1979–84, Sen. Lectr, 1984–88, Dept of Educn; Res. Dir, Centre for Social Ethics and Policy, 1986–; Reader in Applied Philosophy, Sch. of Educn, 1988–90; Prof. of Bioethics and Applied Philosophy, 1990–97; Dir, Inst. of Medicine, Law and Bioethics, 1996–. Series Ed., Social Ethics and Policy, 1985–; Founder and a Gen. Ed., Issues in Biomedical Ethics series, 1994–. Member: Adv. Cttee on Genetic Testing, 1997–99; Human Genetics Commn, 1999–; Ethics Cttee, BMA, 1991–97 and 1999–. Chm., Values and Attitudes Wkg Party, Age Concern, 1996–99. Mem., Romanian Acad. Med. Scis, 1994–. FMedSci 2001. *Publications:* Violence and Responsibility, 1980; The Value of Life, 1985; (ed with S. Hirsch) Consent and the Incompetent Patient, 1988; (ed with A. Dyson) Experiments on Embryos, 1990; Wonderwoman and Superman: ethics and human biotechnology, 1992; (ed with A. Dyson) Ethics and Biotechnology, 1994; Clones, Genes and Immortality, 1998; (ed jtly) AIDS: ethics, justice and European policy, 1998; (ed with S. Holm) The Future of Human Reproduction, 1998; (ed jtly) A Companion to Genethics: philosophy and the genetic revolution, 2001; (ed.) Bioethics, 2001; On Cloning, 2004; Enhancing Evolution, 2007. *Recreations:* cooking, walking, argument, Italy. *Address:* School of Law, University of Manchester, Oxford Road, Manchester M13 9PL. *T:* (0161) 275 3473.

HARRIS, His Honour John Percival, DSC 1945; QC 1974; a Circuit Judge, 1980–95; *b* 16 Feb. 1925; *o s* of late Thomas Percival Harris and Nora May Harris; *m* 1959, Janet Valerie Douglas; one *s* two *d*. *Educ:* Wells Cathedral Sch.; Pembroke Coll., Cambridge. BA 1947. Served in RN, 1943–46: Midshipman, RNVR, 1944, Sub-Lt 1945. Called to the Bar, Middle Temple, 1949, Bencher 1970. A Recorder of the Crown Court, 1972–80; Dep. Sen. Judge, Sovereign Base Areas, Cyprus, 1983–2000 (Acting Sen. Judge, 1995). *Recreations:* golf, reading, Victorian pictures. *Address:* Tudor Court, Fairmile Park Road, Cobham, Surrey KT11 2PP. *T:* (01932) 864756. *Clubs:* Royal St George's Golf (Sandwich); Woking Golf, Rye Golf.

HARRIS, (John Robert) William, FRCP, FRCPI; Consultant in Genito-Urinary Medicine, Imperial College Healthcare NHS Trust (formerly St Mary's Hospital NHS Trust), since 1976; *b* 25 Sept. 1943; *s* of William James Smyth Harris and Anne (*née* Glass); *m* 1st, 1968, Mary Elizabeth Keating (marr. diss. 1992; remarried 1994); one *s* one *d. Educ:* Ballymena Acad.; Queen's Univ., Belfast (MB). FRCP 1985; FRCPI 1996. Postgrad. trng, Royal Victoria Hosp., Belfast and Liverpool Sch. of Tropical Medicine, 1968–72; Consultant and Hon. Sen. Lectr, Sheffield Royal Infirmary, 1972–74; Consultant, King's Coll. Hosp., 1974–75; Med. Dir, St Mary's Hosp. NHS Trust, 1991–97. Lock Lectr, RCPSG, 1993. Internat. Health Award, 1973; Scott-Heron Medal, Royal Victoria Hosp., Belfast, 1985. *Publications:* Recent Advances in Sexually Transmitted Diseases, 1975, 4th edn 1991; papers on sexually transmitted diseases, AIDS and prostatitis. *Recreations:* walking, cinema, travel. *Address:* 75 Harley Street, W1G 8QL. *T:* (020) 7486 4166. *Club:* Athenæum.

HARRIS, Jonathan David, CBE 2002 (OBE 1993); FRICS; President, Royal Institution of Chartered Surveyors, 2000–01; *b* 28 Sept. 1941; *s* of Wilfred Harris and Ann Harris (*née* Godel); *m* 1964, Jeniffer Cecilia Fass; one *s* three *d. Educ:* Haberdashers' Aske's Sch. FRICS 1964. Pepper Angliss & Yarwood, Chartered Surveyors, 1959–94 (Sen. Partner, 1974–94); Director: Cardinal Group, 1973–; Carlisle Gp, 1987–99; Cressida Gp, 1996–; Babraham Bioscience Technologies Ltd, 2002–04. Mem. Bd, Plymouth Develt Corp., 1993–96; Dep. Chm., UN Real Estate Adv. Gp, 2001–06. Committee Member: Sackville Property Unit Trust, 1974–99; Langbourn Income Growth & Property Unit Trust, 1984–. Member: Property Adv. Gp, Bank of England, 1999–2001; Professions Wkg Gp, Council for Excellence in Mgt and Leadership, 2000–02. Founder and Pres., Continuing Professional Develt Foundn, 1980–; Founder and Chm., Inst. of Continuing Professional Develt, 1997. Treas., Prison Reform Trust, 1998–2001. Trustee: Enterprise Education Trust (formerly Understanding Industry, subseq. businessdynamics), 1997– (Dep. Chm., 2006–); LPO Trust, 1996–; Chm. of Trustees, Employment Resource Centre, 2004–. Governor: Univ. of Westminster (formerly Poly. of Central London), 1988–99; Manor Lodge Sch., 2002–07. Mem., Counselors of Real Estate, USA, 2005. Liveryman: Co. of Chartered Surveyors, 1977; Co. of Basketmakers, 1962. Hon. DLitt Westminster, 1998. *Recreations:* golf, bridge, grandchildren. *Address:* 24 Hays Mews, W1J 5PY. *T:* (020) 7495 3132.

HARRIS, Prof. Jose Ferial, PhD; FBA 1993; Professor of Modern History, University of Oxford, 1996–2008; Fellow, St Catherine's College, Oxford, since 1978 (Vice-Master, 2003–05); *d* of Leonard Cecil Chambers and Freda Ellen Chambers (*née* Brown); *m* 1968, Prof. James William Harris, FBA (*d* 2004); one *s. Educ:* Dame Alice Harpur Sch., Bedford; Newnham Coll., Cambridge (MA, PhD). Res. Fellow, Nuffield Coll., Oxford, 1966–69; Lectr, 1969–74, Sen. Lectr, 1974–78, Dept of Social Sci. and Admin, LSE; Reader in Modern History, Oxford Univ., 1990–96. Vis. Res. Fellow, Princeton, 1985–86. Ford Lectr in English History, Oxford Univ., 1996–97; Leverhulme Res. Prof., Oxford Univ., 1998–2002. *Publications:* Unemployment and Politics: a study in English social policy, 1972, 2nd edn 1984; William Beveridge: a biography, 1977, 2nd edn 1997; Private Lives, Public Spirit: a social history of Britain 1870–1914, 1993, 2nd edn 1994; Ferdinand Tönnies: community and civil society, 2001; Civil Society in British History, 2003. *Recreations:* the lesser arts, walking, river boats, family life. *Address:* 5 Belbroughton Road, Oxford OX2 6UZ.

HARRIS, Joseph Hugh; Vice Lord-Lieutenant of Cumbria, 1994–2007; *b* 3 June 1932; *s* of late John Frederick Harris and of Gwendolen Arden Harris; *m* 1957, Anne, *d* of Brig. Leslie Harrison McRobert, CBE. *Educ:* Aysgarth Sch.; Harrow; Royal Agric. Coll. (MRAC). Lieut, 11th Hussars, PAO. Chairman: Cumbrian Newspapers Ltd, 1987–2002; Grasmere Sports (Dir, 1977). Member: Northern Regl Panel, MAFF, 1977–83; Rural Develt Commn, 1989–. Royal Agricultural Society: Sen. Steward, 1960–77; Dep. Pres., 1987; Trustee, 1992–; Hon. Dir, Royal Show, 1978–82. High Sheriff of Cumbria, 1976–77; DL 1984, JP 1971–2002, Cumbria. Chm., Penrith and Alston Bench, 1991–95. Chm. of Govs, Aysgarth Sch., 1975–78; Gov., RAC, Cirencester, 1987–90. Liveryman, Farmers' Co., 1973–. *Recreations:* shooting, country sports, conservation. *Address:* West View, Bowscar, Penrith, Cumbria CA11 9PG. *T:* and *Fax:* (01768) 885661.

HARRIS, Air Cdre Joy; *see* Harris, I. J.

HARRIS, Dr Keith Murray, CBiol, FIBiol, FRES; Director, International (formerly Commonwealth) Institute of Entomology, 1985–92; *b* 26 Nov. 1932; *s* of Clifford Murray Harris and Doris (*née* Cottam); *m* 1957, Elizabeth Harrison; one *s* one *d. Educ:* Lewis Sch., Pengam; Univ. of Wales, Aberystwyth (BSc, DSc); Selwyn Coll., Cambridge (DipAgricSci); Imperial Coll. of Tropical Agric., Trinidad (DipTA). FRES 1960; FIBiol 1985. Entomologist, then Sen. Entomologist, Federal Dept of Agricl Res., Nigeria, 1955–62; Sen. Res. Fellow, BM (Natural History), 1962–66; Entomologist and Sen. Scientist, RHS, Wisley, 1966–74; Principal Taxonomist, Commonwealth Inst. of Entomology, 1974–85. *Publications:* (jtly) Collins Guide to the Pests, Diseases and Disorders of Garden Plants, 1981, 3rd edn (as Collins Photoguide to the Pests, Diseases and Disorders of Garden Plants), 2005; scientific research papers and articles on pests of cultivated plants, esp. pests of African cereal crops, and on taxonomy and biol. of gall midges. *Recreations:* walking, cycling, gardening, music. *Address:* 81 Linden Way, Ripley, Woking, Surrey GU23 6LP. *T:* (01483) 224963.

HARRIS, Leonard John; Commissioner, and Director, VAT Policy (formerly Internal Taxes), Customs and Excise, 1991–96; *b* 4 July 1941; *s* of Leonard and May Harris; *m* 1st, 1965, Jill Christine Tompkins (marr. diss.); one *s* two *d*; 2nd, 1986, Jennifer Dilys Biddiscombe (*née* Barker). *Educ:* Westminster City Sch.; St John's Coll., Cambridge. BA 1964 (Eng. Lit.), MA 1967. HM Customs and Excise: Asst Principal, 1964; Private Sec. to Chairman, 1966–68; Principal, 1969; CS Selection Bd, 1970; HM Customs and Excise, 1971; Cabinet Office, 1971–74; First Sec., UK Rep. to EEC, 1974–76, Counsellor, 1976–77; Asst Sec., HM Customs and Excise, 1977–80, Cabinet Office, 1980–83; Under Sec., 1983; Comr of Customs and Excise, 1983–87; Under Sec., MPO, 1987; Under Sec., HM Treasury, 1987–91. *Recreations:* cooking, music, naturism. *Address:* 2 Greens Row, Laundry Lane, Aston, Oxon OX18 2DG. *Club:* Oxford Naturist (Oxford).

HARRIS, Mark; Assistant Treasury Solicitor, Department for Education (formerly Education and Science), 1988–94; *b* 23 Feb. 1943; *s* of late Solomon Harris and Eva (*née* Lazarus); *m* 1972, Sharon Frances Colin; one *d. Educ:* Central Foundation Boys' Grammar Sch., London; London School of Economics and Political Science, London Univ. (LLB Hons). Solicitor of the Supreme Court, 1967. Entered Solicitor's Office, Dept of Employment, as Legal Asst, 1968; Sen. Legal Asst, 1973; Asst Solicitor, 1978; Legal Advr, 1987–88. Vol. mem. mgt cttee and journalist, Essex Jewish News. *Publications:* numerous short stories, magazine and newspaper articles. *Recreations:* travel, walking, short-story writing, theatre, choral singing (first tenor, London Cantorial Singers).

HARRIS, Mark Philip Allen; Chief Executive, National Lottery Commission, since 1999; *b* 29 July 1961; *s* of Roy Allen Harris and Vivienne Harris; *m* 1993, Patricia Mary Allen; one *s* one *d. Educ:* Bishop's Stortford Coll.; Nottingham Univ. (LLB Hons). CPFA 1987. Audit Examr, 1983–88, Manager, 1988–91, Sen. Manager, 1991–94, District Audit; Associate Controller, Audit Commn, 1994–97; Exec. Consultant, Hammersmith Hosps NHS Trust, 1997–98; Associate Dir (Strategic Develt), Audit Commn, 1998–99. *Recreations:* family, driving, hill walking, mountaineering literature. *Address:* National Lottery Commission, Second Floor, 101 Wigmore Street, W1U 1QU. *T:* (020) 7016 3434.

HARRIS, Prof. Sir Martin (Best), Kt 2000; CBE 1992; DL; President, Clare Hall, Cambridge, since 2008; Director, Office for Fair Access, since 2004; *b* 28 June 1944; *s* of William Best Harris and Betty Evelyn (*née* Martin); *m* 1966, Barbara Mary (*née* Daniels); two *s. Educ:* Devonport High Sch. for Boys, Plymouth; Queens' Coll., Cambridge (BA, MA; Hon. Fellow, 1992); Sch. of Oriental and African Studies, London (PhD). Lecturer in French Linguistics, Univ. of Leicester, 1967; University of Salford: Sen. Lectr in French Linguistics, 1974; Prof. of Romance Ling., 1976–87; Dean of Social Sciences and Arts, 1978–81; Pro-Vice-Chancellor, 1981–87; Vice-Chancellor: Essex Univ., 1987–92; Manchester Univ., 1992–2004. Chairman: CVCP, 1997–99 (Vice-Chm., 1995–97); NW Univs Assoc., 1999–2000; Univs Superannuation Scheme Ltd, 2006– (Dir, 1991–; Dep. Chm., 2004–06). Member: Internat. Cttee for Historical Linguistics, 1979–86; UGC, 1984–87; HEFCE Review of Univ. Libraries, 1992–93; Chairman: NI Sub Cttee, UFC (formerly UGC), 1985–91; Nat. Curriculum Wkg Gp for Modern Foreign Langs, 1989–90; HEFCE/CVCP Review of Postgrad. Educn, 1995–96; Clinical Standards Adv. Gp, 1996–99; DfEE Careers Review, 2000. Member: Commn for Health Improvement, 1999–2002; NW Develt Agency Bd, 2001–08 (Dep. Chm., 2002–08). Chm., Manchester: Knowledge Capital, 2004–08. Mem. Council, Philological Soc., 1979–86, 1988–92. Chm. of Govs, Centre for Inf. on Lang. Teaching, 1990–96; Vice Chm. of Governors, Parrs Wood High Sch., 1982–86; Gov., Colchester Sixth Form Coll., 1988–92; Member Governing Body: Anglia Polytechnic Univ. (formerly Anglia Poly.), 1989–93; SOAS, London Univ., 1990–93; Plymouth Univ., 2004–; Mem. High Council, Eur. Univ. Inst., 1992–96. Mem. Editorial Board: Journal Linguistics, 1982–91; Diachronica, 1983–92; French Studies, 1987–93; Jt Gen. Editor, Longman Linguistics Library, 1982–96. MAE 1991; AcSS 2001. DL Greater Manchester, 1998. Hon. Fellow: Bolton Inst., 1996; Univ. of Central Lancashire, 1999; Hon. RMCM 1996; Hon. FRCP 2005; Hon. FRCSE 2005. Hon. LLD QUB, 1992; DUniv: Essex, 1993; Keele, 2006; Hon. DLitt: Salford, 1995; Manchester Metropolitan, 2000; Leicester, Lincoln, 2003; Ulster, Manchester, UMIST, 2004; Exeter, 2008. *Publications:* (ed) Romance Syntax: synchronic and diachronic perspectives, 1976; The Evolution of French Syntax: a comparative approach, 1978; (ed with N. Vincent) Studies in the Romance Verb, 1982; (ed with P. Ramat) Historical Development of Auxiliaries, 1987; (ed with N. Vincent) The Romance Languages, 1988; about 35 articles in appropriate jls and collections. *Recreations:* gardening, travel, wine. *Address:* The President's House, Clare Hall, 1 Herschel Road, Cambridge CB3 9AL. *T:* (01223) 332360.

HARRIS, Maurice Kingston, CB 1976; Secretary, Northern Ireland Ministry of Home Affairs, 1972, seconded to Northern Ireland Office, 1974–76; *b* 5 Oct. 1916; *s* of Albert Kingston Harris and Annie Rebecca Harris; *m* 1948, Margaret, *d* of Roderick Fraser and Gertrude McGregor; one *s* three *d. Educ:* The Perse Sch.; London Univ. 1st cl. Hons Mod. Langs, 1939. Served in Indian Army, 8th Punjab Regt, 1942–46. Colonial Office, 1946–47. Entered Northern Ireland Civil Service, 1947, and served in various Ministries; retired 1976. *Recreations:* music, walking. *Address:* Apt 1, Marlborough Manor, 48 Marlborough Park South, Belfast BT9 6HS. *T:* (028) 9068 1409.

HARRIS, Mervyn Leslie Richard; a District Judge (Magistrates' Courts) (formerly Stipendiary Magistrate), Nottinghamshire, since 1991; *b* 9 Aug. 1942; *s* of Albert Leslie Harris and Gladys Mary (*née* Plummer); *m* 1967, Marcia Jane Tomblin; one *s* one *d. Educ:* King Henry VIII Sch., Coventry; University Coll. London (LLB 1964). Admitted solicitor, 1969; Partner, Hughes & Masser, solicitors, Coventry, 1969–91. Chm. (part-time), Social Security Appeals Tribunal, 1985–91; Actg Stipendiary Magistrate, 1987–91. Clerk to local charities in Coventry and Atherstone. *Recreations:* walking, railways, railway history, watching football, Rugby and cricket.

HARRIS, Michael David, FRCO; Organist and Master of the Music, St Giles' Cathedral, Edinburgh, since 1996; organ recitalist, conductor and adjudicator; *b* 29 Dec. 1958; *s* of David John Harris and Muriel Harris (*née* Pearson); *m* 1987, Brigitte Johanne Hannelore Schröder; one *d. Educ:* King's Sch., Gloucester; Reading Sch.; St Peter's Coll., Oxford (MA); Royal Coll. of Music (ARCM); FRCO 1980. Sub Organist, Leeds Parish Church, 1982–86; Asst Dir of Music, Leeds Grammar Sch., 1982–86; Asst Organist, Canterbury Cathedral, 1986–96; Organist, King's Sch., Canterbury, 1986–96; Lectr in Music, Napier Univ., Edinburgh, 1996–; Director: Scottish Chamber Choir, 1997–; Edinburgh Organ Acad., 1998–. Numerous CD recordings with Canterbury Cathedral and St Giles' Cathedral, Edinburgh. *Recreations:* railways, cooking. *Address:* St Giles' Cathedral, Edinburgh EH1 1RE.

HARRIS, Hon. Michael Deane; Senior Business Advisor, Goodmans LLP, since 2002; consultant and advisor to various Canadian companies, since 2002; Premier of Ontario, 1995–2002; *b* 23 Jan. 1945; *s* of Sidney Deane Harris and Hope Gooding Harris (*née* Robinson). *Educ:* Algonquin High Sch.; North Bay Teachers' Coll. ICD.D 2005. Formerly: entrepreneur (owned and operated ventures incl. tourist resort and ski center); sch. teacher (Trustee, 1975–81, Chm., 1977–81, Nipissing Bd of Educn). MPP (PC) for Nipissing, Ontario, 1981; Parly Asst to Minister of the Envmt; Minister of Natural Resources and Minister of Energy, 1985. House Leader, 1986–89, Leader, 1990–2002, Ontario Progressive Conservative Party. Director: Magna Internat. Inc., 2003–; Canaccord Capital Inc., 2004–; FirstService Corp., 2006–; Chm., Englobe Corp., 2004–. Chm. of Trustees, Chartwell Seniors Housing Real Estate Investment Trust, 2003–; Director: Tim Horton Children's Foundn, 2002–; Mount Royal Coll. Foundn, 2004–. Sen. Fellow, Fraser Institute, 2002. Freedom Medal, Nat. Citizens Coalition, Canada, 1996; E. P. Taylor Award of Merit, Jockey Club of Canada, 2000; Cam Fella Award, Standardbred Canada, 2000. *Address:* Goodmans LLP, 250 Yonge Street, Suite 2400, Toronto, ON M5B 2M6, Canada.

HARRIS, His Honour Sir Michael (Frank), Kt 2008; a Circuit Judge, 1992–2007; *b* 11 Jan. 1942; *s* of Joseph Frank Harris and Edna Harris; *m* 1969, Veronica Brend; one *s* one *d. Educ:* St Bartholomew's Grammar Sch., Newbury; Merton Coll., Oxford (BA). Called to the Bar, Middle Temple, 1965, Bencher, 2003; a Recorder, 1990–92. Chief Social Security Comr and Chief Child Support Comr, 2001–03. President: Social Security, Medical, Disability and Child Support Appeal Tribunals, 1998–99; The Appeals Service, 1999–2007. *Recreations:* piano playing, amateur dramatics, walking, music, theatre, travel, reading.

HARRIS, Rear-Adm. Michael George Temple; JP; Clerk to the Clothworkers' Co. of the City of London and Secretary to the Clothworkers' Foundation, 1992–2001; *b* 5 July 1941; *s* of late Comdr Antony John Temple Harris, OBE, RN and Doris Drake Harris; *heir-pres.* to Baron Harris, *qv*; *m* 1970, Katrina Chichester; three *d*. *Educ:* Pangbourne Coll.; RNC Dartmouth; Open Univ. (BA, Dip. Spanish 2004). FRGS 1978–2002; FNI 1988–2002. Qualified Submarines, 1963, TAS 1968; commanded HM Submarines: Osiris, 1970–72; Sovereign, 1975–77 (N Pole, 1976); 3rd Submarine Sqn, 1982–85; commanded HM Ships: Cardiff, 1980–82 (Falkland Is, 1982); Ark Royal, 1987–89; ACDS (NATO/UK), 1989–92. Exchange service with USN, 3rd Fleet Staff, 1972–75. Younger Brother of Trinity House, 1989–. Trustee, 1984–, Chm., 1995–, Belmont House, Kent; Trustee, Emmaus Hampshire, 2005–. Mem., Ancient Soc. of Coll. Youths, 1995–. Liveryman, Clothworkers' Co., 1997– (Mem., Ct of Assistants, 2001–). Gov., Pangbourne Coll., 1997–2007. JP NW Hants, 2002. *Recreations:* riding, fishing, bell-ringing, monumental brasses, reading. *Address:* c/o Clothworkers' Hall, Dunster Court, Mincing Lane, EC3R 7AH. *Clubs:* Naval and Military; Band of Brothers.

HARRIS, Michael John; Co-founder and Chairman, Garlik, since 2006; Chairman, Group Innovation, Royal Bank of Scotland, since 2006; *b* 10 March 1949; *s* of John Melton and Ivy May Harris; *m* 1971, Susan Cooper; one *s* one *d*. *Educ:* Dudley Grammar Sch.; University Coll. London (BSc Chemistry). Variety of positions in IT, incl. Head of Systems Develt for Retail Bank, Midland Bank, 1972–86; Dir, Space-Time Systems, 1986–88; Chief Executive: Firstdirect, 1988–91; Mercury Communications Ltd, 1991–95; Prudential Banking, then Egg, 1995–2000; Vice Chm., Egg plc, 2000–05. *Recreations:* tennis, walking, theatre, photography, watching Aston Villa.

HARRIS, Rear Adm. Nicholas Henry Linton, CB 2006; MBE 1987; Clerk to Merchant Taylors' Company, since 2006; *b* 26 Feb. 1952; *s* of Peter N. Harris and Theodora M. F. Harris (*née* Patterson); *m* 1974, Jennifer Mary Peebles; two *d*. *Educ:* Malvern Coll.; BRNC Dartmouth. Joined RN, 1969; CO, HMS Oberon, 1985–86, HMS Sovereign, 1988–90; US Naval War Coll., 1991–92; Naval Staff, Washington, 1992–94; on staff, MoD, 1994–97; Captain, Second Submarine Sqdn, 1997–99; Dep. Flag Officer, Submarines, 1999–2000; Naval Attaché, Washington, 2000–03; FO Scotland, Northern England and NI, 2003–06. *Recreations:* cricket, golf. *Address:* c/o Merchant Taylors' Hall, 30 Threadneedle Street, EC2R 8JB. *T:* (020) 7450 4440. *Clubs:* Royal Navy of 1765 and 1785, Army and Navy; RN Cricket; Broadhalfpenny Brigands Cricket (Hambledon).

HARRIS, Patricia Ann, (Mrs J. N. K. Harris); Central President, The Mothers' Union, 1989–94 (Vice-President, 1986–88); *b* 29 May 1939; *m* 1963, Rev. James Nigel Kingsley Harris, BA; one *s* one *d*. *Educ:* Trinity Coll., Carmarthen (Hon. Fellow, 1995). Teaching Dip. Teacher, 1959–63; pt-time special needs teacher, 1963–88; vol. teacher, Gloucester Prison, 1978–85. Member: Glos Dio. Synod, 1980–2001; C of E General Synod, 1985–2000 (Mem. Exec., 1991–2001, Vice Chm., 1996–2001, Chm., Trust Funds, 1996–2001, Bd of Mission); Bishops' Council, 1985–2001; Cttee, Partnership for World Mission, 1993–2000; Women's Nat. Commn, 1994–96; USPG Council, 1994–96; Cttee, Black Anglican Concerns, 1995–96; Council, 1996–, Publications Cttee, 1997–, Bible Reading Fellowship. Mothers' Union: Young Wives Leader, 1963–65; Enrolling Mem., 1967–76; Presiding Mem., 1969–74; Diocesan Social Concern Chm., 1974–80; Pres., Glos dio., 1980–85; Mem., Worldwide Council, 1995–. Hon. Lay Canon, Gloucester Cathedral, 2001–. Mem., Archbishops' Bd of Examiners, 1996–99. Paul Harris Fellow, Rotary Internat., 1995. Cross of St Augustine, 1995. *Recreations:* swimming, watching Rugby, cooking, craft work. *Address:* 14 Shalford Close, Cirencester, Glos GL7 1WG. *T:* (01285) 885641.

HARRIS, Rt Rev. Patrick Burnet; Assistant Bishop, diocese of Europe, since 1999; Hon. Assistant Bishop, Diocese of Gloucester, since 2005; *b* 30 Sept. 1934; *s* of Edward James Burnet Harris and Astrid Kendall; *m* 1968, Valerie Margaret Pilbrow; two *s* one *d*. *Educ:* St Albans School; Keble Coll., Oxford (MA). Asst Curate, St Ebbe's, Oxford, 1960–63; Missionary with S American Missionary Soc., 1963–73; Archdeacon of Salta, Argentina, 1969–73; Diocesan Bishop of Northern Argentina, 1973–80; Rector of Kirkheaton and Asst Bishop, Dio. Wakefield, 1981–85; Sec., Partnership for World Mission, 1986–88; Asst Bishop, Dio. Oxford, 1986–88; Bishop of Southwell, 1988–99. Asst Bp, Dio. Lincoln, 1999–2005. Mem., South Atlantic Council, 1986–. Chairman: Bible Reading Fellowship, 1995–98; Council, Ridley Hall, 1994–2003; Internat. Anglican Family Network, 2007–; Pres., S Amer. Mission Soc., 1993–; Vice-Pres., TEAR Fund, 1994–2003. Mem., H of L, 1996–99. *Recreations:* ornithology, S American Indian culture, music, harvesting. *Address:* Apt B, Ireton House, Pavilion Gardens, The Park, Cheltenham, Glos GL50 2SP.

HARRIS, Prof. Paul Lansley, DPhil; FBA 1998; Professor of Education, Harvard University, since 2001; *b* 14 May 1946; *s* of Joseph and Betty Harris; *m* Pascale Torracinta; three *s*. *Educ:* Chippenham Grammar Sch.; Sussex Univ. (BA Psychol.); Linacre Coll., Oxford (DPhil Psychol. 1971). Research Fellow: Center for Cognitive Studies, Harvard Univ., 1971–72; in Exptl Psychol., Oxford Univ., 1972–73; Lectr, Dept of Psychol., Lancaster Univ., 1973–76; Reader, Free Univ., Amsterdam, 1976–79; Lectr, Dept of Social Psychology, LSE, 1979–81; Oxford University: Lectr in Exptl Psychol., 1981–96; Reader, 1996–98; Prof. of Develtl Psychol., 1998–2001; Fellow, St John's Coll., 1981–2001, now Emeritus. Fellow, Center for Advanced Study in Behavioral Scis, Stanford, USA, 1992–93; John Simon Guggenheim Meml Foundn Fellow, 2005. Foreign Mem., Norwegian Acad. of Sci. and Letters, 2006–. *Publications:* Children and Emotion, 1989; The Work of the Imagination, 2000; articles in learned jls, incl. Child Development, and Developmental Psychology. *Recreations:* cooking, writing. *Address:* 503A Larsen Hall, Harvard Graduate School of Education, Appian Way, Cambridge, MA 02138, USA.

HARRIS, Dame Pauline (Norma), DBE 2004; DL; company director; *b* 5 Jan. 1942; *d* of Bertie William Chumley and Constance Chumley (*née* Woolett); *m* 1960, Philip Charles Harris (*see* Baron Harris of Peckham); three *s* one *d*. *Educ:* St Helen's Sch., Streatham. Chairman: Organising Cttee, Children's Royal Variety Performance, 1985–88; Appeal Cttee, Birthright, 1988–91; Kingdom Appeal, Foetal Res. Unit, KCH, 1991–93; Co-Chm., Mencap Opera, 1993–96; Vice President: Friends of Guy's Hosp., 1991–; Mencap, 1995–; Pres., Harris HospisCare, 1997–. Dir and Mem., Special Educnl Needs Sub-cttee, Harris City Technol. Coll., Croydon, 1988–; Mem. Council, Harris Manchester Coll., Oxford, 1994–; Dir and Gov., Harris Girls' Acad., E Dulwich, 2006–; Dir, Harris Fedn of S London Schs, 2007–. Hon. Fellow: Oriel Coll., Oxford, 1994; RVC, S Mimms, 1994; Harris Manchester Coll., Oxford, 1996; Lucy Cavendish Coll., Cambridge, 1996. Trustee: Dyslexia Educn Trust, 1986–; Bacon City Technol. Coll., Bermondsey, 1990–; Mem. Cttee, Specialist Schs Trust, 2001–06; Trustee and Gov., Acad. of Peckham, 2002–. Gov., Kemnal Technol. Coll., Sidcup, 1994–. Patron: Nat. Eczema Soc., 1989–; Lewisham Children's Hosp., 1992–. Mem., British Showjumping Assoc., 1958–. DL Kent, 2005. Hon. DHL Richmond, London, 2002. *Recreations:* historic car rallying, dressage. *Address:* c/o Philip Harris House, 1A Spur Road, Orpington, Kent BR6 0PH. *T:* (01689) 886886, *Fax:* (01689) 886887; *e-mail:* dame.pauline@harrisventures.co.uk.

HARRIS, Group Captain Peter Langridge, CBE 1988; AE 1961 (Clasp 1971); CEng, FIET; ADC to the Queen, 1984–88; Inspector, Royal Auxiliary Air Force, 1983–88; *b* 6 Sept. 1929; *s* of Arthur Langridge Harris and Doris Mabel (*née* Offen); *m* 1955, (Yvonne) Patricia Stone (*d* 2003); two *d*. *Educ:* St Edward's Sch., Oxford; Univ. of Birmingham (BSc). CEng, FIET (FIEE 1976). Served: RAF, 1947–49; RAFVR, 1949–60; RAuxAF, 1960–78 and 1982–88; commanded 1 (Co. Hertford) Maritime HQ Unit, 1973–78; Air Force Mem., 1978–94, Vice-Chm. (Air), 1988–94, TA&VRA for Greater London; Gp Captain 1983. Elliott Bros (London) Ltd, 1952–55; Decca Navigator Co. Ltd, 1955–59; GEC plc, 1959–89; retired, 1989. Mem. Bd, Milton Keynes Business Venture, 1983–89. Mem. Bd of Management, 1990–2003, Mem., Adv. Bd, 2003–05, Princess Marina House, Rustington. Chm., Hatfield Dist IEE, 1979–80. Mem., Council, Reserve Forces Assoc., 1989–95. Pres., 1 Maritime HQ Unit Old Comrades Assoc., 1990–. Patron, Cerebral Palsy Centre, Portsmouth, 2003–. Liveryman, GAPAN, 2005– (Freeman, 1987). DL Greater London, 1986–98. KMJ 2003 (CMJ 1998; Chevalier, OSMTH, 1994; Grand Chancellor, NATO Grand Priory, 2005–07). *Recreation:* travel. *Address:* 10 Dolphin Court, St Helens Parade, Southsea, Hants PO4 0QL. *T:* (023) 9281 7602; *e-mail:* plharris-southsea@supanet.com. *Clubs:* Royal Air Force; Royal Naval and Royal Albert Yacht (Portsmouth).

HARRIS, Peter Michael; Official Solicitor to the Supreme Court, 1993–99; *b* 13 April 1937; *m* 1963, Bridget Burke; one *s* two *d*. *Educ:* Cirencester Grammar School; Britannia Royal Naval College, Dartmouth. Cadet, RN, 1953; Lieut Comdr 1967; retired from RN 1972. Called to the Bar, Gray's Inn, 1971; Lord Chancellor's Department: Legal Asst, 1974; Circuit Administrator, Northern Circuit, 1986–93. Trustee, reunite, 2003–. Chairman: Dorothy Pamela Smith Trust, 1999; Grandparents' Assoc., 2003–; Friends of the Belorussian Children's Hospice UK, 2007–. *Publications:* The Children Act 1989: a procedural handbook, 1991; The Expert Witness Pack, 1997. *Recreations:* reading, walking, swimming, gardening. *Address:* 23 Rook Wood Way, Little Kingshill, Great Missenden, Bucks HP16 0DF.

HARRIS, Philippa Jill Olivier, (Pippa); film and television producer; Co-Founder and Director, Neal Street Productions, since 2003; *b* Oxford, 27 March 1967; *d* of Dr Anthony Harris and Angela M. O. Harris (*née* Richards); *m* 1997, Richard McBrien; one *d*. *Educ:* Oxford High Sch.; Robinson Coll., Cambridge (BA Hons English 1989). Prodn asst, Jacaranda Prodns, 1989–91; Drama Ed., Carlton TV, 1993–97; BBC: Develt Exec., Films, 1997–99; Exec. Producer, Drama Serials, 1999–2001; Hd, Drama Commng, TV, 2001–03; producer/executive producer: Warriors, 1999 (BAFTA and RTS Awards); Care, 2000 (BAFTA and Prix Italia Awards); Other People's Children, 2000; The Sleeper, 2000; Love in a Cold Climate, 2001; The Cazalets, 2001; The Way We Live Now, 2001 (BAFTA and BPG Awards); The Inspector Lynley Mysteries, 2001–02; The Key, 2003; The Young Visiters, 2003; Jarhead, 2005; Starter for Ten, 2006; Stuart: A Life Backwards, 2007 (Banff World TV and RTS Awards; Best TV Film, Reims Internat. TV Fest.); Things We Lost in the Fire, 2007; Revolutionary Road, 2008. Mem., Council, 2008–, Film Cttee, 2008–, BAFTA. *Publication:* Song of Love: the letters of Rupert Brooke and Noel Olivier, 1991. *Recreations:* theatre, cinema, reading, contemporary art. *Address:* Neal Street Productions, 26–28 Neal Street, WC2H 9QQ. *T:* (020) 7240 8890; *e-mail:* post@nealstreetproductions.com.

HARRIS, Phillip, FRCSE, FRCPE, FRCSGlas; FRSE; former Consultant Neurosurgeon; formerly Deputy Director, Department of Surgical Neurology, Royal Infirmary and Western General Hospital, Edinburgh; Senior Lecturer, Edinburgh University, 1955–87; Member, MRC Brain Metabolism Unit, University of Edinburgh, 1952–80; Editor, Paraplegia, later Spinal Cord, 1980–97, now Emeritus Editor; *b* Edinburgh, 28 March 1922; *s* of late Simon Harris, Edinburgh; *m* 1949, Sheelagh Shèna (*née* Coutts); one *s* one *d*. *Educ:* Royal High Sch., Edinburgh; Edinburgh Univ.; Sch. of Med. of Royal Colls, Edinburgh. Medallist in Anatomy, Physiol., Physics, Materia Medica and Therapeutics, Med., Midwifery and Gynaec., and Surgery. LRCP and LRCSE, LRCPSGlas 1944; FRCSE 1948; MRCPE 1954; FRCPE 1959; FRCSGlas 1964 (*ad eundem*). Capt., RAMC, 1945–48. Past Chm., Sch. of Occupational Therapy, Edinburgh. Sometime Vis. Prof./Guest Chief in Neurosurg., USA, Canada, Europe, S America, Far East, Middle East and Russia; Lectures: Sydney Watson-Smith, RCPE, 1967; Honeymoon-Gillespie, Edinburgh Univ., 1968. Mem., WHO Cttee for Prevention of Neurotrauma, 1985. Past Chm., Professional and Linguistics Assessments Bd, GMC. World Federation of Neurosurgical Societies: past Sen. UK Deleg. in Neurosurg.; Hon. Vice-Pres., 1977–94; Mem. Exec., Neurotraumatol. Cttee and Archivist and Historian; Founder, Internat. Conf. of Recent Advances in Neurotraumatol.; Founder and Past Chairman: Epilepsy Soc., SE Scotland; Scottish Assoc. of Neurol Scis; Scottish Sports Assoc. for Disabled (Hon. Pres.); Past Member of Council: Soc. of British Neurolog. Surgs; Neurol Sect., RSocMed; Past Pres., British Cervical Spine Soc. Past Director, Epilepsy Internat.; Dir and Trustee, Scottish Trust for Physically Disabled; Mem. Council, Thistle Foundn. President: Royal High Sch. FP Club, 1978; Edinburgh Rotary Club, 1991–92. Inventor of neurosurg. instruments and apparatus. Medal, Internat. Med. Soc. of Paraplegia, 1985; Dr A. S. Lakshumpathi Medal and Prize, Madras, 1986. *Publications:* (ed jtly) Epilepsy, 1971; (ed jtly) Head Injuries, 1971; chapters in books on neurological surgery; over 100 papers in scientific jls on various neurosurgical topics. *Recreations:* sport, music, travel. *Address:* 4/5 Fettes Rise, Edinburgh EH4 1QH. *T:* (0131) 552 8900. *Club:* New (Edinburgh).

HARRIS, Ven. (Reginald) Brian; Archdeacon of Manchester, 1980–98; a Residentiary Canon of Manchester Cathedral, 1980–98, Sub-Dean 1986–98; *b* 14 Aug. 1934; *s* of Reginald and Ruby Harris; *m* 1959, Anne Patricia Hughes; one *s* one *d*. *Educ:* Eltham College; Christ's College, Cambridge (MA); Ridley Hall, Cambridge. Curate of Wednesbury, 1959–61; Curate of Uttoxeter, 1961–64; Vicar of St Peter, Bury, 1964–70; Vicar of Walmsley, Bolton, 1970–80; RD of Walmsley, 1970–80. *Recreations:* walking, painting, music. *Address:* 9 Cote Lane, Hayfield, High Peak SK22 2HL. *T:* (01663) 746321.

HARRIS, Rhian Sara; Director, Foundling Museum, since 2001; *b* 4 Dec. 1967; *m* 2001, Jonathan Hourigan; one *s*. *Educ:* Essex Univ. (BA Hons Art Hist. and Theory); City Univ. (MA Mus. and Gall. Mgt). Res. Asst, 1990–93, Sen. Picture Cataloguer, 1993–95, Wellcome Inst. for Hist. of Medicine; Curator, Foundling Mus., 1995–2001. Member, Advisory Committee: Hogarth Gp, 2004–; 19 Princelet St (Mus. of Immigration), 2004–. *Publications:* (ed jtly and contrib.) Enlightened Self-Interest, 1997; (ed) The Foundling Museum Guidebook, 2004. *Recreations:* contemporary Welsh art, cinema, dance, music, travelling, pilates, gardening. *Address:* The Foundling Museum, 40 Brunswick Square, WC1N 1AZ. *T:* (020) 7841 3600, *Fax:* (020) 7841 3601.

HARRIS, Richard Reader; *b* 4 June 1913; *s* of Richard Reader Harris; *m* 1940, Pamela Rosemary Merrick Stephens; three *d*. *Educ:* St Lawrence Coll., Ramsgate. Called to the

Bar, 1941. Fire Service, 1939–45. MP (C) Heston and Isleworth, 1950–70. *Recreations:* squash, tennis.

HARRIS, Robert Dennis; writer; *b* 7 March 1957; *s* of late Dennis Harris and Audrey (*née* Hardy); *m* 1988, Gillian, *d* of Sir Derek Hornby, *qv* and Margaret (*née* Withers); two *s* two *d*. *Educ:* King Edward VII Sch., Melton Mowbray; Selwyn Coll., Cambridge (BA Hons English). Pres., Cambridge Union, 1978. Joined BBC TV Current Affairs Dept, 1978; Reporter, Newsnight, 1981–85, Panorama, 1985–87; Political Editor, Observer, 1987–89; Political Columnist, Sunday Times, 1989–92, 1996–97; Columnist, Daily Telegraph, 2001–02. Patron, Bletchley Park Trust, 2001–. Mem., BAFTA, 2002. Columnist of the Year, British Press Awards, 2003. FRSL 1996. *Publications: novels:* Fatherland, 1992 (filmed 1994); Enigma, 1995 (filmed 2001); Archangel, 1998 (televised 2005); Pompeii, 2003; Imperium, 2006; The Ghost, 2007; *non-fiction:* (with Jeremy Paxman) A Higher Form of Killing: the history of gas and germ warfare, 1982; Gotcha! the media, the government and the Falklands crisis, 1983; The Making of Neil Kinnock, 1984; Selling Hitler: the story of the Hitler diaries, 1986 (televised, 1991); Good and Faithful Servant: the unauthorized biography of Bernard Ingham, 1990; The Media Trilogy, 1994. *Recreations:* collecting books, walking. *Address:* The Old Vicarage, Kintbury, Berks RG17 9TR. *T:* (01488) 658073. *Club:* Garrick.

HARRIS, Robert K.; *see* Kirby-Harris.

HARRIS, Robert Malcolm; HM Diplomatic Service, retired; Governor of Anguilla, 1997–2000 (Acting Governor, 1996–97); *b* 9 Feb. 1941; *m* 1984, Mary Lavinia Allmark (*née* Taggart). Joined Foreign Office, 1960, Archives Clerk, 1960–62; Istanbul, 1962–63; Cento, Ankara, 1963–65; Blantyre, 1965–69; FCO, 1969; Moscow, 1970–72; FCO, 1972–75; Second Sec., Dublin, 1975–79; Nat. Defence Coll., Latimer, 1979–80; First Sec., FCO, 1980–84; Hd of Chancery, Brunei, 1984–89; Consul, Lyon, 1989–90; First Sec., FCO, 1990–92; Chargé d'Affaires, Almaty, 1992–93; First Sec., FCO, 1993–96. *Recreations:* golf, music, gardening. *Address:* Le Bourg, 46500 Miers, France. *Club:* Golf de Montal.

HARRIS, Robin (David Ronald), CBE 1988; writer; *b* 22 June 1952; *s* of Ronald Desmond Harris and Isabella Jamieson Harris. *Educ:* Canford Sch.; Exeter Coll., Oxford (Stapeldon Schol., MA History, DPhil). Desk Officer, Conservative Res. Dept, 1978–81; Special Adviser: to Financial Sec. to the Treasury, 1981–83; to Home Secretary, 1983–85; Dir, Conservative Res. Dept, 1985–89; Mem., Prime Minister's Policy Unit, 1989–90; Advr to Baroness Thatcher, 1990–2003. Consultant Dir, Politeia, 2003–. *Publications:* Valois Guyenne: a study of politics, government and society in medieval France, 1994; (ed) Margaret Thatcher: the collected speeches, 1997; Dubrovnik: a history, 2003; Beyond Friendship: the future of Anglo-American relations, 2006; Talleyrand: betrayer and saviour of France, 2007. *Recreations:* reading, travel. *Club:* Oxford and Cambridge.

HARRIS, Rolf, CBE 2006 (OBE 1978; MBE 1968); AM 1989; entertainer; *b* 30 March 1930; *s* of C. G. Harris and A. M. Harris (*née* Robbins); *m* 1958, Alwen Hughes, sculptress; one *d*. *Educ:* Bassendean State Sch.; Perth Modern Sch.; Univ. of WA; Claremont Teachers' Coll. Jun. backstroke champion, Australia, 1946; teacher, Perth; paintings exhibited: RA, London, 1954, 1955; Nat. Gall., London, 2002; 80th birthday portrait of HM Queen, 2005; *television* includes: Rolf Harris Show, 1967–71; Rolf on Saturday-OK, 1977–79; Cartoon Time, 1984–89; Rolf's Cartoon Club, 1989–93; Animal Hospital, 1994–; Rolf's Amazing Animals, 1997–; Rolf on Art, 2001–; Rolf's Golden Jubilee, 2003; Rolf Harris' Star Portraits, 2004–; *recordings* include: Tie Me Kangaroo Down Sport, 1960; Sun Arise, 1962; Two Little Boys, 1969; Stairway to Heaven, 1993. *Publications:* Write Your Own Pop Song, 1968; Rolf Goes Bush, 1975; Picture Book of Cats, 1978; Looking at Pictures, 1978; Instant Music, 1980; Your Cartoon Time, 1986; Catalogue of Comic Verse, 1988; Every Picture Tells a Story, 1989; Win or Die: the making of a King, 1989; Your Animation Time, 1991; Personality Cats, 1992; Me and You and Poems Too, 1993; Can You Tell What it is Yet? (autobiog.), 2001; Rolf on Art, 2002. *Address:* c/o Billy Marsh and Associates, 76A Grove End Road, NW8 9ND.

HARRIS, Rosemary Jeanne; author; *b* 20 Feb. 1923; *yr d* of Marshal of the RAF Sir Arthur Harris, 1st Bt, GCB, OBE, AFC, LLD, and of Barbara Kyrle Money. *Educ:* privately; Thorneloe Sch., Weymouth; St Martin's, Central and Chelsea Schs of Art. Red Cross Nursing Auxiliary, London, Westminster Div., from 1941. Student, 1945–48; picture restorer, 1949; student at Courtauld Inst. (Dept of Technology), 1950; Reader, MGM, 1951–52; subseq. full-time writer. Reviewer of children's books for The Times, 1970–73. Television plays: Peronik, 1976; The Unknown Enchantment, 1981. *Publications:* The Summer-House, 1956; Voyage to Cythera, 1958; Venus with Sparrows, 1961; All My Enemies, 1967; The Nice Girl's Story, 1968; A Wicked Pack of Cards, 1969; The Double Snare, 1975; Three Candles for the Dark, 1976; *for children:* The Moon in the Cloud, 1968 (Carnegie Medal); The Shadow on the Sun, 1970; The Seal-Singing, 1971; The Child in the Bamboo Grove, 1971; The Bright and Morning Star, 1972; The King's White Elephant, 1973; The Lotus and the Grail, 1974; The Flying Ship, 1974; The Little Dog of Fo, 1976; I Want to be a Fish, 1977; A Quest for Orion, 1978; Beauty and the Beast, 1979; Greenfinger House, 1979; Tower of the Stars, 1980; The Enchanted Horse, 1981; Janni's Stork, 1982; Zed, 1982; (adapted) Heidi, by Johanna Spyri, 1983; Summers of the Wild Rose, 1987; (ed) Poetry Anthology: Love and the Merry-Go-Round, 1988; Colm of the Islands, 1989; Ticket to Freedom, 1991; The Wildcat Strike, 1995; The Haunting of Joey M'basa, 1996. *Recreations:* music, theatre.

HARRIS, Rosina Mary; Consultant, Taylor Joynson Garrett, 1989–95; Partner, Joynson-Hicks, Solicitors, 1954–89 (Senior Partner, 1977–86); *b* 30 May 1921; *d* of late Alfred Harris, CBE, DSO, and Rosa Alfreda Harris. *Educ:* St Swithun's Sch., Winchester; Oxford Univ. (BA 1946, MA; BCL 1947). Joined American Ambulance of GB, 1940. Member, Whitford Committee (a Cttee set up under the Chairmanship of Hon. Mr Justice Whitford to enquire into and report as to copyright law), 1973. Silver Jubilee Medal, 1977. *Recreations:* theatre, riding. *Address:* 16 Upper Wimpole Street, W1G 6LT.

HARRIS, Prof. Roy, MA, DPhil, PhD; Professor of General Linguistics, University of Oxford, 1978–88, now Emeritus; Fellow of Worcester College, Oxford, 1978–88; *b* 24 Feb. 1931; *s* of Harry and Emmie J. Harris; *m* 1955, Rita Doreen Shulman; one *d*. *Educ:* Queen Elizabeth's Hospital, Bristol; St Edmund Hall, Oxford (MA, DPhil; Hon. Fellow 1987); SOAS, London (PhD). Lecteur, Ecole Normale Supérieure, Paris, 1956–57; Asst Lectr, 1957–58, Lectr, 1958–60, Univ. of Leicester; Exeter Coll., Oxford, 1960–76; Keble Coll., Oxford, 1960–67; Magdalen Coll., Oxford, 1960–76; New Coll., Oxford, 1960–67; Faculty of Medieval and Modern Languages, Oxford, 1961–76; Fellow and Tutor in Romance Philology, Keble Coll., Oxford, 1967–76; Prof. of the Romance Langs, Oxford Univ., and Fellow of Trinity Coll., 1976–77; Prof. of English Language, Univ. of Hong Kong, 1988–91; Dir d'études associé, Ecole Pratique des Hautes Etudes, Paris, 1991–92; Fellow, Univ. Professors, Boston, 1993–95. Visiting Professor: Jawaharlal Nehru Univ., New Delhi, 1986; State Univ. of NY, 1987; Overseas Res. Fellow, Univ. of Cape Town, 1996; Dist. Vis. Schol., Univ. of Adelaide, 1997, 1999. Council Member, Philological Soc., 1978–82. Editor, Language & Communication, 1980–. FRSA. Scott Moncrieff prize, Translators' Assoc. (Soc. of Authors), 1984. *Publications:* Synonymy and Linguistic Analysis, 1973; Communication and Language, 1978; The Language-Makers, 1980; The Language Myth, 1981; (trans.) F. de Saussure: Course in General Linguistics, 1983; (ed) Approaches to Language, 1983; (ed) Developmental Mechanisms of Language, 1985; The Origin of Writing, 1986; Reading Saussure, 1987; Language, Saussure and Wittgenstein, 1988; (ed) Linguistic Thought in England 1914–1945, 1988; (with T. J. Taylor) Landmarks in Linguistic Thought: the Western tradition from Socrates to Saussure, 1989, 2nd edn 1997; La sémiologie de l'écriture, 1993; Signs of Writing, 1995; The Language Connection, 1996; Signs, Language and Communication, 1996; Introduction to Integrational Linguistics, 1998; Rethinking Writing, 2000; Saussure and his Interpreters, 2001; The Necessity of Artspeak, 2003; The Linguistics of History, 2004; The Semantics of Science, 2005; Integrationist Notes and Papers, 2006; (with C. M. Hutton) Definition in Theory and Practice, 2007; The Great Debate about Art, 2008; Mindboggling, 2008; contribs to Analysis, Behavioral and Brain Sciences, Encounter, Essays in Criticism, French Studies, History and Philosophy of Logic, International Jl of Moral and Social Studies, Jl of Linguistics, Language Sciences, Linguistics, Medium Ævum, Mind, Revue de linguistique romane, Semiotica, Studies in Eighteenth-Century Culture, Theoria, TLS, Zeitschrift für romanische Philologie. *Recreations:* cricket, modern art and design. *Address:* 2 Paddox Close, Oxford OX2 7LR. *T:* (01865) 554256.

HARRIS, Russell James; QC 2003; *b* 10 Nov. 1961; *s* of Donald Harris and Jean Harris (*née* Hall); *m* 1999, Nicola Richards; one *s* two *d*. *Educ:* Heolddu Comprehensive Sch., Bargoed; St John's Coll., Cambridge (MacMahon Schol., Pres. JCR, Lamour Prize, MA 1984); City Univ. (Dip Law 1985). Called to the Bar, Gray's Inn, 1986; in practice as a barrister, specialising in planning and public law, 1986–. series advr, The Welsh in London (BBC Wales TV), 2006. *Publications:* (jtly) Environmental Law, 2001; various articles in Jl of Planning and Envmtl Law. *Recreations:* family, Wales (especially Ramsey Sound and the Farmer's Arms, St Davids). *Address:* Landmark Chambers, 180 Fleet Street, EC4A 2HG. *T:* (020) 7430 1221; *e-mail:* russellharrisqc@Mortonhouse.co.uk. *Clubs:* London Welsh Rugby Football; St Davids Rugby Football (Vice-Pres., 2006–).

HARRIS, Sheila Lesley; *see* Scales, S. L.

HARRIS, Terence Victor; Keeper of Japanese Antiquities, British Museum, 1997–2002; *b* 3 Aug. 1942; *s* of William Victor Clayton Harris and Theresa Harris (*née* Bingham); *m* 1974, Kazuko Yanagawa; one *d*. *Educ:* Bancroft's Sch., Essex (Drapers' Co. Schol.); Birmingham Univ. (BSc Mech. Engrg). Lectr, Komazawa Univ., Tokyo, 1968–71; self-employed, Japanese Engineering Translation and Consultancy, 1971–78; British Museum: Res. Asst, Dept of Oriental Antiquities, 1978–87; Asst Keeper of Japanese Antiquities, 1987–97. Vis. Prof., Meiji Univ., Tokyo, 2005. Consultant, Japanese Dept, Christie's, 2005–. Pres., Tokenkai of GB, 1999. Trustee, Chiddingstone Castle until 2002. Mem., HAC. Hon. Librarian, Japan Soc., 2006–; Hon. Curator, Khalili collection of Japanese Art, 2006–. Jubilee Medal. *Publications:* A Book of Five Rings, 1974 (trans. several languages); Swords of the Samurai, 1990; Kamakura: the renaissance of Japanese sculpture, 1991; Japanese Imperial Craftsmen, 1994; Netsuke: the Hull Grundy collection, 1987; (jtly) Masterpieces of Japanese Art, 1991; (ed) Shinto: the sacred art of ancient Japan, 2001; (jtly) William Gowland: the father of Japanese archeology (Japanese/English), 2002; Cutting Edge: Japanese swords in the British Museum collection. *Recreation:* Kendo-Japanese sword-fencing.

HARRIS, (Theodore) Wilson, CCH 1991; *b* 24 March 1921; *m* 1st, 1945, Cecily Carew; 2nd, 1959, Margaret Whitaker (*née* Burns). *Educ:* Queen's Coll., Georgetown, British Guiana. Studied land surveying, British Guiana, 1939, and subseq. qualified to practise; led many survey parties (mapping and geomorphological research) in the interior; Senior Surveyor, Projects, for Govt of British Guiana, 1955–58. Came to live in London, 1959. Writer in Residence, Univ. of West Indies and Univ. of Toronto, 1970; Commonwealth Fellow, Leeds Univ., 1971; Vis. Prof., Univ. of Texas at Austin, 1972; Guggenheim Fellow, 1973; Henfield Fellow, UEA, 1974; Southern Arts Writer's Fellowship, 1976; Guest Lectr, Univ. of Mysore, 1978; Vis. Lectr, Yale Univ., 1979; Writer in Residence: Univ. of Newcastle, Australia, 1979; Univ. of Qld, Australia, 1986; Vis. Prof., Univ. of Texas at Austin, 1981–82; Regents' Lectr, Univ. of California, 1983. Hon. DLit Univ. of West Indies, 1984; Hon. DLitt: Kent at Canterbury, 1988; Essex, 1996; Macerata (Italy), 1999; Liège, 2001. Guyana Prize for Fiction, 1985–87; Premio Mondello dei Cinque Continenti, 1992. *Publications:* Eternity to Season (poems, privately printed), 1954; Palace of the Peacock, 1960, 4th edn 1998; The Far Journey of Oudin, 1961; The Whole Armour, 1962; The Secret Ladder, 1963; Heartland, 1964; The Eye of the Scarecrow, 1965; The Waiting Room, 1967; Tradition, the Writer and Society: Critical Essays, 1967; Tumatumari, 1968; Ascent to Omai, 1970; The Sleepers of Roraima (a Carib Trilogy), 1970; The Age of the Rainmakers, 1971; Black Marsden, 1972; Companions of the Day and Night, 1975; Da Silva da Silva's Cultivated Wilderness (filmed, 1987), and Genesis of the Clowns, 1977; The Tree of the Sun, 1978; Explorations (essays), 1981; The Angel at the Gate, 1982; The Womb of Space: the cross-cultural imagination, 1983; Carnival, 1985; The Infinite Rehearsal, 1987; The Four Banks of the River of Space, 1990; The Radical Imagination (essays), 1992; Resurrection at Sorrow Hill, 1993; Jonestown, 1996; Selected Essays, 1999; The Dark Jester, 2001; The Mask of the Beggar, 2003; The Ghost of Memory, 2006. *Address:* c/o Faber and Faber, 3 Queen Square, WC1N 3AU.

HARRIS, Thomas, (Tom); MP (Lab) Glasgow South, since 2005 (Glasgow, Cathcart, 2001–05); *b* 20 Feb. 1964; *s* of Tom Harris and Rita Harris (*née* Ralston); *m* 1998. *Educ:* Garnock Acad., Kilbirnie, Ayrshire; Napier Coll., Edinburgh (SHND Journalism). Trainee Reporter, E Kilbride News, 1986–88; Reporter, Paisley Daily Express, 1988–90; Press Officer: Labour Party in Scotland, 1990–92; Strathclyde Regl Council, 1993–96; Sen. Media Officer, Glasgow CC, 1996; PR Manager, E Ayrshire Council, 1996–98; Chief PR and Marketing Officer, Strathclyde PTE, 1998–2001. Parly Under-Sec. of State, DfT, 2006–08. *Recreations:* tennis, astronomy, hill walking, cinema. *Address:* Queen's Park Football Club, Somerville Drive, Glasgow G42 9BA. *T:* (0141) 649 9780.

HARRIS, Sir Thomas (George), KBE 2002; CMG 1995; HM Diplomatic Service, retired; Vice Chairman, Standard Chartered Bank Ltd, since 2004; *b* 6 Feb. 1945; *s* of late Kenneth James Harris and of Dorothy Harris; *m* 1967, Mei-Ling Hwang; three *s*. *Educ:* Haberdashers' Aske's School; Gonville and Caius College, Cambridge. MA. Board of Trade, 1966–69; British Embassy, Tokyo, 1969–71; Asst Private Sec. to Minister for Aerospace, 1971–72; Dept of Trade, 1972–76; Cabinet Office, 1976–78; Principal Private Sec. to Sec. of State for Trade, 1978–79; Asst Sec., Dept of Trade, 1979–83; HM Diplomatic Service: Counsellor (Commercial), British Embassy, Washington, 1983–88; Head of Chancery, Lagos, 1988–90; Dep. High Comr, Nigeria, 1990–91; Head, East African Dept, 1991–92, African Dept (Equatorial), 1992–94, FCO; Ambassador, Repub. of Korea, 1994–97; Dir-Gen., Export Promotion, DTI, 1997–99 (on secondment); Dir-Gen., Trade and Investment in the US, and Consul-Gen., NY, 1999–2004. Special Advr, Center for Strategic and Internat. Studies, Washington, 2004–. Chairman: Pakistan Britain Trade and Investment Forum, 2006–; Taiwan Britain Business Council, 2007–; Trade Policy Adv. Gp, British Bankers' Assoc., 2007–. Member: Indonesian British Business

Council, 2004–; UK-Korea Forum for the Future, 2004–; Philippine-British Business Council, 2004–; Korea Britain Business Council, 2007–; Saudi British Business Council, 2005–; Singapore British Business Council, 2005–. Non-executive Director: Biocompatibles plc, 2004–; ISFL Ltd, 2007–. Trustee: Imperial War Mus., 2005–; Asia House, London, 2005–. *Address:* 18 Telfords Yard, 6–8 The Highway, E1W 2BQ. *Club:* Oxford and Cambridge.

HARRIS, (Walter) Frank; retired 1982; *b* 19 May 1920; *m* Esther Blanche Hill; two *s* two *d*. *Educ:* King Edward's Sch., Birmingham; University of Nottingham (BCom (Hons) 1949); BSc (1st cl. Hons) Open Univ., 1994. Served Royal Air Force, 1939–46. University, 1946–49. Ford Motor Company, 1950–65; Principal City Officer and Town Clerk, Newcastle upon Tyne, 1965–69. Comptroller and Dir, Admin, Massey-Ferguson (UK), 1969–71; Finance Dir, Dunlop SA Ltd, 1972–79; Business Planning Exec., Dunlop Ltd (UK Tyre Gp), 1979–81. *Recreation:* astrophysics. *Address:* Acomb High House, Northumberland NE46 4PH. *T:* (01434) 602844.

HARRIS, William; *see* Harris, J. R. W.

HARRIS, Prof. William Anthony, PhD; FRS 2007; Professor of Anatomy, Cambridge University, since 1997; Fellow, Clare College, Cambridge, since 1997; *b* 26 Nov. 1950; *s* of Louis Jacob Harris and Helen Gallendar Harris; *m* 1983, Christine Elizabeth Holt; one *s* one *d*. *Educ:* Univ. of Calif, Berkeley (BA); California Inst. Technol. (PhD 1976). Jun. Fellow, Harvard Univ., 1977–80; Faculty Mem., Univ. of Calif, San Diego, 1980–97; engaged in res. on genetic and molecular basis of neural develt. Co-founder, DanioLabs, 2002–. FMedSci 2007. *Publications:* Genetic Neurobiology, 1982; Development of the Nervous System, 2000, 2nd edn 2005. *Recreations:* ice-hockey, painting. *Address:* Department of Physiology, Development and Neuroscience, Cambridge University, Downing Street, Cambridge CB2 3DY. *T:* (01223) 766137.

HARRIS, Wilson; *see* Harris, T. W.

HARRIS, Winifred Anne Charlotte, (Lady Normington), CBE 2007; Director, Joint International Unit, Department for Work and Pensions, Department for Innovation, Universities and Skills, and Department for Children, Schools and Families (formerly Department for Education and Skills), since 2006; *b* 1 Jan. 1947; *d* of Leslie Frank Harris and Winifred Maisie Bissett Harris (*née* Wilson); *m* 1985, David John Normington (*see* Sir D. J. Normington). *Educ:* Univ. of Aberdeen (MA Hons Hist. 1969). Private Sec. to Sec. of State for Employment, 1974; First Sec. (Labour), British Embassy, Brussels, 1980–84; Area Manager (W London), MSC, 1985–86; Dir, Individual Conciliation, ACAS, 1986–88; Hd, Financial Mgt Services, 1988–91, Regl Dir, London, 1992–96, Dept for Employment; Hd, EU Div., DFEE, 1997–2003; Dep. Dir, Internat., Home Office, 2003–06. MCIPD 1987. *Recreations:* opera, ballet, music, walking, gardening, reading, collecting antique fans. *Address:* Joint International Unit, Caxton House (Level 5), 6–12 Tothill Street, SW1H 9NA. *T:* (020) 7340 4020.

HARRISON, family name of **Baron Harrison**.

HARRISON, Baron *cr* 1999 (Life Peer), of Chester in the county of Cheshire; **Lyndon Henry Arthur Harrison;** *b* 28 Sept. 1947; *s* of late Charles William Harrison and Edith (*née* Johnson); *m* 1980, Hilary Anne Plank; one *s* one *d*. *Educ:* Oxford Sch.; Univ. of Warwick (BA Hons 1970); Univ. of Sussex (MA 1971); Univ. of Keele (MA 1978). Part time Lectr, N Staffs Polytechnic, 1973–75; Research Officer, Students' Union, UMIST, 1975–78; Union Manager, NE Wales Inst. of Higher Educn, Wrexham, 1978–89. Cheshire County Councillor, 1981–90 (Chairman: Libraries and Countryside Cttee, 1982, 1984–89; Further Educn, 1984–89; Tourism, 1985–89). Dep. Chm., NW Tourist Bd, 1987–89. MEP (Lab) Cheshire W, 1989–94, Cheshire W and Wirral, 1994–99. European Parliament: Lab spokesman on monetary union, and on ASEAN and Korea, 1994–99; Vice-President: Tourism Intergp, 1995–99; Small and Med. Size Enterprises Intergp, 1995–99. Vice Chm., ACC, 1990–. Liaison Peer, NI Office, 2000–02; Mem., H of L Cttee on Common Foreign and Security Policy, 2000–03, on Social Policy, 2003–; Mem., Hybrid Instruments Cttee, 2003–. *Recreations:* chess, bridge, the arts, sport. *Address:* House of Lords, SW1A 0PW.

HARRISON, Prof. Alan, TD 1983 (Bar 1989, 2nd Bar 1995); PhD; FDSRCS; FDSRCSE; Professor of Dental Care of the Elderly, University of Bristol, 1987–2004, now Emeritus; *b* 24 July 1944; *s* of Lt-Col John Thomas West Harrison and Mona Evelyn (*née* Gee); *m* 1st, 1967, Pauline Lilian (*née* Rendell) (marr. diss. 1980); one *s* one *d*; 2nd, 1982, Margaret Ann (*née* Frost); two *d*. *Educ:* Rydal Sch., Colwyn Bay; Univ. of Wales (BDS, PhD). FDS RCS; FDSRCSE *ad hominem*; FADM. Lectr, Dental Sch. Cardiff, 1970–78; Sen. Lectr and Hon. Consultant, Univ. of Leeds, 1978–87. Vis. Asst Prof., Univ. of South Carolina, 1974–75. Mem., Inst. for Learning and Teaching in Higher Educn, 2002–. OC 390 Field Dental Team (V), 1971–73; CO 308 Evacuation Hosp. RAMC(V), 1989–94; CO 306 Field Hosp. RAMC(V), 1994–95; Hon. Col Comdt RADC, 1996–2001; Col RADC(V), 1989–2005. QHDS 1996–99. Hon. Fellow, Cardiff Univ., 2006. *Publications:* Overdentures in General Dental Practice, 1988, 3rd edn 1993; Complete Dentures: problem solving, 1999; over 160 publications in scientific jls. *Recreations:* walking, woodworking. *Address: e-mail:* alan.harrison@bristol.ac.uk. *Club:* Fowey Gallants Sailing.

HARRISON, (Alastair) Brian (Clarke); DL; *b* 3 Oct. 1921; *s* of late Brig. E. F. Harrison, Melbourne; *m* 1952, Elizabeth Hood Hardie, Oaklands, NSW, Aust.; one *s* one *d*. *Educ:* Geelong Grammar Sch.; Trinity Coll., Cambridge. Capt. AIF. MP (C) Maldon, Essex, 1955–Feb. 1974; Parliamentary Private Secretary to: Minister of State, Colonial Office, 1955–56; Sec. of State for War, 1956–58; Minister of Agriculture, Fisheries and Food, 1958–60. Mem. Victoria Promotion Cttee (London); Mem. One Nation Gp which published The Responsible Society, and One Europe; toured USA on ESU Ford Foundation Fellowship, 1959; Commonwealth Parliamentary Assoc. Delegations: Kenya and Horn of Africa, 1960; Gilbert and Ellice Islands, New Hebrides and British Solomon Islands Protectorate. Chm., Standing Conf. of Eastern Sport and Physical Recreation, 1974–. Organizer (with Univ. of WA), expedns to Nepal studying human physiol., 1979–87. High Sheriff, 1979, DL 1980, Essex. *Publications:* (jtly) The cumulative effect of High Altitude on Motor Performance: a comparison between caucasian visitors and native highlanders, 1985; (jtly) Entrainment of respiratory frequency to exercise rhythm during hypoxia, 1987. *Recreations:* photography, gardening. *Address:* Green Farm House, Copford, Colchester, Essex CO6 1DA. *Clubs:* Carlton, Pratt's; Melbourne (Melbourne); Weld (Perth).

HARRISON, Alistair; *see* Harrison, W. A.

HARRISON, (Anne) Victoria, (Lady Harrison), DPhil; Policy Director, DIPEx Charity, since 2008 (Director, 2007–08); *d* of Lawrence Greggain and Amy Isabel Greggain (*née* Briggs); *m* 1967, Brian Howard Harrison (*see* Sir Brian Harrison). *Educ:* Workington GS; Milham Ford Sch., Oxford; St Anne's Coll., Oxford (BA 1st Cl. Hons Animal Physiology 1965; Theodore Williams Schol. 1965; MA 1970; DPhil 1970). Exec. Editor, Internat. Abstracts of Biological Scis, 1971–72; MRC HQ Office, 1972–83, PSO, 1974; seconded to Science and Technology Secretariat, Cabinet Office, 1983–85, Dep. to Chief Scientific Advr, 1984–85; Head of Secretariat, MRC, 1985–89; Head of Policy Div., AFRC, 1989–94; Dir of Policy and Assessment, BBSRC, 1994–97; Exec. Sec., Wolfson Foundn, 1997–2006. Mem. Bd, Inst. of Sports and Exercise Medicine, 2007–. Trustee: Comparative Clinical Sci. Foundn, 2007–; UCL Hosps Charity, 2007–. Freeman, Guild of Educators, 2005. *Recreations:* phoning friends from the bath, armchair gardening. *Address:* The Book House, Yarnells Hill, Oxford OX2 9BG. *Club:* Royal Society of Medicine.

HARRISON, Air Vice-Marshal Anthony John, CB 1997; CBE 1992 (OBE 1986); JP; Executive Vice-President and General Manager, Singapore, BAE SYSTEMS (formerly British Aerospace) plc, 1998–2005; *b* 9 Nov. 1943; *s* of Jack and Jean Harrison; *m* 1965, Glynn Dene Hyland-Smith; one *s* one *d*. *Educ:* Woodbridge Sch., Suffolk. Commnd RAF, 1963; Commanding Officer: 617 Sqdn (The Dambusters), 1982–85; RAF Bruggen, 1989–92; Dir, Jt Warfare, MoD, 1992–94; ACDS (Ops), MoD, 1994–97. Upper Freeman, GAPAN, 1985. Pres., Woodbridge RAF Assoc., 1994. FRAeS. JP Devon, 2007. *Recreations:* golf, tennis, aviation history. *Address:* Chudleigh Knighton, Devon. *Clubs:* Royal Air Force; Tanglin (Singapore).

HARRISON, Brian; *see* Harrison, A. B. C.

HARRISON, Brian; *see* Harrison, F. B.

HARRISON, Sir Brian (Howard), Kt 2005; DPhil; FBA 2005; FRHistS; Emeritus Fellow of Corpus Christi College, Oxford, since 2004 (Fellow, 1967–2004); Titular Professor of Modern History, University of Oxford, 1996–2004; *b* 9 July 1937; *s* of Howard Harrison and Mary Elizabeth (*née* Savill); *m* 1967, Anne Victoria Greggain (*see* A. V. Harrison). *Educ:* Merchant Taylors' Sch., Northwood; St John's Coll., Oxford (BA 1st Cl. Hons Mod. Hist. 1961; MA 1966; DPhil 1966). FRHistS 1973. Nat. Service, 2nd Lieut, Malta Signal Sqdn, 1956–58. Oxford University: Sen. Schol., St Antony's Coll., 1961–64; Jun. Res. Fellow, Nuffield Coll., 1964–67; Tutor in Modern Hist. and Pols, 1967–2000, Sen. Tutor, 1984–86 and 1988–90, Vice-Pres., 1992, 1993 and 1996–98, CCC; Univ. Reader in Modern British History, 1990–2000. Editor, Oxford DNB, 2000–04. Visiting Professor: Univ. of Michigan (Ann Arbor), 1970–71; Harvard Univ., 1973–74; Visiting Fellow: Melbourne Univ., 1975; ANU, 1995. *Publications:* Drink and the Victorians, 1971, 2nd edn 1994; Separate Spheres: the opposition to women's suffrage in Britain, 1978; (ed with P. Hollis) Robert Lowery: Chartist and lecturer, 1979; Peaceable Kingdom: stability and change in modern Britain, 1982; (with C. Ford) A Hundred Years Ago: Britain in the 1880s in words and photographs, 1983; Prudent Revolutionaries: portraits of British feminists between the wars, 1987; (ed and contrib.) The History of the University of Oxford, Vol. 8: The Twentieth Century, 1994; (ed) Corpuscles: a history of Corpus Christi College, Oxford, 1994; The Transformation of British Politics 1860–1995, 1996; (ed jtly and contrib.) Civil Histories: essays presented to Sir Keith Thomas, 2000. *Recreations:* looking at architecture, listening to classical music. *Address:* The Book House, Yarnells Hill, Oxford OX2 9BG.

HARRISON, Prof. Bryan Desmond, CBE 1990; PhD; FRS 1987; FRSE; Professor of Plant Virology, University of Dundee, 1991–96, now Professor Emeritus; *b* 16 June 1931; *s* of John William and Norah Harrison; *m* 1968, Elizabeth Ann Latham-Warde; two *s* one *d*. *Educ:* Whitgift Sch., Croydon; Reading Univ. (BSc Hons Agric. Bot. 1952); London Univ. (PhD 1955). FRSE 1979. Postgraduate student, ARC, 1952; Scottish Hort. Res. Inst., Dundee, 1954; Rothamsted Exp. Station, 1957; Head, Virology Section, 1966, Dep. Dir, 1979, Scottish Hort. Res. Inst.; Head, Virology Dept, Scottish Crop Res. Inst., 1981–91. Visiting Professor: Japan Soc. for Promotion of Science, 1970; Organization of American States, Venezuela, 1973; Hon. Prof., Univ. of St Andrews, 1986–99; Hon. Vis. Prof., Univ. of Dundee, 1988–91; Hon. Res. Fellow, Scottish Crop Res. Inst., 1991–; Vis. Prof., Univ. of Zhejiang, China, 2001–. Pres., Assoc. of Applied Biologists, 1980–81. Life Mem., Internat. Cttee for Taxonomy of Viruses, 1997. Hon. Member: Assoc. of Applied Biologists, 1989; Soc. for Gen. Microbiol., 1990; Phytopathological Soc. of Japan, 1992; For. Associate, US Nat. Acad. of Scis, 1998. Hon. DAgrFor Univ. of Helsinki, 1990. *Publications:* Plant Virology: the principles (with A. J. Gibbs), 1976 (trans. Russian and Chinese); research papers and reviews on plant viruses and virus diseases. *Recreations:* growing garden crops, foreign travel. *Address:* Scottish Crop Research Institute, Invergowrie, Dundee DD2 5DA. *T:* (01382) 562731, *Fax:* (01382) 562426.

HARRISON, Bryan James; management consultant; non-executive Director, Barnet Primary Care Trust, since 2004; *b* 30 Oct. 1947; *s* of late James Harrison and of Doris (*née* Burnham); *m* 1st, 1973 (marr. diss. 1988); two *d*; 2nd, 1990, Valerie Mayo; one *d*. *Educ:* Southmoor Sch., Sunderland; Exeter Univ. (BA Politics). DHSS, 1971–81; seconded to Camden and Islington AHA, 1981–82; Dist Administrator, Islington HA, 1982–84; District General Manager: Islington HA, 1984–88; Bloomsbury HA, 1988–90; Bloomsbury and Islington HA, 1990–92; Regl Gen. Manager, NE Thames RHA, 1992–94; Chief Exec., Forest Healthcare NHS Trust, 1995–99; Special Advr, Workforce and Develt, NHS Exec., 1999–2001. Trustee and Mem. Council, Marie Curie Cancer Care, 2002–. *Recreations:* reading, music, history, soccer.

HARRISON, Rev. Cameron Elias; international consultant on education policy; Director, Harrison Leimon Associates, since 2002; *b* 27 Aug. 1945; *s* of Elias Harrison and Herries Harrison; *m* 1968, Pearl Leimon; one *s* one *d*. *Educ:* Cumnock Acad.; Strathclyde Univ. (BSc Hons Physics); Stirling Univ. (MEd). Physics Teacher, Greenock Acad., 1968–71; Head of Physics, Graeme High Sch., 1971–79; Depute Rector, Kirkcudbright Acad., 1979–82; Rector, The Gordon Schools, 1982–91; Chief Exec., Scottish Consultative Council on the Curriculum, 1991–98. Sec.-Gen., Consortium of Instns for Develt & Res. in Educn in Europe, 1993–97; Dir of Educnl Policy, Open Soc. Inst., Budapest, 1998–2002. Ordained, C of S, 2006. FRSA. *Publication:* Managing Change, 1989. *Recreations:* Rugby, walking, singing, talking, listening, teaching, learning. *Address:* Woodfield House, Prior Muir, St Andrews, Fife KY16 8LP; *e-mail:* cameron@harrisonleimon.co.uk.

HARRISON, Claude William, RP 1961; artist; portrait painter and painter of conversation pieces, imaginative landscapes and murals, etc; *b* Leyland, Lancs, 31 March 1922; *s* of Harold Harrison and Florence Mildred Ireton; *m* 1947, Audrey Johnson (*d* 2005); one *s*. *Educ:* Hutton Grammar Sch., Lancs. Served in RAF, 1942–46. Royal Coll. of Art, 1947–49; Studio in Ambleside, 1949–52. Exhibited since 1950 at: RA; RSA; Royal Society Portrait Painters; New English Art Club, etc. Hon. RP 1990. *Publication:* The Portrait Painter's handbook, 1968. *Recreation:* painting. *Address:* 1 Rue Palmaro, 06500 Menton, France. *T:* (4) 93419721.

HARRISON, Sir Colin; *see* Harrison, Sir R. C.

HARRISON, Rev. Fr Crispin; *see* Harrison, Rev. Fr M. B. C.

HARRISON, Sir David, Kt 1997; CBE 1990; FREng; Fellow, since 1957, and Master, 1994–2000, Selwyn College, Cambridge; *b* 3 May 1930; *s* of Harold David Harrison and Lavinia Wilson; *m* 1962, Sheila Rachel Debes; one *s* one *d* (and one *s* decd). *Educ:* Bede Sch., Sunderland; Clacton County High Sch.; Selwyn Coll., Cambridge (1st Cl. Pts I and II Natural Sciences Tripos, BA 1953, PhD 1956, MA 1957, ScD 1979). CEng, FREng (FEng 1987); FRSC (FRIC 1961), FIChemE 1968. 2nd Lieut, REME, 1949. Cambridge University: Research student, Dept of Physical Chemistry, 1953–56; Univ. Asst Lectr in Chem. Engrg, 1956–61; Univ. Lectr, 1961–79; Sen. Tutor, Selwyn Coll., 1967–79; Mem., Council of the Senate, 1967–75; Mem., Univ. Council, 1995–2000; Dep. Vice-Chancellor, 1995–2000; Pro-Vice-Chancellor, 1997; Chm., Faculty Bd of Educn, 1976–78, of Engrg, 1994–2001; Vice-Chancellor: Univ. of Keele, 1979–84; Univ. of Exeter, 1984–94. Visiting Professor of Chemical Engineering: Univ. of Delaware, USA, 1967; Univ. of Sydney, 1976. Chm., Adv. Cttee on Safety in Nuclear Installations, 1993–99; Mem., Engineering Council, 1994–96. Hon. Editor, Trans Instn of Chemical Engrs, 1972–78; Member Council: Lancing Coll., 1970–82; Haileybury, 1974–84; St Edward's, Oxford, 1977–89; Bolton Girls' Sch., 1981–84; Shrewsbury Sch., 1983–2003 (Chm., 1989–2003); Taunton Sch., 1986–89; Fellow, Woodard Corporation of Schools, 1972–94; Chairman: Bd of Trustees, Homerton Coll., Cambridge, 1979–; UCCA, 1984–91; Voluntary Sector Consultative Council, 1984–88; Southern Univs Jt Bd, 1986–88; Church and Associated Colls Adv. Cttee, PCFC, 1988–91; CVCP, 1991–93; Bd of Management, Northcott Theatre, 1984–94; Eastern Arts Bd, 1994–98 (Mem., Arts Council of England, 1996–98); Council, RSCM, 1996–2005; Ely Cathedral Council, 2000–. Pres., IChemE, 1991–92 (Vice-Pres., 1989–91); Dir, Salters' Inst. of Industrial Chemistry, 1993–. Mem., Marshall Aid Commemoration Commn, 1982–89. FRSA 1985; FRSCM 2005; CCMI (CBIM 1990). Freeman, City of London, 1998; Liveryman, Salters' Co., 1998. DUniv: Keele, 1992; York, 2008; Hon. DSc Exeter, 1995. George E. Davis Medal, IChemE, 2001. *Publications:* (with J. F. Davidson) Fluidised Particles, 1963; (also with J. F. Davidson) Fluidization, 1971, rev. edn (with J. F. Davidson and R. Clift) 1985; numerous articles in scientific and technological jls. *Recreations:* music, tennis, hill walking, good food. *Address:* 7 Gough Way, Cambridge CB3 9LN. *T:* (01223) 359315. *Clubs:* Athenæum, Oxford and Cambridge; Federation House (Stoke-on-Trent).

HARRISON, Prof. David James, MD; FRCPath, FRCPE, FRCSE; Professor of Pathology and Head, Division of Pathology, since 1998, and Director, Breakthrough Breast Cancer Research Unit, since 2007, University of Edinburgh; Honorary Consultant in Histopathology, Royal Infirmary of Edinburgh, since 1991; *b* Belfast, 24 March 1959. *Educ:* Campbell Coll., Belfast; Univ. of Edinburgh (BSc Hons 1980; MB ChB 1983; MD 1990). FRCPath 1998; FRCPE 2003; FRCSE 2003. University of Edinburgh: Lectr, 1986–91, Sen. Lectr, 1991–97, Reader, 1997–98, in Pathol.; Dir, Cancer Res. Centre, 2005–08; Clin. Dir, Pathol. Directorate, Lothian Univ. Hosps Div., 2001–04. Adjunct Professor: in Medicinal Chemistry, Univ. of Florida, Gainesville, 2003–; of Pathol. and Forensic Educn, Univ. of Canberra, 2004–. Member: Biomed. and Therapeutics Res. Cttee, Chief Scientist Office, Scotland, 1998– (Dep. Chm.); DoH Gene Therapy Adv. Cttee, 2000– (Vice-Chm., 2006–); DoH Cttee on Carcinogenicity of Chemicals in Food, Consumer Products and the Envmt, 2000–; Food Standards Agency/DoH Cttee on Toxicity of Chemicals in Food, Consumer Products and the Envmt, 2007–. MRC Coll. of Experts Physiological Systems and Clin. Scis Bd, 2004–; Member: CRUK Strat. Adv. Gp, 2006–; Scientific Adv. Bd, Med. Res. Scotland, 2007–; Scientific Adv. Cttee, Yorks Cancer Research, 2007–. Trustee, Melville Trust for Care and Cure of Cancer, 2008. *Publications:* (ed jtly) Muir's Textbook of Pathology, 14th edn 2008; contrib. chapters in books and jls. *Recreations:* EMMS Nazareth charity (Chm. 2002–) which operates a hospital and nursing school in the Middle East, music, hill walking. *Address:* Cancer Research Centre, University of Edinburgh, Crewe Road South, Edinburgh EH4 2XR. *T:* (0131) 777 3500, *Fax:* (0131) 777 3520.

HARRISON, Denis Byrne; Local Government Ombudsman, 1974–81 and Vice-Chairman, Commission for Local Administration, 1975–81; *b* 11 July 1917; *y s* of late Arthur and Priscilla Harrison; *m* 1956, Alice Marion Vickers (*d* 1989), *e d* of late Hedley Vickers. *Educ:* Birkenhead Sch.; Liverpool Univ. (LLM). Legal Associate Mem. RTPI, 1949. Articled to E. W. Tame, OBE (Town Clerk of Birkenhead); admitted Solicitor, 1939. Served War, 1939–46: 75th Shropshire Yeo. (Medium Regt) RA; 168 Field Regt RA; Combined Ops Bombardment Unit landing in Normandy on D-Day with an assault bn of 3rd Canadian Div.; Staff Captain at HQ of OC, Cyprus. First Asst Solicitor, Wolverhampton Co. Borough, 1946–49; Dep. Town Clerk of Co. Boroughs: Warrington, 1949–57; Bolton, 1957–63; Sheffield, 1963–66; Town Clerk and CEO, Sheffield, 1966–74. Member: Advisory Council on Noise, 1970–79; Cttee on the use of valuers in the public service, 1972–73. Mem. Council, 1975–82, Pro-Chancellor, 1980–82, Univ. of Sheffield. Hon. Sec., Trustees, building of Crucible Theatre. JP City of London, 1976–86. *Recreations:* reading, music, walking (London-Ventimiglia, 1989, London-Milan, 1990). *Address:* 2 Leicester Close, Henley-on-Thames, Oxon RG9 2LD. *T:* (01491) 572782.

HARRISON, (Desmond) Roger (Wingate); Chairman, Toynbee Hall, 1990–2002; Deputy Chairman, Capital Radio, 1991–2000 (Director, 1975–2000); *b* 9 April 1933; *s* of late Maj.-Gen. Desmond Harrison, CB, DSO and Kathleen Harrison (*née* Hazley); *m* 1965, Victoria Lee-Barber, MVO, *d* of Rear-Adm. John Lee-Barber, CB, DSO; three *d* (and one *s* one *d* decd). *Educ:* Rugby School; Worcester College, Oxford (MA); Harvard Univ. Business Sch. Writing freelance, principally for The Times, 1951–57; joined staff of The Times, 1957–67; The Observer: joined 1967; Dir, 1970–92; Jt Managing Dir, 1977–84; Chief Exec., 1984–87. Dir, The Oak Foundn, 1987–89. Chairman: Greater Manchester Cablevision, 1990–93; Sterling Publishing, 1993–96; Director: LWT and LWT (Holdings), 1976–94; Sableknight, 1981–; Trinity International Holdings, 1991–2003. Chairman: Asylum Aid, 1991–98; Royal Acad. of Dancing, 1993–2006. Governor, Sadler's Wells, 1984–95. *Recreations:* theatre, country pursuits, tennis. *Address:* Itchen Stoke Mill, Alresford, SO24 0RA. *Clubs:* Beefsteak, Flyfishers', Queen's.

HARRISON, Edward Peter Graham, (Ted), PhD; broadcaster, television producer, writer and cartoonist; *b* 14 April 1948; *s* of Rev. Peter Harrison and Joan Harrison; *m* 1968, Helen Grace Waters; one *s* one *d*. *Educ:* Grenville Coll., Bideford, Devon; University of Kent at Canterbury (PhD 1998). Graduate trainee, Kent Messenger, 1968–72; Reporter: Morgan-Grampian Magazines, 1972; Southern Television, 1970–73; BBC World Service, Radio 4 You and Yours, 1972–80; BBC Radio 4 Sunday, 1972–88; BBC TV Scotland Current Account, 1981–83; Presenter and Reporter, BBC Radio Scotland News and Current Affairs, 1980–85; Reporter: BBC Radio 4 World Tonight, 1981–83; BBC Radio 4 World at One and PM, 1983–87; Presenter: Radio 4 Opinions, 1986–87; Radio 4 Sunday, 1986–88 and Soundings, 1985–88; ITV series The Human Factor, 1986–92; Channel 4 series on Lambeth Conf., 1988; BBC Religious Affairs Corresp., 1988–89; presenter, Does He Take Sugar?, Radio 4, 1991–95; series ed., Ultimate Questions, ITV, 2000; dir, animation series, Wise and Wonderful, 2002; producer: Redcoats, ITV, 2003–04; Essentials of Faith, ITV, 2005; Mosque, ITV, 2005. Dir, Pilgrim Productions, Canterbury, 1992–2008; Founder, Unst Animation Studio, 2000. Contested (L) gen. elections: Bexley, 1970; Maidstone, Feb. 1974. London exhibition of caricatures, 1977; exhibition of watercolours, Oxford, Canterbury, 1981. *Publications:* Modern Elizabethans, 1977; (jtly) McIndoe's Army, 1978; Marks of the Cross, 1981; Commissioner Catherine, 1983; Much Beloved Daughter, 1984; The Durham Phenomenon, 1985; Living with kidney failure, 1990; Kriss Akabusi—on track, 1991; The Elvis People, 1992; Members Only, 1994; Stigmata: a medieval mystery for a modern age, 1994; Letters to a friend I never knew, 1995; Disability: rights and wrongs, 1995; Tanni, 1996; Defender of the Faith, 1996; Diana: icon and sacrifice, 1998; Beyond Dying, 2000; Will the next Archbishop please stand up?, 2002; Diana: myth and reality, 2006; Duncan Dared, 2008. *Recreation:* drawing caricatures of friends and foes. *Club:* Athenæum.

HARRISON, Sir Ernest (Thomas), Kt 1981; OBE 1972; FCA; Chairman, Racal Electronics Plc, 1966–2000 (Chief Executive, 1966–92); Director, Camelot Group plc, 1993–2000; *b* 11 May 1926; *s* of late Ernest Horace Harrison and Gertrude Rebecca Gibbons Harrison; *m* 1960, Phyllis Brenda Knight (Janie); three *s* two *d*. *Educ:* Trinity Grammar Sch., Wood Green, London. Qualified as Chartered Accountant, 1950; served Articles with Harker Holloway & Co.; joined Racal Electronics as Secretary and Chief Accountant, when company commenced manufacturing, 1951; Director, 1958, Dep. Man. Dir, 1961. Chairman: Racal Telecom, then Vodafone Gp, Plc, 1988–98; Chubb Security, 1992–97. Active in National Savings movement, 1964–76, for which services awarded OBE. Chm., Royal Free Cancer Research (formerly Ronald Raven Chair in Clinical Oncology, subseq. Ronald Raven Cancer Research) Trust, 1991–2006. Mem., Jockey Club, 1990–. Mem., RSA. Liveryman, Scriveners' Co. CompIERE 1975; CCMI (CBIM 1976); FIET (CompIEE 1978). Sch. Fellowship, Royal Free Hosp. Sch. of Medicine, 1995. Hon. FCGI 1990; Hon. FREng (Hon. FEng 1997); Hon. Fellow, UCL, 2006. Hon. DSc: Cranfield, 1981; City, 1982; DUniv: Surrey, 1981; Edinburgh, 1983. Businessman of the Year, 1981; Founding Society's Centenary Award, ICA, 1990; Mountbatten Medal, Nat. Electronic Council, 1992. *Recreations:* horse racing (owner), gardening, wild life, sport, espec. soccer.

HARRISON, (Fred) Brian, CBE 1982; FCA; *b* 6 March 1927; *s* of Fred Harrison and Annie Harrison; *m* 1950, Margaret Owen (*d* 1995); two *s*. *Educ:* Burnley Grammar Sch. FCA 1960 (ACA 1950). East Midlands Div., NCB, 1953–67 (Chief Accountant, No 1 Area, 1962–67); Chief Accountant, N Derbyshire Area, NCB, 1967–68; Finance Dir, Coal Products Div., NCB, 1968–71; Dep. Man. Dir, Coal Products Div., NCB, subseq. Dep. Chief Exec., NCB (Coal Products) Ltd, 1971–76, Chm., 1978–83. Mem., NCB, 1976–85. Chm., British Investment Trust, 1978–85. Master, Chartered Accountants' Co., 1994–95; Mem., Ct of Assistants, Fuellers' Co., 1996– (Master, 2000–01). *Recreations:* music, theatre. *Address:* 11 Hillcrest, King Harry Lane, St Albans, Herts AL3 4AT. *T:* (01727) 46938.

HARRISON, George; *see* Harrison, S. G.

HARRISON, (George) Michael (Antony), CBE 1980; Chief Education Officer, City of Sheffield, 1967–85; *b* 7 April 1925; *s* of George and Kathleen Harrison; *m* 1951, Pauline (*née* Roberts); two *s* one *d*. *Educ:* Manchester Grammar Sch.; Brasenose Coll., Oxford. MA (Lit. Hum.); DipEd. Military service, Lieut, 3rd Recce and Parachute Regt, 1947. Asst Master, Bedford Modern Sch., 1951–53; Admin. Asst, W Riding CC, Education Dept, 1953–55; Asst Educn Officer, Cumberland CC Educn Dept, 1955–64; Dep. Educn Officer, Sheffield, 1965–67. Advr, Educn and NVQ Programmes, Dept of Employment, 1985–96. Hon. Research Fellow, Leeds Univ., 1985–89; Associate Prof., Sheffield Univ., 1991–95. Member various cttees, incl.: Taylor Cttee of Enquiry on Govt in Schools, 1975–77; UK Nat. Commn for Unesco Educn Adv. Cttee, 1977–83; Yorkshire and Humberside Econ. Planning Council, 1978–79; Technician Educn Council, 1979–83; Engineering Council, 1982–87; Board, Nat. Adv. Body on Local Authority Higher Educn, 1981–83. Pres., Soc. of Educn Officers, 1976; Vice-Pres., Standing Conf. on Schools' Science and Technology, 1980– (Chm. 1975–79). Vice-Pres., St William's Foundn, York, 1992–95. Hon. LLD Sheffield, 1988. *Recreation:* foreign travel. *Address:* Keeper's Cottage, Rigmaden Court, Mansergh, Kirkby Lonsdale, Cumbria LA6 2ET. *T:* (015242) 76335; *e-mail:* mh.rigmaden@virgin.net.

HARRISON, Jessel Anidjah; President, Slimma Group Holdings Ltd, retired 1989; *b* 28 May 1923; *s* of Samuel Harrison and Esta (*née* Romain); *m* 1st, 1943, Irene (*née* Olsberg) (marr. diss. 1956); one *s* one *d*; 2nd, 1961, Doreen Leigh. *Educ:* Vernon House Preparatory Sch.; Brondesbury Coll.; Macauley Coll., Cuckfield, Sussex. Chairman: Slimma Ltd, 1964; Slimma (Wales) Ltd, 1971; Emu Wool Industries, later Slimma Gp Hldgs, 1973; Dir, Tootals Clothing Div., 1977–89. Member: European Trade Cttee, 1975–; Clothing Industry Productivity Resources Agency, 1978–85; British Overseas Trade Adv. Council, 1978–85. Vice Pres., Clothing Export Council of Great Britain, 1977 (Chm., 1973); Chm., British Overseas Trade Group for Israel, 1978–83, Vice-Pres., 1987–. Pres., Clothing Institute, 1978. *Recreations:* golf, walking. *Address:* 113 Abbotsbury Road, W14 8EP. *T:* (020) 7603 7468. *Club:* Royal Automobile.

HARRISON, Surgeon Vice-Adm. Sir John (Albert Bews), KBE 1982; FRCP, FRCR; Medical Director General (Naval), 1980–83; *b* 20 May 1921; *s* of late Albert William Harrison and Lilian Eda Bews, Dover, Kent; *m* 1943, Jane (*née* Harris) (*d* 1988); two *s*. *Educ:* Queens' Coll., Cambridge; St Bartholomew's Hosp. Surg. Lt RNVR, transf. RN, 1947; served, 1947–83: RM Infirmary, Deal, 1948; HMS Sparrow, Amer. WI stn, 1949; RN Hosp., Plymouth, 1951; HMS Ganges, 1952; Admiralty Med. Bd and St Bartholomew's Hosp., 1953; RN Hosps, Hong Kong, 1955, Chatham, 1958, Haslar, 1959; St Bart's and Middlesex Hosps, 1961; RN Hosps Malta, 1962, Haslar, 1964–75; Adviser in Radiol., 1967–79; Dep. Med. Dir Gen. and Dir Med. Personnel and Logistics, 1975–77; Dean of Naval Medicine and Surgeon Rear-Adm., Inst. of Naval Medicine, 1977–80. Mem., Council for Med. Postgrad. Educn of Eng. and Wales, 1977–79. Pres., Section of Radiology, RSM, 1984–85. Fellow: RSM; MedSocLond (Pres. 1985–86). CStJ 1983. QHP 1976–83. *Publications:* Hyperbaric Osteonecrosis et al, 1975; articles in med. press on sarcoidosis, tomography, middle ear disease, and dysbaric osteonecrosis. *Recreations:* fishing, cricket, countryman. *Address:* Alexandra Cottage, Swanmore, Hampshire SO32 2PB. *Club:* MCC.

HARRISON, John Clive, LVO 1971; HM Diplomatic Service, retired; High Commissioner, Mauritius, 1993–97; *b* 12 July 1937; *s* of Sir Geoffrey Harrison, GCMG, KCVO; *m* 1967, Jennifer Heather Burston; one *s* two *d*. *Educ:* Winchester Coll.; Jesus Coll., Oxford. BA. Entered Foreign Office, 1960; Rangoon, 1961; Vientiane, 1964; FO, 1964; Second, later First, Sec. (Information), Addis Ababa, 1967; Ankara, 1971; seconded to Cabinet Office, 1973; First Sec., FCO, 1976; First Sec., Head of Chancery and Consul, Luxembourg, 1978; Counsellor and Head of Chancery, Lagos, 1981–84; Counsellor, attached to Protocol Dept, FCO, 1984; Hd of Consular Dept, FCO, 1985–89; Dep. High Comr, Islamabad, 1989–93. *Recreations:* gardening, tennis, golf, family holidays. *Address:* Wymering, Sheet Common, Petersfield, Hants GU31 5AT. *Clubs:* Royal Over-Seas League; Petersfield Golf.

HARRISON, Prof. John Fletcher Clews, PhD; Emeritus Professor of History, University of Sussex, since 1985 (Professor of History, 1970–82; Hon. Professor of

History, 1982–85); *b* 28 Feb. 1921; *s* of William Harrison and Mary (*née* Fletcher); *m* 1945, Margaret Ruth Marsh; one *s* one *d*. *Educ*: City Boys' Sch., Leicester; Selwyn Coll., Cambridge (Schol. and Prizeman; Goldsmiths' Open Exhibnr in History, BA 1st Cl. Hons 1942, MA 1946); PhD Leeds. Served Army, 1941–45 (overseas 1942–45): commnd, Leics Regt and seconded to KAR, 1942; Captain and Adjt, 17th Bn, KAR, 1943–44; Staff Captain, GSOIII, E Africa Comd, 1944–45. Lectr, Dept of Adult Educn and Extra-Mural Studies, Univ. of Leeds, 1947–58; Dep. Dir, Extra-Mural Studies and Dep. Head of Dept, Univ. of Leeds, 1958–61; Prof. of History, Univ. of Wisconsin, USA, 1961–70. Research and teaching (Fulbright Award), Univ. of Wisconsin, 1957–58; Faculty Res. Fellow, SSRC, USA, 1963–64; Vis. Professorial Res. Fellow, ANU, 1968–69 and 1977; Res. Fellow, Harvard Univ., 1972–73; Social Sci. Res. Fellow, Nuffield Foundn, 1975; Vice-Chancellor's Cttee Visitor, NZ, 1977; Herbert F. Johnson Res. Prof., Univ. of Wisconsin, 1977–78; Hon. Prof. of History, Warwick Univ., 1987–92. Vice-Pres., Soc. for Study of Labour History, 1984– (Sec., 1960–61; Chm., 1974–81); Mem., Adv. and Editorial Bds, Victorian Studies, 1963–. Hon. Mem., Phi Beta Kappa, Wisconsin, 1978. *Publications*: A History of the Working Men's College 1854–1954, 1954; Social Reform in Victorian Leeds: The Work of James Hole 1820–1895, 1954; Learning and Living 1790–1960: A Study in the History of the English Adult Education Movement, 1961, Toronto 1961; (ed) Society and Politics in England 1780–1960, NY 1965; (ed) Utopianism and Education: Robert Owen and the Owenites, NY 1968; Quest for the New Moral World: Robert Owen and the Owenites in Britain and America, 1969, NY 1969 (Walter D. Love Meml Prize, USA, 1969); The Early Victorians 1832–1851, 1971, NY 1971; The Birth and Growth of Industrial England 1714–1867, 1973; (ed) Eminently Victorian, 1974; (with Dorothy Thompson) Bibliography of the Chartist Movement 1837–1976, 1978; The Second Coming: Popular Millenarianism 1780–1850, 1979, NJ 1979; The Common People, 1984; Late Victorian Britain 1875–1901, 1990; Scholarship Boy: a personal history of the mid-twentieth century, 1995; *festschriften*: New Views of Co-operation, ed S. Yeo, 1988; Living and Learning, ed I. Dyck and M. Chase, 1996; articles and reviews in Victorian Studies, TLS and usual academic history jls. *Recreations*: walking, gardening, book collecting. *Address*: Mill Cottage, Sandford Mill Close, Cheltenham, Glos GL53 7QZ. *T*: (01242) 510205.

HARRISON, Kristina, (Mrs J. Pattinson); a District Judge (Magistrates' Courts), since 2005; *b* 5 June 1957; *d* of late John, (Jack), Harrison and of Sybil Mary Harrison; *m* 1985, John Pattinson; one *s* two *d*. *Educ*: Manchester Poly. (BA Hons Law, 1978). Founded Kristina Harrison, Solicitors, Manchester, 1985, specialising in criminal law. *Recreations*: endlessly renovating old houses, all aspects of interior design, collecting handbags. *Address*: Doncaster Magistrates' Court, PO Box 49, The Law Courts, College Road, Doncaster, S Yorks DN1 3HT.

HARRISON, Michael; *see* Harrison, G. M. A.

HARRISON, Dr Michael; JP; Chairman and Medical Director, Midlands Health Consultancy Network Ltd, since 1996; *b* 1 March 1939; *s* of Frank Harrison and Ruby Wilhelmina (*née* Proctor); *m* 1962, Ann Haiser; two *d*. *Educ*: Leamington Coll.; Univ. of London (St Mary's Hosp.) (MB BS, BA). LRCP, MRCS, DPH, FFPH, MHSM, FRSH. Hosp. med. appts, 1964–66; health MO appts, 1966–70; Birmingham RHB, 1971–74; specialist in community medicine, W Midlands RHA, 1974–76; Area MO, Sandwell AHA, 1976–83; Dist MO, 1983–88, Dist Gen. Manager, 1985–88, Sandwell HA; Sen. Clinical Lectr, Univ. of Birmingham, 1988; Regl Dir of Public Health and Regl MO, 1988–93, Exec. Dir, 1990–94, Dep. Chief Exec., 1993–94, West Midlands RHA. Cons. Advr, WHO, 1989. Pres., Assoc. for Industrial Archaeology, 1998. Pres., Droitwich Spa Saltway Rotary Club, 2001–02. FCMI. SBStJ. JP Birmingham, 1980. *Recreations*: sailing, photography, industrial archaeology. *Address*: 19 Sandles Close, Droitwich Spa, Worcs WR9 8RB. *T*: (01905) 798308.

HARRISON, Michael Anthony; Director, Kettle's Yard, University of Cambridge, since 1992; *b* 30 April 1947; *s* of late William Harrison and Gweneth Harrison (*née* Cooke); *m* 1973, Marie-Claude Bouquet; three *s* one *d*. *Educ*: Newcastle Royal GS; Aylesbury GS; Oxford Coll. of Tech.; Univ. of Nottingham (BA Hons Fine Art/Art Hist.). Arts Council: Regl Art Officer, 1971–73; Exhibn Organiser, 1973–77; Asst Dir for Regl Exhibns, Arts Council, 1977–88, South Bank Centre, 1988–90; Head of Fine Art, Winchester Sch. of Art, 1990–92. *Publications*: numerous exhibn catalogues. *Recreations*: art, places, books, cinema, music, more art. *Address*: Kettle's Yard, Castle Street, Cambridge CB3 0AQ. *T*: (01223) 352124.

HARRISON, Rev. Fr (Michael Burt) Crispin, CR; Superior of the Community of the Resurrection, Mirfield, 1998–2003; *b* 26 April 1936. *Educ*: Univ. of Leeds (BA Phil. with Hist. 1959); Trinity Coll., Oxford (BA Theol. 1962; MA 1966); Coll. of the Resurrection, Mirfield. Ordained deacon 1963, priest 1964; Curate: St Aidan, W Hartlepool, 1963–64; All Saints, Middlesbrough, 1964–66; licensed to officiate: Dio. Wakefield, 1966–69, 1978–87 and 1998–; Dio. Christ the King, SA, 2003–; professed, CR, 1968; Tutor, St Peter's Coll. and Lectr, Federal Theol Seminary, S Africa, 1970–77; Tutor, Coll. of the Resurrection, 1978–84; Vice-Principal, 1984–87; Provincial and Prior, St Peter's Priory, Johannesburg, 1987–97; Canon Theologian, Dio. of Christ the King, S Africa, 1990–97. *Address*: House of the Resurrection, Mirfield, W Yorks WF14 0BN. *T*: (01924) 483337, *Fax*: (01924) 490489.

HARRISON, Hon. Sir Michael (Guy Vicat), Kt 1993; a Judge of the High Court of Justice, Queen's Bench Division, 1993–2004; *b* 28 Sept. 1939; *s* of late Hugh Francis Guy Harrison and Elizabeth Alban Harrison (*née* Jones); *m* 1966, Judith (*née* Gist); one *s* one *d*. *Educ*: Charterhouse; Trinity Hall, Cambridge (MA). Called to the Bar, Gray's Inn, 1965, Bencher, 1993; QC 1983; a Recorder, 1989–93. Dep. Chm., Parly Boundary Commn for England, 1996–2004 (Asst Comr, 1981–93). Chm., Panel for Examination of Structure Plans, Somerset, 1981, Isles of Scilly, 1982; W Sussex, 1986. *Recreations*: tennis, sailing, fishing.

HARRISON, Prof. Michael Jackson; Vice-Chancellor, University of Wolverhampton, 1992–98 (Director, Wolverhampton Polytechnic (formerly The Polytechnic, Wolverhampton), 1985–92); *b* 18 Dec. 1941; *s* of Jackson Harrison and Norah (*née* Lees); *m* 1974, Marie Ghislaine Félix. *Educ*: Guildford Tech. Coll.; Univ. of Leicester (BA, MA). Lecturer in Sociology: Enfield Coll. of Technol., 1966–67; Univ. of Leeds, 1967–68; Sen. Lectr, Enfield Coll. of Technol., 1968–72; Principal Lectr, Sheffield City Polytechnic, 1972–76; Head of Dept, Hull Coll. of Higher Educn, 1976–81; Asst Dir, 1982–84, Dep. Dir, 1985, The Polytechnic, Wolverhampton. Vis. Lectr, Univ. of Oregon, 1971. Governor: Bilston Community Coll.; Thomas Telford CTC. FCMI (FBIM 1983). *Publications*: (jtly) A Sociology of Industrialisation, 1978; contribs to learned jls. *Recreations*: cinema, travelling, music. *Address*: 34 Mount Road, Penn, Wolverhampton WV4 5SW. *T*: (01902) 338807.

HARRISON, Sir Michael James Harwood, 2nd Bt *cr* 1961, of Bugbrooke; JP; Director of private companies; *b* 28 March 1936; *s* of Sir (James) Harwood Harrison, 1st Bt, TD, MP (C) Eye, Suffolk 1951–79, and Peggy Alberta Mary (*d* 1993), *d* of late Lt-Col V. D.

Stenhouse, TD; *S* father, 1980; *m* 1967, Rosamund Louise, *d* of Edward Clive; two *s* two *d*. *Educ*: Rugby. Served with 17th/21st Lancers, 1955–56. Member of Lloyd's. Mem. Council, Sail Training Assoc.; Vice-Pres., Assoc. of Combined Youth Clubs. Patron and Lord of the Manor, Bugbrooke, Northampton, 1980–. Master, Mercers' Co., 1986–87; Freeman of the City of London. JP London, 1993. *Recreations*: sailing, ski-ing, riding. *Heir s* Edwin Michael Harwood Harrison, *b* 29 May 1981. *Address*: Rise Cottage, Hasketon, near Woodbridge, Suffolk IP13 6JA. *T*: (01394) 382352. *Clubs*: Boodle's.

HARRISON, Norman, CChem; Chief Executive Officer, United Kingdom Atomic Energy Authority, since 2007; *b* 25 Jan. 1952; *s* of Robert and Elsie Harrison; *m* 1973 Jacqueline Ogden. *Educ*: John Dalton Poly. Coll., Manchester; Blackburn Tech. Coll. (DMS). CChem, 1981; MRSC 1981. British Energy plc (formerly Central Electricity Generating Board, then Nuclear Electric plc): Commng Team Mem., Heysham 1 Nuclear Power Stn, 1981–85; Control Room Supervisor, Heysham 2 Nuclear Power Stn, 1985–93; Shift Manager, 1993–95, Tech. and Safety Manager, 1995–96, Hartlepool Nuclear Power Stn; Ops Manager, 1996–99, Dir, 1999–2000, Heysham 1 Nuclear Power Stn; Dir, Sizewell B Nuclear Power Stn, 2000–03; Dir, Dounreay Div., UKAEA 2003–07. FRSA. *Recreations*: travel, opera, gardening. *Address*: The Manor Court, Chilton, Oxon OX11 0RN. *T*: (01235) 431999, *Fax*: (01235) 431963; *e-mail*: norman.harrison@ukaea.co.uk.

HARRISON, Patricia Mary, DCNZM 2001; QSO 1987; Member, Otago Regional Council, 1996–2004; *b* 6 Sept. 1932; *d* of Hugh and Catherine Thomson; *m* 1957, Arthur Keith Harrison; one *s* two *d*. *Educ*: Otago Girls' High Sch.; Dunedin Teachers' Coll. Otago Univ. (MA Hons Philosophy; James Clark Meml Prize in Philosophy 1955). Hd of English, Burnside High Sch., 1973–75; Principal, Queen's High Sch., Dunedin, 1975–94. Chm., Otago Youth Wellness Trust, 1996–. Chm., Otago Regl Access Employment Council, 1985–87. Mem. Council, Univ. of Otago, 1985–96. Board Member: YWCA 1970–80; Southern Th. Trust, 1987–90. Commemoration Medal (NZ), 1990; Suffrage Medal (NZ), 1993. *Publication*: Magic, Myth and Legends: a supplementary English text, 1974. *Recreations*: gardening, bridge, walking. *Address*: 31 Gladstone Road, Dalmore, Dunedin North, New Zealand. *T*: (3) 4738606.

HARRISON, Patrick Kennard, CBE 1982; Secretary, Royal Institute of British Architects, 1968–87; *b* 8 July 1928; *e s* of late Richard Harrison and Sheila Griffin; *m* 1955, Mary Wilson, *y d* of late Captain G. C. C. Damant, CBE, RN; one *d*. *Educ*: Lord Williams's Sch., Thame; Downing Coll., Cambridge (Exhbnr in English). Asst Principal, Dept of Health for Scotland, 1953; Private Sec. to Deptl Sec. and to Parly Secs, Scottish Office, 1958–60; Principal, Scottish Develt Dept and Regional Develt Div., Scottish Office, 1960–68. Dir, Building Mus. Project, 1990–97. Hon. Mem., Amer. Inst. of Architects, 1978. Hon. FRIAS, 1987; Hon. FRIBA, 1988. *Recreations*: gardening, travel, reading, music. *Address*: 28B Moray Place, Edinburgh EH3 6BX. *T*: (0131) 225 5342; Upper Stewarton, Eddleston, Peebles EH45 8PP. *T*: (01721) 730602. *Clubs*: Reform; New (Edinburgh).

HARRISON, Prof. Paul Jeffrey, FRCPsych; Professor of Psychiatry, University of Oxford, since 2000; Fellow, Wolfson College, Oxford, since 1997; *b* 18 Oct. 1960; *s* of Walford John Harrison and Bridget Ann Harrison; *m* 1984, Sandra Hallett; three *d*. *Educ*: City of London Sch.; Balliol Coll., Oxford (BA 1982; BM BCh 1985; MA 1987); DM Oxon 1991. MRCPsych 1989, FRCPsych 2001. MRC Trng Fellow, St Mary's Hosp. Med. Sch., 1988; University of Oxford: Clinical Lectr in Psychiatry, 1991–94; Wellcome Trust Sen. Res. Fellow, 1995–97; Clinical Reader in Psychiatry, 1997–2000. Collegium Internationale Neuro-Psychopharmacologicum Schizophrenia Award, 1998; Sen. Clinical Prize, Brit. Assoc. for Psychopharmacol., 1999; A. E. Bennett Award, Soc. for Biol Psychiatry, 2004; Joel Elkes Award, Amer. Coll. of Neuropsychopharmacol., 2005. *Publications*: Lecture Notes on Psychiatry, 8th edn 1998, 9th edn 2005; The Neuropathology of Schizophrenia, 2000; Shorter Oxford Textbook of Psychiatry, 5th edn 2006; articles on schizophrenia, depression and Alzheimer's disease. *Recreations*: sport, music. *Address*: University Department of Psychiatry, Warneford Hospital, Oxford OX3 7JX. *T*: (01865) 223730.

HARRISON, Prof. Peter Duncan, PhD; Andreas Idreos Professor of Science and Religion, and Fellow of Harris Manchester College, University of Oxford, since 2007; *b* 29 Nov. 1955; *s* of Duncan and Jean Harrison; *m* 1994, Carol Taylor; one *s* one *d*. *Educ*: Yeronga Infants Sch.; Bundaberg State High Sch.; Univ. of Queensland (BSc; BA Hons; PhD 1989); Yale Univ. (MA). Bond University: Asst Prof., 1989–93, Associate Prof., 1994–2000, of Philos.; Prof. of Hist. and Philos., 2001–06. Hon. Res. Consultant, Dept of Studies in Religion, Univ. of Queensland, 1990–. *Publications*: Religion and the Religions in the English Enlightenment, 1990, 2nd edn 2002; The Bible, Protestantism and the Rise of Natural Science, 1998, 2nd edn 2002; The Fall of Man and the Foundations of Science, 2007. *Address*: Harris Manchester College, Mansfield Road, Oxford OX1 3TD.

HARRISON, Peter John; QC 2006; a Recorder, since 2007; *b* 14 Feb. 1965; *s* of Robin Harrison and Paddy Harrison (*née* Smith); *m* 2000, Kate Belinda Tucker. *Educ*: Warden Park Comprehensive Sch., Cuckfield; Haywards Heath VIth Form Coll.; Durham Univ. (BA Hons). Called to the Bar, Inner Temple, 1987. Member: SE Circuit Planning and Envmt Bar Assoc., 1990–; Criminal Bar Assoc., 1992–; Admin. Law Bar Assoc., 1994–. Mem. Faculty, SE Circuit Keble Internat. Advocacy trng course, 2003–. Church Comr, 2008–. Lectures in field of regulatory and envmtl crime. *Publication*: (with F. Darroch) Environmental Crime, 1999. *Recreations*: ceroc dancing, English cookery. *Address*: 6 Pump Court, Temple, EC4Y 7AR. *T*: (020) 7797 8400; *e-mail*: peterharrison@ 6pumpcourt.co.uk.

HARRISON, Ven. Peter Reginald Wallace; Archdeacon of the East Riding, 1999–2006; *b* 22 June 1939; *s* of Gilbert V. W. Harrison and Mary L. W. Harrison (*née* Blair); *m* 1970, Elizabeth Mary Byzia; one *s* one *d*. *Educ*: Charterhouse; Selwyn Coll., Cambridge (BA Theol 1962); Ridley Hall, Cambridge. Ordained deacon 1964, priest 1965; Curate, St Luke's, Barton Hill, Bristol, 1964–69; Youth Worker and Chaplain, Greenhouse Trust, London, 1969–77; Dir, Northorpe Hall Trust, Mirfield, 1977–84; Team Rector, Drypool Team Ministry, Hull, 1984–98. *Recreations*: reading, voluntary community work. *Address*: 10 Priestgate, Church Street, Sutton, Hull HU7 4QR. *T*: (01482) 797110.

HARRISON, Philippa Mary; Editorial Director, Ed Victor Literary Agency, since 2002; *b* 25 Nov. 1942; *d* of Charles Kershaw Whitfield and Alexina Margaret Whitfield; *m* 1968 (marr. diss. 1976). *Educ*: Walthamstow Hall; Bristol Univ. (BA Hons). Courtauld Inst. Promotions Organiser, Associated Book Publishers, 1963–66; reader and editor, Jonathan Cape, 1967–73; Editl Dir, Hutchinson, 1974–78; Jt Editor-in-Chief, Penguin, 1979–80; Editl Dir, Michael Joseph, 1980–85; Man. Dir and Publisher, Macmillan London, 1986–88; Managing Director: V&A Enterprises, 1990–91; Macdonald & Co., subseq. Little, Brown & Co. (UK), 1991–96; Chief Exec. and Publisher, 1996–2000, non-exec. Chm., 2000–01, Little, Brown & Co. (UK). Director: Royal Acad. of Arts Enterprise Bd,

1999–; British Mus. Co., 2002–. Member: Freedom to Publish Cttee, 1985–88; Bd, Book Marketing Council, 1983–88; Booker Mgt Cttee, 1987–89; Literature Panel, Arts Council, 1988–92. Mem. Council, Publishers' Assoc., 1995–2002 (Pres., 1998–99). Dir, Book Tokens Ltd, 1996–. Trustee, Eric & Salome Estorick Foundn, 1996–99. CCMI (CIMgt 1987; Mem. Bd, 1999–2005); FRSA 1992. *Recreations:* walking, gardening, theatre, politics, looking at pictures, friends. *Address:* 3B Connaught House, Clifton Gardens, W9 1AL. *T:* (020) 7289 8808. *Club:* Groucho.

HARRISON, Sir (Robert) Colin, 4th Bt *cr* 1922; *b* 25 May 1938; *s* of Sir John Fowler Harrison, 2nd Bt, and Kathleen (*d* 1993), *yr d* of late Robert Livingston, The Gables, Eaglescliffe, Co. Durham; *S* brother, 1955; *m* 1963, Maureen, *er d* of late E. Leonard Chiverton, Garth Corner, Kirkbymoorside, York; one *s* two *d*. *Educ:* St Peter's Coll., Radley; St John's Coll., Cambridge. Commissioned with Fifth Royal Northumberland Fusiliers (National Service), 1957–59. Chm., John Harrison (Stockton) Ltd, 1963–2006. Chm., Young Master Printers Nat. Cttee, 1972–73. *Heir:* *s* John Wyndham Fowler Harrison, *b* 14 Dec. 1972. *Address:* Stearsby Hall, Stearsby, York YO61 4SA. *T:* (01347) 888226.

HARRISON, Robert Michael; QC 1987; a Recorder, since 1985; a Deputy High Court Judge, 1997; *b* 3 Nov. 1945; *s* of Robert William and Bertha Harrison; *m* 1974, Jennifer Armstrong; one *s*. *Educ:* Heckmondwike Grammar School; Hull Univ. (LLB). Called to the Bar, Gray's Inn, 1969. *Address:* Park Court Chambers, 16 Park Place, Leeds LS1 2SJ. *T:* (0113) 243 3277.

HARRISON, Robert Montagu G.; *see* Graham-Harrison.

HARRISON, Roger; *see* Harrison, D. R. W.

HARRISON, Prof. Roy Michael, OBE 2004; PhD, DSc; FRSC, FRMetS; Queen Elizabeth II Birmingham Centenary Professor of Environmental Health, since 1991, and Head, Division of Environmental Health & Risk Management, since 1999, University of Birmingham; *b* 14 Oct. 1948; *s* of Wilfred Harrison and Rosa (*née* Cotton); *m* 1st, 1981, Angela Copeman (marr. diss.); one *s* one *d*; 2nd, 1989, Susan Sturt; one *s*. *Educ:* Henley Grammar Sch.; Univ. of Birmingham (BSc; PhD 1972; DSc 1988). FRMetS 1982; FRSC 1988. Res. Asst, Imperial Coll., Univ. of London, 1972–74; Lectr, Lancaster Univ., 1974–84; Reader, Univ. of Essex, 1984–91. Margary Lectr, RMetS, 1994; John Jeyes Lectr, RSC, 1995. Department of the Environment: Mem., Photochem. Oxidants Rev. Gp, 1986–97; Chairman: Quality of Urban Air Rev. Gp, 1991–97; Airborne Particles Expert Gp, 1997–99; Vice-Chm., Expert Panel on Air Quality Standards, 2003– (Mem., 1992–2002); Member: Adv. Cttee on Hazardous Substances, 2001–06; Air Quality Expert Gp, 2002–; Department of Health: Member: Cttee on Med. Effects of Air Pollution, 1993–2003, 2006–; Health Adv. Gp on Chem. Contamination Incidents, 1994–. Hon. Consulting Envmtl Toxicologist, Nat. Poisons Inf. Service, Birmingham Centre and W Midlands Poisons Unit, 1994–99. Mem., HEFCE Panel, 2001 and 2008 RAEs. Chm., Envmt Gp, RSC, 1990–91; Theme Leader for Envmt, Pollution and Human Health, NERC, 2007–. Hon. FFOM 1998; Hon. MFPHM 1997. *Publications:* (with D. P. H. Laxen) Lead Pollution: causes and control, 1981; Pollution: causes, effects and control, 1983, 4th edn 2001; (with R. Perry) Handbook of Air Pollution Analysis, 2nd edn 1986; (jtly) Acid Rain: scientific and technical advances, 1987; (with S. Rapsomanikis) Environmental Analysis using Chromatography Interfaced with Atomic Spectroscopy, 1989; (jtly) Introductory Chemistry for the Environmental Sciences, 1991, 2nd edn (with S. J. de Mora) 1996; (with R. S. Hamilton) Highway Pollution, 1991; (jtly) Handbook for Urban Air Improvement, 1992; Understanding Our Environment: an introduction to environmental chemistry and pollution, 1992, 3rd edn 1999; (with M. Radojevic) Atmospheric Acidity: sources, consequences and abatement, 1992; (with F. E. Warner) Radioecology after Chernobyl: biogeochemical pathways of artificial radionuclides, SCOPE 50, 1993; (jtly) Urban Air Quality in the United Kingdom, 1993; (jtly) Diesel Vehicle Emissions and Urban Air Quality, 1993; (jtly) Airborne Particulate Matter in the United Kingdom, 1996; (with R. Van Grieken) Atmospheric Particles, 1998; (jtly) Source Apportionment of Airborne Particulate Matter in the United Kingdom, 1999; An Introduction to Pollution Science, 2006; Principles of Environmental Chemistry, 2007; many papers to learned jls. *Recreations:* mowing and other outdoor pursuits. *Address:* Division of Environmental Health & Risk Management, University of Birmingham, Edgbaston, Birmingham B15 2TT. *T:* (0121) 414 3494.

HARRISON, Shirley Margaret; JP; Chair, Human Tissue Authority, since 2007; *b* 26 March 1949; *d* of Colin and Ena Gunn; *m* 1990, Robert Harrison; one *s*. *Educ:* Univ. of Kent (BA Philosophy 1970); Univ. of Sheffield (MBA 1989). Mktg exec. and advertising copywriter, 1970–73; homelessness worker, 1973–76; student welfare officer, 1976–82; conf./event mktg exec., 1982–86; Chief Officer (PR Dir), Sheffield CC, 1986–92; Lectr, Leeds Business Sch., 1992–2001. Chair: S Yorks Probation Bd, 2005–07; HFEA, 2007. Patient rep., Cancer Res. Networks, 2001–07; non-exec. Dir, Sheffield Teaching Hospitals NHS Foundn Trust, 2007–. JP Sheffield, 1998. FRSA. *Publications:* Public Relations: an introduction, 1995, 2nd edn 2000; Disasters and the Media, 1999; contrib. chapters in books; articles in acad. jls on PR and communications, business ethics, etc. *Recreations:* walking the dog, learning the piano, going to the pictures, gardening, cooking and eating. *Address:* c/o Human Tissue Authority, Finlaison House, 15–17 Furnival Street, EC4A 1AB; *e-mail:* shirley.harrison@hta.gov.uk.

HARRISON, (Stanley) George, CBE 2003; a District Judge, Chester County Court and District Registry of High Court, 1985–2008; *b* 16 Aug. 1937; *s* of Stanley George Harrison and Elizabeth Avril Meff (*née* Walker); *m* 1963, Jennifer Lorna Harrow; one *s* one *d*. *Educ:* Wellington Coll.; Univ. of Manchester (LLB Hons). Commnd Lancs Regt (2nd Lt), 1956–58. Admitted solicitor, 1964; Partner, Wayman Hales, Chester, 1967–82; Registrar, Liverpool Co. Court, 1982–85. Mem., Lord Chancellor's Adv. Cttee on Delay in Public Law, 2002. Sec., 1985–2000, Pres., 2002, Assoc. of Dist Judges. Chm., Muir Housing Gp Assoc., 1986–2002. Dir, CLS Care Services, 1991–2001. *Recreations:* fishing, cricket, grass. *Address:* Boothsdale House, Willington, Tarporley, Cheshire CW6 0NH. *Club:* Chester City.

HARRISON, Ted; *see* Harrison, E. P. G.

HARRISON, Sir Terence, Kt 1995; DL; FREng; FIMechE, FIMarEST; Chairman, Alfred McAlpine plc, 1996–2002 (Director, 1995–2002); *b* 7 April 1933; *s* of late Roland Harrison and of Doris (*née* Wardle); *m* 1956, June (*née* Forster); two *s*. *Educ:* A. J. Dawson Grammar Sch., Co. Durham; West Hartlepool and Sunderland Tech. Colls. BSc(Eng) Durham. CEng 1964; FIMechE 1984; FIMarEST (FIMarE 1973); FREng (FEng 1988). Marine engrg apprenticeship, Richardson's Westgarth, Hartlepool, 1949–53; commnd REME, service in Nigeria, 1955–57; Clarke Chapman, Gateshead (Marine Division): Res. Engr, 1957; Chief Mechanical Engr, 1967; Man. Dir, 1969; Man. Dir, Clarke Chapman Ltd, Gateshead, 1976; Northern Engineering Industries plc: Dir, 1977; Man. Dir, UK Ops, 1980–83; Chief Exec., 1983–86; Exec. Chm., 1986–93; Rolls-Royce: Dir, 1989; Chief Exec., 1992–96. Director: Barclays Bank (Regl Bd), 1986–98; T&N, 1995–98. Member: ACOST, 1987; Engrg Council, 1990–93. Pres., BEAMA, 1989–90. Pres., NEC Inst., 1988. DL Tyne and Wear, 1989. Hon. DEng Newcastle, 1991; Hon. DTech Sunderland, 1995; Hon. DSc Durham, 1996. *Publications:* technical papers to mechanical, marine and mining societies. *Recreations:* golf, fell walking. *Address:* 2 The Garden Houses, Whalton, Northumberland NE61 3HB. *T:* (01670) 775400.

HARRISON, Tony; poet; *b* 30 April 1937; *s* of Harry Ashton Harrison and Florrie (*née* Wilkinson-Horner). *Publications:* Earthworks, 1964; Aikin Mata, 1966; Newcastle is Peru, 1969; The Loiners (Geoffrey Faber Meml Prize), 1970; The Misanthrope, 1973; Phaedra Britannica, 1975; Palladas: poems, 1975; The Passion, 1977; Bow Down, 1977; From The School of Eloquence and other poems, 1978; The Bartered Bride, 1978; Continuous, 1981; A Kumquat for John Keats, 1981; US Martial, 1981; The Oresteia, 1981; Selected Poems, 1984, expanded edn 1987; The Mysteries, 1985; Dramatic Verse 1973–85, 1985; v., 1985; The Fire-Gap, 1985; Theatre Works 1973–85, 1986; The Trackers of Oxyrhynchus, 1990; v. and other poems, 1990; A Cold Coming: Gulf War poems, 1991; The Common Chorus, 1992; The Gaze of the Gorgon (Whitbread Award for Poetry), 1992; Square Rounds, 1992; Black Daisies for the Bride, 1993; Poetry or Bust, 1993; A Maybe Day in Kazakhstan, 1994; The Shadow of Hiroshima, 1995; Permanently Bard, 1995; Plays Three: The Kaisers of Carnuntum, The Labourers of Herakles, Poetry or Bust, 1996; The Prince's Play, 1996; Prometheus, 1998 (also Dir, film, 1999); Plays One: The Mysteries, 1999; Laureate's Block and Other Poems, 2000; Plays Two: The Oresteia, The Common Chorus, The Trojan Women, 2001; Plays Four: The Misanthrope, Phaedra Britannica, The Prince's Play, 2001; Plays Five: The Trackers of Oxyrhynchus, Square Rounds, 2004; Hecuba, 2005; Under the Clock: new poems, 2005; Collected Poems, 2007; Collected Film Poetry, 2007. *Address:* c/o Gordon Dickerson, 2 Crescent Grove, SW4 7AH.

HARRISON, Valerie, (Mrs D. M. Harrison); *see* Caton, V.

HARRISON, Victoria; *see* Harrison, A. V.

HARRISON, Rt Hon. Walter; PC 1977; JP; *b* 2 Jan. 1921; *s* of Henry and Ada Harrison; *m* 1948, Enid Mary (*née* Coleman) (*d* 1990); one *s* one *d*; *m* 1991, Jane Marguerite Richards (*d* 2000). *Educ:* Dewsbury Technical and Art Coll. Served RAF, 1940–45. Electrical Inspector and Electrical Foreman, Electricity Supply Industry, 1937–64; Welfare Personnel Officer, Civil and Engrg Industry, 1945–48. MP (Lab) Wakefield, 1964–87. Asst Govt Whip, 1966–68; a Lord Comr of the Treasury, 1968–70; Dep. Chief Opposition Whip, 1970–74 and 1979–83; Treasurer of HM Household and Dep. Chief Govt Whip, 1974–79. Held several positions in the Trade Union and Labour movements. West Riding CC, 1958–64; Alderman, Castleford Borough Council, 1959–66 (Councillor, 1952–59); JP West Riding Yorks, 1962. Hon. Freeman, City of Wakefield, 2003. *Address:* 1 Milnthorpe Drive, Sandal, Wakefield WF2 7HU. *T:* (01924) 255550.

HARRISON, (William) Alistair, CVO 1996; HM Diplomatic Service; High Commissioner to Zambia, 2005–08; *b* 14 Nov. 1954; *s* of William Kent Harrison and late Alice Rita Harrison; *m* 1st, 1981, Theresa Mary Morrison (marr. diss. 1991); 2nd, 1996, Sarah Judith Wood; one *s* two *d*. *Educ:* Newcastle Royal Grammar Sch.; University Coll., Oxford (BA 1977; MA 1980); Birkbeck Coll., London (DipEcon 1995). Joined FCO, 1977: Third, later Second Sec., Warsaw, 1979–82; First Sec., FCO, 1982–84; Private Sec. to Parly Under-Sec., FCO, 1984–86; First Sec., UK Mission to UN, NY, 1987–92; Deputy Head: ME Dept, FCO, 1992–95; of Mission, Warsaw, 1995–98; Foreign Policy Advr to Dir-Gen. for External Relations, EC, Brussels, 1998–2000; Hd of Chancery and Pol Counsellor, UKMIS to UN, NY, 2000–03; Hd, UN (later Internat. Orgns) Dept, FCO, 2003–05. *Recreations:* music, mathematics. *Address:* c/o Foreign and Commonwealth Office, King Charles Street, SW1A 2AH.

HARRISS, Gerald Leslie, DPhil; FBA 1986; Fellow and Tutor, Magdalen College, Oxford, 1967–92, Emeritus Fellow, since 1992; Reader in Modern History, Oxford University, 1990–92; *b* 22 May 1925; *s* of Walter and Mabel Harriss; *m* 1959, Margaret Anne Sidaway; two *s* three *d*. *Educ:* Chigwell Sch.; Magdalen Coll., Oxford (BA 1st Cl. History, MA, DPhil). Service in RNVR, 1944–46. Research Fellow, Durham Univ., 1953–55; Asst Lectr, Manchester Univ., 1955–56; Lectr 1956, Sen. Lectr 1965, Reader 1965–67, Durham Univ. *Publications:* King, Parliament and Public Finance in Medieval England, 1975; (ed) Henry V: the practice of kingship, 1985; Cardinal Beaufort, 1988; (ed) K. B. McFarlane, Letters to Friends, 1997; Shaping the Nation: England 1360–1461, 2005; numerous articles on late medieval English history. *Address:* Fairings, 2 Queen Street, Yetminster, Dorset DT9 6LL.

HARROD, Dominick Roy; journalist and broadcaster; Programme Director, St George's House, Windsor Castle, 1994–98; President, Institute of Journalists, 1994–95; *b* 21 Aug. 1940; *s* of Sir Roy Forbes Harrod, FBA and Wilhelmine Harrod (*née* Cresswell), OBE; *m* 1974, Christina Hobhouse (*d* 1996); one *s*. *Educ:* Dragon Sch., Oxford; Westminster Sch.; Christ Church, Oxford (MA Modern Greats). Sunday Telegraph, 1962–66; Daily Telegraph: Washington corresp., 1966–69; Economics corresp., 1969–71; BBC Economics corresp., 1971–78; Dir of Information, Dunlop Ltd, 1979; Economics Editor, BBC Radio, 1979–93; City Editor, The Yorkshire Post, 1993–94. Member: Council, SCF, 1988–96; Bd for Social Responsibility, C of E, 1996–2000. Founder Mem., Norfolk Churches Trust, 1973; Chm., Friends of Morston Church, 2003. FJI 1990; FRSA 1992. *Publications:* The Politics of Economics, 1978; Making Sense of the Economy, 1983; War, Ice and Piracy, 2000; (contrib.) The Turn of the Tide, 2005. *Recreations:* reading, sailing. *Address:* 4 Duke's Avenue, W4 2AE. *Club:* Garrick.

HARROD, Dr Tanya Olivia; design historian; *b* 7 July 1951; *d* of Peter Kingsmill Ledger and Maria Martha Ledger (*née* Sax); *m* 1977, Henry Mark Harrod; one *s* one *d*, and two step *s*. *Educ:* St Felix Sch., Southwold; Univ. of York (BA Hist.); St Hilda's Coll., Oxford (DPhil 1978). Tutor, Open Univ., 1978–88; Architecture and Design corresp., Independent on Sunday, 1989–94; Vis. Fellow, Sch. of World Art and Museology, UEA, 1995–97. Vis. Prof., Sch. of Humanities, RCA, 2000–. Member, Advisory Board: Jl Design History, 1996–; Interpreting Ceramics, 2003–; Burlington Magazine, 2006–. Mem., Internat. Assoc. of Art Critics, 1992–. Jt Editor, Jl of Modern Craft, 2006–08. *Publications:* (ed) Obscure Objects of Desire: reviewing the crafts in the Twentieth Century, 1997; The Crafts in Britain in the 20th Century, 1999; (contrib.) Contemporary Art and the Home, 2002; Michael Cardew: a life, 2008; contribs to Burlington Mag., TLS, Spectator. *Recreation:* lake, river and sea bathing. *Address:* 51 Campden Hill Square, W8 7JR. *T:* (020) 7727 8485.

HARROLD, Roy Mealham; farmer, 1947–91; *b* 13 Aug. 1928; *s* of John Frederick Harrold and Ellen Selena Harrold (*née* Mealham); *m* 1968, Barbara Mary, *yr d* of William and Florence Andrews; one *s* one *d*. *Educ:* Stoke Holy Cross Primary Sch.; Bracondale Sch., Norwich. County Chm., Norfolk Fedn of Young Farmers' Clubs, 1956–57; Mem., Nat. Council of Young Farmers, 1957–60; Mem. Council, Royal Norfolk Agric. Assoc., 1972–75, 1980–83, 1987–89; Mem., Press Council, 1976–83. Mem., UK Shareholders Assoc., 1993–. Lay Chm., Norwich East Deanery Synod, 1970–79; Member: Norwich

Dio. Synod, 1970–96; Norwich Dio. Bd of Patronage, 1970–82; Norwich Dio. Bd of Finance, 1983–96; Pastoral Asst, St Peter Mancroft, Norwich, 1991– (Church Warden, 1978–82, 1988–92). *Recreations:* music, opera, ballet. *Address:* Salamanca Farm, Stoke Holy Cross, 118 Norwich Road, Norwich NR14 8QJ. *T:* (01508) 492322.

HARROP, Sir Peter (John), KCB 1984 (CB 1980); Second Permanent Secretary, Department of the Environment, 1981–86; *b* 18 March 1926; *s* of late Gilbert Harrop, OBE; *m* 1975, Margaret Joan, *d* of E. U. E. Elliott-Binns, CB; two *s*. *Educ:* King Edward VII Sch., Lytham, Lancs; Peterhouse, Cambridge. MA (Hist. Tripos). Served RNVR, 1945–48 (Sub-Lt). Min. of Town and Country Planning, 1949; Min. of Housing and Local Govt, 1951; Dept of the Environment, 1970 (Chm., Yorks and Humberside Economic Planning Bd, and Regional Dir, 1971–73); Under-Sec., HM Treasury, 1973–76; Deputy Secretary: DoE, 1977–79, 1980–81; Cabinet Office, 1979–80. Chm., National Bus Co., 1988–91; non-executive Director: Nat. Home Loans Hldgs plc, 1987–92; Municipal Mutual Insurance Ltd, 1988–2001; Thames Water plc, 1989–95 (Mem., Thames Water Authority, 1986–89). Chm., UK Cttee, European Year of the Environment, 1986–88. Chairman: Richmond upon Thames Housing Trust, 1990–96; River Thames Boat Project, 2001–06. Chm. of Govs., Richmond upon Thames Coll., 1993–96. Hon. Trustee, British Mus., 1987–97. *Recreation:* golf. *Address:* 19 Berwyn Road, Richmond, Surrey TW10 5BP. *Clubs:* Oxford and Cambridge, Roehampton.

HARROW, John Michael; His Honour Judge Harrow; a Circuit Judge, since 2003; *b* 30 March 1946; *s* of Henry John and Edith Harrow; *m* 2000, Maria Liddle; two *s* one *d*. *Educ:* Hemsworth Grammar Sch.; Coll. of Law, Guildford. Admitted solicitor, 1969; a Recorder, 1996–2003. Chm. (pt-time), 1986–96, Dist Chm., 1996–2003, Appeals Service. *Publication:* (contrib.) Butterworth's Road Traffic Service, annually 1991–94. *Recreations:* running, cinema, architecture, war history. *Address:* Courts of Justice, Deansleigh Road, Bournemouth BH7 7DS. *T:* (01202) 502800; *e-mail:* HHJudge.Harrow@judiciary.gsi.gov.uk.

HARROWBY, 8th Earl of, *cr* 1809; **Dudley Adrian Conroy Ryder;** Baron Harrowby, 1776; Viscount Sandon, 1809; chartered surveyor; *b* 18 March 1951; *s* of 7th Earl of Harrowby, TD and Jeanette Rosalthé (*née* Johnston-Saint); *S* father, 2007; *m* 1st, 1977, Sarah Nichola Hobhouse Payne (*d* 1994), *d* of Captain Anthony Payne; three *s* one *d*; 2nd, 1998, Mrs Caroline J. Coram James (*née* Marks). *Educ:* Eton; Univ. of Newcastle upon Tyne; Magdalene Coll., Cambridge (MA). FRICS 1992. Exec. Dir, Compton Street Securities Ltd, 1988–. Mem., Governing Council, Goldsmiths Coll., Univ. of London, 2003– (Mem., Finance and Resources Cttee, 2004–); Governor: John Archer Sch., Wandsworth, 1986–88; Dean Close Sch., Cheltenham, 2004–. President: Staffordshire Soc., 1995–97; Stafford Historical and Civic Soc., 2008–; Vice Pres., Glos Co. Br., CPRE, 2008–. Mem., NFU, 1975–. Patron: Guild of Handicraft Trust, 1991–; N Staffs Co. RBL, 2008–. Liveryman, Co. of Goldsmiths, 1997. *Recreations:* travel, fell walking, music, study of fine art and architecture. *Heir:* *s* Viscount Sandon, *qv*. *Address:* Sandon Estate Office, Sandon, Stafford ST18 0DA.

HARROWER, Rt Rev. John Douglas; *see* Tasmania, Bishop of.

HARSENT, David, FRSL; poet, novelist, dramatist, librettist; *b* 9 Dec. 1942; *s* of Albert and Mary Harsent; *m* 1989, Julia Watson; one *d*, and two *s* one *d* from former marriage. *Educ:* trifling! Hon. Res. Fellow, Royal Holloway, Univ. of London, 2005–; Dist. Writing Fellow, Sheffield Hallam Univ., 2005–. Commns from Royal Opera House and Proms; performances at S Bank Centre, Kammeroper, Vienna and Carnegie Hall, NY; *words for music:* music by Harrison Birtwistle: Gawain, libretto for an opera, 1991; The Woman and the Hare, song cycle, 1999; The Ring Dance of the Nazarene, song setting, 2003; The Minotaur, libretto for an opera, 2008; Serenade and the Silkie, music by Julian Grant, 1994; When She Died, libretto for an opera, music by Jonathan Dove, 2002. FRSL 1999. *Publications: fiction:* From an Inland Sea, 1985; *poetry:* Truce, 1973; After Dark, 1973; Dreams of the Dead, 1977; A Violent Country, 1979; Mister Punch, 1984; Selected Poems, 1989; Gawain: a libretto, 1991; Storybook Hero, 1992; News From the Front, 1993; The Sorrow of Sarajevo: versions of poems by Goran Simic, 1996; The Potted Priest, 1997; Sprinting from the Graveyard: versions of poems by Goran Simic, 1997; A Bird's Idea of Flight, 1998; Marriage, 2002; Legion (Forward Prize for best poetry collection), 2005; Selected Poems 1969–2005, 2007; *editor:* (with M. Susko) Savramena Britanska Poezija, 1988; Another Round at the Pillars: Festschrift for Ian Hamilton Cargo, 1999; Raising the Iron, 2004. *Recreation:* re-inventing the past for future use. *Address:* c/o United Agents, 12–26 Lexington Street, W1F 0LE.

HARSTON, Julian John Robert Clive; HM Diplomatic Service, retired; Assistant Secretary General, Head of Mission for the Referendum in Western Sahara and Special Representative of the Secretary-General in Western Sahara, United Nations, since 2007; *b* 20 Oct. 1942; *s* of late Col Clive Harston, ERD, and of Kathleen Harston; *m* 1966, Karen Howard Oake (*née* Longfield) (marr. diss. 2000); one *s*. *Educ:* King's Sch., Canterbury; Univ. of London (BSc). British Tourist Authority, 1965–70; FCO, 1970; Consul, Hanoi, 1973; 1st Secretary: Blantyre, 1975; Lisbon, 1982; Counsellor, Harare, 1984–88; FCO, 1988–91; Counsellor, UK Mission, Geneva, 1991–95; Head, Political and Civil Affairs, UN Peace Forces, Zagreb, former Yugoslavia, 1995–96; Dir, UN Liaison Office, Belgrade, Fed. Repub. of Yugoslavia, 1996; Rep. of Sec.-Gen. and Hd of Mission, UN Civilian Police Mission, Haiti, 1998–99; Dep. Special Rep. of UN Sec.-Gen. to Bosnia Herzegovina, 1999–2001; Dir, UN Dept of Peace Keeping, NY, 2001–04; Dir, UN, Belgrade, 2004–07. *Recreations:* photography, travel. *Address:* c/o United Nations, United Nations Plaza, New York, NY 10017, USA. *Clubs:* East India, Royal Automobile; Gremio Literario (Lisbon); Harare (Zimbabwe).

HART, family name of **Baron Hart of Chilton**.

HART OF CHILTON, Baron *cr* 2004 (Life Peer), of Chilton in the County of Suffolk; **Garry Richard Rushby Hart;** Special Adviser to Secretary of State for Justice (formerly for Constitutional Affairs) and Lord Chancellor, 1998–2007; *b* 29 June 1940; *s* of late Dennis George Hart and of Evelyn Mary Hart; *m* 1st, 1966, Paula Lesley Shepherd (marr. diss. 1986); two *s* one *d*; 2nd, 1986, Valerie Elen Mary Davies; twin *d*. *Educ:* Northgate Grammar Sch., Ipswich; University Coll. London (LLB; Fellow 2001). Admitted solicitor (Hons) 1966; Herbert Smith: Articled Clerk, 1962–65; Solicitor, 1966–70; Partner, 1970–98; Hd, Property Dept, 1988–97. Member: Partnership Council, 1988–97; Law Soc. (Mem., Specialist Planning Panel). Freeman, City of London, 1981; Liveryman, Solicitors' Co., 1981–. Trustee: Architecture Foundn, 1996–2005 (Dep. Chm., 1997–2005); British Architectural Liby Trust, 2001–. Member: Almeida Develt Bd, 2007– (Trustee, 1997–2005, Chm., 1997–2002, Almeida Th.); Buildings Strategy Cttee, V & A Mus., 2007–. Mem. Council, UCL, 2004–; Chancellor, Univ. of Greenwich, 2008–. Vice-Patron, Ipswich Soc. for the Blind, 2008–. FRSA 1998. Hon. FRIBA 2000. *Publications:* (ed jtly) Blundell & Dobry's Planning Applications Appeals and Proceedings, 4th edn 1990, 5th edn 1996. *Recreations:* conservation, theatre, talking. *Address:* House of Lords, SW1A 0PW. *Clubs:* Reform, Garrick, Beefsteak.

HART, Alan; broadcasting consultant, since 1991; Director, Global AMG, 1995–200 Executive Director, Eurosport Consortium, 1997–2004 (Trustee, since 2004); *b* 17 Apr 1935; *s* of late Reginald Thomas Hart and Lillian Hart; *m* 1961, Celia Mary Vine; two one *d*. *Educ:* Pinnerwood Primary Sch.; University College Sch., Hampstead. Reporte Willesden Chronicle and Kilburn Times, 1952–58; Newcastle Evening Chronicle, 195 London Evening News, 1958–59; Editorial Asst, BBC Sportsview, 1959–61; Televisio Sports Producer, BBC Manchester, 1962–64; Asst Editor, Sportsview, 1964–65; Edito Sportsview, 1965–68; Editor, Grandstand, 1968–77; Head of Sport, BBC Televisio 1977–81; Controller, BBC1 Television, 1981–84; Special Asst to Dir Gen., BBC, 198 Controller, Internat. Relations, BBC, 1986–91. Dir, Eurosport, 1991–97 (Chm 1989–91); Chm., British Eurosport, 1997–99. Advr on management of E Europea broadcasting services, EBU, 1991–93; Trustee, EBU sub-licence scheme, 2005–. Chm Inventure Trust, 2003–07; Dir, Give Them a Sporting Chance, 2003–. Gov., S Devo Coll., 2005–. FRTS 1983. *Recreations:* sport, music, walking. *Address:* Cutwellwall Avonwick, near South Brent, Devon TQ10 9HA.

HART, Alexander Hendry; QC (Canada) 1969; Agent General for British Columbia i the United Kingdom and Europe, 1981–87; *b* Regina, Sask, 17 July 1916; *s* of Alexande Hart and Mary (*née* Davidson); *m* 1948, Janet MacMillan Mackay; three *s* one *d*. *Edu* Dalhousie Law School (LLB). Served War, Royal Canadian Artillery, 1939–45; retire with rank of Major. Read law with McInnis, Mcquarrie and Cooper; called to Bar c Nova Scotia, 1947. Vice-Pres., Marketing, 1967–71; Sen. Vice-Pres., Canadian Na Rlwys, 1971–81. Dep. Internat. Pres., Pacific Basin Economic Council, 1980–81; Pres Canada-UK Chamber of Commerce, 1983; Past Pres., Vancouver Board of Trade; Pa Chm., Western Transportation Adv. Council; Past Mem., University Council of Britis Columbia; Past Pres., Canada Japan Soc. of Vancouver. *Recreation:* golf. *Address:* 151 Dorcas Point Road, Nanoose Bay, BC V9P 9B4, Canada. *Clubs:* Royal & Ancient Go (St Andrews); Vancouver, Men's Canadian, Shaughnessy Golf and Country (Vancouver).

HART, Anelay Colton Wright; Partner in Appleby, Hope & Matthews, 1963–95; *b* March 1934; *s* of Anelay Thomas Bayston Hart and Phyllis Marian Hart; *m* 1979, Margar Gardner (*née* Dewing). *Educ:* Stamford Sch.; King's Coll., London (LLB). Solicitor, retc Advisory Director, World Society for the Protection of Animals, 1982–2003; RSPCA Mem. Council, 1969–95; Hon. Treasurer, 1974–81; Chm. of Council, 1981–8 1985–86, 1988–90; Vice-Chm. Council, 1983–84, 1986–88; Queen Victoria Silve Medal, 1984. President, Rotary Club of South Bank and Eston, 1972–73. *Recreation* walking. *Club:* Royal Over-Seas League.

HART, Anthony; *see* Hart, T. A. A.

HART, Anthony John, OBE 1995; DSC 1945; JP; Chairman, Cunningham Hart & C Ltd, 1985–87 (Senior Partner, 1972–85), retired; *b* 27 Dec. 1923; *s* of Cecil Victor Ha and Kate Winifred Hart (*née* Boncey); *m* 1st, 1947, E. Penelope Morris (*d* 2001); one *s* on *d*; 2nd, 2003, Mrs Mary Eggleton. *Educ:* King's College Sch., Wimbledon; Dauntsey Sch. ACII, FCILA. RN, 1942–46 (Ordinary Seaman to Lieut). Joined Hart & Co., 194 Partner 1952, Senior Partner 1969; on merger name changed to Cunningham Hart & C Mem. Council, CILA, 1964, Pres., 1970–71. Chm., Medic Alert Foundn in UK 1971–83; Governor, Dauntsey's Sch., 1982–93; Mem. Council, Mansfield Hous University Settlement, 1975–90. Liveryman, 1960, Master, 1976–77, Broderers' Co Liveryman, 1979, Mem. Court, 1986, Insurers' Co. Alderman, Ward of Cheap, City c London, 1977–84. FRSA. JP City of London, 1977 (Vice-Chm. of Bench, 1991–93 *Recreation:* golf. *Address:* Dove Barn, Chapel Lane, Minchinhampton, Stroud, Glos GL 9DL. *T:* (01453) 882154. *Clubs:* Army and Navy; Minchinhampton Golf.

HART, Hon. Sir Anthony (Ronald), Kt 2005; **Hon. Mr Justice Hart;** a Judge of th High Court, Northern Ireland, since 2005; *b* 30 April 1946; *s* of Basil and Hazel Hart; 1971, Mary Morehan; two *s* two *d*. *Educ:* Portora Royal Sch., Enniskillen; Trinity Coll. Dublin (BA Mod.); Queen's Univ., Belfast. Called to the Bar of NI, 1969, Bencher 1995 Treas. 2007; called to the Bar, Gray's Inn, 1975; QC (NI) 1983. Jun. Crown Counsel fo Co. Londonderry, 1973–75 and for Co. Down, 1975–79; Asst Boundary Comr, 1980–81 part-time Chm. of Industrial Tribunals, 1980–83; Dep. County Court Judge, 1983–85 County Court Judge, 1985–2005; Recorder of Londonderry, 1985–90; Recorder o Belfast, 1997–2005; Presiding Judge, County Courts, NI, 2002–05. Member: Council o Legal Educn (NI), 1977–83; Review Cttee on Professional Legal Educn in NI, 1984–85 Standing Adv. Commn on Human Rights, 1984–85; Judicial Studies Bd for NI, 1993–97 Criminal Justice Issues (formerly Criminal Justice Consultative) Gp for NI, 1993–99; Civi Justice Reform Gp, 1998–99; Chairman: Council of HM Co. Court Judges in N 1995–98 (Hon. Sec., 1989–95); County Court Rules Cttee (NI), 1997–2005. Chancello Dio. Clogher, C of I, 1990–. Pres., Irish Legal History Soc., 1991–94. *Publications:* History of the King's Serjeants at Law in Ireland: honour rather than advantage?, 200 (Consultant Ed.) Valentine on Criminal Procedure in Northern Ireland, 1989; (contrib. Brehons, Serjeants and Attorneys: studies in the history of the Irish legal profession, 1990 (contrib.) Explorations in Law and History: Irish legal history society discourse 1989–1994, 1995. *Recreation:* reading. *Address:* Royal Courts of Justice, Chichester Street Belfast BT1 3JF.

HART, Sir David (Michael), Kt 2006; OBE 1988; General Secretary, Nationa Association of Head Teachers, 1978–2005; *b* 27 Aug. 1940; *s* of Edwin Henry Hart an Freda Muriel Hart; *m* 1st (marr. diss.); two *s*; 2nd, 1996, Frances Katrina Morton. *Educ* Hurstpierpoint Coll., Sussex. Solicitor 1963, Herbert Ruse Prizeman. Editor, Heads' Lega Guide, 1984. Hon. FCollP 1986; FRSA 1990. Hon. Dr UCE, 1999. *Recreations:* tennis walking, riding. *Address:* Whinby Cottage, Haltcliffe, Hesket Newmarket, Wigton Cumbria CA7 8JT. *T:* (01697) 478318.

HART, David Timothy Nelson; QC 2003; *b* 18 Nov. 1958; *s* of Timothy Norman Har and late Margaret Jane Hart; *m* Rosalind Catherine English; one *s* one *d*. *Educ:* Oundl Sch.; Trinity Coll., Cambridge (BA Classics and Law 1981). Called to the Bar, Middl Temple, 1982; in practice as barrister, 1983–. Mem., Area Cttee, Legal Aid Bd/Lega Services Commn, 1995–; Appeals Officer, EU Emission Trading Scheme, 2005–. Mem. Local Res. Ethics Cttee, St Thomas' Hosp., 2002–. *Publications:* (contrib.) Introduction t Human Rights and the Common Law, ed English and Havers; numerous contribs o envmtl law issues, esp. human rights. *Recreations:* walking through vineyards, sailing, skiing, conversation. *Address:* Lapwing House, Glebe Lane, Burnham Overy Staithe, Norfol PE31 8JQ; *e-mail:* david.hart@lcor.com. *Club:* Overy Staithe Sailing; Downhill Only (Wengen).

HART, Most Rev. Denis James; *see* Melbourne, Archbishop of, (RC).

HART, Edwina, MBE 1998; Member (Lab) Gower, National Assembly for Wales, sinc 1999; Minister for Health and Social Services, since 2007; *b* 26 April 1957; *d* of Eric G Thomas and late Hannah J. Thomas; *m* 1976, Robert B. Hart; one *d*. Member Employment Appeal Tribunal, 1992–99; Broadcasting Council for Wales, 1995–99; Adv Cttee Wales, EOC, 1998–99. Nat. Pres., BIFU, 1992–94; Chair, Wales TUC, 1997–98

National Assembly for Wales: Sec. for Finance, 1999–2000; Minister for Finance, Local Govt and Communities, 2000–03, for Social Justice and Regeneration, 2003–07. Chm., Equal Opportunity Cttee, 2000–02; Mem., SW Wales Regl Cttee, 1999–. Non-executive Director: Chwarae Teg, 1994–99; Wales Millennium Centre, 1997–99. Mem., Council, 1998–99, Ct of Govs, 2000–, Univ. of Wales, Swansea. *Recreations:* reading, music, cookery. *Address:* National Assembly for Wales, Crickhowell House, Cardiff CF99 1NA. *T:* (029) 2089 8400.

HART, Dr (Everard) Peter, CChem, FRSC; Rector, Sunderland Polytechnic, 1981–90; *b* 16 Sept. 1925; *s* of Robert Daniel Hart and Margaret Stokes; *m* Enid Mary Scott; three *s* one *d. Educ:* Wyggeston Grammar Sch., Leicester; Loughborough Coll.; London Univ. (BSc, PhD). Asst Lectr, Lectr and Sen. Lectr, Nottingham and Dist Technical Coll., 1951–57; Sunderland Technical College, later Sunderland Polytechnic: Head of Dept of Chemistry and Biology, 1958–69; Vice-Principal, 1963–69; Dep. Rector, 1969–80. Member: Cttee for Sci. and Technol., CNAA, 1974–77; Gen. Council, Northern Arts, 1982–90. Royal Institute of Chemistry: Mem. Council, 1963–65, 1970–73; Vice-Pres., 1973–75. FRSA 1985. Hon. DCL Sunderland, 1994. *Recreations:* music, opera, theatre, travel. *Address:* Redesdale, The Oval, North End, Durham City DH1 4NE. *T:* (0191) 384 8305.

HART, Sir Graham (Allan), KCB 1996 (CB 1987); Permanent Secretary, Department of Health, 1992–97; *b* 13 March 1940; *s* of Frederick and Winifred Hart; *m* 1964, Margaret Aline Powell; two *s. Educ:* Brentwood Sch.; Pembroke Coll., Oxford (Hon. Fellow 1997). Assistant Principal, 1962, Principal, 1967, Ministry of Health; Asst Registrar, General Medical Council, 1969–71; Principal Private Sec. to Secretary of State for Social Services, 1972–74; Asst Sec., 1974, Under Sec., 1979, DHSS; Under Sec., Central Policy Review Staff, 1982–83; Dep. Sec., DHSS, then DoH, 1984–89; Sec., Home and Health Dept, Scottish Office, 1990–92. Chairman: King's Fund, 1998–2004; Citizens Advice (formerly NACAB), 1999–2004 (Chm., Governance Rev. Gp, 1998–99); Pharmacy Practice Res. Trust, 1999–2005; Appts Cttee, GDC, 2002–; NI Hospice Review Team, 2003; Mem., Audit Commn, 1999–2004. Dir, NHBC, 2004–. *Address:* 1 Priory Lodge, Priory Park, SE3 9UY. *T:* (020) 8297 6537.

HART, Guy William Pulbrook, OBE 1985; HM Diplomatic Service, retired; *b* 24 Dec. 1931; *s* of late Ernest Guy Hart and Muriel Hart (*née* Walkington); *m* 1954, Elizabeth Marjorie (*née* Bennett); one *s* two *d. Educ:* Cranleigh School. Commissioned, Intelligence Corps, 1951–60. British Cellophane Ltd, 1960–62; CRO, 1962; Consular Officer, Kuala Lumpur, 1963–67; Hungarian Language Course, 1967; Second Sec. (Inf.), Budapest, 1968–71; News Dept, FCO, 1971–74; Second Sec. (Econ.), later First Sec. (Inf.), British Mil. Govt, Berlin, 1974–78; First Sec. (Comm.), Port of Spain, 1978–82, Budapest, 1982–85; Asst Head, Inf. Dept, FCO, 1986; Ambassador to the Mongolian People's Republic, 1987–89; High Comr to Seychelles, 1989–91; Head of British delegn, EC monitor mission, Zagreb, 1993–94; Mem., UN Observer mission, SA election; CSCE observer, election in former Yugoslav republic of Macedonia, 1994. *Publication:* White Month's Return: Mongolia comes of age, 1993. *Recreations:* Alpine sports, shooting, painting. *Address:* 1 Marsh Mill, Wargrave Road, Henley on Thames, Oxon RG9 3JD.

HART, Dr James Maurice, CBE 2007; QPM 1999; Commissioner, City of London Police, 2002–06; law enforcement and security consultant; *b* 10 Sept. 1947; *s* of late Lewis Hart and Beatrice Withington; *m* 1993, Julie Anne Russell; two *s. Educ:* Wayneflete Sch., Esher; Kingston Coll.; City Univ. (BSc Hons Systems and Mgt; PhD 1995). Joined Surrey Police, 1966; transf. to Metropolitan Police, as Chief Inspector, 1983; posts at Heathrow Airport, New Scotland Yard and Notting Hill; Chief Superintendent, 1989; Divl Comdr, Wandsworth, 1990–94; Hd, Diplomatic Protection Br., 1994; Asst Chief Constable, Surrey Police, 1994–98: Head: Support Services, 1994–95; Territorial Policing, 1995–96; Specialist Ops, 1997–98; City of London Police: Asst Comr, 1998–2002; Dep. to Comr and Operational Hd, 1998–99; Head, Support Services, 2000–01. Association of Chief Police Officers: Chm., Firearms Licensing Cttee, 1999–2002; Chm., Econ. Crime Cttee, 2002–06. FCMI (FIMgt 1998). Hon. DSc City, 2004. *Publication:* (jtly) Neighbourhood Policing: theoretical basis for community sector policing, 1981. *Recreations:* ski-ing, creating home and garden, walking, cooking and eating.

HART, Matthew Jason; dancer, choreographer, singer and actor; *b* 13 July 1972; *s* of Colin Dennis Hart and Susan Jean Hart (now Rose). *Educ:* Arts Educational Sch., London; Royal Ballet Sch., London. Dancer: London Fest. Ballet, 1984–87; Royal Ballet, 1991–96; Rambert Dance Co., 1996–2000; George Piper Dances, 2001–03; freelance, 2003–; choreographer: Nat. Youth Dance, 1990; Royal Ballet, 1991–2000; Royal Ballet Sch., 1992–98; Birmingham Royal Ballet, 1993; London City Ballet, 1995–96; English Nat. Ballet, 1996; Dance Umbrella, 1996; English Nat. Ballet Sch., 1999; Ballet Deutsche Oper am Rhein, 2000; Hong Kong Ballet, 2001; London Studio Centre, 2002, 2007; George Piper Dances, 2002; K Ballet Co., Tokyo, 2003; Millennium Dance, 2000, 2005, 2006. Created rôles as: (for Royal Opera House 2): Toad, in Wind in the Willows, 2002; The Devil, in The Soldier's Tale, 2004; Oswald Alving, in Ghosts, 2005; Pinocchio (title rôle), 2005; (for Arc Dance Co.) The Prince, in The Anatomy of a Storyteller, 2004; other appearances include: On Your Toes (musical), 2004; Mrs Henderson Presents (film), 2005; Riot at the Rite (film for BBC2), 2006; Babes in Arms (musical), Chichester Fest. Th., 2007; A Midsummer Night's Dream, Regent's Park, 2008; dance appearances include: Betrothal in a Monastery (opera), Glyndebourne, 2006; The Prince in Matthew Bourne's Swan Lake, 2006; Viva La Diva, 2007. Dance coach and critic, Strictly Dance Fever, BBC, 2006. *Address:* c/o Conway Van Gelder Grant Ltd, 18–21 Jermyn Street, SW1Y 6HP. *T:* (020) 7287 0077.

HART, Michael, CBE 1990; MA; Education Consultant, European Commission, 1990–93; *b* 1 May 1928; *yr s* of late Dr F. C. Hardt; *m* 1956, Lida Dabney Adams, PhD (Wisconsin Univ.). *Educ:* Collège Français, Berlin; Landerziehungsheim Schondorf; Keble Coll., Oxford (Exhib.; 1st Cl. Hons History, 1951). Administrative Asst, UNRRA, 1945–47; Asst Master and Head of History, Sherborne Sch., 1951–56; Head of History, 1956–61, and Housemaster of School House, 1961–67, Shrewsbury Sch.; Headmaster of Mill Hill Sch., 1967–74; HM Inspector of Schs, DES, 1974–76; Headmaster, European Sch., Mol, Belgium, 1976–80; Headmaster, European Sch., Luxembourg, 1980–89; Dir, European Classes, Alden Biesen, Belgium, 1989–92. FRSA. Commandeur de l'Ordre de Mérite (Luxembourg), 1989. *Publications:* The EEC and Secondary Education in the UK, 1974; The European Dimension in Primary and Secondary Education, 1992; contrib. to Reader's Digest World Atlas and Atlas of British Isles. *Recreations:* dogs, history, music, bridge. *Address:* 13 St Luke's Court, Hyde Lane, Marlborough, Wilts SN8 1YU.

HART, Prof. Michael, CBE 1993; FRS 1982; FInstP; Professor of Physics, University of Manchester, 1984–93, now Emeritus; Chairman, National Synchrotron Light Source, Brookhaven National Laboratory, 1995–2000; *b* 4 Nov. 1938; *s* of Reuben Harold Victor Hart and Phyllis Mary (*née* White); *m* 1963, Susan Margaret (*née* Powell); three *d. Educ:* Cotham Grammar Sch., Bristol; Bristol Univ. (BSc, PhD, DSc). FInstP 1971. Research Associate: Dept of Materials Science and Engrg, Cornell Univ., 1963–65; Dept of Physics, Bristol Univ., 1965–67; Lectr in Physics, 1967–72, Reader in Physics, 1972–76, Bristol Univ.; Sen. Resident Res. Associate of Nat. Research Council, Nat. Aeronautics and Space Admin Electronics Research Center, Boston, Mass, 1969–70; Special Advisor, Central Policy Review Staff, Cabinet Office, 1975–77; Wheatstone Prof. of Physics and Head of Physics Dept, KCL, 1976–84; Science Programme Co-ordinator (part-time, on secondment), Daresbury Lab., SERC, 1985–88. Prof. of Applied Physics, De Montfort Univ., 1993–98; Hon. Prof. in Engrg, Warwick Univ., 1993–98; Vis. Prof. in Physics, Bristol Univ., 2000–. Amer. Crystallographic Assoc.'s Bertram Eugene Warren Award for Diffraction Physics (jtly with Dr U. Bonse), 1970; Charles Vernon Boys Prize of Inst. of Physics, 1971. *Publications:* numerous contribs to learned jls on x-ray optics, defects in crystals and synchrotron radiation. *Recreations:* tennis, cookery, flying kites. *Address:* 2 Challoner Court, Merchants Landing, Bristol BS1 4RG. *T:* (0117) 921 5291; *e-mail:* michael.hart8@btopenworld.com.

HART, Michael, FCII; non-executive Chairman, Furness Building Society, since 2005 (Director, since 2000); *b* 28 Sept. 1937; *s* of William and Kathleen Hart; *m* (separated); two *s* two *d.* FCII 1971. Man. Dir, 1987–94, Chm., 1994–95, Provincial Insurance plc; Chief Exec., Sun Life and Provincial (Hldgs) plc, 1995–97, retired. Non-exec. Chm., Flemings European Fledgeling Investment Trust plc, 1998–2006; Director: Inter American Insurance Ltd, 1998–2001; Active Languages Ltd, 1999–; Time Group Ltd, 2001–04; PremierLine Ltd, 2003–06; Home & Legacy Holdings Ltd, 2003–06. Mem. Council, Lancaster Univ., 1998–2006. Chm. Trustees, Brewery Arts Centre, 1997–. *Recreations:* walking, wine. *Address:* Holly Tree Barn, Mewith, High Bentham LA2 7AY. *T:* (015242) 62568.

HART, Prof. Oliver Simon D'Arcy, PhD; Professor of Economics, since 1993, and Andrew E. Furer Professor, since 1997, Harvard University; *b* 9 Oct. 1948; *s* of late Philip Montagu D'Arcy Hart, CBE and Ruth Hart; *m* 1974, Rita Goldberg (who retains maiden name); two *s. Educ:* University Coll. Sch.; Univ. of Cambridge (BA 1969); Univ. of Warwick (MA 1972); Princeton Univ. (PhD 1974). Lectr in Econs, Univ. of Essex, 1974–75; Asst Lectr in Econs, subseq. Lectr, Univ. of Cambridge, 1975–81; Fellow of Churchill Coll., Cambridge, 1975–81; Prof. of Economics, LSE, 1982–85; Prog. Dir, Centre for Economic Policy Res., 1983–84; Prof. of Economics, MIT, 1985–93. Centennial Vis. Prof., LSE, 1997–. Sec.-Treas., Amer. Law and Econs Assoc., 2004–05 (Pres., 2006–07); Vice-Pres., AEA, 2006–07. Fellow: Econometric Soc., 1979 (Mem. Council, 1982–); Amer. Acad. of Arts and Scis, 1988; Eur. Corporate Governance Inst., 2002. Corresp. FBA 2000. Editor, Review of Economic Studies, 1979–83. Dr *hc:* Free Univ. of Brussels, 1992; Univ. of Basel, 1994. *Publications:* Firms, Contracts, and Financial Structure, 1995; articles on economic theory in Econometrica, Rev. of Econ. Studies, Jl of Pol Economy. *Recreations:* playing and watching tennis. *Address:* Department of Economics, Harvard University, Cambridge, MA 02138, USA.

HART, Peter; *see* Hart, E. P.

HART, Roger Dudley, CMG 1998; HM Diplomatic Service, retired; Ambassador to Peru, 1999–2003; *b* 29 Dec. 1943; *s* of Alfred John Hart and Emma Jane Hart; *m* 1968, Maria de Los Angeles (Angela) de Santiago Jimenez; two *s. Educ:* St Olave's Grammar Sch., London; Univ. of Birmingham (BA 1965). Entered FO 1965; served British Mil. Govt W Berlin, Bahrain and FCO; First Sec. (Aid), Nairobi, 1975–78; First Sec. (Commercial), Lisbon, 1978–83; FCO, 1983–85; RCDS 1985; BNSC, 1986; Consul-Gen., Rio de Janeiro, 1986–90; Dep. Hd of Mission, Mexico City, 1990–93; Head of Nationality, Treaty and Claims Dept, FCO, 1993–95; Ambassador to Angola, and (non-resident) to São Tomé and Príncipe, 1995–98. Citizen, 1989, Pedro Ernesto Medal, 1990, Rio de Janeiro. *Recreations:* travel, classical music, old silver. *Address:* 7 Rosscourt Mansions, 4 Palace Street, SW1E 5HZ. *Club:* Canning.

HART, Simon Anthony; Chief Executive, Countryside Alliance, since 2003; *b* 15 Aug. 1963; *s* of Anthony Hart and Judith Hart (*née* Christie); *m* 1998, Abigail Kate Holland; one *s* one *d. Educ:* Radley Coll., Oxon; RAC Cirencester (Rural Estate Mgt). MRICS (ARICS 1985–99). Llewellyn Humphreys, Chartered Surveyors, 1988–98; Balfour, Burd & Benson, Chartered Surveyors, 1998–99; Regl Public Relns Officer, 1999, Dir of Campaign for Hunting, 1999–2003, Countryside Alliance. Master and Huntsman, S Pembrokeshire Hunt, 1988–99. Trustee, Sundorne Estate, 1995–. *Recreations:* all aspects of country sports, cricket, piano. *T:* (020) 7840 9210; *e-mail:* simon-hart@countryside-alliance.org. *Clubs:* Farmers; Cresselly Cricket.

HART, (Thomas) Anthony (Alfred), MA; Headmaster, Cranleigh School, 1984–97; *b* 4 March 1940; *er s* of Rev. Arthur Reginald Hart and Florence Ivy Hart; *m* 1971, Daintre Margaret Withiel (*née* Thomas); one *s* one *d. Educ:* City of Bath Sch.; New Coll., Oxford (2nd Cl. Hons PPE; MA); Pres., Oxford Union, 1963. Served with VSO, Mzuzu Secondary Sch., Nyasaland, 1959–60. Asst Principal and Principal, Min. of Transport, 1964–69; seconded to Govt of Malaŵi as Transport Adviser, 1969–70; Principal, DoE and CSD, 1970–73; Head, Voluntary Services Unit, Home Office, 1973–75; Asst Sec., CSD and HM Treasury, 1975–84. *Recreation:* enjoying Cyprus. *Address:* PO Box 59340, Pissouri, 4607, Cyprus. *T:* (25) 222802; *e-mail:* daintrecyprus@cytanet.com.cy.

HART-DAVIS, Dr Adam John; freelance photographer, writer and broadcaster, since 1994; *b* 4 July 1943; *yr s* of Sir Rupert Hart-Davis; *m* 1965, Adrienne Alpin (marr. diss. 1995); two *s. Educ:* Eton; Merton Coll., Oxford (BA 1st Cl. Hons Chemistry 1966; Hon. Fellow 2006); York Univ. (DPhil 1968). Post-doctoral Research: Univ. of Alberta, Edmonton, 1969–71; Univ. of Oxford, 1971; College Science Editor, Clarendon Press (OUP), 1971–77; Researcher, 1977–83, Producer, 1983–94, Yorkshire Television. Presenter: TV series: Local Heroes, 1992–2000; Hart-Davis on History, 1998, 1999; Secret City, 2000; What the Romans Did for Us, 2000; What the Victorians Did for Us, 2001; Science Shack, 2001, 2003; Adam Hart-Davis says Come to Your Senses, 2001; Tomorrow's World, 2002; What the Tudors Did for Us, 2002; What the Stuarts Did for Us, 2002; Industrial Nation, 2003; What the Ancients Did for Us, 2005; How London Was Built, 2005, 2006, 2007; The Cosmos: a beginner's guide, 2007; Just Another Day, 2007; How Britain Was Built, 2008; radio series: Inventors Imperfect, 1999–2003; High Resolution, 2001; Elements of Surprise, 2001; Engineering Solutions, 2004, 2006, 2007; Eureka Years, 2004, 2005, 2007, 2008. Pres., Wandle Valley Mapping project; Member: Bureau of Freelance Photographers; Newcomen Soc.; Patron: Wrexham Science Fest., 1998; Cycle West, 2000; Brede Steam Engine Soc., 2002; Theatre Odyssey, 2002; The Garden Sci. Trust, 2003; Museum of Sci. and Industry, Manchester, 2003; ACT, 2003; Ideas 21; Assoc. of Lighthouse Keepers, 2003; Bognor Birdman, 2004; Holgate Windmill Preservation Soc., 2004; Crank It Up, 2004; Life Pres., Ellenroad Trust, 2004. Hon. Member: British Toilet Assoc.; Associates of Discovery Museum, 2003. CompILE. Hon. Fellow, Soc. of Dyers and Colourists, 2005; Hon. FRSC 2007; Hon. FRPS 2007. DUniv: York, 2000; Brunel, 2007; Hon DTech: Loughborough, 2001; UWE, 2005; Hon. DSc: Sheffield, Bradford, 2001; Birmingham, 2002; Bristol, Sheffield Hallam, Leicester, 2003; QUB, 2004; Hon. DCL Northumbria, 2002; Hon. DLitt Bath, 2004. Gerald Frewer Meml Trophy, Instn of Engrg Designers, 1999; first medal for public promotion of engrg, Royal Acad. of Engrg, 2002; Sir Henry Royce Meml Medal, IIE, 2003; Judges' Award for Educnl TV, RTS, 2003. *Publications:* Don't Just Sit There!, 1980; (with Hilary Lawson)

Where There's Life..., 1982; Scientific Eye, 1986; Mathematical Eye, 1989; World's Weirdest "True" Ghost Stories, 1991; (with Susan Blackmore) Test Your Psychic Powers, 1995; Thunder, Flush and Thomas Crapper, 1997; Science Tricks, 1997; (with Paul Bader) The Local Heroes Book of British Ingenuity, 1997; (with Paul Bader) More Local Heroes, 1998; Amazing Math Puzzles, 1998; Eurekaaargh!, 1999; (with Paul Bader) The Local Heroes Book of DIY Science, 2000; Chain Reactions, 2000; What the Victorians Did for Us, 2001; (with Emily Troscianko) Henry Winstanley and the Eddystone Lighthouse, 2002; What the Tudors and Stuarts Did for Us, 2002; Talking Science, 2004; What the Past Did for Us, 2004; Why Does a Ball Bounce?, 2005; (with Emily Troscianko) Taking the Piss, 2006; Just Another Day, 2006; (with Paul Bader) The Cosmos: a beginner's guide, 2007; (ed) History: the definitive visual guide, 2007. *Recreations:* cycling, ping pong, photography, drinking wine.

See also P. D. Hart-Davis.

HART-DAVIS, (Peter) Duff; author and journalist; *b* 3 June 1936; *er s* of Sir Rupert Hart-Davis; *m* 1961, Phyllida Barstow; one *s* one *d*. *Educ:* Eton; Worcester Coll., Oxford (BA 1960). Nat. Service, Coldstream Guards, 1955–57. Joined Sunday Telegraph, 1961; Editor, News Background page, 1966–70; feature writer, 1971–75; Literary Editor, 1975–76; Asst Editor, 1976–78. Country Columnist, Independent, 1986–2001. *Publications:* Ascension, 1972; Peter Fleming, 1974; Monarchs of the Glen, 1978; Hitler's Games, 1986; (ed) The Letters and Journals of Sir Alan Lascelles: Vol. 1, End of an Era, 1986; Vol. 2, In Royal Service, 1989; Armada, 1988; Country Matters, 1989; The House the Berrys Built, 1990; Wildings: the secret garden of Eileen Soper, 1991; Further Country Matters, 1992; When the Country Went to Town, 1997; Raoul Millais, 1998; Fauna Britannica, 2002; Audubon's Elephant, 2003; (ed) Pavilions of Splendour, 2004; Honorary Tiger, 2005; (ed) King's Counsellor, 2006; *fiction:* The Megacull, 1968; The Gold of St Matthew, 1970; Spider in the Morning, 1972; The Heights of Rimring, 1980; Level Five, 1982; Fire Falcon, 1983; The Man-eater of Jassapur, 1985; Horses of War, 1991. *Recreations:* opera, wine, cutting and splitting firewood, deer. *Address:* Owlpen Farm, Uley, Glos GL11 5BZ. *T:* (01453) 860239.

See also A. J. Hart-Davis.

HART DYKE, Captain David, CBE 1990; LVO 1980; RN; Clerk to Worshipful Company of Skinners, 1990–2003; *b* 3 Oct. 1938; *s* of Comdr Rev. Eric Hart Dyke and Mary Hart Dyke; *m* 1967, Diana Margaret, *d* of Sir William Luce, GBE, KCMG; two *d*. *Educ:* St Lawrence College, Ramsgate; BRNC Dartmouth. RN 1958; served Far East and Middle East; navigation specialist; Exec. Officer, HMS Hampshire, 1974–76; Staff, RN Staff Coll., 1976–78; Comdr, HM Yacht Britannia, 1978–80; Captain HMS Coventry; action in Falklands, 1982; ACOS to C-in-C Fleet, 1982–84; Asst Naval Attaché, Washington, 1985–87; Dir, Naval Recruiting, 1987–89. ADC to the Queen, 1988–89. *Publication:* Four Weeks in May: the loss of HMS Coventry - a captain's story, 2007. *Recreations:* water-colouring, garden design, military history, tennis. *Address:* Hambledon House, Hambledon, Hants PO7 4RU. *T:* (023) 9263 2380.

HART DYKE, Sir David (William), 10th Bt *cr* 1677, of Horeham, Sussex; journalist; *b* 5 Jan. 1955; *s* of Sir Derek William Hart Dyke, 9th Bt and Dorothy Moses; *S* father, 1987. *Educ:* Ryerson Polytechnical Institute (BA). *Recreations:* portage camping, ice hockey, reading. *Heir: uncle* (Oliver) Guy Hart Dyke [*b* 9 Feb. 1928; *m* 1974, Sarah Alexander, *d* of late Rev. Eric Hart Dyke; one *s* one *d*]. *Address:* 28 King Street West, Apt 14B, Stoney Creek, ON L8G 1H4, Canada.

HART-LEVERTON, Colin Allen; QC 1979; a Recorder of the Crown Court, since 1979; *b* 10 May 1936; *s* of Monty Hart-Leverton and Betty (*née* Simmonds); one *s*; *m* 1990, Kathi Jo, *d* of Hal and Jan Davidson. *Educ:* Stowe; self-taught thereafter. Mem., Inst. of Taxation, 1957 (youngest to have ever qualified); called to the Bar, Middle Temple, 1957 (youngest to have ever qual.). Contested (L): Bristol West, 1959 (youngest cand.); Walthamstow West, 1964. Prosecuting Counsel, Central Criminal Court, 1974–79; Dep. Circuit Judge, 1975; Attorney-at-Law, Turks and Caicos Islands, Caribbean, 1976. Occasional television and radio broadcasts. *Recreations:* table-tennis, jazz. *Address:* 1 Mitre Court Buildings, Temple, EC4Y 7BS. *T:* (020) 7452 8900.

HARTE, (Catherine) Miriam; DL; Director, Beamish, North of England Open Air Museum, 2001–07; *b* 3 Aug. 1960; *d* of Joseph and Mary Harte. *Educ:* Trinity Coll., Dublin (BA Law 1981). Chartered Accountant, 1985; FCA 1995. Trainee, Arthur Andersen & Co., 1981–86; Finance Manager, UK and Europe/US, Procter & Gamble, 1986–97; freelance trng/consulting, 1997–98; Dir, Bede's World, 1998–2001. Board Member: MLA NE (formerly NE MLAC), 2001–07; NE Tourism Adv. Bd, 2004–07. Dir, Audiences NE, 2004–. Non-exec. Dir, Sunderland City Hosps Trust, 2007–. DL Co. Durham, 2007. *Recreations:* riding, walking, cooking, theatre, travelling. *Address:* Thorn Cottage, 125 Kells Lane, Low Fell, NE9 5XY. *T:* (0191) 487 9258; *e-mail:* miriamharte@gmail.com.

HARTE, Julia Kathleen; *see* McKenzie, J. K.

HARTE, Dr Michael John; consultant in information technology, since 1995; Director General Information Technology Systems, Ministry of Defence, 1994–95; *b* 15 Aug. 1936; *s* of late Harold Edward Harte and Marjorie Irene Harte; *m* 1st, 1962, Diana Hayes (marr. diss. 1971); 2nd, 1975, Mary Claire Preston; four step *d*. *Educ:* Charterhouse; Trinity Coll., Cambridge (BA); University Coll., London (PhD; Dip. in Biochem. Engrg). Sen. Scientific Officer, Micro-biol Res. Estab., MoD, 1963; Principal, MoD, 1967; Private Sec. to Minister of State for Def., 1972; Asst Sec., Central Policy Rev. Staff, 1973; Asst Sec., MoD, 1975–77; Counsellor, Budget and Infrastructure, UK Delegn to NATO, 1977–81; Chm., NATO Civil and Mil. Budget Cttees, 1981–83; Asst Sec., MoD, 1983–85; Assistant Under Secretary of State: (Dockyard Planning Team), MoD, 1985–87; (Personnel) (Air), MoD, 1987–90; (Resources), MoD, 1990–93. Non-exec. Dir, GlaxoChem., 1988–91. FRSA 1995. *Publications:* Wadhurst Then and Now, 2003; The Day Wadhurst Changed, 2006. *Recreations:* local history and local website. *Address:* Greenman Farm, Wadhurst, E Sussex TN5 6LE. *T:* (01892) 783292.

HARTE, Miriam; *see* Harte, C. M.

HARTER, Caryl, (Mrs David Harter); *see* Churchill, C.

HARTILL, Edward Theodore, OBE 2004; FRICS; Business Development Advisor, Corderoy, international chartered quantity surveyors and cost consultants, since 2008; City Surveyor, City of London Corporation (formerly Corporation of London), 1985–2008; *b* 23 Jan. 1943; *s* of late Clement Augustus Hartill and Florence Margarita Hartill; *m* 1975, Gillian Ruth Todd; two *s*, and two *s* from previous marr. *Educ:* Priory Sch. for Boys, Shrewsbury; Coll. of Estate Management, London Univ. BSc (Estate Management); FRICS 1978. Joined Messrs Burd and Evans, Land Agents, Shrewsbury, 1963; Estates Dept, Legal and Gen. Assce Soc., 1964–73; Property Investment Dept, Guardian Royal Exchange Assce Gp, 1973–85 (Hd Office Manager, 1980–85). Vis. Lectr in Law of Town Planning and Compulsory Purchase, Hammersmith and W London Coll. of Advanced Business Studies, 1968–78. Royal Institution of Chartered Surveyors: Member: Gen Practice Divl Council, 1989–97 (Pres., 1992–93); Governing Council, 1990–2004; Hon Treas., 2000–04. Mem., Assoc. of Chief Estates Surveyors and Property Managers in Local Govt (formerly Local Authority Valuers Assoc.), 1985–2007 (Mem., Nat. Council 1988–2007; Pres., 1996–97); Mem. Steering Gp, 1992–99, and Chm., Property Services Sub-Gp, 1992–99, Construction Industry Standing Conf.; Founder Mem. and Chm. Property Services NTO, 1999–2004; Vice-Chm., Asset Skills, 2004–07 (Chm., 2003). Mem. Council, Univ. of London, 2004–08 (Dep. Chm., Estates Cttee, 2006–08; Mem. Bd of Trustees, 2008–). Gov. and Trustee, Coram (formerly Coram Family), 2006– (Vice Chm., 2007–08; Chm., 2008–). Hon. Mem., Investment Property Forum, 1995. Hon Associate, Czech Chamber of Appraisers, 1992. Mem., British Schs Exploring Soc. FRSA 1993. Liveryman, Worshipful Co. of Chartered Surveyors, 1985– (Mem., Court of Assistants, 1991–; Master, 2003–04). *Publications:* occasional lectures and articles on professional topics. *Recreations:* hill walking, travel, cars and GT racing. *Address:* 215 Sheen Lane, East Sheen, SW14 8LE. *T:* (020) 8878 4494.

See also R. J. Hartill.

HARTILL, Rosemary Jane; independent broadcaster, writer, and non-executive director; Religious Affairs Correspondent, BBC, 1982–88; *b* 11 Aug. 1949; *d* of late Clement Augustus Hartill and Florence Margarita Ford. *Educ:* Wellington Girls' High Sch., Salop; Bristol Univ. (BA (Hons) English). Editor: Tom Stacey (Publishing) Ltd 1970–73; David and Charles Ltd, 1973–75; Sen. Non-fiction Editor, Hamish Hamilton Children's Books Ltd, 1975–76; freelance journalist and broadcaster, 1976–82; freelance book and ballet reviewer, TES, 1976–80; Religious Affairs Reporter, BBC, 1979–82 Reporter: BBC Everyman Prog., 1987; ITV Human Factor series, 1989–92; Presenter BBC Woman's Hour (NE edns), 1989–90; Meridian Books (BBC World Service), and numerous other progs. Founder, Rosemary Hartill & Associates, 1996; Co-Founder Voyager TV Ltd, 1997; non-executive Director: Shared Interest, 1996–2005; Ethical Investment Res. Service, 1997–2001. Board Member: Nat. Probation Service Northumbria, 2001–07; (non-exec.) Northumberland Tyne and Wear Strategic HA 2002–05; Courts Bd, Northumbria, 2004–07; Youth Justice Bd for England and Wales 2004–. Trustee, Alternatives to Violence Project, 1997–2000 (Facilitator, 1996–) Facilitator, Barter Books bookgp, Alnwick, 2003–. Mem., Soc. of Friends (Mem., Former Yugoslavia Project Mgt Gp, 2000–02). FRSA 2001. Hon. DLitt: Hull, 1995; Bristol 2000. Sandford St Martin Trust personal award for outstanding contrib. to religious broadcasting, 1994, and other awards. *Publications:* (ed) Emily Brontë: poems, 1973; Wild Animals, 1978; In Perspective, 1988; Writers Revealed, 1989; Were You There?, 1995 (ed) Florence Nightingale, 1996. *Recreations:* wildlife, modern art and architecture, being in Northumberland. *Address:* Old Post Office, Eglingham, Alnwick, Northumberland NE66 2TX.

See also E. T. Hartill.

HARTING, Henry Maria Robert Egmont M.; *see* Mayr-Harting.

HARTINGTON, Marquess of; courtesy title of heir of Duke of Devonshire, not used by current heir.

HARTLAND, Michael; *see* James, M. L.

HARTLAND-SWANN, Julian Dana Nimmo, CMG 1992; HM Diplomatic Service retired; Thai-Europe business consultant, since 1997; *b* 18 Feb. 1936; *s* of late Prof. J. J Hartland-Swann and of Mrs Kenlis Hartland-Swann (*née* Taylour); *m* 1st, 1960, Ann Deirdre Green (*d* 2000); one *s* one *d*; 2nd, 2004, Julie Katherine Ryan. *Educ:* Stowe Lincoln Coll., Oxford (History). HM Forces, 1955–57. Entered HM Diplomatic Service 1960; 3rd Sec., Brit. Embassy, Bangkok, 1961–65; 2nd, later 1st Sec., FO, 1965–68; 1st Sec., Berlin, 1968–71; 1st Sec. and Head of Chancery, Vienna, 1971–74; FCO, 1975–77 Counsellor, 1977; Ambassador to Mongolian People's Republic, 1977–79; Counsellor and Dep. Head of Mission, Brussels, 1979–83; Head of SE Asian Dept, FCO, 1983–85 Consul Gen., Frankfurt, 1986–90; Ambassador to Burma (Myanmar), 1990–95; Exec. Dir Eur. Business Inf. Centre, Delegn of the EC to Thailand, 1995–97. *Recreations:* French food, sailing, restoring ruins. *Address:* Résidence Hof Ten Berg, Clos Hof Ten Berg 30 1200 Brussels, Belgium.

HARTLEY, Prof. Brian Selby, PhD; FRS 1971; Chairman, BioConversion Technologies Ltd, since 2006; Professor of Biochemistry, Imperial College, University of London, 1974–91, Emeritus Professor, 1991; Director, 1982–91, Senior Research Fellow 1991–94, Centre for Biotechnology; *b* 16 April 1926; *s* of Norman and Hilda Hartley; *m* 1949, Kathleen Maude Vaughan; three *s* one *d*. *Educ:* Queens' Coll., Cambridge (BA 1947, MA 1952); Univ. of Leeds (PhD 1952). ICI Fellow, Univ. of Cambridge, 1952 Helen Hay Whitney Fellow, Univ. of Washington, Seattle, USA, 1958; Fellow and Lect in Biochemistry, Trinity Coll., Cambridge, 1964; Scientific Staff, MRC Laboratory of Molecular Biology, 1961–74. Chm., Agrol Ltd, 1993–2000. Mem. Council: EMBO (European Centre for Molecular Biology), 1978–84; Royal Soc., 1982–84. Hon. Mem. Amer. Soc. of Biological Chemists, 1977. British Drug Houses Medal for Analytical Biochemistry, 1969. *Publications:* papers and articles in scientific jls and books. *Recreations* fishing, gardening. *Address:* Grove Cottage, Smith Street, Elsworth, Cambridge CB3 8HY.

HARTLEY, Caroline Mary; *see* Rookes, C. M.

HARTLEY, David Fielding, PhD; CEng; FBCS, CITP; Fellow, Clare College Cambridge, since 1987 (Steward, 2002–05); *b* 14 Sept. 1937; *s* of late Robert M. Hartley and Sheila E. Hartley, LRAM; *m* 1960, Joanna Mary (*d* 1998), *d* of late Stanley and Constance Bolton; one *s* two *d*. *Educ:* Rydal Sch.; Clare Coll., Cambridge (MA, PhD 1963). FBCS 1968; CEng 1990; CITP 2004. University of Cambridge: Sen. Asst in Research, Mathematical Lab., 1964–65; Asst Dir of Research, 1966–67; Univ. Lectr 1967–70; Dir, Univ. Computing Service, 1970–94; Jun. Research Fellow, Churchill Coll., Cambridge, 1964–67; Fellow, Darwin Coll., Cambridge, 1969–86; Chief Exec. UK Educn and Res. Networking Assoc., 1994–97; Exec. Dir, Cambridge Crystallographic Data Centre, 1997–2002. British Computer Society: Mem. Council 1970–73, 1977–80, 1985–90, 1998–2002; Vice Pres. (Technical), 1985–87, (External Relns), 1987–90; Dep. Pres., 1998–99; Pres., 1999–2000. Chairman: Inter-University Cttee on Computing, 1972–74; Computer Conservation Soc., 2007–; Mem., Computer Board for Univs and Research Councils, 1979–83; Mem. Council of Management Numerical Algorithms Gp Ltd, 1979–2006 (Chm., 1986–97); adviser to Prime Minister, Information Technology Adv. Panel, 1981–86; DTI Hon. Adviser in Information Technology (on sabbatical leave), 1983; Mem. various Govt, Res. Council and Industry cttees and consultancies. Mem., BBC Science Consultative Gp, 1984–87. Dir, CADCentre Ltd, 1983–94. Governor, Rydal Sch., 1982–88. Medal of Merits, Nicholas Copernicus Univ., Poland, 1984. *Publications:* papers in scientific jls on operating systems, programming languages, computing service management. *Address:* Clare College, Cambridge CB2 1TN.

HARTLEY, Prof. Frank Robinson; DL; CChem, FRSC; Vice-Chancellor, Cranfield University (formerly Cranfield Institute of Technology), 1989–2006; *b* 29 Jan. 1942; *s* of Sir Frank Hartley, CBE; *m* 1964, Valerie Peel; three *d*. *Educ:* King's College Sch., Wimbledon (Sambrooke Schol.; Fellow, 2003); Magdalen Coll., Oxford (Demy; BA, MA, DPhil, DSc). FRAeS 1996. Post-doctoral Fellow, Commonwealth Scientific and Industrial Research Organisation, Div. of Protein Chemistry, Melbourne, Aust., 1966–69; Imperial Chemical Industries Research Fellow and Tutor in Physical Chemistry, University Coll. London, 1969–70; Lectr in Inorganic Chemistry, Univ. of Southampton, 1970–75; Professor of Chemistry and Head of Dept of Chemistry and Metallurgy, 1975–82, Acting Dean, 1982–84, Principal and Dean, 1984–89, RMCS, Shrivenham. Chm., Cranfield IT Inst., 1989–90 (Dir, 1986–89); Man. Dir, CIT (Holdings) Ltd, 1993–2006 (Dir, 1989–93); Chm., CIM Inst., 1990–2006; Dir, Cranfield Ventures Ltd, 1990–2006 (Man. Dir, 2000–06); non-executive Director: T & N, 1989–98; Eastern Regl Adv. Bd, National Westminster Bank, 1990–92; Kalon, 1994–99; Kenwood, 1995–99; Hunting-BRAE Ltd, 1999–2000; Bedfordshire TEC, 1994–96. Sen. Travelling Fellow, ACU, 1986. Special Advr to Prime Minister on defence systems, 1988–91; Special Advr to H of L Select Cttee on Sci. and Technol., 1994–95; Mem., Parly Scientific Cttee, 1986– (Mem. Council and Gen. Purposes Cttee, 1992–98; Vice-Pres., 1995–98). Member: Internat. Adv. Bd, Kanagawa Acad. of Sci. and Technol., Japan, 1989–98; Bd, Internat. Foundn for Artificial Intelligence, 1990–98. Chm., Lorch Foundn, 1995–2006; Dir, Shuttleworth Trust, 1994–97. Member: Council, IoD, 2000–; Eastern Regl Bd, CBI, 2000–06. Gov., Welbeck Coll., 1984–89; Mem. Court, Bath Univ., 1982–89. DL Beds, 2005. Mem., Oxford Union. FRSA 1988. Editor-in-Chief, Brassey's New Battlefield Weapons Systems and Technology series, 1988–. *Publications:* The Chemistry of Platinum and Palladium (Applied Science), 1973; Elements of Organometallic Chemistry (Chemical Soc.), 1974, Japanese edn 1981, Chinese edn 1989; (with C. Burgess and R. M. Alcock) Solution Equilibria, 1980, Russian edn 1983; (with S. Patai) The Chemistry of the Metal—Carbon Bond, vol. 1 1983, vol. 2 1984, vol. 3 1985, vol. 4 1987, vol. 5 1989; Supported Metal Complexes, 1985, Russian edn 1987; The Chemistry of Organophosphorus Compounds, vol. 1, 1990, vol. 2, 1992, vol. 3, 1994, vol. 4, 1996; Chemistry of the Platinum Group Metals, 1991; papers in inorganic, coordination and organometallic chemistry in major English, Amer. and Aust. chemical jls. *Recreations:* gardening, swimming, cliff walking, reading. *Clubs:* Institute of Directors; Shrivenham.

HARTLEY, His Honour Gilbert Hillard; retired; a Circuit Judge (formerly Judge of County Courts), 1967–82; *b* 11 Aug. 1917; *s* of late Percy Neave Hartley and Nellie Bond Hartley (*née* Hillard); *m* 1948, Jeanne, *d* of late C. W. Gall, Leeds; one *s* two *d*. *Educ:* Ashville, Harrogate; Exeter Coll., Oxford. Called to the Bar, Middle Temple, 1939. Served with Army, 1940–46. Recorder of Rotherham, 1965–67; Dep. Chm., WR of Yorkshire QS, 1965–71. *Address:* 3 Rossett Beck, Harrogate HG2 9NT.

HARTLEY, John Robert; Headteacher, Saffron Walden County High School, since 2004; *b* 4 Oct. 1955; *s* of Peter and Josephine Hartley; *m* 1982, Susanna Newton; two *s* one *d*. *Educ:* Oundle Sch.; St Catharine's Coll., Cambridge (BA 1977, PGCE). Physics teacher, Aylesbury GS, 1978–83; Sen. Physicist, Hazelwick Sch., Crawley, 1983–87; Hd of Sci., St Joseph's RC Comprehensive Sch., Swindon, 1988–90; Dep. Headteacher, Moulsham High Sch., Chelmsford, 1991–97; Headteacher, Notley High Sch., Braintree, 1997–2003. *Recreations:* fell-walking, cycling, local and social history. *Address:* Saffron Walden County High School, Audley End Road, Saffron Walden, Essex CB11 4UH. *T:* (01799) 513030, *Fax:* (01799) 513031; *e-mail:* jhartley@saffronwalden.essex.sch.uk.

HARTLEY, Prof. Keith, PhD; Professor of Economics, since 1987, and Director, Centre for Defence Economics, since 1990, University of York; *b* 14 July 1940; *s* of Walter and Ivy Hartley; *m* 1966, Winifred Kealy; one *s* two *d*. *Educ:* Univ. of Hull (BSc Econs; PhD 1974). Dir, Inst. for Res. in Social Scis, Univ. of York, 1982–94. NATO Res. Fellow, 1977–79 and 1986–87. *Publications:* Political Economy of NATO, 1999; (with T. Sandler) Economics of Defense, 2001; (with T. Sandler) Economics of Conflict, 2003; (with T. Sandler) Handbook of Defense Economics, vol. 2, 2007; (with C. Tisdell) Microeconomic Policy, 2008. *Recreations:* walking, angling, football, reading. *Address:* Centre for Defence Economics, University of York, York YO10 5DD. *T:* (01904) 433753.

HARTLEY, Richard Anthony; QC 2008; a Recorder, since 2002; *b* Crewe, 7 Nov. 1962; *s* of Dr Tony Hartley and Renée Hartley; *m* 1987, Clare Meeke; two *s* two *d*. *Educ:* Haslington Co. Primary Sch.; Sandbach Sch.; Liverpool Univ. (LLB Hons 1984). Called to the Bar, Middle Temple, 1985; in practice as barrister, Manchester, specialising in personal injury and clinical negligence cases, 1985–. *Recreations:* football (Manchester City), squash, snowboarding, classic cars, pottering in workshop, hill walking. *Address:* Cobden House Chambers, 19 Quay Street, Manchester M3 3HN. *T:* (0161) 833 6000.

HARTLEY, Richard Leslie Clifford; QC 1976; *b* 31 May 1932; *s* of late Arthur Clifford Hartley, CBE and Nina Hartley. *Educ:* Marlborough Coll.; Sidney Sussex Coll., Cambridge (MA). Called to the Bar, Gray's Inn, 1956, Bencher, 1986. Former Chm., Appeal Bd, Jockey Club; Chm., Appeal Bd, HRA. *Recreations:* golf, tennis, horse racing. *Address:* 15 Chesham Street, SW1X 8ND. *T:* (020) 7235 2420. *Clubs:* Garrick, MCC; Woking Golf; Rye Golf; St Enodoc Golf; New Zealand Golf (Weybridge).

HARTMANN, Dr Peter, Hon. KBE 1992; Ambassador of Germany to France, 1998–2001; *b* 9 Oct. 1935; *m* Baroness Lonny von Blomberg-Hartmann. *Educ:* Frankfurt; Papal Univ., Rome (LPH); Cologne; Fribourg Univ. (DPhil). Foreign Service, 1965; Washington, 1966; Karachi, 1968; EC Brussels, 1971; Buenos Aires, 1978; Head, Foreign Relations Office, CDU, 1981–84; Federal Chancellery: Head, European Policy, 1984–87; Asst Under-Sec., Foreign, Security and Develt Policy, 1987–90; Dep. Under-Sec., Foreign Security Policy, and Advr to Federal Chancellor, 1991–93; Ambassador to UK, 1993–95; Under Sec. of State, Foreign Min., Germany, 1995–98. *Address:* 53343 Wachtberg, Auf dem Reeg 19, Germany.

HARTNACK, Paul Richard Samuel, CB 1999; Comptroller General and Chief Executive, The Patent Office, 1990–99; *b* 17 Nov. 1942; *s* of Carl Samuel and Maud Godden Hartnack; *m* 1966, Marion Quirk; two *s*. *Educ:* Hastings Grammar Sch. Clerical and Exec. posts, BoT, 1961–67; Asst Sec., Cttee of Enquiry into Civil Air Transport, 1967–68; Second Sec., British Embassy, Paris, 1969–71; Exec. posts, DTI, 1972–78; Asst Sec., NEB, 1978–80; Sec., Brit. Technology Gp, 1981–85; Asst Sec., Finance and Resource Management Div., DTI, 1985–89. *Recreation:* gardening. *Address:* 24 Benslow Rise, Hitchin, Herts SG4 9QX. *T:* (01462) 457312.

HARTNETT, David Anthony, CB 2003; a Commissioner and Director General, HM Revenue and Customs, since 2005; *b* 25 Feb. 1951; *s* of George Peter Hartnett and Mary Christine Hartnett (*née* O'Donoghue); *m* 1977, Aileen Patricia Mary O'Dempsey; two *s* one *d*. *Educ:* Hampton Sch.; Birmingham Univ. (BA Hons Latin). Inland Revenue, 1976–2005: Inspector of Taxes, 1976–86; Investigation Manager, 1986–91; Dir, Financial Intermediaries and Claims Office, 1991–96; Asst Dir, Personal Tax Div., 1996–98; Dir, Savings and Investment and Capital and Valuation Divs, 1998–99; Dir, Capital and Savings Div., 1999–2000; a Comr, 2000–05; a Dep. Chm., 2003–05. *Recreations:* food, wine, Marcus Tullius Cicero. *Address:* HM Revenue and Customs, 100 Parliament Street, SW1A 2BQ. *T:* (020) 7147 2180.

HARTNOLL, Mary Charmian, CBE 1990; Director of Social Work, Glasgow City Council, 1996–98; *b* 31 May 1939; *d* of Rev. Sydney W. Hartnoll and Margaret Hartnoll. *Educ:* Colston's Girls' Grammar Sch., Bristol; Bedford Coll., Univ. of London (BA Hons); Univ. of Liverpool (HO Cert. in Child Care). Child Care Officer, Dorset CC, 1961–63; various posts, County Borough of Reading, 1963–74; Asst Dir, Berks CC, 1974–75; Divl Officer, Reading, 1975–77; Dir of Social Work: Grampian Regl Council, 1978–93; Strathclyde Regl Council, 1993–96. Chm., E Park, Glasgow, 2000–01; Convener, Scottish Commn for Regulation of Care, 2001–06. Hon. LLD Robert Gordon Univ., 1993. *Recreations:* natural history, walking, music, theatre going. *Address:* 36 Norfolk Road, Aberdeen AB10 6JR.

HARTOP, Barry; Chief Executive, Telenor Business Solutions (formerly Nextra (UK) Ltd), 2001–03; *b* 15 Aug. 1942; *s* of Philip William Hartop and Constance Winifred (*née* Drew); *m* 1966, Sandra Swan; one *s* one *d*. *Educ:* Durham Univ. (BSc Hons Chem. Engrg). Prodn and technical mgt, Lever Bros Ltd, 1965–72; Unilever PLC: Chm., Cost Reduction and R&D, 1972–80; Man. Dir, European Business Centre, 1980–83; Chm. and Man. Dir, Lever Industrial Ltd, 1983–89; Man. Dir, Gestetner Hldgs, 1989–92; Chief Executive: WDA, 1994–96; Millennium Exhibn, 1996; Man. Dir, Norsk Data, 1997–2001. Chairman: Hammicks Bookshops Ltd, 1994–98; Locum Gp Ltd, 1997–2002; Reed Health Gp plc, 2003–06. Gov., Royal Grammar Sch., Guildford, 1991– (Chm., RGS Foundn, 2004–). *Recreations:* tennis, keep fit, gardening. *Address:* Linton House, Snowdenham Links Road, Bramley, Guildford, Surrey GU5 0BX. *T:* (01483) 890612. *Club:* County (Guildford).

HARTRIDGE, David Charles, CMG 2001; Senior Director, White and Case International Trade, Geneva, since 2002; *b* 22 April 1939; *s* of Sidney George Hartridge and Mabel Kate (*née* Hunt); *m* 1965, Dorothy Ann Ling (marr. diss. 1997); two *d*. *Educ:* Windsor Grammar Sch.; Oriel Coll., Oxford (MA). BoT, 1961–71; First Sec., UK Mission, Geneva, 1971–75; Asst Sec., DTI, 1977–79; Counsellor, UK Repn to EEC, Brussels, 1979–80; Chef de Cabinet, GATT, 1980–85; Dir, GATT and WTO, 1985–2001, Dir, Services Div., 1993–2001, Dir-in-Charge, May–Sept. 1999; Special Advr to DG, WTO, 2001–02. *Recreations:* bird watching, music, history. *Address:* 23 Route de Sauverny, Grilly 01220, France. *T:* (4) 50201993; Hollow Stones, Nailsworth Hill, Nailsworth, Stroud, Glos GL6 0AW. *T:* (01453) 836 884.

HARTWELL, Sir (Francis) Anthony (Charles Peter), 6th Bt *cr* 1805, of Dale Hall, Essex; marine consultant; Director, International Diamond Drilling, West Africa, since 1999; survey and inspection assignments, oil, gas and shipping services, Lagos, Nigeria, since 2000; *b* 1 June 1940; *o s* of Sir Brodrick William Charles Elwin Hartwell, 5th Bt and of his 1st wife, Marie Josephine Hartwell, *d* of S. P. Mullins; *S* father, 1993; *m* 1968, Barbara Phyllis Rae (marr. diss. 1989), *d* of H. Rae Green; one *s*. *Educ:* Thames Nautical Coll., HMS Worcester. Cadet, RNR. Master's Foreign Going (Cl. 1) Cert. MNI, MRIN. Captain (Master Mariner), 1972. Sea Service Navigating Officer, Asst Nautical Inspector, then Cargo Supt (Overseas Containers Ltd) London, P&O Group, 1958–71; Chief Officer/Master, North Sea ops, Ocean Inchcape Ltd, 1972–73; P&O Cadet Trng Officer, 1973–75; overseas port management, Nigeria, Papua New Guinea and Saudi Arabia, 1975–87; Branch Manager, Lloyds Agency, Dammam, Saudi Arabia, 1987–89; marine surveyor and nautical consultant, Saudi Arabia, The Maldives, Nigeria, Cyprus, 1989–93; Man. Dir, Universal UKI Ltd, Nigeria, 1999. *Recreations:* ocean sailing, scuba diving, photography. *Heir:* *s* Timothy Peter Michael Charles Hartwell [*b* 8 July 1970; *m* 2002, Diana Katherine, *d* of Ronald McKelvie Sinclair, Edinburgh; one *s*]. *Clubs:* Cachalots-Southampton Master Mariners'; Old Worcester's Association.

HARTWELL, Prof. Leland Harrison, PhD; Professor, University of Washington, Seattle, since 1973; President and Director, Fred Hutchinson Cancer Research Center, Seattle, since 1997; *b* Los Angeles, 30 Oct. 1939; *s* of Marjorie Hartwell (*née* Taylor); *m* Theresa Naujack. *Educ:* CIT (BS 1961); MIT (PhD 1964). Fellow, Salk Inst., 1964–65; Asst Prof., 1965–67, Associate Prof., 1967–68, Univ. of Calif, Irvine; Associate Prof., 1968–73, Univ. of Washington. Res. Prof., American Cancer Soc., 1990–. (Jtly) Nobel Prize for Physiol. or Medicine, 2001. *Publications:* articles in learned jls. *Address:* Fred Hutchinson Cancer Research Center, 1100 Fairview Avenue N, D1–060, PO Box 19024, Seattle, WA 98109–1024, USA.

HARTY, Bernard Peter, CBE 1998; Chairman, Imerys (UK) Pension Fund (formerly English China Clay Pension Fund), 2000–08; *b* 1 May 1943; *s* of William Harty and Eileen Nora (*née* Canavan); *m* 1965, Glenys Elaine Simpson; one *d*. *Educ:* St Richards Coll., Droitwich; Ullathorne Grammar Sch., Coventry. CPFA 1966. Accountant, Coventry CBC, 1961–69; Forward Budget Planning Officer, Derbyshire CC, 1969–72; Chief Accountant, Bradford CBC, 1972–74; Chief Finance Officer, Bradford MDC, 1973–76; County Treasurer, Oxfordshire CC, 1976–83; Chamberlain, 1983–99, and Town Clerk, 1996–99, City of London Corp.; Man. Dir, Barbican Centre, 1994–95. Chm., London Pension Fund Authy, 1999–2001. Dir, Dexia Public Finance Bank, 1994–2000; Chairman: London Processing Centre Pension Fund, 2001–03; Alstom Pension Trust, 2004–05. Mem. Nat. Cttee, Information Technol. Year 1982 (IT82); Chm., IT82 Local Govt Cttee, 1982. Chm., Foundn for IT in Local Govt, 1988–91. Chm., Treasury Management Panel, 1991–94, Superannuation Investments Panel, 1994–95, CIPFA; Member: Local Govt Sub Gp, Financial Law Panel, 1993–95; HM Treasury Cttee on Local Authy Borrowing, 1994–95. Freeman, City of London, 1983; Liveryman, Worshipful Co. of Tallow Chandlers, 1984; Founder Mem., Co. of Information Technologists (Hon. Liveryman, 1997). Hon. DPhil London Guildhall Univ., 1997. Commander, Nat. Order of Merit (France), 1996. *Publications:* papers in professional jls. *Recreations:* theatre, music, National Trust, sport. *Address:* *e-mail:* bernardharty@aol.com.

HARVERSON, Patrick Richard; Communications Secretary to the Prince of Wales, since 2004, and to the Duchess of Cornwall, since 2005; *b* 8 Nov. 1962; *s* of John and Quinn Harverson. *Educ:* London Sch. of Econs (BSc (Econ) Internat. Relns). Financial Times, 1988–2000: stockmarket reporter; economics writer; NY Correspondent; Sports Correspondent; Dir of Communications, Manchester United FC, 2000–04. *Recreation:* football. *Address:* The Prince of Wales's Office, Clarence House, SW1A 1BA. *T:* (020) 7024 5506, *Fax:* (020) 7925 0795.

HARVEY, family name of **Baron Harvey of Tasburgh**.

HARVEY OF TASBURGH, 2nd Baron *cr* 1954, of Tasburgh, Norfolk; **Peter Charles Oliver Harvey,** FCA; Bt 1868; *b* 28 Jan. 1921; *er s* of 1st Baron Harvey of Tasburgh, GCMG, GCVO, CB, and Maud Annora (*d* 1970), *d* of late Arthur Watkin Williams-Wynn; *S* father, 1968; *m* 1957, Penelope Anne (*d* 1995), *d* of Lt-Col Sir William Makins, 3rd Bt; two *d*. *Educ:* Eton; Trinity College, Cambridge. Served 1941–46 with Royal Artillery, Tunisia, Italy. Bank of England, 1948–56; Binder Hamlyn & Co., 1956–61; Lloyds Bank International Ltd (formerly Bank of London and South America), 1961–75;

English Transcontinental Ltd, 1975–78; Brown, Shipley & Co., 1978–81. *Recreations:* sailing, music. *Heir: nephew* Charles John Giuseppe Harvey, *b* 4 Feb. 1951. *Address:* Crownick Woods, Restronguet, Mylor, Falmouth, Cornwall TR11 5ST. *Clubs:* Brooks's; Royal Cornwall Yacht.

HARVEY, Alan James, (Tim), RDI 1991; production designer, film and television; *b* 14 Oct. 1936; *s* of Ernest Harvey and Ida Harvey; *m* 1958, Sheila Todd; one *s* one *d*. *Educ:* Hampton Grammar Sch.; Manchester Univ. (BA Hons Architecture). Designer: BBC TV N Region, 1960–64; Telefis Eireann, 1964–66; BBC Scotland, 1966–69; BBC London, 1969–88; freelance film designer, 1988–; *films* include: Henry V, 1989; Much Ado About Nothing, 1993; Mary Shelley's Frankenstein, 1994; Othello, 1995; Hamlet, 1996; The Magic Flute, 2006; Sleuth, 2007. US Emmy Award, 1974, 1976; BAFTA Design Awards, 1976, 1985, 1987; Design Award, RTS, 1982. *Recreations:* football, Italian language and culture, family. *Address:* 2 Cambridge Court, Clevedon Road, Twickenham, Middx TW1 2HT.

HARVEY, Prof. Andrew Charles, FBA 1999; Professor of Econometrics, University of Cambridge, since 1996; Fellow, Corpus Christi College, Cambridge, since 1996; *b* 10 Sept. 1947; *s* of Richard Arthur Harvey and Margaret Frances Harvey (*née* Clark); *m* 1969, Lavinia Mary Young; one *s* one *d*. *Educ:* Leeds Modern Sch.; Univ. of York (BA); LSE (MSc). Economist and statistician, Central Bureau of Stats, Nairobi, 1969–71; Lectr, Univ. of Kent at Canterbury, 1971–77; Vis. Prof., Univ. of British Columbia, 1977–78; London School of Economics: Sen. Lectr, 1978–81; Reader, 1981–84; Prof. of Econometrics, 1984–96. Fellow, Econometric Soc., 1990. *Publications:* The Econometric Analysis of Time Series, 1981, 2nd edn 1990; Time Series Models, 1981, 2nd edn 1993; Forecasting, Structural Time Series Models and the Kalman Filter, 1989. *Recreations:* football, opera. *Address:* Faculty of Economics, Sidgwick Avenue, Cambridge CB3 9DD.

HARVEY, Anne Caroline Ballingall, (Mrs John Harvey); *see* McIntosh, A. C. B.

HARVEY, Rev. Canon Anthony Ernest, DD; Canon of Westminster, 1982–99, and Sub-Dean, 1987–99, Canon Emeritus, 1999; *b* 1 May 1930; *s* of Cyril Harvey, QC, and Nina (*née* Darley); *m* 1957, Julian Elizabeth McMaster; four *d*. *Educ:* Dragon Sch., Oxford; Eton Coll.; Worcester Coll., Oxford (BA, MA, DD 1983); Westcott House, Cambridge. Curate, Christ Church, Chelsea, 1958–62; Research Student, Christ Church, Oxford, 1962–69; Warden, St Augustine's Coll., Canterbury, 1969–76; Univ. Lectr in Theology and Fellow of Wolfson Coll., Oxford, 1976–82; Chaplain, The Queen's Coll., 1977–82; Librarian, Westminster Abbey, 1983–98. Examining Chaplain to Archbishop of Canterbury, 1975–90; Six Preacher, Canterbury Cathedral, 1977–82; Bampton Lectr, 1980. Member: Gen. Synod Doctrine Commn, 1977–86; Archbishop's Commn on Urban Priority Areas, 1983–85; Worcester Cathedral Fabric Adv. Cttee, 2001–06. Chm., Jedidiah Foundn, 2004–. Fellow, George Bell Inst., 1997–. *Publications:* Companion to the New Testament (New English Bible), 1970, 2nd edn 2004; Priest or President?, 1975; Jesus on Trial, 1976; Something Overheard, 1977; (ed) God Incarnate: story and belief, 1981; Jesus and the Constraints of History, 1982; Believing and Belonging, 1984; (ed) Alternative Approaches to New Testament Study, 1985; (ed) Theology in the City, 1989; Strenuous Commands, 1990, 2nd edn 1996; Retaliation, 1992; Promise or Pretence?: a Christian's guide to sexual morals, 1994; (ed) The Funeral Effigies of Westminster Abbey, 1994; Renewal through Suffering: a study of 2 Corinthians, 1996; Marriage, Divorce and the Church, 1997; Demanding Peace: Christian responses to war and violence, 1999; By What Authority?: the churches and social concern, 2001; articles in classical and theological jls. *Recreations:* music, walking. *Address:* Mendelssohn Cottage, Broadway Road, Willersey, Broadway, Worcs WR12 7PH. *T:* (01386) 859260.

HARVEY, Anthony Peter; Chairman, The Broad Oak Consultancy, since 1991; *b* 21 May 1940; *s* of late Frederick William Henry Harvey and Fanny Evelyn Harvey (*née* Dixon); *m* 1963, Margaret Hayward; three *s* one *d*. *Educ:* Hertford Grammar Sch. MCLIP. Dept of Oriental Printed Books, British Museum, 1958–60; British Museum (Natural History): Dept of Palaeontology, 1960–75; Librarian, 1963–75; Head, Dept of Library Services, 1981–88; Co-ordinator of Planning and Development, 1985–88; Head of Marketing and Develt, 1988–91. Dir, Natural History Mus. Develt Trust, 1990–91. Chm., Heathfield Partnership, 1997–99; Dir, Welshpool Partnership, 2002–. Chm., Geology Inf. Gp, 1975–78, Liby Cttee, 1981–84, Geol Soc.; Chm., N Powys DFAS, 2005–08; Member: Printing Hist. Soc., 1965–; Garden Hist. Soc., 1988–; Soc. for Hist. of Natural Hist., 1963– (Treas., 1964–2004; Hon. Mem., 2004–). Trustee: Britain Australia Bicentennial Trust, 1988–; Montgomery Co. Regeneration Assoc., 2002–; Oriel Davies Gall., 2003– (Chm., 2005–); Montgomeryshire Wildlife Trust, 2004–08 (Sec., 2006); Trustee and Dir, Gwasg Gregynog (Gregynog Press), 2006– (Hon. Treas., 2007–). Councillor, Welshpool Town Council, 2004–. Freeman, City of London, 1985; Liveryman, Co. of Marketors, 1991. *Publications:* (ed) Secrets of the Earth, 1967; (ed) Directory of Scientific Directories, 1969, 4th edn 1986; Prehistoric Man, 1972; Guide to World Science, vol. 1, 1974; (ed) Encyclopedia of Prehistoric Life, 1979; European Sources of Scientific and Technical Information, 1981, 7th edn 1986; numerous contribs to learned jls, ref. works and periodicals. *Recreations:* garden history and design, transport history bibliography. *Address:* Oak Cottage, 23 High Street, Welshpool, Powys SY21 7JP. *T:* (01938) 559087.

HARVEY, Arthur Douglas; Assistant Under-Secretary of State, Ministry of Defence, 1969–76; *b* 16 July 1916; *o s* of late William Arthur Harvey and Edith Alice; *m* 1940, Doris Irene Lodge (*d* 1997); one *s* (and one *s* decd). *Educ:* Westcliff High Sch.; St Catharine's Coll., Cambridge. Wrangler, Maths Tripos, 1938. Entered War Office, 1938; served in Army, 1940–45; Princ. 1945; Registrar, Royal Military College of Science, 1951–54; Asst Sec. 1954; Under-Sec. 1969. *Address:* 36b Lovelace Road, Long Ditton, Surrey KT6 6ND. *T:* (020) 8399 0587.

HARVEY, Barbara Fitzgerald, CBE 1997; FSA 1964; FBA 1982; Fellow of Somerville College, Oxford, 1956–93, now Emeritus Fellow; Reader (*ad hominem*) in Medieval History, Oxford University, 1990–93; *b* 21 Jan. 1928; *d* of Richard Henry Harvey and Anne Fitzgerald (*née* Julian). *Educ:* Teignmouth Grammar Sch.; Bishop Blackall Sch., Exeter; Somerville Coll., Oxford (Schol.). First Cl. Final Honour Sch. of Modern History, Oxford, 1949; Bryce Student, Oxford Univ., 1950–51; BLitt Oxon 1953. Assistant, Dept of Scottish History, Edinburgh Univ., 1951–52; Asst Lectr, subseq. Lectr, Queen Mary Coll., London Univ., 1952–55; Tutor, Somerville Coll., Oxford, 1955–93; Vice-Principal, 1976–79, 1981–83. Assessor, Oxford Univ., 1968–69. Ford's Lectr, Oxford, 1989. Mem., Royal Commn on Historical MSS, 1991–97. Pres., Henry Bradshaw Soc., 1997–2007. Hon. Vice-Pres., RHistS, 2003–. Gen. Editor, Oxford Medieval Texts, 1987–99. *Publications:* Documents Illustrating the Rule of Walter de Wenlok, Abbot of Westminster 1283–1307, 1965; Westminster Abbey and its Estates in the Middle Ages, 1977; (ed with L. C. Hector) The Westminster Chronicle 1381–94, 1982; Living and Dying in England 1100–1540: the monastic experience, (jtly, Wolfson Foundn History Prize), 1993; (ed) The Twelfth and Thirteenth Centuries: short Oxford history of the British Isles, 2001; The Obedientiaries of Westminster Abbey and their Financial Records *c* 1275 to 1540, 2002; contribs to Economic History Rev., Trans Royal Historical Soc., Bulletin of Inst. of Historical Research, etc. *Address:* 66 Cranham Street, Oxford OX2 6DD. *T:* (01865) 554766.

HARVEY, Prof. Brian Wilberforce; Professor of Law, University of Birmingham 1973–98, now Emeritus; *b* 17 March 1936; *s* of Gerald and Noelle Harvey. *Educ:* Clifton Coll., Bristol; St John's Coll., Cambridge (Choral Schol., MA, LLM). Solicitor, 1961 Lectr, Birmingham Univ., 1962–63; Sen. Lectr, Nigerian Law Sch., 1965–67; Lectr, Sen Lectr and Prof. of Law, QUB, 1967–73; University of Birmingham: Dir, Legal Studies 1973–76; Dean, Faculty of Law, 1982–85; Pro-Vice-Chancellor, 1986–91; Founding Dir Legal Office, 1990–98. Vis. Prof., Univ. of Singapore, 1985–86. Chairman: Gt Birmingham Social Security Appeal Tribunals, 1982–99; Medical Appeals Tribunals 1985–99; Disability Appeal Tribunals, 1992–99. Member: Statute Law Cttee (NI) 1972–73; Cttee on Legal Educn (NI), 1972–73; Adviser, Council of Legal Educn (NI) 1976–79. Mem., British Hallmarking Council, 1989–91. FRSA 2005. *Publications:* Law of Probate Wills and Succession in Nigeria, 1968; (jtly) Survey of Northern Ireland Land Law, 1970; Settlements of Land, 1973; (ed) Vocational Legal Training in UK and Commonwealth, 1975; (ed) The Lawyer and Justice, 1978; The Law of Consumer Protection and Fair Trading, 1978, 6th edn 2000; (jtly) Consumer and Trading Law Cases and Materials, 1985, 2nd edn 1998; (jtly) Law and Practice of Auctions, 1985, 3rd edn 2006; (jtly) The Law and Practice of Marketing Goods and Services, 1990; Violin Fraud: deception, forgery, theft and the law, 1992, 2nd edn (jtly) 1997; The Violin Family and its Makers in the British Isles: an illustrated history and directory, 1995; Buying and Selling Art and Antiques—The Law, 1998; (ed jtly) Edward Heron-Allen's Journal of the Great War, 2002; (jtly) Elgar, Vicat Cole and the Ghosts of Brinkwells, 2007. *Recreations:* performing and listening to music. *Address:* Pear Tree Cottage, Evesham Road, Cookhill Alcester, Warwicks B49 5LJ. *T:* (01789) 400132.

See also J. D. Harvey.

HARVEY, Caroline; *see* Kerr, C.

HARVEY, Caroline; *see* Trollope, Joanna.

HARVEY, Prof. Charles Richard Musgrave, (3rd Bt *cr* 1933, but does not use the title) *b* 7 April 1937; *s* of Sir Richard Musgrave Harvey, 2nd Bt, and Frances Estelle (*d* 1986) *er d* of late Lindsay Crompton Lawford, Montreal; *S* father, 1978; *m* 1967, Celia Vivien *d* of late George Henry Hodson; one *s* one *d*. *Educ:* Marlborough; Pembroke Coll. Cambridge (BA 1960, MA 1964). Fellow, Institute of Development Studies, Sussex 1972–2002; Sen. Res. Fellow, Botswana Institute for Development Policy Analysis Gaborone, 1996–2001. *Heir: s* Paul Richard Harvey, *b* 1971.

HARVEY, Christopher John, (Kit), H.; *see* Hesketh Harvey.

HARVEY, (Christopher) Paul (Duncan), CMG 2004; HM Diplomatic Service International Security Directorate, Foreign and Commonwealth Office, since 2005; *b* 2 July 1956; *s* of late Prof. William John Harvey and of Margaret Anne Harvey; *m* 1989 Anasaini Kamakorewa; one *s* one *d*. *Educ:* Royal Belfast Academical Instn; University Coll., Oxford (MA); Downing Coll., Cambridge. Tutor in Geog., Cambridge Centre for 6th Form Studies, 1982–85; joined FCO, 1986: 2nd Sec., Suva, 1988–90; 1st Sec. Brussels, 1990–94; FCO, 1995–98; UK Rep. to Sierra Leone Peace Talks, Lome, 1999 UK Special Rep. for Peace in Sierra Leone, 1999–2000; Deputy High Comr, Kenya 2000–03; on secondment to Coalition Provisional Authy, Iraq, 2003–04; liaison officer Operation Bracknell, 2005. *Recreations:* books, organic gardening. *Address:* c/o Foreign and Commonwealth Office, King Charles Street, SW1A 2AH.

HARVEY, Clare; *see* Harvey, M. F. C.

HARVEY, Prof. David Robert, FRCP, FRCPCH; Professor of Paediatrics and Neonatal Medicine, Imperial College Faculty of Medicine (formerly Royal Postgraduate Medical School) at Hammersmith Hospital, 1995–2002, now Emeritus; Consultant Paediatrician, Queen Charlotte's and Chelsea (formerly Queen Charlotte's Maternity Hospital, 1970–2002; *b* 7 Dec. 1936; *s* of Cyril Francis Harvey and Margarita Harvey (*née* Cardew Smith); partner 1970, Teck Ong. *Educ:* Dulwich Coll.; Guy's Hosp. Med. Sch (MB BS 1960). MRCP 1963, FRCP 1976; FRCPCH 1997. House Officer: Guy's Hosp 1960–61; Central Middx Hosp., 1961–62; Amer. Hosp., Paris, 1963; Neonatal House Officer, 1964, Neate Res. Fellow, 1964–65, Hammersmith Hosp.; House Officer, Hosp for Sick Children, Gt Ormond St, 1966; Paediatric Registrar, Hammersmith and Hillingdon Hosps, 1966–68; Nuffield Res. Fellow, Oxford, 1968–69; Paediatric Sen Registrar, Hammersmith Hosp., 1969–70; Consultant Paediatrician: St Charles' Hosp. London, 1970–87; St Mary's Hosp., London, 1987–92; Sen. Lectr, RPMS, 1992–95 Hon. Secretary: Neonatal Soc., 1975–79; BPA, 1979–84. Handcock Prize, RCS, 1960 *Publications:* (ed jtly) Biology of Play, 1977; (jtly) The Sick Newborn Baby, 1981; (ed jtly) Child Health, 1985; (ed) New Parents, 1988; (ed jtly) The Baby under 1000 grams, 1989 (ed jtly) The Stress of Multiple Births, 1991; (jtly) Colour Guide: Neonatology, 1991; (ed jtly) Community Child Health and Paediatrics, 1995; contrib. to professional jls *Recreations:* listening to opera, learning Chinese.

HARVEY, Prof. David William, PhD; Distinguished Professor of Anthropology Graduate Center, City University of New York, since 2001; *b* 31 Oct. 1935; *s* of Frederick and Doris Harvey. *Educ:* St John's Coll., Cambridge (BA (Hons), MA, PhD). Lectr, Univ of Bristol, 1961–69; Prof. of Geography, Johns Hopkins Univ., 1969–86; Oxford University: Halford Mackinder Prof. of Geography, 1987–93; Fellow, St Peter's Coll 1987–93; Supernumerary Res. Fellow, St John's Coll., 2001–; Prof. of Geography, Johns Hopkins Univ., 1993–2001. Guggenheim Meml Fellow, 1976–77. Corresp. FBA 1998 Dr (*hc*): Buenos Aires, 1997; Roskilde, 1997; Uppsala, 2000. Outstanding Contributor Award, Assoc. of Amer. Geographers, 1980; Gill Meml Award, RGS, 1982; Anders Retzius Gold Medal, Swedish Soc. for Anthropology and Geography, 1989; Patron's Medal, RGS, 1995; Vautrin Lud Internat. Prize in Geography, 1995. *Publications:* Explanation in Geography, 1969, 4th edn 1978; Social Justice and the City, 1973, 3rd edn 1989; The Limits to Capital, 1982, 2nd edn 1984; The Urbanisation of Capital, 1985 Consciousness and the Urban Experience, 1985; The Urban Experience, 1989; The Condition of Postmodernity, 1989; Justice, Nature and the Geography of Difference 1996; Spaces of Hope, 2000; Spaces of Capital, 2001; Paris, Capital of Modernity, 2003 The New Imperialism, 2003; A Brief History of Neoliberalism, 2005; Spaces of Global Capitalism, 2006. *Address:* PhD Program in Anthropology, Graduate Center, City University of New York, 365 Fifth Avenue, New York, NY 10016, USA.

HARVEY, DeAnne Shirley; *see* Julius, D. S.

HARVEY, Diane Catherine; *see* Redgrave, D. C.

HARVEY, Rt Rev. Donald Frederick; Bishop of Eastern Newfoundland and Labrador 1993–2004; Moderator, Anglican Network in Canada, since 2004; *b* St John's Newfoundland, 13 Sept. 1939; *s* of Robert Joseph and Elsie May Harvey (*née* Vaters); *m* 1964, Gertrude, *d* of George and Jessie Hiscock. *Educ:* St Michael's Sch., 1956; Memorial

Univ. (BA 1985; MA 1987); Queen's Theol Coll. (MDiv 1986). Sch. teacher, 1956–57; ordained deacon, 1963, priest, 1964; served in parishes: Portugal Cove, 1963–64, 1973–76; Twillingate, 1965; King's Cove, 1965–68; Happy Valley, Labrador, 1968–73; St Michael & All Angels, St John's, 1976–83; Anglican Chaplain, Meml Univ. of Newfoundland, 1984–87; Rector, and Dean, Cathedral of St John the Baptist, St John's, 1989–92. Rural Dean of Labrador, 1968–73. Lectr in Pastoral Theol., Queen's Coll., 1984–94; Sessional Lectr, English, Meml Univ. of Newfoundland, 1985–89. Hon. DD Huron Coll., 1996. *Address:* 501–7 Tiffany Lane, St John's, NL A1A 4B7, Canada.

HARVEY, Estella Jacqueline, (Mrs J. G. Harvey); *see* Hindley, E. J.

HARVEY, Dr Helen Lesley; Headmistress, St Swithun's School, since 1995; *b* 7 April 1950; *d* of George Frederick Cox and Olive Cox; *m* 1975, Dr H. Hale Harvey (marr. diss. 1999); one *s* one *d*. *Educ:* Lordswood Sch., Birmingham; Bedford Coll., Univ. of London (BSc); Chester Beatty Cancer Res. Inst., Surrey (PhD). Asst Mistress, Greylands Coll., IoW, 1975–76; Asst Mistress, 1976–89, Dep. Headmistress, 1989–90, Headmistress, 1990–94, Upper Chine Sch., Shanklin, IoW. *Recreations:* sailing, walking. *Address:* The Cottage, 154 Alresford Road, Winchester, Hants SO21 1HB.

HARVEY, Jack; *see* Rankin, I. J.

HARVEY, Prof. Jake Burns, RSA 1989 (ARSA 1977); Head, School of Sculpture, since 1998, and Professor of Sculpture, since 2001, Edinburgh College of Art; *b* 3 June 1948; *s* of George and Nan Harvey; *m* 1971, Penelope F. Proctor; one *s* two *d*. *Educ:* Edinburgh Coll. of Art (DA). *Recreation:* fishing. *Address:* Maxton Cross, Maxton, Melrose, Roxburghshire TD6 0RL. *T:* and *Fax:* (01835) 822650; *e-mail:* j.harvey@eca.ac.uk.

HARVEY, Prof. Jonathan Dean; composer; Professor of Music, Stanford University, 1995–2000; *b* 3 May 1939; *s* of Gerald and Noelle Harvey; *m* 1960, Rosaleen Marie Barry; one *s* one *d*. *Educ:* St Michael's Coll., Tenbury; Repton; St John's Coll., Cambridge (MA, DMus; Hon. Fellow, 2002); Glasgow Univ. (PhD). Lectr, Southampton Univ., 1964–77; Sussex University: Reader, 1977–80; Prof. of Music, 1980–95; Hon. Prof., 1995. Bloch Prof., Univ. of California, Berkeley, 1995; Vis. Prof., Imperial Coll., London, 1999–2002. Harkness Fellow, Princeton Univ., 1969–70. Composer in association with: Sinfonia 21, 1996–; Ictus Ensemble, 1997–; BBC Scottish SO, 2004–. Works performed at most festivals and international centres. Mem., Academia Europaea, 1989. FRCM 1995; FRSCM 2000. Hon. RAM 2002. Hon. DMus: Southampton, 1990; Bristol, 1994; Sussex, 2000. Composer Award, British Acad., 2003; Giga-Hertz Prize, 2007. *Publications:* The Music of Stockhausen, 1975; Music and Inspiration, 1999; In Quest of Spirit, 1999; *compositions:* Persephone Dream, for orch., 1972; Inner Light (trilogy), for performers and tape, 1973–77; Smiling Immortal, for chamber orch., 1977; String Quartet, 1977; Magnificat and Nunc Dimittis, for choir and organ, 1978; Album, for wind quintet, 1978; Hymn, for choir and orch., 1979; Be(com)ing, for clarinet and piano, 1979; Concelebration, instrumental, 1979, rev. 1981; Mortuos Plango, Vivos Voco, for tape, 1980; Passion and Resurrection, church opera, 1981; Resurrection, for double chorus and organ, 1981; Bhakti, for 15 insts and tape, 1982; Easter Orisons, for chamber orch., 1983; The Path of Devotion, for choir and orch., 1983; Nachtlied, for soprano, piano and tape, 1984; Gong-Ring, for ensemble with electronics, 1984; Song Offerings, for soprano and players, 1985 (Britten Award for Composition, 1993); Madonna of Winter and Spring, for orch., synthesizers and electronics, 1986; Lightness and Weight, for tuba and orch., 1986; Forms of Emptiness, for choir, 1986; Tendril, for ensemble, 1987; Timepieces, for orch., 1987; From Silence, for soprano and players with electronics, 1988; Valley of Aosta for 13 players, 1988; String Quartet No 2, 1989; Ritual Melodies, for tape, 1990; Cello Concerto, 1990; Serenade in Homage to Mozart, for wind, 1991; Inquest of Love (opera), 1992; Lotuses, 1992; Scena, 1992; The Riot, for trio, 1993; One Evening, for 2 singers, instruments and electronics, 1994; String Quartet No 3, 1996; Percussion Concerto, 1997; Ashes Dance Back, for choir with electronics, 1997; Wheel of Emptiness, for ensemble, 1997; Calling Across Time, for chamber orch., 1998; Tranquil Abiding, for orch., 1998; White as Jasmine, for soprano and orch., 1999; Mothers Shall Not Cry, for voices, orch. and electronics, 2000; Bird Concerto with Pianosong, 2001; The Summer Cloud's Awakening, for choir and instruments with electronics, 2001; Songs of Li Po, for voice and chamber orch., 2002; Chu, for soprano and two instruments, 2002; String Quartet No 4 (with electronics), 2003; Jubilus, for viola and ensemble, 2003; Two Interludes for an Opera, 2004; String Trio, 2004; Towards a Pure Land, for orch., 2005 (Royal Philharmonic Soc. Award, 2007); Wagner Dream (opera), 2006; Body Mandala, for orch., 2007; Messages, for orch. and chorus, 2007; Speakings, for orch. and electronics, 2008. *Recreations:* tennis, walking, meditation. *Address:* c/o Faber Music, 3 Queen Square, WC1N 3AU. *T:* (020) 7833 7911.

See also B. W. Harvey.

HARVEY, Kenneth George; Chairman, Pennon Group (formerly South West Water) plc, since 1997; *b* 22 July 1940; *s* of George Harvey and Nellie Harvey (*née* Gilmore); *m* 1st, 1963, Wendy Youldon (*d* 1982); one *s* one *d*; 2nd, 1990, Anne Model. *Educ:* Urmston Grammar Sch., Manchester; City Univ. (BSc, 1st Cl. Hons Elec. Eng). Student Apprentice, Westinghouse, 1958–63; Southern and London Electricity Boards, 1963–81; London Electricity Board: Engineering Dir, 1981–84; Dep. Chm., 1984–89; Chm. and Chief Exec., NORWEB plc (formerly North Western Electricity Bd), 1989–95. Chairman: Greater Manchester Buses South Ltd, 1993–95; Intercare Gp plc, 1996–2004; Comax plc, 1997–99; Beaufort Group plc, 1998–2004; non-executive Director: Lattice Gp, 2000–02; Nat. Grid plc (formerly Nat. Grid Transco), 2002– (Sen. Ind. Dir, 2006–). Pres., Electricity Assoc., 1992–93. Chm., Royal Exchange Theatre Co., Manchester, 1994–98. *Recreations:* sport, gardening, DIY, theatre. *Address:* c/o Pennon Group plc, Peninsula House, Rydon Lane, Exeter EX2 7HR.

HARVEY, Prof. Leonard Patrick; Senior Research Associate, Oxford Centre for Islamic Studies, since 2002 (Fellow, 1994–2001); Cervantes Professor of Spanish, King's College, University of London, 1973–84, now Professor Emeritus; *b* 25 Feb. 1929; *s* of Francis Thomas Harvey and Eva Harvey; *m* 1954, June Rawcliffe; two *s*. *Educ:* Alleyn's Sch., Dulwich; Magdalen Coll., Oxford. 1st cl. hons BA Mod. Langs 1952; 2nd cl. Oriental Studies 1954; MA 1956; DPhil 1958. Lectr in Spanish, Univ. of Oxford, 1957–58; Univ. of Southampton, 1958–60; Queen Mary Coll., Univ. of London: Lectr, 1960–63; Reader and Head of Dept, 1963; Prof. of Spanish, 1967–73; Dean of Faculty of Arts, 1970–73; Dean of Faculty of Arts, KCL, 1979–81; FKC 1992. Vis. Prof., Univ. of Victoria, BC, 1966; Vis. Fellow, Oxford Centre for Islamic Studies, 1993–94. Mem. UGC, 1979–83. Chm., Educn Cttee, Hispanic and Luso-Brazilian Council, 1984–87. *Publications:* Islamic Spain 1250–1500, 1990; Muslims in Spain, 1500 to 1614, 2005; Ibn Battuta, 2007; articles in Al-Andalus, Bulletin of Hispanic Studies, Nueva Revista de Filología Española, Al-Masāq, Al-Qantara, etc. *Address:* Oxford Centre for Islamic Studies, George Street, Oxford OX1 2AR. *T:* (01865) 278730.

HARVEY, (Mary Frances) Clare, (Mrs D. R. Feaver), MA; Headmistress, St Mary's Hall, Brighton, 1981–88; *b* 24 Aug. 1927; *e d* of late Rev. Oliver Douglas Harvey and Frances Hilda Harvey (*née* Howes); *m* 1988, Rt Rev. Douglas Russell Feaver (*d* 1997). *Educ:* St Mary's Sch., Colchester; St Hugh's Coll., Oxford (BA, Final Honour Sch. of Mod. Hist., 1950; Diploma in Educn, 1951; MA 1954). History Mistress, St Albans High Sch., 1951; Head of History Dept, Portsmouth High Sch., GPDST, 1956; Headmistress: Sch. of St Clare, Penzance, 1962–69; Badminton Sch., Westbury on Trym, Bristol, 1969–81. Governor, Bristol Cathedral Sch., 1978–81; Foundn Gov. and Trustee, Sexey's Sch., Bruton, 1994–95. *Recreations:* music, travel, reading, needlework. *Address:* Blackman House, Canon Lane, Chichester, West Sussex PO19 1PX.

HARVEY, Michael, MBE 2001; freelance lettering designer, since 1955; *b* 11 Nov. 1931; *s* of Leslie Arthur Harvey and Betty Eileen Harvey; *m* 1956, Patricia Evelyn Hills; three *d*. *Educ:* Ewell Castle Sch. Engrg draughtsman, 1947–55; Asst to Reynolds Stone, inscription carving, 1955–61. Pt-time Lectr, Bournemouth & Poole Coll. of Art & Design, 1961–80; Vis. Lectr, Dept of Typography & Graphic Communication, Univ. of Reading, 1993–2001. Co-Founder, Fine Fonts, 2000. *Work* includes: inscription carving, book jacket design, type design (Monotype, Adobe, Dutch Type Library); collaboration with Ian Hamilton Finlay on carved poetry, sundials, graphic works; design and carving of inscriptions, Sainsbury Wing, Nat. Gall., London, 1990. Mem., Royal Mint Adv. Cttee, 1991–2005. Gov., Arts Inst. at Bournemouth, 1998–2001 (Hon. Fellow, 2001). *Publications:* Lettering Design, 1975; Creative Lettering: drawing & design, 1985; Carving Letters in Stone & Wood, 1987; Calligraphy in the Graphic Arts, 1988; Reynolds Stone: engraved lettering in wood, 1992; Creative Lettering Today, 1996. *Recreations:* reading, listening to jazz, photography, cycling. *Address:* 4 Valley Road, Bridport, Dorset DT6 4JR. *T:* (01308) 422777; *e-mail:* perdido@dircon.co.uk. *Club:* Double Crown.

HARVEY, Michael Llewellyn Tucker; QC 1982; a Recorder, since 1986; a Deputy High Court Judge; *b* 22 May 1943; *s* of late Rev. Victor Llewellyn Tucker Harvey and Pauline Harvey (*née* Wybrow); *m* 1972, Denise Madeleine Neary; one *s* one *d*. *Educ:* St John's Sch., Leatherhead; Christ's Coll., Cambridge (BA Hons Law, LLB, MA). Called to the Bar, Gray's Inn, 1966 (Uthwatt Schol. 1965, James Mould Schol. 1966; Bencher, 1991). *Publication:* joint contributor of title 'Damages' in Halsbury's Laws of England, 4th edn 1975. *Recreations:* shooting, golf. *Address:* 2 Crown Office Row, Temple, EC4Y 7HJ. *T:* (020) 7797 8100. *Clubs:* Athenæum; Hawks (Cambridge); Burhill Golf.

HARVEY, Neil; Head of Business Statistics Division, Central Statistical Office, 1989–93; *b* 10 Feb. 1938; *s* of Edward Felters and Lucy Felters (*née* Graves; she *m* 2nd, Frederick Harvey); *m* 1963, Clare Elizabeth Joscelyne; two *s*. *Educ:* Eton House Sch., Essex; LSE. BSc(Econ). Economist/Statistician, Kuwait Oil Co., 1959–62; Statistician, Midland Bank Economics Dept, 1962–65; Asst Statistician/Statistician, DEA, 1965–69; Statistician, HM Treasury, 1969–73; Chief Statistician, Inland Revenue, 1973–77; Controller, Statistical Office, HM Customs and Excise, 1977–84; Under Sec., Statistics Div. 1, DTI, 1984–89. *Recreation:* reading.

HARVEY, Nicholas Barton; MP (Lib Dem) Devon North, since 1992; *b* 3 Aug. 1961; *s* of Frederick Barton Harvey and Christine Diana Rosalind (*née* Gildea); *m* 2003, Kate Fox; one *s* one *d*. *Educ:* Queen's Coll., Taunton; Middlesex Poly. (BA Hons). Communications and Marketing Consultant: Profile Public Relns, 1984–86; Dewe Rogerson Ltd, 1986–91; Westminster Consortium, 1991–92. Lib Dem spokesman: on transport, 1992–94; on trade and industry, 1994–97; on regions, 1997–99; on health, 1999–2001; on culture, media and sport, 2001–03; on defence, 2006–. Chair, Lib Dem Campaigns and Communications, 1994–99. Mem., Parly Assembly, Council of Europe, 2005–07. *Recreations:* travelling, walking, playing piano, soccer enthusiast. *Address:* House of Commons, SW1A 0AA. *T:* (020) 7219 6232.

HARVEY, Paul; *see* Harvey, C. P. D.

HARVEY, Prof. Paul Dean Adshead, FBA 2003; FSA, FRHistS; Professor Emeritus, University of Durham, since 1985; *b* 7 May 1930; *s* of John Dean Monroe Harvey and Gwendolen Mabel Darlington (*née* Adshead); *m* 1968, Yvonne Crossman. *Educ:* Bishop Feild Coll., St John's, Newfoundland; Warwick Sch.; St John's Coll., Oxford (BA 1953; MA; DPhil 1960); FRHistS 1961, FSA 1963. Asst Archivist, Warwick County Record Office, 1954–56; Asst Keeper, Dept of Manuscripts, British Museum, 1957–66; Lectr, 1966–70, Sen. Lectr, 1970–78, Dept of History, Univ. of Southampton; Prof. of Mediaeval Hist., Univ. of Durham, 1978–85. Mem., Adv. Council on Public Records, 1984–89. Vice-President: Surtees Soc., 1978–; British Records Assoc., 2005– (Chm., 1995–2000). Hon. Fellow, Portsmouth Polytechnic, 1987. Jt Gen. Editor, Southampton Records Series, 1966–78; Gen. Editor, Portsmouth Record Series, 1969–2002. *Publications:* (with H. Thorpe) The printed maps of Warwickshire 1576–1900, 1959; A medieval Oxfordshire village: Cuxham 1240–1400, 1965; (ed with W. Albert) Portsmouth and Sheet Turnpike Commissioners' minute book 1711–1754, 1973; (ed) Manorial records of Cuxham, Oxfordshire, circa 1200–1359, 1976; The history of topographical maps: symbols, pictures and surveys, 1980; (ed) The peasant land market in medieval England, 1984; Manorial records, 1984; (ed with R. A. Skelton) Local maps and plans from medieval England, 1986; Medieval maps, 1991; Maps in Tudor England, 1993; (with A. McGuinness) A guide to British medieval seals, 1996; Editing historical records, 2001; contribs to: The Victoria History of the County of Oxford, vol. 10, 1972; History of Cartography, vol. 1, 1987; Agrarian History of England and Wales, vol. 3, 1991; articles in learned jls and periodicals. *Recreations:* British topography and topographical writings. *Address:* Lyndhurst, Farnley Hey Road, Durham DH1 4EA. *T:* (0191) 3869396. *Club:* Athenæum.

HARVEY, Prof. Paul H., CBE 2008; DPhil, DSc; FRS 1992; Professor in Zoology, and Fellow of Jesus College, since 1996, Head of Department of Zoology, since 1998, Oxford University; *b* 19 Jan. 1947; *s* of Edward Walter Harvey and Eileen Joan (*née* Pagett); *m*; two *s*. *Educ:* Queen Elizabeth's Grammar Sch., Hartlebury; Univ. of York (BA 1st Cl. Hons, DPhil); Univ. of Oxford (MA, DSc). Lectr in Biology, Univ. of Wales, Swansea, 1971–73; University of Sussex: Lectr in Biology, 1973–84; Reader, 1984–85; Oxford University: Lectr in Zoology, 1985–89; Reader, 1989–96; Fellow, Merton Coll., 1985–96. Vis. Lectr in Biology, Harvard Univ., 1978–79; Visiting Professor: Harvard Univ., 1980; Univ. of Washington, Seattle, 1982; Princeton Univ., 1984–85. Sec., Zoological Soc. of London, 2000–. Scientific Medal, Zool Soc., 1986; J. Murray Luck Award, Nat. Acad. of Scis, USA, 1997. *Publications:* The Comparative Method in Evolutionary Biology, 1991; edited books; scientific papers. *Recreations:* walking, aggressive gardening. *Address:* Department of Zoology, University of Oxford, South Parks Road, Oxford OX1 3PS. *T:* (01865) 271260.

HARVEY, Peter, CB 1980; Consultant, Solicitor's Office, Department of Trade and Industry, 1994–96 and 1997–99; *b* 23 April 1922; *o s* of Rev. George Leonard Hunton Harvey and Helen Mary (*née* Williams); *m* 1950, Mary Vivienne (*d* 2006), *d* of John Osborne Goss and Elsie Lilian (*née* Bishop); one *s* one *d*. *Educ:* King Edward VI High Sch., Birmingham; St John's Coll., Oxford (MA, BCL). RAF, 1942–45. Called to the Bar, Lincoln's Inn, 1948. Entered the Home Office as a Legal Assistant, 1948; Principal Asst Legal Advr, 1971–77; Legal Advr, DES, 1977–83; Consultant, Legal Advr's Br., Home Office, 1983–86; Asst Counsel to the Speaker, H of C, 1986–94. Mem., Legal Affairs

Cttee, Inst. for Citizenship Studies, 1992–94. *Publications:* contributor to Halsbury's Laws of England (3rd and 4th edns). *Recreations:* history, genealogy, walking. *Address:* Mannamead, Old Avenue, Weybridge, Surrey KT13 0PS. *T:* (01932) 845133.

HARVEY, Peter Kent; DL; Chairman, Poole Hospital NHS Foundation Trust, since 2001; *b* 1 Feb. 1946; *s* of John Alan Harvey and late Joan Harvey; *m* 1976, Wendy Anne Wills; one *d*. *Educ:* Bishop Wordsworth's Sch., Salisbury; Liverpool Univ. (LLB Hons). Articled Clerk, 1968–71, Asst Solicitor, 1971, IoW CC; Asst Solicitor, Bournemouth BC, 1971–73; Dorset County Council: Sen. Asst Solicitor, 1973; Actg Asst Clerk, 1973–74; Dep. County Solicitor, 1974–85; County Solicitor and Dep. Chief Exec., 1985–91; Chief Exec., and Clerk to the Dorset Lieutenancy, 1991–99. Clerk to Dorset Fire Authy, 1991–99, to Dorset Police Authy, 1991–2006. Director: Dorset TEC, 1991–99; Dorset Business Link, 1997–99; Chairman: Dorset Strategic Bd of Young Enterprise, 1996–99; Poole Bay Primary Care Trust, 2001–01; Trustee, Dorset Health Trust, 2000– (Chm., 2000–06). Trustee and Sec., Police Partnership Trust, 1997–2005. DL Dorset, 1999. *Recreations:* golf, sailing. *Address:* Poole Hospital NHS Trust, Longfleet Road, Poole, Dorset BH15 2JB.

HARVEY, Richard John, FIA; Group Chief Executive, Aviva (formerly CGNU) plc, 2001–07 (Deputy Group Chief Executive, 2000–01); *b* 11 July 1950; *s* of Lester Harvey and Jean Rose Harvey; *m* 1971, Karen Vowles; one *s* two *d*. *Educ:* Univ. of Manchester (BSc Hons Maths). FIA 1975. Personal Pensions Manager, Phoenix Assurance, 1983–85; Mkting Manager, Sun Alliance, 1985–87; Gen. Manager, Sun Alliance Life (NZ), 1987–92; Chief Exec., Norwich Union Hldgs (NZ), 1992–93; Norwich Union: Gen. Manager (Finance), 1993–94; Actuary, 1994; Gp Finance Dir, 1995–97; Dep. Gp Chief Exec., 1997; Gp Chief Exec., 1998–2000. Chm., ABI, 2003–05. Advocate, Concern Universal. *Recreations:* theatre, ski-ing, squash.

HARVEY, Robert Lambart; author and journalist; *b* 21 Aug. 1953; *s* of Hon. John and Elena Harvey; *m* 1981, Jane Roper; one *s*. *Educ:* Eton; Christ Church, Oxford (BA 1974, MA 1978). Staff Correspondent, The Economist, 1974–81, Asst Editor, 1981–83; Columnist and Leader Writer, Daily Telegraph, 1987–91. MP (C) SW Clwyd, 1983–87. Mem., House of Commons Select Cttee on Foreign Affairs, 1984–87. Mem., Wilton Park Council, 1984–88; For. Sec.'s Rep., Adv. Bd for Woodrow Wilson Chair of Internat. Politics, 1985–92. *Publications:* Portugal: birth of a democracy, 1978; Fire Down Below: a study of Latin America, 1988; (ed) Blueprint 2000, 1989; The Undefeated: a study of modern Japan, 1994; The Return of the Strong: the drift to global disorder, 1995, rev. edn as Global Disorder, 2003; Clive: the life and death of a British Emperor, 1998; Liberators: Latin America's struggle for independence 1810–1830, 2000; Cochrane: the life and exploits of a fighting captain, 2000; A Few Bloody Noses: the American War of Independence, 2001; The Fall of Apartheid, 2002; Comrades: the rise and fall of world Communism, 2003; The War of Wars: the epic struggle between Britain and France 1789-1815, 2007. *Recreations:* the arts, films, music, swimming, walking. *Clubs:* Brooks's, Lansdowne.

HARVEY, Sheila Elizabeth; *see* Healy, S. E.

HARVEY, Stephen Frank; QC 2006; *b* 2 Nov. 1951; *s* of Frank George Harvey and Muriel Irene Harvey (*née* Stancombe); *m* 1973, Felicity Anne Murphy (marr. diss. 2000); one *s* two *d*. *Educ:* University Coll. London (LLB Hons); Inns of Court Sch. of Law. ACIArb. Mech. engrg industry, 1968–70; NHS, 1970–72; legal dept, local authy, 1972–78; called to the Bar, Gray's Inn, 1979; Asst Prosecutor, Essex CC, 1979–82; in private practice as a barrister, 1982–. *Recreations:* sailing, fishing. *Address:* 18 Red Lion Court, EC4A 3EB. *T:* (020) 7520 6000, *Fax:* (020) 7520 6248/9; *e-mail:* stephen.harvey@18rlc.co.uk.

HARVEY, Tim; *see* Harvey, A. J.

HARVEY, William Graeme; naturalist; *b* 15 Jan. 1947; *s* of Jack Harvey and late Grace (*née* Wilson); *m* 1999, Pauline Maria Hayes; one *s* two *d* by former marriage. *Educ:* Simon Langton Grammar Sch., Canterbury; University Coll., Oxford (BA Geography; MA). British Council, 1969–2000: Tanzania, 1970–73; Indonesia, 1974–76; Personnel, 1976–80; Madras, 1980–83; Educnl Contracts, 1983–86; Rep., Bangladesh, 1986–90; Gen. Manager, Tech. Co-operation Trng, 1990–92; Regl Dir, Eastern and Central Africa, and Dir, Kenya, 1993–98; Dir, Internat. Partnerships, 1998–2000. MBOU. *Publications:* Birds in Bangladesh, 1990; A Photographic Guide to the Birds of India, 2002; Tails of Dilli (children's stories), 2004; Atlas of the Birds of Delhi and Haryana, 2006; contrib. UK, African and Asian ornithol and conservation jls and books. *Recreations:* bird watching, conservation, gardening, poetry, pop music, Coronation Street. *Address:* Pound Farm, Blackham, Tunbridge Wells TN3 9TY. *Club:* Madras (Chennai) (Life Mem.).

HARVIE, Prof. Christopher; PhD; Member (SNP) Scotland Mid and Fife, Scottish Parliament, since 2007; *b* 21 Sept. 1944; *s* of George Harvie and Isobel Harvie (*née* Russell); *m* 1980, Virginia Roundell (*d* 2005); one *d*. *Educ:* Kelso High Sch.; Royal High Sch., Edinburgh; Univ. of Edinburgh (BA 1st Cl. Hons Hist. 1966; PhD 1972). Lectr, then Sen. Lectr in Hist., Open Univ., 1969–80; Prof. of British and Irish Studies, Eberhard-Karls Univ., Tübingen, 1980–2007, now Emeritus. Hon. Professor: of Politics, Univ. of Wales, Aberystwyth, 1996; of Hist., Strathclyde Univ., 1999. Has made broadcasts and TV films. *Publications:* The Lights of Liberalism, 1976; Scotland and Nationalism, 1977, 4th edn 2004; Scotland since 1914, 1981, 4th edn 2009; The Centre of Things: British political fiction, 1991; Cultural Weapons, 1992; The Rise of Regional Europe, 1993; Fool's Gold: the story of North Sea oil, 1993; Travelling Scot, 1999; The Oxford Short History of Scotland, 2002; Scotland's Transport, 2002; Mending Scotland, 2004; Floating Commonwealth: the Atlantic world, 2008; articles in learned jls, Scotsman, Guardian, etc. *Recreations:* walking, painting, music, travel by train and ship. *Address:* Scottish Parliament, Holyrood, Edinburgh EH99 1SP. *T:* (0131) 348 6765, *Fax:* (0131) 348 6767; *e-mail:* christopher.harvie.msp@scottish.parliament.uk.

HARVIE, Sir John (Smith), (Sir Jack), Kt 1997; CBE 1992; Senior Partner, J. S. Harvie & Co., since 1993; *b* 9 Aug. 1936; *s* of Alexander Wood Harvie and Margaret Isabella Smith Harvie; *m* 1958, Elizabeth Maxwell; one *s* two *d*. *Educ:* Ibrox Secondary Sch., Glasgow. Served HLI, 1954–57; Founder, J. S. Harvie & Co., 1959; Chairman: Central Building Contractors (CBC) Ltd, 1971–; Hugh Muirhead & Son Ltd, 1972–; T. W. Scott Ltd, 1974–; City Link Developments (Glasgow) Ltd, 1984–. *Recreations:* travel, reading. *Address:* Auchencraig, Mugdock, Milngavie, Glasgow G62 8EJ.

HARVIE, Jonathan Alexander; QC 1992; *b* 21 March 1950; *s* of late Anthony Bedford Harvie and of Winifred Jean Harvie (*née* Treliving); *m* 1981, Antonia Mary Lea, *d* of late Rev. His Honour Christopher Gerald Lea, MC; two *s* one *d*. *Educ:* King's Sch., Canterbury; Brasenose Coll., Oxford (BA Jurisprudence). Called to the Bar: Middle Temple, 1973 (Bencher, 2003); Bahamas, 2004. An Asst Recorder, 1994–2000; a Recorder, 2000–02. Life Mem., Internat. Soc. of Dendrologists. *Recreations:* gardening, racing, golf, music. *Address:* Blackstone Chambers, Blackstone House, Temple, EC4Y 9BW. *T:* (020) 7583 1770; 1 Garden Court, Temple, EC4Y 9BJ. *Clubs:* White's, Pratt' Swinley Forest Golf; Vincent's (Oxford).

HARVIE, Patrick; Member (Green) Glasgow, Scottish Parliament, since 2003; *b* 1 March 1973; *s* of Dave and Rose Harvie. *Educ:* Dumbarton Acad.; Manchest Metropolitan Univ. Youth Worker, then Develt Worker, PHACE West, subseq. PHAC Scotland, 1997–2003. *Recreations:* computing, reading, cinema, food and drink. *Addres* Scottish Parliament, Edinburgh EH99 1SP. *T:* (0131) 348 6365; *e-ma* patrick.harvie.msp@scottish.parliament.uk.

HARVIE-WATT, Sir James, 2nd Bt *cr* 1945, of Bathgate, Co. Lothian; FCA; compar director; *b* 25 Aug. 1940; *s* of Sir George Harvie-Watt, 1st Bt, QC, TD and Bettie, *o d* Paymaster-Capt. Archibald Taylor, OBE, RN; *S* father, 1989; *m* 1966, Roseline, *d* of La Baron Louis de Chollet, Fribourg, Switzerland, and Frances Tate, Royal Oak, Marylan USA; one *s* one *d*. *Educ:* Eton; Christ Church, Oxford (MA). FCA 1975 (ACA 1965 Lieut London Scottish (TA), 1959–67. With Coopers & Lybrand, 1962–70; Executiv British Electric Traction Co. Ltd, and Director of subsid. companies, 1970–78; Man. D Wembley Stadium Ltd, 1973–78; Chairman: Cannons Sports & Leisure Ltd, 1990–93; H Ball Gp, then Langley & Johnson, then Medi@Invest, 1995–2002; Oliver & Saunde Gp, 1997–. Director: Lake & Elliot Industries Ltd, 1988–93; Penna Consulting plc, 1995 US Smaller Companies Investment Trust PLC, 1998–2000; Wellington Mgt Portfoli (Ire.), 2000–02, and other cos. Mem. Executive Cttee, London Tourist Board, 1977–8 Member: Sports Council, 1980–88 (Vice-Chm., 1985–88); Mem. Sports Counc enquiries into: Financing of Athletics in UK, 1983; Karate, 1986); Indoor Tennis Initiativ Bd, 1986–89. Chm., Crystal Palace Nat. Sports Centre, 1984–88; Dir, National Centre Bd, 1987–88. Member Management Cttee: Nat. Coaching Foundn, 1984–88; Holm Pierrepont Nat. Water Sports Centre, 1985–88; Mem., Stella Artois Tournament Ctte 1988–95; International Tennis Hall of Fame: Dir, 1996–2005; Chm., Exec. Ctte 2001–05 and 2006–; Chm., Internat. Council, 2007–. Mem. Council, NPFA, 1985–9 FRSA 1978. OStJ 1964, and Mem. London Council of the Order, 1975–84. *Recreation* shooting, tennis, golf, photography, walking. *Heir:* *s* Mark Louis Harvie-Watt [*b* 19 Au 1969; *m* 1996, Miranda, *d* of Martin Thompson; two *s* one *d*]. *Address:* 15 Somers Square, Addison Road, W14 8EE. *T:* (020) 7602 7353; *e-mail:* jhw@dial.pipex.cor *Clubs:* White's, Pratt's, Queen's (Vice-Chm., 1987–90; Chm., 1990–93; Dir, 1987–2006 Swinley Forest Golf.

HARWERTH, Noël, JD; Deputy Chairman, Sumitomo Mitsui Bank Europe, since 200 *b* 16 Dec. 1947; *d* of Ben and Ira Vida Harwerth; *m* 1976, Seth Melhado. *Educ:* Univ. Texas (BS); Univ. of Texas Sch. of Law (JD). Chief Tax Officer: Kennecott Copper Co 1978–82; Dun & Bradstreet, NY, 1982–88; Citigroup, NY, 1988–98; Chief Operatin Officer, Citibank Internat. plc, London, 1998–2003. Partnership Dir, Londo Underground, 2003–; non-executive Director: Royal & SunAlliance plc, 2004–; Cor Gp, 2005–. Non-exec. Mem., Horserace Totalisator Bd, 2006–. *Recreations:* golf, horse racing, shooting, opera. *Address:* Sumitomo Mitsui Bank Europe, Temple Court, 1 Queen Victoria Street, EC4N 4TA. *Clubs:* University, Cosmopolitan (New York Wentworth Golf; Millbrook Golf (New York); Saratoga Golf and Polo.

HARWOOD, John Warwick; DL; Chairman, CfBT Education Trust (formerly CFBT since 2004; Chief Executive, Food Standards Agency, 2006–08; *b* 10 Dec. 1946; *s* of lat Dennis G. and Mrs W. G. Harwood, West Camel, Somerset; *m* 1967, Diana, *d* of la Harford Thomas; one *s* one *d*. *Educ:* Univ. of Kent at Canterbury (BA Hons); Univ. London (MA). Admin. Officer, GLC, 1968–73; Private Sec. to Leader of ILEA, 1973–7 Head of Chief Exec.'s Office, London Bor. of Hammersmith and Fulham, 1977–79; As Chief Exec., London Bor. of Hammersmith and Fulham, 1979–82; Chief Exec., Londo Bor. of Lewisham, 1982–89; Hon. Clerk, S London Consortium, 1983–89; Chief Exec Oxfordshire CC, 1989–2000; Clerk, Lieutenancy for Oxfordshire, 1989–2001; Chi Exec., Learning and Skills Council, 2000–03; Interim Chief Exec., Cumbria CC, 2004 Sen. Associate Fellow, Warwick Business Sch., Univ. of Warwick, 2004–07. Director: N Oxfordshire Business Venture Ltd, 1989–98; Thames Business Advice Centre Lt 1989–99; Heart of England TEC, 1990–2001 (Chm., 2000–01); South East Regiona Investment Ltd, 1998–2000. Member: Commn on Future of Voluntary Sector, 1995–9 Business Link Accreditation Adv. Bd, 1996–2000. Chair, Local Authorities Rac Relations Information Exchange, 1990–2000; Mem. Exec. Cttee, TCPA, 1981–8 Chm., Parrott & Lee Foundn, 1998–; Trustee: Oxfordshire Community Foundr 1996–2004; Oxfordshire Victoria County History Trust Appeal, 1997–; Northmoo Trust, 2003– (Chm.). Mem. Ct, Oxford Brookes Univ., 1999–. DL Oxfordshire, 2001 CCMI. Hon. MA Kent, 1995. *Publications:* (contrib.) The Renaissance of Loc Government, 1995; (contrib.) Understanding British Institutions, 1998. *Recreation* walking, cooking, gardening. *Address:* West End House, Wootton, Oxon OX20 1DL. *T* (01993) 810471. *Club:* Reform.

HARWOOD, Ronald, CBE 1999; FRSL; writer; *b* 9 Nov. 1934; *s* of late Isaac Horwit and Isobel Pepper; *m* 1959, Natasha Riehle; one *s* two *d*. *Educ:* Sea Point Boys' High Sch Cape Town; RADA. FRSL 1974. Actor, 1953–60. Artistic Dir, Cheltenham Festival o Literature, 1975; Presenter: Kaleidoscope, BBC, 1973; Read All About It, BBC TV 1978–79. Visitor in Theatre, Balliol Coll., Oxford, 1986. TV plays include: The Barber o Stamford Hill, 1960; (with Casper Wrede) Private Potter, 1961; The Guests, 1972 Breakthrough at Reykjavik, 1987; Countdown to War, 1989; adapted several of Roal Dahl's Tales of the Unexpected for TV, 1979–80; TV series, All the World's a Stage, 1984 screenplays include: A High Wind in Jamaica, 1965; One Day in the Life of Iva Denisovich, 1971; Evita Perón, 1981; The Dresser, 1983; Mandela, 1987; The Brownin Version, 1994; Cry, The Beloved Country, 1995; Taking Sides, 2002; The Pianist, 200 (Academy Award, 2003); Being Julia, 2004; The Diving Bell and the Butterfly, 200 (BAFTA Award, 2008); Love in the Time of Cholera, 2007; An English Tragedy, 2008 Directed: The Odd Couple, 1989; Poison Pen, 1993, Royal Exchange, Mancheste Another Time, Steppenwolf Theatre, Chicago, 1991. Chairman: Writers Guild of Gi 1969; Council, RSL, 2001–04 (Mem., 1998–2001); Member: Lit. Panel, Arts Council o GB, 1973–78; Cttee, Royal Literary Fund, 1995–2005 (Pres., 2005–); Cttee, Englis PEN, 1987–93 (Pres., 1989–93); Pres., Internat. PEN, 1993–97. Gov., Central Sch. o Speech and Drama, 1993–98. Trustee, Booker Foundn, 2002. Hon. DLitt Keele, 2002 Stefan Mitrov Ljubiša Prize, Budva Festival, Montenegro, for services to Europea literature and human rights, 2000. Chevalier, Nat. Order of Arts and Letters (France 1996. *Publications:* novels: All the Same Shadows, 1961; The Guilt Merchants, 1963; Th Girl in Melanie Klein, 1969; Articles of Faith, 1973; The Genoa Ferry, 1976; Cesar an Augusta, 1978; Home, 1993 (Jewish Qly prize for fiction, 1994); short stories: One Interior. Day.—adventures in the film trade, 1978; (co-ed) New Stories 3, 1978; biography Sir Donald Wolfit, CBE—his life and work in the unfashionable theatre, 1971; (ed) Th Ages of Gielgud, 1984; (ed) Dear Alec: Guinness at seventy-five, 1989; essays: (ed) A Nigh at the Theatre, 1983; (ed) The Faber Book of Theatre, 1993; plays: Country Matters 1969; The Ordeal of Gilbert Pinfold (from Evelyn Waugh), 1977; A Family, 1978; Th Dresser, 1980 (New Standard Drama Award; Drama Critics Award); After the Lion 1982; Tramway Road, 1984; The Deliberate Death of a Polish Priest, 1985; Interpreters

1985; J. J. Farr, 1987; Ivanov (from Chekhov), 1989; Another Time, 1989; Reflected Glory, 1992; Poison Pen, 1993; The Collected Plays of Ronald Harwood, 1993; Ronald Harwood: Plays 2, 1995; Taking Sides, 1995; The Handyman, 1996; Goodbye Kiss, 1997; Equally Divided, 1998; Quartet, 1999; Mahler's Conversion, 2001; An English Tragedy, 2008; Collaboration, 2008; *screenplays*: The Pianist, and Taking Sides, 2002; *musical libretto*: The Good Companions, 1974; *historical*: All the World's a Stage, 1983. *Recreation*: watching cricket. *Address*: c/o Judy Daish Associates, 2 St Charles Place, W10 6EG. *T*: (020) 8964 8811. *Clubs*: Garrick, Beefsteak, MCC.

HASAN, Wajid Shamsul; Adviser to Hon. Benazir Bhutto, 1997; *b* 5 Jan. 1941; *s* of late Shamsul Hasan and Amir Begum; *m* Zarina Wajid Hasan; one *s*. *Educ*: Karachi Univ. (LLB 1964); Master in Internat. Relations 1962. Freelance journalist, 1960; joined Jang Group of Newspapers, 1962; Editor, The News (English lang. daily), 1969; Founding Editor, MAG (English Weekly), 1981. Chm., Nat. Press Trust, 1989–90. Press Adviser to Hon. Benazir Bhutto, 1991–94; High Comr for Pakistan in London, 1994–97. *Recreation*: reading. *Address*: Flat 2, 122 Finchley Road NW3 5HT. *Clubs*: Royal Over-Seas League, Travellers.

HASELER, Prof. Stephen Michael Alan, PhD; author; Director, Global Policy Institute, since 2007, and Professor of Government, since 1986, London Metropolitan University (formerly City of London Polytechnic, then London Guildhall University); *b* 9 Jan. 1942; *m* 1967, Roberta Alexander. *Educ*: London School of Economics (BSc(Econ), PhD). Contested (Lab): Saffron Walden, 1966; Maldon, 1970. Chm., Labour Political Studies Centre, 1973–78. Mem. GLC, 1973–77, Chm. General Purposes Cttee, 1973–75. Founder Mem., SDP, 1981. Sen. Res. Fellow, Federal Trust, London, 2002–. Visiting Professor: Georgetown Univ., Washington DC, 1978; Johns Hopkins Univ., 1984; Maryland Univ., 1984–. Founder and Co-Chm., Radical Soc., 1988–; Chm., Republic, 1992–; Dir, Euro Res. Forum, 1997–2006. MInstD 1987. *Publications*: The Gaitskellites, 1969; Social-Democracy—Beyond Revisionism, 1971; The Death of British Democracy, 1976; Eurocommunism: implications for East and West, 1978; The Tragedy of Labour, 1980; Anti-Americanism, 1985; Battle for Britain: Thatcher and the New Liberals, 1989; The Politics of Giving, 1992; The End of the House of Windsor: Birth of a British Republic, 1993; The English Tribe: identity, nation and Europe, 1996; The Super-Rich: the unequal world of global capitalism, 2000; Super-State: the new Europe and its challenge to America, 2004; Sidekick: British global strategy from Churchill to Blair, 2007. *Recreations*: cricket, American politics. *Address*: 2 Thackeray House, Ansdell Street, W8 5HA. *T*: (020) 7937 3976, (office) (020) 7320 1152.

HASELHURST, Rt Hon. Sir Alan (Gordon Barraclough), Kt 1995; PC 1999; MP (C) Saffron Walden, since July 1977; Chairman of Ways and Means and Deputy Speaker, since 1997; *b* 23 June 1937; *s* of late John Haselhurst and Alyse (*née* Barraclough); *m* 1977, Angela (*née* Bailey); two *s* one *d*. *Educ*: King Edward VI Sch., Birmingham; Cheltenham Coll.; Oriel Coll., Oxford. Pres., Oxford Univ. Conservative Assoc., 1958; Sec., Treas. and Librarian, Oxford Union Soc., 1959–60; Nat. Chm., Young Conservatives, 1966–68. MP (C) Middleton and Prestwich, 1970–Feb. 1974. PPS to Sec. of State for Educn, 1979–82. Mem., H of C Select Cttee on European Legislation, 1982–97, on Catering, 1991–97, on Transport, 1992–97; Hon. Sec., All Party Parly Cricket Gp, 1993–. Chm., Rights of Way Review Cttee, 1983–93. Chairman: Manchester Youth and Community Service, 1974–77; Commonwealth Youth Exchange Council, 1978–81; Chm. Trustees, Community Development (formerly Projects) Foundn, 1986–97. *Publications*: Occasionally Cricket, 1999; Eventually Cricket, 2001; Incidentally Cricket, 2003. *Recreations*: gardening, theatre, music, watching cricket. *Address*: House of Commons, SW1A 0AA; *e-mail*: haselhursta@parliament.uk. *Clubs*: MCC; Essex CC (Mem., Exec. Cttee, 1996–2008).

HASELOCK, Rev. Canon Jeremy Matthew, FSA; Residentiary Canon and Precentor, since 1998, Vice Dean, since 2004, Norwich Cathedral; *b* 20 Sept. 1951; *s* of Kenneth Pool Haselock and Pamela Haselock (*née* Bolus). *Educ*: Univ. of York (BA Hons History 1973); Univ. of York Centre for Mediaeval Studies (BPhil 1974); St Stephen's House, Oxford (BA Theol. 1982, MA 1985). Deacon 1983, priest 1984; Asst Curate, St Gabriel, Pimlico, 1983–86; Asst Priest, St John, Lafayette Sq., Washington, 1985; Asst Curate, St James, Paddington, 1986–88; Domestic Chaplain to Bp of Chichester, 1988–91; Vicar of Boxgrove, 1991–98; Chichester Dio. Liturgical Advr, 1991–98; Preb. of Fittleworth and Canon of Chichester Cathedral, 1994–2000. Proctor in Convocation and Mem., Gen. Synod, 1995–. Chm., Norwich Dio. Liturgical Cttee, 1998–; Member: C of E Liturgical Commn, 1996–2006; C of E Liturgical Publishing Gp, 2001–03; Chichester DAC for Care of Churches, 1991–98; Norwich DAC for Care of Churches, 1998–; Pubns Cttee, 1988–93, Archaeol Working Party, 1997–99, Council for Care of Churches; Cathedrals Fabric Commn for England, 2003–; Bishoprics and Cathedrals Cttee, Church Comrs, 2006–; Council, Guild of Church Musicians, 2001– (Sub-Warden, 2005–). Chm. of Govs, Boxgrove Sch., 1991–98; Gov., Norwich Sch., 1998–. Freeman, Glaziers' Co., 2002. Chaplain Gen., 2001–04, Chancellor, 2005–, Order of St Lazarus of Jerusalem. FSA 2007. *Publications*: (with Roger Greenacre) The Sacrament of Easter, 1989, 3rd edn 1995; chapters in works on history, art and architecture of English cathedrals; articles, reviews and papers on liturgical and artistic matters. *Recreations*: foreign travel, collecting Oriental porcelain, music and theatre, especially opera, reading, church crawling, conversation, cooking and entertaining, wine. *Address*: 34 The Close, Norwich NR1 4DZ. *T*: (01603) 619169. *Club*: Athenæum.

HASHMI, Dr Farrukh Siyar, OBE 1974; FRCPsych; Consultant Psychiatrist: All Saints' Hospital, Birmingham, 1969–92; Woodbourne Priory Hospital (formerly Woodbourne Clinic), Edgbaston, 1992–2007; Psychotherapist, HM Prison, Stafford, 1973–92; *b* Gujrat, Pakistan, 12 Sept. 1927; *s* of Dr Ziaullah Qureshi and Majida Qureshi; *m* 1972, Shahnaz; one *s* two *d*. *Educ*: King Edward Med. Coll., Lahore (Punjab Univ.). MB BS; MRCPsych; DPM; FRCPsych 1979. Mayo Hosp. and King Edward Med. Coll., Lahore, March–Sept. 1953; New End Hosp., Hampstead, 1954; Children's Hosp., Birkenhead, 1954–55; Sen. House Officer, Brook Gen. Hosp., Woolwich, 1955–56; Snowdon Road Hosp., Bristol, 1956; Asst MOH, Co. Berwicks, 1957; Scholar, Volkart Foundn, Switzerland, 1958–60; psychiatric medicine: Registrar, Uffculme Clinic and All Saints Hosp., Birmingham, 1960–63, Sen. Registrar, 1966–69; Research Fellow, Dept of Psychiatry, Birmingham Univ., 1963–66. Chairman: Psychiatric Div., West Birmingham Health Dist, 1977–83 and 1988–92; Woodbourne Clinic Hosp. Management Team, 1989–2003; Member: Race Relations Bd, W Midlands Conciliation Cttee, 1968–81; Community Relations Working Party, NAYC, 1968–81; Home Secretary's Adv. Cttee on Race, 1976–81 (formerly Mem., HO Adv. Cttee on Race Relations Research); CRE, 1980–86; Working Party on Community and Race Relations Trng, HO Police Trng Council, 1982–83; Wkg Gp on Ethnic Minorities, W Midlands RHA, 1982–92; Mental Health Services Cttee, RHA, 1976–92; Council, Mind (NAMH), 1976–81; UK Cttee, World Fedn for Mental Health, 1978–81; Health and Welfare Adv. Panel, NCCI, 1966–81; Cttee of Inquiry into Educn of Children from Ethnic Minority Gps (Swann Cttee), 1982–85; Warley Area Social Services Sub-Cttee, 1973–81; Central DHA, Birmingham, 1982–90; BBC Regl Adv. Council, 1970–77; GMC, 1979–84 (GMC Mem., Tribunal on Misuse of Drugs,

1983–84); Parole Board, 1981–85; Alternate Mem., Economic Social Cttee, EEC, 1985; Advisory Consultant, C of E Bd for Social Responsibility, 1984–87; consultant psychiatrist in eating disorders, St Michael's Hosp., Warwick, 1994–98. President: Pakistan Med. Soc., UK, 1974–76; Overseas Doctors Assoc., UK, 1975–79; Founder and Chm., Iqbal Acad., Coventry Cathedral, 1972–86. Member Editorial Board: New Community, 1972–82; Medicos, 1977–81. Involved in clinical trials and psycho-pharmacological studies, *eg* assessing effects of drugs in anxiety states and neurotic illness, incl. antidepressants. *Publications*: Pakistan Family in Britain, 1965; Mores, Migration and Mental Illness, 1966; Psychology of Racial Prejudice, 1966; Community Psychiatric Problems among Birmingham Immigrants, 1968; In a Strange Land, 1970; Measuring Psychological Disturbance in Asian Immigrants to Britain, 1977. *Recreations*: writing, reading, music. *Address*: Shahnaz, 5 Woodbourne Road, Edgbaston, Birmingham B15 3QJ.

HASKARD, Sir Cosmo (Dugal Patrick Thomas), KCMG 1965 (CMG 1960); MBE 1945; *b* 25 Nov. 1916; *o c* of late Brig.-Gen. J. McD. Haskard, CMG, DSO and Alicia, *d* of S. N. Hutchins, Ardnagashel, Bantry, Co. Cork; *m* 1957, Phillada, *o c* of late Sir Robert Stanley, KBE, CMG and Lady Stanley (*née* Ursula Cracknell); one *s*. *Educ*: Cheltenham; RMC Sandhurst; Pembroke Coll., Cambridge (MA). Served War of 1939–45 (MBE); 2nd Lieut. TA (Gen. List), 1938; emergency Commn, Royal Irish Fusiliers, 1939; seconded KAR, 1941; served 2nd Bn, E Africa, Ceylon, Burma; Major 1944. Apptd Colonial Service cadet, Tanganyika, 1940, but due to war service did not take up duties until 1946 in which yr transf. to Nyasaland; Dist Comr, 1948; served on Nyasaland-Mozambique Boundary Commn, 1951–52; Provincial Commissioner, 1955; acting Secretary for African Affairs, 1957–58; Sec. successively for Labour and Social Development, for Local Government, and for Natural Resources, 1961–64; Governor and C-in-C, Falkland Islands, and High Comr for the British Antarctic Territory, 1964–70. Trustee, Beit Trust, 1976–2003. *Address*: Tragariff, Bantry, Co. Cork, Ireland.

HASKARD, Prof. Dorian Oliver, DM; FRCP; British Heart Foundation Sir John McMichael Professor of Cardiovascular Medicine, and Professor of Rheumatology, National Heart and Lung Institute, Imperial College London (formerly Royal Postgraduate Medical School, then Imperial College School of Medicine) at Hammersmith Hospital, since 1995; *b* 8 July 1951; *s* of Oliver Patrick Miller Haskard and Anna Caroline (*née* Worthington); *m* 1980, Kathleen Ann Keitzman; three *s*. *Educ*: Eton Coll.; St Edmund Hall, Oxford (MA; DM 1989); Middlesex Hosp. Med. Sch. FRCP 1994. Res. Fellow, Southwestern Med. Sch., Dallas, 1984–86; Wellcome Trust Sen. Res. Fellow in Clinical Sci., UMDS, Guy's Hosp., 1987–90; Royal Postgraduate Medical School, Hammersmith Hospital: Sen. Lectr in Rheumatology, 1990–94; Reader, 1994. FMedSci 2001. *Publications*: papers on rôle of blood vessels in inflammation. *Recreation*: gardening. *Address*: National Heart and Lung Institute, Imperial College London, Hammersmith Hospital, Du Cane Road, W12 0NN. *T*: (020) 8383 3064.

HASKEL, family name of **Baron Haskel**.

HASKEL, Baron *cr* 1993 (Life Peer), of Higher Broughton in the Metropolitan County of Greater Manchester; **Simon Haskel**; *b* Kaunas, Lithuania, 9 Oct. 1934; *s* of late Isaac and Julia Haskel; *m* 1962, Carole Lewis, New York, USA; one *s* one *d*. *Educ*: Salford Coll. of Advanced Technol. (BSc Textile Technol.). ATI. Nat Service commn, RA, 1959. Joined Perrotts Ltd, 1961; Chm., Perrotts Gp and associated cos, 1973–97. An opposition whip, H of L, 1994–97; an opposition spokesman on trade and industry, 1995–97; a Lord in Waiting (Govt Whip), 1997–98; front bench spokesman on trade and industry, on treasury, and on social security, 1997–98. Mem., Select Cttee on Sci. and Technol., 1995–97, 1999–2003, 2007–; Dep. Chm. of Cttees, H of L, 2002–; Dep. Speaker, H of L, 2002–. Labour Party: Sec., 1972 Industry Gp, 1976–81; Sec., 1981–90, Chm., 1990–96, Finance and Industry Gp. Chm., Thames Concerts Soc., 1982–90; Pres., Inst. of Jewish Policy Res. (formerly Inst. of Jewish Affairs), 1998–. Chm. Trustees, The Smith Inst., 1999–. Hon. President: Envmtl Industries Commn, 2000–04; Technitex Faraday, 2002–; Materials UK, 2006–. Patron: Soc. of Ops Engrs, 2000–04; Chronic Disease Res. Foundn, 2000–. FRSA 1979. *Recreations*: music, cycling. *Address*: House of Lords, SW1A 0PW. *T*: (020) 7219 4076.

HASKELL, (Donald) Keith, CMG 1991; CVO 1979; international affairs consultant and lecturer; HM Diplomatic Service, retired; *b* 9 May 1939; *s* of Donald Eric Haskell and Beatrice Mary Haskell (*née* Blair); *m* 1966, Maria Luisa Soeiro Tito de Morais; two *s* two *d* (and one *s* one *d* decd). *Educ*: Portsmouth Grammar Sch.; St Catharine's Coll., Cambridge (BA 1961, MA 1964). Joined HM Foreign Service, 1961; served in: London, Lebanon, Iraq, Libya; HM Consul, Benghazi, 1969–70; First Sec., Tripoli, 1970–72; Foreign and Commonwealth Office, 1972–75; Chargé d'Affaires and Consul-Gen., Santiago, 1975–78; Counsellor and Consul-Gen., Dubai, 1978–81; Hd, Nuclear Energy Dept, FCO, 1981–83; Hd, Middle East Dept, FCO, 1983–84; Hd of Chancery, Bonn, 1985–88; on secondment as an advr to industry, 1988–89; Ambassador: to Peru, 1990–95; to Brazil, 1995–99. Dr *hc* Nat. Univ. of Peruvian Amazonia, Iquitos, 1992. Foundation Medal, Soka Univ. of Japan, 1975. Grand Cross, Order of Rio Branco (Brazil), 1997. *Recreations*: rifle shooting (captained Cambridge Univ. Rifle Assoc., 1960–61; represented England and GB in shooting competitions on various occasions), ski-ing, wine and food. *Address*: Barn Cottage, Brightstone Lane, Farringdon, Alton, Hants GU34 3DP. *Club*: Hawks (Cambridge).

HASKELL, Peter Thomas, CMG 1975; PhD, CBiol, FIBiol; Research Consultant, School of Pure and Applied Biology, University of Wales College of Cardiff, 1992–94, Fellow, 1994, retired; *b* 21 Feb. 1923; *s* of late Herbert James and Mary Anne Haskell; *m* 1st, 1946; one *s*; 2nd, 1979, Aileen Kirkley. *Educ*: Portsmouth Grammar Sch.; Imperial Coll., London. BSc, ARCS, PhD. Asst Lectr, Zoology Dept, Imperial Coll., London, 1951–53; Lectr, 1953–55; Sen. Sci. Officer, Anti-Locust Research Centre, Colonial Office, 1955–57; Principal Sci. Officer, 1957–59; Dep. Dir, 1959–62; Dir, Anti-Locust Research Centre, ODM, 1962–71; Dir, Centre for Overseas Pest Res. and Chief Advr on Pest Control, ODA, 1971–83; Dir, Cleppa Park Field Res. Stn, UC Cardiff, later Univ. of Wales Coll. of Cardiff, 1984–91. Consultant: FAO, UN, 1962–; UNDP, 1970–; WHO, 1973–91; OECD, 1975–; UNEP, 1976–91; Agricl and Vet. Adv. Cttee, British Council, 1976–90; Plants and Soils Res. Cttee, AFRC, later Plants and Envmt Res. Cttee, 1988–91; IFAD, 1995–; Mem., UNDP/FAO Special Adv. Cttee on Desert Locust, 1990–. Vice-Pres., Inst. of Biology, 1982. Professorial Res. Fellow, University Coll. Cardiff, 1971–83. Mem., Bd of Governors, Internat. Centre for Insect Physiology and Ecology, Kenya, 1972– (Vice-Chm., 1978; Chm., 1979–). Vis. Prof., Univ. of Newcastle, 1977. Thamisk Lectr, Royal Swedish Acad. of Scis, 1979. Van Den Brande Internat. Prize, 1982. Chief Editor, Tropical Pest Management, 1985–92; Mem., Editorial Bd, Review of Applied Entomol., 1988–91. *Publications*: Insect Sounds, 1962; The Language of Insects, 1962; Pesticide Application: principles and practice, 1985; Ecotoxicology: pesticides and beneficial organisms, 1998; many papers and articles in scientific and literary jls. *Recreations*: gardening, reading. *Address*: 14 Maddox Drive, Worth, W Sussex RH10 7PQ.

HASKINS, family name of **Baron Haskins**.

HASKINS, Baron *cr* 1998 (Life Peer), of Skidby in the co. of the East Riding of Yorkshire; **Christopher Robin Haskins;** Chairman: Northern Foods, 1986–2002; Express Dairies plc, 1998–2002; *b* 30 May 1937; *s* of Robin and Margaret Haskins; *m* 1959, Gilda Horsley; three *s* two *d*. *Educ:* Trinity Coll., Dublin (BA Mod). Ford Motor Co., Dagenham, 1960–62; Northern Foods, formerly Northern Dairies, 1962–2002. Chm., Better Regulation Task Force, 1997–2002; Mem., New Deal Task Force, 1997–2001. Mem. Bd, Yorks and Humber Regl Develt Agency, 1998–. Member: Culliton Irish Industrial Policy Review Gp, 1991–92; Commn for Social Justice, 1992–94; UK Round Table on Sustainable Develt, 1995–98; Hampel Cttee on Corporate Governance, 1996–97. Mem., H of L Europe Sub-Cttee D, 2003–06, Sub-Cttee A, 2007–; Chm., European Movement, 2004–06. Trustee: Runnymede Trust, 1989–98; Demos, 1993–2000; Civil Liberties Trust, 1997–99; Legal Assistance Trust, 1998–2004; Lawes Agricl Trust, 1999–. Pro-Chancellor, Open Univ., 2005–. Hon. LLD: Hull, 1999; Dublin, 2000; Nottingham, Huddersfield, 2002; DU: Leeds Metropolitan, 1998; Essex, 2000; Hon. DSc: Cranfield, 2000; Lincoln, 2003; Bradford, 2005. *Recreations:* writing, week-end farm relief-man, cricket. *Address:* Quarryside Farm, Main Street, Skidby, near Cottingham, East Yorks HU16 5TG. *T:* (01482) 842692.

HASKINS, Sam, (Samuel Joseph); photographic designer; *b* 11 Nov. 1926; *s* of Benjamin G. Haskins and Anna E. Oelofse; *m* 1952, Alida Elzabé van Heerden; two *s*. *Educ:* Helpmekaar Sch.; Witwatersrand Technical Coll.; Bolt Court Sch. of Photography. Freelance work: Johannesburg, 1953–68; London, 1968–. One-man Exhibitions: Johannesburg, 1953, 1960; Tokyo, 1970, 1973, 1976, 1981, 1985, 1987–88, 1990, 1992, 1993, 1996, 1999; London, 1972, 1976, 1978, 1980, 1987, 1999; Paris, 1973; Amsterdam, 1974; NY, 1981; San Francisco, 1982; Toronto, 1982; Bologna, 1982; Auckland, 1991; Sydney, 1991; Hong Kong, 1991; Taipei, 1991; Singapore, 1991; Osaka, 1990, 1992, 1993, 1997, 2000; Prague, 1993; Palermo, 1993; Glasgow, 1997; Berlin, 2000; Australian Nat. Portrait Gall., Canberra, 2006. *Publications:* Five Girls, 1962; Cowboy Kate and other stories, 1964 (Prix Nadar, France, 1964), rev. repr. 2006; November Girl, 1966; African Image, 1967 (Silver Award, Internat. Art Book Contest, 1969); Haskins Posters, 1972 (Gold Medal, New York Art Directors Club, 1974); Photo-Graphics, 1980 (Kodak Book Award); Cowboy Kate—Director's Cut, 2006; portfolios in most major internat. photographic magazines. *Recreations:* sculpting, books, music. *Address: e-mail:* sam@haskins.com; *web:* www.haskinsblog.com.

HASLAM, Christopher Peter de Landre; HM Diplomatic Service, retired; Ambassador (non-resident) to Marshall Islands, Micronesia and Palau, 2000–03; Deputy High Commissioner to Fiji Islands, Tuvalu, Kiribati and Nauru, 2000–03; *b* 22 March 1943; *s* of late Jack Harold Haslam and Molly Patricia Haslam; *m* 1969, Lana Whitley; two *s*. *Educ:* Ashley Co. Secondary, Hants. Admiralty, 1960–66; joined HM Diplomatic Service, 1966: Jakarta, 1969–72; Attaché, Sofia, 1972–74; FCO, 1974–78; Canberra, 1978–82; Second Sec. (Commercial), Lagos, 1982–86; FCO, 1986–89; First Sec. (Commercial), Copenhagen, 1989–93; FCO Inspectorate, 1993–96; First Sec. (Commercial and Econ.), Colombo, 1996–99. *Recreations:* reading, table tennis, tennis, amateur novelist. *Address: e-mail:* chris@christopherhaslam33.wanadoo.co.uk.

HASLAM, David Antony, CBE 2004; FRCP, FRCGP; President, Royal College of General Practitioners, 2006–Nov. 2009; General Practitioner, Ramsey Health Centre, Huntingdon, since 1976; National Clinical Adviser, Healthcare Commission, since 2005; *b* 4 July 1949; *s* of Norman and Mary Haslam; *m* 1974, Barbara Flannery; one *s* one *d*. *Educ:* Monkton Combe Sch.; Birmingham Univ. (MB ChB 1972). DObstRCOG 1974; MRCGP (Dist.) 1976, FRCGP 1989; DFFP 1998; FFPH 2003; FRCP 2004. Vis. Prof. in Primary Health Care, De Montfort Univ., Leicester, 2000–. Chm. of Council, RCGP, 2001–04. Mem., Postgrad. Medical Educn and Trng Bd, 2003–; Co-Chm., Modernising Med. Careers Prog. Bd, 2007–. *Publications:* Sleepless Children, 1984 (also US, Dutch, German, Spanish, Finnish, Swedish, Indonesian, Hebrew, Hungarian, Chinese and Bulgarian edns); Eat It Up, 1986 (also Dutch and Hungarian edns); Travelling With Children, 1987 (also Dutch edn); Parent Stress, 1989 (also Dutch, Finnish and Polish edns); The Expectant Father, 1990, 2nd edn 1998; Bulimia: a guide for sufferers and their families, 1994 (also US and Czech edns); Food Fights, 1995 (also US, German and Chinese edns); Coping with a Termination, 1996; Your Child's Symptoms Explained, 1997 (also Czech, Polish, Romanian and Greek edns); Stress Free Parenting, 1998 (also Bulgarian and Russian edns); A–Z Guide to Children's Health, 1999; (ed) The Guide to Your Child's Symptoms, 1999; (ed) Not Another Guide to Stress in General Practice, 2000; contrib. numerous articles and papers to med. jls. *Recreations:* music, photography, travel; ran London Marathon, 2006. *Address:* 35 Biggin Lane, Ramsey, Huntingdon, Cambs PE26 1NB. *T:* (01487) 813033; *e-mail:* davidhaslam@hotmail.com.

HASLAM, Rear Adm. Sir David William, KBE 1984 (OBE 1964); CB 1979; President, Directing Committee, International Hydrographic Bureau, Monaco, 1987–92; *b* 26 June 1923; *s* of Gerald Haigh Haslam and Gladys Haslam (*née* Finley). *Educ:* Ashe Prep. Sch., Etwall; Bromsgrove Sch., Worcs. FRGS, FRIN, FRICS. Special Entry Cadet, RN, 1941; HMS Birmingham, HMAS Quickmatch, HMS Resolution (in Indian Ocean), 1942–43; specialised in hydrographic surveying, 1944; HMS White Bear (surveying in Burma and Malaya), 1944–46; comd Survey Motor Launch 325, 1947; RAN, 1947–49; HMS Scott, 1949–51; HMS Dalrymple, 1951–53; i/c RN Survey Trng Unit, Chatham, 1953–56; HMS Vidal, 1956–57; comd, HMS Dalrymple, 1958; comd, HMS Dampier, 1958–60; Admty, 1960–62; comd, HMS Owen, 1962–64; Exec. Officer, RN Barracks, Chatham, 1964–65; Hydrographer, RAN, 1965–67; comd, HMS Hecla, 1968–70; Asst Hydrographer, MoD, 1970–72; comd, HMS Hydra, 1972–73; Asst Dir (Naval) to Hydrographer, 1974–75; sowc 1975; Hydrographer of the Navy, 1975–85. Acting Conservator, River Mersey, 1985–87; Advr on Port Appts, Dept of Transport, 1986–87. Underwriting Mem., Lloyd's, 1986–93. Pres., Hydrographic Soc., 1977–79. Vice-Pres., Bromsgrove Sch., 1997– (Gov., 1977–97). President: English Schs Basketball Assoc., 1973–96; Derbyshire CCC, 1991–92. Liveryman, Chartered Surveyors' Co., 1983–. FRSA. *Address:* 146 Worcester Road, Bromsgrove, Worcs B61 7AS. *T:* (01527) 574068.

HASLAM, (Gordon) Edward; Chairman, Talvivaara Mining Company plc, since 2007; Chief Executive Officer, Lonmin plc, 1999–2004; *b* 17 April 1944; *s* of Eric and Marjorie Haslam; *m* 1972, Caroline Rosemary Harrington; three *s*. *Educ:* King Edward VII Grammar Sch., Sheffield. Man. Dir, Western Platinum Ltd, SA, 1997–99. Pres., Internat. Platinum Assoc., 1990. FInstD 1995; CCMI 2002. *Publication:* Platinum Group Metals and the Quality of Life, 1989. *Recreations:* aviation (holds Private Pilot's Licence), sailing (qualified Yachtmaster).

HASLAM, Rev. Gregory Paul; Minister, Westminster Chapel, Buckingham Gate, since 2002; *b* Liverpool, 13 June 1953; *s* of late Wilfred Haslam and Jean Elizabeth Haslam (*née* Stackhouse); *m* 1975, Ruth Carson Munro; three *s*. *Educ:* Bootle Grammar Sch., Liverpool; Newton-le-Willows Grammar Sch., Merseyside; Bede Coll., Durham Univ. (BA 1975); Padgate Coll. (PGCE 1976); London Theol Seminary. Religious Educn Teacher, Hindley High Sch., Wigan, 1976–78; Minister, Winchester Family Church, Hants, 1980–2002. *Publications:* Chosen for Good, 1986; Could You Fall Away?, 1988; Elisha - a sign and a wonder, 1995; Preach the Word!, 2006; Let My People Grow, 2006; A Radical Encounter with God, 2007; Moving in the Prophetic, 2009; articles in Evangelicals Now, New Frontiers, Christianity, Cover to Cover Every Day, Closer to God, Daily Bread. *Recreations:* reading, cinema, cycling, motor cycling, walking, apologetics. *Address:* c/o Westminster Chapel, Buckingham Gate, SW1E 6BS. *T:* (020) 7834 1731, *Fax:* (020) 7931 8600; *e-mail:* office@westminsterchapel.org.uk.

HASLAM, Rev. John Gordon; non-stipendiary Church of England priest; a Chaplain to the Queen, 1989–2002; *b* 15 July 1932; *s* of Ernest Henry Haslam and Constance Mabel (*née* Moore); *m* 1st, 1957, Margaret Anne Couse (*d* 1985); two *s* one *d*; 2nd, 1987, Marian Kidson Clarke. *Educ:* King Edward's Sch., Birmingham; Birmingham Univ. (LLB); Queen's Coll., Birmingham. National Service, RA, 1956–58 (2nd Lieut). Solicitor's Articled Clerk, Johnson & Co., Birmingham, 1953–56; Asst Solicitor, 1958–62, Partner, 1962–75, Pinsent & Co., Solicitors, Birmingham; a Chm. of Industrial Tribunals, 1976–92, Regl Chm., 1992–96, part-time Chm., 1996–2001. Ordained deacon and priest, Birmingham dio., 1977; Hon. Curate: St Michael's, Bartley Green, Birmingham, 1977–79; St Mary's, Moseley, Birmingham, 1980–96; Hon. Hosp. Chaplain, 1980–88; temp. service as priest in many Birmingham parishes, 1983–96; licensed to officiate, Hereford dio., 1996–. *Recreations:* gardening, steam railways, fell walking. *Address:* 16 Mill Street, Ludlow, Salop SY8 1BE. *T:* (01584) 876663.

HASLAM, Jonathan, CBE 1997; Managing Director, Haslamedia Ltd, since 2005; *b* 2 Oct. 1952; *s* of Arthur and Irene Florence; *m* 1981, Dawn Rachel Saunders; two *s*. *Educ:* Cowbridge Grammar Sch., Glam; Plymouth Poly. (BSc Hons Geog. 1975); Croydon Coll. of Art and Technol. (HNC Business Studies). MCIPR 1997. Mgt Trainee, National Westminster Bank, 1975–79; Information Officer: COI, 1979–82; Dept of Industry, 1982–84; Sen. Inf. Officer, Home Office, 1984–86; Chief Press Officer, then Dep. Hd of Inf., Dept of Employment, 1986–89; Dep. Dir of Inf., Home Office, 1989–91; Dep. Press Sec. to Prime Minister, 1991–95; Head of Inf. and Press Sec. to Minister, Min. of Agriculture, 1995–96; Chief Press Sec. to Prime Minister, 1996–97; Dir of Communications, DFEE, 1997; Dir of Corporate Affairs, London Metal Exchange, 1997–2003; Gp Dir of Communications, Jarvis plc, 2003–05; Chm., The Spokesman, 2003–06. Chm., Friends of Dulwich Coll., 2007– (Dep. Chm., 2006–07); Gov., Bishop Challoner Sch., 2007–. *Recreations:* golf, music, cinema, travel, photography, reading.

HASLAM, Michael Trevor, MD; retired consultant psychiatrist and medical director; *b* 7 Feb. 1934; *s* of Gerald Haslam and Edna Beatrice Haslam (*née* Oldfield); *m* 1959, Shirley Dunstan Jefferies; one *s* two *d*. *Educ:* Sedbergh Sch.; St John's Coll., Cambridge (MA 1960, MD 1971); St Bartholomew's Hosp; Univ. of Leeds (MA (Theol) 2003). FRCP(Glas.) 1979; FRCPsych 1980. Captain, RAMC, 1960–62; hosp. posts, York, 1962–64, Newcastle upon Tyne, 1964–67; Consultant Psychiatrist: Doncaster, 1967–70; York, 1970–89; Medical Director: Harrogate Clinic, 1989–91; SW Durham Mental Health NHS Trust, 1993–96; S Durham Health Care NHS Trust, 1996–98. Former Chm., Soc. of Clinical Psychiatrists; former Cttee Chm., RCP. Freeman, City of London, 1973; Liveryman, Soc. of Apothecaries, 1973. *Publications:* Psychiatric Illness in Adolescence, 1975; Sexual Disorders, 1978 (trans. Spanish, 1980); Psychosexual Disorders, 1979; Psychiatry Made Simple, 1982, 2nd edn 1990 (trans. Polish, 1997); Transvestism, 1993; Clifton Hospital: an era, 1997; Close to the Wind, 2006; articles in learned jls. *Recreations:* writing, music, fives, squash, croquet, travel. *Address:* Chapel Garth, Crayke, York YO61 4TE. *T:* (01347) 823042.

HASLAM, Miranda Jayne; *see* Moore, M. J.

HASLAM, Richard Michael, FSA; writer on architecture; buildings consultant; painter; *b* 27 Sept. 1944; *s* of Cecil Henry Cobden Haslam and Sylvia Lois Haslam (*née* Assheton); *m* 1980, Charlotte Sophia Dorrien Smith (*d* 1997); two *s* one *d*. *Educ:* Eton Coll. (Oppidan Schol.); New Coll., Oxford (BA 1966, MA 1967); Courtauld Inst. of Art (MA 1969). FSA 1987. Res. Asst to Sir Nikolaus Pevsner, 1969–71; Statistician, 1971–72, and Mem., Lloyd's. Curator, Clough Williams-Ellis exhibn, Heinz Gall., RIBA, 1997. National Trust: Member: Architectl Panel, 1979–; Cttee for Wales, 1980–88; Properties Cttee, 1985–2005; Council, 2005–; Member: Historic Buildings Council for Wales, 1980–98; Royal Commn on Ancient and Historical Monuments of Wales, 1986–98; Friends' Cttee, Centro Internazionale di Studi di Architettura 'A. Palladio', 1995–; Prize Jury, Premio Dedalo Minosse for commng a building, 1998– (Chm., 2008–). Trustee, Venice in Peril Fund, 1992–. *Publications:* The Buildings of Wales: Powys, 1979; From Decay to Splendour: the repair of church treasures, 1985; Clough Williams-Ellis's Drawings, 1996; (contrib.) Pevsner Architectural Guides: Gwynedd, 2009; articles in Country Life, Arte Lombarda, Perspectives on Architecture and other jls. *Recreations:* walking, reading, family life. *Address:* Bramley Grange, Bramley, Tadley, Hants RG26 5DJ; Parc, Llanfrothen, Gwynedd LL48 6SP.

HASLETT, Prof. Christopher, OBE 2004; FRCP, FRCPE, FMedSci; FRSE; Professor of Respiratory Medicine and Director, Rayne Laboratories, University of Edinburgh, since 1990; Hon. Consultant Physician, Lothian Acute Hospitals Trust, since 1990; *b* 2 April 1953; *s* of James and Elizabeth Haslett; *m* 1973, Jean Margaret Hale; one *s* one *d*. *Educ:* Wirral Grammar Sch.; Univ. of Edinburgh Med. Sch. (BSc 1st Cl. Hons Pathology 1974; MB ChB Hons 1974; Ettles Schol.; Leslie Gold Medal for most distinguished grad. 1977). MRCP 1979, FRCP 1991; FRCPE 1988. Jun. med. posts, Edinburgh, 1977–79; Rotating Med. Registrar, Ealing Hosp. and Hammersmith Hosp., 1980–82; MRC Travelling Fellow, Nat. Jewish Hosp., Denver, 1982–85; MRC Sen. Clin. Fellow and Sen. Lectr, Dept of Medicine, RPMS, Hammersmith Hosp., 1986–90; Associate Dean (Res.), 1996–, and Head, Div. of Clin. Sci. and Community Health, 1998–, Univ. of Edinburgh. Vice-Chairman: Res. Cttee, Nat. Asthma Campaign, 1990–94; MRC Molecular and Cellular Medicine Bd, 1994–98; Mem., MRC Systems A Grants Cttee, 1990–92; Chairman: Lung Injury Section, European Respiratory Soc., 1994–98 (Sec., 1991–94); MRC ROPA Infection and Immunity Panel, 1995, 1996. Medal and Prize for Sci., Saltire Soc., 1996; Gilston Lecture and Medal, Intensive Care Soc., 1998; numerous lectures in UK and abroad. FMedSci 1998. *Publications:* (Sen. Ed.) Davidson's Textbook of Medicine, 17th edn 1995, 18th edn 1999; (ed jtly) ARDS—Acute Respiratory Distress Syndrome in Adults, 1997; numerous articles in learned jls concerning inflammatory cell biology and inflammatory lung disease. *Recreations:* Rugby Union (spectating only, these days), contemporary fiction, cooking, eating and drinking (not necessarily in that order). *Address:* Department of Medical and Radiological Sciences, Royal Infirmary, Lauriston Place, Edinburgh EH3 9YW. *T:* (0131) 536 2263; *e-mail:* C.Haslett@ed.ac.uk.

HASSALL, Prof. Cedric Herbert, FRS 1985; CChem, FRSC; Hon. Visiting Professor, London Metropolitan University (formerly University of North London), since 1999; *b* 6 Dec. 1919; *s* of late H. Hassall, Auckland, NZ; *m* 1st, 1946, H. E. Cotti (marr. diss. 1982); one *d* (and one *s* decd); 2nd, 1984, J. A. Mitchelmore. *Educ:* Auckland Grammar Sch., NZ; Auckland Univ. (MSc); Univ. of Cambridge (PhD, ScD). Lectr, Univ. of Otago, NZ, 1943–45; Sen. studentship, Royal Commn for 1851, Cambridge, 1946–48; Foundn Prof. of Chem., Univ. of WI, 1948–56; Carnegie and Rockefeller Fellowships in USA, 1950, 1956; Head, Dept of Chemistry, Univ. Coll., of Swansea, UCW, 1957–71; Dir of

Research, Roche Products Ltd, 1971–84. Comr, Royal Univ. of Malta, 1964–71; Planning Adviser: Univ. of Jordan, 1965–71; Univ. of Aleppo, 1965; Abdul Aziz Univ., Jedda, 1966, 1968. Visiting Professor: Univ. of Kuwait, 1969, 1979, 1997; Aligarh Univ., India (Royal Soc.), 1969–70; Univ. of Liverpool, 1971–79; UCL, 1979–85; Warwick Univ., 1985–95; Hon. Visiting Professor: UC, Cardiff, 1985–92; Imperial Coll., London, 1989–97. Pres., Chem. Section of British Assoc., 1987; Member: various cttees of Royal Soc. Chem., 1959– (Pres., Perkin Div., 1985–87); Council, British Technol. Gp, 1986–92; various Govt cttees relating to sci. affairs; Co-ordinator, Molecular Recognition Initiative, SERC, 1987–90; ODA Advr on science, technology and educn in India, China and Indonesia, 1989–. Chm., Steering Cttee, Oxford Centre for Molecular Scis, 1988–92. Chm., Mother and Child Foundn, 1995–2001; Dir, IMET 2000, 2001–. Hon. Fellow, UC of Swansea, 1986. Hon. DSc West Indies, 1975. *Publications:* papers on aspects of organic chemistry, largely in Jl of Chemical Soc. *Recreation:* travel. *Address:* 2 Chestnut Close, Westoning, Beds MK45 5LR. *T:* (01525) 712909, *Fax:* (01525) 752550; *e-mail:* cedric.hassall@btinternet.com.

HASSALL, Craig Steven; Managing Director, English National Ballet, since 2005; *b* Australia, 2 Dec. 1964; *s* of Frank Hassall and Brenda Hassall (*née* Zell, now Millan). *Educ:* Univ. of Sydney (BEc). Corporate Inf. Manager, 1987–90, Planning Manager, 1990–92, Opera Australia; Man. Dir, Bell Shakespeare Co., 1993–94; Mktg Dir, Opera Australia, 1995–97; Hd, Cultural Olympiad, Sydney 2000 Olympic Games, 1997–2001; Dep. Gen. Manager, Sydney Theatre Co., 2002–05. *Recreations:* theatre, music, heritage. *Address:* English National Ballet, Markova House, 39 Jay Mews, SW7 2ES. *T:* (020) 7581 1245; *e-mail:* craig.hassall@ballet.org.uk.

HASSALL, Eric Ronald, CBE 1999; FIMMM, FRICS, FGS; Deputy Chairman, Coal Authority, 1997–2000; Chairman, British Geological Survey Board, 1994–2001; *b* 16 Nov. 1930; *s* of George Arthur Hassall and Margaret Hassall; *m* 1953, Joan Wilson; two *s* three *d. Educ:* Leigh Grammar Sch.; Wigan Mining Coll.; Coll. of Estates Management, Manchester Business Sch. CEng. National Coal Bd, 1947–72; Wardell Armstrong: Partner, 1972–81; Sen. Partner, 1981–91; Chairman, 1991–94. Crown Mineral Agent, 1988–92. Mem., NERC, 1993–98. Dep. Pro-Chancellor, Keele Univ., 2003–. Pres., IMinE, 1997–99. Hon. DSc Staffordshire, 1995. *Publications:* contribs on mining technology. *Recreations:* golf, sport, reading, engineering, science, painting, family, local history. *Address:* 33 Sneyd Avenue, Newcastle under Lyme, Staffs ST5 2PZ. *T:* (01782) 619835; *e-mail:* erhjh@hotmail.co.uk. *Clubs:* Newcastle under Lyme Golf; Little Aston Golf; Abersoch Golf.

HASSALL, Tom Grafton, OBE 1999; FSA; archaeologist; Secretary and Chief Executive, Royal Commission on Historical Monuments of England, 1986–99; Fellow, St Cross College, Oxford, since 1974; *b* 3 Dec. 1943; *s* of late William Owen Hassall and Averil Grafton Beaves; *m* 1967, Angela Rosaleen Goldsmith; three *s. Educ:* Dragon Sch., Oxford; Lord Williams's Grammar Sch., Thame; Corpus Christi Coll., Oxford (BA History). FSA 1971. Asst local ed., Victoria County History of Oxford, 1966–67; Director: Oxford Archaeological Excavation Cttee, 1967–73; Oxfordshire Archaeological Unit, 1973–85; Associate Staff Tutor, Oxford Univ. Dept for External Studies, 1978–85; Res. Associate, Inst. of Archaeol., Oxford, 1999–2005. Vis. Fellow, Kellogg Coll., Oxford, 1999–2007. Trustee, Oxford Preservation Trust, 1973–; Chairman: Standing Conf. of Archaeol Unit Managers, 1980–83; British Archaeological Awards, 1983–88; Victoria History of Oxfordshire Trust, 1997–2003; Kelmscott Mgt Cttee, 2000–05; Adv. Cttee on Historic Wreck Sites, 2002–; President: Council for British Archaeology, 1983–86; Oxfordshire Architectural and Historical Soc., 1984–92; ICOMOS, UK, 1997–2003 (Chm., World Heritage Cttee, 2002–07); Mem., Ancient Monuments Adv. Cttee, Historic Buildings and Monuments Commn, 1984–93. Guest Lectr, Swan Hellenic Cruises, 1981–. Crew mem., Athenian Trireme, 1987. Hon. MIFA 1999. *Publications:* Oxford: the city beneath your feet, 1972; specialist articles on archaeology. *Recreation:* boating. *Address:* 4 Whitefriars, Back Lane, Blakeney, Norfolk NR25 7NR. *T:* (01263) 741369. *Club:* Athenæum.

HASSAN, Dame Anna (Patricia Lucy), DBE 2006; Headteacher, 1993–2008, Executive Headteacher, since 2008, Millfields Community School, Hackney; Executive Headteacher, Daubeney Primary School, Hackney, since 2008; *b* 16 March 1946; *d* of Angelo and Rosa Fusco; *m* 1971, Nevzat Hassan; one *s. Educ:* Assumption Convent, Ballynahinch, Co. Down; Coloma Teacher Trng Coll. (Teaching Cert.); NE London Poly. (BEd); London Univ. Inst. of Educn (NPQH). St Joseph's Primary Sch., Rotherhithe, 1969–72; restaurateur, 1973–79; teacher: St Mary's Primary Sch., Banbridge, 1976–79; Baden Powell Sch., Hackney, 1980–85; Headteacher, Grasmere Primary Sch., Hackney, 1986–93. Tutor, NPQH course, London Univ. Inst. of Educn, 2001–. Hon. Fellow, Gloucestershire Univ., 2005. *Publications:* (contrib.) Improving Schools, Improve Communities, 2003; contrib. educnl jls and pubns. *Recreations:* singing, listening to opera mostly and other music genre, reading historical novels. *Address:* c/o Millfields Community School, Hilsea Street, Hackney, E5 0SH. *T:* (020) 8985 7898.

HASSAN, Mamoun Hamid; independent producer/director; Dean (formerly Director) of Editing, International Film and Television School, Cuba, 1997–2002; *b* Jedda, 12 Dec. 1937; *s* of late Dr Hamid Hassan and of Fatma Hassan (*née* Sadat); *m* 1966, Moya Jacqueline Gillespie, MA Oxon; two *s*. Formerly script writer, editor and director; Head of Production Board, British Film Inst., 1971–74; Head of Films Branch, UNRWA, Lebanon, 1974–76; Bd Mem., 1978–84, Man. Dir, 1979–84, Nat. Film Finance Corp. Member: Cinematograph Films Council, 1977–78; Scottish Film Production Fund, 1983–87; Advr, European Script Fund, 1989–90; Sen. Consultant for UNESCO, Harare, Zimbabwe, 1991–93; Hd of Editing, Nat. Film and Television Sch., 1993–97 (Gov., 1983–92). Visiting Lecturer: UCLA; California Inst. of the Arts; Europ. Film Coll.; Satyajit Ray Inst. of Film & Television, Calcutta. Films produced include: No Surrender, 1985; co-writer and co-prod., Machuca, 2004. Producer and presenter, Movie Masterclass, C4 series, 1988, 2nd series, 1990. *Publications:* articles in THES. *Address:* High Ridge, 9 High Street, Deddington, Oxford OX15 0SJ.

HASSELL, Barry Frank; Chief Executive, Independent Healthcare Consultants Ltd, since 2004; *b* 26 Sept. 1944; *s* of late Edgar Frank Hassell and of Rosetta Ethel Hassell (*née* Townsend); *m* 1971, Sylvia Booth; two step *s. Educ:* Swanscombe County Secondary Sch. (Head Boy); London Business Sch. (London Exec. Prog.). FCMI. Accounting, marketing and directors appts, UK, Scandinavia, Africa, 1959–73; Management Consultant, 1973–85; Special Projects Exec., Spastics Soc., 1980–85; Chief Exec., Tadworth Court Trust, 1983–92; Chief Exec., Ind. Healthcare Assoc., 1992–2003. Dir, Project Bombay, 1983–88. Vice Pres., Union of European Private Hosps, 1997, 2000 (Hon. Sec., 1993–97). Gov., Nat. Inst. for Social Work, 1998–2004. FRGS. *Publications:* articles on health and social care issues. *Recreations:* travel, photography, ski-ing. *Address:* Independent Healthcare Consultants Ltd, 2 Perry Avenue, East Grinstead, W Sussex RH19 2DJ. *T:* (01342) 326768.

HASSELL, Julia Elizabeth; *see* Simpson, J. E.

HASSELL, Prof. Michael Patrick, CBE 2002; FRS 1987; Professor of Insect Ecology, Imperial College London, since 1979; *b* 2 Aug. 1942; *s* of Albert Marmaduke Hassell and Gertrude Hassell (*née* Loeser); *m* 1st, 1966, Glynis Mary Everett (marr. diss. 1981); two *s*; 2nd, 1982, Victoria Anne Taylor; one *s* one *d. Educ:* Whitgift School; Clare College, Cambridge (BA 1964, MA); Oriel College, Oxford (DPhil 1967); DSc Oxford 1980. NERC Research Fellow, Hope Dept of Entomology, Oxford, 1968–70; Imperial College London: Lectr, 1970–75, Reader, 1975–79, Dept of Zoology and Applied Entomology; Dep. Head, 1984–92, Head, 1993–2001, Dept of Biology; Dir, Silwood Park, 1988–2004; Principal, 2001–04, Dean, 2004–07, Faculty of Life Scis. Vis. Lectr, Univ. of California, Berkeley, 1967–68; Storer Life Sciences Lectr, Univ. of California, Davis, 1985. Non-exec. Dir, Ealing, Hammersmith and Hounslow HA, 1996–98. Mem., NERC, 1991–94. Trustee, Natural Hist. Mus., 1999–2008. MAE 1998. Scientific Medal, Zoological Soc., 1981; Gold Medal, British Ecol Soc., 1994; Wheldon Prize, Oxford Univ., 1995. *Publications:* Insect Population Ecology (with G. C. Varley and G. R. Gradwell), 1973; The Dynamics of Competition and Predation, 1975; The Dynamics of Arthropod Predator-Prey Systems, 1978; The Spatial and Temporal Dynamics of Host-Parasitoid Interactions, 2000; research papers and review articles on dynamics of animal populations, esp. insects. *Recreations:* natural history, hill walking. *Address:* Barnside, Buckland Brewer, Bideford, Devon EX39 5NF.

HASSELL, Hon. William Ralph Boucher, AM 2000; JP; Proprietor, Hassell Advisory Services, consultants and advisers on community issues and campaigns, 1992–94, and since 1996; Director, Antares Energy Ltd, since 2004; *b* 6 June 1943; *s* of John Boucher Hassell and Dorothy Leslie Hassell (*née* Wright); *m* 1974, Susan Vicki Long; one *s* two *d. Educ:* Western Australian govt schs; Hale Sch., Perth; Univ. of Western Australia (LLB); Univ. of Reading, UK (MA). Barrister and Solicitor; Partner in law firm, Lohrmann, Tindal and Guthrie, WA, 1967–80. MP (L) Cottesloe, WA, 1977–90; Minister for Police and Traffic, 1980–83, for Community Welfare, 1980–82, for Employment and Trng, 1982–83; Leader of the Opposition, 1984–86. Agent Gen. for WA, London, 1994–96; Official Rep., Britain and Europe, Govt of WA, 1997. Dir, Govt Employees Superannuation Bd, WA, 2000–03. Member: Engrg and Manufg Cttee, Commonwealth Industry R&D Bd, 2000–; Commonwealth Superannuation Complaints Tribunal, 2003–; Industry R&D Bd (Commonwealth), 2005–06 (Chm., Automotive Cttee, 2005–). Chm., Liberal Party of Western Australia Pty Ltd, 2006–. Member: Appeal Cttee, Archbp's Appeal for Anglicare, 1987– (Chm., 1991–94); Bd, Multiple Sclerosis Soc. of WA (Vice-Pres), 1990–94 and 1997–; Adv. Bd, Constitutional Centre of WA, 1997–. Hon. Consul for Germany, WA, 1998–. JP WA, 1994–. Centenary Medal, Australia, 2003. *Publications:* Parliamentary newsletter, 1987–90; various articles. *Recreations:* bridge, tennis, reading. *Address:* 20 Loneragan Street, Nedlands, WA 6009, Australia. *T:* (8) 93809991, *Fax:* (8) 93809997; *e-mail:* hassell@arach.net.au. *Clubs:* Weld (Perth); Dalkeith Tennis.

HASTE, Norman David, OBE 1997; FREng; FICE; Chief Operating Officer, Laing O'Rourke Middle East and South Asia, since 2006; *b* 4 Nov. 1944; *s* of Jack Haste and Edith Eleanor Haste (*née* Jarvis); *m* 1968, Judith Ann Graham; two *d. Educ:* Royal Coll. of Advanced Technol., Salford. FICE 1984; FREng (FEng 1996); FIHT 1996. Contracts Manager, McConnell Dowell SE Asia (Singapore), 1981–84; John Laing Construction Ltd: Dir, Special Projects, 1984–85; Project Director: Main Civil Engrg Works, Sizewell B Power Station, 1985–90; Second Severn Crossing, 1990–95; Terminal 5, Heathrow Airport, 1996–2002; Chief Exec., Cross London Rail Links, 2002–05; Ops Dir, High-Point Rendel, 2005–06. Chm., Severn River Crossing PLC, 2000–06. Dir, Transnet, South Africa, 2006–. Hon. DEng West of England, 1997; Hon. DSc Salford, 1998. *Recreations:* golf, music, theatre.

HASTERT, Hon. (John) Dennis; Speaker, House of Representatives, United States of America, 1999–2007; *b* 2 Jan. 1942; *m* 1973, Jean Kahl; two *s. Educ:* Wheaton Coll., Ill (BA 1964); Northern Illinois Univ. (MS 1967). Teacher, Yorkville High Sch., Ill, 1964–80; partner, family restaurant business. Mem. for Springfield, Illinois House of Reps, 1980–86; Mem. (Republican) Illinois, US Congress, 1987–2007. *Address:* c/o Office of the Speaker, H–232 The Capitol, Washington, DC 20515, USA.

HASTERT, Roger Joseph Leon, Grand Cross, Order of Adolphe de Nassau, Luxembourg; Hon. CMG 1972; Dr-en-Droit; Hon. Maréchal de la Cour, Luxembourg, since 1986; *b* Luxembourg City, 10 July 1929; *m* Eléonore Heijmerink; one *s* one *d*. Barrister-at-law, Luxembourg, 1956–59; joined Diplomatic Service, 1959 (Political Affairs); First Sec. and Consul Gen., Brussels, 1963–69; Dir of Protocol and Juridical Affairs, Min. of Foreign Affairs; Pres., Commn Internationale de la Moselle; and Mem., Commn de Contrôle des Comptes des Communautés Européennes, 1969–73; Ambassador to The Netherlands, 1973–1978; Ambassador to UK and Perm. Rep. to Council of WEU, 1978–85, concurrently Ambassador to Ireland and Iceland. *Address:* 44 rue de Mersch, 8181 Kopstal, Luxembourg.

HASTIE, Prof. Nicholas Dixon, CBE 2006; PhD; FMedSci; FRS 2002; FRSE; Member, Scientific Staff, since 1982, Director, since 1994, Medical Research Council Human Genetics Unit, Edinburgh; Director, Edinburgh Institute of Genetics and Molecular Medicine, since 2007; *b* 29 March 1947; *s* of Duncan Sidney Hastie and Eleanor Stella Hastie; *m* 1975, Alison Clayton Todd; one *s* one *d. Educ:* Colwyn Bay Grammar Sch.; Univ. of Liverpool (BSc 1969); King's Coll., Cambridge (PhD 1973). FRSE 1993. Res. Fellow, Edinburgh Univ., 1973–75; Cancer Res. Scientist and Associate Res. Prof., Roswell Park Meml Inst., Buffalo, USA, 1975–82. Hon. Prof., Univ. of Edinburgh, 1993; Internat. Res. Schol., Howard Hughes Med. Inst., 1992–97. Eur. Ed., Genes & Develt, 1991–97. Mem., EMBO, 1990. Member: Scientific Adv. Bd, Inst. of Molecular Pathol., Vienna, 1993–2000; Molecular and Cellular Medicine Bd, 1996–2000, Strategy Develt Gp, 1996–99, MRC; Scientific Adv. Cttee, Lister Inst., 1997–; Internat. Scientific Adv. Bd, Develtl Genetics Prog., Sheffield, 2000–; Cancer Res. UK Scientific Exec. Bd, 2002–; Chairman, Scientific Advisory Board: Wellcome Trust Centre for Human Genetics, Oxford, 2000–; Wellcome Trust, Sanger Inst., 2004–; Chm., Adv. Bd, Cambridge Inst. of Medical Res., 2000–. Numerous distinguished lectures. Charter Fellow, Molecular Medicine Soc., 1996; FMedSci 1998. Gov., Beatson Cancer Res. Inst., 1999–. Hon. DSc Edinburgh, 2005. Genetics Soc. Medal, 2008. *Publications:* contrib. numerous papers to various internat. jls incl. Nature, Cell and Science. *Recreations:* reading, gardening, cooking, travelling, walking, gym. *Address:* MRC Human Genetics Unit, Western General Hospital, Crewe Road, Edinburgh EH4 2XU. *T:* (0131) 467 8401.

HASTIE, Sir Robert Cameron, KCVO 2008; CBE 1983; RD 1968 (Bar 1978); JP; Chairman, Bernard Hastie & Co. Ltd, UK and Australia, since 1973; Lord-Lieutenant, West Glamorgan, 1995–2008 (Vice Lord-Lieutenant, 1991–95); *b* Swansea, 24 May 1933; *s* of B. H. C. Hastie and M. H. Hastie; *m* 1961, Mary Griffiths; two *s* one *d. Educ:* Bromsgrove Sch. Joined RN, National Service, 1951; Midshipman 1953; qual. RNR Ocean comd, 1963; progressive ranks to Captain RNR, 1974, in comd HMS Cambria, 1974–77; Aide-de-Camp to the Queen, 1977; Commodore RNR 1979. Pres., Swansea Unit Sea Cadet Corps, 1982–96. Chairman: Mumbles Lifeboat Station Cttee, 1987–95; Milford Haven Port Authy, 1994–2000. Mem., W Wales Cttee, CBI, 1982–96; Vice

Pres., RNLI, 1999– (Mem. Council, 1991–2006; Trustee and Dep. Treas., 1999–2004). President: Glam W Area Scout Council, 1995–2008 (Chm., 1989–96); RFCA Wales, 2005–08. DL West Glamorgan, 1974; JP Swansea, 1989; High Sheriff of W Glamorgan County, 1977–78. KStJ 2006 (CStJ 1996). *Recreations:* farming, sailing, shooting. *Address:* Upper Hareslade Farm, Bishopston, Swansea SA3 3BU. *T:* (01792) 232957; (day) (01792) 651541. *Clubs:* Naval; Royal Naval Sailing Association (Portsmouth); Bristol Channel Yacht (Swansea); Royal Sydney Yacht Squadron (Sydney, Aust.).

HASTIE-SMITH, Richard Maybury, CB 1984; FIPD 1986; Chairman: Incorporated Froebel Educational Institute, 1993–2003; Templeton Estates Ltd, 1994–2003; *b* 13 Oct. 1931; *s* of Engr-Comdr D. Hastie-Smith and H. I. Hastie-Smith; *m* 1956, Bridget Noel Cox; one *s* two *d. Educ:* Cranleigh Sch. (Schol.); Magdalene Coll., Cambridge (Schol.; MA). HM Forces, commnd Queen's Royal Regt, 1950–51. Entered Administrative Class, Home CS, War Office, 1955; Private Sec. to Permanent Under-Sec., 1957; Asst Private Sec. to Sec. of State, 1958; Principal, 1960; Asst Private Sec. to Sec. of State for Defence, 1965; Private Sec. to Minister of Defence (Equipment), 1968; Asst Sec., 1969; RCDS, 1974; Under-Sec., MoD, 1975, Cabinet Office, 1979–81; Dep. Under-Sec. of State, MoD, 1981–91. Mem., Civil Service Appeal Bd, 1992–99; Non-Service Mem., Home Office Assessment Consultancy Unit for police, prison and fire services, 1992–2003. Chm. Council, Cranleigh and Bramley Schs, 1993–99; Mem. Council, Surrey Univ. Roehampton (formerly Roehampton Inst.), 1993–2003. Chm., 1983–94, Vice-Pres., 1994–, Magdalene Coll. Assoc. *Address:* 18 York Avenue, East Sheen, SW14 7LG. *T:* (020) 8876 4597.
See also Rev. T. M. Hastie-Smith.

HASTIE-SMITH, Rev. Timothy Maybury; Headmaster, Dean Close School, Cheltenham, 1998–Aug. 2009; Principal, Kettering-Montagu Academy, from Sept. 2009; *b* London, 8 March 1962; *s* of Richard Maybury Hastie-Smith, *qv*; *m* 1987, Joanne Elizabeth, *e d* of David and Marion Ide; one *s* two *d. Educ:* Cranleigh Sch. (St Nicholas Scholar); Magdalene Coll., Cambridge (BA 1984); Wycliffe Hall, Oxford (Cert. Theol. 1988). Lay Chaplain, Felsted Sch., 1984–85; Asst Curate, St Ebbe's with Holy Trinity and St Peter-le-Bailey, Oxford, 1988–91; Sen. Chaplain and Admissions Tutor, Stowe Sch., 1991–98. Dir, Knockout Ltd, 1987–90. Chairman: TISCA, 2001–07; HMC West, 2007–08; HMC, 2008–Sept. 2009. Mem., Gloucester Dio. Bd of Educn, 2001–. Governor: St Hugh's Sch., Woodhall Spa, 1995–2001; Orwell Park Sch., 1997–2003; Aldro Sch., 1997–; Hatherop Castle Sch., 1998–; Blue Coat Sch., Birmingham, 1999–2006; Beachborough Sch., 2000–07; Swanbourne House Sch., 2000–; Winterfold House, 2004–08. Fellow, Univ. of Gloucestershire, 1998. *Recreations:* theatre, reading, psephology, cinema, chicken husbandry, Gloucester RUFC, travel, politics, Tottenham Hotspur. *Address:* (until Aug. 2009) Dean Close House, Lansdown Road, Cheltenham, Glos GL51 6QD. *T:* (01242) 267401; *e-mail:* headmaster@deanclose.org.uk. *Club:* East India.

HASTILOW, Michael Alexander; Director, Glynwed Ltd, 1969–81; *b* 21 Sept. 1923; *s* of late Cyril Alexander Frederick Hastilow, CBE, MSc, BCom, FRIC, and Doreen Madge, MA; *m* 1953, Sheila Mary Tipper (*née* Barker); one *s* one *d* (and one *d* decd). *Educ:* Mill Hill Sch.; Birmingham Univ. (Pres., Guild of Undergrads; BSc Civil Engrg, BCom). Served in Fleet Air Arm, RNVR, 1944–46. Commercial Manager, J. H. Lavender & Co. Ltd, 1948–54; Birmid Industries Ltd, 1954–57: Asst Gen. Man., Birmidal Developments Ltd, 1956–57; Commercial Man., Birmetals Ltd, 1957; Commercial and Gen. Sales Man., Bilston Foundries Ltd, 1957–63; Dir, Cotswold Buildings Ltd, 1963–64; Glynwed Ltd, 1964–81: Dir, The Wednesbury Tube Co. Ltd, 1966–81 (Man. Dir, 1968–74; Chm., 1973–76); dir or chm. of various Glynwed divs and subsids. British Non-Ferrous Metals Federation: Mem. Council, 1973–81; Vice Pres., 1975–79; Pres., 1979–80; Chm., Tube Gp, 1975–77. National Home Improvement Council: Mem. Council, 1975–84; Mem. Bd, 1975–84; Vice Chm., 1979–80; Chm., 1980–81. Member: Commn for New Towns, 1978–86; Construction Exports Adv. Bd, 1975–78; Exec. Cttee, 1973–84, and Council, 1974–84, Nat. Council for Bldg Material Producers; EDC for Building, 1980–82. Hon. Treasurer, Midlands Club Cricket Conf., 1970–81, Pres., 1981–82. *Recreations:* cricket, railways. *Address:* The Mount, 3 Kendal End Road, Rednal, Birmingham B45 8PX. *T:* (0121) 445 2007. *Clubs:* MCC, Old Millhillians.
See also N. G. Hastilow.

HASTILOW, Nigel Graham; West Midlands Regional Director, Institute of Chartered Accountants, since 2001; Columnist, Wolverhampton Express & Star, since 2004; *b* 22 Feb. 1956; *s* of Michael Alexander Hastilow, *qv*; *m* 1980, Fiona Mary Findlay. *Educ:* Mill Hill Sch.; Birmingham Univ. (BA 2nd Cl. Hons Eng. Lang. and Lit.). Reporter: Solihull News, 1978–80; Evening Mail, Birmingham, 1980–85; Mktg Manager, Birmingham Post & Mail Ltd, 1985–87; Birmingham Post: Political Editor, 1987–90; Asst Editor, 1990–91; Dep. Editor, 1991–92; Exec. Editor, 1992–93; Editor, 1993–99; W Midlands Dir, Inst. of Dirs, 2000–01; Editl Dir, Heart Media Gp, 2003–05. Contested (C), Birmingham, Edgbaston, 2001. *Publications:* The Last of England, 2004; Tomorrow's England, 2008. *Recreations:* usual sporting and cultural interests, air guitar. *Address:* Corner Cottage, Manor Road, Wickhamford, Worcs WR11 7SA.

HASTINGS; *see* Abney-Hastings, family name of Earl of Loudoun.

HASTINGS, family name of **Baron Hastings of Scarisbrick**.

HASTINGS, 23rd Baron *cr* 1290; **Delaval Thomas Harold Astley;** Bt 1660; *b* 25 April 1960; *er s* of 22nd Baron Hastings and Catherine Rosaline Ratcliffe (*née* Hinton); *S* father, 2007; *m* 1987, Veronica, *er d* of Richard Smart; one *s* two *d. Educ:* Radley; Durham Univ. *Heir: s* Hon. Jacob Addison Astley, *b* 5 Sept. 1991.

HASTINGS OF SCARISBRICK, Baron *cr* 2005 (Life Peer), of Scarisbrick in the County of Lancashire; **Michael John Hastings,** CBE 2002; Global Head of Citizenship and Diversity, KPMG, since 2006; *b* 29 Jan. 1958; *s* of Petain and Olive Hastings; *m* 1990, Jane; one *s* two *d. Educ:* Scarisbrick Hall Sch., Lancs; London Bible Coll. (BA (Hons)); Westminster Coll., Oxford (PGCE). Teacher (Hd of Religious Studies), 1981–85; Govt Policy Consultant, 1985–90; presenter and reporter: TV AM and GMTV, 1990–94; BBC SE, 1994–95; Hd of Public Affairs, BBC, 1996–2003; Hd of Corporate Social Responsibility, 2003–06. Non-exec. Dir, British Telecom (Community Support Cttee), 2004–. Comr, CRE, 1993–2001. Trustee: Crime Concern, 1988–2008 (Chm., 1995–2008); Vodafone Gp Foundn, 2008–. Patron: Springboard for Children, 2005– (Chm., 1992–98); ZANE, 2005–. *Recreations:* cycling, country walking, cinema, friends. *Address:* House of Lords, SW1A 0PW.

HASTINGS, Alfred James, CB 1999; Clerk of the Journals, House of Commons, 1991–2001; *b* 10 Feb. 1938; *s* of William Hastings and Letitia (*née* Loveridge); *m* 1972, Susan Edge; three *s. Educ:* Leamington College; New College, Oxford (MA). A Clerk of the House of Commons, 1960–2001: Registrar of Members' Interests, 1987–91; Clerk of the Cttee of Privileges, and subseq. of the Cttee on Standards and Privileges, 1991–97; Commons Clerk, Jt Cttee on Parly Privilege, 1997–99. *Recreations:* music, high fidelit sound reproduction. *Address:* 26 Feilden Grove, Headington, Oxford OX3 0DU.

HASTINGS, Alison Jane; media consultant, since 2002; Trustee, BBC Trust, since 2006 *b* 14 Aug. 1965; *d* of Len and Jackie Hastings; one *d*; *m* 2007, Dr David Fleming, *qv*; on *d*, and two step *s* one step *d. Educ:* Folkestone Girls' Grammar Sch.; Canterbury Coll Harlow Coll. (Nat. Council for Trng in Journalism). Hd, Editl Staff Devlt, Thomso Regl newspapers, 1994–95; Dep. Ed., 1995–96, Ed., 1996–2002, Newcastle Evenin Chronicle. Mem., Press Complaints Commn, 1998–2002. *Recreations:* time with family travelling, reading, sleeping, watching the West Wing collection on DVD. *Address: e-mai* ajh@alisonhastings.demon.co.uk.

HASTINGS, Sir Max (Macdonald), Kt 2002; FRSL; author and journalist; *b* 28 Dec 1945; *s* of Macdonald Hastings and Anne Scott-James, *qv*; *m* 1st, 1972, Patricia Mar Edmondson (marr. diss. 1994); one *s* one *d* (and one *s* decd); 2nd, 1999, Mrs Penny Grade *Educ:* Charterhouse (Scholar); University Coll., Oxford (Exhibnr). Researcher, BBC T Great War series, 1963–64; Reporter, Evening Standard, 1965–67; Fellow, US Worl Press Inst., 1967–68; Roving Correspondent, Evening Standard, 1968–70; Reporte BBC TV Current Affairs, 1970–73; Editor, Evening Standard Londoner's Diary, 1976–77 Columnist, Daily Express, 1981–83; contributor, Sunday Times, 1985–86; Editor, Th Daily Telegraph, 1986–95; Dir, 1989–95, Editor-in-Chief, 1990–95, The Dail Telegraph plc; Editor, The Evening Standard, 1996–2002; contributor, Daily Mail, 2002– As War Correspondent, covered Middle East, Indochina, Angola, India-Pakistan, Cyprus Rhodesia and S Atlantic. Mem., Press Complaints Commn, 1991–92. TV documentaries Ping-Pong in Peking, 1971; The War about Peace, 1983; Alarums and Excursions 1984; Cold Comfort Farm, 1985; The War in Korea (series), 1988; We Are All Gree Now, 1990; Spies, in series Cold War, CNN, 1998; Hitler's Germany, 2000; Th Falklands: reluctant heroes, 2002; Winston's War, 2003. A Vice Pres., Game Conservancy 1992–; Pres., CPRE, 2002–07. Trustee, Nat. Portrait Gall., 1995–2004. Liddell-Ha Lecture, KCL, 1994; Mountbatten Lecture, Edinburgh Univ., 2004. FRHistS 1988 FRSL 1996. Hon FKC, 2004. Hon. DLitt: Leicester, 1992; Nottingham, 2005. Journali of the Year, British Press Awards, 1982 (cited 1973 and 1980); What The Papers Say Granada TV: Reporter of the Year, 1982; Editor of the Year, 1988; Duke of Westminste Medal for military writing, RUSI, 2008. *Publications:* America 1968: the fire this time 1968; Ulster 1969: the struggle for civil rights in Northern Ireland, 1970; Montrose: th King's champion, 1977; Yoni: the hero of Entebbe, 1979; Bomber Command, 197 (Somerset Maugham Prize for Non-Fiction, 1980); (with Len Deighton) The Battle o Britain, 1980; Das Reich, 1981; (with Simon Jenkins) The Battle for The Falklands, 198 (Yorkshire Post Book of the Year Award); Overlord: D-Day and the battle for Normandy 1984 (Yorkshire Post Book of the Year Award); Victory in Europe, 1985; (ed) Oxfor Book of Military Anecdotes, 1985; The Korean War, 1987; Outside Days, 1989; Scattere Shots, 1999; Going to the Wars, 2000; Editor, 2002; Armageddon, 2004; Warriors, 2005 Country Fair, 2005; Nemesis, 2007. *Recreations:* shooting, fishing. *Address:* c/o PFD Drury House, 34–43 Russell Street, WC2B 5HA. *Club:* Brooks's.

HASTINGS, Michael; playwright; *b* 2 Sept. 1938; *s* of Max Emmanuel Gerald and Mari Catherine Hastings; *m* 1975, Victoria Hardie; two *s*, and one *d* by a previous marriage *Educ:* various South London comprehensive schools. Bespoke tailoring apprentice London, 1953–56. FRGS. *Plays:* Don't Destroy Me, 1956; Yes and After, 1957; Th World's Baby, 1962; Lee Harvey Oswald: 'a far mean streak of indepence brought on b negleck', 1966; The Cutting of the Cloth (unperformed autobiographical play), 1969; Th Silence of Saint-Just, 1971; For the West (Uganda), 1977; Gloo Joo, 1978; Full Fronta 1979; Carnival War a Go Hot, 1980; Midnite at the Starlite, 1980; Molière's The Mise (adaptation), 1982; Tom and Viv, 1984, new version, 2006; Stars of the Roller State Disc (Brixton community play), 1985; The Emperor (adapted with Jonathan Miller), 1987; A Dream of People, 1990; Roberto Cossa's La Nona (translation), 1991; Unfinishe Business, 1994; Calico, 2004; *for film and television:* For the West (Congo), 1963; Blue a his Eyes the Tin Helmet He Wore, 1966; The Search for the Nile (6 parts, with Dere Marlowe), 1972; The Nightcomers, 1972; Auntie Kathleen's Old Clothes, 1977; Murde Rap, 1980; Midnight at the Starlight, 1980; Michael Hastings in Brixton, 1980; Stars o the Roller State Disco, 1984; The Emperor (dir. by Jonathan Miller), 1988; Tom and Viv 1994; adaptations for television: Absolute Hell, 1991; La Nona (also trans.), 1992; Si Characters in Search of an Author (also trans.), 1994. *Publications: plays include:* Three Plays 1965; Three Plays, 1968; Two Plays, 1972; Tom and Viv, 1985; Three Political Plays 1990; Unfinished Business and Other Plays, 1994; Dance of the Mexican Rattlesnake 2003; Calico, 2004; *novels:* The Game, 1957; The Frauds, 1960; Tussy is Me, 1968; Th Nightcomers, 1971; And in the Forest the Indians, 1975; *stories:* Bart's Mornings and othe Tales of Modern Brazil, 1975; *libretti:* Man and Boy: Dada (opera by Michael Nyman) 2003; Love Counts (opera by Michael Nyman), 2006; *poems:* Love me Lambeth, 1959 *criticism:* Rupert Brooke, The Handsomest Young Man in England, 1967; Sir Richar Burton: a biography, 1978. *Address:* 2 Helix Gardens, Brixton Hill, SW2 2JP; *e-mail* 113132.624@compuserve.com.

HASTINGS, Lady Selina (Shirley); writer; *b* 5 March 1945; *d* of 15th Earl o Huntingdon and Countess of Huntingdon, (Margaret Lane). *Educ:* St Paul's Girls' Sch.; S Hugh's Coll., Oxford (MA). Daily Telegraph, 1968–82; Literary Ed., Harper's & Queen 1987–95. *Publications:* Nancy Mitford: a biography, 1985; Evelyn Waugh, 1994 Rosamond Lehmann, 2002. *Address:* c/o Rogers, Coleridge & White, 20 Powis Mew W11 1JN. *T:* (020) 7221 3717.

HASTINGS BASS, family name of **Earl of Huntingdon**.

HASWELL, (Anthony) James (Darley), OBE 1985; Insurance Ombudsman, 1981–89 Chairman, Appeals Tribunals, Financial Intermediaries, Managers and Brokers Regulator Association, 1989; *b* 4 Aug. 1922; *s* of Brig. Chetwynd Henry Haswell, CIE, and Doroth Edith (*née* Berry); *m* 1957, Angela Mary (*née* Murphy) (*d* 2004); three *s* one *d. Educ* Winchester Coll.; St John's Coll., Cambridge (MA). Solicitor of the Supreme Court Admitted Solicitor, 1949; RAC Legal Dept, 1949; private practice, London and Cornwall 1950–51; commnd, Army Legal Services Staff List (Captain), 1952; Temp. Major 1956 Lt-Col 1967; retired from Army Legal Corps, 1981. Dep. Chm., Money Mgt Council 1994–99. Freeman, City of London, 1987; Liveryman, Insurers' Co., 1987. *Publications* Insurance Ombudsman Bureau annual reports for years 1981–88; miscellaneous articles in industry jls. *Recreations:* writing, chamber music, theatre, drawing, woodwork, Londo Phoenix (formerly Insurance) Orchestra (formerly Chm. and playing member). *Address* 31 Chipstead Street, SW6 3SR. *T:* (020) 7736 1163.

HASZELDINE, Dr Robert Neville, ScD; FRS 1968; CChem, FRSC; scientifi consultant; Professor of Chemistry, 1957–82, Head of Department of Chemistry 1957–76, and Principal, 1976–82, University of Manchester Institute of Science an Technology (Faculty of Technology, The University of Manchester); *b* Manchester, May 1925; *s* of late Walter Haszeldine and Hilda Haszeldine (*née* Webster); *m* 1954 Pauline Elvina Goodwin (*d* 1987); two *s* two *d. Educ:* Stockport Grammar Sch.; Universit of Birmingham (John Watt Meml Schol., 1942; PhD 1947; DSc 1955); Sidney Susse

Coll., Cambridge (MA, PhD 1949); Queens' Coll., Cambridge (ScD 1957). University of Cambridge: Asst in Research in Organic Chemistry, 1949; University Demonstrator in Organic and Inorganic Chemistry, 1951; Asst Dir of Research, 1956; Fellow and Dir of Studies, Queens' Coll., 1954–57, Hon. Fellow, 1976. Chm., Chemical and Biol Defence Bd, Mem., Defence Scientific Adv. Cttee, and mem. of various govt and other cttees, 1957–89. Tilden Lectr, 1968; Vis. Lectr at universities and laboratories in the USA, Russia, Switzerland, Austria, Germany, Japan, China, Israel, S America and France. Chm., Langdales Soc., 1987–93 (Pres., 1998); Lord of the Manor of Langdale, 1988. Meldola Medal, 1953; Corday-Morgan Medal and Prize, 1960; Prix Henri Moissan, 1994. *Publications:* numerous scientific publications in chemical jls. *Recreations:* mountaineering, gardening, natural history, good food, wine, wilderness travel. *Address:* Copt Howe, Chapel Stile, Great Langdale, Cumbria LA22 9JR. *T:* (01539) 437685.

HATCH, Prof. David John, FRCA; Professional Standards Advisor, Royal College of Anaesthetists, since 2001; Professor of Paediatric Anaesthesia (first chair), University of London, 1991–2002, now Emeritus; *b* 11 April 1937; *s* of James Frederick Hatch and Marguerite Fanny (*née* Forge); *m* 1960, Rita Goulter; two *s* two *d. Educ:* Caterham Sch.; University Coll. London (MB BS 1961). MRCS, LRCP 1960; FRCA 1965. Fellow in Anesthesiology, Mayo Clinic, USA, 1968–69; Consultant in Anaesthesia and Respiratory Measurement, Gt Ormond St Children's Hosp., 1969–91. Pres., Assoc. Paediatric Anaesthetists, 1993–95; Vice-Pres., RCAnaes, 1991–93; Member: Med. Soc. of London, 1990–2002; GMC, 1994–2003 (Chm., Cttee on Professional Performance, 1999–2004; Chm., Assessment Gp, 2003–). Hewitt Lectr, RCAnaes, 1999. John Snow Medal, Assoc. of Anaesthetists of GB and Ire., 2001; Gold Medal, RCAnaes, 2003. *Publications:* (with E. Sumner) Neonatal Anaesthesia and Intensive Care, 1981, 3rd edn 1995; Paediatric Anaesthesia, 1989, 2nd edn 1999; contribs on paediatric anaesthesia, intensive care and professional self-regulation. *Recreations:* sailing, badminton. *Address:* Royal College of Anaesthetists, 35 Red Lion Square, WC1R 4SG. *T:* (020) 7092 7695.

HATCH, Lionel; Co-founder and Creative Director, The Chase, since 1986; *b* 20 Aug. 1949; *s* of Douglas Hatch and Clarice Hatch (*née* Aldred); *m* Vivien Smith (marr. diss. 1984); one *s. Educ:* Bolton Coll. of Art and Design. Jun. Art Dir, Royds, 1970–71; Art Director: Rileys, 1971–72; Cogent Elliott, 1972–73; Stowe Bowden, 1973–75; McDonalds, 1975–77; Yeoward Taylor Bonner, 1977–79; Creative Gp Hd, J Walter Thompson, 1979–80; graphic design consultant, 1980–86. Projects, drawings and design effectiveness studies exhibited internationally; exhibitions include: Twelve International Lettering Artists, 1983; New York Type Directors Club, 1984. Best in Show, The Roses Awards, 1987; Grand Global Award, NY Advertising Fest., 1994; DBA Design Effectiveness Award, 2003. *Publications:* The Chase by The Chase: how a design consultancy thinks it thinks, 1993; completed projects, drawings and design effectiveness studies in books. *Recreations:* writing first novel, landscape design, pondering enthusiastically. *Address:* The Chase, 1 North Parade, Parsonage Gardens, Manchester M3 2NH. *T:* (0161) 832 5575; *e-mail:* lionel.hatch@thechase.co.uk.

HATCH, Dr Marshall Davidson, AM 1981; FRS 1980; FAA 1975; Chief Research Scientist, 1970–97, Hon. Research Fellow, 1997–2006, Division of Plant Industry, CSIRO, Canberra; *b* 24 Dec. 1932; *s* of Lloyd Davidson Hatch and Alice Endesby Hatch (*née* Dalziel); *m* 1st (marr. diss.); two *s*; 2nd, 1983, Lyndall P. Clarke. *Educ:* Newington Coll., Sydney; Univ. of Sydney (BSc, PhD). FAA 1975. Res. Scientist, Div. of Food Res., CSIRO, 1955–59; Post Doctoral Res. Fellow, Univ. of Calif., Davis, 1959–61; Res. Scientist, Colonial Sugar Refining Co. Ltd, Brisbane, 1961–66 and 1968–69 (Reader in Plant Biochemistry, Univ. of Queensland, Brisbane, 1967). Foreign Associate, Nat. Acad. of Sciences, USA, 1990. Rank Prize, Rank Foundn, UK, 1981; Internat. Prize for Biology, Japan Soc. for Promotion of Science, 1991. *Publications:* 164 papers, reviews and chaps in scientific jls and text books in field of photosynthesis and other areas of plant biochemistry. *Recreations:* ski-ing, cycling, reading. *Address:* PO Box 480, Jamison, ACT 2614, Australia. *T:* (2) 62515159.

HATCH, Tasmin; *see* Little, T.

HATCHER, Prof. (Melvyn) John, PhD, LittD; Professor of Economic and Social History, since 1995, and Chairman of the Faculty of History, since 2005, University of Cambridge; Fellow, since 1976, and Vice-Master, since 2001, Corpus Christi College, Cambridge; *b* 7 Jan. 1942; *s* of John Edward Hatcher and Lilian Florence Hatcher (*née* Lepper); *m* 1967, Janice Miriam Ranson; two *d. Educ:* Owens GS, Islington; London School of Economics, London Univ. (BSc(Econ), PhD); MA, LittD 1994, Cantab. Salesman, Reckitt and Coleman Ltd, 1960–63; Res. Fellow, Inst. of Historical Research, London, 1966–67; Lectr, 1967–74, Sen. Lectr, 1974–75, in History, Univ. of Kent; Vis. Prof., Univ. of Colorado at Boulder, USA, 1975–76; Lectr in History, 1976–86, Reader in Economic and Social History, 1986–95, Univ. of Cambridge. Vice-Chm., ESRC Econ. Affairs Cttee, 1979–84. Fellow, Huntington Liby, Calif, USA, 1986. AcSS 2001. Editor, Economic History Review, 1996–2001. *Publications:* Rural Economy and Society in the Duchy of Cornwall 1300–1500, 1970; English Tin Production and Trade before 1550, 1973; A History of British Pewter, 1974; Plague, Population and the English Economy 1348–1530, 1977; (jtly) Medieval England: rural society and economic change 1086–1348, 1978; (contrib.) The Agrarian History of England and Wales, vol. II 1042–1350, 1988; The History of the British Coal Industry: before 1700, 1993; (jtly) Medieval England: towns, commerce and crafts 1086–1348, 1995; (jtly) Modelling the Middle Ages, 2001; The Black Death: an intimate history, 2008; articles in learned jls. *Recreations:* jazz, football. *Address:* Corpus Christi College, Cambridge CB2 1RP. *T:* (01223) 338000.

HATENDI, Rt Rev. Ralph Peter; Bishop of Harare, 1981–95; *b* 9 April 1927; *s* of Fabian and Amelia Hatendi; *m* 1954, Jane Mary Chikumbu; two *s* three *d. Educ:* St Peter's Coll., Rosettenville, S Africa (LTh); King's Coll. London (DD; AKC). School teacher, 1952–; clergyman, 1957–; Seminary Tutor, 1968–72; Executive Secretary, 1973–75; Distribution Consultant, 1976–78; Suffragan Bishop of Mashonaland, 1979–80. Chm., Electoral Supervisory Commn., 1998–2000. *Publications:* Sex and Society, 1971; Shona Marriage and the Christian Churches, in Christianity South of the Zambezi, 1973. *Recreation:* poultry. *Address:* 16 Kenny Road, Avondale, Harare, Zimbabwe. *Club:* Harare (Zimbabwe).

HATFIELD, Richard Paul, CBE 1991; Personnel Director, Ministry of Defence, since 2001; *b* 8 Feb. 1953; *m* 1982, Penelope Charlotte Bratton. *Educ:* Whitgift Sch., Croydon; University Coll., Oxford (MA). Admin. trainee, MoD, 1974; Private Secretary to: Under Sec. of State (Army), 1978–80; Cabinet Sec., 1982–85; Ministry of Defence: Asst Private Sec. to Defence Sec., 1986; Head: Defence Lands, 1986–88; Overseas Div., 1988–91; Programme and Policy Div., 1991–93; Dir Gen., Mgt and Orgn, 1993–96; Dep. Under Sec. of State (Policy), subseq. Policy Dir, 1996–2001. *Address:* c/o Ministry of Defence, Main Building, Whitehall, SW1A 2HB.

HATFULL, Martin Alan; HM Diplomatic Service; Ambassador to Indonesia, since 2008; *b* 7 June 1957; *s* of late Alan Frederick Hatfull; *m* 1980, Phyllis Julia Mary Morshead; two *s. Educ:* Dulwich Coll.; Worcester Coll., Oxford (BA Lit.Hum. 1980). Joined Foreign and Commonwealth Office, 1980; Second, later First, Sec., Tokyo, 1982–86; EU Dept (External), FCO, 1987–88; Private Sec. to Parly Under Sec. of State, FCO, 1988–91; First Sec., UK Rep. to EU, Brussels, 1991–95; Dep. Head, EU Dept (External), FCO, 1995–96; Head, Commonwealth Co-ordination Dept, FCO, 1996–98; Counsellor (Economic and Commercial), Rome, 1998–2002; Minister, Tokyo, 2003–08. *Address:* BFPO 5445, HA4 6EP.

HATHERTON, 8th Baron *cr* 1835; **Edward Charles Littleton;** agronomist; *b* 24 May 1950; *s* of Mervyn Cecil Littleton (*d* 1970) (*g s* of 3rd Baron) and Margaret Ann (*d* 2000), *d* of Frank Sheehy; *S* cousin, 1985; *m* 1974, Hilda Maria, *d* of Rodolfo Robert; one *s* two *d. Heir: s* Hon. Thomas Edward Littleton, *b* 7 March 1977. *Address:* PO Box 1341–2150, Moravia, Costa Rica.

HATT, Anthony Faun; Vice President, Immigration Appeal Tribunal, 1996–2001; *b* 23 Aug. 1931; *m* 1954, Norma Irene Stotesbury; one *s* one *d. Educ:* Chiswick Grammar Sch.; Westminster Coll. of Commerce. Nat. Service and TA, 1949–62, retd with rank of Captain, transf. to RARO. Admitted solicitor, 1965; solicitor in private practice, 1965–88; Immigration Appeal Adjudicator, part-time 1980–88, full-time 1988–93, Regl Adjudicator, 1993–96; Dep. Metropolitan Stipendiary Magistrate, 1983–85; part-time Legal Chairman: Social Security Appeal Tribunal, 1985–93; Disability Appeal Tribunal, 1992–93; Legal Chm., Immigration Appeal Tribunal, 1995–96; Legal Mem., Special Immigration Appeals Commn, 1998–2001. Mem., Internat. Assoc. of Refugee Law Judges, 1998–2001. *Recreations:* golf, swimming, walking. *Clubs:* Royal Automobile; Royal Automobile Country (Epsom).

HATT, Paul William David; Secretary, Royal Hospital Chelsea, since 2007; *b* 21 Nov. 1949; *s* of late William Oliver Hatt and of Henrietta Hatt (*née* McGregor); *m* 1975, Cecilia Anne Freeman; two *s* two *d. Educ:* Sir Joseph Williamson's Sch., Rochester; Lincoln Coll., Oxford (Schol., BA Hons English Lang. and Lit., PGCE, MA); Nat. Defence Coll. Joined Ministry of Defence, 1973: Principal, 1980–85; on secondment to FCO, as First Sec., UK Delegn to NATO, Brussels, 1985–89; Asst Sec., 1990; Head, Defence Lands, 1990–92; Dir, Proliferation and Arms Control Secretariat, 1992–97; Head, Resources and Programmes (Army), 1997–98; Asst Under Sec., 1998; Comd Sec., RAF Logistics Comd, 1998–2000; Fellow, Center for Internat. Affairs, Harvard Univ., 2000–01; Comd Sec. to Second Sea Lord and C-in-C Naval Home Comd, and Asst Under-Sec. of State (Naval Personnel), MoD, 2001–06; Project Dir, Royal Naval Museum, 2006. *Recreations:* sedentary pursuits, including family, literature and music. *Address:* c/o Royal Hospital Chelsea, SW3 4SR.

HATTER, Sir Maurice, Kt 1999; Chairman, IMO Precision Controls Ltd, since 1970; *b* 6 Nov. 1929; *s* of Ralph and Sarah Hatter; *m* 1999, Irene Noach. Royal Signals, 1949. Formed an electronics manufacturer sold to Thorn, 1968. Pres., World ORT, 2004–08, Pres. Emeritus, 2008. Founded Hatter Inst. of Cardiology, at UCH, 1990. Hon. Life Pres., Charlton Athletic FC, 2000. Hon. Fellow, UCL, 1995. Hon. PhD Haifa, Israel, 1996. *Recreations:* tennis, boating, underwater archaeology. *Address:* IMO Precision Controls Ltd, 1000 North Circular Road, Staples Corner, NW2 7JP.

HATTERSLEY, Baron *cr* 1997 (Life Peer), of Sparkbrook in the co. of West Midlands; **Roy Sydney George Hattersley;** PC 1975; Deputy Leader of the Labour Party, 1983–92; *b* 28 Dec. 1932; *s* of Frederick Roy Hattersley, Sheffield; *m* 1956, Molly Hattersley, *qv. Educ:* Sheffield City Grammar Sch.; Univ. of Hull (BSc (Econ). Journalist and Health Service Executive, 1956–64; Mem. Sheffield City Council, 1957–65 (Chm. Housing Cttee and Public Works Cttee). MP (Lab) Birmingham, Sparkbrook, 1964–97. PPS to Minister of Pensions and National Insurance, 1964–67; Jt Parly Sec., DEP (formerly Min. of Labour), 1967–69; Minister of Defence for Administration, 1969–70; Labour Party spokesman: on Defence, 1972; on Educn and Sci., 1972–74; Minister of State, FCO, 1974–76; Sec. of State for Prices and Consumer Protection, 1976–79; principal opposition spokesman on environment, 1979–80, on home affairs, 1980–83, on Treasury and economic affairs, 1983–87, on home affairs, 1987–92. Visiting Fellow: Inst. of Politics, Univ. of Harvard, 1971, 1972; Nuffield Coll., Oxford, 1984–. Dir, Campaign for a European Political Community, 1966–67. Columnist: Punch; The Guardian; The Listener, 1979–82; Columnist of the Year, Granada, 1982. Hon. DSc Sheffield Hallam; Hon. DCL: Hull; West Midlands. *Publications:* Nelson, 1974; Goodbye to Yorkshire (essays), 1976; Politics Apart, 1982; Press Gang, 1983; A Yorkshire Boyhood, 1983; Choose Freedom: the future for Democratic Socialism, 1987; Economic Priorities for a Labour Government, 1987; Who Goes Home? 1995; 50 Years On, 1997; Blood & Fire, 1999; A Brand from the Burning: the life of John Wesley, 2002; The Edwardians, 2004; Campbell-Bannerman, 2007; Borrowed Time: the story of Britain between the wars, 2007; *novels:* The Maker's Mark, 1990; In That Quiet Earth, 1991; Skylark Song, 1994; Between Ourselves, 1994. *Address:* House of Lords, SW1A 0PW. *Clubs:* Reform, Garrick.

HATTERSLEY, Lady; *see* Hattersley, E. M.

HATTERSLEY, Edith Mary, (Molly Hattersley); educational consultant, since 1990; Visiting Fellow, Institute of Education, University of London (Management Development Centre), 1990–97; *b* 5 Feb. 1931; *d* of Michael and Sally Loughran; *m* 1956, Roy Sydney George Hattersley (*see* Baron Hattersley). *Educ:* Consett Grammar Sch.; University College of Hull. BA Hons English (London), CertEd (Hull). Assistant Mistress at schools in Surrey and Yorkshire, 1953–61; Sen. Mistress, Myers Grove Sch., Sheffield, 1961–64; Dep. Headmistress, Kidbrooke Sch., SE3, 1965–69; Headmistress, Hurlingham Sch., SW6, 1969–74; Headmistress, Creighton Sch., N10, 1974–82; Asst Educn Officer, then Dep. Dir of Educn, ILEA, 1983–90. Advr on educnl matters to Trustees of BM, 1978–86. Chairman of Cttee, Assoc. of Head Mistresses, 1975–77; Pres., Secondary Heads Assoc., 1980–81; Chm., Soc. of Educn Consultants, 1994–96. Mem. Ct of Governors, LSE, 1970–99. FRSA 1982. *Recreation:* reading.

HATTO, Prof. Arthur Thomas, MA; FBA 1991; Head of the Department of German, Queen Mary College, University of London, 1938–77; *b* 11 Feb. 1910; *s* of Thomas Hatto, LLB and Alice Walters; *m* 1935, Margot Feibelmann (decd); one *d. Educ:* Dulwich Coll.; King's Coll., London (Fellow, 1971); University Coll. London. BA (London) 1931; MA (with Distinction), 1934. Lektor für Englisch, University of Berne, 1932–34; Asst Lectr in German, KCL, 1934–38; Queen Mary Coll., University of London, 1938 (Head of Dept of German). Temp. Sen. Asst, Foreign Office, 1939–45; part-time Lectr in German, University Coll., London, 1944–45; returned to Queen Mary Coll., 1945; Reader in German Language and Literature, 1946, Prof. of German Language and Literature, 1953, University of London. Governor: SOAS, Univ. of London, 1960 (Foundn Day Lecture, 1970; Hon. Fellow, 1981); QMC, Univ. of London, 1968–70 (Hon. Fellow, QMW, 1992). Chairman: London Seminar on Epic; Cttee 'A' (Theol. and Arts), Central Research Fund, Univ. of London, 1969. Fellow: Royal Anthropological Institute; Royal Asiatic Society (lecture: Plot and character in Kirghiz epic poetry of the mid 19th cent., 1976); Leverhulme Emeritus Fellow (heroic poetry in Central Asia and Siberia), 1977–. Lectr, Rheinisch-Westfälische Akad. der Wissenschaften, Düsseldorf,

1990. Corresp. Mem., Finno-Ugrian Soc., 1978; Associate Mem., Seminar für Sprach- und Kulturwissenschaft Zentralasiens, Univ. of Bonn, 1984. *Publications:* (with R. J. Taylor) The Songs of Neidhart von Reuental, 1958; Gottfried von Strassburg, Tristan (trans. entire for first time) with Tristran of Thomas (newly trans.) with an Introduction, 1960; The Niblungenlied: a new translation, with Introduction and Notes, 1964; editor of Eos, an enquiry by fifty scholars into the theme of the alba in world literature, 1965; (ed for first time with translation and commentary) The Memorial Feast for Kökötöy-khan: a Kirghiz epic poem, 1977; Essays on Medieval German and Other Poetry, 1980; Parzival, Wolfram von Eschenbach, a new translation, 1980; gen. editor, Traditions of Heroic and Epic Poetry, vol. I 1980, vol. II 1989; (re-ed with trans. and commentary) The Manas of Wilhelm Radloff, 1990; The Mohave Epic of Inyo-kutavêre, 1999; articles in learned periodicals. *Recreations:* reading, gardening.

HATTON; *see* Finch Hatton, family name of Earl of Winchilsea.

HATTON, David William; QC 1996; a Recorder, since 1994; *b* 29 May 1953; *s* of Thomas William Hatton and Margery Hatton; *m* 1994, Janet Elizabeth Bossons; one *s* one *d*. *Educ:* Bolton Sch.; Univ. of Bristol (LLB Hons). Called to the Bar, Gray's Inn, 1976, Bencher, 2005. *Recreations:* reading, music, walking, football. *Club:* Bolton Wanderers Football.

HAUGH, Leslie John; independent consultant, since 2002; Principal Finance Officer, Home Office, 2000–02; *b* 20 Aug. 1947; *s* of John Lamont Haugh and Robina Speed Haugh (*née* Stenhouse); one *s* one *d*. *Educ:* Buckhaven High Sch. ACMA 1980; FCCA 1998. HM Treasury, 1964; MPBW, 1965–67; BoT, then DTI, 1967–76; Dept of Employment, 1976–84; Dep. Accountant and Comptroller Gen., HM Customs and Excise, 1984–92; Accounting Advr, Home Office, 1992–98; seconded to Systems Union, 1998–2000. *Recreations:* golf (badly), bridge (badly), saying no. *Club:* Crail Golfing Society.

HAUGHEY, family name of **Baron Ballyedmond**.

HAUGHEY, Denis; Member (SDLP) Ulster Mid, Northern Ireland Assembly, 1998–2003; *b* 3 Oct. 1944; *s* of Henry Haughey and Elizabeth Falls; *m* 1970, Maureen McCarron; one *s* two *d*. *Educ:* St Patrick's Coll., Armagh; Queen's Univ., Belfast (BA Hons Modern History and Pol Sci.). Mem., Northern Ireland Assembly, 1982–86; Minister, Office of First and Dep. First Ministers, NI Assembly, 1999–2000, 2001–02. Mem., Cttee of the Regions, EU, 1994–. Social Democratic and Labour Party: Founder Mem., 1970; Vice-Chair, 1971–73; Chair, 1973–78; Internat. Sec., 1978–. *Recreations:* reading (history, biography), music, travel. *Address:* 66 Fairhill Road, Cookstown, Co. Tyrone BT80 8DE. *T:* (028) 8676 3349.

HAUPTMAN, Prof. Herbert Aaron, PhD; President, Hauptman-Woodward Medical Research Institute, Inc. (formerly Medical Foundation of Buffalo), since 1986; *b* 14 Feb. 1917; *s* of Israel Hauptman and Leah Hauptman (*née* Rosenfeld); *m* Edith Citrynell; two *d*. *Educ:* City Coll., NY (BS 1937); Columbia Univ. (MA 1939); Univ. of Maryland (PhD 1955). Census Bureau, 1940–42; Electronics Instructor, USAF, 1942–43, 1946–47; Aerology Officer, USNR, 1943–46; Naval Research Laboratory: Physicist-Mathematician, 1947–70; Rep. of Univ. of Maryland Math. Dept, 1966–70, and part-time Prof., Univ. of Maryland; Head, Mathematical Physics Br., 1965–67; Acting Supt, Math. and Inf. Scis. Div., 1967–68; Head, Applied Math. Br., Math. Div., 1968–69; Head, Math. Staff, Optical Scis Div., 1969–70; Medical Foundation of Buffalo: Head, Math. Biophysics Lab., 1970–72; Dep. Res. Dir, 1972; Exec. Vice-Pres., and Res. Dir, 1972–85; Res. Prof. of Biophysical Scis, State Univ. of NY at Buffalo, 1970–. Mem., US scientific instns. Holder of numerous honours and awards; Hon. DSc: Maryland, 1985; City Coll. of NY, 1986; D'Youville Coll., 1989; Bar-Ilan Univ., Israel, and Columbia Univ., NY, 1990; Technical Univ. of Lodz, Poland, 1992; Queen's Univ., Kingston, Ont, 1993; Niagara Univ., 1996; Univ. of Toledo, 1999; Hon. Dr Chem., Univ. of Parma, 1998. Nobel Prize in Chemistry (with Jerome Karle), 1985. *Publications:* Solution of the Phase Problem (with J. Karle), 1953; Crystal Structure Determination, 1972; (ed) Direct Methods in Crystallography (procs 1976 Intercongress Symposium), 1978; numerous articles on crystallography in learned jls. *Recreations:* stained glass art, swimming, hiking. *Address:* Hauptman Woodward Medical Research Institute, 700 Ellicott Street, Buffalo, NY 14203–1196, USA. *Clubs:* Cosmos (Washington); Saturn (Buffalo).

HAUSER, Dr Hermann Maria, Hon. CBE 2002; Founder Director, Amadeus Capital Partners Ltd, since 1997; Director, Globespan-Virata Inc. (formerly ATM Ltd, later Virata), 2001–03 (Chairman, 1992–2001); *b* 23 Oct. 1948; *s* of Hermann Hauser and Gerti Pizl; *m* 1982, Pamela Raspe; one *s* one *d*. *Educ:* Vienna Univ. (MA Physics); Cavendish Lab., Univ. of Cambridge (PhD Physics 1977). Co-founder, Acorn (BBC) Computers, 1978 (500,000 BBC micro computers sold by 1984); Founder, IQ (Bio) Ltd, 1982; Vice-Pres. Research, Olivetti, Italy, 1986–88; Dir, Harlequin Ltd, 1986–99; Founder, IXI Ltd, 1987; formation of ARM Ltd (jt venture between Acorn and Apple), 1987; Founder and Chm., Active Book Co., 1988; Co-Chm., CTO of EO Inc., 1991; Founder: Vocalis Ltd, 1992; Electronic Share Information Ltd, 1993; Advanced Rendering Technology Ltd, 1995; Founder/Chairman: SynGenix Ltd, 1993; Advanced Displays Ltd, 1993–94; Advanced Telecommunications Modules Ltd, 1993; UK Online Ltd, 1994; Entertainment Online Ltd, 1995. Hon. DSc Bath, 1990; Hon. DSc Loughborough, 1998. *Recreations:* tennis, squash, ski-ing, swimming, piano. *Address:* (office) Mount Pleasant House, 2 Mount Pleasant, Cambridge CB3 0RN. *T:* (01223) 707000.

HAUSER, Wolfhart Gunnar; Chief Executive, since 2005 and Board Director, since 2002, Intertek Group plc; *b* 5 Dec. 1949; *s* of Josef Hauser and Eva Bargenda; *m* 1981, Dr Susanne Sandhagen; two *s*. *Educ:* Ludwig Maximilians Univ., Munich (MD 1978). Chief Executive Officer: TÜV Product Service GmbH, 1988–1997; TÜV Süd AG, 1998–2002. *Recreations:* ski-ing, tennis, golf. *Address:* Intertek Group plc, 25 Savile Row, W1S 2ES. *T:* (020) 7396 3400, *Fax:* (020) 7396 3480; *e-mail:* info@intertek.com. *Club:* Rotary (Munich).

HAVARD, Dai; MP (Lab) Merthyr Tydfil and Rhymney, since 2001; *b* 7 Feb. 1950; *m* 1986, Julia Watts (separated). *Educ:* Univ. of Warwick (MA). Union studies tutor, 1971–75; researcher, 1975–79; Educn Officer, 1975–82; Official, MSF, 1989–2001. *Address:* (office) Unit 4, Triangle Business Park, Pentrebach, Merthyr Tydfil CF48 4TQ. *T:* (01685) 379247, *Fax:* (01685) 387563; c/o House of Commons, SW1A 0AA.

HAVARD, John David Jayne, CBE 1989; MD; Secretary, British Medical Association, 1980–89; Chairman, Commonwealth Medical Trust, 2001–05 (Hon. Secretary, Commonwealth Medical Association, 1986–2001); *b* 5 May 1924; *s* of late Dr Arthur William Havard and Ursula Jayne Vernon Humphrey; *m* 1st, 1950, Margaret Lucy Lumsden Collis (marr. diss. 1982); two *s* one *d*; 2nd, 1982, Audrey Anne Boutwood, FRCOG, *d* of Rear Adm. L. A. Boutwood, CB, OBE. *Educ:* Malvern Coll.; Jesus Coll., Cambridge (MA, MD, LLM); Middlesex Hosp. Med. Sch. FRCP 1994. Called to the Bar, Middle Temple, 1953. Professorial Med. Unit, Middlesex Hosp., 1950; National Service, RAF, 1950–52; general practice, Lowestoft, 1952–58 (Sec., E Suffolk LMC, 1956–58).

British Medical Assoc.: Asst Sec., 1958–64; Under-Sec., 1964–76; Dep. Sec., 1976–79 Short-term Cons., Council of Europe, 1964–67, OECD 1964–69, WHO 1967–89, o Road Accident Prevention. Dep. Chm., Staff Side, Gen. Whitley Council for the Heal Services, 1975–89; Sec., Managerial, Professional and Staffs Liaison Gp, 1978–8 Member: various Govt Working Parties on Coroners' Rules, Visual Standards for Driving Licensing of Professional Drivers, etc. Chm., Internat. Driver Behaviour Res. Assoc 1971–94. Pres., British Acad. of Forensic Scis, 1984–85. Mem., GMC, 1989–94 (Mem Professional Conduct and Standards Cttee, 1989–94). Lectr, Green Coll., Oxford, 198 Governor, Malvern Coll., 1984. Hon. FRCGP 1997. Gold Medal, Inter-Scandinavia Union for Non-Alcoholic Traffic, 1962; Stevens Lectr and Gold Medallist, 198 Widmark Award, Internat. Cttee on Alcohol, Drugs and Traffic Safety, 1989; BMA Gol Medal for Dist. Merit, 1990. Pres., CUAC, 1945–46; Captain United Hosps AC 1946–47; London Univ. Record for 100 yards, 1947. Member, Editorial Boar Blutalkohol, 1968–90; Forensic Science Rev. 1989–. *Publications:* Detection of Secre Homicide (Cambridge Studies in Criminology), 1960; Research on Effects of Alcohol an Drugs on Driving Behaviour (OECD), 1968; chapters in textbooks on legal medicin research advances on alcohol and drugs, etc; many articles in med., legal and sci. periodic lit.; several WHO reports. *Recreations:* history, English countryside. *Address:* 1 Wilto Square, N1 3DL. *T:* (020) 7359 2802, *Fax:* (020) 7354 9690. *Clubs:* Oxford an Cambridge; Achilles.

HAVEL, Václav; writer; President of Czech Republic, 1993–2003; *b* Prague, 5 Oct. 1936 *s* of Václav M. Havel and Božena Havel (*née* Vavrečková); *m* 1st, 1964, Olga Šplíchalov (*d* 1996); 2nd, 1997, Dagmar Veskrnova. *Educ:* Faculty of Economy, 1955–5 (unfinished); Drama Dept, Acad. of Arts, Prague, 1966. Chemical Lab. Technicia 1951–55; in Czechoslovak army, 1957–59; stagehand, ABC Theatre, Prague, 1959–60 Theatre on the Balustrade, Prague: stagehand, 1960–61; Asst to Artistic Dir, 1961–6 Literary Manager, 1963–68 (play, Zahradní slavnost [The Garden Party], 1963); Residen Playwright, 1968; Editl Bd, Tvář, 1965; freelance work, 1969–74; labourer, Trutno Brewery, N Bohemia, 1974; freelance work, 1975–89; Co-Founder, Charter 77 (huma rights movement), 1977, and one of its first three spokesmen; Co-Founder, Cttee fc Defence of Unjustly Prosecuted (VONS), 1978; under house arrest, 1978–79; imprisone Oct. 1979–March 1983; Editl Bd and regular contributor, Lidové noviny, 1987–8 imprisoned, Jan.–May 1989; Co-Founder, Civic Forum, 1989; Pres. of Czech and Slova Federal Republic, 1989–92. Chm., Young Writers, Czechoslovak Writers Assoc 1965–69; Member: Czechoslovak Helsinki Cttee, 1989–; Czech Pen Club, 1989–. Hol hon. degrees from many institutions. Awards received include: Austrian State Prize fc European Literature, 1969; Erasmus Prize, 1986; Olof Palme Prize, 1989; Simon Boliva Prize, UNESCO, 1990. *Publications:* plays in translation: The Garden Party, 1969; Th Increased Difficulty of Concentration, 1972; The Memorandum, 1980; Selected Plays b Václav Havel, 1991; *others in translation:* Letters to Olga, 1988; Disturbing the Peace, 1990 Open Letters: selected writings 1965–1990, 1991; Summer Meditations, 1992; Toward Civil Society, 1994; The Art of the Impossible, 1997; To the Castle and Back, 2008; essay in New York Rev. of Books, Granta, Index on Censorship, Independent, etc.

HAVELANGE, Dr Jean Marie Faustin Godefroid, (João); President, Fédératio Internationale de Football Association, 1974–98, now Hon. President; Membe International Olympic Committee, since 1963; *b* 8 May 1916; *m* Anna Maria; one *d*. *Edu* Univ. of Rio de Janeiro (Dr jur). Has practised law, 1936–. Pres., COMETA SA, Brazi Man. Dir, several cos in Brazil. Olympic Games participant, swimming, 1936, and wate polo, 1952. Hon. Citizen, Chicago, 1994. Order of Special Merit in Sports (Brazil), 197 Kt, Order of Vasa (Sweden), 1959; Commandeur de l'Ordre du Lion (Senegal), 197 Gran Cruz de Isabel la Católica (Spain), 1982; Commendatore dell' Ordine de Repubblica Italiana (Italy), 1980; Commandeur de la Légion d'Honneur (France), 199 *Recreation:* swimming. *Address:* Avenida Rio Branco 89–B, conbine 602 Centro 20040–004 Rio de Janeiro RJ, Brazil.

HAVELOCK-ALLAN, Alison Lee Caroline, (Lady Havelock-Allan); *see* Foster, A L. C.

HAVELOCK-ALLAN, Sir (Anthony) Mark (David), 5th Bt *cr* 1858, of Lucknow; Q 1993; **His Honour Judge Havelock-Allan;** a Senior Circuit Judge, Bristol Mercanti Court, since 2001; *b* 4 April 1951; *s* of Sir Anthony James Allan Havelock-Allan, 4th B and Valerie Babette Louise Hobson, actress (who *m* 2nd, J. D. Profumo, CBE; she *d* 1998 *S* father, 2003; *m* 1st, 1976, Lucy Clare (marr. diss. 1984), *y d* of late Alexander Plantagene Mitchell-Innes; 2nd, 1986, Alison Lee Caroline Foster, *qv;* one *s* two *d*. *Educ:* Eton Durham Univ. (BA Hons Law 1972); Trinity Coll., Cambridge (LLB 1974; Dip. i Internat. Law, 1976). FCIArb 1991. Called to the Bar, Inner Temple, 1974, Benche 1995; Asst Recorder, 1993–96; a Recorder, 1997–2001. *Recreations:* salmon fishing an foreign travel (preferably combined). *Heir:* s Henry Caspar Francis Havelock-Allan, *b* Oct. 1994. *Address:* The Law Courts, Small Street, Bristol BS1 1DA. *T:* (0117) 910 6706 *Fax:* (0117) 910 6727. *Clubs:* Garrick, Royal Automobile.

HAVENHAND, Martin Stephen; Chairman, National Metals Technology Centre, sinc 2006; *b* 14 Oct. 1950; *s* of Mark Havenhand and Jessie Brough; *m;* two *s* one *d*. *Edu* Sheffield Business Sch. Centre for Managing Change, London (MSc Managing Change Asst Chief Officer (Recreation, Culture and Health), S Yorks MCC, 1980–85; Dir o Leisure Services, then of Envmt, Trafford MBC, 1985–93; Chief Executive: Bassetlaw DC, 1993–99; Yorkshire Forward, 1999–2006; Exec. Dir, Yorkshire 2012, 2006– *Recreations:* sport, lifelong learning. *Address:* NAMTEC, Swinden House, Moorgate Road Rotherham, S Yorks S60 3AR.

HAVERGAL, Giles Pollock, CBE 2002 (OBE 1987); director and actor; Directo Citizens' Theatre Glasgow, 1969–2003; *b* 9 June 1938; *s* of Henry McLeod Havergal an Margaret Graham Hyacinth Havergal (*née* Chitty). *Educ:* Harrow Sch.; Christ Church Oxford (MA). Trainee Dir, Oldham Repertory, 1963; Director: Her Majesty's Theatre Barrow-in-Furness, 1964; Palace Theatre, Watford, 1965–69. FRSAMD 1988; FRSI 1994. Hon. DLitt: Glasgow, 1987; Strathclyde, 1996. DDra RSAMD, 1997. St Mung Prize, City of Glasgow, 1995. *Address:* c/o Alan Brodie Representation Ltd, 6th Floo Fairgate House, 78 New Oxford Street, WC1A 1HB. *T:* (020) 7079 7990.

HAVERS, Hon. Nigel (Allan); actor; *b* 6 Nov. 1951; *yr s* of Baron Havers, PC, and o Carol Elizabeth (who *m* 1993, C. F. Hughesdon, *qv*); *m* 1st, 1974, Carolyn Cox (mar diss. 1989); one *d*; 2nd, 1989, Polly Bloomfield (*d* 2004); 3rd, 2007, Georgiana Bronfman *Educ:* Arts Educational Sch. Researcher, Jimmy Young Programme, BBC Radio 2 *Television* includes: The Glittering Prizes; Nicholas Nickleby; A Horseman Riding B Upstairs Downstairs; Don't Wait Up, 1983–90; Strangers and Brothers, 1984; Th Charmer, 1987; Proof, 1987; A Perfect Hero, 1991; Sleepers, The Good Guys, 1992; Th Heart Surgeon, 1997; Dangerfield, 1998 and 1999; The Gentleman Thief, 200 Manchild, 2002, 2003; *films* include: Chariots of Fire, 1981; A Passage to India, 1985; Th Whistle Blower; Empire of the Sun, 1988; *theatre* includes: The Importance of Bein Earnest, NT, 1982; Art, 2001; See You Next Tuesday, Albery, 2003; Rebecca, nat. tou 2004–05; Single Spies, nat. tour, 2008; *radio* includes, Mrs Dale's Diary. *Publication*

Playing with Fire (autobiog.), 2006. *Address:* 28 Bramham Gardens, SW5 0HE. *Club:* Garrick.

See also Hon. P. N. Havers.

HAVERS, Hon. Philip Nigel; QC 1995; *b* 16 June 1950; *s* of Baron Havers, PC and of Carol Elizabeth (*née* Lay) (who *m* 1993, C. F. Hughesdon, *qv*); *m* 1976, Patricia Frances Searle; one *s* one *d*. *Educ:* Eton Coll.; Corpus Christi Coll., Cambridge. Called to the Bar, Inner Temple, 1974, Bencher, 2001. A Recorder, 1990–2000; a Dep. High Ct Judge, 2002–. *Recreations:* tennis, music, wine, gardening, travel. *Address:* 1 Crown Office Row, Temple, EC4Y 7HH. *T:* (020) 7797 7500. *Club:* Garrick.

See also Hon. N. A. Havers.

HAVERY, His Honour Richard Orbell; QC 1980; a Judge of the Technology and Construction Court of the High Court, 1998–2007; *b* 7 Feb. 1934; *s* of late Joseph Horton Havery and Constance Eleanor (*née* Orbell). *Educ:* St Paul's; Magdalen Coll., Oxford (MA 1961). Called to the Bar, Middle Temple, 1962, Bencher, 1989; an Asst Recorder, 1982–86; a Recorder, 1986–93; a Circuit Judge and Official Referee, 1993–98. *Publication:* (with D. A. McI. Kemp and M. S. Kemp) The Quantum of Damages: personal injury claims, 3rd edn, 1967. *Recreations:* music, croquet, steam locomotives. *Clubs:* Athenæum, Garrick, Hurlingham.

HAVILLAND; *see* de Havilland.

HAWARD, Birkin Anthony Christopher, RIBA; Joint Principal, van Heyningen and Haward Architects, since 1982; *b* 28 Sept. 1939; *s* of Birkin Haward and Muriel Haward (*née* Wright); *m* 1st, 1963, Rose Hargreaves Heap (marr. diss. 1975; she *d* 1993); one *s* one *d*; 2nd, 1977, Joanna van Heyningen, *qv*; one *s* one *d*. *Educ:* Northgate Grammar Sch., Ipswich; Architectural Assoc. RIBA 1969. Dir, Foster Associates, 1969–83; formed van Heyningen and Haward Architects, 1982. Studio teacher: Cambridge Univ. Sch. of Architecture, 1969–75; Bartlett Sch. of Architecture, 1976–81; RCA, 1981–84. Vis. critic, Univ. of Pennsylvania, 1976, and most UK architectural schs. Award-winning buildings include: Haward House, London, 1976; Newnham Coll. Rare Books Liby, Cambridge, 1981; 2nd Haward House, London, 1986; Clovelly Visitor Centre, 1989; Wilson Court, Cambridge, 1994; Jacqueline du Pré Music Bldg, Oxford, 1995; King Alfred's Sch., London, 1997; Gateway to the White Cliffs (NT), Dover, 1999; West Ham Station, Jubilee Line Extension, 1999; Nat. Centre for Early Music, York, 2000; Polhill Inf. Centre, Bedford, 2000; Khoan and Michael Sullivan Chinese Painting Gall., Ashmolean Mus., Oxford, 2001; Sutton Hoo Visitor Centre (NT), 2002; Music Res. Centre, Univ. of York, 2004; Trinity Centre, Ipswich, 2005; Kaleidoscope, Lewisham, 2006; RSPB Centre, Rainham Marshes, 2007. Ext. Examr, 1984–87, Mem., Steering Cttee, 1991–96, RIBA. Member: Architectural Panel, NT, 1995–; Council, AA, 2000–03; Fabric Adv. Cttee, St Paul's Cathedral, 2003–. Assessor, Heritage Lottery Fund, 1996–99; Architectural Advr, Arts Council Lottery Panel, 1996–2001. Trustee, William Morris Gall., 2003–. Exhibitions: Kent Design, Maidstone, 2000; University Challenge: buildings for higher educn, Building Centre, 2001; New Connections, Municipal Arts Soc. of NY, 2001; Winning Designs, Bristol Arch. Centre, RIBA, London and Cube Gall., Manchester, 2002; Diverse City, RIBA, London, 2003; Celebration of Architectural Competitions, Cube Gall., Manchester, 2003, RIAS, Edinburgh, 2004. *Publications:* contribs to major newspaper and architectural jls. *Recreations:* drawing, painting, theatre, church-crawling, 19th and 20th century stained glass, gardening. *Address:* van Heyningen and Haward Architects, Burghley Yard, 106 Burghley Road, NW5 1AL. *T:* (020) 7482 4454, *Fax:* (020) 7284 0632; *e-mail:* birkin@vhh.co.uk.

HAWARD, Joanna; *see* van Heyningen, J.

HAWARD, John Anthony William; consultant; *b* 8 Feb. 1958; *s* of Anthony Ivor Haward and Joan Haward; partner, Janie Wilson; one *d*. *Educ:* City of London Sch. Joined: DoE, 1977; Spastics Soc., 1987; Mgt Advr and Hd of Chief Exec.'s Office, Berks CC, 1988; Dir of Corporate Strategy, Southwark Council, 1994; Advr, UN Mission to Kosovo, 1999; Chm., Local Govt Modernisation Team, DETR, subseq. ODPM, 2000–03; Dir of Local Govt Practice SE, ODPM, then DCLG, 2004–07. *Publications:* Impact of Advanced Information Systems, 1984; Devolved Management, 1989; Project Management, 1991. *Recreations:* walking, reading, buildings, food and too much wine, holidays, life with teenager. *Address:* 74 Blenheim Crescent, South Croydon CR2 6BP; *e-mail:* johnhaward@omail.co.uk.

HAWARDEN, 9th Viscount (Ire.), *cr* 1793; **Robert Connan Wyndham Leslie Maude;** Bt 1705; Baron de Montalt 1785; *b* 23 May 1961; *s* of 8th Viscount and Susannah Caroline Hyde, *d* of late Maj. Charles Phillips Gardner; *S* father, 1991; *m* 1995, Judith Anne, *y d* of late John Bates; one *s* two *d*. *Educ:* St Edmund's Sch., Canterbury; RAC Cirencester. *Heir:* *s* Hon. Varian John Connan Eustace Maude, *b* 1 Sept. 1997. *Address:* Great Bossington Farm House, Bossington, Adisham, near Canterbury, Kent CT3 3LN.

HAWES, Ven. Arthur John; Archdeacon of Lincoln, and Canon and Prebendary of Lincoln Cathedral, 1995–2008; *b* 31 Aug. 1943; *s* of late John and Sylvia Hawes; *m* 1969, Melanie Harris; one *s* one *d*. *Educ:* City of Oxford High Sch. for Boys; Chichester Theol Coll.; Univ. of Birmingham (Dip. in Pastoral Studies, 1972; Dip. in Liturgy and Architecture, 1975); Univ. of E Anglia (BA Hons 1986). Ordained deacon 1968, priest 1969; Asst Curate, St John the Baptist, Kidderminster, 1968–72; Priest-in-charge, St Richard's, Droitwich, 1972–76; Rector: Alderford with Attlebridge and Swannington, 1976–92; St Faith's, Gaywood, King's Lynn, 1992–95. Chaplain, Hellesdon and David Rice Hosps, Yare Clinic, 1976–92; Rural Dean of Sparham, 1981–91; Hon. Canon of Norwich Cathedral, 1988–95. Mem., General Synod, 2000–08 (Mem., Mission and Public Affairs Council, 2000–; Chm., Mental Health Adv. Cttee, 1995–). Chm., Norwich Diocesan Bd for Social Responsibility, 1990–95. Mental Health Act Comr, 1986–94. Pres., Lincs Rural Housing Assoc., 1998–2007; Chm., East Midlands Develt Centre, 2003–05; non-exec. Dir, Lincolnshire Partnership Trust, 2002–06; Mental Health Act Advr to Lincolnshire Partnership Foundn Trust, 2006–08. Patron, MIND, 1995–2008. *Publications:* (ed jtly) The Ann French Memorial Lectures, 1996; contribs to theol jls. *Recreations:* golf, Romanesque art and architecture, theatre, music. *Address:* 49 Thamespoint, Fairways, Teddington, Middx TW11 9PP. *Club:* Sleaford Golf.

HAWKE, family name of **Baron Hawke**.

HAWKE, 11th Baron *cr* 1776, of Towton; **Edward George Hawke,** TD; FRICS; *b* 25 Jan. 1950; *s* of 10th Baron and of his 2nd wife, Georgette Margaret, *d* of George S. Davidson; *S* father, 1992; *m* 1993, Bronwen, *d* of William James, MRCVS; one *s* one *d*. *Educ:* Eton. 2nd Lt, 1st Bn Coldstream Guards, 1970–73; Territorial Army, Queen's Own Yeomanry, 1973–93 (Major). Hon. Col, Cheshire Yeomanry, 1998–2005. Trustee, Edward Mayes Trust. Governor, Terra Nova Sch. *Heir:* *s* William Martin Theodore Hawke, *b* 23 June 1995.

HAWKE, Hon. Robert James Lee, AC 1979; business consultant; Adjunct Professor, Research School of Pacific Studies and Social Sciences, Australian National University, 1992–95; Prime Minister of Australia, 1983–91; *b* 9 Dec. 1929; *m* 1st, 1956, Hazel Masterson (marr. diss. 1995); one *s* two *d* (and one *s* decd); 2nd, 1995, Blanche d'Alpuget. *Educ:* Univ. of Western Australia (LLB, BA(Econ)); Oxford Univ. (BLitt; Hon. Fellow, University Coll., 1984). Research Officer and Advocate for Aust. Council of Trade Unions, 1958–69. Pres., ACTU, 1970–80. MP (Lab) Wills, Melbourne, 1980–92; Australian Labor Party: Mem., Nat. Exec., 1971–91; Pres., 1973–78; Leader, 1983–91. Leader of the Opposition, Feb.–March 1983. Member: Governing Body of Internat. Labour Office, 1972–80; Board, Reserve Bank of Australia, 1973–80; Aust. Population and Immigration Council, 1976–80; Aust. Manufacturing Council, 1977–80. Chm., Cttee of Experts on Membership of Educn Internat., 1993–. Hon. Vis. Prof., Univ. of Sydney, 1992–97. Mem. Adv. Bd, Inst. for Internat. Studies, Stanford Univ. Hon. DLitt W Australia, 1984; Hon. Dr Nanjing, 1986; Hon. DPhil Hebrew Univ. of Jerusalem, 1987; Hon. LLD Univ. of NSW, 1987. *Publication:* The Hawke Memoirs, 1994. *Recreations:* tennis, cricket, reading, golf, horse racing, snooker.

HAWKEN, Lewis Dudley, CB 1983; a Deputy Chairman of the Board of Customs and Excise, 1980–87; *b* 23 Aug. 1931; *s* of late Richard and Doris May Evelyn Hawken; *m* 1954, Bridget Mary Gamble (*d* 1989); two *s* one *d*. *Educ:* Harrow County Sch. for Boys; Lincoln Coll., Oxford (MA). Comr of Customs and Excise, 1975. *Recreation:* collecting wood engravings. *Address:* 21 Sherleys Court, Wood Lane, Ruislip, Middx HA4 6DH. *T:* (01895) 632405. *Clubs:* Oxford and Cambridge, MCC.

HAWKER, Ven. Alan Fort; Archdeacon of Malmesbury, since 1999; *b* 23 March 1944; *s* of Albert Hawker and Florence Lilian Hawker (*née* Fort); *m* 1968, Jeanette Dorothy Law; one *s* three *d*. *Educ:* Buckhurst Hill County High Sch.; Hull Univ. (BA Hons Soc. Studies 1965); Clifton Theol Coll. (DipTh 1968). PACTA 1973. Asst Curate, St Leonard and St Mary, Bootle, 1968–71; Asst Curate (with charge), St Paul, Fazakerley, 1971–73; Vicar, St Paul, Goose Green, 1973–81; Team Rector, St Mary, Southgate (Crawley), 1981–98; Canon and Prebendary, Chichester Cathedral, 1991–98; Proctor in Convocation, 1990–; RD of E Grinstead, 1993–98; Archdeacon of Swindon, 1998–99. Chm., Gen. Synod Working Party on Clergy Discipline and Reform of Ecclesiastical Courts, 1994–2001; Member: Gen. Synod Standing Cttee, 1995–98; Gen. Synod Business Cttee, 2000–; C of E Clergy Discipline Commn, 2003–. CEDR Accredited Mediator, 1996–. Vice Chair, Council, Glos Univ., 2002–08. *Publication:* Under Authority, 1996. *Recreations:* walking, railways, theatre, reading, music. *Address:* Church Paddock, Church Lane, Kington Langley, Chippenham, Wilts SN15 5NR. *T:* (01249) 750085, *Fax:* (01249) 750086; *e-mail:* alan.hawker@bristol5.gotadsl.co.uk.

HAWKER, David Gordon; Director General of Children, Education, Lifelong Learning and Skills, Welsh Assembly Government, since 2008; *b* 11 Feb. 1954; *s* of Gordon Hawker and Peggy Hawker (*née* Lewis); *m* 1987, Judy Tongue; one *s* one *d*. *Educ:* Whitgift Sch., Croydon; Northampton Grammar Sch.; Wadham Coll., Oxford (BA Hons French and German; PGCE). Teacher, 1976–85; Exams Officer, Oxford Schs Exams Bd, 1985–86; Exams Sec., Inst. of Linguists, 1986–89; Schs Advr, Calderdale MBC, 1989–92; Sen. Professional Officer, Sch. Exams and Assessment Council, 1992–93; Asst Chief Exec., SCAA, 1994–97; Hd, Curriculum and Assessment, QCA, 1997–99; Dir of Educn, 1999–2002, Dir of Children's Services, 2002–2007, Brighton & Hove City Council; Dep. Chief Exec., Westminster City Council, 2007–08. Chm., Assoc. of Dirs of Educn and Children's Services, 2004–07 (Chm., Standards, Performance and Inspection Cttee, 2007–). Consultant to OECD, World Bank and British Council on educnl evaluation and assessment, 2000–; Mem., Gen. Educn Sub-Bd, Open Soc. Inst. Prof., College of Teachers, 2007–. Trustee, 4Children. *Publications:* Core Skills Framework for Modern Languages, 1990; Review of Assessment and Testing, 1995; A Higher Vision for LEAs, 2001; Methodological Recommendations for a Quality Monitoring Framework for the Russian Education System, 2002; (contrib.) Contemporary Issues in the Early Years, 4th edn 2006. *Recreations:* music, squash, travel. *Address:* Department for Children, Education, Lifelong Learning and Skills, Welsh Assembly Government, Cathays Park, Cardiff CF10 3NQ. *T:* (02920) 823284; *e-mail:* david.hawker@btconnect.com.

HAWKER, Hon. David Peter Maxwell; MP (L) Wannon, Vic, since 1983; Deputy Chairman, Joint Standing Committee on Foreign Affairs, Defence and Trade, Australia, since 2008; *b* Adelaide, 1 May 1949; *s* of David Hawker and Pamela Gavin Hawker (*née* Anderson); *m* 1973, Penelope Ann Ahern; three *s* one *d*. *Educ:* Geelong Grammar Sch.; Univ. of Melbourne (BEng). Man. Dir, Newlands Pty Ltd (agricl business), 1973–83. Shadow Minister for Land Transport, 1990–93; Opposition Whip, 1994–96; Mem., Speaker's panel, 1998–2004; Speaker, House of Reps, 2004–08. House of Representatives Standing Committees: Dep. Chm., Industry, Sci. and Technol., 1989–90; Chairman: Finance, Admin and Public Admin, 1996–98; Econs, Finance and Public Affairs, 1998–2004; Chm., Defence Sub-cttee, Jt Standing Cttee on Foreign Affairs, Defence and Trade, 1999–2001; Mem., Jt Select Cttee on Republic Referendum, 1999, on Intelligence Services, 2001–02; Chm., Govt Members Wool Cttee, 1996–2004. Chm., Liberal Party Fed. Rural Cttee, 1987–90. *Publications:* Who Reaps the Benefits?: a chronicle of the wheat debate, 1989; (jtly) The Heart of Liberalism, 1994; Striking a Balance: the lack of adequate and comparable services for regional Australia, 1996. *Recreations:* shooting, golf, cycling. *Address:* 190 Gray Street, Hamilton, Vic 3300, Australia. *Clubs:* Melbourne, Adelaide; Royal Melbourne Golf.

HAWKER, Graham Alfred, CBE 1999; DL; Chief Executive, Hyder (formerly Welsh Water) plc, 1993–2000; *b* 12 May 1947; *s* of Alfred Hawker and Sarah Rebecca (*née* Bowen); *m* 1967, Sandra Ann Evans; one *s* one *d*. *Educ:* Bedwelty Grammar Sch. CIPFA 1969; FCCA 1981. Trainee Acctnt, Caerphilly DC, 1964–66; Abercarn District Council: Acctnt, 1966–67; Chief Acctnt, 1967–68; Dep. Treas., 1968–70; Chief Auditor, Taf Fechan Water Bd, 1970–74; Welsh Water Authority: Audit Manager, 1974–78; Div. Finance Manager, 1978–84; Chief Acctnt, 1984–86; Dir, Planning and Develt, 1986–87; Dir, Finance, 1987–89; Welsh Water, later Hyder, PLC: Dir, Finance, 1989–91; Gp Man. Dir, 1991–93. A Dir, Bank of England, 1998–2000. Chairman: Dŵr Cymru Ltd, 1993–2000; Hyder Consulting (formerly Acer), 1993–2000; Swalec, 1996–2000. Dep. Chm., 1998–2000, Chief Exec., 2000–04, Welsh Develt Agency. Chairman: BITC (Wales), 1994–2000; New Deal Task Force Adv. Cttee (Wales), 1997–98; Member: CBI Council for Wales, 1994–97; New Deal Adv. Cttee (UK), 1997–98; Prince of Wales' Review Cttee on Queen's Awards, 1999. Prince of Wales Ambassador's Award for Corporate Social Responsibility, 1999. CCMI; FRSA. DL Gwent, 1998. Hon. Fellow, Univ. of Wales, Cardiff, 1999. Hon. Dr Glamorgan, 1996. *Recreations:* family, walking, wine. *Address:* St Teilo House, Llantilio Pertholey, Abergavenny NP7 6NY.

HAWKER, Stephen, CB 2005; FIET; Senior Civil Servant, Ministry of Defence, retired 2006; company director; National Security Adviser to Defence Strategy & Solutions, since 2006; *b* 1948; *s* of Derek Hawker and Pamela Hawker (*née* Holland); *m* 1989; one *s* one *d*. *Educ:* Worksop Coll.; Pembroke Coll., Oxford (MA 1970); Univ. of Nottingham (PGCE 1971). FIET (FIEE 2004). Hd of Dept, King James's Coll. of Henley, 1971–78; MoD, 1978–2006; on secondment: to NI Office, 1981–83 and 1998–2000; to Cabinet Office, 1989–92. Strategic Advr, Detica plc, 2007–; Fujiku Services Defence and Security

Adv. Gp, 2007– Vis. Prof., Cranfield Univ., 2006–. Lay Mem. Council, Reading Univ., 2007–. *Address: e-mail:* stephen.hawker@tiscali.co.uk.

HAWKES, David, MA, DPhil; Research Fellow, All Souls College, Oxford, 1973–83, now Emeritus; *b* 6 July 1923; *s* of Ewart Hawkes and Dorothy May Hawkes (*née* Davis); *m* 1950, Sylvia Jean Perkins; one *s* three *d*. *Educ:* Bancroft's Sch. Open Scholarship in Classics, Christ Church, Oxford, 1941; Chinese Hons Sch., Oxford, 1945–47; Research Student, National Peking Univ., 1948–51. Formerly University Lecturer in Chinese, Oxford; Prof. of Chinese, Oxford Univ., 1959–71. *Publications:* Ch'u Tz'ŭ, Songs of the South, 1959, rev. edn as The Songs of the South: an Ancient Chinese Anthology of Poems by Qu Yuan and Other Poets, 1985; A Little Primer of Tu Fu, 1967, repr. 1987; The Story of the Stone, vol. 1, 1973, vol. 2, 1977, vol. 3, 1980; Classical, Modern and Humane: essays in Chinese Literature (ed J. Minford and Siu-kit Wong), 1989; Liu Yi and the Dragon Princess: a thirteenth-century Zaju play by Shang Zhongxian, 2003.

HAWKES, Prof. David John, PhD; FREng; CPhys, FInstP; FIPEM; Professor of Computational Imaging Science, and Director, Centre of Medical Image Computing, University College London, since 2005; *b* 16 Jan. 1953; *s* of Roy and Joyce Hawkes; *m* 1978, Elizabeth Anne Nicholson; two *d*. *Educ:* Christ Church, Oxford (BA 2nd cl. Hons Natural Scis (Physics)); Univ. of Birmingham (MSc Radiobiol.); Univ. of Surrey (PhD 1982). FIPEM 1993; CPhys, FInstP 1997. Principal Physicist and Hd, Imaging and Med. Physics, St George's Hosp., London, 1984–88; Sen. Lectr, 1988–93, Reader in Radiol Scis, 1993–98, Guy's Hosp.; Prof. of Computational Imaging Sci., 1998–2004, and Chm., Div. of Imaging Scis, Sch. of Medicine, 2002–04, KCL. Dir, Interdisciplinary Res. Collaboration in Med. Images and Signals, 2003–. Hon. Consultant Physicist, Guy's and St Thomas' NHS Trust, 1989–. FREng 2003; Business Fellow, London Technol. Network, 2003. *Publications:* (ed with A. Colchester) Information Processing in Medical Imaging, 1991; (ed jtly) Medical Image Registration, 2000; numerous papers in scientific jls on med. imaging. *Recreations:* sailing, windsurfing, hill-climbing, mountain biking, scuba-diving, expeditions, kayaking, travel, conversation lubricated with good wine and beer. *Address:* Centre of Medical Image Computing, Department of Medical Physics, University College London, Gower Street, WC1E 6BT.

HAWKES, (John) Garry, CBE 1999; company director; Chief Executive, Gardner Merchant, 1978–98; Director, Trusthouse Forte, 1983–1993; *b* 26 Aug. 1939; *s* of John and Joyce Hawkes; *m* 1963, Peggy Lee; one *d*. *Educ:* Rowlinson Sch., Sheffield; Huddersfield Coll. of Technology. Joined Gardner Merchant, 1963; Regl Dir, 1972–76; European Man. Dir, 1976; Man. Dir, Gardner Merchant Ltd, 1977–95. Directeur Général, Sodexho SA, 1995–98; Chm., Cheese Cellar Co., 2000–; Vice-Chm., Accord plc, 2005– (Dir, 2000–); Dir, Investors in People, 2000–. Chairman: Nat. Council, NTO, 1997–2001; British Trng Internat., 1997–2001; ARAMARK UK, 2000–04; Edexcel, 2000–05; Basic Skills Agency, 2002–; Guidance Accreditation Bd, 2002–05; Vice Chm., London Qualifications, 2003–05. Pres., Hospitality Action, 1996–04. Chm., Edge Foundn, 2004–. FIH (FHCIMA 1982). Hon. Fellow: Huddersfield Univ., 1996; Oxford Brookes Univ., 1997. *Recreations:* theatre, modern design, travel. *Address:* Coalpit, Rookery Way, Haywards Heath, W Sussex RH16 4RE; Flat 7, 8–9 Rose & Crown Yard, St James's, SW1Y 6RE.

HAWKES, Michael John; Deputy Chairman, Kleinwort, Benson Group plc, 1988–90; *b* 7 May 1929; *s* of Wilfred Arthur Hawkes and Anne Maria Hawkes; *m* 1st, 1957, Gillian Mary Watts; two *s* two *d*; 2nd, 1973, Elizabeth Anne Gurton. *Educ:* Bedford School; New College, Oxford (Exhibnr; MA); Gray's Inn. Kleinwort Sons & Co. Ltd, 1954; Kleinwort, Benson Ltd: Director, 1967; Vice Chm., 1974; Dep. Chm., 1982; Chm., 1983–87; Director, Kleinwort, Benson, Lonsdale plc, 1974–88; Chairman: Sharps Pixley Ltd, 1971–89; Kleinwort Benson Investment Trust, 1984–89. Mem., Management Bd, Sovereign (formerly W Berks) Housing Assoc., 1988–97. Gov., The Willink Sch., 1988–96. *Recreations:* long distance walking, golf, gardening. *Address:* Brookfield House, Burghfield Common, Berks RG7 3BD. *T:* (0118) 983 2912; White Bays, Daymer Lane, Trebetherick, N Cornwall PL27 6SA. *T:* (01208) 862280. *Club:* Leander (Henley on Thames).

HAWKES, Nigel John Mytton, CBE 1999; Health Editor, The Times, since 2000; *b* 1 Sept. 1943; *s* of late R. W. Hawkes, MBE and K. M. Hawkes; *m* 1971, Jo Beresford; two *s* one *d*. *Educ:* Sedbergh Sch.; St Catherine's Coll., Oxford (MA). Mem., editl staff, Nature, 1966–69; Sci. Editor, Science Jl, 1969–70; Associate Editor, Telegraph Mag., 1970–72; The Observer: Sci. Corresp., 1972–81; Foreign News Editor, 1981–83; Diplomatic Corresp., 1983–87; Diplomatic Editor, 1987–90; Science Editor, The Times, 1990–2000. Gov., British Nutrition Foundn, 1999–2006 (British Nutrition Foundn Award, 1992). Chm., Friends of Woodchurch Windmill, 2002–06. Health Journalist Award, MJA, 2007. *Publications:* The Computer Revolution, 1971; Early Scientific Instruments, 1978; (ed and contrib.) Tearing Down the Curtain, 1989; Structures, 1991; Man on the Move, 1992; numerous science and technology titles for children and teenagers. *Recreations:* walking, opera. *Address:* Well House, Front Road, Woodchurch, Kent TN26 3QE. *T:* (01233) 860518.

HAWKESBURY, Viscount; Luke Marmaduke Peter Savile Foljambe; with Savills PLC (formerly FPDSavills Ltd), since 2001; *b* 25 March 1972; *s* and *heir* of 5th Earl of Liverpool, *qv*. *Educ:* Ampleforth; Roehampton Inst. With Property Vision Ltd, 1999–2001. *Recreations:* golf, field sports. *Clubs:* Turf; Old Amplefordian Golf Soc.

HAWKESWORTH, Prof. Christopher John, DPhil; FRS 2002; Professor of Earth Sciences, Bristol University, since 2000; *b* 18 Dec. 1947; *s* of Desmond and Ann Hawkesworth; *m* 1972, Elizabeth Celia Williams; one *d*. *Educ:* Trinity Coll., Dublin (BA Hons); St Edmund Hall, Oxford (DPhil). NERC Res. Fellow, Univ. of Leeds, 1975–78; Open University: Lectr, 1978–83; Sen. Lectr, 1983–88; Prof., 1988–2000. Internat. Sec., Geochemical Soc., 1995–97; Mem., NERC Earth Scis and Technology Bd, 1996–99; Pres., European Assoc. for Geochemistry, 1997–98; Sci. Sec., Geol Soc. of London, 1999–2002; Vice-Pres., European Union of Geosciences, 2001–03. Fellow: American Geophysical Union, 2000; Geochemical Soc., 2001. Maj. John Coke Medal, Geol Soc. of London, 1996; Schlumberger Medal, Mineralog. Soc., 2002. Hon. DSc Copenhagen, 2000. *Publications:* edited jointly: Continental Basalts and Mantle Xenoliths, 1983; Mantle Metasomatism, 1987; Understanding the Earth, II, 1992; Chemical Geology, festschrift for A. W. Hofmann, 1997; 240 scientific papers. *Recreations:* hill walking, sports, photography, reading predominantly non-fiction, gardening. *Address:* Woodbine Cottage, Kirtlington, Oxon OX5 3HA. *T:* (01869) 350304, *Fax:* (01869) 351004; *e-mail:* C.J.Hawkesworth@bristol.ac.uk.

HAWKESWORTH, Gareth; *see* Hawkesworth, W. G.

HAWKESWORTH, (Thomas) Simon (Ashwell); QC 1982; **His Honour Judge Hawkesworth;** a Circuit Judge, since 1999; *b* 15 Nov. 1943; *s* of late Charles Peter Elmhirst Hawkesworth and Felicity Hawkesworth; *m* 1st, 1970, Jennifer Lewis (marr. diss. 1989); two *s*; 2nd, 1990, Dr May Bamber, MD, MRCP; twin *s*. *Educ:* Rugby Sch.; The Queen's Coll., Oxford (MA). Called to the Bar, Gray's Inn, 1967, Bencher 1990; a Recorder, 1982–99. *Address:* Combined Court Centre, Leeds LS1 3BG.
See also W. G. Hawkesworth.

HAWKESWORTH, (Walter) Gareth; His Honour Judge Gareth Hawkesworth; a Circuit Judge, since 1999; *b* 29 Dec. 1949; *s* of late Charles Peter Elmhirst Hawkesworth and of Felicity Hawkesworth (*née* Ashwell); *m* 1982, Barbara Joyce Tapper; one *s* one *d* and one step *d*. *Educ:* Rugby Sch.; Magdalene Coll., Cambridge (Schol.; BA 2nd Cl. Hons Law, MA); Council of Legal Educn. Called to the Bar, Gray's Inn, 1972; joined Fenners Chambers, Cambridge, 1974; a Recorder, 1995–99. *Recreations:* gardening, theatre, travel.
See also T. S. A. Hawkesworth.

HAWKHEAD, Anthony Gerard, CBE 2003; Chief Executive, Groundwork UK, since 1996; *b* 7 Oct. 1957; *s* of Harry and Mary Hawkhead; *m* 1981, Marion Small; one *d* (one *s* decd). *Educ:* Whitefriars Sch., Cheltenham. Various policy and finance jobs, MoD 1978–87; HEOD, Inner Cities Unit, DTI, 1987–88; Leader, Govt's N Peckham Task Force, 1988–89; Hd, Business and Econ. Develt, LDDC, 1989–91; Chief Exec., E London Partnership, 1991–96. MInstD 1998. Hon. FCIWEM 2005. *Recreations:* tennis cricket, music, wine, France. *Address:* Groundwork UK, Lockside, 5 Scotland Street, Birmingham B1 2RR. *T:* (0121) 236 8565, *Fax:* (0121) 236 7356; *e-mail:* info@groundwork.org.uk. *Clubs:* Mandarins Cricket; Olton and W Warks Sports.

HAWKING, Prof. Stephen William, CH 1989; CBE 1982; FRS 1974; Fellow of Gonville and Caius College, Cambridge; Lucasian Professor of Mathematics, Cambridge University, since 1979; *b* 8 Jan. 1942; *s* of Dr F. and Mrs E. I. Hawking; *m* 1st, 1965, Jane Wilde (marr. diss. 1995); two *s* one *d*; 2nd, 1995, Elaine Mason (marr. diss. 2007). *Educ:* St Albans Sch.; University Coll., Oxford (BA), Hon. Fellow 1977; Trinity Hall Cambridge (PhD), Hon. Fellow 1984. Research Fellow, Gonville and Caius Coll. 1965–69; Fellow for distinction in science, 1969–; Mem. Inst. of Theoretical Astronomy Cambridge, 1968–72; Research Asst, Inst. of Astronomy, Cambridge, 1972–73 Cambridge University: Research Asst, Dept of Applied Maths and Theoretical Physics 1973–75; Reader in Gravitational Physics, 1975–77, Professor, 1977–79. Fairchild Distinguished Schol., Calif Inst. of Technol., 1974–75. Mem., Pontifical Acad. of Scis 1986–; Foreign Member: Amer. Acad. of Arts and Scis, 1984; Amer. Philosophical Soc. 1985. Hon. Mem., RAS (Can), 1985. Hon. DSc: Oxon, 1978; Newcastle, Leeds, 1987 Cambridge, 1989; hon. degrees: Chicago, 1981; Leicester, New York, Notre Dame Princeton, 1982. (Jtly) Eddington Medal, RAS, 1975; Pius XI Gold Medal, Pontifical Acad. of Scis, 1975; Dannie Heinemann Prize for Math. Phys., Amer. Phys. Soc. and Amer. Inst. of Physics, 1976; William Hopkins Prize, Cambridge Philosoph. Soc., 1976 Maxwell Medal, Inst. of Physics, 1976; Hughes Medal, Royal Soc., 1976; Albert Einstein Award, 1978; Albert Einstein Medal, Albert Einstein Soc., Berne, 1979; Franklin Medal Franklin Inst., USA, 1981; Gold Medal, RAS, 1985; Paul Dirac Medal and Prize, Inst. of Physics, 1987; (jtly) Wolf Foundn Prize for Physics, 1988; Britannica Award, 1989; Prince of Asturias Foundn Award, Spain, 1989; James Smithson Bicentennial Medal, Smithsonian Inst., Washington, 2005; Copley Medal, Royal Soc., 2006. *Publications:* (with G. F. R. Ellis) The Large Scale Structure of Space-Time, 1973; (ed W. W. Israel) General Relativity: an Einstein centenary survey, 1979; (ed with M. Roček) Superspace and Supergravity, 1981; (ed jtly) The Very Early Universe, 1983; (with W. Israel) 300 Years of Gravitation, 1987; A Brief History of Time, 1988; Black Holes and Baby Universes, 1993; The Universe in a Nutshell, 2001; A Briefer History of Time, 2005; (with Lucy Hawking) George's Secret Key to the Universe (for children), 2007; (ed) A Stubbornly Persistent Illusion: the essential writings of Albert Einstein, 2008. *Address:* Department of Applied Mathematics and Theoretical Physics, Centre for Mathematical Sciences, Wilberforce Road, Cambridge CB3 0WA. *T:* (01223) 337843.

HAWKINS, Very Rev. Alun John; Dean of Bangor, since 2004; *b* 28 May 1944; *m* 1971, Ann Deborah Williams, HMI; two *s*. *Educ:* King's Coll. London (BA, AKC 1966); Univ of Wales, Bangor (BD 1981); St Deiniol's, Hawarden. Lecturer: in English and Drama, St Mary's Coll. of Educn, Bangor, 1969–77; in Educn, UCNW, Bangor, 1977–79; Chief Examiner, Drama and Th. Arts, Associated Examg Bd, 1971–76. Ordained deacon, 1981, priest, 1982; Curate, Dwygyfylchi, 1981–84; Rector, Llanberis, 1984–89; Tutor, Diocesan NSM Course, 1985–90, Dir of Ordinands, 1986–90, Dio. Bangor; Vicar, Knighton and Norton, 1989–93; Canon Residentiary and Missioner, Bangor Cathedral, and Vicar in Bangor Rectorial Benefice, 1993–2000; Archdeacon of Bangor, 2000–04. Chaplain, Knighton Hosp., 1989–93. Archbishop's Commissary, 2004. *Address:* The Deanery, Cathedral Close, Bangor LL57 1LH.

HAWKINS, Prof. Anthony Donald, CBE 2000; PhD; FRSE; Professor of Marine Resource Management, University of Aberdeen, since 2002; Chairman, North Sea Commission Fisheries Partnership, since 2002; Managing Director, Loughine Ltd, since 2002; *b* 25 March 1942; *s* of Kenneth St David Hawkins and Marjorie Lillian Hawkins; *m* 1966, Susan Mary Fulker; one *s*. *Educ:* Poole Grammar Sch.; Bristol Univ. (BSc 1st Cl. Hons Zoology, 1963; PhD 1968). Dept of Agriculture and Fisheries for Scotland: Scientific Officer, Marine Lab., Aberdeen, 1965, Chief Scientific Officer, 1987; Dir of Fisheries Res., Scottish Office Agriculture and Fisheries Dept, subseq. Dir of Fisheries Res. Services, Scottish Exec., 1987–2002; Hon. Res. Prof., Univ. of Aberdeen, 1987–2002. Consultant to FAO, Peru, 1975; Hon. Lectr, Univ. of St Andrews, 1983. Rapporteur, North Sea Regl Adv. Council, 2004–. FRSE 1988. A. B. Wood Medal and Prize, Inst. of Acoustics, 1978. *Publications:* (ed and contrib.) Sound Reception in Fish, 1976; (ed and contrib.) Aquarium Systems, 1981; pubns on marine science, fish physiology and salmon biology. *Recreations:* angling, riding, whippet breeding. *Address:* Kincraig, Blairs, Aberdeen AB12 5YT. *T:* (01224) 868984; *e-mail:* a.hawkins@btconnect.com.

HAWKINS, Catherine Eileen, CBE 1992; World Health Organisation Consultant to Middle Eastern Sector, since 1993; debt consultant; *b* 16 Jan. 1939; *d* of Stanley Richard Hawkins and Mary-Kate Hawkins. *Educ:* La Retraite High Sch., Clifton. SRN, CMB (Pt 1), HVCert, DN London, Queen's Inst. of Nursing Cert, IRCert, DipIT. General nursing, student, 1956–59; Staff Nursing, Charing Cross Hosp., SRN, 1960–61; Pt 1 midwifery, St Thomas' Hosp., 1961; Health Visitor Student, LCC, RCN, 1961–62; LCC Health Visitor, 1962–63; Bristol CC HV, 1963–64; Project Leader, Bahrain Public Health Service, 1964–66; Field Work Teacher, HV, 1966–68; Health Centre Administrator, 1968–71; Administrator, Res. Div., Health Educn Council, 1971–72; Sen. Nursing Officer, Community Services, 1972–74; Area Nurse Service Capital Planning, Avon AHA, 1974–79; Dist Nursing Officer, Bristol and Weston DHA, 1979–82; Chief Nursing Officer, Southmead DHA, 1982–84; Regional Nursing Officer, 1984, Regl Gen. Manager, 1984–93, SW RHA. Non-exec. Dir, N Bristol NHS Trust, 1999–2003. *Address:* Sunraker, Church Road, Colaton Raleigh, Sidmouth, Devon EX10 0LH.

HAWKINS, Christopher James; Deputy Chairman, Black Country Development Corporation, 1992–98; non-executive chairman of a number of cos, 1988–99; *b* 26 Nov. 1937; *s* of Alec Desmond Hawkins and Christina Barbara; *m* Susan Ann Hawkins; two *d*. *Educ:* Bristol Grammar Sch.; Bristol Univ. BA (Hons) Economics. Joined Courtaulds Ltd, Head Office Economics Dept, 1959; seconded to UK aid financed industrial and economic survey of Northern Nigeria, 1960; similar mission to Tunisia to work on 5 year plan, 1961; Research Div. Economist, Courtaulds Ltd, 1961–66, Building Develt Manager, 1965–66; Lectr in Economics, 1966, Sen. Lectr, 1973–83, Univ. of Southampton. MP (C) High Peak, 1983–92. *Publications:* Capital Investment Appraisal, 1971; Theory of the Firm, 1973; The British Economy: what will our children think?, 1982; Britain's Economic Future: an immediate programme for revival, 1983; articles in Jl of Industrial Economics, Amer. Economic Review. *Recreations:* reading, music, sailing.

HAWKINS, Rt Rev. David John Leader; *see* Barking, Area Bishop of.

HAWKINS, Air Vice-Marshal David Richard; *see* Hawkins-Leth.

HAWKINS, Air Vice-Marshal Desmond Ernest, CB 1971; CBE 1967; DFC and Bar, 1942; *b* 27 Dec. 1919; *s* of Ernest and Lilian Hawkins; *m* 1947, Joan Audrey (*née* Munro); one *s*, and one step *s*. *Educ:* Bancroft Sch. Commissioned in RAF, 1938. Served War of 1939–45: Coastal Command and Far East, commanding 36, 230 and 240 Sqdns, 1940–46 (despatches). Commanded RAF Pembroke Dock, 1946–47 (despatches). Staff appts, 1947–50; RAF Staff Coll., 1950; Staff appts, 1951–55; commanded 38 Sqdn, OC Flg, RAF Luqa, 1955–57; jssc, 1957; Staff appts, 1958–61; SASO 19 Gp, 1961–63; commanded RAF Tengah, 1963–66; idc 1967; commanded RAF Lyneham, 1968; SASO, HQ, RAF Strike Command, 1969–71; Dir-Gen., Personal Services (RAF), MoD, 1971–74; Dep. Man. Dir, Services Kinema Corp., 1974–80. *Recreation:* sailing. *Clubs:* Royal Air Force, Royal Cruising; Royal Lymington Yacht.

HAWKINS, Prof. Eric William, CBE 1973; Director, Language Teaching Centre, University of York, 1965–79, now Professor Emeritus; *b* 8 Jan. 1915; *s* of James Edward Hawkins and Agnes Thompson (*née* Clarie); *m* 1938, Ellen Marie Thygesen, Copenhagen; one *s* one *d*. *Educ:* Liverpool Inst. High Sch.; Trinity Hall, Cambridge (Open Exhibn). MA, CertEd, FCIL. War Service, 1st Bn The Loyal Regt, 1940–46 (despatches 1945); wounded N Africa, 1943; Major 1945. Asst Master, Liverpool Coll., 1946–49; Headmaster: Oldershaw Grammar Sch., Wallasey, 1949–53; Calday Grange Grammar Sch., Ches, 1953–65. Member: Central Adv. Council for Educn (England) (Plowden Cttee), 1963–66; Rampton Cttee (educn of ethnic minorities), 1979–81. Hon. Prof., University Coll. of Wales, Aberystwyth, 1979–89. Comenius Fellow, Centre for Inf. on Lang. Teaching, 2000. Hon. DLitt Southampton, 1997. Gold Medal, Inst. Linguists, 1971. Comdr, Ordre des Palmes Académiques (France), 1986. *Publications:* (ed) Modern Languages in the Grammar School, 1961; (ed) New Patterns in Sixth Form Modern Language Studies, 1970; A Time for Growing, 1971; Le français pour tout le monde, vols 1–5, 1974–79; Modern Languages in the Curriculum, 1981; Awareness of Language: an introduction, 1984; (ed) Intensive Language Teaching and Learning, 1988; (ed) 30 Years of Language Teaching, 1996; Listening to Lorca, 1999. *Recreation:* walking.
See also M. R. Jackson.

HAWKINS, James Bruce, MA; Head Master, Norwich School, since 2002; *b* Sussex, 10 Dec. 1965; *s* of Dr Philip John Clare Hawkins and José Phyllis Hawkins (*née* Thorneloe); *m* 1999, Zoë Antonia Neeves; one *d*. *Educ:* King Edward VI Sch., Camp Hill, Birmingham; Brasenose Coll., Oxford (MA Maths; PGCE). Asst Master, Radley Coll., 1988–92; Hd of Maths, Forest Sch., 1992–97; Dep. Hd, Chigwell Sch., 1997–2002. Trustee: Compassion UK, 2002–; Norman's Foundn, 2003–. Governor: Old Sch., Henstead, 2003–; The Open Acad., Norwich, 2008–. *Recreations:* music, films, cafés, crosswords, regattas. *Address:* Norwich School, 70 The Close, Norwich NR1 4DD. *T:* (01603) 728442, *Fax:* (01603) 728491; *e-mail:* hm@norwich-school.org.uk. *Club:* Norfolk (Norwich).

HAWKINS, Dr John, OBE 2001; JP; Programme (formerly Project) Manager, Knowledge and Learning Centres, British Council, 2001–04; *b* 13 Oct. 1944; *s* of Maurice and Anna Hawkins; *m* 1968, Pamela June Donnelly; one *s* one *d*. *Educ:* Reading Univ. (BSc Physical Properties of Materials; PhD); Univ. of East Anglia (MA Develt Studies, 1994). Joined British Council, 1971; served Lahore, Islamabad, Bogotá, and Buenos Aires; Budget Department: Management Accountant, 1980–85; Dir, 1985–91; Manager, HQ Relocation Project, 1991–92; Head, Accommodation Services, 1992–93; Regl Dir, W Africa, 1994–97; Dir, Africa and S Asia, 1997–2000; Acting Dir of Finance, 2000; Special Projects, 2000–01. Work for charities, DISCET UK and Kings Church, Wokingham, 2004–. JP Reading, 2006. *Recreations:* running, walking, carpentry. *Address:* 50 Gipsy Lane, Earley, Reading RG6 7HD.

HAWKINS, Prof. John Alan, PhD; Professor of English and Applied Linguistics, University of Cambridge, since 2004. *Educ:* Trinity Hall, Cambridge (BA 1970; PhD 1975). Lectr, Univ. of Essex, 1973–77; Univ. of Southern Calif, 1977–2004, latterly as Prof. of Linguistics; Max Planck Inst. for Psycholinguistics, Nijmegen, 1982–85. *Publications:* Definiteness and Indefiniteness, 1978; Word Order Universals, 1983; A Comparative Typology of English and German, 1986; A Performance Theory of Order and Constituency, 1994; Efficiency and Complexity in Grammars, 2004. *Address:* Research Centre for English and Applied Linguistics, University of Cambridge, 9 West Road, Cambridge CB3 9DP.

HAWKINS, Prof. John David, FBA 1993; Professor of Ancient Anatolian Languages, School of Oriental and African Studies, University of London, 1993–2005, now Emeritus; *b* 11 Sept. 1940; *s* of John and Audrey Hawkins. *Educ:* Bradfield Coll.; University Coll., Oxford (BA 1962; MA 1965); Inst. of Archaeol., Univ. of London (Postgrad. Dip. 1964). School of Oriental and African Studies, University of London: Res. Fellow, 1964–67; Lectr, then Sen. Lectr, 1967–93. *Publications:* The Hieroglyphic Inscription of the Sacred Pool Complex at Boğazköy-Hattusa, 1995; Corpus of Hieroglyphic Luwian Inscriptions, vol. I, parts 1–3, 2000. *Recreations:* gardening, political cartoons, caricature. *Address:* School of Oriental and African Studies, University of London, Thornhaugh Street, WC1H 0XG. *T:* (020) 7734 5409.

HAWKINS, John Mark; HM Diplomatic Service; Ambassador to Qatar, since 2008; *b* 30 April 1960; *s* of John Clement Hawkins and Diana Margaret Hawkins (*née* Townsend); *m* 1991, Rosemarie Anne Kleynhans; two *s*. *Educ:* Bedford Sch.; New Coll., Oxford (MA Modern Hist.). Mgt trainee, J. Sainsbury plc, 1981–82; joined HM Diplomatic Service, 1982; FCO, 1982–84; Third, later Second, Sec. (Chancery), Pretoria/Cape Town, 1984–88; FCO, 1989–93; First Sec. (Commercial), New Delhi, 1993–96; Internat. Dir, Invest in Britain Bureau, 1997–99; Counsellor and Dir, Trade and Investment Promotion for Spain, Madrid, 2000–04; Consul Gen., Dubai, 2004–08. *Recreations:* travel, family, sport. *Address:* c/o Foreign and Commonwealth Office, King Charles Street, SW1A 2AH. *Club:* Mandarins Cricket.

HAWKINS, Dr Kevin Howard, OBE 2004; Director General, British Retail Consortium, 2004–08; *b* 25 Aug. 1947; *s* of Jack and Mary Hawkins; *m* 1972, Doreen Margaret Duff. *Educ:* Keighley Boys' Grammar Sch.; Gonville and Caius Coll., Cambridge (BA 1968, MA 1972); Univ. of Bradford (MSc 1970; PhD 1981); Nuffield Coll., Oxford (BLitt 1971). Lectr in Industrial Relns, Univ. of Bradford Mgt Centre, 1970–82; Director: CBI W Midlands, 1982–84; Public Affairs, Lucas Industries plc, 1984–89; Corporate Affairs, WH Smith Gp plc, 1989–95; Dir of Communications, Safeway plc, 1995–2004. Member: MLC, 2002–; Better Regulation Commn (formerly Task Force), 2002–06; Scottish Food and Health Council, 2004–06; Retail Policy Forum, DTI, 2004–08; Food Industry Better Regulation Gp, 2006–08, Food Industry Sustainability Strategy Gp, 2006–08, DEFRA; Nat. Retail Crime Steering Gp, 2007–08. *Publications:* Unemployment, 1978, 3rd edn 1987; The Management of Industrial Relations, 1978; Trade Unions, 1980; Case Studies in Industrial Relations, 1982. *Recreations:* golf, military history, keep fit. *Address:* c/o British Retail Consortium, 21 Dartmouth Street, SW1H 9BP.

HAWKINS, Nicholas John; Legal Director, Danoptra Holdings Ltd, since 2007; *b* 27 March 1957; *s* of Arthur Ernest Hawkins, PhD, FInstP, CPhys and Patricia Jean Hawkins, BSc, BA (*née* Papworth); *m* 1st, 1979, Angela Margaret Turner, MA Oxon, CPFA (marr. diss. 2000); two *s* one *d*; 2nd, 2001, Jenny Cassar; one step *s* one step *d*. *Educ:* Bedford Modern Sch.; Lincoln Coll., Oxford (MA); Inns of Court Sch. of Law. ACIArb. Called to the Bar, Middle Temple, 1979 (Harmsworth Sen. Scholar). Practised from chambers in Birmingham and Northampton, 1979–86; worked in construction and recruitment, 1986–87; Company Legal Advr, Access, 1987–89; Gp Legal Advr, Lloyds Abbey Life plc, 1989–92; Corporate Lawyer, AMJ internat. law firm, Sultanate of Oman, 2005–06; Barrister: Harris Hagan, Solicitors, 2006–07; Gambling Governance, 2006–07; Advr, Plus Mkts, 2006–07. Mem., Bar Council, 1988–95; Chm., Bar Assoc. for Commerce, Finance and Industry, 1994–95. Contested (C) Huddersfield, 1987. MP (C) Blackpool S, 1992–97, Surrey Heath, 1997–2005. PPS to Ministers of State, MoD, 1995–96, to Sec. of State for Nat. Heritage, 1996–97; opposition frontbench spokesman: on legal affairs, 1999–2001, 2002–03; on home affairs, 2000–03; on internat. develt, 2001–02. Member: Transport Select Cttee, 1993–95; Home Affairs Select Cttee, 1998–99; DCMS Select Cttee, 2004–05; Sec., Cons. backbench Educn Cttee, 1993–95; Vice Chairman: Cons. backbench Culture, Media and Sport (formerly Nat. Heritage) Cttee, 1997–2005; Cons. backbench Home Affairs Cttee, 1997–2005; Chm., Cons. backbench Sports Cttee, 1994–2005; Vice-Chairman: All-Party Sports Cttee, 1997–2005; All-Party Gp on Insurance and Financial Services, 1995–2005. Chm., W Lancs Support Gp, Marie Curie Cancer Care, 1992–96. *Publications:* booklets and articles on Conservative policy, transport hist., sport, and legal and employment matters. *Recreations:* cricket, music, theatre, transport history, Rugby, soccer, swimming. *Address:* Danoptra, The Mill, Low Lane, Horsforth, Leeds, W Yorks LS18 4ER. *Clubs:* MCC; Surrey CC; Lord's Taverners.

HAWKINS, Sir Richard Caesar, 9th Bt *cr* 1778, of Kelston, Somerset; *b* 29 Dec. 1958; *yr s* of Sir Humphry Hawkins, 7th Bt and of Anita, *d* of C. H. Funkey; *S* brother, 1999; *m* 1992, Ernestine Ehrensperger; one *s*. *Educ:* Hilton Coll., Natal; Witwatersrand Univ. Chartered Accountant (SA). Manager, 5 casinos, Sun International, SA, 2001–. Gov., Pridwin Prep. Sch., 2002–. *Heir: s* Jonathan Caesar Hawkins, *b* 23 June 1992. *Address:* PO Box 410838, Craighall, 2024, South Africa.

HAWKINS, Richard Graeme; QC 1984; **His Honour Judge Hawkins;** a Circuit Judge, since 1989; *b* 23 Feb. 1941; *s* of late Denis William Hawkins and Norah Mary (*née* Beckingsale); *m* 1969, Anne Elizabeth, *d* of late Dr and Mrs Glyn Edwards, The Boltons, Bournemouth; one *s* one *d*. *Educ:* Hendon County Sch.; University College London (LLB Hons 1962). Called to the Bar, Gray's Inn, 1963, Bencher, 2003. A Recorder, 1985–89. Mem., Hon. Soc. of Gray's Inn, 1959–. Liveryman, Curriers' Co., 1995–. *Recreation:* sailing. *Address:* Central Criminal Court, EC4M 7EH. *T:* (020) 7248 3277. *Club:* Royal Thames Yacht.

HAWKINS, Rt Rev. Richard Stephen; Suffragan Bishop of Crediton, 1996–2004; Assistant Bishop, diocese of Exeter, since 2005; Chapter Canon, Exeter Cathedral, since 2006; *b* 2 April 1939; *s* of late Ven. Canon John Stanley Hawkins and Elsie Hawkins (*née* Briggs); *m* 1966, Valerie Ann Herneman; one *s* one *d* (and one *s* one *d* decd). *Educ:* Exeter School; Exeter Coll., Oxford; St Stephen's House, Oxford. MA (Oxon); BPhil (Exeter Univ.); CQSW. Asst Curate, St Thomas, Exeter, 1963–66; Team Vicar of Clyst St Mary, Clyst Valley Team Ministry, 1966–78; Bishop's Officer for Ministry and Joint Director, Exeter-Truro Ministry Training Scheme, 1978–81; Team Vicar, Central Exeter Team Ministry, 1978–81; Diocesan Director of Ordinands, Exeter, 1979–81; Priest-in-charge, Whitestone with Oldridge, 1981–87; Archdeacon of Totnes, 1981–88; Suffragan Bishop of Plymouth, 1988–96. *Address:* 3 Westbrook Close, Whipton, Exeter EX4 8BS. *T:* (01392) 462622.

HAWKINS, Prof. Robert Edward, PhD; FRCP; Cancer Research UK Professor, and Director of Medical Oncology, Christie Hospital NHS Trust, Manchester, and University of Manchester, since 1998; *b* 10 Nov. 1955; *s* of George Edward Russell Hawkins and Rosemary Anne Hawkins; *m* 1989, Gek Kee Lim; one *s*. *Educ:* Trinity Coll., Cambridge (BA (Maths) 1977); UCL (MB BS 1984); MRC Lab. of Molecular Biol., Cambridge (PhD 1994). MRCP 1988, FRCP 1999. MRC Trng Fellow, 1989–92, CRC Sen. Res. Fellow, 1992–96, MRC Lab. of Molecular Biol., Cambridge; Prof. of Oncology, Univ. of Bristol, 1996–98; Hon. Consultant, Christie Hosp. NHS Trust, Manchester, 1998–. Co-ordinator, EU Framework Prog. 6: ATTACK (Adoptive engineered T-cell Targeting to Activate Cancer Killing) Project. Clinical Ed., British Jl of Cancer, 1996–2003. *Publications:* over 50 papers on cancer res. with emphasis on antibody technology, gene and immunotherapy. *Recreation:* golf. *Address:* Medical Oncology, Paterson Institute for Cancer Research, Wilmslow Road, Manchester M20 4BX. *T:* (0161) 446 3208, *Fax:* (0161) 446 3269; *e-mail:* RHawkins@picr.man.ac.uk.

HAWKINS, Prof. Stephen John, PhD; CBiol; Professor of Natural Sciences, and Head, College of Natural Sciences, Bangor University, since 2007; *b* 12 Jan. 1956; *s* of Kenneth and Marjorie Hawkins; *m* 1997, Dr Elspeth Jack. *Educ:* Univ. of Liverpool (BSc Marine Biology 1976; PhD 1980). MIBiol 1980. NERC Post-doctoral Fellow, Marine Biological Assoc., Plymouth, 1979–80; Lectr in Zoology, Univ. of Manchester, 1980–87; Lectr, 1987–90, Sen. Lectr, 1990–95, in Marine Biology, Univ. of Liverpool; University of Southampton: Dir, Centre for Envmtl Scis, 1995–99; Hd, Biodiversity and Ecology Div., 1996–99; Prof. of Envmtl Biology, 1995–2006 (pt-time, 1999–2006); Dir and Sec., Marine Biol Assoc. of UK, 1999–2007; Prof. of Marine Biol., Univ. of Plymouth, 2006–07. Vice-Pres., European Marine Res. Stations Network, 2000–07. Trustee, Nat. Biodiversity Network, 2000–04. *Publications:* (with H. D. Jones) Marine Field Course Guide: Rocky Shores, 1992; (with D. Raffaelli) Intertidal Ecology, 1996, 2nd edn 1999; 180 peer-reviewed papers. *Recreations:* cricket, ski-ing, fishing, sailing, occasional fieldwork. *Address:* College of Natural Sciences, Bangor University, Bangor, Gwynedd LL57 2UW. *Clubs:* Robin Hood (Plymouth); Braunton Cricket (Vice-Pres., 1995–); Barnstaple Rugby Football.

HAWKINS-LETH, Air Vice-Marshal David Richard, CB 1992; LVO 2007; MBE 1975; DL; Co-Founder and Chief Executive Officer, Safe Waste and Power Ltd, since 2003; non-executive Chairman and Director, DBeye Ltd, since 2005; Extra Gentleman Usher to the Queen, since 2007 (Gentleman Usher, 1994–2007); *b* 5 April 1937; 2nd *s* of late Gp Capt. Charles Richard John Hawkins, OBE, AFC and Norah (*née* Terry); *m* 1st,

1965, Wendy Elizabeth Harris (marr. diss. 1981); one *s* one *d*; 2nd, 1982, Elaine Kay Nelson (marr. diss. 1997); 3rd, 1998, Dr Karen Hansen-d'Leth. *Educ:* Worth; Downside Sch.; RMA Sandhurst. Commnd RAF Regt, 1959; Flt Comdr Cyprus and Singapore, 1960–62; ADC to CAS, Air Chief Marshal Sir Charles Elworthy, 1963–65; jun. RAF Regt instructor, RAF Coll., Cranwell, 1965–68; 2nd i/c 63 Sqdn, Singapore, 1968–69; Sqdn Ldr, 1969; Jt Thai/US Mil. R&D Centre as airfield defence specialist, Bangkok, 1969–71; CO, 37 Sqdn, UK, NI and Belize, 1971–74; CO, Queen's Colour Sqdn of RAF, 1974–76; Wing Comdr, on staff of Comdt-Gen., RAF Regt, MoD, 1976–79; Chief, Survivability Br., HQ AAFCE, 1979–82; Sen. Comd RAF Regt Officer, HQ Strike Comd/HQ UK Air, 1982–86; Gp Capt., 1982; CO, RAF Catterick, RAF Regt Depot, 1986–88; NATO Defence Coll., Rome, 1988–89; Dir, RAF Personal Services 1, MoD, 1989–90; Air Cdre, 1989; Dir, RAF Regt, MoD, 1990–91; Comdt-Gen., RAF Regt, and Dir-Gen., RAF Security, 1991–93; Yeoman Usher of the Black Rod and Dep. Serjeant-at-Arms, H of L, 1994–99. Parachute Wings: UK, 1969; Thai Army (Master), 1970; Thai Police (Master), 1970; US Army (1st class), 1971. Vice-Chm. (Air), TA&VRA, Gtr London, 1994–2003. Trustee, Battle of Britain Meml Trust, 1998–. Freeman, City of London, 1992. DL Gtr London, 1994. *Recreations:* golf, ski-ing, walking, shooting. *Club:* Royal Air Force.

HAWKSLEY, (Philip) Warren; Director, Society for the Prevention of Solvent and Volatile Substance Abuse, since 1998; *b* 10 March 1943; *s* of late Bradshaw Warren Hawksley and Monica Augusta Hawksley; *m* 1999, Kathleen Margaret (*née* Lloyd). *Educ:* Denstone Coll., Uttoxeter. Employed by Lloyd's Bank after leaving school. Dir, Edderton Hall, 1989–97. Member: Salop County Council, 1970–81; West Mercia Police Authority, 1977–81. MP (C) The Wrekin, 1979–87; contested (C) same seat, 1987; MP (C) Halesowen and Stourbridge, 1992–97; contested (C) Stourbridge, 1997. Member: Select Cttee on Employment, 1986–87 and 1994–97; Home Affairs Select Cttee, 1996–97; Jt Sec., Cons. Back bench Cttee for New Town and Urban Affairs, 1984–87; Sec., W Midlands Cons. Parly Gp, 1992–97. Hon. Pres., Catering Industries Liaison Council, 1992–98. *Recreations:* collecting political memorabilia, shooting, good food and wines.

HAWKSWORTH, Prof. David Leslie, CBE 1996; DSc; FIBiol, FLS; mycologist and environmental biologist; Professor of Biology, University of Gloucestershire, since 2007; Research Professor, Universidad Complutense de Madrid, since 2001; Hon. Research Associate, Natural History Museum, London, since 2006; Director, MycoNova, since 1998; *b* Sheffield, 5 June 1946; *e s* of late Leslie Hawksworth and Freda Mary (*née* Dolamore); *m* 1st, 1968, Madeleine Una Ford (marr. diss. 1998); one *s* one *d*; 2nd, 1999 (marr. diss. 2008). *Educ:* Herbert Strutt Grammar Sch., Belper; Univ. of Leicester (BSc 1967; PhD 1970; DSc 1980). FIBiol 1982; FLS 1969. Mycologist, Commonwealth Mycological Inst., Kew, 1969–81; sci. asst to Exec. Dir, CAB, 1981–83; Dir, Internat. Mycol Inst., CAB Internat., 1983–97. Visiting Professor: Univ. of Riyadh, 1978; Univ. of Reading, 1984–; Univ. of Assiut, 1985; Univ. of Kent 1990–; Univ. of London, 1992–; Univ. Complutense, Madrid, 2000–01; Hon. Res. Fellow, Birkbeck Coll., London, 2004–. Mem. Council, English Nature, 1996–99. President: British Lichen Soc., 1986–87 (Hon. Mem., 1997); Eur. Congress of Mycologists, 1989; Br. Mycol Soc., 1990 (Centenary Fellow, 1996); Internat. Mycol Assoc., 1990–94 (Sec.-Gen., 1977–90; Hon. Pres., 1994–); Internat. Union of Biol Sci., 1994–97; Vice-Pres., Linnean Soc., 1985–88; Treasurer and Editor-in-Chief, Systematics Assoc., 1972–86; Treas., Internat. Congress of Systematic and Evolutionary Biol., 1989–96; Chairman: Internat Commn on Taxonomy of Fungi, 1982–2002; Ruislip-Northwood Woods Adv. Working Party, 1979–82; Internat. Cttee on Bionomenclature, 1994–; Chief Rapp., CAB Internat. Review Confs, 1985, 1990, 1993, 1996. FRSA 1997. Hon. Member: Soc. Lichenologica Italiana, 1989; Ukrainian Botanical Soc., 1992; Mycol Soc. of America, 1994; Assoc. Latinoamericana de Micología, 1996; Japanese Soc. for Lichenology, 2002. FD *hc* Umeå, 1996. First Bicent. Medal, Linnean Soc., 1978; Acharius Medal, Internat. Assoc. for Lichenology, 2002. Editor: The Lichenologist, 1970–90; Systema Ascomycetum, 1986–98; Mycosystema, 1987–; Sen. (formerly Exec.) Editor, Mycological Research, 2000–08; Editor-in-Chief, Biodiversity and Conservation, 2006–. *Publications:* (jtly) Dictionary of the Fungi, 6th edn 1971 to 8th edn 1995; (ed jtly) Air Pollution and Lichens, 1973; Mycologist's Handbook, 1974; (ed) The Changing Flora and Fauna of Britain, 1974; (jtly) Lichens as Pollution Monitors, 1976; (ed jtly) Lichenology: progress and problems, 1976; (jtly) Lichenology in the British Isles 1568–1975, 1977; (jtly) Key Works to the Fauna and Flora of the British Isles and Northwestern Europe, 4th edn 1978, 5th edn 1988; (ed) Advancing Agricultural Production in Africa, 1984; (jtly) The Lichen-Forming Fungi, 1984; (jtly) The British Ascomycotina, 1985; (ed jtly) Coevolution and Systematics, 1986; (ed jtly) Coevolution of Fungi with Plants and Animals, 1988; (ed jtly) Living Resources for Biotechnology, 1988; (ed) Prospects in Systematics, 1988; (jtly) International Mycological Directory, 1990; (ed) Frontiers in Mycology, 1991; (ed) Improving the Stability of Names, 1991; (ed) The Biodiversity of Microorganisms and Invertebrates: their role in sustainable agriculture, 1991; (jtly) Lichen Flora of Great Britain and Ireland, 1992; (jtly) Biodiversity and Biosystematic Priorities: microorganisms and invertebrates, 1993; (jtly) IMI: retrospect and prospect, 1993; (ed) Identification and Characterization of Pest Organisms, 1994; Glossary of Terms Used in Bionomenclature, 1994; (ed) Ascomycete Systematics: problems and perspectives in the nineties, 1994; (jtly) The Biodiversity of Microorganisms and the Role of Microbial Resource Centres, 1994; (ed jtly) Microbial Diversity and Ecosystem Function, 1995; (ed jtly) Biodiversity Information: needs and options, 1997; (ed) The Changing Wildlife of Great Britain and Ireland, 2001; (ed jtly) International Code of Botanical Nomenclature (Vienna Code), 2006; (ed jtly) Arthropod Diversity and Conservation, 2006; (ed jtly) Forest Diversity and Management, 2006; (ed jtly) Human Exploitation and Biodiversity, 2006; (ed jtly) Marine, Freshwater and Wetlands Biodiversity Conservation, 2006; (ed jtly) Vertebrate Conservation and Biodiversity, 2007; Plant Conservation and Biodiversity, 2007; Biodiversity and Conservation in Europe, 2008; numerous papers on biodiversity, biol nomenclature, fungi (including lichens). *Recreations:* lichenicolous fungi, bionomenclature, Huxley brothers, second-hand books. *Address:* Milford House, The Mead, Ashtead, Surrey KT21 2LZ; *e-mail:* d.hawksworth@nhm.ac.uk.

HAWLEY, Prof. Christine Elizabeth, CBE 2008; RIBA; Professor of Architectural Studies, since 1993, and Dean and Head of The Bartlett, the Faculty of the Built Environment, 1999–July 2009, University College London; *b* 3 Aug. 1949; *d* of John and Margaret Hawley; *m* 1973, Clyde; two *s* one *d*. *Educ:* City of London Sch. for Girls; Architectural Assoc. (AADipl 1975). Lectr, AA, 1978–86; Hd, Sch. of Architecture, Univ. of East London, 1986–93. Recent built work includes: social housing for Internat. Bau Austellung, Berlin, 1989; Kantine, Städel Acad., Frankfurt, 1992; exhibn pavilions, Osaka and Nagoya Expo, 1993; social housing for Gifu, Japan; mus. for Roman remains at Camuntum, Lower Austria, 1997. Advr, CABE, 2001–04. FRSA. *Publications:* articles in a number of prof. jls inc. GA, Architecture and Urbanism and Architects' Jl. *Recreations:* swimming, reading, film. *Address:* The Bartlett, Faculty of the Built Environment, University College London, Gower Street, WC1E 6BT.

HAWLEY, Henry Nicholas, (8th Bt *cr* 1795); *S* father, 1988, but does not use the title and his name is not on the Official Roll of Baronets.

HAWLEY, James Appleton, TD 1969; Lord-Lieutenant of Staffordshire, since 1993; *b* 28 March 1937; *s* of late John J. Hawley and Mary Hawley, JP; *m* 1961, Susan, *d* of Alan Stott, JP, DL; one *s* two *d*. *Educ:* Uppingham; St Edmund Hall, Oxford (MA Jurisp.) Called to the Bar, Middle Temple, 1961. Nat. Service, 2nd Lieut South Staffs Regt, Cyprus; Lieut to Major, Staffs Yeomanry Regt (QORR). Chairman: John James Hawley (Speciality Works) Ltd, 1961–98; J. W. Wilkinson & Co., 1970–98; Dir, Stafford Railway Building Soc., 1985–2003. Pres., Made-Up Textiles Assoc., 1984–85; Chm., Camping Trade Assoc., 1977–78. Patron: Staffs Young Enterprise, 1994–; Stafford Br., 2004–, S Staffs, 2006–, RBL; Lichfield Sci. and Engrg Soc., 2005–. President: St John Council for Staffs, 1993–; Staffs CPRE, 1993–; Staffs Scouts, 1994–; Staffs SSAFA, 1994–; Staffs and Birmingham Agricl Soc., 2004–05; Walsall Soc. for the Blind, 2001– (Chm., 1977–92); Lichfield Fest., 2006–; Vice President: RFCA W Midlands, 1994– (Pres., 1998–2004); Nat. Meml Arboretum, 1997–; Chm. Council, Lichfield Cathedral, 2000–; Trustee, Armed Forces Meml, 2003–; also Pres., Vice-Pres., and Patron, other organisations and charities in Staffs. Mem. Court, Keele Univ., 1994. Freeman, City of London, 1986; Liveryman, Saddlers' Co., 1986–. JP Staffs 1969; High Sheriff, Staffs, 1976–77; DL Staffs 1978. DUniv Staffordshire, 2003. KStJ 1993. *Recreations:* family, Staffordshire, outdoor pursuits. *Address:* Lieutenancy Office, Martin Street, Stafford ST16 2LH. *T:* (01785) 276805, *Fax:* (01785) 276115. *Club:* Oxford and Cambridge.

HAWLEY, Ven. John Andrew; Archdeacon of Blackburn, since 2002; *b* 27 April 1950; *s* of Willie and Constance May Hawley. *Educ:* King's Coll., London (BD, AKC 1971); Wycliffe Hall, Oxford. Ordained deacon, 1974, priest, 1975; Asst Curate, Holy Trinity, Hull, 1974–77; Sen. Curate, Bradford Cathedral, 1977–80; Vicar, All Saints, Woodlands, Doncaster, 1980–91; Team Rector, Dewsbury, 1991–2002. Proctor in Convocation, 1996–2002; Chm., Wakefield Diocesan House of Clergy, 2000–02. Hon. Canon, Wakefield Cathedral, 1998. *Recreations:* cricket, golf, fell walking, long distance walking, quiet holidays in Scotland. *Address:* 19 Clarence Park, Blackburn BB2 7FA. *T:* (01254) 262571, 07980 945035, *Fax:* (01254) 263394; *e-mail:* johnhawley@milestonenet.co.uk.

HAWLEY, Dr Robert, CBE 1997; FREng, FIET, FIMechE, FInstP; FRSE; Chairman: Engineering Council, 1999–2002; Particle Physics and Astronomy Research Council 1998–2001; *b* 23 July 1936; *s* of William and Eva Hawley; *m* 1st, Valerie (*née* Clarke) (marr. diss. 2002); one *s* one *d*; *m* 2nd, 2002, Pamela Elizabeth (*née* Neesham). *Educ:* Wallasey Grammar Sch.; Wallasey Technical Coll.; Birkenhead Technical Coll.; Durham Univ. (BSc 1959; PhD 1963); Newcastle upon Tyne Univ. (DSc 1976). FIET (FIEE 1970); FREng (FEng 1979); FIMechE 1987; FInstP 1971. FRSE 1997. Student apprentice, BICC, Prescot, 1952–55; C. A. Parsons & Co. Ltd: Head of Res. Team, 1961–64; Chief Elec. Engr, 1970–74; Dir of Prodn and Engrg, 1974–76; Man. Dir, NEI Parsons Ltd, 1976–84; NEI plc: Man. Dir, Power Engrg Gp, 1984–89; Man. Dir, 1989–92; Chm., NEI ABB Gas Turbines Ltd, 1990–92; Chief Executive: Nuclear Electric plc, 1992–96; British Energy plc, 1995–97. Mem. Bd, Rolls-Royce plc, 1989–92. Non-executive Chairman: Rotork plc, 1997–98; INBIS Group plc, 1997–2000; ERAtech Ltd, 1997–2000; Taylor Woodrow plc, 1999–2003; Rocktron, 2001–05; Berkeley Resources Ltd, 2006–; Lister Petter Investment Hldgs Ltd, 2006–; Carron Acquisition Co. Ltd, 2006–; non-executive Director: W. S. Atkins Ltd, 1994–97; Tricorder Technology, 1997–2001; Colt Telecom Gp, 1998–; Rutland Trust, 2001–07; Consultant, ABB Ltd, 1993–97; Advr, SEMA Gp, 1995–97; Adv. Dir, HSBC Investment Bank, 1998–. Member: NE Indust. Develt Bd DTI, 1989–92; Bd, Northern Develt Co., 1989–92; Industrial Develt Adv. Bd, DTI 1994–2000; Pres., Partnership Korea, DTI, 1995–2002. Chairman: Hawley Cttee on Corporate Governance Information Management, 1993–98; Hawley Gp on Engrg Profession, DTI and Engrg Council, 1999–2001. Mem., Annual Review Sub-group, and Chm., Energy Wkg Pty, 1986–87, ACARD; Member: DFEE Women's Issues Wkg Gp 1996–97; Mgt and Leadership in the Professions, DFEE, 2000–. Institution of Electrical Engineers: Vice Pres., 1991–95; Dep. Pres., 1995–96; Pres., 1996–97. Member Council, Fellowship of Engrg, 1981–84; Foundn for Sci. and Technol., 1999–2001 (Dep. Chm., 2002–); Royal Instn, 2000–; Mem., Council for Industry and Higher Educn, 2000–. Pres., Energy Industries Club, 1989–91. Mem., Boat and Shoreworks Cttee, RNLI, 1992–95. Trustee, Daphne Jackson Trust, 2000–. Chm., 2002–07, Pres., 2007–, Anglo-Korean Soc Lectures include: C. A. Parsons Meml, IEE and Royal Soc., 1977; Hunter Meml, IEE, 1990; Blackadder, NEC Inst., 1992; Wilson Campbell Meml, Univ. of Newcastle upon Tyne, 1994; Bowden, UMIST, 1994; J. G. Collier Meml, Univ. of Brunel, 1997, Higginson, 1998, Temple Chevallier, 2001, Durham; Armstrong, 2001, Newcastle upon Tyne; Royce, IIE, 2001; Mountbatten, IEE, 2002; Bridge, Engineers' Co., 2002. Blumein, IEE, 2005. Member: Court, Univ. of Newcastle upon Tyne, 1979–; Bd of Advrs, Elec. Engrg, Univ. of London, 1982–86; Court, Loughborough Univ., 2003–; Chm., Council, Univ. of Durham, 1997–2002; Vice-Chancellor, World Nuclear Univ., 2006–. Freeman, City of London, 1985; Master, Engrs' Co., 2005–06. Mem., Nat. Acad. of Engrg of Korea, 2001. FRSE 1997; FCGI 2003. Hon. FINucE 1994; Hon. FIEE 2003. Hon. Fellow, Liverpool John Moores Univ., 2002. Hon. DSc: Durham, 1996; City, 1998; Cranfield, 2002; Hon. DEng: South Bank, 1997; West of England, 1997; Newcastle upon Tyne, 2002; UMIST, 2002; Hon. DTech: Staffordshire 2000; Abertay Dundee, 2001; Robert Gordon, Aberdeen, 2002. DUniv Surrey, 2002. Waverley Gold Medal, RSA, 1960; Achievement Medal, for outstanding contribs to power engrg, IEE, 1989. Premio Vicente Lecuna Medal, Venezuela, 1997; Order of Diplomatic Service Kwongda Medal, Korea, 1999. *Publications:* (with A. Maitland) Vacuum as an Insulator, 1967; (with A. A. Zaky): Dielectric Solids, 1970; Conduction and Breakdown in Mineral Oil, 1973; Fundamentals of Electromagnetic Field Theory, 1974; technical papers on electrical breakdown in vacuum, liquids and solids, electrical machine design and power generation. *Recreations:* gardening, writing, philately. *Address:* Summerfield, Rendcomb, near Cirencester, Glos GL7 7HB. *T:* (01285) 831610, *Fax:* (01285) 831801. *Clubs:* Athenæum; New (Edinburgh).

HAWORTH, Baron *cr* 2004 (Life Peer), of Fisherfield in Ross and Cromarty; **Alan Robert Haworth;** Secretary, Parliamentary Labour Party, 1992–2004; *b* 26 April 1948; *s* of late John Haworth and Hilma Haworth (*née* Westhead); *m* 1st, 1973, Gill Cole; 2nd, 1991, Maggie Rae. *Educ:* Barking Regl Coll. of Technol. (BScSoc London Univ. ext.). Cttee Officer, 1975–85, Sen. Cttee Officer, 1985–92, Parly Labour Party. *Publication:* (ed jtly) Men Who Made Labour, 2006. *Recreations:* hill walking, mountaineering. *Address:* House of Lords, SW1A 0PW.

HAWORTH, Glennis; *see* Haworth, S. G.

HAWORTH, Graham Thomas, RIBA; Director, Haworth Tompkins Architects, since 1991; *b* 15 Jan. 1960; two *s* one *d*. *Educ:* Univ. of Nottingham (BArch); Jesus Coll., Cambridge (DipArch). RIBA 1989. Architect: Skidmore Owings Merrill, 1986–87, Bennetts Associates, 1988–90. Projects include: Royal Court Th., 2000; Coin Street Housing, 2001; Hayward Gall. extension, 2003; Young Vic Th., London Liby, 2005. *Recreations:* contemporary arts, theatre, walking, fishing, painting. *Address:* Haworth Tompkins, 19 Great Sutton Street, EC1V 0DR. *T:* (020) 7250 3225, *Fax:* (020) 7250 3226; *e-mail:* graham.haworth@haworthtompkins.com.

HAWORTH, John Leigh W.; *see* Walker-Haworth.

HAWORTH, (John) Martin, PhD; Headmaster, Wallington County Grammar School, since 1990; *b* 22 Jan. 1949; *s* of Reginald and Hilda Haworth; *m* 1973, Brenda Dawe; two *d. Educ:* London Bible Coll. (BD 1972); Univ. of Birmingham (MA 1973; PhD 1982); Univ. of Warwick (MEd 1984). RE teacher, Plymstock Sch., 1973–77; Hd, RE and Hd, 6th Form, Coundon Court Sch., 1977–84; Dep. Hd, Wisewood Sch., 1985–90. FRSA. *Recreations:* karate (1st Dan), running, church, theatre, concerts, opera. *Address:* Wallington County Grammar School, Croydon Road, Wallington, Surrey SM6 7PH. *T:* (020) 8647 2235, *Fax:* (020) 8254 7921; *e-mail:* mhaworth@suttonlea.org.

HAWORTH, Jonathan Mayo; His Honour Judge Jonathan Haworth; a Circuit Judge, since 1996; *b* 5 Oct. 1948; *s* of George Henry Haworth and Elsa Sophia Haworth; *m* 1973, Brigitte Ilse Müller; one *s* one *d. Educ:* King Edward VII Grammar Sch., Sheffield; King's Coll., London (LLB Hons). Called to the Bar, Middle Temple, 1971; practised from Fenners Chambers, Cambridge, 1973–96. *Recreations:* reading, computers, music, cricket. *Address:* c/o Cambridge Crown Court, 83 East Road, Cambridge CB1 1BT.

HAWORTH, Martin; *see* Haworth, J. M.

HAWORTH, Peter; Master of the Supreme Court Costs Office, since 2006; *b* 27 March 1951; *s* of Arthur Haworth and Mary Haworth (*née* Aynge); *m* 1975, Margaret Elaine Knowles; three *d. Educ:* Towneley High Sch., Burnley; Univ. of Liverpool (LLB 1972). Admitted as solicitor, 1975; Partner, Southerns Solicitors, 1978–2003; a Dep. District Judge, Northern Circuit, 1992–; Solicitor Advocate, 1998; Dep. Master and Costs Judge, 2002–06. Mem., Civil Procedure Rule Cttee, 1996–99; Solicitor Mem. and Chm., Solicitors' Disciplinary Tribunal, 1999–2006. A Lieut Bailiff of Guernsey, 2003–. *Publication:* (contrib. ed) Jordan's Civil Court Service 1999, 12th edn 2006. *Recreations:* yachting, ski-ing, hot air ballooning, fell walking, theatre. *Address:* Supreme Court Costs Office, Fetter Lane, EC4A 1DQ. *T:* (020) 7947 6192; *e-mail:* master.haworth@judiciary.gsi.gov.uk. *Clubs:* Royal Ocean Racing, Royal London Yacht.

HAWORTH, Sir Philip, 3rd Bt *cr* 1911, of Dunham Massey, Co. Chester; farmer; *b* 17 Jan. 1927; *s* of Sir Arthur Geoffrey Haworth, 2nd Bt, and Emily Dorothea, (Dorothy) (*d* 1980), *er d* of H. E. Gaddum; *S* father, 1987; *m* 1951, Joan Helen, *d* of late S. P. Clark, Ipswich; four *s* one *d. Educ:* Dauntsey's; Reading Univ. BSc (Agric.) 1948. *Recreations:* music, art, ornithology. *Heir: s* Christopher Haworth [*b* 6 Nov. 1951; *m* 1994, Susan Rachel, *d* of David Ives and *widow* of Jonathan Dent; one *s* one *d*, and two step *s*]. *Address:* Free Green Farm, Over Peover, Knutsford, Cheshire WA16 9QX. *Club:* Farmers'.

HAWORTH, His Honour Richard James; a Circuit Judge, 1993–2008; *b* 1 Dec. 1943; *s* of late Richard Arthur Haworth and Lily Haworth; *m* 1974, Jane Seren, *y d* of His Honour John Glyn Burrell, QC and of Dorothy Burrell. *Educ:* Ampleforth. Called to the Bar, Inner Temple, 1970; practised on SE Circuit, 1970–93; a Recorder, 1990–93. Mem., Inner Temple Bar Liaison Cttee, 1987–93. *Recreations:* music, English naive paintings, walking. *Club:* Thames Ditton Cricket.

HAWORTH, Prof. (Sheila) Glennis, (Mrs L. F. H. Busk), CBE 2007; MD; FRCP, FRCPath; FRCPCH; FMedSci; British Heart Foundation Professor of Developmental Cardiology, Institute of Child Health, University College London, since 1990; Lead Clinician of the UK Pulmonary Hypertension Service for Children, since 2001; *b* 31 May 1939; *d* of Richard and Elizabeth Haworth; *m* 1st, 1970, Prof. T. J. McElwain (*d* 1990); 2nd, 1993, Maj.-Gen. Leslie Francis Harry Busk, *qv. Educ:* Royal Free Hosp. Sch. of Medicine, Univ. of London (MB BS 1964; MD 1976). FRCP 1981; FRCPath 1991; FRCPCH 1997. Fellow in Fetal Physiol. and Neonatol., Columbia Univ., NY, 1967–69; Med. Registrar, RPMS, 1970; Registrar, then Sen. Lectr, Royal Brompton Hosp., London, 1971–76; Hospital for Sick Children, Great Ormond Street: Hon. Consultant in Paediatric Cardiol., 1976–; Sen. Lectr, 1976–82; Reader, 1982–88; Prof. of Paediatric Cardiol., 1989–90; Sub-Dean, Inst. of Child Health, 1982–85. FACC 1986; FMedSci 1999. *Publications:* clinical and basic science papers on the develt of the pulmonary circulation, the pathogenesis and treatment of pulmonary hypertension in childhood and paediatric cardiology. *Recreations:* playing the piano, opera, travel. *Address:* Institute of Child Health, 30 Guilford Street, WC1N 1EH. *T:* (020) 7813 8459; *e-mail:* s.haworth@ich.ucl.ac.uk.

HAWTHORN, Ven. Christopher John; Archdeacon of Cleveland, 1991–2001, now Archdeacon Emeritus; *b* 29 April 1936; *s* of late Rev. John Christopher Hawthorn and Susan Mary Hawthorn; *m* 1964, Elizabeth Margaret Lowe; three *s* one *d. Educ:* Marlborough Coll.; Queens' Coll., Cambridge (MA Hons); Ripon Hall, Oxford. Deacon 1962, priest 1963; Asst Curate, Sutton-in-Holderness, 1962–66; Vicar: St Nicholas, Hull, 1966–72; Christ Church, Coatham, 1972–79; St Martin's-on-the-Hill, Scarborough, 1979–91; RD Scarborough, 1982–91. Proctor in Convocation, 1987–90; Canon of York, 1987–2001, now Canon Emeritus. *Recreations:* gardening, fell walking, sport. *Address:* 43 Barley Rise, Strensall, York YO32 5AB. *T:* (01904) 492060.

HAWTHORN, Prof. Geoffrey Patrick; Professor of International Politics, University of Cambridge, 1998–2007, now Emeritus; Fellow, Clare Hall, Cambridge, since 1982; *b* 28 Feb. 1941; *s* of Kathleen Mary Hawthorn (*née* Candy); *m* 1st, 1969, Ruth Legg (marr. diss. 1986); two *s*; 2nd, 1987, Gloria Carnevali; one *s. Educ:* Jesus Coll., Oxford (BA); London Sch. of Economics. Lectr in Sociology, Univ. of Essex, 1964–70; University of Cambridge: Lectr in Sociology, 1970–85; Reader in Sociology and Politics, 1985–98; Fellow, Churchill Coll., 1970–76. Vis. Prof. of Sociology, Harvard Univ., 1973–74, 1989–90; Vis. Mem., IAS, Princeton, 1989–90. *Publications:* The Sociology of Fertility, 1970; Enlightenment and Despair, 1976, 2nd edn 1987; (ed) Population and Development, 1977; (ed) The Standard of Living, 1987; Plausible Worlds, 1991; The Future of Asia and the Pacific, 1998; articles and reviews in learned jls and other periodicals. *Recreations:* ornithology, music. *Address:* 19 St Luke's Street, Cambridge CB4 3DA.

HAWTHORNE, Prof. Sir William (Rede), Kt 1970; CBE 1959; MA; ScD; FRS 1955; FREng, FIMechE; Master of Churchill College, Cambridge, 1968–83; Hopkinson and ICI Professor of Applied Thermodynamics, University of Cambridge, 1951–80; Head of Department of Engineering, 1968–73; *b* 22 May 1913; *s* of William Hawthorne, MInstCE, and Elizabeth C. Hawthorne; *m* 1939, Barbara Runkle (*d* 1992), Cambridge, Massachusetts, USA; one *s* two *d. Educ:* Westminster Sch.; Trinity Coll., Cambridge (Hon. Fellow, 1995); Massachusetts Institute of Technology, USA. Development Engineer, Babcock & Wilcox Ltd, 1937–39; Scientific Officer, Royal Aircraft Establishment, 1940–44; seconded to Sir Frank Whittle, Power Jets, 1940–41; British Air Commission, Washington, 1944; Dep. Dir Engine Research, Min. of Supply, 1945; Massachusetts Institute of Technology: Associate Prof. of Mechanical Engineering, 1946; George Westinghouse Prof. of Mechanical Engineering, 1948–51; Jerome C. Hunsaker Prof. of Aeronautical Engineering, 1955–56; Vis. Inst. Prof., 1962–69; Mem. Corporation, 1969–74. Chairman: Home Office Scientific Adv. Council, 1967–76; Defence Scientific Adv. Council, 1969–71; Adv. Council for Energy Conservation, 1974–79; Member: Energy Commn, 1977–79; Standing Commn on Energy and the Environment, 1978–81. Director: Dracone Developments Ltd, 1958–87; Cummins Engine Co. Inc., 1974–86. Governor, Westminster Sch., 1956–76. A Vice-Pres., Royal Soc., 1969–70 and 1979–81; Mem. Council, 1968–70, 1979–81 (Royal Medal, 1982). Foreign Associate: US Nat. Acad. of Sciences, 1965; US Nat. Acad. of Engrg, 1976. Fellow, Imperial Coll., London Univ., 1983. Hon. FAIAA; Hon. FRAeS; Hon. FASME; Hon. FRSE 1983. Hon. DEng: Sheffield, 1976; Liverpool 1982; Hon. DSc: Salford, 1980; Strathclyde, 1981; Bath, 1981; Oxon, 1982; Sussex, 1984. Medal of Freedom (US), 1947. *Publications:* papers in mechanical and aeronautical journals. *Address:* Churchill College, Cambridge CB3 0DS. *Club:* Athenæum.

See also J. O'Beirne Ranelagh.

HAWTIN, Brian Richard, CB 1997; Deputy Director General, Technical Secretariat, Organisation for the Prohibition of Chemical Weapons, 2003–06; *b* 31 May 1946; *s* of late Dick Hawtin and Jean (*née* Middleton); *m* 1969, Anthea Fry; two *d. Educ:* Portsmouth Grammar Sch.; Christ Church, Oxford (MA). Ministry of Defence, 1967–2002: Asst Private Sec. to Permt Under Sec. of State, 1970; seconded to FCO as First Sec., UK Delegn to NATO, Brussels, 1978–80; Asst Sec., 1981; RCDS 1987; Private Sec. to Sec. of State for Defence, 1987–89; Asst Under Sec. of State (material/naval), 1989–92, (Progs), 1992–94, (Home and Overseas), 1994–96, (Policy), 1997–99; Fellow, Center for Internat. Affairs, Harvard Univ., 1996–97; Dir Gen., Internat. Security Policy, 1999–2002. *Recreations:* walking, antiques, grandchildren.

HAWTIN, Rt Rev. David Christopher; Bishop Suffragan of Repton, 1999–2006; an Assistant Bishop, Diocese of Sheffield, since 2007; *b* 7 June 1943; *m* 1968, Elizabeth Ann (*née* Uden); one *s* two *d. Educ:* King Edward VII Sch., Lytham St Annes; Keble Coll., Oxford (BA 1965; MA 1970); William Temple Coll., Rugby; Cuddesdon Coll., Oxford. Ordained deacon, 1967, priest 1968; Curate: St Thomas, Pennywell, Sunderland, 1967–71; St Peter's, Stockton, 1971–74; Priest in charge, St Andrew's, Leam Lane, Gateshead, 1974–79; Rector, Washington (incl. LEP), 1979–88; Diocesan Ecumenical Officer, Durham, 1988–92; Archdeacon of Newark, 1992–99. Member: Gen. Synod, 1983–99 (Mem., Bd for Mission and Unity, 1986–91); BCC, 1987–90; Churches Together in England, 1990–2006 (Enabling Gp, 1991–99; Dep. Moderator, CTE Forum, 1995–99); Council of Churches for Britain and Ireland, 1990–2006; Chairman: Diocesan Bd of Educn, Southwell, 1993–99; E Midlands Consortium for Educn and Trng for Ministry, 1996–2001; Derby Diocesan Council for Mission and Unity, 1999–2001; Derby Diocesan Pastoral Cttee, 1999–2006; E Midlands Ministry Trng Course, 2002–06. Churches Project Co-ordinator, Nat. Garden Fest., Gateshead, 1988–91. Local Unity Advr, Durham Ecumenical Relations Gp, 1991–92; Consultant: Council for Christian Unity, 1991–96; CCU Local Unity Panel, 2007– (Mem., 1999–; Chm., 2003–06). Member: N Notts and N Derbys Coalfield Alliance Bd, 1999–2003; Derbys Partnership, 2001. *Address:* 162 Greenhill Avenue, Greenhill, Sheffield S8 7TF.

HAWTIN, Michael Victor; Director, Underwriting Group, Export Credits Guarantee Department, 1992–95; *b* 7 Sept. 1942; *s* of Guy and Constance Hawtin; *m* 1966, Judith Mary Eeley; one *s* one *d. Educ:* Bournemouth Sch.; St John's Coll., Cambridge (MA); Univ. of Calif, Berkeley (MA). Asst Principal, 1964–69, Principal, 1969–77, HM Treasury; seconded to Barclays Bank, 1969–71; Asst Sec., HM Treasury, 1977–83, Under Sec. (Principal Finance Officer), PSA, 1983–86; Under Sec., HM Treasury, 1986–88; Dir, Resource Management Gp and Principal Establishment and Finance Officer, ECGD, 1988–92. *Recreations:* music, travel.

HAWTON, Prof. Keith Edward, DSc, DM; FRCPsych; Consultant Psychiatrist, Oxfordshire and Buckinghamshire Mental Health NHS Trust (formerly Oxfordshire Mental Healthcare Unit, then Oxfordshire Mental Healthcare NHS Trust), since 1984; Professor of Psychiatry, since 1996, and Director, Centre for Suicide Research, since 1998, University of Oxford; *b* 23 Dec. 1942; *s* of Leslie William Hawton and Eliza Hawton; *m* 1978, Joan Kirk; two *d. Educ:* Balliol Coll., and Med. Sch., Oxford (MB 2001; BChir 1969; DM 1980; DSc 2001); St John's Coll., Cambridge (MA 1970). FRCPsych 1990. Trng in psychiatry, 1970–73; Res. Psychiatrist, Clin. Lectr and Clin. Tutor in Psychiatry, Dept of Psychiatry, Oxford Univ., 1974–84. Boerhaave Vis. Prof., Leiden Univ., 1990–91. Stengel Res. Award, Internat. Assoc. for Suicide Prevention, 1995; Dublin Award, Amer. Assoc. Suicidology, 2001; Res. Award, American Foundn for Suicide Prevention, 2002. *Publications:* Attempted Suicide: a practical guide, 1982, 2nd edn 1987; Sex Therapy: a practical guide, 1985; Cognitive Behaviour Therapy for Psychiatric Problems, 1989; Suicide and Stress in Farmers, 1998; The International Handbook of Suicide and Attempted Suicide, 2000; Prevention and Treatment of Suicidal Behaviour: from science to practice, 2005; (jtly) By Their Own Young Hand: deliberate self-harm and suicidal ideas in adolescents, 2006. *Recreations:* fishing, cricket, wines, golf. *Address:* Centre for Suicide Research, University Department of Psychiatry, Warneford Hospital, Oxford OX3 7JX. *T:* (01865) 226258.

HAY, family name of **Earls of Erroll** and **Kinnoull,** and of **Marquis of Tweeddale**.

HAY, Lord; Harry Thomas William Hay; *b* 8 Aug. 1984; *s* and *heir* of Earl of Erroll, *qv*.

HAY, Prof. Allan Stuart, PhD; FRS 1981; Tomlinson Professor of Chemistry, McGill University, Montreal, 1997–2000, now Emeritus (Professor of Polymer Chemistry, 1987–97); *b* 23 July 1929; *s* of Stuart Lumsden and Verna Emila Hay; *m* 1956, Janet Mary Keck; two *s* two *d. Educ:* Univ. of Alberta (BSc Hon, MSc); Univ. of Illinois (PhD). General Electric Research and Development Center, Schenectady, NY: Research Associate, 1955; Manager, Chemical Laboratory, 1968; Research and Develt Manager, Chemical Labs, 1980–87. Adjunct Professor, Polymer Science and Engineering Dept, Univ. of Massachusetts, 1975. Hon. DSc Alberta, 1987. Soc. of Plastics Engrs Internat. award in Plastics Science and Engineering, 1975; Achievement award, Industrial Res. Inst., 1984; Chemical Pioneer, Amer. Inst. of Chemists, 1985; Carothers Award, ACS, 1985; Macromolecular Sci. and Engrg Award, Canadian Inst. of Chem., 1998. *Publications:* numerous papers and contribs to learned jls. *Recreations:* philately, reading, swimming. *Address:* 5015 Glencairn Avenue, Montreal, QC H3W 2B3, Canada.

HAY, Dame Barbara (Logan), DCMG 2008 (CMG 1998); LVO 2008; MBE 1991; HM Diplomatic Service; Consul-General, and Director of Trade and Investment Promotion, Istanbul, since 2004; *b* 20 Jan. 1953; *d* of late Alfred Hay and Isa Hay (*née* Burgon). *Educ:* Boroughmuir Sen. Secondary Sch., Edinburgh. Joined Diplomatic Service, 1971; Russian language training, 1974–75; served Moscow and Johannesburg, 1975–80; Asst Private Sec. to Perm. Under-Sec. and Head of Diplomatic Service, 1981–83; FCO and Montreal, 1983–88; First Sec. (Inf.), Moscow, 1988–91; Consul-Gen., St Petersburg, 1991–92; Jt Assistance Unit (Central Europe), FCO, 1992–94; Ambassador, Republic of Uzbekistan and (non-res.), Republic of Tajikistan, 1995–99; Counsellor, FCO, 1999–2000; Consul-Gen., St Petersburg, 2000–04. FRSA. *Recreations:* theatre, travel, Scottish country dancing, music, keeping in touch with friends. *Address:* c/o Foreign and Commonwealth Office, SW1A 2AH. *Club:* University Women's.

HAY, Sir David (Osborne), Kt 1979; CBE 1962; DSO 1945; retired public servant; *b* 29 Nov. 1916; 2nd *s* of late H. A. Hay, Barwon Heads, Victoria; *m* 1944, Alison Marion Parker Adams (*d* 2002); two *s*. *Educ:* Geelong Grammar Sch.; Brasenose Coll., Oxford; Melbourne Univ. Joined Commonwealth Public Service, 1939. Australian Imperial Force, 1940–46: Major, 2nd Sixth Infantry Bn; served in Western Desert, Greece, New Guinea. Rejoined External Affairs Dept, 1947; Imp. Def. Coll., 1954; Minister (later Ambassador) to Thailand, 1955–57; High Comr in Canada, 1961–64; Ambassador to UN, New York, 1964–65; First Asst Secretary, External Affairs, 1966; Administrator of Papua and New Guinea, 1967–70; Sec., Dept of External Territories, Canberra, 1970–73; Defence Force Ombudsman, 1974–76; Sec., Dept of Aboriginal Affairs, 1977–79. *Publications:* The Delivery of Services financed by the Department of Aboriginal Affairs, 1976; Nothing Over Us: the story of the 2nd Sixth Australian Infantry Battalion, 1985; The Life and Times of William Hay of Boomanoomana 1816–1908, 1990. *Address:* Boomanoomana Homestead, via Mulwala, NSW 2647, Australia. *Clubs:* Australian, Melbourne (Melbourne).

HAY, Sir David (Russell), Kt 1991; CBE 1981; FRCP; FRACP; (first) Medical Director, National Heart Foundation of New Zealand, 1977–92; Cardiologist, Canterbury Hospital (formerly North Canterbury Hospital) Board, 1964–89; Hon. Consulting Physician, Canterbury District Health Board, since 1990; *b* 8 Dec. 1927; twin *s* of Sir James Lawrence Hay, OBE, and Lady (Davidina Mertel) Hay; *m* 1958, Dr Jocelyn Valerie Bell; two *d*. *Educ:* St Andrew's Coll., Christchurch; Otago Univ., Univ. of New Zealand (MB, ChB; MD). FRACP 1965; FRCP 1971. Resident appts, Christchurch, Royal South Hants, Hammersmith, Brompton and National Heart Hosps, 1951–55; Sen. Registrar, Dunedin and Christchurch Hosps, 1956–59; Physician, N Canterbury Hosp. Bd, 1959–64; Head of Dept of Cardiology, 1969–78; Chm. of Medical Services and Hd of Dept of Medicine, 1978–84. Chm., Christchurch Hosps Med. Staff Assoc., 1983–85; Clin. Lectr, Christchurch Clinical Sch., Univ. of Otago, 1973–80; Clin. Reader, 1980–88. Pres., Nat. Heart Foundn of NZ, 1996–99 (Councillor, 1968–92, 1996–99; Mem. Scientific Cttee, 1968–92); Vice-Pres., RACP, 1988–92 (Councillor, 1964–66, 1987–88; Examiner, 1974–75; Censor, 1975–79, and 1990–92); Mem. Specialist Adv. Cttee on Cardiology, 1980–90; Chm., Central Specialists Cttee of BMA, 1967–68; Pres., Canterbury Div. of BMA, 1972. Cardiac Society of Australia and New Zealand: Chm., NZ Reg. and Councillor, 1977–81; Life Mem., 1992; Fellow, 2004. Overseas Regl Advr, 1987–2000, Emeritus Internat. Advr, 2000, RCP. Member: Resuscitation Cttee of Nat. Cttee on Emergency Care, 1979–87; Health Promotion Forum of NZ, 1984–91; NZ Govt Adv. Cttee on Prevention of Cardiovascular Disease, 1985–86; NZ Govt Adv. Cttee on Smoking and Health, 1974–88; Ethics Cttee, Southern Regl HA, Canterbury, 1994–97; WHO Expert Adv. Panel on Tobacco or Health, 1977–2003; WHO Working Gp on Tobacco or Health in Western Pacific Reg., Manila, 1994; Hypertension Task Force, 1988–89; Life Mem., Nat. Heart Foundn, 1992. Speaker: World Conf. on Smoking and Health, Stockholm, 1979; Internat. Soc. and Fedn of Cardiology Workshop, Jakarta, 1982; Internat. Congress on Preventive Cardiology, Washington, 1989; World Congress of Cardiology, Manila, 1990. Nat. Heart Foundn Lecture, 1992; Charles Burns Oration, 1992. Trustee: J. L. Hay Charitable Trust, 1959–2004; W. H. Nicholls Charitable Trust, 1975–2003; Edna and Winifred White-Parsons Charitable Trust, 1986–2003; Keith Laugesen Charitable Trust, 1991–2002. College Medal, RACP, 1993; WHO Tobacco or Health Medal, 1995; Sir David Hay Medal, NZ Resuscitation Council, 2003. Commemoration Medal, NZ, 1990. *Publications:* (ed) Coronary Heart Disease: prevention and control in NZ, 1983; Heart Sounds, 2005; 100 sci. papers in various med. jls, mostly on smoking and health and preventive cardiology. *Recreations:* golf, writing. *Address:* 20 Greers Road, Christchurch 8041, New Zealand. *T:* 3585482. *Club:* Christchurch Golf.
See also Sir H. G. Hay, Dame M. L. Salas.

HAY, Rt Rev. Mgr George Adam; Canon, Plymouth Cathedral Chapter, since 1994; Parish Priest, Church of the Holy Spirit, Bovey Tracey, since 2003; *b* 14 Nov. 1930; *s* of late Sir William Rupert Hay, KCMG, KCIE, CSI, and late Sybil Ethel, *d* of Sir Stewart Abram. *Educ:* Ampleforth College, York; New Coll., Oxford (BA History, MA); Venerable English Coll., Rome (STL). National Service as Midshipman RNVR, 1949–50; student, Oxford, 1950–53; Venerable English Coll., Rome, 1953–60. Ordained priest at Rome, 1959; Curate, Sacred Heart Church, Exeter, and part-time RC Chaplain to students at Exeter Univ., 1960; Chaplain to students at Exeter Univ. and Priest-in-charge, Crediton, 1966–78; Rector, Venerable English Coll., Rome, 1978–84; Parish Priest: St John the Baptist, Dartmouth, 1984; Sacred Heart and St Teresa, Paignton, 1984–91; St Boniface, Okehampton and Holy Family, Chagford, 1991–97; Our Lady and St Denis, St Marychurch, Torquay, 1997–2003. *Recreations:* fly fishing, mountain walking. *Address:* The Presbytery, Ashburton Road, Bovey Tracey, Devon TQ13 9BY.

HAY, Sir Hamish (Grenfell), Kt 1982; JP; Mayor of Christchurch, New Zealand, 1974–89; Director: Canterbury Development Corporation, 1983–96; Christchurch International Airport Ltd, 1988–96; *b* 8 Dec. 1927; twin *s* of Sir James Lawrence Hay, OBE, and Lady (Davidina) Hay; *m* 1955, Judith Leicester Gill (QSO 1987; CNZM 1998); one *s* four *d*. *Educ:* St Andrew's Coll., Christchurch; Univ. of Canterbury, NZ (BCom). FCA(NZ). Councillor: Christchurch City Council, 1959–74; Canterbury Regl Council, 1995–2003 (Dep. Chm., 1998–2001). Member: Victory Park Bd, 1974–89; Lyttelton Harbour Bd, 1983–89. Chairman: Christchurch Town Hall Board of Management, 1962–92; Canterbury Museum Trust Bd, 1981–84; Canterbury United Council, 1983–86; Museum of New Zealand, Wellington, 1992–98 (Chm., 1992–94). President: Christchurch Aged People's Welfare Council, 1974–89; Christchurch Civic Music Council, 1974–89; Christchurch Symphony Orchestra, 1982–88; Chm., Christchurch Arts Festival, 1965–74; past Mem., Queen Elizabeth II Arts Council. Chm., New Zealand Soc. of Accountants (Canterbury Br.), 1958; Dep. Man. Dir, Haywrights Ltd, 1962–74. Mem. Council, Univ. of Canterbury, 1974–89 (Mem., Foundn Patrons Gp); Chm. of Governors, McLean Inst., 1974–89; Governor, St Andrew's Coll., 1986–92. Vice-Pres., Municipal Assoc. of NZ, 1974–88. Trustee, Canterbury Savings Bank, 1962–88 (Pres., 1974–75); Dir, Trust Bank Canterbury Ltd, 1988–95. Mem., Charles Upham Trust, 1986– (Dep. Chm., 1990–); Trustee: J. L. Hay Charitable Trust, 1959–; Trust Bank Canterbury Community Trust, 1988–96; Christchurch City Mission Foundn, 1999–. Paul Harris Fellow, Rotary Internat., 1997; Emeritus Fellow, Nat. Bd, NZ Inst. of Management. JP New Zealand, 1990. Silver Jubilee Medal, 1977; Commemoration Medal, NZ, 1990; Order of the Rising Sun (with Gold Rays), Japan, 1990. *Publication:* Hay Days (autobiog.), 1989. *Recreations:* gardening, listening to good music. *Address:* PO Box 36224, Merivale, Christchurch 8005, New Zealand. *T:* (3) 3047102; 95 Rue Balguerie, Akaroa, New Zealand. *Club:* Christchurch Rotary (New Zealand).
See also Sir D. R. Hay, Dame M. L. Salas.

HAY, Lady (Helen) Olga; *see* Maitland, Lady H. O.

HAY, John Anthony, AC 2004; Vice-Chancellor and President, University of Queensland, 1996–2007, now Professor Emeritus; *b* Perth, 21 Sept. 1942; *s* of John Ernest and Neva Moy Ellis Hay; *m* 1965, Barbara McKenna; three *s* one *d* (incl. twin *s*). *Educ:* Perth Modern Sch.; Univ. Western Australia (BA Hons 1964; PhD 1976); Pembroke Coll., Cambridge (BA 1966; MA 1969). University of Western Australia: Lectr, Sen. Lect and Prof. of English, 1967–87; Dep. Chm., Acad. Bd, 1985; Monash University: Dean Faculty of Arts, 1987–88; Sen. Dep. Vice-Chancellor, 1988–91; Vice-Chancellor an Pres., Deakin Univ., 1992–95. Editor, Aumla, Jl of Australasian Univs Lang. and Lit Assoc., 1985–92. Chairman: Carrick Inst. for Learning and Technol. in Higher Educn 2004–; R. L. Martin Inst., 2007–. Mem. Council, Nat. Liby of Australia, 2005–. Chm Springfield Health City, 2008–. Trustee, Qld Art Gall., 2008–. Hon. LittD Deakin, 1995 Hon. DLitt Western Australia; Hon. LLD Queensland; DUniv Queensland Univ. o Technol. *Publications:* Spectrum I, II & III, 1971–79; Directions in Australian Secondar English, 1975; Testing English Comprehension, 1979; K. S. Pritchard, 1984; Western Australian Literature: a bibliography, 1985; European Relations, 1985; The Early Imprint at New Norcia, 1986; Australian Studies in Tertiary Institutions, 1987; Western Australia Writing, 1989; Narrative Issues, 1990; Bibliography of Australian Literature, I & II, 1995 Bibliography of Australian Literature, vol. I (A-E), 2001, vol. II (F-J) 2004, vol. III (K-O 2007. *Recreations:* walking, cinema, reading, art museums, architecture. *Address:* 37 Laure Avenue, Chelmer, Qld 4068, Australia; c/o University Librarian's Office, University o Queensland, Qld 4072, Australia. *Club:* Queensland.

HAY, Sir John (Erroll Audley), 11th Bt *cr* 1663 (NS) of Park, Wigtownshire; *b* 3 Dec 1935; *o s* of Sir Arthur Thomas Erroll Hay, 10th Bt, ISO, ARIBA and his 1st wife, Herth Hedwig Paula Louise (*d* 1994), *d* of Ludwig Stölzle, Nagelberg, Austria; *S* father, 1993 *Educ:* Gordonstoun; St Andrews Univ. (MA). *Heir:* none.

HAY, Sir John Hugh D.; *see* Dalrymple-Hay.

HAY, Peter; Strategic Director, Adults and Communities (formerly Social Care an Health), Birmingham City Council, since 2003; *b* 17 July 1962; *s* of Martin and Ann Hay *m* 1989, Carmel Corrigan; one *s* two *d* (and one *s* decd). *Educ:* UC, Swansea (BA Hon 1983); Univ. of Exeter (BPhil 1985); Open Univ. (MBA 1995). CQSW 1985 Humberside County Council: Social worker, 1985–88; Team Ldr Assessment, Grimsby 1988–89; Prin. Practitioner, Scunthorpe, 1989–92; Area Manager, Grimsby, 1992–96 North East Lincolnshire Council: Asst Dir, Child Care, 1996–97; Acting Dir of Socia Services, 1997–98, Dir, 1998–2002; Dir of Community Care, 2002–03. *Recreations:* all tha encompasses family life, gardening, a good book and a whole range of music. *Address* Birmingham City Council, Louisa Ryland House, 44 Newhall Street, Birmingham B 3PP. *T:* (0121) 303 2992, *Fax:* (0121) 303 4383; *e-mail:* peter.hay@birmingham.gov.uk.

HAY, Rev. Richard, CMG 1992; Vicar, St Paul's, Addlestone, 1999–2007; Rural Dea of Runnymede, 2002–07; *b* 4 May 1942; *s* of Prof. Denys Hay, FBA, FRSE and Saral Gwyneth Morley; *m* 1969, Miriam Marguerite Alvin England; two *s*. *Educ:* Georg Watson's Coll., Edinburgh; Edinburgh Univ.; Balliol Coll., Oxford (BA Hons, Mod Hist.); Cranmer Hall, Durham. Assistant Principal, HM Treasury, 1963–68; Secretary West Midlands Economic Planning Council, 1966–67; Private Sec. to Financial Sec. Treasury, 1967–68; Principal, Treasury, 1968–73; European Commission: Member Cabinet of Sir Christopher (later Lord) Soames, Vice-Pres., 1973–75; Dep. Chef d Cabinet, 1975–77; Chef de Cabinet to Mr Christopher (now Lord) Tugendhat, Member 1977–79; Dir, Economic Structures and Community Interventions, Directorate-Gen. fo Economic and Financial Affairs, 1979–81; Dep. Dir-Gen., 1981–86, Dir-Gen., 1986–91 Directorate-General for Personnel and Admin, EC; Special Advr, EC, 1991. Consultant Sharing of Ministries Abroad, 1992–94. Ordained deacon, 1996, priest, 1997; Curate, S Clement and All Saints, Hastings, 1996–99. *Address:* 15 Fox Close, Pyrford, Surrey GU2 8LP.

HAY, Robert Colquhoun, CBE 1988; WS; Sheriff Principal of North Strathclyde 1989–98; *b* 22 Sept. 1933; *s* of late J. B. Hay, dental surgeon, Stirling and Mrs J. Y. Hay *m* 1958, Olive Black; two *s* two *d*. *Educ:* Univ. of Edinburgh (MA, LLB). Legal practice 1957–63, 1968–76; Depute Procurator Fiscal, Edinburgh, 1963–68; Temp. Sheriff 1984–89; Chm., 1976–81, Pres., 1981–89, Industrial Tribunals for Scotland. Mem. Sheriff Court Rules Council, 1989–95 (Chm., 1993–95). Comr, Northern Lighthouse Bd, 1989–98 (Vice-Chm., 1991–92; Chm., 1992–93). Hon. Sheriff, Dumbarton, 1999 Comr for Clan Hay, 1995–2002. *Publication:* contrib. Laws of Scotland: Stair Memoria Encyclopedia, 1988. *Recreations:* walking, sailing. *Address:* Rocklee, Cove, Argyll & Bute G84 0NN. *T:* (01436) 842269. *Club:* Royal Highland Yacht (Oban).

HAY, Robin William Patrick Hamilton; a Recorder, 1985–2005; barrister; *b* 1 Nov 1939; *s* of William R. Hay and Dora Hay; *m* 1969, Lady Olga Maitland, *qv*; two *s* one *d* *Educ:* Eltham; Selwyn Coll., Cambridge (MA, LLB). Called to the Bar, Inner Temple 1964. Legal Assessor, GMC, 2002–; Legal Advisor: Disciplinary Panel, Inst. and Faculty o Actuaries, 2006–; Statutory Cttees, RPSGB, 2006–. Legal Mem., Res. Ethics Cttee, Nat Hosp for Neurology and Neurosurgery, 2001–; Chm., Appeal Panel, Postgrad. Med Educn and Trng Bd, 2005–; Legal Assessor, Nursing and Midwifery Council, 2007–. Chm., Nat. (formerly Young) Musicians Symphony Orchestra, 1990–2001. *Recreations* church tasting, gastronomy, choral singing. *Address:* Lamb Chambers, Lamb Building Temple, EC4Y 7AS. *Club:* Garrick.

HAY, Prof. Roderick James, DM; FRCP, FRCPath, FMedSci; Professor o Dermatology, Queen's University Belfast, 2002–07, now Emeritus; Chairman International Foundation for Dermatology, since 2002; Consultant Dermatologist, King's College Hospital NHS Trust, since 2008; *b* 13 April 1947; *s* of Kenneth Stuart Hay and Margery Geidt (*née* Winterbotham); *m* 1973, Delyth Price; two *d*. *Educ:* Wellington Coll. Merton Coll., Oxford (BA 1968; BM BCh 1971; MA 1979; DM 1980); Guy's Hosp Med. Sch. MRCP 1974, FRCP 1981; MRCPath 1981, FRCPath 1992. House physician and surgeon, SHO and Dermatol. Registrar, Guy's Hosp., 1971–75; London School o Hygiene and Tropical Medicine: Wellcome Res. Fellow, 1975–77; Lectr, 1977–79; Sen Lectr, 1979–83; Reader in Clinical Mycology, 1983–89; Vis. Prof., 2001–; Hon. Cons Dermatologist, 1979–2002, Dean, 1993–2000, St John's Inst. of Dermatol.; Prof., UMDS later Guy's, King's and St Thomas' Hosps' Med. Sch. of KCL, 1989–2002; Mary Dunhill Prof. of Cutaneous Medicine, London Univ., 1990–2002; Clinical Dir, Dermatology Guy's and St Thomas' NHS Trust, 1996–2000; Dean for Ext. Affairs, GKT, 1998–2002 Queen's University Belfast: Dean, Fac. of Medicine and Health Scis, 2002–05; Hd, Sch. of Medicine and Dentistry (formerly Sch. of Medicine), 2002–07. Non-exec. Dir, Eastern Health and Social Services Bd, 2002–. FMedSci 2000. *Publications:* Clinicians Guide to Fungal Disease, 1981; Medical Mycology, 1996; contribs to med. and scientific jls on immunology and treatment of fungal infections and epidemiology of skin disease. *Recreations:* gardening, music. *Address:* International Foundation for Dermatology, Willan House, 4 Fitzroy Square, W1P 5HQ. *T:* (020) 7388 6515; Hunters Moon, Plum Lane, Shipton under Wychwood, Oxon OX7 6DZ.

HAY, Sir Ronald Frederick Hamilton, 12th Bt *cr* 1703, of Alderston; *b* 1941; *s* of Sir Ronald Nelson Hay, 11th Bt and Rita, *d* of John Munyard; *S* father, 1988, but his name does not appear on the Official Roll of the Baronetage; *m* 1978, Kathleen, *d* of John Thake; two *s* one *d*. *Heir:* *s* Alexander James Hay, *b* 1979.

HAY, William; Member for Foyle, and Speaker, since 2007, Northern Ireland Assembly; *b* 16 April 1950; *m* (marr. diss.); three *s* two *d*. *Educ*: Newbuildings Primary Sch.; Faughen Valley High Sch. Mem. (DemU), Derry CC, 1981–. Mem. for Foyle, NI Assembly, 1998– (DemU, 1998–2007, when elected Speaker). Contested (DemU) Foyle, 2001, 2005. *Address*: (constituency office) 9 Ebrington Terrace, Waterside, Londonderry BT47 1JS.

HAY-CAMPBELL, (Thomas) Ian, LVO 1994; HM Diplomatic Service, retired; Deputy Head of Mission, Oslo, 2001–05; *b* 19 May 1945; *s* of Thomas Neil Hay-Campbell and Anthea Joan Hay-Campbell (*née* Carey); *m* 1970, Margaret Lorraine (*née* Hoadley); four *s*. *Educ*: Wanganui Collegiate Sch., NZ; Victoria Univ. of Wellington (BA Hons History). Radio Journalist, NZBC, Wellington, 1969–72; Radio Producer, subseq. Editor, BBC World Service, 1972–84; joined FCO, 1984; First Sec., FCO, 1984–87; Dep. Head of Mission, Kinshasa, 1987–90; FCO, 1990–94; Head of Press and Public Affairs Section, Moscow, 1994–97; Dep. High Comr, Harare, 1998–2001. *Recreations*: modern history, family history research, reading, tennis, trams. *Address*: High House, Bucknell, Shropshire SY7 0AA. *T*: (01547) 530750.

HAY DAVISON, Ian Frederic; *see* Davison.

HAY-PLUMB, Paula Maria; non-executive Director, Skipton Building Society, since 2006; *b* 18 March 1960; *d* of Henry Sephton Green and Eileen Green (*née* Millburn); *m* 1984, Martin Hay-Plumb; one *s* one *d*. *Educ*: Univ. of Exeter (BSc Hons 1980). ACA 1983; MCT 1989. Qualified as chartered accountant with Peat, Marwick, Mitchell; Marks and Spencer plc, 1984–88; Olympia & York Canary Wharf Ltd, 1989–93; Finance Dir, 1994–96, Man. Dir (Ops), 1996–99, Chief Exec., 1999–2002, English Partnerships; Corporate Finance and Gp Reporting Dir, Marks and Spencer plc, 2003–05. Chairman: DETR Coalfields Task Force, 1997–98 (reported 1998); Nat. Australia Gp Common Investment Fund Trustee Ltd, 2007–; non-exec. Dir, Forensic Science Service Ltd, 2006–. Trustee, Coalfields Regeneration Trust, 1999–. *Recreations*: music, theatre.

HAYASHI, Sadayuki, Hon. GCVO 1998; Ambassador of Japan to the Court of St James's, 1997–2001; *b* 10 Nov. 1937; *s* of Tomohiko and Ayako Hayashi; *m* 1969, Chieko Kumazawa; three *d*. *Educ*: Univ. of Tokyo (BA 1960); St John's Coll., Oxford (BA 1962). Entered Ministry of Foreign Affairs, Japan, 1960; Attaché, London, 1962–64; First Secretary: Kuala Lumpur, 1970–72; Washington, 1972–74; Private Sec. to Chief Cabinet Sec., Prime Minister's Office, 1976; Dep. Consul-Gen., Hong Kong, 1978–81; Counsellor, Permt Mission of Japan to UN, NY, 1981–84; Dir, Financial Affairs Div., Minister's Secretariat, 1984–86; Dep. Dir-Gen., UN Bureau, 1986; Minister, Permt Mission of Japan to Internat. Orgns, and concurrently Consul-Gen., Geneva, 1987–89; Director-General: Econ. Affairs Bureau, 1989–92; for Inspection (rank of ambassador), 1992; Dep. Vice-Minister, 1992–94; Dep. Minister, 1994, Vice Minister, 1995–97, for Foreign Affairs. *Recreations*: trekking, walking, collecting classic cameras. *Address*: c/o Embassy of Japan, 101–104 Piccadilly, W1J 7JT. *T*: (020) 7465 6500.

HAYCOCKS, Myra Anne; *see* Kinghorn, M. A.

HAYDAR, Dr Loutof Allah; Syrian Ambassador to the People's Republic of China, 1990–99; *b* 22 March 1940; *s* of Haydar and Mary; *m* 1968, Hayat Hassan; one *s* three *d*. *Educ*: Damascus Univ. (BA English Literature 1964); Moscow State Univ. (PhD 1976). Joined Foreign Office, 1965; served at Syrian Embassy: London, 1965–67; Bonn, 1967–68; Moscow, 1970–75; served with Syrian Delegation to UN, New York, 1978–82; Syrian Ambassador to UK, 1982–86. *Publications*: The Ancient History of Palestine and the Middle East (PhD Thesis), 1976; The Grand Spring: a collection of literary short stories, 1997; The Hut and the Mermaid, 2003.

HAYDAY, Anthony Victor; HM Diplomatic Service, retired; Ambassador to Madagascar, 1987–90; *b* 1 June 1930; *s* of Charles Leslie Victor Hayday and Catherine (*née* McCarthy); *m* 1966, Anne Heather Moffat (*d* 1995); one *s* one *d*. *Educ*: Beckenham and Penge Grammar School. Royal Air Force, 1949–50; HM Foreign (later Diplomatic) Service, 1950; Brazzaville, 1953; British Information Services, New York, 1955; FO, 1958; Vice Consul, Houston, 1961; 2nd Secretary, Algiers, 1962; FO (later FCO), 1966; 1st Secretary, New Delhi, 1969; Head of Chancery, Freetown, 1973; on secondment to Commonwealth Secretariat, 1976–80; Dep. High Comr, Calcutta, 1981–85; Consul-Gen., Cleveland, 1985–87. *Recreations*: birdwatching, athletics. *Address*: Meadow Cottage, Swillbrook, Minety, Malmesbury, Wilts SN16 9QA. *Clubs*: Blackheath Harriers; Bengal (Calcutta).

HAYDEN, Ven. David Frank; Archdeacon of Norfolk, since 2002; *b* 25 Jan. 1947; *s* of Donald and Margaret Hayden; *m* 1968, Ruby Cowles; two *d*. *Educ*: Tyndale Hall, Bristol (DipTh 1969, BD 1971); London Univ. Ordained deacon, 1971, priest, 1972; Curate: St Matthew's, Silverhill, 1971; Galleywood Common, 1975; Rector, Redgrave cum Botesdale with Rickinghall, 1979–84; RD, Hartismere, 1981–84; Vicar, Cromer, 1984–2002; Hosp. Chaplain (pt-time), 1984–2000; RD, Repps, 1995–2002. Hon. Canon, Norwich Cathedral, 1996–2002. *Recreations*: spending time with wife, children and grandchildren; being on, in, or near water. *Address*: 8 Boulton Road, Thorpe St Andrew, Norwich NR7 0DF. *T*: (01603) 702477.

HAYDEN, Hon. William George, AC 1989; cattle farmer, Brisbane Valley; Governor-General of Australia, 1989–96; *b* Brisbane, 23 Jan. 1933; *s* of G. Hayden, Oakland, Calif, USA; *m* 1960, Dallas, *d* of W. Broadfoot; one *s* two *d*. *Educ*: Brisbane State High Sch.; Univ. of Qld (BEcon). Public Service, Qld, 1950–52; Police Constable in Queensland, 1953–61. MHR (Lab) for Oxley, Qld, 1961–88. Parly Spokesman on Health and Welfare, 1969–72; Minister for Social Security, Australian Govt, 1972–75; Federal Treasurer, June–Nov. 1975; Leader of Australian Labor Party and the Opposition, 1977–83; spokesman on defence, 1976–77 and on economic management, 1976–83; Minister for Foreign Affairs, 1983–87, and for Trade, 1987–88. Adjunct Prof., Qld Univ. of Technol., Brisbane, 1996. Chm., Editl Cttee, Quadrant Jl, 1998–2004. Res. Vis. Fellow, Jane Franklin Hall, Univ. of Tasmania, 2000. Patron: (Qld Br.) Australian Inst. Internat. Affairs; (Qld Br.) Australian Fabian Soc.; Gen. Sir John Monash Foundn. Hon. FRACP 1995. Hon. Dr: Griffith Univ., 1990; Univ. of Central Qld, 1992; Hon. LLD Univ. of Qld, 1990; Hon. DLitt Univ. of S Qld, 1997. Australian Humanist of the Year, 1996. Kt, Order of St John in Australia, 1989. Gwanghwa Medal, Order of Diplomatic Merit, Korea. Commander, Order of Three Stars (Latvia). *Publication*: Hayden: an autobiography, 1996. *Address*: PO Box 7829, Waterfront Place, Brisbane, Qld 4001, Australia.

HAYDEN, William Joseph, CBE 1976; Chairman and Chief Executive, Jaguar plc, 1990–92; *b* 19 Jan. 1929; *s* of George Hayden and Mary Ann Hayden (*née* Overhead); *m* 1954, Mavis Ballard; two *s* two *d*. *Educ*: Romford Tech. College. Served Army, 1947–49. Ford Motor Co.: Briggs Motor Bodies, Dagenham, 1950–57; financial staff, Dagenham, 1957–63; Div. Controller, Ford Chassis, Transmission and Engine Div., Dagenham, 1963–67; Gen. Ops Manager, Transmission, Chassis and Truck Mfg Ops, 1967–71; Vice-President: Truck Mfg Ops, 1971; Power Train Ops, 1972; Mfg Ford of Europe, Inc.,

1974–90. Director (non-executive): Hawtell Whiting, 1992–96; Trans Tec. 1993–96. *Recreations*: golf, gardening, soccer. *Address*: Buckley Green Farm, Buckley Green, Henley in Arden, Warwickshire B95 5QF. *Clubs*: Thorndon Park Golf; Stratford on Avon Golf.

HAYDON, Francis Edmund Walter; HM Diplomatic Service, retired; *b* 23 Dec. 1928; *s* of late Surgeon Captain Walter T. Haydon, RN and Maria Christina Haydon (*née* Delahoyde); *m* 1959, Isabel Dorothy Kitchin; two *s* two *d*. *Educ*: Downside School; Magdalen College, Oxford. BA (1st cl. Modern History) 1949. Asst London diplomatic correspondent, Agence France-Presse, 1951–52; Asst diplomatic correspondent, Reuters, 1952–55; joined Foreign Office, 1955; Second Sec., Benghazi, 1959, Beirut, 1962; First Sec., Blantyre, 1969, Ankara, 1978; Counsellor, FCO, 1981–87. *Recreations*: lawn tennis, cricket, bridge, travel, enjoying the countryside. *Address*: Le Picachon, La Rue des Bouillons, Trinity, Jersey JE3 5BB. *T*: (01534) 863155.

HAYE, Colvyn Hugh, CBE 1983; Commissioner for Hong Kong, 1984–87; *b* 7 Dec. 1925; 3rd *s* of Colvyn Hugh Haye and Avis Rose Kelly; *m* 1949, Gloria Mary Stansbury; two *d*. *Educ*: Sherwood Coll.; Univ. of Melbourne (BA, Teachers' Cert.); Christchurch Coll., Oxford (Overseas Service Trng Course). Served War, RNVR, Midshipman and Sub-Lt, 1944–46. Victorian State Educn Service, 1947–52; joined Colonial Service, now HMOCS, Hong Kong Government: Educn Officer, 1953; Sen. Educn Officer, 1962 (world tour, educnl estabs, and trng at Centre for Educnl Television Overseas, London, 1964); Asst Dir and Head of Educnl Television Service, 1969; Dep. Dir, 1975; Dir of Educn and Official Mem., Legislative Council, 1980; Sec., Administrative Service and Comr, London Office, 1984. Jardine Educn Foundn Visitor, Univs of Oxford and Cambridge, 1990–97. Mem. Council, Overseas Service Pensioners' Assoc., 1988–97. JP Hong Kong, 1971–87. *Recreations*: reading, writing, talking, walking. *Address*: Balmenoch, Gwydyr Road, Crieff, Perthshire PH7 4BS. *T*: and *Fax*: (01764) 656626. *Club*: Hong Kong (Hong Kong).

HAYES, Sir Brian, Kt 1998; CBE 1992; QPM 1985; security consultant, since 1998; Deputy Commissioner of Metropolitan Police, 1995–98; *b* 25 Jan. 1940; 2nd *s* of James and Jessie Hayes; *m* 1960, Priscilla Rose Bishop; one *s* three *d*. *Educ*: Plaistow County Grammar Sch.; Sheffield Univ. (BA Hons 1st Cl. Mod. Langs). Metropolitan Police, 1959–77; seconded Northern Ireland, 1971–72; Police Adviser, Mexico, 1975 and 1976, Colombia, 1977 and 1993; British Police representative, EEC, 1976–77; Asst Chief Constable, Surrey Constabulary, 1977–81; Dep. Chief Constable, Wiltshire Constabulary, 1981–82; Chief Constable, Surrey Constabulary, 1982–91; Inspector of Constabulary for SE England, 1991–95. Vice-Pres., ACPO, 1990–91. Chm., Police Athletic Assoc., 1989–91 (Nat. Sec., 1984–88); Pres., Union Sportive des Polices d'Europe, 1990–92. Special Advr on Security to FA, 1997–2002; Security Consultant, TRI-MEX Internat. Ltd, 1999–2002. Freeman, City of London, 1998. OStJ 1987. Police Long Service and Good Conduct Medal, 1981; Cruz al Merito Policial (Spain), 1998. *Recreations*: martial arts, running, sailing, golf.

HAYES, Sir Brian (David), GCB 1988 (KCB 1980; CB 1976); Permanent Secretary, Department of Trade and Industry, 1985–89, retired (Joint Permanent Secretary, 1983–85); *b* 5 May 1929; *s* of late Charles and Flora Hayes, Bramerton, Norfolk; *m* 1958, Audrey Jenkins; one *s* one *d*. *Educ*: Norwich Sch.; Corpus Christi Coll., Cambridge. BA (Hist.) 1952, PhD (Cambridge) 1956. RASC, 1947–49. Joined Min. of Agriculture, Fisheries and Food, 1956; Asst Private Sec. to the Minister, 1958; Asst Sec., 1967; Under-Sec., Milk and Poultry Gp, 1970–73; Dep. Sec., 1973–78; Permanent Sec., 1979–83. Director: Guardian Royal Exchange, 1989–99; Tate & Lyle, 1989–98; Adv. Dir, Unilever plc, 1990–99. Chm., CBI Educn Foundn, 1991–96. Dir, SANE, 1990–2007. Lloyd's Members' Ombudsman, 1994–2007. *Recreations*: reading, television, opera.

HAYES, Christine; *see* Farnish, C.

HAYES, Most Rev. James Martin; Archbishop (RC) of Halifax (NS), 1967–90, now Archbishop Emeritus; *b* 27 May 1924; *s* of late L. J. Hayes. *Educ*: St Mary's Univ., Halifax; Holy Heart Seminary, Halifax; Angelicum Univ., Rome. Asst, St Mary's Basilica, 1947–54; Chancellor and Sec. of Archdiocese of Halifax, 1957–65; Rector, St Mary's Basilica, 1963–65; Auxil. Bp of Halifax, 1965–66; Apostolic Administrator of Archdiocese of Halifax, 1966–67. Pres., Canadian Conf. of Catholic Bishops, 1987–89. Hon. DLitt St Anne's Coll., Church Point, NS, 1966; Hon. DTh King's Coll., Halifax, NS, 1967; Hon. DHL Mount St Vincent Univ., Halifax, 1985; Hon. LLD: St Mary's Univ., Halifax, 1985; St Thomas Univ., 1989; Hon. DD Atlantic Sch. of Theol., Halifax, 1986. *Address*: Catholic Pastoral Centre, Archdiocese of Halifax, PO Box 1527, 1531 Grafton Street, Halifax, NS B3J 2Y3, Canada.

HAYES, Jeremy Joseph James; barrister; freelance journalist and broadcaster; *b* 20 April 1953; *s* of Peter and Daye Hayes; *m* 1979, Alison Gail Mansfield; one *s* one *d*. *Educ*: Oratory Sch.; Chelmer Inst. LLB London. Called to the Bar, Middle Temple, 1977. Formerly Political Ed., Punch mag.; freelance columnist and restaurant reviewer, London Paper, 2006–. MP (C) Harlow, 1983–97; contested (C) same seat, 1997. PPS to Minister of State, NI Office, 1992–94, DoE, 1994–97. Member, Select Committee: on Social Services, 1987–90; on Health, 1990–91; on National Heritage, 1996–97; formerly: Member: All Party Parly Gp on Human Rights; All Party Parly Gp on Race Relations; Vice Chm., All Party AIDS Cttee; Chm., All Party ASH Gp. Promoter: Parents' Aid (No 2) Bill; Sexual Offences Bill; Sponsor: Video Recordings Act; Protection of Children against Tobacco Act; Freedom of Information (Medical Records) Act. Member: FRAME; Amnesty Internat. Fellow, Industry and Parliament Trust. Hon. Dir, State Legislative Leaders Foundn, USA. Gov., Oratory Sch.; Vice Pres., Wendens Ambo Cricket Club. Freeman, City of London. *Recreations*: banker and taxi driver for my children. *Address*: 2 Paper Buildings, Temple, EC4Y 7ET. *Clubs*: Carlton, Savile; Essex.

HAYES, John Henry; MP (C) South Holland and The Deepings, since 1997; *b* 23 June 1958; *s* of late Henry John Hayes and Lily Hayes; *m* 1997, Susan Jane Hopewell; two *s*. *Educ*: Colfe's Grammar Sch., London; Univ. of Nottingham (BA Hons (Politics), PGCE). Joined The Data Base Ltd, 1983, Dir, 1986–99. Mem., Nottinghamshire CC, 1985–98. Contested (C) Derbyshire NE, 1987, 1992. Opposition front-bench spokesman on educn and employment, 2000–01; an Opposition Pairing Whip, 2001–02; Shadow Agriculture and Fisheries Minister, 2002–03; Shadow Housing and Planning Minister, 2003–05; Shadow Transport Minister, 2005; Shadow Minister: for Vocational Educn and Skills, 2005–07; for Lifelong Learning, Further and Higher Educn, 2007–. Member, Select Committee: Agriculture, 1997–99; Educn and Employment, 1998–99; Administration, 2001–02; Mem., Cttee of Selection, 2001–02. A Vice-Chm., Cons. Party, 1999–2000. Adjunct Associate Prof., Richmond, The American Internat. Univ. in London, 2002–. *Recreations*: the arts (particularly English painting, poetry and prose), good food and wine, many sports (including darts), studying history, gardening, making jam, antiques, architecture, aesthetics. *Address*: House of Commons, SW1A 0AA. *T*: (020) 7219 1389. *Clubs*: Carlton; Spalding, Spalding Gentlemen's Soc. (Lincs).

HAYES, John William, CBE 1995; Chairman: Actuarial Profession Disciplinary Board, since 2004; Disciplinary Appeals Committee, Chartered Institute of Public Finance Accountants, since 2001; *b* 10 Feb. 1945; *s* of late Dick Hayes and of Bridget Isobel Hayes; *m* 1970, Jennifer Hayes (*née* Harvey); two *s* one *d*. *Educ:* Nottingham High Sch.; Morecambe Grammar Sch.; Victoria Univ. of Manchester (LLB). Solicitor. Articled Thomas Foord, 1966–69; Worthing Borough Council, 1966–69; Nottingham County Borough Council, 1969–71; Somerset CC, 1971–74; Asst, Dep. Clerk and Dep. Chief Exec., Notts CC, 1974–80; Clerk and Chief Exec., Warwicks CC, 1980–86; Sec.-Gen., Law Soc., 1987–96; Chm., OPRA, 1996–2001. Chm., Local Govt Gp, Law Soc., 1981–82; Sec., Warwicks Probation Cttee, 1983–86; Clerk to Warwicks Magistrates' Courts' Cttee, 1983–86; Clerk to Lord Lieut of Warwicks, 1980–86. Chm., Ind. Inquiry into River Vessel Safety, 1992. Chm., Law Soc. Pension Scheme, 2002–. Chm., Coventry Dio. Church Urban Fund, 1989–91; Member: Bishop of Coventry's Board of Social Responsibility, 1981–86; Inner Cities' Task Force, 1985–86. Mem., Ind. Remuneration Panel, 2001–04, Ind. Mem., Standards Cttee, 2001– (Chm., 2006–), W Sussex CC. Legal Assessor, British Council of Osteopathy, 1998–2003. Mem. Council, Warwick Univ., 1980–90; Gov., Univ. of Chichester (formerly UC Chichester), 2001–07. Gov., Kingsley School, 1986–92. Hon. LLD De Montfort, 1996. *Recreations:* cricket, music, idleness. *Club:* Sussex CC.

HAYES, Patricia Jane; Director, Road and Vehicle Safety and Standards, Department for Transport, since 2007; *b* 9 June 1966; *d* of William and Emily Rennie; *m* 1992, Andrew Hayes; three *s*. *Educ:* Armagh Girls' High Sch.; Pembroke Coll., Oxford (BA PPE 1987, MA). Various posts, Dept of Transport and DETR, 1987–96; First Sec., Transport, British Embassy, Washington, 1996–99; Sec., Sustainable Develt Commn, 2000–02; Department for Transport: Hd, Charging and Local Transport Div., 2002–04; Hd, NW East Midlands Div., 2004–06; Hd, Talent Mgt and People Develt, 2006–07. *Address:* Department for Transport, Great Minster House, 76 Marsham Street, SW1P 4DR. *T:* (020) 7944 8300.

HAYES, Dr Peter Richard; HM Diplomatic Service; High Commissioner, Sri Lanka, since 2008; *b* 11 April 1963; *s* of late Jasper Terrence Hayes and of Greta Louvaine Hayes; *m* 2002, Christine, (Kirsty), Paton; one *s* one *d*. *Educ:* County Sch., Ashford, Surrey; Univ. of Surrey (BSc Physics); King's Coll. London (PhD 1989). Post-doctoral res. associate, KCL, 1989–90; SSO, NPL, 1990–93; Team Leader, Mgt and Technology Services, DTI, 1993–94; Head of Competition Issues, Cabinet Office, 1994–96; Asst Dir, Internat., OST, 1997–98; Dep. Hd, Envmt, Sci. and Energy, FCO, 1998–2000; Dir, Nuclear Decommng, DTI, 2000–01; Counsellor, then Consul Gen., Washington, 2001–05; Principal Private Sec. to Sec. of State for Foreign and Commonwealth Affairs, 2005–07. *Publications:* contrib. to acad. physics pubns and jls. *Recreation:* family. *Address:* c/o Foreign and Commonwealth Office, King Charles Street, SW1A 2AH. *Club:* Farmers.

HAYES, Dr William; President, St John's College, University of Oxford, 1987–2001 (Hon. Fellow, 2001); Senior Research Fellow, Clarendon Laboratory, Oxford University, since 1987; Pro-Vice-Chancellor, University of Oxford, 1990–2001; *b* 12 Nov. 1930; *s* of Robert Hayes and Eileen Tobin; *m* 1962, Joan Ferriss (*d* 1996); two *s* one *d*. *Educ:* University Coll., Dublin (MSc, PhD); Oxford Univ. (MA, DPhil). St John's College, Oxford: 1851 Overseas Schol., 1955–57; Official Fellow and Tutor, 1960–87; Principal Bursar, 1977–87; University Lectr, Oxford Univ., 1962–87; Dir and Head of Clarendon Lab., Oxford, 1985–87. Oxford University: Mem., Gen. Bd of the Faculties, 1985–88; Mem., Hebdomadal Council, 1989–2000; Chm., Curators of Univ. Chest, 1992–2000; Delegate, OUP, 1991–2001. Temporary research appointments at: Argonne Nat. Lab., 1957–58; Purdue Univ., 1963–64; RCA Labs, Princeton, 1968; Univ. of Illinois, 1971; Bell Labs, 1974. Mem., Physics Cttee, SERC, 1982–85. Hon. MRIA 1998. Hon. DSc: NUI, 1988; Purdue Univ., 1996. *Publications:* (ed) Crystals with the Fluorite Structure, 1974; (with R. Loudon) Scattering of Light by Crystals, 1978; (with A. M. Stoneham) Defects and Defect Processes in non-metallic Solids, 1985; contribs to Procs of Royal Soc., Jl of Physics, Physical Rev., etc. *Recreations:* walking, reading, listening to music. *Address:* St John's College, Oxford OX1 3JP. *T:* (01865) 277300.

HAYES, William; General Secretary, Communication Workers Union, since 2001; *b* 8 June 1953; *s* of William and Margaret Hayes; *m* 1995, Dian Lee; one *s* one *d*. *Educ:* St Swithin's Secondary Modern; Univ. of Liverpool (Dip. Trade Union Studies). Fitter-welder, 1968–71; factory worker, 1971–73; unemployed, 1973–74; joined Post Office, 1974, Postman; Lay Official, Union of Post Office Workers, subseq. UCW, then CWU, 1992; Nat. Official, CWU, 1992–2001. *Recreations:* films, music, books, Liverpool FC. *Address:* Communication Workers Union, 150 The Broadway, Wimbledon, SW19 1RX.

HAYHOE, family name of **Baron Hayhoe**.

HAYHOE, Baron *cr* 1992 (Life Peer), of Isleworth in the London Borough of Hounslow; **Bernard John Hayhoe, (Barney),** Kt 1987; PC 1985; CEng, FIMechE; Chairman, Guy's and St Thomas' NHS Trust, 1993–95; *b* 8 Aug. 1925; *s* of late Frank Stanley and Catherine Hayhoe; *m* 1962, Anne Gascoigne Thornton, *o d* of Bernard William and Hilda Thornton; two *s* one *d*. *Educ:* State schools; Borough Polytechnic. Tool Room Apprentice, 1941–44; Armaments Design Dept, Ministry of Supply, 1944–54; Inspectorate of Armaments, 1954–63; Conservative Research Dept, 1965–70. Heston and Isleworth, 1970–74, MP (C) Brentford and Isleworth, 1974–92; PPS to Lord President and Leader of House of Commons, 1972–74; an additional Opposition Spokesman on Employment, 1974–79; Parly Under Sec. of State for Defence for the Army, 1979–81; Minister of State: CSD, 1981; HM Treasury, 1981–85; (Minister for Health) DHSS, 1985–86. Member: Select Cttee on Race Relations and Immigration, 1971–73; Select Cttee on Defence, 1987–92; H of C Commn, 1987–92; Public Accounts Commn, 1987–92; H of L Select Cttee on Public Service, 1997–98; Hon. Sec., 1970–71, Vice-Chm., 1974, Cons. Parly Employment Cttee; Jt Hon. Sec., 1970–73, Vice-Chm., 1973–76, Cons. Gp for Europe; Vice-Chm., Cons. Party Internat. Office, 1973–79. Mem., Trilateral Commn, 1977–79. Chm., Hansard Soc., 1990–94. Governor, Birkbeck Coll., 1976–79. Pres., Help the Hospices, 1992–98; Trustee: British Brain and Spine Foundn, 1992–2001; Foundn for Liver Res. (formerly Liver Res. Trust), 1994–2006. *Address:* 20 Wool Road, SW20 0HW. *T:* (020) 8947 0037. *Club:* Garrick.
See also F. G. J. Hayhoe.

HAYHOE, Prof. Frank George James, MD, FRCP, FRCPath; Leukaemia Research Fund Professor of Haematological Medicine, University of Cambridge, 1968–88; Fellow, Darwin College, Cambridge, since 1964, Vice-Master, 1964–74; *b* 25 Oct. 1920; *s* of late Frank Stanley and Catherine Hayhoe; *m* 1945, Jacqueline Marie Marguerite (*née* Dierkx); two *s*. *Educ:* Selhurst Grammar Sch.; Trinity Hall, Cambridge; St Thomas's Hospital Medical Sch. BA Cantab 1942; MRCS, LRCP 1944; MB, BChir Cantab 1945; MRCP 1949; MA Cantab 1949; MD Cantab 1951; FRCP 1965; FRCPath 1971. Captain RAMC, 1945–47. Registrar, St Thomas' Hosp., 1947–49. Elmore Research Student, Cambridge Univ., 1949–51; Royal Soc. Exchange Res. Schol., USSR, 1962–63; Lectr in Medicine, Cambridge Univ., 1951–68; Mem. Council of Senate, 1967–71. Member: Bd of Governors, United Cambridge Hospitals, 1971–74; Cambs AHA, 1974–75; GMC, 1982–88. Lectures: Langdon Brown, RCP, 1971; Cudlip Meml, Ann Arbor, 1967; vis. lectr at med. schs in N and S America, Europe, Middle East, Africa, India. Hon. MI L'Aquila, 1992; Montpellier, 1993. G. F. Götz Foundn Prize, Zürich Univ., 1974; Suni Rana Panja Gold Medal, Calcutta Sch. of Trop. Med., 1979. *Publications:* (ed) Lectures i Haematology, 1960; Leukaemia: Research and Clinical Practice, 1960; (jtly) Cytology an Cytochemistry of Acute Leukaemia, 1964; (ed) Current Research in Leukaemia, 196 (with R. J. Flemans) An Atlas of Haematological Cytology, 1969, 3rd edn 1992; (with C. Cawley) Ultrastructure of Haemic Cells, 1973; (jtly) Leukaemia, Lymphomas an Allied Disorders, 1976; (jtly) Hairy Cell Leukaemia, 1980; (with D. Quaglin Haematological Cytochemistry, 1980, 3rd edn 1994; (ed with D. Quaglino) Th Cytobiology of Leukaemias and Lymphomas, 1985; (with D. Quaglino) Haematologic Oncology, 1992; contribs to med. and scientific jls, on haematological topics, especiall leukaemia. *Address:* 20 Queen Edith's Way, Cambridge CB1 7PN. *T:* (01223) 248381.
See also Baron Hayhoe.

HAYMAN, family name of **Baroness Hayman**.

HAYMAN, Baroness *cr* 1995 (Life Peer), of Dartmouth Park in the London Borough Camden; **Helene Valerie Hayman;** PC 2001; Lord Speaker, House of Lords, sinc 2006; *b* 26 March 1949; *d* of late Maurice Middleweek and Maude Middleweek; *m* 197 Martin Hayman; four *s*. *Educ:* Wolverhampton Girls' High Sch.; Newnham Coll Cambridge (MA). Pres., Cambridge Union, 1969. Worked with Shelter, Nat. Campaig for the Homeless, 1969; Camden Council Social Services Dept, 1971; Dep. Dir, Na Council for One Parent Families, 1974. Vice-Chairman: Bloomsbury HA, 1988–9 (Mem., 1985–90); Bloomsbury and Islington HA, 1991–92 (Mem., 1990–91); Chm Whittington Hosp. NHS Trust, 1992–97. Contested (Lab) Wolverhampton SW, Feb 1974; MP (Lab) Welwyn and Hatfield, Oct. 1974–1979. Parliamentary Under-Secretar of State: DETR, 1997–98; DoH, 1998–99; Minister of State, MAFF, 1999–200 Member: Select Cttee on the Assisted Dying for the Terminally Ill Bill, 2004–0 Constitution Cttee, 2005–06. Chairman: Cancer Res. UK, 2001–05; Human Tissu Authy, 2005–06. Mem., Human Fertilisation and Embryology Authy, 2005–06. Membe RCOG Ethics Cttee, 1982–96; UCL/UCH Cttee on Ethics of Clinical Investigatio 1987–96 (Vice-Chm., 1990–96); Council, UCL, 1992–97; Review Cttee, Ant Terrorism, Crime and Security Act, 2002–03; Bd, Roadsafe, 2002–06. Trustee: Roy Botanical Gardens, Kew, 2002–06; Tropical Health and Educn Trust, 2005–06.

HAYMAN, Andrew Christopher, CBE 2006; QPM 2004; security commentato analyst and adviser, since 2008; Assistant Commissioner, Special Operations, in charge c counter terrorism, royalty and diplomatic protection and security of London, 2005–08; 31 July 1959; *s* of Geoffrey and Valerie Hayman; *m* 1993, Jane Nicola Corbett; two *Educ:* Exeter Univ. (MA); Fitzwilliam Coll., Cambridge (Postgrad. Dip. in Applie Criminology). Joined Essex Police, 1978; Chief Inspector, Ops, 1993–95; Divl Comd Supt and Chief Supt, 1995–98; Metropolitan Police: Comdr, i/c Drugs and Crim 1998–2001; Dep. Asst Comr, Anti Corruption, and Dep. to Dep. Comr, 2001–02; Chi Constable, Norfolk Constabulary, 2002–05. Security commentator, ITV, NBC and Th Times, 2008–. Mem., Adv. Council on Misuse of Drugs, 2001–06; Chm., Drugs Ctte 2001–06, Terrorism Cttee, 2006–08, Security Advr, 2008–, ACPO. Ext. Exam Cambridge Univ., 2001–. Gov., Anglia Ruskin Univ., 2000–. *Recreations:* gardenin theatre, reading, keeping fit. *Address:* *e-mail:* andy.hayman2@googlemail.com.

HAYMAN, (Anne) Carolyn, OBE 2003; Chief Executive: Peace Direct, since 2004; Th Foyer Federation, since 1996; *b* 23 April 1951; *d* of Walter Kurt Hayman, *qv* and lat Margaret Riley Crann; *m* 1980, Peter John Bury; two *d*. *Educ:* Putney High Sch. for Girl Newnham Coll., Cambridge (BA Classics and Philosophy); Sch. of Oriental and Africa Studies (MSc Econ). Admin Trainee, ODM, 1975–78; Advr, Central Policy Review Staf 1978–80; Senior Consultant, Office Automation: EOSYS, 1980–82; Coopers & Lybranc 1982–83; Jt Man. Dir, Korda & Co., 1983–95; Exec. Dir, Rutherford Ventures, 1995–9 Chairman: Cambridge Animation Systems, 1990–96; Atraverda, 1992–97. Di Technology & Law, 1982–85. Member: Commonwealth Develt Corp., 1994–9 Working Gp on 14–19 Reform, 2003–04. Member: Council, Pitcom, 1981–83; Counc for Industry and Higher Educn, 1992–97; Board, Industrial Res. and Tech. Uni 1995–97. Editor, Work and Society, 1984–86. *Recreations:* music, swimming, cycling *Address:* 36 Lawford Road, NW5 2LN. *T:* (020) 7916 2689; (office) 56–64 Leonard Street EC2A 4JX. *T:* (020) 7549 0285.

HAYMAN, His Honour John David Woodburn; a Circuit Judge, 1976–92; *b* 24 Aug 1918; *m* Jane (*née* Davison); two *s* four *d*. *Educ:* King Edward VII Sch., Johannesburg; S John's Coll., Cambridge (MA, LLM). Served with S African Forces, 1940–42. Called t the Bar, Middle Temple, 1945. Sometime Lecturer in Law: University Coll. of Wales Aberystwyth; Leeds Univ.; Cambridge Univ.

HAYMAN, Prof. Walter Kurt, MA; ScD (Cambridge); FRS 1956; FIC; Professor o Pure Mathematics, University of York, 1985–93, now Emeritus; Senior Research Fellow Imperial College, London, since 1995; *b* 6 Jan. 1926; *s* of late Franz Samuel Haymann an Ruth Therese (*née* Hensel); *m* 1st, 1947, Margaret Riley Crann (*d* 1994), MA Cantab, of Thomas Crann, New Earswick, York; three *d*; 2nd, 1995, Dr Waficka Katifi (*d* 2001) 3rd, 2007, Marie Jennings, MBE. *Educ:* Gordonstoun Sch.; St John's Coll., Cambridge Lecturer at King's Coll., Newcastle upon Tyne, 1947, and Fellow of St John's Coll. Cambridge, 1947–50; Lecturer, 1947, and Reader, 1953–56, Exeter; Prof. of Pure Maths 1956–85, and Dean of RCS, 1978–81, Imperial Coll., London (FIC 1989). Visitin Lecturer at Brown Univ., USA, 1949–50, at Stanford Univ., USA (summer) 1950 an 1955, and to the American Mathematical Soc., 1961. Co-founder with Mrs Hayman o British Mathematical Olympiad; Vice-Pres., London Mathematical Soc., 1982–84 Foreign Member: Finnish Acad. of Science and Letters; Accademia Nazionale dei Lincei Rome; Corresp. Mem., Bavarian Acad. of Science. Hon. DSc: Exeter, 1981; Birmingham 1985; NUI, 1997; Hon. Dr rer. nat. Giessen, 1992; Hon. DPhil Uppsala, 1992. 1st Smith Prize, 1948, shared Adams Prize, 1949, Cambridge Univ.; Jun. Berwick Prize, 1955, Sen Berwick Prize, 1964, de Morgan Medal, 1995, London Mathematical Soc. *Publications* Multivalent Functions (Cambridge, 1958, 2nd edn 1994) Meromorphic Function (Oxford, 1964); Research Problems in Function Theory (London, 1967); Subharmoni Functions, vol. I, 1976, vol. II, 1989; papers in various mathematical journals. *Recreations* music, travel. *Address:* Department of Mathematics, Imperial College London, SW7 2AZ Cadogan Grange, Bisley, Stroud, Glos GL6 7AT.
See also A. C. Hayman.

HAYMAN-JOYCE, Lt-Gen. Sir Robert (John), KCB 1996; CBE 1989 (OBE 1979) DL; Chairman: Raytheon Systems Ltd, since 2000; March Security Ltd, since 2006; *b* 1 Oct. 1940; *s* of late Major T. F. Hayman-Joyce and B. C. Bruford; *m* 1968, Diana Livingstone-Bussell; two *s*. *Educ:* Radley Coll.; Magdalene Coll., Cambridge (MA) Commnd 11th Hussars (PAO), 1963; CO Royal Hussars (PWO), 1980–82; Comdr RAC 1 (BR) Corps, 1983–85; Dir, UK Tank Programme, 1988; Dir Gen., Fighting Vehicle and Engr Equipment, later Land Fighting Systems, MoD (PE), 1989–92; Dir, RAC 1992–94; Military Sec., MoD, 1994–95; MGO, 1995–98, and Dep. Chief of Defence Procurement (Ops), 1996–98. Non-exec. Dir, Alvis plc, 1999–2004. Col Comdt RAC

1995–99; Hon. Col, Royal Yeomanry, 2002–. Chairman: Trustees, Tank Mus., 1995–2002; Monmouthshire Hunt, 1998–2002. Patron: Retired Officers Assoc., 2000–; Soc. for Welfare of Horses and Ponies, 2003–. DL Gwent, 1997. FCIPS 1997. Hon. DSc Cranfield, 1998. *Recreations:* ski-ing, horses. *Address:* Raytheon Systems Ltd, Harman House, 1 George Street, Uxbridge UB8 1QQ; Ty Isha, Mamhilad, Pontypool, Monmouthshire NP4 0JE. *Clubs:* Cavalry and Guards; Leander (Henley-on-Thames).

HAYMES, Rev. Dr Brian; Minister, Bloomsbury Central Baptist Church, 2000–05; *b* 8 Dec. 1940; *s* of Reginald and Ella Haymes; *m* 1965, Jennifer Christine Frankland; two *d. Educ:* King's Coll. Sch., Wimbledon; Univ. of Bristol (BA 1965); Univ. of Exeter (MA 1973; PhD 1976). Baptist Minister: St George, Bristol, 1965–69; South Street, Exeter, 1969–77; Mansfield Road, Nottingham, 1977–81; Tutor, 1981–85, Principal, 1985–94, Northern Baptist Coll., Manchester; Principal, Bristol Baptist Coll., 1994–2000. Lecturer (part-time) in Christian Ethics: Univ. of Manchester, 1983–93; Univ. of Bristol, 1996–2000. Pres., Baptist Union of GB, 1993–94. *Publications:* The Concept of the Knowledge of God, 1986; (jtly) On Being the Church, 2008. *Recreations:* walking, watching cricket and Rugby. *Address:* 1 Colville Grove, Timperley, Altrincham, Cheshire WA15 6NA. *T:* (0161) 374 0813.

HAYNES, Alison Wendy; *see* Hampton, A. W.

HAYNES, Dana Rebecca; *see* Arnold, D. R.

HAYNES, Ernest Anthony, (Tony), CIGEM; Regional Chairman, British Gas plc, East Midlands, 1983–87; *b* 8 May 1922; *s* of Joseph Ernest Haynes and Ethel Rose (*née* Toomer); *m* 1946, Sheila Theresa (*née* Blane); two *s* two *d. Educ:* King Edward VI Grammar Sch., Totnes, S Devon. Joined Devonshire Regt, 1940; RMC Sandhurst, 1941; commnd Hampshire Regt, 1941; served in N Africa, Italy and NW Europe; Captain, 1945. Govt rehabilitation course for ex-officers, 1947–48; joined Torquay and Paignton Gas Co., 1949; appts with: West Midlands and Northern Gas Boards; Gas Council; Eastern; Dep. Chm., North Eastern, 1977–78; Dep. Chm., North Thames Gas, 1979–82. Vice-Pres., Internat. Colloquium about Gas Marketing, 1983–84. Silver Medal, IGasE, for paper, Energy Conservation—a marketing opportunity. *Recreations:* golf, flyfishing.

HAYNES, John Harold, OBE 1995; Chairman, Haynes Publishing Group plc, since 1979 (Chief Executive, 1960–79); *b* 25 March 1938; *s* of Harold and Violet Haynes; *m* 1963, Annette Constance Coleman-Brown; three *s. Educ:* Sutton Valence Sch. Nat. Service, Flt Lieut, RAF, 1957. Wrote first car manual, Building an Austin 750 Special, at age of 16; founded J. Haynes & Co., 1960; Haynes Publishing Group plc, floated on London Stock Exchange, 1979. Founder, Haynes Motor Mus., Sparkford. Mem., Guild of Motoring Writers, 1974. *Publications:* numerous books on motors and motoring, incl. Haynes Owners Workshop Manuals. *Recreations:* reading, walking, motor car rallying, Haynes Motor Museum, opened 1985. *Address:* Haynes Publishing Group plc, Sparkford, near Yeovil, Som BA22 7JJ. *T:* (01963) 440635. *Club:* Royal Automobile.

HAYNES, Lawrence John; Chief Executive, White Young Green Plc, since 2007; *b* 6 Dec. 1952; *s* of Donald H. Haynes and Irene E. Haynes (*née* Langford); *m* 1978, Carol Anne Nelson; one *d*, and two step *d. Educ:* Heriot-Watt Univ. (BA Hons Business Law 1983). FIHT 1995; FCILT (FCIT 1996). RAF technician, 1969–78; Head of Contracts, British Aerospace (Space Systems), 1983–89; Legal Dir, 1989–90, Man. Dir, 1990–91, Microtel Communications; Man. Dir, British Aerospace Communications, 1991–92; Project Dir, British Aerospace, 1992–94; Chief Exec., Highways Agency, 1994–99; Partner and Hd of Ops, Eur. BPO, PricewaterhouseCoopers, 1999–2000; Chief Executive: 186k Ltd, 2000–02; Govt Services Gp, British Nuclear Fuels plc, 2003–04; British Nuclear Gp, 2004–07; Dir, BNFL plc, 2005–07. FRSA 1994. *Recreations:* sailing, ski-ing. *Address:* White Young Green Plc, Arndale Court, Headingly, Leeds LS6 2UJ.

HAYNES, Very Rev. Peter; Dean of Hereford, 1982–92, now Dean Emeritus; Vicar, St John Baptist, Hereford, 1983–92; *b* 24 April 1925; *s* of Francis Harold Stanley Haynes and Winifred Annie Haynes; *m* 1952, Ruth (*d* 2004), *d* of late Dr Charles Edward Stainthorpe, MRCS, LRCP, Brunton Park, Newcastle upon Tyne; two *s. Educ:* St Brendan's Coll., Clifton; Selwyn Coll., Cambridge (MA); Cuddesdon Theol Coll., Oxford. Staff of Barclays Bank, 1941–43; RAF, 1943–47. Deacon 1952, Priest 1953. Asst Curate, Stokesley, 1952–54; Hessle, 1954–58; Vicar, St John's Drypool, Hull, 1958–63; Bishop's Chaplain for Youth and Asst Dir of Religious Educn, Dio. Bath and Wells, 1963–70; Vicar of Glastonbury, 1970–74 (with Godney from 1972); Archdeacon of Wells, Canon Residentiary and Prebendary of Huish and Brent in Wells Cathedral, 1974–82. Proctor in Convocation, 1976–82. Mem., Dioceses Commn, 1978–86. *Recreations:* sailing, model engineering. *Address:* 5 St John Street, Hereford HR1 2NB. *T:* (01432) 342271.

HAYNES, Prof. Peter Howard, PhD; Professor of Applied Mathematics, since 2001, and Head, Department of Applied Mathematics and Theoretical Physics, since 2005, University of Cambridge; Fellow, Queens' College, Cambridge, since 1986; *b* 23 July 1958; *s* of late Bernard Archibald Haynes and of Stella Iris Haynes (*née* Whitehead); *m* 1989, Kathleen Mary Crease; two *s. Educ:* Royal Grammar Sch., Guildford; Queens' Coll., Cambridge (BA 1979, MA 1983, PhD 1984). Res. Associate, Dept of Atmospheric Scis, Univ. of Washington, 1984–85; University of Cambridge: Royal Soc. Meteorol Office Res. Fellow, 1986–90; Asst Dir of Res., 1991; Lectr, 1991–99, Reader in Atmospheric Sci., 1999–2001. Mem., Atmospheric Scis Peer Review Cttee, NERC, 1997–2001. Mem. and Chm. Steering Cttee, Prog. on Transport in Atmosphere and Ocean, ESF, 1996–2000. MAE 1998. *Publications:* contribs to Jl Fluid Mechanics, Jl Atmospheric Scis, Jl Geophysical Res., Qly Jl Royal Meteorol Soc. *Recreations:* orienteering, running, reading, family. *Address:* Department of Applied Mathematics and Theoretical Physics, Centre for Mathematical Sciences, Wilberforce Road, Cambridge CB3 0WA. *T:* (01223) 337862, *Fax:* (01223) 765900; *e-mail:* phh@damtp.cam.ac.uk.

HAYNES, Timothy Hugh Penzer; Headmaster, Tonbridge School, since 2005; *b* 2 April 1955; *s* of Barry and Felicia Haynes; *m* 1987, Charlotte Southall; two *s. Educ:* Shrewsbury Sch.; Univ. of Reading (BA Hist.); Pembroke Coll., Cambridge (PGCE). Assistant Master: Hampton Sch., 1980–82; St Paul's Sch., London, 1982–95 (Surmaster, 1992–95); Headmaster, Monmouth Sch., 1995–2005. *Address:* Tonbridge School, Tonbridge, Kent TN9 1JP. *Club:* East India.

HAYS, Irene; *see* Lucas, I.

HAYTER, 4th Baron *cr* 1927, of Chislehurst, Kent; **George William Michael Chubb;** Bt 1900; *b* 9 Oct. 1943; *s* of 3rd Baron Hayter, KCVO, CBE and of Elizabeth Anne Chubb (*née* Rumbold); *S* father, 2003; *m* 1983, Waltraud, *yr d* of J. Flackl, Sydney; one *s. Educ:* Marlborough; Nottingham Univ. (BSc). Managing Director: Chubb Malaysia, 1972–79; Chubb Australia, 1979–82; Dir, Business Develt for Physical Security, Chubb Security plc, 1982–89; in Australia, 1989–90; Man. Dir, William Chubb Associates, 1991–. Liveryman, Weavers' Co. (Mem., Ct of Assts; Upper Bailiff, 1999–2000). *Heir: s* Hon. Thomas Frederik Flackl Chubb, *b* 23 July 1986.

HAYTER, Dianne; Chair, Consumer Panel, Bar Standards Board, since 2006; Member: Insolvency Practices Council, since 2006; Board for Actuarial Standards, Financial Reporting Council, since 2006; *b* 7 Sept. 1949; *d* of late Alec Hayter and late Nancy Hayter; *m* 1994, Prof. (Anthony) David Caplin. *Educ:* Trevelyan Coll., Durham Univ. (BA Hons Sociology and Social Admin); Univ. of London (PhD 2004). Research Assistant: General and Municipal Workers Union, 1970–72; European Trade Union Confedn (ETUC), Brussels, 1973; Research Officer, Trade Union Adv. Cttee to OECD (TUAC-OECD), Paris, 1973–74; Fabian Society: Asst Gen. Sec., 1974–76; Gen. Sec., 1976–82; Mem. Exec. Cttee, 1986–95; Chm., 1992–93; Journalist, A Week in Politics, Channel Four, 1982–84; Dir, Alcohol Concern, 1984–90; Chief Exec., European PLP, 1990–96; Dir of Corporate Affairs, Wellcome Trust, 1996–99; Chief Exec., Pelican Centre, 1999–2001. Res. Student, QMW, 2001–04. Member: Royal Commn on Criminal Procedure, 1978–80; Bd, Nat. Patient Safety Agency, 2001–04; Dr Foster Ethics Cttee, 2001–; Financial Services Consumer Panel, 2001–05 (Vice Chm., 2003–05); Bd, NCC, 2001–08; Determinations Panel, Pensions Regulator, 2005–; Surveyors Ombudsman Service Bd, 2007–. Chair, Camden Alcoholics Support Assoc., 1996–2003, Vice-Chair, 2003–. Member: Exec. Cttee, London Labour Party, 1977–83; Nat. Constitution Cttee, Labour Party, 1987–98; Labour Party NEC, 1998– (Vice-Chm., 2006–07; Chm., 2007–08); Chm., Holborn & St Pancras Labour Party, 1990–93. Member: Labour Party; Soc. of Labour Lawyers; Socialist Health Assoc.; GMB; Jewish Labour Movt; Co-op. Party; Labour Arab Gp; Socialist Educn Assoc. JP Inner London, 1976–90. *Publications:* The Labour Party: crisis and prospects (Fabian Soc.), 1977; (contrib.) Labour in the Eighties, 1980; (contrib.) Prime Minister Portillo and Other Things that Never Happened, 2003; Fightback: Labour's Traditional Right in the 80s, 2005; (ed jtly) Men Who Made Labour, 2006. *Recreations:* reading, politics. *Address: e-mail:* d.hayter@btinternet.com.

HAYTER, Sir Paul (David Grenville), KCB 2007; LVO 1992; Clerk of the Parliaments, House of Lords, 2003–07; *b* 4 Nov. 1942; *s* of late Rev. Canon Michael George Hayter and Katherine Patricia Hayter (*née* Schofield); *m* 1973, Hon. Deborah Gervaise, *d* of Baron Maude of Stratford-upon-Avon, TD, PC; two *s* one *d. Educ:* Eton (King's Scholar); Christ Church, Oxford (MA). Clerk, Parlt Office, House of Lords, 1964; seconded as Private Sec. to Leader of House and Chief Whip, House of Lords, 1974–77; Clerk of Cttees, 1977; Principal Clerk of Cttees, 1985–90; Prin. Finance Officer, 1991–94; Reading Clerk, 1991–97; Principal Clerk of Public Bills, subseq. Clerk of Legislation, 1994–2003; Clerk Asst, 1997–2003. Sec., Assoc. of Lord-Lieutenants, 1977–91. Chm., Northants, CPRE, 2007–. *Recreations:* music, gardening, botanising, local history, archery, painting. *Address:* Walnut House, Charlton, Banbury OX17 3DR.

HAYTHORNE, John; *see* Parsons, Sir R. E. C. F.

HAYTHORNTHWAITE, Richard Neil; Managing Director, Star Capital Partners Ltd, since 2006; Chair, Risk and Regulation Advisory Council, since 2008; *b* 17 Dec. 1956; *s* of Christopher Scott Haythornthwaite and Angela Mary Haythornthwaite (*née* Painter); *m* 1979, Janeen Marie Dennis; one *s* one *d. Educ:* Colston's Sch., Bristol; Queen's Coll., Oxford (MA Geol.); Massachusetts Inst. of Technol. (SM Mgt). With BP, 1978–95, Pres., BP Venezuela, 1993–95; Commercial Dir, Premier Oil, 1995–97; Blue Circle Industries: Chief Exec., Heavy Bldgs Materials, Europe and Asia, 1997–99; Gp CEO, 1999–2001; Chief Exec., Invensys plc, 2001–05. Non-executive Director: Cookson Gp plc, 1999–2003; ICI plc, 2001–08; Lafarge SA, 2001–03; Mastercard Inc., 2006– (Chm., 2006–). Chair, Better Regulation Commn, 2006–08. Chairman: Centre for Creative Communities, 1996–2006; Almeida Theatre, 2001–08; South Bank Centre, 2008–. Trustee: NMSI, 2002–07; British Council, 2003–08. *Recreations:* ski-ing, travel, visual arts. *Club:* Royal Automobile.

HAYTON, Hon. David John; Justice of the Caribbean Court of Justice, since 2005; *b* 13 July 1944; *s* of Arthur Hayton and Beatrice (*née* Thompson); *m* 1979, Linda Patricia Rae; one *s. Educ:* Newcastle Royal GS; Univ. of Newcastle upon Tyne (LLB 1st Cl. Hons 1966; LLD 1980); MA 1973, LLD 2006, Cantab. Called to the Bar, Inner Temple, 1968, and Lincoln's Inn *aeg* (Bencher, 2004). Lectr, Sheffield Univ., 1966–69; private practice, Lincoln's Inn, 1970–2005; Lectr, QMC, London, 1970–73; Lectr, Univ. of Cambridge and Fellow of Jesus Coll., 1973–87; Prof. of Law, 1987–2005, Dean, Law Faculty, 1988–90, KCL; FKC 2005; Chm., London Univ. Bd of Studies in Law, 1992–95. Vis. Lectr, Inns of Court Sch. of Law, 1971–84, Hon. Reader, 1984–96. An Asst Recorder, 1984–92; a Recorder, 1992–2000; Actg Justice, Supreme Ct, Bahamas, 2000, 2001. Dep. Chm., Trust Law Cttee, 1994–2005; Mem., Law Panel, 2001 RAE, HEFCE. Chm., Council, Pension Trustees Forum, 1992–95. Hon. Sec., SPTL, 1996–2001. Head of UK Delegns to The Hague Confs on Private Internat. Law, 1984, 1988. *Publications:* Registered Land, 1973, 3rd edn 1981; Law of Trusts, 1989, 4th edn 2003; Hayton & Marshall: Cases & Commentary on Trusts, 6th edn 1975 to 12th edn 2005; Underhill & Hayton: Law of Trusts and Trustees, 13th edn 1979 to 17th edn 2007; Hayton Report on Financial Services and Trust Law, 1990; (ed) European Succession Laws, 1991, 3rd edn 2002; (ed) Principles of European Trust Law, 1999; (ed) Modern International Developments in Trust Law, 1999; (ed) Extending the Boundaries of Trust and Similar Ring-fenced Funds, 2002; contribs to chapters in books on trusts, tax and estate planning; articles in learned jls. *Recreations:* health club, watching Rugby and cricket, reading novels, wine tasting. *Address:* Caribbean Court of Justice, 134 Henry Street, Port of Spain, Trinidad, West Indies. *T:* 6259118. *Clubs:* Athenæum, Royal Commonwealth Society, MCC.

HAYTON, Philip John; Newscaster, BBC TV News, 1985–2005; *b* 2 Nov. 1947; *s* of Austin and Jennie Hayton; *m* 1972, Thelma Gant; one *s* one *d. Educ:* at various schs in USA and UK. Pirate radio disc jockey, 1967; joined BBC, 1968; reporter: Radio Leeds, 1968–71; and newscaster, TV Leeds, 1971–74; TV News: reporter, 1974–80; Foreign Corresp., 1980–83; reporter and newscaster, 1983–2005, Six O'clock and Nine O'clock News, World News and News 24. *Recreations:* theatre, walking, investment, foreign travel. *Address: e-mail:* hayton@talk21.com.

HAYWARD, Alexander; Keeper of Science and Technology, National Museums of Scotland, since 2005; *b* 26 Nov. 1960; *s* of Peter and Nikki Hayward; *m* 1990, Rosy Nicholson; one *s* one *d. Educ:* Univ. of Sydney (BA 1982, MA 1986); Univ. of Leicester (MSc 1989). LTCL 1982; AMA 1993. Curator, Science Mus., London, 1990–98; Suffolk County Council: Mus Officer, 1998–2001; Hd of Heritage, 2001–05. Expert Advr (pt time), Heritage Lottery Fund, 2000–04; Scottish Rep., UK Science, Technology and Industry Subject Specialist Network, 2005–; Founding Chm., Scottish Technology and Industry Collections Knowledge Network, 2006–; Member: BT Connected Earth Consulting Gp, 2006–07; Cttee, Scottish Museums Council Collections Recognition Scheme, 2006–. FRSSA 2007. *Publications:* articles on engrg history and conservation in various learned jls. *Recreations:* enjoying the history of technology, flute, pipe organ, music of G. F. Handel, vintage motor cars and steam traction engines. *Address:* Department of Science and Technology, National Museums of Scotland, Chambers Street, Edinburgh EH1 1JF. *T:* (0131) 247 4456, *Fax:* (0131) 247 4312; *e-mail:* a.hayward@nms.ac.uk.

HAYWARD, Anthony Bryan, PhD; Group Chief Executive, BP plc, since 2007; *b* Slough, 21 May 1957; *s* of Bryan and Mary Hayward; *m* 1985, Maureen Fulton; one *s* one *d*. *Educ:* Univ. of Birmingham (BSc); Univ. of Edinburgh (PhD Geol 1982). Joined BP, 1982; BP Exploration, 1982–99: various tech. and commercial posts, London, Aberdeen, France, China and Glasgow; Exploration Manager, Colombia; Pres., Venezuela, 1995–97; Dir, 1997–99; Gp Vice Pres. and Mem. Upstream Exec. Cttee, 1999–2000; Gp Treas., 2000–02; Exec. Vice Pres. and Chief Exec., Exploration and Prodn, 2003–07; Exec. Dir, 2003–07. Non-executive Director: (and Sen. Indep. Dir), Corus Gp; Tata Steel. Mem., Business Council for Britain, 2007–. Mem. Adv. Bd, Sch. of Econs and Mgt, Tsinghua Univ.; Chm., GLOBE CEO Forum for Climate Change. CCMI. *Recreations:* sailing, ski-ing, triathlons, watching sport. *Address:* BP plc, 1 St James's Square, SW1Y 4PD. *T:* (020) 7496 4000, *Fax:* (020) 7496 4626; *e-mail:* liz.gordon@bp.com.

HAYWARD, Sir Anthony (William Byrd), Kt 1978; *b* 29 June 1927; *s* of Eric and Barbara Hayward; *m* 1955, Jenifer Susan McCay; two *s* two *d*. *Educ:* Stowe Sch., Buckingham; Christ Church, Oxford. Served RNVR, 1945–48. With family business in Calcutta, 1948–57; Shaw Wallace & Co. Ltd, India, 1957–78; Man. Dir, Guthrie Berhad, Singapore, 1978–81; Pres. and Chief Exec. Officer, Private Investment Co. for Asia (PICA) SA, 1982–84. Pres., Associated Chambers of Commerce and Industry of India, 1977–78. *Recreations:* golf, photography, reading. *Address:* Manwood House, Sandwich, Kent CT13 9HX. *T:* (01304) 612244. *Clubs:* Oriental; Royal St George's Golf.
See also Ven. J. D. R. Hayward.

HAYWARD, Ven. Derek; *see* Hayward, Ven. J. D. R.

HAYWARD, Gerald William; HM Diplomatic Service, retired; *b* 18 Nov. 1927; *s* of late Frederick William Hayward and Annie Louise (*née* Glasscock); *m* 1956, Patricia Rhonwen (*née* Foster Hall); one *s* three *d*. *Educ:* Tottenham Grammar School; London and Hong Kong Univs. HM Forces, 1946–57. Joined HM Foreign (subseq. HM Diplomatic) Service, 1957; served Bangkok, Hong Kong, Copenhagen, Kuala Lumpur; FCO, 1980–82; (part-time), Cabinet Office, 1984–92. *Address:* Fosters, 9 Ashley Road, Sevenoaks, Kent TN13 3AW. *T:* (01732) 451227.

HAYWARD, Sir Jack (Arnold), Kt 1986; OBE 1968; Chairman, Grand Bahama Development Co. Ltd and Freeport Commercial and Industrial Ltd, since 1976; *b* Wolverhampton, 14 June 1923; *s* of late Sir Charles Hayward, CBE and Hilda, *d* of John and Alexandra Arnold; *m* 1948, Jean Mary Forder; two *s* one *d*. *Educ:* Northaw Prep Sch.; Stowe Sch., Buckingham. Volunteered RAF, 1941; flying training in Clewiston, Florida, USA; active service as officer pilot in SE Asia Comd, demobilised as Flt-Lt, 1946. Joined Rotary Hoes Ltd, 1947; served S Africa branch until 1950. Founded USA operations Firth Cleveland Gp of Companies, 1951; joined Grand Bahama Port Authority Ltd, Freeport, Grand Bahama Island, 1956. President: Lundy Field Soc.; Wolverhampton Wanderers FC; Vice-Pres., SS Great Britain project; Hon. Life Vice-Pres., Maritime Trust, 1971. FRGS 1989. Freeman, City of Wolverhampton, 2003; Hon. Freeman, City of Bristol, 2003. Hon. LLD Exeter, 1971; Hon. DBA Wolverhampton, 1994. Paul Harris Fellow (Rotary), 1983; William Booth Award, Salvation Army, 1987. *Recreations:* promoting British endeavours, mainly in sport; watching cricket; amateur dramatics; preserving the British landscape, keeping all things bright, beautiful and British. *Address:* Seashell Lane (PO Box F-40099), Freeport, Grand Bahama Island, Bahamas. *T:* (242) 3525165. *Clubs:* MCC (Hon. Life Mem.), Pratt's, Royal Air Force, Royal Automobile (Sen. One Hundred); Surrey CC (Hon. Life Mem.).

HAYWARD, Prof. Jack Ernest Shalom, FBA 1990; Research Professor of Politics, University of Hull, since 1999; *b* 18 Aug. 1931; *s* of Menahem and Stella Hayward; *m* 1965, Margaret Joy Glenn; one *s* one *d*. *Educ:* LSE (BSc Econ 1952; PhD 1958). Asst Lectr and Lectr, Univ. of Sheffield, 1959–63; Lectr and Sen. Lectr, Univ. of Keele, 1963–73; Prof. of Politics, Univ. of Hull, 1973–92; Prof. of Politics and Dir, European Studies Inst. and Centre for European Politics, Econs and Soc., Univ. of Oxford, and Fellow, St Antony's Coll., Oxford, 1993–98, now Prof. and Fellow Emeritus. Sen. Res. Fellow, Nuffield Coll., Oxford, 1968–69; Vis. Prof., Univ. of Paris III, 1979–80; Elie Halévy Vis. Prof., Inst. d'Etudes Politiques, Paris, 1990–91. Political Studies Association: Chm., 1975–77; Pres., 1979–81; Vice-Pres., 1981–. Editor, Political Studies, 1987–93. Chevalier de l'Ordre National du Mérite (France), 1980; Chevalier de la Légion d'Honneur (France), 1996. *Publications:* Private Interests and Public Policy, 1966; The One and Indivisible French Republic, 1973; The State and the Market Economy, 1986; After the French Revolution, 1991; De Gaulle to Mitterrand, 1993; Industrial Enterprise and European Integration, 1995; Governing the New Europe, 1995; The Crisis of Representation in Europe, 1995; Elitism, Populism and European Politics, 1996; The British Study of Politics in the Twentieth Century, 1999; Governing From the Centre, 2002; Governing Europe, 2003; Etre gouverné; Fragmented France: two centuries of disputed identity, 2007; Leaderless Europe, 2008. *Recreations:* music, reading, walking. *Address:* Hurstwood, 17C Church Lane, Kirk Ella, Hull HU10 7TA. *Club:* Royal Commonwealth Society.

HAYWARD, Ven. (John) Derek (Risdon), OBE 2000; Vicar of Isleworth, 1964–94; General Secretary, Diocese of London, 1975–93; Archdeacon of Middlesex, 1974–75, now Archdeacon Emeritus; *b* 13 Dec. 1923; *s* of late Eric Hayward and of Barbara Olive Hayward; *m* 1965, Teresa Jane Kaye; one *d* (one *s* decd). *Educ:* Stowe; Trinity Coll., Cambridge (BA 1956, MA 1964). Served War of 1939–45, Lieut 27th Lancers, Middle East and Italy, 1943–45 (twice wounded). Man. Dir, Hayward Waldie & Co., Calcutta (and associated cos), 1946–53. Trinity Coll., Cambridge, 1953–56, Westcott House, Cambridge, 1956–57. Asst Curate, St Mary's Bramall Lane, Sheffield, 1957–58; Vicar, St Silas, Sheffield, 1959–63. Mem., General Synod, 1975–90. Chm., SCM Press, 1992–98 (Dir, 1985–99); Trustee: Church Urban Fund, 1987–94; Bath Preservation Trust, 1996–2007; Herschel Mus., Bath, 1997– (Chm., 1997–2007). Chm. Council, St Luke's Hosp. for the Clergy, 1991–2001. Bronze Star (US) 1945. *Recreations:* walking, playing with my computer. *Address:* 29a Great Pulteney Street, Bath BA2 4BU. *T:* (01225) 336305, *Fax:* (01225) 421862; *e-mail:* derekhayward@tantraweb.co.uk.
See also Sir Anthony Hayward.

HAYWARD, Richard Michael; His Honour Judge Hayward; a Circuit Judge, since 1996; *b* 12 July 1946; *s* of George Michael Hayward and Esmé Mary Florence Hayward (*née* Howard); *m* 1969, Laura Louise Buchan; two *s* one *d*. *Educ:* Highgate Sch.; Inns of Court Sch. of Law. Called to the Bar, Middle Temple, 1969; in practice at the Bar, 1970–96; Asst Recorder, 1990–94; Recorder, 1994–96. *Recreations:* golf, painting, horses, gardening. *Club:* Rye Golf.

HAYWARD, Robert Antony, OBE 1991; Chief Executive, British Beer and Pub Association (formerly Brewers and Licensed Retailers), since 1999; *b* 11 March 1949; *s* of late Ralph and of Mary Hayward. *Educ:* Abingdon Sch.; Maidenhead Grammar Sch.; University Coll. of Rhodesia; BSc Econ Hons London (external). Personnel Officer, Esso Petroleum, 1971–75; Personnel Manager: Coca Cola Bottlers (S & N) Ltd, 1975–79; GEC Large Machines, 1979–82; Dir Gen., British Soft Drinks Assoc., 1993–99. MP (C) Kingswood, 1983–92; contested (C): Kingswood, 1992, Christchurch, July 1993. PPS t Minister for Corporate and Consumer Affairs, 1985–87, to Minister for Industr 1986–87, to Sec. of State for Transport, 1987–89. Mem., Commons Select Cttee c Energy, 1983–85. Chm., Trade Assoc. Forum, CBI, 2007. Dir, Stonewall Gp, 1997–200 Pres., King's Cross Steelers RFC, 1999–2003. *Recreations:* Rugby, psephology. *Addre* (office) Market Towers, 1 Nine Elms Lane, SW8 5NQ. *T:* (020) 7627 9162, *Fax:* (02 7627 9179; *e-mail:* rhayward@beerandpub.com; 11 Grosvenor Park, SE5 0NQ.

HAYWARD SMITH, Rodger; QC 1988; **His Honour Judge Hayward Smith;** Circuit Judge, since 2002; *b* 25 Feb. 1943; *s* of late Frederick Ernest Smith and Heath Hayward (*née* Rodgers); *m* 1975, Gillian Sheila (*née* Johnson); one *s* one *d*. *Edu* Brentwood Sch.; St Edmund Hall, Oxford (MA). Called to the Bar, Gray's Inn, 1967; Recorder, 1986–2002 (Asst Recorder, 1981–86); a Deputy High Ct Judge, 1990–2002. Legal Assessor, GMC, 2000–02. *Publications:* (ed jtly and contrib.) Jackson's Matrimoni Finance and Taxation, 5th edn 1992 to 7th edn 2002; various articles on family lav *Address:* The Crown Court, New Street, Chelmsford, CM1 1EL.

HAYWOOD, Sir Harold, KCVO 1988; OBE 1974; DL; Chairman, BBC/ITC Centr Appeals Advisory Committee, 1989–93; Chairman, YMCA, 1989–93; *b* 30 Sept. 1923; of Harold Haywood and Lilian (*née* Barrett); *m* 1944, Amy (*née* Richardson); three *s*. *Edu* Guild Central Sch., Burton-on-Trent; Westhill Coll. of Educn, Selly Oak, Birmingha (Certificate of Educn, 1948). Organiser, St John's Clubland, Sheffield, 1948–51; Tuto Westhill Coll. of Educn, 1951–53; Regional Organiser, Methodist Youth Dept, 1954–5 Dir of Education and Trng, 1955–66, Dir of Youth Work, 1966–74, NAYC; Gen. Sec Educnl Interchange Council, 1974–77; Dir, Royal Jubilee and Prince's Trusts, 1977–8 Chm., Assoc. of Charitable Foundns, 1989–92; Trustee, Charities Aid Foundn, 1988–9 (Chm., Grants Council, 1989–97); Patron, Kids Internat. UK, 1994–; Vice-Presider Commonwealth Youth Exchange Council, 1988–; Derbys Community Foundn, 1998– Patron, Multi-Faith Campaign, Univ. of Derby, 2001– (Chm., 1999–2001); Pres., RBI Oakwood, Derbys, 2000–. DL Greater London, 1983. FRSA. *Recreations:* the garde books. *Clubs:* Athenæum, Civil Service.

HAYWOOD, Nigel Robert, CVO 2006; HM Diplomatic Service; Ambassador t Estonia, 2003–07; *b* 17 March 1955; *yr s* of late Leslie Haywood and of Peggy Haywoo (*née* Webb, now Sewell); *m* 1979, Mary Louise Smith; three *s*. *Educ:* Truro Sch.; Nev Coll., Oxford (MA, MPhil). MCIL (MIL 1988). Lt, RAEC, 1977–80. Joined HN Diplomatic Service, 1983: Second, later First, Sec., Budapest, 1985–89; FCO, 1989–9 Dep. Consul-Gen., Johannesburg, 1992–96; Counsellor and Dep. Head, UK Delegn t OSCE, Vienna, 1996–2000; Asst Dir (Personnel), FCO, 2000–03. Member: Philologica Soc., 1981–; Golden Scale Club, 1982– (Hon. Pres., 2002–); Council, Angler Conservation (formerly Co-operative) Assoc., 1990–96. Bard of Cornish Gorsedd, 197 *Publications:* (contrib.) The One That Got Away, 1991; occasional articles and reviews i angling press. *Recreations:* fishing (especially saltwater fly fishing), marathon runnin *Address:* c/o Foreign and Commonwealth Office, King Charles Street, SW1A 2AH. *Club* Oxford and Cambridge; Falmouth Sports.

HAZAREESINGH, Dr Sudhir Kumar, FBA 2006; Lecturer in Politics, University c Oxford, since 1990; Fellow and Tutor in Politics, Balliol College, Oxford, since 1990; 18 Oct. 1961; *s* of late Kissoonsingh Hazareesingh and of Thara Hazareesingh; partner, D Karma Nabulsi, Fellow of St Edmund Hall, Oxford. *Educ:* Balliol Coll., Oxford (BA 1s Cl. Hons Politics and Phil. 1984; MPhil Internat. Relns 1986); DPhil Politics Oxon 199 University of Oxford: Open Prize Res. Fellow, Nuffield Coll., 1987–90; Lectr in Politics Exeter Coll., 1989–90; Sen. Tutor, Balliol Coll., 1997–2001. Prof. Invité, Inst. des Etude Politiques, Paris, 2006; British Acad. Res. Reader, 2001–03; Acad. Visitor, Dept of Pc Sci., Princeton Univ., 2002; Dir d'Etudes Invité, Ecole des Hautes Etudes en Scis Sociales Paris, 2003; Vis. Fellow, Remarque Inst., NY Univ., 2004. Maître de Conférences, Ecol Pratique des Hautes Etudes, Paris (Section 4), 2000. Chevalier, Ordre des Palme Académiques (France), 2003; Grand Prix du Mémorial and Medal of Honour, Ajacci (France), 2006. *Publications:* Intellectuals and the French Communist Party: disillusion an decline, 1991; Political Traditions in Modern France, 1994; From Subject to Citizen: th Second Empire and the emergence of modern French democracy, 1998; (with V. Wright Francs-Maçons sous le Second Empire: le Grand Orient de France à la veille de l Troisième République, 2001; Intellectual Founders of the Republic: five studies i Nineteenth-Century French political thought, 2001; (ed and contrib.) The Jacobin Legac in Modern France, 2002; The Saint-Napoleon: celebrations of sovereignty in 19th centur France, 2004; The Legend of Napoleon, 2004 (trans. French 2006). *Recreations* swimming, cinema, reading, listening to music. *Address:* Balliol College, Oxford OX1 3B *T:* (01865) 277758, *Fax:* (01865) 277803; *e-mail:* sudhir.hazareesingh@balliol.ox.ac.uk.

HAZEL, George McLean, OBE 2005; PhD; CEng; Director, MRC McLean Hazel Lt (formerly McLean Hazel Ltd), since 2000; *b* 27 Jan. 1949; *s* of George McLean Hazel an Agnes Steven Hazel (*née* Willins); *m* 1974, Fiona Isabella Gault; one *s* two *d*. *Educ:* Heriot-Watt Univ. (BSc Civil Engrg; MSc Transportation); Cranfield Inst. of Technol. (PhD 1986). CEng 1975, MICE 1975. Transportation engr, Lothian Regl Council an Edinburgh CC, 1971–79; Prof. and Hd of Civil Engrg, Napier Univ., 1979–89; Dir Oscar Faber Ltd (transport consultancy), 1989–93; Dir of Transportation, 1993–96, o City Develt, 1996–2000, Edinburgh CC. Vis. Prof., Robert Gordon Univ., 2000–. Pres. Instn of Highways and Transportation, 2003–04. FIHT 1976; FILT 1978. Member Mercedes-Benz Owners Club; Triumph TR6 Owners Club. *Publication:* (with Roge Parry) Making Cities Work, 2004. *Recreations:* ski-ing, gardening, restoring vintage cars *Address:* MRC McLean Hazel Ltd, 3 Hill Street, Edinburgh EH2 3JP. *T:* (office) (0131) 226 1045, (home) (0131) 444 2492, *Fax:* (office) (0131) 225 9087; *e-mail:* george.hazel@ mrcmh.com.

HAZELL, Bertie, CBE 1962 (MBE 1946); Chairman, Special Programme Board, North Yorkshire, Manpower Services Commission, 1978–83; *b* 18 April 1907; *s* of John and Elizabeth Hazell; *m* 1936, Dora A. Barham; one *d*. *Educ:* various elementary schs in Norfolk. Agricultural worker, 1921; apptd Sec. and Agent to E Norfolk Divisional Labour Party, Sept. 1933; District Organiser, Nat. Union of Agricl Workers, 1937–64, Pres., 1966–78; Mem. W Riding of Yorks, War Agricultural Executive Cttee, 1939 (Chm. several of its Cttees, throughout war period). Contested (Lab) Barkston Ash Parliamentary Division, 1945 and 1950 Gen. Elections; MP (Lab) North Norfolk, 1964–70. Chairman: E and W Ridings Regional Bd for Industry, 1954–64; N Yorks AHA, 1974–82; York DHA, 1981–84; Vice-Chm., Agricultural, Horticultural and Forestry Trng Bd, 1972–74; Member: E Riding Co. Agricultural Exec. Cttee, 1946–64; Agricultural Wages Board, 1946–78; Leeds Regional Hosp. Board, 1948–74 (Chm. Works and Buildings Cttee); Potato Marketing Bd, 1970–79. Magistrate, City of York, 1950–; Chairman: York and District Employment Cttee, 1963–74; N Yorks District Manpower Cttee, 1975–80; Vice-Chm., Leeds Regional Hosp. Bd, 1967–74. Mem. Council, Univ. of E Anglia. MUniv York, 1984. *Recreation:* gardening.

HAZELL, Ven. Frederick Roy; Archdeacon of Croydon, 1978–93; *b* 12 Aug. 1930; *s* of John Murdoch and Ruth Hazell; *m* 1st, 1956, Gwendoline Edna Armstrong (*née* Vare) (*d*

1993), *widow* of Major J. W. D. Armstrong; (one step *s* decd); 2nd, 1994, Norma Irene Palmer (*née* Gardner). *Educ:* Hutton Grammar School, near Preston; Fitzwilliam Coll., Cambridge (MA); Cuddesdon Coll., Oxford. HM Forces, 1948–50. Asst Master, Kingham Hill School, 1953–54; Asst Curate, Ilkeston Parish Church, 1956–59; Priest-in-charge, All Saints', Marlpool, 1959–62; First Vicar of Marlpool, 1962–63; Chaplain, Univ. of the West Indies, 1963–66; Asst Priest, St Martin-in-the-Fields, 1966–68; Vicar of Holy Saviour, Croydon, 1968–84; Rural Dean of Croydon, 1972–78; Priest-in-charge: Chard Furnham with Chaffcombe, Knowle St Giles and Cricket Malherbie, 1995–99; St Bartholomew, Tardebigge, 2000–04; Advr in Pastoral Care and Counselling, Dio. of Bath and Wells, 1994–99. Hon. Canon of Canterbury, 1973–84. *Recreations:* music, history, numismatics. *Address:* 1 Chapelside, Clapton Row, Bourton on the Water GL54 2DN. *T:* (01451) 821140.

HAZELL, Malcolm John, CVO 1988; Official Secretary to the Governor-General of Australia, since 2003; Secretary, Order of Australia, since 2003; *b* 17 Dec. 1948; *s* of Neville John and Joan Nell Hazell; *m* 1976, Rhondda Leonie Scells; two *s*. *Educ:* C of E Grammar Sch., Brisbane; Univ. of Qld (BA Hons); Templeton Coll., Oxford. Admin. Trainee, Public Service Bd, 1972; Exec. Officer to Comr, Nat. Capital Develt Commn, 1973–74; Private Sec., then Sen. Private Sec., to Prime Minister, Aust., 1975–79, 1980–81; Sen. Private Sec. to Minister for Aviation and Minister Assisting Prime Minister, 1982–83; various sen. mgt positions, Dept of Prime Minister and Cabinet, Canberra, 1982–85; Commonwealth Dir, Bicentennial Royal Visits to Aust., 1986–89; Asst Sec. and Hd, Internat. Div., Office of Security and Intelligence Coordination, 1989–94; Hd, S Pacific Forum Task Force, 1994; Asst Sec. and Hd, Cabinet Secretariat, Dept of Prime Minister and Cabinet, 1994–98; Sen. Advr to Prime Minister, 1998–2003. Secretary: Official Estabts Trust, 1985–87, 1995–96; Australian Bravery Decorations Council, 2003–. Hon. Sec., Royal Australian Inst. of Public Admin, 1973–75. Mem., Australian Inst. Company Dirs, 2007–. Vice Pres., Canberra Grammar Sch. Foundn, 1993–96; Dir, Canberra Grammar Sch., 1994–2006 (Vice Chm., 2005–06); Foundn Chm., Anglican Dio. Canberra and Goulburn, Diocesan Schs Council, 1998–2002. Hon. Lay Canon, St Saviour's Cathedral, Goulburn, 2002. CStJ 2004. *Recreations:* music, cricket, family. *Address:* Government House, Canberra, ACT 2600, Australia. *T:* (2) 62833533, *Fax:* (2) 62813760; *e-mail:* malcolm.hazell@gg.gov.au. *Clubs:* Commonwealth, University House (Canberra).

HAZELL, Peter Frank; Chairman, Argent Group plc, since 2001; *b* 4 Aug. 1948; *s* of Frank Henry Hazell and Kathleen Hazell; *m* 1972, Maureen Pamela Church; one *s* one *d*. *Educ:* Hertford Coll., Oxford (MA PPE 1969; BPhil Econs 1971). Partner: Deloitte Haskins & Sells, 1980–90; Coopers & Lybrand, 1990–98; UK Managing Partner, PricewaterhouseCoopers, 1998–2000. Non-executive Director: UK Coal, 2003–; Smith & Williamson, 2004–; Brit Insce, 2004–. Member: Competition Commn, 2002–; NERC, 2004–. *Recreations:* cricket, Rugby, opera, ballet, theatre, hill walking. *Address:* Argent Group plc, 5 Albany Courtyard, Piccadilly, W1V 9RB. *Club:* MCC.

HAZELL, Prof. Robert John Davidge, CBE 2006; Founder and Director, Constitution Unit, since 1995, and Professor of Government and the Constitution, since 1998, University College London; *b* 30 April 1948; *s* of Peter Hazell and Elizabeth Complin Fowler; *m* 1981, Alison Sophia Mordaunt Richards; two *s*. *Educ:* Eton (King's Schol.); Wadham Coll., Oxford (Minor Schol.; MA Hons). Called to the Bar, Middle Temple, 1973; Barrister, 1973–75; Lay Magistrate, Highbury Corner, 1978–96. Home Office, 1975–89, working in Immigration Dept, Policy Planning Unit, Gaming Bd, Race Relns, Broadcasting, Police and Prison Depts; CS travelling fellowship to investigate freedom of inf. in Australia, Canada, NZ, 1986–87; Dir, Nuffield Foundn, 1989–95. Vice-Chm., Assoc. of Charitable Foundns, 1992–95. Mem. Council, Hansard Soc., 1997– (Vice-Chm., Commn on Scrutiny Role of Parlt, 1999–2001). Vice-Chm., Ind. Commn on Proportional Repn, 2002–Dec. 2003. Trustee, Citizenship Foundn. 1991–2000; Mem. Exec., Justice, 1995–. FRSA 1991. Haldane Medal, RIPA, 1978. *Publications:* Conspiracy and Civil Liberties, 1974; (ed) The Bar on Trial, 1978; An Assembly for Wales, 1996; (ed) Constitutional Futures, 1999; (ed) The State and the Nations, 2000; (ed) The State of the Nations 2003, 2003; (ed) Devolution, Law Making and the Constitution, 2005; (ed) The English Question, 2006; (ed) Constitutional Futures 2, 2008; articles in legal and govt jls. *Recreations:* bird-watching, badgers, opera, canoeing. *Address:* 94 Constantine Road, NW3 2LS. *T:* (020) 7267 4881; (office) The Constitution Unit, School of Public Policy, University College London, 29/30 Tavistock Square, WC1H 9QU. *T:* (020) 7679 4971, *Fax:* (020) 7679 4978; *e-mail:* r.hazell@ucl.ac.uk.

HAZLERIGG, family name of **Baron Hazlerigg**.

HAZLERIGG, 3rd Baron *cr* 1945, of Noseley; **Arthur Grey Hazlerigg;** Bt 1622; *b* 5 May 1951; *s* of 2nd Baron Hazlerigg, MC, TD and Patricia, *d* of John Pullar; *S* father, 2002; *m* 1999, Shan (*née* McIndoe); one *s* three *d* (incl. twin *d*) by previous marriage. *Heir:* *s* Hon. Arthur William Grey Hazlerigg, *b* 13 May 1987. *Address:* Noseley Hall, Billesdon, Leics LE7 9EH. *T:* (0116) 259 6487, *Fax:* (0116) 259 6989; *e-mail:* arthur@noseley.demon.co.uk. *Clubs:* MCC; Leicester Tigers Rugby Football.

HAZLEWOOD, Prof. Arthur Dennis; Research Professor in Commonwealth Studies, Oxford University, 1986–88, now Emeritus; Professorial Fellow, Pembroke College, Oxford, 1979–88, now Emeritus; *b* 24 April 1921; *s* of Harry Arthur Sinclair Hazlewood and Miriam Esther Maltby; *m* 1954, Tamara Oszpicyn (*d* 1998); one *d*. *Educ:* Finchley County Sch.; LSE (BSc Econ 1948); The Queen's Coll., Oxford (BPhil 1950; MA 1954). Post Office engineer, 1938–48 (RAF radar stations, 1940–44); Oxford University, 1950–88: Tutor to Colonial Service courses, 1950–56; research staff, Inst. of Economics and Statistics, 1956–79; Pembroke College: tutorial fellow, 1961–79; Domestic Bursar, 1970–79; Vicegerent, 1978–79; Warden, Queen Elizabeth House, Dir, Inst. of Commonwealth Studies, 1979–86. Adviser, Nyasaland Govt on Central African Fedn, 1962; Mem., UK Economic Mission to Malawi, 1965; Dir, Common Market Secretariat, President's Office, Kenya, 1965–66; Dir, Trade and Finance Div., Commonwealth Secretariat and Special Adviser, Commonwealth Fund for Technical Co-operation, 1975–76. *Publications:* (jtly) Nyasaland: the economics of federation, 1960; The Economy of Africa, 1961; (jtly) An Econometric Model of the UK, 1961; Rail and Road in East Africa, 1964; (ed) African Integration and Disintegration, 1967; Economic Integration: the East African experience, 1975; (jtly) Aid and Inequality in Kenya, 1976; The Economy of Kenya, 1979; (jtly) Irrigation Economics in Poor Countries, 1982; Education, Work, and Pay in East Africa, 1989; articles in jls and symposia. *Address:* 14 Fyfield Road, Oxford OX2 6QE. *T:* (01865) 559119.

HAZLEWOOD, Charles Matthew Egerton; conductor; *b* 14 Nov. 1966; *s* of Rev. Canon Ian Hazlewood and Helen Hazlewood; *m* 1993, Henrietta Lang; three *s* one *d*. *Educ:* Christ's Hosp.; Keble Coll., Oxford (Organ Schol.; BA Hons). ARCO 1985. Founder and Music Dir, Excellent Device! (formerly Eos), 1991–; Music Director: Broomhill Opera, 1993–2001; Wiltons Music Hall, 1999–2003; and Co-founder, Dimpho di Kopane, 2000– (composer and Music Dir, The Mysteries, Beggar's Opera, The Snow Queen); and Founder, Harmonieband, 2002–; Principal Guest Conductor, BBC Concert Orch., 2005–. Début at Carnegie Hall, 2003, BBC Proms, 2006. Author, conductor and presenter of television films: Vivaldi Unmasked, 2001; The Genius of Mozart, 2003; Beethoven, 2005; Tchaikovsky, 2007; How Pop Songs Work, 2008; The History of British Music, 2009; music dir and conductor of film, U-Carmen E-Khayelitsha, 2005 (Golden Bear for best film, Berlin Film Fest.); conductor and presenter, BBC radio programmes: Discovering Music; The Charles Hazlewood Show. First Prize, Conducting Comp., EBU, 1995; Sony Award, 2005, 2006. *Recreations:* cooking, film. *Address:* c/o Theia Nankivell, KBJ Management, 7 Soho Street, W1D 3DQ. *T:* (020) 7434 6767; *e-mail:* theia@kbjmgt.co.uk; *web:* www.charleshazlewood.com.

HEAD, family name of **Viscount Head**.

HEAD, 2nd Viscount *cr* 1960, of Throope; **Richard Antony Head;** *b* 27 Feb. 1937; *s* of 1st Viscount Head, GCMG, CBE, MC, PC, and Dorothea, Viscountess Head (*d* 1987), *d* of 9th Earl of Shaftesbury, KP, GCVO, CBE, PC; *S* father, 1983; *m* 1974, Alicia Brigid, *er d* of Julian Salmond; two *s* one *d*. *Educ:* Eton; RMA Sandhurst. The Life Guards, 1957–66 (Captain), retd. Trainer of racehorses, 1968–83. *Recreations:* shooting, golf. *Heir:* *s* Hon. Henry Julian Head, *b* 30 March 1980. *Address:* Throope Manor, Bishopstone, Salisbury, Wilts SP5 4BA. *T:* (01722) 718318. *Club:* White's.

HEAD, His Honour Adrian Herbert; a Circuit Judge, 1972–96; *b* 4 Dec. 1923; *s* of late Judge Head and late Mrs Geraldine Head (*née* Pipon); *m* 1947, Ann Pamela, *d* of late John Stanning and late Mrs A. C. Lewin, of Leyland and Njoro, Kenya; three *s*. *Educ:* RNC Dartmouth (invalided, polio); privately; Magdalen Coll., Oxford (BA; MA). Arden Scholar, Gray's Inn, 1947. Called to Bar, Gray's Inn, 1947 (subseq. *ad eundem* Inner Temple). Chm., Agricultural Land Tribunals (SE Region), 1971; Dep. Chm., Middlesex QS, 1971. Chm., Norfolk Lavender Ltd, and Chilvers & Son Ltd, 1958–71 (Dir, 1953–71). Mem., Law Adv. Bd, UEA, 1979–98. Tredegar Memorial Lectr, RSL, 1948. Licensed Reader, C of E, 1961. Co-founder and subseq. Sen. Trustee, Norfolk Family Conciliation Service, 1983–96; Pres., W Norfolk and Fenland, Marriage Guidance Council, now Relate, 1984–95. Hon. DCL UEA, 1987. *Publications:* (contrib.) Oxford Poetry 1942–1943, 1943; The Seven Words and The Civilian, 1946; contrib. Essays by Divers Hands, 1953; Safety Afloat (trans. from Dutch of W. Zantvoort), 1965; Consumer Credit Act Supplement to McCleary's County Court Precedents, 1979; Poems in Praise, 1982, 2nd edn 1987; Freundschaft und Andenken (Dichtung), 1989; (devised and general ed., 1985–87, consulting ed., 1987–, and contrib.) Butterworths County Court Precedents and Pleadings, 1985, later Butterworths Civil Court Precedents. *Recreations:* painting, writing, trees. *Address:* Overy Staithe, King's Lynn, Norfolk PE31 8TG. *T:* (01328) 738312; 5 Raymond Buildings, Gray's Inn, WC1R 5BP. *T:* (020) 7405 7146. *Clubs:* Jersey Soc.; Norfolk (Norwich) (Pres., 1995–96); Royal Naval Sailing Association, Cruising Association.

HEAD, Alan Kenneth, AO 1992; PhD, DSc; FAA 1971; FRS 1988; Hon. Research Fellow, Commonwealth Scientific and Industrial Research Organization, Australia, since 1990 (Chief Research Scientist, 1969–90); *b* 10 Aug. 1925; *s* of Rowland Henry John Head and Elsie May (*née* Burrell); *m* 1951, Gwenneth Nancy Barlow. *Educ:* Ballarat Grammar Sch.; Scotch Coll.; Univ. of Melbourne (BA, BSc, DSc); Univ. of Bristol (PhD). Research Scientist: CSIR Div. of Aeronautics, 1947–50; Aeronautical Res. Labs, 1953–57; CSIRO Division: of Tribo Physics, 1957–81; of Chemical Physics, 1981–86; of Materials Science, 1987. Visiting Professor: Brown Univ., 1961–62; Univ. of Florida, 1971; Christensen Fellow, 1986, Vis. Fellow, 1990–, St Catherine's Coll., Oxford. *Publications:* Computed Electron Micrographs and Defect Identification, 1973, Chinese edn 1979; numerous contribs to sci. jls. *Address:* 10 Ellesmore Court, Kew, Vic 3101, Australia. *T:* (office) (3) 95452861, *T:* (home) (3) 98530673, *Fax:* (office) (3) 95441128.

HEAD, Audrey May; Member, Monopolies and Mergers Commission, 1986–89; Director, 1973–85, Managing Director, 1976–85, Hill Samuel Unit Trust Managers Ltd; *b* 21 Jan. 1924; *d* of Eric Burton Head and Kathleen Irene Head. *Educ:* St Catherine's Sch., Bramley, Surrey. Chartered Auctioneers' and Estate Agents' Institute, 1949–58; Hill Samuel Group, 1958–85, a Manager, 1968; Director: Hill Samuel Investment Management, 1974–86; Hill Samuel Life Assurance, 1983–86; Trade Union Unit Trust Managers Ltd, 1983–85. Chm., Unit Trust Assoc., 1983–85. Non-exec. Mem., Royal Surrey and St Luke's NHS Trust, 1991–93. Chm. Governing Body, St Catherine's Sch., Bramley, 1988–96. Nominated as Business Woman of the Year, 1976. Silver Jubilee Medal, 1977. *Recreations:* golf, gardening. *Address:* West Chantry, 4 Clifford Manor Road, Guildford, Surrey GU4 8AG. *T:* (01483) 561047.

HEAD, John Philip Trevelyan; His Honour Judge Head; a Circuit Judge, since 2004; *b* 6 July 1953; *s* of Walter Raleigh Trevelyan Head and Rosemary Constance Beatrice Head (*née* Borwick); *m* 1983, Erica Lesley Cox; one *s* one *d*. *Educ:* Marlborough Coll.; Merton Coll., Oxford (MA); Univ. of Virginia (LLM). Fulbright Schol., 1974–75. Called to the Bar, Middle Temple, 1976; Asst Recorder, 1996–2000, Recorder, 2000–04. Mem., Parole Bd for Eng. and Wales, 2006–. Oxford Univ. Hockey Blue, 1974. *Recreations:* travel, books. *Address:* Leicester Crown Court, 90 Wellington Street, Leicester LE1 6HG. *Clubs:* Savile, Sette of Odd Volumes.

HEAD, Michael Edward, CVO 1991; UK Member, European Commission on Racism and Intolerance (Council of Europe), since 1996 (Chairman, 2001–05); Member, Surrey Probation Board, 2001–07; *b* 17 March 1936; *s* of Alexander Edward Head and Wilhelmina Head; *m* 1963, Wendy Elizabeth, *d* of R. J. Davies; two *s* two *d*. *Educ:* Leeds, Kingston, and Woking Grammar Schools; University College London (BA; Pollard Prize for History); Univ. of Michigan (MA). 2nd Lieut, Royal Artillery (Nat. Service), 1958–60. Home Office, 1960; Private Sec. to Parly Under Secs of State, 1964–66; Sec., Deptl Cttee on Liquor Licensing (Erroll), 1971–72; Asst Sec., 1974–84: Probation and After Care Dept; Community Programmes and Equal Opportunities Dept; Criminal Dept; Asst Under Sec. of State, General Dept, 1984, Criminal Justice and Constitutional Dept (Registrar of the Baronetage), 1986, Broadcasting Dept, 1991, Equal Opportunities and Gen. Dept, 1991 (Head of Dept, 1991–96). Dir, Rehab UK, 1996–2005. Mem., Surrey Probation Cttee, 1997–2001. Vice Chm., Woking Community Leisure Ltd, 1996–98. *Recreations:* theatre, reading. *Address:* Rustlings, Castle Road, Horsell, Woking, Surrey GU21 4ET. *T:* and *Fax:* (01483) 772929; *e-mail:* mhead90120@aol.com. *Clubs:* County (Guildford); Rotary (Woking Dist).

HEAD, Peter Richard, OBE 1998; FREng, FICE, FIStructE; Director and Head of Global Planning, Arup, since 2004; *b* 27 Feb. 1947; *s* of Robert Cyril Head and Vera Alice (*née* Kent); *m* 1970, Susan Florence East; one *s* one *d*. *Educ:* Tiffin Boys' Sch., Kingston-upon-Thames; Imperial Coll., London (BSc 1st Cl. Hons Eng 1969). FREng (FEng 1996); FICE 1995; FIStructE 1995; FIHT 1995. Freeman Fox & Partners, 1969–80: team leader for design of: Avonmouth Bridge, M5, 1971–74; Myton Swing Bridge, Hull, 1974–75 (Dep. Resident Engr, construction of Myton Bridge, 1977–80); Section Engr, construction of Friarton Bridge, Perth, 1975–77; G. Maunsell & Partners subseq. Maunsell, later part of AECOM Gp, then FaberMaunsell, 1980–2004: designer of bridges over docks on Dockland Light Rly, London, 1981–84; Project Director: Second Severn

Crossing, 1984–96; design and construction, Kap Shui Mun Bridge, Hong Kong, 1994–96; Dir responsible for studies and choice of bridge for third crossing of Forth Estuary, 1993–2004; Man. Dir, 1995–2001; Chief Exec., Europe, 1997–2001; Corporate Develt Dir, 2001–04; Dir for supervision of construction, Rion Antirion Bridge, Greece, 1997–2004; Maunsell Structural Plastics Ltd, 1984–97: Dir and designer, Aberfeldy Bridge, 1992 and Bonds Mill Bridge, Stonehouse, Glos, 1994; inventor, Advanced Composite Construction System and Spaces bridge concept; Proj. Dir, Dongtan Eco-city, Shanghai, 2005–. Chm., London First Sustainability Unit, 2000; Comr, GLA Sustainable Develt Commn, 2002–; Chm., Steel Construction Inst., 2003–06 (Dep. Chm., 1999–2003); Vice-Pres., Construction Industry Res. Assoc., 1999–2004; Mem., 2012 Olympics Construction Task Force, 2005–. Vis. Prof., Univ. of Surrey, 2000–05. FCGI 2001; FRSA 2006. Hon. Dr Bristol, 2008. Premier Gold Award/PRW Award for Excellence in Design, 1993; Silver Medal, Royal Acad. Engrg, 1995; Laureate Award of Merit Internat. Assoc. of Bridge and Structural Engrg, 1998; Telford Prize, ICE, 2006; Frank Whittle Medal, RAEng, 2008. *Publications:* numerous papers in learned jls and conf. proc. covering sustainability, major bridge projects and pioneering work in advanced composite materials. *Recreations:* hill-walking, gardening, painting. *Address:* Arup, 13 Fitzroy Street, W1T 4BQ. *T:* (020) 7755 4121; *e-mail:* peter.head@arup.com; Parkside, 11 Manor Way, Beckenham, Kent BR3 3LH. *T:* (020) 8658 2901.

HEAD, Philip John, FRICS; Director, Infrastructure and Property Services, Learning and Skills Council, since 2002; *b* 24 Nov. 1951; *s* of Dennis George Head and Marjorie Head; *m* 1974, Barbara Fox; two *s*. *Educ:* Surbiton Grammar Sch.; Univ. of Reading (BSc Hons Estate Management). FRICS 1985. Estates Surveyor, 1973–77, Sen. Commercial Surveyor, 1977–78, Milton Keynes Develt Corp.; Welsh Development Agency, 1978–93: Develt and Funding Manager, 1981–83; Dep. Commercial Dir, 1983–84; Commercial Dir, 1984–87; Exec. Dir, Property and Regional Services, 1987–91; Chief Exec., 1991–93; Hd of Property Services, 1994–98, Asst Dir, 1998–2001, FEFCE; Asst Dir, LSC, 2001–02. Hon. Sec., Coventry Phoenix Rotary Club, 2001–03. *Recreations:* Rotary, gardening, family. *Address:* Learning and Skills Council, Cheylesmore House, Quinton Road, Coventry CV1 2WT; *e-mail:* Philip.Head@lsc.gov.uk.

HEAD, Sir Richard (Douglas Somerville), 6th Bt *cr* 1838, of Rochester, Kent; Assistant Gardener, RHS Garden, Wisley, since 1979; *b* 16 Jan. 1951; *s* of Major Sir Francis Head, 5th Bt, and of Susan, Lady Head (*née* Ramsay); *S* father, 2005; *m* 1991, Edwina Mansell (marr. diss. 1999). *Educ:* Eton; Bristol Poly. (BA Fine Arts 1974); London Univ. Inst. of Educn (PGCE 1975); RA Schs (David Murray Landscape Studentship). Artist in pen and ink, gouache, oil paint, drypoint. Mixed and solo exhibitions: Michael Parkin Fine Arts, 1988; Eton Artists, 1990; Sally Hunter Fine Arts, 1997; The First Gallery, Southampton, 2005. *Recreations:* music, painting, drawing. *Heir: uncle* John Kenelm Somerville Head [*b* 30 April 1918; *m* 1942, Lilah Doreen Prittie Wingfield Perry, FRCS (*d* 2006); two *s* two *d* (of whom one *s* one *d* are twins)]. *Address:* 6 Viscount Gardens, West Byfleet, Surrey KT14 6HE.

HEADFORT, 7th Marquis of, *cr* 1800; **Thomas Michael Ronald Christopher Taylour;** Bt 1704; Baron Headfort, 1760; Viscount Headfort, 1762; Earl of Bective, 1766; Baron Kenlis (UK), 1831; Director: Bective Leslie Marsh (formerly Bective Davidson) Ltd, London, since 2003 (property consultant, 1995–2003); Central London Estate Agents Ltd; *b* 10 Feb. 1959; *o s* of 6th Marquis of Headfort and of Hon. Elizabeth Nall-Cain, *d* of 2nd Baron Brocket; *S* father, 2005; *m* 1987, Susan Jane (*d* 2008), *er d* of late C. A. Vandervell and of Mrs Vandervell; two *s* two *d*. *Educ:* Harrow; RAC Cirencester. Estate agent with John D. Wood & Co., London, 1981–87. Mem., Irish Peers Assoc. *Heir: s* Earl of Bective, qv. *Address:* Shipton Manor, Shipton on Cherwell, Oxon OX5 1JL; (office) One Cadogan Street, SW3 2PP. *T:* (020) 7589 6677. *Clubs:* Lansdowne; Royal Dublin Society (Dublin).

HEAF, Peter Julius Denison, OBE 2002; MD; FRCP; Chairman, Medical Sickness Annuity and Life Insurance Society Ltd, 1988–93; *b* 1922; *s* of late Prof. F. R. G. Heaf, CMG; *m* 1947, Rosemary Cartledge; two *s* two *d*. *Educ:* Stamford Sch., Lincs; University Coll., London, Fellow 1973. MB, BS 1946; MD London 1952; MRCP 1954; FRCP 1965. House Physician and Surg., also RMO, University Coll. Hosp., and Capt. RAMC, 1947–49; Research Asst, Brompton Hosp., 1953–54; Sen. Registrar, St Thomas' Hosp., 1955–58; Consultant Physician, UCH, 1958–86, retired. Hon. Med. Cons to RBL, 1980–2002. *Publications:* papers on chest disease and pulmonary physiology, in Lancet, etc. *Recreations:* painting, gardening. *Address:* Ferrybrook House, Chalmore Gardens, Wallingford, Oxon OX10 9EP. *T:* (01491) 839176.

HEAL, Prof. (Barbara) Jane, PhD; FBA 1997; Professor of Philosophy, University of Cambridge, since 1999; Fellow, St John's College, Cambridge, since 1986 (President, 1999–2003); *b* 21 Oct. 1946; *d* of William Calvert Kneale and Martha Kneale (*née* Hurst); *m* 1968, John Gauntlett Benedict Heal (marr. diss. 1987); one *s* one *d*. *Educ:* Oxford High Sch. for Girls; New Hall, Cambridge (BA 1968; PhD 1973). Sarah Smithson Res. Fellow, Newnham Coll., Cambridge, 1971–74; Harkness Fellow, Commonwealth Fund of NY, and Vis. Fellow, Princeton Univ. and Univ. of Calif at Berkeley, 1974–76; Lectr in Philosophy, Univ. of Newcastle upon Tyne, 1976–86; Univ. Asst Lectr, 1986–91, Lectr, 1991–96, Reader, 1996–99, in Philosophy, Univ. of Cambridge. *Publications:* Fact and Meaning, 1989; Mind, Reason and Imagination, 2003; articles in Mind, Philosophical Qly, etc. *Recreations:* reading, walking. *Address:* St John's College, Cambridge CB2 1TP. *T:* (01223) 338668.

HEAL, Oliver Standerwick; furniture restorer, since 2004; *b* 18 April 1949; *s* of late Anthony Standerwick Heal; *m* 1990, Annik Coatalen; one *s*. *Educ:* Leighton Park Sch., Reading; Bucks Chiltern UC (BA Hons (Furniture Conservation and Restoration) 2004). Joined Heal's, 1970; Dir, Heal & Son Ltd, 1974–83, Chm., 1977–83; Chm., Heal & Son Holdings PLC, 1981–83 (Dir, 1975–83); Dir, Staples & Co. Ltd, 1981–84; Chm., Heal Textil GmbH, 1984–90; VRP multi-carte, France, 1990–91; Commercial Dir, Faïenceries de Quimper, France, 1992–94; sales agent, furnishing fabrics, France, 1994–2000. *Publication:* article in Jl of Furniture History Soc. *Recreation:* vintage cars. *Club:* Vintage Sports Car (Chipping Norton).

HEAL, Sylvia Lloyd; JP; MP (Lab) Halesowen and Rowley Regis, since 1997; First Deputy Chairman of Ways and Means, and a Deputy Speaker, House of Commons, since 2000; *b* 20 July 1942; *d* of late John Lloyd Fox and Ruby Fox; *m* 1965, Keith Heal; one *s* one *d*. *Educ:* Elfed Secondary Modern School, Buckley, N Wales; Coleg Harlech; University College Swansea (BSc Econ 1968). Social worker, health service and Dept of Employment, 1968–70 and 1980–90; Nat. Officer, Carers Nat. Assoc., 1992–97. MP (Lab) Mid Staffordshire, March 1990–1992; contested (Lab) Mid Staffordshire, 1992. PPS to Sec. of State for Defence, 1997–2000. Mem., Select Cttee on Educn, Sci. and Arts, 1990–92; opposition spokesperson on health and women's issues, 1991–92. Mem. Council, ASA, 1992–97; Mem., Exec. Council, SSAFA, 1990–91. Hon. Fellow, Univ. of Wales, 2003. JP Surrey, 1973. *Recreations:* walking, theatre, listening to male voice choirs, gardening. *Address:* House of Commons, SW1A 0AA.

HEALD, Bill; *see* Heald, R. J.

HEALD, Oliver; MP (C) North East Hertfordshire, since 1997 (North Hertfordshire 1992–97); *b* 15 Dec. 1954; *s* of late John Anthony Heald and of Joyce Heald; *m* 1979 Christine Whittle; one *s* two *d*. *Educ:* Reading Sch.; Pembroke Coll., Cambridge. Called to the Bar, Middle Temple, 1977; practice in E Anglia and London, 1979–95 and 1997–2001. Contested (C) Southwark and Bermondsey, 1987. PPS to Minister of Agric Fisheries and Food, 1994–95; Parly Under-Sec. of State, DSS, 1995–97; an Opposition Whip, 1997–2000; Opposition spokesman: on home affairs, 2000–01; on health, 2001–02 on work and pensions, 2002–03; Shadow Leader, H of C, 2003–05; Shadow Sec. of State for Constitutional Affairs, and Shadow Chancellor of Duchy of Lancaster, 2005–07 Member: Employment Select Cttee, 1992–94; Admin Select Cttee, 1998–2000; Select Cttee on Modernisation of H of C, 2003–05; Select Cttee on Work and Pensions, 2007– Cttee on Standards in Public Life, 2008–; Vice-Chm., Cons. Backbench Employment Cttee, 1992–94. *Recreations:* sports, family. *Address:* House of Commons, SW1A 0AA.

HEALD, Prof. Richard John, (Bill), OBE 1998; FRCS, FRCSE; Surgical Director Pelican Cancer Foundation, Basingstoke, since 2000; *b* 11 May 1936; *o s* of late Jack and Muriel Heald, St Albans; *m* 1969, Denise (*née* Boncey); three *d*. *Educ:* Gonville and Caius Coll., Cambridge (BA 1st Cl. Hons 1957 (Coll. Prize); MA 1960; MB 1960, MCh 1965); Guy's Hosp., London. FRCSE 1964; FRCS 1965. Consultant Surgeon: N Hants Hosp., Basingstoke, 1973–; specialist in colorectal cancer surgery and internat. teacher of surgical technique. Personal Chair, Univ. of Southampton, 1998–. Mem. Council, RCS 1989–2001 (Vice-Pres., 1996–98); Pres., Sections of Coloproctol. and of Surgery, RSocMed. Hon. FRSocMed 2001; Hon. Fellow: Assoc. of Coloproctol. of GB and Ireland, 2001; German Surgical Soc., 2004; Austrian Surgical Soc., 2004; Assoc. Française de Chirurgie. Hon. Dr Linkoping, Sweden, 1997. Gold Medal in Surgery, Assoc. of Surgery of Netherlands, 2001; Centenary Medal, French Cancer Soc., 2005. *Publications:* contrib. papers on rectal cancer surgery, particularly total mesorectal excision for rectal cancer to jls incl. Jl RSocMed, Lancet. *Recreation:* sailing. *Address:* Pelican Cancer Foundation, The Ark, North Hampshire Hospital, Aldermaston Road, Basingstoke, Hants RG24 9NA. *T:* (01256) 314848. *Club:* Royal Southampton Yacht.

HEALD, His Honour Thomas Routledge; a Circuit Judge (formerly County Court Judge), 1970–95; *b* 19 Aug. 1923; *s* of late John Arthur Heald and Nora Marion Heald; *m* 1950, Jean, *d* of James Campbell Henderson; two *s* one *d* (and one *d* decd). *Educ:* Merchant Taylors' Sch.; St John's Coll., Oxford (Fish Schol., 1941; BA (Jurisprudence) 1947; MA 1949). Lieut, RAC, 1943–45. Called to Bar, Middle Temple, 1948; Midland Circuit Prosecuting Counsel to Inland Revenue (Midland Circuit), 1965–70; Deputy Chairman QS: Lindsey, 1965–71; Notts, 1969–71; Notts designated Family Judge, 1991–96. Council of HM Circuit Judges: Asst Sec., 1980–83; Sec., 1984–85; Vice-Pres., 1986–87; Pres 1988–89; Member: Matrimonial Rules Cttee, 1980–83; President's Cttee on Adoption 1983–95; President's Family Cttee, 1984–93. Mem., Senate of Inns of Court, 1984–86 Chairman: Notts Children's and Families Mediation Service, 1995–2000; Notts Guardia Ad Litem/Reporting Officers Panel, 1995–98. Mem. Council, Nottingham Univ. 1974–93 (Chm., Physical Recreation Adv. Cttee, 1979–85; Chm., Law Adv. Cttee 1976–84; Chm., Estates and Buildings Cttee, 1985–89); Chm., Law Adv. Cttee, Trent Polytechnic, 1979–84. *Recreations:* golf, local history, family history. *Address:* Rebbu House, Nicker Hill, Keyworth, Nottingham NG12 5ED. *T:* (0115) 937 2676. *Club:* Nott Golf.

HEALD, Timothy Villiers, FRSL; writer and freelance journalist, since 1972; *b* 28 Jan 1944; *s* of Villiers Archer John Heald, CVO, MBE, MC and Catherine Eleanor Jean Heald (*née* Vaughan); *m* 1st, 1968, Alison Martina Leslie (marr. diss. 1997); two *s* two *d* 2nd, 1999, Penelope Byrne. *Educ:* Sherborne Sch.; Balliol Coll., Oxford (MA). Atticu column, Sunday Times, 1965–67; Features Ed., Town Mag., 1967; feature writer, Daily Express, 1967–72; Associate Ed., Weekend Mag., Toronto, 1977–78; Pendennis, The Observer, 1990. Chm., Crime Writers' Assoc., 1987–88. FRSL 2000. Pres., Old Shirburnian Soc., 2000–04. *Publications:* fiction: Unbecoming Habits, 1973; Blue Blood Will Out, 1974; Deadline, 1975; Let Sleeping Dogs Die, 1976; Just Desserts, 1977 Caroline R, 1980; Murder at Moose Jaw, 1981; Masterstroke, 1982; Red Herrings, 1983 Class Distinctions, 1984; Brought to Book, 1988; (ed) The Rigby File, 1989; Business Unusual, 1989; (ed) A Classic English Crime, 1990; (ed) A Classic Christmas Crime, 1995 Stop Press, 1998; Death and the Visiting Fellow, 2004; Death and the D'Urbervilles, 2005 A Death on the Ocean Wave, 2007; *non-fiction:* It's a Dog's Life, 1971; The Making of Space 1999, 1976; John Steed: the authorised biography, vol. 1, 1977; (with Mayo Mohs) HRH The Man Who Would be King, 1979; Networks (who we know and how we us them), 1983; The Character of Cricket, 1986; (ed) The Newest London Spy, 1988; By Appointment: 150 years of the Royal Warrant and its holders, 1990; (ed) My Lord's, 1990 The Duke: a portrait of Prince Philip, 1991; Honourable Estates, 1992; A Life of Love the biography of Barbara Cartland, 1994; Denis: the authorised biography of the incomparable Compton, 1994, revd edn as Denis Compton: life of a sporting hero, 2006 Brian Johnston: the authorised biography, 1995; Beating Retreat: Hong Kong under the last Governor, 1997; A Peerage for Trade, 2001; Village Cricket, 2004; Princess Margaret a life unravelled, 2007. *Recreations:* talking, walking, wine, food, Real tennis. *Address:* The Esplanade, Fowey, Cornwall PL23 1JA. *T:* (01726) 832781, *Fax:* (01726) 833246 *e-mail:* tim@timheald.com. *Clubs:* MCC, Army and Navy, Groucho, Detection; Roya Tennis (Hampton Court); Royal Fowey Yacht.

HEALE, Simon John Newton; Chief Executive, London Metal Exchange, 2001–06; *b* 27 April 1953; *s* of James Newton Heale and Ruth Elizabeth Heale; *m* 1982, Catrion Jean, *d* of Lt-Gen. Sir Robin Carnegie, qv; one *s* two *d*. *Educ:* Winchester Coll.; Orie Coll., Oxford (BA 1975). Chartered Accountant, 1978. Finance Dir, Swire Japan 1982–85; Pres., Oceanroutes Inc., 1985–88; Gen. Manager Cargo, Cathay Pacific 1988–90; Chief Operating Officer, Dragonair, 1990–94; Dep. Man. Dir, Cathay Pacific Airways, 1994–97; Jardine Fleming: Gp Finance Dir, 1997–99; Chief Operating Officer 1999–2001. Non-executive Director: LCH.Clearnet Gp Ltd, 2003–06; The Morga Crucible Co. plc, 2005–; Kazakhmys plc, 2007–; Panmure Gordon & Co. plc, 2007–; PZ Cussons, 2008–. Chief Exec., China Now Fest., 2007–08. *Recreations:* travel, reading walking, labradors. *Club:* Hong Kong (Hong Kong).

HEALEY, family name of **Baron Healey.**

HEALEY, Baron *cr* 1992 (Life Peer), of Riddlesden in the County of West Yorkshire **Denis Winston Healey,** CH 1979; MBE 1945; PC 1964; *b* 30 Aug. 1917; *s* of late William Healey, Keighley, Yorks; *m* 1945, Edna May Edmunds (see Lady Healey); one two *d*. *Educ:* Bradford Grammar Sch.; Balliol Coll., Oxford (Hon. Fellow, 1979). First Cl Hons Mods 1938; Jenkyns Exhib. 1939; Harmsworth Sen. Schol., First Cl. Lit. Hum., BA 1940; MA 1945. War of 1939–45; entered Army, 1940; served N Africa, Italy. Major RE 1944 (despatches). Contested (Lab) Pudsey and Otley Div., 1945; Sec., International Dept Labour Party, 1945–52. MP (Lab) SE Leeds, Feb. 1952–1955, Leeds E, 1955–92; Shadow Cabinet, 1959–64, 1970–74, 1979–87; Secretary of State for Defence, 1964–70 Chancellor of the Exchequer, 1974–79; opposition spokesman on Foreign and

Commonwealth Affairs, 1980–87; Dep. Leader of Labour Party, 1980–83. Mem. Brit. Delegn to Commonwealth Relations Conf., Canada, 1949; British Delegate to: Consultative Assembly, Council of Europe, 1952–54; Inter Parly Union Conf., Washington, 1953; Western European Union and Council of Europe, 1953–55. Chm., IMF Interim Cttee, 1977–79. Mem. Exec. Fabian Soc., 1954–61. Mem., Labour Party Nat. Exec. Cttee, 1970–75. Councillor: RIIA, 1948–60; Inst. of Strategic Studies, 1958–61. Pres., Birkbeck Coll., 1993–99. Freeman, City of Leeds, 1992. FRSL 1993. Hon. Fellow, Leeds Polytechnic, 1987. Hon. DLitt Bradford, 1983; Hon. LLD Sussex, 1991. Grand Cross of Order of Merit, Germany, 1979. *Publications:* The Curtain Falls, 1951; New Fabian Essays, 1952; Neutralism, 1955; Fabian International Essays, 1956; A Neutral Belt in Europe, 1958; NATO and American Security, 1959; The Race Against the H Bomb, 1960; Labour Britain and the World, 1963; Healey's Eye, 1980; Labour and a World Society, 1985; Beyond Nuclear Deterrence, 1986; The Time of My Life (autobiog.), 1989; When Shrimps Learn to Whistle (essays), 1990; My Secret Planet, 1992; Denis Healey's Yorkshire Dales, 1995; Healey's World, 2002. *Recreations:* travel, photography, music, painting. *Address:* Pingles Place, Alfriston, East Sussex BN26 5TT.

HEALEY, Lady; Edna May Healey; writer; *b* 14 June 1918; *d* of Rose and Edward Edmunds; *m* 1945, Baron Healey, *qv*; one *s* two *d. Educ:* Bell's Grammar School, Coleford, Glos; St Hugh's College, Oxford (BA, Dip Ed; Hon. Fellow, 2003). Taught English and History: Keighley Girls' Grammar School, 1940–44; Bromley Girls' High Sch., 1944–47; freelance lecturer, England and America; television writer and presenter; radio writer and broadcaster. *Publications:* Lady Unknown: life of Angela Burdett-Coutts, 1978; Wives of Fame, 1986; Coutts & Co. 1692–1992: the portrait of a private bank, 1992; The Queen's House: a history of Buckingham Palace, 1997; Emma Darwin, 2001; Part of the Pattern (memoir), 2006. *Recreations:* gardening, listening to music.

HEALEY, Sir Charles Edward C.; *see* Chadwyck-Healey.

HEALEY, Edna May; *see* Healey, Lady.

HEALEY, Rt Hon. John; PC 2008; MP (Lab) Wentworth, since 1997; Minister of State (Minister for Local Government), Department for Communities and Local Government, since 2007; *b* 13 Feb. 1960; *s* of Aidan Healey, OBE and Jean Healey; *m* 1993, Jackie Bate; one *s. Educ:* Christ's Coll., Cambridge (schol., BA 1982). Charity campaigner, 1984–90; Campaigns Manager, Issue Communications, 1990–92; Head of Communications, MSF, 1992–94; Campaigns Dir, TUC, 1994–97. PPS to Chancellor of the Exchequer, 1999–2001; Parly Under-Sec. of State, DFES, 2001–02; Econ. Sec., 2002–05, Financial Sec., 2005–07, HM Treasury. Contested (Lab) Ryedale, 1992. *Address:* House of Commons, SW1A 0AA; *e-mail:* healeyj@parliament.uk.

HEALY, Bernadine P., (Mrs F. Loop), MD; Member, President's Council of Advisors on Science and Technology, USA, since 2001; medical and health columnist, US News and World Report, since 2002; *b* 2 Aug. 1944; *d* of Michael J. Healy and Violet (*née* McGrath); *m* 1985, Floyd Loop; two *d. Educ:* Vassar Coll. (AB *summa cum laude* 1965); Harvard Med. Sch. (MD *cum laude* 1970). Intern in medicine, 1970–71, asst resident, 1971–72, Johns Hopkins Hosp., Balt.; Staff Fellow, Sect. Pathology, Nat. Heart, Lung and Blood Inst., NIH, 1972–74; Johns Hopkins University School of Medicine: Fellow, Cardiovascular Div., Dept of Medicine, 1974–76; Fellow, Dept of Pathology, 1975–76; Asst Prof. of Medicine and Pathology, 1976–81; Associate Prof. of Medicine, 1977–82; Asst Dean for Postdoctoral Programs and Faculty Develt, 1979–84; Associate Prof. of Pathology, 1981–84; Prof. of Medicine, 1982–84; Active Staff, Medicine and Pathology, 1976, Dir, Coronary Care Unit, 1977–84, Johns Hopkins Hosp.; Dep. Dir, Office of Sci. and Technol. Policy, Exec. Office of Pres., White House, Washington, 1984–85; Chm., Res. Inst., Cleveland Clinic Foundn, 1985–91; Dir, NIH, 1991–93; Sen. Policy Advr, Page Center for Health and Science Policy, Cleveland Clinic Foundn, 1993–95; Dean, Coll. of Medicine, Ohio State Univ., 1995–99; Pres. and CEO, American Red Cross, 1999–2001. *Publication:* A New Prescription for Women's Health, 1996.

HEALY, Prof. John Francis, MA, PhD; Professor of Classics, London University, 1966–90, now Professor Emeritus; Chairman of Department, Royal Holloway and Bedford New College, 1985–88 (Head of Department, Royal Holloway College, 1966–85); *b* 27 Aug. 1926; *s* of late John Healy and Iris Maud (*née* Cutland); *m* 1st, 1957, Carol Ann McEvoy; one *s*; 2nd, 1985, Barbara Edith Henshall. *Educ:* Trinity Coll., Cambridge (Open Exhbn in Classics 1943; Classical Prelim. Cl. 1 1944; Classical Tripos: 1st Cl. Pt I 1949, 1st Cl. Pt II 1950 (dist. Cl. Archaeol.); Sen. Schol. 1950; BA 1950, MA 1952, PhD 1955). War service, 1944–48; Captain, Intelligence Corps, 1946–48. Walston student, Brit. Sch. of Archaeol., Athens, 1950; G. C. Winter Warr Schol., Cambridge, 1951; Manchester University: Asst Lectr in Classics, 1953–56; Lectr in Classics and Class. Archaeol., 1956–61; London University: Reader in Greek, Bedford Coll., 1961–66; Chm., Bd of Studies in Classics, 1979–81; Dean of Faculty of Arts, Royal Holloway Coll., 1978–81. Chm. Finance Cttee, Inst. of Classical Studies, London, 1967–88. FRNS 1950; FRSA 1971; MRI 1979. *Publications:* contrib. (A. Rowe) Cyrenaican Expeditions of the University of Manchester, 1955–57; Mining and Metallurgy in the Greek and Roman World, 1978, rev. and trans. edn, Miniere e Metallurgia nel Mondo Greco e Romano, 1993; Sylloge Nummorum Graecorum, vol. VII, The Raby and Güterbock collections in Manchester University Museum, 1986; Pliny the Elder, Natural History, 1991; Pliny the Elder, On Science and Technology, 1999; articles and reviews in Jl of Hellenic St., Numismatic Chron., Nature, Amer. Num. Soc.'s Mus. Notes, Jl of Metals, Class. Rev., Gnomon. *Recreations:* travel, music, creative gardening. *Club:* Cambridge Union Society.

HEALY, Maurice Eugene, OBE 2001; Director, National Consumer Council, 1987–91; *b* 27 Nov. 1933; *s* of late Thomas Healy and Emily Healy (*née* O'Mahoney); *m* 1958, Jose Barbara Speller Dewdney; two *d* (and one *d* decd). *Educ:* Downside School; Peterhouse, Cambridge (BA Classics). Nat. service, Royal Artillery, 1954–56. BoT, 1956–60; Consumers' Assoc., working on Which?, 1960–76; Head of Editl Dept and Editor of Which?, 1973–76; Nat. Consumer Council, 1977–91. Chairman, Consumer Policy Committee: BSI, 1993–98; ISO, 1996–98; Member: Council, Bureau Européen des Unions de Consommateurs, 1977–91; Council, Insurance Ombudsman Bureau, 1991–2001 (Chm., 1996–2001); Code of Banking Practice Review Cttee, 1991–99; Indep. Management Cttee, Optical Consumer Complaints Service, 1992–99; Bd, Jazz Services Ltd, 1992–2001; Consumer Panel, PIA, 1993–98; Council, Funeral Ombudsman Service, 2001–03; Assessor to Auld Cttee on reform of shop hours, 1984. Chm., Patients' Assoc., 1991–93. Trustee, European Res. Inst. for Consumer Affairs, 1990–2007. Chm. of Governors, Highgate Wood School, 1983–86. Chm., Friends of Queens Wood, 2000–08. Cruse bereavement counsellor, 2006–. FRSA. Hon. Mem., Inst. of Consumer Affairs. *Publications:* contribs to Which? and Nat. Consumer Council and other jls and conf. papers. *Recreations:* jazz, Irish music, Shona sculpture. *Address:* 15 Onslow Gardens, Muswell Hill, N10 3JT. *T:* (020) 8883 8955. *Clubs:* Ronnie Scott's, Burmese Cat.

HEALY, Sheila Elizabeth; Chief Executive, Cornwall County Council, since 2006; *b* 20 Oct. 1954; *m* 2007, Richard Harvey; one *s*, and one step *s* one step *d. Educ:* Trinity Coll., Dublin (BA Hons, MA Econs and Social Studies). Residential Social Worker, Brent LBC, 1978–80; Community Worker, Pensioners' Link, 1980–83; Policy Officer, GLC, 1983–85; Hd, Urban Prog., and Hd, Policy and Performance, Wolverhampton MBC, 1985–90; Asst City Sec., Quality and Business Services, Nottingham CC, 1990–92; Chief Exec., City Challenge and Dir of Envmt, Walsall MBC, 1992–97; Corporate Dir, Envmt and Econ., 1997–2000, Community Governance, 2000–03, Bor. of Telford & Wrekin; Regl Associate, W Midlands, IDeA, 2003–04; Regl Dir, Local Govt, ODPM, 2004–06. Dir and Vice-Chm., Ikon Gall., Birmingham, 2000–04. Chair, Audiences Central, W Midlands, 2000–06. Member: Friends of Heligan; Cornwall Garden Soc.; Friends of Hall for Cornwall; Friends of Tate Galls. *Recreations:* walking, theatre, reading, cinema, travel, contemporary and modern art. *Address:* Cornwall County Council, County Hall, Truro TR1 3AY. *T:* (01872) 322100, *Fax:* (01872) 323836; *e-mail:* chiefexec@cornwall.gov.uk.

HEALY, Prof. Thomas Edward John, MD; FRCA; Professor of Anaesthesia, University of Manchester, 1981–97, now Emeritus; *b* 11 Dec. 1935; *s* of late Thomas Healy and Gladys May Healy; *m* 1966, Lesley Edwina Sheppard; one *s* three *d. Educ:* Guy's Hosp. Med. Sch., London Univ. (BSc 1st Cl. Hons 1961; MB BS 1964; MD 1975); Manchester Univ. (MSc 1982); Cardiff Univ. (LLM 1999). LRCP 1963; MRCS 1963; DA 1967; FRCA (FFARCS 1968). Consultant Anaesthetist i/c Intensive Care, Gen. Hosp., then Queen's Med. Centre, Nottingham, 1971–81; designed and commissioned Intensive Care Unit, Gen. Hosp., 1972, Queen's Med. Centre, 1975; Reader in Anaesthesia, Univ. of Nottingham, 1974–81. Mem., Med. Adv. Bd, Med. Litigation, 2000–08. Editor-in-Chief, European Jl Anaesthesiology, 1994–99; Mem. Editl Bd, Jl Evaluation in Clinical Practice, 1995–99. Mem., S Manchester HA, 1981–89. Mem. and Chm., tribunal and appeals cttees. Royal College of Anaesthetists: examr for Fellowship exam, 1976–89; Mem. Council, 1989–97; Chm., Professional Standards Cttee, 1994–97; Section of Anaesthesia, Royal Society of Medicine: Mem. Council, 1985–; Hon. Sec., 1986–88; Pres., 1996–97; Member Council: Assoc. Anaesthetists GB and Ireland, 1973–76; Anaesthetic Res. Soc., 1978–81; Postgrad. Med. Fellowship, 1991–94; Academician, 1980, Mem., Senate and Exec. Cttee, 1984–2005, European Acad. Anaesthesiology. Special Visitor, Shanghai Med. Coll., 1994–. Gov., Linacre Centre for Health Care Ethics, 1999–2005. Hon. Mem., Romanian Soc. Anaesthesiology, 1995. Chm., Fundraising Cttee, ReachOut, 1998–. Freeman, City of London, 1978. *Publications:* Aids to Anaesthesia 1: the basic sciences, 1980 (trans. Spanish, Italian), 3rd edn 1991; Aids to Anaesthesia 2: clinical practice, 1984, 2nd edn 1999; (ed) Anaesthesia for Day Case Surgery, 1990; (ed) Wylie and Churchill-Davidson's A Practice of Anaesthesia, 6th edn 1995 (BMA best textbook in a surgical subject, 1995–96), 7th edn 2003; *chapters in*: Medicine for Lawyers, 2005; Encyclopedia of Forensic and Legal Medicine, 2005; numerous scientific papers. *Recreations:* walking, cycling, reading, keep fit, sleeping. *Address:* Department of Anaesthesia, Manchester Royal Infirmary, Oxford Road, Manchester M13 9WL.

HEALY, Tim T.; *see* Traverse-Healy.

HEANEY, Seamus Justin, FBA; MRIA; Professor of Poetry, Oxford University, 1989–94; Boylston Professor of Rhetoric and Oratory at Harvard University (formerly Visiting Professor), 1985–97; Ralph Waldo Emerson Poet in Residence, Harvard University, 1998–2007; *b* 13 April 1939; *s* of Patrick and Margaret Heaney; *m* 1965, Marie Devlin; two *s* one *d. Educ:* St Columb's College, Derry; Queen's University, Belfast (BA first cl. 1961). Teacher, St Thomas's Secondary Sch., Belfast, 1962–63; Lectr, St Joseph's Coll. of Educn, Belfast, 1963–66; Lectr, Queen's Univ., Belfast, 1966–72; free-lance writer, 1972–75; Lectr, Carysfort Coll., 1975–81. Corresp. FBA, 1999. Hon. DLitt Oxon, 1997. Bennett Award, 1982; Nobel Prize for Literature, 1995. *Publications:* Preoccupations: Selected Prose 1968–1978, 1980; The Government of the Tongue, 1988; The Cure at Troy (a version of Sophocles' Philoctetes), 1990; The Redress of Poetry, 1995; (jtly) Homage to Robert Frost, 1998; Finders Keepers: selected prose 1971–2001, 2002; *poetry:* Eleven Poems, 1965; Death of a Naturalist, 1966 (Somerset Maugham Award, 1967; Cholmondeley Award, 1968); Door into the Dark, 1969; Wintering Out, 1972; North, 1975 (W. H. Smith Award; Duff Cooper Prize); Field Work, 1979; Selected Poems, 1965–1975, 1980; (ed with Ted Hughes) The Rattle Bag, 1982; Sweeney Astray, 1984, rev. edn as Sweeney's Flight, (with photographs by Rachel Giese), 1992; Station Island, 1984; The Haw Lantern, 1987 (Whitbread Award, 1987); New Selected Poems 1966–1987, 1990; Seeing Things, 1991; The Spirit Level (Whitbread Book of the Year), 1996; (ed with Ted Hughes) The School Bag, 1997; Opened Ground: poems 1966–1996, 1998; trans., Beowulf (Whitbread Book of the Year), 1999; Electric Light, 2001; trans., The Burial at Thebes, 2004; District and Circle, 2006 (T. S. Eliot Prize, 2007). *Address:* c/o Faber & Faber, 3 Queen Square, WC1N 3AU.

HEAP, Sir Brian; *see* Heap, Sir R. B.

HEAP, Sir Peter (William), KCMG 1995 (CMG 1987); HM Diplomatic Service, retired; *b* 13 April 1935; *s* of Roger and Dora Heap; *m* 1st, Helen Wilmerding; two *s* two *d*; 2nd, Dorrit Breitenstein; 3rd, 1986, Ann Johnson; one step *s* one step *d. Educ:* Bristol Cathedral Sch.; Merton Coll., Oxford. 2nd Lt Glos Regt and RWAFF, 1954–56. Joined Diplomatic Service, 1959; Third Sec., Dublin, 1960; Second Sec., Ottawa, 1960; First Sec., Colombo, 1963–66; seconded to MoD, 1966–68; FO, 1968–71; Dep. Dir-Gen., British Information Services, New York, 1971–76; Counsellor, Caracas, 1976–80; Head of Energy, Science and Space Dept, FCO, 1980–83; High Comr to the Bahamas, 1983–86; Minister and Dep. High Comr, Lagos, 1986–89; British Trade Comr, Hong Kong, and Consul-Gen., Macau, 1989–92; Ambassador to Brazil, 1992–95. Advr to Bd, HSBC Investment Bank, 1995–98; Consultant: Amerada Hess plc, 1996–2006; BOC Gp, 1997–2001; Adv. Bd, CFS Partners, 2001–; Dep. Chm., RCM Gp, 2001–05; non-exec. Dir, D. S. Wolf Internat., 1998–99; non-exec. Chm., Regal Petroleum plc, 2005–06. Chairman: Brazilian Chamber of Commerce in GB, 1996–; Britain Brazil Business Forum, 1998–2003; Labour Finance and Industry Gp, 2003–. Mem., Internat. Cttee, CBI, 1997–2002. Member, Council: Anglo Brazil Soc., 1999–; Friends of the Bahamas, 2000–. Chm., Maria Nobrega Charitable Trust, 2003–. Gov., Greycoat Hosp. Sch., 2001–. Freeman, City of London, 2001. *Address:* (home) 6 Carlisle Mansions, Carlisle Place, SW1P 1HX.

HEAP, Sir (Robert) Brian, Kt 2001; CBE 1994; FRS 1989; FRSC; FIBiol; Master, St Edmund's College, Cambridge, 1996–2004 (Hon. Fellow, since 2003); *b* 27 Feb. 1935; *s* of late Bertram Heap and Eva Mary Heap (*née* Melling); *m* 1961, Marion Patricia Grant; two *s* one *d. Educ:* New Mills Grammar Sch.; Univ. of Nottingham (BSc, PhD); King's Coll., Cambridge (MA, ScD). Univ. Demonstrator, Cambridge, 1960; Lalor Res. Fellow, ARC Babraham, Cambridge, 1963; Staff Mem., AFRC Babraham, 1964–95: Hd, Dept of Physiology, 1976; Hd, Cambridge Res. Station, 1986; Dir, Inst. of Animal Physiol. and Genetics Res., Cambridge and Edinburgh, 1989–93; Dir of Science, AFRC, 1991–94; Dir, AFRC Babraham Inst., 1993–94. Vis. Prof., Univ. of Nairobi, 1974; Vis. Res. Fellow, Murdoch Univ., 1976; Special Prof., Univ. of Nottingham, 1988–; Vis. Prof., Univ. of Guelph, 1990; Vis. Sen. Fellow, Sch. of Clin. Medicine, Univ. of Cambridge, 1994–2001; Res. Associate, Faraday Inst., St Edmund's Coll., Cambridge, 2006–. Mem., Scientific Adv. Bd, Merck, Sharp and Dohme, 1990–98; Principal Scientific Advr,

ZyGEM, NZ, 2005–. UK Rep. NATO Sci. Cttee, Brussels, 1998–2005. Member: Exec. Council, ESF, 1994–97; Council, Royal Soc., 1994–2001 (Foreign Sec. and Vice-Pres., 1996–2001); Nuffield Council on Bioethics, 1997–2001; Chair: Governing Council, Cambridge Theological Fedn, 2006–; Cambridge Genetics Knowledge Park, 2002–07; Vice-Chm., European Acads Sci. Adv. Council, 2004–08. Member Committee: Soc. for Study of Fertility, 1967–72; Jls of Reproduction and Fertility Ltd; Bibliography of Reproduction, 1967–70; Soc. and Jl of Endocrinology, 1980–84; Placenta; Oxford Reviews of Reproductive Biology, 1981–94; Exec. Editor, Philosophical Trans of Royal Soc., 2004–07. Consultant: WHO, Geneva, 1975–82; China, 1981–85. Chairman: Ciba Foundn Symposium, 1978; Harden Conf., 1984. President: Inst. of Biol., 1996–98; Internat. Soc. Sci. and Religion, 2006–08 Judge: Templeton Prize, 2001–04; Kilby Awards, 2002. Mem. Adv. Bd, John Templeton Foundn, 2004–06; Trustee: Cambridge Overseas Trust, 2002–; European Trust, 2002–; Commonwealth Trust, 2003–; Sense about Science, 2004–; Chm. Trustees, Academia Europaea, 2003–. Vice-Pres., Queen Mother Meml Fund, 2003–04. Lectures: Hammond, Soc. for Study of Fertility, 1986; Linacre, Oxford Univ., 1993; Annual, RASE, 1995; Robinson Meml, Univ. of Nottingham, 1997; Rutherford Meml, South Africa, 1999. Hon. FZS 2007; Hon. Foreign Fellow, Korean Acad. of Sci. and Technol., 1998. Hon. Fellow, Green Coll., Oxford, 1997. Hon. DSc: Nottingham, 1994; York, 2001; St Andrews, 2007. Research Medallist, RASE, 1976; Inventor's Award, AFRC, 1980. *Publications:* books and sci. papers on reproductive biology, endocrinology, biotechnology and sustainability, in various biol and med. jls. *Recreations:* music, hiking, kite flying. *Address:* St Edmund's College, Cambridge CB3 0BN.

HEAPS, Jeremy David P.; *see* Pickett-Heaps.

HEAPS, John Edward; Chief Executive, Britannia Building Society, 1993–99; *b* 24 Feb. 1939; *m* 1985, Shirley (*née* Jones); two *d*; one *s* one *d* from previous marr. *Educ:* Caldy Grange Grammar Sch., W Kirby; Oldershaw Grammar Sch., Wallasey. FCIB (FCBSI 1992). Colne Building Society: Sec., 1972; Chief Exec., 1972–80; Chief Exec. and Dir, 1980–83; Britannia Building Society: Dep. Gen. Manager, 1983–87; Gen. Manager, 1987–91; Inf. Systems Dir, 1991; Dep. Man. Dir, 1991–93. Chm., BSA, 1998–99 (Mem. Council, 1994; Dep. Chm., 1996–98); Dir, Bldg Socs Trust, 1997–99. Non-exec. Dir, Police Mutual Assurance Soc., 2001–. Dir, Staffs TEC, 1996–99. Trustee, Keele Develt Trust, 1996–2001. Mem. Court, Univ. of Keele, 1994–. MCMI. *Recreations:* family pursuits. *Address:* Top House Farm, Dodsleigh, Stoke on Trent, Staffs ST10 4QA.

HEARD, Peter Graham, CB 1987; FRICS; IRRV; Deputy Chief Valuer, Valuation Office, Board of Inland Revenue, 1983–89; *b* 22 Dec. 1929; *s* of late Sidney Horwood Heard and Doris Winifred Heard, MBE; *m* 1953, Ethne Jean Thomas; two *d*. *Educ:* Exmouth Grammar School. Articled to W. W. Needham, 1946; joined Valuation Office, 1950; served in Exeter, Kidderminster, Dudley, Leeds; District Valuer, Croydon, 1971; Superintending Valuer, Chief Valuer's Office, 1973; Asst Sec., Bd of Inland Revenue, 1975; Superintending Valuer, Midlands, 1977; Asst Chief Valuer, 1978. *Recreations:* cricket, golf, countryside, walking the dog, theatre. *Address:* Romany Cottage, High Street, Lindfield, Sussex RH16 2HR. *T:* (01444) 482095. *Clubs:* MCC, Civil Service.

HEARN, Barry Maurice William, FCA; Chairman, Matchroom Sport (formerly Matchroom) Ltd, since 1982; *b* 19 June 1948; *s* of George Sydney and Barbara Winifred Hearn; *m* 1970, Susan Clark; one *s* one *d*. *Educ:* Buckhurst Hill Grammar School. Owner and Chm., Leyton Orient FC, 1995–. Chm., Professional Darts Corp., 2001–. *Publication:* The Business, 1990. *Recreations:* football, fishing, poker, golf. *Address:* Matchroom Sport Ltd, Mascalls, Mascalls Lane, Brentwood, Essex CM14 5LJ. *T:* (01277) 359900.

HEARN, David Anthony; General Secretary, Broadcasting Entertainment Cinematograph Theatre Union, 1991–93 (General Secretary, 1987–90, Joint General Secretary, 1984–87, Broadcasting and Entertainment Trades Alliance); Chairman, Litho and Digital Impressions Ltd, since 1997; *b* 4 March 1929; *s* of James Wilfrid Laurier Hearn and Clara (*née* Barlow); *m* 1952, Anne Beveridge; two *s*. *Educ:* Trinity Coll., Oxford (MA). Asst to Gen. Sec., Assoc. of Broadcasting Staff, 1955; subseq. Asst Gen. Sec., then Dep. Gen. Sec.; Gen. Sec., Assoc. of Broadcasting and Allied Staffs, 1972–84. Dir, Nat. Campaign for the Arts Ltd, 1986–93. Chm., Film and Electronic Media Cttee, Fedn of Entertainment Unions, 1991–93; Mem., British Screen Adv. Council, 1987; President: Internat. Fedn of Audio Visual Unions, 1991–93 (Gen. Sec., W European Sect., 1984–91); Eur. Cttee of Trade Unions in Arts, Mass Media and Entertainment, 1992–93. Sen. Res. Fellow, Nuffield Coll., Oxford, 1970–71. *Address:* 4 Stocks Tree Close, Yarnton, Kidlington, Oxon OX5 1LU. *T:* (01865) 374613.

HEARN, Donald Peter; Bursar and Fellow of Clare College, Cambridge, since 2001; *b* 2 Nov. 1947; *s* of late Peter James Hearn and Anita Margaret Hearn; *m* 1973, Rachel Mary Arnold; two *d*. *Educ:* Clifton College; Selwyn College, Cambridge (MA). FCA. Ernst & Whinney, 1969–79; Group Financial Controller, Saga Holidays, 1979–83; Chief Financial Officer, Lee Valley Water Co., 1983–86; Finance Dir, 1986–2001, Sec., 1989–2001, RHS; Gen. Comr for Taxes, 1990–. Mem., F and GP Cttee, RPMS, Univ. of London, 1991–97; Imperial College: Chm., Audit Cttee, 1996–2005; Mem. Court, 1998–2005; Chm., House Cttee, 1998–2001; Gov., 2001–05; Member: Selwyn Coll. Assoc. Cttee, 1997–2001; Cambridge Univ. Audit Cttee, 2002–07; Trustee, Cambridge Univ. Staff Pension Scheme, 2002– (Chm., Investments Cttee, 2002–). Dir, Fitzwilliam Museum Enterprise, 2003–. Trustee: Chelsea Physic Gdn, 2002– (Treas., 2003–); Cambridge Univ. Botanic Gdn, 2003–. Governor, Woldingham Sch., 1990–93. Hon. FRHS. *Recreation:* gardening. *Address:* Clare College, Cambridge CB2 1TL. *T:* (01223) 333221.

HEARN, Rt Rev. George Arthur; Bishop of Rockhampton, 1981–96; Vicar of Canterbury, diocese of Melbourne, 1996–2001; *b* 17 Nov. 1935; *s* of Albert Frederick and Edith Maxham Hearn; *m* 1957, Adele Taylor (*d* 2006); two *s* one *d*. *Educ:* Northcote High School; University High School; Latrobe Univ., Melbourne. BA, ThL 1965, DipRE, ThSchol Aust. Coll. of Theology; MACE. Deacon 1964, priest 1965, Diocese of Gippsland; Curate of Traralgon, 1964–66; Vicar of Omeo, 1966–69; Rector of Wonthaggi, 1969–73; Rector of Kyabram, dio. Bendigo, 1973–77; Field Officer, Dept of Christian Education, Diocese of Melbourne, 1977–79; Dir, Gen. Bd of Religious Education, 1978–81. *Recreations:* gardening, reading, golf, music. *Address:* 2 Arthur Street, Doncaster, Vic 3108, Australia.

HEARN, Prof. John Patrick, PhD; Deputy Vice-Chancellor (Academic and International), University of Sydney, since 2004; *b* Limbdi, India, 24 Feb. 1943; *s* of late Lt-Col Hugh Patrick Hearn, Barrister, and Cynthia Ellen (*née* Nicholson); *m* 1967, Margaret Ruth Patricia McNair; four *s* one *d*. *Educ:* Crusaders' Sch., Headley, Hants; St Mary's Sch., Nairobi, Kenya; University Coll., Dublin (BSc, MSc); ANU, Canberra (PhD). Lectr in Zool., 1967–69, and Dean of Science, 1968–69, Strathmore Coll., Nairobi; Res. Scholar, ANU, 1969–72; scientist, MRC Reproductive Biology Unit, Edinburgh, 1972–79; Consultant Scientist, WHO Special Prog. of Res. in Human Reproduction, Geneva, 1978–79; Zoological Society of London: Dir, Wellcome Labs of Comparative Physiology, 1979–80; Dir of Science and Dir, Inst. of Zool., 1980–87; Dep. Sec., AFRC, 1987–90; Dir, MRC/AFRC Comparative Physiology Res. Gp, 1983–89; Dir, Wisconsin Regl Primate Res. Center and Prof. in Physiol., Med. Sch., Univ. of Wisconsin-Madison, 1989–96; Consultant Scientist, WHO Res. Prog. in Family and Reproductive Health, Geneva, 1996–98; Australian National University: Dir, Res. Sch. of Biol Scis, 1998–2001; Dep. Vice-Chancellor (Res.), 2001–04. Rapporteur, WHO Asia Pacific Regl Panel in Reproductive Health, 1999–. Chm., Australian Biotechnol. Adv. Council, 2001–. Vis. Prof. in Biology (formerly in Zoology), UCL, 1979–93; Vis. Prof. New England Primate Res. Center, Harvard Univ. Med. Sch., 1989–91; Hon. Res. Fellow, CSIRO Wildlife and Ecology, 1999–. Pres., Internat. Primatological Soc. 1984–88; Chm., Soc. for Reproductive Biology, 2000–04. Scientific Medal, Zool Soc. London, 1983; Osman Hill Medal, Primate Soc. of GB, 1986. *Publications:* (ed with H. Rothe and H. Wolters) The Biology and Behaviour of Marmosets, 1978; (ed) Immunological Aspects of Reproduction and Fertility Control, 1980; (ed) Reproduction in New World Primates, 1982; (ed) Advances in Animal Conservation, 1985; (ed) Reproduction and Disease in Captive and Wild Animals, 1988; (ed) Conservation of Primate Species studied in Biomedical Research, 1994; papers on develtl and reproductive physiol. in scientific jls. *Recreations:* wildlife, running, swimming. *Address:* University of Sydney, NSW 2006, Australia. *T:* (2) 93514461, *Fax:* (2) 93514462; *e-mail:* j.hearn@vcc.usyd.edu.au. *Club:* Athenæum.

HEARN, Sarah Penelope; *see* Chambers, S. P.

HEARNDEN, Dr Arthur George, OBE 1990; General Secretary, Independent Schools Joint Council, 1985–97; *b* 15 Dec. 1931; *s* of Hugh and Violet Hearnden; *m* 1962, Josephine McNeill; one *s* two *d*. *Educ:* Methodist Coll., Belfast; Christ's Coll., Cambridge (MA); Wadham Coll., Oxford (DPhil). Teacher, Friends' Sch., Lisburn, 1952–55; N short service commn, Royal Signals, 1955–57; teacher, various schs, incl. Aldenham (1959–67), and in exchange posts, Lycée d'Aix-les-Bains and Bunsengymnasium Heidelberg, 1957–68; Res. Officer, Oxford Univ., 1969–71; Lectr in Comparative Education, Inst. of Education, Univ. of London, 1972–74; Secretary: Standing Conf. on Univ. Entrance, 1975–84; Overseas Res. Students Awards Scheme, 1982–84. Chairman Internat. Cttee, Soc. for Res. in Higher Educn, 1977–81; Internat. Baccalaureate Feasibility Study, 1979–80. Member: DES Adv. Cttee on AS level, 1985–91; Hanover Univ./VW Commn on German Univ. Hist., 1985–91; Sch. Exams and Assessment Council, 1988–91; Funding Agency for Schs, 1994–98 (Chm. of Finance, 1997–98); Pres Complaints Commn, 1999–2005. Educnl Advr, Royal Ballet Sch., 2001–03. Pres., Ind Schs Assoc., 1997–2002; Hon. Vice Pres., Council of British Internat. Schs (formerly Indep. Schs in EC), 1997–; Chm., HSBC Bursary Fund, 1998–2002; Trustee: Hall Sch Charitable Trust, 1988– (Chm, 1998–); Youth for Britain-Worldwide Volunteering 1993–2000 (Chm., 1995–2000); Millwood Educn Trust, 2002– (Chm., 2007–). Governor: Wychwood Sch., 1983–90; Abbotsholme, 1985–92; Oxford High Sch 1985–92; Abingdon Sch., 1988–99; Dunottar Sch., 1990–92; Newton Prep. Sch., 1992– Sec., Hethe PCC, 1998–2005; Mem., Hethe Parish Council, 2003–05. *Publications:* Path to University, 1973; Bildungspolitik in der BRD und DDR, 1973 (trans. Education in the Two Germanies, 1974); Education, Culture and Politics in West Germany, 1974 Methods of Establishing Equivalences, 1976; (ed) The British in Germany, 1978; (ed) From School to University, 1980; Red Robert, a Life of Robert Birley, 1984; A Flying Start: the story of the Manor, 2007; reports and articles in learned jls. *Recreations:* family hill walking, theatre. *Address:* Hethe House, Hethe, Bicester, Oxon OX27 8ES. *T:* (01869) 277985, *Fax:* (01869) 278445. *Club:* Athenæum.

HEARNE, Sir Graham (James), Kt 1998; CBE 1990; Chairman: Catlin Group Ltd since 2003; Enterprise Oil plc, 1991–2002 (Chief Executive, 1984–91); *b* 23 Nov. 1937 *s* of Frank Hearne and Emily (*née* Shakespeare); *m* 1961, Carol Jean (*née* Brown); one *s* two *d* (and one *d* decd). *Educ:* George Dixon Grammar Sch., Birmingham. Admitted solicitor 1959: Pinsent & Co., Solicitors, 1959–63; Fried, Frank, Harris, Shriver & Jacobson Attorneys, NYC, 1963–66; Herbert Smith & Co., Solicitors, 1966–67; IRC, 1967–68; N M. Rothschild & Sons Ltd, 1968–77; Finance Dir, Courtaulds Ltd, 1977–81; Chief Exec Tricentrol, 1981–83; Gp Man. Dir, Carless, Capel and Leonard, 1983–84. Non-executive Director: N. M. Rothschild & Sons Ltd, 1970–; Northern Foods, Ltd, 1976–82; BP Industries, 1982–91; Reckitt & Colman, 1990–97; Courtaulds, 1991–98; Wellcome 1991–95; The Wellcome Foundn, 1991–95; Gallaher Gp plc, 1997–2007 (Dep. Chm 1997–2007); BTR plc, 1998–99; Invensys (formerly BTR Siebe) plc, 1999–2003 Braemar Seascope Gp plc (formerly Seascope Shipping Hldgs plc), 1999– (Chm., 2002–) Wellstream Internat. Ltd, 2003–; Stratic Energy Corp., 2005– (Chm., 2005–); Chairman Caradon, then Novar, plc, 1999–2005; Rowan Cos Inc., 2004–; part-time Member British National Oil Corp., 1975–78; Dover Harbour Bd, 1976–78. Chm., Brindex (Assoc. of British Indep. Oil Exploration Cos), 1986–88. Trustee: Philharmonia Orch Trust, 1982–; Chichester Fest. Theatre Trust, 1988–98; Hayward Foundn, 1992–2002 High Sheriff, Greater London, 1995. *Address:* 5 Crescent Place, SW3 2EA. *Clubs:* Reform Brooks's, MCC.

HEARNE, Peter Ambrose, FREng; Chairman, GEC Avionics, 1992–94; *b* 14 Nov. 1927; *e s* of late Arthur Ambrose Hearne, MD, and Helen Mackay Hearne; *m* 1952 Georgina Gordon Guthrie; three *s*. *Educ:* Sherborne Sch., Dorset; Loughborough Coll. of Technol. (DLC); Cranfield Inst. of Technol. (MSc); MIT. Design Engr, Saunders Roe 1946–47; Ops Develt Engr, BOAC, 1949–54; Helicopter Proj. Engr, BEA, 1954–58 Marketing Manager, British Oxygen, 1958–59; Divl Man., Guided Weapons, Elliott F Automation, 1959; Asst Gen. Man., 1960, Dir and Gen. Man., 1966–87, Marconi (late GEC) Avionics; Asst Man. Dir, 1987–90, Pres., US Ops, 1990–92, GEC Marconi. Vis Prof., Cranfield Inst. of Technol., 1981–82. Chm., Cranfield Soc., 1965–67, Pres 1981–85; Pres., Royal Aeronautical Society, 1980–81 (Vice-Pres., 1976–79; Hon. FRAe 1990; Wright Bros Lectr, 1991); Vice Chm., 1997–99, Vice Pres., 1999–, British Gliding Assoc. FREng (FEng 1984); FRIN 1999. John Curtis Sword, Aviation Week, 1982 Diamond C badge, 1988. *Publications:* (ed) Pilot's Summer, 2nd edn 2000; papers in Jl of RAeS and NATO Agard series. *Recreations:* flying sailplanes, model railways. *Address:* The Limes, Wateringbury, Kent ME18 5NY. *Clubs:* Royal Air Force; Surrey and Hants Gliding; Aero Alpin (Gap).

HEARST, Stephen, CBE 1980; FRSA; independent television producer and consultant since 1986; *b* Vienna, Austria, 6 Oct. 1919; *m* 1948, Lisbeth Edith Neumann; one *s* one *d*. *Educ:* Vienna Univ.; Reading Univ. (Dip. Hort.); Brasenose Coll., Oxford (MA). Free lance writer, 1949–52; joined BBC as producer trainee, 1952; Documentary television script writer, 1953–55; writer producer, 1955–65; Exec. Producer, Arts Programmes Television, 1965–67; Head of Arts Features, Television, 1967–71; Controller, Radio 3 1972–78; Controller, Future Policy Gp, 1978–82; Special Adviser to Dir-Gen., BBC 1982–86. Vis. Fellow, Inst. for Advanced Studies, Edinburgh Univ., 1988. FRSA 198 *Publications:* Two Thousand Million Poor, 1965; Artistic Heritage and its Treatment by Television, 1982; (contrib.) The Third Age of Broadcasting (ed Wenham), 1982 (contrib.) Television and the Public Interest (ed Jay G. Blumler), 1991; (contrib.) Literacy is not enough (ed Brian Cox), 1998. *Recreations:* gardening, swimming, reading, listenin to music. *Address:* c/o British Academy of Film and Television Arts, 195 Piccadilly, W1V 9LG.

HEARTH, John Dennis Miles, CBE 1983; Chief Executive, Royal Agricultural Society of England, 1972–89 and 1991–92; *b* 8 April 1929; *s* of late Cyril Howard Hearth, MC, and Dr Pauline Kathleen Hearth, MB, BCh; *m* 1959, Pamela Anne (*née* Bryant); two *s* (one *d* decd). *Educ:* The King's Sch., Canterbury; Brasenose Coll., Oxford (MA). Called to the Bar, Gray's Inn, 1962. Administrative Officer, HM Overseas Civil Service, 1953–61; Editor, Fairplay Shipping Journal, Fairplay Publications Ltd, 1961–66; Cunard Steam-Ship Co. Ltd, 1966–71 (various appts and Main Board Joint Ventures Director, 1969–71). Mem., Gen. Adv. Council, BBC, 1990–95; Chairman: Rural and Agricl Affairs Cttee, BBC, 1990–96; Nat. Rural Enterprise Centre, RASE, 1988–94; British Food and Farming Ltd, 1989–2004; Management Cttee, Nat. Fedn of Young Farmers' Clubs, 1989–95. Pres., British Pig Assoc., 1990–93. Mem. Council, Conservation Foundn, 1987–94; Dep. Chm., Rural Housing Trust (formerly NAC Rural Trust), 1992–2004 (Trustee, 1987–2004); Chm., English Villages Housing Assoc., 1995–97 (Mem., 1990–2004; Chm. Finance Cttee, 1990–97); Chm., English Rural Housing Assoc., 1999–2003 (Mem. Cttee, 1993–2003); Mem., Rural Adv. Gp, Housing Corp., 1999–2004. Governor, RAC, Cirencester, 1975–92; Mem., 1985–98, Treasurer, 1989–98, Warwick Univ. Council; Director: Univ. of Warwick Science Park Ltd, 1990–98; Warwick Univ. Trng Ltd, 1998–2004; Warwick Univ. Services Ltd, 1998–2004; Trustee, Univ. of Warwick Foundn, 2001–04. CCMI (CBIM 1980); FRSA 1989. Hon. FRASE 1989. Hon. LLD Warwick, 1999. *Recreations:* travel, history, theatre, photography, golf. *Address:* Sheen Farmhouse, Temple End, Harbury, Leamington Spa, Warwicks CV33 9NE. *T:* (01926) 612238. *Club:* Royal Anglo-Belgian.

HEARTY, Michael John; Director of Finance, Department for Children, Schools and Families, since 2007 (Deputy Director, Financial Accounting, 2006–07); *b* Blackpool, 28 May 1959; *s* of Patrick Brian and Joan Hearty; *m* 1990, Janet Holden; one *d*. *Educ:* Holy Family Prim Sch.; St Thomas of Canterbury Sec. Mod. Sch.; Victoria Univ. of Manchester (BA Hons Econs 1983); Liverpool John Moores Univ. (CPFA 1994). Department of Health and Social Security, subseq. Department of Social Security, later Benefits Agency, then Department for Work and Pensions: Clerical grades, 1975–77; Exec. Officer, 1984–90; Higher Exec. Officer (Trainee Accountant), 1990–94; Sen. Exec. Officer (Accountant), 1994–99; Prin. Accountant, 1999–2002; Head: Accounting Gp, 2002–04; Finance, Planning and Performance, 2004–05; Business Mgt Div., 2005–06; Dep. Dir, Gp Finance Directorate, 2005–06. Non-exec. Dir, Audit Cttee, DoH, 2007–. Chm. of Govs, Carr Head Prim. Sch., Poulton-le-Fylde, 2006–. *Recreations:* season ticket holder of Everton FC (with daughter, Rachael), playing guitar. *Address:* Department for Children, Schools and Families, Castle View House, PO Box 12, Runcorn WA7 2GJ. *T:* (01928) 794368; *e-mail:* michael.hearty@dcsf.gsi.gov.uk.

HEASLIP, Rear-Adm. Richard George, CB 1987; Director-General, English-Speaking Union, 1987–90; *b* 30 April 1932; *s* of Eric Arthur Heaslip and Vera Margaret (*née* Bailey); *m* 1959, Lorna Jean Grayston, Halifax, NS, Canada; three *s* one *d* (incl. twin *s* and *d*). *Educ:* Royal Naval Coll., Dartmouth. CO HMS Sea Devil, 1961–62; Exec. Officer, HMS Dreadnought (1st British nuclear submarine), 1965–66; CO HMS Conqueror (nuclear submarine), 1971–72; CO Second Submarine Sqdn, 1975–77; Staff, SACLANT, 1980–82; Staff, CDS, 1982–84; Dep. Asst COS (Ops), Staff of SACEUR, 1984; Flag Officer Submarines, and Comdr Submarine Forces Eastern Atlantic, 1984–87. ADC 1984–85. Member: European Atlantic Gp Cttee, 1988–89; Bureau, Standing Conf. of Atlantic Orgns, 1988–89. Chm., RN Football Assoc., 1976–84; President: London Submarine Old Comrades Assoc., 1987–2007; Conqueror Assoc., 2003–. Mem., Ferndown Town Council, 2006–08. *Publication:* End to End, 2007. *Recreations:* walking (Land's End to John O'Groats, 2002); music, gardening. *Address:* 2 Longfield Drive, West Parley, Dorset BH22 8TY; *e-mail:* rgheaslip@hotmail.com.

HEATH, Angela; *see* Heath, L. A.

HEATH, Prof. Anthony Francis, PhD; FBA 1992; Professor of Sociology, University of Oxford, since 1996; Fellow of Nuffield College, Oxford, since 1987; *b* 15 Dec. 1942; *s* of Ronald John Heath and Cicely Florence (*née* Roberts); *m* 1983, Dr Mary-Jane Pearce, MRCGP, FRCPsych; two *s* one *d*. *Educ:* Merchant Taylors', Crosby; Trinity Coll., Cambridge (BA 1st cl. Classics pt I, 1st cl. Econs pt II; PhD 1971). Asst Principal, HM Treasury, 1965–66; Fellow of Churchill Coll., 1967–70, Asst Lectr, Faculty of Econs, 1968–70, Cambridge Univ.; Univ. Lectr and Fellow of Jesus Coll., Oxford, 1970–86. Dir, 1983, 1987, 1992 and 1997 British Election Studies, and Co-Dir, Centre for Res. into Elections and Social Trends, 1994–, ESRC. *Publications:* Rational Choice and Social Change, 1976; (jtly) Origins and Destinations, 1980; Social Mobility, 1981; (jtly) How Britain Votes, 1985; (jtly) Understanding Political Change, 1991; (jtly) Labour's Last Chance, 1994; (jtly) The Rise of New Labour, 2001; (jtly) Unequal Chances: ethnic minorities in Western labour markets, 2007; contribs to Jl of Royal Stat. Soc., Amer. Jl of Sociol., Eur. Sociol Rev., Eur. Jl of Sociol., Eur. Jl of Pol Res., Sociology, British Jl of Pol. Sci.; Electoral Studies, Acta Sociologica, Oxford Rev. of Educn. *Recreations:* piano playing, cross-country running. *Address:* 72 Lonsdale Road, Oxford OX2 7EP. *T:* (01865) 553512. *Clubs:* Achilles; Hawks (Cambridge).

HEATH, Bernard Oliver, OBE 1980; CEng, FRAeS; Professor of Aeronautical Engineering (British Aerospace Integrated Chair), Salford University, 1983–89; *b* 8 March 1925; *s* of Bernard Ernest Heath and Ethel May Heath; *m* 1948, Ethel Riley; one *s*. *Educ:* Derby Sch.; Bemrose Sch., Derby; University Coll. of Nottingham (BSc Univ. of London 1944); Imperial Coll. of Science and Technology (DIC 1945). CEng 1966; FRAeS 1978. English Electric Co.: Stressman (loading and stressing of Canberra), 1945; Aerodynamicist, Lightning, 1948; Aerostructures Gp Leader (Lightning loading and aeroelasticity), 1951; Chief Proj. Engr, 1957; Asst Chief Engr, Canberra and TSR2, 1959; British Aircraft Corporation: TSR2 Proj. Manager (Devclt), 1963; Special Dir, 1965; Leader, Jaguar Technical Team, 1965; Proj. Manager, AFVG, 1966; Panavia: Dir, Systems Engrg (Warton), 1969–81; Dir, MRCA, 1970; Dir of Engrg, 1974; British Aerospace: Technical Dir, Warton Div., 1978–81; Divisional Dir of Advanced Engrg, 1981–84. Chm., SBAC Technical Bd, 1980–82. Hon. MIED 1975. RAeS Silver Medal (for outstanding work over many yrs on design and develt of mil. aircraft), 1977; (jtly) Internat. Council of Aeronautical Sciences Von Karman Award (for successful internat. co-operation on Tornado), 1982; Corresp. Mem., Deutsche Ges. für Luft und Raumfahrt, 1993. *Publications:* papers to AGARD, Internat. Council of Aeronautical Sciences Congresses, RAF Histl Soc.; contrib. RAeS Jl, Flight, The Times, R & D Mgt and Aircraft Engrg. *Recreation:* history of transport. *Address:* c/o Company Secretary, BAE Systems, Warton Aerodrome, Preston, Lancs PR4 1AX.

HEATH, David William St John, CBE 1989; MP (Lib Dem) Somerton and Frome, since 1997; *b* 16 March 1954; *s* of Eric Heath and Pamela Heath; *m* 1987, Caroline Netherton; one *s* one *d*. *Educ:* Millfield Sch.; St John's Coll., Oxford (MA Physiological Scis); City Univ. FADO 1979. In practice as optician, 1979–86. Somerset County Council: Councillor (Lib Dem), 1985–97; Leader, 1985–89; Chm., Educn Cttee, 1996–97. Vice Chm., Assoc. of County Councils, 1993–97. Chm., Avon & Somerset Police Authy, 1993–96; Vice Chm., Cttee of Local Police Authorities, 1993–97. Mem., Audit Commn, 1995–97. Contested (Lib Dem) Somerton and Frome, 1992. Lib Dem spokesman on European affairs, 1997–98, on foreign affairs, 1999–2001, on work, family and pensions, 2001–03, on home and legal affairs, 2003–05; on constitutional affairs, and shadow to Leader of the House, 2005–07, shadow to Sec. of State for Justice and Lord Chancellor, 2007–. Mem., Witham Friary Friendly Soc., 1984–. FRSA 1995. *Recreations:* cricket, Rugby football, pig breeding until recently. *Address:* The Yard, Witham Friary, near Frome, Somerset BA11 5HF. *T:* (01749) 850458. *Club:* National Liberal.

HEATH, Prof. John Baldwin; management consultant; Secretary General, International Council for Peace, Reconciliation and Recovery, 1996–99; *b* 25 Sept. 1924; *s* of late Thomas Arthur Heath and late Dorothy Meallin; *m* 1st, 1953, Wendy Julia Betts (marr. diss. 1995); two *s* one *d*; 2nd, 2000, Chris Michell. *Educ:* Merchant Taylors' Sch.; St Andrews Univ.; Cambridge Univ. RNVR, 1942–46. Spicers Ltd, 1946–50; Lecturer in Economics, Univ. of Manchester, 1956–64; Rockefeller Foundation Fellowship, 1961–62; Dir, Economic Research Unit, Bd of Trade, 1964–67; Dir, Economic Services Div., BoT, 1967–70; Prof. of Economics, London Business Sch., 1970–86; Dir, London Sloan Fellowship Programme, 1983–86. Chm., EXE Ltd, 1982–93; Dir, Health Policy Unit, 1994–95. Member: Mechanical Engrg EDC, 1971–76; British Airports Authy, 1980–86; Economic Adviser, CAA, 1972–78. *Publications:* Public Enterprise at the Crossroads, 1990; Revitalizing Socialist Enterprise, 1993; Tibet and China in the 21st Century, 2005; articles in many learned jls on competition and monopoly, productivity, cost-benefit analysis. *Recreations:* music, walking.

HEATH, John Moore, CMG 1976; HM Diplomatic Service, retired; *b* 9 May 1922; *s* of late Philip George and Olga Heath; *m* 1952, Patricia Mary Bibby; one *s* one *d*. *Educ:* Shrewsbury Sch.; Merton Coll., Oxford (MA). Served War of 1939–45, France, Belgium and Germany: commnd Inns of Court Regt, 1942; Capt. GSO3 11th Armoured Div., 1944–45 (despatches). Merton Coll., 1940–42, 1946–47. Entered Foreign Service, 1950; 2nd Sec., Comr-Gen.'s Office, Singapore, 1950–52; 1st Sec. (Commercial), Jedda, 1952–56; 1st Sec., FO, 1956–58; Nat. Def. Coll., Kingston, Ont., 1958–59; Head of Chancery and HM Consul, Brit. Embassy, Mexico City, 1959–62; Head of Chancery, Brit. Embassy, Kabul, Afghanistan, 1963–65; Counsellor and Head of Establishment and Organisation Dept, FCO (formerly DSAO), 1966–69; Counsellor (Commercial), Brit. Embassy, Bonn, 1969–74; Overseas Trade Advr, Assoc. of British Chambers of Commerce, on secondment, 1974; Consul-Gen., Chicago, 1975–79; Ambassador to Chile, 1980–82. Dir Gen., Canning House (Hispanic and Luso-Brazilian Council), 1982–87. Chm., Anglo-Chilean Soc., 1987–89. FRPSL 1999. Orden al Merito por Servicios Distinguidos, Peru, 1984; Orden al Merito, Gran Oficial, Chile, 1991. *Publications:* The British Postal Agencies in Mexico 1825–1876, 1969; The Heath family engravers 1779–1878, 3 vols, 1993–98; Mexican Maritime Mail from Colonial Times to the Twentieth Century, 1997; Mexico - The 1868 Issue, 2004. *Recreations:* book collecting, Mexican philately, walking. *Address:* 6 Cavendish Crescent, Bath, N Somerset BA1 2UG. *Club:* Naval and Military.

HEATH, (Lettyce) Angela; non-executive Director, The North West London Hospitals (formerly Northwick Park and St Mark's) NHS Trust, 1996–2002; *b* 27 May 1944; *d* of late Frank Buchanan Ryde and Emily Rose Ryde (*née* Davies); *m* 1st, 1966, Gareth Thomas (marr. diss. 1975); 2nd, 1985, Roger Heath; two step *d*. *Educ:* Birmingham Univ. (BA 1966; MA 1968); Birkbeck Coll., London (MSc 1999). Department of the Environment, 1971–96: Admin. Trainee, 1971; Private Sec. to Minister of Housing, 1979; Asst Sec., 1983; Central Policy Planning Unit, 1983–85; Local Govt Div., 1985–87; Personnel Management, 1987–90; Housing Corp. Finance, 1990–91; Under-Sec., 1992; Regl Dir for London, 1992–94; Dir, Regeneration Progs, Govt Office for London, 1994–95; Dir, Local Govt, 1995–96. Vis. Sen. Fellow, Sch. of Public Policy, Univ. of Birmingham, 1997–99. JP Middlesex, 1997–2003. FRSA 1995. *Address:* 6 High View, Pinner, Middx HA5 3PA.

HEATH, Air Vice-Marshal Michael Christopher, CBE 1998; FRAeS; Special Adviser to Commander, US Central Command, 2005–07; *b* 21 Dec. 1950; *s* of late Stanley Frank Heath and Mary Bridget Heath; *m* 1978, Margaret Bolton; one *s* one *d*. *Educ:* St John's Coll., Southsea. Commnd, 1969; qualified navigator, 1971; Electronic Warfare Instructor, RN, 1974; Staff Navigation Instructor, 1978; qwi 1979; OC 20 Sqn (Tornado), 1991–92; Station Comdr, RAF Benson, 1996–97; rcds, 1998; Dir, Targetting and Inf. Ops, 1999–2003; Sen. British Mil. Advr to US Central Comd, 2003–05. FRAeS 2000. *Recreations:* gliding, golf, walking. *Address:* c/o Lloyds Bank TSB, Cox's & King's Branch, 7 Pall Mall, SW1Y 5NA. *Club:* Royal Air Force.

HEATH, Michael John, MBE 2001; freelance cartoonist, since 1956; Cartoons Editor, The Spectator, since 1989; *b* 13 Oct. 1935; *s* of George Heath and Alice (Queenie) Stewert Morrison Bremner; *m* 1st, 1959, Hanne Sternkopf (marr. diss. 1992); two *d*; 2nd, 2003, Martha Swift; two *d*. *Educ:* no education to speak of (Devon, Hampstead and Brighton); Brighton Art Coll. Trained as animator, Rank Screen Services, 1955; started placing cartoons in Melody Maker, 1955; contributed to: Lilliput; Tatler; John Bull; Man about Town; Men Only; Honey; Punch, 1958–89; Spectator, 1958–; Private Eye, 1964– (strips include The Gays, The Regulars, Great Bores of Today, Baby); Sunday Times, 1967–; London Standard, 1976–86, 1995–96; Mail on Sunday, 1985–; The Independent, 1986–97 (Political Cartoonist, 1991–96), 2003–; London Daily News, 1987. Pocket Cartoonist of the Year, Cartoonist Club of GB, 1977; Glen Grant Cartoonist of the Year, 1978; What the Papers Say Cartoonist of the Year, 1982; Pont Award for drawing the British Character, 2001. *Publications:* Private Eye Cartoon Library, 1973, 2nd edn 1975; The Punch Cartoons of Michael Heath, 1976; Book of Bores, No 1, 1976, No 2, Star Bores, 1979, No 3, Bores Three, 1983; Love All, 1982; Best of Heath (foreword by Malcolm Muggeridge), 1984; Welcome to America, 1985; Heath's Nineties, 1997. *Recreations:* listening to Charlie Parker and Thelonious Monk, walking, ballet. *Club:* Colony Room.

HEATH, Michael John; His Honour Judge Heath; a Circuit Judge, since 1995; Resident Judge, Lincoln Combined Court Centre, since 2000; *b* Grimsby, 12 June 1948; *s* of late Norman Heath and Dorothy Heath; *m* 1972, Heather, *d* of late Christopher Croft and of Mrs D. Croft, Hetton-le-Hole; two *s*. *Educ:* Barcroft County Sch., Wintringham; Grammar Sch., Grimsby; Leeds Univ. (LLB). FCIArb. Asst Solicitor, R. A. C. Symes and Co., Scunthorpe, 1975, Partner, 1977; Dep. Dist Judge, 1987–95; a Recorder, 1993–95; Solicitor Advocate (All Courts), 1994; Ethnic Minorities Liaison Judge, Lincolnshire, 1995–; Resident Judge, Grimsby Crown Court, 1999–2001; Magistrates' Liaison Judge, 2004–. Chm., Humberside Area Criminal Justice Strategy Cttee, 2000–03; Member: Courts Bd, Lincolnshire, 2004–; Lincolnshire Probation Bd, 2004–06. Hon. Recorder, City of Lincoln, 2001–. *Recreation:* keeping a low profile. *Address:* Lincoln Combined Court Centre, 360 High Street, Lincoln LN5 7RL. *T:* (01522) 883000.

HEATH, Maj.-Gen. Michael Stuart, CB 1994; CBE 1991; CEng, FIET; Director of Corporate Strategy, NXT plc, 2000–01; *b* 7 Sept. 1940; *s* of late Bernard Stuart Heath and of Blanche Dorothy Ellen Heath (*née* Fairey); *m* 1965, Frances Wood; one *s* one *d*. *Educ:* St Albans Sch.; Welbeck Coll.; Royal Military Coll. of Science (BSc Eng Upper 2nd cl. Hons London). Commissioned REME, 1961; served Malaya, BAOR, Edinburgh, to 1971; RMCS and Staff Coll., 1972–73; Armour Sch., Bovington, 1974–75; Comd 7 Field Workshop, BAOR, 1976–77; Nat. Defence Coll., 1978; Berlin Field Force, 1978–80; Comd Maint., HQ 2 Armd Div., BAOR, 1981–82; MoD, 1982–85; RCDS, 1986; Dir, Support Planning (Army), MoD, 1987–89; Comd Maint., HQ BAOR, 1990–91; Dir Gen., Electrical and Mechanical Engrg. subseq. Equipment Support (Army), MoD, 1991–93; Team Leader, Army Costs Study Team, 1994. Dir Gen., Engrg Council, 1995–98. Chm., 20/20 Speech Ltd, 1999–2000. *Recreations:* walking, music, photography, DIY. *Address:* c/o Barclays Bank, 167 High Street, Bromley, Kent BR1 1NL. *Club:* Army and Navy.

HEATH, Samantha Louise; Chief Executive Officer, London Sustainability Exchange, since 2006; *b* 6 June 1960; *d* of Harvey and Gillian Heath; *m*; one *s*. *Educ:* Heriot-Watt Univ. (BSc Hons); Univ. of Greenwich (PGCE 1999). Civil engineer, Sir Robert McAlpine & Sons Ltd, 1982–92; Sen. Lectr in Construction, Univ. of Greenwich, 1992–2000. Mem. (Lab) Wandsworth BC, 1994–2000; Mem. (Lab), 2000–04 and Dep. Chm., 2003–04, London Assembly, GLA (Chm., Envmt Cttee, 2000–04). Mem., 2002–, Mayor's Rep. on Energy Taskforce, 2002–04, Co-Chair, 2004–06, London Sustainable Develt Commn. Dep. Chm., Sustainable Energy Action, 2004–; Member: London Waste Action, 2003–06; London Energy Partnership; London Climate Change Partnership, 2005–. *Recreations:* reading, music. *Address:* c/o London Sustainability Exchange, Overseas House, 19–23 Ironmonger Row, EC1V 3QN.

HEATH-BROWN, Prof. David Rodney, (Roger), PhD; FRS 1993; Professor of Pure Mathematics, and Fellow of Worcester College, University of Oxford, since 1999; *b* 12 Oct. 1952; *s* of Basil Heath-Brown and Phyllis Joan (*née* Watson); *m* 1992, Ann Louise Sharpley; two *d*. *Educ:* Welwyn Garden City Grammar Sch.; Trinity Coll., Cambridge (BA, MA, PhD). Jun. Res. Fellow, Trinity Coll., Cambridge, 1977–79; Oxford University: Fellow and Tutor in Pure Maths, Magdalen Coll., 1979–98, Emeritus Fellow, 1999; Reader in Pure Maths, 1990–98. Corresp. Mem., Akad. der Wissenschaften, Göttingen, 1999. Jun. Berwick Prize, 1981, Sen. Berwick Prize, 1996, London Math. Soc. *Publications:* numerous mathematical papers in learned jls. *Recreations:* field botany, bridge, gardening. *Address:* Mathematical Institute, 24–29 St Giles', Oxford OX1 3LB. *T:* (01865) 273535.

HEATHCOAT-AMORY, Rt Hon. David (Philip); PC 1996; FCA; MP (C) Wells, since 1983; *b* 21 March 1949; *s* of late Roderick and Sonia Heathcoat-Amory; *m* 1978, Linda Adams; one *s* one *d* (and one *s* decd). *Educ:* Eton Coll.; Oxford Univ. (MA PPE). Qual. as Chartered Accountant with Price Waterhouse & Co., 1974; FCA 1980. Worked in industry, becoming Asst Finance Dir of British Technology Gp, until 1983 when resigned to fight Gen. Election. PPS to the Financial Sec. to the Treasury, 1985–87, to the Home Secretary, 1987–88; an Asst Govt Whip, 1988–89; a Lord Comr of HM Treasury, 1989; Parly Under Sec. of State, DoE, 1989–90, Dept. of Energy, 1990–92; Dep. Govt Chief Whip and Treasurer, HM Household, 1992–93; Minister of State, FCO, 1993–94; HM Paymaster General, 1994–96; Shadow Chief Sec. to HM Treasury, 1997–2000. *Recreations:* fishing, shooting, music, growing trees. *Address:* 12 Lower Addison Gardens, W14 8BQ. *T:* (020) 7603 3083. *Clubs:* Avalon (Glastonbury); Wells Conservative.

HEATHCOAT AMORY, Sir Ian, 6th Bt *cr* 1874; DL; *b* 3 Feb. 1942; *s* of Sir William Heathcoat Amory, 5th Bt, DSO, and Margaret Isabel Dorothy Evelyn (*d* 1997), *yr d* of Sir Arthur Havelock James Doyle, 4th Bt; *S* father, 1982; *m* 1972, Frances Louise, *d* of J. F. B. Pomeroy; four *s*. *Educ:* Eton. Chairman: Lowman Manufacturing Co. Ltd, 1976–; DevonAir Radio Ltd, 1983–90; Dir, Watts Blake Bearne & Co. PLC, 1984–88. Mem., Devon CC, 1973–85. JP Devon, 1980–93; DL Devon, 1981. *Heir: s* William Francis Heathcoat Amory, *b* 19 July 1975. *Address:* Calverleigh Court, Tiverton, Devon EX16 8BB.

HEATHCOTE, Dr (Frederic) Roger, CBE 2005; Chief Executive, Employment Tribunals Service, 2000–04; *b* 19 March 1944; *s* of late Frederic William Trevor Heathcote and Kathleen Annie Heathcote; *m* 1st, 1970, Geraldine Nixon (marr. diss. 1986); 2nd, 1986, Mary Campbell Syme Dickson; one *s* one step *d*. *Educ:* Bromsgrove Sch.; Birmingham Univ. (BSc (Hons) Physics, PhD). Res. Associate, Birmingham Univ., 1969–70; joined CS as Asst Principal, Min. of Technology (later DTI), 1970; Private Secretary to: Secretary (Industrial Develt), 1973; Permanent Under Sec. of State, Dept of Energy, 1974; Department of Energy: Principal, 1974; Asst Sec., 1978; Dir of Resource Management (Grade 4), 1988; Under Sec., Coal Div., 1989–91; Prin. Estabt and Finance Officer, 1991–92; Hd of Services Mgt Div., DTI, 1992–96; Dir, Export Control and Non-Proliferation, DTI, 1996–2000; UK Gov., IAEA, and UK Rep., Exec. Council of Orgn for the Prohibition of Chemical Weapons, 1996–2000. Non-exec. Dir, Trafalgar House Property Ltd, 1988–94. Gov., British Coll. of Osteopathic Medicine, 2004– (Chm., 2006–). *Recreations:* reading, gardening, painting. *Address:* 8B The Crescent, Surbiton, Surrey KT6 4BN.

HEATHCOTE, Brig. Sir Gilbert (Simon), 9th Bt *cr* 1733; CBE 1964 (MBE 1941); *b* 21 Sept. 1913; *s* of Col R. E. M. Heathcote, DSO (*d* 1970), Manton Hall, Rutland and Millicent Heathcote (*d* 1977), *d* of William Walton, Horsley Priory, Nailsworth, Glos; *S* to baronetcy of 3rd Earl of Ancaster, KCVO, 1983; *m* 1st, 1939, Patricia Margaret (*née* Leslie) (marr. diss. 1984); one *s* one *d*; 2nd, 1984, Ann, *widow* of Brig. J. F. C. Mellor, DSO, OBE. *Educ:* Eton; RMA Woolwich. Commnd RA, 1933, War Service in Europe, 1939–44; Comdr RA, 1960–62; Chief of Staff, Middle East Comd, 1962–64; retd. *Recreations:* writing, travel. *Heir: s* Mark Simon Robert Heathcote, OBE [*b* 1 March 1941; *m* 1975, Susan, *d* of late Lt-Col George Ashley; two *s*]. *Address:* The Coach House, Tillington, near Petworth, Sussex GU28 0RA. *Clubs:* Garrick, Army and Navy.

HEATHCOTE, Roger; *see* Heathcote, F. R.

HEATHCOTE, Sir Timothy Gilbert, 12th Bt *cr* 1733, of Hursley, Hampshire; *b* 25 May 1957; *er s* of Sir Michael Heathcote, 11th Bt and of Victoria (*née* Wilford); *S* father, 2007. Is in remainder to Earldom of Macclesfield. *Heir: b* George Benjamin Heathcote [*b* 2 Feb. 1965; *m* 1999, Dr Kate Rogers].

HEATHCOTE-DRUMMOND-WILLOUGHBY, family name of **Baroness Willoughby de Eresby**.

HEATHER, Stanley Frank, CBE 1980; Comptroller and City Solicitor, City of London Corporation, 1974–80; Attorney and General Counsel, City of London (Arizona) Corporation, 1974–81; *b* 8 Jan. 1917; *s* of Charles and Jessie Heather; *m* 1946, Janet Roxburgh Adams (*d* 1989), Perth; one *s* one *d*. *Educ:* Downhills Sch.; London Univ. Commnd Reconnaissance Corps, RAC, 1941; India/Burma Campaign, 1942–45. Admitted Solicitor, 1959. Asst Solicitor, City of London, 1963; Dep. Comptroller and City Solicitor, 1968. Captain, Sussex Professional Golfers' Union, 1985–86; Patron, Southern Reg., PGA. Freeman, City of London, 1964; Liveryman, Solicitors' Co., 1965–; Hon. Liveryman: Clothworkers' Co., Engineers' Co., 1983; Scriveners' Co., 1993; Hon. Freeman, Water Conservators' Co., 1995. FRSA 1981. *Recreations:* golf, fishing. *Address:* 11 Farebrothers, Church Street, Warnham, W Sussex RH12 3DZ. *T:* (01403) 267724. *Clubs:* City Livery, Guildhall.

HEATHERWICK, Thomas Alexander, RDI 2004; Director, Heatherwick (formerly Thomas Heatherwick) Studio, since 1994; *b* 17 Feb. 1970; *s* of Hugh Heatherwick and Stefany (*née* Tomalin). *Educ:* Manchester Metropolitan Univ. (BA Hons 1992); Royal Coll. of Art (MA Three Dimensional Design 1994). Founded Thomas Heatherwick Studio, 1994, to combine architecture, product design and sculpture in single practice; projects include: B of the Bang, Manchester, largest sculpture in UK, 2004; Rolling Bridge, Paddington Basin, 2005; Longchamp flagship store, NY, 2006; E Beach Café, Littlehampton, 2007. Ext. Exmnr, RCA, 2003–05. Sen. FRCA 2004. Hon. FRIBA 2008; DUniv Sheffield Hallam, 2005; Hon. Dr Manchester Metropolitan, 2007; Hon. LLD Dundee, 2007. *Address:* Heatherwick Studio, 16 Acton Street, WC1X 9NG. *T:* (020) 7833 8800, *Fax:* (020) 7833 8400; *e-mail:* studio@heatherwick.com.

HEATLEY, Brian Antony; Policy Co-ordinator and Member, National Executive, Green Party, since 2004; *b* 20 April 1947; *s* of Thomas Russell Heatley and Margaret Ros[e] (*née* Deacon); *m*; one *d*. *Educ:* Sheen Grammar Sch.; St John's Coll., Cambridge (BA); Balliol Coll., Oxford; Warwick Univ. (MPhil). Volunteer teacher, Ethiopia, 1969–71; Department of Trade and Industry, 1974–89: appts include Financial Services, Consume[r] Protection and Radio Communications; Head, Small Firms and Enterprise Br., 1989–90; Head, Resource Planning Br., 1990–93, Dept of Employment; Head of Adults and Trng Strategy, Dept of Employment, then DFEE, 1993–96. Student teacher, Sheffield Univ., 1996–97; Maths teacher, Graveney Sch., Tooting, 1997–2001. *Recreations:* walking, history, photography, food. *Address:* Lorton Barn, Lorton Lane, Weymouth, Dorset DT[3] 5QH.

HEATLY, Sir Peter, Kt 1990; CBE 1971; DL; Chairman, Commonwealth Game[s] Federation, 1982–90; *b* 9 June 1924; *s* of Robert Heatly and Margaret Ann Heatly; *m* 1st, 1948, Jean Robertha Hermiston (*d* 1979); two *s* two *d*; 2nd, 1984, Mae Calder Cochran[e] (*d* 2003). *Educ:* Leith Academy; Edinburgh Univ. (BSc). CEng, FICE. Chm., Scottish Sports Council, 1975–87. DL City of Edinburgh, 1984. Dr *hc* Edinburgh, 1992; Hon. DLitt Queen Margaret Coll., 1994; DUniv Stirling, 1998. *Recreations:* swimming, golf, gardening. *Address:* Lanrig, Balerno, Edinburgh EH14 7AJ. *T:* (0131) 449 3998.

HEATON, Clive William; QC 2006; a Recorder, since 2003; *b* 20 July 1957; *s* o[f] William and Dilys Heaton; *m* 1980, Susan Margaret Taylor (*d* 2007); two *s*. *Educ:* Huddersfield New Coll.; Keble Coll., Oxford (MA); Chester Coll. of Law. Admitted solicitor, 1982; called to the Bar, Gray's Inn, 1992; in practice, specialising in family and child care law. Mem., Standards Cttee, Bar Standards Bd. *Publication:* (with Heathe[r] Swindells) Adoption: the modern procedure, 2006. *Address:* Zenith Chambers, 10 Park Square, Leeds LS1 2LH. *T:* (0113) 245 5438; *e-mail:* clerks@zenithchambers.co.uk.

HEATON, David, OBE 1993; Consultant, Museums and Galleries Commission, 1984–93; *b* 22 Sept. 1923; *s* of late Dr T. B. Heaton, OBE, MD; *m* 1961, Joan, *d* of Group Captain E. J. Lainé, CBE, DFC; two *s* one *d*. *Educ:* Rugby Sch. Served RNVR, 1942–46; Ghana, 1948–58; Cabinet Office, 1961–69; Home Office, 1969–83; Under Sec. of State, 1976–83. *Address:* 53 Murray Road, SW19 4PF. *T:* (020) 8947 0375.
See also R. N. Heaton.

HEATON, Frances Anne; Director, Legal & General Group plc, since 2001; *b* 11 Aug. 1944; *d* of John Ferris Whidborne and Marjorie Annie (*née* Maltby); *m* 1969, Marti[n] Heaton; two *s*. *Educ:* Queen Anne's, Caversham; Trinity Coll., Dublin (BA, LLB). Called to the Bar, Inner Temple, 1967. Dept. of Econ. Affairs, 1967–70; HM Treasury, 1970–80; seconded to S. G. Warburg & Co. Ltd, 1977–79; Lazard Brothers & Co. Ltd, 1980–2001; Dir, 1987–2001; seconded as Dir Gen., Panel on Takeovers and Mergers, 1992–94; Director: W. S. Atkins, 1990–2003 (Dep. Chm., 1996–2003); Bank of England, 1993–2001; Elementis plc (formerly Harrisons & Crosfield), 1994–99; Commercial Union, 1994–98; BUPA, 1998–2001; AWG plc, 2002–07; Jupiter Primadona Growth Trust, 2005–; BMT Gp, 2007–. Mem., Cttee on Standards in Public Life, 1997–2003. *Recreations:* riding, gardening, bridge.

HEATON, Richard Nicholas; Director-General, Legal Services, Department for Work and Pensions and to Department of Health, since 2007; *b* 5 Oct. 1965; *s* of David Heaton, *qv*. *Educ:* Rugby Sch.; Worcester Coll., Oxford (BA 1987). Called to the Bar, Inner Temple, 1988. Home Office, 1991–96; Legal Secretariat to the Law Officers, 1996–98; Home Office, 1998–2000; Cabinet Office, 2000–01; Lord Chancellor's Dept, subseq. DCA, 2001–06, Legal Advr, 2004–06. *Address:* Department for Work and Pensions, New Court, Carey Street, WC2A 2LS.

HEATON, (William) John; consultant to the betting industry, since 2004; Chief Executive, Betting & Gaming Consultancy Ltd, since 2004; *b* 12 Jan. 1954; *s* of Ronald and Hilda Heaton; *m*; one *s* two *d*. *Educ:* Wigan Grammar Sch.; Sheffield Univ. (LLB). Admitted Solicitor, 1975. Principal Solicitor, Manchester CC, 1976–83; Horserace Totalisator Board: Co. Sec. and Solicitor, 1983–96; Chief Exec., 1997–2004. *Recreations:* Rugby, golf, horseracing. *Address:* 49 Richmond Park Road, SW14 8JU; *e-mail:* john@heaton.co.uk. *Clubs:* Richmond Rugby; Royal Mid Surrey Golf.

HEATON, Sir Yvo (Robert) Henniker-, 4th Bt *cr* 1912; *b* 24 April 1954; *s* of Sir (John) Victor) Peregrine Henniker-Heaton, 3rd Bt, and of Margaret Patricia, *d* of late Lieut Perc[y] Wright, Canadian Mounted Rifles; *S* father, 1971; *m* 1978, Freda, *d* of B. Jones; one *s* one *d*. Mem., North West Leics DC, 1987–95. Chm., Kegworth Cons. Assoc., 1988–94. Gov., Ashby Willesley Sch., 1996–. *Publication:* Corporate Computer Insurance, 1990. *Heir: s* Alastair (John) Henniker-Heaton, *b* 4 May 1990. *Address:* Airedale House, Murphy Drive, Bagworth, Leics LE67 1HR.

HEATON-HARRIS, Christopher; Member (C) East Midlands, European Parliament, since 1999; *b* 28 Nov. 1967; *s* of David Barry Heaton-Harris and Ann Geraldine Heaton-Harris; *m* 1990, Jayne Yvonne Carlow; two *d*. *Educ:* Tiffin Grammar Sch. for Boys, Kingston upon Thames. Dir, What 4 Ltd, 1995–2003. Contested (C) Leicester South, 1997, July 2004. *Recreation:* grade 5 soccer referee. *Address:* (office) Boswell House, 9 Prospect Court, Courteenhall Road, Blisworth, Northants NN7 3DG.

HEATON-WARD, Dr (William) Alan, FRCPsych; Lord Chancellor's Medical Visitor, 1978–89; *b* 19 Dec. 1919; *s* of Ralph Heaton-Ward, MA, and Mabel Orton; *m* 1st, 1945, Christine Edith Fraser (marr. diss. 2005); two *d*; 2nd, 2006, Betty Edgar. *Educ:* Sefton Park Jun. Sch.; Queen Elizabeth's Hosp., Bristol; Univ. of Bristol Med. Sch. MB, ChB, 1944; DPM 1948; Foundn FRCPsych 1971. Jun. Clerk, Messrs W. D. & H. O. Wills, 1936–38; House Phys., Bristol Royal Inf., 1944–45; MO, Littlemore Mental Hosp., 1945–46; served RNVR, 1946–48: Surg. Lt-Comdr; Neuropsychiatrist, Nore Comd; Sen. Registrar, St James Hosp., Portsmouth, 1948–50; Dep. Med. Supt, Hortham Brentry Gp;

1950–54; Stoke Park Hosp. Group: Consultant Psych., 1954–78, Hon. Consultant Psych., 1978–; Med. Supt, 1954–61; Cons. Psych. i/c, 1963–74; Clinical Teacher in Mental Health, Univ. of Bristol, 1954–78; Cons. Psych., Glos Royal Hosp., 1962–67. Mem., SW Mental Health Review Tribunal, 1960–78, 1985–92. Hon. Cons. Adviser: NAMH, 1966–73; CARE, 1970–78; British Council Vis. Lectr, Portugal, 1971. Royal Coll. of Psychiatrists: Vice Pres., 1976–78; Blake Marsh Lectr, 1976; Burden Res. Gold Medal and Prize Winner, 1978; José Jancar Meml Lectr, 2003. Pres., Brit. Soc. for Study of Mental Subnormality, 1978–79; Vice-President: Fortune Centre of Riding Therapy, 1980–; RESCARE, Nat. Soc. for Mentally Handicapped People in Residential Care, 1995–2005; Avon Riding Centre for the Disabled, 1997–; Mem. Council, Inst. of Mental Subnormality, 1972–76; Hon. Mem., Amer. Assoc. of Physician Analysts, 1976–. Mem., Adv. Council, Radio Bristol, 1985–88. *Publications:* Notes on Mental Deficiency (jtly), 1952, 3rd edn 1955; Mental Subnormality, 1960, 5th edn, (jtly) as Mental Handicap, 1984; Left Behind, 1977; papers on all aspects of care and treatment of mentally handicapped people and on gen. psychiatric topics; book revs. *Recreations:* following all forms of outdoor sport, gardening, seeking the sun, philately, asking Why? *Address:* Bala Netty, 27 Withey Close West, Westbury on Trym, Bristol BS9 3SX. *T:* (0117) 968 1940. *Club:* Savages (Bristol).

HEAVEN, Derick R.; Chief Executive Officer, Sugar Industry Authority, Jamaica, since 2002; *b* 19 Dec. 1940; *m* 1966, Thyra Reid; two *s* one *d*. *Educ:* Cornwall Coll.; Jamaica Sch. of Agriculture. Mem., St Catherine Parish Council, 1974–76; MP for South St Catherine, 1976–80; Parly Sec., Min. of Foreign Affairs, then Minister of Trade and Commerce, 1980; involved in farming and business interests, 1980–89; Consul-General, New York, 1989–92; Ambassador to Japan and (non-resident) to People's Republic of China and Republic of Korea, 1992–94; High Comr for Jamaica in London, 1994–99, and Ambassador (non-resident) to Scandinavia, Spain and Portugal; CEO, Sugar Co. of Jamaica Ltd, 1999–2002. Chm., Commonwealth Fund for Tech. Co-operation, 1996–99. *Recreations:* reading, travelling, sports.

HEBBLETHWAITE, Rev. Dr Brian Leslie; University Lecturer in Divinity, Cambridge, 1977–99, and Life Fellow of Queens' College, since 1994; *b* 3 Jan. 1939; *s* of Alderman Cyril Hebblethwaite and Sarah Anne Hebblethwaite; *m* 1991, Emma Sîan (marr. diss. 2003), *d* of John Ivor Disley, *qv*; one *d*. *Educ:* Clifton Coll.; Magdalen Coll., Oxford (BA LitHum 1961; MA 1967); Magdalene Coll., Cambridge (BA Theol 1963; MA 1968; BD 1984; DD 2006); Westcott House, Cambridge; Univ. of Heidelberg. Curate, All Saints', Elton, Bury, 1965–68; Cambridge University: Bye-Fellow and Chaplain, 1968, Fellow and Dean of Chapel, 1969–94, Queens' Coll.; Univ. Asst Lectr in Divinity, 1973–77; Sen. Proctor, 1998–99; Examng Chaplain to Bishop of Manchester, 1977–98; Canon Theologian, Leicester Cathedral, 1982–2001. Pres., Soc. for Study of Theology, 1989–91. Lectures: Teape, Delhi, Calcutta and Bangalore, 1983–84; (jtly) Gifford, Glasgow, 2001; Hensley Henson, Oxford, 2002. Editor for Ethics, Theologische Realenzyklopädie, 1980–. *Publications:* Evil, Suffering and Religion, 1976, rev. edn 2000; The Problems of Theology, 1980; (ed jtly) Christianity and Other Religions, 1980, rev. edn 2001; The Adequacy of Christian Ethics, 1981; (ed jtly) The Philosophical Frontiers of Christian Theology, 1982; The Christian Hope, 1984; Preaching Through the Christian Year 10, 1985; The Incarnation, 1987; The Ocean of Truth, 1988; (ed jtly) Divine Action, 1990; The Essence of Christianity, 1996; Ethics and Religion in a Pluralistic Age, 1997; Philosophical Theology and Christian Doctrine, 2004; In Defence of Christianity, 2005; (ed jtly) The Human Person in God's World, 2006; The Philosophical Theology of Austin Farrer, 2007; *festschrift:* Truth, Religious Dialogue and Dynamic Orthodoxy, ed by J. J. Lipner, 2005. *Recreations:* fell-walking, opera, cathedral and church architecture, books. *Address:* The Old Barn, 32 High Street, Stretham, Ely, Cambs CB6 3JQ. *T:* (01353) 648279. *Club:* Athenæum.

HEBDITCH, Maxwell Graham, CBE 1994; Director, Museum of London, 1977–97; *b* 22 Aug. 1937; *s* of late Harold Hebditch, motor engr, Yeovil, and Lily (*née* Bartle); *m* 1963, Felicity Davies; two *s* one *d*. *Educ:* Yeovil Sch.; Magdalene Coll., Cambridge. MA, FSA, FMA. Field Archaeologist, Leicester Museums, 1961–64; Asst Curator in Archaeology, later Curator in Agricultural and Social History, City Museum, Bristol, 1965–71; Dir, Guildhall Mus., London, 1971–74; Dep. Dir, Mus. of London, 1974–77. Hon. Curator, Lyme Regis Mus., 2000–08. Chm., Mus. Trng Inst., subseq. Cultural Heritage NTO, 1997–2004 (Bd Mem., 1990–). Co-Dir, Mus. Leadership Prog., UEA, 1994–2000. Mem., EC Cttee of Cultural Consultants, 1990–92. Chm., UK Nat. Cttee, ICOM, 1981–87; Pres., Museums Assoc., 1990–92 (Vice-Pres., 1988–90). Hon. DLitt City, 1992. *Publications:* contribs to archaeological and museological jls and books. *Recreation:* archaeology. *Address:* The Garden House, Fons George Road, Taunton TA1 3JU.

HEBER-PERCY, Algernon Eustace Hugh; Lord-Lieutenant for Shropshire, since 1996 (Vice Lord-Lieutenant, 1990–96); *b* 2 Jan. 1944; *s* of Brig. A. G. W. Heber-Percy, DSO and Daphne Wilma Kenyon (*née* Parker Bowles); *m* 1966, Hon. Margaret Jane Lever, *y d* of 3rd Viscount Leverhulme, KG, TD; one *s* three *d*. *Educ:* Harrow; Mons OTC. Lieut Grenadier Guards, 1962–66. Farmer and landowner. Chm., Mercia Regional Cttee, Nat. Trust, 1990–99; Trustee, Nat. Gardens Scheme, 1990–2005. Pres., Shropshire and Mid Wales Hospice, 1988–; Chm., Walker Trust Cttee, 1990– (Mem., 1990–). Hon. Colonel: 5th Bn, Shropshire and Herefordshire LI (Vol.), 1998–99; W Midlands Regt, 1999–2005. Gov., Shrewsbury Sch., 2004–. DL Shropshire, 1986; High Sheriff of Shropshire, 1987. *Recreations:* gardening, country sports. *Address:* Hodnet Hall, Hodnet, Market Drayton, Shropshire TF9 3NN. *T:* (01630) 685202. *Club:* Cavalry and Guards.

HECKMAN, Prof. James Joseph, PhD; Henry Schultz Distinguished Service Professor, University of Chicago, since 1974; *b* 19 April 1944; *s* of John Jacob Heckman and Bernice Irene Medley Heckman; *m* 1st, 1964, Sally Lentz (marr. diss. 1971); 2nd, 1979, Lynne Pettler; one *s* one *d*. *Educ:* Colorado Coll. (BA Math 1965); Princeton (MA Econ 1968; PhD Econ 1971). Instructor-Associate Prof., Columbia Univ., 1970–74: Associate Prof., 1973–77, Prof. of Econs, 1977–, Univ. of Chicago; Yale Univ. (on leave), 1988–90. Guggenheim Fellow, 1977–78; Fellow, Center for Advanced Study in Behavioral Sci., 1977–78. Member: Amer. Acad., 1985–; NAS, 1992–; Fellow: Econometric Soc., 1980; American Statistical Assoc., 2001; Soc. of Labor Economics, 2004. Hon. MA Yale, 1989; Hon. PhD Colorado Coll., 2001; Hon. LLD: Chile, 2002; Univ. Autónoma del Estado de México, 2003; Montreal, Bard Coll., 2004. John Bates Clark Medal, American Econ. Soc., 1983; Nobel Prize for Economics, 2000; Jacob Mincer Award for Lifetime Achievement, Soc. of Labor Economics, 2005. *Publications:* Longitudinal Analysis of Labor Market Data, 1985; Inequality in America: what role for human capital policies?, 2003; (with E. Leamer) Handbook of Econometrics, vol. 5 2001, vol. 6A 2007 and vol. 6B 2007; other books and over 200 articles. *Recreations:* hiking, bicycling, reading. *Address:* 4807 S Greenwood, Chicago, IL 60615, USA. *T:* (773) 2684547; (office) Dept of Economics, University of Chicago, 1126 E 59th Street, Chicago, IL 60637, USA.

HECTOR, Alistair Gordon; Headmaster, George Heriot's School, Edinburgh, since 1998; *b* 5 Oct. 1955; *s* of Gordon Matthews Hector, CMG, CBE; *m* 1980, Rosemary Ann Craig; two *s* one *d*. *Educ:* Edinburgh Acad.; Univ. of St Andrews (MA); Univ. of Erlangen, Germany. Lektor in English, Univ. of Erlangen, 1978–80; Head of German, Merchiston Castle Sch., Edinburgh, 1980–85; Head of Dept, German, 1986–89, Modern Langs, 1989–95, King Edward's Sch., Bath; Dep. Headmaster, Warwick Sch., 1995–97. *Recreations:* sport, walking, music, travel, family. *Address:* George Heriot's School, Lauriston Place, Edinburgh EH3 9EQ. *T:* (0131) 229 7263.

HEDGECOE, Prof. John, Dr RCA; FCSD; Professor of Photography, Royal College of Art, London, 1975–94, now Emeritus; Pro Rector, 1981–93, Acting Rector, 1983–84; *b* 24 March 1937; *s* of William Hedgecoe and Kathleen Don; *m* 1st, 1960, Julia Mardon (marr. diss. 1995); two *s* one *d*; 2nd, 2001, Jennifer M. Ogilvie Hogg, *d* of Col D. O. Hogg, OBE, MC, TD, JP, DL. *Educ:* Gulval Village Sch., Cornwall; Guildford Sch. of Art. Staff Photographer, Queen Magazine, 1957–72; Freelance: Sunday Times and Observer, 1960–70; most internat. magazines, 1958–; Portrait, HM the Queen, for British and Australian postage stamps, 1966; photographed The Arts Multi-Projection, British Exhibn, Expo Japan Show, 1970. Royal College of Art: started Photography Sch., 1965: Head of Dept and Reader in Photography, 1965–74; Fellow, 1973; awarded Chair of Photography, 1975; started Audio/Visual Dept, 1980; Chm., Student Fund Awards, 1981–93; started Holography Unit, 1982; Managing Trustee, 1983; Sen. Fellow, 1992. Vis. Prof., Norwegian Nat. Television Sch., Oslo, 1985. Associate Ed., Country Illustrated, 2006–. Chm., Abacus Ltd (furniture stores), 1962–66; Managing Director: Lion & Unicorn Press Ltd, 1986–94; Mobius Books Internat. Ltd, 1986–92; Director: John Hedgecoe Ltd, 1965–95; Perennial Pictures Ltd, 1980, 1991. Mem. Photographic Bd, CNAA, 1976–78; Gov., W Surrey Coll. of Art (and Mem. Acad. Adv. Bd), 1975–; Acad. Gov., Richmond Coll., London; Trustee, The Minories Victor Batte-Lay Trust, 1985–88. Consultant, English Heritage, 1995–98 (Head of External Pubns). Has illustrated numerous books, 1958–; has contributed to numerous radio broadcasts. Television: Tonight, Aust. TV, 1967; Folio, Anglia, 1980; 8 progs on Photography, Channel Four, 1983, repeated 1984; Winners, Channel Four, 1984; Light and Form, US Cable TV, 1985. Exhibitions: London, Sydney, Toronto, Edinburgh, Venice, Prague; one-man exhibitions: RCA, 2000; Nat. Portrait Gall., 2000; Sainsbury Centre for Visual Arts, UEA, 2000; Westcliffe Gall., Sheringham, 2000, 2002; Waterside Gall., Norfolk, 2000; Guild House Gall., Guildford, 2001; Christchurch Mansion Wolsey Art Gall., Ipswich, 2001; Royal Cornwall Mus., 2003; Poetry-next-the-Sea, Wells, Norfolk, 2003; Gables Yard, Norwich, 2003; Wells, 2004; St Paul's Sch., London, 2005; Beijing, Nanjing and Shanghai, China (rep. GB), 2005; Reflections, Horning, Norwich, 2008; gp exhibn, Fifty Years of Modern British Art, Robert Sandelson Gall., London, 2008; permanent exhibn, Grove Clinic, Norfolk & Norwich Univ. Hosp.; collections: V&A Museum; Art Gall. of Ontario; Nat. Portrait Gall., London; Citibank, London; Henry Moore Foundn; Museum of Modern Art, NY; Leeds City Art Gall.; Ministry of Culture, Morocco. FRSA. Hon. FIIPC. Laureate and Medal for contribution to photography, Govt of Czechoslovakia, 1989; Lente de Plata Photography, Govt of Mexico, 2002. *Publications:* Henry Moore, 1968 (prize best art book, world-wide, 1969); (jtly) Kevin Crossley-Holland book of Norfolk Poems, 1970; Sculptures of Picasso, 1970; (jtly) Photography, Material and Methods, 1971–74 edns; Henry Moore, Energy in Space, 1973; The Book of Photography, 1976, new edn 2007; Handbook of Photographic Techniques, 1977, 3rd edn 1992; The Art of Colour Photography, 1978, new edn 2007 (Kodak Photobuchpreis Stuttgart 1979; Grand Prix Technique de la Photographie, Musée Français de la Photographie, Paris 1980); Possessions, 1978; The Pocket Book of Photography, 1979; Introductory Photography Course, 1979; Master Classes in Photography: Children and Child Portraiture, 1980; (illus.) Poems of Thomas Hardy, 1981; (illus.) Poems of Robert Burns, 1981; The Book of Advanced Photography, 1982; What a Picture!, 1983; The Photographer's Work Book, 1983, new edn 1997; Aesthetics of Nude Photography, 1984; The Workbook of Photo Techniques, 1984, 2nd edn 1997; The Workbook of Darkroom Techniques, 1984, 2nd edn 1997; Pocket Book of Travel and Holiday Photography, 1986; Henry Moore: his ideas, inspirations and life as an artist, 1986, new edn 1999; The Three Dimensional Pop-up Photography Book, 1986; (with A. L. Rowse) Shakespeare's Land, 1986; Photographer's Manual of Creative Ideas, 1986, new edn 1999; (with A. L. Rowse) Rowse's Cornwall, 1987; Practical Portrait Photography, 1987, 2nd edn 2000; Practical Book of Landscape Photography, 1988, 2nd edn 2000; Hedgecoe on Video, 1988; Hedgecoe on Photography, 1988; Complete Photography Guide, 1990; Video Photographer's Handbook, 1992; Zillij, 1992; John Hedgecoe's Complete Guide to Video, 1992; (jtly) The Art of Moroccan Ceramics, 1993; John Hedgecoe's Basic Photography, 1993; The New Book of Photography, 1994, 3rd edn 2004; Black and White Photography, 1994; Camcorder Basics, 1995; John Hedgecoe—a Complete Introductory Guide to Video, 1995; Breakfast with Dolly (novel), 1996; Figure and Form, 1996; John Hedgecoe's New Introductory Photography Course, 1996; The Spirit of the Garden, 1997; England's World Heritage, 1997; A Monumental Vision: the sculpture of Henry Moore, 1998; The Art of Colour Photography, 1998; Photography Sourcebook of Creative Ideas, 1998; John Hedgecoe's 35mm Photography, 1999; Portraits by John Hedgecoe, 2000; Photographing your Children, 2000; How to Take Great Photographs, 2001; (with Marie Pacheco) Dark Night of the Soul, 2001; Photographing Babies, 2002; How to Take Great Vacation Photography, 2003; New Manual of Photography, 2003 (trans. 37 lang), 2nd edn 2005 (German and Russian rev. edns); The Art of Digital Photography, 2006. *Recreations:* sculpture, building, gardening. *Address:* c/o Dorling Kindersley, Penguin Books, 80 Strand, WC2R 0RL. *Clubs:* Arts; Norfolk (Norwich).

HEDGELAND, Air Vice-Marshal Philip Michael Sweatman, CB 1978 OBE 1957 (MBE 1948); CEng, FIET; *b* 24 Nov. 1922; *s* of Philip and Margaret Hedgeland, Maidstone, Kent; *m* 1946, Jean Riddle Brinkworth (*d* 2006), *d* of Leonard and Anne Brinkworth, Darlington, Co. Durham; two *s*. *Educ:* Maidstone Grammar Sch.; City and Guilds Coll., Imperial Coll. of Science and Technology, London. BSc(Eng), ACGI (Siemens Medallist). Served War: commnd into Technical Br., RAF, 1942; despatches, 1943; Radar Officer, Pathfinder Force and at TRE, Malvern. Radar Develt Officer, Central Bomber Estabt, 1945–48; Radio Introd. Unit Project Officer for V-Bomber Navigation and Bombing System, 1952–57; Wing Comdr Radio (Air) at HQ Bomber Comd, 1957–60; jssc 1960; Air Ministry Technical Planning, 1961–62; aws 1963; Dir of Signals (Far East), Singapore, 1963–65; commanded RAF Stanbridge (Central Communications Centre), 1966–67; SASO, HQ Signals Comd/90 Gp, 1968–69; IDC, 1970; MoD Procurement Exec., Project Dir for Airborne Radar, 1971–74; Vice-Pres., Ordnance Bd, 1975–77, Pres., 1977–78. FCGI 1977. Pres., Pathfinder Assoc., 1985–87. *Address:* 34 Castle Court, Hadlow Road, Tonbridge, Kent TN9 1QU. *T:* (01732) 350196. *Club:* Royal Air Force.

HEDGER, Eric Frank, CB 1979; OBE 1960; Under Secretary, Director General of Defence Contracts, Ministry of Defence, 1969–80; *b* 15 Sept. 1919; *s* of late Albert Frank Hedger and Ellen Agnes Hedger (*née* Laffey); *m* 1945, Joan Kathleen Bernas (*d* 2005); two *s* one *d*. *Educ:* St Luke's, Southsea. War Service, 1939–46 (despatches 1945): Adjutant, 10 Air Formation Signals; Adjutant, then 2nd i/c, 7 Indian Air Formation Signals. Secretary, Admiralty Awards Council, 1946–49; Admin. Staff Coll., 1958; Dir of Navy Contracts, 1968. Mem. of Council and Bd of Management, Inst. of Purchasing and Supply, 1974–75. Advr, Defence Manufacturers Assoc., 1983–88. FInstPS. *Recreations:* music, reading, gardening. *Address:* Helere House, Ridgeway Mead, Sidmouth, Devon EX10 9DT. *T:* (01395) 577741.

HEDGER, John Clive, CB 1998; Chairman, Lifelong Learning UK (formerly Shadow Sector Skills Council for Lifelong Learning), 2004–07; *b* 17 Dec. 1942; *s* of late Leslie John Keith Hedger and of Iris Hedger (*née* Friedlos); *m* 1966, Jean Ann Felstead; two *s* one *d*. *Educ:* Quirister Sch., Winchester; Victoria Coll., Jersey; Univ. of Sussex (BA 1965; MA 1966). Dept of Educn and Science, 1966; Asst Private Sec., 1970; Sec., Cttee of Enquiry on Educn of Handicapped, 1974–76; Under Sec., DES, 1988–92; Dep. Sec., Dept for Educn, 1992–95; Dir of Ops, DFEE, 1995–2000. Associate, Finance and Education Services Ltd, 2000–. Trustee:, Rathbone Training (formerly Rathbone CI), 2000–; Nat. Foundn for Educnl Research, 2004–. Mem. Council, Radley Coll., 1998–2007; Gov., Mary Hare Sch., 2006–. *Recreations:* coarse acting, walking, coarse sailing, growing things. *Address:* Mallard Court, Worster Road, Cookham, Berks SL6 9JG. *T:* (01628) 523911.

HEDGES, Anthony (John); Reader in Composition, University of Hull, 1978–95; *b* 5 March 1931; *s* of late S. G. Hedges; *m* 1957, Delia Joy Marsden; two *s* two *d*. *Educ:* Bicester Grammar Sch.; Keble Coll., Oxford. MA, BMus, LRAM. National Service as solo pianist and arranger Royal Signals Band, 1955–57. Teacher and Lecturer, Royal Scottish Academy of Music, 1957–63. During this period became a regular contributor to Scotsman, Glasgow Herald, Guardian, Musical Times, etc. Lecturer in Music, Univ. of Hull, 1963, Sen. Lectr, 1968. The Composers' Guild of Great Britain: Chm., Northern Br., 1966–67; Mem. Exec. Cttee of Guild, 1969–73, 1977–81, 1982–87; Chm. of Guild, 1972, Jt Chm., 1973. Member: Council, Central Music Library, Westminster, 1970; Council, Soc. for Promotion of New Music, 1974–81; Music Bd, CNAA, 1974–77; Music Panel, Yorks Arts Assoc., 1974–75, Lincs and Humberside Arts Assoc., 1975–78; Founder-conductor, The Humberside Sinfonia, 1978–81. Hon. DMus Hull, 1997. Wrote regularly for Yorkshire Post, 1963–78, and contributed to many jls, incl. Composer, Current Musicology, etc, and also broadcast on musical subjects. *Publications include: (works): orchestral:* Comedy Overture, 1962 (rev. 1967); Overture, October '62, 1962 (rev. 1968); Sinfonia Semplice, 1963; Expressions for Orchestra, 1964; Prelude, Romance and Rondo, strings, 1965; Concertante Music, 1965; Four Miniature Dances, 1967; A Holiday Overture, 1968; Variations on a theme of Rameau, 1969; Kingston Sketches, 1969; An Ayrshire Serenade, 1969; Four Diversions, strings, 1971; Celebrations, 1973; Symphony no 1, 1972–73; Festival Dances, 1976; Overture, Heigham Sound, 1978; Four Breton Sketches, 1980; Sinfonia Concertante, 1980; Scenes from the Humber, 1981; A Cleveland Overture, 1984; Concertino for Horn and String Orchestra, 1987; Sinfonia Giovanile, 1992; Showpiece, 1995; Symphony no 2, 1997; Trumpet Concerto, 2000; Fidlers Green, 2001; *choral:* Gloria, unaccompanied, 1965; Epithalamium, chorus and orch. (Spencer), 1969; To Music, chorus and orch. (various texts), 1972; Psalm 104, 1973; A Manchester Mass, chorus, orch. and brass band, 1974; A Humberside Cantata, 1976; Songs of David, 1978; The Temple of Solomon, 1979; I Sing the Birth: canticles for Christmas, 1985; I'll make me a world, 1990; The Lamp of Liberty, 2005; *chamber music:* Five Preludes, piano, 1959; Four Pieces, piano, 1966; Rondo Concertante, violin, clarinet, horn, violoncello, 1967; Sonata for violin and harpsichord, 1967; Three Songs of Love, soprano, piano (from Song of Songs), 1968; String Quartet, 1970; Rhapsody, violin, piano, 1971, revd 1988; piano sonata, 1974; Song Cycle, 1977; Piano Trio, 1977; Fantasy for Violin and Piano, 1981; Sonatinas for Flute, Viola, Cello, 1982; Wind Quintet, 1984; Flute Trios, 1985, 1989; Fantasy Sonata for bassoon and piano, 1986; Clarinet Quintet, 1987; Flute Sonata, 1988; Five Aphorisms, piano, 1990; In such a night, string quartet, 1990; Bassoon Quintet, 1991; Piano Quartet, 1992; Trombone Sonata, 1994; Six Song Cycles, 1997–2006; Ten Bagatelles, piano, 2006; *opera:* Shadows in the Sun (lib. Jim Hawkins), 1976; *musical:* Minotaur (lib. Jim Hawkins), 1978; *miscellaneous:* many anthems, partsongs, albums of music for children; music for television, film and stage. *Recreations:* reading, crosswords, walking. *Address:* Malt Shovel Cottage, 76 Walkergate, Beverley, HU17 9ER. *T:* (01482) 860580.

HEDGES, Rev. Canon Jane Barbara; Canon of Westminster Abbey, since 2006; *b* 6 April 1955; *d* of John William Henry Taylor and Elizabeth Taylor; *m* 1982, Christopher Hedges; two *s*. *Educ:* Durham Univ. (BA Hons). Ordained deaconess, 1980, deacon 1987, priest 1994; Deaconess, Holy Trinity with St Columba, Fareham, 1980–83; Team Vicar, Southampton City Centre Team, 1983–88; Stewardship Advr, Portsmouth Dio., 1988–93; Residentiary Canon, Portsmouth Cathedral, 1993–2001; Team Rector, Honiton Team Ministry, 2001–06. Hon. LLD Portsmouth, 2006. *Recreations:* walking, listening to classical music, animal welfare, sporting events with sons, touring abroad/pilgrimages. *Address:* 2 Little Cloister, Dean's Yard, Westminster Abbey, SW1P 3PL. *T:* (020) 7654 4815; *e-mail:* jane.hedges@westminster-abbey.org.

HEDGES, (Jonathan) Mark; Editor, Country Life, since 2006; *b* 24 Feb. 1964; *s* of John and Mary Hedges; *m* 1989, Stacey Ann Estella; two *s* one *d*. *Educ:* Radley Coll., Abingdon; Univ. of Durham (BSc Geol. 1985). Tattersalls, Newmarket, 1985–88; Ed., Shooting Times, 1998–2000; Publisher, The Field, Shooting Times, Sporting Gun and Anglers' Mail, 2000–02; Ed., Horse & Hound, 2002–03, 2004; Editor-in-Chief, Country and Leisure Media, IPC, 2002–06. *Publication:* Dog, 2000. *Recreations:* shooting, fly fishing, leaning on a fork, the countryside. *Address:* Country Life, Blue Fin Building, 110 Southwark Street, SE1 0SU. *T:* (020) 3148 4420; *e-mail:* mark_hedges@ipcmedia.com.

HEDGES, Michael Irving Ian, CBE 2005; QPM 1995; Chief Constable, South Yorkshire Police, 1998–2004; *b* 27 Jan. 1948; *s* of Arthur and Helen Hedges; *m* 1968, Beryl Janet Smith; one *s*. *Educ:* Holyrood Sch., Chard, Som.; King's College, London (LLB). Constable, Somerset and Bath Police, 1967–72; transf. to Metropolitan Police, 1972–87; Chief Superintendent, Thames Valley Police, 1987–88; Asst Chief Constable, Avon and Somerset Police, 1988–93; Dep. Chief Constable, South Yorkshire Police, 1993–98. RHS Medal for Gallantry, 1968. *Recreations:* swimming, reading, golf, fly fishing, gardening; an active Rotarian.

HEDLEY, Prof. Anthony Johnson, MD; JP; FRCPE, FRCPGlas, FRCP, FFPH; Professor of Community Medicine, University of Hong Kong, since 1988; *b* 8 April 1941; *s* of Thomas Johnson Hedley and Winifred Duncan; *m* 1st, 1967, Elizabeth-Anne Walsh (marr. diss. 1992); 2nd, 1996, Andrea Marilyn Miller (marr. diss. 2007); 3rd, 2008, Sarah Morag Harrigan McGhee. *Educ:* Rydal Sch.; Aberdeen Univ. (MB, ChB 1965; MD 1972); Edinburgh Univ. (Dip. Soc. Med. 1973). MRCP 1973; FRCPE 1981; FRCPGlas, 1985; FRCP 1987; FFPH (FFCM 1981; MFCM 1975). Lectr in Community Medicine, Univ. of Aberdeen, 1974–76; Sen. Lectr in Community Health, Univ. of Nottingham, 1976–83; Titular Prof. in Community Medicine, 1983–84, Henry Mechan Prof. of Public Health, 1984–88, Univ. of Glasgow. Med. Adviser (Thailand), ODA, 1977–. Chm., HK Council on Smoking and Health, 1997–2002. JP Hong Kong, 1998. Hon. MD Khon Kaen Univ., 1983. WHO Medal for services to public health, 1999. Bronze Bauhinia Star, HKSAR, 2000; Dist. Service Award, Food and Health Bureau, HKSAR, 2007. *Publications:* papers and chapters on endocrine disease, surveillance of chronic disease, air pollution, tobacco control and on med. educn. *Recreations:* long-distance running, photography, rifle shooting, flying (private pilot's licence, 1992). *Address:* Flat 16B, Block 2, Tam Towers, 25 Sha Wan Drive, Victoria Road, Pok fu Lam, Hong Kong. *T:* 28757832, *Fax:* 28194708. *Clubs:* Aberdeen Boat, Foreign Correspondents, Hong Kon[g] Aviation (Hong Kong).

HEDLEY, Rev. Charles John Wykeham, PhD; Rector of St James's, Piccadilly, sinc[e] 1999; *b* 26 June 1947; *s* of Harry and Elisabeth Hedley. *Educ:* Christ's Hospital, Horsham; Royal Holloway Coll., Univ. of London (BSc; PhD 1973); Fitzwilliam Coll., Cambridg[e] (MA); Westcott House, Cambridge. Deacon 1976, priest 1977; Asst Curate, St Anne', Chingford, 1976–79; Curate, St Martin-in-the-Fields, 1979–86; Chaplain, Christ's Coll., Cambridge, 1986–90; Team Rector of Gleadless, Sheffield, 1990–99. *Recreations:* walking, squash, classical music. *Address:* St James's Rectory, 197 Piccadilly, W1J 9LL. *T:* (020) 7734 4511, *Fax:* (020) 7734 7449.

HEDLEY, Hon. Sir Mark, Kt 2002; **Hon. Mr Justice Hedley;** a Judge of the Hig[h] Court, Family Division, since 2002; *b* 23 Aug. 1946; *s* of late Peter and Eve Hedley; *m* 1973, Erica Britton; three *s* one *d*. *Educ:* Framlingham College; Univ. of Liverpool (LL[B] Hons). Called to the Bar, Gray's Inn, 1969, Bencher, 2002; VSO, Sudan, 1969–70; practice at Liverpool Bar, 1971–92; Head of Chambers, 1983–92; a Recorder, 1988–92; a Circuit Judge, 1992–2001. Chancellor, Dio. Liverpool, 2002–. Reader in C of E, 1975–. Hon. LLD Liverpool, 2003; Hon. Fellow, Liverpool John Moores Univ., 2005. *Recreations:* cricket, railways. *Address:* Royal Courts of Justice, Strand, WC2A 2LL.

HEDLEY, Prof. Ronald; Director, Trent Polytechnic, Nottingham, 1970–80 (no[w] Nottingham Trent University), Emeritus Professor, 1980; *b* 12 Sept. 1917; *s* of Franc[is] Hedley, Hebburn, Co. Durham; *m* 1942; one *s* one *d*. *Educ:* Jarrow Grammar Sch.; Durham Univ. (MA, DipEd); Ecole Normale d'Instituteurs, Evreux. Various appts in teaching and educational administration, 1947–64; Dep. Dir of Education, Nottingham, 1964–70. Chm., Regional Acad. Bd, Regional Adv. Council for Further Educn in [E.] Midlands, 1972–76; Member: Central Council for Educn and Trng in Social Work, 1971–77; Nat. Adv. Council for Educn for Ind. and Commerce, 1973–77; Centr[al] Council for Educn and Trng of Health Visitors, 1972–77; Cttee for Arts and Socia[l] Studies, CNAA, 1974–76; Personal Social Services Council, 1974–78; Cttee o[n] Recreation Management Training, 1977–80; Local Govt Trng Bd, 1978–81; Adv. Ctte[e] for Supply and Educn of Teachers, 1980–81, Chm., Local Cttee for Teacher Educn, Kin[g] Alfred's Coll., Winchester, 1986–89. FRSA 1970. Hon. Fellow: Trent Polytechnic, 1980; Nottingham Trent, 1992. Hon. Senator, Fachhochschule, Karlsruhe, Germany, 1980; Hon. LLD Nottingham, 1981; DUniv Nottingham Trent, 1993. *Address:* The Ced[ar] House, Avington, Winchester, Hants SO21 1DE. *T:* (01962) 791177.

HEDLEY-MILLER, Dame Mary (Elizabeth), DCVO 1989; CB 1983; Ceremoni[al] Officer, Cabinet Office, 1983–88; *b* 5 Sept. 1923; *d* of late J. W. Ashe; *m* 1950, Roge[r] Latham Hedley-Miller (*d* 2004); one *s* two *d*. *Educ:* Queen's Sch., Chester; St Hugh['s] Coll., Oxford (MA). Joined HM Treasury, 1945; served in UK Treasury Deleg[n] Washington DC, 1947–49; Under-Sec., HM Treasury, 1973–83. Alternate Dir, Moneta[ry] Cttee, EEC, and Alternate Exec. Dir, European Investment Bank, 1977–83. *Recreation[s]:* family, including family music; reading. *Address:* 48 Elms Road, SW4 9EX. *T:* (020) 762[?] 8834. *Club:* Oxford and Cambridge.

HEDWORTH, (Alan) Toby; QC 1996; a Recorder, since 1995; *b* 23 April 1952; *s* [of] late John William Swaddle Hedworth and Margaret Ena Hedworth (*née* Dodds); *m* 198[?] Kathleen Mary (*née* Luke); two *d*. *Educ:* Kings Sch., Tynemouth; Royal Grammar Sch., Newcastle upon Tyne; St Catharine's Coll., Cambridge (MA). Called to the Bar, Inne[r] Temple, 1975; Head, Trinity Chambers, Newcastle upon Tyne, 1999–. Vice Chm., Northumberland and Newcastle Soc., 1997–. *Recreations:* Newcastle United, the Englis[h] Lake District, motoring, the built environment. *Address:* The Custom House, Quaysid[e], Newcastle upon Tyne NE1 3DE. *T:* (0191) 232 1927. *Club:* Northern Counti[es] (Newcastle upon Tyne).

HEEGER, Prof. Alan Jay, PhD; Presidential Chair, since 2003, and Professor of Physic[s] since 1982, and Professor of Materials, since 1987, University of California, Santa Barbar[a]; *b* 22 Jan. 1936; *s* of Peter Jacob Heeger and Alice Minkin Heeger; *m* 1957, Ru[th] Chudacroft; two *s*. *Educ:* Univ. of Nebraska (BS 1957); Univ. of Calif, Berkeley (Ph[D] 1961). University of Pennsylvania: Prof. of Physics, 1962–82; Director: Lab. for Res. o[n] Structure of Matter, 1974–80; Inst. for Polymers and Organic Solids, 1983–99. Founde[r] 1990, Chm., 1990–99, Uniax Corp. Member: NAS; NAE. Holds numerous hon. degree[s]. Buckley Prize, APS, 1983; Balzan Foundn Prize, 1995; Nobel Prize in Chem., 2000. *Recreations:* ski-ing, walking. *Address:* Physics Department, University of California [at] Santa Barbara, Santa Barbara, CA 93106, USA. *T:* (805) 8933184, *Fax:* (805) 893475[?]; *e-mail:* ajh@physics.ucsb.edu.

HEFFER, Simon James; Associate Editor and columnist, Daily Telegraph, since 2005; *b* 18 July 1960; *er s* of late James Heffer and of Joyce Mary Heffer (*née* Clements); *m* 198[?] Diana Caroline, *d* of Sqdn Ldr P. A. Clee; two *s*. *Educ:* King Edward VI Sch., Chelmsfor[d]; Corpus Christi Coll., Cambridge (BA 1982; MA 1986). Medical journalist, 1983–8[?]; Leader Writer and Parly Sketch Writer, Daily Telegraph, 1986–91; Dep. Ed. and Politic[al] Corresp., Spectator, 1991–94; Dep. Ed., Daily Telegraph, 1994–95; columnist, Dai[ly] Mail, 1993–94 and 1995–2005. Mem. Bd, Britten Sinfonia, 2005–. *Publications:* Mor[al] Desperado: a life of Thomas Carlyle, 1995; Power and Place: the political consequence[s] of King Edward VII, 1998; Like the Roman: the life of Enoch Powell, 1998; Nor Sha[ll] My Sword: the reinvention of England, 1999; Vaughan Williams, 2000; Great Britis[h] Speeches, 2007. *Recreations:* cricket, music, bibliophily, my family. *Address:* The Dail[y] Telegraph, 111 Buckingham Palace Road, SW1W 0DT. *T:* (020) 7931 2000. *Club[s]:* Beefsteak, Garrick, MCC.

HEGARTY, Frances; *see* Fyfield, Frances.

HEGARTY, Dr John, FInstP; Provost of Trinity College Dublin, since 2001; *b* Mayo, 1[?] April 1948; *s* of John and Delia Hegarty; *m* 1975, Neasa Ní Chinnéide; two *s*. *Edu[c]:* National Univ. of Ireland, Maynooth (BSc 1969; Higher DipEd 1971); National Univ. [of] Ireland, Galway (PhD 1976); Trinity Coll. Dublin (DSc 2001). FInstP 1986. Re[s.] Associate, Univ. of Wisconsin-Madison, 1977–80; Res. Scientist, Bell Labs, Murray Hi[ll], NJ, 1980–86; Prof. of Laser Physics, TCD, 1986–2001. Adjunct Prof., Univ. of Georgi[a], Athens, USA, 1990. Founder and Dir, Optronics Ireland, 1989–2000. Coordinator, Eu[r.] Consortium on Microcavities, 1993–2000. Member: Bd, Nat. Res. Support Fun[d] Ireland, 1995–98; Higher Educn Authy, Ireland, 1998–2001; Tech. Adv. Panel o[n] Information and Communications Technol., Sci. Foundn Ireland, 2000–01. Chm., Dea[ns] and Vice Presidents for Res. under CHIU, 2000. Fellow, TCD. MRIA; MIEEE. Member: Amer. Physical Soc.; Amer. Optical Soc. Hon. LLD QUB, 2008. *Publication[s]:* contribs to jls incl. Physical Rev., Optical and Quantum Electronics, IEEE Jl Quantu[m] Electronics, Applied Physics Letters, Jl Luminescence, Jl Crystal Growth, Optics Letter[s], Electronics Letters. *Recreations:* voracious reader of all forms of literature from biograph[y] to novels which enrich the soul and ease me to sleep at night, sailing and a love of th[e] power and unpredictability of the sea, cycling for leisure, especially around W Kerry

Address: Provost's Office, Trinity College, Dublin 2, Ireland. *T:* (1) 8961558, *Fax:* (1) 8962302; *e-mail:* provost@tcd.ie.

HEGARTY, Sir John (Kevin), Kt 2007; Worldwide Creative Director, since 1982, and Chairman, 1991, Bartle Bogle Hegarty Ltd; *b* 20 May 1944; *s* of Matthew and Anne Hegarty; *m* (separated); one *s* one *d*. *Educ:* Challoner Grammar Sch.; Hornsey Sch. of Art; London Coll. of Printing. Junior Art Dir, Benton & Bowles, 1965–66; Art Director: John Collings and Partners, 1966–67; Cramer Saatchi, 1967–70; Saatchi & Saatchi: Founding Shareholder, 1970; Dep. Creative Dir, 1971–73; Founding Partner and Creative Dir, TBWA, London, 1973–82. Hon. Prof., London Inst., 1998. FRSA 1992. Wine maker, Domaine de Chamans. *Recreations:* tennis, ski-ing. *Address:* (office) 60 Kingly Street, W1B 5DS. *Clubs:* Groucho; Century.

HEGARTY, Seamus, PhD; Director, National Foundation for Educational Research, 1994–2005; *b* 19 Oct. 1945; *s* of James Hegarty and Mary Hegarty; *m* 1972, Carol Halls; two *s* one *d*. *Educ:* St Colman's Coll., Fermoy; University Coll., Dublin (BSc, HDipEd); Univ. of London Inst. of Educn (PhD 1975). Mgt trng, 1969–70; teaching, 1970–75; research, 1975–94. Visiting Professor: Reading Univ., 1996; London Univ. Inst. of Educn, 1996–; Univ. of Warwick; Univ. of Manchester; QUB; Univ. of Wales, Aberystwyth. Pres., Consortium of Instns for Develt and Res. in Educn in Europe, 2000–02; Chm., Internat. Assoc. for the Evaluation of Educnl Achievement, 2005–. Hon. Dr: Free Univ. of Brussels, 1997; Oxford Brookes, 2001; London, 2006; DUniv York, 1999. MInstD 1994. Ed., Educnl Res., 1983–; Founder Ed., European Jl Special Needs Educn, 1986–. *Publications:* Able to Learn?: the pursuit of culture-fair assessment, 1978; Educating Pupils with Special Needs in the Ordinary School, 1981; Integration in Action, 1982; Recent Curriculum Development in Special Education, 1982; The Making of a Profession, 1983; Training for Management in Schools, 1983; Research and Evaluation Methods in Special Education, 1985; Meeting Special Needs in Ordinary Schools, 1987, 2nd edn 1993; Developing Expertise: INSET for special educational needs, 1988; Review of the Present Situation of Special Education, 1988; Boosting Educational Achievement, 1989; Educating Children and Young People with Disabilities: principles and the review of practice, 1993; New Perspectives in Special Education: a six-country study of integration, 1994; Review of the Present Situation in Special Needs Education, 1995; The Role of Research in Mature Education Systems, 1997; (with M. Alur) Education and Children with Special Needs: from segregation to inclusion, 2002. *Recreations:* contemporary fiction, music, board games, golf. *Club:* West Middlesex Golf.

HEGARTY, Most Rev. Séamus; *see* Derry, Bishop of, (RC).

HEGARTY, Thomas Brendan; QC 1992; **His Honour Judge Hegarty;** a Circuit Judge, since 1996; *b* 6 June 1943; *s* of Thomas Hegarty and Louise (*née* Conlan); *m* 1972, Irene Letitia Hall; one *s* one *d*. *Educ:* St Joseph's Coll., Dumfries; St John's Coll., Cambridge (BA 1964; LLB 1965; MA 1970). Called to the Bar, Middle Temple, 1970; a Recorder, 1988–96. *Address:* 8 King Street, Manchester M2 6AQ. *Club:* Manchester Tennis and Racquet.

HEGGESSEY, Lorraine Sylvia; Chief Executive, talkbackThames, since 2005; *b* 16 Nov. 1956; *d* of Sam and Doris Heggessey; *m* 1985, Ronald de Jong, musician and composer; two *d*. *Educ:* Durham Univ. (BA Hons English Lit.). BBC: News Trainee and Sub Editor, 1979–83; Producer: Panorama, 1983–86; This Week, 1986–91; Editor, Biteback, 1991–92; Series Producer, The Underworld, 1992–94; Exec. Producer, BBC Science (QED, Animal Hospital, The Human Body, Minders), 1994–97; Head of Children's Programmes, 1997–99; Dep. Chief Exec., BBC Productions, 1999–2000; Controller, BBC1, 2000–05. *Recreations:* ski-ing, theatre, gym, my daughters, having fun and laughing. *Address:* talkbackThames, 20–21 Newman Street, W1T 1PG.

HEGGS, Geoffrey Ellis; Chairman of Industrial Tribunals, 1977–97, Regional Chairman, London North, 1990–97; a Recorder of the Crown Court, 1983–97; *b* 23 Oct. 1928; *s* of George Heggs, MBE and Winifred Grace Heggs; *m* 1953, Renée Fanny Madeleine Calderan (*see* R. F. M. Heggs); two *s* one *d*. *Educ:* Elizabeth Coll., Guernsey; LLB London. Admitted Solicitor, 1952. Rotary Foundn Fellow, Yale Univ., 1953–54; LLM Yale; Asst Sec., Law Soc., 1956–58; practised as solicitor in London, 1958–77. Mem., City of London Solicitors' Company. *Recreations:* military history, music, painting, sailing. *Address:* 12 Audley Road, Ealing, W5 3ET. *T:* (020) 8997 0305; *e-mail:* g.heggs@ntlworld.com. *Club:* Royal Over-Seas League.

HEGGS, Renée Fanny Madeleine, (Miguette); a Social Security Commissioner, 1981–2002; a Child Support Commissioner, 1993–2002; *b* 29 Nov. 1929; *d* of Emilio and Graziella Calderan; *m* 1953, Geoffrey Ellis Heggs, *qv*; two *s* one *d*. *Educ:* Notting Hill and Ealing High Sch., GPDST; LLB (London) 1952. Admitted Solicitor, 1955; practising Solicitor, 1955–81. Chm., Nat. Insce Local Tribunal, 1976–81; pt-time Chm. of Industrial Tribunals, 1978–81; Pres., Appeal Tribunal under London Building Acts, 1979–81; Legal Mem., 1985–2000, Dep. Regl Chm., 1995–2000, Mental Health Review Tribunal. Liveryman, City of London Solicitors' Co., 2005–. *Recreations:* music, travelling. *Address:* 12 Audley Road, Ealing, W5 3ET. *T:* (020) 8997 0305. *Club:* Royal Over-Seas League.

HEGINBOTHAM, Prof. Christopher John; Professor of Mental Health Policy and Management, since 2005, and Co-Director, Institute for Philosophy, Diversity and Mental Health, since 2006, University of Central Lancashire; *b* 25 March 1948; *s* of Joseph William and Marjorie Heginbotham; *m* 1988, Barbara Joyce, *d* of Charles and Lois-Ella Gill, Cincinnati, Ohio (marr. diss. 2008); two *d*. *Educ:* Univ. of Birmingham (BSc Hons); Univ. of Essex (MSc); MA Wales 1989; MPhil Cambridge 2001. Area Manager, Circle Thirty Three Housing Trust, 1977–80; Assistant Borough Housing Officer, London Borough of Haringey, 1980–82; Nat. Dir, MIND (Nat. Assoc. for Mental Health), 1982–88; Fellow in Health Services Management, King's Fund Coll., London, 1989–93; Chief Executive: Riverside Mental Health NHS Trust, 1993–96; E and N Herts HA, 1996–2000; Chm. and Chief Exec., Eastern Region Specialised Commissioning Gp, 2000–01; Chief Exec., S Warwicks Gen. Hosps NHS Trust, 2001–03; Chief Exec., Mental Health Act Commn, 2003–08. Member: Hampstead DHA, 1981–87; Waltham Forest DHA, 1989–92 (Vice-Chm., 1991–92); Chm., Redbridge and Waltham Forest FHSA, 1992–93. Member: Nat. Adv. Council on Employment of Disabled People, 1983–90; Bd, World Fedn for Mental Health, 1985–89 (rep., UN Commn on Human Rights, 1985–91); Bd, Internat. Acad. of Law and Mental Health, 1987–89. Vis. Res. Fellow, Univ. of Glasgow Inst. of Law and Ethics in Medicine, 1987–91; Vis. Sen. Fellow, Health Services Mgt Centre, Univ. of Birmingham, 1994–2001; Hon. Prof., Univ. of Warwick, 2005–. *Publications:* Housing Projects for Mentally Handicapped People, 1981; Promoting Residential Services for Mentally Handicapped People, 1982; Webs and Mazes: approaches to community care, 1984; The Rights of Mentally Ill People, 1987; Return to Community, 1990; (with T. Campbell) Mental Illness: prejudice, discrimination and the law, 1990; (with C. Ham) Purchasing Dilemmas, 1992; Philosophy, Psychiatry and Psychopathy, 2000. *Recreations:* art history, walking, cycling. *Address:* University of Central Lancashire, Harrington Building, Preston, Lancs PR1 2HE.

HEGINBOTHAM, Prof. Wilfred Brooks, OBE 1978; FREng; Director General, Production Engineering Research Association of Great Britain (PERA), Melton Mowbray, 1979–84; *b* 9 April 1924; *s* of Fred and Alice Heginbotham; *m* 1957, Marjorie Pixton; three *d*. *Educ:* Manchester Univ. (UMIST). BScTech 1949; MScTech 1950; PhD (Manchester) 1956; DSc (Manchester) 1979. FIProdE; MIMechE; FREng (FEng 1985); FRSA. Started in industry as wood pattern maker; part-time courses to HNC, 1938–46; Walter Preston Schol., Manchester Coll. of Tech., 1946; joined staff, 1951; Lectr in Production Engineering subjects, UMIST, 1951–58; industrial experience for 10 years; Nottingham University: Sen. Lectr, 1958; started first BSc course in Prod. Engrg in UK, 1961; Head of Dept of Prod. Engrg and Prod. Management, 1961–63; Cripps Prof., 1963–79; Dean, Faculty of Applied Science, 1967–71; Special Prof. of Prodn Engrg, 1983–86; Prof. Emeritus, 1990. Hon. Prof., Dept of Engrg, Univ. of Warwick, 1984–89; Vis. Prof., Univ. of RI, USA, 1987; Vis. Sen. Res. Fellow, Dept of Mech. Engrg, Univ. of Birmingham, 1989–. Developed group to study Automatic Assembly Systems and Industrial Robot devices, including computer vision and tactile sense, and co-operated with industry in development of advanced automation equipment. Chm. Org. Cttee for establishment of Brit. Robot Assoc., 1977, Chm. of Council, 1977–80, Pres., 1980–84. Editor-in-Chief: The Industrial Robot; Assembly Automation; Advanced Manufacturing Technology Journal. Hon. DTech Scis Eindhoven, 1981; Hon. DSc Aston, 1983. Engelberger Award, Robot Inst. of America, 1983. *Publications:* Programmable Assembly, 1984; (ed with D. T. Pham) Robot Grippers, 1986; contribs to Encyc. Brit. on Robot Devices and to prof. pubns on metal cutting, automated assembly, industrial robots, artificial intelligence and production processes. *Recreations:* gliding, model aircraft construction and operation (radio controlled). *Address:* 7 Paddocks View, Eaton Grange, Long Eaton, Notts NG10 3QF. *T:* (0115) 946 3250.

HEGLAND, David Leroy, DFC 1944; Director: Kemtron Ltd; Galena; Massey-Ferguson Holdings (Australia) Ltd; Carlton and United Breweries Holdings Ltd; Plessey Pacific Pty Ltd; cattle grazier; *b* 12 June 1919; *s* of Lee and Jennie Hegland; *m* 1944, Dagmar Cooke; two *s* one *d*. *Educ:* Whitman Coll., Washington, USA (BA). Served War, 1942–45; USN aircraft pilot in Pacific Ocean areas; Lt Comdr USNR, 1945. Managing Director: GM International, Copenhagen, 1956–58; GM South African, Port Elizabeth, 1958–61; GM Holden's Pty Ltd, Melbourne, 1962–65; Chm. and Man. Dir, Vauxhall Motors Ltd, Luton, 1966–70; Dir, General Motors Ltd, London, 1966–70; Chm., GKN Australia Ltd, and Dir, Ajax GKN Holdings Pty Ltd, and Guest, Keen & Nettlefolds (Overseas) Ltd, 1972–80. Member: Albury-Wodonga Develt Corp., 1980–81; Industry Forum, Aust. Acad. of Science, 1972; Aust. Inst. of Dirs; Delta Sigma Rho. FIMI. Richard Kirby medal for production engrg, 1964. *Recreations:* flying, tennis, riding. *Address:* 300 Hot Springs Road #A30, Santa Barbara, CA 93108–2038, USA. *Clubs:* Royal & Ancient Golf (St Andrews); Melbourne, Victoria Racing (Melbourne); Albury (Albury, NSW).

HEGLEY, John Richard; freelance poet and performer; *b* 1 Oct. 1953; *s* of René Robert Hegley and Joan Hegley; one *d*. *Educ:* Univ. of Bradford (BSc Hons Social Scis (European Lit./Hist. of Ideas)). Actor/musician: Inter-action Prof. Dogg's Troup, 1978; Soapbox Children's Th., 1979; John Peel Radio sessions, 1983–84; presenter, Word of Mouth, TV poetry series, 1990; BBC on-line Poet-in-Residence, 1998; played Vernon Hines in Pyjama Game, 1999; Hearing with Hegley, BBC Radio series, 1997–99; performed, 21st Edinburgh Fest., 2004. Hon. LLD Luton 2000. *Publications:* Glad to Wear Glasses, 1990; Can I Come Down Now, Dad?, 1992; Five Sugars, Please, 1993; Love Cuts, 1995; The Family Pack, 1997; Beyond Our Kennel, 1998; Dog, 2000; My Dog is a Carrot, 2002; The Sound of Paint Drying, 2003; Uncut Confetti, 2006. *Address:* Troika, 3rd Floor, 74 Clerkenwell Road, EC1M 5QA.

HEIDEN, Paul; Chief Executive, FKI plc, since 2003; *b* 3 Feb. 1957; *s* of Ronald Joseph and Hilda Primrose Heiden; *m* 1979, Susan; one *s* one *d*. *Educ:* Stratford Grammar Sch.; Imperial Coll., London (BSc 1st cl. Hons Biol.). ARCS; ACA. Accountant, Peat Marwick Mitchell, 1979–84; Financial Controller: Mercury Communications, 1984–88; Hanson plc, 1988–92; Rolls-Royce: Finance Dir, Aerospace, 1992–97; Bd Dir, 1997–2002; Man. Dir, Industrial Businesses, 1997–99; Finance Dir, 1999–2002. Non-executive Director: Bunzl, 1999–2005; Filtrona, 2005–06; United Utilities plc, 2006–. *Recreations:* golf, ski-ing, spectator sports. *Address:* FKI plc, 86 Fetter Lane, EC4A 1EN. *T:* (020) 7832 0000; *e-mail:* paul.heiden@fkiplc.com. *Clubs:* Nottingham Golf (Hollinwell); Ratcliffe on Trent Golf.

HEIGL, Peter Richard; HM Diplomatic Service, retired; Resident Deputy High Commissioner, Republic of Kiribati, 2004–06; *b* 21 Feb. 1943; *s* of late Joseph William Heigl and Violet Heigl (*née* Gatti); *m* 1965, Sally Lupton; three *s* one *d*. *Educ:* Worthing Technical High Sch. Min. of Power, 1963–66; Min. of Technology, 1966–70; DTI, 1970–74; FCO, 1974; served: Kuala Lumpur, 1974–78; Accra, 1978–81; FCO, 1981–84; 1st Sec., Riyadh, 1984–86; Consul (Commercial), Jedda, 1986–89; FCO, 1989–91; Dep. Head of Mission, Khartoum, 1991–93; Chargé, Phnom Penh, 1994; Dep. Head of Mission, Kathmandu, 1994–99; High Comr to the Bahamas, 1999–2003. *Recreations:* family, travel, swimming, reading, local history. *Address:* c/o Foreign and Commonwealth Office, King Charles Street, SW1A 2AH.

HEILBRON, Hilary Nora Burstein; QC 1987; *b* 2 Jan. 1949; *d* of Dr Nathaniel Burstein and Dame Rose Heilbron, DBE. *Educ:* Huyton College; Lady Margaret Hall, Oxford (MA). Called to the Bar, Gray's Inn, 1971; Bencher, 1995. DTI Inspector into Blue Arrow plc, 1989–91. Chairman: London Common Law and Commercial Bar Assoc., 1992–93; Jt Gen. Council of Bar and Law Soc. indep. working party into civil justice, 1993. Dir, The City Disputes Panel Ltd, 1994– (Chm., 2006–07). Vice-Chm., Marshall Aid Commemoration Commn, 1998–2002; Member: Adv. Council, Centre for Dispute Resolution, 1996–2002; Civil Justice Council, 1998–2002; Bar Assoc. of NSW. *Publication:* A Practical Guide to International Arbitration in London, 2008. *Recreations:* travel, gardening. *Address:* Brick Court Chambers, 7–8 Essex Street, WC2R 3LD. *T:* (020) 7379 3550.

HEIM, Paul Emil, CMG 1988; Chairman, Taxation Disciplinary Board (formerly Tribunal), 2000–04 (Vice Chairman, Appeal Committee, 2004–08); Visiting Professor, Leicester University, since 1988; *b* 23 May 1932; *s* of George Heim and Hedy Heim (*née* Herz); *m* 1962, Elizabeth, *er d* of late Lt-Col G. M. Allen, MBE; one *s* two *d*. *Educ:* Prince of Wales School, Nairobi; King's Coll., Univ. of Durham (LLB). Called to the Bar, Lincoln's Inn, 1955, Bencher, 1986. Dep. Registrar, Supreme Court of Kenya, then Sen. Dep. Registrar, Magistrate and Acting Registrar (HMOCS), 1954–65; admitted Advocate, Supreme Court, 1959; Administrator, European Court of Human Rights, Strasbourg, 1965, European Commn of Human Rights, Strasbourg, 1966; Principal Administrator, Political Directorate, Council of Europe, 1967, Dep. Head, Private Office, 1969; Head of Div., then Dir, European Parlt, 1973–81; Registrar, European Court of Justice, 1982–88; Pres., Heads of Admin of EC Instns, 1986–88; Special Advr, European Court of Justice, 1988–89; a Chairman: Financial Services Tribunal, 1988–2002; Value Added Tax Tribunal, 1989–2003; Pres., FIMBRA Appeal Tribunals, 1990–2001; a Dep. Chm., PIA Appeal Tribunal, 1994–2002. Hon. Res. Fellow, Univ. of Exeter, 1988–. Chm., George

Heim Meml Trust, 1998–; Dep. Chm., Luxembourg Soc., 1999–; Chm., Langport Area Develt Trust (formerly Langport Forum), 2007– (Dep. Chm., 2001–06). Grand Officer, Order of Merit (Luxembourg), 1998. *Address:* Wearne Wyche, Langport, Somerset TA10 9AA.

HEIN, Prof. Jotun John; Professor of Bioinformatics, University of Oxford, and Fellow of University College, Oxford, since 2001; *b* Denmark, 19 July 1956; *s* of Piet Hein and Gerd Erikson; *m* 2001, Anne-Mette Pedersen; two *d. Educ:* Aarhus Univ. (Licentiate in Sci. 1990). Asst Prof., 1990–94, Associate Prof., 1994–2001, Aarhus Univ. *Recreations:* reading, golf, tennis, badminton. *Address:* Department of Statistics, University of Oxford, 1 South Parks Road, Oxford OX1 3TG. *T:* (01865) 272860.

HEINE, Prof. Volker, FRS 1974; Professor of Theoretical Physics, University of Cambridge, 1976–97; Fellow of Clare College, Cambridge, since 1960; *b* 19 Sept. 1930; *m* 1955, M. Daphne Hines; one *s* two *d. Educ:* Otago Univ. (MSc, DipHons); Cambridge Univ. (PhD). FInstP. Demonstrator, Cambridge Univ., 1958–63, Lectr 1963–70; Reader in Theoretical Physics, 1970–76. Vis. Prof., Univ. of Chicago, 1965–66; Vis. Scientist, Bell Labs, USA, 1970–71. For. Mem., Max-Planck Inst., Stuttgart, 1980–. Fellow, Amer. Phys. Soc., 1987. Maxwell Medal, Inst. of Physics, 1972; Royal Medal, Royal Soc., 1993; Paul Dirac Medal, Inst. of Physics, 1993; Max Born Medal, Inst. of Physics and German Physical Soc., 2001. *Publications:* Group Theory in Quantum Mechanics, 1960; (jtly) Solid State Physics Vol. 24, 1970, Vol. 35, 1980; articles in Proc. Royal Soc., Jl Physics, Physical Review, etc. *Address:* Cavendish Laboratory, 19 J. J. Thomson Avenue, Cambridge CB3 0HE.

HEINEY, Paul; freelance writer and broadcaster; *b* 20 April 1949; *s* of Norbert Wisniewski and Evelyn Mardlin; name changed to Heiney by Deed Poll, 1971; *m* 1980, Elizabeth Mary Purves, *qv;* one *d* (one *s* decd). *Educ:* Parson Cross Primary Sch., Sheffield; High Storrs Grammar Sch. for Boys. Stagehand, Birmingham Rep. Th., 1968; electrician, Mermaid Th., 1969; BBC: asst film recordist, 1969–71; Radio Humberside, 1971–74; television presenter, programmes include: That's Life!, 1978–82; In at the Deep End, 1982–85; Travel Show, 1984–87; Food and Drink, 1991; Watchdog, 2003–05; Trading Places, ITV, 1988–2000; Victorian Farming Year, ITV, 2002–05; BBC Radio, includes: reporter: Newsbeat, Radio 1, 1974–76; Today, Radio 4, 1976–78; Radio 2 (occasionally), 1984–96; End of the Line, Radio 4, 1993–94; A Year in Harness, Radio 4, 1996; Home Truths, 2005. Patron, Wolverstone Project. Hon. DCL East Anglia, 2006. *Publications:* The Sailing Weekend Book, 1984 (Best Book of the Sea, King George's Fund for Sailors); The English and their Horses, 1987; In at the Deep End, 1989; Farming Times, 1993; Second Crop, 1994; George Soper's Horses, 1997; Ham and Pigs, 1998; Domino's Effect (novel), 1999; Golden Apples (novel), 1999; The Nuts and Bolts of Life, 2003; The Traditional Farming Year, 2004; Can Cows Walk Upstairs?, 2005; Maritime Britain, 2005. *Recreations:* sailing, ploughing with Suffolk Punches. *Address:* c/o Jo Gurnett Management, 2 New Kings Road, SW6 4SA. *T:* (020) 7736 7828; *e-mail:* pheiney@mac.com. *Clubs:* Royal Cruising; Suffolk Horse Society.

HEISBOURG, François; Special Adviser, Fondation pour la Recherche Stratégique, Paris, since 2005 (Director, 2001–05); *b* 24 June 1949; *s* of Georges Heisbourg, *qv; m* 1989, Elyette, *d* of Georges Levy; two *s. Educ:* Landon School, Bethesda, Maryland; Collège Stanislas, Paris; Inst. d'Etudes Politiques, Paris; Ecole Nationale d'Administration, Paris. French Foreign Ministry: Asst to Head of Economics Dept, 1978; Mem., Policy Planning Staff, 1979; 1st Sec., French Mission to UN, NY, 1979–81; Diplomatic Adviser to Minister of Defence, 1981–84. Vice-Pres., Thomson SA, Paris, 1984–87; Dir, IISS, 1987–92; Sen. Vice-Pres., Matra Défense-Espace, Paris, 1992–98; Hd, French Interministerial gp on study of internat. relations and strategic affairs, 1999–2000; Prof., Inst. d'Etudes Politiques, Paris, 1999–2001. Chairman: Geneva Centre for Security Policy, 1998–; IISS, 2001–. Numerous foreign orders. *Publications:* Emiliano Zapata et la Révolution mexicaine, 1978; (with P. Boniface) La Puce, les Hommes et la Bombe, 1986; (contrib.) The Conventional Defence of Europe, 1986; (contrib.) Conventional Arms Control and East-West Security, 1989; (ed) The Changing Strategic Landscape, 1989; (ed) The Strategic Implications of Change in the Soviet Union, 1990; (contrib.) The Shape of the New Europe, 1992; (contrib.) Western Europe and the Gulf War, 1992; Les Volontaires de l'An 2000, 1995; Warfare, 1997; European Defence: making it work, 2000; Hyperterrorisme: la nouvelle guerre, 2001; La Fin de l'Occident? L'Amerique, l'Europe et le Moyen-Orient, 2005; (with J. L. Marret) Le Terrorisme en France Aujourd'hui, 2006; L'Épaisseur du Monde, 2007; Iran: le choix des armes?, 2007; contribs to internat. jls. *Recreations:* hiking, old atlas collecting. *Club:* Travellers (Paris).

HEISBOURG, Georges; Ambassador of Luxembourg, retired; *b* 19 April 1918; *s* of Nicolas Heisbourg and Berthe (*née* Ernsterhoff); *m* 1945, Hélène Pinet; two *s* one *d. Educ:* Athénée, Luxembourg; Univs of Grenoble, Innsbruck and Paris. Head of Govt Press and Information Office, Luxembourg, 1944–45; Attaché 1945–48, Sec. 1948–51, of Legation, London; Head of Internat. Organisations Section, Dir of Political Affairs, Min. of For. Affairs, Luxembourg, 1951–58; Luxembourg Ambassador to USA, Canada and Mexico, 1958–64; Perm. Rep. to UN, 1958–61; Luxembourg Ambassador: to Netherlands, 1964–67; to France, 1967–70; Perm. Rep. to OECD, 1967–70; Sec. Gen., WEU, 1971–74; Ambassador to USSR, Finland, Poland and Outer Mongolia, 1974–77; Perm. Rep. to Council of Europe, 1978–79; Ambassador to Fed. Rep. of Germany and to Denmark, 1979–83. Médaille de l'Ordre de la Résistance, Grand Officer, Nat. Order of Crown of Oak, 1980 (Chevalier, 1958), Comdr, Order of Adolphe de Nassau, 1963, and Grand Officer, Order of Merit, 1976, Luxembourg; also holds decorations from Austria, Belgium, France, Germany, Italy, Mexico, and the Netherlands. *Publication:* Le Gouvernement Luxembourgeois en exil 1940, Vol. I, 1986, Vol. II, 1987, Vol. III, 1989, Vol. IV, 1991. *Recreation:* swimming. *Address:* 9A Boulevard Joseph II, 1840 Luxembourg.
  See also F. Heisbourg.

HEISER, Sir Terence Michael, (Sir Terry), GCB 1992 (KCB 1987; CB 1984); Permanent Secretary, Department of the Environment, 1985–92; *b* 24 May 1932; *s* of David and Daisy Heiser; *m* 1957, Kathleen Mary Waddle; one *s* two *d. Educ:* Grafton Road Primary Sch., Dagenham; London Evacuee Sch., Sunninghill, Berks; Windsor County Boy's Sch., Berks; Birkbeck Coll., Univ. of London; BA (Hons English). Served in RAF, 1950–52; joined Civil Service 1949, served with Colonial Office, Min. of Works, Min. of Housing and Local Govt; Principal Private Sec. to Sec. of State for the Environment, 1975–76; Under Secretary: Housing Directorate, 1976–79; Local Govt Finance Directorate, 1979–81; Dep. Sec., DoE, 1981–85. Non-exec. Director: Abbey National plc, 1992–2001; Sainsbury plc, 1992–2000; Wessex Water plc, 1993–98. Mem. Bd, PIA, 1994–2000; Mem., Senior Salaries Review Bd, Office of Manpower Econs, 1998–2003. Chm., Gen. Adv. Council, BBC, 1992–96. Mem., Adv. Panel on Spoliation, DCMS, 2000–. Mem., Exec. Cttee, 1993–2002, Southern Region Cttee, 2003–04, Nat. Trust; Mem., V&A Theatre Mus. Cttee, 2004–06 (Trustee, V&A Mus., 1993–2003); Trustee, Prince of Wales Phoenix Trust, 1996–2001. Governor, Birkbeck Coll., London, 1990–2002; Mem. Council, Sussex Univ., 1999–2008. Freeman, City of London, 1990.

Hon. Fellow, Birkbeck Coll., London, 1988. Hon. DLitt Bradford, 1988. *Recreations:* reading, walking, talking. *Club:* Garrick.

HELAISSI, Sheikh Abdulrahman Al-, Hon. GCVO; retired; Saudi Arabian Ambassado to the Court of St James's, 1966–76; *b* 24 July 1922. *Educ:* Universities of Cairo an London. Secretary to Embassy, London, 1947–54; Under-Sec., Min. of Agricultur 1954–57; Head of Delegn to FAO, 1955–61; Ambassador to Sudan, 1957–6 Representative to UN, and to various confs concerned with health and agricultur Delegate to Conf. of Non-aligned Nations, Belgrade, 1961; Ambassador: Italy and Austri 1961–66; UK and Denmark (concurrently), 1966–76. Versed in Islamic Religious Lav *Publication:* The Rehabilitation of the Bedouins, 1959. *Address:* PO Box No 806 Riyadh-11482, Saudi Arabia.

HELE, Desmond George K.; *see* King-Hele.

HELE, James Warwick, CBE 1986; High Master of St Paul's School 1973–86; *b* 24 Jul 1926; *s* of John Warwick Hele, Carlisle; *m* 1948, Audrey Whalley; four *d. Educ:* Sedberg Sch.; Hertford Coll., Oxford; Trinity Hall, Cambridge (Schol., MA). 1st cl. hons Histor Tripos 1951. 5th Royal Inniskilling Dragoon Guards, 1946–48. Asst Master, Kin College Sch., Wimbledon, 1951–55; Rugby School: Asst Master, 1955–73; Housemaste Kilbracken, 1965–73; 2nd Master, 1970–73. Chairman: Headmasters' Conference, 198 (Chm., Acad. Cttee, 1979–81); Indep. Schs Adv. Cttee, 1983–88; Member: Seconda Exams Council, 1986–88; Exec. Cttee, GBA, 1988–97. Chairman: Westminster Cent for Educn, 1991–97; Combined Trusts Scholarship Trust, 1986–2003. Mem., Dors FHSA, 1990–92. Trustee, Brathay Hall, 1977–91. Governor: Rossall Sch., 1985–9 Uppingham Sch., 1986–92; Port Regis Sch., Shaftesbury, 1986–2001; Sherborne Sch 1986–96 (Chm. Govs, 1990–96); Chm., Clouds House, East Knoyle, 1992–200 *Recreations:* Rugby football (Oxford Univ. XV 1944), hill walking. *Address:* 2 John Woc House, Cathedral Views, Crane Bridge Road, Salisbury, Wilts SP2 7TW. *T:* (0172 322690. *Club:* East India, Devonshire, Sports and Public Schools.

HELLARD, Rebecca Jane; Strategic Director Corporate Services, Bradford Ci Council, since 2007; *b* 11 July 1966; *d* of Hugh Somerled Matheson Macdonald and Sar Jane Macdonald (*née* Tuffs); *m* 2000, Grant Hellard; one *s* one *d. Educ:* Cambridge Co of Arts and Technol. (BA Hons Econs). ACCA 1995. Philips Financial Services, 1991–9 Manager, PricewaterhouseCoopers, 1994–97; Breckland Council: Finance ar Performance Manager, 1997–99; Finance Dir, 1999–2002; Dep. Chief Exec., 2002–0 Chief Exec., 2004–06. *Recreations:* sports - gym, walking, swimming. *Address:* Bradfo City Council, City Hall, Bradford BD1 1HY. *T:* (01274) 432800, 432236, *Fax:* (0127 7300337; *e-mail:* becky.hellard@bradford.gov.uk.

HELLAWELL, Keith, QPM 1990; writer and broadcaster; Expert Adviser to Hom Secretary on international drugs issues, 2001–02; Director, Huddersfield Rugby Leagu Club, since 2002; *b* 18 May 1942; *s* of Douglas Hellawell and Ada Alice Hellawell (n Battye); *m* 1963, Brenda Hey; one *s* two *d. Educ:* Kirkburton Sec. Mod. Sch.; Dewsbu Tech. Coll.; Barnsley Coll. of Mining; London Univ. (LLB 1972); Cranfield Inst. of Tecl (MSc 1982); Police Staff Coll. Huddersfield Borough Police, 1962; seconded to Hom Office, 1975–78, incl. service in NI; Asst Chief Constable, W Yorks Police, 1983; De Chief Constable, Humberside Police, 1985; Chief Constable: Cleveland Police, 1990; Yorks Police, 1993–98; UK Anti-Drugs Co-ordinator, 1998–2001. Advr, Crimestoppe Trust, 1994–. Chairman: Catapult Presentation plc, 2001–; Sterience Ltd; Howe Associates; Goldshield Gp plc; non-executive Director: Evans of Leeds plc, 1998–9 Universal Vehicles Gp plc, 2001; Dalkia plc, 2002–; Universal Vehicles Modula Member: Adv. Council on Misuse of Drugs, 1994–98; Bd, Northern Counties Housir Assoc. Ltd, 1996–98; St John's Council, W Yorks, 1983–85 and 1993–; Council, NSPC (Trustee, 1993–2000); Chm., Services to Children's Cttee, 1996–); Trustee, Children i Crisis. Mem., Editl Bd, Forensic Medicine Jl, 1996–. Hon. LLD Bradford, 1998; Ho DSSc Leeds, 1998; Hon. DCL Huddersfield, 1998. OStJ 1996. *Publication:* The Outsid (autobiog.), 2002. *Recreations:* design, gardening, reading, sport.

HELLER, Angela Mary; *see* Flowers, A. M.

HELLER, Lucy Lauris; Managing Director, ARK Schools, since 2004; *b* London, 8 Fe 1959; *d* of late Lukas Heller and Caroline Carter; *m* 1990, Sir Charles (Abraham Grierso Elton, Bt, *qv* (marr. diss. 2007); one *s* one *d;* partner, Adrian Frederick Melhuish Smit *qv. Educ:* Hampstead Comp. Sch.; Lady Margaret Hall, Oxford (BA Hons PPE). Banke Bankers Trust, 1981–87; Man. Dir, Capital Mkts Gp, Manufacturers Hanover, 1987–9 Gp Treas., Booker, 1990–95; Exec. Chm., Verso, 1995–98; Gen. Manager, Th Observer, Guardian Media Gp, 1998–99; Jt Man. Dir, TSL Education, 2000–03. Mem Marshall Aid Commn, 2002–. Mem. Bd, Bush Th., 1989–2005. *Publication:* Eu Commercial Paper, 1988. *Address:* ARK Schools, 15 Adam Street, WC2N 6AH. *T:* (02 7395 2081; *e-mail:* lucy.heller@arksonline.org.

HELLIER, Maj.-Gen. Eric James, CBE 1977 (OBE 1970, MBE 1967); Region Manager, International Military Services, 1981–92; *b* 23 July 1927; *s* of Harry an Elizabeth Hellier; *m* 1952, Margaret Elizabeth Leadeham; one *s* one *d* (and one *s* dec *Educ:* Hugh Saxons Sch.; Cardiff Univ. Served, 1945–66: Exec. Officer, RNVR; re duty, Royal Signals; Staff Coll. and Jt Services Staff Coll; GSO2 WO; DAA&QMG Inf. Bde; CO, 24 Signals Regt, 1967–69; GSO1 Plans (Operational Requirements) MoI 1970; Col A/Q HQ 4 Div., 1971–72; Comd Bde Royal Signals and Catterick Garriso 1973–74; RCDS, 1975; Brig A/Q HQ 1(BR), Corps, 1976–79; Maj. Gen. Admi UKLF, 1979–81. Col Comdt, 1981–87, Rep. Col Comdt, 1983, Royal Corps of Signa Chairman: Gen. Purposes Cttee, Regular Forces Employment Assoc., 1983–91; Roy Signals Instn, 1984–89; Fund Raising Cttee, Nat. Mus. of Army Communication 1991–97; Trustee, Royal Signals Mus., 1998–2005. *Recreations:* golf, squash, ski-in *Address:* Goddards, 27 Church Street, Wherwell, Hants SP11 7JJ. *T:* (01264) 860710.

HELLINGA, Dr Lotte, FBA 1990; Secretary, Consortium of European Researc Libraries, 1994–2002; a Deputy Keeper, Humanities and Social Sciences, British Librar 1986–95; *b* 9 Sept. 1932; *d* of Arie Querido and Catharina Geertruida Querido (n Nagtegaal); *m* Wytze Hellinga (*d* 1985); one *s. Educ:* Univ. of Amsterdam. Lectr, then Se Lectr, Univ. of Amsterdam, 1967–76; Asst Keeper, British Liby, 1976–86. Vice Pres Bibliographical Soc., 1996–. Correspondent, Royal Netherlands Acad. of Scis, 1989– Gutenberg Preis, Mainz, 1989. *Publications:* The Fifteenth Century Printing Types of th Low Countries, 1966; Caxton in Focus, 1982; (ed jtly) The Cambridge History of th Book in Britain, vol. III, 1999; Catalogue of Books printed in the XVth century now i the British Library, vol. XI (England), 2006; Impresores, editores, correctores y cajist Siglo XV, 2006; numerous articles in learned jls. *Address:* 40A Canonbury Square, N 2AW. *T:* (020) 7359 2083.

HELLIWELL, Prof. John Richard, DPhil, DSc; FInstP, FRSC, FIBiol; Professor o Structural Chemistry, University of Manchester, since 1989; *b* 19 Sept. 1953; *s* of Henr Smith Helliwell and Amy (*née* Southam); *m* 1978, Madeleine Berry; two *s* one *d. Edu*

Ossett Sch.; Univ. of York (BSc 1st cl. Hons Physics 1974; DSc 1996); Balliol Coll., Univ. of Oxford (DPhil Molecular Biophysics 1978). CPhys, FInstP 1986; CChem, FRSC 1995; CBiol, FIBiol 1998. MRC Res. Asst and Jun. Res. Fellow, Linacre Coll., Oxford, 1978; Lectr in Biophysics, Keele Univ., jtly with SERC Daresbury Lab., 1979–83; SSO, then PSO, SERC Daresbury Lab., 1983–85; Lectr in Physics, York Univ., 1985–88; part-time with SERC, subseq. CCLRC, then STFC, Daresbury Lab., 1985–93, 2001–06, Hon. Scientist, 2007–; CCLRC Dir of Synchrotron Radiation Sci., Daresbury Lab., 2002. Vis. Res. Scholar, Cornell Univ., 1994; Visiting Professor: Univ. of Chicago, 1994; of Crystallography, Birkbeck Coll., London Univ., 2002–. Mem., Internat. Adv. Cttee, Centre for Coherent X-ray Sci., Melbourne, 2006–. Pres., Eur. Crystallographic Assoc., 2006–. Leader, UK Delegn, World Congress of Biophysics, New Delhi, 1999; Internat. Union of Crystallography Rep. to Internat. Council of Scientific and Tech. Inf., 2005–. Conference Lectures: Yugoslav-Italian Crystallographic Assoc., 1989; Soc. of Crystallographers of Australia, 1994 (1987 Fellow (Hon.), 1994); British Crystallographic Assoc., 1995; 2nd Internat. Conf. on Life Science, Japan, 1996; other Lectures: Ilyas Haneef Meml, Univ. of Leeds, 1993; Herzenberg Symposium, Yale Univ., 1995; Chem. Dept Dedication, Univ. of Toledo, 1998; K. Banerjee Meml, and Silver Medal, Indian Assoc. for Cultivation of Sci., Calcutta, 2000; 150th Anniv. W. L. Bragg, Univ. of Manchester, 2001; Weizmann Inst., Israel, 2002; Royal Instn, 2004; US Nat. Liby of Medicine, Bethesda, 2006. Transactions Symposium Orgnr, Amer. Crystallographic Assoc., 1999. Mem. Court, Univ. of Manchester, 2004– (UMIST, 1996–2004). Hon. Mem., Nat. Inst. of Chem., Slovenia, 1997–. Editor-in-Chief, Internat. Union of Crystallography's Jls, 1996–2005; Co-Editor: Jl Applied Crystallography, 1995–; Crystallography Reviews, 2006–. *Publications:* Macromolecular Crystallography with Synchrotron Radiation, 1992; (ed jtly) Time-resolved Macromolecular Crystallography, 1992; (ed jtly) Synchrotron Radiation in the Biosciences, 1994; (ed jtly) Time-resolved Diffraction, 1997; original res. papers and reviews in scientific jls. *Recreations:* family, squash, cycling, walking the dog. *Address:* School of Chemistry, University of Manchester, Oxford Road, Manchester M13 9PL. *T:* (0161) 275 4970, *Fax:* (0161) 275 4598; *e-mail:* john.helliwell@manchester.ac.uk.

HELLYER, Hon. Paul Theodore; PC (Canada) 1957; FRSA 1973; Syndicated Columnist, Toronto Sun, 1974–84; *b* Waterford, Ont, Canada, 6 Aug. 1923; *s* of A. S. Hellyer and Lulla M. Anderson; *m* 1st, 1945, Ellen Jean (*d* 2004), *d* of Henry Ralph, Toronto, Ont; two *s* one *d*; 2nd, 2005, Sandra Dorothy Bussiere. *Educ:* Waterford High Sch., Ont; Curtiss-Wright Techn. Inst. of Aeronautics, Glendale, Calif; University of Toronto (BA). Fleet Aircraft Mfg Co., Fort Erie, Ont. Wartime service, RCAF and Cdn Army. Propr Mari-Jane Fashions, Toronto, 1945–56; Treas., Curran Hall Ltd, Toronto, 1950 (Pres., 1951–62). Elected to House of Commons, 1949; re-elected, 1953; Parly Asst to Hon. Ralph Campney, Minister of Nat. Defence, 1956; Associate Minister of Nat. Defence, 1957; defeated in gen. elections of June 1957 and March 1958; re-elected to House of Commons in by-election Dec. 1958 and again re-elected June 1962, April 1963, Nov. 1965, June 1968, and Oct. 1972; defeated gen. election July 1974; Minister of National Defence, 1963–67; Minister of Transport, 1967–69, and Minister i/c Housing, 1968–69; resigned 1969 on question of principle relating to housing. Chm., Federal Task Force on Housing and Urban Develt, 1968. Served as a Parly Rep. to NATO under both L and C administrations. Joined Parly Press Gallery, Oct. 1974. Distinguished visitor, York Univ., 1969–70. Founder and Leader, Action Canada party, 1971; joined Progressive Cons. Party, 1972; Candidate for leadership of Progressive Cons. Party, Feb. 1976; re-joined Liberal Party, Nov. 1982, resigned Dec. 1996; Leader, Canadian Action Party, 1997–2004. Exec. Dir, The Canada Uni Assoc., 1991–92. *Publications:* Agenda: a Plan for Action, 1971; Exit Inflation, 1981; Jobs for All—Capitalism on Trial, 1984; Canada at the Crossroads, 1990; Damn the Torpedoes, 1990; Funny Money: a common sense alternative to mainline economics, 1994; Surviving the Global Financial Crisis: the economics of hope for Generation X, 1996; Arundel Lodge: a little bit of old Muskoka, 1996; The Evil Empire: globalization's darker side, 1997; Stop: think, 1999; Goodbye Canada, 2001; One Big Party: to keep Canada independent, 2003. *Recreations:* philately, music. *Address:* Suite 506, 65 Harbour Square, Toronto, ON M5J 2L4, Canada. *Club:* Ontario.

HELM, Marie Theresa C.; *see* Conte-Helm.

HELMER, Roger; Member (C) East Midlands, European Parliament, since 1999; *b* 25 Jan. 1944; *s* of Charles Henry Helmer and Nellie Ethel Helmer; *m* 1st, 1967, Veronica Logan (marr. diss. 1984); one *s* one *d*; 2nd, 1987, Sara Thomas (*née* Winterbottom). *Educ:* King Edward VI Sch., Southampton; Churchill Coll., Cambridge (BA, MA). Various mkting and gen. mgt posts with major multinationals, Procter & Gamble, Readers' Digest, and Guinness Plc, UK and overseas, especially E and SE Asia, 1965–98. Hon. Chm., Freedom Assoc., 2007–. *Recreation:* walking the dog. *Address:* Boswell House, 9 Prospect Court, Courteenhall Road, Blisworth, Northants NN7 3DG. *T:* (01604) 859746, *Fax:* (01604) 859329.

HELMORE, Roy Lionel, CBE 1980; Principal, Cambridgeshire College of Arts and Technology, 1977–86; Fellow of Hughes Hall, Cambridge, 1982–94, now Emeritus Fellow; *b* 8 June 1926; *s* of Lionel Helmore and Ellen Helmore (*née* Gibbins); *m* 1969, Margaret Lilian Martin. *Educ:* Montrose Academy; Edinburgh Univ. (BScEng); MA (Cantab). FIET. Crompton Parkinson Ltd, 1947–49; Asst Lectr, Peterborough Techn. Coll., 1949–53; Lectr, subseq. Sen. Lectr, Shrewsbury Techn. Coll., 1953–57; Head of Electrical Engrg and Science, Exeter Techn. Coll., 1957–61; Principal, St Albans Coll. of Further Education, 1961–77. Association of Principals of Colleges: Hon. Sec., 1968–71; Pres., 1972–73; Hon. Treasurer, 1983–86; Chm., of Council, Assoc. of Colls of Further and Higher Educn, 1987–88. Member: BBC Further Educn Adv. Council, 1967–73; Air Transport and Travel ITB, 1967–73; Technician Educn Council, 1973–79 (Vice-Chm.); Manpower Services Commn, 1974–82; RAF Trng and Educn Adv. Cttee, 1976–79; Chm., Trng and Further Educn Cons. Gp, 1977–82. JP St Albans, 1964–78. *Publication:* CCAT—a brief history, 1989. *Recreations:* gardening, watercolours, bowls. *Address:* 5 Beck Road, Saffron Walden, Essex CB11 4EH. *T:* (01799) 523981.

HELTAY, Laszlo Istvan; Founder and Music Director, Academy of St Martin in the Fields Chorus, 1975–99; Director, Chorus of Radio Televisión Española SA (RTVE), Madrid, 1998; *b* Budapest, 5 Jan. 1930; *s* of Laszlo Heltay and Gizella Somogy; *m* 1964, Hilary Nicholson. *Educ:* Franz Liszt Acad. of Music, Budapest (MA); Merton Coll., Oxford (MLitt; Hon. Fellow, 1997). Associate Conductor, NZBC Symphony Orchestra and Dir, NZ Opera Co., 1964–67; Conductor, Phoenix Opera Co., 1970–73; Founder and Music Dir, Brighton Fest. Chorus, 1968–95; Dir of Music, Royal Choral Soc., 1985–95. Has conducted major orchestras including: Philharmonia, Royal Philharmonic, London Philharmonic, Dresden Philharmonic, Dallas Symphony, Budapest Philharmonic; also radio orchestras and choirs. Choral music for film, Amadeus, 1984. Has made recordings. Hon. DMus Sussex, 1995. Internat. Kodaly Medal, 1982. *Recreations:* chess, tennis, swimming.

HELY-HUTCHINSON, family name of **Earl of Donoughmore**.

HELY HUTCHINSON, Hon. Timothy Mark; Chief Executive, Hachette Livre UK, since 2004; *b* 26 Oct. 1953; *s* of Earl of Donoughmore, *qv* and late Sheila (*née* Parsons). *Educ:* Eton Coll. (Oppidan Schol.); Magdalen Coll., Oxford (William Doncaster Schol.; MA Mod. Langs and Phil.). Various appts, Macmillan Publishers, 1975–82; Managing Director: Macdonald & Co. (Publishers) Ltd, 1982–86; Headline Book Publishing PLC, 1986–93; Chief Exec., Hodder Headline Ltd, 1993–2004. Director: WH Smith plc, 1999–2004; Inflexion plc, 2000–03; Chm., WH Smith News, 2001–04. Dir, Publishers Assoc., 1998–2004. Venturer of the Year Award, Brit. Venture Capital Assoc., 1990. *Recreations:* opera, horse-racing, bridge. *Address:* Hachette Livre UK Ltd, 338 Euston Road, NW1 3BH. *Club:* Groucho.

HEMANS, Simon Nicholas Peter, CMG 1992; CVO 1983; HM Diplomatic Service, retired; Partner, Cranmore Co., 1997–2001; *b* 19 Sept. 1940; *s* of late Brig. Peter Rupert Hemans, CBE, and Margaret Estelle Hemans (*née* Melsome); *m* 1970, Ursula Martha Naef; three *s* one *d*. *Educ:* Sherborne; London School of Economics (BScEcon). Joined Foreign Office, 1964; British Embassy, Moscow, 1966–68; FO, 1968–69; Dep. Commissioner, Anguilla, March–Oct. 1969; FO, 1969–71; UK Mission to UN, New York, 1971–75; British Embassy, Budapest, 1975–79; FO, 1979–81; Dep. High Comr, Nairobi, 1981–84; Head of Chancery, Moscow, 1985–87; Head of Soviet Dept, FCO, 1987–90; Asst Under-Sec. of State (Africa), FCO, 1990–92; Ambassador, Ukraine, 1992–95; High Comr to Kenya, 1995–97. *Publication:* trans., Savchuk, The Streets of Kiev, 1996. *Recreation:* travel. *Address:* 73 Cranmore Lane, Aldershot, Hants GU11 3AP.

HEMERY, David Peter, CBE 2003 (MBE 1969); Founding Partner, Performance Consultants, since 1989; Deputy Chairman, Performance Consultants International Ltd, since 2006; Director, Developing Potential Ltd, since 1997; *b* 18 July 1944; *s* of Peter Ronald Bentley Hemery and Eileen Beatrice Price; *m* 1981, Vivian Mary Bruford; two *s*. *Educ:* Boston Univ. (BSc Internat. Business 1968; DEd Social Psychology 1984); St Catherine's Coll., Oxford (CertEd 1970); Harvard Univ. (MEd 1972). Commonwealth Games: Gold Medal, 110m Hurdles, 1966, 1970; Captain, England Team, 1970; Olympic Games: Gold Medal, 400m Hurdles, 1968 (World Record); Bronze Medal, 400m Hurdles, 1972; Silver Medal, 4×400m, 1972. Teacher, Coach and Housemaster, Millfield Sch., 1970–71 and 1972–73; Dir, Sobell Sports Centre, 1973–75; Teacher and Coach, Boston Univ., 1976–83; coaching course for Nat. Coaching Foundn, 1983–85; mgt trng. Mem., Nat. Cttee, 1999–, and Exec., 2001– (Vice Chm., 2004–), BOA; Pres., UK Athletics, 1998–2002; Chm., Confedn of British Sport, 2006–. Pres., Marlborough AC, 2003–. Coach and Advr, sch. to internat. level. *Publications:* Another Hurdle (autobiog.), 1975; The Pursuit of Sporting Excellence, 1986, 2nd edn as Sporting Excellence: what makes a champion, 1991; Athletics in Action, 1987; Winning without Drugs, 1989; How to Help Children Find the Champion Within Themselves, 2005. *Recreations:* family, human potential and purpose, sport, walking and running. *Address:* White Acre, Fyfield, Marlborough, Wilts SN8 1PX. *T:* (01672) 861645.

HEMINGFORD, 3rd Baron *cr* 1943, of Watford; **Dennis Nicholas Herbert;** Deputy Chief Executive, Westminster Press, 1992–95 (Editorial Director, 1974–92); *b* 25 July 1934; *s* of 2nd Baron Hemingford and Elizabeth McClare (*d* 1979), *d* of Col J. M. Clark, Haltwhistle, Northumberland; *S* father, 1982; known professionally as Nicholas Herbert; *m* 1958, Jennifer Mary Toresen Bailey (OBE 1997), DL, *d* of F. W. Bailey, Harrogate; one *s* three *d*. *Educ:* Oundle Sch.; Clare Coll., Cambridge (MA). Reuters Ltd, 1956–61; The Times: Asst Washington Corresp., 1961–65; Middle East Corresp., 1965–68; Dep. Features Editor, 1968–70; Editor, Cambridge Evening News, 1970–74. Vice-Pres., Guild of British Newspaper Editors, 1979, Pres., 1980–81. Mem. Bd, Assoc. of British Editors (Hon. Sec., 1985–95), 1985–95. Member: Council, Europa Nostra, 1999–2005; Culture Cttee, UK Commn, UNESCO, 2000–04; Council, Friends of British Library, 2005–; Chm., East Anglia Regl Cttee, Nat. Trust, 1990–2000. Pres., Huntingdonshire Family History Soc., 1985–. Trustee: Bell Educnl Trust, 1985–90; Ely Cathedral Restoration Trust, 1993–. *Heir:* *s* Hon. Christopher Dennis Charles Herbert, *b* 4 July 1973. *Address:* Old Rectory, Hemingford Abbots, Huntingdon PE28 9AN. *T:* (01480) 466234. *Club:* Royal Commonwealth Society.

See also Lady Goodhart, H. T. Moggridge.

HEMINGWAY, Prof. Janet, PhD; FMedSci; Professor of Insect Molecular Biology and Director, School of Tropical Medicine, University of Liverpool, since 2001; Chief Executive Officer, Gates Foundation Innovative Vector Control Consortium, since 2005; *b* 13 June 1957; *d* of Brian Hemingway and Mollie Hemingway; one *d*. *Educ:* Sheffield Univ. (BSc 1st cl. Genetics); LSHTM, London Univ. (PhD). Lectr, Univ. of California, Riverside, 1981–82; MRC Res. Fellow, 1982–84, Royal Soc. Jun. Res. Fellow and Sen. Lectr, 1984–94, LSHTM; Prof. of Molecular Entomology, Cardiff Univ., 1994–2001. FMedSci 2006. Sci. and Technol. Award, Welsh Woman of the Year, 2000; Public service, BT Merseyside Woman of the Year 2003. *Publications:* over 200 articles in scientific jls. *Recreations:* breaking and riding Arabian horses, squash, tennis, ski-ing, reading. *Address:* Liverpool School of Tropical Medicine, Pembroke Place, Liverpool L3 5QA; *e-mail:* hemingway@liverpool.ac.uk.

HEMINGWAY, Peter, FCA; Director and Chief General Manager, Leeds Permanent Building Society, 1982–87; *b* 19 Jan. 1926; *s* of William Edward and Florence Hemingway; *m* 1952, June Maureen, *d* of Maurice and Lilian A. Senior. *Educ:* Leeds College of Commerce. With John Gordon, Walton & Co., Chartered Accountants, Leeds, 1941–62, Partner 1959–62; Director, Provincial Registrars Ltd, 1955–62; joined Leeds Permanent Bldg Soc. as Secretary, 1962. Local Dir (Leeds), Royal Insurance (UK) Ltd, 1983–93; Dir, Homeowners Friendly Soc., 1983–86. Hon. Sec. 1970–82, Vice-Chm. 1982–84, Chm. 1984–86, Yorkshire and North Western Assoc. of Building Societies; Vice Pres., Northern Assoc. of Building Socs, 1988–96; Mem. Council: Building Societies Assoc., 1981–87; Chartered Building Societies Inst., 1982–87. *Recreations:* travel, motor racing, music, gardening. *Address:* Old Barn Cottage, Kearby, near Wetherby, Yorks LS22 4BU. *T:* (0113) 288 6380.

HEMINGWAY, Wayne Andrew, MBE 2006; Co-Founder and Partner, HemingwayDesign, since 1999; *b* 19 Jan. 1961; *s* of Billy Two Rivers and Maureen Hemingway; *m* 1982, Gerardine Astin (MBE 2006); two *s* two *d*. *Educ:* University Coll. London (BSc Hons Geog. and Town Planning); Surrey Univ. (MA Fashion). Co-Founder (with Gerardine Hemingway), Red or Dead, 1982, sold, 1999 (Designer of the Year, 1996, 1997, 1998). Chm., Building for Life, 2002–. Vis. Prof. of Urban Studies, Northumberland Univ., 2004–. Hon. DA Wolverhampton, 2005. *Publications:* Just Above the Mantelpiece, 1998; Mass Market Classics - The Home, 2000. *Recreations:* running, general sport, my kids. *Address:* HemingwayDesign, 15 Wembley Park Drive, Wembley HA9 8HD. *T:* and *Fax:* (020) 8903 1074; *e-mail:* info@hemingwaydesign.co.uk.

HEMINSLEY, Stephen John; Director, Corporate Services, Healthcare Commission, since 2008; *b* 19 Dec. 1951; *s* of John and Joyce Margaret Heminsley; *m* 1980, Yvonne Lesley Stephenson; one *s* one *d*. *Educ:* Joseph Leckie Sch., Walsall. CIPFA 1986. Department of Health and Social Security, later Department of Social Security: Office Supervisor, 1972–77; Internal Auditor, 1977–88; Project Manager, DSS Financial Systems

Strategy, 1988–90; Director of: Finance (Contributions Agency), 1990–95; Business Planning (CSA), 1995–97; Strategy and Planning (Benefits Agency), 1997–2000; Pensions, subseq. Children and Pensioners, 2000–01; Dir, Nat. Services, 2001–04, Acting Dir Gen., Service Delivery, 2004, Bd of Inland Revenue; Dir, Orgnl Design, subseq. Orgnl Develt, 2004–07, Dir, Finance Transformation, 2007–08, HMRC. *Recreations:* walking, Rugby Union, family. *Address:* Healthcare Commission, 14th Floor, 103–105 Bunhill Row, EC1Y 8TG. *Club:* Handsworth Rugby Union Football.

HEMM, Amanda Jane; *see* Roocroft, A. J.

HEMMING, John Alexander Melvin; MP (Lib Dem) Birmingham Yardley, since 2005; *b* 16 March 1960; *s* of Melvin John and Doreen Hemming; *m* 1981, Christine Margaret (*née* Richards); one *s* two *d*; one *d* by Emily Rohaise Cox. *Educ:* King Edward's Sch., Birmingham; Magdalen Coll., Oxford (MA Physics 1981). Founded: John Hemming & Co., subseq. JHC plc, 1983; MarketNet, 1994; Music Mercia International, 1997. Mem., Birmingham CC, 1990–2008 (Dep. Leader, 2004–05; Leader, 1998–2005, Chm., 2005–, Lib Dem Gp). Contested: (L) Birmingham Hall Green, 1983; (L/All) Birmingham Small Heath, 1987; (Lib Dem) Birmingham Yardley, 1992, 1997, 2001. *Recreation:* jazz piano. *Address:* House of Commons, SW1A 0AA; *e-mail:* hemmingj@parliament.uk.

HEMMING, John Henry, CMG 1994; DLitt; FSA; Joint Chairman, Hemming Group Ltd (formerly Municipal Publications Ltd), since 1976 (Director, since 1962; Deputy Chairman, 1967–76); Director and Secretary, Royal Geographical Society, 1975–96; *b* 5 Jan. 1935; *s* of late Henry Harold Hemming, OBE, MC, and Alice Louisa Weaver, OBE; *m* 1979, Sukie, *d* of late M. J. Babington Smith, CBE; one *s* one *d*. *Educ:* Eton Coll.; McGill Univ.; Magdalen Coll., Oxford (Hon. Fellow, 2004); DLitt Oxon 1981. FSA 1998. Chairman: Brintex Ltd, 1979– (Man. Dir, 1963–70, Dep. Chm. 1976–78); Newman Books, 1979–. Member, Iriri River Expedition, Brazil, 1961; Leader, Maracá Rainforest Project, Brazil, 1987–88; Co-Chm., Jordan Badia R&D Prog., 1992–2004. Member Bd, British Council, 1993–2002; Chm., Anglo-Peruvian Soc., 1996–; Member Council: Anglo-Brazilian Soc., 1963–2006; Pro Natura Internat., 1991–; Hakluyt Soc., 1996–. Corres. Mem., Academia Nacional de la Historia, Venezuela. Dep. Chm., Lepra, 1998–; Sponsor, Survival International; Trustee: Gilchrist Educnl Trust, 1988–; Rainforest Foundn, 1997–; John Ellerman Foundn, 1998–; Global Diversity Foundn, 1999–; Cusichaca Trust, 1999–; Earthwatch Trust, 2004–; Chairman: British Empire and Commonwealth Mus. Trust, 1990–99; Rainforest Club, 1997–2002; Greencard Trust, 1997– (Mem. Council, 1989–); Patron: Earth Love Fund, 1996–; Wilderness Trust, 2003–. Hon. DLitt Warwick, 1989; DUniv Stirling, 1991. Mungo Park Medal, RSGS, 1988; Founder's Medal, RGS, 1990; Washburn Medal, Boston Mus. of Sci., 1990; Citation of Merit, Explorers' Club, NY, 1997; Special Award, Instituto Nacional de Cultura, Peru, 1997. Orden al Mérito (Peru), 1986 (now Grand Cross); Order of Cruzeiro do Sul (Brazil), 1998. *Publications:* The Conquest of the Incas, 1970 (Robert Pitman Literary Prize, 1970, Christopher Award, NY, 1971); (jt) Tribes of the Amazon Basin in Brazil, 1972; Red Gold: The Conquest of the Brazilian Indians, 1978; The Search for El Dorado, 1978; Machu Picchu, 1981; Monuments of the Incas, 1982; The New Incas, 1983; (ed) Change in the Amazon Basin (2 vols), 1985; Amazon Frontier: the defeat of the Brazilian Indians, 1987; Maracá, 1988; Roraima: Brazil's northernmost frontier, 1990; Maracá Rainforest Island, 1993; (ed) The Rainforest Edge, 1994; The Golden Age of Discovery, 1998; Die If You Must, 2003; Tree of Rivers: the story of the Amazon, 2008. *Recreations:* writing, travel. *Address:* 10 Edwardes Square, W8 6HE. *T:* (020) 7602 6697. *Clubs:* Boodle's, Beefsteak (Chm., 2002–04), Geographical.
See also L. A. Service.

HEMMING, Martin John, CB 2003; Director General Legal Services and Legal Adviser, Ministry of Defence, since 1998; *b* 29 May 1949; *s* of late Albert Reuben Hemming and Constance Rosaline Hemming; *m* 1976, Kathleen Siân Davies; one *s* one *d*. *Educ:* Tudor Grange Grammar Sch., Solihull; Fitzwilliam Coll., Cambridge (BA 1971; MA 1976); London School of Economics and Political Science (LLM 1973). Called to the Bar, Gray's Inn, 1972, Bencher, 2006; practising barrister, 1974–82; Sen. Legal Asst, Treasury Solicitor's Dept, 1982–85; Legal Advr (Grade 6), MoD, 1985–88; Asst Treasury Solicitor, 1988–98. *Address:* Ministry of Defence, Whitehall, SW1A 2HB. *T:* (020) 7218 0723.

HEMPHILL, 5th Baron *cr* 1906, of Rathkenny and Cashel; **Peter Patrick Fitzroy Martyn Martyn-Hemphill;** *b* 5 Sept. 1928; *o s* of 4th Baron Hemphill and Emily, *d* of F. Irving Sears, Webster, Mass; *S* father, 1957; *m* 1952, Olivia Anne, *er d* of Major Robert Francis Ruttledge, MC, Cloonee, Ballinrobe, County Mayo; one *s* two *d*; assumed surname of Martyn in addition to Hemphill, 1959. *Educ:* Downside; Brasenose Coll., Oxford (MA Jurisp.). Sen. Steward, Irish Turf Club, 1985–88; Steward, Irish Nat. Hunt Steeplechase Cttee, 1973–76 and 1978–81. Chm., Galway Race Cttee, 1971–77. *Heir: s* Hon. Charles Andrew Martyn Martyn-Hemphill [*b* 8 Oct. 1954; *m* 1985, Sarah J. F., *e d* of Richard Lumley; two *s* three *d*]. *Address:* Dunkellin, Kiltulla, Co. Galway, Eire.

HEMPLEMAN-ADAMS, David, LVO 2007; OBE 1998 (MBE 1994); DL; company director; explorer and mountaineer; *b* 10 Oct. 1956; *m* Claire; three *d*. *Educ:* Writhlington Comp. Sch.; Manchester Univ.; Bristol Poly (post-grad. Business Studies). Ascents: Mt McKinley, Alaska Range, 1980; Kilimanjaro, Tanzania, 1981; Mt Everest, Himalayas, 1993; Vinson Massif, Antarctica, 1994; Aconcagua, Andes, 1994; Mt Carstensz, Indonesia, 1995. Arctic/Antarctic expeditions: first solo unsupported expedition to magnetic North Pole, 1984; leader of first unsupported gp expedition to geomagnetic North Pole, 1992; first Briton to walk solo and unsupported to South Pole, 1996; first person to climb highest peaks of all seven continents and trek to magnetic and geographic North and South Poles, 1998; first person to walk solo and unaided by new route to geomagnetic North Pole, 2003. Hot-air balloon flights: first to cross Andes, 1998; first to cross North-West Passage, 1999; first to fly solo to North Pole, 2000; first to fly solo across Arctic Ocean, 2000; first to cross Atlantic in open wicker-basket, 2003. Director: Hempleman Investments; Global Resins; Ultimate Adventures. Founder, Mitchemp Trust. DL Wilts, 2004. Member: RGS; RSGS; GAPAN; Royal Soc. Hon. DSc Leicester, 1998. Forty awards. *Publications:* Race Against Time: North Geomagnetic Pole expedition, 1993; Toughing it Out, 1996; Walking on Thin Ice, 1998; At the Mercy of the Winds, 2000. *Clubs:* Royal Automobile, Alpine; Explorers (NY).

HEMPSALL, Dr David Stuart, MA; Headmaster, Queen Elizabeth's Grammar School, Blackburn, 1995–2007; *b* 4 Jan. 1947; *s* of Harold and Freda Hempsall; *m* 1st, 1969, Patricia Land (*d* 2004); one *s* one *d*; 2nd, 2006, Diane Ewart-Jones. *Educ:* Manchester GS; Sidney Sussex Coll., Cambridge (MA); Univ. of Kent (PhD). Assistant Master: Sir William Nottidge Sch., Whitstable, 1971–72; Rugby Sch., 1973–85 (Head of History, 1977–85); Headmaster, Scarborough Coll., 1985–95. Hon. Treas., HMC, 2002–07. FRSA. *Publications:* articles in hist. and educnl learned jls. *Recreations:* do-it-yourself, hill-walking, music, sport, reading. *Address:* c/o Queen Elizabeth's Grammar School, West Park Road, Blackburn BB2 6DF. *T:* (01254) 686300.

HEMSLEY, Thomas Jeffrey, CBE 2000; free-lance opera and concert singer; Professor: Guildhall School of Music and Drama, since 1987; Trinity College of Music, 1988–93; *b* 12 April 1927; *s* of Sydney William Hemsley and Kathleen Annie Hemsley (*née* Deacon); *m* 1960, Hon. Gwenllian Ellen James, *d* of 4th Baron Northbourne; three *s*. *Educ:* Ashby de la Zouch Grammar Sch.; Brasenose Coll., Oxford (MA). Vicar Choral, St Paul's Cathedral, 1950–51; Prin. Baritone, Stadttheater, Aachen, 1953–56; Deutsche Oper am Rhein, 1957–63; Opernhaus, Zurich, 1963–67; Glyndebourne, Bayreuth, Edinburgh Festivals, etc. Dir of Opera, Dartington Internat. Summer Sch., 1988–. Vis. Prof., RCM, 1986; Guest Prof., Royal Danish Acad. of Music, 1990–91. Mem., Roy. Philharmonic Soc., 1968–. Recordings of operas, lieder and melodies. FGSM 1996; Hon. RAM 1974; Hon. FTCL 1988. FRSA 1991. *Publication:* Singing & Imagination, 1998. *Address:* 10 Denewood Road, N6 4AJ. *T:* (020) 8348 3397. *Club:* Garrick.

HENDER, John Derrik, CBE 1986; DL; public sector consultant; Chief Executive, West Midlands Metropolitan County Council, 1973–86; *b* 15 Nov. 1926; *s* of late Jessie Peter and Jennie Hender; *m* 1949, Kathleen Nora Brown; one *d*. *Educ:* Great Yarmouth Grammar School. IPFA, FCA. Deputy Borough Treasurer: Newcastle-under-Lyme, 1957–61; Wolverhampton County Borough, 1961–64; City Treas. 1965–69, Chief Exec. and Town Clerk 1969–73, Coventry County Borough. FCMI. DL West Midlands, 1975. *Publications:* numerous articles relating to various aspects of local govt and related matters. *Recreation:* gardening. *Address:* Endwood, South Avenue, Thorpe St Andrew, Norwich NR7 0EZ.

HENDERSON, family name of **Baron Faringdon.**

HENDERSON, Andrew David Forbes; HM Diplomatic Service; Ambassador to Algeria, since 2007; *b* 12 July 1952; *s* of James Porteous Henderson and Patricia Margaret Henderson; *m* 1987, Julia Margaret King; two *d*. *Educ:* Crypt Sch., Gloucester. Entered FCO, 1971; Latin American Floater, 1975–77; Vice Consul, Rio de Janeiro, 1977–80; Second Sec. (Political), Oslo, 1980–84; Asst Private Sec. to Minister of State, 1985–87; Consul (Political), NY, 1987–88; First Sec. (Political), Washington, 1988–91; Dep. Hd of Mission, Luanda, 1992–94; First Sec. (Aid/Econ.), later Hd, Commercial Section, Cairo, 1994–98; Hd, Parly Relns Dept, FCO, 1998–99; Consul-Gen., Jeddah, 2000–03; Consul-Gen., São Paulo, and Dir, Trade and Investment, Brazil, 2003–07. *Recreations:* golf, tennis, Rugby, cricket, music. *Address:* c/o Foreign and Commonwealth Office, King Charles Street, SW1A 2AH; *e-mail:* Andrew.Henderson@fco.gov.uk.

HENDERSON, Anne Frances; *see* Milton, A. F.

HENDERSON, Barry; *see* Henderson, J. S. B.

HENDERSON, Bernard Vere, CBE 1987; Chairman: Anglian Water, 1981–94; British Waterways Board, 1994–99; *b* 8 July 1928; *s* of late Percy Cecil and Ruth Elizabeth Henderson; *m* 1952, Valerie Jane Cairns; two *s* one *d*. *Educ:* Ampleforth Coll.; Harvard Business Sch. Served Army, RE, 1946–48. P. C. Henderson Group, 1949–80 (Man. Dir, 1958–80). Chm., Water Services Assoc., 1990–91. Chm., Australia and NZ Trade Adv. Cttee, 1994–95. *Recreations:* countryside, narrow boat cruising. *Address:* Lessudden Bank, St Boswells, Melrose TD6 0DU.

HENDERSON, Charles Edward, CB 1992; FIA; Chairman: Total Holding UK (formerly Total Oil Holdings, then TotalFinalElf Holding UK), 1998–2005; Total Exploration and Production UK (formerly Total Oil Marine, then TotalFinalElf Exploration UK), 1998–2005; *b* 19 Sept. 1939; *s* of late David Henderson and of Giorgiana Leggatt Henderson; *m* 1966, Rachel Hilary Hall, *d* of late Dr Stephen Hall, FRCP and Dr Mary Hall; one *d* one *s*. *Educ:* Charterhouse; Pembroke Coll., Cambridge (MA). FIA 1965. Actuarial Trainee, subseq. Asst Investment Sec., Equity & Law Life Assurance Soc., 1960–70; ECGD, 1971–73; DTI, 1973–74; Dept of Energy, 1974–88: Asst Sec., 1975; Under Sec., 1982; Atomic Energy Div., 1982; Oil Div., 1985; Prin. Estabt and Finance Officer, 1986–88; Head, Office of Arts and Libraries, 1989–92; Dep. Sec., DTI, 1992–96. Mem., Competition (formerly Monopolies and Mergers) Commn, 1998–2007. Dir, Aluminium Corp. Ltd, 1981–84. Sen. Associate, Cambridge Energy Res. Associates, 1998–2002. President: Soc. for Underwater Technology, 1999–2001; Inst. of Petroleum, 2000–02. *Recreations:* making and listening to music, mountaineering, golf. *Address:* 17 Sydney House, Woodstock Road, W4 1DP. *T:* (020) 8994 1345.
See also Julian Hall.

HENDERSON, David; *see* Henderson, P. D.

HENDERSON, Sir Denys (Hartley), Kt 1989; Chairman: Imperial Chemical Industries PLC, 1987–95; ZENECA Group plc, 1993–95; The Rank Group Plc (formerly Rank Organisation), 1995–2001; Chairman and First Crown Estate Commissioner, 1995–2002; *b* 11 Oct. 1932; *s* of John Hartley Henderson and Nellie Henderson (*née* Gordon); *m* 1957, Doreen Mathewson Glashan, *o d* of Robert and Mary Glashan; two *d*. *Educ:* Aberdeen Grammar School; Univ. of Aberdeen (MA, LLB). Solicitor; Mem., Law Soc. of Scotland. Joined ICI as lawyer in Secretary's Dept, London, 1957; Chm., ICI Paints Div., 1977; ICI Main Bd Dir, 1980; Dep. Chm., 1986–87. Non-executive Director: Dalgety plc, 1981–87 and 1996–98 (Chm., 1997–98); Barclays Bank, 1983–97; RTZ Corp., 1990–96; MORI, 1995–2001; Schlumberger Ltd, 1995–2001; QinetiQ plc, 2003–05; Mem., Eur. Adv. Bd, Carlyle Gp, 1997–2005. Member: CBI President's Cttee, 1987–96; Adv. Council, Prince's Youth Business Trust, 1986–99; Adv. Cttee on Business Appointments, 1994–2001; Greenbury Cttee on Directors' Remuneration, 1994–95. Mem., European Round Table, 1992–94. Pres., Soc. of Business Economists, 1990–94. Pres. and Chm. Bd, British Quality Foundn, 1993–97. Trustee, Natural Hist. Mus., 1989–98. Chancellor, Bath Univ., 1993–98; Mem. Court of Governors, Henley Management Coll., 1986–96 (Chm., 1989–96); Chm., Univ. of Aberdeen Quincentenary Appeal Cttee, 1993–96. Hon. Vice-Pres., Chartered Inst. of Marketing, 1989–95. CCMI (CBIM 1981); FInstM 1987. Hon. FCGI 1990. DUniv: Brunel, 1987; Strathclyde, 1993; Hon. LLD: Aberdeen, 1987; Nottingham, 1990; Manchester, 1991; Bath, 1993; Hon. DSc: Cranfield Inst. of Technol., 1989; Teesside, 1993. Centenary Medal, SCI, 1993. *Recreations:* family life, reading, travel. *Club:* Athenæum.

HENDERSON, Derek, FDSRCS; Senior Consultant Oral and Maxillo-facial Surgeon, St Thomas' Hospital, 1975–93; Consultant, St George's Hospital, 1975–86; Emeritus Consultant in Oral and Maxillo-facial Surgery, Guy's and St Thomas' Hospital NHS Trust, since 1993; *b* 9 April 1935; *s* of Robert Henderson and Dorothy Edith Henderson; *m* 1961, Jennifer Jill Anderson; one *s* one *d*. *Educ:* Dulwich Coll.; London Univ. (BDS Hons 1956, MB, BS Hons 1963). FDSRCS (Eng) 1960 (LDS 1956); MRCS, LRCP 1963. Dental and med. trng, KCH, London, 1952–56 and 1959–63 (Prizeman); house surg. appts, KCH and Royal Dental Hosp., 1956–59; King's Coll. Hospital: Lectr in Dental Materials, 1958–65; ENT House Officer, and Casualty Off., 1964; Registrar in Oral Surg., Queen Mary's Hosp., Roehampton, and Westminster Hosp., 1965; Sen. Registrar in Oral Surg., United Cardiff Hosps, 1965–67; Consultant Oral Surgeon to Eastern Reg. Hosp. Bd, Scotland, and Dundee Dental Hosp., 1967–69 (Hon. Sen. Lectr, Univ. of Dundee); Consultant i/c Reg. Maxillo-facial Service to Glasgow and West of Scotland, based on Canniesburn Plastic and Oral Surg. Unit, Glasgow, 1969–75 (Hon.

Clinical Teacher, Glasgow Univ.); Consultant, Royal Dental Hosp., 1975–85. Recognised Teacher, London Univ., 1977–93; Hon. Consultant, Charing Cross Hosp., 1977–93; Hon. Civilian Consultant: Queen Elizabeth Mil. Hosp., Woolwich (formerly Queen Alexandra Mil. Hosp., Millbank), 1976–81; in Oral Surgery, RN, 1971–93, Army, 1981–93; Hon. Sen. Lectr in Oral Surg., Royal Dental Sch., London, 1977–85. Vis. Prof. and Lectr, Brazil, Argentina, Chile, USA, Spain, Venezuela, Australia, Holland, Saudi Arabia, Uruguay, Italy, SA, NZ. Mem. Senate, Royal Surgical Colls of GB and Ire., 1993–96; Royal College of Surgeons: Hunterian Prof., 1975–76; Mem. Council, 1984–86 (Collyer Gold Medal, 1995); Kelsey Fry Adviser in Postgraduate Educnl Trng, 1975–80, Mem. Bd, 1978–86, Mem. Exec. Cttee, 1983–86, and Vice-Dean, 1984–85, Faculty of Dental Surgery (also Examr, FDSRCS). Member: Central Cttee for Hospital Dental Services, 1978–85 (Mem. Exec. Cttee, 1980–85); Central Cttee for Univ. Dental Teachers and Research Workers, 1978–81; Negotiating Subcttee, CCHMS, 1980–85; European Assoc. for Maxillo-Facial Surg.; BMA; Craniofacial Soc. (Mem. Council, 1973–77); Oral Surgery Club GB (Pres., 1992–93). Fellow: BAOMS (Pres., 1994–95; Mem. Council, 1974–76, 1977–80, 1984–86; Downs Prize, 1992). Internat. Assoc. of Oral Surgeons. Hon. Mem., Amer. Assoc. of Oral Surgeons in Europe; Hon. Associate Life Mem., Soc. of Maxillo-facial and Oral Surgeons of SA; Hon. Pres., Inst. of Maxillo-Facial Technol., 1977–78. *Publications:* An Atlas and Textbook of Orthognathic Surgery, 1985 (Astra Prize, Soc. of Authors, 1986); contribs on general oral surgery to British Jl of Oral Surgery and British Dental Jl, and especially on surgery of facial and jaw deformity to Brit. Jl of Oral Surg. and Brit. Jl of Plastic Surg. *Recreation:* fly fishing. *Address:* La Soleille, Route de Beaulieu, Beynat 19190, France. *Club:* Royal Navy Medical.

HENDERSON, Dr Derek Scott, FRSSAf; Principal and Vice-Chancellor, Rhodes University, Grahamstown, South Africa, 1975–96; *b* 28 Oct. 1929; *s* of late Ian Scott and Kathleen Elizabeth Henderson (*née* White); *m* 1958, Thelma Muriel, *d* of W. E. B. Mullins; two *d. Educ:* St John's Coll., Johannesburg; Rhodes University Coll. (BSc); Oxford Univ. (MA); Cambridge Univ. (MA); Harvard Univ. (PhD). FRSSAf 1995. Exec. Trainee, Anglo American Corp. of S Africa, 1953–56; Engr, Advanced Systems Develt, IBM Corp., Poughkeepsie, NY, 1960–62; Univ. of the Witwatersrand: Dir of Computer Centre, 1964–69; Prof. of Computer Science, 1967–75; Dean of Science Faculty, 1974–75. Chm., J. L. B. Smith Inst. of Ichthyology, 1976–96; Mem. Council, CSIR, 1982–87; Mem., Scientific Adv. Council, 1988–93; Mem. Bd, SABC, 1990–93; Vice-Chm., Leather Res. Inst., 1976–96; Mem. Council, Grahamstown (formerly 1820) Foundn (Vice-Chm., 1976–89; Exec. Dir, 1999–2002); Pres., SA Council of Automation and Computation, 1974. Chairman: Hillbrow Br., Progressive Party, 1964–65; Johannesburg Br., Kolbe Assoc. of Catholic Graduates, 1964; Mem. Council, St Andrew's Coll., 1986–2003; Trustee, SA Foundn, 1976–96; Patron, All Saints Coll., Bisho, 1986–96. Dir, Sabinet, 1983–88. Fellow, Computer Soc. of SA, 1974. Hon. LLD Rhodes 1997. *Recreation:* golf. *Address:* 1 Ross Street, Grahamstown, 6139, S Africa. *T:* (46) 6223908. *Club:* Port Elizabeth (Port Elizabeth, S Africa).

HENDERSON, Douglas John; MP (Lab) Newcastle upon Tyne North, since 1987; *b* 9 June 1949; *s* of John and Joy Henderson; *m* 1st, 1974, Janet Margaret Graham (marr. diss.); one *s*; 2nd, 2002, Geraldine Daly; one *d. Educ:* Waid Academy, Anstruther, Fife; Central Coll., Glasgow; Univ. of Strathclyde. Apprentice, Rolls Royce, 1966–68; Clerk, British Rail, 1969; Research Officer, GMWU, 1973–75; Regional Organiser, GMWU, then GMB, 1975–87. Mem. Exec., Scottish Council, Labour Party, 1979–87 (Chm., 1984–85). Opposition spokesman on trade and industry, 1988–92, on local govt, 1992–94, on public service, 1994–95, on home affairs, 1995–97; Minister of State: (Europe), FCO, 1997–98; (Minister for the Armed Forces), MoD, 1998–99. Sec., All Party Athletes Gp, 2002–; Chairman: Northern Gp of Lab MPs, 2000–01; GMB Parly Gp, 2002– (Sec., 1987–97); Mem. UK Delegn to Council of Europe and WEU, 2005–. *Recreations:* athletics, mountaineering. *Address:* House of Commons, SW1A 0AA. *T:* (constituency office) (0191) 286 2024. *Clubs:* Elswick Harriers, Lemington Labour, Newburn Memorial, Dinnington, Union Jack (Newcastle).

HENDERSON, Fergus, MBE 2005; Chef and Owner, St John Restaurant, London, since 1994; *b* 31 July 1963; *s* of Brian and Elizabeth Henderson; *m* 1993, Margot Clayton; one *s* two *d. Educ:* King Alfred's Sch.; Architectural Assoc. RIBA pt 2. Chef, French House Dining Room, 1992–94. *Publications:* Nose to Tail Eating: a kind of British cooking, 1999, 4th edn 2004; (jtly) Beyond Nose to Tail, 2007. *Recreation:* cooking. *Address:* St John Restaurant, 26 St John Street, EC1M 4AY. *T:* (020) 7251 4080, *Fax:* (020) 7251 4090; *e-mail:* kirsty@stjohnrestaurant.com. *Club:* Groucho.

HENDERSON, Gavin Douglas, CBE 2004; Principal, Central School of Speech and Drama, University of London, since 2007; *b* 3 Feb. 1948; *s* of Magnus Reg Henderson and Sybil (*née* Horton); *m* 1st, 1973, Jane Williams (marr. diss. 1977); 2nd, 1983, Carole Becker (marr. diss. 1992); two *s*; 3rd, 1992, Mary Jane Walsh. *Educ:* Brighton Coll.; Brighton Coll. of Art; Kingston Art Coll.; University Coll. London; Slade Sch. of Fine Art. Leader and Dir, Henderson Brass Consort, 1968–75; Principal Trumpet, Worthing Municipal and Concert Orchs, 1969–70; Dep. Front of House and Publicity Manager, Victoria Theatre, Stoke-on-Trent, 1970–71; Founder and Dir, Crawley Fest., 1971–73; Artistic Director: York Fest. Mystery Plays, 1972–76; Portsmouth Fest., 1974–76; Chief Exec., New Philharmonia and Philharmonia Orchs, 1975–78; Dir, S Hill Park Arts Centre and Founder, Wilde Theatre, Bracknell, 1979–84; Artistic Director: Brighton Internat. Fest., 1983–94; Dartington Internat. Summer Sch., 1985–; Court in the Act, Royal Acad. of Arts, 1993; Mem., Adv. Bd, London Contemporary Dance Trust, 1986–87; Pres. and Artistic Advr, Bournemouth Fest., 1996–98 (Artistic Dir, 1994–96); Principal, Trinity Coll. of Music, 1994–2005; Principal and Chief Exec., Trinity Laban, 2005–06. Chairman: Clarion Concert Agency, 1972–75; Palindrome Prodns Ltd, 1994–; World Circuit Arts, 1995–2000; Nat. Foundn for Youth Music (formerly Youth Music Trust), 1998–2007. Writer and presenter, A View of …, BBC TV Series, 1983. Member: Music Panel and Opera Cttee, 1973–75, Regl Cttee, 1981–84, Arts Council of GB; Arts Council of England, 1994–98 (Chm., Music Panel, 1994–2003); Arts Cttee, RSA, 1991–94; Chairman: British Arts Fests Assoc., 1994– (Dep. Chm., 1987–94); Brighton Youth Orch. Trust, 1998–2005; Regency Soc., 1999–2006; Member: Exec. Cttee, SE Arts Assoc., 1982–89 (Chm., Festival Panel, 1986–89); Exec. Bd, European Fests Assoc., 1988–94 (Vice Pres., 1994–2003, Pres., 2003–); Southern Arts Bd, 1990–93; Arts Initiative in Mgt Cttee, Gulbenkian Foundn, 1982–83. Trustee: Electro-Acoustic Music Soc., 1984–90; Brighton Early Music Fest., 2005–. Judge: Prudential Awards, 1992; Audi Young Musician of the Year, 1993; Barclays New Stages, 1994; British Gas Working for Cities, 1995; Olivier Awards, 2001–02; Chm., Royal Over-Seas League Music Competition, 2007–. Pres., Nat. Piers Soc., 1986–. One-man exhibitions: Gall. 185, Brighton, 1968; Mulberry Gall., Lancaster, 1969. Mem. Bd, Trinity Coll., London, 1994–; Governor: Brighton Univ. (formerly Poly.), 1987–95; Chetham's Sch., Manchester, 1994–; Foeffee, Chetham's Hosp., 2007–. Hon. Fellow: Univ. of Sussex, 1991; Univ. of Brighton, 1993; Laban, 2000; Hon. FTCL 1998; Hon. FRCM 2002; Hon. FRNCM 2003; Hon. CTL 2007. Hon. MA Sussex, 1992. Europe Award, E Sussex CC, 1992; Sir Charles Groves Award, 2005; BACS Gold Award, 2007. *Publications:* Picasso and the Theatre, 1982; articles for Resurgence, Classical Music, Tempo, Musical Times, Stage, and Listener.

Recreations: seaside pierage, cooking seafood, vintage motor-racing. *Address:* Central School of Speech and Drama, Embassy Theatre, Eton Avenue, NW3 3HY. *Clubs:* Garrick, Savile, Royal Over-Seas League (Hon. Mem.).

HENDERSON, Prof. George David Smith, FSA; Professor of Medieval Art, Cambridge, 1986–96, then Emeritus; Fellow of Downing College, Cambridge, 1974–94; *b* 7 May 1931; *yr s* of late Very Rev. Prof. George David Henderson, DLitt, DTh, DD and Jenny Holmes McCulloch Henderson (*née* Smith); *m* 1957, Isabel Bisset Murray, OBE, Hon. FSAScot; one *s* one *d. Educ:* Aberdeen Grammar Sch.; Univ. of Aberdeen (MA 1953); Courtauld Inst., Univ. of London (BA 1956); Trinity Coll., Cambridge (MA, PhD 1961). Research Fellow, Barber Inst. of Art, Univ. of Birmingham, 1959–60; Graham Robertson Research Fellow, Downing Coll., Cambridge, 1960–63; University of Manchester: Asst Lectr in History of Art, 1962–64; Lectr, 1964–66; University of Edinburgh: Lectr in Fine Arts, 1966–71; Reader in Fine Arts, 1971–73; University of Cambridge: Lectr in History of Art, 1974–79; Head of Dept, 1974–88; Reader in Medieval Art, 1979–86; a Syndic, Fitzwilliam Museum, 1974–98. Mem., Ely Cathedral Fabric Adv. Cttee, 1990–98. *Publications:* Gothic, 1967; Chartres, 1968; Early Medieval, 1972, repr. 1993; (ed with Giles Robertson) Studies in Memory of David Talbot Rice, 1975; Bede and the Visual Arts (Jarrow Lect.), 1980; Losses and Lacunae in Early Insular Art (Garmonsway Lect.), 1982; Studies in English Bible Illustration, 1985; From Durrow to Kells, 1987; (contrib.) The Eadwine Psalter, 1992; (contrib.) Emulation and Innovation in Carolingian Culture, 1993; Vision and Image in Early Christian England, 1999; (with Isabel Henderson) The Art of the Picts: sculpture and metalwork in early medieval Scotland, 2004 (a Historians of British Art Book Prize, 2006); articles in UK and Amer. jls and papers in procs of internat. confs; *Festschrift:* New Offerings, Ancient Treasures: studies in medieval art for George Henderson, ed. P. Binski and W. Noel, 2001. *Recreations:* listening to Wagner, porphyrology, looking for agates. *Address:* The Old Manse, Nigg by Tain, Ross and Cromarty IV19 1QR. *Club:* Oxford and Cambridge.

HENDERSON, Giles Ian, CBE 1992; Master, Pembroke College, Oxford, since 2001; *b* 20 April 1942; *s* of late Charles David Henderson and Joan K. Firmin; *m* 1971, Lynne Fyfield; two *s* one *d. Educ:* Michaelhouse, Natal; Univ. of Witwatersrand (BA); Magdalen Coll., Oxford (Sen. Mackinnon Scholar; MA, BCL). Fulbright Award, 1966–67. Associate in Law, Univ. of California at Berkeley, 1966–67; joined Slaughter and May, 1968; admitted Solicitor, 1970; Partner, Slaughter and May, 1975, Sen. Partner, 1993–2001. Member: Hampel Cttee on Corporate Governance, 1995–98; Financial Reporting Council, 1998–2001; Chm., Law Gp, UK-China Forum, 1997–2000. Non-executive Director: Land Securities plc, 2000–2002; Standard Life Assurance Co., 2001–03. Chairman: Nuffield Med. Trust, 2003–; Conf. of Oxford Colls, 2007–; Dir, Cumberland Lodge, 2007–. *Recreations:* sport, opera, ballet. *Address:* The Master's Lodgings, Pembroke College, Oxford OX1 1DW. *T:* (01865) 276403.

HENDERSON, Prof. Graham; Vice-Chancellor and Chief Executive, University of Teesside, since 2003; *b* 23 Aug. 1952; *s* of Thomas and Elizabeth Henderson; *m* 1987, Joan Younger; two *s* one *d. Educ:* Heaton Grammar Sch.; Lanchester Poly. (BSc Hons); City Univ. (MSc with Dist.); Nene Coll. (FE Teachers' Cert.). Trainee Accountant, 1970–71, Trainee Operational Res. Scientist, 1973–74, NCB; Lectr, Sch. of Maths, Mgt and Business Studies, Nene Coll., Northampton, 1975–79; Lectr, then Sen. Lectr, then Prin. Lectr, Sch. of Business Analysis, Newcastle Poly., 1979–89; Asst Dir, Newcastle Poly., later Newcastle Business Sch., Univ. of Northumbria, 1989–97; Dir, Sunderland Business Sch., Univ. of Sunderland, 1997–99; Dep. Vice-Chancellor, Univ. of Teesside, 1999–2003. Member: CBI Regl Council, 2003–; Council, NE Chamber of Commerce, 2005–; Nat. Exec., Million+ (formerly Campaign for Mainstream Univs), 2005–; Chm., Univs for the NE, 2005–. Member, Corporation Board: Hartlepool Coll., 1999–2004; Laurence Jackson Sch., 1999–2003; Darlington Coll. of Technology, 1999–2006. Director: Middlesbrough Town Centre Co., 2003–06; Durham and Tees Valley LSC, 2005–; NE Regl LSC, 2007–; Bd Mem., Tees Valley Unlimited, 2006–. Trustee: Capt. Cook Birthplace Trust, 2003–; Trincomalee Trust, 2003–07. FSS 1977; FRSA 2000. *Recreations:* Rugby Union and football (spectator), walking, bridge. *Address:* University of Teesside, Middlesbrough, Tees Valley, TS1 3BA. *T:* (01642) 342002, *Fax:* (01642) 342000; *e-mail:* graham.henderson@tees.ac.uk.

HENDERSON, Rear Adm. Iain Robert, CB 2001; CBE 1991; DL; Registrar and Secretary, Order of the Bath, since 2006 (Gentleman Usher of the Scarlet Rod, 2002–06); *b* 1 April 1948; *s* of John and Christina Henderson; *m* 1976, Rosalind Margaret Arkell; two *s* two *d. Educ:* Epsom Coll. BRNC 1965; qualified as: rotary wing pilot, 1971; fixed wing pilot, 1974; Exec. Officer, HMS Plymouth, 1980–82; CO, HMS Ariadne, 1984–85, HMS Charybdis, 1985; Trng Comdr, BRNC, 1986–87; Directorate of Naval Officer Appointments (Seaman) (Air), 1988–90; CO, HMS London, 1990–91; AD Warfare Directorate of Naval Plans, 1991–93; CO, RNAS Yeovilton, 1993–96; Comdr, Naval Base, Portsmouth, 1996–98; FONA, 1998–2000; AOC No 3 Gp and FOMA, 2000–01. ADC to the Queen, 1996–98. Chief Exec., Sue Ryder Care, 2001–07. Freeman, City of London, 1992; Liveryman, Co. of Upholders, 1996–; Mem., Ct of Assts, Guild of Freemen, City of London, 1997–2003. DL Hants, 2006. *Recreations:* equestrian and country pursuits.

HENDERSON, Ian James, CBE 2001; FRICS; non-executive Director, Liberty International PLC, since 2005; Chief Executive, Land Securities Group PLC, 1997–2004; *b* 18 July 1943; *s* of Robert and Sheila Henderson; *m* 1972, Sheila Sturrock; one *s* one *d. Educ:* BSc (Estate Mgt). FRICS 1978. Joined Land Securities, 1971. Chm., New West End Co. Ltd, 2000–08; Vice-Chm., London Regl Bd, Royal & Sun Alliance, 1998–; Mem., President's Cttee, London First, 2002–07. Chm., London Mayoral Commn into W End Central Retail Area Planning and Develt Policy, 2006–07. Non-executive Chairman: Dawnay Day Treveria, 2005–; Ishaan Real Estate PLC, 2006–; non-exec. Dir, Evans Property Gp, 2006–; consultant, Quintain Estates and Development plc, 2005–. Chm., St Martin-in-the-Fields Develt Trust, 2005–; Vice Chm., Bd of Mgt, Central and Cecil Housing Trust, 1992–2007 (Vice Pres., 2007–). Pres., British Property Fedn, 2002–03. Comr, Commonwealth War Graves Commn, 2002–. Trustee, Natural Hist. Mus., 2005–; Council Mem., Royal Albert Hall, 2005–; Gov., Dolphin Square Charitable Foundn, 2005–. Pres., Lighthouse Club, 2005–08. *Clubs:* Brooks's, Naval and Military, Farmers'.

HENDERSON, Ivan John; public affairs consultant; *b* 7 June 1958; *s* of Margaret Bloice and step *s* of late Michael Bloice; *m* 1992, Jo'anne Atkinson; one *s*; one *s* one *d* from a previous marriage. *Educ:* Sir Anthony Deane Comprehensive Sch., Harwich. British Rail, Sealink, 1975–97: dock operative; Union Orgnr, Docks, and Exec. Officer, RMT, 1991–94. Member (Lab): Harwich Town Council, 1986–97; Tendring DC, 1995–97. MP (Lab) Harwich, 1997–2005; contested (Lab) same seat, 2005. PPS to Minister of State: Home Office, 2001–02; ODPM, 2002–03; PPS to Sec. of State, DWP, 2003–04; PPS to Paymaster-General, HM Treasury, 2004–05. Member: All Party Cancer Gp; All Party Maritime Gp; All Party Town Centre Mgt Gp; All Party Gp against Drug Abuse; All Party China Gp; All Party India Gp; All Party Gp on Animal Welfare; All Party Gp on Child Abduction; Labour Parly TU Gp; Seaside Gp, Labour MPs; Chm., All Party Parly Sea

Cadets Gp, 2004–05; Vice Chm., All Party Parly Gp Ports and Shipping, 2001–05. Parly Spokesman for Clacton, 2006–. *Recreations:* football, golf. *Address:* Harwich, Essex. *T:* 07889 367822; *web:* www.ivanhenderson.labour.co.uk. *Clubs:* Harwich and Parkeston Football; Harwich and Dovercourt Cricket (Vice Pres., 1997).

HENDERSON, James Frowyke; a District Judge (Magistrates' Courts), since 2004; *b* 17 Dec. 1954; *s* of James Murray Henderson and Myrtle Elizabeth Jean Henderson; *m* 1989, Jane Elisabeth; one *s*. *Educ:* King's Sch., Tynemouth; Univ. of Newcastle upon Tyne (LLB); Univ. of Northumbria (LLM 2006). Called to the Bar, Middle Temple, 1984; Tutorial Studentship, 1980–83, Lectr in Laws, 1984–86, KCL; barrister in criminal practice, 1986–2004; Actg Stipendiary Magistrate, 1999–2000; Dep. Dist Judge (Magistrates' Courts), 2000–04. Occasional Lectr, British Acad. of Forensic Sci., 1980–83; Lectr (pt-time), PCL, 1983–84. Member: Heraldry Soc. of Scotland; Scotch Malt Whisky Soc. *Publications:* contrib. numerous academic articles on criminal law and evidence to King's Coll. Law Jl, Criminal Bar Assoc. Newsletter, 4 Brick Court Chambers Law Review. *Recreations:* playing mandolin and guitar and various sized recorders, 4th Dan Black Belt Instructor in Goshin-Do (a modern Ju-Jitsu style). *Address:* Highbury Corner Magistrates' Court, 51 Holloway Road, N7 8JA.

HENDERSON, (James Stewart) Barry; management consultant; *b* 29 April 1936; *s* of James Henderson, CBE and Jane Stewart Henderson (*née* McLaren); *m* 1961, Janet Helen Sprot Todd; two *s*. *Educ:* Lathallan Sch.; Stowe Sch. Nat. Service, Scots Guards, 1954–56; electronics and computer industries, 1957–65; Scottish Conservative Central Office, 1966–70; computer industry, 1971–74; management consultant, 1975–86; paper industry, 1987–90; Dir, British Paper and Board Industry Fedn, 1990–92; Partner, Henderson Consulting, 1993–. Contested (C): E Edinburgh, 1966; E Dunbartonshire, 1970; Fife NE, 1987. MP (C): East Dunbartonshire, Feb.–Sept. 1974; E Fife, 1979–83; Fife NE, 1983–87. PPS to Economic Sec. to HM Treasury, 1984–87. Member: Select Cttee on Scottish Affairs, 1979–87; H of C Chairmen's Panel, 1981–83; Chm., Scottish Cons. Back Bench Cttee, 1983–84; Vice-Chm., PITCOM, 1986–87. Member: Extra Parly Panel for Scottish Private Legislation, 1996–; ODPM Right to Manage review, 2001–04. Area Bd Mem., CityWest Homes, 2003–05. Comr, Strathclyde Tram Public Inquiry, 1996. Trustee, St Andrews Links Trust, 1979–87. Comr, Gen. Assembly of Church of Scotland, 1986. Sec., 1997–2000, Vice-Chm., 2000–02, Pimlico Village Housing Co-op; Chm., Westminster Soc., 2004–. *Publications:* pamphlets on Scottish, European and environmental issues. *Address:* 33 Longleat House, 18 Rampayne Street, SW1V 2TG. *T:* (020) 7828 0056.

HENDERSON, Jane Elisabeth, CB 2004; Strategic Adviser on Sustainable Communities, Improvement and Development Agency, since 2005; *b* 2 May 1952; *m* 1979, Clive Abbott; one *s* one *d*. *Educ:* Tunbridge Wells Grammar Sch.; Somerville Coll., Oxford (BA 1973; BPhil 1975); Birkbeck Coll., Univ. of London (MSc 1983). Joined NI Office, 1975, Pvte Sec. to Perm. Sec., 1977–79; HM Treasury, 1979–81; CSSB, 1984–85; Industrial Econs Div., HM Treasury, 1985–86; Dept of Employment, 1986–88; SW Regl Dir, Employment Service, 1988–92; Trng, Enterprise and Educn Directorate, Dept of Employment, 1992–94; Dir of Finance, HEFCE, 1994–96; Dir of Resources, Rural Develt Commn, 1996–97; Regl Dir, Govt Office for the SW, 1998–2005. *Address:* Improvement and Development Agency, Layden House, 76–86 Turnmill Street, EC1M 5LG.

HENDERSON, Ven. Janet, (Mrs D. M. Challoner); Archdeacon of Richmond, since 2007; *b* 12 May 1957; *d* of John Wilson Henderson and Megan (*née* Williams); *m* 1996, David Michael Challoner. *Educ:* Addenbrooke's Sch. of Nursing, Cambridge (RGN 1982); Durham Univ. (BA Hons 1988). Staff Nurse, Cambridge AHA, 1982–85; ordained deacon, 1988, priest, 1994; Asst Curate, St Peter and St Paul, Wisbech, 1988–90; Parish Deacon, Bestwood Team Ministry, Nottingham, 1990–93; Lectr, St John's Coll., Nottingham, 1993–97; Associate Priest NSM, St Michael and All Angels, Bramcote, Nottingham, 1994–97; Lectr, Cambridge Theol Fedn, and Tutor, Ridley Hall Theol Coll., 1997–2001; Dean, Women's Ministry, Dio. of Southwell, 2001–07; Priest-in-Charge, St Patrick's, Nuthall, 2001–07. *Publications:* (ed jtly) Pastoral Prayers, 1996; articles in British Jl of Theological Educn, Anvil. *Recreations:* playing the double bass and piano, walking. *Address:* Hoppus House, Smith Lane, Hutton Conyers, Ripon HG4 5DX. *T:* (01765) 601316; *e-mail:* janeth@riponleeds-diocese.org.uk.

HENDERSON, Dame Joan; *see* Kelleher, Dame J.

HENDERSON, Sir (John) Nicholas, GCMG 1977 (KCMG 1972; CMG 1965); KCVO 1991; HM Diplomatic Service, retired; re-appointed, Ambassador to Washington, 1979–82; author and company director; *b* 1 April 1919; *s* of Prof. Sir Hubert Henderson; *m* 1951, Mary Xenia Barber (*née* Cawadias) (OBE 1988) (*d* 2004); one *d*. *Educ:* Stowe Sch.; Hertford Coll., Oxford (Hon. Fellow 1975). Mem. HM Diplomatic Service. Served Minister of State's Office, Cairo, 1942–43; Asst Private Sec. to the Foreign Sec., 1944–47; HM Embassy, Washington, 1947–49; Athens, 1949–50; Permanent Under Secretary's Dept, FO, 1950–53; HM Embassy, Vienna, 1953–56; Santiago, 1956–59; Northern Dept, FO, 1959–62; Permanent Under Secretary's Dept, 1962–63; Head of Northern Dept, Foreign Office, 1963; Private Sec. to the Sec. of State for Foreign Affairs, 1963–65; Minister in Madrid, 1965–69; Ambassador to Poland, 1969–72, to Federal Republic of Germany, 1972–75, to France, 1975–79. Lord Warden of the Stannaries, Keeper of the Privy Seal of the Duke of Cornwall, and Mem. of Prince's Council, 1985–90. Mem., BBC General Adv. Council, 1983–87; Chm., Channel Tunnel Gp, 1985–86; Director: Foreign & Colonial Investment Trust, 1982–88; M&G Reinsurance, 1982–90; Hambros, 1983–89; Tarmac, 1983–89; F&C Eurotrust, 1984–; Eurotunnel, 1986–88; Supervisory Bd, Fuel-Tech NV, 1987–; Sotheby's, 1989–. Trustee, Nat. Gallery, 1985–89. Pres., Hertford Soc., 1984–89. Romanes Lectr, 1986. Hon. DCL Oxford, 1987. *Publications:* Prince Eugen of Savoy (biography), 1964; The Birth of Nato, 1982; The Private Office, 1984; Channels and Tunnels, 1987; Mandarin: the diaries of Nicholas Henderson, 1994; Old Friends and Modern Instances (memoirs), 2000; The Private Office Revisited, 2001; various stories and articles in Penguin New Writing, Horizon, Apollo, Country Life, The Economist and History Today. *Recreation:* gardening. *Address:* 6 Fairholt Street, SW7 1EG. *T:* (020) 7589 4291. *Clubs:* Brooks's, Pratt's.

See also Earl of Drogheda.

HENDERSON, Ven. Julian Tudor; Archdeacon of Dorking, since 2005; *b* 23 July 1954; *s* of Ian Tudor Henderson and Susan Blundell Henderson; *m* 1984, Heather Gwenllian Lees; one *s* one *d*. *Educ:* Radley Coll.; Keble Coll., Oxford (MA Theol.). Ordained deacon, 1979, priest, 1980; Curate, St Mary's, Islington, 1979–83; Vicar: Emmanuel and St Mary in the Castle, Hastings, 1983–92; Holy Trinity, Claygate, 1992–2005. Hon. Canon, Guildford Cathedral, 2001–. *Recreations:* gardening, reading, walking. *Address:* The Old Cricketers, Portsmouth Road, Ripley, Woking, Surrey GU23 6ER; *e-mail:* julian.t.henderson@gmail.com.

HENDERSON, Hon. Sir Launcelot (Dinadan James), Kt 2007; **Hon. Mr Justice Henderson;** a Judge of the High Court of Justice, Chancery Division, since 2007; *b* 20 Nov. 1951; *er s* of Baron Henderson of Brompton, KCB; *m* 1989, Elaine Elizabeth Webb; two *s* one *d*. *Educ:* Westminster Sch.; Balliol Coll., Oxford (MA). Fellow of All Soul Coll., Oxford, 1974–81 and 1982–89. Called to the Bar, Lincoln's Inn, 1977, Bencher 2004; practised as Barrister (Chancery), 1978–2006; Standing Junior Counsel: to Inland Revenue (Chancery), 1987–91; to Inland Revenue, 1991–95; QC 1995; a Dep. High Court Judge, Chancery Div., 2001–07. Trustee, Samuel Courtauld Trust, 2005–. *Recreations:* botany, art, music, books. *Address:* Royal Courts of Justice, Strand, WC2A 2LL.

See also Bishop of Tuam, Killala and Achonry.

HENDERSON, Leslie Edwin, CBE 1982; Director of Contracts, Property Service Agency, 1978–82, retired; *b* 16 Dec. 1922; *s* of Thomas Edwin and Mabel Mar Henderson; *m* 1946, Marjorie (*née* Austin); two *s*. *Educ:* Ealing County Sch., London Entered Civil Service (BoT) as Clerical Officer, 1939; Min. of Shipping, 1939; served in RAF, 1941–46; Min. of War Transport, 1946; subsequently in: Min. of Transport and Civil Aviation, MoT, DoE; Head of Contracts, Highways, Dept of Transport, 1968–78 *Recreations:* gardening, do-it-yourself. *Address:* Greenacres, The Rookery, Scotter, Linc DN21 3FB. *T:* (01724) 763850.

HENDERSON, Mark; lighting designer, since 1981; *b* 26 Sept. 1957; *s* of Gordon Henderson and Margaret Henderson (*née* Moakes); two *s*. *Educ:* Sherwood Hall Tech Grammar Sch., Mansfield. Chief electrician for Kent Opera, English Music Th., London Contemporary Dance, Sadler's Wells and Opera North, 1978–; lighting designs for *theatre:* numerous West End productions including: Grease, Follies, Carmen Jones, Rowan Atkinson in Revue, Home, Design for Living; Passion, 1996; West Side Story, 1998 Spend, Spend, Spend, 1999; The Real Thing, 2000; Sunset Boulevard, 2001; A Few Good Men, 2005; The Sound of Music, 2006; RNT productions include: Cat on a Hot Tin Roof (also Broadway), 1988; Hamlet, 1989; The Oedipus Plays, 1996; Amy's View Copenhagen, Antony and Cleopatra, 1998; Battle Royal, 1999; All My Sons, 2001; The History Boys, 2004 (also NY; Tony Award for Lighting Design (Play), 2006); The Alchemist, 2006; RSC productions include: Macbeth, Kiss Me Kate, The Lion, the Witch and the Wardrobe; Almeida Theatre productions include: Phèdre, The Ice Man Cometh 1998; Vassa, Plenty, 1999; Richard II, Coriolanus, 2000; Lulu, 2001; *opera* productions include: The Flying Dutchman (Royal Opera); Anna Karenina, The Silver Tassie, 2000 ENO; Otello, Glyndebourne, 2001; *dance* productions include: Agora, Shadows in the Sun (London Contemp. Dance Th.); Quicksilver (Rambert Dance Co.); Tales of Beatrix Potter, The Judas Tree, Daphnis and Chloë, Sleeping Beauty (Royal Ballet); The Nutcracker, 1999; *films* include: The Tall Guy, 1988; Under Milk Wood, 1992. Olivier Awards: Lighting Designer of the Year, 1992; Best Lighting Designer, 1995, 2000, 2002 *Address:* 34 Indigo Mews, Carysfort Road, N16 9AE.

HENDERSON, Mark; Chief Executive, Northumberland County Council, since 2003 *b* 12 Oct. 1962; *s* of Ralph and Mary Henderson; *m* 1987, Lindsey Robertson; one *s* one *d*. *Educ:* Univ. of Dundee (BSc Hons). Planning Technician: Dunfermline DC, 1979–87 Dundee DC, 1987–91; Strategic Policy Manager, Clackmannanshire, 1994–96 Partnership Funding Officer, Angus Council, 1996–97; Asst Dir (Regeneration), N Linc Council, 1997–2000; Dir of Ops, One Northeast, 2000–03. Mem., Dundee DC 1992–96. *Recreations:* motorsports, family activities, following Dunfermline Athletic FC *Address:* Northumberland County Council, County Hall, Morpeth, Northumberland NE61 2EF. *T:* (01670) 533101, *Fax:* (01670) 533071; *e-mail:* markhenderson@northumberland.gov.uk.

HENDERSON, Michael John Glidden, FCA; Chairman, Advisory Board, Quexco Inc (USA), since 2005 (Executive Vice-Chairman, 2002–05); *b* 19 Aug. 1938; *s* of William Glidden Henderson and Aileen Judith Henderson (*née* Malloy); *m* 1965, Stephanie Maria Dyer; four *s*. *Educ:* St Benedict's Sch., Ealing. FCA 1971. Took articles with William Dyson Jones & Co., 1956; qual. as chartered accountant, 1961; Whinney Smith & Whinney & Co., 1963; Goodlass Wall & Lead Industries, later Cookson Group plc, 1965 Cookson Group: Dir, 1975; Man. Dir, 1979; Chief Exec., 1984–90; Chm. and Chief Exec., 1990–91; Exec. Dir, Ronar Services Ltd, 1991–2006. Chm., Henderson Crossthwaite, subseq. Investec Henderson Crossthwaite, Hldgs Ltd, 1995–2000; Dir Tioxide Gp, 1987–90; Exec. Dir, 1998–2007, non-exec. Dir, 2007–, Cyril Sweett Gp PLC (formerly Cyril Sweett Ltd); non-executive Director: Guinness Mahon Holdings 1988–2000; Three Counties Financial Mgt Services Ltd, 1991–; ECO-BAT Technologies, 1999–2002. Mem., Innovation Adv. Bd, DTI, 1988–93. Trustee, Natural History Mus. Develt Trust, 1990–2000. FRSA 1989. Governor: St George's Coll. Weybridge, 1990– (Dep. Chm., 2002–; Chm., F and GP Cttee, 1991–); Cranmore Sch. W Horsley, 1992– (Dep. Chm., 1998–; Chm., F and GP Cttee, 1992–); St Teresa' Convent, Effingham, 2002– (Chm., F and GP Cttee, 2003–). KHS 2005. *Recreations* tennis, golf, watching all sports. *Address:* Langdale, Woodland Drive, East Horsley, Surrey KT24 5AN. *T:* (01483) 283844, *T:* and *Fax:* (office) (01483) 284464; *e-mail* mike.henderson3@btopenworld.com. *Clubs:* MCC, Queen's; Wisley Golf (Dir 2002–07; Dep. Chm., 2004-07); Horsley Sports; Thurlestone Golf; Salcombe Yacht Kingsbridge Tennis.

HENDERSON, Sir Nicholas; *see* Henderson, Sir J. N.

HENDERSON, Nicholas John; National Hunt racehorse trainer, since 1978; *b* 10 Dec 1950; *s* of late John Ronald Henderson, CVO, OBE; *m* 1978, Diana Amanda Thorne three *d*. *Educ:* Eton. Amateur rider, 1970–78 (rode 75 winners, incl. Imperial Cup Sandown and Liverpool Foxhunters); Asst Trainer to Fred Winter, 1973–78. Trained over 1,000 winners, incl. See You Then (Champion Hurdle, 1985, 1986, 1987), Brown Windsor (Whitbread Gold Cup), Remittance Man (Champion Chase). Leading Nat Hunt trainer, 1986–87, 1987–88; Piper Heidsieck Trainer of the Year, 1986, 1987, 1988 *Address:* Seven Barrows, Lambourn, Hungerford, Berks RG17 8UH.

HENDERSON, (Patrick) David, CMG 1992; economist, author and consultant Visiting Professor, Westminster Business School; *b* 10 April 1927; *s* of late David Thomson Henderson and late Eleanor Henderson; *m* 1960, Marcella Kodicek; one *s* one *d*. *Educ* Ellesmere Coll., Shropshire; Corpus Christi Coll., Oxford. Fellow and Tutor in Economics, Lincoln Coll., Oxford, 1948–65 (Hon. Fellow, 1991); Univ. Lectr in Economics, Oxford, 1950–65; Commonwealth Fund Fellow (Harvard), 1952–53; Junior Proctor, Oxford Univ., 1955–56; Economic Adviser, HM Treasury, 1957–58; Chief Economist, Min. of Aviation, 1965–67; Adviser Harvard Development Advisory Service (Athens and Kuala Lumpur), 1967–68; Vis. Lectr, World Bank, 1968–69; Economist World Bank, 1969–75, Dir of Economics Dept 1971–72; Prof. of Political Economy UCL, 1975–83; Hd of Econs and Stats Dept, OECD, 1984–92. Mem., Commn on Environmental Pollution, 1977–80; Special Adviser, Sec. of State for Wales, 1978–79 Member: Nat. Ports Council, 1979–81; Bd, Commonwealth Develt Corp., 1980–83 Formerly Visiting Fellow or Professor: OECD Develt Centre, Paris; Centre for Eur Policy Studies, Brussels; Fondation Nationale des Sciences Politiques, Paris; Monash Univ., Melb.; Univ. of Melb.; NZ Business Roundtable; Melb. Business Sch. Reith Lectr BBC, 1985; Copland Meml Address, 1989; Shapiro Lectr, LSE, 1993; Downing Oration Melbourne Univ., 1995; Hibberd Lectr, Melb. Business Sch., 1997; Wincott Lecture

2000; Lang Hancock Lecture, 2002. *Publications:* India: the energy sector, 1975; Innocence and Design: the influence of economic ideas on policy, 1986; The Changing Fortunes of Economic Liberalism, 1998; (jointly) Nyasaland: The Economics of Federation, 1960; ed and contrib.: Economic Growth in Britain, 1965; contrib: The British Economy in the 1950's, 1962; Public Enterprise, 1968; Public Economics, 1969; Unfashionable Economics, 1970; The World Bank, Multilateral Aid and the 1970's, 1973; The Economic Development of Yugoslavia, 1975; Contemporary Problems of Economic Policy, 1983; Protectionism and Growth, 1985; Economic Policies for the 1990s, 1991; (ed jtly) Trade Blocs: the future of regional integration, 1994; Misguided Virtue, 2001; The Role of Business in the Modern World, 2004; articles in economic and other jls. *Address:* Westminster Business School, 35 Marylebone Road, NW1 5LS.

HENDERSON, Prof. Paul, CBE 2003; DPhil; Director of Science, Natural History Museum, 1995–2003; *b* 7 Nov. 1940; *s* of Thomas William Henderson and Dorothy Violet (*née* Marriner); *m* 1966, Elizabeth Kathryn Ankerson; one *s* one *d*. *Educ:* King's Coll. Sch., Wimbledon; Univ. of London (BSc 1963); Univ. of Oxford (DPhil 1966). FGS 1990; CGeol 1990; FLS 1997. Asst Lectr in Chemistry, Glasgow Univ., 1967–68; Lectr in Geochem., Chelsea Coll., Univ. of London, 1968–76; British Museum (Natural History), subseq. Natural History Museum: PSO, 1977, Grade 6, 1984, Dep. Keeper, 1987, Keeper, 1989–95, Dept of Mineralogy; Associate Dir, Earth Scis, 1992–95. Visiting Professor: Univ. of Bern, Switzerland, 1989; UCL, 1990–98 (Hon. Prof., 1999–). Pres., Mineralogical Soc., 1989–91 (Mem. Council, 1974–76 and 1986–89); Vice-Pres., Geol Soc., 2002–08; Member Council: Eur. Assoc. for Geochem., 1986–94; Internat. Mineralog. Assoc., 1989–94. Member: Sci. Adv. Bd, 1994–99, Expert Commn, 2001–02, Museum für Naturkunde, Berlin; Sci. Adv. Cttee, 2000–01, Conseil Scientifique, 2002–06, Muséum Nat. d'Histoire Naturelle, Paris. Trustee, Horniman Mus. and Public Park Trust, 2004–. Fourmarier Medal, Belgian Geol Soc., 1989. *Publications:* Inorganic Geochemistry, 1982; (ed) Rare Earth Element Geochemistry, 1984; contribs to jls on geochem. and mineral chem. *Recreations:* music, mineralogy, history, Paris, wine. *Address:* Department of Earth Sciences, University College London, Gower Street, WC1E 6BT; *e-mail:* p.henderson@btinternet.com.

HENDERSON, Air Vice-Marshal Peter William, CB 2000; MBE 1982; CEng, FRAeS; aerospace consultant; *b* 5 Nov. 1945. *Educ:* King's Sch., Macclesfield; RAF Coll. Cranwell (BSc CNAA). Inspectorate of Flight Safety, 1975; RAF Germany, 1978; RAF Staff Coll., 1982; RAF Abingdon, 1982–84; Dept of Air Mem. for Supply and Orgn, 1984–87; Mem., Ordnance Bd, 1987; Stn Comdr, Abingdon, 1990–92; Logistic Comd Project Sponsor, HQ RAF Support Comd, 1992–95; Dir 1995–97, Dir Gen., 1997–99, RAF Support Mgt; Dir Gen., Equipment Support (Air), Mem., Defence Logistics Mgt Bd, and Mem., Air Force Bd, Defence Council, 1999–2000, retd. *Recreations:* golf, music, sailing. *Clubs:* Royal Air Force; Truro Golf; St Mawes Sailing; Morgan Sports Car.

HENDERSON, Dr Richard, FRS 1983; Member of the Scientific Staff, Medical Research Council Laboratory of Molecular Biology, Cambridge, since 1973 (Director, 1996–2006); Fellow of Darwin College, Cambridge, since 1981; *b* 19 July 1945; *s* of late John and Grace Henderson; *m* 1st, 1969, Penelope FitzGerald (marr. diss. 1988); one *s* one *d* (and one *d* decd); 2nd, 1995, Jade Li. *Educ:* Hawick High Sch.; Boroughmuir Secondary Sch.; Edinburgh Univ. (BSc); Corpus Christi Coll., Cambridge (Hon. Fellow, 2005); PhD Cantab 1970. Helen Hay Whitney Fellow, Yale Univ., 1970–73. Founder FMedSci 1998. Foreign Associate, Acad. of Sci., USA, 1998. William Bate Hardy Prize, Cambridge Phil Soc., 1978; Ernst Ruska Prize for Electron Microscopy, Ernst Ruska Foundn, 1981; Lewis S. Rosenstiel Award, Brandeis Univ., 1991; Louis Jeantet Award, Jeantet Foundn, Geneva, 1993; Gregori Aminoff Prize, Royal Swedish Acad. of Scis, 1999. *Publications:* research pubns and reviews in scientific jls. *Recreations:* canoeing, wine-tasting. *Address:* MRC Laboratory of Molecular Biology, Hills Road, Cambridge CB2 0QH. *T:* (01223) 248011.

HENDERSON, Rt Rev. Richard Crosbie Aitken; *see* Tuam, Killala and Achonry, Bishop of.

HENDERSON, Richard Mitchell, CB 2007; WS; Solicitor to the Scottish Executive, and Head of the Government Legal Service for Scotland, 1999–2007; President, Law Society of Scotland, 2007–May 2009 (Vice-President, May-Aug. 2007); *b* 17 April 1947; *s* of Thomas Alex Henderson and Hester Susan England Henderson (*née* Mitchell); *m* 1970, Frances Lesley Eadie; one *s* one *d*. *Educ:* Cellardyke Primary Sch., Anstruther; Strathallan Sch.; Univ. of Edinburgh (LlB Hons 1969). Admitted Solicitor, 1971; WS 2006; Solicitor to the Sec. of State for Scotland, 1998. *Recreations:* golf (occasional and erratic), walking, being in the fresh air.

HENDERSON, Sir Richard (Yates), KCVO 2006; TD 1966; JP; Lord-Lieutenant of Ayrshire and Arran, 1991–2006; *b* 7 July 1931; *s* of late John Wishart Henderson and Dorothy (*née* Yates); *m* 1957, Frances Elizabeth Chrystal; two *s* one *d* (and one *s* decd). *Educ:* Rugby; Hertford Coll., Oxford (BA); Glasgow Univ. (LLB). Served Royal Scots Greys, 1950–52; Ayrshire Yeomanry TA, 1953–69. Partner, Mitchells Roberton, Solicitors, Glasgow, 1958–90; Trustee, TSB, Glasgow, 1966–74; Dir, West of Scotland TSB, 1974–83. Hon. Sheriff, S Strathclyde, Dumfries and Galloway at Ayr, 1997. Ensign, Royal Company of Archers, Queen's Body Guard for Scotland, 2004–. Hon. Col, Ayrshire Yeo. Sqn, Scottish Yeo., 1992–97; Pres., Lowlands TAVRA, 1996–2000. DL Ayrshire, 1970–90. *Recreations:* shooting, tennis, golf. *Address:* Blairston, by Ayr KA7 4EF. *T:* (01292) 441601. *Club:* Western (Glasgow).

HENDERSON, Robert Ewart; QC (Scot.) 1982; *b* 29 March 1937; *s* of William Ewart Henderson and Agnes Ker Henderson; *m* 1st, 1958, Olga Sunter (marr. diss. 1978); one *s* two *d*; 2nd, 1982, Carol Black (marr. diss. 1988); one *s*; 3rd, 1995, Carolyn Gell. *Educ:* Larchfield Sch., Helensburgh; Morrison's Acad., Crieff; Glasgow Univ. (BL 1962). Admitted to Faculty of Advocates, 1963. National Service, 2nd Lieut RA, 1956–58. Hon. Sheriff-Substitute, Stirling, Dunbarton and Clackmannan, 1968; Standing Jun. Counsel in Scotland, DTI, 1970–74, Dept of Trade, 1974–77; Temp. Sheriff, 1978. Pres., Glasgow Univ. Law Soc., 1961–62; Chairman: NHS Appeal Tribunal, 1972; Medical Appeal Tribunal (Scotland), 1985–93; War Pensions Appeal Tribunal, 1986–2004. Contested (C) Inverness-shire, Feb. and Oct. 1974. *Recreations:* golf, sailing. *Address:* The Old Schoolhouse, Gullane, East Lothian EH31 2AF. *T:* (01620) 842012. *Clubs:* New (Edinburgh); Hon. Company of Edinburgh Golfers (Muirfield); Royal St George's Golf (Sandwich).

HENDERSON, Roger Anthony; QC 1980; a Recorder of the Crown Court, since 1983; a Deputy High Court Judge, since 1987; *b* 21 April 1943; *s* of late Dr Peter Wallace Henderson, MC and Dr Stella Dolores Henderson; *m* 1968, Catherine Margaret Williams; three *d* (and one *d* decd). *Educ:* Radley Coll.; St Catharine's Coll., Cambridge (Scholar; 1st Cl. Hons degree in Law, MA; Adderley Prize for Law, 1964). Inner Temple: Duke of Edinburgh Award, 1962; Major Scholarship, 1964; called to the Bar, 1964; Bencher, 1985. Counsel to King's Cross Inquiry, 1988. Mem., Bar Council, 1988–91; Chm., Public Affairs Cttee of Bar, 1989–90. Chm., Civil Service Arbitration Tribunal, 1994–; Member: Exec. Council, British Acad. of Forensic Sciences, 1977–90 (Pres., 1986–87); Council of Legal Educn, 1983–90. Chm., Assoc. of Regulatory and Disciplinary Lawyers, 2003–; Vice Pres., Health and Safety Lawyers' Assoc., 2005–. Gov., London Hosp. Med. Coll., 1989–96 (Chm., Council, 1993–96); Chm., Special Cttee, St Peter's Hosps, 1989–92; Mem. Council, QMW, 1993–2005. FRSA 1994. Hon. Fellow, QMC, London, 2006. *Recreations:* fly-fishing, gardening, shooting. *Address:* 2 Harcourt Buildings, Temple, EC4Y 9DB. *T:* (020) 7583 9020; 9 Brunswick Gardens, W8 4AS; Holbury Mill, Lockerley, Romsey, Hants SO51 0JR. *T:* (01794) 340583. *Club:* Boodle's.

HENDERSON, Victor Joseph, CMG 2000; HM Diplomatic Service, retired; Senior Consultant, MEC International Ltd; *b* 10 Jan. 1941; *s* of Frederick Ilwyn Henderson and Mary Elizabeth Henderson; *m* 1966, Heather Winifred Steed; one *s* one *d*. *Educ:* Rhondda Co. Grammar Sch. for Boys; King's Coll., London (BA Hons Spanish 1961). Joined HM Diplomatic Service, 1966: MECAS, Lebanon, 1967–69; Third Sec. (Commercial), Jedda, 1969–72; Second Sec. (Commercial), Bahrain, 1972–75; FCO, 1975–78; Second, later First Sec., Caracas, 1978–82; Consul, Jerusalem, 1982–87; FCO, 1987–90; First Sec. (Political, later Commercial), Helsinki, 1990–94; Dep. Head, Jt Export Promotion Directorate, FCO/DTI, 1995–97; Ambassador to the Yemen, 1997–2001. Chm., British Yemeni Soc. *Recreations:* watching cricket, reading, listening to music (especially jazz). *Address:* c/o MEC International Ltd, Granville House, 132-135 Sloane Street, SW1X 9AX.

HENDERSON-SELLERS, Prof. Ann, PhD, DSc; Director, World Climate Research Programme, World Meteorological Organisation, since 2006; *b* 7 March 1952; *d* of Thomas William Futtit and Ruth Forester Fielding; *m* 1974, Prof. Brian Henderson-Sellers. *Educ:* Sheffield Girls' High Sch.; Pate's, Cheltenham; Univ. of Bristol (BSc Hons Maths); Univ. of Leicester (PhD 1976, DSc 1999). University of Liverpool: Lectr, 1977–82; Sen. Lectr, 1982–86; Reader, 1986–88; Personal Chair in Physical Geography, 1988; Prof. of Physical Geog., and Dir, Climatic Impacts Centre, Macquarie Univ., 1988–96; Dep. Vice-Chancellor, R&D, RMIT, 1996–98; Dir, Envmt, Australian Nuclear Sci. and Technol. Orgn, 1998–2005. Vis. Lectr, Univ. of Witwatersrand, S Africa, 1979; Vis. Res. Fellow, NASA Goddard Inst. for Space Studies, 1981–82; Vis. Prof., Univ. of Louvain-la-Neuve, Belgium, 1983; Vis. Scientist, Nat. Center for Atmospheric Res., USA, 1985–2003. *Publications:* (jtly) Atmospheric Pollution, 4th edn 1981; The Origin and Evolution of Planetary Atmospheres, 1983; Satellite Sensing of a Cloudy Atmosphere, 1984; (jtly) Contemporary Climatology, 1986, 2nd edn 1999; (jtly) A Climate Modelling Primer, 1987, 3rd edn 2004; (jtly) The Greenhouse Effect: living in a warmer Australia, 1989; (ed jtly) Vegetation and Climate Interactions in Semi-Arid Regions, 1991; (ed jtly) Climate Change Atlas, 1995; (ed) Future Climates of the World: a modelling perspective, 1995; (ed jtly) Climate Change: developing Southern Hemisphere perspectives, 1996; (ed jtly) Assessing Climate Change, 1997; articles in tech. jls. *Recreation:* collecting Winnie the Pooh books in different languages. *Address:* c/o World Meteorological Organisation, 7 bis Avenue de la Paix, Case Postale No 2300, 1211 Geneva 2, Switzerland. *T:* (22) 7308246, *Fax:* (22) 7308036; *e-mail:* ahenderson-sellers@wmo.int.

HENDERSON-STEWART, Sir David (James), 2nd Bt *cr* 1957; *b* 3 July 1941; *s* of Sir James Henderson-Stewart, 1st Bt, MP, and of Anna Margaret (*née* Greenwell); *S* father, 1961; *m* 1972, Anne, *d* of Count Serge de Pahlen; three *s* one *d*. *Educ:* Eton Coll.; Trinity Coll., Oxford. *Heir: s* David Henderson-Stewart [*b* 2 Feb. 1973; *m* 1997, Xenia Yagello; two *s* two *d* (of whom one *s* one *d* are twins)]. *Address:* 90 Oxford Gardens, W10 5UW. *T:* (020) 8964 4356.

HENDON, David Anthony, CBE 2006; FREng, FIET; Director, Business Relations, Department for Business, Enterprise and Regulatory Reform (formerly Department of Trade and Industry), since 2003; *b* 19 Oct. 1949; *s* of Anthony Leonard Hendon and Constance Audrey Hendon (*née* Clayton); *m* 1976, Gillian Anne Iles; one *s* two *d*. *Educ:* Royal Grammar Sch., Guildford; Southampton Univ. (BSc Eng 1972). FIET (FIEE 2000); FREng 2002. MoD, 1973–84 (Principal, 1981–84); Asst Dir (Engrg), Home Office, 1984–88; Dep. Dir, 1988–92, Dir, 1992–98, Technol., Policy, Communications and Inf., Industries Directorate, DTI; Chief Exec., Radiocommunications Agency, 1998–2002; Hd of Communications and Inf. Industries Directorate, DTI, 2002–03. Chm. Bd, Eur. Telecommunications Standards Inst., 1995–99. Chm., Radio Spectrum Internat. Consulting Ltd, 1998–2002. Member: PPARC, 2002–06; EPSRC, 2006–. Spastics Society, later Scope: Mem. Council, 1987–96; Vice-Chm., 1991–93; Chm., Audit Cttee, 1993–; Hon. Life Mem., 1996. Chm., White Lodge Centre, Chertsey, 1980–85. Gov., Guildford Co. Sch., 1994–98. *Recreations:* reading, red wine, the Internet. *Address:* Department for Business, Enterprise and Regulatory Reform, 1 Victoria Street, SW1H 0ET. *T:* (020) 7215 1839.

HENDRICK, Mark Phillip, CEng; MP (Lab and Co-op) Preston, since Nov. 2000; *b* 2 Nov. 1958; *s* of Brian Francis Hendrick and Jennifer (*née* Chapman). *Educ:* Liverpool Poly. (BSc Hons Electrical and Electronic Engrg); Univ. of Manchester (MSc Computer Sci.; Cert Ed). CEng 1987. Trainee Technician, Signal and Telecommunications, BR, 1975–78; Student Engr, 1979–81; RSRE Malvern, MoD, 1979; Special Systems Unit, STC plc, 1980; AEG Telefunken, Seligenstadt, Germany, 1981; Design Engr, Daresbury Lab., SERC, 1982–84 and 1985–88; Lectr, Stockport Coll., 1989–94. MEP (Lab and Co-op) Lancashire Central, 1994–99; contested (Lab) NW Reg., 1999. PPS to Sec. of State, DEFRA, 2003–06, FCO, 2006–07, to Minister of Justice, 2007–. *Recreations:* football supporter (Manchester City and Preston North End), travel, chess, German and French. *Address:* c/o House of Commons, SW1A 0AA; 6 Sedgwick Street, Preston, Lancs PR1 1TP. *T:* (01772) 883575. *Clubs:* Deepdale Labour; Penwortham Sports and Social (Preston).

HENDRICKS, Barbara; American soprano; *b* 20 Nov. 1948; *d* of Rev. M. L. Hendricks and Della Hendricks; *m*; one *s* one *d*. *Educ:* Univ. of Nebraska (BS Chem. and Math. 1969); Juilliard Sch. of Music, NY (Schol.; BM); studied under Jennie Tourel. Début, l'Incoronazione di Poppea, San Francisco Opera, 1976; has appeared with opera cos of Berlin, Boston, Florence, Glyndebourne, Hamburg, La Scala, Milan, LA, Royal Opera, Covent Garden, etc; concert performances with major orchestras; numerous recordings. Launched own record label, Arte Verum, 2005. Goodwill Ambassador, UN High Commn for Refugees, 1987. Hon. Dr Juilliard, NY, 2000. Prince of Asturias Prize, 2000. Commandeur des Arts et des Lettres (France), 1986; Chevalier de la Légion d'Honneur (France), 1993; St George's Cross (Catalonia, Spain), 2006.

HENDRICKS, Rt Rev. Paul Joseph; Auxiliary Bishop in Southwark, (RC), since 2006; *b* 18 March 1956; *s* of Gerald Hendricks and Grace Hendricks (*née* Deacon). *Educ:* Holy Innocents Primary Sch., Orpington; St Mary's Grammar Sch., Sidcup; Corpus Christi Coll., Oxford (BA Physics 1977, MA); Gregorian Univ., Rome (PhL 1985). Ordained deacon, 1983, priest, 1984; Asst Priest, St Boniface Church, Tooting, 1985–89; Lectr in Philosophy, St John's Seminary, Wonersh, 1989–99; Parish Priest, Our Lady of Sorrows, Peckham, 1999–2006. *Recreations:* reading, walking, sailing, music (playing clarinet and piano). *Address:* 95 Carshalton Road, Sutton SM1 4LL. *T:* (020) 8643 8007; *e-mail:* p.hendricks@btinternet.com.

HENDRICKSE, Prof. Ralph George, MD; FRCP, FRCPE; Professor of Tropical Paediatrics and International Child Health, 1988–91, now Professor Emeritus, Head of Department of Tropical Paediatrics, 1974–91, and Dean, 1988–91, Liverpool School of Tropical Medicine; *b* 5 Nov. 1926; *s* of William George Hendrickse and Johana Theresa Hendrickse (*née* Dennis); *m* 1948, Begum Johanara Abdurahman; one *s* four *d*. *Educ:* Livingstone High Sch.; Univ. of Cape Town (MD). FMCPaed (Hon. Foundn Fellow). Res. MO, McCord Zulu Hosp., Durban, 1949–54, incl. secondment to Willis F. Pierce Meml Hosp., S Rhodesia, as MO i/c, 1951; postgrad. studies, Glasgow and Edinburgh, 1955; Sen. Registrar, UCH, Ibadan, Nigeria, 1955–57; Sen. Lectr, Univ. of Ibadan, 1957–62, and Hon. Consultant Paediatrician, UCH, 1957–69; Prof. and Head of Paediatrics, Univ. of Ibadan, 1962–69; Dir, Inst. of Child Health, 1964–69; Sen. Lectr, 1969–74, Prof. of Tropical Paediatrics, 1974–87, Liverpool Univ. Sch. of Trop. Med. Mem., Standing Panel of Experts in Public Health Medicine, Univ. of London, 1990–. Hon. Vis. Prof., Santo Tomas Univ., Philippines. Hon. Founder FRCPCH 1996; Hon. Member: BPA, 1995; Philippines Paed. Soc. Founder and Editor-in-Chief, Annals of Tropical Paediatrics, 1981–2004. Hon. DSc (Med.) Cape Town, 1998. Frederick Murgatroyd Prize, RCP, 1970. *Publications:* Paediatrics in the Tropics: current review, 1981; (ed and contrib.) Paediatrics in the Tropics, 1991; papers in learned jls. *Recreations:* photography, sketching, theatre, swimming, travel. *Address:* Beresford House, 25 Riverbank Road, Heswall, Wirral, Merseyside CH60 4SQ. *T:* (0151) 342 5510.

HENDRIE, Dr Gerald Mills; musicologist, composer, harpsichordist and organist; Professor of Music, The Open University, 1969–90; *b* 28 Oct. 1935; *s* of James Harold Hendrie and Florence Mary MacPherson; *m* 1st, 1962, Dinah Florence Barsham, BMus, PhD (*d* 1985); two *s*; 2nd, 1986, Dr Lynette Anne Maddern, MB, BS. *Educ:* Framlingham Coll., Suffolk; Royal Coll. of Music; Selwyn Coll., Cambridge (MA, MusB, PhD). FRCO, ARCM. Director of Music, Homerton Coll., Cambridge, 1962–63; Lectr in the History of Music, Univ. of Manchester, 1963–67; Prof. and Chm., Dept of Music, Univ. of Victoria, BC, Canada, 1967–69; Reader in Music, subseq. Prof., The Open Univ., 1969–90; Dir of Studies in Music, St John's Coll., Cambridge, 1981–84, Supervisor, 1977–84. Vis. Fellow in Music, Univ. of WA, 1985. *Publications:* Musica Britannica XX, Orlando Gibbons: Keyboard Music, 1962, 3rd rev. edn 2009; G. F. Handel: Anthems für Cannons, 3 vols, 1985, 1987, 1991; Anthems für die Chapel Royal, 1992; Utrecht Te Deum und Jubilate, 1998; articles for Die Musik in Geschichte und Gegenwart; musical compositions include: Five Bagatelles for piano, 1980; Four Excursions for piano, 1983; Three Pieces for flute and piano, 1985; Specula Petro for organ, 1988; Quintet for Brass, 1988; Choral: Hommage à César Franck for organ, 1990; Le Tombeau de Marcel Dupré (for organ): Toccata and Fugue, 1991; Prelude and Fugue, 1991; Prelude and Fugue on the name BACH, 1992; Two Sketches on the name BACH, 1993; In Praise of St Asaph, 1994; Sonata: In Praise of Reconciliation, for organ, 1998, for piano, 1998; Requiem, for soprano, chorus, organ, 1998; Premier Livre d'Orgue, 1999; Deuxième Livre d'Orgue, 2000; Missa Aquitaniae, for soprano, chorus, organ, 2003; Sonate en Trio, for organ, 2006; much church music. *Recreations:* walking, gardening. *Address:* Au Village, 32190 Caillavet, France. *T:* 562644104.

HENDRIE, Robert Andrew Michie; HM Diplomatic Service, retired; Ambassador to Uruguay, 1994–98; *b* 4 May 1938; *s* of John Hendrie, Edinburgh and Effie Campbell (*née* Mackay); *m* 1964, Consuelo Liaño Solórzano; two *d*. *Educ:* Bradford Grammar Sch.; Trinity Hall, Cambridge (BA, MA). Joined HM Diplomatic Service, 1961; MECAS, Beirut, 1961–62; Political Residency, Bahrain, 1962–65; Tehran, 1965–68; Tripoli, 1968–69; Latin America Dept, FCO, 1969–73; Lima, 1973–75; Buenos Aires, 1975–80; Asst Hd, Central Africa Dept, ME Dept and Inf. Dept, FCO, 1980–86; Consul-General: Lille, 1986–90; Dubai, UAE, 1990–94. MCIL (MIL 1987). *Recreations:* reading, walking, watching Rugby, languages. *Address:* c/o Foreign and Commonwealth Office, King Charles Street, SW1A 2AH. *Clubs:* Canning, Roehampton.

HENDRON, Joseph Gerard; Member (SDLP) Belfast West, Northern Ireland Assembly, 1998–2003; *b* 12 Nov. 1932; *m* 1974, Sally (*née* Lennon); three *s* one *d*. *Educ:* St Malachy's Coll.; Queen's Univ., Belfast (MB 1957). FRCGP 1987. GP, W Belfast. Mem. (SDLP) Belfast CC, 1981–93. MP (SDLP) Belfast W, 1992–97; contested (SDLP) same seat, 1983, 1987, 1997. Chm., Health, Social Services and Public Safety Cttee, NI Assembly. Mem., Parades Commn, 2006–.

HENDRY, Prof. Arnold William; Professor of Civil Engineering, University of Edinburgh, 1964–88, now Emeritus; *b* 10 Sept. 1921; *s* of late Dr George Hendry, MB, ChB, Buckie, Scotland; *m* 1st, 1946, Sheila Mary Cameron Roberts (*d* 1966), Glasgow; one *d* (two *s* decd); 2nd, 1968, Elizabeth Lois Alice Inglis (*d* 2003), Edinburgh. *Educ:* Buckie High Sch.; Aberdeen Univ. Civil engineer with Sir William Arrol & Co. Ltd, Bridge builders and Engineers, Glasgow, 1941–43; Asst in Engineering, University of Aberdeen, 1943–46; Lecturer in Civil Engineering, 1946–49; Reader in Civil Engineering, Univ. of London, King's Coll., 1949–51; Prof. of Civil Engrg and Dean of Fac. of Engrg, Univ. of Khartoum, 1951–57; Prof. of Building Science, University of Liverpool, 1957–63. *Publications:* An Introduction to Photo-Elastic Analysis, 1948; (with L. G. Jaeger) The Analysis of Grid Frameworks, 1958; The Elements of Experimental Stress Analysis, 1964, 2nd edn 1977; Structural Brickwork, 1981; An Introduction to the Design of Load Bearing Brickwork, 1981; Structural Masonry, 1990, 2nd edn 1998; (ed) Reinforced and Prestressed Masonry, 1991; (with B. P. Sinha and S. R. Davies) Design of Masonry Structures, 1997; (with F. M. Khalaf) Masonry Wall Construction, 2000; A Career in Ivory Towers, 2001; The Edinburgh Transport Saga, 2002; over 150 papers and articles in professional and technical jls. *Recreations:* walking, reading. *Address:* Apartment 44 Regents Court, 29 Park Road West, Southport, Merseyside PR9 0JU.

HENDRY, Charles; MP (C) Wealden, since 2001; *b* 6 May 1959; *s* of late Charles William Righton Hendry and of Margaret Anne Hendry; *m* 1995, Mrs Sallie A. Moores; two *s*, and one step *s* one step *d*. *Educ:* Rugby Sch.; Univ. of Edinburgh (BCom Hons 1981). Account Dir, Ogilvy and Mather PR, 1983–86; Burson-Marsteller: Associate Dir (PR), 1986–88; Sen. Counsellor, Public Affairs, 1990–92. Non-executive Chairman: Agenda Gp Ltd, 2001–05 (Dir and Chief Exec., 1999–2001); IncrediBull Ideas Ltd, 2003–04. Special Adviser to: Rt Hon. John Moore, 1988; Rt Hon. Anthony Newton, 1988–89; Chief of Staff to Leader of Cons. Party, 1997; Hd of Business Liaison, Cons. Party, 1997–99. Vice-Chm., Battersea Cons. Assoc., 1981–83. Contested (C): Clackmannan, 1983; Mansfield, 1987; MP (C) High Peak, 1992–97; contested (C) same seat, 1997. PPS to Sec. of State for Educn and Employment, 1995; a Vice Chm., Cons. Party, 1995–97; an Opposition Whip, 2001–02; Shadow Minister: for youth affairs, 2002–05; for industry and enterprise, 2005; for energy, science and technology, 2005–07; for Energy, Industry and Postal Affairs, 2007–; Dep. Chm., Cons. Party, 2003–05. Member, Select Committee: on Procedure, 1992–94; on NI Affairs, 1994–97; on Culture, Media and Sport, 2003–04. Secretary: Conservative Back bench Social Services Cttee, 1992–94; Cons. Back bench Home Improvement Sub-Cttee, 1993–94; Cons. Back bench Urban Affairs Cttee, 1994; Jt Chm., All-Party Parly Gp on Homelessness, 1992–96; Vice Chm., All Party Parly Internet Gp, 2005–; Chm., British-Swiss Parly Gp. Sec., E Midlands Area Cons. MPs, 1992–97. Pres., British Youth Council, 1992–97; Trustee: Drive for Youth, 1989–99; Friends of NACAB, 1992–95; Big Issue Foundn, 1995–97 (Patron, 1997–). *Recreation* family, opera, ski-ing. *Address:* House of Commons, SW1A 0AA.

HENDRY, Prof. David Forbes, PhD; FBA 1987; FRSE; Professor of Economic University of Oxford, since 1982; Fellow, Nuffield College, Oxford, since 1982; *b* March 1944; *s* of Robert Ernest Hendry and Catherine Helen (*née* Mackenzie); *m* 196 Evelyn Rosemary (*née* Vass); one *d*. *Educ:* Aberdeen Univ. (MA 1st Cl. Hons); LSE (MS Distinction, PhD). Fellow, Econometric Soc., 1975; FRSE 2002. London School Economics: Lectr, 1969; Reader, 1973; Prof. of Econometrics, 1977–82; Leverhulm Personal Res. Prof. of Econs., Univ. of Oxford, 1995–2000. Vis. Professor: Yale Univ 1975; Univ. of Calif, Berkeley, 1976; Catholic Univ. of Louvain, 1980; Univ. of Cali San Diego, 1981, 1989–90; Vis. Research Prof., Duke Univ., 1987–91. Chm., Re Assessment Panel in Econs, HEFC, 1996. Pres., Royal Economic Soc., 1992–95 (Ho Vice Pres., 1995–). Fellow, Jl of Econometrics, 1997. Hon. Fellow, Internat. Inst. Forecasters, 2001. Hon. Foreign Member: Amer. Economic Assoc., 1991; Amer. Acad. Arts and Scis, 1994. Hon. LLD: Aberdeen, 1987; St Andrews, 2002; Hon. DS Nottingham, 1998; Hon. DPhil Norwegian Univ. of Sci. and Technol., 2001; Hon. D Oec St Gallen, 2001; Hon. DrPhil Lund, 2006. Guy Medal in Bronze, Royal Statistic Soc., 1986. Editor: Rev. of Econ. Studies, 1971–75; Econ. Jl, 1976–80; Oxford Bulleti of Economics and Statistics, 1983–. *Publications:* (ed with K. F. Wallis) Econometrics an Quantitative Economics, 1984; PC-GIVE, 1989; (with A. J. Neale and N. R. Ericsso PC-NAIVE, 1991; Econometrics: alchemy or science?, 1993, 2nd edn 2000; (jtl Cointegration, Error Correction and the Econometric Analysis of Non-stationary Dat 1993; Dynamic Econometrics, 1995; (ed with M. S. Morgan) The Foundations Econometric Analysis, 1995; (with J. A. Doornik) Empirical Econometric Modellin 1996; (with J. A. Doornik) An Interface to Empirical Modelling, 1996; (with J. Doornik) Modelling Dynamic Systems using PcFiml, 1997; (with M. P. Clement Forecasting Economic Time Series, 1998; (with M. P. Clements) Forecasting Non Stationary Economic Time Series, 1999; (ed with N. R. Ericsson) Understandin Economic Forecasts, 2001; (with H. M. Krolzig) Automatic Econometric Mod Selection, 2001; (with J. A. Doornik) Econometric Modelling Using PcGive (3 vols 2001; (with J. A. Doornik) Interactive Monte Carlo Experimentation in Econometric Using PcNaive, 2001; (ed with M. P. Clements) Companion to Economic Forecastin 2002; (with B. Nielson) Econometric Modelling: a likelihood approach, 2007; papers econometrics, statistics and economics jls. *Recreation:* golf. *Address:* Nuffield Colleg Oxford OX1 1NF; 26 Northmoor Road, Oxford OX2 6UR. *T:* (01865) 515588.

HENDRY, Ian Duncan, CMG 1996; HM Diplomatic Service, retired; Deputy Leg Adviser, Foreign and Commonwealth Office, 1999–2005; *b* 2 April 1948; *s* of Dunca William Hendry and Edna Beatrice Hendry (*née* Woodley); *m* 1st, 1973, Elizabeth Ann Southall (marr. diss.); one *s* one *d*; 2nd, 1991, Sally Annabel Hill. *Educ:* Uppingham Sch King's Coll., London (LLB, LLM). Called to the Bar, Gray's Inn, 1971; Asst Legal Adv FCO, 1971–82 and 1985–86; Legal Advr, BMG, Berlin, 1982–85; Legal Counsello FCO, 1986–91; UK Perm. Representation to EC, 1991–95; FCO, 1995–99. *Publication* (with M. C. Wood) The Legal Status of Berlin, 1986; (jtly) The External Relations of th European Communities, 1996; articles in Internat. and Comparative Law Qly an German Yearbook of Internat. Law. *Recreations:* travel, cricket, percussion, the exoti *Address:* Woodlands Cottage, Sturmer, Haverhill, Suffolk CB9 7UW.

HENDRY, Stephen Gordon, MBE 1993; professional snooker player, since 1986; *b* 1 Jan. 1969; *s* of Gordon John Hendry and Irene Agnes (*née* Anthony); *m* 1995, Amand Elizabeth Theresa Tart; one *s*. *Educ:* Inverkeithing High Sch. Embassy World Champio 1990, 1992, 1993, 1994, 1995, 1996, 1999 (record number of wins); Benson & Hedg Masters Champion, 1989, 1990, 1991, 1992, 1993, 1996; UK Professional Champio 1989, 1990, 1994, 1995, 1996; World Doubles Champion, 1987. *Publication:* Remembe My Name, 1989. *Recreations:* golf, music, cars. *Address:* Stephen Hendry Snooker Lt Kerse Road, Stirling FK7 7SG. *T:* (01786) 462634, *Fax:* (01786) 450068. *Club:* Lord Taverners (Scotland).

HENDY, John Giles; QC 1987; *b* 11 April 1948; *s* of late Jack and of Mary Hendy; *m* three *d*. *Educ:* Ealing Technical College (LLB); Queen's Univ., Belfast (DipLL, LLM Called to the Bar, Gray's Inn, 1972; Bencher, 1995. Dir, Newham Rights Centr 1973–76; Lectr, Middlesex Polytechnic, 1976–77; Barrister, 1977–. Vis. Prof., Sch. Law, KCL, 1999–. Chairman: Inst. of Employment Rights, 1989–; Employment Law B Assoc., 2003–05. Member, Editorial Committee: Encyc. of Employment Law, 1990– *Publications:* (jtly) Personal Injury Practice, 2nd edn 1993, 3rd edn 1999; Redgrave Health and Safety, 2nd edn 1994, 3rd edn 1998; (jtly) Munkman on Employer's Liability 12th edn 1995 to 14th edn 2006; (jtly) The Right to Strike: from the Trade Disputes A 1906 to a Trade Union Freedom Bill 2006, 2006. *Address:* Old Square Chambers, 10–1 Bedford Row, WC1R 4BU. *T:* (020) 7269 0300, *Fax:* (020) 7405 1387.
See also P. G. Hendy.

HENDY, Peter Gerard, CBE 2006; Commissioner of Transport for London, since 200 *b* 19 March 1953; *s* of Jack Hendy and Hon. Mary Hendy; *m* 1999, Sue Pendle; one *s* o *d*. *Educ:* Univ. of Leeds (BA Econs and Geog.). London Transport, 1975–89, Dist O Manager, 1986–89; Man. Dir, Centre W London Buses Ltd, 1989–98; Divl Dir, First G 1997–98; Dir, New World First Bus, Hong Kong, 1998–99; Dep. Dir, UK Bus for Fir Gp plc, 1998–2001; Man. Dir, Surface Transport, Transport for London, 2001–06. Chai Commn for Integrated Transport, 2005– (Mem., 2004–05). Member: Industri Tribunals, 1993–98; Council, Confedn of Passenger Transport, 1994–2000. FCIL (FCIT 1985); MCIPD 1992; FIHT 2005; FRSA 2006. *Recreations:* all forms of trave cycling, bus driving, walking, reading, my family. *Address:* Transport for London, Windso House, 42–50 Victoria Street, SW1H 0TL. *Club:* Reform.
See also J. G. Hendy.

HENEAGE, James Arthur; Managing Director, Ottakar's plc, 1988–2006; *b* 31 Oc 1957; *s* of Simon and Elizabeth Heneage; *m* 1987, Charlotte Shott; two *s* two *d*. *Edu* Worth Abbey. Commnd Grenadier Guards, 1977–82. Advertising Executive: D'Arc Macmanus Masius, 1982–84; Ogilvy & Mather, 1984–87; founded Ottakar's, 1987. Chm. Cheltenham Lit. Fest. Dir, Prince's Rainforest Project. *Recreations:* history, cartoonin playing piano in a band, Tintin. *Address:* Buddens House, Bowerchalke, Salisbury, Wilt SP5 5BN.

HENES, John Derek; Head, UK Delegation to UK/French Channel Tunne Intergovernmental Commission, 1997–2006; *b* 8 June 1937; *s* of Frederick Willia Kingaby Henes and Joan Elizabeth Henes (*née* Colbourne); *m* 1981, Virginia Elizabet Evans; one *s* one *d*. *Educ:* Christ's Hospital; Gonville and Caius College, Cambridge (MA) Ministry of Aviation, 1963; Dept of Trade, 1971; Private Sec. to Christopher Chataway 1973–74, to Lord Beswick, 1974–75; Asst Sec., 1975; Dept of Transport, 1983–96; Unde Sec., 1989. *Recreations:* reading, music, walking the dog. *Address:* 1e Cambridge Road Twickenham, Middx TW1 2HN.

HENHAM, His Honour John Alfred; a Circuit Judge, 1983–95; *b* 8 Sept. 1924; *s* of Alfred and Daisy Henham; *m* 1946, Suzanne Jeanne Octavie Ghislaine Pinchart (*d* 1972); two *s*. Stipendiary Magistrate for S Yorks, 1975–82; a Recorder of the Crown Court, 1979–82.

HENIG, family name of **Baroness Henig**.

HENIG, Baroness *cr* 2004 (Life Peer), of Lancaster in the County of Lancashire; **Ruth Beatrice Henig,** CBE 2000; DL; PhD; Chairman, Security Industry Authority, since 2007; *b* 10 Nov. 1943; *d* of Kurt and Elfriede Munzer; *m* 1st, 1966, Stanley Henig, *qv* (marr. diss. 1993); two *s*; 2nd, 1994, Jack Johnstone. *Educ:* Wyggeston Girls' Grammar Sch., Leicester; Bedford Coll., London (BA Hons 1st cl. (Hist.) 1965); Lancaster Univ. (PhD 1978). Lancaster University: Lectr, then Sen. Lectr, in Hist., 1968–2002; Hd, Hist. Dept, 1995–97; Dean, Arts and Humanities, 1997–2000. Mem. (Lab) Lancaster E, 1981–2005, Chm., 1999–2000, Lancs CC. Chm., Lancs Police Authy, 1995–2005. Chm., Assoc. Police Authorities, 1997–2005. DL Lancs, 2002. *Publications:* The League of Nations, 1973; Versailles and After, 1984, 2nd edn 1995; Origins of the Second World War, 1985; Origins of the First World War, 1989, 3rd edn 2002; (with Chris Culpin) Europe 1870–1945, 1997; The Weimar Republic, 1998; (with Simon Henig) Women and Political Power, 2000. *Recreations:* bridge, fell-walking, real ale, wine appreciation, gardening, travel. *Address:* House of Lords, SW1A 0PW; Roeburn House, Wray, Lancaster LA2 8QD. *T:* (01524) 221280; *e-mail:* ruthhenig@aol.com. *Club:* Lancaster Bridge.

HENIG, Prof. Stanley; Professor of European Politics, 1982–97 and Head of Department of European Studies, 1990–97, University of Central Lancashire (formerly Preston, then Lancashire, Polytechnic); Deputy Pro-Chancellor, University of Lancaster, since 2006; *b* 7 July 1939; *s* of Sir Mark Henig and Grace (*née* Cohen); *m* 1st, 1966, Ruth Beatrice Munzer (*see* Baroness Henig) (marr. diss. 1993); two *s*; 2nd, 2002, Christine Carole Swann. *Educ:* Wyggeston Grammar Sch.; Corpus Christi Coll., Oxford. BA 1st Cl. Hons, 1961; MA 1965 Oxon. Teaching Asst, Dept of Politics, Univ. of Minnesota, 1961; Research Student, Nuffield Coll., 1962; Lecturer in Politics, Lancaster Univ., 1964–66; MP (Lab) Lancaster, 1966–70; Lectr in Politics, Warwick Univ., 1970–71; Lectr, Civil Service Coll., 1972–75; Preston, subseq. Lancashire, Polytechnic: Head of Div. of Social Admin, later Sch. of Social Studies, 1976–82; Dean, Faculty of Social Studies, 1985–90. Sen. Res. Fellow, Federal Trust, 2001–. Mem., Lancaster CC, 1981–99 (Leader, 1991–99); Dep. Ldr, Lab. Gp, ADC, 1995–97; Sec., Lab. Gp, LGA, 1997–99. Governor, British Inst. of Recorded Sound, 1975–80. Secretary: Historic Masters Ltd, 1983–; Historic Singers Trust, 1985–. Chm., Court, RNCM, 1986–89. Asst Editor, Jl of Common Market Studies, 1964–72, Editor, 1973–76. *Publications:* (ed) European Political Parties, 1969; External Relations of the European Community, 1971; (ed) Political Parties in the European Community, 1979; Power and Decision in Europe, 1980; Uniting of Europe, 1997; (jtly) Enrico Caruso—Recollections and Retrospective, 1999; (ed) The Kosovo Crisis, 2001; (ed) Modernizing Britain: central, devolved, federal, 2002; Modernising British Government: constitutional challenges and federal solutions, 2006. *Recreation:* collector of old gramophone records. *Address:* 10 Yealand Drive, Lancaster LA1 4EW. *T:* (01524) 69624.

HENLEY, 8th Baron *cr* 1799 (Ire.); **Oliver Michael Robert Eden;** Baron Northington (UK) 1885; *b* 22 Nov. 1953; *er s* of 7th Baron Henley and of Nancy Mary, *d* of Stanley Walton, Gilsland, Cumbria; *S* father, 1977; *m* 1984, Caroline Patricia, *d* of A. G. Sharp, Mackney, Oxon; three *s* one *d*. *Educ:* Clifton; Durham Univ. (BA 1975). Called to the Bar, Middle Temple, 1977. A Lord in Waiting (Govt Whip), 1989; Parliamentary Under-Secretary of State: DSS, 1989–93; Dept of Employment, 1993–94; MoD, 1994–95; Minister of State, DFEE, 1995–97; Opposition spokesman on home affairs, 1997–98, on legal affairs, 2005–; Opposition Chief Whip, H of L, 1998–2001; elected Mem., H of L, 1999. Mem., Cumbria CC, 1986–89. Chm., Penrith and the Border Conservative Assoc., 1987–89. Pres., Cumbria Assoc. of Local Councils, 1981–89. Pres., Cumbria Trust for Nature Conservation, 1988–89. *Heir: s* Hon. John Michael Oliver Eden, *b* 30 June 1988. *Address:* Scaleby Castle, Carlisle, Cumbria CA6 4LN. *Clubs:* Brooks's; Pratt's.

HENLEY, Rt Rev. Michael Harry George, CB 1991; Bishop of St Andrews, Dunkeld and Dunblane, 1995–2004; *b* 16 Jan. 1938; *s* of Eric Edward Henley and Evelyn Agnes Henley (*née* Lilly); *m* 1965, Rachel Jean (*née* Allen); two *d*. *Educ:* St Marylebone Grammar Sch.; St John's Hall, London (LTh). Ordained deacon, 1961, priest, 1962; Curate, St Marylebone Parish Ch, 1961–64; Chaplain: RN, 1964–68; St Andrews Univ., 1968–72; Royal Hosp. Sch., 1972–74; RN, 1974–93 (Chaplain of the Fleet, Archdeacon for RN and Dir Gen. Naval Chaplaincy Services, 1989–93; Archdeacon Emeritus of the Fleet); Priest i/c, Holy Trinity, Pitlochry, 1994–95. Hon. Canon, Holy Trinity Cathedral, Gibraltar, 1989–93. QHC 1989–93. *Recreations:* golf, fishing. *Address:* West Chattan, Mavis Haugh, 108 Hepburn Gardens, St Andrews, Fife KY16 9LT. *Clubs:* Army and Navy; Royal and Ancient Golf (St Andrews).

HENMAN, Timothy Henry, OBE 2004; tennis player; *b* 6 Sept. 1974; *s* of Anthony and Jane Henman; *m* 1999, Lucy, *d* of Prof. Richard John, (Bill), Heald, *qv*; three *d*. *Educ:* Reeds Sch., Cobham. Professional tennis player, 1993–2007; Mem., British Davis Cup Team, 1995–2004, 2007. Winner: Nat. Championships, 1995, 1996, 1997, (doubles) 1999; Silver Medal (doubles), Olympic Games, 1996; Sydney Internat. Tournament, 1997; President's Cup, Tashkent, 1997, 1998; Swiss Indoor Championships, (doubles) 1997, 1998, 2001; Monte Carlo Open, (doubles) 1999, 2004; CA Trophy, Vienna, 2000; Samsung Open, Brighton, 2000; Copenhagen Open, 2001; Australian Hardcourt Championships, 2002; Legg Mason Classic, Washington, 2003; BNP Paribas Masters, Paris, 2003. Most Improved Player of the Year Award, ATP, 1996. *Address:* c/o IMG, McCormack House, Burlington Lane, W4 2TH.

HENN, Charles Herbert; Assistant Under Secretary of State, Ministry of Defence, 1979–88; *b* 11 July 1931; *s* of Herbert George Henn and Ellen Anne Henn; *m* 1955, Ann Turner; one *s* one *d*. *Educ:* King's Coll. Sch., Wimbledon; Queen's Coll., Oxford (BA). National Service, REME, 1952–54 (2/Lieut). Scientific Officer, WO, 1954; Sen. Scientific Officer, 1957; Principal, 1964; Private Sec. to Minister of State for Defence, 1969; Asst Sec., 1972. *Recreations:* walking, running, listening to music.

HENNESSY, family name of **Baron Windlesham**.

HENNESSY, Sir James (Patrick Ivan), KBE 1982 (OBE 1968; MBE 1959); CMG 1975; HM Diplomatic Service, retired; *b* 26 Sept. 1923; *s* of late Richard George Hennessy, DSO, MC; *m* 1947, Patricia, *o d* of late Wing Comdr F. H. Unwin, OBE; five *d* (one *s* decd). *Educ:* Bedford Sch.; King's Coll., Newcastle; Sidney Sussex Coll., Cambridge; LSE. Served RA, 1942–44; seconded IA, 1944–46, Adjt and Battery Comdr, 6th Indian Field Regt. Apptd to HM Overseas Service, Basutoland, District Officer, 1948; Judicial Comr, 1953; Dist Comr, 1954–56; Jt Sec., Constitutional Commn, 1957–59; Supervisor of Elections, 1959; Sec. to Exec. Council, 1960; seconded to Office of High Comr, Cape Town/Pretoria, 1961–63; Perm. Sec. for local govt, 1964; MLC, 1965; Sec. for External Affairs, Defence and Internal Security, 1967; Prime Minister's Office, 1968. Retired, later apptd to HM Diplomatic Service; FO, 1968–70; Chargé d'Affaires, Montevideo, 1971–72; High Comr to Uganda and Ambassador (non-resident), Rwanda, 1973–76; Consul-Gen., Cape Town, 1977–80; Governor and C-in-C, Belize, 1980–81; HM Chief Inspector of Prisons for England and Wales, 1982–87. Mem., Parole Bd, 1988–91. Trustee, Butler Trust, 1988–98. *Address:* Slogarie House, by Castle Douglas, DG7 2NL. *Club:* Royal Commonwealth Society.

HENNESSY, Brig. Mary Brigid Teresa, (Rita), CBE 1988 (MBE 1967); RRC 1982; Matron-in-Chief, Queen Alexandra's Royal Army Nursing Corps, 1985–89 and Director of Defence Nursing Service, 1986–89; *b* 27 Jan. 1933; *d* of late Bartholomew and Nora Agnes Hennessy. *Educ:* Convent of Mercy, Ennis, Co. Clare; Whittington Hosp., Highgate, London; Victoria Maternity Hosp., Barnet. SRN; SCM. Joined QARANC, 1959; service in Britain, Singapore, Malaya, Germany; various hosp. appts, 1959–74; seconded to office of Chargé d'affaires, Peking, 1965–67; Dep. Matron, Hongkong, 1976; Lt-Col 1979; Col 1982; Brig., Matron-in-Chief and Dir of Army Nursing Services, 1985. QHNS 1985–89. *Recreations:* music, theatre, gardening.

HENNESSY, Patrick James; Political Editor, Sunday Telegraph, since 2004; *b* 10 July 1963; *s* of Thomas Michael Hennessy and Elizabeth Anne Hennessy; *m* 2000, Kate Giemre; one *s* one *d*. *Educ:* Colet Court Sch.; Eton Coll.; Lady Margaret Hall, Oxford (BA Hons 1985). Reporter: Express and Echo, Exeter, 1985–88; The Sun, 1988–92; Political Corresp., Daily Express, 1992–96; Dep. Political Ed., Evening Standard, 1996–2004. Judge, Spectator Parliamentarian of Year Awards, 2006–. *Recreations:* football, music, reading. *Address:* c/o Sunday Telegraph, Press Gallery, House of Commons, SW1A 0AA. *T:* (020) 7219 6116; *e-mail:* patrick.hennessy@telegraph.co.uk. *Club:* Chelsea Football.

HENNESSY, Prof. Peter John, FBA 2003; FRHistS; AcSS; Attlee Professor of Contemporary British History, since 2001, and Director, Mile End Institute of Contemporary British Government, Intelligence and Society, since 2006, Queen Mary, University of London; *b* 28 March 1947; *s* of William Gerald and Edith Hennessy; *m* 1969, Enid Mary Candler; two *d*. *Educ:* Marling Sch., Stroud; St John's Coll., Cambridge (BA 1969), PhD Cantab 1990; LSE (Hon. Fellow, 2000); Harvard, 1971–72 (Kennedy Meml Scholar). FRHistS 1993. Reporter, THES, 1972–74, The Times, 1974–76; Lobby corresp., Financial Times, 1976; Whitehall corresp., The Times, 1976–82; journalist, The Economist, 1982; home leader writer and columnist, The Times, 1982–84; columnist: New Statesman, 1986–87; The Independent, 1987–91; Director, 1989–93; The Tablet, 2003–; Prof. of Contemporary History, QMW, Univ. of London, 1992–2000; Chm., Kennedy Meml Trust, 1995–2000. Co-Founder and Co-Dir, 1986–89, Mem. Bd, 1989–98, Inst. of Contemporary British Hist. (Hon. Fellow, 1995). Vis. Prof. of Govt, Strathclyde Univ., 1989–2004; Gresham Prof. of Rhetoric, 1994–97; Vis. Lectr, Dept of Politics, Univ. of Strathclyde, 1983–84 (Hon. Res. Fellow, 1985–89); Visiting Fellow: Policy Studies Inst., 1986–91 (Sen. Fellow, 1984–85; Council Mem., 1991–97); Univ. Depts of Politics, Reading 1988–94, Nottingham 1989–95; RIPA, 1989–92; Hon. Res. Fellow, Dept of Politics and Sociology, Birkbeck Coll., London, 1990–91; Vis. Scholar, Centre for Australian Public Sector Management, Griffith Univ., Brisbane, 1991. Member: Steering Gp, Sharman Review of Audit and Accountability for Central Govt, 2000–01; Cabinet Office Adv. Gp on Security and Intelligence Records, 2004–. Vice-President: Politics Assoc., 1985–90; RHistS, 1996–2000; Pres., Johnian Soc., 1995. Trustee: Attlee Foundn, 1985–98 (Patron, 1998–); Geffrye Mus., 2002–04; Orwell Meml Trust, 2002–04. Mem. Bd, Inst. of Histl Res., 1992–97; Mem. Council, Gresham Coll., 1996–97 (Fellow, 1997); Gov., Ditchley Foundn, 2001–. Dir, The Tablet, 2003–. FRSA 1992. Founding AcSS, 1999. Presenter: Under Fire, TV, 1985–87; Radio 4 Analysis programme, 1986–92; writer and presenter, What Has Become of Us, TV, 1994; numerous other radio and TV productions. Curator, Secret State exhibn, Nat. Archives, 2004. Hon. Fellow, St Benet's Hall, Oxford, 2008. Hon. DLitt: Univ. of W England, 1995; Univ. of Westminster, 1996; Kingston, 1998; Strathclyde, 2005. *Publications:* (with Keith Jeffery) States of Emergency, 1983; (with Michael Cockerell and David Walker) Sources Close to the Prime Minister, 1984; What the Papers Never Said, 1985; Cabinet, 1986; (ed with Anthony Seldon) Ruling Performance, 1987; Whitehall, 1989, rev. edn 2001; Never Again: Britain, 1945–51, 1992 (Duff Cooper Prize, 1993; NCR Book Award for Non-Fiction, 1993); The Hidden Wiring: unearthing the British Constitution, 1995; Muddling Through: power, politics and the quality of government in postwar Britain, 1996; The Prime Minister: the office and its holders since 1945, 2000; The Secret State, 2002; Having It So Good: Britain in the fifties (Orwell Prize for Political Writing), 2006; (ed) The New Protective State: government, intelligence and terrorism, 2007; Cabinets and the Bomb, 2007. *Recreations:* reading, listening to music, searching for the British Constitution, watching West Ham. *Address:* Department of History, Queen Mary, Mile End Road, E1 4NS. *T:* (020) 7882 8350. *Clubs:* Savile, Grillions.

HENNESSY, Richard Patrick, FCA; Chief Financial Officer, The Really Useful Group Ltd, since 2004; *b* 16 Nov. 1953; *s* of Graham Harold Hennessy and Dolores Hennessy (*née* Ellul); *m* 1979, Angela Carthew; one *s* one *d*. *Educ:* Newcastle Univ. (BA Hons Econs and Accounting). FCA 1979. Manager, Peat Marwick Mitchell, London, 1976–80; Sen. Manager, Peat Marwick Mitchell & Co., Hong Kong, 1980–82; Gp Financial Accountant, Hongkong & Shanghai Banking Corp. Ltd, 1982–84; Financial Controller, Saudi British Bank, 1984–88; Sen. Gp Financial Accountant, Hongkong & Shanghai Banking Corp. Ltd, 1988–92; Gp Chief Accountant, HSBC Holdings plc, 1992–95; Chief Financial Officer, Midland, subseq. HSBC, Bank plc, 1996–2003. Mem. Banking Sub-Cttee, ICAEW, 1993–2003. Mem., Soc. of London Theatre, 2004–. *Recreations:* family, motor sport, music, walking, swimming. *Address:* (office) 22 Tower Street, WC2H 9TW.

HENNIG, Dr Georg, Hon. LVO 1969; Austrian Ambassador to the UK, 1993–96; retired, 1999; *b* 3 Sept. 1937; *s* of late Max Hennig and Eva (*née* Weinberger); *m* 1968, Ilona Esterhazy; one *s*. *Educ:* Schottengymnasium, Vienna; Univ. of Vienna (Dr jur 1960); Bologna Centre, Sch. of Advanced Internat. Studies, Johns Hopkins Univ. (Dip.). Protocol Div., Legal Dept, Federal Min. for Foreign Affairs, Vienna, 1961–63; Perm. Mission to UN, NY, 1963–66; Personal Asst to Foreign Minister, 1966–70; First Sec., Madrid, 1970–71; Sen. Dir, Office of Sec.-Gen. of UN, 1972–75; Minister, Hd of Office of Sec.-Gen. for Foreign Affairs, Vienna, 1976–79; Ambassador to: India, and accredited to Bangladesh, Sri Lanka and Nepal, 1979–83; Japan, and accredited to Republic of Korea, 1983–86; Special Advr to Federal Pres. of Austria, 1987–92; Ambassador at Federal Min. for Foreign Affairs, Vienna, 1992–93. Dir Gen., Office of Federal Pres., Austria, 1996–99. Grand Decoration of Honour in Gold (Austria), 1992. *Recreations:* reading, shooting. *Address:* Akademiestrasse 2, 1010 Vienna, Austria. *Club:* St Johann's (Vienna).

HENNIKER, 9th Baron *cr* 1800 (Ire.); **Mark Ian Philip Chandos Henniker-Major;** Bt 1765; Baron Hartismere (UK) 1866; *b* 29 Sept. 1947; *s* of 8th Baron Henniker and Margaret Osla (*née* Benning); *S* father, 2004; *m* 1st, 1973, Lesley Antoinette Masterton-Smith (*née* Foskett) (marr. diss. 1995); one *s* three *d* (and one *s* decd); 2nd, 1996, Bente Tofte. *Educ:* Eton; Trinity Coll., Cambridge (MA); LLM (London). FCIArb; MRAeS. Solicitor. *Heir: s* Hon. Edward George Major Henniker-Major, *b* 1985.

HENNIKER, Sir Adrian Chandos, 9th Bt *cr* 1813, of Newton Hall, Essex; *b* 18 Oct. 1946; *s* of Brig. Sir Mark Chandos Auberon Henniker, 8th Bt, CBE, DSO, MC and Kathleen Denys (*d* 1998), *d* of John Anderson; *S* father, 1991, but his name does not appear on the Official Roll of the Baronetage; *m* 1971, Ann, *d* of Stuart Britton; twin *d*. *Educ:* Marlborough. *Heir:* none. *Address:* The Coach House, Llwyndu, Abergavenny, Gwent NP7 7HG.

HENNIKER HEATON, Sir Yvo Robert; *see* Heaton.

HENNIKER-MAJOR, family name of **Baron Henniker**.

HENRIQUES, Hon. Sir Richard (Henry Quixano), Kt 2000; **Hon. Mr Justice Henriques;** a Judge of the High Court of Justice, Queen's Bench Division, since 2000; Presiding Judge, North Eastern Circuit, 2001–04; *b* 27 Oct. 1943; *s* of late Cecil Quixano Henriques and Doreen Mary Henriques; *m* Joan Hilary, (Toni), (*née* Senior); one *s* and one step *s*. *Educ:* Bradfield Coll., Berks; Worcester Coll., Oxford (BA). Called to the Bar, Inner Temple, 1967; Bencher, 1994. A Recorder, 1983–2000; QC 1986; Mem., Northern Circuit (Leader, 1995–98). Member: Gen. Council of the Bar, 1993–98; Criminal Justice Liaison Cttee, 1993–95; Northern Circuit Exec. Cttee, 1993–98. Council Mem., Rossall Sch., 1985–95. *Recreations:* bridge, golf, the Turf. *Address:* Royal Courts of Justice, Strand, WC2A 2LL. *Club:* Royal Lytham and St Anne's Golf.

HENRY, Rt Hon. Sir Denis (Robert Maurice), Kt 1986; PC 1993; a Lord Justice of Appeal, 1993–2002; *b* 19 April 1931; *o s* of late Brig. Maurice Henry and Mary Catherine (*née* Irving); *m* 1963, Linda Gabriel Arthur; one *s* one *d* (and one *d* decd). *Educ:* Shrewsbury; Balliol Coll., Oxford (MA). 2nd Lieut, KORR, 1950–51. Called to the Bar, Inner Temple, 1955, Bencher, 1985; QC 1977; a Recorder, 1979–86; a Judge of the High Court, QBD, 1986–93. Chm., Judicial Studies Bd, 1994–99. Part-time Tutor, New Coll., Oxford, 1985–90. Mem., Civil Justice Council, 1998–99. *Recreation:* golf. *Address:* c/o Royal Courts of Justice, Strand, WC2A 2LL.

HENRY, Prof. (Diana) Kristin, (Mrs G. G. Blakey), FRCP, FRCPath; Professor of Histopathology, Imperial College School of Medicine (formerly Charing Cross and Westminster Medical School), London University, 1987–98, now Emeritus Professor; Hon. Consultant Pathologist, Charing Cross Hospital, since 1984; *b* 13 Dec. 1934; *d* of late Colin Neil Thorburn Henry and of Vera (*née* Christensen); *m* 1st, 1960, Charles Michael Yates (marr. diss.); 2nd, 1967, George Gavin Blakey; one *s* one *d*. *Educ:* Malvern Girls' Coll.; St Thomas's Hosp. (MB BS). MRCP 1963, FRCP 1982; MRCPath 1965, FRCPath 1977. Junior appts at Lambeth Hosp., Chelsea Hosp. for Women and Brompton Hosp., 1956–64; Res. Registrar, Bd of Governors, Hosp. of Diseases of the Chest, 1964–66; MRC Fellow in Immunology, Middx Hosp., 1966–69; Reader, 1974–82, Prof. of Histopathology, 1982–84, Westminster Med. Sch., London Univ.; Prof. of Histopathology, Charing Cross & Westminster Med. Sch., 1984–87. Mem., Editl Bd, Histopathology, 1975–2003; Founding Ed., Current Diagnostic Pathology, 1993–; Asst Ed., Internat. Jl of Surgical Pathology, 1999–. External Examiner in Final Examination in Pathology to: Leicester Univ., 1987–89; UMDS, 1990–92; RCSI Med. Sch., 1993–96; Birmingham Univ. Med. Sch., 1996–99. British Council Lectr and Foundn Lectr to Coll. of Pathologists, Sri Lanka, 1987; First Cooray Meml Oration and Gold Medal, Sri Lanka, 1987; First Daphne Attegale Meml Oration and Gold Medal, Sri Lanka, 1998. Member: Thymic Tumour Panel, MRC, 1974–79; Pathology Panel, Brit. Nat. Lymphoma Investigation, MRC, 1975–87 (Expert Pathologist representing BNLI in Nat. Cancer Inst. (USA) study of lymphomas, 1976–81 (report pubd 1982)). Mem., Kettering Prize Award Cttee, Gen. Motors Cancer Res. Foundn, 1981–82. Founder Member: British Lymphoma Pathology Gp, 1974–; Eur. Bone Marrow Pathology Gp, 1992–; Member: Eur. Assoc. Haematopathology, 1986–; Melanoma Study Gp, 1989–. Treas., 1981–94, Pres., 1994–96, Cunningham Gold Medal, British Div., Internat. Acad. of Pathology; Vice-Pres. for Europe, Internat. Acad. of Pathology, 1999– (Chm., Educn Cttee, 2000–); Founder, Arab British Sch. of Pathology, 2001. *Publications:* (contrib.) Pathology of Myasthenia Gravis, 1969; Systematic Pathology, vol. 7: 2nd edn, The Thymus Gland (contrib.), 1978; 3rd edn, The Thymus, Lymph Nodes, Spleen and Lymphatics (ed with W. St C. Symmers and contrib.), 1992; (with G. Farrer-Brown) A Colour Atlas of Thymus and Lymph Node Pathology with Ultrastructure, 1981; (contrib.) The Human Thymus in Disease, 1981; (contrib.) Ultrastructure of the Small Intestine, 1982; (contrib.) Bone Marrow Transplantation in Mucopolysaccharidoses, 1984; contrib. to: Recent Advances in Pathology, 9th edn 1975, 10th edn 1978; Recent Results in Cancer Research, 1978; numerous contribs to learned jls in field of haematopathology (incl. Lymphoma Study Gp pubns), and oncology. *Recreations:* painting, driving, animal welfare. *Address:* Imperial College London at Charing Cross Hospital, Fulham Palace Road, W6 8RF. *T:* (020) 8846 7133; Quorn House, Hingham, Norfolk NR9 4AF. *T:* (01953) 851475. *Club:* Royal Over-Seas League.

HENRY, Sir Geoffrey (Arama), KBE 1992; Deputy Prime Minister, Cook Islands, 2002 and 2004–05 (Prime Minister, 1983, and 1989–99); *b* Aitutaki, Cook Is, 16 Nov. 1940; *s* of Arama Henry and Mata Uritaua; *m* 1965, Louisa Olga Hoff; three *s* two *d* (and one *s* decd). *Educ:* St George's Prep. Sch., Wanganui, NZ; Wanganui Collegiate Sch.; Victoria Univ., Wellington, NZ (BA English and Educn). School Teacher, 1965–67; entered politics, 1965–68; public service, 1970–72; returned to politics, and Cabinet Minister, 1972–78; Leader of Opposition, 1978–83, 1983–84; Dep. Prime Minister in Coalition Govt, 1984; Leader of Opposition, 1985–89, 1999–2002, 2003–04. Chm., Standing Cttee, Pacific Is Develt Prog. (EWC), 1989; Organiser, Jt Commercial Commn, USA and Pacific Is, 1990; Chm., Econ. Summit of Small Island States, 1992. Chancellor, Univ. of S Pacific, 1992. Chambellan de l'Ordre des Coteaux de Champagne, 1991. Silver Jubilee Medal, 1977; NZ Commemoration Medal, 1990. *Recreations:* golf, Rugby, Rugby league, other sports, reading, music. *Address:* PO Box 281, Rarotonga, Cook Islands. *Clubs:* Rarotonga Golf, Rarotonga Bowling, Rarotonga Fishing, Lions, Rarotonga (Cook Islands).

HENRY, Hugh; Member (Lab) Paisley South, Scottish Parliament, since 1999; *b* 12 Feb. 1952; *s* of Joseph and Mary Henry; *m* Jacqueline (*née* Muldoon); one *s* two *d*. *Educ:* Glasgow Univ. (BAcc). Worked in accountancy, teaching and social work. Member (Lab): Renfrew DC, 1985–96; Renfrewshire Council, 1995–99 (Leader, 1995–99). Scottish Executive: Dep. Minister for Health and Community Care, 2001–02, for Social Justice, 2002–03, for Justice, 2003–07; Minister for Educn and Young People, 2007; Convenor, European Cttee, Scottish Parlt, 1999–. Mem., Cttee of the Regions, EU. *Address:* Scottish Parliament, Edinburgh EH99 1SP.

HENRY, John Philip; Chairman, Cheltenham Civic Society, since 2001; non-executive Director and Vice-Chairman, Gloucestershire Hospitals NHS Trust, since 2002; *b* 8 Oct. 1946; *s* of late L. Henry, MD, FRCS and P. M. Henry, MB, ChB; *m* 1992, Gillian Mary Richardson; one *s* one *d*. *Educ:* Cheltenham Coll.; Queen's Coll., Oxford (MA). Psychologist, Road Research Lab., 1968; Admin Trainee, DoE, 1972; Principal, 1976; Private Sec., Minister for Housing and Construction, 1981–83; Asst Sec., 1983–89; Regl Dir, Yorks and Humberside Regl Office, Depts of the Envmt and Transport, 1990–94; Prin. Finance Officer, Property Hldgs, DoE, 1994–95; Hd of Agencies Gp, OPS, Cabin Office, 1995–96. Non-exec. Dir, E Glos NHS Trust, 2000–02. Chm., Holst Birthpla Trust, 1999–2001. Chm. Govs, St James' Primary Sch., Cheltenham, 2001–. *Recreatio* arts, architecture, literature. *Address:* 19 Montpellier Terrace, Cheltenham, Glos GL 1UX.

HENRY, Rt Hon. John (Steele), DCNZM 2001; PC (NZ) 1996; Judge, Court Appeal, New Zealand, 1995–2000; *b* 3 July 1932; *s* of Hon. Sir Trevor Ernest Henry ar Audrey Kate (*née* Sheriff); *m* 1957, Jennefer Lynne Stevenson; one *s* two *d*. *Educ:* King Coll., Auckland; Auckland Univ. (LLB 1955). QC (NZ) 1980; High Court Judg 1984–95. Commemoration Medal (NZ), 1990. *Recreations:* fishing, tramping. *Address:* 3 Riddell Road, Glendowie, Auckland 1071, New Zealand. *T:* (9) 5758526. *Cl* Northern (Auckland).

HENRY, Keith Nicholas, FREng; Chairman, Regal Petroleum plc, since 2008; *b* March 1945; *s* of Kenneth G. Henry and Barbara Henry; *m* 1974, Susan Mary Horsburg two *d*. *Educ:* Bedford Sch.; London Univ. (BSc Hons Civil Engrg (ext.) 1967 Birmingham Univ. (MSc Foundn Engrg 1969). With Internat. Mgt and Engrg Gp Lt 1969–71; Project Engr, then Manager, Brown & Root, 1971–77; Engrg Manager, Brow & Root Far East, 1977–80; Brown & Root (UK) Ltd: Engrg Manager, 1980–8 Commercial Dir, 1984–85; Technical Dir and Chief Engr, 1985–88; Managing Directo Brown & Root Vickers Ltd, 1987–89; Brown & Root Marine, 1989; Chief Executiv Brown & Root Ltd, 1990–95; Nat. Power plc, 1995–99; Gp Exec. Vice-Pres. and Chi Exec., Engrg and Construction, Kvaerner E&C PLC, 2000–03; Dep. Chm., Petroleur Geo Services ASA, 2003–06; Chm., Burren Energy plc, 2006–08 (Dir, 2005–08); Chm Petrojarl ASA, 2006. Non-executive Director: Enterprise Oil, 1995–2002; Emera Energy plc, 2004–; South East Water Ltd, 2005–07; High Point-Rendel Ltd, 2006–; Fir Calgary Petroleums Ltd, 2008–. FREng (FEng 1988). *Recreations:* shooting, sailin *Address:* (office) Regal Petroleum plc, 11 Berkeley Street, W1J 8DS; *e-mail:* keithhenry(btinternet.com. *Club:* Royal Automobile.

HENRY, Dr Kenneth Ross, AC 2007; Secretary to the Treasury, Department of th Treasury, Australia, since 2001; *b* 27 Nov. 1957; *s* of John Desmond Henry and Heath Audrey McKay; *m* 1979, Naomi Jayne Smith; one *s* one *d*. *Educ:* Chatham High Sch Taree; Univ. of New South Wales (BCom Hons); Univ. of Canterbury, NZ (PhD Econs Res. Officer, Australian Bureau of Stats, 1979–80; Asst Lectr, 1980–81, Lectr, 1982–8 Univ. of Canterbury, NZ; Department of the Treasury, Australia: Sen. Finance Office 1984–85, Chief Finance Officer, 1985–86, Taxation Policy Div.; Private Sec., Office Treas., 1986–89; Sen. Advr to Treas., 1989–91; Principal Advr, 1991–92; Minister (Eco and Financial Affairs), Australian Delegn to OECD, Paris, 1992–93; First Asst Sec Taxation Policy Div., 1994–97; Chair, Taxation Taskforce, 1997–98; Exec. Dir, Eco Gp, 1998–2001. Mem., Econ. Soc. of Australia, 1999. *Recreations:* care of native faun reading, music. *Address:* The Treasury, Langton Crescent, Parkes, ACT 2600, Australi *Club:* Commonwealth (Canberra).

HENRY, Kristin; *see* Henry, D. K.

HENRY, Lenworth George, (Lenny), CBE 1999; stand-up comedian, since 197 actor; *b* 29 Aug. 1958; *s* of late Winston Henry and Winifred Henry; *m* 1984, Dawn R French; one adopted *d*. *Educ:* Bluecoat Secondary Mod. Sch.; W. R. Tewson Sch Preston Coll.; BA Open Univ. Trustee, Comic Relief, 1987–. Won New Faces Tale Show, 1975; stand-up show, Have You Seen This Man, tour, 2001–02; So Much Thing To Say, Wyndhams, 2003; Where You From?, tour, 2007; *TV appearances* includ Fosters, 1976–77; Tiswas, 1978–81; 3 of a Kind, 1981–84; The Lenny Henry Show, 198 1985, 1987, 1988, 1995, 2004; Lenny Henry Tonight, 1986; Xmas Specials, 1987, 198 1994, 1995; Chef, 1992, 1994, 1996; Lenny's Big Amazon Adventure, 1997; Lenny Go to Town, 1998; Hope and Glory, 1999, 2000; Lenny's Big Atlantic Adventure, 200 Lenny Henry in Pieces, 2002, 2003; This Is My Life, 2003; Lenny's Britain, Lenny Henr So Much Things to Say, 2007; *films:* Coast to Coast, 1984; Work Experience, 1989; Aliv and Kicking, 1990; True Identity, 1990. Lifetime Achievement Award, British Comed Awards, 2003. *Publications:* Quest for the Big Woof; Charlie and the Big Chill, 1995; (jtly Charlie, Queen of the Desert, 1996. *Recreations:* huge fan of R'n'B, hiphop, funk, avi reader, tennis, comics, enjoying my family. *Address:* c/o PBJ Management Ltd, 7 Soh Street, W1D 3DQ. *T:* (020) 7287 1112. *Clubs:* Groucho, Soho House.

HENRY, Patricia; *see* Robertson, P.

HENRY, Sir Patrick (Denis), 3rd Bt *cr* 1923, of Cahore, co. Londonderry; businessma *b* 20 Dec. 1957; *s* of Denis Valentine Henry (*d* 1983), *yr s* of 1st Bt, and of Elizabeth Henr (*née* Walker); *S* uncle, 1997, but his name does not appear on the Official Roll of th Baronetage; *m* 1997, Georgina Ravenscroft (marr. diss.). *Educ:* Corpus Christi Coll. Oxford (BA (Hons) Modern History 1978). *Club:* Blackburn Rovers.

HENRY, Wendy Ann; Foster Dog Co-ordinator, Battersea Dogs' and Cats' Home, sinc 2001; *d* of Bernard and Elsa Henry; *m* 1980, Tim Miles; one *d*. *Educ:* Queen Mary School Lytham. Reporter, Daily Mail, Manchester, 1975–76, News of the World, 1976–79 Features Editor, Woman Magazine, 1979–81; Asst Editor, The Sun, 1981–85; Editor Sunday Magazine, 1985–86; The News of the World, 1986–88; Dep. Editor, The Sun 1988; Editor, The People, 1988–89; Ed.-in-Chief, The Globe, Florida, 1990–93; Man Ed., current affairs TV Prog., 1993–95; Ed., weekend section, Daily News, NY, 1995–97 Ed.-in-Chief, Successful Slimming, and Editl Dir, New Publications, Glob Communications, USA, 1997–99; Ed., Real Homes mag., 1999–2001; Launch Ed., Parkhill Publishing, 2001. Mem., Women in Journalism. *Recreations:* husband, dogs sleeping. *Address:* c/o Battersea Dogs' and Cats' Home, 4 Battersea Park Road, SW8 4AA.

HENSCHEL, Ruth Mary; *see* Ashton, R. M.

HENSHALL, Dr Christopher Harry; Pro Vice-Chancellor for External Relations University of York, since 2005; *b* 16 Feb. 1954; *s* of late Henry James Henshall and Edna Geraldine Henshall (*née* Watkins). *Educ:* Barnard Castle Sch., Co. Durham; Gonville and Caius Coll., Cambridge (BA Natural Sciences 1975; PhD 1983); Univ. of Nottingham (MA in Child Development 1976). Lectr in Psychol., Univ. of Warwick, 1981–84; Res. Fellow, Univ. of Southampton, 1984–85; Prog. Dir, Health Promotion Res. Trust, 1985–88; Sec., Health Services Res. Cttee, MRC, 1988–91; Research and Development Division, Department of Health: Sen. Principal, 1991; Asst Sec., 1993; Dep. Dir, R&D, 1996–2001; Dir, Sci. and Engrg Base Gp, OST, DTI, 2001–04. Hon. Prof., Dept of Public Health and Policy, LSHTM, 2001–05. Pres., Health Technology Assessment Internat., 2003–05. *Recreations:* hill walking (Munroist number 3053), opera, music, wine. *Address:* University of York, Heslington, York YO10 5DD. *T:* (01904) 433492, *Fax:* (01904) 433490; *e-mail:* ch523@york.ac.uk.

HENSHALL, Rt Rev. Michael; Bishop Suffragan of Warrington, 1976–96; an Hon. Assistant Bishop, Diocese of York, since 1999; *b* 29 Feb. 1928; *m* Ann Elizabeth (*née* Stephenson); two *s* one *d*. *Educ:* Manchester Grammar Sch.; St Chad's Coll., Durham (BA

1954, DipTh 1956). Deacon 1956, priest 1957, dio. York; Curate of Holy Trinity, Bridlington and of Sewerby, 1956–59; Priest-in-charge, All Saints, Conventional District of Micklehurst, 1959–62; Vicar, 1962–63; Vicar of Altrincham, 1963–75; Proctor in Convocation, 1964–75; Mem., Terms of Ministry Cttee, General Synod, 1970–75; Hon. Canon of Chester, 1972–75; Secretary, Chester Diocesan Advisory Board for Ministry, 1968–75; Canon Emeritus of Chester Cathedral, 1979. Chairman: Northern Ordination Course Council, 1985–96; Churches Gp NW, Industry Year, 1985–90; Council, St Chad's Coll., Univ. of Durham, 1992–2000; Vice-Chm., National Soc., 1994–96; Mem. Council, Coll. of Preachers, 1989– (Ed., Journal, 1998–). *Publication:* Dear Nicholas, 1989. *Recreations:* military history, old battlefields, etc. *Address:* Brackenfield, 28 Hermitage Way, Eskdaleside, Sleights, Whitby, N Yorks YO22 5HG. *T:* (01947) 811233.

HENSHAW, Sir David (George), Kt 2004; Chief Executive, Liverpool City Council, 1999–2006; Chairman, North West Strategic Health Authority, since 2006; *b* 7 March 1949; *s* of George Ronald Henshaw and Irene Henshaw; *m* 1st 1978, Rosemary St C. Herbert (marr. diss. 2000); two *s*; 2nd, 2000, Alison Joy Jones. *Educ:* Sheffield Poly. (BA Public Admin 1973); Univ. of Birmingham (MScSoc 1975). Corporate Planning Officer, S Yorks MCC, 1974–84; Prin. Asst County Clerk, then Asst Chief Exec., Essex CC, 1984–89; Chief Exec., Knowsley MBC, 1989–99. Clerk to Merseyside Police Authy, 1989–2000. Dir and Dep. Chm., Mersey Partnership, 1993–2006; Mem. Bd, Improvement and Develt Agency for Local Govt, 2001–03. Exec. Chm., Reconsulting Ltd, 2007–. Non-executive Director: Albany Investment Trust plc, 2004–; Hedra plc, 2006–. Dep. Chm., Nat. Task Force on Crime Reduction, 2000–02; non-exec. Dir, Home Office Correctional Services Bd, 2002–05; Hd, Redesign of CSA, 2006–07; Member: Independent Rev. of Higher Educn Pay and Conditions, 1999; Strategy Gp, Civil Service Mgt Bd, 2002–03; Bd, Council for Museums, Libraries and Archives, 2004–06; Public Services Productivity Panel, HM Treasury, 2005–07. Advr, Prime Minister's Delivery Unit, 2001–04. Jt Chm., SOLACE Enterprises, 1998–2005; Pres., SOLACE, 2000–01. Chm., Faenol Festival Trust, 2007–. Gov., NE Wales Inst. of Higher Educn, 2008–. Fellow, Liverpool Univ., 1998; Vis. Fellow, Royal Inst. of Technol., Melbourne, Aust., 1997–2002. FRSA 2005. Hon. Fellow, Liverpool John Moores Univ., 2004. Hon Dr Sheffield Hallam, 2006. *Recreations:* golf, opera, walking. *Clubs:* Royal Automobile; Athenæum (Liverpool); Royal Liverpool Golf; Royal St Davids Golf (Harlech).

HENSHAW, Prof. Denis Lee, PhD; Professor of Physics, University of Bristol, since 1995; *b* 4 May 1946; *s* of late Frederick Henshaw and Evelyne May (*née* Fox); *m* 1994, Wassana. *Educ:* Westfield Coll., Univ. of London (BSc 1969); Univ. of Nottingham (PhD 1974). Teacher, Mundella GS, 1969–70; University of Bristol: Res. Associate, 1973–82; Res. Fellow, 1982–90; Sen. Res. Fellow, 1990–95. Dir, Track Analysis Systems Ltd, Bristol, 1984–. Member, Editorial Board: Physics in Medicine and Biol., 1994–97; Internat. Jl Radiation Biol., 1995–. *Publications:* numerous scientific papers in learned jls. *Recreations:* hot-air ballooning, Italian language and culture. *Address:* H. H. Wills Physics Laboratory, University of Bristol, Tyndall Avenue, Bristol BS8 1TL. *T:* (0117) 926 0353.

HENSHAW, Frank Charles, CBE 1993; DL; FRICS; General Manager, Milton Keynes Development Corporation, 1980–92; *b* 28 Aug. 1930; *s* of Frank and Edith Annie Henshaw; *m* 1966, Patricia Jane McDonald; one *s* one *d*. *Educ:* Towcester Grammar Sch.; Coll. of Estate Management. FRICS 1959. Nat. service, RAF, 1948–50. Quantity Surveyor: Northants CC, 1947–53; Coventry City Council, 1953–63; Prin. Quantity Surveyor, Midlands Housing Consortium, 1963–65; Chief Quantity Surveyor: Runcorn Develt Corp., 1965–70; Sheffield City Council, 1970–71; Milton Keynes Development Corporation: Chief Quantity Surveyor, 1971–74; Exec. Dir, 1974–78; Dep. Gen. Manager, 1978–80. Chm., Milton Keynes Housing Assoc., 1985–88; Dep. Chm., Central Milton Keynes Shopping Man. Co., 1978–89. Pres., Milton Keynes and N Bucks TEC, 1992–95 (Dir, 1990–92). DL Bucks, 1995. Hon. Fellow, De Montfort Univ., 1993. DUniv Open, 1994. OON 1989. *Recreations:* golf, travel. *Club:* Woburn Golf and Country.

HENSHER, Dr Philip Michael, FRSL; novelist; *b* 20 Feb. 1965; *s* of R. J. Hensher and M. Hensher. *Educ:* Tapton Sch., Sheffield; Lady Margaret Hall, Oxford (BA); Jesus Coll., Cambridge (PhD 1992). Clerk, H of C, 1990–96. Chief Book Reviewer, Spectator, 1994–; Art Critic, Mail on Sunday, 1996–; columnist, The Independent. Associate Prof. of English, Univ. of Exeter, 2005–. Mem., Booker Prize Jury, 2001. FRSL 1998 (Mem. Council, 2000–). *Publications:* Other Lulus, 1994; Kitchen Venom, 1996 (Somerset Maugham Prize); Pleasured, 1998; The Bedroom of the Master's Wife, 1999; The Mulberry Empire, 2002; The Fit, 2004; The Northern Clemency, 2008. *Recreations:* dancing, sleeping. *Address:* 83A Tennyson Street, SW8 3TH. *Club:* Trade.

HENSON, Judith Rosalind; *see* Mackrell, J. R.

HENSON, Marguerite Ann, (Mrs Nicky Henson); *see* Porter, M. A.

HENSON, Nicholas Victor Leslie, (Nicky); actor; *b* 12 May 1945; *s* of Leslie Henson and Billie Collins; *m* 1st, 1968, Una Stubbs (marr. diss.); two *s*; 2nd, 1986, Marguerite Porter, *qv*; one *s*. *Educ:* St Bede's, Eastbourne; Charterhouse. Formerly popular song writer; Founder Mem., Young Vic; first stage appearance, 1962; *London stage:* All Square, Vandeville, 1963; Camelot, Drury Lane, 1964; Passion Flower Hotel, Prince of Wales, 1965; Canterbury Tales, Phoenix, 1968; Ride Across Lake Constance, Mayfair, 1973; Hamlet, Greenwich, 1973; Midsummer Night's Dream, Regent's Park, 1973; Cinderella, Casino, 1973; Mardi Gras, Prince of Wales, 1976; Rookery Nook, Her Majesty's, 1980; Noises Off, Savoy, 1982; The Relapse, Lyric, 1983; Sufficient Carbohydrate, Albery, 1984; Journey's End, Whitehall, 1986; The Three Sisters, Royal Court, 1990; Matador, Queen's, 1991; Reflected Glory, Vaudeville, 1992; An Ideal Husband, Globe, 1993, NY, 1996, Australia, 1997; Rage, Bush, 1994; Enter the Guardsman, Donmar, 1997; Alarms and Excursions, Gielgud, 1998; Passion Play, Comedy, 2000; Frame 312, Donmar, 2002; Jumpers, Piccadilly, 2003, NY, 2004; *Young Vic:* Scapino, Waiting for Godot, She Stoops to Conquer, Taming of the Shrew, Measure for Measure, Soldier's Tale, Oedipus, Romeo and Juliet, The Maids, Look Back in Anger, Rosencrantz and Guildenstern are Dead, Charley's Aunt; *National Theatre:* Cherry Orchard, Macbeth, The Woman, The Double Dealer, A Fair Quarrel, Browning Version, Provok'd Wife, Elephant Man, Mandragola; *Royal Shakespeare Co.:* Man and Superman, Merry Wives of Windsor, As You Like It, Twelfth Night; *television series:* Life of Balzac, 1976; Seagull Island, 1981; Happy Apple, 1983; Thin Air, 1988; The Green Man, 1990; The Healer, 1994; Preston Front, 1994; Shine on Harvey Moon, 1994; Blue Dove, 2002; 30 films, incl. Vera Drake, 2004, Syriana, 2005. *Recreation:* music. *Address:* c/o Richard Stone, 2 Henrietta Street, WC2E 8PS. *T:* (020) 7497 0849; *web:* www.nickyhenson.me.uk.

HENTON, (Margaret) Patricia, FRSE; FCIWEM; CGeol, FGS; Director of Environment Protection, Environment Agency, since 2005; *b* 30 Oct. 1949; *d* of Robert Stuart Sanderson and Lois Lindsay Sanderson; *m* 1971, Richard George Henton; one *s* one *d*. *Educ:* George Watson's Coll., Edinburgh; Univ. of Manchester (BSc Hons Geol./Geog. 1970). FGS 1974; FCIWEM 1979; FCIWM 2006 (MInstWM 1981); CGeol 1990. Geologist, Associated Portland Cement Manufacturers, 1970–71; Hydrogeologist, Clyde River Purification Bd, 1972–75; Geologist, NCB Opencast Exec., 1975; Inspector, 1975–79, Hydrologist, 1979–83, Forth River Purification Bd; Associate, 1983–85, Sen. Associate, 1985–90, Dir, Scotland and NI, 1990–95, Aspinwall & Co. Ltd; Dir, Envmtl Strategy, 1995–2000, Chief Exec., 2000–02, SEPA. Dir, Scotland and NI Forum for Envmtl Res., 1996–2002. Member: Sec. of State for Scotland's Adv. Gp on Sustainable Develt, 1993–98; Regulatory Agencies Strategy Bd, DEFRA, 2003–05 (Chm., 2004–05). Chm., Adv. Panel, Forestry Commn, 2003–05; Mem. Council, NERC, 1999–2001; Additional Mem., Water Panel, Competition Commn, 1998–2000. Member: Adv. Cttee for Scotland, 2000–, Council, 2003–, RSPB. Pres., CIWEM, 1995–96. Mem., Audit Cttee, Heriot-Watt Univ., 2003–05. FRSE 2002. *Recreations:* travel, ornithology, the Levant, hill-walking, gardens. *Address:* 4 Jeffrey Avenue, Edinburgh EH4 3RW.

HENTY, Jonathan Maurice; Commissioner of Social Security and Child Support, 1993–2006; *b* 22 Dec. 1933; *s* of Richard Iltid Henty and Lettice Ellen (*née* Moore Gwyn); *m* 1st, 1956, Margaret Louise Sadler (*d* 1972); one *s* one *d* (and one *s* decd); 2nd, 1977, Veronica Mary Francis Miller; two *d*. *Educ:* Eton; New Coll., Oxford (MA). Called to the Bar, Lincoln's Inn, 1957, Bencher, 1989. Chancellor, Dio. Hereford, 1977–2000; Deputy Chancellor: Dio. Lincoln, 1994–98; Dio. Chelmsford, 1997–2000; Dio. London, 1997–2000. *Recreations:* books, art and architecture. *Address:* Fisher Hill House, Northchapel, Petworth, W Sussex GU28 9EJ. *Club:* Athenæum.

HENWOOD, John Philip, MBE 1998; Chairman: Jersey Telecom Group Ltd, since 2002; Byerley Ltd, since 2000; *b* 27 Aug. 1945; *s* of late Snowdon William Henwood and Amy Doris Henwood (*née* Stickley); *m* 1970, Sheila Patricia Renault (marr. diss. 1994). *Educ:* St Lawrence Sch.; Victoria Coll., Jersey. Joined Channel Television Ltd, later Channel Television Group, then ComProp Ltd, 1962: ops trainee, 1962–64; cameraman, 1964–65; Hd of Studio, 1965–66; Dep. Ops Manager, 1966–70; Producer/Dir (setting up commercial prodn unit), 1970–77; Hd, News and Features, 1977–83; Programme Controller, 1983–86; Dir of Progs, 1986–87; Chief Exec. and Man. Dir, 1987–2000; Dir, 1986–2004. Director: Jersey Finance, 2001–; Kleinwort Benson Channel Islands Ltd, 2003–; Kleinwort Benson Private Bank; Flying Brands Ltd. Mem., States of Jersey Review Panel of Machinery of Govt, 1999–2001. Sen. Steward, CI Racing and Hunt Club, 1998; Pres., Jersey Race Club, 1998–2001; Mem., Horserace Writers and Photographers Assoc. President, Jersey Branch: CIM; IoD, 2005 (Chm., 2001–02). Trustee, Durrell Wildlife Conservation Trust, 2006–. *Recreations:* horse racing, the thoroughbred, writing, ski-ing, old motor cars, gardening. *Clubs:* Victoria (Jersey), MG Owners.

HENZE, Hans Werner; composer; Professor of Composition, Royal Academy of Music, 1987–91; *b* 1 July 1926; *s* of Franz Gebhard Henze and Margarete Geldmacher. *Educ:* Bünde i/W; Bielefeld i/W; Braunschweig. Studying music in Heidelberg, 1945; First Work performed (Chamber Concerto), at Darmstadt-Kranichstein, 1946; Artistic Dir of Ballet, Hessian States Theatre, Wiesbaden, 1950; Prof. of Composition, Acad. Mozarteum, Salzburg, 1962–67. Definite departure for Italy; Artistic Director: Internat. Art Workshop, Montepulciano, Tuscany, 1976–80, 1989–; Philharmonic Acad., Rome, 1981–82; Munich Biennale, Internat. Fest. of New Music Theatre, 1988, 1990, 1992, 1994, 1996; Prof. of Composition, Hochschule für Musik, Cologne, 1980–91; Composer-in-Residence, Berlin Philharmonic Orchestra, 1991–92. Member: German Acad. of Arts, Berlin; Philharmonic Acad., Rome; Acad. Scientiarum et Artium Europaea, Salzburg, 1992. Hon. Member: Deutsche Oper, Berlin, 1982; AAIL, 1982; Internat. Soc. for New Music, 1991; Nat. Acad. of Santa Cecilia, Rome, 1995. Hon. FRNCM 1998. Hon. DMus: Edinburgh, 1970; Univ. of Osnabrück, 1996. Robert Schumann Prize, 1951; Prix d'Italia, 1953; Nordrhein-Westfalen Award, 1957; Berlin Prize of Artists, 1959; Great Prize for Artists, Hanover, 1961; Louis Spohr Prize, Brunswick, 1976; Bach Prize, Hamburg, 1983; Siemens Prize, 1990; Duisburg Music Award, Köhler Osbahr Foundn, 1995; Special Cultural Award, Munich, 1996; Annette von Droste Hülshoff Prize, Landschaftsverband Westfalen-Lippe, 1996; Hans von Bülow Medal, Berlin Philharmonic Orch., 1997; Bavarian Order of Maximilian for Science and Art, 1998. Grand Cross, Order of Merit (Germany), 1991. *Compositions:* 10 symphonies; 13 full length operas, 3 one-act operas, 1 children's opera, 2 radio-operas; ballets; chamber music; choral works; concerti for piano, violin, viola, violoncello, double bass, oboe, clarinet, trumpet, guitar and harp; various symphonic works; song cycle; music theatre works incl. The Magic Theatre, Boulevard Solitude, The Prince of Homburg, Elegy for Young Lovers, The Bassarids, The Young Lord, Natascha Ungeheuer, Moralities, La Cubana, Das Verratene Meer, Venus and Adonis; L'Upapa and the Triumph of Filial Love, 2003. *Publications:* Undine, Diary of a Ballet, 1959; Essays, 1964; (with H. Enzenberger) El Cimarrón: ein Werkstattbericht, 1971; Musik und Politik, 1975, 1984; Neue Aspekte der musikalischen Ästhetik: vol. I, Zwischen den Kulturen, 1979; vol. II, Die Zeichen, 1981; vol. III, Lehrgänge, 1986; vol. IV, Chiffren, 1990; vol. V, Musik und Mythos, 1997; The English Cat, 1983; Reiselieder mit böhmischen Quinten (autobiog.), 1996 (trans. English as Bohemian Fifths, 1998); Komponieren in der Schule, 1998. *Address:* Schott Musik International, Weihergarten 5, 55116 Mainz, Germany; Chester Music, 14–15 Berners Street, W1T 3LJ.

HEPBURN, James Douglas; Member (SNP) Scotland Central, Scottish Parliament, since 2007; *b* 21 May 1979; *s* of Iain Hepburn and Mary (*née* Irvine, now Hunter); *m* 2006, Julie Shackleton. *Educ:* Univ. of Glasgow (MA 2002; Sen. Vice-Pres., Students' Rep. Council, 1999–2000). Front of house asst, Citizens' Th., Glasgow, 2001–02; temp. data processor, Scottish Power, 2002; Res. Asst to Alex Neil, MSP, 2002–07. *Recreations:* football, reading, writing, cinema. *Address:* Scottish Parliament, Holyrood, Edinburgh EH99 1SP. *T:* (0131) 348 6573, *Fax:* (0131) 348 6979; *e-mail:* jamie.hepburn@snp.org.

HEPBURN, Sir John Alastair Trant Kidd B.; *see* Buchan-Hepburn.

HEPBURN, John William; Director of Establishments, Ministry of Agriculture, Fisheries and Food, 1996–98; *b* 8 Sept. 1938; *s* of late Dugald S. Hepburn and Margarita R. Hepburn; *m* 1972, Isla Marchbank (*d* 2006); one *s*. *Educ:* Hutchesons' Grammar Sch.; Glasgow Univ. (MA); Brasenose Coll., Oxford. Assistant Principal, 1961, Principal, 1966, MAFF; First Secretary, UK Delegn to European Communities, Brussels, 1969–71; Private Sec. to Minister of Agriculture, Fisheries and Food, 1971–73; Asst Sec., 1973–81, Under Sec., 1982–96, MAFF. *Recreation:* golf.

HEPBURN, Prof. Ronald William; Professor of Moral Philosophy, University of Edinburgh, 1975–96 (Professor of Philosophy, 1964–75), now Professor Emeritus; *b* 16 March 1927; *s* of late W. G. Hepburn, Aberdeen; *m* 1953, Agnes Forbes Anderson; two *s* one *d*. *Educ:* Aberdeen Grammar Sch.; University of Aberdeen. MA 1951, PhD 1955 (Aberdeen). National service in Army, 1944–48. Asst, 1952–55, Lecturer, 1955–60, Dept of Moral Philosophy, University of Aberdeen; Visiting Associate Prof., New York University, 1959–60; Prof. of Philosophy, University of Nottingham, 1960–64. Stanton Lecturer in the Philosophy of Religion, Cambridge, 1965–68. *Publications:* (jtly) Metaphysical Beliefs, 1957; Christianity and Paradox, 1958; Wonder and Other Essays: eight studies in aesthetics and neighbouring fields, 1984; The Reach of the Aesthetic:

collected essays, 2001; contrib. to books and learned journals; broadcasts. *Address:* 8 Albert Terrace, Edinburgh EH10 5EA.

HEPBURN, Stephen; MP (Lab) Jarrow, since 1997; *b* 6 Dec. 1959; *s* of Peter and Margaret Hepburn. *Educ:* Springfield Comprehensive Sch., Jarrow; Newcastle Univ. Former Res. Asst to Donald Dixon, MP. Mem. (Lab) S Tyneside MBC, 1985– (Chair: Finance Cttee, 1989–90; Tyne & Wear Pensions, 1989–97; Dep. Leader, 1990–97). Member: Defence Select Cttee, 2000–01; NI Affairs Select Cttee; Chairman: All Party Parly Shipbuilding and Ship Repair Gp; All Party Parly Mexico Gp. President: Bilton Hall Boxing Club; Jarrovians RFC; Jarrow FC. *Recreation:* sports. *Address:* House of Commons, SW1A 0AA. *T:* (constituency office) (0191) 420 0648. *Clubs:* Neon (Jarrow); Iona (Hebburn).

HEPBURNE-SCOTT, family name of **Lord Polwarth**.

HEPHER, Michael Leslie; Chief Executive, 1996–98, and Chairman, 1997–98, Charterhouse plc; *b* 17 Jan. 1944; *s* of Leslie and Edna Hepher; *m* 1st, 1971, Janice Morton (marr. diss. 2004); one *s* two *d*; 2nd, 2006, Raissa Chtcherbakova. *Educ:* Kingston Grammar School. FIA; Associate, Soc. of Actuaries; FLIA. Provident Life Assoc., UK, 1961–67; Commercial Life Assurance, Canada, 1967–70; Maritime Life Assurance Co., Canada, 1970–79; Chm. and Man. Dir, Abbey Life Group, UK, subseq. Lloyds Abbey Life, 1980–91; Gp Man. Dir, BT, 1991–95. Non-executive Chairman: HambroFraserSmith, 1999–2000; Telecity plc, 2000–05; Lane Clark and Peacock LLP, 2003–05; non-executive Director: Kingfisher, 1997–; Canada Life Assurance Co., 1999–; Catlin Gp Ltd, 2003–; Great-West Life, 2006–. *Recreations:* reading, golf. *Address:* (office) 54 Jermyn Street, SW1Y 6LX. *T:* (020) 7292 3792, *Fax:* 0870 124 7245.

HEPPELL, John; MP (Lab) Nottingham East, since 1992; Vice-Chamberlain of HM Household, 2005–07; *b* 3 Nov. 1948; *m* 1974, Eileen Golding; two *s* one *d*. *Educ:* Rutherford Grammar Sch.; SE Northumberland Technical Coll.; Ashington Technical Coll. Fitter: NCB, 1964–70; various cos, 1970–75; diesel fitter, 1975–78, workshop supervisor, 1978–89, British Rail. Mem. (Lab) Nottinghamshire CC, 1981–93. PPS to Leader of House of Lords, 1997–98; PPS to Dep. Prime Minister and Sec. of State for Envmt, Transport and the Regions, 1998–2001; a Lord Comr of HM Treasury (Govt Whip), 2001–05. *Address:* House of Commons, SW1A 0AA.

HEPPELL, (Thomas) Strachan, CB 1986; Consultant, Department of Health, 1995–2000; Chairman, Management Board, European Medicines Evaluation Agency, 1994–2000; *b* 15 Aug. 1935; *s* of late Leslie Thomas Davidson Heppell and Doris Abbey Heppell (*née* Potts); *m* 1963, Felicity Ann Rice; two *s*. *Educ:* Acklam Hall Grammar Sch., Middlesbrough; The Queen's Coll., Oxford. National Assistance Board, Ministry of Social Security/DHSS: Asst Principal, 1958; Principal, 1963–73 (seconded to Cabinet Office, 1967–69); Asst Director of Social Welfare, Hong Kong, 1971–73; Asst Sec., DHSS, 1973–78 (Social Security Adviser, Hong Kong Govt, 1977); Under Sec., DHSS, 1979–83; Dep. Sec., DHSS, later DoH, 1983–95. Chm., Family Fund Trust, 1997–2003; Mem., Broadcasting Standards Commn, 1996–2003; Expert Mem., Fairness Cttee, OFCOM, 2003–04; Mem., Adv. Bd, Institut des Sciences de la Santé, 2004–06; Chair: Audit Adv. Cttee, EMEA, 2004–; Eur. Inst. for Health. 2006–07. Vis. Fellow, LSE, 1997–2000. *Publications:* contribs on health, social welfare and regulatory affairs. *Recreations:* gardening, travelling.

HEPPLE, Prof. Sir Bob Alexander, Kt 2004; FBA 2003; Master of Clare College, Cambridge, 1993–2003, now Emeritus; Professor of Law, University of Cambridge, 1995–2001, now Emeritus; Judge, UN Administrative Tribunal, since 2007; *b* 11 Aug. 1934; *s* of late Alexander Hepple and Josephine Zwarenstein; *m* 1st, 1960, Shirley Goldsmith; one *s* one *d*; 2nd, 1994, Mary Coussey (CBE 2007). *Educ:* Univ. of Witwatersrand (BA 1954, LLB *cum laude* 1957); Univ. of Cambridge (LLB 1966; MA 1969; LLD 1993). Attorney, S Africa, 1958; Lectr in Law, Univ. of Witwatersrand, 1959–62; Advocate, S Africa, 1962–63. Left S Africa after detention without trial for anti-apartheid activities, 1963. Called to Bar, Gray's Inn, 1966, Bencher, 1996; Lectr in Law, Nottingham Univ., 1966–68; Fellow of Clare Coll., Cambridge and Univ. Lectr in Law, 1968–76; Prof. of Comparative Social and Labour Law, Univ. of Kent, 1976–77 (Hon. Prof., 1978–83); Prof. of English Law, 1982–93, Dean of Faculty of Laws and Head of Dept of Laws, 1989–93, UCL; Chm., Cttee of Heads of Univ. Law Schs, 1992–93. Chairman: Industrial Tribunals (England and Wales), pt-time 1975–77 and 1982–93, full-time 1977–82; Cttee, Justice Report on Industrial Tribunals, 1987. Member: Judicial Studies Bd (Tribunals Cttee), 1988–93; Lord Chancellor's Adv. Cttee on Legal Educn and Conduct, 1994–99; Commn on Future of Multi-Ethnic Britain, 1998–2000; Legal Services Consultative Panel, 2000–01; Mem., Nuffield Council on Bioethics, 2000– (Chm., 2003–07); Chm., Appointing Authy for Phase 1 Ethics Cttees, 2007–. Mem., CRE, 1986–90. Chairman: Univ. of Cambridge Local Exams Syndicate, 1994–98; Septemviri, Univ. of Cambridge, 1995–98; Managers, Smuts Fund, Cambridge, 1995–2003. Expert consultant to EC Commn, 1974–, and to ILO, 1990–; Advr to Russian Fedn, 1992, to S African Govt, 1994–96. Trustee, Canon Collins Educnl Trust for SA, 1990–. Chm., European Roma Rights Centre, 2001–07; Board Member: Internat. Centre for Protection of Human Rights, 2005–; Equal Rights Trust, 2006–. Leverhulme Emeritus Fellow, 2003–05; Nuffield Foundn New Career Develt Fellow, 2003–06. Hon. QC 1996. Hon. Prof., Univ. of Cape Town, 1999–2005. Hon. LLD: Witwatersrand, 1996; UCL, 2005; Cape Town, 2006. *Publications:* (with M. Coussey) Independent Review of Enforcement of UK Anti-Discrimination Legislation, 2000; Labour Laws and Global Trade, 2005; Rights at Work (Hamlyn Lectures), 2005; various books and articles on labour law, race relations, law of tort, etc; Founding Editor, Industrial Law Jl, 1972–77; Gen. Ed (jtly) Encyclopedia of Labour Relations Law, 1972–90; Chief Editor, International Encyclopedia of Comparative Law, Vol. XV, Labour Law, 1979–. *Address:* c/o Clare College, Cambridge CB3 9AJ.

HEPPLEWHITE, Rosalind Mary Joy, (Ros); Chair, Leicestershire and Rutland Probation Board, 2001–04; *b* 20 Dec. 1952; *d* of Anne and Anthony Phillips; *m* 1971, Julian Hepplewhite; one *s* one *d*. *Educ:* University College London (BA Hons). Asst House Governor, 1980–83, and Hosp. Sec., 1983–84, Bethlem Royal and Maudsley Hosps; Unit Administrator (Mental Health), Hammersmith and Fulham HA, 1984–85; Unit Gen. Manager (Mental Health and Mental Handicap), 1985–88, Dir, Corporate Develt, 1988–89, Brighton HA; Nat. Dir, MIND (Nat. Assoc. of Mental Health), 1989–91; Chief Exec., CSA, 1992–94; Chief Exec. and Registrar, GDC, 1996–2000. Mem., Council on Tribunals, 2002–05. JP Leicester, 2002–05. *Recreation:* home and family.

HEPWORTH, Rear-Adm. David, CB 1976; retired from RN, 1976; *b* 6 June 1923; *s* of Alfred Ernest Hepworth and Minnie Louisa Catherine Bennet Tanner (*née* Bowden); *m* 1st, 1946, Brenda June Case (marr. diss. 1974); one *s* one *d*; 2nd, 1975, Eileen Mary Macgillivray (*née* Robson). *Educ:* Banbury Grammar School. Boy Telegraphist, RN, 1939; HMS Ganges, 1939–40; served in Atlantic, Mediterranean and E Indies Fleets; commnd 1944; submarines and midget submarines, 1945–50; CO HMS Tudor, 1951–52; CO HMS Thorough, 1954–55; CO HMS Truncheon, 1956–58; Sen. Officer Submarines Londonderry and CO HMS Stalker, 1959–61; CO HMS Ashanti, 1961–64; jssc 1964; Dep. Dir Undersea Warfare, MoD, 1964–66; idc 1967; CO HMS Ajax and Captain (D) 2nd Far East Destroyer Sqdn, 1968–69; Dir RN Tactical Sch. and Maritime Tactical Sch., 1969–71; Dir Naval Warfare, MoD, 1971–73; Staff of Vice-Chief of Naval Staff, 1973–76; Lt-Comdr 1952; Comdr 1958; Captain 1964; Rear-Adm. 1974. Naval Advr to Imperial Iranian Navy, 1974–76. Naval Advr to Internat. Military Services Ltd, 1977–83. *Recreations:* home and garden. *Address:* Garden House, Lower Heyford, Oxon OX25 5PD. *T:* (01869) 347460.

HEPWORTH, Noel Peers, OBE 1980; Chairman, CIPFA International, since 2002; Director, Chartered Institute of Public Finance and Accountancy, 1980–96; *b* 22 Dec. 1934; *m* 1963, Jean Margaret Aldcroft; one *s* three *d*. *Educ:* Crewe County Grammar Sch.; London Univ. CPFA (IPFA 1958); DPA 1963. Nat. Service, RAF, 1953–55. NW Gas Bd, 1951–58; Asst City Treasurer, Manchester, 1965–72; Dir of Finance, Croydon, 1972–80. Chm., Inst. of Public Finance Ltd, 1996–2002. Financial Advr to London Boroughs Assoc. and AMA, 1972–80; Mem., London Treasurers' Adv. Body, 1972–80. Member: Dept of Envmt Property Adv. Group, 1980–88; Audit Commn, 1983–91; Adv. Bd, Treasury Solicitor Agency, 1996–99. Pres., Internat. Consortium on Governmental Financial Management, 1987–92; Proj. Dir, Eur. Fedn of Accountants single Eur. currency project, 1996–2001. Chm., FEE Public Sector Cttee, 1988–2003. FRSA 1985. Freeman, City of London, 1991. Hon. DSc (Econ) Hull; Hon. LLD Brighton; Hon. DS City. *Publications:* Finance of Local Government, 1970, 7th edn 1984, Japanese edn 1983; Housing Rents, Costs and Subsidies, 1978, 2nd edn 1981; contribs to technical and financial jls, local govt press and nat. and internat. press. *Recreations:* gardening, walking. *T:* (020) 8667 1144; *e-mail:* Noel.Hepworth@cipfa.org.uk.

HERALD, John Pearson; Sheriff of North Strathclyde, since 1992; *b* 12 July 1946; *s* of Andrew James Herald and Martha Wilson or Herald; *m* 1969, Catriona McDougal Anderson; one *d*. *Educ:* Hillhead High Sch., Glasgow; Univ. of Glasgow (LLB). Partner, Carlton Gilruth, Dundee, 1971–91; Dir, William Halley & Sons, Dundee, 1988–91; Depute Town Clerk, Newport-on-Tay, 1970–75; Temp. Sheriff, 1984–91; Chm. Industrial Tribunals, 1984–91. Sec., Angus Legal Aid Cttee, 1979–87; Mem., Legal Aid Central Cttee, 1981–87; Chm., Dundee CAB, 1972–79 and 1982–91. *Recreations:* reading, golf, soccer. *Address:* Sheriff's Chambers, Sheriff Court House, 1 Nelson Street, Greenock PA15 1TR. *T:* (01475) 787073.

HERBECQ, Sir John (Edward), KCB 1977; a Church Commissioner, 1982–96; *b* 29 May 1922; *s* of late Joseph Edward and Rosina Elizabeth Herbecq; *m* 1947, Pamela Filby; one *d*. *Educ:* High Sch. for Boys, Chichester. Clerical Officer, Colonial Office, 1939; Asst Principal, Treasury, 1950; Private Sec. to Chm., UK Atomic Energy Authority, 1960–62; Asst Sec., Treasury, 1964; Asst Sec., 1968, Under Sec., 1970, Dep. Sec., 1973, Second Permanent Sec., 1975–81, CSD. Dep. Chm., Review Body for Nursing Staff, Midwives, Health Visitors and Professions Allied to Medicine, 1986–91 (Mem., 1983–91); Chm. Malaŵi Civil Service Review Commn, 1984–85. Member: C of E Pensions Bd, 1985–89; Chichester Diocesan Bd of Finance, 1983–97 (Chm., 1989–97). *Recreations:* Scottish country dancing (ISTD Supreme Award with Hons), walking, watching cricket. *Address:* 2 The Stables, Mill Lane, Prestbury, Cheltenham, Glos GL52 3NE. *T:* (01242) 571291.

HERBERT, family name of **Earls of Carnarvon, Pembroke,** and **Powis,** and **Baron Hemingford**.

HERBERT, 19th Baron *cr* 1461; **David John Seyfried Herbert;** *b* 3 March 1952, *s* of late John Beeton Seyfried and Lady Cathleen Blanche Lily Eliot, *d* of 6th Earl of St Germans and *g d* of 9th Duke of Beaufort; Herbert Barony, in abeyance since death of 10th Duke of Beaufort, 1984, called out of abeyance in his favour, 2002; *co-heir* to Barony of Botetourt 1305; assumed additional surname of Herbert by Royal Licence, 2002; *m* 1975, Jane, *d* of Dr Ian Francis Bishop; one *s* one *d*. *Educ:* Harrow. *Heir:* *s* Dr the Hon. Oliver Richard Seyfried Herbert [*b* 17 June 1976; *m* 2003, Sarah, (Sally), *d* of Ian Fergusson, FRCS; one *s* two *d*]. *Address:* 39 Chiddingstone Street, SW6 3TQ.

HERBERT, Alfred James; British Council Representative, Portugal, 1980–84, retired; *b* 16 Oct. 1924; *s* of Allen Corbyn Herbert and Betty Herbert; *m* 1st, 1958, Helga Elberling (*d* 1981); two *s*; 2nd, 1982, Dr Wanda Wolska. *Educ:* Royal Masonic Schs; University Coll. London (BA 1950, MA 1952). Guest Prof. of English Lit., Univs of Yokohama and Tokyo, 1958–60; Lectr, English Dept, Birmingham Univ., 1960–62; joined British Council, 1962: Sierra Leone, 1962–65; Brazil, 1965–68; Representative: Somalia, 1968–70; Pakistan, 1974–77; Poland, 1977–80. *Publications:* Modern English Novelists (Japan), 1960; Structure of Technical English, 1965. *Recreations:* travelling, reading. *Address:* Quinta do Val do Riso, São Simão, Azeitão, 2900 Setubal, Portugal.

HERBERT, Dr Andrew James, FBCS; FREng; Managing Director, Microsoft Research, Cambridge, since 2003; Fellow, Wolfson College, Cambridge, since 2001; *b* 3 March 1954; *s* of Edward James Herbert and Catherine Beatrice Herbert (*née* Blaxley); *m* 1976, Jane Elizabeth Cherry; two *s* one *d*. *Educ:* Gillingham Grammar Sch.; Univ. of Leeds (BSc Hons 1st cl. (Computational Sci.) 1975); St John's Coll., Cambridge (PhD (Computer Sci.) 1978). Asst Lectr, 1978–83, Lectr 1983–85, Computer Lab., Cambridge Univ.; Technical Dir, APM Ltd, Cambridge, 1985–98; Chief Architect, ANSA Project, 1985–98; Chief Tech. Officer, Digitivity Inc., 1996–98; Dir, Advanced Technol., Citrix Systems Inc., 1998–2000; Asst Dir, Microsoft Res., Cambridge, 2001–03. Mem., EPSRC, 2006–. FBCS 2005; FREng 2007. *Publications:* The Cambridge Distributed Computing System, 1982; (ed with K. Spärk Jones) Computer Systems: theory, technology and applications, 2004. *Recreations:* general aviation (private pilot's licence and IMC rating), sailing, steam railways. *Address:* (office) 7 JJ Thomson Avenue, Cambridge CB3 0FB.

HERBERT, Brian Douglas; Director of Performance Review, East Anglian Regional Health Authority, 1989–91; *b* 29 May 1930; *s* of Stanley and Kathleen Herbert; *m* 1st, 1952, Linda (marr. diss.); two *s* one *d*; 2nd, 1973, Lila; one *d*. *Educ:* Ipswich School. IPFA. Local Govt Finance, 1946–63; Health Service: Asst Treasurer, NW Metropolitan RHB, 1963; Group Treasurer, SW Middlesex HMC, 1967; Area Treasurer, Ealing Hammersmith and Hounslow AHA(T), 1973; Regional Treasurer, 1981, Dir of Finance and Administration, 1985, E Anglian RHA. *Address:* 3 Dane Drive, Cambridge CB3 9LP. *T:* (01223) 574305.

HERBERT, Rt Rev. Christopher William; *see* St Albans, Bishop of.

HERBERT, (Elizabeth) Jane; Director, Frontline Consultants, since 2004; *b* 17 July 1956; *d* of Reginald John Herbert and Elsa Herbert (*née* Drake). *Educ:* Durham Univ. (BSc 1977); Bath Univ. (MBA 1991). Factory Manager, Clarks Shoes, 1986–91; Unit Gen. Manager, Greater Glasgow Health Bd, 1991–92; Chief Executive, W Glasgow Hosp. Univ. NHS Trust, 1993–98; S Manchester Univ. Hosps NHS Trust, 1998–2002; Chief Exec., Beds and Herts Strategic HA, 2002–03. *Recreations:* sailing, ornithology, music. *Address:* Frontline Consultants, 9 Staple Inn, Holborn, WC1V 7QH.

HERBERT, Frederick William; Emeritus Fellow in Industrial Relations, International Management Centre, Buckingham, 1985–92; Chairman, NALGO Insurance Association Ltd, 1981–93; *b* London, 18 Dec. 1922; *s* of late William Herbert and Alice Herbert; *m* 1948, Nina Oesterman; two *d*. *Educ:* Ealing Boys' Grammar Sch. Served RAFVR, 1942–46. Local Govt Finance, Middx CC, 1939–65; Greater London Council: Local Govt Finance, 1965–72; Personnel Management, Estabt Officer, 1972–77; Asst Dir of Personnel, 1977–80; Head of Industrial Relations, 1980–82; Controller of Personnel, 1982–84. Parly Correspondent, Eurotunnel (UK), 1986–87. FRSA 1986. *Recreations:* cricket, music (classical and jazz), theatre, Antient Society of Cogers (debating). *Address:* 20 Priory Hill, Wembley, Middx HA0 2QF. *T:* (020) 8904 8634. *Clubs:* Royal Over-Seas League, MCC.

HERBERT, James; author; *b* 8 April 1943; *s* of Herbert Herbert and Catherine (*née* Riley); *m* 1967, Eileen O'Donnell; three *d*. *Educ:* Our Lady of Assumption Sch., Bethnal Green; St Aloysius Coll., Highgate; Hornsey Coll. of Art. Typographer, paste-up artist, general dogsbody for John Collings Advertising, 1962–65; Art director, later group head and associate dir, Charles Barker Advertising, 1965–77. Mem., Lloyd's, 1983–89. Avoriaz Grand Prize for Literature Fantastique, 1977. *Publications:* The Rats, 1974 (filmed, 1982); The Fog, 1975; The Survivor, 1976 (filmed, 1986); Fluke, 1977 (filmed, 1995); The Spear, 1978; Lair, 1979; The Dark, 1980; The Jonah, 1981; Shrine, 1983; Domain, 1984; Moon, 1985; The Magic Cottage, 1986; Sepulchre, 1987; Haunted, 1988 (filmed, 1995); Creed, 1990; Portent, 1992; James Herbert: haunted by horror (ed S. Jones), 1992; James Herbert's Dark Places, 1993; The City, 1993; The Ghosts of Sleath, 1993; '48, 1996; Others, 1999; Once, 2001; Nobody True, 2003; The Secret of Crickley Hall, 2006; *relevant publication:* James Herbert: devil in the dark (biog.), by Craig Cabell, 2003. *Recreations:* playing guitar, piano, painting, sketching, photography, study of unnatural phenomena and the paranormal, swimming, reading, films, people. *Address:* c/o Bruce Hunter, David Higham Associates, 5–8 Lower John Street, Golden Square, W1R 4HA. *T:* (020) 7437 7888.

HERBERT, Jane; *see* Herbert, E. J.

HERBERT, Jeffrey William, FREng, FIMechE; EurIng; engineer and industrialist; Deputy Chairman, House of Fraser plc, since 2001; *b* 21 July 1942; *s* of Alexander William John Herbert and Amy (*née* Whitwell); *m* 1965, Sheila Heane; one *s* two *d*. *Educ:* Loughborough Univ. (DLC, BEng Mech. and Prodn Engrg; Hon. DTech 1999). MIET (MIEE 1968); FIMechE 1992; CEng, FREng (FEng 1993). Managing Director: Rover-Triumph Cars Ltd, 1976–81; GEC Diesels Ltd, 1981–85; Exec. Dir, Industry, Charter Consolidated PLC, 1985–89; Chief Exec., 1990–96, Chm., 1996–2001, Charter plc. Chairman: Cape plc, 1985–96; Anderson Gp plc, 1987–95; Esab AB, 1994–2001; British South Africa Co., 1996–2001; Howden Gp plc, 1997–2001; Howden Africa Hldgs Ltd, 1997–2001; Claverham Ltd, 1998–2000; Concentric Gp, 1999–2004; Deputy Chairman: Vickers plc, 1997–2000 (non-exec. Dir, 1991–); House of Fraser plc, 2001–06; non-executive Director: M & G Investment Trust, 1992–2002; F. T. Everard & Sons, 2002–; Tendring Hundred Water Services Ltd, 2003– (Chm., 2005–). Mem. Council, 1995–2003, Hon. Treas., 1997–2003, Royal Acad. of Engrg. Trustee, Thrombosis Res. Inst., 2004–. CCMI; FRSA 1993. Freeman, City of London, 1993; Liveryman, Wheelwrights' Co., 1993. *Recreations:* shooting, walking, wine, veteran and classic cars, living in Portugal. *Address:* Baytrees, Long Road West, Dedham, Colchester, Essex CO7 6EL.

HERBERT, Mark Jeremy; QC 1995; *b* 12 Nov. 1948; *yr s* of late Kenneth Falkner Herbert and of Kathleen Ellis Herbert; *m* 1977, Shiranikha Pullenayegum. *Educ:* Lancing Coll.; King's Coll., London (BA). Called to the Bar, Lincoln's Inn, 1974, Bencher, 2004; in practice at Chancery Bar, 1975–. *Publications:* (contrib.) Whiteman on Capital Gains Tax, 4th edn 1988; Drafting and Variation of Wills, 1989. *Recreations:* bell-ringing, theatre, travel. *Address:* 5 Stone Buildings, Lincoln's Inn, WC2A 3XT. *T:* (020) 7242 6201.

HERBERT, Nicholas; *see* Hemingford, 3rd Baron.

HERBERT, Nicholas Lequesne, (Nick); MP (C) Arundel and South Downs, since 2005; *b* 7 April 1963. *Educ:* Haileybury; Magdalene Coll., Cambridge (BA Hons 1985). British Field Sports Soc., 1990–96, latterly Dir of Political Affairs; Chief Exec., Business for Sterling, 1998–2000; Dir, Reform, 2002–05. Contested (C) Berwick-upon-Tweed, 1997. *Address:* House of Commons, SW1A 0AA.

HERBERT, Adm. Sir Peter (Geoffrey Marshall), KCB 1983; OBE 1969; *b* 28 Feb. 1929; *s* of A. G. S. Herbert and P. K. M. Herbert; *m* 1953, Ann Maureen (*née* McKeown); one *s* one *d*. *Educ:* Dunchurch Hall; RN Coll., Dartmouth. Specialised in submarines, 1949; served in submarines, 1950–68: Comd HM Submarines Scythian, Porpoise and Excalibur, 1956–60; Submarine Staff, 1960–62; Comd nuclear submarine, HMS Valiant, 1963–68; Comd HMS Venus, 1964; Dep. Dir, Naval Equipment, 1969; Comd 10th (Polaris) Submarine Squadron, 1970–72; COS to Flag Officer Submarines, 1972–74; Comd HMS Blake, 1974–75; Dep. Chief, Polaris Exec., 1976–78; Flag Officer Carriers and Amphibious Ships, 1978–79; Dir Gen., Naval Manpower and Training, 1980–81; Flag Officer Submarines and Comdr Submarines Eastern Atlantic, 1981–83; VCDS (Personnel and Logistics), 1983–85. Non-exec. Dir, Radamec Gp plc, 1985–2004. Chm., SSAFA, 1985–93; President: Glos Br., King George's Fund for Sailors, 1990–; North Cotswold RNLI, 1990–2004. Governor: Cheam School, 1987–2000 (Chm., 1992–2000); Cheltenham Ladies' Coll., 1993–2001. CCMI; MINucE. *Recreations:* woodwork, gardening. *Club:* Army and Navy.

HERBERT, Prof. Robert Louis, PhD; Alumnae Foundation Professor of Art, 1990–96, Andrew W. Mellon Professor of Humanities, 1996–97, now Emeritus, Mount Holyoke College, Mass; *b* 21 April 1929; *s* of John Newman Herbert and Rosalia Harr Herbert; *m* 1953, Eugenia Randall Warren; one *s* two *d*. *Educ:* Wesleyan Univ., Middletown, Conn (BA 1951); Yale Univ. (MA 1954, PhD 1957). Fulbright Scholar, Paris, 1951–52; Faculty, Yale Univ., 1956–90: Associate Prof., 1963; Prof., 1966; Departmental Chm., 1965–68; Robert Lehman Prof. of Hist. of Art, 1974–90. Guggenheim Fellow, 1971–72; Slade Prof. of Fine Art, Oxford, 1978. Organizer of exhibitions: Barbizon Revisited, Boston Museum of Fine Arts and others, 1962–63; Neo-Impressionism, Solomon R. Guggenheim Mus., 1968; J. F. Millet, Musées Nationaux, Paris, and Arts Council, London, 1975–76; Léger's Le Grand Déjeuner, Minneapolis Inst. of Arts and Detroit Inst. of Arts, 1980; Seurat, Musées Nationaux, Paris and Metropolitan Mus., NY, 1991; Peasants and 'Primitivism': French prints from Millet to Gauguin, Mount Holyoke Coll., RI Sch. of Design, and Univ. of Chicago, 1995–96; Seurat and the Making of La Grande Jatte, Art Inst. of Chicago, 2004. Fellow, Amer. Acad. of Arts and Sciences, 1978; Mem., Amer. Philosophical Soc., 1993. Chevalier, 1976, Officier, 1990, Ordre des Arts et des Lettres. *Publications:* Barbizon Revisited, 1962–63; Seurat's Drawings, 1963; The Art Criticism of John Ruskin, 1964; Modern Artists on Art, 1964, rev. edn 2000; Neo-Impressionism, 1968; David, Voltaire, 'Brutus' and the French Revolution, 1972; J. F. Millet, 1975; (ed jtly) Société Anonyme and Dreier Bequest at Yale University: a catalogue raisonné, 1984; Impressionism: art, leisure and Parisian society, 1988; Monet on the Normandy Coast, 1994; Nature's Workshop: Renoir's writings on the decorative arts, 2000; Seurat: Drawings and Paintings, 2001; From Millet to Léger, 2002; Seurat and the Making of "La Grande Jatte", 2004; articles in learned jls.

HERBERT, Robin Arthur Elidyr, CBE 1994; DL; JP; President Emeritus, Royal Horticultural Society, since 1994; Chairman, Leopold Joseph Holdings PLC, 1978–2004; *b* 5 March 1934; *s* of late Sir John Arthur Herbert, GCIE and Lady Mary Herbert; *m* 1st, 1960, Margaret Griswold Lewis (marr. diss. 1988); two *s* two *d*; 2nd, 1988, Philippa Harriet King. *Educ:* Eton; Christ Church, Oxford (MA); Harvard Business School (MBA). MRICS. 2nd Lieut Royal Horse Guards, 1953–54; Captain Royal Monmouthshire RE, 1962–68. Chairman: Union Discount Co. of London, later Union PLC, 1990–96 (Director, 1989–96); Lands Improvement Holdings PLC; Foreign & Colonial Income Growth Investment Trust, 1994–2004; Director: Nat. Westminster Bank, 1972–92; Agricl Mortgage Corp., 1985–93; Marks & Spencer, 1986–91; Consolidated Gold Fields, 1986–89 (Dep. Chm., 1988–89); F&C Smaller Companies Investment Trust, 1985–2001; Federated Aggregates, 1991–95; SWOAC Holdings, 1990–98. Financial Advisor: Water Superannuation Fund, 1986–89; Nat. Rivers Authy, 1989–96. Mem. Council, BBA, 1992–98. Dep. Chm., Countryside Commn, 1971–80; Member: Council, National Trust, 1969–87 (Mem., Exec. Cttee, 1969–84; Chm. Cttee for Wales, 1969–84); Nat. Water Council, 1980–83; Welsh Develt Agency, 1980–86; Darwin Initiative Adv. Cttee, 1993–99; Royal Parks Agency Adv. Gp, 1993–2000. Royal Horticultural Society: Mem. Council, 1971–74 and 1979–94; Pres. and Chm. Council, 1984–94. Trustee: Royal Botanic Gardens, Kew, 1987–97 (Chm., 1991–97); Nat. Botanic Gdn of Wales, 1994–2007; Botanic Gdns Conservation Internat., 1991–. Chm., Flowers & Plants Assoc., 1998–2006. DL 1968, JP 1964, High Sheriff 1972, Monmouthshire. *Recreations:* dendrology, walking. *Address:* Neuadd, Llanbedr, Crickhowell, Powys NP8 1SP. *T:* (01873) 812164. *Clubs:* Brooks's, Pratt's.

HERBERT, William Penry Millwarden; Member, Cardiff City Council, 1970–96; Lord Mayor of Cardiff, 1988–89; *b* 31 March 1921; *s* of William John Herbert and Esabella Marinda Francis; *m* 1945, Ellen Vera McCarthy; two *d* (one *s* decd). *Educ:* Argoed Elementary Sch., Blackwood, Monmouthshire. Cert. of Professional Competence, Transport, 1977. Miner, 1934–37; Railwayman, 1937–45. Served RE, 1945–47. 1947–78: Guest Keen Iron and Steel Works; Guest Keen and Baldwins British Steel Corp.; Plant Supervisor, Traffic Foreman, Transport Manager. *Recreations:* dancing, gardening, reading, travel. *Address:* 27 Wellwood Avenue, Llanedeyrn, Cardiff, South Glamorgan CF23 9JP. *Club:* City Social (Cathays, Cardiff).

HERBERT-JONES, Hugh Jarrett, (Hugo), CMG 1973; OBE 1963; HM Diplomatic Service, retired; company director; *b* 11 March 1922; *s* of late Dora Herbert-Jones (*née* Rowlands), MBE and Captain Herbert-Jones; *m* 1954, Margaret (*d* 1996), *d* of Rev. J. P. Veall; one *s* two *d*. *Educ:* Bryanston; Worcester Coll., Oxford. History Scholar. Commnd Welsh Guards, 1941; served NW Europe and Middle East; wounded 1944; demobilised 1946 (Major). Entered Foreign (later Diplomatic) Service, 1947; served: Hamburg, 1947; Berlin, 1949; Hong Kong, 1951; Phnom Penh, 1955; Saigon, 1956; Nairobi, 1959; Pretoria/Cape Town, 1963; FCO, 1966; Paris, 1973; FCO, 1975–79; Internat. Affairs Dir, CBI, 1979–87. Pres., Aldeburgh Soc., 1997–99; Chm., Aldeburgh Community & Sports Trust, 2000–07. Mayor of Aldeburgh, 2007–08. *Recreations:* sailing, golf, shooting, music, spectator sports. *Address:* Prior's Hill, 48 Park Road, Aldeburgh, Suffolk IP15 5ET. *T:* and *Fax:* (01728) 453335; *e-mail:* hugo@herbertjones.fsnet.co.uk. *Clubs:* Garrick, MCC; London Welsh Rugby Football; Aldeburgh Yacht.

HERBISON, Nancy Maureen; *see* Argenta, N. M.

HERCUS, Hon. Dame (Margaret) Ann, DCMG 1988; international consultant; *b* 24 Feb. 1942; *d* of Horace Sayers and Mary (*née* Ryan); *m* John Hercus; two *s*. *Educ:* Victoria Univ. of Wellington; Univs. of Auckland (BA) and Canterbury (LLB). Lawyer and Staff Training Officer, Beath & Co., Christchurch, 1969–70; Mem., Price Tribunal and Trade Practices Commn, 1973–75; Dep. Chm., Commerce Commn, 1975–78; Chm., Consumer Rights Campaign, 1975; MP (Lab) Lyttleton, 1978–87; in opposition, 1978–84; Minister of Social Welfare, Police and Women's Affairs, 1984–87; Ambassador to UN, 1988–90; internat. consultant, 1991–98; Chief of Mission, UN Force in Cyprus, 1998–99. *Address:* 82A Park Terrace, Christchurch 8001, New Zealand.

HERD, Frederick Charles; Assistant Under-Secretary of State (Civilian Management, General), Ministry of Defence, 1970–75; *b* 27 April 1915. *Educ:* Strode's Sch., Egham; Sidney Sussex Coll., Cambridge. Asst Principal, Admiralty, 1937; Principal, 1941; Asst. Sec., 1950; Asst Under-Sec. of State, 1964. *Recreations:* music, country walking, bridge. *Address:* Room 201, Sunrise, Frognal House, Frognal Avenue, Sidcup, Kent DA14 6LF.

HERDAN, Bernard Laurence, CB 2007; CEng; Executive Director for Service Planning and Delivery, Identity and Passport Service, since 2006; *b* 23 Nov. 1947; *s* of Dr Gustav Herdan and late Estelle Muriel Innes Herdan (*née* Jackson); *m* 1971, Janet Elizabeth Hughes; one *d* (and one *d* decd). *Educ:* Bristol Grammar Sch.; Churchill Coll., Cambridge (BA Hons 1969, MA); Bath Univ. (DMS 1972). CEng, MIET (MIEE 1971). Systems Designer, BAe, 1969–73; Prog. Manager, ESA, 1973–84; Managing Consultant, BIS Mackintosh, 1984–85; Man. Dir, Defence Technology Enterprises, 1985–89; Commercial Dir, Meteorological Office, 1990–95; Chief Exec., Driving Standards Agency, 1995–99; Chief Exec., UK Passport Agency and Criminal Records Bureau, subseq. Passport and Records Agency, then UK Passport Service, 1999–2006. MInstD 1986. Editor-in-Chief, Space Communication and Broadcasting, 1982–86. *Publications:* papers in professional jls. *Recreations:* horse riding, ski-ing, foreign travel, theatre, the arts. *Address:* Identity and Passport Service, Globe House, 89 Eccleston Square, SW1V 1PN. *T:* (020) 7901 2400.

HERDMAN, (John) Mark (Ambrose), CBE 1990; LVO 1979; HM Diplomatic Service, retired; *b* 26 April 1932; *s* of late Comdr Claudius Alexander Herdman, DL, RN, and Joan Dalrymple Herdman (*née* Tennant); *m* 1963, Elizabeth Anne Dillon; one *s* two *d*. *Educ:* St Edward's Sch., Oxford; Trinity Coll., Dublin (BA, MA); Queen's Coll., Oxford (postgrad.). HMOCS, Kenya, 1954–64; joined HM Diplomatic Service, 1964; Second, later First Sec., CRO, 1964–65; ODM, 1965; MECAS, 1965–66; Amman, 1966–68; FCO, 1969–71; Lusaka, 1971–74; Hd of Chancery, Jedda, 1974–76; FCO, 1976–78; Lilongwe, 1978–81; FCO, 1981–83; Dep. Governor, Bermuda, 1983–86; Gov., British Virgin Is, 1986–91; Hd of British Delegn to EC Monitoring Mission in Yugoslavia, 1991–92. *Recreations:* fishing, watching cricket, philately. *Address:* Tullywhisker House, Berry Lane, Fox Corner, Worplesdon, Surrey GU3 3PU. *T:* (01483) 232900. *Clubs:* Ebury Court; Surrey CC.

HERDON, Christopher de Lancy, OBE 1971; HM Diplomatic Service, retired; freelance journalist, since 1983; news editor, The Tablet, 1986–2004; *b* 24 May 1928; *s* of late Wilfrid Herdon and Clotilde (*née* Parsons); *m* 1953, Virginia Grace; two *s* two *d* (and one *s* decd). *Educ:* Ampleforth; Magdalen Coll., Oxford. Foreign Office, 1951; Vienna, 1953; 2nd Sec., Baghdad, 1957; Beirut, 1961; 1st Sec., Amman, 1962; FO, 1965; Aden,

1967; FCO, 1970; Counsellor: Rome, 1973; FCO, 1977; retired 1983. RC Observer, BCC, 1984–90; Mem., Assembly of Council of Churches for Britain and Ireland, 1990–94. *Recreations:* painting, music, sailing, long-distance walking. *Address:* Broomhill Cottage, Lodsworth, W Sussex GU28 9DG. *T:* (01798) 861701. *Club:* Reform.

HEREFORD, 19th Viscount *cr* 1550; **Charles Robin de Bohun Devereux;** Bt 1611; Premier Viscount of England; *b* 11 Aug. 1975; *s* of 18th Viscount Hereford and Susan Mary, *o c* of Major Maurice Godley. *Educ:* Stowe; UEA (BA Hons Hist. of Art and Architecture). Valuer, 1998–, Departmental Dir, 2007–, Bonhams Auctioneers. *Heir: b* Hon. Edward Mark de Breteuil Devereux, *b* 8 June 1977. *Address:* 8 Vauxhall Bridge Road, SW1V 2SD; Yew Tree Farm, Ascott, Shipston on Stour, Warwickshire CV36 5PP. *Club:* White's.

HEREFORD, Bishop of, since 2004; **Rt Rev. Anthony Martin Priddis;** *b* 15 March 1948; *s* of Ted and Joan Priddis; *m* 1973, Kathy Armstrong; two *s* one *d*. *Educ:* Corpus Christi Coll., Cambridge (BA 1969; MA 1973); New Coll., Oxford (DipTh 1971; MA 1975); Cuddesdon Coll., Oxford. Ordained deacon, 1972, priest, 1973; Asst Curate, New Addington, 1972–75; Chaplain, Christ Church, Oxford, 1975–80; Team Vicar, High Wycombe, 1980–86; Priest-in-charge, 1986–90, Rector, 1990–96, Amersham; RD of Amersham, 1992–96; Suffragan Bp of Warwick, 1996–2004. Chm., Rural Bishops' Panel, 2006–. Lay Mem. Bd, CEM (formerly FAEM), 2002–; Mem., W Midlands Cultural Consortium, 2002–05. Co-Chm., Family Life and Marriage Educn Network, 2001–06. Hon. FCEM (Hon. FFAEM 2005). *Publications:* (contrib.) Study of Spirituality, 1986. *Recreations:* walking the dogs, music, golf, gardening, watching sport. *Address:* Bishop's House, Hereford HR4 9BN. *T:* (01432) 271355, *Fax:* (01432) 373346; *e-mail:* bishop@hereford.anglican.org.

HEREFORD, Dean of; *see* Tavinor, Very Rev. M. E.

HEREFORD, Archdeacon of; *see* Colmer, Ven. M. J.

HERFT, Most Rev. Roger Adrian; *see* Perth (Australia), Archbishop of.

HERITAGE, John Langdon, CB 1991; Director, Chesham Building Society, 1989–2001 (Chairman, 1992–97); *b* 31 Dec. 1931; *s* of Frank and Elizabeth Heritage; *m* 1956, Elizabeth Faulkner, *d* of Charles and Ethel Robertson; two *s* one *d*. *Educ:* Berkhamsted Sch., Exeter Coll., Oxford (MA). Called to the Bar, Middle Temple, 1956. National Service, Royal Hampshire Regt and Royal W African Frontier Force. Legal Asst, Treasury Solicitor's Office, 1957, Sen. Legal Asst 1964; Asst Solicitor, Lord Chancellor's Dept, 1973; Sec., Royal Commn on Legal Services, 1976–79; Under Sec., 1983; Circuit Administrator, South Eastern Circuit, 1983–88; Hd of Judicial Appts, Lord Chancellor's Dept, 1989–92. *Publications:* articles in legal jls. *Recreation:* amateur physiotherapy. *Address:* Hurdle House, 1 Chestnut Lane, Amersham, Bucks HP6 6EN. *Club:* Oxford and Cambridge.

HERITAGE, Robert, CBE 1980; RDI 1963; DesRCA, FCSD; Professor, School of Furniture Design, Royal College of Art, 1974–85; *b* 2 Nov. 1927; *m* Dorothy; two *s* one *d*. *Educ:* Royal College of Art, RCA, 1950; freelance designer, 1961. *Recreations:* tennis, fishing. *Address:* 12 Jay Mews, Kensington Gore, SW7 2EP.

HERLIE, Eileen; actress; *b* Glasgow, 8 March 1920; *d* of Patrick Herlihy (Irish) and Isobel Cowden (Scottish); *m* 1st, 1942, Philip Barrett (marr. diss.); 2nd, 1951, Witold Kuncewicz (marr. diss.). *Educ:* Shawlands Academy, Glasgow. First stage appearance, Lyric, Glasgow, 1938; first London appearance, as Mrs de Winter in Rebecca, Ambassadors', 1942; varied repertoire with own company, 1942–44; Old Vic Co., Playhouse, Liverpool, 1944–45, including: Lady Sneerwell in The School for Scandal, Doll Common in The Alchemist; Lyric, Hammersmith, 1945–46, including: Andromache in The Trojan Women, Alcestis in Thracian Horses, Queen in The Eagle Has Two Heads; title rôle in Medea, Globe, 1948; Paula in The Second Mrs Tanqueray, Haymarket, 1950; Mrs Marwood in The Way of the World, Belvidera in Venice Preserv'd, Lyric, Hammersmith, 1953; Irene in A Sense of Guilt, King's, Glasgow, 1953; Mrs Molloy in The Matchmaker, Haymarket, 1954, transf. NY, 1955; Emilia Marty in The Makropoulos Secret, NY, 1957; Paulina in The Winter's Tale, Beatrice in Much Ado About Nothing, Stratford, Ont, 1958; Ruth Gray in Epitaph for George Dillon, NY, 1958; Lily in Take Me Along (musical), NY, 1959; Elizabeth Hawkes-Bullock in All American (musical), NY, 1962; Stella in Photo Finish, NY, 1963; Queen Gertrude in Hamlet, NY, 1964; Lady Fitzbuttress in Halfway up the Tree, NY, 1967; Martha in Who's Afraid of Virginia Woolf?, Chicago, 1971; Countess Matilda Spina in Emperor Henry IV, 1973; Queen Mary in Crown Matrimonial, NY, 1973. *Films:* Hungry Hill, 1947; Hamlet, 1948; Angel with the Trumpet, 1949; Gilbert and Sullivan, 1952; Isn't Life Wonderful?, 1952; She Didn't Say No!, 1958; Freud, 1962; The Seagull, 1968. *Television:* Myrtle Fargate in All My Children, ABC TV, 1976–. *Recreations:* riding, reading, music. *Address:* Apt 13P, 405 East 54th Street, New York, NY 10022, USA.

HERMAN, David Joseph; Consultant on Eastern Europe, General Motors Corporation, 2002; Vice President, Russia and the Commonwealth of Independent States, General Motors, 1998–2002; *b* 14 Jan. 1946; *m* Isabel Roehrenbach; two *d*. *Educ:* New York Univ. (BA Govt Affairs 1967); LSE; Harvard Univ. Grad. Sch. (JD 1971). Attorney, Legal Staff, General Motors, NY, 1973; Manager, Sales Develt (USSR), GM Internat. Ops, 1976; Special Asst to Man. Dir, GM España, 1979–82; Managing Director: GM Chile, Santiago, 1982; GM Colombia, 1984–86; GM Continental, Antwerp, 1986–88; Exec. Dir, Europ. Parts & Accessories, GM Europe, 1988–89; Pres. and Chief Exec. Officer, SAAB Automobile, 1989–92; Chm. and Man. Dir, Adam Opel AG, 1992–98. Vice Pres., Gen. Motors Corp., 1992–2002. Dir, Golden Telecom, 2002–. *Recreations:* golf, opera, bridge. *Address:* c/o General Motors Corporation, PO Box 33170, Detroit, MI 48232-5170, USA.

HERMANN, Alexander Henry Baxter; HM Diplomatic Service, retired; *b* 28 Dec. 1917; *m* Rita Rosalind Fernandes. Joined Foreign Service, 1939; served 1942–55; Peking, Ahwaz, Chengtu, Chungking, Shanghai, Quito, Panama, Tamsui; Foreign Office, 1956; Commercial Counsellor and Consul-General, Rangoon, 1957–61; HM Consul-General at Marseilles, also to Monaco, 1961–65; Diplomatic Service Inspector, 1965–66; Counsellor, Hong Kong Affairs, Washington, 1967–70, 1974–77; Consul-General, Osaka, 1971–73. *Address:* 32 Old Place, Aldwick, Sussex PO21 3AX.

HERMER, Julius; solicitor; Consultant with: Howard Palser Grossman Hermer & Partners, 1996–99; Robertsons, since 1999; Lord Mayor of Cardiff, 1987–88; *b* 18 Nov. 1933; *s* of Saul and Cissie Hermer; *m* 1960, Gloria Cohen; three *s* one *d*. *Educ:* St Illtyd's Coll., Cardiff; Peterhouse, Cambridge (BA, MA). Partner, 1959–95, Grossman & Hermer, subseq. Crowley, Grossman & Hermer, Grossman, Hermer & McCarthy, and Grossman, Hermer Seligman. Member: Cardiff City Council, 1964–88, 1991–96 (Chm., Planning Cttee, 1980–84; Dep. Lord Mayor of Cardiff, 1979–80, 1986–87); S Glam CC, 1974–96 (Vice-Chm. of Council and Dep. Leader of Cons. Party, 1977–78). Pres., Cardiff W Cons. Assoc., 1999–2002 (Dep. Chm., 1985). Chm., S Glam Appeal, Sir Geraint Evans Wales Heart Res. Inst., 1991–97. Pres., Cardiff Independent Citizens, 2005–. Chm., Card Masonic Hall Co. Ltd, 1989–. *Recreations:* Freemasonry, sport, wine, food, travel, politic *Address:* 28 Palace Road, Llandaff, Cardiff CF5 2AF. *T:* (029) 2056 6198.

HERMITAGE, Peter Andrew, QPM 1996; management consultant on securit government and police matters, since 2000; *b* 26 Sept. 1948; *s* of late Thomas Hen Hermitage and Freda Helen Hermitage; *m* 1971, Brenda Howard; one *s* one *d*. *Edu* Chatham House GS, Ramsgate. Joined Kent Constabulary, 1968: numerous operation investigative and organisational roles, incl. Dir, Jun. Comd Course, Police Staff Col Bramshill, 1986–87; Asst Chief Constable, Kent, 1990–94; Asst Inspector of Constabular Home Office, 1994–96; Dir, Nat. Police Training (with rank of Chief Constabl 1996–99. Mem. Bd, Security Industry Authy, 2003–06 (Acting Chm., 2003–04; Chn 2004–06). Non-exec. Dir, Perpetuity Res. and Consultancy Internat., 2006–. Chm., Kent Hosps NHS Trust, 2000–03. Ed., Police Jl, 1997–99. Vice-Pres., Police Mutu Assce Soc., 1997–99. Gov., Canterbury Christ Church Univ. (formerly UC), 1999– (Vi Chm., 2003–; Dep. Pro-Chancellor, 2005–). MRSH 1992; FCIPD (FIPD 1997); MInst 1999. *Recreations:* Rugby, fly fishing, painting water colours, family. *Address:* 4 Ealha Close, Canterbury, Kent CT4 7BW.

HERMON, Sir John (Charles), Kt 1982; OBE 1975; QPM 1988; Chief Constab Royal Ulster Constabulary, 1980–89; *b* 23 Nov. 1928; *s* of late William Rowan Hermo and Agnes Hermon; *m* 1954, Jean Webb (*d* 1986); one *s* one *d*; *m* 1988, Sylvia Paisley (*s* Sylvia Hermon); two *s*. *Educ:* Larne Grammar Sch. Accountancy training and busine 1946–50; joined RUC, 1950. Pres., Internat. Professional Security Assoc., 1993–96. CS 1984. *Publication:* Holding the Line: an autobiography, 1997.

HERMON, Peter Michael Robert; Head of Information Systems, CL-Alexanders Lair and Cruickshank Holdings Ltd, 1989–90; *b* 13 Nov. 1928; British; *m* 1954, Norma Stua Brealey; two *s* two *d*. *Educ:* Nottingham High Sch.; St John's Coll., Oxford (1st cl. ho Maths; Univ. Maths Prize, 1953); Merton Coll., Oxford. Leo Computers Ltd, 1955–5 Manager, Management and Computer Divs, Dunlop Co., 1959–65; Informatic Handling Dir, BOAC, 1965–68; Management Services Dir, BOAC, and Mem. Bd Management, 1968–72; Mem. of Board, BOAC, 1972; British Airways: Gp Manageme Services Dir, 1972–78; Board Mem., 1978–83; Management Services Dir, 1978–82; Ma Dir, European Services Div., 1982–83. Man. Dir, Tandem Computers Ltd, 1983–84; D Tandem UK, 1983–85; Head of Systems and Communications, Lloyd's of Londo 1984–86; Informations Systems Dir, Harris Queensway, 1986–88. Mem. Bd of Di Internat. Aeradio Ltd, 1966–83, Chm., 1982–83; Chm., Internat. Aeradio (Caribbea Ltd, 1967–83; Mem. Bd, SITA, 1972–83, Chm., 1981–83. *Publications:* Hill Walking Wales, 1991; (jtly) User-Driven Innovation: the world's first business computer, 199 Lifting the Veil: a plain language guide to the Bible, 2006. *Recreations:* hill walking, musi cats. *Address:* White Flints, Quentin Way, Wentworth, Virginia Water, Surrey GU25 4PS

HERMON, Sylvia, (Lady Hermon); MP (UU) Down North, since 2001; *b* 11 Au 1955; *d* of Robert and Mary Paisley; *m* 1988, Sir John (Charles) Hermon, *qv*; two *s*. *Edu* UCW, Aberystwyth (LLB 1st Cl. Hons); Coll. of Law, Chester. Lectr in Law, QU 1978–88; PR Consultant, 1993–96. *Publication:* A Guide to EEC Law in Northern Irelan 1986. *Recreations:* swimming, fitness-training, proof reading, ornithology. *Address:* Hou of Commons, SW1A 0AA.

HERMON-TAYLOR, Prof. John, FRCS; Professor of Surgery, St George's Hospit Medical School, 1976–2002, now Professor Emeritus; Visiting Professor, School Biomedical and Health Sciences, King's College London; *b* 16 Oct. 1936; *s* of la Hermon Taylor, FRCS; *m* 1971, Eleanor Ann Pheteplace, of Davenport, Iowa; one *s* or *d*. *Educ:* Harrow Sch. (Shepherd-Churchill Open Major Entrance Schol.); St John's Col Cambridge (travelling schol., 1955; BA 1957, MB BChir 1960, MChir 1968); Londo Hosp. Med Coll. (Open Entrance Schol., 1957, prizes in Med., Path., and Obst.). FRC 1963 (Hallett Prize, 1962). Training in surgery, 1962–68; MRC Travelling Fellow Mayo Clinic, USA, 1968–69 (Vis. Prof., 1980, 1985); Senior Lectr, 1970, Reader Surgery, 1971–76, London Hosp. Med. Coll. Pearce-Gould Vis. Prof., Middlesex Hosp 1982; Vis. Prof., Pakistan Inst. of Med. Scis, Islamabad, 1989. Hon. Consultant in Ge Surgery to RN, 1989–2002. Mem. Council, Assoc. of Surgeons of GB and Irelan 1981–84; Dir, James IV Assoc. of Surgeons, 1983–86. Member: Council, Actic Research, 1988–97; Scientific Cttee, British Digestive Foundn, 1991–95; Medical Ad Cttee, British Liver Trust, 1995–96; Health Services Res. and Clin. Epidemiol. Ad Cttee, Wellcome Trust, 1996–2001 (Mem., Clinical Panel, 1985–88); wking gp c Crohn's disease and paratuberculosis, Scientific Cttee on Animal Health and Anim Welfare, EC, 1998–2000. Dir, BioScience Internat. Inc., 1987–. Mem., numero professional bodies, UK and overseas. Innovator of the Year award, Times Newspape Barclays Bank, 1988. *Publications:* scientific papers on purification and biochem. enteropeptidase, diseases of pancreas, peptide chem., enzymeactivation in gastric disorde on causation and specific treatment of Crohn's disease, mycobacterial genetic epidemiology of breast cancer, biolog. res. on common solid tumours. *Recreations:* fishin sailing, shooting, growing soft fruit and vegetables. *Address:* Division of Nutritio Sciences, School of Biomedical and Health Sciences, Franklin-Wilkins Building, King College London, Stamford Street, SE1 9NH. *T:* (020) 7848 4552.

HERN, Jane Carolyn; Registrar, Royal College of Veterinary Surgeons, since 1997; *b* 2 Sept. 1954; *d* of George Kenneth Hern and Elizabeth Ellen Hern (*née* Byford). *Edu* Girton Coll., Cambridge (BA Hons Law 1976; MA). Articles with Lovell, White & Kin 1977–79; admitted as solicitor, 1979; LCD, 1979–87, Law Commn, 1981–86; Law Soc 1987–96: Asst Sec.-Gen., 1992–95; Dir, Management and Planning Directorate, 1995–9 Actg Sec.-Gen., 1996. Chm., UK Inter-Professional Gp, 2005–. *Recreations:* eatin drinking, reading crime thrillers, visiting places of historic interest. *Address:* (offic Belgravia House, 62–64 Horseferry Road, SW1P 2AF. *T:* (020) 7222 2001.

HERNANDEZ, David Anthony; His Honour Judge Hernandez; a Circuit Judg since 2004; *b* 15 Sept. 1953; *s* of Andrew and Daphne Hernandez; *m* 1987, Lesley Newto *qv*; one *s* one *d*. *Educ:* Bury Grammar Sch.; St Catherine's Coll., Oxford (M Jurisprudence). Called to the Bar: Lincoln's Inn, 1976; Trinidad and Tobago, 198 barrister, practising family law, 1976–2004; Jt Head, Young Street Chambers, Mancheste 2001–04. Asst Recorder, 1996–2000, Recorder, 2000–04. Chm., Rent Assessment Ctte (Northern Panel), 1984–2004. *Recreations:* Tai Chi, listening to jazz, travel. *Addre* Manchester Crown Court, Courts of Justice, Crown Square, Manchester M3 3FL. (0161) 954 1800.

HERON, Sir Conrad (Frederick), KCB 1974 (CB 1969); OBE 1953; Permane Secretary, Department of Employment, 1973–76; *b* 21 Feb. 1916; *s* of Richard Fost Heron and Ida Fredrika Heron; *m* 1948, Envye Linnéa Gustafsson; two *d*. *Educ:* Sou Shields High Sch.; Trinity Hall, Cambridge. Entered Ministry of Labour, 1938; Princip Private Secretary to Minister of Labour, 1953–56; Under-Secretary, Industrial Relatio Dept, 1963–64 and 1965–68, Overseas Dept, 1964–65; Dep. Under-Sec. of State, De of Employment, 1968–71; Dep. Chm., Commn on Industrial Relations, 1971–72; Secor

Permanent Sec., Dept of Employment, 1973. *Address:* Old Orchards, West Lydford, Somerton, Somerset TA11 7DG. *T:* (01963) 240387.

HERON, Sir Michael (Gilbert), Kt 1996; Chairman, Post Office, 1993–97; *b* 22 Oct. 1934; *s* of Gilbert Thwaites Heron and Olive Lilian (*née* Steele); *m* 1958, Celia Veronica Mary Hunter; two *s* one *d* (and one *d* decd). *Educ:* St Joseph's Acad., Blackheath; New Coll., Oxford (MA Hist.). Lieut RA, 1953–55. Dir, BOCM Silcock, 1971–76; Chm., Batchelors Foods, 1976–82; Dep. Co-ordinator, Food & Drinks Co-ordination, Unilever, 1982–86; Dir, Unilever, 1986–92. Food and Drink Federation: Mem. Cttee, 1986–92; Mem. Council, 1986–92; Chm., Food Policy Res. Cttee, 1987–92. Mem., Armed Forces Pay Rev. Bd, 1981–82. Dep. Chm. and Mem. Bd, BITC, 1991–95; Member: Policy Steering Bd, BESO, 1992–93; CBI Council, 1992–95; Dep. Chm., NACETT, 1993–95; Chairman: NCVQ, 1994–97; Council for Industry and Higher Educn, 1999–2004. Chm., N London, Prince's Trust Business Div. formerly PYBT), 1999–2004. Chm. Council, St George's Hosp. Med. Sch., 1992–98; Mem., Governing Body, Douai Abbey, 1991–97. *Recreation:* avid Rugby football watcher. *Address:* 43 Albion Gate, Albion Street, W2 2LG. *T:* (020) 7262 8091.

HERON, Raymond, CBE 1984; retired; Deputy Director, Propellants, Explosives and Rocket Motor Establishment, Ministry of Defence (Procurement Executive), 1977–84; *b* 10 April 1924; *s* of Lewis and Doris Heron; *m* 1948, Elizabeth MacGathan; one *s* one *d*. *Educ:* Heath Grammar Sch., Halifax; Queen's Coll., Oxford (BA Physics). Shell Refining and Marketing Co., 1944–47; RN, Instructor Branch, 1947–52; Rocket Propulsion Estabt, Min. of Supply (later Min. of Technology), 1952–67; Cabinet Office, 1967; Asst Dir, Min. of Technology, 1967–73; Dep. Dir, Explosives Research and Development Estabt, MoD, 1973; Special Asst to Sec. (Procurement Exec.), MoD, 1973–74; Head of Rocket Motor Exec. and Dep. Dir/2, Rocket Propulsion Estabt, MoD (PE), 1974–76. *Publications:* articles in scientific and technical jls. *Recreations:* music, hill walking, golf. *Address:* 9 Grange Gardens, Wendover, Aylesbury, Bucks HP22 6HB. *T:* (01296) 622921. *Club:* Ashridge Golf.

HERON, Robert, CVO 1988; MA; Director, Duke of Edinburgh's Award Scheme, 1978–87; *b* 12 Oct. 1927; *s* of James Riddick Heron and Sophie Leathem; *m* 1953, Patricia Mary Pennell; two *s* one *d*. *Educ:* King Edward's Sch., Birmingham; St Catharine's Coll., Cambridge. Housemaster: Strathallan, Perthshire, 1952–59; Christ Coll., Brecon, 1959–62; Headmaster, King James I Sch., IOW, 1962–66. Head of Educational Broadcasting, ATV Network Ltd, 1966–69, responsible for production of TV programme series in the scis, langs, soc. documentary, leisure interests, music, drama; Deleg., EBU study gps on educnl broadcasting, 1967–69; Programme Dir, The Electronic Video Recording Partnership (CBS Inc. USA/ICI/Ciba-Geigy UK), 1970–77; Managing Dir, EVR Ltd, 1974–77, and of EVR Enterprises Ltd, 1975–77. Freeman, City of London, 1981. Formerly 6/7th Bn, The Black Watch (RHR) TA. *Recreations:* travel, sport. *Clubs:* Rugby; Hawks (Cambridge); Achilles.

HERON-MAXWELL, Sir Nigel (Mellor), 10th Bt *cr* 1683; *b* 30 Jan. 1944; *s* of Sir Patrick Ivor Heron-Maxwell, 9th Bt and D. Geraldine E., *yr d* of late Claud Paget Mellor; *S* father, 1982; *m* 1972, Mary Elizabeth Angela, *o d* of late W. Ewing, Co. Donegal; one *s* one *d*. *Educ:* Milton Abbey. *Heir:* *s* David Mellor Heron-Maxwell, *b* 22 May 1975. *Address:* 50 Watlington Road, Old Harlow, Essex CM17 0DY.

HERRIDGE, Michael Eric James; HM Diplomatic Service, retired; Deputy High Commissioner to South India, 1999–2003; *b* 23 Sept. 1946; *s* of late Robert James Herridge and Mary Herridge (*née* Beckitt); *m* 1968, Margaret Elizabeth Bramble; one *d*. *Educ:* Ashley Sch., Hampshire; Bournemouth Coll. Joined HM Diplomatic Service, 1966; Prague, 1969–72; Nairobi, 1972–75; FCO, 1975–79; Second Sec., Lagos, 1979–82; Second, then First, Sec., UKMIS NY, 1982–86; FCO, 1986–90; First Sec., Madrid, 1990–95; FCO, 1995–99. *Recreations:* genealogy, gardening, country pursuits. *Address:* Puzzelcombe House, Dulverton, Som TA22 9NB.

HERRIES OF TERREGLES, Lady (14th in line, of the Lordship *cr* 1490); **Anne Elizabeth Fitzalan-Howard;** *b* 12 June 1938; *e d* of 16th Duke of Norfolk, KG, GCVO, GBE, TD, PC, and Lavinia Duchess of Norfolk, LG, CBE (*d* 1995); *S* to lordship upon death of father, 1975; *m* 1985, Colin Cowdrey (Baron Cowdrey of Tonbridge, CBE; *d* 2000). Racehorse trainer. *Recreations:* riding, golf, breeding spaniels. *Heir:* sister Lady Mary Katharine Mumford, *qv. Address:* Angmering Park, Littlehampton, West Sussex BN16 4EX. *T:* (01903) 871421.

HERRING, Cyril Alfred; management consultant; Senior Partner, Cyril Herring & Associates, since 1978; Chairman and Managing Director, Southern Airways Ltd, since 1978; *b* Dulwich, 17 Jan. 1915; *s* of Alfred James Herring and Minnie Herring (*née* Padfield); *m* 1939, Helen (*née* Warnes); three *s*. *Educ:* Alleyn's Sch.; London School of Economics. BSc(Econ); FCMA; JDipMA; IPFA; FCILT. Chief Accountant, Straight Corporation Ltd, 1936–46; joined BEA, 1946; Chief Accountant, 1951–57; Personnel Director, 1957–65; Financial Director, 1965–71; Executive Board Member, 1971–74; Mem., British Airways Bd, 1972–78; Chief Executive, British Airways Regional Div., 1972–74; Finance Dir, 1975–78; Chm. and Man. Dir, British Air Services Ltd, 1969–76; Chairman: Northeast Airlines Ltd, 1969–76; Cambrian Airways Ltd, 1973–76; London Rail Adv. Cttee, 1976–80; CIPFA Public Corporations Finance Group, 1976–78. Member Council: Chartered Inst. of Transport, 1971–74; Inst. of Cost and Management Accountants, 1967–77 (Vice-Pres., 1971–73, Pres., 1973–74); CBI, 1975–78 (Mem. Financial Policy Cttee, 1975–78; Finance and General Purposes Cttee, 1977–78). Freeman, City of London; Liveryman, GAPAN. *Recreations:* flying, motoring, boating. *Address:* Cuddenbeake, St Germans, Cornwall PL12 5LY. *Club:* Reform.

HERRINGTON, Air Vice-Marshal Walter John, CB 1982; Royal Air Force, retired; *b* 18 May 1928; *s* of Major H. Herrington, MBE, MM and Daisy Restal Gardiner; *m* 1958, Joyce Maureen Cherryman; two *s*. *Educ:* Woking Grammar Sch.; RAF Coll., Cranwell. Commnd RAF, 1949, Pilot; 1950–69: Long Range Transp. Sqdns 24, 53, 99; ADC to C-in-C Bomber Comd; Reconnaissance Sqdns; RAF Staff Coll.; Exchange Officer, USAF Acad., Colo; Comd 100 Sqdn; Jt Services Staff Coll.; Air Sec.'s Dept; Stn Comdr RAF Honnington, 1969–71; Ops Dept, MoD, 1971–73; RCDS (student) 1974; Defence Attaché, Paris, 1975–77. Hon. ADC to the Queen, 1971–74; Senior RAF Mem., Directing Staff, RCDS, 1978–80; Dir of Service Intelligence, 1980–82. Aviation Advr, Internat. Mil. Services, 1982–89; aviation and security consultant, 1989–95. Member: European Security Study Gp, 1982–83; Central Council, TA&VRA, 1984–90; Council, Officers Pensions Soc., 1983–89. *Publications:* The Future for the Defence Industry, 1991; text books for courses on air power for USAF Academy. *Recreations:* reading, international affairs, sport. *Club:* Royal Air Force.

HERRMANN, Georgina, OBE 2001; DPhil; FBA 1999; Reader in the Archaeology of Western Asia, University College London, 1993–2002, Hon. Professor, 2002–08; *b* 20 Oct. 1937; *d* of John Walker Thompson and Gladys Elaine Thompson; *m* 1965, Prof. Luke John Herrmann; two *s*. *Educ:* Inst. of Archaeology, Univ. of London (post-grad. dip.

1963); St Hugh's Coll., Oxford (DPhil 1966). FSA 1968. Sec., Foreign Office, 1956–61; J. R. MacIver Jun. Res. Fellow, Oxford, 1966–68; Calouste Gulbenkian Fellow, Cambridge, 1974–76; Regents' Prof., Univ. of Calif at Berkeley, 1986; Leverhulme Res. Fellow, 1989–91; part-time Lecturer: Inst. of Archaeology, London Univ., 1985–91; in Mesopotamian Archaeology, UCL, 1991–93. Dir, excavations at Merv, Turkmenistan, 1992–2001. Hon. Foreign Mem., Amer. Inst. of Archaeology, 1997. Editor, Iran (jl of British Inst. of Persian Studies), 1966–81. Laureate, Rolex Award for Enterprise, 1996. *Publications:* Ivories from Nimrud, III (with M. Mallowan), 1974, IV, 1986, V, 1992; The Iranian Revival, 1977; Iranische Denkmaler (recording Sasanian rock reliefs), 8–11, 1977–83, and 13, 1989; (ed) Furniture of Western Asia, Ancient and Traditional, 1996; Monuments of Merv I, 1999. *Recreations:* planting trees, labradors, walking. *Address:* The Old Vicarage, Penrhos, Raglan, Usk, Mon NP15 2LE. *T:* (01600) 780524.

HERROD, His Honour Donald; QC 1972; a Circuit Judge, 1978–95; *b* 7 Aug. 1930; *o s* of Wilfred and Phyllis Herrod, Doncaster; *m* 1959, Kathleen Elaine Merrington, MB, ChB; two *d*. *Educ:* grammar schs, Doncaster and Leeds. Called to the Bar, 1956. A Recorder of the Crown Court, 1972–78. Member: Parole Bd, 1978–81; Judicial Studies Bd, 1982–86. *Recreation:* golf.

HERRON, Michael; Director, Business Delivery Services, Department for Transport, since 2004; *b* 7 Jan. 1954; *s* of John Herron and Eileen Herron (*née* Mann); *m* 1989, Tessa Garland; two *s*. *Educ:* North East London Polytech. (BA Hons). Mgt trainee, Aérospatiale, 1978; Sales Manager, MM Electronics, 1979–80; Gen. Manager, York Mill Ltd, 1981–86; DTI, 1986–95; Cabinet Office, 1995–2004. *Recreations:* cooking, wine, motor-cycling, rock 'n roll music, ski-ing, golf. *Address:* Department for Transport, 105 Victoria Street, SW1E 6DT. *Club:* Royal Automobile.

HERSCHBACH, Prof. Dudley Robert; Baird Research Professor (formerly Baird Professor) of Science, Harvard University, since 1976; Professor of Physics, Texas A&M University, since 2005; *b* 18 June 1932; *s* of Robert D. Herschbach and Dorothy E. Herschbach; *m* 1964, Georgene L. Botyos; two *d*. *Educ:* Campbell High School; Stanford Univ. (BS Math 1954, MS Chem 1955); Harvard Univ. (AM Physics 1956, PhD Chem Phys 1958). Junior Fellow, Soc. of Fellows, Harvard, 1957–59; Asst Prof., 1959–61, Associate Prof., 1961–63, Univ. of California, Berkeley; Prof. of Chemistry, Harvard Univ., 1963–76. Hon. DSc: Univ. of Toronto, 1977; Dartmouth Coll., 1992; Charles Univ., Prague, 1993; Wheaton Coll., 1995; Franklin & Marshall Coll., 1998. (Jtly) Nobel Prize for Chemistry, 1986; US Nat. Medal of Sci., 1991; Heyrovský Medal, Czech Acad. of Scis, 1992; Walker Prize, Boston Mus. of Sci., 1994. *Publications:* over 350 research papers, chiefly on quantum mechanics, chemical kinetics, reaction dynamics, molecular spectroscopy, collision theory, in Jl of Chemical Physics. *Recreations:* hiking, canoeing, chess, poetry, viola. *Address:* 116 Conant Road, Lincoln, MA 01773, USA. *T:* (home) (781) 2591386; (office) (617) 4953218.

HERSCHELL, family name of **Baron Herschell.**

HERSCHELL, 3rd Baron *cr* 1886; **Rognvald Richard Farrer Herschell;** late Captain Coldstream Guards; *b* 13 Sept. 1923; *o s* of 2nd Baron and Vera (*d* 1961), *d* of Sir Arthur Nicolson, 10th Bt, of that Ilk and Lasswade; *S* father, 1929; *m* 1948, Lady Heather, *d* of 8th Earl of Dartmouth, CVO, DSO; one *d*. *Educ:* Eton. Page of Honour to the King, 1935–40. Served World War II, 1942–45. *Heir:* none. *Address:* Westfield House, Ardington, Wantage, Oxon OX12 8PN. *T:* (01235) 833224.

See also Lt-Gen. Sir J. P. Kiszely.

HERSEY, David Kenneth; lighting designer; founder Chairman, DH Design Ltd, since 1972; *b* 30 Nov. 1939; *s* of Ella Morgan Decker and C. Kenneth Hersey; *m* Demetra Maraslis; one *s* two *d*. *Educ:* Oberlin Coll., Ohio. Left NY for London, 1968; lighting designer for theatre, opera and ballet cos, incl. Royal Opera House, ENO, Glyndebourne, Ballet Rambert, London Contemporary Dance, Scottish Ballet; lighting consultant to Nat. Theatre, 1974–84; many productions for RSC. Chm., Assoc. of Lighting Designers, 1984–86. *Designs include:* Evita, 1978 (Tony award, 1980); Nicholas Nickleby, 1980; Cats, 1981 (Tony and Drama Desk awards, 1983); Song and Dance, 1982; Guys and Dolls, 1982; Starlight Express, 1984; Les Misérables, 1985 (Tony award, 1987); Porgy and Bess, 1986; Chess, 1986; Miss Saigon, 1989 (Drama Desk award, 1991); Oliver, 1995; Martin Guerre, Jesus Christ Superstar, 1996; My Fair Lady, 2001; South Pacific, The Coast of Utopia, Anything Goes, 2002; Love's Labours Lost, 2003; The Dark, 2004; Porgy and Bess, 2006; Equus, 2007. Hon. Dr Middx, 2002. Olivier Award for best lighting designer, 1995. *Recreation:* sailing (Millennium Odyssey Round the World Yacht Rally, 1998–2000). *Address:* DH Design Ltd, 65 New Cavendish Street, W1G 7LS.

HERSHKO, Avram, PhD, MD; Research Professor, Department of Biochemistry, Technion - Israel Institute of Technology; *b* 31 Dec. 1937; *s* of Moshe Hershko and Shoshana Hershko; *m* 1963, Judith Leibowitz; three *s*. *Educ:* Hebrew Univ., Jerusalem (MD 1965; PhD 1969). (Jtly) Nobel Prize in Chemistry, 2004. *Publications:* articles in learned jls. *Address:* Department of Biochemistry, Ruth and Bruce Rappaport Faculty of Medicine, Technion - Israel Institute of Technology, PO Box 9649, Haifa 31096, Israel.

HERSOV, Gregory Adam; Artistic Director, Royal Exchange Theatre, Manchester, since 1987; *b* 4 May 1956; *s* of Dr Lionel Hersov and Zoe (*née* Henell). *Educ:* Bryanston; Mansfield Coll., Oxford (MA). Regl dirs trainee, Thames TV, Redgrave Th., Farnham, 1976–78; Royal Exchange Theatre: asst dir, 1980–83; Associate Dir, 1983–85; Associate Artistic Dir, 1985–87; productions include: One Flew Over the Cuckoo's Nest, 1982; Death of a Salesman, 1985; A Doll's House, 1987; The Alchemist, 1987; All My Sons, 1988; The Voysey Inheritance, 1989; The Crucible, 1990; Blues for Mr Charlie, 1992; Romeo and Juliet, 1992; Venice Preserv'd, 1994; Animal Crackers, Royal Exchange Th. Internat. Fest. and Lyric, 1995–99; King Lear, 1999; Uncle Vanya, 2001; The Seagull, 2003; Harvey, 2005; Cyrano de Bergerac, 2006; The Tempest, 2007; Look Back in Anger, RNT, 1999. *Address:* Royal Exchange Theatre, St Ann's Square, Manchester M2 7DH. *T:* (0161) 615 6704, *Fax:* (0161) 832 0881; *e-mail:* greg.hersov@royalexchange.co.uk.

HERTFORD, 9th Marquess of, *cr* 1793; **Henry Jocelyn Seymour;** Baron Conway of Ragley 1703; Baron Conway of Killultagh 1712; Earl of Hertford, Viscount Beauchamp 1750; Earl of Yarmouth 1793; *b* 6 July 1958; *s* of 8th Marquess of Hertford and of Comtesse Louise de Caraman Chimay; *S* father, 1997; *m* 1990, Beatriz, *d* of Jorge Karam; two *s* two *d*. *Heir:* *s* Earl of Yarmouth, *qv.*

HERTFORD, Bishop Suffragan of, since 2001; **Rt Rev. Christopher Richard James Foster;** *b* 7 Nov. 1953; *s* of Joseph James Frederick Foster and Elizabeth Foster (*née* Gibbs); *m* 1st, 1982, Julia Marie Jones (*d* 2001); one *s* one *d*; 2nd, 2006, Rev. Sally Elizabeth Davenport. *Educ:* University Coll., Univ. of Durham (BA 1975); Univ. of Manchester (MA (Econ.) 1977); Trinity Hall, Cambridge (BA 1979, MA 1983); Westcott House, Cambridge. Lectr in Economics, Univ. of Durham, 1976–77; ordained deacon, 1980, priest, 1981; Asst Curate, Tettenhall Regis, Wolverhampton, 1980–82; Chaplain, Wadham Coll., Oxford and Asst Priest, Univ. Church of St Mary, with St Cross and St

Peter in the East, Oxford, 1982–86; Vicar, Christ Church, Southgate, London, 1986–94; CME Dir, Edmonton Episcopal Area, 1988–94; Sub Dean and Canon Residentiary, Cathedral and Abbey Church of St Alban, 1994–2001. Chm., F and GP Cttee, Univ. of Herts, 2007–. *Address:* Hertford House, Abbey Mill Lane, St Albans, Herts AL3 4HE. *T:* (01727) 866420, *Fax:* (01727) 811426; *e-mail:* bishophertford@stalbans.anglican.org.

HERTFORD, Archdeacon of; *see* Jones, Ven. T. P.

HERTRICH, Rainer; Co-Chief Executive Officer, European Aeronautic Defence and Space Company, 2000–05; *b* 6 Dec. 1949. *Educ:* apprenticeship and business training, Siemens AG; Technical Univ. of Berlin; Univ. of Nuremberg (Bachelor of Commerce). Messerschmitt-Bölkow-Blohm GmbH: Information Processing Supervisor, Controlling Dept, Mil. Aircraft Div., 1977; Hd, Controlling Dept, 1978, CFO, 1983, Service Div. (Ottobrunn); Hd, Controlling and Finance Dept, Dynamics Div., 1984; CFO and Mem. Div. Mgt, Marine and Special Products Div., 1987; DaimlerBenz Aerospace, subseq. DaimlerChrysler Aerospace AG: Hd of Divl Controlling, Central Controlling Section, Deutsche Aerospace AG, 1990; Sen. Vice Pres., Corporate Controlling, 1991; Hd, Aeroengines business unit, 1996; Mem., Exec. Cttee, 1996; Pres. and CEO, 2000; President and CEO, Motoren und Turbinen Union München GmbH, 1996.

HERTZELL, David John; a Law Commissioner, since 2007; *b* London, 26 Nov. 1955; *s* of Clifford and Barbara Hertzell; *m* 1984, Anne Tootill; one *s* two *d. Educ:* George Abbot Sch., Guildford; Brasenose Coll., Oxford (BA Mod. Hist.); Guildford Coll. of Law. Davies Arnold Cooper Solicitors: trainee, 1981; admitted solicitor, 1983; Partner, 1989–2007; Man. Partner, 1992–96, 2000–06. *Recreations:* squash, sailing (anything). *Address:* Law Commission, Steel House, 11 Tothill Street, SW1H 9LJ. *T:* (020) 3334 0200; *e-mail:* david.hertzell@lawcommission.gsi.gov. uk.

HERVEY, family name of **Marquess of Bristol**.

HERVEY, Rear Adm. John Bethell, CB 1982; OBE 1970; independent naval consultant; *b* 14 May 1928; *s* of late Captain Maurice William Bethell Hervey, RN, and Mrs Joan Hervey (*née* Hanbury); *m* 1950, (Audrey) Elizabeth Mote; two *s* one *d. Educ:* Marlborough Coll., Wilts. Joined RN, 1946; specialised in submarines, 1950, nuclear submarines, 1968; command appointments: HMS Miner VI, 1956; HMS Aeneas, 1956–57; HMS Ambush, 1959–62; HMS Oracle, 1962–64; Sixth Submarine Div., 1964–66; HMS Cavalier, 1966–67; HMS Warspite, 1968–69; Second Submarine Sqdn, 1973–75; HMS Kent, 1975–76; staff appointments: Course Officer, Royal Naval Petty Officers Leadership Sch., 1957–59; Submarine Staff Officer to Canadian Maritime Comdr, Halifax, NS, 1964–66; Ops Officer to Flag Officer Submarines, 1970–71; Def. Op. Requirements Staff, 1971–73; Dep. Chief of Allied Staff to C-in-C Channel and C-in-C Eastern Atlantic (as Cdre), 1976–80; Comdr British Navy Staff, and British Naval Attaché, Washington, and UK Nat. Liaison Rep. to SACLANT, 1980–82, retired. Comdr 1964, Captain 1970, Rear Adm. 1980. Marketing Vice-Pres., Western Hemisphere, MEL, 1982–86. Pres., HMS Cavalier Assoc., 1995–; Chm., Friends of RN Submarine Mus., 1995–99. FCMI (FBIM 1983). *Publication:* Submarines, 1994. *Recreations:* walking, talking, reading. *Address:* c/o National Westminster Bank, 208 Piccadilly, W1A 2DG. *Clubs:* Army and Navy, Royal Navy of 1765 and 1785, Anchorites (Pres., 1988).

HERVEY, Sir Roger Blaise Ramsay, KCVO 1991; CMG 1980; HM Diplomatic Service; Ambassador to Mexico, 1992–94; *b* 3 Oct. 1934. HM Forces, 1953–55. Joined Diplomatic Service, 1958; Bonn, 1958; FO, 1961; Prague, 1963; First Sec., FO, 1965; Office of Political Advr, Singapore, 1968; FCO, 1970; First Sec. and Head of Chancery, Bogotá, 1974; Counsellor, FCO, 1976; Counsellor, The Hague, 1979; Minister, Madrid, 1982; Asst Under Sec. of State (Protocol) and Vice Marshal of Diplomatic Corps, 1986. *Address:* c/o Foreign and Commonwealth Office, SW1A 2AH.

HERVEY-BATHURST, Sir Frederick John Charles Gordon; *see* Bathurst.

HERZBERG, Charles Francis; consultant; Chairman, Unique Business Services Ltd (formerly Newcastle upon Tyne Polytechnic Products Ltd), 1988–95; *b* 26 Jan. 1924; *s* of Dr Franz Moritz Herzberg and Mrs Marie Louise Palache; *m* 1956, Ann Linette Hoare; one *s* two *d. Educ:* Fettes Coll., Edinburgh; Sidney Sussex Coll., Cambridge (MA). CEng 1954; FIMechE 1964; MIGEM (MIGasE 1967). Alfred Herbert Ltd, 1947–51; Chief Engr and Dir, Hornflowa Ltd, Maryport, 1951–55; Chief Engr, Commercial Plastics Gp of Cos, and Dir, Commercial Plastics Engrg Co. at Wallsend on Tyne, North Shields, and Cramlington, Northumberland, 1955–66; Corporate Planning Dir, Appliance Div., United Gas Industries, and Works Dir, Robinson Willey Ltd, Liverpool, 1966–70; Man. Dir and Chief Exec., Churchill Gear Machines Ltd, Blaydon on Tyne, 1970–72; Regional Industrial Director, Dept of Industry, N Region, 1972–75; Dir of Corporate Develt, Clarke Chapman Ltd, 1975–77; Gp Industrial Planning Adviser, 1977–84, Dir Industrial Planning, 1984–88, Northern Engineering Industries plc; Dir, Northern Investors Co. Ltd, 1984–89; Pres., Tyne & Wear Chamber of Commerce and Industry, 1989–90 (Vice-Pres., 1986–89). Gov., Univ. of Northumbria (formerly Newcastle upon Tyne Poly.), 1986–96 (Hon. Fellow, 1991). *Recreations:* shooting, gardening. *Address:* 3 Furzefield Road, Gosforth, Newcastle upon Tyne NE3 4EA. *T:* (0191) 285 5202. *Club:* East India, Devonshire, Sports and Public Schools.

HERZOG, Roman, Hon. GCB 1998; President of the Federal Republic of Germany, 1994–99; *b* 5 April 1934; *m* 1958, Christiane Krauss (*d* 2000); two *s*; *m* Alexandra Freifrau von Berlichingen. *Educ:* Munich, Berlin and Tübingen Univs. DJur. Lecturer: in Law, Munich Univ., 1958–66; in Law and Politics, Free Univ. of Berlin, 1966–69 (Dean, Faculty of Law, 1967–68); Prof. of Politics, 1969–73, Rector, 1971–73, Postgrad. Sch. of Admin. Scis, Speyer. Rep. of Rhineland-Palatinate, Bundestag, 1973–78; Minister for Culture and Sport, 1978–80, for the Interior, 1980–83, Baden-Württemberg; Vice-Pres., 1983–87, Pres., 1987–94, Federal Constitutional Court. Mem. Federal Cttee, CDU, 1979–83. DCL Oxon, 1997. *Publications:* (jtly) Kommentar zur Grundgesetz, 1966, 3rd edn 1987; Allgemeine Staatslehre, 1971; Staaten der Frühzeit, 1988; Ursprünge und Herrschaftsformen, 1988; Staat und Recht im Wandel, 1993; Preventing the Clash of Civilizations: a peace strategy for the 21st century, 1999; vols of collected speeches. *Address:* (office) Prinzregentenstrasse 89, 81675 Munich, Germany.

HESELTINE, family name of **Baron Heseltine**.

HESELTINE, Baron *cr* 2001 (Life Peer), of Thenford in the County of Northamptonshire; **Michael Ray Dibdin Heseltine,** CH 1997; PC 1979; Chairman, Haymarket Publishing Group, since 1999 (Director, since 1997); *b* 21 March 1933; *s* of late Col R. D. Heseltine, Swansea, Glamorgan; *m* 1962, Anne Harding Williams (*see* Lady Heseltine); one *s* two *d. Educ:* Shrewsbury Sch.; Pembroke Coll., Oxford (BA PPE; Hon. Fellow 1986). Pres. Oxford Union, 1954. National Service (commissioned), Welsh Guards, 1959. Director of Bow Publications, 1961–65; Chm., Haymarket Press, 1966–70. Contested (C): Gower, 1959; Coventry North, 1964. MP (C): Tavistock, 1966–74; Henley, 1974–2001. Vice-Chm., Cons. Parly Transport Cttee, 1968; Opposition Spokesman on Transport, 1969; Parly Sec., Min. of Transport, June-Oct. 1970; Parly Under-Sec. of State, DoE, 1970–72; Minister for Aerospace and Shipping, DTI, 1972–74; Opposition Spokesman on: Industry 1974–76; Environment, 1976–79; Sec. of State for the Environment, 1979–83 an 1990–92, for Defence, 1983–86; Pres., BoT, 1992–95; First Sec. of State and Dep. Prim Minister, 1995–97. Pres., Assoc. of Conservative Clubs, 1978; Vice-Pres., 1978, Pres 1982–84, Nat. Young Conservatives; Pres., Conservative Gp for Europe, 2001. Mem Council, Zoological Soc. of London, 1987–90. Patron, Nat. Centre for Competitivenes Univ. of Luton, 2001. Hon. Fellow: Leeds Polytechnic, 1988; Univ. of Wales, Swanse 2001. Hon. FRIBA 1991; Hon. FCIM 1998 (Pres., 2006–08). Hon. LLD Liverpoo 1990. *Publications:* Reviving the Inner Cities, 1983; Where There's a Will, 1987; Th Challenge of Europe, 1989; Life in the Jungle (memoirs), 2000. *Address:* c/o House o Lords, SW1A 0PW. *Clubs:* Brooks's, Carlton, Pratt's, White's.

HESELTINE, Lady; Anne Edna Harding Heseltine; a Trustee, National Gallery, sinc 2008; *b* London, 23 Oct. 1934; *d* of William and Edna Williams; *m* 1962, Michael Ra Dibdin Heseltine (*see* Baron Heseltine); one *s* two *d. Educ:* Bedford Coll., Univ. of Londo (BA Hons 1956). Career in publishing and art dealing at Victor Gollancz Ltd, Cran Kalman Gall. and Bury St Gall. Mem., Bd of Visitors, Ashmolean Mus., Oxfor 1987–2006, Fellow, 2006; Distinguished Friend, Univ. of Oxford, 1999; Trustee: Imperi War Mus., 1990–97; V & A Mus., 1997–2002; Burlington Mag., 2003–; former Mem Council, Attingham Foundn. *Recreations:* travelling, art history, collecting, gardens, fo and stag hunting. *Address:* c/o Haymarket Media Group, 174 Hammersmith, W6 7JP.

HESELTINE, Rt Hon. Sir William (Frederick Payne), GCB 1990 (KCB 1986; C 1978); GCVO 1988 (KCVO 1982; CVO 1969; MVO 1961); AC 1988; QSO 1990; P 1986; Deputy Chairman, P & O Australia Ltd, 1998–2001 (Director, 1990–2001); *b* Fremantle, W Australia, 17 July 1930; *s* of late H. W. Heseltine; *m* 1st, Ann Elizabeth (1957), *d* of late L. F. Turner, Melbourne; 2nd, Audrey Margaret, *d* of late S. Nola Sydney; one *s* one *d. Educ:* Christ Church Grammar Sch., Claremont, WA; University o Western Australia (1st class hons, History). Prime Minister's dept, Canberra, 1951–62 Private Secretary to Prime Minister, 1955–59; Asst Information Officer to The Quee 1960–61; Acting Official Secretary to Governor-General of Australia, 1962; Asst Feder Director of Liberal Party of Australia, 1962–64; attached to Household of Princess Marin for visit to Australia, 1964; attached to Melbourne Age, 1964; Asst Press Secretary to th Queen, 1965–67, Press Secretary, 1968–72; Assistant Private Secretary to the Quee 1972–77, Dep. Private Secretary, 1977–86, Private Sec., and Keeper of the Queen Archives, 1986–90. Chm., NZI Insurance Australia Ltd, 1992–98 (Dep. Chm., 1991–92) Director: West Coast Telecasters Ltd, 1991–96; NZI Insurance NZ, 1996–98. Pres Royal Western Australian Histl Soc., 1998–2001. Senator, Murdoch Univ., 2000–06 *Address:* PO Box 35, York, WA 6302, Australia. *Club:* Weld (Perth).

HESFORD, Stephen; MP (Lab) Wirral West, since 1997; *b* 27 May 1957; *s* of Bernar and Nellie Hesford; *m* 1984, Elizabeth Anne Henshall; two *s. Educ:* Univ. of Bradfor (BScSoc Econs/Politics 1978); Poly. of Central London (Post-grad. Dip. in Law 1980 Called to the Bar, Gray's Inn, 1981. Contested (Lab) S Suffolk, 1992. PPS to Leader of H of L, 2005–07, to Solicitor Gen., 2007–, and to Minister of State, MoJ. Mem., Healt Select Cttee., 1999–2001. Founder: and Sec., All-Party Parly Gp on Primary Care an Public Health, 1998–; and Vice-Chm., All-Party Parly Gp on Autism. Mem. Bd, Mind 1998–2001. FRIPH (FRIPHH 1998); Fellow, Soc. of Public Health; FRSA 2006 *Recreations:* watching football, reading. *Address:* House of Commons, SW1A 0AA. T (020) 7219 6227. *Club:* Lancashire County Cricket (Life Mem.).

HESKETH, 3rd Baron *cr* 1935, of Hesketh; **Thomas Alexander Fermor-Hesketh** KBE 1997; PC 1991; Bt 1761; Chairman, British Mediterranean Airways, 1994–2007 Treasurer, Conservative Party, 2003–05; *b* 28 Oct. 1950; *s* of 2nd Baron and Christia Mary, OBE 1984, *o d* of Sir John McEwen, 1st Bt of Marchmont, DL, JP; *S* father, 1955 *m* 1977, Hon. Claire, *e d* of 3rd Baron Manton; one *s* two *d. Educ:* Ampleforth. A Lord i Waiting (Govt Whip), 1986–89; Parly Under-Sec. of State, DoE, 1989–90; Minister c State, DTI, 1990–91; Capt. of Gentlemen-at-Arms (Govt Chief Whip in H of L) 1991–93. Chm., Cons. Party Foundn, 2003–. Non-exec. Dep. Chm., Babcock Internat. 1993–; indep. Dir, Air Astana JSC, 2007–; Chm., Towcester Racecourse. President British Racing Drivers' Club, 1994–99; Remote Sensing and Photogrammetry Soc 1995–2002. Hon. FSE; Hon. FIET 1982. *Heir: s* Hon. Frederick Hatton Fermor-Hesketh *b* 13 Oct. 1988. *Address:* 33 King Street, SW1Y 6RJ. *T:* (020) 7389 3839. *Clubs:* White's Turf, Pratt's.

HESKETH, Ven. Ronald David, CB 2004; Chaplain-in-Chief and Archdeacon, Roya Air Force, 2001–06; *b* 16 June 1947; *s* of William Ronald Hesketh and Mary Haga Hesketh; *m* 1971, Vera Ruth Taylor; one *s* one *d. Educ:* King David Sch., Liverpool; Bed Coll., Univ. of Durham (BA Hons 1968); Ridley Hall, Cambridge; St Michael's Coll. Llandaff (DPS 1971); Dip in Reformation Studies, Open Univ., 1977. Ordained deaco 1971, priest, 1972; Curate, Southport, 1971–73; Asst Chaplain, Mersey Mission t Seamen, 1973–75; RAF Chaplain, 1975–98; Command Chaplain, 1998–2001; Canon Lincoln Cathedral, 2001–06; Vocations Officer, Worcester Dio., 2006–. Mem., Gen Synod of C of E, 2001–05. QHC 2001–06. Mem. Council, RAF Benevolent Fund 2001–04. FRGS 2002; FCMI 2006. *Recreations:* theatre, travel, philately, antiquaria books. *Address:* The Old Police Station, Bredon Road, Tewkesbury, GL20 5BZ. T (01684) 299773; *e-mail:* ron@hesketh.org.uk. *Club:* Royal Air Force.

HESKETH HARVEY, Christopher John, (Kit); writer, broadcaster and cabare performer; *b* Zomba, Nyasaland, 30 April 1957; *s* of Noel Harvey and Susan Mary Harve (*née* Ford); *m* 1986, Catherine, (Kate), Rabett; one *s* one *d. Educ:* Cathedral Choir Sch. Canterbury; Tonbridge Sch.; Clare Coll., Cambridge (BA English Lit. 1978); S Catherine's Coll., Oxford (Postgrad. Th. Studies). Staff producer, Music and Arts, BB TV, 1980–85; *lyricist and star* (at Vaudeville Th.): Kit and the Widow: Lavishly Mounted 1991; January Sale, 1994; Salad Days, 1996; Meat on the Bone, 1998; starred with Joa Rivers, Haymarket Th. and London Palladium, 2002 and 2006; *plays:* Five O'clock Ange Hampstead Th., 1998; The Caribbean Tempest, Barbados, 2000; *screenwriter:* Mauric 1986; Birkin, 1994; Hans Christian Andersen, 2000; *opera translations* include: Barter Bride, Royal Opera, 2001; Il Turco in Italia, 2002, La Belle Hélène, 2006, ENO Bluebeard, 2007; *librettist* (with James Connel): Orlando, Barbican, 1988 (Vivian Elli Award); Killing Rasputin, Bridewell, 1998; *television* includes: co-writer, Vicar of Dible 1994; Lavishly Mounted; Mounting the Hustings; *radio* includes: Cocktails; panellist, Jus a Minute, 1996–. *Recreations:* mushrooming, surfing, playing the piano execrably. *Address* Park House, Stoke Ferry, King's Lynn, Norfolk PE33 9SF; c/o PBJ Management, 7 Soh Street, W1D 3DQ. *T:* (020) 7287 1112. *Clubs:* Garrick, Saints and Sinners.

HESLAM, (Mary) Noelle, (Mrs David Heslam); *see* Walsh, M. N.

HESLOP, David Thomas, OBE 1987; CompIGasE; Regional Chairman, British Gas pl Southern, 1989–94; *b* 16 Sept. 1932; *s* of late John Heslop and Frances Mary (*née* Brooks) *m* 1952, Barbara Mary Seddon; one *s* one *d. Educ:* Henley Management Coll. (GM 1974); Harvard Business Sch. (AMP 1981). CompIGasE 1990. Commercial Sales Officer Scottish Gas, 1960; Marketing Develt Man., West Midlands Gas, 1965; Sales Man., Sout

Eastern Gas, 1972; Dir of Sales, North Western Gas, 1976; HQ Dir of Sales, British Gas, 1982. Pres., Internat. Gas Marketing Colloquium, 1986–89. FCIM 1977; CCMI (CBIM 1990). *Recreations:* chess, choral singing, walking, Rugby. *Address:* Prestolee, Rhinefield Road, Brockenhurst, Hants SO42 7SR.

HESLOP, Martin Sydney; QC 1995; a Recorder of the Crown Court, since 1993; *b* 6 Aug. 1948; *s* of late Sydney Heslop and of Patricia (*née* Day); *m* 1994, Aurea Jane (*née* Boyle). *Educ:* St George's Coll., Weybridge; Bristol Univ. LLB Hons 1971. Called to the Bar, Lincoln's Inn, 1972; Jun. Treasury Counsel, 1987; First Jun. Treasury Counsel, 1992–93; Sen. Treasury Counsel, 1993–95. An Asst Recorder, 1989–93. *Recreations:* sailing, travel, photography, fine wine and food. *Address:* 2 Hare Court, Temple, EC4Y 7BH. *T:* (020) 7353 5324. *Clubs:* Naval, Royal London Yacht, Bar Yacht.

HESLOP, Sean Martin, MA; Headmaster, Tiffin School, Kingston, since 2004; *b* 31 Oct. 1967; *s* of late Roy Heslop and of Eileen Heslop; *m* 2005, Céline Gagnon. *Educ:* Queens' Coll., Cambridge (BA 1989); King's Coll., London (PGCE); Inst. of Educn, Univ. of London (MA Dist.). Teacher of English, Queen Elizabeth's Sch., Barnet, 1994–97; Hd of English, St Olave's Sch., Orpington, 1997–2000; Dep. Headteacher, Ravens Wood Sch., Bromley, 2000–04. Res. Associate, Nat. Coll. of Sch. Leadership, 2003–. Consultant, Thinking & Learning Schs Alliance, 2002–04. FRSA 2007. *Publications:* contrib. articles on social capital, knowledge capital and change process to educn mgt jls. *Recreations:* walking, reading, bird-watching. *Address:* Tiffin School, Queen Elizabeth Road, Kingston upon Thames, Surrey KT2 6RL. *T:* (020) 8546 4638, *Fax:* (020) 8546 6365; *e-mail:* office@tiffin.kingston.sch.uk.

HESS, Nigel John; composer and conductor for television, film and theatre; *b* 22 July 1953; *s* of John and Sheila Hess; *m* 1996, Lisa Claire Telford; one *d. Educ:* Weston-super-Mare Grammar Sch. for Boys; St Catharine's Coll., Cambridge (MA). House Composer for Royal Shakespeare Co., 1981–85; scores for: *theatre,* including: Troilus and Cressida, Julius Caesar, Much Ado About Nothing and Cyrano de Bergerac (NY Drama Desk Award, 1985), Comedy of Errors, Hamlet, Love's Labour's Lost, Othello, The Winter's Tale, The Swan Down Gloves, A Christmas Carol, Twelfth Night (all for RSC); The Secret of Sherlock Holmes; The Merry Wives of Windsor, Globe; *television,* including: A Woman of Substance; Deceptions; Anna of the Five Towns; All Passion Spent; Vanity Fair; Campion; Testament (Novello Award for Best TV Theme, 1988); Summer's Lease (TRIC Award for Best TV Theme, 1989); The London Embassy; The One Game; Titmuss Regained; Maigret; Growing Pains; Classic Adventure (Music from the Movies Mag. Award for Best BBC Theme Music, 1992); Dangerfield; Just William; Wycliffe (Music from the Movies Mag. Award for Best ITV Theme Music, 1995); Hetty Wainthropp Investigates (Novello Award for Best TV Theme, 1997); Badger; Ballykissangel; New Tricks; Stick with Me Kid; *films,* including: An Ideal Husband, 1999; Ladies in Lavender, 2004; *concert music,* including: Thames Journey; East Coast Pictures, 1985; The Way of Light, 1985; Global Variations, 1990; Stephenson's Rocket, 1991; The Winds of Power, 1993; Scramble!, 1994; To the Stars!, 1996; The TV Detectives, 1998; Monck's March, 2002; New London Pictures, 2003; The Food of Love, 2005; Piano Concerto (commnd by Prince of Wales), 2007; *ballet,* The Old Man of Lochnagar, 2007. Creator, vocal gp, Chameleon (Music Retailers Assoc. Award for Best MOR Vocal Album, 1991). Has made numerous recordings. Mem., British Acad. Composers and Songwriters, 1985–. *Recreations:* travel, photography. *Address:* c/o Bucks Music Ltd, Onward House, 11 Uxbridge Street, W8 7TQ. *T:* (020) 7221 4275, *Fax:* (020) 7229 6893; *e-mail:* nigel@myramusic.co.uk.

HESSAYON, Dr David Gerald, OBE 2007; gardening author; Chairman: Expert Publications Ltd, since 1988; Hessayon Books, since 1993; *b* 13 Feb. 1928; *s* of Jack and Lena Hessayon; *m* 1951, Joan Parker Gray (*d* 2001); two *d. Educ:* Salford Grammar Sch.; Leeds Univ. (BSc 1950); Manchester Univ. (PhD 1954). FRMS 1960; FRES 1960; FRSA 1970; FIBiol 1971; FIHort 1986. Res. Fellow, UC of Gold Coast, 1953. Pan Britannica Industries Ltd: Technical Man., 1955–60; Tech. Dir, 1960–64; Man. Dir, 1964–91; Chm., 1972–93; Chm., Turbair Ltd, 1972–93. Chm., British Agrochemicals Assoc., 1980–81. Vice-Patron, Royal Nat. Rose Soc., 1987–; Patron, Essex Gardens Trust, 1996–. Mem., Guild of Freemen, City of London, 1977–; Liveryman, Gardeners' Co., 1985. FCMI (FBIM 1972). Hon. DSc: Manchester, 1990; Hertfordshire, 1994. Lifetime Achievement Trophy, Nat. British Book Awards, 1992; Veitch Gold Meml Medal, RHS, 1992; Lifetime Achievement Award, Garden Writers' Guild, 2005. *Publications:* Be Your Own Gardening Expert, 1959, rev. edn 1977; Be Your Own House Plant Expert, 1960; Potato Growers Handbook, 1961; Silage Makers Handbook, 1961; Be Your Own Lawn Expert, 1962, rev. edn 1979; Be Your Own Rose Expert, 1964, rev. edn 1977; (with J. P. Hessayon) The Garden Book of Europe, 1973; Vegetable Plotter, 1976; Be Your Own House Plant Spotter, 1977; Be Your Own Vegetable Doctor, 1978; Be Your Own Garden Doctor, 1978; The House Plant Expert, 1980, rev. edn 1991; The Rose Expert, 1981, rev. edn 1996; The Lawn Expert, 1982, rev. edn 1997; The Cereal Disease Expert, 1982; The Tree and Shrub Expert, 1983; The Armchair Book of the Garden, 1983; The Flower Expert, 1984, rev. edn 1999; The Vegetable Expert, 1985; The Indoor Plant Spotter, 1985; The Garden Expert, 1986; The Gold Plated House Plant Expert, 1987; The Home Expert, 1987; Vegetable Jotter, 1989; Rose Jotter, 1989; House Plant Jotter, 1989; The Fruit Expert, 1990; Be Your Own Greenhouse Expert, 1990; The Bio Friendly Gardening Guide, 1990; The Bedding Plant Expert, 1991, rev. edn 1996; The Garden DIY Expert, 1992; The Rock and Water Garden Expert, 1993; The Flowering Shrub Expert, 1994; The Greenhouse Expert, 1994; The Flower Arranging Expert, 1994; The Container Expert, 1995; The Bulb Expert, 1995; The Easy-care Gardening Expert, 1995; The Vegetable & Herb Expert, 1997; The Evergreen Expert, 1998; The Pocket Flower Expert, 2001; The Pocket Tree & Shrub Expert, 2001; The Pocket Garden Troubles Expert, 2001; The Pocket House Plant Expert, 2002; The Pocket Vegetable Expert, 2002; The Garden Revival Expert, 2004; The House Plant Expert Book 2, 2005; The Pest & Weed Expert, 2007; The Orchid Expert, 2008. *Recreations:* American folk music, The Times crossword. *Address:* c/o Transworld Publishers, 61–63 Uxbridge Road, W5 5SA.

HESSE, Prof. Joachim Jens, PhD; Founding Director, European Centre for Comparative Government and Public Policy, Berlin, 1997–2001; Chairman, International Institute for Comparative Government and European Policy, Berlin; *b* 20 Nov. 1942; *s* of Joachim Hesse and Frieda Hesse (*née* Madrowski); *m* 1981, Irmgart Wethmar-von Hagen; one *s* one *d. Educ:* Schadow Gymnasium, Berlin; Univ. of Goettingen; Univ. of Kiel; Univ. of Berlin (Dipl. Volkswirt. 1967); Univ. of Cologne (PhD Econs 1972). Res. Associate, German Inst. of Urbanism, Berlin, 1968–73; Professor of Pol and Admin. Scis, Univ. of Constance, 1973–77; Pol Sci. and Comparative Govt, Duisburg, 1978–83; Exec. Dir, Rhine-Ruhr Inst. for Social Res. and Public Policy Studies, 1980–84; Prof. of Pol and Admin. Scis, German Post-Grad. Sch. of Admin. Scis, Speyer, 1984–90; Prof. of Eur. Politics and Comparative Govt, and Fellow of Nuffield College, Oxford Univ., 1991–97. Vis. Prof., Coll. of Europe, Bruges, 1987–90; Visiting Scholar: Harvard Univ., 1984–85; Oxford Univ., 1988–89. Consultant: OECD, 1970–; EU (formerly EEC), 1988–; UN, 1991–; ILO, 1992–; World Bank, 1995–. Managing Editor: Staatswissenschaften und Staatspraxis, 1990–98; Zeitschrift für Staats und Europawissenschaften, 2003–; Internat.

Editor, Public Admin., 1992–95; General Editor: Jahrbuch zur Staatswissenschaft und Staatspraxis, 1987–; European Yearbook on Comparative Govt and Public Admin., 1994–. *Publications:* include: (with A. Benz) Die Modernisierung der Staatsorganisation, 1990; (ed) Administrative Transformation in Central and Eastern Europe, 1993; (with T. Ellwein) Der überforderte Staat, 1994, 2nd edn 1997; (ed with N. Johnson) Constitutional Policy and Change in Europe, 1995; (ed with V. Wright) Federalizing Europe?: the costs and benefits of federal political systems, 1996; (ed) Regions in Europe, 2 vols, 1996–97; (jtly) Zur Neuordnung der Europäischen Union: die Regierungskonferenz 1996/97, 1997; (ed with C. Hood and B. G. Peters) Paradoxes in Public Sector Reform, 2003; (with T. Ellwein) Das Regierungssystem der Bundesrepublik Deutschland (2 vols), 9th edn, 2004; (with F. Grotz) Europa professionalisieren, 2004; Vom Werden Europas, 2004. *Address:* International Institute of Comparative Government and European Policy, Behrenstrasse 34, 10117 Berlin, Germany.

HESSE, Mary Brenda, MA, MSc, PhD; FBA 1971; Professor of Philosophy of Science, University of Cambridge, 1975–85; Fellow of Wolfson College (formerly University College), Cambridge, 1965–92, subseq. Hon. Fellow; *b* 15 Oct. 1924; *d* of Ethelbert Thomas Hesse and Brenda Nellie Hesse (*née* Pelling). *Educ:* Imperial Coll., London; University Coll., London. MSc, PhD (London); DIC; MA (Cantab). Lecturer: in Mathematics, Univ. of Leeds, 1951–55; in Hist. and Philosophy of Science, UCL, 1955–59; in Philosophy of Science, Univ. of Cambridge, 1960–68; Reader in Philosophy of Sci., Cambridge Univ., 1968–75; Vice-Pres., Wolfson Coll., 1976–80. Member: Council, British Acad., 1979–82; UGC, 1980–85. Visiting Professor: Yale Univ., 1961; Univ. of Minnesota, 1966; Univ. of Chicago, 1968. Stanton Lectr, Cambridge, 1977–80; Joint Gifford Lectr, Edinburgh, 1983. Pres., Cambridge Antiquarian Soc., 1996–98. Mem., Academia Europaea, 1989. Hon. DSc: Hull, 1984; Guelph, Ontario, 1987; Hon. ScD Cantab, 2002. Editor, Brit. Jl for the Philosophy of Science, 1965–69. *Publications:* Science and the Human Imagination, 1954; Forces and Fields, 1961; Models and Analogies in Science, 1963; The Structure of Scientific Inference, 1974; Revolutions and Reconstructions in the Philosophy of Science, 1980; (jtly) The Construction of Reality, 1987; articles in jls of philosophy and of the history and philosophy of science. *Recreations:* walking, landscape history and archaeology. *Address:* Wolfson College, Cambridge CB3 9BB.

HESSELL TILTMAN, Sir John, KCVO 2003 (LVO 1997); Member of Board, Parliamentary Estate, since 2006; *b* 27 Aug. 1942; *s* of Henry Hessell Tiltman and Rita Florence Hessell Tiltman; *m* 1969, Monique Yvonne Françoise Louge; one *s* one *d. Educ:* Brighton Coll.; Brighton Coll. of Art (DipArch 1965). ARIBA 1968. Project Architect, GLC, 1965–68; Property Services Agency, Department of the Environment, 1969–90: Project Architect, 1969–76; Project Manager: PO and BT works, 1976–82; RN works, 1982–85; Chief Architect, work in RN Trng Estabts, 1985–88; Hd of Royal Palaces Gp, 1988–90; Dep. Dir, 1991–96, Dir, 1996–2003, Property Services, HM Household; Project Dir, reconstruction of fire-damaged areas of Windsor Castle, 1993–97; Dir, Time and Space Project, Nat. Maritime Mus., Greenwich, 2004–06. *Recreations:* performing and visual arts, oil painting, bridge, travel. *Address:* 18 rue Sainte Anne, 31000 Toulouse, France.

HESTER, Prof. Ronald Ernest, DSc, PhD; CChem, FRSC; Professor of Chemistry, University of York, 1983–2001, now Emeritus; *b* 8 March 1936; *s* of Ernest and Rhoda Hester; *m* 1958, Bridget Ann Maddin; two *s* two *d. Educ:* Royal Grammar Sch., High Wycombe; London Univ. (BSc; DSc 1979); Cornell Univ. (PhD 1962). CChem 1975; FRSC 1971. Res. Fellow, Cambridge Univ., 1962–63; Asst Prof., Cornell Univ., 1963–65; University of York: Lectr, 1965–71; Sen. Lectr, 1971–76; Reader, 1976–83. Science and Engineering Research Council: Chm., Chemistry Cttee, 1988–90; Mem., Science Bd, 1988–90; Mem., Council, 1990–94. Chm., Envmt Group, RSC, 1982–85. European Editor, BioSpectroscopy, 1994–2003; Mem., Editorial Bd, Biopolymers, 2004–06. *Publications:* (jtly) Inorganic Chemistry, 1965; (ed with R. J. H. Clark) Advances in Infrared and Raman Spectroscopy, 12 vols, 1975–85; (ed with R. J. H. Clark) Advances in Spectroscopy, 14 vols, 1986–98; (ed with R. M. Harrison) Issues in Environmental Science and Technology, 27 vols, 1994–2008; 350 research papers. *Recreations:* tennis, golf, ski-ing, travel. *Address:* Department of Chemistry, University of York, York YO10 5DD. *T:* (01904) 432557.

See also S. A. M. Hester.

HESTER, Stephen Alan Michael; Chief Executive, The British Land Company plc, since 2004; *b* 14 Dec. 1960; *m* 1991, Barbara Abt; one *s* one *d. Educ:* Lady Margaret Hall, Oxford (BA PPE). Credit Suisse First Boston, 1982–2001: various posts, including: Co-Hd, European Investment Banking, 1993–96; Mem. Exec. Bd, 1996–2001; Chief Financial Officer, 1996–2000; Hd, Fixed Income Div., 2000–01; Abbey National plc: Finance Dir, 2002; Chief Operating Officer, 2003–04. Non-exec. Dep. Chm., Northern Rock, 2008–. *Recreations:* ski-ing, country sports, horticulture. *Address:* (office) York House, 45 Seymour Street, W1H 7LX. *T:* (office) (020) 7486 4466.

HETHERINGTON, Roger Rooke; His Honour Judge Hetherington; a Circuit Judge, since 2003; *b* 2 April 1951; *s* of Dr Stephen Hetherington and Jeanette Hetherington; *m* 1976, Charlotte Elizabeth Bourne; one *s* two *d. Educ:* Sherborne Sch.; Trinity Coll., Cambridge (BA Hons). Called to the Bar, Middle Temple, 1973; in practice as barrister, 1973–2003; Asst Recorder, Western Circuit, 1997–2000; Recorder, 2000–03. *Recreations:* golf, National Hunt racing. *Address:* Portsmouth Combined Court Centre, Courts of Justice, Winston Churchill Avenue, Portsmouth PO1 2EB. *Clubs:* Royal Naval (Portsmouth); Huntercombe Golf.

HETHERINGTON, Stephen; Chairman, HQ Theatres, since 2007; *b* 20 May 1949; *s* of Jack Hetherington and Constance Alice, (Billie), Hetherington (*née* Harper); three *d. Educ:* Northern Sch. of Music; Royal Acad. of Music; Warwick Univ. (MA). Trumpeter, with symphony orchs, 1969–75. Formed Hetherington Seelig (with J. Seelig), 1981; Dir, Hetherington Seelig Theatres Ltd, 1981–2007: co. presented opera, ballet, theatre and music worldwide; consultant to govts and cultural instns; formed business plans for Lowry Project (Nat. Landmark Millennium Project for the Arts), 1995, Chief Exec., 1996–2001; led Birmingham CC's bid to become European Capital of Culture 2008; currently working on major urban regeneration projects. *Recreations:* sailing, flying. *Address:* e-mail: stephen@hetherington.biz.

HETZEL, Phyllis Bertha Mabel, (Mrs R. D. Hetzel, jr); Registrar of the Roll, and Bye-Fellow, Newnham College, Cambridge, 1993–98; President, Lucy Cavendish College, Cambridge, 1979–84; *b* 10 June 1918; *d* of Stanley Ernest and Bertha Myson; *m* 1st, 1941, John Henry Lewis James (*d* 1962); one *d*, 2nd, 1974, Baron Bowden (marr. diss. 1983, he *d* 1989); 3rd, 1985, Ralph Dorn Hetzel (*d* 1994). *Educ:* Wimbledon High Sch.; Newnham Coll., Cambridge (MA). Commonwealth (now Harkness) Fellow, 1957–58. BoT, 1941; Principal 1947; Asst Sec., 1960; DEA, 1964–69; Min. of Technology, 1969–70; Dept of Trade and Industry, 1970–75; Asst Under-Sec. of State 1972; Regional Dir, NW Region, DTI, subseq. DoI, 1972–75. Member: Monopolies and Mergers Commn, 1975–78; Local Govt Boundary Commn for England, 1977–81; W Midlands

Cttee, National Trust, 1976–81. Chm., Manchester, Marriage Guidance Council, 1976–79. Member: Court, Manchester Univ., 1976–83; Court and Council, UMIST, 1978–80; Council of Senate, Cambridge Univ., 1983–84; Bd, American Friends of Cambridge University Inc., 1985–98. Vice-Pres., Oxford and Cambridge Club of Los Angeles, 1986–92. *Publications:* The Concept of Growth Centres, 1968; Gardens through the Ages, 1971; Regional Policy in Action, 1980; contrib. Public Administration, Cambridge Review, Encycl. Britannica, Oxford DNB. *Recreations:* landscape painting, conservation, writing, piano, family. *Address:* 18 Trafalgar Road, Cambridge CB4 1EU. *T:* (01223) 369878; Newnham College, Cambridge CB3 9DF.

HEWES, Robin Anthony Charles; Chief Executive, New Millennium Experience Co., 2001 (Finance Director, 2000–01); *b* 15 April 1945; *s* of late Leslie Augustus Hewes and Lily Violet Hewes (*née* Norfolk); *m* 1967, Christine Diane Stonebridge; one *s* two *d*. *Educ:* Colchester Royal Grammar School; Bristol Univ. (LLB Hons 1966). Inspector of Taxes, 1966; Department of Industry, 1974; Cabinet Office (Management and Personnel Office), 1985–87; Dir, Enterprise and Deregulation Unit, DTI, 1987–88; Lloyd's of London: Head, later Dir, Regulatory Services, 1988–94 (nominated Member, Council of Lloyd's and Lloyd's Regulatory Bd, 1993–94); Dir, Finance and Mem., Lloyd's Mkt Bd, 1994–2000. Non-exec. Dir, Comforto-Vickers (formerly Vickers Business Equipment Div.), 1984–88. Lloyd's Silver Medal, 1996. *Address:* 38 Plovers Mead, Wyatts Green, Brentwood, Essex CM15 0PS. *T:* (01277) 822891.

HEWETSON, Ven. Christopher; Archdeacon of Chester, 1994–2002, now Archdeacon Emeritus; *b* 1 June 1937; *s* of Edward and Mary Hewetson; *m* 1963, Alison Mary Croft; four *d*. *Educ:* Shrewsbury Sch.; Trinity Coll., Oxford (MA); Chichester Theol Coll. Assistant Master: Dragon Sch., Oxford, 1960–64 and 1966–67; The Craig, Windermere, 1964–66. Ordained deacon, 1969, priest, 1970; Assistant Curate: SS Peter and Paul, Leckhampton, 1969–71; All Saints, Wokingham, 1971–73; Vicar, St Peter's, Didcot, 1973–82; Rector, All Saints, Ascot Heath, 1982–90; Chaplain, St George's Sch., Ascot, 1985–88; RD, Bracknell, 1986–90; Priest i/c, Holy Trinity, Headington Quarry, 1990–94; Hon. Canon, Christ Church, Oxford, 1992–94; RD, Cowley, 1994. Mem., Chester Cath. Chapter, 2001–02. Bishop's Advr for Spirituality, dio. Exeter, 2003–07. *Recreations:* fell walking, old houses, opera. *Address:* The Old Estate House, The Square, North Molton, South Molton, Devon EX36 3HP.

HEWETSON, Sir Christopher (Raynor), Kt 1984; TD 1967; DL; Partner, Lace Mawer (formerly Laces), Solicitors, Liverpool, 1961–95; President, Law Society, 1983–84; *b* 26 Dec. 1929; *s* of Harry Raynor Hewetson and Emma Hewetson; *m* 1962, Alison May Downie, *d* of late Prof. A. W. Downie, FRCP, FRS; two *s* one *d*. *Educ:* Sedbergh Sch.; Peterhouse, Cambridge (MA). National Service, 2nd Lieut 4th RHA, 1951–53; Territorial Service, 1953–68: Lt-Col commanding 359 Medium Regt, RA, TA, 1965–68. Qualified as solicitor, 1956. Mem. Council, Law Society, 1966–87; Vice-Pres., 1982–83; President, Liverpool Law Society, 1976. Gov., Coll. of Law, 1969–94 (Chm., 1977–82). Hon. Col, 33 Signal Regt (V), 1992–94. DL Merseyside, 1986, High Sheriff, Merseyside, 1998. *Recreations:* golf, walking, music. *Address:* 24c Westcliffe Road, Birkdale, Southport, Merseyside PR8 2BU. *T:* (01704) 567179. *Clubs:* Army and Navy; Athenæum (Pres., 1997–98) (Liverpool); Royal Birkdale Golf (Capt., 1993–94) (Southport).

HEWETT, Sir Richard Mark John, 7th Bt *cr* 1813, of Nether Seale, Leicestershire; Senior software engineer, WesternGeco, since 2000; *b* 15 Nov. 1958; *er s* of Sir Peter John Smithson Hewett, 6th Bt, MM and of Jennifer Ann Cooper Hewett (*née* Jones); *S* father, 2001. *Educ:* Bradfield Coll.; Jesus Coll., Cambridge (BA Nat. Scis 1980). Career in geophysical software develt; Seismograph Service Ltd, 1980–91; Schlumberger Geco-Prakla, 1991–2000; WesternGeco, 2000–. *Recreations:* filk music, SF, choral singing, folk harp, astronomy. *Heir: b* David Patrick John Hewett [*b* 24 June 1968; *m* 1997, Kate Elizabeth Ormand; two *s* one *d*]. *Address:* Orpington, Kent.

HEWETT, Major Richard William; Senior Vice President and Director, International Operations, Reader's Digest Association Inc., 1986–88; *b* 22 Oct. 1923; *s* of late Brig. W. G. Hewett, OBE, MC, and Louise S. Hewett (*née* Wolfe); *m* 1954, Rosemary Cridland; two *d*. *Educ:* Wellington Coll., Berks. Enlisted RA, 1941; commnd RA, 1943; regular commn 1944: served Normandy, India, UK, Malaya; regtl duty, flying duties Air OP, Instr, OCTU, Mons, 1954; sc 1955; Staff and regtl duties, Germany, 1956–59; Mil. Mission, USA, 1959–61. Joined Reader's Digest Assoc. Ltd, 1962; Dir 1976; Man. Dir, 1981–84; Chm. and Man. Dir, 1984–86. *Recreations:* tennis, fishing, travelling.

HEWISH, Prof. Antony, MA, PhD; FRS 1968; FInstP; Professor of Radioastronomy, University of Cambridge, 1971–89, now Emeritus (Reader, 1969–71); Fellow of Churchill College, since 1961; *b* 11 May 1924; *s* of late Ernest William Hewish and Frances Grace Lanyon Pinch; *m* 1950, Marjorie Elizabeth Catherine Richards; one *s* (one *d* decd). *Educ:* King's Coll., Taunton; Gonville and Caius Coll., Cambridge (BA 1948, MA 1950, PhD 1952; Hamilton Prize, Isaac Newton Student, 1952; Hon. Fellow, 1976). FInstP 1998. RAE Farnborough, 1943–46; Research Fellow, Gonville and Caius Coll., 1952–54; Asst Dir of Research, 1954–62; Fellow, Gonville and Caius Coll., 1955–61; Lectr in Physics, Univ. of Cambridge, 1962–69. Dir, Mullard Radio Astronomy Observatory, Cambridge, 1982–87. Visiting Prof. in Astronomy, Yale, 1963; Prof. of the Royal Instn, 1977; Vikram Sarabhai Prof., Physical Res. Lab., Ahmedabad, India, 1988. Lectures: Karl Schwarzschild, Bonn, 1971; Lindsay Meml, Maryland, 1972; Larmor, Cambridge, 1973; Harland, Exeter, 1974; Kelvin, IEE, 1975; Halley, Oxford, 1979; Selby, Cardiff, 1983; Krishnan Meml, New Delhi, 1989; Gold, Cornell, 1992; Saha Meml, Calcutta, 1993; Birla Meml, Hyderabad, 1993; Waynick Meml, Penn State, 2000. MAE 1993. Foreign Mem., Belgian Royal Acad., 1990; Foreign Hon. Mem., Amer. Acad. of Arts and Sciences; Foreign Fellow, Indian Nat. Sci. Acad., 1982; Hon. Fellow: Instn of Electronics and Telecommunication Engrs, India, 1985; Tata Inst. of Fundamental Sci., Bombay, 1996. Hon. DSc: Leicester, 1976; Exeter, 1977; Manchester, 1989; Santa Maria, Brazil, 1989; Univ. Teknologi Malaysia, 1997; Hon. ScD Cambridge, 1996. Eddington Medal, Royal Astronomical Soc., 1969; Charles Vernon Boys Prize, Inst. of Physics and Physical Soc., 1970; Dellinger Gold Medal, Internat. Union of Radio Science, 1972; Michelson Medal, Franklin Inst., 1973; Hopkins Prize, Cambridge Phil Soc., 1973; Holweck Medal and Prize, Soc. Française de Physique, 1974; Nobel Prize for Physics (jtly), 1974; Hughes Medal, Royal Soc., 1977; Vainu Bappu Prize, Indian Nat. Sci. Acad., 1996. Hon. Citizen, Kwangju, S Korea, 1995. *Publications:* Papers in Proc. Royal Society, Phys. Soc., Mon. Not. Royal Astr. Soc., etc. *Recreations:* music, gardening, cliff-walking. *Address:* Pryor's Cottage, Kingston, Cambridge CB3 7NQ. *T:* (01223) 262657; *e-mail:* ah120@mrao.cam.ac.uk.

HEWISON, Erica Jane; *see* Bolton, E. J.

HEWISON, Prof. Robert Alwyn Petrie, DLitt; cultural historian; Theatre Critic, Sunday Times, since 1981; Professor of Cultural Policy and Leadership Studies, City University, since 2006; *b* 2 June 1943; *s* of Robert John Petrie Hewison and Nancy Courtenay (*née* Henderson); *m* 1st, 1981, Jackie Staples (marr. diss. 1986); one *d*; 2nd, 1986, Erica Jane Bolton, *qv*; two *d*. *Educ:* Bedford Sch.; Ravensbourne Coll. of Art and Design; Brasenose Coll., Oxford (BA 1965; MA 1970; MLitt 1972; DLitt 1989). Grad. trainee, Southern Television, 1966; independent writer and critic, 1967–. Guest Curator: J. B. Speed Art Mus., Louisville, Ky, 1978; Museo Correr, Venice, 1983; Ashmolean Mus., Oxford, 1996; Tate Gall., London, 2000. Vis. Prof., De Montfort Univ., 1993–95; Prof. in Literary and Cultural Studies, 1995–2000, pt-time Prof., Dept of English, 2001, Hon. Prof., 2002, Univ. of Lancaster; Slade Prof. of Fine Art, Oxford Univ., 1999–2000. Mem., Writers' Guild of GB, 1968–. Associate, Demos think-tank, 2003–. *Publications:* John Ruskin: the argument of the eye, 1976; Under Siege: literary life in London 1939–45, 1977, rev. edn 1988; Ruskin and Venice, 1978; Irreverence, Scurrility, Profanity, Vilification and Licentious Abuse: Monty Python, the case against, 1981, 2nd edn 1990; (ed) New Approaches to Ruskin: 13 essays, 1981; In Anger: culture in the Cold War 1945–60, 1981, rev. edn 1988; (ed) The Ruskin Art Collection at Oxford: the rudimentary series, 1984; Footlights!: a hundred years of Cambridge comedy, 1986; The Heritage Industry: Britain in a climate of decline, 1987; Too Much: art and society in the Sixties 1960–75, 1988; Future Tense: a new art for the Nineties, 1990; Culture and Consensus: England, art and politics since 1940, 1995, rev. edn 1997; Ruskin and Oxford: the art of education, 1996; (ed) Ruskin's Artists: studies in the Victorian visual economy, 2000; (jtly) Ruskin, Turner and the Pre-Raphaelites, 2000; Ruskin's Venice, 2000; (with John Holden) Experience and Experiment: the UK branch of the Gulbenkian Foundation 1956–2006, 2006; John Ruskin, 2007. *Recreation:* gardening. *Address:* c/o Peters, Fraser & Dunlop, Drury House, 34–43 Russell Street, WC2B 5HA.

HEWITT, family name of **Viscount Lifford**.

HEWITT, Angela Mary, OC 2000; OBE 2006; FRSC 2006; concert pianist; Artistic Director, Trasimeno Music Festival, since 2005; *b* 26 July 1958; *d* of Godfrey Hewitt and Marion Hewitt (*née* Hogg). *Educ:* Royal Conservatory of Music, Toronto (ARCT 1972); Univ. of Ottawa (BMus 1977). First recital at age 9; American début, Kennedy Center, Washington, 1976; Wigmore Hall début, 1985; Proms début, 1990; recitals and concerto appearances throughout N America, Europe, Far East, Australia, NZ, Mexico, etc; numerous radio and TV broadcasts, UK and overseas; has made numerous recordings, incl. all the major keyboard works of J. S. Bach. Winner of competitions, in N America and Europe, incl. First Prize, Toronto Internat. Bach Piano Comp., 1985. Hon. DMus Ottawa, 1995; Hon. LLD Queen's, Kingston, 2002; DUniv Open, 2006. Juno Award, Canada, for Best Instrumental Recording of Year, 1999, 2001, 2004; Governor Gen.'s Award for Performing Arts, Canada, 2002; Listeners' Award, BBC Radio 3, 2003; Artist of the Year, Gramophone Awards, 2006. *Recreations:* travelling, cooking wheat-free meals, seeing friends. *Address:* c/o Intermusica, 16 Duncan Terrace, N1 8BZ. *T:* (020) 7278 5455, *Fax:* (020) 7278 8434; *e-mail:* mail@intermusica.co.uk.

HEWITT, Prof. (Brian) George, PhD; FBA 1997; Professor of Caucasian Languages, School of Oriental and African Studies, London University, since 1996; *b* 11 Nov. 1949; *s* of late Thomas Douglas Hewitt and Joan (*née* Cousins); *m* 1976, Zaira Kiazimovna Khiba; two *d*. *Educ:* Doncaster Grammar Sch. for Boys; St John's Coll., Cambridge (BA 1972; Dip. in Linguistics 1973; MA 1976; PhD 1982). Open Henry Arthur Thomas Schol. in Classics, 1969–72; John Stewart of Rannoch Univ. Schol. and Coll. Graves Prize, 1971; Warr Classical Student, 1972–73; British Council Exchange Postgrad. Student, Tbilisi, Georgia, 1975–76, 1979–80; Marjory Wardrop Scholar for Georgian Studies, 1978–81. Lectr in Linguistics, Hull Univ., 1981–88; Lectr in Linguistics and Caucasian Langs, 1988–92, Reader in Caucasian Langs, 1992–96, SOAS. Member, Editorial Board: Revue des Etudes Géorgiennes et Caucasiennes, 1985–; Central Asian Survey, 1993–. Mem. Council, Philological Soc., 1985–90; First Pres., Societas Caucasologica Europaea, 1986–88 and 1988–90. Hon. Rep. for Republic of Abkhazia in UK, 1993–. Hon. Member: Internat. Cherkess Acad. of Scis, 1997–; Abkhazian Acad. of Scis, 1997; Writers' Union of Abkhazia, 2003–. Mem. Bd of Managers, Marjory Wardrop Fund, Oxford, 1983–. Honour and Glory of Abkhazia Medal, 2004. *Publications:* Lingua Descriptive Studies 2: Abkhaz, 1979; Typology of Subordination in Georgian and Abkhaz, 1987; (ed and contrib.) Indigenous Languages of the Caucasus 2: North West Caucasus, 1989; (ed and contrib.) Caucasian Perspectives, 1992; (ed and contrib. jtly) Subject, Voice and Ergativity: selected essays, 1995; Georgian: a learner's grammar, 1995, 2nd edn 2005; Georgian: a structural reference grammar, 1995; A Georgian Reader, 1996; (with Zaira Khiba) Abkhaz Newspaper Reader (with supplements), 1998; (ed and contrib.) The Abkhazians: a handbook, 1998; The Languages of the Caucasus: scope for study and survival (inaugural lecture), 1998; Introduction to the Study of the Languages of the Caucasus, 2004; Abkhazian Folktales, 2005; articles on Caucasian langs and politics in encycs, Central Asian Survey, Bedi Kartlisa, Revue des Etudes Géorgiennes et Caucasiennes. *Recreations:* classical music, growing fuchsias. *Address:* Department of Near and Middle East, School of Oriental and African Studies, Thornhaugh Street, Russell Square, WC1H 0XG. *T:* (020) 7898 4332; *e-mail:* gh2@soas.ac.uk.

HEWITT, Prof. (Charles) Nicholas, PhD; FRMetS; CChem; Professor of Atmospheric Chemistry, Lancaster University, since 1993; *b* 23 Sept. 1953; *s* of Peter Hewitt and Amanda Hewitt (*née* Rodwell); *m*; one *s* one *d*. *Educ:* Queen Elizabeth's Grammar Sch. for Boys, Barnet; Lancaster Univ. (BA 1976; PhD 1985). FRMetS 1985; CChem 1985; MRSC 1985. Lancaster University: New-Blood Lectr, 1985–91; Sen. Lectr, 1991–93; Hd, Dept of Envmtl Scis, 1996–99. Vis. Fellow and Fulbright Schol., Univ. of Colo, Boulder, 1988–89; Vis. Scientist, Nat. Center for Atmospheric Res., Boulder, Colo, 1994–95. Member: Photochemical Oxidant Rev. Gp, DoE, 1991–99; Scientific Steering Cttee, Eurotrac-2 (a Eureka project), 1996–2002. Chm., Envmtl Chemistry Gp, RSC, 1996–98. *Publications:* Instrumental Analysis of Pollutants, 1991; Methods of Environmental Data Analysis, 1992; (with W. T. Sturges) Global Atmospheric Chemical Change, 1993; (with G. Davison) Air Pollution in the United Kingdom, 1997; Reactive Hydrocarbons in the Atmosphere, 1999; (with A. Jackson) Handbook of Atmospheric Science, 2003; numerous articles in learned jls. *Recreation:* being outdoors. *Address:* Lancaster Environment Centre, Lancaster University, Lancaster LA1 4YQ. *T:* (01524) 593931.

HEWITT, Sir (Cyrus) Lenox (Simson), Kt 1971; OBE 1963; company chairman and director; *b* 7 May 1917; *s* of Cyrus Lenox Hewitt and Ella Louise Hewitt; *m* 1943, Alison Hope (*née* Tillyard); one *s* two *d* (and one *d* decd). *Educ:* Scotch Coll., Melbourne; Melbourne Univ. (BCom). FCPA, FCIS, LCA. Broken Hill Proprietary Co. Ltd, 1933–46; Asst Sec., Commonwealth Prices Br., Canberra, 1939–46; Economist, Dept of Post War Reconstruction, 1946–49; Official Sec. and Actg Dep. High Comr, London, 1950–53; Commonwealth Treasury: Asst Sec., 1953–55; 1st Asst Sec., 1955–62; Dep. Sec., 1962–66; Chm., Australian Univs Commn, 1967; Secretary to: Prime Minister's Dept, 1968–71; Dept of the Environment, Aborigines and the Arts, 1971–72; Dept of Minerals and Energy, 1972–75. Lectr, Econs and Cost Accountancy, Canberra UC, 1940–49, 1954. Acting Chairman: Pipeline Authority, 1973–75; Petroleum and Minerals Authority, 1974–75; Chairman: Qantas Airways Ltd, 1975–80 (Dir, 1973–80); Qantas Wentworth Hldgs Ltd, 1975–80; QH Tours Ltd, 1975–80 (Dir, 1974–80); Petroleum and Minerals Co. of Aust. Pty Ltd, 1975; Austmark Internat. Ltd, 1983–88; Northern Mining Corp. NL, 1984–85; State Rail Authority of NSW, 1985–88; Director: East/Aust.

Pipeline Corp. Ltd, 1974–75; Mary Kathleen Uranium Ltd, 1975–80; Aust. Industry Develt Corp., 1975; Santos Ltd, 1981–82; Pontello Constructions Ltd, 1980–82; Aberfoyle Ltd, 1981–89; Endeavour Resources Ltd, 1982–86; Ansett Transport Industries Ltd, 1982–88; Short Brothers (Australia) Ltd, 1981–91; Airship Industries PLC, 1984–88; Qintex Australia Ltd, 1985–90; British Midland Airways (Australia) Pty Ltd, 1985–; Universal Telecasters Securities Ltd, 1986–90; Mirage Management Ltd, 1986–91; Qintex Ltd, 1987–90; Qintex America Ltd, 1987–90; Fortis Pacific Aviation Ltd, 1987–; Fortis Aviation Group Ltd, 1988–2001; Hope Downs Ltd, 1993–; Hancock Minerals Ltd, 1993–. Dep. Chm., Aust. Atomic Energy Commn, 1972–77; Chairman: Exec. Cttee, IATA, 1976–77 (Mem., 1975–80); Orient Airlines Assoc., 1977; State Rail Authority of NSW, 1985–88; Mem., Judicial Commn of NSW, 1986–89. *Recreation:* farming. *Address:* (office) Level 1, 70 Pitt Street, Sydney, NSW 2000, Australia. *T:* (2) 92313233. *Clubs:* Brooks's; Melbourne (Melbourne); Union (Sydney).

See also Rt Hon. P. H. Hewitt.

HEWITT, Prof. David Sword, PhD; FRSE; Regius Professor of English Literature, University of Aberdeen, since 2007; *b* 22 April 1942; *s* of Rev. George Hewitt and Elisabeth Hewitt; *m* 1967, Angela Williams; one *s* one *d. Educ:* Melrose Grammar Sch.; George Watson's Coll.; Univ. of Edinburgh (MA 1964); Univ. of Aberdeen (PhD 1969). University of Aberdeen: Asst Lectr, Lectr, Sen. Lectr, then Reader in English, 1964–94; Prof. of Scottish Literature, 1994–2007. Treas., Assoc. of Scottish Literary Studies, 1972–96. Elder, 1969–, Session Clerk, 2001–, Cathedral Church of St Machar, Old Aberdeen. FRSE 1990; FEA 1996. Pres., Edinburgh Sir Walter Scott Club, 1988–89. Ed.-in-Chief, Edinburgh Edition of the Waverley Novels, 1987–. *Publications:* (ed) Scott on Himself, 1981; editions of Scott novels: The Antiquary, 1995; (jtly) Redgauntlett, 1997; (jtly) The Heart of Midlothian, 2004; Rob Roy, 2007; contrib. Oxford DNB. *Recreations:* listening to classical music and opera, visiting churches and art galleries, literature and drama. *Address:* 21 Ferryhill Place, Aberdeen AB11 7SE. *T:* (01224) 580834; *e-mail:* david.hewitt@abdn.ac.uk.

HEWITT, Francis Anthony; Chief Executive, Northern Ireland Chamber of Commerce, 2002–08; *b* 1 July 1943; *s* of Joseph and Mary Hewitt; *m* 1st, 1968, Carol Burch; two *d*; 2nd, 2003, Wendy Austin. *Educ:* Queen's Univ., Belfast (BScEcon). FCIM. NI Min. of Agriculture, 1961–63; HM Customs and Excise, 1963–72; NI Min. of Commerce Rep. in W Germany, 1973–78; NI Dept of Commerce, 1978–82; HM Consulate-Gen., LA, 1982–84; Industrial Development Board for Northern Ireland: Exec. Dir, Marketing, 1984–88; Dep. Chief Exec., 1988–96; Chief Exec., NI Growth Challenge, 1996–2000; Dep. Perm. Sec., NI Dept of Culture, Arts and Leisure, 2000–02; Mem., NI Legal Services Commn, 2003–. Non-exec. Dir, Invest Northern Ireland, 2008–. Non-exec. Chm., NI Sci. Park, 2008–. Trustee, Grand Opera Hse, Belfast, 2007–. Hon. Consul, Federal Republic of Germany, 2002–. *Recreations:* music, walking, gun dogs, classic cars.

HEWITT, Gavin Wallace, CMG 1995; Chief Executive, Scotch Whisky Association, since 2003; *b* 19 Oct. 1944; *s* of George Burrill and Elisabeth Murray Hewitt; *m* 1973, Heather Mary Clayton; two *s* two *d. Educ:* George Watson's Coll., Edinburgh; Edinburgh Univ. (MA). Min. of Transport, 1967–70; on secondment from MoT as Third, later Second, Sec. to UK Delegn, EEC, Brussels, 1970–72; FCO, 1972–73; First Sec., British High Commn, Canberra, 1973–78; FCO, 1978–81; First Sec. and Head of Chancery, HM Embassy, Belgrade, 1981–84; Mem., Jt FCO/BBC Review Gp, BBC External Services, 1984; Counsellor on loan to Home Civil Service, 1984–87; Counsellor, Head of Chancery and Dep. Perm. Rep., UK Mission to UN, Geneva, 1987–91; Head, SE Asia Dept, FCO, 1992–94; Ambassador: to Croatia, 1994–97; to Finland, 1997–2000; to Belgium, 2001–03. Mem., Exec. Gp, Scotland Food and Drink, 2008–. Member: Bd of Geneva English Sch., 1989–91 (Vice-Chm., 1990–91); Gen. Convocation, Heriot-Watt Univ., 2005–; Patron, British Sch. of Brussels, 2001–03. *Recreations:* music, tinkering, walking. *Address:* Scotch Whisky Association, 20 Atholl Crescent, Edinburgh EH3 8HF. *T:* (0131) 222 9201, *Fax:* (0131) 222 9203; *e-mail:* ghewitt@swa.org.uk.

HEWITT, Prof. Geoffrey Frederick, FRS 1989; FREng; Courtaulds Professor of Chemical Engineering, 1993–99, now Emeritus, and Senior Research Fellow, since 1999, Imperial College of Science, Technology and Medicine (Professor of Chemical Engineering, 1985–93); *b* 3 Jan. 1934; *s* of Frederick and Elaine Hewitt; *m* 1956, Shirley Foulds; two *d. Educ:* Boteler Grammar School, Warrington; UMIST (BScTech, PhD). CEng, FREng (FEng 1984); FIMechE, FIChemE, CChem, FRSC. Scientist, Group Leader, Div. Head, Harwell Lab., specialising in heat transfer and fluid flow in multiphase systems, 1957–90. Pres., IChemE, 1989–90. Foreign Associate, US Nat. Acad. Engrg, 1998. FCGI. Hon. DSc Louvain, 1988; Hon. DEng: Heriot-Watt, 1995; UMIST, 1998. Max Jakob Award, ASME, 1995; Nusselt-Reynolds Prize, Assembly of World Conf. on Expertl Heat Transfer, Fluid Mechs and Thermodyns, 1997; Senior Multiphase Flow Award, 2007; Global Energy Prize, 2007. *Publications:* (with N. S. Hall Taylor) Annular Two Phase Flow, 1970; (co-author) Two Phase Flow, 1973; Measurement of Two Phase Flow Parameters, 1978; (with J. G. Collier) Introduction to Nuclear Power, 1986, 2nd edn 2000; (jtly) Process Heat Transfer, 1994; (ed) International Encyclopedia of Heat and Mass Transfer, 1997; contribs to books, numerous papers. *Recreations:* bridge, music. *Address:* Department of Chemical Engineering and Chemical Technology, Imperial College of Science, Technology and Medicine, Prince Consort Road, SW7 2BY. *T:* (020) 7589 5111.

HEWITT, George; *see* Hewitt, B. G.

HEWITT, Harry Ronald, FREng; Chairman, Johnson Matthey PLC, 1983–84; retired; *b* 12 April 1920; *s* of Charles William Hewitt and Florence Hewitt; *m* 1954, Rosemary Olive, *d* of Walter George Hiscock and Olive Mary Hiscock; two *s* one *d. Educ:* City of Leeds High Sch.; Leeds Coll. of Technol. (BSc London 1941). FREng (FEng 1982); MIChemE 1949; MRSC 1944; CBIM 1983 (MBIM 1947). Jun. Chemist, Joseph Watson & Sons, soap manufrs, Leeds, 1936–41; Chemist, Royal Ordnance Factories (explosive manuf.), 1941–45; Control Officer, Chemical Br., Control Commn, Germany, 1945–47; Works Manager, Consolidated Zinc Corp., Avonmouth and Widnes, 1947–58; Johnson Matthey: Gen. Man., 1958–62; Exec. Dir, 1962–76; Gp Man. Dir, 1976–83. Freeman, City of London, 1979; Liveryman, Worshipful Co. of Clockmakers, 1979. FRSA. *Recreations:* golf, tennis, ski-ing, music. *Address:* 6 Loom Lane, Radlett, Herts WD7 8AD. *T:* (01923) 5243.

HEWITT, Sir Lenox; *see* Hewitt, Sir C. L. S.

HEWITT, Michael Earling; central banking and financial markets consultant; *b* 28 March 1936; *s* of late Herbert Erland Hewitt and Dorothy Amelia Hewitt; *m* 1st, 1961, Elizabeth Mary Hughes Batchelor (marr. diss. 2000); one *s* one *d*; 2nd, 2004, Galina Andreevna Ulkina. *Educ:* Christ's Hospital; Merton College, Oxford (Chancellor's Prize for Latin Prose, 1958; MA (Modern Hist.)); BSc Econ London. Bank of England, 1961–94: Economic Adviser, Govt of Bermuda, 1970–74; Financial Forecaster, 1976–78; Adviser, Financial Instns, 1981–83; Head of Financial Supervision, Gen. Div., 1984–87; Head of Finance and Industry Area, 1987–88; Senior Advr, Finance and Industry, 1988–90; Dir of Central Banking Studies, 1990–94; Project Manager (IMF), EC Technical Assistance for CIS Trng Prog. for Central Bank of Russian Fedn, 1994–99, and Nat. Bank of Ukraine, 1997–98; Resident Advr, Egyptian Capital Mkt Authy, 2000–02; Expert: Banking Sector Reform Project, Macedonia, 2003–04; Accounting Reform Project, Nat. Bank of Romania, 2006; Advr to Gov., Nat. Bank of Macedonia, 2004–05. Chm., OECD Gp of Experts on Systemic Risks in Securities Markets, 1988–90. *Recreations:* chess, wine, travel. *Address:* Villiers Lodge, 5A Villiers Road, Southsea, Hants PO5 2HG.

HEWITT, Nicholas; *see* Hewitt, C. N.

HEWITT, Sir Nicholas Charles Joseph, 3rd Bt *cr* 1921; *b* 12 Nov. 1947; *s* of Sir Joseph Hewitt, 2nd Bt and Marguerite, *yr d* of Charles Burgess; *S* father, 1973; *m* 1969, Pamela Margaret, *o d* of Geoffrey J. M. Hunt, TD; two *s* one *d. Heir: s* Charles Edward James Hewitt [*b* 15 Nov. 1970; *m* 2002, Alison, *d* of Peter Brown, Hobart, Tas]. *Address:* Colswayn House, Huttons Ambo, Yorks YO60 7HJ. *T:* (01653) 696557.

HEWITT, Rt Hon. Patricia Hope; PC 2001; MP (Lab) Leicester West, since 1997; *b* 2 Dec. 1948; *d* of Sir (Cyrus) Lenox (Simson) Hewitt, *qv*, and Alison Hope Hewitt; *m* 1981, William Jack Birtles, *qv*; one *s* one *d. Educ:* C of E Girls' Grammar Sch., Canberra; Australian Nat. Univ.; Newnham Coll., Cambridge (MA). MA Oxon; AMusA (piano). Public Relations Officer, Age Concern (Nat. Old People's Welfare Council), 1971–73; Women's Rights Officer, Nat. Council for Civil Liberties, 1973–74, Gen. Secretary 1974–83; Press and Broadcasting Sec., 1983–88, Policy Co-ordinator, 1988–89, to Leader of Opposition; Sen. Res. Fellow, 1989, Dep. Dir, 1989–94, Inst. for Public Policy Res.; Head, then Dir, of Research, Andersen Consulting, 1994–97. Associate, Newnham Coll., Cambridge, 1984–97; Vis. Fellow, Nuffield Coll., Oxford, 1992–2001. Trustee: Cobden Trust, 1974–83; Areopagitica Trust, 1981–84; Member: Sec. of State's Adv. Cttee on Employment of Women, 1977–84; Unofficial Cttee of Enquiry into Southall, 23 April 1979; National Labour Women's Cttee, 1979–83; Labour Party Enquiry into Security Services, 1980–81; Council, Campaign for Freedom of Information, 1983–89; Bd, Internat. League for Human Rights, 1984–97; Exec. Cttee, Fabian Soc., 1988–93; Co-Chm., Human Rights Network, 1979–81; Dep. Chair, Commn on Social Justice, 1993–95; Vice-Chairman: Healthcare 2000, 1995–96; British Council, 1997–98. Contested (Lab) Leicester East, 1983. Economic Sec., HM Treasury, 1998–99; Minister of State, DTI, 1999–2001; Sec. of State for Trade and Industry, and Minister for Women, 2001–05; Sec. of State for Health, 2005–07. Mem., Select Cttee on Social Security, 1997–98. Mem. Council, Inst. for Fiscal Studies, 1996–98. Mem., Editorial Adv. Panel, New Socialist, 1980–90. FRSA 1992. *Publications:* Your Rights (Age Concern), 1973; Rights for Women (NCCL), 1975; Civil Liberties, the NCCL Guide (co-ed 3rd edn), 1977; The Privacy Report (NCCL), 1977; Your Rights at Work (NCCL), 1978, 2nd edn 1981; The Abuse of Power, 1981; (jtly) Your Second Baby, 1990; About Time: the revolution in work and family life, 1993. *Recreations:* reading, theatre, music, gardening. *Address:* Ground Floor Front, 5 Frog Island, Leicester LE3 5AG.

HEWITT, Penelope Ann, CBE 2003; Senior District Judge (Chief Magistrate), Bow Street Magistrates' Court, 2000–03; *b* 4 May 1932; *d* of late William Mottershead, JP, MB ChB and Eileen Mottershead; *m* 1954, Peter Nisbet Hewitt; one *s* two *d. Educ:* Howell's Sch., Denbigh; BA Open Univ., 1975. Called to the Bar, Gray's Inn, 1978, Bencher, 2001; in practice, Liverpool, 1978–90; Mem., Northern Circuit; District Judge (Magistrates' Courts) (formerly Stipendiary Magistrate), Leeds, 1990–2000. Lay Chm., Bolton Deanery Synod, 1984–90. Member: British Acad. of Forensic Scis, 1979–2005; Magisterial Cttee, Judicial Studies Bd, 1993–98. FRSA 2003. JP Bolton, 1968–90. *Recreations:* music, reading, opera, embroidery.

HEWITT, Peter John, CBE 2008; Chief Executive, Arts Council England (formerly Arts Council of England), 1998–2008; *b* 17 Nov. 1951; *m* 1977, Joan Coventry; three *d. Educ:* Barnard Castle Sch.; Leeds Univ. (BA, MA). Inter-action, Kentish Town, 1976; Arts Officer, N Tyneside MBC, 1977–82; Northern Arts, 1982–97 (Chief Exec., 1992–97); Corporate Affairs Dir, Tees HA, 1997–98. *Recreations:* arts, walking, Middlesbrough FC. *Address:* c/o Arts Council England, 14 Great Peter Street, SW1P 3NQ.

HEWITT, Peter McGregor, OBE 1967; Regional Director, East Midlands, Departments of the Environment and Transport, 1984–89; *b* 6 Oct. 1929; *e s* of late Douglas McGregor Hewitt and Audrey Vera Hewitt; *m* 1962, Joyce Marie Gavin; three *d. Educ:* De Aston Sch., Market Rasen, Lincs; Keble Coll., Oxford (MA). National Service (Army), 1947–49. HM Overseas Civil Service, 1952–64: served in Malaya and N Borneo; HM Diplomatic Service, 1964–71: served in FO, Shanghai and Canberra; Home Civil Service: Principal, 1971–77; Asst Sec., 1977–83; Grade 4, 1984. *Recreations:* cricket, music, gardening. *Address:* 14 Dovedale Road, West Bridgford, Nottingham NG2 6JA. *Club:* Royal Commonwealth Society.

HEWITT, Sarah Louise; *see* Singleton, S. L.

HEWITT, Sheila Iffat; JP; Regional Chairman, Eastern and Southern Areas, Legal Services Commission (formerly Legal Aid Board), 1998–2004; *b* Pakistan, 6 Oct. 1952; *m* 1973, Anthony Hewitt; two *s. Educ:* London Sch. of Econs and Pol Sci. (BSc Econ). ACIB 1975. Member: London Rent Assessment Panel, 1985–2002; Immigration Appeals Tribunal, 1992–; Appeal Tribunal Competition Commn, 2000–; Ind. Assessor, OCPA, 2000–. Mem., Radio Authority, 1998–2003. Non-exec. Bd Mem., Mid Surrey HA, 1992–95; Chm., Surrey Heartlands NHS Trust, 1995–98. Mem., GMC, 2001–. JP Surrey, 1987. *Recreations:* mountain trekking, tennis. *Address:* Calderwood, Wilmerhatch Lane, Epsom, Surrey KT18 7EH. *T:* (01372) 273730, *Fax:* (01372) 271762. *Club:* Royal Automobile.

HEWLETT, Rev. David Jonathon Peter, PhD; Principal, Queen's Foundation for Ecumenical Theological Education, since 2003; *b* 8 Feb. 1957; *s* of Vincent and Daphne Hewlett; *m* 1978, Penelope Skilton; three *s* one *d. Educ:* Durham Univ. (BA 1st cl. Hons 1979; PhD 1984). Ordained deacon, 1983, priest, 1984; Asst Curate, St James, New Barnet, 1983–86; Lectr in Systematic Theol., C of I Theol Coll., Dublin, and TCD, 1986–90; Jt Dir, SW Ministry Trng Course, and Priest i/c, Feock, dio. Truro, 1990–95; Principal, SW Ministry Trng Course, 1995–2003. Hon. Fellow, Dept of Theol., Exeter Univ., 1995–2003. *Recreation:* music. *Address:* Queen's Foundation for Ecumenical Theological Education, Somerset Road, Edgbaston, Birmingham B15 2QH. *T:* (0121) 454 1527, *Fax:* (0121) 454 8171; *e-mail:* d.hewlett@queens.ac.uk.

HEWLETT, Stephen Edward; writer, broadcaster and media consultant; Director of Programmes, Carlton Television, 1998–2004; Managing Director, Carlton Productions, 2001–04; *b* 8 Aug. 1958; *s* of Lawrence Edward Hewlett and Vera Mary Hewlett; partner, Karole Anne Lange; three *s. Educ:* Harold Malley Grammar Sch. for Boys, Solihull; Solihull Sixth Form Coll.; Univ. of Manchester (BSc Hons Liberal Studies in Sci. 1981). Researcher, Panorama, Nationwide and Watchdog, BBC, 1981–82; Producer and Dir, Diverse Reports and The Friday Alternative, Channel 4, 1982–87; BBC: Producer: Brass

Tacks, 1987–88; Taking Liberties, 1988–90; Inside Story, 1990–92; Exec. Producer, Children's Hosp., The Skipper, Rough Justice, States of Terror, The Diamond Empire, 25 Bloody Years and The Dead (Best Single Documentary Award, RTS, 1994), 1992–94; Ed., Inside Story, 1992–94 (Best Single Documentary Award, BAFTA, 1994); Ed., Panorama and Exec. Ed., Special Projects, 1995–97; Hd, Factual Programmes, Channel 4, 1997–98. Non-exec. Dir, Tiger Aspect TV, 2004–. Gov., Sir John Lawes Sch., Harpenden, 2003–. FRTS 2002. Hon. MA Salford, 1999. Interview of Year and Journalist of Year Awards, RTS, 1995. *Recreations:* cricket, swimming, sailing (occasionally). *Address: e-mail:* lange.hewlett@btinternet.com.

HEWLETT-DAVIES, Mrs Janet Mary; journalist; public affairs consultant; *b* 13 May 1938; *d* of Frederick Charles and Margaret Ellen Hewlett; *m* 1964, Barry Davies. *Educ:* King Edward VI High School for Girls, Birmingham. Journalist, West Midlands 1956–59; BBC, 1959–65; Films Division, Central Office of Information, 1966–67; Press Officer: Prime Minister's Office, 1967–72; HM Customs and Excise, 1972–73; Principal Information Officer, Dept of Trade and Industry, 1973–74; Dep. Press Secretary to Prime Minister, 1974–76; Head of Information, Dept of Transport, 1976–79; Director of Information: DoE, 1979–82; DHSS, 1982–86; Dir of Public Affairs, Pergamon, BPCC and Mirror Gp of Cos, 1986–87. Vice-Chm., WHO Working Gp on Information and Health, 1983. *Recreations:* Shakespeare's Globe, Brighton, acting. *Address:* 44 Sussex Square, Brighton BN2 1GE. *T:* (01273) 693792. *Club:* Reform.

HEWSON, John Robert, AM 2001; PhD; investment banker and company director; Chairman, Pisces Group, since 2008; *b* 28 Oct. 1946; *s* of Donald Hewson and late Eileen Isabella Hewson (*née* Tippett); *m* 1st, Margaret; two *s* one *d*; 2nd, 1988, Carolyn Judith Somerville; one *d*. *Educ:* Univ. of Sydney (BEc Hons); Univ. of Saskatchewan (MA 1969); Johns Hopkins Univ. (MA, PhD 1971). Economist, IMF, 1971–74; Res. Economist, Reserve Bank of Australia, 1976; Economic Advr to Fed. Treas., 1976–82; University of New South Wales: Prof. of Econs, 1978–87; Head, Sch. of Econs, 1983–86; Dir, Japanese Econs Management Studies Centre, 1984–87. Dir, Macquarie Bank, 1985–87. MP (L) Wentworth, NSW, 1987–95; Shadow Minister for Finance, 1988–89; Shadow Treas., 1989–90; Leader of the Opposition, Australian Parlt, 1990–94; Shadow Minister for Industry, Commerce, Infrastructure and Customs, 1994–95. Prof. of Mgt and Dean, Macquarie Grad. Sch. of Mgt, 2002–04. Chairman: John Hewson Gp Pty Ltd, 1995–; Gold and Resources Develt Ltd, 1996–98 (Dir, 2000–04); Australian Bus Manufacturing Co., 1999–; Universal Bus Co. Pty Ltd, 2000–; Global Renewables Ltd, 2000–04; Belle Property Pty Ltd, 2000–03; Strategic Capital Mgt Pty Ltd, 2000–04; X Capital Health, 2004–; Vice-Chm., Qingdao Pacific Coach Co., 2001–; Mem., Adv. Council, ABN AMRO Australia Ltd, 1998–2004 (Chm., 1996–98). Chm., RepuTex Rating Cttee, 2003–04. Chairman: Leadership Foundn Pty, 1998–2003; Investment Adv. Cttee, Australian Olympic Foundn, 2001–; Foundn for New England Regl Art Mus., 2001–03; Adv. Cttee, Dunmore Lang Coll. Foundn, 2002–03; Business Leaders Forum on Sustainable Develt, 2003–; Member, Advisory Group: Gp Training Australia, 2003–; Australia Worldwide, Solutions for a Sustainable Future, 2003–. Chairman: Osteoporosis Australia Council, 1997–; Arthritis Res. Taskforce Ltd, 2003–; Director: Exec. Bd, Asia-Aust. Inst., 1999–; Positive Ageing Foundn, 1999–2003; Pres., Arthritis Foundn of Australia, 1997–2002. Chm., Freehand Gp, 2004–. Columnist, Australian Financial Review, 1998–. *Publications:* Liquidity Creation and Distribution in the Eurocurrency Market, 1975; (jtly) The Eurocurrency Markets and their Implications, 1975; Offshore Banking in Australia, 1981. *Recreations:* jazz, sport, cars, theatre, motor sports. *Address: e-mail:* john.hewson@horwath.com.au. *Clubs:* Australian; Australian Golf, Royal Sydney Golf.

HEWSON, Paul David, (Bono); singer and songwriter; *b* 10 May 1960; *s* of late Robert Hewson and of Iris Hewson; *m* 1982, Alison Stewart; two *s* two *d*. *Educ:* Mount Temple Sch., Dublin. Co-founder and lead singer, U2, 1978–; nat. and internat. tours. *Albums include:* Boy, 1980; October, 1981; War, 1983; Under a Blood Red Sky, 1983; The Unforgettable Fire, 1984; Wide Awake in America, 1985; The Joshua Tree, 1987; Rattle and Hum, 1988; Achtung Baby, 1991; The Fly, 1991; Zooropa, 1993; Pop, 1997; All That You Can't Leave Behind, 2000; How to Dismantle an Atomic Bomb, 2004. Dir, Elevation Partners, 2004–. Co-founder and Dir, Debt, AIDS, Trade, Africa, 2002–. *Address:* c/o Regine Moylett Publicity, 2C Woodstock Studios, Woodstock Grove, W12 8LE.

HEWSTONE, Prof. Miles Ronald Cole, DPhil, DSc; FBA 2002; AcSS; Professor of Social Psychology, University of Oxford, and Fellow, New College, Oxford, since 2001; *b* 4 Aug. 1956; *s* of Ronald Keith and Audrey Cole Hewstone; *m* 1986, Claudia Maria Hammer; one *s* one *d*. *Educ:* Univ. of Bristol (BSc 1st Cl. Hons Psychol. 1978); Trinity Coll., Oxford (DPhil 1981); Univ. of Tübingen, Germany (Habilitation); Univ. of Oxford (DSc 2007). University of Bristol: Lectr in Psychol., 1985–88; Reader in Social Psychol., 1988–91; Prof. of Social Psychol. (Personal Chair), 1991–92; Ordinarius Prof. of Social Psychol., Univ. of Mannheim, 1992–94; Prof. of Psychol., UWCC, 1994–2001. Invited Fellow, Center for Advanced Study in Behavioral Scis, Stanford, Calif, 1987–88 and 1999–2000. Fellow: Soc. for Personality and Social Psychol., 2000; Soc. for Psychol Study of Social Issues, 2000. AcSS 2000. Hon. FBPsS 2003 (FBPsS 1986). Spearman Medal, 1987, Presidents' Award, 2001, BPsS. *Publications:* Understanding Attitudes to the European Community: a social psychological study in four member states, 1986; (ed jtly) Contact and Conflict in Intergroup Encounters, 1986; Causal Attribution: from cognitive processes to collective beliefs, 1989; (ed with A. Manstead) The Blackwell Encyclopedia of Social Psychology, 1995; (ed jtly) Psychology, 2005. *Address:* New College, Oxford OX1 3BN; *e-mail:* miles.hewstone@psy.ox.ac.uk.

HEY, Prof. Anthony John Grenville, CBE 2005; DPhil; FREng; Corporate Vice-President for External Research, Microsoft Corporation (Vice-President for Technical Computing, 2005); *b* 17 Aug. 1946; *s* of Colin Grenville Hey and late Phyllis Gwendolen Rhodes; *m* 1969, Jessie Margaret Nancy; two *s* one *d*. *Educ:* King Edward's Sch., Birmingham; Worcester Coll., Oxford (Open Schol.; BA Physics 1967); St John's Coll., Oxford; DPhil Oxon. CEng; FBCS; FIET; FREng 2001. University of Southampton: Lectr in Physics, 1974–86; Prof. of Computation, Sch. of Electronics and Computer Sci., 1986–2005; Dir, UK e-Science Core Prog., EPSRC, 2001–05 (on secondment). Sabbaticals at CIT, MIT and IBM Research. Former Mem., PPARC. *Publications:* (with Ian Aitchison) Gauge Theories in Particle Physics, 1982, 3rd edn 2004; (with Patrick Walters) The New Quantum Universe, 1987, 2nd edn 2003; (with Patrick Walters) Einstein's Mirror, 1997. *Recreations:* reading, writing, hill-walking, long-term supporter of Southampton FC. *Address:* Microsoft Corporation, One Microsoft Way, Redmond, WA 98052, USA.

HEY, Prof. John Denis; Professor of Economics and Statistics, University of York, since 1984, part-time since 1997; Professore Ordinario, Luiss Guido Carli, Italy, since 2006; *b* 26 Sept. 1944; *s* of George Brian Hey and Elizabeth Hamilton Hey (*née* Burns); *m* 1968, Margaret Robertson Bissett (marr. diss. 1998); one *s* two *d*. *Educ:* Manchester Grammar Sch.; Cambridge Univ. (MA); Edinburgh Univ. (MSc). Econometrician, Hoare & Co., 1968–69; Lectr in Economics, Univ. of Durham, 1969–73, Univ. of St Andrew 1974–75; Lectr in Social and Economic Statistics, Univ. of York, 1975–81, Sen. Lec 1981–84; Prof. Ordinario, Univ. of Bari, 1998–2006. Co-Dir, Centre for Experiment Economics, Univ. of York, 1986–. Economic Consultant, Wise Speke & Co., 1972–8 Editor: Bulletin of Economic Research, 1984–87; Economic Journal, 1986–9 *Publications:* Statistics in Economics, 1974; Uncertainty in Microeconomics, 1979; Britai in Context, 1979; Economics in Disequilibrium, 1981; Data in Doubt, 1983; (ed jtl Surveys in the Economics of Uncertainty, 1987; (ed) Current Issues in Microeconomic 1989; (ed jtly) A Century of Economics, 1990; Experiments in Economics, 1991; (ed) Th Future of Economics, 1992; (ed jtly) Recent Developments in Experimental Economic 1993; (ed) The Economics of Uncertainty, 1997; Intermediate Microeconomics, 200 Microeconomia, 2007; articles in academic economics jls. *Recreations:* spinning, cyclin opera. *Address:* Department of Economics and Related Studies, University of York Heslington, York YO1 5DD. *T:* (01904) 433786; Luiss Guido Carli, Viale Romania 3 Rome 00197, Italy.

HEYES, David Alan; MP (Lab) Ashton under Lyne, since 2001; *b* 2 April 1946; *s* Harold and Lilian Heyes; *m* 1968, Judith Gallagher; one *s* one *d*. *Educ:* Open Univ. (BA Local govt manager, Manchester, 1962–86; trade union organiser, 1986–87; local go manager, Oldham, 1987–90; self employed, computer graphics business, 1990–9 manager, CAB, Manchester, 1995–2001. *Address:* House of Commons, SW1A 0AA.

HEYGATE, Sir Richard John Gage, 6th Bt *cr* 1831, of Southend, Essex; Chairma Welford Technology Partners, since 2005; *b* 30 Jan. 1940; *s* of Sir John Edward Nour Heygate, 4th Bt and his 2nd wife, Gwyneth Eliot (*d* 1994), 2nd *d* of J. E. H. Lloyd; brother, 1991; *m* 1st, 1968, Carol Rosemary (marr. diss. 1972), *d* of Comdr Richa Michell; 2nd, 1974, Jong Ja (marr. diss. 1988), *d* of In Suk, Seoul; one *d*; 3rd, 1988, Susa Fiona, *d* of late Robert Buckley; two *s*. *Educ:* Repton; Balliol Coll., Oxford. IBM (UK Ltd, 1967–70; McKinsey & Company Inc., 1970–77; Director: Olaf Foods, 1977–8 Index Gp, 1985–87; Principal, McKinsey and Co. Inc., 1987–98; CEO, Sophron Partne Ltd, 1998–2005. Director: Isis Technology, 1999–2000; Propero Ltd, 2000–0 Chairman: Storks Nest Wine, 2003–04; Mouse Smart Software, 2004–06. Mem., Financ Cttee, Cancer Res., 1992–98. *Heir: s* Frederick Carysfort Gage Heygate, *b* 28 June 198 *Address:* 8 Brynmaer Road, SW11 4ER.

HEYHOE, David Charles Ross, CB 1998; Director, Greenwich Hospital, 1998–200 *b* 29 June 1938; *s* of late Cecil Ross Heyhoe and Clara Beatrice (*née* Woodard Knight); 1972, Pauline Susan (*née* Morgan); one *s* one *d*. *Educ:* Beckenham and Penge Gramma Sch.; Worcester Coll., Oxford (Schol.; MA Lit.Hum). Served HM Forces, RAEC 1957–59. Asst Principal, War Office, 1963; Asst Private Sec. to Minister (Army), 196 Principal, MoD, 1967; Asst Sec., 1975; Res. Associate, Inst. for Strategic Studies, 1975–7 Private Sec. to Leader of H of C, 1981–84; Asst Under Sec. of State, MoD, 1986–9 Mem., Royal Patriotic Fund Corp., 1998–2002. *Recreation:* golf. *Address:* 4 Westmoreland Road, Barnes, SW13 9RZ. *Clubs:* Roehampton, Rosslyn Park FC.

HEYHOE, Rosemary; Director, Human Resources Operations, Department of Trad and Industry, 2003–05; *b* 17 Sept. 1946; *d* of Herbert Arthur Mears and Mabel Mears (*ne* Foster); *m* 1978, Richard John Heyhoe; two *d*. *Educ:* Wallington County Sch. for Girl Bd of Trade, 1965–70; NEDO, 1970–73; DTI, 1973–74; Metrication Bd, 1974–7 Private Sec., Parly Under-Sec. of State, Dept of Prices and Consumer Protectio 1975–77; Personnel, DTI, 1977–82; privatisation team, Nat. Maritime Inst., 1982; intern consultancy, 1982–92; office of Principal Establishment and Finance Officer, DTI 1992–97; Dir of Resources and Services, OFT, 1997–2001; Dir resp. for Civil Emergenc Planning, DTI, 2001–03. *Recreations:* family, opera, travel. *Address:* 50 Tachbrook Stree Pimlico, SW1V 2NA.

HEYHOE FLINT, Rachael, OBE 2008 (MBE 1972); DL; public relations and spor marketing consultant; journalist, broadcaster, public speaker, sportswoman; *b* 11 Jun 1939; *d* of Geoffrey Heyhoe and Roma (*née* Crocker); *m* 1971, Derrick Flint, BSc; one and one step *s* two step *d*. *Educ:* Wolverhampton High Sch. for Girls; Dartford Coll. c Physical Educn (Dip. in Phys. Educn). Head of Phys. Education: Wolverhampto Municipal Grammar Sch., 1960–62; Northicote Sch., 1962–64; US Field Hockey Assoc Coach, 1964 and 1965; Journalist, Wolverhampton Express & Star, 1965–72; Spor Editor, Wolverhampton Chronicle, 1969–71; first woman Sports Reporter, ITV, 1972 Daily Telegraph Sports Writer, 1967–90; Vice-Chm., 1981–86, and Public Relation Officer, 1982–86, Women's Cricket Assoc.; Consultant, La Manga Club, Southern Spain 1983–; PR Exec., Wolverhampton Wanderers Football Club, 1990– (Dir, 1997–2004) England Hockey rep., 1964 (goalkeeper); Mem., England Women's Cricket team 1960–83, Captain, 1966–77. Hit first 6 in Women's Test Cricket 1963 (England Australia, Oval); scored highest test score by England player in this country, 1976 (highes in world, 1976, now fourth highest) (179 runs for England *v* Australia, Oval). Pres., Lad Taverners Charity, 2000–. DL W Midlands, 1997. Hon. Fellow, Univ. o Wolverhampton, 2002. Hon. BSc Bradford, 2003; Hon. DSc Greenwich, 2003; Hon. D Sports Sci. Leeds Metropolitan, 2006. Best After Dinner Speakers Award, Guild o Professional Toastmasters, 1972. *Publications:* Just for Kicks, (Guide to hocke goalkeeping), 1966; Women's Hockey, 1975; (with Netta Rheinberg) Fair Play, Th Story of Women's Cricket, 1976; (autobiog.) "Heyhoe!", 1978. *Recreations:* golf, cricket former county squash player (Staffs). *Address:* Danescroft, Wergs Road, Tettenhall Wolverhampton, West Midlands WV6 9BN. *Clubs:* MCC (Hon. Life Mem., 1999; firs woman Cttee Mem., 2004–), Lord's Taverners; Patshull Park Golf; South Staffs Golf; L Manga (Spain).

HEYLIN, Angela Christine Mary, (Mrs M. Minzly), LVO 2008; OBE 1997; non-executive Director, Austin Reed Group plc, 2001–06; *b* 17 Sept. 1943; *d* of Bernar Heylin and Ruth Victoria Heylin; *m* 1971, Maurice Minzly; one *s*. *Educ:* Apsley Gramma Sch.; Watford Coll. Charles Barker plc: Chief Exec., 1989–92; Chm., 1992–97; UK Pres. BSMG Worldwide, 1997–2000. Non-executive Director: Provident Financial 1997–2003; Mothercare plc, 1997–2004. Mem. Adv. Bd, Mercer Delta Consulting 2004–06. Prime Minister's Adv. Panel, Citizen's Charter, 1993–97. Trustee, Histori Royal Palaces, 1998–2007. Chm., Public Relations Consultants' Assoc., 1990–92. Chm. House of St Barnabas, 2001–04. *Publication:* Putting it Across, 1991. *Recreations:* theatre entertaining, music. *Address:* 46 St Augustine's Road, NW1 9RN. *T:* (020) 7485 4815 *e-mail:* angela@heylin.com.

HEYMAN, Prof. Jacques, MA, PhD; FICE; FSA; FREng; Professor of Engineering 1971–92, and Head of Department of Engineering, 1983–92, University of Cambridge now Emeritus Professor; Fellow of Peterhouse, 1949–51, and 1955–92, now Emeritus Fellow; *b* 8 March 1925; *m* 1958, Eva Orlans (*d* 1982); three *d*. *Educ:* Whitgift Sch.; Peterhouse, Cambridge. Senior Bursar, Peterhouse, 1962–64; University Demonstrator Engineering Dept, Cambridge Univ., 1951, University Lectr, 1954, Reader, 1968. Vis. Professor: Brown Univ., USA, 1957–58; Harvard Univ., 1966. Consultant Engineer: Ely Cathedral, 1972–2005; St Albans Cathedral, 1978–2000; Lichfield Cathedral, 1986–91; Worcester Cathedral, 1986–90; Gloucester Cathedral, 1989–90. Member: Architectural

Adv. Panel, Westminster Abbey, 1973–98; Cathedrals Fabric Commn (formerly Cathedrals Adv. Commn) for England, 1981–2001; Council, ICE, 1960–63 and 1975–78; Smeatonian Soc. of Civil Engrs, 1982– (Pres., 2004); Fabric Adv. Cttee, Ely Cathedral, 2005–. Hon. FRIBA 1998. Hon. DSc Sussex, 1975; Dr *hc* Univ. Politécnica de Madrid, 2008. James Watt Medal, 1973. Cross of St Augustine, 2005. *Publications:* The Steel Skeleton, vol. 2 (with Lord Baker, M. R. Horne), 1956; Plastic Design of Portal Frames, 1957; Beams and Framed Structures, 1964, 2nd edn 1974 (trans. Spanish, 2002); Plastic Design of Frames, vol. 1, 1969 (paperback 1980), vol. 2, 1971; Coulomb's Memoir on Statics, 1972, reprinted 1997 (trans. Italian, 1999); Equilibrium of Shell Structures, 1977; Elements of Stress Analysis, 1982; The Masonry Arch, 1982; Estructuras de Fábrica (collection of papers on masonry construction, trans. Spanish), 1995; The Stone Skeleton, 1995 (trans. Spanish, 1999); Elements of the Theory of Structures, 1996; Arches, Vaults and Buttresses, 1996; Structural Analysis, a Historical Approach, 1998 (trans. Spanish, 2004); The Science of Structural Engineering, 1999 (trans. Spanish, 2001); Basic Structural Theory, 2008; articles on plastic design, masonry construction and general structural theory. *Address:* 3 Banhams Close, Cambridge CB4 1HX. *T:* (01223) 357360.

HEYMANN, Amanda; *see* Rowlatt, A.

HEYTESBURY, 7th Baron *cr* 1828; **James William Holmes à Court;** Bt 1795; *b* 30 July 1967; *s* of 6th Baron Heytesbury and of Alison Jean (*née* Balfour); *S* father, 2004; *m* 1995, Polly Jane Kendrick. *Educ:* Bryanston; Southampton Univ. (BSc Hons). *Heir: cousin* Peter Michael Hamilton Holmes à Court [*b* 1968; *m* 1995, Divonne Jarecki; two s (twins)].

HEYWOOD, Dr Ann, FRICS; Principal, College of Estate Management, Reading, since 2007; *b* 9 March 1955; *d* of Philip Tassell and Mary (*née* Wicks). *Educ:* Maidstone Grammar Sch. for Girls; Bedford Coll., Univ. of London (BSc 1975); Coll. of Estate Mgt; PhD Salford Univ. 2003. FRICS 1987. MAFF, 1975–81; Rural Planning Services, 1981–86; Founder and Man. Partner, CPM, 1986–99; owner, Principal Purpose, sustainability consultancy, 2003–. Specialist Advr to H of C Select Cttee, 1987–88. Chair, Presidential Commn for Sustainability, RICS, 2005–07. FRGS 1982; MCMI (MBIM 1983). Green Surveyor of the Year, RICS, 1998–99. *Recreations:* sailing, walking, cinema, travel. *Address:* College of Estate Management, Whiteknights, Reading, Berks RG6 6AW. *T:* (0118) 921 4643, *Fax:* (0118) 986 9878; *e-mail:* a.heywood@cem.ac.uk.

HEYWOOD, Barry; *see* Heywood, R. B.

HEYWOOD, Geoffrey, MBE (mil.) 1945; JP; Consulting Actuary; *b* 7 April 1916; *s* of Edgar Heywood and Annie (*née* Dawson), Blackpool; *m* 1941, Joan Corinna Lumley; one *s* one *d*. *Educ:* Arnold Sch., Blackpool; Open Univ. (BA Hons). Served War, 1940–46: Royal Artillery, N Africa, Italy, Greece; commissioned, 1941, Major, 1944; despatches, 1945. Refuge Assce Co. Ltd, 1933–40; Duncan C. Fraser & Co. (Consulting Actuaries), 1946–86 (Sen. Partner, 1952–86). Pres., Manchester Actuarial Soc., 1951–53; Chm., Assoc. of Consulting Actuaries, 1959–62; Founder Chm., Internat. Assoc. of Consulting Actuaries, 1968–72; Pres., Inst. of Actuaries, 1972–74 (Vice-Pres., 1964–67). Mem. Page Cttee to Review National Savings. Dep. Chm., Mersey Docks & Harbour Co., 1975–85; Mem., Nat. Bus Co., 1978–85. Chm., Merseyside Cable Vision, 1982–90; Director: Barclays Bank Trust Co., 1967–86; Liverpool Bd Barclays Bank, 1972–86; Barclays Unicorn Gp, 1977–85; Universities Superannuation Scheme, 1974–86. Hon. Vice-Pres., Royal Patriotic Corp., 2004. Corresp. Mem., Assoc. des Actuaires Suisses, 1973. FFA 1939; FIA 1946; FRAS 1982; FRSA 1986. Founder Master, Actuaries Co., 1979; Liveryman, Clockmakers' Co. JP Liverpool 1962. *Publications:* contribs to Jl Inst. Actuaries. *Recreation:* antiquarian horology. *Address:* Drayton, 46 Croft Drive East, Caldy, Wirral, Merseyside CH48 1LS. *T:* (0151) 625 6707. *Club:* Army and Navy.

HEYWOOD, Jeremy John, CB 2002; CVO 2003; Permanent Secretary, Prime Minister's Office, since 2008; *b* 31 Dec. 1961; *s* of Peter Andrew Heywood and Brenda Heywood (*née* Swinbank); *m* 1997, Dr Suzanne Elizabeth Cook; two *s* one *d* (of whom one *s* one *d* are twins). *Educ:* Bootham Sch., York; Hertford Coll., Oxford (BA Hons Modern Hist. and Econs); London Sch. of Econs (MSc Econ); Harvard Business Sch. (PMD 1994). Econ. Asst, HSE, 1983–84; HM Treasury: Econ. Asst, 1984–85; Private Sec. to Financial Sec., 1986–88; Asst to UK Dir, IMF, Washington, 1988–90 (on secondment); HM Treasury: Private Sec. to Chief Sec., 1990–91; Principal Private Sec. to Chancellor of the Exchequer, 1991–94; Head, Corporate and Mgt Change, 1994–95; Head, Securities and Markets Policy, 1995–97; Private Sec., 1997–99, Principal Private Sec., 1999–2003, to the Prime Minister; Man. Dir, Mergers and Acquisitions, subseq. Man. Dir and Co-Head, UK Investment Banking Div., Morgan Stanley, 2004–07; Hd of Domestic Policy and Strategy, Cabinet Office, 2007–08. *Recreations:* child-care, modern art, cinema, Manchester United. *Address:* 10 Downing Street, SW1A 2AA.

HEYWOOD, Matthew David, RIBA; Director, Matthew Heywood Architecture, since 2003; *b* 26 Dec. 1970; *s* of late David Main Heywood and of Patricia Ann Heywood, *qv*; *m* 2002, Sarah Elizabeth Casemore; one *s*. *Educ:* Dundee Univ. (BSc Architecture, BArch Hons). RIBA 1996. Architect: T. P. Bennett Partnership, 1994–96; Future Systems, 1996–2003 (Associate Dir, 2001–03). *Recreation:* member of St Mark's Church, Battersea Rise, London. *Address:* Matthew Heywood Architecture, 1 Munro Terrace, SW10 0DL. *T:* (020) 7352 7583, *Fax:* 0871 242 4667; *e-mail:* email@matthewheywood.com.

HEYWOOD, Patricia Ann, OBE 2007; World Wide President, Mothers' Union, 2001–06; *b* 8 Feb. 1943; *d* of George and Joan Robinson; *m* 1965, David Main Heywood (*d* 1999); two *s*. *Educ:* Kendal High Sch.; Whitelands Coll., London. Teacher, 1964–68 and 1975–81. Joined, Mothers' Union, 1973; Diocesan Pres., St Andrew's, Dunkeld and Dunblane, and Mem., Central Executive, 1992–95; Provincial Pres. for Scotland and Mem., Trustee Bd, 1995–2000. *Recreations:* reading, gardening, walking, crafts. *Address:* Sunshine Cottage, 246 Barnett Wood Lane, Ashtead, Surrey KT21 2BY.

See also M. D. Heywood.

HEYWOOD, Sir Peter, 6th Bt *cr* 1838, of Claremont, Lancashire; company director; *b* 10 Dec. 1947; *s* of Sir Oliver Kerr Heywood, 5th Bt and Denise Wymondham, 2nd *d* of late Jocelyn William Godefroi; *S* father, 1992; *m* 1970, Jacqueline Anne, *d* of Sir Robert Frederick Hunt, CBE; two *d*. *Educ:* Bryanston Sch.; Keble Coll., Oxford (BA Hons). *Heir:* twin *b* Michael Heywood [*b* 10 Dec. 1947; *m* 1972, Caroline Awdry Greig; one *s* one *d*].

HEYWOOD, Dr (Ronald) Barry; Director, British Antarctic Survey, 1994–97; *b* 28 Sept. 1937; *s* of Ronald Heywood and Edith Henrietta Heywood (*née* Bradbury); *m* 1965, Josephine Despina Panagopoulos; two *d*. *Educ:* Ashby Grammar Sch., Leics; Birmingham Univ. (BSc 1959; MSc 1961); Queen Mary Coll., London Univ. (PhD 1970). MIBiol 1967. British Antarctic Survey: Biologist, 1961–68; Hd, Freshwater Res., 1968–83; Chief Scientist, Offshore Biol Prog., 1978–86; Hd, Marine Life Scis Div., 1986–87; Dep. Dir, 1988–94. UK Delegate: IOC Regl Cttee for Southern Ocean, 1987–97; SCAR, 1995–97 (Mem., Wkg Gp on Human Biol and Medicine, 1995–97); Council of Managers of Nat. Antarctic Progs, 1994–97. Chairman: Eur. Bd for Polar Sci., 1995–97; Jt Exec., Eur. Bds for Marine and Polar Sci., 1995–97; Mem., British Nat. Cttee Antarctic Res., 1994–97. Hon. Associate, RHC, 1981. Polar Medal, 1967 and Clasp, 1986. *Publications:* University Research in Antarctica, 1993; papers on freshwater and marine physics and biol. *Recreations:* walking, music. *Address:* Magdalene House, Glapthorn Road, Oundle, Peterborough PE8 4JA. *Club:* Antarctic.

HEYWOOD, Prof. Vernon Hilton; Emeritus Professor, University of Reading, since 1988; *b* 24 Dec. 1927; *s* of Vernon William and Marjorie Elizabeth Heywood; *m* 1st, 1952, María de la Concepción Salcedo Manrique; four *s*; 2nd, 1980, Christine Anne Brighton. *Educ:* George Heriot's Sch., Edinburgh; Edinburgh Univ. (BSc, DSc); Pembroke Coll., Cambridge (PhD). Lecturer 1955–60, Sen. Lectr 1960–63, Reader 1963–64, Professor 1964–68, Dept of Botany, Univ. of Liverpool; University of Reading: Prof. of Botany and Hd of Dept of Botany, 1968–88; Dean, Faculty of Science, 1978–81. Dir, 1987–92, Consultant Dir, 1993, Botanic Gardens Conservation Internat.; Chief Scientist (Plant Conservation), IUCN, 1988–92; Exec. Editor, Global Biodiversity Assessment, UNEP, 1993–98. Hon. Professor: Botanical Inst., Nanjing, 1989–; Univ. Juan Agustín Maza, Mendoza, Argentina, 1997–; Hon. Fellow, Royal Botanic Garden, Edinburgh, 1995–. Storer Lectr, Univ. of California, Davis, 1990; Regents' Lectr, Univ. of Calif, Riverside, 1998. Chm., European Plants Specialist Gp, Species Survival Commn of IUCN, 1984–87; Pres. Emeritus, Internat. Council on Medicinal and Aromatic Plants, 2003– (Pres., 1994–2003); Member of Board: Genetic Resources Communications Systems Inc., 1990–94; Yves Rocher Foundn, 1991–; Conservatoire Botanique National, Porquerolles, 1991–, Bailleul, 1993–, Nancy, 1996–. Trustee: Royal Botanic Gardens, Kew, 1983–87; IUCN, UK, 1993–2005. Corresponding Mem., Botanical Soc. of Amer., 1987–. Hon. FLS 1999. Councillor of Honour, Consejo Superior de Investigaciones Científicas, Spain, 1970. Linnean Medal, Linnean Soc. of London, 1987; Hutchinson Medal, Chicago Hortl Soc., 1989. Order of the Silver Dog, 1989, Insignia de Oro, 2003 (Gran Canaria). *Publications:* Principles of Angiosperm Taxonomy (with P. H. Davis), 1963, 2nd edn 1965; (ed jtly) Flora Europaea: vol. 1 1964 (2nd edn 1993), vol. 2 1968, vol. 3 1972, vol. 4 1976, vol. 5 1980; Plant Taxonomy, 1967, 2nd edn 1976; Flowering Plants of the World, 1978, 2nd edn 1985; (jtly) Our Green and Living World, 1984; Las Plantas con Flores, 1985; (jtly) Botanic Gardens and the World Conservation Strategy, 1987; The Botanic Gardens Conservation Strategy, 1989; (jtly) International Directory of Botanic Gardens V, 1990; (jtly) Conservation of Medicinal Plants, 1991; (jtly) Conservation Techniques in Botanic Gardens, 1991; (jtly) Tropical Botanic Gardens: their role in conservation and development, 1991; (jtly) Proceedings of the International Symposium on Botanical Gardens, 1991; (jtly) Conservation des ressources végétales, 1991; (jtly) Centres of Plant Diversity: a guide and strategy for their conservation: vol. 1 1994, vol. 2 1995, vol. 3 1996; (ed) Global Biodiversity Assessment, 1995; Les Plantes à Fleurs, 1996; (jtly) Conservation of the Wild Relatives of Cultivated Plants Native to Europe, 1997; Use and Potential of Wild Plants in Farm Households, 1998; (jtly) *In situ* Conservation: a critical review of good practices, 2006; (ed jtly) Do Conservation Targets Help?, 2006; (jtly) Flowering Plant Families of the World, 2007; over 500 papers in sci. jls. *Recreations:* cooking, travel, music, writing. *Address:* White Mead, 22 Wiltshire Road, Wokingham RG40 1TP. *T:* (0118) 978 0185.

HEYWOOD, Victoria Mary Taylor, (Mrs C. W. Jones); Executive Director, Royal Shakespeare Company, since 2003; *b* 25 June 1956; *d* of Kenneth Heywood Taylor and Gillian Dorothea Taylor (*née* Black); *m* 1st, 1988, Christopher Wright (marr. diss. 1994); one *s*; 2nd, 2004, Clive William Jones, *qv*. *Educ:* Truro High Sch.; Fortismere Sch.; Central Sch. of Speech and Drama (Dip. Drama). Stage manager, 1977–84; Gen. Manager, London Bubble Th. Co., 1986–89; Exec. Dir, Contact Th., Manchester, 1989–93; Gen. Manager, London Internat. Fest. of Th., 1994; Exec. Dir, English Stage Co. (Royal Court Th.), 1994–2001. Vice-Chairman: Lyric Th., Hammersmith, 1999–2004; Young Vic Th., 2002–06. Mem., Soc. of London Theatres, 1995–. Trustee, Shakespeare Birthplace Trust, 2004–. FRSA 2005. *Recreations:* sleeping, eating, reading. *Address:* Royal Shakespeare Co., Waterside, Stratford upon Avon CV37 6BB. *T:* (01789) 296655.

See also M. O. J. Taylor.

HEYWOOD-LONSDALE, Lt-Col Robert Henry, MBE 1952; MC 1945; Vice Lord-Lieutenant for Oxfordshire, 1989–96; *b* 18 Dec. 1919; *s* of Col John Pemberton Heywood-Lonsdale, DSO, OBE, TD and Hon. Helen Annesley; *m* 1952, Hon. Jean Helen Rollo, *d* of 12th Lord Rollo; one *s* three *d*. *Educ:* Eton. Grenadier Guards, 1938–56; Royal Wilts Yeo., 1961–67. Farmer. Co. Comr for Scouts, Oxfordshire, 1981–86. High Sheriff, Wilts, 1975; DL Wilts, 1972, Oxon, 1983. *Recreation:* country pursuits. *Address:* Mount Farm, Churchill, Oxon OX7 6NP. *T:* (01608) 658316. *Club:* Boodle's.

HEYWORTH, Michael Paul, MBE 2007; PhD; Director, Council for British Archaeology, since 2004; *b* 30 July 1961; *s* of Allan Keith Heyworth and Jean Barbara Heyworth (*née* Kersey); *m* 1995, Dr Catherine Jane Mortimer; one *s* one *d*. *Educ:* Univ. of Sheffield (BA Hons Prehist. and Archaeol. 1982); Univ. of Bradford (MA Scientific Methods in Archaeol. 1983; PhD 1991); OU Business Sch. (Professional Cert. in Mgt 2003). MIFA 1984; FSA 2001. Res. Asst, 1983–86, Postgrad. res. student, 1986–87, Univ. of Bradford; SO, 1987–89, Higher SO, 1989–90, Ancient Monuments Lab., English Heritage; Council for British Archaeology: Sen. Bibliographer, British and Irish Archaeol Bibliography, 1990–92; Inf. Officer, 1992–94; Dep. Dir and Inf. Officer, 1994–2002; Dep. Dir, 2002–04. Institute of Field Archaeologists: Mem. Council, 1985–88; Hon. Treas., 1986–88; Ed., Technical Papers, 1989–94. Co-Dir, Internet Archaeology, electronic jl, 1995–; Vice Chm., Archaeology Data Service, 1998–; Chm., Archaeology Trng Forum, 2005–. Vice Pres., Europ. Forum of Heritage Assocs, 1993–98. Trustee: York Archaeol Trust, 1996–2007; Yorks Philosophical Soc., 2003–06; Heritage Link, 2005–. MCMI 2003. *Publications:* (jtly) The Hamwic Glass, 1998; compiled and edited: British Archaeological Bibliography (with I. Holroyd), 1990, 1991, 1992; Archaeology in Britain, 1992; British Archaeological Yearbook 1995–96; various papers, articles and reports; over 40 Ancient Monuments Lab. tech. reports on wide variety of technol material. *Recreations:* football, current affairs, local issues. *Address:* Council for British Archaeology, St Mary's House, 66 Bootham, York YO30 7BZ. *T:* (01904) 671417, *Fax:* (01904) 671384; *e-mail:* mikeheyworth@britarch.ac.uk.

HIBBARD, Prof. Bryan Montague, MD, PhD; FRCOG; Professor of Obstetrics and Gynaecology, University of Wales College of Medicine (formerly Welsh National School of Medicine), 1973–91, now Emeritus Professor; *b* 24 April 1926; *s* of Montague Reginald and Muriel Irene Hibbard; *m* 1955, Elizabeth Donald Grassie. *Educ:* Queen Elizabeth's Sch., Barnet; St Bartholomew's Hosp. Med. Coll., London (MD); PhD (Liverpool). MRCS 1950; FRCOG 1965. Formerly: Sen. Lectr, Liverpool Univ.; Consultant Obstetrician and Gynaecologist, Liverpool RHB, and Univ. Hosp. of Wales. Chairman, Joint Standing Committee: Obstetric Anaesthesia, RCOG/RCAnaes, 1988–91; RCOG/RCM, 1988–91; Member: Cttee on Safety of Medicines, 1979–83; Maternity Services Adv. Cttee, 1981–85; Council, RCOG, 1982–88, 1989–92; S Glam HA, 1983–88; Medicines Commn, 1986–89. President: Welsh Obst. and Gynaecol Soc., 1985–86; History of Medicine Soc. of Wales, 1995–96. Hon. Curator of Museum, RCOG, 1986–2000 (Hon. Librarian, 1992–94). Mem. Editl Bd, Confidential Enquiries into Maternal Deaths, 1985–96 (Chm., Clinical Sub-Group, 1990–96). Hon. FRANZCOG

1997. *Publications:* Principles of Obstetrics, 1988; The Obstetric Forceps, 1988; The Obstetrician's Armamentarium, 2000; numerous contribs to world medical literature. *Recreations:* collecting 18th century drinking glasses, fell walking, coarse gardening. *Address:* The Clock House, Cathedral Close, Llandaff, Cardiff CF5 2ED. *T:* (029) 2056 6636.

HIBBERT; *see* Holland-Hibbert, family name of Viscount Knutsford.

HIBBERT, Rev. Barrie Edward; Associate Minister, Flinders Street Baptist Church, Adelaide, 2000–03; *b* 9 June 1935; *s* of Joseph and Eva Hibbert, Gisborne, NZ; *m* 1957, Ellen Judith Eade; one *s* two *d. Educ:* Victoria Univ. of Wellington, NZ (BA); Melbourne Coll. of Divinity, Vic, Australia (LTh); NZ Baptist Theol Coll. Minister: Baptist churches in Gore, Tawa and Dunedin, NZ, 1962–79; Flinders St Baptist Church, Adelaide, SA, 1979–87; Bloomsbury Central Baptist Church, London, 1987–99. *Address:* 1/9 Elizabeth Avenue, Plympton, SA 5038, Australia. *T:* (8) 82978558.

HIBBERT, Christopher, MC 1945; author; *b* 5 March 1924; *s* of late Canon H. V. Hibbert; *m* 1948, Susan Piggford; two *s* one *d. Educ:* Radley; Oriel Coll., Oxford (MA). Served in Italy, 1944–45; Capt., London Irish Rifles. Partner in firm of land agents, auctioneers and surveyors, 1948–59. Fellow, Chartered Auctioneers' and Estate Agents' Inst., 1948–59. Pres., Johnson Soc., 1980. FRSL, FRGS. Hon. DLitt Leicester, 1996. Heinemann Award for Literature, 1962; McColvin Medal, LA, 1989. *Publications:* The Road to Tyburn, 1957; King Mob, 1958; Wolfe at Quebec, 1959; The Destruction of Lord Raglan, 1961; Corunna, 1961; Benito Mussolini, 1962; The Battle of Arnhem, 1962; The Roots of Evil, 1963; The Court at Windsor, 1964; Agincourt, 1964; (ed) The Wheatley Diary, 1964; Garibaldi and His Enemies, 1965; The Making of Charles Dickens, 1967; (ed) Waterloo: Napoleon's Last Campaign, 1967; (ed) An American in Regency England: The Journal of Louis Simond, 1968; Charles I, 1968; The Grand Tour, 1969; London: Biography of a City, 1969; The Search for King Arthur, 1970; (ed) The Recollections of Rifleman Harris, 1970; Anzio: the bid for Rome, 1970; The Dragon Wakes: China and the West, 1793–1911, 1970; The Personal History of Samuel Johnson, 1971; (ed) Twilight of Princes, 1971; George IV, Prince of Wales, 1762–1811, 1972; George IV, Regent and King, 1812–1830, 1973; The Rise and Fall of the House of Medici, 1974; (ed) A Soldier of the Seventy-First, 1975; Edward VII: a portrait, 1976; The Great Mutiny: India 1857, 1978; Disraeli and His World, 1978; The Court of St James's, 1979; (ed) Boswell's Life of Johnson, 1979; The French Revolution, 1981; (ed) Greville's England, 1981; Africa Explored: Europeans in the Dark Continent, 1769–1889, 1982; (ed with Ben Weinreb) The London Encyclopaedia, 1983; Queen Victoria in Her Letters and Journals, 1984; Rome, Biography of a City, 1985; Cities and Civilizations, 1986; The English: A Social History 1066–1945, 1987; A Guide to Royal London, 1987; The Grand Tour, 1987; London's Churches, 1988; (ed) The Encyclopaedia of Oxford, 1988; Venice: biography of a city, 1988; Redcoats and Rebels: the war for America 1770–1781, 1990; The Virgin Queen: the personal history of Elizabeth I, 1990; (ed) Captain Gronow: his reminiscences of Regency and Victorian Life 1810–60, 1991; The Story of England, 1992; Cavaliers and Roundheads: the English at war 1642–1649, 1993; Florence: biography of a city, 1993; Nelson: a personal history, 1994; No Ordinary Place: Radley College and the public school system, 1997; Wellington: a personal history, 1997; George III: a personal history, 1998; Queen Victoria: a personal history, 2000; The Marlboroughs: John and Sarah Churchill 1650–1744, 2001; Napoleon: his wives and women, 2002; Disraeli: a personal history, 2004. *Recreations:* gardening, travel, cooking, crosswords. *Address:* 6 Albion Place, West Street, Henley-on-Thames, Oxon RG9 2DT. *Club:* Army and Navy.

HICHENS, Antony Peverell, RD 1969; Chairman, D. S. Smith (formerly David S. Smith (Holdings)) plc, 1999–2006; *b* 10 Sept. 1936; *s* of late Lt-Comdr R. P. Hichens, DSO (and Bar), DSC (and 2 Bars), RNVR, and Catherine Gilbert Enys; *m* 1963, Sczerina Neomi Hobday, DL; one *d. Educ:* Stowe; Magdalen Coll., Oxford (MA Law); Univ. of Pennsylvania, Wharton Sch. (MBA). Midshipman, RNVR, 1954–56. Called to Bar, Inner Temple, 1960. Rio Tinto-Zinc Corp., 1960–72; Financial Dir, Redland, 1972–81; Man. Dir and Chief Financial Officer, Consolidated Gold Fields, 1981–89; Chairman: Y. J. Lovell (Holdings), 1990–94; Caradon, 1990–98; Lasmo plc, 2000–01; Dep. Chm., Candover Investments plc, 1989–. Mem. (non-exec.), British Coal Corp., 1992–97. Mem., Takeover Panel, 2001–. Waynflete Fellow, Magdalen Coll., Oxford, 1997–. *Publication:* Gunboat Command: the biography of Lieutenant Commander Robert Hitchens DSO* DSC** RNVR, 2007. *Recreations:* travel, wine, shooting. *Address:* Slape Manor, Netherbury, near Bridport, Dorset DT6 5LH. *T:* (01308) 488232. *Clubs:* Brooks's, Naval.

HICK, Prof. John Harwood; Danforth Professor, 1979–92, and Director of Blaisdell Programs in World Religions and Cultures, 1983–92, Claremont Graduate School, California, now Professor Emeritus, Claremont Graduate University; *b* 20 Jan. 1922; *s* of Mark Day Hick and Mary Aileen (Hirst); *m* 1953, (Joan) Hazel, *d* of F. G. Bowers, CB, CBE, and Frances Bowers; two *s* one *d* (and one *s* decd). *Educ:* Bootham Sch., York; Edinburgh Univ. (MA 1948 (1st cl. hons Philos); DLitt 1974); Oriel Coll., Oxford (Campbell-Fraser schol.; DPhil 1950); Westminster Coll., Cambridge. Friends' Ambulance Unit, 1942–45. Ordained, Presb. C of E, 1953; Minister, Belford Presb. Church, Northumberland, 1953–56; Asst Prof. of Philosophy, Cornell Univ., 1956–59; Stuart Prof. of Christian Philosophy, Princeton Theolog. Seminary, 1959–64; S. A. Cook Bye-Fellow, Gonville and Caius Coll., Cambridge, 1963–64; PhD by incorporation; Lectr in Divinity, Cambridge Univ., 1964–67; H. G. Wood Prof. of Theology, Univ. of Birmingham, 1967–82, now Emeritus. Guggenheim Fellow, 1963–64, and 1985–86; Leverhulme Res. Fellow, 1976; Scholar-in-residence, Rockefeller Foundn Research Center, Bellagio, Italy, 1986; Fellow, Inst. for Advanced Res. in Arts and Social Scis (formerly the Humanities), Birmingham Univ., 1988–; Hon. Prof., Univ. of Wales, Lampeter, 1995–2003. Lectures: Mead-Swing, Oberlin Coll., USA, 1962–63; Mary Farnum Brown, Haverford Coll., USA 1964–65; James W. Richard, Univ. of Virginia, 1969; Distinguished Vis., Univ. of Oregon, 1969; Arthur Stanley Eddington Meml, 1972; Stanton, Cambridge Univ., 1974–77; Teape, Delhi, Calcutta and Madras, 1975; Ingersoll, Harvard, 1977; Hope, Stirling, 1977; Younghusband, London, 1977; Mackintosh, East Anglia, 1978; Riddell, Newcastle, 1978–79; Berkeley, TCD, 1979; Greenhoe, Louisville Pres. Sem., 1979; Potter, Washington State Univ., 1980; Montefiore, London, 1980; Brooks, Univ. of S California, 1982; Mars and Shaffer, Northwestern Univ., 1983; Niebuhr, Elmhurst Coll., 1986; Gifford, Edinburgh, 1986–87; Kegley, Calif State Univ.; Bakersfield, 1988; Suarez, Spring Hill Coll., 1988; Gates, Grinnell Coll., 1989; Birks, McGill Univ., 1989; Fritz Marti, Univ. of Southern Illinois, 1989; Brooke Anderson, Brown Univ., 1990; Eliot, Reed Coll., 1990; Resler, Ohio State Univ., 1991; Showers, Univ. of Indianapolis, 1993; McMartin, Ottawa Univ., 1993; Auburn, Union Theol Seminary, NY, 1994; Lily Montagu, London Soc. of Jews and Christians, London, 1994; Killeen, St Norbert Coll., Wis, 1995; Anne Spencer, Bristol Univ., 1996; Whyte, Oxford, 1998; Alister Hardy, World Congress of Faiths, 2005. Visiting Professor: Banares Hindu Univ., 1971; Visva Bharati Univ., 1971; Punjabi Univ., Patiala, 1971; Goa Univ., 1990; Visiting Fellow: British Acad. Overseas, 1974 and 1990; Univ. of Sri Lanka, 1974. Hulsean Preacher, Cambridge Univ., 1969; Select Preacher, Oxford Univ., 1970. Chairman: Religious and Cultural Panel, Birmingham Community Relations Cttee, 1969–74; Co-ordinating Working Party, Statutory Conf. for Revision of Agreed Syllabus of Religious Educn, Birmingham, 1971–74; Birmingham Inter-Faiths Council, 1975; President: Soc. for the Study of Theology, 1975–76; All Faiths for One Race, 1980–85 (Chm., 1972–7., 1978–80); Vice-President: World Congress of Faiths, 1993–; British Soc. for Philosophy of Religion, 1994– (Mem., 1990–); Member: Amer. Acad. of Religion, 1980–94; Ad. Bd, Inst. for Philosophy and Religion, Boston Univ., 1984–; Internat. Bd, Global Ethic and Religion Forum, Calif, 1998–; Member Emeritus: Amer. Soc. for the Study of Religion, 1992 (Mem., 1983); Amer. Philosophical Assoc., 1992 (Mem., 1980). Internat. Consultant, Internat. Interfaith Centre, Oxford, 1996–. Mem. Council, Selly Oak Coll. 1967–80; Governor, Queen's Coll., Birmingham, 1972–80. Mem. Editl Bd, The Encyclopedia of Philosophy. Hon. Teol. Dr Uppsala, 1977; Hon. DD Glasgow, 200. Louisville Grawemeyer Award in Religion, Univ. of Louisville and Louisville Theo. Seminary, 1991. *Publications:* Faith and Knowledge, 1957, 2nd edn 1966; Philosophy of Religion, 1963, 4th edn 1990 (also Spanish, Portuguese, Chinese, Japanese, Korean, Finnish, Polish, Farsi, Hindi and Swedish edns); (ed) Faith and the Philosophers, 1963; (ed) The Existence of God, 1963; (ed) Classical and Contemporary Readings in the Philosophy of Religion, 1963, 3rd edn 1990; Evil and the God of Love, 1966, 3rd edn 2007 (trans. Korean); (ed) The Many-Faced Argument, 1967; Christianity at the Centre, 1968, 2nd edn as The Centre of Christianity, 1977 (trans. Dutch, Korean and Chinese); Argument for the Existence of God, 1971 (trans. German, Polish); Biology and the Soul, 1972; God and the Universe of Faiths, 1973; (ed) Truth and Dialogue, 1974; Death and Eternal Life 1976 (trans. Dutch); (ed) The Myth of God Incarnate, 1977 (trans. German and Arabic) God has Many Names, 1980 (trans. German, Japanese, Korean); (ed with Brian Hebblethwaite) Christianity and Other Religions, 1980; The Second Christianity, 198 (trans. Japanese); (with Michael Goulder) Why Believe in God?, 1983; Problems of Religious Pluralism, 1985 (trans. Japanese, Chinese, Farsi); (ed with Hasan Askari) The Experience of Religious Diversity, 1985; An Interpretation of Religion, 1989, 2nd edn 2004 (trans. German, Chinese, Farsi); (ed with Edmund Meltzer) Three Faiths—One God, 1989; (ed with Lamont Hempel) Gandhi's Significance for Today, 1989; (ed with Paul Knitter) The Myth of Christian Uniqueness, 1992 (trans. Japanese, Italian); Disputed Questions in Theology and the Philosophy of Religion, 1993; The Metaphor of God Incarnate, 1993 (trans. Japanese, Chinese, Portuguese, Spanish, Korean); The Rainbow of Faiths, 1995 (trans. Japanese, Chinese, Portuguese, Turkish); The Fifth Dimension, 199. 2nd edn 2004 (trans. Chinese, Japanese, Russian, Danish, Polish, Farsi, Indonesian) Dialogues in the Philosophy of Religion, 2001; John Hick: an autobiography, 2003 (trans. Japanese); The New Frontier of Religion and Science, 2006; Who or What is God?, 200. *Address:* 144 Oak Tree Lane, Selly Oak, Birmingham B29 6HU.

HICKEY, Most Rev. Barry James; *see* Perth (Australia), Archbishop of, (RC).

HICKEY, Christopher John; Director, British Council, Spain, since 2003; *b* 8 Nov. 1951; *s* of late William Joseph Hickey and Evelyn Mary Hickey; *m* 1984, Pauline Donovan; one *s* one *d. Educ:* Monmouth Sch.; Univ. of Sheffield (BA French and Spanish); Univ. of Leeds (PGCE); University Coll. London (MPhil French Lit.); London Business Sch. (Sen. Exec. Prog.). Dip. TEFL (RSA). English Teacher, Univ. of Rennes and Franco-American Inst., 1975–78; joined British Council, 1978: English teaching ass. 1978–80; Asst English Lang. Officer, Morocco, 1981–83; Regl Lang. Advr, London 1983–86; First Sec. (Educn), British Embassy, Abidjan, 1986–90; English Lang. Officer Barcelona, 1990–93; Hd, Educnl Enterprises, Madrid, 1993–95; Dep. Dir, 1996–99, Dir 1999–2000, Educnl Enterprises, London; Dir, Greece, 2000–03. Chm., British Nat. Cttee for Cultural Olympiad, 2002–04. *Recreations:* literature, languages, the arts, watching football, restaurants. *Address:* British Council, 31 Martinez Campos, 28010 Madrid, Spain *T:* (91) 3373590, *Fax:* (91) 3373573; *e-mail:* chris.hickey@britishcouncil.es.

HICKEY, Dr Stephen Harald Frederick; Director General, Safety, Service Delivery and Logistics Group, Department for Transport, since 2007; *b* 10 July 1949; *s* of late Rev. Dr James Peter Hickinbotham and Ingeborg Hickinbotham; name changed by Deed Poll to Hickey, 1976; *m* 1976, Dr Janet Elizabeth Hunter; three *s. Educ:* St Lawrence Coll. Ramsgate; Corpus Christi Coll., Oxford (BA, MA); St Antony's Coll., Oxford (DPhil) Joined DHSS, 1974; Asst Sec., DHSS, later DSS, 1985–94; seconded to Rank Xerox (UK), 1989–90; Chief Exec., Civil Service Coll., 1994–98; Prin. Finance Officer 1998–2002, Dir, Corporate Services, 2000–02, Dir, Corporate Develt Gp, 2002–03, DSS then DWP; Acting Chief Exec., Highways Agency, 2003; Dir Gen., Driver, Vehicle Operator Gp, DfT, 2003–07. *Publication:* Workers in Imperial Germany: the miners of the Ruhr, 1985. *Recreations:* music, tennis, walking, history. *Address:* Department for Transport, Zone 2/11, Great Minster House, 76 Marsham Street, SW1P 4DR.

HICKFORD, Rev. Canon Michael Francis; Hospital and Community Health Care Chaplain, NHS Highland, since 2004; *b* 7 Oct. 1953; *s* of Frank Hickford and Cherry Wendy Rosalind (*née* Mitchell). *Educ:* Gravesend Grammar Sch.; Edinburgh Theological Coll. Chaplain, St John's Cathedral, Oban, 1986–89; Rector, St Mungo, Alexandria Dunbartonshire, 1989–95; Priest i/c, St James the Great, Dingwall with St Anne Strathpeffer, 1995–2003; Dean of Moray, Ross and Caithness, 1998–2003; Provost and Rector, 2003–04, Hon. Canon, 2007, St Andrew's Cathedral, Inverness. *Recreations:* hill walking, music, cookery, theatre.

HICKINBOTTOM, Hon. Sir Gary Robert, Kt 2009; FCIArb; **Hon. Mr Justice Hickinbottom;** a Judge of the High Court of Justice, Queen's Bench Division, from Jan. 2009; Judge, Supreme Court, Falkland Islands, since 2006; *b* 22 Dec. 1955; *s* of Samuel Geoffrey Hickinbottom and Jean Irene Hickinbottom (*née* Greaney); *m* 1st, 1982 (marr. diss. 2001); two *s* two *d*; 2nd, 2004, Georgina Caroline Hamilton. *Educ:* Queen Mary's Grammar Sch., Walsall; University Coll., Oxford (MA); DipICArb, 1997. FCIArb 1995. Lectr, Poly. of Central London, 1980–81; admitted Solicitor, 1981; Partner, McKenna & Co., subseq. Cameron McKenna, 1986–2000; Lectr, University Coll., Oxford, 1987–89. Registered Mediator, 1991; Parking Adjudicator, Parking Appeals Service and Nat. Parking Adjudication Service, 1994–2000; Asst Recorder, 1994–98; Recorder 1998–2000; Circuit Judge, 2000–08; Dep. High Ct Judge, 2001–08; Solicitor Advocate (all Courts), 1997; Chief Social Security Comr and Child Support Comr, 2003–; Chief Pensions Appeal Comr, 2005–; Designated Civil Judge: for S and W Wales, 2005–07; for Wales, 2007–08; Dep. Sen. Pres. of Tribunals, 2008–. Asst Comr, Boundary Commn for England, 2000. Member: Gen. Council of Bar and Law Soc. Jt Wkg Party on Civil Courts 1992–93; Law Soc. Wkg Party on Gp Actions, 1994–2000; Judicial Technol. Bd 2004–05. *Publications:* various articles on law and legal procedure. *Recreations:* choral singing, opera, ballet, sport. *Address:* Royal Courts of Justice, Strand, WC2A 2LL. *Club:* London Welsh.

HICKMAN, Claire Josephine, MA; Principal, Chetham's School of Music, since 1999; *b* 2 Aug. 1958; *d* of late Peter Alfred White and of Eileen Beatrice White (*née* Kidston); *m* 1st, 1982, John Moreland (marr. diss. 1999); one *s*; 2nd, 2004, Richard Hickman. *Educ:* Devonport High Sch. for Girls; St Hugh's Coll., Oxford (MA Modern Langs, PGCE). Asst teacher, Sevenoaks Sch., 1981–84; Hd of German, Croydon High Sch. for Girls

1984–88; Rugby School: asst teacher, 1988–92; Housemistress, 1992–97; Dep. Head, 1997–99. *Publication:* Schreib mir Bitte, 1982. *Recreations:* literature, music, finding silver linings. *Address:* Chetham's School of Music, Long Millgate, Manchester M3 1SB. *T:* (0161) 834 9644. *Clubs:* University Women's, East India.

HICKMAN, Sir Glenn; *see* Hickman, Sir R. G.

HICKMAN, Sir (Richard) Glenn, 4th Bt *cr* 1903; *b* 12 April 1949; *o s* of Sir Alfred Howard Whitby Hickman, 3rd Bt, and of Margaret Doris (*d* 1996), *o d* of Leonard Kempson; *S* father, 1979; *m* 1981, Heather Mary Elizabeth, *er d* of late Dr James Moffett, Swindon, and late Dr Gwendoline Moffett; two *s* one *d. Educ:* Eton. *Heir: s* Charles Patrick Alfred Hickman, *b* 5 May 1983. *Address:* Manor Farm House, Liddington, Wilts SN4 0HD. *Club:* Turf.

HICKMAN, Richard Michael, CBE 2002; Chief Inquiry Reporter, Scottish Executive (formerly Scottish Office), 1997–2002; *b* 30 April 1942; *m* 1st, 1964, Lorna Dixon (marr. diss. 1992); two *s*; 2nd, 1993, Sandie Jane Randall; one step *s* one step *d. Educ:* Kingswood Sch., Bath; LSE (BA Hons Geog.); Regent St Polytechnic (DipTP); Univ. of British Columbia (MA Community and Regional Planning). MRTPI 1966. Planning Depts of LCC, 1963–65, of GLC, 1965–67; Scottish Develt Dept, 1969–78; Scottish Office Inquiry Reporters' Unit, 1979–2002. *Recreations:* walking, sailing, travel.

HICKMET, Richard Saladin; barrister-at-law; *b* 1 Dec. 1947; *s* of Ferid Hickmet and late Elizabeth Hickmet; *m* 1973, Susan (*née* Ludwig); three *d. Educ:* Millfield Sch.; Sorbonne; Hull Univ. (BA). Called to the Bar, Inner Temple, 1974. Mem., Wandsworth Borough Council, 1978–83 (Chm., Leisure and Amenities Cttee, 1980–83; privatised street cleansing, refuse collection, parks maintenance). Contested (C): Glanford and Scunthorpe, 1987; Eastbourne, Oct. 1990. MP (C) Glanford and Scunthorpe, 1983–87. *Recreations:* squash, hunting. *Address:* The Chantry, Rhode, North Petherton, Somerset TA5 2AD. *T:* (01278) 663388, *Fax:* (01278) 663981; *e-mail:* law@richardhickmet.co.uk.

HICKOX, Richard Sidney, CBE 2002; FRCO(CHM); conductor; Music Director: City of London Sinfonia, since 1971; City of London Sinfonia (formerly Richard Hickox) Singers, since 1971; London Symphony Chorus, since 1976; Opera Australia, since 2005; Associate Conductor, London Symphony Orchestra, since 1985; *b* Stokenchurch, Bucks, 5 March 1948; *m* 1976, Frances Ina Sheldon-Williams (marr. diss.); one *s*; *m* 1995, Pamela Helen Stephen; one *s* one *d. Educ:* in organ, piano and composition, Royal Acad. of Music (LRAM); Queens' Coll., Cambridge (Organ Scholar; MA; Hon. Fellow, 1996). Début as professional conductor, St John's Smith Square, 1971; Organist and Master of the Music, St Margaret's, Westminster, 1972–82; Prom début, 1973; Principal Conductor, BBC Nat. Orch. of Wales, 2000–06, subseq. Conductor Emeritus. Artistic Director: Wooburn Fest., 1967–89; St Endellion Fest., 1974–; Christ Church Spitalfields Fest., 1978–94; Truro Fest., 1981–; Chester Summer Fest., 1989–; Northern Sinfonia, 1982–90 (Conductor Emeritus, 1996–); City of London Fest., 1994; Music Dir, Bradford Festival Choral Soc., 1978–98; Principal Guest Conductor: Dutch Radio Orch., 1980–84; Associate Conductor, San Diego Symphony Orch., 1983–84; also regularly conducts Philharmonia, RPO, Bournemouth Symphony Orch. and Sinfonietta, Royal Liverpool Phil. Orch., BBC Symphony, Concert, Scottish and Welsh Orchs, BBC Singers, Hallé Orch.; San Francisco Symphony Orch.; Detroit Symphony Orch.; Houston Symphony Orch.; National Symphony Orch., Washington; Rotterdam Philharmonic; Oslo Philharmonic; Turku Philharmonia; Salzburg Mozarteum; Suisse Romande; Stockholm Philharmonic. Conducted: ENO, 1979, 1996, 2000; Opera North, 1982, 1986, 1995; Scottish Opera, 1985, 1987; Royal Opera, 1985, 1999, 2001; has appeared at many music festivals incl. Proms, Flanders, Bath and Cheltenham. Co-founder, Opera Stage, 1985. Many recordings of choral and orchestral music. *Address:* c/o Intermusica Artists' Management, 16 Duncan Terrace, N1 8BZ.

HICKS; *see* Joynson-Hicks.

HICKS, Dr Brendan Hamilton, FRCP; Regional Postgraduate Dean Director, NHS Kent, Surrey and Sussex (formerly South East Region), 1996–2004; *b* 22 Feb. 1942; *s* of Bryan Hamilton Hicks and Winifriede (*née* O'Leary); *m* 1966, Jackie Ann Box; one *s* one *d. Educ:* St Brendan's Coll., Bristol; Guy's Hosp. Med. Sch., Univ. of London (BSc 1962; MB BS 1965; MD 1976). FRCP 1982. Jun. med. posts, Guy's Hosp., RPMS and Brompton Hosp., 1965–67; Governors' Res. Schol. and Lectr in Medicine, Guy's Hosp. Med. Sch., 1967–72; NIH Internat. Fellow (US Public Health Service/MRC), Univ. of Michigan, Ann Arbor, 1972–73; Sen. Lectr in Medicine, Undergrad. Tutor and Hon. Consultant Physician, Guy's Hosp. and Med. Sch., 1974–80; Sen. Lectr in Medicine, UMDS of Guy's and St Thomas' Hosps, and Consultant Physician to Guy's and St Thomas' and Lewisham Hosps, 1981–95; Postgrad. Dean and Trust Dir, Postgrad. Med. and Dental Educn, Guy's and St Thomas' Hosp., 1985–95. Hon. Prof., Univ. of Brighton, 2002–. Hon. DSc Brighton, 2005. *Publications:* contrib. chapter in: A Short Textbook of Medicine, ed jtly, biennially, 1978–92; Principles of Clinical Medicine, ed Rees and Williams, 1995; contrib. papers in Metabolism, Diabetic Medicine, Clin. Endocrinol., etc. *Recreations:* books, theatre, music, narrow-boating, sailing, cocker spaniels. *Address:* 60 Greenwich Park Street, SE10 9LT. *T:* (020) 8858 7363; *e-mail:* brendan.hicks@btinternet.com.

HICKS, Dr Colin Peter, CB 2007; CChem, FRSC; Director General, British National Space Centre, 1999–2006; *b* 1 May 1946; *s* of George Stephen Frederick Hicks and Irene Maud (*née* Hargrave); *m* 1967, Elizabeth Joan Payne; two *d. Educ:* Rutlish Grammar Sch., Merton; Univ. of Bristol (BSc, PhD). Lectr in Chemistry, Univ. of W Indies, Jamaica, 1970–73; ICI Res. Fellow, Univ. of Exeter, 1973–75; DTI, 1975–2006; NPL, 1975–80; Laboratory of Govt Chemist, 1984–87; Sec., Ind. Develt Adv. Bd, 1988–90; Hd, Res. and Technol. Policy Div., 1990–94; Hd of Envmt and Energy Technologies Div., 1994–96; Dir, Envmt, 1996–99. Mem., NERC, 2002–06. Pres., Eurisy, 2006–. Mem. Council, BUGB, 2006–. *Address:* 41 Teddington Park, Teddington TW11 8DB.

HICKS, Group Captain (Harry) David, MBE 1967; Director General, English-Speaking Union, 1990–91 (Deputy Director General, 1985–90); *b* 13 July 1923; *s* of Walter Hicks and Clara Ann (*née* Jagger); *m* 1948, Jane Irene Mary Tibbs; one *s* one *d. Educ:* Grange Grammar Sch., Bradford; London Univ. (BA Hons 1947); Nottingham Univ. (PGCE 1948). Served War, 1942–45, as Pilot, 149 Sqdn, Bomber Comd. Schoolmaster, Surbiton Grammar Sch., 1948–49; Royal Air Force: Educn Br., 1950–54; Admin. Br., 1954–76, finally as Dep. Dir, Recruiting; Dir of Educn, E-SU, 1976–85; Gen. Dir, Internat. Shakespeare Globe Centre, 1991–92. Special Consultant to BBC English, 1991–95; German Language Consultant to Callon Sch., 1992. *Recreations:* golf, tennis, playing piano.

HICKS, His Honour John Charles; QC 1980; a Judge of the Technology and Construction Court of the High Court (formerly the Official Referees' Courts), 1993–2000; a Circuit Judge, 1988–2000; *b* 4 March 1928; *s* of late Charles Hicks and late Marjorie Jane Hicks; *m* 1957, Elizabeth Mary, *o d* of late Rev. J. B. Jennings; one *d* (one *s* decd). *Educ:* King Edward VI Grammar Schs, Chelmsford and Totnes; London Univ. LLM 1954. Served RA (National Service), 1946–48. Admitted solicitor, 1952; called to the Bar, Middle Temple, 1966; a Recorder, 1978–88. Legal Dept, Thomas Tilling Ltd, 1953–54; Partner in Messrs Burchells, solicitors, 1955–65; Methodist Missionary Soc., Caribbean, 1965–66. Jl Sec., Methodist Conf., 1989–97. *Publications:* (ed jtly) The Constitution and Discipline of the Methodist Church in the Caribbean and the Americas, 1967, with annual supplements to 1987; (ed) The Constitutional Practice and Discipline of the Methodist Church, 6th edn 1974, 7th edn 1988, with annual supplements, 1974–97; articles in Mod. Law Rev., Cambridge Law Jl, Conveyancer, and Epworth Rev. *Recreations:* music, theatre, opera, the Methodist Constitution. *Address:* Flat 3, 17 Montagu Square, W1H 2LE. *T:* (020) 7935 6008; *e-mail:* john.hicks@montagusquare.net.

HICKS, Maureen Patricia; Tour Director, Town Centre Manager and Consultant, Stratford-upon-Avon, since 2001; *b* 23 Feb. 1948; *d* of Ron and Nora Cutler; *m* 1973, Keith Hicks; one *s* one *d. Educ:* Ashley Secondary School; Brockenhurst Grammar School; Furzedown College of Education. Teacher's Cert. Secondary Teacher, Drama and English, 1969–70; Marks & Spencer Management, 1970–74; Asst Area Educn Officer, 1974–76; Dir, Motor Museum, 1976–82; Project Dir, Stratford-upon-Avon Visitor Mgt Nat. Pilot Project, 1992–96; Dir of Fundraising and Marketing, Myton Hamlet Hospice, Warwick, 1997–2001. Mem., Stratford DC, 1979–84. MP (C) Wolverhampton North East, 1987–92; contested (C) Wolverhampton NE, 1992. PPS to Minister of State and Parly Under-Sec. of State, FCO, 1991–92; Sec., H of C Tourism Cttee, 1987–92. Non-executive Director: David Clarke Associates, 1992–96; S Warwicks Combined Care (formerly Mental Health Services) NHS Trust, 1994–2002. Hon. Fellow, Wolverhampton Univ., 1992. *Recreations:* music, golf, travel.

HICKS, Maj.-Gen. Michael; *see* Hicks, Maj.-Gen. W. M. E.

HICKS, Sir Robert, Kt 1996; Chairman, Resound Health Ltd, since 2004; *b* 18 Jan. 1938; *s* of W. H. Hicks; *m* 1st, 1962, Maria Elizabeth Ann Gwyther (marr. diss. 1988); two *d*; 2nd, 1991, Mrs Glenys Foote. *Educ:* Queen Elizabeth Grammar Sch., Crediton; University Coll., London; Univ. of Exeter. Taught at St Austell Grammar Sch., 1961–64; Lecturer in Regional Geography, Weston-super-Mare Technical Coll., 1964–70. MP (C): Bodmin, 1970–Feb. 1974, Oct. 1974–1983; Cornwall SE, 1983–97. An Asst Govt Whip, 1973–74; Member: Select Cttee of House of Commons, European Legislation, 1973, 1976–97; Speaker's Panel, 1992–97; Vice-Chm., Cons. Parly European Affairs Cttee, 1979–81; Chairman: Cons. Parly Agric. Cttee, 1988–90 (Vice-Chm., 1972–73 (Chm., Horticultural Sub-Cttee), and 1974–82); Westcountry Gp of Cons. MPs, 1976–77; UK Gp, Parly Assoc. for Euro-Arab Co-operation, 1982–97; Vice-Chm., Cons. Party ME Council, 1992–97 (Treasurer, 1980–92); Parly Adviser to British Hotels, Restaurants and Caterers Assoc., 1974–97, to Milk Marketing Bd, 1985–97. Chairman: Westcountry Enterprises, 1997–2003; Midas Consortium, 2003–05. Pres., Plymouth Albion RFC, 1991–96. Chm., Silvanus Trust, 1999–. Trustee, Peninsula Med. Sch. Foundn, 1997–2002. Chm., Bd of Govs, Plymouth Coll., 2004–. *Recreations:* cricket, gardening, golf. *Address:* Burndoo, Luckett, Callington, Cornwall PL17 8NH. *Clubs:* Farmers', MCC.

HICKS, Robin Edgcumbe; Member, Management Board, Royal Smithfield Show, 1998–2004; *b* 6 Dec. 1942; *s* of late Ronald Eric Edgcumbe Hicks and Fredrica Hicks; *m* 1970, Sue (*née* Dalton); one *s* one *d. Educ:* Bancrofts' Sch.; Seale Hayne Coll. (NDA; Dip. Farm Management); Univ. of Reading (DipAgric Extension). ARAgS 1995. Farm worker, 1961–63; Agricl Advr, MAFF, 1967–69; Producer/Presenter, BBC Farming Today, 1969–71; Churchill Fellow, 1973; various production posts, radio and television, 1971–77; Hd of Marketing and Develt, RASE, 1977–79; Hd of Network Radio, BBC South and West, 1979–88; Chief Exec., RASE, 1989–91; Dir, Royal Smithfield Show, 1992–98; Chief Exec., Consortium of Rural TECs, 1998–99; Dir, Expocentric.com, 1999–2001. Ed., blablablah, 2006–. Consultant, Landscape '99. Mem., Bristol and Weston HA, 1986–88; Vice-Chm., Radio Acad., 1986–88; Trustee: St George's Music Trust, 1981–88; Rural Housing Trust, 1990–92; Member: Exec. Cttee, SW Arts, 1981–85; SW Concerts Bd, 1981–88; Trustee, Head Injury Recovery Trust, 1986–94. Hon. Life Mem., Royal Smithfield Club, 2005–. Freeman, City of London, 1977; Liveryman, Drapers' Co., 1981. *Recreations:* family, gardening, theatre. *Address:* Pigeonnier de Senaux, 34320 Roujan, France. *Clubs:* Farmers'; Midi Cricket (Pres., 2005–).

HICKS, Thomas; *see* Steele, Tommy.

HICKS, William David Antony; QC 1995; *b* 11 June 1951; *s* of Maj.-Gen. William Michael Ellis Hicks, *qv*; *m* 1982, Jennifer Caroline Ross; one *s* two *d. Educ:* Eton Coll.; Magdalene Coll., Cambridge (MA Econs). Called to the Bar, Inner Temple, 1975. *Recreations:* fishing, Real tennis, ski-ing, walking. *Address:* Landmark Chambers, 180 Fleet Street, EC4A 2HG. *Clubs:* Flyfishers', MCC.

HICKS, Maj.-Gen. (William) Michael (Ellis), CB 1982; OBE 1967; Secretary, Royal College of Defence Studies, 1983–93; *b* 2 June 1928; *s* of late Group Captain William Charles Hicks, AFC, and Nellie Kilbourne (*née* Kay); *m* 1950, Jean Hilary Duncan; three *s. Educ:* Eton Coll.; RMA Sandhurst. Commnd 2 Lieut Coldstream Guards, 1948; served, 1948–67: regtl service, UK, Tripoli and Canal Zone; Instr, Sch. of Inf. (Captain); Staff Coll. (Major); GSO2 (Ops) HQ 4 Div.; regtl service, BAOR, UK and Kenya; JSSC; GSO (DS) Staff Coll.; GSO1 MO1, MoD, 1967–70 (Lt-Col); CO 1st Bn Coldstream Guards, 1970–72; RCDS, 1973 (Col); comd 4th Guards Armoured Bde, 1974–76 (Brig.); BGS Trng HQ UKLF, 1977–79; BGS (Author) attached to DMO, MoD, 1979; GOC NW Dist, 1980–83, retd. *Recreation:* gardening. *Address:* c/o Lloyds TSB, Cox's & King's, PO Box 1190, 7 Pall Mall, SW1Y 5NA.

See also W. D. A. Hicks.

HICKS BEACH, family name of **Earl St Aldwyn.**

HIDDEN, Hon. Sir Anthony (Brian), Kt 1989; a Judge of the High Court of Justice, Queen's Bench Division, 1989–2003; *b* 7 March 1936; *s* of late James Evelyn Harold Hidden, GM and Gladys Bessie (*née* Brooks); *m* 1982, Mary Elise Torriano Pritchard (marr. diss. 2000), *d* of R. C. Pritchard of Barton Abbotts, Tetbury, Glos; three *s* one *d. Educ:* Reigate Grammar Sch.; Emmanuel Coll., Cambridge (BA Hons 1957, MA 1960). 2nd Lieut, 1st Royal Tank Regt, Far East Land Forces, Hong Kong, 1958–59. Called to the Bar, Inner Temple, 1961, Bencher, 1985; Mem., Hon. Soc. of Inner Temple, 1956–, and of Lincoln's Inn (*ad eundem*), 1973–. QC 1976; a Recorder, 1977–89; Leader, SE Circuit, 1986–89. Inspector, Clapham Junction Railway Accident, 1988. *Recreations:* reading, playing bad golf.

HIDE, Prof. Raymond, CBE 1990; FRS 1971; Senior Research Investigator, Department of Mathematics, Imperial College, University of London, since 2000; Emeritus Professor of Physics, Oxford University, since 1994 (Research Professor, Departments of Physics and Earth Sciences, 1992–94); *b* 17 May 1929; *s* of late Stephen Hide and Rose Edna (*née* Cartlidge); *m* 1958, (Phyllis) Ann Licence; one *s* two *d. Educ:*

Percy Jackson Grammar Sch., near Doncaster; Manchester Univ. (BSc 1st cl. hons Physics, 1950); Gonville and Caius Coll., Cambridge (PhD 1953, ScD 1969; Hon. Fellow, 2001). CPhys, FInstP, 1998. Res. Assoc. in Astrophysics, Univ. of Chicago, 1953–54; Sen. Res. Fellow, AERE Harwell, 1954–57; Lectr in Physics, Univ. of Durham (King's Coll., Newcastle), 1957–61; Prof. of Geophysics and Physics, MIT, 1961–67; Hd of Geophysical Fluid Dynamics Lab., Met. Office, 1967–90 (CSO 1975); Fellow, Jesus Coll., Oxford, 1983–96 (Hon. Fellow, 1997); Dir, Robert Hooke Inst. and Vis. Prof., Dept of Physics, Oxford Univ., 1990–92. Short-term vis. appts at Princeton Inst. for Advanced Study, 1954, MIT and UCLA, 1960, CIT, 1993 (Fairchild Schol.); Visiting Professor: UCL, 1967–84; Reading Univ., 1976–91; Leeds Univ., 1986–91; Gresham Prof. of Astronomy, Gresham Coll., City of London, 1985–90; Adrian Fellow, Univ. of Leicester, 1980–83. Distinguished Vis. Scientist, Jet Propulsion Lab., CIT, 1985–97; Hon. Sen. Res. Fellow, Inst. of Oceanographic Scis Deacon Lab., 1990–; Hon. Scientist, Rutherford Appleton Lab., 1992–. Member Council: RAS, 1969–72 and 1983–86 (Pres., 1983–85); Royal Meteorological Soc., 1969–72 and 1974–77 (Pres., 1974–76; Hon. Mem., 1989); NERC, 1972–75; Eur. Geophysical Soc., 1981–85 (Pres., 1982–84, Hon. Mem., 1988); Royal Soc., 1988–90. Lectures: Symons Meml, RMetS, 1970; R. A. Fisher Meml, 1977; Halley, Oxford, 1980; Jeffreys, RAS, 1981; Union, Internat. Union of Geodesy and Geophysics, Hamburg, 1983; Scott, Cambridge, 1984; Thompson, Toronto, 1984; Lindsay, NASA, 1988; Courtauld, Manchester Lit. & Phil Soc., 1996; Schuster, Manchester Univ., 1998; Starr, MIT, 2001. MAE 1988; Mem., Pontifical Acad. of Scis, 1996; Fellow: Amer. Acad. of Arts and Sciences, 1964; Amer. Geophys. Union, 1967. Hon. DSc: Leicester, 1985; UMIST, 1994; Paris, 1995. Charles Chree Medal, Inst. Physics, 1975; Holweck Medal, Soc. Franç. de Physique, 1982; Gold Medal, RAS, 1989; William Bowie Medal, Amer. Geophysical Union, 1997; Hughes Medal, Royal Soc., 1998; Richardson Medal, European Geophys. Soc., 1999; Symons Gold Medal, RMetS, 2003. *Publications:* papers in scientific jls. *Address:* Department of Mathematics, Imperial College, 180 Queen's Gate, SW7 2RH.

HIDER, David James; Director, Internal Communications Project, British Gas, 1994–95; *b* 5 Nov. 1934; *s* of Edward James Hider and Marguerite Noel Hider (*née* James); *m* 1963, Margaret Gilbert Macdonald Watson; two *s* one *d*. *Educ:* Roan Sch., Greenwich; King Edward VII Nautical Coll., Poplar. Master Mariner; DMS; CIGEM. Merchant Navy, 1952–67 (to Chief Officer); South Eastern Gas: Commercial Asst, 1967; Conversion Unit Manager, 1969; Area Service Manager, Sussex, 1973; Regl Service Manager, 1976; Dir of Marketing, 1981; British Gas: Dir of Service, 1983; Dir of Domestic Marketing, 1990; Regl Chm., British Gas S Western, 1990–94. Mem., SW IDB, 1997–99; Vice Chm., Bristol Regeneration Partnership, 2000–03; Chm., Bristol Partnership Regeneration Progs Mgt Gp (formerly Bristol Regeneration Partnership), 2003–04. Chm., Avon Youth Assoc., 1996–. Chm. and Man. Dir, St Peter's Hospice Enterprises, 2000–; Trustee, CLIC, 2000–04. Gov., UWE, 1993–2004. *Publications:* contribs to Jl IGasE. *Recreations:* squash, swimming, walking, cooking, flying.

HIDER, Prof. Robert Charles, PhD; CChem, FRSC; Professor of Medicinal Chemistry, King's College, London, since 1987; *b* 14 Aug. 1943; *s* of Charles Thomas Hider and Josephine Mary (*née* Breitbach); *m* 1967, Shirley Christine Nickels; one *s* one *d*. *Educ:* King's Coll., London (BSc Chem. and Physics 1964; PhD Chem. 1967; FKC 1997). Wellcome Res. Fellow, St Thomas' Hosp., 1967–70; Lectr, then Reader, Dept of Chem., Essex Univ., 1970–87; King's College, London: Head, Sch. of Life, Basic Med. and Health Scis, then of Health & Life Scis, 1994–2000; Head, Dept of Pharmacy, 2000–03; Head, Sch. of Biomed. Scis, subseq. Sch. of Biomed. and Health Scis, 2002–07. Associated with develt of medicines for thalassaemia, anaemia, and renal failure. Vis. Prof., Dept of Biochem., Univ., of Calif, Berkeley, 1977 and 1980. Hon. MRPharmS, 1995. Member, Editorial Board: Toxicon, 1986–98; Biometals, 1990–; Biochem. Jl, 1996–2001; Jl Pharm. Sci., 2002–; Eur. Jl Pharm. Sci., 2002–. *Publications:* contrib. articles on pharmaceutically active peptides and metal chelating agents to pharmaceutical, biochem. and chem. jls. *Recreations:* arachnology, natural history, Australian philately. *Address:* 257 Point Clear Road, St Osyth, Essex C016 8JL. *T:* (01255) 821335.

HIELSCHER, Sir Leo (Arthur), AC 2004; Kt 1987; Chairman, Queensland Treasury Corporation, since 1988; *b* 1 Oct. 1926; *s* of Leslie Charles Hielscher and Elizabeth Jane Petersen; *m* 1948, Mary Ellen Pelgrave; one *s* one *d* (and one *s* decd). *Educ:* Brisbane State High Sch.; Univ. of Queensland (BComm, AAUQ). FCPA; FAIM. Queensland Public Service, 1942; RAAF, 1945–47; Asst Under Sec. (Budget), Qld Treasury, 1964–69, Dep. Under Treasurer, 1969–74; Under Treas. of Qld (CS Hd of Treasury Dept of Qld Govt), 1974–88. Eisenhower Exchange Fellow, 1973. Chairman: Independent Superannuation Preservation Fund Pty Ltd; Autsafe Ltd. *Recreations:* golf, fishing, boating, theatre. *Address:* 8 Silverash Court, Capalaba, Brisbane, Qld 4157, Australia. *T:* (home) (7) 32060104, *Fax:* (7) 32064241, *T:* (business) (7) 38424620, *Fax:* (7) 32100262. *Clubs:* Brisbane, Tattersalls (Brisbane).

HIGGINBOTHAM, Prof. James Taylor, PhD; FBA 1995; Linda MacDonald Hilf Professor of Philosophy, since 2004, Distinguished Professor of Philosophy and Linguistics, since 2006, and Chair, Department of Linguistics, since 2006, University of Southern California; *b* 17 Aug. 1941; *s* of William Rufus Higginbotham and Eunice Taylor Higginbotham; *m* 1st, 1972, Jenni W. Caldwell (marr. diss. 1988); two *s*; 2nd, 1988, Nancy L. Roberts; two *s* two *d*. *Educ:* Columbia Univ., NY (BS 1967; PhD 1973). Columbia University, New York: Instructor in Philosophy, 1970–73; Asst Prof., 1973–80; Fellow in Humanities, 1975–77 and 1979–80; Massachusetts Institute of Technology: Vis. Associate Prof. of Philosophy, 1980–82; Associate Prof., 1982–87; Prof. of Philosophy and Linguistics, 1987–93; Prof. of Gen. Linguistics, Univ. of Oxford, 1993–2000; Fellow, Somerville Coll., Oxford, 1993–2000; University of Southern California: Prof. of Philosophy and Linguistics, 2000–04; Prof. of Linguistics, 2004–06; Dir, Sch. of Philosophy, 2000–06. *Publications:* articles in Jl Philosophy, Linguistic Inquiry, Mind and Language, Linguistics and Philosophy; contribs to several collections in linguistics and in philosophy. *Recreations:* chess, music. *Address:* School of Philosophy, University of Southern California, 3709 Trousdale Parkway, Los Angeles, CA 90089–0451, USA. *T:* (213) 8212308; (Jan.–June 2009) Somerville College, Oxford OX2 6HD.

HIGGINS, family name of **Baron Higgins**.

HIGGINS, Baron *cr* 1997 (Life Peer), of Worthing, in the co. of West Sussex; **Terence Langley Higgins,** KBE 1993; PC 1979; DL; *b* 18 Jan. 1928; *s* of late Reginald and Rose Higgins, Dulwich; *m* 1961, Dame Rosalyn Higgins, *qv*; one *s* one *d*. *Educ:* Alleyn's Sch., Dulwich; Gonville and Caius Coll., Cambridge (BA (Hons) 1958; MA 1963; Pres. Cambridge Union Soc., 1958). Brit. Olympic Team (athletics) 1948, 1952. NZ Shipping Co., 1948–55; Lectr in Economic Principles, Dept of Economics, Yale Univ., 1958–59; Economist with Unilever, 1959–64. Dir, 1980–92, Consultant, 1992–2003, Lex Service Group (Chm., Lex Pension Fund Trustees, 1994–2002); Dir, First Choice Holidays (formerly Owners Abroad) plc, 1992–97. MP (C) Worthing, 1964–97. Opposition Spokesman on Treasury and Economic Affairs, 1966–70; Minister of State, Treasury, 1970–72; Financial Sec. to Treasury, 1972–74; Opposition Spokesman: on Treasury and Econ. Affairs, 1974; for Trade, 1974–76; Principal Opposition Spokesman, H of L, on social security, 1997–2001, on work and pensions, 2001–06. Chairman: Select Cttee on Procedure, 1980–83; Select Cttee on Treasury and CS, 1983–97 (Mem., 1980–97); House of Commons Liaison Cttee, 1984–97; Sec., Cons. Parly Finance Cttee, 1965–66; Chm. Cons. Parly Cttee on Sport, 1979–81, on Transport, 1979–91; Member: Public Account Commn, 1984–97 (Chm., 1996–97); Exec. Cttee, 1922 Cttee, 1980–97. Member: H of L Select Cttee on Speakership of H of L, 2005; Jt Cttee on the Conventions of Parlt, 2006 Mem., Claims Resolution Tribunal for Dormant Accounts in Switzerland, 1998–2002 Member: Council, RIIA, 1979–85; Council, IAM, 1979–98. Governor: NIESR, 1989– Dulwich Coll., 1980–95; Alleyn's Sch., 1995–99. Special Fellow, PSI, 1986 (Mem Council, 1989–95); Trustee, Industry and Parlt Trust, 1985–91; Hon. Mem., Keyne College, Univ. of Kent, 1976–. DL W Sussex, 1989. *Address:* House of Lords, SW1A 0AA. *Clubs:* Reform, Yale; Hawks (Cambridge); Royal Blackheath Golf, Koninklijke Haagsche Golf.

HIGGINS, Andrew James, PhD; MRCVS; Chairman, Strata Technology Ltd, since 2002; *b* 7 Dec. 1948; *s* of late Edward James Higgins and of Gabrielle Joy, *d* of late Sir John Kelland; *m* 1981, Nicola, *d* of late Peter Eliot and of Jenifer Eliot; one *s* three *d*. *Educ:* St Michael's Coll., Leeds; Royal Veterinary Coll., Univ. of London (BVetMed 1973; PhD 1985); Centre for Tropical Med., Univ. of Edinburgh (MSc 1977). CBiol 1993; FIBiol 1993. Commnd RAVC 1973. Vet. Officer to Sultan of Oman, 1975–76; Vet. Advr, ME and N Africa, Wellcome Foundn, 1977–82; Scientific Dir and Chief Exec., Animal Health Trust, 1988–99. Cons., FAO 1981–86. Mem., Lord Chancellor's Adv. Sub-cttee for W Suffolk, 1999–. Member: Conservation and Welfare Cttee, 1987–96, Ethics Cttee, 1994– Welfare Cttee, 1998–, Zool Soc. of London; Vet. Res. Club, 1989–; Vet. Panel, BEF 1993– (Chm., 2004–); Govt Adv. Cttee on Quarantine, 1997–98; Trustee: Dogs Trust (formerly Nat. Canine Defence League), 1999–; RCVS Trust, 2001–06; Animals in War Meml Fund, 2001–08; Scientific Advr, Internat. League for the Protection of Horses 2006–. Fédération Equestre Internationale: Hon. Scientific Advr, 1990–; Chm. Medication Adv. Gp, 2005–, Welfare Sub-Cttee, 2005–; Mem., Vet. Cttee, 2006– Editor-in-Chief, The Vet. Jl (formerly British Vet. Jl), 1991– (Dep. Ed., 1990–91) Scientific Fellow, Zool Soc.; MRSocMed 1994. Univ. of London Laurel, 1971; Ciba-Geigy Prize for Res. in Animal Health, 1985; Equine Veterinary Jl Open Award and medal, 1986; Centenary Prize, Central Vet. Soc., 1986; George Fleming Prize, British Vet Jl, 1987; President's Award, Vet. Mktg Assoc., 1997. *Publications:* (contrib.) An Anatomy of Veterinary Europe, 1972; (ed and contrib.) The Camel in Health and Disease, 1986 (ed) The Equine Manual, 1995, 2nd edn 2005; papers in sci. and gen. pubns and communications to learned socs. *Recreations:* ski-ing, riding, opera, camels. *Address:* PO Box 274, Bury St Edmunds, Suffolk IP29 5LW. *Fax:* (01284) 725463. *Club:* Buck's.

HIGGINS, Christopher; *see* Higgins, J. C.

HIGGINS, Prof. Christopher Francis, PhD; FRSE, FMedSci; DL; Vice-Chancellor and Warden, Durham University, since 2007; *b* 24 June 1955; *s* of Prof. Philip John Higgins and Betty Ann Higgins (*née* Edmonds); *m* 1st, 1978, Elizabeth Mary Joy (marr. diss. 1994), two *d*; 2nd, 1994, Suzanne Wilson Higgins (marr. diss. 2001); three *d*. *Educ:* Univ. of Durham (BSc 1st Cl. Hons Botany 1976; PhD 1979). FRSE 1989. NATO-SERC postdoctoral Fellow, Univ. of California, Berkeley, 1979–81; University of Dundee Lectr, 1981–87; Reader and Prof. of Molecular Genetics, 1987–89; Lister Inst. Res. Fellow, 1983–89; Oxford University: Principal Scientist, ICRF, and Dep. Dir, ICRF Labs, Inst. of Molecular Medicine, 1989–93; Fellow, Keble Coll., 1989–93; Nuffield Prof. of Clin. Biochemistry, and Fellow, Hertford Coll., 1993–97; Dir, MRC Clinical Scis Centre, and Prof. and Hd of Div. of Clinical Scis, Imperial Coll. London, 1998–2007. Howard Hughes Internat. Res. Scholar; Fellow, EMBO, 1988. Mem., BBSRC, 1997–2000; Mem., Governing Council, John Innes Centre, 1994–2000; Mem. Exec. Council, AMRC, 2003–07. Chairman: Spongiform Encephalopathy Adv. Cttee, 2004–; Scientific Adv. Bd, Microscience; Mem., Nat. Expert Panel on New and Emerging Infections; Scientific Advr, Select Cttee on Stem Cells, H of L, 2001–02; Mem., Human Genetics Commn, 2005–. Charity Trustee: Future Harvest, 2001–05; 2 Higher Ground 2001–04; Kennedy Inst. for Rheumatology, 2004–07. Founding Editor and Editor-in-Chief, Molecular Microbiology, 1987–2003. Mem. Bd, One NorthEast RDA, 2008–. DL Co. Durham, 2008. Founder FMedSci 1998 (Mem., Council, 2000–03); FRSA. Hugh Bean Prize, RCM, 1970; Fleming Medal, Soc. for Gen. Microbiol., 1987; CIBA Medal and Prize, Biochemical Soc., 1995. *Publications:* numerous research papers in learned jls. *Recreations:* five daughters, classical music and opera, playing the violin. *Address:* University Office, Durham University, Old Elvet, Durham DH1 3HP. *T:* (0191) 334 6214, *Fax:* (0191) 334 6213.

HIGGINS, Clare Frances Elizabeth; actress; *d* of James Stephen Higgins and Paula Cecilia (*née* Murphy). *Educ:* St Philomena's Convent Sch., Derbys; Ecclesbourne Sch., Derbys; LAMDA. *Theatre includes:* A View from the Bridge, Harrogate; The White Devil, Oxford Playhouse; Beethoven's Tenth, Vaudeville; Jenkin's Ear, Royal Court; Ride Down Mount Morgan, Wyndhams; A Letter of Resignation, Comedy, 1997; Heartbreak House, 2000, The Secret Rapture, 2001, Chichester; Royal Exchange, Manchester: Measure for Measure; Rollo; Blood Black and Gold; The Deep Man; Greenwich: Time and the Conways; The Rivals; A Streetcar Named Desire; Royal Shakespeare Company: A Midsummer Night's Dream, 1989; Hamlet, 1989; Antony and Cleopatra, 1992; Royal National Theatre: The Futurists, 1986; The Secret Rapture, 1988; Richard III, 1990; King Lear, 1990; Napoli Milionaria, 1991; The Absence of War, 1993 (televised, 1996); The Children's Hour, 1994 (Critics' Circle Award, 1995); Sweet Bird of Youth, 1995 (Olivier Award, Critics' Circle Award, Time Out Award, 1995); The Walls, 2001; Vincent in Brixton, 2002 (Olivier Award, Evening Standard Award, Critics' Circle Award, 2003); Major Barbara, 2008; A Slight Ache, 2008; The Seagull, Present Laughter, W Yorks Playhouse, 1998; Who's Afraid of Virginia Woolf, Bristol Old Vic, 2002; Hecuba, 2004 (Olivier Award, 2005), Phaedra, 2006, Donmar Warehouse; Death of a Salesman, The Night of the Iguana, Lyric, 2005. *Television includes:* Pride and Prejudice; Unity; Byron; The Concubine; Mitch; The Citadel; Cover Her Face; Foreign Body; Beautiful Lies; After the War; Downtown Lagos; Circle of Deceit; Man of the Month. *Films include:* 1919; Hellraiser; Hellbound; The Fruit Machine; Bad Behaviour, 1993; Let it Come Down, 1995; Easter House, 1995; Small Faces, 1996; House of Mirth, 1999; The Libertine, 2004; The Golden Compass, 2007. *Address:* c/o Conway van Gelder Grant Ltd, 18–21 Jermyn Street, SW1Y 6HP.

HIGGINS, Daniel John P.; *see* Pearce-Higgins.

HIGGINS, David Edward Alexander; His Honour Judge Higgins; a Circuit Judge, since 2003; *b* 15 Dec. 1945; *s* of Edward and Rena Higgins; *m* 1971, Roberta Jane Reading; two *d*. *Educ:* St Peter's Sch., York; Newcastle Univ. (LLB). Partner, Herbert Smith (Solicitors), 1976–2003; a Recorder of the Crown Court, 2000–03. *Recreations:* opera, equine sports, Italy. *Address:* c/o Circuit Secretariat, Rose Court, 2 Southwark Bridge, SE1 9HS.

HIGGINS, Jack; *see* Patterson, Harry.

HIGGINS, Prof. James, PhD; FBA 1999; Professor of Latin American Literature, University of Liverpool, 1988–2004, now Emeritus; *b* 28 May 1939; *s* of Peter and Annie Higgins; *m* 1962, Kirstine Anne Atwell; two *s*. *Educ:* Our Lady's High Sch., Motherwell; Univ. of Glasgow (MA); Univ. of Lyons (LèsL); PhD Liverpool 1968. Department of Hispanic Studies, Liverpool University: Asst Lectr, 1964–67; Lectr, 1967–73; Sen. Lectr, 1973–83; Reader, 1983–88; Head of Dept, 1988–97. Visiting Professor: Univ. of Pittsburgh, 1968; Univ. of Waterloo, Ont, 1974; Univ. of West Indies, Trinidad, 1979; Univ. of Wisconsin-Madison, 1990; Hon. Professor: Univ. of San Marcos, Lima, 1984; Univ. of Stirling, 2006. Corresp. Fellow, Peruvian Acad., 2002. Comdr, Order of Merit (Peru), 1988. *Publications:* Visión del hombre y de la vida en las últimas obras poéticas de César Vallejo, 1970; César Vallejo: an anthology of his poetry, 1970; The Poet in Peru, 1982; A History of Peruvian Literature, 1987; César Vallejo: a selection of his poetry (with trans), 1987; César Vallejo en su poesía, 1990; Cambio social y constantes humanas: la narrative corta de J. R. Ribeyro, 1991; Hitos de la poesía peruana, 1993; Myths of the Emergent: social mobility in contemporary Peruvian fiction, 1994; The Literary Representation of Peru, 2002; Lima: a cultural and literary history, 2005; Historia de la literatura peruana, 2006; numerous articles. *Recreations:* reading, gardening, walking, football, whisky. *Address:* Flat 6, Carlton House, 15 Snowdon Place, Stirling FK8 2NR. *T:* (01786) 470641.

HIGGINS, Prof. Dame Joan (Margaret), DBE 2007; PhD; Professor of Health Policy, 1992–2004, now Emerita, and Director, Manchester Centre for Healthcare Management, 1998–2004, University of Manchester; Chairman, NHS Litigation Authority, since 2007; *b* 15 June 1948; *d* of Kenneth and Kate Higgins; *m* 1983, John P. Martin (*d* 1997); three step *s*. *Educ:* Rutherford Coll. of Advanced Technol. (BA Hons (Sociol.), London Univ. (ext.), 1969); Univ. of York (Dip. Soc. Admin 1971); Univ. of Southampton (PhD 1979). Res. Asst, then Lectr, Portsmouth Poly., 1971–74; University of Southampton: Lectr, 1974–86, Sen. Lectr, 1986–89, in Social Policy; Prof. of Social Policy, 1989–92. Chm., Christie Hosp. NHS Trust, Manchester, 2002–07. Chairman: Manchester FHSA, 1992–96; Manchester HA, 1996–99; Patient Information Adv. Gp, 2001–; Regl Chm., NHS Exec. NW, 1999–2001; Interim Chm., Nat. Treatment Agency for Substance Misuse, 2001; non-executive Director: Southampton and SW Hampshire HA, 1981–90; Wessex Regl HA, 1990–92. Member: Care Record Develt Bd, 2004– (Chm., Ethics Adv. Gp, 2004–); Queen's Counsel Selection Panel, 2005–. Pres., European Health Mgt Assoc., 2001–03. *Publications:* The Poverty Business: Britain and America, 1978; States of Welfare: comparative analysis in social policy, 1981; (jtly) Government and Urban Poverty, 1983; The Business of Medicine: private health care in Britain, 1988. *Recreations:* travel, gardening, walking, classical music, reading, cooking, wine, theatre, sailing. *Address:* 28 Woodbridge Street, EC1R 0HP.

HIGGINS, John Andrew; Assistant Auditor General, National Audit Office, 1989–99; *b* 19 Feb. 1940; *s* of George Henry and Mildred Maud Higgins; *m* 1965, Susan Jennifer Mathis; one *s*. *Educ:* Hendon County Sch.; Hastings Grammar Sch. ARCO. Exchequer and Audit Department: Asst Auditor, 1958; Auditor, 1968; Sen. Auditor, 1971; Chief Auditor, 1977; Dep. Dir, 1981; Office of Auditor Gen. of Canada, 1983–84; Dir, Nat. Audit Office, 1984. Treas., Crawley and Horsham Dist Organists' Assoc., 1994–2006; Trustee and Treas., Crawley Open House, 1999–. *Recreations:* classical organ playing, golf, bridge, gardening, supporting Crystal Palace. *Address:* Zaria, 65 Milton Mount Avenue, Pound Hill, Crawley, Sussex RH10 3DP. *T:* (01293) 417075. *Clubs:* Ifield Golf and Country; Crawley Bridge.

HIGGINS, Prof. (John) Christopher; Director of Management Centre, University of Bradford, and Professor of Management Sciences, 1972–89, Emeritus Professor, since 1992; *b* 9 July 1932; *s* of Sidney James Higgins and Margaret Eileen Higgins (*née* Dealtrey); *m* 1960, Margaret Edna Howells; three *s*. *Educ:* Gonville and Caius Coll., Cambridge (MA); Univ. of London (BSc, MSc); PhD Bradford. Short service commission, RAF, 1953–56; 1956–70: Electronics Industry; Dept of Chief Scientist (RAF) in MoD; management consultancy; Director of Economic Planning and Research for IPC Newspapers Ltd. Member: Final Selection Bd for Civil Service Commn, 1976–91; Defence Scientific Adv. Council's Assessments Bd, 1976–83 (Chm. of its Cttee on Operational Analysis, 1980–83); UGC Sub-Cttee on Management and Business Studies, 1979–85; Yorks, Humberside and Midlands Industrial Develt Bd, 1988–91; Chm., Social Sciences Res. Council's Accountancy Steering Cttee and Member of its Management and Industrial Relns Cttee, 1976–80. Vis. Fellow, Wolfson Coll., Cambridge, 1985; Vis. Prof., Open Business School, Open Univ., 1991–97. *Publications:* Information Systems for Planning and Control: concepts and cases, 1976, new edn as Computer-Based Planning Systems, 1985; Strategic and Operational Planning Systems: Principles and Practice, 1980; numerous papers and articles on corporate planning, information systems and management educn. *Recreations:* violin/viola (ex National Youth Orchestra of Great Britain), cricket, fell-walking.

HIGGINS, John Stuart, CBE 2005; Director General, Intellect, since 2002; *b* 26 June 1954; *s* of Robert Brian Higgins and Josephine Mary Higgins; *m* 1977, Ailsa Elizabeth Ann Gibson; three *d*. *Educ:* Cardinal Langley Sch., Middleton; Univ. of East Anglia (BSc Hons Maths and Phys); CDipAF. Systems Analyst, then Project Manager, London Brick Co., 1976–81; Business Manager, Triad Computing Systems, 1982–85; Director: Wilkins Computer Systems, 1986–90; Softwright Systems, then SSA, 1991–96; CEO, Res Rocket Surfer, CA, 1997–98; Dir Gen., Computing Services and Software Assoc., 1998–2002. Chairman: IAP GRID Computing Task Force, 2004; IP Forum Business Opportunities Gp, 2005. Vice-Pres., Europ. Information, Communications and Consumer Electronics Technology Industry Assoc., 2006–08. Lay Mem. Council, Univ. of Warwick, 2003–08. FRSA. *Recreations:* tennis, the outdoors, music, theatre. *Address:* Intellect, Russell Square House, 10–12 Russell Square, WC1B 5EE. *T:* (020) 7331 2000, *Fax:* (020) 7331 2040; *e-mail:* john.higgins@intellectuk.org.

HIGGINS, Dame Julia (Stretton), DBE 2001 (CBE 1996); DPhil; FRS 1995; FREng; Professor of Polymer Science, Imperial College London, since 1989; *b* 1 July 1942; *d* of late George Stretton Downes, CBE and Sheilah D. M. Downes (*née* Gavigan). *Educ:* Somerville Coll., Oxford (MA, DPhil 1968; Hon. Fellow, 1996). CChem 1991, FRSC 1991; CEng 1994, FREng 1999; FIM 1994; FCGI 1994; FInstP 1996; FIChemE 1997. Physics teacher, Mexborough Grammar Sch., 1966–68; Dept of Chemistry, Univ. of Manchester, 1968–72; Res. Fellow, Centre de Recherche sur les Macromolecules, Strasbourg, 1972–73; physicist, Inst Laue-Langevin, Grenoble, 1973–76; Imperial College, London: Dept of Chem. Engrg, 1976–; Dean, City and Guilds Coll., 1993–97; Dir, Graduate Sch. of Engrg and Physical Scis, 2002–06; Principal, Faculty of Engrg, 2006–07. Vis. Academic, Institut für Makromolekulare Chemie, Freiburg, 1988. Trustee, Nat. Gall., 2001–. Chm., EPSRC, 2003–07 (Mem., 1994–2000); Science and Engineering Research Council: Member: Neutron Beam Res. Cttee, 1979–83 and 1988–91; Polymers and Composites Cttee, 1989–94 (Chm., 1991–94); Materials Commn, 1991–94; Facilities Commn, 1993–94; Member: CCLRC, 1995–2000; Sci. and Engrg Cttee, British Council, 1993–98; Council for Sci. and Technol., 1998–2004. Foreign Sec. and Vice Pres., Royal Soc., 2001–06; President: IChemE, 2002–03; BAAS, 2003–04. Foreign Associate, Nat. Acad. Engrg, USA, 1999. Hon. DSc: Nottingham, 1999; QUB, Leicester, 2002; Oxon, Sheffield, 2003; Kent, Exeter, Leeds, Sheffield Hallam, 2004; Bath, 2005; Keele, 2006; Birmingham, 2007; Hon. DEng Heriot-Watt, 2000. *Publications:* (with H. Benoît) Polymers and Neutron Scattering, 1994; contrib. articles on polymer science to learned jls. *Address:* Department of Chemical Engineering, Imperial College of Science, Technology and Medicine, Prince Consort Road, SW7 2BY. *T:* (020) 7594 5565.

See also G. P. S. Downes.

HIGGINS, Rt Hon. Sir Malachy (Joseph), Kt 1993; PC 2007; **Rt Hon. Lord Justice Higgins;** a Lord Justice of Appeal, Supreme Court of Judicature, Northern Ireland, since 2007; *b* 30 Oct. 1944; *er s* of late James and May Higgins; *m* 1980, Dorothy Ann, *d* of Dr Leslie Grech, Malta; three *d*. *Educ:* St MacNissi's Coll., Garron Tower; Queen's Univ., Belfast (LLB); Middle Temple (BL). Called to NI Bar, 1969 (Bencher, 1993), to Irish Bar, 1978; QC (NI), 1985; County Court Judge, 1988–93; Recorder of Londonderry, 1990–93; County Court Judge for Co. Armagh, 1993; Judge of the High Court of Justice, NI, 1993–2007 (Family Div., 1996–2001); Sen. Judge, QBD, 2004–07. Judge in Residence, 1999–2001, Chm. Bd of Visitors, 2005–, QUB. Chm., Children Order Adv. Cttee, 1996–2001. *Recreations:* gardening, golf, sailing, walking. *Address:* Royal Courts of Justice, Belfast BT1 3JF; Ashdene, Comber, Co. Down. *Clubs:* Royal Ulster Yacht, Royal Belfast Golf.

HIGGINS, Very Rev. Michael John, OBE 2003; Dean of Ely, 1991–2003, now Emeritus; *b* 31 Dec. 1935; *s* of Claud John and Elsie Higgins; *m* 1976, Bevyl Margaret Stringer; one *d*. *Educ:* Whitchurch Grammar Sch., Cardiff; Univ. of Birmingham (LLB 1957); Gonville and Caius Coll., Cambridge (LLB 1959, PhD 1962); Harvard Univ.; Ridley Hall, Cambridge. Lectr in English Law, Univ. of Birmingham, 1961–63. Ordained, 1965; Curate, Ormskirk Parish Church, dio. of Liverpool, 1965–68; Selection Sec., ACCM, 1968–74; Vicar, Frome and Priest-in-charge of Woodlands, dio. of Bath and Wells, 1974–80; Rector of Preston, and Leader of Preston Town Centre Team Ministry, dio. of Blackburn, 1980–91. *Publication:* The Vicar's House, 1988. *Recreations:* music, walking, travel. *Address:* Twin Cottage, Great Dunham, Norfolk PE32 2LR.

HIGGINS, Michael Selwyn L.; *see* Longuet-Higgins.

HIGGINS, Prof. Peter Matthew, OBE 1987; Bernard Sunley Professor and Chairman of Department of General Practice, United Medical Schools of Guy's and St Thomas' Hospitals (formerly Guy's Hospital Medical School), University of London, 1974–88, now Emeritus Professor; *b* 18 June 1923; *s* of Peter Joseph Higgins and Margaret Higgins; *m* 1952, Jean Margaret Lindsay Currie; three *s* one *d*. *Educ:* St Ignatius' Coll., London; UCH, London. MB, BS; FRCP, FRCGP. House Phys., Medical Unit, UCH, 1947; RAMC, 1948–49; House Phys., UCH, St Pancras, 1950; Resident MO, UCH, 1951–52; Asst Med. Registrar, UCH, 1953; Gen. Practice, Rugeley, Staffs, 1954–66, and Castle Vale, Birmingham, 1966–68; Sen. Lectr, Guy's Hosp. Med. Sch., 1968–74. Regl Advr in General Practice, SE Thames, 1970–88; Vice-Chm., SE Thames RHA, 1976–92; Chm., Kent FHSA, 1990–92. Mem., Attendance Allowance Bd, 1971–74; Chairman: Inquiry into A&E Dept, KCH, 1992; Review of Arrangements for Emergency Admissions, Ealing Hosp., 1994. Mem., National Council, 1985–95, Nat. Exec. Cttee, 1991–95, Family Service Units. Vice Chm. Governors, Linacre Centre for the Study of Medical Ethics, 1983–86; Mem. Court, Kent Univ., 1984–98. Hon. DSc Greenwich, 1998. *Publications:* articles in Lancet, BMJ, Jl RCGP, Epidemiology and Infection, British Jl of Psychiatry. *Address:* Wallings, Heathfield Lane, Chislehurst, Kent BR7 6AH. *T:* (020) 8467 2756.

HIGGINS, Phillip John; Corporate Director (formerly Corporate Manager), Cardiff County Council, 1999–2006; *b* 9 May 1946; *s* of Eugene Oswald Higgins and Dorothy Mary Higgins; *m* 1969, Anne Elizabeth Watkin; one *s* two *d*. *Educ:* Stand Grammar Sch., Manchester; Coll. of Commerce, Manchester. CIPFA (IMTA 1972). Accountant, Halifax CBC, 1972–74; Sen. Accountant, West Yorks CC, 1974–76; Gp Accountant, 1976–80, Principal Asst, loans and investments, 1980–82, Principal Asst, technical, 1982–85, Gtr Manchester Council; Asst Co. Treas., S Glamorgan CC, 1985–88; Dir of Finance, Cardiff Bay Develt Corp., 1988–99. Treas., S Wales Magistrates' Courts Cttee, 1999–2006. FCMI (FIMgt 1996). *Recreations:* reading political history, the countryside. *Address:* Wisteria Cottage, Llantrithyd, Cowbridge, Vale of Glamorgan CF71 7UB. *T:* (01446) 781676.

HIGGINS, Dame Rosalyn, DBE 1995; JSD; FBA 1995; QC 1986; a Judge, since 1995, and President, since 2006, International Court of Justice; *b* 2 June 1937; *d* of Lewis Cohen and Fay Inberg; *m* 1961, Terence Langley Higgins (*see* Baron Higgins); one *s* one *d*. *Educ:* Burlington Grammar Sch., London; Girton Coll., Cambridge (Scholar; BA 1958, 1st Cl. Law Qualifying 1, 1st Cl. Tripos Pt II; 1st Cl. LLB 1959); Yale Law Sch., (JSD 1962). UK Intern, Office of Legal Affairs, UN, 1958; Commonwealth Fund Fellow, 1959; Vis. Fellow, Brookings Instn, Washington, DC, 1960; Jun. Fellow in Internat. Studies, LSE, 1961–63; Staff Specialist in Internat. Law, RIIA, 1963–74; Vis. Fellow, LSE, 1974–78; Professor of International Law: Univ. of Kent at Canterbury, 1978–81; LSE, London Univ., 1981–95. Gen. course, Hague Acad. of Internat. Law, 1991. Visiting Professor of International Law: Stanford Univ., 1975; Yale Univ., 1977. Bencher, Inner Temple, 1989. Mem., UN Cttee on Human Rights, 1984–95. Hague Lectures on Internat. Law, 1982. Vice Pres., Amer. Soc. of Internat. Law, 1972–74 (Certif. of Merit, 1971, 1995). Membre de l'Institut de Droit International, 1993 (Associé, 1987). Hon. doctorates include: Dr *hc* Univ. of Paris XI, 1980; Hon. LLD: LSE, 1995; Cambridge, 1996; Hon. DCL Oxford, 2002. Manley Hudson Medal, 1998; Balzan Prize, Internat. Balzan Foundn, 2007. Membre de l'Ordre des Palmes Académiques (France), 1988. *Publications:* The Development of International Law through the Political Organs of the United Nations, 1963; Conflict of Interests: international law in a divided world, 1965; The Administration of the United Kingdom Foreign Policy through the United Nations, 1966; (ed with James Fawcett) Law in Movement—essays in memory of John McMahon, 1974; UN Peacekeeping: documents and commentary: Vol. I, Middle East, 1969; Vol. II, Asia, 1971; Vol. III, Africa, 1980; Vol. IV, Europe, 1981; Problems and Process, 1994; articles for law jls and jls of internat. relations. *Recreations:* golf, cooking, eating. *Address:* International Court of Justice, Carnegieplein 2, 2517 KJ The Hague, Netherlands. *T:* (70) 3022323.

HIGGINSON, Sir Gordon (Robert), Kt 1992; DL; PhD; FREng; Vice-Chancellor, 1985–94, Emeritus Professor of Engineering, 1994, University of Southampton; *b* 8 Nov. 1929; *s* of Frederick John and Letitia Higginson; *m* 1954, Marjorie Forbes Rannie (*d* 1996); three *s* two *d*. *Educ:* Leeds Univ. (BSc, PhD). FICE; FIMechE; FREng (FEng 1991). Scientific Officer, then Sen. Scientific Officer, Min. of Supply, 1953–56; Lectr, Leeds Univ., 1956–62; Associate Prof., RMCS, Shrivenham, 1962–65; Durham University: Prof. of Engrg, 1965–85; Dean of Faculty of Science, 1972–75. Non-executive Director: Rolls-Royce, 1988–99; Pirelli General, 1995–2002; Pirelli UK Tyres, 1997–2002. DL Hants, 1994. Hon. FRCP 1992. Hon. DSc: Durham, 1991; Southampton, 1995; Bournemouth, 1997; Loughborough, 2002; Hon. DSc (Eng) London, 1997; Hon. DEng Portsmouth, 1993; Hon. LLD Leeds, 1994. IMechE James Clayton Fund Prize, 1963 and 1979; Gold Medal, Brit. Soc. of Rheology, 1969. *Publications:* Elastohydrodynamic Lubrication (with D. Dowson), 1966, 2nd edn 1977;

Foundations of Engineering Mechanics, 1974; papers on mechanics in various jls. *Address:* 61 Albany Park Court, Westwood Road, Southampton SO17 1LA.

HIGGINSON, Lucy Amanda; Editor, Horse & Hound, since 2002 (Deputy Editor, 2002); *b* 13 March 1970; *d* of Keith Higginson and Judith Britain; *m* 1999, Dr Alexis Warnes; one *d*. *Educ:* Manchester High Sch. for Girls; Univ. of Durham (BA Hons). Deputy Editor, The Field, 1996–2002. *Recreations:* riding across country, spaniel walking, fraternising with rowers (sometimes even in a boat). *Address: e-mail:* Lucy_higginson@ipcmedia.com. *Club:* Farmers'.

HIGGS, Air Vice-Marshal Barry, CBE 1981; Assistant Chief of Defence Staff (Overseas), 1985–87; *b* 22 Aug. 1934; *s* of late Percy Harold Higgs and of Ethel Eliza Higgs; *m* 1957, Sylvia May Wilks; two *s*. *Educ:* Finchley County Secondary Grammar Sch. Served with Nos 207, 115, 138, 49 and 51 Sqdns, 1955–70; sc 1968; Forward Policy (RAF), 1971–73; ndc 1974; Comd No 39 (PR) Sqdn, 1975–77; Asst Dir Defence Policy, 1978–79; Comd RAF Finningley, 1979–81; RCDS 1982; Dep. Dir of Intelligence, 1983–85. Dir Gen., Fertiliser Manufacturers Assoc., 1987–98. ARAgS 1998. Francis New Meml Medal, Internat. Fertiliser Soc., 1999. *Recreations:* cruising, bridge, gardening, the outdoors, theatre. *Address:* 33 Parsonage Street, Cambridge CB5 8DN. *T:* (01223) 473282. *Club:* Royal Air Force.

HIGGS, Brian James; QC 1974; a Recorder of the Crown Court, 1974–98; Barrister-at-Law; *b* 24 Feb. 1930; *s* of James Percival Higgs and Kathleen Anne Higgs; *m* 1st, 1953, Jean Cameron DuMerton; two *s* three *d*; 2nd, 1980, Vivienne Mary Johnson; one *s*. *Educ:* Wrekin Coll.; London Univ. Served RA, 1948–50 (2nd Lieut). Called to Bar, Gray's Inn, 1955, Bencher, 1986; Mem., Hon. Soc. of Inner Temple (*ad eundem*), 1987. Contested (C) Romford, 1966. *Recreations:* gardening, golf, wine, chess, bridge. *Address:* 5 King's Bench Walk, Temple, EC4Y 7DN. *T:* (020) 7353 5638.

HIGGS, Prof. Douglas Roland, DSc; FRCP, FRCPath; FRS 2005; Professor of Haematology, since 1996 and Director, MRC Molecular Haematology Unit, since 2001, University of Oxford; *b* 13 Jan. 1951. *Educ:* Alleyn's Sch.; King's Coll. London; King's Coll. Hosp. Med. Sch. (MB BS 1974); DSc London 1990. FRCP 1993; FRCPath 1994. SHO, 1975, Registrar in Haematol., 1976, King's Coll. Hosp., London; University of Oxford: MRC Trng Fellow, Nuffield Dept of Clinical Medicine, 1977–80; Scientific Officer (Clinical), MRC Molecular Haematol. Unit, 1980–2001; Hon. Consultant in Haematol., John Radcliffe Hosp., Oxford, 1985–. FMedSci 2001. *Address:* MRC Molecular Haematology Unit, Weatherall Institute of Molecular Medicine, John Radcliffe Hospital, Headington, Oxford OX3 9DS.

HIGGS, Elizabeth Ann; *see* Williamson, E. A.

HIGGS, Prof. Peter Ware, PhD; FRS 1983; FRSE; Professor of Theoretical Physics, University of Edinburgh, 1980–96, now Emeritus; *b* 29 May 1929; *s* of Thomas Ware Higgs and Gertrude Maud (*née* Coghill); *m* 1963, Jo Ann, *d* of Jo C. and Meryl Williamson, Urbana, Ill; two *s*. *Educ:* Cotham Grammar Sch., Bristol; King's Coll., Univ. of London (BSc, MSc; PhD 1954). FRSE 1974. Royal Commn for Exhibn of 1851 Sen. Student, KCL, 1953–54 and Univ. of Edinburgh, 1954–55; Sen. Res. Fellow, Univ. of Edinburgh, 1955–56; ICI Res. Fellow, UCL, 1956–57 and Imperial Coll., 1957–58; Lectr in Maths, UCL, 1958–60; Lectr in Mathematical Physics, 1960–70, and Reader in Math. Physics, 1970–80, Univ. of Edinburgh. FKC 1998. Hon. Fellow, Swansea Univ., 2008. Hon. FInstP 1998. Hon. DSc: Bristol, 1997; Edinburgh, 1998; Glasgow, 2002. Hughes Medal, Royal Soc., 1981; Rutherford Medal, 1984, Paul Dirac Medal, 1997, Inst. of Physics; James Scott Prize, 1993, Royal Medal, 2000, RSE; High Energy Particle Physics Prize, Eur. Physical Soc., 1997; Wolf Prize in Physics, 2004. *Publications:* papers on molecular vibrations and spectra, classical and quantum field theories, and on spontaneous breaking of gauge symmetries in theories of elementary particles. *Recreations:* walking, swimming, listening to music. *Address:* 2 Darnaway Street, Edinburgh EH3 6BG. *T:* (0131) 225 7060.

HIGHAM, Catherine Mary; *see* Ennis, C. M.

HIGHAM, Prof. Charles Franklin Wandesforde, PhD, ScD; FRSNZ; FRAS; FSA; FBA; Research Professor, University of Otago, New Zealand, since 2005 (Professor of Anthropology, 1968–2003; James Cook Fellow, 2003–05); *b* 19 Oct. 1939; *s* of Ernest Harry Hamilton Higham and Eileen Florence Emily Higham (*née* Woodhead); *m* 1964, Pauline Askew; two *s* two *d*. *Educ:* Raynes Park Co. Grammar Sch.; St Catharine's Coll., Cambridge (Rugby blue, 1961–62; BA, MA; PhD 1966; ScD 1991; Hon. Fellow, 2008). FSA 1984; FRAS 1986. Lectr in Prehist., Univ. of Otago, 1967–68. Vis. Prof., Univ. of London, 1978; Benians Fellow, St John's Coll., Cambridge, 1991–92; Vis. Scholar, St Catharine's Coll., Cambridge, 2003–. Mortimer Wheeler Lectr, 1983, Reckitt Lectr, 2002, British Acad. FRSNZ 1992; Corresp. FBA 2000. Mem. editl bds various learned jls. *Publications:* The Archaeology of Mainland Southeast Asia, 1989; (with R. Bannanurag) The Excavation of Khok Phanom Di: Vol. I, The Excavation, Chronology and Human Burials, 1990; (ed with R. Bannanurag) The Excavation of Khok Phanom Di: Vol. II, The Biological Remains Part I, 1991; The Bronze Age of Southeast Asia, 1996; The Civilisation of Angkor, 2001; Early Cultures of Mainland Southeast Asia, 2002; The Encyclopaedia of Ancient Asian Civilizations, 2004; (with R. Thosarat) The Excavation of Khok Phanom Di: Vol. VII, Summary and Conclusions, 2004; (ed) The Origins of the Civilization of Angkor: Vol. II, The Excavation of Noen U-Loke and Non Muong Kao, 2007; edited with R. Thosarat: Khok Phanom Di: Vol. III: The Material Culture Part I, 1993; Khok Phanom Di: prehistoric adaptation to the world's richest habitat, 1994; The Excavation of Khok Phanom Di: Vol. IV, The Biological Remains, Part II, 1996; The Excavation of Nong Nor, a Prehistoric Site in Central Thailand, 1998; Prehistoric Thailand: from first settlement to Sukhothai, 1998; The Excavation of Khok Phanom Di: Vol. V, The People, 1999; The Excavation of Khok Phanom Di: Vol. VI, The Pottery, 2004; The Origins of the Civilization of Angkor: Vol. I, The Excavation of Ban Lum Khao, 2005. *Recreation:* classical guitar. *Address:* Department of Anthropology, PO Box 56, Dunedin, New Zealand. *T:* (3) 4798750; 1 Newbury Street, Company Bay, Dunedin, New Zealand. *T:* (3) 4761056. *Club:* Hawks (Cambridge).

HIGHAM, Geoffrey Arthur; Chairman, Rugby Group PLC, 1986–96 (Director, 1979–96); Director and Trustee, Building Centre Group, 1982–2001 (Chairman, 1984–88); *b* 17 April 1927; *s* of Arthur Higham and Elsie Higham (*née* Vickerman); *m* 1st, 1951, Audrey Hill (*d* 2006); one *s* and *d*; 2nd, 2007, Jenny Voice (*née* Cummins). *Educ:* King William Coll., IOM; St Catharine's Coll., Cambridge (MA MechScis). Served RE, 1945–48. Metal Box Co., 1950–64; Montague Burton, 1964–65; Cape Industries, 1965–85: Man. Dir, 1971–80; Chm., 1980–85; Industrial Dir, Charter Consolidated, 1980–87; Director: Pirelli Gen., 1987–2006; Pirelli UK, 1997–2006; Travers Morgan, 1988–91; Try Gp, 1989–99; Vale Housing Assoc., 1998–; Sovereign Housing Assoc., 2007–. Chm., BIM Foundn, 1981–83; Vice Chm., Council, BIM, 1984–88; Mem. Council, CBI, 1994–96; Mem. Council, 1978–88, Chm., 1980–82, UK S Africa Trade Assoc. Trustee, Mansfield Coll., Oxford, 1988–95. CCMI (CBIM 1975); FRSA 1989. *Recreations:* music, cricket, gardening. *Address:* 32 East St Helen Street, Abingdo Oxfordshire OX14 5EB. *Clubs:* Army and Navy, Middlesex CC.

See also N. G. Higham.

HIGHAM, John Arthur; QC 1992; Partner, White & Case, since 2004; a Recorder, sin 2000; *b* 11 Aug. 1952; *s* of late Frank Greenhouse Higham and of Muriel (*née* King); 1st, 1982, Francesca Mary Antonietta Ronan (decd); one *s* two *d*; 2nd, 1988, Catherir Mary Ennis, *qv*; two *s* one *d*. *Educ:* Shrewsbury Sch.; Churchill Coll., Cambridge (schola MA, LLM). Called to the Bar, Lincoln's Inn, 1976; an Asst Recorder, Midland and Oxfo Circuit, 1998–2000; admitted solicitor and authorised as solicitor advocate, 199 Consultant, 1999–2000, Partner, 2000–04, Stephenson Harwood, solicitors. *Publication* (ed jtly) Loose on Liquidators, 2nd edn 1981; (ed jtly) The Law and Practice of Corpora Administration, 1994, 2nd edn as Corporate Administrations and Rescue Procedure 2005. *Recreations:* opera, cricket, gardening. *Address:* White & Case, 5 Old Broad Stree EC2N 1DW. *T:* (020) 7532 1000, *Fax:* (020) 7532 1001; *e-mail:* jhigham(whitecase.com.

HIGHAM, Comdr Michael Bernard Shepley, CVO 1999; RN; Grand Secretar United Grand Lodge of England, 1980–98; Secretary, Grand Charity, 1981–98; *b* 7 Jur 1936; *s* of late Anthony Richard Charles Higham, TD, FRCS and Mary Higham (*n* Shepley); *m* 1st, 1970, Caroline Verena Wells (marr. diss. 1996); one *s* one *d*; 2nd, 199 Andrea Svedberg, *d* of late Elias Svedberg and Astrid Svedberg. *Educ:* Epsom Coll. Joine RN, 1954; served: HM Ships Triumph (twice), Eagle, Cavendish and Chichester; offices of: C-in-C Portsmouth and C-in-C Plymouth; Flag Officers Plymouth, Scotlar and NI; Adm. Comdg Reserves; on staff of C-in-C Fleet; retd RN, 1977. Called to th Bar, Middle Temple, 1968. Grand Secretary's Office, 1977–98, Dep. Grand Sec 1978–80; Past Jun. Grand Warden, 1986–2005; Past Sen. Grand Warden, 2006. Mem RNSA. *Publication:* Freemasonry from Craft to tolerance, 1985. *Recreation:* sailing. *Addres* Oyster Shell, Restronguet Passage, Mylor, Falmouth, Cornwall TR11 5ST. *Club:* Roy Cornwall Yacht (Falmouth).

HIGHAM, Nicholas Geoffrey; correspondent, BBC News, since 1988; *b* 1 June 1954; of Geoffrey Arthur Higham, *qv*; *m* 1981, Deborah Starling; one *s* one *d*. *Educ:* Bradfiel Coll., Berks; St Catharine's Coll., Cambridge (BA Hons English 1975). Freelanc journalist, 1978–88; BBC: Media Correspondent, 1988–91; Arts and Med Correspondent, 1991–2003; analyst and roving reporter, BBC News 24, 2003- Columnist, Marketing Week, 1990–2006. *Recreations:* theatre, armchair history. *Addres* c/o BBC News, BBC Television Centre, Wood Lane, W12 7RJ. *T:* (020) 8743 800 *e-mail:* nick.higham@bbc.co.uk.

HIGHAM, Prof. Nicholas John, PhD; FRS 2007; Richardson Professor of Applie Mathematics, University of Manchester, since 1998; *b* Salford, 25 Dec. 1961; *s* of Kennet Frederick Higham and Doris Higham (*née* Wilson); *m* 1998, Françoise Marie Louis Tisseur; two *s*. *Educ:* Univ. of Manchester (BSc Hons Maths 1982; MSc Numeric Analysis and Computing 1983; PhD Numerical Analysis 1985). University of Mancheste Lectr, 1985–89; Sen. Lectr, 1989–92; Reader, 1992–96; Prof. of Applied Maths, 1996–9 Vis. Asst Prof. of Computer Sci., Cornell Univ., 1988–89; Nuffield Foundn Sci. Re Fellow, 1991–92; Royal Soc. Leverhulme Trust Sen. Res. Fellow, 1999–2000; Royal So Wolfson Res. Fellow, Royal Soc., 2003–08. Alston S. Householder Award VI, 198 Leslie Fox Prize, IMA, 1988; Jun. Whitehead Prize, LMS, 1999. *Publications:* Handboo of Writing for the Mathematical Sciences, 1993, 2nd edn 1998; Accuracy and Stability Numerical Algorithms, 1996, 2nd edn 2002; (with D. J. Higham) MATLAB Guide, 200 2nd edn 2005; Functions of Matrices: theory and computation, 2008; contrib. numerou scientific papers. *Recreations:* photography, playing keyboards. *Address:* School Mathematics, University of Manchester, Manchester M13 9PL. *T:* (0161) 275 5822, *Fa* (0161) 275 5819.

HIGHAM, Norman, OBE 1984; Librarian, University of Bristol, 1966–89; *b* 14 Jun 1924; *s* of John Henry Higham, MM, and Edith Fanny (*née* Hubbard); *m* 1954, Jea Elizabeth (MBE 2006), *d* of Frederick William and Isabel Traylen; one *s* one *d*. *Educ:* Firt Park Grammar Sch., Sheffield; Univ. of Sheffield (BA 1st Cl. Hons English, Philos Spanish); MA Leeds 1961. Served RNVR, 1942–46 (Lieut Coastal Forces). Assistar Librarian: Univ. of Sheffield, 1953–57; Univ. of Leeds, 1957–62; Librarian Loughborough Coll. of Advanced Technology, 1962–63; Dep. Librarian, Univ. of Leeds 1963–66. Mem. Council, Standing Conf. on Nat. and Univ. Libraries, 1972–75 an 1979–86 (Chm., 1976–79); Pres., LA, 1983 (Mem. Council, 1975–86, Chm., 1978–8 and 1985–87); Member: UGC Steering Gp on Liby Res., 1977–83; Brit. Liby Bc 1986–89 (Adv. Council, 1976–79, and 1990–94); Liby and Inf. Services Counc (England), 1977–83; Sci. Inf. Cttee, Royal Soc., 1982–91; Standing Cttee on Librarie CVCP, 1982–89; Nat. Cttee on Regl Liby Co-operation, 1985–89; Council, Liby an Inf. Co-operation Council, 1989–94 (Chm., 1989–92). Mem. Council and Trustee Oxfam, 1973–79 and 1980–86. Hon. DLitt Bristol, 1989. *Publications:* A Very Scientifi Gentleman: the major achievements of Henry Clifton Sorby, 1963; Computer Needs fc University Library Operations, 1973; The Library in the University: observations on service, 1980; articles and reviews in librarianship and history of science. *Recreation* literature and the arts, music. *Address:* 30 York Gardens, Clifton, Bristol BS8 4LN. *T* (0117) 973 6264. *Club:* Royal Commonwealth Society.

HIGHFIELD, Ashley Gilroy Mark, CEng; Chief Executive, Project Kangaroo, sinc 2008; *b* 3 Oct. 1965; *s* of Roy Highfield and Sheila Highfield; *m* 2005, Charlotte Emil Payter. *Educ:* Elizabeth Coll., Guernsey; Royal Grammar Sch., High Wycombe; Cit Univeristy, London (BSc (Hons) Business Computing Systems). MBCS. Mgt Consultant Coopers and Lybrand, 1988–94; Hd of IT and New Media, NBC Europe, 1994–95; Man Dir, Flextech Interactive, Flextech Television, 1996–2000; Dir, Future (formerly New Media and Technol., BBC, 2000–08. Non-executive Director, 1999–2000: Xrefer.cor Ltd; Multimap.com Ltd; Improveline.com Ltd; WayAheadGroup (ticketing) Ltd. FRSA FRTS. *Recreations:* motor racing, reading, architecture, music, film. *Club:* Soho House.

HIGHFIELD, Dr Roger Ronald, FIBiol; Editor, New Scientist, since 2008; Griffithstown, Wales, July 1958; *s* of Ronald and Dorothea Highfield; *m* 1992, Juli Brookes; one *s* one *d*. *Educ:* Chase Side Primary Sch., Enfield; Christ's Hosp., Horsham Pembroke Coll., Oxford (Domus Schol.; MA Chem. 1980); DPhil Oxon 1983. FIBic 2004. Clin. reporter, Pulse mag. for GPs, 1983–84; news ed., Nuclear Engrg Internat 1984–86; Technol. Corresp., 1986, Technol. Ed., 1987–88, Sci. Ed., 1988–2008, Dail Telegraph. Visiting Sabbatical Fellow: Queen Elizabeth Hse, Oxford Univ., 1989; Ballic Coll., Oxford, 1994. Former contributor to Economist, Guardian, New Scientist, Sunda Times, Observer; sci. ed., Esquire, 1996–98; contrib. High Life, Spectator, Conde Nas Traveller and Science. Contrib. BBC radio, incl. Scope, Acid Test, Sci. Now and Leadin Edge. Member: Communications and Public Engagement Cttee, RAEng; Healt Protection and Society Adv. Gp, HPA; Bioscis Futures Forum. Hon. Fellow, BAAS Science Writers' Award, Assoc. of British Sci. Writers, 1987, 1995, 1997, 1998; Britis Press Award, 1988; Medical Journalism Award, 1998, 2007. *Publications:* The Arrow o Time: the quest to solve time's greatest mystery, 1990; The Private Lives of Alber

Einstein, 1993; Frontiers of Complexity: the search for order in a chaotic world, 1995; Can Reindeer Fly?: the science of Christmas, 1998; The Science of Harry Potter: how magic really works, 2002; After Dolly: the uses and misuses of human cloning, 2006; (ed) A Life Decoded, by Craig Venter, 2007. *Recreations:* watching bad TV, cooking, dodgy DIY, Wii boxing. *Address:* New Scientist, Lacon House, Theobalds Road, WC1X 8NS; *web:* www.rogerhighfield.com.

HIGHTON, David Peter; Managing Director, Clinicenta Ltd (formerly Patient Choice Partners), since 2003; *b* 22 May 1954; *s* of Allan Peter Highton and May Comrie Highton (*née* Doughty); *m* Wendy Ann Attree; one *d*. *Educ:* Borden Grammar Sch., Sittingbourne; Univ. of Bristol (BSc Hons Econs 1975). ACA 1978, FCA 1989. Chartered Accountant, Turquands Barton Mayhew, 1975–79; Financial Accountant, Tunnel Avebe Starches Ltd, 1979–81; Financial Controller: R. P. Martin plc, 1981–83; Grand Metropolitan Brewing, 1983–87; Regl Finance Dir, Prudential Property Services, 1987–90; Dir of Finance and Chief Exec., Ealing HA, 1990–92; Dir of Finance, Riverside Hosps, 1992–94; Chief Executive: Chelsea and Westminster Hosp., 1994–2000; Oxford Radcliffe Hosps NHS Trust, 2000–03; Man. Dir, Hyperium Consulting, 2003. Non-exec. Director: Healthwork UK, 2000–05 (Chm., 2001–05); Skills for Health, 2007– (Chm., 2002–03). *Publications:* contribs to health mgt jls. *Recreations:* Rugby, books, films, good food. *Address:* White Cottage, New Yatt, Witney, Oxon OX29 6TF. *Clubs:* Sittingbourne Rugby (Pres.), Imperial Medicals Rugby (Vice Pres.).

HIGNETT, John Mulock, FCA; Chairman, Schroder Income Growth Fund plc, 1995–2005; *b* 9 March 1934; *s* of late Reginald and Marjorie Hignett; *m* 1961, Marijke Inge de Boer; one *s* one *d*. *Educ:* Harrow Sch.; Magdalene Coll., Cambridge (MA). Kemp Chatteris & Co., 1958–61; Deloitte & Co., 1961–63; joined Lazard Brothers & Co. Ltd, 1963; Manager, Issues Dept, 1971; Dir, 1972; Head of Corporate Finance Div., 1980; Man. Dir, 1984–88; Glaxo Holdings plc: Finance Dir, 1988–92; Man. Dir, Corporate Funds, 1992–94. Non-executive Director: TI Group plc, 1989–2000; Sedgwick Group plc, 1993–99; Alfred McAlpine plc, 1994–98; Smiths Gp plc, 2000. Director-General: Panel on Take-Overs and Mergers, 1981–83; Council for the Securities Industry, 1983. Dep. Chm., Internat. Shakespeare Globe Centre Ltd, 1990–. *Clubs:* Royal Thames Yacht, MCC; Hawks (Cambridge).

HIGNETT, Peter George; Regional Veterinary Officer, People's Dispensary for Sick Animals, 1982–90, retired; *b* 3 June 1925; *s* of Harry Sutton Hignett and Annie Hignett; *m* 1st, 1948, Patricia Bishop (marr. diss. 1988); two *s* one *d*; 2nd, 1997, Janet McCully. *Educ:* Pontesbury C of E Sch.; King Edward VI Sch., Birmingham; Univ. of Liverpool (MRCVS). General practice, 1947–49; Wellcome Veterinary Res. Station, 1949–54; Reader in Veterinary Reproduction, Univ. of Glasgow, 1954–76; Gen. Man., Hampshire Cattle Breeders' Soc., 1976–82. Mem. Council, RCVS, 1972–96, Pres., 1981–82; President: Soc. for Study of Animal Breeding, 1966–68; Southern Counties Veterinary Soc., 1983–84; Secretary: Associated AI Centres, 1977–82; Edgar Meml Trust, 1977–82; Member: Trehane Cttee, 1979–82; Scientific Adv. Cttee, Animal Health Trust, 1983–85; Banner Cttee on Ethics of Emerging Technologies in Animal Breeding, 1993–95. Gov., Berks Coll. of Agric., 1990–93. Hon. FRCVS 1998. *Publications:* scientific papers on fertility in domestic animals. *Recreations:* gardening, sailing, music. *Address:* 70 Stonerock Cottages, Chilgrove Park Road, Chichester, W Sussex PO18 9NA. *T:* (01243) 535330.

HIGTON, Dennis John, CEng, FIMechE, FRAeS; aeronautical mechanical engineer, retired; *b* 15 July 1921; *s* of John William and Lillian Harriett Higton; *m* 1945, Joy Merrifield Pickett; one *s* one *d*. *Educ:* Guildford Technical Sch.; RAE Farnborough Technical Sch. Mid-Wessex Water Co., 1937–38. RAE Engineering Apprentice, 1938–42; RAE Aerodynamics Dept (Aero Flight), 1942–52; learned to fly at No 1 EFTS RAF Panshanger, 1946; A&AEE Boscombe Down, Head of Naval Test and Supt of Performance, 1953–66; British Defence Staff, Washington DC, USA, 1966–70; MoD(PE) Anglo-French Helicopter Production, 1970–72; Director Aircraft Production, 1972–75; Under-Sec. and Dir-Gen. of Mil. Aircraft Projects, MoD, 1976–79, of Aircraft 4, 1979–80, of Aircraft 3, 1980–81; Hd, Engrg Profession, Air Systems Controllerate, MoD, 1976–81; aeronautical consultant and company dir, 1981–93. Chm., Technology Div., CS Commn, 1984–89. Mem., Fleet Air Arm Officers Assoc., 1960–. Chm., S Wilts and Salisbury Br., NSPCC, 1982–96; Vice Pres., Boscombe Down Br., RAeS, 2002–. Mem., Exec. Cttee, Salisbury Gp of Artists, 1987–92. Associate, Empire Test Pilots' Sch., 2003–. *Publications:* research and memoranda papers mainly on aerodynamic flight testing, early jet propulsion and control of jet borne flight. *Recreations:* sailing, gardening, enjoying Salisbury Plain, painting (Diploma in Fine Art, Southampton Inst. of Higher Educn, 1994). *Address:* Jasmine Cottage, Rollestone Road, Shrewton, Salisbury, Wiltshire SP3 4HG. *T:* (01980) 620276.

HILBORN, Rev. Dr David Henry Kyte; Director of Studies, North Thames Ministerial Training Course, since 2006; *b* 4 Jan. 1964; *s* of Edwin Henry and Constance May Hilborn; *m* 1988, Mia Alison Kyte (*see* Rev. M. A. K. Hilborn); one *s* one *d*. *Educ:* Langley Park Sch. for Boys; Nottingham Univ. (BA English; PhD Theol. and English); Mansfield Coll., Oxford (MA Theol.). Ordinand, Mansfield Coll., Oxford, 1985–89; Minister, Keyworth URC, 1989–92; research and teaching, Nottingham Univ., 1992–94; Minister: City Temple URC, 1994–99 (Jt Minister, 1997–99); Queen's Park URC, 2000–02; Theol Advr, then Head of Theology, Evangelical Alliance (UK), 1997–2006; ordained deacon and priest, C of E, 2002; Curate, St Mary's, Acton, 2002–06. *Publications:* Picking Up the Pieces: can Evangelicals adapt to contemporary culture?, 1997; (ed) Faith, Hope and Homosexuality, 1998; (ed) The Nature of Hell, 2000; (jtly) One Body in Christ: the history and significance of the Evangelical Alliance, 2001; (ed) 'Toronto' in Perspective, 2001; (ed) God and the Generations, 2002; (contrib.) Evangelicalism and the Orthodox Church, 2002; (contrib.) Faith, Health and Prosperity, 2003; (ed) Movement for Change: evangelicals and social transformation, 2004; articles in theological books and jls. *Recreations:* cricket, poetry. *Address:* North Thames Ministerial Training Course, The Crypt, St George-in-the-East, 16 Canon Street Road, E1 0BH. *T:* (020) 7481 9477.

HILBORN, Rev. Mia Alison Kyte; Hospitaller, Head of Spiritual Health Care and Chaplaincy Team Leader, Guy's and St Thomas' Hospital NHS Foundation Trust (formerly NHS Trust), since 2001; *b* 7 March 1963; *d* of late Harry Stephen Broadbelt and Jean Margaret Broadbelt; *m* 1988, Rev. David Henry Kyte Hilborn, *qv*; one *s* one *d*. *Educ:* City Univ. (BSc (Hons) Econs and Psychol.); Mansfield Coll., Oxford (MA Theol.). Ordination, URC, 1989; Minister, Friary URC, West Bridgford, Nottingham, 1989–94; City Temple URC, 1994–2000, Jt Minister, 1997–99; Free Church Chaplain, St Bart's Hosp., and Children's Chaplain, Bart's and The London NHS Trust, 1997–2001; Associate Minister, Queen's Park URC, 2000–02; ordained deacon, and priest, C of E, 2002; Hon. Asst Curate, N Lambeth Parish, 2002–. Gov., Evelina Hosp. Sch. *Recreations:* reading, theatre, knitting. *Address:* The Chaplaincy, St Thomas' Hospital, Lambeth Palace Road, SE1 7EH.

HILBORNE, Stephanie Vera; Chief Executive, The Wildlife Trusts, since 2004; *b* 3 March 1968; *d* of Derek Vance Hilborne and Mary Elizabeth Hilborne (*née* Drewett); *m* 1997, Jeremy Iain Wallace; one *s* one *d*. *Educ:* Lady Eleanor Holles Sch.; Bristol Univ. (BSc 1st Cl. Hons Biol.); University Coll. London (MSc Conservation 1993). Principal Officer, Wildlife and Countryside Link, 1994–97; Asst CEO, 1998–2000, CEO, 2000–04, Notts Wildlife Trust. FRSA 1996. *Recreations:* walking/rambling, swimming, badminton. *Address:* The Wildlife Trusts, The Kiln, Waterside, Mather Road, Newark, Notts NG24 1WT. *T:* (01636) 677711, *Fax:* (01636) 670001.

HILDEBRAND, Peter; Regional Employment Judge, London South, since 2008; *b* Lurgan, Co. Armagh, 28 June 1954; *s* of William Robert Perry Hildebrand and Olive Hildebrand; *m* 1980, Ann Purdon; one *s* two *d*. *Educ:* Campbell Coll., Belfast; Pembroke Coll., Cambridge (BA 1975). Admitted solicitor, 1978; Sacker and Partners, 1976–80, 1981–86; Stephenson Harwood, 1980–81; Burd Pearse, Exeter, 1986–97; Fee Paid Chm., Exeter, 1993–97, Salaried Chm., Leeds, 1997–2008, Employment Tribunal. *Recreations:* amateur radio (Mem., York Radio Club), languages, running. *Address:* Regional Office of Employment Tribunals, Montague Court, 101 London Road, W Croydon CR2 0RF. *Club:* Reform.

HILDITCH, David William; Member (DemU) Antrim East, Northern Ireland Assembly, since 1998; *b* 23 July 1963; *m* 1987, Wilma McCalmont; two *s*. *Educ:* Carrickfergus Grammar Sch. Carrickfergus Borough Council: Mem. (DemU), 1991–; Dep. Mayor, 1994–96; Mayor, 1997–98. Dist Master, Carrickfergus, Loyal Orange Instn, 1993–2000. *Address:* 130 Salia Avenue, Carrickfergus, Co. Antrim BT38 8NE. *T:* (028) 9335 1090; (office) 31 Lancasterian Street, Carrickfergus, Co. Antrim BT38 1AB. *T:* (028) 9332 9980.

HILDRETH, (Henry) Jan (Hamilton Crossley); independent consultant; Chairman: South West London and St George's Mental Health (formerly Pathfinder) NHS Trust, 1994–2004; High Performance Sports Ltd, since 1995; *b* 1 Dec. 1932; *s* of Maj.-Gen. Sir (Harold) John (Crossley) Hildreth, KBE, and late Mrs Joan Elise Hallett (*née* Hamilton); *m* 1958, Wendy Moira Marjorie, *d* of late Arthur Harold Clough, CMG, OBE and Marjorie Violet Clough; two *s* one *d*. *Educ:* Wellington Coll.; The Queen's Coll., Oxford (Hon. Mods (Nat. Sci.), BA PPE 1956, MA). National Service in RA, BAOR, 1952–53; 44 Parachute Bde (TA), 1953–58. Baltic Exchange, 1956; Royal Dutch Shell Group, 1957: served Philippines (marketing) and London (finance); Kleinwort, Benson Ltd, 1963; NEDO, 1965; Member of Economic Development Cttees for the Clothing, the Hosiery and Knitwear, and the Wool Textile industries; Mem., London Transport Bd, subseq. LTE, 1968–72: main responsibilities Finance, Marketing, Corp. Plan, Data Processing, and Estates; Asst Chief Exec., John Laing & Son Ltd, 1972–74; Dir-Gen., Inst. of Directors, 1975–78. Director: Minster Trust Ltd, 1979–94; Monument Oil and Gas plc, 1984–88; non-exec. dir of several cos, 1983–96; Chairman: Carroll Securities Ltd, 1986–91; Sea Catch PLC, 1987–94; Scallop Kings PLC, 1987–97. Member: Cttee, GBA, 1978–86 and 1997–2000; Council, ISIS, 1979–82; Exec. Cttee, Industrial Soc., 1973–84 (Hon. Life Mem., 1984); Council, British Exec. Service Overseas, 1975–91; Council, SCOPE (formerly Spastic Soc.), 1980–83, 1985– (Chm. Audit Cttee, 1990–92; Hon. Treas., 1992–97); Review Body for Nursing and Midwifery Staff and Professions Allied to Medicine, 1989–95; Council, St George's Hosp. Med. Sch., 1995–2002; Dir, Contact A Family, 1980–89. Constituency Chm., 1986–89, Pres., 1989–92, Wimbledon Cons. Assoc. Governor: Wellington Coll., 1974–2003; Eagle House Sch., 1986–2003. FCILT. FRSA. *Recreations:* cross-country, mountain and road running (London Marathon, 1981–2005), photography, water mills, and others. *Address:* 50 Ridgway Place, Wimbledon, SW19 4SW. *Clubs:* Athenæum; Vincent's (Oxford); Thames Hare and Hounds.

HILDREW, Bryan, CBE 1977; FREng; Managing Director, Lloyds Register of Shipping, 1977–85; *b* 19 March 1920; *s* of Alexander William Hildrew and Sarah Jane (*née* Clark); *m* 1950, Megan Kathleen Lewis; two *s* one *d*. *Educ:* Bede Collegiate Sch., Sunderland; Technical Coll., Sunderland; City and Guilds, Imperial Coll., London (MSc, DIC). FIMechE, FIMarEST; FREng (FEng 1976). Engineer Officer, RN, 1941–46. Lloyds Register of Shipping: Research Surveyor, 1948–67 (Admiralty Nuclear Submarine Project, 1956–61); Chief Engineer Surveyor, 1967–70; Technical Dir, 1970–77. Chm., Abbeyfield, Orpington, 1985–2004. President: IMechE, 1980–81; IMarE, 1983–85; Chm., CEI, 1981–82. FCGI 1990. Hon. DEng Newcastle, 1987; DUniv Surrey, 1994. *Recreations:* orienteering, walking. *Address:* 8 Westholme, Orpington, Kent BR6 0AN. *T:* (01689) 825451.

HILDYARD, Marianna Catherine Thoroton, (Lady Falconer of Thoroton); QC 2002; a Recorder, since 1999; *b* 24 Nov. 1955; *d* of Sir David Hildyard, KCMG, DFC; *m* 1985, Charles Leslie Falconer (*see* Baron Falconer of Thoroton); three *s* one *d*. *Educ:* Council of Legal Educn. Called to the Bar, Inner Temple, 1977. Asst Recorder, 1999. Ambassador, Nat. Aids Trust. Gov., local sch. *Recreations:* gardening, my children. *Address:* 4 Brick Court, Temple, EC4Y 9AD.

HILDYARD, Robert Henry Thoroton; QC 1994; Attorney General, Duchy of Lancaster, since 2006; *b* 10 Oct. 1952; *s* of Sir David (Henry Thoroton) Hildyard, KCMG, DFC and Millicent Hildyard, *d* of Sir Edward Baron; *m* 1980, Isabella Jane Rennie; two *d* (and one *d* decd). *Educ:* Eton Coll.; Christ Church, Oxford (BA Hons Hist.). Called to the Bar, Inner Temple, 1977; Bencher, Lincoln's Inn, 2005. Jun. Counsel to Crown (Chancery), 1992–94; a Deputy High Court Judge, 2002–. Mem., Financial Reporting Review Panel, 2002–. *Recreations:* family, tennis, shooting, opera, writing doggerel. *Address:* 4 Stone Buildings, Lincoln's Inn, WC2A 3XT. *T:* (020) 7242 5524. *Club:* Hurlingham.

HILHORST, Rosemary, OBE 2003; Director, Russia, British Council, since 2008; *b* 10 April 1954; *d* of late Raymond Bowditch and of June Ebdon; *m* 1981, Francis Hilhorst; one *s* one *d*. *Educ:* UCL (BSc Hons (Physics) 1975); Chelsea Coll. Centre for Sci. Educn, London (PGCE (Integrated Sci.) 1976); London Business Sch. (Sen. Exec. Prog. 2003). Sci. teacher and hd of sci. depts, Sussex, Dorset, Italy and Tanzania, 1976–85; British Council, 1985–: Asst Dir, Sudan, 1986–89; mgt posts, HQ, London, 1989–91, and 1994–97; Director: Slovakia, 1991–94; Tanzania, 1997–2000; Central and E Europe, 2000–01; Connecting Futures, 2002–03; Dir, Portugal, 2003–08. Member: Exec. Cttee, Tanzania Br., Britain-Tanzania Assoc., 1997–2000; Selection Cttee, Tanzania Bd, 1997–2000, Portuguese Bd, 2003–08, United World Colls; Governing Body, British Assoc. for Central and Eastern Europe, 2000–02. *Recreations:* gardening, running, family. *Club:* Gremio Literária (Lisbon).

HILL; *see* Clegg-Hill, family name of Viscount Hill.

HILL; *see* Erskine-Hill.

HILL, family name of **Marquess of Downshire** and **Baron Sandys**.

HILL, 9th Viscount *cr* 1842; **Peter David Raymond Charles Clegg-Hill;** Bt 1727; Baron Hill 1814; *b* 17 Oct. 1945; *s* of Major Hon. Frederick Raymond Clegg-Hill, 2nd *s* of 6th Viscount and of Alice Dorothy (*née* Chapman); *S* cousin, 2003; *m* 1973, Sharon Ruth Deane, NZ (marr. diss. 2000; she changed her name to Savanna Dawson; they remarried 2002); one *s* five *d* (and one *s* decd, Paul Andrew Raymond Clegg-Hill, *b* 1979, *d* 2003). *Heir: s* Hon. Michael Charles David Clegg-Hill, *b* 29 Feb. 1988.

HILL, Prof. Adrian Vivian Sinton, DPhil, DM; FRCP; Director, The Jenner Institute, since 2005, and Professor of Human Genetics, since 1996, University of Oxford; Fellow, Magdalen College, Oxford, since 2004; *b* 9 Oct. 1958; *s* of late Fergus Hill and of Helen (*née* O'Donovan); *m* 1994, Sunetra Gupta, *qv*; two *d. Educ:* Belvedere Coll., Dublin; Trinity Coll., Dublin (Foundn Scholar); Magdalen Coll. and Lincoln Coll., Oxford (BA 1979; BM BCh 1982; MA 1982; DPhil 1986; DM 1993). FRCP 1999. University of Oxford: Research Fellow: Exeter Coll., 1983–86, 1994–99; St John's Coll., 1988–90; Balliol Coll., 1990–93; Wellcome Trust Principal Res. Fellow, Wellcome Trust Centre for Human Genetics, 1995–; Chm., Centre for Clinical Vaccinology and Tropical Medicine, 2005–. Hon. Consultant Physician, Oxford Radcliffe Hosps, 1993–. FMedSci 1999. *Publications:* research papers on human genetics, vaccines and infectious diseases, esp. malaria. *Recreations:* music, travel. *Address:* The Jenner Institute, Roosevelt Drive, Oxford OX3 7DQ. *T:* (01865) 617610; *e-mail:* adrian.hill@well.ox.ac.uk. *Club:* Oxford and Cambridge.

HILL, Prof. Alan Geoffrey, MA; FBA 1994; Professor of English Language and Literature in the University of London at Royal Holloway and Bedford New College (formerly Royal Holloway College), 1980–96, now Emeritus; *b* 12 Dec. 1931; *yr s* of Thomas Murton Hill and Alice Marion Hill (*née* Nunn); *m* 1960, Margaret Vincent Rutherford, MA; three *d. Educ:* Dulwich Coll. (Sen. Foundn Schol.); St Andrews Univ. (MA 1st Cl. Hons English Lang. and Lit.); Merton Coll., Oxford (BLitt). Asst Lectr/Lectr in English, Exeter Univ., 1958–62; Lectr in English, St Andrews Univ., 1962–68; Sen. Lectr in English, Dundee Univ., 1968–80. Vis. Professor of English, Univ. of Saskatchewan, 1973–74; British Acad./Royal Soc. of Canada Vis. Lectr, Canadian univs, 1997; Hon. Fellow, Inst. for Advanced Res. in Humanities, Birmingham Univ., 1996–. External Examiner in English: Univ. of Buckingham, 1986–90; Nat. Univ. of Singapore, 1996–98. Lectures: Crowsley, Charles Lamb Soc., 1981; Warton, British Acad., 1986; Newman Centenary, Univ. of Malta, 1990; Lambeth Palace Library, 1992; Tewkesbury Abbey, 2000. Founded Centre for Study of Victorian Art, RHC, 1981. Trustee, Dove Cottage, subseq. Wordsworth, Trust, 1969–2001, now Life Fellow; General Editor, The Letters of William and Dorothy Wordsworth, 1979–. Member: Editl Bd, Forum for Modern Language Studies, 1964–69; Publications Bd, Tennyson Res. Bulletin, 1993–2001. *Publications:* The Letters of William and Dorothy Wordsworth, vol. III, The Middle Years, Part 2, 1812–1820, 2nd edn (rev. and ed with Mary Moorman), 1970; vol. IV, The Later Years, Part 1, 1821–1828, 2nd edn (rev. and ed), 1978; vol. V, The Later Years, Part 2, 1829–1834, 2nd edn (rev. and ed), 1979; vol. VI, The Later Years, Part 3, 1835–1839, 2nd edn (rev. and ed), 1982; vol. VII, The Later Years, Part 4, 1840–1853, 2nd edn (rev. and ed), 1988; vol. VIII, A Supplement of New Letters, 1993; (ed) Selected Letters of Dorothy Wordsworth, 1981; (ed) Selected Letters of William Wordsworth, 1984; (ed) John Henry Newman, Loss and Gain, 1986; Wordsworth's Grand Design, 1987; (ed with Ian Ker) Newman After A Hundred Years, 1990; (ed) Ford Madox Ford, The Soul of London, 1995; Tennyson, Wordsworth, and the 'Forms' of Religion, 1997; Newman's Idea of a University, Revisited, 1998; Lyrical Ballads (1800), a Bicentenary Celebration, 2000; (ed) Newman, Callista, 2001; contrib. DNB, Oxford DNB, articles and reviews in literary, historical and theological jls. *Recreations:* music, fine arts, ecclesiology, travel. *Address:* 4 Lawnside House, Albert Road South, Malvern, Worcs WR14 3AH. *Club:* Savile.

HILL, Alastair Malcolm, OBE 2000; QC 1982; *b* 12 May 1936; *s* of Prof. Sir Ian George Wilson Hill, CBE, LLD, FRCP, FRSE and Lady (Audrey) Hill; *m* 1969, Elizabeth Maria Innes; one *s* one *d. Educ:* Trinity Coll., Glenalmond; Keble Coll., Oxford (Stevenson-Chatterton Schol.; BA Hons Jurisp. 1959). Nat. Service, RHA, 1954–56. Called to the Bar, Gray's Inn, 1961; South Eastern Circuit; a Recorder, 1982. Trustee, Disability Law Service. *Recreations:* collecting prints and watercolours, opera, fly-fishing.

HILL, Allen; *see* Hill, H. A. O.

HILL, Andrea; Chief Executive, Suffolk County Council, since 2008; *b* 12 Feb. 1964; *d* of Michael and Sheila Large; *m* 1984, Phil Hill; three *s. Educ:* N London Poly. (BA 1st Cl. Hons Modern Studies); Univ. of Birmingham (MBA Public Sector). Thurrock Borough Council: Policy Performance Rev. Officer, 1985–87; Principal Asst, 1987–90; Hd of Strategy Planning, 1990–94; Asst Chief Exec., Cambridge CC, 1994–99; Dir of Policy and Community, 1999–2000, Dep. Chief Exec., 2000–01, N Herts DC; Chief Executive: Colchester BC, 2001–04; Bedfordshire CC, 2004–08. Mem. Bd, Living East, Regl Cultural Consortium for E of England, 2002–07. *Recreations:* marathon running, ski-ing, sailing, windsurfing. *Address:* c/o Suffolk County Council, Endeavour House, 8 Russell Road, Ipswich, Suffolk IP1 2BX.

HILL, Prof. (Anthony) Edward, PhD; Director, National Oceanography Centre, Southampton, since 2005; Professor of Oceanography, University of Southampton, since 2007; *b* 30 Dec. 1959; *s* of Anthony Sidney Hill and Philomena Hill (*née* Ward); *m* 1989, Jacqueline Patricia Caukwell; two *s. Educ:* Bishop Wulstan RC High Sch., Rugby; Univ. of Sheffield (BSc (Applied Maths) 1st class 1981); UCNW, Bangor (MSc 1983; PhD (Physical Oceanography) 1987). Lectr in Oceanography, 1986–95, Sen. Lectr, 1995–99, UCNW, Bangor, subseq. Univ. of Wales, Bangor; Dir, Proudman Oceanographic Lab., NERC, 1999–2005. Hon. Vis. Prof., Univ. of Liverpool, 1999–2004; Hon. Prof., Univ. of Southampton, 2005–07. Chm. Bd, Nat. Centre for Ocean Forecasting, 2005–07; Mem. Exec. Bd, NERC, 2001–. FIMarEST, CMarSci 2006. *Publications:* numerous res. contribns on oceanography of continental shelf seas to acad. jls. *Recreations:* oil painting, visiting historical monuments, walking. *Address:* National Oceanography Centre, University of Southampton, Waterfront Campus, European Way, Southampton SO14 3ZH.

HILL, Antony James de Villiers; consultant; *b* 1 Aug. 1940; *s* of James Kenneth Hill and Hon. Yvonne Aletta Hill, *d* of 2nd Baron de Villiers; *m* 1974, Gunilla Els-Charlotte Emilie (Elsa) Nilsson; one *d. Educ:* Sydney Grammar School; Sydney Univ. (BA Hons); Boston Univ. (MEd). Law Clerk, 1962–64; Antarctic Expedition, 1964–65; Master, Canberra Grammar Sch., 1965–66; Instructor, Himalayan Mountaineering Inst., Darjeeling, 1967–68; Master, Sydney C of E Grammar Sch., 1967–72, 1977; Mem. Faculty: Phillips Acad., Andover, Mass, 1972–74; Boston Univ., 1974–76; Senior Master, King's Sch., Parramatta, 1977–81; Headmaster: Christ Church Grammar Sch., WA, 1982–87; Melbourne C of E Grammar Sch., later Melbourne Grammar Sch., 1988–94; St Mark's Sch., Southborough, Mass, 1994–2006; Dir, Wesley College Inst. for Educnl Innovation, Melbourne, 2006. *Recreations:* running, climbing, sailing, theatre, music, reading. *Address:* 22 Dartmouth Street, Boston, MA 02116, USA. *T:* (617) 8696935, *Fax:* (857) 2334633. *Clubs:* Weld (Perth, WA); Savage (Melbourne).

HILL, Sir Arthur (Alfred), Kt 1989, CBE 1980; Chairman, Walsall District Health Authority, 1982–92; *b* 14 May 1920; *s* of Arthur James Hill and Phoebe Mary Hill (*née* Prees); *m* 1947, Alma M. E. Bate (CBE 1981); one *s* two *d. Educ:* Langley High Sch.; Halesowen Technical Coll. Served RAFVR, 1939–45. Joint Company Director: Arth Brook Cars Ltd, 1948–68; Abro Finance Ltd, 1950–65; Cradley Heath Motor Co. L 1956–65. Trainer/Man., Dudley Council Voluntary Services, 1980–82. Chm., CF 1969–72; Treas., 1973–76, Chm., 1976–79, Pres., 1985–88, W Midlands Area Co Council; Mem., Cons. Nat. Union, 1966–80; Chairman: Kidderminster Cons. Assc 1964–67; Walsall S Cons. Assoc., 1981–84. Mem., Rowley Regis BC, 1948–57. Chı Bd of Govs, Rowley Regis Grammar Sch., 1961–64. *Recreations:* travelling, golf. *Addre* 1 Mellish Road, Walsall, West Midlands WS4 2DQ. *T:* (01922) 634949.

HILL, Sir Brian (John), Kt 1989; FRICS; FCIOB; Chairman, Great Ormond Str Hospital, 1992–97 (Governor, subsequently Director, 1985–97, Special Trust 1990–2000); *b* 19 Dec. 1932; *s* of Doris Winifred Hill and Gerald Aubrey Hill, OBE; 1959, Janet J. Newman; two *s* one *d. Educ:* Stowe School; Emmanuel Colleg Cambridge. BA (Land Economy); MA. Managing Director, Higgs and Hill Building L 1966–78; Higgs and Hill plc: Group Managing Dir, 1972–83; Chm. and Chief Exe 1983–89; Exec. Chm., 1989–91; non-exec. Chm., 1991–92. Director: Etonbro Properties, 1991–93; Southern Reg. Nat. Westminster Bank, 1990–92; Chairma Goldsborough Healthcare plc, 1993–97; Sackville Property Unit Trust, 1999–20(Threadneedle Property Unit Trust, 2002–; Longmartin Properties Ltd, 2008–. Preside London Region, Nat. Fedn of Building Trades Employers, 1981–82; CIOB, 1987–8 Building Employers Confedn, 1992–95; Chairman: Vauxhall Coll. of Building a Further Educn, 1976–86; Nat. Contractors Group, 1983–84; Director: Building Centr 1977–85; LDDC, 1994–98. Property Services Agency: Mem. Adv. Bd, 1981–86; Me Bd, 1986–88. Mem. Cttee, Lazard Property Unit Trust, 1982–98. Ext. Examnr, Readi Univ., 1993–97. Chm., Children's Trust, Tadworth, 1998–; Trustee, Falkland Is Me Trust, 1997–2007. Governor: Aberdour Sch., 1988–2007; Pangbourne Coll., 2000–(Hon. FIStructE; Hon. FCGI; Hon. Fellow, Inst. of Child Health, 1996. Hon. D Westminster, 1994; Hon. LLD South Bank, 1995. *Recreations:* travelling, tenn gardening, amateur dramatics. *Address:* Corner Oak, 5 Glen Close, Kingswood, Surr KT20 6NT. *T:* (01737) 832424. *Club:* Royal Automobile.

HILL, Charles; *see* Hill, R. C.

HILL, Charles Edward; HM Diplomatic Service; Deputy Head of Mission, Muscat, sin 2004; *b* 31 March 1963; *s* of Anthony and Jennifer Hill; *m* 1996, Suzanne Victoria Stoc one *s* one *d. Educ:* Royal Holloway Coll., Univ. of London (BA Hist.). Joined H Diplomatic Service, 1990; Third Sec. (Chancery), Doha, 1993–96; Dep. Hd of Missio Almaty, 1997–2000; Parly Clerk, FCO, 2000–02; Hd, Central Asia and S Caucas Section, FCO, 2002–04. *Recreations:* travel, tennis, backgammon, CFC, struggling wi Arabic! *Address:* c/o Foreign and Commonwealth Office, King Charles Street, SW1 2AH; British Embassy Muscat, PO Box 185, Mina Al Fahal-PC 116, Sultanate of Oma *T:* 24609000, *Fax:* 24609013; *e-mail:* charles.hill@fco.gov.uk.

HILL, Rt Rev. Christopher John; *see* Guildford, Bishop of.

HILL, Prof. Christopher John, DPhil; FBA 2007; Sir Patrick Sheehy Professor International Relations, University of Cambridge, since 2004; *b* 20 Nov. 1948; *s* of Pet Alan Hill and Sylvia Dawn Hill; *m* 1970, Maria McKay; one *s* one *d. Educ:* Merton Col Oxford (BA 1st Cl. Hons Modern History 1970); Nuffield Coll., Oxford (DPhil 1979 London School of Economics and Political Science: Noel Buxton Student in Interna Relns, 1973–74; Lectr, 1974–90, Sen. Lectr, 1990–91, in Internat. Relns; Montagu Burton Prof. of Internat. Relns, 1991–2004; Convenor, Dept of Internat. Relns, 1994–9 Vice Chm., Academic Bd, 1999–2002. Vis. Prof., Dartmouth Coll., NH, 1985; Visitir Fellow: RIIA, 1980–81; Woodrow Wilson International Centre for Schola Washington, 1984; European University Inst., Florence, 1992–93, 1998; UCSD, 200 Univ. of Siena, 2003. *Publications:* (ed) National Foreign Policies and European Politic Co-operation, 1983; Cabinet Decisions in Foreign Policy, 1991; (ed jtly) Two Worlds International Relations, 1994; (ed) The Actors in Europe's Foreign Policy, 1996; (ed jtl European Foreign Policy: key documents, 2000; The Changing Politics of Foreign Polic 2003; (ed jtly) The European Union in International Relations, 2005; many articles learned jls and contribs to books. *Recreations:* Wolverhampton Wanderers FC, the visu arts. *Address:* Centre of International Studies, 17 Mill Lane, Cambridge CB2 1RX. (01223) 767230; *e-mail:* cjh68@cam.ac.uk.

HILL, Ven. Colin, PhD; Archdeacon of West Cumberland, since 2004; *b* 4 Sept. 1942; of William Albert Hill and Annie Hill; *m* 1965, Kathleen Chadbourne; three *d. Edu* Leicester Univ. (BSc (Maths) 1964); Ripon Hall, Oxford; Open Univ. (PhD (Sociol. Religion) 1988). Ordained deacon, 1966, priest, 1967; Assistant Curate: Ch of th Martyrs, Dio. Leicester, 1966–69; St Crispin's Ch, Braunstone, 1969–71; Lect Ecumenical Inst., Teesside, 1971–72; Vicar, St Thomas and St James, Worsbrough 1972–78; Chs' Develt Officer for Mission and Ministry for Telford, Dios Lichfield an Hereford, 1978–96; Canon Res., and Canon Treas., Carlisle Cathedral, and Diocesa Sec., Carlisle, 1996–2004; Vice Dean, Carlisle Cathedral, 2004. Rural Dean: Telford, Dic Lichfield, 1980–96; Telford Severn Gorge, Dio. Hereford, 1980–96; Preb., Herefor Cathedral, 1983–96. *Publications:* (contrib.) A Workbook in Popular Religion, 198((contrib.) A Deanery Workbook, 1988; What's Good for the Organisation: apprais schemes, 1991; (contrib.) Religious Movements in a Neo-Weberian Perspective, 1992 Loosing the Apron Strings: devolution to deaneries, 1996; Appointing the Rural Dean 2004; Deans and Deaneries: lessons from Norway, 2006. *Recreations:* Scandinavian travel cultivation of bonsai, walking. *Address:* 50 Stainburn Road, Workington, Cumbria CA1 1SN. *T:* (01900) 66190.

HILL, Rev. Canon Colin Arnold Clifford, OBE 1996; Vicar of Croydon and Chaplai to Archbishop Whitgift Foundation, 1973–94; Chaplain to the Queen, 1990–99; *b* 13 Feb 1929; *s* of William and May Hill; *m* 1st, 1957, Shirley (*d* 1961); one *s*; 2nd, 1971, Iren Chamberlain; one step *s. Educ:* Reading Sch.; Bristol Univ.; Ripon Hall Theol Coll. Oxford; Univ. of Wales, Bangor (MPhil 2003). Ordained deacon, Sheffield Cathedral 1957, priest, 1958; Rotherham Parish Church; Vicar of Brightside, 1960; Rector c Easthampstead, Bracknell, 1964; Chaplain, RAF Staff Coll., Bracknell, 1968. Hon Canon, Canterbury, 1975, Canon Emeritus, 1984; Hon. Canon, Southwark, 1984, Canor Emeritus, 1994. Proctor in Convocation and General Synod, Dio. Oxford, 1970–73, Dio of Canterbury and Southwark, 1980–84. Religious Advr, London Borough of Croydon 1973–94; Chairman: Church Tenements Trust, 1973–94; Croydon Industrial Mission 1975–94. Chm., Croydon Crime Prevention Initiative, 1989–94; Vice Chm., Croydo Police Consultative Cttee, 1985–94. Founder, Bracknell Samaritans, 1968; Founde Chm., Croydon Youth Counselling Agency, 1974–94. *Recreations:* boating, walking reading. *Address:* Silver Birches, 70 Preston Crowmarsh, Wallingford, Oxon OX10 6SL *T:* and *Fax:* (01491) 836102. *Club:* Leander.

HILL, Damon Graham Devereux, OBE 1997; motor racing driver, retired; Chairman Damon Hill BMW, Warwick, since 2001; P1 International Ltd, since 2001; *b* 17 Sept 1960; *s* of late Graham Hill, OBE and of Bette Hill; *m* 1988, Georgie Hill; two *s* two *d Educ:* Haberdashers' Aske's Sch. Began motorcycle racing, 1979; Formula 3, 1986

Formula 3000, 1988; Formula 1, 1992–99: Brabham team, 1992; with Williams Team, 1991–96: test driver, 1991; driver, 1993–96; Grand Prix wins: 3 in 1993, 6 in 1994, 4 in 1995, 8 in 1996 (Argentina, Australia, Brazil, Canada, France, Germany, Japan, San Marino), 1 in 1998; Drivers' World Championship, 1996; with Arrows team, 1997; with Jordan team, 1998–99. Numerous awards incl. BBC Sports Personality of the Year, 1994 and 1996. *Publications:* Grand Prix Year, 1994; Championship Year, 1996. *Address:* P1 International Ltd, Unit C, Imperial Park, Randalls Way, Leatherhead, Surrey KT22 7AT. *Club:* British Racing Drivers' (Pres., 2006–).

HILL, David Neil, MA, FRCO; Musical Director, Bach Choir, since 1998; Chief Conductor, BBC Singers, since 2007; *b* 13 May 1957; *s* of James Brian Greatrex Hill and Jean Hill; *m* 1st, 1979, Hilary Llystyn Jones (marr. diss.); one *s* one *d*; 2nd, 1994, Alice Mary Wills; one *s* one *d*. *Educ:* Chetham's School of Music, Manchester; St John's College, Cambridge (organ student; toured Aust. 1977, USA and Canada, 1978, Japan, 1979; MA). Sub-Organist, Durham Cathedral, 1980–82; Organist and Master of Music: Westminster Cathedral, 1982–88; Winchester Cathedral, 1988–2002; Organist and Dir of Music, St John's Coll., Cambridge, 2003–07. Conductor: Alexandra Choir, 1979–87; Waynflete Singers, Winchester, 1988–2002; Associate Chorus Master, 1987–98, Artistic Dir, 1992–98, Philharmonia Chorus; Principal Conductor, Southern Sinfonia, 2003–; Principal Conductor, Leeds Philharmonic, 2005–. Dir, Southern Cathedrals' Fest., triennially 1990–2002. Mem. Council, RCO, 1984–; President: Cathedral Organists' Assoc., 2006–07; IAO, 2007–. Recordings with choirs and orchs incl. Westminster Cathedral Choir (Gramophone award, 1985); concerts and tours abroad, including tours to Australia, USA and Philippines. Hon. DMus Southampton, 2003. *Recreations:* food, wine, cricket, golf, cars. *Address:* c/o Caroline Phillips Management, The Old Brushworks, 56 Pickwick Road, Corsham, Wilts SN13 9BX. *Club:* Athenæum.

HILL, David Rowland; Director, Bell Pottinger Group, since 2007; *b* 1 Feb. 1948; *s* of Rowland Foster Hill and Rita Maud Hill; *m* 1974, Janet Gibson (marr. diss. 1992); one *s* one *d*. *Educ:* King Edward VI Sch., Birmingham; Brasenose Coll., Oxford Univ. (BA PPE). Unigate Ltd, 1970–72; Asst to Rt Hon. Roy Hattersley, MP, 1972–76; Political Advr, Dept of Prices and Consumer Protection, 1976–79; Head of Staff: Rt Hon. Roy Hattersley, 1979–83; Dep. Leader of Labour Party's Office, 1983–91; Dir of Campaigns and Communications, Lab Party, 1991–93; Chief Spokesperson for Labour Party, 1993–98; Dir, Bell Pottinger Good Relations, subseq. Good Relations, 1998–2003; Man. Dir, Keith McDowall Associates, subseq. Good Relations Political Communications, 2000–03; Dir of Communications, Prime Minister's Office, 2003–07. *Recreations:* cinema, watching sport, foreign travel. *Address:* Bell Pottinger Group, Holborn Gate, 330 High Holborn, WC1V 7QD.

HILL, Edward; *see* Hill, A. E.

HILL, Rev. Mgr Edward Peter; Parish Priest, St Andrew's Church, Tenterden, since 2003; *b* 8 Aug. 1943; *s* of Leslie John Hill and Constance Irene Hill. *Educ:* Holy Family RC Primary Sch., Morden; John Fisher Independent Sch., Purley; St Joseph's Jun. Seminary, Mark Cross, Sussex; St John's Seminary, Wonersh. Ordained priest, 1968; Assistant Priest: St Saviour, Lewisham, 1968–72; St Thomas of Canterbury, Wandsworth, 1972–78; St Peter, Woolwich, 1978–82; served as RAF Chaplain, 1982–2000: Cranwell, Wildenrath, Brampton, Brize Norton, Rheindahlen; Asst Principal Chaplain, Support Command, Brampton, and Personnel and Trng Comd, Innsworth; Prin. RC Chaplain and Dir, Chaplaincy Services 2, RAF, 1997–2000; held rank of Gp Captain; QHC 1997–2000; Officiating Chaplain (RC), RAF Brize Norton, 2000–03. Prelate of Honour to the Pope, 1997. *Recreations:* most sports (interest in, only now, as spectator and studier). *Club:* Royal Air Force.

HILL, Air Cdre Dame Felicity (Barbara), DBE 1966 (OBE 1954); Director of the Women's Royal Air Force, 1966–69; *b* 12 Dec. 1915; *d* of late Edwin Frederick Hill and late Mrs Frances Ada Barbara Hill (*née* Cocke). *Educ:* St Margaret's Sch., Folkestone. Joined WAAF, 1939; commnd, 1940; served in: UK, 1939–46; Germany, 1946–47; Far East Air Force, 1949–51; other appts included Inspector of WRAF, 1956–59; OC, RAF Hawkinge, 1959–60; OC, RAF Spitalgate, 1960–62; Dep. Dir, 1962–65. Hon. ADC to the Queen, 1966–69. *Address:* 24 Lions Hall, St Swithun Street, Winchester, Hants SO23 9HW. *Club:* Royal Air Force.

HILL, Prof. Geoffrey (William); poet and critic; University Professor, and Professor of Literature and Religion, Boston University, 1988–2006, now Emeritus; *b* 18 June 1932; *s* of William George Hill and Hilda Beatrice Hill (*née* Hands); *m* 1st, 1956, Nancy Whittaker (marr. diss. 1983); three *s* one *d*; 2nd, 1987, Alice Goodman; one *d*. *Educ:* County High Sch., Bromsgrove; Keble Coll., Oxford (BA 1953, MA 1959; Hon. Fellow, 1981). Mem., academic staff, Univ. of Leeds, 1954–80 (Prof. of Eng. Lit., 1976–80); Univ. Lectr in English and Fellow of Emmanuel College, Cambridge, 1981–88; founding Co-Dir, Editorial Inst., Boston Univ., 1998–2004. Churchill Fellow, Univ. of Bristol, 1980; Associate Fellow, Centre for Res. in Philosophy and Literature, Univ. of Warwick, 2004. Lectures: Bateson Meml, Corpus Christi Coll., Oxford, 1984; Clark, Trinity Coll., Cambridge, 1986; Warton, British Acad., 1998; Tanner, Brasenose Coll., Oxford, 2000; Ward-Phillips, Univ. of Notre Dame, 2000; Empson, Univ. of Cambridge, 2005; Goldsmith, Univ. of Leeds, 2006. English version of Ibsen's Brand produced at National Theatre, London, 1978. FRSL 1972; Fellow, Amer. Acad. of Arts and Scis, 1996. Hon. Fellow, Emmanuel Coll., Cambridge, 1990. Hon. DLitt: Leeds, 1988; Warwick, 2007. Whitbread Award, 1971; RSL Award (W. H. Heinemann Bequest), 1971; Loines Award, Amer. Acad. and Inst. of Arts and Letters, 1983; Ingram Merrill Foundn Award in Literature, 1985; T. S. Eliot Prize, Ingersoll Foundn, USA, 2000. *Publications: poetry:* For the Unfallen, 1959 (Gregory Award, 1961); King Log, 1968 (Hawthornden Prize, 1969; Geoffrey Faber Meml Prize, 1970); Mercian Hymns, 1971 (Alice Hunt Bartlett Award, 1971); Somewhere is Such a Kingdom: Poems 1952–1971, 1975; Tenebrae, 1978 (Duff Cooper Meml Prize, 1979); The Mystery of the Charity of Charles Péguy, 1983; Collected Poems, 1985; New and Collected Poems 1952–1992, 1994; Canaan, 1996; The Triumph of Love, 1998 (Cholmondeley Award, 1999; Heinemann Award, 2000); Speech! Speech!, 2000; The Orchards of Syon, 2002; Scenes from Comus, 2005; Without Title, 2006; Selected Poems, 2006; A Treatise of Civil Power, 2007; *poetic drama:* Henrik Ibsen, Brand: a version for the English Stage, 1978, 3rd edn 1996; *criticism:* The Lords of Limit, 1984; The Enemy's Country, 1991; Style and Faith, 2003; Collected Critical Writings, 2008. *Address:* 316 Histon Road, Cambridge CB4 3HS.

HILL, Graham Chadwick, FRSC; Headmaster, Dr Challoner's Grammar School, Amersham, 1993–2001, Trustee, since 2001; *b* 11 Jan. 1942; *s* of Harold Hill and Harriet (*née* Chadwick); *m* 1964, Elizabeth Wadsworth; three *d*. *Educ:* Bacup and Rawtenstall Grammar Sch.; Trinity Coll., Cambridge (BA, MA, PGCE Dist, AdvDipEd). FRSC 1985. Asst Science Master, Marlborough Coll., 1965–70; Sen. Chemistry Master, 1970–75, Sen. Science Master, 1975–78, Bristol Grammar Sch.; Dep. Headmaster, Dr Challoner's Grammar Sch., 1978–86, 1989–93; Sen. Fellow, Univ. of York, 1986–87. Chm., 1987–89, Trustee, 1991–93 and 2001–06, ASE. FRSA 1993. Guinness Award for Sci. Teachers, 1968; Bronze Medallion, RSC, 1986. *Publications:* Chemistry in Context, 1978, 5th edn 2000; Chemistry in Context Laboratory Manual and Study Guide, 1982, 5th edn 2001; Chemistry Counts, 1986, 3rd edn 2003; Letts Revise Science, 1990; Science Scene (booklets, books and teachers' guides), 1990–92; Materials, 1992; Science for GCSE, 1998, 2nd edn 2001; Foundation Science for GCSE, 2001; Synoptic Skills in A level Chemistry, 2003; AQA GCSE Science, 2006; AQA GCSE Additional Science, 2007; co-author and editor: AQA GCSE Chemistry, 2007; AQA GCSE Physics, 2007; AQA GCSE Biology, 2007; contribs to learned jls. *Recreations:* walking, gardening, theatre.

HILL, Graham Starforth; Resident Consultant, office in Rome 1992–94, and in Milan, 1990–94, Frere Cholmeley, later Frere Cholmeley Bischoff, solicitors; Consultant: to Monaco office, Frere Cholmeley, later Frere Cholmeley Bischoff, solicitors, 1984–94; to Rodyk and Davidson, solicitors, Singapore, 1985–96; *b* 22 June 1927; *s* of late Harold Victor John Hill and Helen Dora (*née* Starforth); *m* 1952, Margaret Elise Ambler (marr. diss.); one *s* one *d*. *Educ:* Dragon Sch., Oxford; Winchester Coll.; St John's Coll., Oxford (MA Hons). Called to the Bar, Grays Inn, 1951; admitted solicitor, 1961; also admitted solicitor Malaysia, Singapore and Hong Kong; Notary Public and Comr for Oaths, Singapore. Flying Officer, RAF, 1948–50. Crown Counsel, Colonial Legal Service, Singapore, 1953–56; Partner, subseq. Sen. Partner, Rodyk and Davidson, Advocates and Solicitors, Singapore, 1957–76. Chm., Guinness Mahon & Co. Ltd, 1979–83 (Dir, 1977–79); non-exec. Dir, Phelan, Lewis and Peat Ltd, 1984–86. Mem., Malayan Bd of Income Tax, 1957–60. Formerly (all Singapore): Hon. Legal Adviser to High Commn; Law Reform Comr; dir of numerous cos; Member: Univ. Faculty of Law; Constitutional Commn; Council, Law Soc. (Pres., 1970–74, Hon. Mem. 1978); Courts Martial Mil. Ct of Appeal; Council, Internat. Bar Assoc.; Discip. Cttee and Appeal Cttee, ICA, 1980–86. Trustee: Southwark Cathedral Develt Trust Fund, 1980–85; Royal Opera House Trust, 1982–85. FRSA. Cavaliere dell'Ordine della Stella della Solidarieta, and Commendatore dell'Ordine al Merito, Italy. *Publications:* co-editor, The Laws of Singapore, revised edition 1970; report of Constitutional Commission of Singapore. *Recreations:* music, Italy. *Address:* 10 St Thomas Street, Winchester, Hants SO23 9HE. *T:* (01962) 854146; *e-mail:* gshill@bigfoot.com. *Club:* Garrick.

See also I. S. Hill.

HILL, Harry Douglas; Chairman, Countrywide plc, since 2007 (Chief Executive, 1988–2007); *b* Yorks, 4 April 1948; *s* of Jack and Kathleen Hill; *m* 1986, Mandy Elizabeth Glenys; five *s*. *Educ:* Barnsley Grammar Sch.; Coll. of Estate Mgt. Chartered surveyor. Director: Jupiter Second Split plc, 2004–; Milton Homes plc, 2008–. *Recreations:* fishing, bird watching, cycling, National Hunt racing, restaurant in Portugal (owner). *Address:* Countrywide plc, Countrywide House, Perry Way, Witham, Essex CM8 3SX. *T:* (01376) 533700, *Fax:* (01376) 520465; *e-mail:* hdh@countrywideplc.co.uk.

HILL, Prof. (Hugh) Allen (Oliver), FRS 1990; CChem, FRSC; Professor of Bioinorganic Chemistry, Oxford, 1992–2004, now Emeritus; Fellow and Praelector, 1965–2004, Hon. Fellow, 2007, The Queen's College, Oxford; *b* 23 May 1937; *s* of Hugh Rankin Stewart Hill and Elizabeth Hill (*née* Burns); *m* 1967, Boglárka Anna Pinter; two *s* one *d*. *Educ:* Royal Belfast Academical Institution; QUB (BSc 1959; PhD 1962); Wadham Coll., Oxford (MA 1964; DSc 1986; Hon. Fellow, 2002). Oxford University: Weir Jun. Fellow, UC, 1964–65; Deptl Demonstrator, 1965–67, Lectr, 1967–90, in Inorganic Chemistry; Reader in Bioinorganic Chemistry, 1990–92; Sen. Proctor, 1976–77. Vis. appts, Harvard, Univ. of Sydney, Univ. of California, 1970–82; Vis. Prof., Harvard Med. Sch., 1996–2002; Pacific Coast Lects, 1981; Robinson Lectr, RSC, 1994. Chm., Davy Faraday Cttee, 1996–98; Mem. Council, Royal Instn, 1995–98. Hon. DSc QUB, 1996. Interdisciplinary Award, RSC, 1987; Chemistry and Electrochemistry of Transition Metals Award, RSC, 1990; Mullard Award, Royal Soc., 1993; Breyer Medal, RACI, 1994. *Publications:* Physical Methods in Advanced Inorganic Chemistry (with P. Day), 1968; papers in professional jls. *Recreations:* gardening, music. *Address:* The Queen's College, Oxford OX1 4AW. *T:* (01865) 279120; *e-mail:* allen.hill@queens.ox.ac.uk.

HILL, His Honour (Ian) Starforth; QC 1969; a Circuit Judge, 1974–94; Resident Judge, Winchester Combined Court Centre, 1992–94; *b* 30 Sept. 1921; *s* of late Harold Victor John Hill; *m* 1st, 1950, Bridget Mary Footner; one *s* two *d*; 2nd, 1982, Greta Grimshaw; 3rd, 1986, Wendy Elizabeth Stavert. *Educ:* Shrewsbury Sch.; Brasenose Coll., Oxford (MA). 11th Sikh Regt, Indian Army, 1940–45, India, Africa, Italy (despatches). Called to Bar, Gray's Inn, 1949; Dep. Chm., Isle of Wight QS, 1968–71; Western Circuit; a Recorder of the Crown Court, 1972–74. Mem., Parole Bd, 1983–84. *Address:* Amberley House, Haig Road, Alresford, Hants SO24 9LX. *T:* (01962) 732131.

See also G. S. Hill.

HILL, Sir James Frederick, 4th Bt *cr* 1917; OBE 2000; DL; Chairman, Specialist Schools and Academies Trust, since 2007 (Member of Council, 2003–07); *b* 5 Dec. 1943; *s* of Sir James Hill, 3rd Bt and Marjory, *d* of late Frank Croft; *S* father, 1976; *m* 1966, Sandra Elizabeth, *o d* of J. C. Ingram; one *s* three *d*. Dir, Yorkshire Bldg Soc., 1972–96. Chairman: British Wool Fedn, 1987–90; Sir James Hill (Wool) Ltd, 1991–. DL West Yorks, 1994. DUniv Bradford, 1997. *Heir: s* James Laurence Ingram Hill [*b* 22 Sept. 1973; *m* 2003, Kate Elizabeth, *d* of T. Horsfield, Silkstone, Yorks]. *Address:* Roseville, Moor Lane, Menston, Ilkley, West Yorks LS29 6AP. *T:* (01943) 874624. *Clubs:* Royal Automobile; Bradford (Yorks).

HILL, James Michael; QC 2006; a Recorder, since 2002; *b* 5 Oct. 1960; *s* of Michael Hill and late Doreen Hill; *m* 1986, Carolyne Dent; two *d*. *Educ:* Durham Johnston Sch.; Manchester Univ. (LLB Hons 1982). Called to the Bar, Inner Temple, 1984; N Eastern Circuit; in practice, specialising in criminal law. *Recreations:* golf, Newcastle United FC. *Address:* Fountain Chambers, Cleveland Business Centre, 1 Watson Street, Middlesbrough TS1 2RQ. *T:* (01642) 804040, *Fax:* (01642) 804060; *e-mail:* amallett@fountainchambers.co.uk. *Club:* Wynyard Golf.

HILL, James William Thomas, (Jimmy), OBE 1995; Chairman, Jimmy Hill & Co., 1972–2008; Presenter, Jimmy Hill's Sunday Supplement, Sky Sports, 2001–07; *m* 1st, 1950, Gloria Mary (marr. diss. 1961); two *s* one *d*; 2nd, 1962, Heather Christine (marr. diss. 1982); one *s* one *d*; 3rd, 1991, Bryony Ruth Jarvis. *Educ:* Henry Thornton School, Clapham. Player, Brentford FC, 1949–52, Fulham FC, 1952–61; Gen. Manager, Coventry City FC, 1961–67, Managing Director, 1975–83, Chm., 1980–83; Chm., Fulham Football Club (1987) Ltd, 1987–97. London Weekend Television: Head of Sport, 1967–72; Controller of Press, Promotion and Publicity, 1971–72; Deputy Controller, Programmes, 1972–73; Soccer analyst, BBC, 1973–98; Presenter, The Last Word, Sky Sports, 1998–2001. Mem., Sports Council, 1971–76. Hon. Chm., The Professional Footballers Assoc., 1957–61. *Publications:* Striking for Soccer, 1961; Improve your Soccer, 1964; Football Crazy, 1985; The Jimmy Hill Story (autobiog.), 1998. *Recreations:* golf, riding, tennis, bridge. *Address:* Goldbridge House, Langton Lane, Hurstpierpoint, West Sussex BN6 9HA. *Club:* All England Lawn Tennis and Croquet.

HILL, Jeremy; *see* Hill, P. J. O.

HILL, Jimmy; *see* Hill, J. W. T.

HILL, John; *b* 28 April 1922; *s* of William Hallett Hill and Emily Hill (*née* Massey); *m* 1952, Hilda Mary Barratt (*d* 2007); one *s.* *Educ:* Merchant Taylors' Sch., Crosby; Liverpool Univ. (BCom); Inst. of Public Finance and Accountancy, 1954. City Treasurer of Liverpool, 1974–82. Mem., Merseyside Residuary Body, 1985–88. Hon. Sen. Res. Fellow, Inst. of Local Govt Studies, Birmingham Univ., 1982–93. *Recreation:* music. *Address:* 325 Northway, Lydiate, Merseyside L31 0BW. *T:* (0151) 526 3699.

HILL, Sir John Alfred Rowley, 11th Bt *cr* 1779, of Brook Hall, Londonderry; *b* 29 Feb. 1940; *s* of Sir George Alfred Rowley Hill, 9th Bt and his 2nd wife, Jessie Anne (*née* Roberts; *d* 1995); *S* half-brother, 1992, but his name does not appear on the Official Roll of the Baronetage; *m* 1966, Diana Anne Walker (marr. diss. 1981); one adopted *s* one adopted *d.* *Heir: kinsman* Allan Claude Hill [*b* 10 Feb. 1936; *m* 1970, Rachel St Just (marr. diss. 1978); one *s* one *d*]. *Address:* 5 Wherry Close, March, Cambs PE15 9BX.

HILL, John Cameron, TD 1959; FRICS; Member, Lands Tribunal, 1987–99; *b* 8 April 1927; *s* of Raymond Cameron Hill and Margaret (*née* Chadwick); *m* 1954, Jane Edna Austin; one *s* one *d.* *Educ:* Trinity Coll., Oxford; College of Estate Management, London Univ. (BSc EstMan). Hillier Parker May & Rowden, 1953–88, Partner, 1962–88. Served TA (Major), 1949–73; Metropolitan Special Constabulary (Comdt), 1973–86. Liveryman, Farriers' Co. *Publications:* (jtly) Valuations: Principles into Practice, 1980, 4th edn 1993; (jtly) Handbook of Rent Review, 1981, rev. edns to 1988. *Recreations:* shooting, DIY. *Address:* Hastoe House, Hastoe, Tring, Herts HP23 6LS. *T:* (01442) 822084. *Club:* Honourable Artillery Company.

HILL, John Lawrence; Chairman, Britannia Building Society, 1990–94; Chief Executive, Loss Prevention Council, 1986–96; *b* 21 July 1934; *s* of late Sidney Hill and Hilda Wardle Hill; *m* 1960, Elizabeth Godfrey; one *s* three *d.* *Educ:* Abbotsholme Sch.; Sidney Sussex Coll., Cambridge (MA). FIMechE. National Service, Royal Corps of Signals, 1953–55. Royal Dutch Shell Group, 1959–67; PA Consulting Group, 1967–86; Director: Britannia Building Soc., 1984–94; Britannia Life, 1989–94. Director: Loss Prevention Certification Bd, 1986–96; Nat. Approval Council for Security Systems, 1990–96. Governor, Inst. of Risk Management, 1987–93. *Recreations:* golf, bridge, music, greyhound rescue. *Address:* 23 Harvey Road, Guildford, Surrey GU1 3LU. *T:* (01483) 566413. *Clubs:* Hawks (Cambridge); Royal & Ancient Golf, Worplesdon Golf.

HILL, Rear-Adm. John Richard; naval historian and analyst; *b* 25 March 1929; *s* of Stanley Hill and May Hill (*née* Henshaw); *m* 1956, Patricia Anne Sales; one *s* two *d.* *Educ:* Royal Naval College, Dartmouth. China Station as midshipman, 1946–47; Sub-Lieut's Courses, 1948–49; Lieut, HM Ships: Gambia, 1950; Chevron, 1950–52; Tintagel Castle, 1952–54; Dryad (Navigation Specialist), 1954; Cardigan Bay, 1954–56; Albion, 1956–58; Roebuck, 1958–59; Lt-Comdr, Pembroke Dock, 1959–60; HMS Duchess, 1960–62; Comdr, MoD, 1963–65 and 1967–69; IDC 1965–67; HMS Dryad, 1969–71; Captain, MoD, 1973–75; Defence and Naval Attaché, The Hague, 1975–77; Cdre, MoD, 1977–80; Rear-Adm. 1981; Flag Officer, Admiralty Interview Bd, 1981–83. Editor, 1983–2002, Reviews Editor, 2002–, The Naval Review. Under-Treas., Middle Temple, 1984–94 (Hon. Bencher, 1994); Sec., Council of Inns of Court, 1987–93. Member: Council, Greenwich Forum, 1983–; Bd of War Studies, London Univ., 1986–94; Council, Foundn for Internat. Security, 1987–; Council, Navy Records Soc., 1993–2001 (Vice Pres., 1997–2001); Council, Soc. for Nautical Res., 1993–99 (Chm., 1994–99). Trustee, Royal Naval Mus., Portsmouth, 1994–99 (Vice Pres., 2002). Defence Fellow, University of London King's College, 1972. *Publications:* The Royal Navy Today and Tomorrow, 1981; Anti-Submarine Warfare, 1984; British Sea Power in the 1980s, 1985; Maritime Strategy for Medium Powers, 1986; Air Defence at Sea, 1988; Arms Control at Sea, 1988; (Gen. Ed.) Oxford Illustrated History of the Royal Navy, 1995; The Prizes of War, 1998; War at Sea in the Ironclad Age, 2000; Lewin of Greenwich, 2000; Maritime Britain, 2005; articles in Survival, Navy International, Brassey's Annual, NATO's 15 Nations, Naval Review, Naval Forces, DNB and Oxford DNB. *Recreations:* bridge, travel, gardening. *Address:* Cornhill House, The Hangers, Bishop's Waltham, Southampton SO32 1EF.

HILL, Jonathan Hopkin, CBE 1995; Founding Director, Quiller Consultants, since 1998; *b* 24 July 1960; *s* of Rowland Louis Hill and Paddy Marguerite (*née* Henwood); *m* 1988, Alexandra Jane Nettelfield; one *s* two *d.* *Educ:* Highgate Sch.; Trinity Coll., Cambridge (MA). RIT & Northern, 1983; Hamish Hamilton, 1984–85; Conservative Research Dept, 1985–86; Special Advr to Rt Hon. Kenneth Clarke at Dept of Employment, DTI and DoH, 1986–89; Lowe Bell Communications, 1989–91; No 10 Policy Unit, 1991–92; Political Sec. to Prime Minister, 1992–94; Sen. Consultant, Bell Pottinger Consultants, 1994–98. Trustee, Nat. Literacy Trust, 1995–; Mem. Adv. Bd, Reform, 2004–. Governor: Highgate Sch., 1995–; Hanford Sch., 2004–. *Publication:* (with Baroness Hogg) Too Close to Call, 1995. *Recreations:* reading, gardening, walking on Exmoor. *Address:* (office) 11–12 Buckingham Gate, SW1E 6LB.

HILL, Rt Hon. Keith; *see* Hill, Rt Hon. T. K.

HILL, Len; *see* Hill, R. K. L.

HILL, Leslie Francis; Chairman: HartHill Partnership Ltd, since 2004; British Music Rights Ltd, 2005–07; ITV, 1994–2002 (Director, 1987–2002); Director, Carlton Communications PLC, 1994–2004; *b* 2 Sept. 1936; *s* of late Elizabeth May and Francis Alfred Hill; *m* 1972, Christine Susan (*née* Bush); two *s.* *Educ:* Cotham Grammar School. FCA. Qualified as Chartered Accountant; with Ware, Ward (now Ernst & Young), 1952–62, Peat, Marwick, Mitchell, 1962–65; IPC Group, 1965–70, finally Finance Director, Music for Pleasure, continuing as such with EMI Group to 1971; EMI Group: Exec. Dir, Rest of World Div., 1972–73; Man. Dir, EMI NZ, 1973–74; Asst Dir, Group Music, 1975–76; Managing Director: EMI Records (UK), 1976–78; EMI Music, Europe, 1979–80; Jt Man. Dir, HAT Group plc, 1980–86; Dir, ITN, 1987–95; Man. Dir, 1987–91, Chm. and Chief Exec., 1991–95, Central Independent Television. *Recreations:* listening to music, reading, fitness, watching cricket.

HILL, Prof. Leslie James, PhD; FBA 2003; Professor of French Studies, University of Warwick, since 1998. *Educ:* Gonville and Caius Coll., Cambridge (BA (Mod. Langs) 1972; MA 1976; PhD (French) 1976). University of Cambridge: Res. Fellow in French, Selwyn Coll., 1974–76; Lectr in French and Dir of Studies in Mod. Langs, Clare Coll., 1976–79; University of Warwick: Lectr in French Studies, 1979–93; Sen. Lectr, 1993–96; Reader, 1996–98. *Publications:* Beckett's Fiction: in different words, 1990; Marguerite Duras: apocalyptic desires, 1993; Blanchot: extreme contemporary, 1997; Bataille, Klossowski, Blanchot: writing at the limit, 2001; The Cambridge Introduction to Jacques Derrida, 2007. *Recreations:* photography, organic vegetable gardening. *Address:* Department of French Studies, University of Warwick, Coventry CV4 7AL; *e-mail:* leslie.hill@warwick.ac.uk.

HILL, Martin Henry Paul; HM Diplomatic Service; Counsellor (Economic, Science and Innovation), Ottawa, since 2006; *b* 17 May 1961; *s* of John and Jacqueline Hill; *m* 1985 Kim Cherie Lydyard; three *d.* *Educ:* Pembroke Coll., Cambridge (BA Langs and Econs MA). Food Standards Div., MAFF, 1983–84; Parly Clerk to Lord Privy Seal, 1985–86 Ministry of Agriculture, Fisheries and Food: Financial Mgt Team, 1986; EC Div., 1987 Sugar, Oils and Fats Div., 1988; Principal Private Sec. to Food Safety Minister, 1989–90 Trade Policy and Tropical Foods Div., 1990–92; First Sec., Agric., Fisheries and Food Bonn, 1993–96; joined HM Diplomatic Service, 1996; SE Asian Dept, FCO, 1996–98 Dep. High Comr, Colombo, 1998–2001; Commercial Counsellor, Bangkok, 2002–05 *Recreations:* squash, travel, reading, diving, music. *Address:* c/o Foreign and Commonwealth Office, King Charles Street, SW1A 2AH.

HILL, Martyn Geoffrey; tenor singer; *b* 14 Sept. 1944; *s* of Norman S. L. Hill and Gwendoline A. M. Hill (*née* Andrews); three *s* one *d*; *m* 2004, Julie Ann Moffat. *Educ:* Sir Joseph Williamson's Mathematical School, Rochester, Kent; King's College, Cambridge Royal College of Music (ARCM); vocal studies with Audrey Langford. On teaching staff Trinity Coll. of Music, 1997–. Concert, oratorio, recital and operatic appearances throughout the world with major orchestras, conductors and choirs; numerous radio, TV and gramophone recordings. *Address:* c/o Owen/White Management, Top Floor, 59 Lansdowne Place, Hove, E Sussex BN3 1FL.

HILL, Max Benjamin Rowland; QC 2008; a Recorder, since 2004; *b* Hatfield, 10 Jan. 1964; *s* of Thomas Rowland Hill and Shirley Ann Hill; *m* 1993, Heather Faith Coombs; two *d.* *Educ:* St Peter's Coll., Oxford (BA Hons Juris. 1986). Called to the Bar, Middle Temple, 1987; in practice as barrister specialising in crime. Chm., Bd of Trustees, Scene and Heard, 2005–. FRSA. *Publication:* (contributing ed.) Practitioner's Guide to Terrorist Trials, 2007. *Recreations:* theatre, tennis, travel. *Address:* 18 Red Lion Court, EC4A 3EB. *T:* (020) 7520 6000, *Fax:* (020) 7520 6248; *e-mail:* max.hill@18rlc.co.uk.

HILL, Rt Rev. Michael Arthur; *see* Bristol, Bishop of.

HILL, Michael Thomas; HM Diplomatic Service; Administrator, Ascension Island, since 2005; *b* 2 Jan. 1945; *s* of late Roland Hill and Anne Hill (*née* McIlwraith); *m* 1977, Elizabeth Louise, *d* of Derrick Charles Carden, CMG; three *s* one *d.* *Educ:* Bathgate Acad. Joined Foreign Office, 1963; served UKMIS NY, Vientiane, Kaduna, Sana'a; Dep. Hd of Mission, Ulan Bator, 1978–81; Consul, Port of Spain, 1981–85; FCO, 1985–88; Asst to Dep. Governor, Gibraltar, 1988–93; First Sec. and Hd of Aid Sect., Nairobi, 1993–96; FCO 1996–2000; High Comr, Vanuatu, 2000–05. *Recreations:* golf, gardening, walking. *Address:* c/o Foreign and Commonwealth Office, King Charles Street, SW1A 2AH.

HILL, Michael William; President, Fédération Internationale d'Information et de Documentation, 1985–90; *b* 1928; *o s* of late Geoffrey William Hill, Ross on Wye and Torquay; *m* 1st, 1957, Elma Jack Forrest (*d* 1967); one *s* one *d*; 2nd, 1969, Barbara Joy Youngman. *Educ:* King Henry VIII Sch., Coventry; Nottingham High Sch.; Lincoln Coll., Oxford (MA, MSc). MRIC 1953; CChem; FCLIP (FIInfSc 1982). Research Chemist, Laporte Chemicals Ltd, 1953–56; Morgan Crucible Group: Laboratory Head, 1956; Asst Process Control Manager, 1958; Group Technical Editor, 1963; Asst Keeper, British Museum, 1964; Dep. Librarian, Patent Office Library, 1965; Keeper, Nat. Ref. Library of Science and Invention, BM, 1968–73; British Library: Dir, Science Ref. Library, 1973–86; Associate Dir, Sci. Technology and Industry, 1986–88. Member: Exec. Cttee, Nat. Central Library, 1971–74; EEC/CIDST Working Parties on Patent documentation, 1973–80, and on Information for Industry, 1976–80; Board, UK Chemical Inf. Service, 1974–77; Adv. Cttee for Scottish Science Reference Library, 1983–87; Chairman: Circle of State Librarians, 1977–79; Council, Aslib, 1979–81; Vice Pres., IATUL, 1976–81; Founder, Western European Round Table on Information and Documentation, subseq. European Council of Information Assocs, 1980. Series Editor (with I. McIlwaine), Guides to Information Sources. *Publications:* Patent Documentation (with Wittmann and Schiffels), 1979; Michael Hill on Science, Technology and Information (ed by P. Ward), 1988; National Information Policies and Strategies, 1994; The Impact of Information on Society, 1998, 2nd edn 2005; papers on librarianship, documentation and information science in jls and conf. proceedings. *Address:* 137 Burdon Lane, Cheam, Surrey SM2 7DB. *T:* (020) 8642 2418. *Club:* Oxford and Cambridge.

HILL, Ven. Peter; Archdeacon of Nottingham, since 2007; *b* Swansea, 4 Feb. 1950; *s* of John and Megan Hill; *m* 1971, Ellen Purvis; one *s* one *d.* *Educ:* UMIST (BSc 1971); Manchester Univ. (PGCE 1973); Wycliffe Hall, Oxford; Nottingham Univ. (MTh 1990). Teacher, Manchester and Cheshire, 1972–78; Dep. Head Teacher, The Beaches Primary Sch., Sale Moor, 1978–81; ordained deacon, 1983, priest, 1984; Asst Curate, St James, Porchester, 1983–86; Vicar, All Saints, Huthwaite, 1986–95; Priest-in-charge, St Wilfred's, Calverton, 1995–2004; Area Dean, Southwell, 1997–2001; Chair, Dio. Bd of Educn, 2001–04; Chief Exec., Dio. of Southwell and Nottingham, 2004–07. Hon. Canon, Southwell Minster, 2001–. Mem., Gen. Synod of C of E, 1993–2004. *Address:* (office) Dunham House, 8 Westgate, Southwell, Notts NG25 0JL. *T:* (01636) 817206; *e-mail:* archdeacon-nottm@southwell.anglican.org; 15 Adams Row, Southwell, Notts NG25 0FF. *T:* (01636) 816445.

HILL, (Peter) Jeremy (Oldham); HM Diplomatic Service, 1982–2007; *b* 17 April 1954; *m* 1981, Katharine Hearn; one *s* one *d.* Joined FCO as Asst Legal Advr, 1982; First Sec. (Legal Advr), Bonn, 1987–90; on loan as Legal Counsellor, Law Officers' Dept, 1991–95; Legal Counsellor, UK Rep., Brussels, 1995–98; Hd, Southern European Dept, FCO, 1999–2001; Ambassador to: Lithuania, 2001–03; Bulgaria, 2004–07.

HILL, Peter Whitehead; Editor, Daily Express, since 2003; *b* 6 April 1945; *s* of Becket and Edith Hill; *m* 1st, 1984, Vera Marshall (marr. diss. 1998); one *d*; 2nd, 2004, Marjorie Francis; one *s.* *Educ:* Hulme Grammar Sch., Oldham; Manchester Univ. Reporter, Colne Valley Guardian, 1961–62; sub-editor: Huddersfield Examr, 1962–63; Manchester Evening News, 1963–65; leader writer, Oldham Evening Chronicle, 1965–67; sub-ed., Daily Telegraph, 1967–74; sub-ed., Daily Mirror, 1974–78; Chief Sub-Ed., Sunday People, 1970–80; Chief Sub-Ed., Night Ed., Associate Ed., and Dep. Ed., 1978–98, Ed., 1998–2003, Daily Star. Mem., Press Complaints Commn, 2003–. *Recreations:* sailing, tennis, ski-ing, conversation, making mischief. *Address:* Daily Express, 10 Lower Thames Street, EC3R 6EN. *T:* (0871) 520 7476. *Clubs:* Harbour; Hollowshore Sailing (Faversham).

HILL, (Robert) Charles; QC (NI) 1974; Member, Standing Advisory Commission on Human Rights under Northern Ireland Constitution Act 1973, 1991–96 (Chairman, 1992–95); *b* 22 March 1936; *s* of Benjamin Morrison Hill and Mary A. Hill (*née* Roche); *m* 1961, Kathleen Allen; three *s* one *d.* *Educ:* St Malachy's Coll., Belfast; Queen's Univ. Belfast (LLB); Trinity Coll., Dublin (MA). Called to the Bar: Inn of Court, NI, 1959, Bencher, 1988; Gray's Inn, 1971; King's Inns, Dublin, 1986; Sen. Counsel, Ireland, 1987. Official Referee under Finance Acts, 1976; Dep. County Court Judge, 1979–80. Chairman: Statutory Body, Pharmaceutical Soc. of NI, 1977–92; Poison Bd of NI, 1982–92. *Recreations:* history of art, forestry, shooting. *Address:* The Bar Library, Royal

Courts of Justice, Chichester Street, Belfast BT1 3JP. *T:* (028) 9024 1523. *Club:* Kildare Street and University (Dublin).

HILL, Sir Robert (Charles Finch), KBE 1991; FREng; reliability consultant; President, Institute of Marine Engineers, 1995–96; *b* 1 May 1937; *s* of late Frances Margaret Hill (*née* Lumsden) and Ronald Finch Hill; *m* 1971, Deborah Mary (*née* Windle); one *s* one *d. Educ:* Nautical Coll., Pangbourne; RNEC Manadon. BSc(Eng); CEng, FREng (FEng 1992). HMS Thermopylae, 1964–65; HMS Repulse, 1967–71; MoD (PE), 1971–74; RNEC Manadon, 1975–77; HMS Cleopatra, 1977–78; Nuclear Power Manager, Chatham, 1979–80; MoD (PE), 1980–84; RCDS 1985; HMS Raleigh in Comd, 1986–87; CSO (Engrg) to C-in-C Fleet, 1987–89; Chief Abovewater Systems Exec., 1989–91; Dep. Controller of the Navy (Vice-Adm.), 1989–93; Dir Gen. Submarines, 1991–93; retd. Independent Director: British Energy plc, 1999–2003; SEA (Group) Ltd, 1999–. Trustee, Th. Royal, Bath, 2003–. Mem. Council, Univ. of Bath, 2000–06. Hon. FIMarEST 2002. Hon. DTech Plymouth, 1995; Hon. DEng Bath, 2005. *Recreations:* rhythm guitar, theatre, sailing. *Club:* Royal Over-Seas League.

HILL, Hon. Robert Murray; Permanent Representative of Australia to the United Nations (with rank of Ambassador), since 2006; *b* 25 Sept. 1946; *s* of C. M. Hill; *m* 1969, Diana Jacka; two *s* two *d. Educ:* Scotch Coll., Mitcham, SA; Univ. of Adelaide (LLB 1968; BA 1982); Univ. of London (LLM 1970). In practice as barrister and solicitor, SA, 1970–. Senator (L) S Australia, 1981–2006; Fed. Shadow Minister for Foreign Affairs, 1989–93, for Defence, 1993, for Public Admin, 1993–94, for Educn, Sci. and Technol., 1994–96; Leader of the Opposition in Senate, 1993–96; Leader of the Govt in Senate, 1996–2006; Minister for the Envmt, 1996–98, for the Envmt and Heritage, 1998–2001, for Defence, 2001–06. Liberal Party of Australia: Campaign Chm., 1975–77; Chm., Constitutional Cttee, 1977–81; Vice-Pres., 1977–79, Pres., 1985–87, SA Div.; Mem., Fed. Exec., 1985–87 and 1990–2006. *Address:* Australian Mission to the United Nations, 33rd Floor, 150 East 42nd Street, New York, NY 10017, USA.

HILL, Robert Williamson, (Robin), CEng, FIGasE; Regional Chairman, British Gas, North Western, 1990–93; *b* 8 Dec. 1936; *s* of William Hill and Mary Duncanson (*née* Williamson); *m* 1961, Janette Margaret (*née* Bald); one *s* two *d. Educ:* Dumbarton Acad.; Strathclyde Univ. (BSc 1st Cl. Hons). CEng, FIGEM (FIGasE 1958). Scottish Gas Board: various appts, 1958–70; Area Service Manager, subseq. Regional Service Manager, 1970–73; British Gas Corporation: Service Ops Manager, 1973–75; Asst Service Dir, 1975–76; Service Dir, 1977–82; Regl Chm., Scotland, 1982–89. Local Govt Staff Comr, 1994–97; Local Govt Property Comr, 1995–97. Pres., Assoc. for Sci. Educn, Scotland, 1985–86. Pres., IGasE, 1989–90 (Vice-Pres., 1987–89). Mem. Court, Heriot-Watt Univ., 1987–93. Hon. Mem., CGLI, 1981. *Recreation:* golf. *Address:* 5 Grange View, Linlithgow, W Lothian EH49 7HY. *T:* (01506) 671173.

HILL, Rodney, FRS 1961; PhD; ScD; Professor of Mechanics of Solids, University of Cambridge, 1972–79 (Reader, 1969–72); Fellow, Gonville and Caius College, since 1972; *b* 11 June 1921; *o s* of Harold Harrison Hill, Leeds; *m* 1946, Jeanne Kathlyn (*d* 2003), *yr d* of C. P. Wickens, Gidea Park; one *d. Educ:* Leeds Grammar Sch.; Pembroke Coll., Cambridge. MA, PhD, ScD Cambridge. Armament Research Dept, 1943–46; Cavendish Laboratory, Cambridge, 1946–48; British Iron and Steel Research Assoc., 1948–50; University of Bristol: Research Fellow, 1950–53, Reader, 1953; Univ. of Nottingham: Prof. of Applied Mathematics, 1953–62; Professorial Research Fellow, 1962–63; Berkeley Bye-Fellow, Gonville and Caius Coll., Cambridge, 1963–69. Hon. DSc: Manchester, 1976; Bath, 1978. Von Karman Medal, ASCE, 1978; Gold Medal and Internat. Modesto Panetti Prize, Accademia delle Scienze di Torino, 1988; Royal Medal, Royal Soc., 1993. Editor, Jl of Mechanics and Physics of Solids, 1952–68. *Publications:* Mathematical Theory of Plasticity, 1950; Principles of Dynamics, 1964; papers on mechanics of solid continua, esp. metals.

HILL, Rev. Roger Anthony John; Bishop's Missioner, Diocese of Manchester, since 2007; Chaplain to the Queen, since 2001; *b* 23 March 1945; *s* of Arthur and Gladys Hill; *m* 1972, Joanna Reading; three *s. Educ:* Univ. of Liverpool; Linacre Coll., Oxford (BA 1969; MA); Ripon Hall, Oxford. Ordained deacon, 1970, priest, 1971; Curate: St Peter, St Helier, Southwark, 1970–74; Dawley Parva, 1974–76; Team Vicar, 1976–81, Rector, 1981–88, Central Telford; Rector: Newark, 1988–2002; St Ann, Manchester, 2002–07. RD Newark, 1990–95; Area Dean, Hulme, 2005–07. Hon. Canon: Southwell Minster, 1998–2002; Manchester Cathedral, 2002–. *Recreations:* walking, travel. *Address:* Bishopscourt, Bury New Road, Manchester M7 4LE. *T:* (0161) 792 2096.

HILL, Roy Kenneth Leonard, (Len), CBE 1983; JP; Chairman, South West Water Authority, 1977–87; *b* 28 May 1924; *m* 1944, Barbara May Kendall. Mem., ASLEF; Plymouth City Councillor, 1961–68, 1970–74 (formerly Dep. Lord Mayor); County Councillor, Devon, 1974 (formerly Leader of Labour Gp). Chm., Water Authorities Assoc., 1983–86. Mem., SW Econ. Planning Council. Chm. Council, Coll. of St Mark and St John, Plymouth; Governor, Plymouth Polytechnic; Mem. Bd of Visitors, Dartmoor Prison. JP Plymouth, 1968. *Address:* 5 Revell Park Road, Plympton, Plymouth PL7 4EH. *T:* (01752) 339125.

HILL, Shaun Donovan; consultant and writer; chef and restaurateur; *b* 11 April 1947; *s* of George Herbert Hill and Molly Hill; *m* 1966, Anja Toivonen; one *s* two *d. Educ:* London Oratory; St Marylebone Grammar Sch. Cook: Carrier's Restaurant, Islington, 1967–71; Gay Hussar, 1971–73; Intercontinental Hotel, London, 1973–75; Head Chef: Montcalm Hotel, London, 1976–77; Capital Hotel, London, 1978; Lygon Arms, Broadway, Worcs, 1979–81; Gidleigh Park, Chagford, 1985–94; Head Chef, Merchant House, Ludlow, 1994–2005. *Publications:* Gidleigh Park Cookery Book, 1990; Shaun Hill's Cookery Book, 1994; (with John Wilkins) Archestratus: the life of luxury, 1994; Shaun Hill's Cooking at the Merchant House, 2000; How To Cook Better, 2004; (with J. Wilkins) Food in Ancient Cultures, 2005; (jtly) Cook, 2005; (jtly) The Cook's Book, 2005. *Recreations:* wine, travel. *Address:* 24 Droitwich Road, Worcester WR3 7LH; *e-mail:* shaunhill@merchanthouse.co.uk.

HILL, Starforth; *see* Hill, Ian S.

HILL, Stephen Guy; Senior Adviser, 3i Quoted Private Equity, since 2006; *b* 19 July 1960; *s* of Michael Lawrence Hill and Joan Florence Hill (*née* Luce). *Educ:* King Edward VII Sch., Lytham; St John's Coll., Cambridge (MA 1st Cl. Hons Law 1982); Harvard Business Sch. (PMD 1991). Consultant, Boston Consulting Gp, 1982–85; Exec. Asst to Chm., Guinness plc, 1985–87; Dir of Strategy, Pearson plc, 1987–92; Managing Director: Watford Observer Newspapers, 1992–93; Oxford & County Newspapers Ltd, 1993–95; Chief Exec., Westminster Press Ltd, 1995–96; Man. Dir, Financial Times Newspaper, 1996–99; Chief Executive: Financial Times Gp Ltd, 1998–2002; Sporting Exchange Ltd (Betfair), 2003–05. Chairman: Interactive Data Corp. (formerly Data Broadcasting Inc.), 2000–02; S. G. Hill Investments Ltd; Mem., Mgt Bd, Pearson plc, 1998–2002; Director: Marketwatch.com Inc., 2000–02; Royal & Sun Alliance Gp plc, 2000–04; RAW Communications Ltd, 2000–02; Psion plc, 2003–06. Mem. Bd, Channel 4, 2006–. Mem. Adv. Bd, Judge Business Sch., Cambridge Univ., 2007–. Mem. Council, Whitechapel Art Gall., 2000–03. Trustee, RNID. *Recreations:* triathlon, gardening, travel. *Club:* Royal Automobile.

HILL, Prof. Stephen Roderick, PhD; Professor of University of London, since 1991; Principal, Royal Holloway, University of London, since 2002; *b* 15 March 1946; *s* of Alan Hill, CBE and Enid Hill (*née* Malin); *m* 1996, Siobahn Rosser; one *s* one *d. Educ:* University College Sch.; Balliol Coll., Oxford (BA Modern Hist.); London Sch. of Econs (MSc Sociol.; PhD 1973). Lectr in Sociol., Bedford Coll., London, 1968–70; London School of Economics: Lectr in Industrial Relns, 1971–74; Lectr, 1974–82, Reader, 1982–91, in Sociol.; Professor: of Sociol., 1991–2001; of Mgt, 2001–02; Pro-Dir, 1996–2001; Dep. Dir, 2001–02. Ed., British Jl Sociol., 1995–2002. Mem., Corporate Social Responsibility Steering Gp, DTI, 2003–04. Board Member: Surrey Bridges, 2002–; Surrey Economic Partnership, 2002–; Chair, Southern Univs Mgt Services, 2003–. *Publications:* The Dockers, 1976; Competition and Control at Work, 1981; with N. Abercrombie and B. S. Turner: The Dominant Ideology Thesis, 1980; The Penguin Dictionary of Sociology, 1984, 4th edn 2000; Sovereign Individuals of Capitalism, 1986; (ed) Dominant Ideologies, 1990; (with M. White, C. Mills and D. Smeaton) Managing to Change?, 2004. *Recreation:* fell-walking. *Address:* Royal Holloway, University of London, Egham, Surrey TW20 0EX. *T:* (01784) 443033; *e-mail:* stephen.hill@rhul.ac.uk.

HILL, Stephen Russell, CB 2004; OBE 1982; Managing Director, Steve Hill Consultancy Ltd, since 2004; Chief Executive, Defence Aviation Repair Agency, 1999–2003; *b* 27 March 1942; *s* of late Henry Rowland Hill and Kathleen Bertha Hill; *m* 1964, Muriel Chisholm; one *s* one *d. Educ:* St Philip's Grammar Sch., Birmingham; Hendon CAT; BA Open Univ. 1980; Dip. Accounting and Finance 1988. CEng 1975; FIMechE 1985; FRAeS 1986. Marine Engr, BP Tanker Co., 1958–65; Civil Engrg projects, BP Refinery, Grangemouth, 1965–66; RAF, 1966–91: appts incl. Chief Engr, RAF Coningsby, 1981–84; Air Cdre, Dir of Support Mgt, 1989–91; Business Develt, BAe, 1991–95; Projects and Technical Dir, Serco Defence, 1995–96; Chief Exec., Naval Aircraft Repair Orgn, 1996–99. FCMI (FIMgt 1987). *Recreation:* hill walking.

HILL, Dr Stuart John; Managing Director, Delta Rail Group Ltd, 2006; *b* 23 March 1950; *s* of late Maurice William Hill and of Dorothy Alice Hill (*née* Raynor); *m* 1st, 1972 (marr. diss. 1991); one *s* one *d*; 2nd, 1994, Frances Irene Susan Entwistle; one step *s. Educ:* Ecclesbourne GS, Duffield, Derbys; Peterhouse, Cambridge (schol.; BA Hons 1st cl. Engrg; Baker Prize; PhD 1975). BR Research Dept, 1975–77; GKN Technology Ltd, 1977–89; Business Develt Exec., GKN Automotive Div., 1989–90; Develt Dir, GKN Powder Metallurgy Div., 1990–91; Dir, Tech. Strategy, BRB, 1991–93; Man. Dir, BR Production Services, 1993–96; Chief Land Registrar and Chief Exec., HM Land Registry, 1996–99; Chief Exec., Housebuilders Fedn, 1999–2000; Managing Director: AEA Technology Envmt, 2000–05; AEA Technology Rail, 2005–06. FRSA 1996. *Publications:* (trans.) F. Schmelz *et al*, Universal Joints and Driveshafts, 1992, 2nd edn 2005; ed and contrib. books and learned jls on driveline components and engrg mgt. *Recreations:* fostering cats, Macintosh computers.

HILL, Sunetra; *see* Gupta, S.

HILL, Susan Elizabeth, (Mrs Stanley Wells); novelist and playwright; *b* 5 Feb. 1942; *d* of late R. H. and Doris Hill; *m* 1975, Prof. Stanley W. Wells, *qv*; two *d* (and one *d* decd). *Educ:* grammar schs in Scarborough and Coventry; King's Coll., Univ. of London. BA Hons English 1963; Fellow, 1978. FRSL 1972. Literary critic, various jls, 1963–; numerous plays for BBC, 1970–; Presenter, Bookshelf, Radio 4, 1986–87. Founder and Publisher, Long Barn Books, 1996; Founder Publisher and Ed., Books and Company, qly mag., 1997–2000. Patron: Family Nurturing Network, 1999–; Prince of Wales Hospice, Pontefract, 2000–. Chm., Chipping Campden Cricket Club, 1999–. *Publications:* The Enclosure, 1961; Do me a Favour, 1963; Gentleman and Ladies, 1969; A Change for the Better, 1969; I'm the King of the Castle, 1970; The Albatross, 1971; Strange Meeting, 1971; The Bird of Night, 1972; A Bit of Singing and Dancing, 1973; In the Springtime of the Year, 1974; The Cold Country and Other Plays for Radio, 1975; (ed) The Distracted Preacher and other stories by Thomas Hardy, 1979; The Magic Apple Tree, 1982; The Woman in Black: a ghost story, 1983 (adapted for stage, 1989); (ed) Ghost Stories, 1983; (ed) People, an anthology, 1983; Through the Kitchen Window, 1984; Through the Garden Gate, 1986; The Lighting of the Lamps, 1987; Lanterns Across the Snow, 1987; Shakespeare Country, 1987; The Spirit of the Cotswolds, 1988; Family (autobiog.), 1989; Air and Angels, 1991; The Mist in the Mirror: a ghost story, 1992; Mrs de Winter, 1993; (ed) Contemporary Women's Short Stories, 1995; (with Rory Stuart) Reflections from a Garden, 1995; Listening to the Orchestra (short stories), 1996; (ed) The Second Penguin Book of Women's Short Stories, 1997; The Service of Clouds, 1998; The Boy Who Taught the Bee-keeper to Read and Other Stories, 2003; The Various Haunts of Men, 2004; The Pure in Heart, 2005; The Risk of Darkness, 2006; The Man in the Picture (novella), 2007; The Vows of Silence, 2008; The Beacon, 2008; *for children:* One Night at a Time, 1984; Mother's Magic, 1986; Can it be True?, 1988; Susie's Shoes, 1989; Stories from Codling Village, 1990; I've Forgotten Edward, 1990; I Won't Go There Again, 1990; (ed) The Walker Book of Ghost Stories, 1990; Pirate Poll, 1991; The Glass Angels, 1991; Beware, Beware!, 1993; King of King's, 1993; The Battle for Gullywith, 2008; *play:* The Ramshackle Company, 1981. *Address:* Longmoor Farm, Ebrington, Chipping Campden, Glos GL55 6NW. *T:* (01386) 593352; *e-mail:* susan@susan-hill.com.

HILL, Rt Hon. (Trevor) Keith; PC 2003; MP (Lab) Streatham, since 1992; *b* 28 July 1943; *s* of late George Ernest Hill and Ena Ida (*née* Dakin); *m* 1972, Lesley Ann Sheppard. *Educ:* Corpus Christi Coll., Oxford (BA, MA); UCW, Aberystwyth (DipEd). Res. Asst in Politics, Univ. of Leicester, 1966–68; Belgian Govt Scholar, Brussels, 1968–69; Lectr in Politics, Univ. of Strathclyde, 1969–73; Res. Officer, Labour Party Internat. Dept, 1974–76; Political Liaison Officer, NUR, subseq. Nat. Union of Rail, Maritime and Tspt Workers, 1976–92. An Asst Govt Whip, 1998–99; Parly Under-Sec. of State, DETR, 1999–2001; Treasurer of HM Household (Dep. Chief Whip), 2001–03; Minister of State (Minister for Housing and Planning), ODPM, 2003–05; PPS to Prime Minister, 2005–07. *Publications:* (contrib.) European Political Parties, 1969; (contrib.) Electoral Behaviour, 1974. *Recreations:* walks, books, films. *Address:* 110 Wavertree Road, Streatham Hill, SW2 3ST. *T:* (020) 8674 0434.

HILL, Prof. William George, OBE 2004; FRS 1985; FRSE 1979; Professor of Animal Genetics, University of Edinburgh, 1983–2002, now Emeritus; *b* 7 Aug. 1940; *s* of late William Hill and Margaret Paterson Hill (*née* Hamilton); *m* 1971, Christine Rosemary Austin; one *s* two *d. Educ:* St Albans School; Wye Coll., Univ. of London (BSc 1961); Univ. of California, Davis (MS 1963); Iowa State Univ.; Univ. of Edinburgh (PhD 1965; DSc 1976). University of Edinburgh: Asst Lectr, 1965–67, Lectr, 1967–74, Reader, 1974–83, in Genetics; Hd, Dept of Genetics, 1989–90; Hd, Inst. of Cell, Animal and Population Biol., 1990–93; Hd, Div. of Biol Scis, 1993–98; Dean and Provost, Faculty of Sci. and Engrg, 1999–2002. Visiting Professor/Research Associate: Univ. of Minnesota, 1966; Iowa State Univ., 1967–78; N Carolina State Univ., 1979, 1985, 1992–2005. Consultant Geneticist: Cotswold Pig Develt Co., 1965–99; British Friesian Cattle Soc.,

1978–88; Holstein Friesian Soc., 1988–98. Chm., Org Cttee, 4th World Congress, 1990, Pres., 5th World Congress, Genetics Applied to Livestock Prodn; Pres., British Soc. Animal Sci., 1999–2000 (Vice-Pres., 1997–99). Chm., Nat. Consultative Cttee, Animal Genetic Resources, 2001–02; Member: Scientific Study Group, Meat and Livestock Commn, 1969–72; Cattle Res. Consultative Cttee, 1985–86; AFRC Animals Res. Grant Bd, 1986–92; Dir's Adv. Gp, AFRC Animal Breeding Res. Orgn, 1983–86; Tech. Cttee, 1992–99 (Chm., 1995–97), Develt Cttee, 1992–98, Animal Data Centre; Inst. Animal Physiology and Genetics Res., 1986–93; Bd Govs, Roslin Inst., 1994–2002; Council, Royal Soc., 1993–94; Commonwealth Scholarship Commn, 1998–2004 (Dep-Chm., 2002–04). Mem. 1996, Chm. 2001, RAE Biol Sci. Panel. Editor: Animal Prodn, 1971–78; Genetics, 1993–94; Livestock Prodn Sci., 1994–95; Genetics Res. (formerly Genetical Res.), 1996–; Proceedings of Royal Soc. B, 2005–08. Hon. DSc N Carolina State, 2003; Dr *hc* Edinburgh, 2005. *Publications:* (ed) Benchmark Papers in Quantitative Genetics, 1984; (ed) Evolution and Animal Breeding, 1989; numerous papers on quantitative and population genetics, biometrics and animal breeding, in sci. jls. *Recreations:* farming, bridge. *Address:* 4 Gordon Terrace, Edinburgh EH16 5QH. *T:* (0131) 667 3680. *Club:* Farmers'.

HILL-NORTON, Vice-Adm. Hon. Sir Nicholas (John), KCB 1991; Chairman, King George's Fund for Sailors, 2003–07; *b* 13 July 1939; *s* of Admiral of the Fleet Baron Hill-Norton, GCB; *m* 1966, Ann Jennifer, *d* of Vice-Adm. D. H. Mason, CB, CVO; two *s* one *d*. *Educ:* Marlborough Coll.; BRNC, Dartmouth; US Naval War Coll., Newport, RI. Royal Navy, 1957–95; commanded: HMS Antelope, 1974–76; Fishery Protection Sqdn, 1978–80; HMS Southampton, 1980–81; HMS Invincible, 1983–85; Flag Officer, Gibraltar, 1987–90; Flag Officer Surface Flotilla and Comdr, Anti-Submarine Warfare Striking Force Atlantic, 1990–92; Dep. Chief of Defence Staff, 1992–95. Defence Adviser: GEC-Marconi, 1995–99; BAE SYSTEMS, 1999–2000; Director: Matra Marconi Space, 1996–99; Marconi N America, 1997–2000; Lear Astronics (USA), 1996–99. Mem., UK Adv. Bd, Tenix Pty (Australia), 2003–07. Chm., British Greyhound Racing Bd, 2000–02. Vice Pres., RUSI, 1999–2003. *Recreations:* greyhound racing, travel, cooking, country sports, tennis, golf, woodland management, being idle. *Clubs:* Farmers', Royal Navy of 1765 and 1785.

HILL-TOUT, Paul Edward; Director, Forestry Commission, since 2003; a Forestry Commissioner, since 2004; *b* 24 Aug. 1957; *s* of Walter Tony Hill-Tout and Evelyn Mary Hill-Tout; *m* 1982, Lin; one *s* five *d*. *Educ:* King's Coll. London (BA Geog.); Christ Church, Oxford (MSc Forestry and Land Mgt). Joined Forestry Commn, 1980; has held various appts across the orgn and GB. *Recreations:* owns and manages a woodland in Devon, hiking, camping, travel, all eras of history. *Address:* Forestry Commission, Great Eastern House, Tenison Road, Cambridge CB1 2DU. *T:* (01223) 346008, *Fax:* (01223) 576732; *e-mail:* lynn.hammans@forestry.gsi.gov.uk.

HILL-TREVOR, family name of **Baron Trevor**.

HILL-WOOD, Sir Samuel Thomas, 4th Bt *cr* 1921, of Moorfield, Glossop, co. Derby; marketing consultant; *b* 24 Aug. 1971; *er s* of Sir David Basil Hill-Wood, 3rd Bt and of Jennifer Anne, *d* of Peter McKenzie-Strang; *S* father, 2002. *Educ:* Wellington Coll.; Kingston Univ. (BA Hons, MA, PG Dip Marketing). Head of Marketing, Arsenal FC, 1996–98; Marketing Director: In2Sport, 1998–2001; Sportacus, 2001–02. *Recreations:* golf, fishing, cricket, football, shooting. *Heir: b* Edward Charles Hill-Wood [*b* 22 April 1974; *m* 2005, Mandy Jane O'Hara; one *s* one *d*]. *Address:* Dacre Farm, Sandpit Lane, Farley Hill, Reading, Berkshire RG7 1XJ; 50 Riverside Court, Nine Elms Lane, SW8 5BY; *e-mail:* shillwood@hotmail.com.

HILLEL, Mira B.; *see* Bar-Hillel.

HILLEN, John Malcolm; His Honour Judge Hillen; a Circuit Judge, since 2005; *b* 13 May 1952; *s* of Clarence Albert and Winifred Hillen; *m* 1985, Monica Lilian Marie Curice; one *s* one *d*. *Educ:* King Edward VI Grammar Sch., Aston; Lincoln Coll., Oxford (MA). Called to the Bar, Middle Temple, 1976; Asst Recorder, 1997–2000; Recorder, 2000–05. *Recreations:* fair-weather gardening, hibernation. *Address:* c/o Blackfriars Crown Court, 1–15 Pocock Street, SE1 0BJ. *T:* (020) 7922 5800.

HILLHOUSE, Prof. Edward William, PhD; FRCP; Professor of Medicine, and Dean, Faculty of Medicine and Health, University of Leeds, since 2002; *b* 16 March 1950; *s* of William and Joan Hillhouse; *m* 1993, Nicola Judith; three *s* three *d*. *Educ:* All Saints Sch., Wimbledon; Rutlish Sch., Merton; St Thomas's Hosp. Med. Sch., Univ. of London (BSc 1st Cl. Hons 1972; PhD 1975; MB BS 1981). FRCP 1995. Res. Fellow, Tufts Univ., Boston, 1986–87; Lectr in Medicine, King's Coll. Hosp., London, 1988–90; Sen. Lectr in Metabolic Medicine, Univ. of Newcastle, 1990–93; Sen. Lectr in Medicine, Univ. of Bristol, 1993–95; Prof. of Medicine, and Dir of Molecular Res. Inst., Univ. of Warwick, 1995–2002. Non-exec. Dir, Leeds Teaching Hosps NHS Trust, 2003. *Publications:* over 150 articles in learned jls. *Recreations:* yoga, tennis, watching Leeds United FC, reading, history, fine wine. *Address:* Faculty of Medicine, University of Leeds, Leeds LS2 9NL; *e-mail:* e.w.hillhouse@leeds.ac.uk.

HILLHOUSE, Sir (Robert) Russell, KCB 1991; FRSE; Permanent Under-Secretary of State, Scottish Office, 1988–98; *b* 23 April 1938; *s* of Robert Hillhouse and Jean Russell; *m* 1966, Alison Janet Fraser; two *d*. *Educ:* Hutchesons' Grammar Sch., Glasgow; Glasgow Univ. (MA). FRSE 1995. Scottish Education Dept, 1962; HM Treasury, 1971; Asst Secretary, Scottish Office, 1974; Scottish Home and Health Dept, 1977; Under Sec. (Principal Finance Officer), Scottish Office, 1980; Under Sec., 1985–87, Sec., 1987–88, Scottish Educn Dept. Director: Bank of Scotland, 1998–2001; Scottish Provident Instn, 1999–2001. Chairman: Hebrides Ensemble, 1999–2003; Upper Deeside Access Trust, 1998–2003. Gov., RSAMD, 2000–08. DUniv Glasgow, 1999; Hon. LLD Aberdeen, 1999; Hon. DLitt Napier, 1999. CCMI (CBIM 1990). FRSA 1992. *Recreations:* making music, enjoying the countryside. *Address:* 12 Russell Place, Edinburgh EH5 3HH. *T:* (0131) 476 0503. *Club:* New (Edinburgh).

HILLIARD, Nicholas Richard Maybury; QC 2008; Senior Treasury Counsel, Central Criminal Court, since 2001; a Recorder, since 2001; *b* 1 May 1959; *s* of His Honour Judge Christopher Richard Hilliard and Anne Margaret Hilliard. *Educ:* Bradfield Coll.; Lincoln Coll., Oxford (MA). Called to the Bar, Middle Temple, 1981, Bencher, 2003; Standing Counsel to DTI, 1993–95; Jun. Treasury Counsel, 1995–2000. Vice-Chm., 2004–05, Chm., 2005–06, Criminal Bar Assoc. Mem., Common Council, City of London, 1994–96, 2005–. Liveryman, Feltmakers' Co. (Mem., Ct of Assts, 2005–). Contrib. Ed., Archbold, Criminal Pleading, Evidence and Practice, 1994–; Ed., Criminal Appeal Reports, 1994–2000. *Address:* 6 King's Bench Walk, Temple, EC4Y 7DR. *T:* (020) 7583 0410. *Clubs:* Garrick, Beefsteak, MCC; Woking Golf.

HILLIER, Andrew Charles; QC 2002; *b* 4 May 1949; *s* of late William Hillier and Rosemary (*née* Dutton); *m* 1971, Dr Geraldine Morris; one *s* one *d*. *Educ:* St Louis Sch.; Beaumont Coll.; Trinity Coll., Dublin (BA Hons). Called to the Bar, Gray's Inn, 1972; in practice, specialising in employment and public law. Mem., Mental Health Act Commn, 1984–88. *Publication:* Tolley's Employment Act, 1982. *Recreation:* gardening in Franc *Address:* 11 King's Bench Walk, Temple, EC4Y 7EQ.

HILLIER, Bevis; author, art historian, journalist; *b* 28 March 1940; *s* of late Jack Ronal Hillier and Mary Louise Hillier (*née* Palmer). *Educ:* Reigate Grammar Sch.; Magdale Coll., Oxford (demy). Gladstone Memorial Prize, 1961. Editorial staff, The Time 1963–68 (trainee, Home News Reporter, Sale Room Correspondent); Editor, Britis Museum Society Bulletin, 1968–70; Guest Curator, Minneapolis Inst. of Arts, USA, 1971 Editor, The Connoisseur, 1973–76; Antiques Correspondent, 1970–84, Dep. Literar Editor, 1980–82, The Times; Editor, The Times Saturday Review, 1982; Features Edito 1982–83, Exec. Editor, 1983–84, Telegraph Sunday Magazine; Associate Editor, Lo Angeles Times, 1984–88; Editor, Sotheby's Preview, 1990–93. Co-founder and fir Chm., Thirties Soc. (now Twentieth Century Soc.), 1979; Pres., Betjeman Soc., 2006 (Vice-Pres., 1988–2006). Commendatore, Order of Merit (Italy), 1976. FRSA 1967 FRSL 1997. *Publications:* Master Potters of the Industrial Revolution: The Turners of Lan End, 1965; Pottery and Porcelain 1700–1914, 1968; Art Deco of the 1920s and 1930s 1968; Posters, 1969; Cartoons and Caricatures, 1970; The World of Art Deco, 1971; 10 Years of Posters, 1972; Travel Posters, 1973; Victorian Studio Photographs, 1974; (jtly Façade, 1974; Austerity/Binge, 1975; Punorama, 1975; Dead Funny, 1975; (ed with Mar Banham) A Tonic to the Nation: The Festival of Britain 1951, 1976; The New Antique 1977; Fougasse, 1978; Ealing Film Posters, 1981; Bevis Hillier's Pocket Guide to Antique 1981; Greetings from Christmas Past, 1982; The Style of the Century 1900–1980, 1983 John Betjeman: a life in pictures, 1984; Mickey Mouse Memorabilia, 1986; Youn Betjeman, 1988; Early English Porcelain, 1992; (jtly) Art Deco Style, 1997; Joh Betjeman: new fame, new love, 2002; Betjeman: the bonus of laughter, 2004; contribute to books, and periodicals incl. The Connoisseur, Apollo, Trans English Ceramic Circle Proc. Wedgwood Soc., etc. *Recreations:* piano, collecting. *Address:* Flat 23, Hospital of S Cross, St Cross Road, Winchester, Hants SO23 9SD. *T:* (01962) 855294. *Club:* Garrick

HILLIER, Malcolm Dudley; designer and author; *b* 1 Aug. 1936. *Educ:* St Paul's School Guildhall School of Music (LGSM). Advertising career, Colman Prentis and Varley; late Dir of Television, S. H. Benson, 1958–74; started garden design co. (with Colin Hilton) and opened flower shop, specialising in dried flowers, 1974; formed design partnership 1992; writer since 1985. *Publications:* Complete Book of Dried Flowers, 1986; Malcolm Hillier's Guide to Arranging Dried Flowers, 1987; Flowers, 1988; Container Gardening 1991; Roses, 1991; Pot Pourri, 1991; Malcolm Hillier's Christmas, 1992; Little Scente Library, 1992; Garlands, 1994; Container Gardening throughout the Year, 1995; Goo Food Fast, 1995; Malcolm Hillier's Colour Garden, 1995; Entertaining, 1997; Cat' Christmas, 1998; Flowers, 2000. *Recreations:* poetry, pottery. *Address: e-mail:* mhillier@ easynet.co.uk. *Club:* PEN.

HILLIER, Meg; MP (Lab and Co-op) Hackney South and Shoreditch, since 2005 Parliamentary Under-Secretary of State, Home Office, since 2007; *b* 14 Feb. 1969; *m* 1997; one *s* one *d*. *Educ:* St Hilda's Coll., Oxford (BA Hons PPE); City Univ. (Dip Newspaper Journalism). Reporter, S Yorks Times, 1991; Petty Officer, P & O Europea Ferries, 1992; PR Officer, Newlon Housing Gp, 1993; reporter, 1994–95, features edito 1995–98, Housing Today; freelance, 1998–2000. Mem. (Lab) Islington BC, 1994–200 (Chair, Neighbourhood Services Cttee, 1995–97); Mayor, Islington, 1998–99. Mem (Lab) NE, London Assembly, GLA, 2000–04. Mem. Bd, Transport for London, 2004–05 PPS to Sec. of State for Communities and Local Govt, 2006–07. Trustee, War Meml Trust, 2001–. *Recreations:* gardening, local history. *Address:* House of Commons, SW1A 0AA.

HILLIER, Paul Douglas, OBE 2006; singer; Chief Conductor, Ars Nova, Copenhagen since 2003; *b* 9 Feb. 1949; *s* of Douglas and Felicity Hillier; *m* 1st, 1977, Lena-Liis Kiesc (marr. diss. 2002); two *d*; 2nd, 2004, Else Torp; two *d*. *Educ:* Guildhall School of Musi and Drama, London (AGSM). Vicar-Choral, St Paul's Cathedral, 1974–76; Musical Di Hilliard Ensemble, 1974–90; Prof. of Music, Univ. of Calif., Davis, 1990–96; Prof. o Music and Dir, Early Music Inst., Indiana Univ., Bloomington, 1996–2003. Artistic D and Principal Conductor, Estonian Philharmonic Chamber Choir, 2001–07; Conductor Western Wind Chamber Choir, 1985–89; Klemetti Inst. Chamber Choir, Finland 1989–93; Dir, Theatre of Voices, 1989–; Artistic Dir, Nat. Chamber Choir of Ireland 2008–. Hon. Prof., Univ. of Copenhagen, 2003–. Gen. Editor, Fazer Editions of Earl Music, Helsinki, 1992–99. Edison Prize (Holland), 1989; Estonian Cultural Prize, 2004 White Star of Estonia, 2007; Grammy Award for Best Choral Perf., 2007. *Publications:* 30 Years of English Partsongs, 1983; Romantic English Partsongs, 1986; The Catch Book 1987; The Music of Arvo Pärt, 1997; (ed) Steve Reich, Writings on Music, 2002; On Pärt 2005. *Recreations:* reading, walking.

HILLIER, Richard, CB 2001; Director, Resources and Planning Division, Health an Safety Executive, 1994–2002. Manpower Policy Div., Dept of Employment; Dir o Systems and Strategy, MSC, subseq. Trng Agency, 1986–89; Dir, Industrial Relations an Europe, subseq. Internat., Directorate, EDG, 1989–94.

HILLIER, Stephen Martin; Director, Skills Group, Department for Innovation Universities and Skills (formerly Department for Education and Skills), since 2006; *b* 30 May 1957; *s* of Alfred Harley and Mabel Hillier; *m* 2004, Gillian Frances Langford; one one *d* (twins). *Educ:* City of London Polytech. (BA Hons); Birkbeck Coll., Univ. o London (MSc). Exec. Officer, Schs Council, 1978–81; Department of Education an Science: Exec. Officer, Curriculum Br., 1981–82; HEO, student loans policy, 1982–85 Private Sec. to Minister of State, 1985–87; Sen. Exec. Officer, Teachers' Br., 1987–88 Teamleader, Grant-Maintained Schs, DfEE, 1988–93; Dep. Chief Exec., Teacher Trng Agency, 1994–99; Department for Education and Skills: Divl Manager, Post-16 Educn and Trng, 1999–2001; Dep. Dir, Sch. Workforce Unit, 2001–03; Dir, Sch. Workforce Gp, 2004–06. *Recreations:* enjoying married life and being a father to our new twins Amélie and Seth. *Address:* Department for Innovation, Universities and Skills, Moorfoot Sheffield S1 4PQ. *T:* (020) 3300 8232; *e-mail:* stephen.hillier@dius.gsi.gov.uk.

HILLIER, William Edward, CEng, FIET; Visiting Industrial Fellow, Engineering Department, Cambridge University, 1996–98 and since 1999; *b* 11 April 1936; *s* o William Edward and Ivy Hillier; *m* 1958, Barbara Mary Thorpe; one *s* one *d*. *Educ:* Acton Grammar School; Open Univ. (BA). FIET (FIEE 1990). Missile Electronics Engineer, De Havilland Propellers, 1958–60; Semiconductor Test Equipment Design and Productior Manager, 1960–64, Semiconductor Production Manager, 1965–70, Texas Instruments Computer Aided Engineering Services Manager, up to Tech. Dir, CAD, Racal Redac 1970–85 (Dep. Man. Dir, 1982–85); Dir, Application of Computers and Manufg Engrg Directorate, 1985–94, and Hd of IT, 1991–94, SERC; Corporate Industrial Marketing EPSRC, 1994–96. Chairman: Computing and Control Div., IEE, 1993–94; Indust. Adv Bd, Sch. of Manufg and Mech. Engrg, Birmingham Univ., 1997–2000. Dir, Heritage Rly Assoc., 2000–. FCMI. *Publications:* articles in professional papers. *Recreation:* railway preservation (company secretary to standard gauge railway operating company Gloucestershire Warwickshire Steam Railway plc). *Address:* 19 Simon de Montfort Drive Evesham, Worcs WR11 4NR. *T:* (01386) 443449.

HILLIER-FRY, (William) Norman, CMG 1982; HM Diplomatic Service, retired; High Commissioner in Uganda, 1980–83; *b* 12 Aug. 1923; *o s* of William Henry and Emily Hillier Fry; *m* 1948, Elizabeth Adèle Misbah; two *s* two *d*. *Educ:* Colfe's Grammar School, Lewisham; St Edmund Hall, Oxford (BA 1946). Served Army, 1942–45; commissioned, Loyal Regt, 1942. HM Foreign Service, 1946; served: Iran, 1947–52; Strasbourg (Delegation to Council of Europe), 1955–56; Turkey, 1956–59; Czechoslovakia, 1961–63; Counsellor, UK Disarmament Delegn, Geneva, 1968–71; Hd of ME Dept, ODA, 1971–74; Consul-Gen., Hamburg, 1974–79; Ambassador to Afghanistan, 1979–80. *Recreations:* music, theatre. *Address:* 127 Coombe Lane West, Kingston-upon-Thames, Surrey KT2 7HF.

HILLMAN, David, RDI 1997; FCSD; FRCA; Director, Studio David Hillman, since 2007; *b* 12 Feb. 1943; *s* of late Leslie Hillman and Marjorie Joan Hillman (*née* Nash); *m* 1st, 1963, Eileen Margaret Griffin (marr. diss. 1968); one *s* one *d*; 2nd, 1983, Jennie Diana Burns; two *s*. *Educ:* Aristotle Central Sch.; London Sch. of Printing and Graphic Art (NDD Graphic Design 1962). AGI 1977; FCSD 1979; Sen. FRCA 2004. Design Asst, Sunday Times mag., 1962–65; Art Editor, London Life, 1965–66; Designer/Editor, Design for Living section, Sunday Times mag., 1966–68; Art Dir and Dep. Editor, Nova, 1968–75; freelance practice, 1975–78; Dir, Pentagram Design, 1978–2007. Mem., Alliance Graphique Internat., 1977– (UK Pres., 1996–2000; Internat. Pres., 2000–03). *Publications:* (ed jtly) Ideas on Design, 1986; Puzzlegrams, 1989; Pentagames, 1992; (ed jtly) Nova, 1993; (ed jtly) The Compendium, 1993; (jtly) Puzzlegrams Too, 1994; (ed jtly) Pentagram, Book 5, 1999; (jtly) Century Makers, 1999; (jtly) Terence Donovan, The Photographs, 2000; (ed jtly) Pentagram Profile, 2004. *Recreations:* ski-ing, modern jazz. *Address:* The Barns, Wortley, Wotton-under-Edge, Glos GL2 7QP. *T:* (01453) 844266.

HILLMAN, Prof. John Richard, PhD; FRSE; FLS, FIBiol, FIHort; consultant in life sciences and industrial biotechnology; Director, Scottish Crop Research Institute, 1986–2005; *b* 21 July 1944; *s* of late Robert Hillman and of Emily Irene (*née* Barrett); *m* 1967, Sandra Kathleen Palmer; two *s*. *Educ:* Chislehurst and Sidcup Grammar Sch. for Boys; University Coll. of Wales, Aberystwyth (BSc 1965; PhD 1968). FRSE, FIBiol 1985; FLS 1982; FIHort 1997. Univ. of Nottingham: Asst Lectr in Physiology and Environmental Studies, 1968; Lectr, 1969; Univ. of Glasgow: Lectr in Botany, 1971; Sen. Lectr, 1977; Reader, 1980; Prof. of Botany, 1982. Visiting Professor: Univ. of Dundee, 1986–; Univ. of Strathclyde, 1986–; Univ. of Edinburgh, 1988–; Univ. of Glasgow, 1991–. Bawden Lectr, Brighton, 1993. Chm., Agric., Hort. and Forestry Sector Panel, UK Technology Foresight Prog., 1995–97 (Chm., Agric., Nat. Resources and Envmt Sector Panel, 1994–95); Dep. Chm., Mylnefield Research Services Ltd, 1993–2005. Pres., Agriculture & Food Sect., BAAS, 2000–. Member: Bd, BioIndustry Assoc., 1998–2005 (Chm., Industrial Biotechnol. Cttee); Court, Univ. of Abertay Dundee, 1998–2005; Res. and Knowledge Transfer Cttee, SFC, 2003–07; Commercial Farmers Gp, 2006–. Vice-Pres., Scotia Agriculture Club, 2005–. FCMI (FBIM 1987); FRSA 1997; FRAgS 2004. Hon. DSc: Strathclyde, 1994; Abertay Dundee, 1996. British Potato Industry Award, 1999; Internat. Potato Industry Award, 2000; Dr Hardie Award, Virus-Tested Stem Cutting Assoc., 2001; Scottish Horticl Medal, Royal Caledonian Horticultural Soc., 2003. *Publications:* (ed) Isolation of Plant Growth Substances, 1978; (ed with A. Crozier) The Biosynthesis and Metabolism of Plant Hormones, 1984; (ed with C. T. Brett) Biochemistry of Plant Cell Walls, 1985; papers on plant physiol. and biotechnol. in learned jls. *Recreations:* landscaping, building renovations, horology, economics. *Address:* c/o Scottish Crop Research Institute, Invergowrie, Dundee DD2 5DA. *T:* (01382) 562731. *Club:* Farmers'.

HILLS, Andrew Worth; Director, BBC Monitoring, 1996–2003; *b* 1 Sept. 1949; *s* of late Roland Frederick Hills and of Margaret Eunice (*née* Johnson); *m* 1st, 1974, Frances Mary Ralston (marr. diss. 1992); three *s*; 2nd, 1992, Mary Sandra Caraffi. *Educ:* Abingdon Sch.; Corpus Christi Coll., Cambridge (BA 1971; MA 1975). United Kingdom Atomic Energy Authority, 1971–96: Gen. Sec., AEE Winfrith, 1981–84; Principal Finance and Programmes Officer, 1984–86; Authority Personnel Officer, 1986–89; Exec. Dir, Finance and Personnel, 1989–91; Mem., UKAEA, 1991–94; Managing Director: Sites and Personnel, 1991–92; Corporate Services, 1992–94; Services Div., 1994–95; Dir, Special Projects, 1995–96. Trustee, Southern Sinfonia, 2003–. *Recreations:* church-crawling, music, reading. *Address:* Craven Lodge, Speen Lane, Newbury RG14 1RJ.

HILLS, Barrington William; racehorse trainer, since 1969; *b* 2 April 1937; *s* of William George Hills and Phyllis (*née* Biddle); *m* 1st, 1959, Maureen (marr. diss. 1977), *d* of late Patrick Newson; three *s* (incl. twins); 2nd, 1977, Penelope Elizabeth May, *d* of John Richard Woodhouse; two *s*. *Educ:* Robston Hall, Gloucester; St Mary's Convent, Newmarket; Mr Whittaker's, Worcester. National Service, King's Troop, RHA. Major race winners include: Prix de l'Arc de Triomphe, 1973 (Rheingold); 1,000 Guineas, 1978 (Enstone Spark); 2,000 Guineas, 1979 (Tap on Wood), 2004 (Haafhd); Irish Derby, 1987 (Sir Harry Lewis); Irish 1,000 Guineas, 1993 (Nicer), 1999 (Hula Angel); St Leger, 1994 (Moonax); Irish Oaks, 1994 (Bolas); Prix Royal-Oak, 1994 (Moonax). *Recreations:* hunting, shooting, golf. *Address:* B. W. Hills Southbank Ltd, Wetherdown House, Lambourn, Hungerford, Berks RG17 8UB. *T:* (01488) 71548; *e-mail:* info@barryhills.com. *Club:* Turf.

HILLS, Air Vice-Marshal David Graeme Muspratt, CB 1985; OBE 1965; Director, Medical Policy and Plans, Ministry of Defence, 1983–85; *b* 28 Feb. 1925; *s* of late Arthur Ernest Hills and Muriel Steinman Hills (*née* Fisher); *m* 1960, Hilary Enid Mary, *d* of Rev. Raymond Morgan Jones and Mary Jones (*née* Ritson); two *s* one *d*. *Educ:* Salisbury Cathedral School; Epsom College; Middlesex Hosp. Medical School. MB BS 1949; MFCM, DPH, AFOM. Commissioned RAF Med. Branch, 1950; served UK, Korea (Casualty Evacuation and MO to 77 Sqn, RAAF; despatches), A&AEE, RAF Stanmore Park, RAF Tengah and MoD, 1951–68; OC RAF Hosp., Muharraq Bahrain, 1968–70; SMO RAF Cranwell, 1970–72; Dep. Dir Medical Personnel, RAF, 1972–75; PMO RAF Germany, 1975–78; Dep. Dir Gen., RAF Medical Services, 1979–83. QHS, 1980–85. Chm. of Council, Coll. of St. Barnabas, Lingfield, 1996–2000. CStJ. *Recreations:* music, painting, gardening, golf. *Club:* Royal Air Force.

HILLS, David Henry, CBE 1993; Director-General of Intelligence, Ministry of Defence, 1988–93; *b* 9 July 1933; *s* of Henry Stanford Hills and Marjorie Vera Lily Hills; *m* 1957, Jean Helen Nichols; one *s* two *d*. *Educ:* Varndean Sch., Brighton; Univ. of Nottingham (BA Econs). Served Army Intell. Corps, 1954–56. Entered MoD, 1956; other appointments include: NBPI, 1967–70; National Indust. Relations Court, 1971–73; Dir of Marketing, Defence Sales Orgn, MoD, 1979–82; Dir of Economic and Logistic Intell., MoD, 1982–88. *Recreations:* gardening, music.

HILLS, Col David Henry, MBE 1986; Under Treasurer, Honourable Society of Lincoln's Inn, since 1997; *b* 23 May 1946; *s* of Air Vice-Marshal (Eric) Donald Hills, *qv*; *m* 1970, Josephine Anne, *d* of Wing Comdr J. W. Abbott; two *s* one *d*. *Educ:* Mount St Mary's Coll.; RMA Sandhurst. Commnd 2nd Lt Royal Highland Fusiliers, 1967; regimental service, Scotland, Singapore, NI, 1967–77; Staff HQ 8 Bde, Londonderry, 1977–79; Staff Coll., Camberley, 1980; regimental service, Germany, 1981–83; MoD, 1983–85; loan service, Zimbabwe, 1985; DCOS HQ 1 Infantry Bde, 1987–88; Comd 1st Bn Royal Highland Fusiliers, 1988–90; Staff, RMA Sandhurst, 1990–93; Dep. COS Rear Support HQ ARRC, Germany and Croatia, 1993–96. Sec., Council of the Inns of Ct, 2007–; Jt Rep., Council of the Inns of Ct to the Bar Standards Bd, 2008–. *Recreations:* tennis, golf, ski-ing, criticising military and legal programmes whilst watching television. *Address:* Treasury Office, The Honourable Society of Lincoln's Inn, WC2A 3TL. *T:* (020) 7405 1393, *Fax:* (020) 7831 1839; *e-mail:* mail@lincolnsinn.org.uk.

HILLS, Air Vice-Marshal (Eric) Donald, CB 1973; CBE 1968 (MBE 1941); SASO Maintenance Command, 1971–73, retired; *b* 26 Jan. 1917; *s* of late Henry James Hills; *m* 1st, 1945, Pamela Mary (*d* 1989), *d* of late Col A. P. Sandeman, Cape Town; one *s* one *d*; 2nd, 1991, Lady Cynthia Way (*d* 2001). *Educ:* Maidstone Grammar Sch. Joined RAF 1939; Group Captain 1962; Dir of Equipment 3 (RAF), 1968–69; Air Cdre 1969; Dir of Equipment (Policy) (RAF), MoD, 1969–71; Air Vice-Marshal 1971. *Recreations:* gardening, sport as spectator. *Club:* Royal Air Force.
See also Col D. H. Hills.

HILLS, Sir Graham (John), Kt 1988; PhD, DSc; FRSE, CChem, FRSC; Principal and Vice-Chancellor of the University of Strathclyde, 1980–91; Scottish Governor of the BBC, 1989–94; *b* 9 April 1926; *s* of Albert Victor Hills and Marjorie Hills (*née* Harper); *m* 1st, 1950, Brenda Stubbington (*d* 1974); one *s* three *d*; 2nd, 1980, Mary Jane McNaughton. *Educ:* Birkbeck Coll., London Univ. (BSc 1946, PhD 1950, DSc 1962; Hon. Fellow 1984). Lecturer in Physical Chemistry, Imperial College, 1949–62; Professor of Physical Chemistry, Univ. of Southampton, 1962–80; Visiting Professor: Univ. of Western Ontario, 1968; Case Western Reserve Univ., 1969; Univ. of Buenos Aires, 1977. Chm., Ness (formerly Highland Psychiatric Res.) Foundn, 1998–2003. President: Internat. Soc. of Electrochemistry, 1983–85; Soc. of Chemical Industry, 1991–93; Design Industries Assoc., 1992–96. Member: ACOST, 1987–93; Council, RSC, 1983–86; Council, CNAA, 1988–93; Design Council, 1989–90; Scottish Enterprise, 1991–93. Non-Executive Director: Scottish Post Office Bd, 1986–99; Scottish Develt Agency, 1988–90; Glasgow Action, 1986–90; Britoil, 1988–90. Chm. Council, Quarrier's Homes, 1992–97. FRSA 1978. Hon. FRSAMD 1988; Hon. Fellow, Polytechnic of E London, 1991; Hon. FRCPSGlas 1992; Hon. FCSD 1996. Hon. ScD Technical Univ. of Łodz, Poland, 1984; Hon. DSc: Southampton, 1984; Lisbon, 1994; Hon. LLD: Glasgow, 1985; Waterloo, Canada, 1991; Strathclyde, 1991; DUniv Paisley, 1993; Hon. DEd Abertay Dundee, 1999. Hon. Medal, Univ. of Pavia, 1988. Commander: Polish Order of Merit, 1984; Royal Norwegian Order of Merit, 1986. *Publications:* Reference Electrodes, 1961; Polarography, 1964; UHI: the making of a university, 2003; contrib. Faraday Transactions, on physical chemistry, espec. electrochemistry. *Recreations:* music, European political history, rocking the boat. *Address:* The Coach House, 2B Strathearn Road, Edinburgh EH9 2AH. *Club:* Athenæum.

HILLS, Jacqueline Sukie; *see* Binns, J. S.

HILLS, Prof. John Robert, CBE 1999; FBA 2002; Professor of Social Policy, and Director, Centre for Analysis of Social Exclusion, London School of Economics, since 1997; *b* 29 July 1954; *s* of Derrick Walter Hills and Valerie Jean Hills (*née* Gribble); *m* 1989, Anne Elizabeth Power. *Educ:* Nottingham High Sch.; Abingdon Sch.; St John's Coll., Cambridge (BA 1976, MA); Birmingham Univ. (MSocSc 1980). Min. of Finance, Botswana, 1976–78; DoE, 1979–80; Treasury Cttee, H of C, 1980–82; Inst. for Fiscal Studies, 1982–84; Commn of Inquiry into Taxation, Zimbabwe, 1984–86; Welfare State Prog., LSE, 1986–97. Mem., Pensions Commn, 2003–06. *Publications:* (ed) The State of Welfare: the welfare state in Britain since 1974, 1990, 2nd edn (jtly), 1998; Unravelling Housing Finance: subsidies, benefits and taxation, 1991; The Future of Welfare, 1993, 2nd edn 1997; (ed jtly) The Dynamic of Welfare, 1995; (ed) New Inequalities: the changing distribution of income and wealth in the UK, 1996; (jtly) Paying for Health, Education and Housing, 2000; (ed jtly) Understanding Social Exclusion, 2002; Inequality and the State, 2004; (ed jtly) A More Equal Society?, 2005; Ends and Means: the future roles of social housing in England, 2007. *Recreation:* fell walking. *Address:* Centre for Analysis of Social Exclusion, London School of Economics, Houghton Street, WC2A 2AE.

HILLS, Philip, CMG 2003; Chief Executive, Project and Export Finance, HSBC, 1990–2004; *b* 10 Feb. 1946; *s* of Frank and Lilian Elizabeth Patricia Hills; *m* 1969, Margaret Elizabeth Susan Harris; four *d*. *Educ:* Colfe's Grammar Sch., London. N. M. Rothschild & Sons Ltd, 1963–76 (Manager, Export Finance, 1969–76); Dir, Export Finance, Grindlay Brandts Ltd, 1976–81; HSBC Gp, 1981–2004. Director: Anthony Gibbs & Sons Ltd, 1981–88; Samuel Montagu & Co. Ltd, 1988–90. Chm., Export and Shipbuilding Policy Cttee, BBA, 1990–2001. *Recreations:* sport, travel, cookery. *Address:* HSBC Bank plc, 8 Canada Square, E14 5HQ.

HILLS, Prof. Richard Edwin; Project Scientist, Atacama Large Millimetre Array, Santiago, since 2007; Fellow of St Edmund's College, Cambridge, since 1993; *b* 30 Sept. 1945; *s* of Ronald Hills and Betty Dorothy Hills (*née* Davies); *m* 1973, Beverly Bevis; two *s*. *Educ:* Bedford Sch.; Queen's Coll., Cambridge (BA Physics); Univ. of California, Berkeley (PhD Astronomy). Research Scientist, Max Planck Inst. for Radio Astronomy, Bonn, 1972–74; Research Associate, 1974–84, Asst Dir of Research, 1984–90, Cavendish Lab., Cambridge; Project Scientist, James Clerk Maxwell Telescope, 1975–87; Prof. of Radio Astronomy, 1990–2007, and Dep. Head, Dept of Physics, 1999–2003, Univ. of Cambridge. FRAS. Jackson-Gwilt Medal, RAS, 1989; MacRobert Award, Fellowship of Engineers, 1990. *Publications:* contribs to professional jls. *Recreations:* travel, DIY, music. *Address:* c/o Cavendish Laboratory, J. J. Thomson Avenue, Cambridge CB3 0HE. *T:* (01223) 337300.

HILLSBOROUGH, Earl of; Edmund Robin Arthur Hill; *b* 21 May 1996; *s* and *heir* of Marquess of Downshire, *qv*.

HILSON, Malcolm Geoffrey, OBE 2001; HM Diplomatic Service, retired; High Commissioner, Vanuatu, 1997–2000; *b* 28 Sept. 1942; *s* of Geoffrey Norman and Mildred Alice Hilson; *m* 1965, Marian Joan Freeman; two *s*. *Educ:* Bedford Modern School. Entered Foreign Office, 1961; served Jakarta, Singapore, Bombay, Kuala Lumpur and FCO; First Sec., Kaduna, 1982–86; FCO, 1986–90; New Delhi, 1990–93; FCO, 1993–97. *Recreations:* gardening, bowls, golf, bell ringing, photography. *Address:* Chestnuts, Long Lane, South Repps, Norfolk NR11 8NL.

HILSUM, Prof. Cyril, CBE 1990; PhD; FRS 1979; FREng, FIET; Visiting Professor of Physics, University College London, since 1988; *b* 17 May 1925; *s* of Benjamin and Ada Hilsum; *m* 1947, Betty Cooper (*d* 1987); one *d* (and one *d* decd). *Educ:* Raines Sch., London; University Coll., London (BSc, PhD). FIET (FIEE 1967); FREng (FEng 1978); FIEEE 1984. Joined Royal Naval Scientific Service, 1945; Admiralty Res. Lab., 1947–50, and Services Electronics Res. Lab., 1950–64, working first on infra-red res., then on semiconductors; Royal Signals and Radar Estab., 1964–83, working first on compound semiconductors, later on flat panel electronic displays; CSO, 1974–83; Chief Scientist, Gen. Electric Co. Res. Labs, 1983–85; Dir of Res., GEC plc, 1985–93. Mem., SERC,

1984–88. Pres., Inst. of Physics, 1988–90; Hon. FInstP 2001 (FInstP 1960). Foreign Associate, US National Acad. of Engrg, 1983. Hon. DEng: Sheffield, 1992; Nottingham Trent, 1997. Max Born Medal and Prize, 1987, Glazebrook Medal and Prize, 1997, Inst. of Physics; Faraday Medal, IEE, 1988; Braun Prize, Soc. for Inf. Display, 1998; Royal Medal, Royal Soc., 2007. *Publications:* Semiconducting III-V Compounds, 1961; over 100 scientific and technical papers. *Recreation:* ballroom dancing. *Address:* 12 Eastglade, Moss Lane, Pinner, Middx HA5 3AN. *T:* (020) 8866 8323.

See also L. Hilsum.

HILSUM, Lindsey; International Editor, Channel 4 News, since 2004 (diplomatic correspondent, 1996–2004); *b* 3 Aug. 1958; *d* of Prof. Cyril Hilsum, *qv* and late Betty Hilsum. *Educ:* City of Worcester Grammar Sch. for Girls; Exeter Univ. (BA Hons Spanish and French). Freelance journalist in Latin America, 1980–82; Information Officer, UNICEF, Nairobi, 1982–86; stringer, BBC and Guardian, Nairobi, 1986–89; producer, BBC World Service, 1989–93; freelance journalist, 1993–96. Specialist Journalist of the Year, 2003, Journalist of the Year, 2005, RTS; James Cameron Award, 2005. *Publications:* contribs to Granta, TLS, Sunday Telegraph, New Statesman, Observer, etc. *Recreations:* horse riding, duck watching. *Address:* ITN, 200 Gray's Inn Road, WC1X 8XZ. *T:* (020) 7430 4606, *Fax:* (020) 7430 4608; *e-mail:* lindsey.hilsum@itn.co.uk.

HILTON OF EGGARDON, Baroness *cr* 1991 (Life Peer), of Eggardon in the County of Dorset; **Jennifer Hilton,** QPM 1989; *b* 12 Jan. 1936; *d* of John Robert Hilton, CMG. *Educ:* Bedales Sch.; Manchester Univ. (BA Hons Psychology 1970; MA (Research) 1971); London Univ. (Dip. Criminology 1972; Dip. History of Art 1982). Joined Metropolitan Police, 1956; Univ. Scholarship, 1967; Police Staff Coll. (Directing Staff), 1973–74; Met. Police Management Services Dept, 1975–76; Supt then Chief Supt, Heathrow Airport, Battersea, Chiswick, 1977–83; New Scotland Yard (Traffic, Courts, Obscene Publications, Planning, Neighbourhood Policing), 1983–87; Comdr, 1984; Head of Training, Metropolitan Police, 1988–90. House of Lords: Opposition Whip, 1991–95; opposition spokesperson on the envmt, 1991–97; Member: EC Sub-Cttee on Envmt, 1991–95 (Chm., 1995–98); Science and Technol. Cttee, 1993–95, 2004–; EC Sub-Cttee on Defence and Foreign Affairs, 2000–03; Chm., Adv. Panel on Works of Art, 1998–2003. Mem., OSCE Election Monitoring Panel, 1998–. *Publications:* The Gentle Arm of the Law, 1967, 2nd edn 1973; (with Sonya Hunt) Individual Development and Social Experience, 1975, 2nd edn 1981; articles in Police Jl, Police Review, etc. *Recreations:* gardening, history, art, travel. *Address:* House of Lords, SW1A 0PW.

HILTON, (Alan) John Howard; QC 1990; a Recorder, since 1986; *b* 21 Aug. 1942; *s* of Alan Howard Hilton and Barbara Mary Campbell Hilton; *m* 1st, 1968, Jasmina Laila Hamzavi; 2nd, 1978, Nicola Mary Bayley, *qv*; one *s*. *Educ:* Haileybury and Imperial Service Coll.; Manchester Univ. (LLB Hons). Called to the Bar, Middle Temple, 1964. *Recreations:* opera, cooking, magic, 19th century paintings of ladies, enjoying adjournments. *Address:* Queen Elizabeth Building, Temple, EC4Y 9BS. *T:* (020) 7583 5766. *Clubs:* Garrick, Les Six.

HILTON, Prof. (Andrew John) Boyd, DPhil; FBA 2007; Professor of Modern British History, University of Cambridge, since 2007; Fellow of Trinity College, Cambridge, since 1974; *b* 19 Jan. 1944; *s* of Kenneth Boyd Hilton and Irene Beryl Hilton; *m* 1971, Mary à Beckett; one *s* two *d*. *Educ:* William Hulme's Grammar Sch., Manchester; New Coll., Oxford (BA 1966; DPhil 1972). Res. Lectr, Christ Church, Oxford, 1969–74; Lectr, 1988–97, Reader, 1997–2007, Faculty of History, Univ. of Cambridge; Trinity College, Cambridge: Tutor, 1978–88, 1990–91, 1994–96; Sen. Tutor, 1985–88; Dean, 1991–93; Steward, 2000. James Ford Special Lectr, Univ. of Oxford, 1995. FRHistS 1986. *Publications:* Corn, Cash, Commerce: the economic policies of the Tory governments 1815–1830, 1969; The Age of Atonement: the influence of evangelicalism on social and economic thought, 1988; A Mad, Bad, and Dangerous People? England 1783–1846: the new Oxford history of England, 2006. *Recreations:* too few to mention. *Address:* 1 Carlyle Road, Cambridge CB4 3DN; Trinity College, Cambridge CB2 1TQ. *T:* (01223) 338425; *e-mail:* ajbh1@cam.ac.uk.

HILTON, Anthony Victor; Financial Editor, Evening Standard, since 2002 (City Editor, 1984–89 and 1996–2002; Managing Director, 1989–95); *b* 26 Aug. 1946; *s* of Raymond Walwork Hilton and Miriam Eileen Norah Hilton (*née* Kydd); *m* 1st, 1969, Patricia Moore; one *s*; 2nd, 1989, Cynthia June Miles; two *s* one *d*. *Educ:* Univ. of Aberdeen (MA Hons Econs 1968). Financial columnist: Guardian, 1968; Observer, 1969; Daily Mail, 1971; Sunday Express, 1972; Editor, Accountancy Age, 1974–79; NY corresp., Sunday Times, 1979–82; City Editor, The Times, 1982–83; Dir, Associated Newspapers, 1989–95. Dir, London Forum, 1993–94; Mem. Council, London First, 1996–98 (Dir, 1993–96). Mem. Cttee, St John's Ambulance Charity Appeal, 1992–94. Vice Pres., Children's Film Unit, 1993–96. *Publications:* How to communicate financial information to employees, 1979; City within a state: a portrait of the City of London, 1987. *Recreations:* canal cruising, cycling, bonfires. *Address:* Priory Hall, Hadleigh, Suffolk IP7 5AZ. *T:* (01473) 823185. *Clubs:* Reform, Lansdowne.

HILTON, Boyd; *see* Hilton, A. J. B.

HILTON, Brian James George, CB 1992; non-executive director of public companies; Deputy Secretary, Department of Trade and Industry, 1994–99; *b* 21 April 1940; *s* of late Percival William Hilton and Gladys Hilton (*née* Haylett); *m* 1965, Mary Margaret Kirkpatrick; one *s* two *d*. *Educ:* St Marylebone Grammar Sch., London. Export Credits Guarantee Dept, 1958–68; Board of Trade, 1968–71; Foreign and Commonwealth Office, 1971–74: First Secretary to UK Delegn to OECD, Paris; Asst Sec., Dept of Industry, 1976–84; RCDS 1981; Hd, Financial Services Div., DTI, 1984–87; Hd, Central Unit (Under Sec.), DTI, 1987–89; Dep. Sec., MAFF, 1989–91; Dir, Citizen's Charter Unit, Cabinet Office, 1991–94. Complaints Ombudsman, LIFFE, 2007–. Foundation Governor, Hampden Gurney Primary Sch., London W1, 1976–; Gov., RAC, Cirencester, 1990–91, 2005–. *Recreations:* cricket, Rugby, music, opera, gardening, fly fishing. *Address:* 1 Lake View, Shoyswell Manor, Sheepstreet Lane, Etchingham, E Sussex TN19 7AZ.

HILTON, John Howard; *see* Hilton, A. J. H.

HILTON, Rear-Adm. John Millard Thomas, FIMechE, FIET; consulting engineer; *b* 24 Dec. 1934; *s* of late Edward Thomas Hilton and Margaret Norah Attrill (*née* Millard); *m* 1st, 1958, Patricia Anne Kirby (marr. diss. 1979); one *s* one *d*; 2nd, 1985, Cynthia Mary Caroline Seddon-Brown (*née* Hargreave); one step *d*. *Educ:* Wyggeston Grammar Sch. for Boys, Leicester; County High Sch., Clacton; RNC Dartmouth; RNEC Manadon; RNC Greenwich; City Univ. (MSc 1968); Imperial Coll. of Science and Technology (DIC 1973). Joined RN 1951; various sea and shore appts, 1951–80; Dep. Chief Naval Signal Officer, MoD, London, 1980–83; Project Dir, ARE Portsdown, 1984–87; Vice-Pres. (Navy), Ordnance Bd, 1987–88; Pres., Ordnance Bd, 1988–90. Dir, Christian Engineers in Develt, 1997– (Chm., 2000–03). Non-exec. Dir, mi2g, 2004–. Hon. Sen. Vis. Fellow, Sch. of Engrg, City Univ., 1993–96. Hon. DSc City, 2000. ADC to the Queen, 1985–88. Master, 2000–01, Hon. Treas., 2001–05, Scientific Instrument Makers' Co. *Publicatio* professional papers. *Recreations:* personal computing, photography, Christian disciplesh family life. *Address:* 29 Grenehurst Way, The Village, Petersfield, Hants GU31 4AZ.

HILTON, Matthew James; Director of Employment Relations, Department Business, Enterprise and Regulatory Reform, since 2007; *b* 25 Jan. 1967; *s* of Ronald a Mary Hilton; *m* 1995, Elizabeth Sarah Jones; two *s* one *d*. *Educ:* St John Fisher High Sc Wigan; Univ. of Sheffield (BA 1988, MA 1989); Imperial Coll., London (MBA 200 English teacher, Prague, 1990–92; joined DTI, 1992; Private Sec. to Sec. of State a Minister for Energy and Industry, 1994–97; Dir, Business Support Rev., 2001– Principal Private Sec. to Sec. of State, 2003–05; Dir of Strategy and Communicatio then Dir of Communications, DTI, subseq. BERR, 2005–07. Trustee, Nat. D Children's Soc., 2006–; Chm., Lewes Mencap, 2007–. *Address:* Department for Busine Enterprise and Regulatory Reform, 1 Victoria Street, SW1H 0ET; *e-m* matthew.hilton@berr.gsi.gov.uk.

HILTON, Nicola Mary; *see* Bayley, N. M.

HILTON, Prof. Peter John, MA, DPhil Oxon, PhD Cantab; Distinguished Professor Mathematics, State University of New York at Binghamton, 1982–93, Emeritus sin 1993; *b* 7 April 1923; *s* of late Dr Mortimer Hilton and Mrs Elizabeth Hilton; *m* 194 Margaret (*née* Mostyn); two *s*. *Educ:* St Paul's Sch.; Queen's Coll., Oxford. Asst Lec Manchester Univ., 1948–51, Lectr, 1951–52; Lectr, Cambridge Univ., 1952–55; Seni Lecturer, Manchester Univ., 1956–58; Mason Prof. of Pure Mathematics, University Birmingham, 1958–62; Prof. of Mathematics, Cornell Univ., 1962–71, Univ. Washington, 1971–73; Beaumont Univ. Prof., Case Western Reserve Univ., 1972–8 Distinguished Prof. of Maths, Univ. of Central Florida, 1994–. Visiting Professor: Corn Univ., USA, 1958–59; Eidgenössische Techn. Hochschule, Zürich, 1966–67, 1981–8 1988–89; Courant Inst., NY Univ., 1967–68; Univ. Aut. de Barcelona, 1989; Erski Fellow, Univ. of Canterbury, NZ, 2001, 2002. Mahler Lectr, Australian Math. Soc., 199 Mathematician-in-residence, Battelle Research Center, Seattle, 1970–82. Chairman: U Commn on Mathematical Instruction, 1971–74; NRC Cttee on Applied Maths Tr 1977–; First Vice-Pres., Math. Assoc. of Amer., 1978–80. Corresp. Mem., Brazilian Aca of Scis, 1979; Hon. Mem. Belgian Mathematical Soc., 1955. Hon. DHum N Michiga 1977; Hon. DSc: Meml Univ. of Newfoundland, 1983; Univ. Aut. de Barcelona, 198 Silver Medal, Univ. of Helsinki, 1975; Centenary Medal, John Carroll Univ., 198 *Publications:* Introduction to Homotopy Theory, 1953; Differential Calculus, 195 Homology Theory (with S. Wylie), 1960; Partial Derivatives, 1960; Homotopy Theo and Duality, 1965; (with H. B. Griffiths) Classical Mathematics, 1970; Gene Cohomology Theory and K- Theory, 1971; (with U. Stammbach) Course Homological Algebra, 1971, 2nd edn 1996; (with Y.-C. Wu) Course in Modern Algeb 1974; (with G. Mislin and J. Roitberg) Localization of Nilpotent Groups and Spaces, 197 (with J. Pedersen) Fear No More, 1983; Nilpotente Gruppen und Nilpotente Räum 1984; (with J. Pedersen) Build Your Own Polyhedra, 1987; (ed) Miscellan Mathematica, 1991; (with D. Holton and J. Pedersen) Mathematical Reflections, 199 Mathematical Vistas, 2002; numerous research articles on algebraic topology, homologic algebra and category theory in British and foreign mathematical journals. *Recreatio* travel, sport, reading, theatre, chess, bridge, broadcasting. *Address:* Department Mathematical Sciences, State University of New York, Binghamton, NY 13902–600 USA.

HILTON, Prof. Sean Robert, MD; FRCGP; Vice-Principal, since 2004, and Profess of General Practice and Primary Care since 1993, St George's (formerly St Georg Hospital Medical School), University of London; *b* 31 Oct. 1949; *s* of Harold and Do Hilton; *m* 1994, Lesley Wood; two *s* one *d*. *Educ:* Weymouth Grammar Sch.; St Georg Hosp. Med. Sch., London (MB BS 1974; MD 1991). FRCGP 1990. NHS GP Princip Kingston-upon-Thames, 1979–; St George's Hospital Medical School, University London: Sen. Lectr in Gen. Practice, 1987–93; Dean of Undergrad. Medicin 1997–2002; non-exec. Dir, St George's Healthcare Trust, 2003–. Gov., Anglo-Europe Coll. of Chiropractic, 2003– (Chm., 2006–); Mem. Council and Exec., Assoc. for Stu of Med. Educn, 2003–. *Publications:* (with M. Levy) Asthma in Practice, 1987, 4th ec 1999; (jtly) Asthma at Your Fingertips, 1993, 3rd edn 2006; more than 100 peer review papers and book chapters on gen. practice, primary care and med. educn. *Recreations:* mus (especially Schubert and songs of Jackson Browne), gardening, football, cricket. *Addre* Division of Community Health Sciences, St George's, Cranmer Terrace, SW17 0RE. (020) 8725 5422, *Fax:* (020) 8767 7697; *e-mail:* shilton@sgul.ac.uk. *Clubs:* MCC; 1942

HILTON, Tessa, (Mrs G. Ball); Editor at Large, Woman and Home; *b* 18 Feb. 1951; of Michael and Phyllis Hilton; *m* 1976, Graham Ball; two *s* one *d*. *Educ:* St Mary's Sch Gerrards Cross. Trainee reporter, Mirror Gp Trng Scheme, Devon, 1970–74; Reporte Sunday Mirror, 1974–78; freelance writer, 1978–85; Editor, Mother mag., 1985–8 Features Editor, then Asst Editor, Today, 1987–91; Femail Editor, Daily Mail, 1991–9 Asst Editor, Sun, 1994; Editor, Sunday Mirror, 1994–96; Dep. Editor, The Express, th Editor, Express on Sunday Magazine, 1996–99. *Publications:* Great Ormond Street Boo of Child Health, 1990; (with Maire Messenger) New Baby and Child Care Boo *Recreation:* family life.

HIME, Martin, CBE 1987; HM Diplomatic Service, retired; *b* 18 Feb. 1928; *s* of Per Joseph Hime and Esther Greta (*née* Howe); *m* 1st, 1960, Henrietta Fehling (marr. diss one *s* three *d*; 2nd, 1971, Janina Christine Majcher (*d* 2002); one *d*. *Educ:* King's Coll. Sch Wimbledon; Trinity Hall, Cambridge (MA; Lawn Tennis blue). Served RA, 1946–4 Called to the Bar, Inner Temple, 1951; Marks and Spencer Ltd, 1952–58; joined H Diplomatic Service, 1960; served in Tokyo, Kobe, Frankfurt and Buenos Aires, 1960–6 2nd Sec., FCO, 1970–72; Consul, Johannesburg, 1972–74; 1st Sec. (Econ.), Pretori 1974–76; Asst Head, S Pacific Dept, FCO, 1976–79; Dep. High Comr in Banglades 1979–82; Consul-General: Cleveland, Ohio, 1982–85; Houston, Texas, 1985–8 Personnel Assessor, FCO, 1988–93. Administrator, NHS Network, 1996–98. Mem. (Wandsworth BC, 2002–06. Gov., Granard Sch., Putney, 1995–2006. *Recreations:* go lawn tennis, books, table games. *Address:* Field House, 248 Dover House Roa Roehampton, SW15 5DA. *Clubs:* All England Lawn Tennis; Hawks (Cambridge); Roy Wimbledon Golf.

HIMSWORTH, Prof. Richard Lawrence, MD; FRCP; Professor of Health Researc and Development, 1993–2002, and Director, Institute of Public Health, 1999–200 Cambridge University; Fellow, Girton College, Cambridge, since 1995; *b* 14 June 193 *s* of Sir Harold Himsworth, KCB, FRS; *m* 1966, Sara Margaret Tattersall; two *s* one *Educ:* Westminster Sch.; Trinity Coll., Cambridge (MB BChir 1961, MD 1971 University Coll. Hosp. Med. Sch.; University Coll. London (MA in History of Medicin 2005). FRCP 1977; FRCPE 1988; FRCPGlas 1990; FFPH (FFPHM 2002). Lectr Medicine, UCH Med. Sch., 1967–71; MRC Travelling Fellow, New York, 1969–7 MRC Scientific Staff, Clinical Res. Centre, 1971–85: Asst Dir, 1978–82; Hea Endocrinology Res. Gp, 1979–85; Consultant Physician, Northwick Park Hosp 1972–85; Regius Prof. of Medicine, Univ. of Aberdeen, and Hon. Consultant Physicia

Aberdeen Royal Infirmary, 1985–93. Hon. Prof., UEA, 1994. Associate Dir, R&D, Anglia and Oxford RHA, 1994–98; Dir, R&D, Eastern (formerly Anglia and Oxford) Region, NHS Exec., DoH, 1998–2002. Member: NW Thames RHA, 1982–85; Scottish Nat. Med. Adv. Cttee, 1990–92; Gen. Council, King Edward's Hosp. Fund for London, 1980– (Mem. London Commns, 1990–92, 1995–97). Mem. Ct, Imperial Coll., London, 2002–. Liveryman, 1976–, Mem. Ct of Assts, 1995–, Prime Warden, 2007–08, Goldsmiths' Co. Hon. DSc Anglia Poly., 2000. *Publications:* scientific and medical papers. *Address:* Park House, 39 High Street, Balsham, Cambridge CB21 4DJ. *T:* (01223) 893975.

HINCE, Dr Trevor Anthony; Director and Secretary, Lister Institute for Preventive Medicine, since 2004; *b* 17 Aug. 1949; *s* of late Gerald Arthur Hince and Beryl Doris Hince (*née* Franklin); *m* 1st, 1972, Carol Jean Tarabella (marr. diss. 1996); 2nd, 1996, Sarah Elizabeth Verrall. *Educ:* Forest Grammar Sch., Winnersh; University Coll. London (BSc Hons 1971); Middlesex Hosp. Med. Sch. (PhD 1976); Brunel Univ./Henley Mgt Coll. (MSc 1988). Middlesex Hospital Medical School: Research Asst, 1971–76; Temp. Lectr in Pathology, 1976–79; Cancer Research Campaign: Asst Scientific Sec., 1980–86; Scientific Sec., 1986–89; Dep. Dir, Scientific Dept, 1989–96; Scientific Dir, 1996–2002; Dep. Dir Gen., 1998–2002; Dir, Res. Mgt and Planning, CRUK, 2002–04. Mem., Inst. of Cancer Res., 2004–. *Publications:* papers in scientific jls. *Recreations:* riding, walking, gardening, music. *Address:* (office) PO Box 1083, Bushey, Herts WD23 9AG.

HINCH, Prof. Edward John, PhD; FRS 1997; Professor of Fluid Mechanics, since 1998, and Fellow of Trinity College, since 1971, University of Cambridge; *b* 4 March 1947; *s* of Joseph Edward Hinch and Mary Grace Hinch (*née* Chandler); *m* 1969, Christine Bridges; one *s* one *d*. *Educ:* Edmonton County Grammar Sch.; Trinity Coll., Cambridge (BA 1968; PhD 1973). Asst Lectr, 1972–75, Lectr, 1975–94, Reader, 1994–98, Univ. of Cambridge.Fellow, APS, 2003. Chevalier de l'ordre national du Mérite (France), 1997. *Publications:* Perturbation Methods, 1991; papers on fluid mechanics and its applications in scientific jls. *Address:* Trinity College, Cambridge CB2 1TQ. *T:* (01223) 338427.

HINCHCLIFFE, Peter Robert Mossom, CMG 1988; CVO 1979; HM Diplomatic Service, retired; Ambassador to Jordan, 1993–97; *b* 9 April 1937; *s* of Herbert Peter and Jeannie Hinchcliffe; *m* 1965, Archbold Harriet Siddall; three *d*. *Educ:* Elm Park, Killylea, Co. Armagh, Prep. Sch.; Radley Coll.; Trinity Coll., Dublin (BA (Hons), MA). Military service, short service commission, W Yorks Regt, 1955–57; TCD, Dublin Univ., 1957–61; HMOCS: West Aden Protectorate, South Arabian Fedn, 1961–67; Admin. Asst, Birmingham Univ., 1968–69; FCO: 1st Sec., Near Eastern Dept, 1969–70; 1st Sec., UK Mission to UN, 1971–74; 1st Sec. and Head of Chancery, Kuwait, 1974–76; Asst Head of Science and Technology and Central and Southern African Depts, FCO, 1976–78; Dep. High Comr, Dar es Salaam, 1978–81; Consul-Gen., Dubai, 1981–85; Hd of Information Dept, FCO, 1985–87; Ambassador to Kuwait, 1987–90; High Comr to Zambia, 1990–93. Chm., Hutton and Paxton Community Council, 2001–05. Hon. Fellow, Edin. Univ., 1997; Hon. Adjunct Fellow, Curtin Univ., WA, 2002. *Publications:* Time to Kill Sparrows (poetry anthology), 1999; (with B. Milton-Edwards): Jordan: a Hashemite Legacy, 2001, 2nd edn 2008; Conflicts in the Middle East since 1945, 2001, 3rd edn 2007; Without Glory in Arabia: the British retreat from Aden, 2006. *Recreations:* golf, tennis, writing poetry. *Address:* The Old Bakery, Willis Wynd, Duns, Berwickshire TD11 4AD. *Clubs:* East India, Devonshire, Sports and Public Schools; Duns Golf; Royal Co. Down Golf (Newcastle, Co. Down).

HINCHCLIFFE, Dr Peter Roy; environmental consultant, since 2004; *b* 27 May 1946; *s* of Herbert Hinchcliffe and Lucy Hinchcliffe (*née* Avis); *m* 1969, Carole Musetti; one *s* one *d*. *Educ:* Liverpool Univ. (BSc; PhD 1970). FCIWEM 1991. Chemist, Lancs and Western Sea Fisheries Cttee, 1970–75; joined Department of the Environment, 1975: Chief Scientist, Marine Pollution Control Unit, 1986–91; Head: Waste Tech. Div., 1991–96; Chemicals and Biotechnol. Div., 1996–2002; Sec., Royal Commn on Envmtl Pollution, 2002–04. Gulf Medal, 1992. *Publications:* contrib. papers on marine pollution to Jl Marine Biol. Assoc. and other jls. *Recreations:* photography, computers, gardening, music. *Address:* 25 Dinorben Close, Fleet, Hants GU52 7SL. *T:* (01252) 684157; *e-mail:* peter@hinchcliffe.me.uk.

HINCHINGBROOKE, Viscount; Luke Timothy Charles Montagu; *b* 5 Dec. 1969; *er s* and *heir* of Earl of Sandwich, *qv*; *m* 2004, Julie, *d* of Thomas L. Fisher, Chicago; one *s*. *Educ:* Westminster Sch.; Columbia Univ., NY. Director: Wide Multimedia, 1997–2001; Metropolitan Film Sch., 2003–. *Heir:* *s* Hon. William James Hayman Montagu, *b* 2 Nov. 2004. *Address:* c/o Mapperton House, Beaminster, Dorset DT8 3NR.

HINCHLIFF, Stephen, CBE 1976; Chairman and Managing Director, Dexion Group, 1976–91, retired; *b* 11 July 1926; *s* of Gordon Henry and Winifred Hinchliff; *m* 1987, Ann Fiona Maudsley; one *d* and one *s* one *d* from a previous marriage. *Educ:* Almondbury Grammar Sch., Huddersfield; Boulevard Nautical Coll., Hull; Huddersfield Coll. of Technology; Cranfield Inst. of Technology (MSc). FIMechE, FIET. Production Engr, Dowty Auto Units Ltd, 1953–54; Dowty Seals Ltd: Chief Prodn Engr, 1953–54; Works Manager, 1954–56; Dir, 1956–76; Dep. Man. Dir, 1966–67; Man. Dir, 1967–76; Dep. Chm., Dowty Gp Ltd, 1973–76; Man. Dir, Dowty Gp Industrial Div., 1973–76. CCMI; FRSA. *Recreation:* reading, spectator sports, family. *Address:* Cedar House, Little Gaddesden, Berkhamsted, Herts HP4 1PE. *T:* (01442) 843728.

HINCHLIFFE, David Martin; *b* 14 Oct. 1948; *s* of late Robert Victor Hinchliffe and Muriel Hinchliffe; *m* 1982, Julia (*née* North); one *s* one *d*. *Educ:* Lawefield Lane Primary Sch., Wakefield; Cathedral C of E Secondary Modern Sch., Wakefield; Leeds Polytechnic (Cert. in Social Work); Bradford Univ. (MA Social Work and Community Work); Huddersfield Polytechnic (Cert Ed). Social Work with Leeds Social Services, 1968–79; Social Work Tutor, Kirklees Metropolitan Borough Council, 1980–87. MP (Lab) Wakefield, 1987–2005. An opposition front bench spokesman on personal social services and community care, 1992–95. Chairman: Health Select Cttee, 1997–2005; Select Cttee on Adoption and Children Bill, 2001 and 2002. *Publications:* Rugby's Class War, 2000; (ed) A Westminster XIII: Parliamentarians and Rugby League, 2002. *Recreations:* Rugby League—supporter of Wakefield Trinity RLFC, inland waterways, genealogy. *Club:* Wakefield Labour.

HIND, Andrew Fleming, FCA; Chief Executive, Charity Commission, since 2004; *b* 29 Sept. 1955; *s* of Andrew Hind and Mary Hind; *m* 1985, Christina; three *s*. *Educ:* Portsmouth Grammar Sch.; Southampton Univ. (BSc). FCA 1979. Ernst & Young, 1976–80; Pannell Kerr Forster, Kenya, 1980–83; Divl Financial Controller, Balfour Beatty Ltd, 1983–86; Dir of Finance, 1986–89, Dep. Chief Exec., 1989–91, ActionAid; Dir of Finance and Corporate Services, Barnardo's, 1992–95; Dir of Finance and Business Develt, 1995–2002, Chief Operating Officer, 2002–04, BBC World Service. Charity Finance Directors' Group: Co-founder, 1988; Mem., Exec. Cttee, 1988–94; Chm., 1992–94. Member: Commn on Effectiveness and the Voluntary Sector, NCVO, 1990; Charity Awards Judges Panel, 2001–04 (Chm., 2003–04); Audit Cttee, Commonwealth Secretariat, 2004–06; Commn on the Future of Volunteering, 2006–08. Chm., Public Sector Adv. Bd., ICAEW, 2007–. Trustee: Internat. Fundraising Gp, 1992–95; VSO, 1995–98; UNICEF UK, 1995–2002 (Treas., 1996–2002); Trustee and Treas., Diana, Princess of Wales Meml Fund, 1999–2004. *Publications:* (ed jtly) Charity Managers and Charity Trustees – Meeting the Challenges of the 1990s, 1993; (ed) The Charity Finance Handbook, 1994; The Governance and Management of Charities, 1995. *Recreations:* running, golf, travel, collecting old books on Africa. *Address:* Charity Commission, Harmsworth House, 13–15 Bouverie Street, EC4Y 8DP. *T:* (0870) 333 0123, *Fax:* (020) 7674 2310; *e-mail:* andrew.hind@charitycommission.gsi.gov.uk.

HIND, Rt Rev. John William; *see* Chichester, Bishop of.

HIND, Kenneth Harvard, CBE 1995; barrister; *b* 15 Sept. 1949; *s* of George Edward and Brenda Hind; one *s* one *d*; partner, Sue Hall, JP. *Educ:* Woodhouse Grove Sch., Bradford; Leeds Univ. (LLB 1971); Inns of Court Sch. of Law. Pres., Leeds Univ. Union, 1971–72. Called to the Bar, Gray's Inn, 1973; practised North Eastern circuit, 1973–83. MP (C) West Lancashire, 1983–92; contested (C): W Lancashire, 1992; Selby, 1997. PPS to Minister of State: for Defence Procurement, 1986–87; for Employment, 1987–89; for Northern Ireland, 1989–90; PPS to Sec. of State for Northern Ireland, 1990–92. Officer, 1995–97, Chm., 1997–2002, Conservative Candidates Assoc. Member: Soc. of Conservative Lawyers, 1983–; Justice, Internat. Commn of Jurists, 1983–. Chm., Ribble Valley Conservative Assoc., 2006–; Mem., Conservative Nat. Convention. Hon. Vice-Pres., Central and West Lancs Chamber of Industry and Commerce, 1983–92. *Recreations:* music, sailing Enterprise, cricket. *Address:* 3 Temple Gardens, Temple, EC4Y 9AU; 15 Winckley Square, Preston PR1 3JJ.

HINDE, Prof. Robert Aubrey, CBE 1988; FRS 1974; FBA; Master of St John's College, Cambridge, 1989–94 (Fellow, 1951–54, 1958–89 and since 1994); *b* 26 Oct. 1923; *s* of late Dr and Mrs E. B. Hinde, Norwich; *m* 1st, 1948, Hester Cecily (marr. diss. 1971), *d* of late C. R. V. Coutts; two *s* two *d*; 2nd, 1971, Joan Gladys, *d* of F. J. Stevenson; two *d*. *Educ:* Oundle Sch.; St John's Coll., Cambridge; Balliol Coll., Oxford (Hon. Fellow, 1986). Served Coastal Comd, RAF, Flt-Lt, 1941–45. Research Asst, Edward Grey Inst., Univ. of Oxford, 1948–50; Curator, Ornithological Field Station (now sub-Dept of Animal Behaviour), Madingley, Cambridge, 1950–65; St John's Coll., Cambridge: Steward, 1956–58; Tutor, 1958–63; Royal Soc. Res. Prof., Cambridge Univ., 1963–89. Hon. Dir, MRC Unit on Develt and Integration of Behaviour, 1970–89. Hitchcock Prof., Univ. of California, 1979; Green Vis. Scholar, Univ. of Texas, 1983. Mem. Council, Royal Soc., 1985–87. Croonian Lect., Royal Soc., 1990. Chm., British Pugwash Gp, 2003–08. Mem., Academia Europaea, 1990. Hon. Member: Assoc. for the Study of Animal Behaviour, 1987; Deutsche Ornithologische Ges., 1988; For. Hon. Mem., Amer. Acad. of Arts and Sciences, 1974; For. Associate, Nat. Acad. of Scis, USA, 1978; Hon. Fellow, Amer. Ornithologists' Union, 1977; Hon. FBPsS 1981; Hon. FRCPsych 1988; Hon. FTCD, 1990; Hon. FBA 2002. Hon. ScD: Univ. Libre, Brussels, 1974; Paris (Nanterre), 1979; Stirling, 1991; Göteborg, 1991; Edinburgh, 1992; Western Ontario, 1996; Oxford, 1998. Scientific Medal, Zoological Soc., 1961; Leonard Cammer Medal in Psychiatry, Columbia Coll., NY, 1980; Osman Hill Award, Primate Soc. of GB, 1980; Albert Einstein Award for Psychiatry, Albert Einstein Coll. of Medicine, NY, 1987; Huxley Medal, RAI, 1990; Distinguished Scientists Award, Soc. for Res. in Child Develt, 1991; Distinguished Career Award, Internat. Soc. for Study of Personal Relationships, 1992; Frink Medal, Zool Soc., 1992; G. Stanley Hall Medal, Amer. Psychol Assoc., 1993; Royal Medal, Royal Soc., 1996; Society's Medal, Assoc. for Study of Animal Behaviour, 1997; Bowlby/Ainsworth Award, Centre for Mental Health Promotion and NY Attachment Consortium, 2003. *Publications:* Animal Behaviour: a synthesis of Ethology and Comparative Psychology, 1966; (ed) Bird Vocalizations: their relations to current problems in biology and psychology, 1969; (ed jtly) Short Term Changes in Neural Activity and Behaviour, 1970; (ed) Non-Verbal Communication, 1972; (ed jtly) Constraints on Learning, 1973; Biological Bases of Human Social Behaviour, 1974; (ed jtly) Growing Points in Ethology, 1976; Towards Understanding Relationships, 1979; Ethology: its nature and relations with other sciences, 1982; (jtly) Defended to Death, 1982; (ed and contrib.) Primate Social Relationships: an integrated approach, 1983; (ed jtly) Social Relationships and Cognitive Development, 1985; Individuals, Relationships and Culture, 1987; (ed jtly) Relationships within Families, 1988; (ed jtly) Aggression and War, 1989; (ed jtly) Education for Peace, 1989; (ed and contrib) The Institution of War, 1991; (ed jtly) Co-operation and Prosocial Behaviour, 1991; (ed jtly) War: a necessary evil? 1994; Relationships: a dialectical perspective, 1997; Why Gods Persist, 1999; Why Good is Good: the bases of morality, 2002; (jtly) War No More, 2003; Bending the Rules, 2007; sundry papers in biological and psychological journals. *Address:* St John's College, Cambridge CB2 1TP. *T:* (01223) 339356; Park Lane, Madingley, Cambridge CB23 8AL. *T:* (01954) 211816.

HINDE, Thomas; *see* Chitty, Sir Thomas Willes.

HINDLEY, Estella Jacqueline; QC 1992; **Her Honour Judge Hindley;** a Circuit Judge, since 1997; *b* 11 Oct. 1948; *d* of Arthur John Hindley and Olive Maud (*née* Stanley); *m* 1980, John Gilbert Harvey; one *s*. *Educ:* Univ. of Hull (LLB Hons). Called to the Bar, Gray's Inn, 1971; a Recorder, 1989–97. Mem., Parole Bd, 1998–. Chm., Birmingham Children's Hosp. NHS Trust, 2000–04. Pres., Birmingham Medico-Legal Soc., 1999–2001; Sec., UK Assoc. of Women Judges, 2006–. *Recreations:* book collecting, music, theatre, painting. *Address:* The Priory Courts, 33 Bull Street, Birmingham B4 6DW. *T:* (0121) 681 3000.

HINDLEY, Michael John; Member (Lab), Lancashire County Council, 2001–05; *b* 11 April 1947; *s* of John and Edna Hindley; *m* 1980, Ewa Agnieszka (*née* Leszczyc-Grabianka); one *d*. *Educ:* Clitheroe Royal Grammar School; London University (BA Hons); Lancaster University (MA); Free University of West Berlin. Labour Councillor, Hyndburn District Council, 1979–84 (Leader, 1981–84); contested (Lab) Blackpool North, 1983. MEP (Lab) Lancashire E, 1984–94, Lancashire S, 1994–99. Mem., Exec. Bd, War on Want, 1999–. Associate Prof., Georgetown Univ., Washington, 1993–. Advr on Ext. Relations, Blackburn Coll., Lancs, 2007–. *Recreations:* walking, reading, music, travel. *Address:* 27 Commercial Road, Great Harwood, Lancs BB6 7HX. *T:* (01254) 887017. *Club:* Reform.

HINDLEY, Stephen Lewis, CBE 2006; FICE, FCIOB; Executive Chairman, Midas Group Ltd, since 2002; *b* 11 March 1949; *s* of Arthur Stanley Hindley and Ann Hindley; *m* 1973, Moira Ann Williamson; two *d*. *Educ:* St Philip's Grammar Sch., Birmingham; Salford Univ. (BSc). FICE 1997; FCIOB 2001. Civil engr, Trafalgar House Gp, 1970–76; Project Manager, John Mowlem plc, 1976–89; Man. Dir, E. Thomas (subsid. co. of John Mowlem), 1989–98; Chief Exec., 1998–2001, Chm. and CEO, 2001–05, Midas Gp Ltd. *Recreations:* running, hill-walking, sailing, golf, classic cars, motor sport. *Address:* Midas Group, Midas House, Pynes Hill, Exeter EX2 5WS. *T:* (01392) 356200, *Fax:* (01392) 8553814; *e-mail:* shindley@midasgroup.co.uk. *Club:* Royal Automobile.

HINDLIP, 6th Baron *cr* 1886; **Charles Henry Allsopp;** Bt 1880; Deputy Chairman, Agnew's, 2003–04; *b* 5 Aug. 1940; *e s* of 5th Baron Hindlip and Cecily Valentine Jane, *o d* of Lt-Col Malcolm Borwick, DSO; *S* father, 1993; *m* 1968, Fiona Victoria Jean

Atherley, *d* of late Hon. William Johnston McGowan, 2nd *s* of 1st Baron McGowan, KBE; one *s* three *d*. *Educ:* Eton. Coldstream Guards, 1959–62; joined Christie's, 1962; Gen. Manager, Christie's New York, 1965–70; Christie, Manson & Woods: Dir, 1970; Dep. Chm., 1985; Chm., 1986–96; Chm., Christie's Internat., 1996–2002. Trustee, Chatham Historic Dockyard, 1989–. *Recreations:* painting, shooting, ski-ing. *Heir: s* Hon. Henry William Allsopp, *b* 8 June 1973. *Address:* Lydden House, King's Stag, Dorset DT10 2AU. *Clubs:* White's, Pratt's; Corviglia Ski.

HINDMARCH, Anya; Founder, and Chief Executive Officer, Anya Hindmarch, since 1987; *b* Burnham, 7 May 1968; *d* of Michael and Susan Hindmarch; *m* 1996, Hugh James Seymour; four *s* one *d*. *Educ:* New Hall Sch. Consultant, British Airways First Cl., 1999–. Mem., Cons. Party New Enterprise Council, 2008–. Co-Chm., Summer Exhibn Preview Party, Royal Acad. of Arts, 2006, 2007, 2008. Chm., Cons. Party Black and White Fundraiser, 2008. Accessories Designer of Year, 2001, Designer Brand of Year, 2007, British Fashion Council; Luxury Briefing Award for Excellence, 2001; Glamour mag. Award, 2006, 2007; Elle Style Awards for Outstanding Achievement, 2008. *Recreations:* art, architecture, graphic design, photography, eating, sleeping, children. *Address:* Anya Hindmarch Ltd, The Stable Block, Plough Brewery, 516 Wandsworth Road, SW8 3JX. *T:* (020) 7501 0177, *Fax:* (020) 7501 0170; *e-mail:* Katejames@anyahindmarch.com.

HINDMARSH, Irene, JP, MA; Principal, St Aidan's College, University of Durham, 1970–88; Second Pro-Vice-Chancellor, University of Durham, 1982–85; *b* 22 Oct. 1923; *d* of Albert Hindmarsh and Elizabeth (*née* White). *Educ:* Heaton High Sch.; Lady Margaret Hall, Oxford (MA Hons French); King's Coll., Univ. of Durham (PGCE). Taught at St Paul's Girls' Sch., London, 1947–49, Rutherford High Sch., Newcastle upon Tyne, 1949–59; Interchange Teacher, Lycée de Jeunes Filles, Dax, Landes, France, 1954–55; Lectr in Educn and French, King's Coll., Durham, 1959–64; Headmistress, Birkenhead High Sch., GPDST, 1964–70. Vis. Prof., New York State Univ., Syracuse, Cornell, Harvard, 1962; Delegate of Internat. Fedn of Univ. Women to UNO, NY, to Commns on Human Rights and Status of Women, 1962; Vis. Professor: Fu-Dan Univ., Shanghai, 1979, and again, 1980; SW China Teachers' Univ., Beibei, Sichuan, and Fu-Dan Univ., Shanghai, 1986. Delegate/Translator to internat. confs of FIPESO, 1963–70; Chairman: Internat. Cttee of Headmistresses' Assoc., 1966–70; Internat. Panel of Joint Four, 1967–70. Mem. of Council, Chillingham Wild Cattle Assoc., 1988–98. Editor, Internat. Bull. of AHM, 1966–70. JP Birkenhead 1966, Durham 1974. FRSA 1989. *Publications:* various articles on educnl topics in AGM papers of Assoc. of Head Mistresses; contribs to prelim. papers of FIPESO meetings; seminar papers to symposia on lit. topics, Sèvres, under auspices of Council of Europe; contrib. re St Aidan's to Durham History from the Air. *Recreations:* travel, music, theatre, films, art, architecture. *Address:* 8 Dickens Wynd, Merryoaks, Elvet Moor, Durham DH1 3QR. *T:* (0191) 386 1881.

HINDS, Prof. Edward Allen, DPhil; FRS 2004; Professor of Physics, Imperial College London, since 2002; *b* 8 Sept. 1949; *s* of Laurence and Ruth Hinds; *m* 1972, Ann Carter; one *s* three *d*. *Educ:* Jesus Coll., Oxford (BA 1971; DPhil 1974). Professor of Physics: Yale Univ., 1977–95; Univ. of Sussex, 1995–2002. Alfred P. Sloan Fellow, 1981–85; Alexander von Humboldt Res. Award, 1998–2003; EPSRC Sen. Res. Fellow, 1999–2004; Royal Soc. Res. Prof., 2006–. *Publications:* articles in academic physics jls. *Recreations:* music, physics. *Address:* 213 The Blackett Laboratory, Imperial College London, Prince Consort Road, SW7 2BW; *e-mail:* ed.hinds@imperial.ac.uk.

HINDS, Lesley Adelaide; Lord Lieutenant and Lord Provost, City of Edinburgh, 2003–07; Chair, Health Scotland, since 2001; *b* Dundee, 3 Aug. 1956; *d* of late Kenneth Nicol and of Ena Nicol; *m* 1977, Martin Hinds; one *s* two *d*. *Educ:* Kirkton High Sch., Dundee; Dundee Coll. of Educn. Primary sch. teacher, Deans Primary, W Lothian, 1977–80. Mem. (Lab), Edinburgh DC, 1984–96 (Leader, 1993–96), City of Edin. Council, 1996–2007. Director: N Edinburgh Area Renewal; N Edinburgh Arts; Pilton Partnership. Formerly Chm., Edinburgh Internat. Conf. Centre; Chair: Edinburgh Fest. Soc., 2003–07; Edinburgh Mil. Tattoo Ltd, 2003–07. *Recreations:* theatre, dance, swimming, travel. *Address:* 4 Easter Drylaw Place, Edinburgh EH4 2QD.

HINDUJA, Gopichand Parmanand; President, Hinduja Group of Companies, since 1962; *b* 29 Feb. 1940; *s* of Parmanand Deepchand Hinduja and Jamuna Parmanand Hinduja; *m* 1963, Sunita Gurnani; two *s* one *d*. *Educ:* Jai Hind Coll., Bombay, India. Joined family business, 1958; Head, Hinduja Gp's ops in Iran, 1958–78; resident in UK, 1982–; jtly (with brother) initiated diversification and expansion of Hinduja Gp. Pres., Hinduja Foundn, 1962–. Member: Adv. Council, Hinduja Cambridge Trust, 1991–; Duke of Edinburgh's Award Fellowship, 1987–. Patron: Balaji Temple, UK; Swaminarayan Hindu Mission, London. Chm., Gurnanak Trust, Teheran. MInstD. Hon. LLD Westminster, 1996; Hon. DEc Richmond Coll., 1997. *Recreations:* Indian music, travel, sailing, yoga. *Address:* Hinduja Group of Companies, New Zealand House, 80 Haymarket, SW1Y 4TE. *T:* (020) 7839 4661. *Clubs:* Royal Automobile, Annabel's.
See also S. P. Hinduja.

HINDUJA, Srichand Parmanand; Chairman, Hinduja Group of Companies, since 1962; *b* 28 Nov. 1935; *s* of Hinduja Parmanand Deepchand and Hinduja Jamuna Parmanand Bajaj; *m* 1963, Madhu Srichand Menda; two *d*. *Educ:* National Coll., Bombay, India; Davar Coll. of Commerce, Mumbai. Joined family business; jtly (with brother) initiated diversification and expansion of Hinduja Gp. Chm., Hinduja Foundn, 1962–. Global Co-ordinator, IndusInd, 1962; Pres., IndusInd Internat. Fedn, 1996. Member, Advisory Council: Dharam Indic Res. Centres, Columbia, USA and Cambridge, UK; Hinduja Cambridge Trust, 1991–; Judge Inst. of Mgt, Cambridge, 1997. Mem., Duke of Edinburgh's Award Fellowship. Patron, Centre of India/US Educn, USA. Mem. Corp., Massachusetts Gen. Hosp. Hon. LLD Westminster, 1996; Hon. DEc Richmond Coll., 1997. *Publications:* Indic Research and Contemporary Crisis, 1995; The Essence of Vedic Marriage for Success and Happiness, 1996. *Recreations:* sports in general, but particularly tennis, volleyball and cricket, Indian classical music. *Address:* Hinduja Group of Companies, New Zealand House, 80 Haymarket, SW1Y 4TE. *T:* (020) 7839 4661. *Clubs:* Royal Over-Seas League, Les Ambassadeurs.
See also G. P. Hinduja.

HINE, Dame Deirdre (Joan), DBE 1997; FRCP, FFPH; Chairman, BUPA Foundation, since 2004; President, British Medical Association, 2005–06; *b* 16 Sept. 1937; *d* of late David Alban Curran and Noreen Mary Curran (*née* Cliffe); *m* 1963, Raymond Hine; two *s*. *Educ:* Heathfield House, Cardiff; Charlton Park, Cheltenham; Welsh Nat. Sch. of Medicine (MB BCh). DPH 1964; FFPH (FFPHM 1978); FRCP 1993. Asst MO, Glamorgan CC, 1963–74; Specialist in Community Medicine, S Glam HA, 1974–82; Sen. Lectr in Geriatric Medicine, Univ. of Wales Coll. of Medicine, 1982–84; Dep. Chief MO, Welsh Office, 1984–87; Dir, Welsh Breast Cancer Screening Service, 1987–90; CMO, Welsh Office, 1990–97. Mem., Audit Commn, 1998–99; Chm., Commn for Health Improvement, 1999–2004. Non-exec. Dir, Dŵr Cymru, 2001–. Pres., RSocMed, 2000–02 (Chm., Press Bd, 2004–). Vice President: Marie Curie Cancer Care, 1998–; British Lung Foundn, 2005–; Chm., No Smoking Day, 1998–2001. *Publications:* papers on health promotion, health care of elderly, breast cancer screening, epidemiol. of old age in jls and text books; Calman-Hine report on cancer services. *Recreations:* travel, theatre reading, canal cruising.
See also P. D. Curran.

HINE, Rt Rev. John Franklin Meldon; Auxiliary Bishop in Southwark, (RC), an Titular Bishop of Beverly, since 2001; *b* 26 July 1938; *s* of Lt Comdr Jack F. W. Hine, RN and Moira E. Hine. *Educ:* Stonyhurst; Mayfield Coll.; Ven. English Coll., Rome Pontifical Gregorian Univ., Rome (PhL 1958; STB 1961). Assistant Priest: Worceste Park, S London, 1963–70; Maidstone, 1970–73; Chatham, 1973–78; Parish Priest Bearsted and Harrietsham, and Sec., subseq Chm., Diocesan Schs' Commn for Kent 1978–86; VG and Chancellor, Southwark Diocese, 1986–2001. Prelate of Honour, 1986 *Recreations:* golf, walking. *Address:* The Hermitage, More Park, West Malling, Kent ME1 6HN.

HINE, Air Chief Marshal Sir Patrick (Bardon), GCB 1989 (KCB 1983); GBE 1991 Air Officer Commanding-in-Chief, RAF Strike Command and Commander-in-Chief United Kingdom Air Forces, 1988–91; Joint Commander, British Forces, Gulf War 1990–91; Military Adviser to British Aerospace plc, 1992–99; *b* 14 July 1932; parents decd *m* 1956, Jill Adèle (*née* Gardner); three *s*. *Educ:* Peter Symonds Sch., Winchester. Served with Nos 1, 93 and 111 Sqns, 1952–60; Mem., Black Arrows aerobatic team, 1957–59 commanded: No 92 Sqn, 1962–64; No 17 Sqn, 1970–71; RAF Wildenrath, 1974–75 Dir, Public Relations (RAF), 1975–77; RCDS 1978; SASO, HQ RAF, Germany, 1979 ACAS (Policy), 1979–83; C-in-C RAF Germany and Comdr, Second Allied Tactical Ai Force, 1983–85; VCDS, 1985–87; Air Mem. for Supply and Orgn, 1987–88. Air ADC to the Queen, 1989–91. King of Arms, Order of the British Empire, 1997–. CCMI; FRAeS Winner, Carris Trophy, Hants, IoW and Channel Islands Golf Championship, an Brabazon Trophy, 1949; English Schoolboy Golf Internat., 1948–49; Inter-Services Golf 1952–57. QCVSA 1960. *Recreations:* golf, ski-ing, caravanning, photography. *Clubs* Royal Air Force; Colonels (Founder Mem.); Royal & Ancient Golf (St Andrews) Brokenhurst Manor Golf, Seniors.

HINES, (Melvin) Barry, FRSL; writer; *b* 30 June 1939; *s* of Richard and Annie Hines; *m* (marr. diss.); one *s* one *d*. *Educ:* Ecclesfield Grammar Sch.; Loughborough Coll. of Educ (Teaching Cert.). FRSL 1977. Teacher of Physical Educn, London, 1960–62 and S Yorks 1962–72; Yorkshire Arts Fellow in Creative Writing, Sheffield Univ., 1972–74; Midlands Arts Fellow in Creative Writing, Matlock Coll. of Higher Educn, 1975–77 Sheffield City Polytechnic: Arts Council Fellow in Creative Writing, 1982–84; Hon Fellow in Creative Writing, 1984; Hon. Fellow, 1985. *Television scripts:* Billy's Last Stand 1971; Speech Day, 1973; Two Men from Derby, 1976; The Price of Coal (2 films), 1977 The Gamekeeper, 1979; A Question of Leadership, 1981; Threads, 1984; Shooting Stars 1990; Born Kicking, 1992; *screenplays:* Kes, 1970; Looks and Smiles, 1981. *Publications* (fiction): The Blinder, 1966; A Kestrel for a Knave, 1968; First Signs, 1972; The Gamekeeper, 1975; The Price of Coal, 1979; Looks and Smiles, 1981; Unfinished Business, 1983; The Heart of It, 1994; Elvis over England, 1998. *Address:* c/o The Agency 24 Pottery Lane, Holland Park, W11 4LZ. *T:* (020) 7229 9216. *Club:* Hoyland Common Workingmen's (near Barnsley).

HINGLEY, Robert Charles Anthony; Director-General, Panel on Takeovers and Mergers, since 2007; *b* 11 May 1960; *s* of Anthony Hingley and Ruth Hingley; *m* 1993 Arabella Ballard; one *s* one *d*. *Educ:* Rugby Sch.; Corpus Christi Coll., Cambridge (BA Hons 1981). Admitted Solicitor, 1984; Articled Clerk/Solicitor, Coward Chance 1982–85; J. Henry Schroder & Co. Ltd, 1985–2000: Dir of Investment Banking, 1994 Hd of German Investment Banking, 1995–96; Hd of Financial Instns Gp, 1997–2000 Citigroup Investment Bank: Man. Dir and Global Co-Hd of Financial Instns Gp 2000–03; Hd of German Investment Banking, 2001–03; Vice-Chm., Lexicon Partners 2005–; Chief Financial Officer, Save the Children, 2007. Trustee: Arvon Foundn, 2006– Save the Children, 2007–. Gov., Rugby Sch., 2007–. *Recreations:* golf, cricket, reading dog-walking. *Address:* c/o Panel on Takeovers and Mergers, 10 Paternoster Square EC4M 7DY. *T:* (020) 7382 9026; *e-mail:* roberthingley@aol.com. *Club:* MCC.

HINKLEY, Prof. David Victor, PhD; Professor of Statistics, University of California at Santa Barbara, since 1995; *b* 10 Sept. 1944; *s* of Eric Samson Hinkley and Edna Gertrude (*née* Alger); *m*; one *s* one *d*. *Educ:* Birmingham Univ. (BSc 1965); Imperial Coll., London (PhD 1969). MA Oxon 1990. Asst Lectr in Maths, Imperial Coll., London, 1967–69; Ass Prof. in Stats, Stanford Univ., 1969–71; Lectr in Maths, Imperial Coll., 1971–73; Associate Prof. and Prof. in Stats, Univ. of Minnesota, 1973–80; Prof. in Maths, Univ. of Texas 1980–91; Prof. of Statistical Sci., and Fellow of St Anne's Coll., Oxford Univ., 1989–95 Editor: Annals of Statistics, 1980–82; Biometrika, 1991–92. *Publications:* Theoretical Statistics, 1973; Problems and Solutions in Theoretical Statistics, 1977; Statistical Theory and Modelling, 1990; Bootstrap Methods and Their Application, 1997; articles in statistical and scientific jls. *Recreations:* photography, tennis, botanical observation. *Address* Department of Statistics and Applied Probability, University of California at Santa Barbara CA 93106–3110, USA. *T:* (805) 8938331.

HINKLEY, Sarah Ann, (Sally), CBE 1995; Executive Director, Professional Standards Institute of Chartered Accountants in England and Wales, 2003–05; *b* 28 March 1950; *d* of Eric David Booth and Mary Booth; *m* 1st, 1980, Nigel Dorling (marr. diss. 1988); one *s*; 2nd, 1998, Alan Hinkley; one step *d*. *Educ:* Kendal High Sch.; Callington Grammar Sch.; Girton Coll., Cambridge (BA 1972; MA). Joined Dept of the Environment, 1974 Private Sec. to Permanent Sec., 1980–81; Principal, 1981–86; Asst Sec., 1987; Hd, Central Policy Planning Unit, 1987–88; Dir of Finance and Resources, Historic Royal Palaces 1989–92; Department of National Heritage, later of Culture, Media and Sport, 1992–99 Hd, Nat. Lottery Div. and Dir of Finance, 1992–94; Hd, Broadcasting Policy Div. 1994–95; Under Sec., 1995; Hd, Libraries, Galls and Museums Gp, 1995–98; Hd, Educn Trng, Arts and Sports Gp, 1998–99; Dir, Performance and Change Mgt Gp, Cabinet Office, 1999–2002. FRSA 1998. *Recreations:* writing, family.

HINKS, Frank Peter; QC 2000; writer and illustrator of children's stories; *b* 8 July 1950 *s* of Henry John Hinks and Patricia May Hinks (*née* Adams); *m* 1982, Susan Mary, *d* of Co J. A. Haire; three *s*. *Educ:* Bromley Grammar Sch.; St Catherine's Coll., Oxford (schol. BA 1st Cl. Hons 1971; BCL 1st Cl. Hons 1972; MA). Called to the Bar, Lincoln's Inn 1973, Bencher, 2008; in practice at the Bar, 1974–. Churchwarden, St Peter and St Paul Shoreham, 1995–2005. Liveryman, Innholders' Co. *Publications:* include: The Vicar's Chickens, 1992; The Land of Lost Hair, 1992; Creatures of the Forest, 1993; The Crystal Key, 1995; Ramion (collected stories), 2003 (trans. Korean, 2006); The Dim Daft Dwarves, 2004; The Bands of Evil, 2004; The Magic Magpie, 2004; The Cruel Count 2004; Realm of Ramion (collected stories), 2004; The Seven Stones of Iliana, 2005; The Black Marchesa, 2005; Gary and the Frog Prince, 2005; The Embodiment of Evil, 2005 Swords of Ramion (collected stories), 2005. *Recreations:* collecting jugs, gardening *Address:* 6 New Square, Lincoln's Inn, WC2A 3QS.

HINTON, Prof. Denys James, FRIBA; Chairman, Redditch New Town Development Corporation, 1978–85; *b* 12 April 1921; *s* of James and Nell Hinton; *m* 1971, Lynette

Payne (*née* Pattinson); one *d*. *Educ:* Reading Sch.; Architectural Assoc. (MSc; AADip.). FRIBA. Asst, Wells Coates, 1950–52; Birmingham Sch. of Architecture: Lectr, 1952–57; Sen. Lectr, 1957–64; Dir, 1964–72; Prof. of Architecture, Univ. of Aston, 1966–81, now Emeritus. Sen. Partner, Hinton Brown Langstone, Architects, Warwick, 1960–86. Chairman: Architects Registration Council of UK, 1983–86; Fabric Adv. Cttee, St Philip's Cathedral, Birmingham, 1992–93; Pres., EC Architects' Directive Adv. Cttee, 1992–93; Vice-Pres. (formerly Vice-Chm.), Exec. Cttee, Internat. New Towns Assoc., 1980–85. *Publications:* Performance Characteristics of the Athenian Bouleterion, RIBA Athens Bursary, 1962; Great Interiors: High Victorian Period, 1967; contrib. RIBA and Architects Jl, papers on architectural education, Inst. Bulletin (worship and religious architecture), Univ. of Birmingham. *Recreations:* travel, moving house, water colours. *Address:* 7 Hill View Road, S Witham, Lincs NG33 5QW. *T:* (01572) 767572.

HINTON, Prof. Geoffrey Everest, FRS 1998; FRSCan; PhD; Professor of Computer Science, since 2001, University Professor, 2006, University of Toronto; *b* 6 Dec. 1947; *s* of Prof. Howard Everest Hinton, FRS and late Margaret Rose Hinton; *m* 1997, Jacqueline Ford; one *s* one *d*. *Educ:* King's Coll., Cambridge (BA Exptl Psychology 1970); Univ. of Edinburgh (PhD Artificial Intelligence 1978). Fellow: Sussex Univ., 1976–78; UCSD, 1978–80; Faculty Mem., Computer Sci. Dept, Carnegie-Mellon Univ., 1982–87; Fellow, Canadian Inst. for Advanced Res. and Prof. of Computer Science and Psychology, Univ. of Toronto, 1987–98; Dir, Gatsby Computational Neurosci. Unit, UCL, 1998–2001. Pres., Cognitive Science Soc., 1992–93. Fellow, Amer. Assoc. for Artificial Intelligence, 1991; FRSCan 1996. Award for contribs to IT, IT Assoc. of Canada/NSERC, 1992. *Publications:* (ed jtly) Parallel Models of Human Associative Memory, 1989; Connectionist Symbol Processing, 1992; (ed jtly) Unsupervised Learning: foundations of neural computation, 1999; numerous papers and articles in learned jls. *Address:* Department of Computer Science, University of Toronto, 6 King's College Road, Toronto, ON M5S 3G4, Canada. *T:* (416) 978 7564, *Fax:* (416) 978 1455.

HINTON, Leslie Frank; Chief Executive Officer, Dow Jones & Company, since 2007; a Director, Press Association, since 1996; *b* 19 Feb. 1944; *s* of late Frank Arthur Hinton and Lilian Amy Hinton (*née* Bruce); *m* 1968, Mary Christine Weadick; four *s* one *d*. *Educ:* British Army schs in Germany, Libya, Egypt, Ethiopia and Singapore. Reporter, Adelaide News, SA, 1960–65; desk editor, British United Press, London, 1965–66; reporter, The Sun, 1966–69; writer editor, Adelaide News, 1969–70; reporter, The Sun, 1971–76; US corresp., News Internat., NYC, 1976–78; news editor, 1978–80, Managing Editor, 1980–82, The Star, NYC; Associate Editor, Boston Herald, 1982–85; Editor-in-Chief, Star Mag., 1985–87; Exec. Vice Pres., 1987–90, Pres., 1990–91, Murdoch Magazines, NYC; Pres. and Chief Exec. Officer, News America Publishing Inc., NYC, 1991–93; Chm. and Chief Exec. Officer, Fox Television Stations Inc. and Fox News Inc., LA, 1993–95; Exec. Chm., News International Ltd, 1995–2007. Director: British Sky Broadcasting plc, 1999–2003; Johnston Press plc, 2005–07. Chairman: Code of Practice Cttee, Press Complaints Commn, 1998–2007; Council, CPU, 1999–2007; Dir, Press Standards Bd of Finance, 2003–07. Mem. Bd of Trustees, Amer. Sch. in London, 1999–2007. *Address:* Dow Jones & Company, 1 World Financial Center, 200 Liberty Street, New York, NY 10281, USA.

HINTON, Michael Herbert, FCA; FFA; *b* 10 Nov. 1934; *s* of late Walter Leonard Hinton and Freda Millicent Lillian Hinton; *m* 1st, 1955, Sarah Sunderland (marr. diss. 1982); one *s* two *d*; 2nd, 1984, Jane Margaret Manley, *d* of Arthur Crichton Howell. *Educ:* Ardingly Coll. Liveryman: Farmers' Co., 1964 (Master, 1981–82); Wheelwrights' Co.; Arbitrators' Co. (Master, 1998–99); Mem. Court of Common Council, 1970–71, Alderman, 1971–79, Ward of Billingsgate; Clerk to Wheelwrights' Co., 1965–71; Sheriff, City of London, 1977–78. JP City of London, 1971. FRSA. *Recreations:* cricket, Association football, theatre, travel. *Address:* 37 Westgate Road, Beckenham, Kent BR3 5DT. *T:* (020) 8650 1996. *Clubs:* Farmers, MCC, City Livery (Pres., 1976–77).

HINTZ, B. Jürgen; Group Chief Executive, Novar plc (formerly Caradon plc), 1998–2006; *b* 3 May 1942; *s* of Karl-Heinz Hintz and Elsbeth Parr; *m* 2nd, 1996, Kirsty MacMaster; one *s* one *d*, and one step *d*. *Educ:* Univ. of N Carolina State (BSc). Physicist, 1964–75; Procter & Gamble Inc.: various positions, 1976–89; Dir, 1989–91; Chief Exec., CarnaudMetalBox, 1991–95. Non-executive Director: Apple Computers Inc., 1994–97; Inchcape plc, 1994–98. Mem., Supervisory Bd, Head NV, 2003–. *Recreations:* ski-ing, tennis. *Address:* Head NV, Rokin 55, 1012 KK Amsterdam, Netherlands.

HIPKIN, John; Head of English, Meridian School, Royston, Herts, 1977–95; *b* 9 April 1935; *s* of Jack Hipkin and Elsie Hipkin; *m* 1963, Bronwyn Vaughan Dewey (marr. diss. 1985); four *s* one *d*; one *d*; *m* 2004, Marie-Louise Holland; one *d*. *Educ:* Surbiton Grammar Sch. for Boys; LSE (BScEcon). Asst Teacher, 1957–65; Research Officer: King's Coll., Cambridge, 1965–68; Univ. of East Anglia, 1968–71; Sec., Schools Council Working Party on Whole Curriculum, 1973–74; Dir, Adv. Centre for Educn, 1974–77. Cambridge City Councillor (Lib Dem), 1992–; Mayor of Cambridge, 2005–06. Historic Envmt Champion for Cambridge, 2005–. Trustee, Winter Comfort for the Homeless, 2000–. *Publications:* (jtly) New Wine in Old Bottles, 1967; The Massacre of Peterloo (a play), 1968, 2nd edn 1974; (ed jtly) Education for the Seventies, 1970. *Recreations:* theatre, foreign travel, history, medieval music. *Address:* 15 Oxford Road, Cambridge CB4 3PH. *T:* (01223) 564126.

HIPKINS, Michael Francis, PhD; Director, Student Finance, Department for Innovation, Universities and Skills (formerly Department for Education and Skills), since 2004; *b* 12 March 1951; *s* of Leonard Sidney Hipkins and Stella Frances Irving Graham; *m* 1977, Barbara Wilson; one *s* (and one *s* decd). *Educ:* Imperial Coll., London (BSc 1972; PhD 1976). MInstP 1987. EMBO Long-term Fellow, CNRS, France, 1976; Lectr, Univ. of Glasgow, 1976–86; Principal, 1988, Grade 5, 1990, DES, subseq. DFE, DFEE then DFES. *Address:* Department for Innovation, Universities and Skills, Kingsgate House, 66–74 Victoria Street, SW1E 6SW. *T:* (020) 3300 8352.

HIRSCH, Prof. Sir Peter (Bernhard), Kt 1975; MA, PhD; FRS 1963; Isaac Wolfson Professor of Metallurgy in the University of Oxford, 1966–92, Emeritus, 1992; Fellow, St Edmund Hall, Oxford, 1966–92, now Emeritus; *b* 16 Jan. 1925; *s* of Ismar Hirsch and Regina Meyerson; *m* 1959, Mabel Anne Kellar (*née* Stephens), *widow* of James Noel Kellar; one step *s* one step *d*. *Educ:* Sloane Sch., Chelsea; St Catharine's Coll., Cambridge (Hon. Fellow, 1982). BA 1946; MA 1950; PhD 1951. Reader in Physics in Univ. of Cambridge, 1964–66; Fellow, Christ's Coll., Cambridge, 1960–66, Hon. Fellow, 1978. Has been engaged on researches with electron microscope on imperfections in crystalline structure of metals and on relation between structural defects and mechanical properties. Chairman: Metallurgy and Materials Cttee (and Mem., Eng. Bd), SRC, 1970–73; UKAEA, 1982–84 (pt-time Mem., 1982–94); Technical Adv. Gp on Structl Integrity, 1993–2002; Member: Elec. Supply Res. Council, 1969–82; Council for Scientific Policy, 1970–72; Tech. Adv. Cttee, Advent, 1982–89; Tech. Adv. Bd, Monsanto Electronic Materials, 1985–88; Chm., Materials, Processes Adv. Bd, Rolls-Royce, 1996–2000. Chm., Isis Innovation Ltd, 1988–96; Director: Cogent Ltd, 1985–89; Rolls-Royce Associates, 1994–97; Oxford Med. Imaging Analysis, OMIA, 2000–01. FIC 1988. Hon. Fellow: RMS, 1977; Japan Soc. of Electron Microscopy, 1979; Japan Inst. of Metals, 1989; Inst. of Materials, 2002. Associate Mem., Royal Acad. of Sci., Letters and Fine Arts, Belgium, 1995; Hon. Member: French Electron Microscopy Soc.; Spanish Electron Microscopy Soc., 1974; Materials Res. Soc., India, 1990; Chinese Electron Microscopy Soc., 1992; For. Hon. Mem., Amer. Acad. of Arts and Scis, 2005; For. Associate, US NAE, 2001; For. Mem., Russian Acad. of Scis, 2006. Hon. DSc: Newcastle, 1979; City, 1979; Northwestern, 1982; Hon. ScD East Anglia, 1983; Hon. DEng: Liverpool, 1991; Birmingham, 1993. Rosenhain Medal, Inst. of Metals, 1961; C. V. Boys Prize, Inst. of Physics and Physical Soc., 1962; Clamer Medal, Franklin Inst., 1970; Wihuri Internat. Prize, Helsinki, 1971; Royal Soc. Hughes Medal, 1973; Metals Soc. Platinum Medal, 1976; Royal Medal, Royal Soc., 1977; A. A. Griffith Medal, Inst. of Materials, 1979; Arthur Von Hippel Award, Materials Res. Soc., 1983; (jtly) Wolf Prize in Physics, Wolf Foundn, 1983–84; Dist. Scientist Award, Electron Microscopy Soc. of America, 1986; Holweck Prize, Inst. of Physics and French Physical Soc., 1988; Gold Medal, Japan Inst. of Metals, 1989; Acta Metallurgica Gold Medal, 1997; Heyn Medal, German Soc. for Materials Sci., 2002; Lomonosov Gold Medal, Russian Acad. of Scis, 2005. *Publications:* Electron Microscopy of Thin Crystals (with others), 1965; (ed) The Physics of Metals, vol. 2, Defects, 1975; (ed jtly) Progress in Materials Science, vol. 36, 1992; (ed) Topics in Electron Diffraction and Microscopy of Materials, 1999; (ed jtly) Fracture, Plastic Flow, and Structural Integrity, 2000; Methods for the Assessment of the Structural Integrity of Components and Structures, 2003; numerous contribs to learned jls. *Recreation:* walking. *Address:* 104A Lonsdale Road, Oxford OX2 7ET.

HIRSCH, Prof. Steven Richard, FRCP; FRCPsych; private practitioner in psychiatry, Priory Hospital, since 2002; Professor of Psychiatry, Imperial College School of Medicine (formerly Charing Cross and Westminster Medical School), 1975–2002, now Emeritus; *b* 12 March 1937; *m* Teresa Hirsch (*d* 2008); one *s* three *d*. *Educ:* Amherst Coll., Mass (BA Hons); Johns Hopkins Univ. (MD); London Univ. (MPhil). Res. worker, MRC Social Psychiatry, 1971–73; Hon. Sen. Registrar, Maudsley Hosp., 1971–73; Lectr in Psychiatry, Inst. of Psychiatry, Univ. of London, 1972–73; Sen. Lectr and Hon. Cons., Depts of Psychiatry, Westminster Hosp. and Queen Mary's Hosp., 1973–75. Dir, Teaching Governance, W London Mental Health NHS Trust, 2002. *Publications:* (ed with M. Shepherd) Themes and Variations in European Psychiatry: an anthology, 1974; (with J. Leff) Abnormalities in parents of schizophrenics: review of the literature and an investigation of communication defects and deviances, (monograph) 1975; (ed with R. Farmer) The Suicide Syndrome, 1980; (ed with P. B. Bradley) The Psychopharmacology and Treatment of Schizophrenia, 1986; Psychiatric Beds and Resources: factors influencing bed use and service planning (report of a working party, RCPsych), 1988; (ed with J. Harris) Consent and the Incompetent Patient: ethics, law and medicine, 1988; (ed with D. Weinberger) Schizophrenia, 1995, 2nd edn 2003; chapters in books and abstracts; numerous contribs to scientific pubns. *Address:* Department of Neuropathology, Division of Neuroscience and Psychological Medicine, Imperial College Faculty of Medicine, Charing Cross Hospital, St Dunstan's Road, W6 8RP. *T:* (020) 8846 7342.

HIRST, Damien; artist; *b* Bristol, 7 June 1965; *s* of Mary Brennan; three *s* by Maia Norman. *Educ:* Goldsmiths' Coll., Univ. of London (BA Fine Art 1989). *Solo exhibitions include:* ICA, 1991; Emmanuel Perrotin, Paris, 1991; Cohen Gall., NY, 1992; Regen Projects, LA, 1993; Galerie Jablonka, Cologne, 1993; Milwaukee Art Mus., 1994; Dallas Mus., 1994; Kukje Gall., Seoul, 1995; White Cube Gall., 1995, 2003, 2007; Max Gandolph-Bibliothek, Salzburg, 1996; Gagosian Gall., NY, 1996; Bruno Bischofberger, Zurich, 1997; Astrup Fearnley, Oslo, 1997; Southampton City Art Gall., 1998; Tate Gall., 1999; retrospective exhibn, Saatchi Gall., 2003; Gagosian Gall., London, 2006; Serpentine Gall., 2006. Gp exhibitions in UK, Europe, USA and Australia. Co-founder and owner, Pharmacy, Notting Hill, 1998–2003 (contemp. restaurant design award, Carlton London Restaurant Awards, 1999); founder, Number 11, The Quay, Ilfracombe, 2004. Turner Prize, 1995. *Publications:* I Want to Spend the Rest of My Life Everywhere, With Everyone, One to One, Always, Forever, Now, 1997; Theories, Models, Methods, Approaches, Assumptions, Results and Findings, 2000; (illus.) Meaningless Static, by Paul Fryer, 2000; (with Gordon Burn) On the Way to Work, 2001; From the Cradle to the Grave: selected drawings, 2004. *Address:* c/o White Cube Gallery, 48 Hoxton Square, N1 6PB.

HIRST, Rt Hon. Sir David (Cozens-Hardy), Kt 1982; PC 1992; a Lord Justice of Appeal, 1992–99; *b* 31 July 1925; *er s* of late Thomas William Hirst and Margaret Joy Hirst, Aylsham, Norfolk; *m* 1951, Pamela Elizabeth Molesworth Bevan, *d* of Col T. P. M. Bevan, MC; three *s* two *d*. *Educ:* Eton (Fellow, 1976–96); Trinity Coll., Cambridge. MA. Served 1943–47; RA and Intelligence Corps, Capt. 1946. Barrister, Inner Temple, 1951, Bencher, 1974, Reader, 1994, Treas., 1995; QC 1965; a Judge of the High Court, QBD, 1982–92. Vice-Chm. of the Bar, 1977–78, Chm., 1978–79. Member: Lord Chancellor's Law Reform Cttee; Council on Tribunals, 1966–80; Cttee to review Defamation Act, 1952, 1971–74; Chm., Spoliation Adv. Panel, 1999–; Hon. Life Mem., Amer. Bar Assoc. *Recreations:* theatre and opera, growing vegetables. *Address:* c/o Royal Courts of Justice, Strand, WC2A 2LL. *Clubs:* Boodle's, Royal Automobile (Chm. Stewards, 2000–05), MCC.

See also J. W. Hirst.

HIRST, David Michael Geoffrey, FBA 1983; Professor of the History of Art, University of London at the Courtauld Institute, 1991–97, now Emeritus Professor of the History of Art; *b* 5 Sept. 1933; *s* of Walter Hirst; *m* 1st, 1960, Sara Vitali (marr. diss. 1970); one *s*; 2nd, 1972, Jane Martineau (marr. diss. 1984); 3rd, 1984, Diane Zervas. *Educ:* Stowe Sch.; New Coll., Oxford; Courtauld Inst. of Art (Hon. Fellow, 1998). Lectr, 1962–80, Reader, 1980–91, Courtauld Inst. Fellow at Villa I Tatti, 1969–70; Mem., Inst. for Advanced Study, Princeton, 1975. Mem., Pontifical Commn for Restoration of Sistine Ceiling, 1987–90. Mem., Florentine Accademia del Disegno; Fellow, Accademia Veneto. Arranged exhibn, Michelangelo Draftsman, Nat. Gall., Washington, 1988, Louvre, Paris, 1989; co-curated exhibn, The Young Michelangelo, Nat. Gall., 1994. Serena Medal for Italian Studies, British Acad., 2001. *Publications:* Sebastiano del Piombo, 1981; Michelangelo and his Drawings, 1988 (Italian edn 1993); Michelangelo Draftsman, Milan, 1988 (French edn 1989); (jtly) The Young Michelangelo, 1994 (Italian edn 1997); many contribs to British and continental books and periodicals. *Address:* 3 Queensdale Place, W11 4SQ.

HIRST, John Raymond, FCA; Chief Executive, Met Office, since 2007; *b* Nicosia, Cyprus, 9 Aug. 1952; *m* Anne; one *s* one *d*. *Educ:* Leeds Univ. (BA). FCA; ACT. ICI plc, 1979–97: CEO, ICI Autocolor, 1990–95; Gp Treas., 1995–96; CEO, ICI Perf. Chemicals, 1996–97; Gp CEO, Premier Farnell plc, 1998–2005. Chm., Asbis, 2006–; non-exec. Dir, Hammerson plc, 2003– (Chm., Audit Cttee). Chm. Trustees, Fund for Epilepsy. CCMI. *Address:* Met Office, Fitzroy Road, Exeter EX1 3PB. *T:* (01392) 884610, *Fax:* (01392) 884400; *e-mail:* john.hirst@metoffice.gov.uk.

HIRST, Jonathan William; QC 1990; a Recorder, since 1997; a Deputy High Court Judge, since 2003; *b* 2 July 1953; *s* of Rt Hon. Sir David (Cozens-Hardy) Hirst, *qv*; *m* 1974,

Fiona Christine Mary Hirst (*née* Tyser); one *s* (and one *s* decd). *Educ:* Eton Coll.; Trinity Coll., Cambridge (MA). Called to the Bar, Inner Temple, 1975; Bencher, 1994; Jt Hd, Brick Court Chambers, 2005–. Mem., Gen. Council of the Bar, 1987–2000 (Vice Chm., 1999, Chm., 2000; Chairman: Law Reform Cttee, 1992–94; Professional Standards Cttee, 1996–98); Chm., Trinity Law Assoc., 2006–. Governor: Taverham Hall Sch., Norfolk, 1991–95; Goodenough Coll., 2001–. *Recreations:* shooting, gardening, other country pursuits. *Address:* Brick Court Chambers, 7–8 Essex Street, WC2R 3LD. *T:* (020) 7379 3550. *Clubs:* Boodle's, Hurlingham; Norfolk (Norwich).

HIRST, Larry, CBE 2007; Chief Executive, IBM United Kingdom and Ireland, since 2001; Chairman, IBM Europe, Middle East and Africa, since 2001; *b* 4 Nov. 1951; *s* of late Harold Hirst and Joan Hirst; *m* 1978, Ellen Alison Lake; one *s* one *d*. *Educ:* Univ. of Hull (BSc Hons Maths 1973). Kodak, 1973–77; IBM, 1977–: Dir Ops, E Europe, Russia, 1989–90; Exec. Asst to Chm., 1992–93; Vice Pres., Financial Services, Europe, Middle East and Africa, 1994–2001; Mem. Bd, SA, 1995–2000; Gen. Manager, IBM UK, Ire. and SA, 2001–; Chm., IBM Netherlands, 2003. Chm., e-skills UK Sector Skills Council for IT and Telecoms, 2001–; Exec. Chm., Information Age Partnership, 2001–03; Mem., President's Cttee, CBI, 2001–; Comr, UK Commn for Employment and Skills, 2007–. *Recreations:* golf, woodland maintenance hopefully not at the same time, reading biographies, gadgets, technology futures. *Address:* IBM United Kingdom Ltd, PO Box 41, North Harbour, Portsmouth PO6 3AU; *e-mail:* hirstl@uk.ibm.com.

HIRST, Sir Michael (William), Kt 1992; LLB, CA; company director; business consultant; Founder, Michael Hirst Associates; Chairman: Pagoda Public Relations Ltd, since 2000; Millstream Associates Ltd, since 2000; *b* 2 Jan. 1946; *s* of late John Melville Hirst and Christina Binning Torrance or Hirst; *m* 1972, Naomi Ferguson Wilson; one *s* two *d*. *Educ:* Glasgow Acad., Glasgow; Univ. of Glasgow (LLB). CA 1970. Exchange Student, Univ. of Iceland, 1967; Partner, Peat, Marwick Mitchell & Co., 1978–83; Consultant, Peat Marwick UK, 1983–92. Pres., Glasgow Univ. Conservative Club, 1967; National Vice-Chm., Scottish Young Conservatives, 1971–73; Chm., Scottish Conservative Candidates Assoc., 1978–81; Vice-Chairman: Pty Organisation Cttee, 1985; Conservative Party in Scotland, 1987–89; Pres., 1989–92, Chm., 1993–97, Scottish Cons. & Unionist Assoc. Contested (C): Central Dunbartonshire, Feb. and Oct. 1974; E Dunbartonshire, 1979; Strathkelvin and Bearsden, 1987 and 1992. MP (C) Strathkelvin and Bearsden, 1983–87. PPS to Parly Under-Secs of State, DoE, 1985–87. Mem., Select Cttee on Scottish Affairs, 1983–87. Director: Children's Hospice Assoc., Scotland, 1993–2005; Erskine Hosp. Ltd (formerly Princess Louise Scottish Hosp.), 1980– (Mem., Exec. Bd, 1997–). Mem., Bd of Trustees, Diabetes UK (formerly British Diabetic Assoc.), 1988–2006 (Hon. Sec., 1993–98; Vice Chm., 1998–2001; Chm., 2001–06); Vice Pres., Internat. Diabetic Fedn, 2006–. Chm., Park Sch. Educnl Trust, 1988–; Mem. Court, Glasgow Caledonian Univ., 1993–98 (Chm., Audit Cttee, 1993–98). Mem. Council, Imperial Soc. of Kts Bachelor, 2002– (Chm. Scottish Div., 2002–). Chm., Friends of Kippen Kirk Trust, 2004–. FRSA 1993; MCIPR (MIPR 2003). Hon. DLitt Glasgow Caledonian, 2004. *Recreations:* golf, walking, ski-ing. *Address:* Glentirran, Kippen, Stirlingshire FK8 3JA. *T:* (01786) 870283. *Clubs:* Carlton; The Western (Glasgow).

HIRST, Neil Alexander Carr; Director, Office for Energy Technology and Research and Development, International Energy Agency, Paris, since 2004; *b* 16 May 1946; *s* of Theodore James Hirst and Valerie Adamson Hirst; *m* 1984, Caroline Rokeby Collins; two *d*. *Educ:* Canford Sch.; Lincoln Coll., Oxford (BA 1st Cl. Hons PPE); Cornell Univ., USA (Telluride Schol., MBA). Jun. reporter, Eastbourne Gazette and Herald Chronicle, 1964–65; entered Civil Service, 1970: Asst Principal, Min. of Technol., 1970–73; Asst Private Sec. to Ministers for Industry and Energy and Sec. of State for Trade, 1973–75; Principal, Oil and Gas Div., then Atomic Energy Div., Dept. of Energy, 1975–80; on secondment to Private Finance Dept, Goldman Sachs, NY, 1981; returned to Dept of Energy for public flotation of Britoil, 1982; Asst Sec., Atomic Energy Div., 1983–85; Counsellor (Energy), Washington DC, 1985–88; Oil and Gas Div., Dept of Energy, 1988–92; Department of Trade and Industry: coal privatisation legislation, 1992–94; Labs Unit (privatisation of Nat. Engrg Lab. and Nat. Chemical Lab.), 1995; Under Sec. and Hd, Atomic Energy Div., 1995; Dir, Nuclear Industries, 1996–98; Dep. Dir Gen., Energy, 1998–2002; Hd, Energy Mkts Unit, 2002–04. Mem., UKAEA, 1996–98; Chm., Nuclear Safety Wkg Gp of the G8 Summit nations, 1998. Mem., Dorset Natural Hist. and Archaeol Soc., 2000. *Recreations:* gardening, music, theatre, walking. *Address:* 3 Stockwell Park Road, SW9 0AP. *T:* (020) 7735 9615; 59 Corfe Road, Stoborough, near Wareham, Dorset BH20 5AE; 5 rue Champfleury, 75007 Paris, France. *Club:* Oxford and Cambridge.

HIRST, Prof. Paul Heywood; Professor of Education, University of Cambridge, 1971–88, now Emeritus, and Fellow of Wolfson College (formerly University College), Cambridge, since 1971; *b* 10 Nov. 1927; *s* of late Herbert and Winifred Hirst, Birkby, Huddersfield. *Educ:* Huddersfield Coll.; Trinity Coll., Cambridge (BA 1948, MA 1952); Cert. Educn Cantab, 1952; DipEd London, 1955; MA Oxon (by incorporation), Christ Church, Oxford, 1955. Asst Master, William Hulme's Grammar Sch., Manchester, 1948–50; Maths Master, Eastbourne Coll., 1950–55; Lectr and Tutor, Univ. of Oxford Dept of Educn, 1955–59; Lectr in Philosophy of Educn, Univ. of London Inst. of Educn, 1959–65; Prof. of Educn, King's Coll., Univ. of London, 1965–71. Visiting Professor: Univ. of British Columbia, 1964, 1967; Univ. of Malawi, 1969; Univ. of Puerto Rico, 1984; Univ. of Sydney, 1989; Univ. of Alberta, 1989; Inst. of Educn, Univ. of London, 1991–96. De Carle Lectr, Univ. of Otago, 1976; Fink Lectr, Univ. of Melbourne, 1976. Vice-Pres., Philosophy of Educn Soc. of GB; Member: UGC Educn Sub-Cttee, 1971–80; Educn Cttee, 1972–82, Academic Policy Cttee, 1981–87, Chm., Research Cttee, 1988–92, CNAA; Swann Cttee of Inquiry into Educn of Children from Ethnic Minorities, 1981–85. Chm., Univs Council for Educn of Teachers, 1985–88. Member Court: Univ. of Derby, 1996–; Univ. of Glos, 2006–. Hon. Mem., Royal Norwegian Soc. of Scis and Letters, 1996. Hon. DEd CNAA, 1992; Hon. DPhil Cheltenham and Gloucester Coll. of Higher Educn, 2000; Hon. DLitt Huddersfield, 2002. *Publications:* (with R. S. Peters) The Logic of Education, 1970; (ed with R. F. Dearden and R. S. Peters) Education and the Development of Reason, 1971; Knowledge and the Curriculum, 1974; Moral Education in a Secular Society, 1974; (ed) Educational Theory and its Foundation Disciplines, 1984; (with V. J. Furlong) Initial Teacher Training and the Role of the School, 1988; (ed with P. A. White) Philosophy of Education: major themes in the analytic tradition, 1998; papers in: Philosophical Analysis and Education (ed R. D. Archambault), 1965; The Study of Education (ed J. W. Tibble), 1965; The Concept of Education (ed R. S. Peters), 1966; Religious Education in a Pluralistic Society (ed M. C. Felderhof), 1985; Education, Values and Mind (ed D. E. Cooper), 1986; Partnership in Initial Teacher Training (ed M. Booth *et al*), 1990; Beyond Liberal Education (ed R. Barrow and P. White), 1993; The Aims of Education (ed R. Marples), 1999; Education in Morality (ed J. M. Halstead and T. H. McLaughlin), 1999; Leaders in Philosophy of Education (ed L. J. Waks), 2008. *Recreation:* music, especially opera. *Address:* Flat 3, 6 Royal Crescent, Brighton BN2 1AL. *T:* (01273) 684118. *Club:* Athenæum.

HISCOCK, Stephen John; HM Diplomatic Service, retired; High Commissioner t Guyana, and (non resident) Ambassador to Suriname, 2002–06; *b* 16 June 1946; *s* of Lion Percy Hiscock and Dorothy Mabel Hiscock (*née* Wright); *m* 1st, 1967, Gillian Denise Ro two *s*; 2nd, 1983, Dee Mary Forster; two *s* one *d*. *Educ:* Devonport High Sch. for Boy Plymouth. With Inland Revenue, 1963–65; entered Foreign Office, 1965; FCC 1965–68; Kuala Lumpur, 1968–72; Lusaka, 1972–76; FCO, 1976–78; Second Sec Islamabad, 1978–82; First Secretary: Seoul, 1982–86; FCO, 1986–88; Dep. High Com Georgetown, 1988–93; FCO, 1993–96; Consul-Gen., Brisbane, 1997–2001; Commerci Counsellor (temp.), Bangkok, 2001–02; Dep. Hd of Mission (temp.), Kabul, March–Ap 2002. Mem., OAS Election Observation Mission to Guyana, 2006. Dir, Commonwealt Boxing Council Ltd, 2008. *Recreations:* Rotary, amateur dramatics, social tennis, messin about in boats. *Address:* 67 Primrose Drive, Kingsnorth, Ashford, Kent TN23 3NP. *Club* Royal Over-Seas League; Rotary (Ashford).

HISCOX, Robert Ralph Scrymgeour; Chairman, Hiscox Ltd (formerly Hiscox plc since 1996; *b* 4 Jan. 1943; *s* of late Ralph Hiscox, CBE and Louisa Jeanie Hiscox (*née* Boal *m* 1st, 1966, Lucy Mills (marr. diss. 1978; she *d* 1996); two *s*; 2nd, 1985, Lady Jul Elizabeth Meade, 3rd *d* of Earl of Clanwilliam; three *s*. *Educ:* Rugby Sch.; Corpus Chris Coll., Cambridge (MA). ACII. Member of Lloyd's, 1967–98 (Dep. Chm., 1993–95; Dep Chm., First Market Bd, 1993–95); Chairman: Lloyd's Underwriting Agents' Assoc., 199 Lloyd's Corporate Capital Assoc., 1998–99; Lloyd's Market Assoc., 1999–2000. Directo Roberts & Hiscox, 1973–98; Hiscox Hldgs Ltd, 1987–99; R. K. Harrison Hldgs Ltc 1990–99; Hiscox Syndicates Ltd, 1991–; Penrose Forbes Ltd, 1992–99; Hiscox Investmer Mgt Ltd, 1995–; Hiscox Insce Co., 1996–; and other cos in Hiscox Gp; Grainger (former Grainger Trust) plc, 2002–. Mem., Mus. and Galls Commn, 1996–2000. Dir, Publi Catalogue Foundn, 2004–. Treasurer and Trustee: Campaign for Museums, 1998–200 24 Hour Mus., 2000–01; Treas., Friends of the Tate Gallery, 1990–93. Trustee: Wil Bobby Van Trust, 1998– (Chm., 2002–); Kenneth Armitage Foundn, 2005–; Bermud Soc., 2007–; AGCIM Ltd, 2007–. *Recreations:* family life, country life, the arts. *Addres* Hiscox Ltd, 1 Great St Helen's, EC3A 6HX. *T:* (020) 7448 6011, *Fax:* (020) 7448 659 *e-mail:* robert.hiscox@hiscox.com; Rainscombe Park, Oare, Marlborough, Wilts SN 4HZ. *T:* (01672) 563491, *Fax:* (01672) 564120. *Clubs:* Boodle's, Queen's.

HISLOP, George Steedman, CBE 1976; PhD; FREng, FIMechE; FRSE; Directo Aviall Airline Services (Caledonian), 1978–94; *b* 11 Feb. 1914; *s* of George Alexande Hislop and Marthesa Maria Hay; *m* 1942, Joan Daphne, *d* of William Beer an Gwendoline Fincken; two *s* one *d*. *Educ:* Clydebank High Sch.; Royal Technical Coll Glasgow (ARTC); Cambridge Univ. (PhD). BScEng London. CEng, FIMechE 194 FRAeS 1955; FREng (FEng 1976); FRSE 1976. A&AEE, RAF Boscombe Dow 1939–45; RAE, Farnborough, 1945–46; BEA, 1947–53; Chief Engr/Dir, Fairey Aviatio Ltd, 1953–60; Westland Aircraft Ltd, 1960–79: Technical Dir (Develt), 1962–66; Dep Man. Dir, 1966–68; Man. Dir, 1968–72; Vice-Chm., 1972–76. Chm., CEI, 1979–8 (Vice-Chm., 1978–79); Mem., Airworthiness Requirements Bd, CAA, 1976–83 (Chm 1982–83). Vis. Prof., Univ. of Strathclyde, 1978–84. Mem. Council, RAeS, 1960–8 (Pres., 1973–74; Hon. FRAeS, 1983); Gov., Inveresk Res. Foundn, 1980–90. FRS 1959; LRPS 1992. Hon. DSc Strathclyde, 1976. *Publications:* contrib. R & M series an RAeS Jl. *Recreations:* hill walking, photography, bird watching. *Address:* Hadley, St John Hill, Old Coulsdon, Surrey CR5 1HD. *T:* (020) 8660 1008. *Clubs:* Royal Air Forc MCC.

HISLOP, Ian David; Editor, Private Eye, since 1986; writer and broadcaster; *b* 13 Jul 1960; *s* of late David Atholl Hislop and Helen Hislop; *m* 1988, Victoria Hamson; one one *d*. *Educ:* Ardingly College; Magdalen College, Oxford (BA Hons Eng. Lang. and Lit Underhill Exhibn; Violet Vaughan Morgan Scholarship). Joined Private Eye, 1981, Dep Editor, 1985–86. Columnist, The Listener, 1985–89; Television critic, The Spectato 1994–96; Columnist, Sunday Telegraph, 1996–2003. *Radio:* Newsquiz, 1985–90; 4t Column, 1992–96; Lent Talk, 1994; (scriptwriter, with Nick Newman) Gush, 199 Words on Words, 1999; The Hislop Vote, 2000; A Revolution in 5 Acts, 2001; The Re Patron Saints, 2002; A Brief History of Tax, 2003; The Choir Invisible, 2003; There'll b Blue Birds over the White Cliffs of Dover, 2004; Are We Offensive Enough?, 200 Looking for Middle England, 2006; *television:* scriptwriter with Nick Newman: Spittin Image, 1984–89; The Stone Age, 1989; Briefcase Encounter, 1990; The Programme 1990–92; Harry Enfield and Chums, 1994–98; Mangez Merveillac, 1994; Dead on Tim 1995; Gobble, 1996; Sermon from St Albions, 1998; Songs and Praise from St Albion 1999; Confessions of a Murderer, 1999; My Dad's the Prime Minister, 2003, 200 performer, Have I Got News For You, 1990–; documentary presenter: Canterbury Tale 1996; School Rules, 1997; Pennies from Bevan, 1998; Great Railway Journeys East t West, 1999; Who Do You Think You Are?, 2004; Not Forgotten, 2005; Not Forgotte shot at dawn, 2007; Scouting for Boys, 2007. Editors' Ed., 1991, Ed. of the Year, 199 British Soc. of Mag. Editors; Award for political satire, Channel 4 Political Awards, 200 Political Comedy Award, Channel 4, 2006. *Publications:* various Private Eye collection 1985–; contribs to newspapers and magazines on books, current affairs, arts an entertainment. *Address:* c/o Private Eye, 6 Carlisle Street, W1V 5RG. *T:* (020) 7437 4017

HITCHCOCK, Dr Anthony John Michael; Head of Safety and Transportatio Department, Transport and Road Research Laboratory, 1978–89; *b* 26 June 1929; *s* of D Ronald W. Hitchcock and Hilda (*née* Gould); *m* 1st, 1953, Audrey Ellen Ashworth (1990); one *s* two *d*; 2nd, 1992, Louise Nickel (*d* 1999). *Educ:* Bedales; Mancheste Grammar Sch.; Trinity Coll., Cambridge; Univ. of Chicago. PhD, BA; MInstP. Ass Univ. of Chicago, 1951–52; AEA, 1953–67; Department of Transport: Head of Traffi Dept, 1967–71, Head of Transport Ops Dept, 1971–75, TRRL; Head, Res. Polic (Transport) Div., DoE/DoT, 1975–78. Vis. Researcher, Program for Advanced Techno on the Highway, Univ. of Calif at Berkeley, 1990–94. Vis. Prof., Transport Studie Cranfield Inst. of Technology, 1978–81. Health and Safety Volunteer, WRVS, 2002–07 *Publications:* Nuclear Reactor Control, 1960; research reports and articles in learned jl *Recreation:* bridge. *Address:* Seal Point, 2 Oakfield Place, Witney, Oxon OX28 4NH.

HITCHEN, Brian, CBE 1990; Chairman, Brian Hitchen Communications Ltd, sinc 1996; Chairman and Publisher, Kerry Life Ltd, since 1996; *b* 8 July 1936; *s* of Fred an Alice Hitchen, Lancs; *m* 1962, Ellen Josephine O'Hanlon, Kildare, Eire; one *s* one *d*. *Educ* Hegginbottom Sch., Ashton-under-Lyne, Lancs, and elsewhere. Served Army, WO Whitehall, 1954–56. Copy Boy, Daily Despatch, 1951; Gen. Reporter, Bury Time 1952–54; Reporter, Manchester Evening News, 1957; Reporter, 1958–63, Foreig Correspondent, Paris Bureau, 1963–64, Daily Mirror; For. Corresp., Mirror US Bureau New York and Washington, 1964–72; Dep. News Editor, Daily Mirror, 1972; New Editor, Daily Express, 1973–76; Asst Editor, National Enquirer, USA, 1976, Europea Bureau Chief, 1977; Asst Editor, Now! magazine, 1978–80; London Editor, The Dail Star, 1981–86; Dep. Editor, Sunday Express, 1986–87; Ed., Daily Star, 1987–94; Ed Sunday Express, Classic mag. and Sunday Express Magazine, 1994–95; Chm. an Publisher, Irish Country Life Ltd, 1996–2000. Director: Airspeed Internat. Corp 1973–93; Express Newspapers, 1988–96; Independent Star, Eire, 1988–95. Member: Pres Complaints Commn, 1991–95; Defence, Press and Broadcasting Adv. Cttee, 1993–96

NPA Code of Conduct Cttee, 1994–95. Internat. Media Consultant to Saudi Arabian Amb. to UK and Ireland, 1996–; Press Officer, Lifeboat, Shoreham-by-Sea, W Sussex. Member, Committee: Friends of Airborne Forces Charity, 1996–; Saudi-British Jt Cultural Cttee, 2001–. *Publications:* Everything off the Mantlepiece, 1997; Eye of the Storm, 2000; Mischief Maker, 2004. *Recreations:* watercolours, fly-fishing, golf. *Address:* 32 Palmeira Square, Hove, East Sussex BN3 2JP. *Club:* Reform.

HITCHENS, Christopher Eric; author and journalist; *b* 13 April 1949; *s* of late Comdr Eric Ernest Hitchens and Yvonne Jean Hitchens (*née* Hickman); *m* 1st, 1981, Eleni Meleagrou; one *s* one *d*; 2nd, 1991, Carol Blue; one *d*. *Educ:* Leys Sch., Cambridge; Balliol Coll., Oxford (BA PPE 1970). Social sci. corresp., THES, 1971–73; writer and Asst Editor, New Statesman, 1973–81; columnist and corresp. in Washington, 1982–; Columnist: The Nation (NY), 1982–2002; Vanity Fair (NY), 1982–; Atlantic Monthly, 2002–. Mellon Prof. of English, Univ. of Pittsburgh, 1997; Prof. of Liberal Studies, New Sch., NY, 2000–. Lannan Literary Award for Non-Fiction, 1992; Nat. Mag. Award, 2007. *Publications:* Karl Marx and the Paris Commune, 1971; James Callaghan, 1976; Hostage to History: Cyprus from the Ottomans to Kissinger, 1984; Imperial Spoils: the curious case of the Elgin Marbles, 1986; Prepared for the Worst: selected essays, 1989; Blood, Class and Nostalgia: Anglo-American ironies, 1990; For the Sake of Argument: selected essays, 1993; When the Borders Bleed: the struggle of the Kurds, 1994; The Missionary Position: Mother Teresa in theory and practice, 1995; No One Left to Lie To, 1999; Unacknowledged Legislation, 2001; The Trial of Henry Kissinger, 2001; Letters to a Young Contrarian: the art of mentoring, 2001; Orwell's Victory, 2002; A Long Short War: the postponed liberation of Iraq, 2003; Blood, Class and Empire: the enduring Anglo-American relationship, 2004; Love, Poverty and War: journeys and essays, 2005; Thomas Jefferson: author of America, 2005; Thomas Paine's Rights of Man, 2006; God Is Not Great: the case against religion, 2007; (ed) The Portable Atheist, 2007. *Recreations:* reading, travel, disputation. *Address:* 2022 Columbia Road NW, Washington, DC 20009–1352, USA. *T:* (202) 3874842.
See also P. J. Hitchens.

HITCHENS, Rear Adm. Gilbert Archibald Ford, CB 1988; Director General Ship Refitting, Ministry of Defence, 1985–87, retired; *b* 11 April 1932; *m* 1961, Patricia Hamilton; one *s* one *d*. BA Hons. Joined Royal Navy, 1950; Commander, 1968; Guided Weapons Staff Officer, Min. of Technology, 1968–70; Exec. Officer, RNEC, 1970–72; Senior Officer while building and Weapon Engineer Officer, HMS Sheffield, 1973–75; MoD (Navy), 1975–77; Naval Attaché, Tokyo and Seoul, 1977–79; Asst Dir, Manpower Requirements, MoD (Navy), 1979–80; Dir, Officers' Appts (Eng.), 1980–82; Captain, HMS Defiance, 1982–84; ADC to the Queen, 1984; CSO Engrg to C-in-C Fleet, 1984–85. Mem., Plymouth DHA, 1989–90. Admiralty Gov., Royal Naval Benevolent Trust, 1989–96. Chairman: RN Ski and Mountaineering Club, 1984–86; Govs, Devonport High Sch. for Boys, 1993–97. Liveryman, Ironmongers' Co., 1994. *Recreation:* any activity in the high hills.
See also T. M. Hitchens.

HITCHENS, Peter Jonathan; Columnist, Mail on Sunday, since 2001; *b* 28 Oct. 1951; *s* of late Comdr Eric Ernest Hitchens and of Yvonne Jean Hitchens (*née* Hickman); *m* 1983, Eve Ross; two *s* one *d*. *Educ:* Leys Sch., Cambridge; Oxford Coll. of Further Educn; Univ. of York (BA 1973). Journalist: Socialist Worker, 1972; Swindon Evening Advertiser, 1973–76; Coventry Evening Telegraph, 1976; Daily Express, 1977–2001: sometime industrial reporter, Labour Corresp., Dep. Pol Ed., Diplomatic Corresp., Moscow Corresp., Washington Corresp., Asst Ed.; resigned 2001. *Publications:* The Abolition of Britain, 1999; (contrib.) The Rape of the Constitution, 2000; Monday Morning Blues, 2000; The Abolition of Liberty, 2004. *Recreations:* long train journeys, second-hand bookshops. *Address:* Mail on Sunday, 2 Derry Street, W8 5TS. *T:* (020) 7938 7073, *Fax:* (020) 7937 6882; *e-mail:* peter.hitchens@mailonsunday.co.uk.
See also C. E. Hitchens.

HITCHENS, Timothy Mark, LVO 1997; HM Diplomatic Service; Minister, Paris, since 2005; *b* 7 May 1962; *s* of Rear Adm. Gilbert Archibald Ford Hitchens, *qv*; *m* 1985, Sara Kubra; one *s* one *d*. *Educ:* Dulwich Coll.; Christ's Coll., Cambridge (BA). Foreign and Commonwealth Office, 1983–; Tokyo, 1985–89; Private Sec. to Minister of State, FCO, 1991–94; Speechwriter to Foreign Sec., 1994–95; First Sec., Islamabad, 1995–97; Asst Pvte Sec. to the Queen, 1998–2002; Hd, Africa Dept (Equatorial), FCO, 2003–05. *Recreations:* walking, gardening. *Address:* c/o Foreign and Commonwealth Office, SW1A 2AH.

HITCHIN, Prof. Nigel James, DPhil; FRS 1991; Savilian Professor of Geometry, University of Oxford, since 1997; Fellow of New College, Oxford, since 1997; *b* 2 Aug. 1946; *s* of Eric Wilfred Hitchin and Bessie (*née* Blood); *m* 1973, Nedda Vejarano Bernal; one *s* one *d*. *Educ:* Ecclesbourne Sch., Duffield; Jesus Coll., Oxford (BA 1968; Hon. Fellow, 1998); Wolfson Coll., Oxford (MA, DPhil 1972). Res. Asst, Inst. for Advanced Study, Princeton, 1971–73; Instructor, Courant Inst., New York Univ., 1973–74; SRC Res. Asst, 1974–77, SRC Advanced Res. Fellow, 1977–79, Oxford Univ.; Fellow and Tutor in Maths, St Catherine's Coll., Oxford, 1979–90; Prof. of Maths, Univ. of Warwick, 1990–94; Rouse Ball Prof. of Maths, Univ. of Cambridge, 1994–97; Fellow of Gonville and Caius Coll., Cambridge, 1994–97 (Hon. Fellow, 2008). Vis. Prof., SUNY, Stony Brook, 1983. Hon. DSc Bath, 2003. London Mathematical Society: Pres., 1994–96; Jun. Whitehead Prize, 1981; Sen. Berwick Prize, 1990; Polya Prize, LMS, 2002; Sylvester Medal, Royal Soc., 2000. *Publications:* Monopoles, Minimal Surfaces and Algebraic Curves, 1987; (with M. F. Atiyah) The Geometry and Dynamics of Magnetic Monopoles, 1988; (with G. B. Segal and R. S. Ward) Integrable Systems: twistors, loop groups and Riemann surfaces, 1999; articles in learned jls. *Address:* 26 Lonsdale Road, Oxford OX2 7EW.

HITCHING, His Honour Alan Norman; a Circuit Judge, 1987–2006; Resident Judge, Blackfriars Crown Court, 1998–2006; *b* 5 Jan. 1941; *s* of late Norman Henry Samuel Hitching and Grace Ellen Hitching; *m* 1st, 1967, Hilda Muriel (*née* King) (*d* 2000); one *d* two *s*; 2nd, 2003, Susan Mary (*née* Banfield), *widow* of Michael Henry Cotton. *Educ:* Forest Sch., Snaresbrook; Christ Church, Oxford (BA 1962; Radcliffe Exhibnr and Dixon Scholar, 1962; BCL 1963; MA). Harmsworth Entrance Scholar, Middle Temple, 1960; Astbury Scholar and Safford Prize, Middle Temple, 1964; called to the Bar, Middle Temple, 1964, Bencher, 2005; Standing Counsel, Inland Revenue, SE Circuit, 1972–87; a Recorder, 1985–87. Cropwood Fellow, Inst. of Criminology, Cambridge, 1990. Vice-Pres., John Grooms Assoc. for the Disabled, 1991–2007 (Chm., 1981–89; Vice-Chm., 1978–81 and 1989–91). Licensed Reader, dio. of Chelmsford, 1987–2001; ordained deacon, 2001, priest, 2002; NSM, High Ongar, Chelmsford, 2001–05; permission to officiate, Chelmsford dio., 2005–. *Recreations:* people, pottery, poetry, preaching. *Address:* c/o Middle Temple, Treasury Office, Middle Temple Lane, EC4Y 9AT.

HITCHINGS, Prof. Roger Alan, FRCS; FRCOphth; Ophthalmic Surgeon, since 1978, Consultant, since 1981, Director, Research and Development, since 2000, Moorfields Eye Hospital; Professor of Glaucoma and Allied Studies, Institute of Ophthalmology, University College London, since 1999; *b* 30 May 1942; *s* of Alan and Mary Hitchings; *m* 1966, Virmati Talwar; two *d*. *Educ:* Steyning Grammar Sch.; Royal Free Hosp. (MB BS). FRCS 1971; FRCOphth 1988. Resident Surgical Officer, Moorfields Eye Hosp., 1969–73; Res. Fellow, Wills Eye Hosp., 1973–75; Sen. Lectr, Univ. of London, 1975–79; Consultant Ophthalmic Surgeon, KCH, 1979–81. Pres., Eur. Glaucoma Soc., 2000–. *Publications:* Atlas of Clinical Ophthalmology, 1984, 3rd edn 2005; The Refractory Glaucomas, 1995; Glaucoma: a practical guide, 2000; contrib. papers on glaucoma and allied subjects. *Recreations:* gardening, travel, food. *Address:* Moorfields Eye Hospital, City Road, EC1V 2PD.

HIVES, family name of **Baron Hives**.

HIVES, 3rd Baron *cr* 1950, of Duffield, co. Derby; **Matthew Peter Hives;** Director of Technology, CPA, Jersey; *b* 25 May 1971; *s* of Hon. Peter Anthony Hives (*d* 1974) and of Dinah (*née* Wilson-North); *S* uncle, 1997. *Educ:* Haileybury; Newcastle Univ. (BEng); Aberdeen Univ. (MSc). MIMechE. Formerly with GEC/ALSTOM. *Heir: uncle* Hon. Michael Bruce Hives [*b* 12 March 1926; *m* 1951, Janet Rosemary (*née* Gee); two *s* one *d*]. *Address:* Gombrette House, La Rue de Gombrette, St John, Jersey JE3 4EF.

HIX, Mark; Owner: Hix Oyster & Chop House, London, since 2008; Hix Oyster and Fish House, Dorset, since 2008; Director of Food, Browns Hotel, London, since 2008; *b* 10 Dec. 1962; *s* of Ernest and Gill Hix; *m* Suzie Hix (marr. diss.); two *d*. *Educ:* Colfox Sch.; Weymouth Coll. Commis Chef, Grosvenor Hse Hotel, 1981–83; Commis Chef, later Chef de Partie, Dorchester, 1983–84; Sous Chef, then Hd Chef, Mr Pontacs/Candlewick Room, 1985–90 (Michelin Red M award); Hd Chef, Le Caprice; Exec. Hd Chef, 1990–2008, Chef Dir, 1992–2008, Caprice Hldgs Ltd, overseeing Le Caprice and The Ivy (Michelin Red M award); Chef Director: J. Sheekey, Covent Gdn, 1998–2008; Daphne's, 2000–08; Bam-Bou, 2000–08; Pasha, 2000–08. Recipe column, Independent on Saturday mag. (Glenfiddich Award, Best Newspaper Cookery Writer, 2003). Best Cookery Writer, Guild of Food Writers, 2005. *Publications:* The Ivy: the restaurant and its recipes, 1997; (with A. A. Gill) Le Caprice: the book, 1999; Eat Up, 2000; British, 2003, 2nd edn 2005; Fish Etc, 2004; (with M. Gluck) The Simple Art of Food and Wine, 2005; British Regional Food: in search of the best British food today, 2006. *Recreations:* fishing, foraging, golf. *Address: e-mail:* mhix@hixfoodetc.co.uk. *Clubs:* Groucho, Soho House; Stoke Park Golf.

HO, Eric Peter, CBE 1981; Chairman, Public Service Commission, Hong Kong, 1987–91, retired; *b* 30 Dec. 1927; *s* of Sai-Ki Ho and Doris (*née* Lo); *m* 1956, Grace Irene, OBE (*d* 2007), *d* of Mr and Mrs A. V. Young; two *s* one *d*. *Educ:* Univ. of Hong Kong (BA 1950). Inspector of Taxes (under training), London, 1950–53; Hong Kong Civil Service, 1954–87: Sec. for Social Services, 1977–83; Sec. for Trade and Industry, 1983–87. RCDS, London, 1976. *Publication:* Times of Change: a memoir of Hong Kong's governance 1950–1991, 2005. *Address:* London, SW15.

HOAD, Air Vice-Marshal Norman Edward, CVO 1972; CBE 1969; AFC 1951 and Bar, 1956; artist; *b* 28 July 1923; *s* of Hubert Ronald Hoad and Florence Marie (*née* Johnson); two *s*. *Educ:* Brighton. Joined RAF, 1941, pilot trng, S Rhodesia; Lancaster pilot until shot down and taken prisoner in Germany, 1944; various flying and instructional duties, 1945–51; Sqdn Ldr 1951; OC No 192 Sqdn, 1953–55; psc 1956; Wing Comdr, HQ 2 ATAF, 1957–59; pfc 1960; OC No 216 Sqdn, 1960–62; jssc 1963; Gp Capt., MoD, 1963–65; idc 1966; Stn Comdr: RAF Lyneham, 1967, RAF Abingdon, 1968; Defence and Air Attaché, British Embassy, Paris, 1969–72; Dir, Defence Policy (A), 1972–74; Chief of Staff, 46 Gp, RAF Strike Comd, April-Oct. 1974; AOC No 46 Group, and Comdr, UK Jt Airborne Task Force, 1974–75; Senior RAF Mem., RCDS, 1976–78. Director, Air League, 1978–82. Founder Mem., Guild of Aviation Artists; Chm., Soc. of Equestrian Artists. MCMI (MBIM 1970). *Address:* Flowerknot, Starr Lane, All Stretton, Shropshire SY6 6HS. *T:* (01694) 723309. *Club:* Royal Air Force.

HOAD, Pamela Joan; *see* Gordon, P. J.

HOAR, Rev. Ronald William Cecil; Chairman, Manchester and Stockport Methodist District, 1979–95; President of the Methodist Conference, 1991–92; *b* 31 Oct. 1931; *s* of Cecil Herbert William and Lilian Augusta Hoar; *m* 1956, Peggy Jean (*née* Stubbington); three *s* two *d*. *Educ:* Shedfield Church of England Primary Sch., Hants; Prices Sch., Fareham, Hants; Richmond Coll., Univ. of London (BD). Methodist Minister: Wells, Somerset, 1955–58; Bermondsey, London, 1958–62; Westminster and Chelsea, 1962–67; Bristol Mission, 1967–76; Great Yarmouth and Gorleston, 1976–79. *Publications:* Methodism in Chelsea to 1963, 1963; A Good Ideal: a history of the Bristol Methodist Mission, 1973; Advertising the Gospel, 1991. *Recreations:* DIY, watching sport, oil painting, gardening. *Address:* 43 Green Lanes, Prestatyn, Denbighshire LL19 7BH. *T:* (01745) 886923.

HOARE, Alexander Simon; private banker; Chief Executive, C. Hoare & Co., since 2001; *b* 1 April 1962; *s* of Christopher E. B Hoare and Sylvia M. Hoare. *Educ:* Winchester Coll.; Univ. of Edinburgh (BComm Hons). ACIB 1990. Consultant Analyst, PA Consulting Gp, 1985–87; joined C. Hoare & Co., 1987–. Non-exec. Dir, Jupiter Green Investment Trust Plc, 2006–. *Address:* C. Hoare & Co., 37 Fleet Street, EC4P 4DQ. *Club:* St Mawes Billiards and Social.

HOARE, Sir Antony; *see* Hoare, Sir C. A. R.

HOARE, Rev. Brian Richard; Methodist Minister, 1971–2000; Methodist Evangelism Secretary, 1996–2000; President of the Methodist Conference, 1995–96; *b* 9 Dec. 1935; *s* of William Charles Hoare and Kathleen Nora Hoare (*née* Thwaites); *m* 1962, Joyce Eleanor Davidson; one *s* one *d*. *Educ:* Southwell Minster Grammar Sch., Notts; Westminster Coll., London (Teacher's Cert.); Richmond Coll., Univ. of London (BD 1971). Ops Clerk, RAF, 1954–56. Teacher, Col Frank Seely Secondary Sch., Calverton, Notts, 1959–62; Travelling Sec., subsequently Nat. Sec., Colls of Educn Christian Union, Inter-Varsity Fellowship, London, 1962–68. Chaplain Hunmanby Hall Sch., Filey, 1971–74; Minister, Hull Methodist Mission, 1974–77; New Testament Tutor, Cliff Coll., Sheffield, 1977–86; Superintendent Minister, Longton Central Hall, Stoke-on-Trent, 1986–88; Divl Sec. 1988–89, Dep. Gen. Sec. 1989–95, Home Mission Div. Member: World Methodist Council, Nairobi, 1986, Singapore, 1991, Rio de Janeiro, 1996; World Methodist Exec. Cttee, Bulgaria, 1992, Estonia, 1994. *Publications:* (ed) Methods of Mission, 1979; Evangelism in New Testament Practice and Methodist Tradition, 1984; Hymns and Songs for Worship, 1985; Celebrate and Sing, 1991; 20 Things to do in a Decade of Evangelism, 1991; By the Way: six studies in incidental evangelism, 1995; New Creation: a full length musical presentation, 1995; Singing Faith, 1998; (ed) Leisure and Mission, 2000; (jtly) More than a Methodist, 2003; Cover to Cover: studies in Revelation, 2006; hymns and songs (words and music) published in a variety of books. *Recreations:* music, literature, travel. *Address:* 5 Flaxdale Close, Knaresborough, N Yorks HG5 0NZ.

HOARE, Sir (Charles) Antony (Richard), (Tony), Kt 2000; FRS 1982; FREng; Senior Researcher, Microsoft Research Ltd, Cambridge, since 1999; *b* 11 Jan. 1934; *s* of late Henry S. M. Hoare and Marjorie F. Hoare; *m* 1962, Jill Pym; one *s* one *d* (and one *s* decd). *Educ:* King's Sch., Canterbury; Merton Coll., Oxford (MA, Cert. Stats; Hon. Fellow, 2003). Computer Div., Elliott Brothers, London, Ltd, 1960–68: successively Programmer, Chief Engr, Tech. Man., Chief Scientist; National Computer Centre, 1968; Prof. of Computer Science, QUB, 1968–77; Oxford University: Fellow, Wolfson Coll., 1977–99; Prof. of Computation, then James Martin Prof. of Computing, 1977–99; Dir, Univ. Computing Lab., 1982–87. Lee Kuan Yew Distinguished Visitor, Singapore, 1992; Einstein Prof., Chinese Acad. of Sci., 2000. Dist. FBCS 1978; MAE 1989; FREng 2005. For. Mem., Accademia Nazionale dei Lincei, 1988; Corresp. Mem., Bavarian Acad. of Scis, 1997; For. Associate, US NAE. Hon. Fellow: Kellogg Coll., Oxford, 1999; Darwin Coll., Cambridge, 2001. Hon. DSc: Southern California, 1979; Warwick, 1985; Pennsylvania, 1986; Belfast, 1987; York, 1989; Essex 1991; Bath, 1993; Oxford Brookes, 2000; QMC, 2005. A. M. Turing Award, Assoc. Comp. Mach., 1980; Harry Goode Meml Award, Amer. Fedn of Inf. Processing Socs, 1981; Faraday Medal, IEE, 1985; Computer Pioneer Award, IEEE, 1991; Kyoto Prize, Inamori Foundn, 2000; F. L. Bauer Prize, 2007. *Publications:* Structured Programming (with O.-J. Dahl and E. W. Dijkstra), 1972; Communicating Sequential Processes, 1985; Essays in Computing Science, 1988; (with He Jifeng) Unifying Theories of Programming, 1998; articles in Computer Jl, Commun. ACM, and Acta Informatica; *festschrift:* A Classical Mind, 1994. *Recreations:* walking, reading, listening to music. *Address:* (office) 7 J J Thomson Avenue, Cambridge CB3 0FB.

HOARE, Sir Charles James, 9th Bt *cr* 1784, of Annabella, Cork; International Secretary, Christian Action Research and Education, since 1998; *b* 15 March 1971; *s* of Sir Timothy Edward Charles Hoare, 8th Bt, OBE and of Felicity Anne (*née* Boddington); *S* father, 2008; *m* 2000, Hon. Eleanor Filumena Flower, *o d* of Viscount Ashbrook, *qv*; one *s* one *d*. *Educ:* Pimlico Sch.; Durham Univ. (BA); London Sch. of Econs (MSc). OStJ. *Heir:* *s* Edward Harry William Hoare, *b* 13 Feb. 2006.

HOARE, Christopher Henry St John, (Toby); Executive Chairman, since 2005, and Chief Executive Officer, Europe, since 2006, J. Walter Thomson Group; *b* 2 Feb. 1960; *s* of J. Michael Hoare and Ann St J. Hoare; *m* 1986, Hon. Sarah Jane Dixon-Smith; two *s* one *d*. *Educ:* Harrow. Distillers Co. Ltd, 1979–80; Express Newspapers, 1980–84; Centaur Communications, 1984–85; Dorland Advertising, 1985–87; Young & Rubicam, 1987–99; Gp Chief Exec., Bates UK Ltd, 1999–2002; Chm., Bates Gp Europe, 2002–04; CEO, Team HSBC, WPP Gp, 2004–05. Governor, Harrow Sch., 2002–. Freeman, City of London, 1987; Liveryman, Co. of Distillers, 1982. *Recreations:* shooting, golf, theatre. *Address:* 17 Stanley Crescent, W11 2NA. *T:* (020) 7221 5159; The Old Rectory, Bradfield St George, Bury St Edmunds, Suffolk IP30 0DH. *Clubs:* Garrick; Royal Newmarket & Worlington Golf.

HOARE, Sir David (John), 9th Bt *cr* 1786, of Barn Elms, Surrey; Managing Partner, C. Hoare & Co., Bankers, since 2006 (Chairman, 2001–06); *b* 8 Oct. 1935; *s* of Sir Peter William Hoare, 7th Bt, and Laura Ray Hoare, *o d* of Sir John Esplen, 1st Bt, KBE; *S* brother, 2004; *m* 1st, 1965, Mary Vanessa Cardew (marr. diss. 1978); one *s*; 2nd, 1984, Virginia Victoria Graham Labes. *Educ:* Eton. Commnd Nat. Service, 1954–56. Joined Hoare's Bank, 1959: Man. Partner, 1964–88; Dep. Chm., 1988–2001. Dir, Mitre Court Property Holding Co., 1964. Chm., Internat. Atlantic Salmon Club, 1988–. Trustee, West Country Rivers Trust, 1996. *Recreations:* fishing, golf, shooting, ski-ing, forestry. *Heir:* *s* Simon Merrik Hoare [*b* 11 Oct. 1967; *m* 1999, Aurélie, *d* of Jean-François Catoire; two *s*]. *Address:* Luscombe Castle, Dawlish, Devon EX7 0PU; C. Hoare & Co., 37 Fleet Street, EC4P 4DQ. *Clubs:* White's; Royal St George's Golf, Swinley Forest Golf.

HOARE, Henry Cadogan; Senior Partner, C. Hoare & Co., Bankers (Chairman, 1988–2001); *b* 23 Nov. 1931; *s* of late Henry Peregrine Rennie Hoare and of Lady Beatrix Fanshawe, *d* of 6th Earl Cadogan, CBE; *m* 1st, 1959, Pamela Bunbury (marr. diss. 1970); two *s* one *d*; 2nd, 1977, Caromy Maxwell Macdonald. *Educ:* Eton; Trinity Coll., Cambridge (MA). Career in banking. *Address:* c/o C. Hoare & Co., 37 Fleet Street, EC4P 4DQ.

HOARE, John Michael; independent consultant, health services management, since 1990; *b* 23 Oct. 1932; *s* of Leslie Frank Hoare and Gladys Hoare; *m* 1963, Brita Hjalte; one *s* one *d*. *Educ:* Raynes Park; Christ's Coll., Cambridge (BA). Asst Sec., United Bristol Hosps, 1961; House Governor, St Stephen's Hosp., 1963; Asst Clerk, St Thomas' Hosp., 1965; Administrator, Northwick Park Hosp., 1967; Wessex Regional Health Authority: Administrator, 1974–84; Gen. Man., 1984–89; Quality Advr, 1989–90. Mem., Defence Medical Services Inquiry, 1971–73. *Recreations:* reading, walking, music, squash.

HOARE, Rt Rev. Rupert William Noel; Dean of Liverpool, 2000–07; *b* 3 March 1940; *s* of Julian Hoare and Edith Hoare (*née* Temple); *m* 1965, Gesine (*née* Pflüger); three *s* one *d*. *Educ:* Rugby School; Trinity Coll., Oxford (BA 1961, MA 1967); Kirchliche Hochschule, Berlin; Westcott House and Fitzwilliam House, Cambridge (BA 1964); Birmingham Univ. (PhD 1973). Deacon 1964, priest 1965, Dio. Manchester; Curate of St Mary, Oldham, 1964–67; Lecturer, Queen's Theological Coll., Birmingham, 1968–72; Canon Theologian of Coventry Cathedral, 1970–75; Rector, Parish of the Resurrection, Manchester, 1972–78; Residentiary Canon, Birmingham Cathedral, 1978–81; Principal, Westcott House, Cambridge, 1981–93; Bishop Suffragan of Dudley, 1993–99. *Publications:* (trans. jtly) Bultmann's St John, 1971; (contrib.) Queen's Sermons, 1973, Queen's Essays, 1980; The Trial of Faith, 1988; articles in Theology. *Recreations:* hill walking, gardening, listening to music. *Address:* 14 Shaw Hall Bank Road, Greenfield, Saddleworth, Oldham OL3 7LD.

HOARE, Toby; *see* Hoare, C. H. St J.

HOBAN, Mark Gerard; MP (C) Fareham, since 2001; chartered accountant; *b* 31 March 1964; *s* of Tom Hoban and Maureen Hoban (*née* Orchard); *m* 1994, Fiona Jane Barrett. *Educ:* London Sch. of Econs (BSc Econs 1985). ACA 1989. With Coopers & Lybrand, then PricewaterhouseCoopers, 1985–2001; Sen. Manager, 1992–2001. Contested (C) South Shields, 1997. An Opposition Whip, 2002–03; Shadow Minister for Educn, 2003–05; Shadow Financial Sec., HM Treasury, 2005–; Shadow Minister for Wearside, 2007–. Mem., Select Cttee on Sci. and Technology, 2001–03. Hon. Vice-Pres., Soc. of Maritime Industries, 2003–. Freeman, City of London, 2003; Liveryman, Fruiterers' Co., 2003. *Recreations:* cooking, entertaining, reading, travel. *Address:* House of Commons, SW1A 0AA.

HOBAN, Russell Conwell, FRSL 1988; writer; *b* 4 Feb. 1925; *s* of Abram Hoban and Jenny Dimmerman; *m* 1st, 1944, Lillian Aberman (marr. diss. 1975; she *d* 1998); one *s* three *d*; 2nd, 1975, Gundula Ahl; three *s*. *Educ:* Lansdale High Sch.; Philadelphia Museum Sch. of Industrial Art. Served US Army, 1943–45: 339th Inf., 85th Div., Italy (Bronze Star Medal, 1945). Various jobs, 1945–56; free-lance illustration, 1956–65; copywriter with Doyle, Dane, Bernbach, New York, 1965–67; resident in London, 1969–. Drama: (television) Come and Find Me, 1980; (stage) The Carrier Frequency, 1984; (radio) Perfect and Endless Circles, Radio 3, 1995; By a River in the Mind, Radio 4, 1999; opera:

The Second Mrs Kong (music by Sir Harrison Birtwistle), Glyndebourne, 1994; stories fo BBC Radio 4. *Publications:* children's books: What Does It Do and How Does It Work 1959; The Atomic Submarine, 1960; Bedtime for Frances, 1960, 2nd edn 1995; Herma the Loser, 1961; The Song in My Drum, 1962; London Men and English Men, 196. Some Snow Said Hello, 1963; A Baby Sister for Frances, 1964, 2nd edn 1993; Nothin To Do, 1964; Bread and Jam for Frances, 1964, 2nd edn 1993; The Sorely Trying Da 1964; Tom and the Two Handles, 1965; The Story of Hester Mouse, 1965; Wh. Happened When Jack and Daisy Tried To Fool the Tooth Fairies, 1965; Goodnigh 1966; Henry and the Monstrous Din, 1966; Charlie the Tramp, 1966; The Little Bru Family, 1966; Save My Place, 1967; The Mouse and His Child, 1967 (filmed, 1977); Th Stone Doll of Sister Brute, 1968; A Birthday for Frances, 1968, 2nd edn 1995; Ugly Bir 1969; Best Friends for Frances, 1969, 2nd edn 1994; Harvey's Hideout, 1969; The Mo Family's Christmas, 1969; A Bargain for Frances, 1970, 2nd edn 1992; Emmet Otter's Jug Band Christmas, 1971 (filmed for TV, 1977); The Sea-Thing Child, 1972, rev. edn 1999 Letitia Rabbit's String Song, 1973; How Tom Beat Captain Najork and His Hire Sportsmen, 1974 (Whitbread Literary Award); Ten What?, 1974; Dinner at Alberta' 1975; Crocodile and Pierrot, 1975; A Near Thing for Captain Najork, 1975; Th Twenty-Elephant Restaurant, 1977; Arthur's New Power, 1978; The Dancing Tiger 1979; La Corona and Other Tin Tales, 1979; Ace Dragon Ltd, 1980; Flat Cat, 1980; Th Serpent Tower, 1981; The Great Fruit Gum Robbery, 1981; They Came from Aargh 1981; The Flight of Bembel Rudzuk, 1982; The Battle of Zormla, 1982; Jim Frog, 198; Big John Turkle, 1983; Charlie Meadows, 1984; Lavinia Bat, 1984; The Rain Door, 198€ The Marzipan Pig, 1986; Ponders, 1988; Monsters, 1989; Jim Hedgehog's Supernatura Christmas, 1989; Jim Hedgehog and the Lonesome Tower, 1990; M.O.L.E. (Muc Overworked Little Earthmover), 1993; The Court of the Winged Serpent, 1994; Monste Film, 1995; Trouble on Thunder Mountain, 1998; Jim's Lion, 2001; *novels:* The Lion c Boaz-Jachin and Jachin-Boaz, 1973; Kleinzeit, 1974; Turtle Diary, 1975 (filmed, 1985 Riddley Walker, 1980 (John W. Campbell Meml Award, 1981, Best Internat. Fictior Aust. Sci. Fiction Achievement Award, 1983; adapted for stage, 1986); Pilgermann, 198: The Medusa Frequency, 1987; Fremder, 1996; The Trokeville Way, 1996; Mr Rinyo Clacton's Offer, 1998; Angelica's Grotto, 1999; Amaryllis Night and Day, 2001; The Ba Tattoo, 2002; Her Name Was Lola, 2003; Come Dance With Me, 2005; Linger Awhile 2006; My Tango with Barbara Strozzi, 2007; *verse:* The Pedalling Man and Other Poem 1968, 2nd edn 1991; Egg Thoughts and Other Frances Songs, 1972, 2nd edn 1994 (contrib.) Six of the Best (ed A. Harvey), 1989; The Last of the Wallendas and Othe Poems, 1997; *anthology:* The Moment Under the Moment, 1992; stories and essays ii Fiction Magazine and Granta; *films:* (also narrated): Deadsy, 1989; Door, 1989. *Recreatio* rewriting yesterday's pages. *Address:* David Higham Associates Ltd, 5–8 Lower John Stree Golden Square, W1R 4HA. *T:* (020) 7434 5900, *Fax:* (020) 7437 1072.

HOBART (Australia), Archbishop of, (RC), since 1999; **Most Rev. Adrian Le Doyle;** *b* 16 Nov. 1936; *s* of George Leo Doyle and Gertrude Mary (*née* O'Donnell, *Educ:* Urbaniana Univ., Rome (ThL, PhL); Gregorian Univ., Rome (DCL). Ordaine priest, Rome, 1961; Parish Priest, Sandy Bay, Tasmania, 1974–90; VG, Archdio. o Hobart, 1997–99; apptd Coadjutor Archbishop of Hobart, 1997, ordained bishop, 1998 Judge: Regl Marriage Tribunal, Victoria and Tasmania, 1968–; Nat. Appeal Tribuna Aust. and NZ, 1974–. *Recreations:* golf, walking, reading. *Address:* GPO Box 62, Hobar Tas 7001, Australia. *T:* (3) 62086222. *Club:* Athenæum (Hobart).

HOBART, David Anthony, CB 2004; Chief Executive, Bar Council, since 2004 Gentleman Usher to the Queen, since 2007; *b* 24 Dec. 1951; *m* 1977, Mandy Wilson; on *s* one *d*. *Educ:* Magdalene Coll., Cambridge (MPhil); LLB Open Univ. rcds; jsdc; psc Various planning and financial programming posts in MoD; promoted to Air Vice Marshal, 2001; ACDS (Policy), 2001–04. *Recreations:* golf, ski-ing, running. *Address:* c/ Bar Council, 289 High Holborn, WC1V 7HZ. *T:* (020) 7242 0082. *Clubs:* Royal Ai Force; Wildernesse (Kent).

HOBART, Sir John Vere, 4th Bt *cr* 1914, of Langdown, Co. Southampton; *b* 9 Apr 1945; *s* of Lt-Comdr Sir Robert Hampden Hobart, 3rd Bt, RN and Sylvia (*d* 1965), *d* c Harry Argo; *heir-pres.* to Earl of Buckinghamshire, *qv*; *S* father, 1988; *m* 1980, Kate, *o d* c late George Henry Iddles; two *s*. *Heir:* *s* George Hampden Hobart, *b* 10 June 1982.

HOBART-HAMPDEN, family name of **Earl of Buckinghamshire**.

HOBBS, Christina; *see* Dodwell, C.

HOBBS, Prof. (Frederick David) Richard, FRCGP, FRCP; FMedSci; FESC Professor and Head of Department of Primary Care Clinical Sciences (formerly Primar Care and General Practice), University of Birmingham, since 1992; *b* 2 Nov. 1953; *s* o Frederick Derek Hobbs and Nancy Elizabeth (*née* Wilde); *m* 1977, Jane Marilyn Porte one *s* one *d*. *Educ:* King Edward VI Camp Hill Sch., Birmingham; Bristol Univ. (MB, ChI 1977). MRCGP 1981, FRCGP 1990; FRCP 2000. House officer posts, Bath Roya United Hosp., 1977–78; Sen. house officer posts, Selly Oak Hosp., Birminghan 1978–80; GP trainee, Univ. Health Centre, Birmingham, 1980–81; Principal in genera practice, Bellevue Med. Centre, Birmingham, 1981– (part-time, 1992–); Birminghan University: part-time Sen. Lectr in General Practice, 1985–92; Asst Dean, Sch. o Medicine, 1993–96; Hd, Div. of Primary Care, Public and Occupational Health 1998–2001; Associate Dean, Sch. of Medicine, 2002–05. FMedSci 2002; FESC 2002 *Publications:* (with M. Drury) Treatment and Prognosis in General Practice, 1990; (with B Stillwell): Nursing in general practice, 1990; Practice Nurse Programme, 1990; (with M Barrowcliffe) Managing Practice Information, 1992; (with L. Beeley) Treatment: handbook of drug therapy, 1993; (with C. Bradley) Prescribing in Primary Care, 1998 over 500 research contribs to learned jls incl. Lancet, BMJ, Brit. Jl Gen. Pract., Famil Practice, Brit. Jl Cardiol., Gut, Jl RSM. *Recreations:* gardening, travel, interests in musi (passive), wine and good food. *Address:* Department of Primary Care Clinical Sciences Primary Care Clinical Sciences Building, University of Birmingham, Edgbaston Birmingham B15 2TT. *T:* (0121) 414 6764.

HOBBS, Jennifer Lynn, MBE 1992; Principal, St Mary's College, Durham University 1999–2007; *b* 5 March 1944; *d* of Henry Edwin Hobbs and Jean Hobbs (*née* Kennedy) *Educ:* St Paul's Girls' Sch., London; Newnham Coll., Cambridge (BA (Hons) Geog 1966 MA 1970). VSO teacher, Malacca Girls' High Sch., Malaysia, 1966–68; Geography Editor, Overseas Educ. Dept, Macmillan Education, 1968–73; British Council, 1973–94 various posts in UK; Nepal, 1979–83; Yugoslavia/Croatia, 1988–92; on secondment Univ. of Durham, 1992–94; Dir, Internat. Office, 1992–2004, Associate Dean for Studen Support Services, 2004–05; Durham Univ. Mem., Durham Cathedral Council, 2001–07 FRSA 2003. Governor: Durham Sch., 1998–2005; Durham High Sch. for Girls, 2007–. *Recreations:* classical music, sport, walking, birdwatching, gardening. *Club:* Roya Commonwealth Society.

HOBBS, Prof. Kenneth Edward Frederick, ChM, FRCS; Professor of Surgery, Roya Free Hospital School of Medicine, University of London, and Consultant Surgeon, Roya Free Hampstead NHS Trust (formerly Royal Free Hospital), 1973–98, then Emeritu

Professor; Chairman, Joint Board of Surgery, University College London Medical School and Royal Free Hospital School of Medicine, 1993–98; Dean, University of London Faculty of Medicine, 1994–98; *b* 28 Dec. 1936; *s* of late Thomas Edward Ernest Hobbs and Gladys May Hobbs (*née* Neave). *Educ:* West Suffolk County Grammar Sch., Bury St Edmunds; Guy's Hosp. Med. Sch., Univ. of London (MB BS 1960). ChM Bristol 1970; FRCS 1964. Lectr in Surgery, Univ. of Bristol, 1966–70; Surgical Res. Fellow, Harvard Univ., 1968–69; Sen. Lectr in Surgery, Univ. of Bristol, 1970–73; University of London: Vice-Dean, Faculty of Medicine, 1986–90; Mem. Senate, then Council, 1985–98; Chm., Acad. Adv. Bd in Medicine, 1986–90; Dep. Chm., Acad. Council Standing Sub-Cttee in Medicine, 1986–90. Mem., Systems Bd, MRC, 1982–86; Chm., Grants Cttee A, MRC, 1984–86; Member: Med. Sub-Cttee, UGC, 1986–89; Med. Cttee, UFC, 1991–92; GMC, 1996–2001 (Dep. Chm., Professional Conduct Cttee, 1999–2001); Mason Med. Res. Foundn, 1988–98 (Chm., 1993–98). Vis. Prof., Univs in China, Ethiopia, S Africa, Europe, USA, West Indies. Secretary: Patey Soc., 1979–82; 1942 Club, 1985–88; Trustee and Bd Mem., Stanley Thomas Johnson Foundn, Berne, 1976–2004 (Chm., 1997–2004). Hon. Fellow, Chinese Univ. of Hong Kong, 2002. Hon. FCSSL 1995. Internat. Master Surgeon, Internat. Coll. of Surgeons, 1994. FRSocMed 1973. *Publications:* chapters on aspects of liver surgery in textbooks; contribs to professional jls. *Recreations:* gourmet cooking and dining, the countryside. *Address:* The Rookery, New Buckenham, Norfolk NR16 2AE. *T:* (01953) 860558. *Club:* Royal Society of Medicine.

HOBBS, Maj.-Gen. Sir Michael (Frederick), KCVO 1998; CBE 1982 (OBE 1979; MBE 1975); Governor, Military Knights of Windsor, since 2000; *b* 28 Feb. 1937; *s* of late Brig. Godfrey Pennington Hobbs and Elizabeth Constance Mary Hobbs; *m* 1967, Tessa Mary Churchill; one *s* two *d*. *Educ:* Eton College. Served Grenadier Guards, 1956–80; Directing Staff, Staff Coll., 1974–77; MoD, 1980–82; Commander 39 Inf. Bde, 1982–84; Dir of PR (Army), 1984–85; Commander, 4th Armoured Div., 1985–87; retired. Director: Duke of Edinburgh's Award, 1988–98; Outward Bound Trust, 1995–2006. *Address:* Mary Tudor Tower, Windsor Castle, Windsor, Berks SL4 1NJ. *T:* (01753) 850802.

HOBBS, Peter Thomas Goddard; HM first lay Inspector of Constabulary, 1993–98; *b* 19 March 1938; *s* of late Reginald Stanley Hobbs, BEM, Gloucester and of Phyllis Gwendoline (*née* Goddard); *m* 1964, Victoria Christabel, *d* of late Rev. Alan Matheson, Clifton Campville, Staffs; one *d*. *Educ:* Crypt Sch., Glos; Exeter Coll., Oxford (Waugh Scholar; MA). Nat. Service, 2nd Lt, RASC, 1957–59; Capt., RCT, TA, 1959–68. With ICI Ltd, 1962–79 (Jt Personnel Manager, Mond Div.); Gp Personnel Dir, Wellcome Foundn and Wellcome PLC, 1979–92. Chemical Industries Association: Dep. Chm., Pharmaceuticals and Fine Chemical Jt Industrial Council, 1979–89; Chairman: Trng Cttee, 1985–89; Employment Affairs Bd, 1989–91; Mem. Council, 1989–92; Chm., Chem. Industry Educn Centre, Univ. of York, 1992–94. Dir, Employment Conditions Abroad Ltd, 1984–91 and 1993. Confederation of British Industry: Member: Task Force on Vocational Educn and Trng, 1989–90; Educn and Trng Cttee, 1990–94; Business in the Community: Member, Target Team: for Industrial/Educn Partnerships, 1988–90; for Priority Hiring, 1988–91; Founder Chm., Employers' Forum on Disability, 1986–93; Member: Nat. Adv. Council on Employment for People with Disabilities, 1991–93; Learning from Experience Trust, 1988– (Chm., 1992–93 and 1998–). Member: Council, Contemporary Applied Arts, 1990–92; Industry Adv. Gp, Nat. Curriculum Council, 1990–92; Personnel Standards Lead Body, 1992–94; Council, EDEXCEL (formerly BTEC), 1995–98. Non-exec. Dir, Forensic Sci. Service, 1996–2006. Director: and Dep. Chm., Roffey Park Inst., 1989–93; Centre for Enterprise, London Business Sch., 1989–92; Mem. Adv. Council, Mgt Centre Europe, Brussels, 1989–97. CCIPD 1988 (Internat. Vice Pres., 1987–89, 1990–91); FInstD 1989 (Mem., Employment Cttee, 1989–93); FRSA 1992. Dr *hc* Internat. Mgt Centres, 2000. *Recreations:* history, topography, opera, turning the soil. *Address:* 105 Blenheim Crescent, W11 2EQ. *T:* (020) 7727 3054, *Fax:* (020) 7221 9542. *Club:* Oxford and Cambridge.

HOBBS, Philip John; racehorse trainer, since 1985; *b* 26 July 1955; *s* of Tony and Barbara Hobbs; *m* 1982, Sarah Louise Hill; three *d*. *Educ:* King's Coll., Taunton; Univ. of Reading (BSc). Rode 160 winners as a jockey; has trained over 1000 winners, 1985–. *Recreations:* ski-ing, shooting. *Address:* Sandhill Racing Stables, Bilbrook, Minehead, Somerset TA24 6HA. *T:* (01984) 640366, *Fax:* (01984) 641124; *e-mail:* racing@pjhobbs.co.uk. *Club:* Sportsman.

HOBBS, Richard; *see* Hobbs, F. D. R.

HOBBS, Prof. Roger Edwin, PhD, DSc; FIStructE, FICE; Director, Tension Technology International, since 1986; Professor of Engineering Structures, Imperial College of Science, Technology and Medicine, London, 1990–2003, now Emeritus; *b* 24 Feb. 1943; *s* of Edwin Daniel Hobbs and Phyllis Eileen (*née* Chapman); *m* 1st, 1965, Barbara Ann Dalton (*d* 1987); one *s* two *d*; 2nd, 1989, Dorinda Elizabeth Mitchell. *Educ:* Imperial Coll., London (PhD 1966; DSc Eng 1996). FIStructE 1990; FICE 1995; FCGI 1996. Imperial College, London: Res. Asst, 1966–70; Lectr in Civil Engrg, 1970–83; Sen. Lectr, 1983–86; Reader in Structural Engrg, 1986–90; Hd, Dept of Civil Engrg, 1994–97. *Publications:* technical papers on steel structures, wire and high strength fibre ropes, offshore pipelines. *Recreations:* walking, France, preferably in combination. *Address:* Civil Engineering Department, Imperial College of Science, Technology and Medicine, University of London, SW7 2AZ. *T:* (020) 7594 5998.

HOBDAY, Sir Gordon (Ivan), Kt 1979; Lord Lieutenant and Keeper of the Rolls for Nottinghamshire, 1983–91; Chancellor, Nottingham University, 1979–92 (President of the Council, 1973–82); *b* 1 Feb. 1916; *e s* of late Alexander Thomas Hobday and Frances Cassandra (*née* Meads); *m* 1st, 1940, Margaret Jean Joule (*d* 1995); one *d*; 2nd, 2002, Patricia Birge. *Educ:* Long Eaton Grammar Sch.; UC Nottingham. BSc, PhD London; FRSC. Joined Boots Co., 1939; Dir of Research, 1952–68; Man. Dir, 1970–72; Chm., 1973–81; Chm., Central Independent Television, 1981–85; Dir, Lloyds Bank, 1981–86. A Dep. Chm., Price Commn, 1977–78. Pres., Portland Coll., 1990–93. DL Notts, 1981. KStJ 1983. Hon. LLD Nottingham, 1977. *Recreations:* handicrafts, gardening. *Address:* Newstead Abbey Park, Nottingham NG15 8GD.

HOBDAY, Peter James; journalist and broadcaster; *s* of Arthur John Hobday and Dorothy Ann Hobday (*née* Lewis); *m* 1st, 1959, Tamara Batcharnikoff (*d* 1984); one *s* one *d*; 2nd, 1996, Victoria Fenwick. *Educ:* St Chad's Coll., Wolverhampton; Leicester Univ. Wolverhampton Express and Star, 1960; Business magazine, 1960–61; The Director, 1961–74; joined BBC, 1970: World Service, 1970–74; Financial World Tonight, 1974–80, Moneybox, 1977–80, Radio 4; Money Programme, 1979–80, Newsnight, 1980–82, BBC TV; Today programme, Radio 4, 1982–96; Masterworks, Radio 3, 1996–2000. Hon. Dr de Montfort, 1996; Hon. DLitt Wolverhampton, 2008. *Publications:* Man the Industrialist, 1970; Saudi Arabia Today, 1974; In the Valley of the Fireflies, 1995; Managing the Message, 2000; The Girl in Rose: Haydn's last love, 2004. *Recreation:* growing olives in Italy. *Address:* 67 Highlever Road, W10 6PR. *Club:* Athenæum.

HOBHOUSE, Sir Charles (John Spinney), 7th Bt *cr* 1812, of Broughton-Gifford, Bradford-on-Avon and of Monkton Farleigh, Wiltshire; *b* 27 Oct. 1962; *s* of Sir Charles Chisholm Hobhouse, 6th Bt, TD and of Elspeth Jean, *yr d* of late Thomas George Spinney; *S* father, 1991; *m* 1993, Katrina (marr. diss. 1997), *d* of Maj.-Gen. Sir Denzil Macarthur-Onslow, CBE, DSO. *Recreations:* sport, travel. *Heir: uncle* John Spencer Hobhouse [*b* 15 Nov. 1910; *m* 1940, Mary, *yr d* of late Llewelyn Robert, MD]. *Address:* Monkton Farleigh Manor, Bradford-on-Avon, Wilts BA15 2QE.

HOBHOUSE, (Mary) Hermione, MBE 1981; FSA; writer and conservationist; General Editor, Survey of London, 1983–94; *d* of late Sir Arthur Lawrence Hobhouse and Konradin, *d* of Rt Hon. Frederick Huth Jackson; *m* 1958, Henry Trevenen Davidson Graham (marr. diss. 1988); one *s* one *d*. *Educ:* Ladies' Coll., Cheltenham; Lady Margaret Hall, Oxford (Hons Mod. Hist.). Researcher/Writer, Associated-Rediffusion TV and Granada TV, 1957–65; Tutor in Architectural History, Architectural Assoc. Sch., London, 1973–78; Sec., Victorian Soc., 1977–82. Member: Royal Commn for Exhibn of 1851, 1983–98; Council, Nat. Trust, 1983–2001; Council, Soc. of Antiquaries, 1984–87; London DAC, 1988–92; Council, Royal Albert Hall, 1988–2004. *Publications:* Thomas Cubitt: Master Builder, 1971 (Hitchcock Medal, 1972), reprinted 1995; Lost London, 1971; History of Regent Street, 1975, 2nd edn 2008; Oxford and Cambridge, 1980; Prince Albert: his life and work, 1983; (ed) Survey of London, vol. 42, Southern Kensington: Kensington Square to Earls Court, 1986, vol. 17, County Hall, 1991, vols 42 and 43, Poplar, Blackwall and the Isle of Dogs, 1994; London Survey'd: the work of the Survey of London 1894–1994, 1994; The Crystal Palace and the Great Exhibition: Art, Science and Productive Industry: the history of the Royal Commission for the Great Exhibition of 1851, 2002; contrib. Architectural Jl, Architectural Review. *Recreations:* gardening, looking at buildings of all periods. *Address:* Westcombe Stables, Evercreech, Shepton Mallet, Somerset BA4 6ES. *T:* (01749) 830465. *Club:* Reform.

HOBHOUSE, Penelope, (Mrs John Malins); gardener, garden writer and garden consultant, since 1976; *b* 20 Nov. 1929; *d* of late Captain J. J. L.-C. Chichester-Clark, DSO and Bar, MP and Marion Chichester-Clark (later Mrs C. E. Brackenbury); *m* 1st, 1952, Paul Hobhouse (marr. diss. 1982; he *d* 1994); two *s* one *d*; 2nd, 1983, Prof. John Malins (*d* 1992). *Educ:* Girton Coll., Cambridge (BA Hons Econs, 1951; MA). National Trust tenant of Tintinhull House garden, 1980–93. Hon. DLitt: Birmingham, 1998; Essex (Writtle Coll.), 1998. VMH 1996. *Publications:* The Country Gardener, 1976, revd edn 1989; The Smaller Garden, 1981; Gertrude Jekyll on Gardening, 1983; Colour in your Garden, 1985; The National Trust: A Book of Gardening, 1986; Private Gardens of England, 1986; Garden Style, 1988; Painted Gardens, 1988; Borders, 1989; The Gardens of Europe, 1990; Flower Gardens, 1991; Plants in Garden History, 1992; Penelope Hobhouse on Gardening, 1994; Penelope Hobhouse's Garden Designs, 1997; Penelope Hobhouse's Natural Planting, 1997; A Gardener's Journal, 1997; Gardens of Italy, 1998; The Story of Gardening, 2002; The Gardens of Persia, 2003. *Recreations:* reading Trollope and Henry James, Italy. *Address:* The Coach House, Bettiscombe, Bridport, Dorset DT6 5NT.

See also Sir R. Chichester-Clark.

HOBKIRK, Michael Dalgliesh; *b* 9 Dec. 1924; *s* of Roy and Phyllis Hobkirk; *m* 1952, Lucy Preble; two *d*. *Educ:* Marlborough Coll.; Wadham Coll., Oxford. BA (Social Studies), MA 1949. Served War of 1939–45: Army (RAC, RAEC, Captain), 1943–47. Civil Service: War Office, 1949–63; MoD, 1963–70; Directing Staff, Nat. Defence Coll., 1970–74; Brookings Instn, Washington, DC, USA, 1974–75; Lord Chancellor's Dept, 1975–80 (Principal Establishment and Finance Officer, 1977–80); Asst Under-Sec. of State, MoD, 1980–82. Sen. Fellow, Nat. Defense Univ., Washington, DC, USA, 1982–83. *Publication:* (contrib.) The Management of Defence (ed L. Martin), 1976; The Politics of Defence Budgeting, 1984; Land, Sea or Air?, 1992. *Address:* 48 Woodside Avenue, Beaconsfield, Bucks HP9 1JH. *Club:* Oxford and Cambridge.

HOBLEY, Brian, FSA; historical and archaeological researcher and writer; Chief Urban Archaeologist, City of London, 1973–89; Director, Hobley Archaeological Consultancy Services Ltd, 1989–92; *b* 25 June 1930; *s* of William Hobley and Harriet (*née* Hobson); *m* (marr. diss. 1992); one *s* one *d*. *Educ:* Univ. of Leicester (BA Hons 1965); Univ. of Oxford (MSt 1994). FSA 1969; AMA 1970. Field Officer, Coventry Corp., 1965; Keeper, Dept Field Archaeology, Coventry Museum, 1970. Lectr, Birmingham Univ. Extra-mural Dept, 1965–74. Chm. Standing Cttee, Arch. Unit Managers, 1986–89; Jt Sec., British Archaeologists and Developers Liaison Gp, 1986–89. MCMI (MBIM 1978); MIFA 1982. *Publications:* (ed jtly) Waterfront Archaeology in Britain and Northern Europe, 1981; Roman Urban Defences in the West, 1983; Roman Urban Topography in Britain and the Western Empire, 1985; Roman and Saxon London: a reappraisal, 1986; British Archaeologists and Developers Code of Practice, 1986; The Rebirth of Towns in the West AD 700–1050, 1988; reports in learned jls incl. Proc. 7th, 8th, 9th and 12th Internat. Congresses of Roman Frontier Studies, Tel Aviv, Univ. Israel and Bucharest Univ., Rumania on excavations and reconstructions at The Lunt Roman fort, Baginton near Coventry. *Recreations:* classical music, chess. *Address:* 30 Turton Way, Kenilworth, Warwicks CV8 2RT.

HOBMAN, Anthony Hugh Burton; Chief Executive, The Pensions Regulator, since 2005; *b* 5 July 1955; *s* of late David Burton Hobman, CBE and of Erica Agatha Hobman (*née* Irwin); *m* 1st, 1978, Catherine Fenton (marr. diss. 1994); one *s* two *d*; 2nd, 2001, Victoria Richards (*née* Maynard); one *d* and two step *s*. *Educ:* De La Salle Coll.; Cardinal Newman Sch., Hove; N Staffs Polytech. (BA Hons (Modern Studies) 1976). Barclays Bank plc: Graduate Mgt Trainee, 1976–81; various roles in Marketing, Project, Change and Service Mgt, 1982–95; Proshare (UK) Ltd: Hd, Private Investor Services, 1996–99; Chief Exec., 1999–2000; Chief Executive: Money Channel plc, 2000–01; Occupational Pensions Regulatory Authy, 2002–05. Member: Consultative Cttee, Co. Law Review, DTI, 1999–2000; Adv. Gp, Employer Task Force on Pensions, DWP, 2003–04. Gov., Pensions Policy Inst., 2005–. Trustee, David Hobman Charitable Trust, 1987–96. *Recreations:* ski-ing, theatre, wine, watching Time Team. *Address:* 20 Wilbury Gardens, Hove, E Sussex BN3 6HY. *T:* (01273) 727183; *e-mail:* tonyhobman@hotmail.com. *Club:* Reform.

HOBSBAWM, Prof. Eric John Ernest, CH 1998; FBA 1976; Emeritus Professor of Economic and Social History, University of London, since 1982; *b* 9 June 1917; *s* of Leopold Percy Hobsbawm and Nelly Grün; *m* 1962, Marlene Schwarz; one *s* one *d*. *Educ:* Vienna; Berlin; St Marylebone Grammar Sch.; Univ. of Cambridge (BA, PhD). Lectr, Birkbeck Coll., 1947; Fellow, King's Coll., Cambridge, 1949–55, Hon. Fellow, 1973; Birkbeck College, London University: Reader, 1959; Prof., 1970–82; Pres., 2002–. Hon. DPhil Univ. of Stockholm, 1970; Hon. DHL: Univ. of Chicago, 1976; New Sch. of Social Res., 1982; Bard Coll., 1986; Hon. LittD: UEA, 1982; York Univ., Canada, 1986; Columbia, 1997; Oxon, 2001; Hon. DLit London, 1993; DU Essex, 1996; D*hc* Univ. of Pisa, 1987; Univ. of Buenos Aires, 1998; Universidad de Artes e Ciencias Sociales, Santiago de Chile, 1998; Univ. of the Republic, Montevideo, 1999; Univ. of Turin, 2000; Univ. of Pennsylvania, 2002; Univ. of Thessaloniki, 2004; Univ. of Vienna, 2008. Foreign

Hon. Mem., American Academy of Arts and Sciences, 1971; Hon. Member: Hungarian Acad. of Sciences, 1979; Japan Acad., 2005; Foreign Mem., Accademia delle Scienze di Torino, 1998. Palmes Académiques (France), 1993; Comdr, Order of Southern Cross (Brazil), 1996; Ehrenkreuz für Wissenschaft und Kunst (Austria), 2007. *Publications:* Labour's Turning Point, 1948; Primitive Rebels, 1959; (*pseud.* F. Newton) The Jazz Scene, 1959; The Age of Revolution, 1962; Labouring Men, 1964; (ed) Karl Marx, Precapitalist Formations, 1964; Industry and Empire, 1968; (with G. Rudé) Captain Swing, 1969; Bandits, 1969; Revolutionaries, 1973; The Age of Capital, 1975; (with T. Ranger) The Invention of Tradition, 1983; Worlds of Labour, 1984; The Age of Empire, 1987; Politics for a Rational Left, 1989; Nations and Nationalism since 1780, 1990; Echoes of the Marseillaise, 1990; Age of Extremes: the short Twentieth Century, 1994; On History, 1997; Uncommon People: resistance, rebellion and jazz, 1998; (with A. Polito) The New Century, 2000; Interesting Times: a twentieth-century life, 2002; Globalisation, Democracy and Terrorism, 2007; contribs to jls. *Recreation:* travel. *Address:* Birkbeck College, Malet Street, WC1E 7HX. *T:* (020) 7631 6299.

See also J. N. Hobsbawm.

HOBSBAWM BAMPING, Julia Nathalie, FCIPR; Founder, Chief Executive and Director, Editorial Intelligence Ltd, since 2003; Chief Executive, Julia Hobsbawm Consulting Ltd, since 2005; *b* 15 Aug. 1964; *d* of Prof. Eric John Ernest Hobsbawm, *qv* and Marlene (*née* Schwarz); *m* 2004, Alaric Bamping; two *s* one *d*, and one step *s* one step *d*. *Educ:* Camden Sch. for Girls; Poly. of Central London. Asst, Martin Dunitz Med. Publrs, 1982; Publicity Officer, Penguin Books, 1983; Head of Publicity, Virago Press, 1985–87; Researcher: Books by my Bedside, Thames TV, 1987–89; Wogan, BBC, 1989–90; Forward Planning Editor, John Gau Productions, 1990–91; Fundraising Consultant, 1000 Club and High Value Donors, Labour Party, 1991–92; founded Julia Hobsbawm Associates, 1992, then, Hobsbawm Macaulay Communications, 1993 (Chair, 1993–2001); Chief Exec., HMC-Hobsbawm Media + Marketing Communications Ltd, 2001–05. Vis. Prof., London College, 2003–. Member: Commng Panel, ESRC Culture of Consumption Res. Panel, 2002–07; Public Value Adv. Panel, Arts Council, 2006–07; President's Panel, CIPR, 2007–. Vice Pres., Hay Fest. of Lit., 2001–. Mem., Nat. Develt Cttee, Treehouse, 2007–. Trustee: Facial Surgery Res. Foundn, 2000–08 (Patron, 2008–); In-Kind Direct, 2003–07; Jewish Community Centre for London, 2004–05. FRSA 2003. *Publications:* (with Robert Gray) The Cosmopolitan Guide to Working in PR and Advertising, 1996; (ed) Where the Truth Lies: trust and morality in PR and journalism, 2006; (with John Lloyd) The Power of the Commentariat: how much do commentators influence politics and public opinion?, 2008; The See-Saw: 100 recipes for work life balance, 2009. *Recreations:* conversation, singing, gardening. *Web:* www.juliahobsbawm.com. *Clubs:* Groucho, Soho House, One Alfred Place.

HOBSLEY, Prof. Michael, TD 1969; PhD; FRCS; David Patey Professor of Surgery, University of London, 1986–94 (Professor of Surgery, 1984–94), now Emeritus Professor; Head, Department of Surgery, University College and Middlesex School of Medicine, University College London, 1984–93; *b* 18 Jan. 1929; *s* of Henry Hobsley and Sarah Lily Blanchfield; *m* 1953, Jane Fairlie Cambell; one *s* three *d*. *Educ:* La Martinière Coll., Calcutta; Sidney Sussex Coll., Cambridge (MA, MB, MChir); Middlesex Hosp. Med. Sch.; PhD London, 1961; DSc London, 1989. FRCS 1958. Training posts in RAMC and at Middlesex, Whittington and Chace Farm Hosps, 1951–68; Comyns Berkeley Fellow, Gonville and Caius Coll., Cambridge and Middx Hosp. Med. Sch., 1965–66; posts at Middx Hosp. and Med. Sch., 1968–: Hon. Consultant Surgeon, 1969–; Reader in Surgical Science, 1970–75; Prof. of Surg. Science, 1975–83; Dir, Dept of Surgical Studies, 1983–88. Howard C. Naffziger Surg. Res. Fellow, Univ. of Calif, 1966; Windermere Foundn Travelling Prof. of Surgery, 1984; Glaxo Visitor, Univ. of Witwatersrand, 1985; Vis. Professor: Univ. of Calif, 1980; Univ. of Khartoum, 1976; McMaster Univ., 1982; Monash Univ., 1984; Univ. of Louisville, 1995. Non-exec. Mem., Enfield HA, 1990–93. Pres., British Soc. of Gastroenterology, 1992–93; Chm., Assoc. of Profs of Surgery, 1990–94. Royal College of Surgeons: Hunterian Prof., 1962–63; Penrose May Tutor, 1973–78; Sir Gordon Gordon-Taylor Lectr, 1980; Examr, 1968–94. Examiner: Univ. of London, 1978–94; Univ. of Nigeria, 1977–94; Univ. of the WI, 1978–94; Univ. of Bristol, 1986–88; Univ. of Cambridge, 1986–94; St Mary's Hosp. Med. Sch., 1989–91; St George's Hosp. Med. Sch., 1990–93; Univ. of Birmingham, 1992–94; Univ. of Newcastle, 1992–94. Mem., Professional and Linguistics Assessment Bd and Chm., Multiple Choice Questions Panel, 1993–97; Trustee, and Chm. Academic Council, Inst. of Sports Medicine, 1995–2004. Hon. Fellow: Assoc. of Surgeons of India, 1983; Amer. Surgical Assoc., 1989. FRSocMed 1960. *Publications:* Pathways in Surgical Management, 1979, 3rd edn (ed with P. B. Boulos), 2002; Disorders of the Digestive System, 1982; Colour Atlas of Parotidectomy, 1983; Physiology in Surgical Practice, 1992; articles in BMJ, Lancet, British Jl of Surgery, Gut, Klinische Wochenschrift. *Recreation:* cricket. *Address:* Fieldside, Barnet Lane, Totteridge, N20 8AS. *T:* (020) 8445 6507. *Clubs:* Athenæum, MCC.

HOBSON, Anthony Robert Alwyn, DLitt; FBA 1992; book historian; *b* 5 Sept. 1921; *s* of Geoffrey Dudley Hobson, MVO and Gertrude Adelaide, *d* of Rev. Thomas Vaughan, Rector of Rhuddlan, Flintshire; *m* 1959, Elena Pauline Tanya (*d* 1988), *d* of Igor Vinogradoff; one *s* two *d*. *Educ:* Eton Coll. (Oppidan Scholar); New Coll., Oxford (MA); DLitt Oxon, 1992. Served Scots Guards, 1941–46, Captain; Italy, 1943–46 (mentioned in despatches). Joined Sotheby & Co., 1947: Dir, 1949–71, Associate, 1971–77. Sandars Reader in Bibliography, Univ. of Cambridge, 1974–75; Franklin Jasper Walls Lectr, Pierpont Morgan Library, NY, 1979; Vis. Fellow, All Souls Coll., Oxford, 1982–83; Rosenbach Fellow, Univ. of Pennsylvania, 1990; Lyell Reader in Bibliography, Univ. of Oxford, 1990–91. President: Bibliographical Soc., 1977–79; Association internationale de Bibliophilie, 1985–99; Hon. Pres., Edinburgh Bibliographical Soc., 1971–; Trustee: Eton Coll. Collections Trust, 1977–97; Lambeth Palace Library, 1984–90. Hon. Fellow, Pierpont Morgan Library, 1983–; For. Associate, Ateneo Veneto, 1987–. Cavaliere Ufficiale, Al Merito della Repubblica Italiana, 1979. *Publications:* French and Italian Collectors and their Bindings, 1953; Great Libraries, 1970; Apollo and Pegasus, 1975; Humanists and Bookbinders, 1989 (Premio Felice Feliciano, Verona, 1991; Triennial Prize, Internat. League of Antiquarian Booksellers, 1991); (with Paul Culot) Italian and French Sixteenth-century Bookbindings, 1990; Renaissance Book Collecting: Jean Grolier and Diego Hurtado de Mendoza, their books and bindings, 1999; (ed) Ronald Firbank: letters to his mother 1920–1924, 2001; contrib. The Library, TLS, etc. *Recreations:* travel, opera, visiting libraries founded before 1800. *Address:* The Glebe House, Whitsbury, near Fordingbridge, Hants SP6 3QB. *T:* (01725) 518221. *Clubs:* Brooks's, Beefsteak, Roxburghe; Grolier (New York); Société des Bibliophiles François (Paris).

HOBSON, David Constable, CBE 1991; Chartered Accountant; Partner, Coopers & Lybrand, 1953–84, Senior Partner, 1975–83; *b* 1 Nov. 1922; *s* of late Charles Kenneth and Eileen Isabel Hobson; *m* 1961, Elizabeth Anne Drury; one *s* one *d*. *Educ:* Marlborough Coll.; Christ's Coll., Cambridge (Scholar). MA. ACA 1950; FCA 1958. Served War, REME, 1942–47 (Captain). Joined Cooper Brothers & Co. (later Coopers & Lybrand), 1947; Mem., Exec. Cttee, Coopers & Lybrand (International), 1973–83. Chairman: Cambrian & General Securities, 1986–89; Fleming High Income Investment Trust, 1991–93 (Dir, 1989–93); Dir, The Laird Gp, 1985–98. Inspector (for Dept of Trade) London & County Securities Group Ltd, 1974; Advr, Prime Minister's Policy Unit 1983–86. Member: Accounting Standards Cttee, 1970–82; City Capital Markets Cttee 1980–84; Nat. Biological Standards Bd, 1983–88; Building Socs Commn, 1986–92; Board Mem. (repr. UK and Ireland), Internat. Accounting Standards Cttee, 1980–85. Hon Treasurer, Lister Inst., 1986–98. Member of Council: Marlborough Coll., 1967–9 (Chm., 1987–92); Francis Holland Schools, 1975–95. *Address:* Magnolia, Chiswick Mall W4 2PR. *T:* (020) 8994 7511. *Club:* Reform.

HOBSON, John; JP; independent policy adviser; Director, Construction Industry Department of Trade and Industry, 2001–02; *b* 30 March 1946; *s* of late John Leslie Hobson and Beatrice Edith Hobson; *m* 1970, Jeanne Gerrish (marr. diss. 1996); one *s* one *d*. *Educ:* Northampton Grammar Sch.; Manchester Grammar Sch.; King's Coll. Cambridge (MA Mathematics). Joined Min. of Transport, 1967; Asst Private Sec. to Sec of State for the Environment, 1970–72; Private Sec. to Head of CS, 1974–78; Assistant Secretary: Dept of Transport, 1979–80; DoE, 1980–86; Under-Sec., subseq. Dir, DoE subseq. DETR, 1986–2001 (Dir of Construction, 1997–2001). Vis. Prof., Sch. of the Buil Envmt (formerly of Construction and Property Mgt), Univ. of Salford, 2003–. Advr, Join Contracts Tribunal, 2005–. Chm., Accelerating Change in Built Envmt Educn and Construction Knowledge Exchange, 2003–. Gov., Bldg Centre Trust, 1998–. JP Warwicks, 2002. Parish Warden, Sheepy Gp of Churches, 2002–.

HOBSON, John Graham; QC 2000; a Recorder, since 2000; *s* of late John Herbert Hobson and Lilian May Hobson (*née* Mott); *m* 1976, Shirley June Palmer; one *s* one *d*. *Educ:* Monkton Combe Sch.; St John's Coll., Cambridge (LLM). Admitted Solicitor 1968; Director: W Stepney Neighbourhood Law Centre, 1973–75; Southwark Law Project, 1975–80; called to the Bar, Inner Temple, 1980; Supplementary Panel of Counsel to Treasury, 1992–2000; Standing Counsel to Rent Assessment Panel, 1997–2000; Asst Recorder, 1999–2000. Special Advr, NI Affairs Cttee for Enquiry into Planning System in NI, H of C, 1995–96. Hon. Standing Counsel, CPRE, 2002–. *Recreations:* playing the 'cello, rowing, fishing, watching football. *Address:* 4–5 Gray's Inn Square, Gray's Inn WC1R 5JP. *Clubs:* Travellers, London Rowing.

HOBSON, Prof. Marian Elizabeth, CBE 2002; FBA 1999; Professor of French, Queen Mary (formerly Queen Mary and Westfield College), University of London, 1992, now Professorial Research Fellow; *b* 10 Nov. 1941; *d* of Baron Hobson and Doris Mary Hobson; *m* 1968, Michel Jeanneret; one *s*. *Educ:* Newnham Coll., Cambridge. Asst Lectr in French, Univ. of Warwick, 1966–71; Maître-assistante, Univ. of Geneva, 1974–76 Fellow of Trinity Coll., Cambridge (first woman Fellow), 1977–92; Univ. Lectr, Univ. of Cambridge, 1985–92. Visiting Professor: Univ. of Calif, 1990; Johns Hopkins Univ. 1995, 2005; Univ. de Paris, 1997; Harvard Univ., 2007; Eugene Freehling Vis. Prof. Univ. of Michigan, 2006; Occasional Lectr, Ren Min Univ., Beijing, 1999, 2004 Chevalier des palmes académiques (France), 1997. *Publications:* The Object of Art, 1982 Jacques Derrida: opening lines, 1998.

HOCHGREB, Prof. Simone, PhD; Professor of Experimental Combustion, University of Cambridge, since 2002; *b* 24 July 1962; *d* of Osmar Hochgreb and Nilce F. Hochgreb *m* 1998, Stephen Vandermark; one *d*. *Educ:* Univ. of São Paulo (BSME 1985); Princeton Univ. (PhD 1991). Asst Prof., MIT, 1991–99; Principal Investigator, Sandia Nat. Labs Calif, 1999–2000; Man. Engr, Exponent, 2000–02. *Publications:* contrib. transactions on combustion and flame. *Address:* Department of Engineering, University of Cambridge, Trumpington Street, Cambridge CB2 1PZ; *e-mail:* sh372@cam.ac.uk.

HOCHHAUSER, Andrew Romain; QC 1997; FCIArb; a Recorder, since 2004; *b* 16 March 1955; *s* of late Jerome Romain, MD, FRCSE and Ruth Hochhauser. *Educ.* Highgate Sch.; Univ. of Bristol (LLB Hons); London Sch. of Econs (LLM Hons). FCIArb 1995. Called to the Bar, Middle Temple, 1977 (Harmsworth Scholar), Bencher, 2000. Part-time Mem., Law Faculty, LSE, 1979–86. Hon. Counsel, Westminster Abbey, 2004. Chm., Dance Umbrella, 2007–. *Recreations:* collecting paintings, swimming with sharks, contemporary dance. *Address:* Essex Court Chambers, 24 Lincoln's Inn Fields, WC2A 3EG. *T:* (020) 7813 8000. *Club:* Reform.

HOCHHAUSER, Victor, CBE 1994; impresario; *b* 27 March 1923; *m* 1949, Lilian Hochhauser (*née* Shields); three *s* one *d*. *Educ:* City of London Coll. Impresario for: David Oistrakh; Sviatoslav Richter; Mstislav Rostropovich; Emil Gilels; Leonid Kogan; Margot Fonteyn; Natalia Makarova; Nureyev Festival; Bolshoi Ballet seasons, 1963, 1969, 1999, 2004, 2005, 2007, 2008, Bolshoi Ballet and Opera, 2006, Covent Garden; Kirov Ballet and Opera, Royal Opera House, 1961, 1966, 1993, 1995, 1997, 1998, 2000, 2001, 2003, 2004, 2005; Birmingham Royal Ballet, 1994–95; Royal Ballet season, London Coliseum, 1998; concerts, Royal Albert Hall, Barbican and Royal Festival Hall; Peking Opera and other Chinese companies, 1972–; presenter, Aida, Earls Court, 1988, Birmingham Arena, 1991. *Recreations:* reading, swimming, sleeping. *Address:* 4 Oak Hill Way, NW3 7LR. *T:* (020) 7794 0987.

HOCKÉ, Jean-Pierre; international consultant; United Nations High Commissioner for Refugees, 1986–89; *b* 31 March 1938; *s* of Charles and Marie Rose Hocké; *m* 1961, Michèle Marie Weber; two *s*. *Educ:* Univ. of Lausanne (grad. Econ. and Business Admin). With commercial firms in Switzerland and Nigeria, 1961–67; joined Internat. Cttee of Red Cross, 1968: Hd of Operations Dept, 1973; Mem., Directorate, 1981. Mem., Jean Monnet Foundn, Lausanne, 1984–; Vice-Chm., CASIN (internat. negotiations inst.), Geneva, 1986–; Chm., Bd, InterAssist, Bern, 1990–2004. Chm., Property Commn refugees and displaced, Bosnia, 1996–2004. Mem., Bd of Dirs, Eur. Centre for Culture, 2004–. Hon. Dr Lausanne, 1987. *Address:* 4 rue Amiral Duquesne, 1170 Aubonne, Switzerland. *T:* (21) 8088583; *e-mail:* jphocke@bluewin.ch.

HOCKIN, Rt Rev. William Joseph; Bishop of Fredericton, 2000–03; *b* 30 Sept. 1938; *m* 1990, Isabelle Jean Deeks. *Educ:* Wilfred Laurier Univ., Waterloo, Ont (BA); Emmanuel Coll., Saskatoon, Sask (LTh). Ordained priest, 1963; Archdeacon of Middlesex, dio. Huron, 1984–86; Rector, St Paul's, Bloor Street, Toronto, Ont, 1986–96; Dean of Fredericton, 1996–98; Bishop Coadjutor of Fredericton, 1998–2000. *Publications:* God for Monday Morning, 1987; Twelve Stories you need to Know, 1994. *Address:* c/o Bishop's Office, Diocese of Fredericton, 115 Church Street, Fredericton, NB E3B 4C8, Canada.

HOCKLEY, (Charles) Dair F.; *see* Farrar-Hockley.

HOCKLEY, Rev. Canon Raymond Alan; Canon Residentiary, Precentor, Succentor Canonicorum and Chamberlain of York Minster, 1976–95, Canon Emeritus, since 1995; *b* 18 Sept. 1929; 2nd *s* of late Henry Hockley and Doris (*née* Stonehouse); unmarried. *Educ:* Firth Park School, Sheffield; Royal Academy of Music, London; Westcott House, Cambridge. MA, LRAM. Macfarren Schol., Royal Acad. of Music, 1951–54; Charles Lucas Medal, William Corder Prize, Cuthbert Nunn Prize, etc; Theodore Holland Award, 1955. Clements Memorial Prize for Chamber Music by a British subject, 1954.

Curate of St Augustine's, Sheffield, 1958–61; Priest-in-charge of Holy Trinity, Wicker, with St Michael and All Angels, Neepsend, 1961–63; Chaplain of Westcott House, Cambridge, 1963–68; Fellow, Chaplain and Dir of Studies in Music, Emmanuel Coll., Cambridge, 1968–76. Compositions performed include: Songs for Tenor, Soprano; String Quartet; Divertimento for piano duet; Cantata for Easter and the Ascension; Symphony; Suite for Orchestra; Mass for Choir and Organ; various anthems and motets; incidental music for plays. Other works include: two more Symphonies, A Woman's Last Word for three sopranos; Mysterium Dei, oratorio; ten Suites for piano; Canticles for Men's Voices. *Publications:* Six Songs of Faith; New Songs for the Church; Intercessions at Holy Communion; contribs to theological and musical jls. *Address:* 26 Buckingham Mews, Sutton Coldfield B73 5PR. *T:* (0121) 354 7083.

HOCKMAN, Stephen Alexander; QC 1990; *b* 4 Jan. 1947; *s* of Nathaniel and Trude Hockman; *m* 1998, Elizabeth St Hill Davies. *Educ:* Eltham Coll.; Jesus Coll., Cambridge (MA). Called to the Bar, Middle Temple, 1970, Bencher, 1996. Leader, SE Circuit, 2000–03. Chm., Bar Council, 2006 (Vice-Chm., 2005). *Recreations:* philosophy, politics, the arts. *Address:* 6 Pump Court, Temple, EC4Y 7AR. *T:* (020) 7797 8400.

HOCKNEY, Damian; Member, London Assembly, Greater London Authority, 2004–08 (UK Ind, 2004–05; Veritas, 2005; One London, 2005–08). Career in publishing. Vice-Chm., UKIP, 2001–03; Dep. Leader, Veritas, Jan.–July 2005; Leader, One London Party, 2005–. Former Mem., Metropolitan Police Authy. Contested (Veritas) Broxtowe, 2005.

HOCKNEY, David, CH 1997; RA 1991 (ARA 1985); artist; *b* Bradford, 9 July 1937; *s* of late Kenneth and Laura Hockney. *Educ:* Bradford Grammar Sch.; Bradford Sch. of Art; Royal Coll. of Art. Lecturer: Maidstone Coll. of Art, 1962; Univ. of Iowa, 1964; Univ. of Colorado, 1965; Univ. of California, Los Angeles, 1966, Berkeley, 1967. One-man shows: Kasmin Ltd, London, 1963, 1965, 1966, 1968, 1969, 1970, 1972; Alan Gallery, New York, 1964–67; Museum of Modern Art, NY, 1964–68; Stedelijk Museum, Amsterdam, 1966; Whitworth Gallery, Manchester, 1969; Louvre, Paris, 1974; Galerie Claude Bernard, Paris, 1975 and 1985; Nicholas Wilder, LA, 1976; Galerie Neundorf, Hamburg, 1977; Warehouse Gall., 1979; Knoedler Gall., 1979, 1981, 1982, 1983, 1984, 1986 and 1988; André Emmerich Gall., 1979, 1980, annually 1982–95; Tate, 1986, 1988; Hayward Gall., 1983 and 1985; L. A. Louver, LA, 1986, 1989 and 1995, etc; Annely Juda, 1997, 2003, 2005, 2006; Nat. Portrait Gall., 2003; touring show of drawings and prints: Munich, Madrid, Lisbon, Teheran, 1977; USA and Canada, 1978; Tate, 1980; Saltaire, Yorks, New York and LA, 1994; drawing retrospective, Hamburg, London, LA, 1996; Retrospective Exhibitions: Whitechapel Art Gall., 1970; LA County Mus. of Art, Metropolitan Mus. of Art, Tate Gall., 1988–89; Manchester City Art Galls, 1996; Centre Georges Pompidou, Paris, 1999; Bonn Mus., 1999; Mus. of Fine Arts, Boston, LA County Mus. of Art, Nat. Portrait Gall., 2006–07. Exhibitions of photographs: Hayward Gall., 1983; Nat. Mus. of Photography, Film and Television, 1991. 1st Prize, John Moores Exhibn, Liverpool, 1967. Designer: The Rake's Progress, Glyndebourne, 1975, La Scala, 1979; The Magic Flute, Glyndebourne, 1978; L'Enfant et les sortilèges and Nightingale, Double Bill, and Varii Capricci, Covent Garden, 1983; Tristan und Isolde, LA, 1987; Turandot, Chicago, San Francisco, 1990; Die Frau ohne Schatten, Covent Garden, 1992, LA, 1993; designing costumes and sets for Parade and Stravinsky triple bills, Metropolitan Opera House, NY, 1981. Films: A Bigger Splash, 1975; A Day on the Grand Canal with the Emperor of China or surface is illusion but so is depth, 1988; television, Secret Knowledge, 2001. Hon. DLitt Oxford, 1995; Hon. DFA Yale, 2005. Shakespeare Prize, Hamburg Foundn, 1983; First Prize, Internat. Center of Photography, NY, 1985; Silver Progress Medal, RPS, 1988; Praemium Imperiale, Japan Art Assoc., 1989; Fifth Annual Gov's Award for Visual Arts in California, 1994. *Publications:* (ed and illustrated) 14 Poems of C. P. Cavafy, 1967; (illustrated) Six Fairy Tales of the Brothers Grimm, 1969; 72 Drawings by David Hockney, 1971; David Hockney by David Hockney (autobiog.), 1976; The Blue Guitar, 1977; David Hockney: Travels with Pen, Pencil and Ink: selected prints and drawings 1962–77, 1978; Paper Pools, 1980; (with Stephen Spender) China Diary, 1982; Hockney Paints the Stage, 1983; David Hockney: Cameraworks, 1984 (Kodak Photography Book Award); David Hockney: A Retrospective, 1988; Hockney on Photography (conversations with Paul Joyce), 1988; Hockney's Alphabet, 1991 (ed Stephen Spender); That's the Way I See It (autobiog.), 1993; Hockney on Art: photography, painting and perspective, 1999; Secret Knowledge: rediscovering the lost techniques of the old masters, 2001, 2006; Hockney's Portraits and People, 2003; Hockney's Pictures, 2004; David Hockney Portraits, 2006. *Address:* c/o 7508 Santa Monica Boulevard, Los Angeles, CA 90046, USA.

HODDER, Elizabeth; Commissioner, Equal Opportunities Commission, 1996–2002 (Deputy Chairwoman, 1996–2000); Chairman, Lifespan Healthcare NHS Trust, 2000–02 (non-executive Director, since 1993); *b* 5 Sept. 1942; *er d* of John Scruton and Beryl Haynes, High Wycombe; *m* 1st, 1962, Barry Quirke (marr. diss. 1970); two *d*; 2nd, 1971, Prof. Bramwell Hodder (*d* 2006); three step *s* two step *d*. *Educ:* High Wycombe High Sch.; Queen Mary Coll., Univ. of London. Member: Nat. Consumer Council, 1981–87; Building Societies Ombudsman Council, 1987–; Code of Banking Practice Review Cttee, 1992–2002; Comr and Chm., Consumers' Cttee, Meat and Livestock Commn, 1992–98. Founder and Hon. Pres., Nat. Stepfamily Assoc., 1985–; several positions in local and national organs. *Publications:* The Step-parents' Handbook, 1985; Stepfamilies Talking, 1989; The Book of Old Tarts, 2001. *Recreations:* Italy, cooking, painting, hill-walking. *Address:* 4 Ascham Road, Cambridge CB4 2BD. *T:* (01223) 301086.

HODDER, Prof. Ian Richard, PhD; FBA 1996; Dunlevie Family Professor, School of Humanities and Sciences, Stanford University, since 2002; *b* 23 Nov. 1948; *s* of late Prof. Bramwell William Hodderand Noreen Victoria Hodder; *m* 1st, 1975, Françoise Marguerite Hivernel; two *s*; 2nd, 1987, Christine Ann Hastorf; two *s*. *Educ:* Inst. of Archaeology, London (BA 1971); Peterhouse, Cambridge (PhD 1975). Lectr, Dept of Archaeology, University of Leeds, 1974–77; University of Cambridge: Univ. Asst, then Univ. Lectr, Dept of Archaeology, 1977–90; Reader in Prehistory, 1990–96; Dir, Cambridge Archaeol. Unit, 1990–2000; Fellow of Darwin Coll., 1990–2000; Prof. of Archaeology, 1996–2000; Prof., Dept of Cultural and Social Anthropology, 1999–2001, Co-Dir, Archaeol. Centre, 1999–2002, Stanford Univ. Adjunct Asst Prof. of Anthropology, SUNY, 1984–89; Visiting Professor: Dept of Anthropology, Univ. of Minnesota (and Adjunct Prof.), 1986–93; Van Giffen Inst. for Pre- and Proto-history, Amsterdam, 1980; Univ. of Paris I, Sorbonne, 1985; Fellow: Centre for Advanced Study in Behavioural Scis, Calif, 1987; McDonald Inst., Univ. of Cambridge, 2001–. *Publications:* Spatial Analysis in Archaeology (with C. Orton), 1976; Symbols in Action, 1982; The Present Past, 1982; Reading the Past, 1986; The Domestication of Europe, 1990; Theory and Practice in Archaeology, 1992; The Archaeological Process, 1999; Archaeology Beyond Dialogue, 2004. *Recreations:* music (playing violin and piano), tennis, golf, sailing, travel. *Address:* Department of Cultural and Social Anthropology, Stanford University, Stanford, CA 94305, USA.

HODDINOTT, Rear-Adm. Anthony Paul, CB 1994; OBE 1979; Chairman, International Legal Assistance Consortium, since 2002; *b* 28 Jan. 1942; *s* of late Comdr Peter Hoddinott, RN and Marjorie Hoddinott (*née* Kent); *m* 1965, Ellen Ruby, (Rue), Burton; one *s* two *d*. *Educ:* St Michael's, Otford; Bloxham; BRNC Dartmouth. Served HM Ships Chawton, Trump, Dreadnought, Repulse, Porpoise; in Comd, HMS Andrew, 1973–75; Staff of Comdr Third Fleet, USN, 1975–76; in Comd, HMS Revenge, 1976–79; Comdr, Submarine Tactics and Weapons Gp, 1979–81; in Comd, HMS Glasgow, 1981–83 (South Atlantic, 1982); Asst Dir, Naval Warfare, 1983–85; NATO Defence Coll., Rome, 1985; Dep. UK Mil. Rep. to NATO, Brussels, 1986–88; COS (Submarines), 1988–90; Naval Attaché and Comdr, British Naval Staff, Washington, 1990–94, retd. Exec. Dir, Internat. Bar Assoc., 1995–2000. Dir, Warship Preservation Trust, 1995–2006; Trustee, RN Submarine Mus., 1999–08 (Chm., Soc. of Friends, 1999–). Liveryman, Fan Makers' Co., 1998– (Mem., Ct of Assistants, 2007–). *Recreations:* theatre, classic Bentley cars, family, travel. *Address:* 45 Oaklands Road, Petersfield, Hants GU32 2EY.

HODDLE, Glenn; Manager, Wolverhampton Wanderers Football Club, 2004–06; *b* 27 Oct. 1957; *s* of late Derek Hoddle and of Teressa (*née* Roberts); *m* 1979, Christine Anne Stirling (marr. diss. 1999); one *s* two *d*; *m* 2000, Vanessa Shean. *Educ:* Burnt Mill Sch., Harlow. Professional football player: Tottenham Hotspur, 1976–86 (won FA Cup, 1981, 1982, UEFA Cup, 1984); AS Monaco, 1986–91 (won French Championship, 1988); Player/Manager: Swindon Town, 1991–93; Chelsea, 1993–96; Coach, England Football Team, 1996–99; Manager: Southampton, 2000–01; Tottenham Hotspur, 2001–03. 53 England caps, 1980–88; represented England in World Cup, Spain, 1982, Mexico, 1986. *Publications:* Spurred to Success (autobiog.), 1998; (with David Davies) Glenn Hoddle: the World Cup 1998 Story, 1998.

HODGE, Hon. Lord; Patrick Stewart Hodge; a Senator of the College of Justice in Scotland, since 2005; *b* 19 May 1953; *s* of George Mackenzie Hodge and Helen Russell Hodge; *m* 1983, Penelope Jane Wigin; two *s* one *d*. *Educ:* Croftinloan Sch.; Trinity Coll., Glenalmond; Corpus Christi Coll., Cambridge (Scholar, BA); Edinburgh Univ. (LLB). Scottish Office, 1975–78; admitted Faculty of Advocates, 1983; Standing Junior Counsel: to Dept of Energy, 1989–91; to Inland Revenue in Scotland, 1991–96; QC (Scot.) 1996; a Judge of Courts of Appeal of Jersey and Guernsey, 2000–05; Procurator to Gen. Assembly of Church of Scotland, 2000–05. Comr (pt time), Scottish Law Commn, 1997–2003. Gov., Merchiston Castle Sch., Edinburgh, 1998–. *Publication:* Scotland and the Union, 1994. *Recreations:* opera, ski-ing. *Address:* 21 Lynedoch Place, Edinburgh EH3 7PY. *T:* (0131) 220 6914. *Club:* Bruntsfield Links Golfing Society.

HODGE, Sir Andrew (Rowland), 3rd Bt *cr* 1921, of Chipstead, Kent; *b* 4 Dec. 1968; *o s* of Sir John Rowland Hodge, 2nd Bt, MBE and of his 4th wife, Vivien Jill, *d* of A. S. Knightley. *Educ:* Stella Maris Coll., Malta; Benjamin Britten High Sch., Suffolk. Estate agent, 1986–91 and 1993–94. *Recreations:* tennis, ski-ing.

HODGE, David Ralph; QC 1997; **His Honour Judge Hodge;** a Circuit Judge, since 2005; Specialist Chancery Judge, Northern Circuit, since 2005; *b* 13 July 1956; *er s* of Ralph Noel Hodge, CBE and Jean Margaret Hodge; *m* 2003, Jane Woosey. *Educ:* St Margaret's, Liverpool; University Coll., Oxford (BA Jurisprudence 1977; BCL 1978). Called to the Bar, Inner Temple, 1979; admitted to Lincoln's Inn, 1980 (Bencher, 2000); in practice at Chancery Bar, 1980–2005; an Asst Recorder, 1998–2000; a Recorder, 2000–05; a Dep. High Ct Judge, 2004–05. Member: Council of Circuit Judges, 2007–; Incorporated Council of Law Reporting, 2008–. Chm., Lincoln's Inn Bar Representation Cttee, 1997–98. *Publication:* contrib. chapter on Chancery Matters to Law and Practice of Compromise, 4th edn, 1996 to 6th edn 2005. *Recreations:* theatre and wife. *Address:* c/o Manchester Civil Justice Centre, 1 Bridge Street West, Manchester M60 9DJ. *Clubs:* Garrick; Athenæum (Liverpool).

HODGE, Hon. Sir Henry (Egar Garfield), Kt 2004; OBE 1993; **Hon. Mr Justice Hodge;** a Judge of the High Court of Justice, Queen's Bench Division, since 2004; President, Asylum and Immigration Tribunal, since 2005; *b* 12 Jan. 1944; *s* of late Raymond Garfield Hodge and Ruth (*née* Egar); *m* 1st, 1971, Miranda Tufnell (marr. diss. 1975); 2nd, 1978, Margaret Eve Hodge (*see* Rt Hon. M. E. Hodge); two *d*, and one step *s* one step *d*. *Educ:* Chigwell Sch., Essex; Balliol Coll., Oxford (BA Law 1965). Admitted solicitor, 1970; Legal Sec., Justice, 1971; Solicitor and Dep. Dir, CPAG, 1972–77; Sen. Partner, Hodge Jones & Allen, Solicitors, 1977–99; Asst Recorder, 1993–97; a Recorder, 1997–99; a Circuit Judge, 1999–2004; Chief Immigration Adjudicator, 2001–04. Mem. (Lab), Islington Borough Council, 1974–78 (Vice-Chm., Housing Cttee, 1976–78). Member: Lord Chancellor's Legal Aid Adv. Cttee, 1977–83; Matrimonial Causes Rules Cttee, 1986–90. Law Society: Mem. Council, 1984–96 (Legal Aid Specialist); Chm., Courts and Legal Services Cttee, 1987–90; Chairman: Race Relns Cttee, 1992–94; Equal Opportunities Cttee, 1994–95. Dep. Chm., Legal Aid Bd, 1996–99; Member: Supplementary Benefits Commn, 1978–80; Social Security Adv. Cttee, 1980–92; Civil Justice Council, 1998–2000. Chairman: NCCL, 1974–75; Nat. CAB Trng Cttee, 1982–84; Camden CAB, 1983–88. Vice-Chm., Soc. of Labour Lawyers, 1992–99; Dep. Vice-Pres., Law Soc. of England and Wales, 1994–95. Contested (Lab) Croydon S, Feb. 1974. Mem. Council, Richmond Fellowship, 2001–05. Gov., Coll. of Law, 1991–2005. Gov., Middx Univ., 1996–2002. *Publications:* Legal Rights, 1974; numerous articles on legal aid and legal rights. *Recreations:* Arsenal supporter, motor-cycling, golf, gardening. *Address:* Royal Courts of Justice, Strand, WC2A 2LL.

HODGE, Sir James (William), KCVO 1996; CMG 1996; HM Diplomatic Service, retired; Chairman, Society of Pension Consultants, since 2007; *b* 24 Dec. 1943; *s* of late William Hodge and Catherine Hodge (*née* Carden); *m* 1970, Frances Margaret, *d* of late Michael Coyne and of Teresa Coyne (*née* Walsh); three *d*. *Educ:* Holy Cross Academy, Edinburgh; Univ. of Edinburgh (MA(Hons) English Lang. and Lit.). Commonwealth Office, 1966; Third Secretary, Tokyo, 1967; Second Secretary (Information), Tokyo, 1970; FCO, 1972; First Sec. (Development, later Chancery), Lagos, 1975; FCO, 1978; First Sec. (Economic), 1981, Counsellor (Commercial), 1982, Tokyo; Counsellor: Copenhagen, 1986; FCO, 1990; RCDS, 1994; Minister, British Embassy, Peking, 1995–96; Ambassador to Thailand and (non-resident) to Lao People's Democratic Republic, 1996–2000; Consul-General, Hong Kong and (non-resident) Macao, 2000–03. MCIL 1990. Hon. DLitt Ulster, 2003; Hon. LLD Liverpool, 2004. Kt Grand Cross (1st cl.), Order of the White Elephant (Thailand), 1996. *Recreations:* books, music. *Clubs:* Oriental, Royal Over-Seas League, MCC; Hong Kong, Foreign Correspondents', China (Hong Kong); Jockey (Macao).

HODGE, John Dennis; President, J. D. Hodge & Co., International Management and Aerospace Consultants, 1987–2003; *b* 10 Feb. 1929; *s* of John Charles Henry Hodge and Emily M. Corbett Hodge; *m* 1952, Audrey Cox; two *s* two *d*. *Educ:* Northampton Engineering Coll., University of London (now City Univ.). Vickers-Armstrong Ltd, Weybridge, England (Aerodynamics Dept), 1950–52; Head, Air Loads Section, Avro Aircraft Ltd, Toronto, Canada, 1952–59; Tech. Asst to Chief, Ops Div., Space Task Group, NASA, Langley Field, Va, USA, 1959; Chief, Flight Control Br., Space Task Group, NASA, 1961; Asst Chief of Flight Control, 1962, Chief, Flight Control Div., Flight Ops Directorate, NASA, MSC, 1963–68; Manager, Advanced Missions Program,

NASA, Manned Spacecraft Centre, 1968–70; Dir, Transport Systems Concepts, Transport Systems Center, 1970; Vice-Pres., R&D, The Ontario Transportation Develt Corp., 1974–76; Department of Transportation, Washington, 1976–82; Chief, R&D Plans and Programs Analysis Div., 1976–77; Actg Dir, Office of Policy, Plans and Admin, 1977–79; Associate Administrator, for Policy, Plans and Program Management, Res. and Special programs Admin, 1979–82; Dir, Space Station Task Force, NASA, Washington, 1982–84; Dep. Associate Administrator for Space Station, NASA, Washington, 1984–85, Actg Associate Administrator, 1985–86. FAIAA 1991. Hon. ScD City Univ., London, Eng., 1966. NASA Medal for Exceptional Service, 1967 and 1969; Dept of Transportation Meritorious Achievement Award, 1974; Special Achievement Award, 1979; Presidential Rank Award of Meritorious Executive, NASA, 1985. *Publications:* contribs to NASA publications and various aerospace jls. *Recreations:* reading, golf. *Address:* 1105 Challendon Road, Great Falls, VA 22066, USA.

HODGE, Rt Hon. Margaret (Eve), MBE 1978; PC 2003; MP (Lab) Barking, since June 1994; *b* 8 Sept. 1944; *d* of late Hans and Lisbeth Oppenheimer; *m* 1st, 1968, Andrew Watson (marr. diss. 1978); one *s* one *d*; 2nd, 1978, Henry Egar Garfield Hodge (*see* Hon. Sir H. E. G. Hodge); two *d*. *Educ:* Bromley High Sch.; Oxford High Sch.; LSE (BSc Econ 1966). Teaching and internat. market research, 1966–73. London Borough of Islington: Councillor, 1973–94; Chair of Housing, 1975–79; Dep. Leader, 1981; Leader, 1982–92. Chair: Assoc. of London Authorities, 1984–92; London Res. Centre, 1985–92; Vice-Chair, AMA, 1991–92. Member: HO Adv. Cttee on Race Relations, 1988–92; Local Govt Commn, 1993–94; Board, Central and Inner London North TEC, 1990–92; Labour Party Local Govt Cttee, 1983–92. Parly Under-Sec. of State, DfEE, 1998–2001; Minister of State, DFES, 2001–05; Minister of State: (Minister for Employment and Welfare Reform (formerly for Work), DWP, 2005–06; DTI, 2006–07; DCMS, 2007–08. Chair: Educn Select Cttee, H of C, 1997–98; London Gp of Labour MPs, 1996–98; former mem., govt and local govt bodies. Sen. Consultant, Price Waterhouse, 1992–94. Director: London First, 1992; (non-exec.) UCH and Middlesex Hosp., 1992–94. Chair: Circle 33 Housing Trust, 1993–96; Fabian Soc., 1997–98. Gov., LSE, 1990–99; Mem. Council, Univ. of London, 1994–98. Hon. Fellow, Polytechnic of North London. Hon. DCL City, 1993. *Publications:* Quality, Equality and Democracy, 1991; Beyond the Town Hall, 1994; Elected Mayors and Democracy, 1997; contribs to numerous jls and newspapers. *Recreations:* family, opera, piano, travel, cooking. *Address:* c/o House of Commons, SW1A 0AA.

HODGE, Michael, MBE 1975; HM Diplomatic Service, retired; *b* 12 June 1944; *s* of late Howard Jack Hodge and Iris Amy Hodge (*née* Treasure); *m* 1966, Wilhelmina Marjorie Glover; one *s* one *d*. *Educ:* Cotham Grammar Sch., Bristol. With Prison Commn, 1961–62; joined HM Diplomatic Service, 1962: FO, 1962–65; Third Sec., Belgrade, 1965–67; Commercial Officer, Paris, 1968–70; Third, later Second, Sec., Bahrain Residency, 1970–72; Second Secretary: (Information), Kaduna, 1972–73; (Commercial), Kampala, 1973–74; FCO, 1974–78; First Sec. (Econ.), Copenhagen, 1978–82; FCO, 1983–87; on loan to ICI Agrochemicals, 1987–89; First Sec. (Commercial), Paris, 1989–92; Head, Services Planning and Resources Dept, FCO, 1992–96; Consul Gen., Chicago, 1996–99. Chm., Battle Meml Hall, 2001–05. Pres., Rotary Club of Battle, 2004–05. Paul Harris Fellow, 2005. Kt, First Class, Order of Dannebrog (Denmark), 1978. *Recreations:* music, organising events, travel, steam railways. *Club:* Royal Commonwealth Society.

HODGE, Michael John Davy V.; *see* Vere-Hodge.

HODGE, Patricia; actress; *b* 29 Sept. 1946; *d* of Eric and Marion Hodge; *m* 1976, Peter Owen; two *s*. *Educ:* Wintringham Girls' Grammar Sch., Grimsby; St Helen's Sch., Northwood, Middx; Maria Grey Coll., Twickenham; London Acad. of Music and Dramatic Art. Theatre début, No-one Was Saved, Traverse, Edinburgh, 1971; *West End theatre* includes: Popkiss, Globe, 1972; Two Gentlemen of Verona (musical), 1973; Pippin, Her Majesty's, 1973; Hair, Queen's, 1974; The Mitford Girls, Globe, 1981 (transf. from Chichester); Benefactors, Vaudeville, 1984; Noël and Gertie, Comedy, 1989–90; Shades, Albery, 1992; Separate Tables, Albery, 1993; The Prime of Miss Jean Brodie, Strand, 1994; National Theatre: A Little Night Music, 1995; Money (Best Supporting Actress, Laurence Olivier Awards, 2000); Summerfolk, 1999; Noises Off, 2000; His Dark Materials, 2003; The Country Wife, Th. Royal, 2007; *other appearances* include: The Beggar's Opera, Nottingham Playhouse, 1975; Pal Joey, and Look Back In Anger, Oxford Playhouse, 1976; Then and Now, Hampstead, 1979; As You Like It, Chichester Fest., 1983; Lady in the Dark, Edinburgh Fest., 1988; Heartbreak House, Almeida, 1997; The Clean House, Crucible Th., Sheffield, 2006; Calendar Girls, UK tour, 2008; *television plays and films* include: The Girls of Slender Means, 1975; The Naked Civil Servant, 1975; Hay Fever, 1984; The Death of the Heart, 1985; Hotel du Lac, 1986; Heat of the Day, 1988; The Shell Seekers, 1989; The Secret Life of Ian Fleming, 1989; The Moonstone, 1997; The Falklands Play, 2002; Marple: The Sittaford Mystery, 2006; Maxwell, 2007; *television series and serials* include: Rumpole of the Bailey, 7 series, 1978–90; Edward and Mrs Simpson, 1978; Holding the Fort, 3 series, 1979–82; The Other 'Arf, 1979–80, 1981; Nanny, 1980; Jemima Shore Investigates, 1982; The Life and Loves of a She-Devil, 1986; Rich Tea and Sympathy, 1991; The Cloning of Joanna May, 1992; The Legacy of Reginald Perrin, 1996; Sweet Medicine, 2003; *films* include: Betrayal, 1983; The Leading Man, 1996; Jilting Joe, 1997; Before You Go, 2002. Hon. DLitt: Hull, 1996; Brunel, 2001; Leicester, 2003. *Address:* c/o Paul Lyon-Maris, Independent Talent Group Ltd, Oxford House, 76 Oxford Street, W1D 1BS. *T:* (020) 7636 6565.

HODGE, Patrick Stewart; *see* Hodge, Hon. Lord.

HODGES, Gerald; Director of Finance, City of Bradford Metropolitan Council, 1974–85; *b* 14 June 1925; *s* of Alfred John Hodges and Gertrude Alice Hodges; *m* 1950, Betty Maire (*née* Brading); one *s* (and one *s* decd). *Educ:* King's Sch., Peterborough. CPFA. Accountancy Asst, Bexley Borough Council, 1941–48, and Eton RDC, 1948–49; Sen. Accountancy Asst, Newcastle upon Tyne, 1949–53; Chief Accountant, Hemel Hempstead, 1953–56; Dep. Treas., Crawley UDC, 1956–70; Treas., Ilkley UDC, 1970–74. Pres., Soc. of Metropolitan Treasurers, 1984–85. Gen. Comr, Inland Revenue, 1985–. Hon. Treasurer: Yorkshire Arts, 1973–86; Univ. of Bradford, 1986–97; Chm., Bradford Flower Fund Homes; Trustee, Bradford Disaster Appeal, 1985. *Publications:* occasional articles in professional jls. *Recreations:* travelling, ornithology, reading. *Address:* 23 Victoria Avenue, Ilkley, West Yorks LS29 9BW. *T:* (01943) 607346.

HODGES, Prof. John Russell, MD; FRCP, FMedSci; MRC Professor of Behavioural Neurology, University of Cambridge, since 1997; *b* 7 Jan. 1952; *s* of Edward and Gwen Hodges; *m* 1952, Dr Carol Ann Gregory; two *s* one *d*. *Educ:* Kingsbridge Sch.; Royal London Hosp. Med. Sch. (MB BS Hons 1975, MD 1988). MRCP 1977, FRCP 1993. Lectr in Medicine, Southampton Univ., 1980–82; Registrar in Neurology, Radcliffe Infirmary, Oxford, 1982–85; MRC Res. Fellow, 1985–86; Lectr in Clinical Neurol., Radcliffe Infirmary, Oxford, 1986–90; MRC Travelling Fellow, UCSD, 1988–89; Lectr., Univ. of Cambridge, 1990–97. Dir, Alzheimer's Res. Trust Centre, Cambridge, 1998–. Chm., British Neuropsychiatric Assoc., 1982–2001; Pres., Res. Gp on Aphasia, World Fedn of Neurol., 1998–. FMedSci 2002. *Publications:* Transient Amnesia, 1991; Cognitive Assessment for Clinicians, 1994; Memory Disorders in Psychiatric Practice, 2000; Early Onset Dementia: a multidisciplinary approach, 2001; contrib. numerous scientific papers to learned jls. *Recreations:* playing the saxophone, cinema, literature, fishing. *Address:* MRC Cognition and Brain Sciences Unit, 15 Chaucer Road, Cambridge CB2 2EF. *T:* (0122 355294, *Fax:* (01223) 359062; *e-mail:* john.hodges@mrc-cbu.cam.ac.uk.

HODGES, John William, CMG 2003; CEng, FICE; development infrastructure consultant, since 2002; *b* 14 Nov. 1942; *s* of John Henry Hodges and Lilian Elizabeth Hodges; *m* 1962, Barbara Park; two *s* (and one *s* decd). *Educ:* Shoreditch Comprehensive Sch.; Brixton Sch. of Building; Westminster Coll. CEng 1968; FICE 1983. Exec. Engr Govt of Zambia, 1965–68; Engr, UK Transport Res. Labs, 1969–73; Overseas Development Administration: Engrg Advr, 1974–84; Sen. Engrg Advr, 1985–86; Head Pacific, 1987–89; Contracts, 1990–93; Chief Engrg Advr, 1994–2002. *Recreations:* restoration and rallying of classic cars. *Address:* 56 Telfords Yard, E1W 2BQ. *T:* (020) 726 1536; *e-mail:* banjo.hodges@btconnect.com.

HODGES, Lew; Director of Finance and Resources, Leadership Foundation, since 2006 *b* 29 Feb. 1956. *Educ:* University Coll. London (BA (Hons) Classics); MBA London Business Sch., 1990. Chartered Accountant 1981. Subsidy Officer, then Asst Dir of Finance, Arts Council, 1981–87; Head of Finance, CNAA, 1987–89; Finance Dir, Arts Council of GB, subseq. of England, 1989–96; Dir, Corporate Services, Sports Council 1996–97; Hd of Finance, RNT, 1997–2000; Dir of Finance and Mgt Resources, London Arts, 2000–01; Dir of Finance and Planning, Arts & Business, 2001–05. Mem., Inner London Probation Cttee, 1996–2001. Board Member: LAMDA, 2002–; English Touring Th., 2002–; Greenwich Fest., 2002–06; Artsadmin, 2002–; Space, 2007–. *Address:* Leadership Foundation, 88 Kingsway, WC2B 6AA.

HODGES, Nicholas Rudy; Chief Executive Officer, London International Group plc 1993–99; *b* 26 Aug. 1939; *s* of Edward William Hodges and Gwendoline Winifred Hayward (*née* Golding); *m* 1st, 1959, Valerie Joyce Dyke (marr. diss. 1988; now Hedges) one *s* two *d*; 2nd, 1988, Christine Winifred Mary Dodd. *Educ:* Colchester Royal Grammar Sch. Salesman and Mktg, Nestlé Ltd, 1961–63; Kimberley Clark Ltd: Salesman, 1963–65 Product and Mktg Manager, 1965–67; Area Manager, 1967–69; Regl Manager, 1969–72 Regl Manager, Golden Wonder Ltd, 1972–74; Sales Dir, Johnson & Johnson Consumer 1974–80; Man. Dir, Sangers, 1980–82; London International Group: Sales/Mktg Dir 1982–88; World Wide Mkt Dir, Hosp. Products, 1988–90; European Man. Dir, 1990–93 Sen. non-exec. Dir and Dep. Chm., Taylor-Nelson Sofres, 1998–2002. Liveryman Glovers' Co., 1986–; Co. of World Traders, 1989– (Mem. Court, 1999–2003). MCIM (MInstM 1972). *Recreations:* good food and wine, golf, fishing. *Address:* PO Box 352, 16 Endicott Loop, Dunsborough, WA 6281, Australia. *Clubs:* Royal Automobile; Royal Dornoch Golf, Burnham Beeches Golf, Busselton Golf, Dunsborough Lakes Golf (Western Australia).

HODGES, Prof. Richard Andrew, OBE 1995; PhD; FSA 1984; Professor of Visual Arts and Director, Institute of World Archaeology, School of World Arts and Museology University of East Anglia, since 1995; Director, University of Pennslyvania Museum Philadelphia, since 2007; *b* 29 Sept. 1952; *s* of Roy Clarence Hodges and Joan (*née* Hartnell); *m* 1976, Deborah Peters (marr. diss. 1998); one *s* one *d*. *Educ:* City of Bath Boys Sch.; Univ. of Southampton (BA, PhD). Sheffield University: Lectr in Prehistory and Archaeology, 1976–86; Sen. Lectr, 1986–93; Prof., 1993–95. Leverhulme Res. Fellow 1980, Dir, 1988–95 (on secondment), British Sch. at Rome; Dir, Prince of Wales's Inst of Architecture, 1996–98. Special Advr to Minister of Culture, Albania, 1999; Mem. Bd Packard Humanities Inst., 2003– (Advr to proj., Albania, 2000–06). Visiting Professor: in Medieval Studies, SUNY-Birmingham, 1983; in Medieval Archaeology, Siena Univ. 1984–87; in Archaeology, Copenhagen Univ., 1987–88; Sheffield Univ., 2006–; Charles Eliot Norton Lectr, Amer. Inst. of Archaeology, 2005. Director: Roystone Grange landscape project, Derbyshire, 1978–88; San Vincenzo excavations, S Italy, 1980–98; co-director: Sheffield-Siena archaeological project, Montarrenti, Tuscany, 1982–87; Butrint excavations, Albania, 1994–. Scientific Dir, Butrint Foundn, 1995–. *Publications:* Walks in the Cotswolds, 1976; The Hamwih Pottery, 1981; (with G. Barker) Archaeology and Italian Society, 1981; Dark Age Economics, 1982, 2nd edn 1989; (with P. Davey) Ceramics and trade, 1983; (with D. Whitehouse) Mohammed, Charlemagne and the origins of Europe, 1983; (with John Mitchell) San Vincenzo al Volturno, 1985; Primitive and Peasant Markets, 1988; (with B. Hobley) Rebirth of the town in the West, 1988; The Anglo-Saxon Achievement, 1989; Wall to Wall History, 1991 (British Archaeological Book of the Year, 1992); (with K. Smith) Recent Developments in the Archaeology of the Peak District, 1991; (ed) San Vincenzo 1, 1993; (ed) San Vincenzo 2, 1995; (with J Mitchell) La Basilica di Iosue a San Vincenzo al Volturno, 1995; Light in the Dark Ages 1997; (with W. Bowden) The Sixth Century, 1998; Towns and Trade in the Age of Charlemagne, 2000; Visions of Rome: Thomas Ashby, archaeologist, 2000; (with R. Francovich) Villa to Village, 2003; (with W. Bowden and K. Lake) Byzantine Butrint, 2004; Goodbye to the Vikings?, 2006; (with L. Bejko) Eternal Butrint, 2006; New Directions in Albanian Archaeology, 2006; (with K. Bowes and K. Francis) Between Text and Territory, 2006; (with I. Hansen) Roman Butrint, 2006. *Recreations:* hill walking, music, watching cricket. *Address:* School of World Arts and Museology, University of East Anglia, Norwich NR4 7TJ.

HODGETTS, Robert Bartley; Clerk to Worshipful Company of Glaziers, 1979–85; *b* 10 Nov. 1918; *s* of late Captain Bartley Hodgetts, MN and Florence Hodgetts (*née* Stagg); *m* 1st, 1945, A. K. Jeffreys; one *d*; 2nd, 1949, Frances Grace (*d* 2007), *d* of late A. J. Pepper, Worcester; two *d*. *Educ:* Merchant Taylors' Sch., Crosby; St John's Coll., Cambridge (Scholar, MA). Served RNVR (A), 1940–45. Asst Principal, Min. of Nat. Insce, 1947; Principal 1951; Asst Sec. 1964; Under-Sec., DHSS, 1973–78. *Recreations:* watching cricket and Rugby football. *Address:* 10 The Close, Winchester, Hants SO23 9LS. *T:* (01962) 890987.

HODGKIN, Sir Howard, CH 2003; Kt 1992; CBE 1977; painter; *b* 6 Aug. 1932; *m* 1955, Julia Lane; two *s*. *Educ:* Camberwell Sch. of Art; Bath Academy of Art. Taught at Charterhouse Sch., 1954–56; taught at Bath Academy of Art, 1956–66; occasional tutor, Slade Sch. of Art and Chelsea Sch. of Art. Vis. Fellow in Creative Art, Brasenose Coll. Oxford, 1976–77. A Trustee: Tate Gall., 1970–76; National Gall., 1978–85. Mem., Exec. Cttee, Nat. Art Collections Fund, 1988–90. One-man exhibitions include: Arthur Tooth & Sons, London, 1962, 1964, 1967; Kasmin Gall., 1969, 1971, 1976; Arnolfini Gall., Bristol, 1970, 1975; Dartington Hall, 1970; Galerie Müller, Cologne, 1971; Kornblee Gall., NY, 1973; Museum of Modern Art, Oxford, 1976, 1977; Serpentine Gall., London and provincial tour, Waddington Gall., 1976; André Emmerich Gall., Zürich and NY, 1977; Third Sydney Biennale, Art Gall. of NSW, 1979; Waddington Galls, 1972, 1980, 1988; Knoedler Gall. NY, 1981, 1982, 1984, 1988, 1990, 1993–94; Bernard Jacobson NY, 1980, 1981, LA, 1981, London, 1982; Tate Gall., 1982, 1985; Bath Fest., 1984; Phillips Collection, Washington DC, 1984; XLI Venice Biennale, 1984; Yale Centre for British Art, New Haven, 1985, 2007, and tour, incl. Fitzwilliam Mus., Cambridge;

Kestner-Gesellschaft, Hanover, 1985; Whitechapel Art Gall., 1985; Michael Werner Gall., Cologne, 1990; Nantes, Barcelona, Edinburgh and Dublin tour, 1990–91; Anthony D'Offay Gall., 1993, 1999–2000; Alan Cristea Gall., London, 1995; Metropolitan Mus. of Art, NY, 1995–96, and tour, incl. Hayward Gall., 1996–97 (retrospective); Gall. Lawrence Rubin, Zurich, 1996, 1997; Gagosian Gall., NY, 1998, 2003; Haas and Fuchs Galerie, Berlin, 1998; Gall. Lawrence Rubin, Milan, 2001; Dulwich Picture Gall., 2001; Dean Gall., Edinburgh, 2002; Gagosian Gall., LA, 2004; Galerie Lutz & Thalmann, Zürich, 2004; Irish Mus. of Modern Art, Dublin, 2006, and tour incl. London and Madrid; Gagosian Gall., London, 2008. Group Exhibitions include: The Human Clay, Hayward Gall., 1976; British Painting 1952–1977, RA, 1977; A New Spirit in Painting, RA, 1981; Hard Won Image, Tate Gall., 1984; An International Survey of Recent Paintings and Sculpture, Mus. of Mod. Art, 1984; NY, Carnegie International, Mus. of Art, Carnegie Inst., 1985–86; British Art in 20th Century, RA, 1987; Here and Now, Serpentine Gall., 1994; and in exhibns in: Australia, Austria, Belgium, Canada, Denmark, France, Germany, GB, Holland, India, Italy, Japan, Malta, Norway, Sweden, Switzerland, USA. Designs for: Pulcinella, Ballet Rambert, 1987; Piano, Royal Ballet, 1989; mural for British Council building, New Delhi, 1992. Works in public collections: Arts Council of GB; British Council, London; Contemp. Arts Soc.; Kettering Art Gall.; Peter Stuyvesant Foundn; São Paulo Museum; Oldham Art Gall.; Tate Gall., London; V&A Museum; Swindon Central Lib.; Bristol City Art Gall.; Walker Art Center, Minneapolis; Nat. Gall. of S Aust., Adelaide; Fogg Art Museum, Cambridge, Mass; BM; Louisiana Museum, Denmark; Museum of Modern Art, Edinburgh; Southampton Art Gall.; Museum of Modern Art, and Metropolitan Mus. of Art, NY; Mus. of Art, Carnegie Inst.; Whitworth Art Gall., Manchester; City of Manchester Art Galls; Govt Picture Collection, London; Saatchi Collection, London; Nat. Gall. of Washington; Museo Nacional Centro de Arte Reina Sofia, Madrid. Hon. Fellow, Brasenose Coll., Oxford, 1988. Hon. DLitt: London, 1985; Oxford, 2000. 2nd Prize, John Moore's Exhibn, 1976 and 1980; Turner Prize, 1985. *Address:* c/o Cristina Colomar, Gagosian Gallery, 6–24 Britannia Street, WC1X 9JD.

HODGKIN, Prof. Jonathan Alan, PhD; FRS 1990; Professor of Genetics, since 2000, and Associate Head, Department of Biochemistry, since 2005, Oxford University; Fellow of Keble College, Oxford, since 2000; *b* 24 Aug. 1949; *s* of Sir Alan Hodgkin, OM, KBE, FRS and of Marion Hodgkin, *d* of late F. P. Rous; *m* 2005, Patricia Etsuko Kuwabara. *Educ:* Bryanston Sch., Dorset; Merton Coll., Oxford (BA; Hon. Fellow, 2001); Darwin Coll., Cambridge (PhD). SRC Res. Fellowship, 1974–76; Staff Scientist, MRC Lab. of Molecular Biology, 1977–2000. Vis. Prof., Univ. of Wisconsin, 1990. Mem., EMBO, 1989. *Publications:* contribs to scientific jls. *Recreations:* archaeology, cooking, cinema. *Address:* 82a Lonsdale Road, Oxford OX2 7ER. *T:* (01865) 552340.

HODGKIN, Mark William Backhouse; Director, Hawkesbury Capital Management Pte Ltd, since 2005; *b* 26 Jan. 1949; *s* of David Kenneth and Brigit Louise Hodgkin; *m* 1978, Madeleine Alison Newton; three *d*. *Educ:* Australian National Univ. (BEc). A. Fifer Ltd, 1972–74; Laurence Prust & Co., 1974–76; Man. Dir, Rivkin & Co. (Overseas), 1976–92; Vice Pres., Bankers Trust, 1992–93; Man. Dir, West Merchant Bank (WestLB Gp), 1993–98; Chief Exec., Panmure Gordon, subseq. WestLB Panmure, Ltd, 1996–2000; CEO, Compass Capital Ltd, 2001–03; Chief Operating Officer, Cross Asset Mgt Ltd, 2003–05. *Recreations:* sailing, theatre, opera.

HODGKINS, David John, CB 1993; Director, Resources and Planning, Health and Safety Executive, 1992–94; *b* 13 March 1934; *s* of late Rev. Harold Hodgkins and Elsie Hodgkins; *m* 1963, Sheila Lacey; two *s*. *Educ:* Buxton Coll.; Peterhouse, Cambridge. BA 1956, MA 1960. Entered Min. of Labour as Asst Principal, 1956; Principal: Min. of Lab., 1961–65; Treasury, 1965–68; Manpower and Productivity Services, Dept of Employment, 1968–70; Assistant Secretary: Prices and Incomes Div., Dept of Employment, 1970–72; Industrial Relns Div., 1973–76; Under Secretary, Overseas and Manpower Divisions, Dept of Employment, 1977–84; Safety Policy Div., HSE, 1984–92. Mem., Employment Appeal Tribunal, 1996–2004. *Publication:* Sir Edward Watkin: the second railway king, 2002. *Recreation:* narrow boating. *Address:* Four Winds, Batchelors Way, Amersham, Bucks HP7 9AJ. *T:* (01494) 725207. *Club:* Royal Commonwealth Society.

HODGKINSON, Sir Derek; *see* Hodgkinson, Sir W. D.

HODGKINSON, Sir Michael Stewart, Kt 2003; Chairman, Post Office, since 2003; Director, Royal Mail, since 2003; *b* 7 April 1944; *s* of Stewart Gordon Hodgkinson and Ruth Phyllis Hodgkinson; *m* 1988, Elspeth Holman; one *s* two *d*. *Educ:* Nottingham Univ. (BA Hons Industrial Econs). ACMA 1969. Finance: Ford of Europe, 1965–69; British Leyland, 1969–75; Finance and Admin Dir, Leyland Cars Engrg, 1975–78; Man. Dir, Land Rover Ltd, 1978–83; Gp Dir, Watney Mann & Truman Brewers, 1983–85; Dep. Chief Exec., Express Dairies, 1985–89; Chief Exec., Grand Metropolitan Foods, Europe, 1989–92; Gp Airports Dir, 1992–99, Chief Exec., 1999–2003, BAA plc. Chm., First Choice plc, 2004–07; Dep. Chm., TUI Travel plc, 2007–. *Recreations:* golf, theatre, travel. *Address:* The Post Office, 80 Old Street, EC1V 9NN.

HODGKINSON, Neil Robert; Editorial Director, Cumbrian Newspapers Ltd, since 2006; *b* 28 May 1960; *s* of Robert Hodgkinson and Faith Hodgkinson; *m* 1st, 1984, Jacqueline Dawn Proctor; 2nd, 1993, Christine Elizabeth Talbot; 3rd, 2000, Emma Louise Schofield; one *s*. *Educ:* Baines Grammar Sch., Poulton-le-Fylde; Central Lancashire Poly. (Dip. Journalism). Trainee journalist to Dep. News Editor, W Lancs Evening Gazette, 1979–87; News Editor, then Dep. Editor, Lancs Evening Post, 1987–92; Dep. Ed., Yorkshire Evening Post, 1992–96; Editor, Lancs Evening Post, 1996–99; Editor and Dir, Yorkshire Evening Post, 1999–2006. *Recreations:* football, cricket, tennis. *Address:* Cumbrian Newspapers Limited, PO Box 7, Newspaper House, Dalston Road, Carlisle, Cumbria CA2 5UA. *T:* (01228) 612617.

HODGKINSON, Terence; Chairman, Yorkshire Forward, since 2003; *b* 30 March 1949; *m* 1973, Anne Simpson; two *d*. *Educ:* Aston Univ. (BSc Hons). CDir 2001. Chm., Magna Hldgs Ltd, 1997–; Dir, Lemmeleg Bldg and Contracting Ltd, 1997–2004. FCIOB 2001. *Address:* Yorkshire Forward, Victoria House, 2 Victoria Place, Leeds LS11 5AE. *T:* (0113) 394 9600, *Fax:* (0113) 394 9780; *e-mail:* terry.hodgkinson@yorkshire-forward.com.

HODGKINSON, Air Chief Marshal Sir (William) Derek, KCB 1971 (CB 1969); CBE 1960; DFC 1941; AFC 1942; *b* 27 Dec. 1917; *s* of late Ernest Nicholls Hodgkinson; *m* 1939, Nancy Heather Goodwin; one *s* one *d*. *Educ:* Repton. Joined RAF 1936; served war of 1939–45, POW Germany, 1942–45; OC 210 and 240 (GR) Sqns; DS Aust. Jt Anti-Sub. Sch. and JSSC, 1946–58; Gp Captain, 1958; OC RAF St Mawgan, 1958–61; Staff of CDS, and ADC to the Queen, 1961–63; Air Cdre, 1963; IDC, 1964; Comdt RAF Staff Coll., Andover, 1965; Air Vice-Marshal, 1966; ACAS, Operational Requirements, 1966–68; SASO, RAF Training Command, 1969; Air Marshal, 1970; AOC-in-C, Near East Air Force, Commander British Forces Near East, and Administrator, Sovereign Base Areas, Cyprus, 1970–73; Air Secretary, 1973–76; Air Chief Marshal, 1974; retired 1976. Report on RAF Officer Career Structure, 1969. Pres., Regular Forces Employment Assoc., 1982–86 (Vice-Chm., 1977–80; Chm., 1980–82). *Recreations:* fishing, cricket. *Clubs:* Royal Air Force, MCC.

HODGSON, family name of **Baron Hodgson of Astley Abbotts**.

HODGSON OF ASTLEY ABBOTTS, Baron *cr* 2000 (Life Peer), of Nash in the co. of Shropshire; **Robin Granville Hodgson,** CBE 1992; Chairman, Johnson Bros & Co. Ltd, Walsall, since 1989 (Director, since 1970); *b* 25 April 1942; *s* of late Henry Edward and of Natalie Beatrice Hodgson; *m* 1982, Fiona Ferelith, *o d* of K. S. Allom, Dorking, Surrey; three *s* one *d* (and one twin *s* decd). *Educ:* Shrewsbury Sch.; Oxford Univ. (BA Hons 1964); Wharton Sch. of Finance, Univ. of Pennsylvania (MBA 1969). Investment Banker, New York and Montreal, 1964–67; Industry in Birmingham, England, 1969–72; Gp Chief Exec., 1979–95, Chm., 1995–2002, Granville plc, then Granville Baird Ltd; Chairman: Rostrum Gp Ltd, 2000–07; Nova Capital Mgt Ltd, 2002–; Carbo plc, 2002–05; RFIB Group Ltd, 2007–; Tenet Gp Ltd, 2007–; Director: Community Hospitals plc, 1982–85 and 1995–2001; Domnick Hunter Gp, 1992–2002; Staffordshire Building Soc., 1995–2005; Wolverhampton and Dudley Breweries plc, 2002–. Mem., W Midlands Industrial Develt Bd, 1989–97. Contested (C) Walsall North, Feb. and Oct. 1974; MP (C) Walsall North, Nov. 1976–1979. Opposition spokesman on trade and industry, H of L, 2002–06. Chm., Birmingham Bow Gp, 1972–73; National Union of Conservative Associations: Mem. Exec. Cttee, 1988–98; Vice Pres., 1995–96; Chm., 1996–98; Chm., W Midlands Area, 1991–94. Dep. Chm., Cons. Party, 1998–2000; Chairman: Nat. Cons. Convention, 1998–2000; Trustees, Cons. Party Pension Fund, 2000–06. Member: Council for the Securities Industry, 1980–85; Securities and Investments Board, 1985–89; Dir, SFA, 1991–2001; Chm., Nat. Assoc. of Security Dealers and Investment Managers, 1979–85. Gov., Shrewsbury Sch. Trustee and Hon. Fellow, St Peter's Coll., Oxford; Associate, St George's House, Windsor. Liveryman, Goldsmiths' Co., 1983. *Publication:* Britain's Home Defence Gamble, 1978. *Recreations:* squash, fishing, theatre. *Address:* 15 Scarsdale Villas, W8 6PT. *T:* (020) 7937 2964; Nash Court, Ludlow, Salop SY8 3DG. *T:* (01584) 811677.

HODGSON, (Adam) Robin; DL; Chief Executive, Hampshire County Council, 1985–95; *b* 20 March 1937; *s* of Thomas Edward Highton Hodgson, CB; *m* 1962, Elizabeth Maureen Linda Bovenizer; one *s* two *d*. *Educ:* William Ellis Sch., London; Worcester Coll., Oxford (MA 1969); BSc Open Univ. 1997. Admitted Solicitor, 1964. Asst Solicitor, LCC and GLC, 1964–66; Sen. Asst Solicitor, Oxfordshire CC, 1966–71; Asst Clerk, Northamptonshire CC, 1972–74; Dep. County Sec., E Sussex CC, 1974–77; Dep. Chief Exec. and Clerk, Essex CC, 1977–85. Chm., Winchester Diocesan Bd of Finance, 1996–2006. Mem. Council, Univ. of Southampton, 1996–2002; Governor, Univ. of Portsmouth, 1996–2003. Mem. Gen. Chiropractic Council, 1996–2004. DL Hampshire, 1996. *Recreations:* music, drama, geology. *Address:* Tara, Dean Lane, Winchester, Hampshire SO22 5RA. *T:* (01962) 862115.

HODGSON, Gordon Hewett; Master of the Supreme Court, Queen's Bench Division, 1983–2000; *b* 21 Jan. 1929; *s* of late John Lawrence Hodgson and Alice Joan Hodgson (*née* Wickham); *m* 1958, Pauline Audrey Gray; two *s*. *Educ:* Oundle School; University College London. LLB (Hons). National Service, RAEC, 1947–49; called to the Bar, Middle Temple, 1953; private practice, South Eastern Circuit, 1954–83; Asst Boundary Commissioner, 1976; Asst Recorder, 1979. Mem. Cttee, Bentham Club, 1987– (Chm., 1990–95). Sec., Dacorum Heritage Trust Ltd, 2003–. FZS 1990. *Publication:* (ed jtly) Supreme Court Practice, 1991, 1995 and 1999. *Recreations:* gardening, enjoying Tuscany. *Address:* PO Box 28, Hemel Hempstead HP3 0XX. *T:* (01442) 833200; *e-mail:* GHHodgson@aol.com. *Clubs:* East India; Bar Yacht.

HODGSON, Guy Andrew Keith; District Judge (Magistrates' Courts) (formerly Stipendiary Magistrate), Bradford, 1993–2000; *b* 19 March 1946; *s* of Herbert and Kathleen Hodgson; *m* 1968, Kay Bampton; three *s*. *Educ:* Pocklington Sch.; Nottingham Poly. (LLB London Ext.). Articled to M. M. Rossfield, Solicitor, York; Legal Asst, Thames Valley Police, 1970–71; Asst Prosecutor, Suffolk Police, 1971–72; Asst Solicitor, Gotelee & Goldsmith, Ipswich, 1972–74; Partner, Close Thornton, Darlington, 1974–93. *Recreations:* travel, reading, painting, hobby farming, vintage tractors, family interests, canal narrow boats.

HODGSON, Howard Osmond Paul; author and scriptwriter; Columnist, Malta Independent on Sunday, since 2007; *b* 22 Feb. 1950; *s* of late Osmond Paul Charles Hodgson and of Sheila Mary (*née* Ward; now Mrs Baker); *m* 1st, 1972, Marianne Denise Yvonne (marr. diss. 1998), *d* of Samuel Katibien, Aix-en-Provence, France; two *s* one *d* (and one *s* decd); 2nd, 1999, Christine Mary, *d* of A. F. Pickles. *Educ:* Aiglon Coll., Villars, Switzerland. DipFD 1970; MBIFD; Affiliated MRSH, 1970. Asst Man., Hodgson & Sons Ltd, 1969–71; life assce exec., 1971–75; acquired: Hodgson & Sons Ltd, 1975 (floated USM, 1986); Ingalls from House of Fraser, 1987; launched Dignity in Destiny Ltd, 1989; merger with Pompes Funèbres Générales, France, Kenyon Securities and Hodgson Hldgs plc to form PFG Hodgson Kenyon Internat. plc, 1989; launched: Bereavement Support Service, 1990; PHKI Nat. Training Sch., 1990; retd, 1991, to pursue career in broadcasting and writing. Chief Executive: Halkin Hldgs, 1993; Hoskins Brewery plc, 1993; Ronson plc, 1995–97 (acquired Ronson plc and LGW plc, 1994, Home Shopping Marketing Ltd and associated cos, the business of DCK Marketing Ltd and Smiths Packaging Ltd, 1995; Group renamed Ronson plc, 1995; resigned, 1997); CEO, Colibri Internat., 1998–2001; Chairman: Memoria Ltd, 2002–; Forte Ltd, 2002–. Presenter, How Euro Are You, BBC2, 1991–92; panellist, Board Game, Radio 4, 1992–2001. Hon. Vice Pres., Royal Soc. of St George, 1989. USM Entrepreneur of the Year, 1987. *Publications:* How to Become Dead Rich, 1992; Six Feet Under, 2000 (film script, 2001); Exhumed Innocent?, 2002; Charles: the man who will be king, 2007. *Recreations:* cricket, yachting, ski-ing, history. *Club:* Royal Motor Yacht.

HODGSON, Prof. Humphrey Julian Francis, DM; FRCP, FMedSci; Dame Sheila Sherlock Professor of Medicine, since 1999, and Director, Royal Free Campus, since 2001, Royal Free and University College Medical School of University College London; *b* 5 April 1945; *s* of late Harold Robinson Hodgson and Celia Frances Hodgson (*née* Hodgson); *m* 1971, Shirley Victoria Penrose; one *s* one *d*. *Educ:* Westminster Sch.; Christ Church, Oxford (BA, BSc); St Thomas's Hosp. Med. Sch. (BM BCh, DM). FRCP 1983. Trng posts at St Thomas' and Royal Free Hosps, 1970–76; Radcliffe Travelling Fellow, University Coll., Oxford, at Massachusetts Gen. Hosp., Boston, 1977; Consultant Physician, Hammersmith Hosp., 1977–99; Royal Postgraduate Medical School, London: Sen. Lectr in Medicine, 1978–89; Reader, 1989–91; Prof. of Gastroenterology, 1991–95; Vice Dean, 1986–97; Prof. of Medicine, RPMS, then ICSM, 1995–99; Jt Med. Dir, Hammersmith Hosps NHS Trust, 1994–97. Acad. Registrar, RCP, 1992–97. Chm., Scientific Co-ordinating Cttee, Arthritis Res. Campaign (formerly Arthritis and Rheumatism Council for Res.), 1996–2003. Pres., British Assoc. for Study of the Liver, 2003–05; Sen. Censor and Vice-Pres., RCP, 2008–. FMedSci 2002. *Publications:* Textbook of Gastroenterology, 1984; Gastroenterology: clinical science and practice, 1994. *Recreations:* walking, reading, academic travel. *Address:* Department of Medicine,

Royal Free and University College Medical School, Rowland Hill Street, NW3 2PF. *T:* (020) 7433 2850; 40 Onslow Gardens, N10 3JU. *T:* (020) 8883 8297.

HODGSON, Keith Stephen, OBE 1997; Director, Management Support Unit, Board of Inland Revenue, 1998–2001; *b* 29 Oct. 1946; *s* of Leonard Arthur and Florence Hodgson; *m* 1969, Jean Moran. *Educ:* Wolverhampton Municipal Grammar Sch. Min. of Transport, 1965–68; Board of Inland Revenue, 1968–2001; Private Sec. to Chm. of Bd, CS Pay Res. Unit, 1978–81; Dep. Controller of Stamps, 1982–90; Dir, Stamp Office, 1990–98. FRSA 1998. *Publications:* (contrib.) Managing Change in the New Public Sector, 1994; (contrib.) Creating a Good Impression: three hundred years of the Stamp Office and Stamp Duties, 1994. *Recreations:* Freemasonry, golf, wine, Rugby, ski-ing. *Address:* Tenterden, Kent; Chandolin, Val d'Anniviers, Valais, Switzerland. *Club:* Tenterden Golf.

HODGSON, Sir Maurice (Arthur Eric), Kt 1979; Chairman, British Home Stores plc, 1982–87, and Chief Executive, 1982–85; *b* 21 Oct. 1919; *s* of late Walter Hodgson and of Amy Hodgson (*née* Walker); *m* 1945, Norma Fawcett (*d* 2002); one *s* one *d*. *Educ:* Bradford Grammar Sch.; Merton Coll., Oxford (Hon. Fellow, 1979). MA, BSc; FREng, FIChemE; CChem, FRSC. Joined ICI Ltd Fertilizer & Synthetic Products Gp, 1942; seconded to ICI (New York) Ltd, 1955–58; Head of ICI Ltd Technical Dept, 1958; Develt Dir, ICI Ltd Heavy Organic Chemicals Div., 1960, Dep. Chm., 1964; Gen. Man., Company Planning, ICI Ltd, 1966; Commercial Dir and Planning Dir, ICI Ltd, 1970; Dep. Chm., ICI Ltd, 1972–78, Chm., 1978–82; Director: Carrington Viyella Ltd, 1970–74; Imperial Chemicals Insce Ltd, 1970–78 (Chm. 1972); Dunlop Holdings plc, 1982–84 (Chm. 1984); Storehouse, 1985–89; Member: Internat. Adv. Bd, AMAX Inc., 1982–85; European Adv. Council, Air Products and Chemicals Inc., 1982–84; Council, Lloyd's of London, 1987–94. Chm., Civil Justice Review Adv. Cttee, 1985–88; Member: Court, British Shippers' Council, 1978–82; Council, CBI, 1978–82; Internat. Council, Salk Inst., 1978–97; Court, Univ. of Bradford, 1979–90. Vis. Fellow, Sch. of Business and Organizational Studies, Univ. of Lancaster, 1970–80. Governor, London Grad. Sch. of Business Studies, 1978–87. DUniv Heriot-Watt, 1979; Hon. DTech Bradford, 1979; Hon. DSc Loughborough, 1981; Hon. FUMIST, 1979. Messel Medal, Soc. of Chemical Industry, 1980; George E. Davis Medal, IChemE, 1982. *Recreations:* horse-racing, swimming, fishing.

HODGSON, Dame Patricia (Anne), (Dame Patricia Donaldson), DBE 2004 (CBE 1995); Principal, Newnham College, Cambridge, since 2006; Member, BBC Trust, since 2007; *b* 19 Jan. 1947; *d* of Harold Hodgson and Pat Smith; *m* 1979, George Donaldson; one *s*. *Educ:* Brentwood High Sch.; Newnham Coll., Cambridge (MA; Associate Fellow, 1994–97); LRAM (Drama) 1968. Conservative Res. Dept, Desk Officer for public sector industries, 1968–70; freelance journalism and broadcasting in UK and USA during seventies; Chm., Bow Gp, 1975–76; Editor, Crossbow, 1976–80. BBC: joined as educn producer for Open Univ. (part of founding team pioneering distance learning techniques), 1970; most of prodn career in educn, specialising in history and philosophy, with spells in current affairs on Today and Tonight; Secretariat, 1982–83, Dep. Sec., 1983–85, The Sec., 1985–87; Hd of Policy & Planning, 1987–92; Dir of Policy & Planning, 1993–2000; Dir of Public Policy, 2000; Chief Exec., ITC, 2000–04. Chm., Higher Educn Regulation Rev. Gp, 2004–06; Mem., HEFCE, 2005–. Non-executive Director: GCAP Media plc, 2004–06; Competition Commn, 2004– (Mem., Monopolies and Mergers, subseq. Competition, Commn, 1993–97); Member: Statistics Commn, 2000–05; Cttee on Standards in Public Life, 2004–. Dir, BARB, 1987–98. Mem., (C) Haringey BC, 1974–77. Mem., London Arts Bd, 1991–96. Trustee, PYBT, 1992–95. Gov., Wellcome Trust, 2004–08; Mem. Adv. Bd, Judge Inst., Cambridge, 1996–2002. Vis. Bye-Fellow, Newnham Coll., Cambridge, 2004. DU Essex, 2001; Hon. DSc City, 2002. *Television series* include: English Urban History, 1978; Conflict in Modern Europe, 1980; Rome in the Age of Augustus, 1981. *Publications:* (ed) Paying for Broadcasting, 1992; (ed) Public Purposes in Broadcasting, 1999; (ed) Culture and Communications, 2003; articles in various newspapers and jls. *Recreation:* quietness. *Address:* c/o Newnham College, Cambridge CB3 9DF. *Club:* Oxford and Cambridge.

HODGSON, Randolph Arthur, OBE 2006; owner, Neal's Yard Dairy, since 1979; *b* 29 Sept. 1956; *s* of Arthur Ralph and Monica Olive Hodgson; *m* 1982, Anita Leroy; two *s* one *d*. *Educ:* Downside Sch.; King's Coll., London (BSc Hons). Chm., Specialist Cheesemakers' Assoc., 1990–94 and 2000–. *Recreation:* cheese-making. *Address:* 19 Randolph Road, W9 1AN. *T:* (020) 7286 6205; *e-mail:* randolph@nealsyarddairy.co.uk.

HODGSON, Robin; *see* Hodgson, A. R.

HODGSON, Sharon; MP (Lab) Gateshead East and Washington West, since 2005; *b* 1 April 1966; *d* of Joan Cohen (*née* Wilson); *m* 1990, Alan Hodgson; one *s* one *d*. *Educ:* Heathfield Sen. High Sch., Gateshead; Newcastle Coll. Payroll/account clerk, Tyneside Safety Glass, 1982–88; Northern Rock Bldg Soc., Gosforth, 1988–92; Payroll administrator, Burgess Microswitch, 1992–94; Administrator, Total Learning Challenge, 1998–99; Lab. Party Organr, 1999–2002; Labour Link Co-ordinator, UNISON, 2002–05. PPS to Minister of State, Home Office, 2006–07, to Minister of State, MoD, 2007–. Mem., Children, Schs and Families Select Cttee, 2007–. *Address:* (office) 10 Morley Terrace, Felling, Gateshead, Tyne and Wear NE10 9HJ; House of Commons, SW1A 0AA; *web:* www.sharonhodgson.org.

HODGSON, Ven. Thomas Richard Burnham; Archdeacon of West Cumberland, 1979–91, now Archdeacon Emeritus; *b* 17 Aug. 1926; *s* of Richard Shillito Hodgson and Marion Thomasina Bertram Marshall; *m* 1952, Margaret Esther, *o d* of Evan and Caroline Margaret Makinson; one *s* one *d*. *Educ:* Heversham Grammar School; London Coll. of Divinity, Univ. of London. BD, ALCD. Deacon 1952, priest 1953, dio. Carlisle; Curate of Crosthwaite, Keswick, 1952–55; Curate of Stanwix, Carlisle, 1955–59; Vicar of St Nicholas', Whitehaven, 1959–65; Rector of Aikton, 1965–67; Vicar of Raughtonhead with Gaitsgill, 1967–73; Hon. Canon of Carlisle, 1973–91; Vicar of: Grange-over-Sands, 1973–79; Mosser, 1979–83. Mem., General Synod of C of E, 1983–90. Domestic Chaplain to Bishop of Carlisle, 1967–73, Hon. Chaplain 1973–79; Director of Ordination Candidates, 1970–74; RD of Windermere, 1976–79; Surrogate, 1962–91. *Publications:* Saying the Services, 1989; Speaking in Church, 2004. *Recreations:* listening to music, watching drama, geology, meteorological observing, drawing and watercolour painting. *Address:* 58 Greenacres, Wetheral, Carlisle CA4 8LD. *T:* (01228) 561159.

HODKINSON, Prof. Henry Malcolm, DM; FRCP; barrister-at-law, Kew Chambers; Barlow Professor of Geriatric Medicine, University College London, 1985–91, now Emeritus; *b* 28 April 1931; *s* of Charles and Olive Hodkinson; *m* 1st (marr. diss.); four *d*; 2nd, 1986, Judith Marie Bryant, *qv*. *Educ:* Manchester Grammar Sch.; Brasenose Coll., Oxford (DM 1975); Middlesex Hospital; Westminster Univ. (Dip. in Law, 2000). FRCP 1974. Consultant Physician in Geriatrics to: Enfield and Tottenham Gps of Hosps, 1962–70; Northwick Park Hosp., 1970–78 (also Mem., Scientific Staff of Clin. Res. Centre); Sen. Lectr in Geriatric Medicine, 1978–79, Prof. of Geriatric Medicine, 1979–84, RPMS. Called to the Bar, Middle Temple, 2001. Vice Pres., Research into Ageing, 1996– (Governor, 1983–96). *Publications:* An Outline of Geriatrics, 1975, 2nd edn 1981 (trans. Spanish, Dutch, German, Italian and Japanese); Common Symptoms of Disease in th Elderly, 1976, 2nd edn 1980 (trans. Turkish); Biochemical Diagnosis of the Elderly, 197 (ed) Clinical Biochemistry of the Elderly, 1984; (with J. M. Hodkinson) Sherratt? A Natural Family of Staffordshire Figures, 1991; approx. 100 papers in learned jls, 1961–. *Recreations:* English glass and ceramics. *Address:* 8 Chiswick Square, Burlington Lan Chiswick, W4 2QG. *T:* (020) 8747 0239.

HODKINSON, James Clifford; Executive Chairman: Furniture Village, since 200 Wyevale Garden Centres, since 2006; non-executive Director of various companies; *b* 2 April 1944; *s* of John and Lily Hodkinson; *m* 1969, Janet Lee; one *d*. *Educ:* Salesian Coll Farnborough. Trainee Manager, F. W. Woolworth Ltd, London, 1962–71; Manager, & Q, Bournemouth, 1972–74; Sales Manager, B & Q (Retail) Ltd, 1974–76; Man. Dir, & Q (Southern) Ltd, 1976–79; Dir, 1976–79, Ops Dir, 1979–84, Ops and Personnel Di 1984–86, B & Q (Retail) Ltd; Man. Dir, 1986–89, Chief Exec., 1989–92, B & Q pl Internat. Develt Dir, Kingfisher plc, 1992–94; Chm. and Chief Exec., B & Q pl 1994–98; Chief Exec., New Look Retailers Ltd, 1998–2000. *Recreations:* shooting, gol *Clubs:* Annabelle's; Parkstone Golf.

HODKINSON, Judith Marie, (Mrs H. M. Hodkinson); *see* Bryant, J. M.

HODSON, Beverley Cliffe, OBE 2003; non-executive Director: First Milk, since 200 Robert Wiseman Dairies, since 2005; Randstad (formerly Vedior NV), since 2006; *b* 1 June 1951; *d* of Clifford Vernon Hodson and Frances Jeanne Hodson; *m* Peter Joh Cottingham. *Educ:* Newnham Coll., Cambridge (BA 1st cl. hons). Boots, 1978–96; Sear 1996–97; Man. Dir, UK Retail, WH Smith Gp, 1997–2004. Non-executive Directo GWR Trent FM Radio, 1990–97; M&G Gp plc, 1998–99; Legal & General, 2000–0 *Recreations:* ski-ing, tennis, reading, theatre, opera, wine, food.

HODSON, Christopher Robert; His Honour Judge Christopher Hodson; a Circu Judge, since 1993; Resident Judge, Warwick and Coventry Crown Courts, since 2007; 3 Nov. 1946; *s* of James and Elizabeth Hodson; *m* 1970, Jean Patricia Anne Dayer; one one *d*. *Educ:* King's Sch., Worcester. Called to the Bar, Lincoln's Inn, 1970; practise Birmingham, 1971–93; a Recorder, 1988–93. Hon. Recorder, City of Coventry, 2007– *Address:* c/o Judicial Team, Midland Circuit, Priory Courts, 33 Bull Street, Birmingha B4 6DW. *T:* (0121) 681 3205.

HODSON, Clive, CBE 1992; FCCA; FCILT; Chairman, LRT Pension Fund Truste Co. Ltd, 1998–2003; *b* 9 March 1942; *s* of late Stanley Louis Hodson and Elsie Ma Hodson (*née* Stratford); *m* 1976, Fiona Mary Pybus; one *s* one *d*. *Educ:* Erith Grammar Sch FCCA 1967; FCILT (FCIT 1969); CTA (ATII 1968). LT, 1960–69; Asst Sec. an Accountant, London Country Bus Services Ltd, 1970–74; Mgt Accountant, LT, 1974–7 London Buses Ltd: Finance Dir, 1978–89; Man. Dir, 1989–95; Chm., 2000; Managin Director: LT Buses, 1994–2000; London Bus Services Ltd, 2000. Chairman: Victor Coach Station Ltd, 1995–2000; London River Services Ltd, 1998–2000. Mem., LT 1995–2000. LT Project Dir, Bus Privatisation, 1993–95; Project Dir, Croydon Tramlink 1995–2000; Dir, Capital Value Brokers Ltd, 2000–04. Freeman, City of London, 199 Liveryman, Co. of Carmen, 1995. *Recreations:* travel, walking, reading.

HODSON, Daniel Houghton, FCT; Chairman: Design and Artists Copyright Societ 1999–2005; Board of Governors, University of Winchester (formerly King Alfred College, Winchester, then University College Winchester), 2001–06; *b* 11 March 1944; of late Henry Vincent Hodson and Margaret Elizabeth (*née* Honey); *m* 1979, Diana Mar Ryde; two *d*. *Educ:* Eton; Merton Coll., Oxford (MA Hons PPE). FCT 1979. Chas Manhattan Bank, 1965–73; joined Edward Bates & Sons Ltd, 1973, Dir 1974–76; Unigat plc: Gp Treas., 1976–81; Gp Finance Dir, 1981–87; Pres., Unigate Inc., 1986–87; Chie Exec., 1987–88, Chm. 1988, Davidson Pearce Gp plc; Dep. Chief Exec., Nationwid Building Soc., 1989–92; Chief Exec., LIFFE, 1993–98. Director: The Post Offic 1984–95; Ransomes plc, 1993–98; Independent Insurance Gp plc, 1995–2003; Londo Clearing House, 1996–98; Rolfe and Nolan plc, 1999–2003; Norland Managed (former Reliance Environmental) Services Ltd, 1999–2006; Berry Palmer and Lyle Hldgs Lt 2000–; Chairman: Medialink Internat., 1999–2003; Insulation and Machining Service Ltd, 2001–07; SVM Global Fund plc, 2004–. Chm., European Cttee, Options and Future Exchanges, 1996–98. Association of Corporate Treasurers: Chm., 1985–86; Pres. 1992–93. Gresham Prof. of Commerce, 1999–2002. Chm., Lokahi Foundn, 2005–. De Chm., Classical Opera Co., 1997–2005. Governor: Yehudi Menuhin Sch., 1984–200 Peter Symonds' Coll., Winchester, 2000–02; St Paul's Girls' Sch., 2006–; Mem. Counci Gresham Coll., 2006–. Founding Editor, Corporate Finance and Treasury Managemen 1984–. Master, Mercers' Co., 2008–. *Recreations:* music, travel, ski-ing, gardening. *Addres* Chepynge House, 22 Maltravers Street, Arundel BN18 9BU. *T:* (01903) 883234. *Clu* Brooks's.

HODSON, Denys Fraser, CBE 1981; Director, Arts and Recreation, Thamesdow Borough Council, 1974–92; *b* 23 May 1928; *s* of late Rev. Harold Victor Hodson, MC and Marguerite Edmée Ritchie; *m* 1954, Julie Compton Goodwin; one *s* one *d*. *Edu* Marlborough Coll.; Trinity Coll., Oxford (MA). After a career in commerce and industr apptd first Controller of Arts and Recreation, Swindon Bor. Council, 1970. Chairma Southern Arts Assoc., 1974–80 and 1985–87; Council, Regional Arts Assocs, 1975–8 Chief Leisure Officers' Assoc., 1974 and 1982–84; Chm., Public Arts Commns Agenc 1993–2000; Vice-Chm., Arts Council of GB, 1989–94 (Mem., 1987–94); a Directo Oxford Playhouse Co., 1974–86; Oxford Stage Co., 1988–89; Chairman: Brewery Art 1994–98; Arts Research Ltd, 1999–2006 (Trustee, 1995–); Vice-Pres., Voluntary Ar Network, 1998– (Vice-Chm., 1992–94; Chm., 1994–98); a Governor: BFI, 1976–8 (Dep. Chm., 1985–87); Wyvern Arts Trust, 1984–95. Chairman: Friends of Fairfor Church, 1998–; Friends of Lydiard Park, 2005–. *Publications:* (contrib.) Arts Centres, 1981 (contrib.) The Future of Leisure Services, 1988; conf. papers and articles. *Recreations:* bird-watching, fishing, the arts. *Address:* Manor Farm House, Fairford, Glos GL7 4AR. *T* (01285) 712462.

HODSON, Prof. Howard Peter, PhD; FREng, FRAeS; FASME; Professor o Aerothermal Technology, Department of Engineering, University of Cambridge, sinc 2000; Fellow, Girton College, Cambridge, since 1984; *b* 18 Feb. 1957; *s* of Edwar Hodson and late Kathleen Janette Hodson; *m* 1978, Dr Jane Brooks. *Educ:* Churchill Coll. Cambridge (BA Engrg 1978, MA 1982; PhD 1983). CEng 1999, FREng 2005; FRAe 1999. Engr, Perkins Engine Co. Ltd, 1978–79; Res. Asst, Whittle Lab., Cambridge 1982–85; Department of Engineering, University of Cambridge: Sen. Asst in Res. 1985–89; Lectr, 1989–98; Reader in Thermofluid Engrg, 1998–2000; Girton College Cambridge: Lectr, 1985–; Dir of Studies, 1985–2000; Actg Bursar, 1994. Dir and Sec. Cambridge Turbomachinery Consultants Ltd, 1983–2005. FASME 2002. *Publications* contrib. papers to jls of ASME, AIAA and IMechE. *Recreations:* gardening, classic vehicl restoration. *Address:* Whittle Laboratory, Department of Engineering, University o Cambridge, Madingley Road, Cambridge CB3 0DY. *T:* (01223) 337588, *Fax:* (01223 337596; *e-mail:* hph@eng.cam.ac.uk.

HODSON, John; Chief Executive, Singer & Friedlander Group, 1993–2004 (Director, 1987–2004; Chairman, 1999–2003); *b* 19 May 1946; *s* of Arthur and Olga Hodson; *m* 1971, Christina McLeod; one *s* two *d*. *Educ:* Worcester Coll., Oxford (PPE). Joined Singer & Friedlander, 1969: Asst Dir, 1974–83; Dir, 1983–2004; Head of Investment Dept, 1985–90. Chm., UBC Media PLC; non-executive Director: Prestbury Gp plc; Domino's Pizza UK & Ireland plc. *Recreations:* tennis, family.

HODSON, Sir Michael (Robin Adderley), 6th Bt *cr* 1789; Captain, Scots Guards, retired; *b* 5 March 1932; *s* of Major Sir Edmond Adair Hodson, 5th Bt, DSO, and Anne Elizabeth Adderley (*d* 1984), *yr d* of Lt-Col Hartopp Francis Charles Adderley Cradock, Hill House, Sherborne St John; *S* father, 1972; *m* 1st, 1963, Katrin Alexa (marr. diss. 1978), *d* of late Erwin Bernstiel, Dinas Powis, Glamorgan; three *d*; 2nd, 1978, Catherine, *d* of late John Henry Seymour, Wimpole St, W1. *Educ:* Eton. *Heir: b* Patrick Richard Hodson [*b* 27 Nov. 1934; *m* 1961, June, *o d* of H. M. Shepherd-Cross; three *s*]. *Address:* Nantyderry House, Nantyderry, Monmouthshire NP7 9DW.

HODSON, Thomas David Tattersall; His Honour Judge Hodson; a Circuit Judge, since 1987; a Senior Circuit Judge and Honorary Recorder of Newcastle upon Tyne, since 1997; *b* 24 Sept. 1942; *s* of late Thomas Norman Hodson and Elsie Nuttall Hodson; *m* 1969, Patricia Ann Vint; two *s* one *d*. *Educ:* Sedbergh Sch.; Manchester Univ. (LLB). Leader Writer, Yorkshire Post, 1964–65; called to the Bar, Inner Temple 1966, Bencher, 2001; in practice on Northern Circuit, 1967–87; Junior, 1969; a Recorder, 1983–87. Mem., Parole Bd, 1996–97; Chm., Northumbria Area Criminal Justice Strategy Cttee, 2001–03. Pres., S Lancs Br., Magistrates' Assoc., 1994–96. Mem. Court, Univ. of Newcastle upon Tyne, 2000–. Dep. Chancellor, Dio. of Newcastle, 2003–. Hon. Mem., N Eastern Circuit, 2007. Hon. LLD Sunderland, 2002. *Publication:* One Week in August: the Kaiser at Lowther Castle, August 1895, 1995. *Recreations:* music, genealogy, fell-walking. *Address:* The Law Courts, The Quayside, Newcastle upon Tyne NE1 3LA. *T:* (0191) 201 2000.

HOEKMAN, Johan Bernard; Knight, Order of Netherlands Lion; Officer, Order of Orange Nassau; Netherlands Ambassador to the Court of St James's, 1990–94, and concurrently to Iceland; *b* 11 Sept. 1931; *m* 1957, Jeanne van Gelder; three *s* one *d*. *Educ:* Univ. of Groningen (degree in Social Geography). Foreign Service, 1961; served Baghdad, Washington, Jeddah; Counsellor, Cairo, 1972–74; Deputy, later Head, Dept for Financial Economic Develt Co-operation, Min. of Foreign Affairs, 1974–80; Ambassador, Dakar, 1980–81, Paramaribo, 1981–84; Dir-Gen. for Internat. Co-operation, 1984–88; Ambassador, Paramaribo, 1988–90. Holds foreign decorations. *Address:* Staten Laan 102, 2582 GV The Hague, Netherlands.

HOERNER, John Lee; Chief Executive, Central European Clothing, Tesco, since 2005; *b* 23 Sept. 1939; *s* of Robert Lee Hoerner and Lulu Alice (*née* Stone); *m* 1st 1959, Susan Kay Morgan (marr. diss. 1971); one *s* one *d*; 2nd, 1973, Anna Lea Thomas. *Educ:* Univ. of Nebraska (BS, BA). Hahnes Department Stores: senior buying and merchandising positions: Hovland Swanson, Lincoln, Neb, 1959–68; Woolf Bros, Kansas City, Mo, 1968–72; Hahnes, NJ, 1972–73; Pres. and Chief Exec. Officer, First 21st Century Corp., Hahnes, 1974–81; Chief Executive Officer: H. & S. Pogue Co., Cincinnati, Ohio, 1981–82; L. S. Ayres & Co., Indianapolis, Ind., 1982–87; Burton Group, subseq. Arcadia Group, 1987–2000: Chairman: Debenhams, 1987–92; Harvey Nichols, 1988–91; Gp Chief Exec., 1992–2000; Chief Exec., Clothing, 2001–04, Clothing and Internat. Sourcing, 2004–05, Tesco. Chm., British Fashion Council, 1996 and 1999. Non-exec. Dir, BAA, 1998–2004. Mem., Council of Trustees, Battersea Dogs' and Cats' Home (formerly Dogs' Home, Battersea), 1991– (Vice-Chm., 1995–2002; Chm., 2002–06). *Publications:* Ayres Adages, 1983; The Director's Handbook, 1991. *Recreations:* riding, flying, dogs. *Address:* Hawling Lodge, Hawling, Cheltenham, Glos GL54 5SY. *T:* (01451) 850223; *e-mail:* john.hoerner@uk.tesco.com. *Clubs:* Groucho; Air Squadron.

HOEY, Catharine Letitia; MP (Lab) Vauxhall, since June 1989; *b* 21 June 1946; *d* of Thomas Henry and Letitia Jane Hoey. *Educ:* Lylehill Primary Sch.; Belfast Royal Acad.; Ulster Coll. of Physical Educn (Dip. in PE); City of London Coll. (BSc Econs). Lectr, Southwark Coll., 1972–76; Sen. Lectr, Kingsway Coll., 1976–85; Educnl Advr, London Football Clubs, 1985–89. PPS to Minister of State (Minister for Welfare Reform), DSS, 1997–98; Parliamentary Under-Secretary of State: Home Office, 1998–99; DCMS (Minister for Sport), 1999–2001. Chm., Countryside Alliance, 2005–. *Recreations:* watching soccer, keeping fit. *Address:* House of Commons, SW1A 0AA. *T:* (020) 7219 3000. *Club:* Surrey CC (Mem. Cttee).

HOFFBRAND, Prof. (Allan) Victor, DM, DSc; FRCP, FRCPath; Professor of Haematology and Honorary Consultant, Royal Free Hospital School of Medicine, 1974–96, now Emeritus Professor, Royal Free and University College Medical School; *b* 14 Oct. 1935; *s* of late Philip Hoffbrand and Minnie (*née* Freedman); *m* 1963, Irene Jill Mellows; two *s* one *d*. *Educ:* Bradford Grammar Sch.; Queen's Coll., Oxford (BA 1956; MA 1960; BM BCh 1959; DM 1972); Royal London Hospital; DSc London 1987. FRCP 1976; FRCPath 1980. Jun. hosp. posts, Royal London Hosp., 1960–62; Res. and Registrar posts, RPMS, 1962–66; MRC Fellow, New England Med. Centre, Boston, 1967–68; Sen. Lectr, RPMS, 1968–74. Visiting Professor: Sanaa, Yemen, 1986; Armed Forces Inst. Path., Rawalpindi, 1988; Royal Melbourne Hosp., 1991. Lectures: Los Braun Meml, Johannesburg, 1978; Sir Stanley Davidson, Edinburgh, 1983; G. Izak Meml, Jerusalem, 1984; K. J. R. Wightman, Toronto, 1988. Chairman: Standing Intercollegiate Cttee on Oncology, 1993–94; Jt Haematology Cttee, RCP, RCPath, 1994–97; Member: Systems Bd, MRC, 1986–89; Council, RCPath, 1987–90; Council, Royal Free Sch. of Med., 1991–94. Medical Advisor: Leukaemia Res. Fund; Hadassah Med. Relief; Children with Leukaemia. Member: Amer. Soc. Hematology; Brit. Soc. Haematology; Eur. Haematology Assoc. (Mem. Council, 1994–99). FMedSci 2000; Hon. FRCPE 1986. Member, Editorial Board: Clinical Haematology; Acta Haematologica. *Publications:* (ed with S. M. Lewis) Postgraduate Haematology, 1972, 5th edn 2005; (ed) Recent Advances in Haematology, 1977, 8th edn 1996; Essential Haematology, 1980, 5th edn 2006; (with J. E. Pettit) Blood Diseases Illustrated, 1987, 4th edn, as Color Atlas of Clinical Hematology, 2008; (with A. B. Mehta) Haematology at a Glance, 2000, 2nd edn 2005; papers on megaloblastic anaemia, iron chelation, leukaemia and related disorders. *Recreations:* music, antiques, gardening, bridge. *Address:* Department of Haematology, Royal Free Hospital, NW3 2QG. *T:* (020) 7435 1547.

HOFFMAN, Dustin Lee; actor; *b* 8 Aug. 1937; *s* of Harry Hoffman and Lillian Hoffman; *m* 1st, 1969, Anne Byrne (marr. diss. 1980); two *d*; 2nd, 1980, Lisa Gottsegen; two *s* two *d*. *Educ:* Santa Monica City Coll.; Pasadena Playhouse. Stage début in Sarah Lawrence Coll. prodn, Yes is For a Very Young Man; Broadway début, A Cook for Mr General, 1961; appeared in: Harry, and Noon and Night, Amer. Place Theatre, NY, 1964–65; Journey of the Fifth Horse, and Star Wagon, 1965; Fragments, Berkshire Theatre Festival, Stockbridge, Mass, 1966; Eh?, 1966–67; Jimmy Shine, Broadway, 1968–69; Death of a Salesman, Broadway, 1984; London début, Merchant of Venice, Phoenix, 1989. Dir, All Over Town, Broadway, 1974. Films: The Graduate, 1967; Midnight Cowboy, John and Mary, 1969; Little Big Man, Who Is Harry Kellerman and Why Is He Saying Those Terrible Things About Me?, 1971; Straw Dogs, Alfredo, Alfredo, 1972; Papillon, 1973; Lenny, 1974; All The President's Men, 1975; Marathon Man, 1976; Straight Time, 1978; Agatha, Kramer vs Kramer (Acad. Award), 1979; Tootsie, 1983; Death of a Salesman, 1985 (Emmy Award); Ishtar, 1987; Rain Man, 1989 (Academy Award; Golden Globe Award); Family Business, 1990; Billy Bathgate, 1991; Hook, 1992; Accidental Hero, 1993; Outbreak, 1995; American Buffalo, Sleepers, 1996; Mad City, Wag the Dog, 1997; Sphere, 1998; Moonlight Mile, Confidence, 2003; Runaway Jury, Finding Neverland, I Heart Huckabees, 2004; Meet the Fockers, 2005; Stranger than Fiction, Perfume, 2006; Mr Magorium's Wonder Emporium, 2007. Record: Death of a Salesman. Obie Award as best off-Broadway actor, 1965–66, for Journey of the Fifth Horse; Drama Desk, Theatre World, and Vernon Rice Awards for Eh?, 1966; Oscar Award nominee for The Graduate, Midnight Cowboy, and Lenny. *Address:* 11661 San Vicente Boulevard, Suite 222, Los Angeles, CA 90049–5110, USA.

HOFFMAN, Gary Andrew; Chief Executive, Northern Rock, since 2008; *b* 21 Oct. 1960; *m* (marr. diss.). *Educ:* Queens' Coll., Cambridge. With Barclays Bank plc, 1982–2008: Man. Dir, Telephone Banking, 1995–98; Chief Exec., UK Retail Banking, 1998; Man. Dir, Customer Service and Delivery, 1999–2001; Chief Exec., 2001–05, Chm., 2005–06, Barclaycard; Exec. Dir, 2004–08; Chm., UK Banking, 2005–06; Gp Vice Chm., 2006–08. *Recreations:* running, watching Coventry City FC.

HOFFMAN, Rev. Canon Stanley Harold, MA; Chaplain in Ordinary to the Queen, 1976–87; Hon. Canon of Rochester Cathedral, 1965–80, now Emeritus; *b* 17 Aug. 1917; *s* of Charles and Ellen Hoffman, Denham, Bucks; *m* 1943, Mary Mifanwy Patricia (*d* 1991), *d* of late Rev. Canon Creed Meredith, Chaplain to the Queen, and Mrs R. Creed Meredith, Windsor; one *s* one *d*. *Educ:* The Royal Grammar Sch., High Wycombe, Bucks; St Edmund Hall, Oxford (BA 1939, MA 1943); Lincoln Theol Coll., 1940–41. Deacon, 1941; Priest, 1942; Curate: Windsor Parish Ch., 1941–44; All Saints, Weston, Bath, 1944–47; Chertsey (in charge of All SS), 1947–50; Vicar of Shottermill, Haslemere, Sy, 1951–64; Diocesan Director of Education, Rochester, 1965–80; Warden of Readers, 1974–80. Proctor in Convocation, Church Assembly, 1969–70; Exam. Chaplain to Bp of Rochester, 1973–80. Member: Kent Educn Cttee, 1965–80; Bromley Educn Cttee, 1967–80; Kent Council of Religious Educn, 1965–80; Archbps' Commn on Christian Initiation, 1970. Vice-Chm., Christ Church Coll., Canterbury, 1973–80. Hon. MA Kent, 1982. *Publications:* Morning Shows the Day: the making of a priest (autobiog.), 1995; part author: A Handbook of Thematic Material, 1968; Christians in Kent, 1972; Teaching the Parables, 1974; contrib. various pubns on Preaching and Religious Educn; numerous Dio. study papers. *Recreations:* music, walking. *Address:* Flat 3, Ramsay Hall, Byron Road, Worthing, W Sussex BN11 3HN. *T:* (01903) 217332.

HOFFMANN, family name of **Baron Hoffmann**.

HOFFMANN, Baron *cr* 1995 (Life Peer), of Chedworth in the County of Gloucestershire; **Leonard Hubert Hoffmann,** Kt 1985; PC 1992; a Lord of Appeal in Ordinary, 1995–May 2009; *b* 8 May 1934; *s* of B. W. and G. Hoffmann; *m* 1957, Gillian Lorna Sterner; two *d*. *Educ:* South African College Sch., Cape Town; Univ. of Cape Town (BA); The Queen's Coll., Oxford (Rhodes Scholar; MA, BCL, Vinerian Law Scholar; Hon. Fellow, 1992). Advocate of Supreme Court of S Africa, 1958–60. Called to the Bar, Gray's Inn, 1964, Bencher, 1984; QC 1977; a Judge, Courts of Appeal of Jersey and Guernsey, 1980–85; a Judge of the High Court of Justice, Chancery Div., 1985–92; a Lord Justice of Appeal, 1992–95. Non-permanent Judge, HK Court of Final Appeal, 1998–. Stowell Civil Law Fellow, University Coll., Oxford, 1961–73 (Hon. Fellow, 1995). Member: Royal Commn on Gambling, 1976–78; Council of Legal Educn, 1983–92 (Chm., 1989–92). Pres., British-German Jurists Assoc., 1991–. Dir, ENO, 1985–90, 1991–94. Chm., Arts Council Adv. Cttee on London Orchs, 1993. Pres., Heath and Hampstead Soc., 2004–. Hon. Fellow, Chartered Inst. of Taxation, 2006. Hon. DCL: City, 1992; UWE, 1995; Gloucestershire, 2003. *Publication:* The South African Law of Evidence, 1963. *Address:* Surrey Lodge, 23 Keats Grove, NW3 2RS.

HOFFMANN, Prof. Roald; Frank H. T. Rhodes Professor of Humane Letters, Cornell University, since 1996; *b* 18 July 1937; *s* of Hillel Safran and Clara (*née* Rosen, who *m* 2nd, Paul Hoffmann); *m* 1960, Eva Börjesson; one *s* one *d*. *Educ:* Columbia Univ. (BA); Harvard Univ. (MA, PhD). Junior Fellow, Society of Fellows, Harvard Univ., 1962–65; Associate Professor, to Professor, 1965–74, John A. Newman Prof. of Physical Science, 1974–96, Cornell Univ. Member: Nat. Acad. of Sciences; Amer. Acad. of Arts and Sciences. Foreign Member: Royal Soc., 1984; Indian Nat. Acad. of Sciences; Royal Swedish Acad. of Sciences; USSR Acad. of Sciences; Finnish Acad. of Sciences. Hon. DTech Royal Inst. of Technology, Stockholm, 1977; Hon. DSc: Yale, 1980; Hartford, 1982; Columbia, 1982; City Univ. of NY, 1983; Puerto Rico, 1983; La Plata, 1984; Uruguay, 1984; State Univ. of NY at Binghamton, 1985; Colgate, 1985; Rennes, 1986; Ben Gurion, 1989; Lehigh Univ., 1989; Carleton Coll., 1989; Maryland, 1990; Athens 1991; Thessaloniki, 1991; Bar Ilan, 1991; St Petersburg, 1991; Barcelona, 1992; Ohio State, 1993. Nobel Prize for Chemistry, 1981. *Publications:* (with R. B. Woodward) The Conservation of Orbital Symmetry, 1970; Solids and Surfaces, 1988; (with V. Torrence) Chemistry Imagined, 1993; The Same and Not the Same, 1995; (with S. Leibowitz Schmidt) Old Wine, New Flasks, 1997; *fiction:* The Metamict State (poetry), 1987; Gaps and Verges (poetry), 1990; Memory Effects (poetry), 1999; (with Carl Djerassi) Oxygen (drama), 2000; Soliton (poetry), 2002; Catalista (poetry), 2002; many scientific articles. *Address:* Department of Chemistry and Chemical Biology, Cornell University, Ithaca, NY 14853–1301, USA.

HOFMANN, Hansgeorg B.; Deputy Chairman, Kleinwort Benson Group plc, 1995–97 (Chairman, Group Executive Committee, 1997); Member, Board of Managing Directors, Dresdner Bank AG, Frankfurt, 1995–97; *b* Munich, 2 June 1943; *m* 1971, Leonor Bahner; two *s*. Merrill Lynch, London and NY, 1979–87; Shearson Lehman Hutton Internat., London, 1987–89; Dresdner Bank AG, Frankfurt, 1989–97. Non-exec. Dir, SGL Carbon AG, 1996; Co-Chm., Supervisory Bd, equinet Gp.

HOFMEYR, Murray Bernard; Member, Executive Committee, Anglo American Corporation of South Africa Limited, 1972; Chairman, Johannesburg Consolidated Investment Co. Ltd, 1987; *b* 9 Dec. 1925; *s* of William and Margareta Hofmeyr; *m* 1953, Johanna Hendrika Hofmeyr (*née* Verdurmen); two *s* two *d*. *Educ:* BA (Rhodes), MA (Oxon). Joined Anglo American Corp., 1962; in Zambia, 1965–72; in England, 1972–80; Man. Dir, 1972–76, Chm. and Man. Dir, 1976–80, Charter Consolidated Ltd. *Recreations:* golf, tennis; Captain Oxford Univ. Cricket, 1951; played Rugby for England, 1950. *Address:* 20 Pinelands, 46 First Road, Hyde Park, Johannesburg 2196, South Africa.

HOFMEYR, Stephen Murray; QC 2000; a Recorder, since 2005; *b* 10 Feb. 1956; *s* of late Jan Murray Hofmeyr and of Stella Mary Hofmeyr (*née* Mills); *m* 1980, Audrey Frances Cannan; two *s* one *d*. *Educ:* Diocesan Coll., Rondesbosch; Univ. of Cape Town (BCom, LLB); University Coll., Oxford (MA Juris.). Advocate, Supreme Court of S Africa; called to the Bar, Gray's Inn, 1982; Attorney and Conveyancer, Supreme Court of S Africa, 1984–85; in practice at the Bar, 1987–. *Recreations:* walking, ski-ing, tennis. *Address:* Acre

Holt, One Tree Hill Road, Guildford GU4 8PJ. *T:* (01483) 834733; 7 King's Bench Walk, Temple, EC4Y 7DS. *Clubs:* Vincent's (Oxford); Clandon Regis (Clandon).

HOGAN, Prof. Brigid Linda Mary, PhD; FRS 2001; George Barth Geller Professor and Chair, Department of Cell Biology, Duke University Medical Center, since 2002; *b* 28 Aug. 1943; *d* of Edmond Hogan and Joyce Hogan (*née* Willcox). *Educ:* Wycombe High Sch. for Girls; Newnham Coll., Cambridge (MA, PhD 1968). Postdoctoral Fellowship, MIT, 1968–70; Lectr, Univ. of Sussex, 1970–74; ICRF, London, 1974–84; NIMR, London, 1985–88; Prof. of Cell Biol., Vanderbilt Univ. Med. Sch., 1988–2002; Investigator, Howard Hughes Med. Inst., 1993–2002. Fellow, Amer. Acad. of Arts and Scis, 2001. *Address:* Department of Cell Biology, Duke University Medical Center, Box 3709, Durham, NC 27710, USA.

HOGAN, Michael Henry; Member, Gaming Board for Great Britain, 1986–94 (Secretary, 1980–86); *b* 31 May 1927; *s* of James Joseph Hogan and Edith Mary Hogan; *m* 1st, 1953, Nina Spillane (*d* 1974); one *s* three *d*; 2nd, 1980, Mollie Burtwell. *Educ:* Ushaw Coll.; LSE. Certif. Social Sci., Certif. Mental Health. Asst Warden, St Vincent's Probation Hostel, 1949–50; London Probation Service, 1953–61; Home Office Inspectorate, 1961–80, Chief Probation Inspector, 1972–80. *Recreation:* golf. *Address:* Yew Tree Cottage, The Street, Capel, Surrey RH5 5LD. *T:* (01306) 711523.

HOGAN, Sir Patrick, KNZM 1999; CBE 1991; Proprietor, Cambridge Stud, since 1975; *b* 20 Oct. 1939; *s* of Thomas Hogan and Sarah Margaret Small; *m* 1961, Justine Alice Heath; two *d*. *Educ:* Goodwood Sch., Cambridge, NZ; St Peter's Convent Sch., Cambridge; Marist Brothers, Hamilton. Partner, with brother, Fencourt Thoroughbred Stud, 1965–75; estabd Cambridge Stud in partnership with wife, 1975. Pres., NZ Thoroughbred Breeders Assoc., 1993–96; Dir, NZ Thoroughbred Mktg Bd, 1997–99. Patron: Cambridge Chamber of Commerce, 1990–; Equine Res. Foundn, 1992; Epilepsy Foundn of NZ Inc., 1995. Formerly Pres., Cambridge Jockey Club Inc. *Recreations:* tennis, Rugby, racing, fishing. *Address:* Discombe Road, Cambridge, New Zealand. *Clubs:* Cambridge, Hautapu Rugby Football (Cambridge); Waikato Racing (Hamilton); Auckland Racing.

HOGAN-HOWE, Bernard, QPM 2003; Chief Constable of Merseyside, since 2004; *b* 25 Oct. 1957; *s* of Bernard Howe and Cecilia Hogan-Howe; partner, Marion White. *Educ:* Hinde House Comprehensive Sch.; Merton Coll., Oxford (MA Juris.); Sheffield Univ. (MBA). Joined S Yorks Police, 1979; Dist Comdr, Doncaster W Area, 1996–97; Merseyside Police: Asst Chief Constable and Hd, Community Affairs, 1997–99; Hd, Area Ops, 1999–2001; Asst Comr, Metropolitan Police, 2001–04. Mem., Cabinet, ACPO, 2001–04. *Recreations:* horse riding, playing football, supporting Sheffield Wednesday FC, opera. *Address:* Merseyside Police Headquarters, Canning Place, Liverpool L69 1JD. *T:* (0151) 777 8000. *Club:* Athenæum (Liverpool).

HOGARTH, Adrian John; Parliamentary Counsel, since 2002; *b* 7 July 1960; *s* of late Prof. Cyril Alfred Hogarth and of Dr Audrey Hogarth, JP, DL; *m* 1996, Archana (*née* Singh). *Educ:* Magdalene Coll., Cambridge (BA Archaeol. and Anthropol. Law 1981; LLM 1982; MA). Called to the Bar, Inner Temple, 1983; Coll. Supervisor, Magdalene Coll., Cambridge, 1983–85; Asst Parly Counsel, 1985–89; Sen. Asst Parly Counsel, 1989–92; Principal Asst Parly Counsel, 1992–94, seconded to Law Commn; Dep. Parly Counsel, 1994–2002. FRSA. *Recreations:* cricket, tennis, travel, reeling. *Address:* Office of the Parliamentary Counsel, 36 Whitehall, SW1A 2AY. *Clubs:* Lansdowne; Cypos? Cricket.

HOGARTH, Andrew Allan; QC 2003; *b* 21 July 1951; *s* of late William Allan Hogarth and Margaret Hogarth; *m* 1975, Elinor Mary Williams; four *s*. *Educ:* Harrow Sch.; Trinity Coll., Cambridge (MA 1973). Called to the Bar, Lincoln's Inn, 1975; in practice as barrister, specialising in employment law, 1975–. Head of Chambers, 2005–. *Address:* 12 King's Bench Walk, Temple, EC4Y 7EL. *T:* (020) 7583 0811; *e-mail:* hogarth@12kbw.co.uk.

HOGBEN, Ven. Peter Graham; Archdeacon of Dorking, 1982–90, now Archdeacon Emeritus; *b* 5 July 1925; *s* of Harold Henry and Winifred Minnie Hogben; *m* 1948, Audree Sayers; two *s*. *Educ:* Harvey Grammar School, Folkestone; Bishops' College, Cheshunt. Served Royal Engineers, 1943–47 (three years in Far East). Office Manager for two firms of Agricultural Auctioneers in Kent and Herts, 1948–59; theological college, 1960–61; ordained, 1961; Asst Curate of Hale, 1961–64; Vicar of Westborough, Guildford, 1964–71; Chaplain to WRAC, 1964–71; Vicar of Ewell, 1971–82; Editor, Guildford Diocesan Leaflet, 1978–82; Hon. Canon of Guildford, 1979–90, Canon Emeritus, 1990. RD of Epsom, 1980–82. *Recreations:* walking, gardening, water colour painting. *Address:* 3 School Road, Rowledge, Farnham, Surrey GU10 4EJ. *T:* (01252) 793533.

HOGBIN, Ann Denise, CBE 2008; Chief Executive, Commonwealth Games England, since 1991; *b* Dover, 20 Dec. 1953; *d* of Gordon and Josephine Hogbin. *Educ:* Dover Grammar Sch. for Girls; Canterbury Tech. Coll. (Adv. Secretarial Course). Proj. Manager, British Olympic Assoc., 1973–94. Member: Team England HQ staff at Commonwealth Games, 1974, 1978, 1986, 1990; Fedn staff, Commonwealth Games, 1982; Team GB HQ staff at Olympics Games, Montreal, 1976, Seoul, 1988, Barcelona, 1992, and at Winter Olympics, Innsbruck, 1976, Sarajevo, 1984, Albertville, 1992; Gen. Team Manager, Commonwealth Games, Victoria, 1994; Chef de Mission: Team England, Commonwealth Games, Kuala Lumpur, 1998, Manchester, 2002, Melbourne, 2006; Team England, Commonwealth Youth Games, Edinburgh, 2000, Bendigo, 2004, Pune, 2008. *Recreations:* cycling, gardening, dining, cooking. *Address:* Commonwealth Games England, PO Box 36288, SE19 2YY. *T:* (020) 8676 3543, *Fax:* (020) 8676 3604.

HOGBIN, Walter, CBE 1990; FREng, FICE; Consultant, Taylor Woodrow, 1997–99; Chairman, Taylor Woodrow International Ltd, 1983–96; *b* 21 Dec. 1937; *s* of Walter Clifford John Hogbin and Mary Hogbin; *m* 1968, Geraldine Anne-Marie Castley; two *s*. *Educ:* Kent Coll., Canterbury; Queens' Coll., Cambridge (MA). Joined Taylor Woodrow, 1961; Taylor Woodrow International Ltd: Divl Dir, 1975–77; Dir, 1977–79; Man. Dir, 1979–85; Dir, 1984–96, Jt Man. Dir, 1988–92, Taylor Woodrow plc; Chm., Taylor Woodrow Construction Supervisory Bd, 1991–93. Vice-Pres., Europ. Construction Industry Fedn, 1992–94; Member: Adv. Council, ECGD, 1983–88; Overseas Projects Bd, 1986–91; Export Gp for Construction Ind., 1980–97 (Chm., 1988–90); Europ. Internat. Contractors Fedn, 1988–97 (Pres., 1994–97). Col, Engr and Logistic (formerly Transport) Staff Corps, RE, 1986–2000. FREng (FEng 1994). FRSA. Telford Gold Medal, ICE, 1979. *Recreations:* golf, gardening. *Address:* Codrington Court, Wapley Road, Chipping Sodbury, S Glos BS37 6RY. *Club:* Athenæum.

HOGG, family name of **Viscount Hailsham** and of **Baron Hogg of Cumbernauld** and **Baroness Hogg**.

HOGG, Baroness *cr* 1995 (Life Peer), of Kettlethorpe, in the county of Lincolnshire; **Sarah Elizabeth Mary Hogg, (Viscountess Hailsham);** Chairman: 3i Group plc, since 2002 (Director, since 1997; Deputy Chairman, 2000–02); Frontier Economics, since 1999; Deputy Chairman, Financial Reporting Council, since 2007 (Member, since 2004); *b* 1 May 1946; *d* of Baron Boyd-Carpenter, PC; *m* 1968, Rt Hon. Douglas Martin Hogg (*s* Viscount Hailsham); one *s* one *d*. *Educ:* St Mary's Convent, Ascot; Lady Margaret Ha Oxford University (1st Cl. Hons PPE; Hon. Fellow, 1994). Staff writer, Economist, 196 Literary Editor, 1970, Economics Editor, 1977; Economics Editor, Sunday Times, 198 Presenter, Channel 4 News, 1982–83; Econs Editor, and Dep. Exec. Editor, Finance an Industry, The Times, 1984–86; Asst Editor, and Business and City Editor, Th Independent, 1986–89; Econs Editor, Daily Telegraph and Sunday Telegraph, 1989–9 Hd, Prime Minister's Policy Unit, 1990–95; Dir, 1995–97, Chm., 1997–99, Londo Economics. Director: London Broadcasting Co., 1982–90; Royal Nat. Theatre, 1988–9 A Gov., BBC, 2000–04. Non-executive Director: Foreign and Colonial Smaller Co Investment Trust, 1995–2002 (Chm., 1997–2002); Nat. Provident Instn, 1996–99; GKN 1996–2006 (Dep. Chm., 2003–06); The Energy Group, 1996–98; Scottish Easter Investment Trust, 1998–99; Martin Currie Portfolio Investment Trust, 1999–2002; P&C 1999–2000; P&O Princess, 2000–03; Carnival Corp., 2003–08; Carnival plc, 2003–0 BG Group, 2005–. Member: Internat. Adv. Bd, Nat. Westminster Bank, 1995–98; Ad Bd, Bankinter, 1995–98. Member: House of Lords Select Cttee on Sci. and Technol 1996–99; H of L Monetary Policy and Econs Cttee, 2000–03. Member: REcon 1996–2000; Council, IFS, 1998–2005; Cemmap, 2002–04. Governor: Centre fo Economic Policy Research, 1985–92; IDS, 1987; Univ. of Lincoln, 2002–05; Fellow Eton Coll., 1996–. Hon. MA Open Univ., 1987; Hon. DLitt Loughborough, 1992; Hon LLD Lincoln, 2001; Hon. DPhil: City, 2002; Cranfield, 2006. Wincott Foundatio Financial Journalist of the Year, 1985. *Publication:* (with Jonathan Hill) Too Close to Cal 1995. *Address:* House of Lords, SW1A 0PW.

See also Hon. Sir T. P. J. Boyd-Carpenter.

HOGG OF CUMBERNAULD, Baron *cr* 1997 (Life Peer), of Cumbernauld in Nort Lanarkshire; **Norman Hogg;** a Deputy Speaker, House of Lords, 2002–05; Lord Hig Commissioner, General Assembly, Church of Scotland, 1998 and 1999; *b* 12 March 193 *s* of late Norman Hogg, CBE, LLD, DL, JP, and Mary Wilson; *m* 1964, Elizabeth McCa Christie. *Educ:* Causewayend Sch., Aberdeen; Ruthrieston Secondary Sch., Aberdeer Local Government Officer, Aberdeen Town Council, 1953–67; District Officer, Nationa and Local Govt Officers Assoc., 1967–79. MP (Lab) Dunbartonshire East, 1979–8 Cumbernauld and Kilsyth, 1983–97. Mem., Select Cttee on Scottish Affairs, 1979–8 Scottish Labour Whip, 1982–83; Chm., Scottish Parly Lab Gp, 1981–82; Dep. Chie Opposition Whip, 1983–87; Scottish Affairs spokesman, 1987–88; Member: Chairman Panel, 1988–97; Public Accounts Cttee, 1991–92. Mem., H of L Select Cttee o Delegated Powers and Regulatory Reform, 1999–2002. Chm., Bus Appeals Body, 2000– Hon. Pres., YMCA Scotland, 1998–2005; Hon. Vice Pres., CCJ, 1997–. Patron, Scottis Centre for Children with Motor Impairments, 1998–. Hon. LLD Aberdeen, 199 *Recreation:* music. *Address:* House of Lords, SW1A 0PW.

HOGG, Sir Christopher (Anthony), Kt 1985; Chairman: Financial Reporting Council since 2006; Reuters Group (formerly Reuters Holdings) PLC, 1985–2004 (Director 1984–2004); GlaxoSmithKline, 2002–04 (Director, SmithKline Beecham, subseq GlaxoSmithKline, 1993–2004); *b* 2 Aug. 1936; *s* of late Anthony Wentworth Hogg an Monica Mary (*née* Gladwell); *m* 1st, 1961, Anne Patricia (*née* Cathie) (marr. diss. 1997) two *d*; 2nd, 1997, Miriam Stoppard, *qv*. *Educ:* Marlborough Coll.; Trinity Coll., Oxfor (MA; Hon. Fellow 1982); Harvard Univ. (MBA). National Service, Parachute Regt 1955–57. Harkness Fellow, 1960–62; IMEDE, Lausanne, 1962–63; Hill, Samuel Ltd 1963–66; IRC, 1966–68; Courtaulds plc, 1968–96: Chief Exec., 1979–91; Chm. 1980–96; Chm., Courtaulds Textiles, 1990–95; Dep. Chm., 1995–96, Chm., 1996–2002 Allied Domecq. Dir, Air Liquide SA, 2000–05. Member: Indust. Develt Adv. Bd 1976–81; Cttee of Award for Harkness Fellowships, 1980–86; Internat. Council, J. P Morgan, 1988–2003; Court, Bank of England, 1992–96. Chm. Bd, RNT, 1995–2004 Trustee, Ford Foundn, 1987–99. For. Hon. Mem., Amer. Acad. of Arts and Scis, 1991 Hon. FCSD 1987; Hon. Fellow, London Business Sch., 1992; Hon. FCGI 1992. Hon DSc: Cranfield Inst. of Technol., 1986; Aston, 1988. BIM Gold Medal, 1986; Centenary Medal, Soc. of Chemical Industry, 1989; Hambro Businessman of the Year, 1993 *Publication:* Masers and Lasers, 1963. *Recreations:* grandchildren, friends, golf.

HOGG, David Alan, CB 1997; Director General, Governance & Security, HM Revenue and Customs, since 2008; *b* 8 Oct. 1946; *s* of Donald Kenneth Hogg and Alwyn Liliar Hogg (*née* Chinchen); *m* 1st, 1969, Geraldine Patricia Smith (marr. diss. 1979); one *s* one *d*; 2nd, 1981, Pauline Pamela Papworth; two *s*. *Educ:* Brighton Coll.; Coll. of Law Admitted solicitor, 1969; in private practice, 1969–78; Treasury Solicitor's Department Sen. Legal Asst, 1978–85; Asst Treasury Solicitor, 1985–89; Dept of Energy, 1989–90 Treasury Solicitor's Department: Principal Asst Solicitor and Hd, Litigation Div. 1990–93; Dep. Treasury Solicitor, 1993–97; Solicitor and Legal Adviser: DETR 1997–2001; DTLR, 2001–02; ODPM and Dept for Transport, 2002–03; ODPM 2003–04; Actg Solicitor, HM Customs and Excise, 2004–05; Gen. Counsel and Solicitor HM Revenue and Customs, 2005–08. *Recreations:* inland waterways, theatre, reading watching sport. *Address:* HM Revenue and Customs, 100 Parliament Street, SW1A 2BQ.

HOGG, Prof. Dorothy, MBE 2001; Professor, 2004–07, and Head, Jewellery and Silversmithing Department, 1985–2007, Edinburgh College of Art, now Professor Emeritus; craft artist in residence, Victoria and Albert Museum, 2008; *b* 19 May 1945; *d* of William Hogg and Alice Hogg (*née* Murdoch); *m* 1973, Lachlan MacColl; one *s*. *Educ:* Glasgow Sch. of Art (Dip of Art); Royal Coll. of Art (Master of Design, Silver Medal for work of special distn); Moray House Coll. of Educn, Edinburgh (CertEd). Freelance designer, 1970–; Lecturer: Glasgow Sch. of Art, 1972–73; Duncan of Jordanstone Coll. of Art, 1974–85; Lectr, 1985–98, Reader, 1998–2004, Edinburgh Coll. of Art. External examr, UK instns. Chm. Contemp. Cttee, and Trustee, Scottish Goldsmiths Trust, 2000–05; Purchase Advr, 1997–2001, and Selected Index Advr, 2000–03, Crafts Council, London; Specialist Advr, Scottish Arts Council, 2003–05. Solo retrospective exhibn, Scottish Gall., Edinburgh, 1994; many group exhibns, UK, Germany, Italy, Japan and USA, 1967–. Work in public and private collections incl. Royal Mus. of Scotland, Crafts Council, Goldsmiths' Co., Aberdeen Art Gall. and Mus., Koch Ring Collection, V&A, and Mus. of Arts and Design, NY. Freeman, City of London, 1998; Mem., Incorporation of Goldsmiths, City of Edinburgh, 1992; Freeman, Co. of Goldsmiths, London, 1997. FRSA 2007. Hon. FRCA 2006. *Recreations:* drawing, gardening, golf. *Address:* c/o The Scottish Gallery, 16 Dundas Street, Edinburgh EH3 6H2. *T:* (0131) 558 1200, *Fax:* (0131) 558 3900; *e-mail:* dorothy_hogg@hotmail.com.

HOGG, Gilbert Charles; author, since 2000; *b* 11 Feb. 1933; *s* of Charles and Ivy Ellen Hogg; *m* 1st, Jeanne Whiteside; one *s* one *d*; 2nd, 1979, Angela Christina Wallace. *Educ:* Victoria University Coll., Wellington, NZ (LLB 1956). Called to the New Zealand Bar and admitted Solicitor, 1957; admitted Solicitor, GB, 1971. Served RNZAC (TF), 1955–62 (Lieut). Partner, Phillips, Shayle-George and Co., Solicitors, Wellington, 1960–66; Sen. Crown Counsel, Hong Kong, 1966–70; Editor, Business Law Summary, 1970–73; Divl Legal Adviser, BSC, 1974–79; British Gas Corporation, subseq. British Gas: Dir of Legal Services, 1979–84; Sec., 1984–90; Dir, Regulatory Ops, 1990–95; solicitor and regulatory consultant, 1995–2000. Mem., Competition Commn (formerly Monopolies and Mergers Commn), 1998–2003. Mem., Professional Ethics Cttee, 1994–97, and Council, Energy Section, 1993–98, Internat. Bar Assoc. Chairman: Phoenix House, 1996–2004; Charterhouse-in-Southwark, 1999–2004; Trustee, IBA Educn Trust, 1995–98. *Publications:* Teaching Yourself Tranquillity, 2005; *novels:* A Smell of Fraud, 1974; The Predators, 2002; Caring for Cathy, 2008. *Address:* 73 Ellerby Street, SW6 6EU. *T:* (020) 7736 8903.

HOGG, Hon. Dame Mary (Claire), (Hon. Dame Mary Koops), DBE 1995; **Hon. Mrs Justice Hogg;** a Judge of the High Court of Justice, Family Division, since 1995; *b* 15 Jan. 1947; *d* of Rt Hon. Baron Hailsham of St Marylebone, PC, KG, CH, FRS; *m* 1987, Eric Koops (LVO 1997); one *s* one *d. Educ:* St Paul's Girls' Sch. Called to the Bar, Lincoln's Inn, 1968 (Bencher, 1995), NI, 1993; QC 1989; Asst Recorder, 1986–90; Recorder, 1990–95. Mem. Council, Children's Soc., 1990–95; Trustee, Harrison Homes, 1983–. Gov., Univ. of Westminster, 1992– (Poly. of Central London, 1983–92). FRSA 1991. Freeman, City of London, 1981. Hon. LLD Westminster, 1995. *Address:* Royal Courts of Justice, Strand, WC2A 2LL.
See also Viscount Hailsham.

HOGG, Sir Michael Edward L.; *see* Lindsay-Hogg.

HOGG, Sir Piers Michael James, 9th Bt cr 1846, of Upper Grosvenor Street, Middlesex; *b* 25 April 1957; *e s* of Sir Michael Hogg, 8th Bt and of Elizabeth Anne Thérèse, *e d* of Sir Terence Falkiner, 8th Bt; *S* father, 2001; *m* 1982, Vivien (marr. diss. 1996), *y d* of Dr Philip Holman; one *s* one *d. Educ:* St Paul's Sch. *Heir:* s James Edward Hogg, *b* 11 Sept. 1985.

HOGG, Rear-Adm. Robin Ivor Trower, CB 1988; FNI; Managing Director: Raidfleet Ltd, since 1988; Shinbond Ltd, since 1998; Robstar Productions Ltd, since 1998; *b* 25 Sept. 1932; *s* of Dudley and Nancy Hogg; *m* 1st, 1958, Susan Bridget Beryl Grantham; two *s* two *d;* 2nd, 1970, Angela Sarah Patricia Kirwan. *Educ:* The New Beacon, Sevenoaks; Bedford School. Directorate of Naval Plans, 1974–76; RCDS 1977; Captain RN Presentation Team, 1978–79; Captain First Frigate Sqdn, 1980–82; Director Naval Operational Requirements, 1982–84; Flag Officer, First Flotilla, 1984–86; COS to C-in-C Fleet, 1986–87, retd. CEO, Colebrand Ltd, 1988–97. Chm., CPRE for Plymouth and South Hams, 2007–. FCMI; FRSA. *Recreation:* private life. *Address:* c/o Barclays Bank, Blenheim Gate, 22/24 Upper Marlborough Road, St Albans AL1 3AL. *T:* (01727) 863315.

HOGGARD, Robin Richard; Director of External Relations, London School of Economics and Political Science, since 2007; *b* 26 Nov. 1956; *s* of George Lawrence Hoggard and Frances Mary Christine Hoggard (*née* Stephenson); *m* 1988, Tonoko Komuro; one *s. Educ:* Cheadle Hulme Sch.; Univ. of Newcastle upon Tyne (BA Hons Politics 1979); SOAS, Univ. of London (MSc 1982). HM Diplomatic Service, 1982–2007; FCO, 1982; Tokyo, 1984–89; FCO, 1989–91; DTI, 1991–93; UK Deleg. to NATO, 1994–98; Counsellor (Mgt) and Consul Gen., Tokyo, 1998–2003; Counsellor, FCO, 2003–04; Hd of Res. Analysts, FCO, 2004–07. *Address:* London School of Economics and Political Science, Houghton Street, WC2A 2AE.

HOGGART, Richard (Herbert), LittD; Warden, Goldsmiths' College, University of London, 1976–84; *b* 24 Sept. 1918; 2nd *s* of Tom Longfellow Hoggart and Adeline Emma Hoggart; *m* 1942, Mary Holt France; two *s* one *d. Educ:* elementary and secondary schs, Leeds; Leeds Univ. (MA, LittD 1978). Served 1940–46, RA; demobilised as Staff Capt. Staff Tutor and Sen. Staff Tutor, University Coll. of Hull and University of Hull, 1946–59; Sen. Lectr in English, University of Leicester, 1959–62; Prof. of English, Birmingham Univ., 1962–73, and Dir, Centre for Contemporary Cultural Studies, 1964–73; an Asst Dir-Gen., Unesco, 1970–75. Vis. Fellow, Inst. of Development Studies, Univ. of Sussex, 1975. Visiting Prof., University of Rochester (NY), USA, 1956–57; Chichele Lectr, All Souls Coll., Oxford 1961; Reith Lectr, 1971. Member: Albemarle Cttee on Youth Services, 1958–60; (Pilkington) Cttee on Broadcasting, 1960–62; Arts Council, 1976–81 (Chm., Drama Panel, 1977–80; Vice-Chm., 1980–82); Statesman and Nation Publishing Co. Ltd, 1977–81 (Chm., 1978–81); Chairman: Adv. Council for Adult and Continuing Educn, 1977–83; European Museum of the Year Award, 1977–95; Broadcasting Research Unit, 1981–91; Book Trust, 1995–97 (Vice-Chm., 1997–); Vice-Chm., Unesco Forum, 1997–; Patron, Nat. Book Cttee, 1998–. Governor, Royal Shakespeare Theatre, 1962–88. Pres., British Assoc. of Former UN Civil Servants, 1979–86. Hon. Professor: UEA, 1984; Univ. of Surrey, 1985; Hon. Fellow: Sheffield Polytechnic, 1983; Goldsmiths' Coll., 1987; DUniv: Open, 1973; Surrey, 1981; Hon DèsL: Univ. of Bordeaux, 1975; Paris, 1987; Hon. LLD: CNAA, 1982; York (Toronto), 1988; Sheffield, 1999; Hon. LittD East Anglia, 1986; Hon. DLitt: Leicester, 1988; Hull, 1988; Keele, 1995; Leeds Metropolitan, 1995; Westminster, 1996; East London, 1998; London Metropolitan, 2003; Hon. DLit London, 2000. *Publications:* Auden, 1951; The Uses of Literacy, 1957; W. H. Auden, 1957; W. H. Auden—A Selection, 1961; chap. in Conviction, 1958; chapter in Pelican Guide to English Literature, 1961; Teaching Literature, 1963; chapter in Of Books and Humankind, 1964; The Critical Moment, 1964; How and Why Do We Learn, 1965; The World in 1984, 1965; Essays by Divers Hands XXXIII; Guide to the Social Sciences, 1966; Technology and Society, 1966; Essays on Reform, 1967; Your Sunday Paper (ed), 1967; Speaking to Each Other: vol. I, About Society; vol. II, About Literature, 1970; Only Connect (Reith Lectures), 1972; An Idea and Its Servants, 1978; (ed with Janet Morgan) The Future of Broadcasting, 1982; An English Temper, 1982; (ed) The Public Service Idea in British Broadcasting: main principles, 1986; Writers on Writing, 1986; (jtly) The British Council and The Arts, 1986; (with Douglas Johnson) An Idea of Europe, 1987; A Local Habitation (autobiog.), 1988; (ed) Liberty and Legislation, 1989; (ed) Quality in Television: programmes, programme makers, systems, 1989; A Sort of Clowning: life and times 1940–59 (autobiog.), 1990; An Imagined Life: life and times 1959–91 (autobiog.), 1992; Townscape with Figures, 1994; The Way We Live Now, 1995; First and Last Things, 1999; Richard Hoggart en France (essays), ed J.-C. Passeron, 1999; Between Two Worlds, 2001; Everyday Language and Everyday Life, 2003; Mass Media in a Mass Society: myth and reality, 2004; Promises to Keep: thoughts in old age, 2005; numerous introductions, articles, pamphlets and reviews. *Recreation:* pottering.
See also S. D. Hoggart.

HOGGART, Simon David; Parliamentary Reporter, The Guardian, since 1993; *b* 26 May 1946; *s* of Richard Hoggart, *qv; m* 1983, Alyson Clare Corner; one *s* one *d. Educ:* Hymer's College, Hull; Wyggeston Grammar Sch., Leicester; King's College, Cambridge. MA. Reporter, The Guardian, 1968–71, N Ireland corresp., 1971–73, political corresp., 1973–81; feature writer, The Observer, 1981–85; political columnist, Punch, 1979–85; US correspondent, 1985–89, columnist, 1989–92, Political Editor, 1992–93, The Observer; television critic, 2000–, wine corresp., 2001–, The Spectator. Chairman, The News Quiz, Radio 4, 1996–2006. *Publications:* (with Alistair Michie) The Pact, 1978; (with David Leigh) Michael Foot: a portrait, 1981; On the House, 1981; Back on the House, 1982; House of Ill Fame, 1985; (ed) House of Cards, 1988; America: a user's guide, 1990; House of Correction, 1994; (with Michael Hutchinson) Bizarre Beliefs, 1995; (with Steve Bell) Live Briefs, 1996; Playing to the Gallery, 2002; Punch Lines, 2003; The Cat

That Could Open the Fridge, 2004; The Hamster That Loved Puccini, 2005; (with Emily Monk) Dear Mum, 2006; The Hands of History, 2007; The Christmas Letters, 2007. *Recreations:* reading, writing, wine. *Address:* Parliamentary Press Gallery, House of Commons, SW1A 0AA. *T:* (020) 7219 4700; *e-mail:* simon.hoggart@guardian.co.uk.

HOGGER, Henry George, CMG 2004; HM Diplomatic Service, retired; Senior Consultant, MEC International Ltd, since 2005; *b* 9 Nov. 1948; *s* of late Rear-Adm. Henry Charles Hogger, CB, DSC and Ethel Mary Hogger; *m* 1972, Fiona Jane McNabb; two *s* two *d. Educ:* Winchester Coll.; Trinity Hall, Cambridge (MA Hons). Joined FCO 1969; MECAS, Lebanon, 1971–72; served Aden, Caracas, Kuwait; FCO, 1978–82; Head of Chancery, Abu Dhabi, 1982–86; FCO, 1986–89; Counsellor and Dep. Head of Mission, Amman, 1989–92; High Comr, Namibia, 1992–96; Head, Latin America, later Latin America and Caribbean Dept, FCO, 1996–2000; Ambassador to Syria, 2000–03; Governorate Co-ordinator for Basra, Coalition Provisional Authy, Iraq, 2003–04 (on secondment). Member: Inst. of Advanced Motorists; RGS. *Recreations:* golf, sailing, music, travel. *Address:* Shop Farm House, Briantspuddle, Dorchester, Dorset DT2 7HY.

HOGGETT, Anthony John Christopher, PhD; QC 1986; a Recorder, 1988–2006; *b* 20 Aug. 1940; *s* of late Christopher Hoggett and Annie Marie Hoggett; *m* 1968, Brenda Marjorie Hale (*see* Baroness Hale of Richmond) (marr. diss. 1992); one *d. Educ:* Leeds Grammar Sch.; Hymers Coll., Hull; Clare Coll., Cambridge (MA, LLB); PhD Manchester. Asst Juridique, Inst. of Comparative Law, Paris, 1962–63; Lectr in Law, Univ. of Manchester, 1963–69; called to Bar, Gray's Inn, 1969, Head of Chambers, 1985–96; Asst Recorder, 1982. Res. Fellow, Univ. of Michigan, 1965–66. Mem., Civil Service Final Selection Bd for Planning Inspectors, 1987–91. Dir, Europ. Youth Parlt Internat., 1993–2003. Mem. Adv. Council, Rural Bldgs Preservation Trust, 1994–2002 (Trustee, 2000–02). Mem. Editl Bd, Envmtl Law Reports, 1992–2006. *Publications:* articles in Criminal Law Rev., Mod. Law Rev. and others. *Recreations:* swimming, music. *Address:* Kings Chambers, 36 Young Street, Manchester M3 3FT.

HOGWOOD, Christopher Jarvis Haley, CBE 1989; harpsichordist, conductor, musicologist, writer, editor and broadcaster; Founder and Director, Academy of Ancient Music, 1973–2006, now Emeritus Director; *b* 10 Sept. 1941; *s* of Haley Evelyn Hogwood and Marion Constance Higgott. *Educ:* Pembroke Coll., Cambridge (MA; Hon. Fellow, 1992); Charles Univ., Prague. With Acad. of St Martin-in-the-Fields, 1965–76; Founder Mem., Early Music Consort of London, 1965–76; Artistic Director: King's Lynn Festival, 1976–80; Handel & Haydn Soc., Boston, USA, 1986–2001 (Conductor Laureate, 2001–); Summer Mozart Fest., Nat. Symphony Orch., USA, 1993–2001; Dir of Music, St Paul Chamber Orchestra, USA, 1987–92, Prin. Guest Conductor, 1992–98; Associate Dir, Beethoven Academie, Antwerp, 1998–2002; Principal Guest Conductor: Kammerorchester Basel, 2000–06; Orquesta Ciudad de Granada, 2001–04; Orch. Sinfonica di Milano Giuseppe Verdi, 2003–06. Internat. Prof. of Early Music Performance, RAM, 1992–; Vis. Prof., KCL, 1992–96; Hon. Prof. of Music, Keele Univ., 1986–90. Keyboard and orchestral recordings. Mem. Editl Bd, Early Music, 1993–97; Chm. Adv. Bd, C. P. E. Bach Complete Works, 1999–. Freeman, Co. of Musicians, 1989. FRSA 1982. Hon. RAM 1995; Hon. Fellow, Jesus Coll., Cambridge, 1989. Hon. DMus: Keele, 1991; Cambridge, 2008. Walter Willson Cobbett Medal, Co. of Musicians, 1986; Distinguished Musician Award, ISM, 1997; Martinu Medal, Bohuslav Martinu Foundn, Prague, 1999; Handel Prize, Halle, Germany, 2008. *Publications:* Music at Court (Folio Society), 1977; The Trio Sonata, 1979; Haydn's Visits to England (Folio Society), 1980; (ed with R. Luckett) Music in Eighteenth-Century England, 1983; Handel, 1984, rev. edn 2007; (ed) Holmes' Life of Mozart (Folio Society), 1991; (ed) The Keyboard in Baroque Europe, 2003; Handel: Water Music and Music for the Royal Fireworks, 2005. *Address:* 10 Brookside, Cambridge CB2 1JE. *T:* (01223) 363975; *e-mail:* chogwood@compuserve.com.

HOLBOROW, Eric John, MD, FRCP, FRCPath; Emeritus Professor of Immunopathology and Honorary Consultant Immunologist, London Hospital Medical College, E1, retired 1983; *b* 30 March 1918; *s* of Albert Edward Ratcliffe Holborow and Marian Crutchley; *m* 1943, Cicely Mary Foister; two *s* one *d. Educ:* Epsom Coll.; Clare Coll., Cambridge; St Bart's Hosp. MA, MD (Cantab). Served War of 1939–45, Major, RAMC. Consultant Bacteriologist, Canadian Hosp., Taplow, 1953; Mem. Scientific Staff, MRC Rheumatism Unit, Taplow, 1957; Director, 1975; Head, MRC Group, Bone and Joint Res. Unit, London Hosp. Med. Coll., 1976–83. Visiting Prof., Royal Free Hosp. Med. Sch., 1975. Bradshaw Lectr, RCP, 1982. Chm., Smith Kline Foundn, 1987–89 (Trustee, 1977–89). Editor, Jl Immunol. Methods, 1971–85. *Publications:* Autoimmunity and Disease (with L. E. Glynn), 1965; An ABC of Modern Immunology, 1968, 2nd edn 1973; (with W. G. Reeves) Immunology in Medicine, 1977, 2nd edn 1983; (with A. Maroudas) Studies in Joint Disease, vol. 1, 1981, vol. 2, 1983; Fingest: stony ground (local history), 1999; books and papers on immunology. *Recreations:* glebe terriers, ecclesiastical records.
See also J. Holborow.

HOLBOROW, Jonathan; Editor, Mail on Sunday, 1992–98; Member, Editorial Integrity Board, Express Newspapers, 2000–02; *b* 12 Oct. 1943; *s* of Prof. Eric John Holborow, *qv* and Cicely Mary (*née* Foister); *m* 1st, 1965, Susan Ridings (*d* 1993); one *s* one *d;* 2nd, 1994, Vivien Ferguson. *Educ:* Charterhouse. Reporter, Maidenhead Advertiser, 1961–65; Lincs Echo, 1965–66; Lincoln Chronicle, 1966–67; Daily Mail, Manchester, 1967–69; Scottish News Editor, Daily Mail, Glasgow, 1969–70; Daily Mail, Manchester: Northern Picture Editor, 1970–72; Northern News Editor, 1972–74; Daily Mail, London: Dep. News Editor, 1974–75; News Editor, 1975–80; Editor, Cambrian News, Aberystwyth, 1980–82; Asst Editor, then Associate Editor, Mail on Sunday, 1982–86; Dep. Editor, Today, 1986–87; Daily Mail: Asst Editor, then Associate Editor, 1987–88; Dep. Editor, 1988–92; Dir, Associated Newspapers Ltd, 1992–98. Chm., Folkestone and Hythe Cons. Assoc., 2004–. *Recreation:* golf.

HOLBOROW, Prof. Leslie Charles, MA; Vice-Chancellor, Victoria University of Wellington, 1985–98, now Emeritus Professor, and Senior Fellow, Centre for Strategic Studies, since 2003; *b* 28 Jan. 1941; *s* of George and Ivah Vivienne Holborow; *m* 1965, Patricia Lynette Walsh; one *s* two *d. Educ:* Henderson High Sch.; Auckland Grammar Sch.; Univ. of Auckland (MA 1st Cl. Hons Philosophy); Oxford Univ. (BPhil). Jun. Lectr, Auckland Univ., 1963; Commonwealth schol. at Merton Coll., Oxford, 1963–65; Lectr, then Sen. Lectr, Univ. of Dundee (until 1967 Queen's Coll., Univ. of St Andrews), 1965–74, Mem. Court, 1972–74; University of Queensland, Brisbane: Prof. of Philosophy, 1974–85; Pres., Academic Bd, 1980–81; Pro-Vice-Chancellor (Humanities), 1983–85. Pres., Qld Br., Aust. Inst. of Internat. Affairs, 1984–85; Nat. Pres., 1987–90; Mem., Standing Cttee, 2002–; NZ Inst. of Internat. Affairs; Member: NZ Cttee for Pacific Economic Co-operation, 1986–97; Bd, Inst. of Policy Studies, 1986–98; Bd, NZ Inst. of Econ. Res., 1986–91; Bd, Victoria Univ. Foundn, 1990–98; NZ Cttee for Security Co-operation in Asia Pacific, 1994–. Chair: NZ Vice-Chancellors' Cttee, 1990, 1996; Cttee on Univ. Academic Progs, 1993–95; Bd, NZ Univs Acad. Audit Unit, 2003–08; Member: Council, ACU, 1990–91, 1996; Educn Sub-Commn, UNESCO Commn for NZ,

1997–2000. Member: Musica Viva Nat. Bd, 1984–85; Bd of Management, Music Fedn of NZ, 1987–90. Trustee: NZ String Quartet, 1990–; Lilburn Residence Trust, 2005–; Chm., NZ String Quartet Foundn, 1999–. Hon. LLD Victoria Univ. of Wellington, 1998. *Publications:* articles on NZ foreign policy, opera reviews, contrib. philosophical and legal jls. *Recreations:* tramping, golf, listening to music. *Address:* 16 Ames Street, Paekakariki, Wellington, New Zealand. *Clubs:* Wellington, Victoria University Staff (Wellington).

HOLBOROW, Lady Mary (Christina); JP; Lord-Lieutenant of Cornwall, since 1994; *b* 19 Sept. 1936; *d* of 8th Earl of Courtown, OBE, TD, DL, and Christina Margaret Tremlett (*née* Cameron); *m* 1959, Geoffrey Jermyn Holborow, OBE; one *s* one *d*. *Educ:* Tudor Hall Sch., Banbury. Mem., Regional Board, TSB, 1981–89; Director: SW Water, 1989–95; Devon and Cornwall TEC, 1990–96; TSW Broadcasting, 1990–91. Vice-Chm., Cornwall and Isles of Scilly HA, 1990–2000; SW Regl Chm., FEFC, 1993–94; Chairman: Cornwall Macmillan Service, 1982–2002; Cornwall Rural Develt Cttee, 1987–99. Patron or Pres., numerous charitable orgns in Cornwall. Hon. LLD Exeter, 1997. JP Cornwall 1970. DStJ 1987 (Comr, St John Ambulance, 1982–87). *Address:* The Coach House, Ladock, Truro, Cornwall TR2 4PL. *T:* (01726) 882274.

HOLBROOK, David Kenneth, FEA; author; *b* 9 Jan. 1923; *o s* of late Kenneth Redvers and late Elsie Eleanor Holbrook; *m* 1949, Margot Davies-Jones; two *s* two *d*. *Educ:* City of Norwich Sch.; Downing Coll., Cambridge (Exhibr). Intell., mines and explosives officer, ER Yorks Yeo., Armd Corps, 1942–45. Asst Editor, Our Time, 1948; Asst Editor, Bureau of Current Affairs, 1949; Tutor organiser, WEA, 1952–53; Tutor, Bassingbourn Village Coll., Cambs, 1954–61; Fellow, King's Coll., Cambridge, 1961–65; Sen. Leverhulme Res. Fellow, 1965; College Lectr in English, Jesus Coll., Cambridge, 1968–70; Compton Poetry Lectr, Hull Univ., 1969 (resigned); Writer in Residence, Dartington Hall, 1970–73 (grant from Elmgrant Trust); Downing Coll., Cambridge: Asst Dir, English Studies, 1973–75; Fellow and Dir of English Studies, 1981–88, Emeritus Fellow, 1988–; Leverhulme Emeritus Res. Fellow, 1988–90. Hooker Distinguished Vis. Prof., McMaster Univ., Ontario, 1984. Founding FEA 2000. Arts Council Writers Grants, 1970, 1976, 1979. Mem. Editorial Bd, New Universities Qly, 1976–86. *Publications: poetry:* Imaginings, 1961; Against the Cruel Frost, 1963; Object Relations, 1967; Old World, New World, 1969; Moments in Italy, 1976; Chance of a Lifetime, 1978; Selected Poems, 1980; Bringing Everything Home, 1999; *fiction:* Lights in the Sky Country, 1963; Flesh Wounds, 1966; A Play of Passion, 1978; Nothing Larger than Life, 1987; Worlds Apart, 1988; A Little Athens, 1990; Jennifer, 1991; The Gold in Father's Heart, 1992; Even If They Fail, 1994; Getting it Wrong with Uncle Tom, 1998; Going Off the Rails, 2003; *on education:* English for Maturity, 1961; English for the Rejected, 1964; The Secret Places, 1964; The Exploring Word, 1967; Children's Writing, 1967; English in Australia Now, 1972; Education, Nihilism and Survival, 1977; English for Meaning, 1980; Education and Philosophical Anthropology, 1987; Further Studies in Philosophical Anthropology, 1988; English in a University Education, 2006; *literary criticism:* Llareggub Revisited, 1962; The Quest for Love, 1965; The Masks of Hate, 1972; Dylan Thomas: the code of night, 1972; Sylvia Plath: poetry and existence, 1976; Lost Bearings in English Poetry, 1977; The Novel and Authenticity, 1987; Images of Woman in Literature, 1989; The Skeleton in the Wardrobe: the fantasies of C. S. Lewis, 1991; Edith Wharton and the Unsatisfactory Man, 1991; Where D. H. Lawrence was Wrong about Woman, 1991; Charles Dickens and The Image of Woman, 1993; Tolstoy, Women and Death, 1997; Wuthering Heights: a drama of being, 1997; A Study of George MacDonald and the Image of Woman, 2000; Lewis Carroll: nonsense against sorrow, 2001; Jane Austen and the Authentic Choice, 2008; *music criticism:* Gustav Mahler and the Courage to Be, 1975; *general:* Children's Games, 1957; Human Hope and the Death Instinct, 1971; Sex and Dehumanization, 1972; The Pseudo-revolution, 1972; (ed) The Case Against Pornography, 1972; Evolution and the Humanities, 1987; (ed) What is it to be Human?: report on a philosophy conference, 1990; Creativity and Popular Culture, 1994; *anthologies:* edited: Iron, Honey, Gold, 1961; People and Diamonds, 1962; Thieves and Angels, 1963; Visions of Life, 1964; (with Elizabeth Poston) The Cambridge Hymnal, 1967; Plucking the Rushes, 1968; (with Christine Mackenzie) The Honey of Man, 1975; *opera libretti:* (with Wilfrid Mellers) Mary Easter, 1957 and The Borderline, 1958, published as Two Scripts for Plays in Music, 2004; (with John Joubert) The Quarry, 1967; *festschrift:* Powers of Being: David Holbrook and his work, ed E. Webb, 1996. *Recreations:* painting, cooking. *Address:* 1 Tennis Court Terrace, Cambridge CB2 1QX.

HOLBROOKE, Richard Charles; Counselor, Council on Foreign Relations, since 2001; United States Representative to the United Nations, 1999–2001; *b* 2 April 1941; *s* of Dan Holbrooke and Trudi (*née* Moos); two *s*; *m* 1995, Kati Marton. *Educ:* Brown Univ. (BA). Foreign Service Officer in Vietnam and related posts, 1962–66; White House Vietnam staff, 1966–67; Special Asst to Under Secs of State Nicholas Katzenbach and Elliot Richardson, and Mem., US Delegn to Paris peace talks on Vietnam, 1967–69; Dir, Peace Corps, Morocco, 1970–72; Man. Dir, Foreign Policy mag., 1972–76; Consultant, President's Commn on Orgn of Govt for Conduct of Foreign Policy, 1974–75; Contrib. Ed., Newsweek, 1974–75; Co-ordinator, Nat. Security Affairs, Carter-Mondale Campaign, 1976; Asst Sec. of State for E Asian and Pacific Affairs, 1977–81; Vice-Pres., Public Strategies, 1981–85; Man. Dir, Lehman Bros, 1985–93; Ambassador to Germany, 1993–94; Asst Sec. of State for Eur. and Canadian Affairs, 1994–96; Vice-Chm., Credit Suisse First Boston Corp., 1996–99; Advr, Baltic Sea Council, 1996–97; Special Presidential Envoy for Cyprus, to Yugoslavia, 1997–98. Numerous hon. degrees, including: Maryland, and Heidelberg, 1994; Georgetown, 1996; Amer. Univ. of Paris, 1996; Central Euro-Atlantic Bucaresti, Romania, 1996; Tufts, 1997; Brown, 1997; Amer. Univ. in Athens, 1998; Lawrence, 1998; Dayton, 1998. Dist. Public Service Award, Dept of Defense, 1994 and 1996; Excellence in Diplomacy Award, Amer. Acad. of Diplomacy, 1996; Gold Medal for Dist. Service to Humanity, Nat. Inst. of Social Scis, 1996; Citation of Honor, USAF Assoc., 1996; Nahum Goldmann Award, World Jewish Congress, 1996; America's First Freedom Award, 1996; Sec. of State's Dist. Service Award, 1996; Manfred Woerner Award, FRG, 1997; Humanitarian of Year Award, American Jewish Congress, 1998; Nat. Diplomatic Award, Foreign Policy Assoc., 1998; Community Service Award, Mt Sinai Med. Center, 1999. *Publications:* (jtly) Counsel to the President, 1991; To End a War, 1998; contrib. various articles and essays. *Recreations:* tennis, ski-ing. *Address:* Council on Foreign Relations, 58 East 68th Street, New York, NY 10021, USA. *T:* (212) 4349644.

HOLCROFT, Sir Peter (George Culcheth), 3rd Bt *cr* 1921; JP; *b* 29 April 1931; *s* of Sir Reginald Culcheth Holcroft, 2nd Bt, TD, and Mary Frances (*d* 1963), *yr d* of late William Swire, CBE; *S* father, 1978; *m* 1956, Rosemary Rachel (marr. diss. 1987), *yr d* of late G. N. Deas; three *s* one *d*. *Educ:* Eton. High Sheriff of Shropshire, 1969; JP 1976. *Recreation:* the countryside. *Heir:* *s* Charles Antony Culcheth Holcroft [*b* 22 Oct. 1959; *m* 1986, Mrs Elizabeth Carter, *y d* of John Raper, Powys; one *s* one *d*]. *Address:* Appartado de Correos 223, 07210 Algaida, Mallorca, Spain.

HOLDAWAY, Prof. Richard, PhD; FREng; Director, Space Science and Technology, Science and Technology Facilities Council (formerly Council for the Central Laboratory of the Research Councils), since 1998; *b* 22 Feb. 1949; *s* of Maurice Holdaway and Margaret Holdaway; two *s*. *Educ:* Univ. of Southampton (BSc Aeronautics/Astronautic Engrg 1970; PhD Astrodynamics 1974). Design Engr, Harrier, Hawker Siddeley Aviation 1970; Proj. Engr, Appleton Lab., 1974–80; Project Engr, then Div. Head (Space) Rutherford Appleton Lab., 1980–98. Visiting Professor: Univ. of Southampton, 1995–; Univ. of Kent, 1996–; Beijing Univ. of Aeronautics and Astronautics, 2006–. FAIAA 1996; FREng 2001. *Publications:* 80 jtly edited books and articles on space technology. *Recreations:* sport (squash, soccer, hockey), season ticket holder and fanatical supporter of Portsmouth Football Club. *Address:* Rutherford Appleton Laboratory, Chilton, Didcot Oxon OX11 0QX. *T:* (01235) 445527, *Fax:* (01235) 446640; *e-mail:* r.holdaway@rl.ac.uk.

HOLDEN, Amanda Juliet; musician, writer; *b* 19 Jan. 1948; *d* of Sir Brian Warren and Dame Josephine Barnes, DBE; *m* 1971, Anthony Holden, *qv* (marr. diss. 1988); three *s*. *Educ:* Benenden Sch.; Lady Margaret Hall, Oxford (MA); Guildhall Sch. of Music and Drama (LGSM); American Univ., Washington (Hall of Nations Schol.; MA); ARCM, LRAM. Music staff: St Michael's Comprehensive, Watford, 1970–72; Watford Sch. of Music, 1971–75; Guildhall Sch., 1973–87; Founder, Music Therapy Dept, Charing Cross Hosp., London, 1973–75. Mem., Opera Adv. Bd, Royal Opera House, 1998; Advr, Opera Genesis Prog., ROH2, 2006–. Has translated *c* 60 opera libretti, 1985–, including Les Boréades (Rameau), Armide (Gluck), Agrippina, Alcina, Ariodante, Partenope (Handel), La finta giardiniera, Il re pastore, Idomeneo, Die Entführung, The Marriage of Figaro, Don Giovanni, The Magic Flute, La Clemenza di Tito, The Barber of Seville, La Cenerentola, l'Elisir d'amore, Maria Stuarda, Lucia di Lammermoor, Beatrice and Benedict, The Bartered Bride, Lohengrin, Rigoletto, A Masked Ball, Aida, Falstaff, Faust, The Pearl Fishers, The Fair Maid of Perth, Carmen, Werther, La Bohème, Tosca, Madam Butterfly, Il Trittico, Francesca da Rimini (Rachmaninov), Volo di notte (Dallapiccola), Experimentum Mundi (Battistelli); *cartoon film script:* Rhinegold, 1995; *play translation* Kleist, Amphitryon; *adaptations for concert hall:* The Epic of Gilgamesh (Martinu); Der Freischütz; *libretti:* The Selfish Giant (after Wilde); The Silver Tassie (after O'Casey) (Outstanding Achievement in Opera (jtly), Laurence Olivier Awards, 2001); Family Matters (after Beaumarchais), The Piano Tuner; Bliss (after Peter Carey). *Publications:* The Magic Flute (arr. for children), 1990; (contrib.) The Mozart Compendium, 1990; (trans.) Lohengrin, 1993; (ed) The Viking Opera Guide, 1993; (ed) The Penguin Opera Guide, 1995, 2nd edn 1997; (ed) The New Penguin Opera Guide, 2001; The Penguin Concise Guide to Opera, 2005. *Recreations:* swimming, singing (London Symphony Chorus). *Address:* Bank Cottage, Cley-next-the-Sea, Holt, Norfolk NR25 7RN.

HOLDEN, Anthony Ivan; writer; *b* 22 May 1947; *s* of late John Holden and Margaret Lois Holden (*née* Sharpe); *m* 1st, 1971, Amanda Juliet Warren (*see* A. J. Holden) (marr. diss. 1988); three *s*; 2nd, 1990, Cynthia Blake, *d* of Mrs George Blake, Brookline, Mass. *Educ:* Tre-Arddur House Sch., Anglesey; Oundle Sch.; Merton Coll., Oxford (MA Hons Eng. Lang. and Lit.; Editor, Isis). Trainee reporter, Thomson Regional Newspapers, Evening Echo, Hemel Hempstead, 1970–73; home and foreign corresp., Sunday Times, 1973–77; columnist (Atticus), Sunday Times, 1977–79; Washington corresp. and US Editor, Observer, 1979–81; Features Editor and Asst Editor, The Times, 1981–82; freelance journalist and author, 1982–85 and 1986–; Exec. Editor, Today, 1985–86; music critic, The Observer, 2002–. Fellow, Center for Scholars and Writers, NY Public Liby, 1999–2000. Broadcaster, radio and TV; TV documentaries include: The Man Who Would Be King, 1982; Charles at Forty, 1988; Anthony Holden on Poker, 1992; Who Killed Tchaikovsky, 1993. Member, Board of Governors: South Bank Centre, 2002–; Northern Shakespeare Trust, 2006–. Young Journalist of 1972; commended for work in NI, News Reporter of the Year, British Press Awards, 1976; Columnist of the Year, British Press Awards, 1977. Opera translations: Don Giovanni, 1986; La Bohème, 1986; The Barber of Seville, 1987. *Publications:* (trans. and ed) Aeschylus' Agamemnon, 1969; (contrib.) The Greek Anthology, 1973; (trans. and ed) Greek Pastoral Poetry, 1974; The St Albans Poisoner, 1974, 2nd edn 1996; Charles, Prince of Wales, 1979; Their Royal Highnesses, 1981; Of Presidents, Prime Ministers and Princes, 1984; The Queen Mother, 1985, 3rd edn 1995; (trans.) Mozart's Don Giovanni, 1987; Olivier, 1988; Charles, 1988; Big Deal, 1990, 3rd edn 2002; (ed) The Last Paragraph, 1990; A Princely Marriage, 1991; The Oscars, 1993; The Tarnished Crown, 1993; (contrib.) Power and the Throne, 1994; Tchaikovsky, 1995; Diana: her life and legacy, 1997; Charles: a biography, 1998; William Shakespeare: his life and work, 1999; (ed jtly) The Mind Has Mountains, 1999; (ed jtly) There are Kermodians, 1999; The Drama of Love, Life and Death in Shakespeare, 2000; Shakespeare: an illustrated biography, 2002; The Wit in the Dungeon: the life of Leigh Hunt, 2005; All In, 2005; The Man Who Wrote Mozart, 2006; Bigger Deal, 2007. *Recreations:* poker, Arsenal FC, Lancashire CC. *Address:* c/o Rogers Coleridge White, 20 Powis Mews, W11 1JN. *T:* (020) 7221 3717.

HOLDEN, Prof. David William, PhD; FRS 2004; FMedSci; Professor of Molecular Microbiology, Imperial College London, since 1997; *b* 3 Nov. 1955; *s* of John and Bronwen Holden; *m* 2000, Belinda Sinclair. *Educ:* George Watson's Coll., Edinburgh; Univ. of Durham (BSc Hons (Botany) 1977); UCL (PhD 1982). Research Fellow: Agriculture Canada, 1982–84; Univ. of Wisconsin, 1985–88; NIMR, London, 1988–90; Royal Postgraduate Medical School, London: Lectr, 1990–93; Sen. Lectr, 1993–95; Prof., 1995–97. Scientific Founder and Consultant, Microscience Ltd, 1997–2005. FMedSci 2002. *Publications:* numerous articles in learned jls; several patents. *Recreations:* climbing, reading. *Address:* Department of Infectious Diseases, Imperial College London, Armstrong Road, SW7 2AZ. *T:* (020) 7594 3073, *Fax:* (020) 7594 3095; *e-mail:* d.holden@imperial.ac.uk.

HOLDEN, His Honour Derek; a Circuit Judge, 1984–2000; a Chairman, Asylum and Immigration Tribunal (formerly Immigration Appeal Tribunal), since 2000; *b* 7 July 1935; *s* of Frederic Holden and Audrey Holden (*née* Hayes); *m* 1961, Dorien Elizabeth Holden (*née* Bell); two *s*. *Educ:* Cromwell House; Staines Grammar Sch. Served Army; Lieut East Surrey Regt, 1953–56. Qualified as Solicitor, 1966; Derek Holden & Co., Staines, Egham, Camberley, Feltham, Basingstoke and Ashford, 1966–84; Consultant, Batt Holden & Co., 1966–84; Principal, Dorien Property Co., 1974–84; Partner, Black Lake Securities, 1978–84. A Recorder, 1980–84; President: Social Security Appeal Tribunals and Medical Appeal Tribunals, Vaccine Damage Tribunals, and Disability Appeals Tribunal, 1990–92; Child Support Tribunal, 1993; Chm., Tribunals Cttee, Judicial Studies Bd, 1991–93; Mem., Criminal Injuries Compensation Appeal Panel, 2000–; Chairman: Indep. Tribunal for Office of Supervision of Standards of Telephone Inf. Services, 2001–; Appeals Panel for Indep. Mobile Classification Body, 2006–. Mem., Royal Yachting Assoc., 1975– (Dept of Trade Offshore Yachtmaster Instr with Ocean Cert.; Advanced Open Water Diving Cert., 2000); Principal, Chandor Sch. of Sailing, Lymington, 1978–85. *Recreations:* sailing, snow-boarding, photography, music, scuba-diving. *Address:* c/o Independent Appeals Body, Independent Committee for the Supervision of Standards of Telephone Information Services, Clove Building, 4 McGuire Street, SE1 2NQ. *Clubs:* Western (Glasgow); Leander, Remenham (Henley); Burway Rowing (Laleham); Eton Excelsior Rowing (Windsor); Staines Boat; Port Solent Yacht.

HOLDEN, Sir John David, 4th Bt *cr* 1919; *b* 16 Dec. 1967; *s* of David George Holden (*d* 1971) (*e s* of 3rd Bt), and of Nancy, *d* of H. W. D. Marwood, Foulrice, Whenby, Brandsby, Yorks; *S* grandfather, 1976; *m* 1987, Suzanne Cummings; three *d*. *Heir: uncle* Brian Peter John Holden [*b* 12 April 1944; *m* 1984, Bernadette Anne Lopez, *d* of George Gerard O'Malley].

HOLDEN, John Stewart; Board Member, Wiltshire Primary Care Trust, since 2006; *b* 23 July 1945; *s* of William Stewart Holden and Jenny Holden (*née* Brelsford); *m* 1st, 1970, Pamela (marr. diss. 1984); 2nd, 1984, Margaret Newport. *Educ:* Merchant Taylors'; Emmanuel Coll., Cambridge (BA Hons Natural Scis/Law 1967; MA). British Petroleum and subsidiaries, 1964–93: Manager, Gas (Western Hemisphere), 1981–84; Area Oil Co-ordinator and Dir, BP (Schweiz) AG, 1984–87; Dir, Alexander Duckham & Co., 1991–93; Manager, European Lubricants & Bitumen, 1991–93; Develt Dir, Electricity Pool, 1994–96; Chief Exec., Companies House and Registrar of Cos for England and Wales, 1996–2002; Registrar of Political Parties, 1998–2000; Board Member: UK Passport Service, 2002–07; Criminal Records Bureau, 2002–06. Mem., Home Office Review of Criminal Records Bureau, 2002. Mem., Audit Cttee, Indep. Police Complaints Commn, 2005–. Mem., Bradford-on-Avon Rotary Club. *Publications:* The Watlington Branch, 1974; The Manchester and Milford Railway, 1979, 2nd edn 2007. *Recreations:* flying, music, history, industrial archaeology.

HOLDEN, Patrick Brian, MA, FCIS; Chairman: Ainsfield PLC, since 1991; Holden Homes (Southern) Ltd, since 1984; Director, Mortimer Growth II plc, since 1997; *b* 16 June 1937; *s* of Reginald John and Winifred Isabel Holden; *m* 1972, Jennifer Ruth (*née* Meddings), MB, BS (marr. diss. 2001). *Educ:* Allhallows Sch. (Major Schol.); St Catharine's Coll., Cambridge (BA Hons Law 1960, MA 1963). FCIS 1965. Served Royal Hampshire Regt, 1955–57 (regular commn), seconded 1 Ghana Regt, RWAFF. Fine Fare Group: Sec., 1960–69; Legal and Property Dir, 1965–69; Pye of Cambridge Gp, 1969–74; Dir, Pye Telecom. Ltd, 1972–74; Dir and Sec., Oriel Foods Gp, 1975–81; Gp Sec., Fisons plc, 1981–83. Sec., New Town Assoc., 1974–75. *Publications:* Map of Tewin and its Rights of Way, 1991; A–Z of Dog Training and Behaviour, 1999; The Old School House: a Dickensian school, 2000; Agility: a step by step guide, 2001. *Recreations:* dogs, bridge, walking, limericks. *Address:* The Old School House, Lower Green, Tewin, Herts AL6 0LD. *T:* (01438) 717573. *Club:* Naval and Military.

HOLDEN, Patrick Hyla, CBE 2005; Director, Soil Association, since 1995; *b* 9 Sept. 1950; *s* of Dr Hyla Montgomery Holden and Joan Elizabeth Holden; *m* 1st, 1977, Louise Richards (marr. diss.); two *s* two *d*; 2nd, 2002, Rebecca Mary Hiscock; four *s*. *Educ:* Dulwich Hamlet Primary Sch.; Alleyn's Sch., Dulwich; Mount Grace Comp. Sch., Potters Bar; Emerson Coll., Sussex (biodynamic agric. course). Farmer, 240-acre mixed organic dairy farm, W Wales, 1973– (pt-time, 1988–); Dir, British Organic Farmers, 1988–92. Mem., UK Register of Organic Food Standards Bd, 1987–97. *Recreations:* Hebridean Islands, all year swimming, tennis, hill walking, Bach. *Address:* The Soil Association, South Plaza, Marlborough Street, Bristol BS1 3NX. *T:* (0117) 929 3202, *Fax:* (0117) 925 2504; *e-mail:* pholden@soilassociation.org. *Club:* Farmers.

HOLDEN, Sir Paul, 7th Bt *cr* 1893, of Oakworth House, Keighley, Yorkshire; *b* 3 March 1923; *s* of Sir Isaac Holden Holden, 5th Bt and Alice Edna Holden (*née* Byrom); *S* brother, 2003; *m* 1950, Vivien Mary Oldham; one *s* two *d*. *Educ:* Leys Sch., Cambridge; Oriel Coll., Oxford. *Recreations:* film making, swimming, diving. *Heir: s* Michael Peter Holden [*b* 19 June 1956; *m* 1990, Irene Yvonne Salmon; three *d*]. *Address:* 122 Clare Park Gardens, Clare Park, Crondall Lane, Farnham, Surrey GU10 5DT. *Club:* Lions (Farnham).

HOLDEN-BROWN, Sir Derrick, Kt 1979; Chairman, Allied-Lyons PLC, 1982–91 (Chief Executive, 1982–88); Director, Allied Breweries, 1967–91 (Chairman, 1982–86); *b* 14 Feb. 1923; *s* of Harold Walter and Beatrice Florence (*née* Walker); *m* 1st, 1950, Patricia Mary Ross Mackenzie (*d* 2001); one *d* (one *s* decd); 2nd, 2005, Farideh Pelham. *Educ:* Westcliff. Mem., Inst. of Chartered Accountants of Scotland. Served War, Royal Navy, 1941–46, Lt RNVR, Coastal Forces. Chartered Accountant, 1948; Hiram Walker & Sons, Distillers, 1949; Managing Director: Cairnes Ltd, Brewers, Eire, 1954; Grants of St James's Ltd, 1960; Dir, Ind Coope Ltd, 1962; Chm., Victoria Wine Co., 1964; Finance Dir, 1972, Vice-Chm., 1975–82, Allied Breweries; Director: Sun Alliance & London Insurance plc, 1977– (Vice Chm., 1983, Dep. Chm., 1985–92); Midland Bank, 1984–88. Chm., FDIC, 1984–85 (Dep. Chm. 1974–76). President: Food and Drink Fedn, 1985–86; Food Manufacturers' Fedn Inc., 1985. Chairman: Brewers' Soc., 1978–80 (Master, Brewers' Co., 1987–88); White Ensign Assoc., 1987–90; Portsmouth Naval Heritage Trust, 1989–. *Recreations:* sailing, offshore cruising. *Address:* 6 Ashburn Gardens, SW7 4DG. *T:* (020) 370 1597. *Clubs:* Boodle's; Royal Yacht Squadron; Royal Lymington Yacht.

HOLDER, Sir (John) Henry, 4th Bt *cr* 1898, of Pitmaston, Moseley, Worcs; Production Director and Head Brewer, Elgood & Sons Ltd, North Brink Brewery, Wisbech, 1975–93, retired; *b* 12 March 1928; *s* of Sir John Eric Duncan Holder, 3rd Bt and Evelyn Josephine (*d* 1994), *er d* of late William Blain; *S* father, 1986; *m* 1st, 1960, Catharine Harrison (*d* 1994), *yr d* of late Leonard Baker; twin *s* one *d*; 2nd, 1996, Josephine Mary, *d* of late A. Elliott and *widow* of G. Rivett. *Educ:* Eton Coll.; Birmingham Univ. (Dip. Malting and Brewing); Dip. in Safety Management, British Safety Council. Diploma Mem., Inst. of Brewing. National Service, RAC; commnd 5th Royal Tank Regt, 1947. Shift Brewer, Mitchells & Butlers Ltd, 1951–53; Brewer, Reffels Bexley Brewery Ltd, 1953–56; Asst Manager, Unique Slide Rule Co., 1956–62; Brewer, Rhymney Brewery Co. Ltd, 1962–75. *Recreations:* sailing, computing. *Heir: er* twin *s* Nigel John Charles Holder, *b* 6 May 1962. *Address:* Westering, Holt Road, Cley next the Sea, Holt, Norfolk NR25 7UA. *Club:* Brancaster Staithe Sailing (King's Lynn).

HOLDERNESS, Sir Martin (William), 4th Bt *cr* 1920, of Tadworth, Surrey; Director, MH Financial Management Ltd, independent financial advisers, since 2002; *b* 24 May 1957; *s* of Sir Richard William Holderness, 3rd Bt and of Pamela Mary Dawsett (*née* Chapman); *S* father, 1998; *m* 1984, Elizabeth Dorothy, BSc, DipHV, Dip Counselling, *d* of Dr William and Dr Maureen Thornton, Belfast; one *s* one *d*. *Educ:* Bradfield Coll., Berkshire; Portsmouth Poly. (BA Accountancy 1979). CA 1983; MSFA 1995. Articled KMG Thomson McLintock, 1978–83; financial adviser, 1984–. *Recreations:* theatre, films, football, family life. *Heir: s* Matthew William Thornton Holderness, *b* 23 May 1990. *Address:* Cuckman's Farm, Ragged Hall Lane, St Albans, Herts AL2 3NP. *Club:* Two Brydges.

HOLDERNESS-RODDAM, Jane Mary Elizabeth, CBE 2004; LVO 1999; Chairman, Riding for the Disabled Association, since 2000; *b* 7 Jan. 1948; *d* of Jack and Anne Bullen; *m* 1974, Timothy David Holderness-Roddam, *qv*. *Educ:* Westwing Sch., Thornbury, Glos. SRN, Middlesex Hosp., London, 1970. Owner, W Kington Stud Farm. Olympic Team Gold Medallist, Equestrian 3 day Event, 1968. President: Fortune Centre of Riding Therapy, 1969–; British Equestrian Trade Assoc., 2004–; British Eventing, 2004– (Chm., 1999–2004). Chm., Nat. Riding Fest., 1999–; Pres., Caspian Horse Soc., 2007–; Patron, Side Saddle Assoc., 2008–. Hon. Freeman, Co. of Loriners, 2001; Yeoman, Co. of Saddlers, 2005. Hon. Dr UWE, 2004. *Publications:* equestrian books include: Competitive Riding, 1988; Complete Book of Eventing, 1988; Showing, 1989; Show Jumping, 1990; Fitness for Horse and Rider, 1993; Practical Cross Country, 1994; The Life of Horses, 1999; Horse Riding in a Weekend, 2004; contrib. to equestrian magazines. *Recreations:* travel, antique collecting. *Address:* Church Farm, West Kington, Chippenham, Wilts SN14 7JE. *T:* (01249) 782050, *Fax:* (01249) 782940; *e-mail:* jhroddam@aol.com.

HOLDERNESS-RODDAM, Timothy David; Director, Abercrombie & Kent Ltd, since 2003; *b* 23 Nov. 1942; *s* of David and Susan Holderness-Roddam; *m* 1974, Jane Mary Elizabeth Bullen (*see* J. M. E. Holderness-Roddam). *Educ:* Radley Coll. Partner, W Kington Farms, 1988–. Man. Dir, UM Gp, 1993–2000; Dep. Chm., Countrywide Farmers plc, 2004–. Chairman: Horse Trials Support Gp, 1974–; British Equestrian Fedn Fund, 2004–. Trustee, Friends of Conservation, 1976–. *Recreations:* travel, shooting, country pursuits. *Address:* Church Farm, West Kington, Chippenham, Wilts SN14 7JE. *T:* (01249) 782050, *Fax:* (01249) 782940; *e-mail:* jhroddam@aol.com. *Club:* Cavalry and Guards.

HOLDGATE, Sir Martin (Wyatt), Kt 1994; CB 1979; PhD; FIBiol; President: Zoological Society of London, 1994–2004; Freshwater Biological Association, since 2002; *b* 14 Jan. 1931; *s* of late Francis Wyatt Holdgate, MA, JP, and Lois Marjorie (*née* Bebbington); *m* 1963, Elizabeth Mary (*née* Dickason), *widow* of Dr H. H. Weil; two *s*. *Educ:* Arnold Sch., Blackpool; Queens' Coll., Cambridge (BA 1952; MA 1956; PhD 1955). FIBiol 1967. Jt Leader and Senior Scientist, Gough Is Scientific Survey, 1955–56; Lecturer in Zoology: Manchester Univ., 1956–57; Durham Colleges, 1957–60; Leader, Royal Society Expedition to Southern Chile, 1958–59; Asst Director of Research, Scott Polar Research Institute, Cambridge, 1960–63; Senior Biologist, British Antarctic Survey, 1963–66; Dep. Dir (Research), The Nature Conservancy, 1966–70; Director: Central Unit on Environmental Pollution, DoE, 1970–74; Inst. of Terrestrial Ecology, NERC, 1974–76; Dep. Sec., 1976, Dir-Gen. of Res., 1976–79, Chief Scientist, 1979–85, Depts of the Environment and of Transport; Dep. Sec., Environment Protection and Chief Envmt Scientist, DoE, and Chief Scientific Advr, Dept of Transport, 1985–88; Dir Gen., IUCN, 1988–94. Hon. Professorial Fellow, UC Cardiff, 1976–83. Member: NERC, 1976–87; SERC (formerly SRC), 1976–87; ABRC, 1976–88; Bd, World Resources Inst., Washington, 1985–94; China Council for Internat. Co-operation on Envmt and Develt, Beijing, 1992–94; Chairman: Review of Scientific Civil Service, 1980; Renewable Energy Adv. Gp, 1992; Energy Adv. Panel, 1993–96; Internat. Inst. for Envmt and Develt, 1994–99; Co-Chm., Intergovtl Panel on Forests, UN Commn on Sustainable Develt, 1995–97; Mem., Royal Commn on Envmtl Pollution, 1994–2002; Trustee, Nat. Heritage Meml Fund and Heritage Lottery Fund, 1995–98. Chm., British Schools Exploring Society, 1967–78; Vice-Pres., Young Explorer's Trust, 1981–90 (Chm., 1972, 1979–81). President: Governing Council, UN Environment Prog., 1983–84; Global 500 Forum, 1992–97; Chm., Commonwealth Expert Gp on Climate Change, 1988–89. Chm., Governing Council, Arnold Sch., 1997–2004. Hon. Mem., IUCN, 2000. Hon. FZS 2005. Hon. Fellow, RHBNC, 1997. Hon. DSc: Durham, 1991; Sussex, 1993; Lancaster, 1995; QMUL, 2006. Bruce Medal, RSE, 1964; UNEP Silver Medal, 1983; UNEP Global 500, 1988; Patron's Medal, RGS, 1992; Livingstone Medal, RSGS, 1993. Comdr, Order of the Golden Ark (Netherlands), 1991. *Publications:* A History of Appleby, 1956, rewritten as The Story of Appleby in Westmorland, 2006; Mountains in the Sea, The Story of the Gough Island Expedition, 1958; (ed jtly) Antarctic Biology, 1964; (ed) Antarctic Ecology, 1970; (with N. M. Wace) Man and Nature in the Tristan da Cunha Islands, 1976; A Perspective of Environmental Pollution, 1979; (ed jtly) The World Environment 1972–82, 1982; (ed jtly) The World Environment 1972–92, 1992; From Care to Action: making a sustainable world, 1996; The Green Web: a union for world conservation, 1999; Penguins and Mandarins: memories of natural and un-natural history, 2003; numerous papers and articles on Antarctica, environment and conservation. *Address:* Fell Beck, Hartley, Kirkby Stephen, Cumbria CA17 4JH. *Club:* Athenæum.

HOLDING, John Francis; HM Diplomatic Service, retired; business adviser and active Rotarian in New Zealand, since 1996; *b* 12 Aug. 1936; *s* of late Francis George Holding, CA, Inland Revenue, and Gwendoline Elizabeth Holding (*née* Jenkins); *m* 1st, 1970, Pamela Margaret Straker-Nesbit (marr. diss. 1984); two *d*; 2nd, 1993, Susan Ann Clark (marr. diss. 1999). *Educ:* Colwyn Bay Grammar Sch.; LSE (externally). Mil. service, 1955–57; Min. of Housing and Local Govt, 1957; CRO (later FCO), 1964; served Karachi, Islamabad and Kinshasa; First Sec., 1973; Canberra, 1973–78; The Gambia, 1978–80; Grenada and Barbados, 1984–87; Dep. High Comr, Dhaka, 1987–90; Consul-General, Auckland, and Dir UK Trade Promotion in NZ, 1990–96. *Recreations:* tennis, walking, photography, pianoforte. *Address:* 36 Bell Road, Remuera, Auckland 1050, New Zealand.

HOLDING, Malcolm Alexander; HM Diplomatic Service, retired; Consul-General, Naples, 1986–90; *b* 11 May 1932; *s* of Adam Anderson Holding and Mary Lillian (*née* Golding); *m* 1955, Pamela Eve Hampshire; two *d*. *Educ:* King Henry VIII Sch., Coventry. Foreign Office, 1949–51; HM Forces, 1951–53; FO, 1953–55; Middle East Centre for Arab Studies, 1956–57; Third Secretary (Commercial), Tunis, 1957–60; Second Sec. (Commercial), Khartoum, 1960–64; Second, later First Sec. (Commercial), Cairo, 1964–68; Consul, Bari, 1969; FCO, 1970–73; First Sec., British Dep. High Commission, Madras, 1973–75; FCO, 1976–78; Canadian National Defence Coll., Kingston, Ontario, 1978–79; Counsellor (Commercial), Rome, 1979–81; Consul-Gen., Edmonton, 1981–85. Commendatore, Order of Merit of the Republic of Italy, 1980. *Recreation:* sailing. *Address:* 18 Strand Court, The Strand, Topsham, Exeter EX3 0AZ.

HOLDRIDGE, Ven. Bernard Lee; Archdeacon of Doncaster, 1994–2001; *b* 24 July 1935; *s* of Geoffrey and Lucy Medlow Holdridge. *Educ:* Grammar Sch., Thorne; Lichfield Theol Coll. Ordained deacon, 1967, priest, 1968; Curate, Swinton, S Yorks, 1967–71; Vicar, St Jude, Hexthorpe, Doncaster, 1971–81; Rector, St Mary, Rawmarsh with Parkgate, 1981–88; RD of Rotherham, 1986–88; Vicar, Priory Church of St Mary and St Cuthbert, Worksop, with St Giles, Carburton and St Mary the Virgin, Clumber Park, dio. of Southwell, 1988–94; permission to officiate, dio. of Guildford, 2006–. Dignitary in Convocation, 1999–2001. Chairman: DAC for Care of Churches and Churchyards, Southwell, 1990–94; ACS, 1998–2003. Guardian, Shrine of Our Lady of Walsingham, 1996–. *Recreations:* foreign travel, reading, theatre, a glass of wine with friends. *Address:* Flat 35, Denehyrst Court, York Road, Guildford, Surrey GU1 4EA. *T:* (01483) 570791.

HOLDSWORTH, Sir (George) Trevor, Kt 1982; CVO 1997; Chairman, GKN plc, 1980–88; *b* 29 May 1927; *s* of late William Albert Holdsworth and Winifred Holdsworth (*née* Bottomley); *m* 1st, 1951, Patricia June Ridler (*d* 1993); three *s*; 2nd, 1995, Jenny Watson. *Educ:* Hanson Grammar Sch., Bradford; Keighley Grammar Sch. FCA 1950. Rawlinson Greaves & Mitchell, Bradford, 1944–51; Bowater Paper Corp., 1952–63 (financial and admin. appts; Dir and Controller of UK paper-making subsids); joined Guest, Keen & Nettlefolds (later GKN plc), 1963; Dep. Chief Accountant, 1963–64; Gp Chief Accountant, 1965–67; General Man. Dir, GKN Screws & Fasteners Ltd, 1968–70; Dir, 1970–88; Gp Controller, 1970–72; Gp Exec. Vice Chm., Corporate Controls and

Services, 1973–74; Dep. Chm., 1974–77; Man. Dir and Dep. Chm., 1977–80. Chairman: Allied Colloids Gp, 1983–96; British Satellite Broadcasting, 1987–90; National Power, 1990–95; Beauford, 1991–99; Lambert Howarth Gp, 1993–98; Industrial Finance Gp, 1997–2002; Director: Equity Capital for Industry, 1976–84; THORN EMI, 1977–87; Midland Bank plc, 1979–88; Prudential Corp., 1986–96 (Jt Dep. Chm., 1988–92); Owens-Corning Fiberglas Corp., 1994–98. Member: AMF Inc. Europ. Adv. Council, 1982–85; European Adv. Bd, Owens Corning Fiberglas Inc., 1990–93; Adv. Bd, LEK, 1992–99. Confederation of British Industry: Mem. Council, 1974–1990; Mem., Econ. and Financial Policy Cttee, 1978–80; Mem., Steering Gp on Unemployment, 1982; Mem., Special Programmes Unit, 1982; Chm., Tax Reform Working Party, 1984–86; Dep. Pres., 1987–88; Pres., 1988–90. Chairman: Review Body on Doctors' and Dentists' Remuneration, 1990–93; Adv. Council, Foundn for Manufacturing and Industry, 1993–99; Inst. for Manufacturing, 1999–2000; Dep. Chm., Financial Reporting Council, 1990–93; Mem., Business in the Community, 1984–92; British Institute of Management: Mem. Council, 1974–84; Vice-Chm., 1978; Mem., Bd of Fellows, 1979; Chm., 1980–82; a Vice-Pres., 1982–; Gold Medal, 1987. Vice Pres., Engineering Employers' Fedn, 1980–88; Jt Dep. Chm., Adv. Bd, Inst. of Occupational Health, 1980; Duke of Edinburgh's Award: Mem., Internat. Panel, 1980 (Chm., 1987); Internat. Trustee, 1987–94; UK Trustee, 1988–96; Member: Exec. Cttee, SMMT, 1980–83; Engineering Industries Council, 1980–88 (Chm., 1985); Court of British Shippers' Council, 1981–89; British-North American Cttee, 1981–85; Council, RIIA, 1983–88; Internat. Council of INSEAD, 1985–92; Eur. Adv. Cttee, New York Stock Exchange, 1985–97. Chm., Wigmore Hall Trust, 1992–99; Member: Council, Royal Opera House Trust (Trustee, 1981–84); Council, Winston Churchill Meml Trust, 1985–96. Hon. Pres., Council of Mechanical and Metal Trade Assocs, 1987. Dir, UK-Japan 2000 Gp, 1987. Trustee: Anglo-German Foundn for the Study of Industrial Society, 1980–92; Brighton Fest. Trust, 1980–90 (Chm. 1982–87); Philharmonia Trust, 1982–93; Thrombosis Res. Trust, 1989–98. Governor, Ashridge Management Coll., 1978; Chancellor, Bradford Univ., 1992–97. Vice-Pres., Ironbridge Gorge Museum Devolt Trust, 1981–. Internat. Counsellor, Conference Bd, 1984. CIEx 1987. FRSA 1988. Freeman, City of London, 1977; Liveryman, Worshipful Co. of Chartered Accountants in England and Wales, 1978. Hon. DTech Loughborough, 1981; Hon. DSc: Aston, 1982; Sussex, 1988; Hon. DEng: Bradford, 1983; Birmingham, 1992; Hon. DBA Internat. Management Centre, Buckingham, 1986. Chartered Accountants Founding Socs' Centenary Award, 1983; Hon. CGIA 1989. *Recreations:* music, theatre. *Club:* Athenæum.

HOLDSWORTH, Ven. Dr John Ivor; Archdeacon of St Davids, Vicar of Steynton, and Canon of St Davids Cathedral, since 2003; *b* 10 Feb. 1949; *s* of Harold Holdsworth and Edith Mary Holdsworth; *m* 1971, Susan Annette Thomas; one *s* one *d*. *Educ:* Leeds Grammar Sch.; University Coll. of Wales, Aberystwyth (BA); University Coll., Cardiff (BD, MTh); St David's University Coll., Lampeter (PhD 1992). Ordained deacon 1973, priest 1974; Curate, St Paul's, Newport, 1973–77; Vicar: Abercrave and Callwen, 1977–86; Gorseinon, 1986–97; Principal and Warden, St Michael's Theol Coll., Llandaff, 1997–2003. Presenter, HTV Wales Religious Affairs, 1988–98. *Publications:* Communication and the Gospel, 2003; Dwelling in a Strange Land, 2003; SCM Study Guide to the Old Testament, 2005; Getting Started with the Bible, 2007. *Recreations:* walking, beekeeping, armchair supporter of Leeds United and Yorkshire County Cricket Club, broadcasting. *Address:* The Vicarage, Steynton, Milford Haven, Pembs SA73 1AW. *T:* (01646) 692876.

HOLDSWORTH, Very Rev. Kelvin; Provost, St Mary's Episcopal Cathedral, Glasgow, since 2006; *b* 22 Oct. 1966; *s* of John Stuart Holdsworth and Joyce Holdsworth (*née* Kew). *Educ:* Manchester Poly. (BSc Hons Computing Sci. and Maths 1989); Univ. of St Andrews (BD Hons Practical Theol. and Christian Ethics 1992); Univ. of Edinburgh (MTh Ministry 1996). Lay Worker, St Benet's Ecumenical Chaplaincy, QMW, 1992–95; ordained deacon, 1997, priest, 1998; Precentor, St Ninian's Cathedral, Perth, 1997–2000; Rector, St Saviour's Ch, Bridge of Allan, 2000–06. Contested (Lib Dem) Stirling, 2005. Dir, Newscan Pubns, 2006–; Mem. Editl Bd, Inspires (mag. of Scottish Episcopal Ch), 2005–. *Recreations:* politics, blogging, sinking other people's yachts. *Address:* St Mary's Episcopal Cathedral, 300 Great Western Road, Glasgow G4 9JB. *T:* (0141) 530 8643; *e-mail:* provost@thecathedral.org.uk. *Club:* Arlington Baths (Glasgow).

HOLDSWORTH, Sir Trevor; *see* Holdsworth, Sir G. T.

HOLDSWORTH HUNT, Christopher; Founder Director and Managing Director, KBC Peel, Hunt Ltd (formerly Peel, Hunt plc), 1989–2004; Chairman, Melchin Japan Investment Trust plc, since 2006; *b* 2 Aug. 1942; *s* of late Peter Holdsworth Hunt and Monica (*née* Neville); *m* 1st, 1969, Charlotte Folin (marr. diss. 1974); 2nd, 1976, Joanne Lesley Starr Minoprio (*née* Reynolds); two *s*. *Educ:* Summer Fields, St Leonards; Eton Coll.; Tours Univ. Commnd Coldstream Guards, 1961–64. Joined Murton & Adams, Stockjobbers, 1964; firm acquired by Pinchin Denny, 1969; Partner, Pinchin Denny, 1971; firm acquired by Morgan Grenfell, 1986; Dir, Morgan Grenfell Securities, 1987–88. *Recreations:* opera, ballet, theatre, golf, tennis, walking. *Address:* Flat 3, 55 Melbury Road, W14 8AD. *T:* (020) 7603 9742. *Clubs:* White's, City of London; Sunningdale Golf; Swinley Forest Golf.

HOLE, Very Rev. Derek Norman; Provost of Leicester, 1992–99, now Emeritus; *b* 5 Dec. 1933; *s* of Frank Edwin Hole and Ella Evelyn Hole (*née* Thomas). *Educ:* Public Central Sch., Plymouth; Lincoln Theological College. Nat. service, RAF, 1952–54. Asst Librarian, Codrington Liby, Oxford, 1954–56. Ordained deacon, 1960, priest, 1961; Asst Curate, St Mary Magdalen, Knighton, 1960–62; Domestic Chaplain to Archbishop of Cape Town, 1962–64; Asst Curate, St Nicholas, Kenilworth, 1964–67; Rector, St Mary the Virgin, Burton Latimer, 1967–73; Vicar, St James the Greater, Leicester, 1973–92; Chaplain to the Queen, 1985–92. Hon. Canon, Leicester Cathedral, 1983–92. Rural Dean, Christianity South, Leicester, 1983–92; Chm., House of Clergy, 1986–94; Vice-Pres., Diocesan Synod, 1986–94; Member: Bishop's Council, 1986–99; Assoc. of English Cathedrals, 1992–99; Cathedral Music Wkg Party, 1993–99. Chaplain to: Lord Mayor of Leicester, 1976–77, 1994–95, 1996–97; High Sheriffs of Leics, 1980–85, 1987, 1999–2000, 2001–02 and 2007–08; Leicester High Sch., 1984–92; Haymarket Theatre, Leicester, 1980–83, 1993–95; Leicester Br., RAFA, 1978–92; Master of Merchant Taylors' Co., 1995–96; Leicester Guild of Freemen, 1996–99; Royal Soc. of St George, 2000–06; Mayor of Oadby and Wigston BC, 2005–06; Leics br., Royal Soc. of St George, 2006–; Leics br., British Korean Veterans Assoc., Leics Br., 2006–. Commissary to Bishop of Wellington, NZ, 1998–. Priest Associate, Actors' Church Union, 1995– (Mem., 1980–95); Vice-Pres., English Clergy Assoc., 1993–. Chm. Leicester Diocesan Redundant Churches Uses Cttee, 1985–99. Dir and Trustee, Leicester Charity Orgn Soc., 2001–05 (Mem., 1983–2001); Trustee: Leicester Church Charities, 1983–; Leics Historic Churches Preservation Trust, 1989–; Bernard Fawcett Meml Trust, 1993–99; North Meml Homes, 1999–; Pres., Leicester Rotary Club, 1987–88; Vice-President: Leics County Scout Council, 1992–99; Leics Guild of the Disabled, 1992–99; Leicester Cathedral Old Choristers' Assoc., 1999–. Patron, Victoria County History of Leics Trust, 2008–; Mem., Victorian Soc., 1986–; Hon. Life Mem., Leics Br., BRCS, 1995; Mem., Bd of Mgt, Britain-Australia Soc., 2001–05 (Chm., Leics Br., 2000–). Governor: Alderman Newton Sch., Leicester, 1976–82; Leicester High Sch., 1983–92; Alderman Newton Foundn 1992–2007; Leicester GS, 1992–99 (Trustee, 1999–2006; Patron, 2006–); St John's C c E Sch., Leicester, 1997–2000. Mem. (Ind.), Burton Latimer UDC, 1971–73. Sen. Fellow De Montfort Univ., 1998–. Freeman, City of London, 2003; Liveryman, Framewor Knitters' Co., 2003– (Chaplain to Master, 2004–05, 2005–06, 2006–April 2009). Hor DLitt De Montfort, 1999; Hon. LLD Leicester, 2005. *Publication:* (contrib.) Century t Millennium: St James the Greater, Leicester 1899–1999, compiled by Dr A. McWhir 1999. *Recreations:* bridge, music, walking, reading biographies and Victorian history *Address:* 25 Southernhay Close, Leicester LE2 3TW. *T:* and *Fax:* (0116) 270 9988; *e-mai* derek.hole@talktalk.net. *Clubs:* Leicestershire (Leicester); Leicestershire Golf; Roya Western Yacht.

HOLES, Prof. Clive Douglas, FBA 2002; Khalid Bin Abdullah Al-Saud Professor for th Study of the Contemporary Arab World, University of Oxford, since 1997; Fellow Magdalen College, Oxford, since 1997; *b* 29 Sept. 1948; *s* of Douglas John Holes an Kathryn Mary (*née* Grafton); *m* 1st, 1980, Gillian Diane Pountain (marr. diss.); two *s*; 2nd 2004, Deidre Margaret Thorn. *Educ:* High Arcal Grammar Sch., Dudley, Worcs; Trinit Hall, Cambridge (BA Hons 1969; MA 1973); Univ. of Birmingham (MA 1972); Wolfso Coll., Cambridge (PhD 1981). UNA volunteer teacher, Bahrain, 1969–71; Britis Council Officer, Kuwait, Algeria, Iraq, Thailand and London, 1971–76 and 1979–8 Lectr in Arabic and Applied Linguistics, Univ. of Salford, 1983–85; Dir, Lang. Centre Sultan Qaboos Univ., Oman, 1985–87; University of Cambridge: Lectr in Islamic Studie 1987–96; Reader in Arabic, 1996; Fellow, Trinity Hall, 1989–96. Fellow: British Soc. fo Middle Eastern Studies, 1989; Anglo-Oman Soc., 1990; Bahrain-British Soc., 199 Mem., Philological Soc., 1984–. *Publications:* Colloquial Arabic of the Gulf and Saud Arabia, 1984, 3rd edn 1992; Language Variation and Change in a Modernising Arab State 1987; Gulf Arabic, 1990; Breakthrough Arabic, 1992; (ed) Perspectives on Arabi Linguistics, Vol. 5, 1993; Modern Arabic: structures, functions and varieties, 199 Dialect, Culture and Society in Eastern Arabia, Vol. I, 2001, Vol. II, 2005; articles i professional jls concerned with Arabic language, culture, society and literature. *Recreation* keeping fit, watching Wolverhampton Wanderers FC, visiting the Middle East. *Address* Magdalen College, Oxford OX1 4AU. *T:* (01865) 278239.

HOLFORD-STREVENS, Bonnie Jean; *see* Blackburn, B. J.

HOLGATE, David John; QC 1997; a Recorder, since 2002; a Deputy High Court Judge since 2008; *b* 3 Aug. 1956; *s* of late John Charles Holgate and of Catherine Philbin Holgat (*née* Rooney); civil partnership 2006, Alexander Nicholas Constantine. *Educ:* Davenan Foundation Grammar Sch., Loughton; Exeter Coll., Oxford (BA Hons 1977). Called t the Bar, Middle Temple, 1978, Bencher, 2004; admitted to Hong Kong Bar, 2001. Mem Supplementary Panel, Jun. Counsel to the Crown (Common Law), 1986–97; Standin Jun. Counsel to the Inland Revenue in rating valuation matters, 1990–97. *Recreations* music, particularly opera, travel, reading. *Address:* Landmark Chambers, 180 Fleet Street EC4A 2HG. *T:* (020) 7430 1221, *Fax:* (020) 7421 6060; *e-mail:* clerks@ landmarkchambers.co.uk. *Club:* Travellers.

HOLGATE, Nicholas Ian; Chief Operating Officer, Department for Culture, Media an Sport, since 2004; *b* 26 March 1962; *s* of late John Holgate and of Josephine Holgate (*né* Neve); *m* 2005, Natalie Cronin. *Educ:* Hall Grove Sch., Bagshot; Charterhouse; Trinity Coll., Cambridge (BA 1984). ACMA. HM Treasury, 1984–2004: Private Secretary: to Chief Sec. to the Treasury, 1991–92; to Sec. of State for Nat. Heritage, 1992–93; Gov Res. Fellow, 1993–94; Team Leader: Strategy, Finance and Purchasing, 1995–98; Educ and Trng, 1998–2001; Dir, Welfare Reform, Budget and Public Finances Directorate 2001–04. *Recreations:* food, film, games. *Address:* Department for Culture, Media and Sport, 2–4 Cockspur Street, SW1Y 5DH.

HOLGATE, Prof. Stephen Townley, MD, DSc; FRCP, FRCPE, FRCPath, FMedSci CBiol, FIBiol; Medical Research Council Clinical Professor of Immunopharmacology University of Southampton, and Hon. Consultant Physician, School of Medicine Southampton General Hospital, since 1987; *b* 2 May 1947; *s* of William Townley Holgate and Margaret Helen (*née* Lancaster); *m* 1972, Elizabeth Karen Malkinson; three *s* one *d* *Educ:* London Univ. (BSc 1968; MB BS 1971; MD 1979); DSc Soton 1991. FRCP 1984 FRCPE 1995; FRCPath 1999; CBiol, FIBiol 1999. House Physician and Surgeon Charing Cross Hosp., 1971–72; Sen. Hse Physician, Nat. Hosp. for Nervous Diseases and Brompton Hosp., 1972–74; Registrar in Medicine, Salisbury and Southampton Gen Hosps, 1974–76; Lectr in Medicine, 1976–80, Sen. Lectr, 1980–86, Reader and Prof (personal Chair), 1986–87, Univ. of Southampton. MRC/Wellcome Trust Res. Fellow Harvard Univ., 1978–80. Mem., Royal Commn on Envmtl Pollution, 2002–. Founder FMedSci, 1998. FRSA 1997. Hon. MD: Ferrara, Italy, 1997; Jagiellonian, Poland, 1999. Rhône Poulenc Rorer World Health Award, 1995; (jtly) King Faisal Internat. Prize in Medicine, 1999. *Publications:* (ed jtly) Asthma and Rhinitis: implications for diagnosis and treatment, 1995, 2nd edn 2000; (jtly) Health Effects of Air Pollutants, 1999; (ed jtly) Allergy, 1999; Difficult Asthma, 1999; (ed jtly) Allergy: principles and practice, 2004. *Recreations:* gardening, jogging. *Address:* Infection, Inflammation and Repair Division Level F South Pathology and Laboratory Block, Southampton General Hospital, Southampton SO16 6YD.

HOLLAMBY, David James; HM Diplomatic Service, retired; Governor and Commander-in-Chief, St Helena and Dependencies, 1999–2004; *b* 19 May 1945; *s* of Reginald William Hollamby and Eva May Hollamby (*née* Ponman); *m* 1971, Maria Helena Guzmán; two step *s*. *Educ:* Albury Manor Sch., Surrey. Joined Foreign Office, 1964: Beirut, 1967–69; Latin American Floater, 1970–72; Third Sec. and Vice Consul, Asunción, 1972–75; Second Sec., FCO, 1975–78; Vice Consul (Commercial), NY, 1978–82; Consul (Commercial), Dallas, 1982–86; First Secretary: FCO, 1986–90; Rome, 1990–94; Asst Hd, Western Eur. Dept, FCO, 1994–96; Dep. Hd, W Indian and Atlantic Dept, FCO, 1996–98; Dep. Hd, Overseas Territories Dept, FCO, 1998–99. *Recreations:* travel, reading, music, golf, ski-ing. *Address:* 42 Oakbark House, High Street, Brentford Lock TW8 8LF.

HOLLAND, Hon. Sir Alan (Douglas), Kt 1995; Judge, High Court (formerly Supreme Court) of New Zealand, 1978–94, retired; *b* 20 June 1929; *s* of Clarence Cyril Holland and Marjorie Evelyn Holland; *m* 1961, Felicity Ann Ower; one *s*. *Educ:* Waitaki Boys' High Sch.; Canterbury Coll., Univ. of New Zealand (LLB). Part-time Lectr in Law and Commerce Faculties of Canterbury Univ., 1953–63; Partner, Wynn Williams & Co., Solicitors, Christchurch, 1956–78. Pres., Canterbury Dist Law Soc., 1973 (Mem. Council, 1963–73); Mem. Council and associated cttees, NZ Law Soc., 1970–74. *Recreations:* general. *Address:* 29 McDougall Avenue, Christchurch 8001, New Zealand. *T:* (3) 3557102. *Club:* Christchurch.

HOLLAND, Rt Rev. Alfred Charles; Bishop of Newcastle, NSW, 1978–92; *b* 23 Feb. 1927; *s* of Alfred Charles Holland and Maud Allison; *m* 1954, Joyce Marion Embling; three *s* one *d*. *Educ:* Raine's Sch., London; Univ. of Durham (BA 1950; DipTh 1952).

RNVR, 1945–47; Univ. of Durham, 1948–52; Assistant Priest, West Hackney, London, 1952–54; Rector of Scarborough, WA, 1955–70; Asst Bishop, Dio. Perth, WA, 1970–77. Chaplain, St George's Coll., Jerusalem, 1993. Life Member: Stirling Rugby Football Club, 1969; Durham Univ. Society, 1984. *Publications:* Luke Through Lent, 1980; (ed) The Diocese Together, 1987; Eyes' Delight, 2001. *Recreations:* reading, painting. *Address:* 52 Windsor Gardens, 244–264 Mowbray Road, Chatswood, NSW 2067, Australia. *Club:* Australian (Sydney).

See also Rt Rev. J. C. Holland.

HOLLAND, Sir Anthony; *see* Holland, Sir J. A.

HOLLAND, Hon. Sir Christopher (John), Kt 1992; a Judge of the High Court of Justice, Queen's Bench Division, 1992–2007; a Judge of the Employment Appeal Tribunal, 1994–2007; *b* 1 June 1937; *er s* of late Frank and Winifred Mary Holland; *m* 1967, Jill Iona Holland; one *s* one *d*. *Educ:* Leeds Grammar Sch.; Emmanuel Coll., Cambridge (MA, LLB). National Service (acting L/Cpl), 3rd Royal Tank Regt, 1956–58. Called to the Bar, Inner Temple, 1963, Bencher, 1985; commenced practice on North Eastern Circuit (Presiding Judge, 1993–97); QC 1978; a Recorder, 1992. Mem., Criminal Injuries Compensation Bd, 1992. Vice Chm., Cttee of Inquiry into Outbreak of Legionnaires' Disease at Stafford, 1985. Chm., Lower Washburn Parish Council, 1975–91. *Address:* c/o Royal Courts of Justice, Strand, WC2A 2LL.

HOLLAND, Sir Clifton Vaughan, (Sir John), AC 1988; Kt 1973; BCE; CPEng, FTSE, Hon. FIEAust, FAIM, FAIB; Chairman, John Holland Holdings Limited, 1963–86; *b* Melbourne, 21 June 1914; *s* of Thomas and Mabel Ruth Elizabeth Holland; *m* 1st, 1942, Emily Joan Atkinson (*d* 1999); three *s* one *d*; 2nd, 2003, Suzanne Wharton, *d* of Hector Desbrowe-Annear and Gladys Heron. *Educ:* Flinders State Sch.; Frankston High Sch.; Queen's Coll., Univ. of Melbourne (BCE); Monash Univ. (Hon. DEng 1978). Junior Engineer, BP, 1936–39. Served War of 1939–45, RAE and 'Z' Special Force, Middle East, SW Pacific (Lt-Col). Construction Engr, BP Aust. 1946–49; Founder, John Holland (Constructions) Pty Ltd, 1949, Man. Dir 1949–73, Chm., 1949–86; Chm., Process Plant Constructions Pty Ltd, 1949–82; Director: T & G Life Soc., 1972–82; Aust. and NZ Banking Gp, 1976–81. Foundn Pres., Australian Fedn of Civil Contractors (Life Mem., 1971); Chm., Nat. Construction Industry Conf. Organising Cttee, 1982; Mem., Construction Industry Res. Bd, 1982. Chm., Econ. Consultative Adv. Gp to the Treasurer, 1975–81; Mem., Rhodes Scholar Selection Cttee, 1970–73; Mem. Bd, Royal Melbourne Hosp., 1963–79; Nat. Chm., Outward Bound, 1973–74, Chm. Victorian Div., 1964–77; Councillor, Inst. of Public Affairs, 1980; Mem., Churchill Fellowship Selection Cttee, 1968–82; Director: Winston Churchill Meml Trust, 1976–82 (Chm., Vic. Br., 1977–82); Child Accident Prevention Foundn of Australia, 1979–81; Chairman: La Trobe Centenary Commemoration Council, 1975–76; Matthew Flinders Bi-Centenary Council, 1973–75; History Adv. Council of Victoria, 1975–85; Loch Ard Centenary Commemoration Cttee, 1976–78; Citizens' Council, 150th Anniversary Celebrations, Victoria, 1979–82; Victorian Cttee for Anzac Awards, 1982–; Nat. Chm., Queen's Silver Jubilee Trust for Young Australians, 1981–87 (Vic. Chm., 1977–80; Life Mem., 1992); Mem., Centenary Test Co-ordinating Cttee, 1976–77. Dep. Chm., Melbourne Univ. Engineering Sch. Centenary Foundn and Appeal Cttee, 1982–90. Director: Corps of Commissionaires (Victoria) Ltd, 1978–89; Australian Bicentenary Celebrations, 1980–82 (Vic. Chm., 1980–82). Pres., Stroke Res. Foundn, 1983–90; Patron: Bone Marrow Foundn, 1992–; Voluntary Euthanasia Soc. of Victoria, 1996–; Children First Foundn, 2000–. Construction projects include: Jindabyne pumping station; Westgate Bridge; Tasman Bridge restoration, New Parliament House. Foundation Fellow, Australian Acad. of Technological Scis. Hon. Fellow, AATSE, 2004. Hon. DEng Monash, 1976. Peter Nicoll Russell Meml Medal, 1974; Kernot Meml Medal, Univ. of Melbourne, 1976; Consulting Engineers Advancement Soc. Medal, 1983; Dist. Constructor Award, Qld Univ. of Technol., 2000; Australian Constructors' Assoc. Medallion, 2000; Australian Centenary Medal, 2003. *Recreations:* golf, music, gardening, cricket. *Address:* Hurst Lodge II, 33 George Road, Flinders, Vic 3929, Australia. *Clubs:* Australian, Naval and Military (Melbourne); Royal Melbourne Golf, Frankston Golf, Flinders Golf.

HOLLAND, Rt Rev. Edward; an Assistant Bishop, diocese of London, and Hon. Assistant Bishop, diocese in Europe, since 2002; *b* 28 June 1936; *s* of Reginald Dick Holland and Olive Holland (*née* Yeoman). *Educ:* New College School; Dauntsey's School; King's College London (AKC). National Service, Worcestershire Regt, 1955–57; worked for Importers, 1957–61; KCL, 1961–65. Deacon 1965, priest 1966, Rochester; Curate, Holy Trinity, Dartford, 1965–69; Curate, John Keble, Mill Hill, 1969–72; Precentor, Gibraltar Cathedral, and Missioner for Seamen, 1972–74; Chaplain at Naples, Italy, 1974–79; Vicar of S Mark's, Bromley, 1979–86; Suffragan Bishop of Gibraltar in Europe, 1986–95; Area Bishop of Colchester, 1995–2001. Mem., Churches Conservation Trust, 1998–2001. *Recreations:* travel, being entertained and entertaining. *Address:* 37 Parfrey Street, Hammersmith, W6 9EW. *T:* (020) 8746 3636.

HOLLAND, Einion; *see* Holland, R. E.

HOLLAND, Frank Robert Dacre; Chairman, C. E. Heath PLC, 1973–84, non-executive Director, 1984–86; *b* 24 March 1924; *s* of Ernest Albert Holland and Kathleen Annie (*née* Page); *m* 1st, 1948, Margaret Lindsay Aird (*d* 2004); one *d*; 2nd, 2005, Charmian Julie Marchal Watford. *Educ:* Whitgift Sch., Croydon. Joined C. E. Heath & Co. Ltd, 1941; entered Army, 1942; Sandhurst, 1943; commissioned 4th Queen's Own Hussars, 1944; served, Italy, 1944–45, Austria and Germany, 1945–47; returned to C. E. Heath & Co. Ltd, 1947; Joint Managing Director, North American Operation, 1965; Director, C. E. Heath & Co. Ltd, 1965, Dep. Chm., 1969. Director: British Aviation Insce Co., 1974–84; Trade Indemnity plc, 1974–86; Greyhound Corp., USA, 1974–87. Liveryman, Insurers' Co., 1980– (Master, 1985–86). *Recreations:* travel, gardening. *Address:* 23 Forest Ridge Circuit, Peregian Springs, Qld 4573, Australia. *Club:* Cavalry and Guards.

HOLLAND, Sir Geoffrey, KCB 1989 (CB 1984); Chairman: South West Museums, Libraries and Archives Council, since 2002; Quality Improvement Agency for Lifelong Learning, since 2006; *b* 9 May 1938; *s* of late Frank Holland, CBE and of Elsie Freda Holland; *m* 1964, Carol Ann Challen. *Educ:* Merchant Taylors' Sch., Northwood; St John's Coll., Oxford (BA 1st cl. Hons; MA; Hon. Fellow, 1991). 2nd Lieut, RTR, 1956–58. Entered Min. of Labour, 1961, Asst Private Sec., 1964–65; Principal Private Sec. to Sec. of State for Employment, 1971–72; Manpower Services Commission: Asst Sec., Hd of Planning, 1973; Dir of Special Progs, 1977; Dep. Sec., 1981; Dir, 1981; Second Perm. Sec., 1986; Perm. Sec., Dept of Employment, subseq. Employment Dept Gp, 1988–93; Perm. Sec., DFE, 1993–94; Vice-Chancellor, Exeter Univ., 1994–2002. Director: Shell UK, 1994–98; Exeter Investment Gp plc, subseq. iimia plc, 2002–06. Mem., Nat. Cttee of Inquiry into Higher Educn, 1996–97. Chairman: Govt's Sustainable Develt Educn Panel, 1998–2003; Learning and Skills Develt Agency, 2003–06. Mem. Bd, MLA, 2004–. Liveryman, Merchant Taylors' Co., 1967– (Master, 2000–01). CCMI (CBIM 1987). Fellow, Eton Coll., 1994–; Hon. Fellow, Polytechnic of Wales, 1986. Hon. FIPD (Hon. FITD 1986; Pres., IPD, 1998–2000); Hon. FCGI 1994. Hon. LLD: Sheffield, 1994; Exeter, 2003. *Publications:* Young People and Work, 1977; many articles on manpower, educn, training, management etc in professional jls. *Recreations:* journeying, opera, exercising the dog. *Address:* 12A Westminster Palace Gardens, Artillery Row, SW1P 1RL. *Club:* East India, Devonshire, Sports and Public Schools.

HOLLAND, Sir John; *see* Holland, Sir C. V.

HOLLAND, Sir (John) Anthony, Kt 2003; Chairman: Northern Ireland Parades Commission, 2000–05; Standards Board for England, 2001–08; Joint Insolvency Monitoring Unit, 2001–05; Complaints Commissioner, Financial Services Authority, since 2004; *b* 9 Nov. 1938; *s* of John and Dorothy Rita Holland; *m* 1963, Kathleen Margaret Anderson; three *s*. *Educ:* Ratcliffe Coll., Leics; Nottingham Univ. (LLB 1959); Financial Planning Cert., Chartered Insce Inst., 1997; MPhil UWE 1998. Admitted Solicitor of Supreme Court, 1962; notary public. Joined Foot & Bowden, 1964, Partner, 1964–90, Sen. Partner, 1990–97; Principal Ombudsman, PIA, 1997–2000. Chairman: Social Security Appeals Tribunal, 1974–97; South Western Regl Adv. Council, BBC, 1984–87; a Chm., SFA, 1993–2001; Access Dispute (formerly Access Dispute Resolution) Cttee, 2002–; Dep. Chm., Regulatory Decisions Cttee, 2002–04; Member: Council, Law Soc., 1976–95 (Vice-Pres., 1989–90; Pres., 1990–91; Chm., Young Solicitors Gp, 1972); Marre Cttee on future of the Legal Profession, 1986–88; Council, Justice, 1991–2003 (Chm., Exec. Bd, 1996–99); Mem. Council, Howard League for Penal Reform, 1992–2002; Hon. Mem., SPTL, 1992. President: Plymouth Law Soc., 1986–87; Cornwall Law Soc., 1988–89. Mem., Plymouth Diocesan Finances Cttee, 1986–94. Chm., Plymouth Chamber of Commerce and Industry, 1994–96. Governor: Plymouth Coll., 1976–93; Coll. of Law, 1991–97. Hon. Mem., Canadian Bar Assoc., 1990. *Publications:* (jtly) Principles of Registered Land Conveyancing, 1966; (jtly) Landlord and Tenant, 1968; (Jt Adv. Ed.) Mines and Quarries Section, Butterworth's Encyclopædia of Forms and Precedents, 1989; (Gen. Ed.) Cordery on Solicitors, 9th edn, 1995–2004. *Recreations:* opera, literature, the cinema. *Address:* 262 Lauderdale Tower, Barbican, EC2Y 8BY. *T:* (020) 7638 5044. *Clubs:* Athenæum; Clifton (Bristol); Royal Western Yacht (Plymouth).

HOLLAND, John Lewis; Managing Director, Herts & Essex Newspapers, 1990–2000; *b* 23 May 1937; *s* of George James Holland and Esther Holland; *m* 1958, Maureen Ann Adams; one *s* one *d*. *Educ:* Nottingham Technical Grammar Sch. Trainee Reporter, Nottingham Evening News, subseq. Jun. Reporter, Mansfield Br. Office, 1953–55; Sports Reporter, Mansfield Reporter Co., 1955–56; Sports Reporter, subseq. Sports Editor, Aldershot News Group, 1956–59; News Editor, West Bridgford & Clifton Standard, Nottingham, 1959–61; Chief Sports Sub Editor, Bristol Evening Post, and Editor, Sports Green 'Un (sports edn), 1961–64; Editor, West Bridgford & Clifton Standard, Nottingham, and Partner, Botting & Turner Sports Agency, Nottingham, 1964–66; Birmingham Evening Mail: Dep. Sports Editor, 1966–71; Editor, Special Projects Unit (Colour Prodn Dept), 1971–75; Editor, 1975–79, and Gen. Man., 1979–81, Sandwell Evening Mail; Marketing/Promotions Gen. Man., Birmingham Post & Mail, 1981–82; Editor, The Birmingham Post, 1982–86. Director: Birmingham Post & Mail Circulation and Promotions, 1986–88; Birmingham Post & Mail Publications and Promotions, 1988–90; Birmingham Convention and Visitor Bureau, 1982–90. President: Chartered Inst. of Marketing, 1989–90; Chiltern Newspaper Proprietors Assoc., 1995–99 (Vice-Pres., 1994–95). Member: Hertford Business Club, 1994–2000; Soc. of Cambs Area Golf Captains, 1999–2007. *Recreations:* journalism, golf, keeping horses, gardening, keep fit. *Address:* Carob Lodge, Marathounda, PO Box 60151, Paphos 8101, Cyprus. *Clubs:* Press (Birmingham); Heydon Grange Golf (Captain, 1998–99) (Royston); Tsada Golf (Captain, 2003–04), Secret Valley Golf (Cyprus).

HOLLAND, Rt Rev. Dr Jonathan Charles; an Assistant Bishop, Diocese of Brisbane, Queensland, since 2006; *b* Perth, 26 Sept. 1956; *s* of Rt Rev. Alfred Charles Holland, *qv*; *m* 1980, Kerry Anne Minchin; two *s* one *d*. *Educ:* Univ. of Western Australia (BA Hons 1978); Queen's Coll., Oxford (BA Hons 1982); Univ. of Queensland (MA 1999; PhD 2007). Ordained deacon, 1982, priest, 1983; Rector: Church of the Ascension, Midland, 1989–93; Christ Church, St Lucia, Qld, 1993–2006. Archbishop's Examining Chaplain, 1995–2006; Canon, St John's Cathedral, 2004–06. *Publication:* Eyes Delight: six paintings and their theological meaning, 1999; Jesus Unbound: the story of Jesus of Nazareth, 2008. *Recreations:* reading, poetry, gardening. *Address:* 63 Cavendish Street, Nundah, Qld 4017, Australia. *T:* (7) 38352213, *Fax:* (7) 32569436; *e-mail:* jholland@anglicanbrisbane.org.au. *Club:* Australian (Sydney).

HOLLAND, Julian Miles, (Jools), OBE 2003; DL; pianist and broadcaster; *b* 24 Jan. 1958; *s* of Derek Holland and June Rose Holland (*née* Lane); one *s* one *d* by Mary Leahy; *m* 2005, Christabel Durham; one *d*. *Educ:* Invicta Sherington Sch.; Shooters' Hill Sch. Keyboard player with Squeeze, 1974–80; band leader, Rhythm & Blues Orch., 1993–; regular tours in UK and USA. Architect: Helicon Mountain, Greenwich; gatehouse, Witton Castle. *Television:* presenter: The Tube, 1981–86; Juke Box Jury, 1989; Sunday Night, 1990; The Happening, 1990; Later with Jools Holland, 1993–; presenter and writer, Jools Holland's Piano, 2002; actor and writer, The Groovy Fellers, 1988; writer and producer: Walking to New Orleans, 1985; Mr Roadrunner, 1991; Beat Route, 1998; Jools Meets the Saint, 1999; *radio:* presenter, The Jools Holland Show; *films:* writer and producer, Spiceworld the Movie, 1997; writer of film score, Milk, 1999. *Solo albums:* A World of his Own, 1990; Full Compliment, 1991; A-Z Geographer's Guide to the Piano, 1993; Solo Piano, 1995; Sex and Jazz and Rock and Roll, 1996; Lift the Lid, 1997; As the Sun Sets Over London, 1999; Hop the Wag, 2000; Small World Big Band, 2001; More Friends, 2002; Friends 3, 2003; jt album, Tom Jones and Jools Holland, 2004. DL Kent, 2006. *Publications:* Beat Route, 1998; (with Dora Loewenstein) Rolling Stones: a life on the road, 1998; Barefaced Lies & Boogie-Woogie Boasts: the autobiography, 2007. *Address:* Helicon Mountain Ltd, 1 Globe House, Middle Lane Mews, N8 8PN.

HOLLAND, Kevin John William C.; *see* Crossley-Holland.

HOLLAND, Norman James Abbott, IEng, FIET; Group Standards Manager, Philips UK, 1983–90; President, British National Electrotechnical Committee, 1993–99; *b* 16 Dec. 1927; *s* of James George Holland and May Stuart Holland; *m* 1951, Barbara Florence Byatt; one *s* one *d*. *Educ:* Sir Walter St John's Grammar Sch.; Regent Street Polytechnic. UK Delegate: IEC Council, 1987–92 (Delegn Leader, 1993–99; Mem. Bd, 1998–99); CENELEC Gen. Assembly, 1987–92 (Delegn Leader, 1993–99); Chm., Electrotechnical Sector Bd, 1993–99, Mem., Standards Bd, 1993–99, BSI. Member: IEC Finance Cttee, 1985–91; Engrg Council, 1985–91; Bd, Electronic Engrg Assoc., 1985–92 (Chm., Standards Policy Gp); NACCB, 1987–92. *Recreation:* golf. *Address:* 12 Pine Road, Chandler's Ford, Hants SO53 1LP.

HOLLAND, Prof. Peter William Harold, PhD, DSc; FRS 2003; Linacre Professor of Zoology, University of Oxford, since 2002; Fellow, Merton College, Oxford, since 2002; *b* 17 Aug. 1963; *s* of late William Harold Bolton and of Christine (*née* Bartrop) and step *s* of Franklin Holland; *m* 1996, Amanda Susan Horsfall; two *s*. *Educ:* Marple Hall Sch.; Queen's Coll., Oxford (MA); NIMR, London (PhD 1987); DSc Reading 2002. University of Oxford: Demonstrator, Dept of Zool., 1987–91; Browne Res. Fellow, Queen's Coll., 1988–91; Royal Soc. Univ. Res. Fellow, 1991–94; Prof. of Zool., Univ.

of Reading, 1994–2002. Member: Cttee, British Soc. Develtl Biol., 1990–95; Genes Develtl Biol. Cttee, BBSRC, 1997–99; Council, Marine Biol. Assoc., 1998–2001 (Gov., 2003–); Funding Panel, NSF, 2002–03; Comparative Genomics Wkg Gp, NIH, 2004–06. FLS 2002. Scientific Medal, Zool Soc. of London, 1996; De Snoo van 't Hoogerhuijs Medal, 1999; Genetics Soc. Medal, 2004; Blaise Pascal Medal, European Acad. of Scis, 2005; Kowalevsky Medal, St Petersburg Soc. of Naturalists, 2006. *Publications:* (ed with C. Stern) Essential Developmental Biology, 1993; (ed jtly) The Evolution of Developmental Mechanisms, 1994; res. papers in scientific jls. *Recreations:* the natural world, Lepidoptera, football, table tennis. *Address:* Merton College, Oxford OX1 4JD.

HOLLAND, Sir Philip (Welsby), Kt 1983; retired; *b* 14 March 1917; *s* of late John Holland, Middlewich, Cheshire; *m* 1943, Josephine Alma Hudson (*d* 1999); one *s*. *Educ:* Sir John Deane's Grammar Sch., Northwich. Enlisted RAF 1936; commissioned 1943. Factory Manager, Jantzen Knitting Mills, 1946–47; Management Research, 1948–49; Manufacturers' Agent in Engineering and Refractories Products, 1949–60. Contested (C) Yardley Div. of Birmingham, Gen. Election, 1955; MP (C): Acton, 1959–64; Carlton, 1966–83; Gedling, 1983–87. PPS: to Minister of Pensions and Nat. Insurance, 1961–62; to Chief Sec. to Treasury and Paymaster-Gen., 1962–64; to Minister of Aviation Supply, 1970; to Minister for Aerospace, 1971; to Minister for Trade, 1972. Pres., Cons. Trade Union Nat. Adv. Cttee, 1972–74. Personnel Manager, The Ultra Electronics Group of Companies, 1964–66; Personnel Consultant to Standard Telephones and Cables Ltd, 1969–81. Chm., Cttee of Selection, H of C, 1979–84; Standing Cttee Chm., 1983–87. Councillor, Royal Borough of Kensington, 1955–59. Rector's Warden, St Margaret's Church, Westminster, 1990–95. *Publications:* The Quango Explosion (jtly), 1978; Quango, Quango, Quango, 1979; Costing the Quango, 1979; The Quango Death List, 1980; The Governance of Quangos, 1981; Quelling the Quango, 1982; (jtly) A–Z Guide to Parliament, 1988; Lobby Fodder?, 1988; St Margaret's Westminster, 1993; The Hunting of the Quango, 1994. *Recreations:* travel, writing. *Address:* 53 Pymers Mead, West Dulwich, SE21 8NH.

HOLLAND, Richard; District Judge (Magistrates' Courts) (formerly Stipendiary Magistrate), Leicestershire, since 1999; *b* 23 Jan. 1951; *s* of Clifford Holland and Mary Holland (*née* Gledhill, now Smithies); *m* 2001, Ann, *d* of Charles and Mavis Mortimer, Wakefield. *Educ:* Colne Valley High Sch., W Yorks; Queen Mary Coll., Univ. of London (BA Hons 1971). Admitted Solicitor 1974. Articled Clerk, Magistrates' Courts Service, WR of Yorks, 1972–74; Sen. Court Clerk, 1974–75, Dep. Justices' Clerk, 1975–79, Oldham; Justices' Clerk, Rochdale, 1979–89; Justices' Clerk, and Clerk to the Magistrates' Courts Cttee, Wakefield Metropolitan Dist, 1990–97; Justices' Clerk and Chief Exec., Leeds City, 1997–99. *Recreations:* birdwatching, canal boating, the sport of Kings, feigning indolence. *Address:* Leicester City Magistrates' Court, PO Box 1, Pocklingtons Walk, Leicester LE1 6BT. *T:* (0116) 255 3666.

HOLLAND, (Robert) Einion, FIA; Chairman: Pearl Assurance PLC, 1983–89; Pearl Group PLC, 1985–89 (Director, since 1985); *b* 23 April 1927; *s* of late Robert Ellis Holland and Bene Holland; *m* 1955, Eryl Haf Roberts (*d* 1988); one *s* two *d*. *Educ:* University Coll. of N Wales, Bangor (BSc). FIA 1957. Joined Pearl Assurance Co. Ltd, 1953: Dir, 1973; Chief Gen. Manager, 1977–83. Chm., Industrial Life Offices Assoc., 1976–78; Director: Aviation & General Insurance Co. Ltd, 1972–89 (Chm. 1976–78, 1984–85); British Rail Property Board, 1987–90; Community Reinsurance Corp. Ltd, 1973–89 (Chm., 1973–76); Crawley Warren Group, 1987–99; Pearl American Corp., 1972–84; Scottish Legal Life Assurance Soc. Ltd, 1995–97. Member: Welsh Develt Agency, 1976–86; CS Pay Research Unit Bd, 1980–81; Council, Univ. of Wales, 1990–95. *Recreations:* golf and Welsh literature. *Address:* 55 Corkscrew Hill, West Wickham, Kent BR4 9BA. *T:* (020) 8777 1861.

HOLLAND, Stuart (Kingsley); political economist; Chief Executive, Alter-Europe, 1998–2003; Director, Associate Research in Economy and Society Ltd, 1993–98; *b* 25 March 1940; *y s* of late Frederick Holland and May Holland, London; *m* 1976, Jenny Lennard; two *c*. *Educ:* state primary schs; Christ's Hosp.; Univ. of Missouri (Exchange Scholar); Balliol Coll., Oxford (Domus Scholar; 1st Cl. Hons Mod. History); St Antony's Coll., Oxford (Sen. Scholar; DPhil Econs). Econ. Asst, Cabinet Office, 1966–67; Personal Asst to Prime Minister, 1967–68; Res. Fellow, Centre for Contemp. European Studies, Univ. of Sussex, 1968–71, Assoc. Fellow and Lectr, 1971–79. Vis. Scholar, Brookings Instn, Washington, DC, 1970. Adviser to Commons Expenditure Cttee, 1971–72; Special Adviser to Minister of Overseas Develt, 1974–75. MP (Lab) Vauxhall, 1979–89; Opposition frontbench spokesman on overseas develt and co-operation, 1983–87, on treasury and economic affairs, 1987–89; Prof. of Econs, Eur. Univ. Inst., Florence, 1989–93. Res. Specialist, RIIA, 1972–74; Associate, Inst. of Develt Studies, 1974– (Gov., 1983–91). Consultant: Econ. and Social Affairs Cttee, Council of Europe, 1973; Open Univ., 1973. Rapporteur, Trades Union Adv. Cttee, OECD, 1977. Chm., Public Enterprise Gp, 1973–75. European Community Commission: Mem., Expert Cttee on Inflation, 1975–76; Consultant to Directorate Gen. XVI, 1989; Dir, Proj. on Econ. and Social Cohesion, 1991–93; Adviser: to Merger Task Force, DG IV, 1991–93; to Region of Tuscany, 1992–96. Member: Council, Inst. for Workers' Control, 1974–; UN Univ. Working Party on Socio-Cultural Factors in Develt, Tokyo, 1977. Lubbock Lectr, Oxford Univ., 1975; Tom Mann Meml Lectr, Australia, 1977. Mem., Labour Party, 1962–; Mem. sub-cttees (inc. Finance and Econ. Policy, Indust. Policy, EEC, Economic Planning, Defence, Development Cooperation, Public Sector), Nat. Exec. Cttee, Labour Party, 1972–89; Executive Member: Labour Coordinating Cttee, 1978–81; European Nuclear Disarmament Campaign, 1980–83; Mem., Economic Cttee, Socialist International, 1984–. Hon. MRTPI 1980. Dr *hc* Roskilde Univ., Denmark, 1992. *Publications:* (jtly) Sovereignty and Multinational Corporations, 1971; (ed) The State as Entrepreneur, 1972; Strategy for Socialism, 1975; The Socialist Challenge, 1975; The Regional Problem, 1976; Capital versus the Regions, 1976; (ed) Beyond Capitalist Planning, 1978; Uncommon Market, 1980; (ed) Out of Crisis, 1983; (with Donald Anderson) Kissinger's Kingdom, 1984; (with James Firebrace) Never Kneel Down, 1984; The Market Economy, 1987; The Global Economy, 1987; The European Imperative: economic and social cohesion in the 1990s, 1993; Towards a New Bretton Woods: alternatives for the global economy, 1994; (with Ken Coates) Full Employment for Europe, 1995; Europe in Question: constitution, cohesion and enlargement, 2004; contrib. symposia; articles in specialist jls and national and internat. press. *Recreation:* singing in the bath.

HOLLAND, Thomas; historian and novelist; *b* Oxford, 5 Jan. 1968; *s* of Martin and Jans Holland; *m* 1992, Sadie Lowry; two *d*. *Educ:* Chafyn Grove Prep. Sch.; Canford Sch.; Queens' Coll., Cambridge (BA 1989). FEA 2008. *Publications:* The Vampire, 1995; Supping with Panthers, 1996; Deliver us from Evil, 1997; The Sleeper in the Sands, 1998; The Bonehunter, 2001; Rubicon, 2003; Persian Fire, 2005; Millennium, 2008. *Recreations:* running a cricket team, walking in Greece and Turkey, despairing of running a cricket team. *Address:* c/o Conville and Walsh, 2 Ganton Street, W1F 7QL.

HOLLAND, Prof. Walter Werner, CBE 1992; MD; FRCP, FRCPE, FRCGP, FRCPath, FFPH; Professor of Public Health Medicine, 1991–94, now Emeritus, and Hon. Director, 1968–94, Social Medicine and Health Service Research Unit, United Medical and Dental Schools of Guy's and St Thomas' Hospitals (formerly St Thomas' Hospital Medical School); *b* 5 March 1929; *s* of Henry Holland and Hertha Zentner; *m* 1964, Fiona Margaret Auchinleck Love; three *s*. *Educ:* St Thomas's Hosp. Med. Sch. London (BSc Hons 1951; MB, BS Hons 1954; MD 1964). FFCM 1972; FRCP 1973; FRCGP 1982; FRCPE 1990; FRCPath 1992. House Officer, St Thomas' Hosp., 1954–56; MRC Clin. Res. Fellow, London Sch. of Hygiene, 1959–61; Lectr, Johns Hopkins Univ., Md, USA, 1961–62; St Thomas's Hospital Medical School, later United Medical and Dental Schools of Guy's and St Thomas' Hospitals: Sen. Lectr, Dept of Medicine, 1962–64; Reader and Chm., Dept of Clin. Epidemiol. and Social Medicine 1965–68; Prof. of Clin. Epidemiol., 1968–91. Fogarty Scholar-in-Residence, NIH Bethesda, Md, 1984–85; Sawyer Scholar-in-Residence, Case Western Reserve Med. Sch. Cleveland, Ohio, 1985. Vis. Prof., LSE, 1998–. Queen Elizabeth, Queen Mother Lectr FPHM, 1995; Harben Lectr, 1995; Rock Carling Lectr, Nuffield Trust, 1997. President Internat. Epidemiol Assoc., 1987–90; Faculty of Public Health (formerly Community Medicine, RCP, 1989–92. Non-exec. Mem., Glos HA, 1992–96. FKC 1999. Life Mem. Soc. of Scholars, Johns Hopkins Univ., 1970; Hon. Mem., Amer. Epidemiol Soc., 1985 Hon. FFPHMI 1993; Hon. Fellow, UMDS, 1996. Dr *hc*: Univ. of Bordeaux, 1981; Free Univ. of Berlin, 1990. *Publications:* Data Handling in Epidemiology, 1970; Air Pollution and Respiratory Disease, 1972; Epidemiology and Health, 1977; Health Care and Epidemiology, 1978; Measurement of Levels of Health, 1979; Evaluation of Health Care 1983; Chronic Obstructive Bronchopathies, 1983; Oxford Textbook of Public Health 1984, 2nd edn 1991; (with Susie Stewart) Screening in Health Care, 1990; (ed jtly) Public Health Policies in the European Union, 1999; Foundations for Health Improvement 2002; (with S. Stewart) Screening for Health Improvement: a good use of resources, 2005 pubns on health services res., epidemiol methods and on respiratory disease. *Recreations* reading, walking. *Address:* South End Cottage, Orleans Road, Twickenham TW1 3BL *Club:* Athenæum.

HOLLAND-HIBBERT, family name of **Viscount Knutsford**.

HOLLAND-MARTIN, Robert George, (Robin); Director, Henderson (formerly Henderson Administration Group) plc, 1983–98; *b* 6 July 1939; *y s* of late Cyril Holland-Martin and Rosa, *d* of Sir Gerald Chadwyck-Healey, 2nd Bt, CBE; *m* 1976, Dominique, 2nd *d* of Maurice Fromaget; two *d*. *Educ:* Eton. Cazenove & Co., 1960–74 (partner 1968–74); Finance Director, Paterson Products Ltd, 1976–86; Consultant: Newmarket Venture Capital plc (formerly Newmarket Co.), 1982–94; Investindustrial Gp of Cos 1997–. Non-executive Director: Dorling Kindersley Hldgs plc, 1992–2000; Fine Art Soc plc, 1995–; Service Point Solutions (formerly Grupo Picking Pack) SA (Spain) 1998–2006; Grapes Direct Ltd, 2000–06. Hon. Dep. Treasurer, Cons. and Unionist Party 1979–82. Mem., Trustee Bd (formerly Council), Metropolitan Hospital-Sunday Fund 1964–2002 (Chm., 1977–2002); Mem. Council, Homoeopathic Trust, 1970–90 (Vice Chm., 1975–90). Victoria & Albert Museum: Mem. Adv. Council, 1972–83; Mem. Cttee, Associates of V&A, 1976–85 (Chm., 1981–85); Dep. Chm., Trustees, 1983–85 Mem., Visiting Cttee for Royal Coll. of Art, 1982–93 (Chm., 1984–93). Trustee: Blackie Foundn Trust, 1971–96 (Chm., 1987–96; Pres., 1998–); King's Med. Res. Trust, 2000–; C&G of London Art Sch., 2001– (Chm., 2002–). Mem., Court of Assts, Fishmongers' Co., 1999–. *Address:* 18 Tite Street, SW3 4HZ. *T:* (020) 7352 7871. *Clubs:* White's, Royal Automobile.

HOLLANDER, Charles Simon; QC 1999; a Recorder, since 2000; *b* 1 Dec. 1955; *s* of Paul and Eileen Hollander; *m* 1986, Heather Pilley; two *s* two *d*. *Educ:* University College Sch.; King's Coll., Cambridge (BA 1977; MA 1981). Called to the Bar, Gray's Inn, 1978; in practice at the Bar, 1978–. *Publications:* Documentary Evidence, 1985, 8th edn 2003, jointly: Phipson on Evidence, 15th edn 2000; Conflicts of Interest and Chinese Walls, 2000, 2nd edn 2004. *Recreations:* tennis, food, wine. *Address:* Brick Court Chambers, 7/8 Essex Street, WC2R 3LD. *T:* (020) 7379 3550.

HOLLANDS, Maj.-Gen. Graham Spencer; *b* 14 Feb. 1942; *s* of Ernest Darrell Hollands and Gwendoline Isobel Hollands (*née* Matheson); *m* 1968, Lesley Clair Billam; one *s* one *d*. *Educ:* King Edward VI Sch., Bath; RMA Sandhurst; RMCS; Staff Coll., Camberley. Commissioned RA, 1963; served BAOR and UK; MoD, 1980–81; CO 25 Field Regt RA, 1981–84; CO 3rd Regt RHA, 1984–85; COS Artillery Div., HQ 1 (BR) Corps, 1985–86; Comdr, British Trng Teams, Nigeria, 1986–87; CRA 2nd Inf. Div., 1987–89; DCOS, HQ BAOR, 1989–92; Comdr Artillery, 1st British Corps, 1992–94. Chief Exec., W Kent Coll., 1994. *Recreations:* golf, ski-ing, country pursuits.

HOLLENDEN, 4th Baron *cr* 1912, of Leigh, Kent; **Ian Hampden Hope-Morley;** part-owner and Trustee, The Hampden Estate; *b* 23 Oct. 1946; *e s* of 3rd Baron Hollenden and of Sonja (*née* Sundt); *S* father, 1999; *m* 1st, 1972, Beatrice (*née* d'Anchald) (marr. diss. 1985); one *s* one *d*; 2nd, 1988, Caroline (*née* Ash); two *s*. *Educ:* Maidwell Hall; Eton Coll. Shipbroker: Asmarine SA, Paris, 1969–72; Eggar Forrester, London, 1972–77; Mktg Mgr, British Shipbuilders, 1977–79; Shipbroker, Galbraith Wrightson, 1979–86; Proprietor, The Hampden Wine Company, Thame, 1988–98. *Recreations:* shooting, ski-ing. *Heir:* *s* Hon. Edward Hope-Morley, *b* 9 April 1981. *Address:* The Estate Office, Great Hampden, Great Missenden, Bucks HP16 9RE. *Club:* Brooks's.

HOLLENWEGER, Prof. Walter Jacob; Professor of Mission, University of Birmingham, 1971–89; *b* 1 June 1927; *s* of Walter Otto and Anna Hollenweger-Spörri; *m* 1951, Erica Busslinger. *Educ:* Univs. of Zürich and Basel. Dr theol Zürich 1966 (and degrees leading up to it). Stock Exchange, Zürich, and several banking appts, until 1948. Pastor, 1949–57; ordained, Swiss Reformed Church, 1961. Study Dir, Ev. Acad., Zürich, 1964–65; Research Asst, Univ. of Zürich, 1961–64; Exec. Sec., World Council of Churches, Geneva, 1965–71; regular guest prof. in Switzerland, Germany and USA. Hon. Fellow, Selly Oak Colls, Birmingham, 1996. Prize for Theol., Sexau, Germany, 1995; Lifetime Achievement Award, Soc. for Pentecostal Studies, USA, 1999. *Publications:* Handbuch der Pfingstbewegung, 10 vols, 1965/66; (ed) The Church for Others, 1967 (also German, Spanish and Portuguese edns); (ed) Die Pfingstkirchen, 1971; Kirche, Benzin und Bohnensuppe, 1971; The Pentecostals, 1972, 1988 (also German and Spanish edns); Pentecost between Black and White, 1975 (also German and Dutch edns); Glaube, Geist und Geister, 1975; (ed) Studies in the Intercultural History of Christianity, 100 vols, 1975–; Evangelism Today, 1976 (also German edn); (with Th. Ahrens) Volkschristentum und Volksreligion in Pazifik, 1977; Interkulturelle Theologie, vol. I, 1979, vol. II, 1982, vol. III, 1988 (abridged French edn); Erfahrungen in Ephesus, 1979; Wie Grenzen zu Brücken werden, 1980; Besuch bei Lukas, 1981; Conflict in Corinth—Memoirs of an Old Man, 1982 (also German, Italian, Indonesian and French edns; musical and drama edn, 1999); Jüngermesse/Gomer: Das Gesicht des Unsichtbaren, 1983 (music edns 1994 and 1995); Zwingli zwischen Krieg und Frieden, 1983, 1988; Das Fest der Verlorenen, 1984; Der Handelsreisende Gottes, 1985 (music edn 1994); Das Wagnis des Glaubens, 1986 (music edn 1993); Weihnachtsoratorium, 1986; Mirjam, Mutter, and Michal: Die Frauen meines Mannes (zwei Monodramen), 1987 (music edn 1994); Bonhoeffer Requiem, 1990 (music edn 1992); Ostertanz der Frauen/Veni Creator Spiritus, 1990; Kommet her zu mir/Die zehn Aussätzigen, 1990; Fontana (musical), 1991; Jona (musical), 1992; Hiob im Kreuzfeuer der Religionen, 1993; Jürg Rathgeb (oratorio), 1993; Der Kommissar auf biblischer Spurensuche, 1993; Ruth, die Ausländerin, 1993; Kamele und Kapitalisten, 1994; Johannestexte, 1995; Scherben, 1996; Pentecostalism, 1997 (also German edn); Maria von Wedemeyer, 1997; Nympha und Onesimus, 1999; Neuer Himmel—neue Erde, 1999; Der Klapperstorch und die Theologie, 2000; Das Kirchenjahr inszenieren, 2002; Petrus, der Pontifex, 2002; Der Freund der Frauen, 2008; Albert Schweitzer, 2008; *relevant publication:* Theology Out of Place: a theological biography of Walter J. Hollenweger, by Lynne Price, 2002. *Address:* 3704 Krattigen, Switzerland. *T:* (33) 6544302.

HOLLEY, Rear Adm. Ronald Victor, CB 1987; FRAeS; Independent Inspector, Lord Chancellor's Panel, 1992–2001; *b* 13 July 1931; *s* of late Mr and Mrs V. E. Holley; *m* 1954, Sister Dorothy Brierley, QARNNS; two *s* twin *d. Educ:* Rondebosch, S Africa; Portsmouth GS; RNEC Manadon; RAFC Henlow (post graduate); Dip. Music Open Univ. 2003. MIMechE, MIET; FRAeS 1988. Served HM Ships Implacable, Finisterre, Euryalus, Victorious, Eagle (899 Sqdn); NATO Defence Coll., Rome, 1968; Naval Plans, 1969–71; Aircraft Dept, 1971–73; Air Engr Officer, HMS Seahawk, 1973–75; Naval Asst to Controller of the Navy, 1975–77; RCDS, 1978; Seaman Officer Develt Study, 1979; Dir, Helicopter Projects, Procurement Exec., 1979–82; RNEC in command, 1982–84; Sen. Naval Mem., Directing Staff, RCDS, 1984–85; Dir Gen. Aircraft (Navy), 1985–87. Tech. Dir, Shell Aircraft, 1987–92. Sec., European Helicopter Operators Cttee, 1988–91. President: RN Volunteer Bands, 1983–87; RN Amateur Fencing Assoc., 1986–87 (Chm., 1983–86). Member: Parly Gp for Engrg Develt, 1993–2007; Parly Mull of Kintyre Gp, 2003–. Henson and Stringfellow Lectr, RAeS, 1987. *Publications:* contribs to Naval Jls, and Seaford House Papers, 1978. *Recreation:* the Philharmonia Orchestra.

HOLLICK, family name of **Baron Hollick**.

HOLLICK, Baron *cr* 1991 (Life Peer), of Notting Hill in the Royal Borough of Kensington and Chelsea; **Clive Richard Hollick;** Partner, Kohlberg Kravis Roberts, since 2006; *b* 20 May 1945; *s* of Leslie George Hollick and Olive Mary (*née* Scruton); *m* 1977, Susan Mary Woodford (*see* Lady Hollick); three *d. Educ:* Taunton's Sch., Southampton; Univ. of Nottingham (BA Hons). Joined Hambros Bank Ltd, 1968, Dir, 1973–96; Chairman: Shepperton Studios Ltd, 1976–84; Garban Ltd (USA), 1983–97; Founder and Chm., Meridian Broadcasting Ltd, 1992–96; Chief Executive: Mills & Allen Internat., subseq. MAI PLC, 1974–96; United News & Media, subseq. United Business Media plc, 1996–2005; Director: Logica plc, 1987–91; Avenir Havas Media SA, 1989–92; Satellite Information Systems Ltd, 1990–94; British Aerospace, 1992–97; Anglia Television, 1994–97; TRW Inc., 2000–02; Diageo plc, 2001– (Sen. Dir, 2004–); Honeywell Inc., 2003–; Nielsen Inc., 2007–; Pro Sieben Media AG, 2007–. Special Advr to Pres. of BoT and Sec. of State for Trade and Industry, 1997–98. Chm., South Bank Centre, 2002–08. Member: Nat. Bus Co. Ltd, 1984–91; Adv. Cttee, Dept of Applied Econs, Univ. of Cambridge, 1989–97; Financial Law Panel, 1993–97; Commn on Public Policy and British Business, 1995–97. Chm., Galleon Trust, 1992–97. Founding Trustee, Inst. for Public Policy Res., 1988–. Gov., LSE, 1997–2003. Hon. LLD Nottingham, 1993. *Recreations:* reading, theatre, music, cinema, golf, countryside.

HOLLICK, Lady; Susan Mary Woodford-Hollick; Chair, London Regional Council, Arts Council England (formerly London Arts Board), since 2000; *b* 16 May 1945; *d* of Ulric Cross and Joan Woodford; *m* 1977, Clive Richard Hollick (*see* Baron Hollick); three *d. Educ:* La Retraite Convent High Sch., London; Univ. of Sussex (BA Hons). Producer/Dir, World in Action, Granada TV, 1969–81; Founding Commissioning Ed. for multicultural progs, Channel 4 TV, 1980–84; Founder and Dir, Bringing Up Baby Ltd, 1989–. Chm., Index on Censorship, 1993–2000. Member: Arts Council England (formerly Arts Council of England), 2002–; Adv. Bd, Tate Modern, 2000–; Chair: Tate Members' Council, 1999–2005. Chair, AMREF UK, 2007–; Dir, ENO, 1999–2001. *Publication:* The Good Nursery Guide, 1992. *Recreations:* the arts, television, cinema, tennis, golf, horse riding. *Address:* Arts Council England, London, 2 Pear Tree Court, EC1R 0DS. *Clubs:* Royal Commonwealth Society; Queenwood Golf (Ottershaw, Surrey).

HOLLIDAY, Sir Frederick (George Thomas), Kt 1990; CBE 1975; FRSE; Chairman, Northumbrian Water Group, 1993–2006 (Director, 1991); *b* 22 Sept. 1935; *s* of late Alfred C. and Margaret Holliday; *m* 1957, Philippa Mary Davidson; one *s* one *d. Educ:* Bromsgrove County High Sch.; Sheffield Univ. BSc 1st cl. hons Zool. 1956; FIBiol 1970, FRSE 1971. Fisheries Research Trng Grant (Develt Commn) at Marine Lab., Aberdeen, 1956–58; Sci. Officer, Marine Lab., Aberdeen, 1958–61; Lectr in Zoology, Univ. of Aberdeen, 1961–66; Prof. of Biology, 1967–75, Dep. Principal, 1972, Acting Principal, 1973–75, Univ. of Stirling; Prof. of Zoology, Univ. of Aberdeen, 1975–79; Vice-Chancellor and Warden, Univ. of Durham, 1980–90. Member: Scottish Cttee, Nature Conservancy, 1969; Council, Scottish Field Studies Assoc., 1970–78 (Pres., 1981–90); Council, Scottish Marine Biol Assoc., 1967–85 (Pres., 1979–85); Scottish Wildlife Trust (Vice-Pres.); Council, Freshwater Biol Assoc., 1969–72, and 1993–2000 (Pres., 1995–2001); NERC Oceanography and Fisheries Research Grants Cttee, 1971; Council, NERC, 1973–79; Nature Conservancy Council, 1975–80 (Dep. Chm., 1976–77, Chm., 1977–80); Scottish Economic Council, 1975–80; Council, Marine Biol Assoc. UK, 1975–78 (Vice-Pres., 1994–); Oil Develt Council for Scotland, 1976–78; Standing Commn on Energy and the Environment, 1978–82; Adv. Cttee, Leverhulme Trust Res. Awards, 1978–95 (Chm., 1989–95); PCFC, 1989–93; Awards Council, Royal Anniv. Trust, 1993–95; Council, Water Aid, 1994–98; Envmtl Cttee, CBI, 1994–2006; Chm., Independent Review of Disposal of Radioactive Waste at Sea, 1984; Ind. Chm., Jt Nature Conservation Cttee, 1991. Dir, Shell UK, 1980–99; Mem., Shell UK Audit Cttee, 1993–94; Chairman: Investors' Cttee, Northern Venture Partnership Fund, 1990–2001; Northern Venture Capital Fund, 1996–; Go-Ahead Gp, 1998–2002 (Dir, 1997–2002); Dep. Chm., Northern Regional Bd, Lloyd's Bank, 1989–91 (Mem., 1985–91; Chm., 1986–89); Director: Northern Investors Ltd, 1984–90; BRB, 1990–94 (Chm., BR (Eastern), 1986–90); Union Railways, 1993–97; Lyonnaise des Eaux SA, 1996–97; Lyonnaise Europe plc, 1996–2000; Suez Lyonnaise des Eaux, 1997–2001; Wisespeke Plc, 1997–98; Brewin Dolphin Gp, 1998–2005 (Chm., 2003–05). Pres., NE Reg. Assoc. for Sci. Educn, 2004–06. Trustee, Nat. Heritage Meml Fund, 1980–91; Vice-Pres., Civic Trust for NE; Mem., Scottish Civic Trust, 1984–87; Pres., British Trust for Ornithology, 1996–2001. Member, Board of Governors: Rowett Res. Inst., 1976–84; Lathallan Sch., 2005–. DUniv Stirling, 1984; Hon. DSc: Sheffield, 1987; Cranfield, 1991; Hon. DCL Durham, 2002. DL Durham, 1985–90. *Publications:* (ed and contrib.) Wildlife of Scotland, 1979; numerous on fish biology and wildlife conservation in Adv. Mar. Biol., Fish Physiology, Oceanography and Marine Biology, etc. *Recreations:* ornithology, microscopy, walking, gardening. *Address:* Northern Venture Managers, Princess Square, Newcastle upon Tyne NE1 8ER. *T:* (0191) 244 6000.

HOLLIDAY, Dr Robin, FRS 1976; Chief Research Scientist, Commonwealth Scientific and Industrial Research Organisation (Australia), 1988–97; *b* 6 Nov. 1932; *s* of Clifford and Eunice Holliday; *m* 1st, 1957, Diana Collet (*née* Parsons) (marr. diss. 1983); one *s* three *d*; 2nd, 1986, Lily Irene (*née* Huschtscha); one *d. Educ:* Hitchin Grammar Sch.; Univ. of Cambridge (BA, PhD); Fulbright Scholar, 1962. Member, Scientific Staff: Dept of Genetics, John Innes Inst., Bayfordbury, Herts, 1958–65; Division of Microbiology, Nat. Inst. for Med. Research, Mill Hill, 1965–70; Head, Div. of Genetics, Nat. Inst. for Med. Research, 1970–88. Mem., EMBO, 1976. FAA 2005. For. Fellow, INSA, 1995. Lord Cohen Medal, 1987. *Publications:* The Science of Human Progress, 1981; Genes, Proteins and Cellular Aging, 1986; Understanding Ageing, 1995; Slaves and Saviours, 2000; Aging: the paradox of life, 2007; over 250 scientific papers on genetic recombination, repair, gene expression and cellular ageing. *Recreations:* sculpture, writing. *Address:* 12 Roma Court, West Pennant Hills, NSW 2125, Australia. *T:* (2) 98733476, *Fax:* (2) 98712159; *e-mail:* randl.holliday@bigpond.com.

HOLLIDAY, Steven John; Chief Executive, National Grid, since 2007; *b* Exeter, 26 Oct. 1956; *s* of Michael and Jean Holliday; *m* 1996, Kate Patterson; three *d. Educ:* Univ. of Nottingham (BSc Mining Engrg 1978). Esso/Exxon, 1978–97: Ops Manager, Fawley Refinery, Esso UK, 1988–92; Supply and Transportation Divl Dir, Esso UK, 1992–94; Regl Vice-Pres. Gas, Exxon Co. Internat., 1994–97; Bd Dir, British Borneo Oil and Gas, 1997–2000; National Grid: Bd Dir responsible for Transmission, 2001–03; Gp Dir responsible for UK Gas Distribution and Business Services, 2003–07. Non-exec. Dir, Marks & Spencer, 2004–. *Recreations:* sports, Rugby, ski-ing, arts. *Address:* National Grid, 1–3 Strand, WC2N 5EH. *T:* (020) 7004 3021, *Fax:* (020) 7004 3022; *e-mail:* steven.holliday@ngrid.com.

HOLLIGER, Heinz; oboist, composer and conductor; *b* Langenthal, Switzerland, 21 May 1939; *m* Ursula Holliger, harpist. *Educ:* Berne Conservatoire; Paris; Basle; studied with Cassagnaud, Lefébure, Veress, Pierlot and Boulez. Played with Basle Orch., 1959–63; Prof. of oboe, Freiburg Music Acad., 1965–2003. Has appeared as soloist and conductor at all major European music festivals, and with Chamber Orch. of Europe, English Chamber Orch., etc; has directed all major Swiss orchs, Cleveland Orch., Philharmonia, Vienna Philharmonic, Vienna SO, CBSO, Berlin Philharmonic, Concertgebouw, etc. Has inspired compositions by Berio, Penderecki, Stockhausen, Henze, Martin and others. *Compositions include:* Der magische Tänzer, Trio, Dona nobis pacem, Pneuma, Psalm, Cardiophonie, Kreis, Siebengesang, H for wind quintet, string quartet Atembogen, Scardanelli-Cycle, Gesänge der Frühe, (S)irato for orch., Violin Concerto, Partita, Puneigä. Has won many international prizes, including: Geneva Competition first prize, 1959; Munich Competition first prize, 1961; Sonning Prize; Frankfurt Music Prize; Ernst von Siemens Prize. *Address:* Konzertgesellschaft, Hochstrasse 51/Postfach, 4002 Basel, Switzerland.

HOLLINGHURST, Alan James, FRSL; writer; *b* 26 May 1954; *s* of James Kenneth Hollinghurst and Elizabeth Lilian Hollinghurst (*née* Keevil). *Educ:* Canford Sch.; Magdalen Coll., Oxford (BA 1975; MLitt 1979). On staff, TLS, 1982–95. Vis. Prof., Univ. of Houston, 1998; Old Dominion Fellow, Princeton Univ., 2004. FRSL 1995. *Publications:* The Swimming-Pool Library, 1988 (Somerset Maugham Award, E. M. Forster Award, AAAL); (trans.) Bajazet, by Jean Racine, 1991; The Folding Star, 1994 (James Tait Black Meml Prize); The Spell, 1998; The Line of Beauty (Man Booker Prize), 2004. *Recreations:* looking at buildings, listening to music. *Address:* 15 Tanza Road, NW3 2UA. *Club:* Cranium.

HOLLINGHURST, Edmund, FREng, FICE, FIStructE; FIHT; Director and Partner, since 1986, now Senior Partner, Gifford & Partners; *b* 27 June 1944; *s* of Rev. Dr George Frederick Hollinghurst and Rachel Hollinghurst (*née* Cooper); *m* 1986, Glenys Helen Davis; three *d. Educ:* Dragon Sch., Oxford; Kingswood Sch., Bath; Sidney Sussex Coll., Cambridge (MA). CEng 1971; FIHT 1985; FICE 1995; FIStructE 1995; FREng (FEng 1997). Trainee, Ove Arup & Partners, 1962–63; Engineer: Ninham Shand, Cape Town, SA, 1965–66; Ove Arup & Partners, London, Africa and Middle East, 1967–70; Kier Ltd, UK and overseas, 1970–73; Gifford & Partners, 1973–86, seconded as staff consultant, Asian Develt Bank, 1978. Mem., Royal Fine Art Commn, 1996–99. Vis. Prof., Univ. of Southampton. Major designs include: Bray Viaduct, Devon; Kwai Chung, Hong Kong; Dee Crossing, Wales; Second Severn Crossing; Camel Estuary Bridge, Cornwall; Kingston Bridge, Glasgow; River Tyne Millennium Bridge. Fédération Internationale de la Précontrainte Design Award, for Bray Viaduct, 1994. *Publications:* contrib. to ICE and IStructE texts. *Recreation:* sailing. *Address:* Gifford & Partners, Carlton House, Ringwood Road, Woodlands, Southampton SO40 7HT. *T:* (023) 8081 3461.

HOLLINGS, Sir (Alfred) Kenneth, Kt 1971; MC 1944; Judge of the High Court of Justice, Family Division (formerly Probate, Divorce and Admiralty Division), 1971–93; *b* 12 June 1918; *s* of Alfred Holdsworth Hollings and Rachel Elizabeth Hollings; *m* 1949, Harriet Evelyn Isabella, *d* of W. J. C. Fishbourne, OBE, Brussels; one *s* one *d. Educ:* Leys Sch., Cambridge; Clare Coll., Cambridge. Law Qualifying and Law Tripos, Cambridge, 1936–39; MA. Served RA (Shropshire Yeomanry), 1939–46. Called to Bar, Middle Temple, 1947 (Harmsworth Schol.); Master of the Bench, 1971. Practised Northern Circuit; QC 1966; Recorder of Bolton, 1968; Judge of County Courts, Circuit 5 (E Lancs), 1968–71; Presiding Judge, Northern Circuit, 1975–78. *Clubs:* Hurlingham; Tennis and Racquets (Manchester).

HOLLINGSWORTH, Michael Charles; Chairman, Venture Television Ltd (trading as Venture Artistes, Venture Broadcasting, and Venture Correspondents), since 2007 (Chief Executive, 1993–2007); Head of Celebrity Liaison, Cancer Research UK, since 2005; *b* 22 Feb. 1946; *s* of Albert George Hollingsworth and Gwendoline Marjorie Hollingsworth; *m* 1st, 1968, Patricia Margaret Jefferson Winn (marr. diss. 1987); one *d*; 2nd, 1989, Anne Margaret Diamond (marr. diss. 1999); four *s* (and one *s* decd). *Educ:* Carlisle Grammar Sch.; Ruskin Coll., Oxford. Programme Editor, Anglia Television, 1964–67; Producer, BBC Local Radio, 1967–74; Northern Editor, Today, Radio Four, 1974–75; Editor, News and Current Affairs: Southern Television Ltd, 1975–79; ATV Network/Central, 1979–82; Sen. Producer, Current Affairs, BBC TV, 1982–84; Dir of Programmes, TV-am Ltd, 1984–86; Man. Dir, Music Box Ltd, 1986–89. Agent and consultant to television and radio cos, and to charities. FRSA. *Recreation:* DIY (house renovation). *Address:* Macready House, 75 Crawford Street, W1H 5LP; *e-mail:* venturemike@btinternet.com.

HOLLINGTON, Robin Frank; QC 1999; a Recorder, since 2004; *b* 30 June 1955; *s* of late Reginald Barrie Hollington and of Eleanor Gwendoline Hollington (*née* Paxton); *m* 1988, Jane Elizabeth Cadogan Gritten; one *s. Educ:* Haileybury; University Coll., Oxford (MA); Univ. of Pennsylvania (LLM). Called to the Bar, Lincoln's Inn, 1979, Bencher, 2007. *Publication:* Minority Shareholders' Rights, 1990, 5th edn as Shareholders' Rights, 2007. *Recreations:* Real tennis, lawn tennis, golf. *Address:* New Square Chambers, 12 New Square, Lincoln's Inn, WC2A 3SW. *T:* (020) 7419 8000. *Clubs:* Royal Automobile, MCC; Walton Heath Golf.

HOLLINGWORTH, Clare, OBE 1984; Correspondent in Hong Kong for Sunday Telegraph, since 1981; Research Associate (formerly Visiting Scholar), Centre of Asian Studies, University of Hong Kong, since 1981; *b* 10 Oct. 1911; *d* of John Albert Hollingworth and Daisy Gertrude Hollingworth; *m* 1st, 1936, Vyvyan Derring Vandeleur Robinson (marr. diss. 1951); 2nd, 1952, Geoffrey Spencer Hoare (*d* 1966). *Educ:* Girls' Collegiate Sch., Leicester; Grammar Sch., Ashby de la Zouch, Leics; Sch. of Slavonic Studies, Univ. of London. On staff, League of Nations Union, 1935–38; worked in Poland for Lord Mayor's Fund for Refugees from Czechoslovakia, 1939; Correspondent in Poland for Daily Telegraph: first to report outbreak of war from Katawice; remained in Balkans as Germans took over; moved to Turkey and then Cairo, 1941–50, covering Desert Campaigns, troubles in Persia and Iraq, Civil War in Greece and events in Palestine; covered trouble spots from Paris for Manchester Guardian, 1950–63, incl. Algerian War, Egypt, Aden and Vietnam (Journalist of the Year Award and Hannan Swaffer Award, 1963); Guardian Defence Correspondent, 1963–67; Daily Telegraph: foreign trouble shooter, 1967–73, covering war in Vietnam; Correspondent in China, 1973–76; Defence Correspondent, 1976–81. Hon. DLitt Leicester, 1993. James Cameron Award for Journalism, 1994. *Publications:* Poland's Three Weeks War, 1940; There's a German Just Behind Me, 1945; The Arabs and the West, 1951; Mao and the Men Against Him, 1984; Front Line, 1990, new edn 2005. *Recreations:* visiting second-hand furniture and bookshops, collecting modern pictures and Chinese porcelain, music. *Address:* 19 Dorset Square, NW1 6QB. *T:* (020) 7262 6923; 302 Ridley House, 2 Upper Albert Road, Hong Kong. *T:* 28681838. *Clubs:* Cercle de l'Union Interalliée (Paris); Foreign Correspondents (Hong Kong and Tokyo).

HOLLINGWORTH, John Harold; *b* 11 July 1930; *s* of Harold Hollingworth, Birmingham; *m* 1969, Susan Barbara (marr. diss. 1985), *d* of late J. H. Walters, Ramsey, IoM. *Educ:* Chigwell House Sch.; King Edward's Sch., Edgbaston. MP (C) All Saints Division of Birmingham, 1959–64; contested (C) Birmingham, All Saints, 1966 and 1970. Chairman: Birmingham Young Conservatives, 1958–62; Edgbaston Div. Conservative Assoc., 1967–72; Vice-Chm., Birmingham Conservative Assoc., 1958–61, 1972–78 (Vice-Pres. 1960–66). Dir and Gen. Manager, Cambridge Symphony Orch. Trust, 1979–82 (Gov., 1982–92); Dir, Thaxted Fest. Foundn, 1987–93. Chm., Elmdon Trust Ltd, 1984–91; dir of other cos; mem. of various charitable activities. Trustee, 1991–98, Hon. Chief Exec., 1992–93, Hon. Treas., 1993–98, British Performing Arts Medicine Trust. Member: Viola d'Amore Soc. of GB; ESU. *Publications:* contributions to political journals. *Recreations:* exercising Rough Collie dogs, planning third British Empire. *Address:* 10 Hamel Way, Widdington, Saffron Walden, CB11 3SJ. *T:* (01799) 542445. *Club:* Lansdowne.

HOLLINGWORTH, Rt Rev. Dr Peter John, AC 2001 (AO 1988); OBE 1976; Governor General of the Commonwealth of Australia, 2001–03; *b* 10 April 1935; *m* 1960, Kathleen Ann Turner; three *d*. *Educ:* Murrumbeena and Lloyd Street State Schools; Scotch Coll., Melbourne; Trinity Coll., Univ. of Melbourne (BA 1958; MA 1980); Australian Coll. of Theol. (ThL 1959); Univ. of Melbourne (Dip. Social Studies, 1970). Commercial Cadet, Broken Hill Pty, 1952–53. Ordained, 1960; Priest in charge, St Mary's, N Melbourne, 1960–64; Brotherhood of St Laurence: Chaplain and Dir of Youth Work, 1964–70; Assoc. Dir, 1970–79; Exec. Dir, 1980–90; Canon, St Paul's Cathedral, Melbourne, 1980; Bishop in the Inner City, dio. of Melbourne, 1985–90; Archbishop of Brisbane and Metropolitan, Province of Queensland, 1990–2001. Chairman: Social Responsibilities Commn, Gen. Synod, Anglican Church of Aust., 1990–98; Nat. Council for the Centenary of Fedn, 2000. Mem., Australian Assoc. of Social Workers, 1970–78. FAIM 1997; Hon. Fellow, Trinity Coll., Melbourne, 1998. Hon. LLD: Monash, 1986; Melbourne, 1990; DUniv: Griffith, 1993; Qld Univ. of Technol., 1994; Univ. of Central Qld, 1995; DLitt Univ. of Southern Qld, 1999; DLitt Lambeth 2001. KStJ 2001; Nat. ChLJ 1998–2001; GCLJ 1998. Australian of the Year, 1991. *Publications:* Australians in Poverty, 1978; The Powerless Poor, 1972; The Poor: victims of affluence, 1975; Public Thoughts of an Archbishop, 1996. *Recreations:* writing, reading, swimming, music, the arts. *Address:* PO Box 18081, Collins Street East, Melbourne, Vic 8003, Australia.

HOLLINS, Rear-Adm. Hubert Walter Elphinstone, CB 1974; marine consultant; *b* 8 June 1923; *s* of Lt-Col W. T. Hollins; *m* 1963, Jillian Mary McAlpin; one *s* one *d*. *Educ:* Stubbington House; Britannia RNC Dartmouth. Cadet RN, 1937; Comdr 1957; Captain 1963; Rear-Adm. 1972; comd HM Ships Petard, Dundas, Caesar and Antrim; Flag Officer, Gibraltar, 1972–74; Admiral Commanding Reserves, 1974–77; Gen. Man., ME Navigation Aids Service, Bahrain, 1977–84. Younger Brother of Trinity House; Mem., Trinity House Lighthouse Bd, 1985–91. Commodore, Bahrain Yacht Club, 1981–83. Master Mariner. Trustee, Royal Merchant Navy Sch., Bearwood, 1985–92; President: Newbury RN Assoc., 1985–90; Newbury Sea Cadet Corps, 1985–91 (Patron, 1991); Milford Haven Sea Cadet Corps, 2003–. Vice Patron, Gallantry Medallists' League, 1995–2003. *Recreation:* fishing. *Address:* Waunllan, Llandyfriog, Newcastle Emlyn, Cardiganshire SA38 9HB. *T:* (01239) 710456; *e-mail:* jandhhollins@onetel.net.

HOLLINS, Peter Thomas; Chief Executive (formerly Director General), British Heart Foundation, since 2003; *b* 22 Oct. 1947; *m* 1973, Linda Pitchford; two *d*. *Educ:* Hertford Coll., Oxford (2nd Cl. Hons Chem.). British Oxygen, 1970–73; ICI UK, 1973–89; ICI Holland, 1989–92; EVC Brussels, 1992–98; Chief Exec., British Energy, 1998–2001. Holds various non-exec. directorships. *Recreations:* fluent in Dutch, German and French, classical music, travelling, Rugby, hill-walking. *Address:* British Heart Foundation, 14 Fitzhardinge Street, W1H 6DH.

HOLLINS, Prof. Sheila Clare, FRCPsych; FRCPCH; FRCP; Professor of Psychiatry of Learning Disability, St George's, University of London (formerly St George's Hospital Medical School), since 1990; *b* 22 June 1946; *d* of late Captain Adrian Morgan Kelly, Bristol, and of Monica Dallas Kelly (*née* Edwards); *m* 1969, Martin Prior Hollins, *s* of late Harry Pryor Hollins; one *s* three *d*. *Educ:* Notre Dame High Sch., Sheffield; St Thomas's Hosp. Med. Sch., London (MB BS). MRCPsych 1978, FRCPsych 1988; FRCPCH, FRCP 2007. Sen. Registrar in Child Psychiatry, Earls Court Child Guidance Unit and Westminster Children's Hosp., 1979–81; Sen. Lectr in Psychiatry of Learning Disability, 1981–90, Hd, Div. of Mental Health, 2003–05, St George's Hosp. Med. Sch.; Winston Churchill Fellow, 1993; Hon. Consultant: Wandsworth Community Health Trust and Richmond, Twickenham and Roehampton Healthcare Trust, 1981–99; SW London Community Health Trust, 1999–2002; SW London and St George's Mental Health Trust, 2002–. On secondment to Policy Div., DoH, as pt-time Policy Advr on learning disability, 1993–94 and 2001–03; Member: Minister's Adv. Gp on Learning Disability, 1999–2001; Learning Disability Task Force, 2001–; Chairman: NHS Wkg Party on Breast and Cervical Screening in Learning Disability, 1999–2000; External Adv. Gp, Nat. Confidential Inquiry into Suicides and Homicides, 2007–; Dep. Chm., Nat. Specialist Commissioning Adv. Gp, 2006–. Royal College of Psychiatrists: Vice-Pres., 2003–04; Pres., 2005–08; Chm., Exec. Cttee, Psychiatry of Learning Disability Faculty, 1994–98; Mem., Ct of Electors, 1999–2005; Mem., Bd of Internat. Affairs, 2001–05. Mem., Acad. of Med. Royal Colls, 2005–08. Mem., Community Care and Disability Sub-cttee, Joseph Rowntree Foundn, 1989–93. FRSocMed. Mem., Lay Community of St Benedict.

Publications: (ed with M. Craft) Mental Handicap: a multi-disciplinary approach, 1985 (with M. Grimes) Going Somewhere: pastoral care for people with mental handicap, 1988 (with J. Curran) Understanding Depression in People with Learning Disabilities, 1996 (with L. Sireling) Understanding Grief, 1999; editor and joint author 33 titles in Book Beyond Words series, including: Hug Me, Touch Me, 1994 (Best Author, Read Easy Awards Book Trust and Joseph Rowntree Foundn); (with J. Bernal) Getting on with Epilepsy, 1999; Looking After My Breasts, 2000; (jtly) George Gets Smart, 2001; with L Sireling: When Dad Died, 1990; When Mum Died, 1990; with V. Sinason: Jenny Speaks Out, 1992; Bob Tells All, 1992; Mugged, 2002; Supporting Victims, 2007; contrib numerous peer-reviewed papers on mental health and learning disability. *Recreations:* family, walking, music. *Address:* Division of Mental Health, St George's, University of London, Cranmer Terrace, SW17 0RE. *T:* (020) 8725 5501, *Fax:* (020) 8672 1070 *e-mail:* s.hollins@sgul.ac.uk.
See also J. M. Kelly.

HOLLIS, family name of **Baroness Hollis of Heigham.**

HOLLIS OF HEIGHAM, Baroness *cr* 1990 (Life Peer), of Heigham in the City o Norwich; **Patricia Lesley Hollis;** PC 1999; DL; DPhil; FRHistS; *b* 24 May 1941; *d* o (Harry) Lesley (George) Wells and Queenie Rosalyn Wells; *m* 1965, (James) Martin Hollis FBA (*d* 1998); two *s*. *Educ:* Plympton Grammar Sch.; Cambridge Univ. (MA); Univ. o California; Columbia Univ., NY; Nuffield Coll., Oxford (DPhil). Harkness Fellow 1962–64; Nuffield Scholar, 1964–67. University of East Anglia: Lectr, 1967, then Reader and Sen. Fellow in Modern Hist.; Dean, School of English and American Studies 1988–90. Councillor: Norwich City Council, 1968–91 (Leader, 1983–88); Norfolk CC 1981–85. Member: Regional Econ. Planning Council, 1975–79; Govt Commn on Housing, 1975–77; RHA, 1979–83; BBC Regional Adv. Cttee, 1979–83; Bd, Pension Adv. Service, 2006–. Vice-President: ADC, 1990–97; AMA, 1990–97; Assoc. of Envmt Health Officers, 1992–97; NFHA, 1993–97. Dir, Radio Broadland, 1983–97. Nat. Comr English Heritage, 1988–91; Mem. Press Council, 1989–90. Contested (Lab) G Yarmouth, Feb. and Oct. 1974, 1979. An opposition whip, 1990–97; oppositio frontbench spokesperson on social security, disability, local govt and housing, 1992–97 Parly Under-Sec. of State, DSS, 1997–2001, DWP, 2001–05. Trustee: Hist. of Parlt Trust 2005–; Policy Studies Inst., 2006–; Pensions Adv. Service, 2006–. Hon. Pres., Women' Local Govt Soc., 2007–. FRHistS. DL Norfolk, 1994. Hon. DLitt: Anglia Poly. Univ. 1995; London Guildhall, 2001; DUniv Open, 2000. *Publications:* The Pauper Press, 1970 Class and Conflict, 1815–50, 1973; Pressure from Without, 1974; Women in Publi 1850–1900, 1979; (with Dr B. H. Harrison) Robert Lowery, Radical and Chartist, 1979 Ladies Elect: women in English local government 1865–1914, 1987; Jennie Lee: a life 1997 (Orwell Prize; Wolfson Hist. Prize, 1998). *Recreations:* boating, singing, domesticity *Address:* House of Lords, SW1A 0PW. *T:* (020) 7219 3000.

HOLLIS, Rt Rev. Crispian; see Portsmouth, Bishop of, (RC).

HOLLIS, Daniel Ayrton; QC 1968; a Recorder of the Crown Court, 1972–96; *b* 30 April 1925; *m* 1st, 1950, Gillian Mary Turner (marr. diss. 1961); one *d* (one *s* decd); 2nd, 1963, Stella Hydleman; one *s*. *Educ:* Geelong Grammar Sch., Australia; Brasenose Coll. Oxford. Served N Atlantic and Mediterranean, 1943–46. Lieut-Commander, RNVR. Called to Bar, Middle Temple, 1949; Bencher, 1975; Treas., 1994; Head of Chambers, 1968–95. A Comr, CCC, 1971; a Dep. High Ct Judge, 1982–93. Mem., Criminal Injuries Compensation Bd, 1995–2000. Mem., Home Sec.'s Adv. Bd on Restricted Patients 1986–92. *Address:* 22 St James's Square, SW1Y 4JH; 8 place Fontaine Vieille, La Garde Freinet 83680, France. *Club:* Travellers.

HOLLIS, Geoffrey Alan; Director, Drew Associates, since 1997; *b* 25 Nov. 1943; *s* of late William John Hollis and of Elsie Jean Hollis (*née* Baker); *m* 1967, Ann Josephine Prentice; two *s*. *Educ:* Hastings Grammar Sch.; Hertford Coll., Oxford (MA); Polytechnic of Central London (Dip. Management Studies). International Computers, 1966; International Publishing Corp., 1967; Gulf Oil, 1969; MAFF, 1974–96; seconded to FCO, First Sec., 1977–80, UK Perm. Rep., EC, Brussels; Under Sec. and Hd of Meat, later Livestock Gp, 1991–96. Non-executive Director: Lucas Ingredients (Dalgety plc), 1991–95; E and H Herts HA, 1998–2001; Mem., Welwyn Hatfield PCT, 2001–06. Chm., Welwyn & Hatfield CAB, 2006–. Admitted to Co. of Clockmakers, 1997. Clocks Advr, St Albans Dio. *Recreations:* chess, golf, horology. *Address:* 12 Lodge Drive, Hatfield, Herts AL9 5HN.

HOLLIS, Keith Martin John; His Honour Judge Hollis; a Circuit Judge, since 2000; *b* 9 June 1951; *s* of Eric and Joan Hollis; *m* 1979, Mariana Roberts; one *s* one *d*. *Educ:* Whitgift Sch., Croydon. Admitted Solicitor, 1975; Partner, Davies Brown & Co., Solicitors, 1976–82; Sole Principal, then Sen. Partner, Hollis Wood & Co., Solicitors, 1982–92; Dist Judge, 1992–2000. Dir of Studies, Commonwealth Magistrates' and Judges' Assoc., 1999–. *Recreations:* music, walking, gardening. *Address:* c/o Hastings County Court, Bohemia Road, Hastings, Sussex TN34 1QX. *Club:* Royal Commonwealth Society.

HOLLIS, Kim; QC 2002; *b* 19 Sept. 1957; *d* of Gurbaksh Singh Salariya and Jean Taylor; *m* 1987, Andrew Charles Hollis; two *s*. *Educ:* Cheltenham Ladies' Coll.; QMC, Univ. of London (LLB Hons). Called to the Bar, Gray's Inn, 1979. Vice Chm., Diversity (formerly Race and Religion) Cttee, Bar Council, 2005–; Hd, Equality and Diversity Cttee, Criminal Bar Assoc., 2004–; Mem., Diversity Gp, Bar Standards Bd, 2007–. (Jtly) Most Successful Lawyers' Award, Soc. of Asian Lawyers, 2005. *Recreation:* ski-ing. *Address:* 25 Bedford Row, WC1R 4HD. *T:* (020) 7067 1500, *Fax:* (020) 7067 1507; *e-mail:* Kimhollis2@msn.com. *Clubs:* National Liberal; Bank of England Sports.

HOLLIS, Posy; see Simmonds, P.

HOLLIS, Most Rev. Reginald; Rector, St Paul's Church, New Smyrna Beach, Florida, 1994–97; *b* 18 July 1932; *s* of Jesse Farndon Hollis and Edith Ellen Lee; *m* 1957, Marcia Henderson Crombie; two *s* one *d*. *Educ:* Selwyn Coll., Cambridge; McGill Univ., Montreal. Chaplain and Lectr, Montreal Dio. Theol Coll., 1956–60; Chaplain to Anglican Students, McGill Univ.; Asst Rector, St Matthias' Church, Westmount, PQ, 1960–63; Rector, St Barnabas' Church, Pierrefonds, PQ, 1963–70; Rector, Christ Church, Beaconsfield, PQ, 1971–74; Dir of Parish and Dio. Services, Dio. Montreal, 1974–75; Bishop of Montreal, 1975; Metropolitan of the Ecclesiastical Province of Canada and Archbishop of Montreal, 1989–90; Asst Bishop, dio. of Central Florida and Episcopal Dir, Anglican Fellowship of Prayer, 1990–94. Hon. DD 1975. *Publication:* Abiding in Christ, 1987. *Address:* 303–1175 Newport Avenue, Victoria, BC V8S 5E6, Canada.

HOLLIS, Richard Graham, RDI 2005; designer and writer; *b* 4 Dec. 1934; *s* of late George Harry Hollis and Mary Dorothy Hollis (*née* Doughty); *m* 1974, Posy Simmonds, *qv*; one *s* (and one *s* decd) from a previous marr. *Educ:* Aldenham Sch.; Chelsea Sch. of Art; Wimbledon Coll. of Art; Central Sch. of Arts and Crafts. Nat. Service, 2nd Lieut, RASC. Lecturer: London Sch. of Printing and Graphic Arts, 1959–61; Chelsea Sch. of

Art, 1961–63; staff designer, Galeries Lafayette, Paris, 1963–64; Hd, Dept of Graphic Design, W of England Coll. of Art, Bristol, 1964–66; Art Ed., New Society weekly, 1966–68; Sen. Lectr, Central Sch. of Art and Design, 1967–69 and 1976–78. Consultant Designer: Sadler's Wells Th., 1959–61; Finmar Ltd, 1962–64; Modern Poetry in Translation, 1964–2003; Whitechapel Art Gall., 1969–72 and 1976–85; Art Ed. and designer, Pluto Press, 1972–76. *Publications:* Graphic Design: a concise history, 1994, rev. and expanded edn 2001; Swiss Graphic Design: the origins and growth of an international style 1920–1965, 2006. *Address:* 22 Lloyd Square, WC1X 9AJ.

HOLLIS, Rt Rev. (Roger Francis) Crispian; *see* Portsmouth, Bishop of, (RC).

HOLLMAN, Arthur, MD; FRCP; FLS; Hon. Consultant Cardiologist, East Sussex Hospitals NHS Trust, since 2002; Consultant Cardiologist, University College Hospital, London, 1962–87, now Consulting Cardiologist; Consultant Cardiologist, Hospital for Sick Children, London, 1978–88, now Consulting Cardiologist; Hon. Senior Lecturer, University College London Medical School (formerly University College and Middlesex School of Medicine), since 1962; *b* 7 Dec. 1923; *s* of W. J. and I. R. Hollman; *m* 1949, Catharine Elizabeth Large (*d* 2006); three *d* (and one *d* decd). *Educ:* Tiffin Boys' Sch., Kingston upon Thames; University Coll. London (Fellow, 1978); UCH Med. Sch. (MD). FRCP 1967. FLS 1983. Jun. hosp. appts, London, Banbury and Taplow, 1946–57; Bilton Pollard Fellow of UCH Med. sch. at Children's Meml Hosp., Montreal, 1951–52; Clinical Asst, National Heart Hosp., 1954–56; Sen. Registrar and Asst Lectr, Royal Postgraduate Med. Sch., 1957–62; Hon. Consultant Cardiologist, Kingston Hosp., 1964–87. Advisor in Cardiology: to Mauritius Govt, 1966–86; to Republic of Seychelles, 1974–94. Councillor, RCP, 1976–79. Thomas Lewis Lectr, British Cardiac Soc., 1981. Member: Adv. Cttee, Chelsea Physic Garden, 1971–98; Council, British Heart Foundn, 1975–80; British Cardiac Soc. (Mem. Council, Asst Sec., and Sec., 1971–76; Archivist, 1993–); Assoc. of Physicians of GB and Ireland. Mem., Pett Parish Council, 2003–. Pres., Osler Club, 1983–84. Curator of herb garden, Barbers' Co., 1995–. President's Medal, RCP, 1998. *Publications:* Plants in Medicine, 1989, 3rd edn 1996; Plants in Cardiology, 1992; Sir Thomas Lewis: pioneer cardiologist and clinical scientist, 1997; (ed jtly) British Cardiology in the 20th Century, 2000; articles on the history of cardiology and medicinal plants. *Recreations:* sea swimming with Nobs Club, gardening, especially medicinal plants; medical history. *Address:* Seabank, Chick Hill, Pett, Hastings, East Sussex TN35 4EQ. *T:* (01424) 813228; *e-mail:* arthur@hollman.co.uk. *Club:* Athenæum.

HOLLOBONE, Philip Thomas; MP (C) Kettering, since 2005; *b* 7 Nov. 1964; *m* 2001, Donna Anne Cooksey. *Educ:* Dulwich Coll.; Lady Margaret Hall, Oxford (MA 1987). Industry res. analyst, 1987–2003. Served TA, 1984–93. Member (C): Bromley BC, 1990–94; Kettering BC, 2003–. Contested (C): Lewisham E, 1997; Kettering, 2001. *Address:* House of Commons, SW1A 0AA.

HOLLOM, Sir Jasper (Quintus), KBE 1975; Chairman: Eagle Star Holdings PLC, 1985–87; Eagle Star Insurance Co. Ltd, 1985–87; *b* 16 Dec. 1917; *s* of Arthur and Kate Louisa Hollom; *m* 1954, Patricia Elizabeth Mary Ellis. *Educ:* King's Sch., Bruton. Entered Bank of England, 1936; appointed Deputy Chief Cashier, 1956; Chief Cashier, 1962–66; Director, 1966–70, 1980–84; Deputy Governor, 1970–80. Director: BAT Industries plc, 1980–87; Portals Hldgs plc, 1980–88. Chairman: Panel on Take-overs and Mergers, 1980–87; Council for the Securities Industry, 1985–86; Commonwealth Develt Finance Co. Ltd, 1980–86; Pres., Council of Foreign Bondholders, 1983–89. *Address:* The Long Barn, Alexanders Lane, Privett, Alton, Hants GU34 3PW. *T:* (01730) 828417.

HOLLOWAY, Adam James Harold; MP (C) Gravesham, since 2005; *b* 1965; *s* of Rev. Roger Holloway, OBE and Anne (*née* Alsop). *Educ:* Cranleigh Sch.; Magdalene Coll., Cambridge (BA Social and Pol Sci. 1987); RMA Sandhurst; Imperial Coll. of Sci. and Technol. (MBA). Spent time with the Afghan Resistance, 1982; classroom asst, Pace Coll., Soweto, S Africa, 1985. Grenadier Guards, 1987–92 (Captain); service in Gulf War, 1991. Presenter, 1992–94: World in Action (incl. living homeless in London for 3 months); Disguises (reports from UK and Balkans); Sen. Reporter, ITN, 1994–97: Bosnia reporter, Sarajevo, 1994; News at Ten Special Reports; Reporter, Tonight with Trevor MacDonald (undercover as asylum seeker), 2001; Iraq War (Northern front) reports for ITN and Sky News, 2003. Mem., Defence Select Cttee, 2005–. Trustee: Christian Aid, 1997–2001; MapAction, 2004–. *Recreation:* being with my family and godchildren. *Address:* House of Commons, SW1A 0AA. *T:* (020) 7219 3000; c/o 440 Strand, WC2R 0QS; *e-mail:* adamholloway@ntlworld.com. *Clubs:* Gravesend Conservative, Northfleet Conservative.

HOLLOWAY, Hon. Sir Barry (Blyth), KBE 1984 (CBE 1974); *b* 26 Sept. 1934; *s* of Archibald and Betty Holloway; *m* 1990, Fua Evelin; one *s* four *d*, and three *s* four *d* by previous marriage. *Educ:* Launceston Church Grammar Sch., Tasmania; Sch. of Pacific Administration, Sydney, 1957; Univ. of Papua New Guinea. Dip., Pacific Admin. District Officer in Papua New Guinea, 1953–64. Elected to first PNG Parliament, 1964; Foundn Mem., Pangu Pati, 1966; MP Eastern Highlands Province. Member of various parliamentary cttees, incl. Public Accounts; Speaker of Parliament, 1972–77; Finance Minister, 1977–80; Minister for Educn, 1982–85. Policy Co-ordinator, Planning, Prime Minister's Dept, 1995–96. Chairman of Constituent Assembly responsible for the formation of Constitution of the Independent State of Papua New Guinea, 1974–75. Consultant, World Bank, to establish Anti-Corruption Commn, PNG, 1997–98; Alternate Exec. Dir, Asian Develt Bank, Manila, Philippines, 1999–. Director of various companies. *Recreations:* reading, agriculture. *Address:* PO Box 6361, Boroko, Papua New Guinea. *T:* 3231611.

HOLLOWAY, Frank, FCA; Managing Director, Supplies and Transport, 1980–83 and Board Member, 1978–83, British Steel Corporation; *b* 20 Oct. 1924; *s* of Frank and Elizabeth Holloway; *m* 1949, Elizabeth Beattie; two *d*. *Educ:* Burnage High Sch., Manchester. Served War, Royal Navy, 1943–46. Various senior finance appts in The United Steel Companies Ltd and later in British Steel Corp., 1949–72. Managing Director: Supplies and Production Control, 1973–76, Finance and Supplies, 1976–80, British Steel Corp. *Recreations:* cricket, collecting books.

HOLLOWAY, Frederick Reginald Bryn; His Honour Judge Holloway; a Circuit Judge, since 1992; *b* 9 Jan. 1947; *s* of William Herbert Holloway and Audrey (*née* Hull-Brown); *m* 1974, Barbara Bradley; two *s*. *Educ:* Mill Mead, Shrewsbury; Wrekin Coll., Wellington, Salop; Coll. of Law. Entered chambers in Liverpool, 1972; Asst Recorder, 1984–89; Recorder, 1989–92. *Recreations:* gardening, Shrewsbury Town FC, cricket, tennis. *Address:* Queen Elizabeth II Law Courts, Derby Square, Liverpool L2 1XA.

HOLLOWAY, James Essex; Director (formerly Keeper), Scottish National Portrait Gallery, since 1997; *b* 24 Nov. 1948; *s* of Roland David Holloway and Nancy Briant Holloway (*née* Evans). *Educ:* Marlborough Coll.; Courtauld Inst. of Art, London Univ. (BA Hons). Res. Asst, Nat. Gall. of Scotland, 1972–80; Asst Keeper, Nat. Mus. of Wales, 1980–83; Dep. Keeper, Scottish Nat. Portrait Gall., 1983–97. *Publications:* The Discovery of Scotland, 1978; James Tassie, 1986; Jacob More, 1987; William Aikman, 1988; Patrons

and Painters: art in Scotland 1650–1760, 1989; The Norie Family, 1994. *Recreations:* motorbikes, India. *Address:* Scottish National Portrait Gallery, 1 Queen Street, Edinburgh EH2 1JD. *T:* (0131) 624 6401. *Clubs:* New, Puffin's (Edinburgh).

HOLLOWAY, Neil John; Vice President, Business Strategy, Microsoft International, since 2007; *b* 14 May 1960; *s* of Jenny Holley; *m*; one *s* one *d*. *Educ:* Univ. of Bath (BSc 1982); Jesus Coll., Cambridge (MPhil 1984). Man. Dir, Migent UK, 1988–90; Microsoft UK, 1990–2003: Dir, 1994–96; Dep. Gen. Manager, 1996–98; Man. Dir, 1998–2003; Vice-Pres., 2000–05 and Vice-Pres., Sales, Marketing and Services, 2003–05, Pres., 2005–07, Microsoft Europe, ME and Africa. *Recreations:* golf, swimming.

HOLLOWAY, Reginald Eric, CMG 1984; HM Diplomatic Service, retired; *b* 22 June 1932; *s* of late Ernest and Beatrice Holloway; *m* 1958, Anne Penelope, *d* of late Walter Robert and Doris Lilian Pawley; one *d*. *Educ:* St Luke's, Brighton. Apprentice reporter, 1947–53; served RAF, 1953–55; journalist in Britain and E Africa, 1955–61; Press Officer, Tanganyika Govt, 1961–63; Dir, British Inf. Service, Guyana, 1964–67; Inf. Dept, FCO, 1967–69 (Anguilla, 1969); 2nd, later 1st Sec., Chancery in Malta, 1970–72; E African Dept, FCO, 1972–74; Consul and Head of Chancery, Kathmandu, 1974–77 (Chargé d'Affaires ai, 1975 and 1976); Asst Head, S Asian Dept, FCO, 1977–79; Counsellor, 1979; Inspector, 1979–81; Consul-Gen., Toronto, 1981–85; Sen. British Trade Comr, Hong Kong, 1985–89, and Consul-Gen. (non-resident), Macao, 1986–89; Consul-Gen., Los Angeles, 1989–92. Business consultant, 1992–97; tree farmer, 1998–2001. Chm., Canadian Urban Inst., 1993–98. *Recreations:* woodworking, old press cameras. *Address:* 1004 Bramble Lane, Rural Route 3, Minden, ON K0M 2K0, Canada.

HOLLOWAY, Rt Rev. Richard Frederick; Bishop of Edinburgh, 1986–2000 and Primus of the Episcopal Church in Scotland, 1992–2000; Chairman: Scottish Arts Council, since 2005; Joint Board, Scottish Arts Council and Scottish Screen, since 2007; *b* 26 Nov. 1933; *s* of Arthur and Mary Holloway; *m* 1963, Jean Elizabeth Kennedy, New York; one *s* two *d*. *Educ:* Kelham Theol Coll.; Edinburgh Theol Coll.; Union Theol Seminary, New York (STM); BD (London). FRSE 1995. Curate, St Ninian's, Glasgow, 1959–63; Priest-in-charge, St Margaret and St Mungo's, Glasgow, 1963–68; Rector, Old St Paul's, Edinburgh, 1968–80; Rector, Church of the Advent, Boston, Mass, USA, 1980–84; Vicar, St Mary Magdalen's, Oxford, 1984–86. Gresham Prof. of Divinity, 1997–2001. Member: Human Fertilisation and Embryo Authority, 1991–97; Broadcasting Standards Commn, 2001–03; Chm., Edinburgh Voluntary Orgns Council, 1991–95. FRSE 1995. DUniv: Strathclyde, 1994; Open, 2005; Hon. DLitt Napier, 2000; Hon. DD: Aberdeen, 1995; Glasgow, 2001. *Publications:* Let God Arise, 1972; New Vision of Glory, 1974; A New Heaven, 1978; Beyond Belief, 1982; Signs of Glory, 1983; The Killing, 1984, 2nd edn as Behold Your King, 1995; (ed) The Anglican Tradition, 1984; Paradoxes of Christian Faith and Life, 1984; The Sidelong Glance, 1985; The Way of the Cross, 1986; Seven to Flee, Seven to Follow, 1987; Crossfire: faith and doubt in an age of certainty, 1988; Another Country, Another King, 1991; Who Needs Feminism?, 1991; Anger, Sex, Doubt and Death, 1992; The Stranger in the Wings, 1994; (jtly) Churches and How to Survive Them, 1994; Limping Towards the Sunrise, 1995; Dancing on the Edge, 1997; Godless Morality, 1999; Doubts and Loves: what is left of Christianity, 2001; On Forgiveness, 2002; Looking in the Distance, 2004; How to Read the Bible, 2006; Between the Monster and the Saint: reflections on the human condition, 2008. *Recreations:* long-distance walking, reading, cinema, music. *Address:* 6 Blantyre Terrace, Edinburgh EH10 5AE.

HOLLOWAY, Prof. Robin Greville, PhD, MusD; composer; Fellow of Gonville and Caius College, Cambridge, since 1969, and Professor of Musical Composition, University of Cambridge, since 2001; *b* 19 Oct. 1943; *s* of Robert Charles Holloway and Pamela Mary Jacob. *Educ:* St Paul's Cathedral Choir Sch.; King's Coll. Sch., Wimbledon; King's Coll., Cambridge (MA 1968; PhD 1972; MusD 1976); New Coll., Oxford. Lectr in Music, 1975–99, Reader in Music, 1999–2001, Cambridge Univ. *Compositions* include: Garden Music, 1962; First Concerto for Orchestra, 1966–69; Scenes from Schumann, 1969–70; Evening with Angels, 1972; Domination of Black, 1973–74; Sea Surface full of Clouds, 1974–75; Clarissa, 1976 (premièred ENO, 1990); Romanza, 1976; The Rivers of Hell, 1977; Second Concerto for Orchestra, 1978–79; Serenade in C, 1979; Aria, 1980; Peer Gynt, 1980–97; Brand, 1981; Women in War, 1982; Second Idyll, 1983; Seascape and Harvest, 1984; Viola Concerto, 1984; Serenade in E flat, 1984; Ballad for harp and orch., 1985; Inquietus, 1986; Double Concerto for clarinet and saxophone, 1988; The Spacious Firmament, 1989; Violin Concerto, 1990; Boys and Girls Come Out to Play, 1992; Gilded Goldbergs, 1992–98; Missa Caiensis, 1993–2001; Third Concerto for Orchestra, 1994; Canterbury Concerto for clarinet and orch., 1997; Scenes from Antwerp, 1998; Double Bass Concerto, 1998; Symphony, 1999; Spring Music, 2002; String Quartet no 1, 2003; String Quartet no 2, 2004; Fourth Concerto for Orchestra, 2006; Five Temperaments, 2008. *Publications:* Wagner and Debussy, 1978; On Music: essays and diversions 1963–2003, 2003; numerous articles and reviews. *Recreation:* playing on two pianos. *Address:* Gonville and Caius College, Cambridge CB2 1TA. *T:* (01223) 335424.

HOLLOWELL, Rt Rev. Barry Craig Bates; Bishop of Calgary, 2000–05; *b* Boston, Mass, 14 April 1948; *m* 1976, Linda Barry (*d* 2008); two *s* one *d*. *Educ:* Valparaiso Univ., Indiana (BA 1970); Westcott House and Fitzwilliam Coll., Cambridge (BA 1972, MA 1976); Episcopal Divinity Sch., Cambridge, Mass (MDiv 1973); St Paul Univ., Ottawa (MPastStudies 1979); Univ. of NB (MA Psychol. 1986). Ordained deacon, 1973, priest, 1974; Deacon, All Saints', Chelmsford, Mass, 1973–74; Asst Curate, Christ Church Cath., Fredericton, NB, 1974–75; pastoral and liturgical work, Christ Church Cath., and Anglican Chaplain, Univ. of NB, 1975–86; pastoral work, St Barnabas, Ottawa, 1978–79; interim Priest-in-charge, St Margaret's Chapel-of-Ease, 1983; Rector, St George's Anglican Ch, St Catharines, Niagara, 1986–2000; Archdeacon, Lincoln, Niagara, 1991–2000. Mem., Gen. Synod, 1989– (Chm., Faith, Worship and Ministry Cttee, 1995–). Rep. Anglican Ch of Canada at signing of Porvoo Agreement, Westminster Abbey, 1996. *Recreations:* photography, music, downhill ski-ing. *Address:* (home) 137 Citadel Circle NW, Calgary, AB T3G 4C2, Canada. *T:* (403) 208 6475.

HOLLOWS, Dame Sharon, DBE 2001; Director, Sharon Hollows Consultancy Ltd, since 2004; consultant on management and leadership, since 2004; *b* 14 Dec. 1958; *d* of Jack and Margaret Hollows; one *s* one *d*. *Educ:* Haslingden Grammar Sch.; W London Inst. of Higher Educn; Greenwich Univ. (MA Ed). Teacher, 1979–93: Furness Jun. Sch. and Manor Special Sch., Brent; St James' Jun. Sch. and Manor Primary Sch., Newham; Head Teacher, Calverton Primary Sch., Newham, 1994–2002; Adv. Head Teacher, Plumcroft Primary Sch., Greenwich, 2002–04. Mem., Standards Task Force, 2000–02. *Recreations:* horse riding, motor cycling, eating. *Address:* The Oast House, Hartfield Road, Edenbridge, Kent TN8 5NH.

HOLM, Sir Ian, Kt 1998; CBE 1989; actor, since 1954; *b* 12 Sept. 1931; *s* of Dr James Harvey Cuthbert and Jean Wilson Cuthbert; *m* 1st, 1955, Lynn Mary Shaw (marr. diss. 1965); two *d*; and one *s* one *d*; 2nd, 1982, Sophie Baker (marr. diss. 1986); one *s*; 3rd, 1991, Penelope Wilton, *qv* (marr. diss. 2002); one step *d*; 4th, 2003, Sophie de Stempel. *Educ:* Chigwell Grammar Sch., Essex. Trained RADA, 1950–53 (interrupted by Nat.

Service); joined Shakespeare Memorial Theatre, 1954, left after 1955; Worthing Rep., 1956; tour, Olivier's Titus Andronicus, 1957; re-joined Stratford, 1958: roles include: Puck; Ariel; Gremio; Lorenzo; Prince Hal; Henry V; Duke of Gloucester; Richard III; The Fool in Lear; Lennie in The Homecoming (also on Broadway, 1966) (Evening Standard Actor of the Year, 1965); left RSC, 1967; Moonlight, Almeida, 1993 (Evening Standard Actor of the Year, Critics Circle Award); King Lear, RNT, 1997 (Olivier award for Best Actor, 1998); The Homecoming, Comedy, 2001. Major film appearances include: Young Winston, The Fixer, Oh! What a Lovely War, The Bofors Gun, Alien, All Quiet on the Western Front, Chariots of Fire (Best Supporting Actor: Cannes, 1981; BAFTA, 1982); Return of the Soldier; Greystoke; Brazil; Laughterhouse; Dance With a Stranger; Wetherby; Dreamchild; Another Woman; Hamlet; Kafka; Naked Lunch; Blue Ice; Mary Shelley's Frankenstein, 1994; The Madness of King George, Big Night, Night Falls on Manhattan, 1995; Lochness, 1996; A Life Less Ordinary, The Sweet Hereafter, The Fifth Element, 1997; Simon Magus, eXistenZ, The Match, Joe Gould's Secret, 1998; Esther Kahn, Beautiful Joe, 1999; Bless the Child, Fellowship of the Ring, 2001; From Hell, 2002; Return of the King, 2003; The Emperor's New Clothes, Garden State, Strangers with Candy, 2004; Chromophobia, Beyond Friendship, The Treatment, Lord of War, 2005. TV series include: J. M. Barrie in trilogy The Lost Boys (RTS Best Actor Award, 1979); We, the Accused, 1980; The Bell, 1981; Game, Set and Match, 1988; other TV appearances include: Lech Walesa in Strike, 1981; Goebbels in Inside the Third Reich, 1982; Mr and Mrs Edgehill, 1985; The Browning Version, 1986; Uncle Vanya, 1990; The Last Romantics, 1991; The Borrowers, 1992; The Deep Blue Sea, 1994; Landscape, 1995; King Lear, 1997; Alice Through the Looking Glass, 1998. *Publication:* (with Steven Jacobi) Acting My Life (autobiog.), 2004. *Recreations:* tennis, walking, general outdoor activities. *Address:* c/o Markham & Froggatt, 4 Windmill Street, W1T 2HZ.

HOLMAN, Hon. Sir (Edward) James, Kt 1995; **Hon. Mr Justice Holman;** a Judge of the High Court of Justice, Family Division, since 1995; *b* 21 Aug. 1947; *o s* of late Dr Edward Theodore Holman and Mary Megan Holman, MBE (*née* Morris), formerly of Ringwood, Hants, and Manaccan, Cornwall; *m* 1979, Fiona Elisabeth, *er d* of late Dr Ronald Cathcart Roxburgh, FRCP; two *s* one *d*. *Educ:* Dauntsey's; Exeter College, Oxford (BA Jurisp., MA). Called to the Bar, Middle Temple, 1971, Bencher, 1995; QC 1991; Western Circuit; in practice, 1971–95; Standing Counsel to HM Treasury (Queen's Proctor), 1980–91; a Recorder, 1993–95; Family Div. Liaison Judge, Western Circuit, 1995–2002. A Legal Assessor, UK Central Council for Nursing, Midwifery and Health Visiting, 1983–95. Member: Family Proceedings Rules Cttee, 1991–95; Supreme Court Procedure Cttee, 1992–95; ex-officio Mem., Bar Council, 1992–95. Chm., Family Law Bar Assoc., 1992–95 (Sec., 1988–92). Mem., Council, RYA, 1980–83, 1984–87, 1988–91. *Recreations:* sailing, ski-ing, music. *Address:* Royal Courts of Justice, Strand, WC2A 2LL. *Clubs:* Royal Ocean Racing (Mem. Cttee, 1984–87); Royal Yacht Squadron.

HOLMAN, Very Rev. Fr Michael Mark, SJ; Provincial Superior, Society of Jesus (British Province), since 2005; *b* 4 Nov. 1954; *s* of Michael and Sonja Holman. *Educ:* Wimbledon Coll.; Heythrop Coll., Univ. of London (BA); Weston Jesuit Sch. of Theol. (MDiv); Fordham Univ., NY (MSc). Entered Society of Jesus, 1974; ordained priest, 1988; Dep. Headmaster, Mt St Mary's Coll., 1992–94; Headmaster, Wimbledon Coll., 1995–2004. *Recreations:* classical music, hill walking, Ignatian spirituality. *Address:* Jesuit Provincial Offices, 114 Mount Street, W1K 3AH.

HOLMAN, Richard Christopher; His Honour Judge Holman; a Senior Circuit Judge, since 2002 (a Circuit Judge, since 1994); Designated Civil Judge, since 1998; *b* 16 June 1946; *s* of Frank Harold Holman and Joan (*née* Attrill); *m* 1969, Susan Whittaker, MBE, DL (*d* 2007); two *s*. *Educ:* Watford Grammar Sch. for Boys; Eton Coll.; Gonville and Caius Coll., Cambridge (MA 1968). Admitted as solicitor, 1971; Partner, Foysters, later Davies Wallis Foyster, 1973–94, Man. Partner, 1988–89; Dep. Dist Registrar of High Court and Dep. Registrar of County Court, 1982–88; Asst Recorder, 1988–92; a Recorder, 1992–94. Member: NW Legal Aid Area Cttee, 1980–94; Civil Procedure Rule Cttee, 1997–2002. Mem. Council, Manchester Law Soc., 1983–90. Gov., Pownall Hall Sch., Wilmslow, 1990–98 (Chm., 1993–98). *Recreations:* golf, gardening, theatre, music. *Address:* Manchester Civil Justice Centre, 1 Bridge Street West, Manchester M3 3FX. *T:* (0161) 240 5000. *Club:* Wilmslow Golf (Captain, 1999).

HOLMBERG, Eric Robert Reginald; Deputy Chief Scientist (Army), Ministry of Defence, 1972–77; *b* 24 Aug. 1917; *s* of Robert and May Holmberg; *m* 1940, Wanda Erna Reich (*d* 2003); one *s* one *d*. *Educ:* Sandown (Isle of Wight) Grammar Sch.; St John's Coll., Cambridge (MA); Imperial Coll., London (PhD). Joined Mine Design Department, Admiralty, 1940; Admiralty Gunnery Establishment, 1945; Operational Research Department, Admiralty, 1950; appointed Chief Supt Army Operational Research Group, 1956; Dir, Army Operational Science and Res., subseq. Asst Chief Scientist (Army), MoD, 1961–72. *Publications:* The Trouble with Relativity, 1986; papers in Proc. Royal Astronomical Society, and Proc. of Physical Interpretations of Relativity Theory.

HOLMES, Prof. Andrew Bruce, AM 2004; FRS 2000; FAA; FTSE; ARC Federation and VESKI Fellow and Professor of Chemistry, University of Melbourne/CSIRO Molecular and Health Technologies, since 2004; Professor of Chemistry, Imperial College, London, since 2004; *b* 5 Sept. 1943; *s* of late Bruce Morell Holmes and Frances Henty Graham Holmes; *m* 1971, Jennifer Lesley; three *s*. *Educ:* Scotch Coll., Melbourne; Univ. of Melbourne (BSc, MSc); University Coll. London (PhD 1971); ScD Cantab 1997. Royal Soc. European Postdoctoral Fellow, ETH Zürich, 1971–72; University of Cambridge: Demonstrator, 1972–77; Lectr, 1977–94; Dir, Melville Lab. for Polymer Synthesis, 1994–2004; Reader in Organic and Polymer Chemistry, 1995–98; Prof. of Organic and Polymer Chemistry, 1998–2004; Fellow, Clare Coll., Cambridge, 1973–; Dir, Cambridge Quantum Fund, 1995–2004; Mem., CUP Syndicate, 2000–04. Principal Ed., Jl Materials Res., 1994–99; Chm., Editl Bd, Chemical Communications, 2000–03; Member: Bd of Editors, Organic Syntheses, Inc., 1996–2001; Publishing Bd, RSC, 2003–06; Publishing Adv. Bd, CSIRO, 2006–; Editl Bd, New Jl of Chemistry, 2000–03; International Advisory Board: Macromolecular Chem. and Physics, 1999–2006; Jl Mater. Chem., 1996–2006; Chemical Communications, 2004–; Chem. World, 2004–; Aust. Jl of Chem., 2004–; Bulletin, Chemical Soc. of Japan, 2004–; Beilstein Jl Organic Chem., 2005–; Angewandte Chemie, 2006–; Associate Ed., Organic Letters, 2006–. Vis. Fellow, La Trobe Univ., 1977; Visiting Professor: Univ. of Calif, Berkeley, 1984; Univ. of Calif, Irvine, 1991; Royal Soc. Leverhulme Sen. Res. Fellow, 1993–94; Wilsmore Fellow, Univ. of Melbourne, 2002–03. Lectures: W. G. Dauben, Univ. of Calif, Berkeley, 1999–2000; Aggarwal, Cornell Univ., 2002; Tilden, RSC, 2003; Merck-Karl Pfister, MIT, 2005; W. Heinlen Hall, Bowling Green State Univ., Ohio, 2006; Merck Res., RSC, 2008. FAA 2006; FTSE 2006. Alfred Bader Award, 1994, Materials Chem. Award, 1995, RSC; Descartes Prize, EU, 2003; Macro Gp Medal, 2004. *Publications:* contribs to various learned chem., physics and materials sci. jls on subject of synthesis of polymeric materials and of natural products. *Recreations:* musical appreciation, walking, ski-ing. *Address:* Bio21 Institute, University of Melbourne, Vic 3010, Australia. *T:* (3) 83442344, *Fax:* (3) 83442384; *e-mail:* aholmes@unimelb.edu.au; CSIRO Molecular and Health Technologies, Box 312, Clayton, Vic 3169, Australia; Department of Chemistry, Imperi College, South Kensington, SW7 2AZ.

HOLMES, Anthony, CBE 1982; Head of Passport Department, Home Office (former Chief Passport Officer, Foreign and Commonwealth Office), 1980–88, retired; *b* 4 Sep 1931; *s* of Herbert and Jessie Holmes; *m* 1954, Sheila Frances Povall. *Educ:* Calday Grang Grammar School. Joined HM Customs and Excise, 1949; served HM Forces, 1950–5 Passport Office, 1955; Dep. Chief Passport Officer, 1977. *Recreations:* golf, sailing. *Addres* Hilbre, Mill Road, West Chiltington, Pulborough, West Sussex RH20 2PZ. *Clubs:* We Sussex Golf (Pulborough); El Paraiso Golf (Estepona, Spain).

HOLMES, Christopher John, CBE 1998; Member: Youth Justice Board, since 200 Housing Corporation Board, since 2004; *b* 13 July 1942; *s* of Gordon Holmes and Dor Holmes (*née* Waite); *m* 1st, 1969, Ann Warden (marr. diss. 1989); one *s* one *d*; 2nd, 200 Hattie Llewelyn-Davies; one *s* one *d*. *Educ:* Clare Coll., Cambridge (MA Hons Eco 1964); Univ. of Bradford (Dip. in Industrial Admin 1966). Asst Gen. Sec., Stude Christian Movement, 1964–65; John Laing Construction, 1966–68; NE Islingto Community Project, then N Islington Housing Rights Project, 1969–74; Dep. Di 1974–76, Dir, 1995–2002, Shelter; Director: Soc. for Co-operative Dwellings, 1976–7 E London Housing Assoc., 1979–82; CHAR, 1982–87; Consultant, Priority Estat Project, 1988–89; Dir of Housing, London Borough of Camden, 1990–95. Mem., Na Consumer Council, 1975–80. *Publications:* The Other Notting Hill, 2004; A New Visio for Housing, 2006. *Recreations:* my family, reading, walking, theatre, cricket. *Address:* Carpenters Yard, Park Street, Tring, Herts HP23 6AR.

HOLMES, David, CB 1985; Director, Corporate Resources, British Airways pl 1996–99; Chairman, British Airways Regional, 1998–99; *b* 6 March 1935; *s* of late Georg A. Holmes and Annie Holmes; *m* 1963, Ann Chillingworth; one *s* two *d*. *Educ:* Doncaste Grammar Sch.; Christ Church, Oxford (MA); Birkbeck Coll., Univ. of London (BA). As Principal, Min. of Transport and Civil Aviation, 1957; Private Sec. to Jt Parly Sec 1961–63; HM Treasury, 1965–68; Principal Private Sec. to Minister of Transpor 1968–70; Asst Sec., 1970, Under Sec., 1976, Dep. Sec., 1982–91, Dept of Transport; Di Govt and Industry Affairs, British Airways, 1991–95. Chm., RAC Foundn, 2003– Trustee, Motorway Archive Trust, 2002–. *Recreations:* history, archaeology, musi *Address:* Dormer Lodge, 31 Little Park Gardens, Enfield, Middx EN2 6PQ. *Club:* Roya Automobile.

HOLMES, David Robert; Registrar, University of Oxford, and Professorial Fellow, S John's College, Oxford, 1998–2006; *b* 2 May 1948; *s* of late Leslie Howard Holmes an Joyce Mary Holmes (*née* Stone); *m* 1st, 1974, Lesley Ann Crone (marr diss. 1989); one one *d*; 2nd, 1989, Susan, *d* of William John and Edna Bayley. *Educ:* Preston GS; Merto Coll., Oxford (MA; Hon. Fellow, 2000; Chancellor's Prize for Latin Prose, Oxford Univ 1968). University of Warwick: Admin. Asst, 1970–74; Asst Registrar, 1974–78; seconde as Asst Registrar, Univ. of Sheffield, 1975–76; Sen. Asst Registrar, 1978–82; University o Liverpool: Acad. Sec., 1982–86; Dep. Registrar and Acad. Sec., 1987–88; Registrar an Sec., Univ. of Birmingham, 1988–98. Member: Council, Univ. of Warwick, 2006– Academic Council, BPP Univ. Coll. of Professional Studies, 2007–. Trustee and Chm Indep. Schs Governing Body, Foundn for Schs of King Edward VI in Birmingham, 2006– Trustee: James Martin 21st Century Foundn; Arthur Thomson Trust. Hon. DCL Oxo 2006. *Publications:* (contrib.) Beyond the Limelight, 1986; Perspectives, Policy and Practic in Higher Education, 1998; The State of UK Higher Education, 2001. *Recreations:* readin the classics, squash, cricket, golf, tennis, music, gardening. *Address:* 20 Goodby Road Moseley, Birmingham B13 8NJ. *T:* (0121) 249 9714.

See also Sir J. E. Holmes.

HOLMES, David Vivian; Member, Broadcasting Complaints Commission, 1987–92; 12 Oct. 1926; *s* of Vivian and Kathleen St Clair Holmes; *m* 1st, 1957, Rhoda Ann, *d* o late Col N. J. Gai; two *d*; 2nd, 1979, Linda Ruth Alexander (*née* Kirk). *Educ:* Ipswich Sch Allhallows Sch. Served KRRC, 1944–47. Evening Standard, 1951–56; Reporter, BB News, 1956–61; BBC political reporter, 1961–72; Asst Head, BBC Radio Talks an Documentary Programmes; launched Kaleidoscope arts programme, 1973; Politica Editor, BBC, 1975–80; Chief Asst to Dir-Gen., BBC, 1980–83; Sec. of the BBC 1983–85. Chm., Parly Lobby Journalists, 1976–77. Member: Council, Hansard Soc 1981–83; MoD Censorship Study Gp, 1983; Exec. Cttee, Suffolk Historic Churche Trust, 1989–90. Founder and Organiser, Blyth Valley Chamber Music concert 1988–2000. *Publication:* An Inglorious Affair, 2002. *Recreations:* history of 17th centur Dissent, gardening. *Address:* 5 Salters Lane, Walpole, Halesworth, Suffolk IP19 9BA. *T* (01986) 784412.

HOLMES, Eamonn; broadcast journalist; presenter, Sunrise, Sky News, since 2005; *b* Dec. 1959; *s* of Leonard Holmes and Josephine Holmes; three *s* one *d*. *Educ:* St Malachy' Coll., Belfast. Reporter, Ulster TV, 1980; presenter of TV programmes including: Goo Evening Ulster, Ulster TV, 1982–86; Open Air, 1986–91, Holiday, 1989–92, Jet Set 2001–, BBC; GMTV, 1993–2005; presenter, Eamonn Holmes Show, BBC Radio Fiv Live, 2004–. Mem. Bd, Manchester United Charitable Foundn. DUniv: Staffs, 2004 QUB, 2006. *Publication:* Eamonn Holmes: this is my life (autobiog.), 2006. *Recreation* watching Manchester United. *Address:* *e-mail:* info@eamonn.tv.

HOLMES, Prof. (Edward) Richard, CBE (mil.) 1998 (OBE (mil.) 1988); TD 1979 (Ba 1985, 2nd Bar 1996); JP; PhD; Professor of Military and Security Studies, since 1995, an Co-Director, Security Studies Institute, since 1989, Cranfield University; *b* 29 Marcl 1946; *s* of Edward William Holmes and Helen Holmes; *m* 1975, Katharine Elizabet Saxton; two *d*. *Educ:* Forest Sch.; Emmanuel Coll., Cambridge (MA; Hon. Fellow) Northern Illinois Univ.; Reading Univ. (PhD 1975). Royal Military Academy, Sandhurst Lectr, Dept of War Studies, 1969–73; Sen. Lectr, 1973–84; Dep. Hd of Dept, 1984–86 Lt Col (non-Regular Perm. Staff), CO 2nd Bn, Wessex Regt (Vols), 1986–88. Writer an presenter, various TV documentaries, including: War Walks, 1996; War Walks 2, 1997 The Western Front, 1999; Battlefields, 2001; Wellington: the Iron Duke, 2002; Rebel and Redcoats, 2003; In the Footsteps of Churchill, 2005. Territorial Army: enlisted Esse Yeo., 1964; commnd 1966; Brig., 1994–2001; Dir, Reserve Forces and Cadets 1997–2000; Col, The Princess of Wales's Royal Regt, 1999–2007. Trustee, Roya Armouries, 2005–. JP Hants, 1989. President: Corps of Drums Soc., 2003–; Battlefield Trust, 2004–; British Commn for Military History, 2006–; Chm., Project Hougoumont Hon. President: Battle of Cheriton Project; Napoleonic Assoc.; Vice-Pres., Sealed Knot 2006–. Patron, Guild of Battlefields Guides, 2003–. Hon. DLitt: Leicester, 2006; Kent 2007. Comdr 1st cl., Order of the Dannebrog (Denmark), 2000. *Publications:* (with P Young) The English Civil War, 1974; The Little Field Marshal: Sir John French, 1984 Firing Line, 1985 (US edn as Acts of War, 1986), 4th edn 1994; (with J. Keegan) Soldiers 1985; Riding the Retreat, 1995; War Walks, 1996; War Walks 2, 1997; The Western Front, 1999; Battlefields, 2001; (Gen. Ed.) The Oxford Companion to Military History 2001; Redcoat, 2001; Wellington: the Iron Duke, 2002; Tommy, 2004; The D-Day Experience, 2004; In the Footsteps of Churchill, 2005; Sahib: the British soldier in India 2005; Dusty Warriors: modern soldiers at war, 2006; The World at War, 2007;

Marlborough: England's fragile genius, 2008. *Recreation:* riding. *Address:* Security and Resilience Centre, Defence College of Management and Technology, Shrivenham, Swindon, Wilts SN6 8LA. *T:* (01793) 785474. *Club:* Naval and Military.

HOLMES, Sir Frank (Wakefield), Kt 1975; JP; company director; consultant; Emeritus Professor, since 1985, and Deputy Chairman, 1984–89, Chairman, 1989–91, Institute of Policy Studies, Victoria University of Wellington; *b* 8 Sept. 1924; *s* of James Francis Wakefield and Marie Esme Babette Holmes; *m* 1947, Nola Ruth Ross; two *s*. *Educ:* Waitaki Boys' Jun. High Sch. (Dux 1936); King's High Sch. (Dux 1941); Otago Univ.; Auckland University Coll. (Sen. Schol. 1948); Victoria University Coll. MA (1st Cl. Hons) 1949. Flying Officer, Royal NZ Air Force, 1942–45 (despatches). Economic Div., Prime Minister's and External Affairs Depts 1949–52; Lectr to Prof., Victoria Univ. of Wellington, 1952–67; Macarthy Prof. of Economics, 1959–67; Dean, Faculty of Commerce, 1961–63; Economics Manager, Tasman Pulp & Paper Co. Ltd, 1967–70; Victoria Univ. of Wellington: Prof. of Money and Finance, 1970–77; Vis. Prof. and Convener, Master of Public Policy Programme, 1982–85. Adviser, Royal Commn on Monetary, Banking and Credit Systems, 1955; Consultant, Bank of New Zealand, 1956–58 and 1964–67; Chm., Monetary and Economic Council, 1961–64 and 1970–72; Jt Sec., Cttee on Universities, 1959; Mem., NZ Council Educnl Research, 1965–77 (Chm. 1970–74); Chairman: Adv. Council on Educnl Planning and Steering Cttee, Educnl Develt Conf., 1973–74; NZ Govt Task Force on Economic and Social Planning, 1976; NZ Planning Council, 1977–82; Asia 2000 Foundn, NZ, 1994–96 (Hon. Advr, 1996–); Cttee Advising on Professional Educn, 1995–98. President: NZ Assoc. of Economists, 1961–63 (Distinguished Fellow 2004); Economic Section, ANZAAS, 1967, Education Section, 1979; Central Council, Economic Soc. of Australia and NZ, 1967–68; NZ Inst. of Internat. Affairs, 1998–2000. Chairman: South Pacific Merchant Finance Ltd, 1985–89 (Dir, 1984–89); Hugo Group Ltd, 1989– (Exec. Dir., 1986–2007); State Insurance Ltd, 1990–94; Norwich Holdings Ltd, 1990–94; Norwich Union Life Insce (NZ) Ltd, 1993–94; Director: National Bank of NZ Ltd, 1982–95; Norwich Union Life Insce Soc. 1983–92; Lloyds Bank NZA Ltd, Sydney, 1992–95. Mem., Internat. Organising Cttee, Pacific Trade and Develt Confs, 1982–. FRSA; FNZIM 1986; Fellow, NZ Inst. of Dirs, 1995 (Distinguished Fellow, 1999). Life Member: Otago Univ. Students' Assoc., 1947; VUW Students' Assoc., 1967; Australia-NZ Business Council, 1998. JP 1960. Hon. LLD Otago, 1997; Hon. DCom Victoria, Wellington, 2004. *Publications:* Money, Finance and the Economy, 1972; Government in the New Zealand Economy, 1977, 2nd edn 1980; Closer Economic Relations with Australia, 1986; Partners in the Pacific, 1988; (ed) Stepping Stones to Freer Trade, 1989; (jtly) Meeting the East Asia Challenge, 1989; Meeting the European Challenge, 1991; NAFTA, CER and a Pacific Basin Initiative, 1992; A New Approach to Central Banking, 1994; CER: Trends and Linkages, 1994; New Zealand and ASEAN, 1995; Trans-Tasman Co-operation, 1996; The Thoroughbred Among Banks in New Zealand, 1999; An Anzac Dollar?, 2000; Banking in New Territory, 2003; Jungle Bomber, 2004; pamphlets and articles on econs, finance, educn and internat. affairs. *Recreations:* dancing, walking, swimming, music. *Address:* 61 Cheviot Road, Lowry Bay, Lower Hutt, New Zealand. *T:* (4) 5684719. *Club:* Wellington (Wellington).

HOLMES, Prof. George Arthur, PhD; FBA 1985; Chichele Professor of Medieval History, University of Oxford, and Fellow of All Souls College, 1989–94; *b* 22 April 1927; *s* of late John Holmes and Margaret Holmes, Aberystwyth; *m* 1953, Evelyn Anne, *d* of late Dr John Klein and Audrey (*née* McFarlane); one *s* two *d* (and one *s* decd). *Educ:* Ardwyn County Sch., Aberystwyth; UC, Aberystwyth; St John's Coll., Cambridge (MA, PhD). Fellow, St John's Coll., Cambridge, 1951–54; Tutor, St Catherine's Society, Oxford, 1954–62; Fellow and Tutor, St Catherine's Coll., Oxford, 1962–89 (Vice-Master, 1969–71; Emeritus Fellow, 1990). Mem., Inst. for Advanced Study, Princeton, 1967–68. Vis. Prof., Harvard Univ. Centre for Italian Renaissance Studies, Florence, 1995–. Chm. Bd, Warburg Inst., London Univ., 1993–95. Chm., Victoria County Hist. Cttee, Inst. of Hist. Res., 1979–89. Jt Ed., English Historical Review, 1974–81; Delegate, Oxford Univ. Press, 1982–91. FRHistS 1956. Ellen MacArthur Prize for Economic Hist., Cambridge Univ., 1957; Serena Medal for Italian Studies, British Acad., 1993. *Publications:* The Estates of the Higher Nobility in Fourteenth-Century England, 1957; The Later Middle Ages, 1962; The Florentine Enlightenment 1400–1450, 1969; Europe: hierarchy and revolt 1320–1450, 1975; The Good Parliament, 1975; Dante, 1980; Florence, Rome and the Origins of the Renaissance, 1986; (ed) The Oxford Illustrated History of Medieval Europe, 1988; The First Age of the Western City 1300–1500, 1990; (ed) Art and Politics in Renaissance Italy, 1993; Renaissance, 1996; (ed) The Oxford Illustrated History of Italy, 1997; articles in learned jls. *Recreations:* walking in the country, looking at pictures. *Address:* Highmoor House, Bampton, Oxon OX18 2HY. *T:* (01993) 850408.

HOLMES, George Dennis, CB 1979; FRSE; Director-General and Deputy Chairman, Forestry Commission, 1977–86, retired; *b* 9 Nov. 1926; *s* of James Henry Holmes and Florence Holmes (*née* Jones); *m* 1953, Sheila Rosemary Woodger; three *d*. *Educ:* John Bright's Sch., Llandudno; Univ. of Wales (BSc (Hons)); FRSE 1982; FICFor. Post-grad Research, Univ. of Wales, 1947; appointed Forestry Commission, 1948; Asst Silviculturist, Research Div., 1948; Asst Conservator, N Wales, 1962; Dir of Research, 1968; Comr for Harvesting and Marketing, 1973. Mem., Scottish Legal Aid Bd, 1989–94. Hon. Prof., Univ. of Aberdeen, 1984–2000. Pres., Capability Scotland, 2003–. Hon. DSc Wales, 1985. *Publications:* contribs to Forestry Commission pubns and to Brit. and Internat. forestry jls. *Recreations:* golf, fishing. *Address:* 7 Cammo Road, Barnton, Edinburgh EH4 8EF. *T:* (0131) 339 7474.

HOLMES, Sir John (Eaton), GCVO 2004 (CVO 1998); KBE 1999; CMG 1997; Under-Secretary General for Humanitarian Affairs, United Nations, since 2007; *b* 29 April 1951; *s* of late Leslie Howard Holmes and Joyce Mary (*née* Stone); *m* 1976, Margaret Penelope Morris; three *d*. *Educ:* Preston Grammar Sch.; Balliol Coll., Oxford (BA 1st Cl. Hons Lit. Hum., MA). HM Diplomatic Service, 1973–2007: FCO, 1973–76; 3rd Sec., then 2nd Sec., Moscow, 1976–78; Near East and N Africa Dept, FCO, 1978–82; Asst Private Sec. to Foreign Sec., 1982–84; 1st Sec. (Economic), Paris, 1984–87; Asst Hd of Soviet Dept, FCO, 1987–89; seconded to Thomas de la Rue & Co., 1989–91; Counsellor, Econ. and Commercial, New Delhi, 1991–95; Head of European Union Dept (External), FCO, 1995; on secondment as Private Sec. (Foreign Affairs), 1996–99 and Principal Private Sec., 1997–99, to the Prime Minister; Ambassador to Portugal, 1999–2001; Ambassador to France, 2001–07. *Recreations:* sport (tennis, squash, cricket, golf), music, reading. *Address:* Office for the Co-ordination of Humanitarian Affairs, United Nations, New York, NY 10016, USA.

See also D. R. Holmes.

HOLMES, Dr John Ernest Raymond; Director, Quality and Performance, United Kingdom Atomic Energy Authority, 1989–90; *b* Birmingham, 13 Aug. 1925; *s* of late Dr John K. Holmes and of Ellen R. Holmes; *m* 1949, Patricia Clitheroe; one *s* one *d*. *Educ:* King Edward's School, Birmingham; University of Birmingham (BSc, PhD). Asst Lectr in Physics, Manchester Univ., 1949–52; Research Scientist, AERE Harwell, 1952–59; Atomic Energy Establishment, Winfrith: Research Scientist, 1959–66; Chief Physicist, 1966–73; Dep. Dir, 1973–86; Dir, 1986–89. *Publications:* technical papers on nuclear power. *Address:* Flat 1, St Antony's School House, Westbury, Sherborne, Dorset DT9 3QF. *T:* (01935) 817335.

HOLMES, Jonathan Roy; Managing Director, Jon Holmes Media Ltd, since 2006; *b* 26 June 1950; *s* of Roy Coulson Holmes and Margery Eleanor Heathcote Holmes (*née* Adams); *m* 1981, Margaret Helen Shipman; one *s* two *d*. *Educ:* Oundle Sch., Northants; Leeds Univ. (BA Hons (Political Studies) 1971). Reporter, Leicester Mercury, 1971–72; Dir, Pointon York Gp, 1972–80; Founder and Man. Dir, Park Associates Ltd, 1981–98; Partner, Benson McGarvey & Co., 1983–2001; Chm. and CEO, SFX Sports Gp, 1998–2006. Non-exec. Dir, Sportech plc, 2007–. Chairman: Leicester City FC, 2003; Cultivate East Midlands, 2006–. Hon. MBA De Montfort, 2005. *Recreations:* theatre, sport, esp. football, cricket and National Hunt racing, causing trouble. *Address:* Jon Holmes Media Ltd, 5th Floor, Holborn Gate, 26 Southampton Buildings, WC2A 1PQ. *T:* (020) 7861 2550, *Fax:* (020) 7861 3067; *e-mail:* jon@jonholmesmedia.com. *Clubs:* Garrick, Groucho, MCC.

HOLMES, Dame Kelly, DBE 2005 (MBE 1998); international athlete, 1993–2005; National Schools Sports Champion, since 2006; *b* 19 April 1970; *d* of Michael Norris and Pamela Thomson. *Educ:* Hugh Christie Sch., Tonbridge. Nursing Asst for mentally handicapped, 1987; served Army, 1988–97. International athlete: winner: Commonwealth Games: Gold, 1994 and 2002, Silver, 1998, 1500m; European Championships: Silver, 1500m, 1994; Bronze, 800m, 2002; World Championships: Silver, 1500m, Bronze, 800m, 1995; Silver, 800m, 2003; Olympic Games: Bronze, 800m, 2000; Gold, 1500m and 800m, 2004; Silver, World Indoor Championships, 2003; 1500m, 1st World Athletics Final, 2004. Performance of Year Award, IAAF, 2004; BBC Sports Personality of Year, 2004; European Athlete of Year, 2004; World Female Athlete of Year, 2004. *Publications:* (with R. Lewis) My Olympic Ten Days, 2004; (with F. Blake) Black, White and Gold: my autobiography, 2005; (with G. Walden) Katy and the Shooting Star, 2008. *T:* (office) (01732) 838800.

HOLMES, Prof. Kenneth Charles, PhD; FRS 1981; Director of the Department of Biophysics, Max-Planck-Institute for Medical Research, Heidelberg, 1968–2003; Professor of Biophysics, Heidelberg University, 1972–99, now Emeritus; *b* 19 Nov. 1934; *m* 1957, Mary Scruby; one *s* three *d*. *Educ:* St John's Coll., Cambridge (MA 1959); London Univ. (PhD 1959). Res. Associate, Childrens' Hosp., Boston, USA, 1960–61; Mem., Scientific Staff, MRC Lab. of Molecular Biology, Cambridge, 1962–68. Mem., EMBO; Scientific mem., Max Planck Gesellschaft, 1972–; Mem., Heidelberg Acad. of Scis, 1991. Corresp. Mem., Soc. Royale des Scis, Liège. *Publications:* (with D. Blow) The Use of X-ray Diffraction in the Study of Protein and Nucleic Acid Structure, 1965; papers on virus structure, molecular mechanism of muscular contraction and the structure of actin. *Recreations:* rowing, singing. *Address:* Biophysics Unit, Max-Planck-Institute for Medical Research, Jahnstrasse 29, 69120 Heidelberg, Germany. *T:* (6221) 486270.

HOLMES, Maurice Colston, OBE 1985; Director, Safety, British Railways Board, 1989–92; *b* 15 Feb. 1935; *s* of Charles Edward Holmes and Ellen Catherine Mary Holmes (*née* Colston); *m* 1985, Margaret Joan Wiscombe. *Educ:* Presentation Coll., Reading. British Rail: Divl Man., Liverpool Street, 1976–79; Chief Operating Man., 1979–80, Dep. Gen. Man., 1980–82, Southern Region; Dir of Operations, BRB, 1982–88. Dir and Trustee, Railway Pension Trustee Co. Ltd, 1994–96. Pres., British Transport Pension Fedn, 1993–. Col, RE, Engrg and Logistic Staff Corps (TA), 1990–2001. *Recreations:* travel, transport, gardens. *Address:* 9 High Tree Drive, Earley, Reading, Berks RG6 1EU. *T:* (0118) 966 8887.

HOLMES, Michael Harry; Chairman, fountains plc, since 2007; *b* 10 March 1945; *s* of Harry Albert Holmes and Doris Rachel (*née* Linihan); *m* 1968, Ellen van Caspel; three *s*. *Educ:* Alleyn's Sch., Dulwich; Gonville and Caius Coll., Cambridge (MA). Costain Civil Engineering Ltd, 1966–70; Ready Mixed Concrete Ltd, 1970–73; Pioneer Concrete Ltd, 1973–77; Rentokil Group plc, 1977–95: Regl Man. Dir, UK Property Services, 1988–91; Regl Man. Dir, N America, Caribbean and E Africa, 1992–95; self-employed, 1995–97; Chief Executive: Chesterton Internat. plc, 1997–2001; Orbis plc, 2002–08. *Recreations:* fishing, sailing, old cars, motorcycles, theatre. *Address:* Beechcroft, Hophurst Hill, Crawley Down, W Sussex RH10 4LW. *T:* (01342) 716101. *Club:* Oriental.

HOLMES, Michael John; Member (Ind) South West Region, England, European Parliament, 1999–2002 (UK Ind, 1999–2000, subseq. non-aligned); retired; *b* 6 June 1938; adopted *s* of Albert and Elsie Holmes; *m* 1974, Carolyn Allen Jee; two *s* one *d*. *Educ:* Sevenoaks Sch. SSC, Royal Warwicks Regt, 1958–60. Sales and Mkting Exec., Sunday Times, Evening Standard, and Observer, 1962–69; Owner Publisher, Independent Gp of Free Newspapers, 1970–87; voluntary and charity work, 1987–99. European Parliament: Voting Member: Fisheries Cttee; Budgetary Control Cttee. Leader, UK Independence Party, 1998–2000. *Recreations:* travel, reading, politics. *Address:* Venards House, North Gorley, Fordingbridge, Hants SP6 2PJ. *T:* (01425) 654117, *Fax:* (01425) 650283.

HOLMES, Prof. Patrick, PhD; Professor of Hydraulics, Imperial College of Science, Technology and Medicine, 1983–2003; Dean, City and Guilds College, 1988–91; *b* 23 Feb. 1939; *s* of Norman Holmes and Irene (*née* Shelbourne); *m* 1963, Olive (*née* Towning); one *s* one *d*. *Educ:* University Coll. of Swansea, Univ. of Wales (BSc 1960, PhD 1963). CEng, MICE. Res. Engr, Harbour and Deep Ocean Engrg, US Navy Civil Engrg Lab., Port Hueneme, Calif, 1963–65; Lectr, Dept of Civil Engrg, Univ. of Liverpool, 1966–72, Sen. Lectr, 1972–74, Prof. of Maritime Civil Engrg, 1974–83. Vis. Prof., Univ. of the WI, Trinidad, 2001. Chm., Environment Cttee, SERC, 1981–85. Pres., Conf. of European Schs of Advanced Engrg Educn and Res., 1993–95. Hon. Mem., C&G, 1992 (FCGI 1999). *Publications:* (ed) Handbook of Hydraulic Engineering (English edn), by Lencastre, 1987; articles on ocean and coastal engineering, wave motion, wave loading, coastal erosion and accretion, and harbour and breakwater design, in Proc. ICE and Proc. Amer. Soc. of Civil Engrs. *Recreations:* golf, yachting, walking, choral music. *Address:* West Winds, The Green, Steeple Morden, near Royston, Herts SG8 0ND. *T:* (01763) 852582.

HOLMES, Paul Robert; MP (Lib Dem) Chesterfield, since 2001; *b* 16 Jan. 1957; *s* of Frank and Dorothy Holmes; *m* 1978, Raelene Palmer. *Educ:* York Univ. (BA Hons Hist); Sheffield Univ. (PGCE). Teacher, Chesterfield Boys' High Sch., 1979–84; Hd of History, Buxton Coll., 1984–90; Hd of Sixth Form, Buxton Community Sch., 1990–2001. Mem., Chesterfield BC, 1987–95, 1999–2002. Lib Dem spokesman on disability, 2001–05, and on work and pensions, 2002–05, on housing, 2007; Shadow Minister for Arts and Heritage, 2006–07. Member: Educn and Skills Select Cttee, 2001–07; Children, Schs and Families Cttee, 2008–. Chm., Lib Dem Parly Party, 2005–07. *Recreations:* reading, walking, history. *Address:* (office) 69 West Bars, Chesterfield S40 1BA. *T:* (01246) 234879.

HOLMES, Peter Rodney; HM Diplomatic Service, retired; *b* 29 July 1938; *m* Anne Cecilia Tarrant; one *s* three *d*. Diplomatic Service: served Strasbourg, Belgrade, Paris, Cento, Ankara; Stockholm, 1974; Consul, Douala, 1978; Dep. Head of Mission, Bahrain,

1983; Commercial Counsellor, Santiago, 1987; Ambassador to Honduras, 1995–98. *Address:* 2 Sandringham Close, Alton, Hampshire GU34 1QF.

HOLMES, Peter Sloan; Chief Executive: Sheridan Group, since 2004 (Director, since 2000); Sheridan Millennium Ltd, since 2000; *b* 8 Dec. 1942; *s* of George H. G. and Anne S. Holmes; *m* 1966, Patricia McMahon; two *s*. *Educ:* Rossall Sch.; Magdalen Coll., Oxford (BA English Lang. and Lit.). Teacher, Eastbourne Coll., 1965–68; Head of English, Grosvenor High Sch., Belfast, 1968–71; Lectr, then Sen. Lectr, Stranmillis Coll. of Educn, Belfast, 1971–75; Department of Education for Northern Ireland: Inspector, 1975–83 (Sen. Inspector, 1980; Staff Inspector, 1982); Asst Sec., 1983–87; Under Sec., 1987; Dep. Sec., 1996–2000. Chm., Arts & Business NI, 2000–06. *Recreations:* singing, cycling, gliding. *Address:* 303 Comber Road, Lisburn, Co. Antrim BT27 6TA. *T:* (028) 9263 9495. *Club:* Oxford and Cambridge.

HOLMES, Richard; *see* Holmes, E. R.

HOLMES, Richard Gordon Heath, OBE 1992; FBA 1997; FRSL; writer; Professor of Biographical Studies, School of English and American Studies, University of East Anglia, 2001–07; *b* 5 Nov. 1945; *s* of late Dennis Patrick Holmes and Pamela Mavis Holmes (*née* Gordon); partner, Rose Tremain, *qv*. *Educ:* Downside Sch.; Churchill Coll., Cambridge (BA). FRSL 1975. Reviewer and historical features writer for The Times, 1967–92. Mem. Cttee, Royal Literary Fund, 1990–. Vis. Fellow, Trinity Coll., Cambridge, 2000, 2002. Lectures: Ernest Jones Meml, British Inst. of Psycho-Analysis, 1990; John Keats Meml, RCS, 1995; Johan Huizinga Meml, Univ. of Leiden, 1997; Seymour Biography, ANU, 2008. Hon. Dr: UEA, 2000; E London, 2001; Kingston, 2008. *Publications:* Thomas Chatterton: the case re-opened, 1970; One for Sorrow (poems), 1970; Shelley: the pursuit, 1974 (Somerset Maugham Award, 1977); Gautier: my fantoms (trans.), 1976; Inside the Tower (radio drama documentary), 1977; (ed) Shelley on Love, 1980; Coleridge, 1982; (with Peter Jay) Nerval: the chimeras, 1985; Footsteps: adventures of a romantic biographer, 1985; (ed) Mary Wollstonecraft and William Godwin, 1987; (ed with Robert Hampson) Kipling: something of myself, 1987; De Feministe en de Filosoof, 1988; Coleridge: vol. 1, Early Visions (Whitbread Book of the Year Prize), 1989, vol. 2, Darker Reflections (Duff Cooper Memorial Prize), 1998; To the Tempest Given (radio drama documentary), 1992; Dr Johnson & Mr Savage, 1993 (James Tait Black Meml Prize, 1994); The Nightwalking (radio drama documentary), 1995 (Sony Award); (ed) Coleridge: selected poems, 1996; Insights: the Romantic poets and their circle, 1997, enlarged edn 2005; Clouded Hills (radio documentary), 1999; Runaway Lives (radio documentary), 2000; Sidetracks: explorations of a romantic biographer, 2000; Romantics and Revolutionaries: Regency portraits, 2002; The Frankenstein Project (radio documentary), 2002; (ed) Classic Biographies (series), 2004; A Cloud in a Paper Bag (radio documentary), 2007; The Age of Wonder, 2008. *Recreations:* sailing, hill-walking, rooftop gardening, stargazing. *Address:* c/o HarperCollins, 77 Fulham Palace Road, W6 8JB.

HOLMES, Robin Edmond Kendall; Head of Judicial Appointments, Lord Chancellor's Department, 1992–98; *b* 14 July 1938; *s* of Roy Frederick George and Kaye Holmes; *m* 1964, Karin Kutter; two *s*. *Educ:* Wolverhampton Grammar Sch.; Clare Coll., Cambridge (BA); Birmingham Univ. (LLM). Articles, Wolverhampton CBC, 1961–64; admitted solicitor, 1964; Min. of Housing and Local Govt, subseq. DoE, 1965–73 and 1976–82; Colonial Secretariat, Hong Kong, 1973–75; Lord Chancellor's Dept, 1982–98; Grade 3, 1983–98; Circuit Administrator, Midland and Oxford Circuit, 1986–92. *Recreation:* travelling. *Club:* Hurlingham.

HOLMES, Roger; Managing Director, Change Capital Partners, since 2005; *b* 21 Jan. 1960. Strategy Consultant, then Principal, McKinsey & Co.; Kingfisher: Finance Dir, B & Q, 1994–97; Man. Dir, Woolworths, 1997–99; Chief Exec., electrical retailing div., 1999–2000; Marks and Spencer plc: Head, UK retailing business, 2001–02; Exec. Dir, 2001–04; Chief Exec., 2002–04. *Address:* e-mail: rholmes@changecapitalpartners.com.

HOLMES, Roger de Lacy, CB 2002; Chief Executive, St John Ambulance, 2002–07; *b* 15 Jan. 1948; *s* of Stephen and Muriel Holmes; *m* 1st, 1970, Jennifer Anne Heal (marr. diss. 2005); one *s* one *d*; 2nd, 2005, Rosalind Joy Halstead. *Educ:* Huddersfield New Coll.; Balliol Coll., Oxford (BA). DTI, 1969–74; Dept of Prices and Consumer Protection, 1974–77; Dept of Industry, 1977–79; Asst to Chm., British Leyland, 1980–82; Company Sec., Mercury Communications, 1982–83; Jt Sec and Dir, Corporate Affairs, ICL, 1984; Exec. Dir, Dunlop Holdings, 1984–85; Euroroute, 1985–86; Chloride Group: Man. Dir, Power Electronics, 1986–88; Corporate Affairs Dir, 1989–92; Dep. Master and Comptroller, Royal Mint, 1993–2001. Non-executive Director: Cygnet Health Care, 1993–2000; Yorks Ambulance Service NHS Trust, 2006–. Mem. Council, Univ. of London, 2003–08. CStJ 2007 (OStJ 2004). *Recreations:* golf, bridge. *Address:* 15 Hansom Place, York YO31 8FJ.

HOLMES, Timothy Charles; HM Diplomatic Service; Consul General, Sydney and Director General, Trade and Investment, since 2004; *b* 26 April 1951; *s* of late Ronald William Holmes and Barbara Jean (*née* Mickleburgh); *m* 1973, Anna-Carin Magnusson; one *s* one *d*. *Educ:* Bec Sch.; Selwyn Coll., Cambridge (MA); Univ. of Aix-Marseille. Joined FCO, 1974; Second, later First, Sec., Tokyo, 1976–80; seconded to Invest in Britain Bureau, Dept of Industry, 1981–83; FCO, 1983–86; First Sec., Islamabad, 1986–90; FCO, 1990–94; Dep. Head of Mission and Commercial and Econ. Counsellor, Seoul, 1994–97; Dep. Hd of Mission, 1997–2002, Consul-Gen., 2000–02, The Hague; Dir, Asia Pacific, Internat. Gp, Trade Partners UK, then UK Trade & Investment, 2002–04. *Publication:* The Wild Flowers of Islamabad, 1990. *Recreations:* botany, ornithology, reading. *Address:* c/o Foreign and Commonwealth Office, King Charles Street, SW1A 2AH.

HOLMES, Prof. William Neil; Professor of Physiology, University of California, since 1964; *b* 2 June 1927; *s* of William Holmes and Minnie Holmes (*née* Lloyd); *m* 1955, Betty M. Brown, Boston, Mass; two *s* two *d*. *Educ:* Adams Grammar Sch., Newport, Salop; Liverpool Univ. (BSc, MSc, PhD, DSc); Harvard Univ., Cambridge, Mass. National Service, 2nd Bn RWF, 1946–48. Visiting Scholar in Biology, Harvard Univ., 1953–55; Post-grad. Research Schol., Liverpool Univ., 1955–56; ICI Fellow, Glasgow Univ., 1956–57; Asst Prof. of Zoology, 1957–63, Associate Prof. of Zoology, 1963–64, Univ. of British Columbia, Canada; John Simon Guggenheim Foundn Fellow, 1961–62; Visiting Professor of Zoology: Univ. of Hull, 1970; Univ. of Hong Kong, 1973, 1982–83 and 1987. Scientific Fellow, Zoological Soc. of London, 1967; External examiner: for undergraduate degrees, Univ. of Hong Kong, 1976–79, 1985–88; for higher degrees, Univs of Hong Kong and Hull, 1976–; Consultant to: Amer. Petroleum Inst., Washington, DC (environmental conservation), 1972–74; US Nat. Sci. Foundn (Regulatory Biology Prog.), 1980–83; US Bureau of Land Management (petroleum toxicity in seabirds), 1982–. Mem. Editorial Bd, American Journal of Physiology, 1967–70. Member: Endocrine Soc., US, 1957–; Soc. for Endocrinology, UK, 1955–; Amer. Physiological Soc., 1960–; Zoological Soc. of London, 1964–. *Publications:* numerous articles and reviews in Endocrinology, Jl of Endocrinology, Gen. and Comp. Endocrinology, Cell and Tissue Res., Archives of Environmental Contamination and Toxicology, Environmental Res., Jl of Experimental Biology. *Recreations:* travel, old map and prints, carpentry and building. *Address:* 117 East Junipero Street, Santa Barbara, C 93105, USA. *T:* (805) 6827256. *Club:* Tennis (Santa Barbara).

HOLMES à COURT, family name of **Baron Heytesbury**.

HOLMES à COURT, Janet Lee, AC 2007 (AO 1985); Chairman, Heytesbury Pty Ltd Australia, since 1991 (Chairman of all companies in the group, including Heytesbury Be Pty, John Holland Group, Vasse Felix Winery); *b* 29 Nov. 1943; *m* 1966, (Michae Robert (Hamilton) Holmes à Court (*d* 1990); three *s* one *d*. *Educ:* Perth Modern Sch Univ. of Western Australia (BSc Chemistry). Former Chemistry Teacher, Perth. Membe Board: Reserve Bank of Australia, 1992–97; Rio Tinto WA Future Fund, 2006–. B Mem., Aust. Res. Council, 2003–05; Bd Dir, Vision 2020 Aust., 2004–. Comr, Tourism WA, 2002–. Chairman: Australian Children's TV Foundn, 1986–; Black Swan Theatr Co., Perth, 1991–2005; WA Symphony Orch., 1998–; Urban Design Centre, WA 2005–. Gov., Sony Foundn Australia, 1999–. Veuve Clicquot Business Woman of th Year, 1996. *Address:* Heytesbury Pty Ltd, PO Box 6847, East Perth, WA 6892, Australia

HOLMES SELLORS, Sir Patrick John; *see* Sellors.

HolmPATRICK, 4th Baron *cr* 1897; **Hans James David Hamilton;** *b* 15 March 195 *s* of 3rd Baron Holmpatrick and Anne Loys Roche (*d* 1998), *o d* of Commander J. E. F Brass, RN (retd); *S* father, 1991; *m* 1984, Mrs Gill du Feu, *e d* of K. J. Harding; one *s* an one step *s*. *Heir:* *b* Hon. Ion Henry James Hamilton, *b* 12 June 1956.

HOLROYD, Andrew, OBE 2003; Partner, Jackson & Canter, Liverpool, since 1977 President, Law Society, 2007–08; *b* 13 April 1948; *s* of Bill Holroyd and Joan Holroyd; *m* 1975, Caroline Skerry; two *d*. *Educ:* Univ. of Nottingham (BA Law 1969). Admitte solicitor, 1974. *Recreations:* music, golf. *Address:* c/o Jackson & Canter, 88 Church Stree Liverpool L1 3HD. *Clubs:* Royal Automobile; Woolton Golf (Liverpool).

HOLROYD, Air Marshal Sir Frank (Martyn), KBE 1989; CB 1985; FREng Chairman, Military Asset Services Ltd, since 2007; *b* 30 Aug. 1935; *s* of George L. Holroy and Winifred H. Holroyd; *m* 1958, Veronica Christine (*d* 2001), *d* of Arthur G. Booth two *s* one *d*. *Educ:* Southend-on-Sea Grammar Sch.; Cranfield Inst. of Technology (MSc FIET; FRAeS; CEng, FREng (FEng 1992). Joined RAF, 1956; Fighter Comd units 1957–60; Blind Landing Development RAE Bedford, 1960–63; Cranfield Inst. of Tech 1963–65; HQ Fighter Comd, 1965–67; Far East, 1967–69; Wing Comdr, MoD 1970–72; RAF Brize Norton, 1972–74; Gp Captain Commandant No 1 Radio School 1974–76; SO Eng. HQ 38 Gp, 1976–77; Air Cdre Director Aircraft Engrg, MoD 1977–80; RCDS 1981; Dir Weapons and Support Engrg, MoD, 1982, Air Vice-Marsha 1982; DG Strategic Electronics Systems, MoD (Procurement Exec.), 1982–86; AO Engrg Strike Comd, 1986–88; Chief Engr, 1988–91, and Chief of Logistics Support, 1989–91 RAF. Chairman: AVR Communications Ltd, 1992–95; Elettronica (UK) Ltd, 1992–95 Composite Technology Ltd, 1992–2004; Troy Court Mgt Ltd, 2003–07; Military Aircra Spares Ltd, 2004–06 (Dep. Chm., 1999–2003); Director: Admiral plc, 1992–2000; Ultr Electronics Hldgs, 1995–2003; REW Communications Ltd, 1995–96; Airinmar Ltd 1996–2000. Engineering Council: Mem., 1990–2000; Chm. of Trustees, Pension Fund 2000–. Pres., RAeS, 1992–93. Member: Court, 1988–, and Council, 1990–97 (Dep Chm., 1997–2005), Inst. of Technology, now Univ., Cranfield; Adv. Council, RMCS Shrivenham, 1988–91; BBC Engrg Adv. Bd, 1984–90. Trustee, Macrobert Award Trus Royal Acad. of Engrg, 1993–98; Mem., Tribology Trust Awards Cttee, IMechE, 1997– Life Vice-Pres., Chelmsford Br., RAFA, 1990–. Patron: Victim Support Somerse 2004–07; Southend-on-Sea High Sch. Develt Project, 2004–. CCMI (Mem., 1991–98 Chm., 1998–99, Companions Bd). Hon. DSc Cranfield, 2006. *Recreations:* travel gardening, maintaining 14th century house, shooting (game birds). *Club:* Royal Air Force

HOLROYD, John Hepworth, CB 1993; CVO 1999; DL; Secretary for Appointmen to the Prime Minister, and Ecclesiastical Secretary to the Lord Chancellor, 1993–99; *b* 1 April 1935; *s* of Harry Holroyd and Annie Dodgshun Holroyd; *m* 1963, Judith Mar Hudson; one *s* one *d*. *Educ:* Kingswood Sch., Bath; Worcester Coll., Oxford (Ope Schol.; BA(Hist.); MA 1987). Joined MAFF, 1959; Asst. Sec., 1969–78; Under Secretary 1978; Resident Chm., Civil Service Selection Bd, 1978–80; Dir of Establishments, MAFF 1981–85; Cabinet Office: Under Sec., European Secretariat, 1985–89; First CS Comr an Dep. Sec., 1989–93. Advr to Assoc. of Lord-Lieutenants, 1999–2007. Governo Kingswood Sch., 1985–2005; King's Sch., Gloucester, 2001–. Lay Reader, Glouceste Cathedral, 2001–. Chm., Wells Cathedral Council, 2000–07. Trustee, St Albans Cathedra Trust, 1980–2001; Gloucester Cathedral Trust, 2002–; Dementia Care Trust, 2002–06 DL Herts, 1999–2001, Glos, 2002. *Recreations:* music, carpentry, managing 4 acres o Cornish woodland, travel. *Address:* The Miller's House, 2 Miller's Green, Gloucester GL 2BN.

See also W. A. H. Holroyd.

HOLROYD, Dame Margaret; *see* Drabble, Dame M.

HOLROYD, Sir Michael (de Courcy Fraser), Kt 2007; CBE 1989; CLit 2004; author *b* London, 27 Aug. 1935; *s* of Basil Holroyd and Ulla (*née* Hall); *m* 1982, Margaret Drabbl (*see* Dame Margaret Drabble). *Educ:* Eton Coll.; Maidenhead Public Library. Vis. Fellow Pennsylvania State Univ., 1979. Chm., Soc. of Authors, 1973–74; Chm., Nat. Book League, 1976–78; Pres., English PEN, 1985–88. Chm., Strachey Trust, 1990–95 Member: BBC Archives Adv. Cttee, 1976–79; Arts Council of England (formerly of GB) 1992–95 (Vice-Chm., 1982–83, Chm., 1992–95, Literature Panel); Chm., Public Lending Right Adv. Cttee, 1997–2000. Vice-Pres., Royal Literary Fund, 1997–. Nat. Gov., Shaw Fest. Theatre, Ontario, 1993–. FRSL 1968 (Mem. Council, 1977–87; Chm. Council 1998–2001; Vice Pres., 2001–03; Pres., 2003–); FRHistS; FRSA. Saxton Mem Fellowship, 1964; Bollingen Fellowship, 1966; Winston Churchill Fellowship, 1971 Hon. DLitt: Ulster, 1992; Sheffield, 1993; Warwick, 1993; East Anglia, 1994; LSE, 1998 Heywood Hill Prize, 2001; David Cohen British Lit. Prize, 2005; Golden Award, PEN 2006. *Publications:* Hugh Kingsmill: a critical biography, 1964; Lytton Strachey, 2 vols 1967, 1968 (Yorkshire Post Prize, 1968), rev. edn 1994 (Prix du Meilleur Livre Etranger 1995); A Dog's Life: a novel, 1969; (ed) The Best of Hugh Kingsmill, 1970; (ed) Lytton Strachey By Himself, 1971; Unreceived Opinions, 1973; Augustus John, 2 vols, 1974 1975, rev. edn 1996; (with M. Easton) The Art of Augustus John, 1974; (ed) The Geniu of Shaw, 1979; (ed with Paul Levy) The Shorter Strachey, 1980; (ed with Rober Skidelsky) William Gerhardie's God's Fifth Column, 1981; (ed) Essays by Divers Hands vol. XLII, 1982; Bernard Shaw: Vol. I, The Search for Love 1856–1898, 1988 (Irish Life Arts Award, 1988); Vol. II, The Pursuit of Power 1898–1918, 1989; Vol. III, The Lure o Fantasy 1918–1950, 1991; Vol. IV, The Last Laugh 1950–1991, 1992; Vol. V, The Shaw Companion, 1992; abridged edn, 1997; Basil Street Blues, 1999; Works on Paper: the craf of biography and autobiography, 2002; Mosaic: portraits in fragments, 2004; A Strange Eventful History, 2008; various radio and television scripts. *Recreations:* listening to stories watching people dance, avoiding tame animals, being polite, music, siestas. *Address:* c/o A. P. Watt Ltd, 20 John Street, WC1N 2DL.

HOLROYD, Robert Anthony; Headmaster, Repton School, since 2003; *b* 9 Dec. 1962; *s* of Anthony Holroyd and Jean Elizabeth Holroyd; *m* 1988, Penelope Claire Riddell; two *d*. *Educ:* Birkenhead Sch.; Christ Church, Oxford (Schol. 1981; BA 1st cl. Hons (Mod. Langs) 1985; MA 1988; PGCE 1989). Asst Master, Oakham Sch., 1985–86; Colegio Anglo Colombiano, Bogota, 1986–88; Hd of Dept and Housemaster, Radley Coll., 1989–2003. *Recreations:* the hills and the classics. *Address:* The Hall, Repton, Derby DE65 6FH.

HOLROYD, William Arthur Hepworth, FHSM; Chief Executive, North Durham Health Authority, 1992–93; *b* 15 Sept. 1938; *s* of late Rev. Harry Holroyd and Annie Dodgshun Holroyd; *m* 1967, Hilary Gower; three *s*. *Educ:* Kingswood Sch., Bath; Trinity Hall, Cambridge (MA History); Manchester Univ. (DSA). Hospital Secretary: Crewe Memorial Hosp., 1963–65; Wycombe General Hosp., 1965–67; secondment to Dept of Health, 1967–69; Dep. Gp Sec., Blackpool and Fylde HMC, 1969–72; Regional Manpower Officer, Leeds RHB, 1972–74; District Administrator, York Health Dist, 1974–82; Regional Administrator, Yorkshire RHA, 1982–85; Dist Gen. Man., Durham HA, 1985–92. Non-exec. Dir, York Waterworks, plc, 1996–99. Member: National Staff Cttee for Admin. and Clerical Staff in NHS, 1973–82; General Nursing Council for England and Wales, 1978–83; English Nat. Board for Nursing, Midwifery and Health Visiting, 1980–87; NHS Trng Authority, 1988–91. Director, Methodist Chapel Aid Ltd, 1978– (Chm., 2000–). Mem. Ind. Monitoring Bd (formerly Bd of Visitors), HM Prison Full Sutton, 1995–. *Publication:* (ed) Hospital Traffic and Supply Problems, 1968. *Recreations:* walking, music, visiting the Shetland Isles.
See also J. H. Holroyd.

HOLROYDE, Geoffrey Vernon; Director, Coventry (formerly Coventry Lanchester) Polytechnic, 1975–87; *b* 18 Sept. 1928; *s* of late Harold Vincent Holroyde and Kathleen Olive (*née* Glover); *m* 1960, Elizabeth Mary, *d* of Rev. E. O. Connell; two *s* two *d*. *Educ:* Wrekin Coll.; Birmingham Univ. (BSc); Birmingham Conservatoire (BMus 1995); ARCO. Royal Navy, 1949–54 and 1956–61; School-master, Welbeck Coll., 1954–56; English Electric, becoming Principal of Staff Coll., Dunchurch, 1961–70; British Leyland, Head Office Training Staff, 1970–71; Head, Sidney Stringer Sch. and Community Coll., Coventry, 1971–75; Higher Educn Adviser to Training Commn, 1987–88; Dir, GEC Management Coll., Dunchurch, 1989–92. Chairman: Industrial Links Adv. Gp to Cttee of Dirs of Polytechnics, 1980–87; National Forum for the Performing Arts in Higher Educn, 1987–91; Develt Training Steering Gp, 1983–88; Mem., W Midlands RHA, 1985–89 (Chm., Non Clinical Res. Cttee; Vice-Chm., AIDS Task Force); Mem., RSA Educn Industry Forum, 1986–90. Dir of Music, St Mary's Church, Warwick, 1962–72; Dir, Coventry Cathedral Chapter House Choir, 1982–95; Asst Dir, Warwickshire County Youth Chorale, 1999–2006. Mem., Exec. Cttee, British Fedn of Young Choirs, 1993–95. Member: Council, Upper Avon Navigation Trust, 1994–2001; Steering Cttee, Assoc. of Inland Navigation Authorities, 1997–2003. Governor, 1978–91, Trustee, 1979–91, Chm., Governing Body, 1984–89, Brathay Hall Trust; Chm. Trustees, St Mary's Hall, Warwick, 1984–90; Governor: Mid Warwicks Coll. of Further Educn, 1976–87; Kings School, Worcester, 1983–88; Coten End Co. Jun. Sch., 2006–. Hon. Life Mem., RSCM, 1970; Hon. Fellow, Birmingham Conservatoire, UCE, 2002. *Publications:* Managing People, 1968; Delegations, 1968; Communications, 1969; Organs of St Mary's Church, Warwick, 1969. *Recreations:* music (organ and choir), canals, sailing, outdoor pursuits. *Address:* 38 Coten End, Warwick CV34 4NP. *T:* (01926) 492329.

HOLROYDE, Timothy Victor; QC 1996; a Recorder, since 1997; *b* 18 Aug. 1955; *s* of Frank Holroyde and Doreen Holroyde; *m* 1980, Miranda Elisabeth Stone; two *d*. *Educ:* Bristol Grammar Sch.; Wadham Coll., Oxford (BA Hons Juris.). Called to the Bar, Middle Temple, 1977, Bencher, 2005; in practice on Northern Circuit, 1978–. *Recreations:* squash, tennis. *Address:* Exchange Chambers, Pearl Assurance House, Derby Square, Liverpool L2 9XX. *T:* (0151) 236 7747; *e-mail:* holroydeqc@exchangechambers.co.uk.

HOLT, Alexis Fayrer B.; *see* Brett-Holt.

HOLT, Dr Andrew Anthony, CBE 2004; Head, Information Services Division, Department of Health, 1990–2005; *b* 4 Jan. 1944; *s* of Josef Holzmann and Livia Holzmann; *m* 1969, Janet Margery; three *s*. *Educ:* Latymer Upper Sch.; University Coll. London (BSc Maths 1965; PhD 1969). ICI Paints Div., 1968–70; entered Civil Service, 1970: Principal, Treasury, 1974–78; Head, Operational Research: Inland Revenue, 1978–87; DHSS, 1987–90. Tutor, Open Univ., 1972–. *Publications:* History of Teddington, 2005; contrib. to jls or society papers.

HOLT, Constance, CBE 1975; Area Nursing Officer, Manchester Area Health Authority (Teaching), 1973–77; *b* 5 Jan. 1924; *d* of Ernest Biddulph and of Ada Biddulph (*née* Robley); *m* 1975, Robert Lord Holt, OBE, FRCS. *Educ:* Whalley Range High Sch. for Girls, Manchester; Manchester Royal Infirmary (SRN); Queen Charlotte's Hosp., London; St Mary's Hosp., Manchester (SCM); Royal Coll. of Nursing, London Univ. (Sister Tutor Dipl.); Univ. of Washington (Florence Nightingale Schol., Fulbright Award). Nursing Officer, Min. of Health, 1959–65; Chief Nursing Officer: United Oxford Hosps, 1965–69; United Manchester Hosps, 1969–73. Pres., Assoc. of Nurse Administrators (formerly Assoc. of Hosp. Matrons), 1972–. Reader licensed by Bishop of Sodor and Man. Hon. Lectr, Dept of Nursing, Univ. of Manchester, 1972. Hon. MA Manchester, 1980. *Publications:* articles in British and internat. nursing press. *Recreations:* reading, gardening, music. *Address:* 3c Princess Towers, The Promenade, Port Erin, Isle of Man IM9 6LH. *T:* (01624) 833509.

HOLT, Prof. David, (Tim), CB 2000; PhD; FSS; President, Royal Statistical Society, 2005–07 (Vice-President, 2003–04); *b* 29 Oct. 1943; *s* of late Ernest Frederick Holt and Catherine Rose (*née* Finn); *m* 1966, Jill Blake; one *s* one *d*. *Educ:* Coopers' Company's Sch.; Exeter Univ. (BSc Maths 1966; PhD Mathematical Stats 1969). FSS 1973. Res. Fellow, Univ. of Exeter, 1969–70; Survey Statistician, Statistics Canada, 1970–73 (Consultant, 1974–75); University of Southampton: Lectr in Social Stats, 1973–80; Leverhulme Prof. of Social Stats, 1980–2005; Dean, Social Sci. Faculty, 1981–83; Dep. Vice Chancellor, 1990–95; Dir, CSO, 1995–96; Hd, Govt Statistical Service, 1995–2000; Dir, ONS, and Registrar Gen. for England and Wales, 1996–2000. Consultant: NZ Dept of Stats, 1981; OPCS, 1983, 1987, 1991; ESRC, 1990; Australian Bureau of Stats, 1990; EU, 2001–02; UN, 2001–02; IMF, 2002; Scientific Advr to Chief Scientist, DHSS, 1983–88. Vis. Fellow, Nuffield Coll., Oxford, 1995–2003. Associate Editor: Jl Royal Statistical Soc. B, 1983–88; Survey Methodology, 1988–2002; Editor: Jl Royal Statistical Soc. A: Stats and Society, 1991–94; Jl Official Stats, 2001–. Vice-President: Internat. Assoc. of Survey Statisticians, 1989–91 (Scientific Sec., 1985–87); UN Statistical Commn, 1997–99; Mem., Internat. Statistical Inst., 1985 (Vice-Pres., 1999–2001); Fellow, Amer. Statistical Assoc., 1990; Founding Academician, Acad. of Social Scis, 1999. Trustee, Newitt Trust, 1990–. Hon. DSc (SocSci) Southampton, 1999. *Publications:* (jtly) Analysis of Complex Surveys, 1989; papers in academic jls. *Recreations:* orienteering, travelling, golf.

HOLT, Denise Mary, CMG 2002; HM Diplomatic Service; Ambassador to Spain, and concurrently (non-resident) to Andorra, since 2007; *b* 1 Oct. 1949; *d* of William Dennis and Mary Joanna Mills; *m* 1987, David Holt; one *s*. *Educ:* New Hall Sch., Chelmsford; Bristol Univ. Res. Analyst, FCO, 1970–84; First Sec., Dublin, 1984–87; Head of Section, FCO, 1988–90; First Sec., Brasilia, 1991–93; Dep. Hd, Eastern Dept, FCO, 1993–94; Asst Dir, Personnel, 1996–98; Dep. Hd of Mission, Dublin, 1998–99; Dir, Personnel, FCO, 1999–2002; Ambassador to Mexico, 2002–05; Dir for Migration, FCO, 2005–07. *Recreations:* reading, cooking, needlework. *Address:* c/o Foreign and Commonwealth Office, King Charles Street, SW1A 2AH.

HOLT, Prof. Douglas Brewster, PhD; L'Oréal Professor of Marketing, University of Oxford, since 2004; Fellow of Worcester College, Oxford, since 2004. *Educ:* Stanford Univ. (AB); Univ. of Chicago (MBA); Northwestern Univ. (PhD). Brand manager: Clorox Co.; Dole Packaged Foods; Assistant Professor: Penn State Univ., 1992–97; Univ. of Illinois, 1997–2000; Associate Prof., Harvard Business Sch., 2000–04. Founding Partner, Amalgamated, advertising agency. *Publications:* (ed jtly) The Consumer Society Reader, 2000; How Brands Become Icons: the principles of cultural branding, 2004; articles in learned jls. *Address:* Saïd Business School, University of Oxford, Park End Street, Oxford OX1 1HP.

HOLT, Sir James (Clarke), Kt 1990; FSA 1967; FBA 1978; Professor of Medieval History, Cambridge University, 1978–88; Master of Fitzwilliam College, Cambridge, 1981–88 (Hon. Fellow, 1988; Life Fellow, 2000); *b* 26 April 1922; *s* of late Herbert Holt and Eunice Holt, BEM; *m* 1950, Alice Catherine Elizabeth Suley (*d* 1998); one *s*. *Educ:* Bradford Grammar Sch.; Queen's Coll., Oxford (Hastings Schol.; BA 1st cl. Modern Hist; MA 1947; Hon. Fellow, 1996); Merton Coll., Oxford (Harmsworth Sen. Schol., 1947; DPhil 1952; Hon. Fellow, 2001). University of Nottingham: Asst Lectr, 1949; Lectr, 1951; Sen. Lectr, 1961; Prof. of Medieval History, 1962; Reading University: Prof. of History, 1966–78; Dean, Faculty of Letters and Soc. Scis, 1972–76; Professorial Fellow, Emanuel Coll., Cambridge, 1978–81 (Hon. Fellow, 1985). Vis. Prof., Univ. of Calif, Santa Barbara, 1977; Vis. Hinkley Prof., Johns Hopkins Univ., 1983; Vis. JSPS Fellow, Japan, 1986. Raleigh Lectr, British Acad., 1975. Mem., Adv. Council on Public Records, 1974–81. President: Royal Historical Soc., 1980–84; Selden Soc., 2003–06; Life Pres., Pipe Roll Soc., 1999; Vice-Pres., British Academy, 1987–89. Corres. Fellow, Medieval Acad. of America, 1983. Hon. DLitt: Reading, 1984; Nottingham, 1996. Comdr, Order of Civil Merit (Spain), 1988. *Publications:* The Northerners: a study in the reign of King John, 1961, 2nd edn 1992; Praestita Roll 14–18 John, 1964; Magna Carta, 1965, 2nd edn 1992; The Making of Magna Carta, 1966; Magna Carta and the Idea of Liberty, 1972; The University of Reading: the first fifty years, 1977; Robin Hood, 1982, 2nd edn 1989; (ed with J. Gillingham) War and Government in the Middle Ages, 1984; Magna Carta and Medieval Government, 1985; (with R. Mortimer) Acta of Henry II and Richard I, 1986; (ed) Domesday Studies, 1987; Colonial England 1066–1215, 1997; (with J. Everard) Jersey 1204: the forging of an island community, 2004; papers in English Historical Review, Past and Present, Economic History Review, Trans Royal Hist. Soc. *Recreations:* mountaineering, cricket, fly-fishing, music. *Address:* 5 Holben Close, Barton, Cambridge CB3 7AQ. *T:* (01223) 264923. *Clubs:* Oxford and Cambridge, National Liberal, MCC; Wayfarers' (Liverpool).

HOLT, (James) Richard (Trist); President, Pensions Appeal Tribunals (England & Wales), 1993–98; *b* 17 Aug. 1924; *s* of George Richard Holt and Gladys Floyd Holt (*née* Bennetts); *m* 1st, 1952, Helen Worswick (marr. diss); one *s* one *d*; 2nd, 1977, Patricia Mary Hartley. *Educ:* Giggleswick Sch.; Queen's Coll., Oxford (MA 1950); London Univ. (ext. LLB 1952). Served Royal Signals, 1942–47, commnd 1945. Articled clerk, 1941; admitted solicitor, 1951; called to the Bar, Gray's Inn, 1973. Part-time Chairman: Med. Appeal Tribunals, 1979–96; Vaccine Damage Tribunals, 1982–96; Pensions Appeal Tribunals, 1985–98; Disability Appeal Tribunals, 1992–96; Immigration Appeals Adjudicator, 1982–90; Mem., Mental Health Act Commn, 1985–86. Contested (C) Rossendale, 1959. *Publication:* contrib. Law Soc. Gazette. *Recreations:* walking, reading history. *Address:* The Hey Farm, Newton-in-Bowland, near Clitheroe, Lancs BB7 3EE. *T:* (01200) 446213. *Club:* Victory Services.

HOLT, John Frederick; His Honour Judge Holt; a Circuit Judge, since 1998; *b* 7 Oct. 1947; *s* of Edward Basil Holt and Monica Holt; *m* 1970, Stephanie Ann Watson; three *s*. *Educ:* Ampleforth; Bristol Univ. (LLB). Called to the Bar, Lincoln's Inn, 1970; barrister, E Anglian Chambers, 1970–98 (Head of Chambers, 1993–98); Asst Recorder, 1989–92; a Recorder, 1992–98. ECB cricket coach. *Recreations:* village cricket, classic motor cars. *Address:* c/o Group Manager, Chelmsford Group of Courts, 1st Floor, Steeple House, Church Lane, Chelmsford CM1 1NH. *Clubs:* Strangers (Norwich); MG Car; Twinstead Cricket.

HOLT, John Michael, MD, FRCP; Consultant Physician, John Radcliffe Hospital (formerly Radcliffe Infirmary), Oxford, 1974–2000, now Emeritus; Fellow, 1968–2000, now Emeritus, and Vice Principal, 1999–2000, Linacre College, Oxford; *b* 8 March 1935; *s* of late Frank Holt, BSc and of Constance Holt; *m* 1959, Sheila Margaret Morton; one *s* three *d*. *Educ:* St Peter's Sch., York; Univ. of St Andrews. MA Oxon; MD St Andrews; MSc Queen's Univ. Ont. Registrar and Lectr, Nuffield Dept of Medicine, Radcliffe Infirmary, Oxford, 1964–66, Cons. Physician 1968; Chm., Medical Staff, Oxford Hosps, 1982–84. University of Oxford: Med. Tutor, 1967–73; Dir of Clinical Studies, 1971–76; Mem., Gen. Bd of Faculties, 1987–91; Chm., Clinical Medicine Bd, 1992–94. Civilian Advr in Medicine, RAF, 1994–2000. Formerly Examiner in Medicine: Univ. of Oxford; Hong Kong; London; Glasgow; Dublin; RCP. Censor, RCP, 1995–97. Member: Assoc. of Physicians; Soc. of Apothecaries; Cttee on Safety of Medicines, 1979–86; Oxford RHA, 1984–88. Pres., Oxford Medical Alumni, 2003–07. Editor, Qly Jl of Medicine, 1975–92. *Publications:* papers on disorders of blood and various med. topics in BMJ, Lancet, etc. *Recreation:* sailing. *Address:* Old Whitehill, Tackley, Oxon OX5 3AB. *T:* (01869) 331241. *Clubs:* Oxford and Cambridge; Royal Cornwall Yacht (Falmouth).

HOLT, Prof. John Riley, FRS 1964; Professor of Experimental Physics, University of Liverpool, 1966–83, now Emeritus; *b* 15 Feb. 1918; *er s* of Frederick Holt and Annie (*née* Riley); *m* 1949, Joan Silvester Thomas (*d* 2001); two *s*. *Educ:* Runcorn Secondary Sch.; University of Liverpool; PhD 1941; British Atomic Energy Project, Liverpool and Cambridge, 1940–45; University of Liverpool: Lectr, 1945–53; Sen. Lectr, 1953–56; Reader, 1956–66. *Publications:* papers in scientific journals on nuclear physics and particle physics. *Recreation:* gardening. *Address:* Rydalmere, Stanley Avenue, Higher Bebington, Wirral CH63 5QE. *T:* (0151) 608 2041.

HOLT, Her Honour Mary; a Circuit Judge, 1977–95; *d* of Henry James Holt, solicitor, and of Sarah Holt (*née* Chapman); unmarried. *Educ:* Park Sch., Preston; Girton Coll., Cambridge (MA, LLB, 1st cl. Hons). Called to the Bar, Gray's Inn, 1949 (Atkin Scholar). Practised on Northern circuit. Former Vice-Chm., Preston North Conservative Assoc.; Member: Nat. Exec. Council, 1969–72; Woman's Nat. Advisory Cttee, 1969–70; representative, Central Council, 1969–71. MP (C) Preston N, 1970–Feb. 1974. Contested (C) Preston N, Feb. and Oct. 1974. Dep. Pres., Lancs Br., BRCS, 1976–95. Freedom of

Cities of Dallas and Denton, Texas, 1987. Badge of Honour, BRCS, 1989. *Publication:* 2nd edn, Benas and Essenhigh's Precedents of Pleadings, 1956. *Recreation:* walking. *Club:* Royal Over Seas League.

HOLT, Sir Michael, Kt 1995; CBE 1981; FCA; Chairman, Eastern Area Conservative Provincial Council, 1992–96; *b* 23 Dec. 1927; *s* of Frank Holt, MM, FCA and Helen Gertrude Holt (*née* Wheeler); *m* 1955, Janet Michelle Simon; two *s* one *d*. *Educ:* Epsom Coll.; Downing Coll., Cambridge (MA, LLM). Called to the Bar, Inner Temple, 1953; qualified as Chartered Accountant, 1958; Sen. Partner, Arthur Goddard & Co., Chartered Accountants, 1966–83. Dir, Lay and Wheeler Gp Ltd, 1983–2002, and other cos. External Mem., Lloyds, 1983–96. Member: NE Essex HA, 1982–89, 1990–93; Bd of Govs, St John's Hosp. for Diseases of the Skin, 1980–82. Conservative Party: Hon. Treas., Colchester Assoc., 1965–76; Chm., 1983–85, Vice Pres., 1985–95, N Colchester Assoc.; Vice Pres., N Essex Assoc., 1995–; Hon. Treas., 1975–80, Vice Chm., then Dep. Chm., 1986–92, Eastern Area Provincial Council; Pres., N Essex and S Suffolk Eur. Constituency Council, 1994–99; Vice Chm., 1985–86, Chm., 1986–90, Pres., 1991–94, NE Essex European Cons. Council; Mem. Exec. Cttee, Nat. Union of Cons. and Unionist Assocs, 1975–83, 1986–98. *Address:* The Tower House, Bildeston, Suffolk IP7 7ER. *T:* (01449) 741313.

HOLT, Oliver Charles Thomas; Chief Sports Writer, The Mirror, since 2002; *b* 22 May 1966; *s* of Thomas and Eileen Holt; *m* 1995, Sarah Llewellyn-Jones; two *d*. *Educ:* Christ Church, Oxford (BA Hons Modern Hist.). Reporter, Daily Post & Echo, Liverpool, 1990–93; The Times: Motor Racing Corresp., 1993–97; Football Corresp., 1997–2000; Chief Sports Corresp., 2000–02. Sports Writer of the Year, British Press Gazette, 2005, 2006. *Publication:* The Bridge, 1998. *Recreations:* Marlon Brando, Bob Dylan, Stockport County. *Address:* c/o The Mirror, 1 Canada Square, Canary Wharf, E14 5AP.

HOLT, Richard; *see* Holt, J. R. T.

HOLT, Stuart; Headmaster, Clitheroe Royal Grammar School, 1991–2004; *b* 12 Sept. 1943; *s* of Alan and Irene Holt; *m* 1968, Valerie Hollows; one *s* one *d*. *Educ:* Leeds Univ. (BSc 2nd Cl. Hons Zool., MPhil); Univ. of Lancaster (MA Educn). Biol. Master, Adwick Sch., Doncaster, 1968–71; Hd of Biol., King's Sch., Pontefract, 1971–73; Hd of Sci., Whitley High Sch., Wigan, 1973–78; Dep. Hd Curriculum, Wright Robinson High Sch., Manchester, 1978–84; Headmaster, Failsworth Sch., Oldham, 1984–91. Mem., Rotary Internat. *Recreations:* Rossendale Male Voice Choir, theatre, photography, Italy, fell-walking, cabinet making. *Address:* c/o Clitheroe Royal Grammar School, York Street, Clitheroe, Lancs BB7 2DJ.

HOLT, Thelma Mary Bernadette, CBE 1994; Managing Director, Thelma Holt Ltd, since 1990; Associate Producer, Royal Shakespeare Company, since 2004; *b* 4 Jan. 1932; *d* of David Holt and Ellen Finagh (*née* Doyle); *m* 1st, 1956, Patrick Graucob (marr. diss. 1968); 2nd, 1969, David Pressman (marr. diss. 1970). *Educ:* St Ann's Sch., Lytham; RADA. Actress, 1953; Founder, Open Space Theatre (with Charles Marowitz), 1968; Dir, Round House Theatre, 1977; Exec. Producer, Theatre of Comedy, 1983; Head of Touring and Commercial Exploitation, Royal Nat. Theatre, 1985 (Laurence Olivier/Observer Award for Outstanding Achievement, 1987); Exec. Producer, Peter Hall Co., 1989; formed Thelma Holt Ltd, 1990, productions include: The Three Sisters, 1990; Tango at the End of Winter, 1991; Electra, Hamlet, Les Atrides, La Baruffe Chiozotte, Six Characters in Search of an Author, The Tempest, 1992; Much Ado About Nothing, 1993; Peer Gynt, The Clandestine Marriage, 1994; The Seagull, A Midsummer Night's Dream, Antony and Cleopatra, The Glass Menagerie, 1995; Observe the Sons of Ulster Marching Towards the Somme, A Doll's House, 1996; The Maids, Les Fausses Confidences, Oh Les Beaux Jours, Shintoku-Maru, 1997; The Relapse, 1998; Macbeth, King Lear, 1999; Miss Julie, 2000; Semi-Monde, 2001; Via Dolorosa, The Tempest, 2002; Pericles, Ghosts, Hamlet, The Taming of the Shrew, 2003; We Happy Few, Hamlet, 2004; Man and Boy, Primo (NT, NY), Twelfth Night, 2005; Hay Fever, Titus Andronicus, 2006; Kean, Coriolanus, The Giant, 2007; for Royal Shakespeare Company: The Jacobeans, 2003; The Taming of the Shrew/The Tamer Tamed, All's Well that Ends Well, Othello, 2004; A Midsummer Night's Dream, 2005; The Crucible, Canterbury Tales, 2006. Member: Arts Council, 1993–98 (Chm., Drama Adv. Panel, 1994–98); Council, RADA, 1985–. Director: Stage One (formerly Theatre Investment Fund) Ltd, 1982–; Citizens Theatre, Glasgow, 1989– (Vice-Pres., 1997–); Almeida Th., 2001–; Chm., Yvonne Arnaud Th., 2002–05. Cameron Mackintosh Vis. Prof. of Contemporary Theatre, Oxford Univ., 1998; Fellow, St Catherine's Coll., Oxford, 1998–2003, then Emeritus. Patron, OUDS, 2001. Companion, Liverpool Inst. for Performing Arts, 2002; Dist. Friend of Oxford Univ., 2006. DUniv Middlesex, 1994; Hon. MA Open, 1988; Hon. DLitt UEA, 2003. Special Award for Individual Achievement, TMA Awards, 2006. Order of the Rising Sun, Gold Rays with Rosette (Japan), 2004. *Recreation:* bargain hunting at antique fairs. *Address:* Noël Coward Theatre, 85 St Martin's Lane, WC2N 4AU. *T:* (020) 7812 7455, *Fax:* (020) 7812 7550; *e-mail:* thelma@dircon.co.uk.

HOLT, Tim; *see* Holt, David.

HOLTAM, Rev. Nicholas Roderick; Vicar of St Martin-in-the-Fields, since 1995; *b* 8 Aug. 1954; *s* of late Sydney Holtam and Kathleen (*née* Freeberne); *m* 1981, Helen Harris; three *s* one *d*. *Educ:* Latymer Grammar Sch., Edmonton; Collingwood Coll., Univ. of Durham (BA Geog.; MA Theol.); King's Coll. London (BD, AKC; FKC 2005); Westcott House, Cambridge. Ordained deacon, 1979, priest, 1980; Asst Curate, St Dunstan and All Saints, Stepney, 1979–82; Tutor, Lincoln Theol Coll., 1983–87; Vicar, Christ Church and St John with St Luke, Isle of Dogs, 1988–95. Hon. DCL Durham, 2005. *Publication:* A Room With a View: ministry with the world at your door, 2008. *Recreations:* walking, cycling, reading, exploring London. *Address:* 6 St Martin's Place, WC2N 4JJ. *T:* (020) 7766 1100; *e-mail:* clergyoffice@smitf.org.

HOLTHAM, Gerald Hubert; Managing Partner, Cadwyn Capital LLP, since 2005; *b* Aberdare, 28 June 1944; *s* of late Denis Arthur Holtham and Dilys Maud Holtham (*née* Bull); *m* 1st, 1969, Patricia Mary Blythin (marr. diss. 1976); one *d*; 2nd, 1979, Edith Hodgkinson; one *s* one *d*. *Educ:* King Edward's Sch., Birmingham; Jesus Coll., Oxford (BA 1st Cl. PPE); Nuffield Coll., Oxford (MPhil Econ). ODI, 1973–75; Economist, OECD, Paris, 1975–82; Head, Gen. Econ. Div., Dept of Econs, OECD, 1982–85; Vis. Fellow, Brookings Inst., Washington, 1985–87; Chief Internat. Economist, Shearson Lehman, 1988–91; Econs Fellow, Magdalen Coll., Oxford, 1991–92; Chief Economist, Lehman Brothers, Europe, 1992–94; Dir, IPPR, 1994–98; Dir, Global Strategy, Norwich Union Investment Mgt, 1998–2000; Chief Investment Officer, Morley Fund Mgt, 2000–04. Visiting Professor: Univ. of Strathclyde, 1990–93; Cardiff Univ. Business Sch., 2004–; Affiliated Prof., London Business Sch., 1992–99. *Publications:* (with Roger Busby) Main Line Kill (novel), 1967; (with Arthur Hazlewood) Aid and Inequality in Kenya, 1975; (jtly) Empirical Macroeconomics for Interdependent Economies, 1988; (with Ralph Bryant and Peter Hooper) External Deficits and the Dollar, 1988; articles on economics in learned jls. *Recreations:* gardening, windsurfing, listening to jazz. *Address:* 13 Lansdowne Gardens, SW8 2EQ. *T:* (020) 7622 8673.

HOLWELL, Peter, FCA; Principal, University of London, 1985–97; *b* 28 March 1936; *s* of Frank Holwell and Helen (*née* Howe); *m* 1959, Jean Patricia Ashman; one *s* one *d*. *Educ:* Palmers Endowed Sch., Grays, Essex; Hendon Grammar Sch.; London Sch. of Econs and Pol Science (BSc Econ). FCA 1972; MBCS 1974; FRSocMed 1991. Articled Clerk 1958–61, Management Consultant, 1961–64, Arthur Andersen and Co.; University of London: Head of Computing, Sch. Exams Bd, 1964–67; Head of University Computing and O & M Unit, 1967–77; Sec. for Accounting and Admin. Computing, 1977–82; Clerk of the Court, 1982–85; Dir, School Exams Council, 1988–94; Mem., Univ. of London Exams and Assessments Council, 1991–96. Chm., UCCA Computing Gp, 1977–82. Chm., City and E London FHSA, 1994–96. Director: Zoo Operations Ltd, 1988–92; London E Anglian Gp Ltd, 1990–93; non-exec. Mem., NE Thames RHA, 1990–94. Consultant: POW Sch. of Architecture and the Bldg Arts, 1998–99; Chatham Historic Dockyard Trust, 1999–2001. FZS, 1988–2001 (Treas., 1991–92). Chm., St Mark's Res. Foundn and Educnl Trust, 1995–2000; Trustee: Samuel Courtauld (formerly Home House) Trust, 1985–97; Leeds Castle Foundn, 2001–03. Mem. Council, Sch. of Pharmacy, Univ. of London, 1996–2001; Vice-Chm., Wye Coll., 1996–2000. *Recreations:* walking, music, horology. *Address:* Hookers Green, Bishopsbourne, Canterbury, Kent CT4 5JB. *Club:* Royal Society of Medicine.

HOLZACH, Dr Robert; Hon. Chairman, Union Bank of Switzerland, 1988–96; *b* 28 Sept. 1922. *Educ:* Univ. of Zürich (Dr of Law). Union Bank of Switzerland: trainee, Geneva, London, 1951–52; Vice-Pres., 1956; Senior Vice-Pres., Head of Commercial Div., Head Office, 1962; Mem., Exec. Board, 1966; Exec. Vice-Pres., 1968; President, 1976; Chm. of Board, 1980–88. *Publication:* Herausforderungen, 1988. *Address:* Erbstrasse 7, 8700 Küsnacht, Switzerland.

HOM, Ken; BBC TV presenter; author; *b* 3 May 1949; *s* of late Thomas Hom and of Ying Fong Hom. *Educ:* Univ. of Calif, Berkeley. Public television producer, 1974–75; cookery teacher, 1975–78; Cookery prof., Calif. Culinary Acad., San Francisco, 1978–82. Presenter, BBC TV series: Ken Hom's Chinese Cookery, 1984; Hot Chefs, 1991; Ken Hom's Hot Wok, 1996; Ken Hom Travels with a Hot Wok, 1998; Foolproof Chinese Cookery, 2000. Hon. Chm., Inst. for Advancement of Sci. and Art of Chinese Cuisine, NY, 1993–. Founding Patron, Oxford Gastronomica, 2007. Hon. Dr Oxford Brookes, 2007. *Publications:* Ken Hom's Encyclopaedia of Chinese Cookery Techniques, 1984 (US edn as Chinese Technique, 1981); Ken Hom's Chinese Cookery, 1984, rev. edn 2001; Ken Hom's Vegetable and Pasta Book, 1987; Ken Hom's East Meets West Cuisine, 1987; Fragrant Harbour Taste, 1988; Asian Vegetarian Feast, 1988; Ken Hom's Quick and Easy Chinese Cookery, 1988; The Taste of China, 1989; The Cooking of China, 1992; Ken Hom's Chinese Kitchen, 1993; Ken Hom's Hot Wok, 1996; Ken Hom's Asian Ingredients and Posters, 1997; Ken Hom Travels with a Hot Wok, 1997; Easy Family Dishes: a memoir with recipes, 1998 (Andre Simon Award, 1999; US edn as Easy Family Recipes from a Chinese-American Childhood, 1998); Ken Hom Cooks Thai, 1999; Foolproof Chinese Cookery, 2000; Quick Wok, 2001; Foolproof Thai Cookery, 2002; Foolproof Asian Cookery, 2003; 100 Top Stir Fries, 2004; Simple Chinese Cookery, 2005; Simple Thai Cookery, 2006; Simple Asian Cookery, 2007. *Recreations:* Bordeaux vintage wine, bicycling, reading, swimming.

HOMA, Peter Michael, CBE 2000; Chief Executive, Nottingham University Hospitals NHS Trust, since 2006; *b* 3 Jan. 1957; *s* of late Karol Anthony Homa and Anne Kathleen Homa (*née* Dixon); *m* 2006, Deborah Hallas; one *s* one *d* from previous marriage. *Educ:* Ernest Bevin Sch., London; Univ. of Sussex (BA Hons Econs 1979); Univ. of Hull (MBA 1993); Henley Management Coll. and Brunel Univ. (DBA 1998). Comp IHM 2003 (MHSM 1985, FHSM 1999). Self-employed, 1979–81; nat. admin. trainee, SW Thames RHA, 1981–82; Operational Services Adminr, St George's Hosp., London, 1983–84; Dep. Unit Adminr, Bristol Children's and Maternity Hosps, 1984–86; Dep. Unit Gen. Manager, Acute Services, Bromsgrove and Redditch HA, 1986–89; Leicester Royal Infirmary: Associate Gen. Manager, 1989–90; Unit. Gen. Manager, 1990–93; Chief Exec., Leicester Royal Infirmary NHS Trust, 1993–98; Hd, Nat. Patients' Access Team, NHS Exec., 1998–99; Chief Executive: Commn for Health Improvement, 1999–2003; St George's Healthcare NHS Trust, 2003–06. Visiting Professor: Univ. of Lincoln, 2006; Univ. of Surrey, 2006. Pres., IHSM, 1998–99 (Vice-Chm., 1996–97; Chm., 1997–98). *Recreations:* running, cycling, reading, writing, picture framing. *Address:* Nottingham University Hospitals NHS Trust, Queen's Medical Centre Campus, Nottingham NG7 2UH.

HOMAN, Maj.-Gen. John Vincent, CB 1980; CEng, FIMechE; Facilities Manager, Matra Marconi Space (formerly Marconi Space Systems), Portsmouth, 1982–92; *b* 30 June 1927; *s* of Charles Frederic William Burton Homan and Dorothy Maud Homan; *m* 1953, Ann Bartlett; one *s* two *d*. *Educ:* Haileybury; RMA Sandhurst; RMCS Shrivenham. BSc (Eng). Commnd, REME, 1948; Lt-Col 1967; Comdr REME 2nd Div., 1968–70; Col 1970; MoD 1970–72; CO 27 Comd Workshop REME, 1972–74; Brig. 1974; Dep. Dir, Electrical and Mechanical Engineering, 1st British Corps, 1974–76; Dir of Equipment Management, MoD, 1976–77; Dir Gen., Electrical and Mechanical Engrg, MoD, 1978–79; Maj.-Gen. 1978; Sen. Army Mem., RCDS, 1980–82. Col Comdt, REME, 1982–88. *Address:* Roedean, 25 The Avenue, Andover, Hants SP10 3EW. *T:* (01264) 351196. *Club:* Army and Navy.

HOMDEN, Dr Carol Ann; Chief Executive, Coram (formerly Coram Family), since 2007; *b* 9 April 1960; *d* of Dick Homden and Beryl Homden (*née* Kinnersley, now Rabbage); partner, Steve Caplin; two *s*. *Educ:* Shrewsbury High Sch.; Univ. of E Anglia (BA Hons English Lit.; PhD 1986). Publicity Asst, Poly. of N London, 1985–86; Polytechnic of Central London, subsequently University of Westminster: PR Officer, 1986–87; Dir, Corporate Communications, 1987–97; Dir, Mktg and Develt, 1997–99; Dir, Mktg and Public Affairs, BM, 1999–2003; Commercial Dir, Prince's Trust, 2003–07. Chair, Avenues Trust, 2005–. *Publication:* The Plays of David Hare, 1986. *Recreation:* cottage in Suffolk. *Address:* Coram, 49 Mecklenburgh Square, WC1N 2QA. *T:* (020) 7520 0304; *e-mail:* carol@coram.org.uk.

HOME; *see* Douglas Home, and Douglas-Home, family name of Baroness Dacre and Earl of Home.

HOME, 15th Earl of *cr* 1605; **David Alexander Cospatrick Douglas-Home,** CVO 1997; CBE 1991; Baron Home 1473; Baron Dunglass 1605; Baron Douglas (UK) 1875; Chairman: Coutts & Co., since 1999; RBS Coutts (formerly Coutts Bank von Ernst), since 2004 (Director, 1999, Chairman, 2000, Coutts (Switzerland); Chairman, Bank von Ernst (Switzerland), 2003); Grosvenor Group Ltd, since 2007 (Deputy Chairman, 2005–07); *b* 20 Nov. 1943; *o s* of Baron Home of the Hirsel (Life Peer), KT, PC (who disclaimed his hereditary peerages for life, 1963) and Elizabeth Hester (*d* 1990), *d* of Very Rev. C. A. Alington, DD; *S* father, 1995; *m* 1972, Jane Margaret, *yr d* of late Col J. Williams-Wynne, CBE, DSO; one *s* two *d*. *Educ:* Eton College; Christ Church, Oxford (BA 1966). Director: Morgan Grenfell & Co. Ltd, 1974–99; Morgan Grenfell Egyptian Finance Co. Ltd, 1975–77; Morgan Grenfell (Scotland), then Deutsche Morgan Grenfell (Scotland) Ltd, 1978–99 (Chm., 1986–99); Morgan Grenfell (Asia) Ltd, 1978–82 (Dep.

Chm., 1979–82); Arab Bank Investment Co., 1979–87; Agricultural Mortgage Corp., 1979–93; Arab-British Chamber of Commerce, 1975–84; Tandem Group (formerly EFG plc), 1981–96 (Chm., 1993–96); Credit for Exports, 1984–94; Deutsche Morgan Grenfell (Hong Kong), 1989–99; Deutsche Morgan Grenfell Asia Pacific Holdings Pte Ltd, 1989–99; Morgan Grenfell Thai Co., 1990–96; K & N Kenanaga Bhd, 1995–99; Kenanga DMG Futures Sdn Bhd, 1995–99; Deutsche Morgan Grenfell Group plc, 1996–99 (Chm., Jan.–March, 1999); Wheatsheaf Investments Ltd (formerly Deva Gp), 1999–; Deva Gp Ltd (formerly Deva Hldgs), 1999–; Dubai Financial Services Authy, 2005–; Chairman: Morgan Grenfell Export Services, 1984–99; Morgan Grenfell Internat. Ltd, 1987–99; Cegelec Controls Ltd, 1991–94; K & N Kenanga Holdings Bhd, 1993–99; Grosvenor Estate Hldgs, 1993–99; MAN Ltd, 2000–; Trustee, Grosvenor Estate, 1993–. Chm., Committee for Middle East Trade, 1986–92 (Mem., 1973–75). Governor: Ditchley Foundn, 1977–; Commonwealth Inst., 1988–98. Trustee, RASE, 1999–2004 (Hon. Trustee, 2004–). Pres., Old Etonian Assoc., 2002–03. Elected Mem., H of L, 1999. *Recreations:* outdoor sports. *Heir:* Lord Dunglass, *qv*. *Address:* 99 Dovehouse Street, SW3 6JZ. *T:* (020) 7352 9060; The Hirsel, Coldstream, Berwickshire TD12 4LP. *T:* (01890) 882345. *Club:* Turf.

HOME, Anna Margaret, OBE 1993; Chief Executive, Children's Film and Television Foundation, since 1998; *b* 13 Jan. 1938; *d* of James Douglas Home and Janet Mary (*née* Wheeler). *Educ:* Convent of Our Lady, St Leonard's-on-Sea, Sussex; St Anne's Coll., Oxford (MA (Hons) Mod. Hist.). BBC Radio Studio Man., 1960–64; Res. Asst, Dir, Producer, Children's TV, 1966–70; Exec. Producer, BBC Children's Drama Unit, 1970–81: responsible for series such as Lizzie Dripping, Bagthorpe Saga, Moon Stallion; started Grange Hill, 1977; Controller of Programmes SE, later Dep. Dir of Programmes, TVS (one of the original franchise gp), 1981–86; Hd of Children's Programmes, BBC TV, 1986–98. Chair: Cinemagic, 1999–2005; Eurokidnet, 2002–06; Children's Television Trust Internat., 2005–; Kidnet, 2006–; Save Kids TV, 2006–; Board Member: Screen South, 2002–; Unicorn Th. for Children, 2004–. Chm., 2nd World Summit on TV for Children, London, 1998. Chm., Showcommotion Children's Media Fest., 2005–. Trustee, Prince of Wales Arts and Kids Foundn, 2005–. FRTS 1987. Pye Award for distinguished services to children's television, 1984; Eleanor Farjeon Award for services to children's literature, 1989; Judges Award, RTS, 1993; Lifetime Achievement Award, Women in Film and TV, 1996; BAFTA Special Award for Lifetime Achievement in Children's Programmes, 1997. *Publication:* Into the Box of Delights: a history of children's television, 1993. *Recreations:* theatre, literature, travel, gardening. *Address:* 3 Liberia Road, N5 1JP.

HOME, Prof. George, BL; FCIBS; Professor of International Banking, Heriot-Watt University, Edinburgh, 1978–85, Professor Emeritus, since 1985; *b* 13 April 1920; *s* of George Home and Leah Home; *m* 1946, Muriel Margaret Birleson; two *s* one *d*. *Educ:* Fort Augustus Village Sch.; Trinity Academy, Edinburgh; George Heriot's Sch., Edinburgh; Edinburgh Univ. (BL 1952). Joined Royal Bank of Scotland, 1936; served RAF, 1940–46; Dep. Man. Dir, Royal Bank of Scotland Ltd, 1973–80; Dep. Gp Man. Dir, Royal Bank of Scotland Gp Ltd, 1976–80; Director: Williams & Glyn's Bank Ltd, 1975–80; The Wagon Finance Corp. plc, 1980–85. Vice-Pres., Inst. of Bankers in Scotland, 1977–80. Chm., George Heriot's Trust, 1989–96. FCMI. *Recreations:* fishing, gardening, reading, travel. *Address:* Bickley, 12 Barnton Park View, Edinburgh EH4 6HJ. *T:* (0131) 312 7648.

HOME, Sir William (Dundas), 14th Bt *cr* 1671 (NS), of Blackadder, Co. Berwick; consultant tree surgeon and horticulturalist; *b* 19 Feb. 1968; *s* of late John Home, *er s* of 13th Bt, and of Nancy Helen, *d* of H. G. Elliott, Perth, WA (she *m* 1993, Rt Hon. Sir John Grey Gorton, GCMG, AC, CH); *S* grandfather, 1992; *m* 1995, Dominique Meryl, *d* of Sydney Fischer, OBE; one *s* one *d*. *Educ:* Cranbrook Sch., Sydney, NSW. Member: Bd, Internat. Soc. of Arboriculture, 1991 (Founding Mem., Australian Chapter, 1997); Aust. Inst. of Horticulture, 1992; Nat. Arborists' Assoc. of Aust., 1999. *Recreations:* golf, scuba diving, fishing, tennis. *Heir:* *s* Thomas John Home, *b* 24 Nov. 1996. *Address:* 53 York Road, Queen's Park, NSW 2022, Australia. *Club:* Royal Sydney Golf (Sydney).

HOME ROBERTSON, John David; Member (Lab) East Lothian, Scottish Parliament, 1999–2007; *b* 5 Dec. 1948; *s* of late Lt-Col J. W. Home Robertson and Mrs H. M. Home Robertson; *m* 1977, Catherine Jean Brewster; two *s*. *Educ:* Ampleforth Coll.; West of Scotland Coll. of Agriculture. Farmer. Mem., Berwicks DC, 1975–78; Mem., Borders Health Bd, 1976–78. Chm., Eastern Borders CAB, 1977. MP (Lab) Berwick and E Lothian, Oct. 1978–83, E Lothian, 1983–2001. Opposition Scottish Whip, 1983–84; opposition spokesman on agric., 1984–87, 1988–90, on Scotland, 1987–88; PPS to Minister of Agriculture, Fisheries and Food, 1997–98; PPS to Minister for Cabinet Office, 1998–99; Member: Select Cttee on Scottish affairs, 1980–83; Select Cttee on Defence, 1990–97; British-Irish Parly Body, 1993–99. Chm., Scottish Gp of Lab MPs, 1983. Dep. Minister for Rural Affairs, Scottish Exec., 1999–2000. Convener, Holyrood Progress Gp, 2000–05. Founder, Paxton Trust, 1989. *Clubs:* East Lothian Labour, Prestonpans Labour.

HOMER, Linda Margaret, CB 2008; Chief Executive, UK Border (formerly Border and Immigration) Agency (formerly Director General, Immigration and Nationality), Home Office, since 2005; *b* 4 March 1957; *d* of John and Jean Risebrow; *m* 1979, Ian James Homer; three *d*. *Educ:* University Coll. London (LLB). Admitted solicitor, 1980; Lawyer, Reading BC, 1979–82; Solicitor, then Asst Chief Exec., 1982–94, Dir, Corporate Services, 1994–97, Herts CC; Chief Executive: Suffolk CC, 1998–2002; Birmingham CC, 2002–05. *Recreations:* ski-ing, alpine walking, gardening. *Address:* Home Office, 1st Floor, Seacole Building, 2 Marsham Street, SW1P 4DF; *e-mail:* lin.homer@homeoffice.gsi.gov.uk. *Club:* University Women's.

HOMMEN, Johannes Henricus Maria, (Jan); Chairman, Reed Elsevier, since 2005; *b* 29 April 1943; *s* of Joseph Hommen and Johanna van Herpen; *m* 1969, Gertrudis, (Tucke), van Enschot; two *s* two *d*. *Educ:* St Jans Lyceum, Gymnasium B, Den Bosch; Univ. of Tilburg (Business 1970). Controller, Lips Aluminium, 1970–74; Financial Dir, Alcoa Nederland, 1974–78; Alcoa, USA: Asst Treas., 1978–86, Vice Pres. Treas., 1986–91; Exec. Vice Pres. and Chief Financial Officer, 1991–97; Philips Electronics: Exec. Vice Pres. and Chief Financial Officer, Netherlands, 1997–2002; Vice Chm. and Chief Financial Officer, 2002–05. Chairman, Supervisory Board: Academic Hosp., Maastricht, 2001–; TNT, 2005–; ING (Mem., 2005–); Tias Nimbas Business Sch., Univ. of Tilberg; Member, Supervisory Board: Ahold, 2003; Campina. Officier, Orde van Oranje Nassau (Netherlands), 2005. *Recreations:* golf, tennis, swimming, reading, music, chess. *Address:* Reed Elsevier, Radarweg 29, 1043 NX Amsterdam, Netherlands. *T:* (20) 4852993, *Fax:* (20) 4852750; *e-mail:* jan.hommen@reedelsevier.com.

HONDERICH, Prof. Edgar Dawn Ross, (Ted), PhD; Grote Professor of the Philosophy of Mind and Logic, University College London, 1988–98, now Emeritus; Visiting Professor, University of Bath, since 2005; Chairman, Royal Institute of Philosophy, since 2006; *b* 30 Jan. 1933; *s* of John William Honderich and Rae Laura Armstrong, Baden, Canada; *m* 1st, 1964, Pauline Ann Marina Goodwin (marr. diss. 1972), *d* of Paul Fawcett Goodwin and Lena Payne, Kildare; one *s* one *d*; 2nd, 1989, Jane Elizabeth O'Grady (marr. diss. 1998), *d* of Major Robert O'Grady and Hon. Joan Ramsbotham, Bath; 3rd, 2003, Ingrid Coggin Purkiss, *d* of Maurice Edward Henry Coggin and Eleonora Illeris, Cambridge. *Educ:* Kitchener Sch., Kitchener, Canada; Lawrence Park Sch., Toronto; University Coll., Univ. of Toronto (BA 1959); University Coll. London (PhD 1968). Literary Editor, Toronto Star, 1957–59; Lectr in Phil., Univ. of Sussex, 1962–64; Lectr in Phil., 1964–73, Reader in Phil., 1973–83, Prof. of Phil., 1983–88, and Head of Dept of Philosophy, 1988–93, UCL; Chm., Bd of Phil Studies, Univ. of London, 1986–89. Vis. Prof., Yale Univ., and CUNY, 1970. Editor: Internat. Library of Philosophy and Scientific Method, 1966–98; Penguin philosophy books, 1967–98; The Arguments of the Philosophers, 1968–98; The Problems of Philosophy: their past and present, 1984–98; radio, television, journalism. *Publications:* Punishment: the supposed justifications, 1969, 5th edn as Punishment: the supposed justifications reconsidered, 2005; (ed) Essays on Freedom of Action, 1973; (ed) Social Ends and Political Means, 1976; (ed with Myles Burnyeat) Philosophy As It Is, 1979; Violence for Equality: inquiries in political philosophy (incorporating Three Essays on Political Violence, 1976), 1980, 3rd edn as Terrorism for Humanity: inquiries in political philosophy, 2003; (ed) Philosophy Through Its Past, 1984; (ed) Morality and Objectivity, 1985; A Theory of Determinism: the mind, neuroscience, and life-hopes, 1988, 2nd edn, as The Consequences of Determinism, 1990; Mind and Brain, 1990; Conservatism, 1990, revd edn as Conservatism: Burke, Nozick, Bush, Blair?, 2005; How Free Are You? The Determinism Problem, 1993, 2nd edn 2002 (trans. German, Japanese, Chinese, Swedish, Italian, Polish, Romanian, French); (ed) The Oxford Companion to Philosophy, 1995, new edn 2005; Philosopher: a kind of life, 2000; After the Terror, 2002, 2nd edn 2003; Political Means and Social Ends: collected papers, 2003; On Consciousness: collected papers, 2004; On Determinism and Freedom: collected papers, 2005; Humanity, Terrorism, Terrorist War (USA edn as Right and Wrong, and Palestine, 9/11, Iraq, 7/7...), 2006; Radical Externalism: Honderich's Theory of Consciousness discussed, ed Anthony Freeman, 2006; phil articles in Amer. Phil Qly, Analysis, Inquiry, Jl of Theoretical Biol., Mind, Phil., Pol Studies, Proc. Aristotelian Soc., Jl of Consciousness Studies, Jl of Ethics, Rechtsphilosophische Hefte, etc. *Recreations:* old house, wine. *Address:* 66 Muswell Hill Road, N10 3JR. *T:* (020) 8350 4936; *e-mail:* t.honderich@ucl.ac.uk. *Club:* Garrick.

HONDROS, Ernest Demetrios, CMG 1996; DSc; FRS 1984; Director: Petten Establishment, Commission of European Communities' Joint Research Centre, 1985–95; Institute of Advanced Materials, Petten (Netherlands) and Ispra (Italy), 1988–95; *b* 18 Feb. 1930; *s* of Demetrios Hondros and Athanasia Paleologos; *m* 1968, Sissel Kristine Garder-Olsen; two *s*. *Educ:* Univ. of Melbourne (DSc MSc); Univ. of Paris (Dr d'Univ.). CEng, FIMMM. Research Officer, CSIRO Tribophysics Laboratory, Melbourne, 1955–59; Research Fellow, Univ. of Paris, Lab. de Chimie Minérale, 1959–62; National Physical Laboratory: Sen. Research Officer, Metallurgy Div., 1962–65; Principal Res. Fellow, 1965–68; Sen. Principal Res. Officer (Special Merit), 1974; Supt, Materials Applications Div., 1979–85. Vis. Prof., Dept of Materials, ICSTM, 1988–2004. Membre d'Honneur, Société Française de Métallurgie, 1986; Mem., Academia Europaea, 1988. Hon. DSc London, 1997. Rosenhain Medallist, Metals Soc., 1976; Howe Medal, Amer. Soc. for Metals, 1978; A. A. Griffiths Medal and Prize, Inst. of Metals, 1987. *Publications:* numerous research papers and reviews in learned jls. *Recreations:* music, literature, walking.

HONE, David; landscape and portrait painter; President, Royal Hibernian Academy of Arts, 1978–83; *b* 14 Dec. 1928; *s* of Joseph Hone and Vera Hone (*née* Brewster); *m* 1962, Rosemary D'Arcy; two *s* one *d*. *Educ:* Baymount School; St Columba's College; University College, Dublin. Studied art at National College of Art, Dublin, and later in Italy. Hon. RA, HRSA (ex-officio). *Recreations:* walking dogs, photography. *Address:* 4 Ailesbury Gardens, Sydney Parade, Dublin 4, Ireland. *T:* (1) 2692809.

HONE, Michael Stuart, OBE 1993 (MBE 1978); JP; HM Diplomatic Service, retired; Ambassador and Consul-General, Iceland, 1993–96; *b* 19 May 1936; *s* of William John Hone and Marguerite (*née* Howe); *m* 1st, 1957; three *s*; 2nd, 1983, Dr Elizabeth Ann Balmer; one *s* one *d*. *Educ:* Westham Secondary Sch. Entered RN 1951; joined CRO, 1961; served Kingston, Nairobi, Lisbon, Bridgetown; FCO 1972; served Beirut, Baghdad, Canberra; Resident British Rep., St Vincent and Grenadines; Chief Secretary, St Helena, 1990. JP Hasting and Rother, 2001. *Recreations:* family, walking. *Address:* Hillcroft, Station Approach, Crowhurst, Sussex TN33 9DB. *T:* (01424) 830444.

HONE, Richard Michael; QC 1997; **His Honour Judge Hone;** a Circuit Judge at the Central Criminal Court, since 2005; *b* 15 Feb. 1947; *s* of Maj. Gen. Sir Ralph Hone, KCMG, KBE, MC, TD, QC and Sybil Mary Hone (*née* Collins); *m* 1st, Sarah Nicholl-Carne (marr. diss.); two *s*; 2nd, Diana Pavel; two *s*. *Educ:* St Paul's Sch. (Schol.); University Coll., Oxford (MA). Called to the Bar, Middle Temple, 1970 (Bencher, 1994; Cocks' Referee, 1988–94); an Asst Recorder, 1987–91; a Recorder, 1991–2004. Mem., Bar Professional Conduct Cttee, 1993–97; Chm., Jt Regulations Cttee, Inns of Court and Bar, 1995–2000; Legal Mem., Mental Health Review Tribunals, 2000–. Freeman, City of London, 2004; Liveryman, Ironmongers' Co., 2008–. KStJ 2000 (Asst Dir of Ceremonies, 1996). *Recreations:* wine, travel, fine art. *Address:* Central Criminal Court, Old Bailey, EC4M 7EH. *T:* (020) 7248 3277. *Clubs:* Boodle's, Pratt's.

HONEY, Elizabeth; *see* Filkin, E.

HONEY, Michael John; Chief Executive, London Ambulance Service, 1996–2000; *b* 28 Nov. 1941; *s* of Denis Honey and Mary Honey (*née* Henderson); four *d*; *m* 1996, Elizabeth Filkin, *qv*. *Educ:* Clifton College; Regent Street Polytechnic (DipArch); Columbia Univ. MArch (Urban Design); MSc (City Planning). City Planner, Boston Redevelopment Authority, 1968–70; Corporate Planning Manager, Bor. of Greenwich, 1970–74; Head, Exec. Office, Bor. of Croydon, 1974–80; Chief Executive: Bor. of Richmond upon Thames, 1980–88; LDDC, 1988–90; Gloucestershire CC, 1990–96. *Recreations:* flying, sailing.

HONEY, Air Vice-Marshal Robert John, CB 1991; CBE 1987; Air Secretary, 1989–94; *b* 3 Dec. 1936; *s* of F. G. Honey; *m* 1956, Diana Chalmers; one *s* one *d*. *Educ:* Ashford Grammar Sch. Joined RAF as pilot, 1954; served: Germany, 1956–59; Singapore, 1961–64; Canada, 1968–69; India, 1982; UK intervening years; Dep. Commander RAF Germany, 1987–89. Dir, RAF Sports Bd, 1994–2001. Mountaineering expedns to Mulkila, India, 1979, Masherbrum, Pakistan, 1981, Greenland, 1998. *Recreations:* climbing, mountaineering, ski-ing.

HONEYBALL, Mary; Member (Lab) London Region, European Parliament, since Jan. 2000; *b* 12 Nov. 1952; *d* of Stanley James Honeyball and Betty Gath Honeyball (*née* Tandy). *Educ:* Pate's Grammar Sch. for Girls, Cheltenham; Somerville Coll., Oxford (MA). Admin. Officer, GLC, 1975–77; Negotiations Officer, Soc. of Civil and Public Servants, 1977–83; Political Organiser, RACS, 1983–85; Gen. Sec., Newham Voluntary Agencies Council, 1986–90; Chief Exec., Gingerbread, 1992–94; Gen. Sec., Assoc. of Chief Officers of Probation, 1994–98; Chief Exec., Nat. Childbirth Trust, 1999–2000. Mem. (Lab) Barnet LBC, 1978–86. Governor: Grahame Park Comprehensive Sch.,

London NW, 1978–84; Sir Francis Drake Primary Sch., SE8, 1986–90; Deptford Green Comprehensive Sch., SE8, 1986–90. *Recreation:* running (NY Marathon 2003). *Address:* 4G Shirland Mews, W9 3DY. *T:* (020) 8964 9815, *Fax:* (020) 8960 0150; *e-mail:* mary@maryhoneyball.net. *Club:* Royal Commonwealth Society.

HONEYCOMBE, Gordon; *see* Honeycombe, R. G.

HONEYCOMBE, (Ronald) Gordon; author, playwright, television presenter, actor and narrator; *b* Karachi, British India, 27 Sept. 1936; *s* of Gordon Samuel Honeycombe and Dorothy Louise Reid Fraser. *Educ:* Edinburgh Acad.; University Coll., Oxford (MA English). National Service, RA, mainly in Hong Kong, 1955–57. Announcer: Radio Hong Kong, 1956–57; BBC Scottish Home Service, 1958; actor: with Tomorrow's Audience, 1961–62; with RSC, Stratford-on-Avon and London, 1962–63; Newscaster with ITN, 1965–77; Newscaster, TV-am, 1984–89. Acted in TV plays, series and shows including: That Was the Week that Was, 1964; The Brack Report, 1982; CQ, 1984; Numbats, 1994; appearances as TV presenter include: (also writer) A Family Tree and Brass Rubbing (documentaries), 1973; The Late Late Show (series), and Something Special (series), 1978; (also ed and jt writer) Family History (series), 1979; appearances as TV narrator include: Arthur C. Clarke's Mysterious World (series), 1980; A Shred of Evidence, 1984; stage appearances include: Play-back 625, Royal Court, 1970; Paradise Lost, York and Old Vic, 1975; Suspects, Swansea, 1989; Aladdin, Wimbledon, 1989–90, Bournemouth, 1990–91; Run For Your Wife!, tour, 1990; The Taming of the Shrew, Perth, WA, 1998; film appearances include: The Medusa Touch; The Fourth Protocol; Let's Get Skase; The Sculptor. Author of stage productions: The Miracles, Oxford, 1960 and (perf. by RSC), Southwark Cath., 1963 and Consett, 1970; The Princess and the Goblins (musical), Great Ayton, 1976; Paradise Lost, York, Old Vic and Edinburgh Fest., 1975–77; Waltz of my Heart, Bournemouth, 1980; Lancelot and Guinevere, Old Vic, 1980; author of TV plays: The Golden Vision, 1968; Time and Again, 1974 (Silver Medal, Film and TV Fest., NY, 1975); The Thirteenth Day of Christmas, 1986; radio dramatisations (all Radio 4): Paradise Lost, 1975; Lancelot and Guinevere, 1976; A King shall have a Kingdom, 1977; devised Royal Gala performances: God save the Queen!, Chichester, 1977; A King shall have a Kingdom, York, 1977. Directed and prod, The Redemption, Fest. of Perth, 1990. *Publications: non-fiction:* Nagasaki 1945, 1981; Royal Wedding, 1981; The Murders of the Black Museum, 1982; The Year of the Princess, 1982; Selfridges, 1984; TV-am's Official Celebration of the Royal Wedding, 1986; More Murders of the Black Museum, 1993; The Complete Murders of the Black Museum, 1995; Australia For Me, 1996; *documentary novels:* Adam's Tale, 1974; Red Watch, 1976; Siren Song, 1992; *fiction:* The Redemption (play), 1964; Neither the Sea nor the Sand, 1969; Dragon under the Hill, 1972; The Edge of Heaven, 1981; Beach, 2005; contrib. national newspapers and magazines. *Recreations:* bridge, crosswords. *Address:* c/o Actors Management, 76 King Street, Perth, WA 6000, Australia. *T:* (8) 9322 6499.

HONEYMAN, Gitta; *see* Sereny, G.

HONEYSETT, Martin; cartoonist and illustrator, since 1969; *b* 20 May 1943; *s* of Donovan Honeysett and Kathleen Ethel Ivy Probert; *m* 1970, Maureen Elizabeth Lonergan (marr. diss. 1988); one *s* one *d* (and one *s* decd). *Educ:* Selhurst Grammar Sch.; Croydon Art Coll. (for one year). After leaving Art Coll., 1961, spent several years in NZ and Canada doing variety of jobs; returned to England, 1968; started drawing cartoons part-time, 1969; became full-time freelance, working for Punch, Private Eye and other magazines and newspapers, 1972; illustrator of series of books by the author/poet, Ivor Cutler. Vis. Prof., Kyoto Seika Univ., Japan, 2005–07. *Publications:* Private Eye Cartoonists No 4, 1974; Honeysett at Home, 1976; The Motor Show Book of Humour, 1978; The Not Another Book of Old Photographs Book, 1981; Microphobia, 1982; The Joy of Headaches, 1983; Fit for Nothing, 1984; Animal Nonsense Rhymes, 1984; The Best of Honeysett, 1985; (with Ivor Cutler): Gruts, 1961, repr. 1986; Life in a Scotch Sitting Room, vol. 2, 1984, 2nd edn 1998; Fremsley, 1987; Glasgow Dreamer, 1990, 2nd edn 1998. *Recreations:* walking, swimming.

HONIGMANN, Prof. Ernst Anselm Joachim, DLitt; FBA 1989; Joseph Cowen Professor of English Literature, University of Newcastle upon Tyne, 1970–89, now Professor Emeritus; *b* Breslau, Germany, 29 Nov. 1927; *s* of Dr H. D. S. Honigmann and U. M. Honigmann (*née* Heilborn); *m* 1958, Dr Elsie M. Packman (*d* 1994); two *s* one *d*. *Educ:* Glasgow Univ. (MA 1948; DLitt 1966); Merton Coll., Oxford (BLitt 1950). Asst Lectr, 1951, Lectr, Sen. Lectr and Reader, 1954–67, Glasgow Univ.; Fellow, Shakespeare Inst., Birmingham Univ., 1951–54; Reader, Univ. of Newcastle upon Tyne, 1968–70. Jt Gen. Ed., The Revels Plays, 1976–2000. *Publications:* The Stability of Shakespeare's Text, 1965; Shakespeare: Seven Tragedies, the dramatist's manipulation of response, 1976, 2nd edn 2002; Shakespeare's Impact on his Contemporaries, 1982; Shakespeare: the lost years, 1985, 2nd edn 1998; John Weever: a biography, 1987; Myriad-minded Shakespeare, 1989, 2nd edn 1998; The Texts of Othello, 1996; Harold Jenkins 1909–2000, 2001; *editor:* King John, 1954; Milton's Sonnets, 1966; The Masque of Flowers, 1967; Richard III, 1968; Twelfth Night, 1971; Paradise Lost, Book 10 (with C. A. Patrides), 1972; Shakespeare and his Contemporaries: essays in comparison, 1986; (with Susan Brock) Playhouse Wills 1558–1642, 1993; British Academy Shakespeare Lectures 1980–1989, 1993; Othello, 1996; Harold Jenkins, Structural Problems in Shakespeare, 2001; Togetherness: episodes from the life of a refugee, 2006. *Recreations:* grandchildren, gardening, travel. *Address:* 18 Wilson Gardens, Newcastle upon Tyne NE3 4JA.

HONORÉ, Prof. Antony Maurice; QC 1987; DCL Oxon; FBA 1972; Regius Professor of Civil Law, University of Oxford, 1971–88; Fellow, 1971–89, Acting Warden, 1987–89, All Souls College, Oxford; *b* 30 March 1921; *o s* of Frédéric Maurice Honoré and Marjorie Erskine (*née* Gilbert); *m* 1st, Martine Marie-Odette Genouville; one *s* one *d*; 2nd, Deborah Mary Cowen (*née* Duncan). *Educ:* Diocesan Coll., Rondebosch; Univ. of Cape Town; New Coll., Oxford (Rhodes Scholar, 1940); DCL Oxon 1969. Union Defence Forces, 1940–45; Lieut, Rand Light Infantry, 1942. BCL 1948. Vinerian Scholar, 1948. Advocate, South Africa, 1951; called to Bar, Lincoln's Inn, 1952, Hon. Bencher, 1971. Lectr, Nottingham Univ., 1948; Rhodes Reader in Roman-Dutch Law, 1957–70, Fellow of Queen's Coll., Oxford, 1949–64, of New Coll., 1964–70. Visiting Professor: McGill, 1961; Berkeley, 1968. Lectures: Hamlyn, Nottingham, 1982; J. H. Gray, Cambridge, 1985; Blackstone, Oxford, 1988; H. L. A. Hart, University Coll., Oxford, 1992; Maccabean, British Acad., 1998. Member: Internat. Acad. of Comparative Law, 1994; Accademia Costantiniana, 1994. Corresp. Member: Bavarian Acad. of Scis, 1992; Serbian Phil. Soc., 1988; Hon. Fellow, Harris Manchester Coll., Oxford, 2000. Hon. LLD: Edinburgh, 1977; South Africa, 1984; Stellenbosch, 1988; Cape Town, 1990; Witwatersrand, 2002. Hon. Citizen, San Ginesio, Italy, 2004. *Publications:* (with H. L. A. Hart) Causation in the Law, 1959, 2nd edn 1985 (trans. Japanese, 1991, Chinese, 2004); Gaius, 1962; The South African Law of Trusts, 1965, 5th edn 2002; Tribonian, 1978; Sex Law, 1978; (with J. Menner) Concordance to the Digest Jurists, 1980; Emperors and Lawyers, 1981, 2nd edn 1994; The Quest for Security, 1982; Ulpian, 1982, 2nd edn 2002; Making Law Bind, 1987; About Law, 1996 (trans. Arabic and Ukrainian, 1999); Law in the Crisis of Empire, 1998; Responsibility and Fault, 1999; *festschriften:* The Legal Mind (ed N. MacCormick and P. Birks), 1986; (also contrib.) Relating to Responsibility (ed P Cane and J. Gardner), 2001. *Address:* 94C Banbury Road, Oxford OX2 6JT. *T:* (0186 559684.

HONOUR, (Patrick) Hugh, FBA; FRSL; writer; *b* 26 Sept. 1927; *s* of late Herbert Perc Honour and Dorothy Margaret Withers. *Educ:* King's Sch., Canterbury; St Catharine Coll., Cambridge (BA). Asst to Dir, Leeds City Art Gall. and Temple Newsam Hous 1953–54. Guest Curator for exhibn, The European Vision of America, National Gall. c Art, Washington, Cleveland Museum of Art, and, as L'Amérique vue par l'Europe, Gran Palais, Paris, 1976. FRSL 1972. Corresp. FBA 1986 (Serena Medal, 1995). *Publication* Chinoiserie, 1961, 2nd edn 1973; Companion Guide to Venice, 1965, rev. edn 199 (with Sir Nikolaus Pevsner and John Fleming) The Penguin Dictionary of Architecture 1966, 5th rev. edn as Penguin Dictionary of Architecture and Landscape Architectur 1998; Neo-classicism, 1968, 4th edn 1977; The New Golden Land, 1976; (with Joh Fleming) The Penguin Dictionary of Decorative Arts, 1977, rev. edn 1989; Romanticism 1979; (with John Fleming) A World History of Art, 1982 (Mitchell Prize, 1982) (USA a The Visual Arts: a history, 7th edn 2005); The Image of the Black in Western Art IV, fro the American Revolution to World War I, 1989 (Anisfield-Wolf Book Award in Rac Relations, 1990); (with John Fleming) The Venetian Hours of Henry James, Whistler an Sargent, 1991; (ed) Edizione Nazionale delle Opere di Antonio Canova, vol. I, Scritt 1994, 2nd edn 2007, (with Paolo Mariuz), vol. XVIII, 1, 2002 and 2, Epistolario, 200 Carnets Khmers, 1998. *Recreation:* gardening.

HONYWOOD, Sir Filmer (Courtenay William), 11th Bt *cr* 1660; FRICS; Regiona Surveyor and Valuer, South Eastern Region, Central Electricity Generating Boar 1978–88; *b* 20 May 1930; *s* of Col Sir William Wynne Honywood, 10th Bt, MC, an Maud Naylor (*d* 1953), *d* of William Hodgson Wilson, Hexgreave Park, Southwell, Notts *S* father, 1982; *m* 1956, Elizabeth Margaret Mary Cynthia (*d* 1996), *d* of Sir Alastair Georg Lionel Joseph Miller of Glenlee, 6th Bt; two *s* two *d*. *Educ:* Downside; RMA Sandhurs Royal Agricultural College, Cirencester (MRAC Diploma). Served 3rd Carabinie (Prince of Wales' Dragoon Guards). Farmed, 1954–64 (Suffolk Co. Dairy Herd Prod Awards, 1955 and 1956); joined Agricl Land Service, MAFF, Maidstone, 1964; Asst Lan Comr, 1966; Surveyor, Cockermouth, Cumbria, 1973–74; Senior Lands Officer, Sout Eastern Region, CEGB, 1974–78; pt time Sen. Valuer, Inland Revenue Valuatio Service, Folkestone, 1989–90. Consultant on agricultural compensation/restoration, U Nirex Ltd, 1988–90; Land Agency consultant, Nuclear Electric plc, 1993–94. Examine in Agriculture: Incorporated Soc. of Estates & Wayleaves Officers, 1989–95; Soc. c Surveying Technicians, 1996–97. *Heir: s* Rupert Anthony Honywood, *b* 2 March 195 *Address:* Greenway Forstal Farmhouse, Hollingbourne, Maidstone, Kent ME17 1QA. *T* (01622) 880418.

HOOD, family name of **Viscounts Bridport** and **Hood**.

HOOD, 8th Viscount *cr* 1796, of Whitley, co. Warwick; **Henry Lyttelton Alexande Hood;** Bt 1778; Baron (Ire.) 1782, GB 1795; Partner, Hunters, Solicitors, since 1991; Lord in Waiting to the Queen, since 2008; *b* 16 March 1958; *e s* of 7th Viscount Hoo and Diana Maud Hood, CVO (*née* Lyttelton); *S* father, 1999; *m* 1991, Flora, *yr d* of Comd M. B. Casement, OBE, RN; three *s* two *d* (of whom one *s* one *d* are twins). *Edu* Edinburgh Univ. (MA 1981). Qualified as solicitor, 1987. *Heir: s* Hon. Archibald Lyttelto Samuel Hood, *b* 16 May 1993.

HOOD, Prof. Christopher Cropper, DLitt; FBA 1996; AcSS; Gladstone Professor o Government, Oxford University, since 2001; Fellow of All Souls College, Oxford, sinc 2001; *b* 5 March 1947; *s* of David White Hood and Margaret Cropper; *m* 1979, Gillia Thackwray White; two *d*. *Educ:* Univ. of York (BA 1968; DLitt 1987); Univ. of Glasgo (BLitt 1971). Lectr in Politics, Glasgow Univ., 1972–77 and 1979–86; Res. Fellow, Univ of York, 1977–79; Prof. of Govt and Public Administration, Univ. of Sydney, 1986–89 Prof. of Public Admin and Public Policy, LSE, 1989–2000. Chair, Politics and Internat Relations Section, British Acad., 2002–05. Vis. Res. Fellow, Zentrum für Interdisziplinär Forschung, Univ. of Bielefeld, 1982 and 1989; Sen. Teaching Fellow, Nat. Univ. o Singapore, 1984–85; Fellow, Sunningdale Inst., 2007–. AcSS 2001. FRSA 2007 *Publications:* Limits of Administration, 1976; (ed jtly) Big Government in Hard Time 1981; (with A. Dunsire) Bureaumetrics, 1981; The Tools of Government, 198 Administrative Analysis, 1986; (ed jtly) Delivering Public Services in Western Europ 1988; (with A. Dunsire) Cutback Management in Public Bureaucracies, 1989; (with M W. Jackson) Administrative Argument, 1991; Explaining Economic Policy Reversal 1994; (ed jtly) Rewards at the Top, 1994; The Art of the State, 1998; (with C. Scott *et al* Regulation inside Government, 1999; (jtly) Telecommunications Regulation, 1999; (wit Henry Rothstein and Robert Baldwin) The Government of Risk: understanding ris regulation regimes, 2001; (ed jtly) Rewards at the Top: Asian and Pacific Rim states, 2003 (ed jtly) Controlling Modern Government, 2004; (with Martin Lodge) Politics of Publi Service Bargains, 2006; (ed with David Heald) Transparency: the key to bette governance?, 2006; (with H. Margetts) The Tools of Government in the Digital Age 2007. *Address:* All Souls College, Oxford OX1 4AL. *T:* (01865) 279379.

HOOD, Rev. (Elizabeth) Lorna; Minister, Renfrew North, since 1979; Chaplain to th Queen in Scotland, since 2008; *b* Irvine, 21 April 1953; *d* of James Mitchell and Elizabet Mitchell (*née* Sharpe); *m* 1979, Peter Hood; one *s* one *d*. *Educ:* Glasgow University (MA 1974; BD 1977). Ordained Minister, C of S, 1978; Moderator, Paisley Presbytery 1995–96; Nominations Convener, Renfrew North, 1996–99; Vice-Covenor, Bd o Ministry, 2005. Mem., Bd of Studies, Inst. of Counselling, Glasgow, 2000–. Gen. Trustee C of S, 2001–. *Recreations:* golf, reading, travel.

HOOD, James; MP (Lab) Lanark and Hamilton East, since 2005 (Clydesdale, 1987–2005); *b* 16 May 1948; *m* 1967, Marion McCleary; one *s* one *d*. *Educ:* Lesmahagow High Sch.; Motherwell Tech. Coll.; Nottingham Univ.; WEA. Miner, Nottingham, 1968–87; NUM official, 1973–87 (Mem., NEC, 1990–92); Leader, Nottingham striking miners, 1984–85. Member: Ollerton Parish Council, 1973–87; Newark and Sherwood Dist Council, 1979–87. Member: Select Cttee on European Legislation, 1987–97 (Chm., 1992–98); Speaker's Panel of Chairmen, 1997–; Chair, European Scrutiny Cttee, 1998–2006; founder Chm., All Party Gp on ME (Myalgic Encephalomyelitis), 1987–92; Chm., Miners' Party Gp, 1991–92; Convenor: Home Affairs Cttee, 1992–97; Scottish Lab. Gp of MPs, 1995–96; sponsor of four Private Members' Bills: on under-age drinking, on ME, on road transport safety and on shops. UK Mem., NATO Parly Assembly, 2005–. *Recreations:* reading, gardening. *Address:* House of Commons, SW1A 0AA. *T:* (020) 7219 4585; Ras-al-Ghar, 57 Biggar Road, Symington, Lanarkshire ML12 6FT. *Club:* Lesmahagow Miners Welfare Social (Hon. Mem.).

HOOD, John A., PhD; Vice-Chancellor, University of Oxford, 2004–Sept. 2009. *Educ:* Westlake Boys' High Sch., Auckland; Univ. of Auckland (BE; PhD 1976); Worcester Coll., Oxford (Rhodes Schol.; MPhil 1978). With Fletcher Hldgs, subseq. Fletcher Challenge, Ltd, 1979–97: Head, Fletcher Challenge Paper, Fletcher Challenge Building, then Fletcher Construction Co.; Vice-Chancellor, Univ. of Auckland, 1999–2004.

Formerly: Chm., Tonkin and Taylor Ltd; Director: ASB Bank Ltd; Fonterra Co-operative Gp Ltd; BG Gp, 2007–. Gov., NZ Sports Foundn. *Address:* University of Oxford, Wellington Square, Oxford OX1 2JD.

HOOD, Sir John Joseph Harold, 3rd Bt *cr* 1922, of Wimbledon, Co. Surrey; *b* 27 Aug. 1952; *e s* of Sir Harold Joseph Hood, 2nd Bt and Hon. Ferelith Rosemary Florence Kenworthy, *o d* of 10th Baron Strabolgi; *S* father 2005, but his name does not appear on the Official Roll of the Baronetage. *Heir: b* Basil Gervase Francis Gerard Hood [*b* 4 Oct. 1955; one *s*; *m* 2001, Alison Susan Williams].

HOOD, Rev. Lorna; *see* Hood, Rev. E. L.

HOOD, (Martin) Sinclair (Frankland), FSA; FBA 1983; archaeologist; *b* 31 Jan. 1917; *s* of late Lt-Comdr Martin Hood, RN, and late Mrs Martin Hood, New York; *m* 1957, Rachel Simmons; one *s* two *d*. *Educ:* Harrow; Magdalen Coll., Oxford. FSA 1953. British Sch. at Athens: student, 1947–48 and 1951–53; Asst Dir, 1949–51; Dir, 1954–62; Vice-Pres., 1996–. Student, British Inst. Archaeology, Ankara, 1948–49. Geddes-Harrower Vis. Prof. of Greek Art and Archaeology, Univ. of Aberdeen, 1968. Took part in excavations at: Dorchester, Oxon, 1937; Compton, Berks, 1946–47; Southwark, 1946; Smyrna, 1948–49; Atchana, 1949–50; Sakca-Gozu, 1950; Mycenae, 1950–52; Knossos, 1950–51, 1953–55, 1957–61, 1973 and 1987; Jericho, 1952; Chios, 1952–55. Hon. Dr, Univ. of Athens, 2000. *Publications:* The Home of the Heroes: The Aegean before the Greeks, 1967; The Minoans, 1971; The Arts in Prehistoric Greece, 1978; various excavation reports and articles. *Address:* The Old Vicarage, Great Milton, Oxford OX44 7PB. *T:* (01844) 279202. *Club:* Athenæum.

HOOD, Nicholas; *see* Hood, W. N.

HOOD, Peter Charles Freeman G.; *see* Gregory-Hood.

HOOD, Prof. Roger Grahame, CBE 1995; DCL; FBA 1992; Professor of Criminology, 1996–2003, and Director of the Centre for Criminological Research, 1973–2003, University of Oxford; Fellow of All Souls College, Oxford, 1973–2003, now Emeritus; *b* 12 June 1936; 2nd *s* of Ronald and Phyllis Hood; *m* 1963, Barbara Blaine Young (marr. diss. 1985); one *d*; *m* 1985, Nancy Stebbing (*née* Lynah). *Educ:* King Edward's Sch., Five Ways, Birmingham; LSE (BSc Sociology); Downing Coll., Cambridge (PhD); DCL Oxon 1999. Research Officer, LSE, 1961–63; Lectr in Social Admin, Univ. of Durham, 1963–67; Asst Dir of Research, Inst. of Criminology, Univ. of Cambridge, 1967–73; Fellow of Clare Hall, Cambridge, 1969–73; Reader in Criminology, Oxford Univ., 1973–96; Sub-Warden, All Souls Coll., Oxford, 1994–96. Vis. Prof., Univ. of Virginia Sch. of Law, 1980–90, and 2005–08; Dist. Vis. Prof., Univ. of Hong Kong, 2003–04; Associate Prof., City Univ., Hong Kong, 2008–. Expert Consultant, UN, on death penalty, 1988, 1995–96, 2000 and 2005. Member: Parole Bd, 1972–73; SSRC Cttee on Social Sciences and the Law, 1975–79; Judicial Studies Bd, 1979–85; Parole System Review, 1987–88; Foreign Secretary's Death Penalty Panel, 1998–. Pres., British Soc. of Criminology, 1986–89. Hon. QC 2000. Sellin-Glueck Award, Amer. Soc. of Criminology, 1986. *Publications:* Sentencing in Magistrates' Courts, 1962; Borstal Re-assessed, 1965; (with Richard Sparks) Key Issues in Criminology, 1970; Sentencing the Motoring Offender, 1972; (ed) Crime, Criminology and Public Policy: Essays in Honour of Sir Leon Radzinowicz, 1974; (with Sir Leon Radzinowicz) Criminology and the Administration of Criminal Justice: a bibliography, 1976; (with Sir Leon Radzinowicz) A History of English Criminal Law, vol. 5, The Emergence of Penal Policy, 1986; The Death Penalty: a world-wide perspective, 1989, 4th edn (with Carolyn Hoyle) 2008; Race and Sentencing, 1992; (with Stephen Shute) The Parole System at Work, 2000; (with Martina Fielzer) Differences or Discrimination?, 2004; (with Stephen Shute and Florence Seemungal) A Fair Hearing?: ethnic minorities in the Criminal Court, 2005; (with Florence Seemungal) A Rare and Arbitrary Fate, 2006. *Address:* 36 The Stream Edge, Fisher Row, Oxford OX1 1HT. *T:* (01865) 243140; *e-mail:* roger.hood@all-souls.ox.ac.uk.

HOOD, Samuel Harold; Director, Defence Operational Analysis Establishment, Ministry of Defence, 1985–86; *b* 21 Aug. 1926; *s* of Samuel N. and Annie Hood; *m* 1959, Frances Eileen Todd; two *s* four *d*. *Educ:* Larne Grammar Sch., Co. Antrim; Queen's Univ., Belfast (BA Hons Maths). Joined Civil Service, staff of Scientific Advr, Air Min., 1948; Staff of Operational Res. Br., Bomber Comd, 1950; Scientific Officer, BCDU, RAF Wittering, 1954; Operational Res. Br., Bomber Comd, 1959; Staff of Chief Scientist (RAF), 1964; joined DOAE, 1965; Supt, Air Div., DOAE, 1969; Dir, Defence Sci. Divs 1 and 7, MoD, 1974; Head, Systems Assessment Dept, RAE, 1981. *Recreations:* walking, gardening, bird watching. *Address:* 29 St James Avenue, Richmond 7020, Nelson, New Zealand.

HOOD, Sinclair; *see* Hood, M. S. F.

HOOD, (William) Nicholas, CBE 1991; Director, since 2000, Deputy Chairman, since 2005, Brewin Dolphin plc; *b* 3 Dec. 1935; *s* of Sir Tom Hood, KBE, CB, TD and of Joan, *d* of Richmond P. Hellyar; *m* 1st, 1963, Angela Robinson (marr. diss. 1990); one *s* one *d*; 2nd, 1994, Ann E. H. Reynolds (marr. diss. 2003); 3rd, 2007, Patricia Lang. *Educ:* Clifton Coll. FIWEM 1992. Served DCLI, 1955–57. NEM General Insce Assoc. Ltd and Credit Insce Assoc. Ltd, 1958–64; G. B. Britton UK Ltd, eventually Sales and Marketing Dir, 1964–70; UBM Gp Plc, eventually Dir of Central Reg., 1970–84; Man. Dir, UBM Overseas Ltd, 1972–82; Dir, HAT Gp Ltd, 1984–86; Chairman: Wessex Water Authy, 1987–89; Wessex Water plc, 1989–99. Director: Bremhill Industries Plc, 1987–93; Winterthur Life UK (formerly Provident Life Assoc.) Ltd, 1988–2007 (Chm., 2002–07); Western Adv. Bd, Nat. Westminster Bank, 1990–92; CU Environmental Trust Plc, 1992–98; APV plc, 1994–97; QHIT plc, 1998–2003; Dep. Chm., Azurix, 1998–99; Chairman: MHIT plc, 1998–2003; Frogmat Ltd, 2001–. Dep. Chm., BITC, 1993–2007. Mem., DTI/DoE Adv. Cttee on Business and the Envmt, 1991–93. Chm., Water Aid Council, 1990–95; Chm., Water Services Assoc., 1995; Pres., IWSA, 1997–99 (Vice-Pres., 1993–97); Life Vice-Pres., Internat. Water Assoc., 2001; Member: Water Trng Council, 1987–99; Foundn for Water Res., 1989–99; Sustainability South West, 2000–02. Director: Harbourside Centre, 1996–99; Harbourside Foundn, 1998–2001; Clifton College Services Ltd, 2000–. Chairman: Bristol 2000, 1995–98; At-Bristol, 1998–2001 (Life Pres., 2002). Mem., Prince of Wales Council for Duchy of Cornwall, 1993–. Chm. Trustees, Penny Brohn Cancer Centre (formerly Bristol Cancer Help Centre), 2000–07; Trustee, West Country Rivers, 2000–. Dir, West of England Philharmonic Orch., 2003–07. Master, Soc. of Merchant Venturers, 2007–08. CCMI (CBIM 1990). Hon. MBA UWE, 2002. *Recreations:* fishing, painting. *Address:* One Queen's Parade, Bath BA1 2NJ. *T:* (01225) 334423. *Clubs:* Army and Navy, Boodle's.

HOODLESS, Donald Bentley, OBE 2005; Chairman: Royal National Orthopaedic Hospital, since 2002; Skills for Care, since 2005; Member Board, Housing Corporation, since 2005; *b* 14 Oct. 1942; *s* of Ernest William Hoodless and Rosina Mary Hoodless; *m* 1965, Elisabeth Marian Anne Frost Plummer (*see* Dame E. M. A. F. Hoodless); two *s*. *Educ:* Univ. of Durham (BA Hons Econs 1964); Central London Poly. (Dip. Public Admin London Univ. 1968). FCIH 1997. Dir, Circle 33 Housing Trust, 1975–86; Chief Executive: Notting Hill Housing Trust, 1986–93; Circle 33 Housing Trust, 1993–2005. Mem., Islington LBC, 1968–82 (Leader, 1982). *Recreations:* golf, Arsenal Football Club, reading. *Address:* 10 Eclipse Building, 26 Laycock Street, N1 1AH. *T:* (020) 7359 0231, *Fax:* (020) 7288 0716; *e-mail:* donald.hoodless@btopenworld.com. *Club:* Highgate Golf.

HOODLESS, Dame Elisabeth (Marian Anne Frost), DBE 2004 (CBE 1992); Executive Director, Community Service Volunteers, since 1986; *b* 11 Feb. 1941; *d* of late Raymond Evelyn Plummer, TD and Maureen Grace Plummer (*née* Frost); *m* 1965, Donald Bentley Hoodless, *qv*; two *s*. *Educ:* Redland High Sch., Bristol; Univ. of Durham (BA (Social Studies) 1962); LSE (DASS, CQSW 1963). Asst Dir, 1963–75, Dep. Dir, 1975–86, CSV. Churchill Fellow, consultant to US Govt VISTA (Volunteers in Service to America) prog., 1966; Commonwealth Youth Fellow, consultant to Govt of Jamaica, Nat. Youth Service prog., 1974. Mem. (Lab) London Borough of Islington, 1964–68. Dep. Chm., Speaker's Commn on Citizenship, 1987–90; Member: Personal Social Services Council, 1973–80; DoH Wkg Gp on Volunteering in the NHS, 1994–96; Sec. of State's Adv. Gp on Citizenship Educn, 1997–98. Member: IBM Community Adv. Bd, 1988–91; Bd, Innovations in Civic Participation, USA, 2001– (Vice-Chm., 2006–); Bd, Attend (formerly Nat. Assoc. of Hosp. and Community Friends), 2002– (Vice Pres., 2006–). Pres., Volonteurope (European Network of Volunteer Agencies), 1988–; Chairman: Nat. Network of Volunteer Involving Agencies, 2004–; Internat. Assoc. for Nat. Youth Service, 2007–. Freeman, City of London, 1992. JP Inner London Youth Courts, 1969– (Chm.). Chm. Govs, Barnsbury Sch. for Girls, 1971–89; Gov., Reeves Foundn, 1981–2003. DUniv Sheffield Hallam, 2004. *Publications:* Getting Money from Central Government, 1981; Managing Innovation, 1997; (contrib.) Any Volunteers for a Good Society, 2002; Citoyenneté active: intégrer la théorie à la pratique par le volontariat, 2002; Senior Volunteers: solutions waiting to happen, 2003. *Recreations:* grandchildren, growing orchids, ballet, shopping. *Address:* 10 The Eclypse Building, 26 Laycock Street, N1 1AH. *T:* (020) 7359 0231, *Fax:* (020) 7837 9621; *e-mail:* ehoodless@csv.org.uk; c/o Community Service Volunteers, 237 Pentonville Road, N1 9NJ.

HOOK, Prof. Andrew Dunnet, PhD; FBA 2002; FRSE; Bradley Professor of English Literature, University of Glasgow, 1979–98, now Professor Emeritus; *b* 21 Dec. 1932; *s* of Wilfred Thomas Hook and Jessie Hook (*née* Dunnet); *m* 1966, Judith Ann Hibberd (*d* 1984); one *s* (and one *s* one *d* decd). *Educ:* Univ. of Edinburgh (MA 1st Cl. Hons 1954); Princeton Univ. (PhD 1960). Asst Lectr in English Lit., 1961–63, Lectr in American Lit., 1963–71, Univ. of Edinburgh; Sen. Lectr in English, Univ. of Aberdeen, 1971–79. Vis. Fellow, Dept of English, Princeton Univ., 1999–2000; Gillespie Vis. Prof., Coll. of Wooster, Ohio, 2001–02; Visiting Professor: Dartmouth Coll., 2003, 2006, 2007; Univ. of St Thomas, St Paul, Minnesota, 2005. FRSE 2000. *Publications:* (ed) Scott: Waverley, 1972; (ed with J. Hook) Charlotte Bronte: Shirley, 1974; (ed) John Dos Passos: Twentieth Century Views, 1974; Scotland and America: a study of cultural relations 1750–1835, 1975; American Literature in Context 1865–1900, 1983; (ed) History of Scottish Literature 1660–1800, 1987; Scott Fitzgerald, 1992; (ed with R. Sher) The Glasgow Enlightenment, 1995; From Goosecreek to Gandercleugh: studies in Scottish-American literary and cultural history, 1999; (ed with D. Mackenzie) Scott: The Fair Maid of Perth, 1999; F. Scott Fitzgerald: a literary life, 2002. *Recreations:* golf, watching sport on TV. *Address:* 5 Rosslyn Terrace, Glasgow G12 9NB. *T:* (0141) 334 0113; *e-mail:* nassau@palio2.vianw.co.uk.

HOOK, David Morgan Alfred, FREng; Managing Director, 1984–88, Deputy Chairman, 1989–90, G. Maunsell & Partners, now retired; *b* 16 April 1931; *m* 1957, Winifred (*née* Brown); two *s* one *d*. *Educ:* Bancroft's School; Queens' College, Cambridge (MA). FICE, FIStructE; FREng (FEng 1985). Holland & Hannen and Cubitts, 1954–58; Nuclear Civil Constructors, 1958–62; G. Maunsell & Partners (Consulting Engineers), 1962–, Partner, 1968–. Liveryman, Engineers' Co., 1985. *Publications:* papers in Jl of IStructE. *Recreations:* golf, bowls, bridge. *Club:* Oxford and Cambridge.

HOOK, Neil Kenneth, MVO 1983; HM Diplomatic Service; Consul-General, Osaka, since 2001; UK Commissioner-General, Expo 2005; *b* 24 April 1945; *s* of George Edward Hook and Winifred Lucy Hook (*née* Werrell); *m* 1973, Pauline Ann Hamilton; one *s* one *d*. *Educ:* Varndean Grammar Sch., Brighton; Sheffield Univ. (Dip. Management Studies). Joined Diplomatic Service, 1968; served FCO, Moscow, Tokyo; Dhaka, 1980–83; S Africa Dept, FCO, 1984; S Asia Dept, FCO, 1985–86; Tokyo, 1987–92; N America Dept, FCO, 1993–95; Ambassador to Turkmenistan, 1995–98; FCO, 1998–99; High Comr, Swaziland, 1999–2001. *Recreations:* ballads, bridge, Hash House Harriers, photography. *Address:* c/o Foreign and Commonwealth Office, SW1A 2AH.

HOOK, Sister Patricia Mary, DCNZM 2001; RSM; Sister of Mercy; *b* 4 Aug. 1921; *d* of Stanley M. and Mary Hook. *Educ:* Dominican Coll., South Is, NZ; Mercy Hosp. Sch. of Nursing, Auckland (Registered Nurse 1947); Wellington (DipNAdmin 1957); Gonzaga Univ., Washington (MA Spiritual Studies 1982). Served War of 1939–45, RNZAF: Section Officer (WAAF) RDF (Filter) Units Central and Northern Gps; discharged 1944. Entered St Mary's Convent, Sisters of Mercy, Auckland, 1948, professed as Sister Mary de Montfort, 1951; Mercy Hospital, Auckland: Registered Nurse, 1947–58; Midwife, 1958–64; Principal Nurse, Hosp. Admin, 1964–79; founder, and Director, Retreat and Spiritual Direction Centre (run by Sisters of Mercy), Epsom, Auckland, 1982–2000. Mem., Nat. Adv. Cttee to Minister of Health, NZ Health Planning, 1975–78. *Recreations:* reading, gardening, tramping. *Address:* St Mary's Convent, PO Box 47025, Ponsonby, Auckland, New Zealand. *T:* (3) 3786795, *Fax:* (3) 3602306.

HOOKER, Prof. Morna Dorothy, DD; Lady Margaret's Professor of Divinity, University of Cambridge, 1976–98; Fellow of Robinson College, Cambridge, since 1976; *b* 19 May 1931; *d* of Percy Francis Hooker, FIA, and Lily (*née* Riley); *m* 1978, Rev. Dr W. David Stacey, MA (*d* 1993); one step *s* two step *d*. *Educ:* Univ. of Bristol (research schol.; MA 1956); Univ. of Manchester (research studentship; PhD 1966); MA Oxford 1970 and Cambridge 1976; DD Cambridge 1993. Research Fellow, Univ. of Durham, 1959–61; Lectr in New Testament Studies, King's Coll., London, 1961–70; Lectr in Theology, Oxford, and Fellow, Linacre Coll., 1970–76 (Hon. Fellow, 1980); Lectr in Theology, Keble Coll., 1972–76. Visiting Fellow, Clare Hall, Cambridge, 1974; Visiting Professor: McGill Univ., 1968; Duke Univ., 1987 and 1989. FKC 1979. Lectures: T. W. Manson meml, 1977; A. S. Peake meml, 1978; Henton Davies, 1979; Ethel M. Wood, 1984; James A. Gray, Duke Univ., 1984; W. A. Sanderson, Melbourne, 1986; Didsbury, Manchester, 1988; Brennan, Louisville, 1989; St Paul's, 1989; Perkins, Texas, 1990; Shaffer, Yale, 1995; John Albert Hall, Victoria, BC, 1996; Smyth, Columbia Decatur, 1996; Chuen King, Hong Kong, 2001; Lund, Chicago, 2003; Newell, Anderson Univ., 2006. Pres., SNTS, 1988–89. Jt Editor, Jl of Theological Studies, 1985–2005. Hon. Fellow, Westminster Coll., Oxford, 1996. Hon. DLitt Bristol, 1994; Hon. DD Edinburgh, 1997. Burkitt Medal for Biblical Studies, British Acad., 2004. *Publications:* Jesus and the Servant, 1959; The Son of Man in Mark, 1967; (ed jtly) What about the New Testament?, 1975; Pauline Pieces, 1979; Studying the New Testament, 1979; (ed jtly) Paul and Paulinism, 1982; The Message of Mark, 1983; Continuity and Discontinuity, 1986;

From Adam to Christ, 1990; A Commentary on the Gospel according to St Mark, 1991; Not Ashamed of the Gospel, 1994; The Signs of a Prophet, 1997; Beginnings, 1997; Paul: a short introduction, 2003; Endings, 2003; (ed) Not in Word Alone, 2003; contribs to New Testament Studies, Jl of Theological Studies, Theology, Epworth Review, etc. *Recreations:* Molinology, walking, music. *Address:* Robinson College, Grange Road, Cambridge CB3 9AN.

HOOKER, Ronald George, CBE 1985; FREng; Chairman: Management & Business Services Ltd, since 1972; London Ventures Ltd, since 1991; company directorships; *b* 6 Aug. 1921; *m* 1954, Eve Pigott; one *s* one *d*. *Educ:* Wimbledon Technical Coll.; London Univ. (external). Hon. FIET (FIProdE 1980); FREng (FEng 1984). CIMgt (CBIM 1972). Apprentice, Philips Electrical Ltd, 1937–41, Develt Engr, 1945–48; FBI, 1948–50; Dir and Gen. Man., Brush Electrical Engineering Co. Ltd, 1950–60; Man. Dir, K & L Steelfounders & Engineers Ltd, 1960–65; Man. Dir, Associated Fire Alarms Ltd, 1965–68; Chm. and Man. Dir, Crane Fruehauf Trailers Ltd, 1968–71; Dir of Manufacture, Rolls Royce (1971) Ltd, 1971–73; Chm. and Man. Dir, John M. Henderson (Holdings) Ltd, 1973–75; Chairman: Thomas Storey Ltd, 1984–96; EAC Ltd, 1993–2006. Dir, Computing Devices Hldgs Ltd, 1986–92. Pres., Engrg Employers' Fedn, 1986–88 (Mem. Management Bd, 1977–); Mem., Engrg Council, 1982–86. Past Pres., IProdE, 1974–75 (Hon. Life MIProdE 1980); CCMI; FRSA. Freeman, City of London. *Publications:* papers on management and prodn engrg to BIM, ICMA, IProdE and IMechE. *Recreations:* gardening, reading, music. *Address:* Loxborough House, Bledlow Ridge, near High Wycombe, Bucks HP14 4AA. *T:* (01494) 481486. *Clubs:* Athenæum, Lansdowne.

HOOKS, Air Vice-Marshal Robert Keith, CBE 1979; CEng, FRAeS; RAF retired; *b* 7 Aug. 1929; *s* of late Robert George Hooks and Phyllis Hooks; *m* 1954, Kathleen (*née* Cooper); one *s* one *d*. *Educ:* Acklam Hall Sch.; Constantine Coll., Middlesbrough; BSc(Eng) London. Comnd RAF, 1951; served at RAF stations West Malling, Fassberg, Sylt, 1952–55; RAF Technical Coll., Henlow, 1956; Fairey Aviation Co., 1957–58; Air Ministry, 1958–60; Skybolt Trials Unit, Eglin, Florida, 1961–63; Bomber Command Armament Sch., Wittering, 1963–65; OC Engrg Wing, RAF Coll., Cranwell, 1967–69; HQ Far East Air Force, 1969–71; Supt of Armament A&AEE, 1971–74; Director Ground Training, 1974–76; Director Air Armament, 1976–80; Vice-Pres. (Air), Ordnance Board, 1980; Dir Gen. Aircraft 2, MoD (Procurement Exec.), 1981–84; Divl Dir (European Business), Westland Helicopters, 1984–85; Projects Dir, Helicopter Div., Westland plc, 1985–87. Dep. Man. Dir, E H Industries Ltd, 1987–94. *Address:* 34 Thames Crescent, Maidenhead, Berks SL6 8EY. *Club:* Royal Air Force.

HOOKWAY, Sir Harry (Thurston), Kt 1978; Pro-Chancellor, Loughborough University of Technology, 1987–93; *b* 23 July 1921; *s* of William and Bertha Hookway; *m* 1956, Barbara Olive (*d* 1991), *o d* of late Oliver and Olive Butler; one *s* one *d*. *Educ:* Trinity Sch. of John Whitgift; London Univ. (BSc, PhD). Various posts in industry, 1941–49; DSIR, 1949–65; Asst Dir, National Chemical Laboratory, 1959; Dir, UK Scientific Mission (North America), Scientific Attaché, Washington, DC, and Scientific Adviser to UK High Comr, Ottawa, 1960–64; Head of Information Div., DSIR, 1964–65; CSO, DES, 1966–69; Asst Under-Sec. of State, DES, 1969–73; Dep. Chm. and Chief Exec., The British Library Bd, 1973–84; Chairman: Publishers Databases Ltd, 1984–87; LA Publishing Ltd, 1986–89. Chairman: UNESCO Internat. Adv. Cttee for Documentation, Libraries and Archives, 1975–79; British Council Libraries Adv. Cttee, 1982–86; President: Inst. of Information Scientists, 1973–76; Library Assoc., 1985. Mem., Royal Commn on Historical Monuments (England), 1981–89. Governor, British Inst. for Recorded Sound, 1981–86. Dir, Arundel Castle Trustees Ltd, 1976–. Hon. FCLIP (Hon. FLA, 1982); Hon. FIInfSc. Hon. LLD Sheffield, 1976; Hon. DLitt Loughborough, 1980. Gold Medal, Internat. Assoc. of Library Assocs, 1985. *Publications:* various contribs to jls of learned societies. *Recreations:* music, travel. *Address:* 3 St James Green, Thirsk, N Yorks YO7 1AF. *Club:* Athenæum.

HOOLE, John George Aldick; Arts and Culture Worker, Oxford Brookes University, since 2003; *b* 3 Feb. 1951; *s* of John Aldick Hoole and Pamela Betty Coleman; *m* 1975, Lindsey G. Rushworth; one *s* one *d*. *Educ:* Univ. of East Anglia (BA Hons History of Art). Asst Keeper of Art, Southampton Art Gall., 1974–78; Asst Dir, Museum of Modern Art, Oxford, 1978–82; Curator, Barbican Art Gall., 1982–98; Dir, Barbican Art Galls, 1998–2001. Chair, Chiltern Sculpture Trust, 2003–. *Recreations:* parenthood, books. *Address:* 54 Western Road, Oxford OX1 4LG. *T:* (01865) 245268.

HOOLEY, Prof. Christopher, FRS 1983; Distinguished Research Professor, School of Mathematics, University of Cardiff (formerly University of Wales, Cardiff), since 1995; *b* 7 Aug. 1928; *s* of Leonard Joseph Hooley, MA, BSc, and Barbara Hooley; *m* 1954, Birgitta Kneip; two *s*. *Educ:* Wilmslow Preparatory Sch.; Abbotsholme Sch.; Corpus Christi Coll., Cambridge (MA, PhD, ScD). Captain, RAEC, 1948–49 (SO III, British Troops in Egypt). Fellow, Corpus Christi Coll., Cambridge, 1955–58; Lectr in Mathematics, Univ. of Bristol, 1958–65; Prof. of Pure Mathematics, Univ. of Durham, 1965–67; University College, Cardiff, subseq. University of Wales, Cardiff: Prof. of Pure Maths, 1967–95; Hd of Dept of Pure Maths, 1967–88; Dean of Faculty of Science, 1973–76; Dep. Principal, 1979–81; Hd of Sch. of Maths, 1988–95; Dep. Principal, 1991–94. Visiting Member: Inst. for Advanced Study, Princeton, 1970–71, and Fall Terms, 1976, 1977, 1982, 1983; Institut des Hautes Etudes Scientifiques, Paris, 1984. Adams Prize, Cambridge, 1973; Sen. Berwick Prize, London Mathematical Soc., 1980. *Publications:* Applications of Sieve Methods to the Theory of Numbers, 1976; (ed with H. Halberstam) Recent Progress in Analytic Number Theory, 1981; memoirs in diverse mathematical jls. *Recreations:* classic cars; antiquities. *Address:* Rushmoor Grange, Backwell, Bristol BS48 3BN. *T:* (01275) 462363.

HOOLEY, Frank Oswald; retired; *b* 30 Nov. 1923; *m* 1945, Doris Irene Snook; two *d*. *Educ:* King Edward's High Sch., Birmingham; Birmingham Univ. Admin. Asst, Birmingham Univ., 1948–52; Sheffield Univ.: Asst Registrar, 1952–65; Sen. Asst Registrar, 1965–66; Registrar, Fourah Bay Coll., Sierra Leone, 1960–62 (secondment from Sheffield); Sen. Admin. Asst, Manchester Poly., 1970–71; Chief Admin. Offr, Sheffield City Coll. of Educn, 1971–74. Res. Asst to John Tomlinson, MEP, 1984–88. MP (Lab) Sheffield, Heeley, 1966–70 and Feb. 1974–1983. Chm., Parly Liaison Gp for Alternative Energy Strategies, 1978; formerly Member, Select Committees on Public Accounts, Estimates, Sci. and Technol., Overseas Aid, Foreign Affairs, and Procedure. Contested (Lab) Stratford-on-Avon, 1983. Vice-Chairman: Sutton Coldfield Lab. Party, 1988–98; Brecon and Radnorshire Lab. Party, 2001–03 (Chm., 2000–01, 2003–04). Chairman: Co-ordinating Cttee, Internat. Anti-Apartheid Year, 1978; Central Reg., UNA, 1994–98; Mem., UK Commn, UNESCO, 1999–2000; Pres., UNA Wales, 2002–07. Governor: Bishop Vesey Sch., 1985–98; Banners Gate Jun. Sch., 1993–98. Trustee, Sutton Coldfield Municipal Charities, 1986–98. Methodist Local Preacher, 1985–. *Address:* 50 Caenbrook Meadow, Presteigne, Powys LD8 2NE. *T:* (01544) 260790.

HOOLEY, John Rouse; DL; Chief Executive, West Sussex County Council, 1975–90; Clerk to the Lieutenancy of West Sussex, 1976–90; *b* 25 June 1927; *s* of Harry and Elsie Hooley; *m* 1953, Gloria Patricia Swanston; three *s* one *d*. *Educ:* William Hulme's Sch., Manchester; Lincoln Coll., Oxford; Manchester Univ. LLB London. Admitted Solicitor (Hons), 1952. Served Lancashire Fusiliers, 1946–48. Asst Solicitor, Chester, Carlisle and Shropshire, 1952–65; Asst Clerk, Cornwall, 1965–67; Dep. Clerk and Dep. Clerk of the Peace, W Sussex, 1967–74; County Sec., W Sussex, 1974–75. Member: Chichester HA, 1990–95 (Chm., 1993–95); W Sussex HA, 1995–96. Chm., Downland Housing Gp, 1990–2003. DL W Sussex, 1991. *Recreations:* gardening, music. *Address:* Bosvigo, Lavant Road, Chichester PO19 5RQ.

HOON, Rt Hon. Geoffrey (William); PC 1999; MP (Lab) Ashfield, since 1992; Secretary of State for Transport, since 2008; *b* 6 Dec. 1953; *s* of Ernest and June Hoon; *m* 1981, Elaine Ann Dumelow; one *s* two *d*. *Educ:* Nottingham High Sch.; Jesus College, Cambridge (MA). Called to the Bar, Gray's Inn, 1978. Labourer at furniture factory, 1972–73; Lectr in Law, Leeds Univ., 1976–82. Vis. Prof. of Law, Univ. of Louisville, 1979–80. In practice at Nottingham, 1982–84. An Opposition Whip, 1994–95; opposition spokesman on IT, 1995–97; Parly Sec., 1997–98, Minister of State, 1998–99, Lord Chancellor's Dept; Minister of State, FCO, 1999; Sec. of State for Defence, 1999–2005; Lord Privy Seal and Leader of H of C, 2005–06; Minister of State for Europe, FCO, 2006–07; Parly Sec. to HM Treasury (Govt Chief Whip), 2007–08. European Parliament: Mem. (Lab) Derbyshire, 1984–94; Mem., Legal Affairs Cttee, 1984–94; President: Standing Delegn to China, 1987–89; Standing Delegn to US, 1989–92. Chm., Friends of Music, 1992–94; Vice-Chm. and Gov., Westminster Foundn, 1994–97. *Recreations:* football, running, cinema, music, cycling. *Address:* House of Commons, SW1A 0AA; 8 Station Street, Kirkby-in-Ashfield, Notts NG17 7AR.

HOOPER, family name of **Baroness Hooper**.

HOOPER, Baroness *cr* 1985 (Life Peer), of Liverpool and of St James's in the City of Westminster; **Gloria Dorothy Hooper,** CMG 2002; *b* 25 May 1939; *d* of late Frances and Frederick Hooper. *Educ:* University of Southampton (BA Hons Law); Universidad Central, Quito, Ecuador (Lic. de Derecho Internacional). Admitted to Law Society, Solicitor, 1973; Partner, Taylor Garrett, 1974–84. MEP (C) Liverpool, 1979–84; contested (C) Merseyside West, European Parly elecn, 1984. Baroness in Waiting, 1985–87; Parly Under Sec. of State, DES, 1987–88, Dept of Energy, 1988–89, DoH, 1989–92; Dep. Speaker, H of L, 1993–. Mem., Parly Delegns to Council of Europe and WEU, 1992–97, 2002–. Pres., Canning House, 1997–2002. FRGS 1982; Fellow, Industry and Parlt Trust, 1983; FRSA 1986. Order of Francisco de Miranda (Venezuela); Order of Boyaca Gran Cruz (Colombia); Order of Merit (Ecuador); Dame, Order of St Gregory the Great (Holy See). *Publications:* Cases on Company Law, 1967; Law of International Trade, 1968. *Recreations:* theatre and walking. *Address:* House of Lords, Westminster, SW1A 0PW. *T:* (020) 7219 3000.

HOOPER, Rt Hon. Sir Anthony, Kt 1995; PC 2004; **Rt Hon. Lord Justice Hooper;** a Lord Justice of Appeal, since 2004; *b* 16 Sept. 1937; *s* of late Edwin Morris Hooper and Greta Lillian Chissim; *m* 1st, Margrethe Frances (*née* Hansen) (marr. diss. 1986); one *s* one *d*; 2nd, Heather Christine (*née* Randall) (*d* 2005); 3rd, Fiona Mary (*née* Baigrie). *Educ:* Sherborne; Trinity Hall, Cambridge (Scholar; MA, LLB). 2nd Lieut, 7th RTR, 1956–57. Called to the Bar, Inner Temple, 1965, Bencher, 1993; admitted to Law Society of British Columbia, 1969; QC 1987; a Recorder, 1986–95; a Judge of the High Ct of Justice, QBD, 1995–2004; Presiding Judge, NE Circuit, 1997–2000. Asst Lectr and Lectr, Univ. of Newcastle upon Tyne, 1962–65; Asst and Associate Prof., Faculty of Law, Univ. of British Columbia, 1965–68; Prof. Associé, Univ. de Laval, 1969–70; Prof., Osgoode Hall Law Sch., York Univ., 1971–73. Visiting Professor: Univ. de Montréal, 1972, 1973; Osgoode Hall, 1984. Mem., Criminal Procedure Rules Cttee, 2004–. Pres., British Acad. of Forensic Scis, 2001–03. Chm. Govs, Inns of Court Sch. of Law, 1996–99. Gen. Ed., Blackstone's Criminal Practice, 2008–. *Publications:* (ed) Harris's Criminal Law, 21st edn, 1968; articles in legal jls. *Address:* Royal Courts of Justice, Strand, WC2A 2LL. *Club:* Athenæum.

See also R. Hooper.

HOOPER, Dr John David, CDir; Chief Executive, Institute of Clinical Research, since 2004; *b* 22 March 1947; *s* of Wilfred John Hooper and Vera Hooper; *m* 1991, Veronica Jane Bligh; one *s* four *d* by previous marriages. *Educ:* Bath Univ. (BSc 1972); Salford Univ. (MSc 1982); Columbia Pacific Univ. (PhD 1985). CEng 1980; CDir 2001. Apprentice engr, UKAEA, 1964–69; Project Engr, United Glass Ltd, 1969–74; Sen. Project Engr, Cadbury Schweppes Ltd, 1974–78; Dep. Gp Chief Engr, Gp Energy Manager and Sales Manager, Glaxo Pharmaceuticals PLC, 1978–85; Chief Exec., Chartered Inst. Building, 1985–87; Dir, Pan European Ops, Carlson Mktg Gp, Inc., 1987–90; Business Strategy Manager, Scottish Hydro Electric PLC, 1990–94; Chief Executive: British Sports Fedn, 1994–97; RoSPA, 1997–2004. Patron, Lifeskills Learning for Living, 1997–. Advr, Business in the Arts, 1993–. FCMI (FBIM 1985); FInstD 1985; FRSA 1999; FRIPH 2002. *Publications:* Heat Energy Recovery in the Pharmaceutical Industry, 1982; Energy Management and Marketing in the Pharmaceutical Industry, 1985; several contribs to jls. *Recreations:* flying light aircraft, DIY. *Address:* 45 Hunsbury Close, Northampton NN4 9UE.

HOOPER, Rt Rev. Michael Wrenford; *see* Ludlow, Bishop Suffragan of.

HOOPER, Noel Barrie; Judge of the High Court, Hong Kong, 1981–93; *b* 9 Nov. 1931; twin *s* of late Alfred Edward Hooper and Constance Violet Hooper; *m* 1959, Pauline Mary (*née* Irwin); two *d*. *Educ:* Prince of Wales Sch., Kenya; St Peter's Hall, Oxford (BA 1954). Called to the Bar, Gray's Inn, 1956. Advocate of High Court, Uganda, 1956–61; Magistrate, Basutoland, 1961–64 and Hong Kong, 1964–68; Sen. Magistrate, Hong Kong, 1968–73; Principal Magistrate, 1973–76; Dist Judge, 1976–81; Comr of the Supreme Court of Brunei, 1983–86, 1986–89, 1990–93, 1994–. *Recreations:* tennis, cricket, golf, reading. *Clubs:* MCC; Corhampton Golf; Forty.

HOOPER, Richard, CBE 2005; Chairman: Informa (formerly T & F Informa) plc, 2005–07; Artilium plc, since 2007; Managing Partner, Hooper Communications, since 1988; *b* 19 Sept. 1939; *s* of late Edwin Morris Hooper and Greta Lillian (*née* Goode); *m* 1964, Meredith Jean Rooney; two *s* one *d*. *Educ:* Sherborne Sch.; Worcester Coll., Oxford (BA German and Russian, 1963; MA). National Service, 2nd Lieut 7th RTR, BAOR, 1958–59. Gen. trainee, BBC, 1963; Radio Producer, BBC Further Educn, 1964–66; Harkness Fellow, USA, 1967–68; Sen. Radio and TV Producer, BBC Open Univ. Prodns, 1969–72; Dir, National Develt Prog. in Computer Assisted Learning, 1973–77; Man. Dir, Mills & Allen Communications, 1978–79; Dir, Prestel, Post Office Telecommunications, 1980–81; Chief Exec., Value Added Systems and Services, BT, 1982–86; Man. Dir, Super Channel, 1986–88. Chm., Radio Authy, 2000–03; Dep. Chm., OFCOM, 2002–05; Chm., Ind. Council of Postal Services Sector, 2008. Non-exec. Chm., IMS Gp plc, 1997–2002; non-executive Director: MAI, 1993–96; United News & Media, 1996–97; LLP Gp plc, 1997–98; Informed Sources Internat., 1997–99; Superscape plc, 2000–02; UK eUniversities Worldwide, 2002–04; Yell Gp plc, 2006–; Sen. non-exec. Dir, Informa Gp plc, 1999–2005. Special Staff Consultant to President

Lyndon Johnson's Commn on Instructional Technology, 1968. Chm., The Pluralists, 1992–. *Publications:* (ed) Colour in Britain, 1965; (ed) The Curriculum, Context, Design and Development, 1971; Unnatural Monopolies, 1991; contrib. to books and jls. *Recreations:* the family, theatre, golf. *Clubs:* Garrick; Vincent's (Oxford).

See also Rt Hon. Sir A. Hooper.

HOOPER, Toby Julien Anderson; QC 2000; **His Honour Judge Hooper;** a Circuit Judge, since 2007; *b* 14 Dec. 1950; *o s* of Lt Col Denys Anderson Hooper and late Paula Hooper (*née* Glascoe); *m* 1981, Anna, *d* of late Dr Brian Locke, FRCR and of Rachel Locke; one *s* two *d. Educ:* Downside Sch.; Durham Univ. (BA Hons 1972). Called to the Bar, Inner Temple, 1973, Bencher, 2000; in practice at the Bar, 1974–2007; Asst Recorder, 1998–2000; a Recorder, 2000–07. Bar Council: Additional Mem., Remuneration Cttee, 1998–2003 (Vice-Chm. (Civil), 2000–03); Mem. (as SE Circuit Rep.), 2000–03; Chm., Pupillage Bd, 2001–03; Mem., General Management Cttee, 2003–05; Chm., Continuing Educn Cttee, Personal Injuries Bar Assoc., 1999–2001; Mem. (co-opted), Costs Sub-Cttee, Civil Justice Council, 2002–04; Mem., Incorporated Council of Law Reporting, 2004–07. Hon. Sec., Incorp. Inns of Court Mission (Gainsford Youth Club, Covent Garden), 1979–90. Hon. Sec., Thomas More Soc., 1994–97. *Publications:* (ed) Inner Temple Advocacy Handbook, 1998, 7th edn 2004; (Gen. Ed.) Bar Council Taxation and Retirement Benefits Handbook, 3rd edn 2000, 4th edn 2002; (contrib.) Butterworth's Professional Negligence Service, 2000–02. *Recreations:* choral singing, walking. *Address:* Worcester Combined Court Centre, The Shirehall, Worcester WR1 1EQ.

HOOSON, family name of **Baron Hooson**.

HOOSON, Baron *cr* 1979 (Life Peer), of Montgomery in the County of Powys and of Colomendy in the County of Clwyd; **Hugh Emlyn Hooson;** QC 1960; a Recorder of the Crown Court, 1972–93 (Recorder of Swansea, 1971); *b* 26 March 1925; *s* of late Hugh and Elsie Hooson, Colomendy, Denbigh; *m* 1950, Shirley Margaret Wynne, *d* of late Sir George Hamer, CBE; two *d. Educ:* Denbigh Grammar Sch.; University Coll. of Wales, Aberystwyth. Called to Bar, Gray's Inn, 1949 (Bencher, 1968; Vice-Treasurer, 1985; Treasurer, 1986); Wales and Chester Circuit (Junior, 1954–55; Leader, 1971–74); Dep. Chm., Flint QS, 1960–71; Dep. Chm., Merioneth QS, 1960–67, Chm., 1967–71; Recorder of Merthyr Tydfil, 1971. MP (L) Montgomery, 1962–79. Leader, 1966–79, Pres., 1983–86, Welsh Liberal Party. Vice-Chm. Political Cttee, North Atlantic Assembly, 1975–79. Dir (non-exec.), Laura Ashley (Holdings), 1985–96 (Chm., 1995–96); Chm., Severn River Crossing, 1991–2000. President: Royal Nat. Eisteddfod of Wales, Newtown, 1965, Denbigh, 2001; Llangollen Internat. Eisteddfod, 1987–93; Wales International, 1995–98. Gov., Inst. of Grassland and Envmtl Res., 1989–92. Hon. Professorial Fellow, Univ. of Wales Aberystwyth (formerly UCW), 1971–. Hon. LLD Wales, 2003. White Bard, Royal Nat. Eisteddfod of Wales, Gorsedd Circle, 1966. *Address:* Summerfield Park, Llanidloes, Powys SY18 6AQ. *T:* (01686) 412298; *T:* (office) (020) 7219 5226; (home) (020) 7405 4160.

HOOTON, Patrick Jonathan; His Honour Judge Hooton; a Circuit Judge, since 1994; *b* 30 June 1941; *s* of late John Charles Hooton, CMG, MBE, QC (Bermuda) and of Patricia Jessica Hooton (*née* Manning); *m* 1st, 1970, Anne Josephine Wells; one *s*; 2nd, 1980, Jocelyn Margaret East; one *s* one *d. Educ:* Downside Sch., Somerset; Trinity Coll., Cambridge. Commonwealth Develt Corp., 1964–68; Van Moppes & Co., 1969–71; called to the Bar, Gray's Inn, 1973; practised on Western Circuit, 1973–94. Mem., Club Taurino, 1994–. *Recreations:* field sports, sailing, ski-ing, Southampton FC and Hampshire CC. *Clubs:* Lawyers' Fishing; Hampshire CC.

HOPCROFT, George William; HM Diplomatic Service, retired; consultant on international relations; *b* 30 Sept. 1927; *s* of late Frederick Hopcroft and Dorothy Gertrude (*née* Bourne); *m* 1951, Audrey Joan Rodd; three *s* one *d. Educ:* Chiswick County Sch. for Boys (sch. 'MP' July 1945); London Univ. (BCom); Brasenose Coll., Oxford; INSEAD, Fontainebleau; Univ. of Miami. Auditor with Wm R. Warner, 1946; entered Export Credits Guarantee Dept, 1946; Asst Trade Comr, Madras, 1953–57; Sen. Underwriter, ECGD, 1957–64; on secondment to HM Treasury, 1964; joined FO, 1965; First Sec. (Commercial), Amman, 1965–69; First Sec. (Econ.), Bonn, 1969–71; First Sec. (Comm.), Kuala Lumpur, 1971–75; FCO, 1975–78; Counsellor (Comm. and Econ.), Bangkok, 1978–81; FCO 1981; Lloyds of London antibiosis underwriter, 1982–92. Founder Mem., Export and Overseas Trade Adv. Panel (EOTAP), 1982–; operational expert in for. affairs, attached to Govt of Belize, 1982–83. Mem., FCO Assoc. *Recreations:* leisure and circumnavigation (Pilot's A Licence, 1956), German and French literature, song, film, sport (Civil Service ½ mile champion, 1947; Venables Bowl for coxless pairs, Amateur Rowing Assoc. of E, Colombo, 1957; double-marathon in 6 hours, 1959 & 1960; Kow Yai sen. marathon, 1979), serendipity. *Clubs:* Civil Service, Royal Commonwealth Society; British (Bangkok).

HOPE, family name of **Barons Glendevon** and **Hope of Craighead, Marquess of Linlithgow** and **Baron Rankeillour**.

HOPE OF CRAIGHEAD, Baron *cr* 1995 (Life Peer), of Bamff in the District of Perth and Kinross; **James Arthur David Hope;** PC 1989; FRSE; a Lord of Appeal in Ordinary, since 1996; *b* 27 June 1938; *s* of late Arthur Henry Cecil Hope, OBE, WS, Edinburgh and Muriel Ann Neilson Hope (*née* Collie); *m* 1966, Katharine Mary Kerr, *d* of W. Mark Kerr, WS, Edinburgh; twin *s* one *d. Educ:* Edinburgh Acad.; Rugby Sch.; St John's Coll., Cambridge (Open Schol. 1956, BA 1962, MA 1978; Hon. Fellow, 1995); Edinburgh Univ. (LLB 1965). FRSE 2003. National Service, Seaforth Highlanders, 1957–59 (Lieutenant 1959). Admitted Faculty of Advocates, 1965; Standing Junior Counsel in Scotland to Board of Inland Revenue, 1974–78; Advocate-Depute, 1978–82; QC (Scotland) 1978; Dean, Faculty of Advocates, 1986–89; Lord Justice-Gen. of Scotland and Lord Pres. of Court of Session, 1989–96. Chm., Med. Appeal Tribunal, 1985–86; Legal Chm., Pensions Appeal Tribunal, 1985–86. Mem., Scottish Cttee on Law of Arbitration, 1986–89. Mem. Bd of Trustees, Nat. Liby of Scotland, 1989–96. Chm. Bd, Inst. of Advanced Legal Studies, 2000–. President: Stair Soc., 1993–; Internat. Criminal Law Assoc., 2000–; Commonwealth Magistrates' and Judges' Assoc., 2003–06. Chm., Sub-Cttee E (Law and Instns), H of L Select Cttee on EU, 1998–2001. Hon. Prof. of Law, Aberdeen, 1994–. Hon. Member: Canadian Bar Assoc., 1987; Soc. of Legal Scholars (formerly SPTL), 1991; Hon. Fellow, Amer. Coll. of Trial Lawyers, 2000. Hon. Bencher: Gray's Inn, 1989; Inn of Court of NI, 1995. Chancellor, Strathclyde Univ., 1998– (Fellow, 2000). Hon. LLD: Aberdeen, 1991; Strathclyde, 1993; Edinburgh, 1995. David Kelbie Award, Inst. Contemporary Scotland, 2007. *Publications:* (ed jtly) Gloag & Henderson's Introduction to the Law of Scotland, 7th edn 1968, asst editor, 8th edn 1980 and 9th edn 1987, (contrib.) 11th edn 2001; (ed jtly) Armour on Valuation for Rating, 4th edn 1971, 5th edn 1985; (with A. G. M. Duncan) The Rent (Scotland) Act 1984, 1986; (contrib.) Stair Memorial Encyclopaedia of Scots Law; (contrib.) Court of Session Practice. *Recreations:* walking, ornithology, music. *Address:* 34 India Street, Edinburgh EH3 6HB. *T:* (0131) 225 8245; House of Lords, SW1A 0PW. *T:* (020) 7219 3202. *Club:* New (Edinburgh).

HOPE OF THORNES, Baron *cr* 2005 (Life Peer), of Thornes in the County of West Yorkshire; **Rt Rev. and Rt Hon. David Michael Hope,** KCVO 1995; PC 1991; DPhil; Vicar, St Margaret's, Ilkley, 2005–06; Archbishop of York, 1995–2005; Hon. Assistant Bishop: of Bradford, since 2005; of Europe, since 2007; of Blackburn, since 2008; *b* 14 April 1940. *Educ:* Nottingham Univ. (BA Hons Theol); Linacre Coll., Oxford (DPhil; Hon. Fellow, 1993). Curate of St John, Tuebrook, Liverpool, 1965–70; Chaplain, Church of Resurrection, Bucharest, 1967–68; Vicar, St Andrew, Warrington, 1970–74; Principal, St Stephen's House, Oxford, 1974–82; Warden, Community of St Mary the Virgin, Wantage, 1980–87; Vicar of All Saints', Margaret Street, 1982–85; Bishop of Wakefield, 1985–91; Bishop of London, 1991–95. Prelate, Order of British Empire, 1991–95; Dean of the Chapels Royal, 1991–95. Hon. DD: Nottingham, 1999; Hull, 2005. *Publications:* The Leonine Sacramentary, 1971; Living the Gospel, 1993; Signs of Hope, 2001; (with Hugh Little) Better to Travel Hopefully, 2007. *Address:* 2 Aspinall Rise, Hellifield, Skipton, N Yorks BD23 4JT.

HOPE, Alan; JP; Leader, West Midlands County Council Opposition Group (C), 1981–86; *b* 5 Jan. 1933; *s* of George Edward Thomas Hope and Vera Hope; *m* 1960, Marilyn Dawson; one *s* one *d. Educ:* George Dixon Grammar Sch., Birmingham. Councillor, Birmingham CC, 1964–73; West Midlands County Council: Councillor, 1973; Leader, 1980–81; Chairman: Trading Standards, 1977–79; Finance, 1979–80. JP Birmingham 1974. *Address:* Whitehaven, 7 Rosemary Drive, Little Aston Park, Sutton Coldfield, West Midlands B74 3AG. *T:* (0121) 353 3011. *Club:* Royal Commonwealth Society.

HOPE, Sir Alexander (Archibald Douglas), 19th Bt *cr* 1628 (NS), of Craighall; Managing Director, Double Negative VFX Ltd, since 1998; *b* London, 16 March 1969; *s* of Sir John Carl Alexander Hope, 18th Bt and of Merle Pringle, *d* of late Robert Douglas; *S* father, 2007; *m* 2002, Emmeline Grace, *d* of Simon H. Barrow; two *s. Educ:* Eton; Univ. of Bristol (BSocSc). *Heir: s* William John Hope, *b* 7 March 2004. *Address: e-mail:* alex@dneg.com. *Club:* Soho House.

HOPE, Antony Derwin; His Honour Judge Hope; a Circuit Judge, since 2002; *b* 22 Aug. 1944; *s* of John and Lorna Hope; *m* 1979, Heidi Saure; one *s* one *d. Educ:* Leighton Park Sch., Reading; Coll. of Estate Mgt (BSc Estate Mgt); Coll. of Law. Called to the Bar, Middle Temple, 1970; in practice as barrister, London and Winchester, 1971–2002. UK Delegate to Internat. Assoc. of Judges. *Publication:* The 1990–91 Planning Acts, 1993. *Recreations:* cricket, walking, studying history, foreign travel. *Address:* c/o Southampton Combined Court, London Road, Southampton SO15 2XQ.

HOPE, Prof. Charles Archibald, DPhil; Director, and Professor of the History of the Classical Tradition, Warburg Institute, University of London, since 2002; *b* 11 April 1945; 2nd *s* of Sir Archibald Philip Hope, 17th Bt, OBE, DFC, AE and of Ruth, *y d* of Carl Davis; *m* 1st, 1977, Jennifer Katharine Hadley (marr. diss.); one *s*; 2nd, 2003, Donatelli Sparti; one *d. Educ:* Eton; Balliol Coll., Oxford (BA 1967; DPhil); Courtauld Inst., London (MA); MA Cantab 1972. Res. Lectr, Christ Church, Oxford, 1968–72; Jun. Res. Fellow, King's Coll., Cambridge, 1972–76; Warburg Institute: Lectr in Renaissance Studies, 1976–92; Sen. Lectr, 1972–2002; Dep. Dir, 1999–2002. Slade Prof. of Fine Art, Oxford Univ., 1985–86. *Publications:* Masterpieces of Renaissance Painting, 1979; Titian, 1980; (ed) Autobiography of Benvenuto Cellini, 1984; contrib. learned jls. *Address:* Warburg Institute, Woburn Square, WC1H 0AB.

HOPE, Christopher David Tully, FRSL; writer; *b* 26 Feb. 1944; *s* of Dennis Tully and Kathleen Mary Hope (*née* McKenna); *m* 1967, Eleanor Klein (marr. diss. 1994); two *s. Educ:* Christian Brothers College, Pretoria; Univ. of Natal (BA Hons 1970); Univ. of Witwatersrand (MA 1973). FRSL 1990. Founder and Dir, Franschhoek Literary Fest., S Africa, 2007–. Pringle Prize, English Acad. of Southern Africa, 1972; Cholmondeley Award, Soc. of Authors, 1974; Arts Council Bursary, 1982; Travelex, Travel Writers' Award, 1997. *Publications:* Cape Drives, 1974; A Separate Development, 1981 (David Higham Prize for Fiction); In the Country of the Black Pig, 1981; Private Parts and Other Tales, 1982 (rev. edn as Learning to Fly and Other Tales, 1990) (Internat. PEN Silver Pen Award); Kruger's Alp, 1984 (Whitbread Prize for Fiction); Englishmen, 1985; The Hottentot Room, 1986; Black Swan, 1987; White Boy Running, 1988 (CNA Award, S Africa); My Chocolate Redeemer, 1989; Moscow! Moscow!, 1990; Serenity House, 1992; The Love Songs of Nathan J. Swirsky, 1993; Darkest England, 1996; (ed jtly) New Writing, 1996; Me, the Moon and Elvis Presley, 1997; Signs of the Heart: love and death in Languedoc, 1999; Heaven Forbid, 2002; Brothers Under the Skin: travels in tyranny, 2003; My Mother's Lovers, 2006; The Garden of Bad Dreams, 2008; contribs to BBC, newspapers, jls. *Recreation:* getting lost. *Address:* c/o Rogers, Coleridge & White, 20 Powis Mews, W11 1JN.

HOPE, Sir Colin (Frederick Newton), Kt 1996; MA; FREng, FIMechE, FIMI; Executive Chairman, T & N plc, 1995–98; *b* 17 May 1932; *s* of Frederick and Mildred Hope; *m* 1959, Gillian Carden; two *s. Educ:* Stowe Sch.; St Catharine's College, Cambridge (MA). CEng, FREng (FEng 1995). Glacier Metal Co., 1963–70; Managing Dir, 1970–73, Exec. Chm., 1973–75, Covrad; Director: Engineering Group, Dunlop, 1975–79; Tyres UK Dunlop, 1979–82; Tyres Europe Dunlop Holdings, 1982–84; Chief Exec., Dunlop Engineering International, 1984–85; Gp Man. Dir, 1985–89, Chm. and Chief Exec., 1989–95, Turner & Newall, subseq. T & N plc. Chairman: Bryant Gp, 1992–2001; Ibstock Johnsen, 1993–97 (Dir, 1989–98). Pres., SMMT, 1991–93. Trustee, Nat. Motor Mus., 1991–2002. Hon. DSc Cranfield, 1998. *Recreations:* theatre, music, vintage motor cars. *Address:* Hornby Cottage, High Street, Welford-on-Avon, Warwickshire CV37 8EF. *T:* (01665) 576142. *Club:* Royal Automobile.

HOPE, Derwin; *see* Hope, A. D.

HOPE, Marcus Laurence Hulbert, OBE 1998; JP; HM Diplomatic Service, retired; Consul-General, Montreal, 1998–2002; *b* 2 Feb. 1942; *s* of late Laurence Frank Hope, OBE; *m* 1980, Uta Maria Luise Müller-Unverfehrt; one *s. Educ:* City of London Sch.; Sydney C of E Grammar Sch.; Univ. of Sydney (BA); Univ. of London (BA Hons); Open Univ. (Dip. Physical Sci. 2006). Joined HM Diplomatic Service, 1965; Third Sec., CRO, 1965; MECAS, 1966; Second Sec., Tripoli, 1968; FCO, 1970; First Sec., 1972; Head of Chancery, Dubai, 1974; First Sec. (Commercial), Bonn, 1976; FCO, 1980; NATO Defence Coll., Rome, 1984; Counsellor, Beirut, 1984–85; Counsellor and Head of Chancery, Berne, 1985–89; Dep. Head of Mission and Counsellor (Commercial and Aid), Jakarta, 1989–92; Hd, Western Europe Dept, FCO, 1992–95; Ambassador to Zaire, also (non-resident) to the Congo, 1996–98. Trustee, Congo Church Assoc., 2002–. FRAS 2004. JP Wandsworth, 2003. *Recreations:* classical guitar, astronomy. *Address:* 29 Narbonne Avenue, SW4 9JR.

HOPE, Philip Ian; MP (Lab and Co-op) Corby, since 1997; Minister of State, Department of Health, since 2008; *b* 19 April 1955; *s* of A. G. Hope and Grace Hope; *m* 1980, Allison, *d* of John and Margaret Butt; one *s* one *d. Educ:* Wandsworth Comp. Sch.; St Luke's Coll., Exeter Univ. (BEd). Teacher, Kettering Sch. for Boys; Youth Policy

Advr, NCVO; Hd, Young Volunteer Resources Unit, Nat. Youth Bureau; Mgt and Community Work Consultant, Framework, 1985–96; Dir, Framework in Print publishing co-operative. Member (Lab and Co-op): Kettering BC, 1983–87; Northants CC, 1993–97. Contested (Lab and Co-op) Kettering, 1992. PPS to Minister of State for Housing and Planning, 1999–2001, to Dep. Prime Minister, 2001–03; Parliamentary Under-Secretary of State: ODPM, 2003–05; DfES, then Dept for Children, Schools and Families, 2005–07; a Parly Sec. and Minister for the Third Sector, Cabinet Office, 2007–08; Minister for the E Midlands, 2008. Member: Public Accounts Select Cttee, 1997–98; NI Grand Cttee, 1997–2005; Cttee of Selection, 1999–2005; Chairman: All-Party Parly Gp for charities and voluntary orgns, 1997–2001; All-Party Lighting Gp, 2001–05. Vice Chm., PLP Social Security Deptl Cttee, 1997–2001; Mem., Leadership Campaign Team with responsibility for educn, 1997–99. *Publications:* Making Best Use of Consultants, 1993; (jtly) Performance Appraisal, 1995; various curriculum and training packs for schs and youthworkers and information booklets for young people. *Recreations:* tennis, juggling, computing, gardening. *Address:* House of Commons, SW1A 0AA.

HOPE, Prof. Ronald Anthony, (Tony), PhD; FRCPsych; Professor of Medical Ethics, University of Oxford, since 2000; Fellow, St Cross College, Oxford, since 1990; *b* 16 March 1951; *s* of Ronald Sidney Hope and Marion Nutall Hope (*née* Whittaker); *m* 1981, Sally Louise Hirsh; two *d*. *Educ:* Dulwich Coll.; New Coll., Oxford (Bosanquet Open Schol. in Medicine; MA, PhD 1978; BM BCh 1980). FRCPsych 1997. W. H. Rhodes Travel Schol., 1969; doctoral res. in neurobiol. at NIMR, 1973–76; preclinical trng, Middx Hosp., 1976–77; clinical trng, Univ. of Oxford, 1977–80; House surgeon, Royal United Hosp., Bath, 1980–81; House physician, John Radcliffe Hosp., Oxford, 1981; SHO-Registrar rotation in Psychiatry, Oxford, 1981–85; Wellcome Trust Trng Fellow in Psychiatry, Oxford hosps, 1985–87; University of Oxford: Clin. Lectr in Psychiatry, 1987–90; Leader, Oxford Practice Skills Project, 1990–95; Lectr in Practice Skills, 1995–2000; Reader in Medicine, 1996–2000; Dir, Ethox (Oxford Centre for Ethics and Communication in Health Care Practice), 1999–2005; Hon. Consultant Psychiatrist, Warneford Hosp. Oxford, 1990–. Chairman: Wellcome Trust Strategy Cttee on Med. Humanities, 2005–08; Wkg Party on Ethics and Dementia, Nuffield Council on Bioethics, 2007–Sept. 2009. Res. Prize and Medal, RCPsych, 1989. *Publications:* Oxford Handbook of Clinical Medicine, 1985 (trans. 9 langs), 4th edn 1998; Essential Practice in Patient-Centred Care, 1995; Manage Your Mind, 1995 (trans. 5 langs), 2nd edn 2007; Medical Ethics and Law: the core curriculum, 2003, 2nd edn 2008; Medical Ethics: a very short introduction, 2004; Empirical Ethics in Psychiatry, 2008; contrib. numerous papers and chapters, mainly in fields of Alzheimer's Disease and med. ethics. *Recreations:* family, literature, wine, walking. *Address:* Ethox Centre, University of Oxford, Old Road Campus, Oxford OX3 7LF. *T:* (01865) 226936; St Cross College, Oxford OX1 3LZ.

HOPE-DUNBAR, Sir David, 8th Bt *cr* 1664; *b* 13 July 1941; *o s* of Sir Basil Douglas Hope-Dunbar, 7th Bt, and of his 2nd wife, Edith Maude Maclaren (*d* 1989), *d* of late Malcolm Cross; *S* father, 1961; *m* 1971, Kathleen, *yr d* of late J. T. Kenrick; one *s* two *d*. *Educ:* Eton; Royal Agricultural College, Cirencester. MRICS (ARICS 1966). Founder, Dunbar & Co., now Allied Dunbar PLC. *Recreations:* fishing, shooting. *Heir: s* Charles Hope-Dunbar, *b* 11 March 1975. *Address:* Banks Farm, Kirkcudbright DG6 4XF. *T:* (01557) 330424.

HOPE JOHNSTONE, family name of **Earl of Annandale and Hartfell**.

HOPE-MORLEY, family name of **Baron Hollenden**.

HOPE-WALLACE, (Dorothy) Jaqueline, CBE 1958; *b* 1909; 2nd *d* of Charles Nugent Hope-Wallace and Mabel Chaplin. *Educ:* Lady Margaret Hall, Oxford. Entered Ministry of Labour, 1932; transferred to National Assistance Board, 1934; Under-Sec., 1958–65; Under-Sec., Min. of Housing and Local Govt, 1965–69, retired. Commonwealth Fellow, 1952–53. Comr, Public Works Loan Bd, 1974–78; Member Board: Corby Develt Corp., 1969–80; Inst. for Recorded Sound, 1971–74, 1979–83 (Chm. 1975–76); Nat. Corp. for Care of Old People (now Centre for Policy on Ageing), 1973–81 (Chm., 1978–80); Mem., Nat. Sound Archive Adv. Cttee, 1983–84. Mem. Bd of Govs, UCH, 1970–74; Pres., Friends of UCH, 1999–2005 (Chm., 1973–85). *Recreations:* arts, travel. *Address:* 17 Ashley Court, Morpeth Terrace, SW1P 1EN.

HOPES, Rt Rev. Alan Stephen; Auxiliary Bishop of Westminster, (RC), since 2003; Titular Bishop of Cuncacestre, since 2003; *b* 17 March 1944; *s* of William Stephen and Ivy Beatrice Hopes. *Educ:* Enfield Grammar Sch.; King's Coll., London (BD, AKC 1966). Ordained deacon, 1967, priest, 1968; Assistant Curate: All Saints, E Finchley, 1967–72; St Alphage, Burnt Oak (in charge of Grahame Park Estate), 1972–78; Vicar, St Paul, Tottenham, 1978–94; Area Dean, E Haringey, 1982–88; Preb., St Paul's Cathedral, 1987–94; ordained priest in the Roman Catholic Church, 1995; Asst Priest, Our Lady of Victories, Kensington, 1995–97; Parish Priest, Holy Redeemer, Chelsea, 1997–2001; VG, Westminster Archdiocese, 2001–03. *Recreations:* books, art, films, classical music, opera, travel. *Address:* Archbishop's House, Ambrosden Avenue, SW1P 1QJ. *T:* (020) 7798 9043, *Fax:* (020) 7931 6058; *e-mail:* alanhopes@rcdow.org.uk.

HOPETOUN, Earl of; Andrew Victor Arthur Charles Hope; *b* 22 May 1969; *s* and *heir* of Marquess of Linlithgow, *qv*; *m* 1993, Skye, *e d* of Major Bristow Bovill; twin *s* two *d*. *Educ:* Eton; Exeter Coll., Oxford. A Page of Honour to the Queen Mother, 1985–87. Mem., Royal Co. of Archers, 2002–. *Heir: s* Viscount Aithrie, *qv*. *Address:* Hopetoun House, South Queensferry, West Lothian EH30 9SL.

HOPEWELL, John Prince; Consultant Surgeon, Royal Free Hospital, 1957–86 (Hon. Consulting Surgeon (Urology), since 1986); *b* 1 Dec. 1920; *s* of Samuel Prince and Wilhelmina Hopewell; *m* 1st, 1959, Dr Natalie Bogdan (*d* 1975); one *s* one *d*; 2nd, 1984, Dr Rosemary Radley-Smith. *Educ:* Bradfield Coll., Berks; King's Coll. Hosp., London. RAMC, 1945–48. Postgrad. education at King's Coll. Hosp. and Brighton, Sussex, and Hosp. for Sick Children, Gt Ormond Street. Formerly Cnslt Surgeon, Putney Hosp. and Frimley Hosp., Surrey. Mem., Hampstead DHA, 1982–85; Chm., Camden Div., BMA, 1985–93; Past Chairman: Med. Cttee, Royal Free Hosp.; N Camden Dist Med. Cttee; Chm., Hon. Med. Staff Cttee, Hosp. of St John and St Elizabeth, 1993–95. Founder Mem., British Transplantation Soc., 1972; Member: Internat. Soc. of Urology; British Assoc. Urol. Surgeons; Past President: Chelsea Clinical Soc.; Section of Urology, RSM, 1982–83; Fellowship of Postgrad. Medicine. Founder Mem., Assoc. of Univ. Hospitals. Hon. Mem., NY Section, AUA. Hunterian Prof., RCS, 1958. Mem. Court of Examiners, RCSE, 1969–75. Member: Friends of St Helena; Soc. of Ornamental Woodturners. *Publications:* Three Clinical Cases of Renal Transplantation, British Medical Jl, 1964, and contribs to various medical journals. *Address:* Old Vicarage, Langrish, Petersfield, Hants GU32 1QY. *T:* (01730) 261354.

HOPGOOD, Richard Simon; Director, Henry Smith Charity, since 2002; *b* 7 Oct. 1952; *s* of Ronald and Daphne Hopgood; *m* 1988, Elizabeth Wakefield; one *d*. *Educ:* Christ's Hosp.; Wadham Coll., Oxford (BA). On staff of Church Comrs, 1977–98 (Dep. Sec., Policy and Planning, 1994–98); Dir of Policy and Dep. Sec.-Gen., Archbishops' Council, 1999–2002. *Recreations:* reading, photography, cycling. *Address:* (office) 6th Floor, 65 Leadenhall Street, EC3A 2AD.

HOPKIN, Sir Bryan; *see* Hopkin, Sir W. A. B.

HOPKIN, Prof. Deian Rhys, PhD; FRHistS; Vice-Chancellor and Chief Executive London South Bank University (formerly South Bank University), since 2001; *b* 1 March 1944; *s* of late Islwyn Hopkin and Charlotte Hopkin (nee Rees); *m* 1st, 1966, Orian Jones (marr. diss. 1989); two *d*; 2nd, 1989, Lynne Hurley; two *s*. *Educ:* Llandovery Coll. University Coll. of Wales, Aberystwyth (BA 1965; PhD 1981). FRHistS 1985. Lectr 1967–84, Sen. Lectr, 1984–91, Hd of Dept, 1989–91, Dept of History, UCW Aberystwyth; Staff Tutor, Open Univ., 1974–76; Dean, Human Scis, 1992–96, Vice-Provost, 1996–2001, City of London Poly., then London Guildhall Univ. Chm., Cityside Regeneration Ltd, 1997–2002. Member: Council, Nat. Liby of Wales, 1975–88; Gen Adv. Council, BBC, 1988–95; Exec., UK Arts and Humanities Service, 1996–2002; Skill for Health UK, 2004–; Bd, Foundn Degree Forward, 2007–; Learning and Skills Council 2007–; Council for Industry and Higher Educn, 2007–. Chm., Univs UK Skills Task Gp 2006–. Member: London Eur. Progs Cttee, 2000–05; Bd, Central London Partnership 2001–; One London Ltd, 2002–05; South Bank Employers Gp, 2005–; Vice Chm. London Higher, 2006–. Member: Hackney Community Coll. Corp., 2000–02; Lambeth Coll. Corp., 2002–05. Freeman: City of London, 2000; Co. of Inf. Technologists, 2000 Guild of Educators, 2004. FRSA 1997. Chm., UNIAID Foundn, 2004–; Vice-Chm. Council for Assisting Refugee Academics, 2005–; Patron, Bishopsgate Inst., 2008– Trustee: Bishopsgate Foundn, 1999–2003; Aldgate and Allhallows Foundn, 2004–06 Hon. Mem., C&G, 2008. Hon. Fellow, Univ. of Wales, Aberystwyth, 2003. Hon. DLitt Glamorgan, 2008. *Publications:* (ed jtly) History and Computing, 1987; (ed jtly) Class Community and the Labour Movement: Wales and Canada 1850–1930, 1989; (ed jtly) The Labour Party in Wales 1900–2000, 2000; Universities in the Modern Economy 2002; contrib. articles to Internat. Rev. Social Hist., Llafur, etc. *Recreations:* music (especially jazz), writing, broadcasting. *Address:* London South Bank University, 103 Borough Road, SE1 0AA. *T:* (020) 7815 6004. *Club:* Athenæum.

HOPKIN, His Honour John Raymond, DL; a Circuit Judge, 1979–2002; a Chairman Mental Health Review Tribunals, 2001–05; *b* 23 June 1935; *s* of George Raymond Buxton Hopkin and Muriel Hopkin; *m* 1965, Susan Mary Limb; one *s* one *d*. *Educ:* King's Sch., Worcester. Called to Bar, Middle Temple, 1958; in practice at the Bar, 1959–79. A Recorder of the Crown Court, 1978–79. A Chm. of Disciplinary Tribunals, Council of Inns of Court, 1987–90. Mem. Bd, Law Sch., Nottingham Trent Univ., 1998–2004 Chm. of Governors, Nottingham High Sch. for Girls, 1992–2006. Mem., Cathedral Council, Southwell Minster, 2005–. DL Notts, 1996. *Recreations:* fell walking and climbing, gardening, golf, the theatre. *Club:* Nottingham and Notts Services.

HOPKIN, Prof. Julian Meurglyn, MD; FRCP, FRCPE, FMedSci; Professor of Medicine, since 1999, and Head, School of Medicine, since 2001, Swansea University (formerly University of Wales, Swansea); *b* 30 Aug. 1948; *s* of Meurglyn Hopkin and Mair Hopkin (*née* Watkins); *m* 1973, Janina Macczak; two *s* one *d*. *Educ:* Maesydderwen Sch., Ystradgynlais; Univ. of Wales (MB BCh; MD 1981); Univ. of Edinburgh (MSc 1978) MA Oxon 1992. FRCP 1988; FRCPE 2000. Med. House Officer and Registrar, Univ Hosps of Wales, Oxford and Edinburgh, 1972–77; MRC Advanced Student and Clinical Scientist, MRC, Edinburgh, 1977–79; Lectr in Medicine, Univ. of Birmingham 1979–84; Clinical Sen. Lectr and Consultant Physician, Oxford, 1984–98; Fellow, Brasenose Coll., Oxford, 1992–98. Visiting Professor: Univ. of Osaka, 1994; Tor Vergata Univ., Rome, 2001; Univ. of Kyoto, 2002. Dir, Allerna Therapeutics, 2007–; non-exec. Dir, Abertawe Bro Morgannwg Univ. NHS Trust, 2008–. FMedSci 2005. (Jtly) Daiwa-Adrian Prize in Medicine, Daiwa Anglo-Japanese Foundn, 2001. *Publications:* Pneumocystis Carinii, 1991; (contrib.) Oxford Textbook of Medicine, 2nd edn 1987 to 4th edn 2003; contribs on clinical medicine, human genetic variation, allergy and infection to Lancet, BMJ, Nature and Science. *Recreation:* the outdoors. *Address:* Hafod, Llanrhidian Gwyr SA3 1EH. *T:* (01792) 390033; *e-mail:* j.m.hopkin@swan.ac.uk.

HOPKIN, Sir Royston (Oliver), KCMG 2005 (CMG 1995); Chairman and Managing Director, Spice Island Beach Resort (formerly Spice Island Inn), since 1987; Owner, Blue Horizons Cottage Hotel, since 1978; *b* 10 Jan. 1945; *s* of late Curtis Hopkin and Audrey Hopkin; *m* 1st, 1975, Floreen Hope (decd); one *s* one *d*; 2nd, 1983, Betty Grell-Hull; one *d*. *Educ:* Grenada Boys' Secondary Sch. British Amer. Insce Co., 1963–65; joined family business, Ross Point Inn, 1965, Manager, 1969–78. Dir, George F. Huggins & Co. Ltd 2001–. Member: Grenada Tourist Bd, 1965–83; Grenada Bd of Tourism, 1998–2001; Pres., Grenada Hotel Assoc., 1969–89; Caribbean Hotel Association: Dir, 1970–; Pres., 1994–96; Chm., 1996–98; Chm., Memship Policy Cttee, 2000–06; Caribbean Tourism Organization: Dir, 1990–98; Exec. Cttee, 1994–98. Chm., Caribbean Alliance (formerly Action) for Sustainable Tourism, 2002– (Vice-Chm., 1996–2002). Mem. Bd of Trustees, Queen Elizabeth Home, Grenada, 1996– (Dep. Chm., 2006–); Trustee, Duke of Edinburgh's Award of Grenada, 2004–. Numerous awards incl. Caribbean Hotelier of the Year, 1991; Special Service Award, Grenada Bd of Tourism, 2006. *Recreations:* reading, tennis. *Address:* Mace Point Villa, True Blue, Box 6, St George's, Grenada, West Indies. *T:* (home) 4444584; (business) 4444258; *e-mail:* roystonhopkin@hotmail.com.

HOPKIN, Sir (William Aylsham) Bryan, Kt 1971; CBE 1961; Hon. Professorial Fellow, Swansea University (formerly University College, Swansea), since 1988; *b* 7 Dec. 1914; *s* of late William Hopkin and Lilian Hopkin (*née* Cottelle); *m* 1938, Renée Ricour (*d* 2002); two *s*. *Educ:* Barry (Glam.) County Sch.; St John's Coll., Cambridge (Hon. Fellow, 1982); Manchester Univ. Ministry of Health, 1938–41; Prime Minister's Statistical Branch, 1941–45; Royal Commn on Population, 1945–48; Econ. Sect., Cabinet Office, 1948–50; Central Statistical Office, 1950–52; Dir, Nat. Inst. of Econ. and Soc. Research, 1952–57; Sec., Council on Prices, Productivity, and Incomes, 1957–58; Dep. Dir, Econ. Sect., HM Treasury, 1958–65; Econ. Planning Unit, Mauritius, 1965; Min. of Overseas Devlt, 1966–67; Dir-Gen. of Economic Planning, ODM, 1967–69; Dir-Gen., DEA, 1969; Dep. Chief Econ. Adviser, HM Treasury, 1970–72; Prof. of Econs, UC Cardiff, 1972–82 (on leave of absence, Head of Govt Economic Service and Chief Economic Advr, HM Treasury, 1974–77). Mem., Commonwealth Develt Corp., 1972–74. Chm., Manpower Services Cttee for Wales, 1978–79. *Address:* Bedford Charterhouse, Kimbolton Road, Bedford MK40 2PU. *T:* (01234) 267757.

HOPKINS, Adrian Mark; QC 2003; *b* 16 May 1961; *s* of Thomas and Brenda Hopkins. *Educ:* Warwick Sch.; St Peter's Coll., Oxford (Exhibnr; BA Hons Juris. 1983). Called to the Bar, Lincoln's Inn, 1984; in practice, specialising in medical law, clinical negligence and professional disciplinary hearings. Member: Supplementary Panel, Counsel to Treasury (Common Law), 1995–99; Attorney Gen.'s London B Panel for Crown's Civil Litigation, 1999–2002. Contributing Ed., Lloyd's Medical Law Reports, 1999–. *Address:* 3 Serjeants' Inn, EC4Y 1BQ. *T:* (020) 7427 5000, *Fax:* (020) 7353 0425.

HOPKINS, Alan Cripps Nind, MA Cantab, LLB Yale; *b* 27 Oct. 1926; *s* of late Rt Hon. Sir Richard V. N. Hopkins, GCB and Lady Hopkins; *m* 1st, 1954, Margaret Cameron (from whom divorced, 1962), *d* of E. C. Bolton, Waco, Texas, USA; one *s*; 2nd, 1962, Venetia, *d* of Sir Edward Wills, 4th Bt; twin *s*. *Educ:* Winchester Coll.; King's Coll., Cambridge; Yale University Law Sch., USA. BA Cantab 1947, MA 1950; LLB Yale 1952. Barrister, Inner Temple, 1948. MP (C and Nat L) Bristol North-East, 1959–66; PPS to Financial Sec. to Treasury, 1960–62. Chm., Wellman Engrg Corp., 1972–83. *Recreation:* travelling. *Address:* 502 Sagittaire, 1972 Anzere, Valais, Switzerland. *T:* (27) 3981651. *Club:* Brooks's.

HOPKINS, Sir Anthony; *see* Hopkins, Sir P. A.

HOPKINS, Anthony Strother, CBE 1996; BSc(Econ); FCA; Chairman, Northern Ireland Higher Education Council, since 2002; *b* 17 July 1940; *s* of Strother Smith Hopkins, OBE, and Alice Roberta Hopkins; *m* 1965, Dorothy Moira (*née* McDonough); one *s* two *d*. *Educ:* Campbell Coll., Belfast; Queen's University of Belfast (BScEcon). Manager, Thomson McLintock & Co., Chartered Accountants, London, 1966–70; Principal, Dept of Commerce, N Ireland, 1970–74; Northern Ireland Development Agency, 1975–82, Chief Executive, 1979–82; Under Secretary, 1982–88, Second Perm. Sec., 1988–92, Dept of Economic Development for N Ireland; Dep. Chief Exec., 1982–88, Chief Exec., 1988–92, Industrial Develt Bd for NI; Sen. Partner, Deloitte & Tonche (formerly Touche Ross & Co.), NI, Chartered Accountants, 1992–2001; Dep. Chm., 1995–96, Chm., 1997–2007, Laganside Corp. Chm., MMB for NI, 1995–2003; Dep. Chm., Probation Bd for NI, 1997–98. Member: NI Tourist Bd, 1992–98; Council, NI Chamber of Commerce and Industry, 1992–95; NI Skills Task Force, 1999–2003. Mem., Bd of Advrs, Crescent Capital (formerly Hambro NI Ventures), 1995–; Dir, QUBIS Ltd, 2002–05. Vis. Prof., Univ. of Ulster, 1992–. Mem. Adv. Bd, Ulster Business Sch., 1992–99. Member, Appeal Committee: Relate, 1994–97; Mencap (NI), 1997–; Mem., Management Cttee, Ulster Garden Village Ltd Charitable Trust, 2003– (Chm., 2006–). Hon. Treas., Prince's Trust NI Appeal, 1995–97. CCMI (CBIM 1990; Chm. NI Regl Bd, 1992–97). *Recreations:* golf, tennis, sailing. *Clubs:* Royal Belfast Golf, Royal Ulster Yacht (Co. Down).

HOPKINS, Antony, CBE 1976; composer and conductor; *b* 21 March 1921; *s* of late Hugh and of Marjorie Reynolds; adopted *c* of Major and Mrs T. H. C. Hopkins since 1925; *m* 1947, Alison Purves (*d* 1991). *Educ:* Berkhamsted Sch.; Royal Coll. of Music. Won Chappell Gold Medal and Cobbett Prize at RCM, 1942; shortly became known as composer of incidental music for radio; numerous scores composed for BBC (2 for programmes winning Italia prize for best European programme of the year, 1952 and 1957). Composed music for many productions at Stratford and in West End. Dir, Intimate Opera Co., 1952–, and has written a number of chamber operas for this group; *ballets:* Etude and Café des Sports, for Sadler's Wells; *films (music) include:* Pickwick Papers, Decameron Nights, Cast a Dark Shadow, Billy Budd; John and the Magic Music Man (narr. and orch.; Grand Prix, Besançon Film Festival, 1976). Regular broadcaster with a series of programmes entitled Talking about Music. Hon. FRCM 1964; Hon. RAM 1979; Hon. Fellow, Robinson Coll., Cambridge, 1980. DUniv. Stirling, 1980. *Publications:* Talking about Symphonies, 1961; Talking about Concertos, 1964; Music All Around Me, 1968; Lucy and Peterkin, 1968; Talking about Sonatas, 1971; Downbeat Guide, 1977; Understanding Music, 1979; The Nine Symphonies of Beethoven, 1980; Songs for Swinging Golfers, 1981; Sounds of Music, 1982; Beating Time (autobiog.), 1982; Pathway to Music, 1983; Musicamusings, 1983; The Concertgoer's Companion: Vol. I, 1984, Vol. II, 1985, one vol. edn, 1993; The Seven Concertos of Beethoven, 1996. *Address:* Woodyard Cottage, Ashridge, Berkhamsted, Herts HP4 1PS. *T:* (01442) 842257.

HOPKINS, Prof. Antony Gerald, PhD; FBA 1996; Walter Prescott Webb Professor of History, University of Texas at Austin, since 2002; *b* 21 Feb. 1938; *s* of George Henry Hopkins and Queenie Ethel (*née* Knight); *m* 1964, Wendy Beech; two *s*. *Educ:* St Paul's Sch.; QMC, Univ. of London (BA); SOAS (PhD). Asst Lectr, Lectr, then Reader, 1964–77, Prof. of Economic History, 1977–88, Univ. of Birmingham; Prof. of Internat. History, Grad. Inst. of Internat. Studies, Univ. of Geneva, 1988–94; Smuts Prof. of Commonwealth History, Univ. of Cambridge, 1994–2002. DUniv Stirling, 1996. Forkosch Prize, Amer. Historical Assoc., 1995. *Publications:* An Economic History of West Africa, 1973, revd 1988; (with P. J. Cain) British Imperialism: innovation and expansion 1688–1914, 1993, (with P. J. Cain) British Imperialism: crisis and deconstruction 1914–90, 1993, joint 2nd edn as British Imperialism 1688–2000, 2001; (ed) Globalization in World History, 2002; (ed) Global History: interactions between the universal and the local, 2006; articles in learned jls. *Recreation:* worrying. *Address:* Department of History, University of Texas, 1 University Station, Garrison Hall, B7000, Austin, TX 78712–1163, USA.

HOPKINS, Prof. Colin Russell, PhD; Professor of Molecular Cell Biology, Imperial College of Science, Technology and Medicine, since 2000; *b* 4 June 1939; *s* of Bleddyn Hopkins and Vivienne Russell (*née* Jenkins); *m* 1964, Hilary Floyd; one *s* one *d*. *Educ:* UC, Swansea, Univ. of Wales (BSc; PhD 1964). University of Liverpool: Asst Lectr, Dept of Physiol., Med. Sch., 1964–66; Lectr, Dept of Histology, 1966–70; Sen. Lectr, Dept of Histology and Cell Biol. (Medical), 1971–75; Fulbright Fellow, Dept of Cell Biol., 1970, Fulbright Travelling Schol. and Vis. Associate Prof., 1971–72, Rockefeller Univ., NY; Prof. and Head, Dept of Medical Cell Biol., Univ. of Liverpool, 1975–86; Rank Prof. of Physiological Biochem., ICSTM, 1986–91; Dir, MRC Lab. for Molecular Cell Biol., UCL, 1991–2000. *Publications:* Cell Structure and Function, 1964; numerous scientific papers. *Recreations:* natural history, music. *Address:* Faculty of Life Sciences, Imperial College of Science, Technology and Medicine, Exhibition Road, SW7 2AZ. *T:* (020) 7594 5220; *e-mail:* c.hopkins@ic.ac.uk.

HOPKINS, David Rex Eugène; Director of Quality Assurance/Administration, Ministry of Defence, 1983–90; *b* 29 June 1930; *s* of late Frank Hopkins and Vera (*née* Wimhurst); *m* 1st, 1955, Brenda Joyce Phillips (*d* 2005); two *s* one *d* (and one *d* decd); 2nd, 2006, Gwyneth Vick (*née* Rees). *Educ:* Worthing High Sch.; Christ Church, Oxford (MA 1950; Dip. in Econs and Pol Science, 1951). National Service Commn, RA, 1952; service in Korea. Asst Principal, WO, 1953; Principal, WO, 1957, MoD 1964; Asst Sec., 1967; Home Office, 1969–70; RCDS, 1971; Defence Equipment Secretariat, 1972; Dir, Headquarters Security, 1975; Financial Counsellor, UK Delegn to NATO, 1981–83. *Recreations:* church life, travel, fell-walking, military history. *Address:* 6 Hitherwood Court, SE19 1UX. *T:* (020) 8670 7504.

HOPKINS, Prof. David William Richard, PhD; HSBC Professor of International Leadership, Institute of Education, University of London, since 2005; *b* 30 Jan. 1949; *s* of David Clifford Hopkins and Thelma Hopkins; *m* 1985, Marloes de Groot; two *s* one *d*. *Educ:* Univ. of Reading (BA Hons Politics 1970); UCNW, Bangor (PGCE 1971); Univ. of Sheffield (MEd 1976); Simon Fraser Univ., BC (PhD 1980). Outward Bound instructor, 1969–72; teacher, Minsthorpe High Sch. and Community Coll., 1973–75; mountain guide and grad. student, 1976–80; Lectr, Simon Fraser Univ., BC, 1980–82; Sen. Lectr, W Glam Inst. for Higher Educn, 1983–85; Tutor, Inst. of Educn, Univ. of Cambridge, 1985–96; Prof., Hd of Sch. and Dean of Educn, Univ. of Nottingham, 1996–2002; now Emeritus; Dir, Standards and Effectiveness Unit, DfES, 2002–05. Hon. Prof., Univ. of Hull, 2002; Professorial Fellow, Univ. of Melbourne, 2005. Chm., Leicester City Partnership Bd, 1999–2002. Chm., Professional Standards Cttee, British Mountain Guides, 1997–2002. Mem., All Souls Gp, 2003. Freeman, Guild of Educators, 2005. IFMGA 1978; FRSA 2002. *Publications:* over 30 books including: A Teacher's Guide to Classroom Research, 1985, 3rd edn 2002; Evaluation for School Development, 1989; (jtly) The Empowered School, 1991; (jtly) Personal Growth through Adventure, 1993; (jtly) School Improvement in an Era of Change, 1994; Improving the Quality of Education for All, 1996, 2nd edn 2002; (jtly) Models of Learning, 1997, 2nd edn 2002; (ed jtly) The International Handbook of Educational Change, 4 vols, 1998; (jtly) Improving Schools: performance and potential, 1999; School Improvement for Real, 2001; Every School a Great School, 2007; contrib. numerous articles on educn. *Recreations:* mountaineering, ski-ing, modern literature, current affairs, friends and family. *Address:* Old Southgate, 47 Luton Road, Harpenden, Herts AL5 2UB; Les Hautes Aiguilles, 74400 Argentière-Mt Blanc, France. *Clubs:* Alpine; Climbers'.

HOPKINS, Elizabeth Ann; Clerk, House of Lords, 1998–2000; *b* 25 Sept. 1941; *d* of Philip G. H. Hopkins and Edith A. I. (Nessie) Hopkins (*née* Holmes). *Educ:* Parkstone Grammar Sch.; King Edward VI High Sch., Birmingham; Lady Margaret Hall, Oxford (BA Hons); Univ. of Ibadan (MSc); Univ. of Sussex (DPhil). Asst Lectr, Univ. of Sussex, 1965–68; Res. Officer, Inst. of Develt Studies, Sussex, 1968–72; Economist, Govt of Zambia, 1972–76; DoE, 1977–86; Dept of Transport (Channel Tunnel; Internat. Aviation), 1986–90; Regl Dir (SW), Depts of the Envmt and of Transport, 1990–93; Dir of Finance, Dept of Transport, 1993–95; Financial Mgt Advr, Dept of Transport, S Africa, 1995–96; Clerk/Advr, H of C Select Cttee on Eur. Legislation, 1997–98. Dep. Chm., FARM-Africa, 2001–07. *Recreation:* travel. *Address:* 33 Barkston Gardens, SW5 0ER. *T:* (020) 7370 7981; *e-mail:* elizabeth.hopkins@btinternet.com.

HOPKINS, John Humphrey David; Golf Correspondent, The Times, since 1993; *b* 26 March 1945; *s* of Leslie Charles Hopkins and late Mary Eileen Hopkins (*née* Ellis); *m* 1970, Suzanne Ernestine Kommenda (marr. diss. 1998); one *s* one *d*. *Educ:* Llandaff Cathedral Sch., Cardiff (Choral Schol.); Wrekin Coll., Telford, Salop. Sunday Times: Rugby Corresp., 1976–80; Golf Corresp., 1980–91; golf and Rugby writer, Financial Times, 1991–93. *Publications:* Life with the Lions, 1977; The British Lions, 1980; Nick Faldo in Perspective, 1985; Golf: the four Majors, 1988; Golfer's Companion, 1990; Golf in Wales: the Centenary 1895–1995, 1995. *Recreations:* squash, golf, Rugby, theatre, reading. *Address:* c/o The Times, 1 Pennington Street, E98 1TT. *T:* (020) 7782 5944. *Clubs:* Royal Automobile, MCC; Jesters; Cardiff and County (Cardiff); Royal and Ancient (St Andrews), Royal Porthcawl.

HOPKINS, Julian; *see* Hopkins, R. J.

HOPKINS, Kelvin Peter; MP (Lab) Luton North, since 1997; *b* 22 Aug. 1941; *s* of late Prof. Harold Horace Hopkins, FRS and Joan Avery Frost; *m* 1965, Patricia Mabel Langley; one *s* one *d*. *Educ:* Nottingham Univ. (BA Hons Politics, Economics, Maths with Stats). Economic Dept, TUC, 1969–70 and 1973–77; Lectr, St Albans Coll. of Further Educn, 1971–73; Policy and Res. Officer, NALGO, then UNISON, 1977–94. Mem., Public Administration Select Cttee, 2002–. Columnist, Socialist Campaign Gp News, 1998–. Gov., Luton Sixth Form Coll., 1993–. Hon. Fellow, Univ. of Luton, 1993. *Publications:* NALGO papers. *Recreations:* music, photography, theatre, wine, collecting antique glassware. *Address:* House of Commons, Westminster, SW1A 0AA. *T:* (020) 7219 6670; (home) (01582) 722913; 3 Union Street, Luton LU1 3AN. *T:* (01582) 488208.

HOPKINS, Sir Michael (John), Kt 1995; CBE 1989; RA 1992; RIBA; RWA; Founding Partner, Hopkins Architects (formerly Michael Hopkins & Partners), since 1976; *b* 7 May 1935; *s* of late Gerald and Barbara Hopkins; *m* 1962, Patricia Ann Wainwright (*see* P. A. Hopkins); one *s* two *d*. *Educ:* Sherborne Sch.; Architectural Assoc. (AA Dip. 1964). RIBA 1966; RWA 1989. Worked in offices of Sir Basil Spence, Leonard Manasseh and Tom Hancock; partnership with Norman Foster, 1969–75 and with Patricia Hopkins, 1976–; *projects include*: own house and studio, Hampstead, 1976 (RIBA Award, 1977; Civic Trust Award, 1979); brewery bldg for Greene King, 1979 (RIBA Award, 1980); Patera Bldg System, 1984; Res. Centre for Schlumberger, Cambridge, 1984 (RIBA and Civic Trust Awards, 1988); infants sch., Hampshire, 1986 (RIBA and Civic Trust Awards, 1988); Mound (formerly Bicentenary) Stand, Lord's Cricket Ground, 1987 (RIBA, Civic Trust Awards, 1988); R&D Centre, Solid State Logic, 1988 (RIBA Award, 1989; Civic Trust Award, 1990); London office and country workshop for David Mellor, 1989 and 1991 (RIBA Award, 1989; Civic Trust Award, 1990; RIBA Award, 1993); redevelt of Bracken House, St Paul's, for Ohbayashi Corp., 1992 (RIBA Award, 1992; Civic Trust Award, 1994); offices at New Square, Bedfont Lakes, 1992; Glyndebourne Opera House, 1994 (RIBA Award, 1994; Civic Trust Award, 1995); Inland Revenue Centre, Nottingham, 1995 (Civic Trust Award, 1997); Queen's Bldg, Emmanuel Coll., Cambridge, 1995 (RIBA Award, 1996); Lady Sarah Cohen House, 1996; Saga Gp HQ, 1999; Jubilee Campus, Nottingham Univ., 1999 (RIBA and BCI Awards); Dynamic Earth, Edinburgh, 1999 (Civic Trust and RIBA Awards); Westminster Underground Station, 1999 (BCI Award, 2000, Civic Trust Award 2002); Portcullis House, Westminster, 2000 (Civic Trust and RIBA Awards); Wildscreen @ Bristol, 2000 (Civic Trust Award); Pilkington Labs, Sherborne Sch., 2000; Housing, Charterhouse, 2000; Parade Ground, Goodwood Racecourse, 2001 (Civic Trust Award 2003); The Forum, Norwich, 2001; Manchester Art Gall., 2002; Haberdashers' Hall, 2002; Nat. Coll. of Sch. Leadership, Nottingham Univ. (RIBA Award), 2002; GEK HQ, Athens, 2003 (RIBA Award, 2004); Norwich Cathedral Refectory, 2004 (RIBA and Civic Trust Award, 2005); Inn The Park, London, 2004 (Civic Trust Award, 2006); Wellcome Trust HQ, London, 2004 (RIBA Award, 2005); Evelina Children's Hosp., London, 2005 (RIBA and Civic Trust Award, 2006); Utopia, Broughton Hall Pavilion, Yorkshire, 2005 (RIBA Award, 2006, Civic Trust Award, 2007); Alnwick Garden Pavilion, Northumberland, 2006; Shin-Marunouchi Towers, Japan, 2007; LTA's Nat. Tennis Centre, Roehampton, 2007; Dubai Gate Village, 2007; Bryanston Sch. Sci. Bldg, 2007; Faculty of Envmtl Studies, Yale Univ., 2008. Pres., Architectural Assoc., 1997–99 (Vice Pres., 1987–93); Trustee, British Mus., 1993–2004. Hon. FAIA 1996; Hon. FRIAS 1996. Hon. Mem., Bund Architekten, 1996. Dr *hc* RCA 1994; Hon. DLitt Nottingham, 1995; Hon. DTech London Guildhall, 1996. RIBA Royal Gold Medal (with Patricia Hopkins), 1994. *Recreations:* Blackheath, sailing, Catureglio. *Address:* 49A Downshire Hill, NW3 1NX. *T:* (020) 7435 1109; (office) 27 Broadley Terrace, NW1 6LG. *T:* (020) 7724 1751.

HOPKINS, Patricia Ann, (Lady Hopkins); Partner, Hopkins Architects (formerly Michael Hopkins & Partners), since 1976; *b* 7 April 1942; *d* of Denys Wainwright, MB, Dsc, FRCS and Dr Shelagh Wainwright, MB, ChB; *m* 1962, Michael John Hopkins (*see* Sir Michael Hopkins); one *s* two *d*. *Educ:* Wycombe Abbey Sch.; Architectural Assoc. (AA Dip. 1968). Own practice, 1968–76; in partnership with Michael Hopkins, 1976–. Buildings include: own house and studio, Hampstead, 1976 (RIBA Award, 1977; Civic Trust Award, 1979); Hopkins office, Marylebone, London, 1985; Fleet Velmead Infants Sch., Hants, 1986 (RIBA Award, Civic Trust Award, 1988); Masterplan, 1988, Raphael Cartoon Gall., 1993, V&A Mus.; Glyndebourne Opera House, 1994 (RIBA Award, Royal Fine Art Commn Award, 1994; Civic Trust Award, FT Award, 1995); Queen's

Bldg, Emmanuel Coll., Cambridge, 1995 (RIBA Award, Royal Fine Art Commn Award, 1996); Jewish Care residential home for the elderly, 1996; Preachers Court, Charterhouse, 2000; Wildscreen @ Bristol, 2000 (Civic Trust, DTLR Urban Design Awards); Haberdashers' Hall, 2002 (Wood Award, 2003); Manchester Art Gall., 2002 (RIBA Award, Civic Trust Award, 2003). Member: Nat. Lottery Bd, Arts Council England (formerly Arts Council of England), 1994–2000; Foundn Campaign Bd, AA, 1994–2000. Trustee, Nat. Gall., 1998–2005. Gov., Queen's Coll., Harley St, 1997–. Hon. FRIAS 1996; Hon. FAIA 1997. Hon. DTech London Guildhall, 1996. *Recreations:* family, friends, Blackheath, Catureglio. *Address:* 49A Downshire Hill, NW3 1NX. *T:* (020) 7435 1109; (office) 27 Broadley Terrace, NW1 6LG. *T:* (020) 7724 1751.

HOPKINS, Sir (Philip) Anthony, Kt 1993; CBE 1987; actor since 1961; *b* Port Talbot, S Wales, 31 Dec. 1937; *s* of late Richard and of Muriel Hopkins; *m* 1st, 1968, Petronella (marr. diss. 1972); one *d*; 2nd, 1973, Jennifer (marr. diss. 2002), *d* of Ronald Lynton; 3rd, 2003, Stella Arroyave. *Educ:* Cowbridge, S Wales; RADA; Cardiff Coll. of Drama. London début as Metellus Cimber in Julius Caesar, Royal Court, 1964; National Theatre: Juno and the Paycock, A Flea in Her Ear, 1966; The Dance of Death, The Three Sisters, As You Like It (all male cast), 1967; The Architect and the Emperor of Assyria, A Woman Killed with Kindness, Coriolanus, 1971; Macbeth, 1972; Pravda, 1985 (Laurence Olivier/Observer Award for outstanding achievements, 1985; (jtly) Best Actor, British Theatre Assoc. and Drama Magazine Awards, 1985; Royal Variety Club Stage Actor Award, 1985); King Lear, 1986; Antony and Cleopatra, 1987. Other stage appearances include: The Taming of the Shrew, Chichester, 1972; Equus, USA, 1974–75, 1977 (Best Actor Award, NY Drama Desk, Amer. Authors and Celebrities Forum Award, Outer Critics Circle Award, 1975; LA Drama Critics' Award, 1977); The Tempest, LA, 1979; Old Times, New York, 1984; The Lonely Road, Old Vic, 1985; M. Butterfly, Shaftesbury, 1989; Director: Dylan Thomas: return journey, Lyric, Hammersmith, 1992; August, Theatr Clwyd, 1994. *Films:* The Lion in Winter, 1968; The Looking Glass War, 1969; Hamlet, 1969; When Eight Bells Toll, 1971; Young Winston, 1972; A Doll's House, 1973; The Girl from Petrovka, 1974; All Creatures Great and Small, 1974; Juggernaut, 1974; Audrey Rose, 1977; A Bridge Too Far, 1977; International Velvet, 1978; Magic, 1978; The Elephant Man, A Change of Seasons, 1980; The Bounty (Variety Club Film Actor Award), 1984; The Good Father, 1986; 84 Charing Cross Road (Best Actor Award, Moscow Film Fest.), 1986; The Dawning, 1988; A Chorus of Disapproval, 1989; Desperate Hours, 1991; The Silence of the Lambs, 1991; (Acad., BAFTA and NY Film Critics Circle, Awards for Best Actor, 1992); Freejack, Howard's End, Chaplin, 1992; Bram Stoker's Dracula, The Trial, The Innocent, The Remains of the Day, 1993 (BAFTA Best Actor Award); Shadowlands, 1994; The Road to Wellville, Legends of the Fall, 1995; Nixon, 1996; August (also dir), 1996; Surviving Picasso, 1996; Amistad, 1998; The Edge, 1998; The Mask of Zorro, 1998; Meet Joe Black, 1999; Instinct, 1999; Titus, 2000; Hannibal, 2001; Hearts in Atlantis, 2002; Bad Company, 2002; Red Dragon, 2002; The Human Stain, 2004; Alexander, 2005; Proof, 2006; The World's Fastest Indian, 2006; Bobby, 2006; All the King's Men, 2006; Fracture, 2007; Beowulf, 2007. *American television films:* QB VII, 1973; Dark Victory, 1975; Bruno Hauptmann in The Lindbergh Kidnapping Case (Emmy Award), 1976; The Voyage of the Mayflower, 1979; The Bunker (Emmy Award, 1981), The Acts of Peter and Paul, 1980; The Hunchback of Notre Dame, 1981; The Arch of Triumph, 1984; Hollywood Wives, 1984; Guilty Conscience, 1984; The Tenth Man, 1988; To Be the Best, 1991; *BBC television:* Pierre Bezukhov in serial, War and Peace (SFTA Best TV Actor award), 1972; Kean, 1978; Othello, 1981; Little Eyolf, 1982; Guy Burgess in Blunt (film), 1987; Donald Campbell in Across the Lake, 1988; Heartland, 1989; Gwyn Thomas: A Few Selected Exits, 1993; Indep. TV performances incl. A Married Man (series), 1983. Fellow, BAFTA, 2008. Hon. Fellow, St David's Coll., Lampeter, 1992. Hon. DLitt Wales, 1988. Commandeur, Ordre des Arts et des Lettres (France), 1996. *Recreations:* reading, walking, piano.

HOPKINS, (Richard) Julian; Director, St Albans Cathedral, 2006; *b* 12 Oct. 1940; *s* of late Richard Robert Hopkins, CBE and Grace Hilda (*née* Hatfield); *m*; two *s* one *d*; *m* 2005, Stella Louise (*née* Marino). *Educ:* Bedford School. Asst Manager, London Palladium, 1963; Central Services Manager, BBC, 1965; joined RSPCA as Accounts Manager, 1972, appointed Admin. and Finance Officer, 1976; Exec. Dir, 1978–82; Gen. Manager, Charity Christmas Card Council, 1982–83; Admin. and Develt Dir, War on Want, 1984–88; Dir, CARE Internat. (UK), 1988–94; Dir, ORBIS USA, ORBIS Internat., NY, 1994–95; Exec. Vice Pres., American SPCA, NY, 1995–2000; Develt Dir, IUCN, Washington, DC, 2000–05. Dir, and Mem. Exec. Cttee, World Soc. for Protection of Animals, 1980–82; Mem., Farm Animal Welfare Council, 1980–83. FCMI. *Publication:* (novel) Conducting Terror, 2007. *Recreations:* all theatre, but especially opera, concert-going, writing, 6 grandchildren. *Address: e-mail:* julianhop@aol.com.

HOPKINS, Russell, OBE 1989; FDSRCS; Consultant Oral and Maxillo-Facial Surgeon, Cardiff Royal Infirmary, 1968–95; Director of Medical Audit, South Glamorgan Health Authority, 1991–95; *b* 30 April 1932; *s* of Charles Albert Hopkins and Frances Doris Hopkins; *m* 1970, Jill Margaret Pexton; two *s* one *d*. *Educ:* Barnard Castle Sch.; King's Coll., Durham Univ. (BDS 1956); Royal Free Hosp., London Univ. LRCP, MRCS 1964; FDSRCS 1961. Gen. dental practice, 1956–58; SHO, Oral Surgery, Nottingham Gen. Hosp., 1958–59; Registrar, Oral Surgery, St Peter's Hosp., Chertsey, 1959–61; Sen. Registrar, Royal Victoria Infirmary, Newcastle upon Tyne, 1965–68; Consultant, 1968–95, Gen. Manager, 1985–91, Univ. Hosp. of Wales, Cardiff. Member: Central Cttee, Hosp. Med. Services, 1975–88; Jt Consultant Cttee, London, 1980–93 (Chm., Welsh Sub-Cttee, 1986–93); Chairman: Med. Bd, S Glamorgan, 1980–82; Welsh Council, BMA, 1991–94 (Chm., Welsh Consultant and Specialist Cttee, 1989–93); BMA Gen. Managers' Gp, 1988–90; Glan-Y-Môr NHS Trust, 1995–99; Brô Morgannwg NHS Trust, 1999–2005 (Lead Chair, 2002–04). Pres., BAOMS 1992–93; Mem., Eur. Assoc. of Max.-Fac. Surgery, 1980–95; Fellow, BMA, 1998. Ext. Examr, Univ. of Hong Kong, 1990–93. *Publications:* Pre-Prosthetic Oral Surgery, 1986; chapters in numerous medical works. *Recreations:* golf, grass cutting, photography, reading. *Address:* 179 Cyncoed Road, Cardiff CF23 6AH. *T:* (home) (029) 2075 2319.

HOPKINS, Sidney Arthur; Managing Director, Guardian Royal Exchange plc, 1990–94; *b* 15 April 1932; *m* 1955, Joan Marion Smith; one *d*. *Educ:* Battersea Grammar Sch. ACII. Joined Royal Exchange Assce, 1948, Man., Organisation and Methods, 1966; Guardian Royal Exchange Assurance Ltd: Chief Claims Man. (UK), 1974; Man., Home Motor, 1976; Asst Gen. Man. (Life), 1979; Guardian Royal Exchange Assurance plc: Asst Gen. Man. (Field Operations), 1983; Gen. Man. (UK), 1985; Guardian Royal Exchange (UK) Ltd: Man. Dir, 1987; Guardian Royal Exchange plc: Dir, 1986; Dep. Chief Exec., 1989. Dir, Residuary MMB, 1994–2002. Freeman, City of London; Liveryman, Company of Insurers. *Recreations:* sports, films. *Address:* Woodlands, 8 Littleworth Lane, Esher, Surrey KT10 9PF. *Club:* Royal Automobile.

HOPKINSON, family name of **Baron Colyton**.

HOPKINSON, Ven. Barnabas John; Archdeacon of Wilts, 1998–2004; *b* 11 May 1939; *s* of Prebendary Stephan Hopkinson and late Mrs Anne Hopkinson; *m* 1968, Esmé Faith (*née* Gibbons); three *d*. *Educ:* Emanuel School; Trinity Coll., Cambridge (MA); Lincol[n] Theological Coll. Curate: All Saints and Martyrs, Langley, Manchester, 1965–67; Great St Mary's, Cambridge, 1967–70; Chaplain, Charterhouse School, 1970–75; Team Vicar [o]f Preshute, Wilts, 1975–81; RD of Marlborough, 1977–81; Rector of Wimborne Minste[r], Dorset, 1981–86; RD of Wimborne, 1985–86; Archdeacon of Sarum, 1986–98; Priest-in-charge, Stratford-sub-Castle, 1987–98. Canon of Salisbury Cathedral, 1983–2004, no[w] Emeritus. *Recreation:* gardening. *Address:* Tanners Cottage, Frog Street, Bampton, Devo[n] EX16 9NT.

HOPKINSON, Prof. Brian Ridley, FRCS; Professor of Vascular Surgery, University [o]f Nottingham, 1996–2003; Consultant General Surgeon, Queen's Medical Centr[e] Nottingham, since 1973; *b* 26 Feb. 1938; *s* of Edward Alban Ernest Hopkinson and Ma[r] Olive Hopkinson (*née* Redding); *m* 1962, Margaret Ruth Bull; three *s* one *d*. *Edu[c]* Birmingham Univ. (MB ChB 1961; ChM 1972). FRCS 1964. Hse Surgeon, 1961–6[2] Resident Surgical Officer, 1964–65, Hallam Hosp., W Bromwich; Registrar, Cardia[c] Surgery, Queen Elizabeth Hosp., Birmingham, 1965–66; Buswell Res. Fellow, Buffal[o] NY, 1966–67; Sen. Surgical Registrar, Birmingham Gen. Hosp. and Wolverhampto[n] Royal Infirmary, 1967–69; Lectr in Surgery, Univ. of Birmingham, 1969–73; Consultan[t] Gen. Surgeon specialising in vascular surgery, Queen's Med. Centre, Nottingham 1973–96. Hon. Prof., Chinese Med. Univ., Shenyang, China, 1999. Various BMA pos[ts] including: Sec. and Chm., Nottingham Div., 1975–83; Chm., Trent Regl Counci[l] 1992–95; Chm., Regl Consultant and Specialist Cttee, 1987–92; Chm., Annual Rep[s] Meeting, 1998–2001. Licensed Lay Reader, C of E, St Jude's, Mapperley. *Publications* Endovascular Surgery for Aortic Aneurysms, 1997; Operative Atlas of Endovascula[r] Aneurysm Surgery, 1999; contrib. Lancet. *Recreations:* swimming, motor caravanning, coa[l] fired steamboats. *Address:* Lincolnsfield, 18 Victoria Crescent, Private Road, Sherwood Nottingham NG5 4DA. *T:* (0115) 960 4167.

HOPKINSON, Bryan; Strategy Co-ordinator, United Nations Mission in Kosovo 2006–08; Political Consultant, Skorgg International, since 2000; *b* 24 Nov. 1956; *s* o[f] Brian Hopkinson and Florance Hopkinson (*née* Richardson), Huddersfield; *m* 1987 Stephanie Burd (*née* Perkins). *Educ:* King James's Grammar Sch., Huddersfield; King' Coll., Cambridge (BA, MA). Joined FCO, 1980; Kampala, 1981–84; songwriter an[d] musician, 1985–87; rejoined FCO, 1987; Lisbon, 1989–93; FCO, 1993–95; Ambassado[r] to Bosnia-Hercegovina, 1995–96; Hon. Dir, British Council, Sarajevo, 1995–9[6] International Crisis Group: Director: Bosnia Proj., Sarajevo, Jan.–July 1999; Kosovo Proj. Pristina, July–Dec. 1999; Montenegro Proj., Podgorica, Jan.–June 2000; Political Di[r] OSCE Mission in Kosovo, 2002–04. *Publications:* numerous Balkans reports. *Recreations* walking, music, board and computer games. *Address:* Apt 206, 1535 The Melting Point Commercial Street, Huddersfield, W Yorks HD1 3DN. *T:* (01484) 469804.

HOPKINSON, Prof. David Albert, MD; Professor of Human Biochemical Genetics University College London, 1993–2000, now Emeritus; Director, Medical Researc[h] Council Human Biochemical Genetics Unit, 1976–2000; *b* 26 June 1935; *s* of Georg[e] Albert and Lily Hopkinson; *m* 1st, 1959, Josephine Manze; two *s* one *d*; 2nd, 1980 Yvonne Edwards. *Educ:* Chesterfield Grammar Sch.; St Catharine's Coll., Cambridge Royal London Hosp. Med. Coll. (MA, MD). Royal London Hospital: House Surgeo[n] and House Physician, 1959–60; Jun. Lectr, Biochem., 1960; Resident Pathologist, 1961 Scientific Staff, MRC Human Biochemical Genetics Unit, 1962–2000. Hon. Life Mem. Internat. Forensic Haemogenetics Soc., 1992. *Publication:* Handbook of Enzym[e] Electrophoresis in Human Genetics, 1976. *Recreations:* vegetable gardening, hill an[d] mountain walking, furniture restoration, watching Rugby. *Address:* Swan Cottage, 4[?] Church Street, Great Missenden, Bucks HP16 0AZ.

HOPKINSON, David Hugh; editorial consultant, The Times, 1995–2005; *b* 9 Jun[e] 1930; *er s* of late C. G. Hopkinson; *m* Patricia Ann Eaton; one *s* one *d*; and three *s* one by previous marriage. *Educ:* Sowerby Bridge Grammar Sch. Entered journalism o[n] Huddersfield Examiner, 1950; Yorkshire Observer, 1954; Yorkshire Evening News 1954; Evening Chronicle, Manchester, 1956; Chief Sub-Editor, Sunday Graphic London, 1957; Asst Editor, Evening Chronicle, Newcastle upon Tyne, 1959; Chief Ass[t] Editor, Sunday Graphic, 1960; Dep. Editor, Sheffield Telegraph, 1961, Editor, 1962–64 Editor, The Birmingham Post, 1964–73; Dir, Birmingham Post & Mail Ltd, 1967–80 Editor, Birmingham Evening Mail, 1974–79; Editor-in-Chief, Evening Mail series 1975–79, Birmingham Post and Evening Mail, 1979–80; The Times: Asst to Editor, 1981 Chief Night Ed., 1982–89; Dep. Man. Ed., 1990–95. Mem., Lord Justice Phillimore' Cttee inquiring into law of contempt. National Press Award, Journalist of the Year, 1963 *Address:* c/o The Times, 1 Pennington Street, E98 1TT.

HOPKINSON, David Hugh Laing, CBE 1986; RD 1965; DL; Deputy Chairman an[d] Chief Executive, M&G Group PLC, 1979–87; Chairman, Harrisons and Crosfield 1988–91 (Deputy Chairman, 1987–88, Director, 1986–91); Deputy Chairman, ECC Group (formerly English China Clays), 1986–91 (Director, since 1975); *b* 14 Aug. 1926 *s* of late Cecil Hopkinson and Leila Hopkinson; *m* 1951, Prudence Margaret Holmes OBE, JP, DL; two *s* two *d*. *Educ:* Wellington Coll.; Merton Coll., Oxford (BA 1949) RNVR and RNR, 1944–65. A Clerk of the House of Commons, 1948–59; Rober[t] Fleming, 1959–62; M&G Investment Management, 1963–87 (Chm., 1975–87); Director Lloyds Bank Southern Regional Board, 1977–88; BR (Southern) Bd, 1978–87 (Chm. 1983–87); Wolverhampton and Dudley Breweries, 1987–96; Mem., Adv. Gp o[n] Governor of Bank of England, 1984. Mem., Housing Corp., 1986–88. Director: English Chamber Orchestra and Music Soc., 1970–89; Charities Investment Managers, 1970–; Merchants Trust, 1976–99; RTZ Pension Trustees, 1993–99; SE Arts Board, 1994–97 Member: General Synod of C of E, 1970–90; Central Bd of Finance, 1970–90; a Church Comr, 1973–82, 1984–94; Mem., Chichester Dio. Bd of Finance, 1970–2001 (Chm. 1977–88); Chm., Chichester Cathedral Finance Cttee, 2000–05. Chm., Church Army Bd 1987–89. Trustee: Nat. Assoc. of Almshouses; Chichester Cathedral Development Trust Pallant House Gall., Chichester, 1992–2002 (Chm. of Trustees); Royal Pavilion Brighton; RAM Foundn; Edward James Foundn, 1990–2002 (Chm.). Governor Sherborne Sch., 1970–96 (Vice-Chm., Bd, 1987–96); Wellington Coll., 1978–96. DL 1986, High Sheriff, 1987–88, W Sussex. Hon. Fellow: St Anne's Coll., Oxford, 1984–, Chichester Univ., 2007–. Dist. Friend, Univ. of Oxford, 2007. *Recreations:* travelling, walking, opera. *Address:* St John's Priory, Poling, Arundel, W Sussex BN18 9PS. *T:* (01903) 882393. *Club:* Brooks's.

HOPKINSON, George William; Deputy Director and Director of Studies, Royal Institute of International Affairs, 1999–2000; retired writer and speaker on international relations; *b* 13 Sept. 1943; *s* of William Hartley Hopkinson and Mary (*née* Ashmore); *m* 1973, Mary Agnes Coverdale (marr. diss. 1997); one *s*. *Educ:* Tupton Hall Grammar Sch.; Pembroke Coll., Cambridge (BA 1965; MA 1969). Inland Revenue, 1965–73; CSD, 1973–81; HM Treasury, 1981–86; Ministry of Defence, 1986–97: Hd, Defence Arms Control Unit, 1988–91; Vis. Fellow, Global Security Programme, Cambridge Univ., 1991–92 (on secondment); Hd, Defence Lands Service, 1992–93; Asst Under-Sec. of State (Policy) 1993–97; Royal Institute of International Affairs: Hd of Internat. Security Prog.,

1997–99. Associate Fellow: RUSI, 1997–2008; RIIA, 2000–03; Sen. Vis. Fellow, WEU Inst., Paris, 2001. *Publications:* The Making of British Defence Policy, 2000; The Atlantic Crises, Britain, Europe and Parting from the United States, 2005; contribs to books on security policy, international affairs and arms control; occasional papers. *Recreations:* reading, walking. *Address:* Gloucester House, The Southend, Ledbury, Herefordshire HR8 2HD. *Club:* Oxford and Cambridge.

HOPKINSON, Giles, CB 1990; Under-Secretary, Departments of the Environment and Transport, 1976–90, retired; *b* 20 Nov. 1931; *s* of late Arthur John Hopkinson, CIE, ICS, and Eleanor (*née* Richardson); *m* 1956, Eleanor Jean Riddell; three *d. Educ:* Marlborough Coll.; Leeds Univ. (BSc). E. & J. Richardson Ltd, 1956–57; Forestal Land, Timber and Rly Co. Ltd, 1957–58; DSIR: Scientific Officer, 1958–61; Sen. Scientific Officer, 1961–64; Private Sec. to Perm. Sec., 1963–64; Principal, MoT, 1964–71; Asst Sec., DoE, 1971; Under-Secretary: DoE (Personnel Mgt and Trng), 1976; Dept of Transport (Ports and Freight Directorate), 1979; Dir, London Region, PSA, DoE, 1983–90. *Recreations:* music, painting, restoration of antique furniture, church bellringing. *Address:* 12 Barn Hill, Stamford, Lincs PE9 2AE. *Club:* Royal Commonwealth Society.

HOPKINSON, Maj.-Gen. John Charles Oswald Rooke, CB 1984; Director, British Field Sports Society, 1984–93; *b* 31 July 1931; *s* of Lt-Col John Oliver Hopkinson and Aileen Disney Hopkinson (*née* Rooke); *m* 1956, Sarah Elizabeth, *d* of Maj.-Gen. M. H. P. Sayers, OBE; three *s* one *d. Educ:* Stonyhurst Coll.; RMA, Sandhurst. sc 1963, jssc 1968, rcds 1979. Commanding Officer, 1st Bn Queen's Own Highlanders, 1972–74 (despatches); Dep. Comdr 2nd Armoured Division, and Comdr Osnabrück Garrison, 1977–78; Director Operational Requirements 3 (Army), 1980–82; Chief-of-Staff, HQ Allied Forces Northern Europe, 1982–84. Colonel, Queen's Own Highlanders, 1983–94. Chm., Wye Salmon Fishery Owners Assoc., 1993–2002; Vice-Chm., Atlantic Salmon Trust, 1995–2004. Dir, Green Bottom Property Co. Ltd, 1995–2007. Trustee, Wye Foundn, 1996–2005. *Recreations:* shooting, fishing, sailing. *Address:* Bigsweir, Gloucestershire. *Club:* Army and Navy.

HOPKINSON, John Edmund; Judge of the High Court, Hong Kong, 1985–89, retired; *b* 25 Oct. 1924; *s* of Captain E. H. Hopkinson, OBE, RN and Mrs E. H. Hopkinson; *m* 1961, Inge Gansel; one *s* one *d. Educ:* Marlborough Coll., Wilts; Pembroke Coll., Cambridge (MA). Called to the Bar, Lincoln's Inn, 1949. Served War, RN, 1943–46: Ordinary Seaman, Midshipman RNVR, 1943; Sub-Lt RNVR, 1944–46. Prudential Assurance Co., 1949–50; Legal Asst, Colonial Office, 1950–55; Resident Magistrate and Crown Counsel, Uganda, 1955–62; Hong Kong, 1962–89: Crown Counsel, 1962; Principal Crown Counsel, 1972; Dist Judge, 1974. *Recreations:* golf, tennis, ski-ing, music. *Address:* 41 Clavering Avenue, SW13 8DX. *Clubs:* Roehampton; Royal Cinque Ports Golf.

HOPKINSON, Simon Charles; restaurateur, chef, writer; *b* 5 June 1954; *s* of Bruce and late Dorothie Hopkinson. *Educ:* St John's Coll. Sch., Cambridge (chorister); Trent Coll., Derbyshire. Normandie Hotel, Birtle, 1972; Hat and Feather Restaurant, Knutsford, 1973; St Non's Hotel, St David's, 1973–74; Druidstone Hotel, Broadhaven, 1974–75; chef and proprietor: Shed Restaurant, Dinas, 1975–77; Hoppy's Restaurant, 1977–78; Egon Ronay Inspector, 1978–80; private chef, London, 1980–83; Hilaire Restaurant, Kensington, 1983–87; co-proprietor, Bibendum, 1987– (head chef, 1987–95). Cookery writer for The Independent and Food Illustrated. Awards: Glenfiddich, 1995, 1997, 1998, 2000; André Simon Meml, 1995. *Publications:* (with Lindsey Bareham) Roast Chicken and Other Stories, 1994; (contrib.) The Conran Cook Book, 1997; (with Lindsey Bareham) The Prawn Cocktail Years, 1997; Gammon & Spinach, 1998; Roast Chicken and Other Stories: Second Helpings, 2001; Week In Week Out, 2007. *Recreations:* poker, wine. *Address:* c/o David Higham Associates, 5–8 Lower John Street, Golden Square, W1R 4HA. *T:* (020) 7437 7888.

HOPKIRK, Jennifer; Vice Lord-Lieutenant for Buckinghamshire, since 2006; *b* 4 Dec. 1941; *d* of Bertie and Lilian Manser; *m* 1967, Paddy Hopkirk; two *s* one *d. Educ:* Clifton High Sch., Bristol; St Godric's, Hampstead. Commercial TV film prodn, 1960–69. Various posts with Central London Cttee, RNLI, 1977–2004; Mem., NSPCC, 1985– (Chm., Penn Dist Cttee, 1994–97; Hon. Sec., S and Mid Bucks Br., 1998–2001; Chm., Bucks Br., 2006–); Co Vice-Chm., British Paraplegic Sports Soc., 1986–94 (London Cttee). Patron: Chilterns MS Centre, 2006–; Buckinghamshire Foundn, 2006–. Ambassador for Bucks, 2005–. High Sheriff, Bucks, 2005–06. *Recreations:* reading, gardening, tennis, bridge, Lucas Terriers, 4 grand-daughters. *Address:* Penn, Buckinghamshire. *Club:* Queen's.

HOPKIRK, Joyce, (Mrs W. J. Lear); *b* 2 March; *d* of Walter Nicholson and Veronica (*née* Keelan); *m* 1st, 1962, Peter Hopkirk; one *d*; 2nd, 1974, William James Lear; one *s. Educ:* Middle Street Secondary Sch., Newcastle upon Tyne. Reporter, Gateshead Post, 1955; Founder Editor, Majorcan News, 1959; Reporter, Daily Sketch, 1960; Royal Reporter, Daily Express, 1961; Ed., Fashion Magazine, 1967; Women's Ed., Sun, 1967; Launch Ed., Cosmopolitan, 1971–72 (launched 1972); Asst Ed., Daily Mirror, 1973–78; Women's Ed., Sunday Times, 1982; Editl Dir, Elle, 1984; Asst Ed., Sunday Mirror, 1985; Ed.-in-Chief, She Magazine, 1986–89; Dir, Editors' Unlimited, 1990–92; Founder Ed., Chic Magazine 1994. Mem., Competition Commn, 1999–2004. Co-Chm., PPA Awards, 1998. Editor of the Year, 1972; Women's Magazines Editor of the Year, 1988. FRSA. *Publications:* Successful Slimming, 1976; Successful Slimming Cookbook, 1978; (jtly) Splash!, 1995; (jtly) Best of Enemies, 1996; (jtly) Double Trouble, 1997; Unfinished Business, 1998; Relative Strangers, 1999; The Affair, 2000. *Recreations:* conversation, sleeping, gardening, ski-ing, boating.

HOPKIRK, Peter; author and traveller; *b* 15 Dec. 1930; *s* of Rev. Frank Stuart Hopkirk and Mary Hopkirk; *m* 1970, Kathleen Partridge; one *s* one *d. Educ:* Dragon Sch., Oxford; Marlborough. Military service, 1949–51: Subaltern, 4th (Uganda) Bn, KAR; served ex-Italian Somaliland and Kenya. Reporter, Sunday Express, London, 1954–56 (Algerian War, 1956); Ed., Drum (W African news mag.), 1956–57; ITN reporter and newscaster, London, 1958–59; foreign corresp., Daily Express, 1959–62: NY Bureau, 1960–61 (imprisoned Havana, 1961, Bay of Pigs invasion); Beirut corresp., 1962 (expelled); various writing assignments abroad, 1962–64, incl. China, Africa (visiting Albert Schweitzer at Lambaréné leper hosp.), and resident corresp., Istanbul; joined IPC newspapers, London, 1964; assigned to open group's first Moscow bureau, but visa blocked by Soviets; staff reporter, The Times, London, 1966–85: (June 1967 War, Cairo); Chief Reporter, later ME and FE specialist (hijacked by Arab terrorists, 1974). Sir Percy Sykes Meml Medal, RSAA, 1999. *Publications:* Foreign Devils on the Silk Road, 1980; Trespassers on the Roof of the World, 1982; Setting the East Ablaze, 1984; The Great Game, 1990; On Secret Service East of Constantinople, 1994; Quest for Kim, 1996; trans of books in 15 langs incl. Russian, Chinese, Turkish and Japanese. *Recreation:* collecting early picture postcards of Middle East and Central Asia. *Address:* c/o John Murray, 50 Albemarle Street, W1X 4BD.

HOPPEN, Prof. (Karl) Theodore, PhD; FBA 2001; FRHistS; Professor of History, University of Hull, 1996–2003; *b* 27 Nov. 1941; *s* of Paul Ernst Theodore Hoppen and Edith Margaretha Hoppen (*née* Van Brussel); *m* 1st, 1970, Alison Mary Buchan (*d* 2002); one *s* two *d*; 2nd, 2007, Anne Patricia Drakeford. *Educ:* Glenstal Abbey Sch., Co. Limerick; University Coll., Dublin (BA 1961; MA 1964); Trinity Coll., Cambridge (PhD 1967). University of Hull: Asst Lectr, 1966–68; Lectr, 1968–74; Sen. Lectr, 1974–86; Reader, 1986–96. Benjamin Duke Fellow, Nat. Humanities Center, NC, 1985–86; Vis. Fellow, Sidney Sussex Coll., Cambridge, 1988; Res. Reader in Humanities, British Acad., 1994–96. FRHistS 1978. *Publications:* The Common Scientist in the Seventeenth Century, 1970, 2nd edn 2008; (ed) Papers of the Dublin Philosophical Society 1683–1709, 1982, 2nd edn 2008; Elections, Politics and Society in Ireland 1832–1885, 1984; Ireland since 1800: conflict and conformity, 1989, 2nd edn 1999; The Mid-Victorian Generation 1846–1886, vol. in New Oxford History of England, 1998; contrib. numerous articles to learned jls. *Recreations:* idleness, bel canto operas. *Address:* 1 Greyfriars Crescent, Beverley HU17 8LR. *T:* (01482) 861343; *e-mail:* K.T.Hoppen@hull.ac.uk. *Club:* Oxford and Cambridge.

HOPPER, Prof. Andrew, CBE 2007; PhD; FRS 2006; FREng, FIET; Professor of Computer Technology and Head of Department, Computer Laboratory, University of Cambridge, since 2004; Fellow, Corpus Christi College, Cambridge, since 1981; *b* Warsaw, Poland, 9 May 1953; *s* of William John Hopper and Maria Barbara Wyrzykowska; *m* 1988, Prof. Alison Gail Smith; one *s* one *d. Educ:* Quintin Kynaston Sch., London; University Coll. of Swansea (BSc); Trinity Hall, Cambridge (PhD 1978). FREng (FEng 1996); FIET (FIEE 1993). University of Cambridge: Res. Asst, 1977–79; Asst Lectr, 1979–83; Lectr, 1983–92; Reader in Computer Technol., 1992–97; Prof. of Communications, Dept of Engrg, 1997–2004; Dir of Studies in Computer Sci., Corpus Christi Coll., 1981–93. Res. Dir, Acorn Computers Ltd, Cambridge, 1979–84; Man. Dir, Olivetti Oracle Res. Lab., Cambridge, subseq. AT&T Labs Cambridge, 1986–2002; Director: Qudos Ltd, Cambridge, 1985–89; Virata Corp. (formerly Advanced Telecommunications Modules Ltd), 1993–2001; Acorn Computer Gp plc, Cambridge, 1996–98; Adaptive Broadband Ltd, 1998–2001; Telemedia Systems Ltd, Cambridge, 2000–03 (Chm., 1995–2003); Real VNC Ltd, 2002– (Chm., 2002–); Solarflare Inc. (formerly Level 5 Networks Ltd), 2002–; Ubisense (formerly Ubiquitous Systems) Ltd, 2003– (Chm., 2006–); Chairman: Cambridge Broadband Ltd, 2000–05; Adventiq Ltd, Cambridge, 2005–; Vice-Pres., Res., Ing. C. Olivetti & C., SpA, Italy, 1993–98. Clifford Paterson Lecture, Royal Soc., 1999. Silver Medal, Royal Acad. of Engrg, 2003; Sigmobile, outstanding contribn award, ACM (USA), 2004; Mountbatten Medal, IEE, 2004. *Publication:* (jtly) Local Area Network Design, 1986. *Recreations:* ski-ing (Univ. of Cambridge Half Blue), flying, farming. *Address:* Computer Laboratory, William Gates Building, J. J. Thomson Avenue, Cambridge CB3 0FD.

HOPPER, Andrew Christopher Graham; QC 2001; *b* 1 Oct. 1948; *s* of late Hugh Christopher Hopper and Doreen Adele Hopper (*née* Harper); *m* 1980, Rosamund Heather Towers. *Educ:* Monkton Combe Sch., Bath. Admitted solicitor, 1972; Higher Courts (Civil) Qualification 1994; Partner, Adams & Black, Cardiff, 1972–88 (Sen. Partner, 1982–88); HM Dep. Coroner for S Glamorgan, 1977–83; estabd own practice, 1988; Consultant: Cartwrights Adams & Black, Cardiff, 1988–2003; Jay Benning & Peltz, 1997–2000; Geoffrey Williams and Christopher Green, Cardiff, 1998–; Radcliffes Le Brasseur (formerly Radcliffes), 2001–; MLM Cartwright (formerly Cartwrights Adams & Black, then Cartwright Black), Cardiff, 2003–. Mem., Disciplinary Prosecuting Panel, Law Soc., 1979–2002. *Publications:* (ed) Cordery on Solicitors, 9th edn, 1995, 10th edn, 1999; (contrib.) Legal Problems in Emergency Medicine, 1996; (ed) Guide to Professional Conduct of Solicitors, 8th edn, 1999; (with Gregory Treverton-Jones) The Solicitor's Handbook, 2008; (ed) Halsbury's Laws of England, 5th edn, 2008. *Recreation:* mostly Burgundy. *Address:* PO Box 7, Pontyclun, Mid Glamorgan CF72 9XN.

HOPPER, Shami; *see* Chakrabarti, S.

HOPPER, Prof. Stephen Donald, PhD; FLS; Director, Royal Botanic Gardens, Kew, since 2006; *b* 18 June 1951; *s* of Donald Arthur Hopper and Patricia Love Hopper; *m* 1975, Christine Rigden; two *s* one *d. Educ:* Univ. of Western Australia (BSc 1st Cl. Hons 1973; PhD 1978). Pt-time music teacher (guitar and mandolin), Zenith Music, Claremont, WA, 1970–75; botany lab. demonstrator, Univ. of WA, 1973–77; contractual botanist, Western Australian Herbarium, Dept of Agriculture, 1977; Res. Officer (flora conservation), Dept of Fisheries and Wildlife, 1977–85; Sen. Res. Scientist, flora conservation, 1985–88, Sen. Principal Res. Scientist and Officer i/c, 1988–92, Dept of Conservation and Land Mgt, Western Australian Wildlife Res. Centre; Dir, Kings Park and Botanic Garden, Perth, WA, 1992–99; CEO, Botanic Gdns and Park Authy (which manages Kings Park and Botanic Gdn and Bold Park), 1999–2004; Foundn Prof. of Plant Conservation Biol., Univ. of WA, 2004–06. Co-presenter, TV prog., The West, 2003. Corresp. Mem., Botanical Soc. of America, 2007. FLS 2007. *Publications:* (jtly) Western Australia's Endangered Flora, 1990; (jtly) Leaf and Branch, 1990; (jtly) The Banksia Atlas, 1991; Kangaroo Paws and Catspaws, 1993; (ed jtly) Gondwanan Heritage, 1996; (with P. Nikulinsky) Life on the Rocks, 1999; (with P. Nikulinsky) Soul of the Desert, 2005; jl articles and scientific papers. *Recreations:* music, walking, photography, travelling. *Address:* Royal Botanic Gardens, Kew, Richmond, Surrey TW9 3AB. *T:* (020) 8332 5112, *Fax:* (020) 8332 5109; *e-mail:* director@kew.org.

HOPPER, William Joseph; Executive Chairman, WJ Hopper & Co. Ltd, investment bankers and placement agents, since 1996; *b* 9 Aug. 1929; *s* of I. Vance Hopper and Jennie Josephine Hopper; one *d* by a former marriage. *Educ:* Langside Elementary Sch., Glasgow; Queen's Park Secondary Sch., Glasgow; Glasgow Univ. (MA 1st Cl. Hons (Mod. Langs) 1953). Educn Officer, RAF, 1953–55. Financial Analyst, W. R. Grace & Co., NY, 1956–59; London Office Manager, H. Hentz & Co., Members, NY Stock Exchange, 1960–66; Gen. Manager, S. G. Warburg & Co. Ltd, 1966–69; Director: Hill Samuel & Co. Ltd, 1969–74; Morgan Grenfell & Co. Ltd, 1974–79 (Adviser, 1979–86) (bond issue for EIB selected as Deal of the Year by Institutional Investor, 1976); Wharf Resources Ltd, Calgary, 1984–87; Manchester Ship Canal Co., 1985–87; Chm., Robust Mouldings, 1986–90; Exec. Chm., Shire Trust, 1986–91; Advr, Yamaichi Internat. (Europe), 1986–88. MEP (C), Greater Manchester West, 1979–84. Co-founder (1969) and first Chm. (now Mem., Exec. Cttee), Inst. for Fiscal Studies, London; Treasurer, Action Resource Centre, 1985–94; Trustee: Nat. Hosp. for Nervous Diseases Develt Fund, 1986–90; Hampstead, Wells and Campden Trust, 1989–2000; Cambodian Arts and Scholarship Foundn, 2004–. Chm. Cttee of Management, Rosslyn Hill Unitarian Chapel, 1995–98. Mem., London Dist and SE Provincial Assembly of Unitarian and Free Christian Churches, 2000–. Governor, Colville Primary Sch., Notting Hill Gate, 1978–80. *Publications:* A Turntable for Capital, 1969; The Puritan Gift: triumph, collapse and revival of an American dream, 2007. *Recreations:* listening to music, garden design. *Address:* 9a Flask Walk, Hampstead, NW3 1HJ. *T:* (020) 7435 6414, *Fax:* (020) 7431 5568; *e-mail:* will.hopper@wjhopper.com. *Clubs:* Garrick, Royal Air Force.

HOPSON, Christopher Ian; Director, Customer Contact, HM Revenue and Customs, since 2008; *b* 9 April 1963; *s* of David Joseph Hopson and Susan Hopson (*née* Buckingham); *m* 1994, Charlotte Gascoigne; two *s. Educ:* Marlborough Coll.; St Andrew's

Sch., Del, USA (ESU Scholarship); Univ. of Sussex (BA Hons Pols 1985); Cranfield Sch. of Mgt (MBA 1992). Social Democratic Party: constituency agent, 1985–87; Researcher to Rosie Barnes, MP, 1987–88; Dir, Elections and Campaigns, 1988–89; Chief Exec. (Nat. Sec.), 1989; consultant, corporate communications strategy, 1989–91; Pol Advr to Sec. of State, Dept of Nat. Heritage, 1992; Granada Media Group: Corp. Affairs Dir, 1993–99; Bd Dir, 1996–99; Man. Dir, Result e-learning business, 1999–2002; Consultant, DfES, 2002–04; HM Revenue and Customs: Dir, Communications and Mktg, 2005–07; Change and Capability, 2007; Bd Dir, 2006–08. Mem. Council, RTS, 1993–97. Trustee, Foyer Fedn, 1999– (Chm. of Trustees, 2004–). *Recreations:* family, reading, theatre, cinema, football (West Ham), good food and wine (not necessarily in that order). *Address:* HM Revenue and Customs, 100 Parliament Street, SW1A 2BQ. *T:* (020) 7147 2347; *e-mail:* chris.hopson@hmrc.gsi.gov.uk.

HOPWOOD, Prof. Anthony George; American Standard Companies Professor of Operations Management, University of Oxford, and Student of Christ Church, Oxford, 1997–Sept. 2009; *b* 18 May 1944; *s* of late George and Violet Hopwood; *m* 1967, Caryl Davies; two *s*. *Educ:* Hanley High School; LSE (BSc Econ); Univ. of Chicago (MBA, PhD). Fulbright Fellow, Univ. of Chicago, 1965–70; Lectr in Management Accounting, Manchester Business Sch., 1970–73; Senior Staff, Admin. Staff Coll., Henley, 1973–76; Professorial Fellow, Oxford Centre for Management Studies, 1976–78; ICA Prof. of Accounting and Financial Reporting, London Business Sch., 1978–85; Arthur Young, subseq. Ernst and Young, Prof. of Internat. Accounting and Financial Management, LSE, 1985–95; Oxford University: Prof. of Management Studies, and Fellow, Templeton Coll., 1995–97; School of Management Studies, later Saïd Business School: Dep. Dir, 1995–98; Dir, then Peter Moores Dean, 1999–2006; Visitor, Ashmolean Mus., 2000–03. Vis. Prof. of Management, European Inst. for Advanced Studies in Management, Brussels, 1972– (Pres., 1995–2003; Hon. Fellow, 2003); Associate Fellow, Industrial Relations Research Unit, Univ. of Warwick, 1978–80; Dist. Internat. Vis. Lectr, 1981, Presidential Schol., 2006, Amer. Accounting Assoc. (Lifetime Achievement Award, 2002, 2008); Distinguished Vis. Prof. of Accounting, Pennsylvania State Univ., 1983–88. Foreign Mem., Swedish Royal Soc. of Scis, 2003. Mem., Management and Industrial Relations Cttee, SSRC, 1975–79; Chm., Management Awards Panel, SSRC, 1976–79; Pres., European Accounting Assoc., 1977–79 and 1987–88 (Academic Leadership Award, 2005); Member: Council, Tavistock Inst. of Human Relations, 1981–91; Research Bd, ICA, 1982–98; Dir, Greater London Enterprise Bd, 1985–87. Accounting Advr, EC, 1989–90; Accounting Cons., OECD, 1990–91. Chm., Prince's Foundn for the Built Envmt, 2006–. Editor-in-Chief, Accounting, Organizations and Society, 1976–. Hon. DEcon: Turku Sch. of Econs, Finland, 1989; Gothenburg, 1992; Hon. DSc Lincolnshire and Humberside, 1999; Hon. Dr Mercaturae. Copenhagen Business Sch., 2000; DUniv Siena, 2003. Dist. Academic Award, BAA, 1998. *Publications:* An Accounting System and Managerial Behaviour, 1973; Accounting and Human Behaviour, 1973; (with M. Bromwich) Essays in British Accounting Research, 1981; (with M. Bromwich and J. Shaw) Auditing Research, 1982; (with M. Bromwich) Accounting Standard Setting, 1983; (with H. Schreuder) European Contributions to Accounting Research, 1984; (with C. Tomkins) Issues in Public Sector Accounting, 1984; (with M. Bromwich) Research and Current Issues in Management Accounting, 1986; Accounting from the Outside: the collected papers of Anthony G. Hopwood, 1988; International Pressures for Accounting Change, 1989; (with M. Page and S. Turley) Understanding Accounting in a Changing Environment, 1990; (with M. Bromwich) Accounting and the Law, 1992; (with P. Miller) Accounting as Social and Institutional Practice, 1994; (with C. Leuz and D. Pfaff) The Economics and Politics of Accounting, 2004; (with C. Chapman and M. Shields) Handbook of Management Accounting Research, 2 vols, 2007; articles in learned and professional jls. *Address:* Saïd Business School, University of Oxford, Park End Street, Oxford OX1 1HP. *T:* (01865) 288800.

HOPWOOD, Sir David (Alan), Kt 1994; FRS 1979; John Innes Professor of Genetics, University of East Anglia, Norwich, 1968–98, now Emeritus Professor of Genetics; Head of the Genetics Department, John Innes Centre, 1968–98, now Emeritus Fellow; *b* 19 Aug. 1933; *s* of Herbert Hopwood and Dora Hopwood (*née* Grant); *m* 1962, Joyce Lilian Bloom; two *s* one *d*. *Educ:* Purbrook Park County High Sch., Hants; Lymm Grammar Sch., Cheshire; St John's Coll., Cambridge (MA, PhD; Hon. Fellow, 2007). DSc (Glasgow). Whytehead Major Scholar, St John's Coll., Cambridge, 1951–54; John Stothert Bye-Fellow, Magdalene Coll., Cambridge, 1956–58 (Hon. Fellow, 1991); Res. Fellow, St John's Coll., 1958–61; Univ. Demonstrator, Univ. of Cambridge, 1957–61; Lectr in Genetics, Univ. of Glasgow, 1961–68. Pres., Genetical Soc. of GB, 1985–87. Foreign Fellow, Indian Nat. Science Acad., 1987. Hon. Professor: Chinese Acad. of Med. Scis, 1987; Insts of Microbiology and Plant Physiology, Chinese Acad. of Scis, 1987; Huazhong Agricl Univ., Wuhan, China, 1989; Jiao Tong Univ., Shanghai, 2004; Guangxi Univ., Nanning, China, 2004. Hon. FIBiol 2001. Hon. Fellow: UMIST, 1990; Magdalene Coll., Cambridge, 1992. Hon. Member: Spanish Microbiol. Soc., 1985; Hungarian Acad. of Scis, 1990; Soc. for Gen. Microbiol., 1990 (Pres., 2000–03); Kitasato Inst., Tokyo, 1997. Hon. DSc: Eidgenössische Technische Hochschule, Zürich, 1989; UEA, 1998. Mendel Medal, Czech Acad. of Scis, 1995; Start Mudd Prize, Internat. Union of Microbiol Socs, 2002; Ernst Chain Prize, Imperial Coll. London, 2003; André Lwoff Prize, Fedn of Eur. Microbiol Socs, 2003. *Publications:* Streptomyces in Nature and Medicine, 2007; numerous articles and chapters in scientific jls and books. *Recreations:* cooking, gardening. *Address:* John Innes Centre, Colney Lane, Norwich NR4 7UH. *T:* (01603) 450000, *Fax:* (01603) 450778.

HORAM, John Rhodes; MP (C) Orpington, since 1992; *b* 7 March 1939; *s* of Sydney Horam, Preston; *m* 1987, Judith Jackson. *Educ:* Silcoates Sch., Wakefield; Univ. of Cambridge. Marketing Executive, Rowntree & Co., 1960–62; leader and feature writer: Financial Times, 1962–65; The Economist, 1965–68; Man. Dir, Commodities Research Unit Ltd, 1968–70 and 1983–92; Dep. Chm., 1992–95, non-exec. Dir, 1997–, CRU Internat. Ltd. MP Gateshead West, 1970–83 (Lab, 1970–81, SDP, 1981–83). Parly Under-Sec. of State, Dept of Transport, 1976–79; Labour spokesman on econ. affairs, 1979–81; Parly spokesman on econ. affairs, SDP, 1981–83; Parly Sec., OPSS, 1995; Parly Under-Sec. of State, DoH, 1995–97. Chm., Envmtl Audit Select Cttee, 1997–2003; Mem., Foreign Affairs Select Cttee, 2005–. Mem. Exec., 1922 Cttee, 2004–07. Joined Conservative Party, Feb. 1987. *Address:* 6 Bovingdon Road, SW6 2AP.

HORBURY, Rev. Prof. William, PhD, DD; FBA 1997; Professor of Jewish and Early Christian Studies, University of Cambridge, since 1998; Fellow of Corpus Christi College, Cambridge, since 1978; *b* 6 June 1942; *m* 1966, Katharine Mary, *d* of late Rt Rev. D. R. Feaver; two *d*. *Educ:* Charterhouse; Oriel Coll., Oxford (MA 1967); Clare Coll., Cambridge (MA 1968; PhD 1971); Westcott House, Cambridge; DD Cantab 2000. Res. Fellow, Clare Coll., Cambridge, 1968–72; ordained deacon, 1969, priest, 1970; Vicar, Great Gransden, and Rector, Little Gransden, 1972–78; Cambridge University: Dean of Chapel, Corpus Christi Coll., 1978–85; Univ. Lectr in Divinity, 1984–96; Reader, 1996–98; Dir, Jewish Inscriptions Project, Divinity Faculty, 1989–95. NSM, St Botolph, Cambridge, 1990–. Pres., British Assoc. for Jewish Studies, 1996. *Publications:* (ed jtly) Suffering and Martyrdom in the New Testament, 1981; (ed jtly) Essays in Honour of Ernst Bammel, 1983; (ed) *Templum Amicitiae*: essays on the Second Temple, 1991; (jtly) Jewis Inscriptions of Graeco-Roman Egypt, 1992; (jtly) The Jewish-Christian Controvers 1996; Jews and Christians in Contact and Controversy, 1998; Jewish Messianism and th Cult of Christ, 1998; (ed) Hebrew Study from Ezra to Ben-Yehuda, 1999; (ed jtly) Th Cambridge History of Judaism, vol. iii, The Early Roman Period, 1999; Christianity i Ancient Jewish Tradition, 1999; Messianism among Jews and Christians: twelve Biblic and historical studies, 2003; Herodian Judaism and New Testament Study, 2006; article in Vetus Testamentum, Jl of Theol Studies, New Testament Studies, Palestine Exploratio Qly, Jewish Studies Qly, and other jls. *Recreations:* railways, cats. *Address:* Corpus Chris College, Cambridge CB2 1RH; 5 Grange Road, Cambridge CB3 9AS. *T:* (0122 363529.

See also W. A. Feaver.

HORD, Brian Howard, CBE 1989; FRICS; company director; chartered surveyo Director General, Bureau of European Building Consultants and Experts, 1991–95; *b* 2 June 1934; *s* of late Edwin Charles and Winifred Hannah Hord; *m* 1960, Christine Maria Lucas; two *s*. *Educ:* Reedham Orphanage.; Purley Co. Grammar Sch. County Plannin Dept, Middx CC, 1950–51; Surveyor, G. L. Hearn & Partners, 1951–57; Nationa Service, RAF, 1957–59; Estates Surveyor, United Drapery Stores, 1959–66; Richar Costain Ltd, 1966–70; Director, Capcount UK Ltd, principal subsid. of Capital & Counties Property Co. Ltd, 1970–75; Partner, Howard Hord & Palmer, Chartere Surveyors, 1975–84. Chm., Bexley HA, 1986–92. Member: London Rent Assessmen Panel, 1985–2005; London Regl Passengers' Cttee, 1997–2000; Chairman: Sevenoak Rail Travellers' Assoc., 2001–02; Bexhill Rail Action Gp, 2005–. Contested (C Darlington, Feb. and Oct. 1974. MEP (C) London West, 1979–84; Whip of Europea Democratic Gp, 1982–83; Mem., Agric. and Budgets Cttees, EP. Vice-Pres., Sevenoak Cons. Assoc., 1997–. *Publication:* (jtly) Rates-Realism or Rebellion. *Recreations* photography, music, theatre, swimming, gardening, walking the S Downs.

HORDEN, Richard, RIBA; Chairman, Horden Cherry Lee Architects Ltd, since 1999 Managing Director, Richard Horden Associates, since 1985; *b* 26 Dec. 1944; *s* of Pete Horden and Irene Horden (*née* Kelly); *m* 1972, Kathleen Gibson Valentine (*d* 1998); on *s* one *d*. *Educ:* Perrott Hill Sch.; Bryanston Sch.; Architectural Assoc. (AA Dip.). RIB 1974. Work with Sir Norman Foster, 1974–84: Design Assistant for the Sainsbury Centr for Visual Arts, UEA; Stansted Airport; estabd Richard Horden Associates, 1985. Di micro compact home ltd, 2005–. RIBA Commendation for Courtyard House, Poole 1974; FT Award and RIBA Nat. Award for Architecture for Queen's Stand, Epsom, 199 Building of the Year Award, Royal Fine Arts Commn, for House on Evening Hill, Poole 2003. *Publications:* Light Tech: towards a light architecture, 1995; Richard Horde architecture and teaching, 1999; Peak Lab, 2003; Sixty Projects, 2004. *Recreation* yachting, ski-ing, running. *Address:* Horden Cherry Lee Architects Ltd, 34 Bruton Place W1J 6NR. *T:* (020) 7495 4119. *Club:* Royal Motor Yacht (Poole).

HORDER, Prof. Jeremy Christian Nicholas, DPhil; a Law Commissioner for Englan and Wales, since 2005; Professor of Criminal Law, University of Oxford, since 2006; *b* 2 Feb. 1962; *s* of John and Sylvia Horder; partner, Joanne R. Moss; one *d*. *Educ:* Felsted Sch Univ. of Hull (LLB Law 1984); Keble Coll., Oxford (BCL, MA; DPhil 1990). Oxfor University: Jun. Res. Fellow, Jesus Coll., 1987–89; Tutorial Fellow, Worcester Coll 1989–2005; Reader in Criminal Law, 2001–06. *Publications:* Provocation an Responsibility, 1992; Excusing Crime, 2004. *Recreations:* supporting Arsenal Footba Club, reading crime fiction. *Address:* Law Commission, Steel House, 11 Tothill Stree SW1H 9LJ. *T:* (020) 3334 0200; *e-mail:* jeremy.horder@lawcommission.gsi.gov.uk.

HORDER, Dr John Plaistowe, CBE 1981 (OBE 1971); FRCP, FRCPE, FRCGP FRCPsych; general practitioner of medicine, 1951–81, retired; Founder, National Centr for the Advancement of Interprofessional Education, 1987 (Chairman, 1987–94); *b* 9 Dec 1919; *s* of Gerald Morley Horder and Emma Ruth Horder; *m* 1940, Elizabeth Jun Wilson; two *s* two *d*. *Educ:* Lancing Coll.; University Coll., Oxford (BA 1945); Londo Hosp. (BM BCh 1948). FRCP 1972 (MRCP 1951); FRCGP 1970 (MRCGP 1957 FRCPsych 1980 (MRCPsych 1975); FRCPE 1982. Consultant, 1959, Travelling Fellow 1964, WHO; Vis. Lectr, London School of Economics and Pol. Sci., 1964–69; Sir Harr Jeffcott Vis. Prof., Univ. of Nottingham, 1975; Visiting Professor: Royal Free Hosp. Me Sch., 1982–91; Zagreb Univ., 1990–. Samuel Gee Lectr, RCP, 1991. Consultant Adviser DHSS, 1978–84. Pres., Medical Art Soc., 1990–93. Pres., RCGP, 1979–82 (John Hun Fellow, 1974–77; Wolfson Travelling Prof., 1978); Hon. FRSocMed 1983 (Vice-Pres. 1987–89; Pres., Sect. of Gen. Practice, 1970). Hon. Fellow: Green Coll., Oxford, 198 QMW, 1997. Hon. MD Free Univ. Amsterdam, 1985; Hon. DSc: Westminster, 200 Kingston, 2001. Hon. Mem., Coll. of Family Physicians of Canada, 1982. *Publications:* e and co-author: The Future General Practitioner—learning and teaching, 1972; Genera Practice under the National Health Service 1948–1997, 1998. *Recreations:* painting, music *Address:* 98 Regent's Park Road, NW1 8UG. *T:* (020) 7722 3804.

HORDERN, His Honour (Alfred) Christopher (Willoughby); QC 1979; a Circui Judge, 1983–2003; *m*; one *s* two *d*. *Educ:* Oxford Univ. (MA). Called to the Bar, Middl Temple, 1961; a Recorder of the Crown Court, 1974–83. *Recreations:* ski-ing, sailing gardening of course. *Address:* Broom House, High House Farm Road, Sudbourne Woodbridge, Suffolk IP12 2BL.

HORDERN, Rt Hon. Sir Peter (Maudslay), Kt 1985; PC 1993; DL; Chairman, Fin (formerly Petrofina (UK)), 1987–98 (Director, 1973–98); *b* 18 April 1929; British; *s* of C H. Hordern, MBE; *m* 1964, Susan Chataway; two *s* one *d*. *Educ:* Geelong Grammar Sch. Australia; Christ Church, Oxford, 1949–52 (MA). Mem. of Stock Exchange, London 1957–74. Chm., Foreign & Colonial Smaller Cos (formerly Foreign & Colonial Allianc Investment), 1986–97 (Dir, 1976–99); Dir, TR Technology, 1975–98. MP (C) Horsham 1964–74 and 1983–97, Horsham and Crawley, 1974–83. Chm., Cons. Parly Financ Cttee, 1970–72; Member: Exec., 1922 Cttee, 1968–97 (Jt Sec., 1988–97); Public Acct Cttee, 1970–97; Public Accounts Commn, 1984–97 (Chm., 1988–97). Mem. Bd, Britis Liby, 1996–99. DL West Sussex, 1988. *Recreations:* golf, reading and travel.

HORE-RUTHVEN, family name of **Earl of Gowrie**.

HORE-RUTHVEN, Hon. Malise Walter Maitland Knox; *see* Ruthven, Hon. M. W M. K. H.

HORLICK, Vice-Adm. Sir Edwin John, (Sir Ted), KBE 1981; FREng, FIMechE MIMarEST; part-time consultant; *b* 28 Sept. 1925; *m* Jean Margaret (*née* Covington) (*d* 1991); four *s*. *Educ:* Bedford Modern Sch. Joined RN, 1943; Sqdn Eng. Officer, 2nd Frigate Sqdn, 1960–63; Ship Dept, MoD, 1963–66; First Asst to Chief Engineer, HM Dockyard, Singapore, 1966–68; Asst Dir Submarines, 1969–72; SOWC 1973; Fleet Marine Engineering Officer, Staff of C-in-C Fleet, 1973–75; RCDS 1976; Dir Project Team Submarine/Polaris, 1977–79; Dir Gen. Ships, 1979–83; Chief Naval Engineer Officer, 1981–83. FREng (FEng 1983). *Recreations:* golf, Rugby administration, DIY. *Address:* Garden Apt, 74 Great Pulteney Street, Bath BA2 4DL.

HORLICK, Sir James Cunliffe William, 6th Bt *cr* 1914, of Cowley Manor, Gloucester; *b* 19 Nov. 1956; *o s* of Sir John James Macdonald Horlick, 5th Bt and June, *d* of Douglas Cory-Wright, CBE; *S* father, 1995; *m* 1st, 1985, Fiona Rosalie (marr. diss. 1998), *e d* of Andrew McLaren; three *s*; 2nd, 1999, Mrs Gina Hudson. *Educ:* Eton. *Heir: s* Alexander Horlick, *b* 8 April 1987.

HORLICK, Sir Ted; *see* Horlick, Sir Edwin John.

HORLOCK, Henry Wimburn Sudell; Underwriting Member of Lloyd's, 1957–2004; Director, Stepping Stone School, 1962–87; *b* 19 July 1915; *s* of Rev. Henry Darrell Sudell Horlock, DD, and Mary Haliburton Laurie; *m* 1960, Jeannetta Robin, *d* of F. W. Tanner, JP. *Educ:* Pembroke Coll., Oxford (MA). Army, 1939–42. Civil Service, 1942–60. Court of Common Council, City of London, 1969–2001 (Chm., West Ham Park Cttee, 1979–82; Chm., Police Cttee, 1987–90); Deputy, Ward of Farringdon Within, 1978–99; Sheriff, City of London, 1972–73; Chm., City of London Sheriffs' Soc., 1985–2003; Liveryman: Saddlers Co., 1937–, Master, 1976–77; Plaisterers' Co. (Hon.), 1975–; Fletchers' Co., 1977–; Gardeners' Co., 1980–; Member: Parish Clerks' Co., 1966–, Master, 1981–82; Guild of Freemen, 1972–, Master, 1986–87; Farringdon Ward Club, 1970–, Pres., 1978–79; United Wards Club, 1972–, Pres., 1980–81; City Livery Club, 1969–, Pres., 1981–82; City of London Br., Royal Society of St George, 1972–, Chm., 1989–90. Commander: Order of Merit, Federal Republic of Germany, 1972; National Order of the Aztec Eagle of Mexico, 1973; Order of Wissam Alouite, Morocco, 1987. *Recreations:* Freemasonry, gardening, travel. *Address:* Copse Hill House, Lower Slaughter, Glos GL54 2HZ. *T:* (01451) 820276. *Clubs:* Athenæum, Guildhall, City Livery.

HORLOCK, Sir John (Harold), Kt 1996; FRS 1976; FREng; Vice-Chancellor, 1981–90, and Fellow, since 1991, Open University; *b* 19 April 1928; *s* of Harold Edgar and Olive Margaret Horlock; *m* 1953, Sheila Joy Stutely; one *s* two *d*. *Educ:* Edmonton Latymer Sch.; (Scholar) St John's Coll., Cambridge (Hon. Fellow 1989). 1st Class Hons Mech. Sci. Tripos, Pt I, 1948, Rex Moir Prize; Pt II, 1949; MA 1952; PhD 1955; ScD 1975. Design and Development Engineer, Rolls Royce Ltd, Derby, 1949–51; Fellow, St John's Coll., Cambridge, 1954–57 and 1967–74; Univ. Demonstrator, 1952–56; University Lecturer, 1956–58, at Cambridge Univ. Engineering Lab.; Harrison Prof. of Mechanical Engineering, Liverpool Univ., 1958–66; Prof. of Engineering, and Dir of Whittle Lab., Cambridge Univ., 1967–74; Vice-Chancellor, Univ. of Salford, 1974–80. Visiting Asst Prof. in Mech. Engineering, Massachusetts Inst. of Technology, USA, 1956–57; Vis. Prof. of Aero-Space Engineering, Pennsylvania State Univ., USA, 1966. Chm., ARC, 1979–80 (Mem., 1960–63, 1969–72); Member: SRC, 1974–77; Cttee of Inquiry into Engineering Profession, 1977–80; Engineering Council, 1981–83; Chm., Adv. Cttee on Safety in Nuclear Installations, 1984–93. Director: BICERA Ltd, 1964–65; Cambridge Water Co., 1971–74; British Engine Insurance Ltd, 1979–84; Gaydon Technology Ltd, 1978–88; Open University Educational Enterprises Ltd, 1981–88; National Grid Co., 1989–94. Chm., Electro-magnetic Field Biol Res. Trust, 1997–. A Vice-Pres., 1981–83, 1992–97, Treas., 1992–97, Royal Soc. Calvin Rice Lectr, ASME, 1994. FREng (FEng 1977); FIMechE; Fellow ASME; Hon. FRAeS 2003. Foreign Associate, US Nat. Acad. of Engrg. Hon. Fellow, UMIST, 1991 (a Pro-Chancellor, 1995–2001). Hon. DSc: Heriot-Watt, 1980; Salford, 1981; CNAA, 1991; de Montfort, 1995; Cranfield, 1997; Hon. ScD East Asia, 1987; Hon. DEng Liverpool, 1987; DUniv Open, 1991. Clayton Prize, 1962, Thomas Hawksley Gold Medal, 1969, Arthur Charles Main Prize, 1997, IMechE; R. Tom Sawyer Award, ASME, 1997; Sir James Ewing Medal, ICE, 2001; Achievement Award, ISABE, 2003. *Publications:* The Fluid Mechanics and Thermodynamics of Axial Flow Compressors, 1958; The Fluid Mechanics and Thermodynamics of Axial Flow Turbines, 1966; Actuator Disc Theory, 1978; (ed) Thermodynamics and Gas Dynamics of Internal Combustion Engines, vol. I, 1982, vol. II, 1986; Cogeneration—Combined Heat and Power, 1987; Combined Power Plants, 1992; (ed) Energy for the Future, 1995; Advanced Gas Turbine Cycles, 2003; An Open Book, 2006; contribs to mech. and aero. engineering jls and to Proc. Royal Society. *Recreations:* music, watching sport. *Address:* 2 The Avenue, Ampthill, Bedford MK45 2NR. *T:* (01525) 841307.

See also T. J. Horlock.

HORLOCK, Timothy John; QC 1997; a Recorder, since 2000; *b* 4 Jan. 1958; *s* of Sir John Horlock, *qv*; *m*; four *s*. *Educ:* Manchester Grammar Sch.; St John's Coll., Cambridge (MA). Called to the Bar, Middle Temple, 1981 (Bencher, 2007); Asst Recorder, 1997–2000. *Recreations:* football, tennis, cricket. *Address:* 9 St John Street, Manchester M3 4DN.

HORN, Bernard Philip; Chairman: Social Finance Ltd, since 2008; Netik Holdings Ltd, since 2002; E-Box, since 2004; Econiq (Ireland), since 2007; *b* 22 April 1946; *s* of late Robert Horn and Margaret Mary Horn; *m* 1988, Clare Margaret Gilbert; one *s* two *d*, and two *s* one *d* by previous marriage. *Educ:* Catholic Coll., Preston; John Dalton Faculty of Technol., Manchester (DMS); Harvard Business Sch. With National Westminster Bank, 1965–2000: Sen. Internat. Exec., Corp. Financial Services, 1986–88; Chief of Staff, 1989–90; Gen. Manager, Gp Strategy and Communications, 1990–91; Chief Exec., Internat. Businesses, 1991–96; Dir, 1995–2000; Exec. Dir, Gp Ops, 1996–2000. Chairman: Eontec Ltd, 2003–04; Commn on Unclaimed Assets, 2005–. Chm., Magic Bus (UK) (Indian charity), 2007–; Trustee, Enham. Freeman, City of London, 2001; Mem., Co. of Information Technologists, 2001–. FCIB 1991; FRSA 1991. *Recreations:* my children, our home, music, theatre. *Address: e-mail:* bph@bernardhorn.com. *Clubs:* Royal Automobile, Hurlingham.

HORN, Prof. Sir Gabriel, Kt 2002; MA, MD, ScD; FRS 1986; Master of Sidney Sussex College, Cambridge, 1992–99, Emeritus Fellow, since 1999; Fellow of King's College, Cambridge, 1962–74, 1978–92 and since 1999; *b* 9 Dec. 1927; *s* of late Abraham and Anne Horn; *m* 1st, 1952, Ann Loveday Dean Soper (marr. diss. 1979); two *s* two *d*; 2nd, 1980, Priscilla Barrett. *Educ:* Handsworth Technical Sch. and Coll., Birmingham (Nat. Cert. in Mech. Engrg); Univ. of Birmingham (BSc Anatomy and Physiology; MD, ChB). MA, ScD Cantab. Served in RAF (Educn Br.), 1947–49. House appts, Birmingham Children's and Birmingham and Midland Eye Hosps, 1955–56; University of Cambridge: Univ. Demonstrator in Anat., 1956–62; Lectr in Anat., 1962–72; Reader in Neurobiology, 1972–74; Prof. and Head of Dept of Anat., Univ. of Bristol, 1974–77; Cambridge University: Prof. of Zoology, 1978–95, now Emeritus Prof.; Hd of Dept, 1979–94; Dep. Vice-Chancellor, 1994–98; Chairman: Core Cttee, Govt Policy Prog., 1998–; Review Cttee on Origin of BSE, 2001. Sen. Res. Fellow in Neurophysiol., Montreal Neurol Inst., McGill Univ., 1957–58; Leverhulme Res. Fellow, Laboratoire de Neurophysiologie Cellulaire, France, 1970–71; Leverhulme Emeritus Fellow, 2002–04. Vis. Prof. of Physiol Optics, Univ. of Calif, Berkeley, 1963; Vis. Res. Prof., Ohio State Univ., 1965; Vis. Prof. of Zool., Makerere University Coll., Uganda, 1966; Dist. Vis. Prof., Univ. of Alberta, Edmonton, Canada, 1988; Vis. Miller Prof., Univ. of Calif, Berkeley, USA, 1989. Charnock Bradley Lectr, Edinburgh Univ., 1988; Crisp Lectr, Univ. of Leeds, 1990. Dir, Cambridge Consultants Ltd, 1966–69; Sen. Consultant, PA Technology, 1976–86; Mem., Scientific Adv. Bd, Parke-Davis, 1988–99 (Chm., 1996). Member: Biol Sciences Cttee, SRC, 1973–75; Jt MRC and SRC Adv. Panel on Neurobiol., 1971–72; Res. Cttee, Mental Health Foundn, 1973–78; Council, Anatomical Soc., 1976–78; Adv. Gp, ARC Inst. of Animal Physiology, Babraham, 1981–87; AFRC, 1991–94; Chairman: Mgt Cttee, Wellcome Trust and CRC Inst. of Cancer and Develtl Biol., 1990–97; BBSRC Wkg Party on Biol. of Spongiform Encephalopathies, 1991–95; Animal Scis and Psychol. Res. Grants Cttee, BBSRC, 1994–96; Wkg Party on Brain Scis, Addiction and Drugs, Acad. of Med. Scis, 2005–08. Dir, Co. of Biologists, 1980–93. Foreign Fellow, Acad. of Scis, Republic of Georgia, 1997; Hon. Member: Anatomical Soc. of GB and Ireland, 1997; Europ. Brain and Behaviour Soc., 2004. Hon. DSc: Birmingham, 1999; Bristol, 2003; Georgian Acad. of Scis, 2004. Kenneth Craik Award in Physiol Psychol., 1962; Royal Medal, Royal Soc., 2001. *Publications:* (ed with R. A. Hinde) Short-Term Changes in Neural Activity and Behaviour, 1970; Memory, Imprinting and the Brain, 1985; (ed with J. R. Krebs) Behavioural and Neural Aspects of Learning and Memory, 1991; contrib. scientific jls, mainly on topics in neurosciences. *Recreations:* walking, cycling, music. *Address:* Sub-Department of Animal Behaviour, University of Cambridge, Madingley, Cambridge CB23 8AA.

HORN, Gyula, PhD; MP (MSzP) Republic of Hungary, since 1990; Prime Minister of Hungary, 1994–98; *b* 5 July 1932; *s* of Geza Horn and Anna Csornyei; *m* Anna Kiraly; one *s* one *d*. *Educ:* Rostow Inst. Econs, USSR; Polit. Acad., Budapest (PhD 1976). Official, Min. of Finance, Budapest, 1954–59; desk officer, Min. of Foreign Affairs, 1959–61; Embassy Secretary, Diplomatic Mission: Sofia, 1961–63; Belgrade, 1963–69; Staff Mem., then Hd, Internat. Dept, Hungarian Socialist Workers Party (MSZMP), Budapest, 1969–85; State Sec., Min. of Foreign Affairs, 1985–89; Minister of Foreign Affairs, 1989–90; Chm., Foreign Affairs Cttee, Hungarian Parlt, 1990–93. Founder, Hungarian Socialist Party (MSzP), 1989 (Pres., 1990–98). Mem., Hungarian Soc. of Political Scis. Mem., European Hon. Senate, 1991–. Glass of Understanding, Kassel; Karl Prize for work towards European unification, Aachen, 1991. Golden Labour Award of Merit (Hungary); Grand Cross (FRG). *Publications:* Development of East-West Relations in the 70s, 1970; Yugoslavia: our neighbour, 1971; Social and Political Changes in Albania since World War II, 1973; Pikes (autobiog.), 1991; Cölöpök, 1991; Freiheit die ich meine, 1991; Those Were the 90s, 1999; books on E-W relations in the Seventies, European security and co-operation and develt of internat. contacts; contrib. numerous articles to professional jls. *Address:* National Assembly, 1055 Budapest, Kossuth Lajos tér 1, Hungary.

HORN, Dr Heinz; Chairman: Executive Board, Ruhrkohle AG, 1985–95; Supervisory Board, Rütgerswerke AG, 1989–95; *b* 17 Sept. 1930; *m*; two *s* two *d*. *Educ:* Univs of Frankfurt and Munster. Financial Dir, Eschweiler Bergwerks-Verein, 1965–68; Member, Executive Board: Krupp Industrie und Stahlbau, 1968–72; Eisen & Metall AG, 1972–74; Mem., Exec. Bd, later Chm., Eschweiler Bergwerks-Verein, 1974–83; Dep. Chm., Exec. Bd, Ruhrkohle AG, 1983–85. *Address:* c/o Ruhrkohle AG, Rellinghauser Strasse 1, 45128 Essen, Germany.

HORN, Helen Margaret, MBE 1994; HM Diplomatic Service; Head, South East Asia Maritime Team, Foreign and Commonwealth Office, 2007; *b* 27 April 1961; *d* of Kenneth and Mary Horn. *Educ:* Dover Grammar Sch. for Girls; Thanet Tech. Coll.; Heidelberg Univ. Former diplomatic postings: Warsaw; Zurich; Dakar; Dubai; Kinshasa; Vienna; Johannesburg; Ambassador to Guinea, 2003–04; Consul-Gen., Brisbane, 2004–05; Pretoria, 2006–07. *Recreations:* African wildlife, outdoor pursuits, swimming. *Address:* Foreign and Commonwealth Office, King Charles Street, SW1A 2AH.

HORN, Dr Pamela Lucy Ray; author; freelance lecturer, since 1991; *b* 2 May 1936; *d* of Gilbert L. Jones and Marjorie H. Jones; *m* 1963, Clifford Alfred Horn. *Educ:* Girls' High Sch., Burton on Trent; Leicester Univ. (BSc Econ. 1964; PhD 1968). Sec., Derbys CC, 1954–58; Assistant Lecturer: Burton on Trent Tech. Coll., 1958–59; Derby & Dist Coll. of Technol., 1959–63; part-time Lectr in Econ. and Social Hist., Oxford Poly., 1967–91. *Publications:* Joseph Arch, 1971; (ed) Agricultural Trade Unionism in Oxfordshire, 1974; The Victorian Country Child, 1974, 3rd edn 1997; The Rise and Fall of the Victorian Servant, 1975, 3rd edn 2004; Labouring Life in the Victorian Countryside, 1976, 2nd edn 1995; Education in Rural England, 1978; (ed) Village Education in 19th Century Oxfordshire, 1979; The Rural World 1780–1850, 1980; The Changing Countryside, 1984; Rural Life in England in the First World War, 1984; Life and Labour in Rural England 1780–1850, 1987; Around Abingdon in Old Photographs, 1987; The Victorian and Edwardian Schoolchild, 1989; Victorian Countrywomen, 1991; Ladies of the Manor, 1991, 2nd edn 1997; High Society, 1992; Children's Work and Welfare 1780–1890, 1994; Women in the 1920's, 1995; The Victorian Town Child, 1997; Pleasures and Pastimes in Victorian Britain, 1999; Life Below Stairs in the Twentieth Century, 2001; Flunkeys and Scullions, 2004; Behind the Counter, 2006; Life as a Victorian Lady, 2007; Life in a Victorian Household, 2007; contributor to several books. *Recreations:* walking, gardening, foreign travel. *Address:* 11 Harwell Road, Sutton Courtenay, Abingdon, Oxon OX14 4BN. *T:* (01235) 847424.

HORN-SMITH, Sir Julian (Michael), Kt 2004; Senior Adviser, UBS, since 2007; non-executive Director, Lloyds TSB Group plc, since 2006; *b* 14 Dec. 1948. *Educ:* London Univ. (BSc Econ); Bath Univ. (MSc). Vodafone, then Vodafone AirTouch, subseq. reverted to Vodafone Gp plc, 1984–2006: Dir, 1996–2006; Chief Exec., Internat., 1999; Chief Operating Officer, 2001–04; Dep. Chief Exec., 2005–06. Non-exec. Dir, Smiths Gp plc, 2000–06; Chm., Sage Gp, 2006–07; Dir, Digicel Gp (Caribbean and Pacific). Chairman: Turkish British Business Council; Altimo Adv. Bd (Alfa Telecoms). Pres., Egyptian Exploration Soc. DLaws Bath. *Address:* c/o Lloyds TSB Group plc, 25 Gresham Street, EC2V 7HN. *Club:* Army and Navy.

HORNBLOWER, Prof. Simon, DPhil; FBA 2004; Professor of Classics and Ancient History, since 1998, and Grote Professor of Ancient History, since 2006, University College London; *b* 29 May 1949; *s* of George Alexander Hornblower and Edith Faith Hornblower. *Educ:* Eton Coll. (Schol.); Jesus Coll., Cambridge (Schol.; 1st cl. (Classical Tripos Pt I) 1969); Balliol Coll., Oxford (BA 1st cl. (Lit.Hum.) 1971); DPhil Oxon 1978. Fellow by Exam., All Souls Coll., Oxford, 1971–77; Lectr in Ancient Hist., Univ. of Oxford, and Tutorial Fellow, Oriel Coll., Oxford, 1978–97; Sen. Lectr, Dept of Greek and Latin and of Hist., UCL, 1997–98. Mem., Inst. for Advanced Study, Sch. of Historical Studies, Princeton, NJ, 1994–95. *Publications:* Mausolus, 1982; The Greek World 479–323 BC, 1983, 3rd edn 2002; Thucydides, 1987; Commentary on Thucydides, 3 vols, 1991, 1996 and 2008; (ed) Greek Historiography, 1994; (ed jtly) Cambridge Ancient History, vol. 6, 1994; (ed jtly) Ritual, Finance, Politics, 1994; (ed jtly) Oxford Classical Dictionary, 3rd edn 1996; (ed jtly) Greek Personal Names: their value as evidence, 2000; Thucydides and Pindar, 2004; (ed jtly) Pindar's Poetry, Patrons and Festivals, 2007. *Address:* Department of History, University College London, Gower Street, WC1E 6BT. *T:* (020) 7679 1340; *e-mail:* s.hornblower@ucl.ac.uk.

HORNBY, Andrew Hedley; Chief Executive, HBOS plc, since 2006; *b* 21 Jan. 1967; *s* of James and Clare Hornby; *m* Catherine. *Educ:* Univ. of Oxford; Harvard Business Sch. (MBA). Boston Consulting Gp; Blue Circle; ASDA, 1996–99: Dir of Corp. Develt; Retail Man. Dir; Man. Dir, George; Halifax, subseq. HBOS plc: Chief Exec., Halifax Retail,

1999–2001; Chief Exec., Retail Div., 2001–05; Chief Operating Officer, 2005–06. Non-exec. Dir, Home Retail Gp. *Address:* HBOS plc, The Mound, Edinburgh EH1 1YZ. *T:* (0131) 243 5533, *Fax:* (0131) 243 5546; *e-mail:* andyhornby@hbosplc.com.

HORNBY, Sir Derek (Peter), Kt 1990; *b* 10 Jan. 1930; *s* of F. N. Hornby and V. M. Pardy; *m* 1st, 1953, Margaret Withers (marr. diss.); one *s* one *d*; 2nd, 1971, Sonia Beesley; one *s* one *d*. *Educ:* Canford School. With Mobil Oil, Mars Industries and Texas Instruments; Xerox Corp., 1973 (Dir, Internat. Ops); Exec. Dir, Rank Xerox, 1980–84; Chm., Rank-Xerox (UK), 1984–90. Mem. Bd, British Rail, 1985–90; Civil Service Comr, 1986–90; Chairman: BOTB, 1990–95 (Mem., 1987–95; Chm., N Amer. Gp, 1987); NACCB, 1980–84. Chairman: Video Arts, 1993–96; Partnership Sourcing Ltd, 1993–98; London & Continental Railways, 1994–98; IRG, 1997–2000; Director: Cogent Elliott, 1988–; London and Edinburgh Insurance Gp, 1989–96; Kode International, 1989–97; Dixons, 1990–97; Sedgwick Group, 1993–98; Pillar Properties plc, 1994–; Morgan Sindall Ltd, 1995–2002 (Chm., 1995–2000). Mem. Bd, Savills, 1988–95. Pres., Shaw Trust, 1995–2002. Chm. Govs, Priors Court Sch. for Autism, 1999–2002. CCMI (Chm., 1990–93). FRSA. Hon. DSc Aston, 1993. *Recreations:* Real tennis, theatre, cricket. *Address:* Badgers Farm, Idlicote, Shipston-on-Stour, Warwicks CV36 5DT. *Clubs:* Garrick, MCC; Leamington Real Tennis.

See also R. D. Harris, J. P. Hornby.

HORNBY, Derrick Richard; *b* 11 Jan. 1926; *s* of late Richard W. Hornby and Dora M. Hornby; *m* 1948, June Steele; two *s* one *d*. *Educ:* University Coll., Southampton (DipEcon). Early career in accountancy; Marketing Dir, Tetley Tea Co. Ltd, 1964–69; Man. Dir, Eden Vale, 1969–74; Chm., Spillers Foods Ltd, 1974–77; Divisional Managing Director: Spillers Internat., 1977–80; Spillers Grocery Products Div., 1979–80; Chm., Carrington Viyella Ltd, 1979. Pres., Food Manufrs Fedn Incorp., 1977–79; Mem., Food and Drinks EDC. Member Council: CBI, to 1979; Food and Drinks Industry Council, to 1979. Chairman: Appeal Fund, Nat. Grocers Benefit Fund, 1973–74; London Animal Trust, 1978–80. FCMI; FIGD, ACommA. *Recreations:* golf, fly-fishing. *Address:* Northside, Romsey Road, Whiteparish, Wilts SP5 2SD.

HORNBY, Prof. James Angus; Professor of Law in the University of Bristol, 1961–85, now Emeritus; *b* 15 Aug. 1922; twin *s* of James Hornby and Evelyn Gladys (*née* Grant). *Educ:* Bolton County Grammar Sch.; Christ's Coll., Cambridge (BA 1944, LLB 1945, MA 1948). Called to Bar, Lincoln's Inn, 1947. Lecturer, Manchester Univ., 1947–61. *Publications:* An Introduction to Company Law, 1957, 5th edn 1975; contribs to legal journals. *Recreations:* listening to music, reading, walking. *Address:* Flat 9, St Monica Court, Cote Lane, Westbury-on-Trym, Bristol BS9 3TL.

HORNBY, Jonathan Peter; Founding Partner, CHI & Partners (formerly Clemmow Hornby Inge Ltd), advertising agency, 2001; *b* Leamington Spa, 29 March 1967; *s* of Sir Derek Peter Hornby, *qv* and Sonia Margaret Hornby (*née* Beesley); two *s* one *d*; *m* 2003, Clare Griffiths; two *d*. *Educ:* Marlborough Coll.; Univ. of Edinburgh (MA Hons). Joined Ogilvy & Mather, 1990, Account Dir, 1993–94; Brand Account Dir, 1995–96, Client Services Dir, 1996–98, Collett Dickenson Pearce & Partners; Jt Man. Dir, TBWA GGT Simons Palmer, 1998–2001. Mem., Mktg Gp of GB. Associate Mem., DAAD. *Recreations:* Real tennis (British Open Handicap champion 1986), sailing. *Address:* CHI & Partners, 7 Rathbone Street, W1T 1LY. *Clubs:* Soho House, George, Thirty.

HORNBY, Keith Anthony Delgado; His Honour Judge Hornby; a Circuit Judge, since 1995; Lead Judge, Bow County Court, since 2007; *b* 18 Feb. 1947; *s* of late James Lawrence Hornby and Naomi Ruth Hornby (*née* Delgado); *m* 1970, Judith Constance Fairbairn; two *s* one *d*. *Educ:* Oratory Sch.; Trinity Coll., Dublin (BA Hons Legal Sci.). Lectr in Commercial Law, PCL, 1969–70; called to the Bar, Gray's Inn, 1970; practised on SE Circuit, 1970–95; Asst Recorder, 1988–92; Recorder, 1992–95. Mem., Equal Treatment Adv. Cttee, Judicial Studies Bd, 2006–. Gov., Oratory Sch., 2007–. *Recreations:* art, theatre, cricket, squash, golf. *Address:* Bow County Court, 96 Romford Road, Stratford, E15 4EG. *T:* (020) 8536 5200. *Club:* Hurlingham.

HORNBY, Sir Simon (Michael), Kt 1988; Director, 1974–94, Chairman, 1982–94, W. H. Smith Group (formerly W. H. Smith & Son (Holdings) plc); Director: Pearson plc (formerly S. Pearson & Son Ltd), 1978–97; Lloyds TSB Group (formerly Lloyds Bank), 1988–99; Lloyds Abbey Life PLC, 1991–97 (Chairman, 1992–97); *b* 29 Dec. 1934; *s* of late Michael Hornby and Nicolette Joan, *d* of Hon. Cyril Ward, MVO; *m* 1968, Sheran Cazalet. *Educ:* Eton; New Coll., Oxford; Harvard Business Sch. 2nd Lieut, Grenadier Guards, 1953–55. Entered W. H. Smith & Son, 1958, Dir, 1965; Gp Chief Exec., W. H. Smith & Son (Holdings), 1978–82. Mem. Exec. Cttee, 1966–93, Property Cttee, 1979–86, Council 1976–2001, National Trust; Mem. Adv. Council, Victoria and Albert Museum, 1971–75; Council, RSA, 1985–90; Trustee, British Museum, 1975–85; Chairman: Design Council, 1986–92; Assoc. for Business Sponsorship of the Arts, 1988–97; Nat. Literacy Trust, 1993–2001 (Pres., 2001–); President: Book Trust, 1990–96 (Dep. Chm., 1976–78, Chm., 1978–80, NBL); Newsvendors' Benevolent Instn, 1989–94; RHS, 1994–2001 (Mem. Council, 1992–2001); Chelsea Soc., 1994–2000. DUniv Stirling, 1992; Hon. DLitt: Hull, 1994; Reading, 1996. *Recreations:* gardening, cooking. *Address:* The Ham, Wantage, Oxon OX12 9JA. *T:* (01235) 770222.

HORNE, Sir (Alan) Gray (Antony), 3rd Bt *cr* 1929; *b* 11 July 1948; *s* of Antony Edgar Alan Horne (*d* 1954) (*o s* of 2nd Bt), and of Valentine Antonia, *d* of Valentine Dudensing; *S* grandfather, 1984; *m* 1980, Cecile Rose, *d* of Jacques Desplanche. *Heir:* none. *Address:* Château du Basty, 24210 Thenon, Dordogne, France.

HORNE, Sir Alistair Allan, Kt 2003; CBE 1992; LittD; author, journalist, lecturer; *b* 9 Nov. 1925; *s* of late Sir (James) Allan Horne and Lady (Auriol) Horne (*née* Hay), *widow* of Capt. Noel Barran; *m* 1st, 1953, Renira Margaret (marr. diss. 1982), *d* of Adm. Sir Geoffrey Hawkins, KBE, CB, MVO, DSC; three *d*; 2nd, 1987, Hon. Mrs Sheelin Eccles. *Educ:* Le Rosey, Switzerland; Millbrook, USA; Jesus Coll., Cambridge (MA); LittD Cantab 1993. Served War of 1939–45: RAF, 1943–44; Coldstream Gds, 1944–47; Captain, attached Intelligence Service (ME). Foreign Correspondent, Daily Telegraph, 1952–55. Founded Alistair Horne Res. Fellowship in Mod. History, St Antony's Coll., Oxford, 1969, Hon. Fellow, 1988. Fellow, Woodrow Wilson Center, Washington, DC, USA, 1980–81 and 2005; Vis. Scholar, Library of Congress, USA, 2005. Lectures: Lees Knowles, Cambridge, 1982; Goodman, Univ. of West Ontario, 1983. Member: Management Cttee, Royal Literary Fund, 1969–; Franco-British Council, 1979–; Cttee of Management, Soc. of Authors, 1979–82; Trustee, Imperial War Museum, 1975–82. FRSL. Chevalier, Légion d'Honneur (France), 1993. *Publications:* Back into Power, 1955; The Land is Bright, 1958; Canada and the Canadians, 1961; The Price of Glory: Verdun 1916, 1962 (Hawthornden Prize, 1963); The Fall of Paris: The Siege and The Commune 1870–71, 1965, rev. 2nd edn 1990; To Lose a Battle: France 1940, 1969, rev. 2nd edn 1990; Death of a Generation, 1970; The Terrible Year: The Paris Commune, 1971; Small Earthquake in Chile, 1972, rev. 2nd edn 1990; A Savage War of Peace: Algeria 1954–62, 1977 (Yorkshire Post Book of Year Prize, 1978; Wolfson Literary Award, 1978), 3rd edn 1996; Napoleon, Master of Europe 1805–1807, 1979; The French Army and Politics 1870–1970, 1984 (Enid Macleod Prize, 1985); Macmillan: the official biography, Vol. 1894–1956, 1988, Vol. 2, 1957–1986, 1989; A Bundle from Britain, 1993; (with Davi Montgomery) The Lonely Leader: Monty 1944–45, 1994; How Far from Austerlitz Napoleon 1805–1815, 1996; (ed) Telling Lives, 2000; Seven Ages of Paris: portrait of city, 2002; Friend or Foe, 2004; Age of Napoleon, 2004; La Belle France, 2004; *contribs books:* Combat: World War I, ed Don Congdon, 1964; Impressions of America, ed R. A Brown, 1966; Marshal V. I. Chuikov, The End of the Third Reich, 1967; Sports an Games in Canadian Life, ed N. and M. L. Howell, 1969; Decisive Battles of the Twentiet Century, ed N. Frankland and C. Dowling, 1976; The War Lords: Military Commande of the Twentieth Century, ed Field Marshal Sir M. Carver, 1976; Regular Armies an Insurgency, ed R. Haycock, 1979; Macmillan: a life in pictures, 1983; contribs variou periodicals. *Recreations:* thinking about ski-ing, painting, gardening, travel, communin with dogs. *Address:* The Old Vicarage, Turville, near Henley-on-Thames, Oxon RG 6QU. *Clubs:* Garrick, Beefsteak.

HORNE, David Oliver, FCA; Chairman and Chief Executive, Lloyds Merchant Bank 1987–92; *b* 7 March 1932; *s* of Herbert Oliver Horne, MBE and Edith Marion Horne (*n* Sellers); *m* 1959, Joyce Heather (*née* Kynoch); two *s* two *d*. *Educ:* Fettes College Edinburgh. Director: S. G. Warburg & Co., 1966–70; Williams & Glyn's Bank, 1970–78 Lloyds Bank International, 1978–85; Managing Dir, Lloyds Merchant Bank, 1985–87 Dep. Chm., Serif, 1993–97; Director: Waterman Partnership Hldgs, 1992–2003; Blac Arrow Gp, 1993–. *Recreation:* golf. *Address:* Four Winds, 5 The Gardens, Esher, Surre KT10 8QF. *T:* (01372) 463510.

HORNE, Frederic Thomas; Chief Taxing Master of the Supreme Court, 1983–8 (Master, 1967–83); *b* 21 March 1917; *y s* of Lionel Edward Horne, JP, Moreton-in-Marsh Glos; *m* 1944, Madeline Hatton; two *s* two *d*. *Educ:* Chipping Campden Grammar Sch Admitted a Solicitor (Hons), 1938. Served with RAFVR in General Duties Branch (Pilot 1939–56. Partner in Iliffe Sweet & Co., 1956–67. Mem., Lord Chancellor's Adv. Ctte on Legal Aid, 1983–91; Chm., Working Party on the Simplification of Taxation, 1980–8 (Horne Report, 1983). Pres., Assoc. of Law Costs Draftsmen, 1991–97. *Publications* Cordery's Law Relating to Solicitors, 7th edn (jtly) 1981, 8th edn 1987; (contrib.) Atkin Encyclopaedia of Court Forms, 2nd edn, 1983; (ed jtly) The Supreme Court Practice 1985 and 1988 edns; (contrib.) Private International Litigation, 1987. *Recreations:* cricke music, archaeology. *Address:* Dunstall, Quickley Lane, Chorleywood, Herts WD3 5AF *Club:* MCC.

HORNE, Sir Gray; *see* Horne, Sir A. G. A.

HORNE, Marilyn (Bernice); mezzo-soprano; Director, Voice Program, Music Academ of the West, Santa Barbara; *b* 16 Jan. 1934; *m* 1960, Henry Lewis (marr. diss.); one *d*. *Educ* Univ. of Southern California. US opera début, 1954; sings at Covent Garden, La Scala Metropolitan Opera and other major venues; rôles include Adalgisa, Amneris, Carmen Eboli, Isabella, Mignon, Orlando, Rosina, Tancredi, concerts and recitals. *Publications* (with J. Scovell): Marilyn Horne - My Life (autobiog.), 1983; Marilyn Horne: the son continues, 2004. *Address:* c/o Colombia Artists Management, 1790 Broadway, 6th Floor New York, NY 10019, USA.

HORNE, Dr Nigel William, FREng, FIET; company director; *b* 13 Sept. 1940; *s* of lat Eric Charles Henry and Edith Margaret Horne; *m* 1965, Jennifer Ann Holton; one *s* tw *d*. *Educ:* John Lyon Sch., Harrow; Univ. of Bristol (BScEng 1962); Univ. of Cambridg (PhD 1968). FREng (FEng 1982); FIET (FIEE 1984). GEC Telecommunications 1958–82: Management Systems Manager, 1970–72; Manufg Gen. Manager, 1972–75; Di and Gen. Manager, Switching, 1976–82; Managing Dir, GEC Inf. Systems, 1982–83 Director: Technical and Corporate Develt, STC, 1983–90; Abingworth, 1985–90; LS Logic, 1986–90; FI Gp, 1992–98; Xansa (formerly FI Gp) Employees Trust, 1998–2004 Wireless Systems Internat. Ltd, 1995–2001; Foresight Technology VCT Plc, 1997–2008 Onyvax Ltd, 1997–2002; Parc Technologies Ltd, 1999–2000; Sarantel Ltd, 2000–02 Aspex Semiconductor (formerly Aspex Technol.), 2002–; Jersey Telecom Gp, 2002– Intergence Systems Ltd, 2006–08; Chm., Alcatel UK Ltd, 1992–2001. IT Partner, KPMC Peat Marwick, 1990–92; Interim Chief Technol. Officer, NATS, 2005. Vis. Prof., Univ of Bristol, 1990–98. Member: Nat. Electronics Council, 1985–90; EC Esprit Adv. Bd 1988–93; ACOST, Cabinet Office, 1989–93; EC Strategy Bd, DGIII, 1994–98; Ind Review, Higher Educn Pay and Conditions, 1998; British N American Cttee, 1998– Chairman: Computing and Control Div., IEE, 1988–89; DTI/SERC IT Adv. Bd 1988–91. FRSA. Freeman, City of London; Liveryman, Inf. Technologists' Co.; Mem. Engineers' Co. Hon. DEng Bristol, 1992; Hon. DSc: Hull, 1992; City, 1995. Caballero del Monasteria de Juste (Spain), 1992. *Publications:* papers in learned jls. *Recreations:* piano walking, gardening. *Club:* Athenæum.

HORNE, Robert Drake; Financial Adviser, Targeted Budget Support Program, Vietnam *b* 23 April 1945; *s* of late Harold Metcalfe Horne and Dorothy Katharine Horne; *m* 1972 Jennifer Mary (*née* Gill); three *d*. *Educ:* Mill Hill Sch.; Oriel Coll., Oxford (MA Classics) Asst Master, Eton Coll., Windsor, 1967–68; DES, later DFE, then DFEE, 1968–97 seconded to Cabinet Office, 1979–80; Under Sec., 1988–97; Dir of Finance and Planning Employment Service, 1995–97; First Asst Sec., Dept of Educn (formerly Employment and Educn), Trng and Youth Affairs, Canberra, 1998–2001. Budget Planning Advr, Dept o Educn, PNG, 2004–06. *Recreations:* cycling, sun-soaking. *Address:* 53 Gulfview Road Blackwood, SA 5051, Australia.

HORNER, Frederick, DSc; CEng, FIET; Director, Appleton Laboratory, Science Research Council, 1977–79; *b* 28 Aug. 1918; *s* of late Frederick and Mary Horner; *m* 1946, Elizabeth Bonsey; one *s* one *d*. *Educ:* Bolton Sch.; Univ. of Manchester (Ashbury Scholar, 1937; Fairbairn Engrg Prize, 1939; BSc 1st Cl. Hons 1939; MSc 1941; DSc 1968) CEng, FIET (FIEE 1959). On staff of DSIR, NPL, 1941–52; UK Scientific Mission Washington DC, 1947; Radio Research Station, later Appleton Lab. of SRC, 1952–79 Dep. Dir, 1969–77; Admin. Staff Coll., Henley, 1959. Delegate: Internat. Union of Radio Science, 1950–90 (Chm., Commn VIII, 1966–69); Internat. Radio Consultative Cttee 1953–90 (Internat. Chm., Study Group 2, 1980–90). Member: Inter-Union Commn on Frequency Allocations for Radio Astronomy and Space Science, 1965–92 (Sec., 1975–82) Electronics Divl Bd, IEE, 1970–76. Mem. Council: RHC, 1979–85 (Vice-Chm. 1982–85); RHBNC, 1985–89; Hon. Associate, Physics, RHC, 1975–85. Diplôme d'Honneur, Internat. Radio Cons. Cttee, 1989. *Publications:* more than 50 scientific papers. *Recreations:* genealogy, gardening, wildlife studies. *Address:* Gordano Lodge Clevedon Road, Weston-in-Gordano, Bristol BS20 8PZ.

HORNSBY, Timothy Richard, CBE 2008; MA; Chairman, Horniman Museum, since 2004; *b* 22 Sept. 1940; *s* of late Harker William Hornsby and Agnes Nora French; *m* 1971, Dr Charmian Rosemary Newton; one *s* one *d*. *Educ:* Bradfield Coll.; Christ Church, Oxford Univ. (MA 1st Cl. Hons Modern History). Harkness Fellow, USA, at Harvard, Columbia, Henry E. Huntington Research Inst., 1961–63; Asst Prof., Birmingham Southern Coll., Alabama, 1963–64; Research Lectr, Christ Church, Oxford, 1964–65; Asst Principal, Min. of Public Building and Works, 1965–67; Private Sec. to Controller

General, 1968–69; HM Treasury, 1971–73; Prin., then Asst Sec., DoE, 1975; Dir, Ancient Monuments and Historic Buildings, 1983–88, and Dir of Rural Affairs, 1984–88, DoE; Dir Gen., Nature Conservancy Council, 1988–91; Dir, Construction Policy Directorate, DoE, 1991; Chief Executive: Royal Bor. of Kingston upon Thames, 1991–95; Nat. Lottery Charities Bd, 1995–2001. A Comr, Nat. Lottery Commn, 2001 (Chm., 2004–05); Ind. Mem., Consumer Council for Water, 2005–; Mem., Adv. Cttee on Consumer Engagement, FSA, 2008–. Chair, Harkness Fellows Assoc., 2002–. Trustee, Charles Darwin Trust, 2002–. Gov., Legacy Trust, 2007–. FRSA. *Recreations:* conservation, ski-ing, talking. *Address:* c/o The Horniman Museum, 100 London Road, Forest Hill, SE23 3PQ; *e-mail:* thornsby@timothyhornsby.freeserve.co.uk. *Club:* Athenæum.

HOROWITZ, Anthony; children's writer; *b* 5 April 1955; *s* of late Mark and of Celia Joyce Horowitz; *m* 1988, Jill Green; two *s*. *Educ:* Rugby Sch.; Univ. of York (BA). Screenwriter: *film:* Stormbreaker, 2006; *television* includes: Robin of Sherwood; Poirot; Midsomer Murders; Murder in Mind; Crime Traveller; (with J. Green) Foyle's War (series), 2002 (Lew Grade People's Award, 2003), 2004. *Publications:* Devil's Doorbell, 1983; Night of the Scorpion, 1985; Groosham Grange, 1989; Myths and Legends, 1991; Granny, 1995; Falcon's Malteser, 1995; The Switch, 1997; Public Enemy No 2, 1997; The Devil and His Boy, 1999; Horowitz Horror, 1999; Unholy Grail, 1999; More Horowitz Horror, 2000; Mindgame (play), 2000; Stormbreaker, 2000; Point Blanc, 2001; Skeleton Key, 2002 (Red House Children's Book Award, 2003); Eagle Strike, 2003; Scorpia, 2004; The Killing Joke (adult novel), 2004; Ark Angel, 2005; Raven's Gate, 2005; Evil Star, 2006; Nightrise, 2007; Snakehead, 2007. *Recreations:* scuba-diving, cinema, walking in Suffolk. *Address:* c/o Greenlit Rights, 14–15 D'Arblay Street, W1F 8DZ. *T:* (020) 7287 3545, *Fax:* (020) 7439 6767; *e-mail:* contact@anthonyhorowitz.com.

HOROWITZ, Michael; QC 1990; **His Honour Judge Horowitz;** a Circuit Judge, since 2004; *b* 18 Oct. 1943; *s* of late David and Irene Horowitz; *m*; one *d* (one *s* decd). *Educ:* St Marylebone Grammar School; Pembroke College, Cambridge (BA 1966; LLB 1967). Pres., Cambridge Union Soc., 1967; English-Speaking Union Debating Tour of USA, 1967. Called to the Bar, Lincoln's Inn, 1968, Bencher, 1997; Asst Recorder, 1987; a Recorder, 1991–2004. Senate of Inns of Court and Bar, 1982–85; Mem., Professional Conduct Cttee, Bar Council, 1997–2000. Dir, Bar Mutual Indemnity Fund, 1999–2004. *Publications:* (contrib.) Rayden on Divorce, 17th edn 1997, 18th edn 2005; Essential Family Practice, 2002. *Recreations:* reading history, listening. *Address:* Milton Keynes County Court, 351 Silbury Boulevard, Witan Gate East, Milton Keynes MK9 2DT.

HOROWITZ, Prof. Myer, OC 1990; EdD; Adjunct Professor of Education, University of Victoria, since 1998; Professor Emeritus of Education, since 1990, President Emeritus, since 1999, University of Alberta; *b* 27 Dec. 1932; *s* of Philip Horowitz and Fanny Cotler; *m* 1956, Barbara, *d* of Samuel Rosen and Grace Midvidy, Montreal; two *d*. *Educ:* High Sch., Montreal; Sch. for Teachers, Macdonald Coll.; Sir George Williams Univ. (BA); Univ. of Alberta (MEd); Stanford Univ. (EdD). Teacher, Schs in Montreal, Sch. Bd, Greater Montreal, 1952–60. McGill University: Lectr in Educn, 1960–63; Asst Prof., 1963–65; Associate Prof., 1965–67; Asst to Dir, 1964–65; Prof. of Educn, 1967–69 and Asst Dean, 1965–69; University of Alberta: Prof. and Chm., Dept Elem. Educn, 1969–72; Dean, Faculty of Educn, 1972–75; Vice-Pres. (Academic), 1975–79; Pres., 1979–89. Hon. Dr: McGill, 1979; Concordia, 1982; Athabasca, 1989; British Columbia, 1990; Alberta, 1990; Victoria, 2000; Brock, 2000; Calgary, 2005. *Address:* A459 MacLaurin Building, University of Victoria, PO Box 3010 STN CSC, Victoria, BC V8W 3N4, Canada.

HORRELL, Roger William, CMG 1988; OBE 1974; HM Diplomatic Service, retired; *b* 9 July 1935; *s* of William John Horrell and Dorice Enid (*née* Young); *m* 1970, Patricia Mildred Eileen Smith (*née* Binns) (marr. diss. 1975); one *s* one *d*. *Educ:* Shebbear College; Exeter College, Oxford. MA. Served in Devonshire Regt, 1953–55; HM Colonial Service, Kenya, 1959–64; joined Foreign Office, 1964; Economic Officer, Dubai, 1965–67; FCO, 1967–70; First Sec., Kampala, 1970–73; FCO, 1973–76; First Sec., Lusaka, 1976–80; Counsellor, FCO, 1980–93. *Recreations:* cricket, reading, walking, bridge. *Address:* 51 Oatlands Drive, Weybridge, Surrey KT13 9LU. *Club:* Reform.

HORRIDGE, Prof. (George) Adrian, FRS 1969; FAA 1971; Professor, Research School of Biological Sciences, Australian National University, 1969–92, Emeritus Professor, since 1993; *b* Sheffield, England, 12 Dec. 1927; *s* of George William Horridge and Olive Stray; *m* 1954, Audrey Anne Lightburne; one *s* four *d*. *Educ:* King Edward VII Sch., Sheffield. Fellow, St John's Coll., Cambridge, 1953–56; on staff, St Andrews Univ., 1956–69; Dir, Gatty Marine Laboratory, St Andrews, 1960–69. Vis. Fellow, Churchill Coll., Cambridge, 1993–94. *Publications:* Structure and Function of the Nervous Systems of Invertebrates (with T. H. Bullock), 1965; Interneurons, 1968; (ed) The Compound Eye and Vision of Insects, 1975; Monographs of the Maritime Museum at Greenwich nos 38, 39, 40, 54, 1979–82; The Prahu: traditional sailing boat of Indonesia, 1982 (Oxford in Asia); Sailing Craft of Indonesia, 1985 (Oxford in Asia); Outrigger Canoes of Bali & Madura, Indonesia, 1986; (contrib.) The Austronesians, 1995; contribs 240 scientific papers to jls, etc, on behaviour and nervous systems of lower animals, and vision of the honeybee. *Recreations:* optics, mathematics, marine biology; sailing, language, arts, boat construction in Indonesia. *Address:* PO Box 475, Canberra City, ACT 2601, Australia.

HORROBIN, James, FWCB; artist blacksmith, since 1966; *b* 22 March 1946; *s* of Harry Horrobin and Betty Mary Horrobin; *m* 1966, Shirley Fitzgerald (marr. diss. 1983); one *s* one *d*; *m* 2007, Gabrielle Ridler. *Educ:* apprenticeship with his father on Exmoor, 1961–66; Hereford Tech. Coll. Set up own workshop, W Somerset, 1969; Lectr, Haystack Sch. of Craft, Maine, and Nat. Ornamental Metal Mus., Memphis, 1984–85. Chm., British Artist Blacksmith Assoc., 1983. Featured artist, Crafts Council exhibn, 1990. Commissions include: gates for Metalwork Gall., V&A Mus., 1981; portcullis and railings, Richmond Terrace, Whitehall, 1986; staircase, Chelsea residence of Charles Saatchi, 1989; screens, gate, address plates and emblem, 66 Cheapside, London, 1991; screens, railings and figure of Koko, Savoy Th., London, 1993; dossal rail, plaques and choir stalls, Church of Heavenly Rest, NY, 1997; lanterns, portico of St Paul's Chapel, Broadway, NY, 1998; gates, summer garden, Antony House, Cornwall, 1999; cloister railings, St John of Lattingtown, NY, 2003; Churchill Meml Screen, St Paul's Cathedral, London, 2003–04. FWCB 1996 (Silver Medal, 1996, Tonypandy Award, 2006, Co. of Blacksmiths). *Recreations:* painting, art history, architecture, reading, swimming, surfing, travel. *Address:* Doverhay Forge Studios, Porlock, Minehead, Somerset TA24 8QB. *T:* and *Fax:* (01643) 862444; *e-mail:* jh@doverhay.co.uk.

HORROCKS, Prof. Geoffrey Charles, PhD; Fellow, St John's College, Cambridge, since 1983; Professor of Comparative Philology, University of Cambridge, since 1997; *b* 3 Feb. 1951; *s* of Roland Horrocks and Marjorie Horrocks (*née* Atkinson); *m* 1973, Gillian Elizabeth Tasker; two *d*. *Educ:* Manchester Grammar Sch.; Downing Coll., Cambridge (BA 1972; PhD 1978). Employee Relns Manager, Mobil North Sea Ltd, 1972–73; Res. Fellow, Downing Coll., Cambridge, 1976–77; Lectr in Linguistics, SOAS, 1977–83; Lectr in Classics, Univ. of Cambridge, 1983–97. *Publications:* Space and Time in Homer, 1981; Generative Grammar, 1987; Greek: a history of the language and its speakers, 1997; (with J. Clackson) The Blackwell History of Latin Language, 2007; contrib. numerous articles in jls of general, theoretical and historical linguistics, and Classics. *Recreations:* travel, guitar, football, gardening, gossip, talking to the members of my family (in no particular order). *Address:* St John's College, Cambridge CB2 1TP. *T:* (01223) 338600.

HORROCKS, Jane; actress; *b* 18 Jan. 1964; *d* of John and Barbara Horrocks; partner, Nick Vivian; one *s* one *d*. *Educ:* Fearns Co. Secondary Sch., Rossendale, Lancs; RADA (Dip.). *Films:* The Dressmaker, 1989; Life is Sweet, 1991 (Best Supporting Actress, LA Critics Award, 1992); Little Voice, 1998; Chicken Run, 2000; The Corpse Bride, 2006; *plays:* The Rise and Fall of Little Voice, RNT and Aldwych, 1992–93; Cabaret, Donmar Warehouse, 1993–94; Sweet Panic, Duke of York's, 2003; Absurd Person Singular, Garrick, 2007; The Good Soul of Szechuan, Young Vic, 2008; *television:* Road, 1987; Storyteller, 1988; Bad Girl, 1992; Suffer the Little Children, 1994 (Best Actress Award, RTS, 1995); Absolutely Fabulous, 1992–94, 2001–04; Mirrorball, 2000; The Street, 2006, 2007; The Amazing Mrs Pritchard, 2006. *Address:* c/o Independent Talent Group Ltd, 76 Oxford Street, W1D 1BS. *Club:* Groucho.

HORROCKS, Paul John; Editor, Manchester Evening News, since 1997; *b* 19 Dec. 1953; *s* of Joe and Eunice Horrocks; *m* 1976, Linda Jean Walton; two *s* one *d*, and one step *d*. *Educ:* Bolton Sch. Reporter, Daily Mail, 1974; Manchester Evening News: gen. reporter, 1975–80; crime corresp., 1980–87; news editor, 1987–91; Asst Editor, 1991–95; Dep. Editor, 1995–97. Dir, Soc. of Editors, 2001–; Mem., PCC, 2002–. Vice-Pres., Community Foundn for Greater Manchester, 2000–; Mem., Organising Council, Commonwealth Games, Manchester 2002, 1998–. Patron, Francis House Children's Hospice, 1999–. *Recreations:* sailing, golf, Rugby Union. *Address:* Manchester Evening News, 164 Deansgate, Manchester M3 3RN.

HORROCKS, Peter John Gibson; Head of Multimedia Newsroom, BBC, since 2007; *b* 8 Oct. 1959; *s* of James Nigel Gibson Horrocks and Ellen Elizabeth Gibson Horrocks; *m* 1987, Katharine Rosemary Rogers; two *s* one *d*. *Educ:* King's Coll. Sch., Wimbledon; Christ's Coll., Cambridge (BA). BBC: Dep. Ed., Panorama, 1988–90; Editor: Election '92; Public Eye, 1992–94; Here and Now, 1994; Newsnight, 1994–97; Election '97; Panorama, 1997–2000; Hd of Current Affairs, 2000–05; Hd of TV News, 2005–07. *Address:* c/o BBC White City, Wood Lane, W12 7RJ.

HORROCKS, Raymond, CBE 1983; Chairman: Owenbell Ltd, 1987–2000; Chloride Group, 1988–99 (Director, 1986–99; Chief Executive, 1989–91); *b* 9 Jan. 1930; *s* of Elsie and Cecil Horrocks; *m* 1953, Pamela Florence Russell; three *d*. *Educ:* Bolton Municipal Secondary School. Textile Industry, 1944–48 and 1950–51; HM Forces, Army, Intelligence Corps, 1948–50; Sales Rep., Proctor & Gamble, 1951–52; Merchandiser, Marks & Spencer, 1953–58; Sub Gp Buying Controller, Littlewoods Mail Order Stores, 1958–63; various plant, departmental and divisional management positions, Ford Motor Co., 1963–72; Regional Dir, Europe and Middle East, Materials Handling Gp, Eaton Corp., 1972–77; Chm. and Man. Dir, Austin Morris Ltd, 1978–80; Man. Dir, BL Cars, 1980–81; Chm. and Chief Exec., BL Cars Gp, 1981–82; Exec. Dir and Bd Mem., BL, 1981–86; Gp Chief Exec., Cars, 1982–86; Chairman: Unipart Group Ltd, 1981–86; Austin Rover Gp Hldgs, 1981–86; Jaguar Cars Holdings Ltd, 1982–84; Kay Consultancy Group, 1989–91; Dir, Nuffield Services, 1982–86; non-executive Director: Jaguar plc, 1984–85; The Caravan Club, 1983–87; Electrocomponents, 1986–99; Lookers, 1986–99; WOL Hldgs Ltd, 1988–89; Burtree Caravans, 1988–96; Applied Hldgs (UK) Pty, 1988–96; Smith Millington Motor Co. Ltd (formerly SMAC Gp), 1988–96 (Chm., 1988–89); Applied Chemicals, 1988–96 (Dep. Chm., 1988–94); Jabiru UK, 1989–96. Member: Council, CBI, 1981–86; Europe Cttee, CBI, 1985–86. FIMI; CCMI. *Recreations:* fly fishing, gardening, walking. *Address:* Far End, Riverview Road, Pangbourne, Reading, Berks RG8 7AU.

HORSBRUGH-PORTER, Sir John (Simon), 4th Bt *cr* 1902; *b* 18 Dec. 1938; *s* of Col Sir Andrew Marshall Horsbrugh-Porter, 3rd Bt, DSO and Bar, and Annette Mary (*d* 1992), *d* of Brig.-Gen. R. C. Browne-Clayton, DSO; *S* father, 1986; *m* 1964, Lavinia Rose, *d* of Ralph Turton; one *s* two *d*. *Educ:* Winchester College; Trinity Coll., Cambridge (BA Hons History). Formerly, School Master. *Recreations:* literature, music. *Heir:* *s* Andrew Alexander Marshall Horsbrugh-Porter [*b* 19 Jan. 1971; *m* 2005, Jennie, *d* of Keith Downing; one *s*]. *Address:* Bowers Croft, Coleshill, Amersham, Bucks HP7 0LS. *T:* (01494) 724596.

HORSBURGH, John Millar Stewart; QC (Scot.) 1980; Sheriff of Lothian and Borders at Edinburgh, since 1990; *b* 15 May 1938; *s* of late Alexander Horsburgh and Helen Margaret Watson Millar or Horsburgh; *m* 1966, Johann Catriona Gardner, MB, ChB, DObst RCOG; one *s* one *d*. *Educ:* Hutchesons' Boys' Grammar Sch., Glasgow; Univ. of Glasgow (MA Hons, LLB). Admitted to Scots Bar, 1965; Advocate-Depute, 1987–89. Part-time Mem., Lands Tribunal for Scotland, 1985–87. *Address:* 8 Laverockbank Road, Edinburgh EH5 3DG. *T:* (0131) 552 5328.

HORSEY, Gordon; JP; a District Judge, 1991–94; *b* 20 July 1926; *s* of late E. W. Horsey, MBE, and of H. V. Horsey; *m* 1951, Jean Mary (*née* Favill); one *d*. *Educ:* Magnus Grammar Sch., Newark, Notts; St Catharine's Coll., Cambridge. BA, LLB. Served RN, 1944–45, RE, 1945–48 (Captain). Admitted solicitor, 1953; private practice in Nottingham, 1953–71; Registrar: Coventry County Court, 1971; Leicester County Court, 1973; a Recorder, 1978–84. JP Leics, 1975. *Recreation:* fly-fishing. *Address:* The Old Woodyard, 55 Swithland Lane, Rothley, Leics LE7 7SG. *T:* (0116) 230 2545.

HORSFALL, Sir Edward (John Wright), 4th Bt *cr* 1909, of Hayfield, Glusburn, co. York; *b* 17 Dec. 1940; *s* of Sir John Horsfall, 3rd Bt, MC, TD and of Cassandra Nora Bernadine Horsfall (*née* Wright); *S* father, 2005; *m* 1965, Rosemary King; three *s*. *Educ:* Uppingham. Dir, Hayfield Textiles Ltd, 1961–78. Mem. (C) Cotswold DC, 2003– (Cabinet Mem., 2004–). *Recreations:* theatre, travel, the arts, music. *Heir:* *e s* David Edward Horsfall [*b* 3 Sept. 1966; *m* 1996, Maria Gloria Sandoval; one *d*]. *Address:* The Gables, North Cerney, Cirencester, Glos GL7 7DA. *T:* (01285) 831369.

HORSFIELD, Maj.-Gen. David Ralph, OBE 1962; FIET; *b* 17 Dec. 1916; *s* of late Major Ralph B. and Morah Horsfield (*née* Baynes); *m* 1948, Sheelah Patricia Royal Eagan; two *s* two *d*. *Educ:* Oundle Sch.; RMA Woolwich; Clare Coll., Cambridge Univ. (MA). Commnd in Royal Signals, 1936; British troops, Egypt, 1939–41; comd Burma Corps Signals, 1942; Instr, Staff Coll., Quetta, 1944–45; comd 2 Indian Airborne Signals, 1946–47; Instr, RMA Sandhurst, 1950–53 (Company Comdr to HM King Hussein of Jordan); comd 2 Signal Regt, 1956–59; Principal Army Staff Officer, MoD, Malaya, 1959–61; Dir of Telecommunications (Army), 1966–68; ADC to the Queen, 1968–69; Deputy Communications and Electronics, Supreme HQ Allied Powers, Europe, 1968–69; Maj.-Gen. 1969; Chief Signal Officer, BAOR, 1969–72; Col Comdt, Royal Signals, 1972–78. Pres., Indian Signals Assoc. of GB, 1978–; Vice Pres., Nat. Ski Fedn, 1978–81. *Recreations:* ski-ing (British Ski Champion, 1949), the visual arts. *Address:* Preybrook Farm, Preywater Road, Wookey, Wells BA5 1LE. *T:* (01749) 673241. *Club:* Ski Club of Great Britain.

HORSFIELD, Peter Muir Francis; QC 1978; *b* 15 Feb. 1932; *s* of Henry Taylor Horsfield, AFC, and Florence Lily (*née* Muir); *m* 1962, Anne Charlotte, *d* of late Sir Piers Debenham, 2nd Bt, and Lady (Angela) Debenham; three *s. Educ:* Beaumont; Trinity Coll., Oxford (BA 1st Cl. Hons Mods and Greats). Served RNR, 1955–57; Lieut RNR, 1960. Called to the Bar, Middle Temple, 1958, Bencher, 1984; in practice at Chancery Bar, 1958–94. Pt-time Chm., VAT Tribunals and Special Comr of Income Tax, 1993–2003. *Recreation:* painting (one-man shows, Cassian de Vere Cole Fine Arts, 1997, Abbott & Holden, 2004). *Club:* Garrick.

HORSHAM, Area Bishop of; *no new appointment at time of going to press.*

HORSHAM, Archdeacon of; *see* Combes, Ven. R. M.

HORSHAM, Jean, CBE 1979; Deputy Parliamentary Commissioner for Administration, 1981–82, retired; Chairman, Solicitors Complaints Bureau, 1986–89; *b* 25 June 1922; *d* of Albert John James Horsham and Janet Horsham (*née* Henderson). *Educ:* Keith Grammar Sch. Forestry Commn, 1939–64, seconded to Min. of Supply, 1940–45; Min. of Land and Natural Resources, 1964–66; Min. of Housing and Local Govt, 1966; Office of Parly Comr for Administration, 1967–82. Member: Subsidence Compensation Review Cttee, 1983–84; Law Soc. Professional Purposes Cttee, 1984–86; Council on Tribunals, 1986–92; Chorus Enquiry at Royal Opera House, 1988–89; Tribunals Cttee, Judicial Studies Bd, 1990–92. *Address:* 14 Cotelands, Croydon, Surrey CR0 5UD. *T:* (020) 8681 0806; *e-mail:* jeanhorsham@onetel.net.uk.

HORSLEY, Rev. Canon Alan Avery Allen; Provost of St Andrew's Cathedral, Inverness, 1988–91; Canon Emeritus, Peterborough Cathedral, since 1986; Hon. Assistant Priest, All Saints', Northampton, since 2003; *b* 13 May 1936; *s* of Reginald James and Edith Irene Horsley; *m* 1966, Mary Joy Marshall, MA; two *d. Educ:* St Chad's Coll., Durham (BA 1958); Birmingham Univ.; Pacific Western Univ., Calif (MA 1984; PhD 1985); Queen's Coll., Birmingham. Ordained deacon 1960, priest 1961, Peterborough; Assistant Curate: Daventry, 1960–63; St Giles, Reading, 1963–64; St Paul's, Wokingham, 1964–66; Vicar of Yeadon, dio. Bradford, 1966–71; Rector of Heyford and Stowe Nine Churches, dio. Peterborough, 1971–78; RD of Daventry, 1976–78; Vicar of Oakham with Hambleton and Egleton (and Braunston and Brooke from 1980), 1978–86; Non-Residentiary Canon of Peterborough Cathedral, 1979–86; Chaplain: Catmose Vale Hosp., 1978–86; Rutland Memorial Hosp., 1978–86; Vicar of Lanteglos-by-Fowey, dio. Truro, 1986–88; Priest in Charge: St Mary in the Fields, Culloden, 1988–91; St Paul, Strathnairn, 1988–91; Vicar, Mill End and Heronsgate with West Hyde, 1991–2001; acting RD, Rickmansworth, 1998–2000, RD, 2000–01. Permission to officiate: dio. Truro, 1998–2005; dio. Peterborough, 2003–. *Publications:* (with Mary J. Horsley) A Lent Course, 1967, 3rd edn 2007; Lent with St Luke, 1978, 3rd edn 1997; Action at Lanteglos and Polruan, 1987; The Parish Church at Mill End, Rickmansworth, Hertfordshire: Pt I, 1999, 2nd edn 2000; Pt II, 2000; Forty-One Men: a biblical course for Lent, 2008; contribs to Rutland Record Soc. Jl. *Recreations:* music, piano and organ, cultivation of flowers, historical research. *Address:* 3 Leicester Terrace, Northampton NN2 6AJ. *T:* (01604) 628868; *e-mail:* alanahorsley@hotmail.co.uk.

HORSLEY, (Christine) Ruth; *see* Mercer, C. R.

HORSLEY, Colin, OBE 1963; FRCM 1973; Hon. RAM 1977; pianist; Professor, Royal College of Music, London, 1953–90; *b* Wanganui, New Zealand, 23 April 1920. *Educ:* Royal College of Music. Debut at invitation of Sir John Barbirolli at Hallé Concerts, Manchester, 1943. Soloist with all leading orchestras of Great Britain, the Royal Philharmonic Soc. (1953, 1959), Promenade Concerts, etc. Toured Belgium, Holland, Spain, France, Scandinavia, Malta, Ceylon, Malaya, Australia and New Zealand. Festival appearances include Aix-en-Provence, International Contemporary Music Festival, Palermo, British Music Festivals in Belgium, Holland and Finland. Vis. Prof., Royal Manchester Coll., later RNCM, 1964–80. Broadcasts frequently, and has made many records. *Recreation:* gardening. *Address:* Belmont, Dreemskerry, Maughold, Isle of Man IM7 1BF. *T:* (01624) 813095.

HORSLEY, Stephen Daril; Director of Public Health, Northamptonshire Teaching Primary Care Trust, since 2007 (Acting Director, 2006–07); *b* 23 June 1947; *s* of Donald Vincent Horsley and Marie Margaret Horsley; *m* 1974, Vivienne Marjorie Lee; one *s* two *d. Educ:* Guy's Hosp.; Manchester Business Sch. (MBSc 1985); Manchester Univ. (MA Health Ethics and Law 2004). FRCP 1988 (MRCP 1976); FFPH. Gen. Hosp. Medicine, Truro, 1971–75; Community Medicine, Yorks RHA, 1975–79; District Community Physician, E Cumbria HA, 1979–82; District MO, S Cumbria HA, 1982–85; Specialist in Community Medicine, Oxford RHA, 1985–86; Regl MO, N Western RHA, 1986–94; Consultant in Public Health, Morecambe Bay HA, 1994–2000; Locum Consultant in Public Health: St Helens and Knowsley DHA, 2000–02; St Helens PCT, April 2002; Dir of Public Health, Northants Heartlands PCT, 2002–06. Hon. Prof. of Public Health, Lancaster Univ., 1997. *Publications:* contribs to BMJ, Community Medicine. *Recreations:* wind surfing, walking. *Address:* Northamptonshire Teaching Primary Care Trust, Bevan House, Kettering Parkway South, Venture Park, Kettering, NN15 6XR.

HORSMAN, Malcolm; *b* 28 June 1933. Director, Slater Walker Securities Ltd, 1967–70; Chairman: Ralli International Ltd, 1969–73; Alice Hoffman Homes Ltd, later Hoffman De Visme Foundn, 1992–98; Director: The Bowater Corporation Ltd, 1972–77; Tozer Kemsley & Millbourn (Holdings) Ltd, 1975–82. Member: Study Group on Local Authority Management Structures, 1971–72; South East Economic Planning Council, 1972–74; Royal Commission on the Press, 1974–77; Institute of Contemporary Arts Ltd, 1975–78; Council, Oxford Centre for Management Studies, 1973–84; Chm., British Centre, Internat. Theatre Inst., 1982–84 (Mem. Exec. Council, 1980–87). Visiting Fellow, Cranfield Univ. (formerly Cranfield Institute of Technology)/The School of Management, 1977–97. Vis. Lectr, Univ. of Transkei, 1977. Chm., Nat. Youth Theatre, 1982–90 (Dep. Chm. 1971–82); Director: Hackney New Variety Ltd (Hackney Empire Trust), 1995–97; Gate Theatre, 1997–2000; Member: Court, RCA, 1977–80; Editorial Bd, DRAMA, 1978–81; Royal Court Develt Cttee, 1995–98; Council, Birthright, 1974–85; Council, Anti-Slavery Internat., 1998–2000. Chm., Open School Trust, 1998–2000. *Club:* Harlequins Rugby Football.

HORSMAN, Michael John; Special Professor, Nottingham University Business School, 2003–06; Independent Member, House of Commons Senior Pay Panel, since 2003; *b* 3 March 1949; *s* of late Graham Joseph Vivian Horsman and of Ruth (*née* Guest); *m* 1977, Dr Anne Margaret Marley; three *s. Educ:* Dollar Acad.; Glasgow Univ. (MA Hist. and Politics, 1st cl. Hons, 1971); Balliol Coll., Oxford (Snell Exhibnr, Brackenbury Scholar). Entered Civil Service, 1974; Private Sec. to Chm., MSC, 1978–79; Dept of Employment, 1979–84, on secondment to Unilever, 1981–82; Dir, PER, 1984–85; Hd, Finance Policy, and Resource Controller, MSC, 1985–87; Hd, Ops Br., Employment Service, 1987–89; Regl Dir, London and SE, Employment Service, 1989–92; Dir, Office of Manpower Economics, 1992–2003. *Recreations:* historical research, literature, cycling.

HORT, Sir Andrew (Edwin Fenton), 9th Bt *cr* 1767, of Castle Strange, Middlesex; *b* 1 Nov. 1954; *e s* of Sir James Fenton Hort, 8th Bt and Joan, *d* of Edward Peat; *S* father, 1995 but his name does not appear on the Official Roll of the Baronetage; *m* 1986, Mary, *d* of Jack Whibley; one *s* one *d. Heir: s* James John Fenton Hort, *b* 26 Nov. 1989. *Address:* Westerlee, 77 Fortis Green, E Finchley, N2 9JD.

HORTON, Geoffrey Robert; Economic Consultant, Horton 4 Consulting, since 1998; *b* 23 July 1951; *s* of late Leonard Horton and Joan Horton; *m* 1991, Dianne Alexandra Craker; two *d. Educ:* Bristol Grammar Sch.; Exeter Coll., Oxford (MA); University Coll. London (MSc Econ). Economic asst, HM Treasury, 1974–76; Lectr in Econs, University Coll. of Swansea, 1976–78; Economic Advr, HM Treasury, 1978–85; Chief Economist, DRI (Europe) Ltd, 1985–88; Sen. Economic Advr, Dept of Energy, 1988–90; Sen. Consultant, Nat. Economic Research Associates, 1990–92; Dir, Regulation and Business Affairs, Office of Electricity Regulation, 1990–95; Dir Gen., Electricity Supply for NI, 1992–95; Dir of Consumer Affairs, OFT, 1995–98. Member: Panel of Experts for Reform of the Water Service in NI, 2003–06; Energy and Climate Security Panel, BERR, later DECC, 2007–. *Publications:* articles and research papers on economics. *Recreations:* reading, cooking, sailing. *Address:* 43 Grove Park, Camberwell, SE5 8LG. *T:* (020) 7733 6587; *e-mail:* Geoff@Horton4.co.uk.

HORTON, Mark Anthony; His Honour Judge Horton; a Circuit Judge, since 2008; *b* Crediton, Devon, 30 Sept. 1953; *s* of Robert Anthony Horton, DFC and Helene Rene Horton; *m* 1986, Madeleine Curry; two *s. Educ:* Blundell's Sch., Tiverton; Birmingham Univ. (LLB Hons). Called to the Bar, Middle Temple, 1976; in practice as barrister specialising in crime and personal injury; Hd, Criminal Dept, St John's Chambers, Bristol; Recorder, 2000–08. *Recreations:* tennis, football, Rugby, languages, French, German, Spanish, Russian. *Address:* N Somerset.

HORTON, Matthew Bethell; QC 1989; *b* 23 Sept. 1946; *s* of Albert Leslie Horton, BSc FRICS and Gladys Rose Ellen Harding; *m* 1972, Liliane Boleslawski (marr. diss. 1984); one *s* one *d. Educ:* Sevenoaks School; Trinity Hall, Cambridge (Open Exhibn, Hist. Squire Law Scholar; 1st Cl. Hons Law 1967; MA 1967; LLM 1968); Astbury Scholar, Middle Temple, 1968. Called to the Bar, Middle Temple, 1969. Western Circuit; Mem. Parly Bar Mess, 1977. Member: Cttee, Jt Planning Law Conf., 1983–97; European Environmental Law Cttee, Internat. Bar Assoc.; Admin. Law Cttee of Justice. *Recreations:* ski-ing, windsurfing, tennis. *Address:* 39 Essex Street, WC2R 3AT. *Club:* Tramp.

HORTON, Dr Richard Charles, FRCP; Editor, The Lancet, since 1995; *b* 29 Dec. 1961; *s* of Ole Bjarne Kverneland and Barbara Gwendoline Beddow, and adopted *s* of Charles Kenneth Horton and Clarice Audrey Ward; *m* 1998, Ingrid Johanna Wolfe; one *d. Educ:* Bristol GS; Univ. of Birmingham (BSc 1st, MB ChB Hons). FRCP 1997. Sen. House Officer, Queen Elizabeth Hosp., Birmingham, 1987–88; Clin. Res. Fellow, Royal Free Hosp., London, 1988–90; Asst Editor, 1990–93, N American Editor (New York), 1993–95, The Lancet. Med. Columnist, The Observer, 1996–98. Lectures: Guggenheim, 1998; Bradford Hill Meml, 1999; Curtis Meinert Hon., 2001; British Jl of Surg., 2002; Chadwick, 2003; King's Dialogues, 2005; William Withering, 2006; Lock, 2006; Lord Cohen, 2007; Otto Wolf, 2007. Visiting Professor: Cleveland Clinic, USA, 1997, 2007; Duke Univ., USA, 2000; Yale Univ., 2000; Arthur Thomson Vis. Prof., Univ. of Birmingham, 2000; Arnold Johnson Vis. Prof., McMaster Univ., Canada, 2000; Mayo Clinic, USA, 2002; Potiker Prof., Cleveland Clinic, USA, 2002; Hon. Professor: LSHTM, 2000–; UCL, 2005–; Univ. of Edinburgh, 2008–. Writer and Presenter, The Citadel (TV), 1998. Member: Exec. Cttee, UK Medical Journalists Assoc., 1991–93, 1995–97; Evaluation Gp, Acheson Ind. Inquiry into Inequalities in Health, 1998; RCP Wkg Party on Defining and Maintaining Professional Values in Medicine, 2004–05; Co-Chair, WHO Scientific Adv. Gp on Internat. Clinical Trials Registration, 2006–; Chair, RCP Wkg Party on Physicians and the Pharmaceutical Industry, 2007–08. President: World Assoc. of Med. Editors, 1995–96; US Council of Science Editors, 2005–06; Foundn Council, Global Forum for Health Res., 2003–06. Patron, Medsin, 2006–. Fellow, Amer. Acad. for Advancement of Sci., 1997; Founder FMedSci 1998. Hon. MD Birmingham, 2008. Med. Pubn of the Year, Med. Journalists' Assoc., 2004; Edinburgh Medal, 2007. *Publications:* Second Opinion: doctors, diseases and decisions in modern medicine, 2003; Doctors in Society, 2005; books and articles on cardiovascular pharmacol., gastroenterol., global health and journalology; reviews and essays in New York Review of Books, London Review of Books, TLS. *Recreation:* horizontal reflection. *Address:* The Lancet, 32 Jamestown Road, NW1 7BY. *T:* (020) 7424 4929.

HORTON, Sir Robert (Baynes), Kt 1997; Director, since 1987, and Member of European Advisory Council, since 1999, Emerson Electric Co.; *b* 18 Aug. 1939; *s* of late William Harold Horton and Dorothy Joan Horton (*née* Baynes); *m* 1962, Sally Doreen (*née* Wells); one *s* one *d. Educ:* King's School, Canterbury; University of St Andrews (BSc); Massachusetts Inst. of Technology (SM; Sloan Fellow, 1970–71). British Petroleum, 1957–92: General Manager, BP Tankers, 1975–76; Gen. Manager, Corporate Planning, 1976–79; Chief Exec. Officer, BP Chemicals, 1980–83; a Man. Dir, 1983–86 and 1988–92; Chm. and Chief Exec. Officer, 1990–92; Chm., Standard Oil, 1986–88; Vice-Chm., BRB, 1992–93; Chairman: Railtrack, 1993–99; Chubb plc, 2002–03; Sporting Exchange Ltd, 2004–06. Director: ICL plc, 1982–84; Pilkington Brothers plc, 1985–86; National City Corp., 1986–88; Partner Re, 1993–2003; Premier Farnell plc, 1995–2004; Estate Incomes Ltd, 1998–2005. Pres., Chemicals Industry Assoc., 1982–84; Vice-Chm., BIM, 1985–91 (CCMI (CBIM 1982)); Member: SERC, 1985–86; UFC, 1989–92; Bd and Management Cttee, Amer. Petroleum Inst., 1986–88; US Business Roundtable, 1986–88; Nat. Petroleum Council, USA, 1986–88. Pres., BESO, 1993–97. Trustee: Cleveland Orchestra, 1986–93; MIT Corp., 1987–97; Case Western Reserve Univ., 1987–93; Chairman: Tate Foundation, 1988–92; Business in the Arts, 1988–96. Chancellor, Univ. of Kent at Canterbury, 1990–95. Gov., King's Sch., Canterbury, 1984–2005 (Gov. Emeritus, 2005–). FCIT 1994; FRSA. Hon. FIChemE 1990; Hon. FCGI 1992. Hon. LLD: Dundee, 1988; Aberdeen, 1992; Hon. DCL Kent, 1990; Hon. DBA N London Poly., 1991; Hon. DSc Cranfield, 1992; DUniv Open, 1993; Hon. DCL Kingston, 1994. Corporate Leadership Award, MIT, 1987; Civic Award, Cleveland, 1988; SCI Gold Medal, 1990. *Recreations:* books, music, country activities. *Address:* Stoke Abbas, South Stoke, Oxon RG8 0JT. *Clubs:* Athenæum; Leander; Huntercombe Golf.

HORTON, Roger Graham; Chief Executive Officer, Taylor & Francis Group, since 2003; *b* 11 June 1957; *s* of late Bertram Horton and of Joan Horton; *m* 1986, Deborah; two *d.* Sales and mktg roles with Internat. Thomson, 1977–87; Editl Dir, McGraw-Hill, Europe, 1987–94; Man. Dir, Taylor & Francis, 1994–2003. *Publications:* business and industry related articles. *Recreations:* Reading FC home games fanatic, rock 'n' roll bass player, occasional barn dance caller, golf. *Address:* c/o Taylor & Francis, 2 Park Square, Abingdon, Oxon OX14 4RN. *T:* (020) 7017 6000; *e-mail:* roger.horton@informa.com. *Club:* Oxfordshire Golf.

HORTON, Sharon Margaret; *see* Bowles, S. M.

HORVITZ, Prof. (Howard) Robert, PhD; Professor of Biology, Massachusetts Institute of Technology, since 1986; *b* 8 May 1947; *s* of late Oscar Horvitz and of Mary Horvitz; *m* 1993, Martha Constantine Paton; one *d.* *Educ:* Massachusetts Inst. of Technol. (BS 1968); Harvard Univ. (MA 1972; PhD 1974). Asst Prof. of Biol., 1978–81, Associate Prof. of Biol., 1981–86, MIT; Investigator, Howard Hughes Med. Inst., 1988–. (Jtly) Nobel Prize in Physiol. or Medicine, 2002. *Address:* Department of Biology, Massachusetts Institute of Technology, 77 Massachusetts Avenue, Cambridge, MA 02139, USA.

HORWELL, Richard Eric; QC 2006; a Recorder, since 2004; *b* 14 Nov. 1953; *s* of John and Edna Horwell; *m* 2002, Lindsay; one *s.* *Educ:* Ewell Castle Sch.; Council of Legal Educn. Jun. Treasury Counsel, 1991–96; Sen. Treasury Counsel, 1996–2002; First Sen. Treasury Counsel, 2002–06. *Recreations:* motor sport, travel, photography, film. *Address:* 39–40 Cloth Fair, EC1A 7NR.

HORWICH, Prof. Alan, PhD; FRCP, FRCR, FMedSci; Professor of Radiotherapy, since 1986, and Dean, since 2005, Institute of Cancer Research and Royal Marsden Hospital; *b* 1 June 1948; *s* of William and Audrey Horwich; *m* 1981, Pauline Amanda Barnes; two *s* one *d.* *Educ:* William Hulme's Grammar Sch., Manchester; University College Hosp. Med. Sch. (MB BS 1971; PhD 1981). MRCP 1974, FRCP 1994; FRCR 1981. Postgrad. medicine, London, 1971–74; Fellowship in Oncology, Harvard, 1975; res. on ribonucleic acid tumour viruses, ICRF, 1976–79; radiation oncology, Royal Marsden Hosp. and Inst. of Cancer Res., 1979–; Dean, Inst. of Cancer Res., 1992–97; Dir, Clinical R&D, Royal Marsden Hosp., 1994–2005. Chm., MRC Testicular Tumour Working Party, 1988–94. Civilian Consultant to RN, 1989–. Warden, RCR, 1998–2002. FMedSci 2003. *Publications:* Testicular Cancer: investigation and management, 1991, 2nd edn 1996; Combined Radiotherapy and Chemotherapy in Clinical Oncology, 1992; Oncology: a multidisciplinary text book, 1995; numerous articles in med. jls on urological cancers and lymphomas. *Address:* Royal Marsden Hospital, Downs Road, Sutton, Surrey SM2 5PT. *T:* (020) 8661 3274.

See also P. G. Horwich.

HORWICH, Prof. Paul Gordon, PhD; Professor of Philosophy, New York University, since 2005; *b* 7 Feb. 1947; *s* of William Horwich and Audrey (*née* Rigby). *Educ:* Brasenose Coll., Oxford (BA Physics); Yale Univ. (MA Physics & Phil.); Cornell Univ. (MA, PhD Phil. 1975). Massachusetts Institute of Technology: Asst Prof. in Philosophy, 1973–80; Associate Prof., 1980–87; Prof. of Philosophy, 1987–95; Prof. of Philosophy, UCL, 1994–2000; Kornblith Prof. of Philosophy, Grad. Center, CUNY, 2000–05. *Publications:* Probability and Evidence, 1982; Asymmetries in Time, 1987; Truth, 1992, 2nd edn 1998; Meaning, 1998; From a Deflationary Point of View, 2004; Reflections on Meaning, 2005. *Recreations:* opera, ski-ing, summers in Tuscany. *Address:* Department of Philosophy, New York University, 5 Washington Place, New York, NY 10003, USA. *Club:* Black's.

See also A. Horwich.

HORWOOD, Martin Charles; MP (Lib Dem) Cheltenham, since 2005; *b* 12 Oct. 1962; *s* of Don Horwood and Nina Horwood; *m* 1995, Dr Shona Arora; one *s* one *d.* *Educ:* Queen's Coll., Oxford (BA 1984). Account Exec., Ted Bates Advertising, 1985–86; Dir of Develt, British Humanist Assoc., 1986–88; Creative Co-ordinator, Help the Aged, 1988–90; Donor Marketing Manager, Oxfam, 1990–95; Dir of Communications and Fundraising, Oxfam (India), 1995–96; Dir of Fundraising, Alzheimer's Soc., 1996–2001; Sen. Consultant, 2001–03, Hd of Consultancy, 2003–05, Target Direct Marketing. Lib Dem spokesman on envmt, 2006–. Member: Select Cttee on Communities and Local Govt (formerly ODPM), 2005–07; Envmtl Audit Select Cttee, 2007–; Sec., All-Party Gp for corporate responsibility, 2005–; Chm., All-Party Gp for tribal peoples, 2007–. *Recreations:* cycling, drawing, astronomy. *Address:* House of Commons, SW1A 0AA. *T:* (020) 7219 4784; *e-mail:* martin@martinhorwood.net. 16 Hewlett Road, Cheltenham, Glos GL52 6AA. *T:* (01242) 224889, *Fax:* (01242) 256658.

HORWOOD-SMART, Rosamund, (Mrs R. O. Bernays); QC 1996; a Recorder, since 1995; *b* 21 Sept. 1951; *d* of late John Horwood-Smart and of Sylvia Horwood-Smart; *m* 1st, 1983, Richard Blackford (marr. diss. 1994); one *s* one *d*; 2nd, 1996, Richard O. Bernays. *Educ:* Felixstowe Coll.; Cambridgeshire High Sch. for Girls; Inns of Court Sch. of Law. Called to the Bar, Inner Temple, 1974, Bencher, 1998. Trustee: Nat. Music Day, 1992–98; Prisoners of Conscience Fund, 1990–2001; Toyota Trevelyan-shi Trust, 1990–2007; Temple Music Trust, 2006–; Handel House, 2008–. Vice Pres., Internat. Students House, 2007–. *Recreations:* music, gardening. *Address:* 18 Red Lion Court, EC4A 3EB. *T:* (020) 7520 6000.

HOSE, John Horsley, CBE 1987; Forest Craftsman, Forestry Commission, 1975–88 (Forest Worker, 1949, Skilled Forest Worker, 1950); President, National Union of Agricultural and Allied Workers, 1978–82; *b* 21 March 1928; *s* of Harry and Margaret Eleanor Hose; *m* 1st, 1967, Margaret Winifred Gaskin (marr. diss. 1987); 2nd, 1987, Linda Sharon Morris. *Educ:* Sneinton Boulevard Council Sch.; Nottingham Bluecoat Sch. Architects' Junior Asst, 1943–46. National Service, with Royal Engineers, 1946–48. Chm., Nat. Trade Gp, Agricultural and Allied Workers/TGWU, 1982–86 (Mem., 1982–89); Mem., Gen. Exec. Council, TGWU, 1986–88. *Recreations:* reading, drinking real ale. *Address:* St Martin's Rectory, St Agnes Close, Wigman Road, Bilborough, Nottingham NG8 4BJ. *T:* (0115) 929 1534.

HOSIE, Stewart; MP (SNP) Dundee East, since 2005; *b* 3 Jan. 1963; *m* 1997, Shona Robison, *qv*; one *d.* *Educ:* Carnoustie High Sch.; Dundee Coll. of Technol. Gp Inf. Systems Manager, MIH, 1988–93; systems analyst, 1993–96; Year 2000/EMU Project Manager, Stakis/Hilton, 1996–2000. Nat. Sec., SNP, 1999–2003. Contested (SNP): Kirkcaldy, 1992, 1997; Kirkcaldy, Scottish Parlt, 1999. *Address:* (office) 8 Old Glamis Road, Dundee DD3 8HP; House of Commons, SW1A 0AA.

HOSKER, Edmund Nigel Ronald; Director, Energy Markets, Department of Energy and Climate Change (formerly Department for Business, Enterprise and Regulatory Reform), since 2008; *b* 25 April 1958; *s* of Ronald Reece Hosker and Hilda Gertrude Hosker (*née* Harrington); *m* 1983, Elizabeth Miranda Thornely; three *d.* *Educ:* Slough Grammar Sch.; St Catharine's Coll., Cambridge (BA Hons English 1979). Joined Department of Trade and Industry, 1979: Private Sec. to Minister for Industry and subseq. to Sec. of State for Trade and Industry, 1983–84; Principal, 1984; on secondment to British Embassy, Washington, 1990–94; Asst Sec., 1994; transf. to Cabinet Office, 1995–97; Dir of Finance, DTI, 1997–2000; Dir, Finance and Resource Mgt, DTI, 2000–02; on secondment to Scottish Power, 2003; Dir, Europe and World Trade, DTI, subseq. BERR, 2003–08. *Recreations:* reading, family life. *Address:* Department of Energy and Climate Change, 1 Victoria Street, SW1H 0ET.

HOSKER, Sir Gerald (Albery), KCB 1995 (CB 1987); HM Procurator General, Treasury Solicitor and Queen's Proctor, 1992–95; *b* 28 July 1933; *s* of Leslie Reece Hosker and Constance Alice Rose Hosker (*née* Hubbard); *m* 1956, Rachel Victoria Beatrice Middleton; one *s* one *d.* *Educ:* Berkhamsted Sch., Berkhamsted, Herts. Admitted Solicitor, 1956; Corporate Secretary 1964; Associate of the Faculty of Secretaries and Administrators 1964. Articled to Derrick Bridges & Co., 1951–56; with Clifford-Turner & Co., 1957–59; entered Treasury Solicitor's Dept as Legal Asst, 1960; Sen. Legal Asst, 1966; Asst Solicitor, 1973; Under Sec. (Legal), 1982; Dep. Treasury Solicitor, 1984–87; Solicitor to the DTI, 1987–92. Conducted enquiry into: Customs and Excise aspects of Simon de Danser case, 1999; C. W. Cheney Pension Fund for DSS, 2001; Public Inquiry Comr, Falkland Is, 1999–2000. Dir, RAFM Investments Ltd, 2003–. Mem. Bd, Inst. of Advanced Legal Studies, Univ. of London, 1992–95; Governor, Lyonsdown Sch., New Barnet, 1996–2006. Trustee, RAF Mus., 1998–; Mem., Governing Bodies Forum, Mus Assoc., 2005–. FRSA 1964. Hon. QC 1991. *Recreations:* the study of biblical prophecy, swimming. *Address:* (office) c/o Treasury Solicitor, One Kemble Street, WC2B 4TS. *Club:* Royal Over-Seas League.

HOSKING, Barbara Nancy, CBE 1999 (OBE 1985); Deputy Chairman, Westcountry Television, 1997–99 (non-executive Director, 1992–99); *b* 4 Nov. 1926; *d* of late William Henry Hosking and Ada Kathleen Hosking (*née* Murrish). *Educ:* West Cornwall School for Girls, Penzance; Hillcroft College, Surbiton; and by friends. Secretary to Town Clerk, Council of Isles of Scilly, and local corresp. for BBC and Western Morning News, 1945–47; Editl Asst, The Circle, Odeon and Gaumont cinemas, 1947–50; Asst to Inf. Officer, Labour Party, 1952–55; Asst to Gen. Manager, Uruwira Minerals Ltd, Tanzania, 1955–57; Res. Officer, Broadcasting Section, Labour Party, 1958–65; Press and Inf. Officer posts, Civil Service, 1965–77; Controller of Inf. Services, IBA, 1977–86; Political Consultant, Yorkshire TV, 1987–92. Mem. (Lab), Islington BC, 1962–64. Non-exec. Dir, Camden and Islington Community Health Services NHS Trust, 1992–93. Pres., Media Soc., 1987–88; Jt Vice-Chm., NCVO, 1987–92. Mem. Council, Family Policy Studies Centre, 1994–97. Trustee: Charities Aid Foundn, 1987–92; 300 Gp, 1988–91; Nat. Literacy Trust, 1993–99. Associate, Women's Advertising Club of London, 1994–. Patron, Clean-Break Theatre Co., 1992–. Hon. Vice Pres., London Cornish Assoc., 1992; Bard, Gorsedd Kernow. Occasional radio broadcaster. FRTS 1988; FRSA (Mem. Council, 1992–96). DUniv Ulster, 1996. Special citation, Internat. Women's Forum, NY, 1983, Boston, 1996. *Publications:* contribs to Punch, New Scientist, Spectator. *Recreations:* opera, lieder, watching politics, watching sport. *Address:* 9 Highgate Spinney, Crescent Road, N8 8AR. *T:* (020) 8340 1853. *Club:* Reform.

HOSKING, Prof. Geoffrey Alan, FBA 1993; FRHistS; Professor of Russian History, 1984–2007, now Emeritus, and Leverhulme Personal Research Professor, 1999–2004, University College London; *b* 28 April 1942; *s* of Stuart William Steggall Hosking and Jean Ross Hosking; *m* 1970, Anne Lloyd Hirst; two *d.* *Educ:* Maidstone Grammar Sch.; King's Coll., Cambridge (MA, PhD); St Antony's Coll., Oxford. FRHistS 1998. Asst Lectr in Government, 1966–68, Lectr in Government, 1968–71, Univ. of Essex; Vis. Lectr in Political Science, Univ. of Wisconsin, Madison, 1971–72; Lectr in History, Univ. of Essex, 1972–76; Sen. Research Fellow, Russian Inst., Columbia Univ., New York, 1976; Sen. Lectr and Reader in Russian History, Univ. of Essex, 1976–84; Dep. Dir, SSEES, London Univ., 1996–98. Vis. Prof., Slavisches Inst., Univ. of Cologne, 1980–81; Mem., IAS, Princeton, 2006–07. BBC Reith Lectr, 1988 (The Rediscovery of Politics: authority, culture and community in the USSR). Member: Council, Writers and Scholars Educnl Trust, 1985–2007; Overseas Policy Cttee, British Acad., 1994–2000; Council, RHistS, 2002–06; Jury, Booker Prize for Russian Fiction, 1993. Member: Internat. Academic Council, Mus. of Contemporary History (formerly Mus. of the Revolution), Moscow, 1994–; Admin. Bd, Moscow Sch. of Pol Studies, 1992–; Exec. Cttee, Britain-Russia Centre, 1994–2000. Trustee, J. S. Mill Inst., 1992–96; Governor, Camden Sch. for Girls, 1989–94. Member: Editl Bd, Jl of Contemporary History, 1988–99; Editl Cttee, Nations and Nationalism, 1994–; Editl Bd, Nationalities Papers, 1997–; Editl Bd, Reviews in History, 1999–2004; Editl Bd, Ab Imperio, 2002–; Editl Bd, Otechestvennaia Istoriia, 2007–. Hon. Dr Russian Acad. Scis, 2000. *Publications:* The Russian Constitutional Experiment: Government and Duma 1907–14, 1973; Beyond Socialist Realism: Soviet fiction since Ivan Denisovich, 1980; A History of the Soviet Union, 1985, 3rd edn 1992 (Los Angeles Times Hist. Book Prize, 1986); The Awakening of the Soviet Union, 1990, 2nd edn 1991; (with J. Aves and P. J. S. Duncan) The Road to Post-Communism: independent political movements in the Soviet Union 1985–91, 1992; Russia: people and Empire 1552–1917, 1997; (ed with George Schöpflin) Myths and Nationhood, 1997; (ed with Robert Service) Russian Nationalism Past and Present, 1998; (ed with Robert Service) Reinterpreting Russia, 1999; Russia and the Russians: a history, 2001 (history prize, Ind. Publisher Book Awards, USA, 2002); Rulers and Victims: the Russians in the Soviet Union, 2006 (Alec Nove Book Prize, 2008). *Recreations:* music, chess, walking. *Address:* School of Slavonic and East European Studies, University College London, Gower Street, WC1E 6BT. *T:* (020) 7267 5543; *e-mail:* geoffreyhosking@mac.com.

HOSKING, John Everard, CBE 1990; JP; DL; Chairman, Agra Europe (London) Ltd, 1989–94 (Director and Chief Executive, 1974–89); Vice-President, Magistrates' Association, since 1990 (Chairman of Council, 1987–90); *b* 23 Oct. 1929; *s* of J. Everard Hosking, OBE and E. Margaret (*née* Shaxson); *m* 1953, Joan Cecily Whitaker, BSc; two *s.* *Educ:* Marlborough Coll.; Wye Coll., London Univ. (BScA 1953). NDA 1954. Farming and forestry in Kent, 1953–69; Man. Dir, Eastes and Loud Ltd, 1965–69; Director: Newgrain-Kent, 1969–74; Ashford Corn Exchange Co., 1965–69; Agroup Ltd, 1987–94; Bureau Européen de Recherches SA, 1987–90; European Intelligence Ltd, 1987–94. Tax Comr, 1980–2004. Chairman: Centre for European Agricultural Studies Assoc., 1977–83; Kent Magistrates' Courts Cttee, 1984–88; Member: Kent Police Authority, 1970–74; Lord Chancellor's Adv. Cttee on the Appointment of Magistrates, 1977–89; Central Council, Magistrates' Courts Cttees, 1980–83; Bar Council Professional Conduct Cttee, 1983–86; Senate of Inns of Court and the Bar Disciplinary Tribunal, 1983–86; Council, Commonwealth Magistrates' and Judges' Assoc., 1989–92; Lord Chief Justice's Working Party on Mode of Trial, 1989; Lord Chancellor's Adv. Cttee on Legal Educn and Conduct, 1991–94. Pres., Kent Magistrates' Assoc., 2001– (Chm., 1973–78). Pres., Wye Coll. Agricola Club, 1995–2004. Vice-Patron, Ashford Community Arts Trust, 2001–. Governor: Ashford Sch., 1976–2006 (Chm., 1994–2001); Wye Coll., Univ. of London, 1995–2000; Mem. Governing Council, Church Schs Co., 1999–2001. JP Kent, 1962 (Chm., Ashford Bench, 1975–85); DL Kent, 1992. British Univs Ploughing Champion, 1952. *Publications:* (ed) Rural Response to the Resource Crisis in Europe, 1981; The Agricultural Industry of West Germany, 1990. *Recreations:* the arts, the countryside. *Address:* Pett House, Charing, Kent. *Club:* Farmers'.

HOSKINS, Sir Brian (John), Kt 2007; CBE 1998; PhD; FRS 1988; Director, Grantham Institute for Climate Change, Imperial College London, since 2008; Professor of Meteorology, University of Reading, since 1981; Royal Society Research Professor, since 2001; *b* 17 May 1945; *s* of George Frederick Hoskins and Kathleen Matilda Louise Hoskins; *m* 1968, Jacqueline Holmes; two *d.* *Educ:* Bristol Grammar Sch.; Trinity Hall, Cambridge (BA 1966; MA, PhD 1970). FRMetS 1970 (Hon. FRMets 2001); Fellow, Amer. Meteorol Soc., 1985. Post-doctoral Fellow, Nat. Center for Atmospheric Res., Boulder, Colo, 1970–71; Vis. Scientist, GFD Program, Univ. of Princeton, 1972–73; Univ. of Reading: Post-doctoral Fellow, 1971–72, Gp Leader, 1973–, Atmospheric Modelling Gp; Reader in Atmospheric Modelling, 1976–81; Head, Dept of Meteorol., 1990–96. Special Advr to Sec. of State for Transport, 1990. Meteorological Office: Chm.,

SAC, 1995–; non-exec. Dir, 2000–. Member: NERC, 1988–94; Jt Scientific Cttee, World Climate Res. Prog., 1995–2004 (Vice Chm., 2000–04); Royal Commn on Envmtl Pollution, 1998–2005; UK Govt Climate Change Cttee, 2008–; Mem. Council, 2000–2001, Chair, Global Envmtl Res. Cttee, 1999–2006, Royal Soc. Pres., IAMAS, 1991–95. Mem., Academia Europaea, 1989; Corresp. Academician, Real Acad. de Ciencias y Artes de Barcelona, 1994; Foreign Associate, US NAS, 2002; Foreign Mem., Chinese Acad. of Scis, 2002. Lectures: Starr Meml, MIT, 1989; Bernard Haurwitz Meml, Amer. Meteorol Soc., 1995; Welsh, Univ. of Toronto, 2006. Hon. DSc Bristol, 2008. Royal Meteorological Society: Pres., 1998–2000; Symons Meml Lecture, 1982; L. F. Richardson Prize, 1972; Buchan Prize, 1976; Symons Medal, 2006; Charles Chree Silver Medal, Inst. of Physics, 1987; Carl-Gustaf Rossby Res. Medal, Amer. Meteorol Soc., 1988; Vilhelm Bjerknes Prize, Eur. Geophys. Soc., 1997. *Publications:* (ed with R. P. Pearce) Large-scale Dynamical Processes in the Atmosphere, 1983; 135 papers in meteorol jls. *Recreations:* music, sport, gardening. *Address:* Anchor House, Green Lane, Pangbourne, Berks RG8 7BG. *T:* (0118) 984 1308.

HOSKINS, Robert William, (Bob); actor; *b* 26 Oct. 1942; *s* of Robert Hoskins and Elsie Lilian Hoskins; *m* 1st, 1970, Jane Livesey; one *s* one *d*; 2nd, 1982, Linda Banwell; one *s* one *d*. *Educ:* Stroud Green School. *Stage:* Intimate Theatre, Palmers Green, 1966; Victoria, Stoke on Trent, 1967; Century Travelling Theatre, 1969; Royal Court, 1972; Doolittle in Pygmalion, Albery, 1974; RSC season, Aldwych, 1976; The World Turned Upside Down, Has Washington Legs?, 1978, True West, Guys and Dolls, 1981, NT; Old Wicked Songs, Gielgud, 1996; As You Desire Me, Playhouse, 2005; *television:* On the Move, 1976; Pennies from Heaven, 1978; Flickers, 1980; The Dunera Boys, 1985; The Changeling, 1993; World War II: When Lions Roared, 1993; David Copperfield, 1999; The Lost World, 2001; *films:* Zulu Dawn, 1980; The Long Good Friday, 1981; The Honorary Consul, 1982; Lassiter, 1984; Cotton Club, 1984; Sweet Liberty, 1986; Mona Lisa, 1986 (Best Actor award, Cannes Fest.; Golden Globe Award); A Prayer for the Dying, 1988; The Raggedy Rawney (writer, dir, actor), 1988; Who Framed Roger Rabbit, 1988; The Lonely Passion of Judith Hearne, 1989; Heart Condition, 1990; Mermaids, 1991; The Favour, the Watch and the Very Big Fish, 1992; Hook, 1992; The Inner Circle, 1992; Super Mario Brothers, 1993; Nixon, 1996; The Rainbow (dir, actor), 1996; Michael, 1996; Cousin Bette, 1996; TwentyFourSeven, 1997; The Secret Agent (producer, actor), 1998; Captain Jack, Parting Shots, Felicia's Journey, 1999; Enemy at the Gates, 2001; Last Orders, 2002; Beyond the Sea, 2004; Vanity Fair, Mrs Henderson Presents, Unleashed, 2005; Hollywoodland, 2006; Sparkle, 2007. *Recreations:* photography, gardening, playgoing. *Address:* c/o Independent Talent Group Ltd, Oxford House, 76 Oxford Street, W1D 1BS.

HOSKYNS, Sir Benedict (Leigh), 16th Bt, *cr* 1676; *b* 27 May 1928; *s* of Rev. Sir Edwyn Clement Hoskyns, 13th Bt, MC, DD and Mary Trym (*d* 1994), *d* of Edwin Budden, Macclesfield; *S* brother 1956; *m* 1953, Ann Wilkinson; two *s* two *d*. *Educ:* Haileybury; Corpus Christi Coll., Cambridge; London Hospital. BA Cantab 1949; MB, BChir Cantab 1952. House Officer at the London Hospital, 1953. RAMC, 1953–56. House Officer at Royal Surrey County Hospital and General Lying-In Hospital, York Road, SE1, 1957–58; DObstRCOG 1958; in general practice, 1958–93. *Heir:* *s* Edwyn Wren Hoskyns [*b* 4 Feb. 1956; *m* 1981, Jane, *d* of John Sellars; one *s* one *d*. *Educ:* Nottingham Univ. Medical School (BM, BS). MRCP, FRCPCH. Cons. Paediatrician, Leicester Gen. Hosp, 1993–]. *Address:* Russell House, Wherry Corner, High Street, Manningtree, Essex CO11 1AP. *T:* (01206) 396432.

HOSKYNS, Sir John (Austin Hungerford Leigh), Kt 1982; Director-General, Institute of Directors, 1984–89; Chairman: The Burton Group plc, 1990–98; Arcadia Group plc, 1998; *b* 23 Aug. 1927; *s* of Lt-Colonel Chandos Benedict Arden Hoskyns and Joyce Austin Hoskyns; *m* 1956, Miranda Jane Marie Mott; two *s* one *d*. *Educ:* Winchester College. Served in The Rifle Brigade, 1945–57 (Captain); IBM United Kingdom Ltd, 1957–64; founded John Hoskyns & Co. Ltd, later part of Hoskyns Group plc (Chm. and Man. Dir), 1964–75; Director: Martin Marietta Data Systems Inc., 1975–79; ICL plc, 1982–84; AGB Research plc, later Pergamon AGB plc, 1983–89; Clerical Medical & General Life Assurance Soc., 1983–98; McKechnie plc, 1983–93; Ferranti Internat. plc, 1986–94; EMAP plc, 1993–98 (Chm., 1994–98). Hd of PM's Policy Unit, 1979–82. Hon. DSc Salford, 1985; DU Essex, 1987. *Publication:* Just In Time: inside the Thatcher revolution, 2000. *Recreations:* opera, shooting. *Address:* c/o Child & Co., 1 Fleet Street, EC4Y 1BD. *Clubs:* Travellers, Green Jackets.

HOSSAIN, Ajmalul; QC 1998; *b* 18 Oct. 1950; *s* of late Asrarul Hossain, barrister and Senior Advocate, Supreme Court of Bangladesh, and Rabia Hossain; *m* 1970, Nasreen Ahmed; two *s*. *Educ:* King's Coll., London (LLB Hons 1976; LLM 1977). FCIArb 1994. Called to the Bar, Lincoln's Inn, 1976 (Buchanan Prize); SE Circuit; in practice at the Bar, Bangladesh, 1977–, England, 1978–; Supreme Court of Bangladesh: enrolled in High Court Div., 1977, Appellate Div., 1986; Senior Advocate, 1998. Pt-time Chm., Southampton Reg., Employment (formerly Industrial) Tribunals, 1995–2005. Member: Internat. Chamber of Commerce Internat. Court of Arbitration, Paris, 2006–; Code of Conduct Commn, Internat. Cricket Council, 2006–. Member: Supreme Court Bar Assoc., Bangladesh, 1986; Chancery Bar Assoc., 2002. Fellow, Soc. for Advanced Legal Studies, 2000. *Recreations:* travelling, bridge. *Address:* Selborne Chambers, 10 Essex Street, WC2R 3AA. *T:* (020) 7420 9500, *Fax:* (020) 7420 9555; *e-mail:* ajmalul.hossain@selbornechambers.co.uk; A. Hossain & Associates, 3B Outer Circular Road, Maghbazar, Dhaka 1217, Bangladesh. *T:* (2) 8311492, *Fax:* (2) 9344356.

HOTHAM, family name of **Baron Hotham**.

HOTHAM, 8th Baron *cr* 1797; **Henry Durand Hotham;** DL; Bt 1621; *b* 3 May 1940; *s* of 7th Baron Hotham, CBE, and Lady Letitia Sibell Winifred Cecil (*d* 1992), *er d* of 5th Marquess of Exeter, KG; *S* father, 1967; *m* 1972, Alexandra Stirling Home, *d* of late Maj. Andrew S. H. Drummond Moray; two *s* one *d*. *Educ:* Eton; Cirencester Agricultural Coll. Late Lieut, Grenadier Guards; ADC to Governor of Tasmania, 1963–66. DL Humberside, 1981. *Heir:* *s* Hon. William Beaumont Hotham [*b* 13 Oct. 1972; *m* 2005, Katrina Heyward; one *s* one *d*]. *Address:* The Dower House, Mere Lane, South Dalton, Beverley, E Yorks HU17 7PL; Scorborough Hall, Driffield, Yorks YO25 9AZ.

HOTHFIELD, 6th Baron *cr* 1881; **Anthony Charles Sackville Tufton;** DL; Bt 1851; *b* 21 Oct. 1939; *s* of 5th Baron Hothfield, TD and Evelyn Margarette (*d* 1989), *e d* of late Eustace Charles Mordaunt; *S* father, 1991; *m* 1975, Lucinda Marjorie, *d* of Captain Timothy John Gurney; one *s* one *d*. *Educ:* Eton; Magdalene Coll., Cambridge (MA). MICE. DL Cumbria, 2004. *Recreations:* Real tennis, lawn tennis, bridge, shooting. *Heir:* *s* Hon. William Sackville Tufton, MD [*b* 14 Nov. 1977; *m* 2006, Elizabeth, *o d* of Robin Burgess]. *Address:* Drybeck Hall, Appleby, Cumbria CA16 6TF. *Clubs:* Hawks (Cambridge); Jesters; almost every Real tennis club.

HOTSPUR; *see* McGrath, J. A.

HOTTEN, Christopher Peter; QC 1994; a Recorder, since 1990; *b* 7 July 1949; *s* of Ala John Hotten and Ida Lydia Hotten; *m* 1973, Lone Elisabeth Nielsen; one *s* two *d*. *Edu* Hornchurch Grammar Sch.; Leicester Univ. (LLB). Called to the Bar, Inner Templ 1972. *Recreations:* golf, going to the gym. *Address:* No5 Chambers, Fountain Cour Steelhouse Lane, Birmingham B4 6DR. *Club:* Stetchford (Birmingham).

HOTUNG, Sir Joseph (Edward), Kt 1993; Chairman, Ho Hung Hing Estates Ltd, sinc 1962; *b* 25 May 1930; *s* of Edward Sai-kim Hotung and Maud Alice (*née* Newman); 1957, Mary Catherine McGinley (marr. diss. 1969); two *s* two *d*. *Educ:* St Francis Xavie Coll., Shanghai; St Louis Coll., Tientsin; Catholic Univ. of America (BA); Univ. c London (LLB ext.). With Marine Midland Bank, 1957–60. Director: HSBC Hldgs pl 1991–98; Hongkong & Shanghai Banking Corp. Ltd, 1991–96; Hongkong Electric Hldg Ltd, 1984–97; China & Eastern Investment Co. Ltd, 1989–98. Member: Judicial Service Commn, Hong Kong, 1990–97; Inland Revenue Bd of Review, Hong Kong, 1989–9 University of Hong Kong: Mem. Council, 1984–96; Chm. and Trustee, Staff Termin Benefits Scheme, 1987–96; Mem. Council, Business Sch., 1990–96; Chm., Arts Deve Council, Hong Kong, 1994–96; Dir, E Asian Hist. of Sci. Foundn, 1991–2001; Membe Governing Body, SOAS, 1997–2005; St George's Hosp. Med. Sch., London Univ 2001–07; IISS, 2002–. Trustee: British Mus., 1994–2004; Asia Soc., NY, 1991–97; MMA NY, 2000– (Chm., Vis. Cttee, Dept of Asian Art, 2005–). Hon. Mem., Freer Gall. of A and Sackler Gall., Washington, 1990. Hon. DLitt Hong Kong, 1997; Hon. DSc Econ London, 2003. NACF Award, 1993. *Recreation:* Oriental art. *Address:* 1203 Prince' Building, 10 Chater Road, Central, Hong Kong. *T:* 25229929. *Clubs:* Reform, Beefsteak Hong Kong (Hong Kong); Century Assoc. (New York).

HOUGH, Prof. James, PhD; FRS 2003; FRSE; CPhys, FInstP; FRAS; Professor c Experimental Physics, since 1986, and Director, Institute for Gravitational Research, sinc 2000, University of Glasgow; *b* 6 Aug. 1945; *s* of Frederick and Lillias Hough; *m* 1972 Anne Park McNab (*d* 2000); one *s* one *d*. *Educ:* Univ. of Glasgow (BSc 1st Cl. Hon Natural Philosophy 1967; PhD 1971). FInstP 1993; CPhys 2002. University of Glasgow Res. Fellow, 1970–72; Lectr in Natural Philosophy, 1972–83; Sen. Lectr, 1983–86. Vi Fellow, JILA, Univ. of Colorado, 1983; PPARC Sen. Fellow, 1997–2000. Mem PPARC, 2005–07. FRAS 1983; FRSE 1991; FAPS 2001. Max Planck Res. Prize, 199 Duddell Medal and Prize, Inst. of Physics, 2004. *Publications:* contribs to learned jls and t books and conf. reports. *Recreations:* sports cars, photography. *Address:* Institute c Gravitational Research, Department of Physics and Astronomy, University of Glasgow Glasgow G12 8QQ. *T:* (0141) 330 4706, *Fax:* (0141) 330 6833; *e-mail:* j.hough@ physics.gla.ac.uk.

HOUGH, Prof. James Harley, PhD; CPhys, FInstP; FRAS; Professor of Astrophysic since 1989, and Director of Astronomy Research, since 2003, University of Hertfordshir (formerly Hatfield Polytechnic); *b* 2 July 1943; *s* of John Harley Hough and Sarah Ann (*né* Lomax); *m* 1966, Monica Jane Dent; one *s* one *d*. *Educ:* Prince Henry's GS, Otley, Yorks Univ. of Leeds (BSc 1st Cl. Hons; PhD 1967). FRAS 1997; FInstP 1998. Res. Fellow Univ. of Calgary, 1967–71; SERC Res. Fellow, Univ. of Durham, 1971–72; Hatfiel Polytechnic, subseq. Univ. of Hertfordshire: Lectr, 1972–83; Reader in Astronomy 1983–89; Hd of Physical Scis, 1987–98; Dean of Natural Scis, 1998–2003. Particle Physic and Astronomy Research Council: Mem. Council 1997–2000; Chm., Educn and Trn Panel, 1998–2001; Mem. or Chm., numerous SERC/PPARC Cttees and Bds, 1980– *Publications:* PPARC reports on future of UK Ground-Based Astronomy; numerou scientific papers in learned jls, mostly on active galaxies, star formation, interstellar dust astronomical polarimetry. *Recreations:* gardening, walking. *Address:* Centre for Astrophysic Research, Science & Technology Research Institute, University of Hertfordshire, Hatfiel AL10 9AB. *T:* (01707) 284500.

HOUGH, John Patrick; Secretary, Institute of Chartered Accountants in England an Wales, 1972–82; *b* 6 July 1928; *s* of William Patrick Hough, MBE, Lt-Comdr RN an Eva Harriet Hough; *m* 1956, Dorothy Nadine Akerman; four *s* one *d*. *Educ:* Purbrool High School. FCA, MIMC, FBCS. Articled M. R. Cobbett & Co., Portsmouth 1950–53; Derbyshire & Co., 1953–54; Turquand Youngs & Co., 1954–57; Compute Specialist, IBM United Kingdom Ltd, 1957–61; Consultant 1961–62, Partner 1962–69 Robson Morrow & Co.; Dep. Sec., Inst. of Chartered Accountants in England and Wales 1969–71. *Recreations:* music, food. *Address:* 5 South Row, Blackheath, SE3 0RY Coastguard Cottage, Newtown, Newport, Isle of Wight PO30 4PA. *Club:* Londor Rowing.

HOUGH, Julia Marie, (Judy); *see* Taylor, Judy.

HOUGH, Stephen; concert pianist; *b* 22 Nov. 1961; *s* of Colin Hough and Annetta (*né* Johnstone). *Educ:* Chetham's Sch. Music, Manchester; Royal Northern Coll. of Musi (Fellow, 1993); Juilliard Sch. Numerous recitals and concerto appearances with LSO LPO, RPO, Philharmonia, Chicago SO, Philadelphia Orchestra, Cleveland Orchestra NY Philharmonic, LA Philharmonic, San Francisco SO; Boston SO, Orchestre Nat. d France, Deutsches Symphonie Orchester, Berlin Philharmonic; festival performances incl. Ravinia, Mostly Mozart, Hollywood Bowl, Blossom, Proms, Le Grange de Meslay, La Roque d'Antheron, Edinburgh, Sapporo, Salzburg, Tanglewood. *Recordings:* Humme Piano Concertos and Sonatas; 3 Liszt Recitals; 3 Piano Albums; Schumann Recital; Brahms Piano Concertos Nos 1 and 2; Complete Britten Piano Music; Schubert Sonatas; Mendelssohn Piano Concertos; (with Robert Mann) Complete Beethoven and Brahms Violin Sonatas; Chopin Ballades and Scherzos; Scharwenka Piano Concerto No 4, and Sauer Piano Concerto No 1 (Gramophone Record of the Year, 1996); (with Steven Isserlis) Cello Sonatas of Grieg, Rachmaninoff, Franck and Rubinstein; Piano Concertos of Lowell Liebermann; Brahms Sonata; (with Michael Collins and Steven Isserlis) Clarinet Trios; Complete Piano and Orchestra Music of Saint-Saens (Gramophone CD of the Year, 2003); Complete Rachmaninoff Piano Concertos; English Piano Album; piano music of York Bowen, Franck and Mompou; Mozart Album; Beethoven and Mozart Piano and Wind Quartets; Spanish Album; music of Corigliano Tsontakis, Copland and Weber. Internat. Chair of Piano Studies, RNCM, 2003– (Dayas Gold Medal, 1981); Vis. Prof. of Piano, RAM, 2002– (Hon. RAM 2002). MacArthur Fellowship, MacArthu Foundn, 2001–. Internat. Terence Judd Award, 1982; Naumburg Internat. Piano Competition, 1983. *Compositions:* Suite R-B and other enigmas, 2003; Three Marian Hymns for children's choir and organ, 2005; On Falla, 2005; Advent Calendar, 2005; 3 Songs From War, 2006; Mass of Innocence and Experience, 2006; The Loneliest Wilderness: elegy for cello and orch., 2006; Missa Mirabilis, 2007; Londinium Magnificat and Nunc Dimittis, 2007; Herbstlieder, 2007; Three Grove Songs, 2007; Un Piccolo Sonatina, 2008. *Publications:* (contrib.) The Way We Are Now, 2006; The Bible as Prayer, 2007; (contrib.) Elgar: an anniversary portrait, 2007; vols of transcriptions incl. Rodgers and Hammerstein, 1999, Franck, Choral No 3, 2000. *Recreations:* reading, painting. *Address:* HarrisonParrott Ltd, 12 Penzance Place, W11 4PA.

HOUGHAM, John William, CBE 1996; Commissioner and Deputy Chairman, Disability Rights Commission, 2000–07; *b* 18 Jan. 1937; *s* of late William George Hougham and of Emily Jane (*née* Smith); *m* 1961, Peggy Edith Grove (*d* 2006); one *s* one *d. Educ:* Sir Roger Manwood's Sch., Sandwich; Leeds Univ. (BA Hons). National Service: commnd 2nd Lieut RA, 1955–57. British Home Stores, 1960–63; Ford Motor Company Ltd, 1963–93: Director: Industrial Relns, Ford España SA, 1976–80; Industrial Relns, Mfg, Ford of Europe Inc., 1982–86; Personnel, and Exec. Bd Mem., 1986–93. Mem. Bd, Personnel Mgt Services Ltd, 1989–93. Chm., ACAS, 1993–2000; Member: Review Body on Doctors' and Dentists' Remuneration, 1992–93; Adv. Bd of CS Occupational Health Service, 1992–96; Employment Appeal Tribunal, 1992–93 and 2000–07. Member: Engrg ITB, 1987–90; IPM Nat. Cttee for Equal Opportunities, 1987–92; CBI Employment Policy Cttee, 1987–93; Council, CRAC, 1988–2000; Bd, Trng and Employment Agency for NI, 1990–93; Council, Engrg Trng Auth., 1990–93; Chairman: Employment Occupational Standards Council, 1994–97; Employment NTO, 1997–2002, subseq. ENTO, 2002–04; Adv. Cttee, ESRC Future of Work Prog., 1998–2005. Vis. Prof., Univ. (formerly Poly.) of E London, 1991–; Vis. Fellow, City Univ., 1991–. Pres., Manpower Soc., 1997–2001; Mem. Adv. Council, Involvement & Participation Assoc., 1997–2000 (Vice-Pres., 1994–97, Hon. Vice-Pres., 1997–); Chm. Disciplinary Cttee, British Health Trades Assoc., 2000–. Governor: St George's C of E Sch., Gravesend, 1990–; Gravesend GS for Boys, 1990–2003. Trustee, Ellenor Lions Hospices (formerly Ellenor Foundn), 2004–. Comdr, St John Ambulance, Kent, 2007–. Reader, dio. of Rochester, 1998–. CCIPD (CIPM 1986); CCMI (CIMgt 1986); FRSA 1998. Freeman, City of London, 1995. Member, Editorial Advisory Board: Human Resource Mgt Jl, 1991–2000; People Mgt Mag., 1993–2003. Hon. LLD Leeds, 1997; Hon. DBA De Montfort, 1997. *Publication:* (contrib.) Legal Intervention in Industrial Relations (ed William McCarthy), 1992. *Recreations:* collecting books on Kent, watching cricket and Rugby football, family history, amateur dramatics. *Address:* 12 Old Road East, Gravesend, Kent DA12 1NQ. *T:* (01474) 352138. *Club:* Harlequin Football.

HOUGHTON, Brian Thomas, CB 1991; Director, International Division (formerly International Tax Policy Division), Inland Revenue, 1987–91; *b* 22 Aug. 1931; *s* of Bernard Charles Houghton and Sadie Houghton; *m* 1953, Joyce Beryl (*née* Williams); three *s* one *d. Educ:* City Boys' Sch., Leicester; Christ's Coll., Cambridge (Scholar; BA (Mod. Langs); MA 1957). Inland Revenue, 1957; Private Sec. to Chief Sec., HM Treasury, 1966–68; Assistant Secretary: Inland Revenue, 1968–75; HM Treasury, 1975–77; Under Sec., 1977, Principal Finance Officer and Dir of Manpower, Inland Revenue, 1977–83; Policy Div. Dir, Inland Revenue, 1983–87. Consultant, OECD, 1991–93. Vis. Professorial Fellow, QMW, 1992–97. *Recreation:* sailing. *Address:* 19 Rookes Lane, Lymington, Hants SO41 8FP. *T:* (01590) 670375.

HOUGHTON, Dr John; Director, Teesside Polytechnic, 1971–79, retired (Principal, Constantine College of Technology, 1961–70); *b* 12 June 1922; *s* of George Stanley Houghton and Hilda (*née* Simpson); *m* 1951, Kathleen Lamb; one *s* one *d. Educ:* King Henry VIII Sch., Coventry; Hanley High Sch.; Coventry Tech. Coll.; King's Coll., Cambridge; Queen Mary Coll., London Univ. BSc (Hons) Engrg 1949; PhD 1952. CEng, MIMechE, FRAeS. Aircraft Apprentice, Sir W. G. Armstrong-Whitworth Aircraft Ltd, 1938–43; design and stress engr, 1943–46; student at univ. (Clayton Fellow), 1946–51; Lectr, Queen Mary Coll., London Univ., 1950–52; Sen. Lectr and Head of Aero-Engrg, Coventry Techn. Coll., 1952–57; Head of Dept of Mech. Engrg, Brunel Coll. Advanced Technology, 1957–61. Freeman, City of Coventry, 1943. JP Middlesbrough, 1962–92. *Publications:* (with D. R. L. Smith) Mechanics of Fluids by Worked Examples, 1959; various research reports, reviews and articles in professional and learned jls. *Recreations:* keen sportsman (triple Blue), do-it-yourself activities, gardening. *Club:* Middlesbrough Rotary.

HOUGHTON, Lt Gen. Sir (John) Nicholas (Reynolds), KCB 2008; CBE 2000 (OBE 1992); Chief of Joint Operations, Ministry of Defence, 2006–March 2009; Vice Chief of Defence Staff (in rank of Gen.), from May 2009; *b* 18 Oct. 1954; *s* of Frank and Margaret Houghton; *m* 1982, Margaret Glover; one *s* one *d. Educ:* Woodhouse Grove Sch., Bradford; RMA, Sandhurst; St Peter's Coll., Oxford (MA). Commissioned, Green Howards, 1974; psct 1985–86; CO, 1 Green Howards, 1991–94; hcsc 1997; Comdr, 39th Inf. Bde (NI), 1997–99; DMO, MoD, 1999–2002; COS HQ ARRC, 2002–04; ACDS (Ops), MoD, 2004–05; Dep. Comdg Gen., Multinational Force, Iraq, 2005–06. Col, Yorks Regt, 2006–; Col Comdt, Intelligence Corps, 2008–. Officer, Legion of Merit (USA), 2006. *Recreations:* golf, shooting, history, family, watching sport, travel. *Address:* RHQ The Yorkshire Regiment, Trinity Church Square, Richmond, N Yorks DL10 4QN. *T:* (01748) 822133.

HOUGHTON, Sir John (Theodore), Kt 1991; CBE 1983; FRS 1972; Chief Executive (formerly Director General) of the Meteorological Office, 1983–91; Chairman, Royal Commission on Environmental Pollution, 1992–98 (Member, 1991–98); *b* 30 Dec. 1931; *s* of Sidney M. Houghton, schoolmaster, and Miriam Houghton; *m* 1st, 1962, Margaret Edith Houghton (*née* Broughton) (*d* 1986), MB, BS, DPH; one *s* one *d*; 2nd, 1988, Sheila Houghton (*née* Thompson). *Educ:* Rhyl Grammar Sch.; Jesus Coll., Oxford (Scholar). BA hons Physics 1951, MA, DPhil 1955. Research Fellow, RAE Farnborough, 1954–57; Lectr in Atmospheric Physics, Oxford Univ., 1958–62; Reader, 1962–76; Professor, 1976–83; Fellow, Jesus Coll., Oxford, 1960–83, Hon. Fellow 1983; on secondment as Dir (Appleton), 1979–83, and Dep. Dir, 1981–83, Rutherford Appleton Laboratory, SERC, Hon. Scientist, 1992–. Member: Astronomy, Space and Radio Bd, SERC (formerly SRC), 1970–73 and 1976–81; Exec. Cttee, WMO, 1983–91 (Vice-Pres., 1987–91); Astronomy and Planetary Sci. Bd, SERC, 1987–93; Meteorological Cttee, 1975–80; Jt Organising Cttee, Global Atmospheric Res. Programme, 1976–79; Exec. Management Bd, British Nat. Space Centre, 1986–91; UK Govt Panel on Sustainable Develt, 1994–2000; Chairman: Jt Scientific Cttee, World Climate Research Programme, 1981–84; Earth Observation Adv. Cttee, ESA, 1982–93; Scientific Assessment, Intergovtl Panel for Climate Change, 1988–2002; Jt Scientific and Tech. Cttee, Global Climate Observing System, 1992–95; John Ray Initiative, 1997–2006 (Pres., 2006–). Pres., RMetS, 1976–78 (Hon. Mem.). Trustee, Shell Foundn, 2000–. MAE 1988; Fellow, Optical Soc. of America; FInstP. Lectures: Cherwell-Simon Meml, 1983–84, Halley, 1992, Templeton, 1992, Oxford Univ.; Bakerian, Royal Soc., 1991. Hon. Mem., Amer. Met. Soc.; Hon. FRIBA 2001. Hon. Fellow: Univ. of Wales, Lampeter, 1994; Univ. of Wales, Bangor, 2003; Univ. of Wales, Aberystwyth, 2006. Hon. DSc: Wales, 1991; UEA, 1993; Leeds, 1995; Heriot-Watt, 1996; Greenwich, 1997; Glamorgan, 1998; Reading, 1999; Birmingham, 2000; Gloucestershire, 2001; Hull, 2002; Oxford, 2006; DUniv Stirling, 1992. Buchan Prize, RMetS, 1966; Charles Chree medal and prize, Inst. of Physics, 1979; (with F. W. Taylor, C. D. Rodgers and G. D. Peskett) Rank Prize for opto-electronics, 1989; Symons Meml Medal, RMetS, 1991; Glazebrook Medal and Prize, Inst. of Phys, 1990; Global 500 Award, UN Envmt Programme, 1994; Gold Medal, RAS, 1995; Internat. Meteorological Orgn Prize, 1998; Japan Prize, Foundn of Sci. and Technol., Japan, 2006; Champion for Wales, Welsh Assembly, 2008. *Publications:* (with S. D. Smith) Infra-Red Physics, 1966; The Physics of Atmospheres, 1977, 3rd edn 2002; (with F. W. Taylor and C. D. Rodgers) Remote Sounding of Atmospheres, 1984; Does God play dice?, 1988; Global Warming: the complete briefing, 1994, 3rd edn 2004; The Search for God: can science help?, 1995; papers in learned jls on atmospheric radiation, spectroscopy, remote sounding from satellites and climate change. *Recreations:* walking, sailing. *Address:* c/o Hadley Centre, Meteorological Office, Fitzroy Road, Exeter EX1 3PB.

HOUGHTON, Lt Gen. Sir Nicholas; *see* Houghton, Lt Gen. Sir J. N. R.

HOUGHTON, Peter; Chief Executive, South West London and St George's Mental Health NHS Trust, since 2006; *b* 7 Dec. 1957; *s* of late Peter Houghton and of Verde Cicely Houghton. *Educ:* Barnsley Grammar Sch.; Keble Coll., Oxford (BA Classics); Aberdeen Univ. (Cert. Health Econs 1988). NHS nat. admin trainee, 1981–83; Dep. Administrator, Royal Nat. Orthopaedic Hosp., London, 1983–85; Gen. Manager, Mental Health and Learning Disability Services, Cambridge, 1985–91; Chief Exec., Hinchingbrooke Healthcare NHS Trust, Huntingdon, 1991–93; Actg Dir of Planning, E Anglian RHA, 1993–94; Director: Strategic Develt, Anglia and Oxford Reg., NHS Exec., 1994–99; Eastern Reg., NHS Exec., DoH, 1999–2002; Chief Exec., Norfolk, Suffolk and Cambs Strategic HA, 2002–05; Dir, NHS Nat. Leadership Network, DoH, 2005–06. Mem., Inst. Health Mgt, 1984. *Recreations:* classical music and opera, travel, gardening, cycling. *Address:* 1 All Saints Close, Gazeley, Newmarket, Suffolk CB8 8WS. *T:* (01638) 750808.

HOUGHTON, Maj.-Gen. Robert Dyer, CB 1963; OBE 1947; MC 1942; DL; *b* 7 March 1912; *s* of late J. M. Houghton, Dawlish, Devon; *m* 1940, Dorothy Uladh (*d* 1995), *y d* of late Maj.-Gen. R. W. S. Lyons, IMS; two *s* one *d. Educ:* Haileybury Coll. Royal Marines Officer, 1930–64; Col Comdt, Royal Marines, 1973–76. Gen. Sec., Royal UK Beneficent Assoc., 1968–78. DL East Sussex, 1977. *Recreations:* gardening, model engineering. *Address:* Vert House, Whitesmith, near Lewes, East Sussex BN8 6JQ. *Club:* Army and Navy.

HOULDEN, Rev. Prof. (James) Leslie; Professor of Theology, King's College, London, 1987–94, now Emeritus; *b* 1 March 1929; *s* of late James and Lily Alice Houlden. *Educ:* Altrincham Grammar Sch.; Queen's Coll., Oxford. Asst Curate, St Mary's, Hunslet, Leeds, 1955–58; Chaplain, Chichester Theological Coll., 1958–60; Chaplain Fellow, Trinity Coll., Oxford, 1960–70; Principal, Cuddesdon Theol Coll., later Ripon Coll., Cuddesdon, 1970–77; King's College, London: Lectr, 1977; Sen. Lectr in New Testament Studies, 1985; Dean, Faculty of Theology and Religious Studies, 1986–88; Head, Dept of Biblical Studies, 1988–89; Actg Dean, 1993–94; FKC 1994. Hon. Canon of Christ Church Oxford, 1976–77. Member: Liturgical Commn, 1969–76; Doctrine Commn of C of E, 1969–76; Gen. Synod of C of E, 1980–90. Editor, Theology, 1983–91. DD Lambeth, 2005. *Publications:* Paul's Letters from Prison, 1970; (ed) A Celebration of Faith, 1970; Ethics and the New Testament, 1973; The Johannine Epistles, 1974; The Pastoral Epistles, 1976; Patterns of Faith, 1977; Explorations in Theology 3, 1978; What Did the First Christians Believe?, 1982; Connections, 1986; Backward into Light, 1987; (ed jtly) The World's Religions, 1988; History, Story and Belief, 1988; (ed jtly) Dictionary of Biblical Interpretation, 1990; Truth Untold, 1991; (ed) Austin Farrer: the essential sermons, 1991; Bible and Belief, 1991; Jesus: a question of identity, 1992; (ed jtly) Austin Farrer, Words for Life, 1993; (ed) The Interpretation of the Bible in the Church, 1995; (ed jtly) Companion Encyclopedia of Theology, 1995; The Public Face of the Gospel, 1997; (ed jtly) The Common Worship Lectionary: a scripture commentary, Year A, 2001, Year B, 2002, Year C, 2003; The Strange Story of the Gospels, 2002; (ed) Jesus in History, Thought and Culture: an encyclopedia, 2003, reissued as Jesus: the complete guide, 2005; (jtly) Services for Weekdays, 2006; (with J. Woodward) Praying the Lectionary, 2007; (ed jtly) Decoding Early Christianity, 2007; *contributed to:* The Myth of God Incarnate, 1977; Incarnation and Myth, 1979; Alternative Approaches to New Testament Study, 1985; The Reality of God, 1986; A New Dictionary of Christian Ethics, 1986; The Trial of Faith, 1988; God's Truth, 1988; Embracing the Chaos, 1990; Tradition and Unity, 1991; Using the Bible Today, 1991; Fundamentalism and Tolerance, 1991; Anchor Bible Dictionary, 1992; The Resurrection of Jesus Christ, 1993; Crossing the Boundaries, 1994; Divine Revelation, 1997; New Soundings, 1997; Theological Liberalism, 2000; The Oxford Bible Commentary, 2001; reviews and articles in learned jls. *Address:* 5 The Court, Temple Balsall, Knowle, Solihull B93 0AN. *Club:* Athenæum.

HOULDER, Bruce Fiddes; QC 1994; Director of Service Prosecutions (Armed Forces), since 2008; *b* 27 Sept. 1947; *s* of late Charles Alexander Houlder and Jessie Houlder (*née* Fiddes); *m* 1974, Stella Catherine Mattinson; two *d. Educ:* Felsted Sch., Dunmow. Called to the Bar, Gray's Inn, 1969, Bencher, 2001. Recorder, 1991–. Bar Council: Mem., 1995–97, 1998–2000, 2003–05; Vice Chm., Professional Standards Cttee, 1996–98; Chairman: Public Affairs Cttee, 1999–2000 (Vice Chm., 1996–98); Equal Opportunities Cttee, 2003; Bar Quality Adv. Panel, 2007–08; Vice-Chm., Bar IT Panel, 2004–08; Judicial Studies Board: Mem., Criminal Cttee, 2003–06; Mem., Working Pty on Criminal Justice Reforms; Chm., Criminal Bar Assoc. of England and Wales, 2001–02 (Vice Chm., 2000–01). Dir, Barco Ltd, 2003–08. Mem., Internat. Bar Assoc. Fellow, Soc. of Advanced Legal Studies. *Recreations:* painting, sailing, walking, theatre, music. *Address:* Hillingdon House, RAF Uxbridge, Hillingdon Road, Uxbridge, Middx UB10 0RU.

HOULDER, John Maurice, CBE 1977 (MBE (mil.) 1941); Lessee and Operator, Elstree Aerodrome, since 1951; *b* 20 Feb. 1916; *m* 1981, Rody, *d* of late Major Luke White. Private Pilot's Licence, 1938–; instrument rating, 1949–. Chm., Houlder Diving Research Facility Ltd, 1978–; Pres., Houlder (formerly Houlder Offshore Engrg) Ltd, 2002– (Chm., 1984–2002). Vis. Prof., Dept of Naval Architecture (formerly Dept of Ship and Marine Technol.), Univ. of Strathclyde, 1982–. Chm., London Ocean Shipowners Joint Dock Labour Piecework Cttee, 1950–60; first Chm., River Plate Europe Freight Conf., 1961–70; Chm., Bulk Cargo Cttee, Continental River Plate Conf., 1954–70. Member: Gen. Cttee, 1970–, Exec. Board, 1970–93, and Technical Cttee, 1970–95, Lloyds Register of Shipping; Light Aircraft Requirements Cttee, CAA, 1955–84; Adv. Cttee on R&D to Sec. of State for Energy, 1987–90. Member, Council: RSPB, 1974–79; RINA, 1981–87; Pres., Soc for Underwater Technology, 1978–80 (President's Award, 1987). Hon. DSc Strathclyde, 1986. Stanley Gray Award, Inst. of Marine Engrs, 1982; Master Air Pilot, GAPAN, 2006. *Recreations:* ski-ing, flying, bird-watching, computer programming. *Address:* 59 Warwick Square, SW1V 2AL. *T:* (020) 7834 2856, *Fax:* (020) 7834 1647. *Clubs:* Air Squadron; Kandahar Ski, 1001.

HOULDSWORTH, Sir Richard (Thomas Reginald), 5th Bt *cr* 1887, of Reddish and Coodham; Farm Manager since 1988; *b* 2 Aug. 1947; *s* of Sir Reginald Douglas Henry Houldsworth, 4th Bt, OBE, TD and Margaret May (*d* 1995), *d* of late Cecil Emilius Laurie; *S* father, 1989; *m* 1st, 1970, Jane Elizabeth (marr. diss. 1982), *o d* of Alistair Orr; two *s*; 2nd, 1992, Ann Catherine Tremayne; one *s. Educ:* Bredon School, Tewkesbury, Glos; Blanerne School, Denholm, Roxburghshire. *Recreations:* shooting, fishing, tennis, squash, horse racing. *Heir: s* Simon Richard Henry Houldsworth, *b* 6 Oct. 1971. *Address:* April Cottage, Naunton, Cheltenham, Glos GL54 3AA.

HOULIHAN, Michael Patrick; Director General, Amgueddfa Cymru—National Museum Wales (formerly National Museums and Galleries of Wales), since 2003; *b* 27 Sept. 1948; *s* of Michael Houlihan and Kathleen (*née* Small); *m* 1969, Jane Hibbert; one *s* one *d. Educ:* St Francis Xavier's Coll., Liverpool; Univ. of Bristol (BA Hons Hist.).

Imperial War Museum: Research Asst, 1971–75, Dep. Keeper, 1975–76, Dept of Exhibits; Keeper, Dept of Permanent Exhibns, 1976–84; Dep. Dir, 1984–94, Dir, 1994–98, Horniman Mus. and Gardens; Dir, subseq. Chief Exec., Nat. Museums and Galls of NI, 1998–2003. Chm., MDA, 2003–. Member: British Commn for Military Hist., 1982–; NI Cttee, British Council, 1998; Bd, NI Mus Council, 1998. Vis. Prof., Ulster Univ., 1999. Trustee: Nat. Self-Portrait Collection of Ireland, 1998–2003; Nat. Coal Mining Mus., 2004–. Mem. Council, Goldsmiths Coll., Univ. of London, 1997–98. *Publications:* Trench Warfare 1914–18, 1974; (with B. Yale) No Man's Land, 1984. *Recreations:* military history, cycling, Romanesque architecture, battlefields. *Address:* Amgueddfa Cymru—National Museum Wales, Cathays Park, Cardiff CF10 3NP.

HOULSBY, Prof. Guy Tinmouth, DSc; FREng; Professor of Civil Engineering, and Fellow of Brasenose College, Oxford, since 1991; *b* 28 March 1954; *s* of late Lt Col Thomas Tinmouth Houlsby, TD and of Vivienne May Houlsby (*née* Ford); *m* 1985, Jenny Lucy Damaris Nedderman; two *s*. *Educ:* Trinity College, Glenalmond; St John's College, Cambridge (MA, PhD); DSc Oxon 2003. CEng 1983, FREng 1999; FICE 1997. Engineer, Binnie and Partners, 1975–76, Babtie Shaw and Morton, 1976–77; Research Student, Cambridge, 1977–80; Oxford University: Jun. Res. Fellow, Balliol Coll., 1980–83; Lectr in Engineering, 1983–91; Fellow, Keble College, 1983–91. *Publications:* (with A. M. Puzrin) Principles of Hyperplasticity, 2006; contribs to learned jls on soil mechanics. *Recreations:* ornithology, woodwork, Northumbrian small pipes, rowing. *Address:* 25 Purcell Road, Marston, Oxford OX3 0HB. *T:* (01865) 722128.

HOULT, Frederick Wilson; JP; Vice Lord-Lieutenant of Tyne and Wear, since 2007; *b* 18 June 1938; *s* of late Frederick Hoult and Beatrice Hoult (*née* Wilson); *m* 1962, Peta Ann Wood; one *s* two *d*. *Educ:* Beadnell Village Sch.; St Mary's Sch., Melrose; Sedbergh Sch., Yorks; Rutherford Coll., Newcastle upon Tyne. Apprentice engr, CA Parsons, Newcastle upon Tyne, 1955–60; joined Hoults Ltd, family removals co., 1960, sold 1983; Chm., Hoults Hldgs Ltd, 1983–. A Tax Comr, 1981–2007. Vice Chm., NHS Supplies Authy, 1991–98. Mem., Newcastle HA, 1986–90; Chm., Freeman Hosp. NHS Trust, 1990–94. Pres., British Assoc. of Removers, 1976–77. Chairman: Tyneside Carr-Gomm, 1988–91; Mowden Hall Sch., 1998–2002. JP 1970, High Sheriff, 1986–87, Tyne and Wear. *Recreations:* family, sailing, ski-ing, tennis, countryside. *Address:* Stavros, 43 The Grove, Gosforth, Newcastle upon Tyne NE3 1NH. *T:* (0191) 285 3456. *Club:* Northern Counties (Newcastle upon Tyne).

HOULT, Helen Isabel; *see* Cleland, H. I.

HOURIGAN, Rhian Sara; *see* Harris, R. S.

HOURSTON, Sir Gordon (Minto), Kt 1997; FRPharmS; Chairman, United Biscuits plc, 1999–2000 (non-executive Director, 1995–99); *b* 24 July 1934; *s* of William A. M. Hourston and Vera W. (*née* Minto); *m* 1962, Sheila Morris; two *s*. *Educ:* Daniel Stewart's Coll., Edinburgh; Heriot-Watt Univ. FRPharmS 1982 (MRPharmS 1957). Joined Boots The Chemists, 1958: Dir, 1978; Dep. Man. Dir, 1984–88; Chm. and Man. Dir, 1988–95; Dir, Boots Co. plc, 1981–95. Chm., Homestyle plc (formerly Roseleys plc), 1996–2004. Chm., Company Chemists' Assoc., 1988–95. Chm., Armed Forces Pay Rev. Body, 1993–99 (Mem., 1989–99); Mem., Sen. Salaries Rev. Body, 1993–99. Trustee, Pharmacy Practice Res. Trust, 1999–2003. Hon. DSc Robert Gordon, 2004. *Recreations:* golf, walking, modern history, reading. *Address:* Tullich Lodge, Ballater, Aberdeenshire AB35 5SB.

HOUSDEN, Peter James; Permanent Secretary, Department for Communities and Local Government (formerly Office of the Deputy Prime Minister), since 2005; *b* 7 Dec. 1950. Teacher, Madeley Court Sch., Telford, 1975–79; Professional Asst, Humberside LEA, 1979–82; Asst Dir of Educn, Notts LEA, 1982–86; Sen. Educn Officer, Lancs LEA, 1986–88; Dep. Chief Educn Officer, Notts LEA, 1988–91; Dir of Educn, 1991–94, Chief Exec., 1994–2001, Notts CC; Dir Gen., Schs, DfES, 2001–05. Mem., Chartermark Panel, 1997–2001. Advr, LGA, 1997–2001. Chm., Nottingham Drug Action Team, 1994–2000; Mem., Adv. Council on Misuse of Drugs, 1998–2003. Associate Fellow, Warwick Univ. Business Sch., 1996–. Trustee, Wall Foundn, 2007–. *Address:* Department for Communities and Local Government, 6/G6 Eland House, Bressenden Place, SW1E 5DU.

HOUSE, Lt-Gen. Sir David (George), GCB 1977 (KCB 1975); KCVO 1985; CBE 1967; MC 1944; Gentleman Usher of the Black Rod, House of Lords, 1978–85; Serjeant-at-Arms, House of Lords, and Secretary to the Lord Great Chamberlain, 1978–85; *b* 8 Aug. 1922; *s* of A. G. House; *m* 1947, Sheila Betty Darwin (*d* 2006); two *d*. *Educ:* Regents Park Sch., London. War service in Italy; and thereafter in variety of regimental (KRRC and 1st Bn The Royal Green Jackets) and staff appts. Comd 51 Gurkha Bde in Borneo, 1965–67; Chief BRIXMIS, 1967–69; Dep. Mil. Sec., 1969–71; Chief of Staff, HQ BAOR, 1971–73; Dir of Infantry, 1973–75; GOC Northern Ireland, 1975–77. Colonel Commandant: The Light Division, 1974–77; Small Arms School Corps, 1974–77. Dir, Yorks and Humberside, Lloyds Bank, 1985–91. *Address:* Dormer Lodge, Aldborough, near Boroughbridge, N Yorks YO5 9EP. *Club:* Army and Navy.

HOUSE, Prof. John Peter Humphry, PhD; Walter H. Annenberg Professor, Courtauld Institute of Art, University of London, since 2002; *b* 19 April 1945; *s* of Madeline Edith Church and Arthur Humphry House; *m* 1968, Jill Elaine Turner; two *s*. *Educ:* Westminster Sch.; New Coll., Oxford (BA); Courtauld Inst. of Art (MA, PhD). Lecturer: UEA, 1969–76; UCL, 1976–80; Lectr, 1980–87, Reader, 1987–95, Prof., 1995–, Dep. Dir, 1996–99, Courtauld Inst., London Univ. Slade Prof. of Fine Art, Univ. of Oxford, 1986–87; British Acad. Res. Reader, 1988–90; Samuel H. Kress Prof., Nat. Gall. of Art, Washington DC, 2008–09. Organiser: Impressionism Exhibn, RA, 1974; Landscapes of France exhibn, Hayward Gall., 1995; Impressionists by the Sea exhibn, RA, 2007; Co-organiser: Post Impressionism exhibn, RA, 1979–80; Renoir exhibn, Arts Council, 1985. *Publications:* Monet, 1977, 2nd edn 1981; Monet: nature into art, 1986; (jtly) Impressionist and Post-Impressionist Masterpieces from the Courtauld Collection, 1987; (jtly) Impressionism for England: Samuel Courtauld as Patron and Collector, 1994; Renoir: la promenade, 1997; Impressionism: paint and politics, 2004; author/co-author, exhibition catalogues; articles in Burlington Magazine, Art History, Art in America. *Recreations:* second hand bookshops, early music. *Address:* Courtauld Institute of Art, University of London, Somerset House, Strand, WC2R 0RN. *T:* (020) 7848 2777; *e-mail:* john.house@courtauld.ac.uk.

See also E. H. O. Parry.

HOUSE, Roger Keith; a District Judge (Magistrates' Courts) (formerly Metropolitan Stipendiary Magistrate), since 1995; Chairman, Youth Court, since 1995; *b* 24 Jan. 1944; *s* of Donald Stuart House and Kathleen Mary House; *m* 1971, Elizabeth Anne Hall; two *s*. *Educ:* Wychwood Prep. Sch.; Sherborne. Admitted Solicitor, 1972; Asst Solicitor with various firms, 1972–76; sole practitioner, 1976–95. *Recreations:* singing, reading, walking the countryside, shooting, surfing. *Address:* Bournemouth Magistrates' Court, Stafford Road, Bournemouth, Dorset BH1 1LA. *T:* (01202) 745309.

HOUSE, (William) Stephen, QPM 2004; Chief Constable, Strathclyde Police, sinc 2007; *b* 19 Oct. 1957; *s* of William Cullingford House and Alice Reid House; *m* 198 Caroline Jose; one *s* two *d*. *Educ:* Kelvinside Acad., Glasgow; University College Sch Hampstead; Aberdeen Univ. (MA Hons Hist./Eng. Lit.); Brunel Univ. (MBA). Joine Sussex Police, 1981; Supt, W Yorks Police, 1994–98; Asst Chief Constable, Staffs Polic 1998–2001; Dep. Asst Comr, 2001–05, Asst Comr, 2005–07, Metropolitan Polic *Recreations:* reading (science fiction and history), running, hill walking. *Address:* Strathclyd Police, 173 Pitt Street, Glasgow G2 4JS.

HOUSLAY, Prof. Miles Douglas, PhD; FRSE; Gardiner Professor of Biochemistr University of Glasgow, since 1984; *b* 25 June 1950; *s* of Edwin Douglas Houslay an Georgina Marie Houslay; *m* 1972, Rhian Mair Gee; two *s* one *d*. *Educ:* UC Cardiff (BS Hons Biochem. 1971); King's Coll., Cambridge (PhD Biochem. 1974). FRSE 1986. IC Res. Fellow, Dept Pharmacol., Univ. of Cambridge, 1974; Res. Fellow, Queens' Coll Cambridge, 1975; Lectr in Biochem., 1976–82, Reader, 1982–84, UMIST. Ed.-in-Chie Cellular Signalling, 1987–. Chairman: Cell Bd Grant Panel, MRC, 1990–93; Proje Grant Panel, Wellcome Trust, 1996–2000, BHF, 1997–99; former Member: Grant Pane for MRC, AFRC, SHHD, Brit. Diabetic Assoc. and Health Res. Bd (Eire); RAE panel HEFC, 1992, 1996. Selby Fellow, Aust. Acad. Scis, 1984. Minshull Meml Lectr, Univ. Edinburgh, 1990. Trustee, BHF, 1997. Consultant at various pharmaceutical cos in UK Europe, USA. FMedSci, 1998. Colworth Medal, Biochem. Soc., 1984; Most Cite Scientist in Scotland, Edinburgh Sci. Fest. Award, 1992. *Publications:* Dynamics c Biological Membranes, 1982; over 390 contribs on cell signalling systems to learned jl *Recreations:* walking (hill, coastal and desert), reading, driving, cooking, music, eating ou *Address:* Division of Biochemistry and Molecular Biology, Wolfson Building, Institute c Biomedical and Life Sciences, University of Glasgow, Glasgow G12 8QQ. *T:* (0141) 33 4624.

HOUSSEMAYNE du BOULAY, (Edward Philip) George, CBE 1985; FRCR FRCP; Professor of Neuroradiology, University of London at Institute of Neurolog 1975–84, now Emeritus; Hon. Research Fellow, Zoological Society of London (Head, X Ray Department, Nuffield Laboratories, Institute of Zoology, 1965–86); Directo Radiological Research Trust, since 1985; *b* 28 Jan. 1922; *yr s* of Philip Houssemayne d Boulay and Mercy Tyrrell (*née* Friend); *m* 1944, Vivien M. Glasson (marr. diss.); four *s* (an two *s* decd); *m* 1968, Pamela Mary Verity; two *d*. *Educ:* Christ's Hospital; King's Coll London; Charing Cross Hosp. (Entrance Schol. 1940; MB, BS, DMRD). Served RA (Medical), 1946–48; Army Emergency Reserve, 1952–57. House appts, Charing Cro Hosp. and Derby City Hosp., 1945–46; Registrar (Radiology), Middlesex Hosp 1948–49; Sen. Registrar (Radiology): St Bartholomew's Hosp., 1949–54; St George Hosp., 1951–52; Consultant Radiologist: Nat. Hosp. for Nervous Diseases, Maida Val 1954–68; Bartholomew's Hosp., 1954–71; Nat. Hosp. for Nervous Diseases, Quee Square, 1968–75 (Head, Lysholm Radiol Dept, 1975–84). Editor, Neuroradiolog 1974–91. Pres., Brit. Inst. of Radiology, 1976–77, Appeal Co-ordinator 1976–84; Ho Member: Société Française de Neuroradiologie; Amer. Soc. of Neuroradiology; Swedis Soc. of Neuroradiology; German Soc. Neuroradiology. Trustee, Nat. Hosp. Deve Foundn. Glyn Evans Meml Lectr, RCR, 1970; Ernestine Henry Lectr, RCP, 1976. Ho FACR. Hon. DSc Leicester Polytechnic, 1992. Barclay Medal, BIR, 1968. *Publication* Principles of X-Ray Diagnosis of the Skull, 1965, 2nd edn 1979; (jtly) 4th edn of A Te Book of X-Ray Diagnosis by British Authors: Neuroradiology Vol. 1, 5th edn 1984; (jtl The Cranial Arteries of Mammals, 1973; (jtly) An Atlas of Normal Vertebral Angiogram 1976; works in specialist jls. *Recreation:* gardening. *Address:* Old Manor House, Brington Huntingdon, Cambs PE28 5AF. *T:* (01832) 710353.

HOUSSEMAYNE du BOULAY, Sir Roger (William), KCVO 1982 (CVO 1972) CMG 1975; HM Diplomatic Service, retired; Vice Marshal of the Diplomatic Corp 1975–82; *b* 30 March 1922; *s* of Charles John Houssemayne du Boulay, Captain, RN, an Mary Alice Veronica, *née* Morgan; *m* 1957, Elizabeth, *d* of late Brig. Home, late RM, an Molly, Lady Pile; one *d*, and two step *s*. *Educ:* Winchester; Oxford. Served RAFVR 1941–46 (Pilot). HM Colonial Service, Nigeria, 1949–58; HM Foreign, later Diplomati Service, 1959; FO, 1959; Washington, 1960–64; FCO 1964–67; Manila, 1967–71 Alternate Director, Asian Development Bank, Manila, 1967–69, and Director, 1969–71 Counsellor and Head of Chancery, Paris, 1971–73; Resident Comr, New Hebride 1973–75. Adviser: Solomon Is Govt, 1986; Swaziland Govt, 1992.

HOUSTON, Anne Catherine; Chief Executive, CHILDREN 1ST, since 2007; *b* 28 Aug 1954; *d* of Robert and Marta Houston. *Educ:* Glasgow Coll. of Technol. (HNC Applie Physics and Electronics 1975); Jordanhill Coll. of Further Educn (CQSW, Dip SW, 1980 OU Business Sch. (mgt of non-profit enterprises 1992). Various sen. mgt posts in soc work related fields; Counselling Manager, 1990–94, Dir, 1994–2006, ChildLine Scotlan Dep. Chief Exec., ChildLine UK, 2003–06, Dir, ChildLine UK within NSPCC, 200 Member: Partnership Drugs Initiative Bd, Lloyds TSB Foundn for Scotland, 2001–; Bd Scotland, Stop It Now!, 2007–. Trustee, Cattanach Trust, 2007–. Mem. Counsellin Team, consultant on Human Relns and Counselling Course, and student tutor, Scottis Inst. of Human Relns, 1989–94; Member: Adv. Cttee on Prison Mgt, Scottish Priso Service, 1994–2000; Cross Party Parly Gp for Children, 2003–06; Vice Chairma Scottish Alliance on Children's Rights, 1999–2005 (Founder Mem.); Scottish Pre-schoo Play Assoc., 2000–06; Anti-bullying Network Adv. Cttee, 2001–06. Treas., Assoc. c Chief Officers of Scottish Voluntary Orgns, 2000–04. *Publications:* Beyond the Limit children living with parental alcohol misuse, 1998; Young People Helping Young People international telephone helpline guidelines, 2000. *Recreations:* reading, music, gardening food and wine. *Address:* c/o CHILDREN 1ST, 83 Whitehouse Loan, Edinburgh EH 1AT. *T:* (0131) 446 2324; *e-mail:* anne.houston@children1st.org.uk.

HOUSTON, Maj.-Gen. David, CVO 2005; CBE 1975 (OBE 1972); Lord-Lieutenan of Sutherland, 1991–2004; *b* 24 Feb. 1929; *s* of late David Houston and late Christin Charleson Houston (*née* Dunnett); *m* 1959, Jancis Veronica Burn; two *s*. *Educ:* Latyme Upper Sch. Commissioned, Royal Irish Fusiliers, 1949; served Korea, Kenya, BAOR, N Africa; Staff Coll., Camberley, 1961; commanded 1 Loyals and newly amalgamated 1s QLR, 1969–71; in comd 8th Inf. Bde, Londonderry, N Ireland, 1974–75; Mem. RCDS 1976; Military Attaché and Commander, British Army Staff, Washington, 1977–79; HQ UKLF, 1979–80; Pres., Regular Commissions Bd, 1980–83; retd 1984. Hon. Col Manchester and Salford Univs OTC (TA), 1985–90; Col, The Queen's Lancashire Regt 1983–92. DL Sutherland, 1991; JP Sutherland, 1991–2007. *Recreations:* fishing, golf *Address:* c/o Bank of Scotland, Dornoch, Sutherland IV25 3ST.

HOUSTON, James Caldwell, CBE 1982; MD, FRCP; Physician to Guy's Hospital 1953–82, now Emeritus Physician; Dean, United Medical and Dental Schools, Guys an St Thomas's Hospitals, 1982–84 (Hon. Fellow, 1993; Dean, Medical and Dental Schools Guy's Hospital, 1965–82); *b* 18 Feb. 1917; *yr s* of late David Houston and Minnie Walke Houston; *m* 1946, Thelma Cromarty Cruickshank, MB, ChB, 2nd *d* of late Joh Cruickshank, CBE; four *s*. *Educ:* Mill Hill Sch.; Guy's Hosp. Medical Sch. MRCS, LRCP 1939; MB, BS (London) 1940; MRCP 1944; MD 1946; FRCP 1956. Late Major RAMC

Medical Registrar, Guy's Hospital, 1946. Asst Ed., 1954, Jt Ed., 1958–67, Guy's Hosp. Reports. Member: Bd of Governors, Guy's Hosp., 1965–74; SE Metropolitan Regional Hosp. Bd, 1966–71; Lambeth, Lewisham and Southwark AHA (Teaching), 1974–78; Court of Governors, London Sch. of Hygiene and Tropical Med., 1969–84; Senate, Univ. of London, 1970–84; Bd of Faculty of Clinical Medicine, Cambridge Univ., 1975–81; Cttee of Vice-Chancellors and Principals, 1977–80; Chm., Collegiate Council, Univ. of London, 1976–79; Special Trustee, Guy's Hosp., 1974–82; Trustee, Hayward Foundn, 1978–2001. Dir, Clerical, Medical & Gen. Life Assurance Soc., 1965–87; Vice-Pres., Medical Defence Union, 1970–92. *Publications:* Principles of Medicine and Medical Nursing (jtly), 1956, 5th edn 1978; A Short Text-book of Medicine (jtly), 1962, 8th edn 1984; articles in Quart. Jl Med., Brit. Med. Bull., Lancet, etc. *Recreations:* golf, gardening. *Address:* Discovery Cottage, 1 Mews Street, E1W 1UG. *T:* (020) 7481 8912.

HOUSTOUN-BOSWALL, Sir (Thomas) Alford, 8th Bt *cr* 1836; founder and Chairman, The Harrodian School, since 1993; international economics and business consultant; *b* 23 May 1947; *s* of Sir Thomas Houstoun-Boswall, 7th Bt, and of Margaret Jean, *d* of George Bullen-Smith; *S* father, 1982; *m* 1st, 1971, Eliana Michele (marr. diss. 1996), *d* of Dr John Pearse, New York; one *s* one *d*; 2nd, 2007, Malgosia, *d* of Grzegorz Stepnik. *Educ:* Lindisfarne College. Partner, Rosedale-Engel, Houstoun-Boswall Partnership, Bermuda; Director, Stair & Co., New York (specialising in fine 18th century English furniture and works of art); Pres., Houstoun-Boswall Inc. (Fine Arts), New York. Lecturer, New York Univ. and Metropolitan Museum of Art, New York. *Heir: s* Alexander Alford Houstoun-Boswall, *b* 16 Sept. 1972. *Address:* The Harrodian School, Lonsdale Road, SW13 9QN; 18 rue Basse, 06410 Biot, France; 11 East 73rd Street, New York, NY 10021, USA.

HOVELL-THURLOW-CUMMING-BRUCE, family name of **Baron Thurlow.**

HOVEN, Helmert Frans van den; Knight, Order of Netherlands Lion, 1978; Commander, Order of Orange Nassau, 1984; Hon. KBE 1980. Chairman, Unilever NV, 1975–84; Vice-Chairman, Unilever Ltd, 1975–84; *b* 25 April 1923; *m* 1st, 1950, Dorothy Ida Bevan (marr. diss. 1981); one *s*; 2nd, 1981, Cornelia Maria van As. *Educ:* Grammar and Trade schs in The Netherlands. Joined Unilever NV, Rotterdam, 1938; transf. to Unilever Ltd, London, 1948, then to Turkey, 1951, becoming Chm. of Unilever's business there, 1958; Chm., Unilever's Dutch margarine business, Van den Bergh en Jurgens BV, 1962; sen. marketing post, product gp, Margarine, Edible Fats and Oils, 1966; Mem. Bds of Unilever, and responsible for product gp, Sundry Foods and Drinks, 1970; Dir, Fidelity Investments, 1984–; non-executive Director: Hunter Douglas NV, 1984–; Colt Telecom Gp plc, 1995–; formerly: Mem. Supervisory Bd of Shell; Chm. Supervisory Bds of ABN/Amro Bank and various other cos; Mem., Eur. Adv. Bd, AT & T and Rockwell. Pres., ICC, Paris, 1984–86. Mem. Council, North Western (Kellogg) Business Sch., 1984–. *Recreations:* summer and winter sports in general.

HOVING, Thomas; President, Hoving Associates, Inc., since 1977; Editor-in-Chief, Connoisseur, 1982–91; *b* 15 Jan. 1931; *s* of late Walter Hoving and Mary Osgood (*née* Field); *m* 1953, Nancy Melissa Bell; one *d*. *Educ:* Princeton Univ. BA Highest Hons, 1953; Nat. Council of the Humanities Fellowship, 1955; Kienbusch and Haring Fellowship, 1957; MFA 1958; PhD 1959. Dept of Medieval Art and The Cloisters, Metropolitan Museum of Art: Curatorial Asst, 1959; Asst Curator, 1960; Associate Curator, 1963; Curator, 1965; Commissioner of Parks, New York City, 1966; Administrator of Recreation and Cultural Affairs, New York City, 1967; Dir, Metropolitan Museum of Art, 1967–77. Distinguished Citizen's Award, Citizen's Budget Cttee, 1967. Hon. Mem. AIA, 1967. Hon. LLD, Pratt Inst., 1967; Dr *hc* Princeton; New York Univ. Middlebury and Woodrow Wilson Awards, Princeton. *Publications:* The Sources of the Ada Group Ivories (PhD thesis), 1959; Guide to The Cloisters, 1962; The Chase and The Capture, 1976; Two Worlds of Andrew Wyeth, 1977; Tutankhamun, the Untold Story, 1978; King of the Confessors, 1981; Masterpiece (novel), 1986; Discovery (novel), 1989; Making the Mummies Dance: inside the Metropolitan Museum of Art, 1993; (introd.) Andrew Wyeth: autobiography, 1995; False Impressions: the hunt for big time art fakes, 1996; Greatest Works of Art of Western Civilization, 1997; Art for Dummies, 1999; The Art of Dan Namingha, 2000; Master Pieces: the curator's game, 2005; articles in Apollo magazine and Metropolitan Museum of Art Bulletin. *Recreations:* sailing, ski-ing, bicycling, flying. *Address:* (office) Hoving Associates, 150 East 73rd Street, New York, NY 10021, USA.

See also C. D. Leventhal.

HOW, Timothy Francis; Chief Executive, Majestic Wine PLC, since 1989; *b* 29 Dec. 1950; *s* of Mervyn Henry How and Margaret Helen How; *m* 1975, Elizabeth Mary Howard; four *d*. *Educ:* Churchill Coll., Cambridge (MA); London Business Sch. (MSc Business Studies). Gen. Manager, Polaroid (UK) Ltd, 1979–83; Man. Dir, Bejam Gp PLC, 1983–89. *Recreation:* sailing. *Address:* 47 Battlefield Road, St Albans, Herts AL1 4DB. *T:* (01727) 857884. *Clubs:* Oxford and Cambridge Sailing, Brancaster Staithe Sailing.

HOWARD; see Fitzalan-Howard.

HOWARD, family name of **Earls of Carlisle, Effingham,** and **Suffolk,** and of **Barons Howard of Penrith, Howard of Rising** and **Strathcona.**

HOWARD DE WALDEN, Baroness (10th in line) *cr* 1597; **Mary Hazel Caridwen Czernin;** *b* 12 Aug. 1935; *e d* of 9th Baron Howard de Walden and 5th Baron Seaford (*d* 1999) and Countess Irene Harrach; *S* to Howard de Walden Barony of father, called out of abeyance in her favour, 2004; *m* 1957, Count Joseph Czernin; one *s* five *d*. *Heir: s* Hon. Peter John Joseph Czernin [*b* 1 Jan. 1966; *m* 1994, Lucinda Wright; one *s* one *d*].

HOWARD OF EFFINGHAM, Lord; Edward Mowbray Nicholas Howard; Director, UK Corporate Sales, Foreign Exchange, Barclays Capital, since 2004; *b* 11 May 1971; *s* and heir of Earl of Effingham, *qv*, and *s* of Anne M. Howard (who *m* 1978, Prof. P. G. Stein, *qv*); *m* 2002, Tatiana Tafur; one *s* one *d* (twins). *Educ:* Oundle; Bristol Univ. Head of Corporate Sales, ANZ Investment Bank, 1998–2003. *Recreations:* boating, ski-ing, shooting. *Heir: s* Hon. Frederick Henry Charles Howard, *b* 19 March 2007. *Address:* Vermont 10, Domaine de la Résidence, Villars, Switzerland.

HOWARD OF PENRITH, 3rd Baron *cr* 1930, of Gowbarrow, co. Cumberland; **Philip Esme Howard;** Chairman, Tarchon (formerly Esperia) Capital Management Ltd, since 1999; *b* 1 May 1945; *e s* of 2nd Baron Howard of Penrith and Anne (*née* Hotham, *widow* of Anthony Bazley); *S* father, 1999; *m* 1969, Sarah Sophia Walker; two *s* two *d*. *Educ:* Ampleforth Coll.; Christ Church, Oxford. Journalist, Scotsman, then Daily Mail, 1967–71; Dir, Deltec Trading Co. Ltd, 1972–77; Partner, Phillips and Drew, 1977–84; Man. Dir, Lehman Brothers, 1984–97. *Heir: s* Hon. Thomas Philip Howard, *b* 8 June 1974. *Address:* 45 Erpingham Road, SW15 1BQ. *T:* (020) 8789 7604. *Clubs:* Turf, Portland.

HOWARD OF RISING, Baron *cr* 2004 (Life Peer), of Castle Rising in the County of Norfolk; **Greville Patrick Charles Howard;** Chairman, Wicksteed Leisure Ltd,

1984–2003; *b* 22 April 1941; *s* of Col Henry and Patience Howard; *m* 1981, Mary Cortlandt (*née* Culverwell); two *s* one *d*. *Educ:* Eton. Private Sec. to Rt Hon. Enoch Powell, MBE, PC, 1968–70. Chm., Fortress Holdings plc, 1995–2004. Dir, Keep Trust, 1980–89. Chm., Nat. Playing Fields Assoc., 2004–. Mem. (C) King's Lynn and W Norfolk DC, 2003–. *Address:* Castle Rising, Norfolk. *Clubs:* White's, Beefsteak.

HOWARD, Alan (Mackenzie), CBE 1998; actor; Associate Artist, Royal Shakespeare Company, since 1967; *b* 5 Aug. 1937; *s* of late Arthur John Howard and of Jean Compton Mackenzie; *m* 1st, Stephanie Hinchcliffe Davies (marr. diss. 1976); 2nd, 2004, Sally Beauman; one *s*. *Educ:* Ardingly Coll. Belgrade Theatre, Coventry, 1958–60; parts incl. Frankie Bryant in Roots (also at Royal Court and Duke of York's); Wesker Trilogy, Royal Court, 1960; A Loss of Roses, Pembroke, Croydon, 1961; The Changeling, Royal Court, 1961; The Chances, and The Broken Heart, inaugural season, Chichester Festival, 1962; Virtue in Danger, Mermaid and Strand, 1963; Bassanio in The Merchant of Venice, Lysander in A Midsummer Night's Dream, in tour of S America and Europe, 1964; Simon in A Heritage and its History, Phoenix, 1965; Angelo in Measure for Measure, Bolingbroke in Richard II, Nottingham, 1965–66; Cyril Jackson in The Black and White Minstrels, Traverse, Edinburgh, 1972, Hampstead, 1973; A Ride Across Lake Constance, Hampstead and Mayfair, 1973; The Silver King, Chichester, 1990; Scenes from a Marriage, Chichester, transf. Wyndhams, 1990; Kings, 1991; Vladimir in Waiting for Godot, Old Vic, 1997; title rôle in King Lear, Old Vic, 1997; the Man in Play about the Baby, Almeida, 1998; Schon in Lulu, Almeida and Washington, 2001; Gabriel in Gates of Gold, Gate Th., Dublin, 2002; *Royal Shakespeare Company:* joined company, 1966, playing Orsino in Twelfth Night, Lussurioso in The Revenger's Tragedy; 1967: Jaques in As You Like It (also LA, 1968), Young Fashion in The Relapse; 1968: Edgar in King Lear, Achilles in Troilus and Cressida, Benedick in Much Ado about Nothing; 1969: Benedick (also in LA and San Francisco), Achilles, Lussurioso, and Bartholomew Cokes in Bartholomew Fair; 1970: Mephistophilis in Dr Faustus, Hamlet, Theseus/Oberon in A Midsummer Night's Dream, Ceres in The Tempest; 1971: Theseus/Oberon (NY debut); 1971–72: Theseus/Oberon, Nikolai in Enemies, Dorimant in The Man of Mode, The Envoy in The Balcony; 1972–73: Theseus/Oberon, in tour of E and W Europe, USA, Japan, Australia; 1974: Carlos II in The Bewitched; 1975: Henry V, Prince Hal in Henry IV parts I and II; 1976: Prince Hal (SWET Award for Best Actor in revival), Henry V in tour of Europe and USA, Jack Rover in Wild Oats (also Piccadilly); 1977: Henry V, Henry VI parts I, II and III, Coriolanus (Plays and Players London Critics Award, SWET Award for Best Actor in revival, Evening Standard Best Actor Award, 1978); 1978: Antony in Antony and Cleopatra; 1979: Coriolanus in tour of Europe, The Children of the Sun; 1980: title rôles in Richard II and Richard III (Variety Club Best Actor Award); 1981–82: Neschastlivsev in The Forest; Good (Standard Best Actor Award, 1981); 1985: Nikolai in Breaking the Silence; *Royal National Theatre:* Prof. Higgins in Pygmalion, 1992; title rôle in Macbeth, 1993; George in Les Enfants Terribles, 1994; Calogero in La Grande Magia, 1995; Player in Rosencrantz and Guildenstern are Dead, 1995; title rôle, Oedipus Plays, 1996; Khludov in Flight, 1998; Sloper in The Heiress, 2000. Best Actor (jt), 1981, Drama (British Theatre Assoc.) awards for Richard II, Good and The Forest. *Films include:* The Heroes of Telemark; Work is a Four Letter Word; The Return of the Musketeers; Secret Rapture; The Cook, The Thief, his Wife and her Lover; The Fellowship of the Ring. *Television appearances include:* The Way of the World; Comet Among the Stars; Coriolanus; The Holy Experiment; Poppyland; Sherlock Holmes, Evensong, Life Story, 1986; A Perfect Spy, 1987; The Dog it Was That Died, 1988; Death in Holy Orders, 2003. *Radio includes:* Soames in Forsyte Chronicles, 1990–91. *Address:* c/o Julian Belfrage Associates, Adam House, 14 New Burlington Street, W1S 3BQ. *T:* (020) 7287 8544.

HOWARD, Ann; freelance opera singer (mezzo-soprano), 1971–99, now teaching privately; *b* 22 July 1936; *d* of William Alfred and Gladys Winifred Swadling; *m* 1954, Keith Giles; one *d*. *Educ:* privately; with Topliss Green, Rodolfa Lhombino (London) and Dominic Modesti (Paris) via scholarship from Royal Opera House, Covent Garden. Principal Mezzo-Soprano, Sadler's Wells Opera, 1964–73. Main rôles: Carmen, Dalila (Samson et Dalila), Azucena (Il Trovatore), Amneris (Aida), Fricka (Das Rheingold and Die Walküre), La Grande Duchesse de Gerolstein, Brangäne (Tristan und Isolde), Kabanicha (Kátya Kabanová), Gingerbread Witch (Hansel and Gretel), Eboli (Don Carlos), Katisha (Mikado), La Belle Hélène, Babulenka (The Gambler), Fairy Queen (Iolanthe), Dulcinée (Don Quichotte), Hérodiade, Klytemnestra (Electra), Isabella (Italian Girl in Algiers), Old Lady (Candide), Prince Orlofsky (Die Fledermaus), Hostess and Marina (Boris Godunov), Step-Mother (Into the Woods), Auntie (Peter Grimes), Baba (Rake's Progress), Emma Jones (Street Scene), Jezi Baba (Rusalka), Lilli Vanessi (Kiss Me Kate), Marcellina (Marriage of Figaro), Ortrud (Lohengrin); world premières: Madam Leda (The Mines of Sulphur), Sadler's Wells, 1965; Mrs Danvers (Rebecca), Opera North, 1983; Caliban (The Tempest), Santa Fé Festival Opera, USA, 1985; Mrs Worthing (The Plumber's Gift), ENO, 1989; 2nd Official (The Doctor of Myddfai), WNO, 1996; British premières: Cassandra (The Trojans, Pts 1 and 2), Scottish Opera, 1969; Mescalina (Le Grand Macabre), ENO, 1982; début Metropolitan Opera, NY, 1994 (Auntie); also performances in France, Italy, Belgium, Austria, Germany, USA (incl. series of Gilbert and Sullivan operas at Performing Arts Center, NY State Univ., 1993–98), Canada, Mexico, Chile, Portugal; many recordings and videos. Sir Charles Santley Meml Award, Musicians' Co., 2002. *Recreations:* gardening, cooking.

HOWARD, Anthony Michell, CBE 1997; journalist and broadcaster; Obituaries Editor, 1993–99, weekly columnist, 1999–2005, The Times; *b* 12 Feb. 1934; *s* of late Canon Guy Howard and Janet Rymer Howard; *m* 1965, Carol Anne Gaynor. *Educ:* Westminster Sch.; Christ Church, Oxford (Hon. Student, 2003). Chm., Oxford Univ. Labour Club, 1954; Pres., Oxford Union, 1955. Called to Bar, Inner Temple, 1956. Nat. Service, 2nd Lieut, Royal Fusiliers, 1956–58; Political Corresp., Reynolds News, 1958–59; Editorial Staff, Manchester Guardian, 1959–61 (Harkness Fellowship in USA, 1960); Political Corresp., New Statesman, 1961–64; Whitehall Corresp., Sunday Times, 1965; Washington Corresp., Observer, 1966–69 and Political Columnist, 1971–72; Asst Editor, 1970–72, Editor, 1972–78, New Statesman; Editor, The Listener, 1979–81; Dep. Editor, The Observer, 1981–88; Presenter: Face the Press, Channel Four, 1982–85; The Editors, Sky News TV, 1989–90; Reporter, BBC TV News and Current Affairs (Panorama and Newsnight), 1989–92; Chief political book reviewer, Sunday Times, 1990–2004. Hon. LLD Nottingham, 2001; Hon. DLitt Leicester, 2003. Gerald Barry Award, What the Papers Say, 1999. *Publications:* (contrib.) The Baldwin Age, 1960; (contrib.) Age of Austerity, 1963; (with Richard West) The Making of the Prime Minister, 1965; (ed) The Crossman Diaries: selections from the Diaries of a Cabinet Minister, 1979; Rab: the life of R. A. Butler, 1987; Crossman: the pursuit of power, 1990; (contrib.) Secrets of the Press, 1999; Basil Hume: the Monk Cardinal, 2005. *Address:* 11 Campden House Court, 42 Gloucester Walk, W8 4HU. *T:* (020) 7937 7313; Dinham Lodge, Ludlow, Shropshire SY8 1EH. *T:* (01584) 878457. *Clubs:* Garrick, Beefsteak.

HOWARD, Charles Anthony Frederick; QC 1999; *b* 7 March 1951; *s* of late Hon. John Algernon Frederick Charles Howard and Naida Howard (later Mrs Geoffrey Royal); *m* 1st, 1978, Geraldine Dorman (marr. diss.); one *s* one *d*; 2nd, 1999, Rosie Boycott, *qv*; one step *d*. *Educ:* Sherborne Sch.; St John's Coll., Cambridge (Open Hist. Schol.); BA 1972;

MA 1976; McMahon Student). Called to the Bar, Inner Temple, 1975. Mem., Family Law Bar Assoc. *Recreations:* cricket, tennis, gardening, walking, films. *Address:* 1 King's Bench Walk, Temple, EC4Y 7DB. *T:* (020) 7736 1500. *Clubs:* Groucho; Somerset CC.
See also Earl of Effingham.

HOWARD, Rear-Adm. Christopher John, (Jack); Chief of Staff, C-in-C Naval Home Command, 1987–89, retired; *b* 13 Sept. 1932; *s* of late Claude Albert Howard and Hilda Mabel Howard (*née* Norton); *m* 1st, 1960, Jean Webster (marr. diss. 1987); two *d*; 2nd, 1987, Hilary Troy; one *s* one *d*. *Educ:* Newton Abbot Grammar School; King's College London; Imperial College, London. MSc, DIC. MIET. Entered RN 1954; served in HM Ships Ocean, Pukaki, Roebuck, Urchin, Tenby; Officer i/c RN Polaris School, 1978–80; Dean, RN Engineering College, 1980–82; Dir, Naval Officer Appts (Instructor), 1982–84; Commodore, HMS Nelson, 1985–87. NDC Latimer, 1975; Chief Naval Instructor Officer, 1987. Consultant, PA Consulting Group, 1989–91; Dir of Ops, Devon and Cornwall TEC, 1992–97. Gov. Maynard Sch., Exeter, 2002–06. *Recreation:* family. *Club:* Army and Navy.

HOWARD, Sir David (Howarth Seymour), 3rd Bt *cr* 1955, of Great Rissington, co. Gloucester; Managing Director, since 1971 and Chairman, since 1999, Charles Stanley & Co., Stockbrokers; Lord Mayor of London, 2000–01; *b* 29 Dec. 1945; *s* of Sir Edward Howard, 2nd Bt, GBE; *S* father, 2001; *m* 1968, Valerie Picton Crosse, *o d* of Derek W. Crosse; two *s* two *d*. *Educ:* Radley Coll., Worcester Coll., Oxford (MA Hons). Director: Assoc. of Pvte Client Investment Managers and Stockbrokers, 2001–; Securities and Investment (formerly Securities) Inst., 2002– (Chm., Exam. Bd, 2003–; Hon. FSI); Financial Services Skills Council, 2004–07. Mem., Sutton BC, 1974–78; Common Councilman, City of London, 1972–86, Alderman, 1986–, Sheriff, 1997–98. Master, Gardeners' Co., 1990–91. Chm., London Gardens Soc., 1996–. Pres., Chartered Mgt Inst., 2008– (Pres., City Br., 2002–). Pro-Chancellor and Chm. Council, City Univ., 2003–08. KStJ 2000. Grand Cordon (1st class), Order of Independence (Jordan), 2001. *Recreation:* gardening. *Heir: s* Robert Picton Seymour Howard, *b* 28 Jan. 1971. *Clubs:* City Livery, United Wards, Lime Street Ward.

HOWARD, Prof. Deborah Janet, PhD; FSA, FSAScot; FRSE; Professor of Architectural History, University of Cambridge, since 2001 (Head, Department of History of Art, 2002–06, and since 2007); Fellow of St John's College, Cambridge, since 1992; *b* 26 Feb. 1946; *d* of Thomas Were Howard, OBE and Isobel Howard (*née* Brewer); *m* 1975, Prof. Malcolm Sim Longair, *qv*; one *s* one *d*. *Educ:* Loughton High Sch. for Girls; Newnham Coll., Cambridge (BA 1st Cl. Hons Architecture and Fine Arts 1968; MA 1972); Courtauld Inst. of Art, Univ. of London (MA 1969; PhD 1973). FSA 1984; FSAScot 1991; FRSE 2004. Leverhulme Fellow in History of Art, Clare Hall, Cambridge, 1972–73; Lectr in History of Art, UCL, 1973–76; pt-time Lectr, 1982–90, Sen. Lectr, 1990–91, Reader, 1991, Dept of Architecture, Univ. of Edinburgh; pt-time Lectr, Courtauld Inst. of Art, Univ. of London, 1991–92; Cambridge University: Librarian, Faculty of Architecture and History of Art, 1992–96; Reader in Architectl History, 1996–2001. Kennedy Prof. of Renaissance Studies, Smith Coll., Mass, 2006; Vis. Prof., Harvard (Villa i Tatti), 2007. Member: Royal Fine Art Commn for Scotland, 1987–95; Royal Commn on Ancient and Historical Monuments of Scotland, 1990–99; Chm., Soc. of Architectl Historians of GB, 1997–2000. Trustee, British Archtl Liby Trust, 2001–. Hon. FRIAS 1995. *Publications:* (jtly) The Art of Claude Lorrain, 1969; Jacopo Sansovino: architecture and patronage in Renaissance Venice, 1975, 2nd edn 1987; The Architectural History of Venice, 1980, 2nd edn 1987, rev. and enlarged edn 2002; (ed and jtly) The Architecture of the Scottish Renaissance, 1990; (ed) William Adam, 1990; (ed) Scottish Architects Abroad, 1991; Scottish Architecture from the Reformation to the Restoration 1560–1660, 1995; (ed) Architecture in Italy 1500–1600 by Wolfgang Lotz, 2nd edn, 1995; (jtly) La Scuola Grande della Misericordia di Venezia, 1999; Venice & the East: the impact of the Islamic world on Venetian architecture, 2000; (ed with L. Moretti) Architettura e musica nella Venezia del Rinascimento, 2006; numerous articles and book reviews in learned jls. *Recreations:* mountain walking, music, photography, gardening. *Address:* Faculty of Architecture and History of Art, University of Cambridge, 1 Scroope Terrace, Cambridge CB2 1PX. *T:* (01223) 332977; St John's College, Cambridge CB2 1TP. *T:* (01223) 339360.

HOWARD, Elizabeth Jane, CBE 2000; FRSL; novelist; *b* 26 March 1923; *d* of David Liddon and Katharine M. Howard; *m* 1st, 1942, Peter M. Scott (marr. diss. 1951; later Sir Peter Scott, CH, CBE, FRS (*d* 1989)); one *d*; 2nd, 1959, James Douglas-Henry; 3rd, 1965, Kingsley Amis (later Sir Kingsley Amis, CBE) (marr. diss. 1983; he *d* 1995). *Educ:* home. FRSL 1994. Trained at London Mask Theatre Sch. Played at Stratford-on-Avon, and in repertory theatre in Devon; BBC, Television, modelling, 1939–46; Sec. to Inland Waterways Assoc., 1947; subsequently writing, editing, reviewing, journalism and writing plays for television, incl. serials of After Julius in three plays and Something in Disguise in six plays. John Llewellyn Rhys Memorial Prize for The Beautiful Visit, 1950. Hon. Artistic Dir, Cheltenham Literary Festival, 1962; Artistic co-Dir, Salisbury Festival of Arts, 1973. Film script, The Attachment, 1986. *Publications:* The Beautiful Visit, 1950; The Long View, 1956; The Sea Change, 1959; After Julius, 1965; Something in Disguise, 1969 (TV series, 1982); Odd Girl Out, 1972; Mr Wrong, 1975; (ed) A Companion for Lovers, 1978; Getting It Right, 1982 (Yorkshire Post Prize) (film script, 1985); (jtly) Howard and Maschler on Food: cooking for occasions, 1987; The Light Years, 1990; Green Shades (anthology), 1991; Marking Time, 1991; Confusion, 1993; Casting Off, 1995; Anthology on Marriage, 1997; Falling, 1999; Slipstream (autobiog.), 2002; Love All, 2008. *Recreations:* music, gardening, enjoying all the arts, natural history. *Address:* c/o Jonathan Clowes, Iron Bridge House, Bridge Approach, NW1 8BD.

HOWARD, Prof. Ian George, RSA 1998; Principal, Edinburgh College of Art, since 2001; Professor, Heriot-Watt University, since 2001; *b* 7 Nov. 1952; *s* of Harold Geoffrey Howard and Violet Howard (*née* Kelly); *m* 1977, Ruth D'Arcy; two *d*. *Educ:* Aberdeen Grammar Sch.; Univ. of Edinburgh; Edinburgh Coll. of Art. MA Hons Fine Art 1975; Post Grad. Dip. 1976. Lectr in Painting, Gray's Sch. of Art, Aberdeen, 1977–86; Head of Painting, Duncan of Jordanstone Coll. of Art, Dundee, 1986–95; Prof. of Fine Art (personal chair), Dundee Univ., 1995–2001; Mem., Faculty of Fine Art, British Sch. at Rome, 1996–2002; Dean, Duncan of Jordanstone Coll. of Art and Design, 1999–2001. Dir, Dundee Contemporary Arts Ltd, 1997–2004. Treas., Royal Scottish Acad., 2008–. Numerous exhibns internationally; work in collections, including: Scottish Arts Council; Arts Council England; Contemporary Art Soc.; Edinburgh City Art Centre; Hunterian Art Gall., Glasgow; Robert Fleming, London; Royal Scottish Acad. *Publications:* Heretical Diagrams, 1995; Emblemata, 1998; Uncertain Histories, 2000. *Recreations:* travel, cooking, picking wild mushrooms. *Address:* Principal's Office, Edinburgh College of Art, Lauriston Place, Edinburgh EH3 9DF. *T:* (0131) 221 6060.

HOWARD, Rear-Adm. Jack; *see* Howard, Rear-Adm. C. J.

HOWARD, James Boag, CB 1972; Assistant Under-Secretary of State, Home Office, 1963–75; *b* 10 Jan. 1915; *yr s* of William and Jean Howard, Greenock; *m* 1943, Dorothy Jean Crawshaw (*d* 2000); two *d*. *Educ:* Greenock High Sch.; Glasgow Univ. (MA, BSc; 1st cl. Hons Mathematics and Natural Philosophy). Asst Principal, Home Office, 1937; Private Sec. to Permanent Sec., Ministry of Home Security, 1940–41; Principal, 1941; Asst Sec., 1948. *Address:* 12 Windhill, Bishop's Stortford, Herts CM23 2NG. *T:* (01279) 651728.

HOWARD, Prof. (James) Kenneth, RA 1991 (ARA 1983); painter; Professor of Perspective, Royal Academy of Arts, since 2004; *b* 26 Dec. 1932; *s* of Frank and Elizabeth Howard; *m* 1st, Ann Howard (*née* Popham), dress designer (marr. diss. 1974); 2nd, 1990 Christa Gaa (*née* Köhler), RWS (*d* 1992); 3rd, 2000, Dora Bertolutti. *Educ:* Kilburn Grammar School; Hornsey School of Art; Royal College of Art (ARCA). NEAC 1962 (Pres., 1998–2003); ROI 1966 (Hon. ROI 1988; Hon. Fellow 2007); RWA 1981; RWS 1983. British Council scholarship to Florence, 1958–59; taught various London Art Schools, 1959–73; Official Artist for Imperial War Museum in N Ireland, 1973, 1978; painted for the British Army in N Ireland, Germany, Cyprus, Hong Kong, Brunei, Nepal, Belize, Norway, Lebanon, Canada, Oman, 1973–; one man exhibitions: Plymouth Art Centre, 1955; John Whibley Gallery, 1966, 1968; New Grafton Gallery, 1971–2000; Jersey, 1978, 1980, 1983; Hong Kong, 1979; Nicosia, 1982; Delhi, 1983; Lowndes Lodge Gall., 1987, 1989, 1990, 1991; Sinfield Gall., 1991, 1993, 1995; Bankside Gall., 1996; Everard Reid Gall., Johannesburg, 1998; Richard Green Gall., 2002, 2003, 2004, 2005, 2006. Works purchased by Plymouth Art Gall., Imperial War Mus., Guildhall Art Gall., Ulster Mus., Nat. Army Mus., Hove Mus., Sheffield Art Gall., Southend Mus.; commissions for UN, BAOR, Drapers' Co., Stock Exchange, States of Jersey, Banque Paribas, Royal Hosp. Chelsea. Freeman: City of London, 2007; Painter-Stainers' Co., 2007 (Liveryman, 2007–). Hon. RBA 1989; RBSA 1991. First Prize: Hunting Group Award, 1982; Sparkasse Karlsruhe, 1985. Gen. Editor, Art Class series, 1988. *Publications:* contribs to: The War Artists, 1983; 60th Vol. of The Old Water-Colour Societies' Club, 1985; Painting Interiors, 1989; Art of Landscape and Seascape, 1989; Visions of Venice, 1990; Venice: the artist's vision, 1990; 20th Century Painters and Sculptors, 1991; Oils Masterclass, 1996; (jtly) Ken Howard: a personal view—Inspired by Light, 1998; Dictionary of Artists in Britain since 1945, 1998; *relevant publication:* The Paintings of Ken Howard, by Michael Spender, 1992. *Recreations:* cinema, opera. *Address:* 8 South Bolton Gardens, SW5 0DH. *T:* (020) 7373 2912; (studio) St Clements Studio, Mousehole, Cornwall TR19 6TR. *T:* (01736) 731596; (studio) Ramo e Corte del Paludo, 6262 Cannaregio, Venice, Italy. *T:* 0415202277. *Clubs:* Arts, Chelsea Arts.

HOWARD, Hon. John (Winston), AC 2008; Prime Minister of Australia, 1996–2007; *b* 26 July 1939; *s* of Lyall F. Howard and Mona Howard; *m* 1971, Alison Janette Parker; two *s* one *d*. *Educ:* Canterbury Boys' High Sch.; Sydney Univ. Solicitor of NSW Supreme Court, 1962. MP (L) for Bennelong, NSW, 1974–2007. Minister for Business and Consumer Affairs, Australia, 1975; Minister assisting Prime Minister, May 1977; Minister for Special Trade Negotiations, July 1977; Federal Treasurer, 1977–83; Dep. Leader of the Opposition, 1983–85; Leader, Parly Liberal Party, and Leader of the Opposition, Australia, 1985–89, 1995–96. Chm., Manpower and Labour Market Reform Gp, 1990–93. Chm., Internat. Dem. Union, 2002–. Hon. LLD Notre Dame. Centenary Medal, Australia, 2003; Gold Olympic Order, IOC, 2003. *Recreations:* cricket, films, reading, golf. *Club:* Australian (Sydney).

HOWARD, Prof. Jonathan Charles, DPhil; FRS 1995; Professor of Genetics, Institute for Genetics, University of Cologne, since 1994; *b* 24 June 1943; *s* of John Eldred Howard and Marghanita (*née* Laski); *m* 1990, Maria Leptin; two *s*. *Educ:* Westminster Sch.; Magdalen Coll., Oxford (BA Zool. 1964; DPhil Medicine 1969). Mem., Scientific Staff, MRC, at Cellular Immunology Res. Unit, Sir William Dunn Sch. of Pathology, Univ. of Oxford, 1968–73; Weir Jun. Res. Fellow, University Coll., Oxford, 1970–73; Babraham Institute, Cambridge: Mem. Staff, Dept of Immunology, 1974–94; Head of Dept, 1985–94; Res. Fellow, Clare Hall, Cambridge, 1975–78; sabbaticals at: Depts of Pathology and Cell Biol., Stanford Univ., 1983, 1987; Div. of Biol., CIT, 1983; EMBL, 1992. Mem., EMBO, 1993. *Publications:* Darwin, 1982; papers in learned jls on immunology and evolution. *Recreation:* fishing. *Address:* Institut für Genetik, Universität zu Köln, Zülpicher Strasse 47, 50674 Köln, Germany. *T:* (221) 4704864; Heinestrasse 19, 50931 Köln, Germany. *T:* (221) 4200320.

HOWARD, Prof. Judith Ann Kathleen, CBE 1996; DPhil; FRS 2002; Professor of Chemistry, University of Durham, since 1991; *b* 21 Oct. 1945; *d* of James and Kathleen Duckworth; *m* 1969, Dr David Jameson Howard. *Educ:* Univ. of Bristol (BSc Hons 1966; DSc 1986); Somerville Coll., Oxford (DPhil 1971). CChem, FRSC 1991; EurChem 1996; CPhys, FInstP 1996. Sen. Res. Fellow, 1987–91, Reader, 1991, Univ. of Bristol; Sen. Fellow, Royal Soc. Leverhulme Trust, 1996–97; Sir Derman Christopherson Fellow, Univ. of Durham, 1997–98; EPSRC Sen. Res. Fellow, 1998–2003. DUniv Open, 1998. *Publications:* (contrib.) Encyclopedia of Inorganic Chemistry, 1994; Crystallographic Instrumentation, 1998; Implications of Molecular and Materials Structure for New Technologies, 1999; over 700 jl articles. *Recreations:* music, reading, hiking, art, swimming. *Address:* Department of Chemistry, University of Durham, Durham DH1 3LE. *T:* (0191) 334 2047, *Fax:* (0191) 384 4737; *e-mail:* j.a.k.howard@durham.ac.uk.

HOWARD, Kenneth; *see* Howard, J. K.

HOWARD, Laurence, OBE 2004; PhD; Lord-Lieutenant of Rutland, since 2003; *b* 29 March 1943; *s* of Henry Lovering Howard and Beryl Cicely Howard; *m* 1966, Christine Mary Kinver; one *s* one *d*. *Educ:* Strode's Sch.; Nottingham Univ. (BSc 1967); Leicester Univ. (PhD Neurophysiol. 1971). Wolfson Fellow, 1970–73; Leicester University: Lectr, 1974, Sen. Lectr, 1988–90, in Physiology; Sub-Dean, Med. Sch., 1990–2003; Associate Lectr in Physiology, 2003–06. Chairman: Bd of Visitors, HM Prison Stocken, 1988–91; Leicester Magistrates' Courts Cttee, 1997–2002; Central Council, Magistrates' Courts Cttees, 2002–03; Pres., Leics and Rutland Magistrates' Assoc., 2004–; Mem., Unified Courts Admin Bd, 2002–04. Freeman, City of London, 1966. JP Rutland, 1979 (Chm. Bench, 1988–94). Hon. Fellow, UC Northampton, 2001. *Publications:* articles on physiology in scientific jls. *Recreations:* travel, horse riding, music. *Address:* Daventry House, Main Street, Whissendine, Rutland LE15 7ET. *T:* (01664) 474662; *e-mail:* howardlc@whiss64.freeserve.co.uk.

HOWARD, Margaret; freelance broadcaster and concert presenter, since 1969; presenter, with Classic FM, 1992–99; *b* 29 March 1938; *d* of John Bernard Howard and Ellen Corwena Roberts. *Educ:* St Mary's Convent, Rhyl, N Wales; St Teresa's Convent, Sunbury; Guildhall Sch. of Music and Drama; Indiana Univ., Bloomington, USA. LGSM; LRAM 1960. BBC World Service Announcer, 1967–69; Reporter: The World This Weekend, BBC Radio 4, 1970–74; Edition, BBC TV, 1971; Tomorrow's World, BBC TV, 1972; Editor and Presenter: Pick of the Week, BBC Radio 4, 1974–91; Classic Reports, Classic FM, 1992–94; Howard's Week, Classic FM, 1994–97; Presenter: It's Your World, BBC World Service, 1981–86; Masterclass, 1994–99, Music and the Mind, concert series with Medici Quartet, 1995, Classic FM; concerts: Haydn's Seven Last Words from the Cross, Medici Quartet, 2001, 2002; Viva Verdi, Opera Nazionale Italiana, UK tour, 2001; Interviewer/Presenter, Strictly Instrumental, occasional BBC series, 1980–85; consultant and recording artist, Classical Communications Ltd, 2003–. Radio critic, The Tablet; columnist, The Universe; record columnist, Chic magazine. Female UK Radio Personality of the Year, Sony Awards, 1984; Sony Radio Awards Roll of Honour, 1988; Voice of the Listener Award for excellence, 1991; Radio Personality of the Year, TRIC Awards, 1996. *Publications:* Margaret Howard's Pick of the Week, 1984; Court Jesting, 1986. *Recreations:* swimming, tasting wine, dog walking. *Address:* 215 Cavendish Road, SW12 0BP. *T:* (020) 8673 7336. *Club:* South London Swimming (Tooting).

HOWARD, Martin Lloyd, CB 2007; Assistant Secretary General (Operations), North Atlantic Treaty Organisation, since 2007; *b* 1 Oct. 1954; *s* of Leonard Lloyd Howard and Joan Mary Howard; *m* 1993, Caroline Jane Delves. *Educ:* Gravesend Grammar Sch. Joined MoD, 1975; apptd Sen. CS, 1993; Dir, Central and Eastern Europe, MoD, 1993–94; Private Sec. to Sec. of State for NI (on loan), 1994–96; Dep. Chief, Assessments Staff, Cabinet Office (on loan), 1996–98; Ministry of Defence: Hd, Overseas Secretariat, 1998–99; Dir of News, 1999–2001; Dir Gen., Corporate Communications, 2001–03; Dep. Chief of Defence Intelligence, 2003–04; Dir Gen., Operational Policy, 2004–07. *Recreations:* classical and contemporary guitar, sailing, reading, music. *Address:* NATO, 1110 Brussels, Belgium. *T:* (2) 7074111.

HOWARD, Rt Hon. Michael; PC 1990; QC 1982; MP (C) Folkestone and Hythe, since 1983; Leader of the Conservative Party and Leader of the Opposition, 2003–05; *b* 7 July 1941; *s* of late Bernard Howard and of Hilda Howard; *m* 1975, Sandra Clare, *d* of Wing-Comdr Saville Paul; one *s* one *d*, and one step *s*. *Educ:* Llanelli Grammar School; Peterhouse, Cambridge. MA, LLB; President of the Union, 1962. Major Scholar, Inner Temple, 1962; called to the Bar, Inner Temple, 1964, Bencher, 1992. Junior Counsel to the Crown (Common Law), 1980–82; a Recorder, 1986. Contested (C) Liverpool, Edge Hill, 1966 and 1970; Chm., Bow Group, 1970–71. PPS to Solicitor-General, 1984–85; Parly Under-Sec. of State, DTI, 1985–87; Minister of State, DoE, 1987–90; Secretary of State for: Employment, 1990–92; the Environment, 1992–93; the Home Dept, 1993–97; Shadow Foreign Sec., 1997–99; Shadow Chancellor, 2001–03. Jt Sec., Cons. Legal Cttee, 1983–84; Jt Vice-Chm., Cons. Employment Cttee, 1983–84; Vice-Chm., Soc. of Cons. Lawyers, 1985. Pres., Atlantic Partnership. *Recreations:* watching football (Swansea, Liverpool) and baseball (New York Mets). *Address:* House of Commons, SW1A 0AA. *T:* (020) 7219 5493. *Clubs:* Carlton, Pratt's, Coningsby (Chm., 1972–73).

HOWARD, Sir Michael (Eliot), OM 2005; CH 2002; Kt 1986; CBE 1977; MC 1943; DLitt; FBA 1970; FRHistS; Emeritus Professor of Modern History, University of Oxford, since 1989; *b* 29 Nov. 1922; *y s* of late Geoffrey Eliot Howard, Ashmore, near Salisbury, and of Edith Julia Emma, *o d* of Otto Edinger; civil partnership 2006, Mark Anthony James. *Educ:* Wellington; Christ Church, Oxford (BA 1946, MA 1948; Hon. Student, 1990). Served War, Coldstream Guards, 1942–45. Asst Lecturer in History, University of London, King's Coll., 1947; Lecturer, 1950; Lecturer, then Reader, in War Studies, 1953–63; Prof. of War Studies, 1963–68; University of Oxford: Fellow of All Souls Coll., 1968–80; Chichele Prof. of History of War, 1977–80; Regius Prof. of Modern History and Fellow of Oriel Coll., 1980–89 (Hon. Fellow, 1990); Robert A. Lovett Prof. of Military and Naval Hist., Yale Univ., 1989–93. Vis. Prof. of European History, Stanford Univ., 1967; Kluge Vis. Prof., Library of Congress, 2003. Ford's Lectr in English History, Oxford, 1971; Radcliffe Lectr, Univ. of Warwick, 1975; Trevelyan Lectr, Cambridge, 1977; Leverhulme Lectr, 1996; Lee Kuan Yew Distinguished Visitor, Nat. Univ. of Singapore, 1996. FKC. Pres. and co-Founder, Internat. Institute for Strategic Studies; Vice-Pres., Council on Christian Approaches to Defence and Disarmament; Pres., Army Records Soc. For. Hon. Mem., Amer. Acad. of Arts and Scis, 1983. Hon. LittD Leeds, 1979; Hon. DLit London, 1988; Hon. DHumLit Lehigh Univ., Pa, USA, 1990. Chesney Meml Gold Medal, RUSI, 1973; NATO Atlantic Award, 1989. *Publications:* The Coldstream Guards, 1920–46 (with John Sparrow), 1951; Disengagement in Europe, 1958; Wellingtonian Studies, 1959; The Franco-Prussian War, 1961 (Duff Cooper Memorial Prize, 1962); The Theory and Practice of War, 1965; The Mediterranean Strategy in the Second World War, 1967; Studies in War and Peace, 1970; Grand Strategy, vol IV (in UK History of 2nd World War, Military series), 1971 (Wolfson Foundn History Award, 1972); The Continental Commitment, 1972; War in European History, 1976; (with P. Paret) Clausewitz On War, 1977; War and the Liberal Conscience, 1978; (ed) Restraints on War, 1979; The Causes of Wars, 1983; Clausewitz, 1983; Strategic Deception in World War II, 1990; The Lessons of History, 1991; (ed with W. R. Louis) The Oxford History of the Twentieth Century, 1998; The Invention of Peace, 2000 (Pol Book Prize, Friedrich Ebert Stiftung); The First World War, 2002; Captain Professor: a life in war and peace (autobiog.), 2006; Liberation or Catastrophe?: reflections on the history of the 20th century, 2007. *Address:* The Old Farm, Eastbury, Hungerford, Berks RG17 7JN. *Clubs:* Athenæum, Garrick, Pratt's.

HOWARD, Michael Newman; QC 1986; a Recorder of the Crown Court, since 1993; *b* 10 June 1947; *s* of late Henry Ian Howard and of Tilly Celia Howard. *Educ:* Clifton College; Magdalen College, Oxford (MA, BCL). Lecturer in Law, LSE, 1970–74; called to the Bar, Gray's Inn, 1971, Bencher, 1995; in practice at Bar, 1971–; Asst Recorder, 1989–1993; Leader of Admiralty Bar, 1999–. Visiting Professor: Law, Univ. of Essex, 1987–92; Maritime Law, UCL, 1996–99. Mem. of Panel, Lloyd's Salvage Arbitrators, 1987–. *Publications:* Phipson on Evidence, ed jtly, 12th edn 1976 to 14th edn 1990, Gen. Ed., 15th edn 2000; *contributions to:* Frustration and Force Majeure, 1991, 2nd edn 1995; *Consensus ad Idem*: essays for Guenter Treitel, 1996; Halsbury's Laws of England, 4th edn (Damages); Butterworth's Commercial Court and Arbitration Pleadings, 2005; articles and reviews in legal periodicals. *Recreations:* books, music, sport. *Address:* Quadrant Chambers, Quadrant House, 10 Fleet Street, EC4Y 1AU. *T:* (020) 7583 4444, *Fax:* (020) 7583 4455; *e-mail:* michael.howard@quadrantchambers.com. *Clubs:* Royal Automobile, Oxford and Cambridge, Garrick.

HOWARD, Philip Nicholas Charles, FRSL; leader writer, columnist, modern manners and word watching, The Times, since 1992; *b* 2 Nov. 1933; *s* of late Peter Dunsmore Howard and Doris Emily Metaxa; *m* 1959, Myrtle, *d* of Sir Reginald Houldsworth, 4th Bt, OBE, TD; two *s* one *d*. *Educ:* Eton Coll. (King's Scholar); Trinity Coll., Oxford (Major Scholar; first cl. Lit. Hum; MA). Glasgow Herald, 1959–64; The Times, 1964–: reporter, writer, columnist; Literary Ed., 1978–92. Member: Classical Assoc. (Pres., 2002); Horatian Soc.; Soc. of Bookmen; Literary Soc.; Flaccidae. Founder Patron, Friends of Classics, 1991. FRSL 1987. Liveryman, Wheelwrights' Co. London Editor, Verbatim, 1977–. *Publications:* The Black Watch, 1968; The Royal Palaces, 1970; London's River, 1975; New Words for Old, 1977; The British Monarchy, 1977; Weasel Words, 1978; Words Fail Me, 1980; A Word in Your Ear, 1983; The State of the Language, English Observed, 1984; (jtly) The Times Bicentenary Stamp Book, 1985; We Thundered Out, 200 Years of The Times 1785–1985, 1985; Winged Words, 1988; Word-Watching, 1988; (jtly) London, The Evolution of a Great City, 1989; A Word in Time, 1990; (ed) The Times Bedside Book, 1991; Reading a Poem, 1992; (ed) The Times Bedside Book, 1992. *Recreations:* walking, reading, talking, music, the classics, beagles not beagling, Jack Russells, stand at Twickenham. *Address:* Flat 1, 47 Ladbroke Grove, W11 3AR. *T:* (020) 7727 1077. *Clubs:* Garrick; Ad Eundem (Oxford and Cambridge); Eton Ramblers; International PEN.

HOWARD, Robert, (Bob); Northern Regional Secretary, Trades Union Congress, 1980–2000; *b* 4 April 1939; *s* of Robert and Lily Howard; *m* 1984, Valerie Stewart; two *s* one *d*. *Educ:* Gregson Lane County Primary Sch.; Deepdale Secondary Modern Sch.; Queen Elizabeth's Grammar Sch., Blackburn, Lancs; Cliff Training Coll., Calver via Sheffield, Derbyshire. British Leyland, Lancs, 1961–68: Member, Clerical and Admin. Workers' Union Br. Exec.; Councillor, Walton le Dale UDC, 1962–65; GPO, Preston, Lancs, 1969–80: Telephone Area UPW Telecomms Representative Member: Jt Consultative Council, Jt Productivity Council, Council of PO Unions Area Cttee, Delegate to Preston Trades Council; Secretary, Lancashire Assoc. of Trades Councils, 1977–79; created 14 specialist cttees for LATC; appointment as N Reg. Sec., TUC, 1980, by Gen. Sec., TUC, first full-time secretary to a TUC region. Member: Industrial Tribunals, 1979–80; Northumbria Regional Cttee, Nat. Trust, 1989–; Council, Northern Exams Assoc., 1986–; Board: Durham Univ. Business Sch., 1987–; Tyneside TEC, 1989–99; Northern Develt Co., 1991–99; Nat. Resource for Innovative Trng Res. and Employment Ltd, later Northern Informatics, 1995–99. Northern Region Coordinator, Jobs March, 1983; Exec. Organiser, Great North Family Gala Day, 1986–90. JP Duchy of Lancaster, 1969–74. *Publications:* North-East Lancashire Structure Plan—The Trades Councils' View (with Peter Stock), 1979; Organisation and Functions of TUC Northern Regional Council, 1980. *Recreations:* fell walking, opera, ballet, classical music, camping, cricket, football, spectating outdoor sports, reading, chess. *Address:* 8 Caxton Way, North Lodge, Chester le Street, County Durham DH3 4BW. *Club:* Durham CC.

HOWARD, Stephen Lee; Chief Executive, Business in the Community, since 2008 (Managing Director, 2005–08); *b* 25 March 1953; *s* of Richard and Marilyn Howard; *m* 1976, Holly Grothe; three *s*. *Educ:* Michigan State Univ. (BA 1975); Univ. of Michigan Law Sch. (JD *cum laude* 1978). In practice as lawyer, Providence, RI, 1978–85; Cookson America Inc.: General Counsel, 1985–86; Vice-Pres., Corporate Develt and General Counsel, 1986–91; Cookson Group plc: Chief Exec., Gp Develt, 1991–92; Dir and Chief Exec., Engineered Prods Div. and Gp Corporate Develt, 1992–94; Chief Exec., Ceramic and Engineered Prods Div. and Gp Corporate Develt, 1994–97; Gp Jt Man. Dir, 1995–97; Gp Chief Exec., 1997–2004; Chief Exec., Novar plc, 2004–05. Non-executive Director: SEGRO plc; Balfour Beatty plc. Dep. Chm., Habitat, Humanity GB. Gov., St George's Coll. *Recreations:* tennis, basketball. *Address:* Business in the Community, 137 Shepherdess Walk, N1 7RQ. *Club:* Royal Automobile.

HOWARD, Victoria; *see* Barnsley, V.

HOWARD-DOBSON, Gen. Sir Patrick John, GCB 1979 (KCB 1974; CB 1973); *b* 12 Aug. 1921; *s* of late Canon Howard Dobson, MA; *m* 1946, Barbara Mary Mills (*d* 2004); two *s* one *d*. *Educ:* King's Coll. Choir Sch., Cambridge; Framlingham College. Joined 7th Queen's Own Hussars, Egypt, Dec. 1941; served in: Burma, 1942; Middle East, 1943; Italy, 1944–45; Germany, 1946; psc 1950; jssc 1958; comd The Queen's Own Hussars, 1963–65 and 20 Armoured Bde, 1965–67; idc 1968; Chief of Staff, Far East Comd, 1969–71; Comdt, Staff Coll., Camberley, 1972–74; Military Secretary, 1974–76; Quartermaster General, 1977–79; Vice-Chief of Defence Staff (Personnel and Logistics), 1979–81; ADC Gen. to the Queen, 1978–81. Col Comdt, ACC, 1976–82. Nat. Pres., Royal British Legion, 1981–87. Virtuti Militari (Poland), 1945; Silver Star (US), 1945. *Recreations:* sailing, golf. *Address:* 1 Drury Park, Snape, Saxmundham, Suffolk IP17 1TA. *Clubs:* Royal Cruising; Senior Golfers' Society.

HOWARD-DRAKE, Jack Thomas Arthur; Assistant Under-Secretary of State, Home Office, 1974–78; *b* 7 Jan. 1919; *o s* of Arthur Howard and Ruby (*née* Cherry); *m* 1947, Joan Mary, *o d* of Hubert and Winifred Crook; one *s* two *d*. *Educ:* Hele's Sch., Exeter. Asst Inspector, Ministry of Health Insurance Dept, 1937–39 and 1946–47. Served War, RA, 1939–46 (Major, despatches). Colonial Office: Asst Principal, 1947; Principal, 1949; Private Sec. to Sec. of State, 1956–62; Asst Sec., 1962; Asst Sec., Cabinet Office, 1963–65; Asst Sec., Home Office, 1965–72; Asst Under-Sec. of State, NI Office, 1972–74. Chairman: Oxfordshire Local History Assoc., 1984–91; Wychwoods Local History Soc., 1984–92. *Publications:* Oxford Church Courts: Depositions 1542–1550, 1991, 1570–1574, 1993, 1581–1586, 1994, 1589–1593, 1997, 1592–1596, 1998, 1603–1606, 1999, 1609–1616, 2003, 1616–1622, 2005, 1629–1634, 2007, 1634–1639, 2008. *Recreations:* gardening, local history. *Address:* 26 Sinnels Field, Shipton-under-Wychwood, Chipping Norton, Oxon OX7 6EJ. *T:* (01993) 830792.

HOWARD-JOHNSTON, Angela Maureen; *see* Huth, A. M.

HOWARD-LAWSON, Sir John (Philip), 6th Bt *cr* 1841, of Brough Hall, Yorkshire; *b* 6 June 1934; *s* of Sir William Howard Lawson, 5th Bt and Joan Eleanor (*d* 1989), *d* of late Arthur Cowie Stamer, CBE; assumed by Royal Licence surname and arms of Howard, 1962, of Howard-Lawson, 1992; *S* father, 1990; *m* 1960, Jean Veronica (*née* Marsh) (*d* 2001); two *s* one *d*. *Educ:* Ampleforth. *Heir: s* Philip William Howard [*b* 28 June 1961; *m* 1st, 1988, Cara Margaret Browne (marr. diss. 1992); 2nd, 1993, Isabel Anne Oldridge de la Hey; one *d*]. *Address:* Hunter Hall, Great Salkeld, Penrith, Cumbria CA11 9NA. *T:* (01768) 897135.

HOWARTH, family name of **Baron Howarth of Newport**.

HOWARTH OF BRECKLAND, Baroness *cr* 2001 (Life Peer), of Parson Cross in the County of South Yorkshire; **Valerie Georgina Howarth**, OBE 1999; founding Chief Executive, ChildLine, 1987–2001; *b* 5 Sept. 1940. *Educ:* Abbeydale Girls' Grammar Sch.; Univ. of Leicester. MBASW; Associate Mem., ADSS. Caseworker, Family Welfare Assoc., 1963–68; London Borough of Lambeth: Sen. Child CareWorker and Trng Officer, 1968–70; Area Co-ordinator, 1970–72; Chief Co-ordinator of Social Work, 1972–76; Asst Dir of Personal Services, 1976–82; Dir of Social Services, London Borough of Brent, 1982–86. Board Member: Food Standards Agency, 2000–07; Nat. Care Standards Commn, 2001–04; Children and Family Courts Adv. and Support Services, 2004–. Founder Member: King's Cross Homelessness Project (first Chm.), 1986–87; London Homelessness Forum, 1986–87; Home Office Steering Gp on Child Witnesses, 1991–97; Telephone Helplines Assoc. (first Chm.); NCH Commn considering Children as Abusers, 1991–92. Dir and Mem. Cttee, ICSTIS, 1988–2000; Mem., NSPCC Professional Adv. Panel, 1993–94; UK Rep., Euro Forum for Child Welfare, 1994–97. Member: Sub cttee G on EU, H of L, 2005–07 (Chm., 2007–); EU Select Cttee, H of L, 2007–. Trustee: John Grooms Assoc. for Disabled People, 1987–2007 (Pres.); Lucy Faithfull Foundn, 1992– (Vice Chm.); NCVCCO, 1990–95 (Vice Chm.); Stop It Now, 1992– (Chm.); Nat. Children's Bureau, 1993–94; Michael Sieff Foundn, 1994–2004; Little Hearts Matter, 2002– (Patron); Children's Internat. Helplines Assoc., 2003–07 (Chm.); Grooms-Shaftesbury, 2007– (Chm.). DUniv Open, 2007. *Recreations:* gardening, reading, walking. *Address:* House of Lords, SW1A 0PW; *e-mail:* howarthv@parliament.uk.

HOWARTH OF NEWPORT, Baron *cr* 2005 (Life Peer), of Newport in the county of Gwent; **Alan Thomas Howarth,** CBE 1982; PC 2000; *b* 11 June 1944; *e s* of late T. E. B. Howarth, MC, TD and Margaret Howarth; *m* 1967, Gillian Martha (marr. diss. 1996), *d* of Mr and Mrs Arthur Chance, Dublin; two *s* two *d. Educ:* Rugby Sch. (scholar); King's Coll., Cambridge (major scholar in History; BA 1965). Sen. Res. Asst to Field-Marshal Montgomery on A History of Warfare, 1965–67; Asst Master, Westminster Sch., 1968–74; Private Sec. to Chm. of Conservative Party, 1975–79; Dir, Cons. Res. Dept, 1979–81; Vice-Chm., Conservative Party, 1980–81. MP: Stratford on Avon, 1983–97, (C) 1983–95, (Lab) 1995–97; (Lab) Newport E, 1997–2005. PPS to Dr Rhodes Boyson, MP, 1985–87; an Asst Govt Whip, 1987–88; Lord Comr of HM Treasury, 1988–89; Parliamentary Under-Secretary of State: DES, 1989–92 (Schools Minister, 1989–90; Minister for Higher Educn and Sci., 1990–92); DFEE, 1997–98 (Employment Minister and Minister for Disabled People); DCMS, 1998–2001 (Minister for the Arts). Secretary: Cons. Arts and Heritage Cttee, 1984–85; PLP Social Security Cttee, 1996–97; Member: Nat. Heritage Select Cttee, 1992–94; Social Security Select Cttee, 1995–97; Intelligence and Security Cttee, 2001–05; Ad Hoc Cttee on Internat. Orgns, 2008–; Chm., All Party Parly Gp on Charities and Vol. Sector, 1992–97; Treas., 1993–97, Vice-Pres., 2002–, All Party Arts and Heritage Gp; Sec., All Party British Brazil Gp, 2005– (Chm., 2007–); Treas., All Party Latin America Gp, 2005–; Co-Chm., All Party Parly Gp on Architecture and Planning, 2005–. Chm., Friends, Huntington's Disease Assoc., 1988–97; Mem. Adv. Council, Nat. Listening Library, 1992–97; Vice-Pres., British Dyslexia Assoc., 1994–97; Chm., UK Literary Heritage Wkg Gp, 2006–; Mem. Bd, Norwich Heritage and Econ. Regeneration Trust, 2006–. Mem. Bd, Poetry Archive, 2006–. Mem. Court: Univ. of Warwick, 1987–97; Univ. of Birmingham, 1992–97. Mem. Bd., Inst. of Historical Res., 1992–97. Gov., Royal Shakespeare Theatre, 1984–97; Chm., Trustees and Govs, Friends of the Royal Pavilion Art Gall. and Museums, Brighton and Hove, 2006–. FSA 2007. *Publications:* (jtly) Monty at Close Quarters, 1985; jt author of various CPC pamphlets. *Recreations:* books, the arts, hill-walking. *Address:* House of Lords, SW1A 0PW.

HOWARTH, David Ross; MP (Lib Dem) Cambridge, since 2005; Reader in Private Law, University of Cambridge, since 2005; *b* 10 Nov. 1958; *s* of George Albert Howarth and Jean Howarth (*née* Rowbotham); *m* 1985, Edna Helen Murphy; two *s. Educ:* Queen Mary's Grammar Sch., Walsall; Clare Coll., Cambridge (BA 1981); Yale Univ. (MA 1982; LLM 1983; MPhil 1985). University of Cambridge: William Sen. Res. Fellow in Comparative Law, 1985–87, Lectr, 1987, Clare Coll.; Univ. Asst Lectr, 1987–92, Univ. Lectr, 1992–2005, Dept of Land Economy. Mem. (Lib Dem), Cambridge CC, 1987–2004 (Leader, 2000–03). *Publications:* Textbook on Tort, 1995; (jtly) Tort: cases and materials, 2000; (jtly) The Law of Tort, 2001; (jtly) The Law of Restitution, 2002; (jtly) Reinventing the State, 2007; numerous articles in learned jls. *Address:* House of Commons, SW1A 0AA. *T:* (020) 7219 8073; *e-mail:* info@davidhowarth.org.uk.

HOWARTH, Elgar; freelance musician; *b* 4 Nov. 1935; *s* of Oliver and Emma Howarth; *m* 1958, Mary Bridget Neary; one *s* two *d. Educ:* Manchester Univ. (MusB); Royal Manchester Coll. of Music (ARMCM 1956; FRMCM 1970). Royal Opera House, Covent Garden (Orchestra), 1958–63; Royal Philharmonic Orchestra, 1963–69; Mem., London Sinfonietta, 1968–71; Mem., Philip Jones Brass Ensemble, 1965–76; freelance conductor, 1970–; Principal Guest Conductor, Opera North, 1985–88; Musical Advisor, Grimethorpe Colliery Brass Band, 1972–. Hon. RAM 1989; FRNCM 1994; FRWCMD (FWCMD 1997); FRCM 1999. Hon. Fellow, UC Salford, 1992. DUniv: Birmingham, 1993; York, 1999; Hon. DMus Keele, 1995; DLitt Salford, 2003. Olivier Award for Outstanding Achievement in Opera (for Die Soldaten, and The Prince of Hamburg, ENO), 1997. *Publications:* various compositions mostly for brass instruments.

HOWARTH, Rt Hon. George (Edward); PC 2005; MP (Lab) Knowsley North and Sefton East, since 1997 (Knowsley North, Nov. 1986–1997); *b* 29 June 1949; *m* 1977, Julie Rodgers; two *s* one *d. Educ:* Liverpool Polytechnic. Formerly: engineer; teacher; Chief Exec., Wales TUC's Co-operative Centre, 1984–86. Former Mem., Huyton UDC; Mem., Knowsley BC, 1975–86 (Dep. Leader, 1982). Parliamentary Under-Secretary of State: Home Office, 1997–99; NI Office, 1999–2001. *Address:* House of Commons, SW1A 0AA.

HOWARTH, (James) Gerald (Douglas); MP (C) Aldershot, since 1997; *b* 12 Sept. 1947; *s* of late James Howarth and of Mary Howarth, Marlow, Bucks; *m* 1973, Elizabeth Jane, *d* of late Michael and of Muriel Squibb, Crowborough, Sussex; two *s* one *d. Educ:* Haileybury and ISC Jun. Sch.; Bloxham Sch.; Southampton Univ. (BA Hons). Commnd RAFVR, 1968. Gen. Sec., Soc. for Individual Freedom, 1969–71; entered internat. banking, 1971; Bank of America Internat., 1971–77; European Arab Bank, 1977–81 (Manager, 1979–81); Syndication Manager, Standard Chartered Bank, 1981–83; Dir, Richard Unwin Internat., 1983–87; Jt Man. Dir, Taskforce Communications, 1993–96. Dir, Freedom Under Law, 1973–77; estabd Dicey Trust, 1976. Mem., Hounslow BC, 1982–83. MP (C) Cannock and Burntwood, 1983–92. Parliamentary Private Secretary: to Parly Under-Sec. of State for Energy, 1987–90; to Minister for Housing and Planning, 1990–91; to Rt Hon. Margaret Thatcher, MP, 1991–92; Shadow Defence Minister, 2002–. Member: Select Cttee on Sound Broadcasting, 1987–92; Home Affairs Select Cttee, 1997–2001; Defence Select Cttee, 2001–03. Chairman: Lords and Commons Family and Child Protection Gp, 1999–2005; All Party RAF Gp, 2005–; Vice-Chairman: Parly Aerospace Gp, 1997–; All-Party Photography Gp, 2004–; Jt Sec., Cons. Parly Aviation Cttee, 1983–87; Vice-Chm., Cons. Parly Envmt, Transport and the Regions Cttee, 1997–99; Jt Vice-Chm., Cons. Parly Home Affairs Cttee, 2000–02. Mem. Exec., 1922 Cttee, 1999–2002; Chm., 92 Gp, 2001–. Pres., Air Display Assoc. Europe, 2002–; Mem. Council, Air League. Trustee, Vulcan to the Sky project, 2006–. CRAeS 2004. Freeman, GAPAN, 2004. Britannia Airways Parly Pilot of the Year, 1988. Contributor to No Turning Back Gp pubns. *Recreations:* flying (private pilot's licence, 1965), photography, walking up hills, normal family pursuits. *Address:* House of Commons, SW1A 0AA. *T:* (020) 7219 5650.

HOWARTH, Judith; soprano; *b* 11 Sept. 1962. *Educ:* Royal Scottish Acad. of Music and Drama. Rôles include: *Royal Opera:* 1985–86: Oscar, in Un Ballo in Maschera (also in Florida); Elvira, in L'Italiana in Algeri; Iris, in Semele; 1989–: Adele, in Die Fledermaus; Ännchen, in Der Freischutz; Gilda, in Rigoletto; Liu, in Turandot; Marguerite de Valois, in Les Huguenots; Marzelline, in Fidelio; Morgana, in Alcina; Musetta, in La Bohème; Norina, in Don Pasquale; *Opera North:* 1992–: Cressida, in Troilus and Cressida; Norina; Susanna, in Le Nozze di Figaro; *English National Opera:* Madame Mao, in Nixon in China; Fiorilla, in Il Turko in Italia; Leila, in Les Pêcheurs des Perles; Butterfly, in Madame Butterfly; other rôles and productions include: Violetta, in La turbidly, Glyndebourne Touring Opera; Anne Trulove, in The Rake's Progress, Brussels; Marie, in La Fille du Régiment, Geneva; Hasse's Solimano and Cavilli's La Didone, Berlin; Countess Olga Sukarev, in Fedora, Washington; Soprano Heroines, in Les Contes d'Hoffmann, Nedda, in I Pagliacci, Florida; Aithra, in Die Ägyptische Helena, Santa Fe; Ellen Orford, in Peter Grimes, Toulouse; Pamina, in Die Zauberflöte, Strasbourg. Many concerts and festival appearances, incl. Salzburg, Aix-en-Provence, Edinburgh.

HOWARTH, His Honour Nigel John Graham; a Circuit Judge, 1992–2006; a Depu Circuit Judge, since 2006; *b* 12 Dec. 1936; *s* of Vernon and Irene Howarth; *m* 1962, Jani Mary Hooper; two *s* one *d. Educ:* Manchester Grammar Sch,; Manchester Univ. (LL LLM). Called to the Bar, Gray's Inn, 1960; private practice at Chancery Bar, Mancheste 1961–92; Actg Deemster, IOM, 1985, 1989; a Recorder, 1989–92. Chm., Northe Chancery Bar Assoc., 1990–92. Pres., Manchester Incorp. Law Library Soc., 1985–8 Vice Pres., Disabled Living, 1993–. *Recreations:* music, theatre, fell walking, Assoc. footb (Altrincham FC).

HOWARTH, Peter Andreas; Managing Director, Show Media Ltd, since 2002; *b* 1 Sept. 1964; three *s*; partner Emma Tucker. *Educ:* Gonville and Caius Coll., Cambrid (BA English 1986). Projects Manager, Paul Smith Ltd, 1986–88; Head of Menswea Nicole Farhi, 1988–91; Style Ed., 1991–93, Style Dir, 1993–95, GQ; Editor: Aren 1995–96; Esquire, 1996–2002. *Publication:* (ed) Fatherhood, 1997.

HOWARTH, Peter James, CBE 1995; Managing Director, Royal Mail, 1992–96, ar Board Member, 1991–96, Post Office; *b* 27 July 1935; *s* of late Sidney and Margar Howarth; *m* 1964, Susan Mary Briggs; one *s* one *d. Educ:* St Joseph's Coll., Blackpo Entered Post Office, 1953; held junior and middle management positions; He Postmaster, Manchester, 1979–85; Chm., NW Postal Bd, 1985–86; Gen. Manager, W and London Letters Territories, 1986–88; Dir Ops, Royal Mail, 1988–91; Asst Man. D Royal Mail, 1991; Man. Dir, Parcelforce, 1991–92. Mem., Billericay Mayflower Rota Club. *Recreations:* golf, fishing, reading. *Address:* Timbers, 38 Stock Road, Billericay, Ess CM12 0BE.

HOWARTH, Robert Lever; Member (Lab), Bolton County Borough, the Metropolitan Borough, Council, 1972–2004 (Leader, Labour Group, 1975–2004; Lead of the Council, 1980–2004); *b* 31 July 1927; *s* of James Howarth and Bessie (*née* Pearson *m* 1952, Josephine Mary Doyle; one *s* one *d. Educ:* Bolton County Grammar Sch.; Bolt Technical Coll. Draughtsman with Hawker Siddeley Dynamics. MP (Lab) Bolton Ea 1964–70. Lectr in Liberal Studies, Leigh Technical Coll., 1970–76; Senior Lectr General Studies, Wigan Coll. of Technology, 1977–87. Dep. Chm., 1986–87, Chm 1987–88 and 2002–03, Manchester Airport. Mem. (Lab), Bolton BC, 1958–60, 1963–6 Freeman, 2001, Hon. Alderman, 2004, Bolton MBC. *Recreations:* gardening, readin walking, films. *Address:* 93 Markland Hill, Bolton, Lancs BL1 5EQ. *T:* (01204) 844121.

HOWARTH, Stephen Frederick; HM Diplomatic Service, retired; UK Permane Representative to Council of Europe, Strasbourg (with personal rank of Ambassador 2003–07; *b* 25 Feb. 1947; *s* of Alan Howarth and Alice Howarth (*née* Wilkinson); *m* 196 Jennifer Mary Chrissop; one *s* two *d. Educ:* Switzerland; Rossall Sch.; Norwich Sch. Joine HM Diplomatic Service, 1966; FCO, 1966–71; Vice Consul, Rabat, 1971–74; Secon Sec., Washington, 1975–80; Second, later First, Sec., Near East and N Africa Dept, FCC 1980–82; seconded to Ecole Nationale d'Admin, Paris, 1982–83; Asst Head, Trac Relations and Export Dept, FCO, 1983–84; Dep. Head of Mission, Dakar, 1984–88; As Head of Cultural Relations Dept, FCO, 1989–90; Counsellor and Dep. Head, Perm Under Sec.'s Dept, FCO, 1990–92; Head of Consular Dept, later Div., 1993–97; Ministe Paris, 1997–2002. *Publications:* contribs to jl of Institut Internat. de l'Admin Public, EN Mensuel, Paris. *Recreations:* books, buildings, landscape, gardens. *Address:* Le Math Caplong, Ste Foy-la-Grande, 33220, France.

HOWATCH, Susan; writer; *b* 14 July 1940; *d* of George Stanford Sturt and Ann Sturt (*n* Watney); *m* 1964, Joseph Howatch (separated 1975); one *d. Educ:* Sutton High Sc GPDST; King's Coll. London (LLB 1961; FKC 1999). Established Starbridge Lectureshi in Theology and Natural Science, Cambridge University, 1992. *Publications:* The Da Shore, 1965; The Waiting Sands, 1966; Call in the Night, 1967; The Shrouded Wal 1968; April's Grave, 1969; The Devil on Lammas Night, 1970; Penmarric, 197 Cashelmara, 1974; The Rich are Different, 1977; Sins of the Fathers, 1980; The Wheel Fortune, 1984; *Starbridge novels:* Glittering Images, 1987; Glamorous Powers, 198 Ultimate Prizes, 1989; Scandalous Risks, 1991; Mystical Paths, 1992; Absolute Truth 1994; *St Benet's trilogy:* A Question of Integrity, 1997, renamed as The Wonder Worke The High Flyer, 1999; The Heartbreaker, 2003. *Recreation:* reading theology. *Address:* c/ Aitken Alexander Associates Ltd, 18–21 Cavaye Place, SW10 9PT. *T:* (020) 7373 8672

HOWATSON, William, FRAgS; freelance rural affairs journalist; Member (Lib Dem Aberdeenshire Council, since 1999; Provost of Aberdeenshire, since 2007; *b* 22 Jan. 195 *s* of William Smith Howatson and Bessie Howatson; *m* 1985, Hazel Symington Paton; tw *d. Educ:* Lockerbie Acad.; Univ. of Edinburgh (MA Hons 1975). Reporter: Scottis Farmer newspaper, 1979–83; Dumfries and Galloway Standard, 1983–84; Agricl Ed. an Leader Writer, 1984–96, columnist, 1996–2005, The Press and Journal, Aberdeen. Chm Guild of Agricl Journalists, 1995. Member: Scottish Water and Sewerage Custome Council, 1995–99; Health Educn Bd for Scotland, 1996–2003, subseq. NHS Healt Scotland, 2003– (Vice Chm., 2003–); E Areas Bd, Scottish Natural Heritage, 1997–200 (Vice Chm., 1999–2003); Bd, SEPA, 1999–2005 (Chm. E Regl Bd, 2003–05); Ra Passenger Cttee for Scotland, 2001–03. Non-exec. Dir, Angus NHS Trust, 1998–99; no exec. Mem., Grampian NHS Health Bd, 2007–. Mem. Bd of Mgt, Angus Coll., 1996– Gov., Macaulay Land Use Res. Inst., 1998–2003. FRAgS 2003. JP S Aberdeenshir 1999–2007. *Publication:* (contrib.) Farm Servants and Labour in Lowland Scotlan 1770–1914, 1984. *Recreations:* gardening, hill-walking, cooking, reading Scottish history *Address:* Stone of Morphie, Hillside, Montrose, Angus DD10 0AA. *T:* (01674) 83074 *Fax:* (01674) 830114; *e-mail:* billhowatson@aol.com. *Club:* Edinburgh Press.

HOWDEN, Alan Percival; Director: Picturedrome Media Ltd, since 2001; UK Film an Television Production Co. Ltd, since 2001; *b* 28 Aug. 1936; *s* of C. P. Howden an Marian Grindell; *m* 1981, Judith South; one *d. Educ:* Sale Grammar Sch.; UMIST (BS Tech Mech. Engrg). Joined BBC, 1964: Exec., 1966–67, Head, 1977–83, Purchase Programmes; Gen. Manager, later Head, Programme Acquisition, 1983–97; Controlle Prog. Acquisition, 1997–99; Advr, Prog. Acquisition, BBC TV, 1999. Mem. Bd, BB Enterprises, 1989–94. British Film Institute: Gov., 1994–2001; Chm., Film Educn Re Cttee for DCMS, 1998–99; British Federation of Film Societies: Vice-Chm., 1965–8 Chm., 1980–82; Vice Pres., 1982–. *Recreations:* theatre, early music, English countrysid *Address: e-mail:* alanhowden@beeb.net. *Club:* Soho House.

HOWDEN, Timothy Simon; Director, SSL International plc, 1999–2005; *b* 2 Apr 1937; *s* of Phillip Alexander and Rene Howden; *m* 1st, 1958, Penelope Mary Wilmo (marr. diss. 1984); two *s* one *d*; 2nd, 1999, Lois Robin Chesney. *Educ:* Tonbridge Sch Served RA, 1955–57, 2nd Lieut. Floor Treatments Ltd, 1957–59; joined Reckitt & Colman, 1962; France, 1962–64; Germany, 1964–70; Dir, Reckitt & Colman Europ 1970–73; Ranks Hovis McDougall, 1973–92: Dir, RHM Flour Mills, 1973–75; Man. Di RHM Foods, 1975–81; Chm. and Man. Dir, British Bakeries, 1981–85; Planning, the Dep. Man. Dir, 1985–89; Man. Dir, 1989–92; Gp Chief Exec. for Europe, The Albe Fisher Group, 1992–96; CEO, Albert Fisher Inc., N America, 1996–97. Director: Finnin Internat. Inc., 1998–2007; Hyperion Insce Gp, 2000–. *Recreations:* ski-ing, scuba diving tennis, sailing. *Club:* Annabel's.

HOWDLE, Prof. Peter David, MD; FRCP; Professor of Clinical Medicine, University of Leeds, since 2006; Consultant Physician, St James's University Hospital, Leeds, since 1987; *b* 16 June 1948; *s* of George Henry Howdle and Mary Jane Howdle (*née* Baugh); *m* 1972, Susan Ruth Lowery. *Educ:* King's Sch., Pontefract; Univ. of Leeds Med. Sch. (BSc 1969; MB ChB 1972; MD 1985). FRCP 1992. Jun. med. appts, St James's Univ. Hosp., Leeds, 1972–82; University of Leeds: Lectr in Medicine, 1982–87, Sen. Lectr, 1987–96; Prof. of Clinical Educn, 1996–2006; Hd, Acad. Unit of Gen. Surgery, Medicine and Anaesthesia, Univ. of Leeds Med. Sch., 1999–2005; Hd, Section of Medicine, Surgery and Anaesthesia, Leeds Inst. of Molecular Medicine, 2005–. Vis. Lectr (Fulbright Schol.), Harvard Univ., 1984–85; Med. Advr to Coeliac UK, 1995–. Vice-Pres., Methodist Conf., 2002–03; Co-Chm., Jt Implementation Commn for the Anglican-Methodist Covenant, 2003–. *Publications:* Comprehensive Clinical Hepatology, 2000; Your Guide to Coeliac Disease, 2007; contrib. articles on gastroenterology. *Recreations:* classical music, modern literature, Methodist history and liturgy. *Address:* Department of Academic Medicine, Clinical Sciences Building, St James's University Hospital, Leeds LS9 7TF. *T:* (0113) 206 5281.

HOWE, family name of **Baron Howe of Aberavon** and **Baroness Howe of Idlicote**.

HOWE, 7th Earl *cr* 1821; **Frederick Richard Penn Curzon;** Baron Howe, 1788; Baron Curzon, 1794; Viscount Curzon, 1802; farmer; Chairman, London and Provincial Antique Dealers' Association, since 1999; *b* 29 Jan. 1951; *s* of Chambré George William Penn Curzon (*d* 1976) (*g s* of 3rd Earl) and Enid Jane Victoria Curzon (*née* Fergusson) (*d* 1997); *S* cousin, 1984; *m* 1983, Elizabeth Helen Stuart, DL; one *s* three *d*. *Educ:* Rugby School; Christ Church, Oxford (MA Hons Lit. Hum.; Chancellor's Prize for Latin Verse, 1973). AIB. Entered Barclays Bank Ltd, 1973; Manager, 1982; Sen. Manager, 1984–87. Director: Adam & Co., 1987–90; Provident Life Assoc. Ltd, 1988–91. A Lord in Waiting (Govt Whip), 1991–92; front bench spokesman, H of L, on employment and transport, 1991, on environment and defence, 1992; Parly Sec., MAFF, 1992–95; Parly Under-Sec. of State, MoD, 1995–97; opposition front bench spokesman on health, H of L, 1997–; elected Mem., H of L, 1999. Governor: King William IV Naval Foundation, 1984–; Milton's Cottage, 1985–; Trident Trust, 1985–; Member: Council, RNLI, 1997– (Pres., Chilterns Br., 1985–); Council of Mgt, Restoration of Appearance and Function Trust, 2000–; President: S Bucks Assoc. for the Disabled, 1984–; Nat. Soc. for Epilepsy, 1986– (Vice-Pres., 1984–86); Penn Country Br., CPRE, 1986–92; Abbeyfield Beaconsfield Soc., 1991–. Patron: Demand, 2000–; Chiltern Soc., 2001–. *Recreation:* spending time with family. *Heir:* *s* Viscount Curzon, *qv*. *Address:* c/o House of Lords, SW1A 0PW.

HOWE OF ABERAVON, Baron *cr* 1992 (Life Peer), of Tandridge, in the County of Surrey; **Richard Edward Geoffrey Howe,** CH 1996; Kt 1970; PC 1972; QC 1965; *b* 20 Dec. 1926; *er s* of late B. E. Howe and Mrs E. F. Howe, JP (*née* Thomson), Port Talbot, Glamorgan; *m* 1953, Elspeth Rosamund Morton Shand (*see* Baroness Howe of Idlicote); one *s* two *d*. *Educ:* Winchester Coll. (Exhibitioner); Trinity Hall, Cambridge (Scholar, MA, LLB; Hon. Fellow, 1992); Pres., Trinity Hall Assoc., 1977–78. Lieut Royal Signals 1945–48. Chm. Cambridge Univ. Conservative Assoc., 1951; Chm. Bow Group, 1955; Managing Dir, Crossbow, 1957–60, Editor 1960–62. Called to the Bar, Middle Temple, 1952, Bencher, 1969, Reader, 1993; Mem. General Council of the Bar, 1957–61; Mem. Council of Justice, 1963–70. Dep. Chm., Glamorgan QS, 1966–70. Contested (C) Aberavon, 1955, 1959; MP (C): Bebington, 1964–66; Reigate, 1970–74; Surrey East, 1974–92. Sec. Conservative Parliamentary Health and Social Security Cttee, 1964–65; an Opposition Front Bench spokesman on labour and social services, 1965–66; Solicitor-General, 1970–72; Minister for Trade and Consumer Affairs, DTI, 1972–74; opposition front bench spokesman on social services, 1974–75, on Treasury and economic affairs, 1975–79; Chancellor of the Exchequer, 1979–83; Sec. of State for Foreign and Commonwealth Affairs, 1983–89; Lord Pres. of the Council, Leader of H of C, and Dep. Prime Minister, 1989–90. Chm., Interim Cttee, IMF, 1982–83. Chm., Framlington Russian Investment Fund, 1994–2003; Director: Sun Alliance & London Insce Co. Ltd, 1974–79; AGB Research Ltd, 1974–79; EMI Ltd, 1976–79; BICC plc, 1991–97; Glaxo Hldgs, 1991–95; Glaxo Wellcome plc, 1995–96. Special Advr, Internat. Affairs, Jones, Day, Reavis and Pogue, 1991–2000; Member: J. P. Morgan Internat. Adv. Council, 1992–2001; Adv. Council, Bertelsmann Foundn, 1992–97; Fuji Wolfensohn Internat. European Adv. Bd, 1996–98; Carlyle Gp Eur. Adv. Bd, 1997–2001; Fuji Bank Internat. Adv. Council, 1999–2002. Member: (Latey) Interdeptl Cttee on Age of Majority, 1965–67; (Street) Cttee on Racial Discrimination, 1967; (Cripps) Cons. Cttee on Discrimination against Women, 1968–69; Chm. Ely Hospital, Cardiff, Inquiry, 1969. Chm. Steering Cttee, Tax Law Rewrite Project, Inland Revenue, 1996–2005. Visitor, SOAS, Univ. of London, 1991–2001; Vis. Fellow, John F. Kennedy Sch. of Govt, Harvard Univ., 1991–92; Herman Phleger Vis. Prof., Stanford Law Sch., Calif, 1993. Member, International Advisory Council: Inst. of Internat. Studies, Stanford Univ., Calif, 1990–2005; Centre for Eur. Policy Studies, 1992–2005; Chm., Adv. Bd, English Centre for Legal Studies, Warsaw Univ., 1992–99; Pres., Acad. of Experts, 1996–2005; Vice-President: RUSI, 1991–; English Coll. Foundn in Prague, 1992–. President: Cons. Political Centre Nat. Adv. Cttee, 1977–79; Nat. Union of Cons. and Unionist Assocs, 1983–84; GB China Centre, 1992–; Jt Pres., Wealth of Nations Foundn, 1991–2004; Chm., Thomson Foundn, 2004–07 (Trustee, 1995–2007); Trustee: Cambridge Commonwealth Trust, 1993–; Cambridge Overseas Trust, 1993–. Mem., Adv. Council, Presidium of Supreme Rada of Ukraine, 1991–97. Mem. Council of Management, Private Patients' Plan, 1969–70; Mem., Steering Cttee, Project Liberty, 1991–97; Patron: Enterprise Europe, 1990–2004; UK Metric Assoc., 1999–. Pres., Which? (formerly Assoc. for Consumer Res.), 1992– (an Hon. Vice-Pres., 1974–92). Freeman, City of London, 2004; Hon. Freeman, Co. of Tax Advisors, 2004. Hon. Fellow: UCW, Swansea, 1996; UCW, Cardiff, 1999; Amer. Bar Foundn, 2000; Chartered Inst. of Taxation, 2000; SOAS, 2003. Hon. Freeman, Port Talbot, 1992. Hon. LLD: Wales, 1988; LSE, 2004; Glamorgan, 2004; Hon. DCL City, 1993. Joseph Bech Prize, FVS Stiftung, Hamburg, 1993; Paul Harris Fellow, Rotary Internat., 1995. Grand Cross, Order of Merit (Portugal), 1987; Grand Cross, Order of Merit (Germany), 1992; Order of Public Service (Ukraine), 2001. *Publications:* Conflict of Loyalty (memoirs), 1994; various political pamphlets for Bow Group and Conservative Political Centre. *Address:* House of Lords, SW1A 0PW. *Clubs:* Athenæum, Garrick.

HOWE OF IDLICOTE, Baroness *cr* 2001 (Life Peer), of Shipston-on-Stour in the County of Warwickshire; **Elspeth Rosamund Morton Howe,** CBE 1999; JP; Chairman: Broadcasting Standards Commission, 1997–99 (Chairman, Broadcasting Standards Council, 1993–97); BOC Foundation for the Environment and Community, 1990–2003; *b* 8 Feb. 1932; *d* of late Philip Morton Shand and Sybil Mary (*née* Sissons); *m* 1953, Baron Howe of Aberavon, *qv*; one *s* two *d*. *Educ:* Bath High Sch.; Wycombe Abbey; London Sch. of Econs and Pol Science (BSc 1985; Hon. Fellow, 2001). Vice-Chm., Conservative London Area Women's Adv. Cttee, 1966–67, also Pres. of the Cttee's Contact Gp, 1973–77; Mem., Conservative Women's Nat. Adv. Cttee, 1966–71. Member: Lord Chancellor's Adv. Cttee on appointment of Magistrates for Inner London Area, 1965–75; Lord Chancellor's Adv. Cttee on Legal Aid, 1971–75; Parole Board, 1972–75. Dep. Chm., Equal Opportunities Commn, 1975–79. Co-opted Mem., ILEA, 1967–70; Member: Briggs Cttee on Nursing Profession, 1970–72; Justice Cttee on English Judiciary, 1992. Chairman: Hansard Soc. Commn on Women at the Top, 1989–90; The Quality of Care, Local Govt Management Bd Inquiry and Report, 1991–92; Archbishop's Commn on Cathedrals, 1992–94. Director: Kingfisher (formerly Woolworth Holdings) PLC, 1986–2000; United Biscuits (Holdings) PLC, 1988–94; Legal & General Group, 1989–97; Chm., Opportunity 2000 Target Team, Business in the Community, 1990–99. President: Peckham Settlement, 1976–; Women's Gas Fedn, 1979–93; Fedn of Personnel Services, subseq. of Recruitment and Employment Services, 1980–94; UNICEF UK, 1993–2002; Member Council: NACRO, 1974–93; PSI, 1983–92; St George's House, Windsor, 1987–92; Vice-Pres., Pre-Sch. Playgroups Assoc., 1979–83. Trustee, Westminster Foundn for Democracy, 1992–96. Has served as chm. or mem. of several sch. governing bodies in Tower Hamlets; Governor: Cumberlow Lodge Remand Home, 1967–70; Wycombe Abbey, 1968–90; Froebel Educn Inst., 1968–75; LSE, 1985–2006; Mem. Bd of Governors, James Allen's Girls' Sch., 1988–93; Mem. Council, Open Univ., 1996–2003 (Vice-Chm. Council, 2001–03). JP Inner London Juvenile Court Panel, 1964–92 (Chm. of Court, 1970–90). Hon. LLD: London, 1990; Aberdeen, 1993; Liverpool, 1994; DUniv: Open, 1993; South Bank, 1996; Hon. DLitt: Bradford, 1990; Sunderland, 1995. *Publication:* Under Five (a report on pre-school education), 1966. *Address:* House of Lords, SW1A 0PW.

HOWE, Bernard H.; *see* Hogan-Howe.

HOWE, Hon. Brian Leslie, AO 2008 (AM 2001); *b* 28 Jan. 1936; *s* of John P. Howe and Lillian M. Howe; *m* 1962, Renate Morris; one *s* two *d*. *Educ:* Melbourne High Sch.; Melbourne Univ. (BA, DipCrim); McCormick Theol Seminary, Chicago (MA). Ordained Minister of Methodist Church, 1963; parishes at Eltham, Morwell and Fitzroy, 1960–69; Dir, Centre for Urban Research and Action, Fitzroy, and Lectr in Sociology, Swinburne Inst. of Technology, 1970–77. Professorial Associate, Centre for Public Policy, Univ. of Melbourne, 1996–; Woodrow Wilson School of Public and International Affairs, Princeton University: Res. Fellow, Centre of Domestic and Comparative Policy Studies, 1997; Frederick H. Schultz Class of 1951 Prof., 1998. MP (ALP) Batman, Vic, 1977–96; Minister: for Defence Support, 1983–84; for Social Security, 1984–89; for Community Services and Health, 1990–91; for Health, Housing and Community Services, 1991–93; for Housing, Local Govt and Community (then Human) Services, 1993–94; for Housing and Regional Develt, 1994–96; Minister assisting the Prime Minister for Social Justice, 1988–93, for Commonwealth-State Relations, 1991–93; Dep. Prime Minister of Australia, 1991–95. Life Mem., ALP, 2005. Bd Mem., Australia & NZ Sch. of Govt, 2003–. Life Mem., Victorian Council of Social Service, 2007. Patron, Royal Melbourne Philharmonic Orch., 1998–. Charter Mem. and Mem. Bd, Brotherhood of St Laurence, 1998– (Life Mem., 2005). Hon. Fellow, Queen's Coll., Univ. of Melbourne, 2000. Hon. FPIA (Hon. FRAPI 1995). *Publications:* Weighing up Australian Values, 2007; numerous papers, contribs to books, jls and conf. procs. *Recreations:* golf, reading, films, Australian Rules football. *Address:* PO Box 459, North Carlton, Vic 3054, Australia.

HOWE, Prof. Christine Joyce, PhD; Professor of Education, University of Cambridge, since 2006; *b* Birmingham, 21 Nov. 1948; *d* of Walter Virgil Howe and Joyce Winifred Howe (*née* Barmby); *m* 1979, William John Robertson; one *s* one *d*. *Educ:* Univ. of Sussex (BA 1st Cl. Hons); Univ. of Cambridge (PhD 1975). Lectr, Sussex Univ., 1974–76; Strathclyde University: Lectr, 1976–90; Sen. Lectr, 1990–95; Reader, 1995–98; Prof. of Psychol., 1998–2006. Mem., ESRC, 2004–08. Chm., Develtl Section, BPsS, 2006–08. AcSS 2008. *Publications:* Learning Language in a Conversational Context, 1983; Language Learning: a special case for developmental psychology, 1993; Group and Interactive Learning, 1994; Gender and Classroom Interaction, 1997; Conceptual Structure in Childhood and Adolescence: the case of everyday physics, 1998. *Recreations:* bridge, tennis, hill-walking, music, theatre. *Address:* Faculty of Education, University of Cambridge, 184 Hills Road, Cambridge CB2 8PQ. *T:* (01223) 767724; *e-mail:* cjh82@cam.ac.uk.

HOWE, Prof. Christopher Barry, MBE 1997; PhD; FBA 2001; Research Professor, School of East Asian Studies, University of Sheffield, since 2006; *b* 3 Nov. 1937; *s* of Charles Roderick Howe and Patricia (*née* Creeden); *m* 1967, Patricia Anne Giles; one *s* one *d*. *Educ:* William Ellis Sch., London; St Catharine's Coll., Cambridge (MA); PhD London. Economic Secretariat, FBI, 1961–63; Sch. of Oriental and African Studies, London Univ., 1963–2006: Head, Contemp. China Inst., 1972–78; Prof. of Economics with ref. to Asia, 1979–2001; Prof., 2001–03, Res. Prof., 2003–06, of Chinese Business Mgt. Member: Hong Kong Univ. and Polytechnic Grants Cttee, 1974–93; UGC, 1979–84; ESRC Res. Develt Gp, 1987–88; Hong Kong Res. Grants Council, 1991–99; HEFCE Wkg Party on Chinese Studies, 1998. Fellow, 48 Gp Club, 2003. *Publications:* Employment and Economic Growth in Urban China 1949–57, 1971; Industrial Relations and Rapid Industrialisation, 1972; Wage Patterns and Wage Policy in Modern China 1919–1972, 1973; China's Economy: a basic guide, 1978; (ed) Studying China, 1979; (ed) Shanghai: revolution and development, 1980; (ed) The Readjustment in the Chinese Economy, 1984; (ed) China and Japan: history, trends and prospects, 1990; The Origins of Japanese Trade Supremacy, 1996; (ed with C. H. Feinstein) Chinese Technology Transfer in the 1990s, 1997; (with R. A. Ash and Y. Y. Kueh) China's Economic Reform, 2003; (with T. Kambara) China and the Global Energy Crisis, 2007. *Recreations:* music, Burmese cats, walking. *Address:* 12 Highgate Avenue, N6 5RX. *T:* (020) 8340 8104.

HOWE, Prof. Daniel Walker, FRHistS; Rhodes Professor of American History, 1992–2002; Fellow of St Catherine's College, Oxford, 1992–2002, now Fellow Emeritus; *b* 10 Jan. 1937; *s* of Maurice Langdon Howe and Lucie Walker Howe; *m* 1961, Sandra Shumway; two *s* one *d*. *Educ:* Harvard (BA); Magdalen Coll., Oxford (MA); Univ. of California at Berkeley (PhD). Lieut, US Army, 1959–60. Yale University: Instructor, 1966–68; Asst Prof., 1968–73; University of California at Los Angeles: Associate Prof., 1973–77; Prof., 1977–92; Chm., History Dept, 1983–87. Harmsworth Vis. Prof., Oxford, 1989–90. Fellow: Charles Warren Center, Harvard, 1970–71; Nat. Endowment for Humanities, 1975–76; Guggenheim Foundn, 1984–85; Res. Fellow, Huntington Library, 1991–92, 2002–03. FRHistS 2002. Amer. Historian Laureate, 2008. *Publications:* The Unitarian Conscience, 1970, 2nd edn 1988; The Political Culture of the American Whigs, 1980; Making the American Self, 1997; What Hath God Wrought, 2007; articles in learned jls. *Recreation:* music. *Address:* St Catherine's College, Oxford OX1 3UJ. *T:* (01865) 271700; 3814 Cody Road, Sherman Oaks, CA 91403, USA.

HOWE, Prof. Denis; Professor of Aircraft Design, 1973–92, College of Aeronautics, Cranfield Institute of Technology, now Professor Emeritus, Cranfield University; *b* 3 Sept. 1927; *s* of Alfred and Alice Howe; *m* 1st, 1954, Audrey Marion Wilkinson; two *s* three *d*; 2nd, 1981, Catherine Bolton. *Educ:* Watford Grammar Sch.; MIT (SM); College of Aeronautics (PhD). CEng, FIMechE, FRAeS. Project Engineer, Fairey Aviation Co., 1945–54; College of Aeronautics, Cranfield Institute of Technology: Lectr, Sen. Lectr and Reader, 1954–73; Head of College, 1986–90; Dean of Engineering, 1988–91. *Publications:* Aircraft Conceptual Design Synthesis, 2000; Aircraft Loading and Structural Layout, 2004; contribs to learned jls. *Recreations:* gardening, church administration. *Address:* 54 Appledore Road, Bedford MK40 3UZ. *T:* (01234) 56747.

HOWE, Derek Andrew, CBE 1991; public affairs and political consultant; company director; *b* 31 Aug. 1934; *o s* of late Harold and Elsie Howe; *m* 1st, 1958, Barbara (*née* Estill); two *d*; 2nd, 1975, Sheila (*née* Digger), MBE (*d* 1990); one *s*; 3rd, 1996, Penny (*née* James). *Educ:* City of Leeds Sch.; Cockburn High Sch., Leeds. Journalist, Yorkshire Evening News, 1951–61; Conservative Central Office, 1962–70; Parliamentary Liaison Officer, 1970–73; Special Adviser, 1973–75; Press Officer, Leader of HM Opposition, 1975–79; special adviser to: Paymaster Gen., 1979–81; Chancellor of Duchy of Lancaster, 1981; Political Secretary, 10 Downing Street, 1981–83 and Special Adviser to Leader of the House of Commons, 1982–83. Chm., Churchill Clinic, 1996–99 (Dep. Chm., 1995–96). Trustee, London Youth Trust, 1985–2005 (Chm. Trustees, 1988–2004). Freeman of the City of London. *Recreations:* gardening, reading, antiques, philately, Freemasonry. *Address:* The Vines, Kimpton, near Andover, Hampshire SP11 8NU.

HOWE, Eric James, CBE 1990; Data Protection Registrar, 1984–94; *b* 4 Oct. 1931; *s* of Albert Henry Howe and Florence Beatrice (*née* Hale); *m* 1967, Patricia Enid (*née* Schollick); two *d*. *Educ:* Stretford Grammar Sch.; Univ. of Liverpool (BA Econs 1954). FIDPM 1990; FBCS 1972. NCB, 1954–59; British Cotton Industry Res. Assoc., 1959–61; English Electric Computer Co., 1961–66; National Computing Centre, 1966–84: Dep. Dir, 1975–84; Mem. Bd of Dirs, 1976–84. Chairman: National Computer Users Forum, 1977–84; Focus Cttee for Private Sector Users, DoI, 1982–84; Member: User Panel, NEDO, 1983–84; Council, British Computer Soc., 1971–74 and 1980–83; NW Regional Council, CBI, 1977–83. Chm. Bd, N Wales Housing Assoc., 2003–05 (Bd Mem., 1997–2006). Rep. UK, Confedn of Eur. Computer Users Assocs, 1980–83. *Recreations:* gardening, golf.

HOWE, Prof. Geoffrey Leslie, TD 1962 (Bars 1969 and 1974); Professor of Oral Surgery and Oral Medicine, 1987–96, and Dean, 1988–96, Jordan University of Science and Technology; *b* 22 April 1924; *e s* of late Leo Leslie John Howe, Maidenhead, Berks; *m* 1st, 1948, Heather Patricia Joan Hambly (*d* 1997); (one *s* decd); 2nd, 2003, Mrs Margaret Samuel (*née* Hall). *Educ:* Royal Dental and Middlesex Hospitals. LDS RCS 1946; LRCP, MRCS 1954; FDS RCS 1955; MDS Dunelm, 1961; FFD RCSI 1964; FICD 1981. Dental and Medical Sch. Prizeman; Begley Prize, RCS, 1951; Cartwright Prize, RCS, 1961. Dental Officer, Royal Army Dental Corps, 1946–49. House appointments, etc., Royal Dental and Middlesex Hospitals, 1949–55. Registrar in Oral Surgery, Eastman Dental Hosp. (Institute of Dental Surgery), 1955–56; Senior Registrar in Oral Surgery, Plastic and Oral Surgery Centre, Chepstow, Mon, 1956; Senior Registrar in Oral Surgery, Eastman Dental Hospital, 1956–59; Professor of Oral Surgery, University of Newcastle upon Tyne (formerly King's Coll., University of Durham), 1959–67; Prof. of Oral Surgery, Royal Dental Hosp., London Sch. of Dental Surgery, 1967–78 (Dean of School, 1974–78); Prof. of Oral Surgery and Oral Medicine, and Dean of Dental Studies, Univ. of Hong Kong, 1978–83; Dir, Prince Philip Dental Hosp., 1981–83. Cons. Oral Surgeon, United Newcastle upon Tyne Hosps, 1959–67; Chm., Central Cttee for Hosp. Dental Services, 1971–73; Vice-Pres., BDA, 1979– (Vice-Chm., 1971–73; Chm., 1973–78); Pres., Internat. Assoc. of Oral Surgeons, 1980–83. Hon. Col Comdt, RADC, 1975–89. OStJ. *Publications:* The Extraction of Teeth, 1961, 2nd edn 1970; Minor Oral Surgery, 1966, 3rd edn 1985; (with F. I. H. Whitehead) Local Anaesthesia in Dentistry, 1972, 3rd edn 1990; Reflections of a Fortunate Fellow (autobiog.), 2002; contribs to: Medical Treatment Yearbook, 1959; Modern Trends in Dental Surgery, 1962, and to numerous medical and dental journals. *Recreations:* sailing; Territorial Army Volunteer Reserve (lately Col, OC 217 (L) Gen. Hosp. RAMC (V), graded Cons. Dental Surgeon RADC, TAVR). *Address:* 70 Croham Manor Road, South Croydon, Surrey CR2 7BF. *Clubs:* Savage, Gents, Oral Surgery; Hong Kong; Hong Kong Yacht.

HOWE, Geoffrey Michael Thomas; Chairman: Jardine Lloyd Thompson Group plc, since 2006 (Director, 2002–04, Joint Deputy Chairman, 2004–06); Nationwide Building Society, since 2007 (Director, since 2005); *b* 3 Sept. 1949; *s* of Michael Edward Howe and Susan Dorothy Howe (*née* Allan); *m* 1995, Karen Mary Webber (*née* Ford); two *d*. *Educ:* Manchester Grammar Sch.; St John's Coll., Cambridge (MA). Solicitor. Stephenson Harwood, 1971–75; joined Clifford Chance, 1975; Partner, Corporate Dept, 1980; Man. Partner, 1989–97; Gen. Counsel and Dir, Robert Fleming Hldgs Ltd, 1998–2000; Chm., Railtrack Gp plc, 2002. Director: Gateway Electronic Components Ltd, 2000–; Investec plc, 2003–. *Recreations:* opera, wine, antiques, paintings.

HOWE, Ven. George Alexander; Archdeacon of Westmorland and Furness, since 2000; *b* 22 Jan. 1952; *s* of Eugene Howe and Olivia Lydia Caroline Howe (*née* Denroche); *m* 1980, Jane Corbould; one *s* one *d*. *Educ:* Liverpool Inst. High Sch.; Univ. of Durham (BA 1973); Westcott House Cambridge. Ordained deacon, 1975, priest, 1976; Curate: St Cuthbert, Peterlee, 1975–79; St Mary, Norton, Stockton-on-Tees, 1979–81; Vicar, Utd Benefice of Hart with Elwick Hall, 1981–85; Rector, St Edmund, Sedgefield, 1985–91; Rural Dean of Sedgefield, 1988–91; Vicar, Holy Trinity, Kendal, 1991–2000; Rural Dean of Kendal, 1994–99. Hon. Canon, Carlisle Cathedral, 1994–. Bishop's Advr for Ecumenical Affairs, dio. of Carlisle, 2001–. Chm., Church and Community Fund, 2007–. *Recreations:* listening to The Archers, walking the dog, good food and wine, cartology. *Address:* The Vicarage, Windermere Road, Lindale, Grange-over-Sands, Cumbria LA11 6LB. *T:* (015395) 34717.

HOWE, Prof. G(eorge) Melvyn, PhD, DSc; FRSE, FRGS, FRSGS, FRMetS; Professor of Geography, University of Strathclyde, 1967–85, now Emeritus; *b* Abercynon, 7 April 1920; *s* of Reuben and Edith Howe, Abercynon; *m* 1947, Patricia Graham Fennell, Pontypridd; three *d*. *Educ:* Caerphilly Boys' Grammar Sch.; UCW Aberystwyth (BSc 1940; BSc 1st cl. hons Geog. and Anthrop., 1947; MSc 1949; PhD 1957); DSc Strathclyde 1974. Served with RAF, 1940–46: Meteorological Br., 1940–42; commnd Intell. (Air Photographic Interpretation) Br., 1942–46, in Middle East Comd. Lectr, later Sen. Lectr, in Geography, UCW Aberystwyth, 1948; Reader in Geog., Univ. of Wales, 1964. Vis. Prof. (Health and Welfare, Canada), 1977. Mem. Council, Inst. of British Geographers (Pres., 1985); Mem. Medical Geography Cttee, RGS, 1960–; British Rep. on Medical Geog. Commn of IGU, 1970–; Mem., British Nat. Cttee for Geography, RGS, 1978–83. Gill Memorial Award, RGS, 1964. *Publications:* Wales from the Air, 1957, 2nd edn 1966; (with P. Thomas) Welsh Landforms and Scenery, 1963; National Atlas of Disease Mortality in the United Kingdom, 1963, 2nd edn 1970; The Soviet Union, 1968, 2nd edn 1983; The USSR, 1971; Man, Environment and Disease in Britain, 1972, 2nd edn 1976; (ed and contrib.) Atlas of Glasgow and the West of Scotland, 1972; (contrib.) Wales (ed E. G. Bowen), 1958; (contrib.) Modern Methods in the History of Medicine (ed E. Clarke), 1970; (ed with J. A. Loraine, and contrib.) Environmental Medicine, 1973, 2nd edn 1980; (contrib.) Environment and Man (ed J. Lenihan and W. W. Fletcher), 1976; (ed and contrib.) A World Geography of Human Diseases, 1977; (ed and contrib.) Global Geocancerology, 1986; People, Environment, Disease and Death in Britain, 1997; articles in geographical, meteorological, hydrological and medical jls. *Recreation:* travel. *Address:* Hendre, 50 Heol Croes Faen, Nottage, Porthcawl CF36 3SW. *T:* (01656) 772377. *Club:* Royal Air Force.

HOWE, John Francis, CB 1996; OBE 1974; Vice-Chairman, Thales UK plc, since 2002; *b* 29 Jan. 1944; *s* of late Frank and Marjorie Howe; *m* 1981, Angela Ephrosini (*né* Nicolaides); one *d* one step *d*. *Educ:* Shrewsbury Sch.; Balliol Coll., Oxford (Scholar; MA). Pirelli General Cable Works, 1964; joined MoD as Asst Principal, 1967; Principal, 1972; Civil Adviser to GOC NI, 1972–73; Private Sec. to Perm. Under-Sec. of State, 1975–78; Asst Sec., 1979; seconded to FCO as Defence Counsellor, UK Delegn to NATO, 1981–84; Head, Arms Control Unit, MoD, 1985–86; Private Sec. to Sec. of State fo Defence, 1986–87; Asst Under-Sec. of State (Personnel and Logistics), 1988–91; Dep Under-Sec. of State (Civilian Management), 1992–96; Dep. Chief of Defenc Procurement (Support), 1996–2000; on secondment to Thomson CSF Racal, subseq Thales, plc, 2000–02, Sen. Defence Advr, 2001–02. *Recreations:* travel, garden labour paintings. *Club:* Athenæum.

HOWE, Air Vice-Marshal John Frederick George, CB 1985; CBE 1980; AFC 1961; Commandant-General, RAF Regiment and Director General of Security (RAF) 1983–85, retired; *b* 26 March 1930; *m* 1961, Annabelle Gowing; three *d*. *Educ:* S Andrew's Coll., Grahamstown, SA. SAAF, 1950–54 (served in Korea, 2nd Sqdn SAAF and 19 Inf. Regt, US Army, 1951); 222 Sqdn, Fighter Comd, 1956; 40 Commando RM Suez Campaign, 1956; Fighter Command: Flt Comdr, 222 Sqdn, 1957; Flt Comdr, 43 Sqdn, 1957–59; Sqdn Comdr, 74 Sqdn, 1960–61; Air Staff, HQ Fighter Command 1961–63; RAF Staff Coll., 1964; USAF Exchange Tour at Air Defence Comd HQ Colorado Springs, 1965–67; 229 Operational Conversion Unit, RAF Chivenor, 1967–68; OC 228 OCU, Coningsby, 1968–69; Central Tactics and Trials Org., HQ Air Suppor Comd, 1969–70; MoD, 1970–72; Station Comdr, RAF Gutersloh, 1973–74; RCDS 1975; Gp Capt. Ops, HQ No 11 Gp, 1975–77; Comdt, ROC, 1977–80; Comdr Southern Maritime Air Region, 1980–83. Hon. Colonel: Field Sqns (Airfield Damage Repair) (Vol.) (South), 1988–93; 77 Engr Regt (Vol.), 1993. American DFC 1951; Air Medal 1951. *Recreations:* country pursuits, ski-ing, sailing. *Club:* Royal Air Force.

HOWE, Josephine Mary O'C.; *see* O'Connor Howe.

HOWE, Martin, CB 1995; PhD; Director, Competition Policy Division, Office of Fair Trading, 1984–96; *b* 9 Dec. 1936; *s* of late Leslie Wistow Howe and Dorothy Vernon Howe (*née* Taylor Farrell); *m* 1959, Anne Cicely Lawrenson; three *s*. *Educ:* Leeds Univ (BCom (Accountancy), PhD). Asst Lectr, Lectr, Sen. Lectr, in Economics, Univ. o Sheffield, 1959–73; Senior Economic Adviser: Monopolies Commn, 1973–77; Office o Fair Trading, 1977–80; Asst Secretary, OFT and DTI, 1980–84. Special Prof., Univ. o Nottingham Business Sch., 1994–2003. Associate, Europe Economics, 1998–2006 *Publications:* Equity Issues and the London Capital Market (with A. J. Merrett and G. D. Newbould), 1967; articles on variety of topics in learned and professional jls. *Recreations* theatre (including amateur dramatics), cricket, gardening. *Address:* 6 Mansdale Road Redbourn, Herts AL3 7DN. *T:* (01582) 792074; *e-mail:* martin.howe@tiscali.co.uk.

HOWE, Martin Russell Thomson; QC 1996; *b* 26 June 1955; *s* of late Colin Howe FRCS and Dr Angela Howe, *d* of Baron Brock, surgeon; *m* 1989, Lynda Barnett; one three *d*. *Educ:* Trinity Hall, Cambridge (BA, Pt I Engrg, Pt II Law; Baker Prize for Engrg 1974; MA). Called to the Bar, Middle Temple, 1978 (Harmsworth Exhibnr); in practice specialising in intellectual property and European law, 1980–. Councillor (C), London Borough of Hammersmith and Fulham, 1982–86 (Chm., Planning Cttee, 1985–86) Contested (C) Neath (S Wales), 1987. Mem., Cons. Party Commn on a Bill of Rights for the UK, 2007–. Chm., Lawyers Against the European Constitution, 2005–. *Publications* Europe and the Constitution after Maastricht, 1992; (ed) Russell-Clarke on Industrial Designs, 6th edn, 1998, 7th edn, as Russell-Clarke & Howe on Industrial Designs, 2005 contrib. Halsbury's Laws of England, 1986, 1995, 2000; Tackling Terrorism: the European Human Rights Convention and the enemy within, 2001, 2nd edn 2003; A Constitution for Europe: a legal assessment of the Treaty, 2003, 2nd edn 2005; numerous articles in legal jls and pamphlets on European constitutional issues and intellectual property law. *Address* c/o National Westminster Bank plc, Law Courts Branch, 217 Strand, WC2R 1AL.

HOWE, Robert Paul Thomson; QC 2008; *b* England, 12 May 1964; *s* of late Colin Howe and of Hon. Angela Howe; *m* 1998, Rosella Albano; two *d*. *Educ:* Trinity Hall, Cambridge (BA 1986); St Edmund Hall, Oxford (BCL). Called to the Bar, Middle Temple, 1988. *Address:* Blackstone Chambers, Blackstone House, Temple, EC4Y 9BW.

HOWE, His Honour Ronald William; Director of Appeals, General Dental Council, 1999–2004; a Circuit Judge, 1991–97 (Deputy Circuit Judge, 1997–2000); *b* 19 June 1932; *s* of William Arthur and Lilian Mary Howe; *m* 1956, Jean Emily Goodman; three *s* one *d*. *Educ:* Morpeth Sch.; Coll. of Law, London. Admitted Solicitor, 1966; partner with Ronald Brooke & Co., Ilford, then Brooke, Garland & Howe, 1966–75; Registrar of County Court, subseq. Dist Judge, 1975–91. Mem., Judicial Studies Bd, 1990–91 (Mem., Civil and Family Cttee, 1988–91; Tutor, 1987–91); Advocacy Trng Advr, Law Soc., 1998–2000. *Recreations:* gardening, IT, golf (an increasing passion), cycling.

HOWE, Stephen Douglas; Director, British Crop Protection Enterprises Ltd, since 2005; *b* 28 Feb. 1948; *m* 1971, Susan Jane Apps; one *s* one *d*. *Educ:* Brymore Sch., Somerset; Seale-Hayne Coll. (DipAgr); NDA, Dip Farm Management. Lectr in Crop Husbandry and Farm Manager, Lackham Coll. of Agric., Wilts, 1969–72; Power Farming magazine: Management Specialist, 1972–82; Managing Editor, 1982–85; Agricultural Machinery Jl, 1985–87; Editor: Crops, 1987–91; Farmers Weekly, 1991–2005; Associate Publisher, Farmers Weekly Gp, 2000–05. Governor: Inst. of Grassland and Environmental Res., 1996–2000; Nat. Fedn of Young Farmers, 1999–2000. Pres., Eurofarm, 1999–2006. ARAgS 2003; Mem. Council, RASE, 2005–. Fellow, Guild of Agricultural Journalists, 1991; Trustee, Guild of Agricultural Journalists' Charitable Trust, 2005– (Chm., 2008–). Hon. Life Mem., Royal Smithfield Club, 2004. Hon. DArts Plymouth, 2000. *Recreations:* gardening, sailing, farming, flying. *Address:* Springfield Cottage, Byers Lane, South Godstone, Surrey RH9 8JH. *T:* (01342) 893018. *Club:* Farmers'.

HOWE, Timothy Jean-Paul; QC 2008; *b* London, 12 June 1963; *s* of Prof. Alan Howe and Mireille Howe; *m* 1990, Katharine Jane Zisman; one *s* two *d*. *Educ:* St Paul's Sch., London (First Foundn Schol.); Magdalen Coll., Oxford (Anne Shaw Open Schol.; BA 1st Cl. Hons Lit.Hum 1985; Editor, Isis, 1983–84); City Univ. (Dip. Law with Dist. 1986). Called to the Bar, Middle Temple, 1987 (Queen Mother's Fund, Astbury and Harmsworth Scholarships); in practice as barrister, specialising in commercial law, 1988–. Sec. and Mem., Exec. Cttee, Commercial Bar Assoc., 1997–; Chm., Member Services Bd, Bar Council, 2008–. CEDR Accredited Mediator, 2004. *Publications:* (ed jtly) Commercial Court Procedure, 2001; (contrib.) Law of Bank Payments, 2004. *Recreations:* collecting modern British art, wine, travel, ballet and opera. *Address:* Fountain Court Chambers, Temple, EC4Y 9DH. *T:* (020) 7583 3335, *Fax:* (020) 7353 0329; *e-mail:* th@ fountaincourt.co.uk. *Club:* Hurlingham.

HOWELL, family name of **Baron Howell of Guildford**.

HOWELL OF GUILDFORD, Baron *cr* 1997 (Life Peer), of Penton Mewsey in the co. of Hampshire; **David Arthur Russell Howell;** PC 1979; journalist and economist; *b* 18 Jan. 1936; *s* of late Colonel A. H. E. Howell, DSO, TD, DL and Beryl Howell, 5 Headfort Place, SW1; *m* 1967, Davina Wallace; one *s* two *d*. *Educ:* Eton; King's Coll., Cambridge (BA 1st class hons 1959). Lieut Coldstream Guards, 1954–56. Joined Economic Section of Treasury, 1959; resigned, 1960. Leader-Writer and Special Correspondent, The Daily Telegraph, 1960–64; Chm. of Bow Gp, 1961–62; Editor of Crossbow, 1962–64; contested (C) Dudley, 1964. MP (C) Guildford, 1966–97. A Lord Comr of Treasury, 1970–71; Parly Sec., CSD, 1970–72; Parly Under-Sec.: Dept of Employment, 1971–72; NI Office, March–Nov. 1972; Minister of State: NI Office, 1972–74; Dept of Energy, 1974; Secretary of State: for Energy, 1979–81; for Transport, 1981–83. Chairman: Select Cttee on Foreign Affairs, 1987–97; H of L Sub-Cttee on EC Foreign and Security Policy, 1999–2000. H of L Opposition spokesman on foreign affairs, 2000–; Dep. Leader of the Opposition, H of L, 2005–. Chairman: Cons. One Nation Gp, 1987–97; UK-Japan 21st Century (formerly 2000) Group, 1990–2001. Sen. Vis. Fellow, PSI, 1983–85; Vis. Fellow, Nuffield Coll., Oxford, 1993–2001. Dir of Conservative Political Centre, 1964–66. Director: Jardine Insurance Brokers, 1991–97; Monks Investment Trust, 1993–2004; John Laing Plc, 1999–2002; Adv. Dir, UBS (formerly SBC Warburg), 1997–2000; Advisor: Japan Central Railway Co., 2001–; Mitsubishi Electric, Europe, BV, 2003–; Kuwait Investment Office, 2003–; Hermitage Global Fund, 2007–. Mem., Internat. Adv. Council, Swiss Bank Corp., 1988–97. Governor, Sadler's Wells Trust, 1995–98; Trustee, Shakespeare Globe Theatre, 2000–. *Publications:* (co-author) Principles in Practice, 1960; The Conservative Opportunity, 1965; Freedom and Capital, 1981; Blind Victory: a study in income, wealth and power, 1986; The Edge of Now, 2000; Out of the Energy Labyrinth, 2007; various pamphlets and articles. *Recreations:* writing, history, gardening. *Address:* House of Lords, SW1A 0PW. *Club:* Beefsteak.

See also G. G. O. Osborne.

HOWELL, Anthony; Chief Education Officer, since 2002, Strategic Director, Children, Young People and Families (formerly Learning and Culture), since 2003, Birmingham City Council; *b* 7 Jan. 1951; *s* of late Bernard Howell and Katherine Howell; *m* 1975, Hilary Helen Ellis; one *s* one *d*. *Educ:* Xaverian Coll., Manchester; Univ. of Liverpool (BSc Zool.); Univ. of Bristol. Teacher, 1975; Chief Advr, Derbys LEA, 1995–2002; Dep. Chief Educn Officer, Birmingham CC, 2002. Bd Mem., Birmingham and Solihull Connexions, 2002–; Bd Mem. and Trustee, Acad. of Youth/Univ. of the First Age, 2002–; BECTA Educn Cttee, 2002–. Pres., Soc. of Chief Inspectors and Advrs, 1999. *Address:* Birmingham City Council, Council House Extension, Margaret Street, Birmingham B3 3BU. *T:* (0121) 303 2550.

HOWELL, Gareth, CBE 1993; PhD; CChem; Director, British Council, Malaysia, 1990–95; *b* 22 April 1935; *s* of Amwel John and Sarah Blodwen Howell; *m* 1957, Margaret Patricia Ashelford; one *s* two *d*. *Educ:* Ferndale Grammar Sch., Rhondda; University College London; Inst. of Education, Univ. of London. BSc, PhD; PGCE London. MRSC. Asst Master, Canford Sch., Wimborne, Dorset, 1957–61; Lectr, Norwich City Coll., 1961–65; British Council: Science Educn Officer, London, 1965–66; Science Educn Officer, Nigeria, 1966–70; Head, Science Educn Section, 1970–74; Director, Science and Technology Dept, 1974; Representative, Malawi, 1974–76; on secondment to Min. of Overseas Development as Educn Adviser, 1976–79; Counsellor and Dep. Educn Adviser, British Council Div., British High Commn, India, 1979–83; Controller: Sci., Technol. and Educn Div., 1983–87; Americas, Pacific and E Asia Div., 1987–90. *Recreations:* photography, philately, gardening, tennis, walking, travel. *Address:* 9 Alderway, West Cross, Swansea SA3 5PD.

HOWELL, Gwynne Richard, CBE 1998; Principal Bass, Royal Opera House, since 1971; *b* Gorseinon, S Wales, 13 June 1938; *s* of Gilbert and Ellaline Howell; *m* 1968, Mary Edwina Morris; two *s*. *Educ:* Pontardawe Grammar Sch.; Univ. of Wales, Swansea (BSc; Hon. Fellow 1986); Manchester Univ. (DipTP); MRTPI 1966. Studied singing with Redvers Llewellyn while at UCW; pt-time student, Manchester RCM, with Gwilym Jones, during DipTP trng at Manchester Univ.; studied with Otakar Kraus, 1968–72. Planning Asst, Kent CC, 1961–63; Sen. Planning Officer, Manchester Corp., 1965–68, meanwhile continuing to study music pt-time and giving public operatic performances which incl. the rôle of Pogner, in Die Meistersinger; as a result of this rôle, apptd Principal Bass at Sadler's Wells, 1968; also reached final of BBC Opera Singers competition for N of Eng., 1967. In first season at Sadler's Wells, sang 8 rôles, incl. Monterone and the Commendatore; appearances with Hallé Orch., 1968 and 1969; Arkel in Pelleas and Melisande, Glyndebourne and Covent Garden, 1969; Goffredo, in Il Pirato, 1969. *Royal Opera House, Covent Garden:* début as First Nazarene, Salome, 1969–70 season; the King, in Aida; Timur, in Turandot; Mephisto, in Damnation of Faust; Prince Gremin, in Eugene Onegin; High Priest, in Nabucco; Reinmar, in Tannhauser, 1973–74 (later rôle, Landgraf); Colline, in La Boheme; Pimen, in Boris Godunov; Ribbing, Un ballo in maschera; Padre Guardiano, in La forza del destino; Hobson, in Peter Grimes, 1975; Sparafucile, in Rigoletto, 1975–76 season; Ramfis in Aida, 1977; Tristan und Isolde, 1978, 1982; Luisa Miller, 1978; Samson et Delilah, 1981; Fiesco in Simon Boccanegra, 1981; Pogner in Die Meistersinger, 1982; Arkel in Pelléas et Mélisande, 1982; Dossifei in Khovanshchina, 1982; Semele, 1982; Die Zauberflöte, 1983; Raimondo, in Lucia di Lammermoor, 1985; Rocco in Fidelio, 1986; Marcel in Les Huguenots, 1991; Daland in Der Fliegende Holländer, 1992; Katya Kabanova, 1994; Stiffelio, 1995; Mathis der Maler, 1995; The Bartered Bride, 1998; Greek Passion, 2000; The Tempest (world première), 2004; *English National Opera:* Don Carlos, Die Meistersinger, 1974–75; The Magic Flute, Don Carlos, 1975–76; Duke Bluebeard's Castle, 1978, 1991; The Barber of Seville, 1980; Tristan and Isolde, 1981; Hans Sachs in Die Meistersinger, 1984; Parsifal, 1986; Don Carlos, 1992; Banquo in Macbeth, 1993; Fidelio, 1996; Mary Stuart, 1998; Silver Tassie (world première), 2000; War and Peace, 2001; Lulu, 2002; Dansker in Billy Budd, 2005; Aida, 2007; *Metropolitan Opera House, New York:* début as Lódovico in Otello, and Pogner in Die Meistersinger, 1985; *Bastille, Paris:* début in Parsifal, 1997; *sacred music:* Verdi and Mozart Requiems, Missa Solemnis, St Matthew and St John Passions; sings in Europe and USA; records for BBC and for major recording companies. *Recreations:* tennis, golf, Rugby enthusiast, gardening. *Address:* 197 Fox Lane, N13 4BB. *T:* and *Fax:* (020) 8886 1981.

HOWELL, Prof. John Bernard Lloyd, CBE 1991; Chairman, Southampton and SW Hampshire District Health Authority, 1983–98; Foundation Professor of Medicine, University of Southampton, 1969–91, now Emeritus (Dean of the Faculty of Medicine, 1978–83); Hon. Consultant Physician, Southampton General Hospital, 1969–91, now Emeritus; *b* 1 Aug. 1926; *s* of late David John Howells and Hilda Mary Hill, Ynystawe, Swansea; *m* 1952, Heather Joan Rolfe; two *s* one *d*. *Educ:* Swansea Grammar Sch.; Middx Hosp. Med. Sch. (Meyerstein Scholar 1946). BSc, MB, BS, PhD; FRCP. House Officer posts, Middx and Brompton Hosps; MO RAMC, 1952–54; Lectr in Physiol Medicine, 1954–56, in Pharmacol Medicine, 1958–60, Middlesex Hosp. Med. Sch.; Manchester Royal Infirmary: Sen. Lectr in Medicine and Hon. Consultant Physician, 1960–66; Consultant Physician, 1966–69. Eli Lilly Travelling Fellow, Johns Hopkins Hospital, 1957–58; Goulstonian Lectr, RCP, 1966. Member: Physiol Soc., 1956–; Med. Res. Soc., 1956–; Assoc. of Physicians of GB and Ire., 1964–; GMC, 1978–83. President: British Thoracic Soc., 1988–89; BMA, 1989–90 (Chm., Bd of Sci. and Educn, 1991–98). Mem. Soc. of Scholars, Johns Hopkins Univ., 1998–. Hon. Life Mem., Canadian Thoracic Soc., 1978; Hon. FACP 1982. Hon. DSc Southampton, 1994. *Publications:* (ed jtly) Breathlessness, 1966; chapters in: Cecil and Loeb's Textbook of Medicine, 13th edn 1970, 14th edn 1974; Recent Advances in Chest Medicine, 1976; Thoracic Medicine, 1981; Oxford Textbook of Medicine, 1982; Respiratory Medicine, 1995; Asthma and Rhinitis, 1995; papers on respiratory physiology and medicine and health care. *Recreations:* France, DIY, wine. *Address:* The Coach House, Bassett Wood Drive, Southampton SO16 3PT. *T:* (023) 8076 8878.

HOWELL, John Frederick; Senior Research Associate, Overseas Development Institute, since 1997 (Director, 1987–97); *b* 16 July 1941; *s* of late Frederick Howell and Glenys Griffiths; *m* 1993, Paula Wade; two *s*, and one step *s*. *Educ:* Univ. of Wales (BA Hons 1963); Univ. of Manchester (MA Econ. Dist. 1965); Univ. of Reading, (external; PhD). Lectr, Univ. of Khartoum, 1966–73; correspondent, Africa Confidential, 1971–75; Sen. Lectr, Univ. of Zambia, 1973–77; Overseas Development Institute, 1977–; seconded as Advr, Min. of Agric. and Land Affairs, S Africa, 1997–2001. Vis Lectr, Mananga Agric. Management Centre, Swaziland, 1978–80; Vis. Prof. in Agricl Develt, Wye Coll., Univ. of London, 1988–96. Consultant on aid and agricl develt: World Bank; EC; FAO; Commonwealth Secretariat; DFID in S Africa, India, Nepal, Nigeria, Brazil, Tanzania, Malaŵi, Sudan; Adviser: All-Party Parly Gp on Overseas Develt, 1985–86; Princess Royal's Africa Review Gp, 1987–89. Mem. Council, VSO, 1991–97. Pres., UK Chapter, Soc. of Internat. Develt, 1991–93. *Publications:* Local Government and Politics in the Sudan, 1974; (ed) Borrowers and Lenders: rural financial markets and institutions in developing countries, 1980; Administering Agricultural Development for Small Farmers, 1981; (ed) Recurrent Costs and Agricultural Development, 1985; (ed) Agricultural Extension in Practice, 1988; (with Alex Duncan) Structural Adjustment and the African Farmer, 1992. *Address:* Overseas Development Institute, 111 Westminster Bridge Road, SE1 7JD.

HOWELL, John Michael, OBE 2000; DPhil; MP (C) Henley, since June 2008; *b* London, 27 July 1955; *s* of Alexander J. Howell and Gladys S. Howell; *m* 1987, Alison Parker; one *s* two *d*. *Educ:* Battersea Grammar Sch.; Univ. of Edinburgh (MA 1978); St John's Coll., Oxford (DPhil 1981). Ernst & Young, 1987–96; Business Presenter, BBC World Service TV, 1996–97; Director: Fifth World Prodns Ltd, 1996–2003; Media Presentation Consultants Ltd, 2005–. Mem. (C), Oxfordshire CC, 2004– (Cabinet Mem. for Change Mgt, 2005–08). *Publications:* Neolithic Northern France, 1983; Understanding Eastern Europe: the context of change, 1994. *Recreations:* music, theatre. *Address:* House of Commons, SW1A 0AA. *T:* (020) 7219 4828, 7219 6676, *Fax:* (020) 7219 2606; *e-mail:* howellJm@parliament.uk; (constituency office) 8 Gorwell, Watlington OX49 5QE. *T:* 0845 230 4026; *e-mail:* info@henleyconservatives.com.

HOWELL, Maj.-Gen. Lloyd, CBE 1972; Consultant, Technical Education Development, University College, Cardiff, 1980–86 (Fellow, 1981); *b* 28 Dec. 1923; *s* of Thomas Idris Howell and Anne Howell; *m* 1st, 1945, Hazel Barker (*d* 1974); five *s* three *d*; 2nd, 1975, Elizabeth June Buchanan Husband (*née* Atkinson); two step *s*. *Educ:* Barry Grammar Sch.; University Coll. of S Wales and Monmouthshire (BSc); Royal Military Coll. of Science. CEng, MRAeS. Commissioned RA, 1944; Field Regt, RA, E Africa, 1945–46; Staff, Divl HQ, Palestine, 1946–47; RAEC 1949; Instr, RMA Sandhurst, 1949–53; TSO II Trials Estabt, 1954–57; SO II (Educn), Divl HQ, BAOR, 1957–59; DS, Royal Mil. Coll. of Science, 1960–64; SEO, Army Apprentices Coll., 1964–67; Headmaster/Comdg, Duke of York's Royal Mil. Sch., 1967–72; Col (Ed), MoD (Army), 1972–74; Chief Educn Officer, HQ UKLF, 1974–76; Dir, Army Educn, 1976–80. Col Comdt, RAEC, 1982–86. Dir (non-exec.), Building Trades Exhibitions Ltd, 1980–93. Mem. Council, CGLI, 1977–90; Mem., Ct of Governors, Cardiff Univ. (formerly UWCC), 1980–. Hon. MA Open Univ., 1980. *Recreations:* gardening, golf, reading. *Address:* c/o HSBC, The Forum, Old Town, Swindon, Wilts SN3 1QT.

HOWELL, Margaret, CBE 2007; RDI 2007; Designer and Creative Director, Margaret Howell Ltd, since 1986; *b* Tadworth, Surrey, 5 Sept. 1946; *d* of Edwin Harris Howell and Gladys Ivy Howell; *m* 1972, Paul Andrew Renshaw (marr. diss. 1987); one *s* one *d*. *Educ:* Goldsmith's Coll., Univ. of London (DipAD). Self-employed clothes designer, 1970–86; founded Margaret Howell Ltd, 1986. *Recreations:* walking, photography. *Address:* 6 Welbeck Way, W1G 9RZ. *T:* (020) 7009 9000, *Fax:* (020) 7009 9001; *e-mail:* admin@margarethowell.co.uk.

HOWELL, Michael Edward, CMG 1989; OBE 1980; HM Diplomatic Service; High Commissioner, Mauritius, 1989–93; *b* 2 May 1933; *s* of Edward and Fanny Howell; *m* 1958, Joan Little; one *s* one *d*. *Educ:* Newport High Sch. Served RAF, 1951–53. Colonial Office, 1953; CRO, 1958; Karachi, 1959; 2nd Secretary: Bombay, 1962; UK Delegn to Disarmament Cttee, Geneva, 1966; 1st Sec. (Parly Clerk), FCO, 1969; Consul (Comm.), New York, 1973; ndc 1975; FCO, 1976; Hd of Chancery, later Chargé d'Affaires, Kabul, 1978; Consul-General: Berlin, 1981; Frankfurt, 1983; High Comr to Papua New Guinea, 1986. *Recreation:* golf. *Address:* c/o Foreign and Commonwealth Office, SW1A 2AH.

HOWELL, Michael William Davis; Chairman, City and Guilds of London Institute, since 2006 (Treasurer, 2003–06); *b* 11 June 1947; *s* of late Air Vice-Marshal Evelyn Michael Thomas Howell, CBE, and Helen Joan Hayes; *m* 1975, Susan Wanda Adie; two *s* one *d*. *Educ:* Chafyn Grove Sch., Salisbury; Charterhouse Sch., Godalming; Trinity Coll., Cambridge (BA 1968, MA 1969); INSEAD, Fontainebleau (MBA 1975); Harvard Business Sch. (MBA 1976). British Leyland Truck and Bus Division: Graduate Trainee, 1969–71; Personnel Manager, Leyland Nat., 1971–74; Cummins Engine Co. Inc.: Asst to Vice-Pres. Internat. (USA), 1976–77; Dir, European Mktg, Brussels, 1977–80; Vice-President: Europe (based in London), 1981–84; Corporate Strategy, 1984–88; Vice-Pres., GE Canada Inc., 1988–89; Gen. Manager, GE Transportation, 1989–91; Dir, Arlington Capital Partners (formerly Mgt) Ltd, 1991–96 (non-exec. Dir, 1996–); Commercial Dir, Railtrack Gp plc, 1996–97; Chm., FPT Gp Ltd, 1998–2002; Chief Exec., Transport Initiatives Edinburgh, subseq. tie ltd, 2002–06. Chm., Evo Electric Ltd, 2007–; Director: Westinghouse Air Brake Technol. Corp. (USA), 2003–; Hutchison China Meditech Ltd, 2006–. Gov., Clothworkers' Foundn, 1999–. *Recreations:* hill-walking, ski-ing, aviation. *Address:* Shawhill, Dundrennan, Kirkcudbright DG6 4QS. *T:* (01557) 500256; *e-mail:* mwdhowell@aol.com. *Club:* Oxford and Cambridge.

HOWELL, Patrick Leonard; QC 1990; *b* 4 Dec. 1942; *s* of Leonard Howell, MC, and Mary Isobel (*née* Adam); *m* 1966, Sandra Marie McColl; two *s* one *d*. *Educ:* Radley; Christ Church, Oxford (MA); London Sch. of Econs and Pol Science (LLM). Called to the Bar: Inner Temple, 1966; Lincoln's Inn, 1968. Teaching Fellow, Osgoode Hall Law Sch., Toronto, 1965–66. Social Security Comr and Child Support Comr, 1994–; a Judge, Employment Appeal Tribunal, 1999–. *Address:* Office of the Social Security Commissioners, Procession House, 55 Ludgate Hill, EC4M 7JW. *T:* (020) 7029 9850.

HOWELL, Paul Frederic; farmer; Director: ESU Group plc, since 2004; ESU Bio-Africa, since 2006; *b* 17 Jan. 1951; *s* of Sir Ralph Howell; *m*; two *s*. *Educ:* Gresham's Sch., Holt,

Norfolk; St Edmund Hall, Oxford (MA Agric. and Econ.). Conservative Research Dept, 1973–75. MEP (C) Norfolk, 1979–94; contested (C) Eur. Parly elecns, 1994. Mem., Agricl, Foreign Affairs and Fisheries Cttees, European Parlt, 1979–94; spokesman for EDG: on youth culture, educn, information and sport, 1984–86; on agriculture, 1989–92; on fisheries, 1989–94; Mem. and EDG spokesman, Regl Cttee, 1992–94; Member, European Parliament's delegation: to Central America, 1987–94; to Soviet Union, 1989–91; to CIS, 1991–94; to Russia, Ukraine, Georgia, Armenia and Azerbaijan, 1993–94; Vice-Chm., Europ. Parlt/Comecon Delegn, 1984; Pres., Council of Centre for Eur. Educn, 1985–87. Chm., Riceman Insurance Investments plc, 1995–99; Special Ops Manager, WRG plc, 2000. Mem. Council, and Trustee, RSPB, 1992–95; Trustee, Nuffield Russia Trust, 1991–. *Recreations:* all sports. *Address:* The White House Farm, Bradenham Road, Scarning, East Dereham, Norfolk NR19 2LA.

HOWELL, Peter Adrian; Senior Lecturer, Department of Classics, Royal Holloway and Bedford New College, University of London, 1994–99 (Lecturer, 1985–94), now Hon. Research Fellow; *b* 29 July 1941; *s* of Lt-Col Harry Alfred Adrian Howell, MBE and Madge Maud Mary, *d* of Major-Gen. R. L. B. Thompson, CB, CMG, DSO. *Educ:* Downside School; Balliol College, Oxford (BA 1963; MA; MPhil 1966). Asst Lectr and Lectr, Dept of Latin, Bedford Coll., Univ. of London, 1964–85. Dep. Chm., Jt Cttee, Nat. Amenity Socs, 1991–93; Member: Cttee, Victorian Soc., 1968–2005 (Chm., 1987–93); Westminster Cathedral Art Cttee, 1974–91, 1993–; Dept of Art and Architecture, Liturgy Commn, RC Bishops' Conf., 1977–84; Churches Cttee, English Heritage, 1984–88; RC Historic Churches Cttee for Wales and Herefordshire, 1995–; Westminster Diocesan Historic Churches Cttee, 1995–99. *Publications:* Victorian Churches, 1968; (with Elisabeth Beazley) Companion Guide to North Wales, 1975; (with Elisabeth Beazley) Companion Guide to South Wales, 1977; A Commentary on Book I of the Epigrams of Martial, 1980; (ed with Ian Sutton) The Faber Guide to Victorian Churches, 1989; (ed and trans.) Martial: the Epigrams Book V, 1995; articles in Architectural History, Country Life. *Recreations:* art, architecture, music. *Address:* 127 Banbury Road, Oxford OX2 6JX. *T:* (01865) 515050.

HOWELL, Rupert Cortlandt Spencer, FIPA; Managing Director, ITV Brand and Commercial, since 2007; *b* 6 Feb. 1957; *s* of late Lt Col F. R. Howell, MBE, RE, and of S. D. L. Howell (*née* McCallum); *m* 1987, Claire Jane Ashworth; one *s* one *d*. *Educ:* Wellington Coll.; Univ. of Warwick (BSc Mgt Scis). FIPA 1995. Mkting trainee, Lucas Service Overseas, 1978; Account Exec., Mathers Advertising, 1979–81; Account Supervisor, Grey Advertising, 1981–83; Young & Rubicam: Account Dir, 1983–84; New Business Dir, 1985–86; Hd, Client Services, 1987; Howell Henry Chaldecott Lury Ltd, subseq. HHCL & Partners: Founder, 1987; Man. Partner, 1987–97; Jt Chief Exec., 1997–98; Chm., 1999–2002; Jt Chief Exec., Chime Communications plc, 1997–2002; Chm., UK & Ireland, and Pres., Europe, Middle E and Africa, Interpublic Gp, subseq. McCann Worldgroup, 2003–07. President: Inst. of Practitioners in Advertising, 1999–2001; Eur. Assoc. of Communication Agencies, 2006–07. Mem., Marketing Gp of GB. FRSA 2008. *Recreations:* golf, shooting, ski-ing, cricket, Rugby Union, soccer. *Address:* ITV plc, 200 Gray's Inn Road, WC1X 8HF. *T:* 08448 818000, *Fax:* 08445 563889. *Clubs:* MCC, Lord's Taverners, Thirty, Solus.

HOWELL, Prof. Simon Laurence, PhD, DSc; Professor of Physiology, since 1985, Director of Research and Development, since 2007, and Guy's Campus Dean, since 2005, King's College London; *b* 29 June 1943; *s* of Laurence James Howell and Joan Kathleen Rosemary (*née* Wheelwright); *m* 1969, Linda Margaret Chapman; one *d*. *Educ:* St John's Sch., Leatherhead; Chelsea Coll., London (BSc Hons 1964); KCL (PhD 1967); DSc London 1983. Res. Fellow, Univ. of Sussex, 1968–78; Lectr, Charing Cross Hosp. Med. Sch., London, 1978–80; Reader, Queen Elizabeth Coll., London, 1980–85; Hd, Biomed. Scis Div., 1988–98, Hd, GKT Sch. of Biomed. Scis, 1998–2003, KCL. Chm., Diabetes UK, 2006– (Vice Chm., 2002–06). Minkowski Prize, Eur. Assoc. Study of Diabetes, 1983. *Publications:* (jtly) Biochemistry of the Polypeptide Hormones, 1985; (jtly) Diabetes and its Management, 5th edn 1996, 6th edn 2003; The Biology of the Pancreatic B Cell, 1999. *Recreations:* gardening, opera. *Address:* King's College London School of Biomedical and Health Sciences, Guy's Campus, SE1 9UL.

HOWELLS, family name of **Baroness Howells of St Davids**.

HOWELLS OF ST DAVIDS, Baroness *cr* 1999 (Life Peer), of Charlton in the London Borough of Greenwich; **Rosalind Patricia-Anne Howells,** OBE 1994; Vice Chair, London Voluntary Services Council; *b* Grenada, WI, 10 Jan. 1931; *m* 1955, John Charles Howells; two *d*. *Educ:* St Joseph's Convent, Grenada; South West London Coll. (Cert. Welfare and Counselling); City Univ., Washington. Formerly Dep. High Comr for Grenada in London; Equal Opportunities Dir, Greenwich Council for Racial Equality, 1980–87; Chair, Lewisham Racial Equality Council, 1994–97; Mem., Commn on Future of Multi-Ethnic Britain. Governor, Avery Hill Coll., later Thames Poly., then Univ. of Greenwich, 1985–97. Trustee: West Indian Standing Conf.; City Parochial Foundn; Museum of Ethnic Arts; Women of the Year Cttee; Stephen Lawrence Charitable Trust. DUniv Greenwich, 1998. *Recreations:* travelling, adventurous food, all types of music. *Address:* c/o House of Lords, SW1A 0PW.

HOWELLS, Anne Elizabeth, FRMCM; opera, concert and recital singer; Professor, Royal Academy of Music, since 1997; *b* 12 Jan. 1941; *d* of Trevor William Howells and Mona Hewart; *m* 1st, 1966, Ryland Davies, *qv* (marr. diss. 1981); 2nd, 1981, Stafford Dean (marr. diss. 1996); one *s* one *d*; 3rd, 1999. *Educ:* Sale County Grammar Sch.; Royal Northern (subseq. Royal Manchester) Coll. of Music (ARMCM; Hon. Fellow); studied under Frederick Cox and Vera Rosza. Three seasons (Chorus), with Glyndebourne, 1964–66; at short notice given star rôle there in Cavalli's L'Ormindo, 1967; rôles there also include: Dorabella in Così fan Tutte; Cathleen in (world première of) Nicholas Maw's Rising of the Moon, 1970; the Composer in Ariadne; Diana in Calisto; under contract, 1969–71, subseq. Guest Artist, Royal Opera, Covent Garden; sings with Scottish Opera, ENO and major orchs in UK; recitals in Brussels and Vienna; operatic guest performances incl. La Scala (Milan), Chicago, Metropolitan (NY), San Francisco, Geneva, Brussels, Salzburg, Amsterdam, Hamburg (W German début), W Berlin, Paris. Rôles include: Lena in (world première of) Richard Rodney Bennett's Victory; Rosina in Barber of Seville; Cherubino in Marriage of Figaro; Zerlina in Don Giovanni; Giulietta in The Tales of Hoffmann; Orsini in Lucrezia Borgia; Ascanius in Benvenuto Cellini; Helen in King Priam; Judit in Bluebeard's Castle; Octavian in Der Rosenkavalier (video recording), 1985; Annius in La Clemenza di Tito (film of Salzburg prodn); Lady Hautdesert in (world première of) Gawain, 1994. *Recreations:* theatre, cinema, reading. *Address:* c/o IMG, The Light Box, 111 Power Road, Chiswick, W4 5PY.

HOWELLS, Sir Eric (Waldo Benjamin), Kt 1993; CBE 1986; farmer and landowner, since 1966; *b* 9 Aug. 1933; *s* of Vincent Vaughan Howells and Amy (*née* Jones); *m* 1960, Margaret Maisie Edwards; one *s* twin *d*. Sec. and Gen. Manager of a limited co., 1959–66; Director: Carmarthen and Pumsaint Farmers Ltd, 1997; Welsh Milk Ltd, 2000–06. Chm., Whitland and Dist Abattoir Cttee, 2001–. Former Chm., Pembrokeshire NFU. Mem., Llanddewi Velfrey Parish Community Council, 1967– (Chm., 1967, 1974, 1981, 1988, 1995, 2001); Chm., 1978–87, Pres., 1987–90, Pembrokeshire Cons. and Unionist Assoc. Wales Area Conservative Party: Treas., 1984–88; Dep. Chm., 1988–90; Chm., 1990–95 Pres., 1996–99; Life Vice-Pres. Chm., Wales Area Cons. European Co-ordinating Cttee 1992–95; Mem. of numerous other local and nat. Cons. and other bodies; regula broadcaster on radio and television in English and Welsh. Deacon and Treas., Bethe Congregational Chapel, Llanddewi Velfry, 1974–. *Recreations:* music, bee keeping, DIY reading, writing. *Address:* Meadow View, Llanddewi Velfrey, Narberth, Pembrokeshir SA67 7EJ. *T:* (01994) 240205.

HOWELLS, Gwyn; Marketing Consultant, Gwyn Howells Marketing, since 2002; *b* 2 May 1949; *s* of late Emrys Howells and Edith Frances (*née* Taylor); *m* 1st, 1976, Margare Anne Farrall (*d* 1995); one *s* one *d*; 2nd, 2003, Virginia Ann McCarthy. *Educ:* Lewis Sch for Boys, Pengam; City of London Poly. (BSc Econs 1970). Sen. Brand Manager, Gallahe Ltd, 1971–82; Dir, Brand and Trade Mktg, Courage Ltd, 1982–89; Marketing Di Reebok UK Ltd, 1989–92; Marketing Dir, 1992–99, Dir Gen., 1999–2002, Meat an Livestock Commn. Liveryman, Butchers' Co., 2001–. *Recreations:* Rugby football, tennis theatre. *Address:* 30 Bewdley Street, N1 1HB. *Clubs:* Farmers; Hampstead Rugby Football, Rhymney Rugby Football.

HOWELLS, Kim Scott, PhD; MP (Lab) Pontypridd, since Feb. 1989; *b* 27 Nov. 1946; of Glanville James and Joan Glenys Howells; *m* 1983, Eirlys Howells (*née* Davies); two one *d*. *Educ:* Mountain Ash Grammar Sch.; Hornsey College of Art; Cambridge Colleg of Advanced Technology (BA (Jt Hons)); Warwick Univ. (PhD). Steel-worker, 1969–70 Coal-miner, 1970–71; Lectr, 1975–79; Research Officer: Swansea Univ., 1979–82 NUM, S Wales Area, 1982–89. Opposition Front bench spokesman on aid and develt 1993–94, on foreign affairs, 1994, on home affairs, 1994–95, on trade and industry 1995–97; Parliamentary Under-Secretary of State: DFEE, 1997–98; DTI, 1998–2001 DCMS, 2001–03; Minister of State: DfT, 2003–04; DfES, 2004–05; (Minister for th Middle East), FCO, 2005–08. Mem., British Mountaineering Council, 1993–. *Recreations* climbing, painting, jazz, cinema, literature, art, growing vegetables. *Address:* House o Commons, SW1A 0AA. *Clubs:* Llantwit Fadre Cricket, Pontypridd Rugby Footba (Pontypridd); Hopkinstown Cricket (Pontypridd).

HOWES, Sir Christopher (Kingston), KCVO 1999 (CVO 1997); CB 1993; Second Commissioner and Chief Executive of the Crown Estate, 1989–2001; non-executive Chairman, Barclays Property Finance Team, since 2005; Member: HRH Prince o Wales's Council, since 1990; Council, Duchy of Lancaster, 1993–2005; *b* 30 Jan. 1942; *y* *s* of late Leonard Howes, OBE and Marion Howes (*née* Bussey); *m* 1967, Clare, *o d* o Gordon and Lillian Cunliffe; one *s* one *d* (and one *s* one *d* decd). *Educ:* Gresham's Sch. Coll. of Estate Management, Univ. of London (BSc 1965); Univ. of Reading (MPhi 1976). ARICS 1967, FRICS 1977. Valuation and Planning Depts, GLC, 1965–67 Partner and Sen. Partner, Chartered Surveyors, Norwich, 1967–79; Department of th Environment: Dep. Dir, Land Economy, 1979–81; Chief Estates Officer, 1981–85; Dir Land and Property Div., 1985–89. Sen. Vis. Fellow, Sch. of Envmtl Scis, UEA, 1975; part time Lectr, Dept of Land Economy, Univ. of Cambridge, 1976–81; Visiting Lecturer Univ. of Reading, 1974–80; Aberdeen 1982; UCLA and UCS Los Angeles, 1983 Harvard, 1985; Univ. N Carolina, Chapel Hill, 1985; Miami, 1985; Vis. Prof., Bartlet Sch. of Architecture and Planning, UCL, 1984–. Member: Sec. of State for the Envmt' Thames Adv. Cttee, 1995–98; CNAA Surveying Bd, 1978–82; OECD Urban Policy Gp 1985–; Planning and Develt Divl Council, RICS, 1983–92; Policy Review Cttee, RICS 1984–90; RIBA Awards Gp, 1997–2002; Council: Norfolk Archaeol Trust, 1979– British Property Fedn, 1992–2001. Jt Chm., World Land Policy Congress, London, 1986 Vis. Speaker, Commonwealth Assoc. of Surveying and Land Economy Conf., Trinidad 1982 and Cyprus, 1984. Hon. Mem., Cambridge Univ. Land Soc., 1989–. Founde Mem., Norwich Third World Centre, 1970; dir of various housing assocs, 1970–80; non executive Director: Norwich & Peterborough Building Soc., 1998–2005; Compco Hldg Ltd, 2004–; Director: Howard de Walden Estate, 2002–; Colville Estates Ltd, 2003– Member, Advisory Board: Barclays Private Banking, 2001–; Three Delta LLP, 2006– Member: Bd, Norwich Theatre Royal Trust, 1969–79; Adv. Bd, Aldeburgh Music 1998–. Steward and Hon. Surveyor to Dean and Chapter, Norwich Cathedral, 1973–79 Trustee: HRH The Prince of Wales's Inst. of Architecture, 1992–99; British Architectura Library Trust, 1997–; Member: Court of Advisers, St Paul's Cathedral, 1980–99; Court UEA, 1992–. Patron, Heatherley Sch. of Fine Art Chelsea, 2008–. Norwich CC 1969–73; JP Norfolk 1973–80. Hon. FRIBA 1995. Hon. LittD E Anglia, 2000. Mem. o various editorial bds. *Publications:* (jtly) Acquiring Office Space, 1975; Value Maps: aspect of land and property values, 1979; Economic Regeneration (monograph), 1988; Urban Revitalization (monograph), 1988; papers on land and property policy in learned jls *Recreations:* music, art, architecture, sailing. *Address:* 8 Millennium House, 132 Grosvenor Road, SW1V 3JY. *T:* (020) 7828 9920, *Fax:* (020) 7821 5813; Westerly House Aldeburgh, Suffolk IP15 5EL. *Clubs:* Athenæum, Garrick; Norfolk (Norwich); Aldeburgh Yacht; Aldeburgh Golf.

HOWES, Sally Ann; actress (stage, film and television); *b* 20 July; *d* of late Bobby Howes *m* 1958, Richard Adler (marr. diss.); *m* 1969, Andrew Maree (marr. diss.). *Educ* Glendower, London; Queenswood, Herts; privately. *Films include:* Thursday's Child 1943; Halfway House, 1943; Dead of Night, 1945; Nicholas Nickleby, 1947; Anna Karenina, 1948; My Sister and I; Fools Rush In; History of Mr Polly, 1949; Stop Press Girl; Honeymoon Deferred; The Admirable Crichton, 1957; Chitty, Chitty Bang Bang 1968. First appeared West End stage in (revue) Fancy Free, at Prince of Wales's, and at Royal Variety Performance, 1950. *Stage Shows include:* Caprice (musical debut); Paint Your Wagon; Babes in the Wood; Romance by Candlelight; Summer Song; Hatful of Rain; My Fair Lady; Kwamina, NY; What Makes Sammy Run?, NY; Brigadoon (revival) NY City Center, 1962; Sound of Music, Los Angeles and San Francisco, 1972; Lover, St Martin's; The King and I, Adelphi, 1973, Los Angeles and San Francisco, 1974; Hans Andersen, Palladium, 1977; Hamlet (tour), 1983; The Dead, NY, 2000. Has appeared on television: in England from 1949 (Short and Sweet Series, Sally Ann Howes Show, etc) in USA from 1958 (Dean Martin Show, Ed Sullivan Show, Mission Impossible, Marcus Welby MD); Play of the Week; Panel Shows: Hollywood Squares; Password; Bell Telephone Hour; US Steel Hour, etc. *Recreations:* reading, riding, theatre.

HOWES, Sally Margaret; QC 2003; *b* 10 Sept. 1959; *d* of Patrick George Howes and Janet Howes. *Educ:* Polam Hall Sch., Co. Durham; Univ. of Newcastle upon Tyne (BA Hons (Classics); Dip. Law). Called to the Bar, Middle Temple, 1983; Judge Advocate (pt–time), 1993–. Specializes in criminal law. *Recreations:* polo, racing, walking the South Downs with my labrador Shamba. *Address:* 23 Essex Street, WC2R 3AA. *T:* (020) 7413 0353, *Fax:* (020) 7413 0374. *Clubs:* National Liberal; Cowdray Park Polo.

HOWESON, Comdr Charles Arthur, RN; Chairman: UK Seafish Industry Authority, since 2007; First Great Western Trains, since 2007; *b* 27 Nov. 1949; *s* of Arthur C. Howeson and Sheila B. Howeson; *m* 1978, Emma Jane Stevenson; one *s* two *d*. *Educ:* Uppingham Sch.; Royal Naval Coll. Dartmouth; Royal Naval Staff Coll. RN 1968–90, Chief of Allied Staffs and Dep. COS (Ops) to Comdr British Forces Gibraltar, 1990;

retired in rank of Comdr, 1991. Exec. Dir, Plymouth Area Groundwork Trust, 1991–93. Mem., Nat. Consumer Council for Water, 2006– (Chm., Western Reg., 2006–). Chm., Horizon Roofing Ltd, 2004–; non-executive Chairman: Rowe Gp of Cos, 2004–; St Piran Homes Ltd, 2004–; Clearwood Joinery Ltd, 2004–; Crownhill Estates Ltd; Eko-Tek Gp of Cos; Buckland Corporate Finance Ltd; non-executive Director: Duchy of Somerset Estates Ltd; First Gt Western Train Co. Ltd, 2007–. Pres., Millfields Community Econ. Develt Trust; Vice-Pres., Plymouth Chamber of Commerce and Industry, 2006–; Chairman: Plymouth Econ. Develt Gp; Plymouth Policing Adv. Bd, 2007–; Seaton Area Residents' Assoc.; Director: Millfields Estate Mgt Co. Ltd; RNH (West End) Ltd; Plymouth Naval Base Visitors' Centre and Mus. Ltd, 2004–. Patron, St Austell Br., Royal Naval Assoc.; Vice-Patron, Tomorrow's People; Chm. Govs, Drake Foundn, 2006–; Trustee, Estates of 19th Duke of Somerset; Hon. Sec. and Treas., Britannia Assoc. Mem., RNSA. MRIN; FInstD; FCMI; FRSA; FFB; FNI. Freeman, City of London; Liveryman, Shipwrights' Co.; Mem., Guild of Freemen; Younger Brother, Trinity House. Governor and Trustee: Plymouth Coll. Sch. SLJ. *Recreations:* adequate but still improving jazz piano, designing and operating substantial 5 gauge garden railways, wine tasting in heavy seas on board friends' yachts. *Address:* Smallack Barn, Smallack Drive, Crownhill, Plymouth PL6 5FB; *e-mail:* charles@smallack.com. *Clubs:* Army and Navy, Naval and Military; Royal Western Yacht.

HOWICK OF GLENDALE, 2nd Baron *cr* 1960; **Charles Evelyn Baring;** a Director, Northern Rock plc (formerly Northern Rock Building Society), 1987–2001; a Managing Director, Baring Brothers & Co. Ltd, 1969–82; *b* 30 Dec. 1937; *s* of 1st Baron Howick of Glendale, KG, GCMG, KCVO, and Lady Mary Cecil Grey, *er d* of 5th Earl Grey; *S* father, 1973; *m* 1964, Clare Nicolette, *y d* of Col Cyril Darby; one *s* three *d*. *Educ:* Eton; New Coll., Oxford. Director: The London Life Association Ltd, 1972–82; Swan Hunter Group Ltd, 1972–79. Member: Exec. Cttee, Nat. Art Collections Fund, 1973–86; Council, Friends of Tate Gall., 1973–78; Adv. Cttee, Westonbirt Arboretum, 1995–. Dir, Chelsea Physic Garden, 1994–. Mem. Council, Baring Foundn, 1982–99; Trustee: Northern Rock Foundn, 1997–2007; Royal Botanic Gdns, Edinburgh, 2001–. *Heir: s* Hon. David Evelyn Charles Baring [*b* 26 March 1975; *m* 2003, Victoria Jane, *d* of Owen and Margaret Sutherland]. *Address:* Howick, Alnwick, Northumberland NE66 3LB. *T:* (01665) 577624.
See also Sir E. H. T. Wakefield.

HOWIE, family name of **Baron Howie of Troon.**

HOWIE OF TROON, Baron *cr* 1978 (Life Peer), of Troon in the District of Kyle and Carrick; **William Howie;** civil engineer, publisher, journalist; Consultant: George S. Hall Ltd, since 2001; PMS Publications Ltd, since 2001 (Director, 1996–2001); *b* Troon, Ayrshire, 2 March 1924; *er s* of late Peter and Annie Howie, Troon; *m* 1951, Mairi Margaret (*d* 2005), *o d* of late Martha and John Sanderson, Troon; two *d* two *s*. *Educ:* Marr Coll., Troon; Royal Technical Coll., Glasgow (BSc, Diploma). Civil engineer in practice, 1944–63, 1970–73; MP (Lab) Luton, Nov. 1963–70; Asst Whip, 1964–66; Lord Comr of the Treasury, 1966–67; Comptroller, HM Household, 1967–68. A Vice-Chm., Parly Labour Party, 1968–70. Gen. Man., 1976–87, Dir (Internal Relns), 1987–96, Thomas Telford Ltd; Dir, SETO, 1996–2000. MICE 1951, FICE 1984; Member: Council, Instn of Civil Engineers, 1964–67; Cttee of Inquiry into the Engineering Profession, 1977–80; President: Assoc. of Supervisory and Exec. Engrs, 1980–85; Assoc. for Educnl and Trng Technol., 1982–93; Indep. Publishers Guild, 1987–93; Vice-President: PPA, 1990–; Combustion Engrg Assoc., 1999–. Member: Governing Body, Imperial Coll. of Science and Technology, 1965–67; Pro-Chancellor, City Univ., 1984–91 (Mem. Council 1968–91). MSocIS (France), 1978. Hon. FIStructE 1995; Hon. FABE 2000. Hon. DSc City Univ., 1992; Hon. LLD Strathclyde, 1994. *Publications:* (jtly) Public Sector Purchasing, 1968; Trade Unions and the Professional Engineer, 1977; Trade Unions in Construction, 1981; (ed jtly) Thames Tunnel to Channel Tunnel, 1987. *Recreation:* opera. *Address:* 34 Temple Fortune Lane, NW11 7UL. *T:* (020) 8455 0492. *Clubs:* St Stephen's; Luton Labour, Lighthouse, Architecture.

HOWIE, Prof. Archibald, CBE 1998; PhD; FRS 1978; Professor of Physics, Cavendish Laboratory, University of Cambridge, 1986–2001, now Emeritus; Fellow of Churchill College, Cambridge, since 1960; *b* 8 March 1934; *s* of Robert Howie and Margaret Marshall McDonald; *m* 1964, Melva Jean Scott; one *d* (one *s* decd). *Educ:* Kirkcaldy High Sch.; Univ. of Edinburgh (BSc); California Inst. of Technology (MS); Univ. of Cambridge (PhD). English Speaking Union, King George VI Memorial Fellow (at Calif. Inst. of Technology), 1956–57; Cambridge University: Research Scholar, Trinity Coll., 1957–60; Research Fellow, Churchill Coll., 1960–61; Cavendish Laboratory: ICI Research Fellow, 1960–61; Demonstrator in Physics, 1961–65; Lecturer, 1965–79; Reader, 1979–86; Hd of Dept of Physics, 1989–97. Visiting Scientist, Nat. Research Council, Canada, 1966–67; Vis. Prof. of Physics, Univ. of Aarhus, Denmark, 1974. Dir, NPL Management Ltd, 1995–2001. Pres., Internat. Fedn of Socs for Electron Microscopy, 1999–2002. Hon. Member: Chinese Electron Microscopy Soc., 2000; Japanese Soc. of Microscopy, 2003. Hon. FRMS 1978 (Pres., 1984–86); Hon. FRSE 1995. Hon. Dr (Physics): Bologna, 1989; Thessaloniki, 1995. Distinguished Scientist Award, Electron Microscopy Soc. of America, 1991; Guthrie Medal, Inst. of Physics, 1992; Royal Medal, Royal Soc., 1999; (jtly with M. J. Whelan): C. V. Boys Prize, Inst. of Physics, 1965; Hughes Medal, Royal Soc., 1988. *Publications:* (co-author) Electron Microscopy of Thin Crystals, 1965, 2nd edn 1977; papers on electron microscopy and diffraction in scientific jls. *Recreations:* gardening, wine-making. *Address:* 194 Huntingdon Road, Cambridge CB3 0LB. *T:* (01223) 570977.

HOWIE, Prof. John Garvie Robertson, CBE 1996; MD, PhD; FRCGP, FRCPE, FMedSci; Professor of General Practice, University of Edinburgh, 1980–2000; *b* 23 Jan. 1937; *s* of Sir James Howie and Isabella Winifred Mitchell, BSc; *m* 1962, Elizabeth Margaret Donald; two *s* one *d*. *Educ:* High School of Glasgow; Univ. of Glasgow (MD); PhD Aberdeen. House officer, 1961–62; Laboratory medicine, 1962–66; General practitioner, Glasgow, 1966–70; Lectr/Sen. Lectr in General Practice, Univ. of Aberdeen, 1970–80. Founder FMedSci 1998. Hon. DSc Aberdeen, 2002. *Publications:* Research in General Practice, 1979, 2nd edn 1989; A Day in the Life of Academic General Practice, 1999; articles on appendicitis, prescribing and general medical practice and education, in various jls. *Recreations:* golf, gardening, music. *Address:* 4 Ravelrig Park, Balerno, Midlothian EH14 7DL. *T:* (0131) 449 6305; *e-mail:* John.Howie00@btinternet.com.

HOWIE, Prof. John Mackintosh, CBE 1993; Regius Professor of Mathematics, University of St Andrews, 1970–97; Dean, Faculty of Science, 1976–79; *b* 23 May 1936; *s* of Rev. David Y. Howie and Janet McD. Howie (*née* Mackintosh); *m* 1960, Dorothy Joyce Mitchell Miller; two *d*. *Educ:* Robert Gordon's Coll., Aberdeen; Univ. of Aberdeen; Balliol Coll., Oxford. MA, DPhil, DSc; FRSE 1971. Asst in Mathematics: Aberdeen Univ., 1958–59; Glasgow Univ., 1961–63; Lectr in Mathematics, Glasgow Univ., 1963–67; Visiting Asst Prof., Tulane Univ., 1964–65; Sen. Lectr in Mathematics, Stirling Univ., 1967–70; Visiting Professor: Monash Univ., 1979; N Illinois Univ., 1988; Univ. of Lisbon, 1996. Mem., Cttee to Review Examination Arrangements (Dunning Cttee), 1975–77; Chairman: Scottish Central Cttee on Mathematics, 1975–82; Cttee to Review Curriculum and Exams in Fifth and Sixth Years (Howie Cttee), Scottish Office Educn Dept, 1990–92. Vice-Pres., London Mathematical Soc., 1984–86. Chm., Bd of Governors, Dundee Coll. of Educn, 1983–87. DUniv Open, 2000. Keith Prize for 1979–81, RSE, 1982. *Publications:* An Introduction to Semigroup Theory, 1976; Automata and Languages, 1991; Fundamentals of Semigroup Theory, 1995; Real Analysis, 2001; Complex Analysis, 2003; Fields and Galois Theory, 2006; articles in British and foreign mathematical jls. *Recreations:* music, gardening. *Address:* Longacre, 19 Strathkinness High Road, St Andrews, Fife KY16 9UA. *T:* (01334) 474103.

HOWIE, Prof. Robert Andrew, PhD, ScD; FGS; FKC; Lyell Professor of Geology, Royal Holloway and Bedford New College, University of London, 1985–87, now Emeritus Professor of Mineralogy; *b* 4 June 1923; *s* of Robert Howie; *m* 1st, 1952, Honor Eugenie (marr. diss. 1998), *d* of Robert Taylor; two *s*; 2nd, 1998, Irene, *d* of G. R. Ancliff. *Educ:* Bedford Sch.; Trinity Coll., Cambridge (MA, PhD, ScD). FGS 1950. Served War, RAF, 1941–46. Research, Dept of Mineralogy and Petrology, Univ. of Cambridge, 1950–53; Lectr in Geology, Manchester Univ., 1953–62; King's College, London: Reader in Geol., 1962–72; Prof. of Mineralogy, 1972–85; Fellow 1980; Dean, Faculty of Science, Univ. of London, 1979–83; Chairman: Academic Council, Univ. of London, 1983–86; Computer Policy Cttee, Univ. of London, 1987–93; Vice-Chm., Bd of Management, Univ. of London Computer Centre, 1989–93. Mem., Commonwealth Scholarships Commn, 1988–96. Geological Society: Mem. Council, 1968–71, 1972–76; Vice-Pres., 1973–75. Mineralogical Society: Mem. Council, 1958–61, 1963–2003; Gen. Sec., 1965; Ed., Mineralogical Abstracts, 1966–2003 (designated Principal Ed., 1971–2003); Vice-Pres., 1975–77; Pres., 1978–80; Managing Trustee, 1978–87; Hon. Life Fellow, 1994. Fellow, Mineral Soc. of America, 1962 (Dist. Public Service Award, 1999). Member: Gemmological Assoc. and Gem Testing Lab. of GB, 1968– (Pres., 1996–2000; Hon. FGA 1996); Council, Internat. Mineral Assoc., 1974–82; Senate, Univ. of London, 1974–78, 1980–90; Court, Univ. of London, 1984–89. Hon. Mem., Mineralogical Soc. of India, 1973, of USSR, 1982, of France, 1986, of Bulgaria, 1991; For. Mem., Accad. Naz. dei Lincei, Rome, 2003. Murchison Medal, Geol Soc., 1976. *Publications:* Rock-forming Minerals (with Prof. W. A. Deer and Prof. J. Zussman), 5 vols, 1962–63 (2nd edn in 10 vols, 1978–); An Introduction to the Rock-forming Minerals, 1966, 2nd edn 1992; scientific papers dealing with charnockites and with silicate mineralogy. *Recreations:* mineral collecting, writing abstracts. *Address:* Ashcroft, Glebe Close, Church Street, Bonsall, Matlock, Derbyshire DE4 2AE. *Club:* Geological.

HOWIE, Robert Bruce McNeill; QC (Scot.) 2000; *b* 24 Aug. 1960; *s* of Dr William Bruce McNeill Howie, OBE, and Dr Theresa Grant or Howie; *m* 1996, Deirdre Elizabeth Hughes Clark or Haigh; one *s*. *Educ:* Aberdeen Grammar Sch.; Aberdeen Univ. (LLB, DLP). Admitted Advocate, 1986. *Address:* 41a Fountainhall Road, Edinburgh EH9 2LN.

HOWITT, Anthony Wentworth; Senior Consultancy Partner, Peat, Marwick, Mitchell & Co., Management Consultants, 1957–84; *b* 7 Feb. 1920; *o s* of late Sir Harold Gibson Howitt, GBE, DSO, MC, and late Dorothy Radford; *m* 1951, June Mary Brent. *Educ:* Uppingham; Trinity Coll., Cambridge (MA). FCA, FCMA, JDipMA, FIMC. Commissioned RA; served in UK, ME and Italy, 1940–46 (Major). With Peat, Marwick, Mitchell & Co., Chartered Accountants, 1946–57. British Consultants Bureau: Vice-Chm., 1981–83; Mem. Council, 1968–75 and 1979–84; led mission to Far East, 1969. Member Council: Inst. of Management Consultants, 1964–77 (Pres., 1967–68); Inst. of Cost and Management Accountants, 1966–76 (Pres., 1972–73; Gold Medal, 1991); Management Consultants Assoc., 1966–84 (Chm., 1976); Mem., Devlin Commn of Inquiry into Industrial Representation, 1971–72. Member: Bd of Fellows of BIM, 1973–76; Adv. Panel to Overseas Projects Gp, 1973–76; Price Commn, 1973–77; Domestic Promotions Cttee, British Invisible Exports Council, 1984. Member Council: Anglo-Jordanian Soc., 1983–96; Anglo-Indonesian Soc., 1991–; Anglo-Arab Assoc., 1993–2004. CCMI. Mem., Court of Assistants, Merchant Taylors' Co., 1971– (Master 1980–81). *Publications:* papers and addresses on professional and management subjects. *Recreations:* fox-hunting, tennis, golf. *Address:* 17 Basing Hill, Golders Green, NW11 8TE. *Clubs:* Army and Navy; MCC; Harlequins.

HOWITT, Richard Stuart; Member (Lab) Eastern Region, England, European Parliament, since 1999 (Essex South, 1994–99); *b* 5 April 1961. *Educ:* Lady Margaret Hall, Oxford (BA); Univ. of Hertfordshire (DMS). Community worker, 1982–94. Mem. (Lab), Harlow DC, 1984–94 (Leader, 1991–94). Contested (Lab) Billericay, 1987. Hon. Pres., SE Econ. Develt Strategy Assoc., 1994– (Chm., 1986–94); Hon. Vice-President: ADC, 1994–97; LGA, 1997–; Trustee, Centre for Local Econ. Strategies, 1994–. Mem., Labour Party Nat. Policy Forum and NEC Local Govt sub-cttee, 1994–. European Parliament: First Vice-Pres., Regl Affairs Cttee, 1997–99 (Mem., 1994–96); Pres., All-Party Disability Gp, 1999–; Rapporteur: Europe and UN Social Summit, 1995; European Funding for Local and Regl Authorities, 1995; European Refugee Policy, 1996; Guidelines for Effective European Projects, 1998; European Code of Conduct for Enterprises, 1999; Corporate Social Responsibility, 2002–03, 2007; Budget, 2002; Participation of Non-state Actors in EC Develt Policy, 2003; Human Right Report, 2006. *Address:* Labour European Office, Unit 3, Frohock House, 222 Mill Road, Cambridge CB1 3NF. *T:* (01223) 240202, *Fax:* (01223) 241900; *e-mail:* richard.howitt@geo2.poptel.org.uk.

HOWKER, David Thomas; QC 2002; *b* 29 Oct. 1959; *s* of Kenneth Howker and late Miriam Howker; *m* 1994, Shani Estelle Barnes, *qv*; two *s* three *d*. *Educ:* Blackpool Grammar Sch.; Birmingham Univ. (LLB); Inns of Court Sch. of Law. Called to the Bar, Inner Temple, 1982; in practice, specialising in criminal law; Standing Counsel to HM Customs and Excise, 1998–2002; a Recorder, 1999. *Address:* 2 Hare Court, Temple, EC4Y 7BH. *T:* (020) 7353 5324, *Fax:* (020) 7353 0667; *e-mail:* clerks@2harecourt.com.

HOWKER, Shani Estelle; *see* Barnes, S. E.

HOWKINS, John Anthony; consultant and writer; *b* 3 Aug. 1945; *s* of Col Ashby Howkins and Lesley (*née* Stops); *m* 1st, 1971, Jill Liddington; 2nd, 1977, Annabel Whittet. *Educ:* Rugby Sch.; Keele Univ.; Architectural Association's Sch. of Architecture (Dip.). Marketing Manager, Lever Bros, 1968–70; founder, TV4 Gp, 1971; TV/Radio Editor, Books Editor, Time Out, 1971–74; Sec., Standing Conf. on Broadcasting, 1975–76; Editor, InterMedia, Journal of Internat. Inst. of Communications, 1975–84; Exec. Dir, Internat. Inst. of Communications, 1984–89. Gov., London Film Sch. (formerly London Internat. Film Sch.), 1976– (Chm., 1979–84); Member: Interim Action Cttee on the Film Industry, DTI, 1980–84; British Screen Adv. Council, DTI, 1985– (Dep. Chm., 1991–); Vice-Chm. (New Media), Assoc. of Independent Producers, 1984–85. Exec. Editor, National Electronics Review, 1981–99; TV Columnist, Illustrated London News, 1981–83. Chairman: Tornado Productions, 2000–03; BOP Consultants, 2007–; Director: Television Investments, 1993–; Equator Gp plc, 1999–2006; HandMade plc, 2006–; Hotbed Media Ltd, 2006–; Screen East, 2006–; Project Dir, World Learning Network, 1996–2005. Dir, Adelphi (formerly Intellectual Property) Charter, RSA, 2004–06. Specialist Advr, Select Cttee on European Communities, House of Lords, 1985–87; Adviser: Broadcasting Reform Commn, Poland, 1989–90; Polish-Radio-and-Television, 1991–94; Minister of Film, Poland, 1991–92; Chm., Adv. Bd, Createc, 1996–2000; Co-ordinator, Eur. Audiovisual Conf., 1997–98. Associate, Coopers Lybrand Deloitte,

1990–91. Special European Consultant, HBO Inc. (and other Time Warner Inc. cos), 1981–85 and 1989–95. Visiting Professor: Lincoln Univ., 2003–; Sch. of Creativity, Shanghai, 2006–; Chm., John Howkins Res. Centre on the Creative Economy, Shanghai, 2006–; Internat. Vice-Pres., Shanghai Theatre Acad., 2006–. UK Rep., Transatlantic Dialogue on Broadcasting and Information Soc., 1998–. *Publications:* Understanding Television, 1977; The China Media Industry, 1980; Mass Communications in China, 1982; New Technologies, New Policies, 1982; Satellites International, 1987; (with Michael Foster) Television in '1992': a guide to Europe's new TV, film and video business, 1989; Four Global Scenarios on Information and Communication, 1997; The Creative Economy, 2001; CODE, 2002. *Address:* E6 Albany, Piccadilly, W1J 0AR. *T:* (020) 7434 1400; *e-mail:* john@johnhowkins.com.

HOWLAND JACKSON, Anthony Geoffrey Clive; Chairman, General Insurance Standards Council, 1999–2005; Director, Hiscox PLC, 1997–2006; *b* 25 May 1941; *s* of late Arthur Geoffrey Howland Jackson and of Pamela (*née* Wauton); *m* 1963, Susan Ellen Hickson; one *s* two *d. Educ:* Sherborne Sch. Chief Executive: H. Clarkson Insurance Hldgs, 1979–81; Clarkson Puckle, 1981–83; Dir, Gill & Duffus plc, 1983–87; Man. Dir, Bain Clarkson Ltd, 1987; Dep. Chm. and Chief Exec., 1987–93, Chm., 1993–94, Hogg Group plc; Chm., Bain Hogg plc, 1994–97. Dir, AON UK Hldgs, 1997–99. Lloyd's: Mem., 1976–97; Mem., Regulatory Bd, 1993–2002; Chm., Lloyd's Insurance Brokers' Cttee, 1996, 1998, 1999. Mem., Worshipful Co. of Insurers, 1981–. *Recreations:* shooting, cricket, racing, golf. *Club:* Turf.

HOWLETT, Elizabeth, (Elizabeth Robson); Professor of Singing, Royal College of Music, since 1989; *b* 17 Jan. 1938; *d* of Walter James Robson and Lizzie Mason Robson (*née* Houston); *m* 1962, Neil Baillie Howlett (marr. diss. 1987); two *d. Educ:* Royal Scottish Acad. of Music (Sir James Caird Jun. and Sen. Scholarships; DRSAMD). Leading Lyric Soprano, Sadler's Wells Opera Co., 1961–65; Leading Soprano, Royal Opera House, Covent Gdn, 1965–70; Soprano, Staatsoper, Hamburg, 1970–74; guest engagements in Europe, S Africa, Japan, Korea, Canada, USA, Scottish Opera, WNO, Opera North, ENO, 1974–. Nat. and Internat. Examr, 1997–; Adjudicator, Festivales Musicales, Buenos Aires, 1995–2004. Mem. (C) Wandsworth BC, 1986– (Chairman: Social Services Cttee, 1989–92; Educn Cttee, 1992–98; Chief Whip, 1999–2000); Mayor of Wandsworth, 1998. Mem. (C) Merton and Wandsworth, London Assembly, GLA, 2000–08. Mem., Inner London Probation Bd, 1995–2001. Non-exec. Dir and Chm., Nat. Hosp. for Neurol. and Neurosurgery, 1990–96. Founder and Trustee, Margaret Dick Award for young Scottish singers, 1982–; Trustee, Foundn for Young Musicians, 1996–2007. Hon. Vice Patron, Ystradgynlais Male Voice Choir, 1985–. JP Wimbledon, 1985–2006. Freeman, City of London, 1999. Eschanson of Roi René Award, Aix-en-Provence, 1970. *Recreations:* walking, theatre, music. *Address: e-mail:* elizabethhowlett@btconnect.com.

HOWLETT, Gen. Sir Geoffrey (Hugh Whitby), KBE 1984 (OBE 1972); MC 1952; Chairman: Leonard Cheshire Foundation, 1990–95; Services Sound & Vision Corporation, 1991–99 (Vice-Chairman, 1989–91); *b* 5 Feb. 1930; *s* of Brig. B. Howlett, DSO, and Mrs Joan Howlett (later Latham); *m* 1955, Elizabeth Anne Aspinal (*d* 2006); one *s* two *d. Educ:* Wellington Coll.; RMA, Sandhurst. Commnd Queen's Own Royal W Kent Regt, 1950; served, 1951–69: Malaya, Berlin, Cyprus and Suez; 3 and 2 Para, 16 Parachute Bde and 15 Para (TA); RAF Staff Coll. and Jt Services Staff Coll.; Mil. Asst to CINCNORTH, Oslo, 1969–71; CO 2 Para, 1971–73; RCDS, 1973–75; Comd 16 Parachute Bde, 1975–77; Dir, Army Recruiting, 1977–79; GOC 1st Armoured Div., 1979–82; Comdt, RMA, Sandhurst, 1982–83; GOC SE District, 1983–85; C-in-C Allied Forces Northern Europe, 1986–89, retd. Colonel Commandant: ACC, 1981–89; Parachute Regt, 1983–90. Comr, Royal Hosp., Chelsea, 1989–95. President: CCF, 1989–2000; Army Benevolent Fund for Dorset, 1992–2000; Regular Forces Employment Assoc., 1993–97 (Vice-Chm., 1989–90; Chm., 1990–93); Army Cricket Assoc., 1984–85; Combined Services Cricket Assoc., 1985; Stragglers of Asia Cricket Club, 1989–94. Visitor, Milton Abbey Sch., 2001–05 (Chm. of Govs, 1994–2000). Liveryman, Cooks' Co., 1991–. Cross of Merit, 1st cl. (Lower Saxony), 1982. *Recreations:* cricket, shooting, racing. *Address:* 58 Hascombe Court, Somerleigh Road, Dorchester DT1 1AG. *Club:* MCC.

HOWLETT, Air Vice-Marshal Neville Stanley, CB 1982; RAF retired, 1982; Member: Lord Chancellor's Panel of Independent Inquiry Inspectors, 1982–95; Pensions Appeal Tribunal, 1988–2000; *b* 17 April 1927; *s* of Stanley Herbert Howlett and Ethel Shirley Howlett (*née* Pritchard); *m* 1952, Sylvia (*d* 2005), *d* of J. F. Foster; one *s* one *d. Educ:* Liverpool Inst. High Sch.; Peterhouse, Cambridge. RAF pilot training, 1945–47; 32 and 64 (Fighter) Squadrons, 1948–56; RAF Staff Coll. Course, 1957; Squadron Comdr, 229 (Fighter) OCU, 1958–59; OC Flying Wing, RAF Coltishall, 1961–63; Directing Staff, RAF Staff Coll., 1967–69; Station Comdr, RAF Leuchars, 1970–72; RCDS, 1972; Dir of Operations (Air Defence and Overseas), 1973–74; Air Attaché, Washington DC, 1975–77; Dir, Management Support of Intelligence, MoD, 1978–80; Dir Gen. of Personal Services (RAF), MoD, 1980–82. Consultant, Defence Intelligence Staff, 1982–93. Vice-Pres., RAFA, 1984–2003 (Chairman: Exec. Cttee, 1990–97; Central Council, 1999–2001). *Recreations:* golf, fishing. *Address:* Milverton, Bolney Trevor Drive, Lower Shiplake, Oxon RG9 3PG. *Clubs:* Royal Air Force; Phyllis Court (Henley); Huntercombe Golf.

HOWLETT, Ronald William, OBE 1986; Managing Director, Cwmbran Development Corporation, 1978–88, retired; *b* 18 Aug. 1928; *s* of Percy Edward Howlett and Lucy Caroline Howlett; *m* 1st, 1954, Margaret Megan Searl (marr. diss. 1990); two *s*; 2nd, 1996, Judith Lloyd Wade-Jones, *d* of Lt-Col N. L. Wade, OBE, TD. *Educ:* East Ham Grammar Sch. for Boys; University Coll. London (BSc Eng (Hons)). CEng; FICE. Nat. Service, Royal Signals, BAOR, 1947–49. Crawley Develt Corp., 1953–56; Exec. Engr, Roads and Water Supply, Northern Nigeria, 1956–61 (Resident Engr, Kaduna River Bridge; Water Engr, Kano); Bor. of Colchester, 1961–64; Cwmbran Develt Corp., 1964–65; Bor. of Slough, 1965–69; Dep. Chief Engr, 1969–74, Chief Admin. Officer, 1974–77, Cwmbran Develt Corp. Major undertakings: design/construction main drainage and waste treatment works; new town residential, commercial, industrial develt. *Recreations:* fishing, music, furniture restoration.

HOWLETT, Stephen William; Chief Executive, Peabody Trust, since 2004; *b* 18 Nov. 1951; *s* of late Ivan William and Marjorie Elsie Howlett; *m* 1989, Jane Elizabeth Everton; two *s* one *d. Educ:* King Edward VI Sch., Bury St Edmunds; Thames Polytech. (BA Hons). Admin. Officer, Housing Corp., 1975–76; Housing Officer, Warden Housing Assoc., 1976–78; London Regl Officer, NFHA, 1978–82; Director: Croydon Churches Housing Assoc., 1982–88; Notting Hill Housing Trust, 1988–92; Chief Executive: Swale Housing Assoc., 1992–99; Amicus, 1999–2004. Member: Bd, Asset Skills, 2004–; Residential Cttee, British Property Fedn, 2005–. A London Leader, London Sustainable Develt Commn, 2007–. Mem. Bd, 1995–2004, Vice-Chm., 1999–2004, Canterbury Coll.; Mem. Court, Univ. of Greenwich, 2008–. Mem., RSA, 2008–. *Recreations:* my children's sporting and musical activities, cinema, opera, sport. *Address:* Peabody Trust, 45 Westminster Bridge Road, SE1 7JB. *T:* (020) 7021 4230, *Fax:* (020) 7021 4070; *e-mai* stephenh@peabody.org.uk. *Club:* MCC.

HOWSON, Peter John; painter, since 1981; *b* 27 March 1958; *s* of Tom and Jane Howson; *m* 1983, Frances Nevay (marr. diss.); *m* 1989, Terry Cullen; one *d. Edu* Glasgow Sch. of Art (BA Hons 1981). Official British War Artist in Bosnia, 1993–95; Th Times War Artist, Kosovo, 1999. DUniv Strathclyde, 1996. *Address:* 6 Royal Terrace Glasgow G3 7NT.

HOY, Christopher Andrew, MBE 2005; Member, Great Britain Cycling Team; *b* 2 March 1976; *s* of David Hoy and Carol Hoy (*née* Reid). *Educ:* George Watson's Coll Edinburgh; Univ. of Edinburgh (BSc Hons Sport Sci.). Olympic Games: Silver Meda team sprint, 2000; Gold Medal, 1km time trial cycling, 2004; Gold Medals, team sprin keirin, and sprint, 2008; world champion: 1 km time trial and team sprint, 2002; 1 kr time trial, 2004, 2005, 2006, keirin and kilo, 2007; Commonwealth champion, 2002 2006; world record holder, 500m; Olympic record holder, 1000m, 2004; Olympic recor holder, sprint, 2008. Dr *hc* Edinburgh, 2005; Hon. Dr Heriot-Watt, 2005. *Wel* www.chrishoy.com.

HOYLAND, John, RA 1991 (ARA 1983); Professor of Painting, Royal Academ Schools, since 2000; *b* 12 Oct. 1934; *s* of John Kenneth and Kathleen Hoyland; *m* 1958 Airi Karkainen (marr. diss. 1968); one *s. Educ:* Sheffield Coll. of Art (NDD 1956); Roya Academy Schs (RA Cert. 1960). Taught at: Hornsey Coll. of Art, 1960–62; Chelsea Sch of Art, 1962–69, Principal Lectr, 1965–69; St Martin's Sch. of Art, 1974–77; Slade Sch. c Art, 1974–77, 1980, 1983, resigned 1989; Charles A. Dana Prof. of Fine Arts, Colga Univ., NY, 1972. Artist in residence: Studio Sch., NY, 1978; Melbourne Univ., 1979 Selector: Hayward Annual, 1979; RA Silver Jubilee exhibn, 1979; organized and curate Hans Hofman exhibn, Lateworks, Tate Gall., 1988. *One-man exhibitions* include Marlborough New London Gall., 1964; Whitechapel Gall., 1967; Waddington Gall 1967, annually 1969–71 and 1973–76, 1978, 1981, 1983, 1985, 1990, 1995; Carlow Ar Fest., Ireland, 1996; Galerie Fine, London, 1999; Nevill Keating Pictures Ltd, Londor 2001; Beaux Art Gall., London, 2001; also in USA, Australia, Netherlands, Canada Norway, France and Austria; retrospectives: Serpentine Gall., 1979; RA, 1999; Graves A Gall., Sheffield, 2001 and in Canada, USA, Brazil, Italy, Portugal, W Germany an Australia. *Group exhibitions* include: Tate Gall., 1964; Hayward Gall., 1974; Walker A Gall., Liverpool (in every John Moores exhibn, 1963–); British Art in the 20th Century Royal Acad., 1987; Waddington Gall., 1987; Tate Gall. of Liverpool, 1993; Barbica Gall., 1993; also in Belgium, France, Japan and Norway. Work in public collections inc RA, Tate Gall., V&A Mus. and other galls and instns in UK, Europe, USA and Australi *TV appearances:* 6 Days in September, BBC TV, 1979; Signals, Channel 4, 1989. Design for Zansa, Ballet Rambert, 1986; designed Mural Mosaic for Metro, Rome, 2001 designed Don Restaurant, London, 2001. Hon. Dr Sheffield Hallam, 2001. Gulbenkia Foundn purchase award, 1963; Peter Stuyvesant travel bursary, 1964; John Moore Liverpool exhibn prize, 1965, 1st prize, 1983; Open Paintings exhibn prize, Belfast, 1966 (jtly) 1st prize, Edinburgh Open 100 exhibn, 1969; 1st prize, Chichester Nat. Art exhibn 1975; Arts Council purchase award, 1979; Athena Art Award, 1987. Order of th Southern Cross (Brazil), 1986. *Relevant publication:* John Hoyland, by Mel Gooding, 1990 *Address:* 41 Charterhouse Square, EC1M 6EA.

HOYLE, family name of **Baron Hoyle**.

HOYLE, Baron *cr* 1997 (Life Peer), of Warrington in the co. of Cheshire; **Eric Dougla Harvey Hoyle;** consultant; *b* 17 Feb. 1930; *s* of late William Hoyle and Leah Ellen Hoyle *m* 1953, Pauline Spencer (*d* 1991); one *s. Educ:* Adlington C of E Sch.; Horwich an Bolton Techn. Colls. Engrg apprentice, British Rail, Horwich, 1946–51; Sales Engr, AE Manchester, 1951–53; Sales Engr and Marketing Executive, Charles Weston Ltd, Salford 1951–74. Mem., Manchester Regional Hosp. Bd, 1968–74; Mem., NW Regional Healt Authority, 1974–75. Contested (Lab): Clitheroe, 1964; Nelson and Colne, 1970 and Feb 1974; MP (Lab): Nelson and Colne, Oct. 1974–1979; Warrington, July 1981–1983 Warrington N, 1983–97. Chm., PLP, 1992–97 (Mem., Trade and Industry Cttee 1987–92); Mem., Select Cttee on Trade and Industry, 1984–92. Mem. Nat. Exec., Labou Party, 1978–82, 1983–85. A Lord in Waiting (Govt Whip), 1997–99. Pres., ASTMS 1977–81, 1985–88 (Vice-Pres., 1981–85), MSF, 1988–91 (Jt Pres., 1988–90; Pres. 1990–91); Chm., ASTMS Parly Cttee, 1975–76. Pres., Adlington Cricket Club, 1974– Chm., Warrington Rugby League Club, 1999–. JP Chorley, 1958. *Recreations:* sport cricket, theatre-going, reading. *Address:* House of Lords, SW1A 0PW.

See also Hon. L. H. Hoyle.

HOYLE, Prof. Eric; Professor of Education, 1971–96, now Professor Emeritus, an Senior Research Fellow, since 1996, Graduate School of Education, University of Bristol *b* 22 May 1931; *s* of Percy and Bertha Hoyle; *m* 1954, Dorothy Mary Morley; one *s* tw *d. Educ:* Preston Grammar Sch.; Univ. of London (BSc Sociology, MA). Taught, Harehill Secondary Sch., Leeds, 1953–58 (Head of English Dept, 1956–58); Head, English Dept Batley High Sch., 1958–60; Lectr and Sen. Lectr in Educn, James Graham Coll., Leeds 1961–64; Lectr and Sen. Lectr in Educn, Univ. of Manchester, 1965–71; Bristo University: Hd, Sch. of Educn, 1971–91; Dean, Faculty of Educn, 1974–77, 1983–86. Vis Prof., Sch. of Management, Univ. of Lincs and Humberside, 1995–2000. Member: Avor Educn Cttee, 1977–80; Educnl Res. Bd, SSRC, 1973–78 (Vice-Chm., 1976–78); Bd o Management, NFER, 1976–94; Council, Exec. Council for Educn of Teachers, 1971 (Mem. Exec., 1978–81, 1987–90); Adviser to Public Schools Commn, 1968–70 consultant and advr on educnl mgt and professional develt of teachers to UNESCO World Bank etc, SE Asia and Africa, 1972–. Editor, World Yearbook of Educn, 1980–86 founding Co-Editor, Research in Educn, 1969. *Publications:* The Role of the Teacher 1969; (with J. Wilks) Gifted Children and their Education, 1974; The Politics of Schoo Management, 1986; (with Peter John) Professional Knowledge and Professional Practice 1995; (with Mike Wallace) Educational Leadership: ambiguity, professionals anc managerialism, 2005; *festschrift:* Teaching: professionalization, development and leadership ed D. Johnson and R. Maclean, 2008; contribs to professional jls. *Recreations:* music reading, collecting first editions, walking, cooking. *Address:* 42 Oakwood Road, Henleaze Bristol BS9 4NT. *T:* (0117) 962 0614; Graduate School of Education, University o Bristol, 35 Berkeley Square, Bristol BS8 1JA. *T:* (0117) 928 3000.

HOYLE, Hon. Lindsay (Harvey); MP (Lab) Chorley, since 1997; *b* 10 June 1957; *s* o Baron Hoyle, *qv*; *m* 1st, Lynda Anne Fowler (marr. diss. 1982); 2nd, Catherine Swindley two *d. Educ:* Adlington County Sch.; Lord's Coll., Bolton. Owner of building co.; Man Dir, textile printing co. Mem. (Lab) Chorley BC, 1980–98 (Dep. Leader, 1995–97; Chair Economic Develt and Tourist Cttee); Mayor, 1997–98. Member: Trade and Industry Select Cttee, 1998–; H of C Catering Cttee, 1997–2005; European Scrutiny Cttee, 2005– All Pty Rugby League Gp, 1997– (Vice Chm., 1997–); All Pty Cricket Gp, 1997– (Treas. 1998–); Vice Chm., All Pty Tourism Gp, 1999–; Chairman: All Pty Gp on Gibraltar 2001–; All Pty BVI Gp, 2007–. Mem., Royal Lancs Agricl Show Soc. Hon. Colonel: C (64) Med. Sqdn (Vols); 5 Gen. Support Med. Regt. *Recreations:* Rugby League (former

Chm., Chorley Lynx), cricket, football. *Address:* House of Commons, SW1A 0AA. *T:* (020) 7219 3000. *Clubs:* Adlington Cricket, Chorley Cricket.

HOYLE, Martin Trevor William Mordaunt; Radio Critic and Media Writer, Financial Times, since 1994; Classical Music and Opera Editor, Time Out, since 1988; *s* of Capt. T. W. Hoyle and Dora Marie (*née* Muller). *Educ:* Egypt and Canada; Clifton Coll.; Wadham Coll., Oxford (BA); Bristol Old Vic Sch.; Poly. of Central London Business Sch. Music Critic, Bristol Evening Post, 1963–67; freelance researcher, BBC TV 1965–; Sub-editor, John Calder Publishers, 1979–82; Theatre Critic, Financial Times, 1983–90; freelance writer on theatre, music, TV, film, books for Financial Times, Time Out, The Times, Mail on Sunday, Herald, The House, Independent on Sunday; reviews for Meridian (BBC World Service). *Publication:* The World of Opera: Mozart, 1996. *Recreation:* shouting at cyclists. *Address:* Financial Times, 1 Southwark Bridge, SE1 9HL. *T:* (020) 7873 3000. *Club:* Chelsea Arts.

HOYLE, Prof. Richard William, DPhil; Professor of Rural History, University of Reading, since 2000; *b* 4 Dec. 1958; *s* of C. and H. M. Hoyle; *m* 1981, Gillian M. Bishop; two *s*. *Educ:* Univ. of Birmingham (BA 1981); Corpus Christi Coll., Oxford (DPhil 1987). Res. Fellow, Magdalen Coll., Oxford, 1985–87; Lectr, Univ. of Bristol, 1987–89; British Acad. Res. Fellow, Magdalen Coll., Oxford, 1989–92; University of Central Lancashire: Lectr, then Sen. Lectr, 1993–96; Reader, 1997; Prof. of Hist., 1998–2000; Dir, Rural Hist. Centre, Univ. of Reading, 2000–03. British Acad. Res. Reader, 2004–06. Mem., Res. Grants Bd, ESRC, 1997–2001. Sec., British Agricl Hist. Soc., 1996–98. Ed., Agricl Hist. Review, 1998–. *Publications:* books include: (ed) The Estates of the English Crown 1558–1640, 1992; The Pilgrimage of Grace and the Politics of the 1530s, 2001; (ed) People, Landscape and Alternative Agriculture, 2004; (with H. French) The Character of English Rural Society: Earls Colne 1550–1750, 2007; (ed) Our Hunting Fathers: field sports in England since 1850, 2007; contrib. articles to Past and Present, English Histl Review, Histl Jl, Econ. Hist. Review, Northern Hist., Yorks Archaeol Jl. *Recreations:* gardening, twentieth-century music, walking. *Address:* School of History, University of Reading, Whiteknights, PO Box 218, Reading, Berks RG6 6AA. *T:* (0118) 378 8147, *Fax:* (0118) 378 6440; *e-mail:* r.w.hoyle@reading.ac.uk.

HOYLE, Susan Linda; Deputy Director, Clore Leadership Programme, since 2003; *b* 7 April 1953; *d* of Roland and Joan Hoyle. *Educ:* Univ. of Bristol (BA Drama and French). Education Officer, London Festival Ballet, 1980–83; Administrator, Extemporary Dance Th., 1983–86; Dance and Mime Officer, 1986–89, Dir of Dance, 1989–94, Arts Council of GB; Dep. Sec.-Gen., Arts Council of England, 1994–97; Head of Arts, British Council, France, 1997–98; Gen. Manager, then Exec. Dir, The Place, 1998–2003. Director: Shobana Jeyasingh Dance Co., 1998–2002; Ricochet Dance Co., 2001–03; DV8 Physical Th., 2003–; LPO, 2003–05; Create KX, 2007–. *Address:* Clore Leadership Programme, South Building, Somerset House, Strand, WC2R 1LA.

HOYLES, Prof. Celia Mary, (Mrs Richard Noss), OBE 2004; PhD; Professor of Mathematics Education, Institute of Education, University of London, since 1984; Director, National Centre for Excellence in the Teaching of Mathematics, since 2006; *b* London, 18 May 1946; *d* of Harold French and Elsie French (*née* Last); *m* 1996, Prof. Richard Noss; one step *s* one step *d*. *Educ:* Univ. of Manchester (BSc 1st Cl. Hons Maths 1967); Univ. of London (PGCE 1971; MEd 1973; PhD 1980). Teacher in London schs, 1967–72; Sen. Lectr, then Principal Lectr, Poly. of N London, 1972–84; Dean of Res. and Consultancy, Inst. of Educn, Univ. of London, 2002–04. Govt Chief Advr for Maths, 2004–07. DUniv Open, 2006; Hon. DSc Loughborough, 2008. Hans Freudenthal Medal for res. in maths educn, Internat. Commn on Mathematical Instruction, 2004. *Publications:* (with R. Sutherland) Logo Mathematics in the Classroom, 1992; (ed with R. Noss) Learning Mathematics and Logo, 1992; (ed jtly) Computers for Exploratory Learning, 1995; (with R. Noss) Windows on Mathematical Meanings: learning cultures and computers, 1996; contrib. res. jls. *Recreations:* tennis, swimming, walking, reading. *Address:* Institute of Education, University of London, 20 Bedford Way, WC1H 0AL. *T:* (020) 7612 6659; *e-mail:* c.hoyles@ioe.ac.uk.

HOYT, Hon. William Lloyd, OC 2007; Chief Justice of New Brunswick, 1993–98; *b* 13 Sept. 1930; *m* 1954, Joan Millier; three *d*. *Educ:* Woodstock High Sch.; Acadia Univ. (BA, MA); Emmanuel Coll., Cambridge (BA, MA; Hon. Fellow, 2001). Called to New Brunswick Bar, 1957; QC (NB) 1972; Associate, Limerick & Limerick, 1957–59; Partner, Limerick, Limerick & Hoyt and successor firm, Hoyt, Mockler, Allen & Dixon, 1959–81; Judge, 1981–84, Court of Appeal, 1984–98, New Brunswick. Mem., Bloody Sunday Tribunal of Inquiry (UK), 1998–. Member: Fredericton Barristers' Soc., 1957–81 (Pres., 1970–71); New Brunswick Barristers' Soc., 1957–81 (Council, 1970–72, 1975–79); Cttee on Canadian Constitution, Canadian Bar Assoc., 1977–78; Director: Canadian Inst. for Admin of Justice, 1979–83; Canadian Judges' Conf., 1985–89; Canadian Inst. of Advanced Legal Studies, 1994–; Chm., New Brunswick Judicial Council, 1993–98 (Vice-Chm., 1988–93). Hon. LLD: St Thomas Univ., Fredericton, 1997; Univ. of New Brunswick, 1998; Hon. DCL Acadia Univ., 2001. *Publications:* Married Women's Property, 1961; Professional Negligence, 1973.

HRUSKA, Dr Jan; Managing Director, LogicIQ Ltd, since 2006; *b* 22 April 1957; *s* of Ivan Hruska and Bozena Bozicek-Ferrari; *m* 2000, Regula Voellm. *Educ:* King's Sch., Canterbury; Downing Coll., Cambridge (BA 1978); Magdalen Coll., Oxford (DPhil 1984). Co-founder, and Technical Dir, 1985–2000, Jt Chief Exec. Officer, 2000–05, non-exec. Dir, 2006–, Sophos Plc. *Publications:* The PC Security Guide, 1988; Computer Security Solutions, 1990; Computer Viruses and Anti-Virus Warfare, 1990, 2nd edn 1992; Computer Security Reference Book, 1992. *Recreations:* sub-aqua diving, running, flying, ski-ing, piano-playing. *Address:* c/o Sophos Plc, The Pentagon, Abingdon, Oxon OX14 3YP. *T:* (01235) 559933, *Fax:* (01235) 559935; *e-mail:* jh@sophos.com.

HU JINTAO; General Secretary, Communist Party of China, since 2002; President, People's Republic of China, since 2003 (Vice-President, 1998–2003); Chairman, Central Military Commission, since 2004 (Vice-Chairman, 1999–2004); *b* Dec. 1942; *m* Liu Yongqing; one *s* one *d*. *Educ:* Tsinghua Univ., Beijing. Engineer; joined Min. of Water Conservancy, 1968, Technician, 1969–74; Gansu Provincial Construction Committee: Sec., 1974–75; Dep. Dir of Design Mgt, 1975–80; Vice-Chm., 1980–82. Communist Youth League of China: Sec., Gansu Provincial Cttee, 1982; Sec., 1982–84; First Sec., 1984–85; Communist Party of China: Mem., Central Cttee, 1985–; Sec., Guizhou, 1985–88, Tibet, 1988–92; Mem., Standing Cttee, Political Bureau, 1992–. *Address:* Office of the President, Zhong Nan Hai, Beijing, People's Republic of China.

HUANG, Prof. Christopher Li-Hur; Professor of Cell Physiology, Cambridge University, since 2002; Fellow, New Hall (from May 2009, Murray Edwards College), Cambridge, since 1979; *b* 28 Dec. 1951; *s* of Rayson Lisung Huang, *qv*. *Educ:* Methodist Boys' Sch., Kuala Lumpur; Nat. Jun. Coll., Singapore; Queen's Coll., Oxford (Singapore President's Scholar; Florence Heale Scholar; Benefactors Prize; BA, BM, BCh, MA; DM 1985; DSc 1995); Gonville and Caius Coll., Cambridge (MA; PhD 1980; MD 1986; ScD 1995). House Physician, Nuffield Dept of Medicine, Oxford Univ., 1977–78; Cambridge

University: MRC Schol., Physiological Lab., 1978–79; Asst Lectr, 1979–84; Lectr in Physiol., 1984–96; Reader in Cellular Physiol., 1996–2002; New Hall, Cambridge: Fellow and Lectr in Physiol., 1979–2002; Dir of Studies in Med. Sci., 1981–; Professorial Fellow, 2002–. Hon. Res. Fellow, RCS, 1985–88; Hon. Sen. Res. Fellow, St George's Hosp. Med. Sch., London Univ., 1991–. Procultura Foundn Vis. Prof., Debrecen Univ., Hungary, 1996; Vis. Prof., 2001–04, Ext. Assessor, 2007, Mount Sinai Med. Sch., NY; Vis. Prof., 2005, Ext. Assessor, 2005–06 and 2008, Univ. of HK; Ext. Assessor, Univ. of Leeds, 2008. Consulting Ed., John Wiley, 1986–; Mem. Editl Bd, 1990–96, Distributing Ed., 1991–94, Jl Physiol.; Chairman, Editorial Board: Monographs of Physiol Soc., 1994–99; Biological Revs, 2000–; Member Editorial Board: BioMed Central Physiology, 2005–; Europace, 2008–. Mem. Ct of Examrs, RCSE, 1999–2004. Council Mem., 1994–, Biol Sec., 2000–08, Adjudicator and convenor, Wm Bate Hardy Prize, 2008, Cambridge Philosophical Soc. Manager, Prince Philip Scholarship Fund, 1986–. Dir, Aw Boon Haw Foundn, 2004–; ind. non-exec. Dir, Hutchison China Meditech Ltd, 2006–. Brian Johnson Prize in Pathology, Univ. of Oxford, 1976; Lepra Award, Brit. Leprosy Relief Assoc., 1977; Rolleston Meml Prize for Physiological Res., Oxford Univ., 1980; Gedge Prize in Physiol., Cambridge Univ., 1981. *Publications:* Companion to Neonatal Medicine, 1982; Companion to Obstetrics, 1982; Companion to Gynaecology, 1985; Research in Medicine: a guide to writing a thesis in the medical sciences, 1990, 2nd edn 1999; Intramembrane Charge Movements in Striated Muscle, 1993; (ed jtly) Applied Physiology for Surgery and Critical Care, 1995; (ed jtly) Molecular and Cellular Biology of Bone, 1998; over 200 original scientific papers and reviews on striated muscle homeostasis and activation, peripheral nerve growth and repair, physiol magnetic resonance imaging, cellular triggering processes in osteoclasts and cardiac arrhythmogenesis. *Recreations:* music, playing the violin (Cambridge String Players, 2001–), reading Shakespeare. *Address:* New Hall (from May 2009, Murray Edwards College), Huntingdon Road, Cambridge CB3 0DF.

HUANG, Rayson Lisung, Hon. CBE 1976; DSc, DPhil; FRCPE; Vice-Chancellor, University of Hong Kong, 1972–86; *b* 1 Sept. 1920; *s* of Rufus Huang; *m* 1949, Grace Wei Li; two *s*. *Educ:* Munsang Coll., Hong Kong; Univ. of Hong Kong (BSc); Univ. of Oxford (DPhil, DSc); Univ. of Chicago. DSc (Malaya) 1956. FRCPE 1984. Demonstrator in Chemistry, Nat. Kwangsi Univ., Kweilin, China, 1943; Post-doctoral Fellow and Research Associate, Univ. of Chicago, 1947–50; Univ. of Malaya, Singapore: Lecturer in Chemistry, 1951–54; Reader, 1955–59; Univ. of Malaya, Kuala Lumpur: Prof. of Chemistry, 1959–69, and Dean of Science, 1962–65; Vice-Chancellor, Nanyang Univ., Singapore, 1969–72. Chm. Council, ACU, 1980–81; Pres., Assoc. of SE Asian Instns of Higher Learning, 1970–72, 1981–83. MLC Hong Kong, 1977–83. Mem. Drafting Cttee (Beijing) and Vice Chm. Consulting Cttee (Hong Kong), for the Basic Law for Special Administrative Region of Hong Kong, 1985–90. Mem. Adv. Bd, IBM China/Hong Kong Corp., 1989–93. Vice Chm. Council, Shantou Univ., China, 1987–94; Life Member: Court, Univ. of Hong Kong; Bd of Trustees, Croucher Foundn, Hong Kong; Life Trustee, Rayson Huang Foundn, Kuala Lumpur, 2001. JP. Hon. DSc Hong Kong, 1968; Hon. LLD East Asia, Macao, 1987. Order of the Rising Sun (Japan), 1986. *Publications:* Organic Chemistry of Free Radicals, 1974 (London); A Lifetime in Academia (autobiog.), 2000; about 50 research papers on chemistry of free radicals, molecular rearrangements, etc, mainly in Jl of Chem. Soc. (London). *Recreations:* music, violin playing. *Address:* Raycrest II, 10 The Stables, Selly Park, Birmingham B29 7JW. *Clubs:* Royal Over-Seas League; Hong Kong.

See also C. L.-H. Huang.

HUBBARD, family name of **Baron Addington**.

HUBBARD, David; *see* Hubbard, R. D. C.

HUBBARD, Ven. Julian Richard Hawes; Archdeacon of Oxford and Residentiary Canon of Christ Church, Oxford, since 2005; *b* 15 Feb. 1955; *m* 1984, Rachel (*née* Ashton); three *s* one *d*. *Educ:* Emmanuel Coll., Cambridge (BA 1976, MA 1981); Wycliffe Hall, Oxford (BA 1980, MA 1985). Ordained deacon, 1981, priest, 1982; Curate, St Dionis, Parson's Green, 1981–84; Tutor, Wycliffe Hall, Oxford, and Chaplain, Jesus Coll., Oxford, 1984–89; Selection Sec., ACCM, 1989–91, Sen. Selection Sec., ABM, 1991–93; Vicar, Bourne, 1993–99; RD, Farnham, 1996–99; Priest-in-charge, Tilford, 1997–99; Canon Residentiary, Guildford Cathedral, and Dir, Ministerial Trng, Dio. Guildford, 1999–2005. *Address:* Archdeacon's Lodgings, Christ Church, Oxford OX1 1DP.

HUBBARD, Michael Joseph; QC 1985; a Recorder of the Crown Court, since 1984; *b* 16 June 1942; *m* 1967, Ruth Ann; five *s*. *Educ:* Lancing College. Admitted Solicitor, 1966; called to the Bar, Gray's Inn, 1972; Western Circuit; Prosecuting Counsel to Inland Revenue, 1983–85. *Recreation:* sailing and messing about in boats in Cornwall and South of France (yacht Wild Confusion).

HUBBARD, (Richard) David (Cairns), OBE 1995; Chairman: London and Manchester Group, 1993–98 (Director, 1989–98); Exco plc, 1996–98 (Deputy Chairman, 1995); *b* 14 May 1936; *s* of late John Cairns Hubbard and Gertrude Emilie Hubbard; *m* 1964, Hannah Neale (*née* Dennison); three *d*. *Educ:* Tonbridge. FCA. Commissioned, Royal Artillery, 1955–57; Peat Marwick Mitchell & Co., 1957–65; Cape Asbestos Co., 1965–74; Bache & Co., 1974–76; Powell Duffryn, 1976–96 (Chm., 1986–96); Chm., Andrew Sykes Group, 1991–94; non-executive Director: Blue Circle Industries, 1986–96; City of London Investment Trust (formerly TR City of London Trust), 1989–2002; Slough Estates, 1994–2001; Medical Defence Union Ltd, 1998–2000; Mem., Southern Adv. Bd, Nat. Westminster Bank, 1988–91. Mem., Bd of Crown Agents for Oversea Govts and Admins, 1986–88. Mem. Council, Inst. of Dirs, 1991–97. Chm., CRC Council, 1996–98 (Council Mem., 1982–98). Liveryman, Skinners' Co.; Freeman, City of London. *Recreation:* golf. *Address:* Meadowcroft, Windlesham, Surrey GU20 6BJ. *T:* (01276) 472198. *Clubs:* Royal & Ancient Golf (St Andrews); Berkshire Golf (Pres., 1999–2004), Lucifer Golfing Society, Elders Golfing Society (Capt., 2002–04; Pres., 2007–).

HUBEL, Prof. David Hunter, MD; Research Professor of Neurobiology, Harvard Medical School, since 2000; *b* Canada, 27 Feb. 1926; US citizen; *s* of Jesse H. Hubel and Elsie M. Hunter; *m* 1953, S. Ruth Izzard; three *s*. *Educ:* McGill Univ. (BSc Hons Maths and Physics, 1947); McGill Univ. Med. Sch. (MD 1951). Rotating Intern, Montreal Gen. Hosp., 1951–52; Asst Resident in Neurology, Montreal Neurol Inst., 1952–53, and Fellow in Electroencephalography, 1953–54; Asst Resident in Neurol., Johns Hopkins Hosp., 1954–55; Res. Fellow, Walter Reed Army Inst. of Res., 1955–58; Res. Fellow, Wilmer Inst., Johns Hopkins Univ. Med. Sch., 1958–59; Harvard Medical School: Associate in Neurophysiology and Neuropharmacology, 1959–60; Asst Prof. of Neurophys. and Neuropharm., 1960–62; Associate Prof. of Neurophys. and Neuropharm., 1962–65; Prof. of Neurophys., 1965–67; George Packer Berry Prof. of Physiol. and Chm., Dept of Physiol., 1967–68; George Packer Berry Prof. of Neurobiol., 1968–82; John Franklin Enders Univ. Prof., 1982–2000, Emeritus, 2002–. George Eastman Vis. Prof., Univ. of Oxford, and Fellow, Balliol Coll., 1990–91. Sen. Fellow, Harvard Soc. of Fellows, 1971–; Mem., Bd of Syndics, Harvard Univ. Press, 1979–83.

Associate, Neurosciences Res. Program, 1974. Fellow, Amer. Acad. of Arts and Sciences, 1965; Member: Amer. Physiol Soc., 1959; National Acad. of Sciences, USA, 1971; Deutsche Akademie der Naturforscher Leopoldina, DDR, 1971; Soc. for Neuroscience, 1970; Assoc. for Res. in Vision and Ophthalmology, 1970; Amer. Philosophical Soc., 1982; Sigma Xi-Scientific Res. Soc., 1995; Foreign Mem., Royal Soc., 1982; Foreign MAE, 1995; Hon. Member: Physiol Soc., 1983; Amer. Neurol Assoc.; Spanish Soc. of Ophth., 1997. Lectures: George H. Bishop, Washington Univ., St Louis, 1964; Bowditch, Amer. Physiol Soc., 1966; Jessup, Columbia Univ., 1970; Ferrier, Royal Soc., 1972; James Arthur, Amer. Mus. of Nat. Hist., 1972; Harvey, Rockefeller Univ., 1976; Grass Foundn, Soc. for Neuroscience, 1976; Weizmann Meml, Weizmann Inst. of Science, Israel, 1979; Vanuxem, Princeton Univ., 1981; Hughlings Jackson, Montreal Neurol Inst., 1982; first David Marr, Cambridge Univ., 1982; first James S. McDonnell, Washington Univ. Sch. of Medicine, 1982; James A. F. Stevenson Meml, Univ. of W Ont, 1982; Keys Meml, Trinity Coll., Toronto, 1983; Nelson, Univ. of Calif. Davis, 1983; Deane, Wellesley Coll., 1983; first James M. Sprague, Univ. of Pa, 1984; Vancouver Inst., Univ. of BC, 1985; Wilder Penfield, Montreal Neurol Inst., 1998; inaugural Frederick Hughes Scott, Univ. of Toronto, 2000; Case Western Reserve Univ., 2000; Corpus Christi Coll., Oxford, 2001. Hon. DSc: McGill, 1978; Manitoba, 1983; Oxford, 1994; Ohio State, 1995; Hon. DHL Johns Hopkins, 1990; Dr *hc*: Madrid, 1997; Miguel Hernandez, 1998; Toronto, 2002; Optometry, SUNY, 2004; McMaster, 2005; Hon. LLD Dalhousie, 1998. Awards: Res. to Prevent Blindness Trustees, 1971; Lewis S. Rosenstiel for Basic Med. Res., Brandeis Univ., 1972; Friedenwald, Assoc. for Res. in Vision and Ophthalmol., 1975; New England Ophthalmol Soc. Annual, 1983; Paul Kayser Internat. Award of Merit for Retina Res., 1989. Prizes: Karl Spencer Lashley, Amer. Phil Soc., 1977; Louisa Gross Horwitz, Columbia Univ., 1978; Dickson in Medicine, Univ. of Pittsburgh, 1979; Ledlie, Harvard Univ., 1980; Nobel in Medicine or Physiol., 1981; Helen Keller, Hellen Keller Eye Res. Foundn, 1995. *Publications:* Eye, Brain and Vision, 1987; (with Torsten N. Wiesel) Brain and Visual Perception: the story of a 25 year collaboration, 2004; articles in scientific jls. *Recreations:* music, photography, astronomy, amateur radio, Japanese. *Address:* Harvard Medical School, Department of Neurobiology, 220 Longwood Avenue, Boston, MA 02115, USA. *T:* (617) 4321655.

HUBER, Prof. Robert; Director, Max-Planck-Institut für Biochemie, and Scientific Member, Max-Planck Society, 1972–2005, now Director Emeritus; *b* 20 Feb. 1937; *s* of Sebastian and Helene Huber; *m* 1960, Christa Essig; two *s* two *d*. *Educ:* Grammar Sch. and Humanistisches Gymnasium, München; Technische Univ., München (Dr rer. nat. 1963). Lecturer, 1968, Associate Prof., 1976–, Technische Univ., München. Scientific Mem., Max-Planck Soc. Editor, Jl of Molecular Biology, 1976–. Visiting Professor: Univ. Autónoma de Barcelona, 2001; Nat. Univ. of Singapore, 2005; Univ. Duisburg-Essen, 2005; Cardiff Univ., 2007. Member: EMBO (also Mem. Council); Deutsche Chem. Ges.; Ges. für Biologische Chem.; Bavarian Acad. of Scis, 1988; Deutsche Akademie der Naturforscher Leopoldina; Accademia Nazionale dei Lincei, Rome; Orden pour le mérite für Wissenschaft und Künste; Corresp. Mem., Croatian Acad. of Scis and Arts; Fellow, Amer. Acad. of Microbiology, 1996; Associate Fellow, Third World Acad. of Scis, 1995; Foreign Associate, Nat. Acad. of Scis, USA, 1995; Foreign Mem., Royal Soc., 1999. Hon. Member: Amer. Soc. of Biolog. Chemists; Swedish Soc. for Biophysics; Japanese Biochem. Soc; Sociedad Española de Bioquimica y Biología Molecular. Hon. Professor: Ocean Univ., Qingdao, 2002; Peking Univ., 2003; Sichuan Univ., Chengdu, 2003; Shanghai Second Med. Univ., 2004; Shanghai Jiao Tong Univ., 2005; Univ. de Sevilla, 2006; Lotte Dist. Prof., Seoul Nat. Univ., 2005. Dr *hc*: Catholic Univ. of Louvain, 1987; Univ. of Ljubljana, Jugoslavia, 1989; Univ. Tor Vergata, Rome, 1991; Univ. of Lisbon, 2000; Univ. of Barcelona, 2000; Tsinghua Univ., Peking, 2003. E. K. Frey Medal, Ges. für Chirurgie, 1972; Otto-Warburg Medal, Ges. für Biolog. Chem., 1977; Emil von Behring Medal, Univ. of Marburg, 1982; Keilin Medal, Biochem. Soc., 1987; Richard Kuhn Medal, Ges. Deutscher Chem., 1987; (jtly) Nobel Prize for Chemistry, 1988; E. K. Frey-E. Werle Gedächtnismedaille, 1989; Kone Award, Assoc. of Clin. Biochemists, 1990; Sir Hans Krebs Medal, FEBS, 1992; Linus Pauling Medal, 1993–94; Distinguished Service Award, Miami Winter Symposia, 1995; Max Tishler Prize, Harvard Univ., 1997; Max Bergmann Medal, 1997. Bayerischer Maximiliansorden für Wissenschaft und Kunst, 1993; Das Grosse Verdienstkreuz mit Stern und Schulterband (Germany), 1997; Röntgenplakette der Stadt Remscheid-Lennep, 2004; Premio Città di Firenze sulle Scienze Molecolari, 2004. *Publications:* numerous papers in learned jls on crystallography, immunology and structure of proteins. *Recreations:* cycling, hiking, ski-ing. *Address:* Max-Planck Institut für Biochemie, Am Klopferspitz 18a, 82152 Martinsried, Germany. *T:* (089) 85782677/8.

HÜBNER, Danuta, PhD; Member, European Commission, since 2004; *b* 8 April 1948; two *d*. *Educ:* Central Higher Sch. of Planning and Statistics, Warsaw (MSc (Econs) 1971; PhD 1974). Researcher, 1971–92, Prof. of Econs, 1992–, Central Higher Sch. of Planning and Statistics, Warsaw, subseq. Warsaw Sch. of Econs; Dep. Dir, Inst. of Develt and Strategic Studies, Warsaw, 1991–94; Under-Sec. of State, Min. of Industry and Trade, 1994–96; Sec. of State for European Integration, 1996–97; Hd, Chancellery of Pres. of Poland, 1997–98; Dep. Exec. Sec., 1998–2000, Exec. Sec., 2000–01, UN Econ. Commn for Europe, Geneva; Sec. of State, Min. of Foreign Affairs, 2001–03; Minister for European Affairs, 2003–04. *Publications:* books and scientific articles. *Address:* European Commission, Rue de la Loi 200, 1049 Brussels, Belgium.

HUCKER, Rev. Michael Frederick, MBE 1970; Principal Chaplain, Church of Scotland and Free Churches, Royal Air Force, 1987–90; Secretary, Forces Board, Methodist Church, 1990–96; *b* 1 May 1933; *s* of William John and Lucy Sophia Hucker; *m* 1961, Katherine Rosemary Parsons; one *s* one *d*. *Educ:* City of Bath Boys' Sch.; Bristol Univ. (MA); London Univ. (BD). Ordained Methodist minister, 1960; commnd as RAF chaplain, 1962. QHC 1987–90. Mem. Bd, Orbit Housing Assoc., 1996–2004, Orbit Housing Gp Ltd, 2004–05. *Recreations:* gardening, music. *Address:* Jeffries Mill, Spring Gardens, Frome, Somerset BA11 2NZ.

HUCKFIELD, Leslie (John); owner of Leslie Huckfield Research (consultancy and facilitation in communities, regeneration and development), since 1997; *b* 7 April 1942; *s* of Ernest Leslie and Suvla Huckfield. *Educ:* Prince Henry's Grammar Sch., Evesham; Keble Coll., Oxford; Univ. of Birmingham. Lectr in Economics, City of Birmingham Coll. of Commerce, 1963–67. Advertising Manager, Tribune, 1983; Co-ordinator, CAPITAL (transport campaign against London Transport Bill), 1983–84. Prin. Officer, External Resources, St Helen's Coll., Merseyside, 1989–93; European Officer, Merseyside Colls, 1994–95; Eur. Funding Manager, Wirral Metropolitan Coll., 1995–97. Contested (Lab) Warwick and Leamington, 1966; MP (Lab) Nuneaton, March 1967–1983. PPS to Minister of Public Building and Works, 1969–70; Parly Under-Secretary of State, Dept of Industry, 1976–79. MEP (Lab) Merseyside E, 1984–89. Member: Nat. Exec. Cttee, Labour Party, 1978–82; W Midlands Reg. Exec. Cttee, Labour Party, 1978–82; Political Sec., Nat. Union Lab. and Socialist Clubs, 1979–81. Chairman: Lab. Party Transport Gp, 1974–76; Independent Adv. Commn on Transport, 1975–76; Pres., Worcs Fedn of Young Socialists, 1962–64; Member: Birmingham Regional Hosp. Bd, 1970–72; Political Cttee, Co-op. Retail Soc. (London Regional), 1981–93. *Publications:* various newspaper and periodical articles. *Recreation:* running marathons. *Address:* PO Box 600 Auchterarder PH3 1YX. *T:* (01764) 660080, *Fax:* 0871 717 1957; *e-mail:* research@huckfield.com.

HUCKLE, Alan Edden; HM Diplomatic Service; Governor of the Falkland Islands an Commissioner for South Georgia and the South Sandwich Islands, since 2006; *b* 15 Jun 1948; *s* of late Albert Arthur Huckle and of Ethel Maud Pettifer Huckle (*née* Edden); 1973, Helen Myra Gibson; one *s* one *d*. *Educ:* Rugby Sch.; Lower Sch. of John Lyon Harrow; Univ. of Warwick (BA 1st Cl. Hons Hist. 1969; MA Renaissance Studies 1970) Leverhulme Trust Schol., 1971; British Sch. at Rome Schol., 1971; Personnel Mgt Div CSD, 1971–74; Asst Private Sec. to Sec. of State for NI, Belfast, 1974–75; Machinery o Govt Div., CSD, 1975–78; Pol Affairs Div., NI Office, Belfast, 1978–80; FCO, 1980–83 Exec. Dir, British Inf. Services, NY, 1983–87; Hd of Chancery, Manila, 1987–90; Dep Hd, Arms Control and Disarmament Dept, FCO, 1990–92; Counsellor and Dep. Hd o Delegn to CSCE, Vienna, 1992–96; Head: Dependent Territories Regl Secretaria Bridgetown, 1996–98; OSCE/Council of Europe Dept, FCO, 1998–2001; Overse Territories Dept, FCO, and Comr (non-resident), British Antarctic Territory and Britis Indian Ocean Territory, 2001–04; Gov. of Anguilla, 2004–06. *Recreations:* hill-walking armchair mountaineering. *Address:* c/o Foreign and Commonwealth Office, King Charle Street, SW1A 2AH. *T:* (Falkland Is) 28200. *Club:* Royal Commonwealth Society.

HUCKSTEP, Prof. Ronald Lawrie, CMG 1971; MD; FRCS, FRCSE, FRACS, FTSE Professor of Traumatic and Orthopaedic Surgery, University of New South Wales 1972–92, now Emeritus Professor and Emeritus Orthopaedic Consultant, Prince o Wales/Prince Henry Hospital Group; Chairman of Departments of Orthopaedic Surger and Director of Accident Services, Prince of Wales and Prince Henry Hospitals, Sydney Australia, 1972–92; Consultant Orthopaedic Surgeon, Royal South Sydney an Sutherland Hospitals, 1972–92; *b* 22 July 1926; *er s* of late Herbert George Huckstep an Agnes Huckstep (*née* Lawrie-Smith); *m* 1960, Margaret Ann, *e d* of late Ronald Græm Macbeth, DM, FRCS; two *s* one *d*. *Educ:* Cathedral Sch., Shanghai, China; Queens' Coll. Cambridge; Middx Hosp. Med. Sch., London. MA, MB, BChir (Cantab) 1952; MI (Cantab) 1957; FRCSE 1957; FRCS 1958; FAOrthA 1972; FRACS 1973. Registrar an Chief Asst, Orthopaedic Dept, St Bartholomew's Hosp., and various surgical appts Midd and Royal Nat. Orthopaedic Hosps, London, 1952–60; Hunterian Prof., RCS, 1959–60 Makerere Univ. Coll., Kampala, Uganda: Lectr, 1960–62, Sen. Lectr, 1962–65 an Reader, 1965–67, in Orthopaedic Surgery, with responsibility for starting orthopaedi dept in Uganda; Prof. of Orthopaedic Surgery, Makerere Univ., Kampala, 1967–72 Became Hon. Cons. Orthopaedic Surgeon, Mulago and Mengo Hosps, and Round Tabl Polio Clinic, Kampala; Adviser on Orthopaedic Surgery, Ministry of Health, Uganda 1960–72. Vis. Prof. of Surgery, Univ. of Sydney, 1995–. Corresp. Editor: Brit. and Amer jls of Bone and Joint Surgery, 1965–72; Jl Western Pacific Orthopædic Assoc.; British J of Accident Surgery. Fellow, British Orthopaedic Assoc., 1967; Hon. Fellow: Wester Pacific Orthopaedic Assoc., 1968; Assoc. of Surgeons of Uganda, 1993. Commonwealt Foundn Travelling Lectr, 1970, 1978–79 and 1982. FRSocMed; FTSE (FTS 1982) Patron Med. Soc., Univ. of NSW; Founder, World Orthopaedic Concern, 1973 (Hon Mem. 1978); Vice-Pres., Australian Orthopaedic Assoc., 1982–83 (Betts Medal, 1983) Pres., Coast Med. Assoc., Sydney, 1985–86; Chairman, Fellow or Mem. various med. soc and of assocs, councils and cttees concerned with orthopaedic and traumatic surgery accident services and rehabilitation of physically disabled. Inventions incl. Huckste femoral fracture nail, hip, knee, shoulder, shoulder staple and circlip. Hon. Mem., Mar Twain Soc., 1978. Hon. MD NSW, 1988. Irving Geist Award, 11th World Congress Internat. Soc. for Rehabilitation of the Disabled, 1969; James Cook Medal, Royal Soc. o NSW, 1984; Sutherland Medal, Australian Acad. of Technological Scis, 1986; Paul Harri Fellow and Medal, Rotary Internat., 1987; Humanitarian Award, Orthopaedics Overseas 1991. Rotary Vocational Service Award, 1994; Centenary Medal, Australia, 2003 *Publications:* Typhoid Fever and Other Salmonella Infections, 1962; A Simple Guide t Trauma, 1970, 5th edn 1995 (trans. Italian 1978, Japanese 1982); Poliomyelitis, A Guid for Developing Countries, Including Appliances and Rehabilitation, 1975 (ELBS and repr edns 1979, 1983, French edn 1983); A Simple Guide to Orthopaedics, 1993; Colour Tes in Orthopaedics and Trauma, 1994; various booklets, chapters in books, papers and film on injuries, orthopaedic diseases, typhoid fever, appliances and implants. *Recreations* photography, designing orthopaedic appliances and implants for cripples in developing an developed countries, swimming, travel. *Address:* 108 Sugarloaf Crescent, Castlecrag Sydney, NSW 2068, Australia. *T:* (612) 99581786, *Fax:* (612) 99672971. *Club:* Australia (Sydney).

HUDD, Roy, OBE 2004; actor; *b* 16 May 1936; *s* of Harold Hudd and Evelyn Barham; *m* 1st, 1963, Ann Lambert (marr. diss. 1983); one *s*; 2nd, 1988, Deborah Flitcroft. *Educ* Croydon Secondary Technical School. Entered show business, 1957, as half of double ac Hudd & Kay; Butlin Redcoats; started as a solo comedian, 1959; first pantomime, Empire Theatre, Leeds, 1959; 4 years' concert party Out of the Blue, 1960–63; first radio broadcas Workers Playtime, 1960; *stage includes:* The Merchant of Venice, 1960; The Give Away 1969; At the Palace, 1970; Young Vic Co. seasons, 1973, 1976, 1977; Oliver!, 1977 Underneath the Arches, 1982 (SWET Actor of the Year); Run For Your Wife, 1986 1989; The Birth of Merlin, Theatre Clwyd, 1989; The Fantasticks, 1990; Midsumme Night's Dream, 1991; Friends Like This, 1998; A Funny Thing Happened on the Way to the Forum, 1999; Hard Times, Haymarket, 2000; Theft, 2001; Roy Hudd's Exceedingly Entertaining Evening, 2005–08; The Solid Gold Cadillac, Garrick, 2006; The Merry Widow, Coliseum, 2008; The Wizard of Oz, RFH, 2008; *films include:* Blood Beas Terror, 1967; Up Pompeii; The Seven Magnificent Deadly Sins; Up the Chastity Belt The Garnet Saga; An Acre of Seats in a Garden of Dreams, 1973; The Sweet Life, 1998 Kind of Hush, 1998; Purely Belter, 2000; *television series include:* Not So Much a Programme, More a Way of Life, 1964; Illustrated Weekly Hudd, 1966–68; Roy Hudd Show, 1971; Comedy Tonight, 1970–71; Up Sunday, 1973; Pebble Mill, 1974–75; Hold the Front Page, 1974–75; The 60 70 80 show, 1974–77; Movie Memories, 1981–85; Halls of Fame, 1985; The Puppet Man, 1985; Cinderella, 1986; Hometown, 1987, 1988–89 What's My Line?, 1990; Lipstick On Your Collar, 1993; Common as Muck, 1994–96 What's My Line, 1994–96; Karaoke, 1996; The Quest, 2002; Coronation Street 2002–04, 2006–; The Quest 2, 2004; The Final Quest, 2005; In the City, 2006; *radio series* The News Huddlines, 1975–2003; Like They've Never Been Gone, 2001–04; Tickling Tunes, 2006; *author of stage shows:* Victorian Christmas, 1978; Just a Verse and Chorus, 1979; Roy Hudd's Very Own Music Hall, 1980; Beautiful Dreamer, 1980; Underneath the Arches, 1982; While London Sleeps, 1983; They Called Me Al, 1987; numerous pantomimes, 1980–. Columnist, Yours magazine, 1991–. Chm., Entertainment Artistes Benevolent Fund, 1980–90. President: British Music Hall Soc., 1992–; TRIC, 2000–01 Trustee, British Actors Equity. King Rat, Grand Order of Water Rats, 1989, 2000. Hon DCL E Anglia, 2007. Variety Club BBC Radio Personality, 1976, 1993; Gold Badge of Merit, BASCA, 1981; Sony Gold Award, 1990; British Comedy Lifetime Achievement, LWT, 1990; EMAP Columnist of the Year, 1995; Crystal Award for services to entertainment, Inst. of Entertainment & Arts Mgt, 1995; Roy Castle Award for outstanding services to variety, 2003. *Publications:* Music Hall, 1976; Roy Hudd's Book of

Music Hall, Variety and Show Biz Anecdotes, 1993; Roy Hudd's Who's Who in Variety 1945–60, 1997; Twice Nightly, 2007. *Recreations:* collecting old songs, sleeping. *Address:* PO Box 604, Ipswich IP6 9WZ. *Club:* Garrick.

HUDGELL, Susan Alison; *see* Pember, S. A.

HUDGHTON, Ian Stewart; Member (SNP) Scotland, European Parliament, since 1999 (Scotland North East, Nov. 1998–1999); *b* 19 Sept. 1951; *m* 1981, Lily M. Ingram; one *s* one *d* (and one *s* decd). *Educ:* Forfar Acad.; Kingsway Technical Coll., Dundee. Partner and Jt Proprietor, then Proprietor, F. Hudghton & Son, Painters and Decorators, 1971–95. Mem., Cttee of Regions, 1998. Member (SNP): Angus DC, 1986–96 (Housing Convener, 1988–96); Angus Council, 1995–99 (Leader, 1995–99); Tayside Regl Council, 1994–96 (Depute Leader, 1994–96). Pres., SNP, 2005–. *Recreations:* family, theatre, music, hill walking. *Address:* (office) 8 Old Glamis Road, Dundee, DD3 8HP. *T:* (01382) 623200.

HUDSON, Andrew Peter; Chief Executive, Valuation Office Agency, since 2004; *b* 22 March 1958; *s* of late John Thomas David Hudson and of Margaret Hudson; *m* 2002, Judith Simpson. *Educ:* King Edward's Sch., Birmingham; New Coll., Oxford (BA Hons). Inland Revenue, 1980–82, 1984–86; HM Treasury: 1982–84; Chancellor of the Exchequer's Office, 1986–89; Local Govt Finance Div., 1989–91; seconded to Interconnection Systems Ltd, 1991–92; Press Sec. to Chancellor of the Exchequer and Hd of Communications, 1992–96; Hd, Health Team, 1996–99; Essex County Council: Asst Chief Exec., 1999–2002; Dep. Chief Exec. (Finance and Performance), 2002–04. *Recreations:* running, walking, watching sport. *Address:* Valuation Office Agency, New Court, Carey Street, WC2A 2JE. *T:* (020) 7506 1901, *Fax:* (020) 7506 1990; *e-mail:* andrew.hudson@voa.gsi.gov.uk.

HUDSON, Prof. Anne Mary, DPhil; FRHistS; FBA 1988; Professor of Medieval English, Oxford, 1989–2003; Fellow of Lady Margaret Hall, Oxford, 1963–2003, now Hon. Fellow; *b* 28 Aug. 1938; *d* of late R. L. and K. M. Hudson. *Educ:* Dartford Grammar Sch. for Girls; St Hugh's Coll., Oxford (BA English cl. I; MA; DPhil 1964). FRHistS 1976. Lectr in Medieval English, 1961–63, Tutor, 1963–91, LMH, Oxford; Oxford University: CUF Lectr, 1963–81; Special Lectr, 1981–83; British Acad. Reader in the Humanities, 1983–86; Lectr in Medieval English, 1986–89. Early English Text Society: Exec. Sec., 1969–82; Mem. Council, 1982–; Dir, 2006–. Sir Israel Gollancz Prize, British Acad., 1985, 1991. *Publications:* (ed) Selections from English Wycliffite Writings, 1978; (ed) English Wycliffite Sermons, i, 1983, iii, 1990, iv and v (with P. Gradon), 1996; Lollards and their Books, 1985; (ed jtly) From Ockham to Wyclif, 1987; The Premature Reformation, 1988; (ed) Two Wycliffite Texts, 1993; (ed jtly) Heresy and Literacy 1000–1500, 1994; (ed) The Works of a Lollard Preacher, 2001. *Address:* Lady Margaret Hall, Oxford OX2 6QA.

HUDSON, Prof. Anthony Hugh, PhD; Professor of Common Law, Liverpool University, 1977–92, now Emeritus (Dean of Faculty of Law, 1971–78 and 1984–91); *b* 21 Jan. 1928; *s* of late Dr Thomas A. G. Hudson and Bridget Hudson; *m* 1962, Joan O'Malley; one *s* three *d*. *Educ:* St Joseph's Coll., Blackpool; Pembroke Coll., Cambridge (LLB 1950, MA 1953); PhD Manchester 1966. Called to Bar, Lincoln's Inn, 1954. Lecturer in Law: Hull Univ., 1951–57; Birmingham Univ., 1957–62; Manchester Univ., 1962–64; Liverpool University: Sen. Lectr, 1964–71; Professor of Law, 1971–77. *Publications:* (jtly) Hood Phillips: A First Book of English Law, 7th edn 1977, 8th edn 1988; (jtly) Pennington Commercial Banking Law, 1978; (jtly) Stevens and Borrie Mercantile Law, 17th edn 1978; Halsbury's Laws of England, 4th edn (contrib. or ed with N. E. Palmer and others) vol. 8 (i) Confidence, 1996, 2003, vol. 12 (i) Damages, 1998, vol. 45 (i) Tort, 1999, vol. 5 (i) Carriers, 2004; Encyclopaedia of Forms and Precedents, 5th edn, vol. 34 Sale of Goods, 2002; contribs on common and commercial law to various legal books and periodicals. *Recreations:* gardening, walking, history. *Address:* 18 Dowhills Road, Blundellsands, Liverpool L23 8SW. *T:* (0151) 924 5830.

HUDSON, Barrie; *see* Hudson, N. B.

HUDSON, (Eleanor) Erlund, RE 1946 (ARE 1938); RWS 1949 (ARWS 1939); ARCA 1937; artist; *b* 18 Feb. 1912; *d* of Helen Ingeborg Olsen, Brookline, Boston, USA, and Harold Hudson. *Educ:* Torquay; Dorking; Royal College of Art (Diploma 1937, Travelling Scholarship 1938). Former Mem. Chicago Print Soc. and Soc. of Artist Print-Makers. Studied and travelled in Italy, summer 1939. Interrupted by war. Exhibited in London, Provinces, Scandinavia, Canada, USA, etc; works purchased by War Artists Advisory Council, 1942–43. Formerly Artistic Dir and designer, Brooking Ballet Sch., W1. *Recreations:* music, country life. *Address:* 6 Hammersmith Terrace, W6 9TS. *T:* (020) 8748 3778; Meadow House, Canute Road, Old Bosham, W Sussex PO18 8JF. *T:* (01243) 573558.

HUDSON, Prof. George, FRCP, FRCPath; Professor of Experimental Haematology, University of Sheffield, 1975–89, now Emeritus; *b* 10 Aug. 1924; *s* of George Hudson, blacksmith, and Edith Hannah (*née* Bennett); *m* 1955, Mary Patricia Hibbert (decd); one *d*. *Educ:* Edenfield C of E Sch.; Bury Grammar Sch.; Manchester Univ. (MSc, MB, ChB); MD, DSc Bristol. House Officer, Manchester Royal Inf., 1949–50; Demonstr in Anatomy, Univ. of Bristol, 1950–51; RAMC, 1951–53; University of Bristol: Lectr, later Reader, in Anatomy, 1953–68; Preclinical Dean, 1963–68; Vis. Prof., Univ. of Minnesota (Fulbright Award), 1959–60; Sheffield University: Admin. Dean, 1968–83; Hon. Clinical Lectr in Haematology, 1968–75; Head, Dept of Haematology, 1981–89; Postgrad. Dean, 1984–91. Hon. Cons. Haematologist, United Sheffield Hosps, 1969–89. Chm., Conf. of Deans of Provincial Med. Schs, 1980–82; Member: Sheffield RHB, 1970–74; Sheffield HA, 1974–84; DHSS Working Party on NHS Adv. and Representative Machinery, 1980–81; Council for Postgraduate Med. Educn for England and Wales, 1980–83. Hon. LLD Sheffield, 1993. *Publications:* papers in medical and scientific jls on haematological subjects. *Recreations:* lay reader since 1953, history of medicine, cavies, garden. *Address:* Box Cottage, Hill Bottom, Whitchurch Hill RG8 7PU. *T:* (0118) 984 2671.

HUDSON, Kathryn Margaret; Deputy Parliamentary and Heath Service Ombudsman, since 2008; *b* 28 March 1949; *d* of William and Annie Stead; *m* 1971, Michael Hudson; two *s*. *Educ:* Univ. of Southampton (BSc Sociol./Law); Univ. of S Bank (MSc Public Sector Mgt 1994); letter of accreditation as Probation Officer, Home Office, 1971. Probation Officer, 1971–75; Youth Worker, ILEA, 1979–83; Social Worker, Bromley, 1983–86; Sen. Social Worker, Greenwich, 1986–90; Team Ldr, Adoption and Fostering, 1990–92, Principal Officer, 1992–94, Bexley; Assistant Director of Social Services: Bexley, 1994–98; Lewisham, 1998–2000 (Actg Dir, 2000); Dir, Social Services, Newham, 2001–04; Nat. Dir for Social Care, DoH, 2004–08. *Address:* Office of the Parliamentary and Health Service Ombudsman, Millbank Tower, Millbank, SW1P 4QP. *T:* (020) 7217 4070; *e-mail:* Kathryn.Hudson@ombudsman.org.uk.

HUDSON, Keith William, FRICS; Technical Secretary, Cost Commission, Comité Européen des Economistes de la Construction, 1989–94; *b* 2 June 1928; *s* of William Walter Hudson and Jessie Sarah Hudson; *m* 1952, Ailsa White; two *s* two *d*. *Educ:* Sir Charles Elliott Sch.; Coll. of Estate Management. FRICS 1945. Served Army, 1948–50 (Lieut). Private practice, 1945–48 and 1950–57; Min. of Works, Basic Grade, 1957–64; Min. of Health (later DHSS), 1964–86: Main Grade, 1964–66; Sen. Grade, 1966–74; Superintending, 1974–76; Dir B, 1976–79; Under Sec., 1979; Dir of Construction and Cost Intelligence, and Chief Surveyor, DHSS, 1979–86, retd. *Publications:* articles in Chartered Surveyor and in Building. *Recreations:* painting, walking.

HUDSON, Kirsty; *see* McLeod, K.

HUDSON, Lucian; HM Diplomatic Service; special assignment on collaborative partnerships, Foreign and Commonwealth Office, since 2008; *b* 5 July 1960; *s* of John and Vanda Hudson; *m* 1982, Margaret Prythergch. *Educ:* Ecole Montalembert, Paris; Lycée Français de Londres; St Catherine's Coll., Oxford (MA (Hons) PPE); London Business Sch. Professional communicator with expertise in corporate strategy, driving collaboration and building teams; launched and managed 10 new content-driven ventures in UK, Europe, N and S America, India, Far East; BBC: producer and sen. producer, Nine O'Clock News, 1988–93; night editor, Breakfast News, news editor, party confs, 1993–94; strand editor, BBC World, 70 live events and breaking news specials inc. first 6 hrs of death of Diana, Princess of Wales, 1994–97; hd of programming, launched new cable channels, BBC Worldwide, 1997–99; Dir of e-Communications Gp, Cabinet Office, 2000–01; seconded to MAFF to run media ops during foot and mouth disease, 2001; Dir of Commns, DEFRA, 2001–04; Dir of Commns, DCA, 2004–06; Dir of Communication and Press Sec., FCO, 2006–08. Founding editorial dir, Justpeople.com, 1999–2000. Chm., Rory Peck Trust, 1998–2000. Chm., Council, Tavistock Inst., 2003–07. MCIPR 2005. *Recreations:* reading, swimming, listening to music. *Address:* Foreign and Commonwealth Office, King Charles Street, SW1A 2AH. *Club:* Royal Automobile.

HUDSON, Mark Henry; Chairman, Game Conservancy Trust Ltd, since 2006; *b* 27 Jan. 1947; *s* of Tom Hudson and Peggy Hudson (*née* Field); *m* 1970, Susan Gordon Russell; two *s*. *Educ:* Sedbergh Sch.; St Catharine's Coll., Cambridge (BA 1969, MA 1974); Wye Coll., Univ. of London (Dip. Farm Business Admin 1970). Dir, 1985–, Chm., 2006–, NWF Gp plc; Principal, Mark Hudson Associates, 1991–. Pres., CLA, 2003–05. Mem. Council, Duchy of Lancaster, 2006–. Chm., Oxford Farming Conf., 1990–91. ARAgS 2007. *Recreations:* family, fishing, golf. *Address:* c/o Game Conservancy Trust Ltd, Burgate Manor, Fordingbridge, Hants SP6 1EF. *Clubs:* Farmers (Chm., 1990), MCC.

HUDSON, (Norman) Barrie, CB 1996; Director, International Development Affairs (formerly Under Secretary, International Division), Overseas Development Administration, 1993–97, retired; *b* 21 June 1937; *s* of William and Mary Hudson; *m* 1963, Hazel (*née* Cotterill); two *s* one *d*. *Educ:* King Henry VIII Sch., Coventry; Univ. of Sheffield (BA Hons 1958); University Coll., London (MScEcon 1960). Economist, Tube Investments Ltd, 1960; Economist, Economist Intell. Unit, 1962; National Accounts Statistician (UK Technical Assistance to Govt of Jordan), 1963; Statistician, ODM, 1966; Econ. Adviser, ME Develt Div., Beirut, 1967; Overseas Development Administration: Econ. Adviser, 1972, Sen. Econ. Adviser, 1973; Head, SE Asia Develt Div., Bangkok, 1974; Asst Sec., 1977; Under Sec. (Principal Establishments Officer), 1981; Under Sec. for Africa, 1986. Trustee, SCF, 1998–2005. *Recreations:* theatre, reading, music, watching football and cricket. *Address:* The Galleons, Sallows Shaw, Sole Street, Cobham, Kent DA13 9BP. *T:* (01474) 814419.

HUDSON, Pamela May; *see* Hudson-Bendersky, P. M.

HUDSON, Peter Geoffrey; Member, Panel of Chairmen, Civil Service Selection Board, 1987–94; *b* 26 July 1926; *s* of late Thomas Albert Hudson and Gertrude Hudson; *m* 1954, Valerie Mary, *yr d* of late Lewis Alfred Hart and Eva Mary Hart; two *s*. *Educ:* King Edward VII Sch., Sheffield; Queen's Coll., Oxford (Hastings Scholar, MA). Gold Medallist, Royal Schs of Music, 1940. Sub-Lt RNVR, 1944–46 (Bletchley Park, 1944–45). Min. of Transport, 1949; Private Sec. to Minister of Transport and Civil Aviation, 1951–53; Principal, Min. of Transport and Civil Aviation, 1953–57; Admin. Staff Coll., Henley, 1957; British Civil Air Attaché, SE Asia and Far East, 1958–61; Asst Sec., Overseas Policy Div. and Estabt Div., Min. of Aviation and BoT, 1963–68; Counsellor (Civil Aviation), British Embassy, Washington, 1968–71; Under-Sec., DTI, 1971–84; Dir of Resources, British Tourist Authority and English Tourist Bd, 1984–86. Indep. Advr to Lady Marre Cttee on Future of Legal Profession, 1987–88. Vice Chm., Bromley CAB, 1989–95. Governor, Coll. of Air Trng, Hamble, 1974–75. *Recreation:* music. *Address:* Candle Hill, Raggleswood, Chislehurst, Kent BR7 5NH. *T:* (020) 8467 1761.

HUDSON, Peter John, CB 1978; Deputy Under-Secretary of State (Finance and Budget), Ministry of Defence, 1976–79; *b* 29 Sept. 1919; *o s* of late A. J. Hudson; *m* 1954, Joan Howard FitzGerald (*d* 1998); one *s* one *d*. *Educ:* Tollington Sch.; Birkbeck Coll., London. Exchequer and Audit Dept, 1938; RNVR, 1940–46 (Lieut); Asst Principal, Air Min., 1947; Private Sec. to Perm. Under Sec. of State for Air, 1948–51; Asst Sec., 1958; Head of Air Staff Secretariat, 1958–61; Imperial Defence Coll., 1962; Head of Programme and Budget Div., MoD, 1966–69; Under-Sec., Cabinet Office, 1969–72; Asst Under-Sec. of State, MoD, 1972–75; Dep. Under-Sec. of State (Air), MoD, 1975–76. *Address:* Folly Hill, Haslemere, Surrey GU27 2EY. *T:* (01428) 642078. *Club:* Royal Air Force.

HUDSON, Prof. Raymond, PhD, DSc; FBA 2006; Professor of Geography, since 1990, and Pro Vice-Chancellor, since 2007, University of Durham; *b* 7 March 1948; *s* of John and Jean Hudson; *m* 1975, Geraldine Holder Jones; one *s* one *d*. *Educ:* Bristol Univ. (BA 1st Cl. Hons 1969; PhD 1974; DSc 1996). University of Durham: Lectr in Geog., 1972–83; Sen. Lectr, 1983–87; Reader, 1987–90; Head of Geog. Dept, 1992–97; Dir, Centre for European Studies, 1990–99; Chair, Internat. Centre for Regl Regeneration and Develt Studies, 1999–2005; Dir, Wolfson Res. Inst., 2003–07. Chairman: Conf. of Heads of Geog. Depts in HE Instns in UK, 1995–99; Human Geog. Subject Area Panel, ESRC, 1999–2001; Mem., Trng and Develt Bd, ESRC, 2002–06. Vice-Pres., RGS with IBG, 1999–2004; Pres., Geog. Sect., BAAS, 2001–02. AcSS 2001; MAE 2007. Editor, European Urban and Regional Studies, 1994–2007. Hon. DSc Roskilde, 1987. Edward Heath Award, 1989, Victoria Medal, 2005, RGS. *Publications:* (with D. Pocock) Images of the Urban Environment, 1978; (contrib. and ed, jtly) Regions in Crisis, 1980; (with D. W. Rhind) Land Use, 1980; (contrib. and ed, jtly) Regional Planning in Europe, 1982; (contrib. and ed, jtly) Redundant Spaces in Cities and Regions, 1983; (jtly) An Atlas of EEC Affairs, 1984; (contrib. and ed, jtly) Uneven Development in Southern Europe, 1985; (with A. Williams) The United Kingdom, 1986; Wrecking a Region, 1989; (with D. Sadler) The International Steel Industry, 1989; (with A. Williams) Divided Britain, 1989; (jtly) A Tale of Two Industries, 1991; (jtly) A Place called Teesside, 1994; (ed and contrib., jtly) Towards a New Map of Automobile Manufacturing in Europe?, 1995; (with M. Dunford) Successful European regions, 1996; (contrib. and ed jtly) Divided Europe, 1998; (jtly) Digging up Trouble: environment, protest and opencast coal mining, 2000; Production, Place and Environment: changing perspectives in economic geography, 2000; (jtly) Coalfields Regeneration: dealing with the consequences of industrial decline, 2000; Producing Places, 2001; (jtly) Placing the Social Economy, 2002; Economic Geographies:

circuits, flows and spaces, 2005; numerous articles in scientific and scholarly jls. *Recreations:* reading, walking, keeping fit, travel. *Address:* 7 Oliver Place, Merryoaks, Durham DH1 3QS. *T:* (0191) 386 2963, *T:* (office) (0191) 334 0070.

HUDSON, Prof. Richard Anthony, FBA 1992; Professor of Linguistics, University College London, 1989–2004, now Emeritus; *b* 18 Sept. 1939; *s* of late Prof. John Pilkington Hudson, CBE, GM and Mary Gretta Hudson (*née* Heath); *m* 1970, Gaynor Evans; two *d. Educ:* Loughborough Grammar Sch.; Corpus Christi Coll., Cambridge (BA); Sch. of Oriental and African Studies, London (PhD). University College London: Research Asst, Linguistics, 1964–70; Lectr 1970, Reader 1980, Dept of Phonetics and Linguistics. *Publications:* English Complex Sentences: an introduction to systemic grammar, 1971; Arguments for a Non-Transformational Grammar, 1976; Sociolinguistics, 1980; Word Grammar, 1984; An Invitation to Linguistics, 1984; English Word Grammar, 1990; Teaching Grammar: a guide for the national curriculum, 1992; Word Meaning, 1995; English Grammar, 1998; Language Networks: the new word grammar, 2007; articles in jls. *Recreations:* walking, cycling, music. *Address:* Department of Phonetics and Linguistics, University College London, Gower Street, WC1E 6BT. *T:* (020) 7380 7172.

HUDSON, Richard Bayliss, RDI 1999; stage designer; *b* 9 June 1954; *s* of Peter Obank Hudson and Ella Joyce Bayliss. *Educ:* Peterhouse Sch., Rhodesia; Wimbledon Sch. of Art (BA Hons 1976). Designer of sets and costumes, 1986–, for major theatre companies in Britain, and for Royal Opera, ENO, Glyndebourne, Chicago Lyric Opera, La Fenice, Vienna State Opera, Bayerische Staatsoper; designs include: King Lear and Candide, Old Vic (Olivier award for season), 1988; A Night at the Chinese Opera, Kent Opera, 1990; The Queen of Spades, 1992, Eugene Onegin, 1994, Manon Lescaut, 1997, Le Nozze di Figaro and Don Giovanni, 2000, Glyndebourne; Die Meistersinger, Royal Opera, 1993; The Cherry Orchard, RSC, 1995; The Lion King, Broadway, 1997 (Tony Award, 1998), also London, Tokyo, Osaka, Toronto, Los Angeles, Hamburg; Samson et Dalila, Met. Opera, New York, 1998; Guillaume Tell and Ernani, Vienna State Opera, 1998; Peter Grimes, Amsterdam, 2000; Pique Dame, Chicago Lyric Opera, 2000; Tamerlano, Maggio Musicale Fiorentino, 2001; The Cunning Little Vixen, Opera North, 2001; Khovanshchina, Opéra de Paris, 2001; Doctor Faustus, Young Vic, 2002; Benvenuto Cellini, Zurich, 2002; Les Vêpres Siciliennes, Opéra de Paris, 2003; Ring Cycle, ENO, 2004–05; Emperor Jones, Gate, 2005; Women Beware Women, 2006, Coriolanus, 2007, RSC; L'après-midi d'un Faune, Jeux, Fall of the House of Usher, Bregenz Fest., 2006; The Makropulos Case, Royal Danish Opera, 2006; Death in Venice (costumes), Aldeburgh Fest., La Bohème, Greek Nat. Opera, 2007; La Forza del Destino, Vienna State Opera, Rushes, Royal Ballet, 2008. British Scenographic Comr, Orgn Internat. des Scénographes, Techniciens et Architectes de Théâtre, 1996–. DUniv Surrey, 2005. Gold Medal for set design, Prague Quadrenniale, 2003. *Address:* c/o Judy Daish Associates, 2 St Charles Place, W10 6EG.

HUDSON, Prof. Robert Francis, PhD; FRS 1982; Professor of Organic Chemistry, University of Kent at Canterbury, 1967–85 (part-time, 1981–85), now Emeritus; *b* 15 Dec. 1922; *s* of late John Frederick Hudson and Ethel Hudson; *m* 1945, Monica Ashton Stray (*d* 2000); one *s* twin *d. Educ:* Brigg Grammar Sch.; Imperial Coll. of Science and Technol., London (BSc, ARCS, PhD, DIC). Asst Lectr, Imperial Coll., London, 1945–47; Consultant, Wolsey Ltd, Leicester, 1945–50; Lectr, Queen Mary Coll., London, 1947–59; Res. Fellow, Purdue Univ., 1954; Gp Dir, Cyanamid European Res. Inst., Geneva, 1960–66. Vis. Professor: Rochester, USA, 1970; Bergen, 1971; CNRS, Thiais, Paris, 1973; Calgary, 1975; Mainz, 1979; Queen's, Kingston, Ont, 1983. Lectures: Frontiers, Case-Western Reserve Univ., USA, 1970; Nuffield, Canada, 1975; Quest, Queen's, Ont, 1983. Vice-Pres., Inst. of Science Technol., 1970–76; Member: Council, Chemical Soc., 1967–70 (Foundn Chm., Organic Reaction Mechanism Gp, 1973); Dalton Council, 1973–76; Perkin Council, 1980–83. *Publications:* (with P. Alexander) Wool—its physics and chemistry, 1954, 2nd edn 1960; Structure and Mechanism in Organophosphorus Chemistry, 1965; papers mainly in Jl of Chem. Soc., Helvetica Chimica Acta and Angewandte Chemie. *Address:* 37 Puckle Lane, Canterbury, Kent CT1 3LA. *T:* (01227) 761340. *Club:* Athenæum.

HUDSON, Thomas Charles, CBE 1975; Chairman, ICL Ltd, 1972–80; Chartered Accountant (Canadian); *b* Sidcup, Kent, 23 Jan. 1915; British parents; *m* 1st, 1944, Lois Alma Hudson (marr. diss. 1973); two *s* one *d*; 2nd, 1986, Susan Gillian van Kan (marr. diss. 2004). *Educ:* Middleton High Sch., Nova Scotia. With Nightingale, Hayman & Co., Chartered Accountants, 1935–40. Served War, Royal Canadian Navy, Lieut, 1940–45. IBM Canada, as Sales Rep., 1946–51 (transf. to IBM, UK, as Sales Manager, 1951, and Managing Dir, 1954–65). Plessey Company: Financial Dir, 1967; Dir, 1969–76; Dir, ICL, 1968. Councillor for Enfield, GLC, 1970–73. *Recreations:* tennis, ski-ing, gardening. *Address:* Hele Farm, North Bovey, Devon TQ13 8RW. *T:* (01647) 440249. *Club:* Carlton.

HUDSON-BENDERSKY, Pamela May, CBE 1988; JP; Regional Nursing Director, North West Thames Regional Health Authority, 1985–88, retired; *b* 1 June 1931; *d* of late Leonard Joshua Hudson and of Mabel Ellen Hudson (now Baker); *m* 1987, David Bendersky, NY State and Kansas City. *Educ:* South West Essex High School. SRN. Nursing Officer, Charing Cross Hosp., 1966–67; Matron, Fulham Hosp., 1967–70; Principal Regl Nursing Officer, SE Thames RHB, 1970–73; Area Nursing Officer, Lambeth, Southwark and Lewisham AHA(T), 1973–82; Regional Nursing Officer, NW Thames RHA, 1982–85. Member, Alcohol Education and Research Council, 1982–87. JP: Inner London SE Div., 1983–88; N Glos (formerly Cheltenham) Petty Sessional Div., 1989–2001 (Chm., 1998–2001). *Publications:* contribs to nursing profession jls. *Recreations:* embroidery, theatre, gardening. *Address:* Uluru, 13 Northcot Lane, Draycott, near Moreton-in-Marsh, Glos GL56 9LR. *T:* (01386) 700142.

HUDSON DAVIES, (Gwilym) Ednyfed; *see* Davies.

HUDSON-WILKIN, Rev. Rose Josephine; Vicar, Holy Trinity, Dalston and All Saints, Haggerston, since 1998; Chaplain to the Queen, since 2008; *b* 19 Jan. 1961; *m* 1983, Rev. Kenneth Wilkin; one *s* two *d. Educ:* Montego Bay High Sch.; Church Army Coll.; W Midlands Ministerial Trng Course; Birmingham Univ. (BPhil Ed 2000). Lay Trng Officer, Anglican Dio. Jamaica, 1982; ordained deacon, 1991, priest, 1994; Curate, St Matthew, Wolverhampton, 1991–94; Priest, Good Shepherd, W Bromwich, 1995–98; Officer for Black Anglican Concerns, Lichfield Dio., 1995–98. Mem., Broadcasting Standards Commn, 1998–2003. Member: Gen. Synod of C of E, 1995–98, 2005– (Chm., Cttee for Minority Ethnic Anglican Concerns, 1999–); Theol Bd, WCC, 1996–98; Chm., Worldwide Cttee, SPCK, 1998–2004. *Recreations:* theatre, cooking, entertaining, tennis. *Address:* The Vicarage, Livermere Road, E8 4EZ.

HUEBNER, Michael Denis, CB 1994; Director General, Judicial Group, and Secretary of Commissions, Lord Chancellor's Department, 1998–2000; Deputy Clerk of the Crown in Chancery, 1993–2000; *b* 3 Sept. 1941; *s* of late Dr Denis William Huebner and Rene Huebner (*née* Jackson); *m* 1965, Wendy Ann, *d* of Brig. Peter Crosthwaite; one *s* one *d. Educ:* Rugby Sch.; St John's Coll., Oxford (BA Modern History). Called to the Bar, Gray's Inn, 1965, Bencher, 1994; Master of the House, 2001–03. Lord Chancellor's Department, 1966–68; Law Officers' Dept, 1968–70; rejoined Lord Chancellor's Dept, 1970: Asst Solicitor, 1978; Under Sec., Circuit Administrator, NE Circuit, 1985–88; Prin. Estabt and Finance Officer, 1988–89; Dep. Sec., Judicial Appts, 1989; Sec. of Commns, 1989–91; Hd of Law and Policy Gps, 1991–93; Head, 1993–95, Chief Exec., 1995–98, Court Service. Pres., Electricity Arbitration Assoc., 2002–. Trustee, St Luke's Community Trust, 2000–07. Liveryman, Clockmakers' Co., 2003–. *Publications:* brief guide to Ormesby Hall (Nat. Trust); contrib. (jtly) Courts, Halsbury's Laws of England, 4th edn 1975; legal articles in New Law Jl. *Recreations:* looking at pictures, architecture, theatre going. *Club:* Athenæum.

HUFFINLEY, Beryl; Vice-President and Vice-Chair, Labour Action for Peace, since 2005 (Chair, 1987–2005); formerly: President, National Assembly of Women; Vice-President, British Peace Assembly; *b* 22 Aug. 1926; *d* of Wilfred and Ivey Sharpe; *m* 1948, Ronald Brown Huffinley. Secretary: Leeds Trades Council, 1966; Yorkshire and Humberside TUC Regional Council, 1974. Chairman: Leeds and York Dist Cttee, T&GWU, 1974; Regional Cttee, T&GWU No 9 Region, 1972. Member: Regional Econ. Planning Council (Yorkshire and Humberside), 1975–79; Leeds AHA, 1977; Press Council, 1978–84; Leeds CC Peace-Link Gp. Trustee Yeadon Trade Council Club. *Address:* Cornerways, 29 South View, Menston, Ilkley, West Yorks LS29 6JX. *T:* (01943) 875115. *Club:* Trades Council (Leeds).

HUFTON, Dame Olwen, DBE 2004; PhD; FBA 1993; Professor of History, University of Oxford, 1997–2003 (Leverhulme Personal Research Professor, 1997–2002); Senior Research Fellow, Merton College, Oxford, 1997–2003, now Fellow Emeritus; *d* of Joseph Hufton and Caroline Hufton; *m* 1965, Brian Taunton Murphy; two *d. Educ:* Hulme Grammar Sch., Oldham; Royal Holloway Coll., Univ. of London (BA 1959; Hon. Fellow, 2000); UCL (PhD 1962; Hon. Fellow, 1999); DLitt Reading, 1999. Lectr, Univ. of Leicester, 1963–66; Reading University: Lectr, then Reader, 1966–75; Prof. of Modern Hist., 1975–88; Vis. Fellow, All Souls Coll., Oxford, 1986–87; Prof. of Modern Hist. and Women's Studies, Harvard Univ., 1987–91; Prof. of History, Eur. Univ. Inst., Florence, 1991–97. *Publications:* Bayeux in the Late Eighteenth Century, 1967; The Poor of Eighteenth Century France, 1974; Europe, Privilege and Protest 1730–1789, 1980, 2nd edn 2001; Women and the Limits of Citizenship in the French Revolution, 1992; The Prospect before Her: a history of women in Western Europe, vol. 1, 1500–1800, 1995; articles in Past and Present, Eur. Studies Rev., and French Hist. Studies. *Address:* 40 Shinfield Road, Reading, Berks RG2 7BW. *T:* (0118) 987 1514.

HUGGINS, family name of **Viscount Malvern**.

HUGGINS, Sir Alan (Armstrong), Kt 1980; Vice-President, Court of Appeal, Hong Kong, 1980–87; *b* 15 May 1921; *yr s* of late William Armstrong Huggins and Dare (*née* Copping); *m* 1st, 1950, Catherine Davidson (marr. diss.), *d* of late David Dick; two *s* one *d*; 2nd, 1985, Elizabeth Low (*d* 2007), *d* of late Christopher William Lumley Dodd, MRCS, LRCP. *Educ:* Radley Coll.; Sidney Sussex Coll., Cambridge (MA). TARO (Special List), 1940–48 (Actg Major); Admiralty, 1941–46. Called to Bar, Lincoln's Inn, 1947. Legal Associate Mem., TPI, 1949–70. Resident Magistrate, Uganda, 1951–53; Stipendiary Magistrate, Hong Kong, 1953–58; District Judge, Hong Kong, 1958–65; Chm., Justice (Hong Kong Br.), 1965–68; Judicial Comr, State of Brunei, 1966–2000 (Pres., Court of Appeal, 2000–02); Judge of Supreme Court, Hong Kong, 1965–76; Justice of Appeal, Hong Kong, 1976–80; Justice of Appeal: Gibraltar, 1988–96; St Helena, 1988–97; British Antarctica, 1988–2002 (Pres., 2000–02); Falkland Is, 1988–2002 (Pres., 1991–2002); Bermuda, 1989–2000; British Indian Ocean Territory, 1991–2002 (Pres.). Mem., Ct of Final Appeal, HKSAR, China, 1997–2003. Hon. Lectr, Hong Kong Univ., 1979–87. Chm., Adv. Cttee on Legal Educn, 1972–87. Diocesan Reader, Dio. of Hong Kong and Macao, 1954–87; Reader, Dio. of Exeter, 1988–. Past Pres., YMCAs of Hong Kong. Hon. Life Governor, Brit. and For. Bible Soc; Hon. Life Mem., Amer. Bible Soc. Liveryman, Leathersellers' Company, 1942–91. *Recreations:* forestry, boating, archery, amateur theatre, tapestry. *Address:* Widdicombe Lodge, Widdicombe, Kingsbridge, Devon TQ7 2EF. *T:* (01548) 580727. *Club:* Royal Over-Seas League.

HUGGINS, Rt Rev. Philip James; an Assistant Bishop, Diocese of Melbourne (Bishop of the North & West Region (formerly Bishop of the Northern Region)), since 2004; *b* 16 Oct. 1948; *s* of Alf Huggins and Mary Nutt; *m* 1976, Elizabeth Cuming; three *s. Educ:* Monash Univ. (BEcon, Grad. Dip. Welfare Admin., MA). Teaching Fellow, Univ. of New England, 1971–74; ordained priest, 1977; worked in parishes, Dio. of Bendigo, 1977–80; Industrial Chaplain, dio. Melbourne, 1980–83; Univ. Chaplain, Monash Univ., 1983–89; Exec. Officer, Archbishop of Melbourne's Internat. Develt Fund, 1990–91; Rector of Williamstown, 1991–95; Archdeacon of Essendon, 1994–95; Regl Bishop, Dio. of Perth, 1995–98; Bishop of Grafton, NSW, 1998–2003; Parish Priest, St Stephen's Anglican Church, Richmond, Vic, 2003–04. ChLJ 1997. *Recreations:* varied sports, poetry, the arts. *Address:* The Anglican Centre, 209 Flinders Lane, Melbourne, Vic 3000, Australia.

HUGH-JONES, Sir Wynn Normington, (Sir Hugh Jones), Kt 1984; LVO 1961; Joint Hon. Treasurer, Liberal Party, 1984–87; *b* 1 Nov. 1923; *s* of Huw Hugh-Jones and May Normington; *m* 1st, 1958, Ann (*née* Purkiss) (marr. diss. 1987); one *s* two *d*; 2nd, 1987, Oswynne (*née* Buchanan). *Educ:* Ludlow; Selwyn Coll., Cambridge (Scholar; MA). Served in RAF, 1943–46. Entered Foreign Service (now Diplomatic Service), 1947; Foreign Office, 1947–49; Jedda, 1949–52; Paris, 1952–56; FO, 1956–59; Chargé d'Affaires, Conakry, 1959–60; Head of Chancery, Rome, 1960–64; FO, 1964–66; Counsellor, 1964; Consul, Elizabethville (later Lubumbashi), 1966–68; Counsellor and Head of Chancery, Ottawa, 1968–70; FCO, 1971, attached Lord President's Office, Cabinet Office, 1972–73; Director-Gen., ESU, 1973–77; Sec.-Gen., Liberal Party, 1977–83. A Vice-Chm., European-Atlantic Gp, 1985–92; Vice-Pres., Lib. Internat. British Gp, 1995–98 (Patron, 1998–). Chm., Avebury in Danger, 1988–89. Gov., Queen Elizabeth Foundn for Disabled People, 1985–2001; Trustee, Wilts Community Foundn, 1991–93. FCMI. *Publications:* Diplomacy to Politics by Way of the Jungle, 2002; Campaigning Face to Face, 2007. *Recreations:* golf, gardening. *Address:* Fosse House, Avebury, Wilts SN8 1RF. *Clubs:* English-Speaking Union; N Wilts Golf.

HUGH SMITH, Sir Andrew (Colin), Kt 1992; Chairman, London Stock Exchange (formerly International Stock Exchange), 1988–94 (Member, 1970, Member of Council, 1981–91); Chairman, Barloworld (formerly Barlow International) Plc, 2000–02; *b* 6 Sept. 1931; *s* of late Lt-Comdr Colin Hugh Smith and Hon. Mrs C. Hugh Smith; *m* 1964, Venetia, *d* of Lt-Col Peter Flower; two *s. Educ:* Ampleforth; Trinity Coll., Cambridge (BA). Called to Bar, Inner Temple, 1956; Hon. Bencher, 1995. Courtaulds Ltd, 1960–68; with Capel-Cure Carden (later Capel-Cure Myers), 1968–85; ANZ Merchant Bank, 1985–88. Chairman: Holland & Holland, 1987–95; Penna plc, then Penna Consulting Plc, 1995–2001; Eur. Adv. Bd, Accenture (formerly Andersen Consulting), 1995–2001; Director: Matheson Lloyds Investment Trust, 1994–97; Barloworld (formerly J. Bibby & Sons, then Barlow Internat.), 1997–2002; Barlow Ltd, 1998–2002. Vice-Chm., GBDA, 1990–2001; Hon. Treas., Malcolm Sargent Cancer Fund for Children, 1992–2002.

Recreations: gardening, shooting, fishing, reading. *Clubs:* Brooks's, Pratt's.
See also H. O. Hugh Smith.

HUGH SMITH, Col Henry Owen, LVO 1976; Defence Adviser to British High Commissioner, Nairobi, 1987–90; *b* 19 June 1937; *s* of Lt-Comdr Colin Hugh Smith and late Hon. Mrs C. Hugh Smith. *Educ:* Ampleforth; Magdalene Coll., Cambridge. BA Hons 1961. Commnd Royal Horse Guards, 1957; Blues and Royals, 1969; psc 1969; served Cyprus and Northern Ireland (wounded); Equerry in Waiting to The Duke of Edinburgh, 1974–76; CO The Blues and Royals, 1978–80; GSO1, MoD, 1980–87. Chm., BLESMA, 1996–. *Recreation:* sailing. *Clubs:* Boodle's, Pratt's; Royal Yacht Squadron, Royal Cruising.
See also Sir A. C. Hugh Smith.

HUGHES, family name of **Baron Hughes of Woodside**.

HUGHES OF WOODSIDE, Baron *cr* 1997 (Life Peer), of Woodside in the City of Aberdeen; **Robert Hughes;** *b* Pittenweem, Fife, 3 Jan. 1932; *m* 1957, Ina Margaret Miller; two *s* three *d. Educ:* Robert Gordon's Coll., Aberdeen; Benoni High Sch., Transvaal; Pietermaritzburg Tech. Coll., Natal. Emigrated S Africa, 1947, returned UK, 1954. Engrg apprentice, S African Rubber Co., Natal; Chief Draughtsman, C. F. Wilson & Co. (1932) Ltd, Aberdeen, until 1970. Mem., Aberdeen Town Council, 1962–70; Convener: Health and Welfare Cttee, 1963–68; Social Work Cttee, 1969–70. Mem., AMICUS (formerly AEU, then AEEU), 1952–. Contested (Lab) North Angus and Mearns, 1959; MP (Lab) Aberdeen North, 1970–97. Member: Standing Cttee on Immigration Bill, 1971; Select Cttee, Scottish Affairs, 1971 and 1992–97; introd. Divorce (Scotland) Bill 1971 (failed owing to lack of time); Parly Under-Sec. of State, Scottish Office, 1974–75; sponsored (as Private Member's Bill) Rating (Disabled Persons) Act 1978; Principal Opposition Spokesman: on agriculture, 1983–84; on transport, 1985–88 (Jun. Opp. Spokesman, 1981–83); Mem., PLP Shadow Cabinet, 1985–88. Chm., Aberdeen City Labour Party, 1961–69. Vice-Chm., Tribune Gp, 1984–85. Founder Mem. and Aberdeen Chm., Campaign for Nuclear Disarmament; Vice-Chm., 1975–76, Chm., 1976–94, Anti-Apartheid Movement; Member: GMC, 1976–79; Movement for Colonial Freedom, 1955 (Chm. Southern Africa Cttee); Scottish Poverty Action Group; Aberdeen Trades Council and Exec. Cttee, 1957–69; Labour Party League of Youth, 1954–57; Chm., 1994–99, Hon. Pres., 1999–, Action for Southern Africa; Hon. Pres., Mozambique Angola Cttee, 2001–; Trustee, Canon Collins Educn Trust for Southern Africa, 1997–2007. Grand Companion, Order of Oliver Tambo (SA), 2004. *Recreation:* golf. *Address:* House of Lords, SW1A 0PW.

HUGHES, Alan; Managing Director, Whitechapel Bell Foundry Ltd (established 1570), since 1982; *b* 25 Aug. 1948; *s* of William A. Hughes and Florence I. Hughes; *m* 1985, Kathryn Smith; two *d. Educ:* Christ's Hosp. Church bell founder, 1966–. Freeman, City of London, 1984; Liveryman, Founders' Co., 2000. *Address:* Whitechapel Bell Foundry Ltd, 32 & 34 Whitechapel Road, E1 1DY.

HUGHES, Prof. Alan; Margaret Thatcher Professor of Enterprise Studies, Judge Business School (formerly Judge Institute of Management Studies), since 1999, and Director, Centre for Business Research, since 1994, University of Cambridge; Fellow, Sidney Sussex College, Cambridge, since 1973; *b* 1 Aug. 1946; *s* of Benjamin Redshaw Hughes and Lilias Hughes; *m* 1968, Jean Braddock; two *s* one *d. Educ:* King's Coll., Cambridge (BA Econs 1968). Sen. Economic Asst, NEDO, 1971–73; University of Cambridge: Univ. Asst Lectr, then Univ. Lectr in Econs, 1973–94; Chm., Faculty Bd of Econs and Pols, 1983–88; Dir, ESRC Small Business Res. Centre, Dept of Applied Econs, 1989–93; Dir of Res., Judge Inst. of Mgt Studies, 2001–04; Dir, Nat. Competitiveness Network Prog., Cambridge-MIT Inst., 2000–03. Member: Commn on Public Policy and British Business, 1995–96; DfES Expert Panel on Educn, Learning and Lifelong Skills, 2000–05; Council for Sci. and Technol., 2004–; Special Advr to UK Govt Interdeptl Wkg Party on Assessing the Impact of Business Support Policies, 1997–2000; Specialist Advr to H of L Select Cttee on EU with ref. to EU Green Paper on Entrepreneurship, 2003. Consultant to Dutch Min. of Econ. Affairs on support policy for high technol. business start-ups, 2003. *Publications:* (ed with D. J. Storey) Finance and the Small Firm, 1994; (ed with S. Deakin) Enterprise and Community: new directions in corporate governance, 1997; edited with A. D. Cosh: The Changing State of British Enterprise: growth, innovation and competitive advantage in SMEs 1986–1995, 1996; Takeovers, 3 vols, 1998; Enterprise Britain: growth innovation and public policy in the small and medium sized enterprise sector 1994–1997, 1998; British Enterprise in Transition: growth innovation and public policy in the small and medium sized enterprise sector 1994–1999, 2000; Enterprise Challenge: policy and performance in the British SME Sector 1999–2002, 2003. *Recreations:* photography, walking, golf, gardening, watching football and Rugby. *Address:* Centre for Business Research, Top Floor, Judge Business School Building, Trumpington Street, Cambridge CB2 1AG. *T:* (01223) 765335, *Fax:* (01223) 765338; *e-mail:* a.hughes@cbr.cam.ac.uk.

HUGHES, Aneurin Rhys; Ambassador and Head of Delegation of European Commission to Australia and New Zealand, 1995–2002; *b* 11 Feb. 1937; *s* of William and Hilda Hughes; *m*; two *s*; *m* 2001, Lisbeth Lindbaeck. *Educ:* University College of Wales, Aberystwyth (BA; Fellow, 2002). President, National Union of Students, 1962–64. Research in S America, 1964–66; HM Diplomatic Service, 1967–73: served, Singapore and Rome; Commission of the European Communities, 1973–2002: Head of Division for Internal Coordination in Secretariat-General, 1973–77; Adviser to Dir. Gen. for Information, 1977–80; Chef de Cabinet to Mr Ivor Richard, Comr responsible for Employment, Social Affairs and Educn, 1981–85; Adviser to Dir Gen. for Information, and Chm., Selection Bd for Candidates from Spain and Portugal, 1985–87; Amb. and Head of Delegn in Norway, 1987–95. *Publication:* Billy Hughes - Founding Father of the Australian Labour Party, 2005. *Recreations:* golf, music.

HUGHES, Rt Hon. Sir Anthony (Philip Gilson), Kt 1997; PC 2006; **Rt Hon. Lord Justice Hughes;** a Lord Justice of Appeal, since 2006; *b* 11 Aug. 1948; *s* of late Patrick and Patricia Hughes; *m* 1972, Susan Elizabeth March; one *s* one *d. Educ:* Tettenhall Coll., Staffs; Van Mildert Coll., Durham (BA 1969). Sometime Lectr, Durham Univ. and QMC. Called to the Bar, Inner Temple, 1970, Bencher, 1997; in practice at the Bar, 1971–97; a Recorder, 1988–97; QC 1990; a Judge of the High Court of Justice, Family Div., 1997–2003, QBD, 2004–06. Presiding Judge, Midland (formerly Midland and Oxford) Circuit, 2000–03. *Recreations:* garden labouring and mechanics, bellringing. *Address:* Royal Courts of Justice, Strand, WC2A 2LL. *Clubs:* Athenæum; Worcester Rowing.

HUGHES, Antony; *see* Hughes, M. A.

HUGHES, Dr Antony Elwyn; consultant, since 1996; Director, Engineering and Science, and Deputy Chief Executive, Engineering and Physical Sciences Research Council, 1994–96; *b* 9 Sept. 1941; *s* of Ifor Elwyn Hughes and Anna Betty Hughes (*née* Ambler); *m* 1963, Margaret Mary Lewis; one *s* two *d* (and one *s* decd). *Educ:* Newport High Sch., Gwent; Jesus Coll., Oxford (MA; DPhil). CPhys; FInstP. Harkness Fellow, Cornell Univ., 1967–69. United Kingdom Atomic Energy Authority, Atomic Energy Research Establishment (Harwell): Scientific Officer, 1963–67; Sen. Scientific Officer, 1969–72; Principal Scientific Officer, 1972–75; Leader: Defects in Solids Gp, 1973; Solid State Sciences Gp, 1978; Individual Merit Appointment, 1975–81; Sen. Personal Appointment, 1981–83; Head, Materials Physics Div., 1983–86; Dir, Underlying Res. and Non-Nuclear Energy Res., 1986–87; Authority Chief Scientist and Dir, Nuclear Res., 1987–88. Science and Engineering Research Council: Dir, Labs, 1988–91; Dir, Progs, and Dep. Chm., 1991–93; acting Chief Exec., 1993–94. Mem., NI Higher Educn Council, 1993–2001. Member Council: Royal Instn of GB, 1995–98; Careers Res. and Adv. Centre, 1994–2007. *Publications:* Real Solids and Radiation, 1975; (ed) Defects and their Structure in Non-Metallic Solids, 1976; review articles in Contemporary Physics, Advances in Physics, Jl of Materials Science, Jl of Nuclear Materials, Reports on Progress in Physics. *Recreations:* walking, watching Rugby and cricket, playing the trumpet, gardening. *Address:* Kingswood, King's Lane, Harwell, Didcot, Oxfordshire OX11 0EJ. *T:* (01235) 835301.

HUGHES, Rt Hon. Beverley (June); PC 2004; MP (Lab) Stretford and Urmston, since 1997; Minister of State, Department for Children, Schools and Families (formerly Department for Education and Skills), since 2005, and Minister for the North West, since 2007; *b* 30 March 1950; *d* of Norman Hughes and Doris Hughes (*née* Gillard); *m* 1973, Thomas K. McDonald; one *s* two *d. Educ:* Manchester Univ. (BSc Hons, MSc); Liverpool Univ. (DSA, DASS). Merseyside Probation Service, 1973; Manchester University: Res. Fellow, 1976; Lectr, Sen. Lectr and Head of Dept of Social Policy and Social Work, 1981–97. Mem. (Lab), Trafford MBC, 1986–97 (Leader, 1995–97). Parly Under-Sec. of State, DETR, 1999–2001, Home Office, 2001–02; Minister of State, Home Office, 2002–04. *Publication:* Community Care and Older People, 1995. *Recreations:* jazz, walking, family. *Address:* House of Commons, SW1A 0AA. *T:* (020) 7219 3000.

HUGHES, Catherine Eva, CMG 1984; HM Diplomatic Service, retired; Principal, Somerville College, Oxford, 1989–96; *b* 24 Sept. 1933; *d* of late Edmund Ernest Pestell and Isabella Cummine Sangster; *m* 1991, Dr (John) Trevor Hughes. *Educ:* Leeds Girls' High Sch.; St Hilda's Coll., Oxford (MA). FO, 1956; Third Sec., The Hague, 1958; Second Sec., Bangkok, 1961; FO, 1964; First Sec., UK Delegn to OECD, Paris, 1969; FCO, 1971; St Antony's Coll., Oxford, 1974; Counsellor, East Berlin, 1975–78; Cabinet Office, 1978–80; Diplomatic Service Inspector, 1980–82; Minister (Economic), Bonn, 1983–87; Asst Under-Sec. (Public Depts), FCO, 1987–89. *Address:* 2 Bishop Kirk Place, Oxford OX2 7HJ. *Club:* Reform.
See also J. E. Pestell.

HUGHES, Hon. Claudia Madeleine; *see* Ackner, Hon. C. M.

HUGHES, Dafydd Lloyd; His Honour Judge Dafydd Hughes; a Circuit Judge, since 2004; Deputy Designated Family Judge, Caernarfon and Rhyl, since 2007; *b* 3 June 1947; *s* of Rev. Elwyn Morris Hughes and Gwen Mai Hughes (*née* Evans); *m* 1971, Ann Tegwen Davies; one *s* two *d. Educ:* Grove Park Grammar Sch. for Boys, Wrexham; University Coll. London (LLB Hons). Admitted solicitor, 1971; Asst Solicitor and Partner, Edmund Pickles & Upton, Solicitors, Wrexham, 1971–90; Co. Court Registrar, later Dist Judge, 1990–2004; Asst Recorder, 1994–98; Recorder, 1998–2004. Mem., Ministerial Steering Gp on Childcare Proceedings Rev., Welsh Assembly Govt, 2006–. Mem., Adv. Cttee, CAFCASS Cymru, 2006–. *Recreations:* theatre, museums and galleries, travel, cookery, developing and refining grandparenting skills. *Address:* Caernarfon County Court, Ffordd Llanberis, Caernarfon, Gwynedd LL55 2DF. *T:* (01286) 684600.

HUGHES, (David Evan) Peter, MA; part-time teacher, Westminster School, since 1994; *b* 27 April 1932; *s* of late Evan Gwilliam Forrest-Hughes, OBE; *m* 1956, Iris (*née* Jenkins); one *s* one *d* (and one *d* decd). *Educ:* St Paul's Sch.; St John's Coll., Oxford (Gibbs Schol. in Chemistry; MA). National Service, 5 RHA, 1954. Assistant Master, Shrewsbury School, 1956; Head of Chemistry, 1958, Science, 1965; Nuffield Foundation, 1967–68; Second Master, Shrewsbury Sch., 1972; Headmaster, St Peter's Sch., York, 1980–84; Head of Science, Westminster Sch., 1984–89; Dir, Understanding Science Project, and Leverhulme Res. Fellow, Imperial Coll. and Westminster Sch., 1989–94. Chief Examr, Univ. of Cambridge Local Exam. Syndicate, 1968–2006. Chm., Friends' Cttee, Imperial Coll., 1992–94. *Publications:* Advanced Theoretical Chemistry (with M. J. Maloney), 1964; Chemical Energetics, 1967; (ed) Awareness of Science, 4 vols, 1993–94; (with P. F. Cann) Chemistry for Advanced Level, 2002; contrib. Oxford DNB; articles in professional jls. *Recreations:* music, bridge, hill-walking. *Address:* Flat 1, 63 Millbank, SW1P 4RW.

HUGHES, David Glyn; National Agent, 1979–88, Senior National Officer, 1986–88, the Labour Party; *b* 1 March 1928; *s* of Richard and Miriam Hughes; *m* 1958, Mary Atkinson (*d* 2002); one *d. Educ:* Darwin St Secondary Modern Sch. Apprentice, later fitter and turner, 1944–52; Labour Party Agent: Northwich, Bolton, Tonbridge, Portsmouth, 1952–69; Asst Regional Organiser, 1969–75, Regional Organiser, 1975–79, Northern Region. *Recreations:* gardening, walking. *Address:* Pembury, 7 Hayes Mead Road, Hayes, Bromley, Kent BR2 7HR. *T:* (020) 8462 1659.

HUGHES, Prof. David John, CEng, FREng, FIMechE; Managing Director, Business Innovation Group LLP, since 2006; Professor of Engineering Management, City University, since 2006; *b* 5 May 1947; *m* 1970, Dawn Anne Newman; two *d. Educ:* Royal Grammar Sch., High Wycombe; Aston Univ. (MSc 1970). CEng 1975, FREng 2001; FIMechE 1996; MIEEE 2000; CDir 2007. Hd, Electrical/Electronic Systems, Ford Motor Co., 1970–91; Director: Advanced Vehicle Systems, Lucas plc, 1991–97; Technol. Planning, GEC plc, 1997–99; Exec. Vice Pres., Marconi plc, 1999–2001; Dir, Special Projects, BAE Systems, 2002; Dir Gen., Innovation Gp, and Chief Scientific Advr, DTI, 2002–06. Member: Technol. and Innovation Cttee, CBI, 1999–2003; EPSRC, 2003–06; Innovation and Engagement Bd, Cardiff Univ., 2005–. *Publications:* articles for various jls and mgt confs. *Recreations:* walking, 20th century British art, antique metalware, African tribal art. *Address:* School of Engineering and Mathematical Sciences, City University, Northampton Square, EC1V 0HB.

HUGHES, His Honour David Morgan; a Circuit Judge, 1972–98; *b* 20 Jan. 1926; *s* of late Rev. John Edward Hughes and Mrs Margaret Ellen Hughes; *m* 1956, Elizabeth Jane Roberts; one *s* two *d. Educ:* Beaumaris Grammar Sch.; LSE (LLB). Army, 1944–48: Captain, Royal Welch Fusiliers; attached 2nd Bn The Welch Regt; Burma, 1945–47. London Univ., 1948–51; Rockefeller Foundn Fellowship in Internat. Air Law, McGill Univ., 1951–52; called to Bar, Middle Temple, 1953; practised Wales and Chester Circuit; Dep. Chm., Caernarvonshire QS, 1970–71; a Recorder, Jan.-Nov. 1972; Dep. Chm., Agricultural Lands Tribunal, 1972; Mem., Mental Health Review Tribunal, 1989–98. Pres., Council, HM Circuit Judges for England and Wales, 1995. *Recreations:* tennis, cricket, gardening. *Address:* Bryn, Kelsall, Cheshire CW6 0PA. *T:* (01829) 751349.

HUGHES, David Richard; Chief Leader Writer, Daily Telegraph, since 2006; *b* 3 April 1951; *s* of John Arfon Hughes and Lilian Elvira Hughes (*née* Jones); *m* 1973, Christine O'Brien; two *s. Educ:* Cowbridge Grammar Sch.; Univ. of Leicester (BA Hons Hist.). Reporter, Merthyr Express, 1973–76; Leader Writer, 1976–79, Political Corresp.,

1979–84, Western Mail; Political Reporter, Daily Mail, 1984–86; Political Corresp., 1986–89, Chief Political Corresp., 1989–92, Sunday Times; Editor, Western Mail, 1992–94; Political Ed., 1994–2005, Leader Writer, 2005–06, Daily Mail. *Recreations:* Rugby, music, family, surfing. *Address:* 7 Southfield Gardens, Strawberry Hill, Twickenham TW1 4SZ. *T:* (020) 8892 5726.

HUGHES, Dr David Treharne Dillon, FRCP; Consultant Physician, Royal London (formerly London) Hospital, 1970–96; Director, Respiratory Medicine, Royal Hospitals NHS Trust, 1994–96; Head, Department of Clinical Investigation, Wellcome Research Laboratories, 1978–93; *b* 31 Oct. 1931; *s* of Maj.-Gen. W. D. Hughes, CB, CBE; *m* 1959, Gloria Anna Bailey; one *s* two *d. Educ:* Cheltenham Coll.; Trinity Coll., Oxford (BSc, MA); London Hosp. Medical Coll. (BM BCh); RPMS. MRCP 1959, FRCP 1972. Jun. hosp. posts, London Hosp., 1957–59; Capt. RAMC, 1959–61 (jun. med. specialist, BMH Hong Kong); Res. Fellow, Univ. of Calif, 1963–64; jun. hosp. appts, London Hosp., 1964–70. Mem., GMC, 1993–96. Past President: Internat. Soc. Internal Medicine; Hunterian Soc. Chm., Bd of Govs, Moving Theatre Trust, 1994–2000. Master, Soc. of Apothecaries, 1992–93. *Publications:* Tropical Health Science, 1967; Human Biology and Hygiene, 1969; Lung Function for the Clinician, 1981; numerous scientific papers on respiratory function and chest disease. *Recreations:* cricket, rowing, horse racing, theatre. *Address:* 94 Overbury Avenue, Beckenham, Kent BR3 6PY. *T:* (020) 8650 3983; Littleport Farm, Sedgeford, Norfolk PE36 5LR. *T:* (01485) 570955. *Clubs:* Savage, Garrick; Leander (Henley-on-Thames).

HUGHES, Dr (Edgar) John; HM Diplomatic Service; Ambassador to Argentina, 2004–08; *b* 27 July 1947; *s* of William Thomas Hughes and Martha Hughes (*née* Riggs); *m* 1982, Lynne Evans; two *s. Educ:* Lewis Sch., Pengam, Wales; LSE (BSc Econ 1969); Lehigh Univ., USA (MA 1970); Pembroke Coll., Cambridge (Univ. of Cambridge Sara Norton Res. Prize in Amer. Hist., 1972; PhD 1973). FCO, 1973–79; on secondment to Cabinet Office, 1979–81; First Sec., UK Delegn to CSCE, Madrid, 1981–82; FCO, 1982–83; First Sec. and Head of Chancery, Santiago, 1983–85, First Sec. (Inf.), Washington, 1985–89; Counsellor and Hd of Aviation and Maritime Dept, FCO 1990–93; Dep. Hd of Mission, Norway, 1993–97 ; Change Manager, FCO, 1997–99; on secondment to BAE Systems, 1999–2000; Ambassador to Venezuela, 2000–03; on secondment to Shell, 2003–04. *Publications:* The Historian as Diplomat (with P. A. Reynolds), 1976; articles in internat. affairs jls. *Recreations:* running, ski-ing, tennis, watching Rugby, reading. *Club:* Rhymney Rugby Football.

HUGHES, Edmwnd Goronwy M.; *see* Moelwyn-Hughes.

HUGHES, Francine Elizabeth; *see* Stock, F. E.

HUGHES, Prof. George Morgan; Professor of Zoology, Bristol University, 1965–85, now Emeritus; *b* 17 March 1925; *s* of James Williams Hughes and Edith May Hughes; *m* 1954, Jean Rosemary, *d* of Rowland Wynne Frazier and Jessie Frazier; two *s* one *d. Educ:* Liverpool Collegiate Sch.; King's Coll., Cambridge (Scholar; Martin Thackeray Studentship, 1946–48; MA, PhD, ScD); Frank Smart Prize, Cambridge Univ., 1946. Cambridge Univ. Demonstrator, 1950–55, Lectr, 1955–65; successively Bye-Fellow, Research Fellow and Fellow of Magdalene Coll., Cambridge, 1949–65; University of Bristol: Head of Dept of Zoology, 1965–70; Head of Res. Unit for Comparative Animal Respiration, 1970–90. Research Fellow, California Inst. of Technology, 1958–59; Visiting Lectr in Physiology, State Univ. of New York, at Buffalo, 1964; Visiting Professor: Duke Univ., 1969; Japan Society for the Promotion of Science, Kochi, Kyoto, Kyushu and Hokkaido Univs, 1974; Univ. of Regensburg, 1977; Univs of Bhagalpur and Bretagne Occidentale, 1979; Kuwait, 1983; Nairobi, 1985. Invited Prof., Nat. Inst. of Physiolog. Sciences, Okazaki, 1980; Hon. Prof., Univ. of Wales Coll. of Cardiff, 1991–99. Mem., Internat. Cœlacanth Expdn, 1972. *Publications:* Comparative Physiology of Vertebrate Respiration, 1963; (jtly) Physiology of Mammals and other Vertebrates, 1965; (jtly) Air-breathing Fishes of India, 1992; (ed) several symposium vols; papers in Jl of Experimental Biology and other scientific jls, mainly on respiration of fishes. *Recreations:* travel, Welsh genealogy, photography; hockey for Cambridge Univ., 1945, and Wales, 1952–53. *Address:* 11 Lodge Drive, Long Ashton, Bristol BS41 9JF. *T:* (01275) 393402.

HUGHES, Very Rev. Geraint Morgan Hugh; Dean of Brecon, 1998–2000; *b* 21 Nov. 1934; *s* of late Ven. Hubert Hughes, Archdeacon of Gower, and late Blodwen Hughes; *m* 1959, Rosemary Criddle; one *s* one *d. Educ:* Brecon Grammar Sch.; Keble Coll., Oxford (BA 1958; MA 1963); St Michael's Coll., Llandaff. Nat. Service, RAF, 1953–55. Ordained deacon, 1959, priest, 1960; Curate: Gorseinon, 1959–63; Oystermouth, 1963–68; Rector: Llanbadarn Fawr Group, 1968–76; Llandrindod with Cefnllys, 1976–98; Canon of Brecon Cathedral, 1989–98; RD of Maelienydd, 1995–98. Chaplain, Mid and West Wales Fire Bde, 1996– (Supervisory Chaplain, 2002–); Mid Wales Regl Chaplain, SJAB, 2003–. Paul Harris Fellow, Rotary Club, 1991. OStJ 2004. *Recreations:* gardening, computing, sheep husbandry, wood turning. *Address:* Hafod, Cefnllys Lane, Penybont, Llandrindod Wells, Powys LD1 5SW. *T:* (01597) 851830.

HUGHES, Rev. Dr Gerard Joseph, SJ; Tutor in Philosophy, since 1998, Master, 1998–2006, Campion Hall, University of Oxford; *b* 6 June 1934; *s* of Henry B. Hughes and Margaret (*née* Barry). *Educ:* Campion Hall, Oxford (MA Greats 1962); Heythrop Coll. (STL 1967); Univ. of Michigan (PhD 1970). Entered Society of Jesus, 1951; ordained priest, 1967; Heythrop College, University of London: Lectr in Philosophy, 1970–98; Head, Dept of Philosophy, 1974–96; Vice-Principal, 1984–98. *Publications:* Authority in Morals, 1978; (ed) The Philosophical Assessment of Theology, 1987; The Nature of God, 1995; Aristotle on Ethics, 2001; Is God to Blame?, 2007. *Recreations:* classical music, gardening. *Address:* Campion Hall, Oxford OX1 1QS. *T:* (01865) 286111.

HUGHES, Glyn Tegai, MA, PhD; Warden of Gregynog, University of Wales, 1964–89; *b* 18 Jan. 1923; *s* of Rev. John Hughes and Keturah Hughes; *m* 1957, Margaret Vera Herbert (*d* 1996), Brisbane, Qld; two *s. Educ:* Newtown and Towyn County Sch.; Liverpool Institute; Manchester Grammar Sch.; Corpus Christi Coll., Cambridge (Schol., MA, PhD). Served War, Royal Welch Fusiliers, 1942–46 (Major). Lector in English, Univ. of Basel, 1951–53; Lectr in Comparative Literary Studies, Univ. of Manchester, 1953–64, and Tutor to Faculty of Arts, 1961–64. Contested (L) Denbigh Div., elections 1950, 1955 and 1959. Mem., Welsh Arts Council, 1967–76; Nat. Governor for Wales, BBC, and Chm., Broadcasting Council for Wales, 1971–79; Member: Bd, Channel Four Television Co., 1980–87; Welsh Fourth TV Channel Authy., 1981–87. Chm., Welsh Broadcasting Trust, 1988–96; Vice-Pres., N Wales Arts Assoc., 1977–94; Chm., Undeb Cymru Fydd, 1968–70. Fellow, Univ. of Wales Aberystwyth, 2000; Hon. Fellow, Univ. of Wales Bangor, 2004. Methodist local preacher, 1942–. *Publications:* Eichendorffs Taugenichts, 1961; Romantic German Literature, 1979; (ed) Life of Thomas Olivers, 1979; Williams Pantycelyn, 1983; (with David Esslemont) Gwasg Gregynog: a descriptive catalogue, 1990; Islwyn, 2003; articles in learned journals and Welsh language periodicals. *Recreation:* book-collecting. *Address:* Rhyd-y-gro, Tregynon, Newtown, Powys SY16 3PR. *T:* (01686) 650609.

HUGHES, Prof. Graham Robert Vivian, MD; FRCP; Professor of Medicine, King' College London, since 2005; Head, London Lupus Centre, London Bridge Hospital, sinc 2005; *b* 26 Nov. 1940; *s* of G. Arthur Hughes and Elizabeth Emily Hughes; *m* 1966 Monica Ann Austin; one *s* one *d. Educ:* Cardiff High Sch. for Boys; London Hosp. Med Coll. (MB BS 1967; MD 1973). Trng posts, London Hosp., 1967–69; Vis. Fellow Columbia Univ., NY, 1969–70; Sen. Registrar, Hammersmith Hosp., 1970–73 Consultant, Univ. Hosp. of WI, Kingston, Jamaica, 1974; Consultant, and Reader i Medicine, Hammersmith Hosp., 1975–85; Consultant, and Hd, Lupus Arthritis Res Unit, subseq. Lupus Unit, St Thomas' Hosp., 1985–2005. Ed., Lupus, 1991–; mem., edit bds of numerous jls. Consultant, RAF, 1985–. Life Pres., Lupus UK, 1985; Chm., Hughe Syndrome Foundn, 2001–. Dr *hc:* Marseilles, 2001; Barcelona, 2004. Rheumatolog World Prize, Internat. League against Rheumatism, 1993; Lifetime Achievement Award Internat. Soc. for Immunology, 2006; Master, Amer. Coll. of Rheumatol., 2006 *Publications:* Connective Tissue Diseases, 1977, 4th edn 1994; Modern Topics i Rheumatology, 1977; Clinics in Rheumatic Diseases: Systemic Lupus Erythematosus 1982; Lupus: a guide for patients, 1985; Lecture Notes in Rheumatology, 1986; Problem in the Rheumatic Diseases: lessons from patients, 1988; Phospholipid Binding Antibodie 1991; Autoimmune Connective Tissue Diseases, 1993; Antibodies to Endothelial Cell and Vascular Damage, 1993; Hughes Syndrome, 1998; Lupus: the facts, 2000; Hughe Syndrome: a patients' guide, 2001; contrib. numerous papers on lupus and related diseases *Recreations:* tennis, golf, sailing, piano (classical and jazz). *Address:* London Lupus Centre London Bridge Hospital, 27–29 Tooley Street, SE1 2PR. *T:* (020) 7234 2155.

HUGHES, (Harold) Paul; Director of Finance, BBC, 1971–84; Director, Lazard Selec Investment Trust Ltd, 1988–2001; *b* 16 Oct. 1926; *o s* of Edmund and Mabel Hughes; *n* 1955, Beryl Winifred Runacres; one *s* one *d. Educ:* Stand Grammar Sch., Whitefield, nea Manchester. Certified Accountant. Westminster Bank Ltd, 1942–45; Royal Marines an Royal Navy, 1945–49; Arthur Guinness Son & Co. Ltd, 1950–58; British Broadcasting Corporation: Sen. Accountant, 1958–61; Asst Chief Accountant, Finance, 1961–69; Chie Accountant, Television, 1969–71; Pension Fund Consultant, 1984–89; Chm., BBC Enterprises Ltd, 1979–82; Chm., Visnews Ltd, 1984–85; Chief Exec., BBC Pension Trus Ltd, 1987–89. Chm., Pan European Property Unit Trust, 1987–96; Director: Kleinwor Benson Farmland Trust (Managers) Ltd, 1976–89; Keystone Investment Co. PLC, late Mercury Keystone Investment Trust PLC, 1988–96. *Recreations:* opera, gardening *Address:* 26 Downside Road, Guildford, Surrey GU4 8PH. *T:* (01483) 569166.

HUGHES, (Harold) Victor, CBE 1989; FRAgS; Principal, Royal Agricultural College, Cirencester, 1978–90, Principal Emeritus 1990; *b* 2 Feb. 1926; *s* of Thomas Brindley Hughes and Hilda Hughes (*née* Williams). *Educ:* Tenby County Grammar Sch.; UCW, Aberystwyth (BSc). FRAgS 1980. Lectr, Glamorgan Training Centre, Pencoed, 1947–49; Crop Husbandry Adv. Officer, W Midland Province, Nat. Agricultural Adv. Service, 1950; Lectr in Agric., RAC, 1950–54; Vice Principal, Brooksby Agricultural Coll., Leics, 1954–60; Royal Agricultural College: Farms Dir and Principal Lectr in Farm Management, 1960–76; Vice Principal and Farms Dir, 1976–78. Hon. MRICS (Hon. ARICS 1984). FIAgrM 1992. *Publications:* articles in learned jls and agric. press. *Recreation:* shooting. *Address:* No 17 Quakers Row, Coates, Cirencester, Glos GL7 6JX.

HUGHES, Henry Andrew Carne M.; *see* Meyric Hughes.

HUGHES, Howard; World Managing Partner, Price Waterhouse, 1992–98; *b* 4 March 1938; *s* of Charles William Hughes and Ethel May Hughes (*née* Howard); *m* 1st, 1964, Joy Margaret Pilmore-Bedford (*d* 1984); two *s* one *d*; 2nd, 1988, Christine Margaret Miles, one *s. Educ:* Rydal School. FCA. Articled Bryce Hanmer & Co., Liverpool, 1955; joined Price Waterhouse, London, 1960: Partner, 1970; Dir, London Office, 1982; Managing Partner, UK, 1985–91; Member: World Bd, 1988–98; World Mgt Cttee, 1990–98. Auditor, Duchy of Cornwall, 1983–98. Mem., Agricl Wages Bd, 1990–99. Chairman: Royal London Soc. for the Blind, 2000–05 (Vice Pres., 2007–); British Heart Foundn, 2006– (Trustee, 1998–). Chairman: Govs, Dorton House Sch., 1998–2001; Utd Westminster Schs, 2002– (Trustee, 2000–); Governor: Westminster City Sch., 1998–; Emanuel Sch., 2002–; Sutton Valance Sch., 2002–. Liveryman, Chartered Accts' Co., 1991–. *Recreations:* golf, music. *Address:* Witham, Woodland Rise, Seal, Sevenoaks, Kent TN15 0HZ. *T:* (01732) 761161, *Fax:* (01732) 763553. *Clubs:* Carlton, MCC; Wildernesse Golf (Sevenoaks).

HUGHES, Iain; QC 1996; **His Honour Judge Iain Hughes;** a Circuit Judge, since 2002; Designated Civil Judge for Hampshire, Isle of Wight, Dorset and Wiltshire, since 2003; *b* 7 Dec. 1950; *s* of late John Sidney Mather and of Jessica Hamilton-Douglas; *m* 1978, Hon. Claudia Madeleine Ackner, *qv*; one *s* one *d* (and one *s* decd). *Educ:* Moseley Hall Grammar Sch., Cheadle; Univ. of Bristol (LLB). Called to the Bar, Inner Temple, 1974; Bencher, 2001. Asst Recorder, 1997–2000; Recorder, 2000–02. Chm., Professional Negligence Bar Assoc., 2000–01 (Vice-Chm., 1997–99). *Publication:* (ed) Jackson and Powell on Professional Negligence, 3rd edn 1992, 4th edn 1997, and annual supplements. *Recreations:* theatre, cinema, pottering in workshop. *Address:* c/o The Law Courts, Winchester SO23 9EL.

HUGHES, Ian Noel; HM Diplomatic Service; Ambassador to Guatemala, El Salvador and Honduras, 2006–09; *b* 5 Dec. 1951; *s* of Robert John Hughes and Sylvia Betty Hughes (*née* Lewis); *m* 1978, Tereasa June Tinguely; two *s* one *d. Educ:* Khormaksar, Aden; St John's, Singapore. FCO, 1971–74; Latin America Floater, 1974–76; Vice-Consul: Kabul, 1976–80; Warsaw, 1980–82; S Pacific Dept, FCO, 1982–85; Second Sec. and Vice-Consul, Tegucigalpa, 1985–88; First Sec. (Political), Berne, 1988–90; News Dept, FCO, 1991–93; First Sec. (Press/Information), New Delhi, 1993–97; Dep. Hd, Near East and N Africa Dept, FCO, 1997–2000; Dep. Hd of Mission and Consul-Gen., Mexico City, 2000–03; Dep. High Comr, Mumbai, 2003–05. *Recreations:* reading, history, travel, playing golf badly. *Address:* c/o Foreign and Commonwealth Office, King Charles Street, SW1A 2AH.

HUGHES, Prof. Ieuan Arwel, FRCP, FRCPCH, FMedSci; Professor and Head of Department of Paediatrics, University of Cambridge, since 1989; Fellow, Fitzwilliam College, Cambridge, since 2007; *b* 9 Nov. 1944; *s* of Arwel Hughes and Enid Phillips (*née* Thomas); *m* 1969, Margaret Maureen Davies; two *s* one *d. Educ:* Univ. of Wales Coll. of Medicine, Cardiff (MB, BCh, MD); MA Cantab, 1991. MRCP 1971, FRCP 1984; FRCPC 1974; FRCPCH 1997; MRSocMed. Medical Registrar, UCH, 1970–72; Senior Paediatric Resident, Dalhousie Univ., Canada, 1972–74; Endocrine Research Fellow, Manitoba Univ., Canada, 1974–76; MRC Fellow, Tenovus Inst., Cardiff, 1976–78; Consultant Paediatrician, Bristol, 1978–79; Senior Lectr in Child Health, 1979–85, Reader in Child Health, 1985–89, Univ. of Wales Coll. of Medicine, Cardiff; Fellow, Clare Hall, Cambridge, 1994–2007. Chm., DoH Cttee on Toxicity of Chemicals in Food, Consumer Products and the Envmt (Phytoestrogen Working Gp). President: European Soc. for Paediatric Endocrinology, 1993– (Sec., 1987–92); Assoc. of Clinical Profs of Paediatrics, 1995–99; Section of Endocrinology, RSocMed, 2005–07; Mem. Council, Soc. for Endocrinology. Perspectives Ed., Archives of Disease in Childhood, 2003–. Mem., Ralph Vaughan Williams Soc. Founder FMedSci 1998. Andrea Prader Prize,

European Soc. for Paediatric Endocrinology, 2006. *Publications:* Handbook of Endocrine Tests in Children, 1986; articles on paediatric endocrine disorders, steroid biochemistry and mechanism of steroid hormone action. *Recreations:* music (choral singing, bassoon, piano, concert-going), travel, hill walking, cycling. *Address:* c/o Department of Paediatrics, Level 8, Addenbrooke's Hospital, Hills Road, Cambridge CB2 2QQ; 4 Latham Road, Cambridge CB2 7EQ.

HUGHES, James Ernest, PhD; FREng; Director, 1973–85 and Managing Director and Chief Executive, 1983–84, Johnson Matthey PLC; *b* 3 Nov. 1927; *s* of Herbert Thomas Hughes and Bessie Beatrice Hughes; *m* 1950, Hazel Aveline (*née* Louguet-Layton); three *d. Educ:* Spring Grove Sch.; Imperial Coll., London Univ., (BSc, ARSM (Bessemer Medalist); DIC); PhD London 1952. FIMMM; FREng (FEng 1981). Associated Electrical Industries, 1952–63; Johnson Matthey PLC, 1963–85. Vis. Professor, Univ. of Sussex, 1974–80. President: Inst. of Metals, 1972–73; Metals Soc., 1981–82; Instn of Metallurgists, 1982–83. FRSA 1978. *Publications:* scientific papers in learned jls. *Recreations:* antiques, music, gardening. *Address:* Beechcroft Farmhouse, Upton Lovell, Warminster, Wilts BA12 0JW.

HUGHES, Janis; Member (Lab) Glasgow Rutherglen, Scottish Parliament, 1999–2007; *b* 1 May 1958; *d* of Thomas Nish and Janet (*née* Cumming); *m* (marr. diss.). *Educ:* Queen's Park Sch., Glasgow; Western Coll. of Nursing, Glasgow. Nursing: Royal Hosp. for Sick Children, Glasgow, 1980–82; Victoria Infirmary, Glasgow, 1982–86; Belvidere Hosp., Glasgow, 1986–88; Health Service Adminr, Renal Unit, Glasgow Royal Infirmary, 1988–99. Steward, 1980–83, Sec., Glasgow Royal Infirmary Br., 1993–99, NUPE, then UNISON. *Recreations:* reading, cooking.

HUGHES, Jeremy Michael; Chief Executive, Breakthrough Breast Cancer, since 2005; *b* 15 Aug. 1957; *s* of Rev. Martyn L. Hughes and Mary D. Hughes; *m* 1989, Caroline Anne Chappell; two *s. Educ:* Harrow Sch.; St Edmund Hall, Univ. of Oxford (BA 1st cl., MA). Man. Dir, LMS Public Relns Ltd, 1983–89; Asst Dir, Nat. Children's Home, 1989–92; Director: Muscular Dystrophy Gp, 1992–93; Leonard Cheshire, 1994–99; BRCS, 1999–2003; Hd, External Relns, Internat. Fedn of Red Cross and Red Crescent Socs, 2003–04. Bd Mem., NCRI, 2007–. Trustee: Ockenden Internat., 2002–06; Sightsavers Internat., 2006–; AMRC, 2006–; Jt Chm., Nat. Voices, 2008–. Mem. Adv. Bd, Foundn for Excellence in Business Practice, Geneva, 2003–05. *Publication:* (contrib.) Sweet Charity: the role and workings of voluntary organisations, 1996. *Recreations:* hill-walking, house renovation. *Address:* Breakthrough Breast Cancer, Weston House, 246 High Holborn, WC1V 7EX. *T:* (020) 7025 2412, *Fax:* (020) 7025 2401; *e-mail:* jeremyh@breakthrough.org.uk.

HUGHES, John; *see* Hughes, E. J. and Hughes, R. J.

HUGHES, John; *b* 29 May 1925; *m* Josephine Brown; two *s. Educ:* Durham. Served with Fleet Air Arm, 1943–45. Apprentice joiner; then miner and mechanic; worked for GEC, and Unipart (TGWU convener). Mem., Coventry City Council, 1974–82; Chm., Coventry NE Lab Party, 1978–81. MP (Lab) Coventry North East, 1987–92; contested (Ind. Lab) Coventry North East, 1992. *Address:* 15 Stafford Close, Bulkington, Bedworth, Nuneaton, Warwicks CV12 9QX.

HUGHES, Prof. John, PhD; FRS 1993; Director, Parke-Davis Neuroscience Research Centre (formerly Parke-Davis Research Unit), Cambridge, 1983–2000; Senior Research Fellow, Wolfson College, University of Cambridge, 1983–2000; *b* 6 Jan. 1942; *s* of Joseph and Edith Hughes; *m* 1967, Madelaine Carol Jennings (marr. diss. 1981); one *d*; three *s* one *d*; *m* 1997, Ann Rosemary Elizabeth, *d* of Joseph and Norma Mutty; one step *s* one step *d. Educ:* Mitcham County Grammar Sch. for Boys; Chelsea Coll., London (BSc); Inst. of Basic Med. Sciences, London (PhD). MA Cantab, 1988. Res. Fellow, Yale Univ. Med. Sch., 1967–69; University of Aberdeen: Lectr in Pharmacology, 1969–77; Dep.-Dir, Drug Res. Unit, 1973–77; Imperial College, London University: Reader in Pharmacol Biochemistry, 1977–79; Prof. of Pharmacol Biochemistry, 1979–82; Vis. Prof., 1983–. Hon. Professor: of Neuropharmacology, Univ. of Cambridge, 1989–; of Pharmacol., Aberdeen Univ., 1998–. Vice-Pres. of Res., Warner-Lambert/Parke-Davis Co., 1988–2000; Founding Mem. and Chm., 2000–02, Chm., Scientific Adv. Bd, 2002–, Cambridge Biotechnology Ltd; Chm., Scientific Adv. Bd, Synaptica Ltd, 2002–. Member: Substance Abuse Cttee, Mental Health Foundn, 1986–; Scientific Cttee, Assoc. of British Pharmaceutical Industry, 1990–95; Bd, Nat. Inst. for Biol Standards and Control, 1999–; Chm., Res. Cttee, Chronic Fatigue Syndrome (formerly Persistent Virus Disease) Res. Foundn, 1992– (Trustee of the Foundn, 1997–). Mem. Council, Internat. Sch. Neuroscience, 1988–. Editor: Brit. Jl Pharmacol., 1977–83; Brain Res., 1976–; Jt Chief Exec. Editor, Neuropeptides, 1980–. J. Y. Dent Meml Lectr, Soc. for Study of Drug Addiction, 1976; Oliver-Sharpey Lectr, RCP, 1980; Gaddum Lectr and Medal, British Pharmacol Soc., 1982. Mem., Royal Acad. of Medicine, Belgium, 1983. Dr *hc* Univ. of Liège, 1978. Sandoz Prize, British Pharmacol Soc., 1975; Pacesetter Award, US Nat. Inst. on Drug Abuse, 1977; Lasker Prize, Albert and Mary Lasker Foundn, NY, 1978; Scientific Medal, Soc. for Endocrinology, 1980; W. Feldberg Foundn Award, 1981; Lucien Dautrebande Prize, Fondation de Pathophysiologie, Belgium, 1983; Lilly Award, European Coll. of Neuropsychopharmacology, 1992. *Publications:* Centrally Acting Peptides, 1978; Opioids Past, Present and Future, 1984; (ed jtly) The Neuropeptide Cholecystokinin (CCK), 1989; articles in Nature, Science, Brit. Jl Pharmacol., and Brain Res. *Recreations:* family, friends, gardening. *Address:* Department of Pharmacology, University of Cambridge, Tennis Court Road, Cambridge CB2 1PD.

HUGHES, Very Rev. John Chester; Vicar of Bringhurst with Great Easton and Drayton, 1978–87; *b* 20 Feb. 1924; *m* 1950, Sybil Lewis McClelland; three *s* two *d* (and one *s* decd). *Educ:* Dulwich Coll.; St John's Coll., Durham (BA 1948; DipTh 1950; MA 1951). Curate of Westcliff-on-Sea, Essex, 1950–53; Succentor of Chelmsford Cathedral, 1953–55; Vicar of St Barnabas, Leicester, 1955–61; Vicar of Croxton Kerrial with Branston-by-Belvoir, 1961–63; Provost of Leicester, 1963–78. ChStJ 1974. *Publication:* The Story of Launde Abbey, 1998. *Address:* 29 High Street, Hallaton, Market Harborough, Leics LE16 8UD. *T:* (01858) 555622.

HUGHES, John Dennis; Consultant, Trade Union Research Unit; Principal, Ruskin College, Oxford, 1979–89 (Tutor in Economics and Industrial Relations, 1957–70, and Vice Principal, 1970–79); *b* 28 Jan. 1927; *m* 1949, Violet (*née* Henderson); four *d. Educ:* Westminster City Sch.; Lincoln Coll., Oxford (MA). Lieut, RAEC, 1949–50. Extramural Tutor, Univs of Hull and Sheffield, 1950–57. Founded, Trade Union Res. Unit, 1970; Dep. Chm., Price Commn, 1977–79. Non-exec. Dir, BRB, 1997–99. Member: Industrial Develt Adv. Bd, 1975–79; Nat. Consumer Council, 1982–94; Ind. Mem., Rail Passengers Council, 2001–05. Governor, London Business Sch., 1979–92. Mem. Council, St George's House, 1978–83; Trustee Dir, NUMAST (formerly Merchant Navy and Airline Officers Assoc.), 1981–. *Publications:* Trade Union Structure and Government, 1968; (with R. Moore) A Special Case? Social Justice and the Miners, 1972; (with H. Pollins) Trade Unions in Great Britain, 1973; Industrial Restructuring: some manpower aspects, 1976; Britain in Crisis, 1981; The Social Charter and the European Single Market, 1991; contrib. Eur. Labour Forum jl. *Recreation:* cycling. *Address:* Rookery Cottage, Stoke Place, Old Headington, Oxford OX3 9BX. *T:* (01865) 763076.

HUGHES, Judith Caroline Anne, (Mrs Inigo Bing); QC 1994; **Her Honour Judge Judith Hughes;** a Circuit Judge, since 2001; a Deputy High Court Judge, since 1997; *b* 13 Oct. 1950; 3rd *d* of Frank and Eva Hughes; *m* 1st, 1977, Mark G. Warwick (marr. diss. 1998); two *d*; 2nd, 2004, Inigo Geoffrey Bing, *qv. Educ:* Univ. of Leeds (LLB 1973). Called to the Bar, Inner Temple, 1974 (Bencher, 1994); Asst Recorder, 1991–95; a Recorder, 1995–2001; a Judicial Mem., Parole Bd, 2002–. Vice Chm., Legal Services Cttee, Bar Council, 1999. Trustee: Gilbert Place Centre, 1995–98; Children's Soc., 1996–2003; Help African Schs to Educate, 2000– (Chm., 2001–); Mem. Cttee, Bottoms Up, 2001–. Hon. Mem., Harrow Rotary Club, 2004. *Publication:* (jtly) Butterworths Guide to Family Law, 1996. *Recreations:* theatre, reading, handicrafts, travel, gardening, philately. *Address:* Gee Street Courthouse, 29–41 Gee Street, EC1V 3RE. *Club:* Reform.

HUGHES, Prof. Leslie Ernest, FRCS, FRACS; Professor of Surgery, University of Wales College of Medicine (formerly Welsh National School of Medicine), 1971–92; *b* 12 Aug. 1932; *s* of Charles Joseph and Vera Hughes; *m* 1955, Marian Castle; two *s* two *d. Educ:* Parramatta High Sch.; Sydney Univ. MB, BS (Sydney); DS (Queensland), 1975; FRCS, 1959; FRACS, 1959. Reader in Surgery, Univ. of Queensland, 1965–71. Hunterian Prof., RCS, 1986. Eleanor Roosevelt Internat. Cancer Fellow, 1970. President: Welsh Surgical Soc., 1991–93; Surgical Res. Soc., 1992–94; Hist. of Medicine Soc. of Wales, 2000. Audio-visual Aid Merit Award, Assoc. of Surgeons of GB and Ireland, 1983, 1986. Educn Editor and Chm., Editl Bd, European Jl of Surgical Oncology, 1992–97. *Publications:* (jtly) Benign Disorders of the Breast, 1988, 3rd edn 2008; numerous papers in medical jls, chiefly on immune aspects of cancer, and diseases of the colon. *Recreations:* music, travel. *Address:* 74 Lake Road East, Roath Park, Cardiff CF23 5NN.

HUGHES, Lewis Harry, CB 1996; consultant in public sector audit, since 2004; Deputy Auditor General for Wales, 2000–04; *b* 6 March 1945; *s* of Reginald Harry Hughes, retired MoD official, and Gladys Lilian Hughes; *m* 1975, Irene June Nash, violinist and teacher; one *s. Educ:* Devonport High Sch. for Boys; City of London Coll. CIPFA. Exchequer and Audit Dept, 1963–83 (Associate Dir, 1982–83); National Audit Office, 1983–2000: Dir of Health Audit and of Defence Audit to 1990; Asst Auditor Gen., 1991–2000. *Recreations:* golf, music, family life. *Address:* 1 Wood End Road, Harpenden, Herts AL5 3EB. *T:* (01582) 764992. *Club:* Redbourn Golf.

HUGHES, Louis Ralph; Chief Executive Officer, GBS Laboratories LLC, since 2004; non-executive Chairman, Maxager Technology Inc., since 2001; *b* Cleveland, Ohio, 10 Feb. 1949. *Educ:* General Motors Inst., Flint (BMechEng); Harvard Univ. (MBA). General Motors Corp., 1973–2000: financial staff, 1973; Asst Treasurer, 1982; Vice-Pres., of Finance, Gen. Motors of Canada, 1985; Vice-Pres. of Finance, General Motors Europe, Zürich, 1987; Chm. and Man. Dir, Adam Opel AG, Rüsselsheim, 1989; Pres., General Motors Europe, 1992; Exec. Vice Pres., 1992–2000; Pres., Internat. Ops, 1994–98; Pres. and Chief Operating Officer, Lockheed Martin Corp., 2000. C of S, Afghanistan Reconstruction Gp, US Embassy, Kabul, 2004–05. *Recreations:* ski-ing, climbing, cuisine, antiques. *Address:* Maxager Technology Inc., 2173 East Francisco Boulevard, San Rafael, CA 94901, USA.

HUGHES, Merfyn; *see* Hughes, T. M.

HUGHES, Michael, CBE 1998; Chief Investment Officer, Baring Asset Management Ltd, 2000–07 (Director, 1998–2000); *b* 26 Feb. 1951; *s* of late Leonard and Gwyneth Mair Hughes; *m* 1978, Jane Ann Gosham; two *d. Educ:* Univ. of Manchester (BA Econs); London School of Economics and Political Science (MSc Econs). Economist, BP Pension Fund, 1973–75; Partner and Chief Economist, de Zoete and Bevan, Stockbrokers, 1976–86; Dir, BZW Securities, 1986–89; Man. Dir, BZW Strategy, 1989–98; Chm., Barclays Capital Pension Fund, 1995–2000. Chm., Financial Panel, Foresight Prog., DTI, 1994–97; Mem., ESRC, 1995–98. Mem. Council, Univ. of Essex, 1997–2006. FRSA 2005. *Recreations:* horses, gardening. *Club:* National Liberal.

HUGHES, (Michael) Antony; His Honour Judge Antony Hughes; a Circuit Judge, South Eastern Circuit, since 2006; Designated Family Judge, Milton Keynes and Oxford, since 2007; Deputy High Court Judge, since 2007; *b* 26 May 1953; *s* of late Joseph Frederick Hughes, MA Oxon, BSc, and Doris Anne Hughes, MBE; *m* 1977, Ann Holdsworth; three *d. Educ:* King's Sch., Canterbury; Coll. of Law. Articled with Cole & Cole, Oxford, 1973–77; admitted as solicitor, 1977; Partner with Linnell & Murphy, then Linnells, subseq. Borneo Linnells, Solicitors, Oxford, 1979–2006; NP, 1985–2006; Dep. Metropolitan Stipendiary Magistrate, 1993–2000; a Recorder, 2000–06. *Recreations:* walking, cycling, growing vegetables. *Address:* Milton Keynes County Court, 351 Silbury Boulevard, Milton Keynes MK9 2DT. *T:* (01908) 302810.

HUGHES, Miranda, PhD; CPsychol; Regional Commissioner, Northern and Yorkshire, Appointments (formerly NHS Appointments) Commission, since 2004; *b* 18 Oct. 1952; *d* of John and Diana Hughes; *m* 1987, Paul Rayner; two *s* one *d. Educ:* Univ. of Keele (BA 1976; PhD 1981); Univ. of Stirling (MSc 1978). CPsychol 1988. Lectr in Psychol., Leeds Univ., 1979–84; Mgt Consultant, KPMG, 1984–87; consultancy and non-exec. appts in private and public sectors, 1987–2001. Chair, W Yorks Probation Bd, 2001–05. *Address:* Appointments Commission, Blenheim House, Duncombe Street, Leeds LS1 4PL. *T:* (0113) 394 2964, *Fax:* (0113) 394 2956; *e-mail:* miranda.hughes@appointments.org.uk.

HUGHES, Nigel Howard, FREng; Director of Technology, Smiths Industries Aerospace and Defence Systems Ltd, 1992–97; *b* 11 Aug. 1937; *s* of late William Howard Hughes and of Florence Hughes (*née* Crawshaw); *m* 1962, Margaret Ann Fairmaner; three *d. Educ:* St Paul's Sch.; Queen's Coll., Oxford (MA). CEng, FIMechE; FRAeS 1993; FREng (FEng 1995). Pilot Officer, RAF, 1956–58. RAE, Bedford, 1961–73; Head of Radio and Navigation Div., 1973–77, Head of Flight Systems Dept, 1977–80, RAE, Farnborough; MoD Central Staffs, 1980–82; Asst Chief Scientific Advr (Projects), MoD, 1982–84; Dep. Chief Scientific Advr, MoD, 1985–86; Dir, RSRE, 1986–89; Chief Exec., Defence Res. Agency, 1989–91. Mem., 1992–98, Chm., 1998–2003, Airworthiness Requirements Bd, CAA. *Recreations:* Rolls-Royce enthusiast; model engineering, amateur radio, music.

HUGHES, Owain Arwel, OBE 2004; orchestral conductor, since 1970; Principal Conductor, Aalborg Symphony Orchestra, Denmark, since 1995; Principal Associate Conductor, Royal Philharmonic Orchestra, since 2003; *b* 21 March 1942; *s* of Arwel Hughes and Enid Hughes (*née* Thomas); *m* 1966, Jean Lewis; one *s* one *d. Educ:* Howardian High Sch., Cardiff; University Coll., Cardiff (BA Hons); Royal Coll. of Music. Has conducted all major UK orchs and their choirs and also orchs throughout Europe; Associate Conductor: BBC Welsh Symphony Orch., 1980–86; Philharmonia Orch., London, 1985–90; Musical Dir, Huddersfield Choral Soc., 1980–86; Founder and Artistic Dir, Annual Welsh Proms, 1986–; Music Dir, NYO of Wales, 2003–; Founder and Music Dir, Camerata, Wales, 2005–; Principal Guest Conductor, Cape Town Philharmonic Orch., S Africa, 2007–. Television: Blodeugerdd (series), BBC Wales,

1974–76; Development of English Choral Tradition, 1975; Music in Camera, 1976–86; Much Loved Music Show, 1977–83; Requiem series, 1987; Easter series, 1988. Has made numerous recordings and videos. Vice-Pres., NCH Action for Children, 1988–. Founding Fellow, George Thomas Soc., 1989. FRWCMD (FWCMD 1995). Hon. Fellow: Univ. of Glamorgan (formerly Poly. of Wales), 1986; UC, Cardiff, 1991; Trinity Coll., Carmarthen, 2004; UC, Lampeter, 2007; UC, Bangor, 2007. Hon. DMus: CNAA, 1986; Wales, 1991. Gold Medal, Welsh Tourist Bd, 1988. *Recreations:* Rugby, cricket, golf. *Address: e-mail:* sinead.ocarroll@btinternet.com.

HUGHES, Paul; *see* Hughes, H. P.

HUGHES, Ven. Paul Vernon; Archdeacon of Bedford, since 2003; *b* 4 Aug. 1953; *s* of Reginald Harry Hughes and Eileen Mary Hughes; *m* 1984, Elizabeth Jane Hawkes; one *s* one *d. Educ:* Ghyll Royd Prep. Sch., Ilkley; Pocklington Sch.; Central London Poly. (Dip. Urban Estate Mgt); Ripon Coll., Cuddesdon. Residential Property Surveyor, Chestertons, 1974–79. Ordained deacon, 1982, priest, 1983; Curate, Chipping Barnet with Arkley, 1982–86; Team Vicar, Dunstable, 1986–93; Vicar, Boxmoor, 1993–2003. RD Hemel Hempstead, 1996–2003. *Recreations:* music, amateur operatics, walking (country and coast), reading. *Address:* 17 Lansdowne Road, Luton, Beds LU3 1EE. *T:* (01582) 730722, *Fax:* (01582) 877354; *e-mail:* archdbedf@stalbans.anglican.org.

HUGHES, Peter; *see* Hughes, D. E. P.

HUGHES, Peter Thomas; QC 1993; **His Honour Judge Peter Hughes;** a Circuit Judge, since 2007; *b* 16 June 1949; *s* of late Peter Hughes, JP, and Jane Blakemore Hughes (*née* Woodward); *m* 1974, Christine Stuart Taylor; one *s* one *d. Educ:* Bolton Sch.; Bristol Univ. (LLB Hons). Called to the Bar, Gray's Inn, 1971, Bencher, 2001; Mem., Wales and Chester Circuit, 1971–2007 (Junior, 1991; Treas., 1999–2000), Northern Circuit, 2007–; Asst Recorder, 1988–92; Recorder, 1992–2007; Dep. High Ct Judge, 2001–07. Chairman: Medical Appeal Tribunals, 1988–93; Registered Homes Tribunals, 1993–2002 (Lead Chm., 2000–02); Mental Health Review Tribunals, 1999–. Mem., Gen. Council of the Bar, 1993–98. Freeman, Co. of Clockmakers, 2005. *Recreations:* fell-walking, books, gardening in a cruel climate. *Address:* Carlisle Combined Court Centre, Earl Street, Carlisle CA1 1DJ. *T:* (01228) 590588. *Clubs:* Army and Navy; Lancashire County Cricket.

HUGHES, Philip; *see* Hughes, R. P.

HUGHES, Philip Arthur Booley, CBE 1982; artist; Director, Thames and Hudson Ltd, since 1991; *b* 30 Jan. 1936; *s* of Leslie Booley Hughes and Elizabeth Alice Hughes (*née* Whyte); *m* 1964, Psiche Maria Anna Claudia Bertini; two *d*, and two step *d. Educ:* Bedford Sch.; Clare Coll., Cambridge (BA). Engineer, Shell Internat. Petroleum Co., 1957–61; Computer Consultant, SCICON Ltd (formerly CEIR), 1961–69; Co-Founder, Logica, 1969: Man. Dir, 1969–72; Chm., 1972–90; Dir, 1990–95. Vis. Prof., UCL, 1981–90. Member: SERC, 1981–85; Nat. Electronics Council, 1981–88. Governor, Technical Change Centre, 1980–88. Mem. Council, RCA, 1988–92. Trustee: Design Museum, 1990–96; Inst. for Public Policy Res., 1988–99; Nat. Gall., 1996–2002 (Chm., Bd of Trustees, 1996–99). Official Vis. Artist to Antarctica, British Antarctic Survey, 2001–02. Exhibn of paintings with Beryl Bainbridge, Monks Gall., Sussex, 1972; exhibited: Contemp. British Painting, Madrid, 1983; Contemp. Painters, Ridgeway Exhibn Museum and Art Gall., Swindon, 1986; exhibitions with: Philip Wolfhagen, Sherman Gall., Sydney, 2002; Keith Grant, Churchill Coll., Cambridge, 2003; with Antoine Poncet, Château la Nerthe, Châteauneuf-du-Pape, 2004; one-man exhibitions: Parkway Focus Gall., London, 1976; Angela Flowers Gall., London, 1977; Gal. Cance Manguin, Vaucluse, France, 1979, 1985, 2000; Francis Kyle Gall., London, 1979, 1982, 1984, 1987, 1989, 1992, 1994, 1997, 2000, 2003, 2006; Gal. La Tour des Cardinaux, Vaucluse, France, 1993; Mus. of Contemp. Art, Monterrey, Mexico, 1997; Mus. Rufino Tamayo, Mexico City, 1998; Tate St Ives, 2000; V&A Mus., 2001; Musée du Châtillonais, Châtillon-sur-Seine, 2002; Star Gall., Lewes, 2004; Watermill Gall., Aberfeldy, 2005; Rex Irwin Gall., Sydney, 2005, 2008; Galerie Pascal Lainé, Ménerbes, Vaucluse, France, 2007; Charleston, E Sussex, 2008; retrospectives: Inverness Mus. and Art Gall., 1990; Ambassade d'Australie, Paris, 1995; Drill Hall Gall., Canberra, 1998, 2002, 2008; Volvo Gall., Sydney, George Adams Gall., Melbourne, 1999; Maison de la Truffe et du Vin, Ménerbes, 2007; Pier Arts Centre, Stromness, Orkney, 2008. CompOR 1985. Hon. Fellow, QMC, 1987. DUniv Stirling, 1985; Hon. DSc: Kent, 1988; London, 2000. *Publications:* Patterns in the Landscape, 1998; articles in nat. press and learned jls on management scis and computing.

HUGHES, Prof. Richard Anthony Cranmer, MD; FRCP; FMedSci; Professor of Neurology, King's College London (formerly Guy's, King's and St Thomas's School of Medicine, King's College London), 1999–2007, now Emeritus; *b* 11 Nov. 1942; *s* of Dr Anthony Chester Cranmer Hughes and Lilian Mildred Hughes; *m* 1968, Coral Stephanie Whittaker; one *s* two *d. Educ:* Marlborough Coll.; Clare Coll., Cambridge (BA Double First); Guy's Hosp. Med. Sch. (MB BChir (Dist. in Pathol.), MD). MRCP 1970, FRCP 1980. Sen. Lectr, Guy's Hosp. Med. Sch., 1975–87; Prof. of Neurol., UMDS, 1987–98, Hd, Div. of Clin. Neuroscis, GKT, 1999–2001. Hon. Consultant Neurologist: Guy's Hosp., 1975–; KCH, 1995–; Nat. Hosp. for Neurol. and Neurosurgery, 1996–. Ed., Jl Neurol., Neurosurgery and Psychiatry, 1989–96; Founding Co-ordinating Ed., Cochrane Neuromuscular Disease Gp, 1998–. Pres., Clinical Neuroscis Section, RSocMed, 2002–03. Mem. Council, Assoc. British Neurologists, 2001–03. Vice-Pres., Eur. Fedn of Neurol Socs, 2001–05. FMedSci 2000. Gov., Highgate Sch., 1991–95. Medal, Assoc. of British Neurologists, 2006. *Publications:* Guillain-Barré Syndrome, 1990; Neurological Emergencies, 1994, 4th edn 2003; European Handbook of Neurological Management, 2006; contrib. numerous articles to New England Jl of Medicine, Lancet, Annals of Neurol., Brain and other jls on neuroimmunol., multiple sclerosis and peripheral neuropathy. *Recreations:* botany, theatre, tennis. *Address:* Department of Clinical Neuroscience, King's College London, Hodgkin Building, Guy's Hospital, SE1 1UL. *T:* (020) 7848 6125, *Fax:* (020) 7848 6123. *Clubs:* Athenæum, Royal Society of Medicine.

HUGHES, Richard John C.; *see* Carey-Hughes.

HUGHES, Robert Gurth; Chief Executive, Association of Optometrists, since 2005; *b* 14 July 1951; *s* of late Gurth Martin Hughes and Rosemary Dorothy Hughes (*née* Brown), JP; *m* 1986, Sandra Kathleen (*née* Vaughan); four *d. Educ:* Spring Grove Grammar Sch.; Harrow Coll. of Technology and Art. Trainee, then Film Producer, BAC Film Unit, 1968–73; News Picture Editor, BBC Television News, 1973–87. Greater London Council: Mem., 1980–86; Opposition Dep. Chief Whip, 1982–86; Opposition spokesman on arts and recreation, 1984–86. MP (C) Harrow West, 1987–97; contested (C) same seat, 1997. PPS to Rt Hon. Edward Heath, 1988–90, to Minister of State, DSS, 1990–92; an Asst Govt Whip, 1992–94; Parly Sec., OPSS, Cabinet Office, 1994–95; Gen. Sec. (subseq. Exec. Dir), Fedn of Ophthalmic and Dispensing Opticians, 1997–2005. National Chm., Young Conservatives, 1979–80. A Governor, BFI, 1990–92. Hon. DSc Anglia Poly. Univ., 1998. *Recreations:* watching cricket, listening to music. *Club:* Heston Catholic Social.

HUGHES, (Robert) John; journalist; Syndicated Columnist, The Christian Scien Monitor, since 1985; Director, International Media Studies Program, 1991–97 (on lea of absence, 1997–2006), Professor of Communications, since 2007, Brigham You University, Utah; *b* Neath, S Wales, 28 April 1930; *s* of Evan John Hughes and Dellis M Hughes (*née* Williams); *m* 1st, 1955, Vera Elizabeth Pockman (marr diss. 1987); one *s* o *d*; 2nd, 1988, Peggy Janeane Chu; one *s. Educ:* Stationers' Company's Sch., Londo Reporter, sub-editor, corresp. for miscellaneous London and S African newspapers a news agencies (Natal Mercury, Durban; Daily Mirror, Daily Express, Reuter, Lond News Agency), 1946–54; joined The Christian Science Monitor, Boston, USA, 195 Africa Corresp., 1955–61; Asst Foreign Editor, 1962–64; Far East Corresp., 1964–7 Man. Editor, 1970; Editor, 1970–76; Editor and Manager, 1976–79; Pres. and Publish Hughes Newspapers Inc., USA, 1979–81, 1984–85; Associate Dir, US Informati Agency, 1981–82; Dir, Voice of America, 1982; Asst Sec. of State for Public Affairs, US 1982–84; Pres., Concord Communications Inc., 1989–91; Asst Sec.-Gen., UN, 1995 (leave of absence); special advr on communications to Sec.-Gen., UN, 1996–; E 1997–2006, and Chief Operating Officer, 1999–2006, Deseret Morning News, Salt La City. Chairman: Presidential Commn on US Govt Internat. Broadcasting, 199 Congressional Commn on Broadcasting to China, 1992. Nieman Fellow, Harvard Uni 1961–62. Pres., Amer. Soc. of Newspaper Editors, 1978–79. Pulitzer Prize for Interna Reporting, 1967; Overseas Press Club of America award for best daily newspaper or wi service reporting from abroad, 1970; Sigma Delta Chi's Yankee Quill Award, 1977. Ho LLD Colby Coll., 1978; Hon. DH Southern Utah, 1995. *Publications:* The New Face Africa, 1961; Indonesian Upheaval (UK as The End of Sukarno), 1967; articles magazines and encyclopaedias. *Recreations:* reading, walking, raising Labrador retrieve *Address:* Department of Communications, Brigham Young University, Provo, UT 846 USA. *Clubs:* Foreign Correspondents' (Hong Kong); Overseas Press (New York).

HUGHES, (Robert) Philip; His Honour Judge Philip Hughes; a Circuit Judge, sin 1998; Liaison Judge (Powys Magistrates), and Diversity and Community Relations Jud (North Wales), since 2007; *b* 4 June 1947; *s* of late Peredur and of Myra Hughes; *m* 197 Kathleen, (Katie), Dolan; two *s. Educ:* Valley Sch., Anglesey; Wrekin Coll., Shropshir Called to the Bar, Gray's Inn, 1971; in practice at the Bar, 1971–98, Hd of Chambe 1994–98; Asst Recorder, 1990–93, a Recorder, 1993–98, Wales and Chester Circu Designated Family Judge at Warrington, 2000–07. Asst Boundary Comr, 1996–98. Me Cttee, Council of HM Circuit Judges, 2007–. *Recreations:* sailing, vegetable gardenin coarse cooking, theatre. *Address:* The Law Courts, Mold, North Wales CH7 1AE. (01352) 707405. *Club:* Holyhead Sailing.

HUGHES, Robert Studley Forrest; Senior Writer (Art Critic), Time Magazine, Ne York, since 1970; *b* Sydney, Aust., 28 July 1938; *s* of Geoffrey E. F. Hughes and Margar Sealey Vidal; *m* (marr. diss. 1981); (one *s* decd); *m* 1981, Victoria Whistler (marr. di 2000). *Educ:* St Ignatius' Coll., Riverview, Sydney; Sydney Univ. (architecture cours unfinished). Contributed articles on art to The Nation and The Observer, Sydne 1958–62; to Europe, 1964, living in Italy until 1966, when moved to London; freelanci for Sunday Times, BBC and other publications/instns, 1966–70. TV credits includ Landscape with Figures, ten-part series on Australian art for ABC, Australia; Caravaggi Rubens and Bernini, for BBC, 1976–77; The Shock of the New, eight-part series f BBC, 1980, 2004; American Visions, BBC, 1996; Visions of Space: Antoni Gaudi, BB 2003. Mem., Amer. Acad. of Arts and Scis, 1993. Hon. Dr Fine Arts, Sch. of Visual Ar NY, 1982; Hon. DLitt Melbourne, 1997. Frank Jewett Mather Award, Coll. Art Asso of America, 1982, 1985; Golden Plate Award, Amer. Acad. of Achievement, 1988; Brusi Prize, Barcelona Olympiad, 1992; Dimbleby Award for lifetime achievement broadcasting, 1997. *Publications:* The Art of Australia, 1966; Heaven and Hell in Weste Art, 1969; The Shock of the New (BBC publication), 1980, rev. edn 1991; The Fa Shore, 1987; Frank Auerbach, 1990; Nothing If Not Critical, 1991; Barcelona, 199 Culture of Complaint: the fraying of America, 1993; American Visions, 1997; A Jerk One End, 1999; Goya, 2003; Things I Didn't Know: a memoir, 2006. *Recreatior* gardening, shooting, river and sea fishing, cooking. *Address:* Time Magazine, 1271 Aven of the Americas, New York, NY 10020, USA.

HUGHES, Robert Valentine, CBE 1999; FCIS; Chairman, Horserace Betting Lev Board, 1998–Sept. 2009; *b* 13 Feb. 1943; *s* of Robert Canning Hughes and Betty Bert Hughes; *m* 1968, Eryl Lumley. *Educ:* Univ. of Birmingham (DMS 1976; MSocSc 197 FCIS 1982. Review Leader (Performance Rev.), W Midlands Co. Transport and Eng Dept, 1977–81; Birmingham District Council: Principal Asst to Chief Exec., 1981–8 Develt and Promotion Officer, 1983–84; Town Clerk and Chief Exec., Great Grims BC, 1984–88; Chief Exec., Kirklees Metropolitan Council, 1988–98. Pres., SOLAC 1997–98. DUniv UCE, 1999. *Recreations:* composing music (jazz), cooking, ski-in horse-racing. *Address:* Horserace Betting Levy Board, 52 Grosvenor Gardens, SW1 0AU. *T:* (020) 7333 0043.

HUGHES, Rodger Grant, FCA; Senior Independent Director, Chime Communicatio plc, since 2007; *b* 24 Aug. 1948; *s* of Eric and Doreen Hughes; *m* 1973, Joan Clare Bark two *s. Educ:* Rhyl Grammar Sch.; Queens' Coll., Cambridge (BA 1970). FCA 197 PricewaterhouseCoopers (formerly Price Waterhouse): joined 1970; Partner, 1982–200 i/c Ind. Business Gp, 1988–91; i/c NW Reg., 1991–95; Mem., Supervisory Bd, 1991–9 Hd, Audit and Business Adv. Services, 1995–2002; Mem., Mgt Bd, 1995–2007; Managi Partner, Clients and Mkts, 2002–06. Auditor to Duchy of Cornwall, 1998–2007. Mem Steering Bd and Chm., Audit Cttee, Companies House, 2008–; non-exec. Mem. Bd a Chm., Audit Cttee, Simmons & Simmons, 2008–. Mem., Educn Leadership Team, BIT 2005–. *Recreations:* old cars, old buildings (arts and crafts).

HUGHES, Ronald Frederick, CEng, FICE; quality management consultant, since 199 Systems Consultant, London Underground Ltd, 1992; *b* 21 Oct. 1927; *s* of Harr Frederick and Kate Hughes; *m* 1957, Cecilia Patricia, *d* of Maurice Nunis, MCS, Sta Treasurer, Malaya, and Scholastica Nunis; two *s* one *d. Educ:* Birmingham Centr Technical College; Bradford College of Technology. Articled pupil, Cyril Boucher an Partners, 1943; Royal Engineers Engineering Cadet, 1946; commissioned RE, 195 service in Malaya, 1950–53. Res. Asst, BISRA, 1954; Civil Engineer, H. W. Evans & C Ltd, Malaya, 1955, Man. Dir, 1958; War Office, 1959; Head of War Office Works Grou Singapore, 1963; Works Adviser to C-in-C, FARELF, 1964; District Civil Enginee Malaya, 1966; Property Services Agency: Regional Site Control Officer, Midland Regio 1969; Principal Engineer, Post Office Services, 1970; Area Works Officer, Birminghar 1977; Asst Dir, 1979, Dir, 1983–87, Civil Engineering Services; Dir and Quality Syster Manager, Mott MacDonald Consultants, 1987–92. Dir, Construction Industr Computing Assoc., 1982–86; Member: Standing Cttee for Structural Safety, 1985–8 Maritime Bd, ICE, 1985–90; Nat. Jt Consultative Cttee for Building, 1986–88; Memb Council: Construction Industry Res. and Inf. Assoc., 1984–88; BSI, 1985; Perm. Interna Assoc. of Navigation Congresses, 1983–94; Parly Maritime Gp, 1988–96; Vice Pres Concrete Soc., 1989–95. *Recreations:* photography, music. *Address:* 9A The Street, We Horsley, Surrey KT24 6AY. *T:* (01483) 282182. *Clubs:* Naval; Effingham (Surrey).

HUGHES, Rosemary Ann, (Rosemary, Lady Hughes); DL; President, Special Educational Needs and Disability Tribunal, 2003–08; *b* 30 June 1939; *d* of Rev. John Pain and Barbara Pain; *m* 1964, Sir David Collingwood Hughes, 14th Bt (*d* 2003); three *s* (and one *s* decd). *Educ:* Girton Coll., Cambridge (BA 1960; LLB 1962). Dep. Metropolitan Stipendiary Magistrate, 1990–95. Chm. (pt-time), Special Educnl Needs and Disability Tribunal, 1995–2003. Lay Canon, Ely Cathedral, 2000–. DL Cambs, 1997. *Recreations:* playing double bass, ski-ing, horse racing, bridge. *Address:* The Coach House, High Street, Wilburton, Ely, Cambs CB6 3RA.

See also Sir T. C. Hughes, Bt.

HUGHES, Prof. Sean Patrick Francis, MS; FRCS, FRCSEd, FRCSI, FRCSEd (Orth); Professor of Orthopaedic Surgery, Imperial College London (formerly at Royal Postgraduate Medical School), University of London, 1991–2006, now Emeritus Professor of Musculoskeletal Surgery; Medical Director, Ravenscourt Park Hospital, 2002–04; Hon. Consultant Orthopaedic Surgeon, Imperial College Healthcare NHS Trust (formerly Hammersmith Hospitals), since 1991; Hon. Consultant, National Hospital for Nervous Diseases, Queen Square, since 1994; *b* 2 Dec. 1941; *s* of late Patrick Joseph Hughes and Kathleen Ethel Hughes (*née* Bigg); *m* 1972, Felicity Mary (*née* Anderson); one *s* two *d*. *Educ:* Downside Sch.; St Mary's Hospital, Univ. of London (MB BS, MS). Senior Registrar in Orthopaedics, Middlesex and Royal National Orthopaedic Hosp., 1974–76; Research Fellow in Orthopaedics, Mayo Clinic, USA, 1975; Sen. Lectr, and Dir Orthopaedic Unit, RPMS, Hammersmith Hosp., 1977–79; George Harrison Law Prof. of Orthopaedic Surgery, Univ. of Edinburgh, 1979–91; Chief of Orthopaedic Service, 1995–98, Clin. Dir, Surgery and Anaesthesia, 1998–2002, Hammersmith Hosps NHS Trust; Hd of Surgery, Anaesthesia and Intensive Care, Imperial Coll. Faculty of Medicine, 1997–2004; Dir, Inst. of Musculoskeletal Surgery, Imperial Coll. London, 2004–06. Hon. Civilian Consultant, RN. Non-exec. Dir, W Middlesex Univ. Hosp. NHS Trust, 1998–2006. Vice President: RCSE, 1994–97 (Mem. Council, 1984–97); Assoc. Res. Circulation Bone, 1994–97; Mem. Council, British Orthopaedic Assoc., 1989–92. Fellow: Brit. Orthopaedic Assoc.; Royal Soc. Med.; Member: Orthopaedic Research Soc.; British Orth. Res. Soc. (Pres., 1995–97); Soc. Internat. de Chirurgie Orth. et de Traumatologie; World Orth. Concern; Internat. Soc. for Study of the Lumbar Spine. *Publications:* Astons Short Text Book of Orthopaedics, 2nd edn 1976 to 5th edn (jtly) 1997; Basis and Practice of Orthopaedics, 1981; Basis and Practice of Traumatology, 1983; Musculoskeletal Infections, 1986; (ed jtly) Orthopaedics: the principles and practice of musculoskeletal surgery, 1987; (ed jtly) Orthopaedic Radiology, 1987; papers on blood flow and mineral exchange, fracture healing, bone scanning, antibiotics and infection in bone, external fixation of fractures, surgery of the lumbar and cervical spine. *Recreations:* walking, ski-ing, music. *Address:* The Old Dairy, Maugersbury, Cheltenham, Glos GL54 1HG. *T:* (01451) 870234. *Clubs:* Athenæum, Naval.

HUGHES, Shirley, (Mrs J. S. P. Vulliamy), OBE 1999; FRSL; free-lance author/illustrator; *b* 16 July 1927; *d* of Thomas James Hughes and Kathleen Dowling; *m* 1952, John Sebastian Papendiek Vulliamy (*d* 2007); two *s* one *d*. *Educ:* West Kirby High Sch. for Girls; Liverpool Art Sch.; Ruskin Sch. of Art, Oxford. Illustrator/author; overseas edns or distribn in France, Spain, W Germany, Denmark, Holland, Sweden, Aust., NZ, Japan, USA, China and Canada. Lectures to Teacher Trng Colls, Colls of Further Educn, confs on children's lit. and to children in schs and libraries; overseas lectures incl. tours to Aust. and USA. Mem., Cttee of Management, 1983–86, Chm., Children's Writers and Illustrators Gp, 1994–96, Soc. of Authors; Member: Public Lending Right Registrar's Adv. Cttee, 1984–88; Library and Information Services Council, 1989–92. FRSL 2000. Hon. FCLIP (Hon. FLA 1997); Hon. Fellow, Liverpool John Moores Univ., 2004. Hon. LittD: UEA, 2004; Liverpool, 2004. Eleanor Farjeon Award for services to children's lit., 1984. *Publications:* illustrated about 200 books for children of all ages; written and illustrated: Lucy and Tom's Day, 1960, 2nd edn 1979; The Trouble with Jack, 1970, 2nd edn 1981; Sally's Secret, 1973, 3rd edn 1976; Lucy and Tom go to School, 1973, 4th edn 1983; Helpers, 1975 (Children's Rights Other Award, 1976), 2nd edn 1978; Lucy and Tom at the Seaside, 1976, 3rd edn 1982; Dogger, 1977 (Kate Greenaway Medal, 1978; Silver Pencil Award, Holland, 1980; Greenaway Picture Book of All Time, 2007), 4th edn 1980; It's Too Frightening for Me, 1977, 4th edn 1982; Moving Molly, 1978, 3rd edn 1981; Up and Up, 1979, 3rd edn 1983; Here Comes Charlie Moon, 1980, 3rd edn 1984; Lucy and Tom's Christmas, 1981; Alfie Gets in First, 1981, 2nd edn 1982; Charlie Moon and the Big Bonanza Bust-up, 1982, 2nd edn 1983; Alfie's Feet, 1982, 2nd edn 1984; Alfie Gives a Hand, 1983; An Evening at Alfie's, 1984; Lucy and Tom's abc, 1984; A Nursery Collection, 6 vols, 1985–86; Chips and Jessie, 1985; Another Helping of Chips, 1986; Lucy and Tom's 123, 1987; Out and About, 1988; The Big Alfie and Annie Rose Story Book, 1988; Angel Mae, 1989; The Big Concrete Lorry, 1989; The Snowlady, 1990; Wheels, 1991; The Big Alfie Out-of-Doors Story Book, 1992; Bouncing, 1993; Giving, 1993; Stories by Firelight, 1993; Chatting, 1994; Hiding, 1994; Rhymes for Annie Rose, 1995; Enchantment in the Garden, 1996; Alfie and the Birthday Surprise, 1997; The Lion and the Unicorn, 1998; Abel's Moon, 1999; Alfie's Numbers, 1999; The Shirley Hughes Collection, 2000; Alfie Weather, 2001; A Life Drawing: recollections of an illustrator (memoirs), 2002; Annie Rose is My Little Sister, 2002; Olly and Me, 2003; Ella's Big Chance, 2003 (Kate Greenaway Medal, 2004); Alfie Wins a Prize, 2004; A Brush with the Past, 2005; Alfie's World, 2006; Alfie and the Big Boys, 2007; Jonadab and Rita, 2008; (ed) Mother and Child Treasury, 1998. *Recreations:* looking at paintings, dressmaking, writing books for children. *Address:* c/o Random House Children's Books, 61–63 Uxbridge Road, W5 5SA.

See also E. S. Vulliamy.

HUGHES, Simon Henry Ward; MP (Lib Dem) Southwark North and Bermondsey, since 1997 (MP Southwark and Bermondsey, Feb. 1983–1997, L, 1983–88, Lib Dem, 1988–97); barrister; *b* 17 May 1951; *s* of late James Henry Annesley Hughes and of Sylvia (Paddy) Hughes (*née* Ward). *Educ:* Llandaff Cathedral Sch., Cardiff; Christ Coll., Brecon; Selwyn Coll., Cambridge (BA 1973, MA 1978); Inns of Court Sch. of Law; Coll. of Europe, Bruges (Cert. in Higher European Studies, 1975). Trainee, EEC, Brussels, 1975–76; Trainee and Mem. Secretariat, Directorate and Commn on Human Rights, Council of Europe, Strasbourg, 1976–77. Called to the Bar, Inner Temple, 1974; in practice, 1978–. Vice-Pres., Southwark Chamber of Commerce, 1987– (Pres., 1984–87). Spokesman: (L), on the environment, 1983–Jan. 1987 and June 1987–March 1988; (Alliance), on health, Jan.–June 1987; (Lib Dem), on education and science, 1988–90, on envmt, 1988–94, on natural resources, 1992–94, on community and urban affairs and young people, 1994–95, on social welfare, 1995–97, on health, 1995–99, on home affairs, 1999–2003, on London, 2003–05, on ODPM affairs, 2005; Lib Dem shadow to Attorney-Gen., 2005–07, to Leader of H of C, 2007–. Mem., Accommodation and Works Select Cttee, 1992–97. Jun. Counsel, Lib. Party application to European Commn on Human Rights, 1978–79; Chm., Lib. Party Adv. Panel on Home Affairs, 1981–83; Vice-Chm., Bermondsey Lib. Assoc., 1981–83. Jt Pres., British Youth Council, 1983–84. President: Young Liberals, 1986–88 (Vice-Pres., 1983–86, Mem. 1973–78); Democrats Against Apartheid, 1988–; Lib Dem Party, 2004–. Vice-President: Union of Liberal Students, 1983–88 (Mem., 1970–73); Southwark Chamber of Commerce, 1987– (Pres., 1984–87); Student Democrats, 1988–; Vice-Chm., Parly Youth Affairs Lobby, 1984–. Member: the Christian Church; Gen. Synod of Church of England, 1984–85; Southwark Area Youth Cttee; Council of Management, Cambridge Univ. Mission, Bermondsey; Anti-Apartheid Movement. Trustee: Salmon Youth Centre, Bermondsey; Rose Theatre Trust; Gov., St James C of E Sch., Bermondsey. Hon. Fellow, South Bank Univ., 1992. Member to Watch Award, 1985. *Publications:* pamphlets on human rights in Western Europe, the prosecutorial process in England and Wales, Liberal values for defence and disarmament. *Recreations:* music (including raves), theatre, sport (Millwall and Hereford FC, Glamorgan CCC, Wales RFU), the open air. *Address:* House of Commons, SW1A 0AA. *T:* (020) 7219 6256; 6 Lynton Road, Bermondsey, SE1 5QR.

HUGHES, Stephen Edward; Chief Executive, Birmingham City Council, since 2006 (Acting Chief Executive, 2005–06); *b* 18 Feb. 1954; *s* of Lawrence Edward Hughes and Dorothy Hughes (*née* Merricks); *m* 1991, Marian Nicholls; one step *s* one step *d*. *Educ:* Lincoln Grammar Sch.; Tettenhall Coll., Wolverhampton; Peterhouse, Cambridge (BA Hons Econs). CPFA 1997. Res. Officer, Internat. Wool Secretariat, 1976–79; Economist, Coventry CC, 1979–81; Principal Officer (Finance), AMA, 1981–84; Dep. Sec., ALA, 1984–90; seconded to Policy Unit, Islington LBC, 1990–92; Principal Asst Dir of Finance, 1992–97, Head of Finance and Property Services, 1997–98, Islington LBC; Divl Manager, Local Govt Taxation, DETR, 1998–99; Dir of Finance, London Bor. of Brent, 1999–2004; Strategic Dir of Resources, Birmingham CC, 2004–05. Dir, Walterton and Elgin Community Homes Ltd, 2001–04. Mem. (Lab), Didcot Town Council, 1987–95 (Chair, Finance Cttee, 1991–93; Dep. Leader, 1991–95). *Publications:* contribs to various local govt jls. *Recreations:* golf, ski-ing, sailing, chess, Go, surfing the net. *Address:* The Council House, Birmingham B1 1BB. *T:* (0121) 303 2000.

HUGHES, Stephen Skipsey; Member (Lab) North East Region, England, European Parliament, since 1999 (Durham, 1984–99); *b* 19 Aug. 1952; *m* 1988, Cynthia Beaver; one *s* one *d*, and one *s* twin *d* by previous marriage. *Educ:* St Bede's School, Lanchester; Newcastle Polytechnic (DMA). European Parliament: Dep. Ldr, Lab. Pty, 1991–93; Substitute Member: Legal Affairs Cttee, 1989–94; Citizens Rights Cttee, 1989–94; Mem., Environment Cttee, 1984–94; former Member: Rules Cttee; Security and Defence Cttee; Mem., Intergroup on Nuclear Disarmament, 1988– (Chm., 1988–90); Chm., 1994–99, Socialist Co-ordinator, 1999–, Social Affairs and Employment Cttee. Vice-President: Fedn of Industrial Develt Authorities, 1990–; Assoc. of District Councils, 1990–. *Address:* (office) County Hall, Durham DH1 5UR; (home) 19 Oakdene Avenue, Darlington, Co. Durham DL3 7HR.

HUGHES, Sir Thomas (Collingwood), 15th Bt *cr* 1773, of East Bergholt, Suffolk; FRCS; consultant in emergency medicine and medical educator; Consultant in Emergency Medicine, John Radcliffe Hospital, Oxford, since 2005; Hon. Clinical Lecturer, University of Oxford; *b* 16 Feb. 1966; *s* of Sir David Collingwood Hughes, 14th Bt and of Rosemary Ann Hughes, *qv*; *S* father, 2003; *m* 1996, Marina Louise Barbour, MB BS, DPhil, MRCP, FRACP, consultant in paediatric cardiology, Gt Ormond St Hosp., *d* of Richard Barbour, Albany, WA; one *s* two *d*. *Educ:* Oundle; Soham Village Coll.; Hills Road Sixth Form Coll.; Univ. of Sheffield (MB ChB); Univ. of Wales Coll. of Medicine (MSc); Open Univ. (MBA). MRCP. PhD student, Univ. of Melbourne. Consultant in Emergency Medicine, Ballarat, 1999–2004. *Heir: s* Alfred Collingwood Hughes, *b* 24 May 2001. *Address: e-mail:* mail@berristead.com.

HUGHES, Thomas George; Sheriff of Tayside, Central and Fife at Dundee, since 2004; *b* 2 Jan. 1955; *s* of Thomas and Patricia Hughes; *m* 1995, Janice Owens; one *s* one *d*. *Educ:* Strathclyde Univ. (LLB). Admitted solicitor, 1979; in practice as solicitor, 1979–2003; pt-time Sheriff, 2003–04. *Recreations:* sport, reading. *Address:* Sheriff Court House, 6 West Bell Street, Dundee DD1 9AD. *T:* (01382) 229961; *e-mail:* sheriffthughes@scotcourts.gov.uk.

HUGHES, Thomas Lowe; Trustee, since 1971, and President Emeritus, since 1991, Carnegie Endowment for International Peace, Washington (President, 1971–91); *b* 11 Dec. 1925; *s* of Evan Raymond Hughes and Alice (*née* Lowe); *m* 1st, 1955, Jean Hurlburt Reiman (*d* 1993); two *s*; 2nd, 1995, Jane Dudley Casey Kuczynski. *Educ:* Carleton Coll., Minn (BA); Balliol Coll., Oxford (Rhodes Schol., BPhil); Yale Law Sch. (LLB, JD). USAF, 1952–54 (Major). Member of Bar: Supreme Court of Minnesota; US District Court of DC; Supreme Court of US. Professional Staff Mem., US Senate Sub-cttee on Labour-Management Relations, 1951; part-time Prof. of Polit. Sci. and Internat. Relations, Univ. of Southern California, Los Angeles, 1953–54, and George Washington Univ., DC, 1957–58; Exec. Sec. to Governor of Connecticut, 1954–55; Legislative Counsel to Senator Hubert H. Humphrey, 1955–58; Admin. Asst to US Rep. Chester Bowles, 1959–60; Staff Dir of Platform Cttee, Democratic Nat. Convention, 1960; Special Asst to Under-Sec. of State, Dept of State, 1961; Dep. Dir of Intelligence and Research, Dept of State, 1961–63; Dir of Intell. and Res. (Asst Sec. of State), 1963–69; Minister and Dep. Chief of Mission, Amer. Embassy, London, 1969–70; Mem., Planning and Coordination Staff, Dept of State, 1970–71. Vis. Sen. Res. Fellow, German Histl Inst., Washington, 1997–. Chm., Nuclear Proliferation and Safeguards Adv. Panel, Office of Technology Assessment, US Congress; Chm., Bd of Editors, Foreign Policy Magazine; Sec., Bd of Dirs, German Marshall Fund of US; Dir, Arms Control Assoc. Chairman: Oxford-Cambridge Assoc. of Washington; US-UK Bicentennial Fellowships Cttee on the Arts. Member Bds of Visitors: Harvard Univ. (Center for Internat. Studies); Princeton Univ. (Woodrow Wilson Sch. of Public and Internat. Affairs); Georgetown Univ. (Sch. of Foreign Service); Bryn Mawr Coll. (Internat. Adv. Bd.); Univ. of Denver (Soc. Sci. Foundn); Atlantic Council of US (Exec. Cttee). Member Bds of Advisers: Center for Internat. Journalism, Univ. of S Calif; Coll. of Public and Internat. Affairs, Amer. Univ., Washington, DC; Washington Strategy Seminar; Cosmos Club Jl (Chm.). Member Bds of Trustees: Civilian Military Inst.; Amer. Acad. of Political and Social Sci.; Amer. Cttee, IISS; Hubert H. Humphrey Inst. of Public Affairs; Amer. Inst. of Contemp. German Studies, Washington, DC; Arthur F. Burns Fellowship Program. Mem. Adv. Bd, Fundacion Luis Munoz Marin, Puerto Rico. Member: Internat. Inst. of Strategic Studies; Amer. Assoc. of Rhodes Scholars; Amer. Political Sci. Assoc.; Amer. Bar Assoc.; Amer. Assoc. of Internat. Law; Amer. For. Service Assoc.; Amer. Acad. of Diplomacy; Internat. Studies Assoc.; Washington Inst. of Foreign Affairs (Pres.); Trilateral Commn; Assoc. for Restoration of Old San Juan, Puerto Rico; Soc. Mayflower Descendants. Arthur S. Flemming Award, 1965. Hon. LLD: Washington Coll., 1973; Denison Univ., 1979; Florida Internat. Univ., 1986; Hon. HLD: Carleton Coll., 1974; Washington and Jefferson Coll., 1979. KStJ 1984. *Publications:* occasional contribs to professional jls, etc. *Recreations:* swimming, tennis, music, 18th century engravings. *Address:* 5636 Western Avenue, Chevy Chase, MD 20815, USA. *T:* (301) 6561420. *Clubs:* Yale, Century Association, Council on Foreign Relations (New York); Cosmos, Chevy Chase (Washington).

HUGHES, (Thomas) Merfyn; QC 1994; **His Honour Judge Merfyn Hughes;** a Circuit Judge, since 2001; *b* 8 April 1949; *s* of John Medwyn Hughes and Blodwen Jane Hughes (*née* Roberts); *m* 1977, Patricia Joan (DL; High Sheriff, Gwynedd, 2002–03), *d* of John Talbot, surgeon, Brentwood; two *s* one *d*. *Educ:* Rydal Sch., Colwyn Bay; Liverpool

Univ. (LLB Hons 1970); Council of Legal Educn. Called to the Bar, Inner Temple, 1971; in practice at the Bar, Chester, 1971–94, Temple, 1994–2001; Asst Recorder, 1987–91; a Recorder, 1991–2001; Leading Counsel to Local Authorities, Waterhouse Tribunal on Child Abuse, 1996–98; Pres., Mental Health Review Tribunal, 1999–; Member: Parole Bd for England and Wales, 2004–; Courts Bd for N Wales, 2005–; N Wales Probation Bd, 2005–. Chm., Chester Bar Cttee, 1999–2001; Mem., Wales and Chester Circuit Mgt Bd, 1999–2001. Contested (Lab) Caernarfon, 1979. *Recreations:* sailing, watching Rugby, golf. *Address:* The Law Courts, The Civic Centre, Mold, Flintshire CH7 1AE. *Clubs:* Royal Anglesey Yacht; Bangor Rugby Union Football.

HUGHES, Sir Trevor Denby L.; *see* Lloyd-Hughes.

HUGHES, Sir Trevor (Poulton), KCB 1982 (CB 1974); FICE; Permanent Secretary, Welsh Office, 1980–85; *b* 28 Sept. 1925; *y s* of late Rev. John Evan and Mary Grace Hughes; *m* 1st, 1950, Mary Ruth Walwyn (marr. diss.); two *s*; 2nd, 1978, Barbara June Davison. *Educ:* Ruthin Sch. RE, 1945–48, Captain 13 Field Survey Co. Municipal engineering, 1948–61; Min. of Transport, 1961–62; Min. of Housing and Local Govt: Engineering Inspectorate, 1962–70; Dep. Chief Engineer, 1970–71; Dir, 1971–72 and Dir-Gen., 1972–74, Water Engineering, DoE; Dep. Sec., DoE, 1974–77; Dep. Sec., Dept of Transport, 1977–80. Mem., British Waterways Bd, 1985–88. Chairman: Building and Civil Engrg Holidays Scheme Mgt Ltd, 1987–99; Building and Civil Engrg Benefits Scheme Trustee Ltd, 1987–99. Vice-Chm., Public Works Congress Council, 1975–89, Chm., 1989–91. Chief British Deleg., Perm. Internat. Assoc. of Navigation Congresses, 1985–91; Mem., Water Panel, Monopolies and Mergers Commn, 1991–97. A Vice-Pres., ICE, 1984–86. Hon. Fellow, Univ. of Glamorgan (formerly Poly. of Wales), 1986. Hon. FCIWEM. *Recreations:* music, gardening, reading. *Address:* Clearwell, 13 Brambleton Avenue, Farnham, Surrey GU9 8RA. *T:* (01252) 714246.

HUGHES, Victor; *see* Hughes, H. V.

HUGHES, William Frederick, QPM 2001; Director General, Serious Organised Crime Agency, since 2006 (Director General designate, 2004–06); *b* Aug. 1950. *Educ:* Univ. of Aston in Birmingham (BSc Hons Mech. Engrg 1973). PC to Supt, Thames Valley Police, 1975–91; Asst Chief Constable, W Yorks Police, 1991–97; Dep. Chief Constable, Herts Constabulary, 1997–2001; Dir Gen., Nat. Crime Squad, 2001–04; seconded to SOCA, 2004. *Recreations:* aviation, personal computers, music. *Address:* Serious Organised Crime Agency, PO Box 8000, SE11 5EN. *T:* (020) 7238 8000.

HUGHES, William Young, CBE 1987; Chairman, Aberforth Smaller Companies Trust plc, 1990–2005; Chief Executive, 1976–98, and Chairman, 1985–98, Grampian Holdings plc; *b* 12 April 1940; *s* of Hugh Prentice Hughes and Mary Henderson Hughes; *m* 1964, Anne Macdonald Richardson; two *s* one *d*. *Educ:* Firth Park Grammar Sch., Sheffield; Univ. of Glasgow (BSc Hons Pharmacy, 1963). MPS 1964. Research, MRC project, Dept of Pharmacy, Univ. of Strathclyde, 1963–64; Lectr, Dept of Pharmacy, Heriot-Watt Univ., 1964–66; Partner, R. Gordon Drummond (group of retail chemists), 1966–70; Man. Dir, MSJ Securities Ltd (subsid. of Guinness Gp), 1970–76; Grampian Holdings, Glasgow, 1977–98 (holding co. in transport, tourism and retail). Dir, Royal Scottish Nat. Hosp. and Community NHS Trust, subseq. Central Scotland Healthcare NHS Trust, 1992–97; Mem. Council, Strathcarron Hospice, 2000–. Chairman: CBI Scotland, 1987–89; Prince's Scottish Youth Business Trust, 2000–07; Prince's Trust—Scotland, 2003–07; Trustee, Prince's Trust (UK), 2003–. Hon. Chm., European Summer Special Olympic Games (1990), Strathclyde, 1988–91. Pres., Right Track (formerly Work Wise), 1994–. Treas., Scottish Conservative Party, 1993–98 (Dep. Chm., 1989–92).

HUGHES-HALLETT, David John, FRICS; chartered surveyor; consultant, since 1999; *b* 19 June 1947; *s* of Peter Hughes-Hallett and Pamela (*née* Marshall); *m* 1976, Anne Mary Wright; two *s* one *d*. *Educ:* Fettes Coll., Edinburgh; Coll. of Estate Mgt, Reading. FRICS 1982. Director: Scottish Landowners' Federation, 1982–89; Scottish Wildlife Trust, 1989–98; main Bd Mem., SEPA, 1995–2002; Bd Mem., 2002–, Depute Convener, 2006–, Loch Lomond and Trossachs Nat. Park Authy; Mem., East Areas Bd, SNH, 2005–; Panel Mem., Waterwatch Scotland, 2006–. Chm., RICS in Scotland, 1987–88; Chm., Balerno High Sch. Bd, 1994–96. *Recreations:* sailing, sea kayaking, cycling, choral singing, Scottish countryside and its wildlife. *Address:* The Old School, Back Latch, Ceres, Fife KY15 5NT. *T:* (01334) 829333; *e-mail:* david@hugheshallett.co.uk.

HUGHES-HALLETT, James Wyndham John, FCA; Chairman, John Swire & Sons Ltd, since 2005; Director: Swire Pacific Ltd, since 1995 (Chairman, 1999–2004); Cathay Pacific Airways Ltd, since 1999; HSBC Holdings plc, since 2005; *b* 10 Sept. 1949; *s* of Michael Wyndham Norton Hughes-Hallett and Penelope Ann Hughes-Hallett (*née* Fairbairn); *m* 1991, Lizabeth Louise Hall; two *d*. *Educ:* Eton Coll.; Merton Coll., Oxford (BA; Hon. Fellow 2007). FCA 1973. Articled Clerk, Dixon, Wilson, Tubbs and Gillett, 1970–73; chartered accountant, 1974–76; various posts in Japan, Taiwan, Hong Kong and Australia, Swire Gp, 1976–2000; Chairman: John Swire & Sons (HK) Ltd, 1999–2004; Cathay Pacific Ltd, 1999–2004. Trustee: Esmée Fairbairn Foundn, 2005–; Dulwich Picture Gall., 2005; China Now, 2006–. Gov., SOAS, Univ. of London, 2005–. Hon. Fellow, Univ. of Hong Kong, 2004. *Address:* c/o John Swire and Sons Ltd, Swire House, 59 Buckingham Gate, SW1E 6AJ. *T:* (020) 7834 7717. *Club:* Hong Kong.
See also T. Hughes-Hallett.

HUGHES-HALLETT, Thomas; Chief Executive, Marie Curie Cancer Care, since 2000; *b* 28 Aug. 1954; *s* of Michael Wyndham Norton Hughes-Hallett and Penelope Ann Hughes-Hallet (*née* Fairbairn); *m* 1979, Juliet, *o d* of Col Anthony Rugge-Price; two *s* one *d*. *Educ:* Eton Coll.; Oriel Coll., Oxford (MA Modern Hist. 1974); Coll. of Law. Called to the Bar, Inner Temple, 1975. J. Henry Schroder Wagg & Co. Ltd, 1978–82; Enskilda Securities, 1982–93 (Chief Exec., Enskilda Corp., London, 1991–93); Robert Fleming & Co. Ltd, 1993–2000: Chm., Robert Fleming Securities, 1993–99; Chm., Fleming Private Asset Mgt, 1999–2000. Sen. Associate on End of Life Care, King's Fund, 2005. Chairman: English Churches Housing Gp, 2000–04; Michael Palin Centre for Stammering Children, 2002–. Special Trustee, Great Ormond St Hosp. Children's Charity, 2004–08. *Recreations:* music, tennis, cooking, walking. *Address:* Marie Curie Cancer Care, 89 Albert Embankment, SE1 7TP. *T:* (020) 7599 7130, *Fax:* (020) 7599 7131.
See also J. W. J. Hughes-Hallett.

HUGHES JONES, Dr Nevin Campbell, FRS 1985; on scientific staff, Medical Research Council, 1954–88; Fellow of Hughes Hall, Cambridge, 1987–90, now Emeritus; *b* 10 Feb. 1923; *s* of William and Millicent Hughes Jones; *m* 1952, Elizabeth Helen Dufty; two *s* one *d*. *Educ:* Berkhampsted Sch., Herts; Oriel Coll., Univ. of Oxford; St Mary's Hosp. Med. School. MA, DM, PhD; FRCP. Medical posts held at St Mary's Hosp., Paddington, Radcliffe Infirmary, Oxford, and Postgrad. Med. Sch., Hammersmith, 1947–52; Member: MRC's Blood Transfusion Unit, Hammersmith, 1952–79 (Unit transferred to St Mary's Hosp. Med. Sch., Paddington, as MRC's Experimental Haematology Unit, 1960); MRC's Mechanisms in Immunopathology (formerly in Tumour Immunity) Unit, Cambridge, 1979–88. *Publication:* Lecture Notes on Haematology, 1970, 7th edn 2004. *Recreations:* making chairs, walking the Horseshoe Path on Snowdon. *Address:* 65 Orchard Road, Melbourn, Royston, Herts SG8 6BB. *T:* (01763) 260471.

HUGHES-MORGAN, Sir (Ian) Parry (David), 4th Bt *cr* 1925, of Penally, co. Pembroke; *b* 22 Feb. 1960; *e s* of His Honour Maj.-Gen. Sir David John Hughes-Morgan, 3rd Bt, CB, CBE and Isabel Jean Hughes-Morgan (*née* Lindsay); *S* father, 2006; *m* 1992, Julia Katrin, *er d* of R. J. S. Ward; three *d*. *Heir:* *b* Jonathan Michael Vernon Hughes-Morgan [*b* 19 Feb. 1962; *m* 1996, Gail Christine Melling; one *s* one *d*].

HUGHES-YOUNG, family name of **Baron St Helens**.

HUGHESDON, Charles Frederick, AFC 1944; FRAeS; *b* 10 Dec. 1909; *m* 1st, 1937, Florence Elizabeth (actress, as Florence Desmond) (*d* 1993), *widow* of Captain Tom Campbell Black; one *s*; 2nd, 1993, Carol Elizabeth, *widow* of Baron Havers, PC; two step *s*. *Educ:* Raine's Foundation School. Entered insurance industry, 1927; learned to fly, 1932; Flying Instructor's Licence, 1934; commnd RAFO, 1934; Commercial Pilot's Licence, 1936. Joined Stewart, Smith & Co. Ltd, 1936; RAF Instructor at outbreak of war; seconded to General Aircraft as Chief Test Pilot, 1939–43; rejoined RAF, 1943–45 (AFC). Rejoined Stewart, Smith & Co. Ltd, 1946; retired as Chm. of Stewart Wrightson 1976. Dir, Aeronautical Trusts Ltd; Chm., The Charles Street Co. Hon. Treas., RAeS, 1969–85. Upper Freeman, City of London; Member: GAPAN; Gunmakers' Guild. Order of the Cedar, Lebanon, 1972. *Recreations:* shooting, horseracing, riding (dressage). *Clubs:* Royal Air Force, Royal Thames Yacht.
See also Hon. N. A. Havers, Hon. P. N. Havers.

HUGHESDON, John Stephen, FCA; Partner, 1977–2004, Consultant, 2004–06, Mazars (formerly Neville Russell); *b* 9 Jan. 1944; *s* of Eric Hughesdon and Olive Mona (*née* Quirk); *m* 1970, Mavis June Eburne; one *s* one *d*. *Educ:* Eltham Coll. ACA 1967, FCA 1977. Articled Clerk, then Manager, Peat Marwick Mitchell, 1962–73; Manager, Neville Russell, 1973–76. Common Councilman, 1991–96, Alderman, 1997–, Sheriff, 2004–05, City of London. Liveryman: Co. of Coopers, 1992– (Master, 2006–07); Co. of Chartered Accountants, 2003–; Freeman: Co. of Parish Clerks, 2001–; Co. of Watermen and Lightermen, 2005–. Trustee: Christ's Hosp. Foundn, 1993–2007 (Trustee, Pension Scheme, 2007–); British and Foreign Bible Soc., 1997– (Trustee, Pension Scheme, 2000–). Chm., Southwark Dio. Welcare, 2005–07; Pres., Boys' Bde London Dist, 2005–; Hon. Treasurer: Girls' Bde Nat. Council for England and Wales, 1979–91; Tear Fund, 1992–96. *Recreations:* family, church, golf, ski-ing. *Address:* 44 Speen Lane, Speen, Newbury, Berks RG14 1RN. *T:* (1635) 43120; *e-mail:* john.hughesdon@cityoflondon.gov.uk. *Clubs:* City Livery, National.

HUGHFF, Victor William, FIA; Chief General Manager, Norwich Union Insurance Group, 1984–89; *b* 30 May 1931; *s* of William Scott Hughff and Alice Doris (*née* Kerry); *m* 1955, Grace Margaret (*née* Lambert) one *s* one *d*. *Educ:* City of Norwich School. Served in RAF, 1951–53; commnd in Secretarial Br., National Service List. Joined Norwich Union Life Insce Soc., 1949; Assistant Actuary, 1966; General Manager and Actuary, 1975; Main Board Director, 1981–89. Director: Stalwart Assurance Group, 1989–93; Congregational & General Insurance, 1989–2001; United Reformed Church Ministers' Pension Trust Ltd, 1993–2005; Norwich Centre Projects Ltd, 1994–2006. CCMI. Liveryman, Actuaries' Co., 1990–. Elder of United Reformed Church, 1972–. *Recreation:* bowls. *Address:* 18 Hilly Plantation, Thorpe St Andrew, Norwich NR7 0JN. *T:* (01603) 434517.

HUGILL, John; QC 1976; a Recorder of the Crown Court, 1972–96; *b* 11 Aug. 1930; *s* of late John A. and Alice Hugill; *m* 1956, Patricia Elizabeth Hugill (*née* Welton); two *d*. *Educ:* Sydney C of E Grammar Sch., NSW; Fettes Coll.; Trinity Hall, Cambridge (MA). 2nd Lieut RA, 1948–49; Capt., RA (T), 1954. Called to the Bar, Middle Temple, 1954 (Bencher, 1984); Northern Circuit, 1954; Assistant Recorder, Bolton, 1971; a Dep. High Court Judge, 1985–96. Chairman: Darryn Clarke Inquiry, 1979; Stanley Royd Inquiry, 1985. Member: Criminal Injuries Compensation Bd, 1998–2000; Criminal Injuries Compensation Appeals Panel, 2000–02. Member: Senate of the Inns of Court and the Bar, 1984–86; Gen. Council of the Bar, 1987–89. Hon. Legal Advr, Clay Pigeon Shooting Assoc., 1992–. *Recreation:* talking and reading about yachting. *Address:* Peel Court Chambers, Sunlight House, Quay Street, Manchester M3 3JZ. *Club:* Army and Navy.

HUGILL, Michael James; Assistant Master, Westminster School, 1972–86; *b* 13 July 1918; 2nd *s* of late Rear-Adm. R. C. Hugill, CB, MVO, OBE, and Winifred (*née* Backwell). *Educ:* Oundle; King's Coll., Cambridge (Exhibitioner; BA 1939; MA 1943). War Service in the RN; Mediterranean, Home and Pacific Fleets, 1939–46; rank on demobilisation, Lieut-Comdr. Mathematics Master, Stratford Grammar Sch., 1947–51; Senior Mathematics Master, Bedford Modern Sch., 1951–57; Headmaster, Preston Grammar Sch., 1957–61; Headmaster, Whitgift School, Croydon, 1961–70; Lectr, Inst. of Education, Keele Univ., 1971–72. *Publication:* Advanced Statistics, 1985. *Address:* 4 Glenmore, Kersfield Road, SW15 3HL. *Club:* Army and Navy.

HUHNE, Christopher Murray Paul; MP (Lib Dem) Eastleigh, since 2005; *b* 2 July 1954; *s* of Peter Ivor Paul Huhne and Ann Gladstone Murray; *m* 1984, Vicky Pryce, *qv*; two *s* one *d*, and two step *d*. *Educ:* Université de Paris-Sorbonne (Certificat 1972); Magdalen Coll., Oxford (BA 1st Cl. Hons PPE 1975). Freelance journalist, India, 1975–76; Liverpool Daily Post and Echo, 1976–77; Brussels Corresp., Economist, 1977–80; Economics Leader Writer, 1980–84, Economics Editor, 1984–90, Guardian; Business Editor and Asst Editor, Independent on Sunday, 1990–91; Economic Columnist and Business and City Editor, Independent and Independent on Sunday, 1991–94; Founder and Man. Dir, sovereign ratings div., Ibca Ltd, 1994–97; Gp Man. Dir, Fitch Ibca Ltd, 1997–99; Vice-Chm., sovereign and internat. public finance, Fitch Ratings Ltd, 1999–2003. Mem. Council, REconS, 1993–98. Contested (SDP/Lib Dem Alliance): Reading E, 1983; Oxford W and Abingdon, 1987. Liberal Democrats: Chair, Press and Broadcasting Policy Panel, 1994–95; Econ. Advr, General Election, 1997; Mem., Econ. Policy Commn, 1998; Mem. Adv. Bd, Centre Forum (formerly Centre for Reform), 1998–; Jt Chair, Policy Panel on Global Stability, Security and Sustainability, 1999–2000; Chairman: Expert Commn on Britain's adoption of Euro, 1999–2000; Commn on public services, 2001–02. MEP (Lib Dem) SE Reg., England, 1999–2005. European Parliament: spokesman: European Lib Dem and Reformist Gp, Econ. and Monetary Affairs Cttee, 1999–2004; Alliance of Liberals and Democrats for Europe, 2004–05; Substitute Mem., Budget Cttee, 1999–2005. Lib Dem dep. Treasury spokesman, 2005–06, spokesman on the envmt, 2006–07, on home affairs, 2007–. Mem., Standing Cttee, Finance Act, 2005. Mem. Council, Britain in Europe, 1999–2005. Mem. Council, Consumers' Assoc., 2002–04. Young Financial Journalist of the Year, 1981, Financial Journalist of the Year, 1990, Wincott Awards. *Publications:* (jtly) Debt and Danger: the world financial crisis, 1984, 2nd edn 1987; Real World Economics, 1990; (jtly) The Ecu Report, 1991; Both Sides of the Coin: the case for the Euro, 1999, 2nd edn 2001. *Recreations:* family, exercise, cinema. *Address:* House of Commons, SW1A 0AA. *T:* (020) 7219 5490. *Clubs:* National Liberal, Hurlingham.

HUHNE, Vicky; *see* Pryce, V.

HUISMANS, Sipko; non-executive Director, Imperial Tobacco, 1996–2006; *b* 28 Dec. 1940; *s* of Jouko and Roelofina Huismans; *m* 1969, Janet; two *s* one *d.* *Educ:* primary sch., Holland; secondary sch., Standerton, S Africa; Stellenbosch Univ., S Africa (BA Com). Shift chemist, Usutu Pulp Co. Ltd, 1961–68; Gen. Man., Springwood Cellulose Co., 1968–74; Man. Dir, Courtaulds Central Trading, 1974–80; Dir, 1980–96, Man. Dir, 1982–84, Courtaulds Fibres; Dir, 1984–96, Man. Dir, 1990–91, Chief Exec., 1991–96, Courtaulds PLC; Chairman: Internat. Paints Ltd, 1987–90; Courtaulds Chemical and Industrial Exec., 1988–96; Special Advr to Chm., Texmaco, Indonesia, 1996–2000. Non-exec. Dir, Vickers, 1996–; Mem., Supervisory Bd, Reemstma, 2002–. *Recreations:* motor racing, sailing, competition. *Clubs:* Royal Lymington Yacht, Royal Southampton Yacht.

HULDT, Prof. Bo Kristofer Andreas; Professor of Strategic Studies, Department of Security and Strategy, Swedish National Defence College, since 2002; *b* 24 April 1941; *s* of Bo and Marta Huldt; *m* Ingrid Mariana Neering; two *d.* *Educ:* Lund Univ., Sweden (PhD Hist.); Augustana Coll., USA (BA); graduate work, Princeton. Asst and Associate Prof. of History, Lund and Växjö Univs, 1974–79; Res. Associate, Secretariat for Future Studies, Swedish Cabinet Office, 1975–78; Swedish Institute of International Affairs: Res. Associate, 1979; Asst Dir, 1983; Dep. Dir and Dir of Studies, 1985; Dir, 1988–97 (on leave of absence, 1992–95); Dir, IISS, 1992–93; Dir, Dept of Security Policy, Strategy and Mil. Hist., Royal Swedish Mil. Staff and War Coll., Stockholm, 1994–95; Prof. of Strategic Studies, 1996–, and Dir, Dept of Strategic Studies, 1997–2001, Swedish Nat. Defence Coll. Hd, Res. Council, Folke Bernadotte Acad., 2006–. Special Consultant to Swedish Dept of Defence, 1981–82. Pres., Swedish Nat. Defence Assoc., 1997–2000. Member: Swedish Royal Acad. of War Sciences, 1984 (Chm., 2006–); Swedish Royal Naval Acad., 1991. Editor: Yearbook of Swedish Inst. of Internat. Affairs, 1983–92; Swedish Nat. Defence Coll. Strategic Yearbook, 2002–. *Publications:* Sweden, the United Nations and Decolonization, 1974; (jtly) Sweden in World Society, 1978; World History 1945–65, Norwegian edn, 1982, Swedish and Finnish edns, 1983, Icelandic edn, 1985, French edn, 1995; contribs to learned jls on history, internat. politics and security. *Recreations:* shooting, literature. *Address:* Swedish National Defence College, Box 27805, 11593 Stockholm, Sweden.

HULINE-DICKENS, Frank William, (Frank Dickens); cartoonist, since 1959; writer; *b* 9 Dec. 1931; *s* of William James Charles Huline-Dickens and Lucy Sarah White; one *d* by Maria del Sagrario. *Educ:* Stationers' Co.'s Sch., London. Creator of cartoons 'Bristow', 1960–2002, 'Patto', 2002–04, Evening Standard. Plays: Fantasyland; No to be in England; three series of Bristow, BBC Radio, 1999–2000. *Publications:* 42 books including: Bristow collections, 1980–98; A Curl Up and Die Day (novel), 1980; Three Cheers for the Good Guys (novel), 1984; The Big Big Big Bristow Book, 2001; A Calmer Sutra, 2002; *for children:* Fly Away Peter (with Ralph Steadman), 1961; The Great Boffo, 1969; Boffo and the Great Motor Cycle Race; Boffo and the Great Air Race; Boffo and the Great Balloon Race; Boffo and the Great Cross Country Race; Teddy Pig; Albert Herbert Hawkins, the Naughtiest Boy in the World, 1971, and the Queen's Birthday, and the Space Rocket, 1978, and the Olympics, 1980; (with Raoul Dufy) Il Violino D'Oro. *Recreations:* cycling, painting. *Address:* Flat 3, 19 Albion Street, Chipping Norton, Oxon OX7 5BL. *T:* (01608) 641650; *e-mail:* frankdickens@lineone.net. *Club:* Unity Cycling (Pres., 2006–08).

HULL, Bishop Suffragan of, since 1998; **Rt Rev. Richard Michael Cokayne Frith;** *b* 8 April 1949; *s* of Roger Cokayne Frith and Joan Agnes Frith; *m* 1st, 1975, Jill Richardson (marr. diss. 2000); two *s* two *d*; 2nd, 2006, Kay Gledhill. *Educ:* Marlborough Coll., Wiltshire; Fitzwilliam Coll., Cambridge (BA 1972; MA 1976); St John's Coll., Nottingham. Ordained deacon, 1974, priest 1975; Asst Curate, Mortlake with East Sheen, Southwark, 1974–78; Team Vicar, Thamesmead, Southwark, 1978–83; Team Rector, Keynsham, Bath and Wells, 1983–92; Archdeacon of Taunton, 1992–98. *Recreations:* cricket, squash, theatre. *Address:* Hullen House, Woodfield Lane, Hessle, East Yorks HU13 0ES. *Club:* MCC.

HULL, Prof. Sir David, Kt 1993; FRCP, FRCPCH; Foundation Professor of Child Health, University of Nottingham, 1972–96; *b* 4 Aug. 1932; *s* of late William and Nellie Hull; *m* 1960, Caroline Elena Lloyd; two *s* one *d.* *Educ:* Univ. of Liverpool (BSc Hons, MB ChB). DCH, DObstRCOG; FRCP 1974; FRCPCH 1996. Lectr in Paediatrics, Oxford, 1963–66; Consultant Paediatrician, Hosp. for Sick Children, London, 1966–72; Sen. Lectr, Inst. of Child Health, Univ. of London, 1966–72. President: Neonatal Soc., 1987–91; British Paediatric Assoc., 1991–94. Hon. FFPH 2000. *Publications:* (with D. I. Johnston) Essential Paediatrics, 1981, 4th edn 1999; (with A. D. Milner) Hospital Paediatrics, 1984, 3rd edn 1997; (with E. F. St J. Adamson) Nursing Sick Children, 1984; (with L. Polnay) Community Paediatrics, 1984, 2nd edn 1993. *Recreations:* gardening, drawing.

See also Derek Hull.

HULL, Air Vice-Marshal David Hugill, FRCP; Dean of Air Force Medicine and Clinical Director, RAF, 1994–96, retired; *b* 21 Aug. 1931; *s* of late T. E. O. and M. E. Hull (*née* Dinsley); *m* 1957, Ann Thornton-Symington; two *d.* *Educ:* Rugby; Trinity Hall, Cambridge; St Thomas' Hosp. MA, MB BChir. Royal Waterloo and Kingston upon Thames Hosps, 1956–57; RAF 1957; Consultant in Medicine, PMRAF Hosp., Akrotiri, 1966–67; RAF Hosp., Cosford, 1967–74; Exchange Consultant, Aeromedical Consultation Service, USAF Sch. of Aerospace Medicine, 1974–77; PARAF Hosp., Wroughton, 1977–82; Consultant Advr in Medicine, RAF, 1983–93; Reader, Clinical Aviation Medicine, RAF IAM, 1981–93. QHS, 1991–96. Lady Cade Medal, RCS, 1973. Hon. Texas Citizen, 1977. OStJ 1997. *Publications:* chapters in books on aviation and aerospace medicine; papers in professional jls. *Recreations:* sailing, gardening, cross-country ski-ing. *Club:* Royal Air Force.

HULL, Prof. Derek, FRS 1989; FREng, FIMMM; Senior Fellow, University of Liverpool, since 1991; Goldsmiths' Professor of Metallurgy, University of Cambridge, 1984–91, now Professor Emeritus; Fellow, Magdalene College, Cambridge, 1984–91; *b* 8 Aug. 1931; *s* of late William and Nellie Hull (*née* Hayes); *m* 1953, Pauline Scott; one *s* four *d.* *Educ:* Baines Grammar School, Poulton-le-Fylde; Univ. of Wales (PhD, DSc). AERE, Harwell and Clarendon Lab., Oxford, 1956–60; University of Liverpool: Senior Lectr, 1960–64; Henry Bell Wortley Prof. of Materials Engineering, 1964–84; Dean of Engineering, 1971–74; Pro-Vice-Chancellor, 1983–84. Dist. Vis. Prof. and Senior Vis. NSF Fellow, Univ. of Delaware, 1968–69; Monash Vis. Prof., Univ. of Monash, 1981; Andrew Laing Lecture, NECInst, 1989. FREng (FEng 1986). Hon. Fellow, University Coll. Cardiff, 1985. Hon. DTech Tampere Univ. of Technology, Finland, 1987. Rosenhain Medal, 1973, A. A. Griffith Silver Medal, 1985, Inst. of Metals; Medal of Excellence in Composite Materials, Univ. of Delaware, 1990. *Publications:* Introduction to Dislocations, 1966, 4th edn 2001; An Introduction to Composite Materials, 1981, 2nd edn 1996; Fractography: observing, measuring and interpreting fracture surface topography, 1999; Celtic and Anglo-Saxon Art: geometric aspects, 2003; numerous contribs to Proc. Royal Soc., Acta Met., Phil. Mag., Jl Mat. Sci., MetalScience, Composites. *Recreations:* golf, music, fell-walking, early Medieval art. *Address:* Department of Engineering, University of Liverpool, Liverpool L69 3BX. *Club:* Heswall Golf.

See also Sir David Hull.

HULL, John Folliott Charles, CBE 1993; Chairman, 1997–98, Deputy Chairman, 1976–97 and 1998–99, Land Securities plc; *b* 21 Oct. 1925; *er s* of Sir Hubert Hull, CBE, and Judith, *e d* of P. F. S. Stokes; *m* 1951, Rosemarie Waring; one *s* three *d.* *Educ:* Downside; Aberdeen Univ.; Jesus Coll., Cambridge (Titular Schol.; 1st cl. hons Law; Keller Prize; MA). RA, 1944–48 (attached Royal Indian Artillery, 1945–48). Called to Bar, Inner Temple, 1952, *ad eund* Lincoln's Inn, 1954. J. Henry Schroder Wagg & Co. Ltd, 1957–72, 1974–85: a Man. Dir, 1961–72; Dep. Chm., 1974–77; Chm., 1977–83; Dir, 1984–85; Schroders plc: Dir, 1969–72, 1974–85; Dep. Chm., 1977–85. Director: Lucas Industries plc, 1975–90; Legal and General Assurance Soc., 1976–79; Legal & General Group plc, 1979–90; Goodwood Racecourse Ltd, 1987–93. Dir-Gen., City Panel on Take-overs and Mergers, 1972–74 (Dep. Chm., 1987–99); Chm., City Company Law Cttee, 1976–79. Lay Mem., Stock Exchange, 1983–84. Mem., Council, Manchester Business Sch., 1973–86. *Recreation:* reading 19th century novelists. *Address:* 33 Edwardes Square, W8 6HH. *T:* (020) 7603 0715. *Club:* MCC.

See also Duke of Somerset.

HULL, His Honour John Grove; QC 1983; a Circuit Judge, 1991–2003; *b* 21 Aug. 1931; *s* of Tom Edward Orridge Hull and Marjory Ethel Hull; *m* 1961, Gillian Ann, *d* of Leslie Fawcett Stemp; two *d.* *Educ:* Rugby School; King's College, Cambridge. BA (1st cl. in Mech. Scis Tripos) 1953, MA 1957; LLB 1954. National Service, commissioned RE, 1954–56; called to the Bar, Middle Temple, 1958 (Cert. of Honour, Bar Final), Bencher, 1989; in practice, common law Bar, 1958–91; a Recorder, 1984–91. *Recreations:* gardening, English literature.

HULL, Leslie David; His Honour Judge Leslie Hull; a Circuit Judge, since 2001; *b* 7 Jan. 1950; *s* of Leslie and Irene Hull; *m* Susanna; two *s* one *d.* *Educ:* Cowley Sch., St Helens; Brasenose Coll., Oxford (MA Juris.). Called to the Bar, Middle Temple, 1972 (Harmsworth Schol.); a Recorder, 1988–2001. *Recreations:* sport, music, wine. *Address:* Great Grimsby Combined Court Centre, Town Hall Square, Great Grimsby, Lincs DN31 1HX.

HULL, Robert; Director, Consultative Work, European Economic and Social Committee, 2002–06; *b* 23 Jan. 1947; *s* of John Whitfield Hull and Marguerite (*née* Stace); *m* 1972, Christine Elizabeth Biffin; one *s* two *d.* *Educ:* Dame Allan's Sch., Newcastle upon Tyne; Univ. of Leicester (BA Hist. 1968); Manchester Business Sch. (MBA 1973); King's Coll. London/RADA (MA 2007). UKAEA, 1968–69; PO Telecommunications, 1969–71; North of England Develt Council, 1973–74; EC Commission, 1974–79: Customs Service, 1974–76; Ext. Relns, SE Asia, 1976–79; Civil Servant, Scottish Office, 1979–82; European Commission, 1982–98: Ext. Relns, ME, 1982–86; Asst to Dir Gen., Financial Instns and Co. Law, 1986–90; Head, Policy Co-ordination Unit for Envmt, 1990–98; Dir, Common Services Orgn, subseq. Jt Services, Eur. Econ. and Social Cttee and Eur. Cttee of Regs, 1998–2002. Contested (C) Durham, EP elecn, 1989. Mem. Council, Univ. of Newcastle, 2006–. FRSA. *Publications:* various articles on EU ext. relns, financial services, envmt and sustainable develt, lobbying the EU. *Recreations:* sailing, ski-ing, music, theatre. *Address:* Maiden Cross, Allendale Road, Hexham, Northumberland NE46 2DH. *T:* (01434) 606192. *Club:* International (Brussels).

HULL, Robert David, (Rob), PhD; consultant; *b* 17 Dec. 1950; *s* of David Archibald Hull and Rosalie Joy Hull (*née* Cave); *m* 1973, Sarah, (Sally), Ann, *d* of Frank Bernard Cockett, *qv*; one *s* one *d.* *Educ:* Royal Grammar Sch., Guildford; Jesus Coll., Cambridge (BA 1st cl. Hons Mathematics; MA; PhD Linguistics 1975). Civil Service Dept, 1974–81; HM Treasury, 1981–82; Dept of Educn and Science, later Dept for Educn, 1982–94; Sec., HEFCE, 1994–98 (on secondment); Dir for Qualifications and Occupational Standards, subseq. for Qualifications and Young People, DFEE, subseq. DFES, 1998–2004. Mem., NIHEC, 1994–98. Chm., E London Advanced Technol. Trng, 2005–. Chm., On Golden Lane, 2007–. Governor: Holloway Sch., 1999–; Richard Cloudesley Sch., 2007–; Prior Weston Sch., 2007–; Cripplegate Foundn, 2008–. FRSA 2007. *Recreations:* chess, writing, photography. *Address:* 27 Myddelton Square, EC1R 1YE. *T:* (020) 7713 5343. *Clubs:* Surrey County Cricket; Cavendish Chess.

HULLAH, Rt Rev. Peter Fearnley; Principal, Northampton Academy, since 2006; *b* 7 May 1949; *s* of Ralph and Mary Hullah; *m* 1971, Hilary Sargent Long (marr. diss. 2008); one *s* one *d*; *m* 2008, Penelope Ann Bristow. *Educ:* Bradford Grammar Sch.; King's Coll., London (BD, AKC); Makerere Univ., Kampala; Cuddesdon Coll., Oxford. Curate, St Michael and All Angels, Summertown, Oxford, 1974–77; Asst Chaplain, St Edward's Sch., Oxford, 1974–77; Chaplain, 1977–82, Housemaster, 1982–87, Internat. Centre, Sevenoaks Sch.; Sen. Chaplain, King's Sch., Canterbury, 1987–92; Headmaster, Chetham's Sch. of Music, 1992–99; Area Bishop of Ramsbury, 1999–2005. Chm., Chaplains' Conf., 1987–92. Canon, Manchester Cathedral, 1995–99. Archbishops' Advr for Secondary Sch. Chaplaincy, 2001–06. Chm. Trustees, Bloxham Project, 2000–06 (Mem., 1979–99, Chm., 1996–99, Steering Cttee). Mem. Council, RSCM, 2002–05; Gov., Marlborough Coll., 2000–08; Trustee, Uppingham, 2008–. FRSA 1993. *Recreations:* pilgrimage, music, reaching the highest point in Africa. *Address:* Northampton Academy, Wellingborough Road, Northampton NN3 8NH. *T:* (01604) 402811; *e-mail:* peter.hullah@northampton-academy.org. *Club:* Athenæum.

HULME, Bishop Suffragan of, since 1999; **Rt Rev. Stephen Richard Lowe;** Bishop for Urban Life and Faith, since 2006; *b* 3 March 1944; *s* of Leonard Ernest Lowe and Marguerite Helen Lowe; *m* 1967, Pauline Amy Richards; one *s* one *d.* *Educ:* Leeds Grammar School; Reading School; Birmingham Poly (BSc London); Ripon Hall, Oxford. Curate, St Michael's Anglican Methodist Church, Gospel Lane, Birmingham, 1968–72; Minister-in-Charge, Woodgate Valley Conventional District, 1972–75; Team Rector of East Ham, 1975–88; Archdeacon of Sheffield, 1988–99. Hon. Canon, Chelmsford Cathedral, 1985–88; Chelmsford Diocesan Urban Officer, 1986–88. A Church Comr, 1992–99, 2001– (Member: Bd of Govs, 1994–99, 2001–; Bishoprics Cttee, 1995–99, Dep. Chm., 2001–); General Synod: Mem., 1991–99, 2000–; Member: Exec., Central Bd of Finance, 1993–96; House of Bishops, 2000–; Urban Bishops' Panel, 2001– (Chm., 2006–); Bd for Social Responsibility, 2000–02. Member: Churches Council for Britain and Ire., 1991–96; Bishoprics and Cathedrals Cttee, 1991– (Dep. Chm., 2002–); Archbishop's Commn on Orgn of C of E, 1994–95; Bishops' Adv. Gp on urban priority areas, 1993–97; Archbishops' Commn on Urban Life and Faith, 2004–06; Trustee, Church Urban Fund, 1991–97 (Chm., Grants Cttee, 1993–96). Chairman: Sheffield Somalian Refugees Trust, 1990–94; William Temple Foundn, 2006–. Mem., Duke of Edinburgh Commonwealth Study Conf., 1989. Travelling Fellowship, Winston Churchill Meml Trust, 1980; Paul Cadbury Travelling Fellowship on Urban Empowerment, 1996. *Publication:* The Churches' Role in the Care of the Elderly, 1974. *Recreations:* watching football, cinema, theatre, travel, photography. *Address:* 14 Moorgate Avenue, Withington, Manchester M20 1HE. *T:* (0161) 445 5922, *Fax:* (0161) 448 9687; *e-mail:* lowehulme@btinternet.com. *Club:* Royal Commonwealth Society.

See also P. M. Lowe.

HULME, Prof. Charles, DPhil; CPsychol, FBPsS; Professor of Psychology, University of York, since 1992; *b* 12 Oct. 1953; *s* of Norman and Edith Hulme; *m* 1995, Margaret Jean Snowling, *qv*; three *d*, and one step *s*. *Educ:* Oriel Coll., Oxford (MA; DPhil 1979). CPsychol 1989; FBPsS 1990. Lectr in Psychol., 1978–88, Reader, 1988–92, Univ. of York. *Publications:* Reading Retardation and Multi-sensory Teaching, 1981; (with S. Mackenzie) Working Memory and Severe Learning Difficulties, 1992. *Recreations:* walking, yoga, music, wine. *Address:* Department of Psychology, University of York, York YO10 5DD. *T:* (01904) 433145, *Fax:* (01904) 433181; *e-mail:* ch1@york.ac.uk.

HULME, Geoffrey Gordon, CB 1984; Chairman, Knowledge Aid for Sierra Leone, since 2001; *b* 8 March 1931; *s* of Alfred and Jessie Hulme; *m* 1956, Shirley Leigh Cumberlidge (*d* 2003); one *s* one *d*. *Educ:* King's Sch., Macclesfield; Corpus Christi Coll., Oxford (MA, 1st Cl Hons Mod. Langs). Nat. Service, Intelligence Corps, 1949–50; Oxford, 1950–53; Ministry of Health, subseq. Department of Health and Social Security, latterly Department of Health: Asst Principal, 1953–59; Principal, 1959–64; Principal Regional Officer, W Midlands, 1964–67; Asst Sec., 1967–74; Under-Sec., 1974–81; Principal Finance Officer, 1981–86; Dep. Sec., 1981–91; seconded to Public Finance Foundn as Dir, Public Expenditure Policy Unit, 1986–91; consultant, Office of Health Econs, CIPFA, 1991–2001. Trustee: Council for Educn in the Commonwealth, 2001–; Disabled Living Foundn, 2001– (Chm., 2001–06). *Recreations:* most of the usual things and collecting edible fungi. *Address:* Stone Farm, Little Cornard, Sudbury, Suffolk CO10 0NW. *Club:* Royal Automobile.

HULME, Margaret Jean; *see* Snowling, M. J.

HULME, Prof. Michael, PhD; Professor of Environmental Science, University of East Anglia, since 2002; Director, Tyndall Centre for Climate Change Research, 2000–07; *b* 23 July 1960; *s* of Ralph Hulme and Shelagh Mary Hulme (*née* Close); *m* 1987, Gillian Margaret Walker; one *d*. *Educ:* Madras Coll., St Andrews; Univ. of Durham (BSc); UC, Swansea (PhD 1985). Lectr in Geog., Univ. of Salford, 1984–88; Sen. Res. Associate, 1988–97, Reader, 1998–2002, UEA. *Publications:* (ed) Climates of the British Isles, 1997; Climate Change Scenarios for the United Kingdom, 1998, 2nd edn 2002; Imagined Memories and the Seductive Quest for a Family History, 2008; Why we Disagree about Climate Change, 2009; contrib. numerous climate-related articles to acad., professional and popular jls. *Recreations:* cricket, modern history, genealogy. *Address:* School of Environmental Sciences, University of East Anglia, Norwich NR4 7TJ. *T:* (01603) 593162, *Fax:* (01603) 593901; *e-mail:* m.hulme@uea.ac.uk; *web:* www.mikehulme.org.

HULME, Rev. Paul; Minister, Petts Wood, Orpington Circuit, since 2003; *b* 14 May 1942; *s* of Harry Hulme and Elizabeth Hulme; *m* 1976, Hilary Frances Martin; three *s*. *Educ:* Hatfield House, Yorks; Didsbury Theological Coll., Bristol (BA). Minister: Bungay, Suffolk, 1968–70; Brighton, (also Chaplain, Sussex Univ.), 1970–75; Newquay, Cornwall, 1975–79; Taunton, 1979–86; Enfield, 1986–88; Supt Minister, Wesley's Chapel, London, 1988–96; Minister, New River Circuit, N London, 1997–2003. Duty Chaplain, Westminster Abbey, 1996–. Mem., BBC Churches Religious Adv. Council, 1992–95. Freeman, City of London, 1990. *Recreations:* walking, music. *Address:* 19 Petts Wood Road, Orpington, Kent BR5 1JT. *T:* (01689) 821956. *Club:* National Liberal.

HULME CROSS, Peter; Member, London Assembly, Greater London Authority, 2004–08 (UK Ind, 2004–05; Veritas, 2005; One London, 2005–08). Computer engr, then trainer. Former Mem., London Fire and Emergency Planning Authy.

HULSE, Christopher, CMG 1992; OBE 1982; HM Diplomatic Service, retired; Ambassador to the Swiss Confederation, and concurrently (non-resident) to the Principality of Liechtenstein, 1997–2001; *b* 31 July 1942; *s* of Eric Cecil Hulse and late Joan Mary Hulse (*née* Tizard); *m* 1966, Dimitra, *d* of Brig. and Mrs D. Karayannakos, Karayanneïka-Trypi, Sparta, Greece; one *d*. *Educ:* Woking Grammar Sch.; Trinity Coll., Cambridge (BA 1964). Entered Foreign Office, 1964; UN Dept, FO, 1964–67; Third Sec., later Second Sec., Prague, 1967–70; Eastern European and Soviet Dept, FCO, 1970–72; First Sec., Bangkok, 1973; Western European Dept, FCO, 1973–77; UK Deleg'n to NATO, Brussels, 1977–80; UK Deleg'n to CSCE Conf., Madrid, 1980–81; Asst Hd, Defence Dept, FCO, 1981–82; Counsellor, NATO Defence Coll., Rome, 1983; Political Counsellor and Consul-Gen., Athens, 1983–88; Hd of Eastern European, subseq. Central European Dept, FCO, 1988–92; Permt Rep., UN, Vienna, 1992–97. *Recreations:* books, music, walking, gardening, carpentry. *Address:* Karayanneïka-Trypi, near Sparta, 23100, Greece.

HULSE, Sir Edward (Jeremy Westrow), 10th Bt *cr* 1739, of Lincoln's Inn Fields; DL; *b* 22 Nov. 1932; *er s* of Sir Westrow Hulse, 9th Bt and his 1st wife Philippa Mabel Hulse (decd) (*née* Taylor, later Lamb); *S* father, 1996; *m* 1957, Verity Ann Pilkington; one *s* one *d*. *Educ:* Eton; Sandhurst. Late Captain, Scots Guards. High Sheriff, Hampshire, 1978; DL Hampshire, 1989. *Recreations:* tennis, shooting. *Heir: s* Edward Michael Westrow Hulse [*b* 10 Sept. 1959; *m* 1986, Doone Brotherton; three *s* three *d*]. *Address:* Breamore House, near Fordingbridge, Hampshire SP6 2DF. *T:* (01725) 512233. *Club:* White's.

HULSE, Dr Russell Alan; Principal Research Physicist, Plasma Physics Laboratory, Princeton University, since 1992; *b* 28 Nov. 1950; *s* of Alan Earle Hulse and Betty Joan Hulse (*née* Wedemeyer). *Educ:* The Cooper Union, NY (BS Physics 1970); Univ. of Massachusetts, Amherst (MS Physics 1972; PhD Physics 1975; DSc 1994). National Radio Astronomy Observatory, 1975–77; Plasma Physics Lab., Princeton Univ., 1977–, Dist. Res. Fellow, 1994. Vis. Prof. of Physics and Sci. Educn, Univ. of Texas at Dallas, 2004–. Fellow, Amer. Physical Soc., 1993. (Jtly) Nobel Prize in Physics, 1993. *Publications:* papers in professional jls and conf. procs in fields of pulsar astronomy, controlled fusion plasma physics and computer modeling. *Recreations:* cross-country ski-ing, canoeing, nature photography, bird watching, other outdoor activities, clay target shooting, music. *Address:* Princeton University, Plasma Physics Laboratory, James Forrestal Research Campus, PO Box 451, Princeton, NJ 08543, USA. *T:* (609) 2432621.

HULYER, Douglas, CBiol; independent adviser on environment and heritage and on environmental communications and learning; Director, Conservation Programmes, Wildfowl and Wetlands Trust, 1997–2005; *b* 13 April 1952; *s* of Charles and Florence Hulyer; *m* 1975, Beth Woodward; two *d*. *Educ:* Colfe's Sch.; Avery Hill Coll. of Educn (Cert Ed Dist.; BEd 1st Cl Hons London). CBiol, MIBiol. Educn Officer, Surrey Wildlife Trust, 1977–84; Wildfowl and Wetlands Trust: Educn Officer, 1984–88; Dir, Educn and Public Affairs, 1988–97. Member: Council for Envmtl Educn, 1998–; Council, English Nature, 2002–06; Bd, Natural England, 2006–. Member: Commn on Educn and Communication, IUCN, 1996–; Learning Panel, NT, 2008–. Trustee: Nat. Heritage Meml Fund, 2006–; Heritage Lottery Fund, 2006–. Vice-Pres., Surrey Wildlife Trust, 2003–. MInstD. *Recreations:* art, gardening, design, music. *Address:* Thornton, Thrupp Lane, Thrupp, Stroud, Glos GL5 2EF; *e-mail:* doug.hulyer@btinternet.com.

HUM, Sir Christopher (Owen), KCMG 2003 (CMG 1996); HM Diplomatic Service, retired; Master of Gonville and Caius College, Cambridge, since 2006; *b* 27 Jan. 1946; *s* of late Norman Charles Hum and Muriel Kathleen (*née* Hines); *m* 1970, Julia Mary, secon*d* of Hon. Sir Hugh Park; one *s* one *d*. *Educ:* Berkhamsted Sch.; Pembroke Coll. Cambridge (Foundn Scholar; 1st Cl. Hons; MA; Hon. Fellow 2004); Univ. of Hong Kong. Joined FCO, 1967; served in: Hong Kong, 1968–70; Peking, 1971–73; Office of the UK Perm. Rep. to the EEC, Brussels, 1973–75; FCO, 1975–79; Peking, 1979–81; Paris, 1981–83; Asst Head, Hong Kong Dept, FCO, 1983–85; Counsellor, 1985; Dep Head, Falkland Is Dept, FCO, 1985–86; Head, Hong Kong Dept, FCO, 1986–89; Counsellor (Political) and Hd of Chancery, UK Mission to UN, New York, 1989–92; Asst Under-Sec. of State (Northern Asia), 1992–94, (Northern Asia and Pacific), 1994–95; Ambassador to Poland, 1996–98; Dep. Under-Sec. of State and Chief Clerk, FCO, 1998–2001; Ambassador to the People's Republic of China, 2002–05. Dir, Laird, plc, 2006–. Adv. Cttee, China Policy Inst., Univ. of Nottingham, 2006–; Exec. Cttee, GB-China Centre, 2006–. Gov., SOAS, 1998–2001. Hon. LLD Nottingham, 2006; Hon PhD London Metropolitan, 2006. *Recreations:* music (piano, viola), walking. *Address:* Gonville and Caius College, Cambridge CB2 1TA. *Club:* Athenæum.

HUMBLE, James Kenneth, OBE 1996; fair trading consultant, since 1998; non-executive Director, Dignity in Dying, since 2007; *b* 8 May 1936; *s* of Joseph Humble and Alice (*née* Rhodes); *m* 1962, Freda (*née* Holden); three *d*. Served RN, 1954–56. Weights and Measures, Oldham, 1952–62; Fed. Min. of Commerce and Industry, Nigeria, 1962–66; Chief Trading Standards Officer, Croydon, 1966–74; Asst Dir of Consumer Affairs, Office of Fair Trading, 1974–79; Dir of Metrication Bd, 1979–80; Dir, Nat. Metrological Co-ordinating Unit, 1980–87; Chief Exec., Local Auths Co-ordinating Body on Food and Trading Standards, 1982–98. Non-exec. Dir, NCC, 1997–2002. Sec. Trade Descriptions Cttee, Inst. of Trading Standards, 1968–73; Examr, Dip. in Trading Standards, 1978–94; Vice Chm., Council of Europe Cttee of Experts on Consumer Protection, 1976–79. Member: Council for Vehicle Servicing and Repair, 1972–75; Methven Cttee, 1974–76; OECD Cttee, Air Package Tours, 1978–79; BSI Divl Council, 1976–79; Eden Cttee on Metrology, 1984; Food Codes Cttee, DoH, 1998–; Group Chairman: World Conf. on Safety, Sweden, 1989; Yugoslavian Conf. on Fair Trading, 1992; Member: European Consumer Product Safety Assoc., 1987–97; W European Legal Metrology Co-operation, 1989–98; European Forum Food Law Enforcement Practitioners, 1990–98; Consumer Congress, 1998–2002. Non-exec. Dir, Wine Standards Bd, 1999–2003. Organiser, First European Metrology Symposium, 1988. Conf. papers to USA Western States Conf. on Weights and Measures, 1989. FITSA 1974– (Vice Pres. 1997–); FRSA 1996. Trustee, Golden Leaves, 2002–. Rugby, Devonport Services, 1954–56; Captain, Oldham Rugby Union, 1957–59; Professional Rugby, Leigh RFC, 1959–65. *Publications:* (contrib.) Marketing and the Consumer Movement, 1978 European Inspection, Protection and Control, 1990; contrib. to various jls. *Recreations:* bridge, golf, opera. *Address:* 153 Upper Selsdon Road, Croydon, Surrey CR2 0DU. *T:* (020) 8657 6170.

HUMBLE, Jovanka, (Joan); JP; MP (Lab) Blackpool North and Fleetwood, since 1997; *b* 3 March 1951; *d* of John and Dora Piplica; *m* 1972, Paul Nugent Humble; two *d*. *Educ:* Lancaster Univ. (BA Hons). DHSS, 1972–73; Inland Revenue, 1973–77. Mem. (Lab) Lancs CC, 1985–97. *Recreations:* gardening, cooking, reading. *Address:* (constituency office) 216 Lord Street, Fleetwood FY7 6SW. *T:* (01253) 877346.

HUME, Gary, RA 2001; artist; *b* 9 May 1962. *Educ:* Goldsmiths' Coll., Univ. of London (BA 1988). Prof. of Drawing, RA, 2004. *Solo exhibitions* include: Karsten Schubert Ltd, 1989, 1991; Galerie Tanja Grünert, Cologne, 1991, 1993; Matthew Marks Gall., NY, 1992, 1994, 1997, 1998, 2001, 2005; White Cube, ICA, Kunsthalle Bern, 1995; Galleria il Ponte, Rome, 1996; Hayward Gall., Sadler's Wells Th., 1998; Whitechapel Art Gall. Dean Gall., Edinburgh, 1999; La Caixa, Barcelona, 2000; White Cube, 2002; MOMA, Dublin, 2003; *group exhibitions* include: Karsten Schubert Ltd, 1990, 1992, 1993, 1995; British Art Show, McLellan Galls, Glasgow, Leeds City Art Gall. and Hayward Gall., 1990; Matthew Marks Inc., NY, 1991; Musée Nat. d'Histoire, Luxembourg, Times Sq., NY, 1993; Stedelijk Mus., Amsterdam, 1995; Venice Biennale, 1995, 1999; Saatchi Gall., 1997, 2000; White Cube², NPG, 2000; Tate Modern, 2001; Tate Liverpool, 2002; Tate Britain, 2004; *work in public collections* including Arts Council, British Council, Saatchi Collection, Tate Gall., Paine Webber Art Collection, NY, DESTE Foundn for Contemp. Art, Athens, and Art Inst. of Chicago. Jerwood Painting Prize, 1997. *Address:* c/o Royal Academy of Arts, Burlington House, Piccadilly, W1J 0BD.

HUME, James Bell; Under-Secretary, Scottish Office, 1973–83; *b* 16 June 1923; *s* of late Francis John Hume and Jean McLellan Hume; *m* 1950, Elizabeth Margaret Nicolson. *Educ:* George Heriot's Sch., Edinburgh; Edinburgh Univ. (MA Hons History, 1st Cl.). RAF, 1942–45. Entered Scottish Office, 1947; Jt Sec., Royal Commn on Doctors' and Dentists' Remuneration, 1958–59; Nuffield Trav. Fellowship, 1963–64; Head of Edinburgh Centre, Civil Service Coll., 1969–73. *Publication:* Mandarin Grade 3, 1993. *Recreations:* dance music, walking, enjoying silence. *Address:* 2/9 Succoth Court, Succoth Park, Edinburgh EH12 6BZ. *T:* (0131) 346 4451. *Club:* New (Edinburgh).

HUME, James Robert; Member (Lib Dem) Scotland South, Scottish Parliament, since 2007; *b* 4 Nov. 1962; *s* of Walter and Joyce Hume; *m* 1986, Lynne White; two *s* one *d*. *Educ:* Selkirk High Sch.; East of Scotland Coll. of Agric. (Dip. Agric. 1982); Univ. of Edinburgh (MBA 1997). Farmer; Partner, John Hume & Son, 1988–. Dir, NFU Scotland, 2004–06 and 2007. Mem. (Lib Dem), Scottish Borders Council, 2007–. Chm., Borders Foundn for Rural Sustainability, 2002–07; Mem. Bd, Scottish Enterprise Borders, 2002–07. Trustee, Borders Forest Trust, 2000–06. *Publication:* (contrib.) Shepherds, by Walter Elliot, 2000. *Recreations:* amateur radio, gardening, motorcycling, conservation work. *Address:* Sundhopeburn, Yarrow, Selkirk TD7 5NF; Scottish Parliament, Holyrood Road, Edinburgh EH99 1SP. *T:* (0131) 348 6705, *Fax:* (0131) 348 6703; *e-mail:* jim.hume.msp@scottish.parliament.uk. *Club:* Cockenzie and Port Seton Amateur Radio.

HUME, Prof. John; Tip O'Neill Professor of Peace Studies, Faculty of Social Sciences, University of Ulster, since 2002; *b* 18 Jan. 1937; *s* of Samuel Hume; *m* 1960, Patricia Hone; two *s* three *d*. *Educ:* St Columb's Coll., Derry; St Patrick's Coll., Maynooth, NUI (MA). Res. Fellow in European Studies, TCD; Associate Fellow, Centre for Internat. Affairs, Harvard, 1976. Pres., Credit Union League of Ireland, 1964–68; MP for Foyle, NI Parlt, 1969–73; Member (SDLP): Londonderry: NI Assembly, 1973–75; NI Constitutional Convention, 1975–76; NI Assembly, 1982–86; Foyle, NI Assembly, 1998–2000; Minister of Commerce, NI, 1974. Mem. (SDLP) NI, European Parlt, 1979–2004. Leader, SDLP, 1979–2001. Mem. (SDLP) New Ireland Forum, 1983–84. Contested (SDLP) Londonderry, UK elections, Oct. 1974. Member: Cttee on Regl Policy and Regl Planning, European Parlt, 1979–2004; ACP-EEC Jt Cttee, 1979–2004; Bureau of European Socialist Gp, 1979–2004. MP (SDLP) Foyle, 1983–2005. Mem., Irish T&GWU (now Services, Industrial, Professional & Technical Union). Hon. DLitt: Massachusetts, 1985; Catholic Univ. of America, 1986; St Joseph's Univ., Philadelphia, 1986; Tusculum Coll., Tennessee, 1988. St Thomas More Award, Univ. of San Francisco, 1991; (jtly) Nobel Peace Prize, 1998; Freedom of Londonderry, 2000. *Address:* Faculty of Social Sciences, University of Ulster, Magee Campus, Londonderry BT48 7JL.

HUME, Dr Robert, FRCPE, FRCPGlas, FRCPI, FRCPath, FRCSE; Consultant Physician, Southern General Hospital, Glasgow, 1965–93; *b* 6 Jan. 1928; *m* 1958, Kathleen Ann Ogilvie; two *s* one *d*. *Educ:* Univ. of Glasgow (MB, ChB, MD, DSc). FRCPGlas 1968; FRCPE 1969; FRCPath 1992; FRCSE 1992; FRCPI 1993. Nat. Service in India and Germany, 1946–48, commnd into Gordon Highlanders. Glasgow University: Hutcheson Res. Scholar, 1955–56; Hall Fellow, 1956–58; Hon. Clinical Sub-Dean, 1985–93. Dir, HCI Internat. Med. Centre, 1996–2002. Pres., RCPSGlas, 1990–92. Chm., Jt Cttee on Higher Med. Trng for UK Colls, 1990–93. Mem., Acad. of Medicine, Malaysia, 1991. Hon. FACP; Hon. FRACP; Hon. FCSSA; Hon. FRCP&S (Canada). *Publications:* on haematological and vascular diseases. *Recreations:* hill-walking, swimming, reading, art appreciation, gardening, talking, golf. *Address:* 6 Rubislaw Drive, Bearsden, Glasgow G61 1PR. *T:* (0141) 586 5249. *Club:* Buchanan Castle Golf.

HUMFREY, Charles Thomas William, CMG 1999; HM Diplomatic Service, retired; Ambassador to Republic of Indonesia, 2004–08; *b* 1 Dec. 1947; *s* of Brian and Marjorie Humfrey; *m* 1971, Enid Thomas; two *s* one *d*. *Educ:* The Lodge Sch., Barbados (Barbados Scholar, 1966); St Edmund Hall, Oxford (Webb Medley Jun. Prize, 1968). FCO 1969; Tokyo, 1971–76; SE Asian Dept, FCO, 1976–79; Private Sec. to Minister of State, 1979–81; UK Mission, NY, 1981–85; Southern African Dept, FCO, 1985–87; Counsellor, Ankara, 1988–90; Counsellor (Econ.), Tokyo, 1990–94; Head of African Dept (Southern), FCO, 1994–95; Minister, Tokyo, 1995–99; Ambassador, Republic of Korea, 2000–03. *Address:* 31 Welford Place, Wimbledon, SW19 5AJ.

HUMM, Robert Peter; Director, Legal Services, Department for Environment, Food and Rural Affairs, since 2004; *b* 8 June 1949; *s* of Joseph Robert Humm and Winifred Maud Humm (*née* Fox). Chartered Sec. Formerly Solicitor to HSC and HSE. *Recreations:* opera, travel. *Address:* Department for Environment, Food and Rural Affairs, 3–8 Whitehall Place, SW1A 2HH.

HUMM, Roger Frederick; Director: Andrew Macdonald (London) Ltd, since 2002; St James and Country Estates Ltd, since 2004; Mount Securities Ltd, since 2006; *b* 7 March 1937; *s* of Leonard Edward Humm, MBE, and Gladys Humm; *m* 1966, Marion Frances (*née* Czechman) (marr. diss.). *Educ:* Hampton Sch., Hampton, Middx; Univ. of Sheffield (BA Hons Econ). Graduate trainee, Ford Motor Co. Ltd (UK), 1960, Sales Manager, 1973; Marketing Dir, 1977, Internat. Gp Dir, N Europe, 1978, Ford of Europe Inc.; Exec. Dir of Sales, 1980, Man. Dir, 1986–90, Ford Motor Co. Ltd; Director: Henry Ford & Son Ltd (Cork), 1978–90; Ford Motor Credit Co. Ltd, 1980–90; Vice-Chm. and Chief Exec., 1992–2000, non-exec. Dir, 2000–02, Alexanders Holdings plc. FRSA 1987; FInstD; FIMI. Liveryman, Worshipful Co. of Carmen, 1986; Freeman, City of London, 1986. *Recreations:* golf, scuba diving, writing. *Address:* The Clock House, Kelvedon, Essex CO5 9DG. *Clubs:* Royal Automobile, Lord's Taverners, Variety Club of Great Britain.

HUMMEL, Frederick Cornelius, MA, DPhil, BSc; Head of Forestry Division, Commission of the European Communities, 1973–80, retired; *b* 28 April 1915; *s* of Cornelius Hummel, OBE, and Caroline Hummel (*née* Riefler); *m* 1st, 1941, Agnes Kathleen Rushforth (marr. diss. 1961); one *s* (and one *s* decd); 2nd, 1961, Floriana Rosemary Hollyer; three *d*. *Educ:* St Stephan, Augsburg, Germany; Wadham Coll., Oxford. District Forest Officer, Uganda Forest Service, 1938–46; Forestry Commn, 1946–73; Mensuration Officer, 1946; Chief, Management Sect., 1956; released for service with FAO as Co-Dir, Mexican Nat. Forest Inventory, 1961–66; Controller, Management Services, Forestry Commn, 1966–68, Comr for Harvesting and Marketing, 1968–73. Hon. Member: Société Royale Forestière de Belgique; Asociación para el Progreso Forestal, Spain; Corresponding Member: Mexican Acad. of Forest Scis; Italian Acad. of Forest Scis; Soc. of Forestry, Finland. Dr *hc* Munich, 1978. Bernard Eduard Fernow Plaquette, (jtly) Amer. Forestry Assoc. and Deutscher Forstverein, 1986; Alexander von Humboldt Gold Medal, 1995. *Publications:* Forest Policy, 1984; Biomass Forestry in Europe, 1988; Forestry Policies in Europe: an analysis, 1989; Memories of Forestry and Travel, 2001. *Address:* Ridgemount, 8 The Ridgeway, Guildford, Surrey GU1 2DG. *T:* (01483) 572383.

HUMPHERSON, Edward Allen; Assistant Auditor General, National Audit Office, since 2007; *b* Salisbury, 2 June 1970; *s* of William Allen Humpherson and Rosemary Elizabeth Humpherson (*née* Arbuthnot); *m* 2004, Fiona Kathryn James; one *s*. *Educ:* Univ. of Edinburgh (MA 1st Cl. Hons Politics and Econ. Hist.). Chartered Accountant 1996. Nat. Audit Office, 1993–2007. *Publications:* National Audit Office reports. *Recreations:* cricket, contemporary art. *Address:* National Audit Office, 151 Buckingham Palace Road, SW1W 9SS. *T:* (020) 7798 7115; *e-mail:* edward.humpherson@nao.gsi.gov.uk.

HUMPHERY-SMITH, Cecil Raymond Julian, OBE 2004; FSA; Principal, Institute of Heraldic and Genealogical Studies, Canterbury, since 1983; *b* 29 Oct. 1928; *s* of Frederick Humphery-Smith, MBE and Agnes Violet (*née* Boxall); *m* 1951, Alice Elizabeth Gwendoline Cogle; one *s* five *d*. *Educ:* Hurstpierpoint Coll.; London Sch. of Hygiene and Tropical Medicine, Univ. of London (BSc 1950); Parma-Piacenza Dept of Agronomy; Univ. of Kent at Canterbury. Consumer Services Manager, H. J. Heinz Corp., 1955–60; UK Rep. and Internat. Consultant, DeRica SpA, 1961–74; Man. Dir, Achievements Ltd, 1961–91; script ed. and writer, Media Internat., 2001–04. Founder and Director: Sch. of Family History, 1957; Inst. of Heraldic and Genealogical Studies, 1961 (Trustee, 1964–). Pt-time Extra Mural Lectr, Univs of Oxford, London and Kent, 1951–2000. Ed., Family History, 1962–. Vis. Prof., Univ. of Minho, 1975. Co-Founder, Fedn of Family Hist. Socs, 1974; formerly Mem. Cttees, Soc. of Genealogists (FSG 1970); Heraldry Society: Mem. Council, 1953–2003; Fellow, 1960; Vice-Pres., 1993; Vice-Pres., Cambridge Univ. Heraldry Soc., 1954; Hon. Vice Pres., Cambridge Univ. Heraldic and Genealogical Soc., 1994. Pres. Emeritus, Confedn Internat. des Sciences Généalogique et Héraldique (Pres., 1986–90); Mem., Bureau Perm. des Congrès internationaux, 1976–; Academician, 1976, Mem. Council, 1994–, Acad. Internat. d'Héraldique; Pres., Internat. Fedn of Schs of Family Hist. Studies, Bologna, 2001. Mem., Governing Council, Rutherford Coll., Univ. of Kent at Canterbury, 1992–2001. FSA 1982. Hon. Fellow, Canterbury Christ Ch Univ., 2008. Freeman, City of London, 1967; Liveryman: Co. of Broderers, 1973–; Co. of Scriveners, 1979– (Hon. Historian, 1983; Mem. Court, 1999). DLit Minho, 1975. Kt of Obedience, SMO Malta, 1977; Founding Co-ordinator, Order of Malta Volunteers, 1974. *Publications:* (jtly) The Colour of Heraldry, 1958; General Armory Two, 1973; Sonnets of Life, 1973; Anglo-Norman Armory, vol. 1, 1973, vol. 2, 1993; Atlas and Index of Parish Registers, 1974, as Phillimore's Atlas and Index of Parish Registers, 1995, 3rd edition 2003; A Genealogist's Bibliography, 1985; Hugh Revel, Master of the Hospital 1257–1277, 1994; Armigerous Ancestors, 1997; (jtly) A History of the Worshipful Company of Scriveners of London, 2001; A Tudor Armorial, 2004; several pamphlets and studies in the heraldry of Canterbury Cathedral; contrib. articles to proc. of internat. congresses and colloquia in genealogy and heraldry; contrib. encyclopedias, DNB, The Coat of Arms, Genealogists Mag., Family History, etc. *Recreations:* music, walking, writing sonnets, enjoying four generations of family. *Address:* Institute of Heraldic and Genealogical Studies, Northgate, Canterbury, Kent CT1 1BA. *T:* (01227) 768664; *e-mail:* principal@ihgs.ac.uk; Saint Michael's, Allan Road, Seasalter, Whitstable, Kent CT5 4AH. *T:* (01227) 275791; *e-mail:* scatterbr@sky.com. *Clubs:* Athenæum; Royal British (Lisbon).

HUMPHREY, Prof. Caroline, (Lady Rees of Ludlow), PhD; FBA 1998; Fellow, King's College, Cambridge, since 1978; Sigrid Rausing Professor of Collaborative Anthropology, University of Cambridge, since 2006; *b* 1 Sept. 1943; *d* of Prof. C. H. Waddington, CBE, FRS and M. J. Waddington; *m* 1st, 1967, Nicholas Humphrey (marr. diss. 1977); 2nd, 1986, Prof. Martin Rees (*see* Baron Rees of Ludlow). *Educ:* St George's High Sch., Edinburgh; Girton Coll., Cambridge (BA 1965; PhD 1973); Leeds Univ. (MA Mongolian Studies 1971). University of Cambridge: Research Fellow, Girton Coll., 1971–74; Sen. Asst in Res., Scott Polar Res. Inst., 1973–78; Asst Lectr, 1978–83; Lectr, 1983–95; Reader, 1995–98; Prof. of Asian Anthropology, 1998–2006. British Acad. Research Reader, 1990–92; Vis. Fellow, Inst. for Humanities, Univ. of Michigan, 1992. MAE 2007. Foreign Mem., Amer. Philosophical Soc., 2004. Staley Prize in Anthropology, Sch. of Amer. Res., USA, 1990. Chevalier, Ordre des Palmes Académiques (France), 2004. *Publications:* Karl Marx Collective: economy, society and religion in a Siberian collective farm, 1983, rev. edn 1998; (with J. Laidlaw) The Archetypal Actions of Ritual, 1994; Shamans and Elders: experience, knowledge and power among the Daur Mongols, 1996; (with D. Sneath) The End of Nomadism?: pastoralism and the state in Inner Asia, 1998; The Unmaking of Soviet Life, 2002. *Recreation:* classical music. *Address:* River Farm House, Latham Road, Cambridge CB2 2EJ. *T:* (01223) 369043.

HUMPHREYS, Prof. Colin John, CBE 2003; FREng, FIMMM, FInstP; Director of Research, Department of Materials Science and Metallurgy, University of Cambridge since 2008 (Goldsmiths' Professor of Materials Science, 1992–2008); Professor of Experimental Physics, Royal Institution of Great Britain, since 1999; Director, Rolls-Royce University Technology Centre, since 1994; Fellow of Selwyn College, Cambridge, since 1990; *b* 24 May 1941; *s* of Arthur William Humphreys and Olive Annie (*née* Harton); *m* 1966, Sarah Jane Matthews; two *d*. *Educ:* Luton Grammar Sch.; Imperial Coll., London (BSc); Churchill Coll., Cambridge (PhD); Jesus Coll., Oxford (MA). Sen. Res. Officer 1971–80, Lectr 1980–85, in Metallurgy and Science of Materials, Univ. of Oxford; Sen. Res. Fellow, Jesus Coll., Oxford, 1974–85; Henry Bell Wortley Prof. of Materials Engrg and Hd of Dept of Materials Sci. and Engrg, Liverpool Univ., 1985–89; Prof. of Materials Sci., 1990–92, Hd, Dept of Materials Sci. and Metallurgy, 1991–95, Univ. of Cambridge. Visiting Professor: Univ. of Illinois, 1982–86; Arizona State Univ., 1979. Lectures: D. K. C. MacDonald Meml, Toronto, 1993; Hume-Rothery Meml, Oxford, 1997; Gladstone, London, 1999; Hatfield Meml, Sheffield, 2000; Royal Acad. of Engrg Sterling, Singapore and Malaysia, 2001; John Matthews Meml, Durban, 2002; Robert Warner, Founders' Co., London, 2002; Sigma Xi, McGill Univ., 2004. Chm., Commn on Electron Diffraction, and Mem. Commn on Internat. Tables, Internat. Union of Crystallography, 1984–87. Member: SERC, 1988–92 (Chm., Materials Sci. and Engrg Commn, 1988–92; Mem., Science Bd, 1990–92); Adv. Cttee, Davy-Faraday Labs, Royal Instn, 1989–92; Scientific Adv. Cttee on Advanced Materials for EC Internat. Scientific Co-opn Prog., 1990–2000; Metallurgy and Materials Panel, RAE 2001, HEFCE; BERR (formerly DTI) Nat. Adv. Cttee on Electronic Materials and Devices, 1999–; Internat. Adv. Panel, Etisalat, UAE, 2003–04; Chairman: Internat. Adv. Bd, Nat. Inst. for Materials Sci., Tsukuba, Japan, 2003–; Internat. Review Panel, Dept of Materials, Technion, Israel, 2004. Member Council: RMS, 1988–89; Inst. of Metals, 1989–91; President: Physics sect., BAAS, 1998–99; Inst. of Materials, 2002 (Mem. Council, 1992–2002; Sen. Vice-Pres., 2000–01); Inst. of Materials, Minerals and Mining, 2002–03 (Chm., Managing Bd, 2004–05); Awards Cttee, Royal Acad. of Engrg, 2003–. Fellow in Public Understanding of Physics, Inst. of Phys, 1997–98; Selby Fellow, Aust. Acad. of Scis, 1997. Hon. Pres., Canadian Coll. for Chinese Studies, 1996–; Member Court: Univ. of Bradford, 1990–92; Univ. of Cranfield, 1992–. Freeman, City of London, 1994; Liveryman: Goldsmiths' Co., 1997– (Freeman, 1992; Mem., Technology and Promotions Cttee, 2002–); Armourers' and Brasiers' Co., 2001– (Freeman, 1998; Mem., Ct of Assts, 2004–; Renter Warden, 2008–). FREng (FEng 1996); MAE 1991. Hon. DSc Leicester, 2001. RSA Medal, 1963; Reginald Mitchell Meml Lecture and Medal, 1989; Rosenhain Medal and Prize, Inst. of Metals, 1989; Templeton Award, 1994; Elegant Work Prize, Inst. of Materials, 1996; Kelvin Medal and Prize, Inst. of Physics, 1999; Gold Medal, Fedn of Eur. Materials Socs, 2001; Robert Franklin Mehl Gold Medal, Minerals, Metals and Materials Soc., USA, 2003. Editor, Reports on Progress in Physics, 2001–. *Publications:* (ed) High Voltage Electron Microscopy, 1974; (ed) Electron Diffraction 1927–77, 1978; Creation and Evolution, 1985 (trans. Chinese 1988); (ed) Understanding Materials, 2002; The Miracles of Exodus, 2003; patents and numerous sci. and tech. pubns mainly on electron microscopy, semiconductors, superconductors and nanometre scale electron beam lithography. *Recreations:* chronology of ancient historical events, contemplating gardening. *Address:* Department of Materials Science and Metallurgy, Pembroke Street, Cambridge CB2 3QZ. *T:* (01223) 334457.

HUMPHREYS, Emyr Owen, FRSL; author; *b* 15 April 1919; *s* of William and Sarah Rosina Humphreys, Prestatyn, Flints; *m* 1946, Elinor Myfanwy, *d* of Rev. Griffith Jones, Bontnewydd, Caerns; three *s* one *d*. *Educ:* University Coll., Aberystwyth; University Coll., Bangor (Hon. Fellow, Univ. of Wales, 1987). Gregynog Arts Fellow, 1974–75; Hon. Prof., English Dept, Univ. Coll. of N Wales, Bangor, 1988. FRSL 1993. Hon. DLitt Wales, 1990. Cymmrodorion Medal, 2003. *Publications:* The Little Kingdom, 1946; The Voice of a Stranger, 1949; A Change of Heart, 1951; Hear and Forgive, 1952 (Somerset Maugham Award, 1953); A Man's Estate, 1955; The Italian Wife, 1957; Y Tri Llais, 1958; A Toy Epic, 1958 (Hawthornden Prize, 1959); The Gift, 1963; Outside the House of Baal, 1965; Natives, 1968; Ancestor Worship, 1970; National Winner, 1971 (Welsh Arts Council Prize, 1972); Flesh and Blood, 1974; Landscapes, 1976; The Best of Friends, 1978; Penguin Modern Poets No 27, 1978 (Soc. of Authors Travelling Award, 1979); The Kingdom of Brân, 1979; The Anchor Tree, 1980; Pwyll a Riannon, 1980; Miscellany Two, 1981; The Taliesin Tradition, 1983 (Welsh Arts Council Non-Fiction Prize, 1984); Jones: a novel, 1984; Salt of the Earth, 1985; An Absolute Hero, 1986; Darn o Dir, 1986; Open Secrets, 1988; The Triple Net, 1988; The Crucible of Myth, 1990; Bonds of Attachment, 1991 (Book of the Year, Welsh Arts Council, 1992); Outside Time, 1991; Brodyr a Chwiorydd, 1994; Unconditional Surrender, 1996; The Gift of a Daughter, 1998 (Book of the Year, Welsh Arts Council, 1999); Collected Poems, 1999; Dal Pen Rheswm, 1999; Ghosts and Strangers, 2001; Conversations and Reflections, 2002; Old People Are a Problem, 2003; The Shop, 2005. *Recreation:* walking. *Address:* Llinon, Penyberth, Llanfairpwll, Ynys Môn, Gwynedd LL61 5YT.

HUMPHREYS, Janet, (Mrs V. W. Humphreys); *see* Anderson, Janet.

HUMPHREYS, Kate; *see* Priestley, K.

HUMPHREYS, Dr Keith Wood, CBE 1992; Chairman, The Technology Partnership plc, since 1998; *b* 5 Jan. 1934; *s* of William and Alice Humphreys; *m* 1964, Tessa Karen Shepherd; three *d*. *Educ:* Manchester Grammar School; Trinity Hall, Cambridge (MA, PhD). FRSC. Managing Dir, Plastics Div., Ciba-Geigy (UK), 1972–78; Jt Managing Dir,

Ciba-Geigy (UK), 1979–82; Managing Dir, 1982–84, Chm. and Man. Dir, 1984–95, May & Baker, later Rhône-Poulenc Ltd. Director: Hickson Internat. plc, 1995–2000; BIP Ltd, 1996–2001. Mem., BBSRC, 1994–98. CCMI. *Recreations:* music, tennis, mountain walking.

HUMPHREYS, Richard William; QC 2006; barrister; *b* 22 Feb. 1963; *s* of Ian Richardson Humphreys and Valerie Thursby Trewin; *m* 1988, Rosalind Julia Birley; one *s* two *d*. *Educ:* Aldwickbury Sch., Wheathampstead; Stowe Sch.; Nottingham Univ. (LLB); Gonville and Caius Coll., Cambridge (LLM 1985). Called to the Bar, Inner Temple, 1986. *Recreations:* history, tennis, ski-ing.

HUMPHRIES, Barry; *see* Humphries, J. B.

HUMPHRIES, Chris, CBE 1998; Chief Executive Officer, UK Commission for Employment and Skills, since 2008; *b* 31 Aug. 1948; *s* of John Joseph Humphries and Neradah Merle Humphries; *m* 1996, Hazel Maxwell Cross; one *s* two *d*. *Educ:* Univ. of NSW (BA 1972). Media Resources Officer, ILEA, 1975–79; Producer, Promedia, 1979–82; IT Prog. Manager, 1982–84, Asst Dir, 1984–87, CET; Production Manager, ICL Interactive Learning Services, 1987–88; Educn Business Unit Manager, Acorn Computers Ltd, 1988–91; Chief Exec., Hertfordshire TEC, 1991–94; Dir, then Chief Exec., TEC Nat. Council, 1994–98; Director General: British Chambers of Commerce, 1998–2001; City & Guilds of London Inst., 2001–07. Chairman: Nat. Skills Task Force, 1998–2000; UK Skills, 2000–; Member: Nat. Learning and Skills Council, 2000–02; Nat. Adult Learning Cttee, 2000–07; Council for Excellence in Leadership and Mgt, 2001–02; BBC Educn Adv. Gp, 2002–; Skills Strategy Steering Gp, 2002–04. Mem. Council, Gresham Coll., 2003–. Bd Mem., NHSU Trust, 2003–05.

HUMPHRIES, David Ernest; defence science consultant; Director, Materials Research Laboratory, Defence Science and Technology Organisation, Melbourne, Australia, 1992–94; *b* 3 Feb. 1937; *er s* of late Ernest Augustus Humphries and Kathleen Humphries; *m* 1959, Wendy Rosemary Cook; one *s* one *d*. *Educ:* Brighton Coll.; Corpus Christi Coll., Oxford (Scholar; MA). RAE Farnborough: Materials Dept, 1961; Avionics Dept, 1966; Head of Inertial Navigation Div., 1974; Head of Bombing and Navigation Div., 1975; Head of Systems Assessment Dept, 1978; Dir Gen. Future Projects, MoD PE, 1981–83; Chief Scientist (RAF) and Dir Gen. of Res. (C), MoD, 1983–84; Dir Gen. Res. Technol., MoD (PE), 1984–86; Asst Chief Scientific Advr (Projects and Research), MoD, 1986–90; Dir, Australian Aeronautical Res. Lab., 1990–92. *Recreations:* music, theatre. *Address:* Lynmouth Cottage, 28 Howard Road, Dorking, Surrey RH4 3HP.

HUMPHRIES, His Honour Gerard William; a Circuit Judge, 1980–2003; *b* 13 Dec. 1928; *s* of late John Alfred Humphries and Marie Frances Humphries (*née* Whitwell), Barrow-in-Furness; *m* 1st, 1957, Margaret Valerie (*d* 1999), *o d* of late W. W. Gelderd and Margaret Gelderd (*née* Bell), Ulverston; four *s* one *d*; 2nd, 2007, Elizabeth Anne Swinburne. *Educ:* St Bede's Coll., Manchester; Manchester Univ. (LLB Hons). Served RAF, 1951–53, Flying Officer. Called to Bar, Middle Temple, 1952; admitted to Northern Circuit, 1954; Asst Recorder of Salford, 1969–71; a Recorder of the Crown Court, 1974–80. Chairman: Medical Appeals Tribunal, 1976–80; Vaccine Damage Tribunals, 1979–80. Charter Mem., Serra Club, N Cheshire, 1963– (Pres. 1968, 1973, 1995–96, 2003–04). Trustee: SBC Educnl Trust, 1979– (Chm., 1979–90); Serra Foundn, 1998–. Foundn Governor, St Bede's Coll., Manchester, 1978–. KCHS 1996, with star 2003 (KHS 1986). *Publication:* The Stations of the Cross: stations for vocation, 1995. *Recreations:* tennis, golf, music, caravanning, gardening, lecturing on New Testament trials and other subjects.

HUMPHRIES, John Anthony Charles, OBE 1980; Senior Partner, Travers Smith Braithwaite, 1980–95; *b* 15 June 1925; *s* of Charles Humphries; *m* 1951, Olga June, *d* of Dr Geoffrey Duckworth, MRCP; four *d*. *Educ:* Fettes; Peterhouse, Cambridge (1st Law). Served War, RNVR, 1943–46. Solicitor (Hons), 1951. Chairman: Water Space Amenity Commn, 1973–83; Southern Council for Sport and Recreation, 1987–92; Vice-Pres., Inland Waterways Assoc., 1973– (Chm., 1970–73); Mem. Inland Waterways Amenity Adv. Council, 1971–89; Adviser to HM Govt on amenity use of water space, 1972; Member: Nat. Water Council, 1973–83; Thames Water Authy, 1983–87. Mem., Sports Council, 1987–88. Chm., Evans of Leeds plc, 1982–97; Mem., London Bd, Halifax Building Soc., 1985–92; Dep. Chm., Environment Council, 1985–94. Chm., Lothbury Property Trust, 1996–99. Vice Chm., Council, Surrey Univ., 1995–99. Governor, Sports Aid Foundn, 1990–96. Trustee, Thames Salmon Trust, 1987–2001. *Publication:* A Lifetime of Verse, 2006. *Recreations:* inland waters, gardening. *Address:* 21 Parkside, Wimbledon, SW19 5NA. *T:* (020) 8946 3764. *Club:* Naval.

HUMPHRIES, (John) Barry, AO 1982; CBE 2007; music-hall artiste and author; *b* 17 Feb. 1934; *s* of J. A. E. Humphries and L. A. Brown; *m* 1959, Rosalind Tong; two *d*; *m* 1979, Diane Millstead; two *s*; *m* 1990, Lizzie, *d* of Sir Stephen (Harold) Spender, CBE, CLit. *Educ:* Melbourne Grammar Sch.; Univ. of Melbourne. Repertory seasons, Union Theatre, Melbourne, 1953–54; Phillip Street Revue Theatre, Sydney, 1956; Demon Barber, Lyric, Hammersmith, 1959; Oliver!, New, 1960, Piccadilly, 1968, London Palladium, 1997; Treasure Island, Mermaid, 1968. One-man shows (author and performer): A Nice Night's Entertainment, 1962; Excuse I, 1965; Just a Show, Australia, 1968, Fortune Theatre, 1969; A Load of Olde Stuffe, 1971; At Least You Can Say That You've Seen It, 1974; Housewife Superstar, 1976; Isn't It Pathetic at His Age, 1979; A Night with Dame Edna, 1979; An Evening's Intercourse with Barry Humphries, 1981–82; Tears Before Bedtime, 1986; Back with a Vengeance, 1987; Look At Me When I'm Talking To You!, 1994; Rampant in Whitehall, Les Patterson Has a Stand Up, 1996; New Edna, the Spectacle, 1998; Edna's Royal Tour, 1998, NY, 2000 (Special Tony Award); Remember You're Out, 1999; Nat. American Tour, 2001; Back to My Roots and Other Suckers, Australia, 2003; Dame Edna Back With a Vengeance, NY, 2004 and US nat. tour, 2005; Back With a Vengeance, a New Effort, Australia, 2006. TV series: The Dame Edna Experience, 1987; Ally McBeal, 2002; The Dame Edna Treatment, 2007. Numerous plays, films, broadcasts and recordings. Exhibition: Wish You Were Here!: travels with a brush, Savill Galls, Melbourne, 2007. Pres., Frans de Boever Soc. (Belgium). DUniv Griffith Univ., Qld, 1994. *Publications:* Bizarre, 1964; Innocent Austral Verse, 1968; (with Nicholas Garland) The Wonderful World of Barry McKenzie, 1970; (with Nicholas Garland) Bazza Holds His Own, 1972; Dame Edna's Coffee Table Book, 1976; Les Patterson's Australia, 1979; Treasury of Australian Kitsch, 1980; A Nice Night's Entertainment, 1981; Dame Edna's Bedside Companion, 1982; The Traveller's Tool, 1985; (with Nicholas Garland) The Complete Barry McKenzie, 1988; My Gorgeous Life: the autobiography of Dame Edna Everage, 1989; The Life and Death of Sandy Stone, 1991; More Please (autobiog.), 1992; Women in the Background (novel), 1995; My Life As Me (autobiog.), 2002. *Recreations:* kissing, inventing Australia, painting beautifully. *Clubs:* Garrick, Beefsteak, Pratt's; Savage (Melbourne).

HUMPHRIES, John Charles Freeman; Founder and Trustee, since 1987, and Director, 1993–2002, British Bone Marrow Donor Appeal; Chief Executive, Cymru Annibynnol Independent Wales Party, 2000–03; *b* 2 Jan. 1937; *s* of Charles Montague Humphries and Lilian Clara Humphries; *m* 1959, Eliana Paola Julia Mifsud; two *s* one *d*. *Educ:* St Julian High Sch., Newport, Gwent. Western Mail: News Editor, 1966–73; Dep. Editor, 1973–80; Thomson Regional Newspapers: European Bureau Chief, 1980–86; London City Editor, 1986–87; Editor, Western Mail, 1988–92; Launch Editor, Wales on Sunday, 1989. Mem., Wales Cttee, Consumer Council for Water, 2005–. *Publications:* The Man From the Alamo: why the Welsh Chartist uprising 1839 ended in a massacre, 2004; Gringo Revolutionary: the amazing adventures of Caryl ap Rhys Pryce, 2005. *Recreations:* walking, opera, reading, Rugby, gardening. *Address:* Cwr y Coed, Usk Road, Tredunnock, Gwent NP5 1PE. *Club:* Cardiff and County.

HUMPHRIES, Prof. Martin James, PhD; FMedSci; Wellcome Trust Principal Research Fellow and Professor of Biochemistry, University of Manchester, since 1995; Director, Wellcome Trust Centre for Cell-Matrix Research, since 2000; *b* 26 Nov. 1958; *s* of Terence and Kathleen Lesley Humphries; *m* 1982, Sandra Ceinwen Jones; two *d*. *Educ:* Nottingham High Sch.; Univ. of Manchester (BSc 1980; PhD 1983). Guest Researcher, Nat. Cancer Inst., NIH, Bethesda, Md, 1983–88; Postdoctoral Res. Associate, 1983–87, Associate Dir for Res., 1987–88, Howard Univ. Cancer Center, Washington; Wellcome Trust Sen. Res. Fellow, Univ. of Manchester, 1988–95. Vice-Chm., 2005–07, Chm., 2008–, Biochemical Soc. FMedSci 2000; MAE 2006. *Publications:* The Extracellular Matrix Factsbook, 1993, 2nd edn 1998; contrib. numerous articles to learned jls. *Recreations:* golf, red wine. *Address:* Faculty of Life Sciences, University of Manchester, Michael Smith Building, Oxford Road, Manchester M13 9PT; *e-mail:* martin.humphries@manchester.ac.uk.

HUMPHRIES, Michael John; QC 2003; *b* 15 June 1959; *s* of Derek James Humphries and Joan Irene Humphries; *m* 1989, Juliet Claire Hampton; one *s* two *d*. *Educ:* Univ. of Leicester (BL). Called to the Bar, Inner Temple, 1982. Sen. Editor, Tottels (formerly Butterworths) Compulsory Purchase and Compensation Service, 1999–. *Recreations:* house in France, music, literature. *Address:* Francis Taylor Building, Temple, EC4Y 7BY. *T:* (020) 7353 8415; *e-mail:* mhumphries@ftb.eu.com. *Club:* Reform.

HUMPHRYES, Jane Carole; QC 2003; a Recorder, since 1999; *d* of Alan John Humphryes and Avril Pamela Gloria Humphryes; *m* Timothy Stephen Robert Wakefield; one *s* four *d*, and one step *s* one step *d*. *Educ:* Univ. of Kent at Canterbury; Council of Legal Educn. Called to the Bar, Middle Temple, 1983. *Recreations:* walking, watercolours, travel, cuisine, theatre, ski-ing. *Address:* 3 Raymond Buildings, Gray's Inn, WC1R 5BH. *T:* (020) 7400 6400; *e-mail:* jh@humphryesqc.com.

HUMPHRYS, John; Presenter: Today Programme, Radio 4, since 1987; On the Ropes, Radio 4, since 1994; Mastermind, BBC TV, since 2003; *b* 17 Aug. 1943; *s* of George and Winifred Humphrys; *m* 1965, Edna Wilding (marr. diss. 1991); one *s* one *d*; partner Valerie Sanderson; one *s*. *Educ:* Cardiff High School. BBC TV: Washington Correspondent, 1971–77; Southern Africa Correspondent, 1977–80; Diplomatic Correspondent, 1980–81; Presenter: 9 o'Clock News, 1981–86; On the Record, 1993–2002. Hon. Fellow, Cardiff Univ., 1998. Hon. DLitt Abertay Dundee, 1996; Hon. MA Wales, 1998; Hon. LLD St Andrews, 1999. *Publications:* Devil's Advocate, 1999; The Great Food Gamble, 2001; Lost for Words: the mangling and manipulation of the English language, 2004; Beyond Words: how language reveals the way we live now, 2006; In God We Doubt: confessions of a failed atheist, 2007. *Recreations:* music, attempting to play the 'cello, hill walking. *Address:* c/o News Centre, BBC TV Centre, W12 7RJ.

HUNJAN, Satinder Pal Singh; QC 2002; a Recorder, since 2003; *b* 5 Nov. 1960; *s* of Nasib Singh Hunjan and Rajinder Kaur Hunjan; *m* 1990, Gurtej Mina Kaur Ghata-Aura; one *s* one *d*. *Educ:* Univ. of Birmingham (LLB Hons). Called to the Bar, Gray's Inn, 1984; specialises in clinical negligence, personal injuries and general insurance law. *Recreations:* travelling, tennis, ski-ing, football, theatre. *Address:* 5 Fountain Court, Steelhouse Lane, Birmingham B4 6DR. *T:* (0121) 606 0500, *Fax:* (0121) 606 1501; *e-mail:* sh@no5.com.

HUNKIN, Timothy Mark Trelawney; artist, cartoonist, engineer; *b* 27 Dec. 1950; *s* of Oliver John and Frances Elizabeth Hunkin; *m* 2005, Meg; one step *d*. *Educ:* St Paul's Sch., Hammersmith; Caius Coll., Cambridge (BA Engrg 1972). Launched Phlegethon Fireworks, staging public displays and building fireworks, 1971; cartoonist, Rudiments of Wisdom (cartoon strip), Observer, 1973–87; worked for Oxfam, Africa, 1980; Osher Fellow, Exploratorium Sci. Centre, San Francisco, 1993; British Council lect. tour, How to Cheat at Art, Australia and USA, 1997; Fellowship, Xerox Parc, 1998; Co-founder, Mongrel Media, designing and building exhibns, 1999; Nesta Dreamtime Fellowship, 2004. Projects include: inflatable pigs and sheep shot from mortar shells, developed for Pink Floyd's Animal tour, 1977; designed and built 50-ft high water clock, Neal's Yd, Covent Gdn, 1982; designed How Television Works (gallery), Nat. Museum of Photography, Bradford, 1986; designed Ride of Life (ride), 1989; created The Secret Life of the Home (gallery), Sci. Mus., London, 1994–95; created, with Mongrel Media, visitor centre, Eden Project, 2000, Science in the Dock (sci. ethics automata show), Glasgow Sci. Centre, 2001; opened Under the Pier Show (amusement arcade of homemade slot machines), Southwold Pier, 2002; interactive exhibits, Nat. Archives and V&A, 2005; public clocks, Hawkins Bazaar and London Zoo, 2007. Exhibitions include: The Disgusting Spectacle (mechanical sculptures), ICA, London, 1981; The Art Gallery (mechanical art gall. spectators), tour of 20 provincial galls, 1983. Researcher, writer and presenter, Channel 4: Secret Life of Machines, series 1, 1988, series 2, 1990; Secret Life of the Office (series), 1992. *Publications:* Mrs Gronkwonk and the Post Office Tower (for children), 1973; Almost Everything There is to Know: the Rudiments of Wisdom cartoons, 1988; Hunkin's Experiments, 2003. *Recreations:* I do things I'm interested in and enjoy; I've never distinguished between work and recreation. *Address:* *e-mail:* hunkin@timhunkin.com.

HUNNINGS, Mary Rosa Alleyne; *see* Berry, M. R. A.

HUNNISETT, Dr Roy Frank, FSA, FRHistS; on staff of Public Record Office, 1953–88; *b* 26 Feb. 1928; *s* of Frank Hunnisett and Alice (*née* Budden); *m* 1st, 1954, Edith Margaret Evans (marr. diss. 1989); 2nd, 1989, Janet Heather Stevenson. *Educ:* Bexhill Grammar Sch.; New Coll., Oxford (1st Cl. Hons Mod. Hist., 1952; Amy Mary Preston Read Scholar, 1952–53; MA, DPhil 1956). FRHistS 1961; FSA 1975. Lectr, New Coll., Oxford, 1957–63. Royal Historical Society: Alexander Prize, 1957; Mem. Council, 1974–77; Vice-Pres., 1979–82; Selden Society: Mem. Council, 1975–84, 1987–; Vice-Pres., 1984–87; Treasurer, Pipe Roll Soc., 1973–87; Literary Dir, Sussex Record Soc., 2003– (Mem. Council, 1992–2003). *Publications:* Calendar of Inquisitions Miscellaneous: (ed jtly) vol. IV, 1957 and vol. V, 1962; (ed) vol. VI, 1963 and vol. VII, 1968; The Medieval Coroners' Rolls, 1960; The Medieval Coroner, 1961; (ed) Bedfordshire Coroners' Rolls, 1961; (ed) Calendar of Nottinghamshire Coroners' Inquests 1485–1558, 1969; (contrib.) The Study of Medieval Records: essays in honour of Kathleen Major, 1971; Indexing for Editors, 1972; Editing Records for Publication, 1977; (ed jtly and contrib.) Medieval Legal Records edited in memory of C.A.F. Meekings, 1978; (ed) Wiltshire Coroners' Bills 1752–1796, 1981; (ed) Sussex Coroners' Inquests 1485–1558, 1985; (ed) Sussex Coroners' Inquests 1558–1603, 1996, and 1603–1688, 1998; (ed) East

Sussex Coroners' Records 1688–1838, 2005; articles and revs in historical and legal jls. *Recreations:* Sussex, music, cricket. *Address:* 23 Byron Gardens, Sutton, Surrey SM1 3QG. *T:* (020) 8661 2618.

HUNSDON OF HUNSDON, Baron; *see* Aldenham, Baron.

HUNSWORTH, John Alfred; Director, Banking Information Service, 1954–81; *b* 23 Dec. 1921; *s* of late Fred Sheard Hunsworth and Lillian Margaret (*née* Wetmon); *m* 1972, Phyllis Sparshatt (*d* 1994). *Educ:* Selhurst Grammar Sch.; LSE (BCom). Served War, 1941–46: commnd E Surrey Regt; served 2nd Punjab Regt, Indian Army, 1942–45. Dep. Editor, Bankers' Magazine, 1948–54. Freeman, City of London. *Publications:* contrib. prof. jls. *Recreations:* gardening, world travel, philately; formerly lawn tennis and Rugby football. *Address:* 29 West Hill, Sanderstead, Surrey CR2 0SB. *T:* (020) 8657 2585. *Clubs:* Reform, Royal Over-Seas League; Surrey County Cricket.

HUNT, family name of Barons Hunt of Chesterton, Hunt of Kings Heath and Hunt of Wirral.

HUNT OF CHESTERTON, Baron *cr* 2000 (Life Peer), of Chesterton in the co. of Cambridgeshire; **Julian Charles Roland Hunt,** CB 1998; PhD; FRS 1989; Professor in Climate Modelling, University College London, 1999–2008, now Emeritus; *b* 5 Sept. 1941; *s* of Roland Charles Colin Hunt, CMG; *m* 1965, Marylla Ellen Shephard; one *s* two *d*. *Educ:* Westminster Sch.; Trinity Coll., Cambridge (BA 1963; PhD 1967); Univ. of Warwick. Post-doctoral res., Cornell Univ., USA, 1967; Res. Officer, Central Electricity Res. Labs, 1968–70; University of Cambridge: Fellow, 1966–, Sen. Res. Fellow, 1998–99, Trinity Coll.; Lectr in Applied Maths and in Engrg, 1970–78; Reader in Fluid Mechanics, 1978–90; Prof., 1990–92, Hon. Prof., 1992–, in Fluid Mechanics; Chief Exec., Meteorol Office, 1992–97. Hon. Dir, Lighthill Inst. for Math. Scis, 2003–06, Acad. Dir, Lighthill Risk Network, 2006–, UCL. Vis. Scientist, 1997, 1998, Pierre Fermat Vis. Prof., 2007, 2008, Cerfacs and Inst de Mécanique des Fluides de Toulouse; Visiting Professor: Colorado State Univ., 1975; NC State Univ., and Envmtl Protection Agency, 1977; Univ. of Colorado, 1980; Nat. Center for Atmospheric Res., Boulder, Colo, 1983; Arizona State Univ., 1997–98, 2007–; Stanford Univ., 1998; J. M. Burgers Prof., Tech. Univ., Delft, 1998–; Mary B. Upson Vis. Prof., Cornell Univ., 2003–06. Founder Dir, 1986–91, Dir, 1997–, Cambridge Envmtl Res. Consultants Ltd. President: IMA, 1993–95 (Hon. Sec., 1984–89; Vice-Pres., 1989–93); Adv. Cttee on Protection of the Sea, 2003– (Chm., 2001–03); Nat. Soc. for Clean Air, 2006–07; Vice Pres., Globe Internat., 2006–. Member: Man. Bd, European Res. Community for Flow Turbulence and Combustion, 1988–95; Exec. Council, WMO, 1992–97; NERC, 1994–96; Stakeholder Adv. Panel, EDF Energy, 2006–. Councillor, Cambridge CC, 1971–74 (Leader, Labour Gp, 1972). Fellow, APS, 2003; Hon. FICE 2003. Hon. DSc: Salford, 1995; Bath, 1996; UEA, 1997; Grenoble, Uppsala, Warwick, 2000; Dundee, 2005. L. F. Richardson Medal, Eur. Geophysical Soc., 2001. *Publications:* (contrib.) New Applications of Mathematics, ed C. Bondi, 1991; (ed) London's Environment, 2005; scientific pubns in Jl of Fluid Mechanics, Atmospheric Envmt, Qly Jl of Royal Meteorol Soc., Proc. Royal Soc., Jl of the Atmospheric Scis. *Address:* Department of Earth Sciences, University College London, Gower Street, WC1E 6BT.

See also Hon. T. J. W. Hunt.

HUNT OF KINGS HEATH, Baron *cr* 1997 (Life Peer), of Birmingham in the co. of West Midlands; **Philip Alexander Hunt,** OBE 1993; Minister of State, Department for Environment, Food and Rural Affairs and Department of Energy and Climate Change, since 2008; *b* 19 May 1949; *s* of Rev. Philip Lacey Winter Hunt and Muriel Hunt; *m* 1st, 1974 (marr. diss.); one *d*: 2nd, 1988, Selina Ruth Helen Stewart; three *s* one *d*. *Educ:* City of Oxford High Sch.; Oxford Sch.; Leeds Univ. (BA). MHSM. Oxford RHB, 1972–74; Nuffield Orthopaedic Centre, 1974–75; Mem., Oxfordshire AHA, 1975–77; Sec. Edgware/Hendon Community Health Council, 1975–78; Asst Sec., 1978–79, Asst Dir, 1979–84, NAHA; Dir, NAHA, then NAHAT, 1984–97; Chief Exec., NHS Confedn, 1997. Chair, Nat. Patient Safety Agency, 2004–05. Sen. Policy Advr, Sainsbury Centre for Mental Health, 1997; Sen. Policy Associate, King's Fund, 1998. Member: Oxford City Council, 1973–79; Birmingham City Council, 1980–82. A Lord in Waiting (Govt Whip), 1998–99; Parly Under-Sec. of State, DoH, 1999–2003, DWP, 2005–06; Minister of State, DoH, 2006–07; Parly Under-Sec. of State, MoJ, 2007–08. Chm., H of L Select Cttee on Merits of Statutory Instruments, 2004; Co-Chm., All-Party Gp on Public Health and Primary Care, 1997–98. Member: Council, Internat. Hosp. Fedn, 1986–91; King's Fund Inst. Adv. Cttee, 1991–93; Council, Assoc. for Public Health, 1992 (Co-Chm., 1994). Pres., FPA, 1998. *Publications:* The Health Authority Member (discussion paper) (with W. E. Hall), 1978; articles in Health Service publications. *Recreations:* music, cycling, swimming, football. *Address:* House of Lords, SW1A 0PW.

HUNT OF WIRRAL, Baron *cr* 1997 (Life Peer), of Wirral in the co. of Merseyside; **David James Fletcher Hunt,** MBE 1973; PC 1990; Chairman, Financial Services and Partner, Beachcroft LLP, solicitors; *b* 21 May 1942; *s* of late Alan Nathaniel Hunt, OBE and Jessie Edna Ellis Northrop Hunt; *m* 1973, Patricia, (Paddy), Margery (*née* Orchard); two *s* two *d*. *Educ:* Liverpool Coll.; Montpellier Univ.; Bristol Univ. (LLB); Guildford Coll. of Law. Solicitor of Supreme Court of Judicature, admitted 1968; Partner: Stanleys & Simpson North, 1977–88; Beachcroft Stanleys, 1988–99; Beachcroft Wansbroughs, 1999–2006; Beachcroft LLP, 2006–; Partner, then Consultant, Stanley Wansbrough & Co., 1965–85; Director: BET Omnibus Services Ltd, 1980–81; Solicitors Indemnity Mutual Insce Assoc. Ltd, 2001–05. Chartered Insurance Institute: Chm., Professional Standards Bd, 2004–06; Dep. Pres., 2006–07; Pres., 2007–08; Chm., Assoc. of Ind. Financial Advisers, 1999–2002. Contested (C) Bristol South, 1970, Kingswood, 1974; MP (C) Wirral, March 1976–1983, Wirral West, 1983–97; contested (C) Wirral West, 1997. PPS to Sec. of State for Trade, 1979–81, to Sec. of State for Defence, 1981; an Asst Govt Whip, 1981–83; a Lord Comr of HM Treasury, 1983–84; Parly Under-Sec. of State, Dept of Energy, 1984–87; Treasurer of HM Household and Dep. Chief Whip, 1987–89; Minister for Local Govt and Inner Cities, DoE, 1989–90; Secretary of State: for Wales, 1990–93; for Employment, 1993–94; Chancellor, Duchy of Lancaster and Minister for Public Service and Sci., 1994–95. Chm., Cons. Shipping and Shipbuilding Cttee, 1977–79; Vice-Chairman: Parly Youth Lobby, 1978–80; Parly War Crimes Gp, 2000–; Vice-Pres., Cons. Group for Europe, 1984–87 (Vice-Chm., 1978–81; Chm., 1981–82); Pres., All Party Parly Gp on Occupational Safety and Health, 1999–. Chm., Inter-Parly Council against Anti-Semitism, 1996–. Chm., Bristol Univ. Conservatives, 1964–65; winner of Observer Mace for British Universities Debating Competition, 1965–66; Nat. Vice-Chm., FUCUA, 1965–66; Chm., Bristol City CPC, 1965–68; Nat. Vice-Chm., YCNAC, 1967–69; Chm., Bristol Fedn of YCs, 1970–71; Chm., British Youth Council, 1971–74 (Pres., 1978–80); Vice-Pres., Nat. YCs, 1986–88 (Chm., 1972–73); Vice-Chairman: Nat. Union of Cons. and Unionist Assocs, 1974–76; Cons. Party, 1983–85. Pres., Tory Reform Gp, 1991–97. Vice-Pres., Nat. Playbus Assoc., 1981–. Member: South Western Economic Planning Council, 1972–76; CBI Council, 1999–2006. Mem. Adv. Cttee on Pop Festivals, 1972–75. Trustee, Holocaust Educnl Trust, 1998–; Chm., ESU, 2005– (Gov., 1999–; Dep. Chm., 2000–05). Mem., Rotary Club, London, 2000–. Fellow, Internat. Inst. of Risk and Safety Mgt, 2002. Hon. FIA 2003; Hon. FCII 2004. *Publications:* pamphlets on political subjects. *Recreations:* cricket, walking. *Address:* Beachcroft LLP, 100 Fetter Lane, EC4A 1BN. *T:* (020) 7894 6066, *Fax:* (020) 7894 6158; *e-mail:* lordhunt@beachcroft.co.uk. *Club:* Hurlingham.

HUNT, Alan Charles, CMG 1990; HM Diplomatic Service, retired; Director, Oxford University Foreign Service Programme, since 2003; *b* 5 March 1941; *s* of John Henry Hunt and Nelly Elizabeth Hunt (*née* Hunter); *m* 1978, Meredith Margaret Claydon; two *d*. *Educ:* Latymer Upper School, Hammersmith; Univ. of East Anglia. First Cl. Hons BA in European Studies. Clerical Officer, Min. of Power, 1958–59; FO, 1959–62; Vice-Consul, Tehran, 1962–64; Third Sec., Jedda, 1964–65; floating duties, Latin America, 1965–67; University, 1967–70; Second, later First Sec., FCO, 1970–73; First Sec., Panama, 1973–76; FCO 1976–77; First Sec. (Commercial), Madrid, 1977–81; FCO, 1981–83; Counsellor (Econ. and Commercial), Oslo, 1983–87; Head of British Interests Section, subseq. Chargé d'Affaires, Buenos Aires, 1987–90; Counsellor, FCO, 1990–91; Consul-Gen., Düsseldorf, and Dir-Gen. of Trade and Investment Promotion in Germany, 1991–95; Sen. Directing Staff (Civilian), RCDS, 1995–96; Dir of Trade and Investment Promotion, FCO, and Dep. Dir-Gen. for Export Promotion, DTI, 1996–97; High Comr, Singapore, 1997–2001. *Recreations:* golf, ski-ing, travel, reading, music. *Club:* Royal Commonwealth Society.

HUNT, Anthony Blair, DLitt; FBA 1999; Fellow and Tutor in French, 1990–Sept. 2009, and Vice Master, 2007–Sept. 2009, St Peter's College, Oxford; Lecturer in Mediaeval French Literature, Oxford University, 1990–Sept. 2009; *b* 21 March 1944; *s* of Norman Blair Hunt and Dorothy Gaskell Hunt (*née* Mottershead). *Educ:* Birkenhead Sch.; Worcester Coll., Oxford (BLitt, MA 1971); St Andrews Univ. (DLitt 1991). University of St Andrews: Asst Lectr, 1968–72; Lectr, 1972–79; Reader, 1979–90; British Acad. Res. Reader, 1986–88. Vis. Prof. of Mediaeval Studies, Westfield Coll., London Univ., 1986–88. FSA 1986. Foreign Mem., Norwegian Acad. of Sci. and Letters, 1999. *Publications:* Rauf de Linham, Kalender, 1983; Chrétien de Troyes, Yvain, 1986; Les giupartiz des eschez, 1986; Plant Names of Medieval England, 1989; Popular Medicine in Thirteenth-Century England, 1990; Teaching and Learning Latin in Thirteenth-Century England, 1991; The Medieval Surgery, 1992; Anglo-Norman Medicine, vol. 1, 1994, vol. 2, 1997; Le Livre de Catun, 1994; Villon's Last Will, 1996; Sermons on Joshua, 1998; Three Receptaria from Medieval England, 2001; Le Chant des Chanz, 2004; Les Paraboles maistre Alain en Françoys, 2005; Les Cantiques Salomon, 2006; Les Proverbez d'Alain, 2006; Miraculous Rhymes: the writing of Gautier de Coinci, 2007; Ovide, Du remede d'amours, 2008; An Old French Herbal, 2009; Three Anglo-Norman Treatises on Falconry, 2009; articles in learned jls, contribs to collective vols, etc. *Recreations:* fell-walking, playing the double bass, opera. *Address:* St Peter's College, Oxford OX1 2DL. *T:* (01865) 278852.

HUNT, Anthony James, CEng, FIStructE; Chairman: Anthony Hunt Associates, 1988–2002; YRM plc, 1993–94; *b* 1932; *s* of late James Edward Hunt and of Joan Margaret (*née* Cassidy); *m* 1st, 1957, Patricia Daniels (marr. diss. 1972; remarried 1975; marr. diss. 1982); one *s* one *d*; 3rd, 1985, Diana Joyce Collett (marr. diss. 2007). *Educ:* Salesian Coll., Farnborough; Westminster Tech. Coll. CEng 1961; FIStructE 1973. Articled via Founders' Co. to J. L. Wheeler Consulting Engr, 1948–51; F. J. Samuely and Partners, Consulting Engrs, 1951–59; Morton Lupton, Architects, 1960–62; founded Anthony Hunt Associates, Consulting Engrs, 1962; acquired by YRM plc, Bldg Design Consultants, 1988; became separate limited co., 1997. Major buildings: Sainsbury Centre for the Visual Arts, Norwich, 1978, 1993; Willis Faber Dumas HQ, Ipswich, 1975; Inmos Micro Electronics Factory, Gwent, 1982; Schlumberger Cambridge Research, 1985; Waterloo Internat. Terminal, 1993; Law Faculty, Cambridge, 1995; Nat. Botanic Gdn, Wales, 1998; New Mus. of Scotland, Edinburgh, 1998; Lloyd's Register of Shipping, London, 1998–99; Eden Project, Cornwall, 1998–99. Willis Vis. Prof. of Architecture, Sheffield Univ., 1994–; Graham Vis. Prof. of Architecture, Univ. of Penn, 2002; Visiting Professor: Chinese Univ. of Hong Kong, 2004; Univ. du Québec, Montreal, 2004–; Inst. Superior Técnico, Lisbon, 2005–. FRSA 1989. Hon. FRIBA 1989. Hon. DLitt Sheffield, 1999; Hon. DEng Leeds, 2003. Gold Medallist, IStructE, 1995. *Publications:* Tony Hunt's Structures Notebook, 1997, 2nd edn 2003; Tony Hunt's Sketchbook, 1999, vol. 2, 2003. *Recreations:* furniture restoration, music, sailing, ski-ing, painting. *Address:* The Studio, Box, Stroud, Glos GL6 9HD. *Clubs:* Chelsea Arts, Oriental.

HUNT, Barbara L.; *see* Leigh-Hunt.

HUNT, Bernard John, MBE 1977; Professional Golfer, Foxhills Golf and Country Club, since 1975; *b* 2 Feb. 1930; *s* of John and Lilian Hunt; *m* 1955, Margaret Ellen Clark; one *s* two *d*. *Educ:* Atherstone Grammar Sch. Mem., Ryder Cup team, 1953, 1957–69 (Captain, 1973, 1975); Winner: H. Vardon Trophy, 1958, 1960, 1965; over 30 major tournaments, incl. Dunlop Masters, 1963, 1965, and German, French, Brazilian and Belgian Opens. Captain, PGA, 1966, 1995, 1996. *Recreations:* golf, badminton. *Address:* Foxhills Golf and Country Club, Stonehill Road, Ottershaw, Surrey KT16 0EL.

HUNT, Christopher H.; *see* Holdsworth Hunt.

HUNT, Christopher John, FSA; Acting Director of Library Services, University of London, 2003–04; Director and University Librarian, John Rylands University Library of Manchester, 1991–2002, now University Librarian Emeritus; *b* 28 Jan. 1937; *s* of Richard John Hunt and Dorothy (*née* Pendleton); *m* 1963, Kathleen Mary Wyatt. *Educ:* Rutlish Sch., Merton; Univ. of Exeter (BA); King's Coll., Univ. of Durham (MLitt). FSA 1995. Asst Librarian, Univ. of Newcastle upon Tyne, 1960–67; Sub Librarian, Univ. of Manchester, 1967–74; University Librarian: James Cook Univ. of N Queensland, 1974–81; La Trobe Univ., 1981–85; Librarian, British Library of Political and Economic Science, LSE, 1985–91. Chairman: Internat. Cttee for Social Sci. Inf. and Documentation, 1989–92; Library Panel, Wellcome Trust, 1993–99 (Mem., 1988–99). Curator of Libraries, Univ. of Oxford, 2000–02; Acting Dir of Library Servs, London Univ., 2003. Academic Gov., LSE, 1989–91; Mem. Council, Univ. of Manchester, 2000–02; Feoffee of Chetham's Hosp. and Library, Manchester, 1993–2005. *Publications:* The Leadminers of the Northern Pennines, 1970; The Book Trade in Northumberland and Durham to 1860, 1975; papers in professional and learned jls. *Recreations:* book collecting, scuba diving, wine. *Address:* 35 South End, Longhoughton, Alnwick, Northumberland NE66 3AW.

HUNT, (David) Peter; His Honour Judge Peter Hunt; a Circuit Judge, since 1997; Designated Family Judge, Leeds County Court (formerly Care Centre), since 2000; *b* 25 April 1951; *s* of late Rev. Charles Christopher Hunt and of Edna Hunt; *m* 1984, Cherryl Janet Nicholson; two *s*. *Educ:* Grangefield Grammar Sch., Stockton-on-Tees; Keble Coll., Oxford (MA). Called to the Bar, Gray's Inn, 1974; in practice at the Bar, 1974–97; Junior, North Eastern Circuit, 1981–82; a Recorder, 1993–97. Mem., Gen. Council of the Bar, 1981–84. Chm., Inquiry into multiple abuse of nursery sch. children, Newcastle, 1993–94. *Publication:* (with M. L. Rakusen) Distribution of Assets on Divorce, 1979, 3rd edn 1990. *Address:* Leeds Combined Court, The Courthouse, 1 Oxford Row, Leeds LS1 3BG. *T:* (0113) 306 2800.

HUNT, David Roderic Notley; QC 1987; a Recorder, since 1991; *b* 22 June 1947; *s* of Dr Geoffrey Notley Hunt and Deborah Katharine Rosamund Hunt; *m* 1974, Alison Connell Jelf; two *s*. *Educ:* Charterhouse School; Trinity College, Cambridge (MA Hons). Called to the Bar, Gray's Inn, 1969, Bencher, 1996. *Recreations:* sailing, ski-ing, golf. *Address:* Blackstone Chambers, Blackstone House, Temple, EC4Y 9BW. *T:* (020) 7583 1770.

HUNT, Derek Simpson; Chairman: MFI Furniture Group Plc, 1987–2000 (Chief Executive, 1987–94); MFI Furniture Centres Ltd, 1987–2000 (Managing Director, 1987–90); *b* 9 June 1939; *s* of late John William Hunt and of Elizabeth (*née* Simpson); *m* 1967, Sandra Phyllis Jones; two *s*. *Educ:* Queen Elizabeth Grammar Sch., Darlington, Co. Durham. Joined MFI as Retail Area Controller, 1972; Branch Ops Controller, 1973; Dir, MFI Furniture Centres, 1974; MFI Furniture Group: Dir, 1976; Man. Dir, 1981; Chm., 1984; during merger with Asda, also Chief Exec. and Dep. Chm., Asda-MFI, 1985–87; returned to MFI and effected management buy-out, 1987. Gov., Ashridge Management Coll., 1986–95. Vice Pres., NCH Action for Children (formerly Nat. Children's Home), 1989–2000. Founding Fellow, Nat. Children's Home George Thomas Soc., 1989. Hon. Fellow, Manchester Polytechnic, 1988. *Recreations:* sailing, Rugby Union, golf.

HUNT, Donald Frederick, OBE 1993; FRCO; Principal, Elgar School of Music, since 1997; Master of the Choristers and Organist, Worcester Cathedral, 1975–96; *b* 26 July 1930; *m* 1954, Josephine Benbow; two *s* two *d*. *Educ:* King's School, Gloucester. ARCM; ARCO 1951; FRCO(CHM) 1954. Asst Organist, Gloucester Cathedral, 1947–54; Director of Music: St John's Church, Torquay, 1954–57; Leeds Parish Church, 1957–75; Leeds City Organist, 1973–75. Chorus Dir, Leeds Festival, 1962–75; Conductor: Halifax Choral Soc., 1957–88; Leeds Philharmonic Soc., 1962–75; Worcester Festival Choral Soc., 1975–97; Worcester Three Choirs Festival, 1975–96; Elgar Chorale, 1980–; Elgar Camerata, 1999–; Guest Conductor, Cape Town Philharmonia, 1997–; Artistic Director: Bromsgrove Festival, 1981–91; N Staffs Triennial Fest., 1999; Artistic Dir and Conductor, Elgar 150th Anniv., Worcester, 2007. Hon. DMus Leeds 1975. *Publications:* S. S. Wesley: cathedral musician, 1990; Festival Memories, 1996; Elgar and the Three Choirs Festival, 1999; *compositions:* Magnificat and Nunc Dimittis, 1972; Missa Brevis, 1973; Versicles and Responses, 1973; God be gracious, 1984; Missa Nova, 1985; Mass for Three Voices, 1986; A Song of Celebration, 1995; Hymnus Paschalis, 1999; anthems and carols. *Recreations:* cricket, poetry, travel. *Address:* 13 Bilford Avenue, Worcester WR3 8PJ. *T:* (01905) 756329; *e-mail:* dhunt2126@aol.com.

HUNT, (Henry) Holman, CBE 1988; Deputy Chairman, 1985–91, Member, 1980–91, Monopolies and Mergers Commission; *b* 13 May 1924; *s* of Henry Hunt and Jessie Brenda Beale; *m* 1954, Sonja Blom; one *s* two *d*. *Educ:* Queens Park Sch., Glasgow; Glasgow Univ. (MA). FCMA, FIMC, FBCS, FInstAM. Caledonian Insce Co., 1940–43; RAF, 1943–46; Glasgow Univ., 1946–50; Cadbury Bros, 1950–51; PA Management Consultants: Consultant, 1952–57; Manager, Office Organisation, 1958–63; Dir, Computer Div., 1964–69; Bd Dir, 1970–83; Man. Dir, PA Computers and Telecommunications, 1976–83. Pres., Inst. of Management Consultants, 1974–75. *Recreations:* music, reading, walking, travel, photography. *Address:* 28 The Ridings, Epsom, Surrey KT18 5JJ. *T:* (01372) 720974. *Club:* Caledonian.

HUNT, Jeremy; MP (C) Surrey South West, since 2005; *b* 1 Nov. 1966; *s* of Adm. Sir Nicholas John Streynsham Hunt, *qv*. *Educ:* Charterhouse; Magdalen Coll., Oxford (BA 1st Cl. Hons PPE 1988). Co-Founder and Man. Dir, Hotcourses, 1991–2005; Co-Founder and Chm., Hotcourses Foundn, 2004–. Shadow Sec. of State for Culture, Media and Sport, 2007–. *Recreation:* Latin music and dancing. *Address:* 23 Red Lion Lane, Farnham, Surrey GU9 7QN. *T:* (01252) 712536, *Fax:* (01428) 607498; *e-mail:* huntj@parliament.uk.

HUNT, Prof. John David, PhD; FRS 2001; Professor of Materials, University of Oxford, 1996–2002; Fellow and Tutor in Metallurgy, St Edmund Hall, Oxford, 1968–2002, now Emeritus Fellow; *b* 12 Dec. 1936; *s* of Frederick John Hunt and Eleanor Hunt; *m* 1961, Ann Mercy Carroll; one *s* one *d* (and one *s* decd). *Educ:* Wellington Sch., Som; Christ's Coll., Cambridge (BA 1960; PhD 1963). Sen. Scientist, Bell Telephone Labs, Murray Hill, NJ, 1963–65; SSO, UKAEA, Harwell, 1965–66; Lectr, Dept of Metallurgy, 1966–90, Reader in Physical Metallurgy, 1990–96, Univ. of Oxford. Hon. Prof., Key Solidification Lab. of China, N Western Poly. Univ., Xian, China, 1996. Mathewson Gold Medal, 1967, Bruce Chalmers Award, 1996, Amer. Inst. Metallurgical Engrs; Rosenhain Medal and Prize, Inst. Metals, 1981; Armourers' and Brasiers' Award, Royal Soc., 2001. *Publications:* numerous contribs on solidification theory and experiment to learned jls. *Recreations:* keeping livestock, growing ferns, walking. *Address:* Church Farm House, Church Road, Northleigh, Witney, Oxon OX29 6TX.

HUNT, Sir John (Leonard), Kt 1989; *b* 27 Oct. 1929; *s* of late William John Hunt and Dora Maud Hunt, Keston, Kent; unmarried. *Educ:* Dulwich Coll. Councillor, Bromley Borough Council, 1953–65; Alderman, Bromley Borough Council, 1961–65; Mayor of Bromley, 1963–64. Contested (C) S Lewisham, 1959. MP (C): Bromley, 1964–74; Ravensbourne, 1974–97. Member: Select Cttee on Home Affairs (and Mem., Sub-Cttee on Race Relations and Immigration), 1979–87; Speaker's Panel of Chairmen, 1980–97. Chm., Indo-British Parly Gp, 1979–91; UK Rep. at Council of Europe and WEU, 1973–77 and 1988–97. Jt Pres., British-Caribbean Assoc., 1998– (Jt Chm., 1968–77 and 1984–97). Mem., BBC Gen. Adv. Council, 1975–87. Pres., Inst. of Administrative Accountants, subseq. of Financial Accountants, 1970–88. Mem. of London Stock Exchange, 1958–70. Freeman, City of London, 1986; Freeman, Haberdashers' Co., 1986. *Recreations:* foreign travel, good food. *Address:* 164 Sutherland Avenue, W9 1HR.

HUNT, John Maitland, MA, BLitt; Headmaster of Roedean, 1971–84; *b* 4 March 1932; *s* of Richard Herbert Alexander Hunt and Eileen Mary Isabelle Hunt (*née* Witt); *m* 1969, Sarah, *d* of Lt-Gen. Sir Derek Lang, KCB, DSO, MC; two *s*. *Educ:* Radley College; Wadham College, Oxford. BA 1956; BLitt 1959; MA 1960. Assistant Master, Stowe School, 1958–70 (Sixth Form tutor in Geography). Chm., Bd of Managers, Common Entrance Exam. for Girls' Schs, 1974–81. *Publications:* Dutch South Africa, 2005; various articles on fine arts and architecture. *Recreations:* estate management, fine arts, writing, travel. *Address:* Logie, Dunfermline, Fife KY12 8QN. *Club:* Royal Commonwealth Society.

HUNT, John Michael Graham, OBE 2000; Chief Executive and Secretary, British Dental Association, 1993–2001; Director, Smile-on Ltd, since 2001; *b* 5 Feb. 1942; *s* of Robert Graham Hunt and Patricia Mary Hunt; *m* 1966, Jill Mason Williams; one *s* two *d*. *Educ:* Guy's Hosp. Dental Sch., Univ. of London (BDS 1965). LDS RCS 1965. Resident House Officer, Guy's Hosp., 1965; Fulbright Travelling Schol., Clinical Dental Fellow, Eastman Dental Centre, NY, 1966–67; London Hospital Dental Institute: Registrar, Conservative Dentistry, 1967–70; Lectr in Oral Surgery, 1968–70; General Dental Practice, Torquay, 1970–80; Clinical Dental Surgeon, Prince Philip Dental Hosp., Univ. of Hong Kong, 1980–84; Dental Officer, 1984–89, Sen. Dental Officer, 1989–93, DoH. Hon. Lectr, London Hosp. Med. Coll., 1989–93; Speaker, FDI, World Dental Fedn, 1999–2005. FRSA. Hon. FFGDP(UK) 2001. *Recreations:* walking, ski-ing, tennis, sailing. *Address:* Beaston, Broadhempston, Totnes, Devon TQ9 6BX. *Club:* Royal Society of Medicine.

HUNT, Rt Hon. Jonathan (Lucas), ONZ 2005; PC 1987; High Commissioner for New Zealand in the United Kingdom, and Ambassador to Eire, 2005–08; *b* 2 Dec. 1938; *s* of Henry Lucas Hunt and Alison Zora Hunt. *Educ:* Auckland Grammar Sch.; Univ. of Auckland (MA Hons). Teacher, Kelston Boys' High Sch., 1961–66; MP NZ, 1966–2005 (MP (Lab) New Lynn, Auckland, 1966–96). New Zealand Parliament: Dep. Speaker, 1974–75; Sen. Opposition Whip, 1980–84; Minister of Broadcasting and Communications, 1984–90; Leader of the House, 1987–90; Speaker, 1999–2005. *Recreations:* music, cricket, wine appreciation, reading. *Club:* Wellington (New Zealand).

HUNT, Judith Anne, OBE 1999; independent consultant and executive coach, since 1999; Board Member, Transport for London, since 2006; *b* 13 Sept. 1945; *d* of late Philip E. Riley and Amy Riley; *m* 1st, 1967, Alan J. Hunt (marr. diss. 1979); two *d*; 2nd, 1988, Daniel W. Silverstone, *qv*. *Educ:* Cheadle Hulme Sch.; Leeds Univ. (BA Hons). Lectr, Stockport Coll. and Salford Coll. of Technology, and teacher, Salford, 1967–74; Nat. Organiser, 1974–80 and Asst Gen. Sec., 1980–82, AUEW (TASS); Equal Opportunities Advr and Dep. Head, Personnel Services, GLC, 1982–84; Dir of Personnel (Staffing), GLC, 1984–86; Acting Dir of Personnel, ILEA, 1986–87; Chief Executive: London Borough of Ealing, 1987–93; Local Govt Mgt Bd, 1993–99. Special Advr, LGA, 1999–. CS Comr, 1995–98; Mem. Adv. Council, CS Coll., 1995–99. Non-exec. Dir, CPS, 2002–05. Chairman: Camden and Islington HA, 2000–02; London Health Observatory, 2002–06. Parent Governor, ILEA; Member: Governing Body, Ruskin Coll.; Exec. Council, Solace; Women's Nat. Commn, 1976–82; ESRC Res. Priorities Bd, 1995–; W London TEC; W London Leadership, 1989–93; London First, 1992–95. Trustee, Common Purpose, 1994–2004. FRSA 1990. *Publications:* Organising Women Workers, 1985; (ed) Jackie West: work, women and the labour market; contribs to jls. *Recreations:* books, gardening, opera, painting.

HUNT, Maj.-Gen. Malcolm Peter John, OBE 1984; Royal Marines retired, 1992; General Secretary, Association of British Dispensing Opticians, 1995–99; *b* 19 Nov. 1938; *s* of Peter Gordon Hunt and Rachel Margaret Hunt (*née* Owston); *m* 1st, 1962, Margaret Peat (*d* 1996); two *s*; 2nd, 2004, Angela Jean Payne (*née* Oats), *widow* of Capt. R. N. E. Payne, RN. *Educ:* St John's Sch., Leatherhead; Staff Coll., Camberley. Joined Royal Marines, 1957; service in Malta, Aden and NI; OC RM Detachment, HMS Nubian, 1966–68; Instructor, Army Staff Coll., 1979–81; CO, 40 Commando RM, 1981–83 (Falklands, NI); Internat. Mil. Staff, HQ NATO, 1984–87; Dir, NATO Defence Commitments Staff, MoD, 1987–90; Comdr, British Forces Falkland Islands, 1990–91. Exec. Dir, Nat. Back Pain Assoc., 1993–94. Member: Metropolitan Police Cttee, 1995–2000; Gen. Optical Council, 1999–2001. Pres., S Atlantic Medal Assoc. 1982, 2002–. Gov., St John's Sch., Leatherhead, 1993–2007 (Vice-Chm., 1997–2006). FRSA 1993. Freeman, City of London, 1999; Liveryman, Co. of Spectacle Makers, 2000. *Recreations:* golf, politics, reading, theatre. *Address:* Gillons Lawn, Woolston, N Cadbury, Somerset BA22 7BP. *T:* (01963) 440929.

HUNT, Margaret Corinna; *see* Phillips, M. C.

HUNT, Martin Robert, RDI 1981; Partner, Queensberry Hunt (formerly Queensberry Hunt Levien), design consultancy, since 1966; *b* 4 Sept. 1942; *s* of Frederick and Frances Hunt; *m* 1st, 1963, Pauline Hunt; one *s* one *d*; 2nd, 1980, Glenys Barton; one *s*. *Educ:* Monmouth. DesRCA, FCSD. Graduated RCA 1966 (Hon. Fellow 1987); formed Queensberry Hunt Partnership, 1966. Part time Tutor, 1968, Head of Glass Sch. 1974–86, Vis. Prof., 1997–2000, Royal Coll. of Art; Vis. Prof., De Montfort Univ. 1997–. Master, Faculty of RDI, 2001–03. *Recreation:* sailing. *Address:* Queensberry Hunt, 63 Penfold Street, NW8 8PQ. *T:* (020) 7535 7120.

HUNT, Maurice William; Deputy Director-General, 1989–97, and Secretary, 1986–97, Confederation of British Industry; *b* 30 Aug. 1936; *s* of Maurice Hunt and Helen Hunt (*née* Andrews); *m* 1960, Jean Mary Ellis; one *s* one *d*. *Educ:* Selhurst Grammar School, Croydon; LSE (BSc Econ). ACIB. Nat. Service, RAF, 1955–57. ANZ Bank, 1953–66; Joint Iron Council, 1966–67; Board of Trade, 1967; Asst Sec., DTI, 1974; RCDS 1982; Dir, Membership, CBI, 1984; Exec. Dir (Ops), CBI, 1987. Dir, Pool Reinsurance Co. Ltd, 1994–2002. *Recreations:* walking, gardening, sailing. *Address:* Hurstbury, Blackhill, Lindfield, W Sussex RH16 2HE. *T:* (01444) 487598.

HUNT, Neil Philip; Chief Executive, Alzheimer's Society, since 2003; *b* 2 May 1954; *s* of Keith Hunt and Doreen Hunt; *m* Tracey Ellen Hassell; two *s* (twins). *Educ:* Univ. of Sussex (BA Hons); Goldsmiths Coll., London (PGCE); Croydon Coll. (DipASS; CQSW). Social worker, 1977–84; Team/Area Manager, London Borough of Lewisham, 1984–89; Divl Manager, Kent CC, 1989–91; NSPCC: Regl Dir, 1991–97; Dir of Child Protection, 1997–2003; on secondment to Home Office, then to DfES, 2002–03. *Recreation:* a new challenge is emerging, namely to persuade my increasingly sceptical sons that I can actually play football! *Address:* Alzheimer's Society, Devon House, 58 St Katherine's Way, E1W 1JX. *T:* (020) 7243 3507; *e-mail:* nhunt@alzheimers.org.uk.

HUNT, Adm. Sir Nicholas (John Streynsham), GCB 1987 (KCB 1985); LVO 1961; DL; Chairman, Ferrero UK Ltd, since 2005; *b* 7 Nov. 1930; *s* of Brig. and Mrs J. M. Hunt; *m* 1966, Meriel Eve Givan; two *s* one *d*. *Educ:* BRNC, Dartmouth. CO HMS Burnaston, HMS Palliser, HMS Troubridge, HMS Intrepid, and BRNC, Dartmouth; Asst Private Sec. to Princess Marina, Duchess of Kent, 1959–62; Executive Officer, HMS Ark Royal, 1969–71; RCDS 1974; Dir of Naval Plans, 1976–78; Flag Officer, Second Flotilla, 1980–81; Dir-Gen., Naval Manpower and Training, 1981–83; Flag Officer, Scotland and NI, and Port Admiral Rosyth, 1983–85; C-in-C, Fleet, and Allied C-in-C, Channel and Eastern Atlantic, 1985–87, retd. Rear-Adm. of the UK, 1994–97, Vice Adm. of the UK and Lt of the Admiralty, 1997–2001. Dep. Man. Dir (Orgn and Develt), Eurotunnel, 1987–89; Dir-Gen., Chamber of Shipping, 1991–97; Chm., Chatham Historic Dockyard Trust, 1998–2005. Chairman: SW Surrey DHA, 1990–95; Nuffield Hosps, 1996–2001. Comr, CWGC, 1988–92. Freeman, City of London, 1988. DL Surrey, 1996. Gov., Sutton's Hosp. in Charterhouse, 2002–06. *Recreation:* family. *Clubs:* Boodle's, Royal Navy of 1765 and 1785; Surrey.

See also Jeremy Hunt.

HUNT, Peter; *see* Hunt, D. P.

HUNT, Peter Lawrence, CMG 2001; HM Diplomatic Service; Consul-General, Los Angeles, 2001–05; *b* 10 June 1945; *s* of late Lawrence Hunt and Catherine Hunt (*née* Bree); *m* 1972, Anne Langhorne Carson; two *s* two *d*. *Educ:* St Anselm's Coll.; Birkbeck Coll., Univ. of London (BA Hons). Joined HM Diplomatic Service, 1962: African floater duties, 1967–69; Managua, 1970–73; FCO, 1973–78; Second Sec., (Commercial), Caracas, 1978–82; First Secretary: FCO, 1982–87; Dep. Head of Mission and Consul, Montevideo, 1987–90; Dep. Head, S Atlantic and Antarctic Dept and Dep. Comr, British

Antarctic Territory, 1990–93; Minister-Counsellor, Dep. Head of Mission, and Consul-Gen., Santiago, 1993–96; Consul-Gen., Istanbul, 1997–2001. *Recreations:* chess, golf, tennis, hill-walking. *Address:* c/o Foreign and Commonwealth Office, King Charles Street, SW1A 2AH.

HUNT, Philip Bodley; Director, Welsh Office Industry Department, 1975–76; *b* 28 July 1916; *s* of Bernard and Janet Hunt; *m* 1940, Eleanor Margaret Parnell (*d* 1989); three *s* one *d*. *Educ:* Sedbergh Sch.; Christ Church, Oxford (Boulter Exhibnr; 1st cl. PPE; MA). Joined Board of Trade, 1946; Trade Commissioner, Montreal, 1952; Principal Trade Commissioner, Vancouver, 1955; Commercial Counsellor, Canberra, 1957; returned Board of Trade, 1962; Dept of Economic Affairs, 1964–65; Director, London & SE Region, BoT, 1968; Dir, DTI Office for Wales, 1972–75. Chm., S Wales Marriage Guidance Council, 1974–83; Mem. Nat. Exec., Nat. Marriage Guidance Council, 1977–83; Dept Mem. of Panel, County Structure Plans of S and W Glamorgan, 1978, of Gwent and Mid Glamorgan, 1979; Vice-Pres., Develt Corporation for Wales, 1980–83. Chm., John Macmurray Fellowship, 1993–2002. Silver Jubilee Medal, 1977. *Publication:* John Macmurray and the BBC: 1930–1941, 1995. *Recreation:* life and works of John Macmurray. *Address:* 3 Allen Gardens, Ecclesfield, Sheffield S35 9TT. *T:* (0114) 245 7758.

HUNT, Sir Rex (Masterman), Kt 1982; CMG 1980; HM Diplomatic Service, retired; Civil Commissioner, Falkland Islands, 1982–Sept. 1985, and High Commissioner, British Antarctic Territory, 1980–85 (Governor and Commander-in-Chief, Falkland Islands, 1980–82; Governor, Oct. 1985); *b* 29 June 1926; *s* of H. W. Hunt and Ivy Masterman; *m* 1951, Mavis Amanda Buckland; one *s* one *d*. *Educ:* Coatham Sch.; St Peter's Coll., Oxford (BA). Served with RAF, 1944–48; Flt Lt RAFO. Entered HM Overseas Civil Service, 1951; District Comr, Uganda, 1962; CRO, 1963–64; 1st Sec., Kuching, 1964–65; Jesselton, 1965–67; Brunei, 1967; 1st Sec. (Econ.), Ankara, 1968–70; 1st Sec. and Head of Chancery, Jakarta, 1970–72; Asst, ME Dept, FCO, 1972–74; Counsellor, Saigon, 1974–75, Kuala Lumpur, 1976–77; Dep. High Comr, Kuala Lumpur, 1977–79. Mem., RAFA. Hon. Air Cdre, City of Lincoln Sqn, RAuxAF, 1987–97. Hon. Freeman: City of London, 1981; Stanley, Falkland Is, 1985. *Publication:* My Falkland Days, 1992. *Recreations:* golf, gardening. *Address:* The Grooms House, Elton, Stockton-on-Tees TS21 1AG.

HUNT, Richard Bruce; Chairman, R. B. Hunt and Partners Ltd, 1966–95; Deputy Chairman, Howe Robinson and Co. Ltd, 1990–97; *b* 15 Dec. 1927; *s* of Percy Thompson Hunt and Thelma Constance Hunt; *m* 1972, Ulrike Dorothea Schmidt; two *d*. *Educ:* Christ's Hospital. FICS. Served Royal Signals, 1946–48; joined Merchant Bankers Ralli Brothers, 1949–66; formed own company, R. B. Hunt and Partners, 1966. Chm., Baltic Exchange Ltd, 1985–87 (Dir, 1977–80, re-elected, 1981–87). Liveryman, Shipwrights' Co. *Recreations:* golf, ski-ing. *Clubs:* Hurlingham, Royal Wimbledon Golf; Royal Lymington Yacht.

HUNT, Sir Richard Timothy; *see* Hunt, Sir Tim.

HUNT, Robert Alan, OBE 1984; QPM 1992; Assistant Commissioner, Territorial Operations Department, Metropolitan Police, 1990–95; *b* 6 July 1935; *s* of Peter and Minnie Hunt; *m* 1956, Jean White; one *s* three *d*. *Educ:* Dulwich Coll.; London Univ. (LLB external 1970). Served in RA. Joined Metropolitan Police, 1955: Chief Superintendent, 1973; Comdr, 1976; Dep. Asst Comr, 1981. *Recreations:* music—traditional and light classical, reading, the family.

HUNT, Sally Colette; General Secretary, University and College Union, since 2007 (Joint General Secretary, 2006–07); *b* 14 July 1964; *d* of Barry Hunt and Catherine Hunt (*née* Cox); *m* 2000, Peter John Sutcliffe; one *d*. *Educ:* Univ. of Sussex (BA Hons Internat. Relns 1987). Researcher, Ind. Union of Halifax Staff, 1990–91; Asst Gen. Sec., Nationwide Gp Staff Union, 1991–95; Association of University Teachers: London Regl Official, 1995–97; Asst Gen. Sec., 1997–2002; Gen. Sec., 2002–06. *Address:* University and College Union, 25–31 Tavistock Place, WC1H 9UT. *T:* (020) 7670 9700.

HUNT, Terence, CBE 1996; Chief Executive (formerly National Director), NHS Supplies, 1991–2000; *b* 8 Aug. 1943; *s* of Thomas John Hunt and Marie Louise Hunt (*née* Potter); *m* 1967, Wendy Graeme George; one *s* one *d*. *Educ:* Huish's Grammar Sch., Taunton. Associate Mem. Inst. of Health Service Management. Tone Vale Group HMC, 1963–65; NE Somerset HMC, 1965–67; Winchester Gp HMC, 1967–69; Lincoln No 1 HMC, 1969–70; Hosp. Sec., Wycombe General Hosp., 1970–73; Dep. Gp Sec., Hillingdon Hosp., 1973–74; Area General Administrator, Kensington and Chelsea and Westminster AHA(T), 1974–77; District Administrator: NW Dist of KCW AHA(T), 1977–82; Paddington and N Kensington, 1982–84; Regl Gen. Manager, NE Thames RHA, 1984–91. Member: Steering Gp on Undergrad. Med. and Dental Educn and Res., 1987–91; NHS Central R&D Cttee, 1991–94; Hosp. Cttee, EEC, 1991–93; Med. Cttee, UFC, 1989–91. Member: Twyford & Dist Round Table, 1975–84 (Chm., 1980–81; Pres., 1988–89); Cttee, Reading Town Regatta, 1984–95 (Treas., 1984–86; Chm., 1989–93); Rotary Club of Reading Maiden Erlegh, 2004–. Member: Council of Govs, London Hosp. Med. Coll., 1985–91; Council, UCL, 1985–91. CCMI. Freeman, 1991, Liveryman, 1998, Barbers' Co. Knight's Cross, Order of Falcon (Iceland), 2001. *Recreations:* motor cycling, cycling, all things practical with metal and wood. *Address:* 36 Old Bath Road, Charvil, Reading, Berks RG10 9QR. *T:* (0118) 934 1062. *Club:* Royal Society of Medicine.

HUNT, Sir Tim, Kt 2006; PhD; FRS 1991; Principal Scientist, Cancer Research UK (formerly Senior Scientist, Imperial Cancer Research Fund), since 1990; *b* 19 Feb. 1943; *s* of Richard William Hunt and Katherine Eva Rowland; named Richard Timothy, named changed by Deed Poll to Tim, 2004; *m* 1st, 1971, Missy Cusick (marr. diss. 1974); 2nd, 1995, Prof. Mary Katharine Levinge Collins; two *d*. *Educ:* Dragon Sch.; Magdalen Coll. Sch., Oxford; Clare Coll., Cambridge (BA Nat. Sci. 1964; PhD 1968; Hon. Fellow, 2002). University of Cambridge: Fellow, Clare Coll., 1968–2002; Univ. Lectr in Biochem., 1981–90; Junior Proctor, 1982–83. Mem., EMBO; MAE 1998. Founder FMedSci 1998. Foreign Hon. Mem., Amer. Acad. of Arts and Scis, 1997; Foreign Associate, US Nat. Acad. of Scis, 1999. (Jtly) Nobel Prize for Physiology or Medicine, 2001. Officier, Légion d'Honneur (France), 2002. *Publications:* Molecular Biology of the Cell Problems (with John Wilson), 1989, 3rd edn 2002; The Cell Cycle: an introduction (with Andrew Murray), 1993; articles in cell and molecular biology jls. *Recreations:* cooking, eating, photography. *Address:* Cancer Research UK, Clare Hall Laboratories, South Mimms, Herts EN6 3LD. *T:* (01707) 625981, *Fax:* (01707) 625803; *e-mail:* tim.hunt@cancer.org.uk.

HUNT, Hon. Tristram Julian William, PhD; FRHistS; Lecturer in Modern British History, Queen Mary, University of London, since 2003; *b* 31 May 1974; *s* of Baron Hunt of Chesterton, *qv*; *m* 2004, Juliet Thornback. *Educ:* University Coll. Sch.; Trinity Coll., Cambridge (BA 1995; PhD 2000); Univ. of Chicago (Exchange Fellow). FRHistS 2005. Sen. researcher, Labour Party election campaign, 1997; Special Advr to Parly Under-Sec. of State, DTI, 1998–2001; Res. Fellow, IPPR, 2001; Associate Fellow, Centre for Hist. and Econs, King's Coll., Cambridge, 2001–02. Vis. Prof., Arizona State Univ., 2004–05. Author and presenter, television: Civil War (series), 2002; Isaac Newton: Great Briton, 2002; British Middle Class, 2005; The Protestant Revolution (series), 2007. Trustee: Heritage Lottery Fund, 2005–; Nat. Heritage Meml Fund, 2005–. *Publications:* The English Civil War, 2002, 3rd edn 2006; Building Jerusalem: the rise and fall of the Victorian city, 2004, 2nd edn 2005; Friedrich Engels: a revolutionary life, 2009; contribs to History Today, Jl Social Hist. *Recreations:* Victorian urban architecture, fresh-water swimming, beach cricket, book-browsing. *Address:* c/o Capel & Land, 29 Wardour Street, W1D 6PS. *T:* (020) 7734 2414, *Fax:* (020) 7734 8101; *e-mail:* Matilda@capelland.co.uk.

HUNT, William George, TD 1988 (and Clasp 1994); Windsor Herald of Arms, since 1999; Registrar, College of Arms, since 2007; *b* 8 Dec. 1946; *s* of Frank Williams Hunt, TD, MA, and late Mary Elizabeth Leyland Hunt (*née* Orton), JP; *m* 1998, Michaela Wedel; two *s*. *Educ:* Liverpool Coll.; Univ. of Southampton (BA); Univ. of Constance; Univ. of Lausanne; Univ. of Caen (Dip.). FCA 1979. Mentor, Salem Sch., 1967–69; Audit Manager, Arthur Young McClelland Moores, 1970–83; Financial Controller and Partnership Sec., Frere Cholmeley, 1983–92; Finance Dir, Hopkins & Wood, 1993–95; Portcullis Pursuivant of Arms, 1992–99. Clerk, HM Commn of Lieutenancy for City of London, 1990–; Mem., Ct of Common Council, City of London, 2004–. Dir, Heraldry Soc., 1997–2006. Treas., HAC Biographical Dictionary (1537–1914) Trust, 1993–. Freeman, City of London; Founder Mem., Treas., 1976–78, Chm., 1978–79, Soc. of Young Freemen of City of London; Maj. and Mem., Ct of Assts, 1988–2000, HAC; Mem., Ct of Assts, 1996–, Master, 2000–01, Co. of Makers of Playing Cards. SBStJ 1999. *Publications:* Guide to the Honourable Artillery Company, 1987; (ed jtly) Dictionary of British Arms, Vol. 1, 1992. *Recreation:* orders and decorations. *Address:* College of Arms, Queen Victoria Street, EC4V 4BT. *T:* (020) 7329 8755. *Club:* City Livery (Clerk, 1996–98, Dep. Clerk, 1998–2003).

HUNT-DAVIS, Brig. Sir Miles (Garth), KCVO 2003 (CVO 1998); CBE 1990 (MBE 1977); Private Secretary, since 1993, and Treasurer, since 2000, to HRH The Duke of Edinburgh (Assistant Private Secretary, 1991–92); *b* Johannesburg, SA, 7 Nov. 1938; *s* of late Lt-Col Eric Hunt-Davis, OBE, ED and Mary Eleanor Turnbull (*née* Boyce); *m* 1965, Anita (Gay) Ridsdale, *d* of Francis James Ridsdale; two *s* one *d*. *Educ:* St Andrew's Coll., Grahamstown, SA. Commnd 6th QEO Gurkha Rifles, 1962; active service in Borneo and Malaya, 1964–66; student, Canadian Land Forces Comd and Staff Coll., 1969–70; Bde Maj., 48 Gurkha Inf. Bde, 1974–76; Comdt, 7th Duke of Edinburgh's Own Gurkha Rifles, 1976–79; School of Infantry: Chief Instructor, Tactics Wing, 1979–80; GSO 1 Tactics, 1980–82; Instr, Staff Coll., Camberley, 1982–83; Commander: British Gurkhas, Nepal, 1985–87; Bde of Gurkhas, 1987–90; retd, 1991. Col, 7th Duke of Edinburgh's Own Gurkha Rifles, 1991–94. Chm., Gurkha Bde Assoc., 1991–2003. Trustee, Gurkha Welfare Trust (UK), 1987–2002. Freeman, City of London, 2002. Yr Brother, Trinity House, 2004. *Publication:* (with Col E. D. Powell-Jones) Abridged History of the 6th Queen Elizabeth's Own Gurkha Rifles, 1974. *Recreations:* golf, elephant polo. *Address:* Nottingham Cottage, Kensington Palace, W8 4PY. *T:* (home) (020) 7937 6258, (office) (020) 7930 4832. *Clubs:* Army and Navy, Beefsteak, Pratt's; Hong Kong Golf.

HUNTER, Air Vice-Marshal Alexander Freeland Cairns, CBE 1982 (OBE 1981); AFC 1978; DL; Deputy Chairman, Annington Holdings plc, since 1996; *b* 8 March 1939; *s* of late H. A. C. and L. E. M. Hunter; *m* 1964, Wilma Elizabeth Bruce Wilson. *Educ:* Aberdeen Grammar Sch.; Aberdeen Univ. (MA 1960, LLB 1962). Commissioned RAFVR 1959; RAF 1962; flying training 1962; Pilot, 81 (PR) Sqn, FEAF, 1964–67; Central Flying Sch., 1967–68; Instructor, Northumbrian Univ. Air Sqn, 1968–69; Asst Air Attaché, Moscow, 1971–73; RAF Staff Coll., 1974; Flight Comdr, 230 Sqn, 1975–77; OC 18 Sqn, RAF Germany, 1978–80; Air Warfare Course, 1981; MoD (Air), 1981; OC RAF Odiham, 1981–83; Gp Captain Plans, HQ Strike Comd, 1983–85; RCDS 1986; Dir of Public Relations (RAF), 1987–88; Comdt, RAF Staff Coll., 1989–90; Comdr British Forces Cyprus and Adminr of Sovereign Base Areas, 1990–93. Chm., Home Housing Assoc., 1995–98; Member, Board: North Housing Assoc. Ltd, 1993–95 (Vice Chm. (NE), 1994); Warden Housing Assoc., 1996–98. Chairman: Home in Scotland Ltd, 1998–2000; Home Gp, 1998–2003; Paramount Homes Ltd, 1998–2003; Kenton Bar Bunker Co. Ltd, 1999–2004; UK Haptics Ltd, 2006–07; Dep. Chm., Annington Trust, 2008–; Dep. Chm., Urban Housing Trust Ltd, 2001–03; Director: Clyde Helicopters Ltd, 1993–95; Newcastle Bldg Soc., 1993–2004; Newcastle Bank (Gibraltar), 1995–99; Great NE Air Ambulance Trading Co. Ltd, 2000–01. Vice-Pres., HMS Trincomalee Trust, 2007–. Chm., N of England, RFCA, 2003–06 (Vice Chm. (Air), 1996–2003); Vice Chm. (Air), Council of RFCAs (formerly TAVRAs), 1999–2004. Hon. Col, Tyne-Tees Regt, 1999–2006; Hon. Air Cdre, No 609 (W Riding) Sqdn, RAuxAF, 2001–06. Gentleman of the Four and Twenty, Rothbury, 2002–. DL Northumberland, 1994. OStJ 1994 (Chm. Council, Northumbria, 1998–2000). *Recreations:* shooting, fishing, hill-walking, military history. *Address:* c/o Clydesdale Bank, Business Banking Centre, Wakefield Road, Carlisle CA3 0HE. *Clubs:* Royal Air Force; Northern Counties (Newcastle upon Tyne); Tanglin (Singapore).

HUNTER, Sir Alistair (John), KCMG 1994 (CMG 1985); DL; HM Diplomatic Service, retired; *b* 9 Aug. 1936; *s* of Kenneth Clarke Hunter and Joan Tunks; *m* 1st, 1963; one *s* two *d*; 2nd, 1978, Helge Milton (*née* Kahle); two step *s*. *Educ:* Felsted; Magdalen Coll., Oxford. Royal Air Force, 1955–57; CRO, 1961–65; Private Sec. to Permanent Under-Sec., 1961–63; 2nd Sec., Kuala Lumpur, 1963–65; 1st Sec. (Commercial), Peking, 1965–68; seconded to Cabinet Office, 1969–70; FCO, 1970–73; 1st Sec., Rome, 1973–75; FCO, 1975–80; Hd of Chancery, Bonn, 1980–85; seconded to DTI as Under Sec., Overseas Trade, 1985–88; Consul-Gen., Düsseldorf, and Dir-Gen. of British Trade and Investment Promotion in FRG, 1988–91; Consul-Gen., NY, and Dir-Gen. of Trade and Investment, USA, 1991–96. Exec. Chm., British-Amer. Chamber of Commerce, London, 1996–98. Chairman: British Music Rights, 1998–2005; E Kent Forum, 1998–2001; Manston Airport Consultative Cttee, 1999–2006; Margate Th. Royal Trust, 2000–07. Dir, PRS, 1996–2002; Dep. Chm., Locate in Kent, 1996–2005. Trustee, Horniman Mus. and Gdns, 1996–99. DL Kent, 2001. *Address:* Bay View House, 2A Bay View Road, Broadstairs CT10 2EA.

HUNTER, Andrew Reid; Headmaster, Merchiston Castle School, since 1998; *b* Nairobi, 28 Sept. 1958; *s* of John Horatio Hunter and Irene Hunter (*née* Fish); *m* 1981, Barbara Gandy Bradford; two *s* one *d*. *Educ:* Univ. of Manchester (BA Hons). Teacher of English, 1983–91, Housemaster, 1991, Worksop Coll.; Housemaster and Teacher of English and Religious Studies, Bradfield Coll., 1991–98. *Recreations:* previously county tennis, hockey and squash player; theatre, literature. *Address:* Merchiston Castle School, Colinton Road, Edinburgh EH13 0PU. *T:* (0131) 312 2203, *Fax:* (0131) 441 6060; *e-mail:* headmaster@merchiston.co.uk. *Club:* New (Edinburgh).

HUNTER, Andrew Robert Frederick Ebenezer; *b* 8 Jan. 1943; *s* of late Sqdn Leader Roger Edward Hunter, MBE, DFC and Winifred Mary Hunter (*née* Nelson); *m* 1972, Janet (*d* 2002), *d* of late Samuel Bourne of Gloucester; one *s* one *d*. *Educ:* St George's Sch., Harpenden; Durham Univ.; Jesus Coll., Cambridge; Westcott House, Cambridge. In industry, 1969; Asst Master, St Martin's Sch., Northwood, 1970–71; Asst Master, Harrow

Sch., 1971–83. Contested: (C) Southampton, Itchen, 1979; (DemU) Lagan Valley, NI Assembly, 2003. MP (C, 1983–2002, Ind. C, 2002–04, DemU, 2004–05) Basingstoke. PPS to Minister of State, DoE, 1985–86. Member: NI Select Cttee, 1994–2001; NI Grand Cttee, H of C, 1996–2005; Chm., Cons. NI Cttee, 1992–97. Chairman: Freedom Assoc., 2005–; Monday Club, 2008–. Mem., Countryside Alliance, 1997–. Commnd TAVR, 1973 (resigned commn as Major, 1984). Hon. Mem., Soc. of the Sealed Knot, 1987–. *Recreations:* horse riding, watching cricket and Rugby football, collecting model soldiers. *Address:* 21 Manor Court, Meeting Street, Moira, Co. Down BT67 0TL. *Clubs:* St Stephen's, Carlton.

HUNTER, Angela Jane; Director of Communications, BP, 2002–07; *b* 29 July 1955; *d* of Arthur John, (Mac), Hunter and Joy Lorraine Hunter; *m* 1st, 1980, Nick Cornwall (marr. diss. 2004); one *s* one *d*; 2nd, 2006, (Thomas) Adam (Babington) Boulton, *qv. Educ:* St Leonard's Sch., St Andrews, Fife; Brighton Poly. (BA 1987). Teacher of English as a foreign language, Academia Britanica, Córdoba, Spain, 1976–78; Legal Asst, Hodge Jones & Allen, then Offenbach & Co., 1978–80; Res. Asst to Tony Blair, MP, 1986–90, Head of Office, 1990–97; Special Asst to Prime Minister, 1997–2001; Dir of Govt Relations, Prime Minister's Office, 2001. Trustee: Snowdon Awards Scheme; Three Faiths Forum. Mem., Bd of Govs, Birmingham Business Sch., 2005–. *Recreations:* diving, ski-ing, horse-riding.

HUNTER, Anthony John; Executive Director, Community Services, Liverpool City Council, since 2004; *b* 9 March 1954; *s* of Robert and Elizabeth Hunter; *m* 1986, Tatyana Fomina; one *s* one *d. Educ:* Doncaster Grammar Sch.; Queen's Coll., Oxford (MA PPE 1976); Nottingham Univ. (MA Applied Social Studies, CQSW, 1980); Sheffield Poly. (DMS 1984). Social Worker and Social Services Manager: Doncaster MBC, 1976–84; Barnsley MBC, 1985–86; Res. and Develt Manager, Barnardo's, 1986–89; Health and Social Care Consultant, Price Waterhouse, 1989–95; Dir of Social Services, Housing and Public Protection, ER of Yorks Council, 1995–2003. Pres., Assoc. of Dirs of Social Services, 2004–05. *Publications:* articles on social care, local govt develt and change mgt issues in social work and local govt jls. *Recreations:* football, rock'n'roll singing, playing computer games with my children. *Address:* (office) 60 Victoria Street, Liverpool L1 6JQ. *T:* (0151) 233 4415, *Fax:* (0151) 233 4496.

HUNTER, Anthony Rex; *see* Hunter, Tony.

HUNTER, Archibald Sinclair; DL; CA; Chairman, Macfarlane Group PLC, since 2004 (Director, since 1998); *b* 20 Aug. 1943; *s* of late John Lockhart Hunter and Elizabeth Hastings (*née* Sinclair); *m* 1969, Patricia Ann Robertson; two *s* one *d. Educ:* Queen's Park Sch., Glasgow. CA 1966. With Mackie & Clark, Glasgow, 1966; joined Thomson McLintock, 1966: Partner, 1974–87; Glasgow Office Managing Partner, 1983–87; Glasgow Office Managing Partner, KPMG Peat Marwick, 1987–92; Sen. Partner, Scotland, 1992–99, Consultant, 1999–2001, KPMG. Pres., ICAS, 1997–98. Non-executive Director: Clydeport plc, 1999–2002; Edinburgh US Tracker Trust, 2003–; Royal Bank of Scotland, 2004–. Dir, Beatson Inst., 1999–. Mem. Court, Univ. of Strathclyde, 1999– (Chm., 2002–). DL Renfrewshire, 1995. DUniv Strathclyde, 2006. *Recreations:* golf, swimming, hill-walking. *Address:* Macfarlane Group, Clansman House, 21 Newton Place, Glasgow G3 7PY. *T:* (0141) 226 5511. *Clubs:* Williamwood Golf (formerly Capt.) (Glasgow); Western Gailes Golf (Ayrshire).

HUNTER, Rt Rev. Barry Russell, AM 1992; Bishop of Riverina, 1971–92; permission to officiate, diocese of Newcastle, NSW, 1996–2001, diocese of Armidale, NSW, since 2001; *b* Brisbane, Queensland, 15 Aug. 1927; *s* of late John Hunter; *m* 1961, Dorothy Nancy, *d* of B. P. Sanders, Brisbane; three *d. Educ:* Toowoomba Grammar Sch.; St Francis' Theological Coll., Brisbane; Univ. of Queensland (BA, ThL). Assistant Curate, St Matthew's, Sherwood, 1953–56; Member, Bush Brotherhood of St Paul, Cunnamulla, Queensland, 1956–61; Rector, St Cecilia's, Chinchilla, 1961–66; Rector, St Gabriel's, Biloela, 1966–71; Archdeacon of the East, Diocese of Rockhampton, 1969–71; Locum Tenens in parish of Cudal, NSW, 1992–96. DLitt (*hc*) Charles Sturt Univ., 1994. *Recreation:* music. *Address:* 90 Calala Lane, Tamworth, NSW 2340, Australia.

HUNTER, Prof. Christopher Alexander, PhD; FRS 2008; Professor of Chemistry, University of Sheffield, since 1997; *b* Dunedin, NZ, 19 Feb. 1965; *s* of John Alexander Hunter and Alice Mary Hunter; *m* 2008, Rosaleen Theresa McHugh; two *s* one *d. Educ:* Churchill Coll., Cambridge (BA 1986; PhD 1989). Lecturer: Dept of Chem., Univ. of Otago, NZ, 1989–91; Dept of Chem., Univ. of Sheffield, 1991–94; Liste Inst. Res. Reader, 1994–97. ESPRC Sen. Res. Fellow, 2005–. *Publications:* contrib. papers to scientific jls. *Address:* Department of Chemistry, University of Sheffield, Sheffield S3 7HF. *T:* (0114) 222 9476, *Fax:* (0114) 222 9346; *e-mail:* c.hunter@shef.ac.uk.

HUNTER, David Peter; Director, Department for Environment, Food and Rural Affairs, 1996–2007; *b* 31 Dec. 1948; *o s* of Mr and Mrs D. Hunter, Southampton; *m* 1973, Judith, *d* of Mr and Mrs G. A. Baker, Worcester; two *s* two *d. Educ:* Regent's Park Sch.; Shirley Sch.; King Edward VI Sch., Southampton; Magdalen Coll., Oxford (MA). MAFF, 1972–82; Cabinet Office, 1982–83; rejoined MAFF, 1983; Head: Beef Div., 1984–87; Trade Policy and Tropical Products Div., 1987–93; Agencies and Citizen's Charter Div., 1993–96; EU and Livestock Gp, 1996–98; Agricl Gp, MAFF, subseq. DEFRA, 1998–2001; Dir, EU and Internat. Policy Directorate, 2001–06, Review of Rural Payments Agency, 2006–07, DEFRA. *Recreations:* theatre, vegetables, Soton FC. *Club:* Lion & Unicorn Players (Petersfield).

HUNTER, Rear-Adm. Ian Alexander, CB 1993; Chief of Naval Staff, New Zealand, 1991–94; *b* 23 Oct. 1939; *s* of late A. A. Hunter and O. R. Hunter; *m* 1965, Hilary R. Sturrock; two *s. Educ:* Christchurch Boys' High Sch.; BRNC Dartmouth. Joined RNZN 1957; served HMNZS Otago, HMS Tabard, USS Arneb, HMNZS Rotoiti (Antarctic), N Ireland Anti-Submarine Sch., HM Ships Torquay and Eastbourne, HMNZ Ships Taranaki, Blackpool, Canterbury, Waikato (Command), Southland (Command); posts with Chief of Naval Staff; RCDS 1985; ACDS (Develt Plans), 1987–88; Commodore Auckland, 1988–91 (concerned with Govt financial reforms for RNZN, restructuring Dockyard, orgn of Whitbread Round the World Yacht Race). Pres., Sea Cadet Assoc. of NZ, 1998–. Patron, Wellington Returned Services Assoc., 2001–. *Address:* 108B Messines Road, Karori, Wellington, New Zealand.

HUNTER, Ian Gerald Adamson; QC 1980; SC (NSW) 1994; a Recorder, 1986–2000; *b* 3 Oct. 1944; *s* of late Gerald Oliver Hunter and Jessie Hunter; *m* 1975, Maggie (*née* Reed) (marr. diss. 1999); two *s*; *m* 2000, Jill (*née* Nichols). *Educ:* Reading Sch.; Pembroke Coll., Cambridge (Open Scholar, Squire Univ. Law Scholar, Trevelyan Scholar, BA (double first in Law), MA, LLB); Harvard Law Sch. (Kennedy Memorial Scholar, LLM). Called to the Bar, Inner Temple, 1967 (Duke of Edinburgh Entrance Scholar, Major Scholar), Bencher, 1986; Mem. Bar, NSW, 1993; Avocat à la cour de Paris, 1995. CEDR Accredited Mediator, 1998–. Chm., Consolidated Regulations and Transfer Cttee, Senate of Inns of Court, 1986–87 (Mem., 1982–85); Member: International Relations Cttee, Bar Council, 1982–90; Exec. Cttee, Bar Council, 1985–86. Mem. and Rapporteur, Internat. Law Assoc. Anti-Trust Cttee, 1968–72; Pres., Union Internat. des Avocats, 1989 (UI Vice-Pres., 1982–86; first Vice Pres., 1986–; Dir of Studies, 1990–91); Vice Pres., Franco British Lawyers Soc., 1996–99; Pres., Anglo-Australasian Lawyers Soc., 1998–; Treas., Ba Pro Bono Unit, 1997–99; Hon. Mem., Canadian Bar Assoc., 1990. *Publications:* articles o public international law. *Recreations:* bebop, other good music, French cooking. *Address:* Essex Court Chambers, 24 Lincoln's Inn Fields, WC2A 3ED. *T:* (020) 7813 8000.

HUNTER, James, CBE 2001; PhD; FRSE; Director, Centre for History, UH Millennium Institute, Dornoch, since 2005; *b* 22 May 1948; *s* of Donald and Jean Hunter *m* 1972, Evelyn Ronaldson; one *s* one *d. Educ:* Oban High Sch.; Aberdeen Univ. (MA Hons 1971); Edinburgh Univ. (PhD 1974). Res. Fellow, Aberdeen Univ., 1974–76 journalist: Press and Jl, 1976–81; Sunday Standard, 1981–82; freelance journalist and broadcaster, 1982–85; Founding Dir, Scottish Crofters' Union, 1985–90. Chairman: Skye and Localsh Enterprise, 1995–98; Highlands and Is Enterprise, 1998–2004 (Bd Mem. 1991–95); Isle of Eigg Heritage Trust, 2004–07; Member: Scottish Tourist Bd, 1995–98 Council, NT for Scotland, 1995–98; Convention of the Highlands and Is, 1996–2004; Bd Scottish Natural Heritage, 2004– (Mem., N Areas Bd, 1992–98). Mem., BBC' Broadcasting Council for Scotland, 1999–2002. FRSE 2007. *Publications:* The Making o the Crofting Community, 1976; For the People's Cause, 1986; Skye: the island, 1986; The Claim of Crofting, 1991; Scottish Highlanders: a people and their place, 1992; A Dance Called America: the Scottish Highlands, the United States and Canada, 1994; On the Other Side of Sorrow: nature and people in the Scottish Highlands, 1995; Glencoe and the Indians, 1996 (US edn as Scottish Highlanders, Indian Peoples); Last of the Free: a millennial history of the Highlands and Islands of Scotland, 1999; Culloden and the Las Clansman, 2001; Scottish Exodus: travels among a worldwide clan, 2005. *Recreations* hillwalking, swimming. *Address:* Rowanbrae, Kiltarlity, Beauly, Inverness-shire IV4 7HT *T:* (01463) 741644; *e-mail:* jameshunter22548@btinternet.com.

HUNTER, His Honour John; a Circuit Judge, 1980–93; *b* 12 April 1921; *s* of Charles and Mary Hunter; *m* 1956, Margaret Cynthia Webb; one *s* two *d. Educ:* Fitzwilliam House, Cambridge (MA). Called to the Bar, Lincoln's Inn, 1952. Served War, Army 1939–46. Industry, 1952–62; practised at the Bar, 1962–80. *Recreations:* sailing, gardening *Address:* 230 Compass House, Smugglers Way, SW18 1DQ. *Club:* London Rowing.

HUNTER, Prof. John Angus Alexander, OBE 1997; MD; Grant Professor o Dermatology, University of Edinburgh, 1981–99, now Emeritus; *b* 16 June 1939; *s* of Dr John Craig Alexander Hunter and Alison Hay Shand Alexander; *m* 1968, Ruth Mary Farrow; one *s* two *d. Educ:* Loretto Sch., Musselburgh; Pembroke Coll., Cambridge (BA 1960); Univ. of Edinburgh (MB ChB 1963; MD 1977 (Gold Medal)). FRCPE 1978. Gen med. posts, Edinburgh, 1963–66; Research Fellow in Dermatology: Inst. of Dermatology, London, 1967; Univ. of Minnesota, 1968–69; Lectr, Dept of Dermatology, Univ. of Edinburgh, 1970–74; Consultant Dermatologist, Lothian Health Bd, 1974–80. Hon. Member: British Assoc. of Dermatologists, 1999; Dermatological Socs of N America, Greece, Germany, Poland, Austria and USA. *Publications:* (jtly) Common Diseases of the Skin, 1983; (jtly) Clinical Dermatology, 1989, 4th edn 2008; (jtly) Skin Signs in Clinical Medicine, 1997; (ed jtly) Davidson's Principles and Practice of Medicine, 18th edn 1999 to 20th edn 2006; (ed jtly) Davidson's Clinical Cases in Medicine, 2008; numerous articles in dermatol jls. *Recreations:* golf, gardening, music. *Address:* Sandy Lodge, Nisbet Road, Gullane, E Lothian EH31 2BQ; *e-mail:* jaa.hunter@virgin.net. *Clubs:* Hawks (Cambridge); Hon. Company of Edinburgh Golfers.

HUNTER, John Garvin, CB 2004; Permanent Secretary, Department of Finance and Personnel, Northern Ireland Civil Service, 2003–07; *b* 9 Aug. 1947; *s* of Garvin and Martha Hunter; *m* 1976, Rosemary Alison Haire; one *s* two *d. Educ:* Merchant Taylors' Sch., Liverpool; Queen's Univ., Belfast (BA); Cornell Univ., NY (MBA). Asst Principal, NICS, 1970; Department of Health and Social Services: Dep. Principal, 1973; Harkness Fellow, 1977–79; Principal Officer, 1979; Asst Sec., 1982; Dir Gen., Internat. Fund for Ireland, 1986; Under Sec., 1988; Chief Exec., Mgt Exec., Health and Personal Social Services, NI, 1990–96; Dir of Personnel, NICS, 1997–99; Perm. Sec., Dept for Social Develt, NICS, 1999–2003. *Publications:* contribs to conf. papers on the conflict in NI and on health service planning. *Recreations:* Corrymeela Community, church, swimming, Belfast Philharmonic Choir.

HUNTER, Prof. John Rotheram, PhD; FSA, FSAScot, FFSSoc; Professor of Ancient History and Archaeology, University of Birmingham, since 1996; *b* 4 Jan. 1949; *s* of William Rotherham Hunter and Stella Maud Hunter (*née* Atthill); *m* 1971, Margaret Suddes; three *s* one *d. Educ:* Merchant Taylors' Sch., Crosby; Univ. of Durham (BA 1970; DipArch 1971; PhD 1977); Univ. of Lund. FSAScot 1980; MIFA 1985; FSA 1986. Lectr, 1974–83, Sen. Lectr, 1983–95, Reader, 1995–96, in Archaeology, Univ. of Bradford. Cathedral Archaeologist, Bradford Cathedral, 1990–99. Registered Forensic Practitioner, 2003–; Dir, Centre for Internat. Forensic Assistance, 2003–05. Mem., Royal Commn on Ancient and Histl Monuments of Scotland, 2004–. *Publications:* Rescue Excavations on the Brough of Birsay, Orkney, 1986; (with I. B. M. Ralston) Archaeological Resource Management in the UK, 1993; (with C. Roberts and A. Martin) Studies in Crime: an introduction to forensic archaeology, 1996; Fair Isle: the archaeology of an island community, 1996; (with I. B. M. Ralston) The Archaeology of Britain: an introduction, 1998; (with M. Cox) Advances in Forensic Archaeology, 2005; Investigations in Sanday, Orkney: vol. 1, Excavations at Pool, Sanday, 2007. *Recreations:* rowing, watching football, walking the dog. *Address:* Institute of Archaeology and Antiquity, University of Birmingham, Birmingham B15 2TT. *T:* (0121) 414 5498.

HUNTER, Keith Robert, OBE 1981; British Council Director, Italy, 1990–96; *b* 29 May 1936; *s* of Robert Ernest Williamson and Winifred Mary Hunter; *m* 1st, 1959, Ann Patricia Fuller (marr. diss. 1989); one *s* two *d*; 2nd, 1991, Victoria Solomonidis. *Educ:* Hymers Coll., Hull; Magdalen Coll., Oxford (MA). Joined British Council, 1962; Lectr, Royal Sch. of Admin, Phnom Penh, 1960–64; Schs Recruitment Dept, 1964–66; SOAS, 1966–67; Asst Rep., Hong Kong, 1967–69; Dir, Penang, 1970–72; Dep. Rep., Kuala Lumpur, 1972–74; London Univ. Inst. of Educn, 1974–75; Rep., Algeria, 1975–78; First Sec. (Cultural), subseq. Cultural Counsellor (British Council Rep.), China, 1979–82; Sec. of Bd, and Hd of Dir-Gen.'s Dept, 1982–85; Controller, Arts Div., 1985–90. Trustee, British Sch. at Rome, 1997–2001. Chm., Parkhouse Award Trust, 1999–. *Recreations:* music, printmaking, restoration. *Address:* 15 Queensdale Road, W11 4SB.

HUNTER, Sir Laurence (Colvin), Kt 1995; CBE 1987; FRSE 1986; Professor of Applied Economics, University of Glasgow, 1970–2003, now Professor Emeritus and Hon. Senior Research Fellow; *b* 8 Aug. 1934; *s* of Laurence O. and Jessie P. Hunter; *m* 1958, Evelyn Margaret (*née* Green); three *s* one *d. Educ:* Hillhead High Sch., Glasgow; Univ. of Glasgow (MA); University Coll., Oxford (DPhil). Asst, Manchester Univ., 1958–59; National Service, 1959–61; Post-Doctoral Fellow, Univ. of Chicago, 1961–62; University of Glasgow: Lectr, 1962; Sen. Lectr, 1967; Titular Prof., 1969; Vice-Principal, 1982–86; Dir of External Relations, 1987–90; Dir, Business Sch., 1996–99. Member: Ct of Inquiry into miners' strike, 1972; Council, Advisory, Conciliation and Arbitration Service, 1974–86; Royal Commn on Legal Services in Scotland, 1976–80; Council,

ESRC, 1989–92; Chairman: Post Office Arbitration Tribunal, 1974–92; Police Negotiating Bd, 1987–99 (Dep. Chm., 1980–86). Pres., Scottish Econ. Soc., 1993–96; Treas., RSE, 1999–2004. DUniv Paisley, 1999. *Publications:* (with G. L. Reid) Urban Worker Mobility, 1968; (with D. J. Robertson) Economics of Wages and Labour, 1969, 2nd edn (with C. Mulvey), 1981; (with G. L. Reid and D. Boddy) Labour Problems of Technological Change, 1970; (with A. W. J. Thomson) The Nationalised Transport Industries, 1973; (with R. B. McKersie) Pay, Productivity and Collective Bargaining, 1973; (with L. Baddon *et al.*) People's Capitalism, 1989; other pubns in economics and industrial relations. *Recreations:* golf, painting, curling. *Address:* 7 Boclair Crescent, Bearsden, Glasgow G61 2AG. *T:* (0141) 563 7135.

HUNTER, Mack Robert; a District Judge (Magistrates' Courts), since 2004; *b* 21 Oct. 1954; *s* of Mack and Joan Hunter; *m* 1996, Margaret (*née* Campbell); one *s* one *d*. *Educ:* Sevenoaks Sch.; Worcester Coll., Oxford (MA). Called to the Bar, Gray's Inn, 1979; in practice as barrister, 1979–2004; Actg Stipendiary Magistrate, then Dep. Dist Judge, 1998–2004. *Recreations:* swimming, tennis, history, spending time with family. *Address:* c/o Chief Magistrates' Office, Westminster City Magistrates' Court, 70 Horseferry Road, SW1P 2AX.

HUNTER, Mark James; MP (Lib Dem) Cheadle, since July 2005; *b* 25 July 1957; *s* of Arthur Brian Hunter and Elizabeth Mary, (Betty), Hunter; *m* 1997, Lesley Graham; one *s* one *d*. *Educ:* Audenshaw Grammar Sch. In newspaper advertising industry, latterly as business develt manager, local newspaper div., Guardian Media Gp. Member (Lib Dem): Tameside MBC, 1980–89; Stockport MBC, 1996–2005 (Chm., Educn Cttee; Dep. Leader, 2001–02; Leader, 2002–05). Contested: (Liberal SDP Alliance) Ashton under Lyne, 1987; (Lib Dem) Stockport, 2001. Lib Dem spokesman on foreign affairs, 2007, dep. spokesperson on transport and PPS to Lib Dem Leader, 2007–08. Mem., Trade and Industry, subseq. BERR Select Cttee. *Address:* (office) Hillson House, 3 Gillbent Road, Cheadle Hulme, Stockport, Cheshire SK8 7LE. *T:* (0161) 486 1359, *Fax:* (0161) 486 9005; *e-mail:* hunterm@parliament.uk; House of Commons, SW1A 0AA.

HUNTER, Prof. Michael Cyril William, FSA; FRHistS; FBA 2007; Professor of History, Birkbeck College, University of London, since 1992; *b* 22 April 1949; *s* of Francis Hunter and Olive Hunter (*née* Williams). *Educ:* Christ's Hospital; Jesus Coll., Cambridge (BA 1971, MA 1975); Worcester Coll., Oxford (DPhil 1975). Research Fellow: Worcester Coll., Oxford, 1972–75; Univ. of Reading, 1975–76; Birkbeck College, University of London: Lectr in History, 1976–84; Reader in History, 1984–92. Longstanding activist on issues concerning historic preservation; also involved in projects for making digital resources available online. *Publications:* John Aubrey and the Realm of Learning, 1975; Science and Society in Restoration England, 1981; The Victorian Villas of Hackney, 1981; (with Annabel Gregory) An Astrological Diary of the Seventeenth Century, 1988; Establishing the New Science, 1989; (jtly) Avebury Reconsidered, 1991; The Royal Society and its Fellows 1660–1700, 1982, rev. edn 1994; Robert Boyle by Himself and his Friends, 1994; Science and the Shape of Orthodoxy, 1995; (ed) Preserving the Past, 1996; (ed) Archives of the Scientific Revolution, 1998; (ed with Edward B. Davis) The Works of Robert Boyle, vols 1–7, 1999, vols 8–14, 2000; Robert Boyle: scrupulosity and science, 2000; (ed jtly) The Correspondence of Robert Boyle, 6 vols, 2001; The Occult Laboratory, 2001; (jtly) London's Leonardo, 2003; The Boyle Papers, 2007; Editing Early Modern Texts, 2007. *Recreations:* book-collecting, motorcycling, historic buildings. *Address:* Exmouth House, Exmouth Place, Hastings, East Sussex TN34 3JA. *T:* (01424) 430727; School of History, Classics and Archaeology, Birkbeck College, Malet Street, WC1E 7HX. *T:* (020) 7631 6299.

HUNTER, Muir Vane Skerrett; QC 1965; MA Oxon; Barrister-at-Law; *b* 19 Aug. 1913; *s* of late H. S. Hunter, Home Civil Service, and Bluebell M. Hunter, novelist; *m* 1st, 1939, Dorothea Eason, JP (*d* 1986), *e d* of late P. E. Verstone; one *d*; 2nd, 1986, Gillian Victoria Joyce Petrie, MA, *d* of late Dr Alexander Petrie, CBE, MD, FRCS, FRCP. *Educ:* Westminster Sch.; Christ Church, Oxford (Scholar). Voluntary war relief work, Spain, 1937. Called to the Bar, Gray's Inn, 1938 (*ad eundem* Inner Temple, 1965); Holker Senior Scholar; Bencher, Gray's Inn, 1975. Served 1940–46: Royal Armoured Corps (Hon. Lt-Col); GS Intelligence, GHQ (India); GSO 1 attd War and Legislative Depts, Mil. Judge of Anti-Corruption Tribunals, Govt of India, 1943–45; returned to the Bar, 1946; standing counsel (bankruptcy) to Bd of Trade, 1949–65; Dep. Chm., Advisory Cttee on Service Candidates, HO, 1960–95; Member: EEC Bankruptcy Adv. Cttee, Dept of Trade, 1973–76; Insolvency Law Review Cttee, Dept of Trade, 1977–82; Advr, Law Reform Commn, Kenya Govt, 1991–96; Consultant on law reform, Govt of The Gambia/USAID, 1992. Visiting Professor of Insolvency Law: Bournemouth Univ., 1997–; Kingston Univ., 2007–. Presenter, Back-Handers (Poulson bankruptcy case), BBC4 documentary, 2006. Founder-Chairman, N Kensington Neighbourhood Law Centre, 1969–71; Mem., Exec. Cttee, British-Polish Legal Assoc., 1991–97; Hon. Mem. of Council, Justice. Amnesty/ICJ International Observer: Burundi, 1962; Rhodesia, 1969; Turkey, 1972. Gov., Royal Shakespeare Theatre, 1964–83, now Hon. Life Gov.; Mem. Council, Royal Shakespeare Theatre Trust, 1978–97; Pres., East Street Poets, Blandford, 1995–97; Sec., Kick Start Poets, Salisbury, 2000–02. Chairman: Gdansk Hospice Fund, 1989–92; Polish Hospices Fund, 1992–2002. Hon. Legal Advr, Nairobi Hospice, Kenya, 1989–92. Hon. Life Mem., Commercial Law League of America, 1985. Mem. Editl Board, Insolvency Law & Practice, 1985–95; Editl Consultant, Sweet & Maxwell Ltd, 1999–2004. (With Gillian Petrie Hunter) Aid and Co-operation Medals, Polish Govt, 1996. Hon. LLD Bournemouth, 2000. *Publications:* Senior Editor, Williams on Bankruptcy, 1958–78, Williams and Muir Hunter on Bankruptcy, 1979–84, Muir Hunter on Personal Insolvency, 1987–; Emergent Africa and the Rule of Law, 1963; Jt Editor: Halsbury's Laws, 4th edn, Vol. 3; Atkins' Forms, Vol. 7; Editor, Kerr, The Law and Practice as to Receivers and Administrators, 17th edn, 1988, 18th edn as Kerr & Hunter, The Law and Practice on Receivers and Administrators, 2004, First Supplement, 2006; Part Editor, Butterworth's Civil Court Precedents (formerly County Court Precedents and Pleadings), 1984–; Going Bust?: how to resist and survive bankruptcy and winding-up, 2007; (contrib.) Tears in the Fence (poetry), 1994; The Grain of My Life (poetry), 1997; contrib. Jl of Business Law, Commercial Law League Jl (US). *Recreations:* writing poetry, theatre, travel, music. *Address:* (chambers) 3–4 South Square, Gray's Inn, WC1R 5HP. *T:* (020) 7696 9900, *Fax:* (020) 7696 9911; Hunterston, Donhead St Andrew, Shaftesbury, Dorset SP7 9EB. *T:* (01747) 828779; *e-mail:* mvshunterqc@aol.com. *Clubs:* Hurlingham; Oxford Union.

HUNTER, Paul Anthony, FRCS, FRCP, FRCOphth; Consultant Ophthalmic Surgeon, King's College Hospital, since 1982; President, Royal College of Ophthalmologists, 2000–03; *b* 22 Nov. 1944; *s* of Gordon Nicholson Hunter and Kathleen Margaret (*née* Tyldesley); *m* 1971, Elizabeth Alex Pearse; one *s* one *d*. *Educ:* Leys Sch., Cambridge; Queens' Coll., Cambridge (BA Hons 1966; MB BChir 1969); Middlesex Hosp. Med. Sch. DO RCP&RCS 1974. FRCS 1977; FRCOphth 1993; FRCP 2002. Resident Surgical Officer, Moorfields Eye Hosp., 1976–79; Sen. Registrar, Middx Hosp., 1980–81; Hon. Lectr, King's Coll. Med. Sch., London Univ., 1982–. *Publications:* (ed jtly) Atlas of Clinical Ophthalmology, 1988, 3rd edn 2005; contribs on cornea and external eye disease to professional jls. *Recreations:* travel, ski-ing, gardening, grandchildren. *Address:* 22a Harley Street, W1G 9BP. *T:* (020) 7636 4326.

HUNTER, Prof. Peter John, DPhil; FRS 2006; FRSNZ; Professor of Engineering Science, since 1997 and Director, Bioengineering Institute, since 2001, University of Auckland; *b* Auckland, NZ, 30 July 1948. *Educ:* Univ. of Auckland (BE 1971; ME 1972); Univ. of Oxford (DPhil 1975). Res. Fellow, Rutherford Lab., 1975–77; Fellow, St Catherine's Coll., Oxford, 1975–77; Lectr in Engrg Sci., Univ. of Auckland, 1978–97. Dir of Computational Physiol., Univ. of Oxford. Co-Chm., Physiome Cttee, IUPS. FRSNZ 1994. *Publications:* articles in learned jls. *Address:* Bioengineering Institute, Faculty of Engineering, University of Auckland, Private Bag 92019, Auckland Mail Centre, Auckland 1142, New Zealand.

HUNTER, Sir Philip John, Kt 2008; CBE 1999; PhD; Chief Schools Adjudicator, since 2002; Director of Education (formerly Chief Education Officer), Staffordshire, 1985–2000; *b* 23 Nov. 1939; *m* Ruth Bailey; two *s* one *d*. *Educ:* Univ. of Durham (BSc 1962); Univ. of Newcastle upon Tyne (PhD 1965). Lectr, Univ. of Khartoum, 1965–67; Senior Scientific Officer: ARC, Cambridge, 1967–69; DES, 1969–71; Course Dir, CS Staff Coll., 1971–73; posts at DES, including science, schools, finance and Private Office, 1973–79; Dep. Chief Educn Officer, ILEA, 1979–85. Dir, Staffs TEC, 1990–2001; Member of Council: Keele Univ., 1987–99; BTEC, 1990–95; Member: Nat. Council for Educnl Technol., 1986–91; Nat. Curriculum Wkg Gp on Design and Technol., 1988–89; Design Council Educn Cttee, 1990–94; Qualifications and Curriculum Authy, 1997–2001. Chm., West Midlands Chief Educn Officers, 1995–97; Pres., Soc. of Educn Officers, 1998–99 (Vice-Pres., 1997). Vis. Prof. of Educn, Keele Univ., 1998–. Hon. DTech Staffs, 1999. *Publications:* (jtly) Terrestrial Slugs, 1970; (jtly) Pulmonates, 1978; (ed) Developing Education: fifteen years on, 1999; papers on ecology of invertebrates; contrib. educnl jls on educn policy matters. *Recreation:* gardening. *Address:* Upmeads, Newport Road, Stafford ST16 1DD.

HUNTER, Prof. Richard Lawrence, PhD; Regius Professor of Greek, Cambridge University, since 2001; Fellow, Trinity College, Cambridge, since 2001; *b* 30 Oct. 1953; *s* of John Lawrence Hunter and Ruth Munro Hunter; *m* 1978, Iris Temperli; one *s* one *d*. *Educ:* Cranbrook Sch., Sydney; Univ. of Sydney (BA Hons 1974); Pembroke Coll., Cambridge (PhD 1979). University of Cambridge: Fellow, 1977–2001, Dir of Studies in Classics, 1979–99, Asst Tutor, 1985–87, Tutor for Admissions, 1987–93, Pembroke Coll.; Univ. Lectr in Classics, 1987–97; Reader in Greek and Latin Lit., 1997–2001; Chm., Sch. of Arts and Humanities, 2007–08. Visiting Professor: Princeton Univ., 1991–92; Univ. of Virginia, 1979, 1984. Fellow, Alexander S. Onassis Public Benefit Foundn, 2006. Ed., Jl of Hellenic Studies, 1995–2000. Corresp. Fellow, Acad. of Athens, 2001; Hon. Fellow, Aust. Acad. of Humanities, 2005. Hon. Dr Phil. Thessaloniki, 2004. Premio Anassilaos, Reggio Calabria, 2006. *Publications:* Eubulus: the fragments, 1983; A Study of Daphnis and Chloe, 1983; The New Comedy of Greece and Rome, 1985; Apollonius of Rhodes, Argonautica III, 1989; The Argonautica of Apollonius, Literary Studies, 1993; trans., Jason and the Golden Fleece (The Argonautica), 1993; Theocritus and the Archaeology of Greek Poetry, 1996; (ed) Studies in Heliodorus, 1998; Theocritus: a selection, 1999; Theocritus, Encomium of Ptolemy, 2003; Plato's Symposium, 2004; (with M. Fantuzzi) Tradition and Innovation in Hellenistic Poetry, 2004 (Italian edn, 2002); (ed) The Hesiodic Catalogue of Women: constructions and reconstructions, 2005; The Shadow of Callimachus, 2006; On Coming After (collected papers), 2008; articles and reviews in learned jls. *Recreation:* travel. *Address:* Faculty of Classics, Sidgwick Avenue, Cambridge CB3 9DA. *T:* (01223) 335960, 335152.

HUNTER, Sir Thomas (Blane), Kt 2005; Chairman: West Coast Capital, since 1998; Hunter Foundation, since 1998; *b* 6 May 1961; *m* 1987, Marion McKillop; two *s* one *d*. *Educ:* Strathclyde Univ. (BA Mktg and Econs). Founder: Sports Div., 1984, sold 1998; Hunter Foundn, 1998; West Coast Capital, 2001. Founder and Mem. Bd, Clinton-Hunter Develt Initiative, 2005–. Beacon Prize, 2004. *Recreations:* ski-ing, water sports, music. *Address:* Marathon House, Olympic Business Park, Drybridge Road, Dundonald KA2 9AE. *T:* (01563) 852226, *Fax:* (01563) 850091.

HUNTER, Dr Tony, (Anthony Rex Hunter), FRS 1987; Professor, Molecular and Cell Biology Laboratory, Salk Institute, San Diego, California, since 1982; concurrently Adjunct Professor of Biology, University of California, San Diego; *b* 23 Aug. 1943; *s* of Ranulph Rex Hunter and Nellie Ruby Elsie Hunter (*née* Hitchcock); *m* 1969, Philippa Charlotte Marrack (marr. diss. 1974); *m* 1992, Jennifer Ann Maureen Price; two *s*. *Educ:* Felsted Sch., Essex; Gonville and Caius Coll., Cambridge (BA, MA, PhD). Research Fellow, Christ's Coll., Cambridge, 1968–71 and 1973–74; Salk Inst., San Diego: Res. Associate, 1971–73; Asst Prof., 1975–78; Associate Prof., 1978–82. American Cancer Soc. Res. Prof., 1992–2008. Assoc. Mem., EMBO, 1992. FRSA 1989; Fellow, Amer. Acad. of Arts and Scis, 1992; For. Associate, US Nat. Acad. of Scis, 1998; Member: Inst. of Medicine, US Nat. Acads, 2004; Amer. Philos. Soc., 2006. Katharine Berkan Judd Award, Meml Sloan-Kettering Cancer Center, 1992; Gairdner Foundn Internat. Award, 1994; Hopkins Meml Medal, Biochemical Soc., 1994; Mott Prize, Gen. Motors Cancer Res. Foundn, 1994; Feodor Lynen Medal, Univ. of Miami, 1999; J. Allyn Taylor Internat. Prize in Medicine, John P. Robarts Res. Inst. and C. H. Stiller Meml Foundn, 2000; Keio Med. Sci. Prize, Keio Univ. Med. Sci. Fund, Tokyo, 2001; Sergio Lombroso Award in Cancer Res., Weizman Inst. Sci., 2003; Amer. Cancer Soc. Medal of Honor, 2004; Kirk A. Landon Amer. Assoc. for Cancer Res. Prize, 2004; Prince of Asturias Award, 2004; Louis Gross Horowitz Prize, 2004; Wolf Prize in Medicine, 2005; Daniel Nathans Meml Award, Van Andel Inst., 2005; Pasarow Award in Cancer, Robert J. and Claire Pasarow Foundn, 2007; Herbert Tabor Award, Amer. Soc. of Biochem. and Molecular Biol., 2007; Clifford Prize for Cancer Res., Inst. of Med. and Veterinary Sci., Adelaide. *Publications:* numerous, in leading scientific jls. *Recreations:* white water rafting, exploring the Baja peninsula. *Address:* Molecular and Cell Biology Laboratory, The Salk Institute, 10010 North Torrey Pines Road, La Jolla, CA 92037, USA. *T:* (858) 4534100, ext. 1385, *Fax:* (858) 4574765; *e-mail:* hunter@salk.edu.

HUNTER, William Hill, CBE 1971; JP; DL; CA; Consultant, McLay, McAlister & McGibbon, Chartered Accountants, since 1991 (Partner, 1946–91); *b* 5 Nov. 1916; *s* of Robert Dalglish Hunter and Mrs Margaret Walker Hill or Hunter; *m* 1947, Kathleen, *d* of William Alfred Cole; one *s* (and one *s* decd). *Educ:* Cumnock Academy. Chartered Accountant, 1940. Served War: enlisted as private, RASC, 1940; commissioned RA, 1941; Staff Capt., Middle East, 1944–46. Director: Abbey National Building Soc. Scottish Adv. Bd, 1966–86; City of Glasgow Friendly Soc., 1966–88 (Pres., 1980–88); J. & G. Grant Glenfarclas Distillery, 1966–92. President: W Renfrewshire Conservative and Unionist Assoc., 1972–99; Scottish Young Unionist Assoc., 1958–60; Scottish Unionist Assoc., 1964–65. Contested (U) South Ayrshire, 1959 and 1964. Chairman: Salvation Army Adv. Bd in W Scotland, 1982–93 (Vice-Chm., 1972–82; Hon. Life Mem., 2001); Salvation Army Housing Assoc. (Scotland) Ltd, 1986–91; Salvation Army hostel named after him, Glasgow, 1991. Hon. Financial Advr and Mem. Council, Erskine Hosp., 1972; Hon. Treasurer, Quarrier's Homes, 1979–94 (Acting Chm., 1989–92). Deacon

Convener, Trades House of Glasgow, 1986–87. Hon. Vice-Pres., Royal Scottish Agricl Benevolent Inst., 1993–; Hon. Pres., Friends of Glasgow Botanic Gardens, 1994–2004. Session Clerk, Kilmacolm Old Kirk, 1967–72. JP 1970, DL 1987, Renfrewshire. Mem., Order of Distinguished Auxiliary Service, Salvation Army, 1981. *Recreations:* gardening, swimming. *Address:* Armitage, Kilmacolm, Renfrewshire PA13 4PH. *T:* (01505) 872444. *Club:* Western (Glasgow).

HUNTER, William John, MB, BS; FRCP, FRCPE, FFOM; Director, Public Health, European Commission, 1999–2000; *b* 5 April 1937; *m*; two *s* one *d*. *Educ:* Westminster Medical Sch. (MB, BS). LRCP 1961, FRCP 1995; FRCPE 1999; MRCS 1961; FFOM 1978. Commission of the European Communities: Principal Administrator, 1974–82; Hd of Div., Industrial Medicine and Hygiene, 1982–88; Dir, Public Health and Safety at Work, 1988–99. Hon. DG, EC, 2000–. Permt Mem., Caducée Gp, Commissariat Gén. du Plan advising Prime Minister of France, 2004–. Internat. Advr, 1998–2007, Mem., European Wkg Gp, 2001–07, RCP. Member: Admin. Bd, Assoc. Internat. des Anciens des Communautés Européennes, 2001–; Adv. Bd, Inst des Scis de la Santé, 2004–06; Admin. Bd, Ribérac Hosp., 2006–. Member, Administrative Board: Cercle d'Histoire et de Généalogie du Perigord, 1998–2005; Ensemble Vocal Arnaut de Mareuil, 2004–05. Hon. FFPH (Hon. FFPHM 1997). OStJ 1993. Ed., Internat. Jl of Integrated Care, 1999–2002. *Publications:* many on public health and safety at work. *Recreations:* swimming, diving, music.

HUNTER, Winston Ronald O'Sullivan; QC 2000; a Recorder, since 2000; *b* 7 Sept. 1960; *m* 1988, Louise Mary Blackwell; three *s*. *Educ:* Leeds Univ. (LLB 1st Cl. Hons). Called to the Bar, Lincoln's Inn, 1985. *Recreations:* cricket, shooting, antiques. *Address:* 12 Byrom Street, Manchester M3 4PP. *T:* (0161) 829 2100.

HUNTER BLAIR, Sir Patrick (David), 9th Bt *cr* 1786, of Dunskey; owner, Blairquhan Estate, Ayrshire; *b* 12 May 1958; *s* of Francis John Hunter Blair and of Joyce Adeline Mary (*née* Graham); *S* cousin, 2006; *m* 1984, Marguerite Catherine O'Neill; three *s* (incl. twins) two *d*. *Educ:* Edinburgh Acad.; Univ. of Aberdeen (BSc Forestry). FICFor. Dir of Policy Standards, NI Forest Service, 1998–2005. Non-executive Director: Forward Scotland, 2005–; Scottish Natural Heritage, 2007–. Mem., S Scotland Regl Forestry Forum. Chm., Professional and Educnl Standards Cttee, Inst. of Chartered Foresters. *Recreations:* family, friends, forestry and fishing. *Heir:* *s* Ronan Patrick Hunter Blair, *b* 10 Feb. 1995. *Address:* Blairquhan, Maybole, Ayrshire KA19 7LZ. *T:* (01655) 770239, *Fax:* (01655) 770278; *e-mail:* enquiries@blairquhan.co.uk.

HUNTER JOHNSTON, David Alan; *b* 16 Jan. 1915; *s* of James Ernest Johnston and Florence Edith Johnston (*née* Hunter); *m* 1949, Philippa Frances Ray (*d* 2008); three *s* one *d*. *Educ:* Christ's Hospital; King's Coll., London. FKC 1970. Royal Ordnance Factories, Woolwich, 1936–39; S Metropolitan Gas Co., 1939–44; Min. of Economic Warfare (Economic and Industrial Planning Staff), 1944–45; Control Office for Germany and Austria, 1945–47; Sec. to Scientific Cttee for Germany, 1946; FO (German Section), Asst Head, German Gen. Economic Dept, 1947–49; HM Treasury, Supply, Estabt and Home Finance Divs, 1949–53. Central Bd of Finance of Church of England: Sec. (and Fin. Sec. to Church Assembly), 1953–59, and Investment Manager, 1959–65; concurrently, Dir, Local Authorities Mutual Investment Trust, 1961–65, and Investment Man. to Charities Official Investment Fund, 1963–65; a Man. Dir, J. Henry Schroder Wagg & Co. Ltd, 1965–74; Chairman: Schroder Executor & Trustee Co. Ltd, 1966–74; Reserve Pension Bd, 1974–75; Assoc. of Investment Trust Cos, 1975–77; Director: Trans-Oceanic Trust, subseq. Schroder Global Trust plc, 1965–88; Clerical, Medical & General Life Assurance Soc., 1970–74; Lindustries Ltd, 1970–79 and of other investment trust cos for many years. Mem., Monopolies Commn, 1969–73. A Reader, 1959–85, licensed in dio. St Albans, dio. Bath and Wells. *Publications:* Stewardship and the Gospel, 1995; Church Synod State and Crown, 1997. *Address:* 49 Oatley House, Cote Lane, Bristol BS9 3TN. *T:* (0117) 9621 435. *Club:* Farmers'.

HUNTER SMART, (William) Norman, CA; Senior Partner, Hays Allan, Chartered Accountants, 1983–86; *b* 25 May 1921; *s* of William Hunter Smart, CA, and Margaret Thorburn Inglis; *m* 1st, 1948, Bridget Beryl Andreae (*d* 1974); three *s* (and one *s* decd); 2nd, 1977, Sheila Smith Stewart (*née* Speirs) (*d* 2000). *Educ:* George Watson's Coll., Edinburgh. Served War, 1939–45; 1st Lothians & Border Horse; Warwickshire Yeomanry; mentioned in despatches. Hays Allan, Chartered Accountants, 1950–86. Chairman: Charterhouse Develt Capital Fund Ltd, 1987–96; C. J. Sims Ltd, 1990–99. Chm., Assoc. of Scottish Chartered Accountants in London, 1972–73; Institute of Chartered Accountants of Scotland: Council Mem., 1970–75; Vice-Pres., 1976–78; Pres., 1978–79. Member: Gaming Bd for GB, 1985–90; Scottish Legal Aid Bd, 1986–89. *Address:* Greenhouse Cottage, Lilliesleaf, Melrose, Roxburghshire TD6 9EP. *Club:* Caledonian.

HUNTING, Richard Hugh; Chairman, Hunting plc, since 1991 (Deputy Chairman, 1989–91); *b* 30 July 1946; *s* of late Charles Patrick Maule Hunting, CBE, TD and Diana, *d* of Brig. A. B. P. Pereira, DSO; *m* 1970, Penelope, *d* of Col L. L. Fleming, MBE, MC; one *s* two *d*. *Educ:* Rugby Sch.; Sheffield Univ. (BEng); Manchester Business Sch. (MBA). Joined Hunting Gp, 1972; worked at Hunting Surveys and Consultants, Field Aviation, E. A. Gibson Shipbrokers, Hunting Oilfield Services, Hunting Engineering; Director: Hunting Associated Industries, 1986–89 (Chm., 1989); Hunting Petroleum Services, 1989; Hunting plc, 1989–. Dir, Yule Catto & Co. plc, 2000–. Non-exec. Dir, Royal Brompton and Harefield NHS Trust, 2007–. Mem. Council, CBI, 1992–97. Comr, Royal Hosp., Chelsea, 2002–08. Trustee: Geffrye Mus., 1995– (Chm., 2000–); Battle of Britain Meml Trust, 1998– (Chm., 2000–); Coronary Artery Disease Res. Assoc., 2001–. Mem. Court, Ironmongers' Co., 1986– (Master, 1996). *Recreations:* arts, ski-ing, family history. *Address:* (office) 3 Cockspur Street, SW1Y 5BQ. *T:* (020) 7321 0123. *Clubs:* Boodle's, Chelsea Arts, Hurlingham, Travellers.

HUNTINGDON, 16th Earl of, *cr* 1529; **William Edward Robin Hood Hastings Bass,** LVO 1999; racehorse trainer, since 1976; *b* 30 Jan. 1948; *s* of Capt. Peter Robin Hood Hastings Bass (who assumed additional surname of Bass by deed poll, 1954) (*d* 1964); *g s* of 13th Earl and of Priscilla Victoria, *d* of Capt. Sir Malcolm Bullock, 1st Bt, MBE; *S* kinsman, 1990; *m* 1989, Sue Warner (marr. diss. 2001). *Educ:* Winchester; Trinity Coll., Cambridge. Trainer, West Ilsley Stables, Berks, 1989–98. *Heir:* *b* Hon. Simon Aubrey Robin Hood Hastings Bass, *b* 2 May 1950. *Address:* Park House, Kingsclere, near Newbury, Berks RG20 5PY.

HUNTINGDON, Bishop Suffragan of, since 2008; **Rt Rev. David Thomson,** DPhil; FSA, FRHistS; *b* 2 Feb. 1952; *s* of Canon Ronald and Coral Thomson; *m* 1974, Jean Elliot Douglas-Jones; two *s* two *d*. *Educ:* Keble Coll., Oxford (MA, DPhil 1978); Selwyn Coll., Cambridge (BA 1980, MA 1984); Westcott House, Cambridge. FSA 2008; FRHistS 2008. Lectr, Wentworth Castle Coll. of Educn, 1976–78. Ordained deacon, 1981, priest, 1982; Curate, Maltby Team Ministry, 1981–84; Team Vicar, Banbury, 1984–94; Team Rector, Cockermouth, 1994–2002; Archdeacon of Carlisle, and Canon Residentiary, 2002–08. Hon. Canon, Ely Cathedral, 2008–. Gov., Trinity Sch., Carlisle, 2002–08 (Chair, 2003–05). Sec., Parish and People, 1984–93. FRSA. *Publications:* A Descriptive Catalogue of Middle English Grammatical Texts, 1979; An Edition of the Middle English Grammatical Texts, 1984; A Journey with John, 2004; Lent with Luke 2005; Christmas by Candlelight, 2006; Ways to Pray, 2007; contribs to collaborative works; articles in learned jls on medieval and theol subjects. *Recreations:* medieval studies detective fiction, fine art. *Address:* 14 Lynn Road, Ely, Cambs CB6 1DA. *T:* (01353) 662137, *Fax:* (01353) 669357; *e-mail:* bishop.huntingdon@ely.anglican.org.

HUNTINGDON AND WISBECH, Archdeacon of; *see* McCurdy, Ven. H. K.

HUNTINGFIELD, 7th Baron *cr* 1796 (Ire.); **Joshua Charles Vanneck;** Bt 1751 Lecturer, Cambridge Enterprise Agency, since 1999; Development Manager, Young Enterprise Cambridgeshire, since 2001; *b* 10 Aug. 1954; *o s* of 6th Baron Huntingfield and of Janetta Lois, *er d* of Captain R. H. Errington, RN; *S* father, 1994; *m* 1982, Arabella Mary, *d* of A. H. J. Fraser, MC; four *s* one *d* (incl. twin *s*). *Educ:* West Downs, Winchester; Eton; Magdalene Coll., Cambridge (MA). ACA. With Gerald Eve & Co., London, 1976; Chestertons, London, 1977–82; Highland Wineries, Inverness, 1982–87; accountant Deloitte Haskin & Sells, later Coopers & Lybrand, Cambridge, 1987–91; NFU Mutual, Cambridge, 1993–96; Stafford & Co., Cambridge, 1996–2001. *Recreations:* family, history. *Heir:* *s* Hon. Gerard Charles Alastair Vanneck, *b* 12 March 1985. *Address:* 69 Barrons Way, Comberton, Cambridge CB3 7EQ. *Club:* Pratt's.

HUNTINGTON-WHITELEY, Sir Hugo (Baldwin), 3rd Bt *cr* 1918; DL; *b* 31 March 1924; *e* surv. *s* of Captain Sir Maurice Huntington-Whiteley, 2nd Bt, RN, and Lady (Pamela) Margaret Huntington-Whiteley (*d* 1976), 3rd *d* of 1st Earl Baldwin of Bewdley, KG, PC; *S* father, 1975; *m* 1959, Jean Marie Ramsay, JP 1973, DStJ; two *d*. *Educ:* Eton. Royal Navy, 1942–47 (despatches). Chartered Accountant; Partner, Price Waterhouse, 1963–83. Mem. Ct of Assts, Goldsmiths' Co., 1982– (Prime Warden, 1989–90). Worcs: High Sheriff 1971; DL 1972. *Recreations:* music, travel. *Heir:* *b* (John) Miles Huntington-Whiteley, VRD, Lieut-Comdr RNR [*b* 18 July 1929; *m* 1960, Countess Victoria Adelheid Clementine Louise, *d* of late Count Friedrich Wolfgang zu Castell-Rudenhausen; one *s* two *d*]. *Address:* Ripple Hall, Tewkesbury, Glos GL20 6EY. *T:* (01684) 592431; 22 Park Close, Ilchester Place, W14 8ND. *T:* (020) 7603 3029. *Club:* Brooks's.

HUNTINGTOWER, Lord; John Peter Grant of Rothiemurchus; DL; *b* 22 Oct. 1946; *s* and *heir* of Countess of Dysart, *qv*; *m* 1971, Wendy Philippa Chance; one *s* two *d*. *Educ:* Gordonstoun. DL Inverness-shire, 1986.

HUNTLEY, Andrew John Mack, FRICS; Chairman, Insignia Richard Ellis (formerly Richard Ellis, Chartered Surveyors), 1993–2001; *b* 24 Jan. 1939; *s* of William Mack Huntley and Murial Huntley (*née* Akehurst); *m* 1963, Juliet Vivien Collum; three *d*. *Educ:* Monkton Coombe Sch., Bath. FRICS 1963. Davis & Son, Bristol, 1956–58; D. Ward & Son, Plymouth, 1958–61; Davige & Partners, London, 1961–65; with Richard Ellis, subseq. Insignia Richard Ellis, 1965–2001. Director: Pillar Property, 2002–05; Miller Gp, 2002–; Charities Official Investment Fund, 2002–. *Recreations:* shooting, tennis. *Address:* Ashurst, Fernhurst, Haslemere, Surrey GU27 3JB. *Club:* Boodle's.

HUNTLEY, Gillian Lesley; *see* Slater, G. L.

HUNTLEY, Maj. Gen. Michael, CB 2005; Director General Logistics (formerly Equipment Support) (Land), 2002–06; *b* 24 Dec. 1950. *Educ:* BSc. Commnd REME, 1972; rcds; psc; hcsc; Dep. COS 1st (UK) Armoured Div.; Dir Equipment Support (Army); Comdr Equipment Support, HQ Land Comd; Dir Support Ops, Equipment Support (Land), until 2002. Col Comdt, REME, 2004–. *Address:* c/o Army Personnel Centre, Kentigern House, 65 Brown Street, Glasgow G2 8EX.

HUNTLY, 13th Marquess of, *cr* 1599 (Scot.); **Granville Charles Gomer Gordon;** Earl of Huntly, 1450; Earl of Aboyne, Baron Gordon of Strathavon and Glenlivet, 1660; Baron Meldrum (UK), 1815; Premier Marquess of Scotland; Chief of House of Gordon; *b* 4 Feb. 1944; *s* of 12th Marquess of Huntly and Hon. Mary Pamela Berry (*d* 1998), *d* of 1st Viscount Kemsley; *S* father, 1987; *m* 1st, 1972, Jane Elizabeth Angela (marr. diss. 1990), *d* of late Col Alistair Gibb and Lady McCorquodale of Newton; one *s* two *d*; 2nd, 1991, Mrs Catheryn Millbourn; one *d*. *Educ:* Gordonstoun. Chm., Cock o' the North Liqueur Co. Ltd, 1998–; Dir, Hintlesham Hldgs Ltd, 1987–. *Heir:* *s* Earl of Aboyne, *qv*. *Address:* Aboyne Castle, Aberdeenshire AB34 5JP. *T:* (01339) 887778.

See also Baron Cranworth.

HUNTON, Christopher John; Global Managing Partner, Young & Rubicam, since 2007; *b* 12 Aug. 1961; *s* of Thomas and Elsie Hunton; *m* 1992, Dr Sara Hunton; one *s* one *d*. *Educ:* Bedford Coll., London (BA Hons); Hughes Hall, Cambridge (PGCE 1983). Teacher, Knox Sch., NY, 1984–85; Asst Housemaster, Wellingborough Sch., Northants, 1985–86; Account Manager, Foote, Cone & Belding, 1986–88; Account Dir, Ayer Barker, 1988–90; Bd Account Dir, Young & Rubicam, 1990–94; Gp Account Dir, Lowe Howard-Spink, 1994–98; CEO, McCann-Erickson, 1998–2004; Man. Dir, Lowe London, 2005–06. *Recreations:* family, sport, musical theatre, fishing.

HUNTSMAN, Peter William, FRICS; FAAV; Principal, College of Estate Management, University of Reading, 1981–92, Hon. Fellow, 1993; *b* 11 Aug. 1935; *s* of late William and Lydia Irene Huntsman (*née* Clegg); *m* 1st, 1961, Janet Mary Bell (marr. diss.); one *s* one *d*; 2nd, 1984, Cicely Eleanor (*née* Tamblin). *Educ:* Hymers Coll., Hull; Coll. of Estate Management, Univ. of London (BSc Estate Man.). Agricultural Land Service, Dorset and Northumberland, 1961–69; Kellogg Foundn Fellowship, Cornell Univ., USA, 1969–70; Principal Surveyor, London, ADAS, 1971–76; Divl Surveyor, Surrey, Middx and Sussex, 1976–81. Liveryman, Chartered Surveyors' Co., 1985; Freeman, City of London, 1985. Hon. FSVA 1993. *Publications:* (contrib.) Walmsley's Rural Estate Management, 6th edn 1978; contribs to professional jls. *Recreations:* sport, Dorset countryside, reading. *Address:* 68 Cauldron Barn Road, Swanage, Dorset BH19 1QF. *T:* (01929) 425857.

HUPPERT, Prof. Herbert Eric, ScD; FRS 1987; Professor of Theoretical Geophysics and Foundation Director, Institute of Theoretical Geophysics, Cambridge University, since 1989; Fellow of King's College, Cambridge, since 1970; *b* 26 Nov. 1943; *er c* of Leo Huppert and Alice Huppert (*née* Neuman); *m* 1966, Felicia Adina Huppert (*née* Ferster), PhD; two *s*. *Educ:* Sydney Boys' High Sch.; Sydney Univ. (BSc 1963); ANU (MSc 1964); Univ. of California at San Diego (MS 1966, PhD 1968); Univ. of Cambridge (MA 1971, ScD 1985). ICI Research Fellow, 1968–70; University of Cambridge: Asst Dir of Research, 1970–81; Lectr in Applied Maths, 1981–88; BP Venture Unit Sen. Res. Fellow, 1983–89; Reader in Geophysical Dynamics, 1988–89. Visiting research scientist: ANU; Univ. of California, San Diego; Canterbury Univ.; Caltech; MIT; Univ. of NSW; Univ. of WA; Univ. of Sydney; Tata Inst., Mumbai; Weizmann Inst. of Sci., Rehovot; Woods Hole Oceanographic Inst.; Vis. Prof., Univ. of NSW, 1991–96. Member: NERC, 1993–98; Council, Royal Soc., 2001–03. Fellow: Amer. Geophysical Union, 2002; APS, 2004. Lectures: Evnin, Princeton, 1995; Midwest Mechanics, 1996–97; Henry Charnock Dist., Southampton Oceanography Centre, 1999; Smiths Industries, Oxford Univ., 1999;

Arthur L. Day (also Prize), Nat. Acad. of Sci., USA, 2005; Dist. Israel Pollak, Technion, 2005. Associate Editor, Jl Fluid Mechanics, 1971–90; Editor, Jl of Soviet Jewry, 1985–; Member, Editorial Board: Philosophical Trans of Royal Soc. (series A), 1994–99; Reports on Progress in Physics, 1997–2003. William Hopkins Prize, Cambridge Philos. Soc., 2005; Wolfson Merit Award, Royal Soc., 2006; Murchison Medal, London Geol Soc., 2007. *Publications:* approximately 200 papers on applied mathematics, crystal growth, fluid mechanics, geology, geophysics, oceanography and meteorology. *Recreations:* my children, squash, tennis, mountaineering, cycling. *Address:* Institute of Theoretical Geophysics, Department of Applied Mathematics and Theoretical Physics, Centre for Mathematical Sciences, Wilberforce Road, Cambridge CB3 0WA. *T:* (office) (01223) 337853, *Fax:* (01223) 765900; 46 De Freville Avenue, Cambridge CB4 1HT. *T:* (01223) 356071; *e-mail:* heh1@esc.cam.ac.uk.

HURD, family name of **Baron Hurd of Westwell**.

HURD OF WESTWELL, Baron *cr* 1997 (Life Peer), of Westwell in the co. of Oxfordshire; **Douglas Richard Hurd,** CH 1996; CBE 1974; PC 1982; Deputy Chairman, Coutts & Co., since 1998; *b* 8 March 1930; *e s* of Baron Hurd (*d* 1966) and Stephanie Corner (*d* 1985); *m* 1st, 1960, Tatiana Elizabeth Michelle (marr. diss. 1982), *d* of A. C. Benedict Eyre, Westburton House, Bury, Sussex; three *s*; 2nd, 1982, Judy, *d* of Sidney and Pamela Smart; one *s* one *d*. *Educ:* Eton (King's Scholar and Newcastle Scholar; Fellow, 1981–96); Trinity Coll., Cambridge (Major Scholar). Pres., Cambridge Union, 1952. HM Diplomatic Service, 1952–66; served in: Peking, 1954–56; UK Mission to UN, 1956–60; Private Sec. to Perm. Under-Sec. of State, FO, 1960–63; Rome, 1963–66. Joined Conservative Research Dept, 1966; Head of Foreign Affairs Section, 1968; Private Sec. to Leader of the Opposition, 1968–70; Political Sec. to Prime Minister, 1970–74. MP (C): Mid-Oxon, Feb. 1974–1983; Witney, 1983–97. Opposition Spokesman on European Affairs, 1976–79; Minister of State, FCO, 1979–83; Minister of State, Home Office, 1983–84; Sec. of State for NI, 1984–85, for Home Dept, 1985–89; Sec. of State for Foreign and Commonwealth Affairs, 1989–95. Dir, NatWest Gp, 1995–99; Dep. Chm., NatWest Markets, 1995–98; Chm., British Invisibles, 1997–2000; Sen. Advr, Hawkpoint, 2000–. Member: Royal Commn on H of L reform, 1999; Appointments Commn, 2000–. Chairman: Prison Reform Trust, 1997–2001 (Hon. Pres., 2001–); CEDR, 2001–04; Canterbury Review Gp, 2000–01. Co-Pres., RIIA, 2001–. Chm., German British Forum, 2000–05. Vis. Fellow, Nuffield Coll., Oxford, 1978–86. Chm. Booker Prize Judges, 1998. High Steward, Westminster Abbey, 2000–. *Publications:* The Arrow War, 1967; An End to Promises, 1979; The Search for Peace (televised), 1997; Ten Minutes to Turn the Devil (short stories), 1999; Memoirs, 2003; Robert Peel, 2007; *novels:* Truth Game, 1972; Vote to Kill, 1975; The Shape of Ice, 1998; Image in the Water, 2001; with Andrew Osmond: Send Him Victorious, 1968; The Smile on the Face of the Tiger, 1969, repr. 1982; Scotch on the Rocks, 1971; War Without Frontiers, 1982; (with Stephen Lamport) Palace of Enchantments, 1985. *Recreation:* writing. *Address:* c/o House of Lords, SW1A 0PW. *Clubs:* Beefsteak, Pratt's, Travellers.
See also N. R. Hurd.

HURD, Nicholas Richard; MP (C) Ruislip Northwood, since 2005; *b* 13 May 1962; *s* of Baron Hurd of Westwell, *qv* and Tatiana Elizabeth Michelle Hurd; *m* 1988, Kim Richards; two *s* two *d*. *Educ:* Eton Coll.; Exeter Coll., Oxford (BA Classics 1985). Investment Manager, Morgan Grenfell, 1985–90; Corporate Finance Exec., Crown Communications, 1990–92; Managing Director: Passport Magazine Directories, 1992–94; Robert Fleming Do Brasil, 1994–2000; Business Develt Dir, Band-X Ltd, 2000–04; COS to Tim Yeo, MP, 2004–05. Shadow Minister for Charities, Social Enterprise and Volunteering, 2008–. Trustee, Greenhouse Sports Charity, 2004–. *Recreations:* sport, music. *Address:* House of Commons, SW1A 0AA. *T:* (020) 7219 6648, *Fax:* (020) 7219 4854; *e-mail:* hurdn@parliament.uk.

HURFORD, Peter (John), OBE 1984; organist; *b* 22 Nov. 1930; *e c* of H. J. Hurford, Minehead and Gladys Winifred Hurford (*née* James); *m* 1955, Patricia Mary Matthews, *e d* of late Prof. Sir Bryan Matthews, CBE, FRS; two *s* one *d*. *Educ:* Blundells Sch.; Royal Coll. of Music; Jesus Coll., Cambridge (MA, MusB; Hon. Fellow, 2006). FRCO. Commnd, Royal Signals, 1954–56. Director of Music, Bablake Sch., Coventry and Conductor, Leamington Spa Bach Choir, 1956–57; Master of the Music, Cathedral and Abbey Church of St Alban, 1958–78; Conductor, St Albans Bach Choir, 1958–78; Founder, Internat. Organ Festival, St Albans, 1963. Artist-in-Residence: Univ. of Cincinnati, 1967–68; Sydney Opera Ho., 1980, 1981, 1982; Acting Organist, St John's Coll., Cambridge, 1979–80; recital and lecture tours throughout Europe, USA, Canada, Japan, Philippines, Taiwan, Australia and NZ, 1960–98; perf. the organ works of J. S. Bach, in 34 progs for BBC, 1980–82, and at 50th Edinburgh Fest., 1997. Vis. Prof. of Organ, Univ. of Western Ontario, 1976–77; Prof., RAM, 1982–88; Betts Fellow, Oxford Univ., 1992–93; Hon. Fellow in Organ Studies, Bristol Univ., 1997–98. Mem. Council, 1963–2003, Pres., 1980–82, RCO; Pres., IAO, 1995–97; Mem., Hon. Council of Management, Royal Philharmonic Soc., 1983–87. Has made numerous LP records and CDs, incl. complete organ works of J. S. Bach (Gramophone Award, 1979; Silver Disc, 1983), F. Couperin, G. F. Handel, P. Hindemith. Hon. FRSCM 1977; Hon. Mem., RAM, 1981; Hon. FRCM 1987. Hon. Dr, Baldwin-Wallace Coll., Ohio, 1981; Hon. DMus Bristol, 1992; Hon. DArts Hertfordshire, 2007. *Publications:* Making Music on the Organ, 1988; Suite: Laudate Dominum; sundry other works for organ; Masses for Series III, and Rite II of Amer. Episcopal Church; sundry church anthems. *Recreations:* walking, wine, silence. *Address:* Broom House, St Bernard's Road, St Albans, Herts AL3 5RA.

HURLEY, Sarah Ruth; *see* Baldock, S. R.

HURN, Sir (Francis) Roger, Kt 1996; Chairman, Prudential plc, 2000–02; Deputy Chairman, Cazenove Group plc, since 2003 (Director, since 2001); *b* 9 June 1938; *s* of Francis James Hurn and Joyce Elsa Hurn (*née* Bennett); *m* 1980, Rosalind Jackson; one *d*. *Educ:* Marlborough Coll. Engrg apprentice, Rolls Royce Motors, 1956; joined Smiths Industries, 1958. National Service, 1959–61. Smiths Industries: Export Dir, Motor Accessory Div., 1969; Man. Dir, Internat. Operations, 1974; Exec. Dir, 1976; Man. Dir, 1978; Chief Exec., 1981–96; Chm., 1991–98; Chm., GEC, subseq. Marconi, 1998–2001; Dep. Chm., Glaxo Wellcome, 1997–2000, GlaxoSmithKline, 2000–03. Non-executive Director: Ocean Transport & Trading, 1982–88; Pilkington, 1984–94; S. G. Warburg Gp, 1987–95; ICI, 1993–2001. Gov., Henley Mgt Coll., 1986–2004 (Chm. Govs, 1996–2004). Liveryman, Coachmakers and Coach Harness Makers' Co., 1979–. *Recreations:* outdoor pursuits, travel. *Address:* Cazenove Group plc, 20 Moorgate, EC2R 6DA.

HURRELL, Sir Anthony (Gerald), KCVO 1986; CMG 1984; HM Diplomatic Service, retired; *b* 18 Feb. 1927; *s* of late William Hurrell and Florence Hurrell; *m* 1951, Jean Wyatt; two *d*. *Educ:* Norwich Sch.; St Catharine's Coll., Cambridge. RAEC, 1948–50; Min. of Labour, 1950–53; Min. of Educn, 1953–64; joined Min. of Overseas Develt, 1964; Fellow, Center for International Affairs, Harvard, 1969–70; Head of SE Asia Develt Div., Bangkok, 1972–74; Under Secretary: Internat. Div., ODM, 1974–75; Central Policy Rev. Staff, Cabinet Office, 1976; Duchy of Lancaster, 1977; Asia and Oceans Div., ODA, 1978–83; Ambassador to Nepal, 1983–86. Pres., St Catharine's Soc., 1993–94. *Recreations:* bird-ringing, bird-watching, digging ponds, music. *Address:* Lapwings, Dunwich, Saxmundham, Suffolk IP17 3DR.

HURRELL, Air Vice-Marshal Frederick Charles, CB 1986; OBE 1968; Director General, Royal Air Force Medical Services and Deputy Surgeon General (Operations), 1986–87; retired 1988; *b* 24 April 1928; *s* of Alexander John Hurrell and Maria Del Carmen Hurrell (*née* De Biedma); *m* 1950, Jay Jarvis; five *d*. *Educ:* Royal Masonic School, Bushey; St Mary's Hosp., Paddington (MB BS 1952). MRCS, LRCP 1952; DAvMed 1970; MFOM 1981, FFOM 1987. Joined RAF 1953; served UK, Australia, Singapore and USA; Dep. Dir, Aviation Medicine, RAF, 1974–77; British Defence Staff, Washington DC, 1977–80; CO Princess Alexandra Hosp., RAF Wroughton, 1980–82; Dir, Health and Research, RAF, 1982–84; PMO Strike Command, 1984–86. Dir of Appeals, RAF Benevolent Fund, 1988–95. Vice Pres., Royal Internat. Air Tattoo, 1997–2003. QHP 1984–88. FRAeS 1987. CStJ 1986. Chadwick Gold Medal, 1970. *Recreations:* painting, photography. *Address:* Hale House, 4 Upper Hale Road, Farnham, Surrey GU9 0NJ. *T:* (01252) 714190. *Club:* Royal Air Force.

HURST, Alan Arthur; *b* 2 Sept. 1945; *s* of George Arthur Hurst and Eva Grace Hurst; *m* 1976, Hilary Caroline Burch; two *s* one *d*. *Educ:* Westcliff High Sch.; Univ. of Liverpool (BA Hons). Admitted Solicitor, 1975; Partner, Law, Hurst & Taylor, 1980–. Member (Lab): Southend BC, 1980–96; Essex CC, 1993–98. MP (Lab) Braintree, 1997–2005; contested (Lab) same seat, 2005. Pres., Southend-on-Sea Law Soc., 1992–93. *Recreations:* bird watching, local history, canvassing. *Address:* 28 Whitefriars Crescent, Westcliff-on-Sea, Essex SS0 8EU. *T:* (01702) 337864.

HURST, Sir Geoffrey Charles, Kt 1998; MBE 1977; Director, Aon Warranty Group (formerly London General Insurance), 1995; Director of Football, McDonald's, UK, since 2002; professional football player, 1957–76; *b* 8 Dec. 1941; *s* of Charles and Evelyn Hurst; *m* 1964, Judith Helen Harries; three *d*. Professional Football Player: West Ham United, 1957–72; Stoke City, 1972–75; West Bromwich Albion, 1975–76; Player-Manager, Telford United, 1976–79; Manager, Chelsea, 1979–81; English Football International, 1966–72. Joined London General Insurance, 1981. *Publications:* The World Game, 1970; (with Michael Hart) 1966 and All That, 2001. *Recreations:* sport in general, family.

HURST, George; conductor; *b* 20 May 1926; Rumanian father and Russian mother. *Educ:* various preparatory and public schs in the UK and Canada; Royal Conservatory, Toronto, Canada. First prize for Composition, Canadian Assoc. of Publishers, Authors and Composers, 1945. Asst Conductor, Opera Dept, Royal Conservatory of Music, Toronto, 1946; Lectr in Harmony, Counterpoint, Composition etc, Peabody Conservatory of Music, Baltimore, Md, 1947; Conductor of York, Pa, Symph. Orch., 1950–55, and concurrently of Peabody Conservatory Orch., 1952–55; Asst Conductor, LPO, 1955–57, with which toured USSR 1956; Associate Conductor, BBC Northern Symphony Orchestra, 1957; Principal Conductor, BBC Northern Symphony Orchestra (previously BBC Northern Orchestra), 1958–68; Artistic Adviser, 1968–73, Staff Conductor, 1968–88, Vice-Pres., 1979, Western Orchestral Soc. (Bournemouth SO and Bournemouth Sinfonietta); Prin. Conductor, Nat. SO of Ireland, 1990–91. Consultant, Nat. Centre of Orchestral Studies, 1980–87; RAM conducting studies consultant, 1983–; Principal Guest Conductor, BBC Scottish Symphony Orchestra, 1986–89. Since 1956 frequent guest conductor in Europe, Israel, Canada. Founder, Conductors' Course, Canford Summer Sch. of Music, 1959. *Publications:* piano and vocal music (Canada). *Recreations:* yachting, horse-riding.

HURST, Henry Ronald Grimshaw; Overseas Labour Adviser, Foreign and Commonwealth Office, 1976–81, retired; *b* 24 April 1919; *s* of Frederick George Hurst and Elizabeth Ellen (*née* Grimshaw); *m* 1st, 1942, Norah Joyce (*d* 1984), *d* of John Stanley Rothwell; one *s* one *d*; 2nd, 1986, Joy Oldroyde (*d* 1991). *Educ:* Darwen and Blackpool Grammar Schs; St Catharine's Coll., Cambridge (MA). Served War, Army, 1940–46. Colonial Service, 1946–70: Permanent Sec., Min. of Labour, Tanzania, 1962–64; Labour Adviser, Tanzania, 1965–68, and Malaŵi, 1969–70; Dep. Overseas Labour Adviser, FCO, 1970–76. *Recreations:* cricket, gardening. *Address:* Flat 1, Meriden, Weston Road, Bath BA1 2XZ. *T:* (01225) 334429. *Club:* Civil Service.

HURST, (Jonathan) Martin (Stuart), PhD; Director, Water, Department for Environment, Food and Rural Affairs, since 2007; *b* 7 Sept. 1960; *s* of John Stuart Hurst and Jeanette Rose Hurst; *m* 2007, Stephanie (*née* Cottrill); one *d*, and one step *d*. *Educ:* Queens' Coll., Cambridge (BA 1982); Univ. of Southampton (MSc 1983; PhD 1989). Economist, HM Treasury, 1985–95; Divl Manager, DETR, 1995–2002; Sen. Policy Advr (envmt, farming, housing, planning), 10 Downing Street, 2002–05; Transformation Dir, Natural England, 2005; Dir, Regulation, DEFRA, 2006–07. Non-exec. Dir, Wandle Housing Assoc. Trustee, Groundwork SE London, 2005–. *Recreations:* hill walking, cricket, choral singing, bird watching. *Address:* Department for Environment, Food and Rural Affairs, Ergon House, Horseferry Road, SW1P 2AL. *T:* (020) 7238 5247; *e-mail:* martin.hurst@defra.gsi.gov.uk.

HURST, Peter Thomas; Senior Costs Judge of England and Wales (formerly Chief Master of the Supreme Court Taxing Office), since 1992 (Master, 1981–92); a Recorder, since 2000; Judicial Taxing Officer: House of Lords, since 2002; Privy Council, since 2005; *b* Troutbeck, Westmorland, 27 Oct. 1942; *s* of Thomas Lyon Hurst and Nora Mary Hurst; *m* 1968, Diane Irvine; one *s* two *d*. *Educ:* Stonyhurst College; LLB 1973, MPhil 2000, London. Admitted as Solicitor of the Supreme Court, 1967; Partner: Hurst and Walker, Solicitors, Liverpool, 1967–77; Gair Roberts Hurst and Walker, Solicitors, Liverpool, 1977–81. Greffier Substitute, Royal Court of Jersey, 2005–. Hon. Bencher, Gray's Inn, 2007. Mem. Sen. Edtl Bd, Civil Procedure (The White Book) (formerly The Supreme Court Practice), 2000– (contrib., 1986–). *Publications:* (ed jtly) Butterworth's Costs Service, 1986–; (contrib.) Cordery on Solicitors, 8th edn 1988; (ed jtly) Legal Aid, 1994, Solicitors, 1995, Halsbury's Laws of England, 4th edn; Civil Costs, 1995, 4th edn 2007; (ed jtly) Legal Aid Practice 1996–97, 1996; (ed jtly) The New Civil Costs Regime, 1999; Criminal Costs, 2007. *Recreation:* music. *Address:* Royal Courts of Justice, Strand, WC2A 2LL. *T:* (020) 7936 6000. *Club:* Athenæum.

HURT, John, CBE 2004; actor, stage, films and television; *b* 22 Jan. 1940; *s* of Rev. Arnould Herbert Hurt and Phyllis Massey; *m* 1984, Donna Peacock (marr. diss. 1990); *m* 1990, Jo Dalton (marr. diss. 1995); two *s*; *m* 2005, Anwen Rees-Myers. *Educ:* The Lincoln Sch., Lincoln; RADA. Started as a painter. *Stage:* début, Arts Theatre, London, 1962; Chips With Everything, Vaudeville, 1962; The Dwarfs, Arts, 1963; Hamp (title role), Edin. Fest., 1964; Inadmissible Evidence, Wyndham's, 1965; Little Malcolm and his Struggle Against the Eunuchs, Garrick, 1966; Belcher's Luck, Aldwych (RSC), 1966; Man and Superman, Gaiety, Dublin, 1969; The Caretaker, Mermaid, 1972; The Only Street, Dublin Fest. and Islington, 1973; Travesties, Aldwych (RSC), 1974; The Arrest, Bristol Old Vic, 1974; The Shadow of a Gunman, Nottingham Playhouse, 1978; The Seagull, Lyric, Hammersmith, 1985; A Month in the Country, Albery, 1994; Krapp's Last Tape, New Ambassadors, 2000, Barbican, 2006; Heroes, Wyndham's, 2005. *Films include:* With

The Wild and the Willing, 1962; A Man for All Seasons, 1966; Sinful Davey, 1967; Before Winter Comes, 1969; In Search of Gregory, 1970; Mr Forbush and the Penguins, (Evans in) 10 Rillington Place, 1971; The Ghoul, Little Malcolm, 1974; East of Elephant Rock, 1977; The Disappearance, The Shout, Spectre, Alien, Midnight Express (BAFTA award, 1978), 1978; Heaven's Gate, 1979; The Elephant Man, 1980 (BAFTA award, 1981); History of the World Part 1, 1981; Partners, 1982; Champions, Nineteen Eighty-Four, The Osterman Weekend, The Hit, 1984; Jake Speed, Rocinate, 1986; Aria, 1987; White Mischief, 1988; Scandal, 1989; Frankenstein Unbound, The Field, 1990; King Ralph, Lapse of Memory, 1991; Dark at Noon, 1992; Second Best, 1994; Even Cowgirls Get the Blues, Rob Roy, 1995; Dead Man, Wild Bill, 1996; Contact, 1997; Love and Death on Long Island, 1998; All the Little Animals, You're Dead, 1999; Night Train, 2000; Lost Souls, Captain Corelli's Mandolin, 2001; Miranda, 2002; Dogville, 2003; Hellboy, 2004; The Skeleton Key, 2005; The Proposition, V for Vendetta, Shooting Dogs, Manderlay, Perfume, 2006; Oxford Murders, Indiana Jones and the Kingdom of the Crystal Skull, 2008. *Television:* The Waste Places, 1968; The Naked Civil Servant, 1975 (Emmy Award, 1976); Caligula, in I Claudius (series), 1976; Treats, 1977; Crime and Punishment (series), 1979; Deadline, 1988; Poison Candy, 1988; Who Bombed Birmingham, 1990; Red Fox, 1991; Six Characters in Search of an Author, 1992; The Alan Clark Diaries, 2004. Dir, United British Artists, 1982. *Address:* c/o Independent Talent Group Ltd, 76 Oxford Street, W1D 1BS.

HURWITZ, His Honour Vivian Ronald; a Circuit Judge, 1974–91; *b* 7 Sept. 1926; *s* of Alter Max and Dora Rebecca Hurwitz; *m* 1963, Dr Ruth Cohen, Middlesbrough; one *s* two *d. Educ:* Roundhay Sch., Leeds; Hertford Coll., Oxford (MA). Served RNVR: Univ. Naval Short Course, Oct. 1944–March 1945, followed by service until March 1947. Called to Bar, Lincoln's Inn, 1952, practised NE Circuit. A Recorder of Crown Court, 1972–74. *Recreations:* bowls, bridge, music (listening), art (looking at), sport—various (watching).

HUSBAND, Dame Janet (Elizabeth Siarey), DBE 2007 (OBE 2002); FRCP, FRCR, FMedSci; Professor of Diagnostic Imaging, Institute of Cancer Research, University of London, 1996–2007, now Emeritus; Consultant Radiologist, Royal Marsden Hospital, 1980–2007; Special Adviser, Royal Marsden NHS Foundation Trust, since 2007; *b* 1 April 1940; *d* of late Ronald Howard Siarey and Clarissa Marian Siarey; *m* 1963, Peter Husband; three *s. Educ:* Headington Sch., Oxford; Guy's Hosp. Med. Sch., Univ. of London (MB BS 1964). MRCS, LRCP 1964; DCH 1966; DObstRCOG 1967; DMRD 1974; FRCR 1976; FRCP 1987. Registrar in Diagnostic Radiol., Guy's Hosp. and KCH (pt-time), 1971–76; Clinical Scientist, MRC Div. of Radiol., Northwick Park Hosp., 1976; Radiol. Res. Fellow, 1977–80, Med. Dir, Clinical Services Div., 2000–03, Royal Marsden Hosp.; Hd, Academic Dept of Radiol., 1985–2007, Med. Dir, 2003–06, Royal Marsden NHS Trust; Co-dir, CRUK (formerly ICRF) Clinical Magnetic Resonance Res. Gp, Inst. Cancer Res., London Univ., 1986–2005. Co-founder and Pres., Internat. Cancer Imaging Soc., 2000–01; President: BIR, 2003–04; RCR, 2004–07. Mem., Soc. of Computed Body Tomography, 1982–2004, now Emeritus. Comr, Royal Hospital Chelsea, 2007–. Hon. Member: Royal Belgian Radiol Soc., 1994; Eur. Soc. for Therapeutic Radiol. and Oncology, 1999. FMedSci 2001. *Publications:* (ed) Computed Tomography Review, 1989; (ed jtly) Imaging in Oncology, 2 vols, 1998, 2nd edn 2004; (jtly) Guide to the Practical Use of MRI in Oncology, 1999; articles in learned jls. *Recreations:* walking, opera, painting. *Address:* 48 Rose Square, The Bromptons, Fulham Road, SW3 6RS. *Club:* Athenæum.

HUSBAND, Prof. Thomas Mutrie, PhD; FREng, FIMechE; Chairman: UKERNA, 1997–2000; East and North Herts NHS Trust, 2000–01; Vice-Chancellor, University of Salford, 1990–97; *b* 7 July 1936; *s* of Thomas Mutrie Husband and Janet Clark; *m* 1st, 1962, Pat Caldwell (*d* 2001); two *s*; 2nd, 2003, Gwen Fox. *Educ:* Shawlands Acad., Glasgow; Univ. of Strathclyde (BSc(Eng), MA, PhD). Weir Ltd, Glasgow: Apprentice Fitter, 1953–58; Engr/Jun. Manager, 1958–62; sandwich degree student (mech. engrg), 1958–61; various engrg and management positions with ASEA Ltd in Denmark, UK and S Africa, 1962–65; postgrad. student, Strathclyde Univ., 1965–66; Teaching Fellow, Univ. of Chicago, 1966–67; Lectr, Univ. of Strathclyde, 1967–70; Sen. Lectr, Univ. of Glasgow, 1970–73; Prof. of Manufacturing Organisation, Loughborough Univ., 1973–81; Prof. of Engrg Manufacture, 1981–90, Dir of Centre for Robotics, 1982–90, Hd of Dept of Mech. Engrg, 1983–90, Imperial Coll., London Univ. Member: Standing Cttee for Educn, Training and Competence to Practise, Royal Acad. of Engrg (formerly Fellowship of Engrg), 1989–93; Engrg Technol. Adv. Cttee, DTI, 1990–93; Council, Engrg Council, 1992–95; Manufacturing Div. Bd, IEE, 1992–95; McRobert Award Cttee, Royal Acad. of Engrg, 2000–05. Mem., Univ. Bd, Bournemouth Univ., 2003–. Non-executive Director: Royal Exchange Theatre, Manchester, 1993–97; Univs and Colls Employers Assoc., 1994–97. FREng (FEng 1988). Hon. DSc: Manchester, 1997; Salford, 1998. *Publications:* Work Analysis and Pay Structure, 1976; Maintenance and Terotechnology, 1977; Education and Training in Robotics, 1986; articles in Terotechnica, Industrial Relations Jl, Microelectronics and Reliability, etc. *Recreations:* watching Arsenal FC, music, theatre. *Address:* 12 Roscrea Drive, Wick Village, Bournemouth BH6 4LU.

HUSBAND, William Anthony, (Tony); freelance cartoonist and writer; *b* 28 Aug. 1950; *s* of Henry Ronald and Vera Husband; *m* 1976, Carole Garner; one *s. Educ:* Holy Trinity Primary Sch., Hyde; Greenfield Secondary Sch., Hyde. Full-time cartoonist, 1984–; works for The Times, The Sun, The Sunday Express, Private Eye, The Spectator, The Oldie, Playboy, Punch, Manchester United Magazine, Golf International, Nursing Standard, Prescriber, Tameside Advertiser, Greenkeeper Internat., The Idler, The Sharp End, TES, Cheshire Life, The Village Link and many more; co-devised and co-wrote: Oink (comic), 1985–88; Round the Bend (children's TV prog.), 1988–90; co-wrote: (with David Wood) Save The Human (play), UK tour, 1991; Hanger 17 (children's TV series), 1993; episode of Chucklevision, 1994; series of greetings cards, Camden, Carlton, Hallmark Cards and Paperhouse; (with Ian McMillan, poet) performs cartoon/poetry event in front of live audiences. Several solo exhibns; exhibn accompanying Lowry's paintings, The Lowry, Salford, 2001; Cartoonist in Residence, The Lowry, 2006–. Awards: Cartoonist Club of GB: Gag Cartoonist, 1985, 1986, 1988; Strip Cartoonist, 1987; Cartoon Arts Trust: Sports Cartoonist, 1995, 2001; Gag Cartoonist, 2000, 2002; Strip Cartoonist, 2000; Pont Award, 2005. *Publications:* Use Your Head, 1985; Bye Bye Cruel World, 1986; Animal Husbandry, 1987; 102 Uses for a Black Lace Album, 1988; The Greatest Story Never Told, 1988; Yobs 1, 1989; Another Pair of Underpants, 1990; Yobs 2, 1993; (with David Day) True Tales of Environmental Madness, 1993; (with David Wood) Save The Human, 1993; (with David Day) The Complete Rhino, 1994; Football Food Guide, 1995; Reduced History of Football, 2004; Reduced History of Cricket, 2005; Reduced History of Golf, 2005; Reduced History of Rugby, 2006; Reduced History of Britain, 2006; The World's Worst Jokes, 2006; Reduced History of Tennis, 2006; (illus.) Private Eye's Coleman Balls, 2006; Reduced History of Sex, 2007; Reduced History of Cats, 2007; Reduced History of Dogs, 2007; 10 books pubd in Germany. *Recreations:* golf (8 handicap), music, photography (Mem., Hyde Photographic Soc.), Manchester United, playing the drums, wine and good food. *Address:* Hicroft, 132 Joel Lane, Gee Cross, Hyde, Cheshire SK14 5LN. *T:* (0161) 366 0262, *Fax:* (0161) 368 8479; *e-mail:* toonyhusband@hotmail.com; *web:* www.tonyhusband.co.uk. *Clubs:* Groucho, Werneth Low Golf (Hyde).

HUSBANDS, Sir Clifford (Straughn), GCMG 1996; KA 1995; CHB 1989; GCM 1986; Governor-General of Barbados, since 1996; President, Privy Council for Barbados since 1996; *b* 5 Aug. 1926; *s* of Adam Straughn Husbands and Ada Augusta (*née* Griffith); *m* 1959, Ruby C. D. Parris; one *s* two *d. Educ:* Parry Sch., Barbados; Harrison Coll. Barbados; Middle Temple, Inns of Court, London. Called to the Bar, Middle Temple 1952, Bencher, 2007; in private practice, Barbados, 1952–54; Actg Dep. Registrar Barbados, 1954; Legal Asst to Attorney Gen., Grenada, 1954–56; Magistrate: Grenada 1956–57; Antigua, 1957–58; Crown Attorney, Magistrate and Registrar, Montserrat 1958–60; Actg Crown Attorney, 1959, Actg Attorney Gen., 1960, St Kitts-Nevis Anguilla; Asst to Attorney Gen., Barbados, 1960–67 (Legal Draughtsman, 1960–63); DPP Barbados, 1967–76; QC Barbados 1968; Judge, Supreme Court, Barbados, 1976–91 Justice of Appeal, 1991–96. Chairman: Community Legal Services, 1985–96; Penal Reform Cttee, Barbados, 1995–96; Mem., Judicial and Legal Service Commn, Barbados 1987–96. Mem. Council, Barbados FPA, 1960–96. Vice-Pres., Barbados LTA, 1970s Pres., Old Harrisonian Soc., 1983–87. Chief Scout, Barbados Boy Scouts Assoc., 2006– Paul Harris Fellowship Award, 2001. KStJ 2004. Silver Jubilee Medal, 1977. *Recreations* music, swimming, photography, cricket. *Address:* Government House, St Michael Barbados. *T:* 4292962/4292646. *Clubs:* Rally, Spartan (Barbados).

HUSH, Prof. Noel Sydney, AO 1993; DSc; FRS 1988; FAA; Foundation Professor and Head of Department of Theoretical Chemistry, University of Sydney, 1971–92, now Professor Emeritus; *b* 15 Dec. 1924; *s* of Sidney Edgar Hush and Adrienne (*née* Cooper) *m* 1949, Thea L. Warman (decd), London; one *s* one *d. Educ:* Univ. of Sydney (BSc 1946 MSc 1948); Univ. of Manchester (DSc 1959). FAA 1977. Res. Fellow in Chemistry Univ. of Sydney, 1946–49; Lectr in Phys. Chem., Univ. of Manchester, 1950–54; Lectr subseq. Reader in Chem., Univ. of Bristol, 1955–71. Visiting Professor: ANU, 1960 Florida State Univ., 1965; Case Western Reserve Univ., 1968; Cambridge Univ., 1981 Stanford Univ., 1987; Vis. Fellow, Cavendish Lab., 1971; Vis. Sen. Scientist, Brookhaven Nat. Lab., USA, 1959–. Mem., Aust. Res. Grants Cttee, 1984–90 (Chm., Chem. Cttee 1987–90). Dir, Molecular Electronics Res. Ltd, 1997–. Adv. Editor, Chemical Physics 1973–; Mem. Bd of Mgt, Quadrant Magazine, 2002–. Foreign Mem., Amer. Acad. of Arts and Scis, 1999. Centenary Medal, RSC, 1990; Flinders Medal, 1994, Inaugural Award David Craig Medal, 2000, Australian Acad. of Science; Centenary Medal, Australia, 2004 Robert A. Welch Award in Chem., Welch Foundn, USA, 2007. *Publications:* (ed) Reactions of Molecules at Electrodes, 1971; papers in Jl of Chemical Physics, Chemical Physics, Jl of Amer. Chemical Soc., etc. *Recreations:* literature, music, travel. *Address:* 170 Windsor Street, Paddington, Sydney, NSW 2021, Australia. *T:* (2) 93281685; Department of Theoretical Chemistry, University of Sydney, Sydney, NSW 2006, Australia. *T:* (2) 96923330. *Clubs:* Athenæum; Union (Sydney).

HUSKINSON, (George) Nicholas (Nevil); His Honour Judge Nicholas Huskinson; a Circuit Judge, since 2003; a Member, Lands Tribunal, since 2006; *b* 7 Dec. 1948; *s* of Leonard and Margaret Huskinson; *m* 1972, Pennant Elfreda Lascelles Iremonger; two *s. Educ:* Eton (King's Schol.); King's Coll., Cambridge (MA). Called to the Bar, Gray's Inn, 1971 (Arden Schol.); Asst Recorder, 1995–99; a Recorder, 1999–2003; a Vice Pres., Immigration Appeal Tribunal, subseq. a Sen. Immigration Judge and Mem., Asylum and Immigration Tribunal, 2003–05. Asst Ed., Woodfall's Law of Landlord and Tenant, 28th edn, 1978–89. *Recreations:* tennis, gardening, walking, cooking. *Address:* Snaresbrook Crown Court, 75 Hollybush Hill, Snaresbrook, E11 1QW. *T:* (020) 8530 0000. *Club:* MCC.

HUSKISSON, Edward Cameron, MD; FRCP; Consultant Rheumatologist, King Edward VII's Hospital Sister Agnes (formerly King Edward VII Hospital for Officers), since 1982; *b* 7 April 1939; *s* of Edward William Huskisson, Northwood, Middx and late Elinor Margot Huskisson (*née* Gibson); *m* 1990, Janice Elizabeth Louden; three *s* one *d. Educ:* Eastbourne Coll.; King's Coll., London (BSc); Westminster Hosp. Med. Sch. (MB BS 1964); MD London 1974. MRCS 1964; LRCP 1964, MRCP 1967, FRCP 1980. Consultant Physician and Head of Rheumatology, St Bartholomew's Hosp., 1976–93. *Publications:* (jtly) Joint Disease: all the arthropathies, 1973, 4th edn 1988; Repetitive Strain Injury, 1992. *Address:* 14A Milford House, 7 Queen Anne Street, W1G 9HN. *T:* (020) 7636 4278, *Fax:* (020) 7323 6829; *e-mail:* edwardhuskisson@aol.com.

HUSSAIN, Karamat, SQA 1983; retired; Councillor (Lab) Mapesbury Ward, London Borough of Brent, 1971–86; Chairman, National Standing Conference of Afro-Caribbean and Asian Councillors, 1980–86 (Founder Member); *b* Rawalpindi, 1926; *m* Shamim. *Educ:* Aligarh Muslim Univ., India (BA Hons Humanities, MPhil). Political Educn Officer, Brent E, 1967–70. Brent Council: Chm., Planning Cttee, 1978–86; Vice Chm., Develt Cttee, 1978–86; Mem., Housing and Finance Cttees, 1978–86; Mayor of Brent, 1981–82 (Dep. Mayor, 1980–81); formerly Mem. and Vice-Chm., Brent Community Relations Council. Former Member: Regl Adv. Council on Higher Technical Educn, London and Home Counties; ASTMS. Gov., Willesden Coll. of Technology, 1971–86. *Recreation:* research in political philosophy. *Address:* Bungalow 14, Tregwilym Road, Rogerstone, Newport, Gwent NP10 9DW. *T:* (01633) 892187.

HUSSAIN, Mukhtar; QC 1992; a Recorder of the Crown Court, since 1989; *b* 22 March 1950; *s* of late Karam Dad and Rehmi Bi; *m* 1972, Shamim Akhtar Ali; three *d. Educ:* William Temple Secondary School. Came to UK, 1964. Called to the Bar, Middle Temple, 1971, Bencher, 2000; Asst Recorder, 1986–89; Head of Chambers, 1992–. Chm., Police Discipline Appeals Tribunal, 1997–; Member: Mental Health Review Tribunal, 2000–; CICB, 2000–; Bar Council, 2001. Presenter, Granada TV, 1982–87. *Recreations:* cricket, squash, bridge, golf, reading. *Address:* Lincoln House, 1 Brazennose Street, Manchester M2 5EL.

HUSSAIN, Nasser, OBE 2002; cricket commentator, Sky Sports, since 2004; *b* Madras, India, 28 March 1968; *s* of Joe Hussain and Shireen Hussain (*née* Price); *m* Karen Birch; two *s. Educ:* Univ. of Durham (BSc). Essex County Cricket Club: first-class début, 1987; county cap, 1989; Vice-Captain, 1995–99; Captain, 1999–2004, retired; England: début, 1990; Vice-Captain, 1998–99; Captain, 1999–2003; toured India, W Indies, Zimbabwe, NZ, Aust., S Africa, Pakistan, Sri Lanka; highest test score 207 *vs* Aust., Edgbaston, 1997. Player of the Series, England *vs* India, 1996. *Publications:* (with Steve Waugh) An Ashes Summer, 1997; Playing with Fire (autobiog.), 2004. *Address:* c/o Essex County Cricket Club, County Ground, New Writtle Street, Chelmsford, Essex CM2 0PG.

HUSSEY, Derek Robert; Member (UU) Tyrone West, Northern Ireland Assembly, 1998–2007; *b* 12 Sept. 1948; *s* of Sidney Robert Hussey and Rachael Hussey (*née* Maguire); *m* 1st (marr. diss.); one *s*; 2nd, Karen (*née* Vaughan); one *s* one *d. Educ:* Model Sch., Omagh; Omagh Acad.; Stranmillis Coll., Belfast (Cert Ed). Head of Business Studies, Castlederg High Sch., 1972–98, retired. Mem. (Ind. U 1989–97, UU 1997–), Strabane DC. Mem., N Ireland Forum, 1996–98. Dep. Whip, UUP, NI Assembly, 1998–99; UU spokesman on victims' issues. Contested (UU) Tyrone West, NI Assembly, 2007.

Recreations: country and western music, soccer, Rugby, ski-ing, Ulster-Scots history and culture. *Address: e-mail:* drhussey@hotmail.com.

HUSSEY, Lady Susan Katharine, DCVO 1984 (CVO 1971); Lady-in-Waiting to the Queen, since 1960; *b* 1 May 1939; 5th *d* of 12th Earl Waldegrave, KG, GCVO; *m* 1959, Marmaduke Hussey (later Baron Hussey of North Bradley) (*d* 2006); one *s* one *d*.
See also Sir Francis Brooke, Bt.

HUSTLER, Dr Margaret Joan; Headmistress, Harrogate Ladies' College, 1996–2007; *b* 1 Nov. 1949; *d* of Harry Hustler and Dorothy (*née* Kaye); *m* 1976, David Thomas Wraight; three *s* five *d*. *Educ:* Marist Convent, London; Westfield Coll., London Univ. (BSc Hons); Royal Holloway Coll., London Univ. (PhD Biochem). Teacher, Lady Eleanor Holles Sch., Hampton, 1977–85; Dep. Headmistress, Atherley Sch., Southampton, 1985–89; Headmistress, St Michael's Sch., Limpsfield, 1989–96. *Recreations:* walking, sewing, knitting, reading.

HUSTON, Felicity Victoria; Commissioner, House of Lords Appointments Commission, since 2000; Commissioner for Public Appointments for Northern Ireland, since 2005; Partner, Huston & Co., Tax Consultants, since 1994; *b* May 1963; *d* of Jim McCormick and Joy McCormick (*née* Day); *m* 1992, Adrian Robert Arthur Huston, JP; two *s*. *Educ:* Strathearn Sch., Belfast; Campbell Coll., Belfast; Nottingham Univ. (BA Hons 1985). HM Inspector of Taxes, 1988–94. Director: Cassandra Consulting (NI) Ltd, 2003–07; Moyle Hldgs Ltd; Moyle Interconnector (Financing) plc, 2003–; Moyle Interconnector plc; NI Energy Hldgs Ltd, 2005–; NI Gas Transmission Ltd, 2005–; Premier Transmission Ltd, 2005–. Gen. Comr of Income Tax, 2002– (Chm., NI Reg., Assoc. of Gen. Comrs of Income Tax, 2005–07). Mem., Industrial Tribunals Panel, 1999–2000. Member: Consumer Panel, PIA, 1996–98; PO Users' Council, NI, 1996–2000; Gen. Consumer Council, 1996–2000 (Dep. Chm., 1999–2000); Chm., NI Consumer Cttee for Electricity, 2000–03. Member Board: NI Charities Adv. Cttee, 1998–2000; Clifton House (Belfast Charitable Soc.), 1995–2007 (Hon. Treas., 2000–05). Dir, Team NI Ltd, 2004–06. Chm., Point Fields Th. Co., 1996. Trustee, Assisi Animal Sanctuary, 2006–. *Recreations:* cookery, family, pets. *Address:* c/o Huston & Co., 481 Upper Newtownards Road, Belfast BT4 3LL. *T:* (028) 9080 6080; *e-mail:* felicity@huston.co.uk.

HUTCHEON, Joy Louise; Head, Zambia, Department for International Development, since 2007; *b* 26 Feb. 1965; *d* of Keith Hutcheon and Margaret (*née* Swindells); partner, Christopher Nuttall. *Educ:* University Coll. London (BA English). Home Office: Private Sec. to Minister of State, 1991–92; Hd, Sentencing Policy, 1992–95; Private Sec. to Perm. Sec., 1995–97; Franchising Exec., Office of Passenger Rail Franchising, 1997–99; Team Leader, Performance and Innovation Unit, Cabinet Office, 1999–2000; Consultant, Caribbean, 2000–03; Hd, Western Asia Dept, 2003–05, Dir, Communication and Knowledge Sharing, 2005–07, DFID. *Publications:* Winning the Generation Game, 2000; Prime Minister's Review of Adoption, 2000; Sentencing for Drug and Drug Related Cases in OECS Magistrates' Courts, 2005. *Recreations:* weekends in Suffolk, playing the saxophone, California. *Address:* DFID Zambia, British High Commission, Independence Avenue, PO Box 50050, Lusaka, Zambia.

HUTCHEON, William Robbie; Editor, The Courier and Advertiser, since 2002 (Deputy Editor, 2001); *b* 19 Jan. 1952; *s* of Alexander Hutcheon and Williamina Hutcheon (*née* Robbie); *m* 1974, Margo Martin; one *s* two *d*. *Educ:* Aberdeen Acad. D. C. Thomson & Co. Ltd: joined as reporter, Aberdeen, 1969; Sports Sub-ed., Dundee, 1970; various posts, The Courier and Advertiser, inc. Sports Ed., Chief Sub-ed., Night News Ed., to 2001. Mem., Editors' Cttee, Scottish Daily Newspapers Soc., 2002– (Chm., 2007–08). *Recreations:* sport, music, travel, computing. *Address:* 42 Ferndale Drive, Broughty Ferry, Dundee DD5 3DF. *T:* (01382) 774552; *e-mail:* billhutcheon@aol.com.

HUTCHESON, Linda Dolores; *see* Cardozo, L. D.

HUTCHINGS, Gregory Frederick; Executive Chairman, Lupus Capital plc, since 2004. *Educ:* Uppingham Sch.; University of Aston (BSc); MBA Aston Mgt Centre. Dir, 1983–2000, Chief Exec., 1984–95, Chm., 1995–2000, Tomkins plc. Bd Mem., RNT, 1996–2002; Gov., Mus. of London, 1999. Hon. DBA Sunderland, 2000. *Address:* PO Box 1119, Kingston and Surbiton, Surrey KT2 7WY.

HUTCHINS, Bonnie; *see* Greer, B.

HUTCHINS, Patricia; freelance writer and illustrator of children's books, since 1964; *b* 18 June 1942; *d* of Edward and Lily Victoria Goundry; *m* 1966, Laurence Edward Hutchins; two *s*. *Educ:* Darlington Art Sch.; Leeds Coll. of Art (NDD). Asst Art Dir, J. Walter Thompson Advertising Agency, 1962–64. Dir and writer, Hutchins Film Co., 1997–; wrote and co-produced 39 ten-minute animated children's films, based on Titch books, for television. Hon. DCL UEA, 2006. Kate Greenaway Medal, 1974. *Publications:* Rosie's Walk, 1968; Tom and Sam, 1968; The Surprise Party, 1968; Clocks and More Clocks, 1970; Changes, Changes, 1971; Titch, 1971; Goodnight Owl, 1972; The Wind Blew, 1974; The Silver Christmas Tree, 1974; The House That Sailed Away, 1975; Don't Forget the Bacon, 1976; Happy Birthday Sam, 1979; Follow That Bus!, 1978; One-Eyed Jake, 1978; The Best Train Set Ever, 1978; The Mona Lisa Mystery, 1981; One Hunter, 1982; King Henry's Palace, 1983; You'll soon Grow into them, Titch, 1983; The Curse of the Egyptian Mummy, 1983; The Very Worst Monster, 1985; The Tale of Thomas Mead, 1986; The Doorbell Rang, 1986; Where's the Baby?, 1987; Which Witch is Which?, 1989; Rats!, 1989; What Game Shall We Play?, 1990; Tidy Titch, 1991; Silly Billy, 1992; My Best Friend, 1992; Little Pink Pig, 1993; Three Star Billy, 1994; Titch and Daisy, 1996; Shrinking Mouse, 1997; It's My Birthday, 1999; Ten Red Apples, 2001; We're Going on a Picnic, 2002; There's only one of me, 2003; Don't Get Lost!, 2004; Bumpety Bump, 2006; Barn Dance, 2007. *Recreations:* music, reading, gardening, cooking. *Address:* Random House Children's Books, 61–63 Uxbridge Road, W5 5SA. *Club:* Chelsea Arts.

HUTCHINSON; *see* Hely-Hutchinson.

HUTCHINSON, family name of **Baron Hutchinson of Lullington**.

HUTCHINSON OF LULLINGTON, Baron *cr* 1978 (Life Peer), of Lullington in the County of E Sussex; **Jeremy Nicolas Hutchinson;** QC 1961; *b* 28 March 1915; *o s* of late St John Hutchinson, KC; *m* 1st, 1940, Dame Peggy Ashcroft (marr. diss. 1966; she *d* 1991); one *s* one *d*; 2nd, 1966, June Osborn (*d* 2006). *Educ:* Stowe Sch.; Magdalen Coll., Oxford. Called to Bar, Middle Temple, 1939, Bencher 1963. RNVR, 1939–46. Practised on Western Circuit, N London Sessions and Central Criminal Court. Recorder of Bath, 1962–72; a Recorder of the Crown Court, 1972–76. Member: Cttee on Immigration Appeals, 1966–68; Cttee on Identification Procedures, 1974–76. Prof. of Law, RA, 1987–2005. Mem., Arts Council of GB, 1974–79 (Vice-Chm., 1977–79); Trustee: Tate Gallery, 1977–84 (Chm., 1980–84); Chantrey Bequest, 1977–99. *Address:* House of Lords, Westminster, SW1A 0PW. *Club:* MCC.

HUTCHINSON, His Honour Arthur Edward; QC 1979; a Circuit Judge, 1984–2000; *b* 31 Aug. 1934; *s* of late George Edward Hutchinson and Kathleen Hutchinson; *m* 1967, Wendy Pauline Cordingley; one *s* two *d*. *Educ:* Silcoates Sch.; Emmanuel Coll., Cambridge (MA). Commissioned, West Yorkshire Regt, 1953; served in Kenya with 5th Fusiliers, 1953–54. Called to Bar, Middle Temple, 1958; joined NE Circuit, 1959; a Recorder, 1974–84. *Recreation:* dreaming.

HUTCHINSON, Elisabeth Helen; *see* Wicksteed, E. H.

HUTCHINSON, (George) Malcolm, CB 1989; CEng, FIET; Chairman, Serco Docklands Ltd, since 2006; *b* 24 Aug. 1935; *s* of Cecil George Hutchinson and Annie Hutchinson; *m* 1958, Irene Mary Mook; four *d*. *Educ:* Pocklington Sch.; Queens' Coll., Cambridge (MA). Develt Engr, Metropolitan Vickers, 1957; short service commn, 1958, regular commn, 1961, REME; RMCS, 1967; sc Camberley, 1968; CO 12 Armd Workshop, REME, 1968–70; Staff appts, 1970–74; British Liaison Officer, USA Army Materiel Comd, 1974–76; Comdr REME 1 British Corps troops, 1977–79; REME staff, 1979–82; Project Man., Software Systems, 1982–85; Dep. to DGEME, 1985–86; Dir Procurement Strategy MoD(PE), 1986–88; Vice Master-Gen. of the Ordnance, 1988–90. Mem., Defence Prospect Team, 1990. Procurement and logistic consultant, 1991–92. Managing Director: DLR, 1992–97; Docklands Rly Mgt Ltd, 1997–99; Chm., Atomic Weapon Estabt Mgt Ltd, 1999–2003; Exec. Chm., Atomic Weapon Estabt plc, 2002–05. Mem., Engrg Council, 1993–99. Pres., IEEIE, 1990–94. Col Comdt, REME, 1991–96. *Recreations:* Rugby, cricket, sailing. *Address:* Rectory Cottage, Little Ann, Andover, Hants SP11 7NR.

HUTCHINSON, Henry; *see* Hutchinson, M. H. R.

HUTCHINSON, (John) Maxwell, PPRIBA; architect, writer, broadcaster; *b* 3 Dec. 1948; *s* of late Frank Maxwell Hutchinson and Elizabeth Ross Muir (*née* Wright); marr. diss. *Educ:* Wellingborough Prep. Sch.; Oundle; Scott Sutherland Sch. of Arch., Aberdeen; Architectural Assoc. Sch. of Arch. (AA Dip. 1972); RIBA 1972. Founder, Hutchinson and Partners, Chartered Architects, 1972, Chm., 1987–93; Dir, The Hutchinson Studio Architects, 1993–. Chm., Permarock Products Ltd, Loughborough, 1985–95; non-exec. Dir, SMC Gp plc, 2005–. Royal Institute of British Architects: Mem. Council, 1978–93, Sen. Vice Pres., 1988–89, Pres., 1989–91; Chairman: East Midlands Arts Bd Ltd, 1991–95; Industrial Bldg Bureau, 1987–89; Vice-Chm., Construction Industry Council, 1990–92. Vis. Prof., Architecture, QUB, 1989–93; Special Prof. of Architecture, Nottingham Univ., 1993–96; Vis. Prof., Westminster Univ., 1998–2000. Founder and Chm., Architects for Aid, 2005–. Chm., British Architectural Library Trust, 1991–99; Mem. Council, RSCM, 1997–2000. Associate Mem., PRS, 1988. Hon. Fellow: Greenwich Univ., 1990; Royal Soc. of Ulster Architects, 1991; UCL, 2008. Hon. DDes, Robert Gordon, 2007. *Compositions:* The Kibbo Kift, Edinburgh Fest., 1976; The Ascent of Wilberforce III, Lyric Hammersmith, 1982; Requiem in a Village Church (choral), 1986; St John's Cantata, 1987. *Publications:* The Prince of Wales: right or wrong?, 1989; Number 57: the storey of a house, 2003. *Recreation:* playing jazz piano. *Address:* Hutchinson Studios, 26 Exmouth Market, EC1R 4QE. *Clubs:* Athenæum, Groucho.

HUTCHINSON, Malcolm; *see* Hutchinson, G. M.

HUTCHINSON, Prof. (Marcus) Henry (Ritchie), PhD; FInstP; Director, Central Laser Facility, CCLRC Rutherford Appleton Laboratory, since 1997; *b* 2 Dec. 1945; *s* of Marcus Henry McCracken Hutchinson and Maud Hutchinson; *m* 1973, Gillian Ruth Harris; one *s* two *d*. *Educ:* Coleraine Academical Instn; Queen's Univ. of Belfast (BSc 1st cl. Hons Physics 1968; PhD Physics 1971). FInstP 1998. Imperial College, London: Lectr in Physics, 1973–83; Sen. Lectr, 1983–86; Reader in Optics, 1986–89; Prof. of Laser Physics, 1989–2002, Vis. Prof., 2002–; Dir, Blackett Lab. Laser Consortium, 1986–97; Associate Dir, Centre for Photomolecular Scis, 1992–97. Chief Scientist, CCLRC, 2004–07. Vis. Res. Prof., Univ. of Illinois at Chicago, 1986; Vis. Prof., Univ. of Oxford, 2003–. Member: SERC Physics Cttee, 1990–92; Wissenschaftliche Rat, Gesellschaft für Schwerionenforschung mbH, Darmstadt, 2001–05 (Chm., Plasma Physics Adv. Cttee, 2004–); UK Mem., European Strategy Forum for Res. Infrastructures, 2005–07. FRSA 2007. *Publications:* contrib. numerous scientific papers and articles in physics. *Recreations:* walking, gardening. *Address:* 16 Chiltern Hills Road, Beaconsfield, Bucks HP9 1PL.

HUTCHINSON, Maxwell; *see* Hutchinson, J. M.

HUTCHINSON, Patricia Margaret, CMG 1981; CBE 1982; HM Diplomatic Service, retired; *b* 18 June 1926; *d* of late Francis Hutchinson and Margaret Peat. *Educ:* abroad; St Paul's Girls' Sch.; Somerville Coll., Oxford (PPE, MA, Hon Fellow, 1980). ECE, Geneva, 1947; Bd of Trade, 1947–48; HM Diplomatic Service, 1948: 3rd Sec., Bucharest, 1950–52; Foreign Office, 1952–55; 2nd (later 1st) Sec., Berne, 1955–58; 1st Sec. (Commercial), Washington, 1958–61; FO, 1961–64; 1st Sec., Lima, 1964–67 (acted as Chargé d'Affaires); Dep. UK Permanent Rep. to Council of Europe, 1967–69; Counsellor: Stockholm, 1969–72; UK Delegn to OECD, 1973–75; Consul-Gen., Geneva, 1975–80; Ambassador to Uruguay, 1980–83; Consul-Gen., Barcelona, 1983–86. Pres., Somerville ASM, 1988–91. *Recreations:* music, reading. *Address:* 118A Ashley Gardens, SW1P 1HL. *Club:* Oxford and Cambridge.

HUTCHINSON, Prof. Philip; DL; FREng; CPhys; Principal, Royal Military College of Science, Cranfield University, 1996–2006, now Emeritus Professor; *b* 26 July 1938; *s* of George and Edna Hutchinson; *m* 1960, Joyce Harrison; one *s* one *d*. *Educ:* King James 1st Grammar Sch., Bishop Auckland, Co. Durham; King's Coll., Univ. of Durham (BSc); Univ. of Newcastle upon Tyne (PhD). MInstP. SO and SSO, Theoretical Phys. Div., AERE, Harwell, 1962–69; Vis. Fellow, Chem. Engrg Dept, Univ. of Houston, Texas, 1969–70; AERE, Harwell: SSO and PSO, Theoretical Phys Div., 1970–75; Hd of Thermodynamics and Fluid Mechanics Gp, Engrg Scis Div., 1975–80; Hd of Engrg Phys Br., Engrg Scis Div., 1980–85; Hd of Engrg Scis Div., 1985–87; Hd, Harwell Combustion Centre, 1980–87; Cranfield Institute of Technology, then Cranfield University: Head, Sch. of Engrg, 1987–2002; Pro Vice-Chancellor, 1996–99; Dep. Vice Chancellor, 1996–2003. Visiting Professor: Imperial Coll., London, 1980–85; Univ. of Leeds, 1985–. Chairman: Exec. Cttee on Fundamental Res. in Combustion, 1977–81, Exec. Cttee on Energy Efficiency and Emissions Reduction in Combustion, 1997–98, Internat. Energy Agency; Combustion Phys Gp of InstP, 1985–89; MRI 1989; Mem., Combustion Inst., 1977–2003; Past Mem., Watt Cttee on Energy, representing InstP and Combustion Inst. respectively; Founding Bd Mem., Europ. Research Community on Flow Turbulence and Combustion, 1988 (Chm., 1994–2000; Treas., 2000–02). 27th Leonardo da Vinci Lectr for IMechE, 1983. Liveryman, Engineers' Co., 2004–. DL Oxon, 2003. FREng (FEng 1997). Hon. DTech Lund, 1999. *Publications:* papers in learned jls on statistical mechanics, fluid mechanics, combustion and laser light scattering. *Recreations:* squash, music, reading, Go, gadgets.

HUTCHINSON, His Honour Richard Hampson; a Circuit Judge, 1974–2000; *b* 31 Aug. 1927; *s* of late John Riley Hutchinson and May Hutchinson; *m* 1954, Nancy Mary (*née* Jones); two *s* three *d*. *Educ:* St Bede's Grammar Sch., Bradford; UC Hull (LLB 1st Cl. Hons London). National Service, RAF, 1949–51. Called to Bar, Gray's Inn, 1949; practised on NE Circuit, 1951–74. Recorder: Rotherham, 1971–72; Crown Court, 1972–74; Hon. Recorder of Lincoln, 1991–2000; Resident Judge, Lincoln Crown Court, 1985–2000. Mem., County Court Rules Cttee, 1990–94; Technical Rep., Central Council of Probation Cttees, 1989–2000. *Recreations:* reading, conversation, history. *Address:* c/o Lincoln Combined Court Centre, 360 High Street, Lincoln LN5 7RL.

HUTCHISON, family name of **Baroness Kennedy of the Shaws**.

HUTCHISON, Rt Rev. Andrew Sandford; Primate of the Anglican Church of Canada, 2004–07; *b* 19 Sept. 1938; *s* of Ralph Burton Hutchison and Kathleen Marian (*née* Van Nostrand); *m* 1960, Lois Arlene Knight; one *s*. *Educ:* Lakefield Coll. Sch.; Upper Canada Coll.; Trinity Coll. Toronto (LTh). Ordained deacon, 1969, priest, 1970; served fifteen years in the dio. of Toronto; Dean of Montreal, 1984–90; Bp of Montreal, 1990–2004, Archbishop, 2002–04; Metropolitan, Ecclesiastical Province of Canada, 2002–04. Pres., Montreal Diocesan Theol Coll., 1990–2004; Visitor, Bishops Univ., Lennoxville, 1990–2004; Chaplain: Canadian Grenadier Guards, 1986–90 (Hon. Chaplain, 1990–2004); 6087 and 22 CAR, 1986–2004; Order of St John of Jerusalem, Quebec, 1987–2004; Bishop Ordinary, Canadian Forces, 1997–2004. Pres., Fulford Residence, Montreal, 1990–2004. Trustee, Lakefield Coll. Sch., 1997–2000. Hon. DD: Montreal Diocesan Theol Coll., 1993; Trinity Coll., Toronto, 1994; Huron Univ. Coll., London, Ont, 2007; Hon. DCL Bishop's Univ., Lennoxville, 2003. OStJ 1991. Ecclesiastical Grand Cross, Order of St Lazarus, 1992.

HUTCHISON, Geordie Oliphant; Managing Director, Calders & Grandidge, timber importers and manufacturers, 1974–96; *b* 11 June 1934; *s* of late Col Ronald Gordon Oliphant Hutchison and of Ruth Gordon Hutchison-Bradburne; *m* 1964, Virginia Barbezat; two *s* one *d*. *Educ:* Eton Coll. Served RN, 1952–54: commnd as aircraft pilot, 1953. Calders Ltd, 1954–59; Calders & Grandidge Ltd, 1959–96: Dir, 1969. Comr, Forestry Commn, 1981–89. High Sheriff, Lincs, 1998. *Recreations:* golf, shooting. *Address:* Riseholme, Stoke Rochford, Grantham, Lincs NG33 5EB. *T:* (01476) 530731. *Club:* Royal and Ancient Golf (St Andrews).

HUTCHISON, Prof. James Douglas, PhD; FRCSE, FRCS, FRCSGlas; Regius Professor of Surgery, since 2000 and Sir Harry Platt Professor of Orthopaedics, since 1995, University of Aberdeen; Hon. Consultant Orthopaedic Surgeon, Aberdeen Royal Infirmary, since 1991; *b* 8 Oct. 1955; *s* of James Hutchison, FRCS and Grace J. J. Holloway, MA; *m* 1985, Catherine, (Kate), MacLeod Douglas; two *s* one *d*. *Educ:* High Sch. of Dundee; Univ. of Dundee (MB ChB 1979); Univ. of Aberdeen (PhD 1988). FRCSE 1984; FRCS 2000; FRCSGlas 2002. Orthopaedic Registrar and Sen. Registrar, Royal Infirmary, Edinburgh, and Princess Margaret Rose Orthopaedic Hosp., 1986–90; Sen. Lectr in Orthopaedics, Univ. of Aberdeen, 1991–95. Speciality Advr in Orthopaedics and Trauma to CMO (Scotland), 1999–. Chairman: Scottish Cttee for Orthopaedics and Trauma, 2000–04; Scottish Hip Fracture Audit, 2004–06; Hip Fracture Delivery Team for Scottish Exec. Health Dept, 2005–; Intercollegiate Specialty Bd in Trauma and Orthopaedic Surgery, 2005–08; Specialty Adv. Bd in Orthopaedics, RCSE. Member: Harveian Soc., 1997 (Pres., 2008); Moynihan Chirurgical Club, 2005; Pres., Aberdeen Medico-Chirurgical Soc., 2005–06. Chm., Bd of Govs, Surgeons Hall Trust, 2007– (Dep. Chm., 2006–07). *Publications:* contribs to scientific and clinical jls incl. Lancet, BMJ, Jl Bone and Joint Surgery. *Recreations:* family, dogs, golf, shooting, art, curling. *Address:* Cowiehillock Cottage, Echt, Skene, Aberdeenshire AB32 6XD. *T:* (01330) 860716; *e-mail:* j.d.hutchison@abdn.ac.uk. *Club:* Royal Northern and University (Aberdeen).

HUTCHISON, Rt Hon. Sir Michael, Kt 1983; PC 1995; a Lord Justice of Appeal, 1995–99; *b* 13 Oct. 1933; *s* of Ernest and Frances Hutchison; *m* 1957, Mary Spettigue; two *s* three *d*. *Educ:* Lancing; Clare College, Cambridge (MA). Called to Bar, Gray's Inn, 1958, Bencher, 1983; a Recorder, 1975–83; QC 1976; a Judge of the High Court, QBD, 1983–95; Judge, Employment Appeal Tribunal, 1984–87; Presiding Judge, Western Circuit, 1989–92. Surveillance Comr, 1998–2006. Member: Judicial Studies Bd, 1985–87; Parole Bd, 1987–89.

HUTCHISON, Sir Peter Craft, 2nd Bt *cr* 1956; CBE 1992; FRSE; Chairman: Hutchison & Craft Ltd, Insurance Brokers, Glasgow, 1979–96; Forestry Commission, 1994–2001; *b* 5 June 1935; *s* of Sir James Riley Holt Hutchison, 1st Bt, DSO, TD, and Winefryde Eleanor Mary (*d* 1988), *d* of late Rev. R. H. Craft; *S* father, 1979; *m* 1966, Virginia, *er d* of late John Millar Colville, Gribloch, Kippen, Stirlingshire; one *s*. *Educ:* Eton; Magdalene Coll., Cambridge. Mem., Scottish Tourist Bd, 1981–87; Mem., 1987–98, Vice-Chm., 1989–98, British Waterways Bd; Chm., Loch Lomond and Trossachs Wkg Party, 1991–92. Dep. Convenor, Loch Lomond and the Trossachs Nat. Park Authy, 2002–. Chm. of Trustees, Royal Botanic Gdn, Edinburgh, 1985–94; Mem. Bd, Scottish Natural Heritage, 1994. Hon. Pres., Royal Caledonian Horticultural Soc., 1994–. Deacon, Incorporation of Hammermen, 1984–85. FRSE 1997. *Heir: s* James Colville Hutchison [*b* 7 Oct. 1967; *m* 1996, Jane, *d* of Peter Laidlaw]. *Address:* Broich, Kippen, Stirlingshire FK8 3EN.

HUTCHISON, Sir Robert, 3rd Bt *cr* 1939, of Thurle, Streatley, co. Berks; independent financial adviser, since 1978; *b* 25 May 1954; *er s* of Sir Peter Hutchison, 2nd Bt and of Mary-Grace (*née* Seymour); *S* father, 1998; *m* 1987, Anne Margaret, *e d* of Sir (Godfrey) Michael (David) Thomas, 11th Bt; two *s*. *Educ:* Orwell Park Sch., Ipswich; Marlborough Coll. With J. & A. Scrimgeour Ltd, 1973–78. *Recreations:* golf, tennis, watching Association Football, family life. *Heir: s* Hugo Thomas Alexander Hutchison, *b* 16 April 1988. *Address:* Hawthorn Cottage, Lower Road, Grundisburgh, Woodbridge, Suffolk IP13 6UQ. *Clubs:* Ipswich & Suffolk (Ipswich), Woodbridge Golf.

HUTCHISON, Robert Edward; Keeper, Scottish National Portrait Gallery, 1953–82, retired; *b* 4 Aug. 1922; *y s* of late Sir William Hutchison; *m* 1946, Heather, *d* of late Major A. G. Bird; one *s* one *d*. *Educ:* Gresham's Sch., Holt. Served War, 1940–46, Infantry and RA; Asst Keeper, Scottish National Portrait Gallery, 1949. Hon. MA Edinburgh, 1972. *Publication:* (with Stuart Maxwell) Scottish Costume 1550–1850, 1958. *Address:* Ivory Court, Langriggs, Haddington, East Lothian EH41 4BY. *T:* (01620) 823213.

HUTH, Angela Maureen, (Mrs J. D. Howard-Johnston); writer; *b* 29 Aug. 1938; *d* of late Harold Edward Strachan Huth and Bridget Huth (*née* Nickols); *m* 1961, Quentin Hugh Crewe (marr. diss. 1970; he *d* 1998); one *d* (one *s* decd); *m* 1978, James Douglas Howard-Johnston; one *d* (one *s* decd). *Educ:* Lawnside, Gt Malvern, Worcs; Beaux Arts, Paris; Annigoni Sch. of Painting, Florence; Byam Shaw Art Sch., London. Harpers Bazaar, 1957–58; Art dept, J. Walter-Thompson, 1958–59; Queen mag., 1959–61; reporter, Man Alive, BBC, 1965–67; BBC TV presenter, How It Is, 1969–70; Kaleidoscope, Radio 4, 1970; freelance, 1968–. Radio and TV: plays: The Drip (radio); I didn't take my mother (radio); Past Forgetting (radio), 2001; Special Co-respondent; The Emperor's New Hat; The Summer House; Virginia Fly is Drowning; Sun Child; documentaries: The English Woman's Wardrobe, 1987; Land Girls, 1995; stage plays: The Understanding, 1982; The Trouble with Old Lovers, 1995. FRSL 1975. *Publications:* Nowhere Girl, 1970; Virginia Fly is Drowning, 1972; Sun Child, 1975; South of the Lights, 1977; Monday Lunch in Fairyland and Other Stories, 1978; The Understanding (play), 1982; Wanting, 1984; The English Woman's Wardrobe (non-fiction), 1986; Eugenie in Cloud Cuckoo Land (for children), 1986; Such Visitors and Other Stories, 1989; Invitation to the Married Life, 1991; Land Girls, 1994; The Trouble with Old Lovers (play), 1995; Another Kind of Cinderella, 1996; Wives of the Fishermen, 1998; Easy Silence, 1999; Of Love and Slaughter, 2002; The Collected Stories of Angela Huth, 2003; (ed) Well Remembered Friends: eulogies on celebrated lives, 2004. *Recreations:* collecting antique paste jewellery, re-visiting favourite places in Britain, tap dancing. *Address:* c/o Caroline Michel, PFD, Drury House, 34–43 Russell Street, WC2B 5HA.

HUTSON, Prof. Jeremy Mark, DPhil; CChem, FRSC; CPhys, FInstP; Professor of Chemistry, University of Durham, since 1996; *b* 7 May 1957; *s* of James Murray Hutson and Margaret Joyce Hutson (*née* Pearson). *Educ:* Brentwood Sch.; Wadham Coll., Oxford (MA); Hertford Coll., Oxford (DPhil 1981). CPhys, MInstP 1994; FInstP 2004; MRSC, CChem 1988; FRSC 1999. NATO/SERC Res. Fellow, Univ. of Waterloo, Canada, 1981–83; Drapers' Co. Res. Fellow, 1983–84, Stokes Res. Fellow, 1984–86, Pembroke Coll., Cambridge; Lectr, 1987–93, Reader, 1993–96, Hd, Dept of Chem., 1998–2001, Univ. of Durham. JILA Vis. Fellow, Univ. of Colo, Boulder, 2001–02. Chairman: EPSRC Collaborative Computational Project on Molecular Quantum Dynamics, 2000–05; ESF Sci. Cttee, EuroQUAM, 2007–. Member: EPSRC Peer Review College, 1994–; Bd, Atomic Molecular and Optical Physics Div., European Physical Soc., 2004–07. Ed., Internat. Rev. in Physical Chem., 2000–. Corday-Morgan Medal, RSC, 1991; Kołos Medal, Univ. of Warsaw and Polish Chemical Soc., 2007; Computational Chem. Award, RSC, 2006. *Publications:* numerous contribs to jls incl. Jl Chem. Physics, Jl Physical Chem., Physical Rev. *Recreations:* hiking, diving, paddling, local history. *Address:* Department of Chemistry, University of Durham, South Road, Durham DH1 3LE; *e-mail:* J.M.Hutson@durham.ac.uk.

HUTSON, John Whiteford, OBE 1966; HM Diplomatic Service, retired; Consul-General, Casablanca, 1984–87; *b* 21 Oct. 1927; *s* of John Hutson and Jean Greenlees Laird; *m* 1954, Doris Kemp; one *s* two *d*. *Educ:* Hamilton Academy; Glasgow Univ. (MA (Hons)). MCIL (MIL 1987). HM Forces, 1949–51; Foreign Office, 1951; Third Secretary, Prague, 1953; FO, 1955; Second Sec., Berlin, 1956; Saigon, 1959; First Sec., 1961; Consul (Commercial) San Francisco, 1963–67; First Sec. and Head of Chancery, Sofia, 1967–69; FCO, 1969; Counsellor, 1970; Baghdad, 1971–72; Inspector, FCO, 1972–74; Head, Communications Operations Dept, FCO, 1974–76; Counsellor (Commercial), Moscow, 1976–79; Consul-Gen., Frankfurt, 1979–83. *Recreations:* British diplomatic oral history project, church yesterday and today, elementary bridge.

HUTT, Ven. David Handley; Canon, 1995–2005, now Emeritus, and Archdeacon, 1999–2005, of Westminster; Steward, 1995–2005, and Sub-Dean, 1999–2005, Westminster Abbey; *b* 24 Aug. 1938; *s* of late Frank and of Evelyn Hutt. *Educ:* Brentwood; RMA Sandhurst; King's College London (Hanson Prize for Christian Ethics; Barry Prize for Theology; AKC). Regular Army, 1957–64. KCL, 1964–68. Deacon 1969, priest 1970; Curate: Bedford Park, W4, 1969–70; St Matthew, Westminster, 1970–73; Priest Vicar and Succentor, Southwark Cathedral, 1973–78; Sen. Chaplain, King's Coll., Taunton, 1978–82; Vicar: St Alban and St Patrick, Birmingham, 1982–86; All Saints, Margaret St, 1986–95. Mem. Court, Sion Coll., 2005–07 (Pres., 1996–97; Fellow and Curator, 2007–). Nat. Co-ordinator, Affirming Catholicism, 1990–98. Mem. Council, ALVA, 2000–05. Trustee, Utd Westminster Schs' Foundn, 2006–; Gov., Sutton Valence Sch., 2007–. Patron, London Parks and Gardens Trust, 2003–. MA Lambeth, 2005. *Publications:* miscellaneous theol articles and reviews. *Recreations:* gardening, cooking, music, theatre. *Address:* 3cc Morpeth Terrace, SW1P 1EW.

HUTT, Sir Dexter (Walter), Kt 2004; Chief Executive (formerly Executive Head), Ninestiles Federation of Schools, Birmingham, since 2004; Executive Leader, Hastings Schools Federation, since 2008; *b* Georgetown, Guyana, 25 July 1948; *s* of Walter and Binks Hutt; *m* 1976, Rosemary Lyn Jones; two *s* one *d*. *Educ:* Birmingham Univ. (BScSoc). Hd, Middle Sch., Holte Sch., Birmingham, 1978–82; Dep. Hd and Actg Hd, Sidney Stringer Sch., Coventry, 1982–88; Headteacher, Ninestiles Sch., Birmingham, 1998–2004. Man. Dir, Ninestiles Plus, 2003–. Comr, Commn for Racial Equality, 2004–07. Trustee, Villiers Park, 2005–. *Recreations:* current affairs, reading novels and biographies, horse-racing, golf. *Address:* Ninestiles School, Hartfield Crescent, Acocks Green, Birmingham B27 7QG. *T:* (0121) 628 1311, *Fax:* (0121) 778 4234; *e-mail:* dexterh@ninestiles.bham.sch.uk.

HUTT, Jane Elizabeth; Member (Lab) Vale of Glamorgan, National Assembly for Wales, since 1999; Minister for Children, Education, Lifelong Learning and Skills, since 2007; *b* 15 Dec. 1949; *d* of late Prof. Michael Stewart Rees Hutt and of Elizabeth Mai Hutt; *m* 1984, Michael John Hillary Trickey; two *d*. *Educ:* Highlands Sch., Eldoret, Kenya; Rosemead Sch., Littlehampton; Univ. of Kent (BA Hons 1970); London Sch. of Econs (CQSW 1972); Bristol Univ. (MSc Mgt Develt and Social Responsibility 1995). Community worker: IMPACT (Town Planners & Architects), Wales, 1972–74; Polypill (Community Projects Foundn), Wales, 1975–77; Co-ordinator, Welsh Women's Aid, 1978–88; Director: Tenant Participation Adv. Service, (Wales), 1988–92; Chwarae Teg (Wales), 1992–99. National Assembly for Wales: Sec., then Minister, for Health and Social Services, 1999–2005; Business Minister and Minister for Children, 2005–07; Minister for Budget and Business, 2007. Hon. Fellow, UWIC, 1996. *Publications:* Opening the Town Hall: an introduction to local government, 1989; Making Opportunities: a guide for women and employers, 1992. *Recreations:* music, reading. *Address:* National Assembly for Wales, Cardiff Bay, Cardiff CF99 1NA. *T:* (029) 2082 5111.

HUTTER, Prof. Otto Fred, PhD; Regius Professor of Physiology, University of Glasgow, 1971–90, now Emeritus; *b* 29 Feb. 1924; *s* of Isak and Elisabeth Hutter; *m* 1948, Yvonne T. Brown; two *s* two *d*. *Educ:* Chajes Real Gymnasium, Vienna; Bishops Stortford Coll., Herts; University Coll., London (BSc, PhD). Univ. of London Postgrad. Student in Physiology, 1948; Sharpey Scholar, UCL, 1949–52; Rockefeller Travelling Fellow and Fellow in Residence, Johns Hopkins Hosp., Baltimore, 1953–55; Lectr, Dept of Physiology, UCL, 1953–61; Hon. Lectr, 1961–70. Visiting Prof., Tel-Aviv Univ., 1968, 1970; Scientific Staff, Nat. Inst. for Medical Research, Mill Hill, London, 1961–70. Hon. Mem., Physiological Soc., 1992. Hon. DSc Glasgow Caledonian, 1994. *Publications:* papers on neuromuscular and synaptic transmission, cardiac and skeletal muscle, in physiological jls. *Address:* 60 Browning Avenue, Bournemouth BH5 1NW.

HUTTON, family name of **Baron Hutton**.

HUTTON, Baron *cr* 1997 (Life Peer), of Bresagh in the county of Down; **James Brian Edward Hutton,** Kt 1988; PC 1988; a Lord of Appeal in Ordinary, 1997–2004; *b* 29 June 1931; *s* of late James and Mabel Hutton, Belfast; *m* 1st, 1975, Mary Gillian Murland (*d* 2000); two *d*; 2nd, 2001, Lindy, *widow* of Christopher H. Nickols; two step *s* one step *d*. *Educ:* Shrewsbury Sch.; Balliol Coll., Oxford (1st Cl. final sch. of Jurisprudence; Hon.

Fellow, 1988); Queen's Univ. of Belfast. Called to the Northern Ireland Bar, 1954; QC (NI) 1970; Bencher, Inn of Court of Northern Ireland, 1974; called to English Bar, 1972. Junior Counsel to Attorney-General for NI, 1969; Legal Adviser to Min. of Home Affairs, NI, 1973; Sen. Crown Counsel in NI, 1973–79; Judge of the High Court of Justice (NI), 1979–88; Lord Chief Justice of NI, 1988–97. Hon. Bencher: Inner Temple, 1988; King's Inns, Dublin, 1988. Mem., Jt Law Enforcement Commn, 1974; Dep. Chm., Boundary Commn for NI, 1985–88. Chm., Inquiry into death of Dr David Kelly, 2003–04. Visitor, Univ. of Ulster, 1999–2004. Hon. LLD: QUB, 1992; Ulster, 2004. *Address:* House of Lords, SW1A 0PW.

HUTTON, Alasdair Henry, OBE 1990 (MBE 1986); TD 1977; writer and narrator of public events, UK and overseas; Convener, Scottish Borders Council, since 2003 (Member (C), since 2002); *b* 19 May 1940; *s* of Alexander Hutton and Margaret Elizabeth (*née* Henderson); *m* 1975, Deirdre Mary Cassels (*see* Dame D. M. Hutton); two *s*. *Educ:* Dollar Academy; Brisbane State High Sch., Australia. Radio Station 4BH, Brisbane, 1956; John Clemenger Advertising, Melbourne, 1957–59; Journalist: The Age, Melb., 1959–61; Press and Journal, Aberdeen, Scotland, 1962–64; Broadcaster, BBC: Scotland, N Ireland, London, Shetland, 1964–79. MEP (C) S Scotland, 1979–89; European Democratic Gp spokesman on regional policy, 1983–87, on budgetary control, 1987–89; contested (C) S Scotland, EP elecn, 1989 and 1994. Contested (C) Roxburgh and Berwickshire, Scottish Parly elecn, 1999. Sen. Consultant, Coutts Career Consultants, Scotland, 1994–97; Sen. Advr, Career Associates, 1998–2003; Sec., Devonshire House Mgt Club, 2002–03. European Adviser: IOM Parlt, 1997–2001; Scottish Police Coll., 1997–2001. Board Member: Scottish Agricl Coll., 1990–95; UK 2000 Scotland, 1991–96. Chm., Crime Concern, Scotland, 1990–95. Member: Internat. Relns Cttee, Law Soc. of Scotland, 1991–99; Church and Nation Cttee, Church of Scotland, 1992–96; Social Security Adv. Cttee, 1996–99. Presenter, The Business Programme, BBC Radio Scotland, 1989–90; Narrator, Edinburgh Mil. Tattoo, 1992–. Mem., Queen's Body Guard for Scotland, Royal Co. of Archers. Hon. Col, Lothian and Borders Bn, ACF, 2006–. Mem., Border Union Agricl Soc.; Vice Pres., John Buchan Soc.; Life Mem., Edinburgh Sir Walter Scott Club. Scottish Chm. and Trustee, Community Service Volunteers, 1985–. Founding Fellow, Inst. of Contemp. Scotland, 2001–. Elder, Kelso N, Church of Scotland. *Publication:* 15 Para 1947–1993, 1993. *Address:* 4 Broomlands Court, Kelso, Roxburghshire TD5 7SR. *T:* (01573) 224369, *Fax:* (01573) 224368; *e-mail:* AlasdairHutton@yahoo.co.uk. *Clubs:* New, Royal Scots (Edinburgh).

HUTTON, Anthony Charles, CB 1995; Executive Director, OECD, Paris, 2001–07; *b* 4 April 1941; *s* of Charles James Hutton and Athene Mary (*née* Hastie); *m* 1963, Sara Flemming; two *s* one *d*. *Educ:* Brentwood School; Trinity College, Oxford (MA). HM Inspector of Taxes, 1962; joined Board of Trade, 1964; Private Sec. to 2nd Perm. Sec., 1967–68; Principal Private Sec. to Sec. of State for Trade, 1974–77; Asst Sec., DoT, 1977, DTI, 1983; Under Sec., 1984–91; Dep. Sec., 1991–96; Principal Estabt and Finance Officer, 1991–97; Dir Gen., Resources and Services, 1996–97; Dir Gen., Trade Policy, DTI, 1997–2000; Dir, Public Mgt Service, OECD, 2000–01. *Recreations:* music, reading, 20th century history. *Club:* Athenæum.

HUTTON, Brian Gerald, PhD; Secretary, 1976–88, Deputy Librarian, 1983–88, National Library of Scotland (Assistant Keeper, 1974–76); *b* Barrow-in-Furness, 1 Nov. 1933; *s* of James and Nora Hutton; *m* 1958, Serena Quartermaine May; one *s* one *d*. *Educ:* Barrow Grammar Sch.; Nottingham Univ. (BA Hons Hist. 1955); University Coll. London (Dip. Archive Admin. and Churchill Jenkinson prizeman, 1959); Oxford Brookes Univ. (LLB 1st Cl. 1996); PhD Brunel 2002. National Service as Russian Linguist, RN, 1955–57. Asst Archivist, Herts County Record Office, 1959–60; Asst Keeper and Dep. Dir, Public Record Office, N Ireland, also Administrator, Ulster Hist. Foundn and Lectr in Archive Admin., Queen's Univ., Belfast, 1960–74; Stagiaire, Archives Nationales, Paris, 1970. County Sec., Bucks CPRE, 1990–93. Chm., Friends of Oxfordshire Museums, 1991–96; Mem. Exec. Cttee, Bucks Record Soc., 1999–; Chm., Bucks Br., Histl Assoc., 2005–. Lectr in local history studies and on legal topics. Commissioned, Kentucky Colonel, 1982. *Publications:* contribs to library, archive and legal hist. jls. *Recreations:* walking in Chilterns, visiting art galleries, listening to music, enjoying the company of grandsons. *Address:* Elma Cottage, The Green, Kingston Blount, Oxon OX39 4SE. *T:* (01844) 354173; La Casa Bianca, Groppoli, Tuscany, Italy. *Club:* New (Edinburgh).

HUTTON, Dame Deirdre (Mary), DBE 2004 (CBE 1998); Chairman, Food Standards Agency, since 2005; *b* 15 March 1949; *d* of Kenneth Alexander Home Cassels and Barbara Kathleen Cassels; *m* 1975, Alasdair Henry Hutton, *qv* (separated 2002); two *s*. *Educ:* Sherborne Sch. for Girls; Hartwell House Coll. Researcher, Glasgow Chamber of Commerce, 1975–80; freelance researcher, 1980–86; Scottish Consumer Council: Mem. Council, 1987–89; Vice Chm., 1990–91; Chm., 1991–99; Vice-Chm., 1997–2000, Chm., 2001–05, Nat. Consumer Council. Dep. Chm., Financial Services Authy, 2004–07 (non-exec. Dir, 1998–2007). Vice Chm., Borders Local Health Council, 1991–94; Chairman: Enterprise Music Scotland Ltd, 1992–95 (also Founder); Rural Forum (Scotland) Ltd, 1992–99; Council, PIA Ombudsman, 1997–2000 (Dep. Chm., 1995–97); DTI Foresight Panel on Food Chain and Crops for Industry, 1999–2000; Steering Gp, Food Chain Centre, 2002–05; Vice-Chm., Scottish Envmt Protection Agency, 1999–2002; Dep. Chm., European Food Safety Authy, 2003–; Member: Music Cttee, Scottish Arts Council, 1985–91; Scottish Consultative Council on the Curriculum, 1987–91; Parole Bd for Scotland, 1993–97; Minister's Energy Adv. Panel, DTI, 1997–99; Sec. of State for Scotland's Constitutional Steering Gp on Scottish Parliament, 1998; Sec. of State's Competitiveness Council, DTI, 1999–2000; Better Regulation Task Force, 1999–2005; Sustainable Develt Commn, 2000–01; Curry Commn on Future of Agriculture and Food, 2001. Bd Mem., Picker Inst. Europe, 2003–06. Non-executive Director: Edinburgh Festival Theatres Ltd, 1997–99; Borders Health Bd, 1997–2002. Honorary Vice-President: Inst. of Food Sci. and Technol., 2007; Trading Standards Inst., 2007. DUniv Stirling, 2000; Hon. DSc: Loughborough, 2005; Cranfield, 2007. *Recreations:* reading, eating, talking, music. *Address:* Food Standards Agency, Aviation House, 125 Kingsway, WC2B 6NH.

HUTTON, His Honour Gabriel Bruce; a Circuit Judge, 1978–2003; *b* 27 Aug. 1932; *y s* of late Robert Crompton Hutton, and Elfreda Bruce; *m* 1st, 1963, Frances Henrietta Cooke (*d* 1963); 2nd, 1965, Deborah Leigh Windus; one *s* two *d*. *Educ:* Marlborough; Trinity Coll., Cambridge (BA). Called to Bar, Inner Temple, 1956; Dep. Chm., Glos QS, 1971. A Recorder of the Crown Court, 1972–77. Liaison Judge for Glos, 1987–2003, and Resident Judge for Gloucester Crown Court, 1990–2003. Chairman: Glos and Wilts Area Criminal Justice Liaison Cttee, 1992–2000; Glos Criminal Justice Strategy Cttee, 2001–03. Chm., Glos Br., CPRE, 1993–2005. *Recreations:* hunting (Chm., Berkeley Hunt, 1973–2005), shooting, fishing. *Address:* Chestal House, Chestal, Dursley, Glos GL11 5AA. *T:* (01453) 543285, *Fax:* (01453) 549998.

HUTTON, Janet; nursing/management adviser, self-employed consultant, 1988–99; *b* 15 Feb. 1938; *d* of Ronald James and Marion Hutton. *Educ:* Gen. Infirmary at Leeds Sch. of Nursing. SRN 1959. Ward Sister, Leeds Gen. Infirmary, 1962–64, 1966–68; Nursing Sister, Australia, 1964–66; Commng Nurse, Lister Hosp., Stevenage, 1968–71; Planning and Develts Nurse, N London, 1971–73; Divl Nursing Officer, Colchester, 1973–79; Dist Nursing officer, E Dorset, 1979–83; Regl Nursing Officer, 1983–88, Quality Assurance Manager, 1986–88, Yorks RHA. Trustee, Sue Ryder Care (formerly Sue Ryder Foundn), 1998–2007 (Vice Chm., 2004–07). *Recreations:* music, needlework, walking, gardening, tennis (spectator). *Club:* Soroptimist International of Harrogate and District (Harrogate).

HUTTON, Rt Hon. John (Matthew Patrick); PC 2001; MP (Lab) Barrow and Furness, since 1992; Secretary of State for Defence, since 2008; *b* 6 May 1955; *m* (marr. diss.); three *s* one *d* (and one *s* decd); *m* 2004, Heather Rogers. *Educ:* Magdalen Coll., Oxford (BA, BCL). Research Associate, Templeton Coll., Oxford, 1980–81; Sen. Lectr, Newcastle Poly., 1981–92. Parly Under-Sec. of State, 1998–99, Minister of State, 1999–2005, DoH; Chancellor, Duchy of Lancaster, 2005; Secretary of State: for Work and Pensions, 2005–07; for Business, Enterprise and Regulatory Reform, 2007–08. Contested (Lab): Penrith and Borders, 1987; Cumbria and Lancs N (European Parlt), 1989. *Publications:* articles on labour law in Industrial Law Jl. *Recreations:* football, cricket, cinema, music, First World War history. *Address:* House of Commons, SW1A 0AA; (office) 22 Hartington Street, Barrow-in-Furness, Cumbria LA14 5SL. *T:* (01229) 431204.

HUTTON, Prof. John Philip, MA; Professor of Economics and Econometrics, 1982–2004, and Head of Department of Economics and Related Studies, 2001–04, University of York; *b* 26 May 1940; *s* of Philip Ernest Michelson Hutton and Hester Mary Black Hutton; *m* 1964, Sandra Smith Reid; one *s* one *d*. *Educ:* Daniel Stewart's Coll., Edinburgh; Edinburgh Univ. (MA 1st Cl.). York University: Junior Research Fellow, 1962; Lecturer, 1963; Sen. Lectr, 1973; Reader, 1976. Economic Adviser, HM Treasury, 1970, 1971; Advr to Malaysian Treasury, 1977, Mem., Technical Assistance Mission, Kenya, 1990, IMF; Consultant to: NEDO, 1963; Home Office, 1966; Royal Commission on Local Govt in England and Wales, 1967; NIESR, 1980. Chairman, HM Treasury Academic Panel, 1980, 1981; Mem. Council, Royal Economic Soc., 1981–86. Jt Managing Editor, Economic Journal, 1980–86; Jt Editor, Bulletin of Economic Research, 1986–91 (Chm., Bd of Trustees, 2000–); Associate Editor, Applied Economics, 1986–. *Publications:* contribs to learned jls, incl. Economic Jl, Rev. of Economic Studies, Oxford Economic Papers. *Recreations:* golf, modern fiction, cinema. *Address:* 1 The Old Orchard, Fulford, York YO10 4LT. *T:* (01904) 638363.

HUTTON, Kenneth; Chairman, Peterborough Development Agency, 1987–92; *b* 11 May 1931; *s* of Wilks and Gertrude Hutton; *m* 1981, Georgia (*née* Hutchinson); one *s*, and two step *s* one step *d*. *Educ:* Bradford Belle Vue Grammar School; Liverpool University (Thomas Bartlett Scholar; BEng). FICE; FIHT. Graduate Asst, Halifax CBC, 1952–54; Royal Engineers, 1954–56; Sen Engineer, Halifax CBC, 1956–59; Sen. Asst Engineer, Huddersfield CBC, 1959–63; Asst Chief Engineer, Skelmersdale Develt Corp., 1963–66; Dep. Chief Engineer, Telford Develt Corp., 1966–68; Chief Engineer, 1968–84, Gen. Manager, 1984–88, Peterborough Develt Corp. Gov., Peterborough Enterprise Programme, 1988–92. *Recreations:* swimming, bridge, woodworking. *Address:* 2 Barkston Drive, Peterborough PE1 4LA.

HUTTON, Prof. Peter, PhD; FRCP, FRCA; CEng, FIMechE; Professor of Anaesthesia, since 1986, and Head, Department of Anaesthesia and Intensive Care, 1986–2001, University of Birmingham; Hon. Consultant Anaesthetist, University Hospital Birmingham NHS Trust, since 1986; President, Royal College of Anaesthetists, 2000–03; *b* 9 Nov. 1947; *s* of Peter Hutton and Lily Hutton (*née* Draper); *m* 1973, Barbara Meriel Johnson; two *s* two *d*. *Educ:* Morecambe GS; Birmingham Univ. (BSc 1st Cl. Hons Mech. Engrg 1969, PhD 1973; MB ChB 1978). FRCA 1982; FRCP 2001; CEng, FIMechE 2003. SERC Res. Fellow, Birmingham Univ., 1969–72; jun. doctor trng posts in anaesthesia and medicine, Birmingham and Bristol, 1978–82; Clinical Lectr in Anaesthesia, Univ. of Bristol and Hon. Sen. Registrar, Avon AHA, 1982–86. Mem., Jt Cttee for Higher Trng in Anaesthesia, 1988–92; Chm., Nat. Clinical Adv. Bd, 2003–04. Pres., Anaesthetic and Recovery Nurses Assoc., 1989–90; Council Member: Assoc. Anaesthetists of GB and Ireland, 1989–92; RCAnaes, 1993– (Sen. Vice Pres., 1999–2000); Chm., Acad. of Med. Royal Colls, 2002–04 (Vice-Chm., 2001–02). Founder FMedSci 1998; FRCPGlas (*ad eundem*) 2003; FRCS 2004; Hon. FCEM (Hon. FFAEM 2003); Hon. FCA(SA) 2003; Hon. Fellow, Coll. of Anaesthetists, RCSI, 2003. *Publications:* (with G. M. Cooper) Guidelines in Clinical Anaesthesia, 1985; (ed. with C. Prys-Roberts) Monitoring in Anaesthesia and Intensive Care, 1994; (ed jtly) Fundamental Principles and Practice of Anaesthesia, 2001; contrib. numerous scientific and rev. papers. *Recreations:* family, woodwork, fell-walking. *Address:* University Department of Anaesthesia, North 5, Queen Elizabeth Hospital, University Hospital Birmingham NHS Trust, Edgbaston, Birmingham B15 2TH. *T:* (0121) 627 2060, *Fax:* (0121) 627 2062. *Club:* Athenæum.

HUTTON, Prof. Ronald Edmund, DPhil; FRHistS, FSA; Professor of History, University of Bristol, since 1996; *b* 19 Dec. 1953; *s* of Geoffrey Edmund Hutton and late Elsa Edwina (*née* Hansen); *m* 1988, Lisa Radulovic (marr. diss. 2003); one *d*. *Educ:* Pembroke Coll., Cambridge (BA 1976; MA 1980); St John's Coll., Oxford (DPhil 1980). FRHistS 1981; FSA 1993. Prize Fellow, Magdalen Coll., Oxford, 1979–81; University of Bristol: Lectr, 1981–89; Reader, 1989–96. *Publications:* The Royalist War Effort 1642–1646, 1981, 2nd edn 1999; The Restoration, 1985; Charles II, 1989; The British Republic, 1990, 2nd edn 2000; The Pagan Religions of the Ancient British Isles, 1991; The Rise and Fall of Merry England, 1994; The Stations of the Sun, 1996; The Triumph of the Moon, 1999; Shamans, 2001; Witches, Druids and King Arthur, 2003; Debates in Stuart History, 2004; The Druids, 2007; Blood and Mistletoe, 2008. *Recreation:* travel with a view to adventure. *Address:* Department of Historical Studies, University of Bristol, 13 Woodland Road, Bristol BS8 1TB. *T:* (0117) 928 7595, *Fax:* (0117) 928 8276; *e-mail:* r.hutton@bristol.ac.uk.

HUTTON, Tracy Jane; *see* Ayling, T. J.

HUTTON, William Nicholas; Chief Executive, The Work Foundation (formerly Industrial Society), since 2000; *b* 21 May 1950; *s* of late William Thomas Hutton and Dorothy Anne (*née* Haynes); *m* 1978, Jane Anne Elizabeth Atkinson; one *s* two *d*. *Educ:* Chislehurst and Sidcup GS; Bristol Univ. (BSocSc); INSEAD (MBA). With Phillips & Drew, Stockbrokers, 1971–77; Sen. Producer, Current Affairs, BBC Radio 4, 1978–81; Dir and Producer, Money Programme, BBC 2, 1981–83; econs corresp., Newsnight, BBC 2, 1983–88; Ed., European Business Channel, 1988–90; The Guardian: Econs Ed., 1990–95; Asst Ed., 1995–96; The Observer: Ed., 1996–98; Ed.-in-Chief, 1998–99; Contributing Ed. and columnist, 2000–. Rapporteur, Kok Gp, 2004. Vis. Fellow, Nuffield Coll., Oxford, 1995; Visiting Professor: Manchester Business Sch., 1996–99; Bristol Univ., 1996–; Univ. of the Arts, 2006. Fellow, Sunningdale Inst., 2006. Chm., Employment Policy Inst., 1995–2002. Hon. Fellow, Mansfield Coll., Oxford. Hon. DLitt: Kingston, 1995; De Montfort, 1996; Strathclyde, London Guildhall, UCE, 1997; Bristol, Glasgow, 2003; DUniv Open, 2001. Political Journalist of Year, What The Papers Say, 1993. *Publications:* The Revolution That Never Was: an assessment of Keynesian economics, 1986; The State We're In, 1995; The State To Come, 1997; The Stakeholding Society, 1998; (with Anthony Giddens) On the Edge: living with global capitalism, 2000;

The World We're In, 2002; The Writing on the Wall, 2007; Staying Ahead: the economic performance of the UK's creative industries, 2007. *Recreations:* family, reading, eating, tennis, cinema, writing. *Address:* The Work Foundation, 21 Palmer Street, SW1H 0AD. *T:* (020) 7976 3500.

HUXLEY, Sir Andrew Fielding, OM 1983; Kt 1974; FRS 1955; MA, Hon. ScD Cantab; Master, 1984–90, Fellow, 1941–60 and since 1990, Trinity College, Cambridge (Hon. Fellow, 1967–90); *b* 22 Nov. 1917; *s* of late Leonard Huxley and Rosalind Bruce; *m* 1947, Jocelyn Richenda Gammell Pease (*d* 2003); one *s* five *d*. *Educ:* University College Sch.; Westminster Sch. (Hon. Fellow, 1991); Trinity Coll., Cambridge (MA). Operational research for Anti-Aircraft Command, 1940–42, for Admiralty, 1942–45. Demonstrator, 1946–50, Asst Dir of Research, 1951–59, and Reader in Experimental Biophysics, 1959–60, in Dept of Physiology, Cambridge Univ.; Dir of Studies, Trinity Coll., Cambridge, 1952–60; Jodrell Prof., 1960–69 (now Emeritus), Royal Soc. Research Prof., 1969–83, UCL (Hon. Fellow, 1980). Lectures: Herter, Johns Hopkins Univ., 1959; Jesup, Columbia Univ., 1964; Alexander Forbes, Grass Foundation, 1966; Croonian, Royal Society, 1967; Review Lectr on Muscular Contraction, Physiological Soc., 1973; Hans Hecht, Univ. of Chicago, 1975; Sherrington, Liverpool, 1977; Florey, ANU, 1982; John C. Krantz Jr, Maryland Univ. Sch. of Medicine, 1982; Darwin, Darwin Coll., Cambridge, 1982; Romanes, Oxford, 1983; Fenn, IUPS XXIX Internat. Congress, Sydney, 1983; Blackett, Delhi, 1984; Green Coll., Oxford, 1986; Tarner, Trinity Coll., Cambridge, 1988; Maulana Abul Kalam Azad Meml, Delhi, 1991; C. G. Bernhard, Stockholm, 1993; Davson Meml, Amer. Physiol. Soc., 1998. Fullerian Prof. of Physiology and Comparative Anatomy, Royal Institution, 1967–73; Cecil H. and Ida Green Vis. Prof., Univ. of British Columbia, 1980. President: BAAS, 1976–77; Royal Soc., 1980–85 (Mem. Council, 1960–62, 1977–79, 1980–85); Internat. Union of Physiological Scis, 1986–93; Vice-Pres., Muscular Dystrophy Gp of GB, 1980–. Member: ARC, 1977–81; Nature Conservancy Council, 1985–87. Trustee: BM (Nat. Hist.), 1981–91; Science Museum, 1984–88. Hon. Member: Physiolog. Soc., 1979; Amer. Soc. of Zoologists, 1985; Japan Acad., 1988; Hon. MRIA, 1986; Foreign Associate: Nat. Acad. of Scis, USA, 1979; Amer. Philosophical Soc., 1975; Foreign Hon. Member: Amer. Acad. of Arts and Sciences, 1961; Royal Acad. of Medicine, Belgium, 1978; Foreign Fellow, Indian Nat. Science Acad., 1985; Hon. MRI, 1981; Associate Mem., Royal Acad. of Scis, Letters and Fine Arts, Belgium, 1978; Mem., Leopoldina Academy, 1964; Foreign Member: Danish Acad. of Sciences, 1964; Dutch Soc. of Sciences, 1984. Hon. Fellow: Imperial Coll., London, 1980; Darwin Coll., Cambridge, 1981; QMW, London, 1987; RHBNC, London, 1994. Hon. FIBiol 1981; Hon. FRSC (Canada) 1982; Hon. FRSE 1983; Hon. FREng (Hon. FEng 1986); Hon. FMedSci 1999. Hon. MD: University of the Saar, 1964; Humboldt, E Berlin, 1985; Ulm, 1993; Charles Univ., Prague, 1998; Hon. DSc: Sheffield, 1964; Leicester, 1967; London, 1973; St Andrews, 1974; Aston, 1977; Western Australia, 1982; Oxford, 1983; Pennsylvania, 1984; Harvard, 1984; Keele, 1985; East Anglia, 1985; Maryland, 1987; Brunel, 1988; Hyderabad, 1991; Glasgow, 1993; Witwatersrand, 1998; Hon. LLD: Birmingham, 1979; Dundee, 1984; DUniv York, 1981; Hon. DHL New York, 1982; Hon. Dr: Marseille Fac. of Medicine, 1979; Toyama Med. and Pharm. Univ., Japan, 1995. Nobel Prize for Physiology or Medicine (jtly), 1963; Copley Medal, Royal Soc., 1973; Swammerdam Medal, Soc. for Natural Sci., Medicine and Surgery, Amsterdam, 1997. Grand Cordon, Order of Sacred Treasure (Japan), 1995. *Publications:* Reflections on Muscle (Sherrington Lectures XIV), 1980; (contrib.) The Pursuit of Nature, 1977; papers in the Journal of Physiology, etc. *Recreations:* walking, designing scientific instruments. *Address:* Manor Field, 1 Vicarage Drive, Grantchester, Cambridge CB3 9NG. *T:* and *Fax:* (01223) 840207; Trinity College, Cambridge. *T:* (01223) 338586.

HUXLEY, Air Vice-Marshal Brian, CB 1986; CBE 1981; Deputy Controller, National Air Traffic Services, 1985–86; retired 1987; *b* 14 Sept. 1931; *s* of Ernest and Winifred Huxley; *m* 1955, Frances (*née* Franklin) (*d* 2007); two *s*. *Educ:* St Paul's Sch.; RAF College, Cranwell. Commissioned 1952; No 28 Sqdn, Hong Kong, 1953–55; qual. Flying Instructor, 1956; Cranwell, Central Flying Sch. and No 213 Sqdn, 1956–65; MoD, 1966–68; Chief Flying Instr, Cranwell, 1969–71; Commanding RAF Valley, 1971–73; RAF Staff Coll., 1973–74; RCDS 1975; Defence Intelligence Staff, 1976–77; AOC Mil. Air Traffic Ops, 1978–80; Dir of Control (Airspace Policy), and Chm., Nat. Air Traffic Management Adv. Cttee, 1981–84. Mem., CAA Ops Adv. Cttee, 1987–99. Chm., Review of Helicopter Offshore Safety and Survival, 1993–94. *Publications:* contribs to Children's Encyclopaedia Britannica, 1970–72, and to Railway Modeller, 1974–83. *Recreations:* flying, model-making. *Club:* Royal Air Force.

HUXLEY, Prof. George Leonard, FSA; MRIA; Hon. Professor, Trinity College Dublin, since 1989 (Research Associate, 1983–89); Professor Emeritus, Queen's University, Belfast, since 1988; Adjunct Professor in Mathematics and Ancient Classics, National University of Ireland, Maynooth, since 2007; *b* Leicester, 23 Sept. 1932; *s* of late Sir Leonard Huxley, KBE and Ella M. C., *d* of F. G. and E. Copeland; *m* 1957, Davina Best; three *d*. *Educ:* Blundell's Sch.; Magdalen Coll., Oxford (2nd Mods, 1st Greats, Derby Scholar 1955). Commnd in RE, 1951, Actg Op. Supt, Longmoor Mil. Rly. Fellow of All Souls Coll., Oxford, 1955–61; Asst Dir, British School at Athens, 1956–58; Prof. of Greek, QUB, 1962–83; Dir, Gennadius Library, Amer. Sch. of Classical Studies, Athens, 1986–89. Harvard University: Vis. Lectr, 1958 and 1961; Loeb Lectr, 1986; Leverhulme Fellow, European Sci. Foundn, 1980–81; Vis. Lectr, St Patrick's Coll., Maynooth, 1984–85 and 1993; Vis. Prof., UCSD, 1990. Mem. of Exec., NI Civil Rights Assoc., 1971–72. Member: Irish Nat. Cttee, Greek and Latin Studies, 1972–86, 1991–99 (Chm., 1976–79); Irish Adv. Cttee, Liverpool Univ. Inst. of Irish Studies, 1996–2004; Exec., Nat. Library of Ireland Soc., 1997–2000; Member, Managing Committee: British Sch. at Athens, 1967–79; Amer. Sch. of Classical Studies, Athens, 1991–; Irish Mem., Standing Cttee on Humanities, European Science Foundn, Strasbourg, 1978–86. Royal Irish Academy: Sec., Polite Literature and Antiquities Cttee, 1979–86; Sen. Vice-Pres., 1984–85 and 1999–2000; Vice-Pres., 1997–98; Hon. Librarian, 1990–94; Special Envoy, 1994–97; Hon. Pres., Classical Assoc. of Ireland, 1999; Mem., Bureau, Fédn Internat. d'Etudes Classiques, 1981–89 (Senior Vice-Pres. 1984–89); Mem., Internat. Commn, Thesaurus Linguae Latinae, Munich, 1999–2001; MAE 1990. Patron, Irish Inst. of Hellenic Studies, Athens, 1998–. Hon. LittD TCD, 1984; Hon. DLit QUB, 1996. Cromer Greek Prize, British Acad., 1963. *Publications:* Achaeans and Hittites, 1960; Early Sparta, 1962; The Early Ionians, 1966; Greek Epic Poetry from Eumelos to Panyassis, 1969; (ed with J. N. Coldstream) Kythera, 1972; Pindar's Vision of the Past, 1975; On Aristotle and Greek Society, 1979; Homer and the Travellers, 1988; articles on Hellenic and Byzantine subjects. *Recreation:* siderodromophilia. *Address:* Department of Classics, Trinity College, Dublin 2, Ireland; Forge Cottage, Church Enstone, Oxfordshire OX7 4NN. *Club:* Athenæum.

HUXLEY, Hugh Esmor, MBE 1948; MA, PhD, ScD; FRS 1960; Professor of Biology, 1987–97, now Emeritus, and Director, 1988–94, Rosenstiel Basic Medical Sciences Research Center, Brandeis University, Boston, Mass; *b* 25 Feb. 1924; *s* of late Thomas Hugh Huxley and Olwen Roberts, Birkenhead, Cheshire; *m* 1966, Frances Fripp, *d* of G. Maxon, Milwaukee; one *d*, and two step *s* one step *d*. *Educ:* Park High Sch., Birkenhead; Christ's Coll., Cambridge (Exhibitioner and Scholar; Hon. Fellow 1981). Natural Science Tripos, Cambridge, 1941–43 and 1947–48 (Pt II Physics); BA 1948, MA 1950, PhD 195 ScD 1964. Served War of 1939–45, Radar Officer, RAF Bomber Command a Telecommunications Research Establishment, Malvern, 1943–47; Mem. Empire A Armaments Sch. Mission to Australia and NZ, 1946. Research Student, MRC Unit f Molecular Biology, Cavendish Lab., Cambridge, 1948–52; Commonwealth Fund Fello Biology Dept, MIT, 1952–54; Research Fellow, Christ's Coll., Cambridge, 1953–5 Mem. of External Staff of MRC, and Hon. Res. Associate, Biophysics Dept, UC 1956–62; Fellow, King's Coll., Cambridge, 1962–67; Scientific Staff, MRC Lab. Molecular Biol., Cambridge, 1962–87, Dep. Dir, 1977–87; Fellow, Churchill Co Cambridge, 1967–87. Ziskind Vis. Prof., Brandeis Univ., 1971; Lectures: Harvey So New York, 1964–65; Hooke, Univ. of Texas, 1968; Dunham, Harvard Med. Sch., 196 Croonian, Royal Soc., 1970; Mayer, MIT, 1971; Penn, Pennsylvania Univ., 197 Carter-Wallace, Princeton Univ., 1973; Adam Muller, State Univ. of NY, 1973; Paulin Stanford, 1980; Jesse Beams, Virginia, 1980; Ida Beam, Iowa, 1981; Staples, Univ. Maine, 1994; Davson, Amer. Physiol. Soc., 1994. Member: Council, Royal So 1973–75, 1984–85; President's Adv. Bd, Rosentiel Basic Med. Scis Center, Brand Univ., 1971–77; Scientific Adv. Council, European Molecular Biol. Lab., 1976–8 Mem., German Acad. of Sci., Leopoldina, 1964; Hon. Member: Amer. Soc. of Bi Chem., 1976; Amer. Assoc. of Anatomy, 1981; Amer. Physiol. Soc., 1981; Amer. Soc. Zoologists, 1986; Foreign Hon. Member: Amer. Acad. of Arts and Scis, 1965; Dani Acad. of Scis, 1971; Foreign Associate, US Nat. Acad. of Scis, 1978. Hon. ScD: Harvar 1969; Leicester, 1989; Hon. DSc: Chicago, 1974; Pennsylvania, 1976. Feldbe Foundation Award for Experimental Medical Research, 1963; William Bate Hardy Pri (Camb. Phil. Soc.) 1965; Louisa Gross Horwitz Prize, 1971; Internat. Feltrinelli Priz 1974; Gairdner Foundn Award, 1975; Baly Medal, RCP, 1975; Royal Medal, 197 Copley Medal, 1997, Royal Soc.; E. B. Wilson Award, Amer. Soc. Cell Biology, 198 Albert Einstein Award, World Cultural Council, 1987; Franklin Medal, Franklin Ins Philadelphia, 1990; Distinguished Scientist Award, Electron Microscope Soc. of Americ 1991. *Publications:* contrib. to learned jls. *Recreations:* ski-ing, sailing. *Address:* Rosenst Basic Medical Sciences Research Center, Brandeis University, Waltham, MA 0245 USA. *T:* (781) 7362490.

HUXLEY, Paul, RA 1991 (ARA 1987); artist; Professor of Painting, Royal College Art, 1986–98, now Emeritus; Treasurer, Royal Academy, since 2000; *b* 12 May 1938; 1st, 1957, Margaret Doria Perryman (marr. diss. 1972); two *s*; 2nd, 1990, Susan Jennif Metcalfe. *Educ:* Harrow Coll. of Art; Royal Acad. Schs (Cert.). Harkness Fellov 1965–67; Vis. Prof., Cooper Union, New York, 1974; Vis. Tutor, RCA, 1974–8 Member: Serpentine Gallery Cttee, 1971–74; Art Panel and Exhibns Sub-Cttee, Ar Council of GB, 1972–76; Trustee, Tate Gall., 1975–82. Mem. Council, British Sch. Rome, 2000–. Commnd by London Transport to design 22 ceramic murals for King Cross Underground Stn, 1984; commnd by Rambert Dance Co. to design sets an costumes for Cat's Eye, 1992. *One-man exhibitions:* Rowan Gall., London, 1963, 196 1968, 1969, 1971, 1974, 1978, 1980; Juda Rowan Gall., London, 1982; Kornblee Gal New York, 1967, 1970; Galeria da Emenda, Lisbon, 1974; Forum Kunst, Rottweil, Germany, 1975; Mayor Rowan Gall., 1989; Galerie zur alten deutschen Schul Switzerland, 1992; Gillian Jason Gall., 1993; Gardner Art Centre, Sussex Univ., 199 Jason & Rhodes Gall., London, 1998; Rhodes & Mann Gall., London, 2001; *gro exhibitions:* Whitechapel Art Gall., London, and Albright-Knox Gall., Buffalo, NY, 196 Paris Biennale, and Marlborough-Gerson Gall., New York, 1965; Galerie Milano, Mila 1966; Carnegie Inst., Pittsburgh, 1967; UCLA, Calif (also USA tour), and touring sho of Mus. of Modern Art, New York, 1968; Mus. am Ostwall, Dortmund (also Eur. tour and Tate Gall., 1969; Walker Art Gall., Liverpool, 1973; Hayward Gall., 1974; São Paul Bienal, and Forum Gall., Leverkusen, 1975; Palazzo Reale, Milan, 1976; Royal Acad 1977; Nat. Theatre, 1979; Arts Council tour, Sheffield, Newcastle upon Tyne and Bristo 1980; Museo Municipal, Madrid, and Eastern Arts 4th Nat. Exhibn and British tour, 198 Juda Rowan Gall., 1985; Kunstlerhaus, Vienna, 1986; Mappin Art Gall., Sheffield, 198 British Council tour, Eastern Europe, 1990–93; South Bank Centre, and Arts Counc tour, 1992–93; Barbican Gall., London, 1993; British Council tour, Africa, 1994–9 Gallery 7, HK, 1996; Gulbenkian Foundn Center for Modern Art, Lisbon, 1997; Pallar House Gall., Chichester, 1998; Kettle's Yard, Cambridge, 1999; Rhodes+Mann, Londor 2000; *works in public collections:* Tate Gall., V&A Mus., Arts Council of GB, British Counci Royal Acad., RCA, Contemp. Arts Soc., Camden Council, Govt Art Collection, Nuffiel Foundn, London; Whitworth Art Gall., Manchester; Graves Art Gall., Sheffield; Walke Art Gall., Liverpool; City Art Gall., Leeds; Creasey Collection of Modern Art, Salisbury Leics Educn Authority; Fitzwilliam Mus., Cambridge; Ulster Mus., Belfast; Art Gall. NSW, and Mus. of Contemp. Art, Sydney; Art Gall. of SA, Adelaide; Albright-Kno Gall., Buffalo, Neuberger Mus., Purchase, and MOMA, NY; Centro Cultural Art Contemporaneo, Mexico City; Art Gall. of Ontario, Toronto; Moroccan Gov Collection, Asilah; Szépmüvészeti Mus., Budapest; Technisches Mus., Vienna. *Publicatio* (ed) Exhibition Road: painters at the Royal College of Art, 1988. *Address:* 2 Dalling Road W6 0JB.

HUXLEY, Dr Peter Arthur, PhD; CBiol; FIBiol; agroforestry education consultant 1992–2002; *b* 26 Sept. 1926; *s* of Ernest Henry Huxley and Florence Agnes (*née* King); 1st, 1954, Betty Grace Anne Foot (marr. diss. 1980); three *s* one *d*; 2nd, 1980, Jennife Margaret Bell (*née* Pollard); one *s* one *d*. *Educ:* Alleyn's Sch.; Edinburgh Univ.; Readin Univ. (BSc, PhD). FIBiol 1970. RNVR, 1944–46. Asst Lectr to Sen. Lectr, Makerer University Coll., Uganda, 1954–64; Dir of Res., Coffee Res. Foundn, Kenya, 1965–6 Prof. of Horticulture, Univ. of Reading, 1969–74; Prof. of Crop Science, Univ. of Dar e Salaam/FAO, 1974–76; Agric. Res. Adviser/FAO, Agric. Res. Centre, Tripoli, 1977–78 International Council for Research in Agroforestry, Nairobi, 1979–92: Dir, Res. Devel Div., 1987–90; Principal Res. Advr, 1991–92. *Publications:* (ed jtly) Soils Research i Agroforestry, 1980; (ed jtly) Plant Research and Agroforestry, 1983; (ed) Manual c Research Methodology for the Exploration and Assessment of Multipurpose Trees, 1983 (ed jtly) Multipurpose trees: selection and testing for agroforestry, 1989; (ed jtly) Tree-cro Interactions: a physiological approach, 1996; (ed jtly) Agroforestry for Sustainabl Development in Sri Lanka, 1996; (ed jtly) Glossary for Agroforestry, 1997; (compiled an ed jtly) Tropical Agroforestry, 1999; approx. 135 pubns in agric., horticult., agroforestry meteorol and agricl botany jls. *Recreations:* cooking, music, philosophy. *Address:* Flat 4, Linton Road, Oxford OX2 6UH. *Club:* Royal Commonwealth Society (Oxford).

HUXTABLE, Gen. Sir Charles Richard, KCB 1984 (CB 1982); CBE 1976 (OBE 1972; MBE 1961); DL; Commander-in-Chief, United Kingdom Land Forces, 1988–90 Aide-de-Camp General to the Queen, 1988–90; *b* 22 July 1931; *m* 1959, (Margaret) Mary (OBE 2002), *d* of late Brig. J. H. C. Lawlor; three *d*. *Educ:* Wellington Coll.; RMA Sandhurst; Staff College, Camberley; psc, jssc. Commissioned, Duke of Wellington's Regt, 1952; Captain, 1958, Major, 1965; GS02 (Ops), BAOR, 1964–65; GS01 Staf College, 1968–70; CO 1 DWR, 1970–72; Col, 1973; MoD, 1974; Brig., Comd Dhofa Bde, 1976–78; Maj.-Gen., 1980; Dir, Army Staff Duties, 1982–83; Comdr, Training and Arms Dirs (formerly Training Estabts), 1983–86; QMG, 1986–88. Colonel: DWR 1982–90; Col, Royal Irish Regt, 1992–96; Colonel Commandant: The King's Div.

1983–88; UDR, 1991–92. Pres., Ex-Services Mental Welfare Soc., 1990–2001. DL N Yorks, 1994. *Address:* c/o Lloyds TSB, 23 High Street, Teddington, Middlesex TW11 8EX.

HYDE, Lord; George Edward Laurence Villiers; Partner, Knight Frank, since 2006; *b* 12 Feb. 1976; *s* and *heir* of 7th Earl of Clarendon, *qv*; *m* 2007, Bryonie, *d* of Maj.-Gen. Anthony de C. L. Leask, *qv*; one *s*. *Educ:* Royal Agricl Coll. (BSc Hons). MRICS. Page of Honour to the Queen, 1987–89. *Heir: s* Hon. Edward George James Villiers, *b* 17 April 2008. *Address:* c/o Holywell House, Swanmore, Hants SO32 2QE. *Club:* Boodle's.

HYDE, Charles Gordon; QC 2006; a Recorder, since 2004; *b* 27 Feb. 1963; *s* of Gordon and Ann Hyde; *m* 2001, Liz Cunningham; two *s* one *d*. *Educ:* Rugby Sch.; Manchester Univ. (LLB Hons). Called to the Bar, Middle Temple, 1988. Mem., Family Procedure Rule Cttee, 2004–. *Recreations:* fly fishing, walking, watching sport, natural history. *Address:* Albion Chambers, Broad Street, Bristol BS1 1DR. *T:* (0117) 927 2144, *Fax:* (0117) 926 2569; *e-mail:* charles.hyde@albionchambers.co.uk.

HYDE, Helen Yvonne, MA; Headmistress, Watford Grammar School for Girls, since 1987; *b* 11 May 1947; *d* of Henry and Tilly Seligman; *m* 1968, Dr John Hyde; two *d*. *Educ:* Parktown Girls' High Sch., Johannesburg; Witwatersrand Univ. (BA 1967; BA Hons 1969); King's Coll., London (MA 1974). Teacher of French, 1970, Head of Modern Languages, 1978, Acland Burghley; Dep. Headmistress, Highgate Wood, 1983. Chm., Foundn and Aided Schs Nat. Assoc. (formerly Assoc. of Heads of Grant Maintained Schs, later Assoc. of Heads of Foundn and Aided Schs), 2006– (Treas., 1995–2006). Accredited Trainer: Edward de Bono Thinking Skills, 2003; Mind Mapping (Buzan), 2004. *Recreations:* tapestry, exercise, cycling, theology. *Address:* Watford Grammar School for Girls, Lady's Close, Watford, Herts WD18 0AE.

HYDE, Margaret Sheila, OBE 2006; Director, Esmée Fairbairn Foundation (formerly Esmée Fairbairn Charitable Trust), 1994–2005; *b* 11 Sept. 1945; *er d* of late Gerry Tomlins and Sheila (*née* Thorpe); *m* 1966, Derek Hyde (marr. diss. 1976). *Educ:* Watford Grammar Sch. for Girls; London Sch. of Econs and Political Science (DSA 1969; BSc Hons Social Admin 1971; Mostyn Lloyd Meml Prize, 1969; Janet Beveridge Award, 1971). Blackfriars Settlement, 1965–67; Home Office, 1972–77: served in Probation, Prison and Gen. Depts, 1972–76; Private Sec. to Perm. Under Sec. of State, 1976–77; Head of Information, NCVO, 1977–85; Chief Exec., Action Resource Centre, 1985–91 (Trustee, 1992–94); Dep. Sec. Gen., Arts Council of GB, 1991–92; Prog. Consultant, Internat. Save the Children Alliance and Save the Children UK, 1992–94. Mem., Exec. Cttee, 300 Gp, 1984–87 (Treas., 1985–87). Member: Exec. Cttee, Assoc. of Charitable Foundns, 1995–99 (Vice Chm., 1997–99); Venturesome Investment Cttee, 2005–; Futurebuilders Adv. Panel, 2005–07; England Cttee, Big Lottery Fund, 2007–; Charity Tribunal, 2008–; Trustee: Peter Bedford Trust, 1983–92 (Chm., 1985–87); Charities Effectiveness Review Trust, 1986–91; New Econs Foundn, 2005–. Mem. Ct of Govs, LSE, 1987–. FRSA 1991 (Mem. Council, 1994–99). *Recreation:* hill walking. *Club:* Reform.

HYDE-CHAMBERS, Fredrick Rignold, OBE 2003; Secretary-General, International Association of Business and Parliament, since 1997; *b* 12 May 1949; *s* of late Derek Christie Hyde-Chambers and Margaret M. Rignold; *m* 1976, Audrey Christine Martin (*née* Smith); two *s*. *Educ:* Buckingham Coll., Harrow; Arts Educnl Sch. Child actor, TV and stage, 1958–64; The Tibet Relief Fund, UK, 1965–68; Gen. Sec., Buddhist Soc., 1968–72; Private Sec. to MPs, 1974–80; Industry and Parliament Trust, 1980–, Dir, 1987–2003. Co-Founder and Hon. Advr, All-Party Parly Tibet Gp. Member: Bd, Inst. of Citizenship; Adv. Bd, State Legis. Leaders' Foundn, USA; Board, Arts Inform; Council, Buddhist Soc.; Chm., Tibet Soc. of UK and Tibet Relief Fund. Script writer and consultant, BBC TV and Channel 4 documentaries. First Novel Award, Authors' Club, 1988; Airey Neave Trust Human Rights Scholarship, 1989. *Publications:* The Mouse King, 1976; (with Audrey Hyde-Chambers) Tibetan Folktales, 1979, repr. 2002 (Japan, 1997); Tibet and China, 1988; Lama, 1988 (also USA, Germany, Sweden, Argentina and France). *Recreations:* carriage driving, my two children. *Address:* International Association of Business and Parliament, 14 Great College Street, SW1P 3RX. *T:* (020) 7878 1036; *e-mail:* frhc@iabp.org; 12 Gloucester Court, Swan Street, SE1 1DQ. *T:* (020) 7407 5244. *Club:* Athenæum.

HYDE-PARKER, Sir Richard William; *see* Parker.

HYDON, Kenneth John; non-executive Director: Reckitt Benckiser plc, since 2003; Tesco plc, since 2004; Pearson plc, since 2006; *b* Leicester, 1944; *s* of John Thomas and Vera Hydon; *m* 1966, Sylvia Sheila Johnson; one *s* one *d*. FCMA 1970; FCCA 1983; FCT 1997. Financial Director: Racal Electronics subsids, 1979–85; Vodafone Gp plc, 1985–2005. Non-exec. Dir, Cellco Partnership (dba Verizon Wireless USA), 2000–05; Mem., Supervisory Bd, Vodafone Deutschland (formerly Mannesman), 2000–03. Non-exec. Dir, Royal Berks NHS Foundn Trust, 2005–. Patron, Dixie GS, 2000–. FRSA. *Recreations:* sailing in dinghy races, playing golf, driving, especially on track days, watching sport, particularly Rugby and horse-racing, gym sessions, cycling. *Address:* Shiplake, Oxon; *e-mail:* ken.hydon@interdefence.com. *Clubs:* Royal Automobile; Leander (Henley-on-Thames).

HYETT, Paul David Etheridge, PPRIBA; Chairman, Ryder HKS (formerly Ryder), since 2001; President, Royal Institute of British Architects, 2001–03; *b* 18 March 1952; *s* of Derek James and Josephine Mable Hyett (*née* Sparks); *m* 1976, Susan Margaret Beavan; three *s*. *Educ:* Architectural Assoc. (AA Dip.); Bartlett Sch. of Planning (MPhil Planning). RIBA 1979; MRTPI 1992; MEWI 1995; FFB 2002. Career Assistant: Cedric Price Architects, 1974–78; Alan Baxter Associates, 1978–80; Partner: Arno Jobst & Paul Hyett Architects, 1981–82; Nicholas Lacey, Jobst and Hyett Architects, 1982–87; Paul Hyett Architects, 1987–97; Hyett Salisbury Whiteley, 1997–2001. Mem., Architectl Assoc., 1972–. Columnist: Architects Jl; RIBA Jl. Hon. DArt Lincoln, 2004. *Publications:* In Practice, 2000; (with B. Edwards) Rough Guide to Sustainability, 2001; (contrib.) Sustaining Architecture in the Anti-Machine Age, 2001; (with John Jenner) Tomorrow's Hospitals, 2004; contribs to Building Design. *Recreations:* trekking, political biographies, history, writing. *Address:* Ryder HKS, 7 Soho Square, W1D 3QB. *T:* (020) 7292 9494, *Fax:* (020) 7292 9495; *e-mail:* phyett@ryderhks.com.

HYLAND, (James) Graham (Keith); QC 1998; a Recorder, since 1996; *b* 11 Jan. 1955; *s* of Reginald Keith Hyland and Evelyn (*née* Graham); *m* 1st, 1979, Angela Lancaster (marr. diss. 1993); one *s*; 2nd, 1995, Jane Alison Davies; one *d*. *Educ:* Heath Grammar Sch., Halifax; Newcastle upon Tyne Poly. (BA Law 1977). Called to the Bar, Inner Temple, 1978, Bencher, 2007. *Recreations:* walking, music, reading, wine, cricket. *Address:* Broadway House, 9 Bank Street, Bradford BD1 1TW. *T:* (01274) 722560; 9 Lincoln's Inn Fields, WC2A 3BP. *Clubs:* Bradford; South Caernarvonshire Yacht.

HYLAND, Susan Margaret; HM Diplomatic Service; Head, Human Rights, Democracy and Governance Group, Foreign and Commonwealth Office, since 2006; *b* 30 Oct. 1964; *d* of Alan and Joan Frances Hyland (*née* Beddow). *Educ:* Somerville Coll., Oxford (MA; BPhil; Nuffield Exhibn Grad. Scholarship); Yale Univ. (Henry Fellowship); Ecole Nationale d'Admin, France (diplôme). Joined HM Diplomatic Service, 1990; Second Sec., Oslo, then UK Mission to the UN, NY, 1992; Second Sec., UK Delegn to the OECD, 1993; Ecole Nationale d'Admin, 1994–95; First Secretary: FCO, 1996; Moscow, 2000; Private Sec. to Perm. Under-Sec., FCO, 2001; seconded to Westminster Foundn for Democracy, 2004; First Sec., Paris, 2005. *Recreations:* theatre, travel, reading. *Address:* Foreign and Commonwealth Office, King Charles Street, SW1A 2AH.

HYLTON, 5th Baron *cr* 1866; **Raymond Hervey Jolliffe,** MA; *b* 13 June 1932; *er s* of 4th Baron Hylton and Perdita Rose Mary (*d* 1996), *d* of late Raymond Asquith and *sister* of 2nd Earl of Oxford and Asquith, *qv*; *S* father, 1967; *m* 1966, Joanna Ida Elizabeth, *d* of late Andrew de Bertodano; four *s* one *d*. *Educ:* Eton (King's Scholar); Trinity Coll., Oxford (MA). MRICS. Lieut R of O, Coldstream Guards. Asst Private Sec. to Governor-General of Canada, 1960–62; Trustee, Shelter Housing Aid Centre 1970–76; Chairman: Catholic Housing Aid Soc., 1972–73; Nat. Fedn of Housing Assocs, 1973–76; Housing Assoc. Charitable Trust; Help the Aged Housing Trust, 1976–82; Hugh of Witham Foundn, 1978–; Vice-Pres., Age Concern (Nat. Old People's Welfare Council), 1971–77; President: SW Reg. Nat. Soc. for Mentally Handicapped Children, 1976–79; NI Assoc. for Care and Resettlement of Offenders, 1989. An indep. mem. of H of L; Member, All Party Parliamentary Group: on Penal Affairs; on Human Rights; British-Russian; British-Armenian; British-Albanian; British-Palestine; elected Mem., H of L, 1999. Vice-Chm., Partners in Hope (formerly St Francis and St Sergius Trust Fund), 2001– (Chm., 1993–2001). Founder and Mem., Mendip and Wansdyke Local Enterprise Gp, 1979–85. Hon. Treas., Study on Human Rights and Responsibilities in Britain and N Ireland, 1985–88. Mem., Nat. Steering Gp, Charter '87, 1987–99; Signatory of Charter '88 and of Charter '99. Trustee: Christian Internat. Peace Service, 1977–82; Acorn Christian Healing Trust, 1983–98; Action around Bethlehem among Children with Disabilities, 1993–2000; Forward Thinking, 2004–; Chm., Moldovan Initiatives Cttee of Mgt, 1993–; Member: Council for Advancement of Arab-British Understanding; RIIA. Gov., Ammerdown Centre, Bath, 1972–. Mem., Frome RDC, 1968–72. DL Somerset, 1975–90. Hon DSc (SocSc) Southampton, 1994. *Heir: s* Hon. William Henry Martin Jolliffe, *b* April 1967. *Address:* c/o House of Lords, SW1A 0PW.

HYMAN, Howard Jonathan; Chairman, Hyman Associates, since 1997; *b* 23 Oct. 1949; *s* of late Joe Hyman and Corrine Irene (*née* Abrahams); *m* 1972, Anne Moira Sowden; two *s* one *d*. *Educ:* Bedales Sch., Hants; Manchester Univ. (MA Hons Econs 1972). ACA 1975, FCA 1982. Price Waterhouse: articled clerk, 1972–75; Partner, 1984; seconded to HM Treasury as specialist privatisation adviser, 1984–87; Founder and Partner i/c of Privatisation Services Dept, 1987–90; Head of Corporate Finance, Europe, 1990; Member: E European Jt Venture Bd, 1990–94; European Mgt Bd, 1991–94; China Bd, 1993–94; World Gen. Council, 1992–94; World Head, Corporate Finance, 1994; Dep. Chm., Charterhouse Bank Ltd, 1994–96; Man. Dir, Charterhouse plc, 1994–96. Freeman, City of London, 1997. *Publications:* Privatisation: the facts, 1988; The Implications of Privatisation for Nationalised Industries, 1988; chapters in: Privatisation and Competition, 1988; Privatisation in the UK, 1988; articles in Electrical Rev., Equities Internat., Public Finance and Accountancy, Business and Govt, Administrator. *Recreations:* Chinese culture and language, walking, golf, watching cricket, reading, gardening, classical music. *Address:* 1 Cato Street, W1H 5HG. *T:* (020) 7258 0404. *Clubs:* Reform, MCC; Cirencester Golf, Richmond Golf.

HYMAN, Robin Philip; publisher; Chairman, Laurence King Publishing Ltd (formerly Calmann & King Ltd), 1991–2004; *b* 9 Sept. 1931; *s* of late Leonard Hyman and Helen Hyman (*née* Mautner); *m* 1966, Inge Neufeld; two *s* one *d*. *Educ:* Henley Grammar Sch.; Christ's Coll., Finchley; Univ. of Birmingham (BA (Hons) 1955). National Service, RAF, 1949–51. Editor, Mermaid, 1953–54; Bookselling and Publishing: joined Evans Brothers Ltd, Publishers, 1955: Dir, 1964; Dep. Man. Dir, 1967; Man. Dir, 1972–77; Chm., Bell & Hyman Ltd, 1977–86, which merged with Allen & Unwin Ltd, 1986, to form Unwin Hyman Ltd, Man. Dir, 1986–88, Chm. and Chief Exec., 1989–90. Mem. Editorial Bd, World Year Book of Education, 1969–73. Publishers' Association: Mem. Council, 1975–92; Treasurer, 1982–84; Vice-Pres., 1988–89, 1991–92; Pres., 1989–91; Member: Exec. Cttee, Educnl Publishers' Council, 1971–76 (Treas., 1972–75); Publishers' Adv. Cttee, British Council, 1989–92; BBC Gen. Adv. Council, 1992–97. Dir, Spiro Inst., 1991–98. Trustee: ADAPT, 1997–2006; Samuel Pepys Award Trust, 2001– (Chm., 2007–). Mem., First British Publishers' Delegn to China, 1978. FRSA. *Publications:* A Dictionary of Famous Quotations, 1962; (with John Trevaskis) Boys' and Girls' First Dictionary, 1967; Bell & Hyman First Colour Dictionary, 1985; Universal Primary Dictionary (for Africa), 1976; (with Inge Hyman) 11 children's books, incl. Barnabas Ball at the Circus, 1967; Runaway James and the Night Owl, 1968; The Hippo who Wanted to Fly, 1973; The Magical Fish, 1974; Peter's Magic Hide-and-Seek, 1982. *Recreations:* theatre, reading, travel. *Address:* 101 Hampstead Way, NW11 7LR. *T:* (020) 8455 7055. *Clubs:* Garrick, MCC.

HYND, Annette, (Mrs Ronald Hynd); *see* Page, Annette.

HYND, Ronald; choreographer; Ballet Director, National Theater, Munich, 1970–73 and 1984–86; *b* 22 April 1931; *s* of William John and Alice Louisa Hens; *m* 1957, Annette Page, *qv*; one *d*. *Educ:* erratically throughout England due to multiple wartime evacuation. Joined Rambert School, 1946; Ballet Rambert, 1949; Royal Ballet (then Sadlers Well's Ballet), 1952, rising from Corps de Ballet to Principal Dancer, 1959; danced Siegfried (Swan Lake), Florimund (Sleeping Beauty), Albrecht (Giselle), Poet (Sylphides), Tsarevitch (Firebird), Prince of Pagodas, Moondog (Lady and Fool), Tybalt (Romeo), etc; produced first choreography for Royal Ballet Choreographic Group followed by works for London Festival Ballet, Royal Ballet, Dutch National Ballet, Munich Ballet, Houston Ballet, Australian Ballet, Tokyo Ballet, Nat. Ballet of Canada, Grands Ballets Canadiens, Santiago Ballet, Cincinnati Ballet, Pact Ballet, Malmö Ballet, Ljubljana Ballet, Northern Ballet, Ballet of La Scala, Milan, Bonn Ballet, Vienna State Ballet, Amer. Ballet Theatre, New London Ballet, Deutsche Oper Berlin, Royal Danish Ballet. *Ballets include:* Le Baiser de la Fée, 1968, new production 1974; Pasiphaë, 1969; Dvorak Variations, 1970; Wendekreise, 1972; In a Summer Garden, 1972; Das Telefon, 1972; Mozartiana, 1973; Charlotte Brontë, 1974; Mozart Adagio, 1974; Galileo (film), 1974; Orient/Occident, 1975; La Valse, 1975; Valses Nobles et Sentimentales, 1975; The Merry Widow, 1975, eleven subseq. prodns incl. Amer. Ballet Th. at Met. Opera, NY, 1997 and Royal Danish Ballet, 1998; L'Eventail, 1976; The Nutcracker (new version for Festival Ballet), 1976, new prodns for Ballet de Nice, 1997, La Scala, 2000; ice ballets for John Curry, 1977; Rosalinda, 1978, eleven subseq. prodns incl. Berlin, 1998; La Chatte, 1978; Papillon, 1979; The Seasons, 1980; Alceste, 1981; Scherzo Capriccioso, 1982; Le Diable a Quatre, 1984; Fanfare fur Tänzer, 1985; Coppelia (new prodn for Festival Ballet), 1985, new prodns for Santiago and Berlin, 2000, Hong Kong Ballet, 2008; Ludwig-Fragmente Eines Rätsels, 1986; The Hunchback of Notre Dame, 1988; Ballade, 1988; Liaisons Amoureuses, 1989; Sleeping Beauty (new prodn for English Nat. Ballet), 1993 and Pacific Northwest Ballet, 2001; *musicals:* Sound of Music, 1981; Camelot, 1982; *TV productions:* The Nutcracker, The Sanguine Fan (Fest. Ballet); The Merry Widow (Nat. Ballet of

Canada and Aust. Ballet); operas, La Traviata and Amahl and the Night Visitors. *Recreations:* the gramophone, garden, travel.

HYNES, Dame Ann Patricia; *see* Dowling, Dame A. P.

HYNES, Prof. Richard Olding, FRS 1989; Daniel K. Ludwig Professor for Cancer Research, Massachusetts Institute of Technology, since 1999; Investigator, Howard Hughes Medical Institute, since 1988; *b* 29 Nov. 1944; *s* of Hugh Bernard Noel Hynes and late Mary Elizabeth Hynes; *m* 1966, Fleur Marshall; two *s. Educ:* Trinity Coll., Cambridge (BA 1966; MA 1970); MIT (PhD Biology 1971). Res. Fellow, Imperial Cancer Res. Fund, 1971–74; Massachusetts Institute of Technology: Asst Prof., 1975–78, Associate Prof., 1978–83, Prof., 1983–, Dept of Biology and Center for Cancer Res.; Associate Hd, 1985–89, Head, 1989–91, of Biology Dept; Dir, Center for Cancer Res., 1991–2001. Hon. Res. Fellow, Dept of Zoology, UCL, 1982–83. Guggenheim Fellow, 1982. Mem., Inst. of Medicine, US NAS, 1995; Mem., US NAS, 1996. FAAAS, 1987; Fellow, Amer. Acad. of Arts and Scis, 1994. Gairdner Internat. Award, Gairdner Foundn, Toronto, 1997. *Publications:* (ed) Surfaces of Normal and Malignant Cells, 1979; (ed) Tumor Cell Surfaces and Malignancy, 1980; Fibronectins, 1990; over 300 articles in professional jls. *Recreations:* reading, music, gardening, ski-ing. *Address:* E17–227, Massachusetts Institute of Technology, Cambridge, MA 02139, USA. *T:* (617) 2536422, *Fax:* (617) 2538357.

HYNES, Prof. Samuel, DFC 1945; PhD; Woodrow Wilson Emeritus Professor of Literature, Princeton University, since 1990; *b* 29 Aug. 1924; *s* of Samuel Hynes and Margaret Turner Hynes; *m* 1944, Elizabeth Igleheart; two *d. Educ:* Univ. of Minnesota (AB 1947); Columbia Univ. (PhD 1956). Pilot, US Marine Corps: 2nd Lieut, 1943–46; Capt., then Major, 1952–53. Instructor to Prof. of English, Swarthmore Coll., 1949–52 and 1954–68; Professor: Northwestern Univ., 1968–76; Princeton Univ., 1976–90. Woodrow Wilson Prof. of Literature, 1977–90. FRSL 1978. Air Medal, 1945. *Publications:* (ed) Further Speculations by T. E. Hulme, 1955; The Pattern of Hardy's Poetry, 1961; The Edwardian Turn of Mind, 1962; William Golding, 1964; (ed) The Author's Craft and Other Critical Writings of Arnold Bennett, 1968; (ed) Romance and Realism, 1970; Edwardian Occasions, 1972; The Auden Generation, 1976; (ed) Complete Poetical Works of Thomas Hardy, Vol. I 1982, Vol. II 1984, Vol. III 1985, Vols IV and V 1995; (ed) Thomas Hardy, 1984; Flights of Passage: reflections of a World War II aviator, 1988; A War Imagined, 1990; (ed) Joseph Conrad: complete short fiction, 4 vols, 1992–93; The Soldiers' Tale: bearing witness to modern war, 1997; The Growing Seasons, 2003. *Address:* 130 Moore Street, Princeton, NJ 08540, USA. *T:* (609) 9211930.

HYSLOP; *see* Maxwell-Hyslop.

HYSLOP, Fiona Jane; Member (SNP) Lothians, Scottish Parliament, since 1999; Cabinet Secretary for Education and Lifelong Learning, since 2007; *b* 1 Aug. 1964; *d* of Thomas Hyslop and Margaret Birrell; *m* 1994; one *s* one *d. Educ:* Ayr Acad.; Glasgow Univ. (MA Hons 1985); Scottish Coll. of Textiles (Post Grad. Dip. 1986). Mkting Manager, Standard Life, 1986–99. Mem., SNP, 1986– (Mem., Nat. Exec., 1990–). Contested (SNP): Edinburgh Leith, 1992; Edinburgh Central, 1997. *Address:* Scottish Parliament, Edinburgh EH99 1SP. *T:* (0131) 348 5920.

HYSLOP, Peter Henry St G.; *see* St George-Hyslop.

HYTNER, Benet Alan; QC 1970; a Recorder of the Crown Court, 1972–97; Judge of Appeal, Isle of Man, 1980–97; *b* 29 Dec. 1927; *s* of late Maurice and Sarah Hytner, Manchester; *m* 1954, Joyce Myers (OBE 2004); three *s* one *d. Educ:* Manchester Grammar Sch.; Trinity Hall, Cambridge (Exhibr; MA). National Service, RASC, 1949–51 (commnd). Called to Bar, Middle Temple, 1952, Bencher, 1977, Reader, 1995; Leader, Northern Circuit, 1984–88. Member: Gen. Council of Bar, 1969–73, 1986–88; Senate of Inns of Court and Bar, 1977–81, 1984–86. *Recreations:* walking, music, theatre, reading. *Address:* 42 Bedford Row, WC1R 4LL.
    See also N. R. Hytner.

HYTNER, Nicholas Robert; theatre and film director; Director, National Theatre, since 2003; *b* 7 May 1956; *s* of Benet Hytner, *qv* and Joyce Hytner, OBE. *Educ:* Manchester Grammar School; Trinity Hall, Cambridge (MA; Hon. Fellow, 2005). Associate Director, Royal Exchange Theatre, Manchester, 1985–89; NT, 1989–97. Vis. Prof. of Contemporary Theatre, Oxford Univ., 2000–01; Emeritus Fellow, St Catherine's Coll., Oxford, 2003. Director of many theatre and opera productions including: *theatre:* As You Like It, 1985, Edward II, 1986, The Country Wife, 1986, Don Carlos, 1987, Royal Exchange; Measure for Measure, 1987, The Tempest, 1988, RSC; Ghetto, National Theatre, 1989; Miss Saigon, Drury Lane, 1989, Broadway, 1991; Volpone, Almeida, 1990; King Lear, RSC, 1990; The Wind in the Willows, NT, 1990; The Madness of George III, NT, 1991; The Recruiting Officer, NT, 1992; Carousel, NT, 1992, Shaftesbury, 1993, NY, 1994; The Importance of Being Earnest, Aldwych, 1993; The Cripple of Inishmaan, NT, 1997; Twelfth Night, NY, 1998; Lady in the Van, Queen's, 1999; Cressida, Albery, 2000; Orpheus Descending, Donmar Warehouse, 2000; The Winter's Tale, Mother Clapp's Molly House, NT, 2001; Sweet Smell of Success, NY, 2002; National Theatre: Henry V, His Dark Materials, 2003; The History Boys, 2004, NY, 2006; Stuff Happens, 2004; Henry IV, Pts 1 and 2, 2005; Southwark Fair, The Alchemist, 2006; The Man of Mode, The Rose Tattoo, Rafta, Rafta, Much Ado About Nothing, 2007; Major Barbara, 2008; *opera:* English National Opera: Rienzi, 1983, Xerxes, 1985 (Laurence Olivier and Evening Standard Awards); The Magic Flute, 1988; The Force of Destiny, 1992; King Priam, Kent Opera, 1983; Giulio Cesare, Paris Opera, Houston Grand Opera, 1987; Le Nozze di Figaro, Geneva Opera, 1989; La Clemenza di Tito, Glyndebourne, 1991; Don Giovanni, Bavarian State Opera, 1994; The Cunning Little Vixen, Paris, 1995; Così fan tutte, Glyndebourne, 2006; Don Carlo, Covent Garden, 2008; *films:* The Madness of King George, 1994 (Evening Standard and BAFTA Awards for Best British Film); The Crucible, 1997; The Object of My Affection, 1998; The History Boys, 2006. Awards for Best Director: Evening Standard, 1989; Critics' Circle, 1989; Olivier, 1993, 2005; Tony, 1994, 2006. *Address:* National Theatre, South Bank, SE1 9PX.

I

IACOBESCU, George, CBE 2003; Chief Executive Officer, Canary Wharf Group plc, since 1997; *b* 9 Nov. 1945; *m* 1976, Gabriela; one *d. Educ:* Lyceum D. Cantemir (BSc 1963); Univ. of Civil & Industrial Engrg, Bucharest (Masters degree in professional engrg 1968). Construction Dir, Homeco Invst, Montreal and Toronto, 1975–78; Project Dir, Olympia Center and Neiman Marcus Bldgs, Chicago, 1981–84; Vice-Pres., Develt and Construction, World Financial Center, 1984–87; Vice-Pres., Construction, 1987–92; Dir, CWL, 1993–95; Dep. CEO, Canary Wharf Gp plc, 1995–97. Co-Chm., Teach First; Director: London First; Gateway to London; Wood Wharf (Gen. Partners) Ltd. Mem. Adv. Bd, UK Acad. of Finance. Trustee, British Mus., 2007–. CCMI. Hon. DBA East London, 2007. *Recreations:* jazz, opera, antiques, football, tennis. *Address:* Canary Wharf Group plc, 1 Canada Square, E14 5AB. *T:* (020) 7418 2209.

IAN, David; *see* Lane, D. I.

IANNUCCI, Armando Giovanni; freelance writer, director and comedy producer; *b* 28 Nov. 1963; *s* of Armando and Gina Iannucci; *m* 1990, Rachael Jones; two *s* one *d. Educ:* St Peter's Primary Sch., Glasgow; St Aloysius Coll., Glasgow; Glasgow Univ.; University Coll., Oxford (MA English Lang. and Lit. 1986). Writer for television: and performer, The Friday Night Armistice, 1995, 1997, 1998; and producer, The Day Today, 1995; and dir, The Armando Iannucci Shows, 2001; and producer, I'm Alan Partridge, 1997 and 2001; deviser and dir, The Thick of It, 2005–07. Columnist: Daily Telegraph, 1998–2005; Sunday Observer, 2006–; Gramophone mag., 2006–. *Publications:* Facts and Fancies, 2000; Alan Partridge: every ruddy word, 2005. *Recreations:* prevaricating, bad piano, astronomy, fearing, re-assuring, theology. *Address:* c/o PBJ Management, 7 Soho Street, W1D 3DQ. *T:* (020) 7287 1112, *Fax:* (020) 7287 1191; *e-mail:* general@pbjmgt.co.uk; c/o Aitken Alexander Associates, 18–21 Cavaye Place, SW10 9PT. *T:* (020) 7373 8672.

IBBETSON, Prof. David John, PhD, DPhil; FBA 2003; Regius Professor of Civil Law, University of Cambridge, and Fellow of Corpus Christi College, Cambridge, since 2000. *Educ:* Corpus Christi Coll., Cambridge (BA 1976; PhD 1980); DPhil Oxon. Formerly Lectr in Law, Univ. of Oxford, and Fellow of Magdalen Coll., Oxford. Hon. Bencher, Gray's Inn, 2008. *Publications:* (ed with A. D. E. Lewis) Roman Law Tradition, 1994; Historical Introduction to the Law of Obligations, 1999. *Address:* Corpus Christi College, Cambridge CB2 1RH.

IBBOTSON, Peter Stamford; broadcasting and media consultant; *b* 13 Dec. 1943; *s* of Arthur Ibbotson and Ivy Elizabeth (*née* Acton); *m* 1975, Susan Mary Crewdson; two *s* (one *d* decd). *Educ:* Manchester Grammar Sch.; St Catherine's Coll., Oxford (BA Modern History). BBC: Editor, Newsweek, 1978–82; Editor, Panorama, 1983–85; Asst Head, Television Current Affairs, 1985–86; Chief Asst to Dir of Programmes, Television, 1986–87; Dep. Dir of Progs, TV, 1987–88; Dir of Corporate Affairs, Carlton Television Ltd, 1991–94. Director: UK Radio Develts Ltd, 1990–94; Film and Television Completions PLC, 1990–98. Corporate Consultant, Channel 4, 1988–91 and 1994–2004; Consultant: to BBC Govs, 2004–06; to Bd, ITV plc, 2007–. Dir, BARB, 1987–88. Gov., ESU, 2000–05. FRTS 1994. *Publication:* (jtly) The Third Age of Broadcasting, 1978. *Recreations:* silviculture, reading, photography. *Address:* Newnham Farm, Wallingford, Oxon OX10 8BW. *T:* (01491) 833111. *Clubs:* Beefsteak, Garrick, Royal Automobile.

IBBOTSON, Rear Adm. Richard Jeffery, CB 2008; DSC 1992; Flag Officer Sea Training, 2007–Feb. 2009; Deputy Commander-in-Chief Fleet and Chief Naval Warfare Officer (in rank of Vice Adm.), from April 2009; *b* 27 June 1954; *s* of Jeffrey Ibbotson and Joan Ibbotson; *m* 1975, Marie; two *d. Educ:* Univ. of Durham (BSc); RNEC Manadon (MSc). CGIA. Capt., First Frigate Sqdn and HMS Boxer, 1998–99; Asst Dir, MoD, 1999–2001; Comdr, British Forces Falkland Is, 2001–02; Comdr, Standing Naval Forces Atlantic, 2003–04; CO, Britannia RNC, 2004–05; Naval Sec. and Dir Gen. Human Resources Navy, 2005–07. *Recreations:* water sports, classic cars. *Address:* Grenville Block, HMS Drake, Devonport, Plymouth PL2 2BG.

IBBOTSON, Roger; His Honour Judge Ibbotson; a Circuit Judge, since 2001; *b* 2 Jan. 1943; *s* of Harry and Lily Ibbotson; *m* 1967, Susan Elizabeth Dalton; three *d. Educ:* Cockburn High Sch., Leeds; Univ. of Manchester (LLB). Articled clerk, Burton and Burton, Leeds, 1963–66; admitted solicitor, 1966; Asst Solicitor, 1966–70, Partner, 1970–2001, Booth & Co., later Addleshaw Booth & Co.; Asst Recorder, 1994–98; Recorder, 1998–2001. Pres., Leeds Law Soc., 1996–97; Council Mem., Law Soc., 1997–2001. *Recreations:* walking, reading. *Address:* Leeds Combined Court Centre, 1 Oxford Row, Leeds LS1 3BG.

IBBOTT, Alec, CBE 1988; HM Diplomatic Service, retired; *b* 14 Oct. 1930; *s* of Francis Joseph Ibbott and Madge Winifred Ibbott (*née* Graham); *m* 1964, Margaret Elizabeth Brown; one *s* one *d.* Joined Foreign (subseq. Diplomatic) Service, 1949; served in HM Forces, 1949–51; FCO, 1951–54; ME Centre for Arab Studies, 1955–56; Second Secretary and Vice Consul, Rabat, 1956–60; Second Secretary, FO, 1960–61; Second Sec. (Information), Tripoli, 1961; Second Sec., Benghazi, 1961–65; First Sec. (Information), Khartoum, 1965–67; First Sec., FO (later FCO), 1967–71; Asst Political Agent, Dubai, 1971; First Secretary, Head of Chancery and Consul: Dubai, 1971–72; Abu Dhabi, 1972–73; First Secretary and Head of Chancery: Nicosia, 1973–74; FCO, 1975–77; Carácas, 1977–79; Counsellor, Khartoum, 1979–82; seconded to IMS Ltd, 1982–85; Ambassador to Liberia, 1985–87; High Comr to the Republic of The Gambia, 1988–90. Chief Exec., Southern Africa Assoc., 1992–95; Gen. Manager, UK Southern Africa Business Assoc., 1994–95. Mem. Council, Anglo-Arab Assoc., 1992–2003. Trustee, Charlton Community Develt Trust, 1995–2003. *Address:* 15a Sanderstead Hill, South Croydon, Surrey CR2 0HD.

IBBS, Sir (John) Robin, KBE 1988; Kt 1982; Chairman: Lloyds TSB Group PLC, 1995–97; Lloyds Bank, 1993–97 (Director, 1985–97; Deputy Chairman, 1988–93); *b* 21 April 1926; *o s* of late Prof. T. L. Ibbs, MC, DSc, FInstP and of Marjorie Ibbs (*née* Bell); *m* 1st, 1952, Iris Barbara (*d* 2005), *d* of late S. Hall; one *d*; 2nd, 2006, Penelope Ann, *d* of late Capt. H. C. Buckland. *Educ:* West House Sch.; Gresham's Sch.; Upper Canada Coll., Toronto; Univ. of Toronto; Trinity Coll., Cambridge (MA Mech. Scis). Instr Lieut, RN, 1947–49. Called to the Bar, Lincoln's Inn, 1952 (Hon. Bencher 1999). C. A. Parsons & Co. Ltd, 1949–51; joined ICI, 1952; Dir, 1976–80 and 1982–88; on secondment as Head, Central Policy Review Staff, Cabinet Office, 1980–82; Advr (pt-time) to Prime Minister on Efficiency and Effectiveness in Govt, 1983–88; Chm., Lloyds Merchant Bank Hldgs, 1989–92; Dep. Chm., Lloyds Bank Canada, 1989–90. Dir, IMI, 1972–76. Chm., Adv. Council, PA Search and Selection, 1997–98. Member: Governing Body and Council, British Nat. Cttee of ICC, 1976–80; Industrial Develt Adv. Bd, DoI, 1978–80; Council, CBI, 1982–87 (Mem. Companies Cttee, 1978–80); Council, CIA, 1976–79, 1982–87 (Vice Pres., 1983–87; Hon. Mem., 1987); Chemicals EDC, NEDO, 1982–88; Council, RIIA, Chatham House, 1983–89; Top Salaries Review Body, 1983–89; Adv. Cttee on Business Appts, 1991–98; second Mem., Sierra Leone Arms Investigation, 1998; Leader, Review of H of C Services, 1990. Pres., Bankers Club, 1994–95. Vice Pres., CIB, 1993–97 (FCIB 1993). Trustee and Dep. Chm., Isaac Newton Trust, 1988–99. Mem. Court, Cranfield Inst. of Technology, 1983–88; Chm. of Council, UCL, 1989–95; Mem. Council, Foundn for Sci. and Technol., 1997–2002. CCMI (CBIM 1985). Hon. Fellow UCL, 1993. Hon. DSc Bradford, 1986; Hon. LLD Bath, 1993. BIM Special Award, 1989. *Address:* c/o Lloyds TSB Group, 25 Gresham Street, EC2V 7HN. *Clubs:* Oxford and Cambridge (Trustee, 1989–2002), Naval and Military, Royal Society of Medicine.

IDDESLEIGH, 5th Earl of, *cr* 1885; **John Stafford Northcote;** Bt 1641; Viscount St Cyres, 1885; *b* 15 Feb. 1957; *s* of 4th Earl of Iddesleigh, and of Maria Luisa Alvarez-Builla y Urquijo (Condesa del Real Agrado in Spain), OBE, DL; S father, 2004; *m* 1983, Fiona Caroline Elizabeth (marr. diss. 1999; she *d* 2006), *d* of P. Wakefield, Barcelona, and Mrs M. Hattrell, Burnham, Bucks; one *s* one *d*; *m* 2000, Maria Ann Akaylar. *Educ:* Downside Sch.; RAC Cirencester. *Heir:* *s* Viscount St Cyres, *qv.*

IDDON, Dr Brian, CChem, FRSC; MP (Lab) Bolton South East, since 1997; *b* 5 July 1940; *s* of John Iddon and Violet (*née* Stazicker); *m* 1st, 1965, Merrilyn Ann Muncaster (marr. diss. 1989); two *d*; 2nd, 1995, Eileen Harrison; two step *s. Educ:* Univ. of Hull (BSc Chem. 1961; PhD Organic Chem. 1964; DSc 1981). FRSC (FCS 1959); CChem 1980. Temp. Lectr in Organic Chem., 1964–65, Sen. Demonstrator, 1965–66, Univ. of Durham; University of Salford: Lectr in Organic Chem., 1966–78; Sen. Lectr, 1978–86; Reader, 1986–97. Vis. Prof., Dept of Chemistry, Liverpool Univ., 2002–. Has lectured worldwide, incl. lect. The Magic of Chemistry presented to schs and univs in UK and Europe, 1968–98. Chm., Bolton Technical Innovation Centre Ltd, 2003–08. Has made TV and radio broadcasts. Mem. (Lab) Bolton MDC, 1977–98 (Vice-Chm., 1980–82, Chm., 1986–96, Housing Cttee). Hon. Mem., SCI, 2003. Hon. Fellow, Univ. of Bolton, 2005. President's Award, RSC, 2006. *Publications:* (jtly) Radiation Sterilization of Pharmaceutical and Biomedical Products, 1974; The Magic of Chemistry, 1985; contrib. chapters in books; numerous papers and reviews and articles in learned jls incl. Jl Chem. Soc., Perkin Trans, Tetrahedron, Chem. Comm., Sch. Sci. Rev., Heterocycles. *Recreations:* gardening, philately, cricket (spectator). *Address:* House of Commons, SW1A 0AA. *T:* (020) 7219 2096, (020) 7219 4064, *Fax:* (020) 7219 2653; *web:* www.brianiddon.org.uk. *Club:* Derby Ward Labour (Life Mem.).

IDIENS, Dale; Depute Director, National Museums of Scotland, 2000–01 and Acting Director, 2001–02; Vice-Chair, Scottish Arts Council, 2002–05 (Member, 1998–2005; Acting Chair, 2004–05); *b* 13 May 1942; *d* of Richard Idiens and Ruth Christine Idiens (*née* Hattersley). *Educ:* High Wycombe High Sch.; Univ. of Leicester. BA (Hons); DipEd. Department of Art and Archaeology, Royal Scottish Museum, later National Museums of Scotland: Asst Keeper in charge of Ethnography, 1964; Dep. Keeper, 1979; Keeper, Dept of Hist. and Applied Art, 1983; Depute Dir (Collections), 1992. Mem. Council, Architectural Heritage Soc. of Scotland, 2003–06. *Publications:* Traditional African Sculpture, 1969; Ancient American Art, 1971; (ed with K. G. Ponting) African Textiles, 1980; The Hausa of Northern Nigeria, 1981; Pacific Art, 1982; (contrib.) Indians and Europe, an Interdisciplinary Collection of Essays, 1987; Cook Islands Art, 1990; (contrib.) No Ordinary Journey: John Rae, Arctic explorer 1813–1893, 1993; articles and papers in Jl of the Polynesian Soc., African Arts, Textile History; reviews and lectures. *Recreations:* travel, film, wine. *Address:* 97/10 East London Street, Edinburgh EH7 4BF. *T:* (0131) 557 8481. *Club:* Naval and Military.

IDLE, Eric; actor and writer; *b* 29 March 1943; *m* 1st, Lynn Ashley (marr. diss.); one *s*; 2nd, Tania Kosevich; one *d. Educ:* Royal Sch., Wolverhampton; Pembroke Coll., Cambridge (BA 1965; Pres., Cambridge Footlights, 1964–65). Pres., Prominent Features. *Stage* includes: I'm Just Wild About Harry, Edinburgh Fest., 1963; Monty Python Live at Drury Lane, 1974; Monty Python Live at the Hollywood Bowl, 1980; The Mikado, ENO, 1987, Houston Opera House, 1989; writer, Spamalot (musical), Chicago, 2004, NY, 2005, Palace Th., 2007; *television* includes: joint writer: The Frost Report, 1967; Marty Feldman, 1968–69; joint writer and actor: Monty Python's Flying Circus, 4 series, 1969–74; Rutland Weekend Television, 1978; actor: Do Not Adjust Your Set, 1968–69; Around the World in 80 Days, 1989; Nearly Departed, 1989; *films* include: joint writer and actor: And Now for Something Completely Different, 1970; Monty Python and the Holy Grail, 1974; Life of Brian, 1978; The Meaning of Life, 1982; Splitting Heirs, 1993; actor: The Adventures of Baron Munchausen, 1988; Nuns on the Run, 1990; Casper, 1995; Wind in the Willows, 1996. *Publications:* The Greedy Bastard Diary, 2005; *novels:* Hello Sailor, 1975; The Road to Mars, 1999; The Pythons Autobiography by the Pythons, 2003.

IDLE, Prof. Jeffrey Robert, PhD; CSci; CChem, FRSC, EurChem; CBiol, FIBiol, EurProBiol; FBPharmacolS; Professor of Pharmacology, Charles University, Prague, since 2004; *b* 17 Sept. 1950; *s* of Robert William Idle and Margaret Joyce Idle (*née* Golightly); *m* Samar El-Sallab (marr. diss.); one *d*. *Educ:* Hatfield Polytechnic (BSc 1972, BSc Hons 1973); St Mary's Hosp. Med. Sch. (PhD 1976). CChem 1987; FRSC 1987; CBiol 1999; FIBiol 1999; EurChem 2000; EurProBiol 2000; CSci 2004; FBPharmacolS 2005. St Mary's Hospital Medical School, London: Lectr in Biochem., 1976; Lectr in Biochemical Pharmacol., 1976–83; Wellcome Trust Sen. Lectr, 1983–88; Reader in Pharmacogenetics, 1985–88; University of Newcastle upon Tyne: Prof. of Pharmacogenetics, 1988–95; Hd, Sch. of Clinical Med. Scis, 1992–95; Hd, Dept of Pharmacol. Scis, 1992–95; Consultant in Med. Genetics, Regl Hosp., Trondheim, 1996–99; Prof. in Medicine and Molecular Biol., Norwegian Univ. of Sci. and Technol., 1996–2004. Vis. Prof., Univ. of Bern, 2003–. Dir, Nivy Blacksmith Music sro, 1999–. Founding Editor and Editor-in-Chief, Pharmacogenetics, 1991–98. Chief Executive: Genotype Ltd, 1993–95; VitOmega Internat., 1995–98. *Publications:* articles in internat. scientific and med. jls. *Recreations:* language and culture of the Middle East, music. *Address:* U Háje 1651, 25263 Roztoky, Czech Republic.

IDRIS, Kamil E., PhD; Director General, World Intellectual Property Organization, since 1997 (Deputy Director General, 1994–97); Secretary General, International Union for the Protection of New Varieties of Plants, since 1997; *b* 26 Aug. 1954. *Educ:* Univ. of Cairo (BA); Univ. of Geneva (PhD Internat. Law); Univ. of Ohio (Master Internat. Affairs); Inst. of Public Admin, Khartoum (DPA); Univ. of Khartoum (LLB). Part-time Journalist, El-Ayam and El-Sahafa (newspapers), Sudan, 1971–79; Lecturer: in Philosophy and Jurisp., Univ. of Cairo, 1976–77; in Jurisp., Ohio Univ., 1978; Asst Dir, Res. Dept, subseq. Dep. Dir, Legal Dept, Min. of Foreign Affairs, Sudan, 1978; Vice-Consul in Switzerland, and Legal Advr, Sudan Perm. Mission to UN Office, Geneva, 1979–82; Sen. Prog. Officer, Develt Co-operation and External Relns Bureau for Africa, 1982–85, Dir, Develt Co-operation and External Relns Bureau for Arab and Central and European Countries, 1985–94, WIPO. Prof. of Public Internat. Law, Univ. of Khartoum. Advocate and Comr of Oaths, Republic of Sudan. Member: UN Internat. Law Commn, 1992–96, 2000–01; Sudan Bar Assoc.; African Jurists Assoc. Comdr, Ordre Nat. du Lion (Senegal), 1998. *Publications:* articles on law, econs, jurisp. and aesthetics in jls. *Address:* (office) 34 Chemin des Colombettes, 1211 Geneva, Switzerland. *T:* (22) 3389111.

IDRIS JONES, Denise; *see* Jones, D. I.

IEMMA, Hon. Morris; MP (ALP) Lakemba, New South Wales, since 1999; Premier of New South Wales, since 2005; *b* July 1961; *s* of George and Maria Iemma; *m* 1997, Santina Raiti; three *s* one *d*. *Educ:* Narwee Boys' High Sch.; Univ. of Technology, Sydney (LLB); Univ. of Sydney (BEc). Industrial Officer, Commonwealth Bank Officers Assoc., 1984–86; Advr to Senator Graham Richardson, Minister for Envmt, Arts, Sport, Tourism and Territories, Australian Nat. Parlt, 1986–91. Government of New South Wales: MP (ALP) Hurstville, 1991–99; Member: Parly Constitutional Fixed Terms Cttee, 1991–92; Parly Regulation Rev. Cttee, 1991–95; Parly Sec. to the Premier, 1995–99; Minister: for Public Works and Services, 1999–2003; Assisting the Premier on Citizenship, 1999–2003; for Sport and Recreation, 2001–03; for Health, 2003–05; for Citizenship, 2005–; for State and Regl Develt, 2006–07; Treasurer, 2005–06. Mem., ALP, 1977–. *Recreations:* all sports, particularly Australian Rules, league and soccer, blues music, cinema. *Address:* Office of the Premier, Level 40, Governor Macquarie Tower, 1 Farrer Place, Sydney, NSW 2000, Australia. *T:* (02) 92285239, *Fax:* (02) 92283935.

IFE, Prof. Barry William, CBE 2000; PhD; Principal, Guildhall School of Music & Drama, since 2004; *b* 19 June 1947; *s* of Bernard Edward Ife and Joan Mary (*née* Thacker); *m* 1st, 1968, Anne Elizabeth Vernon (marr. diss. 1985); 2nd, 1986, Christine Mary Whiffen (marr. diss. 1998); two *s*; partner, Dr Trudi Laura Darby. *Educ:* King's Coll., London (BA Hons 1968; FKC 1992); Birkbeck Coll., London (PhD 1984). ALCM 1965. Asst Lectr in Spanish, 1969–71, Lectr, 1971–72, Univ. of Nottingham; Lectr in Spanish, Birkbeck Coll., London, 1972–88; King's College, London: Cervantes Prof of Spanish, 1988–2004; Hd, Sch. of Humanities, 1989–96; Vice-Principal, 1997–2003; Actg Principal, 2003–04. Leverhulme Res. Fellow, 1983–85. Trustee: Boise Foundn, 2004–; Mendelssohn Scholarship Foundn, 2004–; Mem. Cttee, City of London Fest., 2004–. Gov., RAM, 1998–2004. Fellow, Birkbeck, Univ. of London, 2007. Hon. FRAM 2001. *Publications:* Dos Versiones de Piramo y Tisbe, 1974; Francisco de Quevedo: La Vida del Buscón, 1977; Anthology of Early Keyboard Methods, 1981; Domenico Scarlatti, 1985; Reading and Fiction in Golden-Age Spain, 1985; Early Spanish Keyboard Music, 1986; Antonio Soler: Twelve Sonatas, 1989; Christopher Columbus: Journal of the First Voyage, 1990; Lectura y Ficción, 1992; Letters from America, 1992; Miguel de Cervantes: Exemplary Novels, 1993; Corpus of Contemporary Spanish, 1995; Don Quixote's Diet, 2000; contrib. articles and reviews to Bull. Hispanic Studies, MLR, Jl Inst. Romance Studies, TLS and others. *Recreations:* music, literature, sorting things out. *Address:* Guildhall School of Music & Drama, Barbican, EC2Y 8DT; *e-mail:* barry.ife@gsmd.ac.uk; Hasketon Grange, Grundisburgh Road, Hasketon, Woodbridge, Suffolk IP13 6HN.

IGGO, Prof. Ainsley, PhD, DSc; FRCPE; FRS 1978; FRSE; Professor of Veterinary Physiology, University of Edinburgh, 1962–90, now Emeritus; *b* 2 Aug. 1924; *s* of late Lancelot George Iggo and late Catherine Josefine Fraser; *m* 1952, Betty Joan McCurdy, PhD, *d* of late Donald A. McCurdy, OBE; three *s*. *Educ:* Gladstone Sch., NZ; Southland Technical High Sch., NZ; Lincoln Coll., NZ (Sen. Scholar; MAgrSc 1947); Univ. of Otago (BSc 1949). PhD Aberdeen, 1954; DSc Edinburgh, 1962. FRSE 1962; FRCPE 1985. Asst Lectr in Physiology, Otago Univ. Med. Sch., 1948–50; NZ McMillan Brown Trav. Fellow, Rowett Inst., 1950–51; Lectr in Physiol., Univ. of Edinburgh Med. Sch., 1952–60; Nuffield Royal Soc. Commonwealth Fellow, ANU, 1959; Royal Soc. Locke Res. Fellow, 1960–62; Dean, Faculty of Veterinary Med., Univ. of Edinburgh, 1974–77 and 1985–90. Vis. Professor: Univ. of Ibadan, Nigeria, 1968; (also Leverhulme Res. Fellow) Univ. of Kyoto, 1970; Univ. of Heidelberg, 1972. Chm., IUPS Somatosensory Commn, 1974–84. Mem. Council: RCVS, 1975–78 and 1985–90; Royal Soc., 1982–83; Pres., Internat. Assoc. for Study of Pain, 1980–83. Governor, E of Scotland Coll. of Agriculture, 1968–77. Hon. DSc Pennsylvania; Hon. DVM&S Edinburgh, 1993. *Publications:* (ed) Sensory Physiology: Vol. II, Somatosensory System, 1973; articles on neurophysiol topics in Jl Physiol., etc. *Recreation:* gardening. *Address:* 5 Relugas Road, Edinburgh EH9 2NE. *T:* (0131) 667 4879.

IGNARRO, Prof. Louis J., PhD; Professor, Department of Molecular and Medical Pharmacology, University of California, Los Angeles, since 1985; *b* 31 May 1941; *m* 1st (marr. diss.); one *d*; 2nd, 1997, Sharon Elizabeth Williams. *Educ:* Long Beach High Sch.; Columbia Univ. (BA 1962); Univ. of Minnesota (PhD 1966). Post-doctoral Fellow, NIH, 1966–68; Hd, Biochem. and Anti-inflammatory Prog., Geigy Pharmaceuticals, 1968–73; Asst Prof., 1973–79, Prof., 1979–85, Dept of Pharmacol., Sch. of Medicine, Tulane Univ. Mem., US Nat. Acad. of Scis. Nobel Prize for Medicine (jtly), 1998. *Publications:* articles in scientific jls. *Address:* Department of Molecular and Medical Pharmacology, University of California, 10833 Le Conte Avenue, Los Angeles, CA 90095, USA.

IGNATIEFF, Prof. Michael, PhD; MP (L) Etobicoke-Lakeshore, Canada, since 200 writer; *b* 12 May 1947; *s* of George Ignatieff and Alison (*née* Grant); *m* 1st, 1977, Susa Barrowclough (marr. diss. 1998); one *s* one *d*; 2nd, 1999, Suzanna Zsohar. *Educ:* Upp Canada Coll., Toronto; Univ. of Toronto (BA 1969); Cambridge Univ. (MA 1978 Harvard Univ. (PhD 1975). Asst Prof. of History, Univ. of BC, 1976–78; Sen. Re Fellow, King's Coll., Cambridge, 1978–84; Vis. Fellow, Ecole des Hautes Etudes, Pari 1985; Alistair Horne Fellow, St Antony's Coll., Oxford, 1993–95; Visiting Professo Univ. of Calif, Berkeley, 1997; LSE, 1998–2000; Carr Prof. of Human Rights Polic Kennedy Sch. of Govt, Harvard Univ., 2000–06. Presenter: Voices, Channel 4, 198 Thinking Aloud, BBC TV Series, 1987–88; The Late Show, BBC TV, 1989–95; Bloo and Belonging, BBC, 1993; Trial of Freedom, C4, 1999; The Future of War, BBC, 200 Editorial Columnist, The Observer, 1990–93. Hon. DPhil Stirling, 1996. *Publications:* Just Measure of Pain, 1978; The Needs of Strangers, 1984; The Russian Album, 198 (Canadian Governor General's Award, 1988; Heinemann Prize, RSL, 1988); Asya, 199 Scar Tissue, 1993; Blood and Belonging, 1993; The Warrior's Honour: ethnic war an the modern conscience, 1998; Isaiah Berlin: a life, 1998; Virtual War: Kosovo and beyon 2000; The Rights Revolution, 2000; Human Rights as Politics and Idolatry, 2001; Empi Lite, 2003; Charlie Johnson in the Flames, 2003; The Lesser Evil: political ethics in an ag of terror, 2004. *Recreations:* walking, talking, wine, theatre, music. *Address:* c/o A. P. Wa Ltd, 20 John Street, WC1N 2DR; House of Commons, Ottawa, ON K1A 0A6, Canada

IKERRIN, Viscount; Arion Thomas Piers Hamilton Butler; *b* 1 Sept. 1975; *s* an *heir* of 10th Earl of Carrick, *qv*.

ILCHESTER, 10th Earl of, *cr* 1756; **Robin Maurice Fox-Strangways;** Baron Ilchest of Ilchester, Somerset, and Baron Strangways of Woodsford, Dorset, 1741; Baron Ilchest and Stavordale of Redlynch, Somerset, 1747; *b* 2 Sept. 1942; *s* of Hon. Raymond Fo Strangways, 2nd *s* of 8th Earl of Ilchester and Margaret Vera (*née* Force); *S* uncle, 2006; 1969, Margaret Elizabeth, *d* of late Geoffrey Miles; one *s* one *d*. *Educ:* Loughborough Col *Heir:* *s* Lord Stavordale, *qv*.

ILERSIC, Prof. Alfred Roman; Emeritus Professor of Social Studies, Bedford Colleg University of London, since 1984 (Professor, 1965–84); *b* 14 Jan. 1920; *s* of late Roma Ilersic and Mary (*née* Moss); *m* 1st, 1944, Patricia Florence Bertram Liddle (marr. dis 1976); one *s* one *d*; 2nd, 1976, June Elaine Browning. *Educ:* Polytechnic Sec. Sch London; London Sch. of Economics. Lectr in Econs, University Coll. of S West, Exete 1947–53; Lectr in Social Statistics, Bedford Coll., 1953; Reader in Economic and Soci Statistics, Bedford Coll., London, 1963. Vis. Prof., Univ. of Bath, 1983–87. Mem., Co of Living Adv. Cttee, 1970–88. Chm., Inst. of Statisticians, 1968–70. Mem., Wilts CC 1989–93. Hon. Mem., Rating and Valuation Assoc., 1968. *Publications:* Statistics, 195 Government Finance and Fiscal Policy in Post-War Britain, 1956; (with P. F. B. Liddl Parliament of Commerce 1860–1960, 1960; Taxation of Capital Gains, 1962; Ra Equalisation in London, 1968; Local Government Finance in Northern Ireland, 196 *Recreations:* listening to music, walking.

ILIC, Fiona Jane; *see* Alexander, F. J.

ILIESCU, Ion; Member of Senate, Romania, 1996–2000 and since 2004; President Romania, 1990–96 and 2000–04; *b* 3 March 1930; *s* of Alexandru and Maria Iliescu; 1951, Elena Şerbănescu. *Educ:* Bucharest Poly. Inst.; Moscow Energy Inst. Design Eng and Researcher, Energy Engrg Inst., Bucharest, 1955–56; Chm., Nat. Water Resourc Council, 1979–84; Dir, Tech. Publishing House, 1984–89. President: Council, Na Salvation Front, 1989–90; Provisional Council for Nat. Unity, 1990; Pres. of Romani 1990–92, then, on first constitutional mandate, 1992–96; Pres., Social Democratic Par (formerly Party of Social Democracy) of Romania, 1996–2000, now Hon. Pre *Publications:* Global Issues: Creativity, 1992; Revolution and Reform, 1993; Romania i Europe and in the World, 1994; The Revolution as I lived it, 1995; Diplomatic Autumn 1995; Moments of History, vol. I 1995, vols II and III 1996; Romanian-America Dialogues, 1998; Political Life Between Dialogue and Violence, 1998; Where to? Romanian Society, 1999; Hope Reborn, 2001; Romanian Revolution, 2001; Integratio and Globalisation, 2003; The Great Shock at the End of a Short Century, 2004; Romania Culture and European Identity, 2005; For Sustainable Development, 2005. *Recreation* reading, theatre, opera, classical music concerts. *Address:* Str. Molière 3, Buchares Romania.

ILIFFE, family name of **Baron Iliffe**.

ILIFFE, 3rd Baron *cr* 1933, of Yattendon; **Robert Peter Richard Iliffe;** DL; Chairman Yattendon Investment Trust PLC, since 1984; *b* Oxford, 22 Nov. 1944; *s* of late Hon. W H. R. Iliffe and Mrs Iliffe; *S* uncle, 1996; *m* 1966, Rosemary Anne Skipwith; three *s* on *d* (of whom one *s* one *d* are twins). *Educ:* Eton; Christ Church, Oxford. Subsidiary cos c Yattendon Investment Trust: Marina Developments Ltd; Cambridge Newspapers Ltd Herts & Essex Newspapers Ltd; Staffordshire Newspapers Ltd; Channel TV Holdings Ltd Yattendon Estates Ltd. Former Chairman: Birmingham Post and Mail Ltd; West Midland Press Ltd; Dillons Newsagents. Member of Council, RASE, 1972– (Chm., 1994–98) Mem., Governing Body, Bradfield Coll., 1996– (Warden, 2001–06). High Sheriff o Warwicks, 1983–84; DL Berks, 2007. *Recreations:* yachting, shooting, fishing, old cars *Heir:* *s* Hon. Edward Richard Iliffe, *b* 13 Sept. 1968. *Address:* Barn Close, Yattendon Thatcham, Berks RG18 0UX. *Clubs:* Boodle's; Royal Yacht Squadron (Cdre, 2005–).

ILIFFE, Prof. John; Professor of African History, University of Cambridge, 1990–2006 now Emeritus; Fellow of St John's College, Cambridge, since 1971; *b* 1 May 1939; 2nd of late Arthur Ross Iliffe and Violet Evelyn Iliffe. *Educ:* Framlingham Coll.; Peterhouse Cambridge (BA 1961; MA; PhD 1965; LittD 1990). Lectr, then Reader, in History, Univ of Dar-es-Salaam, 1965–71; University of Cambridge: Asst Dir of Res. in Hist., 1971–80 Reader in African Hist., 1980–90. FBA 1989–2006. *Publications:* Tanganyika unde German Rule, 1969; A Modern History of Tanganyika, 1979; The Emergence of Africa Capitalism, 1983; The African Poor: a history, 1987; Famine in Zimbabwe, 1989 Africans: the history of a continent, 1995, 2nd edn 2007; East African Doctors: a history of the modern profession, 1998; Honour in African History, 2005; The African Aid Epidemic: a history, 2006. *Recreation:* cricket. *Address:* St John's College, Cambridge CB2 1TP. *T:* (01223) 338714. *Club:* MCC.

ILLINGWORTH, David Gordon, CVO 1987 (LVO 1980); MD, FRCPE; retired Surgeon Apothecary to HM Household at Holyrood Palace, Edinburgh, 1970–86; *b* 22 Dec. 1921; *yr s* of Sir Gordon Illingworth; *m* 1946, Lesley Beagrie, Peterhead; two *s* one *d*. *Educ:* George Watson's Coll.; Edinburgh University. MB, ChB Edinburgh, 1943 MRCPE 1949; MD (with commendation) 1963; FRCPE 1965; FRCGP 1970. Nuffield Foundn Travelling Fellow, 1966. RN Medical Service, 1944–46 (2nd Escort Gp); medica appts, Edinburgh Northern Hosps Group, 1946–82. Dep. CMO, Scottish Life Assurance Co., 1973–92. Hon. Sen. Lectr in Rehabilitation Studies, Dept of Orthopaedic Surgery Edinburgh Univ., 1977–82; Lectr in Gen. Practice Teaching Unit, Edinburgh Univ. 1965–82. Member: Cancer Planning Group, Scottish Health Service Planning Council

1976–81; Tenovus, Edinburgh, 1978–92; ASH, Royal Colleges Jt Cttee, 1978–82; Specialty Sub-Cttee on Gen. Practice, 1980–82; Nat. Med. Cons. Cttee, 1980–82. AFOM, RCP, 1980. Mem., Harveian Soc. Life Governor, Imperial Cancer Res. Fund, 1978. *Publications:* Practice (jtly), 1978; (contrib.) By Royal Command, ed H. Buckton, 1997; The Bridge With Broken Arches (autobiog.), 2003; contribs to BMJ, Jl of Clinical Pathology, Gut, Lancet, Medicine. *Recreations:* golf, gardening. *Address:* 19 Napier Road, Edinburgh EH10 5AZ. *T:* (0131) 229 8102. *Clubs:* University (Edinburgh); Bruntsfield Links Golfing Soc.

ILLINGWORTH, David Jeremy, FCA; Partner, 1975–2001, Senior Adviser, 2001–04, KPMG (formerly KMG Thomson McLintock); President, Institute of Chartered Accountants in England and Wales, 2003–04; *b* Stockport, Cheshire, 28 April 1947; *s* of late Prof. Charles Raymond Illingworth and Joan Ellen Mary Illingworth; *m* 1968, Annie Vincenza Bailey; two *d. Educ:* Stockport Sch.; Emmanuel Coll., Cambridge (BA 1968). ACA 1971, FCA 1972. Trainee, KMG Thomson McLintock, 1968–71. Non-exec. Dir, Nuclear Decommng Authy, 2004– (Chm., Audit Cttee). Indep. Chm., Trinity Retirement Benefit Scheme, 2006–. Mem., Cttee, Manchester Soc. of Chartered Accountants, 1983–2004 (Pres., 1992–93); Mem. Council, 1997–2006, Vice-Pres., 2001–02, Dep. Pres., 2002–03, Chm., NW Regl Bd, 2004–07, ICAEW. NW Regl Council Mem., CBI, 1993–2003. Mem. Cttee, Duke of Westminster Awards for Business and Industry in the NW, 1995–2001. Mem. Council, 2006–, Trustee and Mem. Exec. Cttee, 2007–, C&G. Governor: Oldham Hulme Grammar Schs (formerly Hulme Grammar Schs, Oldham), 1992– (Chm., 2008–); Withington Girls Sch., 2006– (Treas., 2007–). FRSA. Liveryman, Co. of Chartered Accountants, 2002– (Mem. Court, 2007–). *Recreations:* travel, golf, music, theatre, opera, walking. *Address:* Alphin, 7 Park Lane, Greenfield, Oldham OL3 7DX. *T:* (01457) 875971. *Clubs:* St James' (Manchester); Saddleworth Golf (Oldham).

ILLINGWORTH, Raymond, CBE 1973; cricketer; Manager, Yorkshire County Cricket Club, 1979–84; Chairman of Selectors, Test and County Cricket Board, 1994–96; and Manager, England Cricket Team, 1995–96; *b* 8 June 1932; *s* of late Frederick Spencer Illingworth and Ida Illingworth; *m* 1958, Shirley Milnes; two *d. Educ:* Wesley Street Sch., Farsley, Pudsey. Yorkshire County cricketer; capped, 1955. Captain: MCC, 1969; Leics CCC, 1969–78; Yorks CCC, 1982–83. Toured: West Indies, 1959–60; Australia twice (once as Captain), 1962–63 and 1970–71. Played in 66 Test Matches (36 as Captain). Hon. MA Hull, 1983; Hon. Dr Leeds Metropolitan, 1997. *Publications:* Spinners Wicket, 1969; The Young Cricketer, 1972; Spin Bowling, 1979; Captaincy, 1980; Yorkshire and Back, 1980; (with Kenneth Gregory) The Ashes, 1982; The Tempestuous Years 1977–83, 1987; One Man Committee, 1996. *Recreations:* golf, bridge. *Address:* The Mistle, 4 Calverley Lane, Farsley, Pudsey, West Yorkshire LS28 5LB.

ILLMAN, John, CMG 1999; HM Diplomatic Service, retired; Ambassador to Peru, 1995–99; *b* 26 Oct. 1940; *s* of Reginald Thomas Illman and Hilda Kathleen Illman (*née* Targett); *m* 1962, Elizabeth Hunter Frame; one *s* two *d. Educ:* Reading Sch.; St Andrews Univ. Joined Foreign Office, 1961: Leopoldville, later Kinshasa, 1963–66; Dublin, 1967–71; Paris, 1971–73; First Sec., FCO, 1973–75; Buenos Aires, 1975–79; Lagos, 1979–82; Commonwealth Co-ordination Dept, FCO, 1982–86; Dep. Head of Mission and Consul-Gen., Algiers, 1986–90; Consul-Gen., Marseilles and for Principality of Monaco, 1990–94. Member: Anglo-Peruvian Trade and Investment Gp, 1997–; Anglo-Peruvian Soc., 1999– (Chm., 2003–04). Freeman, City of London, 2000. Chairman: BCT Peru, 1998–; MS Yavari Trust, 2006– (Trustee, 2002–). Pres., Old Redingensians Assoc., 2003. *Recreations:* squash, tennis, Rugby, cricket, amateur dramatics. *Clubs:* Royal Commonwealth Society, Candlewick Ward.

ILLSLEY, Anthony Kim; non-executive Chairman: Plastic Logic Ltd, since 2006; Velocix Ltd, since 2007; *b* 8 July 1956. *Educ:* Loughborough Grammar Sch.; Bath Univ. (BSc Business Admin). Mktg and Sales Trainee, subseq. Gp Brand Manager, Colgate Palmolive, 1979–84; joined Pepsico, 1984: European Mktg Manager, subseq. Ops Dir, Pepsicola International; resp. for business in France, Belgium and Scandinavia, Pepsi-Cola; President: Pepsicola Japan; Asia Pacific Div., Hong Kong; Walkers Snack Foods UK Ltd, 1995–98; CEO, Telewest Communications, 1998–2000. Non-executive Chairman: Leisure Link Hldgs Ltd, 2002–05; Power Paper Ltd, 2005–06; non-executive Director: EasyJet, 2000–05; GCap Media plc (formerly Capital Radio), 2000–; Northern Foods plc, 2006–; Sepura plc, 2007–.

ILLSLEY, Eric Evlyn; MP (Lab) Barnsley Central, since 1987; *b* 9 April 1955; *s* of John and Maude Illsley; *m* 1978, Dawn Webb; two *d. Educ:* Barnsley Holgate Grammar Sch.; Leeds Univ. (LLB Hons 1977). NUM, Yorkshire Area: Compensation Officer, 1978–81; Asst Head of General Dept, 1981–84; Head of Gen. Dept and Chief Admin. Officer, 1984–87. An Opposition Whip, 1991–94; Opposition spokesperson: on health, 1994–95; on local govt, April–Oct. 1995; on NI, 1995–97. Member, Select Committee: on televising proceedings of H of C, 1988–91; on Energy, 1987–91; on Procedure, 1991–; on Foreign Affairs, 1997–; Mem., Speaker's Panel of Chairmen, 1999–; Chm., All Party Parly Packaging Manufg Industry Gp, 2005–; Jt Chm., All Party Parly Glass Gp, 1992–2002; Vice Chm., All Party Parly Gp on Occupnl Pensions, 1997– (Treas., 1993–97); Mem., Parly and Scientific Cttee, 1987– (Jt Hon. Sec., 1994–95; Jt Dep. Chm., 1995–98; Vice-Pres., 1998–2001). Sec., Barnsley Constit. Lab. Pty, 1980–83 (Treas., 1979–80); Sec. and Election Agent, Yorks S Eur. Constit. Lab. Pty, 1983–87; Treas., Yorks Gp of Lab. MPs, 1988–. Member Executive Committee: CPA, 1997–; IPU, 1997–. *Recreation:* golf. *Address:* House of Commons, Westminster, SW1A 0AA. *T:* (020) 7219 4863, (office) (01226) 730692.

ILLSLEY, Prof. Raymond, CBE 1979; PhD; Professorial Fellow in Social Policy, University of Bath, 1984–2003; *b* 6 July 1919; *s* of James and Harriet Illsley; *m* 1948, Jean Mary Harrison; two *s* one *d. Educ:* St Edmund Hall, Oxford (BA 1948); PhD Aberdeen 1956. Served War, 1939–45: active service in GB and ME, 1939–42; PoW, Italy and Germany, 1942–45. Econ. Asst, Commonwealth Econ. Cttee, London, 1948; Social Res. Officer, New Town Develt Corp., Crawley, Sussex, 1948–50; Sociologist, MRC, working with Dept of Midwifery, Univ. of Aberdeen, as Mem., Social Med. Res. Unit and later Mem., Obstetric Med. Res. Unit, 1951–64; Prof. of Sociology, Univ. of Aberdeen, 1964–75, Prof. of Medical Sociology, 1975–84. Dir, MRC Medical Sociology Unit, 1965–83. Vis. Prof., Cornell Univ., NY, 1963–64; Vis. Scientist, Harvard Univ., 1968; Sen. Foreign Scientist, National Sci. Foundn, Boston Univ., 1971–72; Vis. Prof., Dept of Sociology, Boston Univ., 1971–72, Adjunct Prof., 1972–76. Chairman: Scottish TUC Inquiry on Upper Clyde Shipbuilders Ltd, 1971; Social Sciences Adv. Panel, Action for the Crippled Child, 1971–76; Health Services Res. Cttee, Chief Scientist's Org., SHHD, 1976–84. Member: Sec. of State's Scottish Council on Crime, 1972–76; Exec. Cttee, Nat. Fund for Res. into Crippling Diseases, 1972–76; Chief Scientist's Cttee, SHHD, 1973–85; EEC Cttee on Med. Res., 1974–77; SSRC, 1976–78 (Chairman: Sociol. and Soc. Admin Cttee, 1976–79; Social Affairs Cttee, 1982–85); Chief Scientist's Adv. Cttee, DHSS, 1980–81; European Adv. Cttee for Med. Res., WHO, 1981–85. Rock Carling Fellow, Nuffield Prov. Hosps Trust, 1980. Hon. DSc Univ. of Hull, 1984; DUniv Stirling, 1987; Hon. dr med. Copenhagen, 1992. *Publications:* Mental Subnormality in the Community: a clinical and epidemiological study (with H. Birch, S. Richardson, D. Baird et al), 1970; Professional or Public Health, 1980; (with R. G. Mitchell) Low Birth Weight, 1984; articles in learned jls on reproduction, migration, social mobility, mental subnormality. *Recreation:* rough husbandry. *Address:* Tisbut House, Box Hill, Wilts SN13 8HG. *T:* (01225) 742313.

ILLSTON, Prof. John Michael, CEng, FICE; Director of the Hatfield Polytechnic, 1982–87, Professor and Professor Emeritus, 1987, Fellow, 1991; *b* 17 June 1928; *s* of Alfred Charles Illston and Ethel Marian Illston; *m* 1951, Olga Elizabeth Poulter; one *s* two *d. Educ:* Wallington County Grammar Sch.; King's Coll., Univ. of London (BScEng, PhD, DScEng; FKC 1985). CEng, FICE 1975. Water engr, then schoolmaster, 1949–59; Lectr, Sen. Lectr and Reader in Civil Engrg, King's Coll., London, 1959–77; Dir of Studies in Civil Engrg, Dean of Engrg, and Dep. Dir, Hatfield Polytechnic, 1977–82. Member: Commonwealth Scholarships Commn, 1983–92; Engrg Bd, SERC, 1983–86; Engrg Council, 1984–90; Council, BTEC, 1986–89; Chm., CNAA Cttee for Engrg, 1987–91; Visitor, Building Res. Stn, 1989–95. Chairman: Govs, Bishop Wordsworth Sch., 1994–98; Salisbury Br., CRUSE Bereavement Care, 1998–2001; Salisbury and Dist, Univ. of Third Age, 2002–05. *Publications:* (with J. M. Dinwoodie and A. A. Smith) Concrete, Timber and Metals, 1979; (ed) Construction Materials, 2nd edn 1994, 3rd edn 2001; contrib. Cement and Concrete Res. and Magazine of Concrete Res. *Address:* 10 Merrifield Road, Ford, Salisbury, Wilts SP4 6DF.

ILVES, Toomas Hendrik, Hon. GCB 2006; President of Republic of Estonia, since 2006; *b* Stockholm, 26 Dec. 1953; *m* Evelin; one *s* two *d. Educ:* Columbia Univ., USA (BA Psychol. 1976); Pennsylvania Univ. (MA Psychol. 1978). Res. Asst, Dept of Psychol., Columbia Univ., 1974–79; Asst Dir and English teacher, Open Educn Center, Englewood, NJ, 1979–81; Dir and Adminr of Art, Vancouver Arts Center, Canada, 1981–83; Lectr in Estonian Lit. and Linguistics, Dept of Interdisciplinary Studies, Simon Fraser Univ., Vancouver, 1983–84; analyst and researcher, res. unit, 1984–88, Hd, Estonian desk, 1988–93, Radio Free Europe, Munich; Ambassador of Estonia to USA, Canada and Mexico, 1993–96; Minister of Foreign Affairs, 1996–98; Chm., N Atlantic Inst., 1998; Minister of Foreign Affairs, 1999–2002; MP Estonia, 2002–04; MEP, 2004–06. Grand Comdr, Légion d'Honneur (France), 2001; Third Cl. Order of the Seal (Estonia), 2004; Three Star Order of Republic (Latvia), 2004; Collar, Order of Cross of Terra Mariana (Estonia), 2006; Order of White Rose (Finland), 2007; Golden Fleece Order (Georgia), 2007; Order of Isabel la Católica (Spain), 2007. *Publication:* Eesti jõudmine: compilation of speeches and writings from 1986–2006, 2006. *Address:* Office of the President, A. Weizenberg 39, 15050 Tallinn, Estonia. *T:* 6316202, *Fax:* 6316250.

IMBERT, family name of **Baron Imbert**.

IMBERT, Baron *cr* 1999 (Life Peer), of New Romney, in the county of Kent; **Peter Michael Imbert,** Kt 1988; CVO 2008; QPM 1980; Lord-Lieutenant of Greater London, 1998–2008; Commissioner, Metropolitan Police, 1987–93 (Deputy Commissioner, 1985–87); *b* 27 April 1933; *s* of late William Henry Imbert and of Frances May (*née* Hodge); *m* 1956, Iris Rosina (*née* Dove); one *s* two *d. Educ:* Harvey Grammar Sch., Folkestone, Kent. Joined Metropolitan Police, 1953; Asst Chief Constable, Surrey Constabulary, 1976, Dep. Chief Constable, 1977; Chief Constable, Thames Valley Police, 1979–85. Metropolitan Police Anti-Terrorist Squad, 1973–75; Police negotiator at Balcome Street siege, Dec. 1975; visited Holland following Moluccan sieges, and Vienna following siege of OPEC building by terrorists, Dec. 1975. Lectures in UK and Europe to police and military on terrorism and siege situations; lecture tours to Australia, 1977, 1980 and 1986, to advise on terrorism and sieges, and to Canada, 1981 re practical effects on police forces of recommendations of Royal Commn on Criminal Procedure; Vis. Internat. Fellow, Australian Police Staff College, 1994 and 1997. Leader, Internat. Criminal Justice Delegn to Russia, 1993. Sec., Nat. Crime Cttee-ACPO Council, 1980–83 (Chm., 1983–85). Non-executive Director: Securicor Gp, 1993–2001; Camelot Gp, 1994–2001; Retainagroup, 1995–; Chm., Capital Eye Security, 1997–. Member: Gen. Advisory Council, BBC, 1980–87; Criminal Justice Consultative Cttee, 1992–93; Mental Health Foundn, Cttee of Inquiry into Care in the Community for the Severely Mentally Ill, 1994; Academic Consultative Cttee, King George VI and Queen Elizabeth Foundn of St Catharine's, Cumberland Lodge, Windsor, 1983–2001; Ministerial Adv. Gp, Royal Parks, 1993–2001; Public Policy Cttee, RAC, 1993–2003. Trustee, Queen Elizabeth Foundn of St Catharine's, 1988–2001. Chm., Surrey CCC Youth Trust, 1993–96; Hon. Life Vice Pres., Surrey CCC, 2004–; Pres., Richmond Horse Show, 1993–99. Gov., Harvey Grammar Sch., 1994–2002. CCMI (CBIM 1982). DL Greater London, 1994. Hon. DLitt Reading, 1987; Hon. DBA IMCB, 1989. *Publications:* occasional articles and book reviews. *Recreations:* bad bridge, coarse golf, talking about my grandchildren. *Address:* House of Lords, SW1A 0PW.

IMBERT-TERRY, Sir Michael Edward Stanley, 5th Bt *cr* 1917, of Strete Ralegh, Whimple, Co. Devon; *b* 18 April 1950; *s* of Major Sir Edward Henry Bouhier Imbert-Terry, 3rd Bt, MC, and of Jean (who *m* 1983, 6th Baron Sackville), *d* of late Arthur Stanley Garton; *S* brother, 1985; *m* 1975, Frances Dorothy, *d* of late Peter Scott, Ealing; two *s* two *d. Educ:* Cranleigh. *Heir: s* Brychan Edward Imbert-Terry, *b* 1975.

IMBODEN, Dr Christoph Niklaus; consultant ecologist; *b* 28 April 1946; *s* of Max Imboden and Elisabeth Imboden-Stahel; *m* 1970, Eve Elisabeth Staub; one *s* one *d. Educ:* Univ. of Basel (PhD). New Zealand Wildlife Service: Sen. Scientist, 1977; Asst Dir (Research), 1978; Dir-Gen., ICBP, later BirdLife Internat., 1980–96; Interim CEO, WWF Switzerland, 2002–03. Mem., Bd of Dirs, Plantlife International. Premio Gaia, Sicily, 1993; RSPB Conservation Medal, 1993. Officer, Order of the Golden Ark (Netherlands), 1996. *Publications:* papers on ornithology, ecology, conservation. *Recreations:* classical music, birdwatching, hill-walking, travelling.

IMISON, Dame Tamsyn, DBE 1998; education strategist; Headteacher, Hampstead School, 1984–2000; *b* 1 May 1937; *m* 1958, Michael Imison; two *d* (one *s* decd). *Educ:* Hitchin Girls' GS; Milham Ford Sch., Oxford; Somerville Coll., Oxford (Hon. Fellow, 1999); Queen Mary Coll., London (BSc Hons Zoology 1964; Hon. Fellow, 2004); Ruskin Sch. of Drawing and Fine Art, Oxford; Inst. of Education, London Univ. (PGCE 1972; Hon. Fellow, 2001); Open Univ. (Cert. of Prof. Develt in Educn 1994; MA Educn 1996). Freelance scientific, exhibn and illustration work for Oxford Mus., British Mus. (Natural History), and Publisher's Editor, Elsevier, 1960–70; Teacher: Brentford Sch. for Girls, 1972–76; Pimlico Sch., 1976–79; Abbey Wood Sch., 1979–84. Member: Secondary Exam. Council, 1986–88 (Chair, A Level and GCSE Biology and Music Cttees); Secondary Heads Council, 1993–98; SHA Exec., 1994–98; various DES Steering Gps; Adv. Gp on Raising Achievement of Ethnic-minority Children; Dir, CRAC Council, 1996–2002; Mem., Nat. Adv. Cttee on Creativity and Cultural Educn, 1997–99; Founder, Nat. Schs Playwright Commning Gp, 1995–2004; Heads' Appraiser, GDST, 1998–2004; Director: Lifelong Learning Foundn, 1999–; 5x5x5=creativity, 2007–; Vice-Pres., Soc. for Promoting the Trng of Women, 2002–; Trustee: Menerva (formerly 300 Gp) Educnl Trust, 1990–99 (Patron, 2001–); Soc. for Furtherance of Critical Philosophy (also Chair), 1994–; I Can (Special Needs charity), 1997–2001. Mem. Council, UCS, 1995–2002. Patron: Students Exploring Marriage, 2001–; Campaign for Learning, 2003–. Scientific Fellow, Zoological Soc. of London, 1966; FRSA 1995. *Publications:* (contrib.) Education 14–19: critical perspectives, 1997; (contrib.) New Teachers in an Urban Comprehensive School, 1997; Managing ICT in the Secondary School, 2001; (contrib.) Enquiring Minds, 2004; scientific illustrations in textbooks. *Recreations:* fun, theatre, painting, gardening, walking, swimming, sailing. *Address:* Magnolia House, Station Road, Halesworth, Suffolk IP19 8BZ. *T:* (01986) 873354; *e-mail:* tamsyn_imison@mac.com.

IMRAN KHAN, (Imran Ahmad Khan Niazi); *see* Khan.

IMRAY, Sir Colin (Henry), KBE 1992; CMG 1983; HM Diplomatic Service, retired; *b* 21 Sept. 1933; *s* of late Henry Gibbon Imray and Frances Olive Imray; *m* 1957, Shirley Margaret Matthews; one *s* three *d*. *Educ:* Highgate Sch.; Hotchkiss Sch., Conn; Balliol Coll., Oxford (2nd cl. Hons PPE, MA). Served in Seaforth Highlanders and RWAFF, Sierra Leone, 1952–54. CRO, 1957; Canberra, 1958–61; CRO, 1961–63; Nairobi, 1963–66; FCO, 1966–70; British Trade Comr, Montreal, 1970–73; Counsellor, Head of Chancery and Consul-Gen., Islamabad, 1973–77; RCDS, 1977; Commercial Counsellor, Tel Aviv, 1977–80; Rayner Project Officer, 1980; Dep. High Comr, Bombay, 1980–84; Asst Under-Sec. of State (Dep. Chief Clerk and Chief Inspector), FCO, 1984–85; High Commissioner: Tanzania, 1986–89; Bangladesh, 1989–93. Order of St John: Sec. Gen., 1993–97; Dir, Overseas Relns, 1997–98. Vice Pres., Royal Over-Seas League, 2005– (Mem., Central Council, 1998–2005; Mem., Exec. Council, 1999–2005; Chm., 1999–2005); Trustee, Jt Commonwealth Societies Trust, 2000–05; Chm., Wallingford Chameleon Arts, 2008–. High Steward, Wallingford, 2002–. KStJ 1993. *Address:* Holbrook House, Reading Road, Wallingford OX10 9DT. *Clubs:* Travellers, Royal Over-Seas League.
See also F. King.

IMRIE, Celia Diana Savile; actress; *b* 15 July 1952; *d* of David and Diana Imrie; one *s*. *Educ:* Guildford High Sch. Advanced Greek Dancing Cert. *Theatre* includes: The Sea, National Th., 1992 (Best Supporting Actress Award); The Royal Family, 2001, Acorn Antiques, 2005, Theatre Royal, Haymarket; *films* include: Highlander, 1986; In the Bleak Midwinter, 1995; The Borrowers, 1997; Hilary and Jackie, 1998; Star Wars: Episode 1, 1999; Bridget Jones's Diary, 2001; Lucky Break, 2001; Calendar Girls, 2003; Wimbledon, 2004; Bridget Jones: The Edge of Reason, 2004; Nanny McPhee, 2005; *television* includes: Bergerac, 1981; Victoria Wood: As Seen on TV, 1985; Acorn Antiques, 1986; Oranges are not the Only Fruit, 1990; The Riff Raff Element, 1993; Blackhearts in Battersea, 1996; The History of Tom Jones, 1997; Dinnerladies, 1998; Gormenghast, 2000; Love in a Cold Climate, 2001; Doctor Zhivago, 2002; Daniel Deronda, 2002; After You've Gone, 2007. *Recreations:* biking by the sea, going to Nice. *Address:* c/o CDA, 125 Gloucester Road, SW7 4TE.

INCH, Thomas David, OBE 2000; CChem, FRSC; Secretary-General, Royal Society of Chemistry, 1993–2000; *b* 25 Sept. 1938; *s* of Thomas Alexander Inch and Sarah Lang Graves Inch; *m* 1964, Jacqueline Vivienne Pudner; one *d*. *Educ:* St Austell Grammar Sch.; Univ. of Birmingham (BSc 1st Cl. Hons Chem. 1960; PhD 1963; DSc 1971). Salters Fellow, Univ. of Birmingham, 1963–64; Vis. Fellow, NIH, USA, 1964–65; Chemical Defence Estabt, MoD, 1965–87 (RCDS 1985); Gen. Manager, Research Business Development, BP Research, 1987–90; Vice-Pres., R&D, BP America, 1990–93. Director: BP Ventures, 1987–89; Edison Polymer Innovation Corp., 1990–92; Ohio Science and Technology Commn, 1992. Chm., Nat. Adv. Cttee, Chemical Weapons Convention, 1997–2005. *Publications:* papers and reviews on chemistry and related topics. *Recreation:* golf. *Address:* 16 Ashlands, Ford, Salisbury SP4 6DY. *Club:* High Post Golf.

INCHBALD, Michael John Chantrey, FCSD; architectural and interior designer; design consultant; *b* 8 March 1920; *s* of late Geoffrey H. E. Inchbald and Rosemary, *d* of Arthur Ilbert and *niece* of Sir Courtenay Ilbert, GCB, KCSI, CIE; *m* 1955, Jacqueline Bromley (*see* J. A. Duncan) (marr. diss. 1964); one *s* one *d*; *m* 1964, Eunice Haymes (marr. diss. 1970). *Educ:* Sherborne; Architect. Assoc. Sch. of Architecture. FCSD (MSIA 1947). Director, Michael Inchbald Ltd, 1953–83. Work exhibited: Triennale, Milan; V & A Mus.; Design Centres London, New York, Helsinki. Design projects for: Bank of America; Crown Estate Comrs; Cunard; Dunhill worldwide; Ferragamo; Imperial Group; Justerini & Brooks; Law Soc.; John Lewis; Manufacturers Hanover Bank; Manufacturers Hanover Trust Bank; John Player; Plessey Co.; Pratt Burnard Engineering; Savoy Group—Berkeley, Claridges and Savoy hotels, and the restaurant complex Stones Chop House; Scottish Highland Industries; Trust House Forte—Post House, London Airport and several restaurants; Wolsey; ships, QE2, Carmania, Franconia and Windsor Castle; royal and private yachts and houses. Consultant to furniture and carpet manufacturers. Consulted *re* changes at Buckingham Palace; other projects, for the Duc de la Rochefoucauld, 13th Duke of St Albans, 8th Marquess of Ailesbury, 6th Marquess of Bristol, 17th Earl of Perth, 9th Earl of Dartmouth, 2nd Earl St Aldwyn, 3rd Baron Gisborough, 6th Baron Kilmarnock, 7th Baron Latymer, and 4th Baron St Levan. Inchbald schs founded under his auspices, 1960. Winner of four out of four nat. design competitions entered, including: Shapes of Things to Come, 1946; Nat. Chair Design Competition, 1955. Freeman, Clockmakers' Co., 1985. Award for outstanding contribution to design, idFX/BIDA, 2005. *Publications:* contrib. Arch. Rev., Arch. Digest, Connaissance des Arts, Connoisseur, Country Life, Harpers/Queen, House & Garden, Internat. Lighting Rev., Tatler, and Vogue. *Recreations:* arts, travel, antiques. *Address:* Stanley House, 10 Milner Street, SW3 2PU. *T:* (020) 7584 8832.

INCHCAPE, 4th Earl of, *cr* 1929; **Kenneth Peter Lyle Mackay,** AIB; Viscount Glenapp 1929; Viscount Inchcape 1924; Baron Inchcape 1911; Director: Glenapp Estate Co. Ltd, since 1980; Inchcape Family Estates (formerly Investments) Ltd, since 1980; Gray Dawes Travel Ltd, since 1996; Assam Oil and Gas Co., since 2006; *b* 23 Jan. 1943; *er s* of 3rd Earl of Inchcape, and of his 1st wife, Mrs Aline Thorn Hannay, *d* of Sir Richard Pease, 2nd Bt; *S* father, 1994; *m* 1966, Georgina, *d* of late S. C. Nisbet and Mrs G. R. Sutton; one *s* two *d*. *Educ:* Eton. Late Lieut 9/12th Royal Lancers. Master, Grocers' Co., 1993–94; Prime Warden, Shipwrights' Co., 1998–99. *Recreations:* shooting, fishing, golf, farming, ski-ing, diving. *Heir: s* Viscount Glenapp, *qv*. *Address:* Manor Farm, Clyffe Pypard, Swindon, Wilts SN4 7PY; 63E Pont Street, SW1X 0BD. *Clubs:* White's, Oriental, Pratt's; New (Edinburgh); Prestwick (Ayrshire); Royal Sydney (Sydney, NSW).
See also Baron Camoys.

INCHIQUIN, 18th Baron of, *cr* 1543; **Conor Myles John O'Brien;** (The O'Brien); Bt 1686; Prince of Thomond; Chief of the Name; *b* 17 July 1943; *s* of Hon. Fionn Myles Maryons O'Brien (*d* 1977) (*y s* of 15th Baron) and of Josephine Reine, *d* of late Joseph Eugene Bembaron; *S* uncle, 1982; *m* 1988, Helen, *d* of Gerald Fitzgerald O'Farrell; two *d*. *Educ:* Eton. Served as Captain, 14th/20th King's Hussars. *Heir: cousin* Conor John Anthony O' Brien, *b* 24 Sept. 1952. *Address:* Thomond House, Dromoland, Newmarket on Fergus, Co. Clare, Ireland.

INCHYRA, 2nd Baron *cr* 1962, of St Madoes, Co. Perth; **Robert Charles Renek Hoyer Millar;** Treasurer, Multiple Sclerosis International Federation, since 2000; *b* April 1935; *er s* of 1st Baron Inchyra, GCMG, CVO and Elizabeth de Marees va Swinderen; *S* father, 1989; *m* 1961, Fiona Mary, *d* of Major E. C. R. Sheffield; one *s* tw *d*. *Educ:* Eton; New Coll., Oxford. J. Henry Schroder Wagg & Co., 1958–64; Barcla Bank, 1964–88: Local Dir, Newcastle upon Tyne, 1967–75; Reg. Gen. Man., 1976–8 Dep. Chm., Barclays Bank Trust Co., 1982–85; Gen. Man. and Dir, UK Financi Services, 1985–88; Sec. (later Dir) Gen., BBA, 1988–94. Chm., European Utilities Tru plc (formerly Johnson Fry, then Legg Mason Investors), 1994–2005; Dir, Wit Investment Co., 1979–2002. Chm., NABC-CYP, subseq. Nat. Assoc. of Clubs for Your People, 1994–2003. *Heir: s* Hon. Christian James Charles Hoyer Millar [*b* 12 Aug. 196 *m* 1992, Caroline, *d* of Robin Swan; one *s* two *d*]. *Address:* Rookley Manor, Kin Somborne, Stockbridge, Hants SO20 6QX. *T:* (01794) 388319. *Clubs:* White's, Pratt's.

IND, Jack Kenneth; Headmaster, Dover College, 1981–91; *b* 20 Jan. 1935; *s* of late Re William Price Ind and Mrs Doris Maud Ind (*née* Cavell); *m* 1964, Elizabeth Olive Toomb two *s* two *d*. *Educ:* Marlborough Coll.; St John's Coll., Oxford (BA Hons Mods, 2nd C Class. Lit. and Lit. Hum.). Teacher: Wellingborough Sch., 1960–63; Tonbridge Sch 1963–81 (Housemaster, 1970–81) and 1991–92; Eastbourne Coll., 1992–93; Gymnásiu Nové Zámky, Slovakia, 1994; Talbot Heath Sch., Bournemouth, 1996–97; Eastbour Coll., 1997–98; Prior Park Coll., Bath, 1999–2001; Eastbourne Coll., 2001–02; (pa time) Brighton Coll., 2002–04; Guildford High Sch., 2004–05; St Catherine's Sch Bramley, 2006–07. Trustee, HMC projects in Central and Eastern Europe, 1997–200 *Recreations:* tennis, Rugby football, music, reading. *Address:* 3 Sheepfold Road, Guildfor Surrey GU2 9TS. *T:* (01483) 832110.

IND, Rt Rev. William; Bishop of Truro, 1997–2008; *b* 26 March 1942; *s* of Willia Robert and Florence Emily Ind; *m* 1967, Frances Isobel Bramald; three *s*. *Educ:* Univ. Leeds (BA); College of the Resurrection, Mirfield. Asst Curate, St Dunstan's, Feltha 1966–71; Priest in charge, St Joseph the Worker, Northolt, 1971–74; Team Vica Basingstoke, 1974–87; Director of Ordinands, dio. of Winchester, 1982–87; Hon. Can of Winchester, 1985–87; Bishop Suffragan of Grantham, 1987–97; Dean of Stamfor 1988–97. *Recreations:* bird watching, cricket watching, orchid finding. *Address:* 15 Dea Close, Melksham, Wilts SN12 7EZ. *T:* (01225) 340979.

INDIAN OCEAN, Archbishop of the, since 2006; **Most Rev. (Gerald James) Ia Ernest,** GOSK 2006; *b* 30 Aug. 1954; *s* of Gerald and Jessie Ernest; *m* 1983, Kam Ramloll; one *s*. *Educ:* Madras Univ., India (BCom 1979); St Paul's Theol Coll., Mauritiu Westhill Coll., Univ. of Birmingham, UK (CPS 1986); Procter Schol., Episcopal Div Sch., Cambridge, Mass and Boston Inst. of Theol., 2005. Ordained priest, 1985; Bisho of Mauritius, 2001–. Mem., 1989–93, Chm., 2001–, Bd of Comrs, Dio. Mauritiu Member: Provincial Standing Cttee and Provincial Electoral Coll., Ch of Province Indian Ocean, 1992–2001; Council of Religious and Spiritual Leaders of Mauritiu 1996–. Convener, Target Gp for Bps Trng, Task Force of Theol Educn for Anglica Communion, 2003–; Mem., Eight Mems Design Gp Cttee, apptd by Archbp Canterbury to prepare for Lambeth Conf. and Anglican Gathering 2008, 2003–. Mai translator of New Testament into Creole, 1987–91; Ed., Anglican Diocesan Mag 1990–95. *Publication:* (jtly) Autonomy for Rodrigues Island. *Recreations:* reading, musi swimming. *Address:* Bishop's House, Dr X. Nalletamby Road, Phoenix, Republic Mauritius. *T:* (home) (230) 6960767, (office) (230) 6865158, *Fax:* (230) 6971096; *e-mai* dioang@intnet.mu.

INGAMELLS, John Anderson Stuart; Senior Fellow, Paul Mellon Centre for Studies i British Art, since 1992; *b* 12 Nov. 1934; *s* of late George Harry Ingamells and Gladys Luc (*née* Rollett); *m* 1964, Hazel Wilson; two *d*. *Educ:* Hastings Grammar School; Eastbour Grammar School; Fitzwilliam House, Cambridge. National Service, Army (Cyprus 1956–58; Art Asst, York Art Gallery, 1959–63; Asst Keeper, Dept of Art, Nation Museum of Wales, 1963–67; Curator, York Art Gallery, 1967–77; Asst to the Directo 1977–78, Director, 1978–92, Wallace Collection. Mem. Exec. Cttee, NACF, 1992–97 *Publications:* The Davies Collection of French Art, 1967; The English Episcopal Portrai 1981; (ed) Dictionary of British and Irish Travellers in Italy 1701–1800, 1997; (ed jtly) Th Letters of Sir Joshua Reynolds, 2001; numerous catalogues, including: Philip Merci (with Robert Raines), 1969; Portraits at Bishopthorpe Palace, 1972; Paintings by Alla Ramsay (ed), 1999; museum catalogues at York, Cardiff, Wallace Collection, Dulwic Picture Gall. and Nat. Portrait Gall.; articles in Apollo, Connoisseur, Burlingto Magazine, Walpole Soc., etc. *Address:* 39 Benson Road, SE23 3RL.

INGE, family name of **Baron Inge.**

INGE, Baron *cr* 1997 (Life Peer), of Richmond in the co. of North Yorkshire; **Fiel Marshal Peter Anthony Inge,** KG 2001; GCB 1992 (KCB 1988); PC 2004; DL; Chi of the Defence Staff, 1994–97; Constable, HM Tower of London, 1996–2001; *b* 5 Aug 1935; *s* of late Raymond Albert Inge and Grace Maud Caroline Inge (*née* Du Rose); 1960, Letitia Marion Beryl, *yr d* of late Trevor and Sylvia Thornton-Berry; two *d*. *Edu* Summer Fields; Wrekin College; RMA Sandhurst. Commissioned Green Howards, 195 served Hong Kong, Malaya, Germany, Libya and UK; ADC to GOC 4 Div., 1960–61 Adjutant, 1 Green Howards, 1963–64; student, Staff Coll., 1966; MoD, 1967–69; Co Comdr, 1 Green Howards, 1969–70; student, JSSC, 1971; BM 11 Armd Bde, 1972 Instructor, Staff Coll., 1973–74; CO 1 Green Howards, 1974–76; Comdt, Junior Div. Staff Coll., 1977–79; Comdr Task Force C/4 Armd Bde, 1980–81; Chief of Staff, HQ (BR) Corps, 1982–83; GOC NE District and Comdr 2nd Inf. Div., 1984–86; Dir Ge Logistic Policy (Army), MoD, 1986–87; Comdr 1st (Br.) Corps, 1987–89; Comd Northern Army Gp, and C-in-C, BAOR, 1989–92; CGS 1992–94. ADC Gen. to th Queen, 1991–94. Colonel, The Green Howards, 1982–94. Col Comdt: RMP, 1987–92 APTC, 1988–97. Non-exec. Dir, Racal Electronics plc, 1997–2000. Comr, Royal Hosp Chelsea, 1998–2004; Trustee, Historic Royal Palaces, 1999–2007. President: Arm Benevolent Fund, 1998–2002; The Pilgrims, 2002–; Member Council: St George' House, Windsor Castle, 1998–2006; Marlborough Coll., 1998–2006. Mem., Hakluy Foundn, 1999–2004; Chm., King Edward VII's Hosp. Sister Agnes, 2004–. DL N Yorks 1994. Hon. DCL Newcastle, 1995. *Recreations:* cricket, walking, music and reading especially military history. *Address:* c/o House of Lords, SW1A 0PW. *Clubs:* Boodle's Beefsteak, Army and Navy, MCC.

INGE, George Patrick Francis, FRICS; Chairman, FPD Savills (formerly Savills Land & Property) Ltd, 1992–2000; *b* 31 Aug. 1941; *s* of late John William Wolstenholme Inge an Alison Lilias Inge; *m* 1977, Joyce (*née* Leinster); one *s* one *d*. *Educ:* Old Malthouse Prep Sch., Dorset; Sherborne Sch. Joined Alfred Savill & Sons, 1960; Partner, 1968; Man Partner, Savills, 1985; Chief Exec., 1987–91, and Chm., 1987–95, Savills Plc. Non-exec Chm., Severn Trent Property Ltd, 1995–2006; non-exec. Dir, Westbury plc, 1995–2003 Governor: Old Malthouse Sch., Dorset, 1977–98 (Chm., 1986–98); Cothill House Sch. 1989–; Nottingham Trent Univ., 1994–96; Downe House Sch., 1996–2004 (Chm. 1999–2004). *Recreations:* shooting, fishing, golf. *Address:* The Old Vicarage, Little Milton, Oxford OX44 7QB. *T:* (01844) 279538. *Clubs:* Buck's, Flyfishers'.

INGE, Rt Rev. John Geoffrey; *see* Worcester, Bishop of.

INGESTRE, Viscount; James Richard Charles John Chetwynd-Talbot; *b* 11 Jan. 1978; *s* and *heir* of 22nd Earl of Shrewsbury and Waterford, *qv*; *m* 2006, Polly Elizabeth, *d* of Henry Blackie. *Educ:* Shrewsbury Sch.; Royal Agricl Coll. MRICS 2002. *Club:* Farmers.

INGHAM, Sir Bernard, Kt 1990; Chairman, Bernard Ingham Communications, since 1990; *b* 21 June 1932; *s* of Garnet and Alice Ingham; *m* 1956, Nancy Hilda Hoyle; one *s*. *Educ:* Hebden Bridge Grammar Sch., Yorks. Reporter: Hebden Bridge Times, 1948–52; Yorkshire Post and Yorkshire Evening Post, Halifax, 1952–59; Yorkshire Post, Leeds, 1959–61; Northern Industrial Correspondent, Yorkshire Post, 1961; Reporter, The Guardian, 1962–65; Labour Staff, The Guardian, London, 1965–67; Press and Public Relns Adviser, NBPI, 1967–68; Chief Inf. Officer, DEP, 1968–73; Dir of Information: Dept of Employment, 1973; Dept of Energy, 1974–77; Under Sec., Energy Conservation Div., Dept of Energy, 1978–79; Chief Press Sec. to Prime Minister, 1979–90; Head, Govt Inf. Service, 1989–90. Columnist: The Express (formerly Daily Express), 1991–98; PR Week, 1994–2001; Yorkshire Post, 2003–. Non-executive Director: McDonald's Restaurants Ltd, 1991–2005 (Mem. Adv. Bd, 2005–); Hill and Knowlton (UK) Ltd, public relations counsel, 1991–2002. Mem. Exec. Cttee, Meml to Women of WWII, 2004–05. Vis. Fellow, Univ. of Newcastle, 1989–2004; Vis. Prof., Middlesex Univ. Business Sch., 1998–. Pres., British Franchise Assoc., 1993–. Sec., Supporters of Nuclear Energy, 1998–. Mem. Council Univ. of Huddersfield, 1994–2000. Hon. DLitt: Buckingham, 1997; Bradford, 2004; DUniv Middlesex, 1999. *Publications:* Kill The Messenger, 1991; Yorkshire Millennium, 1999; Yorkshire Castles, 2001; Yorkshire Villages, 2001; The Wages of Spin, 2003; Yorkshire Greats, 2005. *Recreations:* walking, gardening, reading. *Address:* 9 Monahan Avenue, Purley, Surrey CR8 3BB. *T:* (020) 8660 8970, 07860 535962, *Fax:* (020) 8668 4357; *e-mail:* bernardinghamcom@aol.com. *Clubs:* Reform; Midgehole Working Mens's, Pennine (Hebden Bridge).

INGHAM, Christopher John, CMG 2002; HM Diplomatic Service, retired; Ambassador to Republic of Uzbekistan and (non-resident) to Republic of Tajikistan, 1999–2002; *b* 4 June 1944; *s* of Dr Roland Ingham and Dorothy Ingham; *m* 1968, Jacqueline Anne Clarke; one *s* two *d*. *Educ:* St John's Coll., Cambridge (MA). Mgt trainee, Cadbury Bros Ltd, 1966–68; joined HM Diplomatic Service, 1968; Moscow, 1972–74; Calcutta, 1974; Kuwait, 1974–76; FCO, 1976–80; Dep. Perm. Rep. to IAEA/UNIDO, Vienna, 1980–85; FCO, 1985–87; Hd, Commercial Section, Mexico City, 1987–89; FCO, 1989–91; Counsellor and Dep. Hd of Mission, Bucharest, 1991–95; Counsellor, EU and Economic, Madrid, 1995–99. Mem., Little Chalfont Parish Council, Bucks, 2007. *Recreations:* hill-walking, choral singing.

INGHAM, Prof. Kenneth, OBE 1961; MC 1946; Professor of History, 1967–84, Part-time Professor of History, 1984–86, now Emeritus Professor, and Head of History Department, 1970–84, University of Bristol; *b* 9 Aug. 1921; *s* of Gladson and Frances Lily Ingham; *m* 1949, Elizabeth Mary Southall; one *s* one *d*. *Educ:* Bingley Grammar Sch.; Keble Coll., Oxford (Exhibitioner). Served with West Yorks Regt, 1941–46 (despatches, 1945). Frere Exhibitioner in Indian Studies, University of Oxford, 1947; DPhil 1950. Lecturer in Modern History, Makerere Coll., Uganda, 1950–56, Prof., 1956–62; Dir of Studies, RMA, Sandhurst, 1962–67. MLC, Uganda, 1954–61. *Publications:* Reformers in India, 1956; The Making of Modern Uganda, 1958; A History of East Africa, 1962; The Kingdom of Toro in Uganda, 1975; Jan Christian Smuts: the conscience of a South African, 1986; Politics in Modern Africa, 1990; Obote: a political biography, 1994; contrib. to Encyclopædia Britannica, Britannica Book of the Year. *Address:* The Woodlands, 94 West Town Lane, Bristol BS4 5DZ.

INGHAM, Rt Rev. Michael; *see* New Westminster, Bishop of.

INGHAM, Prof. Philip William, DPhil; FMedSci; FRS 2002; FIBiol; Professor of Developmental Genetics and Director, MRC Centre for Developmental and Biomedical Genetics (formerly Centre for Developmental Genetics), University of Sheffield, since 1996; Deputy Director, Institute of Molecular and Cell Biology, Singapore, since 2006; *b* 19 March 1955; *s* of late George Philip Ingham and of Dorothy Ingham; *m* 1993, Anita Maria Taylor; one *s* two *d*. *Educ:* Queens' Coll., Cambridge (BA, MA); Univ. of Sussex (DPhil 1981). FIBiol 2000. Res. Scientist, MRC, 1986; Imperial Cancer Research Fund: Res. Scientist, 1986–91; Sen. Scientist, 1991–94; Principal Scientist, 1994–96. Chm., British Soc. for Develtl Biol., 1999–. Mem., EMBO, 1995. FMedSci 2001. Hon. FRCP 2007. Genetics Soc. Medal, 2005. *Publications:* contrib. scientific papers to Cell, Nature, Science, Genes and Develt, Develt, Develtl Biol. *Recreations:* music, playing tennis, walking, gardening, watching football and Rugby, reading. *Address:* MRC Centre for Developmental and Biomedical Genetics, Department of Biomedical Science, Firth Court, Western Bank, Sheffield S10 2TN. *T:* (0114) 222 2710, *Fax:* (0114) 276 5413; *e-mail:* p.w.ingham@sheffield.ac.uk.

INGHAM, Stuart Edward; Chief Executive, United Leeds Teaching Hospitals NHS Trust, 1991–98; *b* 9 Oct. 1942; *s* of Edward Ingham and Dorothy Mary (*née* Pollard); *m* 1969, Jane Stella Wilkinson; one *s* one *d*. *Educ:* Canon Slade Grammar Sch., Bolton. AHSM 1970. Bolton and District HMC: Trainee in Hosp. Admin, 1965–66; HCO, 1966–67; Dep. Gen. Supt, Ancoats Hosp., 1967–69; Sen. Admin Asst, Royal Bucks and Associated HMC, 1969–70; Hospital Secretary: Harefield Hosp., 1970–73; St James's Univ. Hosp., Leeds, 1973–74; Leeds Area Health Authority (Eastern): General Administrator, 1974–77; Dist Administrator, 1977–82; York Health Authority: Dist Administrator, 1982–84; Dist Gen. Manager, 1985–88; Dist Gen. Manager, Leeds Western HA, 1988–90. *Recreation:* equestrian sports. *Address:* The Turnings, Woodacre Crescent, Bardsey, Leeds LS17 9DQ.

INGILBY, Sir Thomas (Colvin William), 6th Bt *cr* 1866; FAAV; managing own estate; *b* 17 July 1955; *s* of Sir Joslan William Vivian Ingilby, 5th Bt, DL, JP, and of Diana, *d* of late Sir George Colvin, CB, CMG, DSO; *S* father, 1974; *m* 1984, Emma Clare Roebuck, *d* of Major R. R. Thompson, Whinfield, Strensall, York; four *s* one *d*. *Educ:* Aysgarth Sch., Bedale; Eton Coll.; Royal Agricultural Coll., Cirencester. MRAC; MRICS; FBII. Joined Army, May 1974, but discharged on death of father; Assistant: Stephenson & Son, York, 1978–80; Strutt & Parker, Harrogate, 1981–83. Chairman: Harrogate Mgt Centre Ltd, 1991–99; Action Harrogate Ltd, 1992–98. Dir, Yorks Tourist Bd, 1997– (Dep. Chm., 2005–). Founder and Nat. Co-ordinator, Stately Homes Hotline, 1988–; Pres., Council for Prevention of Art Theft, 1991–2001; Chm., Yorkshire's Great Houses, Castles and Gardens, 1995–; Chm., Great Inns of Britain, 1996–. Chm., Bd of Govs, Cundall Manor Sch., Helperby, 2007–. President: Nidderdale Amateur Cricket League, 1979–; Harrogate Gilbert and Sullivan Soc., 1988–. Internat. Hon. Citizen, New Orleans, 1979. *Publication:* Yorkshire's Great Houses: behind the scenes, 2005. *Recreations:* cricket, tennis, reading, writing, lecturing. *Heir: s* James William Francis Ingilby, *b* 15 June 1985. *Address:* Ripley Castle, Ripley, near Harrogate, North Yorkshire HG3 3AY. *T:* (01423) 770152; *e-mail:* enquiries@ripleycastle.co.uk.

INGLE, Alan Richmond, CMG 2000; HM Diplomatic Service, retired; *b* 16 Oct. 1939; *s* of late Henry Ingle and of Helen Ingle (*née* Keating); *m* 1963, Gillian Hall; one *s* one *d*. *Educ:* Stand Grammar Sch. and Prince Rupert Sch., Wilhelmshaven. Entered BoT, 1957; Accra (Trade Commn Service), 1961–65; FO, 1965–66; Kingston, 1966–70; Third Sec., Christchurch, 1970–74; Second Secretary: FCO, 1974–77; (Commercial), Singapore, 1977–81; First Sec., FCO, 1981–83; Consul and Dir, British Inf. Services, NY, 1983–88; First Sec., FCO 1988–93; Counsellor (Mgt), Lagos and Abuja, 1993–96; Hd of Delegn, Jt Mgt Office, Brussels, 1996–99; Counsellor: FCO, 2000; UK Mission to UN, NY, 2001. *Address:* Martins Cottage, Furley, Axminster, Devon EX13 7TR. *T:* (01404) 881735. *Club:* Royal Over-Seas League.

INGLEBY, 2nd Viscount *cr* 1955, of Snilesworth; **Martin Raymond Peake;** landowner; Director, Hargreaves Group Ltd, 1960–80; *b* 31 May 1926; *s* of 1st Viscount Ingleby, and Joan, Viscountess Ingleby (*d* 1979); *S* father, 1966; *m* 1st, 1952, Susan (*d* 1996), *d* of late Henderson Russell Landale; four *d* (one *s* decd); 2nd, 2003, Dobrila, d of late Radomir Radović. *Educ:* Eton; Trinity Coll., Oxford (MA). Called to the Bar, Inner Temple, 1956. Sec., Hargreaves Group Ltd, 1958–61. Administrative Staff Coll., 1961. CC Yorks (North Riding), 1964–67. Mem., N Yorks Moors Nat. Park Planning Cttee, 1968–78. *Heir:* none. *Address:* Shepherd Hill House, Shepherd Hill, Swainby, Northallerton, North Yorks DL6 3DL.

INGLEDOW, Anthony Brian, OBE 1969; HM Diplomatic Service, retired; Counsellor, Foreign and Commonwealth Office, 1983–93; *b* 25 July 1928; *s* of Cedric Francis Ingledow and Doris Evelyn Ingledow (*née* Worrall); *m* 1956, Margaret Monica, *d* of Sir Reginald Watson-Jones, FRCS; one *s* one *d*. *Educ:* St Bees School; London Univ. Served HM Forces, 1947–49. Joined Colonial Administrative Service, Nigeria, 1950; District Officer: Auchi, 1954; Oyo, 1956; Secretariat, Ibadan, 1958, retired 1960; joined HM Diplomatic Service, 1961; 2nd Secretary, Khartoum, 1962; FO, 1964; 1st Secretary, Aden, 1966; Lagos, 1967; FCO, 1970; Dakar, 1972; FCO, 1975. *Recreations:* reading, travel. *Address:* c/o Lloyds TSB, 8–10 Waterloo Place, SW1Y 4BE. *Club:* Athenæum.

INGLESE, Anthony Michael Christopher, CB 2008; General Counsel and Solicitor, HM Revenue and Customs, since 2008; *b* 19 Dec. 1951; *s* of Angelo Inglese and Dora Inglese (*née* Di Paola); *m* 1974, Jane Elizabeth Kerry Bailes; one *s* one *d*. *Educ:* Salvatorian Coll., Harrow Weald; Fitzwilliam Coll., Cambridge (MA, LLB). Called to the Bar, Gray's Inn, 1976, Bencher, 2002; Legal Advr's Br., Home Office, 1975–86; Legal Secretariat to Law Officers, 1986–88; Legal Advr's Br., Home Office, 1988–91; Legal Dir, OFT, 1991–95; Legal Advr, MoD (Treasury Solicitor's Dept), 1995–97; Dep. Treasury Solicitor, 1997–2001; Solicitor and Dir Gen., Legal Services, DTI, later BERR, 2002–08. *Recreation:* writing theatricals. *Address:* HM Revenue and Customs, 100 Parliament Street, SW1A 2BQ.

INGLEWOOD, 2nd Baron *cr* 1964; **(William) Richard Fletcher-Vane;** DL; *b* 31 July 1951; *e s* of 1st Baron Inglewood, TD and Mary (*d* 1982), *e d* of Major Sir Richard George Proby, 1st Bt, MC; *S* father, 1989; *m* 1986, Cressida, *y d* of late Desmond Pemberton-Pigott, CMG; one *s* two *d*. *Educ:* Eton; Trinity Coll., Cambridge (MA); Cumbria Coll. of Agriculture and Forestry. MRICS. Called to the Bar, Lincoln's Inn, 1975. Member: Lake Dist Special Planning Bd, 1984–90 (Chm., Develt Control Cttee, 1984–89); NW Water Authority, 1987–89. Pres., Cumbria Tourist Bd, 2004–. Dir, CN Group, 1997– (Chm., 2002–); non-exec. Dir, Carr's Milling Industries, 2004– (Chm., 2005–). Chm., Reviewing Cttee on Export of Works of Art, 2002–. Contested (C) Houghton and Washington, 1983; Durham, EP elecns, 1984; MEP (C) Cumbria and Lancashire N, 1989–94; contested (C) same reg., 1994; MEP (C) NW Reg., England, 1999–2004. Cons. spokesman on legal affairs, EP, 1989–94 and 1999–2004, on constitutional affairs, 2001–04; Dep. Whip, EDG, 1992–94, Chief Whip, 1994. A Lord in Waiting (Govt Whip), 1994–95; Captain of HM Yeomen of the Guard (Dep. Govt Chief Whip), 1995; Parly Under-Sec. of State, DNH, 1995–97; elected Mem., H of L, 1999. FSA 2002. DL Cumbria, 1993. *Heir: s* Hon. Henry William Frederick Fletcher-Vane, *b* 24 Dec. 1990. *Address:* Hutton-in-the-Forest, Penrith, Cumbria CA11 9TH. *T:* (01768) 484500, *Fax:* (01768) 484571. *Clubs:* Pratt's, Travellers.

INGLIS, Sir Brian Scott, AC 1988; Kt 1977; FTSE; Chairman: Optus Communications, 1992–96; Scalzo Automotive Research Ltd, 1986–95; *b* Adelaide, 3 Jan. 1924; *s* of late E. S. Inglis, Albany, WA; *m* 1953, Leila, *d* of E. V. Butler; three *d*. *Educ:* Geelong Church of England Grammar School; Trinity Coll., Univ. of Melbourne (BSc; Mem. Council, 1985). Served War of 1939–45; Flying Officer, RAAF, 453 Sqdn, 1942–45. Director and Gen. Manufacturing Manager, 1963–70, first Australian Man. Dir, Ford Motor Co. of Australia Ltd, 1970–81, Vice-Pres., 1981–83, Chm. 1981–85; Chm., Ford Asia-Pacific Inc., 1983–84. Chairman: Newcrest Mining (formerly Newmont Holdings), 1985–94; Aerospace Technologies of Aust. Pty Ltd, 1987–94; Amcor, 1989–94 (Dep. Chm., 1988–89; Dir, 1984–94); non-exec. Dir, Australian Paper, 1994–98. Chm., Defence Industry Cttee, 1984–87 (Mem., 1982–87). Chm., Centre for Molecular Biology and Medicine, Monash Univ. Hon. LLD Monash. James N. Kirby Medal, IProdE, 1979; Kernot Medal, Faculty of Engrg, Univ. of Melbourne, 1979. Légion d'Honneur (France), 2005. *Address:* 10 Bowley Avenue, Balwyn, Victoria 3103, Australia. *Clubs:* Australian (Melbourne); Barwon Heads Golf.

INGLIS, George Bruton; Senior Partner, Slaughter and May, 1986–92; *b* 19 April 1933; *s* of late Cecil George Inglis and Ethel Mabel Inglis; *m* 1968, Patricia Mary Forbes; three *s*. *Educ:* Winchester College; Pembroke College, Oxford (MA). Solicitor. Partner, Slaughter and May, 1966–92. *Recreation:* gardening.

INGLIS, Heather Hughson; *see* Swindells, H. H.

INGLIS, Ian Grahame, CB 1983; Chairman, State Grants Commission, Tasmania, 1990–2001; *b* 2 April 1929; *s* of late William and Ellen Jean Inglis; *m* 1952, Elaine Arlene Connors; three *s* one *d*. *Educ:* Hutchins Sch., Hobart; Univ. of Tasmania (BCom). Agricl Economist, Tasmanian Dept. of Agric., 1951–58; Economist, State Treasury, 1958–69; Chairman: Rivers and Water Supply Commn, and Metropolitan Water Bd, 1969–77; NW Regl Water Authority, 1977; State Under Treasurer, Tas, 1977–89. Dir, TGIO Ltd (formerly Tasmanian Govt Insce Bd), 1989–96. Chm., Retirement Benefits Fund Investment Trust, 1989–95. Member: Ambulance Commn of Tasmania, 1959–65; Tasmanian Grain Elevators Bd, 1962–65; Clarence Municipal Commn, 1965–69; Motor Accidents Insurance Bd, 1991–95. Dir, Comalco Aluminium (Bell Bay) Ltd, 1980–95. *Recreations:* yacht-racing, gardening, bridge. *Address:* 5 Sayer Crescent, Sandy Bay, Hobart, Tas 7005, Australia. *T:* (3) 62231928. *Clubs:* Tasmanian, Royal Yacht of Tasmania (Hobart).

INGLIS, Prof. Kenneth Stanley, AO 2003; DPhil; Professor of History, Australian National University, 1977–94, retired; *b* 7 Oct. 1929; *s* of S. W. Inglis; *m* 1st, 1952, Judy Betheras (*d* 1962); one *s* two *d*; 2nd, 1965, Amirah Gust. *Educ:* Univ. of Melbourne (MA); Univ. of Oxford (DPhil). Sen. Lectr in History, Univ. of Adelaide, 1956–60; Reader in History, 1960–62; Associate Prof. of History, Australian National Univ., 1962–65; Prof.,

1965–66; Prof. of History, Univ. of Papua New Guinea, 1966–72, Vice-Chancellor, 1972–75; Professorial Fellow in Hist., ANU, 1975–77. Vis. Prof. of Australian Studies, Harvard, 1982; Vis. Prof., Univ. of Hawaii, 1985; Vis. Fellow, St John's Coll., Cambridge, 1990–91. Hon. DLitt Melbourne, 1996. Jt Gen. Editor, Australians: a historical library, 1987–88. *Publications:* Hospital and Community, 1958; The Stuart Case, 1961, 2nd edn 2002; Churches and the Working Classes in Victorian England, 1963; The Australian Colonists, 1974; This is the ABC: the Australian Broadcasting Commission, 1932–1983, 1983; The Rehearsal: Australians at War in the Sudan 1885, 1985; (ed and introduced) Nation: the life of an independent journal 1958–1972, 1989; Sacred Places: war memorials in the Australian landscape, 1998; Anzac Remembered: selected writings, 1998; Observing Australia, 1959–1999, 1999; Whose ABC?: the Australian Broadcasting Corporation 1983–2006, 2006. *Address:* 1 Dundas Lane, Albert Park, Vic 3206, Australia.

INGLIS, Richard Anthony Girvan; His Honour Judge Inglis; a Circuit Judge, since 1996; *b* 28 Dec. 1947; *s* of Angus Inglis and Kathleen Flora Inglis; *m* 1976, Heather Hughson Swindells, *qv*; one *s*. *Educ:* Marlborough Coll.; Selwyn Coll., Cambridge (BA 1969). Called to the Bar, Middle Temple, 1971; Jun., Midland and Oxford Circuit, 1984; Recorder, 1993–96; Hon. Recorder of Newark, 2002–. *Recreations:* garden, music, church bell ringing. *Address:* Nottingham County Court, 60 Canal Street, Nottingham NG1 7EJ.

INGLIS of Glencorse, Sir Roderick (John), 10th Bt *cr* 1703 (then Mackenzie of Gairloch); MB, ChB; *b* 25 Jan. 1936; *s* of Sir Maxwell Ian Hector Inglis of Glencorse, 9th Bt and Dorothy Evelyn (*d* 1970), MD, JP, *d* of Dr John Stewart, Tasmania; *S* father, 1974; *m* 1960, Rachel (marr. diss. 1975), *d* of Lt-Col N. M. Morris, Dowdstown, Ardee, Co. Louth; twin *s* one *d* (and *e s* decd); *m* 1975 (marr. diss. 1977); one *d*. *Educ:* Winchester; Edinburgh Univ. (MB, ChB 1960). *Heir: s* Ian Richard Inglis [*b* 9 Aug. 1965; *m* 1st, 1990, Lesley Margaret Moss (marr. diss. 1994); one *s*; 2nd, 2000, Yvonne Rossina Hird; one *s* one *d*].

INGLIS, Dr Stephen Charles; Director, National Institute for Biological Standards and Control, since 2002; *b* 1 Sept. 1952; *s* of John Reid Inglis and Joan Inglis (*née* Devear); *m* 1975, Moira Margaret Hunter; two *s* one *d*. *Educ:* Aberdeen Grammar Sch.; Aberdeen Univ. (BSc Hons Biochem. 1974); Churchill Coll., Cambridge (PhD 1978). University of Cambridge: Res. Fellow, Churchill Coll., 1978–80; Demonstrator, 1979–84, Lectr, 1984–90, Dept of Pathol.; Fellow, Darwin Coll., 1984–90; Hd, Molecular Scis, 1990–95, Res. Dir, 1995–2001, Cantab Pharmaceuticals, subseq. Xenova PLC. Chm., Phogen, 1997–2001. Member: Molecular and Cellular Medicine Bd, MRC, 1996–2000; Biologicals Subcttee, Cttee for Safety of Medicines, 2002–05; Jt Cttee on Vaccines and Immunisation, 2002–; Biologicals and Vaccines Expert Adv. Gp, Commn for Human Medicines, 2006–; Measurement Bd, BERR, 2007–. MInstD 1997. *Publications:* contrib. scientific papers to professional jls in fields of virology, molecular biol., vaccine develt. *Recreations:* music: jazz piano, saxophone and bagpipes (occasionally), sport: tennis, ski-ing, diving. *Address:* National Institute for Biological Standards and Control, Blanche Lane, South Mimms, Potters Bar, Herts EN6 3QG. *T:* (01707) 641400.

INGLIS-JONES, Nigel John; QC 1982; Barrister-at-Law; *b* 7 May 1935; 2nd *s* of Major John Alfred Inglis-Jones and Hermione Inglis-Jones; *m* 1st, 1965, Lenette Bromley-Davenport (*d* 1986); two *s* two *d*; 2nd, 1987, Ursula Culverwell; one *s*. *Educ:* Eton; Trinity Coll., Oxford (BA). Nat. Service with Grenadier Guards (ensign). Called to the Bar, Inner Temple, 1959, Bencher, 1981. A Recorder, 1976–93. Dep. Social Security Comr, 1993–2002; Gen. Comr of Income Tax, 1992–2005. *Publication:* The Law of Occupational Pension Schemes, 1989. *Recreations:* gardening, fishing, collecting English drinking glass. *Address:* 21 Elms Crescent, SW4 8QE. *T:* (020) 7622 3043.

INGMAN, David Charles, CBE 1993; Chairman, British Waterways Board, 1987–93; *b* 22 March 1928; *s* of Charles and Muriel Ingman; *m* 1951, Joan Elizabeth Walker; two *d*. *Educ:* Grangefield Grammar Sch., Stockton-on-Tees; Durham Univ. (BSc, MSc). Imperial Chemical Industries, 1949–85: Dir, then Dep. Chm., Plastics Div., 1975–81; Gp Dir, Plastics and Petrochemicals Div., 1981–85; Chm. and Chief Exec., Bestobell, 1985–86. Dir, Engineering Services Ltd, 1975–78; Alternative Dir, AECI Ltd, SA, 1978–82; non-exec. Dir, Negretti-Zambra, 1979–81. Mem., Nationalised Industries Chairmen's Gp, 1987–93. *Recreations:* golf, walking, travel.

INGOLD, Cecil Terence, CMG 1970; DSc 1940; Professor of Botany in University of London, Birkbeck College, 1944–72; Vice-Master, Birkbeck College, 1965–70, Fellow, 1973; *b* 3 July 1905; *s* of late E. G. Ingold; *m* 1933, Leonora Mary Kemp; one *s* three *d*. *Educ:* Bangor (Co. Down) Grammar Sch.; Queen's Univ., Belfast. (BSc 1925). Asst in Botany, QUB, 1929; Lectr in Botany, University of Reading, 1930–37; Lecturer-in-charge of Dept of Botany, University Coll., Leicester, 1937–44; Dean of Faculty of Science, London Univ., 1956–60. Dep. Vice-Chancellor, London Univ., 1966–68, Chm. Academic Council, 1969–72. Chm., University Entrance and School Examinations Council, 1958–64; Vice-Chm., Inter-Univ. Council for Higher Educn Overseas, 1969–74. Chm., Council Freshwater Biolog. Assoc., 1965–74; Pres., Internat. Mycological Congress, 1971. Hooker Lectr, Linnean Soc., 1974. Hon. FLS 2000 (FLS 1934). Hon. DLitt Ibadan, 1969; Hon. DSc Exeter, 1972; Hon. DCL Kent, 1978. Linnean Medal (Botany), 1983; de Bary Medal (Mycology), Internat. Mycological Assoc., 1996; Millennium Gold Medal, 15th Internat. Botanical Congress, 1999. *Publications:* Spore Discharge in Land Plants, 1939; Dispersal in Fungi, 1953; The Biology of Fungi, 1961; Spore Liberation, 1965; Fungal Spores: their liberation and dispersal, 1971. *Address:* The Old Vicarage, 26 Cottage Road, Wooler, Northumberland NE71 6AD.

See also T. Ingold.

INGOLD, Dr Keith Usherwood, OC 1994; FRS 1979; FRSC 1969; Distinguished Research Scientist, National Research Council, Canada, since 1991; *b* Leeds, 31 May 1929; *s* of Christopher Kelk Ingold and Edith Hilda (*née* Usherwood); *m* 1956, Carmen Cairine Hodgkin; one *s* one *d* (and one *s* decd). *Educ:* University Coll. London (BSc Hons Chem., 1949; Fellow, 1987); Univ. of Oxford (DPhil 1951). Emigrated to Canada, 1951; Post-doctorate Fellow (under Dr F. P. Lossing), Div. of Pure Chem., Nat. Res. Council of Canada, 1951–53; Def. Res. Bd Post-doctorate Fellow (under Prof. W. A. Bryce), Chem. Dept, Univ. of BC, 1953–55; National Research Council of Canada: joined Div. of Appl. Chem., 1955; Head, Hydrocarbon Chem. Section of Div. of Chem., 1965; Associate Dir, Div. of Chemistry, 1977–90. Adjunct Professor: Brunel Univ., 1983–94; Univ. of Guelph, 1985–87; Carleton Univ., 1991–; Van Arkel Vis. Prof., Leiden Univ., Holland, 1992; Vis. Lectr, Japan Soc. for Promotion of Science, 1982. Hon. Treas., RSC, 1979–81; Canadian Society for Chemistry: Vice-Pres., 1985–87, Pres., 1987–88. Hon. Mem., Argentinian Soc. for Res. in Organic Chem., 1997. Lectures: Frontiers in Chem., Case Western Res. Univ., and Frank Burnett Dains Meml, Univ. of Kansas, 1969; J. A. McRae Meml, Queen's Univ., Ont, 1980; Canadian Industries Ltd, Acadia Univ., NS, Imperial Oil, Univ. of Western Ont, and Douglas Hill Meml, Duke Univ., NC, 1987; Rayson Huang, Univ. of Hong Kong, 1988; 3M University, Univ. of Western Ont, Peter de la Mare Meml, Univ. of Auckland, and Gilman, Iowa State Univ., 1993; Marjorie Young Bell, Mount Allison Univ., NB, and Bergman, Yale Univ., 1994; Weissberger-Williams, Kodak Res. Center, Rochester, NY, and Stanley J. Cristol, Univ. of Colorado, 1995; (first) Cheves Walling, Gordon Res. Conf., 1997; Max T. Rogers, Michigan Stat Univ., 2000. Hon. FRSE 2001. Hon. DSc: Univ. of Guelph, 1985; St Andrews, 198 Carleton, 1992; McMaster, 1995; Hon. LLD: Mount Allison, New Brunswick, 198 Dalhousie, 1996; Dr *hc* Ancona, 1999. Awards: American Chemical Society: Award i Petroleum Chem., 1968; Pauling Award, 1988; Arthur C. Cope Scholar Award, 199 James Flack Norris Award in Physical Organic Chem., 1993; Award in Kinetics an Mechanism, Chem. Soc., 1978; Chemical Institute of Canada: Medal, 1981; Synte Award for Physical Organic Chem., 1983; Royal Society of Canada: Centennial Meda 1982; Henry Marshall Tory Medal, 1985; Humboldt Res. Award, Alexander vo Humboldt Foundn, W Germany, 1989; Alfred Bader Award in Organic Chem., Canadia Soc. for Chem., 1989; Sir Christopher Ingold Lectureship Award, Royal Soc. of Chem 1989; VERIS Award, Vitamin E Res. Inf. Services, 1989; Lansdowne Visitor Awar Univ. of Victoria, Canada, 1990; Mangini Prize in Chem., Univ. of Bologna, 1990; Roy Society: Davy Medal, 1990; Royal Medal A, 2000; Izaak Walton Killam Meml Priz Canada Council, 1992; Angelo Mangini Medal, Italian Chem. Soc., 1997; Canada Gol Medal for Sci. and Engrg, Natural Scis and Engrg Res. Council of Canada, 1998. Silve Jubilee Medal, 1977; Golden Jubilee Medal, 2002. *Publications:* over 500 scientific pape in field of physical organic chemistry, partic. free-radical chemistry. *Recreation:* ski-ing *Address:* 72 Ryeburn Drive, Ottawa ON K1V 1H5, Canada. *T:* (613) 8221123, (office (613) 9900938.

INGOLD, Prof. Timothy, PhD; FBA 1997; FRSE; Professor of Anthropolog University of Aberdeen, since 1999; *b* 1 Nov. 1948; *s* of Cecil Terence Ingold, *qv*; *m* 197 Anna Kaarina Väli-Kivistö; three *s* one *d*. *Educ:* Churchill Coll., Cambridge (BA 1st c Hons 1970; PhD Social Anthropol. 1976). Department of Social Anthropolog University of Manchester: Lectr, 1974–85; Sen. Lectr, 1985–90; Prof., 1990–99 (Ma Gluckman Prof. of Social Anthropology, 1995–99); Hd of Dept, 1993–97. Britis Academy Res. Readership, 1997–99; ESRC Professorial Fellowship, 2005–Sept. 200 Adjunct Prof., Univ. of Tromsø, Norway, 1997–2000. Corresp. Mem., Finnish Litera Soc., 1993. FRSE 2000. Rivers Meml Medal, RAI, 1989; Jean-Marie Delwart Found Award, Royal Belgian Acad. of Scis, 1994; Anders Retzius Gold Medal, Swedish Soc. fo Anthropol. and Geog., 2004. *Publications:* The Skolt Lapps today, 1976; Hunter pastoralists and ranchers, 1980; Evolution and social life, 1986; The appropriation o nature, 1986; (ed) What is an animal?, 1988; (ed jtly) Hunters and gatherers, 2 vols, 198 (ed jtly) Tools, language and cognition in human evolution, 1993; (ed) Companio encyclopedia of anthropology, 1994; (ed) Key debates in anthropology, 1996; Th Perception of the Environment, 2000; (ed jtly) Creativity and Cultural Improvisatio 2007; Lines, 2007; (ed jtly) Ways of Walking, 2008; articles in academic books and learne jls. *Recreation:* music ('cello and piano). *Address:* Department of Anthropology, Universit of Aberdeen, Aberdeen AB24 3QY. *T:* (01224) 274350.

INGRAHAM, Rt Hon. Hubert Alexander; PC 1993; Prime Minister, Commonwealt of the Bahamas, 1992–2002 and since 2007; Member, National Assembly, since 197 (PLP, 1977–86, Ind, 1987–90, FNM, since 1990); *b* 4 Aug. 1947; *m* Delores Velma Mille five *c*. *Educ:* Cooper's Town Public Sch.; Southern Senior Sch.; Govt High Sch. Evenin Inst., Nassau. Called to Bahamas Bar, 1972; Sen. Partner, Christie, Ingraham & Co Formerly: Mem., Air Transport Licensing Authy; Chm., Real Property Tax Tribuna Chm., Bahamas Mortgage Corp., 1982. Mem., Progressive Liberal Party, 1975–8 Minister of Housing, Nat. Insurance and Social Services, 1982–84; Leader, Free Nationa Movement, 1990–; Leader of Opposition, 1990–92, 2002–07. *Address:* c/o Free Nationa Movement, PO Box N–10713, Nassau, Bahamas.

INGRAM, Adam Hamilton; Member (SNP) South of Scotland, Scottish Parliament since 1999; Minister for Children and Early Years, since 2007; *b* 1 May 1951; *m* 1977 Gerry; three *s* one *d*. *Educ:* Kilmarnock Acad.; Paisley Coll. (BA Hons Busines Economics, 1980). Family bakery business, 1971–76; Sen. Economic Asst, Manpowe Services Commn, 1985–86; Researcher and Lectr, Paisley Coll., 1987–88; Hd of Res. Development Options Ltd; Economic Develt consultant, 1990–99. Joined SNP, 198 (Mem., Nat. Exec. Cttee, 1994–99). *Address:* Scottish Parliament, Edinburgh EH99 1SP.

INGRAM, Rt Hon. Adam (Paterson); PC 1999; MP (Lab) East Kilbride, Strathave and Lesmahagow, since 2005 (East Kilbride, 1987–2005); *b* 1 Feb. 1947; *s* of Bert Ingran and Lousia Paterson; *m* 1970, Maureen Georgina McMahon. *Educ:* Cranhill Secondar School. Commercial apprentice, 1965, computer programmer, 1966–69, J. & P. Coats Glasgow; programmer/analyst, Associated British Foods, 1969–70; programmer/system analyst, SSEB, 1970–77; Trade Union Official, NALGO, 1977–87. Sec., Jt Trades Unio Side, Gas Staffs and Senior Officers, Scottish Gas, 1978–82; Chair, East Kilbrid Constituency Labour Party, 1981–85; Councillor, E Kilbride DC, 1980–87, Leader 1984–87. An Opposition Whip, Feb.–Nov. 1988 (responsible for Scottish business an Treasury matters); PPS to Leader of the Opposition, 1988–92; front bench spokesman o social security, 1993–95, on sci. and technol., 1995–97; Minister of State: NI Office 1997–2001; MoD, 2001–07. Mem., Select Cttee on Trade and Industry, 1992–93; Vice-Chm., British-Japanese All-Party Parly Gp, 1992–97; Sec., British-Singapore All-Part Parly Gp, 1992–97; Vice-Chm., All-Party Parly Gp on Nuclear Energy, 2007–. *Recreations:* fishing, cooking, reading. *Address:* House of Commons, SW1A 0AA. *T:* (020 7219 4093.

INGRAM, Christopher John; Chairman, Ingram Enterprise, since 2007; Foundin Partner, Ingram (formerly The Ingram Partnership Ltd), 2003–07; *b* 9 June 1943; *s* o Thomas Frank Ingram and Gladys Agnes Ingram; *m* 1964, Janet Elizabeth Rye; one *s* on *d*. *Educ:* Woking Grammar Sch. KMP, 1970–72; Man. Dir, TMD Advertising, 1972–76; founded Chris Ingram Associates (CIA), later Tempus Group plc, 1976, Chm. 1976–2002; Partner, Genesis Investments, 2002–. Chm., Woking FC Hldgs, 2002–; Director: Vitesse Media plc, 2004–; Consumer Dynamics, USA, 2005–; The Brand Co., Hong Kong, 2006–. Dep. Chm., Foundn for Entrepreneurial Mgt, London Business Sch.; Chm., Centre for Creative Business, 2005–. Chm., Azzurri Sport and Leisure, 2008–. Vice Pres., Shelter, 2001–. Trustee, Ingram Trust, 1992–. *Recreations:* theatre, football, moder British art, eating out, travel in cold climates. *Address:* (office) 1 Dorset Street, W1U 4EG.

INGRAM, Prof. David Stanley, OBE 1999; botanist; Hon. Professor: University o Edinburgh, since 1992; University of Glasgow, since 2005; Master, St Catharine's College, Cambridge, 2000–06; *b* 10 Oct. 1941; *s* of Stanley Arthur Ingram, toolmaker and Vera May Ingram (*née* Mansfield); *m* 1965, Alison Winifred Graham; two *s*. *Educ:* Yardley Grammar School, Birmingham; Univ. of Hull (BSc, PhD); MA, ScD Cantab. CBiol, FIBiol 1986; FLS 1991; FRSE 1993; FIHort 1997; FRCPE 1998. Research Fellow, Univ. of Glasgow Dept of Botany, 1966–68; ARC Unit of Develt Botany, Cambridge, 1969–74; University of Cambridge: Research Fellow, Botany Sch., 1968–69; Univ. Lectr, 1974–88; Reader in Plant Pathology, 1988–90; Mem. Gen. Board, 1984–88; Fellow, Downing Coll., Cambridge, 1974–90 (Dean, 1976–82; Tutor for Graduate Students, 1982–88; Dir of Studies in Biology, 1976–89; Hon. Fellow, 1998); Regius Keeper, Royal Botanic Garden, Edinburgh, 1990–98 (Hon. Fellow, 1998); Advr to Univ. of Edinburgh on public engagement with science, 1998– (Mem. Adv. Cttee, Div. of Biol Scis, 1991–98);

Cambridge University: Chairman: Cttee for Interdisciplinary Envmtl Studies, 2001–03; Colls Cttee, 2003–05; Mem., Council, 2003–05. Visiting Professor: Univ. of Glasgow, 1991–2005; of Envmtl Sci. and Horticulture, Napier Univ., 1998–2005; Prof. of Horticulture, RHS, 1995–2000; Vis. Sen. Res. Fellow, ESRC Genomics Forum, Edinburgh, 2006– (Mem. Adv. Cttee, 2005–). Chairman: Scientific Council, Sainsbury Lab. for Plant Pathology, 1990–92; Science and Plants for Schools Trust, 1991–98; Science and Plants for Schs, Scotland, 1998–2000; Scientific and Horticultural Advice Cttee, RHS, 1995–2000 (Mem., Scientific Cttee, 1992–95); Adv. Cttee, Darwin Initiative for Survival of the Species, 1999–2005; Prog. Convener and Chair, Sci. and Soc. Steering Gp, RSE, 2005–; Member: Adv. Cttee, St Andrews Botanic Garden, 1990–95; Exec. Cttee, Scotland's Nat. Gardens Scheme, 1990–96; Adv. Cttee on SSSI in Scotland, 1992–98; Council, Linnean Soc., 1992–95 (Vice Pres., 1993–94); Council, Internat. Assoc. of Botanic Gardens; main Bd and Scientific Adv. Cttee, Scottish Natural Heritage, 1999–2000; Jt Nature Conservation Cttee, 1999–2000 and 2002– (Dep. Chm., 2006–); Forestry Commn Adv. Panel, 2004–06. Member: Editl Cttee, Flora of China, 1992–98; Editorial Board: Biol Revs, 1984–98, 2001–05; Annals of Botany, 1992–2001; Advances in Plant Path., 1992–95. Trustee: Grimesthorpe and Drummond Castle Trust, 1990–98; John Fife Meml Trust, 1990–98; Younger Botanic Garden Trust, 1990–2000; Royal Botanic Garden (Sibbald) Trust, 1990–98; Botanic Gardens Conservation International, 1991–98; Scottish Sci. Trust, 1998–99 (Mem. Scientific Adv. Cttee, 1999–2002); Dynamic Earth Proj., 1998–2000; World Conservation Monitoring Centre 2000, 2001–04. President: 7th Internat. Congress of Plant Pathology, 1994–98; British Soc. for Plant Pathology, 1998 (Hon. Mem., 2008); Hon. Vice-Pres., Royal Caledonian Horticultural Soc., 1990. Hon. Fellow: Myerscough Coll., 2001; Worcester Coll., Oxford, 2003; St Catharine's Coll., Cambridge, 2006. Hon. FRSGS 1998. DUniv Open, 2000. VMH 2004. *Publications:* (with D. N. Butcher) Plant Tissue Culture, 1974; (with J. P. Helgeson) Tissue Culture Methods for Plant Pathologists, 1980; (with A. Friday) Cambridge Encyclopedia of Life Sciences, 1985; (with P. H. Williams) Advances in Plant Pathology, vol. 1, 1982 to vol. 9, 1993; (with A. Hudson) Shape and Form in Plants and Fungi, 1994; (with N. F. Robertson) Plant Disease, 1999; (with D. Vince-Prue and P. J. Gregory) Science and the Garden, 2002, 2nd edn 2008; many papers dealing with research in plant pathology, plant tissue culture and botany, in learned jls. *Recreations:* listening to classical music and jazz, theatre, ceramics, gardening, reading, strolling around capital cities. *Address:* Town End House, 56 High Street, Burton-in-Lonsdale LA6 3JP; c/o Royal Society of Edinburgh, 22–26 George Street, Edinburgh EH2 2PQ. *Club:* New (Edinburgh).

INGRAM, Edward John W.; *see* Winnington-Ingram.

INGRAM, Sir James (Herbert Charles), 4th Bt *cr* 1893; *b* 6 May 1966; *s* of (Herbert) Robin Ingram (*d* 1979) and of Shiela, *d* of late Charles Peczenik; *S* grandfather, 1980; *m* 1998, Aracea Elizabeth, *d* of Graham Pearce. *Educ:* Eton; Cardiff Univ. *Heir: half b* Nicholas David Ingram, *b* 12 June 1975.

INGRAM, Sir John (Henderson), Kt 1994; CBE 1984; FIMechE, Dist. FIPENZ; company director; *b* 3 Sept. 1924; *s* of John Garden Ingram and Irene Caro Ingram (*née* Simpson); *m* 1952, Rosemary Clara Cuningham; three *d*. *Educ:* Nelson Coll., NZ; Canterbury Univ., Christchurch, NZ (BE; Dist. Alumnus, 1999). FIPENZ (FNZIE 1969; Dist. FIPENZ 1997); FAusIMM 1975; FIMechE 1991. Served RNZAF, NZ and Pacific, 1943–45. Man. Dir, NZ Steel Ltd, 1969–86; Dir, Nat Bank of NZ, 1983–95; Chm., Auckland Uniservices Ltd, 1988–99. Chm., Youth Skills NZ, 1989–97; Mem., Auckland HA, 1990–91. President: Inst. of Professional Engrs, NZ, 1976–77; Auckland Manufacturers' Assoc., 1989–91. Mem., Waitangi Tribunal, 1993–98. Mem. Council, 1979–96, Pro Chancellor, 1982–83 and 1995–96, Fellow, 1997, Univ. of Auckland. Dist. FInstD 2003. Commemoration Medal, NZ, 1990. *Publications:* contrib. papers in Inst. of Professional Engrs, NZ Jl, Conf. papers IISI, Inst. of Engrs, Australia, Aust. Inst. of Metals. *Recreations:* garden, ski-ing. *Address:* 6 Glenbrook Street, Remuera, Auckland 5, New Zealand. *T:* (9) 5200167. *Club:* Northern (Auckland).

INGRAM, Paul; Head of Agricultural Services, Barclays Bank plc, 1988–94; *b* 20 Sept. 1934; *s* of John Granville Ingram and Sybil Ingram (*née* Johnson); *m* 1957, Jennifer (*née* Morgan) (*d* 1988); one *s* one *d*. *Educ:* Manchester Central High School; University of Nottingham (BSc 1956). Dept of Conservation and Extension, Fedn of Rhodesia and Nyasaland, 1956–63; Nat. Agricl Adv. Service, later ADAS, MAFF, 1965–88; County Livestock Officer, Lancs, 1969–70; Policy Planning Unit, MAFF, 1970–72; Farm Management Adviser, Devon, 1972–76; Regional Farm Management Adviser, Wales, 1976–77; Dep. Sen. Livestock Advr, 1977–79, Sen. Agricl Officer, 1979–85, Chief Agricl Officer, 1985–87, Dir of Farm and Countryside Service, 1987–88, ADAS. *Address:* 36 Ceylon Road, W14 0PY.

INGRAM, Robert Alexander; Chief Operating Officer, and President, Pharmaceutical Operations, 2000–02, Special Advisor, since 2002, GlaxoSmithKline; *b* 6 Dec. 1942; *s* of Myra L. Ingram; *m* 1962, Carolyn Jean Hutson; three *s*. *Educ:* Eastern Illinois Univ. (BSc Business Admin); Lumpkin Coll. of Business. Sales rep., 1965; Merrell Dow Pharmaceuticals: various sales mgt, then govt and public affairs posts; Vice Pres., Public Affairs, until 1985; Vice Pres., Govt Affairs, Merck & Co. Inc., 1985–88; Pres., Merck Frosst Canada Inc., 1988–90; joined Glaxo Inc., 1990: Exec. Vice Pres., Admin and Regulatory Affairs, 1990–93; Exec. Vice Pres., then Pres. and Chief Operating Officer, 1993–94; Pres. and CEO, 1994–99; Chm., Glaxo Wellcome Inc., and Chief Exec., Glaxo Wellcome plc, 1997–2000; Chm., Glaxo Inc., 1999–2000. Director: Wachovia Corp., 1997–; TheraCom, 1998–; Northern Telecom Ltd (NORTEL), 1999–2006. Hon. LLD: Eastern Illinois, 1988; Univ. of Scis, Philadelphia, 1999. *Recreations:* Formula One motor racing, Porsche restoration. *Address:* GlaxoSmithKline, Five Moore Drive, PO Box 13398, Research Triangle Park, NC 27709–3398, USA. *Club:* Royal Automobile.

INGRAM, Stanley Edward; solicitor; *b* 5 Dec. 1922; *o s* of late Ernest Alfred Stanley Ingram and Ethel Ann Ingram; *m* 1948, Vera (*née* Brown); one *s* one *d*. *Educ:* Charlton Central School. Articled clerk with Wright & Bull, Solicitors; admitted Solicitor, 1950. Served RAF, 1942–46. Legal Asst, Min. of Nat. Insurance, 1953; Sen. Legal Asst, Min. of Pensions and Nat. Insurance, 1958; Asst Solicitor, 1971, Under Sec. (Legal), 1978–83, DHSS. Member Council: Civil Service Legal Soc. and of Legal Section of First Division Assoc., 1971–82; Mem., Salaried Solicitors' Cttee of Law Society, 1978–81. Secretary: Romsey Gp, CS Retirement Fellowship, 1989–97; Test Valley Croquet Club, 1995–2002 (Treas., 1994–95); Winchester Croquet Club, 1998–2006; Romsey Abbey Probus Club, 2000– (Vice-Pres., 1996; Pres., 1997). *Recreations:* gardening, playing croquet. *Address:* 2 Little Woodley Farm, Winchester Hill, Romsey, Hants SO51 7NU. *Club:* Law Society.

INGRAM, Tamara; Executive Managing Director, and Leader, Team P&G, WPP, since 2007; *b* 1 Oct. 1960; *d* of John Ingram and Sonia (*née* Bolson); *m* 1989, Andrew Millington; one *s* one *d*. *Educ:* Queen's Coll., Harley St; Univ. of E Anglia (BA Hons Eng.). Joined Saatchi & Saatchi, 1985: Account Exec., 1985–87; Supervisor, 1987–88; Dir, 1988–89; Bd Account Dir, 1989–90; Gp Account Dir, 1990–93; Exec. Bd Dir, 1993–95; Saatchi & Saatchi Advertising Ltd: Jt CEO, 1995–99; Chief Exec., 1999–2001; Chm., 2001; Chm. and Chief Exec., McCann-Erickson London, 2002; Pres., Added Value, Henley Centre, and Fusion5, Kantar Div., WPP, 2003–05; CEO, Grey Gp UK, WPP, 2005–07. Chm., Visit London, 2002–; Mem. Bd, London Develt Agency, 2000–06. Member Council: IPA, 1995–; Mktg Soc., 1995–. *Recreations:* theatre, football, tennis, family.

INGRAM, Timothy Charles William; Chief Executive, Caledonia Investments plc, since 2002; *b* 18 June 1947; *s* of Stanley Ingram and Sheila Ingram; *m* 1975, Christine Cooper; three *s*. *Educ:* Harrow Sch.; Churchill Coll., Cambridge (MA Econs); INSEAD Business Sch. (MBA). Gen. Manager, ANZ Bank, 1985–91; First National Finance Corporation: Finance Dir, 1992–94; Chief Exec., 1994–2002; Man. Dir, Abbey National plc, 1996–2002. Non-executive Director: Hogg Robinson plc, 1999–2000; Sage Group plc, 2002–; Savills plc, 2002–; ANZ Bank (Europe) Ltd, 2004–. *Recreations:* ski-ing, opera, travel. *T:* (020) 7802 8451; *e-mail:* tim.ingram@caledonia.com. *Clubs:* Reform, Hurlingham.

INGRAMS, family name of **Baron Darcy de Knayth**.

INGRAMS, Richard Reid; journalist; Editor, Private Eye, 1963–86, Chairman, since 1974; Editor, The Oldie, since 1992; *b* 19 Aug. 1937; *s* of late Leonard St Clair Ingrams and Victoria (*née* Reid); *m* 1962, Mary Morgan (marr. diss. 1993; she *d* 2007); one *s* (and one *s* one *d* decd). *Educ:* Shrewsbury; University Coll., Oxford. Joined Private Eye, 1962; columnist: Observer, 1988–90, 1992–2005; The Independent, 2005–. *Publications:* (with Christopher Booker and William Rushton) Private Eye on London, 1962; Private Eye's Romantic England, 1963; (with John Wells) Mrs Wilson's Diary, 1965; Mrs Wilson's 2nd Diary, 1966; The Tale of Driver Grope, 1968; (with Barry Fantoni) The Bible for Motorists, 1970; (ed) The Life and Times of Private Eye, 1971; (as Philip Reid, with Andrew Osmond) Harris in Wonderland, 1973; (ed) Cobbett's Country Book, 1974; (ed) Beachcomber: the works of J. B. Morton, 1974; The Best of Private Eye, 1974; God's Apology, 1977; Goldenballs, 1979; (with Fay Godwin) Romney Marsh and the Royal Military Canal, 1980; (with John Wells) Dear Bill: the collected letters of Denis Thatcher, 1980; (with John Wells) The Other Half: further letters of Denis Thatcher, 1981; (with John Wells) One for the Road, 1982; (with John Piper) Piper's Places, 1983; (ed) The Penguin Book of Private Eye Cartoons, 1983; (with John Wells) My Round!, 1983; (ed) Dr Johnson by Mrs Thrale, 1984; (with John Wells) Down the Hatch, 1985; (with John Wells) Just the One, 1986; John Stewart Collis: a memoir, 1986; (with John Wells) The Best of Dear Bill, 1986; (with John Wells) Mud in Your Eye, 1987; The Ridgeway, 1988; You Might As Well Be Dead, 1988; England (anthology), 1989; (with John Wells) Number 10, 1989; On and On…, 1990; (ed) The Oldie Annual, 1993; (ed) The Oldie Annual 2, 1994; Malcolm Muggeridge: the authorized biography, 1995; (ed) I Once Met, 1996; (ed) The Oldie Annual 3, 1997; (ed) Jesus: authors take sides (anthology), 1999; (ed) The Oldie Annual 4, 1999; The Life and Adventures of William Cobbett, 2005; My Friend Footy: a memoir of Paul Foot, 2005. *Recreation:* piano. *Address:* c/o The Oldie, 65 Newman Street, W1T 3EG.

INJIA, Hon. Sir Salamo, Kt 2005; Deputy Chief Justice of Papua New Guinea, since 2003; *b* 12 Sept. 1958; *s* of Kapo Injia and Anna Injia; *m* 1994, Peam; three *s* two *d*. *Educ:* Univ. of Papua New Guinea (LLB); Harvard Law Sch. (LLM). Dep. Public Solicitor, 1989–90; private legal practice, 1991–93; a Judge of the Nat. and Supreme Courts, PNG, 1993–2003. *Publication:* (jtly) Criminal Law and Practice in Papua New Guinea, 3rd edn, 2001. *Recreation:* social golf. *Address:* PO Box 1300, Waigani, Papua New Guinea. *T:* 3245715, *Fax:* 3257732; *e-mail:* sinjia@pngjudiciary.gov.pg.

INKIN, Sir Geoffrey (David), Kt 1993; OBE 1974 (MBE 1971); Member, Judicial Appointments Commission, since 2006; Chairman, Cardiff Bay Development Corporation, 1987–2000; *b* 2 Oct. 1934; *e s* of late Noel D. Inkin and Evelyn Margaret Inkin; *m* 1st 1961, Susan Elizabeth Sheldon (marr. diss. 1998); three *s*; 2nd, 1998, Mrs Susan Inglefield (*née* Turcan). *Educ:* Dean Close Sch.; RMA, Sandhurst; Staff Coll., Camberley; Royal Agricl Coll., Cirencester. Commnd The Royal Welch Fusiliers, 1955; served Malaya, 1955–57 and Cyprus, 1958–59 (despatches); commanded 1st Bn The Royal Welch Fusiliers, 1972–74. Member: Gwent CC, 1977–83; Gwent Police Authority, 1979–83; Mem. Bd, 1980–83, Chm., 1983–87, Cwmbran Develt Corp.; Chm., Land Authy for Wales, 1986–98; Mem. Bd, Welsh Devlt Agency, 1984–87. Gov., Haberdashers' Monmouth Schs, 1977–90; Mem. Bd, WNO, 1987–91, 1993–95; Member Council: UWIST, 1987–88; Cardiff Univ., 1988–2002. Patron, Butler Trust, 1996–2005. Parly Cand. (C) Ebbw Vale, 1977–79. Hon. MRICS 2002. Gwent: DL, 1983–91; High Sheriff, 1987–88. Hon. Consul for Hungary, 2000–. Hon. Dr Univ. of Glamorgan, 1996. *Address:* Castle Upon Alun, St Brides Major, Bridgend CF32 0TN. *T:* (01656) 880298. *Clubs:* Brooks's, Army and Navy; Cardiff and County (Cardiff); Royal Porthcawl Golf.

INKSTER, Nigel Norman, CMG 2003; Counsellor, Foreign and Commonwealth Office, 1998. Entered FCO, 1975; Third Secretary: FCO, 1975; Kuala Lumpur, 1976; Third, later Second Sec., FCO, 1976–79; Second, later First Sec., Bangkok, 1979–82; First Secretary: FCO, 1982–83; Peking, 1983–85; Buenos Aires, 1985–89; FCO, 1989–92; Counsellor: Athens, 1992–94; Hong Kong, 1994–98. *Address:* c/o Foreign and Commonwealth Office, King Charles Street, SW1A 2AH.

INMAN, His Honour Derek Arthur; a Circuit Judge, 1993–2008; *b* 1 Aug. 1937; *s* of Arthur and Marjorie Inman; *m* 1st, 1963, Sarah Juliet Cahn (marr. diss. 1982); one *s* two *d*; 2nd, 1983, Elizabeth (*née* Dickinson), *widow* of Lt-Col C. Thomson. *Educ:* Roundhay Sch., Leeds; RNC, Dartmouth. RN; served in HM Ships Sheffield, Belfast and Bulwark; Staff of C-in-C Home Fleet; Sec. to Comdr Naval Forces Gulf and HMS Hermione; retired as Lieut Comdr, 1974. Called to the Bar, Middle Temple, 1968; in Chambers at 2 Harcourt Bldgs, 1974–93. *Recreations:* watching cricket and Rugby, compulsory gardening. *Address:* c/o Lloyds TSB, High Street, Godalming, Surrey GU7 1AT.

INMAN, Edward Oliver, OBE 1998; FRAeS; Chief Executive, South Bank Employers' Group, since 2004; *b* 12 Aug. 1948; *s* of John Inman and Peggy Inman (*née* Beard); *m* 1st, 1971, Elizabeth (*née* Douglas) (marr. diss. 1982); one *s* one *d*; 2nd, 1984, Sherida (*née* Sturton) (marr. diss. 2005); one *d*, and two step *d*. *Educ:* King's College Sch., Wimbledon; Gonville and Caius Coll., Cambridge (MA); School of Slavonic and East European Studies, London (MA). FRAeS 1999. Joined Imperial War Museum as Res. Asst, 1972; Asst Keeper 1974; Keeper of Exhibits (Duxford) 1976; Dir, Imperial War Mus., Duxford, 1978–2004. Trustee, American Air Mus. in Britain, 2004–. Bd Mem., Lambeth First, 2006–. *Address:* South Bank Employers' Group, 103 Waterloo Road, SE1 8UL. *T:* (020) 7202 6900, *Fax:* (020) 7202 6904; *e-mail:* email@southbanklondon.com.

INMAN, Melbourne Donald; QC 1998; **His Honour Judge Melbourne Inman;** a Circuit Judge, since 2007; *b* 1 April 1957; *s* of Melbourne and Norah Inman. *Educ:* Bishop Vesey's Grammar Sch.; Regent's Park Coll., Oxford (MA). Called to the Bar, Inner Temple, 1979, Bencher, 2002. Asst Recorder, 1996–99; Recorder, 1999–2007. Hd of Advocacy Trng and Continuing Professional Develt, Midland Circuit, 1998–2007.

Recreations: ski-ing, listening to the piano. *Address:* Queen Elizabeth II Law Courts, 1 Newton Street, Birmingham B4 7NA.

INMAN, Roger, OBE (mil.) 1945 (MBE (mil.) 1944); TD 1945; Vice Lord-Lieutenant of South Yorkshire, 1981–90; Joint Managing Director, since 1951, and Chairman, since 1997, Harrison Fisher Group; *b* 18 April 1915; *y s* of S. M. Inman, Sheffield; *m* 1939, Christine Lucas, *e d* of Lt-Col J. Rodgers, Sheffield; two *s*. *Educ:* King Edward VII Sch., Sheffield. Commissioned into 71st (WR) Field Bde, RA TA, 1935; served War, with RA and General Staff, Western Desert, Middle East, Italy, 1939–46; released, 1946, with rank of Lt-Col; reformed and commanded 271 (WR) Fd Regt, RA TA, 1947–51; Brevet Col 1953; Hon. Col, Sheffield Artillery Volunteers, 1964–70; Member, W Riding T&AFA, 1947–; Vice-Chm., Yorkshire and Humberside TA&VRA, 1973–80. JP 1954 (Chm. Sheffield City Bench, 1974–80), DL 1967, West Riding. General Commissioner of Income Tax, 1969–90; Chm. of Comrs, Don Div. of Sheffield, 1975–90. Chm., Guardians of Standard of Wrought Plate within the Town of Sheffield, 1988–98. *Recreation:* golf. *Address:* Flat 1, Mayfield View, 15 Whitworth Road, Sheffield S10 3HD. *Club:* Hallamshire Golf (Sheffield).

INNES, Alistair Campbell M.; *see* Mitchell-Innes.

INNES of Coxton, Sir David (Charles Kenneth Gordon), 12th Bt *cr* 1686 (NS); consultant in electronics for petro-chemical and power generation fields; *b* 17 April 1940; *s* of Sir Charles Innes of Coxton, 11th Bt and Margaret Colquhoun Lockhart (*d* 1992), *d* of F. C. L. Robertson; *S* father, 1990; *m* 1969, Majorie Alison, *d* of E. W. Parker; one *s* one *d*. *Educ:* Haileybury Coll.; City & Guilds Coll. of Imperial Coll., London Univ. BSc(Eng); ACGI. Technical Dir, Peak Technologies, 1974–78; Man. Dir, Peak Combustion Controls, 1978–81. *Recreations:* electronics, aeronautics, astronomy. *Heir: s* Alastair Charles Deverell Innes, *b* 17 Sept. 1970. *Address:* 28 Wadham Close, Shepperton, Middlesex TW17 9HT. *T:* (01932) 228273.

INNES of Edingight, Sir Malcolm (Rognvald), KCVO 1990 (CVO 1981); Orkney Herald of Arms Extraordinary, since 2001; *b* 25 May 1938; 3rd *s* of late Sir Thomas Innes of Learney, GCVO, LLD, and Lady Lucy Buchan, 3rd *d* of 18th Earl of Caithness; *m* 1963, Joan, *o d* of Thomas D. Hay, CA, Edinburgh; three *s*. *Educ:* Edinburgh Acad.; Univ. of Edinburgh (MA, LLB). WS 1964. Falkland Pursuivant Extraordinary, 1957–58; Carrick Pursuivant, 1958–71; Lyon Clerk and Keeper of the Records, 1966–81; Marchmont Herald, 1971–81; Lord Lyon King of Arms, 1981–2001; Sec., Order of the Thistle, 1981–2001. Mem., Queen's Body Guard for Scotland (Royal Company of Archers), 1971. Fellow, Heraldry Socs of Scotland, Canada and NZ. Grand Officer of Merit, SMO Malta. *Recreation:* visiting places of historic interest. *Clubs:* New, Puffins (Edinburgh).

INNES, Sir Peter (Alexander Berowald), 17th Bt *cr* 1628, of Balvenie; *b* 6 Jan. 1937; *s* of Lt-Col Sir (Ronald Gordon) Berowald Innes, 16th Bt, OBE and Elizabeth Haughton (*d* 1958), *e d* of late Alfred Fayle; *S* father, 1988; *m* 1959, Julia Mary, *d* of A. S. Levesley; two *s* one *d*. *Educ:* Prince of Wales School, Nairobi, Kenya; Bristol Univ. (BSc). Scott Wilson Kirkpatrick and Partners, then Scott Wilson Kirkpatrick & Co. Ltd, Consulting Engineers, 1964–2000: Associate, 1982–87; Partner, 1987–95; Dir, 1995–2000; responsible for several airport projects in UK, Africa and Middle East, including major military airbases. Lt-Col Engr and Logistic (formerly Transport) Staff Corps, RE (TA). *Heir: s* Alexander Guy Berowald Innes, *b* 4 May 1960. *Club:* S Winchester Golf.

INNES, Peter Maxwell; HM Diplomatic Service, retired; Consul-General, Melbourne, 1998–2001; *b* 9 Aug. 1941; *s* of James Innes and Agnes Margaret Innes (*née* Dea); *m* 1965, Robina Baillie Walker; one *s* one *d*. *Educ:* Morrison's Acad., Crieff. Min. of Aviation, 1960–72; Department of Trade and Industry, 1972–77; Asst Airport Manager, Aberdeen Airport, 1972–73; on secondment to British Embassy, Washington, 1973–76; joined FCO, 1977; Seoul, 1979–83; FCO, 1983–85; First Sec. (Agric.), Dublin, 1985–89; FCO, 1989–92 (EC Monitoring Mission in Bosnia, 1991); Dir, British Information Services, NY, 1992–97; FCO, 1997–98. Member: Probus Club, Comrie; 30 Club, Crieff. *Recreations:* reading, walking, travel, watching most sports. *Address:* Alberton, South Crieff Road, Comrie, Perthshire PH6 2HF. *Clubs:* Royal Over-Seas League; Comrie Golf.

INNES, Sheila Miriam; consultant (education and media); *b* 25 Jan. 1931; *d* of late Dr James Innes, MB, ChB, MA and of Nora Innes. *Educ:* Talbot Heath School, Bournemouth; Lady Margaret Hall, Oxford (Exhibnr; BA Hons Mod. Langs; MA). BBC Radio Producer, World Service, 1955–61; BBC TV producer: family programmes, 1961–65; further education, 1965–73; exec. producer, further education, 1973–77; Head, BBC Continuing Educn, TV, 1977–84; Controller, BBC Educnl Broadcasting, 1984–87; Dir, BBC Enterprises Ltd, 1986–87; Chief Exec., 1987–89, Dep. Chm., 1989–92, Open Coll. Non-exec. Dir, Brighton Health Care NHS Trust, 1993–96. Chairman: Cross-Sector Cttee for Development and Review, BTEC, 1986–87; Cross-Sector Cttee for Product Develt, BTEC, 1989–92; British Gas Training Awards, 1988–92. Member: Gen. Board, Alcoholics Anonymous, 1980–; Board of Governors, Centre for Information on Language Teaching and Research, 1981–84; Council, Open Univ., 1984–87; Council for Educational Technology, 1984–87; EBU Educational Working Party, 1984–87; Educn Cttee, 1990–95, Women's Adv. Gp, 1992–95, RSA; Standing Conf. on Schools' Science and Technol., 1990–93 (Mem. Council, 1993–98); Age Concern Training Validation (later Quality) Cttee, 1992–94; IMgt Management Develt Proj., 1992–95. Vice-Pres., Educn Sect., BAAS, 1990–. Mem., Clothing and Allied Products ITB Management 2000 Cttee of Enquiry, 1989. Patron, One World Broadcasting Trust, 1988–98. Gov., Talbot Heath Sch., Bournemouth, 1989–95. Vice-Pres., Abbeyfield Eastbourne Soc., 2005–. Mem., RTS, 1984; FRSA 1986; FITD 1987; CCMI (CIMgt 1987). Hon. DLitt South Bank, 1992. *Publications:* BBC publications; articles for language jls and EBU Review. *Recreations:* music (classical and jazz), country pursuits, sketching, photography, travel, languages. *Address:* Wychwood, Barcombe, East Sussex BN8 5TP. *T:* (01273) 400268. *Clubs:* Reform, Royal Commonwealth Society; Oxford Society.

INNES, William James Alexander; Assistant Under Secretary of State, 1985–94, Head of Fire and Emergency Planning Department, 1992–94, Home Office, retired; *b* 11 Oct. 1934; *s* of late William Johnstone Innes and Helen Margaret Meldrum Porter; *m* 1st, 1959, Carol Isabel Bruce (marr. diss. 1983); one *s* one *d*; 2nd, 1992, Mrs Ann Harrold. *Educ:* Robert Gordon's Coll., Aberdeen; Aberdeen Univ. (MA). Served Royal Air Force, 1956, Officer Commanding 45 Sqdn, 1967–70. Principal, Home Office, 1972; Private Sec. to Home Sec., 1974–76; Asst Sec., 1977; Asst Under Sec. of State, seconded to NI Office, 1985–88; Dir of Operational Policy, Prison Dept, Home Office, 1988–90; Dir of Custody, Prison Service HQ, Home Office, 1990–92. *Recreations:* opera, theatre, golf. *Address:* Nightingales, Nightingale Lane, Maidenhead, Berks SL6 7QL. *Club:* Royal Air Force.

INNES-KER, family name of **Duke of Roxburghe**.

INSALL, Donald William, CBE 1995 (OBE 1981); FSA, RWA, FRIBA, FRTPI; architect and planning consultant; Director, Donald Insall Associates Ltd (formerly Donald W. Insall & Associates), since 1958 (Founder, 1958; Principal, 1958–81; Chairma 1981–98); *b* 7 Feb. 1926; *o s* of late William R. Insall and Phyllis Insall, Henleaze, Brist *m* 1964, Amy Elizabeth, MA, *er d* of Malcolm H. Moss, Nanpantan, Leics; two *s* one *Educ:* Bristol Univ.; RA; Sch. of Planning, London (Dip. (Hons)); SPAB Lethaby Scho 1951. FRIBA 1968, FRTPI 1973. Coldstream Guards, 1944–47. Architectural ar Town-Planning Consultancy has included town-centre studies, civic and univ., churc domestic and other buildings, notably in conservation of historic towns and buildings (in restoration of ceiling, House of Lords, and Windsor Castle after fire, 1992); Medal (Mi of Housing and Local Govt), Good Design in Housing, 1962. Visiting Lecturer: RC 1964–69; Coll. d'Europe, Bruges, 1976–81; Catholic Univ. of Leuven, 1982–200 Adjunct Prof., Univ. of Syracuse, 1971–81. Mem., Council of Europe Working Part 1969–70; Nat. Pilot Study, Chester: A Study in Conservation, 1968; Consultant, Chest Conservation Programme, 1970–87 (EAHY Exemplar; European Prize for Preservatic of Historic Monuments, 1981; Europa Nostra Medals of Honour, 1983 and 198 Member: Historic Buildings Council for England, 1971–84; Grants Panel, EAHY, 197 Council, RSA, 1976–80 (FRSA, 1948); Council, SPAB, 1979–2007; Ancie Monuments Bd for England, 1980–84; UK Council, ICOMOS, 1998–; Royal Parks Ad Bd, 2000–02; Comr, Historic Bldgs and Monuments Commn, 1984–89; Membe Standing Adv. Cttee, Getty Grant Program, 1988–92; EC Expert Cttee on Architectur Heritage, 1990, 1993–; DNH Inquiry into Fire Protection at Royal Palaces, 1993; Arch Adv. Cttee, World Monuments Fund in Britain, 1996–; Vice-Chm., Conf. on Trng Architectural Conservation, 1990–2000 (Hon. Sec., 1959–89); Vice-President: Bl Crafts and Conservation Trust, 1994–; City of Winchester Trust, 2002–. Member: Arch Adv. Cttee, Westminster Abbey, 1993–98; Fabric Adv. Cttee, Southwark Cathedra 1992–, Canterbury Cathedral, 1997–. Patron: Kew Soc., 2001–; Envmtl Trust f Richmond-on-Thames, 2001–; Bedford Park Soc., 2001–. RIBA: Banister Fletch Medallist, 1949; Neale Bursar, 1955; Examnr, 1957; Competition Assessor, 197 Conferences: White House (Natural Beauty), 1965; Historic Architectural Interiors, US 1988, 1993; Singapore, 1994. Lecture tours: USA, 1964, 1972 (US Internat. Reg. Con on Conservation), 2003; Mexico, 1972; Yugoslavia, 1973; Canada, 1974, 199 Argentina, 1976; India, 1979; Portugal, 1982. Hon. Freeman, City of Chester, 2000. Ho LLD Bristol, 2004. European Architectural Heritage Year Medal (for Restoration Chevening), 1973; Harley J. McKee Award, Assoc. for Preservation Technol. Interna 1999; People in Conservation Award, RICS, 1999; Europa Nostra Medal of Honou 2000; Plowden Medal, Royal Warrant Holders' Assoc., 2001. Silver Jubilee Medal, 197 *Publications:* (jtly) Railway Station Architecture, 1966; (jtly) Conservation Areas 1967; Th Care of Old Buildings Today, 1973; Historic Buildings: action to maintain the experti for their care and repair, 1974; Conservation in Action, 1982; Conservation in Cheste 1988; Living Buildings, Architectural Conservation: philosophy, principles and practic 2008; contrib. to Encyclopædia Britannica, professional, environmental and internat. j *Recreations:* visiting, sketching, photographing and enjoying places; appreciatir craftsmanship; Post-Vintage Thoroughbred Cars (Mem., Rolls Royce Enthusiasts' Club *Address:* 73 Kew Green, Richmond, Surrey TW9 3AH; (office) 19 West Eaton Plac Eaton Square, SW1X 8LT. *T:* (020) 7245 9888. *Club:* Athenæum.

INSCH, Elspeth Virginia, OBE 1998; DL; Headmistress, King Edward VI Handswort School, Birmingham, since 1989; *b* 21 Aug. 1949; *d* of John Douglas Insch and Isabel Elizabeth Campbell (*née* Brodie). *Educ:* Newarke Girls' Sch., Leicester; Birkbeck Coll Univ. of London (BSc); Univ. of Edinburgh (MPhil, DipEd, PGCE). CGeog 200 Demonstrator, Univ. of Edinburgh, 1970–73; Teacher: Abington High Sch., Leic 1974–77; Nottingham High Sch. for Girls (GPDST), 1977–84; Dep. Head, Kesteven ar Sleaford High Sch. for Girls, 1984–89. Consultant, Springbank Sand and Gravel Co. Lt 1970–79. Pres., Assoc. of Maintained Girls' Schools, 1999–2000; Mem. Cttee, Na Grammar Schools Assoc., 1990–. FRGS 1968 (Mem., 1994–, Chm., 2003–06, Educ Cttee; Vice Pres., 2003–06). Fellow, Winston Churchill Meml Trust, 1980; Truste Grantham Yorke Trust, 1990–. DL W Midlands, 2008. Hon. DSc Aston, 2006. *Addre* King Edward VI Handsworth School, Rose Hill Road, Birmingham B21 9AR.

INSHAW, Maj. Gen. Timothy Gordon; Director General Training and Educatio since 2007; *b* Hong Kong, 14 Aug. 1957; *s* of Gordon Henry William Inshaw and Ri Inshaw; *m* 1982, Sally Patricia Roe; three *s*. *Educ:* Wilsthorpe Comp. Sch.; Welbeck Coll RMA Sandhurst; RMCS (BSc 1981). CE, MIET 2000. SO3 Comms HQN1, 1985–8 Instructor, Sch. of Signals, 1987; Army Staff Coll., 1988–89; OC 212 (12 Armoured Bd Signal Sqn, 1990–92; Instructor, JSDC, 1992–93; SO2 Operational Requirements, 199 S01 Mgt Plans, DGCIS, 1995; CO 9th Signal Regt (Radio), 1995–98; Dep. Dir Defenc Resources and Plans, 1998–2000; rcds 2001; Comdr 1st Signal Bde, 2002–04; D Capability Integration (Army), 2004–07. Col Comdt, Royal Corps of Signals, 2007– *Recreations:* cricket (playing and watching), gardening. *Address:* Main Building, Ministry c Defence, Whitehall, SW1A 2HB.

INSKIP, family name of **Viscount Caldecote**.

INSOLE, Douglas John, CBE 1979; Marketing Director, Trollope & Colls Ltd, 1975–9 *b* 18 April 1926; *s* of John Herbert Insole and Margaret Rose Insole; *m* 1948, Barbara Haz Ridgway (*d* 1982); two *d* (and one *d* decd). *Educ:* Sir George Monoux Grammar Sch.; S Catharine's Coll., Cambridge (MA). Cricket: Cambridge Univ., 1947–49 (Captair 1949); Essex CCC, 1947–63 (Captain, 1950–60); played 9 times for England; Vice Captain, MCC tour of S Africa, 1956–57. Chairman: Test Selectors, 1965–68; TCCE later ECB, 1975–78 (Chm., Cricket Cttee, 1968–87; Chm., Internat. Cttee, 1988–2000 Mem., MCC Cttee, 1955–94; Manager, England cricket team, Australian tours, 1978–7 and 1982–83. Soccer: Cambridge Univ., 1946–48; Pegasus, and Corinthian Casual Amateur Cup Final medal, 1956. Member: Sports Council, 1971–74; FA Council, 1979 (Life Vice-Pres., 1999). Pres., Essex CCC, 1994–. JP Chingford, 1962–74. *Publicatior* Cricket from the Middle, 1960. *Recreations:* cricket, soccer. *Address:* 8 Hadleigh Cour Crescent Road, Chingford, E4 6AX. *T:* (020) 8529 6546. *Club:* MCC (Trustee, 1988–94 Hon. Life Vice Pres., 1995; Pres., 2006–07).

INSTANCE, Caroline Mary; Chief Executive, Actuarial Profession, since 2002; *b* 4 Ma 1957; *d* of William Henry and late Hilary Willatt; *m* 1st (marr. diss. 1995); one *s* one *d* 2nd, 1998, John Instance; two step *d*. *Educ:* Henley Grammar Sch.; Sheffield Univ. (BS Hons Psychol. 1978). MIPD. With Rank Orgn, 1978–82; United Friendly, 1982–9 (Human Resources Dir, 1993–96); Chief Exec., OPRA, 1996–2002. *Recreations:* famil life, enjoying countryside, theatre, cinema, good food and wine, teasing lawyers an actuaries. *Address:* Faculty and Institute of Actuaries, Staple Inn Hall, High Holborn WC1V 7QJ. *T:* (020) 7632 2115; *e-mail:* caroline.instance@actuaries.org.uk.

INVERDALE, John Ballantyne; sports presenter, BBC; *b* 27 Sept. 1957; *s* of Capt. Joh Ballantyne Inverdale, CBE, RN and Stella Norah Westlake (*née* Richards); *n* Jacqueline Elizabeth Knight; two *d*. *Educ:* Clifton Coll.; Univ. of Southampton (BA Hons). Journalist, Lincolnshire Echo, 1979–82; BBC Radio Lincs, 1982–85; BBC Radi 2, 1985–88; presenter: Sport on 5 (formerly Sport on 2), BBC Radio, 1988–94 Drivetime, BBC Radio 5 Live, 1994–97, and Rugby Special, BBC TV, 1994–; Onside

1997–, Grandstand, 1999–, BBC TV. Hon. DLitt Soton. *Address:* c/o BBC Television, Wood Lane, W12 7RJ.

INVERFORTH, 4th Baron *cr* 1919, of Southgate; **Andrew Peter Weir;** *b* 16 Nov. 1966; *s* of 3rd Baron Inverforth and of Jill Elizabeth, *o d* of late John W. Thornycroft, CBE; *S* father, 1982; *m* 1992, Rachel Sian Shapland Davies. *Educ:* Marlborough College; Trinity Coll., Cambridge; London Hosp. Med. Coll. MB BS 1994.

INVERNESS (St Andrew's Cathedral), Provost of; *see* Gordon, Very Rev. A. R.

INWOOD, Rt Rev. Richard Neil; *see* Bedford, Bishop Suffragan of.

ION, Dr Susan Elizabeth, OBE 2002; FREng, FIMMM, FINucE; Vice-President, Royal Academy of Engineering, since 2002; *b* 3 Feb. 1955; *d* of Lawrence James Burrows and Doris Burrows (*née* Cherry); *m* 1980, John Albert Ion. *Educ:* Penwortham Girls' Grammar Sch., Preston, Lancs; Imperial Coll., London (BSc 1st Cl. Hons, DIC; PhD Materials Sci./Metallurgy 1979). FREng (FEng 1996). British Nuclear Fuels Ltd: Hd, R & D, Fuel Div., 1990–92; Dir, Technol. Develt, 1992–96; Dir of Technol., 1996–2006; Mem., Company Executive, 1996–2006. Member: PPARC, 1994–2000; Council for Sci. and Technol., 2004–; EPSRC, 2005–. Vis. Prof., Imperial Coll. London, 2006–. Pres., British Nuclear Soc., 2004–06. Gov., Univ. of Manchester, 2004–. Hinton Medal for Outstanding Contribn to Nuclear Engrg, INucE, 1993. *Recreations:* ski-ing, fell walking, playing the violin. *Address:* Royal Academy of Engineering, 3 Carlton House Terrace, SW1Y 5DG.

IPGRAVE, Ven. Michael Geoffrey, PhD; Archdeacon of Southwark, since 2004; *b* 18 April 1958; *s* of Geoffrey William Ipgrave and Ellen Ruth Ipgrave; *m* 1981, Julia Dawn Bailey; three *s*. *Educ:* Magdalen College Sch., Brackley; Oriel Coll., Oxford (BA 1978, MA 1994); Ripon Coll., Cuddesdon; St Chad's Coll., Durham (PhD 1999); SOAS, Univ. of London (MA 2005). Ordained deacon, 1982, priest, 1983; Asst Curate, All Saints, Oakham, 1982–85; Asst Priest, Ch of the Resurrection, Chiba, Japan, 1985–87; Team Vicar, The Ascension, Leicester, 1987–90; Team Vicar, 1990–95, Team Rector, 1995–99, The Holy Spirit, Leicester; Inter Faith Relns Advr, Archbishops' Council, and Sec., Chs' Commn on Inter Faith Relns, 1999–2004. *Publications:* Christ in Ten Thousand Places, 1994; Trinity and Inter Faith Dialogue, 2003; The Road Ahead: Christian-Muslim dialogue, 2003; (ed) Scriptures in Dialogue, 2004; (ed) Bearing the Word, 2005. *Recreations:* walking, all things Japanese. *Address:* Trinity House, 4 Chapel Court, Borough High Street, SE1 1HW. *T:* (020) 7939 9409, *Fax:* (020) 7939 9465; *e-mail:* michael.ipgrave@southwark.anglican.org.

IPSWICH, Viscount; Henry Oliver Charles FitzRoy; *b* 6 April 1978; *s* and *heir* of Earl of Euston, *qv*. *Educ:* Harrow Sch.; Edinburgh Univ.; RAC, Cirencester.

IPSWICH, Bishop of; *see* St Edmundsbury and Ipswich.

IPSWICH, Archdeacon of; *no new appointment at time of going to press.*

IRBY, family name of **Baron Boston**.

IRBY, Charles Leonard Anthony, FCA; Director, since 1999, and Chairman, since 2000, Aberdeen Asset Management plc; *b* 5 June 1945; *s* of Hon. Anthony P. Irby and Mary Irby (*née* Apponyi); *m* 1971, Sarah Jane Sutherland; one *s* one *d*. *Educ:* Eton Coll. FCA 1979. Binder Hamlyn & Co., Chartered Accountants, 1965–69; Joseph Sebag & Co., Stockbrokers, 1971–74; Baring Brothers & Co. Ltd, 1974–95 (Dir, 1985–95); Baring Brothers Asia Ltd, 1976–79; Dir, Baring Brothers Internat. Ltd, 1995–99 (Dep. Chm., 1997–99); Man. Dir, 1995–99, Sen. UK Advr, 1999–2001, ING Barings. Director: E. C. Harris, 2001–05; QBE Insurance Group Ltd, 2001–; N Atlantic Smaller Cos Investment Trust, 2002–; Great Portland Estates Plc, 2004–. Mem., Panel on Takeovers and Mergers, 1998–99. Chm., Corporate Finance Cttee, London Investment Bankers' Assoc., 1998–99. Mem. Council, King Edward VII's Hosp. Sister Agnes, 2000–. FRSA. *Recreations:* travel, photography. *Address:* 125 Blenheim Crescent, W11 2EQ. *T:* (020) 7221 2979. *Clubs:* Boodle's, City of London.

See also Viscount Combermere.

IREDALE, Peter, PhD; FInstP, FIET; Chairman: Oxfordshire Health Authority, 1996–2001; Four Counties Public Health Resources Unit, 1997–2000; *b* Brownhills, Staffs, 15 March 1932; *s* of late Henry and Annie Iredale; *m* 1957, Judith Margaret (*née* Marshall); one *s* three *d*. *Educ:* King Edward VIth Grammar Sch., Lichfield; Univ. of Bristol (BSc, PhD). AERE Harwell (subseq. Harwell Laboratory), 1955–92: research: on Nuclear Instrumentation, 1955–69; on Non Destructive Testing, 1969–70; Computer Storage, 1970–73; Commercial Officer, 1973–75; Gp Leader, Nuclear Instrumentation, 1975–77; Dep. Hd, Marketing and Sales Dept, 1977–79; Hd of Marine Technology Support Unit, 1979–81; Chm., UK Wave-Energy Steering Cttee, 1979–84; Dir, Engrg, 1981–84; Dir, Engrg and Non Nuclear Energy, 1984–86; Dep. Dir, 1986–87, Dir, 1987–90, Harwell Lab.; Dir, Culham/Harwell Sites, UKAEA, 1990–92. Chairman: Oxfordshire DHA, 1992–96; Develt Bd, Oxford Inst. of Health Scis, 1993–2001; Elliot-Smith Clinic, 2002–. Supernumerary Fellow, 1991–99, Mem. of Common Room, Wolfson Coll., Oxford, 1999–. Hon. DSc Oxford Brookes, 1993. *Publications:* papers on high energy physics, nuclear instrumentation. *Recreations:* family, music, working with wood, gardening. *Address:* 25 Kirk Close, Oxford OX2 8JL.

IREDALE, Prof. Roger Oliver, PhD; Professor of International Education, 1993–96, now Professor Emeritus, and Director (formerly Dean), Faculty of Education, 1994–96, University of Manchester; *b* 13 Aug. 1934; *s* of Fred Iredale and Elsie Florence (*née* Hills); *m* 1968, Mavis Potter; one *s* one *d*. *Educ:* Harrow County Grammar Sch.; Univ. of Reading (BA 1956, MA 1959, PhD 1971; Hurry Medal for Poetry; Early English Text Soc's Prize; Seymour-Sharman Prize for Literature; Graham Robertson Travel Award); Peterhouse Coll., Univ. of Cambridge (Cert. Ed. 1957). Teacher, Hele's Sch., Exeter, 1959–61; Lectr and Senior Lectr, Bishop Otter Coll., Chichester, 1962–70; British Council Officer and Maître de Conférences, Univ. of Algiers, 1970–72; Lectr, Chichester Coll. of Further Educn, 1972–73; British Council Officer, Madras, 1973–75; Dir of Studies, Educl Admin., Univ. of Leeds, 1975–79; Educn Adviser, 1979–83, Chief Educn Advr, 1983–93, ODA. Sen. Consultant, Iredale Develt Internat., 1996–2003. Member: Commonwealth Scholarship Commn, 1984–93; Unesco-Unicef Jt Cttee, 1991–96; VSO Educn Adv. Cttee, 2002–04; Comr, Sino-British Friendship Scholarship Scheme Commn, 1986–96. Governor: Sch. of Oriental and African Studies, 1983–95; Queen Elizabeth House, Oxford, 1986–87; Commonwealth of Learning, 1988–93; Sidcot Sch., 2001–03. Trustee, 1993–98, non-exec. Dir, 1998–2007, CfBT Educn Services, subseq. CfBT Educn Trust; Chm., CfBT LLC, Abu Dhabi, 2006–. Trustee: War on Want, 1998–2000; BookPower, 1999–2006. Hon. FCP 1995. Poetry Society's Greenwood Prize, 1974. *Publications:* Turning Bronzes (poems), 1974; Out Towards the Dark (poems), 1978; articles in The Times, Guardian, Comparative Education and other jls; poems for BBC Radio 3 and in anthologies and jls. *Recreations:* poetry writing, championing the oppressed. *Address:* Northsyde House, 17 High Street, West Coker, Yeovil BA22 9AP. *T:* (01935) 864422.

IRELAND, Norman Charles; Chairman, BTR, 1993–96 (Director, 1969–96); *b* 28 May 1927; *s* of Charles and Winifred Ireland; *m* 1953, Gillian Margaret (*née* Harrison) (*d* 2001); one *s* one *d*. *Educ:* England, USA, India. CA (Scot.); Chartered Management Accountant. With Richard Brown & Co., Edinburgh, 1944–50; Brown Fleming & Murray, London, 1950–54; Avon Rubber Co., Melksham, 1955–64; Chief Accountant, United Glass, 1964–66; Finance Dir, BTR, 1967–87; Chm., Bowater plc, 1987–93. Chairman: The Housing Finance Corp., 1988–93; Intermediate Capital Gp, 1989–93; Dir, Meggitt, 1987–93. *Recreations:* gardening, ballet, opera, music.

IRELAND, Patrick Gault de C.; *see* de Courcy-Ireland.

IRELAND, Ronald David; QC (Scot.) 1964; Sheriff Principal of Grampian, Highland and Islands, 1988–93; *b* 13 March 1925; *o s* of William Alexander Ireland and Agnes Victoria Brown. *Educ:* George Watson's Coll., Edinburgh; Balliol Coll., Oxford (Scholar; BA 1950, MA 1958); Edinburgh Univ. (LLB 1952). Served Royal Signals, 1943–46. Passed Advocate, 1952; Clerk of the Faculty of Advocates, 1957–58; Aberdeen University: Prof. of Scots Law, 1958–71; Dean of Faculty of Law, 1964–67; Hon. Prof., Faculty of Law, 1988–; Sheriff of Lothian and Borders (formerly Lothians and Peebles) at Edinburgh, 1972–88. Governor, Aberdeen Coll. of Education, 1959–64 (Vice-Chm., 1962–64). Comr, under NI (Emergency Provisions) Act, 1974–75. Member: Bd of Management, Aberdeen Gen. Hosps, 1961–71 (Chm., 1964–71); Departmental Cttee on Children and Young Persons, 1961–64; Cttee on the Working of the Abortion Act, 1971–74; Hon. Sheriff for Aberdeenshire, 1963–88. Member: North Eastern Regional Hosp. Bd, 1964–71 (Vice-Chm. 1966–71); After Care Council, 1962–65; Nat. Staff Advisory Cttee for the Scottish Hosp. Service, 1964–65; Chm., Scottish Hosps Administrative Staffs Cttee, 1965–72. Dir, Scottish Courts Admin, 1975–78. Hon. LLD Aberdeen, 1994. *Address:* 6A Greenhill Gardens, Edinburgh EH10 4BW. *Clubs:* New (Edinburgh); Royal Northern and University (Aberdeen); Highland (Inverness).

IRELAND, (William) Seith (Stanners); Sheriff of North Strathclyde at Kilmarnock, since 2004; *b* 5 April 1956; *s* of Samuel Ireland and Isobel Ireland (*née* Stanners); *m* 2006, Elizabeth Crombie. *Educ:* High Sch. of Glasgow; Univ. of Glasgow (LLB Hons 1979). Admitted as solicitor, 1982; asst solicitor, 1982–85; founded own practice, Ireland & Co., 1986–2003. Temp. Sheriff, 1999; Sheriff (pt-time), 2000–03; Floating Sheriff, 2003–04. Pres., Glasgow Bar Assoc., 1993–94; Mem. Council, Law Soc. of Scotland, 1995–98. Mem. Business Cttee, Gen. Council, Univ. of Glasgow, 2005–. *Recreations:* golf, cinema, cooking. *Address:* Sheriff's Chambers, Sheriff Court House, Kilmarnock, Ayrshire KA1 1ED. *T:* (01563) 550024, *Fax:* (01563) 543568; *e-mail:* sheriffwsireland@scotcourts.gov.uk.

IRENS, Nicholas James, FCA; Chairman, Sporting Index Ltd, since 2006; *b* 6 Oct. 1946; *s* of late Gp Capt. Henry James Irens and of Helen Margaret Irens; *m* 1972, Fiona Mary Walker; three *s* one *d*. *Educ:* Blundell's Sch., Tiverton. FCA 1970. Partner, Turner Easdale & Co., Chartered Accountants, 1970–78; Finance Director: Juliana's Hldgs plc, 1979–87; First Leisure Corp. plc, 1988–92; Chm., Cannons Gp plc, 1992–2001. Non-exec. Chm., James Hull Gp Ltd, 2006–; non-exec. Dir, Evolution Gp plc, 2004–. *Recreations:* bridge, cricket, racing, Chelsea FC. *Address:* Whitegates Farm, Grants Lane, Limpsfield, Surrey RH8 0RQ. *T:* (01883) 730505, *Fax:* (01883) 723453; *e-mail:* nirens@btopenworld.com. *Clubs:* Portland, Turf, MCC, Middlesex CC.

IRETON, Barrie Rowland, CB 2000; Director, Copperbelt Development Foundation, since 2002; *b* 15 Jan. 1944; *s* of Philip Thomas Ireton, CBE, and Marjorie Rosalind Ireton; *m* 1965, June Collins; one *s* one *d* (and one *s* decd). *Educ:* Alleyn's Grammar Sch., Stevenage; Trinity Coll., Cambridge (MA); London School of Economics (MSc 1970). Economic Statistician, Govt of Zambia, 1965–68; Economist, Industrial Develt Corp., Zambia, 1968–69; Development Sec., The Gambia, 1970–73; Overseas Development Administration: Economic Advr, 1973–76; Sen. Economic Advr, 1976–84; Asst Sec., 1984–88; Under Sec., 1988–96; Principal Finance Officer, 1988–93; Dir, Africa Div., 1993–96; Dir-Gen., Progs, subseq. Internat. and Resources, ODA, FCO, then DFID, 1996–2003. Sen. Fellow, Inst. of Commonwealth Studies, 2005–. Director: Zambia Copper Investments, 2002–05; European Investment Bank, 2002–05; Dir, 2002–05, Business Advr, 2006–, Konkola Copper Mines. *Recreations:* tennis, gardening, walking. *Address:* 11 Eynella Road, SE22 8XF.

IRONS, Jeremy; actor; *b* 19 Sept. 1948; *s* of late Paul Dugan Irons and of Barbara Anne Brereton (*née* Sharpe); *m* 1st (marr. diss.); 2nd, 1978, Sinead Cusack; two *s*. *Educ:* Sherborne; Bristol Old Vic Theatre Sch. *Theatre* appearances include: Bristol Old Vic Theatre Co., 1968–71; Godspell, Round House, transf. Wyndham's, 1971; The Taming of the Shrew, New Shakespeare Co., Round House, 1975; Wild Oats, RSC, 1976–77; The Rear Column, Globe, 1978; The Real Thing, Broadway, 1984 (Tony Award for Best Actor); The Rover, Mermaid, 1986; A Winter's Tale, RSC, 1986; Richard II, RSC, 1986; A Little Night Music, NY, 2003; Camelot, Hollywood Bowl, 2004; Embers, Duke of York, 2006; Never So Good, Lyttelton, 2008; *television* appearances include: The Pallisers; Love for Lydia; Brideshead Revisited, 1981; The Captain's Doll, 1983; Longitude, 2000; Elizabeth I, 2005 (Best Supporting Actor, Emmy Awards, 2006, Golden Globe Awards, 2007); *films* include: The French Lieutenant's Woman, 1981; Moonlighting, 1982; Betrayal, 1982; Swann in Love, 1983; The Wild Duck, 1983; The Mission, 1986; A Chorus of Disapproval, 1988; Dead Ringers, 1988 (Best Actor, New York Film Critics Circle Awards, 1988, Genie Awards, 1989); Danny Champion of the World, 1988; Reversal of Fortune, 1990 (Academy Award for Best Actor, 1991); Australia, 1991; Kafka, 1992; Waterland, 1992; Damage, 1993; M. Butterfly, 1994; The House of the Spirits, 1994; Die Hard: with a vengeance, 1995; Stealing Beauty, 1996; Lolita, 1997; The Man in the Iron Mask, 1998; Chinese Box, 1998; Dungeons and Dragons, And Now Ladies and Gentlemen, Callas Forever, Last Call, 2001; The Time Machine, 2002; Being Julia, 2004; Merchant of Venice, 2004; Kingdom of Heaven, 2005; Casanova, Eragon, Inland Empire, 2006. Member: Gaia Foundn; European Film Acad.; Patron: Prison Phoenix Trust; Archway Foundn. *Address:* c/o Hutton Management, 4 Old Manor Close, Askett, Bucks HP27 9NA.

IRONS, Norman MacFarlane, CBE 1995; DL; CEng; Lord Provost and Lord Lieutenant of Edinburgh, 1992–96; Partner, IFP Consulting Engineers, 1983–2006; *b* 4 Jan. 1941; *s* of Dugald Paterson Irons and Anne Galbraith Irons (*née* Rankin); *m* 1966, Anne Wyness Buckley; one *s* one *d*. *Educ:* George Heriot's Sch.; Borough Road Coll.; Napier Tech. Coll. CEng; MCIBSE 1968; MIMechE 1973. Building Services Engr, 1962–. Mem. (SNP) City of Edinburgh Council, 1976–96. JP 1983, DL 1988, Edinburgh. Pres., Lismore RFC, 1989–94. Hon. Consul for Denmark, 1999. Paul Harris Fellow, Rotary Internat., 1996; Hon. Mem. Rotary Club of Edinburgh, 2007. Hon. FRCSE 1994. Hon. DLitt Napier, 1993; DUniv Heriot-Watt, 1997. Royal Order of Merit (Norway), 1994. *Recreations:* enjoying life with his wife, Rugby. *Address:* 141 Saughtonhall Drive, Edinburgh EH12 5TS. *T:* (0131) 337 6154. *Club:* New (Edinburgh).

IRONSIDE, family name of **Baron Ironside**.

IRONSIDE, 2nd Baron *cr* 1941, of Archangel and of Ironside; **Edmund Oslac Ironside;** Defence Consultant, Rolls-Royce Industrial Power Group, 1989–95; *b* 21 Sept. 1924; *o s* of 1st Baron Ironside, Field Marshal, GCB, CMG, DSO, and Mariot Ysabel Cheyne (*d* 1984); *S* father, 1959; *m* 1950, Audrey Marigold, *y d* of late Lt-Col Hon. Thomas Morgan-Grenville, DSO, OBE, MC; one *s* one *d*. *Educ:* Tonbridge Sch. Joined Royal Navy, 1943; retd as Lt, 1952. Marconi Co., 1952–59; English Electric Leo Computers, 1959–64; Cryosystems Ltd, 1964–68; International Research and Development Co., 1968–84; Market Co-ordinator (Defence), NEI plc, 1984–89. Mem., EC Select Cttee, H of L, 1974–90; Vice-Pres., Parly and Scientific Cttee, 1977–80 and 1983–86 (Dep. Chm., 1974–77); Treas., All Party Energy Studies Gp, 1979–92; Chm., All Party Defence Study Gp, 1994–99 (Hon. Sec., 1992–94). Mem., Organising Cttee, British Library, 1972–74. President: Electric Vehicle Assoc., 1975–83; European Electric Road Vehicle Assoc., 1980–82; Vice-Pres., Inst. of Patentees and Inventors, 1976–90; Chm., Adv. Cttee, Science Reference Lib., 1975–85. Member: Court, 1975–94, Council, 1986–88, City Univ.; Court, 1982–, Council, 1984–87, Essex Univ. Pres., Sea Cadet Corps, Chelmsford, 1959–88. Mem. Ct Assts, Skinners' Co. (Master, 1981–82). Hon. FCGI (CGIA 1986). *Publication:* (ed) High Road to Command: the diaries of Major-General Sir Edmund Ironside, 1920–22, 1972. *Heir: s* Hon. Charles Edmund Grenville Ironside [*b* 1 July 1956; *m* 1st, 1985, Hon. Elizabeth Law (marr. diss. 2000), *e d* of Lord Coleraine, *qv*; one *s* two *d*; 2nd, 2001, Katherine Rowley; one *d*]. *Address:* Priory House, Old House Lane, Boxted, Colchester, Essex CO4 5RB. *Club:* Royal Ocean Racing.

IRONSIDE, Gordon Douglas; Headmaster, Sutton Grammar School, since 1990; *b* 11 Aug. 1955; *s* of Douglas William Ironside and Doreen Grant Ironside; *m* 1979, Rachael Elizabeth Ann Golder; two *s* one *d*. *Educ:* Pembroke Coll., Cambridge (BA 1977; Scholar); Durham Univ. (PGCE). CMath; FIMA. Hd of Maths, 1983–89, Dep. Headmaster, 1987–90, Sutton Grammar Sch. *Recreations:* tennis, golf, Rotary, mathematics. *Address:* Sutton Grammar School, Manor Lane, Sutton SM1 4AS. *T:* (020) 8642 3821; *e-mail:* gironside@aol.com. *Clubs:* Sutton Rotary (Pres., 1998–2000); Cuddington Golf; Surrey Racquets.

IRONSIDE, Prof. James Wilson, CBE 2006; FRCPath, FRCPE; FMedSci; Professor of Clinical Neuropathology, National CJD Surveillance Unit, University of Edinburgh, since 2000; *b* 18 Nov. 1954; *s* of James F. Ironside and Jessie C. Ironside (*née* Moir); *m* 1979, Janet A. D. Cruickshank (marr. diss. 1992); one *s* one *d*. *Educ:* Univ. of Dundee (BMSc, MB ChB). FRCPath 1997; FRCPE 1999. Lectr in Pathology, Univ. of Leeds, 1986–90; Consultant Neuropathologist, Western Gen. Hosp., Edinburgh, 1990–; Sen. Lectr in Pathology, 1994–98, Reader, 1998–2000, Univ. of Edinburgh. Hon. Consultant Neuropathologist, Lothian Univ. Hosps NHS Trust, 1994–. FMedSci 2002; FRSA 2007. *Publications:* (jtly) Neuropathology: a color atlas and text, 1994; (jtly) Intraoperative Diagnosis of CNS Tumours, 1997; (jtly) Diagnostic Pathology of Nervous System Tumours, 2002; numerous contribs to scientific jls. *Recreations:* singing (Scottish Chamber Orchestra Chorus), early music, piano, Renaissance Art, wine, Francophile. *Address:* National CJD Surveillance Unit, Western General Hospital, Crewe Road, Edinburgh EH4 2XU. *T:* (0131) 537 3109, *Fax:* (0131) 537 3056; *e-mail:* james.ironside@ed.ac.uk.

IRONSIDE, Leonard, CBE 2003; JP; Area Development Officer, North of Scotland, since 2003, and Information and Support Manager for Scotland, Parkinson's Disease Society; *b* 16 Feb.; *s* of Alexander and Olive Ironside; *m* 1992, Wendy Anita Cook; two *d*. *Educ:* Hilton Acad., Aberdeen. Professional Lightweight Wrestler, 1973–91 (Commonwealth Middleweight Champion, 1981–91). Department of Social Security, Aberdeen: Welfare Benefits Manager, 1976–79; Manager, Pensions Section, 1980–85; Adjudication Officer, 1985–87; Nat. Insce Inspector, 1987–99; Nat. Minimum Wage Officer, 1999–2000. Convention of Scottish Local Authorities: social works spokesman, 1997–99; Chm., Urban Affairs, 1999–2001. Columnist, Aberdeen Independent, 2000–. Aberdeen City Council: Mem. (Lab) 1996–; Dep. Leader and Convener, Social Work Cttee, 1996–99; Leader, 1999–2003; Leader, Lab. Gp and Opposition, 2003–. Chm., Grampian Initiative, 1990–94. Mem. Bd, NHS Grampian, 2001–03. Member: Bd, Aberdeen Exhibn and Conf. Centre, 1986–96; Aberdeen Voluntary Service, 1995–99; Bd of Govs, Robert Gordon Univ., 1999–2008. Chm., Aberdeen Internat. Youth Fest., 1995–2003. Mem., Granite City Chorus, 2008–. FRSA 2003. JP Aberdeen, 1995. Rose Bowl Award for services to disabled sport, Scottish Sports Council, 1990. *Publications:* When You're Ready Boys… Take Hold, 2008; articles in local govt mags, local press, etc. *Recreations:* tennis, yoga, walking, cycling, being with my family, coaching people with disabilities in athletics, swimming and weightlifting. *Address:* 42 Hillside Terrace, Portlethen, Aberdeen AB12 4QG. *T:* (01224) 780929; *e-mail:* ironside@ifb.co.uk.

IRRANCA-DAVIES, (Ifor) Huw; MP (Lab) Ogmore, since Feb. 2002; Parliamentary Under-Secretary of State, Department for Environment, Food and Rural Affairs, since 2008; *b* 22 Jan. 1963; *s* of Gethin Davies and Anne Teresa Davies; *m* 1991, Joanna Teresa Irranca; three *s*. *Educ:* Crewe and Alsager Coll. (BA Hons Combined Studies); Swansea Inst. of Higher Educn (MSc Eur. Leisure Resource Mgt (Univ. of Wales Award)). Recreation Asst, then Duty Manager, Lliw Valley BC, 1986–89; Manager, CLM Ltd and Serco Ltd, 1989–92; Facilities Manager, Swansea Coll., 1994–96; Sen. Lectr, Swansea Inst. of Higher Educn, 1996–2002. An Asst Govt Whip, 2006–07; Parly Under-Sec. of State, Wales Office, 2007–08. *Recreations:* family activities, hill-walking, cycling, reading biographies and historical fiction, Rugby. *Address:* House of Commons, SW1A 0AA. *T:* (020) 7219 2952.

IRVIN, Albert, RA 1998; painter; *b* 21 Aug. 1922; *s* of Albert Henry Jesse Irvin and Nina Lucy Irvin; *m* 1947, Beatrice Olive Nicolson; two *d*. *Educ:* Northampton Sch. of Art; Goldsmiths' Coll. Sch. of Art (NDD (Painting); Hon. Fellow, 2002). Navigator, RAF, 1941–46. Lectr, Goldsmiths' Coll. Sch. of Art, 1962–83; visitor at art schs, Britain and abroad. *Solo exhibitions* include: New Art Centre, London, 1961, 1963, 1965, 1971, 1973; Acme Gall., London, 1980; Gimpel Fils, London, 1982, 1984, 1986, 1990, 1992, 1994, 1996, 1998, 2002, 2004, 2007; Aberdeen Art Gall., 1976, 1983; Third Eye Centre, Glasgow, 1983; Ikon Gall., Birmingham, 1983; Talbot Rice Gall., Edinburgh, 1989; Serpentine Gall., London, 1990; Oriel and Chapter, Cardiff, 1990; RHA, Dublin, 1995; RWA, Bristol, 1999; Stühler Galerie, Berlin, 2002; Lancaster Univ. and Storey Galls, Lancaster, 2003; Peppercanister Gall., Dublin, 2003, 2006, 2008; Advanced Graphics, London 2005; Tate Britain, 2008; King's Place, London, 2008; also at galls and museums in USA, Australia, Austria, Germany, France, Belgium, Spain, Saudi Arabia, etc; *group exhibitions* include: British Art, Hayward, 1974; British Art, Royal Acad., 1977; Hayward, 1980; Presence of Painting, Mappin Gall., Sheffield and tour, 1988; Experience of Painting, Laing Art Gall., Newcastle and tour, 1989; Great British Art Show, Glasgow, 1990; Here and Now, Serpentine, 1994; "1979", Bloomberg SPACE, London, 2005; Réalités Nouvelles, Paris, 2006; Dreischritt, Galerie Parterre, Berlin, 2006; Royal Acad., 2006, 2007; 10 Royal Academicians, Dubai, 2006; *work in public collections* including: Tate Gall.; Royal Acad.; V&A; British Council; Arts Council; also in other British and internat. collections; *commissions* include: painting for Homerton Hosp., Hackney, 1987; design for Diversions Dance Co., 1994; painting for Chelsea and Westminster Hosp., 199 *Television:* A Feeling for Paint, 1983; Off the Wall: the Byker Show, 1994; Albert Irvi artist at work, 2000; Albert Irvin: portrait (France), 2003; radio interviews. Arts Counc Awards, 1968, 1975, 1980; Prizewinner, John Moores Liverpool Exhibn, 198 Gulbenkian Award for Printmaking, 1983; Giles Bequest Prize, V&A and British Mu 1986; Korn/Ferry Internat. Premier Award, Royal Acad., 1989. *Relevant publicatio* Albert Irvin: life to painting, by Paul Moorhouse, 1998. *Recreation:* music. *Address:* 1 Gorst Road, SW11 6JB. *T:* (020) 7228 2929; 71 Stepney Green, E1 3LE. *Clubs:* Chelse Arts, Arts.

IRVINE, family name of **Baron Irvine of Lairg**.

IRVINE OF LAIRG, Baron *cr* 1987 (Life Peer), of Lairg in the District of Sutherlan **Alexander Andrew Mackay Irvine;** PC 1997; Lord High Chancellor of England ar Wales, 1997–2003; *b* 23 June 1940; *s* of Alexander Irvine and Margaret Christina Irvin *m* 1974, Alison Mary, *y d* of Dr James Shaw McNair, MD, and Agnes McNair, MA; tw *s*. *Educ:* Inverness Acad.; Hutchesons' Boys' Grammar Sch., Glasgow; Glasgow Uni (MA, LLB); Christ's Coll., Cambridge (Scholar; BA 1st Cl. Hons with distinction; LL 1st Cl. Hons; George Long Prize in Jurisprudence; Hon. Fellow, 1996). Called to the Ba Inner Temple, 1967, Bencher, 1985; QC 1978; a Recorder, 1985–88; Dep. High Cou Judge, 1987–97. Univ. Lectr, LSE, 1965–69. Contested (Lab) Hendon North, 197 Opposition spokesman on legal and home affairs, 1987–92; Shadow Lord Chancellor, of L, 1992–97. Joint President: Industry and Parlt Trust, 1997–; British-Amer. Parly G 1997–; IPU, 1997–; CPA, 1997–; Pres., Magistrates' Assoc. Church Comr. Trustee, Joh Smith Meml Trust, 1992–97; Foundn Trustee, Whitechapel Art Gall., 1990–97; Truste Hunterian Collection, 1997–. Mem. Cttee, Friends of the Slade, 1990–. Vice-Patro World Fedn of Mental Health, 1998–. Hon. Bencher, Inn of Court of NI, 1998. Fellov US Coll. of Trial Lawyers, 1998; Hon. Fellow: Soc. for Advanced Legal Studies, 199 LSE, 2000. Hon. Mem., Polish Bar, 2000. Hon. LLD: Glasgow, 1997; Siena, 200 *Recreations:* cinema, theatre, collecting paintings, reading, travel. *Address:* House of Lord SW1A 0PW. *Club:* Garrick.

IRVINE, Alan Montgomery, RDI 1964; DesRCA, ARIBA; architect in privat practice; *b* 14 Sept. 1926; *s* of Douglas Irvine and Ellen Marler; *m* 1st, 1955; one *s*; 2n 1966, Katherine Mary Buzas; two *s*. *Educ:* Regent Street Polytechnic, Secondary Sch. an Sch. of Architecture; Royal College of Art. RAF (Aircrew), 1944–47. Worked in Mila with BBPR Gp, 1954–55. In private practice since 1956, specialising in design of interior museums and exhibitions; partnership Buzas and Irvine, 1965–85. Accredite correspondent to NASA, Apollo 13 Mission, 1970. Work has included interior design f Schroder Wagg & Co., Lazards, Bovis, S Australian Govt, Nat. Enterprise Bd; Mem. design team for QE2, 1966. Various exhibns for V&A Museum, Tate Gallery, Roy Academy, Imperial War Museum, RIBA, British Council, British Museum, Wellcom Inst., Olivetti, Fiat etc including: Treasures of Cambridge, 1959; Book of Kells, 196 Internat. Exhibn of Modern Jewellery, 1961; Architecture of Power, 1963; Mello Collection, 1969; Art and the E India Trade, 1970; Age of Charles I, 1972; Interna Ceramics, 1972; Pompeii AD79, 1976; Gold of El Dorado, 1978; The Medal: Mirror History, 1979; Horses of San Marco (London, NY, Milan, Berlin), 1979–82; Great Japa Exhibition, 1981; Art and Industry, 1982; Cimabue Crucifix (London, Madrid, Munich 1982–83; Treasures of Ancient Nigeria, 1983; The Genius of Venice, 1983; Leonardo d Vinci: studies for the Last Supper (Milan, Sydney, Toronto, Barcelona, Tokyo), 1984; A of the Architect, 1984; Re dei Confessori (Milan, Venice), 1985; C. S. Jagger: War an Peace Sculpture, 1985; Queen Elizabeth II: portraits of 60 years, 1986; Eye for Industry 1986; Glass of the Caesars (London, Cologne, Rome), 1988; Michaelangelo Drawing Louvre, 1989; Conservation Today, 1989; Paul de Lamerie, 1990; Lion of Venic (London, Amsterdam), 1991; David Smith Medals, 1991; Leonardo and Venezia, Venice 1992. Museum work includes: Old Master Drawings Gallery, Windsor Castle, 1965; Nev Galleries for Royal Scottish Museum, 1968; Crown Jewels display, Tower of London 1968; Heinz Gallery for Architectural Drawings, RIBA, London, 1972; Museum and A Gallery for Harrow School, 1975; Heralds' Museum, London, 1980; Housesteads Roma Fort Mus., 1982; Al Shaheed Museum, Baghdad, 1983; Cabinet War Rooms, London 1984; West Wing Galls, Nat. Maritime Mus., Greenwich, 1986; Beatrix Potter Museum Cumbria, 1988; George III Gall., Science Mus., 1993; English Sculpture Gall., V&A Mus 1999; Fleming Collection Gall., London, 2001; Project, Monumental Tower, Bologn Airport, 2003; Treasuries at: Winchester Cathedral, 1968; Christ Church, Oxford, 197 Winchester Coll., 1982; Lichfield Cath., 1993. Retrospective personal exhibitions: RIB Heinz Gall., 1989; Portraits from Detroit: US cars 1940s–60s, photographs by Alan Irvine RCA, 1996. Consultant designer to Olivetti, Italy, 1979–89; Consultant architect t British Museum, 1981–84. Mem., Crafts Council, 1984–86. Liveryman, Worshipful Co of Goldsmiths. Hon. Fellow, RCA. *Recreations:* travel, photography. *Address:* 2 Aubre Place, St John's Wood, NW8 9BH. *T:* (020) 7328 2229. *Club:* London Collie.

See also J. M. Irvine.

IRVINE, Rev. Canon Christopher Paul; Canon Librarian, Canterbury Cathedral, sinc 2007; *b* 17 Dec. 1951; *s* of Joseph Ernest Irvine and Phyllis Irvine; *m* 1978, Rosemar Hardwicke; two *d*. *Educ:* Univ. of Nottingham (BTh); Univ. of Lancaster (MA); Kelha Theol Coll. Ordained deacon and priest, 1976; Asst Curate, St Mary, Stoke Newington 1977–80; Anglican Chaplain, Sheffield Univ., 1980–85; Chaplain, St Edmund Hal Oxford, 1985–90; Tutor, 1985–90, Vice-Principal, 1991–94, St Stephen's House Oxford; Vicar, Cowley St John, Oxford, 1994–98; Principal, Coll. of the Resurrection Mirfield, 1998–2007. Chm., Soc. of Liturgical Study, 1998–2002; Consultant, C of Liturgical Commn, 2006–. *Publications:* Worship, Church and Society, 1993; (ed Celebrating the Easter Mystery, 1996; (ed) They shaped our Worship, 1998; (with Ann Dawtry) Art and Worship, 2002; The Art of God: the making of Christians and th meaning of worship, 2005; (ed) The Use of Symbols in Worship, 2007. *Recreations:* ar galleries and exhibitions, poetry, gardening, film. *Address:* 19 The Precincts, Canterbury Kent CT1 2EP. *T:* (01227) 865226; *e-mail:* irvinec@canterbury-cathedral.org.

IRVINE, Sir Donald (Hamilton), Kt 1994; CBE 1987 (OBE 1979); MD; FRCGP Principal in General Practice, Ashington, 1960–95; Regional Adviser in General Practice University of Newcastle, 1973–95; President, General Medical Council, 1995–2002; *b* 2 June 1935; *s* of late Dr Andrew Bell Hamilton Irvine and Dorothy Mary Irvine; *m* 1st, 1960, Margaret McGuckin (marr. diss. 1983); two *s* one *d*; 2nd, 1986, Sally Fountair (marr. diss. 2004); 3rd, 2007, Cynthia Rickitt, MBE. *Educ:* King Edward Sixth Gramma Sch., Morpeth; Medical Sch., King's Coll., Univ. of Durham (MB BS); DObstRCOG 1960; MD Newcastle 1964; FRCGP 1972 (MRCGP 1965). House Phys. to Dr C. N Armstrong and Dr Henry Miller, 1958–59. Chm. Council, RCGP, 1982–85 (Vice-Chm., 1981–82); Hon. Sec. of the College, 1972–78; Jt Hon. Sec., Jt Cttee on Postgrad. Trng for Gen. Practice, 1976–82; Fellow, BMA, 1976; Member: GMC, 1979– (Chm., Cttee on Standards and Medical Ethics, 1985–95); UKCC, 1983–93; Vice Chm., Dr Foste Ethics Cttee, 2002–; Gov., MSD Foundn, 1982–89 (Chm., Bd of Govs, 1983–89). Chm., Picker Inst., Europe, 2002–. Vice-Pres., Medical Defence Union, 1974–78. Vis. Prof. in Family Practice, Univ. of Iowa, USA, 1973; (first) Vis. Prof. to RACGP, 1977; Vis. Cons.

on Postgrad. Educn for Family Medicine to Virginia Commonwealth Univ., 1971, Univ. of Wisconsin-Madison, 1973, Med. Univ. of S Carolina, 1974. 30th Sir William Osler Lectr, McGill Univ., 2006. Mem., Audit Commn, 1990–96. Mem., Internat. Adv. Council, Pfizer Inc., 2004–. Chm., Adv. Bd for Medicine, Univ. of Warwick, 2003–. Founder FMedSci 1998. Hon. FRCP 1997; Hon. FRCPE 1997; Hon. FPHM 1998; Hon. FRCS 2000. Hon. DSc: Exeter, 1997; Leicester, 1998; Durham, 2002; Hon. DCL: Newcastle, 2002; Northumbria at Newcastle, 2002; DUniv York, 1997. *Publications:* The Future General Practitioner: learning and teaching, (jtly), 1972 (RCGP); Managing for Quality in General Practice, 1990; (ed jtly) Making Sense of Audit, 1991, 2nd edn 1997; (with Sally Irvine) The Practice of Quality, 1996; The Doctors' Tale: professionalism and public trust, 2003; chapters to several books on gen. practice; papers on clinical and educnl studies in medicine, in jls incl. BMJ, Lancet, Jl of RCGP. *Recreations:* bird watching, gardening, walking, watching television. *Address:* Mole End, Fairmoor, Morpeth NE61 3JL.

IRVINE, Hazel Jane; broadcast journalist and television presenter, BBC Sport, since 1990; *b* 26 May 1965; *d* of William and Norma Irvine. *Educ:* St Andrews Univ. (MA Hons Art Hist.). Prodn asst, Radio Clyde, 1986–87; sports broadcaster and journalist: Scottish Television, 1987–90; BBC Scotland, 1990–99; based in London, 1999–. *Recreations:* golf, hill-walking, travelling, playing piano. *Address:* c/o David John Associates Artiste Representation, 16a Winton Drive, Glasgow G12 0QA. *T:* (0141) 357 0532; *e-mail:* info@davidjohnassociates.co.uk.

IRVINE, James Montgomery, RDI 2004; industrial designer; Founder: Studio James Irvine, 1988; James Irvine Srl, 2003; *b* London, 29 Dec. 1958; *s* of Alan Montgomery Irvine, *qv* and Betty Middleton-Sandford; *m* 2005, Marialaura Rossiello; one *s. Educ:* Kingston Poly. (BA Hons 1981); Royal Coll. of Art (DesRCA 1984). Moved to Milan, 1984; Consultant for industrial products with Olivetti Design Studio, Milan, 1984–92; exchange designer with Toshiba Design Studio, Tokyo, 1987–88; returned to Milan and opened own design office specialising in product design, 1988; Partner, Sottsass Associati, with resp. for industrial design gp, Milan, 1993–97. Work includes new city bus for Hanover transport system, 2000 (131 built by Mercedes Benz); other clients include: Alias, Artemide, B&B Italia, Canon Japan, Muji, Thonet, WMF, Olivetti and Zumtobel. Hon. DDes Kingston Univ., 2007. *Recreations:* travel, Italian food, classic British motorcycles. *Address:* James Irvine Srl, Via Vigevano 8, 20144 Milan, Italy. *T:* (02) 89059980; *e-mail:* info@james-irvine.com. *Club:* BSA Owners.

IRVINE, Very Rev. John Dudley; Dean of Coventry, since 2001; Priest-in-charge, St Francis's, North Radford, since 2006; *b* 2 Jan. 1949; 3rd *s* of Rt Hon. Sir Arthur Irvine, QC, MP and Eleanor Irvine; *m* 1972, Andrea Mary Carr; three *s* one *d. Educ:* Haileybury Coll. (Hd of Sch.); Sussex Univ. (BA (Hons) Law, 1970); Wycliffe Hall, Oxford (BA (Hons) Theol., 1980; MA 1985). Called to the Bar, Middle Temple, 1973; in practice, Inner Temple, 1973–78. Ordained deacon, 1981, priest, 1982; Curate, Holy Trinity, Brompton with St Paul's, Onslow Sq., 1981–85; Priest i/c, 1985–95, Vicar, 1995–2001, St Barnabas, Kensington. *Recreations:* travel, film, theatre, walking. *Address:* The Deanery, 11 Priory Row, Coventry CV1 5EX. *T:* (024) 7652 1227, *Fax:* (024) 7652 1220; *e-mail:* dean@coventrycathedral.org.uk.

See also M. F. Irvine.

IRVINE, John Ferguson, CB 1983; financial consultant to local charities, 1995–2002; Chief Executive, Industrial Therapy Organisation (Ulster), 1984–94; *b* 13 Nov. 1920; *s* of Joseph Ferguson Irvine and Helen Gardner; *m* 1st, 1945, Doris Partridge (*d* 1973); one *s* one *d*; 2nd, 1980, Christine Margot Tudor; two *s* and two step *s. Educ:* Ardrossan Acad.; Glasgow Univ. (MA). RAF, 1941–46; Scottish Home Dept, 1946–48; NI Civil Service, 1948–66; Chief Exec., Ulster Transport Authority, 1966–68; Chief Exec., NI Transport Holding Co., 1968; NI Civil Service, 1969–83; Dep. Sec., DoE, NI, 1971–76; Permanent Secretary: attached NI Office, 1977–80; Dept of Manpower Services, 1980–81; DoE for NI, 1981–83. Chm. Management Cttee, 1974–75, and Vice-Chm. General Council, 1975, Action Cancer; Chm., Down Care and Aftercare Cttee, 1992–2000 (Mem. Cttee, 2000–07); Member: NI Marriage Guidance Council (Chm., 1976–78); Council, PHAB (NI), 1984–86; Council, PHAB (UK), 1984–86; Trustee, Heart Fund, Royal Victoria Hosp., Belfast, 1986–88. Mem., Downpatrick Inter-Church Caring Project, 1996–2002. *Recreations:* yoga, Majorca, football. *Address:* 11 Quarry Hill, Strawberry Fields, Strangford, Co. Down BT30 7GZ. *T:* (028) 4488 1613.

IRVINE, John Jeremy; Washington Correspondent, ITN, since 2006; *b* 2 June 1963; *s* of Dr Kenneth Irvine and Jacqueline Irvine; *m* 1992, Libby McCann; one *s* one *d. Educ:* Brackenber House Prep. Sch., Belfast; Campbell Coll., Belfast. Reporter: Tyrone Constitution, Omagh, 1983–87; Ulster TV, Belfast, 1987–94; Ireland Corresp., 1994–2000, Middle East Corresp., 2000–03, Asia Corresp., 2003–06, ITN. *Recreation:* golf. *Address:* c/o ITN, 200 Gray's Inn Road, WC1X 8XZ. *Clubs:* Malone Golf (Belfast); Royal County Down Golf (Newcastle).

IRVINE, Prof. (John) Maxwell, PhD; CPhys, FInstP; FRAS; FRSE; Professor of Physics, University of Manchester, since 2001; *b* 28 Feb. 1939; *s* of John MacDonald Irvine and Joan Paterson (*née* Adamson); *m* 1962, Grace Ritchie; one *s. Educ:* George Heriot's Sch., Edinburgh; Edinburgh Univ. (BSc Math. Phys. 1961); Univ. of Michigan (MSc 1962); Univ. of Manchester (PhD 1964). FInstP 1971; CPhys 1985; FRAS 1986; FRSE 1993. English-Speaking Union Fellow, Univ. of Michigan, 1961–62; Asst Lectr, Univ. of Manchester, 1964–66; Res. Associate, Cornell Univ., 1966–68; University of Manchester: Lectr, 1968–73; Sen. Lectr, 1973–76; Reader, 1976–83; Prof. of Theoretical Physics, 1983–91; Dean of Science, 1989–91; Principal and Vice-Chancellor, Aberdeen Univ., 1991–96; Vice-Chancellor and Principal, Univ. of Birmingham, 1996–2001. Chairman: CVCP Information Systems Sector Gp, 1996–98; Cttee of Scottish Univ. Principals, 1994–96; W Midlands Regl Innovation Strategy Gp, 1996–2001; Jt Information Systems Cttee, 1998–2003; RSE Inquiry into Energy Issues for Scotland, 2005–. Advr to Cttee on Radioactive Waste Mgt, 2005–06. Director: Grampian Enterprise Ltd, 1992–96; Rowett Res. Inst., 1992–96. Member: Nuclear Physics Bd, SERC, 1983–88 (Chm., Nuclear Structure Cttee, 1984–88); Bd, Scottish Council for Develt and Industry, 1992–96; Scottish Econ. Council, 1993–96; Scottish Cttee, British Council, 1994–96; BT Scottish Forum, 1994–96; Bd, HEQC, 1994–97; Univ. and Colls Employers Assoc., 1995–2001; UCAS, 1995–2001; Bd, PHLS, 1998–2005; Quality Mgt Panel, European Univs Assoc., 1999–; Commonwealth Scholarship Commn, 2002–06; Educnl Consultancy Service, 2002–03; Nursing and Midwifery Council, 2005–06; Energy Steering Gp, Eur. Acads Sci. Adv. Cttee, 2005–. Member Council: ACU 1994–2004 (Chm., 1995; Treas., 1998–2004); CVCP, 1996–2001; NERC, 1998–2001. Vice-Pres., 1982–87, Mem. Council, 1981–87, 1988–94, Inst. of Physics. Gov., ESU, 1999–2005. Sen. Advr, Oxford Round Table, 2001–. FRSA 1993; CCMI (CIMgt 1996). DL West Midlands, 1999–2001. Hon. FRCSEd 1995. Hon. DSc: Coll. of William and Mary in Va, 1995; Aston, 2002; Hon. DEd Robert Gordon Univ., 1995; DUniv: Edin., 1995; Birmingham, 2001; Hon. LLD Aberdeen, 1997. *Publications:* The Basis of Modern Physics, 1967 (trans. Dutch and French, 1969); Nuclear Structure Theory, 1972; Heavy Nuclei, Superheavy Nuclei and Neutron Stars, 1975; Neutron Stars, 1978; research articles on nuclear physics, astrophysics and condensed matter physics. *Recreations:* hill walking, tennis, bridge. *Address:* 27 Belfield Road, Manchester M20 6BJ.

IRVINE, Maxwell; *see* Irvine, J. M.

IRVINE, Michael Fraser; barrister; *b* 21 Oct. 1939; *s* of Rt Hon. Sir Arthur Irvine, PC, QC, MP, and Eleanor Irvine. *Educ:* Rugby; Oriel College, Oxford (BA). Called to the Bar, Inner Temple, 1964. Sen. Legal Assessor, Nursing and Midwifery Council, 2004–06. Contested (C): Bishop Auckland, 1979; Ipswich, 1992; MP (C) Ipswich, 1987–92. PPS to Attorney-Gen., 1990–92. Pres., Ipswich Cons. Assoc., 1998–. *Recreation:* hill walking in Scotland. *Address:* 48 Alder Road, SW14 8ER. *T:* (020) 8878 3162.

See also Very Rev. J. D. Irvine.

IRVINE, Prof. Robin Francis, FRS 1993; Royal Society Research Professor, Department of Pharmacology, University of Cambridge, since 1996; *b* 10 Feb. 1950; *s* of Charles Donald Irvine and June (*née* Ievers); *m* 1973, Sandra Jane Elder; two *s. Educ:* Stroud Sch., Romsey; Sherborne Sch., Dorset; St Catherine's Coll., Oxford (MA Biochem. 1972); Corpus Christi Coll., Cambridge (PhD Botany 1976). SRC Res. Student, ARC Unit of Developmental Botany, Cambridge, 1972–75; Beit Meml Fellow, ARC Inst. of Animal Physiol., Babraham, 1975–78; Mem. of Scientific Staff, 1978–95, UG5, 1993–95, AFRC Inst. of Animal Physiol. and Genetics Res., subseq. AFRC Babraham Inst., Cambridge. Mem., Wellcome Trust Cell and Molecular Panel, 1989–92. Mem. Council, Royal Soc., 1999–2001. Morton Lectr, Biochem. Soc., 1994. FIBiol 1998; Founder FMedSci 1998. Member Editorial Board: Biochemical Jl, 1988–96; Cell, 1994–; Current Biology, 1994–; Molecular Pharmacology, 2000–. *Publications:* (ed) Methods in Inositide Research, 1990; contribs to Nature, Biochem. Jl and other scientific jls. *Recreations:* playing the lute and guitar, music (especially pre-1650), ornithology, reading. *Address:* Department of Pharmacology, Tennis Court Road, Cambridge CB2 1PD. *T:* (01223) 339683.

IRVINE, Sarah Frances; *see* Beamish, S. F.

IRVING, Edward, CM 2002; ScD; FRS 1979; FRSC 1973; Research Scientist, Pacific Geoscience Centre, Sidney, BC, 1981–92, Emeritus since 1992; *b* 27 May 1927; *s* of George Edward and Nellie Irving; *m* 1957, Sheila Ann Irwin; two *s* two *d. Educ:* Colne Grammar Sch.; Cambridge Univ., 1948–54 (BA, MA, MSc, ScD). Served Army, 1945–48. Research Fellow, Fellow and Sen. Fellow, ANU, 1954–64; Dominion Observatory, Canada, 1964–66; Prof. of Geophysics, Univ. of Leeds, 1966–67; Res. Scientist, Dominion Observatory, later Earth Physics Br., Dept of Energy, Mines and Resources, Ottawa, 1967–81; Adjunct Professor: Carleton Univ., Ottawa, 1975–81; Univ. of Victoria, 1985–94. FRAS 1958; Fellow: Amer. Geophysical Union, 1976 (Walter H. Bucher Medal, 1979); Geological Soc. of America, 1979 (Arthur L. Day Medal, 1997); For. Associate, NAS, US, 1998. Hon. FGS 1989. Hon. DSc: Carleton, 1979; Memorial Univ. of Newfoundland, 1986; Victoria, 1999. Gondwanaland Medal, Mining, Geological and Metallurgical Soc. of India, 1962; Logan Medal, Geol Assoc. of Canada, 1975; J. T. Wilson Medal, Canadian Geophys. Union, 1984; Alfred Wegener Medal, European Geoscience Union, 1995; Wollaston Medal, Geol Soc. of London, 2005. Golden Jubilee Medal, 2002. *Publications:* Paleomagnetism, 1964; numerous contribs to learned jls. *Recreations:* gardening, carpentry, choral singing. *Address:* Pacific Geoscience Centre, 9860 West Saanich Road, Box 6000, North Saanich, BC V8L 4B2, Canada. *T:* (250) 3636508; 9363 Carnoustie Crescent, North Saanich, BC V8L 5G7, Canada. *T:* (250) 6569645; *e-mail:* tirving@pgc-gsc.nrcan.gc.ca.

IRVING, Gillian; QC 2006; *b* 1 Nov. 1958; *d* of Roger Irving and Mary Holliday Irving; *m* 1988, Peter Cadwallader. *Educ:* Caldew Comprehensive Sch., Dalston; Trent Poly., Nottingham (BA Hons Law); Inns of Court Sch. of Law. Called to the Bar, Inner Temple, 1984; in practice specialising in family law and community and mental health law. Part-time Chairman: Registered Homes Tribunal, 1997–2000; Care Standards Tribunal, 2000–; pt-time Legal Pres., Mental Health Rev. Tribunal, 1998–. *Recreations:* gardening, keeping fit, ski-ing, being outdoors in all weathers, animal husbandry. *Address:* 9 St John Street, Manchester M3 4DN. *T:* (0161) 955 9000, *Fax:* (0161) 955 9001; *e-mail:* clerks@9stjohnstreet.co.uk.

IRVING, John Winslow; novelist; *b* Exeter, New Hampshire, 2 March 1942; *s* of Colin Franklin Newell Irving and Frances Winslow Irving; *m* 1st, 1964, Shyla Leary (marr. diss. 1981); two *s*; 2nd, 1987, Janet Turnbull; one *s. Educ:* Phillips Exeter Acad., USA; Univ. of New Hampshire (BA 1965); Univ. of Iowa (MFA 1967). Professor of English: Windham Coll., 1967–72; Univ. of Iowa, 1972–75; Mount Holyoke Coll., 1975–78; Brandeis Univ., 1978–79. Wrestling Coach: Northfield Mt Hermon Sch., 1981–83; Fessenden Sch., 1983–86; Vermont Acad., 1987–89. Rockefeller Foundn grantee, 1971–72; Nat. Endowment for the Arts Fellow, 1974–75; Guggenheim Fellow, 1976–77. Mem., AAAL, 2001. *Publications:* Setting Free the Bears, 1968; The Water-Method Man, 1972; The 158-Pound Marriage, 1974; The World According to Garp, 1978 (Nat. Book Award, USA, 1979); The Hotel New Hampshire, 1981; The Cider House Rules, 1985 (screenplay, 1999; Best Screenplay Award, Nat. Bd of Review, 1999; Academy Award for best adapted screenplay, 2000); A Prayer for Owen Meany, 1989; A Son of the Circus, 1994; Trying to Save Piggy Sneed, 1996; A Widow for One Year, 1998; My Movie Business: a memoir, 1999; The Fourth Hand, 2001; Until I Find You, 2005. *Address:* c/o The Turnbull Agency, POB 757, Dorset, VT 05251, USA.

IRVING, Prof. Malcolm, PhD; FRS 2003; Professor of Biophysics, since 1998, and Director, Randall Division of Cell and Molecular Biophysics, since 2003, King's College London; *b* 23 July 1953. *Educ:* Emmanuel Coll., Cambridge (BA 1974); University Coll. London (MSc 1976; PhD 1979). Research Fellow: UCLA, 1979–80; Yale Univ., 1980–81; King's College London: Res. Asst, 1982–83; Royal Soc. Univ. Res. Fellow, 1983–91; Lectr in Biophysics, 1991–94; Reader in Biophysics, 1994–98. FMedSci 2006. *Address:* Randall Division of Cell and Molecular Biophysics, King's College London, New Hunt's House, Guy's Campus, SE1 1UL.

IRVING, Sir Miles (Horsfall), Kt 1995; MD; FRCS, FRCSE; Professor of Surgery, University of Manchester, 1974–99, now Emeritus; Chairman: Newcastle upon Tyne NHS Hospitals Trust, 1998–2006; NHS Innovations (North), since 2004; *b* 29 June 1935; *s* of Frederick William Irving and Mabel Irving; *m* 1965, Patricia Margaret Blaiklock; two *s* two *d. Educ:* King George V Sch., Southport; Liverpool Univ. (MB, ChB 1959; MD 1962; ChM 1968); Sydney Univ., Australia; MSc Manchester Univ., 1977. FRCS 1964; FRCSE 1964. Robert Gee Fellow, Liverpool Univ., 1962; Phyllis Anderson Fellow, Sydney Univ., 1967; St Bartholomew's Hospital, London: Chief Asst in Surgery, 1969–71; Reader in Surgery, Asst Dir of Professorial Surgical Unit, and Hon. Consultant Surgeon, 1972–74. Hon. Consultant Surgeon: Hope Hosp., Salford, 1974–99; Manchester Royal Infirmary, 1993–95; to the Army, 1989–2002. Hunterian Prof., 1967, Hunterian Orator, 1993, RCS; Sir Gordon Bell Meml Orator, NZ, 1982. Regl Dir of R&D, N Western RHA, 1992–94; Chm., Standing Gp on Health Technol., DoH,

1993–99; Nat. Dir, NHS Health Technol. Prog., 1994–99; Member: Expert Adv. Gp on AIDS, DoH, 1991–96; MRC Health Services and Public Health Res. Bd, 1993–96. Member: Council, RCS, 1984–95; GMC, 1989–92; President: Ileostomy Assoc. of GB and Ireland, 1982–92; Assoc. of Surgeons of GB and Ireland, 1995–96; Internat. Surgical Gp, 1995–96; Section of Coloproctology, RSM, 1997–98; Assoc. of Coloproctology of GB and Ireland, 1998–99; Manchester Med. Soc., 1999–2000. Mem. Bd, Imperial War Mus., 2006–. Mem. Council, Newcastle Univ., 2001–. Chm. Council, Northumbria, Order of St John, 2007–. Founder FMedSci 1998. Hon. Fellow: Amer. Assoc. for Surgery of Trauma, 1985; Amer. Surgical Assoc., 2000; Hon. FCEM (Hon. FFAEM 1995); Hon. FRCSCan; FRCSGlas *ad eund*; Hon. FACS 2000. Hon. Member: Assoc. Française de Chirurgie, 1996; Romanian Soc. of Surgeons. Hon. DSc Salford, 1996; DSc (*hc*) Sibiu Univ., Romania, 1997; Hon. DCL Northumbria, 2007. Moynihan Medal, Assoc. of Surgeons of GB and Ire., 1968; Pybus Medal, N of England Surgical Soc., 1986; John Loewenthal Medal, Sydney Univ., 1993; Canet Medal, Inst. of Mech. Incorp. Engrs, 1995; Bryan Brooke Medal, Ileostomy Assoc. of GB and Ire., 1996; Presidents Medal, British Soc. of Gastroenterology, 1999; Guthrie Medal, RAMC, 2005. Hon. Col 201 (Northern) Fd Hosp. Vol., 1999–2006. *Publications:* Gastroenterological Surgery, 1983; Intestinal Fistulas, 1985; ABC of Colorectal Diseases, 1993; Introduction to Minimal Access Surgery, 1995; 100 Years of the RVI, 2006. *Recreations:* thinking about and occasionally actually climbing mountains, reading, opera. *Address:* Juniper, The Old Stables, Aydon Road, Corbridge, Northumberland NE45 5EH. *T:* (01434) 634243.

IRWIN, Lord; James Charles Wood; *b* 24 Aug. 1977; *s* and *heir* of 3rd Earl of Halifax, *qv*; *m* 2006, Georgia E. Clarkson. *Educ:* Eton; Keble Coll., Oxford. *Address:* Garrowby, York YO41 1QD.

IRWIN, Lt Gen. Sir Alistair (Stuart Hastings), KCB 2002; CBE 1994 (OBE 1987); Adjutant General, 2003–05; *b* 27 Aug. 1948; *s* of late Brig. Angus Digby Hastings Irwin, CBE, DSO, MC and of Elizabeth Bryson Irwin (*née* Cumming); *m* 1972, Nicola Valentine Blomfield Williams; one *s* two *d*. *Educ:* Wellington Coll.; St Andrews Univ. (MA); Univ. of Baluchistan (BSc Hons 1980). Commnd The Black Watch (RHR), 1970; Staff Coll., Quetta, Pakistan, 1980; CO 1st Bn, The Black Watch, 1985–88 (despatches, 1987); Instructor, Staff Coll., Camberley, 1988–92; Comd, 39 Inf. Bde, 1992–94; Dir Land Warfare, MoD, 1994–95; Prog. Dir, PE, MoD, 1996; Comdt, RMCS, 1996–99; Military Sec., 1999–2000; GOC NI, 2000–03. Mem., Commonwealth War Graves Commn, 2006–. President: RBL Scotland, 2006–; Earl Haig Fund for Scotland, 2006–; Officers' Assoc. Scotland, 2006–; (Army) Officers' Assoc., 2006–; Veterans Scotland, 2006–; Chm., Christina Mary Hendrie Trust, 2006–. Col, The Black Watch, 2003–06. Col Comdt, Scottish Div., 2000–04; Hon. Col Tayforth Univs OTC, 1998–. Officer, Royal Co. of Archers (Queen's Bodyguard for Scotland), 1989–. Pres., Army Angling Fedn, 1997–2005. Vice-Pres., Royal Caledonian Schs Trust, 2007–; Patron, Annan Juvenile Pipe Band, 2007–. *Recreations:* shooting, fishing, walking, photography, bad golf. *Address:* c/o Adam & Co. plc, 22 Charlotte Square, Edinburgh EH2 4DF. *Clubs:* Boodle's, Caledonian; Highland Brigade.

IRWIN, David; Partner, Irwin Grayson Associates (consultants in enterprise and economic development), since 2002; *b* 5 Sept. 1955; *s* of Hew Irwin and Ann (*née* Tattersfield); *m* 1983, Jane Christine Kinghorn (separated 2002); one *s* one *d*; one *s* with Penny Hawley. *Educ:* Worksop Coll.; Durham Univ. (BSc (Hons) Engrg Sci and Mgt 1977); Cambridge Univ. (Adv. Course Prodn Methods and Mgt 1978); Newcastle Univ. (MBA 1986). Develt Engr, Hydraulic Hose Div., Dunlop, 1978–80; Co-founder and Dir, Project North East, 1980–2000; Chief Exec., Small Business Service, 2000–02; Chm., Cobweb Information Ltd, 2002–. Dir, Inst. for Small Business and Entrepreneurship, 2004–08. FIBC (Fellow, Inst. of Business Advisers, 1989; FCMC 1993); FRSA 1993. *Publications:* Financial Control, 1991; Planning to Succeed in Business, 1995; Financial Control for Non Financial Managers, 1995; Make Your Business Grow, 1998; On Target, 1999. *Recreations:* squash, photography. *Club:* Northern Rugby Football (Newcastle upon Tyne).

IRWIN, Flavia; *see* de Grey, F.

IRWIN, Helen Elizabeth; Clerk of Committees, House of Commons, 2005–08; *b* 21 April 1948; *d* of late Walter William Taylor and Kathleen Taylor (*née* Moffoot); *m* 1972, Robert Graham Irwin; one *d*. *Educ:* Whalley Range Grammar Sch., Manchester; King's Coll., London (BA Hons Hist. 1969); SSEES, Univ. of London (MA Soviet Studies 1970). Asst Clerk, H of C, 1970–72; Admin Asst, Univ. of St Andrews, 1972–75; a Clerk, House of Commons, 1977–2008: Cttee of Public Accounts, 1977–81; served in Table Office, 1981–85; Social Services Cttee, 1985–89; Health Cttee, 1989–91; Foreign Affairs Cttee, 1991–94; Principal Clerk, Committee Office, 1994–99; Clerk of Bills, 1999–2001; Principal Clerk, Table Office, 2001–05. Mem. Council, Hansard Soc., 1990–99. Fellow, Industry and Parlt Trust. *Publications:* occasional contribs to books on parliamentary practice and procedure. *Recreations:* family, friends, travel.

IRWIN, Ian Sutherland, CBE 1982; Executive Chairman (formerly also Chief Executive), Scottish Transport Group, 1987–2002; *b* Glasgow, 20 Feb. 1933; *s* of Andrew Campbell Irwin and Elizabeth Ritchie Arnott; *m* 1959, Margaret Miller Maureen Irvine; two *s*. *Educ:* Whitehill Sen. Secondary Sch., Glasgow; Glasgow Univ. (BL). CA, IPFA, FCILT. Commercial Man., Scottish Omnibuses Ltd, 1960–64; Gp Accountant, Scottish Bus Gp, 1964–69; Gp Sec., 1969–75, Dep. Chm. and Man. Dir, 1975–87, Scottish Transport Gp; Chairman: Scottish Bus Gp Ltd, 1975–2002; Caledonian MacBrayne Ltd, 1975–90; STG Properties Ltd (formerly Scottish Transport Investments Ltd), 1975–2002; STG Pension Funds, 1975–2002. Dir, Scottish Mortgage & Trust plc, 1986–99. Pres., Bus and Coach Council, 1979–80; Hon. Vice-Pres., Internat. Union of Public Transport; Member Council: CIT, 1978–87 (Vice Pres., 1984–87); CBI, 1987–93; Mem., Nationalised Industries Chairmen's Gp, 1987–91. Hon. Col, 154 Regt RCT (V), 1986–93. FInstD; CCMI. *Publications:* various papers. *Recreations:* golf, foreign travel, walking, swimming, reading. *Address:* 10 Moray Place, Edinburgh EH3 6DT. *T:* (0131) 225 6454. *Club:* Bruntsfield Links Golfing Soc.

IRWIN, Dr Michael Henry Knox; Chairman, Voluntary Euthanasia Society, 1996–99 and 2001–03 (Vice-Chairman, 1995 and 1999–2001); *b* 5 June 1931; *s* of late William Knox Irwin, FRCS and of Edith Isabel Mary Irwin; *m* 1958, Elizabeth Naumann (marr. diss. 1982); three *d*; partner, Angela Farmer. *Educ:* St Bartholomew's Hosp. Med. Coll., London (MB, BS 1955); Columbia Univ., New York (MPH 1960). House Phys. and House Surg., Prince of Wales' Hosp., London, 1955–56; MO, UN, 1957–61; Dep. Resident Rep., UN Technical Assistance Bd, Pakistan, 1961–63; MO, 1963–66, SMO, 1966–69, and Med. Dir, 1969–73, United Nations; Dir, Div. of Personnel, UNDP, 1973–76; UNICEF Rep., Bangladesh, 1977–80; Sen. Advr (Childhood Disabilities), UNICEF, 1980–82; Sen. Consultant, UN Internat. Year of Disabled Persons, 1981; Med. Dir, UN, UNICEF and UNDP, 1982–89; Director: Health Services Dept, IBRD, 1989–90; Westside Action, 1991–93. Founder, Doctors for Assisted Dying, 1998. Pres., Assistance for Blind Children Internat., 1978–84. Consultant, Amer. Assoc. of Blood Banks, 1984–90; Advr, ActionAid, 1990–91; Vice Pres., UNA, 1999– (Vice-Chm., 1995–96; Chm., 1996–98); Chm., UK Cttee, UNHCR, 1997–2002; Vice Pres., N Peace Council, 1996–2000. Dir, World Fedn of Right-to-Die Socs, 2004–06 (Vice-Pr 2000–02; Pres., 2002–04). Co-ordinator, Secular Med. Forum, 2006–08. Contes (Living Will Campaign) Kensington and Chelsea, Nov. 1999. Mem. Editl Adv. Pa Medicine and War, 1985–95. Officer Cross, Internat. Fedn of Blood Do Organizations, 1984. *Publications:* Check-ups: safeguarding your health, 19 Overweight: a problem for millions, 1964; Travelling without Tears, 1964; Viruses, Co and Flu, 1966; Blood: new uses for saving lives, 1967; The Truth About Cancer, 19 What Do We Know about Allergies?, 1972; A Child's Horizon, 1982; Aspirin: curr knowledge about an old medication, 1983; Can We Survive Nuclear War?, 1984; Nucl Energy: good or bad?, 1985; Peace Museums, 1991; Pro-Choice Living Will, 20 Psyche-Anima, 2004; What Survives?, 2005; Tilting at Windmills, 2007; *novel:* Tal 1990. *Recreations:* politics, metaphysics. *Address:* 9 Waverleigh Road, Cranleigh, Sur GU6 8BZ.

IRWIN, Rear-Adm. Richard Oran, CB 1995; Member, Criminal Inju Compensation Appeals Panel, since 2000; *b* 3 Sept. 1942; *s* of Lt Col Richard Art Irwin, TD and Catherine Millicent (*née* Palmer); *m* 1st, 1965, Coreen Jill Blackham (m diss. 2005), *d* of Rear-Adm. J. L. Blackham, CB; one *s* one *d*; 2nd, 2005, Rosemary Syl Helen Groves, PhD, *widow* of Richard Groves, and *d* of R. E. Storrar. *Educ:* Sherbor Dartmouth; RN Engrg Coll., Manadon (BSc Engrg). FIET (FIEE 1986). Served in 7 3rd and 10th Submarine Sqdns, 1968–78; on Naval Staff, 1978–81; on staff of Flag Offic Submarines, 1981–83; on staff, Strategic Systems Exec., 1983–86; RCDS, 1987; D Nuclear Systems, 1988–91; Captain, HMS Raleigh, 1991–92; Chief, Strategic Syste Exec., MoD, 1992–95; RN retd, 1996. Mem., DFEE Panel of Ind. Assessors, 1996–20 Panel of Ind. Assessors, DCMS, 2004–08. Ind. Investigator, Financial Servi Compensation Scheme, 2002–08. Chm., W Sussex HA, 1996–2000. Non-exec. D Halmatic Ltd, 1996–98. Chm., Queen Alexandra Hosp. Home, 1998–. Trustee, Ro Naval Mus., 2003– (Chm., Friends of RN Mus. and HMS Victory, 1999–). Memb RNSA; Assoc. of Retired Naval Officers. Gov., Kingsham Primary Sch., 1996–20 Pres., Old Shirburnian Soc., 1999–2000. Officer, Legion of Merit (US), 1996. *Recreatio* sailing, squash, tennis, ski-ing, bridge. *Address:* Deep Thatch, Gracious Street, Selbor Hants GU34 3JB. *Clubs:* Lansdowne; Ocean Cruising.

IRWIN, Hon. Sir Stephen (John), Kt 2006; **Hon. Mr Justice Irwin;** a Judge of High Court of Justice, Queen's Bench Division, since 2006; Presiding Judge, Northe Circuit, since 2008; *b* 5 Feb. 1953; *s* of late John McCaughey Irwin and of Norma Gord Irwin; *m* 1978, Deborah Rose Ann Spring; one *s* two *d*. *Educ:* Methodist Coll., Belf Jesus Coll., Cambridge (BA Hons 1975). Called to the Bar: Gray's Inn, 1976 (Bench 2002); Northern Ireland, 1997; QC 1997; a Recorder, 2000–06. Chm., Bar Coun 2004. *Publications:* Medical Negligence: a practitioner's guide, 1995; legal articles learned jls. *Recreations:* walking, Irish history, music, verse. *Address:* Royal Courts Justice, Strand, WC2A 2LL.

ISAAC, Anthony Eric, FCMA; Chief Executive, The BOC Group, 2000–06; *b* 24 N 1941; *m* Janice Donovan; one *s* one *d*. Finance Director: GEC Ples Telecommunications, 1988–90; Arjo Wiggins Appleton plc, 1990–94; Exec. Dir, BO Gp, 1994–2006. Non-executive Director: International Power plc, 2000–; Schlumberg 2003–. Mem. Adv. Bd, Ian Jones & Partners, 2001–.

ISAAC, Anthony John Gower, CB 1985; fiscal consultant; a Deputy Chairman, Boa of Inland Revenue, 1982–91 (a Commissioner of Inland Revenue, 1973–77 a 1979–91); *b* 21 Dec. 1931; *s* of Ronald and Kathleen Mary Gower Isaac; *m* 1963, O Elizabeth Sibley; one *s* two *d* (and two *d* decd). *Educ:* Malvern Coll.; King's Co Cambridge (BA). HM Treasury, 1953–70: Private Sec. to Chief Sec. to Treasu 1964–66; Inland Revenue, 1971; on secondment to HM Treasury, 1976–78. Mem., T Law Rev. Cttee, 1994–2006. *Publications:* A Local Income Tax, 1992; A Comment on t Viability of the Allowance for Corporate Equity, 1997. *Recreations:* gardening, fishir grandchildren.

ISAAC, James Keith, CBE 1985; FCILT; Hon. President, International Union of Pub Transport, since 1997 (Vice-President, 1989–93; President, 1993–97); Director, Lond Transport Buses Ltd, 1994–99; *b* 28 Jan. 1932; *s* of late Arthur Burton Isaac and Dore (*née* Davies); *m* 1957, Elizabeth Mary Roskell; two *d*. *Educ:* Leeds Grammar Sch. Me Inst. of Traffic Admin; FCILT (FCIT 1978). Asst to Traffic Manager, Aldershot and D Traction Co. Ltd, 1958–59; Asst Traffic Man., Jamaica Omnibus Services Ltd, Kingsto Jamaica, 1959–64; Dep. Traffic Man., Midland Red (Birmingham and Midland Mot Omnibus Co. Ltd), Birmingham, 1965–67; Traffic Manager: North Western Road C Co. Ltd, Stockport, Cheshire, 1967–69; Midland Red, Birmingham, 1969–73; Dir Ops, 1973–77, Dir Gen., 1977–86, W Midlands Passenger Transp. Exec., Birmingha Man. Dir, 1986–90, Chief Exec., 1986–92, Chm., 1986–94, West Midlands Travel Lt Chm., Bus and Coach Services Ltd, 1986–90. Chm., Internat. Commn on Transp Economics, 1981–88; President: Omnibus Soc., 1982; Bus and Coach Council, 1985–8 Mem. Council, CIT, 1982–85. *Recreations:* golf, walking, reading, travel, grandchildre *Address:* 24B Middlefield Lane, Hagley, Worcs DY9 0PX. *T:* (01562) 884757. *Clu* Army and Navy; Rotary of Hagley (Worcs); Churchill and Blakedown Golf (ne Kidderminster).

ISAAC, Maurice Laurence Reginald, MA; Headmaster, Latymer Upper Scho Hammersmith, W6, 1971–88; *b* 26 April 1928; *s* of late Frank and Lilian Isaac; *m* 195 Anne Fielden (*d* 2003); three *d*. *Educ:* Selhurst Grammar Sch., Croydon; Magdalene Co Cambridge. BA Hist. Tripos, 1950; MA 1955, Cambridge; Certif. in Educn, 1952. A Master: Liverpool Collegiate Sch., 1952–56; Bristol Grammar Sch., 1956–62; Head History, Colchester Royal Grammar Sch., 1962–65; Headmaster, Yeovil Sch., 1966–7 Mem. Council, Francis Holland Schools Trust, 1982–95. *Publications:* A History Europe, 1870–1950, 1960; contributor to The Teaching of History, 1965. *Address:* Askew Grove, Repton, Derbyshire DE65 6GR. *T:* (01283) 702899.

ISAACS, family name of **Marquess of Reading**.

ISAACS, Dr Anthony John; Consultant Endocrinologist, London Medical Lond Diabetes (formerly London Diabetes and Lipid Centre), since 2002; *b* 22 Oct. 1942; *s* Benjamin H. Isaacs, BSc and late Lily Isaacs (*née* Rogol); *m* 1st, 1971, Jill Kathleen Ele three *s*; 2nd, 1986, Dr Edie Friedman; one *d*. *Educ:* Wanstead County High Sch.; Hertfo Coll., Oxford (Open Exhibnr; Domus Scholar; BA Animal Physiology, 1st Cl. Ho 1965; MA 1968; BM, BCh 1968); Westminster Med. Sch. (Barron Schol.); MSc (Publ Health Medicine), London, 1992. MRCP 1971, FRCP 1997. House posts, Westminste Whittington and Hammersmith Hosps, 1968–70; Med. Registrar, Westminster Hosp 1971–73; Research Fellow (Endocrinology), Royal Free Hosp., 1973–75; Sen. Me Registrar, Westminster Hosp., 1975–84; SMO, Medicines Div., 1984–85, PMO, ar Med. Assessor, Cttee on Safety of Medicines, 1985–86, SPMO/Under Sec., and Hd, Me Manpower and Educn Div., 1986–91, DHSS, subseq. DoH; Regl Consultant (Servi Policy and Clinical Audit), NE Thames, later N Thames RHA, 1993–95; Consulta

Endocrinologist: Charing Cross Hosp., 1993–95; Chelsea & Westminster Hosp., 1993–2003, Emeritus, 2003–. Sen. Med. Assessor, Medicines and Healthcare products Regulatory (formerly Medicines Control) Agency, 2002–08. Consultant in Clinical Audit, Educn and Trng, Barnet HA, 1995–2001; Hon. Consultant Physician, Barnet, Enfield and Haringey HA, 2001–02. Hon. Consultant Phys. (Endocrinology), UC and Middx Hosps, 1986–96. Vice-Chm., Jt Planning Adv. Cttee, 1986–91; Member: Steering Gp for Implementation of Achieving a Balance (and Co-Chm., Technical sub-gp), 1986–91; 2nd Adv. Cttee on Med. Manpower Planning, 1986–89; Steering Gp on Undergrad. Med. and Dental Educn and Res., 1987–91 (Chm., Implementation Task Gp, 1989–90 and Working Gp, 1990–91); Ministerial Gp on Junior Doctors' Hours, 1990–91; Fitness to Practise Panel, GMC, 2006–. Chairman: Barnet Health Promoting Schs, later Barnet Healthy Schs Scheme, Steering Gp, 1995–2002; Barnet Cardiovascular Strategy Steering Gp (formerly Barnet Coronary Heart Disease, Stroke and Smoking Focus Gp), 1995–2001; Barnet Adv. Gp on Palliative Care Services, 1996–2000. Hon. Vis. Fellow, LSHTM, 1992–93; Associate Prof., Sch. of Health, Biol and Envmntl Scis, subseq. of Health and Social Scis, Middlesex Univ., 2002–05 (Hon. Vis. Prof., 2001–02, 2006–). Chm., New End Sch. PTA, 1983–85; Parent Governor, 1987–92, Partnership (formerly First) Gov., 1992–, Chm. Governing Body, 2003–, Hendon Sch. Mem., Soc. for Endocrinology, 1998–. DFPHM 1999. FRSocMed 1971 (Hon. Treas., 2001–03, Hon. Sec., 2003–05, Vice-Pres., 2005–07, Section of Endocrinol. and Diabetes). *Publications:* Anorexia Nervosa (with P. Dally and J. Gomez), 1979; papers in med. jls on rheumatol and endocrinol topics. *Recreations:* music, cinema, table tennis, chess, travel. *Address:* London Medical London Diabetes, 49 Marylebone High Street, W1U 5HJ.

ISAACS, Jane; Partner, ATM Consulting, since 2006; *b* 12 Dec. 1954; *d* of Tom and Mabel Scott; *m* 1978, Edward Isaacs; two *d*. *Educ:* Edinburgh Univ. (MA); Wolverhampton Business Sch. (DMS, MBA). Associate Lectr, Open Univ. Business Sch., 1996–. Non-exec. Dir, Wolverhampton HA, 1994–98; Chm., Wolverhampton Healthcare NHS Trust, 1998–2001; Regl Appts Comr, W Midlands, NHS Appts Commn, 2001–05. Chm., Wolverhampton Voluntary Sector Council, 1992–95; non-exec. Dir, Wolverhampton TEC, 1993–95. Mem., Regl Panel, Nat. Lottery Charities Bd, 1995–97. *Recreations:* reading, gardening, cooking. *Address:* Woodside, 3 Lapley Hall Cottages, Stretton Road, Lapley, Staffs ST19 9JR.

ISAACS, Sir Jeremy (Israel), Kt 1996; General Director, Royal Opera House, Covent Garden, 1988–97 (Member, Board of Directors, 1985–97); Chief Executive, Jeremy Isaacs Productions, 1998–2008; *b* 28 Sept. 1932; *s* of Isidore Isaacs and Sara Jacobs; *m* 1st, 1958, Tamara (*née* Weinreich) (*d* 1986), Cape Town; one *s* one *d*; 2nd, 1988, Gillian Mary Widdicombe. *Educ:* Glasgow Acad.; Merton Coll., Oxford (MA; Hon. Fellow 2006). Pres. of the Union, Hilary, 1955. Television Producer, Granada TV (What the Papers Say, All Our Yesterdays), 1958; Associated-Rediffusion (This Week), 1963; BBC TV (Panorama), 1965; Controller of Features, Associated Rediffusion, 1967; with Thames Television, 1968–78: Controller of Features, 1968–74; Producer, The World at War, 1974; Director of Programmes, 1974–78; Chief Exec., Channel Four TV Co., 1981–87; TV programmes: A Sense of Freedom, STV; Ireland, a Television History, BBC; Cold War, CNN; Millennium, CNN; Millennium Minds, Channel 4; Artists At Work, Artsworld, 2001; interviewer, Face to Face, BBC. Chm., Artsworld Channels Ltd, 2000–03. Dir, Glasgow 1999, 1996–99. Chairman: DCMS Adv. Panel, European Capital of Culture UK Nomination for 2008, 2002–03; EU Selection Panel, European Capitals of Culture 2010, 2006. Chm., Salzburg Festival Trust, 1997–2001; Trustee, IPPR, 1989–99. Member: Somerset House Trust, 1997–2003; Council, UEA, 1997–2000; Trustee: European Opera Centre, 1996–2008; Children's Music Workshop, 1997–2007. Dir, Open College, 1987–92. Governor, BFI, 1979–84 (Chm., BFI Production Bd, 1979–81). President: RTS, 1997–2000; Merton Soc., 2005–07. Organised A Statue for Oscar Wilde, Adelaide Street, 1998. James MacTaggart Meml Lectr, Edinburgh TV Fest., 1979. FRSA 1983; Fellow: BAFTA, 1985; BFI, 1986; FRSAMD 1989; FGSM 1989. Hon. FRIBA 2004. Hon. DLitt: Strathclyde, 1984; CNAA, 1987; Bristol, 1988; Hon. LLD Manchester, 1999. Desmond Davis Award for outstanding creative contrib. to television, 1972; George Polk Meml Award, 1973; Cyril Bennett Award for outstanding contrib. to television programming, RTS, 1982; Lord Willis Award for Distinguished Service to Television, 1985; Directorate Award, Internat. Council of Nat. Acad. of TV Arts and Scis, NY, 1987; Lifetime Achievement Award, Banff, 1988. Commandeur de l'Ordre des Arts et des Lettres (France), 1988; Mem., Ordre pour le Mérite (France), 1993. *Publications:* Storm over Four: a personal account, 1989; (jtly) Cold War, 1998, 2nd edn 2008; Never Mind the Moon: my time at the Royal Opera House, 1999; Look Me in the Eye: a life in television, 2006. *Recreations:* reading, walking. *Club:* Garrick.

ISAACS, Stuart Lindsay; QC 1991; a Recorder, since 1997; a Deputy High Court Judge, since 2004; *b* 8 April 1952; *s* of late Stanley Leslie Isaacs and of Marquette Isaacs; *m* 2000, Melodie, *e d* of Mannie and Judy Schuster; two *s* one *d*. *Educ:* Haberdashers' Aske's Sch., Elstree; Downing Coll., Cambridge (Law, Double 1st cl. Hons); Univ. Libre de Bruxelles (License spécial en droit européen, grande distinction). Called to the Bar, Lincoln's Inn, 1975, Bencher, 1999; admitted NY Bar, 1985. An Asst Recorder, 1992–97. Member: Internat. Panel of Arbitrators, Singapore Internat. Arbitration Centre, 1998–; Restricted Patients Panel, Mental Health Review Tribunal, 2000–04; Internat. Panel of Mediators, Singapore Mediation Centre, 2007–. Mem. Law Adv. Cttee, British Council, 1996–99. Consultant Editor: Butterworth's EC Case Citator, 1991–; Banking Law Reports, 1996–98. *Publications:* EC Banking Law, 1985, 2nd edn 1994; Banking and the Competition Law of the EEC, 1978; (ed jtly) The EC Insolvency Regulation, 2003. *Recreations:* family, travel, languages. *Address:* 3–4 South Square, Gray's Inn, WC1R 5HP. *T:* (020) 7696 9900, *Fax:* (020) 7696 9911; *e-mail:* stuartisaacs@southsquare.com.

ISAACS, Tamara Margaret; *see* Finkelstein, T. M.

ISAACSON, Laurence Ivor, CBE 1998; Joint Founder and Deputy Chairman, Groupe Chez Gérard PLC, 1986–2002; *b* 1 July 1943; *s* of Henry Isaacson and Dorothy (*née* Levitt). *Educ:* London Sch. of Econs (BSc Econ). FIH (FHCIMA 1996). Mgt trainee, Unilever, London and Rotterdam, 1964–67; Doyle Dane Bernbach Advertising, 1967–70; Foote Cone & Belding Advertising, 1970–72; Jt Founder and Man. Dir, Creative Business Ltd, 1972–83; Dir, Kennedy Brookes Plc, 1983–86. Chm., MAP Travel-Canada, 2001–04; Dir, Paris Commune LLC, 2005–. Mem. Adv. Bd, UK in NY, 2001. Chairman: Contemp. Dance Trust, 1988–94; BOC Covent Gdn Fest. of Opera and Music Theatre, 1993–2001; London Restaurant Week, 1999; Dir and Mem. Council, Arts & Business (formerly ABSA), 1987–2002. Royal Shakespeare Co.: Director: RSC Foundn, 1998–2000; Main Bd, 2003–; RSC America Inc., 2004–; Gov., 2000–; Chm., Actors' Circle, 2001–; non-exec. Dir, Ambassador Theatre Gp, 2000–. Dir, London Tourist Bd, 1994–2002; Mem., London First Visitors Council, 1994–98. Dir, Crusaid, 1994–; Dir and Trustee, World Cancer Res. Fund (UK), 2003–. Patron, Cardiff Internat. Fest. of Music Theatre, 2001–. FRSA 1997. *Address:* 5 Chalcot Crescent, NW1 8YE. *T:* (020) 7586 3793; 30 Crosby Street, Soho, New York, NY 10013, USA. *T:* (212) 4318545; *e-mail:* laurencei@aol.com. *Clubs:* Garrick, Groucho, Home House (Founding Partner, and Dir, 1999–2005).

ISAACSON, Prof. Peter Gersohn, DM, DSc; FRCPath; Professor of Morbid Anatomy, University College London, 1982–2002, now Emeritus; Consultant Histopathologist, University College London Hospitals NHS Foundation Trust, since 2002; *b* 24 Nov. 1936; *s* of Robert and Freda Isaacson; *m* 1959, Maria de Lourdes Abranches Pinto; one *s* three *d*. *Educ:* Prince Edward Sch., Salisbury, Rhodesia; Univ. of Cape Town (MB ChB); DM Southampton, 1980; DSc London, 1992. FRCPath 1972. Sen. Lectr, then Reader, Southampton Univ. Med. Sch., 1974–82. Founder FMedSci 1998. Hon. MD: Free Univ. of Berlin, 1998; Universidade Nova de Lisboa, 2005. San-Salvatore Prize, Lugano, 1999. *Publications:* Biopsy Pathology of the Lymphoreticular System, 1983; Oxford Textbook of Pathology, 1993; Extranodal Lymphoma, 1994; numerous contribs to med. jls. *Address:* Department of Histopathology, Rockefeller Building, University Street, WC1E 6JJ. *T:* (020) 7679 6045.

ISAAMAN, Gerald Michael, OBE 1994; journalist and consultant; Editorial Consultant, Home Counties Newspapers plc, 1994–99; Editor, 1968–94, and General Manager, 1990–94, Hampstead and Highgate Express; *b* 22 Dec. 1933; *s* of Asher Isaaman and Lily Finklestein; *m* 1962, Delphine Walker, *e d* of Cecile and Arnold Walker; one *s*. *Educ:* Dame Alice Owen's Grammar School. Reporter, North London Observer Series, 1950, Hampstead and Highgate Express, 1955. Director: Pipistrel Retail Solutions, 1994–; Pipistrel Education Systems, 1994–; Health Independent Ltd, 2002–; non-exec. Dir, Whittington Hosp. NHS Trust, 1994–98. Founder Trustee, Arkwright Arts Trust, 1971; Chairman: Camden Arts Trust Management Board, 1970–82; Exhibns Cttee, Camden Arts Centre, 1971–82; Russell Housing Soc., 1976–82; Trustees, King's Cross Disaster Fund, 1987–89; Dep. Chm., Assoc. of British Editors, 1996–2000 (Mem. Council, 1985–93); Member: Press Complaints Commn, 1993–95; Bd, Camden Trng Centre, 1997–2001; Camden Festival Trust, 1982–; Cheltenham Literary Fest. Cttee, 1998–; Patron and Trustee, Hamden Trust, 1995–; Patron, Ledbury Poetry Fest., 1997–. FRSA 1992. Special presentation, for distinguished services to journalism, British Press Awards, 1994. *Recreations:* cooking breakfast, listening to jazz, work. *Address:* 13 George Lane, Marlborough, Wilts SN8 4BX. *T:* (01672) 519375; *e-mail:* gerald@isaaman.com. *Club:* Garrick.

ISCHINGER, Wolfgang Friedrich; Chairman, Munich Security Conference, since 2008; *b* 6 April 1946; *s* of Karl and Margarete Ischinger; *m* 2002, Jutta Falke; one *s* two *d* (and one *s* decd). *Educ:* German Law Sch.; Fletcher Sch. of Law and Diplomacy, Medford, Mass. (MA 1973). Joined German Foreign Service, 1975; Policy Planing Staff, Foreign Ministry, Bonn, 1977–79; Washington, 1979–82; Pvte Sec. to Foreign Minister, 1982–90; Minister, Paris, 1990–93; Dir, Policy Planning Staff, 1993–95, Political Dir, 1995–98, State Sec., 1998–2001, Foreign Ministry; Ambassador to USA, 2001–06; Ambassador to UK, 2006–08. Holds numerous foreign decorations incl. Comdr, Légion d'Honneur (France), 1999. *Publications:* numerous contribs on foreign and security policy issues. *Recreations:* mountaineering, ski-ing. *Address:* Munich Security Conference, Heidemannstrasse 50, 80939 Munich, Germany. *T:* (89) 15982125; *e-mail:* office@securityconference.de.

ISENBERG, Prof. David Alan, MD; FRCP; Arthritis Research Campaign's Diamond Jubilee Professor of Rheumatology and Academic Director of Rheumatology, University College London, since 1996; *b* 20 Oct. 1949; *s* of Harry and Sheila Isenberg; *m* 1975, Lucy Fischel; one *s* one *d*. *Educ:* St Bartholomew's Hosp. Med. Coll. (MB BS 1973); MD London 1984. MRCS 1973; LRCP 1973, MRCP 1976, FRCP 1990. Various trng posts in internal medicine, N London hosps, 1976–79; Sir Jules Thorn Res. Fellow, UCL, 1979–81; Sir Stanley Thomas Johnson Res. Fellow, Tufts–New England Med. Center, Boston, 1982–83; University College London: Consultant Rheumatologist, Middlesex Hosp., 1984–; Sen. Lectr, Middlesex Hosp., 1984–92; Prof. of Rheumatology, 1992–95. Pres., British Soc. of Rheumatology, 2004–06. FMedSci 2006. *Publications:* (jtly) Autoimmune Rheumatic Disease, 1987, 2nd edn 1999; (ed jtly) Oxford Textbook of Rheumatology, 1993, 3rd edn 2004; (jtly) Friendly Fire: explaining autoimmune disease, 1995; (ed jtly) Controversies in Rheumatology, 1997; (ed jtly) Adolescent Rheumatology, 1998; (ed jtly) Imaging in Rheumatology, 2002. *Recreations:* playing tennis and guitar, writing short stories, watching football, going to the theatre and classical music concerts. *Address:* Room 331, The Windeyer Building, University College London, 46 Cleveland Street, W1T 4JF. *T:* (020) 7679 9684; *e-mail:* d.isenberg@ucl.ac.uk.

ISEPP, Martin Johannes Sebastian; Head of Music, Opera Akademie, Royal Danish Opera, Copenhagen, since 2006; Head of Music Studies, National Opera Studio, 1979–95; Chief Guest Coach, Glyndebourne Festival Opera, since 1994; *b* Vienna, 30 Sept. 1930; *s* of Sebastian and Helene Isepp; *m* 1966, Rose Henrietta Harris; two *s*. *Educ:* St Paul's Sch.; Lincoln Coll., Oxford; Royal Coll. of Music, London (ARCM 1952). Studied piano with Prof. Leonie Gombrich, 1939–52. English Opera Gp, 1954–57; Glyndebourne Fest. Opera, 1957– (Head of Music Staff, 1973–93); Head of Opera Trng Dept, Juilliard Sch. of Music, New York, 1973–78; Hd, Acad. of Singing, Banff Sch. of Fine Arts, Alberta, Canada, 1982–93. As accompanist, began career accompanying mother, Helene Isepp (the singer and voice teacher); has accompanied many of the world's leading singers and instrumentalists, notably Elisabeth Schwarzkopf, Elisabeth Söderström, Janet Baker and John Shirley-Quirk; harpsichordist with Handel Opera Soc. of New York in most of their Handel Festivals, 1966–; master classes in opera and song at Amer. univs, incl. Southern Calif, Ann Arbor, Maryland, Minnesota and Colorado, 1975–; lieder courses, Britten-Pears Sch. for Advanced Musical Studies, Aldeburgh, 1988–; coached Peking Opera and Peking Conservatory in Mozart operas, 1983; opera prodns, Centre de la Voix, Fondation Royaumont, France, 1992–; annual opera course (Music Dir), Walton Foundn, Ischia, Italy, 1992–95; classes in opera and song, Pacific Music Fest., Sapporo, Japan, 1995–98; classes at New Nat. Opera, Tokyo, 2001–. As conductor: Le Nozze di Figaro, Glyndebourne Touring Op., 1984; Don Giovanni, Glyndebourne Touring Op., 1986; Abduction from the Seraglio, Washington Op., 1986–87; Asst Conductor, Met. Op., NY, 1994–. Hon. DMus Wake Forest, NC, 2001. Carroll Donner Stuchell Medal for Accompanists, Harriet Cohen Internat. Musical Foundn, 1965. *Recreations:* photography, walking. *Address:* 55 Parliament Hill, NW3 2TB. *T:* (020) 7722 3085.

ISH-HOROWICZ, Dr David, FRS 2002; Principal Scientist, Cancer Research UK (formerly Imperial Cancer Research Fund), since 1987; *b* 2 Aug. 1948; *s* of Moshe Ish-Horowicz and Hava Ish-Horowicz (*née* Berman); *m* 1988, Rosamund Diamond. *Educ:* Manchester Grammar Sch.; Pembroke Coll., Cambridge (BA 1969); Darwin Coll., Cambridge/MRC Lab. of Molecular Biol. (PhD 1973). Post-doctoral Res. Fellow, Basel Univ., Switzerland, 1973–76; Imperial Cancer Research Fund: Res. Scientist, 1977–81; Sen. Res. Scientist, 1981–87. Hon. Prof., UCL, 1997–. Mem., EMBO, 1985. *Publications:* contrib. papers to research jls. *Recreations:* swimming, ski-ing, reading bridge columns, music, eating wife's cooking. *Address:* Developmental Genetics Laboratory, Cancer Research UK, PO Box 123, 44 Lincoln's Inn Fields, WC2A 3PX. *T:* (020) 7269 3053, *Fax:* (020) 7269 3417.

ISHAM, Sir Ian (Vere Gyles), 13th Bt *cr* 1627; *b* 17 July 1923; *s* of Lt-Col Vere Arthur Richard Isham, MC (*d* 1968) and Edith Irene (*d* 1973), *d* of Harry Brown; *S* cousin, Sir

Gyles Isham, 12th Bt, 1976. Served War of 1939–45, Captain RAC. *Heir: b* Norman Murray Crawford Isham, OBE [*b* 28 Jan. 1930; *m* 1956, Joan, *d* of late Leonard James Genet; two *s* one *d*]. *Address:* 50 Willow Court, Ackender Road, Alton, Hants GU34 1JW.

ISHERWOOD, John David Gould, CMG 2001; Chairman, Hampshire Archives Trust, since 2001; consultant solicitor, 1991–2002; *b* 8 Feb. 1936; *s* of Frank Hilton Isherwood and Beatrice Marion Isherwood (*née* Gould); *m* 1967, Anne Isobel Inglis; one *s* one *d*. *Educ:* Cheltenham Coll.; Merton Coll., Oxford (MA 1963; MSt 1997); Stanford Univ., California. Lieut, RA, 1954–56. Admitted Solicitor, 1964; VSO, 1964–68; Solicitor, 1969, Sen. Partner, 1985–91, Barker, Son & Isherwood, Andover. Mem., Law Soc. Trustee: Oxfam 1968–98 (Chm., Exec. Cttee, 1979–85); Wateraid, 1981–2001 (Chm., 1995–2001); NCVO, 1996–2003. Trustee, SE Museums, Libraries and Archives Council, 2003–. Patron, Charities' Technology Trust, 2002–. *Recreations:* local history, theatre, travel. *Address:* Chalcot, Penton Mewsey, Andover, Hants SP11 0RQ.

ISHERWOOD, Mark; Member (C) Wales North, National Assembly for Wales, since 2003; *b* 21 Jan. 1959; *s* of Rodney Isherwood and Patricia McLean; *m* 1985, Hilary Fleming; two *s* four *d*. *Educ:* Univ. of Newcastle-upon-Tyne (BA Hons Politics). Trainee Manager, subseq. Br. Manager, Cheshire Building Soc., 1981–89; Commercial Business Develt Manager, NWS Bank, 1989–90; Wirral Area Manager, 1990–94, N Wales Area Manager, 1994–2003, Cheshire Building Soc. Mem., Treuddyn Community Council, 1999–2004 (Vice-Chm., 2002–03). Bd Mem., Venture Housing Assoc., 1992–2003. Gov., Ysgol Parc-y-Llon, 1996–2004. Contested (C) Alyn and Deeside, 2001. Mem., Mold Round Table, 1984–. ACIB. *Recreations:* sailing, spending time with family. *Address:* National Assembly for Wales, Cardiff Bay, Cardiff CF99 1NA. *T:* (029) 2089 8730, *Fax:* (029) 2089 8323; *e-mail:* mark.isherwood@wales.gov.uk; (constituency office) 5 Halkyn Street, Holywell, Flintshire CH8 7TX.

ISHIGURO, Kazuo, OBE 1995; FRSL; author; *b* 8 Nov. 1954; *s* of Shizuo and Shizuko Ishiguro; *m* 1986, Lorna Anne MacDougall; one *d*. *Educ:* Univ. of Kent (BA English/Philosophy); Univ. of East Anglia (MA Creative Writing). Began publishing short stories, articles, in magazines, 1980; writer of TV plays, 1984–; filmscripts: (jtly) The Saddest Music in the World, 2004; The White Countess, 2006. Mem. Jury, Cannes Film Festival, 1994. FRSL 1989. Hon. DLitt: Kent, 1990; UEA, 1995; St Andrews, 2003. Premio Scanno for Literature, Italy, 1995; Premio Mantova, Italy, 1998. Chevalier de l'Ordre des Arts et des Lettres (France), 1998. *Publications:* A Pale View of Hills, 1982 (Winifred Holtby Prize, RSL); An Artist of the Floating World, 1986 (Whitbread Book of the Year, Whitbread Fiction Prize); The Remains of the Day, 1989 (Booker Prize; filmed 1993); The Unconsoled, 1995 (Cheltenham Prize, 1995); When We Were Orphans, 2000; Never Let Me Go, 2005 (Premio Serono, Italy, Corine Internat. Book Prize, Germany, Casino de Santiago Eur. Novel Award, Spain, 2006). *Recreations:* music; playing piano and guitar. *Address:* c/o Faber & Faber, 3 Queen Square, WC1N 3AU.

ISLE OF MAN, Archdeacon of; *see* Smith, Ven. B.

ISLE OF WIGHT, Archdeacon of; *see* Baston, Ven. C.

ISLES, Maj.-Gen. Donald Edward, CB 1978; OBE 1968; DL; *b* 19 July 1924; *s* of Harold and Kathleen Isles; *m* 1948, Sheila Mary Stephens (formerly Thorpe); three *s* one *d*. *Educ:* Roundhay; Leeds Univ.; RMCS. jssc 1961. Italian campaign, Palestine, Egypt, Sudan, Syria, with 1st Bn, Duke of Wellington's Regt, 1944–47; Asst Mil. Attaché, Paris, 1963–65; CO, 1DWR, BAOR and UN Forces in Cyprus, 1965–67; AMS, MoD, 1968; Col GS, MoD, 1968–71; Dir of Munitions, Brit. Defence Staff Washington, 1972–75; Dir-Gen. Weapons (Army), 1975–78, retired. Dep. Man. Dir, British Manufacture & Res. Co., 1979–89. Col, The Duke of Wellington's Regt, 1975–82; Col Comdt, The King's Div., 1975–79; Vice-Chm., Yorks and Humberside TA&VRA, 1984–87. Hon. Colonel: 3rd Bn, Yorkshire Volunteers, 1977–83; Leeds Univ. OTC, 1985–90. Mem., Court, Leeds Univ., 1987–95. Pres., Lincs and S Humberside RBL, 1990–96; Patron, Lincs RBL, 1996–2004. DL Lincs, 1990. *Recreation:* shooting. *Club:* Army and Navy.

ISON, Very Rev. David John, PhD; Dean of Bradford, since 2005; *b* 15 Sept. 1954; *s* of Richard Lea Ison and Maureen Jean Ison; *m* 1977, Hilary Margaret Powell; two *s* two *d*. *Educ:* Univ. of Leicester (BA 1976); Univ. of Nottingham (BA 1978); St John's Coll., Nottingham (DPS 1979); King's Coll. London (PhD 1985). Ordained deacon, 1979, priest, 1980; Asst Curate, St Nicholas and St Luke, Deptford, 1979–85; Tutor, Church Army Trng Coll., 1985–88; Vicar, Potters Green, Coventry, 1988–93; Officer for Contg Ministerial Educn, Dio. Exeter, 1993–2005. *Publications:* (ed) Pilgrim Guide to Exeter Cathedral, 1999; (ed) The Vicar's Guide, 2005. *Recreations:* building a car, bodgery. *Address:* The Deanery, 1 Cathedral Close, Bradford BD1 4EG. *T:* (01274) 777722, *Fax:* (01274) 777730; *e-mail:* dean@bradford.anglican.org.

ISRAEL, Prof. Jonathan Irvine, DPhil; FBA 1992; Professor of Modern History, Institute for Advanced Study, Princeton, since 2000; *b* 22 Jan. 1946; *s* of David and Miriam Israel; *m* 1985, Jenny Tatjana Winckel; one *s* one *d*. *Educ:* Kilburn Grammar Sch.; Queens' Coll., Cambridge; St Antony's Coll., Oxford (DPhil 1972). Lectr, Hull Univ., 1972–74; Lectr, 1974–81, Reader, 1981–84, Prof. of Dutch History and Instns, 1985–2000, UCL. *Publications:* Race, Class and Politics in Colonial Mexico, 1975; The Dutch Republic and the Hispanic World, 1982; European Jewry in the Age of Mercantilism 1550–1750, 1985; Dutch Primacy in World Trade 1585–1740, 1989; Empires and Entrepots: the Dutch, the Spanish monarchy and the Jews 1585–1713, 1990; (ed) The Anglo-Dutch Movement: essays on the Glorious Revolution and its world impact, 1991; The Dutch Republic, 1995; Conflicts of Empires: Spain, the Low Countries and the struggle for world supremacy 1585–1713, 1997; Radical Enlightenment: philosophy and the making of modernity 1650–1750, 2001; Enlightenment Contested, 2006. *Address:* School of Historical Studies, Institute for Advanced Study, Einstein Drive, Princeton, NJ 08540, USA.

ISRAEL, Prof. Werner, OC 1994; FRS 1986; Adjunct Professor of Physics, University of Victoria, since 1997; *b* 4 Oct. 1931; *s* of Arthur Israel and Marie Kappauf; *m* 1958, Inge Margulies; one *s* one *d*. *Educ:* Cape Town High Sch.; Univ. of Cape Town (BSc 1951, MSc 1954); Dublin Inst. for Advanced Studies; Trinity Coll., Dublin (PhD 1960). Lectr in Applied Maths, Univ. of Cape Town, 1954–56; University of Alberta: Asst Prof., 1958; Associate Prof., 1964; Prof. of Maths, 1968–71; Prof. of Physics, 1972–96; Univ. Prof., 1985–96. Sherman Fairchild Dist. Schol., CIT, 1974–75; Vis. Prof., Dublin Inst. for Advanced Studies, 1966–68; Sen. Visitor, Dept of Applied Maths and Theoretical Physics, Univ. of Cambridge, 1975–76; Maître de Recherche Associé, Inst. Henri Poincaré, Paris, 1976–77; Visiting Professor: Berne, 1980; Kyoto, 1986, 1998; Vis. Fellow, Gonville and Caius Coll., Cambridge, 1985. Fellow, Canadian Inst. for Advanced Research, 1986–. Pres., Internat. Soc. of Gen. Relativity and Gravitation, 1998–2001. Hon. DSc: Queen's, Kingston, Ont, 1987; Victoria, BC, 1999; Dr *hc* Tours, 1994. *Publications:* (ed) Relativity, Astrophysics and Cosmology, 1973; (ed with S. W. Hawking) General Relativity: an Einstein centenary survey, 1979; (ed with S. W. Hawking) 300 Years of Gravitation, 1987; numerous papers on black hole physics, general relativity, relativistic statistical mechani *Recreation:* music. *Address:* Department of Physics and Astronomy, University of Victor Victoria, BC V8W 3P6, Canada. *T:* (250) 7217708.

ISRAELACHVILI, Prof. Jacob Nissim, FRS 1988; FAA; Professor of Chemic Engineering and Materials Science, Department of Chemical Engineering and Materi Department, University of California, Santa Barbara, since 1986; *b* 19 Aug. 1944; *s* Haim and Hela Israelachvili; *m* 1971, Karina (*née* Haglund); two *d*. *Educ:* Univ. Cambridge (MA; PhD 1972). FAA 1982. Post-doctoral res. into surface forces, Cavendi Lab., Cambridge, 1971–72; EMBO Res. Fellow, Biophysics Inst., Univ. of Stockholr 1972–74; Res. Fellow, subseq. Professorial Fellow, Res. Sch. of Physical Scis, Inst. Advanced Studies, ANU, Canberra, 1974–86. Council Mem., 1983–87, Vice-Pre 1986–87, Internat. Assoc. of Colloid and Interface Scientists. Foreign Associate, US NA 1996; Fellow, APS, 2004; MNAS 2004. Pawsey Medal, 1977, Matthew Flinders Lec medallist, 1986, Aust. Acad. of Sci.; (jtly) David Syme Res. Prize, 1983; (jtly) Medal, U Materials Res. Soc., 2004. *Publications:* Intermolecular and Surface Forces: wi applications to colloidal and biological systems, 1985, 2nd edn 1991; about 300 pubns learned jls, incl. Nature, Science, Procs Royal Soc. *Recreation:* history of science. *Addre* 2233 Foothill Lane, Santa Barbara, CA 93105, USA. *T:* (residence) (805) 9639545, (offic (805) 8938407.

ISSERLIS, Steven John, CBE 1998; 'cellist; *b* 19 Dec. 1958; *s* of George and late Cynth Isserlis; lives with Pauline Mara; one *s*. *Educ:* City of London School; International 'Cel Centre; Oberlin College. London recital début, Wigmore Hall, 1977; London concer début, with English Chamber Orchestra, 1980; concerts in Europe, N America, Australi 1978–; tours in USSR, later Russia, 1984–; débuts, 1990–, in New York, Paris, Berli Vienna, Tokyo, Sydney, Seoul, Taipei, etc; numerous recordings. Awards for recordin include: Gramophone Award (Contemporary Music), for John Tavener's The Protectir Veil, 1992; Deutsche Schallplattenpreis, for Schumann Cello Concerto, 1998; Classic C Award, for Haydn Concertos, 1999; Gramophone Award (Instrumental Recording) ar CD of the Year, BBC R3 CD Review, for Bach Cello Suites, 2007. Piatigorsky Arti Award, USA, 1993; Instrumentalist Award, Royal Philharmonic Soc., 1993; Schumar Prize, City of Zwickau, 2000; Red F Award, Classic FM, 2002; Classical Artist of tl Year, Time Out, 2002. *Publications:* for children: Why Beethoven Threw the Stew, 200 Why Handel Waggled His Wig, 2006. *Recreations:* talking on the telephone, e-mailir everybody I know (usually for no good reason), eating too much, regretting it, watchir videos, reading, panicking about upcoming concerts, sleeping, jet-lag, telling people ho tired I am, wondering if I should have any more worthwhile recreations. *Address:* c/o IM Artists, The Light Box, 111 Power Road, W4 5PY. *T:* (020) 7957 5800.

ISSING, Dr Otmar; Member, Executive Board, European Central Bank, 1998–2006; 27 March 1936. *Educ:* Univ. of Würzburg (BA Econs; PhD 1961). Res. Asst, Inst. Econs and Social Scis, 1960–66, Lectr, 1965–66, Univ. of Würzburg; Temp. Prof., Uni of Marburg, 1965–66; Professor: Faculty of Econs and Social Scis, and Dir, Inst. fo Internat. Econ. Relns, Univ. of Erlangen-Nuremberg, 1967–73 (Temp. Prof., 1966–67 of Econs, Monetary Affairs and Internat. Econ. Relns, Univ. of Würzburg, 1973–90 (Ho Prof., 1991–); Mem. Directorate, Deutsche Bundesbank, 1990–98. Co-founder and Ed., WiSt (scientific jl), 1972–90. Hon. doctorates from: Bayreuth, 1996; Constanc 1998; Frankfurt am Main, 1999. *Publications* include: Leitwährung und internationa Währungsordnung, 1965; Indexklauseln und Inflation, 1973; Einführung in d Geldtheorie, 1974, 14th edn 2006 (trans. Chinese and Bulgarian); Investitionslenkung i der Marktwirtschaft?, 1975; (jtly) Kleineres Eigentum: Grundlage unserer Staats- un Wirtschaftstordnung, 1976; Einführung in die Geldpolitik, 1981, 6th edn 199 Internationale Währungsordnung, 1991; Von der D-Mark zum Euro, 1998; (jtl Monetary Policy in the Euro Area, 2001; contrib. learned jls. *Address:* Georg Sittig Stras 8, 97074 Würzburg, Germany.

ISTEAD, Maj.-Gen. Peter Walter Ernest, CB 1989; OBE 1978; GM 1966; DL; Chi Executive, Institute of Brewing, 1990–96; *b* 7 Aug. 1935; *s* of Walter and Marie Istead; 1961, Jennifer Mary Swinson; one *s* one *d*. *Educ:* Whitgift Trinity Sch., Croydon. Enliste as boy soldier into Scots Guards, 1952; commnd Queen's Royal Regt, 1954; seconded t KAR, 1954–56; transf. RAOC, 1957; HQ 16 Parachute Bde, 1958–62; sc 1968; Directin Staff, Staff Coll., Camberley, 1971–73; DCS, 4 Armd Div., 1978–81; RCDS, 1982; Di Admin. Planning (Army), 1983–86; Comdr Supply, BAOR, 1986–87; Dir Gen., Logisti Policy (Army), 1987–90. Hon. Col Comdt, RAOC, 1989–92. Freeman, City of Londo 1986. DL Greater London, 1997. *Recreation:* angling. *Address:* Wandsworth, London.

IUUL, Michael Christian Stig; Managing Director and Chief Executive Office Carlsberg Asia Ltd, Singapore, 2001–03; *b* Copenhagen, 26 Jan. 1943; *s* of Stig A. Iuul an Grethe (*née* Gerlach); *m* Annie Ingeborg Scavenius; two *s*. *Educ:* Herlufsholm Sch.; Univ of Copenhagen (MA Econs); Univ. of Paris; Univ. of Rome. International Bank fo Reconstruction and Development: Planning Consultant, 1970–74; Industrial Economis then Chief Economist, projects in Ghana, 1971, and Malaysia, 1972–74; joined Carlsber A'S, Copenhagen, 1974: Manager, Sinebrychoff AB, Helsinki, 1975–76; Man. Di Carlsberg Brewery Ltd, Northampton, 1977–85; Gp Man. Dir and CEO (Internat. Ops 1985–2001. Chm., Carlsberg-Tetley Ltd; Director: Th. Wessel & Vett Ltd. Ridder Dannebrog (Denmark). *Recreations:* tennis, ski-ing, yachting. *Address:* Grosvenor Road SW1.

IVANYI, Prof. Juraj, MD; PhD; Head (formerly Director), Tuberculosis and Relate Infections Unit, MRC Clinical Sciences Centre, 1984–97; Professor Mycobacteriological Immunology, Royal Postgraduate Medical School, University o London, 1990–97; *b* 20 June 1934; *s* of Dr Arnold Ivanyi and Maria (*née* Keszner); *m* 1960 Dr Ludmila Svobodova (*d* 2002). *Educ:* Charles Univ., Prague (MD); Acad. of Scis, Pragu (PhD 1963). Czechoslovak Acad. of Scis, Prague, 1961–68; Wellcome Res. Lab Beckenham, 1969–84; MRC, Hammersmith Hosp., 1984–97. Hon. Prof., Dept o Clinical and Diagnostic Scis, KCL at Guy's Hosp. (formerly Dept of Oral Med. an Pathology, Guy's, King's and St Thomas's Hosp. Med. and Dental Sch.), 1998–. Hon Mem., Slovak Soc. for Immunology, 1995. Garnet Immunoglobulin Award, Czec Immunology Soc., 2006. *Publications:* numerous in field of immunology. *Recreation* theatre, ski-ing. *Address:* 3 Grotes Place, Blackheath, SE3 0QH. *T:* (020) 8318 1088.

IVE, Jonathan Paul, CBE 2006; RDI 2003; Senior Vice President and Head of Design Apple, since 1996; *b* London, 1967; *m*; twin *s*. *Educ:* Newcastle upon Tyne Poly. (BA 1s Cl. Hons Industrial Design 1989). Partner, Tangerine, design consultancy, London 1989–92; joined Apple, 1992. *Designs* include: ceramic-ware, electrical appliance consumer electronics, computers (incl. iMac, PowerBook, iBook, iPod, iPhone Inaugural medal, RSA, 1999; Designer of Year, Design Mus., 2003; Benjamin Frankli Medal, RSA, 2004; President's Award, D&AD, 2005, and Royal Acad. of Engrs, 2005 *Address:* c/o Apple, 1 Infinite Loop, Cupertino, CA 95014, USA. *T:* (408) 9961010.

IVEAGH, 4th Earl of, *cr* 1919; **Arthur Edward Rory Guinness;** DL; Bt 1885; Baro Iveagh 1891; Viscount Iveagh 1905; Viscount Elveden 1919; *b* 10 Aug. 1969; *s* of 3rd Ear of Iveagh and of Miranda Daphne Jane, *d* of Maj. Michael Smiley; *S* father, 1992; *m* 2001, Clare Hazell; two *s*. DL Suffolk, 2008. FIAgrM. *Heir: s* Viscount Elveden, *qv. Address:* The Estate Office, Elveden, Thetford, Norfolk IP24 3TQ.

IVENS, Martin Paul; Deputy Editor, Sunday Times, since 1996; *b* London, 29 Aug. 1958; *s* of Michael William and Rosalie Joy Evans; *m* 1994, Anne McElvoy; two *s* one *d. Educ:* Finchley Catholic High Sch.; St Peter's Coll., Oxford (BA 1st Cl. Modern Hist.). Foreign Ed., Sunday Telegraph, 1986–88; The Times: Foreign News Ed., 1988–90; Foreign Ed., 1990–94; Exec. Ed. (News and Comment), 1994–96. Directory Trustee, Social Mkt Foundn. *Recreations:* mediaeval and modern history, running, classical music. *Address:* The Sunday Times, 1 Pennington Street, E98 1ST. *Club:* Travellers.

IVERSEN, Prof. Leslie Lars, PhD; FRS 1980; Professor of Pharmacology and Director, Wolfson Centre for Age-Related Diseases, King's College London, 1999–2004; *b* 31 Oct. 1937; *s* of Svend Iversen and Anna Caia Iversen; *m* 1961, Susan Diana (*née* Kibble) (*see* S. D. Iversen); one *s* one *d* (and one *d* decd). *Educ:* Trinity Coll., Cambridge (BA Biochem, PhD Pharmacol). Harkness Fellow, United States: with Dr J. Axelrod, Nat. Inst. of Mental Health, and Dr E. Kravitz, Dept of Neurobiology, Harvard Med. Sch., 1964–66; Fellow, Trinity Coll., Cambridge, 1964–84; Locke Research Fellow of Royal Society, Dept of Pharmacology, Univ. of Cambridge, 1967–71; Dir, MRC Neurochemical Pharmacology Unit, Cambridge, 1971–82; Dir, Merck, Sharp & Dohme Neurosci. Res. Centre, Harlow, 1982–95; Sen. Vis. Scientist, Dept of Pharmacology, 1995–96, Vis. Prof. of Pharmacol., 1996–, Oxford Univ. Foreign Associate, Nat. Acad. of Scis (USA), 1986. *Publications:* The Uptake and Storage of Noradrenaline in Sympathetic Nerves, 1967; (with S. D. Iversen) Behavioural Pharmacology, 1975, 2nd edn 1981; The Science of Marijuana, 2000; Speed, Ecstasy, Ritalin: the science of amphetamines, 2007. *Recreations:* reading, gardening. *Address:* Department of Pharmacology, University of Oxford, Mansfield Road, Oxford OX1 3QT.

IVERSEN, Prof. Susan Diana, CBE 2005; PhD, ScD; FMedSci; Professor of Psychology, 1993–2005, now Emeritus, and Pro-Vice-Chancellor (Planning and Resource Allocation), 2000–05, Oxford University; Fellow of Magdalen College, Oxford, 1993–2005, now Emeritus; *b* 28 Feb. 1940; *d* of Jack Bertram Kibble and Edith Margaret Kibble; *m* 1961, Leslie Lars Iversen, *qv;* one *s* one *d* (and one *d* decd). *Educ:* Girton Coll., Cambridge (BA Zoology, PhD Exp. Psych, ScD). NATO Science Fellow, Nat. Inst. Mental Health and Dept of Pharmacology, Harvard Med. Sch., 1964–66; Fellow: Girton Coll., Cambridge, 1964–75; Jesus Coll., Cambridge, 1981–93; Dept of Exp. Psychology, Cambridge, 1966–83; Merck Sharp & Dohme, Neuroscience Research Centre, Harlow, 1983–93; Oxford University: Prof. and Head of Dept of Experimental Psychol., 1993–2000; Pro-Vice-Chancellor (Res.), 1998–2000. Oxford University Press: Psychology Delegate, 1994–2005; Chm., Finance Cttee, 2001–05. Member: Council, SERC, 1991–94; BBSRC, 1994–97. Member: Animal Procedures Cttee, Home Office, 1989–98; Mental Health and Neurosci. Grant Cttee, Wellcome Trust, 1990–98 (Chm. Panel, 1995–98); Health and Life Scis Panel, 1993–98, Brain Sci., Addiction and Drug Project Panel, 2004–, Foresight. President: British Assoc. of Psychopharmacol., 1984–86; Experimental Psychol. Soc., 1988–90; Med. Sect., 1989, Psychol. Sect., 1997, BAAS; Chm., Brain Res. Assoc., 1994–96. Member Council: Acad. of Med. Scis, 2004–; Bioscis Fedn, 2004–; Inst. for Animal Health, 2004–; GDST, 2005–. Chm., Internat. Adv. and Scientific Bd, Inst. of Neurosci., TCD; Mem. Adv. Bd, Brain, Mind and Behavior Prog., J. S. McDonnell Foundn, St Louis, USA, 1999–. A. Vibert Douglas Fellow, Internat. Fedn of Univ. Women, 1964–65. FMedSci 1999. Hon. Fellow, Cardiff Univ., 1999. Hon. DSc St Andrews, 2005. K. M. Stott Prize, Newnham Coll., Cambridge, 1972; Spearman Medal, BPsS, 1974; Lifetime Achievement Award, British Assoc. for Psychopharmacol., 2003. Receiving Ed., Science, 1994–99; Chief Ed., Neuropsychologia, 1997–2000. *Publications:* (with L. L. Iversen) Behavioural Pharmacology, 1975, 2nd edn 1981; (ed with L. L. Iversen and S. H. Snyder) Handbook of Psychopharmacology, 20 vols. *Recreations:* history, wildlife, modern art, theatre. *Address:* University Offices, Wellington Square, Oxford OX1 2JD.

IVES, Charles John Grayston, (Bill); Informator Choristarum, Organist, and Tutor in Music, Magdalen College, Oxford, since 1991; Fellow of Magdalen College, since 1991; *b* 15 Feb. 1948; *s* of Harold James Ives and Catherine Lilla Ives; *m* 1st, 1972, Bethan Eleri Jones (marr. diss. 1986); one *s* one *d*; 2nd, 1988, Janette Ann (*née* Buqué). *Educ:* King's Sch., Ely; Selwyn Coll., Cambridge. Asst Dir of Music, Reed's Sch., Cobham, 1971–76; Lectr in Music, Coll. of Further Educn, Chichester, 1976–78; tenor, The King's Singers, 1978–85; freelance composer, 1985–91. Examr, Associated Bd of Royal Schs of Music, 1988–2006. Hon. FRSCM 2008. *Publications:* (as Grayston Ives) musical compositions of sacred choral music, including Canterbury Te Deum (commnd for Enthronement of Archbishop George Carey, Canterbury Cathedral, 1991) and The Gift of Grace (commnd for Nat. Commemoration Service, Westminster Abbey, 2007). *Recreations:* books, wine, travel. *Address:* Magdalen College, Oxford OX1 4AU. *T:* (01865) 276007.

IVES, Prof. Kenneth James, CBE 1996; FREng; FICE; Chadwick Professor of Civil Engineering, University College London, 1984–92, retired; *b* 29 Nov. 1926; *s* of Walter Ives and Grace Ives (*née* Curson); *m* 1952, Brenda Grace Tilley; one *s* one *d. Educ:* William Ellis Grammar School, London; University College London (BSc Eng, PhD, DSc Eng; Fellow, 1996). FREng (FEng 1986); FICE 1983. Junior Engineer, Metropolitan Water Board, London, 1948–55; Lectr, Reader, Prof., University Coll. London, 1955–92. Research Fellow, Harvard Univ., 1958–59; Visiting Professor: Univ. of North Carolina, 1964; Delft Technical Univ., 1977; Consultant Expert Adviser, WHO, 1966–92. Mem., Badenoch Cttee on Cryptosporidium in Water Supplies, 1989–95. For. Associate, NAE, US, 2003. Gans Medal, Soc. for Water Treatment, 1966; Gold Medal, Filtration Soc. Internat., 1983; Jenkins Medal, IAWPRC, 1990; Freese Award, ASCE, 1994. *Publications:* Scientific Basis of Filtration, 1975; Scientific Basis of Flocculation, 1978; Scientific Basis of Flotation, 1984; contribs to sci. and eng. jls on water purification. *Recreation:* ballroom dancing. *Address:* Department of Civil and Environmental Engineering, University College London, Gower Street, WC1E 6BT.

IVISON, David Malcolm; Director, British Metallurgical Plant Constructors' Association, 1994–2002; *b* 22 March 1936; *s* of John and Ruth Ellen Ivison; *m* 1961, Lieselotte Verse; one *s* one *d. Educ:* King Edward VI School, Lichfield; RMA Sandhurst; Staff College, Camberley. Army, Gurkha Transport Regt, 1955–83 (Lt-Col). Tate & Lyle, 1984–85; Chief Exec., Inst. of Road Transport Engrs, 1985–89. Mem. (C) Surrey CC, 2005–. *Recreations:* learning languages, tennis, reading. *Address:* 1 Dundaff Close, Camberley, Surrey GU15 1AF. *T:* (01276) 27778.

IVORY, Sir Brian (Gammell), Kt 2006; CBE 1999; CA; Chairman of Trustees, National Galleries of Scotland, since 2000; *b* 10 April 1949; *s* of late Eric James Ivory and Alice Margaret Joan, *d* of Sir Sydney James Gammell; *m* 1981, Oona Mairi Macphie Bell-MacDonald (*see* O. M. M. Ivory); one *s* one *d. Educ:* Eton College; Magdalene College, Cambridge (MA). The Highland Distilleries Co., subseq. Highland Distillers plc: Dir, 1978–99; Man. Dir, 1988–94; Gp Chief Exec., 1994–97; Exec. Chm., 1997–99. Chairman: Macallan Glenlivet plc, 1996–99; Scottish Amer. Investment Co. plc, 2001–; Retec Digital plc, 2006–; Director: Rémy Cointreau SA, 1991–; Bank of Scotland, 1998–07; HBOS plc, 2001–07; Retec Interface Ltd, 2001–06; Orpar SA, 2003–; Insight Investment Mgt Ltd, 2003–; Synesis Life Ltd, 2007–; Marathon Asset Management Ltd, 2007–. Vice-Chm., Scottish Arts Council, 1988–92; Mem., Arts Council of GB, 1988–92. Founder and Chm., Nat. Piping Centre, 1996–. Mem., Royal Co. of Archers (Queen's Body Guard for Scotland), 1996–. FRSA 1993; FRSE 2001. Freeman, City of London, 1996. *Recreations:* the arts, farming, hill walking. *Address:* 12 Ann Street, Edinburgh EH4 1PJ. *Club:* New (Edinburgh).

IVORY, James Francis; film director; Partner in Merchant Ivory Productions, since 1961; *b* 7 June 1928; *s* of Edward Patrick Ivory and Hallie Millicent De Loney. *Educ:* Univ. of Oregon (BA Fine Arts); Univ. of Southern California (MFA Cinema). Guggenheim Fellow, 1974. Collaborator with Ruth Prawer Jhabvala and Ismail Merchant on the following films: The Householder, 1963; Shakespeare Wallah, 1965; The Guru, 1969; Bombay Talkie, 1970; Autobiography of a Princess, 1975; Roseland, 1977; Hullabaloo over Georgie and Bonnie's Pictures, 1978; The Europeans, 1979; Jane Austen in Manhattan, 1980; Quartet, 1981; Heat and Dust, 1983; The Bostonians, 1984; A Room With a View, 1986; Mr and Mrs Bridge, 1990; Howards End, 1992; The Remains of the Day, 1993; Jefferson in Paris, 1995; Surviving Picasso, 1996; A Soldier's Daughter Never Cries, 1998; The Golden Bowl, 2000; Le Divorce, 2003; The City of Your Final Destination, 2008; collaborator with Ismail Merchant (producer) on: (with Nirad Chaudhuri) Adventures of a Brown Man in Search of Civilization, 1971; (with George W. S. Trow and Michael O'Donoghue) Savages, 1972; (with Walter Marks) The Wild Party, 1975; (with Kit Hesketh-Harvey) Maurice, 1987; (with Tama Janowitz) Slaves of New York, 1989; (with Kazuo Ishiguro) The White Countess, 2006; other films: (with Terrence McNally) The Five Forty Eight, 1979; documentaries: Venice, Theme and Variations, 1957; The Sword and the Flute, 1959; The Delhi Way, 1964. D. W. Griffith Award, Directors Guild of America, 1995. Commandeur, Ordre des Arts et des Lettres (France), 1996. *Publication:* Autobiography of a Princess (Also Being the Adventures of an American Film Director in the Land of the Maharajas), 1975. *Recreation:* looking at pictures. *Address:* PO Box 93, Claverack, NY 12513, USA. *T:* (office) (212) 5828049.

IVORY, Oona Mairi Macphie, (Lady Ivory); DL; Founder and Director, since 1996 and Deputy Chairman, since 1999, National Piping Centre; *b* 21 July 1954; *d* of late Archibald Ian Bell-Macdonald and Mary Rae (*née* Macphie); *m* 1981, Brian Gammell Ivory (*see* Sir B. G. Ivory); one *s* one *d. Educ:* Royal Scottish Acad. of Music and Drama; King's Coll., Cambridge (MA); Royal Acad. of Music. ARCM. Dir, 1988–97, Chm., 1995–97, Scottish Ballet; Dir, RSAMD, 1989–2002. Dir, Glasgow Internat. Piping Fest., 2004–. FRSA 1993. DL Edinburgh, 1998. *Recreations:* the arts, sailing, wild places. *Address:* 12 Ann Street, Edinburgh EH4 1PJ.

IVORY, Thomas Peter Gerard; QC 1998; *b* 29 Sept. 1956; *s* of late Patrick Ivory and of Rosaleen Ivory; *m* 1985, Deborah Mary Stinson. *Educ:* St Patrick's Coll., Knock, Belfast; St Catharine's Coll., Cambridge (BA 1977; MA). Called to the Bar, Lincoln's Inn, 1978. Fellow, St Catharine's Coll., Cambridge, 1983–90. *Recreation:* golf. *Address:* 1 Essex Court, Temple, EC4Y 9AR. *T:* (020) 7583 2000.

IWAN, Dafydd; President, Plaid Cymru, since 2003 (Vice-President, 2001–03); *b* 24 Aug. 1943; *s* of Rev. Gerallt Jones and Elizabeth Jane Jones; *m* 1988, Bethan; two *s* and two *s*, one *d* from previous marriage. *Educ:* Welsh Sch. of Architecture, Cardiff (BArch 1968). Chair, Cymdeithas yr Iaith Gymraeg, 1968–71; Dir, 1969–, Man. Dir, 1982–2004, Sain Recording Co. Organiser, Tai Gwynedd Housing Assoc., 1974–82. Mem., Gwynedd Council, 1996– (Leader, Develt Portfolio, 2004–). Hon. Fellow: Univ. of Wales, Bangor; Univ. of Wales, Aberystwyth. Hon. Mem., Gorsedd of Bards. Hon. LLD Wales, 2004. *Publications:* First Autobiography, 1983; Holl Ganeuon (song collection), 1992; Cân Dros Gymru (autobiog.), 2002; Pictorial Biography, 2005. *Recreations:* writing poetry, composing, art, Rugby. *Address:* Carrog, Rhos-Bach, Caernarfon, Gwynedd LL55 2TF. *T:* (01286) 676004; *e-mail:* dafyddiwan@cymru1.net.

IZZA, Michael Donald McCartney, FCA; Chief Executive, Institute of Chartered Accountants in England and Wales, since 2006; *b* 13 Dec. 1960; *s* of late Salvatore Izza and of Jean Izza (*née* McCartney); *m* 1991, Gillian Johnston; one *s* one *d. Educ:* Thornleigh Salesian Coll., Bolton; Durham Univ. (BA Hons Law). ACA 1987, FCA 2007. Coopers & Lybrand, 1983–89; John Labatt Ltd, 1989–96 (Man. Dir, John Labatt Retail, 1992–96); Spring Group plc, 1996–2000: Man. Dir, Spring Skills, 1996–97; Divl Man. Dir, 1997–98; Actg Gp Finance Dir, 1999–2000; Divl Dir, Professional Services and Exec. Dir, Support Services, Carlisle Support Services, 2001; Institute of Chartered Accountants in England and Wales, 2002–: Exec. Dir, Finance and Ops, 2002–03; Chief Operating Officer, 2004–06. *Recreations:* running, hill walking, gardening, Bolton Wanderers FC, history. *Address:* Institute of Chartered Accountants in England and Wales, Chartered Accountants' Hall, PO Box 433, Moorgate Place, EC2P 2BJ. *T:* (020) 7920 8419; *e-mail:* michael.izza@icaew.com.

J

JABALÉ, Rt Rev. (John) Mark; *see* Menevia, Bishop of, (RC).

JACK, Hon. Sir Alieu (Sulayman), Grand Commander, 1972, and Chancellor, 1972–83, National Order of The Gambia; Kt 1970; Speaker, House of Representatives of the Republic of The Gambia, 1962–72, and 1977–83, retired; *b* 14 July 1922; *m* 1946, Yai Marie Cham; four *s* four *d* (and one *d* decd). *Educ:* St Augustine's School. Entered Gambia Civil Service, 1939; resigned and took up local appt with NAAFI, 1940–44; Civil Service, 1945–48; entered commerce, 1948; Man. Dir, Gambia National Trading Co. Ltd, 1948–72. Mem., Bathurst City Council, 1949–62. Minister for Works and Communications, The Gambia, 1972–77. Represented The Gambia Parlt at various internat. gatherings. Comdr, National Order of Senegal, 1967; Comdr, Order of Merit of Mauritania, 1967; Commander, Order of Fed. Republic of Nigeria, 1970; Kt Grand Band, Liberia, 1977. *Recreation:* golf. *Address:* PO Box 376, Banjul, The Gambia. *T:* (home) 4392204, (office) 4227486. *Club:* Bathurst (Banjul).

JACK, Sir David, Kt 1993; CBE 1982; PhD; FRS 1992; FRSE; pharmacologist; *b* 22 Feb. 1924; *s* of Andrew Jack and Mary McDougal Jack (*née* Maiden); *m* 1952, Lydia Downie Brown; two *d*. *Educ:* Markinch and Buckhaven Schools, Fife; Univ. of Glasgow (BSc); Univ. of London (PhD); Royal Technical Coll., Glasgow. FRSC, FIBiol, FRPharmS; FRSE 1978. Lectr in Pharmacology, Glasgow Univ. and RTC Glasgow, 1948–51; Scientist, Glaxo Labs, 1951–53; Head of Product Develt, Smith Kline and French, 1953–61; Res. Dir, Allen & Hanburys, 1961–78; R&D Dir, Glaxo Holdings, 1978–87; associated with new medicines for the treatment of asthma (salbutamol, salmeterol, beclomethasone dipropionate, fluticasone propionate), peptic ulcer (ranitidine), migraine (sumatriptan), and controlling side-effects of cancer chemotherapy (ondansetron). Hon. DL Dundee, 1991. Hon. DSc: Strathclyde, 1982; Bath, 1987; CNAA, 1987; Liverpool, 1998; London, 1999; Glasgow, 2001. Medicinal Chem. Medal, RSC, 1980; Award for Drug Discovery, Soc. for Drug Research, 1985; Lilly Prize Medal, British Pharm. Soc., 1989; Mullard Medal, Royal Soc., 1991; Galen Medal, Soc. of Apothecaries, 1995; Host-Madsen Medal, Internat. Pharmaceutical Fedn, 1995; Royal Medal, RSE, 2006; Hanbury Meml Award, RPSGB, 2006. *Publications:* papers in Br. Jl Pharmacology etc. *Recreations:* theatre, gardening, golf. *Address:* 6 The Slype, Gustard Wood, Wheathampstead, Herts AL4 8RY. *T:* (01582) 832241.

JACK, David M.; *see* Morton Jack.

JACK, Ian Grant; writer and editor; Editor, Granta, 1995–2007; *b* 7 Feb. 1945; *s* of Henry Jack and Isabella Jack (*née* Gillespie); *m* 1st, 1979, Aparna Bagchi (marr. diss. 1992); 2nd, 1998, Rosalind Sharpe; one *s* one *d*. *Educ:* Dunfermline High School, Fife. Trainee journalist, Glasgow Herald, 1965; reporter, Cambuslang Advertiser and East Kilbride News, 1966; journalist, Scottish Daily Express, 1966–70; Sunday Times, 1970–86; Observer and Vanity Fair (NY), 1986–88; Dep. Editor, 1989–91, Exec. Editor, 1991–92, Editor, 1992–95, Independent on Sunday. Journalist of the Year, Granada TV What The Papers Say award, 1985; Colour Magazine Writer of the Year, 1985, Reporter of the Year, 1988, British Press Awards; Nat. Newspaper Editor of the Year, Newspaper Focus Awards, 1992. *Publications:* Before the Oil Ran Out, 1987; The Crash That Stopped Britain, 2001. *Address:* c/o Rogers, Coleridge and White, 20 Powis Mews, W11 1JN. *Club:* India International Centre (New Delhi).

JACK, Prof. (James) Julian (Bennett), PhD; FRS 1997; Professor of Physiology, 1996–2003, and Fellow of University College, since 1966, University of Oxford; *b* Invercargill, NZ, 25 March 1936. *Educ:* Univ. of Otago (MMedSc, PhD); Magdalen Coll., Oxford (BM 1963; MA). Rhodes Scholarship, 1960–63; House Officer, Radcliffe Infirmary, Oxford, 1963–64; Foulerton Gift Res. Fellow, Royal Soc., 1964–68; University of Oxford: Weir Jun. Res. Fellow in Natural Sci., UC, 1966; Lectr in Physiology, 1970–94; Reader in Cellular Neurosci., 1994–96. Vis. Prof., UCL, 2003–. Mem. Council, Action Res., 1988–91; Chm. Res. Panel, Multiple Sclerosis Soc., 2001–; Gov., Wellcome Trust, 1987–2004 (Dep. Chm. of Govs, 1994–99); Trustee, Brain Res. Trust, 2006–. Founder FMedSci 1998; FRCP 1999. Hon. FRSNZ 1999. *Address:* 24 Claylands Road, SW8 1NZ. *T:* (020) 7582 3085.

JACK, Rt Hon. (John) Michael; PC 1997; MP (C) Fylde, since 1987; *b* 17 Sept. 1946; *m* 1976, Alison Jane Musgrave; two *s*. *Educ:* Bradford Grammar Sch.; Bradford Tech. Coll.; Leicester Univ. BA(Econs); MPhil. Shipping, subseq. Advertising, Depts, Procter & Gamble, 1970–75; PA to Sir Derek Rayner, Marks & Spencer, 1975–80; Sales Dir, L. O. Jeffs Ltd, 1980–87. Mem., Mersey RHA, 1984–87. Contested (C) Newcastle upon Tyne Central, Feb. 1974. PPS to Minister of State, DOE, 1988–89, to Minister of Agric., Fisheries and Food, 1989–90; Parly Under Sec. of State, DSS, 1990–92; Minister of State: Home Office, 1992–93; MAFF, 1993–95; Financial Sec. to HM Treasury, 1995–97; Opposition front bench spokesman on health, 1997, on agric., fisheries and food, 1998. Member: Agriculture Select Cttee, 2000–01; Envmt, Food and Rural Affairs Select Cttee, 2001–07 (Chm., 2003–); Tax Law Rewrite Steering Cttee, 1999–; Exec., 1922 Cttee, 2000–03. Sec., Cons. Back-bench Transport Cttee, 1987–88; Chm., Cons. Back-bench sub-cttee on Horticulture and Markets, 1987–88; Sec., Cons. NW Members Gp, 1988–90. Nat. Chm., Young Conservatives, 1976–77. Trustee: MedAlert, 1990–; Lytham Community Sports Assoc., 1997. Vice-Pres., Think Green, 1989–90. President: Clifton Hosp. League of Friends, 1991–; Lytham St Annes ATC 2486 Sqdn, 1991–; Friends of Trinity Hospice, Lytham St Annes Br., 1995–; Lytham St Annes Road Runners Club, 1999–. *Recreations:* dinghy sailing, running, vegetable growing, motor sport, boule. *Address:* House of Commons, SW1A 0AA; *web:* www.michaeljackmp.org.uk.

JACK, Julian; *see* Jack, (James) J. B.

JACK, Prof. Kenneth Henderson, OBE 1997; PhD, ScD; FRS 1980; CChem, FRSC Professor of Applied Crystal Chemistry, University of Newcastle upon Tyne, 1964–8 now Emeritus Professor, and Director of Wolfson Research Group for High-Strengt Materials, 1970–84; Leverhulme Emeritus Fellow, 1985–87; *b* 12 Oct. 1918; *e s* of lat John Henderson Jack, DSC, and Emily (*née* Cozens), North Shields, Northumberland; 1942, Alfreda Hughes (*d* 1974); two *s*. *Educ:* Tynemouth Municipal High Sch.; King Coll., Univ. of Durham, Newcastle upon Tyne (BSc 1939, DThPT 1940, MSc 1944 Fitzwilliam Coll., Univ. of Cambridge (PhD 1950, ScD 1978). Experimental Office Min. of Supply, 1940–41; Lectr in Chemistry, King's Coll., Univ. of Durham, 1941–4 1949–52, 1953–57; Sen. Scientific Officer, Brit. Iron and Steel Res. Assoc., 1945–4 research at Crystallographic Lab., Cavendish Laboratory, Cambridge, 1947–49; Researc Engr, Westinghouse Elec. Corp., Pittsburgh, Pa, 1952–53; Research Dir, Therma Syndicate Ltd, Wallsend, 1957–64. Consultant, Cookson Group, 1986–94. Hon. Prof. c Materials Engrg, Univ. of Wales Swansea, 1996–. Lectures: J.W. Mellor Meml, Bri Ceramic Soc., 1973; Harold Moore Meml, Metals Soc., 1984; W. Hume-Rothery Mem Oxford Metallurgical Soc., 1986; Sosman Meml, Amer. Ceramic Soc., 1989. Fellow Amer. Ceramic Soc., 1984 (Dist. Life Mem., 2007); Membre d'Honneur, Sociét Française de Métallurgie, 1984; Mem., Internat. Acad. of Ceramics, 1990; Hon. Membe Materials Res. Soc. of India, 1991; Ceramic Soc. of Japan, 1991. Saville-Shaw Medal, So of Chem. Industry, 1944; Sir George Beilby Meml Award, Inst. of Metals, RIC and So of Chem. Industry, 1951; Kroll Medal and Prize, Metals Soc., 1979; (with Dr R.J. Lumby Prince of Wales Award for Industrial Innovation and Production, 1984; Armourers & Brasiers' Co. Award, Royal Soc., 1988; World Materials Congress Award, ASM Internat 1988; A. A. Griffith Silver Medal and Prize, Inst. of Metals, 1989; Centennial Awar Ceramic Soc. of Japan, 1991. *Publications:* papers in scientific jls and conf. proc. *Addres* 147 Broadway, Cullercoats, Tyne and Wear NE30 3TA. *T:* (0191) 257 3664.

JACK, Dr Malcolm Roy; Clerk and Chief Executive of the House of Commons, sinc 2006; *b* 17 Dec. 1946; *s* of late Iain Ross Jack and Alicia Maria Eça da Silva, Hong Kong *Educ:* school in Hong Kong; Univ. of Liverpool (Hong Kong Govt Scholar; BA Hons 1s Class); LSE, Univ. of London (PhD). A Clerk, House of Commons, 1967–; Private Sec to Chm. of Ways and Means, 1977–80; Clerk to Agriculture Select Cttee, 1980–88; Clerl of Supply, 1989–91; Clerk of Standing Cttees, 1991–95; Sec. to H of C Commn 1995–2001; Clerk of the Journals, 2001–03; Clerk to Jt Cttee on H of L Reform 2002–03; Clerk of Legislation, 2003–06. Presidential Advr, OSCE Parly Assembly 1992–96. Chm., Beckford Soc., 1996–; Sec., Johnson Club, 1998–. *Publications:* Th Social and Political Thought of Bernard Mandeville, 1987; Corruption and Progress: th eighteenth-century debate, 1989; (ed with Anita Desai) The Turkish Embassy Letters o Lady Mary Wortley Montagu, 1993; (ed) Vathek and Other Stories: a William Beckfor Reader, 1993; (ed) The Episodes of Vathek of William Beckford, 1994; William Beckford an English Fidalgo, 1996; Sintra: a glorious Eden, 2002; Lisbon: city of the sea, 2007 articles and essays in books, learned and literary jls; reviews in TLS, APN Lisbon *Recreations:* thinking for oneself (Enlightenment), empires adrift, Johnsoniana, orienta ceramics, Africana, escaping southwards. *Address:* House of Commons, SW1A 0AA. *Club* East India.

JACK, Rt Hon. Michael; *see* Jack, Rt Hon. J. M.

JACK, Hon. Sir Raymond (Evan), Kt 2001; **Hon. Mr Justice Jack;** a Judge of th High Court, Queen's Bench Division, since 2001; *b* 13 Nov. 1942; *s* of Evan an Charlotte Jack; *m* 1976, Elizabeth Alison, *d* of Rev. Canon James Seymour Denis Mansel KCVO; one *s* two *d*. *Educ:* Rugby; Trinity Coll., Cambridge (MA). Called to Bar, Inne Temple, 1966, Bencher, 2000; QC 1982; a Recorder, 1989–91; a Circuit Judge 1991–2001; Judge of the Bristol Mercantile Court, 1994–2001. *Publication:* Documentary Credits, 1991, 3rd edn 2000. *Recreations:* words and wood. *Address:* Royal Courts o Justice, Strand, WC2A 2LL.

JACK, Prof. Robert Barr, CBE 1988; Partner, McGrigor Donald, Solicitors, Glasgow Edinburgh and London, 1957–93 (Joint Senior Partner, 1986–90; Senior Partner 1990–93); *b* 18 March 1928; *s* of Robert Hendry Jack and Christina Alexandra Jack; *m* 1958, Anna Thorburn Thomson; two *s*. *Educ:* Kilsyth Acad.; High Sch., Glasgow Glasgow Univ. MA 1948, LLB 1951. Admitted a solicitor in Scotland, 1951; Prof. o Mercantile Law, Glasgow Univ., 1978–93. Member: Company Law Cttee of Law Society of Scotland, 1971–95 (Convener, 1978–85); Scottish Law Commn, 1974–77. Scottisl observer on Dept of Trade's Insolvency Law Review Cttee, 1977–82; Mem., DoT Adv Panel on Company Law, 1980–83; Chm., Review Cttee on Banking Services Law 1987–89. Lay Member: Council for the Securities Industry, 1983–85; Stock Exchange Council, 1984–86; Independent Mem. Bd, Securities Assoc., later SFA, 1987–94; Mem Bd, SIB, 1994–97; UK Mem., Panel of Arbitrators, ICSID, 1989–95; Member: Takeover Panel, 1992–2001; Financial Law Panel, 1993–2001; MSI 1993. Chairman: Brownlee plc Timber Merchants, Glasgow, 1984–86 (Dir, 1974–86); Joseph Dunn (Bottlers) Ltd, Soft Drink Manufacturers, Glasgow, 1983–2003; Scottish Mutual Assce 1992–98 (Dir 1987–98); Dep. Chm., Scottish Metropolitan Property, 1991–98 (Dir, 1980–98); Director: Clyde Football Club Ltd, 1980–96; Bank of Scotland, 1985–96; Gartmore Scotland Investment Trust, 1991–2001; Glasgow Develt Agency, 1992–97. Pres., Scottish Nat. Council of YMCAs, 1983–98 (Chm., 1966–73). Mem., SHEFC, 1992–96. Chm., The Turnberry Trust, 1983–; Mem., Cttee of Mgt, Malin Housing Assoc., Turnberry, 1971–; Governor, Hutchesons' Educational Trust, Glasgow, 1978–87 (Chm. 1980–87), Mem. Bd of Govs, Beatson Inst. for Cancer Res., Glasgow, 1989–2004; Chm., Audit Cttee, Glasgow Univ., 1996–2003. Mem., W of Scotland Adv. Bd, Salvation Army, 1995–. Trustee, Football Trust, 1998–2000. DUniv Glasgow, 2001. *Publications:* lectures on various aspects of company, insolvency and banking law and financial services regulation law. *Recreations:* golf (now unhappily on a non-playing basis), hopeful support of one of Scotland's less fashionable football teams; an erstwhile dedicated lover of Isle of Arran. *Address:* 50 Lanton Road, Newlands, Glasgow G43 2SR. *T:* (0141) 637 7302; *e-mail:* Robertjack75@aol.com. *Clubs:* Caledonian; Western (Glasgow); Pollok Golf; Shiskine Golf and Tennis (Isle of Arran) (Captain 1973–75).

JACK, Simon Michael; His Honour Judge Jack; a Circuit Judge, North Eastern Circuit, since 2004; *b* 29 Oct. 1951; *s* of Donald Fingland Jack and Hilary Jack (*née* Gresham); *m* 1973, Christine Anne King (separated 2003); one *s* two *d*. *Educ:* Richard Hale Sch., Hertford; Winchester Coll.; Trinity Coll., Cambridge (BA (Langs and Law) 1973). Called to the Bar, Middle Temple, 1974; in practice as barrister, N Eastern Circuit, 1975–2003 (specialized in criminal and family law, and civil actions involving police). *Recreations:* cycling, running, flying, sailing, ski-ing, cinema. *Address:* Kingston upon Hull Combined Court Centre, Lowgate, Hull HU1 2EZ. *Clubs:* Sherburn Aero (Yorks), Meribel Aero.

JACK, Stuart Duncan Macdonald, CVO 1994; HM Diplomatic Service; Governor, Cayman Islands, 2005–Nov. 2009; *b* 8 June 1949; *s* of William Harris Jack and Edith Florence Jack (*née* Coker); *m* 1977, Mariko Nobechi; one *s* two *d*. *Educ:* Westcliff High Sch. for Boys; Merton Coll., Oxford (BA 1971). VSO, Laos, 1971; joined HM Diplomatic Service, 1972: Eastern European and Soviet Dept, FO, 1972–73; Tokyo, 1974–79; Far Eastern Dept, FCO, 1979–81; Moscow, 1981–84; on secondment with Bank of England, 1984–85; Tokyo, 1985–89; Overseas Inspector, 1989–92; Consul Gen., St Petersburg, 1992–95; Hd of Research and Analysis, FCO, 1996–99; Minister, Tokyo, 1999–2003; FCO, 2003–05. *Recreations:* reading, photography, music. *Address:* c/o Foreign and Commonwealth Office, King Charles Street, SW1A 2AH.

JACK, Dr William Hugh, CB 1988; management consultant, 1994–2005; Comptroller and Auditor General, Northern Ireland Audit Office, 1989–94; *b* 18 Feb. 1929; *s* of John Charles Jack and Martha Ann Jack; *m* 1953, Beatrice Jane Thompson; three *s* one *d*. *Educ:* Ballymena Acad.; Univ. of Edinburgh (BSc(For); PhD); Queen's Univ., Belfast (BSc (Econ)). MICFor 1959. Min. of Agriculture for NI, 1948–49; Colonial Forest Service, Gold Coast/Ghana, 1949–59 (Conservator of Forests, 1957); Dept of Agriculture for NI, 1959–89 (Permanent Sec., 1983). CCMI. *Publications:* various articles in forestry research and economic jls. *Recreations:* walking, reading. *Address:* 22 Viewfort Park, Belfast BT17 9JY.

JACKAMAN, Michael Clifford John; Chairman of Grand Appeal, Royal Hospital for Sick Children, Bristol, 1995–2001; Chairman, Allied Domecq (formerly Allied-Lyons) plc, 1991–96 (Vice-Chairman, 1988–91); *b* 7 Nov. 1935; *s* of Air Cdre Clifford Thomas Jackaman, OBE and Lily Margaret Jackaman (*née* Turner); *m* 1960, Valerie Jane Pankhurst; one *s* one *d*. *Educ:* Felsted Sch., Essex; Jesus Coll., Cambridge (MA Hons). Lieut RA, 1955–56. Dep. Man. Dir, Harveys of Bristol, 1976–78; Marketing Dir, Allied Breweries, 1978–83; Dir, Allied Domecq (formerly Allied Lyons) plc, 1978–96; Chairman: Showerings Vine Products and Whiteways, 1983–86; Hiram Walker Allied Vintners, 1986–91; John Harvey & Sons Ltd, 1983–93; Mem., Council of Admin, Château Latour, 1983–93; Director: Fintex of London Ltd, 1986–92; Rank Orgn, 1992–97; Kleinwort Benson Gp, 1994–98. Governor, Bristol Polytechnic, 1988–91. Dir, Th. Royal, Bath, 1999–2005. Founder Mem., Wine Guild of UK. Vice Pres., Internat. Wine and Spirits Comp. Liveryman, Distillers' Co.; Grand Master, Keepers of the Quaich (Scotland), 1996; Commanderie des Bontemps du Médoc et des Graves (France); Confraria do Vinho do Porto (Portugal). Hon. DBA UWE, 1993. *Publications:* contribs to periodicals, incl. Arts Review. *Recreations:* stoneware pottery, painting, etching, theatre, walking. *Club:* Army and Navy.

JACKLIN, Anthony, CBE 1990 (OBE 1970); professional golfer, 1962–85 and 1988–99; Director of Golf, San Roque Club, 1988–90; *b* 7 July 1944; *s* of Arthur David Jacklin; *m* 1st, 1966, Vivien (*d* 1988); two *s* one *d*; 2nd, 1988, Astrid May Waagen; one *s*, one step *s* one step *d*. Successes include: British Assistant Pro Championship, 1965; Pringle Tournament, 1967; Dunlop Masters, 1967; Greater Jacksonville Open, USA, 1968; British Open Championship, 1969; US Open Championship, 1970; Benson & Hedges, 1971; British Professional Golfers Assoc., 1972, 1982; Gtr Jacksonville Open, 1972; Bogota Open, 1973 and 1974; Italian Open, 1973; Dunlop Masters, 1973; Scandinavian Open, 1975; Kerrygold International, 1976; English National PGA Championship, 1977; German Open, 1979; Jersey Open, 1981; PGA Champion, 1982; Ryder Cup player, 1967–80, Team Captain, Europe, 1983–89. Life Mem., PGA (Hon. Life Mem., European Tournament Players Div.). Inducted, World Golf Hall of Fame, 2002. *Publications:* Golf with Tony Jacklin, 1969; The Price of Success, 1979; (with Peter Dobereiner) Jacklin's Golfing Secrets, 1983; Tony Jacklin: the first forty years, 1985; (with Bill Robertson) Your Game and Mine, 1990; Tony Jacklin: my autobiography, 2006. *Recreation:* shooting. *Address:* 1175 51st Street West, Bradenton, FL 34209, USA. *Clubs:* Royal & Ancient Golf (Hon. Mem., 2002); Potters Bar Golf; Hon. Mem. of others.

JACKLIN, Susan Elizabeth; QC 2006; a Recorder, since 1998; *b* 4 Aug. 1958; *d* of Joseph and Alice Jacklin. *Educ:* Winckley Sq. Convent Sch., Preston; Univ. of Durham (BA Hons Law); Inns of Court Sch. of Law. Called to the Bar, Inner Temple, 1980; in practice at the Bar, 1982–. Advocacy Trainer: Western Circuit, 1996–; Hon. Soc. of Inner Temple, 2003–. Ext. Examr, Bar Vocational Course, UWE, 2002–06. *Recreations:* international travel, walking, cooking and entertaining. *Address:* St John's Chambers, 101 Victoria Street, Bristol BS1 6PU. *T:* (0117) 921 3456; *e-mail:* susan.jacklinqc@stjohnschambers.co.uk. *Club:* Athenæum.

JACKLIN, William, (Bill), RA 1991 (ARA 1989); *b* 1 Jan. 1943; *s* of Harold and Alice Jacklin; *m* 1st, 1979, Lesley Sarina Berman (marr. diss. 1993); 2nd, 1993, Janet Ann Russo. *Educ:* Walthamstow Sch. of Art; Royal College of Art (NDD, MARCA). Part-time Lectr at various art colleges, 1967–75; Arts Council Bursary, 1975; lives and works in New York and Newport, RI, 1985–; Artist in Residence, British Council, Hong Kong, 1993–94. One man exhibns, London galleries, 1970–, USA, 1985–, Hong Kong, 1995; retrospective exhibn, Mus. of Modern Art, Oxford, 1992; frequent shows in internat. exhibns; works in major collections including Arts Council, British Mus., Metropolitan Mus. NY, Mus. of Modern Art NY, Tate Gall., V&A. *Publications:* catalogues to one man exhibns, London and New York; *relevant publication:* Bill Jacklin (monograph), by John Russell-Taylor, 1997. *Recreation:* planting trees. *Address:* c/o Marlborough Fine Art, 6 Albemarle Street, W1X 4BY. *T:* (020) 7629 5161. *Club:* Chelsea Arts.

JACKLING, Sir Roger Tustin, KCB 2001 (CB 1995); CBE 1982; Director, Defence Academy of the UK, 2002–05; *b* 23 Nov. 1943; *s* of Sir Roger Jackling, GCMG and late Joan (*née* Tustin) (Lady Jackling); *m* 1976, Jane Allen Pritchard; two *s*. *Educ:* Wellington Coll.; New York Univ. (BA); Jesus Coll., Oxford. Asst Principal, MoD, 1969, Principal, 1972; London Executive Prog., London Business Sch., 1974; Sec. of State's Office, MoD, 1976–79; Asst Sec. and Hd of DS11, 1979–82; Prime Minister's Office, 1983; Head of DS7/Resources and Programmes (Army), MoD, 1983–85; Fellow, Center for Internat. Affairs, Harvard Univ., 1985–86; Principal, CS Coll., 1986–89; Asst Under-Sec. of State (Progs), MoD, 1989–91; Dep. Under-Sec. of State (Resources, Progs and Finance), MoD, 1991–96; Second Perm. Under Sec. of State, MoD, 1996–2002. Visiting Professor: War Studies Dept, KCL, 2002–; Durham Business Sch., 2003–; Cranfield Univ. at Shrivenham, 2003–. Trustee: Imperial War Mus., 1997–2003; RAF Mus., 2002–. Member Council: RIPA, 1987–92; RUSI, 1993–2005; Chairman: Toc H, 2004–; Internat. Military Services, 2005–; Council of Voluntary Welfare Work, 2005–; non-exec. Dir, Moorfield Eye Hosp., 2008–. Member, Advisory Board: Durham Business Sch., 1999–; Kent Business Sch., 2005–. *Recreations:* books, theatre, opera, playing golf, watching cricket. *Clubs:* Garrick; Highgate Golf, Faversham Golf, Tandridge Golf.

JACKSON, Adam Edward; Director, Climate Change Programme, Tesco, since 2008; *b* 5 March 1969; *s* of Michael and Patricia Jackson. *Educ:* University Coll. London (BA Modern Hist.; MA Legal and Pol Theory). Industry and Consumer Affairs Attaché, UK Perm. Repn to EU, Brussels, 1994–96; Number Portability Manager, Oftel, 1996–97; Department of Trade and Industry: Asst Dir, Regl Policy, 1997–99; Hd, Strategic Communications and Speechwriting, 2000–02; Dep. Dir, Sen. Staff Mgt, 2002–03; Dir, Business Planning, 2003–05; Dir of Finance, 2005–06; Dir of Public Policy, Tesco, 2006–08. Mem. Bd, London Retail Consortium, 2007–. *Recreations:* horse riding, cooking and eating, balcony gardening, walking Bessie the dog with Holly. *Address:* Tesco Stores Ltd, New Tesco House, Delamare Road, Cheshunt, Herts EN8 9SL. *T:* (01992) 806588; *e-mail:* adam.jackson@uk.tesco.com. *Club:* Bournemouth Exiles (Bournemouth FC Supporters).

JACKSON, Alan Robert, AO 1991; Chairman: Australian Trade Commission, 1996–2001; Austrim Nylex (formerly Austrim) Ltd, 1990–2001 (Chief Executive, 1990–2001); *b* 30 March 1936; *m* 1962, Esme Adelia Giles; four *d*. FCA, FASA, FAIM, FCPA. Accountant to Man. Dir, Mather & Platt, 1952–77; Man. Dir, 1977–90, Chm., 1990–97, BTR Nylex Ltd; Man. Dir and Chief Exec. Officer, BTR plc, 1991–95. Director: Australia Reserve Bank, 1990–2001; Seven Network Ltd, 1995–2001; Titan Petrochemicals and Polymers Berhad (Malaysia), 1997–2001. Dir, St Frances Xavier Cabrini Hosp., 1995–2001. *Recreations:* tennis, golf.

JACKSON, Albert Leslie Samuel; JP; Chairman, Birmingham Technology Ltd (Aston Science Park), 1984–2005; *b* 20 Jan. 1918; *s* of Bert Jackson and Olive Powell; *m* Gladys Burley; one *s* one *d*. *Educ:* Handsworth New Road Council Sch. War service, Radio Mechanic, RAF. Mem., Birmingham CC, 1952–86; Lord Mayor, 1975–76, Dep. Lord Mayor, 1978–79, Birmingham. Dir and Cttee Chm., NEC, 1984–87; Dir, National Exhibition Centre (Developments) PLC, 1997–2006. JP 1968. Hon. DSc Aston, 1999. *Recreations:* chess, sailing. *Address:* Dickies Meadow, Dock Lane, Bredon, near Tewkesbury GL20 7LG. *T:* (01684) 772541.

JACKSON, Alison Mary; artist, photographer, film-maker; *b* 15 May 1960; *d* of George Hulbert Mowbray Jackson and Catherine Mary Jackson (*née* Harvey Kelly). *Educ:* Chelsea Coll. of Art (BA Hons Fine Art Sculpture); Royal Coll. of Art (MA Fine Art Photography). *Solo art exhibitions* include: Richard Salmon Gall., London, 1999, 2000, 2003; Jerwood Space, London, 2001; Musée de la Photographie à Charleroi, Brussels, 2002; Le Mois de la Photo, Montreal, Photo London, Pro-gram Gall., 2004; Julie Saul Gall., NY, 2005; M&B Gall., Los Angeles, 2007; Hamiltons Gall., London, 2008; F2 Gall., Beijing, 2008; *group art exhibitions* include: Edinburgh Fest., Art 2000, London, 2000; Paris Photo, Louvre, Photographers' Gall./Julie Saul Gall., NY, 2002–05; Internat. Center of Photography (ICP), NY, Musée de l'Eysée, Lausanne, 2003; Photo London, Hayward Gall., London, 2004; KunstForum, Vienna, 2005–06. *Television:* creator, writer, dir, Doubletake, 2002, 2003 (BAFTA Award for Innovation, 2002); producer/dir, Saturday Night Live, USA, 2004–05; writer and director: Royal Wedding Special, 2005; The Secret Election, 2005; Sven: the coach, the cash and his lovers, 2006; dir, Tony Blair Rock Star, 2006. Schweppes advertising campaign, 2001–03 (Best of the Best Award for Photography, IPA, 2002, 2003; Creative Circle Award, 2002). Photographers' Gall. Award, London, 1999; Infinity Award for Photography, ICP, NY, 2004. *Publications:* Private, 2003; Alison Jackson: confidential, 2007. *Recreation:* tennis. *Address:* c/o Paul Stevens, Independent Talent Group Ltd, 76 Oxford Street, W1D 1BS. *T:* (020) 7636 6565; c/o Kevin Cooper, CAA, 2000 Avenue of the Stars, Los Angeles, CA, USA. *T:* (424) 2884545.

JACKSON, Alison Muriel; Team Leader, Public Issues, Methodist Church, since 2005; Director, Wales Office, 1999–2005; *b* 24 Sept. 1947; *d* of John McIntyre and Muriel McIntyre (*née* Brookes); *m* 1970, Alan D. Jackson; one *s*. *Educ:* Sydenham High Sch., GPDST; St Anne's Coll., Oxford (BA (Lit. Hum.) 1970, MA 1976); Bristol Univ. (Dip. Adult Educn (ext.) 1982). Land Registry, Gloucester, 1983–86; Welsh Office: Local Govt Finance, 1986–88; Private Sec. to Perm. Sec., 1988–90; Urban Affairs Div., 1990–93; Agric. Div., 1993–98. Panel Chair, Judicial Appts Commn, 2005–. Methodist Lay Preacher, 1976–. *Recreations:* horse-riding, walking, cooking.

JACKSON, Anthony Geoffrey Clive H.; *see* Howland Jackson.

JACKSON, Sir Barry (Trevor), Kt 2001; MS, FRCS; Serjeant Surgeon to The Queen, 1991–2001; Consultant Surgeon: St Thomas' Hospital, 1973–2001; Queen Victoria Hospital, East Grinstead, 1977–98; King Edward VII Hospital for Officers, 1983–2002; President, Royal Society of Medicine, 2002–04; *b* 7 July 1936; *er s* of Arthur Stanley Jackson and Violet May (*née* Fry); *m* 1962, Sheila May Wood; two *s* one *d*. *Educ:* Sir George Monoux Grammar Sch.; King's College London; Westminster Med. Sch. (Entrance Scholar). MB, BS 1963; MRCS, LRCP 1963; MS 1972; FRCS 1967; FRCP 1999; FRCSGlas 1999. Down Bros Ltd, 1952–54; RAF 1954–56; junior surgical appts, Gordon Hosp., St James' Hosp., Balham, St Peter's Hosp., Chertsey, St Helier Hosp., Carshalton, St Thomas' Hosp. Surgeon to the Royal Household, 1983–91; Hon. Consultant in Surgery to the Army, 1990–2006. Royal College of Surgeons: Arris & Gale Lectr, 1973; Vicary Lectr, 1994; Bradshaw Lectr, 1998; Examr Primary FRCS, 1977–83; Mem. Court of Examrs, 1983–89; Mem. Council, 1991–2001; Pres., 1998–2001; Mem., Court of Patrons, 2008; Asst Editor 1984–91, Editor, 1992–97, Annals RCS; Pres., Assoc. of Surgeons of GB and Ireland, 1994–95 (Mem. Council, 1982–85; Hon. Sec., 1986–91; Vice Pres., 1993–94); Mem. Council, RSocMed, 1987–92 (Pres., Sect. of Coloproctology, 1991–92; Steven's Lect. for the Laity, 2001; Stuart Lectr, 2005); Mem., GMC, 1999–2003. Pres., British Acad. Forensic Scis, 2005–07. External examr in surgery: Khartoum, 1981, 1997; Ibadan, 1982; Colombo, 1984, 1988; Abu Dhabi, 1989. Mem., W Lambeth HA, 1982–83; Special Trustee: St Thomas' Hosp., 1982–84, 1994–99; Guy's Hosp., 1996–99; Trustee, Smith & Nephew Foundn, 1995–2002; Chm., SE Thames Regional Med. Adv. Cttee, 1983–87. Mem. Council of Govs, UMDS of Guy's and St Thomas' Hosps, 1989–94. President: Royal Med. Benevolent Fund, 2002–08; Med. Artists Assoc. of GB, 2005–. Liveryman, Barbers' Co. (Master, 2003–04; Charles Bernard Lectr, 2007). Hon. FRCSI, 1999; Hon. FRCSEd, 1999; Hon. FDSRCS, 1999; Hon. FACS, 2000; Hon. FRACS, 2000; Hon. FRCSCan, 2003; Hon. FRSocMed 2005. Hon. DSc Hull, 2001. *Publications:* contribs to surgical jls and textbooks (surgery of gastro-intestinal tract). *Recreations:* book collecting, reading, medical history, music, especially opera, cryptic crosswords. *Address:* Westminster Bridge Consulting Rooms, St Thomas' Hospital, SE1 7EH. *T:* (020) 7188 1610. *Club:* Garrick.

JACKSON, Betty, CBE 2007 (MBE 1987); RDI 1988; Designer Director, Betty Jackson Ltd, since 1981; *b* 24 June 1949; *d* of Arthur and Phyllis Gertrude Jackson; *m* 1985, David Cohen; one *s* one *d*. *Educ:* Bacup and Rawtenstall Grammar Sch.; Birmingham Coll. of Art (DipAD fashion and textiles). Freelance fashion illustrator, 1971–73; design asst, 1973–75; chief designer, Quorum, 1975–81. Part-time Tutor, 1982–90, Vis. Prof., 1998–, RCA. Fellow: Birmingham Polytechnic, 1989; Univ. of Central Lancs, 1992. Hon. Fellow, RCA, 1989. Trustee, V&A Mus., 2005–. Awards include: British Designer of the Year, Harvey Nichols and British Fashion Council, 1985; Viyella, 1987; Fil d'Or, Internat. Linen, 1989; Contemporary Designer of the Year, British Fashion Awards, 1999. *Address:* Betty Jackson Ltd, 1 Netherwood Place, Netherwood Road, W14 0BW. *T:* (020) 7602 6023; Betty Jackson Retail, 311 Brompton Road, SW3 2DY. *T:* (020) 7589 7884; *e-mail:* info@bettyjackson.com. *Club:* Groucho.

JACKSON, Very Rev. Brandon Donald; Dean of Lincoln, 1989–97, now Emeritus; *b* 11 Aug. 1934; *s* of Herbert and Millicent Jackson; *m* 1958, Mary Lindsay, 2nd *d* of John and Helen Philip; two *s* one *d*. *Educ:* Stockport School; Liverpool Univ.; St Catherine's Coll. and Wycliffe Hall, Oxford (LLB, DipTh). Curate: Christ Church, New Malden, Surrey, 1958–61; St George, Leeds, 1961–65; Vicar, St Peter, Shipley, Yorks, 1965–77; Provost of Bradford Cathedral, 1977–89. Mem., Gen. Synod, 1970–77, 1980–89. Religious Adviser to Yorkshire Television, 1969–79; Church Commissioner, 1971–73; Mem., Marriage Commn, 1975–78; Examining Chaplain to Bishop of Bradford, 1974–80. Chm., Wensleydale CPRE. Member Council: Wycliffe Hall, Oxford, 1971–85; St John's Coll., Nottingham, 1987–89; Governor: Harrogate College, 1974–86; Bradford Girls' GS, 1977–81; Bradford Grammar Sch., 1977–89; Bishop Grosseteste Coll., Lincoln, 1989–97; Lincoln Christ's Hosp. Sch., 1989–97. Hon. DLitt Bradford, 1990. *Recreations:* sport (mainly watching), fell-walking, fishing, enjoying grandchildren, routine house maintenance and repair, wooding, reading, thinking, speaking. *Address:* 6 Logan Crescent, Market Harborough, Leics LE16 9QT. *T:* (01858) 445527; *e-mail:* bdj1@mlj2.freeserve.co.uk.

JACKSON, Caroline Frances; Member (C) South West Region, England, European Parliament, since 1999 (Wiltshire, 1984–94; Wiltshire North and Bath, 1994–99); *b* 5 Nov. 1946; *d* of G. H. Harvey; *m* 1975, Robert Victor Jackson, *qv*; one *s* decd. *Educ:* School of St Clare, Penzance; St Hugh's and Nuffield Colleges, Oxford. MA, DPhil. Elizabeth Wordsworth Research Fellow, St Hugh's College, Oxford, 1972. Oxford City Councillor, 1970–73; contested (C) Birmingham, Erdington, 1974. European Parliament: Secretariat of Cons. Group, 1974–84; Chm., Envmt, Consumer Protection and Public Health Cttee, 1999–2004. Chm., Inst. for European Envmt Policy, 2006–. Dir, Peugeot Talbot (UK) Ltd, 1987–99. Mem., Nat. Consumer Council, 1982–84. *Publications:* A Student's Guide to Europe, 1988; Europe's Environment, 1989; The End of the Throwaway Society, 1998; Playing by the Green Rules, 2000; Britain's Waste: the lessons we can learn from Europe, 2006. *Recreations:* walking, painting, tennis, golf. *Address:* c/o European Parliament, 60 rue Wiertz, 1047 Brussels, Belgium. *T:* (2) 2845255, *Fax:* (2) 2849255.

JACKSON, Christopher Murray; Chairman: CJA Consultants Ltd, 1995–2002 (Director, since 1995); Wellmeade Ltd, since 1998; *b* 24 May 1935; *s* of Rev. Howard Murray Jackson and Doris Bessie Jackson (*née* Grainger); *m* 1971, Carlie Elizabeth Keeling; one *s* one *d*. *Educ:* Kingswood Sch., Bath; Magdalen Coll., Oxford (Open Exhibnr, BA Hons (Physics) 1959, MA 1964); Goethe Univ., Frankfurt; London Sch. of Economics. National Service, commnd RAF, Pilot, 1954–56. Unilever, 1959–69, Sen. Man., 1967; Save and Prosper Gp, 1969–71; D. MacPherson Gp, 1971–74; Dir of Corporate Development, Spillers Ltd, 1974–80; Chairman: Natural Resources Internat. Ltd, 1997–2003; European Broadcasting Network plc, 1997–99. Contested (C): East Ham South, 1970; Northampton North, Feb. 1974. MEP (C) Kent E, 1979–94; contested (C) Kent E, EP elecns, 1994; Hon. MEP, 1994–; European Parliament: spokesman on develt and co-op., 1981–87, on foreign affairs, 1991–92, on econ. affairs, 1992–94; Cons. spokesman on agric., 1987–89; Chm., Intergroup on Frontier Controls, 1987–94; Co-Pres., Working Gp on Population and Develt, 1990–94; Mem., Bureau of EDG, 1984–91; Dep. Ldr, Cons. MEPs, 1989–91; Rapporteur-General, ACP-EEC Jt Assembly, 1985–86. Chm., Countryside (formerly Nat. Agricl and Countryside) Forum, 1995–98. Mem., Cons. Nat. Union Exec. Cttee, 1995–98. Dir, Politics International Ltd, 1995–98. Vice President: Assoc. of Dist Councils, 1980–95; Assoc. of Local Councils, 1984–95; Assoc. of Port Health Authorities, 1989–99. Member: RIIA; Inst. of Dirs. Treas., St Martin-in-the-Fields, 1975–79. Pres. Kent Hotels and Restaurants Assoc., 1988–94. Chm., Bd of Govs, Bethany Sch., Goudhurst, 1999–. *Publications:* Towards 2000—people centred development, 1986 (major report); (ed) Your European Watchdogs, 1990; Shaking the Foundations: Britain and the New Europe, 1991; The Maastricht Summit, 1992; Whose Job is it Anyway?—decentralisation (or subsidiarity) and the EC, 1992; Working for the European Community, 1990, 2nd edn 1992; (ed) Industrial Property Rights, 1997 (official EC pubn); pamphlets on Britain and Europe. *Recreations:* music, tennis, walking, travel, sailing. *Address:* Flackley Ash Farmhouse, Peasmarsh, Rye, E Sussex TN31 6TB. *T:* (01797) 230660; *e-mail:* c.jackson@btconnect.com. *Clubs:* Athenæum; Rye Lawn Tennis.

JACKSON, Colin Ray, CBE 2003 (OBE 2000; MBE 1990); former athlete; broadcaster and television presenter; *b* Cardiff, 18 Feb. 1967. *Educ:* Llanederyn High Sch., Cardiff. Gold Medals won in 110m hurdles: European Cup, 1989, 1993, 1998; Commonwealth Games, 1990, 1994; European Championships, 1990, 1994, 1998, 2002; World Cup, 1992; World Championships, 1993, 1999; also Silver Medal, Olympic Games, 1988; Gold Medals won in 60m hurdles: European Indoor Championships, 1989, 1994, 2002; World Indoor Championships, 1999; set world record for 110m hurdles (12.91 secs), 1993, and 60m indoor hurdles (7.30 secs), 1994. Silver Medal for 4 x 100m relay, World Championships, 1993. *Publication:* Colin Jackson: the autobiography, 2003. *Address:* c/o MTC (UK) Ltd, 20 York Street, W1U 6PU.

JACKSON, Daphne Diana; Assistant Personnel Officer, City Engineer's Department, City of Birmingham, 1986–93; *b* 8 Oct. 1933; *d* of Major Thomas Casey, MC, South Lancs Regt, and Agnes Nora Casey (*née* Gradden); *m* 1953, John Hudleston Jackson. *Educ:* Folkestone County Grammar School for Girls; South West London College. ACIS. Westminster Bank, 1951–53; Kent Educn Cttee, 1953–57; Pfizer Ltd, Sandwich, 1957–67; Southern Transformer Products, 1967–68; Borough of Hounslow, 1968–86, Personnel and Central Services Officer, Borough Engr and Surveyor's Dept, 1978–86. Mem., NACRO Employment Adv. Cttee, 1984–86; Chm., Gen. Adv. Council to IBA, 1985–89 (Mem., 1980). Mem., Soroptimists International (Pres., Stratford-upon-Avon, 1995–96). Mem., Cleeve Prior PCC, 1991–; Gov., Cleeve Prior C of E Controlled First Sch., 1989–2005; Chm. Mgt Cttee, Cleeve Prior Meml Village Hall, 1994–97. Freeman, City of London, 1980; Liveryman, Chartered Secretaries and Administrators Co., 1980. *Recreations:* bereavement counselling, learning about antiques, reading. *Address:* 3 Manor Court, Bidford Road, Cleeve Prior, Evesham, Worcs WR11 8HZ. *T:* (01789) 772817.

JACKSON, Prof. David Cooper; Chairman, Immigration Appeal Tribunal, 1996–200 (Vice-President, 1984–96); Professor of Law (part time), 1984–98, now Emeritus, an Director, Institute of Maritime Law, 1987–90, University of Southampton; *b* 3 Dec. 1931 *s* of late Rev. James Jackson and Mary Emma Jackson; *m* Roma Lilian (*née* Pendergast *Educ:* Ashville Coll., Harrogate; Brasenose Coll., Oxford. MA, BCL; Senior Hulm Scholar, 1954; LLD Southampton, 1997. Called to the Bar, Inner Temple, 1957, an Victoria, Australia, 1967. Bigelow Fellow, Univ. of Chicago, 1955; Fellow, Assoc. of Ba of City of New York, 1956; National Service, 1957–59; Senior Lectr, Univ. of Singapore 1963–64; Sir John Latham Prof. of Law, Monash Univ., 1965–70 (Carnegie Travellin Fellow, 1969); Prof. of Law, Southampton Univ., 1970–83 (Dean of Law, 1972–75 1978–81; Dep. Vice-Chancellor, 1982–83); Consultant, UNCTAD, 1980, 1983. Visitin Professor: Queen Mary Coll., London, 1969; Arizona State Univ., 1976; Melbourn Univ., 1976. JP Hants 1980–84. Editor, World Shipping Laws, 1979– (and contrib.). *Publications:* Principles of Property Law, 1967; The Conflicts Process, 1975; Enforcemen of Maritime Claims, 1985, 4th edn 2005; Civil Jurisdiction and Judgments: maritim claims, 1987; Immigration Law and Practice, 1996, 2nd edn 1999, (loose-leaf), 2001–05 articles in legal jls, Australia, UK, USA. *Recreations:* walking, travel, theatre.

JACKSON, David Richard Holmes, CBE 2004; JP; Chief Executive, Bradfor Teaching Hospitals NHS Foundation Trust (formerly Bradford Hospitals NHS Trust) 1992–2005; *b* 24 Sept. 1948; *s* of Samuel Horace Jackson and Pauline Jackson (né Blockey); *m* 1973, Frances Bush; two *s* two *d*. *Educ:* Kingswood Sch., Bath; Univ. of Leed (LLB). DipHSM 1978. Trainee and Dep. Hosp. Sec., Leeds (St James) Univ. HMC 1970–73; Sen. Adminr, Hull A Gp HMC, 1973–74; Dep. Dist Adminr, Gen. Infirmary Leeds, 1974–78; Dist Adminr, Beverley Health Dist, 1978–82; Grimsby Health Authority Dist Adminr, 1982–85; Dist Gen. Manager, 1985–92. JP Bradford, 1998. *Recreations* walking, travelling, good living. *Address:* 10 Southway, Ilkley LS29 8QG. *T:* (01943 609521; *e-mail:* davidrhjackson@hotmail.com. *Club:* Ilkley Bowling.

JACKSON, Donald, MVO 1985; artist calligrapher; Scribe to Crown Office, since 1964 *b* 14 Jan. 1938; *s* of Wilfred Jackson and Helena Ruth Jackson (*née* Tolley); *m* 1962, Mabe Elizabeth Morgan; one *s* one *d*. *Educ:* Bolton Sch. of Art; City & Guilds, London; Centra Sch. of Art; Goldsmiths' Coll. FSSI 1960 (Chm., 1973). Preparer of Letters Patent an Royal Charters under Great Seal, incl. 1974 redesignated Royal Cities, towns an boroughs in England and Wales; Dir, Calligraphy Centre, 1984–97; Artistic Dir, The S John's Bible (handwritten and illuminated Bible in seven vols to mark Millennium, for S John's Univ. and Benedictine Abbey, Minn), 1997–. Vis. Lectr, Camberwell Sch. of Ar 1958–75; Vis. Prof. of Art, California State Univ., 1976–77; lectr in USA and Australia 30-year personal retrospective exhibn, Painting with Words, in USA, Puerto Rico, Hon Kong, Europe, 1988–91; exhibition series, Illuminating the Word: the St John's Bible incl. Minneapolis Inst. of Arts, 2005, Joslyn Mus., Omaha, V&A, Mus. of Biblical Imag and Art, NY, Liby of Congress, Washington, and Tyler Art Mus., Texas, 2006, Naples Ar Mus., Fla, and Phoenix Art Mus., Arizona, 2007; work in public and private collections Founding Trustee, Irene Wellington Educnl Trust, 1987. Presenter, and producer with Jeremy Bennett, Alphabet (film series), 1979. Liveryman, Scriveners' Co., 1973 (Master 1997–98). *Publications:* The Story of Writing, 1980, 3rd edn 1994; (jtly) The Calligraphers Handbook, 1985; (jtly) More than Fine Writing, 1986; Gospel and Acts (facsimile edn) 2005; Psalms (facsimile edn), 2006, Pentateuch (facsimile edn), 2006; Prophets (facsimil edn), 2007. *Recreations:* people watching, travel, graphic arts, architecture, country sports *Address:* The Hendre Hall, The Hendre, Monmouth NP25 5HB. *T:* (01600) 716565.

JACKSON, Francis Alan, CBE 2007 (OBE 1978); Organist and Master of the Music York Minster, 1946–82, Organist Emeritus, since 1988; *b* 2 Oct. 1917; *s* of W. A. Jackson *m* 1950, Priscilla, *d* of Tyndale Procter; two *s* one *d*. *Educ:* York Minster Choir Sch.; Si Edward Bairstow. Chorister, York Minster, 1929–33; ARCO, 1936; BMus Duneln 1937; FRCO (Limpus Prize), 1937; DMus Dunelm 1957. Organist Malton Parish Church, 1933–40. Served War of 1939–45, with 9th Lancers in Egypt, N Africa and Italy 1940–46. Asst Organist, York Minster, 1946; Conductor York Musical Soc., 1947–82 Conductor York Symphony Orchestra, 1947–80. Pres. Incorp. Assoc. of Organists 1960–62; Pres., RCO, 1972–74. Hon. FRSCM 1963; Hon. Fellow, Westminster Choi. Coll., Princeton, NJ, 1970; Hon. FRNCM, 1982; Hon. FGCM 2005; Hon. FGMS DUniv York, 1983. Order of St William of York, 1983. *Publications:* Piano Trio, 2001 organ music, including 6 sonatas, 2 duets, symphony, organ concerto, church music songs, monodramas. *Recreation:* gardening. *Address:* Nether Garth, East Acklam, Malton N Yorks YO17 9RG. *T:* (01653) 658395.

JACKSON, Prof. Frank Cameron, AO 2006; Professor of Philosophy, Australian National University, 1986–90 and 1992–2007; Research Professor, La Trobe University since 2008; *b* 31 Aug. 1943; *s* of Allan Cameron Jackson and Ann Elizabeth Jackson; *m* 1966, Morag Elizabeth Fraser; two *d*. *Educ:* Melbourne Univ. (BA, BSc, 1966); LaTrobe Univ. (PhD 1975). Temp. Lectr, Adelaide Univ., 1967; Lectr, Sen. Lectr, then Reader LaTrobe Univ., 1968–77; Prof., Monash Univ., 1978–86 and 1991; Australian Nationa University: Dir, Inst. of Advanced Studies, 1998–2001; Dir, Res. Sch. of Soc. Scis, 2004–07. Vis. Prof., Princeton Univ., 2007–. Corresp. FBA 2000. *Publications:* Perception, 1977; Conditionals, 1987; (with D. Braddon-Mitchell) Philosophy of Mind and Cognition, 1996; From Metaphysics to Ethics, 1998; Mind, Method, and Conditionals, 1998. *Recreations:* reading, tennis. *Address:* 75 Napier Crescent, Montmorency, Vic 3094, Australia. *Club:* Turner Tennis (Canberra).

JACKSON, Glenda May, CBE 1978; MP (Lab) Hampstead and Highgate, since 1992; *b* Birkenhead, 9 May 1936; *d* of Harry and Joan Jackson; *m* 1958, Roy Hodges (marr. diss. 1976); one *s*. *Educ:* West Kirby Co. Grammar Sch. for Girls; RADA. Actress, 1957–92; with various repertory cos, 1957–63, stage manager, Crewe Rep.; joined Royal Shakespeare Co., 1963. Dir, United British Artists, 1983. Parly Under-Sec. of State, DETR, 1997–99. Pres., Play Matters (formerly Toy Libraries Assoc.), 1976–. *Plays:* All Kinds of Men, Arts, 1957; The Idiot, Lyric, 1962; Alfie, Mermaid and Duchess, 1963; Royal Shakespeare Co.: Theatre of Cruelty Season, LAMDA, 1964; The Jew of Malta, 1964; Marat/Sade, 1965, NY and Paris, 1965; Love's Labour's Lost, Squire Puntila and his Servant Matti, The Investigation, Hamlet, 1965; US, Aldwych, 1966; Three Sisters, Royal Ct, 1967; Fanghorn, Fortune, 1967; Collaborators, Duchess, 1973; The Maids, Greenwich, 1974; Hedda Gabler, Australia, USA, London, 1975; The White Devil, Old Vic, 1976; Stevie, Vaudeville, 1977; Antony and Cleopatra, Stratford, 1978; Rose, Duke of York's, 1980; Summit Conference, Lyric, 1982; Great and Small, Vaudeville, 1983; Strange Interlude, Duke of York's, 1984; Phedra, Old Vic, 1984, Aldwych, 1985; Across from the Garden of Allah, Comedy, 1986; The House of Bernarda Alba, Globe, 1986; Macbeth, NY, 1988; Scenes from an Execution, Almeida, 1990; Mother Courage, Mermaid, 1990; *films:* This Sporting Life, 1963; Marat/Sade, 1967; Negatives, 1968; Women in Love (Oscar Award, 1971), 1970; The Music Lovers, 1971; Sunday, Bloody Sunday, 1971; The Boyfriend, 1972; Mary, Queen of Scots, 1972; Triple Echo, 1972; Il Sorviso de Grande Tentatore (The Tempter), 1973; Bequest to the Nation, 1973; A Touch of Class (Oscar Award, 1974), 1973; The Maids, 1974; The Romantic Englishwoman, 1974; Hedda Gabler, 1975; The Incredible Sarah, 1976; House Calls,

1978; Stevie, 1978; The Class of Miss MacMichael, 1978; Lost and Found, 1979; Hopscotch, 1980; Return of the Soldier, 1982; Health, 1982; Giro City, 1982; Sacharov, 1983; Turtle Diary, 1985; Business as Usual, 1987; Beyond Therapy, 1987; Salome's Last Dance, 1988; The Rainbow, 1989; The Secret Life of Sir Arnold Bax, 1992; *TV:* Elizabeth in Elizabeth R, 1971; The Patricia Neal Story (Amer.). Best film actress awards: Variety Club of GB, 1971, 1975, 1978; NY Film Critics, 1971; Nat. Soc. of Film Critics, US, 1971. *Recreations:* cooking, gardening, reading Jane Austen. *Address:* c/o House of Commons, SW1A 0AA.

JACKSON, Gordon; *see* Jackson, W. G.

JACKSON, Helen Margaret; Trustee/Director, South Yorkshire Women's Development Trust, 2005–06; Member, Women and Pensions Network, Equality and Human Rights Commission, since 2006 (voluntary outreach worker on women and pensions, Equal Opportunities Commission, 2005–06); *b* 19 May 1939; *d* of Stanley Price and Katherine (*née* Thornton); *m* 1960, Keith Jackson (marr. diss. 1998); two *s* one *d*. *Educ:* St Hilda's Coll., Oxford (BA Hons Mod. Hist., MA); C. F. Mott Coll. of Educn, Prescot (Cert Ed 1972). Asst Librarian, 1961; mother, housewife and voluntary worker, 1961–72; teacher, 1972–80; City Cllr, Sheffield, 1980–91 (Chm., Public Works and Econ. Develt Cttees). Founder Mem. and Chair, Centre for Local Economic Strategies, 1986–91. MP (Lab) Sheffield, Hillsborough, 1992–2005. PPS to Sec. of State for NI, 1997–2001. Member: Envmt Select Cttee, 1992–97; Modernisation of H of C Select Cttee, 1997–2001; Transport, Local Govt and the Regions Select Cttee, 2001–03; Chair: All-Party Parly Water Gp, 1993–97; Parly Envmt Gp, 1997–2005; All-Party Parly Gp on S Africa, 1997–2005; Founder and Chair, All-Party Parly Steel Gp, 2002–05; Co-Chair, PLP Women's Gp, 1992–97; Sec., PLP Gp on Envmtl Protection, 1995–97; Vice-Chair, PLP, 2001–02 (Mem., Parly Cttee, Labour Party, 2001–05); Mem., NEC, Labour Pty, 1999–2005. UK Parly Rep., Assoc. of Eur. Parliamentarians for Africa, 1997–2005. Vice Chair, Fawcett Soc., 2007–. Pres., Sheffield Homestart, 2005–; Trustee, Age Concern, Sheffield, 2005–. *Publication:* The Active Citizen, 2007. *Recreations:* walking, music. *Address:* 2 Topside, Grenoside, Sheffield S35 8RD.

See also Christopher Price.

JACKSON, Prof. James Anthony, PhD; FRS 2002; Professor of Active Tectonics, since 2002, and Head, Department of Earth Sciences, since 2008, Cambridge University; Fellow, Queens' College, Cambridge, since 1979; *b* 12 Dec. 1954; *s* of Richard Owen Jackson and Honor (*née* Thomason); *m* 1984, Susan Elliott; one *s* one *d*. *Educ:* Cranleigh Sch.; Queens' Coll., Cambridge (BA 1976, PhD 1980). Res. Fellow, NERC, 1979–82; Asst Lectr, 1984–88, Lectr, 1988–96, Reader, 1996–2002, Dept of Earth Scis, Cambridge Univ. Allan Cox Vis. Prof., Stanford Univ., 1990–91; Visiting Professor: CIT, 2006; CNRS Grenoble, 2006. Royal Instn Christmas Lects, Planet Earth: an Explorer's Guide, 1995. Fellow, Amer. Geophys. Union, 2003. Pres.'s Award, 1985, Bigsby Medal, 1997, Geol. Soc. London. *Publications:* contribs to professional jls in earth scis. *Recreations:* violin making, hill-walking. *Address:* Bullard Laboratories, Madingley Road, Cambridge CB3 0EZ. *T:* (01223) 337197, *Fax:* (01223) 360779; *e-mail:* jackson@esc.cam.ac.uk.

JACKSON, Jane Thérèse, (Tessa); international cultural development consultant, since 2002; Artistic Director, Artes Mundi Prize, since 2002; *b* 5 Nov. 1955; *d* of John Nevill Jackson and Viva Christian Thérèse Jackson (*née* Blomfield). *Educ:* Univ. of East Anglia (BA Hons Fine Art); Univ. of Manchester (Dip. Museum Studies); Univ. of Bristol (MA Film and TV Prodn), 1998. Art Editor, OUP, 1979–80; Exhibns Organiser, SPAB, 1981–82; Curator, Eyemouth Museum, 1982; Curator, Collins Gallery, Univ. of Strathclyde, 1982–88; Visual Arts Officer, Glasgow 1990—European City of Culture, 1988–91; Director: Arnolfini, Bristol, 1991–99; Scottish Arts Council, 1999–2001. Consultant, Arts Council England Rev. of Presentation of Contemporary Visual Arts, 2005. *Publications:* (with John R. Hume) George Washington Wilson and Victorian Glasgow, 1983; (jtly) Signs of the Times: art and industry in Scotland 1750–1985, 1985; (ed jtly) A Platform for Partnership (Glasgow City Council), 1991. *Recreations:* travel, walking, architecture. *Address: e-mail:* TessaJackson@aol.com.

JACKSON, John Bernard Haysom; Chairman: Xenova Group plc, 1990–2005; Oxford Technology Venture Capital Trusts plc, since 1997; *b* 26 May 1929; *m* 1st, 1955, Ann Nichols (marr. diss. 1984); one *s* two *d*; 2nd, 1984, Rowena Thomas. *Educ:* King's School, Canterbury; Queens' Coll., Cambridge (BA, LLB). Called to the Bar, Inner Temple, 1954. Philips Electronics, 1952–80 (Dir, 1966–94); Dir, 1980–2001, Vice-Chm., 1991–94, Chm., 1994–2001, Hilton Gp. Non-solicitor Chm., Mishcon de Reya, 1992–; Chairman: Celltech Gp, 1982–2003; Wyndeham Press Gp plc, 1990–2003; Dep. Chm., BHP Billiton plc, 2001–02; Director: WPP Group plc, 1993–2004 (Founding Mem., Adv. Bd, 2004–); Instore (formerly Brown & Jackson) plc, 1994–; Billiton plc, 1997–2001; Opendemocracy Ltd, 2000–. Chairman: Countryside Alliance, 1999–2005; Rural Regeneration Unit, 2003–06; Trustee, One World Action, 1998–2005. Chm. and co-owner, History Today magazine, 1981–. *Publications:* A Bucket of Nuts and a Herring Net, 1979, 2nd edn as A Little Piece of England: a small holding from scratch, 2000; (contrib.) Even Paranoids have Enemies, 1998. *Recreations:* growing rare plants, breeding butterflies, fishing, painting, writing.

JACKSON, John Henry; Clerk to the Governors, Dulwich College, 1998–2007; Company Secretary, BG plc (formerly British Gas), 1990–97; *b* 7 Aug. 1948; *s* of late John and of May Jackson; *m* 1975, Patricia Mary Robinson; one *s* one *d*. *Educ:* Trinity School, Croydon; St Catherine's College, Oxford (MA). FCIS. Joined SE Gas Board, 1970; Asst Sec., 1977, Sen. Asst Sec., 1983, British Gas Corp., later British Gas plc. Mem., Solicitors Disciplinary Tribunal, 2002–. Assessor, Nat. Clinical Assessment Service (formerly Authy), 2003–07. Mem., Indep. Monitoring Bd, HMP High Down, 2004–05; Independent Member: Parole Bd, 2005–; CIPFA Disciplinary Cttee, 2007–. Mem. UK and Internat. Councils, ICSA, 1996–2002 (a Chief Examr, 1997–2000). Non-exec. Dir, Queen Victoria Hosp. NHS Trust, E Grinstead, 1996–98. Clerk to Govs, Alleyn's Sch., 1998–2004.

JACKSON, (John) Patrick; Director, Portugal, British Council, 1993–96; *b* 18 Sept. 1940; *s* of Godfrey Jackson and Mary Jackson (*née* Worthington); *m* 1st, 1963, Marieliese de Vos van Steenwyk (marr. diss.); three *d* (and one *d* decd); 2nd, 1978, Hélène Mellotte; two *d*. *Educ:* Worksop Coll.; Midhurst Grammar Sch.; New Coll., Oxford (MA); Moscow Univ. (postgrad. studies); London Univ. Inst. of Educn (postgrad. Cert Ed). British Council, 1963–96: English Language Teaching Inst., London, 1964–66; Asst Dir, Bahrain, 1966–69; Asst Cultural Attaché, Moscow, 1969–71; Dep. Dir, Higher Educn Dept, 1971–73; Regl Dir, Calcutta, 1973–75; Dir, N Europe Dept, 1975–79; Rep., Senegal, 1979–83; Regl Dir, São Paulo, 1983–88; Dep. Controller, Home Div., 1988–91; Dir, Exchanges and Training Div., 1991–93; early retirement, 1996; kidney transplant, 1997; Baggage Agent, Gatwick Handling Ltd, 1997–2000; Homesearch consultant, 2000–04. *Recreations:* birdwatching, languages, bridge, spreadbetting. *Address:* Two Houses, Hollow Lane, East Grinstead, W Sussex RH19 3PS.

JACKSON, Judith Mary; QC 1994; *b* 18 Sept. 1950; *d* of Thomas Worthington Jackson and Betty Jackson (*née* Kinsey); one *d*. *Educ:* Queen Mary College, London. LLB, LLM. Called to the Bar, Inner Temple, 1975; Bencher, Lincoln's Inn, 2001. Dir, Bar Mutual Insce Fund Ltd, 1999–. Chm., Young Barristers' Cttee, 1984–85. *Recreations:* music, cycling, trekking in the Andes. *Address:* Maitland Chambers, 7 Stone Buildings, Lincoln's Inn, WC2A 3SZ. *T:* (020) 7406 1200.

JACKSON, Prof. Julian Timothy, PhD; FBA 2003; FRHistS; Professor of Modern French History, Queen Mary, University of London, since 2003; *b* 10 April 1954; *s* of Edward Francis Jackson and Marion Marianne Marris (*née* Ellinger). *Educ:* Peterhouse, Cambridge (BA 1976; PhD 1982). Res. Asst to Robert Rhodes James, MP, for biog. of Eden, 1983; University College of Swansea, subseq. University of Wales, Swansea: Lectr, 1983–90, Sen. Lectr, 1990–95, Reader, 1995–2000, in Hist.; Prof. of Hist., 2000–03. FRHistS 1985. *Publications:* The Politics of Depression in France, 1985 (trans. Japanese 2001); The Popular Front in France: defending democracy, 1988 (trans. Japanese 1992); De Gaulle, 1990; France: the dark years 1940–44, 2001 (trans. French 2004); The Fall of France, 2003; De Gaulle, 2003 (trans. French 2004). *Recreations:* cinema, theatre, opera, travel. *Address:* Department of History, Queen Mary, University of London, Mile End Road, E1 4NS. *T:* (020) 7727 9930, *Fax:* (020) 8980 8400; *e-mail:* j.t.jackson@qmul.ac.uk.

JACKSON, Sir Kenneth Joseph, (Sir Ken), Kt 1999; Chairman, Nirex Ltd, 2001–05. *Educ:* St Joseph's Sch., Wigan. Electrical technician, RAF, 1956–61; joined ETU, 1966: Br. Sec., Wigan; area officer, Preston; officer, Merseyside and NW; Exec. Councillor, EETPU, 1987; Pres., EETPU section, 1992–96, Gen. Sec., 1996–2003, AEEU.

JACKSON, (Kenneth) Robin, PhD; Chief Executive and Secretary, British Academy, since 2006; *b* 7 Oct. 1949; *s* of Kenneth and Lily Jackson; *m* 1985, Joanna Motion; one *s*. *Educ:* RGS Newcastle upon Tyne; Pembroke Coll., Oxford (MA Lit.Hum. 1973); Princeton Univ. (PhD Classical Philos. 1982). Classics Fellow, Marlboro Coll., Vermont, 1973–75; Seymour Reader in Greek Philos., Ormond Coll., and Lectr, then Sen. Lectr, in Classics, Univ. of Melbourne, 1977–94; Associate Dir, QAA, 1995–98; Res. Policy Advr, UUK, 1998–2002; Regl Consultant, London, 2002–06, Actg Dir, Corporate Resources, 2006, HEFCE. *Publications:* Olympiodorus: commentary on Plato's Gorgias, 1998; articles on Greek philosophy; policy papers on higher educn funding and res. policy. *Recreations:* listening to music, reading, walking in London. *Address:* British Academy, 10 Carlton House Terrace, SW1Y 5AH. *T:* (020) 7969 5255, *Fax:* (020) 7969 5413; *e-mail:* r.jackson@britac.ac.uk. *Clubs:* Athenæum; Newcastle United Football.

JACKSON, (Kevin) Paul; Director, Entertainment and Comedy, ITV plc, since 2006; *b* 2 Oct. 1947; *s* of late T. Leslie Jackson and of Jo (*née* Spoonley); *m* 1981, Judith Elizabeth Cain; two *d*. *Educ:* Gunnersbury Grammar Sch.; Univ. of Exeter (BA 1970); Stanford Univ. (Exec. Program 1993). Stage manager: Marlowe Theatre, Canterbury, 1970; Thorndike Theatre, Leatherhead, 1971. BBC Television: Production Assistant, 1971–79; Producer, 1979–82: programmes include: The Two Ronnies, Three of a Kind (BAFTA Award 1982), Carrot's Lib, The Young Ones (BAFTA Award 1984), Happy Families; freelance producer and director, 1982–84: programmes include: Cannon & Ball, Girls On Top; Producer and Chm., Paul Jackson Prodns Ltd, 1984–86: programmes include: Red Dwarf, Don't Miss Wax, Saturday Live; Man. Dir, Noel Gay TV, 1987–91: progs include The Appointments of Dennis Jennings (Oscar for Best Live Action Short, 1989); Dir of Progs, 1991–93, Man. Dir, 1993–94, Carlton TV; Man. Dir, Carlton UK Productions, 1994–96; Head, then Controller, BBC Entertainment, 1997–2000; Man. Dir, Granada Media Australia and Chief Exec., Red Heart Prodns, 2000–02; Dir, Internat. Prodn and Entertainment, Granada, London, 2002; CEO, Granada America, 2002–06; Chm., Granada Productions (Australia), 2002–06 (CEO, 2000–02). Chairman: RTS, 1994–96; Comic Relief, 1985–98; Charity Projects, 1992–98; Trustee, Pilotlight, 1996–2003 (Chm., 1996–2000); Chm. Trustees, 1999–, Patron, 2000–, Timebank. Academic Visitor, 1996–2004, Vis. Prof., 2004–, Exeter Univ. FInstD 1992; FRTS 1993. Hon. Fellow, Exeter Univ., 1999. Hon. LLD Exeter, 2004. *Recreations:* my family, theatre, Rugby, travel, food and wine. *Address:* c/o Capel and Land Ltd, 29 Wardour Street, W1D 6PS. *Clubs:* Garrick, Groucho.

JACKSON, Michael; Founder, and Chairman, Shaping Tomorrow Ltd, since 2003; *b* 12 March 1948; *s* of Stanley Jackson and Maisie Joan Jackson. *Educ:* Salford Univ. (BSc Electronics). Hawker Siddeley, 1970–73; Vice Pres., Citibank NA, 1973–86; Sen. Vice Pres., Bank of America, 1986–90; Chief Exec., Birmingham Midshires Bldg Soc., 1990–98; Chm., Results Plus Ltd, 1998–2004. Non-exec. Dir, GallifordTry plc, 1997–. Hon. DBA Wolverhampton, 1997. *Recreations:* genealogy, music, sport. *Address:* The Habit, Blackladies, Kiddemore Green Road, Brewood, Staffs ST19 9BH.

JACKSON, Gen. Sir Michael David, (Sir Mike), GCB 2005 (KCB 1998; CB 1996); CBE 1992 (MBE 1979); DSO 1999; DL; Chairman: Benchmark Search Gp Ltd, since 2007; Silk Route Resources Ltd, since 2007; *b* 21 March 1944; *s* of George Jackson and Ivy (*née* Bower); *m* 1985, Sarah Coombe; two *s* one *d*. *Educ:* Stamford Sch.; RMA Sandhurst; Birmingham Univ. (BSocSc 1967). Commnd Intelligence Corps, 1963; transf. to Parachute Regt, 1970; Staff Coll., 1976; Bde Major, Berlin, 1977–78; ndc 1981; Directing Staff, Staff Coll., 1981–83; Comd 1st Bn Parachute Regt, 1984–86; Sen. DS, Jt Service Defence Coll., 1986–88; Services Fellow, Wolfson Coll., Cambridge, 1989; Comdr, 39 Inf. Bde, 1990–92; Dir Gen. Personal Services (Army), MoD, 1992–94; GOC 3 (UK) Div., 1994–95; Comdr, Implementation Force Multinat. Div. SW, Bosnia Herzegovina, 1995–96; Dir Gen., Develt and Doctrine, MoD, 1996–97; Comdr, ACE Rapid Reaction Corps, 1997–2000; Comdr, Kosovo Force, March–Oct. 1999; C-in-C, Land Comd, 2000–03; ADC Gen. to the Queen, 2001–06; CGS, 2003–06. Dir, Risk Advisory Gp, 2007–; Sen. Advr, PA Consulting Gp, 2007–; Consultant, Numis Securities, 2007–; Mem. Internat. Adv. Bd, Rolls-Royce, 2007–. Col Comdt, Parachute Regt, 1998–2004; Hon. Col, Rifle Vols, TA, 1999–2007. DL Wilts, 2007. Hon. LLD: Birmingham, 2000; Sheffield, 2005. Freeman, City of London, 1988. *Publication:* Soldier: the autobiography, 2007. *Recreations:* travel, music, ski-ing, tennis. *Address:* Flagstaff House, Napier Road, Colchester, Essex CO2 7SW. *Clubs:* Army and Navy, Buck's, Garrick; St Moritz Tobogganing.

JACKSON, Rt Rev. Michael Geoffrey St Aubyn; *see* Clogher, Bishop of.

JACKSON, Michael Richard; President of Programming, IAC, since 2006; *b* 11 Feb. 1958; *s* of Ernest Jackson and Margaret (*née* Kearsley). *Educ:* King's Sch., Macclesfield; Poly. of Central London (BA (Hons) Media Studies). Organiser, Channel Four Gp, 1979; Producer, The Sixties, 1982; Independent Producer, Beat Productions Ltd, 1983–87, produced Whose Town is it Anyway?, Open the Box, The Media Show; joined BBC Television; Editor: The Late Show (BFI Television Award), 1988–90; Late Show Productions, 1990–91, progs incl. The Nelson Mandela Tribute, Tales from Prague (Grierson Documentary Award), Moving Pictures, The American Late Show (PBS), Naked Hollywood (BAFTA Award, Best Factual Series); Head of Music and Arts, BBC Television, 1991–93; Controller, BBC 2, 1993–96; Controller, BBC 1 and BBC Dir of

Television, 1996–97; Dir of Progs, 1997–98, Chief Exec., 1997–2001, C4; Chm., Film Four Ltd, 1997–2001; Pres. and Chief Exec., USA Entertainment, 2001–02; Chm., Universal Television Gp, 2002–04; Exec. Producer, The Genius of Photography (series), BBC, 2005. Non-exec. Dir, EMI Gp, 1999–2002; Dir, DIC Entertainment, 2006–. Chm., Photographers' Gall., 2001–02. FRTS 1997. Hon. DLitt Westminster, 1995. *Recreations:* reading, films, collecting photography, walking.

JACKSON, Air Vice-Marshal Michael Richard, CB 1998; independent consultant, since 2004; Deputy Chairman, Alpha Intelligence Management Ltd, since 2007; Director General, Ministry of Defence, 1996–98; *b* 28 Dec. 1941; *s* of Felix Ralph Jackson and Margaret Jackson (*née* Marshall); *m* 1967, Kay Johnson; two *s*. *Educ:* Cardinal Vaughan Sch.; RAF Coll., Cranwell. Joined RAF, 1965: sqdn flying duties, 1965–69; navigation instructor, 1969–70; Exchange Officer, USA, 1971–74; RAF Staff Coll., 1974; Sqdn Comdr, 1975–77; Mem., Directing Staff, Army Staff Coll., Camberley, 1977–80; Ops Wing Comdr, 1981–84; Defence and Air Attaché, Warsaw, 1985–87; Unit Comdr, 1987–89; Defence Fellow, Rand Corp. and Cambridge Univ., 1989–90; Dir, MoD Central Staffs, 1991–95. Exec. Dir, Oracle Corp., 1998–2004; Dir, Market Develt, Silicon Graphics, 2002–04. *Recreations:* music, walking, gardening. *Address:* c/o RAF Record Office, High Wycombe, Bucks HP14 4UE. *Club:* Royal Air Force.

JACKSON, (Michael) Rodney; Consultant, Sandersons, Solicitors, 2001–05; a Recorder, 1985–2001; *b* 16 April 1935; *s* of John William Jackson and Nora Jackson (*née* Phipps); *m* 1968, Anne Margaret, *d* of Prof. E. W. Hawkins, *qv*; two *s*. *Educ:* King Edward VII Sch., Sheffield; Queen Elizabeth Grammar Sch., Wakefield; Queens' Coll., Cambridge (MA, LLM). Admitted Solicitor of the Supreme Court, 1962; Notary Public, 1967; Solicitor Advocate, 1996–2005. Partner, 1964–94, Sen. Partner, 1992–94, Consultant, 1994–2001, Andrew M. Jackson & Co., Solicitors. *Recreations:* reading, rail travel. *Address:* 11 The Paddock, Swanland, North Ferriby, E Yorks HU14 3QW. *T:* (01482) 633278.

JACKSON, Sir Michael (Roland), 5th Bt *cr* 1902; MA; CEng, MIET; *b* 20 April 1919; *s* of Sir W. D. Russell Jackson, 4th Bt, and Kathleen (*d* 1975), *d* of Summers Hunter, CBE, Tynemouth; *S* father 1956; *m* 1st, 1942, Hilda Margaret (marr. diss. 1969), *d* of late Cecil George Herbert Richardson, CBE, Newark; one *s* one *d*; 2nd, 1969, Hazel Mary, *d* of late Ernest Harold Edwards. *Educ:* Stowe; Clare Coll., Cambridge. Served War of 1939–45; Flt-Lieut, Royal Air Force Volunteer Reserve. *Heir: s* Thomas St Felix Jackson [*b* 27 Sept. 1946; *m* 1980, Victoria, *d* of late George Scatliff, Wineham, Sussex; two *d*]. *Address:* Jolliffe's House, Stour Row, Shaftesbury, Dorset SP7 0QW.

JACKSON, Michael Walter; Under Secretary and Head of Marine Directorate, Department of Transport, 1993–94, retired; *b* 5 April 1934; *s* of late William Henry Jackson and Nellie Jackson; *m* 1963, Mary Bruce Hope Sinclair; one *s* one *d*. *Educ:* Queen Elizabeth Grammar Sch., Wakefield; Queen's Coll., Oxford (MA Lit.Hum.). UKAEA, 1959–68; joined MoT, 1968; Assistant Secretary: MoT, 1973–76; PSA, 1976–80; Dept of Transport, 1980–93. *Recreations:* hill-walking, opera. *Address:* Tranby Croft, Greystoke Gill, Penrith, Cumbria CA11 0UQ. *T:* (017684) 83848.

JACKSON, Mike; *see* Jackson, R. M.

JACKSON, Sir Neil Keith, 9th Bt *cr* 1815, of Arlsey, Bedfordshire; *b* 12 May 1952; *s* of Sir Keith Arnold Jackson, 8th Bt and of Pauline Mona (*née* Climo); *S* father, 2000, but his name does not appear on the Official Roll of the Baronetage; *m* 1973, Sandra Whitehead (marr. diss.); two *s*. *Heir: s* Stephen Keith Jackson, *b* 27 Sept. 1973.

JACKSON, Sir Nicholas (Fane St George), 3rd Bt *cr* 1913; organist, harpsichordist and composer; Director, Concertante of London, since 1987; *b* 4 Sept. 1934; *s* of Sir Hugh Jackson, 2nd Bt, and Violet Marguerite Loftus (*d* 2001), *y d* of Loftus St George; *S* father, 1979; *m* 1972, Nadia Françoise Genevieve (*née* Michard); one *s*. *Educ:* Radley Coll.; Wadham Coll., Oxford; Royal Acad. of Music. LRAM; ARCM. Organist: St Anne's, Soho, 1963–68; St James's, Piccadilly, 1971–74; St Lawrence, Jewry, 1974–77; Organist and Master of the Choristers, St David's Cathedral, 1977–84. Musical Dir, St David's Cathedral Bach Fest., 1979; Dir, Bach Festival, Santes Creus, Spain, 1987–89. Organ recitals and broadcasts: Berlin, 1967; Paris, 1972, 1975; USA (tour), 1975, 1978, 1980 and 1989; Minorca, 1977; Spain, 1979; Madrid Bach Festival, 1980; RFH, 1984; Croatia (tour), annually, 2002–08; concert tours of Spain and Germany, annually 1980–. Début as harpsichordist, Wigmore Hall, 1963; directed Soho Concertante, Queen Elizabeth Hall, 1964–72. Mem. Music Cttee, Welsh Arts Council, 1981–84. Examiner, Trinity Coll. of Music, 1985–99. Lectr on work of Sir Thomas Graham Jackson incl. Venice, 2008. Recordings: Mass for a Saint's Day, 1971; organ and harpsichord music, incl. works by Arnell, Bach, Couperin, Langlais, Mozart, Vierne and Walther; Spanish organ music; own organ music, recorded at Chartres Cath., 2000; Requiem and other choral music, 2006. Hon. Patron, Hertford Coll. Music Soc., 1996–. Master, Drapers' Co., 1994–95; Liveryman, Musicians' Co., 1985. Hon. Fellow, Hertford Coll., Oxford, 1995. *Publications:* (ed) Sir Thomas Graham Jackson, Recollections: the life and travels of a Victorian architect, 2003; Requiem, 2007; *compositions:* Mass for a Saint's Day, 1966; 20th Century Merbecke, 1967; 4 Images (for organ), 1971; Divertissement (organ), 1983; Organ Mass, 1984; 2 Organ Sonatas, 1985; Suite, for brass quintet and organ, 1986; The Reluctant Highwayman (opera), 1992 (world première, 1995); (completed) Bach's Fugue, BWV 906, 1996; Missa Cum Jubilo. *Recreations:* sketching, writing. *Heir: s* Thomas Graham St George Jackson, *b* 5 Oct. 1980.

JACKSON, Patrick; *see* Jackson, J. P.

JACKSON, Patrick; *see* Jackson, W. P.

JACKSON, Paul; *see* Jackson, K. P.

JACKSON, Paul Edward; Managing Director (International) (Amex), Ogilvy Group, 2006–07; *b* 8 July 1953; *s* of George Edward Jackson and Joan (*née* Barry); *m* 2000, Elaine Claire Adams; two *s*. *Educ:* Taunton Sch.; Watford Sch. of Art; Canterbury Coll. of Art (BA Hons Graphic Design); Bradford Univ. Mgt Centre. MIPA 1987. Account Executive: Saatchi & Saatchi, 1978–80; Mathers, 1980–81; Account Supervisor, Fletcher Shelton Delaney, 1981–83; Account Manager, Publicis, 1983–85; Bd Dir, BSB Dorland, 1985–92; Man. Dir, Kevin Morley Mktg, 1992–95; Exec. Man. Partner and Vice Chm., Ammirati Purlis Lintas, 1995–97; Client Service Dir, Dewe Rogerson, 1997–99; Ogilvy & Mather: Exec. Mgt Dir, 1999–2002; CEO, 2002–06. Non-exec. Dir, Aga Rangemaster Gp (formerly AGA Foodservice) plc, 2005–. MInstD 1992. FRSA 1993. *Recreations:* sailing, fly fishing.

JACKSON, Peter Arthur Brian; QC 2000; a Recorder, since 2000; *b* 9 Dec. 1955; *s* of late Guy Jackson and of Amanda Jackson (now Park); *m* 1983, Deborah Sanderson; two *d*. *Educ:* Marlborough Coll.; Brasenose Coll., Oxford (BA Hons). Called to the Bar, Inner Temple, 1978; barrister specialising in family law, 1978–. Gov., Camden Sch. for Girls, 2000–. *Address:* 4 Paper Buildings, Temple, EC4Y 7EX. *T:* (020) 7583 0816.

JACKSON, Peter John; Chairman, Kingfisher plc, since 2006; *b* 16 Jan. 1947; *s* of Ja and Joan Jackson; *m* 1974, Anne Campbell; two *s* one *d*. *Educ:* Leeds Univ. (BA Econ Industrial Relations Officer, BSC, 1968–71; Res. Officer, Commn on Industrial Rel 1971–73; Personnel Manager, Guthrie Industries Europe, 1973–76; Perkins Engin Indust. Relns Manager, 1976–80; Personnel Dir, 1980–83; Man. Dir, Rolls Roy Diesels, 1983–84; Dir and Gen. Manager, Gp Parts and Distribn, 1985–87; join Associated British Foods, 1987; British Sugar plc: Exec. Dir, 1987–88; Dep. Man. D 1988–89; Chief Exec., 1989–99; Chief Exec., Associated British Foods, 1999–2005. No exec. Dir, Smiths Group plc, 2003–. Chm., Disabilities Trust, 2007–. *Recreations:* garde golf, Sheffield United. *Address:* c/o Kingfisher plc, 3 Sheldon Square, Paddington, W 6PX. *Club:* Farmers'.

JACKSON, Peter (Michael); Senior Lecturer in Industrial Studies, Institute of Extr mural Studies, National University of Lesotho, 1980; *b* 14 Oct. 1928; *s* of Leona Patterson Jackson; *m* 1961, Christine Thomas. *Educ:* Durham Univ.; University Co Leicester. Lecturer, Dept of Sociology, University of Hull, 1964–66; Fellow, Univ. Hull, 1970–72; Tutor, Open Univ., 1972–74; Senior Planning Officer, S Yorks C 1974–77. MP (Lab) High Peak, 1966–70; contested (Lab) Birmingham North, Europe Parly elecns, 1979. Member: Peak Park Jt Planning Bd, 1973–77, 1979–82; Derby C 1973–77. *Recreations:* numismatics, book collecting, ski-ing. *Address:* 82 Vandon Cou Petty France, SW1H 9HG. *Club:* Maseru (Lesotho).

JACKSON, Peter Robert, CNZM 2002; film producer, director, writer and actor; Pukerua Bay, NZ, 31 Oct. 1961; *s* of late Bill and Joan Jackson; *m* 1987, Frances Wals one *s* one *d*. Formerly photographer, Evening Post, Wellington, NZ; Founder ar Partner: WingNut Films Ltd (acquired Nat. Film Unit, NZ, 2000); Weta Ltd; Three Fo Six Ltd, 1999–. *Films:* producer, director, co-writer and actor: Bad Taste, 198 Braindead, 1992; Heavenly Creatures, 1994; Forgotten Silver, 1995; The Frightene 1997; The Lord of the Rings trilogy: The Fellowship of the Ring, 2001 (BAFTA Awar for Best Film and Best Dir, 2002); The Two Towers, 2002; The Return of the King, 20 (Acad. Awards for Best Dir, Best Picture and Best Adapted Screenplay, 2004); prod., and co-writer: Meet the Feebles, 1989; King Kong, 2005; prod. and co-writer, Ja Brown Genius, 1994; prod. and actor, The Long and Short of it, 2003; prod., Valley the Stereos, 1992.

JACKSON, Philip Henry Christopher, FRBS; DL; sculptor; *b* 18 April 1944; *s* Humphrey Hoskins Jackson and Margaret Jackson (*née* Edwards); *m* 1979, Jean Barba Welch; two *s* one *d*, and one step *s* one step *d*. *Educ:* Farnham Sch. of Art. Vice Pres., RB 1991–93; Pres., W Sussex Art Soc., 2001–; Mem., Art Workers Guild, 1988–. *Maj commissions* include: Manchester Peace Gp, St Peters Sq., Manchester, 1988; Falklands W Monument, Portsmouth, 1992; The Young Mozart, Orange Sq., London, 199 Liberation Sculpture Jersey, St Helier, 1995; Sir Matt Busby, Manchester United F Manchester, 1996; Wallenberg Monument, Great Cumberland Place, London, 199 Minerva Sculpture, Chichester Fest. Th., 1997; Gurkha Monument, Horse Guards Av London, 1997; Constantine the Great, York Minster, 1998; Christ in Judgement, 1998, Richard, 2000, Chichester Cath.; Empress Elizabeth of Austria, Geneva, 199 Wallenberg Monument, Buenos Aires, 1998; The In Pensioner, Royal Hosp. Chelse London, 2000; King George VI, RNC, Dartmouth, 2002; Champions, the World Cu Sculpture, West Ham, London, 2003; equestrian sculpture of HM the Queen, Winds Great Park, 2003; Terence Cuneo, Waterloo Station, London, 2003; Bobby Moo Sculpture, new Wembley Stadium; Queen Mother Meml, The Mall, London, 2007; Lo Glenconner sculpture, Mustique, 2008; United Trinity sculpture, Manchester United F 2008; Sir Alf Ramsey sculpture, New Wembley Stadium, 2008. DL W Sussex, 2008. Ho MA UC Chichester. Silver Medal, 1990, Sir Otto Beit Medal for Sculpture, 1991, 199 and 1993, RBS. *Publication:* Philip Jackson: sculptures since 1987, 2002. *Recreation* messing about in boats, being taken for walks by our black labrador Louis. *Address:* Edwar Lawrence Studios, Petersfield Road, Midhurst, West Sussex GU29 9RL. *T:* (0173 816872, *Fax:* (01730) 812618; *e-mail:* jacksonj@btconnect.com. *Club:* Athenæum.

JACKSON, Ralph S.; *see* Seymour-Jackson.

JACKSON, Prof. Richard James, PhD; FRS 2006; Professor of RNA Biochemistr University of Cambridge, 2000–07, now Emeritus; Fellow of Pembroke Colleg Cambridge, 1967–2007, now Emeritus; *b* 1 July 1940; *s* of James Rufus Jackson and Edit Winifred Jackson (*née* Clark); *m* 1967, Wiltrud Elfriede Klippel; two *d*. *Educ:* Bryansto Sch., Blandford Forum; Pembroke Coll., Cambridge (BA Natural Scis (Biochem.) 196 PhD 1966). Res. Fellow, Dept of Molecular Biol., Univ. of Geneva, 1966–67; Universit of Cambridge: Res. Fellow, Pembroke Coll., 1967–70; Univ. Demonstrator, 1970–7 Lectr, 1973–94; Reader in the Biochem. of Nucleic Acids, 1994–2000. Roche Re Fellow, Dept of Molecular Biol., Univ. of Geneva, 1977 (on sabbatical). Mem. EMBO 1990. Jubilee Lect. and Harden Medal, Biochem. Soc., 2005. *Publications:* articles, esp. o the mechanism and regulation of mammalian protein biosynthesis, in scientific jl *Recreations:* walking, bird watching, travel, music, reading. *Address:* Department c Biochemistry, University of Cambridge, 80 Tennis Court Road, Cambridge CB2 1GA *T:* (01223) 333682, *Fax:* (01223) 766002; *e-mail:* rjj@mole.bio.cam.ac.uk.

JACKSON, Richard Michael, (Mike), CVO 1983; HM Diplomatic Service, retire Ambassador to Costa Rica, 1995–97; *b* 12 July 1940; *s* of Richard William Jackson an Charlotte (*née* Wrightson); *m* 1961, Mary Elizabeth Kitchin; one *s* one *d*. *Educ:* Quee Elizabeth Grammar Sch., Darlington; Paisley Grammar Sch.; Glasgow Univ. (MA Hon 1961). Joined Home Civil Service, 1961; Scottish Office, 1961–70; seconded to MAFF 1971–72; seconded to FCO and served in The Hague, 1973–74; trans. to HM Diplomati Service, 1974; European Integration Dept (External), FCO, 1975–76; Panama City 1976–79; Arms Control and Disarmament Dept, FCO, 1979–81; Buenos Aires, 1981–82 Falkland Islands Dept, FCO, 1982; Stockholm, 1982–87; Dep. Head of Mission, Seoul 1987–91; Ambassador to Bolivia, 1991–95. *Recreations:* conservation, birdwatching, rea ale. *Address:* *e-mail:* mollieandmike@yahoo.com.

JACKSON, Robert Victor; *b* 24 Sept. 1946; *m* 1975, Caroline Frances Harvey (*see* C. F Jackson); one *s* decd. *Educ:* Falcon Coll., S Rhodesia; St Edmund Hall, Oxford (H. W. C Davis Prize, 1966; 1st Cl. Hons Mod. Hist. 1968); President Oxford Union, 1967. Priz Fellowship, All Souls Coll., 1968 (Fellow, 1968–86). Councillor, Oxford CC, 1969–71 Political Adviser to Sec. of State for Employment, 1973–74; Member, Cabinet of Si Christopher Soames, EEC Commn, Brussels, 1974–76; Chef de Cabinet, President o EEC Economic and Social Cttee, Brussels, 1976–78; Mem. (C) Upper Thames, Europear Parlt, 1979–84; Special Adviser to Governor of Rhodesia (Lord Soames), 1979–80 European Parlt's Rapporteur-Gen. on 1983 European Community Budget. MP Wantage 1983–2005 (C, 1983–2005, Lab, 2005). Parly Under Sec. of State, DES, 1987–90, Dep of Employment, 1990–92, Office of Public Service and Sci., 1992–93. Mem., Select Ctte on Sci. and Technol., 1999–2001. Mem., Adv. Cttee on Works of Art, H of C; Treas. Cons. Mainstream Parly Gp. Mem., UK Delegn, Council of Europe and WEU, 2000–01 Contested (C) Manchester Central Div., Oct. 1974. Co-Chm., CAABU, 2001–. Trustee Hattori Foundn; Hattori Trust Co. Ltd. Editor: The Round Table: Commonwealth Jl o

Internat. Relations, 1970–74; International Affairs (Chatham House), 1979–80. *Publications:* South Asian Crisis: India, Pakistan, Bangladesh 1972, 1975; The Powers of the European Parliament, 1977; The European Parliament: Penguin Guide to Direct Elections, 1979; Reforming the European Budget, 1981; Tradition and Reality: Conservative philosophy and European integration 1982; From Boom to Bust?—British farming and CAP reform, 1983; Political Ideas in Western Europe Today, 1984. *Recreations:* reading, music, walking. *Address:* New House, Hanney Road, Southmoor, Abingdon OX13 5HR.

JACKSON, Ven. Robert William; Archdeacon of Walsall, since 2004; *b* 21 June 1949; *s* of Joseph William and Mary Edith Jackson; *m* 1973, Anne Christine Day; one *s* one *d* (and one *s* decd). *Educ:* King's Coll., Cambridge (MA 1973); Univ. of Manchester (MA 1973); Univ. of Nottingham (DipTh). Govt Economic Advr, 1972–78. Ordained deacon, 1981, priest, 1982; Curate, Christ Church, Fulwood, 1981–84; Vicar: St Mark's, Grenoside, 1984–92; St Mary, Scarborough, 1992–2001; Springboard Res. Missioner, 2001–04. *Publications:* Matthew, 1987, 2nd edn 1993; Godspeed, 1994; Till the Fat Lady Sings, 1996; Higher than the Hills, 1999; Hope for the Church, 2002; The Road to Growth: towards a thriving church, 2005; Going for Growth, 2006. *Recreations:* tennis, cricket, walking, trains. *Address:* 55B Highgate Road, Walsall WS1 3JE. *T:* (01922) 620153; *e-mail:* archdeacon.walsall@lichfield.anglican.org.

JACKSON, Robin; *see* Jackson, K. R.

JACKSON, Rodney; *see* Jackson, M. R.

JACKSON, Sir Roland; *see* Jackson, Sir W. R. C.

JACKSON, Rosemary Elizabeth; QC 2006; a Recorder, since 2002; *b* 16 April 1958; *d* of Douglas and Pauline Jackson; *m*; one *s* one *d*. *Educ:* King's Coll. London (LLB Hons 1980; AKC 1980). Called to the Bar, Middle Temple, 1981; Accredited, 2001, Registered, 2003, Mediator. *Address:* Keating Chambers, 15 Essex Street, WC2R 3AA. *T:* (020) 7544 2600, *Fax:* (020) 7544 2700.

JACKSON, Prof. Roy, DSc; FRS 2000; Class of 1950 Professor of Engineering and Applied Science, Princeton University, 1983–98, now Professor Emeritus; *b* 6 Oct. 1931; *s* of Harold and Ellen Jackson; *m* 1957, Susan Margaret Birch (*d* 1991); one *s* one *d*. *Educ:* Trinity Coll., Cambridge (BA 1954, MA 1959); Univ. of Edinburgh (DSc 1968). ICI Ltd, 1955–61; Reader in Chemical Engrg, Univ. of Edinburgh, 1961–68; A. J. Hartsook Prof. of Chemical Engrg, Rice Univ., 1968–77; Prof. of Chemical Engrg, Univ. of Houston, 1977–82; Sherman Fairchild Dist. Schol., CIT, 1982–83. Alpha Chi Sigma Award, 1980, Thomas Baron Award, 1993, AIChE. *Publications:* Transport in Porous Catalysts, 1977; The Dynamics of Fluidized Particles, 2000. *Recreations:* sailing, water colour painting. *Address:* 311 Johnson Street, New Bern, NC 28560, USA. *T:* (252) 5142493.

JACKSON, Roy Arthur; Assistant General Secretary, Trades Union Congress, 1984–92; *b* 18 June 1928; *s* of Charles Frederick Jackson and Harriet Betsy (*née* Ridewood); *m* 1956, Lilian May Ley; three *d*. *Educ:* North Paddington Central Sch.; Ruskin Coll., Oxford (DipEcon Pol Sci (Distinction)); Worcester Coll., Oxford (BA Hons, PPE). Post Office Savings Bank, 1942; RN, Ord. Signalman, 1946–48. Trades Union Congress: joined Educn Dept, 1956; Dir of Studies, 1964; Head of Educn, 1974–84. Member: Albemarle Cttee of Youth Service, 1958–60; Open Univ. Cttee on Continuing Educn, 1975–76; Adv. Cttee for Continuing and Adult Educn, 1977–83; Schools Council Convocation, 1978–82; Further Educn Unit, DES, 1980–; Employment Appeal Tribunal, 1992–99; TUC Comr, MSC, 1987–88. Non-exec. Dir, Remploy Ltd, 1992–99. *Recreations:* walking, reading, gardening. *Address:* 27 The Ryde, Hatfield, Herts AL9 5DQ. *T:* (01707) 890566.

JACKSON, Rt Hon. Sir Rupert (Matthew), Kt 1999; PC 2008; **Rt Hon. Lord Justice Jackson;** a Lord Justice of Appeal, since 2008; *b* 7 March 1948; *s* of late George Henry Jackson and Nancy Barbara Jackson (*née* May); *m* 1975, Claire Corinne Potter; three *d*. *Educ:* Christ's Hospital; Jesus College, Cambridge (MA, LLB). Pres., Cambridge Union, 1971. Called to the Bar, Middle Temple, 1972, Bencher, 1995; QC 1987; a Recorder, 1990–98; a Dep. High Court Judge, 1993–98; a Judge of the High Court of Justice, QBD, 1999–2008; Judge in charge of Technol. and Construction Ct, 2004–07. Chm., Professional Negligence Bar Assoc., 1993–95. Editor, Jackson and Powell on Professional Negligence, 1982–99, consultant editor, 2000–. *Address:* Royal Courts of Justice, Strand, WC2A 2LL. *Club:* Reform.

JACKSON, Prof. Stephen Philip, PhD; FRS 2008; Frederick James Quick Professor of Biology, Department of Zoology, Cambridge University, since 1995; Senior Scientist, since 1996, Head, Cancer Research UK Laboratories, since 2004, Wellcome Trust/Cancer Research UK Gurdon Institute (formerly Wellcome/CRC Institute of Cancer and Developmental Biology), Cambridge University; *b* 17 July 1962; *s* of Philip George Jackson and Marian Margaret (*née* Smith); *m* 1991, Teresa Margaret Clarke; two *s*. *Educ:* Univ. of Leeds (BSc 1st Cl. Hons Biochem. 1983); Univ. of Edinburgh (PhD Molecular Biol. 1987). Postgraduate research: Imperial Coll., London, 1983–85; Univ. of Edinburgh, 1985–87; Postdoctoral Fellow, Univ. of Calif, Berkeley, 1987–91; Research Gp Leader, 1991–95, Dep. Dir, then Dep. Chm., 2001–04, Wellcome/CRC Inst., subseq. Wellcome Trust/CRUK Gurdon Inst., Univ. of Cambridge. Founder, and CSO, KuDOS Pharmaceuticals Ltd, 1997–. Tenovus Medal Lecture, Tenovus-Scotland, 1997. FMedSci 2001; Mem. EMBO, 1997–. Eppendorf European Investigator Award, 1995; Colworth Medal, 1997, GlaxoSmithKline Award, 2008, Biochemical Soc.; Anthony Dipple Carcinogenesis Young Investigator Award, 2002. *Publications:* over 200 research papers and review articles in leading scientific jls, particularly in areas of DNA repair. *Recreations:* my children, gardening, travel. *Address:* Wellcome Trust/Cancer Research UK Gurdon Institute, University of Cambridge, Tennis Court Road, Cambridge CB2 1QN. *T:* (office) (01223) 334102.

JACKSON, Stewart James; MP (C) Peterborough, since 2005; *b* 31 Jan. 1965; *s* of Raymond Thomas Jackson and Sylvia Alice Theresa Jackson; *m* 1999, Sarah O'Grady; one *d*. *Educ:* Royal Holloway Coll., Univ. of London (BA Hons (Econs and Public Admin) 1988); Thames Valley Univ. (MA Human Resource Mgt). MCIPD 2001. Pres., Univ. of London, 1988–89. Retail Banker, Lloyds TSB, 1993–98; Business Services Manager, AZTEC (Trng and Enterprise Council for SW London), 1998–2000; Business Advr, Human Resources, Business Link for London, 2000–05. Mem. (C) Ealing BC, 1990–98. Contested (C) Brent S, 1997, Peterborough, 2001. *Recreations:* family, cinema, travel, biographies, local history. *Address:* House of Commons, SW1A 0AA. *T:* (020) 7219 8286; *e-mail:* jacksonsj@parliament.uk. *Club:* Peterborough Conservative.

JACKSON, Dr Sylvia; Member (Lab) Stirling, Scottish Parliament, 1999–2007; *b* 3 Dec. 1946; *d* of Herbert Edward Woodforth and Lucy Franklin; *m* 1970, Michael Peart Jackson (*d* 2001); one *s* one *d*. *Educ:* Brigg Girls' High Sch.; Univ. of Hull (BSc Hons Chemistry; PGCE; BPhil Educn); Univ. of Stirling (PhD Educn). Teacher of chemistry and physics, schools in Hull, Alva, Stirling, Cumbernauld and Kirkintilloch; Asst Sci. Advr, Edinburgh CC and Lothian Regl Council; Res. Fellow, Univ. of Stirling; Lectr, Moray House Inst. of Educn, Univ. of Edinburgh. Scottish Parliament: Dep. Convenor, Local Govt Cttee, 2000; Convenor, Subordinate Legislation Cttee, 2003–07; Mem., Local Govt and Transport Cttee, 2003–07; Cross Party Groups: Convenor, Animal Welfare; Co-Convenor, Affordable Housing; Vice Convenor, Drugs and Alcohol, 2004–07. Exec. Mem., CPA, 2003–07. *Publications:* Introducing Science (series of 12 pupil books and 6 teacher guides); contribs to jls, mainly dealing with professional develt of teachers. *Recreations:* walking, photography.

JACKSON, Tessa; *see* Jackson, J. T.

JACKSON, (Walter) Patrick, CB 1987; FRHistS; Under-Secretary, Department of Transport, 1981–89, retired; *b* 10 Feb. 1929; *m* 1952, Kathleen Roper; one *s* one *d*. *Educ:* University Coll., Oxford. John Lewis Partnership, 1952–66; Principal, Min. of Transport and DoE, 1966–72; Asst Sec., DoE, 1972–78; Under Sec. and Regional Dir (E Midlands), DoE and Dept of Transport, 1978–81. FRHistS 2001. *Publications:* The Last of the Whigs, 1994; Education Act Forster, 1997; Harcourt and Son, 2004; Enigma Variation, 2004; Loulou, 2006. *Recreations:* concert- and theatre-going, historical research.

JACKSON, (William) Gordon; QC (Scot) 1990; Member (Lab) Glasgow Govan, Scottish Parliament, 1999–2007; *b* 5 Aug. 1948; *s* of Alexander Jackson and Margaret Shillinglaw or Jackson; *m* 1972, Anne Stevely; one *s* two *d*. *Educ:* Ardrossan Academy; St Andrews Univ. (LLB). Advocate, 1979; called to the Bar, Lincoln's Inn, 1989; Advocate Depute, Scotland, 1987–90.

JACKSON, Sir (William) Roland (Cedric), 9th Bt *cr* 1869, of The Manor House, Birkenhead; DPhil; Chief Executive, British Association for the Advancement of Science, since 2002; *b* 9 Jan. 1954; *s* of Sir (William) Thomas Jackson, 8th Bt and Gillian Malise (*née* Stobart); *S* father, 2004; *m* 1977, Nicola Mary, MA, DPhil, *yr d* of Prof. Peter Reginald Davis, PhD, FRCS; three *s*. *Educ:* Wycliffe Coll.; St Peter's Coll., Oxford (MA); Exeter Coll., Oxford (DPhil). Hd of Science, Backwell Sch., 1986–89; Educn Advr, ICI, 1989–93; Science Museum: Hd of Learning, 1993–2002; Hd of Mus., 2001–02. Trustee: UK Sierra Leone Cultural Foundn; Mather-Jackson Library. *Recreations:* collecting and reading mountaineering and rock-climbing literature and occasionally repeating some of the feats described therein, contributing to the preservation of the cultural heritage of Sierra Leone. *Heir: s* Adam William Roland Jackson, *b* 19 May 1982. *Clubs:* Athenæum, Alpine.

JACKSON, Yvonne Brenda, OBE 1985; DL; Chairman, West Yorkshire Metropolitan County Council, 1980–81; *b* 23 July 1920; *d* of Charles and Margaret Wilson; *m* 1946, Edward Grosvenor Jackson; twin *s* one *d*. *Educ:* Edgbaston C of E Coll., Birmingham; Manchester Teachers' Trng Coll. (Dip. Domestic Science and qualified teacher). School Meals Organizer, West Bromwich, Staffs, 1942–45. Mem., W Riding CC, 1967–73 (local govt reorganisation); Mem. W Yorks CC, 1973–86; Chm., Fire and Public Protection Cttee, 1977–80; Deputy Leader and Shadow Chairman: Fire Cttee, 1981–86; Trading Standards Cttee, 1981–86; Police Cttee, 1982–86. Chm., Yorks Electricity Consultative Council, 1982–90; Mem., Yorks RHA, 1982–87. Mem. Exec. Cttee, Nat. Union of Cons. Assocs, 1981–88 (Dep. Chm., Yorks Area Finance and Gen. Purposes Cttee, 1982–88; Divl Pres., Elmet, 1985–93). Mem. Council and Court, Leeds Univ. DL W Yorks, 1983, High Sheriff, 1986–87. *Recreations:* badminton, fishing; formerly County hockey and tennis player; former motor rally driver (competed in nat. and internat. events incl. Monte Carlo, Alpine and Tulip rallies). *Address:* East Garth, School Lane, Collingham, W Yorks LS22 5BQ. *T:* (01937) 573452.

JACKSON-LIPKIN, Miles Henry, (Li Pak-Kim); QC (Hong Kong) 1974; SC 1997; JP; a Judge of the High Court of Hong Kong, 1981–87; *b* Liverpool, 24 May 1924; *s* of late I. J. Jackson-Lipkin, MD and F.A. Patley; *m* Lucille Yun-Shim Fung, DCLJ, barrister; one *s*. *Educ:* Harrow; Trinity Coll., Oxford. FCIArb 1986; Mem., HKIArb; Chartered Arbitrator, Canada, Hong Kong and UK. Called to the Bar, Middle Temple, 1951; admitted Hong Kong Bar, 1963, NSW Bar, 1980. Comr, Supreme Court of Negara Brunei Darussalam, 1984–87. Panel Member: Inland Revenue Bd of Review, Hong Kong, 1975; London Court of Internat. Arbitration, 1994; WIPO, 1995; British Columbia Arbitration Mediation Inst., 1995; Hong Kong Internat. Arbitration Centre Mediation Gp, 1996. Chief Legal Advr, Hope and Lee (Consultants) Ltd, 1988. Chm. Exec. Cttee, and Man. Dir, Hong Kong Children and Youth Services, 1978. Member: Medico-Legal Soc., 1952; Justice, 1956; Council of Honour, Monarchist League, 1969; Council, Constitutional Monarchy Assoc., 1995; Founder Member: Hong Kong Br., Justice, 1963; Hong Kong Medico-Legal Soc., 1974 (Mem. Cttee, 1976). Hon. Advr, China North-West Coll. of Law. Vice-Chm., Hong Kong Island Br., Internat. Wine and Food Soc. Hon. Mem., Chinese Soc. for Wind Engrg. Delegate, HKSAR, Order of St Lazarus of Jerusalem, 1999. Liveryman: Meadmakers' Co. (Edinburgh), 1984; Arbitrators' Co., 1986; Freeman, City of London, 1986. JP Hong Kong, 1977. GLJ 1998 ((Grand Priory of Lochore); KCLJ 1983; KLJ 1977; CLJ 1973). *Publications:* The Beaufort Legitimation, 1957; Scales of Justice, 1958; Israel Naval Forces, 1959. *Recreations:* gardening, heraldry, classical music, philately, walking. *Address:* 309 The Capilano, 2024 Fullerton Avenue, West Vancouver, BC V7P 3G4, Canada; *e-mail:* lipakkim@netvigator.com. *Clubs:* Naval and Military, MCC; Hong Kong, Hong Kong Cricket, Hong Kong Golf, Hong Kong Jockey, American, Arts, Classic Car, (Hon.) Shanghai Fraternity Assoc. (Hong Kong).

JACKSON-NELSON, Marjorie, AC 2001; CVO 2002; MBE 1953; Governor, South Australia, 2001–07; *b* 13 Sept. 1931; *d* of William Alfred Jackson and Mary Jackson; *m* 1953, Peter Nelson (*d* 1977); one *s* two *d*. *Educ:* Lithgow High Sch., NSW. Athlete (the Lithgow Flash): holder, Australian 100 yards, 100 metres, 220 yards and 200 metres sprint titles, 1950–54; broke world sprint records on ten occasions; Olympic Gold Medals for 100m and 200m, Helsinki, 1952; 7 Commonwealth Games Gold Medals. Australian Commonwealth Games teams: Women's Section Manager, Auckland, 1982, Edinburgh, 1986, Auckland, 1990; Gen. Team Manager, Victoria, Canada, 1994; Athletes' Liaison Officer, Malaysia, 1998. Member Board: S Australian Govt's Sports Inst., 1985–90; Sydney Organising Cttee for 2000 Olympic Games, 1998–2000. Launched Peter Nelson Leukaemia Res. Fellowship, 1977; has raised over Aust. $4 million to sponsor research into fighting leukaemia; funds raised have sponsored a leukaemia lab. in Adelaide. Hon. Dr, Charles Sturt, NSW, 2001. Australian Sports Medal, 2000.

JACKSON-STOPS, Timothy William Ashworth, FRICS; Chairman, 1978–98, Consultant, since 1998, Jackson-Stops & Staff; *b* 1942; *s* of late Anthony and Jean Jackson-Stops; *m* 1987, Jenny MacArthur; two *s*. *Educ:* Eton; Agricultural Coll., Cirencester. Jackson-Stops & Staff, 1967–: Dir, 1974. *Recreations:* ski-ing, sailing, shooting. *Address:* Wood Burcote Court, Towcester, Northants NN12 7JP. *T:* (01327) 350443.

JACOB, David Oliver L.; *see* Lloyd Jacob.

JACOB, Prof. François; Croix de la Libération; Grand-Croix de la Légion d'Honneur; biologist; Head of Cellular Genetics Unit, Pasteur Institute, 1960–91; Professor of Cellular Genetics, at the College of France, 1964–91; *b* Nancy (Meurthe & Moselle), 17 June 1920; *m* 1st, 1947, Lysiane Bloch (*d* 1984); three *s* one *d*; 2nd, 1999, Geneviève Barrier. *Educ:* Lycée Carnot, France. DenM 1947; DèsS 1954. Pasteur Institute: Asst, 1950–56; Head of Laboratory, 1956–60; Prof., 1960–; Pres., 1982–88. Member: Acad. of Scis, Paris, 1977; Acad. Française, Paris, 1996. Charles Léopold Mayer Prize, Acad. des Sciences, Paris, 1962; Nobel Prize for Medicine, 1965. Foreign Member: Royal Danish Acad. of Letters and Sciences, 1962; Amer. Acad. of Arts and Sciences, 1964; Nat. Acad. of Scis, USA, 1969; Royal Soc., 1973; Acad. Royale de Médecine, Belgique, 1973; Acad. of Sci., Hungary, 1986; Royal Acad. of Sci., Madrid, 1987. Holds hon. doctorates from several univs, incl. Chicago, 1965. *Publications:* La Logique du Vivant, 1970 (The Logic of Life, 1974); Le Jeu des Possibles, 1981 (The Possible and the Actual, 1982); La Statue Intérieure, 1987 (The Statue Within, 1988); La Souris, la Mouche et l'Homme, 1997 (Of Flies, Mice and Men, 1998); various scientific. *Recreation:* painting. *Address:* Institut Pasteur, 25 rue du Dr Roux, 75724 Paris, Cedex 15, France.

JACOB, Rt Hon. Sir Robert Raphael Hayim, (Sir Robin), Kt 1993; PC 2003; **Rt Hon. Lord Justice Jacob;** a Lord Justice of Appeal, since 2003; *b* 26 April 1941; *s* of Sir Isaac Hai, (Sir Jack) Jacob, QC; *m* 1967, Wendy Jones; three *s*. *Educ:* King Alfred Sch., Hampstead; Mountgrace Secondary Comprehensive Sch., Potters Bar; St Paul's Sch.; Trinity Coll., Cambridge (BA, MA); LSE (LLB; Hon. Fellow, 2005). Called to the Bar, Gray's Inn, 1965 (Atkin Scholar; Bencher, 1989; Vice-Treas., 2006; Treas., 2007); teacher of law, 1965–66; pupillage with Nigel Bridge (later Lord Bridge of Harwich), 1966–67, with A. M. Walton, 1967; entered chambers of Thomas Blanco White, 1967; Junior Counsel to Treasury in Patent Matters, 1976–81; QC 1981; a Judge of the High Court of Justice, Chancery Div., 1993–2003. Dep. Chm., Copyright Tribunal, 1989–93; apptd to hear appeals to Sec. of State under the Trade Marks Acts, 1988–93. Mem. Adv. Bd, Centre for European Law, KCL, 2002–. Governor: LSE, 1994–; Expert Witness Inst., 1996–2006. Hon. Vis. Prof. of Law, Univ. of Birmingham, 1999–; Dist. Judicial Visitor, UCL, 2002–. Hon. President: Assoc. of Law Teachers, 2002–; Licensing Exec. Soc., 2003–. Hon. Fellow, St Peter's Coll., Oxford, 1998. Jt Editor, Encyclopedia of UK and European Patent Law, 1977–. *Publications:* Kerly's Law of Trade Marks (ed jtly), 1972, 1983 and 1986 edns; Patents, Trade Marks, Copyright and Designs (ed jtly), 1970, 1978, 1986; Editor, Court Forms Sections on Copyright (1978), Designs and Trade Marks (1975–86); section on Trade Marks (ed jtly), 4th edn, Halsbury's Laws of England, 1985, 1995; Guidebook of Intellectual Property, 1993, 5th edn 2004. *Recreations:* Arsenal FC, photography, country garden. *Address:* Royal Courts of Justice, Strand, WC2A 2LL.

JACOB, Ven. William Mungo, PhD; Archdeacon of Charing Cross, since 1996; Rector, St Giles-in-the-Fields, since 2000; A. J. Jones Professor of Pastoral Theology, University of Wales, Lampeter, since 2006; *b* 15 Nov. 1944; *s* of John William Carey Jacob and Mary Marsters Dewar. *Educ:* King Edward VII School, King's Lynn; Hull Univ. (LLB); Linacre Coll., Oxford (MA); Exeter Univ. (PhD). Deacon 1970, priest 1971; Curate of Wymondham, Norfolk, 1970–73; Asst Chaplain, Exeter Univ., 1973–75; Lecturer, Salisbury and Wells Theological Coll., 1975–80, Vice-Principal, 1977–80; Sec. to Cttee for Theological Education, ACCM, 1980–86; Warden, Lincoln Theol Coll., 1986–96; Canon of Lincoln Cathedral, 1986–96. Ed., Theology, 1998–2008. *Publications:* (ed with P. Baelz) Ministers of the Kingdom, 1985; (contrib.) Religious Dissent in East Anglia, 1991; (contrib.) The Weight of Glory, 1991; (ed with N. Yates) Crown and Mitre, 1993; Lay People and Religion in the Early Eighteenth Century, 1996; The Making of the Anglican Church Worldwide, 1997; (contrib.) The National Church in Local Perspective, 2003; (contrib.) Studies in Church History, vols 16, 28, 31, 38, 40, 42; (contrib.) Anglicanism and the Western Tradition, 2003; (contrib.) The Pastor Bonus, 2004; (contrib.) St Paul's: the Cathedral Church of London 604–2004, 2004; (contrib.) Cambridge History of Libraries in Britain and Ireland, vol. 2, 2006; The Clerical Profession in the Long Eighteenth Century, 1680–1840, 2007. *Address:* 15A Gower Street, WC1E 6HW. *T:* (020) 7323 1992.

JACOBI, Sir Derek (George), Kt 1994; CBE 1985; actor; *b* 22 Oct. 1938; *s* of Alfred George Jacobi and Daisy Gertrude Masters. *Educ:* Leyton County High Sch.; St John's Coll., Cambridge (MA Hons; Hon. Fellow, 1987). Artistic Associate, Old Vic Co. (formerly Prospect Theatre Co.), 1976–81; associate actor, RSC; Artistic Dir, Chichester Fest. Th., 1995–96. Vice-Pres., Nat. Youth Theatre, 1982–. *Stage:* Birmingham Repertory Theatre, 1960–63 (first appearance in One Way Pendulum, 1961); National Theatre, 1963–71; Prospect Theatre Co., 1972, 1974, 1976, 1977, 1978; Hamlet (for reformation of Old Vic Co., and at Elsinore), 1979; Benedick in Much Ado About Nothing (Tony Award, 1985), title rôle in Peer Gynt, Prospero in The Tempest, 1982, title rôle in Cyrano de Bergerac, 1983 (SWET Award; Plays and Players Award), RSC; Breaking the Code, Haymarket, 1986, Washington and NY 1987; Dir, Hamlet, Phoenix, 1988; title rôle in Kean, Old Vic, 1990; title rôle in Becket, Haymarket, 1991; Byron, in Mad, Bad and Dangerous to Know, Ambassadors, 1992; Macbeth, RSC, 1993; title rôle in Hadrian VII, Playing the Wife, Chichester, 1995; Uncle Vanya, Chichester, 1996, NY, 2000; God Only Knows, Vaudeville, 2001; The Tempest, Old Vic, 2003; Don Carlos, Gielgud, 2005; A Voyage Round My Father, Wyndham's, 2006; *appearances include: TV:* She Stoops to Conquer, Man of Straw, The Pallisers, I Claudius, Philby, Burgess and Maclean, Richard II, Hamlet, Inside the Third Reich, Mr Pye, Cadfael; The Gathering Storm, 2002; The Jury, 2002; The Long Firm, 2004; The Old Curiosity Shop, 2007; *films:* 1971–: Odessa File; Day of the Jackal; The Medusa Touch; Othello; Three Sisters; Interlude; The Human Factor; Charlotte; The Man Who Went Up in Smoke; Enigma; Little Dorrit (Best Actor Award, Evening Standard); Henry V; The Fool; Dead Again; Hamlet; Love is the Devil (Best Actor Award, Evening Standard); Gladiator; The Body; Gosford Park; A Revenger's Tragedy; Nanny McPhee; The Golden Compass. *Awards:* BAFTA Best Actor, 1976–77; Variety Club TV Personality, 1976; Standard Best Actor, 1983. *Address:* c/o Independent Talent Group Ltd, Oxford House, 76 Oxford Street, W1D 1BS.

JACOBI, Sir James (Edward), Kt 1989; OBE 1978; Medical Practitioner (private practice), since 1960; *b* 26 Aug. 1925; *s* of Edward William Jacobi and Doris Stella Jacobi; *m* 1946, Joy; one *s* two *d*; *m* 1974, Nora Maria; two *s*. *Educ:* Maryborough State High School; Univ. of Queensland (MB, BS, PhC). Clerk, Public Service, 1941; RAAF, 1943–46; served navigator-wireless operator, Beaufighter Sqdn, SW Pacific. Apprentice pharmaceutical chemist, 1946–50; pharm. chem., 1950–54, and Univ. student, 1954–60; Resident MO, Brisbane, 1961; MO, Dept of Health, Papua New Guinea, 1962–63; GP Port Moresby, 1963–. *Recreation:* Past President, PNG Rugby Football League. *Address:* Jacobi Medical Centre, Box 1551, Boroko, Papua New Guinea. *T:* 3255355. *Clubs:* United Services (Brisbane); City Tattersalls, NSW Leagues (Sydney); Brisbane Polo; Papua (Port Moresby).

JACOBS, family name of **Baron Jacobs**.

JACOBS, Baron *cr* 1997 (Life Peer), of Belgravia in the City of Westminster; **Dav Anthony Jacobs,** Kt 1988; FCA; *b* Nov. 1931; *s* of Ridley and Ella Jacobs; *m* 19 Evelyn Felicity Patchett; one *s* one *d*. *Educ:* Clifton Coll.; London Univ. (BCon Chairman: Nig Securities Gp, 1957–72; Tricoville Gp, 1961–90, 1992–94; British Sch. Motoring, 1973–90. Contested (L) Watford, Feb. and Oct. 1974. Jt Treas., Liberal Par 1984–87; Vice-Pres., Soc. & Lib. Dem., 1988; Chm., Federal Exec., Soc. & Lib. Der 1988. *Recreations:* golf, reading, theatre, opera, travel. *Address:* 9 Nottingham Terrac NW1 4QB. *T:* (020) 7486 6323. *Clubs:* Coombe Hill Golf (Surrey); Palm Beach Count (USA).

JACOBS, David Lewis, CBE 1996; DL; radio and television broadcaster; *b* 19 May 192 *s* of David Jacobs and Jeanette Victoria Jacobs; *m* 1st, 1949, Patricia Bradlaw (marr. di 1972); three *d* (one *s* decd); 2nd, 1975, Caroline Munro (*d* 1975); 3rd, 1979, Mrs Linds Stuart-Hutcheson. *Educ:* Belmont Coll.; Strand Sch. RN, 1944–47. First broadcast, Na Mixture, 1944; Announcer, Forces Broadcasting Service, 1944–45; Chief Announc Radio SEAC, Ceylon, 1945–47; Asst Stn Dir, Radio SEAC, 1947; News Reader, BB Gen. Overseas Service, 1947, subseq. freelance. Major radio credits include: Book Verse, Housewives' Choice, Journey into Space, Dateline London, Grande Gingol Curioser and Curioser, Puffney Post Office, Follow that Man, Man about Town, Ja Club, Midday Spin, Music Through Midnight, Scarlet Pimpernel, Radio 2 DJ Show, Pi of the Pops, Saturday Show Band Show, Melodies for You (12 years), Saturday S Sounds, Any Questions (Chm. for 17 years), Any Answers; Internat. Fest. of Light Mus TV credits incl.: Focus on Hocus, Vera Lynn Show, Make up your Mind, Tell the Tru Juke Box Jury, Top of the Pops, Hot Line, Miss World, Top Town, David Jacobs' Wor and Music, Sunday Night with David Jacobs, Little Women, There Goes that Song Agai Make a Note, Where are they Now, What's My Line, Who What or Where, Fra Sinatra Show, Mario Lanza Show, Walt Disney Christmas Show, Wednesday Sho Wednesday Magazine, Eurovision Song Contest, TV Ice Time, Twist, A Song for Europ Ivor Novello Awards, Aladdin, Airs and Graces, Tell Me Another, Those Wonderful T Times, Blankety Blank, Come Dancing, Questions (TVS), Primetime, Countdow Holiday Destinations (Sky). Numerous film performances incl. Golden Disc, You Mu Be Joking, It's Trad Dad, Stardust; former commentator, British Movietone News. Royal Command Performances; 6 yrs Britain's Top Disc Jockey on both BBC and Rad Luxembourg; Variety Club of Gt Brit., BBC TV Personality of Year, 1960, and BB Radio Personality of the Year, 1975; Sony Gold Award for Outstanding Contribution Radio over the Years, 1984; RSPCA Richard Martin Award, 1978. Chairman: Kingsto FM, 1994–95; Thames FM, 1995–. Director: Duke of York's Theatre, 1979–85; Man the Moon (UK) Ltd, 1986–; Video Travel Guides, 1990–91; Tom Smith Cracke 1997–98; private banking section, Guinness Mahon, 1997–98. Dir, Kingston Theat Trust, 1991– (Chm., 1990–2008); Pres., Kingston Th. Appeal, 1992–; Dir, College Driver Educn, 1991–96. Vice-President: Stars Organisation for Spastics (Past Chm.); Sc of Stars, 1996–; Mem. Council, RSPCA, 1969–77, Vice-Chm. 1975–76; Vice-Pres., T St John Ambulance London (Prince of Wales's), 1985–97. Past Pres., Nat. Children Orch.; Vice-Pres., Wimbledon Girls Choir. Chm., Think British Council, 1985–89 (De Chm., 1983–85); Vice-Pres., Invest in Britain Campaign, 1992– (Chm., 1989–92 President: Kingston upon Thames Royal British Legion, 1984–2008; SW London Are SSAFA 1995–2008; Jt Pres., SW London Community Foundn, 1994–; Vice-Presiden Royal Star and Garter Home, Richmond, 1988–; Friends of Chelsea and Westminst Hosp., 1993–; Patron: Age Resource, 1990–; Kingston Wel-Care Assoc., 1995; Quee Alexandra Hosp. Home. Pres., Kingston Alcohol Adv. Service, 1993–; Vice Pres Kingston Arts Council; Trustee, Dine-a-Mite, 1994–. Life Gov., ICRF, 1995. DL Great London, 1983, Kingston upon Thames, 1984–2001 (representative); High Stewar Kingston upon Thames, 2001. DUniv Kingston, 1994. *Publications:* (autobiog.) Jacob Ladder, 1963; Caroline, 1978; (with Michael Bowen) Any Questions?, 1981. *Recreation* talking and listening, hotels. *Address:* Wyncombe Hill Cottage, The Fleet, Fittlewort Pulborough, W Sussex RH20 1HN. *Clubs:* St James', Chelsea Arts.

JACOBS, Edward John; Social Security and Child Support Commissioner, since 1998; 20 Nov. 1952; *m* Jill, *d* of W. J. Langford. *Educ:* Paston Sch.; Univ. of Southampto Called to the Bar, Inner Temple, 1976. *Publications:* Effective Exclusion Clauses, 199 (with M. Jones) Company Meetings: law and procedure, 1991; (with G. Douglas) Chi Support: the legislation, 1993, 8th edn 2007; contrib. articles to legal jls. *Recreation* ancient and medieval murder, cross-country ski-ing. *Address:* Commissioners' Offic Third Floor, Procession House, 55 Ludgate Hill, EC4M 7JW.

JACOBS, Rt Hon. Sir Francis (Geoffrey), KCMG 2006; PC 2005; Professor of Lav since 2006, and President, Centre of European Law, since 2007, King's College Londo an Advocate General, Court of Justice of the European Communities, 1988–2006; *b* June 1939; *s* of late Cecil Sigismund Jacobs and Louise Jacobs (*née* Fischhof); *m* 1st, 196 Ruth (*née* Freeman); one *s*; 2nd, 1975, Susan Felicity Gordon (*née* Cox); one *s* three *Educ:* City of London Sch.; Christ Church, Oxford; Nuffield Coll., Oxford. MA, DPhi Called to the Bar, Middle Temple, 1964, Bencher, 1990; in part-time practice, 1974–8 2006–; QC 1984; Lectr in Jurisprudence, Univ. of Glasgow, 1963–65; Lectr in Law, LSI 1965–69; Secretariat, European Commn of Human Rights, and Legal Directorat Council of Europe, Strasbourg, 1969–72; Legal Sec., Court of Justice of Europea Communities, Luxembourg, 1972–74; Prof. of European Law, Univ. of Londor 1974–88; Dir, Centre of Eur. Law, 1981–88, Vis. Prof., 1989–2006, KCL. Hon. Sec., U Assoc. for European Law, 1974–81 (a Vice-Pres., 1988–); Trustee, British Inst. of Interna and Comparative Law, 2006–. Chm., Eur. Maritime Law Orgn, 2005–. Cooley Lect 1983, Bishop Lectr, 1989, LeRoy Fellow, 1993, 2002, Jean Monnet Fellow, 2002, Univ of Mich.; Hamlyn Lectr, 2006. Marcel Storme Prof., Univ. of Ghent, 2005–06; Jea Monnet Prof., KCL, 2006–; Prof., Coll. of Europe, Bruges, 2006–. Governor: British Ins of Human Rights, 1985–; Inns of Court Sch. of Law, 1996–2001. Patron, UK Envm Law Assoc., 2007–; Pres., Missing Children Europe, 2007–. FKC, 1990. Hon. Fellow Soc. for Advanced Legal Studies, 1998; Hon. Mem., Soc. of Legal Scholars, 2003; Foreig Mem., Royal Flemish Acad. of Belgium for Sci. and Arts, 2005. Hon. LLD: Birmingham 1996; Glasgow, 2006; Hon. DCL City, 1997; Hon. Dr Ghent, 2007. Hon. Texan, 200 Commandeur de l'Ordre de Mérite, Luxembourg, 1983. Founding Editor, Yearbook c European Law, 1981–88; Mem. Editl Bd, Yearbook of European Law and many lav reviews. Gen. Ed., Oxford EC Law Library (formerly Oxford European Community Lav series), 1986–. *Publications:* Criminal Responsibility, 1971; The European Convention o Human Rights, 1975, 2nd edn (with Robin C. A. White), 1996; (jtly) References to th European Court, 1975; (ed) European Law and the Individual, 1976; (jtly) The Court c Justice of the European Communities, 1977; (jtly) The European Union Treaty, 198 (joint editor): The European Community and GATT, 1986; The Effect of Treaties i Domestic Law, 1987; Liber Amicorum Pierre Pescatore, 1987; European Communit Law in English Courts, 1998; (contrib.) de Smith, Woolf and Jowell, Judicial Review c Administrative Action, 1995; The Sovereignty of Law: the European way, 2007 *Recreations:* family life, books, music, nature, travel. *Address:* Wayside, 15 St Alban Gardens, Teddington, Middx TW11 8AE. *T:* (020) 8943 0503; *e-mail:* francis.jacobs@ kcl.ac.uk; Fountain Court, Temple, EC4Y 9DH.

JACOBS, Prof. Ian Jeffrey, MD; Professor of Women's Health and Director, Institute for Women's Health, University College London, since 2004; Consultant Gynaecological Oncologist, University College London Hospital, since 2004; *b* 6 Oct. 1957; *s* of Sidney and Shirleen Jacobs; *m* 1988, Chris Steele; two *s* one *d. Educ:* Trinity Coll., Cambridge (BA 1980, MA 1983); London Univ. (MB BS 1983; MD 1991). MRCOG 1990. Consultant Gynaecological Oncologist, Bart's and the London NHS Trust, 1996–2004; Prof. of Gynaecological Oncology, 1999–2004, and Dir, Cancer Inst., 2002–04, Bart's and the London, Queen Mary's Sch. of Medicine. Hon. Consultant, Royal Marsden Hosp., 1996–. *Publications:* Ovarian Cancer, 2002; numerous contribs to med. and scientific jls, incl. Lancet, BMJ and Cancer Res. *Recreations:* Arsenal football fan, dogs, family life. *Address:* Institute for Women's Health, 1st Floor, Maple House, 149 Tottenham Court Road, W1T 7NF.

JACOBS, Rabbi Irving, PhD; Principal, Jews' College, London, 1990–93; *b* 2 Aug. 1938; *s* of Solomon Jacobs and Bertha (*née* Bluestone); *m* 1963, Ann Klein; one *s* three *d. Educ:* Jews' Coll., London; Univ. of London (BA, PhD); Rabbinical Dip. Jews' College, London: Res. Fellow, 1966–69; Lectr, 1969–75; Sen. Lectr, 1975–84; Dean, 1984–90. *Publications:* The Midrashic Process, 1995; articles on Midrash Apocryphal lit. and Jewish liturgy in scholarly jls. *Address:* 28 Elmstead Avenue, Wembley, Middx HA9 8NX. *T:* (020) 8248 5777.

JACOBS, Jeffrey, CB 2002; Senior Advisor to Mayor of London, since 2007; Chief Executive, Government Olympic Executive, Department for Culture, Media and Sport, 2006–07; *b* 20 July 1949; *s* of late Sydney and Jane Jacobs; *m* 1974, Mary Jane Whitelegg; one *s* one *d. Educ:* Enfield Grammar Sch. Joined Ministry of Housing and Local Government, later Department of the Environment, 1965: Asst Private Sec. to Sec. of State for Envmt, 1979–82; Head: Housing Policies Studies Div., 1987–90; Envmt Agency Project Team, 1990–92; Manchester Olympic Unit, 1992–94; Regeneration Div., 1994–97; Principal Private Sec. to Dep. Prime Minister, 1997–98; Dir, Planning Directorate, DETR, 1998–2001; Exec. Dir, Policy and Partnerships, GLA, 2001–04; Dir Gen., Children and Young People and Communities, DCMS, 2004–06. Fellow, Hubert H. Humphrey Inst., Minneapolis, 1986–87. *Recreations:* sport, walking.

JACOBS, John Robert Maurice, OBE 1997; golf entrepreneur; *b* 14 March 1925; *s* of Robert and Gertrude Vivian Jacobs; *m* 1949, Rita Wragg; one *s* one *d. Educ:* Maltby Grammar School. Asst Professional Golfer, Hallamshire Golf Club, 1947–49; Golf Professional: Gezira Sporting Club, Cairo, 1949–52; Sandy Lodge Golf Club, 1952–64; Man. Dir, Athlon Golf, 1967–75; Professional Golfers' Association: Tournament Dir-Gen., 1971–76, Advr to Tournament Div., 1977; European Ryder Cup Captain, 1979–81 (player, 1955); Golf Instructor: Golf Digest Magazine Schs, 1971–76; Golf Magazine Schs, US, 1977. Adviser to: Walker Cup Team; Spanish and French nat. teams; Past Adviser to: Curtis Cup Team; English Golf Union team; Scottish Union team; German, Swedish and Italian teams. Golf Commentator, ITV, 1967–87. Currently associated with John Jacobs' Practical Golf Schools, based in USA. Golf adviser to Golf World Magazine, 1962–86. President: PGA of Europe, 1999–2000; Orgn of Golf Range Owners, 2002–; Founder Mem., Professional Golfers' Architects Assoc.; Vice-Pres., Assoc. of Golf Writers, 1996– (Michael Williams Award, 2003). Legends in Golf Award, Irish Legends Golf Soc., 1994; Medal of Merit, Spanish Royal Golf Fedn, 1995; 5-Star Professional Award, PGA of Europe, 1996; Lifetime Achievement Award, 1996; Geoffrey Dyson Trophy, Sportscoach UK, 2002; Lindberg Bowl for services to European golf, 2005; PGA Master Professional, 2006. Inducted World Golf Hall of Fame, 2000, World Golf Teaching Hall of Fame, 2001. *Publications:* Golf, 1961; Play Better Golf, 1969; Practical Golf, 1973; John Jacobs Analyses the Superstars, 1974; Golf Doctor, 1979; The Golf Swing Simplified, 1993; Golf in a Nutshell, 1995; 50 Greatest Golf Lessons of the Century, 1999; 50 Years of Golfing Wisdom, 2005. *Recreations:* shooting, fishing. *Address:* Stable Cottage, Chapel Lane, Lyndhurst, Hants SO43 7FG. *T:* (023) 8028 2743. *Clubs:* Royal and Ancient Golf (St Andrews), Sandy Lodge Golf, New Forest Golf, Brokenhurst Manor Golf, Bramshaw Golf, Burley Golf, Hamptworth Golf and Country, Wellow Golf (Vice Pres., 2002–), Walton Heath Golf; Lake Nona Golf and Country (Florida).

JACOBS, Hon. Sir Kenneth (Sydney), KBE 1976; Justice of High Court of Australia, 1974–79; *b* 5 Oct. 1917; *s* of Albert Sydney Jacobs and Sarah Grace Jacobs (*née* Aggs); *m* 1952, Eleanor Mary Neal (*d* 2002); one *d. Educ:* Knox Grammar Sch., NSW; Univ. of Sydney (BA, LLB); University Coll. London (MA Ancient History 2006). Admitted to NSW Bar, 1947; QC 1958; Supreme Court of NSW: Judge, 1960; Judge of Appeal, 1966; Pres., Court of Appeal, 1972. *Publication:* Law of Trusts, 1958. *Address:* 261 Latymer Court, Hammersmith Road, W6 7LB.

JACOBS, Nigel Robert; QC 2006; barrister and arbitrator; *b* 31 May 1960; *m* 1993, Suzanne Tanchan; two *d. Educ:* Highgate Sch.; Pembroke Coll., Cambridge (BA 1982); Trinity Coll., Cambridge (LLM 1984). Called to the Bar, Middle Temple, 1983. *Recreations:* tennis, theatre, cinema. *Address:* Quadrant Chambers, 10 Fleet Street, EC4Y 1UA. *T:* (020) 7583 4444, *Fax:* (020) 7583 4455.

JACOBS, Prof. Patricia Ann, OBE 1999; FRS 1993; Director, Wessex Regional Genetics Laboratory, 1988–2001; *b* 8 Oct. 1934; *d* of Cyril Jacobs and Sadie Jacobs (*née* Jones); *m* 1972, Newton Ennis Morton; three step *s* two step *d. Educ:* St Andrews Univ. (BSc 1st Cl. Hons 1956; D'Arcy Thomson Medal 1956; DSc 1966; Sykes Medal 1966). FRSE 1977; FRCPath 1987; FRCPE 1998; FRCOG 1999. Res. Asst, Mount Holyoke Coll., USA, 1956–57; Scientist, MRC, 1957–72; Prof., Dept of Anatomy and Reproductive Biology, Univ. of Hawaii Sch. of Medicine, 1972–85; Prof. and Chief of Div. of Human Genetics, Dept of Pediatrics, Cornell Univ. Med. Coll., 1985–87. Hon. Prof. of Human Genetics, Univ. of Southampton Med. Sch., 1993. Mem., MRC, 1996–98. Founder FMedSci 1998. Hon. DSc St Andrews, 2002. Allan Award, Amer. Soc. of Human Genetics, 1981; Regents Medal, Univ. of Hawaii, 1983; Premio Phoenix Anni-Verdi, 1998; Mauro Baschivotto Award, European Soc. of Human Genetics, 1999. *Publications:* numerous articles in learned jls. *Recreations:* walking, botany, gardening. *Address:* Wessex Regional Genetics Laboratory, Salisbury District Hospital, Salisbury SP2 8BJ. *T:* (01722) 429080.
See also Peter A. Jacobs.

JACOBS, Peter Alan; non-executive Chairman: L. A. Fitness (formerly L. A. Leisure), 1999–2005; W. T. Foods, 2002–05; *b* 22 Feb. 1943; *s* of Cyril and Sadie Jacobs; *m* 1966, Eileen Dorothy Naftalin; twin *s* one *d. Educ:* Glasgow Univ. (BSc Hons MechEng); Aston Univ. (Dip. Management Studies). Tube Investments: grad. trainee, 1965–67; Production Controller, Toy Div., 1968–70; Pedigree Petfoods: Production Shift Manager, 1970–72; Purchasing Dept, 1972–81; Production Manager, 1981–83; Sales Dir, Mars Confectionery, 1983–86; Berisford International: Man. Dir, British Sugar, 1986–89; Chief Exec., Berisford and Chm., British Sugar, 1989–91; Chief Exec., BUPA, 1991–98; non-executive Chairman: Healthcall Ltd, 1998–2001; Hillsdown Holdings plc, 1999–2000; abc Media, 2005–; non-executive Director: Allied Domecq, 1998–2004; Bank Leumi (UK), 1999–2003; Virtual Communities Inc., 1999–2000; RAF Strike Command, 2002–. *Recreations:* tennis, theatre, music. *Address:* Garden Flat, 29 Daleham Gardens, NW3 5BY. *Club:* Royal Automobile.
See also Patricia A. Jacobs.

JACOBS, Peter John; His Honour Judge Jacobs; a Circuit Judge, since 1997; *b* 16 April 1943; *s* of Herbert Walter Jacobs and Emma Doris Jacobs; *m* 1975, Dr Ruth Edwards; two *s. Educ:* King Edward VII Sch., King's Lynn; University Coll., Cardiff (BA Hons 1964). Schoolmaster: Barry Boys' Grammar Sch., 1965–68; Cathays High Sch., 1968–72; called to the Bar, Gray's Inn, 1973; practice, 1973–97; Standing Counsel to Inland Revenue, 1995–97; Resident Judge, Norwich Crown Court, 2004–. Mem. (L), Barry Borough Council, 1966–69. Pres., Old Lennensians Assoc., 2006–. Hon Recorder of Norwich, 2008. *Recreations:* watching Norwich City Football Club, fine art, Norfolk railways and churches. *Address:* Norwich Crown Court, The Law Courts, Bishopgate, Norwich NR3 1UR. *Clubs:* Norfolk (Norwich); Norwich City Football; Norwich Wanderers Cricket (Vice Pres.).

JACOBS, Richard David; QC 1998; a Recorder, since 2002; *b* 21 Dec. 1956; *s* of late Elliott Jacobs, chartered accountant, and of Ruth Jacobs (*née* Ellenbogen); *m* 1990, Pamela Fine; one *s* two *d. Educ:* Highgate Sch.; Pembroke Coll., Cambridge. Called to the Bar, Middle Temple, 1979. Vis. Fellow, LSE, 2003. *Publication:* (jtly) Liability Insurance in International Arbitration: the Bermuda form, 2004. *Recreations:* tennis, Arsenal FC, theatre, piano. *Address:* Essex Court Chambers, 24 Lincoln's Inn Fields, WC2A 3ED. *T:* (020) 7813 8000. *Clubs:* MCC, Royal Automobile.

JACOBSON, Prof. Dan; novelist, critic; Professor Emeritus, University College London, since 1994; *b* 7 March 1929; *s* of Michael Hyman Jacobson and Liebe Jacobson (*née* Melamed); *m* 1954, Margaret Dunipace Pye; two *s* one *d. Educ:* Kimberley Boys' High Sch., SA; Univ. of Witwatersrand, Johannesburg (BA 1949). Fellow in Creative Writing, Stanford Univ., Calif, 1956–57; University College London: Reader in English, 1979–86; Prof. of English, 1986–94. Vis. Prof., Syracuse Univ., NY, 1965–66; Visiting Fellow: State Univ. of NY, 1972; Humanities Research Centre, ANU, 1981. Lectures: Ernest Jones Meml, British Inst. of Psycho-Analysis, 1988; Ethel M. Wood, Univ. of London, 1990; Bernard Krikler Meml, Wiener Liby, 1995; Lord Northcliffe, UCL, 2001. FRSL 1974–99. Hon. DLitt Witwatersrand, 1997. Llewellyn Rhys Award, Book Trust, 1958; W. Somerset Maugham Award, Soc. of Authors, 1962. Mary Elinore Smith Poetry Prize, Amer. Scholar, 1992. *Publications: fiction:* The Trap, 1955; A Dance in the Sun, 1956; The Price of Diamonds, 1957; The Evidence of Love, 1960; The Beginners, 1966; The Rape of Tamar, 1970; Inklings: selected stories, 1973; The Wonder-Worker, 1973; The Confessions of Josef Baisz, 1977 (H. H. Wingate Award, Jewish Chronicle, 1979); Her Story, 1987; Hidden in the Heart, 1991; The God-Fearer, 1992; All For Love, 2005; *criticism:* The Story of the Stories, 1982; Adult Pleasures, 1988; *autobiography:* Time and Time Again, 1985 (J. R. Ackerley Prize, PEN, 1986); *travel:* The Electronic Elephant, 1994; *memoir:* Heshel's Kingdom, 1998; *translation:* H. van Woerden, A Mouthful of Glass, 2000; *interview:* Ian Hamilton in Conversation with Dan Jacobson, 2002. *Recreations:* tennis, walking, reading, talking. *Address:* c/o A. M. Heath & Co., 6 Warwick Court, WC1R 5DJ. *T:* (020) 7242 2811. *Club:* Athenæum.

JACOBSON, Howard Eric; novelist; critic; *b* 25 Aug. 1942; *s* of Max Jacobson and Anita (*née* Black); *m* 1st, 1964, Barbara Starr (marr. diss.); one *s*; 2nd, 1978, Rosalin Sadler (marr. diss.); 3rd, 2005, Jenny De Yong. *Educ:* Stand Grammar Sch., Whitefield; Downing Coll., Cambridge (BA, MA). Lectr in English Lit., Univ. of Sydney, Australia, 1965–67; Tutor in English, Selwyn Coll., Cambridge, 1968–72; Sen. Lectr, Wolverhampton Poly., 1974–80. Writer and presenter, TV documentaries: Into the Land of Oz, 1991; Yo, Mrs Askew, 1991; Roots Schmoots, 1993; Sorry, Judas, 1993; Seriously Funny, 1997; Howard Jacobson Takes on the Turner, 2000; Why the Novel Matters: a South Bank Show Special, 2002; contrib. to Late Show, 1989–, Late Rev., 1995–. TV critic, The Correspondent, 1989–90; columnist, The Independent, 1998–. Mem. Editl Bd, Modern Painters, 1990–. *Publications:* (with W. Sanders) Shakespeare's Magnanimity, 1978; In the Land of Oz, 1987; Roots Schmoots, 1993; Seeing with the Ear (Peter Fuller Meml Lecture), 1993; Seriously Funny, 1997; *novels:* Coming from Behind, 1983; Peeping Tom, 1984; Redback, 1986; The Very Model of a Man, 1992; No More Mister Nice Guy, 1998; The Mighty Walzer, 1999; Who's Sorry Now?, 2002; The Making of Henry, 2004; Kalooki Nights, 2006; The Act of Love, 2008. *Address:* c/o Curtis Brown, Haymarket House, 28–29 Haymarket, SW1Y 4SP. *T:* (020) 7393 4400. *Clubs:* Chelsea Arts, Groucho.

JACOBUS, Prof. Mary Longstaff, DPhil; Professor of English (Grace 2), and Fellow of Churchill College, since 2000, and Director, Centre for Research in the Arts, Social Sciences and Humanities, since 2006, University of Cambridge; *b* 4 May 1944; *d* of Marcus Jacobus and Diana (*née* Longstaff); *m* 1981, A. Reeve Parker; one *s* one *d. Educ:* Oxford High Sch. for Girls, GPDST; Lady Margaret Hall, Oxford (BA 1st Cl. Hons English 1965, MA; DPhil 1970; Hon. Fellow, 2000). Oxford University: Randall McIver Jun. Res. Fellow, 1968–70, Fellow and Tutor in English, 1971–80, Lady Margaret Hall; Lectr, English Faculty, 1972–80; Lectr, Manchester Univ., 1970–71; Cornell University: Associate Prof. of English, 1980–82; Prof. of English, 1982–89; John Wendell Anderson Prof. of English and Women's Studies, 1989–2000. Hon. Res. Fellow, LMH, Oxford, 1980–2000. Guggenheim Fellow, 1988–89. *Publications:* Tradition and Experiment in Wordsworth's Lyrical Ballads (1798), 1976; (ed) Women Writing and Women Writing About Women, 1979; Reading Woman: essays in feminist criticism, 1986; (ed jtly) Body/Politics: women and the discourse of science, 1989; Romanticism, Writing and Sexual Difference: essays on The Prelude, 1989; First Things: the maternal imaginary in literature, art and psychoanalysis, 1996; Psychoanalysis and the Scene of Reading, 1999; The Poetics of Psychoanalysis: in the wake of Klein, 2005. *Address:* Faculty of English, University of Cambridge, 9 West Road, Cambridge CB39DP. *T:* (01223) 335070.

JACOMB, Sir Martin (Wakefield), Kt 1985; Chairman: Share plc, since 2001; Canary Wharf Group PLC, since 2003 (Director, since 1999); *b* 11 Nov. 1929; *s* of Hilary W. Jacomb and Félise Jacomb; *m* 1960, Evelyn Heathcoat Amory (MBE 2007); two *s* one *d. Educ:* Eton Coll.; Worcester Coll., Oxford (MA Law 1953; Hon. Fellow, 1994). 2nd Lieut, RA, 1948–49. Called to the Bar, Inner Temple, 1955; practised at the Bar, 1955–68. Kleinwort Benson Ltd, 1968–85; Dep. Chm., Barclays Bank PLC, 1985–93; Chairman: Barclays de Zoete Wedd, 1986–91; Postel Investment Management, 1991–95; Delta plc, 1993–2003; Prudential Corp., 1995–2000 (Dir, 1994–2000); Director: The Telegraph plc (formerly Daily Telegraph), 1986–95; Rio Tinto plc (formerly RTZ Corp.), 1988–2000; Marks and Spencer, 1991–2000. A Dir, Bank of England, 1986–95. Chm., British Council, 1992–98. External Mem., Finance Cttee, OUP, 1971–95. Mem., Nolan Cttee on Standards in Public Life, 1994–97. Director, Oxford Playhouse Trust, 1999–2006. Trustee, Nat. Heritage Meml Fund, 1982–97. Chancellor, Univ. of Buckingham, 1998–. Hon. Bencher, Inner Temple, 1987. Hon. FKC 2007. Hon. Dr: Humberside, 1993; Buckingham, 1997; Hon. DCL Oxford, 1997. *Recreations:* theatre, family bridge, the outdoors.

JACQUES, Dr David Lawson; garden historian; Programme Director, Conservation (Landscape and Gardens), Architectural Association, 2000–06; *b* 29 Sept. 1948; *s* of late

Greville Lawson Jacques and Anne Grace Jacques; *m* 1st, 1973, Rosalind Catherine Denny (marr. diss. 1993); two *d*; 2nd, 2004, Karen Sims-Neighbour. *Educ:* Univ. of Leeds (MSc Transportation Engrg 1972); Poly of N London (DipTP 1977); Courtauld Inst., Univ. of London (PhD 1999). MIHT 1977; MRTPI 1981. Land Use Consultants, 1973–76; Jacques Miller Partnership, 1977–78; Associate, Travers Morgan Planning, 1978–87; Inspector of Historic Parks and Gardens, English Heritage, 1987–93; Consultant on historic landscapes, parks and gardens, 1993– (eg. Privy Garden, Hampton Court); Lectr (pt-time) Landscapes and Gardens, Dept of Archaeol., Univ. of York, 1994–98. Vis. Prof., De Montfort Univ., 1999–2003. Mem. Council, 1975–2001, Chm., 1998–2000, Garden Hist. Soc.; International Council on Monuments and Sites: Co-ordinator, Landscapes Wkg Gp, 1991–95; Corresp. Mem., Internat. Cttee for Gdns and Sites, 1991–; Chm., UK Historic Gdns and Landscapes Cttee, 1993–98. Trustee and Chm., Gdns Cttee, Castle Bromwich Hall Gdns Trust, 1985–87; Chm., Bishop's Park Co-ordinating Gp, 1985–87; Trustee: Landscape Design Trust, 1994–; Chiswick House & Garden Trust, 2005–. Chairman: Staffs Gdns and Parks Trust, 1994–97; Friends of the William Salt Liby, 2004–. Chm., Hammersmith and Fulham Liberal Democrats, 1987–93. *Publications:* Georgian Gardens: the reign of nature, 1983, repr. 1990; (with A. J. Van der Horst) The Gardens of William and Mary, 1988; Strategic Guidance for Heritage Land in London, 1988; Essential to the pracktick part of phisick: the London apothecaries 1540–1617, 1994; The Millennial Landscape, 2006; contrib. chapters in books and articles to jls incl. Jl Gdn Hist. Soc., Landscape Design, Country Life, Jl Envmtl Mgt, Jl RTPI, Monuments Historiques, English Heritage Conservation Bull., Die Gartenkunst, Arte dei Giardini, Internat. Jl Heritage Studies, Jl Architectural Conservation, Schriftenreihe des Deutschen Rates fur Landespflege, Tuinjournaal and Architectural Hist. *Recreations:* narrow boats, croquet, visiting historic gardens. *Address:* Sugnall Hall, Sugnall, Stafford ST21 6NF. *T:* (01785) 851711. *Club:* Farmers'.

JACQUES, Peter Roy Albert, CBE 1990; Secretary, TUC Social Insurance and Industrial Welfare Department, since 1971; *b* 12 Aug. 1939; *s* of George Henry Jacques and Ivy Mary Jacques (*née* Farr); *m* 1965, Jacqueline Anne Sears; one *s* one *d*. *Educ:* Archbishop Temple's Secondary Sch.; Newcastle upon Tyne Polytechnic (BSc Sociology); Univ. of Leicester. Building labourer, 1955–58; market porter, 1958–62; Asst, TUC Social Insce and Industrial Welfare Dept, 1968–71. Member: Industrial Injuries Adv. Council, 1972; Nat. Insce Adv. Cttee, 1972–78; Health and Safety Commn, 1974–95; Royal Commn on the Nat. Health Service, 1976–79; EEC Cttee on Health-Safety, 1976; NHS London Adv. Cttee, 1979; Social Security Adv. Cttee, 1980–95; Health Educn Council, 1984–87; Civil Justice Review Adv. Cttee, 1985–; Royal Commn on Envmtl Pollution, 1989–95; Employment Appeal Tribunal, 1996–. Jt Sec., BMA/TUC Cttee, 1972; Secretary: TUC Social Health and Envmt Protection Cttee (formerly Social Insurance and Industrial Welfare Cttee), 1972–93; TUC Health Services Cttee, 1979–; TUC Special Advr, 1992–95. Vice-Chm., Redbridge and Waltham Forest HA, 1996–99. Mem. Exec. Cttee, Royal Assoc. for Disability and Rehabilitation, 1975–. *Publications:* responsible for TUC pubns Health-Safety Handbook; Occupational Pension Schemes. *Recreations:* reading, yoga, walking, camping, vegetable growing. *Address:* 8 Osborne Road, Buckhurst Hill, Essex IG9 5RR. *T:* (020) 8257 7757.

JAEGER, Prof. Leslie Gordon, CM 2002; FRSE 1966; Research Professor of Civil Engineering and Applied Mathematics, Technical University of Nova Scotia, 1988–92, Emeritus 1992; *b* 28 Jan. 1926; *s* of Henry Jaeger; *m* 1st, 1948, Annie Sylvia Dyson; two *d*; 2nd, 1981, Kathleen Grant. *Educ:* King George V Sch., Southport; Gonville and Caius Coll., Cambridge. PhD, DSc (Eng) London. Royal Corps of Naval Constructors, 1945–48; Industry, 1948–52; University College, Khartoum, 1952–56; Univ. Lectr, Cambridge, 1956–62; Fellow and Dir of Studies, Magdalene Coll., Cambridge, 1959–62; Prof. of Applied Mechanics, McGill Univ., Montreal, 1962–65; Regius Prof. of Engineering, Edinburgh Univ., 1965–66; Prof. of Civil Engineering, McGill Univ., 1966–70; Dean, Faculty of Engineering, Univ. of New Brunswick, 1970–75; Academic Vice-Pres., Acadia Univ., NS, 1975–80; Vice-Pres. (Res.), Technical Univ. of NS, 1980–88. Pres., Canadian Soc. for Civil Engrg, 1992–93. Hon. Prof. of Civil Engrg, Tong Ji Univ., Shanghai, 1987; Hon. Rector, Usman Inst. of Technol., Karachi, 1993. DEng *hc* Carleton Univ., Ottawa, 1991; Meml Univ., Newfoundland, 1994; Technical Univ. of NS, 1995; LLD *hc* Dalhousie, 2005. Telford Premium, ICE, 1959; A. B. Sanderson Award, 1983, P. L. Pratley Award, 1994, Horst Leipholz Medal, 2007, Canadian Soc. for Civil Engrg; Gzowski Medal, 1985, Julian C. Smith Medal, 1996, Engrg Inst. of Canada. *Publications:* The Analysis of Grid Frameworks and Related Structures (with A. W. Hendry), 1958; Elementary Theory of Elastic Plates, 1964; Cartesian Tensors in Engineering Science, 1965; (with B. Bakht) Bridge Analysis Simplified, 1985; (with B. Bakht) Bridge Analysis by Microcomputer, 1989; various papers on grillage analysis in British, European and American Journals. *Recreations:* golf, curling, contract bridge. *Address:* PO Box 1000, Halifax, NS B3J 2X4, Canada. *T:* (902) 4779571. *Club:* Saraguay (Halifax, Canada).

JAFFÉ, David Andrew, FSA; Senior Curator, National Gallery, since 1998; *b* 7 July 1953; *s* of Peter John Jaffé and Patricia Willis Jaffé (*née* Andrew); *m* 1988, Elizabeth Kate Stephen; two *s*. *Educ:* Geelong Grammar Sch.; Melbourne Univ. (BSc); Courtauld Inst. of Art, Univ. of London (MA). Lectr, Univ. of Qld, 1979–81; Curator, Australian Nat. Gall., 1982–90; engaged in research, 1990–94; Curator of Paintings, J. Paul Getty Mus., 1994–98. FSA 1989. Hon. Life Mem., Art Exhibns Australia, 2005. Commendatore, Stella della Solidarietà (Italy), 2004. *Publications:* Rubens: self portrait in focus, 1988; Rubens and the Italian Renaissance, 1992; Titian, 2003; Rubens: the making of a master, 2005; contrib. articles to jls incl. Apollo, Burlington mag., Jl Warburg and Courtauld Insts. *Recreations:* tennis, gymnastics. *Address:* National Gallery, Trafalgar Square, WC2N 5DN. *T:* (020) 7747 2802, *Fax:* (020) 7747 2472; *e-mail:* david.jaffe@ng-london.org.uk. *Club:* Melbourne (Melbourne).

JAFFERJEE, Aftab Asger; QC 2008; Senior Treasury Counsel, Central Criminal Court, since 2001; *b* 25 June 1956; *s* of Asger Jafferjee and Tara Kajiji; *m* 2002, Nazli Javeri; two *d*. *Educ:* St Paul's Sch., Darjeeling; Rugby Sch.; Durham Univ. (BA Hons). Called to the Bar, Inner Temple, 1980; Jun. Treasury Counsel, 1997–2001. Member: Professional Conduct Cttee of Bar (of England and Wales), 1994–96; Cttee, Criminal Bar Assoc., 1995–97. *Recreations:* cuisine, travel, theatre (Founder, Castle Th. Co., Durham, 1977). *Address:* 2 Harcourt Buildings, Temple, EC4Y 9DB. *T:* (020) 7353 2112.

JAFFRAY, Alistair Robert Morton, CB 1978; Deputy Under-Secretary of State, Ministry of Defence, 1975–84; *b* 28 Oct. 1925; *s* of late Alexander George and Janet Jaffray; *m* 1st, 1953, Margaret Betty Newman (decd); two *s* one *d*; 2nd, 1980, Edna Mary, *e d* of late S. J. Tasker, Brasted Chart. *Educ:* Clifton Coll.; Corpus Christi Coll., Cambridge. BA First Cl. Hons., Mod. Langs. Served War, RNVR, 1943–46. Apptd Home Civil Service (Admty), 1948; Private Sec. to First Lord of Admty, 1960–62; Private Sec. to successive Secretaries of State for Defence, 1968–70; Asst Under-Sec. of State, MoD, 1971, Dep. Sec. 1975; Sec. to Admty Bd, 1981–84. Governor, Clifton Coll., 1980–; Chm. Management Cttee, Royal Hospital Sch., Holbrook, 1985–91. *Address:* Okeford, 10 Lynch Road, Farnham, Surrey GU9 8BZ.

JAFFRAY, Sir William Otho, 5th Bt *cr* 1892; *b* 1 Nov. 1951; *s* of Sir William Edmun Jaffray, 4th Bt, TD, JP, DL and of Anne, *d* of Captain J. Otho Paget, MC, Thorp Satchville, Leics; *S* father, 1953; *m* 1981, Cynthia Ross Corrington (marr. diss. 1997) three *s* one *d*. *Heir:* *s* Nicholas Gordon Alexander Jaffray, *b* 18 Oct. 1982. *Address:* c/o 7 Carter Lane, EC4V 5EP.

JAFFREY, Saeed, OBE 1995; actor and writer; *b* 8 Jan. 1929; *s* of late Dr Hamid Hussai Joffrey and Hadia Begum Joffrey; *m* 1st, 1958, Madhur Bahadur (marr. diss. 1966); thre *d*; 2nd, 1980, Jennifer Irene Sorrell. *Educ:* Allahabad Univ. (MA Medieval Hist. 1950) Catholic Univ., Washington DC (MFA Drama 1958). First Indian actor to tour USA i Shakespeare, 1958, and to appear on Broadway, in A Passage to India, 1962; *films* include The Wilby Conspiracy, 1974; The Man Who Would Be King, 1975; The Chess Players 1977 (Best Actor Awards, Filmfare, and Filmworld, 1978); Touch Wood, 1981; Masoom 1982; Gandhi, 1982; My Beautiful Laundrette, 1985 (BAFTA award, 1986); A Passage t India, 1985; Ram Teri Ganga Maili, 1985; Henna, 1989; Masala (Canadian Acad. Award 1992; *television* includes: Gangsters, 1975–77; Jewel in the Crown, Staying On, 1980–82 Far Pavilions, 1985; Partition, Tandoori Nights, 1985–87; Love Match, 1986; Killing o the Exchange, 1986; Rumpole, 1990; Little Napoleons, 1994–95; Common as Muck 1996–97; Ravi Desai in Coronation Street, 1998–99; *theatre* includes: Captai Brassbound's Conversion, 1972; Midsummer Night's Dream, 1989; White Chameleon 1991; My Fair Lady, 1997; The King & I, 2001; *radio* includes: wrote and presented firs programme on India in America, Reflections of India, 1961–63; numerous plays incl. Ar of Love (Kama Sutra), The Pump, Shakuntala, Savitri, A Suitable Boy, and The Silve Castle. *Publication:* Saeed: an actor's journey, 1998. *Recreations:* snooker, cartooning an caricatures, watching cricket and tennis. *Address:* Jaffrey Management Ltd, The Doubl Lodge, Pinewood Studios, Pinewood Road, Iver Heath, Bucks SL0 0NH. *T:* (01753 785162.

JAGAN, Janet, OE 1993; President, Republic of Guyana, 1997–99; *b* Chicago, 20 Oct 1920; *d* of Charles and Kathryn Roberts; *m* 1943, Dr Cheddi Jagan (*d* 1997), forme President of Guyana; one *s* one *d*. *Educ:* Univ. of Detroit; Wayne Univ.; Michigan Stat Coll. Founder Mem., 1946, Political Affairs Cttee, which became People's Progressiv Party, Guyana, in 1950: Exec. Mem., 1950–; Gen. Sec., 1950–70; Editor, Thunder (part jl), 1950–57, 2005–; Internat. Affairs Sec., 1970–80. First woman elected to Georgetow CC, 1950; MP Guyana, 1953, 1957–61, 1963–64, 1976–97; Dep. Speaker, House o Assembly, 1953; imprisoned for six months, Sept. 1954–Feb. 1955; Minister of Labour Health and Housing, 1957–61, of Home Affairs, 1963–64; Prime Minister of Guyana May–Dec. 1997. Mem., Elections Commn, 1967–68. Pres., Union of Guyanes Journalists, 1970–90. Mem., Council of Women World Leaders, 1999–. Trustee, Chedd Jagan Res. Centre, 2000–. Editor, Mirror newspaper, 1973–97. Gandhi Gold Medal fo Democracy, Peace and Women's Rights, UNESCO, 1997. Order of the Liberato (Venezuela), 1998. *Publications:* History of the PPP, 1960; Army Intervention in 197 Elections, 1973; *for children:* When Grandpa Cheddi was a Boy, 1993; Patricia the Baby Manatee and other stories, 1995; Children's Stories of Guyana's Freedom Struggles, 1995 Anastasia the Anteater and other stories, 1997; The Dog Who Loved Flowers, 2000; Th Alligator Ferry Service and other stories from Guyana, 2001; (ed) Anthology of Children' Stories by Guyanese Writers, 2002. *Recreation:* swimming. *Address:* 65 Plantation Bel Air Georgetown, Guyana; HQ of People's Progressive Party, 41 Robb Street, Georgetown Guyana. *T:* 72095.

JAGDEO, Bharrat; President and Commander-in-Chief of the Armed Forces, Republi of Guyana, since 1999; *b* 23 Jan. 1964; *m* 1998, Varshnie Jagdeo. *Educ:* Gibson Primar Sch.; Mahaica Multilateral Sch.; Univ. of Moscow (MSc Econs 1990). Economist, Macro-economic Planning Div., State Planning Secretariat, 1990–92; Special Advr to Minister o Finance, 1992–93; Jun. Minister of Finance, 1993–95; Minister of Finance, 1995–2001 Director: Guyana Water Authy; Nat. Bank of Industry and Commerce; Governor: IMF World Bank; Caribbean Develt Bank (Dir); Inter American Develt Bank (Chm. Caribbean Gp of Govs). Nat. Authorising Officer, EU. *Address:* Office of the President New Garden Street and South Road, Georgetown, Guyana.

JAGGER, Ven. Ian; Archdeacon of Durham and Canon Residentiary of Durham Cathedral, since 2006; *b* 17 April 1955; *m* 1993, Ruth Green; one *s*. *Educ:* Huddersfield New Coll.; King's Coll., Cambridge (BA 1977, MA 1981); St John's Coll., Durham (BA 1980, MA 1987). Ordained deacon, 1982, priest, 1983; Curate, St Mary, Twickenham, 1982–85; Team Vicar, Willen, Milton Keynes, 1985–94; Team Rector, Fareham, 1994–98; RD Fareham, 1996–98; Canon Residentiary, Portsmouth Cathedral, 1998–2001; Archdeacon of Auckland, Dio. Durham, 2001–06. *Address:* 15 The College, Durham DH1 3EQ.

JAGGER, Jonathan David, FRCS, FRCOphth; Surgeon-Oculist to the Queen, since 2002; Consultant Ophthalmologist: Royal Free Hospital, since 1986; King Edward VII's Hospital for Officers, since 1995; St Luke's Hospital for the Clergy, since 2000; *b* 12 April 1951; *s* of Lt-Col Derek Bourne Jagger and Pamela (*née* Jarratt); *m* 1977 Sarah Elisabeth Lee; one *s* one *d*. *Educ:* Uppingham; St Thomas' Hosp., London (MB, BS 1974); DO 1979. FRCS 1981; FRCOphth 1989. Registrar, Westminster Hosp., 1979–80; Resident Surgical Officer, 1980–83, Sen. Resident, 1983, Moorfields Eye Hosp.; Sen. Registrar, Western Ophthalmic Hosp. and Moorfields Eye Hosp., 1983–86; Cons. Ophthalmic Surgeon, UCH and Middx Hosp., 1986–89; Surgeon-Oculist to HM Household, 1999–2002. Cons. Ophthalmologist, Assoc. of Royal Naval Officers, 1998–. Mem. Council, RCOphth, 1990–94; Mem., Ophthalmic Qualifications Cttee, 1993–. FRSocMed. *Publications:* articles on cataract surgery, lasers, retinal disorders. *Recreations:* travel, ski-ing, DIY. *Address:* 149 Harley Street, W1G 6DE.

JAGGER, Sir Michael Philip, (Sir Mick), Kt 2002; singer, songwriter and film producer; *b* Dartford, Kent, 26 July 1943; *s* of late Basil Fanshawe, (Joe), Jagger and Eva Jagger; *m* 1st, 1971, Bianca Rose Pérez Morena de Macías (marr. diss. 1979); one *d*; 2nd, 1990, Jerry Hall (marr. diss. 1999); two *s* two *d*; one *d* by Marsha Hunt; one *s* by Luciana Gimenez Morad. *Educ:* Dartford Grammar Sch.; LSE. Lead singer, Rolling Stones, 1962–; tours worldwide, 1964–. *Records include: albums:* The Rolling Stones, 1964; The Rolling Stones No 2, 1965; Out of Our Heads, 1965; Aftermath, 1966; Between the Buttons, 1967; Their Satanic Majesties Request, 1967; Beggars' Banquet, 1968; Let It Bleed, 1969; Get Yer Ya-Ya's Out!, 1970; Sticky Fingers, 1971; Exile on Main Street, 1972; Goat's Head Soup, 1973; It's Only Rock 'n' Roll, 1974; Black and Blue, 1976; Some Girls, 1978; Emotional Rescue, 1980; Tattoo You, 1981; Still Life, 1982; Undercover, 1983; Dirty Work, 1986; Steel Wheels (also prod.), 1989; Flashpoint, 1991; Voodoo Lounge, 1994; Bridges to Babylon, 1997; Bent, 1997; No Security, 1998; Forty Licks, 2002; A Bigger Bang, 2005; *solo albums:* She's the Boss, 1985; Primitive Cool, 1987; Wandering Spirit, 1993; Goddess in the Doorway, 2001. *Films include:* Performance, 1970; Ned Kelly, 1970; Freejack, 1992; Shine a Light, 2008; producer, Enigma, 2001. Founded film prodn co., Jagged Films. *Address:* c/o Project Associates, Queens House, 1 Leicester Place, WC2H 7BP.

JAGLAND, Thorbjørn; MP (Lab) Norway, since 1993; President of Storting, since 2005; *b* 5 Nov. 1950; *m* 1975, Hanne Grotjord; two *s*. *Educ:* Univ. of Oslo. Leader, Labour Youth League, 1977–81; Labour Party of Norway: Res. and Analysis Sec., 1981–86; Party Sec., 1986–92; Leader, 1992–2002. Prime Minister of Norway, 1996–97; Minister of Foreign Affairs, 2000–01. Chm., Standing Cttee on Foreign Affairs, 2001–05. *Publications:* My European Dream, 1990; New Solidarity, 1993; Letters, 1995. *Recreations:* ski-ing, outdoor activities, literature. *Address:* Stortinget, 0026 Oslo, Norway.

JAGO, David Edgar John; Communar of Chichester Cathedral, 1987–92; *b* 2 Dec. 1937; *s* of late Edgar George Jago and of Violet Jago; *m* 1st, 1963, Judith Lissenden, DPhil (*d* 1995); one *s* one *d*; 2nd, 1997, Gertraud Marianne, (Gerty), Apfelbeck. *Educ:* King Edward's Sch., Bath; Pembroke Coll., Oxford (MA). National Service, RA, 1956–58. Asst Principal, Admiralty, 1961; Private Sec. to Permanent Under Sec. of State (RN), 1964–65; Principal 1965; Directing Staff, IDC, 1968–70; Private Sec. to Parly Under Sec. of State for Defence (RN), 1971–73; Ministry of Defence: Asst Sec., 1973; Asst Under Sec. of State: Aircraft, 1979–82; Naval Staff, 1982–84; Under Sec., Cabinet Office, 1984–86. Gov., Bedgebury Sch., 1996–2000. *Recreations:* theatre, opera, military history, supporting Arsenal FC. *Club:* Oxford and Cambridge.

JAGPAL, Jagdip; executive search consultant, since 2007; *b* London, 22 Nov. 1964; *d* of late Darshan Singh and of Jaswant. *Educ:* London Sch. of Econs and Pol Sci. (LLB Hons); Coll. of Law. Man. Ed., Butterworths Ltd, 1986–91; Solicitor, Rubinstein Callingham Polden & Gale, 1992–95; BBC Radio: lawyer, 1995–96; Chief Asst to Controller, Radio 4, 1996–99; Man. Dir, Network Television Prodn, SMG plc, 1999–2002; Chief Exec., Cloisters, 2004–07. Non-executive Director: Franklin Rae Communications Ltd, 2002–; Noel Gay Artists Ltd, 2004–. Trustee, Wallace Collection, 2007–. *Recreations:* museums, cinema, swimming, cycling, London, fashion, opera, watching sport and Columbo. *Address:* 9 Hepworth Court, Gatliff Road, SW1W 8QN; *e-mail:* jagdip@mac.com.

JAHN, Dr Wolfgang; Managing Director, Commerzbank AG, Düsseldorf, 1969–84; *b* 27 Sept. 1918; *s* of Dr Georg Jahn and Ella (*née* Schick); *m* 1949, Gabriele (*née* Beck); two *s* one *d*. *Educ:* Zürich Univ.; Berlin Univ.; Heidelberg Univ. (DrEcon). Industrial Credit Bank, Düsseldorf, 1949–54; IBRD, Washington, 1954–57; Commerzbank AG, Düsseldorf, 1957–84. *Address:* c/o Commerzbank AG, PO Box 101137, 40002 Düsseldorf, Germany.

JAHODA, Prof. Gustav, FBA 1988; FRSE; Professor of Psychology, University of Strathclyde, 1964–85, now Emeritus Professor; *b* 11 Oct. 1920; *s* of late Olga and Leopold Jahoda; *m* 1950, Jean Catherine (*née* Buchanan) (*d* 1991); three *s* one *d*. *Educ:* Vienna, Paris, Univ. of London. MScEcon, PhD. FRSE 1993. Tutor, Oxford Extra-Mural Delegacy, 1946–68; Lectr, Univ. of Manchester, 1948–51; Univ. of Ghana, 1952–56; Sen. Lectr, Univ. of Glasgow, 1956–63. Visiting Professor, Universities of: Ghana, 1968; Tilburg, 1984; Kansai, Osaka, 1985; Ecole des Hautes Etudes, Paris, 1986; Saarbrücken, 1987; New York, 1987; Geneva, 1990. Fellow, Netherlands Inst. of Advanced Studies, 1980–81; Hon. Fellow, Internat. Assoc. for Cross-Cultural Psychology (Pres., 1972–74); Membre d'Honneur, Assoc. pour la Recherche Inter-culturelle, 1986. *Publications:* White Man, 1961, 2nd edn 1983; The Psychology of Superstition, 1969, 8th edn 1979; Psychology and Anthropology, 1982 (French edn 1989; Japanese edn 1992); (with I. M. Lewis) Acquiring Culture, 1988; Crossroads between Culture and Mind, 1992; Images of Savages, 1999; A History of Social Psychology, 2007; contribs to learned jls. *Recreations:* fishing, gardening. *Address:* c/o Department of Psychology, University of Strathclyde, Glasgow G1 1RD. *Club:* University of Strathclyde Staff.

JAINE, Tom William Mahony; Proprietor, Prospect Books, since 1993; freelance writer; *b* 4 June 1943; *s* of William Edwin Jaine and Aileen (*née* Mahony); *m* 1st, 1965, Susanna F. Fisher; 2nd, 1973, Patience Mary Welsh (decd); two *d*; 3rd, 1983, Sally Caroline Agnew; two *d*. *Educ:* Kingswood Sch., Bath; Balliol Coll., Oxford (BA Hons). Asst Registrar, Royal Commn on Historical Manuscripts, 1967–73; Partner, Carved Angel Restaurant, Dartmouth, 1974–84; publisher, The Three Course Newsletter (and predecessors), 1980–89; Petits Propos Culinaires; Editor, Good Food Guide, 1989–94. Wine and Food Writer of the Year, Glenfiddich Awards, 2000. *Publications:* Cooking in the Country, 1986; Cosmic Cuisine, 1988; Making Bread at Home, 1995; Building a Wood-Fired Oven, 1996; contribs Sunday Telegraph, etc. *Recreations:* baking, buildings. *Address:* Allaleigh House, Blackawton, Totnes, Devon TQ9 7DL.

JAKEMAN, Prof. Eric, FRS 1990; Professor of Applied Statistical Optics, University of Nottingham, 1996–2004, now Professor Emeritus; *b* 3 June 1939; *s* of Frederick Leonard Jakeman and Hilda Mary Hays; *m* 1968, Glenys Joan Cooper; two *d*. *Educ:* Brunts Grammar Sch., Mansfield; Univ. of Birmingham (BSc, PhD). FInstP 1979. Asst Res. Physicist, UCLA, 1963–64. DRA (formerly RRE, subseq. RSRE), 1964–95 (DCSO, 1985–95). Hon. Sec., Inst. of Physics, 1994–2003 (Vice-Pres. for Publications, 1989–93); Mem. Exec. Cttee, European Physical Soc., 1990–94. Fellow, Optical Soc. of America, 1988. Maxwell Medal and Prize, Inst. of Physics, 1977; (jtly) MacRobert Award, 1977; (jtly) Instrument Makers' Co. Award. *Publications:* numerous contribs to learned jls. *Recreations:* gardening, music, beekeeping. *Address:* University of Nottingham, University Park, Nottingham NG7 2RD.

JALLOH, Sulaiman T.; *see* Tejan-Jalloh.

JAMES; *see* Streatfeild-James.

JAMES, family name of **Baron Northbourne**.

JAMES OF BLACKHEATH, Baron *cr* 2006 (Life Peer), of Wildbrooks in the County of West Sussex; **David Noel James,** CBE 1992; Chairman, Litigation Control Group Ltd, 2002–06; *b* 7 Dec. 1937; *m* 2004, Caroline Webster. Lloyds Bank, 1959–64; Chairman: Eagle Trust plc, 1989–97; Davies & Newman, 1990–92; New Millennium Experience Co., 2000–01; Racecourse Holdings Trust, 2003–05. *Address:* House of Lords, SW1A 0PW.

JAMES OF HOLLAND PARK, Baroness *cr* 1991 (Life Peer), of Southwold in the County of Suffolk; **Phyllis Dorothy White, (P. D. James),** OBE 1983; JP; FRSL; author; *b* 3 Aug. 1920; *d* of Sidney Victor James and Dorothy Amelia James (*née* Hone); *m* 1941, Connor Bantry White (*d* 1964); two *d*. *Educ:* Cambridge Girls' High Sch. Administrator, National Health Service, 1949–68; Civil Service: apptd Principal, Home Office, 1968; Police Dept, 1968–72; Criminal Policy Dept, 1972–79. Associate Fellow, Downing Coll., Cambridge, 1986. A Gov., BBC, 1988–93; Member: BBC Gen. Adv. Council, 1987–88; Arts Council, 1988–92 (Chm., Literature Adv. Panel, 1988–92); Bd, British Council, 1988–93 (Mem., Literature Cttee, 1988–93). Chm., Booker Prize Panel of Judges, 1987. Pres., Soc. of Authors, 1997– (Chm., 1984–86); Mem., Detection Club. JP: Willesden, 1979–82; Inner London, 1984. FRSL 1987; FRSA. Hon. Fellow: St Hilda's Coll., Oxford, 1996; Downing Coll., Cambridge, 2000; Girton Coll., Cambridge, 2000. Hon. DLitt: Buckingham, 1992; Hertfordshire, 1994; Glasgow, 1995; Durham, 1998; Portsmouth, 1999; Hon. DLit London, 1993; DU Essex, 1996. Awarded many major prizes for crime writing in GB, America, Italy and Scandinavia; Grand Master award, Mystery Writers of America, 1999. *Publications:* Cover Her Face, 1962 (televised 1985); A Mind to Murder, 1963 (televised 1995); Unnatural Causes, 1967 (televised 1993); Shroud for a Nightingale, 1971 (televised 1984); (with T. A. Critchley) The Maul and the Pear Tree, 1971; An Unsuitable Job for a Woman, 1972 (filmed 1982; televised 1998); The Black Tower, 1975 (televised 1986); Death of an Expert Witness, 1977 (televised 1983); Innocent Blood, 1980; The Skull beneath the Skin, 1982; A Taste for Death, 1986 (televised 1988); Devices and Desires, 1989 (televised 1991); The Children of Men, 1992; Original Sin, 1994 (televised 1997); A Certain Justice, 1997 (televised 1998); A Time to be in Earnest: a fragment of autobiography, 1999; Death in Holy Orders, 2001 (televised 2003); (ed with Harriet Harvey Wood) Sightlines, 2001; The Murder Room, 2003; The Lighthouse, 2005; The Private Patient, 2008. *Recreations:* exploring churches, walking by the sea. *Address:* c/o Greene & Heaton Ltd, 37 Goldhawk Road, W12 8QQ.

JAMES, Anne Eleanor S.; *see* Scott-James.

JAMES, (Arthur) Walter; Principal, St Catharine's, Windsor, 1974–82 (Hon. Fellow, 2006); *b* 30 June 1912; *s* of late W. J. James, OBE; *m* 1st, 1939, Elisabeth (marr. diss. 1956), *e d* of Richard Rylands Howroyd; one *d*; 2nd, 1957, Ann Jocelyn (*d* 2004), *y d* of late C. A. Leavy Burton; one *d* and one adopted *s* two adopted *d*. *Educ:* Uckfield Grammar Sch.; Keble Coll., Oxford (Scholar); 1st Cl. Mod. Hist.; Liddon Student; Arnold Essay Prizeman. Senior Demy of Magdalen Coll., 1935; Scholar in Mediæval Studies, British School at Rome, 1935; Editorial staff, Manchester Guardian, 1937–46. NFS 1939–45. Contested (L) Bury, Lancs, 1945. Dep. Editor, The Times Educational Supplement, 1947–51, Editor, 1952–69; Special Advisor on Educn, Times Newspapers, 1969–71; also Editor, Technology, 1957–60. Reader in Journalism, Univ. of Canterbury, NZ, 1971–74. Member: BBC Gen. Advisory Council, 1956–64; Council of Industrial Design, 1961–66; Council, Royal Society of Arts, 1964; Cttee, British-American Associates, 1964; Governor, Central School of Art and Design, 1966. Woodard Lecturer, 1965. *Publications:* (Ed.) Temples and Faiths 1958; The Christian in Politics, 1962; The Teacher and his World, 1962; A Middle-class Parent's Guide to Education, 1964; (contrib.) Looking Forward to the Seventies, 1967. *Recreation:* gardening. *Address:* 1 Cumberland Mews, The Great Park, Windsor, Berks SL4 2JD. *T:* (01784) 431377. *Club:* National Liberal.

JAMES, Basil; Special Commissioner, 1963–82, Presiding Special Commissioner, 1982–83; *b* 25 May 1918; *s* of late John Elwyn James, MA (Oxon.), Cardiff, and Mary Janet (*née* Lewis), Gwaelodygarth, Glam; *m* 1943, Moira Houlding Rayner, MA (Cantab.), *d* of late Capt. Benjamin Harold Rayner, North Staffs Regt, and Elizabeth (*née* Houlding), Preston, Lancs; one *s* twin *d*. *Educ:* Llandovery Coll.; Canton High Sch., Cardiff; Christ's Coll., Cambridge (Exhibnr). Tancred Law Student, Lincoln's Inn, 1936; Squire Law Scholar, Cambridge, 1936. BA 1939; MA 1942. Called to Bar, Lincoln's Inn, 1940. Continuous sea service as RNVR officer in small ships on anti-submarine and convoy duties in Atlantic, Arctic and Mediterranean, 1940–45. King George V Coronation Scholar, Lincoln's Inn, 1946. Practised at Chancery Bar, 1946–63. Admitted to Federal Supreme Court of Nigeria, 1962. *Publications:* contrib. to Atkin's Court Forms and Halsbury's Laws of England. *Recreations:* music, gardening.

See also J. E. R. James.

JAMES, Cecil; *see* James, T. C. G.

JAMES, Charles Edwin Frederic; His Honour Judge Charles James; a Circuit Judge, since 1993; *b* 17 April 1943; *s* of Frederic Crockett Gwilym James and Marjorie Peggy James (*née* Peace); *m* 1968, Diana Mary Francis (*née* Thornton); two *s*. *Educ:* Trent College, Long Eaton, Derbyshire; Selwyn College, Cambridge. MA 1968. Called to the Bar, Inner Temple, 1965; practised on Northern Circuit, 1965–93; Jun. of Northern Circuit, 1966. A Recorder, 1982–93. *Recreation:* family pursuits. *Clubs:* Cambridge University Cricket; Royal Liverpool Golf, Royal Mersey Yacht.

JAMES, Christopher John; Deputy Chairman, R. Griggs Group Ltd, 1994–2000 (Director, 1993–2000); *b* 20 March 1932; *s* of John Thomas Walters James, MC and Cicely Hilda James; *m* 1958, Elizabeth Marion Cicely Thomson; one *s* one *d*. *Educ:* Clifton Coll., Bristol; Magdalene Coll., Cambridge (MA). Served RA, 2nd Lieut, 1951–52; TA, 1952–60. Admitted Solicitor, 1958; Partner, Johnson & Co., Birmingham, 1960–87 (Sen. Partner, 1985–87); Dep. Sen. Partner, Martineau Johnson, 1987–89, Sen. Partner, 1989–94. Director: Birmingham Building Soc., then Birmingham Midshires Building Soc., 1980–96 (Dep. Chm., 1988–90; Chm., 1990–96); Police Mutual Assurance Soc., 1996–2001. Gen. Comr for Income Tax, 1974–82. Pres., Birmingham Law Soc., 1983–84. Chm., Kalamazoo Trust, 1997–2001. Mem. Council, Edgbaston High Sch. for Girls, 1980–90 (Chm., 1987–90); Gov., Clifton Coll., 1980–99. *Recreations:* photography, railways, trying to get the better of my computer, water colour painting.

JAMES, His Honour Christopher Philip; a Circuit Judge, 1980–97; *b* 27 May 1934; *yr s* of late Herbert Edgar James, CBE, and Elizabeth Margaret James (*née* Davies). *Educ:* Felsted School; Magdalene Coll., Cambridge (MA). Commnd RASC, 1953. Called to the Bar, Gray's Inn, 1959; a Recorder of the Crown Court, 1979; Judge of Woolwich County Court, 1982–92, of Lambeth County Court, 1992–97. *Address:* Flat 8, 93 Elm Park Gardens, SW10 9QW. *Club:* Oxford and Cambridge.

JAMES, Clive Vivian Leopold, AM 1992; writer and broadcaster; Director, clivejames.com, since 2005; *b* 7 Oct. 1939; *s* of Albert Arthur James and Minora May (*née* Darke). *Educ:* Sydney Technical High Sch.; Sydney Univ. (BA Hons); Pembroke Coll., Cambridge (MA). President of Footlights when at Cambridge. Dir, Watchmaker Prodns, 1994–99. Record albums as lyricist for Pete Atkin: Beware of the Beautiful Stranger; Driving through Mythical America; A King at Nightfall; The Road of Silk; Secret Drinker; Live Libel; The Master of the Revels; Touch has a Memory, 1991; Midnight Voices, the Clive James-Pete Atkin Songbook Vol. 1, 2008. Song-book with Pete Atkin: A First Folio. *Television series:* Cinema, Up Sunday, So It Goes, A Question of Sex, Saturday Night People, Clive James on Television, The Late Clive James, The Late Show with Clive James, Saturday Night Clive, The Talk Show with Clive James, Clive James—Fame in the Twentieth Century, Review of the Year, Sunday Night Clive, The Clive James Show, Clive James on Television (1997); Clive James Talking; *television documentaries:* Shakespeare in Perspective: Hamlet, 1980; The Clive James Paris Fashion Show, Clive James and the Calendar Girls, 1981; The Return of the Flash of lightning, 1982; Clive James Live in Las Vegas, 1982; Clive James meets Roman Polanski, 1984; The Clive James Great American Beauty Pageant, 1984; Clive James in Dallas, 1985; Clive James Meets Katherine Hepburn, 1986; Clive James on Safari, 1986; Clive James and the Heroes of San Francisco, 1987; Clive James in Japan, 1987; Clive James meets Jane Fonda, Clive James on the 80s, 1989; Clive James meets Damon Hill, The Clive James Formula One Show, 1997; Clive James meets Mel Gibson, 1998; Clive James meets the Supermodels, 1998; Postcard series, 1989–: Rio, Chicago, Paris, Miami, Rome, Shanghai, Sydney, London, Cairo, New York, Bombay, Berlin, Buenos Aires, Nashville, Hong Kong, Mexico City, Las Vegas, Havana. Hon. Fellow, Australian Acad. of the Humanities, 2006. Hon. DLitt: Sydney, 1999; UEA. Philip Hodgkins Meml Medal, 2003. *Publications:*

non-fiction: The Metropolitan Critic, 1974, 2nd edn 1994; The Fate of Felicity Fark in the Land of the Media, 1975; Peregrine Prykke's Pilgrimage through the London Literary World, 1976; Britannia Bright's Bewilderment in the Wilderness of Westminster, 1976; Visions Before Midnight, 1977; At the Pillars of Hercules, 1979; First Reactions, 1980; The Crystal Bucket, 1981; Charles Charming's Challenges on the Pathway to the Throne, 1981; From the Land of Shadows, 1982; Glued to the Box, 1982; Flying Visits, 1984; Snakecharmers in Texas, 1988; On Television, 1991; The Dreaming Swimmer, 1992; Fame, 1993; Reliable Essays, 2001; Even As We Speak, 2001; The Meaning of Recognition: new essays 2001–2005, 2005; Cultural Amnesia, 2007; *fiction:* Brilliant Creatures, 1983; The Remake, 1987; Brrm! Brrm!, 1991; The Silver Castle, 1996; *verse:* Fan-Mail, 1977; Poem of the Year, 1983; Other Passports: poems 1958–85, 1986; The Book of my Enemy: collected verse 1958–2003, 2003; *autobiography:* Unreliable Memoirs, 1980; Falling Towards England: Unreliable Memoirs II, 1985; May Week Was in June: Unreliable Memoirs III, 1990; Always Unreliable, 2001; North Face of Soho: Unreliable Memoirs IV, 2006.

JAMES, Rt Rev. Colin Clement Walter; Bishop of Winchester, 1985–95; *b* 20 Sept. 1926; *yr s* of late Canon Charles Clement Hancock James and Gwenyth Mary James; *m* 1962, Margaret Joan, (Sally), Henshaw (*d* 2001); one *s* two *d. Educ:* Aldenham School; King's College, Cambridge (MA, Hons History); Cuddesdon Theological College. Assistant Curate, Stepney Parish Church, 1952–55; Chaplain, Stowe School, 1955–59; BBC Religious Broadcasting Dept, 1959–67; Religious Broadcasting Organizer, BBC South and West, 1960–67; Vicar of St Peter with St Swithin, Bournemouth, 1967–73; Bishop Suffragan of Basingstoke, 1973–77; Canon Residentiary of Winchester Cathedral, 1973–77; Bishop of Wakefield, 1977–85. Member of General Synod, 1970–95; Chairman: Church Information Cttee, 1976–79; C of E's Liturgical Commn, 1986–93. Chm., BBC and IBA Central Religious Adv. Cttee, 1979–84. President: Woodard Corp., 1978–93; RADIUS, 1980–93. Chm., USPG, 1985–88. Hon. DLitt Southampton, 1996. *Recreations:* theatre, travelling. *Address:* 3 Back Street, Winchester SO23 9SB. *T:* (01962) 868874.

JAMES, Colin John Irwin, FIPD; producer, television documentaries, since 2005; Chief Executive, Roads Service, Northern Ireland, 1999–2002; *b* 17 Sept. 1942; *s* of William and Evelyn James; *m* 1968, Monica Jean Patston; one *s* one *d. Educ:* Royal Belfast Academical Instn; Queen's Univ., Belfast (BSc Hons 1965); University Coll. London (MPhil 1967). FIPD 1988; MCIH 1992; MIHT 1999. GLC, 1967–71; DoE (NI), 1971–73; NI Housing Exec., 1973–94; joined Defence Housing Exec., 1994, Chief Exec., 1995–99. *Recreations:* cycling, photography. *Address:* 10 Fort Road, Helens Bay, Co. Down BT19 1LA.

JAMES, Sir Cynlais Morgan, (Sir Kenneth), KCMG 1985 (CMG 1976); HM Diplomatic Service, retired; Director General, Canning House, 1987–92; *b* 29 April 1926; *s* of Thomas James and Lydia Ann James (*née* Morgan); *m* 1953, Mary Teresa, *d* of R. D. Girouard and Lady Blanche Girouard; two *d. Educ:* Trinity Coll., Cambridge (MA). Service in RAF, 1944–47. Cambridge 1948–51. Entered Senior Branch of Foreign Service, 1951; Foreign Office, 1951–53; Third Sec., Tokyo, 1953–56; Second Sec., Rio de Janeiro, 1956–59; First Sec. and Cultural Attaché, Moscow, 1959–62; FO, 1962–65; Paris, 1965–69; promoted Counsellor, 1968; Counsellor and Consul-General, Saigon, 1969–71; Head of W European Dept, FCO, 1971–75; NATO Defence Coll., Rome, 1975–76; Minister, Paris, 1976–81; Ambassador to Poland, 1981–83; Asst Under Sec. of State, FCO, 1983; Ambassador to Mexico, 1983–86. Director: Thomas Cook, 1986–91; Latin American Investment Trust, 1990–96; Foreign and Colonial Emerging Markets, 1993–96; Polish Investment Trust, 1996–2002; Consultant, Darwin Instruments, 1986–; Advr, Amerada Hess Ltd, 1997–. Chairman: British-Mexican Soc., 1987–90; British Inst. in Paris, 1988–2000; Bd, Inst. of Latin American Studies, 1992–98; Mem., Franco-British Council, 1986–99. Hon. Dr Mexican Acad. of Internat. Law, 1984. Order of the Aztec, 1st cl. (Mexico), 1985; Order of Andres Bello, 1st cl. (Venezuela), 1990; Order of Merit (Chile), 1991; Chevalier, Legion of Honour (France), 1995. *Recreation:* tennis. *Address:* 64 The Atrium, 30 Vincent Square, SW1P 2NW. *Clubs:* Brooks's, Beefsteak, Pratt's, MCC; Travellers (Paris).

JAMES, Rt Rev. David Charles; *see* Bradford, Bishop of.

JAMES, Prof. David Edward; Professor (formerly Director) of Adult Education, 1969–2002, University Professor, and Special Adviser to the Vice-Chancellor on Regional Academic Affairs, 2002–05, University of Surrey; *b* 31 July 1937; *s* of Charles Edward James and Dorothy Hilda (*née* Reeves); *m* 1963, Penelope Jane Murray; two *s* one *d. Educ:* Universities of Reading, Oxford, Durham, London (Bsc Hons Gen., BSc Hons Special, MEd, DipEd, DipFE); FRSH; FITD 1992. Lectr in Biology, City of Bath Tech. Coll. 1961–63; Lectr in Sci. and Educn, St Mary's Coll. of Educn, Newcastle upon Tyne, 1963–64; University of Surrey: Lectr in Educnl Psych., 1964–69; Hd, Dept of Educnl Studies, 1982–93; Dean of Associated Instns, 1996–2002. FRSA. *Publications:* A Student's Guide to Efficient Study, 1966, Amer. edn 1967; Introduction to Psychology, 1968, Italian edn 1972. *Recreation:* farming. *Address:* 30 Glendale Drive, Burpham, Guildford, Surrey GU4 7HZ.

JAMES, Dr (David) Geraint, FRCP; Consultant Ophthalmic Physician, St Thomas' Hospital, London, since 1973; Teacher, University of London, since 1979; *b* 2 Jan. 1922; *s* of David James and Sarah (*née* Davies); *m* 1951, Sheila Sherlock, (Dame Sheila Sherlock, DBE, FRS; *d* 2001); two *d. Educ:* Jesus Coll., Cambridge (MA 1945); Middx Hosp. Med. Sch., London (MD 1953); Columbia Univ., NYC. FRCP 1964. Consultant Physician, Royal Northern Hosp., 1959–86 (Dean, 1968–86). Adjunct Prof. of Medicine, Univ. of Miami, Fla, 1973–, and Prof. of Epidemiology, 1981–; Adjunct Prof., Royal Free Hosp. Med. Sch., 1987–; Consulting Phys. to RN, 1972–86; Hon. Consultant Phys., US Veterans' Admin, 1978–; Hon. Consulting Phys., Sydney Hosp., Australia, 1969–79. President: Internat. Cttee on Sarcoidosis, 1987–99 (World Exec. Sec., 1980–86); Italian Congress on Sarcoidosis, 1983; World Assoc. of Sarcoidosis, 1987–; Vice-Pres., Fellowship of Postgrad. Medicine; Past President: Med. Soc. of London; Harveian Soc.; Osler Club (Hon. Fellow); Pres., London Glamorgan Soc., 1989–; Vice-Pres., Cymmrodorion Soc., 2004–. Lectures: Tudor Edwards, RCP and RCS, 1983; George Wise Meml, New York City, 1983. Foreign Corresponding Mem., French Nat. Acad. of Medicine, 1987; Hon. Corresp. Mem., Thoracic Socs of Italy, France, Dominican Republic and Portugal; Hon. FACP 1990; Hon. FRCOphth, 1994. Editor, Internat. Rev. of Sarcoidosis, 1984–95. Freeman, City of London, 1961. Hon. LLD Wales, 1982. Chesterfield Medal, Inst. of Dermatology, London, 1957; Gold Medal, Barraquer Inst. of Ophthalmology, 1958; Carlo Forlanini Gold Medal, Italian Thoracic Soc., 1983. Gold Medal, Milan, 1987. Kt of Order of Christopher Columbus (Dominican Republic), 1987. *Publications:* Diagnosis and Treatment of Infections, 1957; Sarcoidosis, 1970; Circulation of the Blood, 1978; Atlas of Respiratory Diseases, 1981, 2nd edn 1992; Sarcoidosis and other Granulomatous Disorders, 1985; Textbook on Sarcoidosis and other Granulomatous Disorders, 1994; The Granulomatous Disorders, 1999. *Recreations:* history of medicine, international Welshness, Rugby football. *Address:* 41 York Terrace East, NW1 4PT. *T:* (020) 7486 4560. *Club:* Athenæum.

JAMES, Dr David Gwynfor; Head of Meteorological Research Flight, Royal Aircra[ft] Establishment, Farnborough, 1971–82; *b* 16 April 1925; *s* of William James and Margar[et] May Jones; *m* 1953, Margaret Vida Gower; two *d. Educ:* Univ. of Wales, Cardiff (BS[c], PhD). Joined Meteorological Office, 1950; Met. Res. Flight, Farnborough, 195[1]; Forecasting Res., Dunstable, 1953; Christmas Island, Pacific, 1958; Satellite Lab., U[S] Weather Bureau, 1961; Cloud Physics Res., Bracknell, 1966; Met. Res. Flight, RA[E], 1971. Fellow, UC Cardiff, 1987. *Publications:* papers in Qly Jl Royal Met. Soc., [Jl] Atmospheric Sciences, Met. Res. Papers, and Nature. *Recreations:* golf, choral singing.

JAMES, Derek Claude, OBE 1989; Director of Social Services, Leeds, 1978–89; *b* [..] March 1929; *s* of Cecil Claude James and Violet (*née* Rudge); *m* 1954, Evelyn (*née* Thomas); one *s* one *d. Educ:* King Edward's Grammar Sch., Camp Hill, Birmingham; Open Univ. (BA). Dip. in Municipal Admin. Local Government: Birmingham, 1946–6[0]; Coventry, 1960–63; Bradford, 1963–69; Leeds, 1969–89. Mem., Yorks and Humberside RHA, 1976–82; Chm., Leeds Area Review Cttee (Child Abuse), 1978–89; Mem., Na[t]. Adv. Council on Employment of Disabled People, 1984–89; Pres., Nat. Assoc. of Nurser[y] and Family Care, 1988–92; Chairman: Nightstop Homeless Persons Project, 1989–92; Nightstop Trust, Leeds, 1993–2000; Disabled Living Centre, Leeds, 1994–2002 (Mem. Exec. Cttee, 2002–); Vice-Chm., Nat. Family Service Units, 1992–96 (Mem. Nat. Cttee 1992–96); Expert Panel Mem., Registered Homes Tribunal, 1990–96; Adviser: AM[A] Social Services Cttee, 1983–89; Physical Disablement Res. Liaison Gp, 1986–8[9]; Sanctuary Housing Association: Chm., North and West Yorks Area Cttee, 1992–2001; Member: North Divl Cttee, 1992–97; North Regl Cttee, 2004–; Central Council 1993–97, 2001–03; Scrutiny Cttee, 2004–; Chm., Care Cttee, 1998–2003; Chairman and non-executive Director: Sanctuary Care Co., 2002–; Sanctuary Home Care Co., 2003–; Non-exec. Dir, Neuroscis and Maxillo-Facial Surgery Subsid. Governing Body, United Leeds Teaching Hosps Trust, 1997–98. *Recreations:* watching sport, garden pottering, acceding to my grandchildren's wishes. *Address:* Hill House, Woodhall Hills, Calverley, Pudsey, West Yorks LS28 5QY. *T:* (0113) 2578044.

JAMES, Hon. Edison Chenfil; MP (UWP) Marigot, Dominica; Leader of th[e] Opposition, since 2000; *b* 18 Oct. 1943; *s* of David and Patricia James; *m* 1970, Wilma; one *s* two *d. Educ:* North East London Poly. (BSc Hons); Univ. of Reading (MSc); Imperial Coll., London (Dip. Pest Management). Teacher, St Mary's Acad., 197[3]; Agronomist, Min. of Agriculture, Dominica, 1974–76; Farm Improvement Officer, Caribbean Develt Bank and Agric. and Indust. Develt Bank, 1976–80; Project Co-ordinator, Coconut Rehabilitation; Gen. Manager, Dominica Banana Marketing Corp. 1980–87; Man. Dir, Agric. Managing Corp., 1987–95. Prime Minister, Dominica 1995–2000. *Recreations:* cricket, football, table tennis, politics, international affairs. *Address:* Parliament of Dominica, Roseau, Dominica, West Indies. *T:* 4482401. *Club:* Rotary Club of Dominica.

JAMES, (Edwin) Kenneth (George); Chairman, Photon plc, 1986–89, retired; Chie[f] Scientific Officer, Civil Service Department, 1970–76; *b* 27 Dec. 1916; *s* of late Edwi[n] and Jessie Marion James; *m* 1941, Dorothy Margaret Pratt (*d* 1998); one *d. Educ:* Latymer Upper Sch.; Northern Polytechnic. BSc London; FRSC; FOR. Joined War Office, 1938; Chem. Defence Exper. Stn, 1942; Aust. Field Exper. Stn, 1944–46; Operational Research Gp, US Army, Md, 1950–54; Dir, Biol and Chem. Defence, WO, 1961; Army (late Defence) Op. Res. Estab., Byfleet, 1965; HM Treasury (later Civil Service Dept), 1968; Chm., PAG Ltd, 1984–87 (Dir, 1977–84). Chm., Maths Cttee, SRC, 1974–77. Mem. Soc. of Authors. Silver Medal, Op. Res. Soc., 1979. *Publications:* Strew on her Roses, Roses (memoir), 2000; Escoffier: the King of Chefs, 2002; A to Z of What to Cook, 2003; A to Z of Puddings, 2004; Sage in May (novel), 2004; Biography of a Century, 2005; A to Z of Starters and Light Lunches, 2006; They Made Us What We Are, 2007. *Recreation:* writing. *Address:* 5 Watersmeet Road, Harnham, Salisbury, Wilts SP2 8JH. *T:* (01722) 334099. *Club:* Athenæum.

JAMES, Eleanor Mary; Lecturer in Mathematics, University College of Wales Aberystwyth, 1957–92; *b* 31 Aug. 1935; *d* of Morris and Violet Mary Jones; *m* 1958, David Bryan James. *Educ:* Ardwyn Grammar Sch., Aberystwyth; University College of Wales Aberystwyth (BSc 1955; PhD 1972). Member: Welsh Consumer Council, 1981–90; CECG, 1982–84; Consumer Develt Sub-Cttee, Nat. Consumer Council, 1983–85; Layfield Cttee of Enquiry, Local Govt Finance, 1974–76; Audit Commn for Local Authorities and NHS, 1988–91; Dyfed-Powys Police Authy, 1994–99. Member: N Wales Area Cttee, NACAB (formerly CAB), 1987–90, 1991–99 (Chm., Aberystwyth, 1988–93, 1998–2000); POUNC, 1991–97 (Chm., Council for Wales, 1991–97); Radioactive Waste Management Adv. Cttee, 1991–94; Wkg Pty, Churches' Enquiry into Unemployment and Future of Work, 1995–97; Chm., Wales Rural Forum, 1994–97; Campaign for the Protection of Rural Wales: Chm., Ceredigion Br., 1992–2000; Mem., Exec. Cttee, 1996–2004; Vice-Chm., 2001–04. National Federation of Women's Institutes: Mem., Envmt and Public Affairs Sub-Cttee, 1981–84; Vice Chm., Fedn of Wales Sub-Cttee, 1991–94; Chm., Dyfed Ceredigion Fedn of WIs, 1993–96 (Treas., 1989–92). University College of Wales: Mem. Council, 1982–86; Mem., Court of Governors, 1982–; Treas., Old Students' Assoc., 1975–. *Publication:* (with T. V. Davies) Nonlinear Differential Equations, 1966. *Recreations:* walking, the WI. *Address:* Dolhuan, Llandre, Bowstreet, Ceredigion SY24 5AB. *T:* (01970) 828362.

JAMES, Rev. Canon Eric Arthur; an Extra Chaplain to HM the Queen, since 1995 (Chaplain, 1984–95); Hon. Director, Christian Action, 1990–96 (Director, 1979–90); *b* 14 April 1925; *s* of John Morgan James and Alice Amelia James. *Educ:* Dagenham County High School; King's Coll. London (MA, BD; FKC 1986). Asst Curate, St Stephen with St John, Westminster, 1951–55; Chaplain Trinity Coll., Cambridge, 1955–59; Select Preacher to Univ. of Cambridge, 1959–60; Vicar of St George, Camberwell and Warden of Trinity College Mission, 1959–64; Director of Parish and People, 1964–69; Proctor in Convocation, 1964–72; Canon Precentor of Southwark Cathedral, 1964–73; Canon Residentiary and Missioner, Diocese of St Albans, 1973–83; Hon. Canon, 1983–90; Canon Emeritus, 1990. Preacher to Gray's Inn, 1978–97; Select Preacher to Univ. of Oxford, 1991–92. Commissary to Bishop of Kimberley, 1965–67, to Archbishop of Melanesia, 1969–93. Examining Chaplain to Bishop of St Albans, 1973–83, to Bishop of Truro, 1983–93. Hon. Bencher Gray's Inn, 1997. FRSA 1992. DD Lambeth, 1993. *Publications:* The Double Cure, 1957, 2nd edn 1980; Odd Man Out, 1962; (ed) Spirituality for Today, 1968; (ed) Stewards of the Mysteries of God, 1979; A Life of Bishop John A. T. Robinson: Scholar, Pastor, Prophet, 1987; (ed) God's Truth, 1988; Judge Not: a selection of sermons preached in Gray's Inn Chapel, 1989; Collected Thoughts: fifty scripts for BBC's Thought for The Day, 1990; (ed) A Last Eccentric: a symposium concerning the Rev. Canon F. A. Simpson: historian, preacher and eccentric, 1991; Word Over All: forty sermons 1985–1991, 1992; The Voice Said, Cry: forty sermons 1990–1993, 1994; A Time to Speak: forty sermons 1993–95, 1997; In Season, Out of Season: sermons 1996–97, 1999; Who Is This?: Holy Week meditations and other sermons 1998–2000, 2001; Collected Thoughts: BBC Radio 4 Thought for the Day broadcasts, 2002; The House of My Friends: memories and reflections, 2003; The Voice of This Calling: twenty-five sermons, 2005; Old Men Ought to be Explorers: the journal of a journey, 2006. *Address:* 11 Denny Crescent, SE11 4UY. *T:* (020) 7582 3068. *Clubs:* Reform, Royal Commonwealth Society.

JAMES, Evan Maitland; *b* 14 Jan. 1911; *er s* of late A. G. James, CBE, and late Helen James (*née* Maitland); *m* 1st, 1939, Joan Goodnow (*d* 1989), *d* of late Hon. J. V. A. MacMurray, State Dept, Washington, DC; one *s* one *d* (and one *d* decd); 2nd, 1992, Miriam Beatriz Porter, *d* of late George and Elizabeth Wansbrough. *Educ:* Durnford; Eton (Oppidan Scholar); Trinity Coll., Oxford (MA). Served War of 1939–45: War Reserve Police (Metropolitan), 1939; BBC Overseas (Propaganda Research) Dept, 1940–41; Ordinary Seaman/Lieut, RNVR, 1941–46. Clerk of the Merchant Taylors' Company, 1947–62; Steward of Christ Church, Oxford, 1962–78. *Address:* Upwood Park, Besselsleigh, Abingdon, Oxon OX13 5QE. *T:* (01865) 390535. *Club:* Travellers.

JAMES, Prof. Frank Arthur John Lord, PhD; FRAS; Professor of the History of Science, since 2004, and Head, Collections and Heritage, since 1998, Royal Institution; *b* 7 March 1955; *s* of Arthur Montague James and Mary Patricia James (*née* Lord); *m* 1986, Joasia Hermaszewska; two *s* one *d*. *Educ:* Chelsea Coll. (BSc); Imperial Coll., London (MSc, DIC; PhD 1981). FRAS 1981. Associate, Univ. of London Inst. of Educn, 1981–82; Royal Institution: Res. Fellow, 1982–86; seconded to Marine Soc. serving in S Atlantic, 1984; Lectr, 1986–97; Reader in Hist. of Sci., 1997–2004. Vis. Res. Fellow, Sci. Studies Centre, Univ. of Bath, 1998–; Visiting Professor: UCL, 2007–; Centro Simão Mathias, São Paulo, 2008. Earnshaw Lectr, QUB, 2004. Mem., Exec. Cttee, COPUS, 1989–97. British Society for History of Science: Officer and Council Mem., 1989–2005; Vice-Pres., 2005–06, 2008–09; Pres., 2006–08; Newcomen Society for History of Engineering and Technology: Mem. Council, 1991–94, 1996–99 and 2005–07; Vice Pres., 1999–2003; Pres., 2003–05; British Association for Advancement of Science: Recorder of Hist. of Sci. Section, 1992–97; Mem. Council, 1995–2000. Jt Ed., History of Technol., 1989–96. *Publications:* (ed jtly) Faraday Rediscovered: essays on the life and work of Michael Faraday, 1791–1867, 1985; Chemistry and Theology in mid-Victorian London: The Diary of Herbert McLeod 1860–1870, 1987; (ed) The Place of Experiment: essays on the development of laboratories in industrial civilisation, 1989; (jtly) Faraday, 1991; (ed) The Correspondence of Michael Faraday, vol. 1 1991, vol. 2 1993, vol. 3 1996, vol. 4 1999, vol. 5 2008; (ed jtly) Renaissance and Revolution: humanists, scholars, craftsmen and natural philosophers in early modern Europe, 1993; (jtly) Science in Art: works in the National Gallery that illustrate the history of science and technology, 1997; (ed) Semaphores to Short Waves, 1998; Guide to the Microfilm edition of the Manuscripts of Michael Faraday (1791–1867) from the Collections of the Royal Institution, Institution of Electrical Engineers and Guildhall Library, 2000–01; (ed) The Common Purposes of Life: science and society at the Royal Institution of Great Britain, 2002; Guide to the Microfilm edition of the Letters of John Tyndall (1820–1893) from the Collections of the Royal Institution, 2003; Christmas at the Royal Institution: an anthology of lectures, 2007; contrib. many articles on nineteenth century science in its social, religious, military and cultural contexts. *Recreations:* swimming, walking in the country, visiting historic buildings, browsing in second hand bookshops. *Address:* Royal Institution, 21 Albemarle Street, W1S 4BS. *T:* (020) 7670 2924; *e-mail:* fjames@ri.ac.uk.

JAMES, Geraint; *see* James, D. G.

JAMES, Geraldine, OBE 2003; actress; *b* 6 July 1950; *d* of Gerald Trevor Thomas and Annabella Doogan Thomas; adopted stage name, Geraldine James, 1972; *m* 1986, Joseph Sebastian Blatchley; one *d*. *Educ:* Downe House, Newbury; Drama Centre London Ltd. *Stage:* repertory, Chester, 1972–74, Exeter, 1974–75, Coventry, 1975; Passion of Dracula, Queen's, 1978; The White Devil, Oxford, 1981; Turning Over, Bush, 1984; When I was a Girl I used to Scream and Shout, Whitehall, 1987; Cymbeline, National, 1988; Merchant of Venice, Phoenix, 1989, NY (Drama Desk Best Actress Award), 1990; Death and the Maiden, Duke of York's, 1992; Lysistrata, Old Vic and Wyndham's, 1993; Hedda Gabler, Royal Exchange, Manchester, 1993; Give Me Your Answer Do!, Hampstead, 1998; Faith Healer, Almeida, 2001; The Cherry Orchard, 2003, Home, 2004, Oxford Stage Co.; UN Inspector, RNT, 2005; The Exonerated, Riverside Studios, 2006; *TV series include:* The History Man, 1980; Jewel in the Crown, 1984; Blott on the Landscape, 1985; Echoes, 1988; Band of Gold, 1994, 1995; Kavanagh QC, 1994, 1995, 1997, 1998; Drover's Gold, 1996; Seesaw, 1998; The Sins, 2000; White Teeth, State of Play, 2002; Jane Hall, 2004; The Amazing Mrs Pritchard, 2006; Time of Your Life, 2007; The Last Enemy, 2008; *TV films include:* Dummy (Best Actress, BPG), 1977; A Doll's House, 1992; Doggin' Around, 1994; Crime and Punishment, 2001; Hound of the Baskervilles, 2002; Hex, 2004; Poirot, 2005; A Harlot's Progress, 2006; The Heist, 2008; *films include:* Sweet William, Night Cruiser, 1978; Gandhi, 1981; The Storm, 1985; Wolves of Willoughby Chase, 1988; The Tall Guy, She's Been Away, (Best actress, Venice Film Festival, 1989), 1989; If Looks Could Kill, The Bridge, 1990; Prince of Shadows, 1991; No Worries Australia, 1993; Words on the Window Pane, 1994; Moll Flanders, 1995; The Man Who Knew Too Little, 1998; All Forgotten, The Testimony of Taliesin Jones, The Luzhin Defence, 2000; An Angel for May, 2001; Calendar Girls, 2002; The Fever, 2003. *Recreation:* music. *Address:* c/o Julian Belfrage Associates, Adam House, 14 New Burlington Street, W1S 3BQ.

JAMES, Rt Rev. Graham Richard; *see* Norwich, Bishop of.

JAMES, Hamilton E.; President, Blackstone Group, since 2002; *b* 3 Feb. 1951; *s* of Hamilton R. James and Waleska Bacon Evans; *m* 1973, Amabel G. Boyce; one *s* two *d*. *Educ:* Harvard Coll. (AB *magna cum laude* 1973); Harvard Business Sch. (MBA with High Dist., Baker Schol. 1975). Chairman: Banking Gp, Donaldson, Lufkin & Jenrette, 1975–2000; Global Investment Banking and Private Equity, Credit Suisse First Boston, 2000–02. Director: Costco Corp., 1988–; Swift River Investments, 2005–; has served on other corporate bds. Member: various cttees, Harvard Univ., 1990–; Subcttee on Technology and Competitiveness, US President's Export Council; Bd, Council for US and Italy. Vice Chairman: Kennedy Center Corporate Fund Bd; Coldwater Conservation Fund, Trout Unlimited. Trustee: (and Chm.) American Ballet Th., 1992–2000; (and Mem., Exec. Cttee) Second Stage Th., 1995–. Trustee: Brearley Sch., 1996–2001; Choate Sch., 2000–. *Recreations:* fly-fishing, hunting, soccer, cycling, ski-ing, racquet sports. *Address:* Blackstone Group, 345 Park Avenue, New York, NY 10154, USA. *T:* (212) 5835455, *Fax:* (212) 5835460; *e-mail:* James@Blackstone.com. *Clubs:* River, Links (NY); Wee Burn Country (Darien, Conn.); Little Harbor (Harbor Springs, MI).

JAMES, Howell Malcolm Plowden, CBE 1997; Permanent Secretary, Government Communications, since 2004; *b* 13 March 1954; *s* of late T. J. and Virginia James. *Educ:* Mill Hill Sch., London. Head of Promotions, Capital Radio, 1978–82; Organiser, Help a London Child Charity, 1979–82; Head of Press and Publicity, TV-am, 1982–85; Special Adviser: Cabinet Office, 1985; Dept of Employment, 1985–87; DTI, 1987; Dir of Corporate Affairs, BBC, 1987–92; Dir of Corporate and Govt Affairs, Cable and Wireless, 1992–94; Pol Sec. to Prime Minister, 1994–97; Dir, Brown Lloyd James, 1997–2004. Mem., Review of Govt Communication, 2003. Dir, Broadcast Audience Res. Bd, 1987–92. Dir, Equilibrium Hotels (Riad El Fenn), 2003–. Director: English Nat. Ballet Sch., 1990–96; Chichester Fest. Th., 2005–. Gov., George Eliot Sch., 1989–92; Mem., Ct of Govs, Mill Hill Sch., 1996–2003. Trustee, Queen Elizabeth's Foundn for Disabled People Develt Trust, 1992–96. *Recreations:* theatre, movies, food. *Address:* Cabinet Office, 70 Whitehall, SW1A 2AS. *T:* (020) 7270 3000. *Clubs:* Garrick, Soho House.

JAMES, Prof. Ioan Mackenzie, FRS 1968; MA, DPhil; Savilian Professor of Geometry, Oxford University, 1970–95, Professor Emeritus, since 1995; Fellow of New College, Oxford, 1970–95, Emeritus Fellow, 1995, Leverhulme Emeritus Fellow, 1996–98, Hon. Fellow, 1999; Editor, Topology, since 1962; *b* 23 May 1928; *o s* of Reginald Douglas and Jessie Agnes James; *m* 1961, Rosemary Gordon Stewart, *qv*; no *c*. *Educ:* St Paul's Sch. (Foundn Schol.); Queen's Coll., Oxford (Open Schol.). Commonwealth Fund Fellow, Princeton, Berkeley and Inst. for Advanced Study, 1954–55; Tapp Res. Fellow, Gonville and Caius Coll., Cambridge, 1956; Reader in Pure Mathematics, Oxford, 1957–69, and Senior Research Fellow, St John's Coll., 1959–69, Hon. Fellow, 1988. Hon. Prof., Univ. of Wales, 1989; Vis. Prof., Univ. of Paris, 1995–97. London Mathematical Society: Treasurer, 1969–79; Pres., 1985–87; Whitehead Prize and Lectr, 1978. Mem. Council, Royal Soc., 1982–83. Gov., St Paul's Schs, 1970–99. Hon. DSc Aberdeen, 1993. *Publications:* The Mathematical Works of J. H. C. Whitehead, 1963; The Topology of Stiefel Manifolds, 1976; Topological Topics, 1983; General Topology and Homotopy Theory, 1984; Aspects of Topology, 1984; Topological and Uniform Spaces, 1987; Fibrewise Topology, 1988; Introduction to Uniform Spaces, 1990; Handbook of Algebraic Topology, 1995; Fibrewise Homotopy Theory, 1998; Topologies and Uniformities, 1999; History of Topology, 1999; Remarkable Mathematicians, 2002; Remarkable Physicists, 2003; Asperger's Syndrome and High Achievement, 2006; The Mind of the Mathematician, 2007; papers in mathematical and historical jls. *Address:* Mathematical Institute, 24–29 St Giles, Oxford OX1 3LB.

JAMES, Irene; Member (Lab) Islwyn, National Assembly for Wales, since 2003; *b* 1952. Formerly special needs teacher, Risca Primary Sch. Agent to Don Touhig, MP, gen. election, 2001. *Address:* National Assembly for Wales, Cardiff CF99 1NA; (constituency office) The Institute, 128 Newport Road, Cwmcarn, Newport NP11 7LZ. *T:* (01495) 272710.

JAMES, Sir Jeffrey (Russell), KBE 2001; CMG 1994; HM Diplomatic Service, retired; UK Special Representative for Nepal, 2003–05; *b* 13 Aug. 1944; *s* of Lewis Charles James and Ruth James; *m* 1965, Mary Longden; two *d*. *Educ:* Whitgift Sch.; Keele Univ. (BA Hons Internat. Relations). FCO 1967; served Tehran and Kabul; Dep. Political Advr, BMG Berlin, 1978; FCO 1982; Counsellor on loan to Cabinet Office, 1984; Counsellor and Head of Chancery, Pretoria/Cape Town, 1986; Counsellor (Economic and Commercial), New Delhi, 1988; Head, Edinburgh European Council Unit, FCO, 1992; Chargé d'Affaires, Tehran, 1993; High Comr, Nairobi, 1997–2001. Lay Mem., Asylum and Immigration Tribunal, 2005–. Director: AMREF (UK), 2006–; Eastern Africa Assoc., 2006–. Mem., RIIA, 2002– (Assoc. Fellow, 2006). Mem. Governing Council, Keele Univ., 2006–. *Recreations:* birding, golf, hill walking. *Address:* 7 Rockfield Close, Oxted, Surrey RH8 0DN. *Clubs:* Royal Commonwealth Society; Tandridge Golf.

JAMES, John Christopher Urmston, OBE 2003; President, European Tennis Federation, since 2002; Vice-President, Lawn Tennis Association, since 2003; Chairman, British Olympic Foundation, since 1989; *b* 22 June 1937; *s* of John Urmston James and Ellen Irene James; *m* 1st, 1959, Gillian Mary Davies (marr. diss. 1982); two *s*; 2nd, 1982, Patricia Mary, *d* of late Arthur Leslie Walter White. *Educ:* St Michael's, Llanelli; Hereford Cathedral Sch. Harrods, 1954; Jaeger, 1961; Pringle, 1972; Asst Sec., 1973–81, Sec., 1981–2002, LTA. Pres., Middx Tennis Assoc., 2003–. Mem., Internat. Council, Tennis Hall of Fame, 2003–. Vice Chm., BOA, 2001–04. International Tennis Federation: Mem., Olympic Cttee; Technical Delegate, Beijing Olympic Games, 2008. Trustee: Torch Trophy Trust, 2003–; British Tennis Foundn, 2003–; Dan Maskell Trust, 2003–. Member: NT; Ealing NT; Friends of Osterley Park; Wetlands Nature Reserve Centre, Barnes; Paignton Zoo. Lay Vice Chm., St Mary's, Osterley PCC. Mem., Lib Dem Party (Pres., Hounslow Lib Dems, 2005–). *Recreations:* tennis, Rugby football, walking, architecture, the countryside, gardening, theatre. *Address:* Parkfield Cottage, Osterley Road, Isleworth, Middx TW7 4PF. *T:* (020) 8232 8683. *Clubs:* All England Lawn Tennis and Croquet, Queen's, London Welsh Rugby Football, International of GB; Cambridge University Tennis (Hon. Vice Pres.); Llanelli Scarlets, Llanelli Lawn Tennis and Squash.

JAMES, John Douglas, OBE 1996; conservationist and gallery owner; *b* 28 July 1949; *s* of late William Antony James, ERD, MA and of Agnes Winifred James (*née* Mitchell); *m* 1971, Margaret Patricia Manton. *Educ:* Spalding Grammar School; Dip. in Co. Direction, Inst. of Dirs, 1994; MBA Nottingham Univ. 1999. Articled pupil, William H. Brown & Son, 1967–68; Marketing Dept, Geest Industries, 1969–71; Marketing Dept, John Player & Sons, 1971–77; Woodland Trust: Nat. Develt Officer, 1977; (first) Director, 1980; Exec. Dir, 1985; Chief Exec., 1992–97. Forestry Comr, 1998–2004 (Mem. Nat. Cttee for England, 2003–04). Co-owner: Focus Gall., Nottingham, 1995–2004; Church Street Gall., Cromer, 2004–. Nottingham Roosevelt Scholar, 1975 (Trustee, Nottingham Roosevelt Scholarship, 1997–2004); Churchill Fellow, 1980. Founder Mem., S Lincs Nature Reserves Ltd, 1968; Mem., Inst. of Charity Fundraising Managers. FRSA 1995. *Publications:* articles in countryside and gardening jls. *Recreation:* woodland walks. *Address:* c/o Church Street Gallery, Cromer NR27 9ER.

JAMES, John Henry; Chief Executive, Kensington & Chelsea and Westminster Health Authority (formerly Commissioning Agency), 1992–2002; *b* 19 July 1944; step *s* of late George Arthur James and *s* of late Doris May James; *m* 3rd, 1987, Anita Mary Stockton, *d* of Brian Scarth, QPM and late Irene Scarth. *Educ:* Ludlow Grammar Sch.; Keble Coll., Oxford (BA Mod. Hist. 1965; postgrad. dip. in Econ. and Pol Sci. 1966). AHSM 1991 (LHSM 1989). Entered Home Civil Service 1966; Asst Principal, Min. of Pensions and Nat. Insurance; Private Sec. to First Perm. Sec., 1969–71, Principal, 1971–74, DHSS; seconded to HM Treasury, 1974–76; Principal, 1976–78, Asst Sec., 1978–86, Under Sec., 1986–91, DHSS, later Dept of Health; Dir of Health Authority Finance, NHS Management Bd, 1986–89; General Manager: Harrow DHA, 1990–92; Parkside DHA, 1991–93. Chm. of reviews and dir of projects, DoH, 2002–05. Co-ordinator, London Cardiac Specialty Rev., 1993. Non-Exec. Dir, Laing Homes Ltd, 1987–89. Member: Adv. Council, King's Fund Inst., 1990–93; NHS Res. Task Force, 1993; NHS Central R&D Council, 1994–99; MRC Health Services and Public Health Res. Bd, 1995–99; NHS Adv. Cttee on Resource Allocation, 1997–99; Accessible Transport Commn for London, 1998–2002; Nat. Strategic Gp tackling Racial Harassment in NHS, 1999–2001. Mem. Editl Bd, Milbank Foundn, NY, 2000–. FRSA 1994. *Publications:* Transforming the NHS, 1994; contributed: Oxford Textbook of Public Health, 1985, 2nd edn 1991; Health Care UK, 1993; Rationing of Health and Social Care, 1993; Information Management in Health Services, 1994; articles in jls. *Recreations:* chess, cricket, travel, food and wine, collecting edible fungi. *Address:* *e-mail:* anj.james@btinternet.com. *Club:* Athenæum.

JAMES, Sir John (Nigel Courtenay), KCVO 1997; CBE 1990; FRICS; Secretary and Keeper of the Records, Duchy of Cornwall, 1993–97; Trustee of the Grosvenor Estate, 1971–2000; a Crown Estate Commissioner, 1984–99; *b* 31 March 1935; *s* of Frank Courtenay James and Beryl May Wilford Burden; *m* 1961, Elizabeth Jane St Clair-Ford; one *s* one *d*. *Educ:* Sherborne Sch., Dorset. Chief Agent and Estate Surveyor, Grosvenor Estate, 1968–71. Director: Sun Alliance & London Insurance Gp, 1972–93 (a Vice-Chm., 1988–93); Woolwich Equitable Building Soc., 1982–89; Williams & Glyn's Bank plc, 1983–85; Royal Bank of Scotland, 1985–93. Member: Commn for the New Towns, 1978–86; Cttee of Management, RNLI, 1980–2005 (Dep. Chm., 1999–2005); Council, Architectural Heritage Fund, 1983–2001 (Chm., 1999–2001); Prince of Wales' Council, 1984–97. Pres., RICS, 1980–81. Trustee, Henry Smith's Charity, 1991–2005. Gov., Sherborne Sch., 1990–2002. *Recreation:* sailing. *Club:* Brooks's.

JAMES, Jonathan Elwyn Rayner; QC 1988; a Recorder, 1998–2002; *b* 26 July 1950; *s* of Basil James, *qv*; *m* 1981, Anne Henshaw (*née* McRae); one *s*. *Educ:* King's College Sch., Wimbledon; Christ's Coll., Cambridge (MA, LLM); Brussels Univ. (Lic. Spécial en Droit Européen 1973). Called to Bar, Lincoln's Inn (Hardwicke Schol.), 1971, Bencher, 1994. Asst Recorder, 1994–98. Mem. Editl Bd, Entertainment Law Rev., 1990. *Publications:* (co-ed) EEC Anti-Trust Law, 1975; (co-ed) Copinger and Skone James on Copyright, 12th edn 1980–14th edn 1998; (jt consulting editor) Encyclopaedia of Forms and Precedents, Vol. 15 (Entertainment), 1989. *Recreations:* DIY, opera, 007, squash, France. *Address:* Hogarth Chambers, 5 New Square, Lincoln's Inn, WC2A 3RJ. *T:* (020) 7404 0404.

JAMES, Sir Kenneth; *see* James, Sir C. M.

JAMES, Kenneth; *see* James, E. K. G.

JAMES, Lawrence Edwin; author, since 1985; *b* 26 May 1943; *s* of Arthur and Laura James; *m* 1967, Mary Charlotte Williams; two *s*. *Educ:* Weston-super-Mare GS; York Univ. (BA 1966); Merton Coll., Oxford (MLitt 1979). Schoolmaster: Merchant Taylors' Sch., Northwood, 1969–76; Sedbergh Sch., Cumbria, 1976–85. *Publications:* Crimea: the war with Russia in contemporary photographs, 1981; The Savage Wars: the British conquest of Africa 1870–1920, 1985; Mutiny, 1987; Imperial Rearguard: wars of empire 1919–1985, 1988; The Golden Warrior: the life and legend of Lawrence of Arabia, 1990, 3rd edn 2005; The Iron Duke: a military biography of the Duke of Wellington, 1992, 2nd edn 2001; Imperial Warrior: the life and times of Field-Marshal Viscount Allenby, 1993; The Rise and Fall of the British Empire, 1994, 2nd edn 1997; Raj: the making and unmaking of British India, 1997; Warrior Race: the British experience of war, 2001; The Middle Class: a history, 2006. *Recreations:* bird watching, pipe smoking, maintenance of a Springer spaniel. *Address:* c/o Little, Brown, 100 Victoria Embankment, EC4Y 0DY. *Club:* Travellers.

JAMES, Linda Elizabeth Blake; *see* Sullivan, L. E.

JAMES, Michael; *see* James, R. M. and Jayston, M.

JAMES, Michael Francis; a District Judge (Magistrates' Courts) (formerly Stipendiary Magistrate), West Midlands, 1991–2002; *b* 30 Oct. 1933; *s* of Francis and Eveline James; *m* 1958, Lois Joy Elcock. *Educ:* King Charles I Grammar Sch., Kidderminster. Admitted solicitor, 1956. National Service: commnd RAF, 1957; qualified as air navigator, 1958. Partner, Ivens Morton & Greville-Smith (later Morton Fisher), 1959–86; Sen. Partner, 1986–91. Part-time ind. prison adjudicator, 2002–08. Vis. Fellow, UWE, 1996–99. *Recreations:* books, wine, walking, music.

JAMES, Michael Leonard, (Michael Hartland); writer and broadcaster, since 1983; *b* 7 Feb. 1941; *s* of late Leonard and Marjorie James; *m* 1975, Jill Elizabeth (marr. diss. 1992), *d* of late George Tarján, OBE and Etelka Tarján; two *d*. *Educ:* Latymer Upper Sch.; Christ's Coll., Cambridge. Entered British govt service, 1963; Private Sec. to Rt Hon. Jennie Lee, MP, Minister for the Arts, 1966–68; DES, 1968–71; Planning Unit of Rt Hon. Margaret Thatcher, MP, Sec. of State for Educn and Science, 1971–73; Asst Sec., 1973; DCSO 1974; served London, Milan, Paris, Tokyo, 1973–78; Director, IAEA, Vienna, 1978–83; Advr on Internat. Relations, CEC, Brussels, 1983–85. Member: CSSB, 1983–93; Immigration Appeal Tribunal, 1987–2005; Asylum and Immigration Tribunal, 2005–; a Chm., Professional Conduct Cttee, GMC, 2000–06. Governor: Colyton Grammar Sch., 1985–90; Sidmouth Community Coll., 1988–2004 (Chm., 1998–2001). Chm., Kennaway House Trust, 2008–. Feature writer and book reviewer for The Times (thriller critic, 1989–90; travel correspondent, 1993–), Daily Telegraph (thriller critic, 1993–), Sunday Times and Guardian, 1986–. Television and radio include: Sonja's Report (ITV), 1990; Masterspy, interviews with Oleg Gordievsky (BBC Radio 4), 1991. FRSA 1982. Hon. Fellow, Univ. of Exeter, 1985. *Publications:* as *M. L. James:* (jtly) Internationalization to Prevent the Spread of Nuclear Weapons, 1980; as *Michael Hartland:* Down Among the Dead Men, 1983; Seven Steps to Treason, 1985 (SW Arts Lit. Award; dramatized for BBC Radio 4, 1990); The Third Betrayal, 1986; Frontier of Fear, 1989; The Year of the Scorpion, 1991; The Verdict of Us All (short stories), 2006; Masters of Crime: Lionel Davidson and Dick Francis, 2006; as *Ruth Carrington:* Dead Fish, 1998. *Address:* Cotte Barton, Branscombe, Devon EX12 3BH. *Clubs:* Athenæum, PEN, Detection; Honiton Working Men's (Devon).

JAMES, Prof. Michael Norman George, DPhil, FRS 1989; FRS(Can) 1985; Professor of Biochemistry, University of Alberta, since 1978, University Professor of Biochemistry, since 1993; Canada Research Chair in Protein Structure and Function, since 2001; *b* 16 May 1940; *s* of Claud Stewart Murray James and Mimosa Ruth Harriet James; *m* 1961, Patricia McCarthy; one *s* one *d*; *m* 1977, Anita Sielecki; *m* 1996, Deborah Brown; one *d*. *Educ:* Univ. of Manitoba (BSc, MSc); Linacre Coll., Oxford (DPhil). Asst Prof., Associate Prof., Univ. of Alberta, 1968–78. Mem., MRC of Canada Group in Protein Structure and Function, 1974. *Publications:* contribs to learned jls. *Address:* Department of Biochemistry, University of Alberta, Edmonton, AB T6G 2H7, Canada. *T:* (403) 4924550.

JAMES, Dame Naomi (Christine), DBE 1979; PhD; author and yachtswoman; *b* 2 March 1949; *d* of Charles Robert Power and Joan Power; *m* 1st, 1976, Robert Alan James (*d* 1983); one *d*; 2nd, 1990, Eric G. Haythorne (marr. diss.), *o s* of G. V. Haythorne, Ottawa, Canada. *Educ:* Rotorua Girls' High Sch., NZ; UC, Cork (BA Philosophy and Eng. Lit. 1997; MA Philosophy 1999; PhD Philosophy 2005). Hair stylist, 1966–71; language teacher, 1972–74; yacht charter crew, 1975–77. Sailed single handed round the world via the three great Capes, incl. first woman solo round Cape Horn, on 53 ft yacht, Express Crusader, Sept. 1977–June 1978; sailed in 1980 Observer Transatlantic Race, winning Ladies Prize and achieving women's record for single-handed Atlantic crossing, on 53 ft yacht Kriter Lady; won 1982 Round Britain Race with Rob James, on multihull Colt Cars GB. Trustee, Nat. Maritime Museum, 1985–92; Council Mem., Winston Churchill Meml Trust, 1986–93. Royal Yacht Sqdn Chichester Trophy, 1978; NZ Yachtsman of the Year, 1978. *Publications:* Woman Alone, 1978; At One with the Sea, 1979; At Sea on Land, 1981; Courage at Sea, 1987. *Recreations:* riding, literature, philosophy. *Address:* Shore Cottage, Currabinny, Carrigaline, Co. Cork, Ireland. *Club* Royal Dart Yacht (Dartmouth); Royal Lymington Yacht (Lymington); Royal Wester Yacht (Plymouth).

JAMES, Prof. Oliver Francis Wintour, FRCP; Professor of Geriatric Medicine, sinc 1985, and Pro Vice Chancellor, since 2004, University of Newcastle upon Tyn Consultant Physician, Freeman Hospital, Newcastle, since 1977; *b* 23 Sept. 1943; *s* Baron James of Rusholme and Cordelia Mary (*née* Wintour); *m* 1965, Rosanna Foster; or *s* one *d*. *Educ:* Winchester; Balliol Coll., Oxford (MA 1964; BM BCh 1967); Middlese Hosp. Med. Sch. Registrar and Fellow, Royal Free Hosp., 1971–74; University Newcastle upon Tyne: First Asst in Medicine, 1974–75; Reader in Medicine (Geriatrics 1975–85; Hd, Sch. of Clin. Med. Scis, 1994–2004. Vis. Prof., Univs of Hong Kon Indianapolis and St Louis. Chairman: Liver Section, EC Concerted Action on Cellul Aging, 1982–86; Jt Cttee for Higher Med. Trng, SAC in Geriatrics, 1992–95. Pres., Bri Assoc. for Study of Liver, 1992–94. Royal College of Physicians: Censor, 1994–96; Se Vice Pres., 1997–2001. Trustee, Help the Aged, 2001–. Founder FMedSci 199 *Publications:* numerous papers and chapters on aspects of liver disease, geriatric medicin and training of physicians. *Recreations:* vegetable growing, wine, golf. *Addres* Sleightholmedale, Kirbymoorside, York YO62 7JG.

JAMES, P. D.; *see* Baroness James of Holland Park.

JAMES, Patrick Leonard, FRCS, FDS RCS; Hon. Consulting Oral and Maxillo-faci Surgeon: Royal London (formerly London) Hospital, Whitechapel (Senior Consulta Surgeon, 1963–91); North East Thames Regional Hospital Board Hospitals (Consulta Surgeon, 1963–91); Recognized Teacher in Oral Surgery, London University, since 196 *b* 7 Jan. 1926; *s* of late John Vincent James and Priscilla Elsie James; *m* 1951, Jean Margare *er d* of Leslie and Ruth Hatcher; one *s* two *d*. *Educ:* King's Coll., London; London Hos FDSRCS 1958; FRCS 1985 (MRCS 1956); LRCP 1956. Served RAF, Flt Lieut, M Comd, 1949–51. Sen. Registrar, Queen Victoria Hosp., E Grinstead, 1959–63; Ho Consulting Oral and Maxillo-facial Surgeon: to London Hosp., Honey Lane Hosp Waltham Abbey, Herts and Essex Hosp., Bishop's Stortford (Consultant Surgeon, 1963 to King George Hosp. (Consultant Surgeon, 1967); St Margaret's Hosp., Eppin (Consultant Surgeon, 1966); Black Notley Hosp. (Consultant Surgeon, 1969); Hon. Civ Consultant (Oral and Maxillo-facial Surgery), RAF, 1989 (Civil Consultant in Or Surgery, 1979–89). Exchange Fellow, Henry Ford Hosp., Detroit, Mich., 196 Hunterian Prof., RCS, 1970–71. Member: Academic Bd, London Hosp. Med. Coll 1968–71; Adv. Cttee in Plastic Surgery, NE Met. Reg. Hosp. Bd, 1969–77; NE Thame Reg. Manpower Cttee, 1975–78. Fellow: BAOS, 1963– (Mem. Council, 1971–74 Internat. Assoc. of Oral Surgs (BAOS Rep. on Council, 1974–78); Chm., Sci. Session, 6t Internat. Congress of Oral Surgs, Sydney, 1977; Associate Mem., Brit. Assoc. of Plasti Surgs, 1958–77. FRSocMed; Mem., Acad. of Expert Witnesses. Member: Counci Chelsea Clin. Soc; Bd of Governors, Eastman Hosp., 1983–84. Liveryman, Soc. Apothecaries, 1969; Freeman, City of London, 1978. *Publications:* (chapter in Or Surgery) Malignancies in Odontogenic Cysts, 1967; (chapter in Oral Surgery) Correctio of Apertognathia with Osteotomies and Bone Graft, 1970; (chapter in Oral Surgery, vo 7) Surgical Treatment of Mandibular Joint Disorders, 1978; numerous articles on surgic treatment of mandibular joint disorders, surgery of salivary glands and maxillo faci surgery in med. and surg. jls. *Recreations:* reading, sailing (Cdre, United Hosps Sailing Club 1968–75), ski-ing. *Address:* Meesden Hall, Meesden, Buntingford, Herts SG9 0AZ; 15 Harley Street, W1G 7LH. *T:* (020) 7935 4444; *e-mail:* patrickjames@btconnect.com *Club:* Boodle's.

JAMES, Peter John; Principal, London Academy of Music and Dramatic Art, since 1994 Joint Principal, Conservatoire for Dance and Drama, since 2007; *b* 27 July 1940; *s* o Arthur Leonard James and Gladys (*née* King); *m* 1st, 1964, Anthea Olive (marr. diss. 1972 one *d*; one *s* by Bernadette McKenna; 2nd, 1999, Alexandra Paisley. *Educ:* Birmingha Univ. (BA Hons English, Philosophy); Bristol Univ. (Postgrad. Cert. Drama). Founde Dir, Liverpool Everyman Theatre, 1964–71; Associate Dir, NT at Young Vic, 1971–73 Director: Crucible Theatre, Sheffield, 1974–81; Lyric Theatre, Hammersmith, 1981–9 (numerous first productions; Theatre Awards, 1986, 1992). Dir of plays, UK and overseas incl. Russia. Former cttee memberships incl. Arts Council, European Theatr Convention, Internat. Theatre Inst. (Award for Excellence, 1990). *Recreations:* cooking watching boxing and football matches. *Address:* LAMDA, 155 Talgarth Road, Baron Court, W14 9DA. *T:* (020) 8834 0500.

JAMES, Philip; *see* James, W. P. T.

JAMES, (Robert) Michael; UK Trade Adviser, International Tropical Timbe Organisation, 1998–2000; *b* 2 Oct. 1934; *s* of late Rev. B. V. James and Mrs D. M. James *m* 1959, Sarah Helen (*née* Bell); two *s* one *d*. *Educ:* St John's, Leatherhead; Trinity Coll. Cambridge (BA Hons History). Schoolmaster: Harrow Sch., 1958–60; Cranleigh Sch. 1960–62; joined CRO, 1962; 3rd Sec., Wellington, NZ, 1963–65; 1st Sec., Colombo, Sr Lanka, 1966–69; FCO, 1969–71; Dep. High Comr and Head of Chancery, Georgetown Guyana, 1971–73; Econ. Sec., Ankara, Turkey, 1974–76; FCO, 1976–80; Commercia Counsellor and Deputy High Commissioner: Accra, 1980–83; Singapore, 1984–87; Dep High Comr, Bridgetown, Barbados, 1987–90. Exec., Timber Trade Fedn, 1990–98; Dir Forests Forever Campaign, 1990–98. *Recreations:* sport (cricket Blue, 1956–58), drawing travel. *Address:* 17 North Grove, Highgate, N6 4SH. *T:* (020) 8245 3763. *Clubs:* MCC Hawks (Cambridge); Hunstanton Golf, Highgate Golf.

JAMES, Rosemary Gordon; *see* Stewart, R. G.

JAMES, Roy Lewis, CBE 1998; independent educational consultant, since 1997; HM Chief Inspector of Schools in Wales, 1992–97; *b* 9 Feb. 1937; *s* of David John and Eleano James; *m* 1962, Mary Williams; one *d*. *Educ:* Llandysul Grammar School; University College of Wales, Aberystwyth (BSc Hons, DipEd). Asst Master, Strode's Grammar Sch., Egham, 1959–60; Head of Maths Dept, Lampeter Comp. Sch., 1960–62; Head of Maths Dept, Cyfarthfa Castle Sch., Merthyr Tydfil, 1962–70; HM Inspector of Schs, 1970–84, seconded as Sec., Schs Council Cttee for Wales, 1975–77; Staff Inspector, 1984–90; Chie Inspector of Schs (Wales), Welsh Office, 1990–92. External Prof., Univ. of Glamorgan, 1997–2002. Chairman: Techniquest (Wales) Educn Adv. Gp, 1997–2002; Awards Pane Wales (Teaching Awards), 2000–06. Trustee, Welsh Dyslexia Proj., 2004–. Admitted to Gorsedd of Bards, Nat. Eisteddfod of Wales, 1997. *Publications:* numerous res. reports and articles on educn policy, curriculum and assessment, and initial trng and continuous professional develt of teachers. *Recreations:* travel, walking, reading, wine, chess, snooker. *Address:* Bryn Cemais, Llanfarian, Aberystwyth SY23 4BX.

JAMES, Shani R.; *see* Rhys-James.

JAMES, Siân Catherine; MP (Lab) Swansea East, since 2005; *b* 24 June 1959; *d* of Melbourne Griffiths and Martha Griffiths (*née* Morgan); *m* 1976, Martin R. James. *Educ:* University Coll. of Wales, Swansea (BA Hons Welsh). Field Officer, Wales, Nat. Fedn of

Young Farmers Clubs, 1990–91; Fundraiser, Wales, SCF, 1991–95; Dep. Public Affairs Manager, Wales, NT, 1995–98; Communications Manager, Securicor, HMP Parc, 1998–99; Assembly Liaison Manager, ATOL, 1999–2003; Dir, Welsh Women's Aid, 2003–05. *Recreations:* dolls houses, model railways, antiques, spending quality time with family. *Address:* (office) 2 Sway Road, Morriston, Swansea SA6 6HT. *T:* (01792) 795100, *Fax:* (01792) 650766; *e-mail:* sianjamesmp@parliament.uk.

JAMES, Sir Stanislaus (Anthony), GCSL 1992; GCMG 1992 (CMG 1990); OBE 1985; Governor General of Saint Lucia, West Indies, 1988–96; *b* 13 Nov. 1919; *s* of Raymond and Theresa James; *m* 1952, Lucille MacDonald; two *s* two *d*. *Educ:* St Mary's Coll., St Lucia; Govt Training Coll., Trinidad; Univ. of Wales, Swansea; Carleton Univ., Ottawa. Educn Dept, St Lucia, 1944–46; Head, Public Relations and Social Welfare Dept, Probation Officer, 1948–50; Chief Clerk, Govt Office, 1954–56; PR and Social Welfare Officer, 1956–65; Perm. Sec., Min. of Trade, Industry, Agric. and Tourism, Min. of Housing, Community, Social Affairs and Labour, Min. of Educn and Health, 1965–74; National Co-ordinator: for Non-Govt Orgns, 1974–88; for Emergency Services, 1979–88. *Recreation:* horticulture. *Address:* Sunny Acres, Choc, Castries, St Lucia, West Indies. *T:* 4519562.

JAMES, Stanley Francis; Head of Statistics Division 1, Department of Trade and Industry, 1981–84; *b* 12 Feb. 1927; *s* of H. F. James; unmarried. *Educ:* Sutton County Sch.; Trinity Coll., Cambridge. Maths Tripos Pt II; Dip. Math. Statistics. Research Lectr, Econs Dept, Nottingham Univ., 1951; Statistician, Bd of Inland Revenue, 1956; Chief Statistician: Bd of Inland Revenue, 1966; Central Statistical Office, 1968; Asst Dir, Central Statistical Office, 1970–72; Dir, Stats Div., Bd of Inland Revenue, 1972–77; Head, Econs and Stats Div. 6, Depts of Industry and Trade, 1977–81. Hon. Treasurer, Royal Statistical Soc., 1978–83. *Recreations:* travel, theatre, gardening. *Address:* 23 Hayward Road, Oxford OX2 8LN. *Club:* Royal Automobile.

JAMES, Stephen Lawrence; Consultant, Simmons & Simmons, Solicitors, 1992–2002 (Partner, 1961; Senior Partner, 1980–92); *b* 19 Oct. 1930; *s* of Walter Amyas James and Cecile Juliet (*née* Hillman); *m* 1st, 1955, Patricia Eleanor Favell James (marr. diss. 1986); two *s* two *d*; 2nd, 1998, Monique Whittome (*née* Borda). *Educ:* Clifton Coll.; St Catharine's Coll., Cambridge (BA History and Law). Mem., Gray's Inn, 1953, Bar finals, 1956; admitted Solicitor: England and Wales, 1959; Hong Kong, 1980. Director: Horace Clarkson PLC (formerly H. Clarkson (Holdings) PLC), 1975–2002; Shipping Industrial Holdings Ltd, 1972–82; Tradinvest Bank & Trust Co. of Nassau Ltd, 1975–85; Nodiv Ltd, 1975–78; Silver Line Ltd, 1978–82; Thompson Moore Associates Ltd, 1984–88; Greycoat PLC, 1994–99; Kiln Capital PLC, 1994–99. Mem., Law Soc., 1961–. *Recreations:* yachting, gardening. *Address:* 39 Markham Square, SW3 4XA; Widden, Shirley Holms, Lymington, Hampshire SO41 8NL. *Clubs:* Royal Thames Yacht; Royal Yacht Squadron; Royal Lymington Yacht.

JAMES, Steven Wynne Lloyd; Circuit Administrator, North-Eastern Circuit, Lord Chancellor's Department, 1988–94; *b* 9 June 1934; *s* of Trevor Lloyd James and Olwen James; *m* 1962, Carolyn Ann Rowlands (*d* 1995), *d* of James Morgan Rowlands and Mercia Rowlands; three *s*. *Educ:* Queen Elizabeth Grammar Sch., Carmarthen; LSE. LLB 1956. Admitted solicitor, 1959. Asst Solicitor in private practice, 1959–61; Legal Asst, HM Land Registry, 1961; Asst Solicitor, Glamorgan CC, 1962–70; Asst Clerk of the Peace, 1970–71; Lord Chancellor's Dept, 1971–94: Wales and Chester Circuit: Courts Administrator, (Chester/Mold), 1971–76; Asst Sec., 1976; Dep. Circuit Administrator, 1976–82; Under Sec., 1982; Circuit Administrator, 1982–88. *Address:* Westlake, 2 Heol-y-Bryn, The Knap, Barry, Vale of Glamorgan CF62 6SY. *T:* (01446) 420677. *Club:* Civil Service.

JAMES, (Thomas) Cecil (Garside), CMG 1966; Assistant Under-Secretary of State, Ministry of Defence, 1968–77; *b* 8 Jan. 1918; *s* of Joshua James, MBE, Ashton-under-Lyne; *m* 1941, Elsie Williams (*d* 2002), Ashton-under-Lyne; one *s* two *d*. *Educ:* Manchester Grammar Sch.; St John's Coll., Cambridge. Prin. Priv. Sec. to Sec. of State for Air, 1951–55; Asst Sec., Air Min., 1955; Civil Sec., FEAF, 1963–66; Chief of Public Relations, MoD, 1966–68. RAF historian. Order of Merit (Poland), 1998. *Publications:* The Battle of Britain, The Official Narrative, 2000; The Growth of Fighter Command 1936–40, 2002. *Address:* 4 The Granary, Wilson Road, Hadleigh, Suffolk IP7 5TJ. *Club:* Royal Air Force.

JAMES, Thomas Garnet Henry, CBE 1984; FBA 1976; Keeper of Egyptian Antiquities, British Museum, 1974–88; *b* 8 May 1923; *s* of late Thomas Garnet James and Edith (*née* Griffiths); *m* 1956, Diana Margaret (*d* 2002), *y d* of late H. L. Vavasseur-Durell; one *s*. *Educ:* Neath Grammar Sch.; Exeter Coll., Oxford (2nd Cl. Lit. Hum. 1947; 1st Cl. Oriental Studies 1950, MA 1948; Hon. Fellow, 1998). Served War of 1939–45, RA; NW Europe; 2nd Lieut 1943; Captain 1945. Asst Keeper, Dept of Egyptian and Assyrian Antiquities, 1951; Dep. Keeper (Egyptian Antiquities), 1974. Laycock Student of Egyptology, Worcester Coll., Oxford, 1954–60; Wilbour Fellow, Brooklyn Museum, 1964; Visiting Professor: Collège de France, 1983; Memphis State Univ., 1990. Vice-Pres., Egypt Exploration Soc., 1990– (Chm., 1983–89); Mem., German Archæological Inst., 1974. Chm. Cttee, Freud Mus., 1986–2003. Foreign Corresp., l'Institut de France, 2000. Editor: Jl of Egyptian Archæology, 1960–70; Egyptological pubns of Egypt Exploration Soc., 1960–89. *Publications:* The Mastaba of Khentika called Ikhekhi, 1953; Hieroglyphic Texts in the British Museum I, 1961; The Hekanakhte Papers and other Early Middle Kingdom Documents, 1962; (with R. A. Caminos) Gebel es-Silsilah I, 1963; Egyptian Sculptures, 1966; Myths and Legends of Ancient Egypt, 1969; Hieroglyphic Texts in the British Museum, 9, 1970; Archæology of Ancient Egypt, 1972; Corpus of Hieroglyphic Inscriptions in the Brooklyn Museum, I, 1974; (ed) An Introduction to Ancient Egypt, 1979; (ed) Excavating in Egypt, 1982; (with W. V. Davies) Egyptian Sculpture, 1983; Pharaoh's People, 1984; Egyptian Painting, 1985; Ancient Egypt: the land and its legacy, 1988; Howard Carter, the Path to Tutankhamun, 1992; Egypt: the living past, 1992; A Short History of Ancient Egypt, 1996; Egypt Revealed, 1997; Tutankhamun: the eternal splendours of the boy Pharaoh, 2000; Ramesses II, 2002; The British Museum Concise Introduction: Ancient Egypt, 2005; contributed to: W. B. Emery: Great Tombs of the First Dynasty II, 1954; T. J. Dunbabin: Perachora II, 1962; Cambridge Ancient History, 3rd edn, Vol. II, i, 1973, Vol III, ii, 1991; Encyclop. Britannica, 15th edn, 1974; (ed English trans.) H. Kees: Ancient Egypt, 1961; articles in Jl Egyptian Arch., etc; reviews in learned jls. *Recreations:* music, cooking. *Address:* 113 Willifield Way, NW11 6YE. *T:* (020) 8455 9221. *Club:* Oxford and Cambridge.

JAMES, Prof. Vivian Hector Thomas; Professor and Head of Department of Chemical Pathology, St Mary's Hospital Medical School, London University, 1973–90, now Professor Emeritus; Hon. Chemical Pathologist, St Mary's NHS Trust (formerly Paddington and North Kensington Health Authority), since 1973; *b* 29 Dec. 1924; *s* of William and Alice James; *m* 1958, Betty Irene Pike. *Educ:* Latymer Sch.; London Univ. BSc, PhD, DSc; FRCPath 1977. Flying duties, RAFVR, 1942–46. Scientific Staff, Nat. Inst. for Med. Res., 1952–56; St Mary's Hospital Medical School, London: Lectr, Dept of Chemical Pathol., 1956; Reader, 1962; Prof. of Chem. Endocrinol., 1967; Chm., Div. of

Pathology, St Mary's Hosp., 1981–85. Emeritus Fellow, Leverhulme Trust, 1991. Mem., Herts AHA, 1974–77. Secretary: Clin. Endocrinol. Cttee, MRC, 1967–72; Cttee for Human Pituitary Collection, MRC, 1972–76 (Chm., 1976–82); Endocrine Sect., RSocMed, 1972–76 (Pres., 1976–78); Gen. Sec., Soc. for Endocrinology, 1979–85 (Treas., 1986–91); Hon. Mem., 2003); Sec.-Gen., European Fedn of Endocrine Socs, 1986–; Chm., UKSport Expert Cttee, 1999–; Mem., Review Bd, Internat. Tennis Fedn, 2007–. Clinical Endocrinology Medal Lectr, Clin. Endocrinol. Trust, 1990; Jubilee Medal, Soc. for Endocrinology, 1992. Hon. MRCP 1989. Hon. Mem., Italian Endocrine Soc., 1980. Freeman, Haverfordwest, 1946. Fiorino d'oro, City of Florence, 1977. Editor, Clinical Endocrinology, 1972–74; Editor-in-Chief, 1993–2000, Founder Editor, 2000–, Endocrine-Related Cancer; Editl Advr, European Jl of Endocrinology, 1994–2002. *Publications:* (ed jtly) Current Topics in Experimental Endocrinology, 1971, 5th edn 1983; (ed) The Adrenal Gland, 1979, 2nd edn 1992; (ed jtly) Hormones in Blood, 1961, 3rd edn 1983; contribs to various endocrine and other jls. *Club:* Royal Society of Medicine.

JAMES, Walter; see James, A. W.

JAMES, Prof. Walter, CBE 1977; Dean and Director of Studies, Faculty of Educational Studies, 1969–77, Professor of Educational Studies, 1969–84, Open University; *b* 8 Dec. 1924; *s* of late George Herbert James and Mary Kathleen (*née* Crutch); *m* 1948, Joyce Dorothy Woollaston; two *s*. *Educ:* Royal Grammar Sch., Worcester; St Luke's Coll., Exeter; Univ. of Nottingham. BA 1955. School teacher, 1948–52; Univ. of Nottingham: Resident Tutor, Dept of Extra-Mural Studies, 1958–65; Lectr in Adult Educn, Dept of Adult Educn, 1965–69. Consultant on Adult Educn and Community Develt to Govt of Seychelles and ODA of FCO, 1973; Adviser: to Office of Educn, WCC, 1974–76; on Social Planning, to State of Bahrain, 1975; Council of Europe: UK Rep., Working Party on Develt of Adult Education, 1973–81; UK Rep. and Project Adviser, Adult Educn for Community Develt, 1982–87, Adult Educn for Social Change, 1988–93. Chairman: Nat. Council for Voluntary Youth Services, 1970–76; Review of Training of part-time Youth and Community Workers, 1975–77; Religious Adv. Bd, Scout Assoc., 1977–82; Inservice Training and Educn Panel for Youth and Community Service, 1978–82; Council for Educn and Trng in Youth and Community Work, 1982–85; Nat. Adv. Council for the Youth Service, 1985–88; Council for Local Non-Stipendiary Ministerial Training, dio. of Southwark, 1992–95; Eastbourne, Seaford and Wealden CHC, 1998–2002; non-exec. Dir, Eastbourne Downs Primary Care Trust, 2002–06. Member: DES Cttee on Youth and Community Work in 70s, 1967–69; ILO Working Party on Use of Radio and TV for Workers' Educn, 1968; Gen. Synod, C of E, 1970–75; Exec. Cttee, Nat. Council of Social Service, 1970–75; Univs' Council for Educn of Teachers, 1970–84; Univs Council for Adult Educn, 1971–76; BBC Further Educn Adv. Council, 1971–75; Exec. Cttee and Council, Nat. Inst. of Adult Educn, 1971–77; Library Adv. Council for England, 1974–76; Adv. Council, HM Queen's Silver Jubilee Appeal, 1976–78; Bd of Educn, Gen. Synod of C of E, 1991–2001; Bd of Govs, S Eastern Museums Service, 1997–2001; SE Arts Bd, 1998. Trustee: Young Volunteer Force Foundn, 1972–77; Trident Educnl Trust, 1972–86; Community Projects Foundn, 1977–90; Community Develt Foundn, 1990–96; President: Inst. of Playleadership, 1972–74; Fair Play for Children, 1979–82; London and SE Regl Youth Work Unit, 1992–94. Councillor (Lib Dem), Eastbourne BC, 1994–98. *Publications:* (with F. J. Bayliss) The Standard of Living, 1964; (ed) Virginia Woolf, Selections from her essays, 1966; (contrib.) Encyclopaedia of Education, 1968; (contrib.) Teaching Techniques in Adult Education, 1971; (contrib.) Mass Media and Adult Education, 1971; (with H. Janne and P. Dominice) The Development of Adult Education, 1980; (with others) The 14 Pilot Experiments, Vols 1–3, 1984; Some Conclusions from the Co-operation of 14 Development Projects, 1985; Handbook on Co-operative Monitoring, 1986; The Uses of Media for Community Development, 1988; (contrib.) Tomorrow is Another Country: education in a postmodern world, 1996; (contrib.) Called to New Life, 1999. *Recreation:* living. *Address:* 25 Kepplestone, Staveley Road, Eastbourne BN20 7JZ. *T:* (01323) 417029.

JAMES, Prof. Wendy Rosalind, (Mrs D. H. Johnson), DPhil; FBA 1999; Professor of Social Anthropology, University of Oxford, 1996–2007; Fellow, St Cross College, Oxford, 1972–2007, now Emeritus; President, Royal Anthropological Institute, 2001–04; *b* 4 Feb. 1940; *d* of William Stanley James and Isabel James (*née* Lunt); *m* 1977, Douglas Hamilton Johnson; one *s* one *d*. *Educ:* Kelsick Grammar Sch., Ambleside; St Hugh's Coll., Oxford (BA 1962; BLitt 1964; DPhil 1970). Lectr in Social Anthropol., Univ. of Khartoum, 1964–69; Leverhulme Res. Fellow, St Hugh's Coll., Oxford, 1969–71; Lectr in Social Anthropol., Univ. of Oxford, 1972–96. Vis. Lectr, Univ. of Bergen, 1971–72. Vice-Pres., British Inst. in Eastern Africa, 2001–. Hon. Dr Scientiarum Anthropologicarum Copenhagen, 2005. *Publications:* 'Kwanim Pa: the making of the Uduk people, 1979; (ed with D. L. Donham) The Southern Marches of Imperial Ethiopia, 1986; The Listening Ebony: moral knowledge, religion and power among the Uduk of Sudan, 1988; (ed with D. H. Johnson) Vernacular Christianity, 1988; (ed) The Pursuit of Certainty: religious and cultural formulations, 1995; (ed jtly) Juan Maria Schuver's Travels in North East Africa 1880–1883, 1996; (ed with N. J. Allen) Marcel Mauss: a centenary tribute, 1998; (ed jtly) Anthropologists in a Wider World: essays on field research, 2000; (ed jtly) Remapping Ethiopia: socialism and after, 2002; The Ceremonial Animal: a new portrait of anthropology, 2003; (ed with D. Mills) The Qualities of Time: anthropological approaches, 2005; (ed jtly) R. G. Collingwood, The Philosophy of Enchantment: studies in folktale, cultural criticism and anthropology, 2005; War and Survival in Sudan's Frontierlands: voices from the Blue Nile, 2007; (ed jtly) Early Human Kinship: from sex to social reproduction, 2008. *Recreations:* travel, vegetarian cookery, gardening. *Address:* c/o Institute of Social and Cultural Anthropology, 51 Banbury Road, Oxford OX2 6PE. *T:* (01865) 274677, 559041.

JAMES, Prof. (William) Philip (Trehearne), CBE 1993; MD, DSc; FRCP, FMedSci; FRSE; FIBiol; Director, Public Health Policy Group, since 1999; Research Professor, Aberdeen University, since 1983; *b* 27 June 1938; *s* of Jenkin William James and Lilian Mary James; *m* 1961, Jean Hamilton (*née* Moorhouse); one *s* one *d*. *Educ:* Ackworth Sch., Pontefract, Yorks; University Coll. London (BSc Hons 1959; DSc 1983); University Coll. Hosp. (MB, BS 1962; MD 1968). FRCP 1978; FRCPE 1983; FRSE 1986; FIBiol 1988. Sen. House Physician, Whittington Hosp., London, 1963–65; Clin. Res. Scientist, MRC Tropical Metabolism Res. Unit, Kingston, Jamaica, 1965–68; Harvard Res. Fellow, Mass Gen. Hosp., 1968–69; Wellcome Trust Res. Fellow, MRC Gastroenterology Unit, London, 1969–70; Sen. Lectr, Dept of Human Nutrition, London Sch. of Hygiene and Trop. Medicine, and Hon. Consultant Physician, UCH, 1970–74; Asst Dir, MRC Dunn Nutrition Unit, and Hon. Consultant Physician, Addenbrooke's Hosp., Cambridge, 1974–82; Dir, Rowett Res. Inst., Aberdeen, 1982–99. Hon. Prof. of Nutrition, LSHTM, 2004–. Advr, Eur. Dirs of Agricl Res. on Diet and Health, 1995–2000. Chairman: FAO Consultation on internat. food needs, 1987; Nat. Food Alliance, 1988–90 (Pres., 1990–98); Coronary Prevention Gp, 1988–95 (Pres., 1999–2008); WHO Consultation on world food and health policies, 1989; DoH Panel on Novel Foods, 1992–98; DoH Task Force on Obesity, 1994; RCPE Wkg Pty on Mgt of Obesity in NHS, 1994–97; Eur. Panel, Eur. Heart Foundn's Analysis of Cardiovascular Risk, 1994; Planning Gp, Eur. Young Nutrition Leadership Courses, 1994–2001; Internat. Obesity Task Force, 1995–;

UN Commn on Food and Health, later Nutrition Needs in new Millennium, 1997–99; Assoc. of Profs of Human Nutrition, 1994–97; Member: MAFF Adv. Cttee on Novel Foods and Processes, 1986–88; EC Scientific Cttee for Food, 1992–95; DoH (formerly MAFF) Nutrition Task Force, 1992–95; DoH Cttee on Med. Aspects of Food Policy, 1990–99; Internat. Panel on Diet and Cancer, World Cancer Res. Fund, 1994–97, 2004–; Independent Member: Scientific Steering Cttee, DGXXIV, Brussels, 1997–2000; BSE Cttee, 2001–02; Sen. Vice-Pres., Internat. Assoc. for Study of Obesity, 2004–06 (Pres. Elect, 2006–). Author, proposals on Food Standards Agency for Prime Minister, 1997 and EU, 1999. Vice-Pres., Internat. Union of Nutritional Scis, 2001–05. Founder FMedSci 1998. Hon. MFPHM 1994. FRSA 1988. Hon. MA Cantab, 1977. *Publications:* The Analysis of Dietary Fibre in Food, 1981; The Body Weight Regulatory System: normal and disturbed mechanisms, 1981; Assessing Human Energy Requirements, 1990; (ed) Human Nutrition and Dietetics, 1992, 2nd edn 1999; documents on European national nutrition policy and energy needs for Scottish Office, DoH, FAO, NACNE and WHO; scientific pubns on energy metabolism, salt handling, obesity and heart disease in Lancet, Nature, Clin. Science. *Recreations:* talking, writing reports; eating, preferably in France. *Address:* 231 North Gower Street, NW1 2NS. *T:* (020) 7691 1900; *e-mail:* jeanhjames@aol.com. *Club:* Athenæum.

JAMESON, Antony; *see* Jameson, G. A.

JAMESON, Derek; news, TV and radio commentator; Co-Presenter, Jamesons, Radio 2, 1992–97; *b* 29 Nov. 1929; *e s* of Mrs Elsie Jameson; *m* 1st, 1948, Jacqueline Sinclair (marr. diss. 1966); one *s* one *d*; 2nd, 1971, Pauline Tomlin (marr. diss. 1978); two *s*; 3rd, 1988, Ellen Petrie. *Educ:* elementary schools, Hackney. Office boy rising to Chief Sub-editor, Reuters, 1944–60; Editor, London American, 1960–61; features staff, Daily Express, 1961–63; Picture Editor, Sunday Mirror, 1963–65; Asst Editor, Sunday Mirror, 1965–72; Northern Editor, Sunday and Daily Mirror, 1972–76; Managing Editor, Daily Mirror, 1976–77; Editor, Daily Express, 1977–79; Editor-in-Chief, The Daily Star, 1978–80; Editor, News of the World, 1981–84. Presenter: Radio 2 Jameson Show, 1986–91; Jameson Tonight, Sky TV, 1989–90. *Publications:* Touched by Angels (autobiog.), 1988; Last of the Hot Metal Men (autobiog.), 1990. *Recreations:* opera, music, reading. *Address:* The Lodge, Broadwater Road, Worthing, Sussex BN14 8HU; *e-mail:* derekjameson333@hotmail.com.

JAMESON, Prof. (Guy) Antony, PhD; FRS 1995; FREng; Thomas V. Jones Professor of Engineering, Stanford University, since 1997; *b* 20 Nov. 1934; *s* of Brig. Guy Oscar Jameson and late Olive Maud Helen Jameson (*née* Turney); *m* 1st, 1964, Catharina Selander (marr. diss.); one *s* one *d*; 2nd, 1985, Charlotte Ansted. *Educ:* Trinity Hall, Cambridge (MA; PhD 1963). FREng 2005. Nat. Service, 2nd Lieut, RE, 1953–55. Research Fellow, Trinity Hall, Cambridge, 1960–63; Economist, TUC, 1964–65; Chief Mathematician, Hawker Siddeley Dynamics, Coventry, 1965–66; Aerodynamics Engineer, Grumman Aerospace, Bethpage, NY, 1966–72; Courant Institute of Mathematical Sciences, New York University: Research Scientist, 1972–74; Prof. of Computer Sci., 1974–80; Prof. of Aerospace Engrg, 1980–82, James S. McDonnell Dist. Univ. Prof. of Aerospace Engrg, 1982–96, Princeton Univ. *Publications:* numerous articles in jls and conference proceedings. *Recreations:* squash, tennis, ski-ing. *Address:* Department of Aeronautics and Astronautics, Stanford University, Durand Building, Stanford, CA 94305, USA.

JAMESON, Brig. Melville Stewart, CBE 1994; Lord-Lieutenant for Perth and Kinross, since 2006; *b* 17 July 1944; *s* of Melville Stewart Jameson and Mary Bowring Jameson; *m* 1973, Sarah Amy Walker-Munro; two *s*. *Educ:* Glenalmond; RMA Sandhurst. Commnd Royal Scots Greys, 1965; CO, Royal Scots Dragoon Guards, 1986–88; Comdr, 51 Highland Bde, 1993–96; Col, Royal Scots Dragoon Guards, 2003–. Chief Exec. and Producer, Edinburgh Mil. Tattoo, 1995–2007. Officer, Royal Co. of Archers, Queen's Body Guard for Scotland, 1983–. Mem., Royal Caledonian Hunt. *Recreations:* shooting, Highland bagpipes, gardening, trees. *Address:* Home HQ, Royal Scots Dragoon Guards, Edinburgh Castle, Edinburgh EH1 2YT. *T:* (0131) 310 5100, *Fax:* (0131) 310 5101; *e-mail:* homehq@scotsdg.org.uk. *Clubs:* Cavalry and Guards, Caledonian; New (Edinburgh).

JAMESON, Rodney Mellor Maples; QC 2003; a Recorder, since 2001; *b* 22 Aug. 1953; *s* of late Denys and of Rosemary Jameson; *m* 1977, Clare Fiona Mary Agius; two *s*. *Educ:* Charterhouse; Univ. of York (BA Hons). Called to the Bar, Middle Temple, 1976. *Recreations:* opera, wine, ski-ing, golf, tennis. *Address:* 6 Park Square, Leeds LS1 2LW; The Old Rectory, Sessay, N Yorks YO7 3LZ.

JAMIESON, Brian George, PhD; research management consultant, since 1997; *b* 7 Feb. 1943; *s* of George and Amy Jamieson; *m* 1966, Helen Carol Scott. *Educ:* Boroughmuir Sch.; Edinburgh Univ. (BSc, PhD). Research Assistant: Brigham Young Univ., Utah, 1967–68; Edinburgh Univ., 1968–70; Natural Environment Res. Council, 1970–73 and 1975–77; Principal, ARC, 1973–75; Cabinet Office, 1977–78; Agricultural and Food Research Council: Asst Sec., 1978–87; Dir, Central Office, 1987–91; Acting Sec., Oct.–Dec. 1990; Dir of Admin, 1991–94; Dep. Chief Exec., BBSRC, 1994–97. Mem., Univ. of Bristol Agriculture Cttee, 1997–2001. Mem., Remuneration Cttee, Royal Soc., 1995–2000. Member: Bd of Mgt, Sarsen Housing Assoc., 1997– (Vice-Chm., 2004–); Bd, Mendip Housing Ltd, 2005–06. Mem. Court, Univ. of Salford, 1996–98. *Publications:* papers on igneous petrology and research management. *Recreations:* running, keeping fit, ski-ing, travelling, family history. *Address:* 8 Orwell Close, Caversham, Reading, Berks RG4 7PU. *T:* (0118) 954 6652; *e-mail:* brianjamieson@compuserve.com. *Club:* Phyllis Court (Henley-on-Thames).

JAMIESON, Cathy; Member (Lab and Co-op) Carrick, Cumnock and Doon Valley, Scottish Parliament, since 1999; *b* 3 Nov. 1956; *d* of Robert and Mary Jamieson; *m* 1976, Ian Sharpe; one *s*. *Educ:* James Hamilton Acad., Kilmarnock; Glasgow Art Sch. (BA Hons Fine Art); Goldsmiths' Coll. (Higher Dip. Art); Glasgow Univ. (CQSW); Glasgow Poly. (Cert. Management). Social Worker, Strathclyde Regl Council, 1980–92; Principal Officer, Who Cares? Scotland, 1992–99. Scottish Executive: Minister: for Educn and Young People, 2001–03; for Justice, 2003–07. Mem., Scottish Exec. Cttee, 1996–, NEC 1998–99, Lab Party. *Address:* Scottish Parliament, Edinburgh EH99 1SP.

JAMIESON, David Charles; transport consultant; President, Motor Cycle Industry Association, since 2005; *b* 18 May 1947; *s* of Frank and Eileen Jamieson; *m* 1971, Patricia Hofton; two *s* one *d*. *Educ:* Tudor Grange Sch., Solihull; St Peter's, Birmingham; Open Univ. (BA). Teacher, Riland Bedford Sch., 1970–76; Head, Maths Dept, Crown Hills Sch., Leicester, 1976–81; Vice-Principal, John Kitto Community Coll., Plymouth, 1981–92. MP (Lab) Plymouth Devonport, 1992–2005. An Asst Govt Whip, 1997–98; a Lord Comr of HM Treasury (Govt Whip), 1998–2001; Parly Under-Sec. of State, DTLR, subseq. DfT, 2001–05. Mem., Select Cttee on Educn, 1992–97. Sponsored Private Mem.'s Bill for Activity Centres (Young Persons' Safety) Act, 1995. Member: Bd, Roadsafe, 2007–; IAM, 2007–. Fellow, Inst. of Couriers. *Recreations:* music, classic cars, gardening. *Address:* *e-mail:* davidcj@hotmail.co.uk.

JAMIESON, Air Marshal Sir (David) Ewan, KBE 1986 (OBE 1967); CB 1981; Chie of Defence Staff, New Zealand, 1983–86, retired; *b* Christchurch, 19 April 1930; *s* o Judge R. D. Jamieson, CMG; *m* 1957, Margaret Elaine, *d* of L. J. Bridge; three *s* one *d*. *Educ:* Christchurch and New Plymouth Boys' High Sch. Joined RNZAF, 1949; OC Flying, Ohakea, 1964; CO Malaysia, 1965–66; Jt Services Staff Coll., 1969; CO Auckland 1971–72; AOC Ops Group, 1974–76; RCDS 1977; Chief of Air Staff, RNZAF 1979–83. *Address:* 14 Hinerau Grove, Taupo, New Zealand.

JAMIESON, Rt Rev. Hamish Thomas Umphelby; Bishop of Bunbury, 1984–2000; 15 Feb. 1932; *s* of Robert Marshall Jamieson and Constance Marzetti Jamieson (*né* Umphelby); *m* 1962, Ellice Anne McPherson; one *s* two *d*. *Educ:* Sydney C of E Gramma Sch.; St Michael's House, Crafers (ThL); Univ. of New England (BA). Deacon 1955 Priest 1956. Mem. Bush Brotherhood of Good Shepherd, 1955–62. Parish of Gilgandra 1957; Priest-in-Charge, Katherine, NT, 1957–62; Rector, Darwin, 1962–67; Canon o All Souls Cathedral, Thursday Island, 1963–67; Royal Australian Navy Chaplain 1967–74; HMAS Sydney, 1967–68; HMAS Albatross, 1969–71; Small Ships Chaplain 1972; HMAS Cerberus, 1972–74; Bishop of Carpentaria, 1974–84. Liaison Bp to the Wes and Chm. Australian Council, Mission to Seafarers (formerly to Seamen), 1992–2000 Chm. Nat. Exec., Anglican Renewal Ministries of Australia, 1984–2000; Exec. Mem. Internat. Charismatic Consultation on World Evangelisation, 1994–2002; Member Anglican Bd of Mission, 1977–98; Bd of Reference, Christian Solidarity Australasia 1990–99; Internat. Bd, Sharing of Ministries Abroad, 1998–2008; Bd, People Alive Praye Ministry, 2001–08; Nat. Advr, Aglow Australia, 2005–07. Mem. Bd, Australian Coll. o Theology, ACT, 1993–97. *Recreations:* reading, music, gardening. *Address:* 17 Bonnydoon Court, Cooloongup, WA 6168, Australia.

JAMIESON, Margaret; *see* Wallace, M.

JAMIESON, Rt Rev. Penelope Ann Bansall, DCNZM 2004; PhD; Bishop o Dunedin, 1990–2004; *b* Chalfont St Peter, Bucks, 21 June 1942; *m* 1964, Ian William Andrew Jamieson; three *d*. *Educ:* St Mary's Sch., Gerrards Cross; High Sch., High Wycombe; Edinburgh Univ. (MA 1964); Victoria Univ., Wellington (PhD 1977); Otago Univ. (BD 1983). Ordained deacon 1982; priest 1983; Asst Curate, St James', Lower Hutt, 1982–85; Vicar, Karori West with Makara, dio. Wellington, 1985–90. *Publication:* Living at the Edge, 1997. *Address:* c/o Diocesan Office, PO Box 13–170, Green Island, 9052, Dunedin, New Zealand.

JAMIESON, Peter Nicholas; Executive Chairman, British Phonographic Industry, 2002–07; *b* 4 April 1945; *s* of William Herbert Jamieson and Mary Elaine Jamieson; *m* 1989, Jane Elinor Dalzell; one *s* two *d*. *Educ:* St George's Coll., Buenos Aires; Eastbourne Coll. Managing Director: EMI-AL Greece, 1972–75; EMI NZ, 1977–79; EMI Australia, 1979–83; EMI Records UK, 1983–86; Chm., RCA BMG UK, 1986–89; Vice-Pres., BMG Asia Pacific, 1989–95; Pres., MTV Asia, 1995–98; CEO, Linguaphone Gp, 1998–2002. Dir, Combe House Hotel, Devon, 1998–. *Recreations:* tennis, golf, amateur dramatics. *Address:* Newlands, South Road, St George's Hill, Surrey KT13 0NA. *T:* 01932 855822; *e-mail:* bearandbat@btinternet.com. *Clubs:* Hurlingham, Royal Automobile; St George's Hill Tennis; Burhill Golf.

JAMIESON, William Bryce; Executive Editor, The Scotsman, since 2000; Director, The Policy Institute, since 2000; *b* 9 June 1945; *s* of John Bryce Jamieson and Anne Jamieson (*née* Leckie); *m* 1971, Elaine Margaret Muller; one *s*. *Educ:* Sedbergh Sch., Yorks; Manchester Univ. (BA Econs). Sub-Editor, Gwent Gazette, 1969–70; Chief Sub-Editor, Celtic Press, 1970–71; Sub-Editor, Western Mail, 1971–73; Thomson Regional Newspapers: City Reporter, 1973–75; Economics Correspondent, 1975–76; City Reporter, Daily Express, 1976–78; City Editor, 1978–86; Dep. City Editor, Today, 1986; Dep. City Editor, 1986–95, Econs Editor, 1995–2000, Sunday Telegraph. *Publications:* Goldstrike: Oppenheimer empire in crisis, 1989; Britain Beyond Europe, 1994; UBS Guide to Emerging Markets, 1997; EU Enlargement: a coming home or poisoned chalice?, 1998; Britain: free to choose, 1998; Illustrated Guide to the British Economy, 1998; A Constitution to Destroy Europe, 2003. *Recreations:* reading, opera, gardening. *Address:* The Scotsman, 108 Holyrood Road, Edinburgh EH8 8AS. *T:* (0131) 620 8361.

JAMISON, Rt Rev. Christopher; *see* Jamison, Rt Rev. P. C.

JAMISON, James Kenneth, OBE 1978; Director, Arts Council of Northern Ireland, 1969–91; *b* 9 May 1931; *s* of William Jamison and Alicia Rea Jamison; *m* 1964, Joan Young Boyd; one *s* one *d*. *Educ:* Belfast College of Art (DA). Secondary school teacher, 1953–61; Art Critic, Belfast Telegraph, 1956–61; Art Organiser, Arts Council of Northern Ireland, 1962–64, Dep. Director, 1964–69. Hon. DLitt Ulster, 1989. *Publications:* miscellaneous on the arts in the North of Ireland. *Recreations:* the arts, travel.

JAMISON, Rt Rev. (Peter) Christopher, OSB; Abbot of Worth, since 2002; *b* 26 Dec. 1951; *s* of John Warren Jamison and Mary Beverley (*née* Allen). *Educ:* Downside Sch.; Oriel Coll., Oxford (MA Mod. Langs 1973); Heythrop Coll., Univ. of London (BA Theol. and Philos. 1977). Entered Worth Abbey, 1973; ordained priest, 1978; Worth School: Head of RE and Housemaster, 1979–93; Headmaster, 1994–2002. Pres., Internat. Commn on Benedictine Educn, 2002–. Founder, The Soul Gym, 2003. *Publications:* (with D. Lundy and L. Poole) To Live is to Change: a way of reading Vatican II, 1994; (with R. Steare) Integrity in Practice, 2003; Finding Sanctuary, 2006; Finding Happiness, 2008; articles in The Tablet. *Address:* Worth Abbey, Paddockhurst Road, Turners Hill, Crawley, W Sussex RH10 4SB. *T:* (01342) 710200, *Fax:* (01342) 710311; *e-mail:* cjamison@worth.org.uk.

JAMMEH, Alhaji Yahya Abdulaziz Jemus Junkung; President, Republic of the Gambia, since 1996; *b* 25 May 1965; *m* 1998, Zineb Yahya Souma. *Educ:* Gambia High Sch. Joined Gambia Nat. Gendarmerie, 1984; commnd 1989; served: Special Intervention Unit, 1984–86; Mobile Gendarmerie Special Guards Unit, 1986–87; Gendarmerie Trng Sch., 1987–89; 2nd Lieut, 1989; OC, Mobile Gendarmerie, Jan.–June 1991; OC, Mil. Police Unit, June–Aug. 1991; Gambia Nat. Army, 1991–93; Lieut, 1992; Mil. Police Officers' Basic Course, Alabama, 1993–94; Capt., 1994; Chm., Armed Forces Provisional Ruling Council and Hd of State, 1994–96; Col, 1996; retd from Army, 1996. Chm., CILLS (Inter-states cttee for control of drought in Sahel), 1997–2000; Vice-Chm., Orgn of Islamic Conf., 2000–. Hon. DCL St Mary's, Halifax, Canada, 1999. Has received numerous awards and decorations from USA, Libya, China, Liberia and Senegal. *Recreations:* tennis, soccer, hunting, reading, correspondence, driving, riding motorcycles, music, movies, world events, animal rearing. *Address:* Office of the President, State House, Banjul, The Gambia.

JANES, Maj.-Gen. Mervyn, CB 1973; MBE 1944; *b* 1 Oct. 1920; *o s* of W. G. Janes; *m* 1946, Elizabeth Kathleen McIntyre; two *d*. *Educ:* Sir Walter St John's Sch., London. Commnd 1942; served with Essex Yeo. (104 Regt RHA), 1942–46, Middle East and Italy; psc 1951; served with 3 RHA, 1952–53; 2 Div., BMRA, 1954–55; Chief Instructor, New Coll., RMAS, 1956–57; Batt. Comd, 3 RHA, 1958–60; Asst Army Instructor

(GSO1), Imperial Defence Coll., 1961–62; comd 1st Regt RHA, 1963–65; Comdr, RA, in BAOR, 1965–67; DMS2 (MoD(A)), 1967–70; GOC 5th Division, 1970–71; Dir, Royal Artillery, 1971–73. Col Comdt, RA, 1973–81. *Recreations:* music, ornithology. *Address:* Lucy's Cottage, North Street, Theale, Reading, Berks RG7 5EX. *Club:* Army and Navy.

JANKOVIĆ, Dr Vladeta; Ambassador of Serbia to the Holy See, since 2007; *b* 1 Sept. 1940; *s* of Dr Dragoslav and Bosiljka Janković; *m* 1970, Slavka Srdić; one *s* one *d*. *Educ:* Univ. of Belgrade (BA 1964; MA 1967; PhD Lit. 1975). University of Belgrade, Faculty of Philology: Asst Lectr, 1970–78; Lectr, 1978–83; Prof. of Classical Lit. and Comparative Hist. of Eur. Drama, 1983–2000; Hd, Dept of Comparative Lit. and Theory of Lit., 1992–2000. Lectr, Univ. of Ann Arbor, and Univ. of Columbia (Fulbright Schol.), 1987–88. Co-founder (with Vojislav Kostunica), Democratic Party of Serbia, 1992. MP Serbia, 1992–93; Mem., Fed. Parlt of Yugoslavia, 1996–2000; Chm., Foreign Affairs Cttee, Upper Chamber of Parlt, 2000–01. Ambassador of Federal Republic of Yugoslavia, then Serbia and Montenegro, to UK, 2001–04; Diplomatic Advr to Prime Minister of Serbia, 2004–07. *Publications:* Menander's Characters and the European Drama, 1978; Terence, Comedies, 1978; The Laughing Animal: on classical comedy, 1987; Comedies of Hroswitha, 1988; Who's Who in Classical Antiquity, 1991, 2nd edn 1996; Myths and Legends, 1995, 5th edn 2006. *Recreation:* tennis. *Address:* 16 Vlajkovićeva, 11000 Belgrade, Serbia.

JANMAN, Timothy Simon; Senior Consultant, Hoggett Bowers, since 2003; *b* 9 Sept. 1956; *s* of Jack and Irene Janman; *m* 1990, Shirley Buckingham (marr. diss. 2000). *Educ:* Sir William Borlase Grammar Sch., Marlow, Bucks; Nottingham Univ. (BSc Hons Chemistry). Ford Motor Co., 1979–83; IBM UK Ltd, 1983–87; Manpower PLC: Nat. Account, subseq. Public Sector Business, Manager, 1993–95; Sen. Nat. Account Manager, 1995–97; Dir, Boyden Internat. Ltd, 1997–2003. Nat. Sen. Vice-Chm., FCS, 1980–81; Vice-President: Selsdon Gp, 1988– (Chm., 1983–87); Jordan is Palestine Cttee, 1988–. Mem., Southampton City Council, May–July 1987. MP (C) Thurrock, 1987–92; contested (C) Thurrock, 1992. Mem., Select Cttee on Employment, 1989–92. Vice-Chm., Cons. Backbench Employment Cttee, 1988–92 (Sec., 1987–88); Sec., Cons. Backbench Home Affairs Cttee, 1989–92. Pres., Thurrock Cons. Assoc., 2002–. *Publications:* contribs to booklets and pamphlets. *Recreations:* restaurants, theatre. *Address:* 35c Weltje Road, Hammersmith, W6 9LS.

JANNER, family name of **Baron Janner of Braunstone**.

JANNER OF BRAUNSTONE, Baron *cr* 1997 (Life Peer), of Leicester in the co. of Leicestershire; **Greville Ewan Janner;** QC 1971; barrister, author, lecturer, journalist and broadcaster; *b* 11 July 1928; *s* of Baron Janner and Lady Janner; *m* 1955, Myra Louise Sheink (*d* 1996), Melbourne; one *s* two *d*. *Educ:* Bishop's Coll. Sch., Canada; St Paul's Sch. (Foundn Schol.); Trinity Hall, Cambridge (Exhibnr; MA); Harvard Post Graduate Law School (Fulbright and Smith-Mundt Schol.); Harmsworth Scholar, Middle Temple, 1955. Nat. Service: Sgt RA, BAOR, War Crimes Investigator. Pres., Cambridge Union, 1952; Chm., Cambridge Univ. Labour Club, 1952; Internat. Sec., Nat. Assoc. of Labour Students, 1952; Pres., Trinity Hall Athletic Club, 1952. Contested (Lab) Wimbledon, 1955. MP (Lab) Leicester NW, 1970–74, Leicester W, 1974–97. Mem., Select Cttee on Employment, 1982–96 (Chm., 1992–96); Co-Chm., All Party Employment Gp, 1996–97; Chairman: All-Party Industrial Safety Gp, 1975–97; All-Party Magic Group, 1991–97; Founder, 1973, and former Chm., All-Party Cttee for Homeless and Rootless People; Founder, 1990, and Vice-Chm., 1990–92, All Party Race and Community Gp; Vice-Chairman: All-Party Parly Cttee for Jews in the Former Soviet Union (formerly Cttee for Release of Soviet Jewry), 1971–97; (Jt), British-Israel Parly Gp, 1983–; British-India Parly Gp, 1991–97 (Jt Vice-Chm., 1987–91); British-Spanish Parly Gp, 1987–97 (Sec., 1986); All-Party British-Romanian Gp, 1990–92; All-Party Parly Cttee for E Europ. Jewry, 1990–97; Sec., All-Party War Crimes Gp, 1987–97, 2000–; Founder and Pres. of World Exec., Inter-Parly Council Against Anti-Semitism, 1990–97. President: National Council for Soviet Jewry, 1979–85; Bd of Deputies of British Jews, 1979–85; Commonwealth Jewish Council, 1983–; Vice-President: Assoc. for Jewish Youth, 1970–; Assoc. of Jewish Ex-Servicemen; IVS, 1983–; World Jewish Congress: European Vice-Pres., 1984–86; Mem. World Exec., 1986–; Vice-Pres., 1990–; Jt Pres., Political Council for Co-existence, 2005–. Partner, JSB Associates, 1984–88; Chm., JSB Gp Ltd, 1988–97 (Hon. Pres., 1997); non-exec. Dir, Ladbroke Plc, 1986–95. Member: Nat. Union of Journalists (Life Mem.); Soc. of Labour Lawyers; Magic Circle; Internat. Brotherhood of Magicians; Pres., REACH, 1982–; Pres., Jewish Museum, 1985–2001; Mem. Bd of Dirs, Jt Israel Appeal, 1985–; Vice-Pres., Guideposts Trust, 1983–; Founder and Pres., Maimonides Foundn, 1992–2002; Chairman: Holocaust Educnl Trust, 1987–; Lord Forte Charitable Foundn, 1995–. Formerly Dir, Jewish Chronicle Newspaper Ltd; Trustee, Jewish Chronicle Trust. Hon. Mem., Leics NUM, 1986–. FIPD (FIPM 1976). Hon. PhD Haifa Univ., 1984; Hon. LLD De Montfort, 1998. Comdr, Order of Grand Duke Gediminas (Lithuania), 2002. *Publications:* 66 books, mainly on employment and industrial relations law, presentational skills, and on public speaking, including: Complete Speechmaker; Janner on Presentation; One Hand Alone Cannot Clap; To Life! (memoirs). *Recreations:* family, magic, languages—speaks nine. *Address:* House of Lords, SW1A 0PW. *Fax:* (020) 7222 2864; *e-mail:* lordj@netcomuk.co.uk.

See also Hon. D. J. M. Janner.

JANNER, Hon. Daniel (Joseph Mitchell); QC 2002; *b* 27 April 1957; *s* of Lord Janner of Braunstone, *qv* and late Myra Jannner, JP; *m* 1983, Caroline Gee; three *d*. *Educ:* University College Sch.; Trinity Hall, Cambridge (MA; Pres., Cambridge Union Soc., 1978). Called to the Bar, Middle Temple (Jules Thorn Scholar), 1980. Accredited Mediator, CIArb, 2004. Dir of Res., Soc. of Conservative Lawyers, 1996–99. Mem., Cttee, Criminal Bar Assoc., 1999–2005. Member: Bd of Deputies of British Jews, 2000–05; Cttee, Dermatrust, 2000–05. Contested (Lab) Bosworth, 1983. Gov., The Hall Sch., Hampstead, 2005–; Chm. Govs, Immanuel Coll., Herts, 2007–. Editor: Litigation Law Jl, 1986–90; Criminal Appeal Reports, 1994–. *Recreations:* swimming, ski-ing, Arsenal Football Club. *Address:* 23 Essex Street, WC2R 3AS. *T:* (020) 7413 0353, *Fax:* (020) 7413 0374.

JANŠA, Janez; Prime Minister of Slovenia, since 2004; *b* 17 Sept. 1958; one *s* one *d*. *Educ:* Univ. of Ljubljana (Defence Studies). Trainee, Republican Secretariat for Defence, 1982; Pres., Cttee for Basic People's Defence and Social Self-Protection, 1983–89; Ed.-in-Chief, Democracy, 1989–90. Minister of Defence and MP (SDZ), Slovenia, 1990–94; MP (Soc. Dem.), 1994–2004; Leader of the Opposition, 1994–2000; Minister of Defence, 2000. Vice Pres., later Pres. Council, Slovene Democratic Alliance (SDZ), 1989–91; Mem., 1992–, Pres., 1993–, Social Democratic Party. *Publications:* On My Own Side, 1988; Movements, 1992; The Barricades, 1994; (jtly) Seven Years Later, 1995. *Address:* Office of the Prime Minister, Gregorčičeva 25, 1000 Ljubljana, Slovenia. *T:* (1) 4781000, *Fax:* (1) 4781140; *e-mail:* gp.kpv@gov.si.

JANSEN, Elly, (Mrs Elly Whitehouse-Jansen), OBE 1980; Founder and Chief Executive Officer: The Richmond Fellowship for Community Mental Health, 1959–91; The Richmond Fellowship International, 1981–2000; Fellowship Charitable Foundation, 1983–93; Richmond Fellowship Foundation International, since 2006; *b* 5 Oct. 1929; *d* of Jacobus Gerrit Jansen and Petronella Suzanna Vellekoop; *m* 1969, Alan Brian Stewart Whitehouse (known as George); three *d*. *Educ:* Paedologisch Inst. of Free Univ., Amsterdam; Boerhave Kliniek (SRN); London Univ. Founded: Richmond Fellowship of America, 1968, of Australia, 1973, of New Zealand, 1978, of Austria, 1979, of Canada, 1981, of Hong Kong, of India, of Israel, 1984, and of the Caribbean, 1987; Richmond Fellowship Internat., 1981; Richmond Fellowship branches in France, Malta, Peru, Bolivia, Uruguay, Costa Rica, Mexico, Ghana, Nigeria, Zimbabwe, Pakistan, Philippines, Nepal and Bangladesh, 1981–93. Organised internat. confs on therapeutic communities, 1973, 1975, 1976, 1979, 1984, 1988 and 1999; acted as consultant to many govts on issues of community care. Fellowship, German Marshall Meml Fund, 1977–78. Templeton Award, 1985. *Publications:* (ed) The Therapeutic Community Outside the Hospital, 1980; (contrib.) Mental Health and the Community, 1983; (contrib.) Towards a Whole Society: collected papers on aspects of mental health, 1985; (contrib.) R. D. Laing: creative destroyer, 1997; contribs to Amer. Jl of Psychiatry, L'Inf. Psychiatrique, and other jls. *Recreations:* literature, music, interior design. *Address:* Clyde House, 109 Strawberry Vale, Twickenham, TW1 4SJ. *T:* (020) 8744 0374, *Fax:* (020) 8891 0500.

JANSEN, Sir Ross (Malcolm), KBE 1989 (CBE 1986); Chairman, Local Government Commission, New Zealand, 1998–2001; Mayor of Hamilton City, New Zealand, 1977–89; *b* 6 Sept. 1932; *m* 1957, Rhyl Robinson; three *s* three *d*. *Educ:* Horowhenua Coll., Levin (Dux *proxime accessit* 1950); Victoria Univ., Wellington (LLB 1957); Univ. of Waikato (DPhil 1994). NZ Univ. Law Moot Prize, 1956. Practised law in partnership. Hamilton, 1958–77. Hamilton City Council: Mem., 1965–74, 1977–89; Chairman: Planning Cttee, 1965–68; Works Cttee, 1968–74; Dep. Mayor, 1971–74. Chairman: Waikato United Council, 1986–89; Hamilton Industrial Develt Prog., 1966–68; NZ Bldg Industry Commn, 1986–89; Lottery Community Facilities Cttee, 1989–91; Waikato Regl Council, 1989–91; Midland Regl HA, 1992–98. President: Municipal Assoc. of NZ, 1984–89; NZ Local Govt Assoc., 1988–89. Mem. Council, Univ. of Waikato, 1977–99. Winston Churchill Trust Fellowship in Town Planning, 1968. FRSA; ACIArb. Hon. Dr Waikato Univ., 1984. Hon. Chieftain of Western Samoa (for services to the Samoan Community). Commemoration Medal, NZ, 1990. *Recreations:* reading (poetry and history), tennis, gardening. *Address:* Apartment 12, 232 Hibiscus Coast Highway, Orewa, Rodney, New Zealand.

JANSON-SMITH, (Peter) Patrick; literary agent, Christopher Little Literary Agency, since 2005; *b* 28 July 1949; *s* of (John) Peter Janson-Smith and (Diana) Mary Janson-Smith (*née* Whittaker); *m* 1st, 1972, Lavinia Jane Priestley (marr. diss.); one *s* one *d*; 2nd, 1987, Pamela Jean Gossage (marr. diss.); two *s*; 3rd, 2006, Anne-Louise Fisher. *Educ:* Cathedral Sch., Salisbury; Cokethorpe Park Sch., Witney. Asst to Export Publicity Manager, Univ. of London Press Ltd, 1967–69; Granada Publishing: asst to Publicity Manager, Panther Books Ltd, 1969–70; ed., 1970–71, 1973–74, press officer, 1971–72, Mayflower Books; Publicity Manager, Octopus Books, 1972; Transworld Publishers: ed., 1974–78, Associate Editl Dir, 1978–79, Corgi Books; Editl Dir, Nationwide Book Service, 1979–81; Publisher: Corgi and Black Swan Books, 1981–95; Adult Trade Div., 1995–2005. Member: Bd, Edinburgh Book Fest., 1994–97; Soc. of Bookmen, 1998–. *Recreations:* book collecting, late 19th and early 20th century illustrations, wine, food. *Address:* Christopher Little Literary Agency, Eelbrook Studios, 125 Moore Park Road, SW6 4PS. *T:* (020) 7736 4455, *Fax:* (020) 7736 4490; *e-mail:* pjs@christopherlittle.net. *Clubs:* Garrick; Century.

JANSONS, Mariss; conductor; Principal Conductor, Royal Concertgebouw Orchestra, Amsterdam, since 2004; Music Director, Bavarian Radio Symphony Orchestra, Munich, since 2003; *b* Riga, Latvia, 14 Jan. 1943; *s* of late Arvid Jansons; *m* 1998, Irina; one *d* from previous marr. *Educ:* Leningrad Conservatory; studied in Vienna with Prof. Hans Swarowsky and in Salzburg with Herbert von Karajan. Leningrad Philharmonic (later renamed St Petersburg Philharmonic): Associate Conductor, 1973–85; Associate Principal Conductor, 1985–; Music Director: Oslo Philharmonic Orch., 1979–2002; Pittsburgh SO, 1997–2004; Principal Guest Conductor, LPO, 1992–. Has conducted leading orchestras of Europe and America incl. Boston and Chicago Symphony Orchestras, Berlin and Vienna Philharmonic, Royal Concertgebouw, etc. Has toured extensively in Europe, America and Japan. Prof. of Conducting, St Petersburg Conservatoire, 1992–2000. Numerous recordings. Hon. RAM 1999; Hon. Mem., Ges. der Musikfreunde, Vienna, 2001. Hon. Dr: Oslo, 2006; Riga, 2006. Eddison Award for recording of Shostakovich's 7th Symphony, Holland, 1989; Dutch Luister Award for recording of Berlioz Symphonie fantastique with Royal Concertgebouw Orch., 1982; Norwegian Culture Prize of Anders Jahre, 1991; Artist of the Year, EMI Classics, 1996, MIDEM, 2006; Grammy Award for Shostakovich's 13th Symphony, 2006. Comdr with Star, Royal Norwegian Order of Merit, 1995; Three Starts Medal (Latvia), 2006. *Address:* c/o Bavarian Radio Symphony Orchestra, Rundfunkplatz 1, 80335 Munich, Germany. *T:* (89) 59004974.

JANUARY, Peter, PhD; HM Diplomatic Service, retired; Head of Private Security Company policy review team, International Security Directorate, Foreign and Commonwealth Office, 2004–08; *b* 13 Jan. 1952; *s* of late Eric Frank January and of Hetty Amelia January (*née* Green); *m* 2000, Catherine Helen Courtier Jones, MBE. *Educ:* Sexey's Sch., Bruton; Univ. of Reading (BA 1st Cl. Hons History and Italian); University Coll. London (PhD Italian History 1983). Asst Master, Chatham Grammar Sch. for Girls, 1975–80; joined FCO, 1983; First Sec. (Commercial), Hungary, 1985–88; FCO, 1988–91; Dep. Head of Mission, Mozambique, 1991–93; FCO, 1993–99; Ambassador to Albania, 1999–2001; Hd, OSCE and Council of Europe Dept, FCO, 2001–04. *Recreations:* spending time with my wife, watching and reading about cricket, Shakespeare, Elizabethan and Jacobean tragedy, European history (articles in progress on military history of the Venetian Republic), medieval English churches, travel in Italy, poetry, English detective novels, British coins, Falkland Island stamps, canine company, Times crossword, English countryside, daydreaming. *Address:* 8 New Road, Trull, Taunton TA3 7NJ. *Club:* Somerset County Cricket.

JANVRIN, family name of **Baron Janvrin**.

JANVRIN, Baron *cr* 2007 (Life Peer), of Chalford Hill in the County of Gloucestershire; **Robin Berry Janvrin,** GCB 2007 (KCB 2003; CB 1997); GCVO 2007 (KCVO 1998; CVO 1994; LVO 1983); QSO 2007; PC 1998; Private Secretary to the Queen and Keeper of the Queen's Archives, 1999–2007; *b* 20 Sept. 1946; *s* of Vice Adm. Sir Richard Janvrin, KCB, DSC; *m* 1977, Isabelle de Boissonneaux de Chevigny; two *s* two *d*. *Educ:* Marlborough Coll.; Brasenose Coll., Oxford (BA 1970; Hon. Fellow, 1999). Royal Navy, 1964–75; joined Diplomatic Service, 1975; First Secretary: UK Delegn to NATO, 1976–78; New Delhi, 1981–84; Counsellor, 1985; Press Sec. to the Queen, 1987–90; Asst Private Sec. to the Queen, 1990–95; Dep. Private Sec. to the Queen, 1996–99. Dep. Chm., HSBC Private Bank (UK), 2008–. *Recreations:* family, painting. *Address:* House of Lords, SW1A 0PW.

JANZON, Mrs Bengt; *see* Dobbs, Mattiwilda.

JAPAN, Emperor of; *see* Akihito.

JARDINE, Sir Andrew (Colin Douglas), 5th Bt *cr* 1916; *b* 30 Nov. 1955; *s* of Brigadier Sir Ian Liddell Jardine, 4th Bt, OBE, MC, and of Priscilla Daphne, *d* of Douglas Middleton Parnham Phillips; *S* father, 1982; *m* 1997, Dr Claire Vyvien Griffith, *d* of Dr William and Dr Vyvien Griffith; one *s* two *d*. *Educ:* Charterhouse; Royal Agricultural Coll., Cirencester; Reading Univ. (BSc Hons 1996). MRICS (ARICS 1998). Commissioned Royal Green Jackets, 1975–78. With C. T. Bowring & Co. Ltd, 1979–81; with Henderson Administration Gp, 1981–92; Dir, Gartmore Investment Trust Management Ltd, 1992–93; with Strutt & Parker, 1996–99; resident land agent, 2000–. MSI 1993. Mem., Queen's Body Guard for Scotland, Royal Company of Archers, 1990–2007. *Heir: s* Guy Andrew Jardine, *b* 15 March 2004. *Address:* Comely Farm, Clapton, Berkeley, Glos GL13 9QX. *T:* (01453) 511780.

See also Sir J. A. G. Baird, Bt.

JARDINE, Sir (Andrew) Rupert (John) Buchanan-, 4th Bt *cr* 1885; MC 1944; DL; landowner and farmer; *b* 2 Feb. 1923; *s* of Sir John William Buchanan-Jardine, 3rd Bt and Jean Barbara (*d* 1989), *d* of late Lord Ernest Hamilton; *S* father, 1969; *m* 1950, Jane Fiona (marr. diss. 1975), 2nd *d* of Sir Charles Edmonstone, 6th Bt; one *s* one *d*. *Educ:* Harrow; Royal Agricultural College. Joined Royal Horse Guards, 1941; served in France, Holland and Germany; Major 1948; retired, 1949. Joint-Master, Dumfriesshire Foxhounds, 1950–2001. JP Dumfriesshire, 1957; DL Dumfriesshire, 1978. Bronze Lion of the Netherlands, 1945. *Recreations:* country pursuits. *Heir: s* John Christopher Rupert Buchanan-Jardine [*b* 20 March 1952; *m* 1975, Pandora Lavinia, *d* of Peter Murray Lee; one *s* five *d*]. *Address:* Dixons, Lockerbie, Dumfriesshire DG11 2PR. *T:* (01576) 202508. *Club:* MCC.

JARDINE, Dr Ian William; Chief Executive, Scottish Natural Heritage, since 2002; *b* 22 May 1959; *s* of William Laing Jardine and Isabel Dakers Jardine (*née* Ferguson); *m* 1986, Anne Scott Daniel; three *s*. *Educ:* Royal High Sch., Edinburgh; Univ. of Durham (BSc Biol. (Ecol.) 1980); Univ. of Leeds (PhD Zool. 1984). Various posts, mainly in urban renewal, housing and industry, Scottish Office, 1984–91; Dir, NE Scotland, Nature Conservancy Council for Scotland, 1991–92; Scottish Natural Heritage, 1992–: Director: NE Scotland, 1992–97; Strategy and Ops, 1997–2002. Mem. Council, RZSScot, 2005–. *Recreations:* natural history, drama, Middle Eastern history. *Address:* Scottish Natural Heritage, Great Glen House, Leachkin Road, Inverness IV3 8NW. *T:* (01463) 725001, *Fax:* (01463) 725044; *e-mail:* ian.jardine@snh.gov.uk.

JARDINE, James Christopher Macnaughton; Sheriff of Glasgow and Strathkelvin, 1979–95; *b* 18 Jan. 1930; *s* of James Jardine; *m* 1955, Vena Gordon Kight; one *d*. *Educ:* Glasgow Academy; Gresham House, Ayrshire; Glasgow Univ. (BL). National Service (Lieut RASC), 1950–52. Admitted as Solicitor, in Scotland, 1953. Practice as principal (from 1955) of Nelson & Mackay, and as partner of McClure, Naismith, Brodie & Co., Solicitors, Glasgow, 1956–69; Sheriff of Stirling, Dunbarton and Clackmannan, later N Strathclyde, at Dumbarton, 1969–79. A Vice-Pres., Sheriffs' Assoc., 1976–79. Sec., Glasgow Univ. Graduates Assoc., 1956–66; Mem., Business Cttee of Glasgow Univ. Gen. Council, 1964–67. Member: Consultative Cttee on Social Work in the Criminal Justice System (formerly Probation) for Strathclyde Region, 1980–94; Professional Advisory Cttee, Scottish Council on Alcoholism, 1982–85. *Recreation:* enjoyment of music and theatre.

JARDINE, Prof. Lisa Anne, CBE 2005; PhD; Centenary Professor of Renaissance Studies, since 2005, and Director, Research Centre for Editing Lives and Letters, since 2002, Queen Mary (formerly Queen Mary and Westfield College), University of London (Professor of Renaissance Studies, 1989–2005); Chair, Human Fertilisation and Embryology Authority, since 2008; *b* 12 April 1944; *d* of Jacob Bronowski and Rita (*née* Coblenz); *m* 1st, 1969, Nicholas Jardine, *qv* (marr. diss. 1979); one *s* one *d*; 2nd, 1982, John Robert Hare; one *s*. *Educ:* Cheltenham Ladies' Coll.; Newnham Coll., Cambridge (BA Maths and English 1966; MA 1968; PhD 1973; Associate 1992); Univ. of Essex (MA 1967). Res. Fellow, Warburg Inst., Univ. of London, 1971–74; Lectr in Renaissance Literature, Univ. of Essex, 1974; Res. Fellow, Cornell Univ., 1974–75; University of Cambridge: Res. Fellow, Girton Coll., 1974–75; Fellow: King's Coll., 1975–76 (Hon. Fellow, 1995); Jesus Coll., 1976–89 (Hon. Fellow, 2006); Lectr in English, 1976–89; Reader in Renaissance English, 1989. Davis Center Fellow, Princeton Univ., 1987–88. Chm., AHRB Wkg Party on public understanding of the arts and humanities, 2002; Mem., AHRC (formerly AHRB), 2003– (Chm., Mus and Collections Cttee, 2004–). Trustee: V & A Mus., 2003– (Chm., Collections Cttee, 2004–; Chm., Bethnal Green Mus. Cttee, 2007–); Artangel, 2006–; Sir Joseph Banks Archive Proj., 2007; Mem. Council, Royal Instn, 2004–; Patron, Nat. Council on Archives, 2007. Presenter, Night Waves, BBC Radio 3, 1992–96. Chair of Govs, Westminster City Sch., 1999–2006; London Dio. Bd for Schs Foundn Gov., St Marylebone Secondary Sch., 2006–. Chair of Judges: Orange Prize for Fiction, 1997; Booker Prize for Fiction, 2002; Mem., Michael Faraday Prize Cttee, Royal Soc., 2003–. FRHistS 1992; FRSA 1992. Hon. Dr: Sheffield Hallam, 2004; Open, 2008; Hon. DLitt St Andrews, 2005. *Publications:* Francis Bacon: discovery and the art of discourse, 1974; Still Harping on Daughters: women and drama in the age of Shakespeare, 1983; (jtly) From Humanism to the Humanities: education and the liberal arts in fifteenth- and sixteenth-century Europe, 1986; (jtly) What's Left? Women In Culture and the Labour Movement, 1989; Erasmus, Man of Letters, 1993; Reading Shakespeare Historically, 1996; Wordly Goods: a new history of the Renaissance, 1996; Erasmus, the Education of a Christian Prince, 1997; (jtly) Hostage to Fortune: the troubled life of Francis Bacon, 1998; Ingenious Pursuits: building the scientific revolution, 1999; Francis Bacon, A New Organon and Other Writings, 1999; (jtly) Global Interests: Renaissance art between East and West, 2000; On a Grander Scale: the outstanding career of Sir Christopher Wren, 2002; The Curious Life of Robert Hooke: the man who measured London, 2003; (jtly) London's Leonardo, 2003; The Awful End of Prince William the Silent, 2005; Going Dutch: how England plundered Holland's glory, 2008; A Point of View, 2008; contribs to newspapers, numerous articles in learned jls. *Recreations:* conversation, cookery, contemporary art. *Address:* 51 Bedford Court Mansions, Bedford Avenue, WC1B 3AA.

JARDINE, Prof. Nicholas, PhD; FBA 2004; Professor of History and Philosophy of the Sciences, University of Cambridge, since 1991; Fellow, Darwin College, Cambridge, since 1975; *b* 4 Sept. 1943; *s* of Michael James Jardine and Jean Caroline (*née* Crook); *m* 1992, Marina Frasca-Spada; two *s* two *d* from previous marriages. *Educ:* Monkton Combe; King's Coll., Cambridge (BA 1965; PhD 1969). Jun. Res. Fellow, 1967–71, Sen. Res. Fellow, 1971–75, King's Coll., Cambridge; Royal Soc. Res. Fellow, 1968–73; University of Cambridge: Lectr, 1975–86; Reader, 1986–91. Mem., Internat. Acad. of Hist. of Sci., 1991–. Editor: Studies in Hist. and Philosophy of Sci., 1982–; Studies in Hist. and Philosophy of Biol and Biomedic. Scis, 1998–. *Publications:* (with R. Sibson) Mathematical Taxonomy, 1971; The Birth of History and Philosophy of Science, 1984, rev. edn 1988; The Fortunes of Inquiry, 1986; (ed jtly) Romanticism and the Sciences, 1990; The Scenes of Inquiry, 1991, 2nd edn 2000; (ed jtly) Cultures of Natural History, 1996; (ed jtly) Books and Sciences in History, 2000; (with A. Segonds) La guerre des astronomes, 2 vols, 2008. *Recreation:* plant hunting. *Address:* 83 Alpha Road, Cambridge CB4 3DQ. *T:* (01223) 313734.

JARDINE, Ronald Charles C.; *see* Cunningham-Jardine.

JARDINE, Sir Rupert Buchanan-; *see* Jardine, Sir A. R. J. B.

JARDINE of Applegirth, Sir William Murray, 13th Bt *cr* 1672 (NS); 24th Chief of the Clan Jardine; *b* 4 July 1984; *s* of Sir Alec Jardine of Applegirth, 12th Bt and of Mary Beatrice, posthumous *d* of Hon. John Cross, 3rd *s* of 2nd Viscount Cross; *S* father, 2008. *Educ:* Strathallan Sch., Perthshire. Outdoor sports educator. *Recreations:* windsurfing, sailing. *Heir: b* John Alexander Cross Jardine, *b* 18 Sept. 1991. *Address:* Ash House, Millom, Cumbria LA18 5HY; *e-mail:* jardinesglobal@aol.com.

JARMAN, Andrew Miles, MA; Headmaster, Lancaster Royal Grammar School, since 2001; *b* 16 May 1957; *s* of Basil Jarman and Josephine Mary Jarman (*née* Lockyer); *m* 1980, Kerstin Maria Bailey; one *s* two *d*. *Educ:* PGCE Oxford 1979; Hertford Coll., Oxford (MA 1992); NPQH 2000. Mathematics teacher: Aylesbury GS, 1979–80; Portsmouth GS, 1980–84; Haberdashers' Aske's Sch., Elstree, 1984–88; Cheltenham College, 1988–2001: Hd of Maths, 1988–92; Dir of Studies, 1992–2001. *Recreations:* golf, family. *Address:* Lancaster Royal Grammar School, East Road, Lancaster LA1 3EF. *T:* (01524) 580600, *Fax:* (01524) 847947; *e-mail:* ajarman@lrgs.org.uk. *Clubs:* East India; Pedagogues Golf Society.

JARMAN, Sir Brian, Kt 1998; OBE 1988; PhD; FRCP, FRCGP, FFPH, FMedSci; Professor of Primary Health Care, Imperial College School of Medicine (formerly St Mary's Hospital Medical School), 1984–98, now Emeritus; President, British Medical Association, 2003–04; *b* 9 July 1933; *m* 1963, Marina Juez Uriel; three *s*. *Educ:* Barking Abbey Sch.; St Catharine's Coll., Cambridge (Open Exhibn; BA Nat. Sci. 1954; MA 1957); Imperial Coll., London (DIC 1957, PhD 1960, Geophysics); St Mary's Hosp. Med. Sch., London Univ. (MB BS 1st Cl. Hons 1969). MRCP 1972, FRCP 1988; MRCGP (Hons) 1978, FRCGP 1984; MFPHM 1994, FFPH (FFPHM 1999). National Service 2nd Lt, 19 Field Regt, RA, 1954–55, Army Opnl Res. Gp, 1955–56. Geophysicist: Royal Dutch Shell Oil Co., 1960–63; Geophysical Services Inc., 1963–64; House appts: St Mary's Hosp., London, 1969; St Bernard's Hosp., Gibraltar, 1970; Beth Israel Hosp., Harvard Med. Sch., 1970; Clin. Fellow, Harvard Univ., 1970; GP, London, 1971–98; St Mary's Hospital Medical School, later Imperial College School of Medicine: pt-time Sen. Lectr, Dept of Gen. Practice, 1973–83; Hd of Community Health Scis Div., 1995–97; Hd, Div. of Primary Care and Population Health Scis, 1997–98; Hd, Dr Foster Unit, 2001–. Med. Advr and Cons., Barnet FHSA, 1991–95. Member: Sci. Consultative Gp, BBC, 1983–89; Health Services Res. Cttee, MRC, 1987–89; Requirements Bd, Advanced Informatics in Medicine, EC, 1989–90; Kensington, Chelsea & Westminster FHSA, 1990–96; Standing Med. Adv. Cttee, 1998–2005. Mem. Council, RCP, 1995–98. Med. Mem., Bristol Royal Infirmary Inquiry, 1999–2001. Sen. Fellow, Inst. for Healthcare Improvement, Boston, USA, 2001–. Trustee, Wytham Hall Unit for the Homeless, 1979–; Chm., Trustees, Anna Freud Centre, 1995–2003. Founder FMedSci 1998. *Publications:* (ed and contrib.) Primary Care, 1988; contribs to books, papers, reviews, articles in med. jls, conf. proceedings. *Recreations:* music, reading, family, travel, squash, friends. *Address:* 62 Aberdare Gardens, NW6 3QD. *T:* (020) 7624 5502.

JARMAN, (John) Milwyn; QC 2001; **His Honour Judge Jarman;** a Specialist Chancery Circuit Judge, since 2007; *b* 30 April 1957; *s* of Thomas Jarman and Mary Elizabeth Jarman; *m* 1983, Caroline Anne Joyce Newman; two *s* one *d*. *Educ:* UCW Aberystwyth (LLB 1st Cl. Hons); Sidney Sussex Coll., Cambridge (LLM). Called to the Bar, Gray's Inn, 1980, Bencher, 2006; in practice, Cardiff, 1981–2007, specialising in chancery, planning and local government, and personal injuries law; Recorder, 2002–07. Treas., Wales and Chester Circuit, 2006–. An Asst Boundary Comr. Hon. Counsel, Welsh Books Council. *Recreations:* ski-ing, snooker, Welsh affairs and sport. *Address:* Civil Justice Centre, 2 Park Street, Cardiff CF10 1ET.

JARMAN, Nicholas Francis Barnaby; QC 1985; barrister; a Recorder of the Crown Court, since 1982; *b* 19 June 1938; *s* of late A. S. Jarman and Helene Jarman; *m* 1st, 1973, Jennifer Michelle Lawrence-Smith (marr. diss. 1978); one *d*; 2nd, 1989, Julia Elizabeth MacDougall (*née* Owen-John). *Educ:* Harrow; Christ Church, Oxford (MA Jurisprudence). Commnd RA, 1956–58 (JUO Mons, 1957). Called to the Bar, Inner Temple, 1965 (Duke of Edinburgh Scholar). Bar Chm., Bucks, Berks and Oxon Jt Liaison Cttee, 1986–96. Pres., Mental Health Appeals Tribunal, 2000–05. *Recreations:* France, fly-fishing. *Address:* Mas Terrier Gibertes, 30700 Flaux, France. *T:* (4) 66030308; 12 Chatsworth Court, W8 6DG. *Clubs:* Garrick, Pilgrims.

JARMAN, Pauline; Member (Plaid Cymru), Rhondda Cynon Taff County Borough Council, since 1995 (Leader, 1999–2004); *b* 15 Dec. 1945; *m* Colin Jarman; two *s*. *Educ:* Mountain Ash Grammar Sch. Export Officer, AB Metals, 1962–65; Export/Import Officer, Fram Filters, 1965–68; self-employed retailer, 1976–88. Member: Cynon Valley BC, 1976–96 (Leader, Plaid Cymru Gp; Mayor, 1987–88); Mid-Glamorgan CC, 1981–96 (Leader, Plaid Cymru Gp; Leader of Council); (Plaid Cymru) S Wales Central, Nat. Assembly for Wales, 1999–2003. *Address:* 3 Middle Row, Mountain Ash, Aberdare CF45 4DN.

JARMAN, Richard Neville; arts consultant; General Director, Britten-Pears Foundation, since 2002; *b* 24 April 1949; *s* of late Dr Gwyn Jarman and of Pauline (*née* Lane). *Educ:* King's Sch., Canterbury; Trinity Coll., Oxford (MA English). Sadler's Wells Opera and ENO, 1971–76; Touring Officer, Dance, Arts Council, 1976–77; Edinburgh International Festival: Artistic Asst, 1978–82; Fest. Adminr, 1982–84; Gen. Adminr, London Fest. and English Nat. Ballet, 1984–90; Gen. Dir, Scottish Opera, 1991–97; Interim Gen. Manager, Arts Theatre, Cambridge, 1997–98; Artistic Dir, Royal Opera House, 1998–2000. Chm., Dance Umbrella, 1997–2007; Dir, Canterbury Fest., 2001–05. Gov., Central Sch. of Speech and Drama, 2000–05. Trustee, British Performing Arts Medicine Trust, 1999–. FRSA. *Publications:* History of Sadler's Wells Opera, 1974; History of London Coliseum Theatre, 1979. *Recreations:* listening to music, going to the theatre, gardening, food and drink, travel, reading. *Address:* 78 Riversdale Road, Highbury, N5 2JZ. *T:* (020) 3227 0086.

JARMAN, Roger Whitney; Under Secretary, Local Government Finance, Housing and Social Services Group, Welsh Office, 1994–95; *b* 16 Feb. 1935; *s* of Reginald Cecil Jarman and Marjorie Dix Jarman; *m* 1959, Patricia Dorothy Odwell; one *s*. *Educ:* Cathays High Sch., Cardiff; Univ. of Birmingham (BSocSc Hons; Cert. in Educn). Recruitment and Selection Officer, Vauxhall Motors Ltd, 1960–64; Asst Sec., Univ. of Bristol Appts Bd, 1964–68; Asst Dir of Recruitment, CSD, 1968–72; Welsh Office: Principal, European Div., 1972–74; Asst Sec., Devolution Div., 1974–78; Asst Sec., Perm. Sec.'s Div., 1978–80; Under Secretary: Land Use Planning Gp, 1980–83; Transport, Highways and Planning Gp, 1983–88; Transport, Planning, Water and Environment Gp, 1988; Housing,

Health and Social Services Policy Gp, 1988–94. Standing Orders Comr, Nat. Assembly for Wales, 1998. Mem. Panel of Chairmen, RAS, 1995–2002; Lay Chm., NHS Complaints Procedure, 1996–2007; Bd Mem., Linc-Cymru (formerly Glamorgan and Gwent) Housing Assoc., 1996–. Mem., Nat. Trust Cttee for Wales, 2000–06. *Recreations:* walking, reading, wine and food. *Club:* Civil Service.

JAROSZEK, Jeremy; Chief Executive, Erewash Borough Council, since 2006; *b* 5 Dec. 1951; *s* of Walenty Jaroszek and Sylvia Jaroszek (*née* Stanley); *m* 1989, Rosemary Moon; one *s* one *d*. *Educ:* Vyners Sch.; Selwyn Coll., Cambridge (MA); Imperial Coll., London (MSc 1974). CPFA 1982. Greater London Council, 1974–85; Camden LBC, 1985–86; Dep. Dir of Finance, London Borough of Hillingdon, 1986–89; Dir of Finance, 1990–99, Strategic Dir of Resources, 1999–2002, London Borough of Barnet; Dir, J. J. Global Ltd, financial consultancy and mgt for local govt, 2002–06. Treas., Middlesex Probation Service, 1990–2001. *Recreations:* ski-ing, stargazing, family pursuits.

JARRATT, Sir Alexander Anthony, (Sir Alex), Kt 1979; CB 1968; DL; Chancellor, University of Birmingham, 1983–2002; Chairman, Centre for Dispute Resolution, 1990–2000, Life President, since 2000; *b* 19 Jan. 1924; *o s* of Alexander and Mary Jarratt; *m* 1946, Mary Philomena Keogh; one *s* two *d*. *Educ:* Royal Liberty Gram. Sch., Essex; University of Birmingham. War Service, Fleet Air Arm, 1942–46. University of Birmingham, BCom, 1946–49. Asst Principal, Min. of Power, 1949, Principal, 1953, and seconded to Treas., 1954–55; Min. of Power: Prin. Priv. Sec. to Minister, 1955–59; Asst Sec., Oil Div., 1959–63; Under-Sec., Gas Div., 1963–64; seconded to Cabinet Office, 1964–65; Secretary to the National Board for Prices and Incomes, 1965–68; Dep. Sec., 1967; Dep. Under Sec. of State, Dept of Employment and Productivity, 1968–70; Dep. Sec., Min. of Agriculture, 1970. Man. Dir, IPC, 1970–73; Chm. and Chief Executive, IPC and IPC Newspapers, 1974; Chm. and Chief Exec., Reed Internat., 1974–85 (Dir, 1970–85); Chm., Smiths Industries, 1985–91 (Dir, 1984–96); a Dep. Chm., Midland Bank, 1980–91; Jt Dep. Chm., Prudential Corp. plc, 1987–91, 1992–94 (Dir, 1985–94); Director: ICI, 1975–91; Thyssen-Bornemisza Group, 1972–89; Mem., Ford European Adv. Council, 1983–88. Confederation of British Industry: Mem., Council, 1972–92; Mem., President's Cttee, 1983–86; Chairman: Economic Policy Cttee, 1972–74; Employment Policy Cttee, 1983–86; Mem., NEDC, 1976–80. President: Advertising Assoc., 1979–83; PPA 1983–85. Chairman: Industrial Soc., 1975–79; Henley: The Management Coll., 1977–89; Gov., Ashridge Management Coll., 1975–91. Vice-Pres., Inst. of Marketing, 1982–92. Pres., Age Concern, Essex, 2000–. FRSA. DL Essex, 1995. Hon. CGIA 1990. Hon. DSc Cranfield, 1973; DUniv: Brunel, 1979; Essex, 1997; Hon. LLD Birmingham, 1982. *Recreations:* walking, the countryside, reading, music. *Address:* Barn Mead, Fryerning, Essex CM4 0NP.

JARRATT, Prof. Peter, CEng; FBCS; FSS; FIMA; Professor of Computing, University of Birmingham, 1975–2000, now Emeritus; *b* 2 Jan. 1935; *s* of Edward Jarratt and Edna Mary Jarratt; *m* 1972, Jeanette Debeir; one *s* two *d*. *Educ:* Univ. of Manchester (BSc, PhD). Programmer, Nuclear Power Plant Co. Ltd, 1957; Chief Programmer, Nuclear Power Gp, 1960; Lectr in Mathematics, Bradford Inst. of Technology, 1962; Asst Dir, Computing Lab., Univ. of Bradford, 1966; Dir, Computing Lab., Univ. of Salford, 1972; University of Birmingham: Dir, Computer Centre, 1975–91; Dep. Dean, Faculty of Science and Engrg, 1984; first Dean of Faculty of Science, 1985–88; Develt Advr to Vice-Chancellor, 1988–93. Director: Birmingham Res. and Develt Ltd, 1986–88; BISS Ltd, 1993–96; Carma Ltd, 1993–; Wang-Inet Ltd, 1996–97; Wang Global Ltd, 1997–99. Chm., Birmingham Inst. for Conductive Educn, 1987–90. Mem., Birmingham Lunar Soc., 1991–93. Gov., Royal Nat. Coll. for the Blind, 1986–95; Patron, Henshaw's Soc. for the Blind, 1993–. *Publications:* numerous res. papers on mathematics, computer sci. and risk mgt. *Recreations:* classical music, mountain walking, gardening, chess. *Address:* c/o The University of Birmingham, Edgbaston, Birmingham B15 2TT. *Club:* Athenæum.

JARRAUD, Michel; Secretary-General, World Meteorological Organization, since 2004; *b* 31 Jan. 1952; *s* of René Jarraud and Simone Blanchet; *m* 1975, Martine Camus; one *s* one *d*. *Educ:* Ecole Polytechnique, Paris; Ecole de la Météorologie Nationale, Paris (Ingénieur de la Météorologie 1976). Researcher in Numerical Weather Prediction: Météo France, Paris, 1976–78; Eur. Centre for Medium-range Weather Forecast, Reading, 1978–85; Dir, French Nat. Forecasting, Météo France, Paris, 1986–89; Hd, Ops Dept, 1990–94, Dep. Dir, 1991–94, ECMWF, Reading; Dep. Sec.-Gen., WMO, 1995–2003. *Address:* World Meteorological Organization, 7bis avenue de la Paix, Case Postale No 2300, 1211 Geneva 2, Switzerland. *T:* (22) 7308200; *e-mail:* sgomm@wmo.int.

JARRE, Maurice Alexis; French composer; *b* 13 Sept. 1924; *s* of André Jarre and Gabrielle Jarre (*née* Boullu); *m* 1984, Khong Fui Fong; two *s* one *d* by previous marriages. *Educ:* Lycée Ampère, Lyons; Univ. of Lyons; Univ. of Paris, Sorbonne; Conservatoire Nat. Supérieur de Musique. Musician, Radiodiffusion Française, 1946–50; Dir of Music, Théâtre Nat. Populaire, 1950–63. Work includes symphonic music, music for theatre and ballet; film scores include: Hôtel des Invalides, 1952; Sur le pont d'Avignon, 1956; Sundays and Cybele, 1962; The Longest Day, 1962; Lawrence of Arabia, 1962 (Acad. Award for best original score); Dr Zhivago, 1965 (Acad. Award for best original score); Gambit, 1966; The Fixer, 1968; Ryan's Daughter, 1970; El Condor, 1970; The Life and Times of Judge Roy Bean, 1972; The Man Who Would Be King, 1975; Jesus of Nazareth, 1977; Shogun, 1980; Firefox, 1982; The Year of Living Dangerously, 1983; A Passage To India, 1985 (Acad. Award for best original score); Mad Max 3, 1985; Witness, 1985; The Mosquito Coast, 1986; Tai-Pan, 1987; Fatal Attraction, 1987; Gorillas in the Mist, 1989; Dead Poets Society, 1989; Ghost, 1990; A Walk in the Clouds, 1995; La Jour et la Nuit, 1997; Sunshine, 1999; I Dreamed of Africa, 2000. Hon. Citizen: Lyon; Lille; Officier, Légion d'honneur (France); Commandeur des Arts et des Lettres (France); Comdr, Ordre Nat. du Mérite (France). *Address:* c/o Sacem, 225 avenue Charles de Gaulle, 92521 Neuilly-sur-Seine, France.

JARRETT, Keith; pianist and composer; *b* Allentown, Penn, 8 May 1945; *s* of Daniel and Irma Jarrett; *m* Margot; two *s*. *Educ:* Berklee Sch. of Music. Pianist with jazz gps led by Art Blakey, 1965, Charles Lloyd, 1966–69, Miles Davis, 1970–71; tours of Europe and numerous recordings; soloist and leader of own gps, 1969–. Concert soloist with various US orchs; numerous recordings of classical music. *Albums include:* Life Between the Exit Signs, 1968; Restoration Ruin, 1968; Birth, 1971; Expectations, 1971; Facing You, 1972; In the Light, 1973; Belonging, 1974; Treasure Island, 1974; Death and the Flower, 1974; Personal Mountains, 1979; Nude Arts, 1979; Invocations, 1981; Standards, 1983; The Cure, 1990; Bye Bye Black Bird, 1991; At the Deer Head Inn, 1992; Bridge of Light, 1993; At the Blue Note, 1994; La Scala, 1995; Tokyo '96, 1998; Expectations, 1999; Melody at Night with You, 1999; Whisper Not, 2000; Inside Out, 2001; Always Let Me Go, 2002. *Compositions include:* Celestial Hawk, 1980; Sonata for Violin and Piano, 1985; Elegy for Violin and String Orchestra, 1985; Sacred Ground, 1985. *Address:* c/o Vincent Ryan, 135 West 16th Street, New York, NY 10011, USA.

JARRETT, Rt Rev. Martyn William; *see* Beverley, Bishop Suffragan of.

JARRETT, Prof. William Fleming Hoggan, FRS 1980; FRSE 1965; Professor of Veterinary Pathology, 1968–91, Senior Research Fellow, 1991, University of Glasgow; *b* 2 Jan. 1928; *s* of James and Jessie Jarrett; *m* 1952, Anna Fraser Sharp; two *d*. *Educ:* Lenzie Academy; Glasgow Veterinary Coll.; Univ. of Glasgow; PhD, FRCVS, FRCPath. Gold Medal, 1949; John Henry Steele Meml Medal, 1961; Steele Bodger Meml Schol. 1955. ARC Research Student, 1949–52; Lectr, Dept of Veterinary Pathology, Univ. of Glasgow Vet. Sch., 1952–53; Head of Hospital Path. Dept of Vet. Hosp., Univ. of Glasgow, 1953–61; Reader in Pathology, Univ. of Glasgow, 1962–65; seconded to Univ. of E Africa, 1963–64; Titular Prof. of Experimental Vet. Medicine, Univ. of Glasgow, 1965. Lectures: Leeuwenhoek, Royal Soc., 1986; McFadyean Meml, RVC, 1986. Fogarty Scholar, NIH, 1985. Hon. FRCPSGlas 1988. Dr *hc* Liège Univ., 1986; DUniv Stirling, 1988; Hon. DSc: East Anglia, 1989; Edinburgh, 1989; Hon. DVSc RVC, London, 1991. Centennial Award, Univ. of Pennsylvania, 1984; Makdougall Brisbane Prize, RSE, 1984; J.T. Edwards Meml Medal, RCVS, 1984; Feldberg Prize, 1987; Tenovus-Scotland Margaret McLellan Award, 1989; Saltire Award, 1989; WSAVA Waltham Internat. Award, 1991. *Publications:* various, on tumour viruses, leukaemia and immunology. *Recreations:* sailing, ski-ing, mountaineering, music. *Clubs:* Clyde Cruising; Glencoe Ski.

JARROLD, Kenneth Wesley, CBE 1997; Senior Consultant, since 2006, Director, since 2007, Dearden Consulting; *b* 19 May 1948; *s* of William Stanley Jarrold and Martha Hamilton Jarrold (*née* Cowan); *m* 1973, Patricia Hadaway (separated 2007); two *s*. *Educ:* St Lawrence Coll., Ramsgate; Sidney Sussex Coll., Cambridge (Whittaker Schol.; BA Hons Hist. 1st cl.; Pres., Cambridge Union Soc.) Dip. IHSM (Hons Standard). E Anglian RHB, 1969–70; Briggs Cttee on Nursing, 1970–71; Dep. Supt, Royal Hosp., Sheffield, 1971–74; Hosp. Sec., Derbyshire Royal Infirmary, 1974–75; Sector Administrator, Nottingham Gen. and Univ. Hosps, 1975–79; Asst Dist Administrator (Planning), S Tees HA, 1979–82; Dist Administrator, 1982–84, Dist Gen. Manager, 1984–89, Gloucester HA; Regl Gen. Manager, Wessex RHA, 1990–94; Dir of Human Resources and Dep. Chief Exec., NHS Exec., 1994–97; Chief Executive: Co. Durham HA, 1997–2002; Co. Durham and Tees Valley Strategic HA, 2002–05. Non-exec. Dir, Serious Organised Crime Agency, 2005–. Chm., Co. Durham Econ. Partnership, 2006–. Member: NHS Training Authy (and Chm., Training Cttee), 1984–87; Nat. Adv. Gp, NHS Leadership Centre, 2002–04; Nat. Mental Health Taskforce, 2003–05; Govt Programme Bd on Health Inequalities, 2004–05; Chairman: Management Educn System by Open Learning Project Group, 1986–89, and 1991–93; Durham and Teesside Workforce Develt Confedn, 2001–02; DoH Wkg Party on Code of Conduct of NHS Managers, 2002; NHS Reference Gp on Health Inequalities, 2003–05; DoH Task Gp on maximising NHS contrib. to Public Health, 2004; Pharmacy Regulation and Leadership Oversight Gp, 2007–. Pres., IHSM, 1985–86 (Mem., Nat. Council, 1977–89. Hon. Visiting Professor: York Univ., 1998–; Salford Univ., 1998–2004; Durham Univ., 2005–. Hon. Fellow, John Snow Coll., Durham Univ., 2006. DUniv Open, 1999. *Publications:* Challenges for Health Services in the 1990s, 1990; (contrib.) Health Care Systems in Canada and the UK, 1994; Minding Our Own Business: healing division in the NHS, 1995; Servants and Leaders, 1998; articles in professional jls. *Address:* 75 Beechwood Road, Eaglescliffe, Stockton-on-Tees TS16 0AE. *Club:* Athenæum.

JARROLD, Nicholas Robert; HM Diplomatic Service, retired; Director, British Association for Central and Eastern Europe, 2004–08; *b* 2 March 1946; *s* of late Albert and Dawn Jarrold; *m* 1972, Anne Catherine Whitworth; two *s*. *Educ:* Shrewsbury Sch.; Western Reserve Acad., Ohio (ESU Scholar); St Edmund Hall, Oxford (Exhibnr, MA). Entered Diplomatic Service, 1968: FCO, 1968–69; The Hague, 1969–72; Dakar, 1972–75; FCO, 1975–79; 1st Sec. and Hd of Chancery, Nairobi, 1979–83; FCO, 1983–89; Counsellor and Dep. Head of Mission, Havana, 1989–91; Vis. Fellow, St Antony's Coll., Oxford, 1991–92; Counsellor (Economic and Commercial), Brussels and Luxembourg, 1992–96; Ambassador to: Latvia, 1996–99; Croatia, 2000–04. *Recreations:* reading history, cricket, the theatre. *Address:* 9 Park Drive, SW14 8RB. *Club:* Athenæum.

JARROW, Bishop Suffragan of, since 2007; **Rt Rev. Mark Watts Bryant;** *b* 8 Oct. 1949; *s* of Douglas William and Kathleen Joyce Bryant; *m* 1976, Elisabeth Eastaugh; two *s* one *d*. *Educ:* St John's Sch., Leatherhead; St John's Coll., Univ. of Durham (BA); Cuddesdon Theol Coll. Ordained deacon, 1975, priest, 1976; Curate, Addlestone, 1975–79; Asst Priest, 1979–83; Vicar, 1983–88, St John Studley, Trowbridge; Chaplain, Trowbridge FE Coll., 1979–83; Dir of Ordinands and Hd, Vocations and Trng Dept, Dio. Coventry, 1988–96; Team Rector, Caludon, Coventry, 1996–2001; Archdeacon of Coventry, 2001–07; Residentiary Canon, Coventry Cathedral, 2006–07. *Recreations:* music, walking, popular television. *Address:* Bishop's House, Ivy Lane, Low Fell, Gateshead NE9 6QD.

JÄRVI, Neeme; Principal Conductor and Music Director, New Jersey Symphony Orchestra, since 2005; Chief Conductor, Residentie Orkest, The Hague, since 2005; Principal Conductor Emeritus, Gothenburg Symphony Orchestra, Sweden (Chief Conductor, 1982–2004); Music Director Emeritus, Detroit Symphony Orchestra (Music Director, 1990–2005); *b* Tallinn, Estonia, 7 June 1937; *s* of August and Elss Järvi; *m* 1961, Liilia Järvi; two *s* one *d*. *Educ:* Estonia-Tallinn Conservatory of Music; Leningrad State Conservatory. Chief Conductor: Estonian Radio Symphony Orch., 1963–77 (Conductor, 1960–63); Estonia opera house, Tallinn, 1963–77; toured USA with Leningrad Phil. Orch., 1973 and 1977; Chief Conductor, Estonian State Symph. Orch., 1976–80; since emigration to USA in 1980 has appeared as Guest Conductor with New York Phil. Orch., Philadelphia Orch., Boston Symph., Chicago Symph., Los Angeles Phil., Met. Opera (New York) and in San Francisco, Cincinnati, Indianapolis, Minneapolis and Detroit; has also given concerts in Vienna, London, Canada, Sweden, Finland, Norway, Denmark, Holland, Switzerland and W Germany; Principal Guest Conductor, CBSO, 1981–84; Musical Dir and Principal Conductor, Scottish Nat. Orch., 1984–88, Conductor Laureate, 1989; First Principal Guest Conductor, Japan Philharmonic SO. 1st Prize, Internat. Conductors Competition, Accademia Santa Cecilia, Rome, 1971. Over 310 CDs including: works by Bartok, Dvorak, Medtner, Barber, Prokofiev (symphonic cycle), Shostakovich; complete works of Sibelius and all symphonies of Nielsen and Mahler (Toblach Prize for best recording, 1993, for No 3); Saul and David, opera by Nielsen; Don Giovanni; Schmidt symphonies. *Recreation:* traveller. *Address:* c/o HarrisonParrott International Artists Management Ltd, 12 Penzance Place, W11 4PA.

JARVIE, Elizabeth (Marie-Lesley); QC (Scot.) 1995; Sheriff of Lothian and Borders at Edinburgh, since 1997; *b* 22 Jan. 1952; *d* of Dr James Leslie Rennie and Marie-Thérèse (*née* Loyseau de Mauléon); *m* 1976, John Jarvie; one *s* four *d*. *Educ:* Larbert High Sch., Stirlingshire; Univ. of Edinburgh (MA Hons, LLB). Apprentice, Biggert Baillie & Gifford WS, 1978–79; admitted to Scots Bar, 1981; Advocate-Depute, 1991–94. Part-time Chm., Social Security Appeal Tribunal, 1986–89. *Recreations:* ski-ing, music, lunching, news. *Address:* Rowallan, Barnton Avenue, Edinburgh EH4 6JJ. *T:* (0131) 336 2117.

JARVIS, Anthony, MA; Headmaster, St Olave's and St Saviour's Grammar School, since 1994; *b* Oxford, 30 March 1945; *s* of Donald Anthony Jarvis and Ida Jarvis (*née* Allmond); *m* Brigit Mary, *d* of Baillie Andrew Convery and Elizabeth Convery; one *s* one *d*. *Educ:*

City of Oxford High Sch.; Brighton Coll. of Educn (Cert Ed); Univ. of Sussex (BEd Hons; MA). Haywards Heath County School: Asst Master, 1968–71; Librarian, 1971–72; Hd, Social Studies, 1972–73; Housemaster, Beckworth Boarding Hse, Lindfield, 1969–72; Oathall School: Hd of Year, 1973–74; Hd, Social Studies and Curriculum Co-ordinator, 1974–79; Hd of English, 1979–84; Dep. Principal and Headmaster of Secondary Sch., St George's English Sch., Rome, 1984–90; Headmaster, Sir Thomas Rich's Sch., Gloucester, 1990–94. PGCE teacher and tutor, Univ. of Sussex, 1975–79. Educn consultancies in UK and Europe, 2004–. Addnl Mem., HMC, 1996–. Headteacher Mem., Army Scholarship Bd, 1997–2001. Woodard Corporation: Fellow, 2002–; Dir, 2006–; Chm., Educn Cttee, 2006–. Governor: Hurstpierpoint Coll., 2001–; Christ's Hosp., Horsham, 2007–. FRSA 1993. *Recreations:* travel and restaurants, books and newspapers, Rugby Union, Italy. *Address:* Headmaster's House, St Olave's, Goddington Lane, Orpington, Kent BR6 9SH. *T:* (01689) 820101; *e-mail:* office@saintolaves.net. *Clubs:* East India and Public Schools (Hon. Mem.); Sir Thomas Rich's Bowling.

JARVIS, Catriona, (Mrs P. St J. Bolton); a Senior Immigration Judge, Asylum and Immigration Tribunal (formerly a Vice-President, Immigration Appeal Tribunal), since 2004; *b* 16 April 1950; *d* of late Stanley and Isabella Jarvis; *m* 1996, Philip St John Bolton; one *s*. *Educ:* Manresa House Coll. of Educn (Cert Ed 1972); Univ. of Paris, Sorbonne (Cert. de Langue Française Degré Supérieur 1975); Univ. of E London (LLM Dist. 2000). Admitted solicitor, 1985; solicitor in private practice and local govt, 1985–92; Immigration Adjudicator (pt-time), 1992–96; Immigration Adjudicator, Immigration Appellate Authy, 1996–2004. Founder Mem., 1997, Dep. Pres., 1997–98, Council of Immigration Judges. Mem. Council, Internat. Assoc. of Refugee Law Judges, 2005–. *Publications:* (contrib.) Security of Residence and Expulsion: protection of aliens in Europe, 2001; contrib. papers and articles on internat. refugee, immigration and human rights law. *Recreations:* literary debate, creative writing, walking, tennis. *Address:* Asylum and Immigration Tribunal, Field House, 15 Breams Buildings, EC4A 1DZ. *T:* (020) 7073 4200. *Club:* Highbury Group.

JARVIS, Frederick Frank, (Fred); General Secretary, National Union of Teachers, 1975–89; Member of General Council, 1974–89, President, 1987, Trades Union Congress (Chairman, 1986–87); *b* 8 Sept. 1924; *s* of Alfred and Emily Ann Jarvis; *m* 1954, Elizabeth Anne Colegrove, Stanton Harcourt, Oxfordshire; one *s* one *d*. *Educ:* Plaistow Secondary Sch., West Ham; Oldershaw Grammar Sch., Wallasey; Liverpool Univ. (Dip. in Social Science with dist.); St Catherine's Society, Oxford (BA Hons PPE; MA). Contested (Lab) Wallasey, Gen. Elec., 1951; Chm., Nat. Assoc. of Labour Student Organisations, 1951; Pres., Nat. Union of Students, 1952–54 (Dep. Pres., 1951–52); Asst Sec., Nat. Union of Teachers, 1955–59; Head of Publicity and Public Relations, 1959–70; Dep. Gen. Sec., NUT, 1970–74 (apptd Gen. Sec. Designate, March 1974). Pres., Eur. Trade Union Cttee for Educn, 1983–84, 1985–86 (Vice-Pres., 1981–83); Chairman, TUC Cttees: Local Govt, 1983–88; Educn Training, 1985–88; Chm., TUC Nuclear Energy Review Body, 1986–88. Member: Central Arbitration Cttee, 1985–94; Franco-British Council, 1986–98. Mem. Council, Nat. Youth Theatre; Trustee, Trident Trust; Mem. Bd, Univ. of First Age, Birmingham. *Photographic exhibitions:* Days of Rallies and Roses, London, Manchester, Norwich and Grantham, 1997; Politicians, Poppies and other Flowers, London, 1998; Monet's Garden and the lesser known Provence, London, Birmingham, 2000, Poole, Edinburgh, Alton, Provence, Oxford, 2001; Homage to the Hammers, London, 2001; Market Day, Provence, 2002; Forty Years On: a year in the life of St Catherine's College, Oxford, 2002; London's Future: the spirit of its schools, London, 2004; Photo Opportunities, London, 2004. FRSA. Hon. FEIS 1980; Hon. FCP 1982. DUniv UCE, 2004. *Publications:* The Educational Implications of UK Membership of the EEC, 1972; Education and Mr Major, 1993; Ed, various jls including: 'Youth Review', NUT Guide to Careers; NUT Univ. and Coll. Entrance Guide. *Recreations:* swimming, cycling, gardening, cinema, theatre, photography. *Address:* 92 Hadley Road, New Barnet, Herts EN5 5QR. *Club:* Ronnie Scott's.

JARVIS, James Roger; His Honour Judge Jarvis; a Circuit Judge, since 2000; *b* 7 Sept. 1944; *s* of Flt Lieut Douglas Bernard Jarvis, DFC, RAF (retd), and Elsie Vanessa Jarvis; *m* 1972, Kerstin Marianne Hall; one *s* two *d*. *Educ:* Latymer Upper Sch.; Brockenhurst County Grammar Sch.; Peter Symonds. Articled Clerk, Bernard Chill & Axtell; admitted Solicitor, 1969; joined Andrews McQueen, later McQueen Yeoman, 1972; Asst Solicitor, 1972–73; Partner, 1973–2000. *Recreations:* jogging, walking, reading. *Address:* c/o Bournemouth Crown and County Courts, Deansleigh Road, Bournemouth BH7 7DS. *T:* (01202) 502800.

JARVIS, John Francis, CVO 2001; CBE 1993; Chairman, Jarvis Hotels plc, since 1990 (Chief Executive, 1990–2002); *b* 15 Feb. 1943; *s* of Thomas Jarvis and Mary Jarvis; *m* 1984, Sally Ann Garrod; one *s* two *d*. *Educ:* Scarborough Grammar Sch.; S Devon Hotel Coll. FIH (FHCIMA 1975). With Rank Orgn, 1965–75; Ladbroke Gp plc, 1975–90: Chairman: Ladbroke Hotels, Holidays and Entertainment, 1975–87; Texas Homecare, 1985–87; Hilton Internat., 1987–90; Prince's Trust-Action, 1993–98; Prince's Trust Trading, 1998–2000; Prince's Foundn, 2001–. Director: Shepperton Hldgs Ltd, 1995–2001; Apollo Leisure Gp, 1998–99; non-exec. Chm., On Board Services Ltd, later Europ. Rail Catering (Hldgs) Ltd, 1995–97. Member: English Tourist Bd, 1983–96; BTA, 1995–2000; Chm., British Hospitality Assoc. Council, 2000–01. Mem., Exec. Bd, Variety Club of GB, 1986–98. *Recreation:* tennis. *Address:* Jarvis Hotels plc, Castle House, Desborough Road, High Wycombe, Bucks HP11 2PR. *T:* (01494) 473800.

JARVIS, Dr John Herbert; Senior Vice President, John Wiley and Sons - Europe, since 1997; *b* 16 May 1947; *s* of Herbert Henry Wood Jarvis and Mabel (*née* Griffiths); *m* 1970, Jean Elizabeth Levy; one *s* one *d*. *Educ:* UC of Swansea (BSc; PhD 1972). Research Fellow: Welsh Nat. Sch. of Medicine, 1972–75; Univ. of Bristol, 1975–77; Ed., Elsevier Sci. Pubns, 1977–79; John Wiley Publishers, 1979–: Publishing Dir, 1987–93; Man. Dir, 1993–97. Dir, STM Publishing Gp, 1999–. Mem. Council, Publishers' Assoc., 1998–. Mem. Bd, Chichester Fest. Th., 2001–04. Gov., Chichester Coll., 2005–. *Publications:* contrib. articles to various med. and biomed. jls on aspects of cancer. *Recreations:* boating, walking, guitar, reading, theatre, hypochondria. *Address:* Chilgrove Barn, Chilgrove, Chichester, West Sussex PO18 9HX. *T:* (01243) 535323, *Fax:* (01243) 770122; *e-mail:* jjarvis@wiley.co.uk. *Club:* Groucho.

JARVIS, John Manners; QC 1989; a Recorder, since 1992; a Deputy High Court Judge, since 1998; *b* 20 Nov. 1947; *s* of late Donald Edward Manners Jarvis and Theodora Brixie Jarvis; *m* 1972, Janet Rona Kitson; two *s*. *Educ:* King's Coll. Sch., Wimbledon; Emmanuel Coll., Cambridge (MA (Law)). Called to Bar, Lincoln's Inn, 1970, Bencher, 1998; practising barrister specialising in Commercial Law, particularly banking; Jt Hd of Chambers, 1999–. An Asst Recorder, 1987–92. Chm., Commercial Bar Assoc., 1995–97 (Treas., 1993–95); Mem., Bar Council, 1995–97. Gov., King's Coll. Sch., Wimbledon, 1987– (Chm., 2008–). Overseas Editor, Jl of Banking and Finance—Law and Practice, 1990–; Consultant Editor, Jl of Internat. Banking and Finance, 2006–. *Publications:* (jtly) Lender Liability, 1993; (contrib.) Banks, Liability and Risk, 2nd edn 1995. *Recreations:* tennis, horse-riding, sailing, ski-ing, cycling, music. *Address:* 3 Verulam Buildings, Gray's Inn, WC1R 5NT. *T:* (020) 7831 8441, *Fax:* (020) 7831 8479; *e-mail:* jjarvis@3vb.con *Club:* Hurlingham.

JARVIS, Surg. Rear Adm. Lionel John, QHS 2006; FRCR; Assistant Chief of Defenc Staff (Health), since 2008; *b* Windsor, 13 May 1955; *s* of Steve Jarvis; *m* 1998, Dr Penelop Gordon; one *s* one *d*. *Educ:* Wellington Coll., Berks; Guy's Hosp., London (MB BS 1977 MRCS, LRCP 1977; FRCR 1988; MIET 2003. Defence consultant advr in radiol 1995–2000; Cons. Radiologist and CO, Royal Hosp., Haslar, 2001–03; rcds 2004; Di Med. Policy, MoD, 2005–08. Diagnostic Imaging Dr of Year, 1999; Crookshank Meda RCR, 2007. Gulf War Medal (with clasp), 1991; Queen's Jubilee Medal, 2002; Iraq W Medal (with clasp), 2003. *Publications:* contribs to med. jls, incl. Lancet, American Radiol., Clinical Radiol. *Recreations:* sailing, ski-ing, riding. *Address:* Midlingto Farmhouse, Droxford, Hants SO32 3PU. *Club:* Army and Navy.

JARVIS, Martin, OBE 2000; actor and director; *b* 4 Aug. 1941; *s* of late Denys Jarvis an of Margot Jarvis; *m*; two *s*; *m* 1974, Rosalind Ayres. *Educ:* Whitgift School; RADA (Hor Dip., 1962, Silver Medal, 1962, Vanbrugh Award, 1962; RADA Associate, 1980). Na Youth Theatre, 1960–62; played Henry V, Sadler's Wells, 1962; Manchester Librar Theatre, 1962–63; *stage:* Life of Galileo, Mermaid, 1963; Cockade, Arts, 1963; Poor Bito Duke of York's, 1963; Man and Superman, Vaudeville, 1966; The Bandwagon, Mermaic 1970; The Rivals, USA, 1973; Hamlet (title rôle), Fest. of British Th., 1973; The Circl Haymarket, 1976; She Stoops to Conquer, Canada, and Hong Kong Arts Festival, 197 Caught in the Act, Garrick, 1981; Importance of Being Earnest, NT, 1982; Victor Station, NT, 1983; The Trojan War Will Not Take Place, NT, 1983; Woman in Min Vaudeville, 1986; The Perfect Party, Greenwich, 1987; Henceforward, Vaudeville, 198 Exchange, Vaudeville, 1990, Los Angeles, 1992; You Say Potato, Los Angeles, 199 Twelfth Night, Playhouse, 1991; Leo in Love, Southampton, 1992; Just Betwee Ourselves, Greenwich, 1992; Make and Break, 1993, Man of the Moment, 1994, Lo Angeles; On Approval, Playhouse, 1994; Table Manners, LA, 1995; The Doctor Dilemma, Almeida, 1998; Skylight, LA, 1999; Passion Play, Donmar, 2000; By Jeeve NY, 2001; recitals of Paradise Lost, Old Vic, Chichester and QEH, 1975–77; Th Queen's Birthday Concert, Royal Festival Hall, 1996; narrator, Peter and the Wol Barbican, 1997; An Audience with Martin Jarvis, RNT, 2003; Gielgud Centenary Gal Gielgud, 2004; Twelfth Night, Regent's Pk, 2005; Honour, Wyndham's, 2006; Dir, Th Life of Galileo, LA, 2008; recitals of Beloved Clara and Odyssey of Love, Chichester an Wigmore Hall, 2007–08; *films:* The Last Escape, Ike, The Bunker, Taste the Blood o Dracula, Buster; The Fool of the World and the Flying Ship, 1991 (Emmy Award Emily's Ghost, 1992; Calliope; Absence of War, 1995; Titanic, 1997; The X-Ray Ki Sex 'n' Death, 1999; Mrs Caldicot's Cabbage War, By Jeeves, 2002; Much Ado Abou Nothing, 2005; Framed, 2006; The Legend of Spyro, 2007; *television series:* The Forsyt Saga, 1967; Nicholas Nickleby, 1968; Little Women, 1969; The Moonstone, 1971; Th Pallisers, 1974; David Copperfield, 1975; Killers, 1976; Rings on Their Fingers, 1978–8 Breakaway, 1980; The Black Tower, 1985; Chelworth, 1988; Countdown, 1990– Murder Most Horrid, 1991; The Good Guys, 1992; Woof!, 1992; Library of Romanc 1992; Girl from Ipanema (British Comedy Award); Scarlet and Black, 1993; Brilla Saverin, 1994; Lovejoy, 1994; Murder She Wrote, 1995; Supply and Demand, 199 Space Island One, 1998; Lorna Doone, 2000; Micawber, 2001; Bootleg, 2002; Psi-Ki (USA), 2003; Doctors, 2004; Numb3rs (USA), 2007; Taking the Flak, 2008; Stargat Atlantis (USA), 2008; *radio:* numerous performances, incl. one-man series, Jarvis's Frayn as Charles Dickens in series, The Best of Times; Gush, 1994; (and prod.) Speak After th Beep, 2 series, 1997; Spies, 2002; productions of plays; script writing and adaptation prod. and dir dramas, BBC R4, 2002–, incl. Dr No, 2008; Jeeves Live, BBC an Cheltenham Fest., 2008; commentaries for TV and film documentaries and for art programmes; has adapted and read over 100 of Richmal Crompton's Just William storie for radio, TV and CD; recorded one-man performance of David Copperfield for cassett 1991; one-man perf., Oscar Wilde, 1996; co-produced cassette 2nd World War Poetry 1993; produced and directed cassettes, Tales from Shakespeare; P. G. Wodehous recordings, 2007–08; Voice of God, OT CD recordings (USA), 2008. Writer/presente Concorde Playhouse, 1994–97. Dir, Children's Film Unit, 1993–2000. Vice-Pres Salamander Oasis Trust, 1990–. Sony Silver Award, 1991; NY Internat. Award, fo contribn to broadcasting, 1994; British Talkies award, 1995, 1997, 1998; US Audi Award, 1999; US Earphones Award, 2003, 2005, 2007; Radio Independents Gp Award for outstanding contribn to broadcasting, 2007. *Publications:* Bright Boy, 1977; Willian Stories: a personal selection, 1992; Meet Just William, 1999; Acting Strangely (autobiog.) 1999; Broadway, Jeeves?, 2003; short stories for radio; contribs to many anthologies articles in The Listener, Punch, Tatler, The Times, Daily Telegraph and Daily Mail *Recreations:* Beethoven, Mozart, growing lemons. *Address:* c/o Amanda Howar Associates, 21 Berwick Street, W1F 0PZ.

JARVIS, Prof. Martin John, OBE 2002; DSc; Principal Scientist, Cancer Research UK (formerly Imperial Cancer Research Fund), 1991–94; Professor of Health Psychology University College London, 1999–2004, now Emeritus; *b* 30 June 1939; s of Richar William Jarvis and Mary May Jarvis (*née* Utting); *m* 1969, Muriel Richardson; one *s* on *d*. *Educ:* Watford Grammar Sch.; Corpus Christi Coll., Cambridge (MA); Birkbeck Coll. London (BA Psychol.); Inst. of Psychiatry (MPhil Clin. Psychol); UCL (DSc Medicin 1997). Res. worker, 1978–89, Sen. Lectr, 1986–89, Addiction Res. Unit, Inst. Psychiatry Sen. Scientist, Health Behaviour Unit, ICRF, 1989–91; Reader in Health Psychol., UCL 1996–99. Mem., CMO's Scientific Cttee on Tobacco and Health, 1994–. Dir, ASH 1996–. Mem., Scientific Cttee on Tobacco Product Regulation, WHO, 2000–. *Publications:* numerous res. papers on tobacco smoking and nicotine addiction. *Recreations* growing vegetables, bee-keeping, walking, gym. *Address:* Department of Epidemiology and Public Health, University College London, 1–19 Torrington Place, WC1E 6BT; 11 Woodwarde Road, SE22 8UT. *T:* (020) 8693 3508; *e-mail:* martin.jarvis@ucl.ac.uk.

JARVIS, Patrick William, CB 1985; CEng, FIET, FIMarEST; RCNC; Deputy Controller (Warships), Ministry of Defence (Procurement Executive), and Head of Roya Corps of Naval Constructors, 1983–86; *b* 27 Aug. 1926; *s* of Frederick Arthur and Marjorie Winifred Jarvis; *m* 1951, Amy (*née* Ryley); two *s*. *Educ:* Royal Naval Coll., Greenwich; Royal Naval Engrg Coll., Keyham, Devonport. BScEng. Trade apprentice HM Dockyard, Chatham, 1942–46; Design Engineer, Admiralty, Bath, 1946–62; Warship Electrical Supt, Belfast, 1962–63; Suptg Engr, MoD(N), Bath, 1963–72; Ship Department, MoD (PE), Bath: Asst Dir and Dep. Dir, 1972–78; Under Sec., 1978; Dir of Naval Ship Production, 1979–81; Dir of Ship Design and Engrg, and Dep. Head of Royal Corps of Naval Constructors, 1981–83; Dep. Sec., 1983. *Address:* Ranworth, Bathampton Lane, Bath BA2 6ST.

JASON, Sir David, Kt 2005; OBE 1993; actor; *b* 2 Feb. 1940; *s* of Arthur and Olwyn White; adopted stage name, David Jason, 1965; *m* 2005, Gill Hinchcliffe; one *d*. Stage career began with a season in repertory, Bromley Rep.; *theatre includes:* Under Milk Wood, Mayfair, 1971; The Rivals, Sadler's Wells, 1972; No Sex Please … We're British!, Strand, 1972; Darling Mr London, tour, 1975; Charley's Aunt, tour, 1975; The Norman Conquests, Oxford Playhouse, 1976; The Relapse, Cambridge Theatre Co., 1978;

Cinderella, 1979; The Unvarnished Truth, Mid/Far East tour, 1983; Look No Hans!, tour and West End, 1985; *films:* Under Milk Wood, 1970; Royal Flash, 1974; The Odd Job, 1978; Only Fools and Horses; Wind in the Willows, 1983; *television includes:* Do Not Adjust Your Set, 1967; The Top Secret Life of Edgar Briggs, 1973–74; Mr Stabbs, 1974; Ronnie Barker Shows, 1975; Open All Hours, 1975; Porridge, 1975; Lucky Feller, 1975; A Sharp Intake of Breath, 1978; Del Trotter in Only Fools and Horses, 1981–91 (Best Light Entertainment Perf., BAFTA, 1990); Porterhouse Blue, 1986; Jackanory, 1988; A Bit of A Do, 1988–89; Single Voices: The Chemist, 1989; Amongst Barbarians, 1989; Pa Larkin in The Darling Buds of May, 1990–93; A Touch of Frost, 1992–; The Bullion Boys, 1993; All the King's Men, 1999; Micawber, 2001; The Quest (also dir), 2002; *voice work:* Dangermouse, Count Duckula, The Wind in the Willows. Awards include Best Actor Award, BAFTA, 1988; Special Recognition Award for Lifetime Achievement in Television, Nat. Television Awards, 1996; Best Comedy Perf. Award, BAFTA, 1997; BAFTA Fellowship, 2003. *Recreations:* diving, flying, motorcycles. *Address:* c/o Richard Stone Partnership, 2 Henrietta Street, WC2E 8PS.

JASPAN, Andrew; Editor-in-Chief, The Age, since 2004; *b* 20 April 1952; *s* of Mervyn and Helen Jaspan; *m* 1991, Karen Jane Grant; two *s. Educ:* Beverley GS; Manchester Univ. (BA Hons Politics). Co-Founder, New Manchester Review, 1976–79; Daily Telegraph features, 1979; Fellowship, Journalists in Europe, Paris, 1980–81; freelance journalist, Daily Mirror and Daily Telegraph, 1982; News Sub-Ed., The Times, 1983–85; Asst News Ed., Sunday Times, 1985–88; Editor: Sunday Times Scotland, 1988–89; Scotland on Sunday, 1989–94; The Scotsman, 1994–95; The Observer, 1995–96; Publr and Man. Dir, The Big Issue, 1996–98; Ed., Sunday Herald, 1999–2004. *Publications:* Exams and Assessment, 1975; Preparing for Higher Education, 1975. *Recreations:* tennis, travelling. *Address:* Age Company Ltd, 250 Spencer Street, Melbourne, Vic 3000, Australia.

JAVACHEFF, Christo; see Christo and Jeanne-Claude.

JAVACHEFF, Jeanne-Claude; see Christo and Jeanne-Claude.

JAWARA, Alhaji Sir Dawda Kairaba, Kt 1966; Hon. GCMG 1974; Grand Master, Order of the Republic of The Gambia, 1972; President of the Republic of The Gambia, 1970–94; Vice-President of the Senegambian Confederation, 1982; *b* Barajally, MacCarthy Island Div., 16 May 1924. *Educ:* Muslim Primary Sch. and Methodist Boys' Grammar Sch., Bathurst; Achimota Coll.; Glasgow Univ. FRCVS 1988 (MRCVS 1953); Dip. in Trop. Vet. Med., Edinburgh, 1957. Veterinary Officer for The Gambia Govt, 1954–57, Principal Vet. Officer, 1957–60. Leader of People's Progressive Party (formerly Protectorate People's Party), The Gambia, 1960; MP 1960; Minister of Education, 1960–61; Premier, 1962–63; Prime Minister, 1963–70. Chairman: Permanent Inter State Cttee for Drought in the Sahel, 1977–79; Organisation pour la Mise en Valeur du Fleuve Gambie Conf., Heads of State and Govt, 1987–88; Authy of Heads of State and Govt, Economic Community of W African States, 1988–89. Patron, Commonwealth Vet. Assoc., 1967–. Hon. LLD Ife, 1978; Hon. DSc Colorado State Univ., USA, 1986. Peutinger Gold Medal, Peutinger-Collegium, Munich, 1979; Agricola Medal, FAO, Rome, 1980. Grand Cross: Order of Cedar of Lebanon, 1966; Nat. Order of Republic of Senegal, 1967; Order of Propitious Clouds of China (Taiwan), 1968; Nat. Order of Republic of Guinea, 1973; Grand Cordon of Most Venerable Order of Knighthood, Pioneers of Republic of Liberia, 1968; Grand Comdr, Nat. Order of Federal Republic of Nigeria, 1970; Comdr of Golden Ark (Netherlands), 1979; Grand Gwanghwa Medal of Order of Diplomatic Service (Republic of Korea), 1984; Nishan-i-Pakistan (Pakistan), 1984; Grand Officer of Nat. Merit, Islamic Republic of Mauritania, 1992; Grand Comdr, Nat. Order of Republic of Portugal, 1993. *Recreations:* golf, gardening, sailing. *Address:* 40 Atlantic Blvd, Fajara, The Gambia.

JAY, family name of **Baroness Jay of Paddington.**

JAY OF EWELME, Baron *cr* 2006 (Life Peer), of Ewelme, in the County of Oxfordshire; **Michael Hastings Jay,** GCMG 2006 (KCMG 1997; CMG 1992); HM Diplomatic Service, retired; Permanent Under-Secretary of State, Foreign and Commonwealth Office, and Head of the Diplomatic Service, 2002–06; *b* 19 June 1946; *s* of late Alan David Hastings Jay, DSO, DSC, RN and of Vera Frances Effa Vickery, MBE; *m* 1975, Sylvia Mylroie (see Lady Jay of Ewelme). *Educ:* Winchester Coll.; Magdalen Coll., Oxford (MA; Hon. Fellow, 2004); School of Oriental and African Studies, London Univ. (MSc 1969). ODM, 1969–73; UK Delegn, IMF-IBRD, Washington, 1973–75; ODM, 1976–78; First Sec., New Delhi, 1978–81; FCO, 1981–85; Counsellor: Cabinet Office, 1985–87; (Financial and Commercial), Paris, 1987–90; Asst Under-Sec. of State for EC Affairs, FCO, 1990–93; Dep. Under-Sec. of State (Dir for EC and Economic Affairs), FCO, 1994–96; Ambassador to France, 1996–2001; Prime Minister's Personal Rep. for G8 Summits, 2005–06. Non-executive Director: Associated British Foods, 2006–; Candover Investments plc, 2008–; Credit Agricole SA, 2007–; Valeo SA, 2007. Chm., Merlin, 2007–. Vice Chm., Business for New Europe, 2006–; Assoc. Mem., BUPA, 2006–. Sen. Associate Mem., St Antony's Coll., Oxford, 1996. *Address:* House of Lords, SW1A 0PW.

JAY OF EWELME, Lady; Sylvia Jay, CBE 2005; Vice-Chairman, L'Oréal (UK) Ltd, since 2005; *b* 1 Nov. 1946; *d* of William Edwin Mylroie and Edie Mylroie (*née* Chew); *m* 1975, Michael Hastings Jay (see Baron Jay of Ewelme). *Educ:* Nottingham Univ. (BA (Hons) Soc. Sci.); London Sch. of Econs. Home Civil Service: Admin. grade, ODA, 1971–87; secondments to French Ministère de la Coopération, 1988–89, to French Trésor, Paris, 1990, to EBRD, London, 1990–93; Clerk to European Union Sub-cttee A, H of L, 1994–96; accomp. husband, Ambassador to France, Paris, 1996–2000; Dir Gen., Food and Drink Fedn, 2001–05. Member Board: Saint-Gobain, 2001–; Carrefour, 2003–05; Lazard Ltd, 2006–; Alcatel-Lucent, 2006–. Chm., Food from Britain, 2006– (Mem., 2003–). Chm., Pilgrim Trust, 2005–; Trustee: Entente Cordiale Scholarships Scheme, 2001–; Prison Reform Trust, 2006–. *Address:* L'Oréal (UK) Ltd, 255 Hammersmith Road, W6 8AZ.

JAY OF PADDINGTON, Baroness *cr* 1992 (Life Peer), of Paddington in the City of Westminster; **Margaret Ann Jay;** PC 1998; Leader of the House of Lords, 1998–2001; Minister for Women, 1998–2001; *b* 18 Nov. 1939; *er d* of Baron Callaghan of Cardiff, KG, PC and late Audrey Elizabeth (*née* Moulton); *m* 1961, Hon. Peter Jay, *qv* (marr. diss. 1986); one *s* two *d; m* 1994, Prof. M. W. Adler, *qv.* Principal Opposition Spokesman on Health, H of L, 1995–97; Minister of State, DoH, 1997–98. Dir, Nat. Aids Trust, 1988–92. Non-executive Director: Carlton Television, 1996–97; Scottish Power, 1996–97; Independent Media Gp, 2001–; BT Gp, 2002–08. Mem., Kensington, Chelsea & Westminster HA, 1992–97; Chm., Nat. Assoc. of Leagues of Hosp. Friends, 1994. Chm., ODI, 2002–. *Address:* c/o House of Lords, SW1A 0PW.

JAY, Sir Antony (Rupert), Kt 1988; CVO 1993; freelance writer and producer, since 1964; Chairman, Video Arts Ltd, 1972–89; *b* 20 April 1930; *s* of Ernest Jay and Catherine Hay; *m* 1957, Rosemary Jill Watkins; two *s* two *d. Educ:* St Paul's Sch. (scholar); Magdalene Coll., Cambridge (major scholar; BA (1st cl. Hons) Classics and Comparative Philology, 1952; MA 1955; Hon. Fellow, 2001). 2nd Lieut Royal Signals, 1952–54. BBC, 1955–64: Editor, Tonight, 1962–63; Head of Talks Features, TV, 1963–64; (with Jonathan Lynn) writer of BBC TV series, Yes, Minister and Yes, Prime Minister, 1980–88. Mem., Cttee on Future of Broadcasting, 1974–77. FRSA 1992; CCMI (CIMgt 1992). Hon. MA Sheffield, 1987; Hon. DBA IMCB, 1988. *Publications:* Management and Machiavelli, 1967, 2nd edn 1987; (with David Frost) To England with Love, 1967; Effective Presentation, 1970; Corporation Man, 1972; The Householder's Guide to Community Defence against Bureaucratic Aggression, 1972; (with Jonathan Lynn): Yes, Minister, Vol. 1 1981, Vol. 2 1982, Vol. 3 1983; The Complete Yes, Minister, 1984; Yes, Prime Minister, Vol. 1 1986, Vol. 2 1987; The Complete Yes, Prime Minister, 1989; Elizabeth R, 1992; (ed) Oxford Dictionary of Political Quotations, 1996, 3rd edn 2006; How to Beat Sir Humphrey, 1997; Not In Our Back Yard, 2005. *Address:* c/o Alan Brodie Representation Ltd, 6th Floor, Fairgate House, 78 New Oxford Street, WC1A 1HB. *T:* (020) 7079 7990.

JAY, John Philip Bromberg; Director, New Star Asset Management, since 2001; *b* 1 April 1957; *s* of late Alec Jay and June (*née* Bromberg); *m* 1st, 1987, Susy Streeter (marr. diss. 1992); 2nd, 1992, Judi Bevan (*née* Leader); one *d. Educ:* University Coll. Sch.; Magdalen Coll., Oxford (BA Hons Mod. Hist.). Journalist, Western Mail, 1979–81; financial journalist: Thomson Regl Newspapers, 1981–84; Sunday Telegraph, 1984–86; City Editor, Sunday Times, 1986–89; City and Business Editor, Sunday Telegraph, 1989–95; Man. Ed., Business News, Sunday Times, 1995–2001. *Publication:* (with Judi Bevan) The New Tycoons, 1989. *Recreations:* ski-ing, cinema, theatre, walking. *Address:* New Star Asset Management, 1 Knightsbridge Green, SW1X 7NE. *T:* (020) 7225 9200.

JAY, Hon. Martin, CBE 2000; DL; Chairman: VT Group (formerly Vosper Thornycroft Holdings) plc, 2002–05 (Chief Executive, 1989–2002); Invensys plc, since 2003; *b* 18 July 1939; *s* of Baron Jay, PC and Margaret Christian Jay; *m* 1969, Sandra Mary Ruth Williams; one *s* two *d. Educ:* Winchester Coll.; New Coll., Oxford (MA). With BP, 1962–69; GEC plc, 1969–85 (Man. Dir, GEC Inf. Services, and Mem., Mgt Bd, 1980–85); Man. Dir, Lewmar plc, 1985–87; Man. Dir, Electronics Components Div., GEC plc, 1987–89. Chm., EADS UK Ltd, 2005–06. Mem., Nat. Defence Industries Council, 1997–; Pres., British Maritime Equipment Council, subseq. Soc. for Maritime Industries, 1997–2003. DL Hants, 2001. Chairman: Rose Rd Children's Appeal, 1997–2003; Tall Ships Youth Trust, 2005–. Hon. DBA Southampton Inst., 2001; Hon. LLD Portsmouth, 2004. *Recreations:* sailing, gardening, tennis. *Address:* Bishops Court, Bishops Sutton, Alresford, Hants SO24 0AN. *T:* (01962) 732193. *Clubs:* Garrick; Royal Yacht Squadron (Cowes); Seaview Sailing.
See also C. I. Arney, Hon. P. Jay.

JAY, Hon. Peter; writer and broadcaster; *b* 7 Feb. 1937; *s* of Baron Jay, PC and Margaret (Peggy) Christian Jay; *m* 1st, 1961, Margaret Ann (see Baroness Jay of Paddington) (marr. diss. 1986), *d* of Baron Callaghan of Cardiff, KG, PC; one *s* two *d;* one *s;* 2nd, 1986, Emma, *d* of late P. K. Thornton, CBE ; three *s. Educ:* Winchester Coll.; Christ Church, Oxford (MA 1st cl. hons PPE, 1960). President of the Union, 1960. Nuffield Coll., 1960. Midshipman and Sub-Lt RNVR, 1956–57. Asst Principal 1961–64, Private Sec. to Jt Perm. Sec. 1964, Principal 1964–67, HM Treasury; Economics Editor, The Times, 1967–77, and Associate Editor, Times Business News, 1969–77; Presenter, Weekend World (ITV Sunday morning series), 1972–77; The Jay Interview (ITV series), 1975–76; Ambassador to US, 1977–79; Dir Economist Intelligence Unit, 1979–83. Consultant, Economist Gp, 1979–81; Chm. and Chief Exec., TV-am Ltd, 1980–83 and TV-am News, 1982–83, Pres., TV-am, 1983; Presenter, A Week in Politics, Channel 4, 1983–86; COS to Robert Maxwell (Chm., Mirror Gp Newspapers Ltd), 1986–89; Supervising Editor, Banking World, 1986–89 (Editor, 1984–86); Economics and Business Editor, BBC, 1990–2001. Non-exec. Dir, Bank of England, 2003–. Presenter, The Road to Riches, BBC TV series, 2000. Chairman: NACRO Working Party on Children and Young Persons in Custody, 1976–77; NCVO, 1981–86 (Vice-Pres., 1986–92); Trustee, Charities Aid Foundn, 1981–86; Chm., Charities Effectiveness Review Trust, 1986–87. Vis. Scholar, Brookings Instn, Washington, 1979–80; Wincott Meml Lectr, 1975; Copland Meml Lectr, Australia, 1980; MacTaggart Meml Lectr, 1981; Shell Lectr, Glasgow, 1985. Hon. Prof., Univ. of Wales, Aberystwyth, 2001–; Exec. Prof. of Political Economy, Henley Mgt Coll., 2006–. Governor, Ditchley Foundn, 1982–; Mem. Council, St George's House, Windsor, 1982–85. Dep. Mayor, 2004–06, Mayor, 2008–, Woodstock. Dir, New Nat. Theater, Washington, DC, 1979–81. Political Broadcaster of Year, 1973; Harold Wincott Financial and Economic Journalist of Year, 1973; RTS Male Personality of Year (Pye Award), 1974; SFTA Shell Internat. TV Award, 1974; RTS Home News Award, 1992. FRGS 1977. Hon. DH Ohio State Univ., 1978; Hon. DLitt Wake Forest Univ., 1979; Berkeley Citation, Univ. of Calif, 1979. *Publications:* The Budget, 1972; (contrib.) America and the World 1979, 1980; The Crisis for Western Political Economy and other Essays, 1984; (with Michael Stewart) Apocalypse 2000, 1987; Road to Riches, or The Wealth of Man, 2000; contrib. Foreign Affairs jl. *Recreation:* sailing. *Address:* Hensington Farmhouse, Woodstock, Oxon OX20 1LH. *T:* (01993) 811222, *Fax:* (01993) 812861; *e-mail:* peter@jay.prestel.co.uk. *Clubs:* Garrick; Royal Naval Sailing Association, Royal Cork Yacht.
See also Hon. M. Jay.

JAY, Robert Maurice; QC 1998; a Recorder, since 2000; *b* 20 Sept. 1959; *s* of late Prof. Barrie Samuel Jay and of Marcelle Ruby Jay; *m* 1997, Deborah Jacinta Trenner; one *d. Educ:* King's Coll. Sch. (Open Schol.); New Coll., Oxford (Open Schol.; BA 1st cl. Hons Jurisp. 1980). Called to the Bar, Middle Temple, 1981, Bencher, 2007; in practice at the Bar, 1981–. Jun. Counsel to the Crown (Common Law), 1989–98. *Recreations:* golf, opera, chess, bridge, politics. *Address:* 39 Essex Street, WC2R 3AT. *T:* (020) 7832 1111. *Clubs:* Royal Automobile; Coombe Hill Golf.

JAYSON, Prof. Malcolm Irving Vivian, MD; FRCP; Professor of Rheumatology and Director, University Centre for the Study of Chronic Rheumatism, University of Manchester, 1977–96, now Emeritus Professor; *b* 9 Dec. 1937; *s* of Joseph and Sybil Jayson; *m* 1962, Judith Tauber; two *s. Educ:* Middlesex Hosp. Med. Sch., Univ. of London (MB, BS 1961); MD Bristol, 1969; MSc Manchester, 1977. FRCP 1976. House Physician, 1961, House Surgeon, 1962, Middlesex Hosp.; House Physician: Central Middlesex Hosp., 1962; Brompton Hosp., 1963; Sen. House Officer, Middlesex Hosp., 1963; Registrar: Westminster Hosp., 1964; Royal Free Hosp., 1965; Lectr, Univ. of Bristol, Royal Nat. Hosp. for Rheumatic Diseases, Bath, and Bristol Royal Infirmary, 1967; Sen. Lectr, Univ. of Bristol, and Consultant, Royal Nat. Hosp. for Rheumatic Diseases, Bath, and Bristol Royal Infirmary, 1979. Visiting Professor: Univ. of Iowa, 1984; Univ. of Queensland, 1985; Univ. of Cairo, 1992. Gen. Sec., Internat. Back Pain Soc., 1986–; President: Soc. of Chiropodists, 1984; Arachnoiditis Self-Help Gp, 1989–; Pres., Internat. Soc. for Study of the Lumbar Spine, 1995–96. *Publications:* (with A. St J. Dixon) Rheumatism and Arthritis, 1974, 8th edn 1991; The Lumbar Spine and Back Pain, 1976, 4th edn 1992; Back Pain: the facts, 1981, 3rd edn 1992; (with C. Black) Systemic Sclerosis: Scleroderma, 1988; Understanding Back Pain, 2001; contribs to Lancet, BMJ and other med. jls. *Recreations:* antiques (especially sundials), trout fishing. *Address:* The Gate House,

8 Lancaster Road, Didsbury, Manchester M20 2TY. *T:* (0161) 445 1729. *Club:* Royal Society of Medicine.

JAYSTON, Michael, (Michael James); actor; *b* 29 Oct. 1935; *s* of Aubrey Vincent James and Edna Myfanwy Llewelyn; *m* 1st, 1965, Lynn Farleigh (marr. diss. 1970); 2nd, 1970, Heather Mary Sneddon (marr. diss. 1977); 3rd, 1978, Elizabeth Ann Smithson; three *s* one *d*. *Educ:* Becket Grammar School, Nottingham; Guildhall Sch. of Music and Drama (FGSM). *Stage:* Salisbury Playhouse, 1962–63 (parts incl. Henry II, in Becket); Bristol Old Vic, 1963–65; RSC, 1965–69 (incl. Ghosts, All's Well That Ends Well, Hamlet, The Homecoming (NY), The Relapse); Equus, NT, 1973, Albery, 1977; Private Lives, Duchess, 1980; The Sound of Music, Apollo, 1981; The Way of the World, Chichester, 1984, Haymarket, 1985; Woman in Mind, Vaudeville, 1987; Dancing at Lughnasa, Garrick, 1992; The Wind in the Willows, NT, 1994; Easy Virtue, Chichester, 1999; Wild Orchids, Chichester, 2001; The Rivals, Moment of Weakness, tour, 2002; The Marquise, tour, 2004; *films include:* Midsummer Night's Dream, 1968; Cromwell, 1969; Nicholas and Alexandra, 1970; *television includes:* Beethoven, 1969; Mad Jack, 1970; Wilfred Owen, 1971; The Power Game, 1978; Tinker, Tailor, Soldier, Spy, 1979; Dr Who, 1986; A Bit of a Do, 1988, 1989; Haggard, 1990; Darling Buds of May, 1992; Outside Edge, 1995, 1996; Only Fools and Horses, 1996; Eastenders, 2001; The Bill, 2005. Life Mem., Battersea Dogs and Cats Home. *Recreations:* cricket, darts, chess. *Address:* c/o Diamond Management, 31 Percy Street, W1T 2DD. *Clubs:* MCC, Lord's Taverners', Cricketers'; Sussex CC, Gedling Colliery CC (Vice-Pres.); Rottingdean CC (Pres.).

JEAFFRESON, David Gregory, CBE 1981; Deputy Chairman, Big Island Holdings (formerly Big Island Contracting) (HK) Ltd, since 1992; *b* 23 Nov. 1931; *s* of late Bryan Leslie Jeaffreson, MD, FRCS, MRCOG and Margaret Jeaffreson; *m* 1959, Elisabeth Marie Jausions; two *s* two *d* (and one *d* decd). *Educ:* Bootham Sch., York; Clare Coll., Cambridge (MA). 2nd Lieut, RA, 1950. Dist Officer, Tanganyika, 1955–58; Asst Man., Henricot Steel Foundry, 1959–60; Admin. Officer, Hong Kong Govt, 1961; Dep. Financial Sec., 1972–76; Sec. for Economic Services, 1976–82; Sec. for Security, 1982–88; Comr, Independent Commn Against Corruption, 1988–92. *Recreations:* history, music, sailing, walking. *Address:* A2 Cherry Court, 12 Consort Rise, Hong Kong. *T:* 28188025. *Club:* Royal Hong Kong Yacht.

JEAN, Rt Hon. Michaëlle, CC 2005; CMM 2005; CD 2005; Governor General of Canada, since 2005; *b* Port au Prince; *m* Jean-Daniel Lafond (CC 2005); one *d*, and two step *d*. *Educ:* Univ. of Montreal (BA Italian and Hispanic Langs and Lit; MA Comparative Lit); Univ. of Perouse; Univ. of Florence; Catholic Univ. of Milan. Worked with Québec shelters for battered women, 1979–86; taught at Faculty of Italian Studies, Univ. of Montreal, 1984–86; Employment and Immigration Canada; Conseil des Communautés culturelles du Québec; joined Radio-Canada, 1988; reporter and host on news and public affairs progs incl. Actuel, Montréal ce soir, Virages and Le Point; presenter of several Réseau de l'Information à Radio-Canada progs, 1995; presenter: The Passionate Eye and Rough Cuts, CBC Newsworld, 1999; weekend edns of Le Téléjournal, 2001, daily edn of Le Téléjournal, Le Midi, 2003, Radio-Canada; own show, Michaëlle, 2004. *Address:* Office of the Governor General, Rideau Hall, 1 Sussex Drive, Ottawa, ON K1A 0A1, Canada.

JEANES, Leslie Edwin Elloway, CBE 1982; Chief of Public Relations, Ministry of Defence, 1978–81, retired; *b* 17 Dec. 1920; *er s* of late Edwin Eli Jubilee Jeanes and of Mary Eunice Jeanes; *m* 1942, Valerie Ruth, *d* of Ernest and Ethel Vidler; one *d*. *Educ:* Westcliff High Sch. Entered Civil Service, 1939; Inf. Officer, DSIR, 1948–65; Chief Press Officer, Min. of Technol., 1965–68; Dep. Head of Inf., MoT, 1968–70; Head of News, DoE, 1970–73; Chief Inf. Officer, MAFF, 1973–78. *Recreations:* gardening, motoring, DIY. *Address:* 14 Whistley Close, Bracknell, Berks RG12 9LQ. *T:* (01344) 429429.
See also R. E. Jeanes.

JEANES, Ronald Eric; Deputy Director, Building Research Establishment, 1981–86; *b* 23 Sept. 1926; *s* of Edwin and Eunice Jeanes; *m* 1951, Helen Field (*née* Entwistle); one *s* one *d*. *Educ:* University Coll., Exeter (BSc 1951). Served HM Forces, 1945–48. Royal Naval Scientific Service, 1951–62; BRE, 1962–86. *Publications:* DoE and BRE reports. *Recreation:* amateur theatre. *Address:* 10 Whybrow Gardens, Berkhamsted, Herts HP4 2GU. *T:* (01442) 870242.
See also L. E. E. Jeanes.

JEANNERET, Marian Elizabeth; *see* Hobson, M. E.

JEANNIOT, Pierre Jean, OC 1988; CQ 2002; Chairman, Thales Canada, since 2003; President and Chief Executive Officer, Jinmag Inc., since 1990; *b* Montpellier, France, 9 April 1933; *s* of Gaston and Renée Jeanniot; *m* 1979, Marcia David; two *s* one *d*. *Educ:* Sir George Williams Univ. (BSc); McGill Univ. (Management Prog.). Sperry Gyroscope, 1952–55; Air Canada, 1955–68; Vice-Pres., Computers and Communications, Québec Univ., 1969; Air Canada: Vice-Pres., Computer and Systems Services, 1970–76; subseq. Exec., sales, marketing, planning subsid. cos; Exec. Vice-Pres. and Chief Operating Officer, 1980; Pres. and CEO, 1984–90; Dir Gen. and CEO, IATA, 1993–2002, Dir Gen. Emeritus, 2002–. Dir of many cos. Pres., Canadian OR Soc., 1966; Chm., Air Transport Assoc. of Canada, 1984; Mem., Exec. Cttee and Chm., Strategic Planning Sub-Cttee, IATA, 1988–90. Chm., Council for Canadian Unity, 1991–94. University of Québec: Chm. Bd, 1972–78; Pres., Foundn, 1978–92; Chancellor, 1995–2008. Chm. and participant, numerous charitable bodies. FRAeS, 2007. Hon. Dr Quebec, 1988; Hon. LLD Concordia, 1997; Hon. DSc McGill, 2006. Airline Business Strategy Award, Airline Business Magazine, 2002. Chevalier, Légion d'Honneur (France), 1991; Independence Medal (First Order) (Kingdom of Jordan), 1995. *Address:* 1010 de la Gauchetière West, Montreal, QC H3B 2N2, Canada.

JEANS, Ven. Alan Paul; Archdeacon of Sarum, since 2003; *b* 18 May 1958; *s* of Brian Edward and Jacqueline Rosemary Jeans; *m* 1981, Anita Gail (*née* Hobbs); two *d*. *Educ:* Bournemouth Sch.; Bournemouth and Poole Coll. (MIAS, MIBC 1983); Southampton Univ. (BTh 1989); Salisbury and Wells Theol Coll.; Univ. of Wales, Lampeter (MA 2002). Building Surveyor, 1976–86. Ordained deacon, 1989, priest, 1990; Curate, Parkstone with Branksea, 1989–93; Priest i/c, Bishop's Cannings, All Cannings and Etchilhampton, 1993–98; Advr for Parish Devel t, 1998–2005, Diocesan Dir of Ordinands, 2007–, Dio. of Salisbury; Rural Dean, Alderbury, 2005–07. Canon, Salisbury Cathedral, 2002–. Asst Chaplain, Dauntsey's Sch., 1995–2007; Chaplain to the Forces (TA), 2002–. Mem., Gen. Synod of C of E, 2000–05. *Recreations:* food, architectural history. *Address:* Southbroom House, London Road, Devizes, Wilts SN10 1LT. *T:* (01380) 729808, *Fax:* (01380) 738096; *e-mail:* adsarum@salisbury.anglican.org.

JEANS, Christopher James Marwood; QC 1997; *b* 24 Jan. 1956; *s* of late David Marwood Jeans and Rosalie Jean Jeans; *m* 1998, Judith Mary Laws; one *d*. *Educ:* Minchenden Sch.; King's Coll. London (LLB 1977); St John's Coll., Oxford (BCL 1979). Called to the Bar, Gray's Inn, 1980, Bencher, 2007; Lectr, City of London Poly., 1981–83; in practice at the Bar, 1983–. Part-time Employment Judge (formerly part-time Chm.), Employment Tribunals, 1998–2008. Mem., Law Panel, The Times, 2007–. Fellow, Inst. of Continuing Professional Develt, 1998. *Recreations:* football (Spurs), cricket, walking, swimming, cinema, theatre, arctic and world travel. *Address:* 11 King's Bench Walk, Temple, EC4Y 7EQ.

JEAPES, Maj.-Gen. Anthony Showan, CB 1987; OBE 1977; MC 1960; retired; Consultant Inspector, Lord Chancellor's Panel of Independent Inspectors, 2003–05 (Member, 1991–2003); *b* 6 March 1935; *s* of Stanley Arthur Jeapes; *m* 1959, Jennifer Clare White; one *s* one *d*. *Educ:* Raynes Park Grammar Sch.; RMA Sandhurst. Commissioned Dorset, later Devonshire and Dorset, Regt, 1955; joined 22 SAS Regt, 1958; attached US Special Forces, 1961; Staff College, 1966; Brigade Major, 39 Inf. Bde, NI, 1967; Sqn Comdr, 22 SAS Regt, 1968; Nat. Defence Coll., 1971; Directing Staff, Staff Coll., Camberley, 1972; CO 22 SAS Regt, 1974; Mem., British Mil. Adv. Team, Bangladesh, 1977; Dep. Comdr, Sch. of Infantry, 1979; Comdr, 5 Airborne Brigade, 1982; Comdr, Land Forces NI, 1985–87; GOC, SW Dist, 1987–90. Vice-Chairman: Romanian Orphanage Trust, 1991–99; European Children's Trust, 1995–99. *Publications:* SAS Operation Oman, 1980; SAS Secret War, 1996. *Recreations:* offshore sailing, country pursuits. *Address:* c/o National Westminster Bank, Warminster, Wilts BA12 9AW.

JEAVONS, (Robert) Clyde (Scott); Curator, National Film and Television Archive, British Film Institute, 1990–97; *b* 30 June 1939; *s* of Frank Rechab Scott-Jeavons and Olive Edith (*née* Robins); *m* 1st, 1963, Hilary Coopey (marr. diss.); one *d*; 2nd, 1977, Orly Yadin (marr. diss.); 3rd, 2007, Shirley Ann Tait. *Educ:* Royal Russell Sch.; University Coll. London (BA Hons Scandinavian Studies). Asst Stage Manager, Det Norske Riksteatret, Norway, 1963; financial journalist, Investors' Rev., 1964; Chief Sub, Features Ed. and book reviewer and film critic, SHE mag., 1964–69; Dep. Curator and Hd, Film and TV Acquisitions, Nat. Film Archive, BFI, 1969–85; freelance author and film programmer, 1986–90. Archive Consultant, London Film Fest. Member: Satyajit Ray Foundn; BAFTA; Critics' Circle; British Cinema and TV Veterans. Hon. Mem., BFI. Mem., Islington Choral Soc. FRSA 1992–2002. Hon. FBKS 1994. *Publications:* (with Michael Parkinson) A Pictorial History of Westerns, 1974; A Pictorial History of War Films, 1975; (with Jeremy Pascall) A Pictorial History of Sex in the Movies, 1976; British Film-Makers of the Eighties, 1990; contrib. Sight & Sound, Monthly Film Bull., Guardian, Sunday Times, etc. *Recreations:* cricket, golf, travel, dining, music, film, choral singing, reading the New Yorker. *Address:* Garden Flat, 110A Highbury New Park, N5 2DR. *T:* (020) 7226 6778. *Clubs:* Union; Brondesbury Cricket, Barnes Cricket (Hon. Mem.), Bushmen Cricket and Dining (Chm.); St Augustine's Golf (Ramsgate).

JEBB, family name of **Baron Gladwyn**.

JEBB, Dom (Anthony) Philip, MA; Prior, Downside Abbey, 1991–2001; Cathedral Prior, Bath, since 2002; Parish Priest, Radstock, 1998–2002; *b* 14 Aug. 1932; 2nd *s* of late Reginald Jebb and Eleanor, *d* of Hilaire Belloc. *Educ:* Downside; Christ's Coll., Cambridge, 1957–60 (MA Classics). Professed at Downside, 1951; priest, 1956; Curate, Midsomer Norton, 1960–62; teaching at Downside, 1960–97; House master, 1962–75; Dep. Head Master, 1975–80; Headmaster, 1980–91; Dir of Sch. Appeal, 1996–98; Guest Master, 2003–07. Archivist and Annalist, English Benedictine Congregation, 1972–; Mem., EBC Theological Commn, 1969–82 (Chm., 1979–82); Delegate to General Chapter, EBC, 1981–2001; Mem., Central Cttee, 1987–88, Chm., SW Div., 1988, HMC; Member: Council, Somerset Records Soc., 1975–97; Cttee, Area 7, SHA, 1984–91; Court, Bath Univ., 1983–85. Trustee, Somerset Archaeol and Natural Hist. Soc., 1989–97 (Pres., 1993–94). Vice-Pres., SW Amateur Fencing Assoc., 1970–. Chaplain of Magistral Obedience, British Assoc., Sovereign Mil. Order of Malta, 1978–; Asst Chaplain, Shepton Mallet Prison, 1995–2001. Gov., St Antony's-Leweston Sch., 1980–97. *Publications:* Missale de Lesnes, 1964; Religious Education, 1968; Widowed, 1973, 2nd edn 1976; contrib. Consider Your Call, 1978, 2nd edn 1979; A Touch of God, 1982; (ed) By Death Parted, 1986; In a Quiet Garden, 1999; contribs to Downside Review, The Way, The Sword. *Recreations:* fencing, archaeology, astronomy, canoeing. *Address:* Downside Abbey, Stratton-on-the-Fosse, Radstock BA3 4RH. *T:* (01761) 235148.

JEEPS, Richard Eric Gautrey, CBE 1977; Chairman, Sports Council, 1978–85; *b* 25 Nov. 1931; *s* of Francis Herbert and Mildred Mary Jeeps; *m* 1954, Jean Margaret Levitt (marr. diss.); three *d*. *Educ:* Bedford Modern Sch. Rugby career: Cambridge City, 1948–49; Northampton, 1949–62 and 1964; Eastern Counties, 1950–62; England, 1956–62 (24 caps); Barbarians, 1958–62; British Lions: SA, 1955; NZ, 1959; SA 1962; 13 Tests. Rugby Football Union: Mem. Cttee, 1962–78; Pres., 1976–77. Formerly: Mem., English Tourist Bd; Trustee, Sports Aid Trust. *Recreations:* Rugby Union football, sport. *Address:* Alcheringa Lodge, 1 Swan Grove, Exning, Suffolk CB8 7HX.

JEEVES, Prof. Malcolm Alexander, CBE 1992; FMedSci, FBPsS; PPRSE; Professor of Psychology, University of St Andrews, 1969–93, Hon. Research Professor, since 1993; *b* 16 Nov. 1926; *s* of Alderman Alexander Frederic Thomas Jeeves and Helena May Jeeves (*née* Hammond); *m* 1955, Ruth Elisabeth Hartridge; two *d*. *Educ:* Stamford Sch.; St John's Coll., Cambridge (MA, PhD). Commissioned Royal Lincs Regt, served 1st Bn Sherwood Foresters, BAOR, 1945–48. Cambridge University: Exhibnr, St John's Coll., 1948, Res. Exhibnr, 1952; Burney Student, 1952; Gregg Bury Prizeman, 1954; Kenneth Craik Res. Award, St John's Coll., 1955. Rotary Foundn Fellow, Harvard, 1953; Lectr, Leeds Univ., 1956; Prof. of Psychology, Adelaide Univ., 1959–69, and Dean, Faculty of Arts, 1962–64; Vice-Principal, St Andrews Univ., 1981–85; Dir, MRC Cognitive Neuroscience Res. Gp, St Andrews, 1984–89. Lectures: Abbie Meml, Adelaide Univ., 1981; Cairns Meml, Aust., 1986; New Coll., Univ. of NSW, 1987; Boyle, 2008. Member: SSRC Psych. Cttee, 1972–76; Biol. Cttee, 1980–84, Science Bd, 1985–89, Council, 1985–89, SERC; MRC Neuroscience and Mental Health Bd, 1985–89; Council, 1984–88, Exec., 1985–87, Vice-Pres., 1990–93, Pres., 1996–99, RSE; ABRC Manpower Sub-Cttee, 1991–93; Pres., Section J, BAAS, 1988. Founder FMedSci 1998. Hon. Sheriff, Fife, 1986–. Hon. DSc: Edinburgh, 1993; St Andrews, 2000; DUniv Stirling, 1999. Editor-in-Chief, Neuropsychologia, 1990–93. *Publications:* (with Z. P. Dienes) Thinking in Structures, 1965 (trans. French, German, Spanish, Italian, Japanese); (with Z. P. Dienes) The Effects of Structural Relations upon Transfer, 1968; The Scientific Enterprise and Christian Faith, 1969; Experimental Psychology: an introduction for Biologists, 1974; Psychology and Christianity: the view both ways, 1976 (trans. Chinese); (with G. B. Greer) Analysis of Structural Learning, 1983; (with R. J. Berry and D. Atkinson) Free to be Different, 1984; Behavioural Sciences: a Christian perspective, 1984; (with D. G. Myers) Psychology—through the eyes of faith, 1987, 2nd edn 2002; Mind Fields, 1994; Human Nature at the Millennium, 1997; (with R. J. Berry) Science, Life and Christian Belief, 1998; (ed and contrib.) From Cells to Souls, 2004; (ed and contrib.) Human Nature, 2005; papers in sci. jls, mainly on neuropsychology and cognition. *Recreations:* music, fly fishing, walking. *Address:* Psychology Laboratory, The University, St Andrews KY16 9JU. *T:* (01334) 462057. *Club:* New (Edinburgh).
See also E. R. Dobbs.

JEEWOOLALL, Sir Ramesh, Kt 1979; Speaker, Mauritius Parliament, 1979–82 and 1996–2000; *b* 20 Dec. 1940; *s* of Shivprasad Jeewoolall; *m* 1971, Usweenee (*née* Reetoo); two *s*. *Educ:* in Mauritius; Inns of Court Sch. of Law. Called to the Bar, Middle Temple, 1968; practising at the Bar, 1969–71; Magistrate, 1971–72; practising at the Bar and Chm., Mauritius Tea Develt Authority, 1972–76. Mem., Mauritius Parlt, 1976–82 and 1987–91; Minister of Housing, Lands, Town and Country Planning and the Envmt, 1987–90; Dep. Speaker, 1977–79. Pres., CPA, 1996–97 (Vice-Pres., 1995–96). Chancellor, Univ. of Mauritius, 2006–. *Recreations:* reading, conversation, chess. *Address:* 92 Belle Rose Avenue, Quatre Bornes, Mauritius. *T:* 4645371.

JEFFCOTT, Prof. Leo Broof, PhD, DVSc; FRCVS; Dean, Faculty of Veterinary Science, University of Sydney, since 2004; *b* 19 June 1942; *s* of late Edward Ian Broof Jeffcott and of Pamela Mary (*née* Hull); *m* 1969, Tisza Jacqueline (*née* Hubbard); two *d*. *Educ:* Univ. of London (BVetMed 1967, PhD 1972); Univ. of Melbourne (DVSc 1989); MA Cantab 1994. FRCVS 1978. Animal Health Trust, Newmarket: Asst Pathologist, 1967–71; Clinician, 1972–77; Head, Clinical Dept, 1977–81; Professor: of Clinical Radiology, Swedish Univ. of Agricl Scis, Uppsala, 1981–82; of Veterinary Clinical Sciences, Univ. of Melbourne, 1982–91; Prof. of Vet. Clin. Studies and Dean of Vet. Sch., 1991–2004, Fellow of Pembroke Coll., 1993–2004, Cambridge Univ. Mem. Council, RCVS, 1992–2004. Chm., Internat. Cttee for 5th Internat. Conf. on Equine Exercise Physiology, 1994–98; Mem. Bureau, FEI, 1998–2006 (Hon. Mem., 2006; Chm., Vet. Cttee, 1998–2006). Lectures: Sir Frederick Hobday Meml, BEVA, 1977; Peter Hernqvist, Swedish Univ. of Agricl Scis, Skara, 1991; Share-Jones, RCVS, 1993. FEI Official Veterinarian: Seoul Olympics, 1988; World Equestrian Games, Stockholm, 1990, The Hague, 1994, Rome, 1998; Jerez, Spain, 2002; Barcelona Olympics, 1992; Atlanta Olympics, 1996; Sydney Olympics, 2000; Athens Olympics, 2004; Beijing Olympics, 2008. Hon. FRVC 1997. VetMedDr *hc* Swedish Univ. of Agricl Scis, 2000. Norman Hall Medal for Research, RCVS, 1978; Internat. Prize of Tierklinik Hochmoor, Germany, 1981; Equine Veterinary Jl Open Award, BEVA, 1982; John Hickman Orthopaedic Prize, BEVA, 1991; Internat. Hall of Fame Award for Equine Res., Univ. of Kentucky, 1991; UK Equestrian Award for Scientific Achievement, 1994; Sefton Award for Services to Equestrian Safety, 1997; Dalrymple-Champneys Cup and Medal, 2001. *Publications:* (with R. K. Archer) Comparative Clinical Haematology, 1977; (ed jtly) Equine Exercise Physiology 3, 1991; (with G. Dalin) Osteochondrosis in the 90s, 1993; (with A. F. Clarke) On to Atlanta '96, 1994; (with A. F. Clarke) Progress towards Atlanta '96: thermoregulatory responses during competitive exercise with performance horse, Vol. I 1995, Vol. II 1996; Equine Exercise Physiology 5, 1999; (ed jtly) Osteochondrosis and Musculoskeletal Development in the Foal Under the Influence of Exercise, 1999; (ed with P. D. Rossdale) A Tribute to Colonel John Hickman, 2001. *Recreations:* swimming, photography, equestrian sports. *Address:* Faculty of Veterinary Science, University of Sydney, Sydney, NSW 2006, Australia.

JEFFERIES, David George, CBE 1990; FREng; Chairman: National Grid Group plc, 1990–99; Viridian Group (formerly Northern Ireland Electricity) plc, 1994–98; *b* 26 Dec. 1933; *s* of Rose and George Jefferies; *m* 1959, Jeanette Ann Hanson. *Educ:* SE Coll. of Technology. FREng (FEng 1989); FIET, FInstE. Southern Electricity Board: Area Manager, Portsmouth, 1967–72; Staff Coll., Henley, 1970; Chief Engr, 1972–74; Dir, NW Region, CEGB, 1974–77; Dir Personnel, CEGB, 1977–81; Chm., London Electricity Bd, 1981–86; Dep. Chm., Electricity Council, 1986–89. Non-exec. Dir, Strategic Rail Authy, 1999–2001; Chairman: 24/Seven Utilities Service Co., 1999–2002; Smartlogik, 2000–02; Costain, 2001–07; Geotrupes, 2004–07. Chm., Electricity Pension Scheme, 1986–97. Chm., Power Sector Working Gp, 1993–2002; Co-Chm., Indo-British Partnership, 1999–2003. President: Energy Industries Club, 1991–93; Inst. of Energy, 1994–96; Electricity Assoc., 1996–97; IEE, 1997–98; Electrical and Electronic Industries Benevolent Assoc., 1998–99. Mem. Bd, Royal Instn, 2000–05. Liveryman, Wax Chandlers' Co., 1984– (Master, 2005–06). CCMI. Hon. DTech Brunel, 1992; Hon. LLD Manchester, 1993. *Recreations:* golf, gardening, music. *Address:* Espada, 30 Abbots Drive, Virginia Water, Surrey GU25 4SE. *Clubs:* Athenæum, Royal Automobile; Wentworth.

JEFFERIES, Roger David; Independent Housing Ombudsman, 1997–2001; *b* 13 Oct. 1939; *s* of George Edward Jefferies and Freda Rose Jefferies (*née* Marshall); *m* 1st, 1962, Jennifer Anne Southgate (marr. diss.); one *s* two *d*; 2nd, 1974, Margaret Sealy (marr. diss.); 3rd, 1984, Pamela Mary Elsey (*née* Holden); one *s*. *Educ:* Whitgift School; Balliol College, Oxford. BA, BCL; solicitor. Member: Law Society, 1965–; British and Irish Ombudsman Assoc., 1997–. Asst Solicitor, Coventry Corporation, 1965–68; Asst Town Clerk, Southend-on-Sea County Borough Council, 1968–70; Director of Operations, London Borough of Hammersmith, 1970–75; Chief Exec., London Borough of Hounslow, 1975–90; Under Secretary, DoE, 1983–85 (on secondment); Chief Exec., London Bor. of Croydon, 1990–93; Housing Assoc. Tenants' Ombudsman, 1993–97. Chm., Discipline Cttees, Lambeth, Southwark and Lewisham HA, 1998–2004. Non-executive Director: Nat. Clinical Assessment Authy, 2001–05; Financial Ombudsman Service, 2002–08; Telecommunications Ombudsman Service, 2002–07. Independent Adjudicator: for Lewisham LBC, 2006–07; for Telecommunications and Energy Ombudsman, 2007–. Member: Regl Planning Bd, Arts Council of GB, 1986–88; Adv. Bd, Lewisham Theatre, 1994–99; Council, RIPA, 1982–88; Bd, Public Finance Foundn, 1987–93; Pres., SOLACE, 1990–91. Clerk: Mortlake Crematorium Bd, 1973–90; W London Waste Authy, 1986–90. Director: Extemporary Dance Co., 1989–91; Croydon Business Venture, 1991–93; Solotec, 1992–93. Hon. Sec., Commn for Local Democracy, 1993–96. Trustee: S African Advanced Educn Project, 1989–96; Barnes Workhouse Fund, 2002–. *Publication:* Tackling the Town Hall, 1982. *Recreations:* the novel, genealogy, the Languedoc.

JEFFERIES, Sheelagh, CBE 1987; Deputy Director General, 1983–87, Acting Director General, Jan.–June 1987, Central Office of Information; *b* 25 Aug. 1926; *d* of late Norman and Vera Jefferies. *Educ:* Harrogate Grammar Sch.; Girton Coll., Cambridge (MA); Smith Coll., Northampton, Mass, USA (MA). FCIPR; FCAM. Archivist, RIIA, 1947–50, 1951–52; COI, 1953–60; Office of Chancellor of Duchy of Lancaster, 1960–61; Press Officer, Prime Minister's Office, 1961–67; Principal Inf. Officer, Privy Council Office, 1967–69; Chief Press Officer, Min. of Housing and Local Govt, 1969–71; Head of Parly Liaison Unit and later Head of News, DoE, 1971–74; Chief Inf. Officer, Dept of Prices and Consumer Protection, 1974–77; Central Office of Information: Dir, Overseas Press and Radio, 1977–78; Controller (Home), 1978–83. Press Consultant, WRVS, 1988–92. *Recreations:* reading, conversation. *Address:* 17 Beaumont Avenue, Richmond, Surrey TW9 2HE. *T:* (020) 8940 9229.

JEFFERIES, Stephen; Artistic Director and Choreographer, Suzhou Kewen Promotion Co., since 2007; *b* 24 June 1951; *s* of George and Barbara Jefferies; *m* 1972, Rashna Homji; one *s* one *d*. *Educ:* Turves Green Sch., Birmingham; Royal Ballet Sch. ARAD (Advanced Hons). Joined Sadler's Wells Royal Ballet, 1969; created 10 leading roles whilst with Sadler's Wells; Principal Dancer, 1973–76 and 1977–79, Sen. Principal Dancer, 1979–95, Character Principal, 1994–95, Royal Ballet; joined National Ballet of Canada as Principal Dancer, 1976; created role of Morris, in Washington Square, 1977; returned to Royal Ballet at Covent Garden, 1977; Rehearsal Dir, Rambert Dance Co., Jan.–July 1995 (on leave of absence); Artistic Dir, Hong Kong Ballet, 1996–2006. *Major roles include:* Prince in Sleeping Beauty, Swan Lake and Giselle, Prince Rudolf in Mayerling, Petruchio in Taming of the Shrew, Romeo and Mercutio in Romeo and Juliet, Lescaut in Manon; lead, in Song and Dance, 1982; *roles created:* Yukinojo (mime role), in world première of Minoru Miki's opera An Actor's Revenge, 1979; male lead in Bolero, Japan (chor. by Yashiro Okamoto), 1980; Antonio in The Duenna, S Africa (chor. by Ashley Killar), 1980; lead, in Dances of Albion (chor. by Glen Tetley), 1980; Esenin in Kenneth Macmillan's ballet, Isadora, Covent Garden, 1981; lead, in L'Invitation au Voyage, Covent Garden (chor. by Michael Corder), 1982; Consort Lessons, and Sons of Horos, 1986, Still Life at the Penguin Café, and The Trial of Prometheus, 1988 (chor. by David Bintley); title role in Cyrano (chor. by David Bintley), 1991. Choreographed ballets: Bits and Pieces, in Canada, 1977; Mes Souvenirs, in London, 1978; Magic Toyshop, 1987; *for Hong Kong Ballet:* Swan Lake, 1996; Giselle, Nutcracker, 1997; Tango Ballet Tango, 2000; Sleeping Beauty, 2002; (and designed) The Legend of the Great Archer, 2004; Suzie Wong, 2006. *Film:* Anna, 1988. *Recreations:* golf, football, gardening, swimming and various other sports. *Address:* 45D Tower 3, Coastal Skyline, 12 Tung Chung Waterfront Road, Hong Kong.

JEFFERISS, Dr Paul Howard; Director of Environmental Policy, BP, since 2006; *b* 29 Oct. 1955; *s* of Leonard James Jefferiss and Elsie Jefferiss (*née* Shenton). *Educ:* Peterhouse, Cambridge (BA Hons Anglo-Saxon, Norse and Celtic 1977, MA 1990); Harvard Univ. (MA Celtic Langs and Lit. 1980; PhD 1991); Tufts Univ. (Cert. Envmtl Mgt 1992; MA Envmtl (and Urban) Policy 1994). Publicity Asst, OUP, 1978–79; Harvard University: Hd Teaching Fellow, 1982–91; Lectr, 1988–91; Asst Sen. Tutor, 1988–91, Tutor, 1991–93, Dunster House; Lectr in Envmtl Mgt, UNEP at Tufts Univ., 1995–97; Dir of Energy, Union of Concerned Scientists, 1994–98; Hd, Envmtl Policy, RSPB, 1998–2000 and 2001–06; Dir, Green Alliance, 2000–01. Member: Renewables Wkg Gp, US President's Initiative on Climate Change Technol. Strategy, 1997; Energy Adv. Panel, 1999–2003, Renewables Adv. Bd, 2006–07, DTI; Envmtl Adv. Gp, Ofgem, 2002–; Envmtl Innovations Adv. Gp, BERR (formerly DTI)-DEFRA, 2003–08; Sustainable Develt Task Force, DEFRA, 2003–05; Bd, Renewable Fuels Agency, 2007–. Non-executive Director: Renewable Energy Policy Project, 1997–98; Carbon Trust, 2001–; Carbon Trust Investments Ltd, 2003–; SITA Trust, 2005–08. Member: Adv. Bd and Annual Assessment Panel, Tyndall Centre for Climate Change Res., 2000–06; Steering Bd, (Univ. of) Sussex Energy Gp, 2005–. Member: Green Globe Network, 2000–; Bd, Eur. Envmtl Bureau, 2000–01 (Chm., EEB-UK, 2000–01); Bd, Low-Carbon Vehicle Partnership, 2003–08. Trustee, Nat. Energy Foundn, 2005–08. *Publications:* (ed with W. J. Mahon) Proceedings of the Harvard Celtic Colloquium, Vol IV 1984, Vol V 1985; reports, briefing papers and articles on sustainable develt, envmt, energy and transport policy, incl. contribs to Science jl. *Recreations:* reading, running, travelling, maintaining a listed building. *Address:* Lyndhurst House, 61 Mill Street, Gamlingay, Sandy, Beds SG19 3JS. *T:* 07770 342123; *e-mail:* paul.jefferiss@bp.com.

JEFFERS, John Norman Richard, CStat; CBiol, FIBiol; FICFor; consultant; Visiting Professor: Mechanical, Materials and Manufacturing, University of Newcastle, since 1994; Mathematical Institute, University of Kent, since 1993; School of Mathematics, Statistics and Computing, University of Greenwich, since 1994; *b* 10 Sept. 1926; *s* of late Lt-Col John Harold Jeffers, OBE, and Emily Matilda Alice (*née* Robinson); *m* 1951, Edna May (*née* Parratt); one *d*. *Educ:* Portsmouth Grammar Sch.; Forestry Commission Forester Trng Sch., 1944–46. Forester in Forestry Commn Research Br., 1946–55; joined Min. of Agriculture, 1955, as Asst Statistician, after succeeding in limited competition to Statistician Class; rejoined Forestry Commn as Head of Statistics Section of Forestry Commn Research Br., 1956; Dir, Nature Conservancy's Merlewood Research Station, 1968; Dep. Dir, Inst. of Terrestrial Ecology, NERC, 1973, Dir, 1976–86. Editor, Internat. Jl of Sustainable Develt and World Ecology, 1994–. Hon. DSc Lancaster, 1988. *Publications:* Experimental Design and Analysis in Forest Research, 1959; Mathematical Models in Ecology, 1972; Introduction to Systems Analysis: with ecological applications, 1978; Modelling, 1982; Practitioner's Manual on the Modelling of Dynamic Change in Ecosystems, 1988; Microcomputers in Environmental Biology, 1990; Research, Ecology and Environment, 2003; numerous papers in stat., forestry and ecolog. jls. *Recreations:* military history and wargaming, amateur dramatics. *Address:* Glenside, Oxenholme, Kendal, Cumbria LA9 7RF. *T:* (01539) 734375. *Club:* Athenæum.

JEFFERSON, Prof. Ann Margaret, FBA 2004; Fellow and Tutor in French, New College, Oxford, since 1987; Professor of French, University of Oxford, since 2006; *b* 3 Nov. 1949; *d* of Antony and Eirlys Jefferson; *m* 1971, Anthony Glees (marr. diss. 1992); two *s* one *d*; partner, Michael Holland. *Educ:* St Anne's Coll., Oxford (BA Hons 1971; MA); Wolfson Coll., Oxford (DPhil 1976). University of Oxford: Jun. Res. Fellow, 1978–82, Lectr in French, 1982–87, St John's Coll.; CUF Lectr in French, Fac. of Mod. Langs, 1987–2006. Officière, Ordre des Palmes Académiques (France), 2001. *Publications:* The Nouveau Roman and the Poetics of Fiction, 1980; (with D. Robey) Modern Literary Theory: a comparative introduction, 1982, rev. edn 1986; Reading Realism in Stendhal, 1988; Nathalie Sarraute, Fiction and Theory: questions of difference, 2000; Stendhal: La Chartreuse de Parme, 2003; Biography and the Question of Literature in France, 2007. *Recreations:* watching films, being in France. *Address:* New College, Oxford OX1 3BN. *T:* and *Fax:* (01865) 279521; *e-mail:* ann.jefferson@new.ox.ac.uk.

JEFFERSON, Bryan; *see* Jefferson, J. B.

JEFFERSON, Sir George Rowland, Kt 1981; CBE 1969; BSc Hons (London); FREng, Hon. FIMechE, FIET, FRAeS; FCGI; Chairman, 1981–87 and Chief Executive, 1981–86, British Telecommunications plc; *b* 26 March 1921; *s* of Harold Jefferson and Eva Elizabeth Ellen; *m* 1943, Irene Watson-Browne (*d* 1998); three *s*. *Educ:* Grammar Sch., Dartford, Kent. Engrg Apprentice, Royal Ordnance Factory, Woolwich, 1937–42; commnd RAOC, 1942; transf. REME, 1942; served 1942–45, Anti-Aircraft Comd on heavy anti-aircraft power control systems and later Armament Design Dept, Fort Halstead, on anti-aircraft gun mounting development; subseq. Mem. Min. of Supply staff, Fort Halstead, until 1952; joined Guided Weapons Div., English Electric Co. Ltd, 1952; Chief Research Engr, 1953; Dep. Chief Engr, 1958; Dir, English Electric Aviation Ltd, 1961 (on formation of co.); British Aircraft Corporation: Dir and Chief Exec., BAC (Guided Weapons) Ltd, 1963 (on formation of Corp.), Dep. Man. Dir, 1964, Mem. Board, 1965–77, Man. Dir, 1966–68, Chm. and Man. Dir, 1968–77; a Dir, British Aerospace, and Chm. and Chief Exec., Dynamics Gp, British Aerospace, 1977–80 (Mem., Organizing Cttee, 1976–77); Chm., Stevenage/Bristol and Hatfield/Lostock Divs, Dynamics Gp, 1978–80; Chm., BAC (Anti-Tank), 1968–78; Dep. Chm., Post Office, 1980; Chm., 1981–87, Chief Exec., 1981–86, British Telecommunications plc. Chairman: Matthew Hall, 1987–88; City Centre Communications, 1988–90; Videotron Corp., 1990–97. Director: British Aerospace (Australia) Ltd, 1968–80; British Scandinavian Aviation AB, 1968–80; Hawker Siddeley Dynamics, 1977–80; Engineering Sciences Data Unit Ltd, 1975–80; Babcock International, 1980–87; Lloyds Bank,

1986–89; AMEC, 1988–91. Member: NEB, 1979–80; NEDC, 1981–84; NICG, 1980–84; Member Council: SBAC, 1965–80; Electronic Engineering Assoc., 1968–72; RAeS, 1977–79 (Vice-Pres., 1979). Freeman of the City of London. FRSA; CCMI. Hon. DSc Bristol, 1984; DUniv Essex, 1985.

JEFFERSON, Joan Ena; *see* Appleyard, J. E.

JEFFERSON, (John) Bryan, CB 1989; CBE 1983; PPRIBA; Architectural Advisor to Department for Culture, Media and Sport (formerly National Heritage), 1993–2001; Visiting Professor, School of Architecture, Sheffield University, 1992–2000; *b* 26 April 1928; *s* of John Jefferson and Marjorie Jefferson (*née* Oxley); *m* 1st, 1954, Alison Gray (marr. diss. 1965); three *s*; 2nd, 1999, Jean Marsden. *Educ:* Lady Manners Sch., Bakewell; Sheffield Univ. DipArch 1954. ARIBA 1954. Morrison and Partners, Derby, 1955–57; established practice in Sheffield and London with Gerald F. Sheard, 1957; Sen. Partner, Jefferson Sheard and Partners, 1957–84; Dir-Gen. of Design, PSA, DoE, 1984–89; Chm., PSA Projects, DoE, 1989–92; Mem., Standing Cttee on Structl Safety, 1991–99. President: Sheffield Soc. of Architects, 1973–74; Concrete Soc., 1977–78; RIBA, 1979–81; Chm., RIBA Yorks Region, 1974–75. Trustee, Civic Trust, 1998–2003. Hon. FRAIC 1980; Hon. Mem., RICS 1987. Hon. DEng Bradford, 1986; Hon. LittD Sheffield, 1992. *Publications:* broadcasts; articles in lay and professional jls. *Recreation:* music. *Address:* 6 St Andrews Mansions, Dorset Street, W1U 4EQ. *Club:* Royal Automobile.

JEFFERSON, Sir Mervyn Stewart D.; *see* Dunnington-Jefferson.

JEFFERSON, William Hayton, OBE 1985; Director, Portugal, British Council, and Cultural Counsellor, Lisbon, 1996–98; *b* 29 July 1940; *s* of late Stanley Jefferson and Josephine (*née* Hayton); *m* 1st, 1963, Marie-Jeanne Mazenq (marr. diss. 1986); three *s*; 2nd, 1986, Fadia Georges Tarraf; one *s*. *Educ:* Nelson-Thomlinson Grammar Sch., Wigton, Cumbria; Wadham Coll., Oxford (MA 1966). Russian teacher, 1963–66; with British Council, 1967–98: Tripoli, 1967–70; Kuwait, 1970–72; Algeria, 1972–75; Director: Qatar, 1975–79; Overseas Co-operation, London, 1979–82; United Arab Emirates, 1982–85; Algeria, 1985–90; Dir, Czechoslovakia, and Cultural Counsellor, Prague, 1990–96. Mem. (Ind), Allerdale Borough Council, Cumbria, 1999–; Chairman: N Allerdale Regeneration Gp, 2001–06; Jt Adv. Cttee, Solway Coast Area of Outstanding Natural Beauty, Cumbria, 2002–; Lake Dist Nat. Park Authy, 2008– (Mem., 2007–). Pres., Cumbria Co. Bowling Assoc., 2005–07. Gold Medal: Czech Scientific Univ., 1995; Palacky Univ., Olomouc, 1996; Silver Medal: Charles Univ., Prague, 1996; Masaryk Univ., Brno, 1996. *Recreations:* Cumbrian local history and dialect, wine, bowls. *Address:* 3 Marine Terrace, Silloth, Cumbria CA7 4BZ. *T:* (01697) 332526. *Club:* Silloth-on-Solway Bowls.

JEFFERSON SMITH, Peter, CB 1992; Trustee, South East London Community Foundation, 1995–2005 (Chair of Trustees, 1995–2000); *b* 14 July 1939; *m* 1964, Anna Willett; two *d*. *Educ:* Trinity College, Cambridge. HM Customs and Excise, 1960; Commissioner, 1980; Dep. Chm., 1988–94. *Address:* 22 Iveley Road, SW4 0EW. *T:* (020) 7622 8285.

JEFFERTS SCHORI, Most Rev. Katharine, PhD; Presiding Bishop, Episcopal Church in the United States of America, since 2006; *b* 26 March 1954; *m* 1979, Richard Miles Schori; one *d*. *Educ:* Stanford Univ. (BS 1974); Oregon State Univ. (MS Oceanography 1977; PhD 1983); Church Divinity Sch. of the Pacific (MDiv 1994). Ordained deacon and priest, 1994; Pastoral Associate, then Asst Rector, Episcopal Ch of the Good Samaritan, Corvallis, Oregon, and Priest-in-charge, El Buen Samaritano, Corvallis, 1994–2001; Bishop of Nevada, 2001–06. *Publication:* A Wing and a Prayer: a message of faith and hope, 2007. *Address:* Episcopal Church Center, 815 Second Avenue, New York, NY 10017, USA.

JEFFERY, Prof. Charles Adrian, PhD; Professor of Politics, University of Edinburgh, since 2004; *b* 27 July 1964; *yr s* of late Frank Jeffery and of June Jeffery (now Addington); *m* 1998, Elke Lieve Versmessen; one *d*. *Educ:* Univ. of Loughborough (BA 1985; PhD 1990). Lecturer: in Eur. Hist., N Staffs Poly., 1988–89; in W Eur. Politics, Leicester Univ., 1989–94; Institute for German Studies, University of Birmingham: Sen. Res. Fellow, 1994–96; Reader, 1996–99; Prof. of German Politics and Dep. Dir, 1999–2004. Joint Editor: Regl and Fed. Studies, 1995–; German Politics, 2001–05. Mem., Res. Adv. Bd, Cttee on Standards in Public Life, 2001–. Specialist Advr, Select Cttee on ODPM, 2004–05. Dir, ESRC Res. Prog. on Devolution and Constitnl Change, 2000–06. Mem., ESRC, 2005–. Chm., Assoc. for Study of German Politics, 1999–2000 and 2005–. AcSS 2004. FRSE 2007. *Publications:* (jtly) German Federalism Today, 1991; Social Democracy in the Australian Provinces 1918–1934, 1995; The Regional Dimension of the European Union, 1997; Recasting German Federalism, 1998; (jtly) Germany's European Diplomacy, 2000; Verfassungspolitik und Verfassungswandel: Deutschland und Grossbritannien im Vergleich, 2001; (jtly) Devolution and Electoral Politics, 2006. *Recreations:* food and cooking, rock music. *Address:* School of Social and Political Studies, Adam Ferguson Building, George Square, Edinburgh EH8 9LL. *T:* (0131) 650 4266; *e-mail:* charlie.jeffery@ed.ac.uk.

JEFFERY, David John, CBE 2000; Chief Executive, British Marine Equipment Council, 2000–01; *b* 18 Feb. 1936; *s* of late Stanley John Friend Jeffery and Sylvia May (*née* Mashford); *m* 1959, Margaret (*née* Yates); one *s* two *d*. *Educ:* Sutton High Sch., Plymouth; Croydon Coll. of Technology. Nat. Service, RAOC, 1954–56; Admiralty Dir of Stores Dept, 1956–66; RN Staff Coll., 1967; MoD, 1968–70; on secondment, 1970–76: Treasury Centre for Admin. Studies, 1970–72; Management Science Training Adviser, Malaysian Govt, Kuala Lumpur, 1972–74; Civil Service Dept, 1974–76; MoD, 1976–83; RCDS, 1983; Dir, Armaments and Management Services, RN Supply and Transport Service 1984–86; Chief Exec. and Bd Mem., PLA, 1986–99. Chm., Estuary Services Ltd, 1988–99. Director: UK Major Ports Ltd, 1993–99; British Ports Industry Trng Ltd, 1993–99 (Chm., 1998–99); Trustee Dir, Pilots' Nat. Pension Fund, 1987–95; Vice-Pres. of Conf., Internat. Assoc. of Ports and Harbors, 1995–97; Chairman: European Sea Ports Orgn, 1997–99; DTI Ports Sector Gp, 1998–; Mem., European Maritime Industries High Level Panel, 1994–95, Marine Foresight Panel, 1997–99. Orgnl Develt Advr, VSO, Kathmandu, 2004–06. Chm., Frome CAB, 2001–04. Gov., Selwood Middle Sch., Frome, 2001–04. Freeman, City of London, 1987; Mem., Co. of Watermen and Lightermen of River Thames, 1987. *Recreations:* theatre, music, travel. *Address:* The Old Coach House, High Street, Nunney, Frome, Somerset BA11 4LZ.

JEFFERY, Prof. Nicholas David, PhD; FRCVS; Professor of Veterinary Clinical Studies, University of Cambridge, since 2006; *b* 1 May 1958; *s* of John and Jill Jeffery; *m* 2005, Kat; three *s*. *Educ:* Bristol Univ. (BVSc); Wolfson Coll., Cambridge (PhD). FRCVS; Dip. ECVN; Dip. ECVS; Dip. SAS. Veterinary Officer, PDSA, 1981–83; Veterinary Surgeon: Citivet, E1, 1983–90; Animal Health Trust, 1990–93; Wellcome Trust Scholarship, Cambridge Univ., 1993–97; Wellcome Trust Fellowship, UCL, 1997–2000; Lectr in Veterinary Neurol., Univ. of Cambridge, 2000–06. *Publications:* Handbook of Small Animal Spinal Surgery, 1995; contrib. veterinary and neurosci. jls. *Recreations:* dog walking in the Fens, TV, crosswords, reading the newspaper. *Address:* Department of Veterinary Medicine, Madingley Road, Cambridge CB3 0ES. *T:* (01223) 339969; *e-mail:* ndj1000@cam.ac.uk.

JEFFERY, Maj.-Gen. (Philip) Michael, AC 1996 (AO (mil.) 1988); CVO 2000; MC 1971; Governor-General of Australia, 2003–08; *b* 12 Dec. 1937; *s* of Philip Frederick Jeffery and Edna Mary Jeffery (*née* Johnson); *m* 1967, Marlena Joy Kerr; three *s* one *d*. *Educ.* Kent Street High Sch., WA; Royal Mil. Coll., Duntroon. Served Infantry, 1958–93: jun. regtl appts, 17 Nat. Service Trng Co. and SAS Regt, 1959–62; Operational Service, Malaya, Borneo and Vietnam, 1962–72; psc 1972; Commanding Officer: 2nd Bn Pacific Islands Regt, PNG, 1974–75; SAS Regt, Perth, 1976–77; jssc 1978; Dir, Special Forces, 1979–81; Comd, 1 Bde, Sydney, 1983–84; rcds 1985; comd, 1 Div., Brisbane, 1986–88; DCGS, Canberra, 1990–91; ACGS Materiel, 1991–93. Gov., WA, 1993–2000. Chm., Future Directions Internat. Ltd, 2001–03. Mem., United Services Inst., Canberra, 1978–. Hon. DTech Curtin, 2000. Citizen of WA, 2000. KStJ 1995. Grand Companion, Order of Logohu (PNG), 2005. *Recreations:* golf, fishing, music. *Address:* c/o Government House, Canberra, ACT 2600, Australia. *Clubs:* Commonwealth (Canberra); Royal Canberra Golf.

JEFFERY, Very Rev. Robert Martin Colquhoun; Canon and Sub-Dean of Christ Church, Oxford, 1996–2002; *b* 30 April 1935; *s* of Norman Clare Jeffery and Gwenyth Isabel Jeffery; *m* 1968, Ruth Margaret Tinling (*d* 1995); three *s* one *d*. *Educ:* St Paul's School; King's Coll., London (BD, AKC). Assistant Curate: St Aidan, Grangetown, 1959–61; St Mary, Barnes, 1961–63; Asst Sec., Missionary and Ecumenical Council of Church Assembly, 1964–68; Sec., Dept of Mission and Unity, BCC, 1968–71; Vicar, St Andrew, Headington, Oxford, 1971–78; RD of Cowley, 1973–78; Lichfield Diocesan Missioner, 1978–79; Archdeacon of Salop, 1980–87; Dean of Worcester, 1987–96, now Dean Emeritus. Mem., Gen. Synod of C of E, 1982–87 and 1988–96 (Member: Standing Cttee, 1990–96; Business Cttee, 1990–96); Mem., Crown Appointments Commn, 1996. Chm. Trustees, Emmaus Oxford, 2003–05. Select Preacher, Univ. of Oxford, 1990, 1997, 1999, 2002. Chm., Churches Together in Oxfordshire, 1997–2000. Gov., Ripon Coll., 1976–2007 (Hon. Fellow, 2007). FRSA 1992. Hon. DD Birmingham, 1999. *Publications:* (with D. M. Paton) Christian Unity and the Anglican Communion, 1965, 3rd edn 1968; (with T. S. Garret) Unity in Nigeria, 1964; (ed) Lambeth Conference 1968 Preparatory Information; Areas of Ecumenical Experiment, 1968; Ecumenical Experiments: A Handbook, 1971; Case Studies in Unity, 1972; (ed) By What Authority?, 1987; Anima Christi, 1994; (contrib.) Ambassadors for Christ, 2004; (contrib.) In Search of Humanity and Deity, 2006; Imitating Christ, 2006; Discovering Tong, 2007. *Recreations:* local history, cooking. *Address:* 47 The Manor House, Bennett Crescent, Cowley, Oxford OX4 2UG. *T:* (01865) 749706; *e-mail:* rmcj@btopenworld.com.

JEFFERY, Thomas Baird, CB 2006; Director General, Children and Families, Department for Children, Schools and Families (formerly Director General, Children, Young People and Families, Department for Education and Skills), since 2003; *b* 11 Feb. 1953; *s* of Herbert George, (Jeff), Jeffery and Margaret (*née* Thornton); *m* 1987, Alison Nisbet; one *s* one *d*. *Educ:* King's Sch., Canterbury; Jesus Coll., Cambridge (MA Eng. Lit.); Centre for Contemporary Cultural Studies, Univ. of Birmingham. Joined DES, 1981; Private Sec. to Perm. Sec., 1984–85; Principal Private Sec. to Sec. of State, 1987–89; Dir, Student Loans Co., 1989–92; Head: Special Educnl Needs Div., 1992–95; Personnel and Related Roles, 1995–98; on secondment to DoH as Hd, Children's Services, 1998–2001; Dir, Children and Families Group, DfES, 2001–03. *Publications:* (contrib.) Impacts and Influences, 1987; (contrib.) Metropolis London, 1989; (contrib.) Splintered Classes, 1990; Mass-Observation: a short history, 1999. *Recreations:* family, walking, cricket, modern history and literature. *Address:* Department for Children, Schools and Families, Sanctuary Buildings, Great Smith Street, SW1P 3BT. *T:* (020) 7925 5510. *Club:* MCC.

JEFFERYS, Dr David Barrington, FFPM, FRCP, FRCPE; Vice President, Global Regulatory Affairs, Eisai Research and Development Co. Ltd, since 2006; Senior Strategic Regulatory Advisor, Eisai Europe, 2005–06; *b* 1 Aug. 1952; *s* of Godfrey B. Jefferys and Joyce E. Jefferys; *m* 1985, Ann-Marie Smith; one *s* one *d*. *Educ:* St Dunstan's Coll.; Guy's Hosp. Med. Sch., Univ. of London (BSc Hons; MB BS 1976; MD 1983). FFPM 1990; FRCPE 1990; FRCP 1992. Medical posts at Guy's and St Thomas' Hosps, 1976–83; locum consultant physician, Tunbridge Wells, 1983–84; SMO, DoH, 1984–86; PMO and Principal Assessor to Cttee on Safety of Medicines, 1986; Medicines Control Agency: Business Manager, Eur. and New Drug Licensing, 1986–94; Dir, Licensing Div., 1994–2000; Chief Exec. and Dir, Medical Devices Agency, 2000–03; Actg Hd, Med. Devices Sector, Medicines and Healthcare products Regulatory Agency, 2003. Vis. Prof. in Medicine, Univ. of Newcastle upon Tyne, 1994. UK Deleg. to Cttee on Proprietary Medicinal Products, 1995–2000. Chm., Mutual Recognition Facilitation Gp, EU, 1997–98. Member: EU Med. Device Expert Gp; Global Harmonisation Task Force Steering Cttee. Mem., British Inst. of Regulatory Affairs, 2000–; Pres., Regulatory Affairs Professional Soc. FRSocMed 2004. *Publications:* chapters in books and articles on medicines regulation, regulatory policy and quality assurance. *Recreations:* sport, ski-ing, theatre, music, art, Church affairs. *Club:* Surrey County Cricket.

JEFFORD, Barbara Mary, OBE 1965; actress; *b* Plymstock, Devon, 26 July 1930; *d* of late Percival Francis Jefford and Elizabeth Mary Ellen (*née* Laity); *m* 1953, Terence Longdon (marr. diss. 1961); *m* 1967, John Arnold Turner. *Educ:* Weirfield Sch., Taunton, Som. Studied for stage, Bristol and Royal Academy of Dramatic Art (Bancroft Gold Medal). *Royal Shakespeare Co.:* Stratford-on-Avon, 1950–54: Isabella in Measure for Measure; Anne Bullen in Henry VIII; Hero in Much Ado About Nothing; Lady Percy in Henry IV parts I and II; Desdemona in Othello; Rosalind in As You Like It; Helena in A Midsummer Night's Dream; Katharina in The Taming of the Shrew; Patsy Newquist in Little Murders, Aldwych, 1967; Volumnia in Coriolanus, 1989 and 1990; Tatyana in Barbarians, 1990; Countess in All's Well That Ends Well, Mistress Quickly in The Merry Wives of Windsor, 1992; Katia in Misha's Party, 1993; Countess Terzky in Wallenstein, 1993–94; *Old Vic Company:* (1956–62) Imogen in Cymbeline; Beatrice in Much Ado About Nothing; Portia in The Merchant of Venice; Julia in Two Gentlemen of Verona; Tamora in Titus Andronicus; Lady Anne in Richard III; Queen Margaret in Henry VI parts I, II and III; Isabella in Measure for Measure; Regan in King Lear; Viola in Twelfth Night; Ophelia in Hamlet; Rosalind in As You Like It; St Joan; Lady Macbeth; Gwendoline in The Importance of Being Earnest; Beatrice Cenci; Lavinia in Mourning Becomes Electra; *for Prospect, at Old Vic:* (1977–79) Gertrude in Hamlet; Cleopatra in All for Love; Cleopatra in Antony and Cleopatra; Nurse in Romeo and Juliet; Anna in The Government Inspector; RSC Nat. Tour, 1980, Mistress Quickly in Henry IV pts 1 and 2; *National Theatre:* Gertrude in Hamlet, Zabina in Tamburlaine the Great, 1976; Mother in Six Characters in Search of an Author, Arina Bazarov in Fathers and Sons, Salathiel in Ting Tang Mine (Clarence Derwent Award, 1988), 1987; Sanctuary, 2002; Anne of Austria in Power, 2003. *Other London stage appearances include:* Andromache in Tiger at the Gates, Apollo, 1955, NY, 1956; Lina in Misalliance, Royal Court and Criterion, 1963; step-daughter in Six Characters in Search of an Author, Mayfair, 1963; Nan in Ride a Cock

Horse, Piccadilly, 1965; Mother Vauzou in Mistress of Novices, Piccadilly, 1973; Filumena, Lyric, 1979; Duchess of York in Richard II, and Queen Margaret in Richard III, Phoenix, 1988–89; Oenone in Phèdre, Albina in Britannicus, Albery, 1998, NY, 1999; Duchess of York in Richard II, and Volumnia in Coriolanus, Almeida at Gainsborough Studios, NY and Tokyo, 2000; Mary in The Old Masters, Comedy, 2004; Hanna in Mary Stuart, Donmar, 2005; *other stage appearances include:* Hedda Gabler, Medea; Phaedra, Oxford Playhouse, 1966; Lady Sneerwell in The School for Scandal, toured UK, 1995; Our Betters, Chichester, 1997; Queen Margaret in Richard III, Crucible Th., Sheffield, 2002; Mrs Higgins in Pygmalion, Th. Royal Bath and tour, 2007, transf. Old Vic, 2008; has toured extensively in UK, Europe, USA, Near East, Far East, Africa, Australia, Russia, Poland and Yugoslavia. *Films:* Ulysses, 1967; A Midsummer Night's Dream, 1967; The Shoes of the Fisherman, 1968; To Love a Vampire, 1970; Hitler: the last ten days, 1973; And the Ship Sails On, 1983; Why the Whales Came, 1988; Reunion, 1988; Where Angels Fear to Tread, 1991; The Ninth Gate, 1999. Has appeared in numerous television and radio plays. Hon. DLitt Exeter, 2004. Pragnell Shakespeare Award, 1994. Silver Jubilee Medal, 1977. *Recreations:* music, swimming, gardening. *Address:* c/o United Agents Ltd, 12–26 Lexington Street, W1F 0LE.

JEFFORD, Nerys Angharad; QC 2008; a Recorder, since 2007; *b* Swansea, 25 Dec. 1962; *d* of John Keith Jefford and Eirlys Rona Jefford. *Educ:* Olchfa Comprehensive Sch.; Lady Margaret Hall, Oxford (Schol.; BA 1984); Univ. of Virginia (Fulbright Schol.; LLM). MCIArb 2006. Called to the Bar, Gray's Inn, 1986 (Lord Justice Holker Schol.; Karmel Schol.), Bencher, 2007; in practice at the Bar, 1988–. Mem., Educn and Trng Cttee, Bar Standards Bd, 2007–. Mem. Council, Soc. of Construction Law, 2002– (Chm., 2007–08). Mem., Adv. Council, Lady Margaret Hall, Oxford, 2006–. *Publications:* Keating on Construction Contracts, 8th edn 2006; (contrib.) Keating on Building Contracts, 5th edn 1991 to 7th edn 2001. *Recreations:* choral singing (London Welsh Chorale; Gray's Inn Chapel Choir), flat racing. *Address:* Keating Chambers, 15 Essex Street, WC2R 3AA. *T:* (020) 7544 2600, *Fax:* (020) 7544 2700; *e-mail:* njefford@keatingchambers.com.

JEFFREY, Joan; *see* MacNaughton, J.

JEFFREY, Dr Robin Campbell, FREng, FIChemE, FIMechE; Chairman and Chief Executive, British Energy, 2001–02; Chairman, Bruce Power, 1999–2002; *b* 19 Feb. 1939; *s* of Robert Stewart Martin Jeffrey and Catherine Campbell McSporran; *m* 1962, Barbara Helen Robinson; two *s* one *d*. *Educ:* Kelvinside Acad.; Royal Technical Coll. (Glasgow Univ.) (BSc); Pembroke Coll., Cambridge (PhD). With Babcock & Wilcox, 1956–79; South of Scotland Electricity Board, later Scottish Power: Engrg Resources Manager, 1964–79; Technical Services Manager, 1979–80; Torness Project Manager, 1980–88; Chief Engr, 1988–89; Man. Dir, Engrg Resources Business, 1989–92; Chief Exec., 1992–95, Chm., 1995–98, Scottish Nuclear Ltd; Dep. Chm., 1996–2001, Exec. Dir, N America, 1998–2001, British Energy. Board Member: London Transport, 1996–98; London Underground Ltd, 1996–98. Former Member: Scottish Council, CBI; Exec., Scottish Council for Develt and Industry. Vis. Prof., Univ. of Strathclyde, 1994–2004. FREng (FEng 1992). *Publications:* (jtly) Open Cycle MHD Power Generation, 1969; pubns on energy related issues. *Recreations:* squash, tennis, ski-ing, playing musical instruments. *Address:* Brambles, Spring Copse, Oxford OX1 5BJ. *Clubs:* Cambridge University Royal Tennis; Hinksey Heights Golf.

JEFFREY, Sir William Alexander, KCB 2008 (CB 2001); Permanent Secretary, Ministry of Defence, since 2005; *b* 28 Feb. 1948; *s* of Alexander and Joyce Jeffrey; *m* 1979, Joan MacNaughton, *qv*. *Educ:* Alan Glen's, Glasgow; Univ. of Glasgow (BSc Hons). Home Office, 1971–94: Private Sec. to Permanent Under Sec. of State, 1975–76; Principal, 1976–84; Assistant Secretary: Criminal Policy Dept, 1984–88; HM Prison Service, 1988–91; Asst Under Sec. of State, Immigration and Nationality Dept, 1991–94; Under Sec., Economic and Domestic Affairs Secretariat, Cabinet Office, 1994–98; Dep. Sec., NI Office, 1998–2002; Dir Gen., Immigration and Nationality, Home Office, 2002–05; Security and Intelligence Co-ordinator and Permanent Sec., Cabinet Office, 2005. *Recreations:* reading, hill-walking, watching football. *Address:* Ministry of Defence, Main Building, Whitehall, SW1A 2HB.

JEFFREYS, family name of **Baron Jeffreys**.

JEFFREYS, 3rd Baron *cr* 1952, of Burkham; **Christopher Henry Mark Jeffreys;** stockbroker, since 1992; Director: Raphael Asset Management, since 1997; Savoy Investment Management Ltd, since 2000; *b* 22 May 1957; *s* of 2nd Baron Jeffreys and of Sarah Annabelle Mary, *d* of late Major Henry Garnett; *S* father, 1986; *m* 1985, Anne Elisabeth Johnson; one *s* one *d*. *Educ:* Eton. With: GNI Ltd, 1985–90; Raphael Zorn Hemsley, 1992–2000. *Recreations:* country sports. *Heir:* *s* Hon. Arthur Mark Henry Jeffreys, *b* 18 Feb. 1989. *Address:* Manor Farmhouse, Edmondthorpe, Melton Mowbray, Leics LE14 2JU. *T:* (01572) 787397.
See also Hon. R. A. Prince.

JEFFREYS, Alan Howard; QC 1996; a Recorder, 1993–2004; *b* 27 Sept. 1947; *s* of late Hugh and Rachel Jeffreys; *m* 1975, Jane Olivia Sadler; one *s* one *d*. *Educ:* Ellesmere Coll.; King's College, London (LLB Hons). Called to the Bar, Gray's Inn, 1970; South Eastern Circuit; Asst Recorder, 1989–93. Mem., Criminal Injuries Compensation Appeals Panel (formerly Criminal Injuries Compensation Bd), 1999–2002. Mem., Exec. Cttee, Personal Injuries Bar Assoc., 2006–. *Recreations:* fishing, chess, music. *Address:* Farrar's Building, Temple, EC4Y 7BD. *T:* (020) 7583 9241. *Club:* Hurlingham.

JEFFREYS, Sir Alec John, Kt 1994; FRS 1986; Wolfson Research Professor of the Royal Society, University of Leicester, since 1991 (Professor of Genetics, since 1987); *b* 9 Jan. 1950; *s* of Sidney Victor Jeffreys and Joan (*née* Knight); *m* 1971, Susan Miles; two *d*. *Educ:* Luton Grammar School; Luton VIth Form College; Merton College, Oxford (Postmaster; Christopher Welch Schol.; BA, MA, DPhil 1975; Hon. Fellow, 1990). EMBO Research Fellow, Univ. of Amsterdam, 1975–77; Leicester University: Lectr, Dept of Genetics, 1977–84; Reader, 1984–87; Lister Inst. Res. Fellow, 1982–91. Member: EMBO, 1983; Human Genome Orgn, 1989. Editor, Jl of Molecular Evolution, 1985. FRCPath 1991; FLS 1994; Founder FMedSci 1998. Hon. FRCP 1993; Hon. FIBiol 1998; Hon. FRSocMed 2001. Fellow, Forensic Sci. Soc. of India, 1989; Hon. Mem., Amer. Acad. of Forensic Scis, 1998. Hon. Fellow, Univ. of Luton, 1995. DUniv Open, 1991; Hon. DSc: St Andrews, 1996; Strathclyde, 1998; Hull, 2004; Oxford, 2004. Colworth Medal for Biochemistry, Biochem. Soc., 1985; Carter Medal, Clinical Genetics Soc., 1987, 2003; Davy Medal, Royal Soc., 1987; Linnean Soc. Bicentenary Medal, 1987; Analytika Prize, German Soc. for Clin. Chem., 1988; Press, Radio and TV Award, Midlander of the Year, 1989; Linnean Medal, 1994; Sir Frederick Gowland Hopkins Meml Medal, Biochem. Soc., 1996; Albert Einstein World of Science Award, World Cultural Council, 1996; Baly Medal, RCP, 1997; SCI Medal, 1997; Sir George Stokes Medal, RSC, 2000; Gold Medal, RCS, 2004. Hon. Freeman, City of Leicester, 1993. UK Patents on genetic fingerprints. *Publications:* research articles on molecular genetics and evolution in Nature, Cell, etc. *Recreations:* walking, swimming, postal history, reading unimproving novels.

JEFFREYS, David Alfred; QC 1981; a Recorder of the Crown Court, 1979–99; *b* 1 July 1934; *s* of late Coleman and Ruby Jeffreys; *m* 1964, Mary Ann Elizabeth Long; one *s* one *d*. *Educ:* Harrow; Trinity Coll., Cambridge (BA Hons). Served, Royal Signals, 1952–54; City, 1958. Called to the Bar, Gray's Inn, 1958, Bencher, 1989; Junior Prosecuting Counsel to the Crown, Central Criminal Court, 1975; Sen. Prosecuting Counsel to the Crown, CCC, 1979–81; Jt Head, Hollis Whiteman Chambers, 1995–99, retd. Mem., Bar Council, 1977–80. *Address:* c/o Queen Elizabeth Building, Temple, EC4Y 9BS.

JEFFREYS, Prof. Elizabeth Mary; Bywater and Sotheby Professor of Byzantine and Modern Greek Language and Literature, University of Oxford, 1996–2006; Fellow of Exeter College, Oxford, since 1996; *b* 22 July 1941; *d* of Lawrence R. Brown and Veronica Thompson; *m* 1965, Michael J. Jeffreys; one *d*. *Educ:* Blackheath High Sch. for Girls (GPDST); Girton Coll., Cambridge (MA (Class. Tripos)); St Anne's Coll., Oxford (BLitt; Hon. Fellow, 1997). Classics Mistress, Mary Datchelor Girls' Sch., 1965–69; Sen. Res. Fellow, Warburg Inst., London Univ., 1969–72; Vis. Fellow, Dumbarton Oaks Centre for Byzantine Studies, 1972–74, 1984; Res. Fellow, Ioannina Univ., Greece, 1974–76; part-time Lectr, univs in Sydney, Australia, 1976–86; Vis. Fellow, Humanities Centre, Canberra, 1978; Res. Fellow, Melbourne Univ., 1987–89; Res. Fellow, 1990–92, Australian Sen. Res. Fellow, 1993–95, Sydney Univ. Fellow, Australian Acad. of Humanities, 1993. *Publications:* Byzantine Papers, 1981; Popular Literature in Late Byzantium, 1983; The Chronicle of John Malalas: a translation, 1986; Studies in John Malalas, 1990; The War of Troy, 1996; Digenis Akritis, 1998; Through the Looking Glass, 2000; Rhetoric in Byzantium, 2003; The Age of the Dromon, 2006. *Recreation:* walking. *Address:* Exeter College, Oxford OX1 3DP.

JEFFREYS, Prof. Paul William, PhD; CPhys; University of Oxford: Professor of Computing, since 2002; Director: e-Horizons Institute, since 2005; Information and Communications Technology, since 2007 (Acting Dir, 2005–07); e-Research Centre, since 2006; Fellow, Keble College, Oxford, since 2001; *b* 4 July 1954; *s* of George Lewis Jeffreys and Naomi Emily Jeffreys; *m* 1985, Linda Christine Pay; two *s* one *d*. *Educ:* Drayton Manor Grammar Sch., Hanwell; Univ. of Manchester (BSc Hons); Univ. of Bristol (PhD 1980); MA Oxon. CPhys 1982; MInstP 1982. CERN Fellow, Geneva, 1979–82; Rutherford Appleton Laboratory: physicist, 1982–95; Hd, Computing and Resource Mgt Div., Particle Physics Dept, 1995–2001; Leader, CCLRC e-Science Centre, 2000–01; Dir, Oxford Univ. Computing Services, 2001–05; Dir, e-Science Centre, Univ. of Oxford, 2001–06. Dir, Digitalspires, 2006–. *Recreations:* family life, ski-ing, squash, running, Real tennis. *Address:* Keble College, Oxford OX1 3PG. *T:* (01865) 273229, *Fax:* (01865) 283346; *e-mail:* paul.jeffreys@odit.ox.ac.uk.

JEFFRIES, Prof. Donald James, CBE 2007; FRCP, FRCPath; Professor of Virology, Barts and the London, Queen Mary's School of Medicine and Dentistry (formerly St Bartholomew's Hospital Medical College), University of London, 1990–2006, now Professor Emeritus; Hon. Consultant in Virology, Barts and the London NHS Trust (formerly St Bartholomew's Hospital), 1990–2006; *b* 29 Aug. 1941; *s* of late Edmond Frederick Jeffries and Eileen Elizabeth (*née* Elton); *m* 1966, Mary Millicent Bray; two *s* one *d*. *Educ:* William Ellis Grammar Sch., Highgate; Royal Free Hosp. Sch. of Medicine (BSc Hons Physiol. 1963; MB BS 1966). MRCPath 1974, FRCPath 1986; FRCP 2001. St Mary's Hospital Medical School: Sen. Registrar in Microbiol., 1970–72; Lectr in Virol., 1972–74; Sen. Lectr in Virol., 1974–87; Reader, 1987–90; Hd, Div. of Virol., 1982–90; Dir, Clinical Studies, 1985–90; Hd, Microbiol. and Virol. Clinical Service, Barts and the London NHS Trust, 1998–2006. Vis. Prof., Univ. of Riyadh, 1988; C. T. Huang Lectr, Hong Kong Univ., 1991; Wellcome Vis. Prof., Coll. of Medicine of S Africa, 1993. Consultant in Virol., St John Ambulance, 1994–. Sen. Examr, Univ. of London, 1993–2000. Chairman: Transmissible Spongiform Encephalopathies Wkg Gp, Adv. Cttee on Dangerous Pathogens, 1999–; Expert Adv. Gp on AIDS, DoH, 2003–05 (Mem., 1992–2002); Steering Gp on Health Care Associated Infections, HPA, 2004–07; Assoc. of British Insurers Expert Wkg Gp on HIV, 2005–; Member: Adv. Cttee on Genetic Modification, HSE, 1988–99; UK Adv. Panel for Health Care Workers infected with blood-borne viruses, 1992–2002; Adv. Cttee on Dangerous Pathogens, 1993–2002; Diagnostics and Imaging Panel, NHS Health Technol. Assessment, 1993–98; CJD Incidents Panel (Dep. Chm., 2000–; Actg Chm., 2003–05); Cttee on Safety of Medicines, 2001–05 (Mem., Biologicals Sub-cttee, 1999–2005, Chm., 2003–05); Nat. Expert Panel on New and Emerging Infections, 2003–07. Royal College of Pathologists: Mem. Council, 1996–2002; Vice-Pres., 1999–2002; Chairman: Virol. Examrs' Panel, 1995–2000; Exams Cttee, 1999–2002; Special Adv. Cttee in Microbiol., 1999–2002; Chm., Jt Cttee on Infection and Tropical Medicine, RCP/RCPath, 1999–2002. Member: Soc. Gen. Microbiol., 1970–; Hosp. Infection Soc., 1980– (Mem. Council, 1980–83 and 1990–93). Ellison Nash Prize, Barts and the London, 2001. *Publications:* Lecture Notes on Medical Virology, 1987; (ed jtly) Current Topics in AIDS, Vol. I 1987, Vol. II 1989: (ed with E. de Clercq) Antiviral Chemotherapy, 1995; (ed with C. N. Hudson) Viral Infections in Obstetrics and Gynaecology, 1999; papers and reviews on aspects of medical virology, especially HIV/AIDS, antiviral drugs, herpes viruses. *Recreations:* hill walking, fly fishing, gardening. *Address:* 63 Manor Park Avenue, Princes Risborough, Bucks HP27 9AS. *T:* (01844) 343821; *e-mail:* d.j.jeffries@qmul.ac.uk.

JEFFRIES, Hon. Sir John (Francis), Kt 1993; Chairman, New Zealand Press Council, 1997–2005; *b* 28 March 1929; *s* of Frank Leon Jeffries and Mary Jeffries; *m* 1951, Joan Patricia Christensen (*d* 2001); one *s* one *d*. *Educ:* St Patrick's Coll., Wellington; Victoria Univ. of Wellington (BA, LLB). Clerical, 1946–50; school teaching, 1950–55; Law, 1956–76; Judge of the High Court of New Zealand, 1976–92; NZ Police Complaints Authority, 1992–97. Chm., Air New Zealand, 1975. Wellington City Council, 1962–74; Dep. Mayor, Wellington, 1971–74. Chm., Nat. Housing Commn, 1973–75. Vice-Pres., NZ Law Soc., 1973–76; Member: Trust for Intellectually Handicapped, 1980–88; NZ Inst. of Mental Retardation, 1984–88. Comr of Security Warrants, 1999–. Hon. Life Mem., Amer. Bar Assoc., 1974. *Recreations:* reading, music, sports generally, playing golf. *Address:* 4/310 Oriental Parade, Oriental Bay, Wellington, New Zealand. *T:* (4) 3859995. *Clubs:* Wellington; Royal Wellington Golf.

JEFFRIES, Lionel Charles; actor since 1949, screen writer since 1959, and film director since 1970; *b* 10 June 1926; *s* of Bernard Jeffries and Elsie Jackson; *m* 1951, Eileen Mary Walsh; one *s* two *d*. *Educ:* Queen Elizabeth's Grammar Sch., Wimborne, Dorset; Royal Academy of Dramatic Art (Dip., Kendal Award, 1947). War of 1939–45: commissioned, Oxf. and Bucks LI, 1945; served in Burma (Burma Star, 1945); Captain, Royal West African Frontier Force. Stage: (West End) *plays:* Carrington VC; The Enchanted; Blood Wedding; Brouhaha; Hello Dolly, Prince of Wales, 1984; See How They Run, Two Into One, Rookery Nook, Shaftesbury, 1985–86; Pygmalion, Broadway, 1987; The Wild Duck, Phoenix, 1990; *films* include: Bhowani Junction, Lust for Life, The Baby and The Battleship, 1956; Colditz Story, Doctor at Large, 1957; Law and Disorder, 1958; The Nun's Story, 1959; Idle on Parade; Two Way Stretch, The Trials of Oscar Wilde, 1960; Fanny, 1961; The Notorious Landlady (Hollywood), The Wrong Arm of the Law, 1962; The First Men in the Moon, 1964; The Truth about Spring, 1965; Arrivederci Baby, The Spy with a Cold Nose, 1966; Camelot (Hollywood), 1967; Chitty, Chitty, Bang Bang,

1968; Baxter, 1973 (also dir; Golden Bear Award for Best Film, Europe); The Prisoner of Zenda, 1979; Eyewitness, 1981; Ménage à Trois; Chorus of Disapproval, 1989; Danny Champion of the World; Ending Up; First and Last. Wrote and directed: The Railway Children, 1970 (St Christopher Gold Medal, Hollywood, for Best Film); The Amazing Mr Blunden, 1972 (Gold Medal for Best Screen Play, Internat. Sci. Fiction and Fantasy Film Fest., Paris, 1974); Wombling Free, 1977; co-wrote and directed: The Water Babies, 1979; *television:* Cream in my Coffee, 1980; Shillingbury Tales, 1981; Father Charlie; Tom, Dick, and Harriet, 1983; Rich Tea and Sympathy, 1991; Look at it This Way, 1993. *Recreations:* painting, writing scripts, articles and a book. *Address:* c/o Liz Hobbs, MBE Management Ltd, 65 London Road, Newark, Notts NG24 1RZ.

JEFFRIES, Michael Makepeace Eugene, RIBA; FICE; Chairman, VT Group plc, since 2005; *b* 17 Sept. 1944; *s* of William Eugene Jeffries and Margaret Jeffries (*née* Makepeace); *m* 1966, Pamela Mary Booth; two *s* two *d*. *Educ:* Poly. of North London (DipArch Hons). RIBA 1973; FICE 2003. Architectural Assistant: John Laing & Sons Ltd, 1963–67; Surrey CC, 1967–68; Gillespie & Steele, Trinidad, 1968–69; Deeks Bousell Partnership, London, 1969–73; Senior Architect: Bradshaw Gass & Hope, Lancs, 1973–75; W. S. Atkins Ltd, 1975–78; Man. Dir, ASFA Ltd, 1978; Dir, W. S. Atkins Gp Consultants Ltd, 1979–92; Mkting and Business Develt Dir, W. S. Atkins Ltd, 1992–95; W. S. Atkins plc: Chief Exec., 1995–2001; Chm., 2001–04. Non-exec. Dir, De La Rue, 2000–07. Chairman: Wembley Nat. Stadium Ltd, 2002–08; Parking Internat. Hldgs Ltd (NCP), 2005–07; NCP Services Ltd, 2008–; GVA Grimley, 2008–. *Publications:* various technical papers in jls. *Recreations:* sailing, golf, water colour painting, antiquarian horology. *Address:* Hethfelton House, Hethfelton, Wareham, Dorset BH20 6HS. *T:* (01929) 401609. *Clubs:* Parkstone Golf, Royal Motor Yacht (Poole).

JEFFS, Julian; QC 1975; author; *b* 5 April 1931; *s* of Alfred Wright Jeffs, Wolverhampton, and Janet Honor Irene (*née* Davies); *m* 1966, Deborah, *d* of Peter James Stuart Bevan; three *s*. *Educ:* Mostyn House Sch.; Wrekin Coll.; Downing Coll., Cambridge (MA; Associate Fellow, 1986). Nat. Service, Naval rating, 1949–50. Sherry Shipper's Asst, Spain, 1956. Barrister, Gray's Inn, 1958 (Bencher 1981), Inner Temple, 1971; Midland and Oxford Circuit; Hong Kong Bar; retired from practice, 1991; a Recorder, 1975–96; a Dep. High Court Judge, Chancery Div., 1981–96. Chm., Patent Bar Assoc., 1980–89; Member: Senate of Inns of Court and Bar, 1984–85; Bar Council, 1988–89. Gen. Comr of Income Tax, 1983–91. Editor, Wine and Food, 1965–67; Mem., Cttee of Management, International Wine & Food Soc., 1965–67, 1971–82; Chm., 1970–72, Vice-Pres., 1975–91, Pres., 1992–96, Circle of Wine Writers. Gen. Editor, Faber's Wine Series, 1985–2002. Dep. Gauger, City of London, 1979. Freeman, City of London. Lauréat de l'Office International de la Vigne et du Vin, 1962 and 2001; Glenfiddich wine writer awards, 1974 and 1978. Mem., Gran Orden de Caballeros del Vino. Encomienda, Orden de Isabel la Católica (Spain), 2004. *Publications:* Sherry, 1961, 5th edn 2004; (an editor) Clerk and Lindsell on Torts, 13th edn 1969 to 16th edn 1989; The Wines of Europe, 1971; Little Dictionary of Drink, 1973; (jtly) Encyclopedia of United Kingdom and European Patent Law, 1977; The Wines of Spain, 1999, 2nd edn 2006; A Short History of the Lodge of Antiquity No 2, 2007; (ed with Jocelyn Hillgarth) Maurice Baring: letters, 2007. *Recreations:* freemasonry, wine, walking, old cars, musical boxes, follies, Iberian things. *Address:* Church Farm House, East Ilsley, Newbury, Berks RG20 7LP. *T:* (01635) 281216, *Fax:* (01635) 281756; *e-mail:* julian.jeffs@btopenworld.com. *Clubs:* Beefsteak, Garrick, Reform, Saintsbury.

JEFFS, Kenneth Peter, CMG 1983; FRAeS; consultant; *b* 30 Jan. 1931; *s* of Albert Jeffs and Theresa Eleanor Jeffs; *m* Iris Woolsey; one *s* two *d*. *Educ:* Richmond and East Sheen County Sch. jssc. National Service, RAF, 1949–51. Entered CS as Clerical Officer, Bd of Control, 1947; Air Min., 1952; Principal, 1964; JSSC, 1966–67; Private Secretary: to Under-Sec. of State (RN), MoD, 1969–71; to Minister of Defence, 1971–72; Asst Sec., Dir Defence Sales, MoD, 1972–75; Counsellor, Defence Supply, Washington, DC, 1976–79; Dir Gen. (Marketing), MoD, 1979–83; Exec. Vice-Pres., (Mil. Affairs), 1984–87, Dir, 1985–87, British Aerospace Inc.; Pres., MLRS Internat. Corp., 1987–92; Dir, Studley Associates, 1994–99. FRAeS 1985. *Recreations:* granddaughters, golf, horse racing. *Address:* Old Studley, Howell Hill Grove, Ewell, near Epsom, Surrey KT17 3ET. *Clubs:* Royal Automobile; Bude and North Cornwall Golf.

JEHANGIR, Sir Cowasji, 4th Bt *cr* 1908, of Bombay; *b* 23 Nov. 1953; *er s* of Sir Hirji Jehangir, 3rd Bt and of Jinoo, *d* of K. H. Cama; *S* father, 2000; *m* 1988, Jasmine, *d* of Beji Billimoria; one *s* one *d*. *Educ:* Cathedral and John Connon Sch., Bombay; Elphinstone Coll., Bombay (BA Econ). National Radio and Electronics Co. Ltd, Bombay, 1976–80. Chm., Jehangir Hosp., Pune, 1989–. Hon. Dir, Centre for Photography as an Art Form, Bombay, 1986–. Mem. Senate, Univ. of Pune, 1992–95. Trustee: Sir Cowasji Jehangir Sch., Bombay, 1976–; Jehangir Art Gall., Bombay, 2000–. *Recreations:* wildlife, photography, jazz, squash. *Heir: s* Cowasji Jehangir, *b* 28 March 1990. *Clubs:* Willingdon Sports, Bombay Gymkhana (Bombay); Royal Western India Turf (Bombay and Pune); Poona (Pune).

JEJEEBHOY, Sir Jamsetjee, 8th Bt *cr* 1857, of Bombay; *b* 16 Nov. 1957; *o s* of Sir Jamsetjee Jejeebhoy, 7th Bt and Shirin J. H. Cama; *S* father, 2006, and assumed name of Jamsetjee Jejeebhoy in lieu of Rustom Jejeebhoy; *m* 1984, Delara Jal Bhaisa; one *s*. *Educ:* Bombay Univ. (BCom 1979; LLM 1984). Dep. Man., Legal, Tata Exports Ltd, 1983–98; Vice Pres., India, Quantum Technologies Inc., 1998–2004. Director: Beaulieu Investment Pvt. Ltd, 1975; Dawn Threads Pvt. Ltd, 1984; Harinagar Holdings & Trading Co. Pvt. Ltd, 1985; Evergreen Stud & Agricultural Farms Pvt. Ltd, 2006. Chairman: Parsi Dhandha Rojgar Fund, 2004; Bombay Panjrapole, 2006; Sett Rustom Jamsetjee Jejeebhoy Gujarati Sch. Fund, 2006; Sir Jamsetjee Jejeebhoy Parsee Benevolent Institution, 2006; Sir Jamsetjee Jejeebhoy Charity Fund, 2006. Trustee: Destitute Eranis Charity Fund, 1990; Zoroastrian Building Fund, 2004. Hon. Freeman and Liveryman, Clockmakers' Co., 2008. *Recreation:* collecting curios. *Heir: s* Jehangir Jejeebhoy, *b* 20 Jan. 1986. *Address:* (residence) Beaulieu, 95 Worli Seaface, Mumbai 400030, India. *T:* 24985026; (office) Sir J J Charity Fund, Kalpataru Heritage Building, 5th Floor, 127 Mahatma Gandhi Road, Mumbai 400001. *T:* 22673843; *e-mail:* qti@vsnl.com. *Clubs:* Willingdon Sports, Royal Western India Turf, Ripon (Mumbai).

JELINEK, Elfriede; writer; *b* Mürzzuschlag, Austria, 20 Oct. 1946; *m* 1974, Gottfried Hüngsberg. *Educ:* Vienna Conservatory; Albertsgymnasium, Vienna; Univ. of Vienna. Writer of plays for radio, and for theatre incl. Raststätte, Das Werk; screenplays: Die Ausgesperrten (TV), 1982; Malina (film), 1991; Das Werk (TV), 2004; opera libretto, Lost Highway, 2003. Nobel Prize for Literature, 2004. *Publications:* Lisas Schatten (poems), 1967; ende: gedichte von 1966–1968, 1980; Die endlose Unschuldigkeit (essays), 1980; Was geschah, nachdem Nora ihren Mann verlassen hatte oder Stützen der Gesellschaften, 1980; Theaterstücke, 1984; Oh Wildnis, oh Schutz vor ihr, 1985; Krankheit oder moderne Frauen, 1987; Isabelle Huppert in Malina, 1991; Sturm und Zwang, 1995; Stecken, Stab und Stangl, 1997; er nicht als er, 1998; Macht nichts: eine kleine Trilogie des Todes, 1999; Der Tod und das Mädchen I–V: Prinzessinnendramen, 2003; *novels:* wir sind lockvögel baby!, 1970; Michael: ein Jugendbuch für die Infantilgesellschaft, 1972; Die Liebhaberinnen, 1975 (Women as Lovers, 1994); bukolit, 1979; Die Ausgesperrten, 198 (Wonderful, Wonderful Times, 1990); Die Klavierspielerin, 1983 (The Piano Teache 1988) (filmed, 2001); Lust, 1989 (Lust, 1992); Die Kinder der Toten, 1995; Gier: e Unterhaltungsroman, 2000 (Greed, 2006); *plays:* Wolken. Heim, 1990; Totenauberg: e Stück, 1991; Ein Sportstück, 1998; Das Lebewohl, 2000; In den Alpen, 2002; Bambilan Babel, 2004; Ulrike Maria Stuart, 2007; also translations of other writers' works. *Addres* c/o Serpent's Tail, 4 Blackstock Mews, N4 2BT.

JELLICOE, family name of **Earl Jellicoe**.

JELLICOE, 3rd Earl *cr* 1925; **Patrick John Bernard Jellicoe;** Viscount Jellicoe of Scap 1918; Viscount Brocas of Southampton, 1925; *b* 29 Aug. 1950; *s* of 2nd Earl Jellicoe, KB DSO, MC, PC, FRS and his 1st wife, Patricia Christine (*née* O'Kane); *S* father, 2007; 1971, separated 1971, marr. diss. 1981; two *s* (*b* 1970, 1977). *Educ:* Eton. Professio engineer. *Heir: b* Hon. Nicholas Charles Joseph John Jellicoe [*b* 23 March 1953; *m* 198 Patricia, *d* of late Count Arturo Ruiz de Castilla; two *d*].

JELLICOE, (Patricia) Ann, (Mrs Roger Mayne), OBE 1984; playwright and directo *b* 15 July 1927; *d* of John Andrea Jellicoe and Frances Jackson Henderson; *m* 1st, 1950, C E. Knight-Clarke (marr. diss. 1961); 2nd, 1962, Roger Mayne; one *s* one *d*. *Educ:* Pola Hall, Darlington; Queen Margaret's, York; Central Sch. of Speech and Drama (Els Fogarty Prize, 1947). Actress, stage manager and dir, London and provinces, 1947–5 privately commnd to study relationship between theatre architecture and theatre practic 1949; founded and ran Cockpit Theatre Club to experiment with open stage, 1952–5 taught acting and directed plays, Central Sch., 1954–56; Literary Manager, Royal Cou Theatre, 1973–75; Founder, 1979, Director, 1979–85 and Pres., 1986, Colway Theat Trust to produce community plays; Life Pres., Dorchester Community Plays Assoc., 199 *Plays:* The Sport of My Mad Mother (also dir with George Devine), Royal Court, 195 (also dir) For Children, 1959; The Knack, Arts (Cambridge), 1961 (also dir with Keit Johnstone), Royal Court, 1962, New York, 1964, Paris, 1967 (filmed, 1965; Palme d'O Cannes, 1965); Shelley or The Idealist (also dir), Royal Court, 1965; The Risin Generation, Royal Court, 1967; The Giveaway, Garrick, 1969; Flora and the Bandits (als dir), Dartington Coll. of Arts, 1976; The Bargain (also dir), SW Music Theatre, 197 *community plays:* (also directed): The Reckoning, Lyme Regis, 1978; The Tide, Seato 1980; (with Fay Weldon and John Fowles) The Western Women, Lyme Regis, 198 Mark og Mønt (Money and Land), Holbæk, Denmark, 1988; Under the God, Dorcheste 1989; Changing Places, Woking, 1992; *plays for children:* (also directed): You'll Neve Guess!, Arts, 1973; Clever Elsie, Smiling John, Silent Peter, Royal Court, 1974; A Goo Thing or a Bad Thing, Royal Court, 1974; *translations:* Rosmersholm, Royal Court, 196 The Lady from the Sea, Queen's, 1961; (with Ariadne Nicolaeff) The Seagull, Queen' 1963; Der Freischütz, Sadlers Wells, 1964; *directed:* Skyvers, 1963; A Worthy Guest, 197 (community plays): The Poor Man's Friend, Bridport, 1981; The Garden, Sherborn 1982; Entertaining Strangers, Dorchester, 1985. *Publications:* Some Unconsciou Influences in the Theatre, 1967; (with Roger Mayne) Shell Guide to Devon, 197 Community Plays: how to put them on, 1987; *plays:* The Sport of My Mad Mother, 195 (USA 1964); The Knack, 1962 (USA 1964; trans. various langs); Shelley or The Idealis 1966; The Rising Generation, 1969; The Giveaway, 1970; 3 Jelliplays, 1975. *Recreatio* enjoying grandchildren. *Address:* Colway Manor, Lyme Regis, Dorset DT7 3HD.

JENCKS, Charles Alexander, PhD; landscape architect, designer and writer; *b* 21 Jur 1939; *s* of Gardner Platt Jencks and Ruth Pearl Jencks; *m* 1st, 1960, Pamela Balding (mar diss. 1973); two *s*; 2nd, 1978, Margaret Keswick (*d* 1995); one *s* one *d*. *Educ:* Harvar University (BA Eng. Lit. 1961; BA, MA Arch. 1965); London University (PhD Arc Hist., 1970). Joined Architectural Association, 1968: Lectr in Architecture, 1970–91; Lec in Arch., 1974–85, Vis. Prof. of Arch., 1985–94, Univ. of Calif at LA Sch. of Arch. Write on Post-Modern architecture, 1975–, Late-Modern architecture, 1978–; designer c furniture, gardens, and sculpture, incl. DNA sculpture for James Watson, Kew Garden and Landform for Scottish Nat. Gall. of Modern Art (Gulbenkian Prize 2004); Parc Portello, Milan, 2006–08; numerous Univ. lectures, incl. Peking, Warsaw, Tokyo, US Paris; house designs incl. The Garagia Rotunda, 1976–77, The Elemental House, 198 The Thematic House, 1984. Fulbright Schol., Univ. of London, 1965–67; Melbourn Oration, Australia, 1974; Bossom Lectr, RSA, 1980; Mem., Cttee for selection c architects, Venice Biennale, 1980; Curator, Post-Modern London, exhibn, 1991. Edit at Academy Editions, 1979–. Member: Architectural Assoc.; RSA. Gold Medal f Architecture, Nara, Japan, 1992; Gardener of the Year, Country Life, 1998. *TV film* (wrote) Le Corbusier, BBC, 1974; (wrote and presented) Kings of Infinite Space (Fran Lloyd Wright and Michael Graves), 1983. *Publications:* Meaning in Architecture, 196 Architecture 2000, 1971; Adhocism, 1972; Modern Movements in Architecture, 197 2nd edn 1985; Le Corbusier and the Tragic View of Architecture, 1974, 2nd edn 198 The Language of Post-Modern Architecture, 1977, 6th edn 1991; Late-Moder Architecture, 1980; Post-Modern Classicism, 1980; Free-Style Classicism, 198 Architecture Today (Current Architecture), 1982, 2nd edn 1988; Abstrac Representation, 1983; Kings of Infinite Space, 1983; Towards a Symbolic Architectur 1985; What is Post-Modernism? 1986, 3rd edn 1989; Post-Modernism—the ne classicism in art and architecture, 1987; The Architecture of Democracy, 1987; Th Prince, The Architects and New Wave Monarchy, 1988; The New Moderns, 1990; (ed The Post Modern Reader, 1992; Heteropolis, Los Angeles, the Riots and the Strang Beauty of Heteroarchitecture, 1993; The Architecture of the Jumping Universe, 199 2nd edn 1997; Frank O. Gehry: cultural conservation and individual imagination, 199 (ed jtly) Theories and Manifestos of Contemporary Architecture, 1997; Ecstati Architecture, 1999; Le Corbusier and the Continual Revolution in Architecture, 200 Architecture 2000 and Beyond, 2001; The New Paradigm in Architecture, 2002; Th Garden of Cosmic Speculation, 2003; Scottish Parliament, 2005; The Iconic Building 2005; Critical Modernism, 2007; articles in Encounter, Connoisseur, l'Oeil, TL Prospect. *Recreations:* travel, collecting Chinese (bullet-hole) rocks. *Address:* 19 Lansdown Walk, W11 3AH; 519 Latimer Road, Santa Monica, CA 90402, USA.

JENKIN, family name of **Baron Jenkin of Roding**.

JENKIN OF RODING, Baron *cr* 1987 (Life Peer), of Wanstead and Woodford in Greate London; **Charles Patrick Fleeming Jenkin;** PC 1973; MA; President, Foundation f Science and Technology, since 2006 (Vice-President, 1996–97; Chairman, 1997–2006); 7 Sept. 1926; *s* of late Mr and Mrs C. O. F. Jenkin; *m* 1952, Alison Monica Graham; tw *s* two *d*. *Educ:* Dragon Sch., Oxford; Clifton Coll.; Jesus Coll., Cambridge (MA 1951 Served with QO Cameron Highlanders, 1945–48. Harmsworth Scholar, Middle Templ 1951; called to the Bar, 1952. Distillers Co. Ltd, 1957–70. Member: Hornsey Boroug Council, 1960–63; London Coun. of Social Service, 1963–67. MP (C) Wanstead an Woodford, 1964–87. An Opposition front bench spokesman on Treasury, Trade an Economics, 1965–70; Jt Vice-Chm., Cons. Parly Trade and Power Cttee, 1966–6 Founder Chm., All Party Parly Group on Chemical Industry, 1968–70; Financial Sec. t the Treasury, 1970–72; Chief Sec. to Treasury, 1972–74; Minister for Energy, 197 Opposition front bench spokesman: on Energy, 1974–76; on Soc. Services, 1976–7

Secretary of State: for Social Services, 1979–81; for Industry, 1981–83; for the Environment, 1983–85. Mem., Select Cttee on Sci. and Technol., H of L, 1996–2001 (Chm., Sub-Cttee II on Sci. and Soc., 1999–2000). Mem., Exec. Cttee, Assoc. of Cons. Peers, 1996–2000. President: National CPC Cttee, 1983–86; Greater London Area, Nat. Union of Cons. Assocs, 1989–93 (Vice-Pres., 1987–89). Chm., Friends' Provident Life Office, 1988–98 (Dep. Chm., Friends' Provident Life Office (Dir, 1986–88) and UK Provident Institution (Dir, 1987–88), 1987–88, when merged). Chm., Forest Healthcare NHS Trust, 1991–97. Director: Tilbury Contracting Gp Ltd, 1974–79; Royal Worcester Ltd, 1975–79; Continental and Industrial Trust Ltd, 1975–79; Chairman: Crystalate Hldgs PLC, 1988–90 (Dir, 1987–90); Lamco Paper Sales Ltd, 1987–93; Consultant, Thames Estuary Airport Co. Ltd, 1994–; Mem. Internat. Adv. Bd, Marsh and McLennan, 1993–98. UK Co-Chm., UK–Japan 2000 Gp, 1986–90 (Bd Mem., 1990–99); Vice-Pres., 1991 Japan Festival Cttee, 1987–91. Adviser: Andersen Consulting, Management Consultants, 1985–96; Sumitomo Trust and Banking Co. Ltd, 1989–; Member: UK Adv. Bd, Nat. Economic Res. Associates Inc., 1985–98; Supervisory Bd, Achmea Hldg NV, Netherlands, 1992–98. Member, Council: UK CEED, 1987–2003; Guide Dogs for the Blind Assoc., 1987–97; ICRF, 1991–97 (Dep. Chm., 1994–97); Royal Instn, 2002–05; Chm., Visual Handicap Gp, 1990–98; Pres., Friends of Wanstead Hosp., 1987–91. Pres., British Urban Regeneration Assoc., 1990–96; Sen. Vice Pres., World Congress on Urban Growth and Develt, 1992–95; Vice President: Nat. Housing Fedn, 1992–2000; LGA, 1997–; Jt Pres., London Councils (formerly Assoc. of London Govt), 1995–. Pres., ASE, 2002–03. Chm. Trustees, Westfield Coll. Trust, 1988–2000 (Gov., Westfield Coll., 1964–70; Fellow, QMW, 1991); Gov., Clifton Coll., 1969– (Mem. Council, 1972–79; Pres. of School, 1994–99; Pres., Old Cliftonian Soc., 1987–89); Mem. Internat. Adv. Bd, Nijenrode Univ., Netherlands, 1994–98. Trustee, Monteverdi Choir, 1992–2001. Patron, St Clare West Essex Hospice Trust, 1991–. Freeman: City of London, 1985; London Bor. of Redbridge, 1988. FRSA 1985. Hon. FRSE 2001; Hon. FCOptom 2003; Hon. Fellow BAAS, 2007. Hon. LLD South Bank, 1997; Hon. DSc Ulster, 2001. *Recreations:* music, gardening, sailing, bricklaying. *Address:* House of Lords, SW1A 0PW. *T:* (020) 7219 6966, *Fax:* (020) 7219 0759; *e-mail:* jenkinp@parliament.uk.

See also Hon. B. C. Jenkin, Rear-Adm. D. C. Jenkin.

JENKIN, Hon. Bernard Christison; MP (C) Essex North, since 1997 (Colchester North, 1992–97); *b* 9 April 1959; *s* of Lord Jenkin of Roding, *qv; m* 1988, Anne Caroline, *d* of late Hon. Charles Strutt; two *s. Educ:* Highgate Sch.; William Ellis Sch.; Corpus Christi Coll., Cambridge (BA Hons Eng. Lit., MA). Ford Motor Co., 1983–86; 3i, 1986–88; Hill Samuel Bank, 1988–89; Legal & General Ventures, 1989–92. Contested (C) Glasgow Central, 1987. PPS to Sec. of State for Scotland, 1995–97; Opposition spokesman on constitutional affairs, 1997–98, on transport, 1998–99; Opposition front bench spokesman on transport, and for London, 1999–2001; Shadow Defence Sec., 2001–03; Shadow Sec. of State for the Regions, 2003–04; Shadow Minister for Energy, 2005; Dep. Chm., Conservative Party (Candidates), 2005–06. Member: Select Cttee on Social Security, 1992–97; Select Cttee on Defence, 2006–; Sec., Cons. Backbench Small Business Cttee, 1992–97; Jt Sec., Cons. Backbench Foreign Affairs Cttee, 1994–95. Pres., Cambridge Union Soc., 1982. *Recreations:* family, music (esp. opera), fishing, shooting, sailing, ski-ing, DIY, arguing the Conservative cause. *Address:* House of Commons, SW1A 0AA. *T:* (020) 7219 3000. *Club:* Colchester Conservative.

See also Baron Rayleigh.

JENKIN, Rear Adm. (David) Conrad, CB 1983; Commandant, Joint Service Defence College (formerly National Defence College), 1981–84, retired; *b* 25 Oct. 1928; *s* of Mr and Mrs C. O. F. Jenkin; *m* 1958, Jennifer Margaret Nowell; three *s* one *d. Educ:* Dragon Sch., Oxford; RNC, Dartmouth. Entered RN at age of 13½, 1942; qual. in Gunnery, 1953; commanded: HMS Palliser, 1961–63; HMS Cambrian, 1964–66; HMS Galatea, 1974–75; HMS Hermes (aircraft carrier), 1978–79; Flag Officer, First Flotilla, 1980–81. President: Hong Kong Flotilla Assoc., 1999–; HMS Cambrian Assoc. *Recreations:* sailing, scale model-making. *Address:* Knapsyard House, West Meon, Hants GU32 1LF. *T:* (01730) 829227.

See also Baron Jenkin of Roding.

JENKIN, Simon William Geoffrey, OBE 2006; education consultant; Chief Education Officer, Devon County Council, 1989–98; *b* 25 July 1943; *s* of Dudley Cyril Robert Jenkin and Muriel Grace (*née* Mather); *m* 1973, Elizabeth Tapsell; two *d. Educ:* Univ. of London (BSc Econs); Jesus Coll., Oxford (DipEd). Lectr, 1967–72, Sen. Lectr, 1972–75, Bournemouth Coll. of Technology; Educn Officer, Essex CC, 1975–80; Area Educn Officer, NE Essex, 1980–83; Principal Educn Officer, Derbys CC, 1983–87; Dep. Chief Educn Officer, Devon CC, 1988–89. Mem., SW Regl Cttee, FEFCE, 1993–98. Director: Cornwall and Devon Careers Co. Ltd, 1995–98; Cambridge Education, 2001–. Advr, LGA, 1991–98. Gov., United World Coll. of the Atlantic, 1991–98. Trustee, Bath Technology Centre, 2006–. FRSA 1992. *Recreation:* my wife. *Address:* Grainge House, 10 Matford Avenue, Exeter EX2 4PW. *T:* (01392) 499798.

JENKINS OF HILLHEAD, Lady; *see* Jenkins, Dame M. J.

JENKINS, Adrian Richard; Director, Bowes Museum, Barnard Castle, since 2001; *b* 23 Jan. 1965; *s* of George and Mary Jenkins; *m* 2006, Lucy Whetstone; one *s* one *d. Educ:* Tasker Milward Comp. Sch.; Univ. of Leicester (BA Hons Ancient Hist. 1986); Barber Inst. of Fine Arts, Univ. of Birmingham (MPhil Art Hist. 1990); Bolton Business Sch. (MBA 2001). Curatorial Asst, English Heritage, 1990–92; Asst Keeper of Art, Laing Art Gall., Newcastle upon Tyne, 1992–96; Sen. Keeper of Fine and Applied Art, Bolton Mus. and Art Gall., 1996–2001. *Publications: catalogues:* (with Lucy Whetstone) Expressionism in Germany 1905–1925, 1999; Painters and Peasants: Henry La Thangue and British Rural Naturalism 1880–1905, 2000; (ed) The Road to Impressionism: Josephine Bowes and painting in nineteenth century France, 2002; (jtly) Creative Tension: British art 1900–1950, 2005; various contribs to jls. *Recreations:* looking at paintings, drainage issues, swimming, celebrating the flair of Welsh Rugby. *Address:* c/o The Bowes Museum, Barnard Castle, Co. Durham DL12 8NP. *T:* (01833) 690606, *Fax:* (01833) 637163; *e-mail:* adrian.jenkins@bowesmuseum.org.uk.

JENKINS, Alan Dominique; Chairman, Eversheds, solicitors, since 2004; *b* 27 May 1952; *s* of Ian Samuel and Jeannette Juliette Jenkins; *m* 1979, Caroline (*née* Treverton Jones); one *s* three *d. Educ:* Clifton Coll., Bristol; New Coll., Oxford (MA Jurisprudence). Admitted solicitor, 1977; Partner, 1983–1998, Man. Partner, 1996–98, Frere Cholmeley Bischoff; Eversheds: Partner, 1998–; Hd of Internat., 2002–. Trustee Foundn for Internat. Envmtl Law and Develt, 1998– (Chm., 2003–05); Internat. Inst. for Envmt and Develt, 2005– (Vice-Chm., 2005–). FInstD (Mem., Council, 2007–). FRSA. *Publication:* (contrib.) International Commercial Fraud, 2002. *Recreations:* ski-ing, tennis, watching sport in general (especially cricket and Rugby), theatre, music. *Address:* Eversheds, Senator House, 85 Queen Victoria Street, EC4V 4JL; *e-mail:* alanjenkins@eversheds.com. *Clubs:* Walbrook, MCC, Roehampton.

JENKINS, Alun; *see* Jenkins, T. A.

JENKINS, (Archibald) Ian; *b* 18 March 1941; *s* of Archibald Jenkins and Margaret (*née* Duncan); *m* 1967, Margery MacKay. *Educ:* Rothesay Acad., Isle of Bute; Glasgow Univ. (MA 1963; DipEd 1964). Teacher of English, Clydebank High Sch., 1964–70; Principal Teacher of English, Peebles High Sch., 1970–99. Mem. (Lib Dem) Tweeddale, Ettrick and Lauderdale, Scottish Parlt, 1999–2003; Lib Dem spokesman on educn, culture and sport, 2000–03. *Recreations:* golf, jazz, watching Rugby, reading. *Address:* 1 South Park Drive, Peebles EH45 9DR. *T:* (01721) 720528.

JENKINS, Prof. Aubrey Dennis; Professor of Polymer Science, University of Sussex, 1971–92, now Emeritus; *b* 6 Sept. 1927; *s* of Arthur William Jenkins and Mabel Emily (*née* Street); *m* 1st, 1950, Audrey Doreen Middleton (marr. diss. 1987); two *s* one *d*; 2nd, 1987, Jitka Horská, *er d* of late Josef Horský and Anna Horská, Hradec Králové, Czechoslovakia. *Educ:* Dartford Grammar Sch.; Sir John Cass Technical Inst.; King's Coll., Univ. of London. BSc 1948, PhD 1951; DSc 1961. FRIC 1957. Research Chemist, Courtaulds Ltd, Fundamental Research Laboratory, Maidenhead, 1950–60; Head of Chemistry Research, Gillette Industries Ltd, Reading, 1960–64 (Harris Research Labs, Washington, DC, 1963–64); University of Sussex, 1964–92: Sen. Lectr in Chemistry, 1964–68; Reader, 1968–71; Dean, Sch. of Molecular Scis, 1973–78. Visiting Professor: Inst. of Macromolecular Chemistry, Prague, 1978 and 1986; Univ. of Massachusetts, Amherst, 1979; ETH Zürich, 2002. Mem. Council, RSC, 2003–05. Member: Internat. Union of Pure and Applied Chemistry, Commn on Macromolecular Nomenclature, 1974– (Chm., 1977–85; Sec., Macromolecular Div., 1985–93); British Assoc. for Central and Eastern Europe (formerly GB/E Europe Centre), 1975–2005; British, Czech and Slovak Assoc., 1990–. Mem., Brighton HA, 1983–90. Examining chaplain to Bishop of Chichester, 1980–90. Hon. Fellow, Soc. of Organic Chemistry of Argentina, 1993. Geza Zemplyen Medal, Budapest, 1984; Heyrovský Gold Medal for Chemistry, Czechoslovak Acad. of Scis, 1990. *Publications:* Kinetics of Vinyl Polymerization by Radical Mechanisms (with C. H. Bamford, W. G. Barb and P. F. Onyon), 1958; Polymer Science, 1972; (with A. Ledwith) Reactivity, Mechanism and Structure in Polymer Chemistry, 1974; (with J. F. Kennedy) Macromolecular Chemistry, Vol. I 1980, Vol. II 1982, Vol. III 1984; Progress in Polymer Science (12 vols), 1967–85; (with J. N. Murrell) Properties of Liquids and Solutions, 1994; papers in learned jls. *Recreations:* music, travel, photography. *Address:* Vixens', 22A North Court, Hassocks, West Sussex BN6 8JS. *T:* (01273) 845410; *e-mail:* polygon@vixens.eclipse.co.uk.

JENKINS, Bethan Maeve; Member (Plaid Cymru) South Wales West, National Assembly for Wales, since 2007; *b* 9 Dec. 1981; *d* of Mike Jenkins and Marie Jenkins; partner, Jonathan Edwards. *Educ:* Ysgol Gyfun Rhydfelen, Pontypridd; Univ. of Wales, Aberystwyth (BScEcon Internat. Pol. and Internat. Hist.). Equal Opportunities Officer, 2003–04, Pres., 2004–05, Aberystwyth Guild of Students; Youth Organiser, Plaid Cymru, 2005–07. *Recreations:* blogging, playing viola, swimming. *Address:* 75 Briton Ferry Road, Neath SA11 1AR. *T:* (01639) 643549; *e-mail:* bethan.jenkins@wales.gov.uk.

JENKINS, Brian David; MP (Lab) Tamworth, since 1997 (SE Staffordshire, April 1996–1997); *b* 19 Sept. 1942; *s* of Hiram Jenkins and Gladys (*née* Morgan); *m* 1963, Joan Dix; one *s* one *d. Educ:* Aston Coll.; Coventry Coll.; Coleg Harlech; London Sch. of Econs (BSc Econ); Wolverhampton Poly. (PGCE). With CEGB, 1963–68; Jaguar Cars, 1968–73; Percy Lane, 1973–75; Lecturer: Isle of Man Coll., 1981–83; Tamworth Coll., 1983–96. Mem., USDAW. Tamworth Borough Council: Mem. (Lab), 1985–96; Dep. Mayor, 1992–93; Mayor, 1993–94; Leader, 1995–96. Contested (Lab) SE Staffs, 1992. Mem., Tamworth Br., RBL. *Recreations:* music, reading, watching sport. *Address:* House of Commons, SW1A 0AA.

JENKINS, Sir Brian (Garton), GBE 1991; FCA; Prior, England and the Islands, Order of St John of Jerusalem, since 2004; *b* 3 Dec. 1935; *s* of late Owen Garton Jenkins and Doris Enid (*née* Webber); *m* 1967, (Elizabeth) Ann Prentice; one *s* one *d. Educ:* Tonbridge; Trinity Coll., Oxford (State Scholar; MA; Hon. Fellow, 1992). FCA 1974. Served RA, Gibraltar, 1955–57 (2nd Lieut). With Cooper Brothers & Co., later Coopers & Lybrand, 1960–95; Chm., Woolwich Bldg Soc., later Woolwich plc, 1995–2000; Dep. Chm., Barclays Bank plc, 2000–04. Pres., ICAEW, 1985–86. Pres., London Chamber of Commerce, 1996–98. Chm., 1998–2003, Pres., 2003–08, Charities Aid Foundn. Vice-Pres., Foundn for Sci. and Technol., 2000–. Alderman, City of London (Ward of Cordwainer), 1980–2004 (Sheriff, 1987–88); Lord Mayor of London, 1991–92; Liveryman: Chartered Accountants' Co., 1980– (Master, 1990–91); Merchant Taylors' Co., 1984– (Master, 1999–2000); Information Technologists' Co., 1985– (Master, 1994–95). Dep. Pres., 1996–97, Pres., 1997–98, BCS. Trustee, Community Service Volunteers, 1987–. Hon. Bencher, Inner Temple, 1992; Hon. Mem., Baltic Exchange, 1993. Hon. DSc City Univ., 1991; Hon. DLitt London Guildhall Univ., 1991; Companion, De Montfort Univ., 1993; Hon. Fellow, Goldsmiths Coll., London, 1998. FBCS. CCMI. FRSA. Centenary Award, Chartered Accountants Founding Socs, 1993. KStJ 1991. Grand Conseiller Tutélaire des Neuf Nations de Bruxelles, 1992. *Publication:* An Audit Approach to Computers, 1978, 4th edn 1992. *Recreations:* garden construction, old books, large jigsaw puzzles, ephemera. *Address:* Vine Cottage, 4 Park Gate, SE3 9XE. *Clubs:* Brooks's, City of London, City Livery.

JENKINS, Lt-Col Charles Peter de Brisay, MBE 1960; MC 1945; Clerk, Worshipful Company of Goldsmiths, 1975–88, retired; *b* 19 Aug. 1923; *s* of late Brig. A. de B. Jenkins and of Mrs Elizabeth Susan Jenkins; *m* 1949, Joan Mary, *e d* of late Col and Mrs C. N. Littleboy, Thirsk; one *s. Educ:* Cheltenham Coll.; Selwyn Coll., Cambridge. Commnd RE, 1943; served in Italy, 1943–45; subseq. Hong Kong, Kenya and Germany; jssc 1960; Instructor, Staff Coll., Camberley, 1961–63; Comdr, RE 1st Div., 1965–67; retd 1967. Asst Clerk, Goldsmiths' Co., 1968. Mem., Hallmarking Council, 1977–88; Vice-Chm., Goldsmiths' Coll. (Univ. of London) Council, 1983–91. Trustee Nat. Centre for Orchestral Studies, 1980–89. *Publication:* Unravelling the Mystery – the Story of the Goldsmiths' Company in the Twentieth Century, 2000. *Recreations:* swimming, gardening, Wagner. *Address:* Oak Hill, South Brent, Devon TQ10 9JL.

JENKINS, Sir Christopher; *see* Jenkins, Sir J. C.

JENKINS, Christopher Dennis Alexander M.; *see* Martin-Jenkins.

JENKINS, Rt Rev. David Edward; Bishop of Durham, 1984–94; an Assistant Bishop, diocese of Ripon and Leeds, since 1994; *b* 26 Jan. 1925; *er s* of Lionel C. Jenkins and Dora (*née* Page); *m* 1949, Stella Mary Peet; two *s* two *d. Educ:* St Dunstan's Coll., Catford; Queen's Coll., Oxford (MA; Hon. Fellow, 1991). EC, RA, 1945–47 (Captain). Priest, 1954. Succentor, Birmingham Cath. and Lectr, Queen's Coll., 1953–54; Fellow, Chaplain and Praelector in Theology, Queen's Coll., Oxford, 1954–69; Dir, Humanum Studies, World Council of Churches, Geneva, 1969–73 (Consultant, 1973–75); Dir, William Temple Foundn, Manchester, 1973–78 (Jt Dir, 1979–84); Prof. of Theology, Univ. of Leeds, 1979–84, Emeritus Prof., 1985; Hon. Prof. of Divinity, Univ. of Durham, 1994–. Exam. Chaplain to Bps of Lichfield, 1956–69, Newcastle, 1957–69, Bristol, 1958–84, Wakefield, 1978–84, and Bradford, 1979–84; Canon Theologian, Leicester, 1966–82, Canon Emeritus, 1982–. Lectures: Bampton, 1966; Hale, Seabury-Western, USA, 1970;

Moorehouse, Melbourne, 1972; Cadbury, Birmingham Univ., 1974; Lindsay Meml, Keele Univ., 1976; Heslington, York Univ., 1980; Drummond, Stirling Univ., 1981; Hibbert, Hibbert Trust, 1985; Hensley Henson, Oxford, 1987; Gore, Westminster Abbey, 1990; Samuel Ferguson, Manchester Univ., 1997. Chm., SCM Press, 1987–92; Trustee, SCM Press Trust, 1992–97. Hon. Fellow: St Chad's Coll., Durham, 1986; Univ. of Sunderland (formerly Sunderland Poly.), 1986. Hon. DD: Durham, 1987; Trinity Coll., Toronto, 1989; Aberdeen, 1990; Birmingham, 1996; Leeds, 1996; Hon. DLitt Teesside, 1994; Hon. DCL Northumbria, 1994. DUniv Open 1996. Jt Editor, Theology, 1976–82. *Publications:* Guide to the Debate about God, 1966; The Glory of Man, 1967; Living with Questions, 1969; What is Man?, 1970; The Contradiction of Christianity, 1976; God, Miracle and the Church of England, 1987; God, Politics and the Future, 1988; God, Jesus and Life in the Spirit, 1988; Still Living with Questions, 1990; (with Rebecca Jenkins) Free to Believe, 1991; Market Whys and Human Wherefores, 2000; The Calling of a Cuckoo (memoirs), 2003; contrib. Man, Fallen and Free, 1969, etc. *Recreations:* music, reading, walking, birdwatching. *Address:* Ashbourne, Cotherstone, Barnard Castle, Co. Durham DL12 9PR.

JENKINS, David Edward Stewart; Managing Consultant, Lateral Research Consultants, since 2003 (Senior Partner, 1994–2003); *b* 9 May 1949; *s* of late William Stephen Jenkins and of Jean Nicol Downie; *m* 1972, Maggie Steele, *d* of Dr C. H. and Mrs J. D. Lack; two *s* one *d*. *Educ:* Univ. of London Goldsmiths' College (BA(Soc) 1977); LSE. Warden, Ellison Hse Adult Probation Hostel, SE17, 1973–74; Lecturer: (part-time) in Sociology, Brunel Univ., 1980–81; (part-time) in Social Administration, LSE and Goldsmiths' Coll., 1980–81; in Criminology, Univ. of Edinburgh, 1981; Dir, Howard League, 1982–86; Res. Fellow, PSI, 1986–87; Res. Consultant to HM Chief Inspector of Prisons, 1987–95. Morris Ginsburg Fellow in Sociology, LSE, 1986–87. *Recreations:* music, swimming, cycling.

JENKINS, David Hugh; Chief Executive, Dorset County Council, since 1999; *b* 28 April 1952; *s* of David Lyndhurst Jenkins and Charlotte Elizabeth Jenkins; *m* 1980, Ethna Geraldine Trafford; one *d*. *Educ:* Barry Boys' Comprehensive Sch.; Jesus Coll., Oxford (MA). Asst Master, Fairfield GS, Bristol, 1973–74; admitted solicitor, 1977; Articled Clerk then Asst Solicitor, Oxon CC, 1975–79; Solicitor, Commn for Local Admin in Wales, 1979–84; Asst Co. Sec., Hants CC, 1984–89; Dorset County Council: Dep. Co. Solicitor, 1989–91; Asst Chief Exec., 1991–93; Co. Solicitor, 1993–96; Dir, Corporate Services, 1996–99. Pres., Dorset Law Soc., 1993–94. Clerk to: Dorset Fire Authy, 1999–; Dorset Lieutenancy, 1999–; Secretary: Dorset Probation Cttee, 1999–; Dorset Strategic Partnership, 2002–. Dep. Chair, Nat. Efficiency Taskforce, 2008–. Board Member: Dorset TEC, 1999–2001; Dorset Business Link, 1999–2001; Bournemouth SO, 2000–; Dorset Connexions Partnership, 2001–06 (Chair, 2005–06). Chair: SW Centre for Excellence Bd, 2004–07; Bd, SW Regl Improvement and Efficiency Partnership, 2007–. Chm., ACCE, 2006–07; Mem. Council, SOLACE, 2005–. *Recreations:* music, theatre. *Address:* County Hall, Dorchester, Dorset DT1 1XJ. *T:* (01305) 224195.

JENKINS, David John, OBE 2004 (MBE 1993); Chairman, National Leadership and Innovation Agency for Healthcare in Wales, since 2007; *b* 21 Sept. 1948; *s* of William and Dorothy Jenkins; *m* 1976, Felicity Anne (*née* Wood); two *s* one *d*. *Educ:* Canton High Sch., Cardiff; Liverpool Univ. (BA Hons); Garnett Coll., London (CertEd). Industrial Sales Organiser, ITT (Distributors), 1970–74; steel worker, GKN, 1974; Lectr, Peterborough Tech. Coll., 1975–78; Wales Trades Union Congress: Research and Admin. Officer, 1978–83; Gen. Sec., 1983–2004. Chm., Health Professions Wales, 2004–06. Pt-time Mem., Competition (formerly Monopolies and Mergers) Commission, 1993–2002; Member: Employment Appeal Tribunal, 1994–; Fitness to Practice Panel, GMC, 2006–. *Recreation:* renovating old quarryworker's cottage in mid-Wales. *Address:* Twyn, Pregge Lane, Brecon Road, Crickhowell, Powys NP8 1SE. *T:* (01873) 812601.

JENKINS, Maj.-Gen. David John Malcolm, CB 2000; CBE 1994; Under-Treasurer, Honourable Society of Gray's Inn, since 2000; *b* 2 Jan. 1945; *m* 1969, Ann Patricia Sharp; one *s* two *d*. *Educ:* Sherborne Sch.; Reading Univ. (BA Hons); Magdalene Coll., Cambridge (MPhil). Commissioned The Queen's Own Hussars, 1964; regimental service, 1964–75; RMCS and Staff Coll., 1976–77; Allied Staff, Berlin, 1983–85; CO, The Queen's Own Hussars, 1985–87; COS, 3 Armd Div., 1988–90; Comdr Armd 1 (Br) Corps, 1990–91; Dir, Military Ops, 1991–93; Commandant, RMCS, 1994–96; DG Land Systems, MoD, 1996–2000; Master Gen. of the Ordnance, 1998–2000. Col Comdt, REME, 1997–2002; Col, Queens Royal Hussars, 1999–2004; Hon. Col, Inns of Court and City Yeomanry, 2003–. *Recreations:* ski-ing, country sports, music, military history. *Address:* Treasury Office, 8 South Square, Gray's Inn, WC1R 5ET. *Clubs:* Beefsteak, Garrick.

JENKINS, Ven. David Thomas Ivor; Archdeacon of Westmorland and Furness, 1995–99, now Emeritus; *b* 3 June 1929; *s* of Edward Evan and Edith Olwen Jenkins; *m* 1st, 1953, Rosemary German (*d* 1990); one *d*; 2nd, 1992, Kathleen Theresa Sidey. *Educ:* King's Coll. London (BD, AKC); Birmingham Univ. (MA (Theol.)). Ordained deacon, 1953, priest, 1954; Asst Curate, St Mark's Bilton, Rugby, 1953–56; Vicar, St Margaret's, Wolston, Coventry, 1956–61; Asst Dir, Religious Educn, dio. of Carlisle, 1961–63; Vicar: St Barnabas, Carlisle, 1963–72; St Cuthbert's, Carlisle, 1972–91; Canon Residentiary, Carlisle Cathedral, 1991–95, Canon Emeritus, 2000. Sec., Carlisle Diocesan Synod and Bishop's Council, 1972–95; Diocesan Synod Sec., 1984–95; Sec., Synod of Convocation of York, 1985–2005. *Recreations:* golf, reading, good food and wine with friends, foreign travel. *Address:* Irvings House, Sleagill, Penrith, Cumbria CA10 3HD. *T:* (01931) 714400.

JENKINS, Prof. Edgar William, CChem, FRSC; Professor of Science Education Policy, University of Leeds, 1993–2000, now Emeritus; *b* 7 Jan. 1939; *s* of Lewis Morgan Jenkins and Eira Gwyn (*née* Thomas); *m* 1961, Isobel Harrison; two *d*. *Educ:* Univ. of Leeds (BSc, MEd). CChem, FRSC 1974. Teacher: Keighley Grammar Sch., 1961–62; Leeds Grammar Sch., 1962–67; University of Leeds: Lectr and Sen. Lectr, 1967–76; Reader in Science Education, 1980–92; Head, Sch. of Education, 1980–84, 1991–95; Dir, Centre for Studies in Science Educn, 1997–2000. Chm., Bd, Grad. Teacher Trng Registry, 1995–2001. JP W Yorks, 1977. Editor: Studies in Science Education, 1986–98; Internat. Jl of Technology and Design Education, 1994–2000. *Publications:* A Safety Handbook for Science Teachers, 1973, 4th edn 1991; From Armstrong to Nuffield, 1979; Inarticulate Science?, 1983; Technological Revolution?, 1985; A Magnificent Pile, 1985; Policy, Practice and Professional Judgement, 1993; Investigations by Order, 1996; Junior School Science Education since 1900, 1998; Learning from Others, 2000; Policy, Professionalism and Change, 2001; Innovations in Science and Technology Education, 2003; Guidelines for Policy-making in Secondary School Science and Technology Education, 2003; books for schools. *Recreations:* choral music, walking, lay administration of justice.

JENKINS, Edward Nicholas; QC 2000; a Recorder, since 2000; *b* 27 May 1954; *m* 1979; one *s* one *d*. *Educ:* Trinity Hall, Cambridge (BA Hons). Called to the Bar, Middle Temple, 1977; Asst Recorder, 1999–2000. *Address:* 5 Paper Buildings, Temple, EC4Y 7HB. *T:* (020) 7583 6117.

JENKINS, Sir Elgar (Spencer), Kt 1996; OBE 1988; Member (C), Bath and North Ea Somerset Council, and Executive Member for Transport, 2003–07; *b* 16 June 1935; *s* late Spencer and Mabel Jenkins. *Educ:* Monmouth Sch.; St Edmund Hall, Oxford (Pres Oxford Univ., Cons. Assoc., 1955); St Luke's Coll., Exeter; Open Univ. (BA, Teachin Cert). Commission, RAF, 1956–59. Asst Master, Bath and Bristol, 1962–73; De Headmaster, Cardinal Newman Sch., then St Gregory's Catholic Comp. Sch., Bat 1973–88. Chairman: Bath and Dist HA, 1989–93; Bath Mental Health Care NHS Trus 1993–97. Member: Local Govt Mgt Bd, 1990–96; Nat. Adv. Cttee on Libraries, 1995–9 Bath City Council: Mem. (C), 1966–72, 1973–96; Mayor, Leader of Council, Chm. Cttees. Association of District Councils: Mem., 1985–96; Leader, Cons. Gp, 1991–9 Dep. Chm., 1991–93; Vice-Chm., 1993–96. Mem., Nat. Exec., Cons. Party, 1994–9 Contested (C) Ebbw Vale, 1970. Mem. Council, 1968–96, Mem. Court, 1968–, Ba Univ. Chm. of Trustees, Bath Postal Mus., 1986–2002; Trustee, Holburne Mus. of Ar 2003–07. Mem., Bath Archaeol Trust, 1994–2005. FRSA. *Recreations:* history, readin theatre. *Address:* 22 Frankley Buildings, Bath BA1 6EG. *T:* (01225) 314834.

JENKINS, Elizabeth, OBE 1981; writer; *b* 31 Oct. 1905. *Educ:* St Christopher's Schoo Letchworth; Newnham College, Cambridge. *Publications:* The Winters, 1931; Lad Caroline Lamb, a Biography, 1932; Harriet (awarded the Femina Vie Heureuse Prize 1934; The Phoenix' Nest, 1936; Jane Austen, a Biography, 1938; Robert and Heler 1944; Young Enthusiasts, 1946; Henry Fielding (The English Novelists Series), 1947; Si Criminal Women, 1949; The Tortoise and the Hare, 1954; Ten Fascinating Womer 1955; Elizabeth the Great (biography), 1958; Elizabeth and Leicester, 1961; Brightnes 1963; Honey, 1968; Dr Gully, 1972; The Mystery of King Arthur, 1975; The Princes i the Tower, 1978; The Shadow and the Light, 1983; A Silent Joy, 1992; The View fror Downshire Hill (memoir, ed by Sir Michael Jenkins), 2004.

JENKINS, Emyr; *see* Jenkins, J. E.

JENKINS, Ffion Llywelyn; *see* Hague, F. L.

JENKINS, Very Rev. Frank Graham; Dean of Monmouth and Vicar of St Woolo 1976–90; *b* 24 Feb. 1923; *s* of Edward and Miriam M. Jenkins; *m* 1950, Ena Doraine Parr two *s* one *d*. *Educ:* Cyfarthfa Sec. Sch., Merthyr Tydfil; Port Talbot Sec. Sch.; St David Coll., Lampeter (BA Hist); Jesus Coll., Oxford (BA Theol., MA); St Michael's Coll Llandaff. HM Forces, 1942–46. Deacon 1950, priest 1951, Llandaff; Asst Curat Llangeinor, 1950–53; Minor Canon, Llandaff Cathedral, 1953–60; CF (TA), 1956–6 Vicar of Abertillery, 1960–64; Vicar of Risca, 1964–75; Canon of Monmouth, 1967–7 Vicar of Caerleon, 1975–76. *Address:* Rivendell, 209 Christchurch Road, Newpor Gwent NP19 7QL. *T:* (01633) 255278.

JENKINS, Prof. George Charles, MB, BS, PhD; FRCPE, FRCPath; Consultan Haematologist, The Royal London (formerly London) Hospital, 1965–92, now Hon Consulting; Hon. Consultant, St Peter's Hospitals, 1972–86; Professor of Haematology i the University of London, 1974–92, now Emeritus; Consultant to the Royal Navy; *b* Aug. 1927; *s* of late John R. Jenkins and Mabel Rebecca (*née* Smith); *m* 1956, Elizabet *d* of late Cecil J. Welch, London; one *s* two *d*. *Educ:* Wyggeston, Leicester; S Bartholomew's Hosp. Med. Coll. MB, BS, PhD; MRCS 1951; LRCP 1951; FRCPat 1975 (MRCPath 1964); FRCPE; FRSocMed. House Phys. and Ho. Surg., St Bart Hosp., 1951–52. Sqdn Ldr, RAF Med. Br., 1952–54. Registrar in Pathology, St Bart Hosp., 1954–57; MRC Research Fellow, Royal Postgraduate Med. Sch., 1957–60; Sen Registrar, Haematology, London Hosp., 1960–63; Cons. Haematologist, N Middlese Hosp., 1963–65. Examiner: Univ. of London, 1971–95; Univ. of Cambridge, 1984–95 Sen. Examiner, RCPath, 1971–92, Mem. Council, 1979–84, Vice-Pres., 1981–8 Member, subcttee on biologicals, 1976–86, cttee on dental and surgical material 1988–92, Cttee on Safety of Medicines. Pres., British Acad. of Forensic Scis, 1990–9 (Mem., 1977–; Chm. Exec. Council, 1985–89); Member: British Soc. for Haematolog 1962– (formerly Hon. Sec.; Pres., 1988–89); Internat. Soc. of Haematology, 1975–95 Assoc. of Clinical Pathologists, 1958–92. Gov. and Mem. Council, Home Farm Trus 1993–2002. *Publications:* (jtly) Advanced Haematology, 1974; (jtly) Infection an Haematology, 1994; papers and contribs to med. and sci. books and jls. *Recreations:* theatre music, talking to people. *Address:* 3 Lambert Jones Mews, Barbican, EC2Y 8DP.

JENKINS, Prof. Geraint Huw, PhD, DLitt; FBA 2002; Director, University of Wale Centre for Advanced Welsh and Celtic Studies, since 1993; *b* 24 Jan. 1946; *s* of Davi Hugh Jenkins and Lilian Jenkins (*née* Phillips); *m* 1972, Ann Ffrancon; three *d*. *Educ* Ardwyn Grammar Sch., Aberystwyth; UCW, Swansea (BA 1st Cl. Hons 1967; Hon Fellow, Univ. of Wales Swansea, 2004); UCW, Aberystwyth (PhD 1974); DLitt Wal 1994. University of Wales, Aberystwyth: Lectr in Welsh Hist., 1968–81; Sen. Lect 1981–88; Reader, 1988–90; Prof. of Welsh Hist., 1990–93; Head of Welsh History 1991–93. Member: Univ. of Wales Bd of Celtic Studies, 1985– (Chm., 1993–2007) Council and Court, Univ. of Wales, Aberystwyth, 1991–2006; Cardiganshire Historica (formerly Antiquarian) Soc. (Chm., 1998–); Council, British Acad., 2007–. Editor Ceredigion, 1985–95; Cof Cenedl, 1986–. *Publications:* Cewri'r Bêl-droed yng Nghymru 1977; Literature, Religion and Society in Wales 1660–1730, 1978; Thomas Jones y Almanaciwr, 1980; Hanes Cymru yn Cyfnod Modern Cynnar, 1983, rev. edn 198 (Welsh Arts Council Prize, 1989); The Foundations of Modern Wales, 1987, rev. ed 1993; (ed jtly) Politics and Society in Wales 1840–1922, 1988; Llunio Cymru Fodern 1989; The Making of Modern Wales, 1989; Cymru Ddoe a Heddiw, 1990; Wale Yesterday and Today, 1990; Cadw Tŷ mewn Cwmwl Tystion, 1990 (Welsh Arts Counci Prize, 1991); Protestant Dissenters in Wales 1639–1689, 1992; The Illustrated History o the University of Wales, 1993; (ed jtly) Merêd: Casgliad o'i Ysgrifau, 1995; (ed) Y Gymraeg yn ei Disgleirdeb, 1997; (ed) The Welsh Language before the Industria Revolution, 1997; (ed jtly) Cardiganshire in Modern Times, 1998; (ed) Iaith Carreg f Aelwyd, 1998; (ed) Language and Community in the Nineteenth Century, 1998; (ed Gwnewch Bopeth yn Gymraeg, 1999; Doc Tom: Thomas Richards, 1999; (ed) Wels and its Social Domains 1801–1911, 2000; (ed jtly) Eu Hiaith a Gadwant?, 2000; (ed jtly Let's Do Our Best for the Ancient Tongue, 2000; (ed) Cymru a'r Cymry 2000, 2001; (e jtly) From Medieval to Modern Wales, 2004; A Rattleskull Genius: the many faces of Iol Morganwg, 2005; A Concise History of Wales, 2007; (ed jtly) The Correspondence o Iolo Morganwg, 2007; (ed jtly) Degrees of Influence, 2008. *Recreations:* music, sport gardening. *Address:* University of Wales Centre for Advanced Welsh and Celtic Studies National Library of Wales, Aberystwyth SY23 3HH. *T:* (01970) 636543.

JENKINS, Hugh Royston, CBE 1996; FRICS, FPMI; Chairman and Chief Executive Prudential Portfolio Managers, and Director, Prudential Corporation, 1989–95 Chairman: Falcon Property Trust, 1995–2003; Development Securities plc, 1999–2003; 9 Nov. 1933; *m* 1988, Mrs Beryl Kirk. *Educ:* Llanelli Grammar Sch.; National Service Royal Artillery, 1954–56. Valuer, London County Council, 1956–62; Assistan Controller, 1962–68, Managing Director, 1968–72, Coal Industry (Nominees) Ltd; Di Gen. of Investments, NCB, 1972–85. Vice Chm., National Assoc. of Pension Funds 1979–80; Chief Exec. Officer, Heron Financial Corp., 1985–86; Gp Investment Dir Allied Dunbar Assce, 1986–89; Dep. Chm. and Chief Exec., Allied Dunbar Unit Trusts

1986–89; Chm., Dunbar Bank, 1988–89; Chm. and Chief Exec., Allied Dunbar Asset Management, 1987–89. Dep. Chm., 1996–97, Chm., 1997–98, Thorn plc; Director: Unilever Pensions Ltd, 1985–89; IBM Pensions Trust PLC, 1985–89; Heron International, 1985–89; EMI, 1995–2003; Rank Gp plc, 1995–2001; Johnson Matthey, 1996–2003. Chm., Property Adv. Gp, DoE, 1990–96; Member: The City Capital Markets Cttee, 1982; Private Finance Panel, 1994–95; Lay Mem. of the Stock Exchange, 1984–85. *Recreation:* golf. *Address:* 15 Walpole Street, SW3 4QP. *Club:* Garrick.

JENKINS, Ian; *see* Jenkins, A. I.

JENKINS, Surg. Vice Adm. Ian Lawrence, CB 2006; CVO 2000; FRCS; Constable and Governor of Windsor Castle, since 2008; *b* 12 Sept. 1944; *s* of Gordon Eaton Jenkins, MBE and Edith Jenkins (*née* Rouse); *m* 1968, Elizabeth Philippa Anne Lane; one *s* one *d*. *Educ:* Howardian Grammar Sch.; Welsh Nat. Sch. of Medicine (MB BCh 1968). FRCS 1973. Joined RN, 1975; HMS Ark Royal, 1975; RN Hosp. Haslar, 1976, 1979; Newcastle Gen. Hosp., 1977–79; OC 1 RN Surg. Support Team (3rd Cdo Bde), 1976–79; RN Hosp. Gibraltar, 1979–82; Consultant Urological Surg., 1982–90, MO i/c, 1990–96, RN Hosp. Haslar; Prof. of Naval Surgery, RN and RCS, 1988–90; Defence Postgrad. Med. Dean and Comdt, Royal Defence Med. Coll., 1996–99; Med. Dir Gen. (Naval), MoD, 1999–2002; Surgeon Gen. to the Armed Forces, 2002–06. QHS 1994–2006. Chm., Portsmouth Cathedral Council, 2001–. Gov., Sutton's Hosp. in Charterhouse, 2006–. Mem. Council, White Ensign Assoc.; Chm., Seafarers UK, 2007–. Patron, COFEPOW, 2005–. CStJ 2000. *Publications:* contribs to med. jls on various urological subjects. *Recreations:* swimming, game fishing, music, painting in watercolour, travel. *Address:* Windsor Castle, Windsor, Berks SL4 1NJ. *Club:* Naval.

JENKINS, Sir (James) Christopher, KCB 1999 (CB 1987); First Parliamentary Counsel, 1994–99; *b* 20 May 1939; *s* of Percival Si Phillips Jenkins and Dela (*née* Griffiths); *m* 1962, Margaret Elaine Edwards, *yr d* of Rt Hon. L. John Edwards and Dorothy (*née* Watson); two *s* one *d*. *Educ:* Lewes County Grammar Sch.; Magdalen Coll., Oxford (Mackinnon Schol.; BA 1st class Hons Jurisprudence 1961; MA 1968). With Slaughter and May, 1962–67, solicitor, 1965. Joined Office of Parly Counsel, 1967; at Law Commn, 1970–72 and 1983–86; Parly Counsel, 1978–91; Second Parly Counsel, 1991–94. Adv. Council, Citizenship Foundn, 1989–; Adv. Law Cttee, British Council, 1998–2001; Adv. Council, Constitution Unit, UCL, 1999–; Council, Statute Law Soc., 2000–02. Hon. QC 1994. *Address:* c/o Parliamentary Counsel Office, 36 Whitehall, SW1A 2AY.

JENKINS, Dame Jennifer; *see* Jenkins, Dame M. J.

JENKINS, John, CMG 2003; LVO 1989; HM Diplomatic Service; Director, Middle East and North Africa, Foreign and Commonwealth Office, since 2007; *b* 26 Jan. 1955; *s* of John Malsbury Jenkins and Mabel Lilleen Norah Jenkins (*née* Gardiner); *m* 1982, Nancy Caroline Pomfret. *Educ:* St Philip's Grammar Sch., Birmingham; Becket Sch., Nottingham; Jesus Coll., Cambridge (BA 1977; PhD 1980). Joined FCO, 1980; Second, later First, Sec., Abu Dhabi, 1983–86; First Sec., FCO, 1986–89; Head of Chancery, Kuala Lumpur, 1989–92; First Sec., FCO, 1992–95; Counsellor and Dep. Head of Mission, Kuwait, 1995–98; Ambassador to Burma (Union of Myanmar), 1999–2002; Consul-Gen., Jerusalem, 2003–06; Ambassador to Syria, 2006–07. *Recreations:* Nottingham Forest FC, strenuous exercise, histrionics, the ancient world, drums. *Address:* c/o Foreign and Commonwealth Office, King Charles Street, SW1A 2AH. *T:* (020) 7270 1500.

JENKINS, John David; QC 1990; a Recorder, since 1990; *b* 7 Dec. 1947; *s* of late Vivian Evan Jenkins, MBE and of Megan Myfanwy Evans; *m* 1972, Susan Elizabeth Wilkinson; two *s*. *Educ:* Ashville Coll., Harrogate; King's Coll. London (LLB Hons). Called to the Bar, Gray's Inn, 1970; in practice at the Bar, Wales and Chester Circuit, 1970–. *Recreations:* football, cricket, psephology. *Address:* (office) 30 Park Place, Cardiff CF10 3BS. *T:* (029) 2039 8421. *Club:* Pentyrch Cricket.

JENKINS, (John) Emyr; Chief Executive, Arts Council of Wales, 1994–98; *b* 3 May 1938; *s* of Llewellyn Jenkins and Mary Olwen Jenkins; *m* 1964, Myra Bonner Samuel; two *d*. *Educ:* Machynlleth County Sch.; UCW, Aberystwyth (BSc Physics). BBC Studio Manager, 1961–63; BBC Announcer and Newsreader, 1963–71; Anchorman, Heddiw (Daily TV Mag.), 1968–69; BBC Wales Programme Organiser, 1971–77; First Dir, Royal Nat. Eisteddfod of Wales, 1978–93; Dir, Welsh Arts Council, 1993–94. Mem., IBA Welsh Adv. Cttee, 1986–90. Foundn Chm., Mudiad Ysgolion Meithrin (Assoc. of Welsh Playgroups), 1971–73; Member: Welsh Lang. Educn Develt Cttee, 1987–88; Council, UCW Aberystwyth, 1982–86; Steering Cttee/Council, Voluntary Arts Network, 1988–94; Voluntary Arts Wales Cttee, 1999–2001; Bd, Univ. of Wales Press, 1999– (Chm., 2003–06). Chairman: Welsh Music Inf. Centre, 2000–05; Sherman Cymru, 2007–. Gov., RWCMD, 1998– (Dep. Chm., 2000–06). FRSA 1992. Hon. FRWCMD (Hon. FWCMD 1997). Hon. MA Wales, 1993. Hon. Mem., Gorsedd of Bards, 1982. Elder, Crwys Presbyterian Church of Wales, 1983. *Recreations:* music, theatre, walking, sport.

See also F. L. Hague.

JENKINS, Dr Karl William Pamp, OBE 2005; FRAM; composer; *b* 17 Feb. 1944; *s* of David and Lily Jenkins; *m* 1973, Carol Barratt, composer; one *s*. *Educ:* Gowerton Grammar Sch.; University Coll. of Wales, Cardiff (BMus); DMus Wales 2006; Royal Acad. of Music (LRAM 1966; ARAM 2001; FRAM 2003). Played saxophone, keyboards and oboe with Ronnie Scott's jazz band, Nucleus (co-founder) and Soft Machine (1972–80); composer of advertising music for Levi's, British Airways, Pepsi, etc (D&AD award for best music, 1985, 1989; Creative Circle Gold Award, 1986). *Compositions:* Adiemus: Songs of Sanctuary, 1995; Cantata Mundi, 1997; Dances of Time, 1998; The Journey, 1999; The Eternal Knot, 2000; Vocalise, 2003; Diamond Music/Palladio, 1996; Imagined Oceans, 1998; Eloise (opera), 1999; The Armed Man: A Mass for Peace (for soloists, chorus and orch.) (commnd by Royal Armouries), 2000; Dewi Sant, 2000; Over the Stone (harp concerto), 2002; In These Stones Horizons Sing, 2004; Requiem, 2005; Quirk (concertante), 2005; Tlep, 2006; film score: River Queen, 2005. FRWCMD (FWCMD 2003); Fellow: Cardiff Univ., 2004; Trinity Coll., Carmarthen, 2005; Swansea Inst., 2005. *Recreations:* travel, food, sport. *Address:* c/o Karl Jenkins Music Ltd, 46 Poland Street, W1F 7NA. *T:* (020) 7434 2225; *e-mail:* info@karljenkins.com.

JENKINS, Katharine Mary; Chairman, Kate Jenkins Associates; *b* 14 Feb. 1945; *d* of late Rev. Dr Daniel Thomas Jenkins and Nell Jenkins; *m* 1967, Euan Sutherland, *qv* (marr. diss. 1995); one *s* one *d*. *Educ:* South Hampstead High Sch.; St Anne's Coll., Oxford (BA Hons); London School of Economics (MScEcon). Called to Bar, Inner Temple, 1971. Asst Principal, 1968, Principal, 1973, Dept of Employment; Central Policy Review Staff, 1976; Asst Sec., Dept of Employment, 1979; Dep. Head of Efficiency Unit, 1984; Hd, Prime Minister's Efficiency Unit, and Under Sec., Cabinet Office, 1986–89; Dir, Personnel, Royal Mail, 1989–91. Member: NHS Policy Bd, 1992–95; Audit Commn, 1993–99; Hansard Soc. Commn on Scrutiny Rôle of Parliament, 1999–2001; Council, Hansard Soc., 2003– (Vice Chm., 2005–). Dir, London and Manchester Gp, 1989–97. Vis. Prof., LSE, 2002–. Special Trustee, St Thomas' Hosp., 1992–95. Member: Barbican Centre Cttee, 2000–06; Council, Spitalfields Fest., 2003–06; St Bartholomew's Hosp. Trust Med. Coll., 2003– (Vice Chm., 2006–). Governor, 1990–, Mem. Council, 2000–03, LSE; Governor, Alleyn's Sch., Dulwich, 1990–98. *Publications:* (with W. J. P. Plowden) Governance and Nationbuilding: the failure of international intervention, 2006; Politicians and Public Services: a clash of cultures, 2008; reports: Making Things Happen: the implementation of government scrutinies, 1985; Improving Management in Government: the next steps, 1988; (with W. J. P. Plowden) Keeping Control: the management of public sector reform programmes, 1995. *Address:* 9 Fournier Street, E1 6QE.

See also Sir S. D. Jenkins.

JENKINS, Dame (Mary) Jennifer, (Lady Jenkins of Hillhead), DBE 1985; Member of Council, National Trust, 1985–90 (Chairman, 1986–90); *b* 18 Jan. 1921; *d* of late Sir Parker Morris; *m* 1945, Baron Jenkins of Hillhead, OM, FBA (*d* 2003); two *s* one *d*. *Educ:* St Mary's Sch., Calne; Girton Coll., Cambridge (scholar). Chm., Cambridge Univ. Labour Club. With Hoover Ltd, 1942–43; Min. of Labour, 1943–46; Political and Economic Planning (PEP), 1946–48; part-time extra-mural lectr, 1949–61; part-time teacher, Kingsway Day Coll., 1961–67. Chairman: Consumers' Assoc., 1965–76; Historic Buildings Council for England, 1975–84; Member: Exec. Bd, British Standards Instn, 1970–73; Design Council, 1971–74; Cttee of Management, Courtauld Inst., 1981–84; Ancient Monuments Bd, 1982–84; Historic Buildings and Monuments Commn, 1984–85 (Chm., Historic Buildings Adv. Cttee, 1984–85); Pres., Ancient Monuments Soc., 1985– (Sec., 1972–75). Chairman: N Kensington Amenity Trust, 1974–77; Royal Parks Review Gp, 1991–96; Architectural Heritage Fund, 1994–97; Adv. Panel, Heritage Lottery Fund, 1995–99; Civic Trust, 2003–04. Trustee, Wallace Collection, 1977–83. Director: J. Sainsbury Ltd, 1981–86; Abbey National plc (formerly Abbey National Building Soc.), 1984–91. Liveryman, Goldsmiths' Co., 1980. Freeman, City of London, 1982. JP London Juvenile Courts, 1964–74. Hon. FRICS 1981; Hon. FRIBA 1982; Hon. MRTPI 1988; Hon. FLI 1995. Hon. LLD: London, 1988; Bristol, 1990; DUniv: York, 1990; Strathclyde, 1993; Hon. DCL: Newcastle, 1992; Oxford, 2003; Hon. DArch Oxford Brookes, 1993; Hon. DLitt Greenwich, 1998; Hon. DSc St Andrews, 2006. *Publications:* (with Patrick James) From Acorn to Oak Tree, 1994; (ed) Remaking the Landscape: the changing face of Britain, 2002. *Address:* St Amand's House, East Hendred, Oxon OX12 8LA.

JENKINS, Sir Michael (Nicholas Howard), Kt 1997; OBE 1991; *b* 13 Oct. 1932; *s* of C. N. and M. E. S. Jenkins; *m* 1957, Jacqueline Frances Jones; three *s*. *Educ:* Tonbridge School; Merton College, Oxford (MA Jurisp.). Shell-Mex & BP, 1956–61; IBM UK, 1961–67; Partner, Robson, Morrow, Management Consultants, 1967–71; Technical Dir, Stock Exchange, 1971–77; Man. Dir, European Options Exchange, Amsterdam, 1977–79; Chief Executive, LIFFE, 1981–92; Chairman: London Commodity Exchange, 1992–96; Futures and Options Assoc., 1993–99; Dir, 1991–2003, Chm., 1996–2003, London Clearing House Ltd. Chm., E-Crossnet Ltd, 1999–2005; Director: Tradepoint Financial Networks plc, 1995–99; British Invisibles, 1998–2001; EasyScreen plc, 1999–2005. Trustee, Brain and Spine Foundn, 1993–. Pres., Merton Soc., 2007–. Gov., Sevenoaks Sch., 1993–2007. Liveryman, Information Technologists' Co., 2004–. *Recreations:* games, classical music and jazz, furniture making. *Club:* Wildernesse (Sevenoaks).

JENKINS, Sir Michael (Romilly Heald), KCMG 1990 (CMG 1984); CRAeS; President, Boeing UK, 2003–05; Commissioner, Royal Hospital Chelsea, since 2007; *b* 9 Jan. 1936; *s* of late Prof. Romilly Jenkins and Juliette Celine Haeglar; *m* 1968, Maxine Louise Hodson; one *s* one *d*. *Educ:* privately; King's Coll., Cambridge (Exhibr, BA). Entered Foreign (subseq. Diplomatic) Service, 1959; served in Paris, Moscow and Bonn; Deputy Chef de Cabinet, 1973–75, Chef de Cabinet, 1975–76, to Rt Hon. George Thomson, EEC; Principal Advr to Mr Roy Jenkins, Pres. EEC, Jan.–Aug. 1977; Head of European Integration Dept (External), FCO, 1977–79; Hd of Central Adv. Gp, EEC, 1979–81; Dep. Sec. Gen., Commn of the Eur. Communities, 1981–83; Asst Under Sec. of State (Europe), FCO, 1983–85; Minister, Washington, 1985–87; Ambassador to the Netherlands, 1988–93; Exec. Dir, 1993–96, Vice-Chm., 1996–2003, Kleinwort Benson Gp, then Dresdner Kleinwort Benson, subseq. Dresdner Kleinwort Wasserstein. Director: Aegon NV, 1995–2001; EO plc, 2000–02; Frontiers Capital, 2006– (Chm., 2008–); GeoPark Hldgs Ltd, 2006–; Chm., Matra Petroleum plc, 2007–; Advr, Sage Internat. Ltd, then SELS, 1998–2001. Member: European Exec. Cttee, Trilateral Commn, 1994–99; President's Adv. Council, Atlantic Council, 1994–. Chairman: Action Centre for Europe, 1995–2004; Dataroam, 2000–01; weComm, 2002–03. Advr, Prince's Trust, 2002–. CRAeS 2004. *Publications:* Arakcheev, Grand Vizier of the Russian Empire, 1969; A House in Flanders, 1992; (ed) The View from Downshire Hill (memoir), by Elizabeth Jenkins, 2004; contrib. History Today. *Address:* c/o Frontiers Capital Ltd, 75 Wells Street, W1T 3QH. *Clubs:* Brooks's, Pilgrims, MCC (Treas., 1999–2000; Chm., 2000–01; Trustee 2001–07), Queen's.

JENKINS, Neil Martin James; opera singer; tenor; music editor; *b* 9 April 1945; *s* of Harry James Jenkins and Mary Morrison Jenkins (*née* Terry); *m* 1st, 1969, Sandra Wilkes; one *s*; 2nd, 1982, Penny (*née* Underwood); one *s*, and two step *s* one step *d*. *Educ:* Westminster Abbey Choir School; Dean Close School (music Scholar); King's College Cambridge (Choral Scholar; MA). Recital début, Kirkman Concert Series, Purcell Room, 1967; operatic début, Menotti's The Consul, Israel Festival, 1968; major rôles with English Music Theatre, Glyndebourne Fest. Opera, Kent Opera, New Sussex Opera, Scottish Opera, WNO; ENO; numerous recordings, film sound tracks and videos. Prof. of Singing, RCM, 1975–76; teacher, summer schools, incl. Canford, Ardingly and Dartington, 1989–. Cummins Harvey Vis. Fellow, Girton Coll., Cambridge, 2003. President: Grange Choral Soc., Hants; Haywards Heath Music Soc., 2000–; Shoreham Oratorio Choir, 2003–; Vice-President: Hunts Philharmonic; Brighton Competitive Music Festival. Geoffrey Tankard Lieder Prize, 1967; NFMS Award, 1972; Sir Charles Santley Award, Musicians' Co., 2004. *Publications: choral music* (edited and arranged): The Carol Singer's Handbook, 1993; O Praise God, 1994; O Holy Night, 1994; Sing Solo Sacred, 1997; works by J. S. Bach: St Matthew Passion, 1997; St John Passion, 1998; Christmas Oratorio, 1999; Magnificat, 2000; B Minor Mass, 2002; Easter Oratorio, 2003; Ascension Oratorio, 2004; articles in: Haydn Soc. of Great Britain Jl, 2005; Göttinger Händel-Beiträge XII, 2008. *Recreations:* visiting ancient monuments, 18th century music research. *Address:* c/o Music International, 13 Ardilaun Road, N5 2QR. *T:* (020) 7359 5813.

JENKINS, Paul, OBE 2001; Chief Executive, Rethink, since 2007; *b* 11 Feb. 1963; *s* of Ifor and Sheila Jenkins; *m* 1989, Catherine Bannister; two *s*. *Educ:* Solihull Sch.; Balliol Coll., Oxford (MA Ancient and Modern Hist.); Manchester Business Sch. (MBA). Admin trainee, DoH, 1985; Project Manager, DoH, 1998–2004: Next Steps Proj. Team, Cabinet Office, 1988–91; Policy Lead for NHS Community and Continuing Care, 1991–96; Dir, Service Develt, NHS Direct, 2004–07. *Recreations:* Welsh language and culture, Rugby, cricket, history, archaeology, hill-walking. *Address:* Rethink, 5th Floor, Royal London House, 22–25 Finsbury Square, EC2A 1DX. *T:* (020) 7330 9104, *Fax:* (020) 7330 9102; *e-mail:* Paul.Jenkins@rethink.org.

JENKINS, Paul Christopher; HM Procurator General, Treasury Solicitor and Head of Government Legal Service, since 2006; *b* 22 Sept. 1954; *s* of late Reginald Turberville Jenkins and Elsie Jenkins (*née* Williams). *Educ:* Harrow County Sch. for Boys; Univ. of Manchester (LLB Hons 1976). Called to the Bar, Middle Temple, 1977, Bencher, 2002; Treasury Solicitor's Dept, 1979–90; Monopolies and Mergers Commn, 1990–92; Legal Adviser: DNH, subseq. DCMS, 1992–98; LCD, 1998–2002; Dir Gen., Legal and Internat. Gp, LCD, subseq. DCA, 2002–04; Solicitor to DWP and to DoH, and Dir Gen., Law, Governance and Special Policy, DWP, 2004–06. Gov., Europäische Rechtsakad., Trier, 2002–05, 2007–; Trustee, Inns of Court and Bar Educnl Trust, 2005–. Dir, Hampstead Theatre, 2006–. *Recreations:* opera, London, theatre. *Address:* Treasury Solicitor's Department, 1 Kemble Street, WC2B 4TS. *Club:* Reform.

JENKINS, Peter Redmond, CMG 2005; HM Diplomatic Service, retired; Special Adviser to the Director, International Institute for Applied Systems Analysis, since 2006; *b* 2 March 1950; *s* of late Denys Arthur Reali Jenkins and Monique Marie-Louise Jenkins; *m* 1990, Angelina Chee-Hung Yang; one *s* one *d*. *Educ:* Downside Sch.; Corpus Christi Coll., Cambridge (BA Hons, MA); Harvard Univ. Graduate Sch. of Arts and Scis (Harkness Fellow). Joined HM Diplomatic Service, 1973: FCO, 1973–75; UK Mission to Internat. Orgns, Vienna, 1975–78; FCO, 1978–82; Private Sec. to HM Ambassador, Washington, 1982–84; FCO, 1984–87; Paris, 1987–91; Minister-Counsellor and Consul Gen., Brasilia, 1992–95; Dep. Perm. Rep., 1996–2001, and Minister, 1998–2001, UK Mission to UN, Geneva; Perm. Rep. to UN and other Internat. Orgns, Vienna, 2001–06; Special Rep. for the Renewable Energy and Energy Efficiency Partnership, 2006–08. Mem. Adv. Bd, Ecoenergen, 2008–. Chm., IAEA Conference on Illicit Trafficking of Nuclear Materials, 2007. *Recreations:* ski-ing, hill/mountain walking, reading, travelling. *Address:* Nussberggasse 7/6/28, 1190 Vienna, Austria; *e-mail:* prjs@post.harvard.edu. *Clubs:* Brooks's, Beefsteak.

JENKINS, Peter White, MBE 2007; County Treasurer, Merseyside County Council, 1973–84; *b* 12 Oct. 1937; *s* of John White Jenkins, OBE, and Dorothy Jenkins; *m* 1961, Joyce Christine Muter; one *s* one *d*. *Educ:* Queen Mary's Grammar Sch., Walsall; King Edward VI Grammar Sch., Nuneaton. CIPFA. Local govt service in Finance Depts at Coventry, Preston, Chester, Wolverhampton; Dep. Treasurer, Birkenhead, 1969–73; Dir of Finance, Welsh Water Authority, 1984–87. Hon. Treas., 1994–98, Chapter Clerk, 2006–, Brecon Cathedral. *Recreations:* walking, gardening, local history, reading. *Address:* 9 Camden Crescent, Brecon, Powys LD3 7BY.

JENKINS, Richard Peter Vellacott; His Honour Judge Richard Jenkins; a Circuit Judge, since 1989; *b* 10 May 1943; *s* of late Gwynne Jenkins and of Irene Lilian Jenkins; *m* 1975, Agnes Anna Margaret Mullan (*d* 2003); one *s* one *d*. *Educ:* Edge Grove School, Aldenham; Radley College; Trinity Hall, Cambridge (MA). Called to the Bar, Inner Temple, 1966; Midland Circuit, 1968–72; Midland and Oxford Circuit, 1972–89 (Remembrancer and Asst Treasurer, 1984–89); a Recorder, 1988–89; Designated Family Judge, Lincoln, 1997–2007. Mem., Humberside Probation Cttee Policy Sub-Cttee, 1996–2000; Mem., Lincs Probation Bd, 2001–03. Chairman: Lincolnshire Family Mediation Service, 1997–2002 (Hon. Pres., 2005–); Lincs Area Criminal Justice Strategy Cttee, 2000–02. Mem. Cttee, Council of Circuit Judges, 2000– (Chm., Family Sub-Cttee, 2003–08; Jun. Vice Pres., 2007; Sen. Vice Pres., 2008). Chm., Adv. Bd, Law Sch., Univ. of Lincoln, 2006–. Mem., Sleaford Music Club. Liveryman, Co. of Barbers, 1967–. Hon. LLD Lincoln, 2004. *Address:* Lincoln Combined Court Centre, 360 High Street, Lincoln LN5 7PS. *T:* (01522) 883000. *Clubs:* MCC, Lansdowne.

JENKINS, Richard Thomas, OBE 1986; HM Diplomatic Service, retired; Ambassador to Georgia, 1998–2001; *b* 19 Aug. 1943; *s* of Vincent Arthur Wood Jenkins and Edna Jenkins (*née* Frith); *m* 1976, Maurizia Marantonio; two *s*. *Educ:* Plaistow Co. GS; Nottingham Univ. (BA Hons 1964); Warsaw Univ.; Glasgow Univ. Entered HM Diplomatic Service, 1967; FCO, 1967–70; Warsaw, 1970; FCO, 1970–76; Second, subseq. First Sec., E Berlin, 1976–79; Res. Dept, FCO, 1979–83; First Sec. (Commercial), Warsaw, 1983–85; Head, Central European Sect., 1985–89, Dep. Head, Jt Assistance Unit (Know How Fund), 1989–94, FCO Res. Dept; Dep. Head of Mission and Consul-Gen., Kiev, 1994–97. Election monitoring for OSCE Office for Democratic Instns and Human Rights: Albania, 2003; Georgia, Macedonia, 2004; Belarus, Tajikistan, Kazakhstan, 2005; Kosovo (Council of Europe), 2006. Mem., Fabian Soc. Freeman, City of London, 1998. Hon. Fellow, Univ. of E London, 1995.

JENKINS, (Sir) Simon David, Kt 2004; columnist, The Guardian and The Sunday Times, since 2005; Chairman, National Trust, since 2008; *b* 10 June 1943; *s* of late Rev. Dr Daniel Thomas Jenkins and Nell Jenkins; *m* 1978, Gayle Hunnicutt; one *s*, and one step *s*. *Educ:* Mill Hill Sch.; St John's Coll., Oxford (BA Hons; Hon. Fellow 2004). Country Life magazine, 1965; Univ. of London Inst. of Educn, 1966; Times Educational Supplement, 1966–68; Evening Standard, 1968–74; Insight Editor, Sunday Times, 1974–75; Dep. Editor, Evening Standard, 1976, Editor, 1976–78; Political Editor, The Economist, 1979–86; The Sunday Times: columnist, 1986–90; editor, Books Section, 1988–89; The Times: Editor, 1990–92; columnist, 1992–2005. Member: British Railways Bd, 1979–90; LRT Bd, 1984–86; South Bank Bd, 1985–90; Calcutt Cttee on Privacy, 1989–90; Grade Cttee on Fear of Crime, 1989; Runciman Cttee on Misuse of Drugs Act 1971, 1998–2000; HFEA, 2001–06. Chm., Commn for Local Democracy, 1994–95. Director: Municipal Journal Ltd, 1980–90; Faber & Faber, 1980–90. Chm., Booker Prize, 2000. Mem. Council, Bow Group, and Editor of Crossbow, 1968–70; Member: Cttee, Save Britain's Heritage, 1976–85; Historic Buildings and Monuments Commn, 1985–90 (Dep. Chm., 1988–90); Millennium Commn, 1994–2000; Mem. Council, Old Vic Co., 1979–81; Chm., Buildings Books Trust, 1994–; Dep. Chm., Thirties Soc., 1979–85; Founder and Dir, Railway Heritage Trust, 1985–90; Trustee: World Monuments Fund, 1995–98; Somerset House Trust, 2003–. Gov., Mus. of London, 1985–87. FSA 2004; FRSL 2004; Hon. RIBA, 1997. Hon. Dr UCE, 1998; Hon. DLitt: London, 2000; City, 2001; Univ. of Wales, Lampeter, 2001; Exeter, 2003; Univ. of London Inst. of Educn, 2005. What The Papers Say Journalist of the Year, 1988; Columnist of the Year, British Press Awards, 1993; Edgar Wallace Trophy for Outstanding Reporting, London Press Club, 1997; David Watt Meml Prize, Rio Tinto, 1998. *Publications:* A City at Risk, 1971; Landlords to London, 1974; (ed) Insight on Portugal, 1975; Newspapers: the power and the money, 1979; The Companion Guide to Outer London, 1981; (with Max Hastings) The Battle for the Falklands, 1983; Images of Hampstead, 1983; (with Anne Sloman) With Respect Ambassador, 1985; The Market for Glory, 1986; The Times Guide to English Style and Usage, 1992; The Selling of Mary Davies, 1993; Against the Grain, 1994; Accountable to None: the Tory nationalization of Britain, 1995; England's Thousand Best Churches, 1999; England's Thousand Best Houses, 2003; Big Bang Localism, 2005; Thatcher and Sons, 2006 (Political Book of the Year, Channel 4, 2007). *Recreations:* London, old buildings. *Address:* c/o The Albany, Piccadilly, W1J 0AU. *Club:* Garrick.
See also K. M. Jenkins.

JENKINS, Stanley Kenneth; HM Diplomatic Service, retired; *b* 25 Nov. 1920; *s* of Benjamin and Ethel Jane Jenkins; *m* 1957, Barbara Mary Marshall Webb (*d* 2004); four *d*. *Educ:* Brecon; Cardiff Tech. Coll. President, Nat. Union of Students, 1949–51. LIOI 1950. Served War, Royal Artillery and Royal Engineers, 1942–46, retiring as Majo Joined Foreign (later Diplomatic) Service, 1951; Singapore, 1953; Kuala Lumpur, 1955 FO, 1957; Singapore, 1959; Rangoon, 1961; FO, 1964; Nicosia, 1967; FO, 1970–78 Counsellor. *Publication:* So Much to Do, So Little Time (autobiog.), 2000. *Recreation* gardening, tennis. *Address:* Willow Cottage, 1 Beehive Lane, Ferring, Worthing, W Susse BN12 5NL. *T:* (01903) 247356. *Club:* Royal Commonwealth Society.

JENKINS, Stephen Lewis; Head of Media Relations, Archbishops' Council of th Church of England, since 1999 (Acting Head of Communications, 2002–04); *b* 1 Dec 1955; *s* of Charles Lewis Jenkins and Marjorie Jenkins (*née* Negus); *m* 1979, Susan Jan Varley; two *s*. *Educ:* Reading Sch.; UCNW, Bangor (BSc Hons (Agric. with Agric Econs)). Technical and news reporter, Big Farm Weekly, 1977–80; Dep. Ed., Big Farm Management, subseq. Farm Business, 1980–84; freelance, 1984–85; tech. journalist, Farr Contractor Mag., 1985–87; Press Officer: Children's Soc., 1987–90; Gen. Synod of C c E, 1991–99. *Recreations:* family life and the search for time. *Address:* Church House, Grea Smith Street, SW1P 3NZ. *T:* (020) 7898 1326, *Fax:* (020) 7222 6672; *e-mai* steve.jenkins@c-of-e.org.uk.

JENKINS, Prof. Stephen Pryse, DPhil; Professor of Economics, since 1994, an Director, since 2006, Institute for Social and Economic Research, University of Essex; 11 June 1956; *s* of David W. P. Jenkins and Katherine E. Jenkins (*née* Gillingham). *Edu* Univ. of Otago, Dunedin (BA 1977); Univ. of York (DPhil 1983). Jun. Lectr, Masse Univ., 1978; Res. Fellow, Univ. of York, 1979–80, 1981–83; Lectr, Univ. of Bath 1983–91; Prof. of Applied Econs, Univ. of Wales, Swansea, 1991–94. *Publications:* (ed jtly The Distribution of Household Welfare and Household Production, 1998; (ed jtly) Th Dynamics of Child Poverty in Industrialized Countries, 2001; numerous articles in learne jls. *Recreations:* music, running, cycling. *Address:* Institute for Social and Economi Research, University of Essex, Colchester CO4 3SQ. *T:* (01206) 873374, *Fax:* (01206 873151; *e-mail:* stephenj@essex.ac.uk.

JENKINS, (Thomas) Alun; QC 1996; a Recorder, since 2000; *b* 19 Aug. 1948; *s* o Seward Thomas Jenkins and Iris, *d* of Alderman W. G. H. Bull, miner and sometim Chm. of Monmouthshire CC; *m* 1971, Glenys Maureen Constant; one *s* two *d*. *Edu* Ebbw Vale Tech. Sch.; Bristol Univ. (LLB Hons 1971). Called to the Bar, Lincoln's Inn 1972; in private practice, Bristol, 1972–, and London, 1996–, specialising in law of seriou crime, esp. large diversion frauds, large scale drug importations, organised crime, an conspiracies; Head of Chambers, Queen Square, Bristol, 1995–. Asst Recorder 1992–2000. *Recreations:* cultural: opera, Shakespeare and literature generally; sport: hors riding, Rugby, motor cars, point to point. *Address:* Queen Square Chambers, 56 Quee Square, Bristol BS1 4PR. *T:* (0117) 921 1966; 2 Bedford Row, WC1R 4BU. *T:* (020 7440 8888.

JENKINS, Thomas Harris, (Tom), CBE 1981; General Secretary, Transport Salarie Staffs' Association, 1977–82; *b* 29 Aug. 1920; *s* of David Samuel Jenkins and Mirian Hughes (*née* Harris); *m* 1946, Joyce Smith; two *d*. *Educ:* Port Talbot Central Boys' Sch. Port Talbot County Sch.; Shrewsbury Technical Coll. (evenings); Pitmans Coll., Londo (evenings). Served War, RAMC, 1941–46 (Certif. for Good Service, Army, Wester Comd, 1946). Railway clerk, 1937–41; railway/docks clerk, 1946–49. Full-time servic with Railway Clerks' Assoc., subseq. re-named Transport Salaried Staffs' Assoc., 1949–82 Southern Reg. Divl Sec., 1959; Western Reg. Divl Sec., 1963; LMR Divl Sec., 1966 Sen. Asst Sec., 1968; Asst Gen. Sec., 1970, also Dep. to Gen. Sec., 1973. Member: Cttee of Transport Workers in European Community, 1976–82; Transport Industry Nationalised Industries, and Hotel and Catering Industry Cttees of TUC, 1977–82 Management and Indus. Relns Cttee, SSRC, 1979–81; Air Transport and Travel Industr Trng Bd, 1976–82; Hotel and Catering Industry Trng Bd, 1978–82; Employment Appea Tribunal, 1982–91; British Railways Midland and NW Reg. Bd, 1982–86; Police Complaints Bd, 1983–85; Central Arbitration Cttee, 1983–90; ACAS Arbitration Bd 1983–90. Mem. Labour Party, 1946–; Mem., Lab. Party Transport Sub-Cttee, 1970–82 *Recreations:* watching cricket, athletics and Rugby football. *Address:* 23 The Chase Edgware, Middx HA8 5DW. *T:* (020) 8952 5314.

JENKINS, Thomas Lawrence; Sports Photographer: The Guardian, since 1990 Observer, since 1993; *b* 1 Jan. 1968; *s* of Richard and Mary Jenkins; *m* 2003, Rosamunc Harris; one *s* one *d*. *Educ:* Sevenoaks Sch.; Gwent Coll. of Higher Educn (BTEC HNL Documentary Photography 1989). Freelance sports photographer: Allsport, 1989; Sunday Telegraph, 1989; Sunday Express, 1990. Young Photographer of the Year, 1990, Sport Photographer of the Year, 2004, 2006, 2007, British Press Awards; Sports Photographe of the Year, 2000, Photograph of the Year, 2004, What the Papers Say; Sport Photographer of the Year, Nikon, 2002, Sports Journalists Assoc., 2003, 2004. *Recreation* spending time with my family. *Address: e-mail:* tom.jenkins@guardian.co.uk.

JENKINSON, Dr David Stewart, FRS 1991; Lawes Trust Senior Fellow, Rothamstec Research (formerly Rothamsted Experimental Station), since 1990; Visiting Professor University of Reading, since 1992; *b* 25 Feb. 1928; *s* of Hugh McLoughlin Jenkinson anc Isabel Frances (*née* Glass); *m* 1958, Moira O'Brien; three *s* one *d*. *Educ:* Armagh Roya Sch.; Trinity Coll., Dublin (BA 1950; BSc 1950; PhD 1954). MRSC 1955. Asst Lectr Univ. of Reading, 1955–57; on scientific staff, Rothamsted Exptl Station, 1957–88 Hannaford Res. Fellow, Univ. of Adelaide, 1976–77; Vis. Scientist, CSIRO, 1977 Lectures: Hannaford, Univ. of Adelaide, 1977; Distinguished Scholars, QUB, 1989; Univ of Kent, 1992; Massey Ferguson Nat. Agricl Award, 1993. Hon. Member: Soil Science Soc. of Amer., 1995; British Soc. of Soil Science, 2007. *Publications:* Nitrogen Efficiency in Agricultural Soils, 1988; numerous papers in jls of soil science, soil biochemistry anc agronomy. *Recreations:* Irish history and literature, low input gardening. *Address:* 15 Topstreet Way, Harpenden, Herts AL5 5TU. *T:* (01582) 715744.

JENKINSON, Eric, OBE 2003; HM Diplomatic Service; High Commissioner, Trinidad and Tobago, since 2007; *b* 13 March 1950; *s* of Horace and Bertha Jenkinson; *m*; two *s*; *m* 2004, Máire Donnelly. Joined FCO, 1967; Protocol Div., FCO, 1967–70; Brussels, 1971–73; Islamabad, 1973–76; full-time language training, 1976–77; temp. duty, then Third Sec., Commercial, Jedda, 1978–80; Second Sec., Commercial, Riyadh, 1980–82; Sci., Energy and Nuclear Dept, FCO, 1982–84; Asst Private Sec., FCO, 1984–86; First Sec., Econ, Bonn, 1986–90; Dep. Consul General, Frankfurt, 1990–91; full-time language training, 1991–92; Dep. Head of Mission, Bahrain, 1992–95; Head, Parly Relns Dept, FCO, 1995–98; First Sec., Commercial/Econ., then Dep. Head of Mission, Tehran, 1999–2002; High Comr, The Gambia, 2002–06. *Recreations:* cooking, photography, Rugby, cricket, reading. *Address:* c/o Foreign and Commonwealth Office, King Charles Street, SW1A 2AH.

JENKINSON, Jeffrey Charles, MVO 1977; Chief Executive, Harwich Haven Authority, 1992–97; *b* 22 Aug. 1939; *s* of late John Jenkinson and Olive May Jenkinson; *m* 1962, Janet Ann (*née* Jarrett); one *s* two *d*. *Educ:* Royal Liberty Sch., Romford; City of London Coll. MCIT. National Service, RN, 1957–59. Port of London Authority: Port operations and gen. management, 1959–71; British Transport Staff Coll., 1972; PLA Sec., 1972–81; Dir of Admin, 1982–86; Bd Mem., 1982–92; Chief Exec., Property, 1987–92; Dir, Placon Ltd and other PLA gp subsid. cos, 1978–92. Dir, E London Small Business Centre Ltd, 1977–92; Mem. Bd, Globe Centre Ltd, 1992–96. Envmt Agency Chm., Essex Area Envmt Gp, 1996–2002; Mem., Anglian (Eastern) Regl Flood Defence Cttee, 2003– (Vice Chm., 2005–). Member: Bd, and Council, London Chamber of Commerce and Industry, 1989–92; Council, British Ports Assoc., 1993–96; Chm., Thames Riparian Housing Assoc., 1986–92; Member: Newham CHC, 1974–80; Committee of Management: Seamen's Gp of Hosps, 1972–74; Seamen's Hosp. Soc., 1974– (Hon. Treas., 1998–2002). Freeman, City of London, 1975; Mem. Ct, Co. of Watermen and Lightermen of River Thames, 1990– (Master, 1997–98). MCMI. *Recreations:* sailing, walking, music.

JENKINSON, Sir John (Banks), 14th Bt *cr* 1661; *b* 16 Feb. 1945; *o s* of Sir Anthony Banks Jenkinson, 13th Bt and Frances (*d* 1996), *d* of Harry Stremmel; *S* father, 1989; *m* 1979, Josephine Mary Marshall-Andrew; one *s* one *d*. *Educ:* Eton; Univ. of Miami. *Heir: s* George Samuel Anthony Banks Jenkinson, *b* 8 Nov. 1980. *Address:* Hawkesbury Home Farm, Hawkesbury, Badminton, S Glos GL9 1AY.

JENKINSON, Kenneth Leslie; Headmaster, Colchester Royal Grammar School, since 2000 (Deputy Headmaster, 1994–2000); *b* 4 Oct. 1955; *s* of Reginald and Margaret Jenkinson; *m* 1979, Jacqueline Anne Loose; two *d*. *Educ:* Danum Grammar Sch., Doncaster; Univ. of Leeds (BA, PGCE); Univ. of Sheffield (MA); NPQH. Teacher, Modern Languages, Hayfield Sch., Doncaster, 1979–88; Head, Modern Languages, Blundell's Sch., Tiverton, 1988–94. *Recreations:* family, travel, sport. *Address:* Colchester Royal Grammar School, Lexden Road, Colchester, Essex CO3 3ND. *T:* (01206) 509100.

JENKINSON, Nigel Harrison; Executive Director, Financial Stability, Bank of England, since 2003; *b* 18 June 1955; *s* of Alan and Jean Jenkinson; *m* 1977, Jeanne Mellalieu; two *s*. *Educ:* Birmingham Univ. (BSocSc 1st cl. Hons Mathematics, Econs and Statistics); London Sch. of Economics (MSc Econometrics and Mathematical Econs (Dist)). Bank of England: Economist, 1977–90; Mem., Economic Unit, Secretariat of Cttee of Govs, European Union Central Banks, 1990–93 (on secondment); Dep. Head, Reserves Mgt, 1993–94; Head, Structural Economic Analysis Div., 1994–98; Dep. Dir, Monetary Analysis and Statistics, 1999–2003. Mem., REconS. *Recreations:* football, cricket, reading. *Address:* Bank of England, Threadneedle Street, EC2R 8AH. *T:* (020) 7601 3000. *Club:* Colchester United Supporters Association.

JENKINSON, Philip; DL; Chairman, Active Devon Sports Partnership, since 2005; *b* 2 June 1948; *s* of Harold Jenkinson and Edith Florence Jenkinson (*née* Phillipson); *m* 1970, Sandra Elizabeth Cornish; four *s*. *Educ:* Manchester Grammar Sch.; Univ. of Exeter (LLB 1st Cl. Hons); Liverpool Poly. Trainee solicitor, Gillingham BC, Kent, 1970–72; admitted solicitor, 1972; Asst Solicitor, Bath CC, 1972–74; Devon County Council: Solicitor, 1974–95; Chief Exec., and Clerk to the Lieutenancy, 1995–2006. Director: Prosper (formerly Devon and Cornwall TEC), 1995–2002; Cornwall and Devon Connexions, 2001–. Gov., Exeter Coll., 2005– (Chm., 2008–). DL Devon, 2006. FRSA. *Recreations:* walking designated footpaths, music.

JENKS, Prof. Christopher, AcSS; sociologist; Vice-Chancellor and Principal, Brunel University, since 2006; *b* 12 June 1947; *y s* of late Arthur Jenks and Alice Elizabeth Jenks; *m* Barbara Read; two *d*. *Educ:* Westminster City Sch.; Univ. of Surrey (BSc 1969); Univ. of London; PGCE 1970, MSc Econ 1971, London Univ. Goldsmiths' College, London University: Lectr, 1971–76, Sen. Lectr, then Reader, 1976–94, in Sociology; Prof. of Sociology, 1995–2004; Pro-Warden, 1995–2000; Prof. of Sociology and Pro-Vice-Chancellor, Brunel Univ., 2004–06. Ed., Childhood jl, 1995–. AcSS 2000. FRSA 2006; FRSocMed 2008. Hon. PhD Univ. of Sci. and Technol., Trondheim, 2005. *Publications:* Rationality, Education and the Social Organization of Knowledge, 1976; (ed jtly) Worlds Apart, 1977; (jtly) Toward a Sociology of Education, 1977; (ed) The Sociology of Childhood, 1982; Culture, 1993, 2nd edn 2005; Cultural Reproduction, 1993; Visual Culture, 1995; Childhood, 1996, 2nd edn 2005; (jtly) Theorizing Childhood, 1998; (ed) Core Sociological Dichotomies, 1998; (jtly) Images of Community: Durkheim, social systems and the sociology of art, 2000; Aspects of Urban Culture, 2001; Culture, 4 vols, 2002; Transgression, 2003; Urban Culture, 4 vols, 2004; Subculture: the fragmentation of the social, 2004; Childhood, 3 vols, 2005; (jtly) Qualitative Complexity, 2006; Transgression, 4 vols, 2006; articles in British Jl of Sociology, Theory, Culture and Society, Cultural Values and others. *Recreations:* cricket, art and literature, previously rock climbing and mountaineering. *Address:* Brunel University, Uxbridge, Middx UB8 3PH. *Clubs:* Athenæum, Chelsea Arts, MCC.

JENKS, Sir (Richard) Peter, 4th Bt *cr* 1932, of Cheape in the City of London; FCA; *b* 28 June 1936; *yr s* of Sir Richard Atherley Jenks, 2nd Bt and of Marjorie Suzanne Arlette Jenks (*née* du Cros); *S* brother, 2004; *m* 1963, Juniper Li-Yung Foo; one *s* two *d*. *Educ:* Charterhouse; Grenoble Univ. FCA 1959. Lieut, Royal Inniskilling Dragoon Guards, 1959–61. Articled chartered accountancy clerk, 1954–59; stockbroking, 1962–88: Partner, Govett Sons & Co.; Partner and Finance Dir, Hoare Govett; Dir, Security Pacific Bank Ltd. *Recreations:* ski-ing, mountaineering, olive farming, butterflies, wine, travel, astronomy, charity work. *Heir: s* Richard Albert Benedict Jenks, *b* 27 Feb. 1965. *Address:* 81 Onslow Square, SW7 3LT. *T:* (020) 7589 6295, *Fax:* (020) 7584 9952; *e-mail:* peter.jenks@virgin.net; Sornanino, Loc. Casafrassi, 53010 Quercegrossa, Siena, Italy.

JENNER, Ann Maureen; Ballet Teacher, Australian Ballet School; Guest Ballet Teacher: Victorian College of the Arts, Melbourne; Australian Ballet; Queensland Ballet, and many other schools in Sydney and Melbourne; also guest choreographer; *b* 8 March 1944; *d* of Kenneth George Jenner and Margaret Rosetta (*née* Wilson); *m* 1980, Dale Robert Baker; one *s*. *Educ:* Royal Ballet Junior and Senior Schools. Royal Ballet Co., 1961–78: Soloist 1964; Principal Dancer 1970. Australian Ballet, 1978–80. Associate Dir, 1987, Dir, 1988–94, Nat. Theater Ballet Sch., Melbourne. Roles include: Lise, Fille Mal Gardée, 1966; Swanhilda, Coppelia, 1968; Cinderella, 1969; Princess Aurora, Sleeping Beauty, 1972; Giselle, 1973; Gypsy, Deux Pigeons, 1974; White Girl, Deux Pigeons, 1976; Juliet, Romeo and Juliet, 1977; Countess Larisch, Mayerling, 1978; Flavia, Spartacus, 1979; Kitri, Don Quixote, 1979; Anna, Anna Karenina, 1980; Poll, Pineapple Poll, 1980; one-act roles include: Symphonic Variations, 1967; Firebird, 1972; Triad, 1973; Les Sylphides; Serenade; Les Patineurs; Elite Syncopations, Concert, Flower Festival Pas de Deux, etc. Guest Teacher, San Francisco Ballet Co. and San Francisco Ballet Sch., 1985.

JENNER, Prof. Peter George, PhD, DSc; FRPharmS; Professor of Pharmacology, King's College London School of Biomedical and Health Sciences (formerly Guy's, King's, and St Thomas' School of Biomedical Sciences), King's College London, since 1989; *b* 6 July 1946; *s* of late George Edwin Jenner and Edith (*née* Hallett); *m*; one *s*. *Educ:* Chelsea Coll., London Univ. (BPharm Hons 1967; PhD 1970; DSc 1987). FRPharmS 1994; FBPharmacolS 2005. Post-grad. Fellow, Dept of Pharmacy, Chelsea Coll., London, 1970–72; Lectr in Biochem., 1972–78, Sen. Lectr, 1978–85, Dept of Neurol., Inst. of Psychiatry, Univ. of London, 1972–78; King's College, London University: Reader in Neurochem. Pharmacol., Inst. of Psychiatry and KCH Med. Sch., 1985–89; Hon. Sen. Lectr, Inst. of Neurol., 1988–2000; Prof. of Pharmacology and Head, Dept of Pharmacology, 1989–98, Head, Div. of Pharmacology and Therapeutics, GKT Sch. of Biomed. Scis, 1998–2004; FKC 2006. Director: Exptl Res. Labs, Parkinson's Disease Soc., 1988–99; Neurodegenerative Diseases Res. Centre, 1993–. Dir, Proximagen Ltd, 2005–. Adjunct Prof. of Neurology, Univ. of Miami, USA, 1997–99. Parkinson's Disease Society: Mem. Council, 1993–99 (Hon. Sec. to Council, 1996–99); Mem., Med. Adv. Panel, 1993–99. Mem., Molecular and Cellular Pharmacol. Gp Cttee, Biochem. Soc., 1993–2000. Mem., Bd of Mgt, Inst. of Epileptology, KCL, 1994–2003. Vice-Pres., Eur. Soc for Clin. Pharmacol., 2001–. Mem., Med. Adv. Bd, Bachman-Strauss Foundn, 2000–05. European Ed., Synapse, 1990–; Series Editor: Neurosci. Perspectives, 1991–96; (jtly) Internat. Review of Neurobiol., 1996–; Handling Editor: Jl of Neurochemistry, 1998–; Neuropharmacology, 2002–; Jl of Neural Transmission; Member, Editorial Board: Jl of Pharmacy and Pharmacology; Polish Jl of Pharmacology, 2002–. *Publications:* (with B. Testa) Drug Metabolism: chemical and biochemical aspects, 1976; (ed with B. Testa) Concepts in Drug Metabolism, Part A 1980, Part B 1981; (ed jtly) Approaches to the Use of Bromocriptine in Parkinson's Disease, 1985; (ed jtly) Neurological Disorders, 1987; (ed) Neurotoxins and their Pharmacological Implications, 1987; (ed jtly) Disorders of Movement, 1989; (ed jtly) Neuroprotection in Parkinson's Disease, vol. 3: beyond the decade of the brain, 1998; (ed jtly) Biomedical and Health Research, vol. 19: dopamine receptor subtypes, 1998; contrib. Lancet, Jl Neurochem., Annals Neurol., Biochem. Pharmacol., Brain Res., Psychopharmacol., Neurosci.; Exptl Neurol.; Jl Pharmacol Exptl Therapeutics; Pharmacol. & Therapeutics; Eur. Jl of Pharmacol.; Clinical Neuropharmacol.; Jl of Neurochem. *Recreations:* gardening, driving. *Address:* Neurodegenerative Diseases Research Centre, Division of Pharmacology and Therapeutics, Hodgkin Building, King's College London School of Biomedical and Health Sciences, Guy's Campus, London Bridge, SE1 1UL. *T:* (020) 7848 6011. *Club:* Athenæum.

JENNER, Air Marshal Sir Timothy (Ivo), KCB 2000 (CB 1996); FRAeS; Senior Advisor, Serco Defence, Science and Technology (formerly Senior Military Advisor, Serco Defence and Aerospace), since 2005; *b* 31 Dec. 1945; *s* of Harold Ivo Jenner and Josephine Dorothy Jenner; *m* 1968, Susan Lesley Stokes; two *d*. *Educ:* Maidstone Grammar Sch.; RAF Coll., Cranwell. Wessex Sqdn Pilot and Instructor, UK, ME and Germany, 1968–75; Puma Pilot and Instructor, 1976–78; MoD Desk Officer, Helicopter, 1979–80; Army Staff Coll., Camberley, 1981; OC 33 Sqdn, 1982–84; Military Assistant to: ACDS (Commitments), 1985; DCDS (Programmes & Personnel), 1986; OC, RAF Shawbury, 1987–88; RCDS 1989; Dep. Dir, Air Force Plans, 1990–91; Dir, Defence Progs, 1992–93; AO Plans, HQ Strike Command, 1993; Asst Chief of Defence Staff (Costs Review), 1993–95; ACAS, 1995–98; COS and Dep. C-in-C, Strike Comd, 1998–2000; Comdr, NATO Combined Air Ops Centre 9, 2000; Dir, European Air Gp, 2000; Strategic Advr, Serco Gp 2001–03; Chm., Serco Defence, then Serco Defence and Aerospace, 2003–05. Advr, Atmaana Ltd, 2006–. Non-exec. Dir, NATS, 1996–98. FRAeS 1997 (Mem. Council, 2001–03; Pres., Coventry Br., 2002–). *Recreations:* gliding, old cars, photography, mountain walking. *Address:* c/o Lloyds TSB, PO Box 1190, 7 Pall Mall, SW1Y 5NA. *Club:* Royal Air Force.

JENNINGS, Alex Michael; actor; *b* 10 May 1957; *s* of Michael Thomas Jennings and Peggy Patricia Jennings (*née* Mahoney); partner, Lesley Moors; one *s* one *d*. *Educ:* Abbs Cross Tech. High Sch., Hornchurch; Univ. of Warwick (BA); Bristol Old Vic Theatre Sch. *Theatre:* début, Orchard Theatre Co., 1980; The Country Wife, Royal Exchange, Manchester, 1986; seasons at York, Cambridge Th. Co., Bristol Old Vic; Associate Actor with RSC, Stratford and London: Measure for Measure, Taming of the Shrew, Hyde Park, 1987–88; Richard II, 1991–92; Peer Gynt (Olivier Award for Best Actor, 1996), Measure for Measure, A Midsummer Night's Dream, 1994–96; Hamlet (also in NY and Washington) (Helen Hayes Award for Best Actor, 1999), Much Ado About Nothing, 1996–98; Associate Actor with Royal National Theatre: Ghetto, 1989; The Recruiting Officer, 1992; The Winter's Tale, The Relapse (Evening Standard Award for Best Actor), 2001; Albert Speer, 2000; His Girl Friday, 2003; Stuff Happens, 2004; The Alchemist, 2006; Present Laughter, 2007; other London appearances include: Too Clever By Half, 1986 (Olivier Award for Best Comedy Performance, London Theatre Critics' Award for Best Actor, 1987), The Liar, 1987, Old Vic; The Wild Duck, Peter Hall Co., 1990; The Importance of Being Earnest, Aldwych, 1993; My Fair Lady, Theatre Royal, Drury Lane (Olivier Award for Best Actor in a Musical), 2002; Candide, ENO, 2008; *films:* War Requiem, 1988; A Midsummer Night's Dream, 1995; Wings of the Dove, 1996; The Four Feathers, 2002; Five Children and It, 2004; Bridget Jones: The Edge of Reason, 2004; The Queen, 2006; Babel, 2007; *television:* Ashenden, 1992; Bad Blood, 1999; Riot at the Rite, 2005; A Very Social Secretary, 2005; State Within, 2006; Cranford, 2007; 10 Days to War, 2008; Hancock and Joan, 2008; *concert work:* Peer Gynt (with Gothenberg SO), 1993; with London Mozart Players: The Soldier's Tale, 2001; The Crocodiamond, 2004; Tamos, King of Egypt, 2006; extensive radio work. Hon. DLitt Warwick, 1999. *Recreations:* books, painting, shopping. *Address:* c/o Independent Talent Group Ltd, Oxford House, 76 Oxford Street, W1D 1BS. *T:* (020) 7636 6565.

JENNINGS, Audrey Mary; Metropolitan Stipendiary Magistrate, 1972–99; *b* 22 June 1928; *d* of Hugh and Olive Jennings, Ashbrook Range, Sunderland; *m* 1961, Roger Harry Kilbourne Frisby, QC (marr. diss. 1980; he *d* 2001); two *s* one *d*. *Educ:* Durham High Sch.; Durham Univ. (BA); Oxford Univ. (DPA). Children's Officer, City and County of Cambridge, 1952–56. Called to Bar, Middle Temple, 1956 (Harmsworth Schol.); practised at Criminal Bar, London, 1956–61 and 1967–72. Occasional opera critic, Musical Opinion. *Recreations:* theatre, music, gardening, writing short stories.

JENNINGS, Colin Brian; Special Professor of Diplomacy, University of Nottingham, since 2006; *b* 27 Nov. 1952; *s* of Brian Jennings and Jean (*née* Thomas); *m* 1978, Jane Barfield. *Educ:* Hereford Cathedral Sch.; Univ. of Leicester (BA 1975; MA 1976). Joined MoD, 1976; Procurement Executive, 1976–78; Defence Secretariat, 1979, Principal, 1982–83; Second Sec., UK Delegn to NATO, 1980–81 (on secondment); HM Diplomatic Service, 1983–2006; Policy Planning Staff, FCO, 1983–86; First Sec. (Economic), Lagos, 1986–89; Asst, Central and Southern Africa Dept, FCO, 1990–92; Dep. High Comr, Nicosia, 1992–96; Chief Exec., Wilton Park Exec. Agency, FCO, 1996–2006. Vice Chair, Diplomatic Service Appeal Bd, 2007–. Occasional Lectr, Inst. of Policy Studies, Rennes, 2007–. *Recreations:* tennis, watching Rugby, walking the fox terrier. *Address:* c/o Wilton Park, Wiston House, Steyning, West Sussex BN44 3DZ.

JENNINGS, Rt Rev. David Willfred Michael; *see* Warrington, Bishop Suffragan of.

JENNINGS, James, OBE 1998; JP; Convener, Strathclyde Regional Council, 1986–90; *b* 18 Feb. 1925; *s* of late Mark Jennings and Janet McGrath; *m* 1st, 1943, Margaret Cook Barclay (decd); three *s* two *d*; 2nd, 1974, Margaret Mary Hughes, JP; two *d*. *Educ:* St Palladius School, Dalry; St Michael's College, Irvine. In steel industry, 1946–79. Member: Ayr County Council, 1958 (Chairman: Police and Law Cttee, 1964–70; Ayrshire Jt Police Cttee, 1970–75; N Ayrshire Crime Prevention Panel, 1970–82); Strathclyde Regional Council, 1974–96 (Chm., Police and Fire Cttee, 1978–82, 1990–96; Vice-Convener,

1982–86); N Ayrshire Unitary Council, 1995– (Chm., Social Work Cttee, 1995–). Convention of Scottish Local Authorities: Rep. for Strathclyde, 1974–96; Chm., Protective Services Cttee, 1977–82; Mem., Exec. Policy Cttee, 1982–96. Chm., Official Side, Police Negotiating Bd, 1986–88, 1992–94 (Vice-Chm., 1984–86). Chm., Garnock Valley Develt Exec., 1988–. Contested (Lab) Perth and East Perthshire, 1966. Hon. Sheriff, Kilmarnock, 1991–. Hon. Vice-President: Royal British Legion Scotland (Dalry and District Branch); Scottish Junior FA, 1994. JP Cunninghame, 1969 (Chm., Cunninghame Justices Cttee, 1974–). Freeman, N Ayrshire, 1997. *Recreation:* local community involvement. *Address:* 4 Place View, Kilbirnie, Ayrshire KA25 6BG. *T:* (01505) 683339. *Club:* Garnock Labour (Chairman).

JENNINGS, Sir John (Southwood), Kt 1997; CBE 1985; PhD; FRSE; Director, Shell Transport and Trading Company plc, 1987–2001 (Chairman, 1993–97); Vice Chairman, Committee of Managing Directors, Royal Dutch/Shell Group of Companies, 1993–97; Managing Director, Royal Dutch/Shell Group of Companies, 1987–97; *b* 30 March 1937; *s* of George Southwood Jennings and Irene Beatrice Jennings; *m* 1961, Gloria Ann Griffiths (marr. diss. 1996); one *s* one *d*; *m* Linda Elizabeth Baston. *Educ:* Oldbury Grammar Sch.; Univ. of Birmingham (BSc Hons Geology, 1958); Univ. of Edinburgh (PhD Geology, 1961); London Business Sch. (Sloan Fellow, 1970–71). Various posts, Royal Dutch/Shell Group, 1962–2001, including: Gen. Man. and Chief Rep., Shell cos in Turkey, 1976–78; Man. Dir, Shell UK Exploration and Prodn, 1979–84; Exploration and Prodn Co-ordinator, Shell Internationale Petroleum Mij., The Hague, 1985–90. Non-executive Director: Robert Fleming Holdings, 1997–2000; Det Norske Veritas, 1997–2001; MITIE Gp, 1997–2007 (Dep. Chm., 1997–2007); Bechtel Gp Internat., 2002–08; Mem., Internat. Adv. Bd, Toyota, 1997–2005; Chairman: Spectron Gp, 2000–05; Intelligent Energy, 2001–05. Vice Chm., Governing Body, London Business Sch., 1993–97 (Mem., 1992–); Vice Pres., Liverpool Sch. of Tropical Medicine, 1991–97; Member Council: RIIA, 1994–97; Exeter Univ., 1997–99. Chancellor, Loughborough Univ., 2003–. FRSE 1992. Hon. FGS 1992. Hon. DSc: Edinburgh, 1991; Birmingham, 1997. Commandeur de l'Ordre National du Mérite (Gabon), 1989. *Recreations:* fly fishing, travel. *Address:* South Kenwood, Kenton, Exeter EX6 8EX. *T:* (01626) 891824. *Clubs:* Brooks's, Flyfishers'.

JENNINGS, Rev. Jonathan Peter; Priest-in-charge, St Augustine's, Gillingham, since 2008; *b* 6 March 1961; *s* of John Harold Jennings and Margaret Jennings (*née* Amps); *m* 1998, Helen Jarvis; two *s* one *d*. *Educ:* Grangefield Grammar Sch., Stockton-on-Tees; Stockton 6th Form Coll.; KCL (BD); Westcott House, Cambridge. Ordained deacon, 1986, priest, 1987; Curate: St Cuthbert Peterlee, 1986–89; St Cuthbert Darlington, 1989–92; Press and Communications Officer, Dio. Manchester, 1992–95; Broadcasting Officer, Gen. Synod of C of E, 1995–98; Hd of Broadcasting, Archbps' Council, 1998–2001; Press Sec. to Archbp of Canterbury, 2001–08. Producer, religious progs, and news and sports journalist, 1987–2000. TA Chaplain to HM Forces, 1993–. *Recreations:* early music, Middlesbrough FC, cricket, sea fishing, steam railways. *Address:* St Augustine's Vicarage, Rock Avenue, Gillingham, Kent ME7 5PW.

JENNINGS, Rev. Peter; educational and interfaith consultant; *b* 9 Oct. 1937; *s* of Robert William Jennings and Margaret Irene Jennings; *m* 1963, Cynthia Margaret Leicester; two *s*. *Educ:* Manchester Grammar Sch.; Keble Coll., Oxford (MA); Hartley Victoria Methodist Theological Coll.; Manchester Univ. (MA). Ordained 1965. Minister: Swansea Methodist Circuit, 1963–67; London Mission (East) Circuit, 1967–78, and Tutor Warden, Social Studies Centre, 1967–74; Gen. Sec., Council of Christians and Jews, 1974–81; Associate Minister, Wesley's Chapel, 1978–81; Asst Minister, Walthamstow and Chingford Methodist Circuit, 1981–82; Superintendent Minister: Whitechapel Mission, 1982–91; Barking and Ilford Methodist Circuit, 1991–93; Dir, N E London Religious Educn Centre, 1993–98; Associate Minister: Cambridge Methodist Circuit, 1998–2003; Welshpool and Bro Hafren Methodist Circuit, 2003–06. Pastoral Tutor, Centre for Jewish-Christian Relns, Wesley House, Cambridge Univ., 1999–2003. *Publications:* papers and articles on aspects of Christian-Jewish relations. *Recreations:* photography, being educated by Tim and Nick. *Address:* 5 Cuffnell Close, Liddell Park, Llandudno LL30 1UX. *T:* (01492) 860449.

JENNINGS, Sir Peter (Nevile Wake), Kt 2000; CVO 1999; Serjeant at Arms, House of Commons, 1995–99; *b* 19 Aug. 1934; *s* of late Comdr A. E. de B. Jennings, RN and Mrs V. Jennings, MBE; *m* 1958, Shirley Anne, *d* of late Captain B. J. Fisher, DSO, RN and Mrs C. C. Fisher; one *s* two *d*. *Educ:* Marlborough College; psc (m)†, osc (US). Commissioned 2/Lt, RM, 1952; retired as Major, 1976. Appointed to staff of House of Commons, 1976. Chairman: Central London Br., SSAFA Forces Help, 2001–; St Martin-in-the-Fields Almshouse Charity, 2004–; Bowles (formerly Bowles Outdoor Centre), 2004–. *Address:* c/o House of Commons, SW1A 0AA.

JENNINGS, Robert Samuel, MBE 2003; DPhil; Principal, Slemish College, Ballymena, since 1996; *b* 29 Aug. 1949; *s* of James and Elizabeth Jennings; *m* 1978, Jennifer Titterington; one *s* one *d*. *Educ:* Stranmillis Coll., Belfast (Cert Ed); London Bible Coll. (BA Hons Theol.); Queen's Univ., Belfast (MTh); Univ. of Ulster (DPhil); Open Univ. (MA). Head of physical educn, 1971–73, and of RE, 1973–75, Antrim High Sch.; Asst Teacher of RE, Wallace High Sch., Lisburn, 1978–80; Head of RE, Rainey Endowed Sch., Magherafelt, 1980–94; Asst Adv. Officer for RE, Western Educn and Library Bd, 1994–96. Pt-time Lectr, Post Grad. Cert. in Expert Teaching, Univ. of Ulster, 1999–. *Publication:* (contrib.) New International Version Thematic Study Bible, 1996. *Recreations:* golf, walking. *Address:* Slemish College, Larne Road, Ballymena BT42 3HA. *T:* (028) 2563 0156, *Fax:* (028) 2563 2944; *e-mail:* info@slemish.ballymena.ni.sch.uk.

JENNINGS, Thomas James, CBE 2004; CEng, FIMechE; Chairman and Managing Director, Rotary Group Ltd, since 1997; *b* 1 March 1954; *s* of Gerald and Dorithia Jennings; *m* 1978, Jane Speers; two *s* one *d*. *Educ:* Queen's Univ. of Belfast (BSc). CEng, FIMechE. Grad. engr, 1975; subseq. held mgt posts; Chm., Cusp Ltd, 2002–. FRSA 2004. *Recreation:* country sports. *T:* (028) 9181 1361; *e-mail:* tj.jennings@rotarygroup.com.

JENSEN, Most Rev. Peter; *see* Sydney, Archbishop of.

JENSEN, Tom Risdahl; Ambassador of Denmark to Sweden, since 2006; *b* 28 Sept. 1947; *s* of Laust and Eva Jensen; *m* 2001, Helle Bundgaard. *Educ:* Univ. of Aarhus, Denmark (BA Scand. Lit. and Langs; MSc Political Sci.). Entered Ministry of Foreign Affairs, Copenhagen, 1977; First Sec., Danish Perm. EU Repn, 1981–84; Hd of Section, 1984–88; Econ. Counsellor, Bonn, 1988–92; Hd of Dept, 1992–97; Under-Sec., 1997–2001; Ambassador to UK, 2001–06. *Address:* Danmarks Ambassade, Jakobs Torg 1, Box 16 119, 103 23 Stockholm, Sweden.

JEPHCOTT, Sir Neil (Welbourn), 3rd Bt *cr* 1962, of East Portlemouth, Devon; retired engineer; *b* 3 June 1929; *yr s* of Sir Harry Jephcott, 1st Bt and Doris Jephcott (*née* Gregory); *S* brother, 2003; *m* 1st, 1951, Mary Denise Muddiman (*d* 1977); two *s* one *d*; 2nd, 1978, Mary Florence Daly. *Educ:* Emmanuel Coll., Cambridge (MA). MIMarEST 1955, CEng 1960, MIMechE 1960. Engine Repair Manager, J. I. Thornycroft & Co., 1956–61; Asst Gen. Manager, Silley Cox & Co., 1961–69; Managing Director: Ocean Aids, 1969–71; W. Visick & Sons, 1972–82; Surveyor to Amer. Bureau of Shipping & Bureau Veritas, 1982–90. *Recreations:* yachting, bellringing. *Heir:* *s* David Welbourn Jephcott, *b* 9 Aug. 1952. *Address:* Thalassa, East Portlemouth, Salcombe, Devon TQ8 8PU. *Clubs:* Royal Society of Medicine, Royal Ocean Racing.

JEREMIAH, Melvyn Gwynne, CB 1994; JP; Chairman, Wages and Salary Commission, Republic of Namibia, 1995–97; *b* 10 March 1939; *s* of Bryn Jeremiah and Evelyn (*née* Rogers); *m* 1960, Lilian Clare (*née* Bailey) (marr. diss. 1966). *Educ:* Abertillery County Sch. Apptd to Home Office, 1958; HM Customs and Excise, 1963–75; Cabinet Office, 1975–76; Treasury, 1976–79; Principal Finance Officer (Under Sec.), Welsh Office, 1979–87; Under Sec., DHSS, later DoH, 1987–95; Chief Exec., Disablement Services Authy, 1987–91, on secondment from DoH. Special Advr to Govt of Repub. of Namibia, 1995–97. Sec., Assoc. of First Div. Civil Servants, 1967–70. Pres., Assoc. of Amateur Heralds, 2006– (Sec., 2002–04); Hon. Secretary: Heraldry Soc., 2002–; Friends of City Churches, 2006–. Chm., White Lion Soc., 2008–. Life FRSA 2005. Freeman, City of London, 2002; Liveryman, Co. of Scriveners, 2002–. JP Inner London, 2002. *Recreations:* heraldry, genealogy. *Clubs:* Reform, Royal Over-Seas League.

JEREMY, David Hugh Thomas; QC 2006; a Recorder, since 1999; *b* 3 March 1955; *s* of Tom and Sarah Jeremy; *m* 1991, Caroline Jacobs; three *s* one *d*. *Educ:* Cheltenham Coll.; Exeter Univ. (LLB). Called to the Bar, Middle Temple, 1977; in practice at the Bar specialising in criminal law. *Recreations:* reading newspapers, studying maps, watching my children play sport, camping, researching cheap red wines. *Address:* Hollis Whiteman Chambers, Queen Elizabeth Building, Temple, EC4Y 9BS. *T:* (020) 7583 5776, *Fax:* (020) 7353 0339; *e-mail:* david.jeremy@holliswhiteman.co.uk.

JERMEY, Dominic James Robert, OBE 2001; HM Diplomatic Service; Managing Director, Sectors Group, UK Trade & Investment, since 2007; *b* 26 April 1967; *s* of Kevin Jermey and Maureen Jermey; *m* 2003, Clare Judith Roberts; one *s* one *d*. *Educ:* Tonbridge Sch.; Clare Coll., Cambridge (BA Hons 1989). Corp. Finance Dept, J. H. Schroder Wagg & Co. Ltd, 1990–93; Foreign and Commonwealth Office, 1993–: Second Sec. (Pol), then First Sec. (Afghanistan), Islamabad, 1995–99; First Sec., Skopje, 1999; British Rep., East Timor, 2000; peacekeeping and crisis related roles, London and Kabul, 2000–03; Hd, British Embassy Office (Tsunami Crisis), Phuket, Jan.–Feb. 2005; Dir of Trade and Investment, 2004–06, and Dep. Hd of Mission, 2007, Madrid. *Recreations:* adventure travel, diving, Hospitalité Notre Dame de Lourdes, entertaining. *Address:* UK Trade & Investment, Kingsgate House, 66–74 Victoria Street, SW1E 6SW. *Clubs:* Commonwealth; Casino de Madrid.

JERRAM, (Jeremy) James, CBE 1995; Chairman, Railways Pension Scheme, since 1996; *b* 7 Aug. 1939; *s* of Lionel Jerram and Kathleen (*née* Cochrane); *m* 1965, Ruth Middleton; four *d*. *Educ:* Selwyn Coll., Cambridge (MA). FCA 1966. Arthur Andersen & Co., 1963–71; Standard Telephones & Cables, 1971–87; finance dir, computer software cos, 1987–90; Bd Mem. for Finance, then Vice-Chm., BRB, 1991–2000. *Address:* Railways Pension Trustee Co., 55 Old Broad Street, EC2M 1LJ. *T:* (020) 7256 8003.

JERSEY, 10th Earl of, *cr* 1697; **George Francis William Child Villiers;** Viscount Grandison of Limerick (Ire.), 1620; Viscount Villiers of Dartford and Baron Villiers of Hoo, 1691; actor; *b* 5 Feb. 1976; *s* of George Henry Child Villiers, Viscount Villiers (*d* 1998), and of his 2nd wife, Sacha Jane Hooper Valpy (now Mrs Raymond Hubbard); *S* grandfather, 1998; *m* 2003, Marianne Simonne, *d* of Peter and Jeannette De Guelle; two *d*. *Educ:* Canford Sch.; Birmingham Sch. of Speech and Drama. *Recreations:* Rugby, squash, tennis, cricket, sailing, shooting. *Heir:* *half-b* Hon. Jamie Charles Child Villiers, *b* 31 May 1994. *Club:* Royal Automobile.

JERSEY, Dean of; *see* Key, Very Rev. R. F.

JERVIS, family name of **Viscount St Vincent**.

JERVIS, Roger P.; *see* Parker-Jervis.

JERVIS, Simon Swynfen, FSA; Director of Historic Buildings (formerly Historic Buildings Secretary), National Trust, 1995–2002; *b* 9 Jan. 1943; *s* of late John Swynfen Jervis and Diana (*née* Marriott); *m* 1969, Fionnuala MacMahon; one *s* one *d*. *Educ:* Downside Sch.; Corpus Christi Coll., Cambridge (schol.). Student Asst, Asst Keeper of Art, Leicester Mus. and Art Gall., 1964–66; Department of Furniture, Victoria and Albert Museum: Asst Keeper, 1966–75; Dep. Keeper, 1975–89; Actg Keeper, 1989; Curator, 1989–90; Dir, Fitzwilliam Mus., Cambridge, 1990–95. Guest Schol., J. Paul Getty Mus., 1988–89, 2003; Ailsa Mellon Bruce Sen. Fellow, Center for Advanced Study in Visual Arts, Nat. Gall. of Art, Washington, 2006–07. Mem., Reviewing Cttee on Export of Works of Art, 2007–. Chairman: Nat. Trust Arts Panel, 1987–95; Furniture Hist. Soc., 1998– (Ed. Furniture Hist., 1987–92); Walpole Soc., 2003–. Dir, Burlington Magazine, 1993– (Trustee, 1996–). Trustee: Royal Collection Trust, 1993–2001; Leche Trust, 1995– (Chm., 2007–); Sir John Soane's Mus., 1999–2002 (Life Trustee, 2002–; Chm. 2008–); Emery Walker Trust, 2003–; Mem., Adv. Council, NACF, 2002–. FSA 1983 (Pres., 1995–2001). Iris Foundn award, Bard Center, NY, 2003. *Publications:* Victorian Furniture, 1968; Printed Furniture Designs Before 1650, 1974; High Victorian Design, 1983; Penguin Dictionary of Design and Designers, 1984; many articles in learned jls. *Address:* 45 Bedford Gardens, W8 7EF. *T:* (020) 7727 8739. *Club:* Brooks's.

JESSEL, Sir Charles (John), 3rd Bt *cr* 1883; farmer; nutrition consultant, since 1987; *b* 29 Dec. 1924; *s* of Sir George Jessel, 2nd Bt, MC, and Muriel (*d* 1948), *d* of Col J. W. Chaplin, VC; *S* father, 1977; *m* 1st, 1956, Shirley Cornelia (*d* 1977), *o d* of John Waters, Northampton; two *s* one *d*; 2nd, 1979, Gwendolyn Mary (marr. diss. 1983), *d* of late Laurance Devereux, OBE, and *widow* of Charles Langer, MA. *Educ:* Eton; Balliol College, Oxford; Northants Inst. of Agric., Moulton, 1952 (Dip with distinction); Dip., Inst. for Optimum Nutrition, 1987. Served War of 1939–45, Lieut 15/19th Hussars (despatches). Chm., Ashford Br., NFU, 1963–64; Mem., Exec. Cttee, Kent Br., NFU, 1960–73; Pres., Kent Br., Men of the Trees, 1979–85, and 1995–. Life Vice Pres., British Soc. of Dowsers, 1994 (Pres., 1987–93). Gov., Inst. for Optimum Nutrition, 1994–98 (Chm., 1997–98). Life Mem., British Inst. for Allergy and Envmtl Therapy; Mem., British Assoc. of Nutritional Therapists, 1997–. Patron, Nutritional Cancer Therapy Trust, 1998–2005. Hon. Fellow, Psionic Med. Soc., 1977 (Pres., 1995–2002; Vice Pres., 2003–). JP Kent 1960–78. *Publication:* (ed) An Anthology of Inner Silence, 1990. *Recreations:* gardening, planting trees, opera. *Heir:* *s* George Elphinstone Jessel [*b* 15 Dec. 1957; *m* 1st, 1988, Rose (marr. diss. 1993), *yr d* of James Coutts-Smith; 2nd, 1998, Victoria, *y d* of Captain A. J. B. Naish, CBE, RN]. *Address:* South Hill Farm, Hastingleigh, near Ashford, Kent TN25 5HL. *T:* (01233) 750325. *Club:* Cavalry and Guards.

JESSEL, Oliver Richard; Chairman of numerous companies in the Jessel Group, 1954–89; *b* 24 Aug. 1929; *s* of late Comdr R. F. Jessel, DSO, OBE, DSC, RN; *m* 1950, Gloria Rosalie Teresa (*née* Holden); one *s* five *d*. *Educ:* Rugby. Founded group of companies, 1954; opened office in City of London, 1960; Chm., London, Australian and

General Exploration Co. Ltd., 1960–75; formed: New Issue Unit Trust and other trusts, 1962–68; Castle Communications, 1983; Standard Financial Holdings, 1987; responsible for numerous mergers, incl. Johnson & Firth Brown Ltd, and Maple Macowards Ltd; Chm., Charles Clifford Industries Ltd, 1978–81; reorganised Belvoir Petroleum Corp., 1987–89; Chm., Thomas Seager PLC, 1993–2000. *Address:* Tilts House, Boughton Monchelsea, Maidstone, Kent ME17 4JE.

JESSEL, Toby Francis Henry; *b* 11 July 1934; *y s* of late Comdr R. F. Jessel, DSO, OBE, DSC, RN; *m* 1st, 1967 (marr. diss. 1973); one *d* decd; 2nd, 1980, Eira Gwen, *y d* of late Horace and Marigwen Heath. *Educ:* Royal Naval Coll., Dartmouth; Balliol Coll., Oxford (MA). Sub-Lt, RNVR, 1954. (Co-opted) LCC Housing Cttee, 1961–65; Councillor, London Borough of Southwark, 1964–66; Mem. for Richmond-upon-Thames, GLC, 1967–73 (Chm., S Area Bd, Planning and Transportation Cttee, 1968–70). Contested (C): Peckham, 1964; Hull North, 1966. MP (C) Twickenham, 1970–97; contested (C) same seat, 1997. Mem., Nat. Heritage Select Cttee, 1992–97. Chairman: Cons. Parly Arts and Heritage Cttee, 1983–97 (Vice-Chm., 1979); Anglo-Belgian Parly Gp, 1983–97; Indo-British Parly Gp, 1991–97 (Hon. Sec., 1972–87; Vice-Chm., 1987); Treas., Anglo-Chilean Parly Gp, 1991–93. Parliamentary delegate: to India and Pakistan, 1971; to India, 1982, 1992, 1994; to Belgium, 1994; Member: Council of Europe, 1976–92; WEU, 1976–92. Hon. Sec., Assoc. of Adopted Cons. Candidates, 1961–66. Hon. Sec., Katyn Meml Fund, 1972–75. Mem. Metropolitan Water Bd, 1967–70; Mem., London Airport Consultative Cttee, 1967–70. Mem. Council, Fluoridation Soc., 1976–83. Dir, Warship Preservation Trust, 1994–2006. Member: Exec. Cttee and Organizing Cttee, European Music Year, 1985; Council, Assoc. of British Orchestras, 1991–94. Liveryman, Worshipful Co. of Musicians. Chevalier, Ordre de la Couronne (Belgium), 1980; Order of Polonia Restituta (Polish Govt in Exile); Commander's Cross with Star, Order of Merit (Liechtenstein), 1979. *Recreations:* music (has performed Mozart, Beethoven and Schumann piano concertos; raised £30,000 for NSPCC, Nov. perf., 1993, and £40,000 Dec. perf., 1995), gardening, croquet (Longworth Cup, 1961, Younger Cup, 2002, 2004, Fox Cup, 2004, Hurlingham), ski-ing. *Address:* Old Court House, Hampton Court, East Molesey, Surrey KT8 9BW. *Clubs:* Garrick, Hurlingham.

See also O. R. Jessel.

JESSELL, Prof. Thomas Michael, PhD; FRS 1996; FMedSci; Professor, Department of Biochemistry and Molecular Biophysics, Columbia University, New York, since 1989; Investigator, Howard Hughes Medical Institute, since 1985; *b* 2 Aug. 1951; *s* of Andre Hubert Jessell and Bettina Maria Anna Jessell (*née* Arndt); *m* 1973, Jennet Ann Priestland (marr. diss. 1981); partner, Jane Dodd; three *d*. *Educ:* Chelsea Coll., Univ. of London (BPharm); Trinity Coll., Cambridge Univ. (PhD 1977). Harkness Fellow, Harvard Univ., 1978–80; Res. Fellow, Trinity Coll., Cambridge, 1979; Royal Soc. Locke Res. Fellow, St George's Hosp., London, 1980–81; Asst Prof., Dept of Neurobiol., Harvard Med. Sch., 1981–85; Associate Prof., Dept of Biochem. and Molecular Biophysics, Columbia Univ., 1985–89. FMedSci 2006. Fellow, Amer. Acad. of Arts and Scis, 1992; Mem., Inst. of Med., 2001; Foreign Assoc., NAS, 2002. Hon. DPhil Umeå, Sweden, 1998; Hon. DSc London, 2004. *Publications:* edited with E. Kandel and J. Schwartz: Principles of Neural Science, 3rd edn 1991, 4th edn 2000; Essentials of Neural Science, 1995; contrib. to scientific jls. *Recreation:* British art. *Address:* Columbia University Medical Center, 701 West 168th Street, New York, NY 10032, USA. *T:* (212) 3051531.

JESSOP, Alexander Smethurst; Sheriff of Grampian, Highland and Islands at Aberdeen, since 1990; *b* 17 May 1943; *s* of Thomas Alexander Jessop and Ethel Marion Jessop; *m* 1967, Joyce Isobel Duncan; two *s* one *d*. *Educ:* Montrose Acad.; Fettes Coll.; Aberdeen Univ. (MA, LLB). Solicitor in private practice, Montrose, 1966–76; Depute Procurator Fiscal, Perth, 1976–78; Asst Solicitor, Crown Office, 1978–80; Sen. Asst Procurator Fiscal, Glasgow, 1980–84; Regional Procurator Fiscal: Aberdeen, 1984–87; Glasgow, 1987–90. Mem., Scottish Legal Aid Bd, 1996–2004. External Examr, Aberdeen Univ., 1998–2004. *Recreation:* sport. *Address:* 1 Hillhead of Hedderwick, Hillside, Montrose DD10 9JS; Sheriff Court, Castle Street, Aberdeen AB10 1WP. *Club:* Royal Montrose Golf (Captain).

JEVONS, Prof. Frederic Raphael, AO 1986; Hon. Professorial Associate, Department of History and Philosophy of Science, University of Melbourne, Australia, since 1996; *b* 19 Sept. 1929; *s* of Fritz and Hedwig Bettelheim; *m* 1956, Grete Bradel; two *s*. *Educ:* Langley Sch., Norwich; King's Coll., Cambridge (Major Schol.). 1st Cl. Hons Nat. Scis Pt II (Biochem.) Cantab 1950; PhD Cantab 1953; DSc Manchester 1966. Postdoctoral Fellow, Univ. of Washington, Seattle, 1953–54; Fellow, King's Coll., Cambridge, 1953–59; Univ. Demonstrator in Biochem., Cambridge, 1956–59; Lectr in Biol Chem., Manchester Univ., 1959–66; Prof. of Liberal Studies in Science, Manchester Univ., 1966–75; Vice-Chancellor, Deakin Univ., Australia, 1976–85, subseq. Emeritus Prof.; consultant on distance educn in southern Africa, 1986–87; Prof. of Science and Technology Policy, Murdoch Univ., Australia, 1988–92. Simon Sen. Res. Fellow, Univ. of Manchester, 1992; Hon. Professorial Fellow, Dept of Mgt, Monash Univ., 1994–96. Chairman: Gen. Studies Cttee, Schools Council, 1974–75; Grad. Careers Council of Aust., 1976–80; Policy Cttee, Victorian Technical and Further Educn Off-Campus Network, 1985–88; Member: Jt Matriculation Bd, Manchester, 1969–75; Jt Cttee, SRC and SSRC, 1974–75; Educn Res. and Develt Cttee, Aust., 1980–81; Council, Sci. Mus. of Vic., 1980–83; Council, Mus. of Vic., 1983–87; Aust. Vice-Chancellors' Exec. Cttee, 1981–82; Standing Cttee on External Studies, Commonwealth Tertiary Educn Commn, Canberra, 1985–87; Aust. Sci. and Technol. Council, 1986–89. Interviewer for Civil Service Commn on Final Selection Bds, 1970–75; Adviser to Leverhulme project on educnl objectives in applied science, Strathclyde Univ., 1972–75; British Council tours in India, E Africa, Nigeria, 1972–75. Mem., Editorial Advisory Boards: R and D Management, 1972–76; Studies in Science Educn, 1974–84; Scientometrics, 1978–; Australasian Studies in History and Philosophy of Science, 1980–86. Life Gov., Geelong Hosp., 1986. DUniv Open, 1985; Hon. DLitt Deakin, 1986; Hon. DSc Manchester, 1986. Inaugural winner, UNESCO prize for science and technology policy, 1992. *Publications:* The Biochemical Approach to Life, 1964, 2nd edn 1968 (trans. Italian, Spanish, Japanese, German); The Teaching of Science: education, science and society, 1969; (ed jtly) University Perspectives, 1970; (jtly) Wealth from Knowledge: studies of innovation in industry, 1972; (ed jtly) What Kinds of Graduates do we Need?, 1972; Science Observed: science as a social and intellectual activity, 1973; Knowledge and Power, 1976; numerous papers on biochem., history of science, science educn and science policy. *Recreations:* music, theatre, reading. *Address:* 250 Richardson Street, Carlton North, Vic 3054, Australia. *T:* (3) 9380 5629; *e-mail:* fredjevons@yahoo.co.uk; 162 B Solomon Street, South Fremantle, WA 6162, Australia.

JEWELL, Prof. Derek Parry, DPhil; FRCP, FMedSci; Professor of Gastroenterology, University of Oxford, since 1999; Fellow, Green Templeton College (formerly Green College), Oxford, since 1995; Consultant Physician, John Radcliffe Hospital, Oxford, since 1980; *b* 14 June 1941; *s* of Ralph Parry Jewell and Eileen Rose Jewell; *m* 1974, Barbara Margaret Lockwood; one *s* one *d*. *Educ:* Bristol Grammar Sch.; Pembroke Coll., Oxford (MA, DPhil 1972). FRCP 1979. Radcliffe Travelling Fellow, 1973; Associate Prof. in Medicine, Stanford Univ., USA, 1973–74; Sen. Lectr in Medicine, Royal Free Sch. of Medicine, 1974–80; Sen. Lectr, 1980–97, Reader, 1997–99, Univ. of Oxford. Pres., British Soc. of Gastroenterology, 2001–02. FMedSci 1999. *Publications:* (with H. C. Thomas) Clinical Gastrointestinal Immunology, 1979; Challenges in Inflammatory Bowel Disease, 2001; (contrib.) Topics in Gastroenterol., 1972, 1980–90; numerous original papers. *Recreations:* music, reading, gardening. *Address:* Radcliffe Infirmary, Oxford OX2 6HA.

JEWELL, John Anthony, (Tony), FRCGP, FFPH; Chief Medical Officer for Wales, since 2006; *b* 6 May 1950; *s* of John and Madelon Jewell; *m* 1978, Jane Rickell; two *s*. *Educ:* Christ's Coll., Cambridge (BA 1972; MB BChir 1976); London Hosp. Med. Coll. DRCOG 1977, DCH 1979; FFPH 1998; FRCGP 2001. Principal in gen. practice, 1989; Consultant, 1994; Director of Public Health: Peterborough, 1996–98; NW Anglia, 1996–98; Cambridgeshire, 1998–2002; Clin. Dir and Dir, Public Health, Norfolk, Suffolk and Cambs SHA, 2002–06. Mem., Tower Hamlets HA, 1982–88. Pres., UK Assoc. of Dirs of Public Health, 2001–06. *Publications:* (with S. Hillier) Healthcare and Traditional Medicine in China 1800–1982, 1984, 2nd edn 2005; (contrib.) Oxford Handbook of Public Health; (contrib.) Perspectives in Public Health; contribs to jls on road traffic injuries, primary care, counselling and politics of the NHS. *Recreation:* travelling with DK guidebooks. *Address:* Welsh Assembly Government, Cathays Park, Cardiff CF10 3NQ. *T:* (029) 2082 3911, *Fax:* (029) 2082 5242; *e-mail:* tony.jewell@wales.gsi.gov.uk.

JEWERS, William George, CBE 1982 (OBE 1976); Managing Director, Finance, and Member, British Gas plc (formerly British Gas Corporation), 1976–87; *b* 18 Oct. 1921; *s* of late William Jewers and Hilda Jewers (*née* Ellison); *m* 1955, Helena Florence Rimmer; one *s* one *d*. *Educ:* Liverpool Inst. High Sch. for Boys. Liverpool Gas Co., 1938–41. Served War: RAFVR Observer (Flying Officer), 1941–46: Indian Ocean, 265 Sqdn (Catalinas), 1943–44; Burma 194 Sqdn (Dakotas), 1945. Liverpool Gas Co./NW Gas Bd, Sen. Accountancy Asst, 1946–52; W Midlands Gas Bd: Cost Acct, Birmingham and Dist Div., 1953–62; Cost Acct, Area HQ, 1962–65; Asst Chief Acct, 1965–66; Chief Acct, 1967; Dir of Finance, 1968; Gas Council, Dir of Finance, 1969–73; British Gas Corp., Dir of Finance, 1973–76. FCMA, FCCA, JDipMA, CompIGasE. *Publications:* papers and articles to gas industry jls. *Recreations:* music, reading. *Address:* 17 South Park View, Gerrards Cross, Bucks SL9 8HN. *T:* (01753) 886169.

JEWITT, (Anselm) Crispin; historian of cartography; researching the history of British military cartography, since 2007; Director, National Sound Archive, British Library, 1992–2007; *b* 30 July 1949; *s* of Vivian Henry Anselm Jewitt and Helen Phyllis Jewitt (*née* Charles); *m* 1970, Mary Lee Lai-ling; two *s* one *d*. *Educ:* Skinners' Sch., Tunbridge Wells; Polytech. of N London. ALA 1974. Curator, Map Liby, 1980–84; Nat. Conspectus Officer, 1984–88, BL; Asst Dir, Nat. Sound Archive, 1988–92. Pres., Internat. Assoc. of Sound and Audiovisual Archives, 1999–2002; Convenor, Co-ordinating Council of Audiovisual Archives Assocs, 2003–07. Advisor: Arkivet för Ljud och bild, 1998; ScreenSound Australia, 2001. Trustee: Nat. Life Stories Collection, 1992–2007; Wildlife Sound Trust, 1992–; Saga Trust, 1999–2007. *Publications:* Maps for Empire, 1992; numerous book reviews and articles in professional jls. *Recreations:* dogs, trees, whisky. *Address: e-mail:* crispinjewitt@hotmail.com.

JEWKES, Sir Gordon (Wesley), KCMG 1990 (CMG 1980); HM Diplomatic Service, retired; Director, Slough Estates plc, 1992–2002; *b* 18 Nov. 1931; *er s* of late Jesse Jewkes; *m* 1954, Joyce Lyons (*d* 2005); two *s*; *m* 2008, Estelle Heime (*née* Houghton). *Educ:* Barrow Grammar Sch.; Magnus Grammar Sch., Newark-on-Trent, and elsewhere. Colonial Office, 1948; commnd HM Forces, Army, 1950–52; Gen. Register Office, 1950–63; CS Pay Res. Unit, 1963–65; Gen. Register Office, 1965–68; transf. to HM Diplomatic Service, 1968; CO, later FCO, 1968–69; Consul (Commercial), Chicago, 1969–72; Dep. High Comr, Port of Spain, 1972–75; Head of Finance Dept, FCO, and Finance Officer of Diplomatic Service, 1975–79; Consul-General: Cleveland, 1979–82; Chicago, 1982–85; Gov., Falkland Is and High Comr, British Antarctic Territory, 1985–88; Dir-Gen. of Trade and Investment, USA, and Consul-Gen., NY, 1989–91. Dir, Hogg Group, 1992–94; Exec. Dir, Walpole Cttee, 1992–96. Member: Council, Univ. of Buckingham, 1996–2001; Marshall Aid Commemoration Commn, 1996–99; London Metropolitan Adv. Bd, Salvation Army, 1996–2002. DUniv Buckingham, 2007. *Recreations:* music, travel, walking. *Address:* 23 Crabtree Close, Beaconsfield, Bucks HP9 1UQ. *T:* (01494) 678564.

JEWSON, Richard Wilson; Lord-Lieutenant of Norfolk, since 2004; Chairman, Archant (formerly Eastern Counties Newspapers Group Ltd), since 1997 (Director, since 1982); *b* 5 Aug. 1944; *s* of Charles Boardman and Joyce Marjorie Jewson; *m* 1965, Sarah Rosemary Spencer; one *s* three *d*. *Educ:* Rugby; Pembroke Coll., Cambridge (MA). Joined Jewson & Sons, 1965, Man. Dir, 1974–86; Meyer International: Dir, 1983–93; Group Man. Dir, 1986–91; Dep. Chm., 1990–91; Chm., 1991–93; Chairman: Danogue (formerly Ideal Hardware, then Inter X) plc, 1994–2002; Anglian Housing Gp Ltd, 1996–2001; Octagon Healthcare (Holdings) Ltd, 1998–2006; Hy-phen.com Ltd, 2000–01; East Port Great Yarmouth Ltd, 2000–07; PFI Infrastructure plc, 2004–07; Raven Russia plc, 2007–; Dep. Chm., Anglian Water, 1994–2002 (Dir, 1991–2002); non-executive Director: Pro Share (UK), 1992–95; Building Centre Gp Ltd, 1992–95; Delian Lloyds Investment Trust, 1993–95; Savills plc, 1994–2004 (Chm., 1995–2004); Queens Moat Houses, 1994–2003 (Chm., 2001–03); Grafton Gp plc, 1995–; Miller Insurance Group Ltd, 1995–96; Angerstein Underwriting Trust, 1995–96; Taverham Hall Educnl Trust Ltd, 1998–2004; Temple Bar Investment Trust plc, 2001–; Anglian Water Services Ltd, 2002–04; Jarrold and Sons Ltd, 2003–; Watts, Blake, Bearne & Co. plc, 2004–07; LexiHoldings Ltd, 2004–06; Clean Energy Brazil plc, 2007–. Mem., CBI London Region Cttee, 1986–93. CCMI. DL Norfolk, 2000. *Recreations:* golf, sailing, Real tennis, horse trials, gardening, opera, visual arts. *Address:* Dades Farm, Barnham Broom, Norfolk NR9 4BT. *T:* (01603) 757909, *Fax:* (01603) 757909. *Clubs:* Boodle's; Royal West Norfolk Golf.

JHABVALA, Mrs Ruth Prawer, CBE 1998; author; *b* in Germany, of Polish parents, 7 May 1927; *d* of Marcus Prawer and Eleonora Prawer (*née* Cohn); came to England as refugee, 1939; *m* 1951, C. S. H. Jhabvala; three *d*. *Educ:* Hendon County Sch.; Queen Mary Coll., London Univ. Started writing after graduation and marriage, alternating between novels and short stories; occasional original film-scripts (with James Ivory and Ismail Merchant), including: Shakespeare-wallah, 1965; The Guru, 1969; Bombay Talkie, 1971; Autobiography of a Princess, 1975; Roseland, 1977; Hullabaloo over Georgie and Bonnie's Pictures, 1978; The Europeans (based on Henry James' novel), 1979; Jane Austen in Manhattan, 1980; Quartet (based on Jean Rhys' novel), 1981; Heat and Dust (based on own novel), 1983; The Bostonians (based on Henry James' novel), 1984; A Room with a View (based on E. M. Forster's novel), 1986 (Academy Award, 1987); Mr and Mrs Bridge (based on Evan Connell's novels), 1991; Howards End (based on E. M. Forster's novel), 1992 (Academy Award, 1993); Remains of the Day (based on Kazuo Ishiguro's novel), 1993; Jefferson in Paris, 1995; Surviving Picasso, 1996; A Soldier's Daughter Never Cries, 1998; The Golden Bowl (based on Henry James' novel), 2000; film script (with John Schlesinger), Madame Sousatzka, 1988. *Publications: novels:* To Whom She Will, 1955; The Nature of Passion, 1956; Esmond in India, 1958; The Householder, 1960; Get Ready for Battle, 1962; A Backward Place, 1965; A New Dominion, 1973; Heat and Dust, 1975 (Booker Prize, 1975); In Search of Love and Beauty, 1983; Three Continents, 1987; Poet and Dancer, 1993; Shards of Memory, 1995; My Nine Lives: chapters of a possible past, 2004; *short story collections:* Like Birds, like Fishes, 1964; A Stronger Climate, 1968; An Experience of India, 1971; How I became a Holy Mother and other Stories, 1976; Out of India: selected stories, 1986; East into Upper East, 1998. *Recreation:* writing film-scripts. *Address:* 400 East 52nd Street, New York, NY 10022, USA.

See also Prof. S. S. Prawer.

JI Chaozhu; Under-Secretary General of the United Nations, 1991–96; *b* Shanxi Province, 30 July 1929; *s* of Dr Chi Kung-Chuan, Commissioner of Education, and Chang Tao-Jan; *m* 1957, Wang Xiangtong; two *s*. *Educ:* Primary and secondary schools in Manhattan; Harvard Univ. (reading Chemistry); Tsinghua Univ. (graduated 1952). English stenographer at Panmunjom, Korea, for Chinese People's Volunteers, 1952–54; English interpreter for Chinese leaders, incl. Chairman Mao, Premier Chou En-Lai, 1954–73; Dep. Dir, Translation Dept, Foreign Ministry, 1970–73; Counsellor, Liaison Office, Washington DC, 1973–75; Dep. Dir, Dept of Internat. Organisations and Confs, Foreign Min., 1975–79; Dep. Dir, Dept of American and Oceanic Affairs, Foreign Min., 1979–82; Minister-Counsellor, US Embassy, 1982–85; Ambassador to Fiji, Kiribati and Vanuatu, 1985–87; Ambassador to UK, 1987–91. Vice Pres., All China Fedn of Returned Overseas Chinese, 1996–2005. *Publication:* The Man on Mao's Right: from Harvard Yard to Tiananmen Square, my life inside China's foreign ministry (autobiog.), 2008. *Recreations:* swimming, music.

JIANG ENZHU; Chairman, Foreign Affairs Committee, National People's Congress, China, since 2003; *b* 14 Dec. 1938; *s* of Jiang Guohua and Yu Wen Guizhen; *m* 1967, Zhu Manli; one *s*. *Educ:* Beijing Foreign Languages Inst. Teacher, Beijing Foreign Languages Inst., 1964; London Embassy, People's Republic of China, 1964–77; Ministry of Foreign Affairs: Dep. Dir, 1978, Dir, 1983, Dep. Dir-Gen. and Dir-Gen., 1984–90, Dept of W European Affairs; Asst Minister, 1990–91; Vice Foreign Minister, 1991–95; Chinese Ambassador to UK, 1995–97; Dir, Xinhua News Agency (Hong Kong Br.), 1997–2000; Minister, Liaison Office of Central People's Govt, HKSAR, 2000–02. Chief Negotiator for People's Republic of China in Sino-British talks over future of Hong Kong, 1993; a Dep. Hd, Prelim. Wkg Cttee of Preparatory Cttee, HKSAR, 1993–95. Res. Fellow, Center for Internat. Affairs, Harvard Univ., and Sen. Vis. Scholar, Brookings Inst., USA, 1981–82. *Address:* Foreign Affairs Committee, National People's Congress, 23 XI Jiao Min Xiang, Beijing 100805, People's Republic of China.

JIANG ZEMIN; President, People's Republic of China, 1993–2003; Chairman, Central Military Commission, 1990–2004; *b* Yangzhou City, Aug. 1926. *Educ:* Jiaotong Univ., Shanghai. Participated in student movement led by underground Party orgns, 1943; joined Communist Party of China, 1946. Associate engr, section chief and power workshop dir, factory Party sec., then First Dep. Dir, Shanghai Yimin No 1 Foodstuffs Factory; First Dep. Dir, Shanghai Soap Factory; Section Chief of electrical machinery, Shanghai No 2 Designing Sub-bureau, First Min. of Machine-building Industry; trainee, Stalin Automobile Plant, Moscow, 1955; Dep. Chief, Power Div., Dep. Chief Power Engr, and Dir, Power Plant, Changchun No 1 Auto Works, 1956–62; Dep. Dir, Shanghai Electric Equipt Res. Inst., 1962; Dir and actg Party sec., Wuhan Thermo-Tech. Machinery Res. Inst.; Dep. Dir, and Dir, Foreign Affairs Bureau, First Min. of Machine-building Industry; Vice-Chm. and Sec.-Gen., State Commns on Admin of Imports and Exports and on Admin of Foreign Investment, 1980–82; Vice Minister and Dep. Sec., Party Gp, later Minister and Sec., Party Gp, Min. of Electronics Industry, 1982–85. Mayor of Shanghai and Dep. Sec., later Sec., Shanghai Municipal Party Cttee, 1985. Communist Party of China Central Committee: Mem., 1982; Mem., Political Bureau, 1987 (Mem., Standing Cttee, 1989, Gen. Sec.); Chm., Military Cttee, 1989. *Address:* 25 Huangsi Dajie, Beijing 100011, People's Republic of China.

JILANI, Asaf; journalist and broadcaster; a pioneer of Urdu journalism in the UK; Senior Producer, South Asia Region (formerly Eastern) Service, BBC World Service, 1983–94; *b* 24 Sept. 1934; *s* of Abdul Wahid Sindhi and Noor Fatima Jilani; *m* 1961, Mohsina Jilani; two *s* one *d*. *Educ:* Jamia Millia, Delhi; Sindh Madrasa, Karachi; Karachi Univ. (MA, Economics). Sub-Editor, Daily Imroze, Karachi (Progressive Papers Ltd), 1952; Political Corresp., Daily Imroze, 1954; Special Corresp., Daily Jang, Karachi (posted in India), 1959–65; first Urdu journalist to be posted as a foreign correspondent; held prisoner in Delhi during India/Pakistan War, 1965; London Editor: Daily Jang (Karachi, Rawalpindi, Quetta); Daily News, Karachi, and Akhbar-Jehan, Karachi, 1965–73; Editor, Daily Jang, London (first Urdu Daily in UK), 1973–82. Iqbal Medal (Pakistan), for journalistic contribution to exposition of Islamic poetic philosopher Dr Mohammed Iqbal, during his centenary celebrations, 1979. *Publications:* Wast Asia, Nai Azadi Nay Challenge (Central Asian Journey, in Urdu; based on 21 prog. series for BBC World Service), 1994; Gaon Gaon Badalti Dunia (Changing Villages, in Urdu; based on 36 prog. series for BBC Urdu Service), 1998. *Recreations:* walking, swimming, painting. *Address:* 17 Leys Gardens, Cockfosters, Herts EN4 9NA.

JILLINGS, Godfrey Frank; Deputy Chairman, Gladedale Holdings plc, since 2000; *b* 24 May 1940; *s* of late Gerald Frank Jillings and Dorothy Marjorie Jillings; *m* 1967, Moira Elizabeth McCoy (*d* 1986); one *s*. *Educ:* Tiffin's Sch., Kingston; Inst. of Personnel Management. DMS; FCIB. S. G. Warburg & Co. Ltd, 1956–58; National Westminster Bank Ltd, 1958–90: Head of Industrial Section, 1983; Sen. Project Manager, 1985–86; Director: County Unit Trust Managers Ltd, 1986–87; Natwest Stockbrokers Ltd, 1986–89; Chief Exec., Natwest Personal Financial Management Ltd, 1987–89; Senior Exec., Group Chief Exec.'s Office, 1989–90; Chief Exec., FIMBRA, 1990–94; Dir, Financial Services Initiative, later Dir, London Office, WDA, 1994–97. A Dep. Chief Exec., PIA, 1992–94. Chm., John Gater Holdings Ltd, 1994–95; Director: DBS Mgt plc, 1994–2001 (Dep. Chm., 1996–2001); Baronsmead VCT plc, 1995–; DBS Financial Management plc, 1997–2001; Baronsmead VCT 2 plc, 1998–; Spring Studios Ltd, 2004– (Chm., 2006–); Chm., Ma Potter's plc, 2002–07. *Recreations:* travel, chess. *Address:* 47 Hurlingham Square, Peterborough Road, SW6 3DZ. *T:* (020) 7736 9083, *Fax:* (020) 7736 9391. *Club:* Royal Automobile.

JINGA, Ion, PhD; Ambassador of Romania to the Court of St James's, since 2008; *b* Daneasa, Romania, 1 Sept. 1961; *s* of Ion Jinga and Viorica Jinga; *m* 1987, Daniela Doina; one *d*. *Educ:* Dinicu Golescu High Sch., Câmpulung-Muscel; Univ. of Bucharest (BSc Physics 1986; BA Law 1992); National Sch. for Pol and Admin. Studies, Bucharest (MA Public Admin 1992); College of Europe, Bruges (MA Eur. Admin 1992); Al. I. Cuza Acad., Bucharest (PhD Law 1999). Teacher: Economic High Sch. no. 4, Bucharest, 1984–85; Secondary Sch. no. 127, Bucharest, 1985–86; Physicist Engr, Nuclear Energy Reactors Inst., Pitesti, 1986–91; Hd of Protocol, Mass Media and External Relns Office, Arges Co. Govt, Pitesti, 1991–92; Third Sec., Directorate for EU Affairs, 1992–94, Second Sec., Minister's Office, 1994–95, Min. of Foreign Affairs, Bucharest; First Sec., 1995–98, Dep. Hd of Mission, 1998–99, Mission of Romania to the EU, Brussels; Counsellor, Directorate for EU Affairs, Min. of Foreign Affairs, 1999–2000; Dep. Hd of Mission, then Chargé d'Affaires ai, Mission of Romania to the EU, Brussels, 2000–01; Mem., Romanian Delegn, and Coordinator of Nat. Secretariat, Convention on the Future of Europe, 2002; Dir Gen. for EU Affairs, Min. of Foreign Affairs, Bucharest, 2002–03; Ambassador of Romania to Belgium, 2003–08. NATO Res. Fellow, 1997–99. Patriarchal Cross, Romanian Orthodox Church, 2005; Hon. Citizen, Câmpalung-Muscel, 2007; Dip. of Excellence and Son of the Arges County, 2007. Officer, Nat. Order for Merit (Romania), 2000; Officier, l'Ordre national du mérite (France), 2003; Grand Cross, Order of the Crown (Belgium), 2008. *Publications:* 5 books and over 30 articles in magazines and newspapers in Romania and Belgium, mainly on the reform of EU instns, Romania's access to the EU, the Constitutional Treaty and EU policies. *Recreations:* literature, history, travelling, tennis, ski-ing. *Address:* Embassy of Romania, Arundel House, 4 Palace Green, W8 4QD. *T:* (020) 7937 9666; *e-mail:* roemb@roemb.co.uk. *Club:* Cercle Gaulois (Brussels).

JINKINSON, Alan Raymond; General Secretary, UNISON, 1993–96; *b* 27 Feb. 1935; *s* of Raymond and Maggie Jinkinson; *m* 1968, Madeleine Gillian Douglas (*d* 1995). *Educ:* King Edward VII Sch., Sheffield; Keble Coll., Oxford (BA Hons). National and Local Government Officers' Association: Education Dept, 1960; District Officer, 1967; District Orgn Officer, 1973; National Officer (Local Govt), 1976; Asst Gen. Sec., 1981; Dep. Gen. Sec., 1983; Gen. Sec., 1990. *Recreations:* cinema, opera, theatre, walking. *Address:* 10 Princethorpe Road, SE26 4PF. *T:* (020) 8778 1098.

JIRIČNA, Eva Magdalena, CBE 1994; RA 1997; RDI 1991; architect; Principal of own practice, since 1984; President, Architectural Association, 2003–05; *b* 3 March 1939; *d* of Josef Jiričny and Eva (*née* Svata); *m* 1963, Martin Holub (marr. diss. 1973). *Educ:* Coll. of Architecture and Town Planners, Univ. of Prague (Engr Architect 1962); Acad. of Fine Arts, Prague (Acad. Architect 1967). Professional practice and management examination, RIBA, 1973. Main projects include: AMEC plc, London HQ; Boodle & Dunthorne (later Boodles), Jewellers, Dublin, London, Chester, Manchester and Liverpool; Prague HQ, Andersen Consulting; Canada Water Bus Stn, Jubilee Line Extension; Orangery, Prague Castle; Hotel Josef, Prague; RA shop, London; V&A Museum: masterplan; Modernism Exhibn; Jewellery Gall.; Canary Wharf penthouses; Selfridges shopfronts, London; Faith Zone, Millennium Dome. Hon. Prof. of Architecture and Design, Univ. of Applied Arts, Prague, 2002. Hon. AIA 2006. *Address:* 3rd Floor, 38 Warren Street, W1T 6AE. *T:* (020) 7554 2400, *Fax:* (020) 7388 8022; *e-mail:* mail@ejal.com.

JOACHIM, Rev. Dr Margaret Jane; Programme Manager, Fujitsu Services Ltd, since 2006; Minister in Secular Employment, Diocese of London, since 1997; *b* 25 June 1949; *d* of late Reginald Carpenter and Joyce Margaret Carpenter; *m* 1970, Paul Joseph Joachim; one *d*. *Educ:* Brighton and Hove High School; St Hugh's College, Oxford (MA Geology); Univ. of Birmingham (PhD Geology); Southern Dioceses Ministerial Trng Scheme. FRES 1983; FGS 1991. Grammar school teacher, 1971–76; post-doctoral research Fellow, Univ. of Birmingham, 1976–79; computer consultant, 1979–84; Futures Database Manager, Rudolf Wolff & Co., 1984–87; EDS (Electronic Data Systems) Ltd: Manager, UK Insurance Services, 1988–91; Leadership and Professional Develt Instr, 1991–93; Sen. Relationship Manager (Insce), 1994–96; Manager, EMEA Year 2000 Services, 1997–2000; Client Delivery Manager, 2000–02; Global Support Manager, 2002–03; UK Applications Prog. Manager, ABN Amro Account, 2003; Prog. Dir, 2003–04, EMEA Allications Delivery Manager (Insce), 2004–05, Applications Develt Manager, EMEA Financial Services Applications Industry Unit, 2005–06, EDS Credit Services Ltd; Asst Dir, Taskforce 2000, 1997 (on secondment). Training Officer, Liberal Parly Assoc., 1979–84; Mem., Exec. Cttee, Women's Liberal Fedn, 1984–85; Chair, Fawcett Soc., 1984–87 (Vice-Chair, 1993–95; Mem. Exec. Cttee, 1990–95); Trustee, Fawcett Trust, 1995–2005; Chair, internat. working gp to set up EEC Women's Lobby, 1988–90; Chair, 1989–90, Vice-Chair, 1990–92, WLD (formerly SLD Women's Orgn). Co-ordinator, Women into Public Life Campaign, 1987–88; Vice-Chair, 1989, Mem. Exec. Cttee, 1989–91, 300 Gp. Contested: (L) West Gloucestershire, 1979; (L/Alliance) Finchley, 1983; (L/Alliance) Epsom and Ewell, 1987. Chair, Lib Dem London Region Candidates' Cttee, 2007–. Ordained deacon, 1994, priest, 1995; Asst Curate (non-stipendiary), St Barnabas, Ealing, 1994–97, St Peter's, Mount Park, Ealing, 1998–. Moderator, CHRISM (Christians in Secular Ministry), 1999–2002, 2007–. Mem., Exec. Cttee, Nat. Traction Engine Club, 1976–79; Founder, Steam Apprentice Club, 1978; Founder, Oxford Univ. Gilbert and Sullivan Soc., 1968. *Publications:* papers in: Studies in the Late-Glacial of North-West Europe, 1980; Holocene Palaeoecology and Palaeohydrology, 1986. *Recreations:* walking, reading, going to traction engine rallies, making jam, running 1954 MG TF. *Address:* 8 Newburgh Road, W3 6DQ. *T:* (020) 8723 4514; *e-mail:* margaret.joachim@london.anglican.org. *Club:* Reform.

JOB, Rev. Canon (Evan) Roger (Gould); Canon Residentiary, Precentor and Sacrist, 1979–94, Vice Dean, 1991–94, Canon Emeritus, since 2003, Winchester Cathedral; *b* 15 May 1936; 2nd *s* of late Thomas Brian and Elsie Maud Job, Ipswich; *m* 1964, Rose Constance Mary, *o d* of late Stanley E. and Audrey H. Gordon, Hooton, Wirral; two *s*. *Educ:* Cathedral Choir School and King's Sch., Canterbury; Magdalen Coll., Oxford; Cuddesdon Theol Coll. BA 1960, MA 1964; ARCM 1955. Deacon 1962, priest 1963. Asst Curate, Liverpool Parish Church, 1962–65; Vicar of St John, New Springs, Wigan, 1965–70; Precentor of Manchester Cath., 1970–74; Precentor and Sacrist of Westminster Abbey, 1974–79; Chaplain of The Dorchester, 1976–79. Chaplain: to first High Sheriff of Gtr Manchester, 1973–74; to High Sheriff of Hampshire, 2004–05. Select Preacher, Univ. of Oxford, 1974, 1991. *Recreations:* gardening, piano. *Address:* Kitwood Farm-house, Ropley, Alresford, Hants SO24 0DB.

JOB, Sir Peter James Denton, Kt 2001; Chief Executive, Reuters Group PLC, 1991–2001; *b* 13 July 1941; *s* of late Frederick Job and of Marion Job (*née* Tanner); *m* 1966, Christine Cobley, *d* of Frederick Cobley; one *s* one *d*. *Educ:* Clifton College; Exeter College, Oxford (BA). Trainee Reuter journalist, 1963; reporter then manager in Paris, New Delhi, Kuala Lumpur, Jakarta and Buenos Aires, 1963–78; Man. Dir, Reuters Asia, based in Hong Kong, 1978–90; Dir, Reuters Gp, 1989–2001; Chm., Visnews Ltd, 1991–92. Non-executive Director: Grand Metropolitan, 1994–97; Glaxo Wellcome, 1997–99; Diageo, 1997–99; Schroders, 1999– (Sen. Ind. Dir, 2004–); GlaxoSmithKline, 2000–04; Instinet, 2000–05; TIBCO Software Inc., 2000– (Presiding Dir, 2007–); Royal Dutch Shell (formerly Shell Transport & Trading), 2001–. Member Supervisory Board: Deutsche Bank AG, 2001–; Bertelsmann AG, 2002–05. Chm., Internat. Adv. Council, NASDAQ, 1999; Member: DTI Multimedia Adv. Gp, 1994–97; DTI Japan Trade Gp, 1994–98; HM Treasury Adv. Panel, 1995; High Level Adv. Gp on Information Society, EU, 1996; FCO Business Panel, 1998; INSEAD UK Nat. Council, 1993–2001. Hon. Fellow, Green Coll., Oxford, 1995. Hon. DLitt Kent, 1998. Comdr, Order of the Lion (Finland), 2001. *Recreations:* boating, golf, tennis, music, gardening, theatre, country sports. *Address:* 505 Rowan House, 9 Greycoat Street, SW1P 2QD. *Clubs:* Garrick, Oriental; Hong Kong (Hong Kong); Tadmarton Golf.

JOBBINS, Robert, OBE 2001; media consultant, since 2001; Director of News, BBC World Service, 1996–2001; *b* 2 Nov. 1941; *s* of Henry Robert Jobbins and Miriam Jeffrey

Jobbins; *m* 1st, 1962, Jenifer Ann Rowbotham (marr. diss. 1991); two *s*; 2nd, 1992, Jacqueline Duff. *Educ:* Rickmansworth Grammar Sch.; Univ. of Essex (MA Art History, 2005). BBC Foreign Correspondent: Cairo, 1977–83; Singapore, 1983–86; Head of BBC Arabic Service, 1986–89; Editor, BBC World Service News and Current Affairs, 1989–96. Ind. Mem., Essex Police Authy, 2001–05. Chm., Rory Peck Trust, 2001–. *Recreations:* walking, medieval art, opera. *Address:* Blue House Cottage, Maldon Road, Bradwell on Sea, Essex CM0 7MR. *T:* (01621) 776507.

JOBLING, Captain James Hobson, RN; Metropolitan Stipendiary Magistrate, 1973–87; *b* 29 Sept. 1921; *s* of late Captain and Mrs J. S. Jobling, North Shields, Northumberland; *m* 1946, Cynthia (*d* 2004), *o d* of late F. E. V. Lean, Beacon Park, Plymouth; one *s* one *d*. *Educ:* Tynemouth High Sch.; London Univ. (LLB Hons, 1971). Entered Royal Navy, 1940; HMS Furious, 1941; HMS Victorious, 1941–45; awarded Gedge Medal and Prize, 1946; called to Bar, Inner Temple, 1955; Comdr, 1960; JSSC course, 1961–62; Dir, Nat. Liaison, SACLANT HQ, USA, 1962–65; Chief Naval Judge Advocate, in rank of Captain, 1969–72; retd, 1973. Planning Inspector, DoE, 1973; a Dep. Circuit Judge, 1976–82. *Recreations:* gardening, walking. *Address:* Pinewell Lodge, Wood Road, Hindhead, Surrey GU26 6PT. *T:* (01428) 604426.

JOBS, Steven Paul; Joint Founder, 1975, Consultant, since 1995, and interim President, since 1997, Apple Computer Inc.; *b* 1955; adopted *s* of Paul and Clara Jobs; one *d*; *m* 1991, Laurene Powell; one *s* one *d*. *Educ:* Homestead High Sch.; Reed Coll. Electronics engr; Video Game Designer, Atari Inc., 1974; Apple Computer Inc.: Jt Designer, Apple I computer, 1976; Chm., 1975–77, 1981–84; Dir, 1995–; Pres., NeXT Inc., 1985–96 (CEO); Chm. and CEO, Pixar Animation Studios, 1986–2006. *Address:* c/o Apple Computer Inc., 1 Infinite Loop, Cupertino, CA 95014–2084, USA.

JOBSON, Roy; Director of Children and Families Department, Edinburgh City Council, 2005–07; *b* 2 June 1947; *s* of James Jobson and Miriam H. Jobson; *m* 1971, Maureen Scott; one *s* two *d*. *Educ:* Bedlington Grammar Sch.; Univ. of Durham; Newcastle and Sunderland Polytechnics. Teacher: King's Sch., Tynemouth, 1970–73; Norham High Sch., 1973–74; Asst Sec., E Midland Regional Examining Bd, 1974–80; Asst Dir of Educn, Gateshead Metropolitan Borough Council, 1980–84; Dep. Chief Educn Officer, 1984–88, Chief Educn Officer, 1988–98, Manchester City Council; Dir of Education, Edinburgh CC, 1998–2005. Adviser: AMA, 1993–97; LGA, 1997–98. Member: Jt Council for GCSE, 1989–93; NEAB, 1992–93; Soc. of Educn Officers, 1988–2007; Chm., ACEO, 1997–98; Pres., Assoc. of Dirs of Educn in Scotland, 2004–05 (Vice-Pres., 2003–04). FRSA 1994. *Recreations:* children, family, church, music, dogs. *Address:* 4 Buckstone View, Edinburgh EH10 6PE. *T:* (0131) 469 3322.

JOCELYN, family name of **Earl of Roden**.

JOCELYN, Viscount; Shane Robert Henning Jocelyn; *b* 9 Dec. 1989; *s* and *heir* of Earl of Roden, *qv*.

JODRELL, Prof. Duncan Ian, DM; Professor of Cancer Therapeutics, University of Cambridge, since 2008; Researcher, Cancer Research UK Cambridge Research Institute, since 2008; *b* Warrington, 8 Oct. 1958; *s* of Ian and Joyce Jodrell. *Educ:* Univ. of Southampton (BM 1982; DM 1990); Univ. of London (MSc 1989). Registrar, Royal Marsden Hosp., London, 1986–87; Clinical Fellow, Inst. of Cancer Res., Univ. of London, 1987–90; Vis. Asst Prof., Univ. of Maryland at Baltimore, 1990–91; Sen. Registrar and Lectr, Beatson Oncol. Centre, Univ. of Glasgow, 1991–94; University of Edinburgh: Sen. Lectr, 1994–98; Reader, 1998–2006; Prof. of Cancer Therapeutics, 2006–08. *Recreations:* golf, hill-walking. *Address:* Department of Oncology, Box 193 (R4), Addenbrookes Hospital, Cambridge CB2 0QQ. *T:* (01223) 769310; *e-mail:* duncan.jodrell@medschl.cam.ac.uk. *Clubs:* Bruntsfield (Edinburgh); Gog Magogs (Cambridge).

JOEL, William Martin, (Billy); singer, pianist and songwriter, since 1972; *b* 9 May 1949; *s* of Howard Joel and Rosalind Joel (*née* Nyman); *m* 1st, 1971, Elizabeth Weber (marr. diss. 1982); 2nd, 1985, Christie Brinkley (marr. diss. 1994); one *d*; 3rd, 2004, Kate Lee. Albums include: Cold Spring Harbor, 1972; Piano Man, 1973; Streetlife Serenade, 1974; Turnstiles, 1976; The Stranger, 1977; 52nd Street, 1978; Glass Houses, 1980; The Nylon Curtain, 1982; An Innocent Man, 1983; The Bridge, 1986; Storm Front, 1989; River of Dreams, 1993; Fantasies and Delusions, 2001. *Publications:* Goodnight, My Angel: a lullabye, 2004; New York State of Mind, 2005. *Address:* c/o Maritime Music, 2E Main Street, Oyster Bay, NY 11771–2406, USA.

JOFFE, family name of **Baron Joffe**.

JOFFE, Baron *cr* 2000 (Life Peer), of Liddington in the County of Wiltshire; **Joel Goodman Joffe,** CBE 1999; Chairman: Oxfam, 1995–2001; The Giving Campaign, 2000–04; *b* 12 May 1932; *s* of Abraham Joffe and Dena Joffe (*née* Idelson); *m* 1962, Vanetta Pretorius; three *d*. *Educ:* Marist Brothers' Coll., Johannesburg; Univ. of Witwatersrand (BCom, LLB). Admitted Solicitor, Johannesburg, 1956; called to the Bar, S Africa, 1962; Human Rights lawyer, 1958–65; Dir and Sec., Abbey Life Assurance Co., 1965–70; Dir, Jt Man. Dir and Dep. Chm., Allied Dunbar Life Assurance Co., 1971–91. Chairman: Swindon Private Hosp., 1982–87; Swindon HA, 1988–93; Swindon and Marlborough NHS Trust, 1993–95. Mem., Royal Commn on Long Term Care for the Elderly, 1997–98. Special Advr to S African Minister of Transport, 1997–98. Trustee, 1980–2000, Hon. Sec., 1982–85, Exec. Cttee Chm., 1985–93, Oxfam; numerous other charitable organisations. *Publications:* The Rivonia Trial, 1995, new edn as The State vs Nelson Mandela, 2007. *Recreations:* tennis, voluntary work.

JOHANNESBURG, Bishop of, since 2000; **Rt Rev. Brian Charles Germond;** *b* 21 Jan. 1947; *s* of Charles Alfred Germond and Dorothy Eileen Germond (*née* Impey); *m* 1971, Susan Patricia Strong; one *s* two *d*. *Educ:* King Edward VII Sch.; Univ. of SA (BA); St Paul's Theol Coll. (DipTh); Univ. of London (BD); McCormack Seminary (DMin). Ordained deacon, 1976, priest, 1977; Curate, St Martin-in-the-Veld, Johannesburg, 1976–80; Rector: St Barnabas Lichtenburg, St Andrews, Lichtenburg, and St John's, Zeerust, 1980–85; St Martin-in-the-Veld, 1987–2000; Archdeacon of Rosebank, 1989–2000. *Recreations:* birdwatching, woodworking. *Address:* PO Box 1131, Johannesburg 2000, RSA. *T:* (011) 3368724.

JÓHANNSSON, Kjartan, PhD; Icelandic Ambassador to the European Union, 2002–05; *b* 19 Dec. 1939; *s* of Johan and Astrid Dahl Thorsteinsson; *m* 1964, Irma Karlsdottir; one *d*. *Educ:* Reykjavik Coll.; Tech. Univ. of Stockholm; Univ. of Stockholm; Illinois Inst. of Tech., Chicago. Consulting Engr, Reykjavik, 1966–78; University of Iceland: Teacher, Faculty of Engrg and Sci., 1966–74; Prof., Faculty for Econs and Business Admin, 1974–78 and 1980–89. Mem., Municipal Council, Hafnarfjördur, 1974–78; Mem. (SDP), Althing (Parlt of Iceland), 1978–89; Speaker, Lower Hse, 1988–89; Minister of Fisheries, 1978–80, also of Commerce, 1979–80; Ambassador and Perm. Rep. to UN and other internat. orgns, Geneva, 1989–94; Sec. Gen., EFTA, 1994–2000; Ambassador, Ministry for Foreign Affairs, Reykjavik, 2000–02. Social Democratic Party: Mem., Party Council and Exec. Council, 1972–89; Vice-Chm., 1974–80; Chm., 1980–84.

JOHANSEN, Lindsay; *see* Nicholson, L.

JOHANSEN-BERG, Rev. John; Founder Member, since 1984, and International Director, since 2001, Community for Reconciliation (Leader, 1986–2001); Moderator, Free Church Federal Council, 1987–88; *b* 4 Nov. 1935; *s* of John Alfred and Caroline Johansen-Berg, Middlesbrough; *m* 1971, Joan, *d* of James and Sally Ann Parnham, Leeds; two *s* one *d*. *Educ:* Acklam Hall Grammar Sch., Middlesbrough; Leeds Univ. (BA Hons Eng. Lit., BD); Fitzwilliam Coll., Cambridge Univ. (BA Theol Tripos, MA); Westminster Theol Coll. (Dip. Theol.). Tutor, Westminster Coll., Cambridge, 1961; ordained, 1962; pastoral charges: St Ninian's Presbyterian Church, Luton, 1962–70 (Sec., Luton Council of Churches); Founder Minister, St Katherine of Genoa Church, Dunstable (dedicated 1968); The Rock Church Centre, Liverpool (Presbyterian, then United Reformed), 1970–77, work begun in old public house, converted into Queens Road Youth Club, new Church Centre dedicated 1972, a building designed for youth, community and church use; Minister: St Andrew's URC, Ealing, 1977–86; Rubery URC, 1992–2001. Convener, Church and Community Cttee of Presbyterian C of E, 1970–72; Chm. Church and Society Dept, URC, 1972–79; Moderator of the Gen. Assembly of the URC, 1980–81. British Council of Churches: Mem., Assembly, 1987–90; formerly Member: Div. of Internat. Affairs; Div. of Community Affairs; Chm. Gp on Violence, Non-violence and Social Change (for Britain Today and Tomorrow Programme, 1977); Convenor, Commission on Non-Violent Action (report published 1973); Mem., Forum of Churches Together in England, 1990–97; Chairman: Reflection Gp, 2000–05, Mgt Gp, 2003–05, Project Gp, 2005–, CTBI Living Spirituality Network. Chm., Christian Fellowship Trust, 1981–87; Trustee, Nat. Assoc. of Christian Communities and Networks, 1989–2001; Mem., Exec., CCJ, 1989–97; Mem. Council, Centre for Study of Judaism and Jewish Christian Relns, 1989–96; Trustee, Fellowship of Reconciliation, 2000– (Chm., 2005–). Co-Convenor, Methodist/URC Gp Report, Peacemaking: A Christian Vocation, 2005–06. Founder Mem. and Sponsor, Christian Concern for Southern Africa, 1972–94; Founder Sponsor, Clergy Against Nuclear Arms, 1982– (Chm., 1986–90); Founder: Romania Concern, 1990; United Africa Aid, 1996; Ecumenical Order of Ministry, 1990; initiated Village India Aid, 2006; Jt Leader, Ecumenical Festivals of Faith in: Putney and Roehampton, 1978; Stroud, 1980; Banstead, 1983; North Mymms, 1985; Guildford, 1986; Jesmond, 1987; Worth Abbey, 1988; Palmers Green, 1990; Poole, and Ballyholme, 1991; Finchley, 1992; South Wallasey, 1994; Rye, 2003. Jt Editor, Jl of Presbyterian Historical Soc. of England, 1964–70. Pro Ecclesia Millennium Award, 2001. *Publications:* Arian or Arminian? Presbyterian Continuity in the Eighteenth Century, 1969; Prayers of the Way, 1987 (rev. edn 1992); Prayers of Pilgrimage, 1988; Prayers of Prophecy, 1990; Prayers for Pilgrims, 1993; A Celtic Collection, 1996; Pilgrims on the Edge, 1997. *Recreations:* mountain walking, golf, drama. *Address:* 12 Rannoch Avenue, Worcester WR5 3UN. *T:* (01905) 767366.

JOHANSON, Capt. Philip, OBE 2002; International Secretary, Church Army International, since 2007; *b* 10 April 1947; *s* of late Stanley Theodore Johanson and Betty Johanson. *Educ:* Alderman Cogan Sch., Hull; Wilson Carlile Coll. of Evangelism, London. Missioner, dio. of Coventry, 1972–75; Church Army: Head of Missions, 1975–83; Dir of Evangelism, 1983–90; Chief Sec., 1990–2006. Patron, African Pastors Trust, 2000– (Chm., 1981–97); Member: C of E Partnership for World Mission Cttee, 1990–2006; Portman House Trust, 1990–2006; Council, Evangelical Alliance, 1991–2003; C of E Board of Mission, 1997–2003; Council, Wilson Carlile Coll. of Evangelism, 2002–06; Council, Christian Enquiry Agency, 2003–07. *Recreations:* theatre, music, travel, reading. *Address:* 10 Ditton Lodge, 8 Stourwood Avenue, Bournemouth BH6 3PN. *T:* (01202) 416917; *e-mail:* p.johanson@churcharmy.org.uk. *Club:* Royal Commonwealth Society.

JOHN, Sir David (Glyndwr), KCMG 1999; Chairman: BSI Group (formerly British Standards Institution), since 2002; Premier Oil plc, since 1998; *b* 20 July 1938; *o s* of William Glyndwr John and Marjorie John (*née* Gaze); *m* 1964, Gillian Edwards; one *s* one *d*. *Educ:* Llandovery Coll., Carms; Christ's Coll., Cambridge (MA); Columbia Univ., NY (MBA); Harvard Univ. (SMP). 2nd Lieut, RA, 1957–59. United Steel Co., 1962–64; Rio Tinto Zinc Corp., 1966–73 (RTZ Consultants, Hardman & Holden); Redland plc, 1973–81 (Land Reclamation Co., Redland Indust. Services, Redland Purle); Inchcape, 1981–95; Main Bd Dir, 1988–95; Develt Dir, later Chief Exec., Gray Mackenzie & Co., Middle East, 1981–87; Chairman: Inchcape Bhd, Singapore, 1990–95 (Chief Exec., 1987–90); Inchcape Middle East, 1991–94; Inchcape Toyota, 1994–95; BOC Group, 1996–2002 (non-exec. Dir, 1993–96); Balfour Beatty, 2003–08 (non-exec. Dir, 2000–03). Non-executive Director: British Biotech plc, 1996–99; The St Paul Cos Inc., Minn, USA, 1996–2003. Dir, WDA, 2001–02; Vice Chm., British Trade Internat., 1999–2002. Vice Pres. and Mem. Bd, POW Business Leaders Forum, 1996–99; Member: President's Cttee, and Chm. Internat. Cttee, CBI, 1996–2002; CBI Internat. Adv. Bd, 2002–; Dir and Trustee, Council for Industry and Higher Educn, 1996–2002; Mem., Wilson Cabinet Cttee on Export Promotion, 1998–99. Gov., SOAS, 1993–; Mem. Bd of Overseers, Columbia Business Sch., NY, 1996–2002; Trustee: Asia House, 2000–04; Llandovery Coll., Carms, 2003–. Freeman, City of London, 1997; Liveryman, Scientific Instrument Makers' Co., 1997–. DUniv Glamorgan, 2003. *Recreations:* walking, gardening, reading. *Address:* c/o HSBC Private Bank (UK) Ltd, 78 St James's Street, SW1A 1JB. *Clubs:* Oxford and Cambridge, Oriental, Travellers; Cardiff and County (Cardiff).

JOHN, Dr David Thomas, (Dai), PhD; Vice Chancellor, University of Luton, 1998–2003; *b* 31 Oct. 1943; *s* of Trevor John and Violet Gwyneth; *m* 1966, Jennifer Christine Morris; one *s* two *d*. *Educ:* Portsmouth (BSc ext. London Univ.); Birkbeck Coll., London (PhD). Kingston Polytechnic: Asst Lectr, 1966–67; Lectr, 1967–70; Sen Lectr, 1970–74; Principal Lectr, 1974–84; Hd of Applied Sci. and Associate Dean of Sci., 1984–86; Vice Principal, NE Surrey Coll. of Technology, 1987–89; Dep. Dir, Luton Coll. of Higher Educn, 1989–93, Dep. Vice-Chancellor, Univ. of Luton, 1993–98. *Publications:* several books and chapters on geology and geomorphology; various sci. papers on Tertiary and Quaternary history of SE England and on soils. *Recreations:* music, reading, travel, squash, Rugby.

JOHN, Sir Elton (Hercules), Kt 1998; CBE 1996; musician; *b* Pinner, Middlesex, 25 March 1947; *s* of late Stanley Dwight and of Sheila (now Farebrother); *né* Reginald Kenneth Dwight; changed name to Elton Hercules John; *m* 1984, Renate Blauel (marr. diss. 1988); civil partnership 2005, David Furnish. *Educ:* Pinner County Grammar Sch.; Royal Acad. of Music, London. Singer, songwriter, musician, began playing piano 1951; joined group, Bluesology, 1965; since 1969 has toured across the world consistently as solo performer and with the Elton John Band; played to over 2 million people across 4 continents, 1984–86; first popular Western singer to perform in USSR, 1979. Appeared: (film) Tommy, 1975; Live Aid, 1985; Freddie Mercury Tribute concert, 1992; Live 8, 2005. Voice (films): The Lion King, 1994; The Road to El Dorado, 2000. Pres., Watford Football Club, 1990– (Chm., 1976–90). Established Elton John AIDS Foundn, 1992;

Patron: Amnesty International, 1997–; Internat. AIDS Vaccine Initiative, 1999–; Terrence Higgins Trust; Globe Theatre; Elton John Scholarship Fund, RAM, 2004–. Chm., Old Vic Trust, 2000–. *Composer: albums:* Empty Sky, 1969; Elton John, Tumbleweed Connection, 1970; 11.17.70, Friends, Madman Across the Water, 1971; Honky Chateau, 1972; Don't Shoot Me, I'm Only the Piano Player, Goodbye Yellow Brick Road, 1973; Caribou, Greatest Hits, 1974; Captain Fantastic and the Brown Dirt Cowboy, Rock of the Westies, 1975; Here and There, Blue Moves, 1976; Greatest Hits vol. II, 1977; A Single Man, 1978; Victim of Love, 1979; 21 at 33, 1980; The Fox, 1981; Jump Up, 1982; Too Low for Zero, 1983; Breaking Hearts, 1984; Ice on Fire, 1985; Leather Jackets, 1986; Live in Australia, 1987; Reg Strikes Back, 1988; Sleeping with the Past, 1989; To Be Continued, 1990; The One, 1992; Duets, 1993; Made in England, 1995; Love Songs, 1996; The Big Picture, 1997; Elton John and Tim Rice's Aida, The Muse, 1999; One Night Only, 2000; Songs From the West Coast, 2001; Greatest Hits—1970–2002, 2002; Peachtree Road, 2004; The Captain & the Kid, 2006; *musical scores:* (film) The Lion King, 1994 (Acad. Award for Best Original Song—Can You Feel the Love Tonight?); Broadway musicals: The Lion King, 1998 (6 Tony Awards); Aida, 2000 (Tony Award for Best Original Score); Lestat, 2006; (West End) Billy Elliot the Musical, 2005; *singles:* co-writer of many international hit songs with Bernie Taupin (and others) including Your Song, Rocket Man, Crocodile Rock, Daniel, Goodbye Yellow Brick Road, Candle in the Wind, Don't Let the Sun Go Down On Me, Philadelphia Freedom, Someone Saved My Life Tonight, Don't Go Breaking My Heart (duet with Kiki Dee), Sorry Seems to be the Hardest Word, The Bitch is Back, Song for Guy, I Guess that's Why They Call It the Blues, I'm Still Standing, Nikita, Sacrifice, Blue Eyes, Circle of Life, Are You Ready for Love?, I Want Love, Electricity. Biggest selling single of all time, Candle in the Wind, re-released 1997 (over 33,000,000 copies sold). Fellow, British Acad. of Songwriters and Composers, 2004. Hon. RAM 1997; Hon. Dr RAM, 2002. Awards include: 11 Ivor Novello Awards, 1973–2000; Brit Award (Best British Male Artist), 1991; inducted into Rock 'n Roll Hall of Fame, 1994;5 Grammy Awards, 1986–2000; Grammy Legend Award, 2001; Kennedy Center Honor, 2004. *Address:* Twenty First Artists Ltd, 1 Blythe Road, W14 0HG. *T:* (020) 7348 4800.

JOHN, Geoffrey Richards, CBE 1991; Chairman, Food From Britain, 1993–99; *b* 25 March 1934; *s* of Reginald and Mabel John; *m* 1st, 1961, Christine Merritt (*d* 2002); two *d*; 2nd, 2004, Eiluned Davies (*née* Edmunds). *Educ:* Bromsgrove School, Worcs; University College Cardiff (BA 1st cl. Hons Econs). Flying Officer, RAF, 1955–57; Cadbury Schweppes, 1957–74; Man. Dir, Spillers Foods, 1974–80; Chief Exec., Foods Div., Dalgety-Spillers, 1980–82; Chm. and Chief Exec., Allied Bakeries, 1982–87; Chm., Dairy Crest, 1988–94; Director: Associated British Foods, 1982–87; Frizzell Gp, 1991–92; Morland plc, 1993–99; NFU Services Ltd, 1999–2004. Mem., ARC, 1980–82; Chm., Meat and Livestock Commn, 1987–93. Dir, Hereford Hosps NHS Trust, 1994–99. Bromsgrove School: Pres., 1994–; Gov., 1965–94 (Chm., 1982–91); Governor: Inst. of Grassland and Envmtl Res., 1996–98; Hereford Cathedral Sch., 1997–2003; Aston Univ., 1999–2003 (Pro-Chancellor, 2003–). *Recreations:* Rugby Football, music. *Address:* 71 Adventurers Quay, Cardiff Bay, Cardiff CF10 4NQ. *Clubs:* Royal Air Force, Harlequin FC.

JOHN, Very Rev. Jeffrey Philip Hywel, DPhil; Dean of St Albans, since 2004; *b* 10 Feb. 1953; *s* of late Howell John and of Dulcie John; civil partnership 2006, Rev. Grant Holmes. *Educ:* Tonyrefail Grammar Sch.; Hertford Coll., Oxford (BA Classics and Modern Langs 1975); St Stephen's House, Oxford (BA Theol. 1977, MA 1978); Brasenose Coll., Oxford; DPhil Oxon 1984. Ordained deacon, 1978, priest, 1979; Curate, St Augustine, Penarth, 1978–80; Asst Chaplain, Magdalen Coll., Oxford, 1980–82; Chaplain and Lectr, Brasenose Coll., Oxford, 1982–84; Fellow and Dean of Divinity, Magdalen Coll., Oxford, 1984–91; Vicar, Holy Trinity, Eltham, 1991–97; Canon Theologian and Chancellor, dio. Southwark, 1997–2004; nominated Bishop Suffragan of Reading, 2003. *Publications:* Living Tradition, 1990; Living the Mystery, 1995; This is Our Faith, 1995, 2nd edn 2001; Permanent, Faithful, Stable, 2000; The Meaning in the Miracles, 2002. *Recreation:* modern European languages. *Address:* The Deanery, Sumpter Yard, St Albans, Herts AL1 1BY.

JOHN, Maldwyn Noel, FREng, FIEEE; Consultant, Kennedy & Donkin, 1994–97 (Chairman, 1987–94); *b* 25 Dec. 1929; *s* of Thomas Daniel John and Beatrice May John; *m* 1953, Margaret Cannell; two *s*. *Educ:* University College Cardiff. BSc 1st Cl. Hons, Elec. Eng. Metropolitan Vickers Elec. Co. Ltd, Manchester, 1950–59; Atomic Energy Authy, Winfrith, 1959–63; AEI/GEC, Manchester, as Chief Engineer, Systems Dept, Chief Engineer, Transformer Div., and Manager, AC Transmission Div., 1963–69; Chief Elec. Engineer, 1969–72, Partner, 1972–86, Kennedy & Donkin. President: IEE, 1983–84; Convention of Nat. Socs of Elec. Engineering of Western Europe, 1983–84; Dir Bd, Nat. Inspection Council for Electrical Installation Contractors, 1988–91; Mem., Overseas Projects Bd, 1987–91. FIEE 1969, Hon. FIET (Hon. FIEE 1998); FIEEE 1985; FREng (FEng 1979). Freeman, City of London, 1987. *Publications:* (jtly) Practical Diakoptics for Electrical Networks, 1969; (jtly) Power Circuit Breaker Theory and Design, 1975, 2nd edn 1982; papers in IEE Procs. *Recreation:* golf. *Address:* 65 Orchard Drive, Horsell, Woking, Surrey GU21 4BS. *T:* (01483) 825755.

JOHN, Stewart Morris, OBE 1992; FREng, FRAeS; Director, Taikoo Aircraft Engineering Company, Xiamen, China, since 1992; *b* 28 Nov. 1938; *s* of Ivor Morgan John and Lilian John; *m* 1961, Susan Anne Cody; one *s* one *d*. *Educ:* Porth Co. Grammar Sch.; N Staffs Tech. Coll.; Southall Tech. Coll. CEng 1977; FREng (FEng 1990); FRAeS 1977. BOAC: apprentice, 1955–60; on secondment to: Kuwait Airways, 1960–63; Malaysia-Singapore Airlines, as Chief Engr, Borneo, 1963–67; Develt Engr, 1967–70; Workshop Superintendent/Manager, 1970–73; Manager Maintenance, American Aircraft Fleet, 1973–77; Cathay Pacific Airways: Dep. Dir, Engrg, Hong Kong, 1977–80; Engrg Dir (Main Bd Mem.), 1980–94; Dep. Chm., Hong Kong Aircraft Engrg Co., 1982–94; Director: Rolls-Royce Commercial Aero Engines Ltd, 1994–98; British Aerospace Aviation Services, 1994–98; British Midland Aviation Services, 1995–2000; Hong Kong Aero Engine Services Ltd, 1996–98; Mem., Adv. Bd, Kingfisher Airlines, 2006–. President: Internat. Fedn of Airworthiness, 1993–96; RAeS, 1997–98. Trustee, Brooklands Mus., 1994–. Chm., Surrey Section, Rolls-Royce Enthusiast Club, 2000–. Liveryman, GAPAN, 1996–. *Recreations:* golf, classic cars, Rugby. *Address:* Wychbury House, Warreners Lane, St George's Hill, Weybridge, Surrey KT13 0LH. *Clubs:* Burhill Golf; Hong Kong, Aviation, Shek O Golf (Hong Kong).

JOHN-CHARLES, Most Rev. Brother; *see* Vockler, Most Rev. J. C.

JOHNS, Vice Adm. Sir Adrian (James), KCB 2008; CBE 2001; Second Sea Lord and Commander-in-Chief Naval Home Command, 2005–08; Flag Aide-de-Camp to the Queen, 2005–08; *b* 1 Sept. 1951; *m* 1976, Susan Lynne; one *s* three *d*. *Educ:* Imperial Coll., London (BSc). In command: HMS Yarnton, 1981–83; Ariadne, 1989–90; HMS Campbeltown, 1995–96; Captain, RN Presentation Team, 1996–97; Asst Dir, Naval Plans, 1997–98; Principal Staff Officer to CDS, 1998–2000; i/c HMS Ocean, 2001–03; ACNS, MoD, 2003–05; Head, FAA, 2003–08. Freeman, City of London, 2002; Liveryman, GAPAN, 2006–; Freeman, Co. of Farriers, 2002. QCVS 2003. *Recreations:* music, cycling.

JOHNS, Prof. David John, CBE 1998; FREng; Chairman, Genetics and Insurance Committee, Department of Health, 2002–08; *b* 29 April 1931. *Educ:* Univ. of Bristol (BSc Eng, MSc Eng, Aeronautical Engineering); Loughborough Univ. of Technology (PhD, DSc). FREng (FEng 1990); FRAeS, FAeSI, FHKIE. Bristol Aeroplane Co., 1950–57 (section leader); Project Officer, Sir W. G. Armstrong Whitworth Co., 1957–58; Lectr, Cranfield Inst. of Technology, 1958–63; Loughborough University of Technology: Reader, 1964–68; Prof. in Aeronautics, 1968–83; Hd, Dept of Transport Technology, 1972–82; Senior Pro-Vice-Chancellor, 1982–83; (Foundation) Dir, City Polytechnic of Hong Kong, 1983–89; Vice-Chancellor and Principal, Univ. of Bradford, 1989–98. Chairman: Prescription Pricing Authy, 1998–2001; N and E Yorks and Northern Lincs Strategic HA, 2002–06. Dir, British Bd of Agrément, 1997–2006. Comr, Commonwealth Scholarships Commn, 2002–08. Member, Council: Hong Kong Instn of Engrs, 1985–88; RAEng, 2000–03; RAeS, 2002–05. Unofficial JP Hong Kong, 1987–89. *Publications:* Thermal Stress Analyses, 1965; contribs to learned jls. *Recreations:* bridge, theatre, music. *Fax:* (01423) 502561. *Clubs:* Royal Air Force; Hong Kong; Hong Kong Jockey.

JOHNS, Derek Ernest; art dealer; *b* 22 July 1946; *s* of Ernest Edward Johns and Evelyn May Johns (*née* Pays); *m* 1st, 1971, Annie Newman; one *s* one *d*; 2nd, 1981, Daphne Ellen Hainworth; one *s* one *d*. *Educ:* City of London Freemans Sch.; Ashtead Park. Dir, and Hd, Old Master Paintings, Sotheby's, London, 1966–81; Chm., Derek Johns Ltd, Fine Paintings, 1981–. Winner, Masterchef, BBC, 1997. Mem., Chirton Parish Council, Wilts, 2003–07. *Recreations:* horticulture, shooting, travel, languages, opera. *Address:* Conock Old Manor, Devizes, Wilts SN10 3QQ. *T:* (office) (020) 7839 7671, *Fax:* (020) 7930 0986; *e-mail:* fineart@derekjohns.co.uk. *Clubs:* Travellers, East India, Beefsteak.

JOHNS, Glynis; actress; *b* Pretoria, South Africa; *d* of late Mervyn Johns and Alice Maude (*née* Steel-Payne); *m* 1st, Anthony Forwood (marr. diss.); one *s*; 2nd, David Foster, DSO, DSC and Bar (marr. diss.); 3rd, Cecil Peter Lamont Henderson; 4th, Elliott Arnold. *Educ:* Clifton and Hampstead High Schs. First stage appearance in Buckie's Bears as a child ballerina, Garrick Theatre, London, 1935. Parts include: Sonia in Judgement Day, Embassy and Strand, 1937; Miranda in Quiet Wedding, Wyndham's, 1938 and in Quiet Weekend, Wyndham's, 1941; Peter in Peter Pan, Cambridge Theatre, 1943; Fools Rush In, Fortune; The Way Things Go, Phœnix, 1950; Gertie (title role), NY, 1952; Major Barbara (title role), NY, 1957; The Patient in Too True to Be Good, NY, 1962; The King's Mare, Garrick, 1966; Come as You Are, New, 1970; A Little Night Music, New York, 1973 (Tony award for best musical actress); Ring Round the Moon, Los Angeles, 1975; 13 Rue de l'Amour, Phœnix, 1976; Cause Célèbre, Her Majesty's, 1977 (Best Actress Award, Variety Club); Hayfever, UK; The Boy Friend, Toronto; The Circle, NY, 1989–90. Entered films as a child. *Films include:* South Riding, 49th Parallel, Frieda, An Ideal Husband, Miranda (the Mermaid), State Secret, No Highway, The Magic Box, Appointment with Venus, Encore, The Card, Sword and the Rose, Personal Affair, Rob Roy, The Weak and the Wicked, The Beachcomber, The Seekers, Poppa's Delicate Condition, Cabinet of Dr Caligari, Mad About Men, Josephine and Men, The Court Jester, Loser Takes All, The Chapman Report, Dear Bridget, Mary Poppins, Zelly and Me, Nuki, While You Were Sleeping. Also broadcasts; television programmes include: Star Quality; The Parkinson Show (singing Send in the Clowns); Mrs Amworth (USA); All You Need is Love; Across a Crowded Room; Little Gloria, Happy at Last; Sprague; Love Boat; Murder She Wrote; The Cavanaughs; starring role, Coming of Age (series). *Address:* c/o A. Morgan Maree, Jr, and Associates, Inc., 1145 Gayley Avenue #303, Los Angeles, CA 90024–3428, USA.

JOHNS, Jasper; painter; *b* 15 May 1930; *s* of Jasper Johns and Jean Riley. *Educ:* Univ. of South Carolina. Works in collections of Tate Gall., NY Mus. of Modern Art, Buffalo, Cologne, Washington, Amsterdam, Stockholm, Dallas, Chicago, Baltimore, Basle, Cleveland, Minneapolis; one-man exhibitions principally in Leo Castelli Gallery, NY; others in UK, USA, Canada, France, Germany, Italy, Japan, Switzerland; retrospective exhibns, NY Mus. of Modern Art, 1996, Scottish Nat. Gall. of Modern Art, 2004. Hon. RA; Mem., Amer. Acad. of Arts and Letters (Gold Medal, 1986); Pittsburgh Internat. Prize, 1958; Wolf Foundn Prize, 1986; Venice Biennale, 1988; Nat. Medal of Arts, 1990; Praemium Imperiale Award, Japan, 1993. Officier, Ordre des Arts et des Lettres (France), 1990. *Address:* c/o Leo Castelli Gallery, 18 East 77th Street, New York, NY 10021, USA.

JOHNS, Michael Alan, CB 2000; Chief Executive, Valuation Office Agency and a Commissioner of Inland Revenue, 1997–2004; *b* 20 July 1946; *s* of John and Kathleen Johns. *Educ:* Judd School, Tonbridge; Queens' College, Cambridge (MA Hist.). Inland Revenue, 1967–79; Central Policy Review Staff, 1979–80; Inland Revenue, 1980–84; seconded to Orion Royal Bank, 1985; Inland Revenue, 1986–; Under Sec., 1987; Dir, Oil and Financial Div., 1988–91; Dir, Central Div., 1991–93; Dir, Business Ops Div., 1993–97. Treasurer, Working Men's College, 1986–90. Hon. RICS 2003. *Recreations:* ski-ing, teaching adults, moral philosophy.

JOHNS, Rev. Patricia Holly, MA; Non-stipendiary Curate, Marlborough Team Ministry, 1994–99; Priest in charge, Mildenhall, Marlborough, 1996–99; *b* 13 Nov. 1933; *d* of William and Violet Harris; *m* 1958, Michael Charles Bedford Johns (*d* 1965), MA; one *s* one *d*. *Educ:* Blackheath High Sch.; Girton Coll., Cambridge (BA 1956, MA 1959, CertEd with distinction 1957). Asst Maths Mistress; Cheltenham Ladies' Coll., 1957–58; Macclesfield Girls' High Sch., 1958–60; Asst Maths Mistress, then Head of Maths and Dir of Studies, St Albans High Sch., 1966–75; Sen. Mistress, and Housemistress of Hopeman House, Gordonstoun, 1975–80; Headmistress, St Mary's Sch., Wantage, 1980–94. Ordained deacon, 1990, priest, 1994. *Recreations:* choral singing, walking, travel. *Address:* Flat 1, Priory Lodge, 93 Brown Street, Salisbury, Wilts SP1 2BX. *T:* (01722) 328007.

JOHNS, Paul; management consultant, since 1994; Director, College of Preachers, since 2006; story writer and teller; *b* 13 March 1934; *s* of Alfred Thomas Johns and Margherita Johns; *m* 1st, 1956, Ruth Thomas (marr. diss. 1973); two *s* one *d*; 2nd, 1984, Margaret Perry. *Educ:* Kingswood School, Bath; Oriel College, Oxford (MA Hons Modern Hist.). Personnel Management, Dunlop Rubber Co., 1958–63 and Northern Foods Ltd, 1963–68; Senior Partner, Urwick Orr & Partners, 1968–83; Dir, Profile Consulting, 1983–89; Man. Dir, Traidcraft, 1988–91; Chief Exec., Fairtrade Foundn, 1992–94. Chairperson, 1985–87, Vice-Chairperson, 1987–88, CND. Consultant, FA Premier League, 1994–2000. Co-Founder, SANA develt agency in Bosnia, 1994–, Dir, 1998–. Lay preacher, Methodist Church. *Recreations:* photography, listening to music, watching football (keen supporter of Nottingham Forest). *Address:* 33 Burleigh Road, West Bridgford, Nottingham NG2 6FP.

JOHNS, Air Chief Marshal Sir Richard (Edward), GCB 1997 (KCB 1994; CB 1991); KCVO 2007 (LVO 1972); CBE 1985 (OBE 1978); FRAeS; Constable and Governor of Windsor Castle, 2000–08; *b* Horsham, 28 July 1939; *s* of late Lt-Col Herbert Edward Johns, RM and of Marjory Harley Johns (*née* Everett); *m* 1965, Elizabeth Naomi Anne Manning; one *s* two *d*. *Educ:* Portsmouth Grammar Sch.; RAF College, Cranwell. FRAeS

1997. Commissioned 1959; Night Fighter and Fighter/Reconnaissance Sqns, UK, Cyprus, Aden, 1960–67; Flying Instructional duties, 1968–71; Flying Instructor to Prince of Wales, 1970–71; OC 3 (Fighter) Sqn (Harrier), 1975–77; Dir, Air Staff Briefing, 1979–81; Station Comdr and Harrier Force Comdr, RAF Gütersloh, 1982–84; ADC to the Queen, 1983–84; RCDS 1985; SASO, HQ RAF Germany, 1985–88; SASO, HQ Strike Comd, 1989–91; AOC No 1 Gp, 1991–93; COS and Dep. C-in-C, Strike Comd and UK Air Forces, 1993–94; AOC-in-C Strike Comd, 1994; C-in-C, Allied Forces NW Europe, 1994–97; Chief of Air Staff, 1997–2000; Air ADC to the Queen, 1997–2000. Hon. Col, 73 Engr Regt (V), 1994–2002; Hon. Air Cdre, RAF Regt, 2000–. Pres., Hearing Dogs for Deaf People, 2005–. Vice-Pres., Royal Windsor Horse Show, 2000–. Chm., Bd of Trustees, RAF Mus., 2000–06. Freeman, City of London, 1999; Liveryman, GAPAN, 1999–. *Recreations:* military history, Rugby, cricket, equitation. *Address:* Dolphin House, Warminster Road, Chitterne, Wilts BA12 0LH. *T:* (01985) 850039. *Club:* Royal Air Force.

JOHNSON, Rt Hon. Alan Arthur; PC 2003; MP (Lab) Kingston-upon-Hull West and Hessle, since 1997; Secretary of State for Health, since 2007; *b* 17 May 1950; *s* of late Lillian May and Stephen Arthur Johnson; *m* 1st, 1968, Judith Elizabeth Cox (marr. diss.); one *s* one d (and one *d* decd); 2nd, 1991, Laura Jane Patient; one *s*. *Educ:* Sloane Grammar School, Chelsea. Postman, 1968; UCW Branch Official, 1976; UCW Exec. Council, 1981; UCW National Officer, 1987–93; Gen. Sec., UCW, 1993–95; Jt Gen. Sec., CWU, 1995–97. PPS to Financial Sec. to the Treasury, 1997–99, to Paymaster General, 1999; Parly Under-Sec. of State, 1999–2001, Minister of State, 2001–03, DTI; Minister of State, DFES, 2003–04; Secretary of State: for Work and Pensions, 2004–05; for Trade and Industry, 2005–06; for Educn and Skills, 2006–07. Mem., Trade and Industry Select Cttee, 1997. Mem. Gen. Council, TUC, 1994–95; Exec. Mem., Postal, Telegraph and Telephone Internat., 1994–97; Mem., Labour Party NEC, 1995–97; Dir, Unity Trust Bank plc. Duke of Edinburgh Commonwealth Study Conf., 1992. Gov., Ruskin Coll., 1992–97. *Recreations:* music, tennis, reading, football, cookery, radio. *Address:* House of Commons, SW1A 0AA.

JOHNSON, Air Vice-Marshal Alan Taylor, FRAeS; Director of Occupational Health, Metropolitan Police, 1991–95; *b* 3 March 1931; *s* of Percy and Janet Johnson; *m* 1954, Margaret Ellen Mee; two *s* three *d* (and one *s* decd). *Educ:* Mexborough Grammar Sch.; Univ. of Sheffield (MB, ChB); DAvMed; FFOM, MFCM. Commnd RAF, 1957; MO, RAF Gaydon, 1957–59; Princess Mary's RAF Hosp., Akrotiri, Cyprus, 1959–61; No 1 Parachute Trng Sch., RAF Abingdon, 1961–65; RAF Changi, Singapore, 1965–67; RAF Inst. of Aviation Medicine, 1967–71; RAF Bruggen, Germany, 1971–74; Med. SO (Air) HQ RAF Support Comd, 1974–77; RAF Brize Norton, 1977–78; Chief of Aerospace Medicine HQ SAC Offutt AFB, USA, 1978–81; Dep. Dir of Health and Res. (Aviation Medicine), 1981–84; OC Princess Alexandra Hosp., RAF Wroughton, 1984–86; Asst Surg.-Gen. (Environmental Medicine and Res.), MoD, 1986; PMO, HQ RAF, Germany, 1986–88; PMO, HQ Strike Comd, RAF High Wycombe, 1988–91; retired. QHS 1986–91. OStJ 1976. *Recreations:* sport parachuting, music, cricket. *Address:* Hoo Cottage, School Lane, Buckden, St Neots, Cambs PE19 5TT. *Club:* Royal Air Force.

JOHNSON, (Alexander) Boris (de Pfeffel); Mayor of London (C), since 2008; *b* 19 June 1964; *s* of Stanley Patrick Johnson, *qv* and Charlotte Johnson (*née* Fawcett); *m* 1st, 1987, Allegra Mostyn-Owen (marr. diss. 1993); 2nd, 1993, Marina Wheeler; two *s* two *d*. *Educ:* Eton (King's Schol.); Balliol Coll., Oxford (Brackenbury Schol.; Pres., Oxford Union). LEK Partnership, one week, 1987; The Times, 1987–88; Daily Telegraph, 1988–99: EC Correspondent, 1989–94; Asst Ed. and Chief Pol Columnist, 1994–99; Ed., The Spectator, 1999–2005. MP (C) Henley, 2001–June 2008. Opposition frontbench spokesman on higher educn, 2005–07. Jt Vice-Chm., Cons. Party, 2003–04. Commentator of the Year, What the Papers Say awards, 1997; Editors' Editor of the Year, 2003; Columnist of the Year, British Press Awards, 2004. *Publications:* Friends, Voters, Countrymen, 2001; Lend Me Your Ears: the essential Boris Johnson, 2003; Seventy Two Virgins (novel), 2004; The Dream of Rome, 2006; Life in the Fast Lane: the Johnson guide to cars, 2007. *Recreations:* painting, cricket. *Address:* Greater London Authority, City Hall, Queen's Walk, SE1 2AA. *Club:* Beefsteak.

JOHNSON, Andrew Robert; Headmaster, Stonyhurst College, since 2006; *b* Lytham St Annes, 1 April 1967; *s* of Robert and Josephine Johnson; *m* 1993, Dawn Bridger; two *s*. *Educ:* Univ. of Bristol (BA Hons Mod. Langs). Asst Teacher, Douai Sch., 1991–93; Winchester College: Asst Teacher, 1993–98; Hd, Mod. Langs, 1998–2002; Dep. Headmaster, Birkdale Sch., Sheffield, 2002–06. *Recreations:* hill-walking, theatre, music. *Address:* Stonyhurst College, Lancs BB7 9PZ. *T:* (01254) 826345; *e-mail:* headmaster@stonyhurst.ac.uk. *Club:* Lansdowne.

JOHNSON, Prof. Anne Mandall, MD; FFPH, FRCP, FRCGP, FMedSci; Professor of Epidemiology, Royal Free and University College Medical School, University College London (formerly University College London Medical School), since 1996; Director, Division of Population Health, University College London, since 2007; *b* 30 Jan. 1954; *d* of Gordon Trevor Johnson and Helen Margaret Johnson; *m* 1996, John Martin Watson; one *s* one *d*. *Educ:* Newnham Coll., Cambridge (BA 1974; MA 1979; Associate, 1996–); Univ. of Newcastle upon Tyne (MB BS 1978; MD with commendation 1992); LSHTM (MSc 1984); MRCGP 1982, FRCGP 2002; FFPH (FFPHM 1993); MRCP 1998, FRCP 2005. House Officer, Newcastle upon Tyne, 1978–79; Sen. House Officer, vocational trng in Gen. Practice, Northumbria, 1979–83; Registrar in Community Medicine, NE Thames RHA, 1983–84; Lectr, Middlesex Hosp. Med. Sch., 1985–88; University College London Medical School, subseq. Royal Free and University College Medical School, University College London: Sen. Lectr in Epidemiology and Hon. Consultant in Public Health Medicine, 1988–94; Reader in Epidemiology, 1994–96; Hd, Dept of Primary Care and Population Studies, 2002–07. Hon. Sen. Lectr, 1990–99, Vis. Prof., 1999–, LSHTM; Hon. Consultant in Public Health Medicine, Camden Primary Health Care (formerly Camden and Islington) NHS Trust, 1995–. Non-exec. Dir, Whittington Hosp. NHS Trust, 2005–. Dir, MRC UK Co-ordinating Centre for Epidemiol Study of HIV and AIDS, 1989–99. Chm., Prison Health Res. Ethics Cttee, 1999–2001 (Mem., 1996–); Member: Council, Inst. of Drug Dependency, London, 1990–98; Specialist Adv. Cttee on antimicrobial resistance, DoH, 2001–; MRC Physiological Medicine and Infections Bd, 2002–04; MRC Infections and Immunity Bd, 2004–06; Public Health Ethical Issues Wkg Party, Nuffield Council on Bioethics, 2006–07. Vis. Scholar, Univ. of Sydney, 1998. Editor, AIDS, 1994–2000. FMedSci 2001. *Publications:* (jtly) Sexual Attitudes and Lifestyles, 1994; Sexual Behaviour in Britain, 1994; articles on HIV/AIDS, sexually transmitted diseases and infectious disease epidemiology. *Recreation:* singing. *Address:* Division of Population Health, University College London, Mortimer Market Centre, off Capper Street, WC1E 6JB.

JOHNSON, Anne Montgomrey; Market Research, Harris Research Centre, 1983–92; *b* 12 June 1922; *y c* of late Frederick Harold Johnson and late Gertrude Le Quesne (*née* Martin). *Educ:* St John's, Bexhill-on-Sea; Queen Elizabeth Hosp. (SRN); Royal Brompton Hosp. (BTA Hons); Simpson Memorial Maternity Pavilion, Edinburgh (SCM). Asst Matron, Harefield Hosp., 1956–59; Dep. Matron, St Mary's Hosp., Paddington, 1959–62; Matron, Guy's Hosp., 1962–68; Mem. Directing and Tutorial Staff, King Edward's Hosp. Fund for London, 1968–71; Regional Dir, Help the Aged, 1971–73; Matron, The Royal Star and Garter Home for Disabled Sailors, Soldiers and Airmen, 1975–82. Sec., King's Fund Working Party, 'The Shape of Hospital Management 1980', 1966–67 (report publd 1967); Member: Jt Cttee of Gen. Synod Working Party 'The Hospital Chaplain' (report publd 1974); Hosp. Chaplaincies Council, 1963–81; Nursing Cttee, Assoc. of Indep. Hosps, 1978–83. Gov., Orleans Park Sch., Twickenham, 1988–97. *Recreations:* straight theatre, travel. *Address:* Flat 5, 6 Cardigan Road, Richmond-on-Thames, Surrey TW10 6BJ.

JOHNSON, WO1 Barry, GC 1990; RAOC; Warrant Officer 1 (Staff Sergeant Major), 1986, retired 1992; *b* 25 Jan. 1952; *s* of Charles William Johnson and Joyce Johnson; *m* 1971, Linda Maria Lane; one *s* one *d*. Mem., Inst. of Explosives Engineers. Army Apprentices College, Chepstow, 1967; Royal Army Ordnance Corps, 1970; served in UK, BAOR, NI, Canada and Belize. *Club:* Victoria Cross and George Cross Association.

JOHNSON, Boris; *see* Johnson, A. B. de P.

JOHNSON, Prof. Brian Frederick Gilbert, PhD; FRS 1991; FRSE; FRSC; Professor of Inorganic Chemistry, University of Cambridge, 1995–2005; Master of Fitzwilliam College, Cambridge, 1999–2005; *b* 11 Sept. 1938; *s* of Frank and Mona Johnson; *m* 1962, Christine Draper; two *d*. *Educ:* Northampton Grammar Sch.; Univ. of Nottingham (BSc, PhD). FRSE 1992; FRSC 1992. Lecturer: Univ. of Manchester, 1965–67; UCL, 1967–70; Cambridge University: Lectr, 1970–78; Reader, 1978–90; Fitzwilliam College: Fellow, 1970–90, and 1995–99, Hon. Fellow, 2005; Pres., 1988–89; Vice Master, 1989–90; Crum Brown Prof. of Inorganic Chem., Univ. of Edinburgh, 1991–95. Mem., EPSRC, 1994–99 (Chm., Public Understanding of Sci., Engrg and Technol. Steering Gp, 1998–). Fellow, European Soc. *Publication:* Transition Metal Clusters, 1982. *Recreations:* chemistry, walking, cycling, travel.

JOHNSON, Bruce Joseph F.; *see* Forsyth-Johnson.

JOHNSON, Charles Ernest; JP; Councillor (Lab), Salford, 1986–2002; *b* 2 Jan. 1918; adopted *s* of Henry and Mary Johnson; *m* 1942, Betty, *d* of William Nelson Hesford, farmer; one *s*. *Educ:* elementary school. Commenced work as apprentice coppersmith, 1932; called up to Royal Navy, 1940, demobilised, 1946. Councillor and Alderman, Eccles Town Council, 1952–73; Mayor, 1964–65; Chm. of various cttees, incl. Housing, for 14 years, and of Local Employment Cttee, for ten years; Councillor, Greater Manchester County Council, 1974–86 (Chairman, 1982–83). Mem., Police Authy, Gtr Manchester, 1986–88. Mem., Assoc. of Municipal Councils, 1958–. JP Eccles, 1965. 1939–45 Medal, Atlantic Medal, Africa Star, Victory Medal; Imperial Service Medal, 1978. *Recreations:* gardening, watching football, swimming. *Address:* 17 Dartford Avenue, Winton, Eccles, Manchester M30 8NF. *T:* (0161) 789 4229.

JOHNSON, Christopher Edmund; Director General, Defence Accounts, Ministry of Defence, 1984–89; *b* 17 Jan. 1934; *s* of late Christopher and Phyllis Johnson; *m* 1956, Janet Yvonne Wakefield (*d* 2007); eight *s* three *d*. *Educ:* Salesian Coll., Chertsey; Collyer's Sch., Horsham. Sub Lt, RNVR, 1952–54. Exec. Officer, 1954–58, Higher Exec. Officer, 1959–65, War Office; Principal, MoD, 1965–71; UK Jt Comd Sec., ANZUK Force, Singapore, 1971–74; Ministry of Defence: Asst Sec., 1974–84; Asst Under Sec. of State, 1984. *Recreations:* gardening, reading. *Address:* 3 Cedric Close, Bath BA1 3PQ. *T:* (01225) 314247.

JOHNSON, Rt Rev. Colin Robert; *see* Toronto, Bishop of.

JOHNSON, Sir (Colpoys) Guy, 8th Bt *cr* 1755, of New York in North America; Director, ClearLine Communications Ltd, since 2002; *b* 13 Nov. 1965; *s* of Sir Peter Colpoys Paley Johnson, 7th Bt and his 1st wife, Clare (*née* Bruce); *S* father, 2003; *m* 1990, Marie-Louise, *d* of John Holroyd; three *s*. *Educ:* Winchester; King's Coll., London (BA Hons); Henley Mgt Coll. (MBA). Midland Bank plc, 1988–90; HSBC Capital Markets, 1990–98; Eurospend.com Ltd, 1999–2001. Hon. Col Comdt, King's Royal Yorkers, Canada, 2003. FRGS. *Recreations:* yacht racing, fly fishing. *Heir: s* Colpoys William Johnson, *b* 28 Dec. 1993. *Address:* Hollygate, Sleepers Hill, Winchester, Hants SO22 4ND. *T:* (01962) 869769. *Club:* Royal Ocean Racing.

JOHNSON, Daniel, PhD; Counsel, McCarthy Tétrault, Barristers and Solicitors LLP, since 1998; *b* Montreal, 24 Dec. 1944; *s* of Daniel Johnson (Premier of Quebec, 1966–68) and Reine (*née* Gagné); *m* 1993, Suzanne Marcil; one *s* one *d* from former marriage. *Educ:* Stanislas Coll., Montreal; Saint-Laurent Coll. (BA Univ. of Montreal); Univ. of Montreal (LLL); University Coll. London (LLM, PhD); Harvard Business Sch. (MBA). A lawyer. Corp. Sec., 1973–81, Vice-Pres., 1978–81, Power Corp. of Canada. Director: Great-West Life Assce Co., 1999–; London Life Insce Co., 1999–; Bombardier Inc., 1999–; iGM Financial Inc., 1999–; Investors Gp, 2003–; Victhom Human Bionics, 2002–; Canada Life Assce Co., 2003–. Mem. (L) Vaudreuil, Quebec Nat. Assembly, 1981–98; Minister of Industry and Commerce, 1985–88; Dep. House Leader, 1985–94; Pres., Treasury Bd and Minister responsible for Admin, 1988–89; Minister responsible for Admin and CS and Chm., Treasury Bd, 1989–94; Prime Minister and Pres. Exec. Council, Jan.–Sept. 1994; Leader of Official Opposition, 1994–98. Leader, Quebec Liberal Party, 1993–98. Hon. Consul for Sweden in Montreal, 2002. *Address:* (office) Suite 2500, 1000 rue de La Gauchetière W, Montreal, QC H3B 0A2, Canada.

JOHNSON, Daniel Benedict; Editor, Standpoint, since 2008; *b* 26 Aug. 1957; *s* of Paul Bede Johnson, *qv*; *m* 1988, Sarah Thompson, *d* of J. W. M. Thompson, *qv*; two *s* two *d*. *Educ:* Langley Grammar Sch.; Magdalen Coll., Oxford (BA 1st Cl. Hons Hist.). Res. Student, Peterhouse, Cambridge, 1978–81; Shakespeare Scholar, Berlin, 1979–80; taught German hist., QMC, 1982–84; Dir of Pubns, Centre for Policy Studies, 1983–84; Daily Telegraph: Leader Writer, 1986–87; Bonn Corresp., 1987–89; Eastern Europe Corresp., 1989; The Times: Leader Writer, 1990–91; Literary Editor, 1991–95; an Asst Editor, 1995–98; an Associate Editor, Daily Telegraph, 1998–2005; a Contrib. Editor, NY Sun, 2005–. *Publications:* White King and Red Queen: how the Cold War was fought on the chessboard, 2007; co-edited: German Neo-Liberals and the Social Market Economy, 1989; Thomas Mann: Death in Venice and other stories, 1991; Collected Stories, 2001; contrib. to Commentary, New Criterion, American Spectator, Weekly Standard, TLS, Lit. Review, Prospect, and other jls. *Recreations:* family, antiquarian book-collecting, music, chess. *Address:* c/o Capel & Land Ltd, 29 Wardour Street, W1D 6PS.

See also L. O. Johnson.

JOHNSON, Darren Paul; Member (Green): London Assembly, Greater London Authority, since 2000; Lewisham Borough Council, since 2002; *b* 20 May 1966; *s* of Alan Johnson and Joyce Johnson (*née* Abram, now Reynolds). *Educ:* Goldsmiths' Coll., Univ. of London (BA 1st Cl. Hons Politics and Econs 1997). Finance and admin posts, 1987–93. Envmt Advr to Mayor of London, 2000–01; Chm., Envmt Cttee, London Assembly, GLA, 2004–. Mem., Green Party, 1987–; Elections Co-ordinator, Nat. Exec., 1993–95;

Principal Speaker, 2001–03. *Recreations:* walking, cycling. *Address:* Greater London Authority, City Hall, Queen's Walk, SE1 2AA. *T:* (020) 7983 4000.

JOHNSON, Ven. David Allan G.; *see* Gunn-Johnson.

JOHNSON, David Bryan; Chief Executive, North and East Yorkshire and Northern Lincolnshire Strategic Health Authority, 2002–06; *b* 27 Feb. 1957; *s* of Audrey and Bernard Johnson; *m* 1980, Gillian Pobgee; one *s*. *Educ:* Sheffield Univ. (BA Hons Politics 1978). Nat. Management Trainee, NHS, 1980–83; Asst, then Dep. Administrator, Manchester Royal Infirmary, 1983–85; Unit Gen. Manager, Pontefract HA Acute and Maternity Services, 1985–90; Dir of Ops, 1990–92, Acting Chief Exec., Feb.–May 1992, St James's Univ. Hosp.; Chief Executive: St James's and Seacroft Univ. Hosps NHS Trust, 1992–98; Leeds Teaching Hosps NHS Trust, 1998–2002. *Recreations:* golf, guitar, reading, cycling, travel.

JOHNSON, David Burnham; QC 1978; commercial arbitrator; a Recorder, 1984–98; *b* 6 Aug. 1930; *s* of late Thomas Burnham Johnson and of Elsie May Johnson; *m* 1968, Julia Clare Addison Hopkinson, *o d* of late Col H. S. P. Hopkinson, OBE; one *s* three *d*. *Educ:* Truro Sch.; Univ. of Wales. Solicitor and Notary Public, Oct. 1952. Commissioned, National Service, with Royal Artillery, 1952–54. Private practice as solicitor, Cardiff and Plymouth, 1954–67; called to Bar, Inner Temple, 1967, Bencher, 1985. *Recreations:* sailing, walking, shooting, reading, music. *Address:* 25 Murray Road, Wimbledon, SW19 4PD. *T:* (020) 8947 9188; (chambers) 20 Essex Street, WC2R 3AL. *T:* (020) 7583 9294. *Clubs:* Lansdowne; Royal Western Yacht (Plymouth).

JOHNSON, David Gordon, CBE 2003; Director, Land Forces Secretariat, since 2007; *b* 1 Aug. 1966; *s* of Gordon Alexander Johnson and Margaret Edith Johnson (*née* Bangay); *m* 1995, Salimata Ouattara; two *s* one *d*. *Educ:* Chesterfield Sch.; Pembroke Coll., Oxford (BA Hons Classics, MA 1992). Ministry of Defence: various posts, 1989–95; Assistant Director: Housing Project Team, 1995–97; Defence Policy, 1997–98; Defence and Overseas Secretariat, Cabinet Office, 1998–2001; Asst Dir, Defence Resources and Plans, 2001–02; Director: Iraq, 2002–04; Human Resources Develt, 2004–06; Dir-Gen., Logistics (Resources), 2006–07. *Recreations:* studying and teaching karate, coaching young cricketers. *Address:* Headquarters Land Command, Erskine Barracks, Wilton, Salisbury, Wilts SP2 0AG.

JOHNSON, David Robert W.; *see* Wilson-Johnson.

JOHNSON, David Timothy; Assistant Secretary of State, Bureau of International Narcotics and Law Enforcement Affairs, United States, since 2007; *b* 28 Aug. 1954; *s* of Weyman T. Johnson and Dixie P. Johnson; *m* 1981, Scarlett M. Swan; one *s* two *d*. *Educ:* Emory Univ. (BA Econs 1976). United States Foreign Service, 1977–: Consul Gen., Vancouver, 1990–93; Dir, State Dept Press Office, 1993–95; Dep. Press Sec., The White House, and Spokesman for Nat. Security Council, 1995–97; Ambassador to OSCE, 1998–2001; Afghan Co-ordinator for US, 2002–03; Dep. Chief of Mission, US Embassy, London, 2003–07. *Address:* Room 7333, Harry S. Truman Building, Department of State, Washington, DC 20520, USA.

JOHNSON, Diana Ruth; MP (Lab) Hull North, since 2005; an Assistant Government Whip, since 2007; *b* 25 July 1966; *d* of late Eric Johnson and Ruth Johnson. *Educ:* Northwich Co. Grammar Sch. for Girls; Sir John Deane's Sixth Form Coll., Cheshire; Queen Mary Coll., Univ. of London (LLB 1988). Paralegal, Herbert Smith Solicitors, 1990; volunteer/locum lawyer, Tower Hamlets Law Centre, 1991–94; lawyer: McCormacks Solicitors, 1994–95; N Lewisham Law Centre, 1995–99; Paddington Law Centre, 1999–2002. Member (Lab): Tower Hamlets LBC, 1994–2002; London Assembly, GLA, March 2003–2004. Mem., Metropolitan Police Authy, 2003–04. Non-executive Director: Newham Healthcare Trust, 1998–2001; Tower Hamlets PCT, 2001–05. Vis. Legal Mem., Mental Health Act Commn, 1995–98. Contested (Lab) Brentwood and Ongar, 2001. PPS to Minister of State, DWP, 2005–06, to Chief Sec. to HM Treasury, 2006–07. *Recreations:* cinema, dog walking, theatre. *Address:* (office) Unit 8, Hull Business Centre, Guildhall Road, Hull HU1 1HJ; *e-mail:* johnsond@parliament.uk; *web:* www.dianajohnson.co.uk;; House of Commons, SW1A 0AA.

JOHNSON, Edwin Geoffrey; QC 2006; barrister; *b* 11 May 1963; *s* of Colin Johnson and Fiona Johnson; *m* 1991, Mary Ann Thorne; two *s* one *d*. *Educ:* Lancing Coll.; Christ Church Coll., Oxford (BA Hons Jurisprudence 1986). Called to the Bar, Lincoln's Inn, 1987; in practice as a barrister, 1988–, specialising in real property and professional negligence. *Publication:* (ed) Snell's Equity, 31st edn 2005. *Recreations:* travel, running, hill walking, scuba diving, ski-ing, reading. *Address:* Maitland Chambers, 7 Stone Buildings, WC2A 3SZ. *T:* (020) 7406 1200, *Fax:* (020) 7406 1300; *e-mail:* ejohnson@maitlandchambers.com.

JOHNSON, Emma Louise, MBE 1996; solo clarinettist and conductor; *b* 20 May 1966; *d* of Roger and Mary Johnson; *m* 1997, Chris West; one *d* (one *s* decd). *Educ:* Newstead Wood Sch.; Sevenoaks Sch.; Pembroke Coll., Cambridge (MA English Lit. and Music 1992; Hon. Fellow, 1999). Concerts and tours in Europe, USA, Far East, Australia and Africa; guest appearances with major orchestras world-wide; compositions commnd from several leading British composers. Dir, chamber music gp; Prof. of Clarinet, RCM, 1997–2002. Numerous recordings, including the concertos of Mozart, Crusell, Weber, Finzi, Arnold and Berkeley; four recital discs. Winner, BBC Young Musicians, 1984; Bronze Medal, Eurovision Young Musicians Competition, 1984; Winner, Young Concert Artists Auditions, NY, 1991. *Publication:* "Encore!": compositions and transcriptions for clarinet and piano, 1994. *Recreations:* theatre, literature, art, gardening, bird watching, travel. *Address:* c/o Nick Curry, Clarion Seven Muses, 47 Whitehall Park N19 3TW. *T:* (020) 7272 4413.

JOHNSON, Air Vice-Marshal Frank Sidney Roland, CB 1973; OBE 1963; *b* 4 Aug. 1917; *s* of Major Harry Johnson, IA, and Georgina Marklew; *m* 1943, Evelyn Hunt; two *s*. *Educ:* Trinity County Secondary Sch., Wood Green. Enlisted, 1935; served in UK and India; commnd, 1943; Germany (Berlin Airlift), 1948; Western Union Defence Organisation, 1955–57; Directing Staff, RAF Staff Coll., 1958–60; comd 113 MU, RAF Nicosia, 1960–63; Chief Instructor Equipment and Secretarial Wing, RAF Coll. Cranwell, 1963–64; Dep. Dir MoD, 1965–66; idc 1967; Chief Supply Officer, Fighter and Strike Comds, 1968–70; Dir-Gen. of Supply, RAF, 1971–73; Supply Manager, BAC, Saudi Arabia, 1974–76; Base Manager, BAC RSAF, Khamis Mushayt, Saudi Arabia, 1976–77, Dhahran, 1978–82. CCMI. *Recreations:* golf, squash, hockey, cricket. *Club:* Royal Air Force.

JOHNSON, Frederick Alistair, PhD; FInstP; consultant, BAE Systems and other companies, since 2000; *b* Christchurch, NZ, 9 April 1928; *s* of Archibald Frederick Johnson and Minnie, *d* of William Frederick Pellew; *m* 1952, Isobel Beth, *d* of Horace George Wilson; two *d*. *Educ:* Christchurch Boys' High Sch.; Univ. of Canterbury, New Zealand (MSc, PhD). Rutherford Meml Fellow, 1952; Lectr, Univ. of Otago, 1952; post graduate research, Bristol Univ., 1953–55. Royal Radar Establishment, 1956–75: Individual Merit Promotion, 1964; Head of Physics Dept, 1968–73; Dep. Director, 1973–75; Dep. Dir, Royal Armament Research & Development Estabt, 1975–77; Dir of Scientific and Technical Intell., MoD, 1977–79; Chief Scientist (Royal Navy) and Dir Gen. Research A, MoD, 1980–84; Dir, Marconi Maritime Applied Res. Lab., and Chief Scientist, Marconi Underwater Systems Ltd, 1985–87; Technical Dir, GEC Research, later GEC-Marconi Res. Centre, 1987–95; Dir, Special Projects, GEC-Marconi, subseq. BAE Systems Res. Centre, 1995–2000. Visiting Professor, Massachusetts Inst. of Technology, 1967–68; Hon. Prof. of Physics, Birmingham Univ., 1969–75. *Publications:* numerous papers on spectroscopy, optics, lattice dynamics and ocean thermal energy conversion in Proc. Physical Soc. and Proc. Royal Soc. *Recreation:* sailing. *Address:* Otia Tuta, Grassy Lane, Sevenoaks, Kent TN13 1PL. *Club:* Athenæum.

JOHNSON, Frederick James Maugham M.; *see* Marr-Johnson.

JOHNSON, Gen. Sir Garry (Dene), KCB 1990; OBE 1977 (MBE 1971); MC 1965; Chairman, International Security Advisory Board, since 1995; *b* 20 Sept. 1937; *m* 1962, Caroline Sarah Frearson; two *s*. *Educ:* Christ's Hospital. psc, ndc, rcds. Commissioned 10th Princess Mary's Own Gurkha Rifles, 1956; Malaya and Borneo campaigns, 1956–67; Royal Green Jackets, 1970; command, 1st Bn RGJ, 1976–79; Comdr, 11 Armoured Brigade, 1981–82; Dep. Chief of Staff, HQ BAOR, 1983; ACDS (NATO/UK), 1985–87; Comdr, British Forces Hong Kong, and Maj.-Gen., Bde of Gurkhas, 1987–89; MEC, Hong Kong Govt, 1987–89; Comdr Trng and Arms Dirs, 1989–91; Inspector Gen. Doctrine and Trng, 1991–92; C-in-C, AFNORTH, 1992–94. Colonel, 10th PMO Gurkha Rifles, 1985–94; Col Comdt, Light Div., 1990–94. Chm., TEC Nat. Council, 1995–99; Vice-Pres., Nat. Fedn of Enterprise Agencies, 1996–99. Chairman: Ogilby Trust, 1991–; Need in Nepal, 1997–2005; Trustee, Gurkha Welfare Trust, 1985–2007 (Chm., 1987–89). Patron, Nat. Malaya & Borneo Veterans Assoc., 2002–. Pres., De Burght Foundn, 2001–07; Member: NACETT, 1995–99; Adv. Council, Prince's Youth Business Trust, 1995–99; NCIHE, 1996–99; Adv. Bd, Centre for Leadership Studies, Exeter Univ., 1998–2005. Treas., Christ's Hosp., 2007–. FRGS 1993; FRAS 1994; FRSA 1994; FRUSI 1999. Hon. DSc Soton 1999. Order of Terra Mariana (Estonia), 1997; Order of Grand Duke Gediminas (Lithuania), 1999; Medal of Merit (Latvia), 2000. *Publications:* Brightly Shone the Dawn, 1979; Inland from Gold Beach, 1999. *Address:* c/o Holt's Branch, Royal Bank of Scotland, Lawrie House, Victoria Road, Farnborough GU14 7NR. *Club:* Army and Navy.

JOHNSON, Prof. Garth Roston, PhD; FREng, FIMechE; Professor of Rehabilitation Engineering, University of Newcastle upon Tyne, since 1995; *b* 23 Jan. 1945; *s* of Daniel Cowan Johnson and Vera Olive Johnson; *m* 1978, Katherine Zaida Cooke; one *s*. *Educ:* Univ. of Leeds (BSc Hons; PhD 1974). CEng 1991, FIMechE 1991; FREng 2000. Res. engr, Adcock & Shipley, machine tool manufrs, Leicester, 1961–71; Res. Fellow, Rheumatology Res. Unit, Dept of Medicine, Univ. of Leeds, 1971–75; Tech. Dir, Orthotics and Disability Res. Centre, Derbys Royal Infirmary, 1975–81; University of Newcastle upon Tyne: William Leech Reader in Biomed. Engrg, Dept of Mechanical, Materials and Manufg Engrg, 1981–95; Tech. Dir, Centre for Rehabilitation and Engrg Studies, 1991–. *Publications:* (ed with M. P. Barnes) Upper Motor Neurone Syndrome and Spasticity, 2001; contrib. to learned jls incl. Proc. IMechE, Jl Biomechanics, Clin. Biomechanics. *Recreation:* music. *Address:* Centre for Rehabilitation and Engineering Studies, University of Newcastle upon Tyne, Stephenson Building, Newcastle upon Tyne NE1 7RU. *T:* (0191) 222 6196.

JOHNSON, Dr Gordon; President, Wolfson College, since 1994, and Deputy Vice-Chancellor, since 2002, University of Cambridge; Provost, Gates Cambridge Trust, since 2000; *b* 13 Sept. 1943; *s* of Robert Johnson and Bessie (*née* Hewson); *m* 1973, Faith Sargent Lewis, New Haven, Conn; three *s*. *Educ:* Richmond Sch., Yorks; Trinity Coll., Cambridge (BA 1964; MA, PhD 1968). Fellow, Trinity Coll., Cambridge, 1966–74; Selwyn College, Cambridge: Fellow, 1974–94; Tutor, 1975–92; Hon. Fellow, 1994; University of Cambridge: Lectr in History of S Asia, 1974–2005; Dir, Centre of S Asian Studies, 1983–2001; Chairman, Faculty of: Oriental Studies, 1984–87; Architecture and History of Art, 1985–2008; Educn, 1994–2005; Member: Library Syndicate, 1978–; Press Syndicate, 1981– (Chm., 1993–); Syndicate on Govt of Univ., 1988–89; Statutes and Ordinances Revision Syndicate, 1990–; Gen. Bd of Faculties, 1979–82 and 1985–90; Council, Senate, 1985–92 and 1999–2000. Lady Margaret Preacher, Univ. of Cambridge, 2006. Trustee: Cambridge Commonwealth Trust, 1983–; Cambridge Overseas Trust, 1989–; Malaysian Commonwealth Studies Centre, 1999–. Governor: Comberton Village Coll., 1991–2001 (Chm., 1992–2001); Gresham's Sch., 2006–. Liveryman, Stationers' Co., 2003–. Editor, Modern Asian Studies, 1971–2008; Gen. Editor, The New Cambridge History of India, 1979–. *Publications:* Provincial Politics and Indian Nationalism, 1973; University Politics: F. M. Cornford's Cambridge and his advice to the young academic politician, 1994; Cultural Atlas of India, 1995; Printing and Publishing for the University: three hundred years of the press syndicate, 1999. *Recreations:* reading, taking exercise. *Address:* Wolfson College, Cambridge CB3 9BB. *T:* (01223) 335900.

JOHNSON, Gordon Arthur; DL; Chief Executive, Lancashire County Council, 1998–2000; *b* 30 Aug. 1938; *y s* of Annie Elizabeth Johnson and William Johnson; *m* 1963, Jennifer Roxane Bradley; two *d*. *Educ:* Bournemouth Sch.; University College London (BA Hons Hist.). Solicitor. Kent CC, 1962–64; Staffs CC, 1964–73; Dep. Dir of Admin, W Yorks MCC, 1973–76; Dep. Clerk, 1977–90, Chief. Exec. Clerk, 1991–98, Lancs CC. Lancs County Electoral Returning Officer, 1991–2000; Clerk: Lancs Lieutenancy, 1991–2000; Lancs Police Authy, 1995–2000; Lancs Combined Fire Authy, 1998–2000; Secretary: Lancs Adv. Cttee, 1991–2000; Lord Chancellor's Adv. Cttee on Gen. Cmrs of Income Tax, 1991–2000; Lancs Probation Cttee; Lancs Cttee, Prince's Trust-Action; Co. Sec., Lancs County Enterprises Ltd, 1991–2000; Mem., MSC Area Manpower Bd, 1986–88; Chm., Soc. of County Secretaries, 1987–88 (Hon. Treasurer, 1977–86); Dir, LAWTEC, 1991–98. Adviser: LGA Policy and Strategy Cttee, 1997–2000; Assoc. of Police Authorities, 1997–2000. Mem. Court, 1991–2000, Dep. Pro-Chancellor, 2002–, Univ. of Lancaster. Constable, Lancaster Castle, 2004–. DL Lancs, 2000. *Recreations:* motor cycling, travel, reading. *Address:* Beech House, 72 Higher Bank Road, Fulwood, Preston, Lancs PR2 8PH.

JOHNSON, Graham Rhodes, OBE 1994; concert accompanist; Senior Professor of Accompaniment, Guildhall School of Music, since 1986; *b* 10 July 1950; *s* of late John Edward Donald Johnson and of Violet May Johnson (*née* Johnson). *Educ:* Hamilton High Sch., Bulawayo, Rhodesia; Royal Acad. of Music, London. FRAM 1984; FGSM 1988. Concert début, Wigmore Hall, 1972; has since accompanied Elisabeth Schwarzkopf, Jessye Norman, Victoria de los Angeles (USA Tour 1977), Dame Janet Baker, Sir Peter Pears, Dame Felicity Lott, Dame Margaret Price (USA Tour 1985), Peter Schreier, John Shirley Quirk, Mady Meslé, Thomas Hampson, Robert Holl, Tom Krause, Sergei Leiferkus, Brigitte Fassbaender, Matthias Goerne, Christine Schäfer. Work with contemporaries led to formation of The Songmakers' Almanac (Artistic Director); has devised and accompanied over 150 London recitals for this group since Oct. 1976. Tours of US with Sarah Walker, Richard Jackson, and of Australia and NZ with The

Songmakers' Almanac, 1981. Writer and presenter of major BBC Radio 3 series on Poulenc songs, and BBC TV programmes on Schubert songs (1978) and the songs of Liszt (1986). Lectr at song courses in Savonlinna (Finland), US and at Pears-Britten Sch., Snape; Artistic advr and accompanist, Alte Oper Festival, Frankfurt, 1981–82; Song Adviser, Wigmore Hall, 1992–; Chm. Jury, Wigmore Hall Internat. Singing Competition, 1997, 1999 and 2001. Festival appearances in Aldeburgh, Edinburgh, Munich, Hohenems, Salzburg, Bath, Hong Kong, Bermuda. Many recordings incl. those with Songmakers' Almanac, Martyn Hill, Elly Ameling, Arleen Auger, Janet Baker, Philip Langridge, Marjana Lipovsek, Ann Murray, Sarah Walker, Anthony Rolfe Johnson, and of complete Schubert Lieder, with various artists, 1987–2005. Hon. Mem., Royal Swedish Acad. of Music, 2000. Gramophone Award, 1989, 1996, 1997 and 2001; Royal Philharmonic Prize for Instrumentalist, 1998; Edison Prize, 2006. Chevalier, Ordre des Arts et des Lettres (France), 2002. *Publications:* (contrib.) The Britten Companion, ed Christopher Palmer, 1984; (contrib.) Gerald Moore, The Unashamed Accompanist, rev. edn 1984; (contrib.) The Spanish Song Companion, 1992; The Songmakers' Almanac: reflections and commentaries, 1996; A French Song Companion, 2000; Britten, Voice and Piano, 2003; Gabriel Fauré: the songs and their poets, 2008, reviews in TLS, articles for music jls. *Address:* c/o Askonas Holt Ltd, Lincoln House, 300 High Holborn, WC1V 7JH.

JOHNSON, Sir Guy; *see* Johnson, Sir C. G.

JOHNSON, Heather Jean; *see* Mellows, H. J.

JOHNSON, Hugh Eric Allan, OBE 2007; author, broadcaster and editor; *b* 10 March 1939; *s* of late Guy Francis Johnson, CBE and Grace Kittel; *m* 1965, Judith Eve Grinling; one *s* two *d.* *Educ:* Rugby Sch.; King's Coll., Cambridge (MA; Fellow Commoner, 2001). Staff writer, Condé Nast publications, 1960–63; Editor, Wine & Food, and Sec., Wine and Food Soc., 1963–65; Wine Corresp., 1962–67, and Travel Editor, 1967, Sunday Times; Editor, Queen, 1968–70; Wine Editor, Gourmet, NY, 1971–72. President: The Sunday Times Wine Club, 1973–; Circle of Wine Writers, 1997–2006. Founder Mem., Tree Council, 1974. Chairman: Saling Hall Press, 1975–; Conservation Cttee, Internat. Dendrology Soc., 1979–86; Winestar Productions Ltd, 1984–2006; The Hugh Johnson Collection Ltd, 1985–; Vice-Pres., Essex Gardens Trust, 1997–; Director: Société Civile de Château Latour, 1986–2001; Coldstream Winemakers Ltd, 1991–94. Editorial Director: Jl of RHS, 1975–89, Editl Cons., 1989–2006; The Plantsman, 1979–94. Wine Editor, Cuisine, New York, 1983–84; Wine Consultant: to Jardine Matheson Ltd, Hong Kong and Tokyo, 1985–2001; to British Airways, 1987–2002; to the Royal Tokaji Wine Co., 1990–; Hon. Trustee, Amer. Center for Wine, Food and the Arts, Calif, 2000–; Hon. Pres., Internat. Wine and Food Soc., 2002–08. Gardening Correspondent, New York Times, 1986–87. Editl Advr, The World of Fine Wine, 2004–. Video, How to Handle a Wine, 1984 (Glenfiddich Trophy, 1984; reissued as Understanding Wine, 1989); TV series: Wine—a user's guide (KQED, San Francisco), 1986; Vintage—a history of wine (Channel 4 and WGBH, Boston), 1989; TV documentary, Return Voyage (Star TV, Hong Kong), 1992. Hon. Chm., Wine Japan (Tokyo exhibn), 1989–94. Hon. Liveryman, Vintners' Co., 2003. Docteur ès Vins, Acad. du Vin de Bordeaux, 1987. DUniv Essex, 1998. Carl-Friedrich von Rumor Gold Ring, German Gastronomic Acad., 1998; Veitch Meml Medal, RHS, 2000. Chevalier, Ordre Nat. du Mérite (France), 2003. *Publications:* Wine, 1966, rev. edn 1974; (ed) Frank Schoonmaker's Encyclopedia of Wine, English edn, 1967; The World Atlas of Wine, 1971, 6th edn (with Jancis Robinson) 2007; The International Book of Trees, 1973, rev. edn 1994; (with Bob Thompson) The California Wine Book, 1976; Hugh Johnson's Pocket Wine Book, annually 1977–; The Principles of Gardening, 1979, rev. edn as Hugh Johnson's Gardening Companion, 1996; Understanding Wine, 1980; (with Paul Miles) The Pocket Encyclopedia of Garden Plants, 1981; Hugh Johnson's Wine Companion, 1983, 6th edn (with Stephen Brook), 2009; How to Enjoy Your Wine, 1985, 2nd edn 1998; The Hugh Johnson Cellar Book, 1986; The Atlas of German Wines, 1986, rev. edn (with Stuart Pigott) 1995; Hugh Johnson's Wine Cellar, (US) 1986; (with Jan Read) The Wine and Food of Spain, 1987; (with Hubrecht Duijker) The Wine Atlas of France, 1987, rev. edn 1997; The Story of Wine, 1989 (ten awards, incl. Glenfiddich Wine Award, 1990, Grand Prix de la Communication de la Vigne et du Vin, 1992), new illus. edn, 2004; Hugh Johnson's Pop-up Wine Book, 1989; (with James Halliday) The Art and Science of Wine, 1992, new edn 2006; Hugh Johnson on Gardening: the best of Tradescant's Diary, 1993; Tuscany and its Wines, 2000; Wine: a life uncorked, 2005; articles on gastronomy, travel and gardening. *Recreations:* trees, travelling, staying at home. *Address:* Saling Hall, Great Saling, Essex CM7 5DT; 73 St James's Street, SW1A 1PH. *Clubs:* Garrick, Brooks's, Saintsbury; Essex.

JOHNSON, Rt Rev. James Nathaniel; Bishop of St Helena, 1985–91, now Bishop Emeritus; Hon. Assistant Bishop, Oxford Diocese, since 2004; *b* 28 April 1932; *s* of William and Lydia Florence Johnson; *m* 1953, Evelyn Joyce Clifford; one *s* one *d.* *Educ:* Primary and Secondary Selective School, St Helena; Church Army College; Wells Theol Coll. Deacon 1964, priest 1965; permission to officiate, Dio. of Europe, 1998; Curate of St Peter's, Lawrence Weston, dio. Bristol, 1964–66; Priest-in-charge of St Paul's Cathedral, St Helena, 1966–69, Vicar 1969–71; Domestic Chaplain to Bishop of St Helena, 1967–71; USPG Area Sec. for Diocese of Exeter and Truro, 1972–74; Rector of Combe Martin dio. Exeter, 1974–80; Hon. Canon of St Helena, 1975–; Vicar of St Augustine, Thorpe Bay, dio. Chelmsford, 1980–85; Rector of Byfield with Boddington and Aston-le-Walls, and Hon. Asst Bishop, dio. Peterborough, 1991–92; Vicar of Hockley, Essex, 1992–97; Asst Bishop, 1992–97, Hon. Asst Bishop, 1997–2004, dio. Chelmsford. Non-residentiary Canon, Chelmsford Cathedral, 1994–97, Canon Emeritus, 1997. *Recreations:* music, gardening, walking. *Address:* St Helena, 28 Molyneux Drive, Bodicote, Oxon OX15 4AP. *T:* (01295) 255357.

JOHNSON, James North, MD; FRCS, FRCP; FDSRCS; Consultant Surgeon, Halton General Hospital, Runcorn, since 1985; Chairman of Council, British Medical Association, 2003–07; *b* 13 Nov. 1946; *s* of Edwin Johnson and Elizabeth Marjorie Johnson (*née* North); *m* 1st, 1972, Dr Gillian Christine Markham (marr. diss. 2002); one *s* one *d*; 2nd, 2006, Fiona Helen Simpson. *Educ:* Liverpool Univ. Med. Sch. (MB ChB 1970, MD 1980). FRCS 1977; FRCP 2000; FDSRCS 2000. Demonstrator, then Lectr in Anatomy, Univ. of Liverpool, 1971–74; Fellow, Merseyside Assoc. for Kidney Res., 1974–75; Registrar and Sen. Registrar trng posts, Mersey Reg., 1975–85; Clinical Lectr in Surgery, Liverpool Univ., 1987–. Vis. Prof. in Anatomy, Univ. of Texas, 1973. British Medical Association: Mem. Council, 1975–80 and 1992–2007; Chairman: Hosp. Jun. Staffs Cttee, 1979–80; Central Consultants and Specialists Cttee, 1994–98 (Vice-Chm., 1990–94). Chm., Jt Consultants Cttee, 1998–2003 (Vice-Chm., 1994–98); Mem., Standing Med. Adv. Cttee, DoH, 1998–2004. Mem., Mgt Cttee, Nat. Counselling Service for Sick Doctors, 1985–2004. *Publications:* contrib. articles on surgical, vascular surgical and medico-political topics, incl. the future rôle of consultant, hospital configuration and appraisal. *Recreations:* travel, fine wine, medical politics. *Address:* Talgarth, 66 View Road, Rainhill, Prescot, Merseyside L35 0LS. *T:* (0151) 426 4306, *Fax:* (0151) 426 6572; *e-mail:* jnjohnson33@hotmail.com. *Club:* Athenæum.

JOHNSON, His Honour John Robin; a Circuit Judge, 1973–93; *b* 5 Nov. 1927; *s* of Sir Philip Bulmer Johnson, Hexham, Northumberland; *m* 1958, Meriel Jean, *d* of H. B. Speke, Aydon, Corbridge; one *s* one *d.* *Educ:* Winchester; Trinity Coll., Cambridge. Called to Bar, Middle Temple, 1950. Dep. Chm., Northumberland QS, 1966–71; a Recorder of the Crown Court, 1972–73. *Address:* Kirk Fenwick, Cambo, Morpeth NE61 4BN.

JOHNSON, Sir John (Rodney), KCMG 1988 (CMG 1981); HM Diplomatic Service, retired; Chairman, Countryside Commission, 1991–95; Visiting Fellow, Kellogg College, Oxford, since 2000; *b* 6 Sept. 1930; *s* of Edwin Done Johnson, OBE and Florence Mary (*née* Clough); *m* 1956, Jean Mary Lewis; three *s* one *d.* *Educ:* Manchester Grammar Sch.; Oxford Univ. (MA). HM Colonial Service, Kenya, 1955–64; Dist Comr, Thika, 1962–64; Administrator, Cttee of Vice-Chancellors and Principals of UK Univs, 1965; First Sec., FCO, 1966–69; Head of Chancery, British Embassy, Algiers, 1969–72; Dep. High Comr, British High Commn, Barbados, 1972–74; Counsellor, British High Commn, Lagos, 1975–78; Head of W African Dept, FCO, and Ambassador (non-resident) to Chad, 1978–80; High Comr in Zambia, 1980–84; Asst Under Sec. of State (Africa), FCO, 1984–86; High Comr in Kenya, 1986–90; Dir, Foreign Service Prog., and specially elected Fellow, Keble Coll., Oxford Univ., 1990–95. Mem., Jt Nature Conservation Cttee, 1991–95. Chairman: Kenya Soc., 1992–98; Chilterns Conservation Bd, 2001–; President: Friends of Lake Dist, 1995–2005; Long Distance Walkers Assoc., 1995–; Vice-President: Royal African Soc., 1995–2005; YHA, 1995–; Chiltern Soc., 1995–; Vice-Chm., Chilterns Conf., 1996–2001. *Publication:* (ed) Colony to Nation: British administrators in Kenya, 2002. *Recreations:* walking, reaching remote places. *Address:* The Gables, 27 High Street, Amersham, Bucks HP7 0DP. *Clubs:* Travellers, Alpine; Climbers; Mombasa.

JOHNSON, Kenneth James, OBE 1966; colonial administrator and industrialist; *b* 8 Feb. 1926; *s* of Albert Percy Johnson and Winifred Florence (*née* Coole); *m* 1951, Margaret Teresa Bontoft Jenkins; three *s* two *d.* *Educ:* Rishworth School, near Halifax; Wadham Coll., Oxford; LSE; SOAS. Indian Army (14 Punjab Regt), 1945–47. Colonial Admin. Service, Nigeria, 1949–61, senior appts in Min. of Finance and Min. of Commerce and Industry; Head of Economic Dept, later Dir of Industrial Affairs, CBI, 1961–70; Courtaulds Ltd, 1970–73: Chm. and Man. Dir, various subsidiary cos; Dep. Chm., Pay Board, 1973–74; Dunlop Group, 1974–85: Personnel Dir, 1974–79; Overseas Dir, Dunlop Holdings plc, 1979–84; Chm., Dunlop International AG, 1984–85; Chm., Crown Agents Pensions Trust, 1984–96. Member: Bd of Crown Agents for Oversea Govts and Administrations, 1980–88; Crown Agents Hldg and Realisation Bd, 1980–88. Chm., Farlington Sch. Trust, 1990–2000. FRSA 1972; FIPM 1976. *Recreation:* book-collecting. *Address:* Snappers Field, Shipley, Horsham, West Sussex RH13 9BQ. *Club:* Oriental.

JOHNSON, Prof. Kenneth Langstreth, PhD; FRS 1982; FREng; Professor of Engineering, Cambridge University, 1977–92, now Emeritus; Fellow of Jesus College, Cambridge, 1957–92, now Emeritus; *b* 19 March 1925; *s* of Frank Herbert Johnson and Ellen Howorth Langstreth; *m* 1954, Dorothy Rosemary Watkins; one *s* two *d.* *Educ:* Barrow Grammar Sch.; Manchester Univ. (MScTech, MA, PhD). FIMechE; FREng (FEng 1987). Engr, Messrs Rotol Ltd, Gloucester, 1944–49; Asst Lectr, Coll. of Technology, Manchester, 1949–54; Lectr, then Reader in Engrg, Cambridge Univ., 1954–77. Hon. FUMIST, 1993. Tribology Trust Gold Medal, IMechE, 1985; Mayo Hersey Award, ASME, 1991; William Prager Medal, Amer. Soc. Engrg Sci., 1999; Royal Medal, Royal Soc., 2003; Timoshenko Medal, ASME, 2006. *Publications:* Contact Mechanics, 1985; contrib. scientific and engrg jls, and Proc. IMechE. *Recreations:* mountain walking, swimming. *Address:* 1 New Square, Cambridge CB1 1EY. *T:* (01223) 355287.

JOHNSON, Dame Louise (Napier), DBE 2003; FRS 1990; David Phillips Professor of Molecular Biophysics, and Professorial Fellow, Corpus Christi College, Oxford, 1990–2007; Director of Life Sciences, Diamond Light Source, since 2003; *b* 26 Sept. 1940; *m*; one *s* one *d.* *Educ:* Wimbledon High Sch. for Girls; University College London (BSc 1962; Fellow, 1993); Royal Institution, London (PhD 1965). Research Asst., Yale Univ., 1966; University of Oxford: Demonstrator, Zoology Dept, 1967–73; Lectr in Molecular Biophysics, 1973–90; Reader, 1990; Additional Fellow, Somerville College, 1973–90, Hon. Fellow, 1991. Member: Council, Royal Soc., 1998–2001; CCLRC, 1998–2001; Scientific Adv. Council, EMBL, 1994–2001 (Chm., 1998–2001). Mem., EMBO, 1991. Trustee, Cambridge Crystallographic Data Base, 1996–2003. Gov., Westminster Sch., 1993–2001. Associate Fellow, Third World Acad. of Scis, 2000; MAE, 2001. Hon. DSc St Andrews, 1992. Kaj Linderström-Lang Prize, 1989; Charmian Medal, Royal Soc. Chem., 1997; Datta Medal, FEBS, 1998. *Publications:* Protein Crystallography (jtly with T. L. Blundell), 1976; papers on lysozyme, glycogen phosphorylase, kinases and cell cycle proteins, protein crystallography, enzyme mechanism and allosteric mechanisms. *Recreations:* family, horses. *Address:* Laboratory of Molecular Biophysics, Rex Richards Building, University of Oxford, South Parks Road, Oxford OX1 3QU; Diamond Light Source Ltd, Harwell Science and Innovation Campus, Diamond House, Chilton, Didcot, Oxon OX11 0DE.

JOHNSON, Luke Oliver; Chairman: Channel 4 Television, since 2004; Risk Capital Partners, since 2001; *b* 2 Feb. 1962; *s* of Paul Bede Johnson, *qv*; *m* 2004, Liza Pickrell; one *s* one *d.* *Educ:* Langley Grammar Sch.; Magdalen Coll., Oxford. Stockbroking Analyst, Grieveson Grant, then Kleinwort Benson, 1983–88; Director: AoD, 1989–92; ICD, 1989–92; Crabtree Gp, 1992–94; PizzaExpress, 1992–95 and 1998–99 (Chm., 1996–98); My Kinda Town, 1994–96; American Port Services, 1995–98; Abacus Recruitment, 1995–99; Integrated Dental Hldgs, 1996–2006; Whittards of Chelsea, 1998–2001; NewMedia SPARK, 1999–2001; Nightfreight, 1999–2001; Acquisitor, 1999–2004; Manager, Intrinsic Value, 1999–2001; Chm., Belgo Gp, subseq. Signature Restaurants Ltd, 1997–2005. Gov., Univ. of the Arts, London (formerly London Inst.), 2000–06. Columnist: Sunday Telegraph, 1997–2006; FT, 2007–. *Publications:* How to Get a Highly Paid Job in the City, 1987; Betting to Win, 1990, 2nd edn 1997; The Maverick: dispatches from an unrepentant capitalist, 2007. *Recreations:* writing, squash, tennis. *Address:* Risk Capital Partners, 32 Beford Row, WC1R 4HE. *T:* (020) 7400 0490. *Clubs:* Royal Automobile, Groucho, Cobden.

See also D. B. Johnson.

JOHNSON, Prof. Margaret Anne, MD, FRCP; Consultant Physician in Thoracic Medicine and HIV Medicine, since 1989, and Clinical Director, HIV/AIDS, since 1992, Royal Free Hampstead NHS Trust; Professor of HIV Medicine, University College London, since 2005; *b* 7 Feb. 1952; *d* of Dr Frederick W. Johnson and Dr Margaret Rosemary Johnson; *m* 1980, Prof. John William Winston Studd, *qv*; one *s* two *d.* *Educ:* Convent of Sacred Heart, Woldingham; Royal Free Hosp. Sch. of Medicine, Univ. of London (MD 1987). FRCP 1993. House Physician, 1976, House Surgeon, 1976–77, Royal Free Hosp.; Senior House Officer: Postgrad. Trng Scheme in Medicine, Whittington Hosp., 1977–78; London Chest Hosp., 1978; Nat. Hosp. for Nervous

Diseases, 1978–79; Registrar Rotation in Gen. Medicine, St Mary's Hosp., W2, 1979–81; Res. Registrar, Royal Brompton Hosp., 1981–83; Sen. Registrar Rotation in Gen. Medicine and Thoracic Medicine, Royal Free Hosp./Royal Brompton Hosp., 1983–89; Med. Dir, Royal Free Hampstead NHS Trust, 2002–06. Chm., British HIV Assoc., 2004–. *Publications:* An Atlas of HIV and AIDS, 1995, 2nd edn 2004; articles concerning clinical mgt of HIV in learned jls. *Address:* Department of HIV Medicine, Royal Free Hospital, Pond Street, NW3 2QG. *T:* (020) 7941 1820, *Fax:* (020) 7941 1830; *e-mail:* margaret.johnson@royalfree.nhs.uk. *Club:* Athenæum.

JOHNSON, Martin; Sports Feature Writer, Daily Telegraph, since 1995; *b* 23 June 1949; *s* of late Basil Johnson and of Bridget Johnson; *m* 1985, Teresa Mary Wright; one *s* one *d*. *Educ:* St Julian's High Sch., Newport, Mon.; Monmouth Sch. Ronald French Advertising Agency, Liverpool, 1970; South Wales Argus, Newport, 1970–73; Leicester Mercury, 1973–86; Cricket Corresp., The Independent, 1986–95. *Publications:* (ed) The Independent World Cup Cricket, 1987; (jtly) Gower: the autobiography, 1992; Rugby and All That: an irreverent history, 2000. *Recreation:* golf. *Address:* 3 Oadby Hill Drive, Oadby, Leicester LE2 5GF. *Club:* Cosby Golf.

JOHNSON, Prof. Martin Hume, PhD; FRCOG; Professor of Reproductive Sciences, University of Cambridge, since 1992; Fellow, since 1969, Vice-Master, since 2007, Christ's College, Cambridge; *b* 19 Dec. 1944; *s* of late Reginald Hugh Ben Johnson and of Joyce Florence Johnson. *Educ:* Cheltenham Grammar Sch.; Christ's Coll., Cambridge (MA, PhD). FRCOG 2005. Jun. Res. Fellow, Christ's Coll., Cambridge, 1969; MRC Jun. Res. Fellow, 1970; Harkness Fellow, 1971; University of Cambridge: Lectr in Anatomy, 1974–84; Reader in Exptl Embryology, 1984–92; Head of Dept of Anatomy, 1995–99. Hon. Sen. Lectr in Obstetrics and Gynaecology, UMDS, 1991–95; Distinguished Vis. Fellow, La Trobe Univ., 1993, 2006; Vis. Prof., Sydney Univ., 1999–2004. Chm., Brit. Soc. for Developmental Biol., 1984–89; Mem., HFEA, 1994–99. Albert Brachet Prize, Belgian Royal Acad. Scis, Letters and Fine Arts, 1989. *Publications:* Essential Reproduction, (with B. J. Everitt) 1980, 6th edn 2007; contrib. to numerous scientific pubns. *Recreations:* opera, music. *Address:* Department of Anatomy, Downing Street, Cambridge CB2 3DY. *T:* (01223) 333777.

JOHNSON, Martin Osborne, CBE 2004 (OBE 1998); Rugby Union football player, retired; Head Coach, England Rugby Football Union Team, since 2008; *b* Solihull, 9 March 1970; *s* of David Johnson and late Hilary Johnson; *m* 2000, Kay Gredrig; one *s* one *d*. *Educ:* Robert Smyth Sch., Market Harborough. Joined Leicester RFU Club Youth team, 1988; played for College Old Boys, King Country, NZ and NZ Under 21s, 1989–90; joined Leicester Tigers, 1989: Captain, 1997–2003, 2004–05; Premiership Champions, 1999, 2000, 2001, 2002; winners, European Cup, 2001, 2002. 1st cap for England, 1993; Capt., 1999–2003; 84 caps, 39 as Capt.; captained Grand Slam side, 2003; has played in 3 World Cup teams, two as Capt.; winners, Rugby World Cup, Australia, 2003; Member, British Lions tours: NZ, 1993; S Africa, 1997 (Capt.); Australia, 2001 (Capt.). *Publications:* Agony and Ecstasy, 2001; Martin Johnson: the autobiography, 2003.

JOHNSON, Melanie Jane; JP; *b* 5 Feb. 1955; *d* of David Guyatt Johnson and Mary Angela Johnson; one *s* twin *d* by William Jordan. *Educ:* University Coll. London (BA Jt Hons Phil. and Ancient Greek); King's Coll., Cambridge (postgrad. res.). Mem. Relns Officer, 1981–88, Retail Admin Manager, 1988–90, Cambridge Co-op. Soc.; Asst Gen. Manager (Quality Assurance), Cambs FHSA, 1990–92; Schools Inspector, 1993–97. Mem. (Lab) Cambs CC, 1981–97. MP (Lab) Welwyn Hatfield, 1997–2005; contested (Lab) same seat, 2005. PPS to Financial Sec., HM Treasury, 1999; Economic Sec., HM Treasury, 1999–2001; Parly Under-Sec. of State, DTI, 2001–03; Parly Under-Sec. of State (Minister for Public Health), DoH, 2003–05. Member: Public Admin. Select Cttee, 1997–98; Home Affairs Select Cttee, 1998–99; Chm., All Party Parenting Gp, 1998–2005. Chm., Customer Impact Panel, ABI, 2006–. Contested (Lab) Cambs, EP elecn, 1994. JP Cambridge, 1994. *Recreations:* family, films, gardening. *Address: e-mail:* melaniejohnson@ntlworld.com.

JOHNSON, Merwyn; *see* Johnson, W. M.

JOHNSON, Michael Robert; graphic designer; Founder, 1992, and Creative Director, since 1992, Johnson Banks Design, graphic design consultancy; *b* 26 April 1964; *s* of late Charles Beverley Johnson and of Shirley Anne Johnson (*née* Fowler); *m* 1995, Elisabeth Schoon; one *s* one *d*. *Educ:* Ecclesbourne Sch., Duffield, Derby; Univ. of Lancaster (BA 1st Cl. Jt Hons Design and Mktg 1985). Junior consultant, Wolff Olins, London, 1985–86; designer, Billy Blue Gp, Sydney, 1986–87; freelance designer, Tokyo, 1987; designer, Emery Vincent Design, Melbourne and Sydney, 1988; Art Dir, Omon Advertising, Sydney, 1988; Sen. Designer, Sedley Place Design, London, 1988–89; Gp Art Dir, Smith and Milton, London, 1990–92. D&AD: Mem., 1991–; Cttee Mem., 1999–2003; Educn Chm., 2001–02; Pres., 2003; Chm., Design Week Awards, 1989, 1999. External Examiner: Glasgow Sch. of Art, 2001–04; Kingston Univ., 2006–; Mem., Re-validation Cttee, Communications course, RCA, 1998. Visiting Lecturer: Kingston Univ.; Nottingham Univ.; Northumbria Univ.; Middlesex Univ.; Falmouth Coll. of Art; Glasgow Sch. of Art; Central St Martins. *Exhibitions* include: *group:* The Power of the Poster (contrib. curator), 1998, Rewind: 40 Years of Design and Advertising (co-curator), 2002, V&A; European Design Biennial, Design Mus., 2003, 2005; Communicate: Independent British Graphic Design since the Sixties, Barbican Gall., 2004–05; *solo:* Words & Pictures, the design work of Michael Johnson + johnson banks, 2004, Jeans Shop Ginza, 2005, Creation Gall., Tokyo. Seven Silver Awards, one Gold Award, D&AD; 11 Design Week Awards; Gold Award, 1991, Silver Award, 2004, NY Art Dirs. *Publications:* Problem Solved: a primer in design and communication, 2002; (contrib.) Rewind: 40 years of design and advertising, 2002. *Recreations:* playing and collecting guitars, music, rollerblading. *Address:* Johnson Banks Design Limited, Crescent Works, Crescent Lane, SW4 9RW. *T:* (020) 7587 6400, *Fax:* (020) 7587 6411; *e-mail:* Michael@johnsonbanks.co.uk.

JOHNSON, Michael York-; *see* York, M.

JOHNSON, Neil Anthony, OBE (mil.) 1989; TD 1985, bar 1992; Chairman, Motability Finance Ltd, since 2001; *b* 13 April 1949; *s* of Anthony and Dilys Johnson, Glamorgan; *m* 1st, 1971 (marr. diss. 1996); three *d*; 2nd, 1996, Elizabeth Jane Hunter Johnston (*née* Robinson); one *d*, and three step *d*. *Educ:* Canton High Sch., Cardiff; RMA Sandhurst. Graduate Trainee, Lex Gp, 1971–73; British Leyland Motor Corp., 1973–82; Dir, Sales and Marketing, Jaguar Cars, 1982–86; MoD, 1986–89; Main Bd Dir, Rover Gp, British Aerospace, resp. for European Ops, 1989–92; Dir-Gen., EEF, 1992–93; Gen. Sec., 1994–99, Chief Exec., 1996–99, RAC; Chief Exec., British and Amer. Chamber of Commerce, 2000–01. Chairman: Hornby plc, 2000–; Cybit plc, 2001–; Tenon plc, 2003–06 (Dir, 2000–06); Autologic plc, 2006–07. Chm., Speedway Control Bd, 1994–96. Territorial Army: Pembroke Yeomanry, 1971; 4th Bn RGJ, 1973; CO, 1986–89; ADC to the Queen, 1990; Hon. Col, 157 Transport Regt, RLC, 1993–2001; Trustee RGJ TA Trust, 1994–; Hon. Col, F Co., London Regt, RGJ, 2000–07. Member: Prime Minister's Panel of Advrs on Citizen's Charter, Cabinet Office, 1995–2003; UK Round Table on Sustainable Develt, 1997–98; Cleaner Vehicles Task Force, 1997–99. Member: Nat. Employers' Liaison Cttee for the Reserve Forces, 1992–98; Nat. Employers' Adv. Bd, 2006–. Trustee, Jaguar Daimler Heritage Trust, 1994–99. FIMI; CCMI (CIMgt 1995); FRSA. Freeman, City of London, 1985. Rep. DL, City of Westminster, 1993–2007. Ordre de l'Encouragement Publique (France), 1987. *Recreations:* town and country pursuits, fast British cars, slow Italian lunches. *Address:* 22 Southwark Bridge Road, SE1 9HB. *Clubs:* Army and Navy, Royal Green Jackets, Royal Automobile, Beefsteak; Cardiff & County (Cardiff); Woodroffe's; Midland Automobile (Shelsley Walsh); Arlberg Ski.

JOHNSON, Prof. Newell Walter, MDSc, PhD; FDSRCS, FRACDS, FRCPath, FMedSci; Foundation Dean and Head, School of Dentistry and Oral Health, Griffith University, Queensland, since 2005; specialist in oral medicine, oral pathology and periodontics; *b* 5 Aug. 1938; *s* of Otto Johnson and Lorna (*née* Guy); *m* 1965, Pauline Margaret Trafford (marr. diss. 1984); two *d*. *Educ:* University High Sch., Melbourne; Univ. of Melbourne (BDSc Hons 1960; MDSc 1963); Univ. of Bristol (PhD 1967). FDSRCS 1964; FRACDS 1966; FRCPath 1982; FFOP (RCPA) 1996; ILTM. Res. Fellow in Pathology, Univ. of Melbourne, 1961–63; Lectr in Dental Surgery, UCL, 1963–64; Scientific Officer, MRC Dental Res. Unit, Bristol, 1964–67; London Hospital Medical College: Reader in Experimental Oral Path., 1968–76; Prof. of Oral Path., 1976–83; Hon. Dir, MRC Dental Res. Unit, 1983–93; Governor, 1983 (Chm., Academic Div. of Dentistry, 1983); Chm., London Hosp. Div. of Dentistry, 1981–83; Nuffield Res. Prof. of Dental Science, RCS, 1984–2003; Dir of Res. and Univ. Postgrad. Educn, Dental Inst., KCL, 1994–95; Prof. of Oral Pathology, King's Coll. Sch. of Medicine and Dentistry, subseq. GKT Dental Inst. of KCL, Univ. of London, 1994–2003; Prof. of Oral Health Scis, GKT Dental Inst., KCL, 2003–05. Hon. Consultant Dental Surgeon: Royal London (formerly London) Hosp., 1968–; King's Healthcare NHS Trust, 1993–2005. Consultant, Fédération Dentaire Internationale, 1984– (Comr, 1996–); Academician, Argentine Acad. of Medicine, 2004. Consultant in Oral Health, WHO, 1984–; Dir, WHO Collaborating Centre for Oral Cancer and Precancer, 1995–2005. Pres., British Soc. of Periodontology, 1992–93. Chm., UK Cttee, Royal Australasian Coll. of Dental Surgeons, 1981–83; FRSocMed (Mem. Council, 2001–; Mem. Council, Section of Odontology, 1972–91 (Pres., 1988–89 and 2004–05)); Founder FMedSci 1998. John Tomes Medal, BDA, 2005; Dist. Scientist Award, Oral Medicine and Pathology, IADR, 2005. Member, Editorial Board: Jl of Oral Pathology, 1982–93; Jl of Periodontal Research, 1986–96 (Associate Ed., 1993–); Jl of Clin. Periodontology, 1990–; Oral Oncology, 1992–; Editor in Chief, Oral Diseases, 1994–. *Publications:* (jtly) The Oral Mucosa in Health and Disease, 1975; (jtly) The Human Oral Mucosa: structure, metabolism and function, 1976; (jtly) Dental Caries: aetiology, pathology and prevention, 1979; (ed jtly) Oral Diseases in the Tropics, 1992; (ed) Detection of High Risk Groups for Oral Diseases, 3 vols, 1991; Oral Cancer, 2000; articles in scientific jls. *Recreations:* music, theatre, visual arts, the environment, the Third World.

JOHNSON, Nichola; Director of Museology, since 1993, Director, Sainsbury Centre for Visual Arts, since 1996, University of East Anglia; *b* 21 May 1945; *d* of John Nicholas Healey and Jessica (*née* Horrocks); *m* 1965, M. D. Johnson (marr. diss. 1971); one *s* one *d*. *Educ:* Ipswich High Sch.; Univ. of Sheffield (BA); Univ. of Essex (MA). Lectr, Dept of Art History, Univ. of Essex, 1980–83; Hd, Dept of Later London History, Mus. of London, 1983–93. Chair: mda, 1998–2003; Univ. Museums Gp, 2003–; Clore Leadership Prog., 2004–. *Publications:* University Museums in the United Kingdom, 2004; contribs to professional jls and edited volumes. *Recreations:* music-making, driving in the USA, long-distance walking. *Address:* Sainsbury Centre for Visual Arts, University of East Anglia, Norwich NR4 7TJ. *T:* (01603) 593193.

JOHNSON, Nicholas Robert; QC 2006; a barrister, since 1987; *b* 28 Aug. 1964; *s* of Rev. Robin E. H. Johnson and Joyce Verry Johnson; *m* 2001, Jane Woodfine; one *s* two *d*. *Educ:* St Paul's Cathedral Choir Sch.; Manchester Grammar Sch.; Leeds Univ. (BA Hist. 1985); Poly. of Central London (Dip. Law 1986). Called to the Bar, Inner Temple, 1987. *Recreation:* catching up. *Address:* 1st Floor, 25–27 Castle Street, Liverpool L2 4TA. *T:* (0151) 227 5661.

JOHNSON, Sir Patrick Eliot, 8th Bt *cr* 1818, of Bath; *b* 11 June 1955; *s* of Sir Robin Eliot Johnson, 7th Bt and of Barbara Alfreda, *d* of late Alfred T. Brown; *S* father, 1989, but his name does not appear on the Official Roll of the Baronetage; *m* 1980, Rose (marr. diss. 1989), *d* of Olav Alfheim; twin *s*. *Heir:* *s* Richard Eliot Johnson, *b* 8 Jan. 1983.

JOHNSON, Prof. Paul A., DPhil; Vice-Chancellor and President, La Trobe University, Australia, since 2007; *b* Bath, 26 Nov. 1956; *s* of Alan and Joyce Johnson; *m* Dr Susannah Morris; one *s* one *d*. *Educ:* St John's Coll., Oxford (BA); Nuffield Coll., Oxford (DPhil). Res. Fellow, Nuffield Coll., Oxford, 1981–84; London School of Economics: Lectr in Social Hist., 1984–94; Reader in Econ. Hist., 1994–99; Prof. of Econ. Hist., 1999–2007; Dep. Dir, 2004–07. *Publications:* Saving and Spending, 1985; Ageing and Economic Welfare, 1992; Twentieth Century Britain, 1994; Old Age: from antiquity to post-modernity, 1998; Cambridge Economic History of Modern Britain, 2004. *Recreation:* my family. *Address:* La Trobe University, Melbourne, Vic 3086, Australia. *T:* (3) 94792000, *Fax:* (3) 94710093; *e-mail:* p.johnson@latrobe.edu.au.

JOHNSON, Paul (Bede); author; *b* 2 Nov. 1928; *s* of William Aloysius and Anne Johnson; *m* 1957, Marigold Hunt, MBE; three *s* one *d*. *Educ:* Stonyhurst; Magdalen Coll., Oxford. Asst Exec. Editor, Réalités, 1952–55; Editorial Staff, New Statesman, 1955, Dir, Statesman and Nation Publishing Co., 1965, Editor of the New Statesman, 1965–70. Member: Royal Commn on the Press, 1974–77; Cable Authority, 1984–90. *Publications:* The Suez War, 1957; Journey into Chaos, 1958; Left of Centre, 1960; Merrie England, 1964; Statesmen and Nations, 1971; The Offshore Islanders, 1972; (with G. Gale) The Highland Jaunt, 1973; Elizabeth I, 1974; A Place in History, 1974; Pope John XXIII, 1975 (Yorkshire Post Book of the Year Award, 1975); A History of Christianity, 1976; Enemies of Society, 1977; The National Trust Book of British Castles, 1978; The Recovery of Freedom, 1980; British Cathedrals, 1980; Ireland: Land of Troubles, 1980; Pope John Paul II and the Catholic Restoration, 1982; A History of the Modern World from 1917 to the 1980s, 1983, rev. edn 1991; The Pick of Paul Johnson, 1985; Oxford Book of Political Anecdotes, 1986; A History of the Jews, 1987; Intellectuals, 1988; The Birth of the Modern: world society 1815–30, 1991; Wake Up Britain! A Latterday Pamphlet, 1994; The Quest for God: a personal pilgrimage, 1996; To Hell With Picasso!: essays from the Spectator, 1996; A History of the American People, 1997; The Renaissance, 2000; Napoleon, 2002; Art: a new history, 2003; Washington, 2003; The Vanished Landscape: a 1930s childhood in the Potteries, 2004; Heroes: from Alexander the Great to Mae West, 2008. *Recreations:* hill-walking, painting. *Address:* 29 Newton Road, W2 5JR. *T:* (020) 7229 3859; The Coach House, Over Stowey, near Bridgwater, Somerset TA5 1HA. *T:* (01278) 732393.

See also D. B. Johnson, L. O. Johnson.

JOHNSON, Paul Gavin; Senior Associate, Frontier Economics Ltd, since 2007; Research Fellow, Institute for Fiscal Studies, since 2007; *b* 5 Jan. 1967; *s* of Robert and Joy Johnson; partner, Lorraine Dearden; four *s*. *Educ:* Keble Coll., Oxford (BA 1st. Cl. Hons PPE);

Birkbeck Coll., London (MSc Econs). Inst. for Fiscal Studies, 1988–98 (Dep. Dir, 1996–98); Hd, Econs of Financial Regulation, FSA, 1999–2000; Chief Economist, and Dir, Analytical Services, DFEE, subseq. DFES, 2000–04; Dir, Public Services, and Chief Micro-Economist, HM Treasury, 2004–07; Dep. Hd, Govt Econ. Service, 2005–07. Mem., ESRC, 2002–07. *Publications:* (jtly) Inequality in the UK, 1996; (jtly) Pension Systems and Retirement Incomes Across OECD Countries, 2001; contrib. numerous articles to econs jls and in press. *Address:* Frontier Economics Ltd, 71 High Holborn, WC1V 6DA.

JOHNSON, Peter Michael; Director, since 1999, and Chairman, since 2007, DS Smith plc (formerly David S. Smith (Hldgs)); *b* 3 July 1947; *s* of late James and Nancy Johnson; *m* 1972, Janet Esther Ashman; two *s* one *d*. *Educ:* Bromley Grammar Sch.; St Edmund Hall, Oxford (MA PPE, BPhil Econs). With Unilever PLC, 1970–73; Redland PLC, 1973–96: Gp Treas., 1978–81; Dir of Planning, 1981–84; Man. Dir, Redland Bricks Ltd, 1984–88; Dir, Redland PLC, 1988–96; Chief Executive: Rugby Gp PLC, 1996–2000; George Wimpey Plc, 2000–06. Mem., Supervisory Bd, Wienerberger AG, 2005–. President: Fédération Européene des Fabricants de Tuiles et de Briques, 1994–96; Nat. Council of Building Material Producers, 1997–2000; Mem., Council for Industry and Higher Educn, 2001–06. *Recreations:* music, tennis, cricket.

JOHNSON, Peter Michael; Headmaster, Millfield School, 1998–2008; *b* 21 Dec. 1947; *s* of Joseph William (Johnnie) Johnson and Dorothy Johnson; *m* 1969, Christine Anne Rayment; two *s*. *Educ:* Bec Grammar Sch.; Mansfield Coll., Oxford (Army Scholarship; MA Geog.; PGCE; Rugby Blue, 1968, 1969, 1970, Judo Blue, 1968, 1969). Commnd Parachute Bde, 1971; served 7 Parachute Regt, RHA, 1971–76 (emergency tours in NI, 1972 and 1974 (GSM)); retd in rank of Captain. Radley College: Asst Master, 1976–91; Housemaster, 1983–91; Headmaster, Wrekin Coll., 1991–98. Oxford Univ. Rep. on RFU Council, 1987–98; Trustee: Nat. Centre for Schs and Youth Rugby, 1992–98; Raleigh Internat., 2003–05; Wells Cathedral, 2004–. Capt., Northampton FC, 1978–79. FRSA. *Recreations:* gardening, music, oenology, golf. *Address:* Borrowdale, Mill Hill, Stoke Gabriel, Devon TQ9 6RY. *Clubs:* East India; Vincent's (Oxford); Free Foresters.

JOHNSON, Peter William; Chairman: Inchcape plc, since 2006 (Chief Executive, 1999–2005); Rank plc, since 2007; *b* 2 Nov. 1947; *s* of Alfred and Emily Johnson; *m* 1973, Ann Gillian Highley; one *s* one *d*. *Educ:* Hull Univ. (BSc Hons Econs). Mgt trainee, 1969, sen. mgt posts, 1970–79, British Leyland; Sales Dir, Austin-Morris, 1980–84; Export Dir, Austin-Rover, 1984–86; Sales Dir, Rover Gp, 1986–88; Chief Executive: Applied Chemicals, 1988–90; Marshall Gp, 1990–94; Inchcape Motors International, 1994–99. Non-executive Director: Wates Gp, 2002–; Bunzl plc, 2006–; Chm., Automotive Skills Ltd, 2003–. Vice Pres., Motor Agents Assoc., 1992–95. FIMI 1984 (Chm., 1991–95); MInstD 1990. *Recreations:* golf, reading, travel. *Address:* Inchcape plc, 22A St James's Square, SW1Y 5LP. *T:* (020) 7546 8418. *Clubs:* Royal Automobile; Redditch Golf.

JOHNSON, Richard; National Hunt jockey; *b* 21 July 1977; *m* 2007, Fiona, *d* of Noel Chance. Equal 10th in list of winning jockeys while still an apprentice, 1995–96; 2nd, 1998–99, 1999–2000, 2002–03, 2005–06, 2006–07 and 2007–08 seasons; winner: Cheltenham Gold Cup on Looks Like Trouble, 2000; Queen Mother Champion Chase on Flagship Uberalles, 2002; Champion Hurdle on Rooster Booster, 2003. Rode 1,000th winner, Stratford, 2003. *Publication:* (with Alan Lee) Out of the Shadows, 2002. *Address:* c/o Nicholas Whittle Communications, Bucklow Hill, Knutsford, Cheshire WA16 6PP.

JOHNSON, Richard John M.; *see* McGregor-Johnson.

JOHNSON, Richard Keith; actor and producer; *b* 30 July; *s* of Keith Holcombe and Frances Louisa Olive Johnson; *m* 1st, 1957, Sheila Sweet (marr. diss); one *s* one *d*; 2nd, 1965, Kim Novak (marr. diss.); 3rd, 1982, Marie-Louise Norlund (marr. diss.); one *s* one *d*. *Educ:* Parkfield School; Felsted School; RADA. RN, 1945–48. 1st stage appearance, Opera House, Manchester, 1944; repertory, Haymarket, 1944–45; *stage:* contract, Royal Shakespeare Theatre, 1957–62; Antony in Antony and Cleopatra, RSC, 1972–73, and 1992–93; NT, 1976–78; The War That Still Goes On, Young Vic, 1991; King, in All's Well that Ends Well, RSC, 1992–93; An Inspector Calls, Aldwych, 1994; The Rivals, Albery, 1994–95; Freddie in Gangster No 1, Almeida, 1995; Tyrone in Long Day's Journey into Night, Young Vic, 1996; Serebyakov in Uncle Vanya, Albery, 1996; Tusker in Staying On, nat. tour, 1997; Atticus in To Kill a Mockingbird, nat. tour, 1997; Sir Leonard Darwin in Plenty, Albery, 1999; Dr Dorn in The Seagull, RSC, 2000; Heinrich Mann in Tales from Hollywood, Donmar, 2001; Mrs Warren's Profession, Strand, 2002; The Hollow Crown, RSC, 2003, 2005; And Then There Were None, Gielgud, 2005; Victory, Th. Royal, Bath, 2007; *films:* MGM contract, 1959–65; acted in: The Haunting; Moll Flanders; Operation Crossbow; Khartoum; The Pumpkin Eater; Danger Route; Deadlier than the Male; Oedipus the King; Hennessy (also wrote original story); Aces High; The Four Feathers; Happy Days, 2000; Tomb Raider, 2001; produced: Turtle Diary; Castaway (Exec. Producer); The Lonely Passion of Judith Hearne; *television:* Rembrandt (title rôle); Hamlet (King); Antony and Cleopatra (Antony); The Member for Chelsea (title rôle); The Camomile Lawn (Oliver); Anglo-Saxon Attitudes (Gerald); Breaking the Code (Knox); The Robinsons (Hector Robinson); Wallis and Edward (Stanley Baldwin). Jt Founder, United British Artists, 1982. Member, Council: BAFTA, 1977–79; RADA, 2000–. *Recreations:* reading, gardening, travelling. *Address:* c/o ConwayVan Gelder Grant Ltd, 18–21 Jermyn Street, SW1Y 6HP.

JOHNSON, Sir Robert (Lionel), Kt 1989; a Justice of the High Court, Family Division, 1989–2004; *b* 9 Feb. 1933; *er s* of late Edward Harold Johnson, MSc, FRIC, and of Ellen Lydiate Johnson, Cranleigh; *m* 1957, Linda Mary, *er d* of late Charles William Bennie and Ena Ethel Bennie, Egglescliffe; one *d* (and one *s* one *d* decd). *Educ:* Watford Grammar Sch. (1940–51); London Sch. of Econs and Polit. Science. 5th Royal Inniskilling Dragoon Guards, 1955–57, Captain; ADC to GOC-in-C Northern Comd, 1956–57; Inns of Court Regt, 1957–64. Called to the Bar, Gray's Inn, 1957, Bencher, 1986; QC 1978; a Recorder, 1977–89. Jun. Counsel to Treasury in Probate Matters, 1975–78; Legal Assessor, GNC, 1977–82. Chairman: Bar Fees and Legal Aid Cttee, 1984–86 (Vice-Chm., 1982–84); Family Law Bar Assoc., 1984–86; Family Law Cttee, Justice, 1990–93; Mem., Bar Council, 1981–88; Vice Chm., 1987, Chm., 1988, Gen. Council of Bar. Member: Supreme Court Procedure Cttee, 1982–87; Law Soc. Legal Aid Cttee, 1981–87; No 1 Legal Aid Area Cttee, 1980–87; Co-Chm., Civil and Family Cttee, Judicial Studies Bd, 1989–94. Pres., English Chapter, Internat. Acad. of Matrimonial Lawyers, 1986–89. Sec., Internat. Cystic Fibrosis Assoc., 1984–90; Trustee: Cystic Fibrosis Res. Trust, 1964–; Robert Luff Charitable Foundn, 1977–. *Publications:* (with James Comyn) Wills & Intestacies, 1970; Contract, 1975; (with Malcolm Stitcher) Atkin's Trade, Labour and Employment, 1975. *Recreations:* charitable work, gardening. *Address:* Forest Gate, Pluckley, Kent TN27 0RU.

JOHNSON, Prof. Roger Paul, FREng; Professor of Civil Engineering, University of Warwick, 1971–98, now Emeritus; *b* 12 May 1931; *s* of Norman Eric Ernest Johnson and Eleanor Florence (*née* Paul); *m* 1958, Diana June (*née* Perkins); three *s*. *Educ:* Cranleigh Sch., Surrey; Jesus Coll., Cambridge (BA 1953; MA 1957). FIStructE 1972; FICE 1979; FREng (FEng 1986). Holloway Bros (London), Civil Engineering Contractor, 1953–55; Ove Arup and Partners, Consulting Engineers, 1956–59; Lectr in Engineering, Cambridge Univ., 1959–71. Visiting Professor: Univ. of Sydney, 1982–83; Univ. of Adelaide, 1995, 1999. Gold Medal, IStructE, 2006. *Publications:* Structural Concrete, 1967; Composite Structures of Steel and Concrete, vol. 1, 1975, 3rd edn 2004, vol. 2 (with R. J. Buckby), 1979, 2nd edn 1986; (with D. Anderson) Designers' Handbook to Eurocode 4, 1994; Designers' Guide to Eurocode 4, Pt 1 (with D. Anderson), 2004, Pt 2 (with C. R. Hendy), 2006; contribs to learned jls. *Recreations:* music, travel, mountain walking. *Address:* School of Engineering, University of Warwick, Coventry CV4 7AL. *T:* (024) 7652 3129.

JOHNSON, Stanley, CBE 1970; FCA; FCIT; Managing Director, British Transport Docks Board, 1967–75; *b* 10 Nov. 1912; *s* of late Robert and Janet Mary Johnson; *m* 1st, 1940, Sheila McLean Bald (*d* 1994); two *s* two *d*; 2nd, 1998, Ellen Elaine Sholten; three step *s* one step *d*. *Educ:* King George V Sch., Southport. Served as Lieut (S) RINVR, 1942–45. Joined Singapore Harbour Board, 1939; Asst Gen. Man. 1952; Chm. and Gen. Man. 1958–59; Chief Docks Man., Hull Docks, 1962; Asst Gen. Man. 1963, Mem. and Dep. Man. Dir 1966, British Transport Docks Board. Chm. Major Ports Cttee, Dock and Harbour Authorities Assoc., 1971–72. Mem., Exec. Council, British Ports Assoc., 1973–75; Vice-Pres., Internat. Assoc. of Ports and Harbours, 1975–77. Vice-Pres., CIT, 1973–75. *Recreations:* walking, reading, travel. *Address:* 2425 20th Street, Apt 113, Vero Beach, FL 32960, USA.

JOHNSON, Stanley Patrick; author and environmentalist; *b* 18 Aug. 1940; *s* of Wilfred Johnson and Irène (*née* Williams); *m* 1st, 1963, Charlotte Offlow Fawcett (marr. diss.); three *s* one *d*; 2nd, 1981, Mrs Jennifer Kidd; one *s* one *d*. *Educ:* Sherborne Sch.; Exeter Coll., Oxford (Trevelyan Schol., Sen. Classics Schol.; Newdigate Prize for Poetry, 1962; MA 1963; Dip. Agric. Econs 1965); Harkness Fellow, USA, 1963–64. World Bank, Washington, 1966–68; Project Dir, UNA-USA Nat. Policy Panel on World Population, 1968–69; Mem. Conservative Research Dept, 1969–70; Staff of Internat. Planned Parenthood Fedn, London, 1971–73; Consultant to UN Fund for Population Activities, 1971–73; Mem. Countryside Commn, 1971–73; Head of Prevention of Pollution and Nuisances Div., EEC, 1973–77; Adviser to Head of Environment and Consumer Protection Service, EEC, 1977–79; MEP (C) Wight and Hants E, 1979–84; Advr to Dir Gen. for Envmt, Civil Protection and Nuclear Safety, EEC, 1984–90; Dir for Energy Policy, EEC, 1990; Special Advr, Coopers & Lybrand, Deloitte, 1991; Dir, Envmtl Resources Mgt, 1992–94. Contested (C) Teignbridge, 2005. Richard Martin Award, RSPCA, 1982; Greenpeace Award, 1984. *Publications:* Life Without Birth, 1970; The Green Revolution, 1972; The Politics of the Environment, 1973; (ed) The Population Problem, 1973; The Pollution Control Policy of the EEC, 1979, 3rd edn 1989; Antarctica—the last great wilderness, 1985; (jtly) The Environmental Policy of the EEC, 1989, 2nd edn 1995; The Earth Summit: the United Nations Conference on Environment and Development, 1993; World Population—turning the tide, 1994; The Politics of Population, 1995; *novels:* Gold Drain, 1967; Panther Jones for President, 1968; God Bless America, 1974; The Doomsday Deposit, 1980; The Marburg Virus, 1982; Tunnel, 1984; The Commissioner, 1987; Dragon River, 1989; Icecap, 1999. *Recreations:* writing, travel. *Address:* Nethercote, Winsford, Minehead, Somerset TA24 7HZ; 34 Park Village East, NW1 7PZ. *T:* (020) 7380 0989. *Clubs:* Beefsteak, Garrick.

See also A. B. de P. Johnson.

JOHNSON, Terry; playwright and director; *b* 20 Dec. 1955; *s* of Harry Douglas Johnson and Winifred Mary Johnson (*née* Wood); one *d* by Marion Bailey. *Educ:* Birmingham Univ. (BA 2nd cl. Drama and Th. Arts). Actor, 1971–75; *playwright:* Amabel, Bush Th., 1972; Insignificance, Royal Court (Most Promising Playwright, Evening Standard Award), 1982 (screenplay, 1985); Unsuitable for Adults, Bush, Cries from the Mammal House, Royal Ct, 1984; (jtly) Tuesday's Child, Stratford Th. Royal, 1986; Imagine Drowning, Hampstead (John Whiting Award), 1991; Hysteria, Royal Ct, 1993 (Meyer-Whitworth Award, 1993; Best Comedy, Olivier Award, and Best Play, Writers' Guild, 1994); (also dir.) Dead Funny, Savoy, 1994 (Best Play, Writers' Guild, 1994; Best New Play, Critics' Circle, and Playwright of the Year, Lloyds Pvte Banking, 1995); adaptation (also dir.), The London Cuckolds, 1997, (also dir.) Cleo, Camping, Emmanuelle and Dick, 1998 (Best Comedy, Olivier Award, 1999), RNT; adaptation (also dir.), The Graduate, Gielgud, 2000; Hitchcock Blonde, Royal Court, 2003; plays also performed in USA, Europe, Australia, Canada and NZ; other *plays directed* include: The Memory of Water, Vaudeville, 1996; The Libertine, Chicago, 1996; Elton John's Glasses, Queen's, 1997; Sparkleshark, RNT, 1999; Entertaining Mr Sloane, Arts, 2001; One Flew Over the Cuckoo's Nest, Gielgud, 2004; Dumb Show, Royal Court, 2004; Piano/Forte, 2006; Whipping It Up, 2006; *television:* (dir.) Way Upstream, 1988; wrote and directed: Blood and Water, 1995; Cor Blimey!, 2000; Not Only But Always, 2004; The Man Who Lost His Head, 2007; screenplay, The Bite, 1994. *Publications:* Insignificance, 1982; Cries from the Mammal House, 1984; Unsuitable for Adults, 1985; Tuesday's Child, 1987; Imagine Drowning, 1991; Hysteria, 1993; Dead Funny, 1994; Johnson: Plays One, 1993; The London Cuckolds, 1997; Johnson: Plays Two, 1998; Cleo, Camping, Emmanuelle and Dick, 1998; The Graduate, 2000; Hitchcock Blonde, 2003; Piano/Forte, 2006.

JOHNSON, Sir Vassel (Godfrey), Kt 1994; CBE 1979 (OBE 1970); JP; Director: Fidelity Bank (Cayman) Ltd (formerly British American Bank), 1983–2005, now Director Emeritus; Monetary Authority, Cayman Islands, 1997–2000; *b* 18 Jan. 1922; *s* of late Charles McKintha Johnson and of Theresa Virginia Johnson (*née* McDoom); *m* 1952, Rita Joanna Hinds; two *s* four *d* (and one *s* decd). *Educ:* Govt Secondary Sch., Grand Cayman; Bennett Coll., England; Wolsey Hall; Sussex Univ. Entered Cayman Is CS, 1942; transferred to Cayman Co. of Jamaica Home Guard, 1942–45; Clerical Officer, Dept of Treasury, Customs and PO, 1945–55; Asst to Dep. Treas., 1955–59; Clerk of Courts, 1959–60; Public Recorder, 1962–76; Treas. and Collector of Taxes, 1965–82; Hd of Exchange Control, 1966–80; Inspector of Banks and Trust Cos, 1966–73; Chm., Cayman Is Currency Bd, 1971–82; Mem., Exec. Council, resp. for Finance and Develt, 1972–82; Actg Gov., Cayman Is, 1977; Chm., Govt Vehicles Funding Scheme, 1977–82; retd from CS, 1983. Chm., Public Service Commn, 1983–84; MLA, George Town, 1984–88; Mem., Exec. Council, resp. for Develt and Nat. Resources, 1984–88. Cayman Airways Ltd: Founding Dir, 1968; Chm., 1971–77 and 1984–85; Chm., Cayman Is Corp. (Airport), 1969–77; Trustee, Swiss Bank & Trust Corp., 1983–97; Man. Dir, Montpelier Properties (Cayman) Ltd, 1983–97. JP Cayman Is, 1977. Chm., Bd of Govs, Cayman Prep. Sch., 1982–84 and 1993–95. Silver Jubilee Medal, 1977. *Publications:* Cayman Islands Economic and Financial Review 1904–1981, 1982; As I See It: how Cayman became a leading financial centre (autobiog.), 2001. *Recreations:* bridge, church work (Senior Elder, United Church). *Address:* PO Box 78G, Grand Cayman, Cayman Islands. *T:* 9499217, *Fax:* 9459326.

JOHNSON, Wendy Rosalind; *see* James, W. R.

JOHNSON, Prof. William, DSc, MA; FRS 1982; FREng, FIMechE; Professor of Mechanics, Engineering Department, Cambridge University, 1975–82, now Professor Emeritus; Professorial Fellow, Fitzwilliam College, Cambridge, 1975–82; *b* 20 April 1922;

er s of James Johnson and Elizabeth Johnson (*née* Riley); *m* 1946, Heather Marie (*née* Thornber) (*d* 2004); three *s* two *d*. *Educ:* Manchester Central High Sch.; Manchester Coll. of Science and Technology (BScTech 1943; DSc 1960); BSc Maths, London (ext.) 1949; UCL (Hist. and Phil. of Sci. MSc course, 1950; Fellow, 1982); MA Cantab. CEng, FREng (FEng 1983). Commnd REME, UK, Italy and Austria, 1943–47. Asst Principal, Administrative Grade, Home Civil Service, 1948–50; Lecturer, Northampton Polytechnic, London, 1950–51; Lectr in Engineering, Sheffield Univ., 1952–56; Senior Lectr in Mechanical Engineering, Manchester Univ., 1956–60; Prof. of Mechanical Engrg, 1960–75, Dir of Medical Engrg, 1973–75, UMIST. Visiting Professor: McMaster Univ., Canada, 1969; Springer Prof., Univ. of Calif, Berkeley, 1980; Singapore, 1982; Allied Irish Banks Prof., Univ. of Belfast, 1983; UMIST, 1983–94; Industrial Engrg Dept, Purdue Univ., Indiana, 1984 and 1985; Taiwan, 1985; United Technologies Dist. Prof. of Engrg, Purdue Univ., 1988 and 1989. Hon. Sec., Yorks Br. of IMechE, 1953–56, and Chm., NW Br., 1974–75; Vis. for DoI to Prodn Engrg Res. Assoc. and Machine Tool Res. Assoc., 1973–75; President: Manchester and Salford Med. Engrg Club, 1971–72; Manchester Assoc. of Engrs, 1972–73; Manchester Technol. Assoc., 1983–84. Founder, and Editor-in-Chief: Internat. Jl Mech. Sciences, 1960–87; Internat. Jl Impact Engineering, 1983–87; Chm., Internat. Jl Mech. Engrg Educn, 1960–84. For. Fellow, Nat. Acad. of Athens, 1982; For. Mem., Russian Acad. of Scis, Ural Br., 1993; Hon. Mem., Indian Nat. Acad. Engrg, 1999; Amer. Biog. Hon. Res. Bd of Advrs. Hon. DTech Bradford, 1976; Hon. DEng: Sheffield, 1986; UMIST, 1995. Premium Award, Jl RAeS, 1956; T. Constantine Medal, Manchester Assoc. of Engrs, 1962; Bernard Hall Prize (jt), IMechE, 1965–66 and 1966–67; James Clayton Fund Prize (jt), IMechE, 1972 and 1978; Safety in Mech. Engrg Prize, (jt) 1980, 1991; Silver Medal, Inst. of Sheet Metal Engrg, 1987; James Clayton Prize, IMechE, 1987; W. Johnson Gold Medal for Lifetime Achievement in Materials Processing Technology, Dublin, 1995; Engr-Historian Award, ASME, 2000; Sustainability Award, 2007. *Publications:* Plasticity for Mechanical Engineers (with P. B. Mellor), 1962; Mechanics of Metal Extrusion (with H. Kudo), 1962; Plane Strain Slip Line Fields (with R. Sowerby and J. B. Haddow), 1970; Impact Strength of Materials, 1972; Engineering Plasticity (with P. B. Mellor), 1973; Lectures in Engineering Plasticity (with A. G. Mamalis), 1978; Crashworthiness of Vehicles (with A. G. Mamalis), 1978; Plane-Strain Slip-Line Fields for Metal-Deformation Processes (with R. Sowerby and R. Venter), 1982; Collected Works on B. Robins and G. Hutton, 2001; Record and Services, Satisfactory (memoir), 2003; papers in mechanics of metal forming, impact engineering, mechanics of sports and games, solids, medical and bioengineering, and history of engineering mechanics. *Address:* 5 Epworth Court, King Street, Cambridge CB1 1LR.

JOHNSON, (Willis) Merwyn; Agent General for Saskatchewan in the United Kingdom, 1977–83; *b* 9 May 1923; *s* of Robert Arthur Johnson and Gudborg Kolbinson; *m* 1946, Laura Elaine Aseltine; two *s* two *d*. *Educ:* McKenzie High Sch., Kindersley; Univ. of Saskatchewan. BSA, BA. Farmer, Saskatchewan. MP for Kindersley, Parliament of Canada, 1953–58. *Recreations:* fishing, golf.

JOHNSON-FERGUSON, Sir Ian (Edward), 4th Bt *cr* 1906, of Springkell, Dumfries, of Kenyon, Newchurch-in-Culceth, Lancaster, and of Wiston, Lanark; *b* 1 Feb. 1932; *s* of Sir Neil Edward Johnson-Ferguson, 3rd Bt, TD and Sheila Marion (*d* 1985), *er d* of Col H. S. Jervis, MC; *S* father, 1992; *m* 1964, Rosemary Teresa, *yr d* of C. J. Whitehead; three *s*. *Educ:* Ampleforth Coll.; Trinity Coll., Cambridge (BA 1953); Imperial Coll., London (DIC Geophysics 1954). Royal Dutch Shell, 1954–62; IBM UK Ltd, 1963–90. *Heir: s* Major Mark Edward Johnson-Ferguson, RE [*b* 14 Aug. 1965; *m* 1995, Dr Julia Catherine, *d* of T. D. Getley; three *d*].

JOHNSON-LAIRD, Prof. Philip Nicholas, FRS 1991; FBA 1986; Stuart Professor of Psychology, Princeton University, since 1994 (Professor of Psychology, since 1989); *b* 12 Oct. 1936; *s* of Eric Johnson-Laird and Dorothy (*née* Blackett); *m* 1959, Maureen Mary Sullivan; one *s* one *d*. *Educ:* Culford Sch.; University Coll. London (Rosa Morison Medal, 1964; James Sully Schol., 1964–66; BA (Hons) 1964; PhD 1967; Fellow, 1994). MBPsS 1962. 10 years of misc. jobs, as surveyor, musician, hosp. porter (alternative to Nat. Service), librarian, before going to university. Asst Lectr, then Lectr, in Psychol., UCL, 1966–73; Reader, 1973, Prof., 1978, in Exptl Psychol., Univ. of Sussex; Asst Dir, MRC Applied Psychology Unit, Cambridge, 1983–89; Fellow, Darwin Coll., Cambridge, 1984–89. Vis. Mem., Princeton Inst. for Advanced Study, 1971–72; Vis. Fellow, Stanford Univ., 1980; Visiting Professor: Stanford Univ., 1985; Princeton Univ., 1986. Member: Psychol. Cttee, SSRC, 1975–79; Linguistics Panel, SSRC, 1980–82; Adv. Council, Internat. Assoc. for Study of Attention and Performance, 1984. Member: Linguistics Assoc., 1967; Exptl Psychol. Soc., 1968; Cognitive Sci. Soc., 1980; Assoc. for Computational Linguistics, 1981; Amer. Philosophical Soc. 2006; Nat. Acad. of Scis, 2007. Hon. DPhil: Göteborg, 1983; Padua, 1997; Madrid, 2000; Dublin, 2000; Ghent, 2002; Palermo, 2005. Spearman Medal, 1974, President's Award, 1985, BPsS; International Prize, Fondation Fyssen, 2002. *Publications:* (ed jtly) Thinking and Reasoning, 1968; (with P. C. Wason) Psychology and Reasoning, 1972; (with G. A. Miller) Language and Perception, 1976; (ed jtly) Thinking, 1977; Mental Models, 1983; The Computer and the Mind, 1988; (with Ruth Byrne) Deduction, 1991; Human and Machine Thinking, 1993; How We Reason, 2006; contribs to psychol, linguistic and cognitive sci. jls, reviews in lit. jls. *Recreations:* talking, arguing, laughing, playing modern jazz. *Address:* Department of Psychology, Princeton University, Princeton, NJ 08544–1010, USA. *T:* (609) 2584432.

JOHNSON SMITH, Rt Hon. Sir Geoffrey, Kt 1982; PC 1996; DL; *b* 16 April 1924; *s* of late J. Johnson Smith; *m* Jeanne Pomeroy, MD; two *s* one *d*. *Educ:* Charterhouse; Lincoln Coll., Oxford. Served War of 1939–45: Royal Artillery, 1942–47; Capt. RA, 1946. BA Hons, Politics, Philosophy and Economics, Oxford, 1949. Mem., Oxford Union Soc. Debating Team, USA, 1949. Information Officer, British Information Services, San Francisco, 1950–52; Mem. Production Staff, Current Affairs Unit, BBC TV, 1953–54; London County Councillor, 1955–58; Interviewer, Reporter, BBC TV, 1955–59. MP (C): Holborn and St Pancras South, 1959–64; East Grinstead, Feb. 1965–1983; Wealden, 1983–2001. PPS, Board of Trade and Min. of Pensions, 1960–63; Opposition Whip, 1965; Parly Under-Sec. of State for Defence for the Army, MoD, 1971–72; Parly Sec., CSD, 1972–74. Chm., Cons. Back-bench Defence Cttee, 1988–93 (Vice-Chm., 1980–88); Chm., Select Cttee on Members' Interests, 1980–95; Vice-Chm., 1922 Cttee, 1988–2001 (Mem. Exec., 1979–2001). A Vice-Chm., Conservative Party, 1965–71. Member: IBA Gen. Adv. Council, 1975–80; N Atlantic Assembly, 1980–2001 (Chm., Military Cttee, 1985–89; Leader, UK Delegn to Assembly, 1987–97; Treas., 1996–2001). Governor, BFI, 1980–88. Trustee, Handicapped Anglers, 1985–; Chm., Salmon and Trout Trust, 1987–2003. Pres., High Weald Area of Outstanding Natural Beauty, 2000. Freeman, City of London, 1980. DL East Sussex, 1986. *Club:* Travellers.

JOHNSTON; *see* Campbell-Johnston.

JOHNSTON; *see* Lawson Johnston.

JOHNSTON, Alexander Graham; Sheriff of Strathkelvin at Glasgow, 1985–2005; part-time Sheriff, since 2005; *b* 16 July 1944; *s* of Hon. Lord Kincraig; *m* 1st, 1972, Susan (marr. diss. 1982); two *s*; 2nd, 1982, Angela; two step *d*. *Educ:* Edinburgh Acad.; Strathallan Sch.; Univ. of Edinburgh (LLB); University Coll., Oxford (BA). Admitted as Solicitor and Writer to the Signet, 1971; Partner, Hagart and Burn-Murdoch, Solicitors, Edinburgh, 1972–82. Sheriff of Grampian, Highland and Isles, 1982–85. Editor, Scottish Civil Law Reports, 1987–92. Hon. Fellow, Inst. of Professional Investigators, 1980. *Recreations:* photography, computing and IT, bridge, puzzles. *Address:* 3 North Dean Park Avenue, Bothwell, Lanarkshire G71 8HH. *T:* (01698) 852177; Kincraig, Elie House, Elie, Fife KY9 1ER; *e-mail:* grahamjohnston1@tiscali.co.uk. *Clubs:* Oxford and Cambridge Golfing Society; Vincent's (Oxford).

JOHNSTON, Angela Maureen Howard-; *see* Huth, A. M.

JOHNSTON, Callum William; Secretary and Chief Executive, Central Arbitration Committee, 1999–2002; *b* 15 Sept. 1946; *s* of James Johnston, OBE, and Mary Johnston (*née* Upchurch); *m* 1974, Sarah Motta; one *s* one *d*. *Educ:* Westcliff High Sch.; King Edward VII Sch., Lytham; Durham Univ. (BA Econs and Law 1968); Indiana Univ. (MBA 1970). Financial journalist and broadcaster, 1970–73; DTI, 1973–79 (Private Sec., 1975–79); Cabinet Office, 1979–86; Department of Trade and Industry: British Steel privatisation, 1986–89; UK and EU Co. Law Policy, 1989–90; on secondment to Leyland DAF plc, 1990–92; UK and EU Technol. and IT Security Policy, 1992–95; Pay Dir, 1995–98; Dir, Small Business Policy, 1998–99. *Recreations:* music, walking, cycling, black and white photography. *Address:* 10 Wontner Road, SW17 7QT.

JOHNSTON, Carey Ann; QC 2003. *Educ:* Univ. of Warwick (LLB, LLM). Called to the Bar, Middle Temple, 1977. Specializes in criminal law. *Address:* (chambers) 18 Red Lion Court, EC4A 3EB. *T:* (020) 7520 6000.

JOHNSTON, Catherine Elizabeth, CB 2000; Parliamentary Counsel, since 1994; *b* 4 Jan. 1953; *d* of Sir Alexander Johnston, GCB, KBE and Betty Joan Johnston (*née* Harris), CBE; *m* 1989, Brendan Patrick Keith; one *s* one *d*. *Educ:* St Paul's Girls' Sch.; St Hugh's Coll., Oxford (Scholar 1970; BA 1974). Admitted as solicitor, 1978; joined Parliamentary Counsel Office, 1980; with Law Commn, 1983–85 and 1990–92; on secondment to Office of Parly Counsel, Canberra, 1987–88. *Address:* Office of the Parliamentary Counsel, 36 Whitehall, SW1A 2AY.

JOHNSTON, Prof. David, MD, ChM; FRCS, FRCSE, FRCSGlas; Professor of Surgery and Head of Department, University of Leeds at Leeds General Infirmary, 1977–98; *b* Glasgow, 4 Sept. 1936; *s* of Robert E. and Jean Johnston; *m* (marr. diss); three *s* one *d*; *m* 1987, Dr Maureen Teresa Reynolds; two *s*. *Educ:* Hamilton Acad.; Glasgow Univ. (MB, ChB Hons; MD Hons, ChM). FRCSE 1963; FRCSGlas 1964; FRCS 1979. House Surgeon, Western Infirmary, Glasgow, 1961–62; Res. Asst and Registrar, Univ. Dept of Surg., Leeds Gen. Infirm., 1962–64; Lectr in Surg., Univ. of Sheffield, 1965–68; Sen. Lectr and Consultant, Univ. Dept of Surg., Leeds Gen. Infirm., 1968–75; Prof. of Surg. and Head of Dept, Univ. of Bristol (Bristol Royal Infirm.), 1975–77. *Publications:* papers on physiology and surgery of the stomach, colon and rectum, and on obesity. *Recreations:* reading, running, tennis, fishing. *Address:* 3 The Coppice, Middleton, Ilkley, N Yorks LS29 0EZ. *T:* (01943) 816349.

JOHNSTON, David Alan H.; *see* Hunter Johnston.

JOHNSTON, David Carr; education consultant, since 2002; Chief Education Officer, Manchester City Council, 1998–2002; *b* 18 March 1944; *s* of William and Sarah Johnston; *m* 1969, Jennifer Anne Hopkinson; two *d*. *Educ:* Didsbury Coll. of Educn (Teacher's Cert. 1965); Sheffield Univ. (DipASE 1971); Sheffield Poly. (Dip Educn Mgt 1975); Leicester Univ. (MEd 1982). Asst Teacher, Trafford, Lancs, 1965–67, Sheffield primary schs, 1967–69; Dep. Hd, Park Hill Jun. Sch., Sheffield, 1969–72; Headteacher: Shirebrook Middle Sch., Sheffield, 1972–74; Ballifield Nursery, First and Middle Sch., Sheffield, 1974–79; School Advr, Derbys CC, 1979–84; Sen. Sch. Inspector, 1984–88, Dep. Chief Educn Officer, 1988–92, Manchester City Council; Dir of Educn and Leisure, Salford City Council, 1992–98. *Publications:* Managing Primary Schools, 1985; Managing Primary Schools in the 1990s, 1990. *Recreations:* music appreciation, fell walking, supporting Manchester City FC. *Address:* Totley Hall Croft, Totley, Sheffield S17 4BE.

JOHNSTON, Dr David Eric Lothian; QC (Scot.) 2005; advocate, since 1992; *b* 10 March 1961; *e s* of Thomas Lothian Johnston, *qv*, and Joan (*née* Fahmy). *Educ:* Daniel Stewart's and Melville Coll., Edinburgh; St John's Coll., Cambridge (BA 1982; MA 1986; PhD 1986; LLD 2001). Research Fellow, 1985–89, Fellow, 1993–99, Christ's Coll., Cambridge; Regius Prof. of Civil Law, Univ. of Cambridge, 1993–99. Visiting Fellow: Univ. of Freiburg, 1985–86; Univ. of Michigan Law Sch., 1987; Univ. of Calif, Berkeley, Law Sch., 1996, 1998; Visiting Professor: Paris I, 1999; Paris V, 2000–03; Univ. of Osaka, 2000; Hon. Prof., Edinburgh Univ. Law Sch., 2000–. *Publications:* On a Singular Book of Cervidius Scaevola, 1987; The Roman Law of Trusts, 1988; Roman Law in Context, 1999; Prescription and Limitation, 1999; (ed with R. Zimmermann) Unjustified Enrichment: key issues, 2002; (contrib.) Gloag and Henderson, The Law of Scotland, 11th edn, 2001; articles in learned jls mainly on Roman law and legal history. *Recreations:* music, travel, wine and food. *Address:* Advocates' Library, Parliament House, Edinburgh EH1 1RF. *T:* (0131) 226 5071.

JOHNSTON, David Lawrence, OBE 1997; CEng, FIET; RCNC; Director General, National Inspection Council for Electrical Installation Contracting, 1989–2001; Chairman, National Quality Assurance Ltd, 1993–2001 (Director, 1989–1993); *b* 12 April 1936; *s* of late Herbert David Johnston and Hilda Eleanor Johnston (*née* Wood); *m* 1959, Beatrice Ann Witten; three *d*. *Educ:* Lancastrian Sch., Chichester; King's Coll., Durham (BSc). FIET (FIEE 1980). Electrical Fitter Apprentice, HM Dockyard, Portsmouth, 1951–56; Short Service Commn (Lieut), RN, 1959–62; joined Ministry of Defence, 1962; Overseeing, Wallsend, 1962–63; switchgear design, Bath, 1963–66; Production and Project Mgt, Devonport Dockyard, 1966–73; Dockyard Policy, Bath, 1973–76; Warship System Design, Bath, 1976–79; Production and Planning, Portsmouth Dockyard, 1979–81; Planning and Production, Devonport Dockyard, 1981–84; Asst Under-Sec. of State, and Man. Dir, HM Dockyard, Devonport, 1984–87; Chm., Devonport Dockyard Ltd, Mgt Buy-out Co., 1985–87; Dep. Chm., Devonport Mgt Ltd, 1987–88; mgt consultant, 1988–89. Dep. Chm., NQA, USA Inc., 1998–2001 (Dir, 1993–98); Dir, UK Accreditation Service, 2000–06. Dir, Nat. Supervisory Council, Intruder Alarms Ltd, subseq. Nat. Approval Council, Security Systems Ltd, 1989–96. Chairman: BASEEFA Adv. Council, subseq. Electrical Equipment Certification Service Product Adv. Cttee, HSE, 1990–2002; Adv. Bd, BASEEFA 2001 Ltd, 2003–; Member: Electrical Equipment Certification Adv. Bd, HSE, 1990–2002; HSE Open Govt Complaints Panel, 1995–2002; IEE Wiring Regulations Policy Cttee, 2001–04. *Recreations:* home, hearth and garden, novice golf, watercolour painting. *Address:* Chinley House, 1 Eaton Park Road, Cobham, Surrey KT11 2JG. *T:* (01932) 588269.

JOHNSTON, Prof. David Lloyd; President and Vice-Chancellor, University of Waterloo, since 1999; *b* 28 June 1941; *s* of Lloyd Johnston and Dorothy Stonehouse Johnston; *m* 1963, Sharon Downey; five *d*. *Educ:* Harvard Univ., Cambridge, Mass; Cambridge Univ.; Queen's Univ. at Kingston, Ont. Asst Prof., Faculty of Law, Queen's Univ., Kingston, 1966–68; Faculty of Law, Univ. of Toronto: Asst Prof., 1968–69; Associate Prof., 1969–72; Prof., 1972–74; Dean and Prof., Faculty of Law, Univ. of Western Ont, 1974–79; Prof. of Law, 1979–99, Principal and Vice-Chancellor, 1979–94, McGill Univ. Chairman: Nat. Round Table on Envmt and the Economy, 1988–92; Information Highway Adv. Council, 1994–97; Canadian Inst. for Advanced Res., 1994–99; NeuroScience Network, 1994–98. LLD *hc* Law Soc. of Upper Canada, 1980. *Publications:* Computers and the Law (ed), 1968; Canadian Securities Regulation, 1977; (jtly) Business Associations, 1979, 2nd edn 1989; (with R. Forbes) Canadian Companies and the Stock Exchange, 1980; (jtly) Canadian Securities Regulation, Supplement, 1982; (jtly) Partnerships and Canadian Business Corporations, 1989; (jtly) If Quebec Goes, 1995; (jtly) Getting Canada Online: understanding the information highway, 1995; (jtly) Cyberlaw and Communication Law, 1997; articles and reports. *Recreations:* jogging, ski-ing, tennis. *Address:* University of Waterloo, Waterloo, ON N2L 3G1, Canada. *T:* (519) 8884400. *Clubs:* University (Toronto); University (Waterloo); Westmount Golf.

JOHNSTON, Hon. Donald (James); PC 1980; QC (Can.) 1985; Secretary-General, Organisation for Economic Co-operation and Development, 1996–2006; *b* 26 June 1936; *s* of Wilbur Austin Johnston and Florence Jean Moffat Tucker; *m* 1965, Heather Bell Maclaren; four *d*. *Educ:* McGill Univ. (BA, BCL; Gold Medallist 1958); Univ. of Grenoble (schol.). Joined Strikeman & Elliott, 1961; founder of law firm, Johnston, Heenan and Blaikie; Counsel, Heenan Blaikie, 1988–96; Lectr, Fiscal Law, McGill Univ., 1963–76; MP (L) St Henri-Westmount, 1978–88; Pres., Treasury Bd of Canada, 1980–82; Minister for Econ. Develt, and Minister of State for Sci. and Tech., 1982–83; Minister of State for Econ. Develt and Tech., 1983–84; Minister of Justice and Attorney-Gen., Canada, 1984. Pres., Liberal Party, 1990–94. Hon. DCL. *Publications:* How to Survive Canada's Tax Chaos, 1974; Up the Hill (political memoirs), 1986; (ed) With a Bang, Not a Whimper: Pierre Trudeau speaks out, 1988. *Recreations:* writing, tennis, piano. *Clubs:* Mount-Royal (Montreal); Montreal Indoor Tennis.

JOHNSTON, Very Rev. Frederick Mervyn Kieran; Dean of Cork, 1967–71, retired; *b* 22 Oct. 1911; *s* of Robert Mills Johnston and Florence Harriet O'Hanlon; *m* 1938, Catherine Alice Ruth FitzSimons; two *s*. *Educ:* Grammar Sch., Galway; Bishop Foy Sch., Waterford; Trinity Coll., Dublin. BA 1933. Deacon, 1934; Priest, 1936; Curate, Castlecomer, 1934–36; Curate, St Luke, Cork, 1936–38; Incumbent of Kilmeen, 1938–40; Drimoleague, 1940–45; Blackrock, Cork, 1945–58; Bandon, 1958–67; Rector of St Fin Barre's Cathedral and Dean of Cork, 1967; Examng Chaplain to Bishop of Cork, 1960–78. *Address:* 24 Lapps Court, Hartlands Avenue, Cork, Republic of Ireland.

JOHNSTON, Frederick Patrick Mair, CBE 1993; Chairman, Johnston Press plc (formerly F. Johnston & Co. Ltd), 1973–2001 (Director, since 1959); *b* Edinburgh, 15 Sept. 1935; *e s* of late Frederick M. Johnston and Mrs M. K. Johnston, Falkirk; *m* 1961, Elizabeth Ann Jones; two *s*. *Educ:* Morrison's Acad., Crieff; Lancing Coll., Sussex; New Coll., Oxford (MA, Mod. Hist.). Commissioned in Royal Scots Fusiliers, 1955; served in E Africa with 4th (Uganda) Bn, KAR, 1955–56. Joined Editorial Dept of Liverpool Daily Post & Echo, 1959; joined The Times Publishing Co. Ltd, as Asst Sec., 1960–62; F. Johnston & Co. Ltd, subseq. Johnston Press plc: Asst Manager, 1962; Company Sec., 1969–73; Managing Dir, 1973–80; Chief Exec., 1980–91; Exec. Chm., 1991–97. Chm., Dunn & Wilson Ltd, 1976–97; Director: Scottish Mortgage and Trust plc, 1991–2002; Lloyds TSB Bank Scotland plc, 1996–2003; The Press Association Ltd, 1997–2001. Dir, FIEJ, 1990–96. President: Young Newspapermen's Assoc., 1968–69; Forth Valley Chamber of Commerce, 1972–73; Scottish Newspaper Proprietors' Assoc., 1976–78; Newspaper Soc., 1989–90; Chm., Newspapers Press Fund Appeal, 1995; Chm., Central Scotland Manpower Cttee, 1976–83; Mem., Press Council, 1974–88; Treasurer: Soc. of Master Printers of Scotland, 1981–86; CPU, 1987–91. Chm., Edinburgh Internat. Book Fest. (formerly Edinburgh Book Fest.), 1996–2001. Chm., Scotland in Europe, 2001–04. Regent, RCSE, 2001–. FRSA 1992. Liveryman, Stationers' and Newspapermakers' Co., 2004–. *Recreations:* reading, travelling. *Address:* Johnston Press plc, 53 Manor Place, Edinburgh EH3 7EG. *Clubs:* Caledonian; New (Edinburgh).

JOHNSTON, Gordon MacKenzie, OBE 1996; HM Diplomatic Service, retired; *b* 24 June 1941; *s* of William Johnston and Betty Isabel Lamond (*née* MacKenzie); *m* 1963, Barbara Glenis Christie; one *s* one *d*. *Educ:* Robert Gordon's Coll., Aberdeen; Dingwall Acad. Joined HM Foreign, later Diplomatic, Service, 1959; FO, 1959–63; Berne, 1963–65; Pro-Consul, Tamsui, 1966–67; FCO, 1967–71; Entry Clearance Officer, Islamabad, 1971; FCO, 1972–74; Commercial Attaché, Paris, 1974–77; Second Sec., Georgetown, 1978–81; Press Officer, FCO, 1981–84; First Secretary: Commercial, Belgrade, 1984–88; Economic, Dublin, 1989–90; FCO, 1990–92; Ambassador, Slovenia, 1992–97; Counsellor (Commercial and Econ.), Stockholm, 1997–98. *Recreations:* golf, tennis, reading.

JOHNSTON, Lt Col Grenville Shaw, OBE 1986; TD (2 clasps) 1975; CA; Senior Partner, W. D. Johnston & Carmichael, 1975–2001 (Consultant, 2001–05); Lord-Lieutenant of Moray, since 2005 (Vice Lord-Lieutenant, 1996–2005); *b* 28 Jan. 1945; *s* of Lt Col William Dewar Johnston, OBE, TD, CA and Margaret Raynor Adeline Johnston (*née* Shaw); *m* 1972, Marylyn Jean Picken; two *d*. *Educ:* Seafield Primary Sch., Elgin; Blairmore Prep. Sch., Huntly; Fettes Coll., Edinburgh. CA 1968. Apprentice with Scott-Moncrieff Thomson & Sheils, Edinburgh, 1963–68; Asst, Thomson McLintock & Co., Glasgow, 1968–70; with W. D. Johnston & Carmichael, 1970–. Mem. Council, ICA Scotland, 1993–98 (Jun. Vice Pres., 1998; Sen. Vice Pres., 1999–2000; Pres., 2000–01). Chm., Grampian & Shetland Cttee, Royal Jubilee and Prince's Trusts, 1980–91; Mem., Grampian Cttee, Prince's Scottish Youth Business Trust, 1989–97. Sec., Moray Local Health Council, 1975–91; Board Member: Moray Enterprise Trust, 1985–93; Moray Badenoch & Strathspey Local Enterprise Co. Ltd, 1990–93; Cairngorm Mountain Ltd, 1999–; Highlands and Is Airports Ltd, 2001–08; Chm., Caledonian Maritime Assets Ltd, 2007–. Trustee, Nat. Museums of Scotland, 1998–2006. Vice-Chm., Gordonstoun Sch., 1985–99. Mem., Highland Area, TAVRA Assoc., 1980–99; Highland Reserve Forces and Cadets Association, 1999–: Chm., Northern Area, 1999–2001; Chm., 2001–05; Vice Pres., 2005–06; Pres., 2007–; Vice Chm. (Army), RFCA, 2003–07. Lt Col, TA, 1982; Hon. Col, 3rd Highlanders, 1997–99. Pres., Moray Scouts, 2005–. DL Moray, 1979. KCSG 1982. *Recreations:* fishing, ski-ing, shooting, hockey. *Address:* Spynie Kirk House, Spynie, Elgin, Moray IV30 8XJ. *T:* (01343) 542578. *Clubs:* New (Edinburgh); Elgin Rotary (Hon. Mem., 2008–).

JOHNSTON, Henry Butler M.; *see* McKenzie Johnston.

JOHNSTON, Hugh Philip, CB 1977; FREng; Deputy Secretary, Property Services Agency, Department of the Environment, 1974–87; *b* 17 May 1927; *s* of late Philip Rose-Johnston and Dora Ellen Johnston; *m* 1949, Barbara Frances Theodoridi; one *s* three *d*. *Educ:* Wimbledon Coll.; Faraday House. DFH (Hons). Air Ministry Works Dept: Asst Engr, 1951; Engr, 1956; Ministry of Public Buildings and Works: Prin. Engr, 1964; Asst Dir, 1969; Dir (Under-Sec.), Dept of Environment and Property Services Agency, Engrg Services Directorate, 1970. Pres., CIBSE, 1987–88. FREng (FEng 1989). *Recreations:* motoring, music. *Address:* 9 Devas Road, Wimbledon, SW20 8PD. *T:* (020) 8946 2021.

JOHNSTON, Ian; *see* Johnston, W. I. R.

JOHNSTON, Ian Alistair, CB 1995; PhD; Vice Chancellor and Principal, Glasgow Caledonian University, 1998–2006; *b* 2 May 1944; *s* of late Donald Dalrymple Johnston and Muriel Joyce Johnston; *m* 1973, Mary Bridget Lube; one *s* one *d*. *Educ:* Royal Grammar Sch., High Wycombe; Birmingham Univ. (BSc, PhD). Joined Dept of Employment as Assistant Principal, 1969; Private Sec. to Permanent Secretary, Sir Denis Barnes, 1972–73; Principal, 1973; First Sec. (Labour Attaché), British Embassy, Brussels, 1976–77; Asst Sec. (Director, ACAS), 1978; Under-Sec. (Dir of Planning and Resources, MSC), 1984; Chief Exec., Vocational Educn Trng Gp, MSC, 1985; Dep. Dir Gen., MSC, subseq. Training Commn, then Training Agency, then Training Enterprise and Education Directorate of Department of Employment, 1987–92; Dir of Resources and Strategy (Dep. Sec.), Dept of Employment, 1992; Dir Gen., TEED, Dept of Employment, 1992–95; Dep. Principal, Sheffield Hallam Univ., 1995–98. Director: Glasgow Chamber of Commerce, 1998–2005; CAPITB plc, 1999–2002. Hon. Treas. and Council Mem., Industrial Soc., 1991–2002. Mem., European Commn Expert Study Gp on Educn and Trng, 1995–2000. Member, Council: BTEC/Univ. of London Exam. Bd, 1995–98; Council for Industry and Higher Educn, 2001–06; Mem., Jt Nat. Council for Higher Educn Staff, 2002–06. Director: Qualification for Industry, 1996–99; Univs and Colls Employers Assoc., 2001–06; Board Member: Scottish Enterprise Glasgow, 2004–06; Lifelong Learning UK, 2005–06. Gov. and Dep. Chm., Sheffield Hallam Univ. (formerly Sheffield City Poly.), 1988–95; Bd Mem., then Dep. Chm., Univ. for Industry, 1998–2003; Trustee, Carnegie Trust for Univs of Scotland, 1998–2006. Mem., Merchants' House of Glasgow, 2005. Hon. Life Mem., Work Foundn, 2002. DL City of Glasgow, 2004–06. CCMI (CIMgt 1993); FCIPD (FIPD 1993); FRSA 1995. DUniv Glasgow Caledonian, 2006. Lord Provost's Medallist for Educn, 2005. *Publications:* contribs to learned jls on atomic structure of metals, 1966–69, and subseq. on public admin and educn and trng strategy, incl. virtual educn. *Recreations:* birding, fishing, travel, tennis. *Address:* Stonecroft, 18 Eaton Drive, Baslow, Bakewell, Derbys DE45 1SE.

JOHNSTON, Prof. Ian Alistair, PhD; CBiol, FIBiol; FRSE; Director, Gatty Marine Laboratory, since 1985, and Chandos Professor, since 1997, School of Biology, University of St Andrews; *b* 13 April 1949. *Educ:* Univ. of Hull (BSc 1st cl. Hons Biological Chem. and Zoology 1970; PhD 1973). CBiol, FIBiol 1997. NERC Res. Fellow, Univ. of Bristol, 1973; University of St Andrews: Lectr, 1976–84, Reader, 1984, in Physiology; Prof., 1985–95; Founding Chm., Dept of Biology and Preclin. Medicine, 1987–91; Head, Sch. of Biological and Med. Scis, 1991–92; Mem. Court, 1997–2002; Founding Head, Div. of Envmtl and Evolutionary Biol., Sch. of Biology, 1997–2004; Dir of Res., Sch. of Biology, 2003–06. Vis. Prof., Univ. of Nairobi, 1993. Mem. Council, NERC, 1995–2000. Pres., Soc. for Experimental Biol., 2007–. FRSE 1987. Scientific Medal, Zool Soc., 1984. *Publications:* (contrib.) Essentials of Physiology, 3rd edn 1991 (trans. Spanish 1987, trans. Italian 1989, trans. French 1990); (ed jtly) Phenotypic and Evolutionary Adaptation of Animals to Temperature, 1996; (jtly) Environmental Physiology of Animals, 2000. *Address:* School of Biology, University of St Andrews, Gatty Marine Laboratory, St Andrews KY16 8LB. *T:* (01334) 463440.

JOHNSTON, Jennifer, (Mrs David Gilliland), FRSL; author; *b* 12 Jan. 1930; *d* of late (William) Denis Johnston, OBE; *m* 1st, 1951, Ian Smyth; two *s* two *d*; 2nd, 1976, David Gilliland, *qv*. *Educ:* Park House Sch., Dublin; Trinity Coll., Dublin. FRSL 1979. Mem., Aosdána. Plays: Indian Summer, performed Belfast, 1983; The Porch, prod Dublin, 1986. Hon. DLitt: Ulster, 1984: TCD, 1992; QUB, 1993; UCD 2005. *Publications:* The Captains and the Kings, 1972; The Gates, 1973; How Many Miles to Babylon?, 1974; Shadows on Our Skin, 1978 (dramatised for TV, 1979); The Old Jest, 1979 (filmed as The Dawning, 1988); (play) The Nightingale and not the Lark, 1980; The Christmas Tree, 1981; The Railway Station Man, 1984; Fool's Sanctuary, 1987; The Invisible Worm, 1991; The Illusionist, 1995; (contrib.) Finbar's Hotel, 1997; Two Moons, 1998; The Gingerbread Woman, 2000; This Is Not a Novel, 2002; Grace & Truth, 2005; Foolish Mortals, 2007. *Recreations:* theatre, cinema, gardening, travelling. *Address:* Brook Hall, Culmore Road, Derry, N Ireland BT48 8JE. *T:* (028) 7135 1297.

JOHNSTON, Mark Steven; racehorse trainer, since 1987; Trainer and Managing Director, Mark Johnston Racing Ltd, since 1988; *b* 10 Oct. 1959; *s* of Ronald and Mary Johnston; *m* 1985, Deirdre Ferguson; two *s*. *Educ:* Glasgow Univ. Vet. Sch. (BVMS 1983). MRCVS 1983. Veterinary practice, 1983–86. MRSocMed 1999. *Recreation:* cycling. *Address:* Kingsley House, Middleham, Leyburn, N Yorks DL8 4PH. *T:* (01969) 622237, *Fax:* (01969) 622484; *e-mail:* mark@markjohnstonracing.com.

JOHNSTON, Lt-Gen. Sir Maurice (Robert), KCB 1982; CVO 2005; OBE 1971; Lord-Lieutenant of Wiltshire, 1996–2004; Deputy Chief of Defence Staff, 1982–83, retired 1984; *b* 27 Oct. 1929; *s* of late Brig. Allen Leigh Johnston, OBE, and Gertrude Geraldine Johnston (*née* Templer); *m* 1960, Belinda Mary Sladen; one *s* one *d*. *Educ:* Wellington College; RMA Sandhurst. rcds, psc. Commissioned RA, 1949; transf. The Queen's Bays, 1954; served in Germany, Egypt, Jordan, Libya, N Ireland, Borneo. Instr, Army Staff Coll., 1965–67; MA to CGS, 1968–71; CO 1st The Queen's Dragoon Guards, 1971–73; Comdr 20th Armoured Brigade, 1973–75; BGS, HQ UKLF, 1977–78; Senior Directing Staff, RCDS, 1979; Asst Chief of Gen. Staff, 1980; Dep. Chief of Defence Staff (Op. Reqs), 1981–82. Col, 1st The Queen's Dragoon Guards, 1986–91. Chairman: Secondary Resources plc, 1988–91; Detention Corp., 1988–94; Managing Director: Freshglen Ltd, Wraxall Gp, 1984–85; Unit Security Ltd, 1985–88; Director: HIAB (formerly Partek Cargotec), 1984–; Shorrock Guards Ltd, 1988–91. Governor: Dauntsey's Sch., Wilts, 1987–2004, St Mary's Sch., Calne, 1988–94. DL Wilts, 1990, High Sheriff, 1993–94. *Recreations:* fishing, shooting, gardening, music, glass engraving. *Address:* Ivy House, Worton, Devizes, Wilts SN10 5RU. *Club:* Army and Navy.

JOHNSTON, Paul Charles; HM Diplomatic Service; Director, International Security, Foreign and Commonwealth Office, since 2008; *b* 29 May 1968; *s* of late Charles Johnston and of Muriel (*née* Hall); *m* 2004, Nicola Carol Maskell. *Educ:* Galashiels Acad.; Univ. of Glasgow (MA Hons). MoD, 1990–93; HM Diplomatic Service, 1993–: Desk Officer, Eastern Adriatic Unit, 1993–95 (Private Sec. to Lord Owen at Internat. Conf. on Former Yugoslavia, 1994); Private Sec. to Ambassador to France, 1995–97; 2nd Sec. (Political), Paris, 1997–99; Foreign and Commonwealth Office: Head: Kosovo Policy Section, 1999–2000; European Defence Section, 2000–01; Dep. Hd, EU Ext. Dept, 2001–02; Hd, Security Policy Dept, FCO, 2002–04; Counsellor (Political), UK Mission to the UN, NY, 2005–08. *Recreations:* cinema, music, walking, idling. *Address:* c/o Foreign and Commonwealth Office, King Charles Street, SW1A 2AH.

JOHNSTON, (Paul) Nicholas, FIMI; *b* 5 Jan. 1948; *s* of Joseph Leo Johnston and Winifred Vera Neale or Johnston; *m* 1st, 1972, Catherine MacPhee (marr. diss. 1993); one *s* two *d*; 2nd, 1993, Anna Jiménez-Olive; two *s*. *Educ:* North Kesteven Grammar Sch.; RMA Sandhurst. Dir, Eastern Hldgs Ltd, 1972–. Mem. (C) Scotland Mid and Fife, Scottish Parlt, 1999–2001. *Recreations:* cookery, history, gardening.

JOHNSTON, Peter Henry; Controller, BBC Northern Ireland, since 2006; *b* 20 Jan. 1966; *s* of Tommy and Edna Johnston; *m* 1991, Jill McAlister; one *s* one *d*. *Educ:* Imperial College, London (MEng Chem. Engrg 1988). Business Consultant, Shell Internat., London, 1988–90; Sen. Associate, Price Waterhouse Coopers Mgt Consultants, Belfast, 1990–94; BBC Northern Ireland, Belfast: Res. and Special Projs Exec., 1994–97; Hd, Mktg and Develt, 1997–2001; Hd, New Media, BBC Nations and Regions, London, 2001–03; Hd, Broadcasting, BBC NI, Belfast, 2003–06. *Recreations:* no longer playing but watching Rugby, being at the North Coast of Northern Ireland, socialising, playing golf badly, playing with the kids. *Address:* BBC Northern Ireland, Broadcasting House, Ormeau Avenue, Belfast BT2 8HQ. *T:* (02890) 338200, *Fax:* (02890) 338800; *e-mail:* peter.johnston@bbc.co.uk.

JOHNSTON, Peter William; consultant, International Federation of Accountants (Chief Executive, 1999–2002, Director, 2002–03, Adviser, 2003–05); *b* 8 Feb. 1943; *s* of late William Johnston and of Louisa Alice Johnston (*née* Pritchard); *m* 1967, Patricia Sandra Macdonald; one *s* one *d*. *Educ:* Univ. of Glasgow (MA, LLB). Partner, MacArthur & Co., Solicitors, Inverness, 1971–76; Procurator Fiscal Depute, Dumfries, 1976–78; Procurator Fiscal, Banff, 1978–86; Senior Procurator Fiscal Depute, Crown Office, Edinburgh, 1986–87; Asst Solicitor, Crown Office, 1987–89; Chief Exec. and Sec., ICAS, 1989–99. Mem. Bd, Risk Management Authy, 2006–. Trustee, Friends of Duff House. FRSA. *Recreations:* music, foreign languages, sailing. *Address:* 13 Scotstown, Banff AB45 1LA.

JOHNSTON, Rita Margaret; Premier, Province of British Columbia, 1991; *b* 22 April 1935; *d* of John and Annie Leichert; *m* 1951, George Johnston; one *s* two *d*. Businesswoman and Mem., Chamber of Commerce. Alderman, Surrey, BC, 1970–83; MLA for Surrey, 1983–91; Parly Sec. to Minister of Energy, Mines and Petroleum Resources, then to Minister of Municipal Affairs, 1983–86; Minister: Municipal Affairs and Transit, 1986–89, also Recreation and Culture, 1988–89; Transportation and Highways, 1989–90; Dep. Premier, 1990–91. *Address:* 480 Rockland Drive, Vernon, BC V1B 2X5, Canada.

JOHNSTON, Robert Alan, AC 1986; Governor, Reserve Bank of Australia, 1982–89; *b* 19 July 1924; *m* 1st, 1948, Verna (*d* 1999), *d* of H. I. Mullin; two *s* two *d*; 2nd, 2000, Judith Ann, *d* of P. A. Lazzarini. *Educ:* Essendon High School; University of Melbourne. BCom. Commonwealth Bank of Australia, 1940–60; RAAF, 1943–46; Reserve Bank of Australia, 1960–89: Dep. Manager and Manager, Investment Dept, 1964–70; Chief Manager, Internat. Dept, 1970–76; Adviser, 1973–82; Chief Representative, London, 1976–77; Exec. Dir, World Bank Group, Washington, 1977–79; Secretary, Reserve Bank of Aust., 1980–82. Director: Australian Mutual Prov. Soc., 1989–97; John Fairfax Gp Pty, 1989–90; Westpac Banking Corp., 1992–96. Pres., Cttee for Econ. Devel of Australia, 1990–94. Hon. DCom Melbourne, 1992.

JOHNSTON, Robert Gordon Scott, CB 1993; Executive Director, United Kingdom Major Ports Group, 1993–99; *b* 27 Aug. 1933; *s* of late Robert William Fairfield Johnston, CMG, CBE, MC, TD; *m* 1960, Jill Maureen Campbell; one *s* one *d*. *Educ:* Clifton; Clare Coll., Cambridge (1st Cl. Hons Classical Tripos, MA). 2/Lieut Scots Guards (National Service), 1955–57. Entered Air Min. as Asst Principal, 1957; Private Sec. to Parly Under Sec. of State for Air, 1959–62; transf. to MPBW, Def. Works Secretariat, 1963; Sec., Bldg Regulation Adv. Cttee, 1964; Principal Private Sec. to successive Ministers of Public Bldg and Works, 1965–68; seconded to Shell Internat. Chemical Co., Finance Div., 1968–70; Asst Dir of Home Estate Management, Property Services Agency, 1970–73; seconded to Cabinet Office, 1973–75; Asst Sec., Railways Directorate, Dept of Transport, 1975–79; Under Sec., DoE, 1979–93; seconded to Price Commn, 1979; Dir of Civil Accommodation, 1979–88, Dir, Defence Services, 1988–90, PSA; Man. Dir, PSA Internat., 1990–93. Rep. of Sec. of State for Envmt on Commonwealth War Graves Commn, 1988–93. Lay Chm., NHS Complaints Panels, 2000–05; Mem., Ind. Review Panel, Healthcare Commn, 2004–07. *Address:* 5 Methley Street, SE11 4AL.

JOHNSTON, Prof. Ronald John, PhD; FBA 1999; AcSS; Professor of Geography, Bristol University, since 1995; *b* 30 March 1941; *s* of Henry Louis Johnston and Phyllis Joyce (*née* Liddiard); *m* 1963, Rita Brennan; one *s* one *d*. *Educ:* Commonweal County Secondary Grammar Sch., Swindon; Univ. of Manchester (BA 1962; MA 1964); Monash Univ. (PhD 1967). Department of Geography, Monash University: Teaching Fellow, 1964; Sen. Teaching Fellow, 1965; Lectr, 1966; University of Canterbury, New Zealand: Lectr, 1967–68; Sen. Lectr, 1969–72; Reader, 1973–74; University of Sheffield: Prof. of Geography, 1974–92; Pro-Vice-Chancellor for Acad. Affairs, 1989–92; Vice-Chancellor, Essex Univ., 1992–95. AcSS 1999. DU Essex, 1996; Hon. LLD Monash, 1999; Hon. DLitt: Sheffield, 2002; Bath 2006. Murchison Award, 1985, Victoria Medal, 1990, RGS; Honors Award for Distinction in Res., Assoc. Amer. Geographers, 1991; Prix Vautrin Lud, Fest. Internat. de Geographie, 1999. *Publications:* (with P. J. Rimmer) Retailing in Melbourne, 1970; Urban Residential Patterns: an introductory review, 1971; Spatial Structures: an introduction to the study of spatial systems in human geography, 1973; The New Zealanders: how they live and work, 1976; The World Trade System: some enquiries into its spatial structure, 1976; (with B. E. Coates and P. L. Knox) Geography and Inequality, 1977; Multivariate Statistical Analysis in Geography: a primer on the general linear model, 1978; Political, Electoral and Spatial Systems, 1979; (with P. J. Taylor) Geography of Elections, 1979; Geography and Geographers: Anglo-American human geography since 1945, 1979, 6th edn 2004; City and Society: an outline for urban geography, 1980; The Geography of Federal Spending in the United States of America, 1980; The American Urban System: a geographical perspective, 1982; Geography and the State, 1982; Philosophy and Human Geography: an introduction to contemporary approaches, 1983, 2nd edn 1986; Residential Segregation, the State and Constitutional Conflict in American Urban Areas, 1984; The Geography of English Politics: the 1983 General Election, 1985; On Human Geography, 1986; Bell-Ringing: the English art of change-ringing, 1986; Money and Votes: constituency campaign spending and election results, 1987; (jtly) The United States: a contemporary human geography, 1988; (with C. J. Pattie and J. G. Allsopp) A Nation Dividing?: the electoral map of Great Britain 1979–1987, 1988; Environmental Problems: nature, economy and state, 1989, 2nd edn 1996; (jtly) An Atlas of Bells, 1990; A Question of Place: exploring the practice of human geography, 1991; (ed) The Dictionary of Human Geography, 1989, 4th edn 2000; (with D. J. Rossiter and C. J. Pattie) The Boundary Commissions, 1999; (jtly) From Votes to Seats, 2001; (with C. J. Pattie) Putting Voters in Their Place, 2006; contrib. chapters in ed vols and numerous papers in learned jls. *Recreation:* bell-ringing. *Address:* School of Geographical Sciences, University of Bristol, Bristol BS8 1SS. *T:* (0117) 928 9116, *Fax:* (0117) 928 7878; *e-mail:* r.johnston@bristol.ac.uk.

JOHNSTON, Sir Thomas Alexander, 14th Bt *cr* 1626, of Caskieben; *b* 1 Feb. 1956; *s* of Sir Thomas Alexander Johnston, 13th Bt, and of Helen Torry, *d* of Benjamin Franklin Du Bois; *S* father, 1984. *Heir: cousin* William Norville Johnston [*b* 11 July 1922; *m* 1952, Kathrine Pauline, *d* of Herbert Sigfred Solberg; three *s* one *d*].

JOHNSTON, Thomas Lothian; DL; Principal and Vice-Chancellor of Heriot-Watt University, 1981–88; President, Royal Society of Edinburgh, 1993–96; *b* 9 March 1927; *s* of late T. B. Johnston and Janet Johnston; *m* 1956, Joan, *d* of late E. C. Fahmy, surgeon; two *s* three *d*. *Educ:* Hawick High Sch.; Univ. of Edinburgh (MA 1951, PhD 1955); Univ. of Stockholm. FRSE 1979; FEIS 1989. Served RNVR, 1944–47 (Sub-Lt). Asst Lectr in Polit. Economy, Univ. of Edinburgh, 1953–55, Lectr 1955–65; Res. Fellow, Queen's Univ., Canada, 1965; Prof. and Hd of Dept of Econs, Heriot-Watt Univ., 1966–76. Visiting Professor: Univ. of Illinois, 1962–63; Internat. Inst. for Labour Studies, Geneva, 1973; Western Australia Inst. of Technol., 1979. Sec., Scottish Econ. Soc., 1958–65 (Pres., 1978–81); Member: Scottish Milk Marketing Bd, 1967–72; Nat. Industrial Relations Court, 1971–74; Scottish Cttee on Licensing Laws, 1971–73; Scottish Telecommunications Bd, 1977–84; Scottish Economic Council, 1977–91; Council for Tertiary Educn in Scotland, 1979–83; Chm., Manpower Services Cttee for Scotland, 1977–80; Economic Consultant to Sec. of State for Scotland, 1977–81. Trustee, Nat. Galls of Scotland, 1989–95. Director: First Charlotte Assets Trust, 1981–92; Universities Superannuation Scheme, 1985–88; Scottish Life Assurance, 1989–97; Hodgson Martin Ltd, 1989–97. A Dir, Edinburgh Sci. Festival, 1989–91. Chairman: Scottish Cttee, Industry Year 1986; Scottish Cttee, Industry Matters, 1987–89; Scottish Cttee, RSA, 1991–95; Univ. Authorities Pay Panel, 1985–88. Chairman: Enquiry into staff representation, London Clearing Banks, 1978–79; Water Workers' Enquiry, 1983; Mem., Review Cttee for NZ Univs, 1987; Arbitrator; Overseas Corresp., Nat. Acad. of Arbitrators, USA. FRSA 1981; CCMI (CBIM 1983); FIPD (FIPM 1986). For. Mem., Swedish Royal Acad. of Engrg Scis, 1985. DL Edinburgh, 1987. Dr *hc* Edinburgh, 1986; Hon. DEd CNAA, 1989; Hon. LLD Glasgow, 1989; DUniv Heriot-Watt, 1989; Hon. DLitt Napier, 1997. Comdr, Royal Swedish Order of the Polar Star, 1985. *Publications:* Collective Bargaining in Sweden, 1962; (ed and trans.) Economic Expansion and Structural Change, 1963; (jtly) The Structure and Growth of the Scottish Economy, 1971; Introduction to Industrial Relations, 1981; numerous translations from Swedish; articles in learned jls. *Recreations:* gardening, walking. *Address:* 14 Mansionhouse Road, Edinburgh EH9 1TZ. *T:* (0131) 667 1439.

See also D. E. L. Johnston.

JOHNSTON, Ven. William Francis, CB 1983; Rector, Winslow with Great Horwood and Addington, diocese of Oxford, 1991–95; *b* 29 June 1930; *m* 1963, Jennifer Morton; two *s* one *d*. *Educ:* Wesley Coll., Dublin; Trinity Coll., Dublin (BA 1955; MA 1969). Ordained 1955; Curate of Orangefield, Co. Down, 1955–59; commissioned into Royal Army Chaplains Dept, 1959; served, UK, Germany, Aden, Cyprus; ACG South East District, 1977–80; Chaplain-Gen. to the Forces, 1980–86; QHC 1980–86; Priest-in-charge, Winslow with Addington, 1987–91. *Recreations:* golf, fishing, gardening. *Address:* Lower Axehill, Chard Road, Axminster, Devon EX13 5ED. *T:* (01297) 33259.

JOHNSTON, (William) Ian (Ridley), CBE 2001; QPM 1995; DL; Chief Constable, British Transport Police, since 2001; *b* 6 Sept. 1945; *s* of late William and Alice Johnston; *m* 1968, Carol Ann Smith; two *s*. *Educ:* Enfield Grammar Sch.; LSE (BSc 1st Cl. Hons). Joined Metropolitan Police 1965; ranks of PC to Chief Supt, 1965–88; Staff Officer to Sir Peter Imbert, 1988–89; Senior Command Course, 1989; Asst Chief Constable, Kent, 1989–92; Dep. Asst Comr, 1992–94, Asst Comr, 1994–2001, Met Police. DL Gtr London, 2007. *Recreations:* jogging, tennis, football, squash. *Address:* British Transport Police HQ, 25 Camden Road, NW1 9LN. *Club:* Orpington Rovers Football.

JOHNSTON, William James; Secretary, Association of Local Authorities of Northern Ireland, 1979–82; Chairman, National House Building Council, Northern Ireland, 1989–95; *b* 3 April 1919; *s* of late Thomas Hamilton Johnston and of Mary Kathleen Johnston; *m* 1943, Joan Elizabeth Nancye (*née* Young) (*d* 2008); two *d*. *Educ:* Portora Royal Sch., Enniskillen. FCA(Ire.). Professional accountancy, 1937–44; Antrim CC, 1944–68, Dep. Sec., 1951–68; Dep. Town Clerk, Belfast, 1968–73, Town Clerk, 1973–79. Dir, NI Adv. Bd, Abbey Nat. Bldg Soc., 1982–89. Member: NI Adv. Council, BBC, 1965–69; Council, ICAI, 1967–71; NI Tourist Bd, 1980–85; Local Govt Staff Commn, 1974–85; Public Service Trng Council (formerly Public Service Trng Cttee), 1974–83 (Chm., 1974–83); Arts Council of NI, 1974–81. Chm., Extra Care for Elderly People (NI) Ltd, 1999–2004. NI Rep., Duke of Edinburgh's Commonwealth Study Conf., Canada, 1962. *Recreations:* golf, live theatre. *Address:* 19A Windsor Avenue, Belfast BT9 6EE. *T:* (028) 9066 9373; 4 Riverside Close, Cushendall, Ballymena BT44 0NR. *T:* (028) 2177 2013. *Club:* Ulster Reform (Belfast).

JOHNSTON, Sir William Robert Patrick K.; *see* Knox-Johnston.

JOHNSTONE; *see* Hope Johnstone, family name of Earl of Annandale and Hartfell.

JOHNSTONE, VANDEN-BEMPDE-, family name of **Baron Derwent**.

JOHNSTONE, Lord; David Patrick Wentworth Hope Johnstone; Master of Annandale and Hartfell; *b* 13 Oct. 1971; *s* and *heir* of Earl of Annandale and Hartfell, *qv*; *m* 2001, Penny, *d* of late John Macmillan; one *s* one *d*. *Educ:* Stowe; St Andrews Univ. (BSc 1994). Director: Scottish Rural Property & Business Assoc., 2004–; Dumfries & Galloway Small Community Housing Trust, 2007–. *Heir: s* Percy John Wentworth Hope Johnstone, Master of Johnstone, *b* 16 Feb. 2002.

JOHNSTONE, Alexander; Member (C) North East Scotland, Scottish Parliament, since 1999; *b* 31 July 1961; *m* 1981, Linda; one *s* one *d*. *Educ:* Mackie Acad., Stonehaven. Farmer, 1981–. *Address:* 25 Evan Street, Stonehaven, Kincardine AB39 2EQ.

JOHNSTONE, David; Director of Social Services, Devon County Council, since 1999; *b* 9 May 1951; *s* of David Armour Johnstone and Veronica Johnstone; *m* 1974, Andra Newton; one *s* two *d*. *Educ:* Middlesex Poly. (BA Hons Social Sci.); Newcastle upon Tyne Univ. (MBA). Joined Social Services Dept, Newcastle upon Tyne, 1974, Asst Dir, 1990–95; Dir of Social Services, Stockton on Tees, 1995–99. Member: Exec. Bd, Assoc. of Dirs of Social Services; Nat. Prog. for IT. *Recreations:* sport, rare breed animal husbandry. *Address:* Devon County Council, County Hall, Topsham Road, Exeter EX2 4QR. *Club:* Teign Corinthian Yacht.

JOHNSTONE, Prof. Eve Cordelia, CBE 2002; MD; FRCPsych, FRCPGlas, FRCPE, FMedSci; FRSE; Professor of Psychiatry, and Head, Department of Psychiatry, University of Edinburgh, since 1989; *b* 1 Sept. 1944; *d* of late William Gillespie Johnstone and Dorothy Mary Johnstone. *Educ:* Park Sch., Glasgow; Univ. of Glasgow (MB ChB 1967; DPM 1970; MD 1976). MRCP 1971; MRCPsych 1972, FRCPsych 1984; FRCPE 1992. House officer posts, 1967–68, trng posts in Psychiatry, 1968–72, Glasgow Hosp.; Lectr in Psychological Medicine, Glasgow Univ., 1972–74; Mem., Scientific Staff, MRC, Clin. Res. Centre and Northwick Park Hosp., Harrow, 1974–89 (Hon. Consultant, 1979–). Mem., MRC, 1996–2002 (Chm., Neuroscience and Mental Health Bd, 1999–2002). Founder FMedSci 1998; FRSE 2005. *Publications:* Searching for the Causes of

Schizophrenia, 1994; (ed) Biological Psychiatry, 1996; (ed jtly) Schizophrenia: concepts and management, 1999; (ed jtly) Companion to Psychiatric Studies, 6th edn 1998, 7th edn 2004; (with C. Frith) Schizophrenia: a very short introduction, 2003; (ed jtly) Schizophrenia: from neuroimaging to neuroscience, 2004; numerous contribs to learned jls mainly relating to schizophrenia and other serious psychiatric disorders. *Recreations:* card-playing, gardening, listening to opera, foreign travel. *Address:* Department of Psychiatry, University of Edinburgh, Kennedy Tower, Royal Edinburgh Hospital, Edinburgh EH10 5HF. *T:* (0131) 537 6267.

JOHNSTONE, Sir Geoffrey (Adams Dinwiddie), KCMG 2002 (CMG 1994); Ambassador (non-resident) of The Bahamas to Chile, Argentina, Uruguay and Brazil, 1995–2002; *b* 19 Sept. 1927; *s* of Bruce Eric Johnstone and Wilhelmina Johnstone; *m* 1954, Winifred Anne Duncombe. *Educ:* Queen's Coll., Nassau, Bahamas; Inns of Court Sch. of Law, London. Called to the Bar: Middle Temple, 1950; Bahamas, as Counsel and Attorney-at-Law, 1950; in practice, 1950–98. MHA (United Bahamian) Bahamas, 1962–72; Cabinet Minister, 1964–67; Leader of Opposition, 1970–71; Dep. to Gov. Gen. of Bahamas on numerous occasions, 1995–2001. Chm., Hotel Corp. of The Bahamas, 1992–94. Silver Jubilee Award (Bahamas), 1998. *Recreations:* shooting, fishing. *Address:* 5 Commonwealth Avenue, Blair Estate, PO Box N3247, Nassau, Bahamas. *T:* 3932586, *Fax:* 3941208; *e-mail:* gjohnstone@coralwave.com. *Club:* Royal Nassau Sailing.

JOHNSTONE, Sir (George) Richard (Douglas), 11th Bt *cr* 1700, of Westerhall, Dumfriesshire; *b* 21 Aug. 1948; *er s* of Sir Frederic Allan George Johnstone, 10th Bt and of Doris Johnstone (*née* Shortridge); *S* father, 1994; *m* 1976, Gwyneth Susan Bailey (marr. diss. 2003); one *s* one *d*. *Educ:* Leeds Grammar Sch.; Magdalen Coll., Oxford (MA; Dip. Physical Anthropology). Production Control Manager, Wolsey Ltd, 1973; Section Head, ITT Consumer Products (UK) Ltd, 1979; Dir, Central Govt Gp, P-E International plc, 1988; Managing Director: DBI Associates Ltd, 1990; Moat House Consultants Ltd. *Recreations:* biking, travel, computing. *Heir: s* Frederic Robert Arthur Johnstone, *b* 18 Nov. 1981.

JOHNSTONE, Iain Gilmour; author and broadcaster; *b* 8 April 1943; *s* of Jack and Gilly Johnstone; *m* 1980, Mo Watson; one *s* two *d*. *Educ:* Campbell College, Belfast; Bristol Univ. (LLB Hons). Newscaster, ITN, 1966–68; Producer, BBC TV, 1968–74; Prof. of Broadcasting, Boston Univ., 1975; Man. Dir, DVD Prodns Ltd (formerly Kensington TV), 1977–; BBC presenter, Film 1983, 1984; film critic, The Sunday Times, 1983–93. Accredited Mediator, ADR Gp. Screenplays: Fierce Creatures (with John Cleese), 1996; The Evening News, 2001; The Bank of San Benedetto, 2002; documentaries: Steven and Stanley, 2001; Policing the Future, 2002; The Flying Con Man, 2003; H. G. Wells, 2005. *Publications:* The Arnhem Report, 1977; The Man With No Name, 1980; Cannes: The Novel, 1990; Wimbledon 2000, 1992; The James Bond Companion, 1999; (contrib.) British Comedy Greats, 2003; Tom Cruise: all the world's a stage, 2006; (with Kathryn Apanowicz) Richard by Kathryn, 2006. *Recreations:* lawn tennis, ski-ing, camel riding. *Address:* Sheil Land Associates Ltd, 52 Doughty Street, WC1N 2LS; *e-mail:* iain.j@uk.com. *Clubs:* Garrick, Queen's.

See also Baron Tollemache.

JOHNSTONE, Isobel Theodora, PhD; Curator, Arts Council Collection, 1979–2004; *b* 1944. *Educ:* James Gillespie's High School; Edinburgh Univ.; Edinburgh Coll. of Art (MA Hons Fine Art); Glasgow Univ. (PhD). Lectr in History of Art, Glasgow School of Art, 1969–73; Scottish Arts Council, 1975–79. Painter. *Publications:* (as Isobel Spencer): Walter Crane, 1975; articles on late 19th century and 20th century British art. *Address:* 28 Elgin Crescent, W11 2JR.

JOHNSTONE, Sir (John) Raymond, Kt 1993; CBE 1988; Chairman, Historic Buildings Council for Scotland, 1995–2002; Chairman, Atrium (formerly Lomond) Underwriting plc, 1994–2003; *b* 27 Oct. 1929; *s* of Henry James Johnstone of Alva, Captain RN and Margaret Alison McIntyre; *m* 1979, Susan Sara Gore, DL; five step *s* two step *d*. *Educ:* Eton Coll.; Trinity Coll., Cambridge (BA Maths). CA. Apprenticed Chiene & Tait, Chartered Accts, Edinburgh, 1951–54; Robert Fleming & Co. Ltd, London, 1955–59; Partner in charge of investment management, Brown Fleming & Murray CA (becoming Whinney Murray CA, 1965), Glasgow, 1959–68; Murray Johnstone Ltd, Glasgow, formed to take over investment management dept of Whinney Murray: Man. Dir, 1968–89; Chm., 1984–94; Pres., 1994–. Chm., Forestry Commn, 1989–94. Chm., Summit Gp, 1989–98; Director: Shipping Industrial Holdings, 1964–75; Scottish Amicable Life Assce Soc., 1971–97 (Chm., 1983–85); Dominion Insurance Co. Ltd, 1973–95 (Chm., 1978–95); Scottish Financial Enterprise, 1986–91 (Chm., 1989–91); Kiln plc, 1995–2002. Hon. Pres., Scottish Opera, 1986–98 (Dir, 1978–86; Chm., 1983–85); Chm., Patrons, Nat. Galls of Scotland, 1996–2003. Member: Scottish Adv. Cttee, Nature Conservancy Council, 1987–89; Scottish Econ. Council, 1987–95. Trustee, Nuclear Trust, 1996–2007; Dir, Nuclear Liabilities Fund (formerly Nuclear Generation Decommissioning Fund) Ltd, 1996–2007 (Chm., 1996–2003). *Recreations:* fishing, music, farming. *Address:* 20 Ann Street, Edinburgh EH4 1PJ. *T:* (01389) 830321.

JOHNSTONE, Paul William, FFPH; Regional Director of Public Health, Yorkshire and Humberside, since 2002; *b* 12 Feb. 1960; *s* of Peter and Pamela Johnstone; *m* Caroline; one *s* two *d*. *Educ:* Southampton Univ. (BM); Liverpool Univ. (DTM&H); LSHTM (MSc Public Health); Glasgow Univ. (DCH). MRCGP 1990; FFPH (FFPHM 2001). Overseas health volunteer, 1988–90; Officer, ODA, 1991–93; public health consultant, 1996–99; Dir of Public Health, Teesside, 2002; Medical Dir, Co. Durham Tees Valley, 2002. Visiting Professor: Teesside Univ., 1999–; Nuffield Inst. for Health, Univ. of Leeds, 2002–. MRSocMed 1990. *Publications:* Management Support for Primary Care, 1994; around 40 peer reviewed articles and monographs. *Recreations:* ski-ing, walking. *Address:* The Beeches, 71 High Street, Great Ayton, Cleveland TS9 6NF. *T:* and *Fax:* (01642) 723427; *e-mail:* paul@johnstone40.fsnet.co.uk.

JOHNSTONE, Peter, CMG 2004; HM Diplomatic Service, retired; Governor of Anguilla, 2000–04; *b* 30 July 1944; *m* 1969, Diane Claxton; one *s* one *d*. Joined FO, 1962; served: Berne, 1965–66; Benin City, 1966–68; Budapest, 1968–69; Maseru, 1969–72; FCO, 1973–77; Dacca, 1977–79; First Sec., Dublin, 1979–82; FCO, 1983–86; First Sec. (Commercial), Harare, 1986–89; Consul Gen., Edmonton, 1989–91; FCO, 1991–95; Counsellor (Commercial Develt), Jakarta, 1995–98; FCO, 1999.

JOHNSTONE, Sir Raymond; *see* Johnstone, Sir J. R.

JOHNSTONE, Sir Richard; *see* Johnstone, Sir G. R. D.

JOHNSTONE, Rev. Prof. William, DLitt; Professor of Hebrew and Semitic Languages, University of Aberdeen, 1980–2001; *b* 6 May 1936; *s* of Rev. T. K. Johnstone and Evelyn Hope Johnstone (*née* Murray); *m* 1964, Elizabeth Mary Ward; one *s* one *d*. *Educ:* Hamilton Academy; Glasgow Univ. (MA 1st Cl. Hons Semitic Langs, BD Distinction in New Testament and Old Testament; DLitt 1998); Univ. of Marburg. University of Aberdeen: Lectr 1962, Sen. Lectr 1972, in Hebrew and Semitic Languages; Dean, Faculty of Divinity, 1984–87; Hd of Dept, Divinity with Religious Studies, 1998–2000. Member, Mission archéologique française: Ras Shamra, 1963, 1964, 1966; Enkomi, 1963, 1965, 1971; Member, Marsala Punic Ship Excavation, 1973–79. Pres., SOTS, 1990. *Publications:* Exodus, 1990; 1 and 2 Chronicles, 1997; Exodus and Chronicles, 1998; (ed and contrib.) William Robertson Smith: essays in reassessment, 1995; (ed and contrib.) The Bible and the Enlightenment: a case study - Dr Alexander Geddes (1737–1802), 2004; *translation:* Fohrer: Hebrew and Aramaic Dictionary of the Old Testament, 1973; *contributions to:* Ugaritica VI, 1969, VII, 1978, Alasia I, 1972; Dictionary of Biblical Interpretation, 1990; Cambridge Companion to Biblical Interpretation, 1998; Eerdmans Commentary on the Bible, 2003; New Interpreter's Dictionary of the Bible, 2006; Festschriften for: W. McKane, 1986; R. Davidson, 1992; G. W. Anderson, 1993; C. H. W. Brekelmans, 1997; E. W. Nicholson, 2003; A. G. Auld, 2006; articles in Aberdeen Univ. Review, Atti del I Congresso Internazionale di Studi Fenici e Punici, Bibliotheca Ephemeridum Theologicarum Lovaniensium, Expository Times, Kadmos, Notizie degli Scavi, Palestine Exploration Qly, Trans. Glasgow Univ. Oriental Soc., Scottish Jl of Theology, Studia Theologica, Theology, Vetus Testamentum, Zeitschrift für die alttestamentliche Wissenschaft, etc. *Recreation:* alternative work. *Address:* 9/5 Mount Alvernia, Edinburgh EH16 6AW; Makkevet Bor, New Galloway, Castle Douglas DG7 3RN.

JOHNSTONE, William Neill, RDI 1989; Founder Chairman, Neill Johnstone Ltd, 1986–2008; former Chairman, Fabric Design Consultants International; *b* 16 May 1938; *s* of Harry McCall Johnstone and Ethel Mary Neill; *m* 1st, (marr. diss.); two *d*; 2nd, 1991, Mara Lukic; one *s* one *d*. *Educ:* Forfar Acad.; Edinburgh Acad.; Univ. of Edinburgh; Scottish Coll. of Textiles; RCA. Designer, then Design Dir, R. G. Neill & Son, 1961–70; Man. Dir and Design Dir, Neill of Langholm, 1970–85; Design Dir, Illingworth Morris Gp and Co-ordinator of design training programme, 1982–85; Internat. Wool Secretariat Design Consultant, 1978–90. Chm., Confedn of British Wool Textiles Ltd Steering Cttee, 1982–85; Industrialist on Selection Panel, Designer Graduate Attachment Scheme, 1982–85. *Recreations:* climbing, hill walking, collecting Inuit carvings, painting.

JOHNSTONE-BURT, Rear Adm. Charles Anthony, (Tony), OBE 1997; Commander, Joint Helicopter Command, since 2008; *b* 1 Feb. 1958; *s* of Comdr Charles Leonard Johnstone-Burt, OBE, RN and Margaret Hilary Johnstone-Burt; *m* 1981, Rachel Ann Persson; three *s* two *d*. *Educ:* Wellington Coll.; Durham Univ. (BA Jt Hons Psychol. and Anthropol. 1980); US Naval War Coll., Rhode Is (MA Internat. Relns and Strategic Studies 1997; UK Res. Fellow). Chartered FCIPD 2002. HMS Active, Falklands War, 1982; helicopter pilot, Fleet Air Arm, and Anti-submarine Warfare Officer; CO HMS Brave, 1994–96; Captain 6th Frigate Sqdn and CO HMS Montrose, 2000–02; Cdre, BRNC, 2002–04; CO HMS Ocean, 2004–05; Dep. Comdr and COS, Jt Helicopter Comd, 2005–06; FO Scotland, England, Wales and NI and FO Reserves, 2006–08. Mem., Windsor Leadership Trust, 1999–. Pres. RN and RM Sport Parachute Assoc., 2006–; Vice Pres., RN RU, 2002–. Younger Brother, Trinity House, 2005–. Freeman: City of London, 1998; Co. of Haberdashers, 1998; Mem., Incorporation of Wrights, Trades House, Glasgow, 2007. *Recreations:* all sports, reading, hill walking. *Address:* Headquarters Joint Helicopter Command, Erskine Barracks, Wilton, Salisbury, Wilts SP2 0AG. *T:* (01722) 433503, *Fax:* (01722) 436380.

JOICEY, family name of **Baron Joicey**.

JOICEY, 5th Baron *cr* 1906, of Chester-le-Street, Co. Durham; **James Michael Joicey;** DL; Bt 1893; *b* 28 June 1953; *s* of 4th Baron and Elisabeth Marion Joicey, MBE (*née* Leslie Melville); *S* father, 1993; *m* 1984, Agnes Harriet Frances Mary, *yr d* of Rev. and Mrs W. M. D. Thompson; two *s* two *d*. *Educ:* Eton Coll.; Christ Church, Oxford. DL Northumberland, 2006. *Heir: s* Hon. William James Joicey, *b* 21 May 1990. *Address:* Etal Manor, Berwick-upon-Tweed TD15 2PU.

JOICEY, Nicholas Beverley; Director International, HM Treasury, since 2008; *b* Guisborough, 11 May 1970; *s* of Harold Beverley and Wendy Joicey. *Educ:* Wintringham Sch., Grimsby; Univ. of Bristol (BA Hons Hist.); Peterhouse, Cambridge (PhD 1996). Journalist, The Observer, 1995–96; HM Treasury: Asst Private Sec. to Chief Sec., 1996–98; Hd, Internat. Instns Br., 1998–99; Private Sec. and Speechwriter to Chancellor of the Exchequer, 1999–2001; Advr, UK Delegn to IMF and World Bank, Washington, 2001–03 (on secondment); Head: EU Policy Team, 2004–06; EU Coordination and Strategy, 2006–07; Dir, Europe, 2007–08. *Recreations:* modern history, film. *Address:* c/o HM Treasury, 1 Horseguards Road, SW1A 2HQ.

JOLL, James Anthony Boyd, FSA; Chairman: Sir Winston Churchill Archive Trust, since 2000; Pearson Group Pension Trustee, since 1988; *b* 6 Dec. 1936; *s* of late Cecil Joll, FRCS and Antonia (*née* Ramsden); *m* 1st, 1963, Thalia Gough (marr. diss. 1973); one *s* two *d*; 2nd, 1977, Lucilla Kingsbury (marr. diss. 2007); two *s*. *Educ:* Eton; Magdalen Coll., Oxford (MA). FSA 2000. 2nd Lieut, 4th Queen's Own Hussars, 1955–57. Editorial staff, Financial Times, 1961–68, Jt Ed., Lex column, 1965–68; N. M. Rothschild & Sons, 1968–80, Dir, 1970–80; Exec. Dir, 1980–96, Finance Dir, 1985–96, Pearson plc. Chairman: AIB Asset Mgt Hldgs, 1997–2004; Atrium Underwriting plc, 2006–07; Dep. Chm., Jarvis Hotels, 1990–2004; Director: The Economist Newspaper, 1995–99; Equitas Hldgs, 1996–2007. Chm., Museums and Galls Commn, 1996–2000; Mem., Urgent Issues Task Force, Accounting Standards Bd, 1991–95. Trustee: Wallace Collection, 1990–2000; Design Museum, 1992–2005; Henry Moore Foundn, 2003–. Mem. Council, RCM, 2000–07. Robinson Medallist, V&A Museum, 2004. *Recreation:* the gothic revival. *Address:* Pearson plc, 80 Strand, WC2R 0RL. *Club:* Boodle's.

JOLLIFFE, family name of **Baron Hylton**.

JOLLIFFE, Sir Anthony (Stuart), GBE 1982; DL; *b* Weymouth, Dorset, 12 Aug. 1938; *s* of late Robert and of Vi Dorothea Jolliffe. *Educ:* Portchester Sch., Bournemouth. Qualified chartered accountant, 1964; articled to Morison Rutherford & Co.; commenced practice on own account in name of Kingston Jolliffe & Co., 1965, later, Jolliffe Cork & Co., Sen. Partner, 1976. Chairman: China Retail Sales Ltd; Jolliffe Internat.; Director: General Mediterranean Holdings; Turbochef Technologies Inc. Adv. and jt venture projects, China, ME; advr on foreign trade to Jinan govt, 2004; advr to Gov. of Shandong Province, China. Chm., Adv. Mission, Yunnan Provincial Govt, 2002–. Chm., Stoke Mandeville NHS Trust, 1994–95. Alderman, Ward of Candlewick, 1975–84; Sheriff, City of London, 1980–81; Lord Mayor of London, 1982–83. Pres., London Chamber of Commerce, 1985–88. Formerly Treasurer: Relate; Britain in Europe. Pres., Soc. of Dorset Men, 1984–. DL Dorset, 2006. KStJ 1983. *Recreations:* yachting, classic cars. *Clubs:* Garrick, City Livery (Pres., 1979–80), Saints and Sinners, Royal Automobile.

JOLLIFFE, Maj.-Gen. David Shrimpton, CB 2003; FRCP; Director General, Army Medical Services, 2000–03; *b* 20 March 1946; *s* of John Hedworth Jolliffe and Gwendoline Frances Angela Jolliffe (*née* Shrimpton); *m* 1969, Hilary Dickinson; two *d*. *Educ:* Ratcliffe Coll., Leicester; King's Coll. Hosp., London (MB). FRCP 1987. Regl MO, 23 Para Field Amb., 1971–73, 2 Para, 1973–74; Cons. Dermatologist, Queen Elizabeth Mil. Hosp., 1980–82; Consultant Advr in Dermatology to the Army, 1982–86; Commanding Officer:

British Mil. Hosp., Hong Kong, 1986–89; Cambridge Mil. Hosp., Aldershot, 1993–94; COS, Army Medical Directorate, 1996–99; Comdr, Med. HQ, Land Command, 1999–2000. QHP 1999–2003. Hon. Med. Advr, Royal Commonwealth Ex-Services League, 2003–. Chm., Hong Kong Locally Enlisted Personnel Trust, 2001–. Gov., Ratcliffe Coll., Leicester, 2001–; Mem., Bd of Mgt and Ct of Govs., LSHTM, 2006– (Chm., Audit Cttee, 2001–). Hon. Col, 207 (Manchester) Field Hosp. (V), 2003–. *Publications:* contrib. papers on general and tropical dermatology to professional jls. *Recreations:* carpentry, computer technology. *Address:* Ness House, 75 Eastgate, Pickering, North Yorkshire YO18 7DY; *e-mail:* red@pennswood.demon.co.uk.

JOLLIFFE, William Orlando, CPFA, FCA; County Treasurer of Lancashire, 1973–85; *b* 16 Oct. 1925; *s* of late William Dibble Jolliffe and Laura Beatrice Jolliffe; *m* 1st (marr. diss.); one *s* one *d*; 2nd, 1975, Audrey (*née* Dale); one step *d*. *Educ:* Bude County Grammar Sch. Chartered Accountant (first place in final exam. of (former) Soc. of Incorporated Accountants, 1956). Joined Barclays Bank Ltd, 1941. Served War of 1939–45 (HM Forces, 1944–48). Subseq. held various appts in Treasurers' depts of Devon CC, Winchester City Council, Doncaster CB Council, Bury CB Council (Dep. Borough Treas.), and Blackpool CB Council (Dep. 1959, Borough Treas., 1962). Mem. Council, Chartered Inst. of Public Finance and Accountancy, 1969–85 (Pres., 1979–80); Financial Adviser, ACC, 1976–85; Mem. Council (Pres. 1974–75), Assoc. of Public Service Finance Officers, 1963–76; Chm., Officers' Side, JNC for Chief Officers of Local Authorities in England and Wales, 1971–76; Mem. Exec. Cttee (Pres. 1970–71), NW Soc. of Chartered Accountants, 1966–76; Chm., NW and N Wales Region of CIPFA, 1974–76; Mem., Soc. of County Treasurers (Mem. Exec. Cttee, 1977–85); Hon. Treas., Lancashire Playing Fields Assoc., 1974–85. Financial Adviser to Assoc. of Municipal Corporations, 1969–74; Mem. (Govt) Working Party on Collab. between Local Authorities and the National Health Service, 1971–74. *Publications:* articles for Public Finance and Accountancy and other local govt jls. *Address:* 12 The Leylands, Lytham St Annes, Lancs FY8 5QS. *T:* (01253) 739358. *Club:* St Annes Old Links Golf.

JOLLY, Sir (Arthur) Richard, KCMG 2001; PhD; development economist; Hon. Professorial Fellow, Institute of Development Studies, University of Sussex; Co-Director, UN Intellectual History Project, Graduate Center, City University, New York, since 2000; *b* 30 June 1934; *s* of late Arthur Jolly and Flora Doris Jolly (*née* Leaver); *m* 1963, Alison Bishop, PhD; two *s* two *d*. *Educ:* Brighton Coll.; Magdalene Coll., Cambridge (BA 1956, MA 1959; Hon. Fellow, 2001); Yale Univ. (MA 1960, PhD 1966). Community Develt Officer, Baringo Dist, Kenya, 1957–59; Associate Chubb Fellow, Yale Univ., 1960–61; Res. Fellow, E Africa Inst. of Social Res., Makerere Coll., Uganda, 1963–64; Res. Officer, Dept of Applied Econs, Cambridge Univ., 1964–68 (seconded as Advr on Manpower to Govt of Zambia, 1964–66); Fellow, 1968–71, Professorial Fellow, 1971–81, Dir, 1972–81, Inst. of Develt Studies, Univ. of Sussex; Dep. Exec. Dir, Programmes, 1982–95, Actg Exec. Dir, 1995, UNICEF, NY; Special Advr to Adminr, UNDP, NY, 1996–2000. Advr on Manpower Aid, ODM, 1968; Sen. Economist, Min. of Develt and Finance, Zambia, 1970; Advr to Parly Select Cttee on Overseas Aid and Develt, 1974–75; ILO Advr on Planning, Madagascar, 1975; Member: Triennial Rev. Gp, Commonwealth Fund for Tech. Co-operation, 1975–76; UK Council on Internat. Develt, 1974–78; UN Cttee for Develt Planning, 1978–81; Special Consultant on N-S Issues to Sec.-Gen., OECD, 1978; sometime member and chief of ILO and UN missions, and consultant to various governments and international organisations. Hon. Chairman: Water Supply and Sanitation Collaborative Council, 1997–2005 (Hon. Lifetime Patron, 2005); UNA-UK, 2001–05. Trustee, Oxfam, 2001–06. Sec., British Alpine Hannibal Expedn, 1959. Member: Founding Cttee, European Assoc. of Develt Insts, 1972–75; Governing Council, 1976–85, and N-S Round Table, SID, 1976– (Vice-Pres., 1982–85; Chm., N-S Round Table, 1988–96). Mem., Editorial Bd, World Development, 1973–. Master, Curriers' Co., 1977–78. Hon. LittD E Anglia, 1988; Hon. DLitt Sussex, 1992; Hon. Dr Inst. of Social Studies, The Hague. *Publications:* (jtly) Cuba: the economic and social revolution, 1964; Planning Education for African Development, 1969; (ed) Education in Africa: research and action, 1969; (ed jtly) Third World Employment, 1973; (jtly) Redistribution with Growth, 1974 (trans. French 1977); (ed) Disarmament and World Development, 1978, 3rd edn 1986; (ed jtly) Recent Issues in World Development, 1981; (ed jtly) Rich Country Interests in Third World Development, 1982; (ed jtly) The Impact of World Recession on Children, 1984; (ed jtly) Adjustment with a Human Face, 1987 (trans. French 1987, Spanish 1987); (ed jtly) The UN and the Bretton Woods Institutions, 1995; (ed jtly) Human Development Report, annually 1996–2000 (trans. French, Spanish); (ed jtly) Development with a Human Face, 1998; (jtly) Ahead of the Curve, 2001; (ed) Jim Grant - UNICEF visionary, 2001; (jtly) UN Contributions to Development Thinking and Practice, 2004; articles in professional and develt jls. *Recreations:* billiards, croquet, nearly missing trains and planes. *Address:* Institute of Development Studies, University of Sussex, Brighton, Sussex BN1 9RE. *T:* (01273) 606261; *e-mail:* r.jolly@ids.ac.uk.

JOLLY, James Falcon; Editor-in-Chief, Gramophone, since 2006 (Editor, 1989–2005); Presenter, Classical Collection, BBC Radio 3, since 2007; *b* 12 Feb. 1961; *s* of late Gordon Jolly, FRCOG and of Enid Jolly; civil partnership 2006, Christopher Peter Davies. *Educ:* Pinewood Sch., Bourton; Bradfield Coll.; Univ. of Bristol (BA Hons); Univ. of Reading (MA). Asst Editor, Gramophone, 1985–88; Producer, BBC Radio 3, 1988–89. *Publications:* contrib. British Music Yearbook, 1986–88, Good CD Guide, Gramophone, Independent, Le Monde de la Musique, New Grove Dictionary of Opera. *Recreations:* food, wine, travel, cinema, gardening. *Address:* The Old White Horse, Sparrows Herne, Bushey, Herts WD23 1FU. *T:* (020) 8950 4552; (office) Teddington Studios, Broom Road, Teddington, Middx TW11 9BE.

JOLLY, Michael Gordon, CBE 2001; Chairman, Park Holidays UK (formerly Cinque Ports Leisure Ltd), since 2006; *b* 21 Sept. 1952; *s* of Ron and Joy Jolly; *m* 1975, Julia Catherine Gordon Sharp; one *s* one *d*. *Educ:* Henley-on-Thames Grammar Sch. Marketing and other positions, Cadbury-Schweppes plc, 1972–83; Tussaud's Group: Head, Marketing, 1983–87; Bd Dir, 1987–91; Chief Operating Officer, 1991–94; CEO, 1994–2000; Chm., 1994–2001; Chief Exec., Penna Consulting plc, 2001–03; Chm., Star Parks SA Europe, 2004–06. Comr, English Heritage, 2002–. *Recreations:* golf, the Arts.

JOLLY, Sir Richard; *see* Jolly, Sir A. R.

JOLLY, Air Cdre Robert Malcolm, CBE 1969; retired; *b* 4 Aug. 1920; *s* of Robert Imrie Jolly and Ethel Thompson Jolly; *m* 1946, Josette Jacqueline (*née* Baindeky); no *c*. *Educ:* Skerry's Coll., Newcastle upon Tyne. Commnd in RAF, 1943; served in: Malta, 1941–45; Bilbeis, Egypt, 1945; Shaibah, Iraq, 1945–46; Malta, 1946–49; Air Cdre 1971; Dir of Personal Services, MoD, 1970–72; Dir of Automatic Data Processing (RAF), 1973–75, retd. Man. Dir, Leonard Griffiths & Associates, 1975–77; Vice-Pres., MWS Consultants Inc., 1978–80; Gen. Man., Diebold Europe SA and Dir, Diebold Research Program Europe, 1983–84. Hon. Archivist, St Paul's Anglican Pro-Cathedral, Malta GC, 1992–. *Address:* Villa Grey Golf, 26 Triq Galata, High Ridge, St Andrews STJ 03, Malta GC. *T:* 370282. *Club:* Royal Air Force.

JOLOWICZ, Prof. John Anthony; QC 1990; Professor of Comparative Law, University of Cambridge, 1976–93; Fellow, Trinity College, Cambridge, since 1952; *b* 11 April 1926; *e s* of late Prof. Herbert Felix Jolowicz and Ruby Victoria Wagner; *m* 1957, Poppy Stanley; one *s* two *d*. *Educ:* Oundle Sch.; Trinity Coll., Cambridge (Scholar; MA; 1st Cl. Hons Law Tripos 1950). Served HM Forces (commnd RASC), 1944–48. Called to the Bar, Inner Temple and Gray's Inn, 1952; Bencher, Gray's Inn, 1978. Univ. of Cambridge: Asst Lectr in Law, 1955, Lectr, 1959; Reader in Common and Comparative Law, 1972. Professeur associé, Université de Paris 2, 1976; Lionel Cohen Lectr, Hebrew Univ. of Jerusalem, 1983. Pres., SPTL, 1986–87. Vice-Pres., Internat. Acad. of Comparative Law, 1994–2006 (Pres., Common Law Gp, 1990–98). Editor, Jl of Soc. of Public Teachers of Law, 1962–80. Corresp., Institut de France, Acad. des Sciences morales et politiques, 1989; MAE 1988. Hon. Dr Universidad Nacional Autónoma de México, 1985; Hon. LLD Buckingham, 2000. Chevalier de la Légion d'Honneur (France), 2002. *Publications:* (ed) H. F. Jolowicz's Lectures on Jurisprudence, 1963; Winfield and Jolowicz on Tort, 1971, 16th edn (ed W. V. H. Rogers) 2002; (with M. Cappelletti) Public Interest Parties and the Active Role of the Judge, 1975; (jtly) Droit Anglais, 1986, 2nd edn 1992; (jtly) Recourse against Judgments in the European Union, 1999; On Civil Procedure, 2000; contrib. to Internat. Encyc. of Comparative Law and to legal jls. *Address:* Trinity College, Cambridge CB2 1TQ. *T:* (01223) 338400; West Green House, Barrington, Cambridge CB22 7SA. *T:* (01223) 870495. *Clubs:* Royal Automobile; Leander (Henley-on-Thames).

JONAH, Samuel Esson, Hon. KBE 2003; Chairman, Jonah Capital; *b* 19 Nov. 1949; *s* of Thomas Jonah and Beatrice Sampson; *m* 1973, Lady Theodora Arthur; two *s* two *d*. *Educ:* Camborne Sch. of Mines (ACSM 1973); Imperial Coll. of Sci. and Technol. (MSc Mine Mgt). CEO, Ashanti Goldfields Co. Ltd, 1986–2005 (non-exec. Dir, AngloGoldAhanti, 2004–). Exec. Chm., Equator Exploration Co.; Director: Lonmin plc, 1992–2004; Anglo American Corp. of SA; Amplats; Standard Banking Gp. Member, International Advisory Council: Pres. of S Africa; Pres. of Ghana; Pres. of Nigeria; Member: Adv. Council of Pres. of African Develt Bank; Adv. Council, IFC; Global Compact Adv. Council of UN Sec.-Gen. Co-Chm., World Econ. Forum, Durban, 2003. Vis. Prof. of Business, Univ. of Witwatersrand Business Sch. of Johannesburg. Trustee, Nelson Mandela Legacy Trust, UK. Hon. DSc Camborne Sch. of Mines and Univ. of Exeter, 1994. Lifetime Achievement Award, Mining Jl, 2004. *Relevant publication:* Sam Jonah and the Re-making of Ashanti, by A. A. Taylor. *Recreation:* fishing. *Address:* PO Box 551, Melrose Arch, 2076 Johannesburg, South Africa. *T:* (11) 2152280, *Fax:* (11) 2686868; *e-mail:* sam@jonahcapital.com.

JONAS, Christopher William, CBE 1994; FRICS; property strategy adviser to large corporations; President, Royal Institution of Chartered Surveyors, 1992–93; *b* 19 Aug. 1941; *s* of late Philip Griffith Jonas, MC and Kathleen Marjory Jonas (*née* Ellis); *m* 1st, 1968, Penny Barker (marr. diss. 1997); three *s* one *d*; 2nd, 2003, Dame Judith Mayhew (*see* Dame Judith Mayhew Jonas). *Educ:* Charterhouse; Coll. of Estate Management; London Business Sch. (Sloan Fellow). TA Inns of Court Regt, 1959–66. Jones Lang Wootton, 1959–67; Drivers Jonas: Partner, 1967–82; Managing Partner, 1982–87; Sen. Partner, 1987–95. Property Adviser, Staffs County Council, 1982–2005. Director: SFA, 1988–91; BITC, 1999–2006; Railtrack Gp plc, 1994–2001; Canary Wharf Gp plc, 1994–2004; England Bd, Bank of Scotland, 1998–2000; Sunrise Senior (formerly Assisted) Living, 1998–; Chairman: Tate Modern develt, 1997–2000, and 2nd stage develt, 2006–; Education Capital Finance plc, 2000–03; Glasgow Harbour Ltd, 2001–03; Henderson Global Property Cos Ltd, 2006–; Sen. Advr, Lazard & Co., 2007–; Board Member: PLA, 1985–99; British Rail Property Bd, 1991–94; BR, 1993–94. Founder, ProHelp, 1989–; Mem., FEFC, 1992–98. Chm., Economics Research Associates, USA, 1987–93; Mem., Counselors of Real Estate, USA, (Gold Medal 2007). Dir, ENO, 1999–2007; Trustee, Westminster Abbey Pension Fund, 2001–. Governor: Charterhouse, 1995–2006; UCL, 1997–2005 (Vice-Chm., 2000–04); Chairman of Council: Roedean, 2004–; Goldsmiths Univ. of London (formerly Goldsmiths Coll.), 2006–. Liveryman: Clothworkers' Co. (Master, 2007–08); Chartered Surveyors' Co. FInstD; FRSA. Hon. DSc De Montfort, 1997. *Recreations:* lieder, opera, playing tennis. *Address:* 25 Victoria Square, SW1 0RB. *T:* (020) 7828 9977; *e-mail:* cwj@kingslodge.com. *Clubs:* Queen's; Toronto (Toronto).
See also R. W. Jonas.

JONAS, Dame Judith M.; *see* Mayhew Jonas.

JONAS, Sir Peter, Kt 2000; CBE 1993; opera company and orchestra director; General Director (Staatsintendant), Bavarian State Opera, 1993–2006; *b* 14 Oct. 1946; *s* of late Walter Adolf Jonas and Hilda May Jonas; *m* 1989, Lucy (marr. diss. 2001), *d* of Christopher and Cecilia Hull. *Educ:* Worth School; Univ. of Sussex (BA Hons); Royal Northern Coll. of Music (LRAM; FRNCM 2000); Royal Coll. of Music (CAMS; Fellow, 1989); Eastman Sch. of Music, Univ. of Rochester, USA. Asst to Music Dir, 1974–76, Artistic Administrator, 1976–85, Chicago Symphony Orch.; Dir of Artistic Admin, Orchestral Assoc. of Chicago (Chicago Symph. Orch., Chicago Civic Orch., Chicago Symph. Chorus, Allied Arts Assoc., Orchestra Hall), 1977–85; Man. Dir, subseq. Gen. Dir, ENO, 1985–93. Member: Adv. Bd, Hypo-Vereinsbank, 1994–2005; Bd of Governors, Bayerische Rundfunk, 1999–2006; Chm., German Speaking Opera Intendants Conf., 2000–05; Lectr, Faculty, Univ. of St Gallen, Switzerland, 2003–; Visiting Lecturer: Univ. of Zürich, 2004–; Bavarian Theatre Acad., Munich, 2006–. Mem., Adv. Bd, Tech. Univ., Munich, 2006–. Member: Bd of Management, Nat. Opera Studio, 1985–93; Council, RCM, 1988–95; Council, London Lighthouse, 1990–94; Supervisory Bd, City of Berlin Opera Trust, 2005–. FRSA 1989. Fellow, Bavarian Acad. of Fine Arts, 2005–. Hon. DrMus Sussex, 1994. Munich Prize for Culture, 2003; German-British Forum Award, 2006. Bavarian Constitutional Medal, 2001; Bayerische Verdienstorden, 2001. *Publications:* (with Mark Elder and David Pountney) Power House, 1992; (jtly) Eliten und Demokratie, 1999. *Recreations:* cinema, old master paintings, cricket, long-distance hiking. *Address:* Einsiedlerstrasse 15A, 8820 Wädenswil, Switzerland. *Club:* Athenæum.

JONAS, Richard Wheen, FRICS; Senior Partner, Cluttons, 1992–2003; *b* 10 April 1943; *s* of late Philip Griffith Jonas, MC and of Kathleen Marjory (*née* Ellis); *m* 1973, Bettina Banton; two *d*. *Educ:* Charterhouse; Royal Agricl Coll. Strutt & Parker, 1965–70; Carter Jonas, 1970–73; Cluttons, 1973–2003: Partner, 1978–2003. Dir, Babraham Bioscience Technologies Ltd, 2003–. Mem. Council, Roedean Sch., 2000–05; Gov., Sutton's Hospital in Charterhouse, 2002–. Liveryman, Clothworkers' Co., 1965– (Warden, 1996). Gold Medal, RASE, 1967. *Recreations:* shooting, golf, ornithology. *Club:* City of London.
See also C. W. Jonas.

JONES; *see* Allen-Jones.

JONES; *see* Armstrong-Jones, family name of Earl of Snowdon.

JONES; *see* Clement-Jones, family name of Baron Clement-Jones.

JONES; *see* Duncan-Jones.

JONES; *see* Garel-Jones.

JONES; *see* Griffith-Jones.

JONES; *see* Gwynne Jones, family name of Baron Chalfont.

JONES; *see* Idris Jones.

JONES; *see* Lloyd Jones and Lloyd-Jones.

JONES; *see* Neville-Jones.

JONES, family name of **Barons Jones** and **Jones of Cheltenham**.

JONES, Baron *cr* 2001 (Life Peer), of Deeside in the County of Clwyd; **Stephen Barry Jones;** PC 1999; *b* 1937; *s* of late Stephen and Grace Jones, Mancot, Flintshire; *m* Janet Jones (*née* Davies); one *s*. MP (Lab): Flint East, 1970–83; Alyn and Deeside, 1983–2001. PPS to Rt Hon. Denis Healey, 1972–74; Parly Under-Sec. of State for Wales, 1974–79; Opposition spokesman on employment, 1980–83; Chief Opposition spokesman on Wales, 1983–87, 1988–92; Mem., Labour Shadow Cabinet, 1983–87 and 1988–92. Member: Speaker's Panel of Chairmen, 1993–2001; Prime Minister's Intelligence and Security Cttee, 1994–2001; Dep. Speaker, Westminster Hall, 2001–; Chm., Speaker's Adv. Cttee on political parties, 1999; Mem., Speaker's Cttee on Electoral Commn, 2001. Mem., WEU and Council of Europe, 1971–74. Member: Govs, Nat. Mus., Wales, 1992–; Court, Univ. of Wales, 1992–; Nat. Liby of Wales, 1992–. Chm., St Asaph Diocesan Bd of Educn and Lifelong Learning, 2004–. President: Deeside Hosp., 2000–; Flintshire Br., Alzheimer's Soc., 2001–; NE Wales Inst. for Higher Educn, 2007–. *Address:* House of Lords, SW1A 0PW.

JONES OF BIRMINGHAM, Baron *cr* 2007 (Life Peer), of Alvechurch and of Bromsgrove in the county of Worcestershire; **Digby Marritt Jones,** Kt 2005; Minister of State for UK Trade and Investment, Department for Business, Enterprise and Regulatory Reform, and Foreign and Commonwealth Office, 2007–08; *b* 28 Oct. 1955; *s* of Derek Alwyn Jones and Bernice Joyce Jones; *m* 1990, Patricia Mary Moody. *Educ:* Bromsgrove Sch.; UCL (LLB Hons 1977; Fellow, 2004). Admitted Solicitor, 1980. Joined Edge & Ellison, Solicitors, 1978; articled clerk, 1978–80; Asst Solicitor, 1980–81; Associate, 1981–84; Partner, 1984–98; Head of Corporate, 1987; Dep. Sen. Partner, 1990–95; Sen. Partner, 1995–98; Vice-Chm., Corporate Finance, KPMG Business Advisors, 1998–99; Dir Gen., CBI, 2000–06. Mem., CRE, 2003–07. Senior Advr to Exec., Deloitte, Barclays Capital, JCB, 2006–07; Corporate and Govtl Affairs Advr to Ford of Europe, 2006–; Corporate Affairs Advr to Bucknall Austin Ltd, 2006–07; Special Advr to Duke of York, Monetise Ltd, 2006–07; Mem., Adv. Bd, Thales (UK) Ltd, 2006–07. Non-executive Director: Alba plc, 2004–07; Leicester Tigers Rugby Club, 2005–. Chm., Tourism Alliance, 2001–05; Dir, VisitBritain, 2003–06. Dir, BITC, 2000–06; Mem., Nat. Learning and Skills Council, 2003–06. UK Skills Envoy, 2006–07. Vice-Pres., UNICEF, 2002–06 (Fellow, 2006). CCMI. DUniv: UCE, 2002; Birmingham, 2002; Herts 2004; Hon. DLitt UMIST, 2003; Hon. Dr: London; Cardiff; Manchester; Middlesex; Sheffield Hallam; Aston; Hull; Warwick; Bradford; Thames Valley; Wolverhampton; QUB. *Recreations:* Rugby, ski-ing, military history, keeping fit by cycling (cycled from John O'Groats to Lands End in June 1998) and running (London Marathon in 5 hours 58 minutes and 26 seconds, 2005). *Address:* House of Lords, SW1A 0PW.

JONES OF CHELTENHAM, Baron *cr* 2005 (Life Peer), of Cheltenham in the county of Gloucestershire; **Nigel David Jones;** *b* 30 March 1948; *m* 1981, Katy Grinnell; one *s* twin *d*. *Educ:* Prince Henry's Grammar Sch., Evesham. With Westminster Bank, 1965–67; computer programmer, ICL Computers, 1967–70; systems analyst, Vehicle and Gen. Insce, 1970–71; systems programmer, Atkins Computing, 1971; systems designer and consultant, ICL Computers, 1971–92. Contested (L) Cheltenham, 1979. MP (Lib Dem) Cheltenham, 1992–2005. Lib Dem spokesman on England, local govt and housing, 1992–93, science and technology, 1993–99, consumer affairs, 1995–97, culture, media and sport, 1997–99, internat. devel t, 1999–2005. *Address:* House of Lords, SW1A 0PW.

JONES OF WHITCHURCH, Baroness *cr* 2006 (Life Peer), of Whitchurch in the County of South Glamorgan; **Margaret Beryl Jones;** Director of Policy and Public Affairs, UNISON, 1995–2006; *b* 22 May 1955; *d* of Bill and Audrey Jones. *Educ:* Whitchurch High Sch., Cardiff; Sussex Univ. (BA Hons Sociol. 1976). Regl Official, 1979–89, Nat. Officer, 1989–95, NUPE, later UNISON. Mem. Bd, Circle Anglia, 2006–; Trustee, Shelter, 2003–; Vice Chm., School Food Trust, 2006–. Mem., Fitness to Practice Panel, GMC, 2006–. Mem. Bd, Waste and Resources Action Prog., 2007–. Chm., RICS Ombudsman Scheme, 2007–. Contested (Lab) Blaenau Gwent, 2005. *Address:* House of Lords, SW1A 0PW.

JONES, Adam M.; *see* Mars-Jones.

JONES, Adrianne Shirley, (Ann), MBE 1969; Women's Team Captain, Lawn Tennis Association, 1990–97; BBC tennis commentator, since 1970; *b* 17 Oct. 1938; *d* of Adrian Arthur Haydon and Doris (*née* Jordan); *m* 1962, Philip Frank Jones (*d* 1993); two *s* one *d*. *Educ:* King's Norton Grammar Sch., Birmingham. Finalist, World Table Tennis Championships: Ladies Doubles, 1954; Singles, Ladies Doubles, Mixed Doubles, 1957; Tennis Championships: Winner, French Open, 1961, 1966; Winner, Italian Open, 1966; Finalist, US, 1961, 1967; Wimbledon: Finalist, Ladies Singles, 1967; Winner, 1969; semi-finalist nine times. Chm., Women's Internat. Professional Tennis Council, 1977–84; Dir, European Ops, Women's Tennis Assoc., 1976–84. Member: Cttee of Mgt, Wimbledon Championships, 1991–; Internat. and Professional Tennis Bd, LTA, 1993–2004. *Publications:* Tackle Table Tennis My Way, 1957; Tennis: a game to love, 1970. *Recreations:* all sports, reading, music. *Address:* 101 Knightlow Road, Harborne, Birmingham B17 8PX. *T:* (0121) 247 5644. *Clubs:* All England Lawn Tennis, Queen's; Edgbaston Priory.

JONES, Alan; *see* Jones, David A.

JONES, Alan; Chief Executive, Somerset County Council, since 2003; *b* 22 Sept. 1952; *s* of Thomas Jones and Ellen Jones; *m* 1974, Susan Fiona Dawn Lovell; two *d*. *Educ:* Univ. of Kent at Canterbury (BA 1st cl. Hons (Sociol.) 1974); Univ. of Liverpool (MCD 1st cl. 1976); Kent Coll. (Dip. Mgt Studies (Distn) 1982). Res. Asst, Merseyside MCC, 1975–76; Area Planning Officer, Maidstone BC, 1976–83; Prin. Planner, Gravesham BC, 1983–84; Develt Control Manager, Reading BC, 1984–86; Hd, Develt and Planning, Stevenage BC, 1986–88; Corporate Dir, Develt Services, Newbury DC, 1988–96; Chief Exec., Test Valley BC, 1996–2003; Interim Change Manager, Watford Council, 2002–03. *Recreations:* cycling, tennis, canoeing, watercolour painting, photography, acoustic guitar, gardening. *Address:* Somerset County Council, County Hall, Taunton, Somerset TA1 4DY. *T:* (01823) 355455, *Fax:* (01823) 355258; *e-mail:* alanjones@somerset.gov.uk.

JONES, Alan David, OBE 1996; Founder Chairman, Team Excellence Ltd, since 2004; *b* 16 June 1947; *s* of late Sydney Jones and Yvette Jones; *m* 1996, Juliet Louise Nance-Kivell Berrisford; one *s* three *d*. *Educ:* Holly Lodge Grammar Sch. for Boys; Staffordshire Coll. of Commerce. CTA 1968; FCCA 1973; FCILT (FCIT 1990); FCIPS 1992. Man. Dir, TNT UK Ltd, 1984–99; Gp Man. Dir, TNT Express, 1999–2003; Mem. Bd of Mgt, TPG NV, 1999–2003; Chief Exec., GSL, 2005–08. Founder Chairman, Midlands Excellence, 1996–. Director: Ardent Productions Ltd, 1994–2002; British Quality Foundn, 1995–99; Services Bd, DTI, 2001–04. Member: Ministerial Adv. Bd for Defence Procurement, 1996–2006; Employment Tribunal System Taskforce, 2002–04. Special Prof., Nottingham Univ. Business Sch., 2003– Founder, Faculty of Freight, 1990, Chm., 1990–91, CIT; Mem. Council, Inst. of Logistics, 1992–94. Mem., Eastern Reg. Council, 1977–78, Nat. Council, 1989–91, CBI; Dep. Chm., Coventry and Warwicks TEC, 1992–99. Freeman, City of London, 1994; Liveryman, Co. of Carmen, 1994–. Guardian, Assay Office, Birmingham, 1998–2000. Chm., In Kind Direct, 1997–2004; Chm., European, Mediterranean and Arab States Reg., and Trustee, Duke of Edinburgh's Award, 2004–. Mem. Ct, Warwick Univ., 1992–96. Hon. Gov., European Foundn for Quality Mgt, 2000–. CCMI (CIMgt 1993); CCQI (CIQA 2004). Hon. MA Coventry, 1996; Hon. DSc Aston, 2002; DUniv UCE 2004. *Recreations:* reading, walking, jazz. *Address:* Cherwell House, Little Tew, near Chipping Norton, Oxon OX7 4JE; TeamExcellence Ltd, 5 Park Town, Oxford OX2 6SN. *Club:* Athenæum.

JONES, Sir Alan (Jeffrey), Kt 2005; Chairman, Toyota Motor Manufacturing (UK) Ltd, 2003–06, now Chairman Emeritus; Executive Vice-President, Toyota Motor Engineering and Manufacturing Europe, 2003–06. *Educ:* Luton Coll. of Higher Educn. Manufacturing Dir, Vauxhall Motors, 1987–90; Dir of Manufacturing, 1990–96, Dep. Man. Dir, 1996–2001, Man. Dir, 2001–03, Toyota Motor Manufacturing (UK) Ltd. Chairman: SMMT Industry Forum, 2002– (Mem. Bd, 1997–); Sci., Engrg and Manufg Technologies Alliance, 2006–.

JONES, Alan Wingate, FREng, FIET; Chairman, Manchester Airports Group, since 2004; *b* 15 Oct. 1939; *s* of Gilbert Victor Jones and Isobel Nairn Jones; *m* 1974, Judi Ann Curtis; one *s* one *d*. *Educ:* Sutton Valence Sch.; King's Coll., Cambridge (MA MechScis). GEC, 1961–73; Plessey Co. Plc, 1973–89: Man. Dir, Plessey Marine, 1975–79; Divl Man. Dir, Plessey Displays and Sensors, 1979–85; Internat. Dir, 1985–87; Man. Dir, Plessey Electronic Systems, 1987–89; Dir, Plessey Plc, 1985–89; Chief Exec., Westland Gp, 1989–95; Dir, GKN, 1994–95; Chief Exec., BICC plc, 1995–99. Chm., Britax Internat., 2001–04; Director: Witan Investment Trust, 1996–; Agusta Westland, 2005–. Mem., Financial Reporting Council, 1998–2001. FREng (FEng 1989); FIET (FIEE 1990); FRAeS 1993; CCMI (CIMgt 1995). *Recreations:* opera, shooting, sailing. *Address:* The Grange, North Cadbury, Yeovil, Somerset BA22 7BY.

JONES, Aled; singer; television and radio presenter; *b* 29 Dec. 1970; *s* of Derek Jones and Nêst Jones; *m* 2001, Claire Fossett; one *s* one *d*. *Educ:* Royal Acad. of Music (ARAM); Bristol Old Vic Theatre Sch. Presenter: Songs of Praise, BBC TV; various radio progs. Recordings include: Walking in the Air, 1985; albums: Aled Jones; Ave Maria; Hear My Prayer; Whenever God Shines His Light, 2002; From the Heart, 2002; Aled, 2002; Higher, 2003; Morning Has Broken, 2003; Sacred Songs, 2004; The Christmas Album, 2004; New Horizons, 2005; You Raise Me Up: the best of Aled Jones, 2006. *Publication:* Aled (autobiog.), 2005. *Address:* *e-mail:* steve.abbott@bedlammanagement.com, giselle.allier@bedlammanagement.com.

JONES, Alexander Martin, (Sandy); Chief Executive, Professional Golfers' Association, since 1991; *b* 9 Dec. 1946; *s* of Henry and Catherine Jones. *Educ:* Stow Coll., Glasgow (qualif. Structl Engr 1968). Structural engineer/computer programmer, 1969–80; Scottish Regl Sec., PGA, 1980–91; Director: Ryder Cup, 1991–; Golf Foundn, 1991–; Chm., PGA of Europe, 1995–. *Recreations:* golf, football (watching). *Address:* Professional Golfers' Association, Centenary House, The Belfry, Sutton Coldfield, W Midlands B76 9PT. *T:* (01675) 470333; *e-mail:* sandy.jones@pga.org.uk. *Clubs:* Caledonian; Loch Lomond Golf, Little Aston Golf.

JONES, Allan William, MBE 2000; Chief Executive Officer (formerly Chief Development Officer), London Climate Change Agency, since 2004; Director, London ESCO Ltd, since 2006; Chief Technologist, London Development Agency, since 2007; *b* 23 Dec. 1948; *s* of Leonard John William Jones and Joan Violet Jones; *m* 1989, Margaret Jane Deeks; one *s* one *d*, and one step *s*. *Educ:* Guildford County Coll. of Technology (CNAA HNC Electrical and Electronic Engrg). IEng, FIET. From Design Engr to Sen. Manager, Dept of Mech. and Elec. Engrg, GLC, 1971–86; Sen. Manager, Dept of Bldg and Property Services, ILEA, 1986–89; Energy Services Manager, Woking BC, 1989–2004; Dir, Thameswey Ltd (Woking BC's energy and envmtl services co.), 1999–2004. FRSA. *Publications:* Woking Park - fuel cell combined heat and power system, 2003; Moving London towards a Sustainable Low-carbon City, 2007; numerous papers incl. for IEE, IMechE, CIBSE, Combined Heat and Power Assoc., Fuel Cell Europe, Renewable Power Assoc., Connecticut Clean Energy Fund, Forum for the Future, Parly Renewable and Sustainable Energy and Warm Homes Gps, London Hydrogen Partnership. *Recreations:* nature, the environment, walking, photography, the family. *Address:* London Climate Change Agency, Palestra, 197 Blackfriars Road, SE1 8AA. *T:* (020) 7593 8122, *Fax:* (020) 7593 8002; *e-mail:* allan.jones@lcca.co.uk.

JONES, Allen, RA 1986 (ARA 1981); artist; *b* 1 Sept. 1937; *s* of William Jones and Madeline Jones (*née* Aveson); *m* 1st, 1964, Janet Bowen (marr. diss. 1978); two *d*; 2nd, 1994, Deirdre Morrow. *Educ:* Ealing Grammar Sch. for Boys; Hornsey Sch. of Art (NDD; ATD); Royal Coll. of Art. Teacher of Lithography, Croydon Coll. of Art, 1961–63; Teacher of Painting, Chelsea Sch. of Art, 1966–68; Tamarind Fellow in Lithography, Los Angeles, 1968; Guest Professor: Hochschule für Bildenden Kunst, Hamburg, 1968–70; Univs of S Florida, 1970, Calif at Irvine, 1973, Los Angeles, 1977; Hochschule für Kunst Berlin, 1983; has travelled extensively. Sec., Young Contemporaries exhibn, London, 1961. First internat. exhibn, Paris Biennale, 1961 (Prix des Jeunes Artistes); first professional exhibn (with Howard Hodgkin), Two Painters, ICA, 1962; first UK mus. exhibn, Decade of Painting and Sculpture, Tate Gall., 1964; *museum and group exhibitions* in UK and abroad include: New Generation, Whitechapel, 1964; London, The New Scene, Minneapolis, 1965; British Drawing/New Generation, NY, 1967; Documenta IV, Kassel, 1968; Pop Art Redefined, Hayward Gall., 1969; British Painting and Sculpture, Washington, 1970; Metamorphosis of Object, Brussels, and tour, 1971; Seibu, Tokyo, 1974; Hyperealist/Realistes, Paris, 1974; Arte Inglese Oggi, Milan, 1976; El color en la pintura Britanica, British Council S American tour, 1977; British Painting 1952–77, Royal Academy, 1977; Arts Council sponsored exhibn tour, UK, 1978, Wales, 1992; British Watercolours, British Council tour, China, 1982; The Folding Image, Washington and Yale, 1984; Pop Art 1955–1970, NY, then Aust. tour, 1985; 40 Years of Modern Art, Tate Gall., 1986; British Art in the Twentieth Century, Royal Academy, then Stuttgart, 1987; Pop Art, Tokyo, 1987; Picturing People, British Council tour, Hong Kong, Singapore, Kuala Lumpur, 1990; New Acquisitions, Kunstmus., Dusseldorf, 1990; Seoul Internat. Art Fest., 1991; BM, 1991, 1997; Pop Art, Royal Academy, 1991, then Cologne, Madrid and Montreal, 1992; From Bacon to Now, Florence; Nat. Portrait Gall., 1994; Centre Georges Pompidou, Paris, 1995; Treasure Island, Gulbenkian Foundn, Lisbon, 1997; The Pop '60s, Centro Cultural de Belém, Lisbon, 1997; Pop Impressions Europe/USA, MoMA NY,

1999; Pop Art: US/UK Connections 1956–1966, Menil Foundn, Houston, 2001; Les années pop, Centre Georges Pompidou, Paris, 2001; Transition: the London art scene in the Fifties, Barbican, 2002; Out of Line: drawings from the Arts Council collection, 2002; Den Haag Sculptuur, 2002; Blast to Freeze, Wolfsburg, 2002; Thinking Big: concepts for 21st century British Sculpture, Peggy Guggenheim Collection, Venice, 2002; Phantom der Lust, Stadtmus., Graz, 2002; Mike Kelley - The Uncanny, Tate Liverpool, 2004; Art and the Sixties: This Was Tomorrow, Tate Britain, 2004 and Birmingham Mus. and Art Gall., 2004–05; Pop Art Portraits, NPG, 2007; Gagosian Gall., London, 2007; exhibited annually at Royal Acad., 1981–; *one-man exhibitions* include: Arthur Tooth and Sons, London, 1963, 1964, 1967, 1970; Richard Feigen Gall., NY, Chicago and LA, 1964, 1965, 1970; Marlborough Fine Art, London, 1972; Arts Council sponsored exhibn tour, UK, 1974; Waddington Galls, London, 1976, 1980, 1982, 1983, 1985, 1993; James Corcoran Gall., LA, 1977, 1987; UCLA Art Galls, LA, 1977; Graphic Retrospective 1958–78, ICA, 1978; first Retrospective of Painting, 1959–79, Walker Art Gall., Liverpool, and tour of England and Germany, 1979; Thorden Wetterling, Gothenburg, 1983; Gall. Kammer, Hamburg, 1983, 1984; Gall. Wentzel, Cologne (sculpture), 1984; Gall. Patrice Trigano, Paris, 1985, 1986, 1989, 1998; Gall. Kaj Forsblom, Helsinki, 1985, 1999; Gall. Hete Hunermann, Dusseldorf, 1987, 1994; Charles Cowles Gall., NY, 1988; Heland Wetterling Gall., Stockholm, 1989; Gall. Wentzel, Cologne, 1992; Gall. Punto, Valencia, 1992; Gall. Levy, Hamburg and Madrid, 1993, 1995, 1997, 1999, 2003; Galerie Hilger, Vienna, 2004; Galerie Terminus, Munich, 2004; Print Retrospective, Barbican Centre and tour, 1995–98; Kunsthalle, Darmstadt, 1996; Galeria Civica, Modena, 1996; Thomas Gibson Fine Art, London, 1997; Trussardi, Milan, 1998; Ars Nova Mus. of Contemp. Art, Turku, 1999; Summerstage (sculpture), Vienna, 1999; Gall. d'Arte Maggiore, Bologna, 1999; Palazzo dei Sette, Orvieto, 2002; Norddeutschen Landesbank, Hanover, 2002; Landeshauptstadt, Schwerin, 2003; Galerie Trigano, Paris, 2006; Galerie Levy, Hamburg, 2006; *dedicated rooms:* RA Summer Exhibn, 2002; paintings and drawings, Tate Britain, 2007–08; water colours, Royal Acad., 2007–08; Galeria Prates, Lisbon, 2007; Alan Cristea Gall., London, 2007; *murals and sculptures for public places* include: Fogal, Basel and Zurich; Liverpool Garden Fest., 1984; Citicorp/Canadian Nat. Bank, London Bridge City, 1987; Milton Keynes, 1990; BAA, Heathrow, 1990; Ivy Restaurant, London, 1990; Chelsea/Westminster Hosp., 1993; LDDC, 1994; Swire Properties, Hong Kong, 1997; Sculpture at Goodwood, 1998; Chatsworth House, 2000; GlaxoSmithKline, London, 2001; Swire Properties, Hong Kong, 2002; Yuzi Paradise Sculpture Parks, Guilin and Shanghai, China, 2006; television and stage sets include: O Calcutta!, for Kenneth Tynan, London and Europe, 1970; Manner Wir Kommen, WDR, Cologne, 1970; Understanding Opera, LWT, 1988; Cinema/Eric Satie, for Ballet Rambert, 1989; Signed in Red, for Royal Ballet, 1996. Television films have been made on his work. Trustee, British Mus., 1990–99. *Publications:* Allen Jones Figures, 1969; Allen Jones Projects, 1971; Waitress, 1972; Sheer Magic, 1979, UK 1980; Allen Jones, 1993; Allen Jones Prints, 1995; Allen Jones, 1997; Allen Jones Works, 2005; articles in various jls. *Recreation:* gardening. *Address:* 41 Charterhouse Square, EC1M 6EA. *Fax:* (020) 7600 1204; *e-mail:* aj@allenjonestheartist.com.

JONES, Alun; *see* Jones, R. A.

JONES, Dr Alun Denry Wynn, OBE 2001; CSci, FInstP; Chief Executive, Institute of Physics, 1990–2002; *b* 13 Nov. 1939; *s* of Thomas D. and Ray Jones; *m* 1964, Ann Edwards; two *d.* *Educ:* Amman Valley Grammar Sch.; Christ Church, Oxford (MA, DPhil). FInstP 1973; CSci 2004. Sen. Student, Commission for Exhibn of 1851, 1964–66; Sen. Research Fellow, UKAEA, 1966–67; Lockheed Missiles and Space Co., California, 1967–70; Tutor, Open Univ., 1971–82; joined Macmillan and Co., Publishers, 1971; Dep. Editor, Nature, 1972–73; British Steel Corp., 1974–77; British Steel Overseas Services, 1977–81; Asst Dir, Technical Change Centre, 1982–85; Dep. Dir, 1986–87, Dir, 1987–90, Wolfson Foundn. British Association for Advancement of Science: Sec. of working party on social concern and biological advances, 1972–74; Mem., Section X Cttee, 1981–92; Council Mem., 1999–2005; Mem., Exec. Cttee, 2001–05; Mem., Audit Cttee, 2005–. British Library: Adv. Council, 1983–85; Document Supply Centre Adv. Cttee, 1986–89; Mem. Council, Nat. Library of Wales, 1987–94 (Gov., 1986–94). Dir, Sci. Council (formerly Council for Sci. and Technol. Insts), 1990–2002 (Chair, Registration Authority, 2005–); Mem. Council, Assoc. of Schs' Sci., Engrg & Technol. (formerly Standing Conf. on Schs' Sci. & Technol.), 1992–2000 (Dep. Chm., 1996–2000). Gov., 1990–92 and 2002–05, Council Mem., 2002–05, UCW, Aberystwyth; Governor: City Univ., 1991–2001; Sir William Perkins's Sch., Chertsey, 2002– (Chair of Govs, 2005–). Fellow, Univ. of Wales, Aberystwyth, 2000. *Publication:* (with W. F. Bodmer) Our Future Inheritance: choice or chance, 1974. *Recreations:* gardening, theatre, cricket. *Address:* 4 Wheatsheaf Close, Woking, Surrey GU21 4BP.

JONES, Alun Ffred; Member (Plaid Cymru) Arfon, National Assembly for Wales, since 2007 (Caernarfon, 2003–07); *b* 29 Oct. 1949; *s* of Rev. Gerallt and Elizabeth Jane Jones; *m* 1981, Alwen Roberts (*d* 2005); two *s* one *d.* *Educ:* University Coll. of N Wales, Bangor (BA). Teacher: Deeside High Sch., 1971–75; Alun High Sch., Mold, 1975–79 (Head of Dept); TV journalist, 1979–81; TV director/producer, 1981–2003. Member: Arfon Borough DC, 1992–96; Gwynedd Council, 1996–2004; Leader, Gwynedd UA, 1996–2003. Chm., Envmt, Agric. and Planning Cttee, Nat. Assembly for Wales, 2003–07. *Address:* Plaid Cymru, 8 Stryd y Castell, Caernarfon, Gwynedd LL55 1SE. *T:* (01286) 672076, *Fax:* (01286) 672003; *e-mail:* alunffred.jones@cymru.gov.uk.

JONES, Angela; *see* Jones, S. A. M.

JONES, Ann; *see* Jones, Adrianne S.

JONES, Ann; Member (Lab) Vale of Clwyd, National Assembly for Wales, since 1999; *b* 4 Nov. 1953; *d* of Charles and Helen Sadler; *m* 1973, Adrian Jones; two *c.* *Educ:* Rhyl Grammar, then High, Sch. Fire Service Emergency Call Operator, 1976–99. Nat. Official, Fire Brigade's Union, 1982–99. Member (Lab): Rhyl Town Council, 1991–99 (Mayor of Rhyl, 1996–97); Denbighshire CC, 1995–99 (Lab spokesman on educn, 1995–98). Mem., N Wales Fire Authy, 1995–99. Welsh Assembly: Chm., Lab Mems, 1999–2000; Member: Econ. Develt Cttee, 1999–; N Wales Regl Cttee, 1999–; Health and Social Services Cttee, 2000–. *Address:* 47 Kinmel Street, Rhyl LL18 1AG. *T:* (01745) 332813.

JONES, Anna Louise; *see* Bradley, A. L.

JONES, Prof. Anne; Founder and Managing Director, Lifelong Learning Systems Ltd, since 2000; Professor of Lifelong Learning, Brunel University, 1995–2001, now Professor Emeritus; *b* 8 April 1935; *d* of Sydney Joseph and Hilda Pickard; *m* 1958, C. Gareth Jones (marr. diss. 1989); one *s* two *d.* *Educ:* Harrow Weald County Sch.; Westfield Coll., London (BA; Fellow, QMW, 1992); DipSoc, PGCE London. Assistant Mistress: Malvern Girls' Coll., 1957–58; Godolphin and Latymer Sch., 1958–62; Dulwich Coll., 1964; Sch. Counsellor, Mayfield Comprehensive Sch., 1965–71; Dep. Hd, Thomas Calton Sch., 1971–74; Head: Vauxhall Manor Sch., 1974–81; Cranford Community Sch., 1981–87; Under Sec. (Dir of Educn), Dept of Employment, 1987–91; management consultant, 1991–93; Brunel University: Prof. of Continuing Educn, 1991–97; Dir of Contg Educn, 1991–93; Hd of Dept of Contg Educn, 1993–97; Dir, Centre for Lifelong Learning, 1995–2001; Mem. of Ct, 2001–. Vis. Prof. of Educn, Sheffield Univ., 1989–91. OFSTED Registered Inspector, 1993–2003. Chm., Parents in a Learning Soc., RSA, 1992–95. Director: CRAC, 1983–94; Grubb Inst. of Behavioural Studies, 1987–94. Occasional Mem., Selection Panel, Cabinet Office, 1993–. Advr, European Trng Foundn, 1995–. Indep. Lay Chair, Complaints, NHS, 1996–2003. Member Council: QMW, 1991–2002; W London Inst. of Higher Educn, 1991–95; NICEC, 1991–95. Chm., Boathouse Reach Mgt, 2005–. Gov., Abbey Sch., Reading, 2004–. Trustee: The Westfield Trust, 1992–; Menerva Educnl Trust, 1993–2004 (Chm., 1993–99). FRSA 1984 (Mem. Council, 1986–94); FCMI (FIMgt 1992) (Chm., Reading Br., 2004–08); FICPD 1998. Hon. FCP 1990. *Publications:* School Counselling in Practice, 1970; Counselling Adolescents in School, 1977, 2nd edn as Counselling Adolescents, School and After, 1984; Leadership for Tomorrow's Schools, 1987; (with Jan Marsh and A. G. Watts): Male and Female, 1974, 2nd edn 1982; Living Choices, 1976; Time to Spare, 1980; contribs to various books. *Recreations:* rambling, travel, boating, gardening, theatre, opera, singing in Henley Choral Society (Chm., 2005–). *Address:* 8 Boathouse Reach, Henley-on-Thames, Oxfordshire RG9 1TJ. *T:* (01491) 578672; *e-mail:* anne.jones@lls.co.uk. *Club:* Phyllis Court (Henley-on-Thames).

JONES, Prof. Anthony Edward, CBE 2003; FRCA; President of the School of Art and Co-Chief Executive Officer, Art Institute of Chicago, 1986–92 and since 1996; *b* 3 Aug. 1944; *s* of late Edward and Violet Jones; *m* 1st, 1972, Gwen Brandt (marr. diss. 1978); one *s*; 2nd, 1989, Patricia Jon Carroll. *Educ:* Goldsmiths' Coll., Univ. of London; Newport Coll. of Art, Newport (DipAD, BA); Tulane Univ., New Orleans (MFA). Artist-in-Residence, Loyola Univ., 1967–68; Teaching Fellow, Gloucester Coll. of Art, Cheltenham, 1968–69; Sen. Lectr and Dep. Head of Sculpture, Glasgow Sch. of Art, 1969–72; Chm., Dept of Art and Art Hist., Texas Christian Univ., 1972–80; Dir, Glasgow Sch. of Art, 1980–86; Rector, Royal Coll. of Art, 1992–96. Fulbright Scholar, USA, 1966–68. Hon. Prof., Univ. of Wales, 2000; Hon. Dir, Osaka Univ. of the Arts, 2002. Exhibn, Liberty Style, Japan tour, 1999–2000, and catalogue, 1999; Exhibn, Painting the Dragon, Nat. Mus. of Wales, 2000 (presenter, BBC TV series, 2001). FRCA 1993; FRSA 1994; Hon. AIA 1991. Hon. DFA Memphis Coll. of Art, 2002. Newbery Medal, Glasgow Univ., 1986; US Nat. Council of Art Administrators Award, 2001; Austrian Cross of Honour for Sci. and the Arts, 2002. *Publications:* Chapel Architecture in the Merthyr Valley, 1964; Welsh Chapels (Capeli Cymru), 1984, 1996; Charles Rennie Mackintosh, 1990; Painting the Dragon, 2000; Living in Wales: David Hurn, 2003; Archibald Knox (essays), 2003; Robert Stewart Design (essays), 2003. *Recreation:* travel, reluctantly! *Address:* School of the Art Institute of Chicago, 37 South Wabash Avenue, Chicago, IL 60603, USA. *Clubs:* Chelsea Arts; University (Chicago).

JONES, Anthony Graham Hume; His Honour Judge Graham Hume Jones; a Circuit Judge, since 1993; Deputy Senior Judge, Sovereign Base Areas, Cyprus, since 1999; Resident Judge, Taunton Crown Court, since 2003; *b* 16 Aug. 1942; *s* of Rt Hon. Sir Edward Jones, PC and Margaret Anne Crosland (*née* Smellie); *m* 1966, Evelyn Ann Brice Smyth (*d* 1998), *o d* of Brice Smyth, Belfast; two *s* one *d.* *Educ:* Trinity Coll., Glenalmond; Trinity Coll., Dublin (BA 1966). Mardon, Son & Hall Ltd, 1966–71; called to the Bar, Gray's Inn, 1971; called to the Bar, NI, 1981; a Recorder, 1990–93. Vice-Pres., Avon Br., SSAFA, 1993–; Mem. Council, RNLI, 2003–. Master, Antient Soc. of St Stephen's Ringers, 1999–2000. *Recreations:* sailing, golf. *Address:* Yeowood, Wrington, Bristol BS40 5NS; Craig-y-Mor, Trearddur Bay, Holyhead, Anglesey LL65 2UP. *Clubs:* Royal Ocean Racing; Trearddur Bay Sailing (Cdre, 1994–96); Royal County Down Golf, Burnham and Berrow Golf, Holyhead Golf.

JONES, Anthony W.; *see* Whitworth-Jones.

JONES, Rt Rev. Arthur Lucas Vivian, OAM 2006; PhD; Bishop of Gippsland, 1994–2001; Rector, Holy Trinity, Dubbo, NSW, 2004–07; *b* 11 Dec. 1934; *s* of Arthur Edmond Jones and Mona Emily Jones; *m* 1979, Valerie Joan Maxwell; one *s* three *d.* *Educ:* St John's Coll., Morpeth, NSW (ThL); ACT (ThSchol); London Univ. (BD ext); Deakin Univ. (BA); Newcastle Univ., NSW (MA Classics); Adelaide Coll. of Adv. Educn (Grad.Dip.RE); Geneva Theol Coll. (ThD); Lambeth Diploma; LaTrobe Univ. (PhD 1998; MCounsHS 2003). Deacon 1966, priest 1967; Curate, Holy Trinity, Orange, NSW, 1966–69; Missionary, Panama, 1970–73 and 1977–80; Rector, St Barnabas, Orange, NSW, 1973–77; Vicar, Corangamite, Vic, 1980–82; Lectr in NT, St John's Coll., Morpeth, 1982–85; Rector, Woy Woy, NSW, 1985–89; Dean, St Paul's Cathedral, Sale, 1989–94; Diocesan Theologian, Gippsland, 1989–94. Lectr in New Testament, Singapore, India, Manila, Peru, PNG, 2001–08. Hon. Res. Associate, Monash Univ., Vic, 2003. *Recreations:* golf, writing. *Address:* 151 Phillip Street, Orange, NSW 2800, Australia.

JONES, Prof. Arthur Stanley, CBE 1997; CBiol, FIBiol; consultant to agricultural and food industries, since 1997; Principal, Royal Agricultural College, Cirencester, 1990–97; *b* 17 May 1932; *s* of John Jones and Anne Jones (*née* Hamilton); *m* 1962, Mary Margaret Smith; three *s* one *d.* *Educ:* Gosforth Grammar Sch.; Durham Univ. (BSc); Aberdeen Univ. (PhD). Commnd Army, 2nd Lieut, 1955–57; Pilot Officer, RAFVR, 1958–62. Rowett Research Institute: Res. Scientist, 1959; Hd, Applied Nutrition Dept, 1966; Chm., Applied Scis Div., 1975; Dep. Dir, 1983; Governor, 1986–90; Strathcona-Fordyce Prof. of Agriculture, Univ. of Aberdeen, 1986–90; Head, Sch. of Agriculture, Aberdeen, and Principal, N of Scotland Coll. of Agriculture, 1986–90; Gov., Aberdeen Centre for Land Use, 1987–90. Mem., House of Lords Rural Econ. Gp, 1992–94. Chairman: Scottish Beef Develts Ltd, 1988–91; RAC Enterprises Ltd, 1992–97; Member: Council, RASE, 1991–97; Bd, Arable Res. Centres, 1992–96. Gov., Henley Coll. of Management, 1996–2003 (Chm. Acad. Adv. Council, 1996–2001). Dir, Clan Grant Centre Trust Ltd, 1998–2006; Mem. Council and Hon. Treas., Clan Grant Soc., 1998–2006. Trustee: Trehane Trust, 1993–2007; Geoffrey Cragghill Meml Scholarship Trust, 1993–99; Ceres Foundn, 1996–. Hon. Prof., Univ. of Prague, 1994–. FRSA; FCMI; FIAgrM; FRAgS. *Publications:* Nutrition of Animals of Agricultural Importance (vol. 17, Internat. Encyc. of Food and Nutrition) (ed D. P. Cuthbertson), 1967; 115 articles in learned jls. *Recreations:* yachting, flying, gardening. *Address:* Begsdell, Caskieben, Kinellar, Aberdeenshire AB21 0TB. *Clubs:* Farmers', Royal Air Force.

JONES, Brinley; *see* Jones, Robert B.

JONES, Bryn Terfel, (Bryn Terfel), CBE 2003; opera singer; bass baritone; *b* 9 Nov. 1965; *s* of Hefin and Nesta Jones; *m* Lesley Halliday; three *s.* *Educ:* Guildhall Sch. of Music and Drama (AGSM). Opera performances in major venues: WNO, 1990–; ENO, 1991–; Salzburg, 1992–; Covent Garden, 1992–; Vienna State Opera, 1993–; NY Metropolitan, 1994–; Sydney Opera House, 1999–; rôles include: Guglielmo, Jochanaan in Salome, Balstrode, Leporello, Figaro, Falstaff, Don Giovanni, Nick Shadow in The Rake's Progress, Wolfram in Tannhauser, Four Villains in Les Contes d'Hoffmann, Dulcamara in L'Elisir d'Amore, Mephistopheles in Gounod's Faust, Wotan in Der Ring des Nibelungen, The Flying Dutchman, Scarpia in Tosca, Sweeney Todd. Hon. Fellow, Univ. of Wales Aberystwyth, 1995; Hon. FRWCMD (Hon. FWCMD, 1995). Hon. DMus Glamorgan, 1997. Queen's Medal for Music, 2006. *Recreations:* golf, supporting

Manchester United, collecting fob watches. *Address:* c/o Harlequin Agency, 203 Fidlas Road, Cardiff CF14 5NA. *T:* (029) 2075 0821.

JONES, Caroline; *see* Dean, C.

JONES, Carwyn Howell; Member (Lab) Bridgend, National Assembly for Wales, since 1999; Counsel General, Leader of the House and Minister for Assembly Business and Communications, since 2007; *b* 21 March 1967; *s* of Caron Wyn Jones and (Katherine) Janice Jones; *m* 1994, Lisa Josephine Murray. *Educ:* Aberystwyth Univ. (LLB). Called to the Bar, Gray's Inn, 1989. Tutor, Centre for Professional Legal Studies, Cardiff, 1997–99. National Assembly for Wales: Sec. for Agric. and Rural Develt, 2000; Minister: for Rural Affairs, 2000–02; for Open Govt and Assembly Business, 2002–03; for Envmt, Planning and Countryside, 2003–07; for Educn, Culture and the Welsh Language, 2007. *Recreations:* sport, reading, travel. *Address:* National Assembly for Wales, Cardiff Bay, Cardiff CF99 1NA. *T:* (029) 2089 8769. *Clubs:* Bridgend United Services; Brynaman Rugby, Bridgend Rugby.

JONES, Ceri Jayne, (Mrs T. C. Cuthbert); business and financial journalist; *b* 3 July 1958; *d* of David and Julie Jones; *m* 1984, Thomas Charles Cuthbert; three *s* one *d*. *Educ:* Keele Univ.; Liverpool Univ. (BA Hons 1982). Ed., Pensions & Employees Benefits, 1986; Ed., Pensions Management, 1986–87, Financial Advr, 1987–94, Financial Times magazines; Ed., Investors Chronicle, 1994–2002; Ed.-in-Chief, Personal Finance Div., Financial Times Business, 1997–2002. *Publications:* Guide to Alternative Investments, 2006; business and financial commentary in various newspapers and magazines. *Recreations:* children, natural history, travel. *Address:* 28 Longfield Drive, Amersham, Bucks HP6 5HE.

JONES, Charles Beynon Lloyd, CMG 1978; Chairman of Directors, David Jones Ltd, 1963–80; Consul General of Finland in Sydney, 1971–88; *b* 4 Dec. 1932; *s* of late Sir Charles Lloyd Jones and Lady (Hannah Beynon) Lloyd Jones, OBE. *Educ:* Cranbrook Sch., Sydney; Univ. of Sydney (not completed). Joined David Jones Ltd, 1951; Alternate Director, 1956; Director, 1957; Joint Managing Director, 1961. President: Retail Traders Assoc., NSW, 1976–78; Bd of Trustees, Art Gall. of NSW, 1980–83 (Trustee, 1972; Vice-Pres., 1976–80). Governor, London House for Overseas Graduates, 1983–92. Officer, Order of Merit, Republic of Italy (Cavaliere Ufficiale); Comdr, Order of the Lion, Finland. *Address:* Summerlees Farm, Yarramalong, NSW 2259, Australia.

JONES, (Charles) Ian (McMillan); education consultant, since 1995; *b* 11 Oct. 1934; *s* of Wilfred Charles Jones and Bessie Jones (*née* McMillan); *m* 1962, Jennifer Marie Potter; two *s*. *Educ:* Bishop's Stortford Coll.; St John's Coll., Cambridge (CertEd 1959; MA 1962). 2nd Lieut RA, 1953–55. Head of Geog. Dept, Bishop's Stortford Coll., 1960–70, Asst to Headmaster, 1967–70; Vice-Principal, King William's Coll., IoM, 1971–75; Head Master, Bedford School, 1975–86; Dir of Studies, BRNC, Dartmouth, 1986–88; Centre for British Teachers, subseq. CfBT Education Services: Project Dir, Brunei Darussalam, 1988–91, Malaysia, 1990–91; Regl Dir, Educn Services, SE Asia, 1991–94; Grants Adminstr, UK, 1995–97. OFSTED Trained Inspector, 1996–2002; ISI Trained Reporting Inspector, 2000–05; Tutor for Nat. Professional Qualification for Head Teachers, 1998–. FCMI; FRSA. Man., England Schoolboy Hockey XI, 1967–74; Man., England Hockey XI, 1968–69; Pres., English Schoolboys Hockey Assoc., 1980–88; Mem. IoM Sports Council, 1972–75. *Publications:* articles in Guardian. *Recreations:* hockey (Captain Cambridge Univ. Hockey XI, 1959; England Hockey XI, 1959–64, 17 caps; Gt Britain Hockey XI, 1959–64, 28 caps), cricket (Captain IoM Cricket XI, 1973–75), golf. *Address:* 9 Phillipa Flowerday Plain, Norwich, Norfolk NR2 2TA. *Clubs:* MCC; Hawks (Cambridge); Royal Norwich Golf; Pantai Mentiri Golf (Brunei).

JONES, Christine L.; *see* Lee-Jones.

JONES, Most Rev. Christopher; *see* Elphin, Bishop of (RC).

JONES, Sir Christopher L.; *see* Lawrence-Jones.

JONES, Clive Lawson, CBE 1997; Secretary General, European Energy Charter Conference, 1991–95; *b* 16 March 1937; *s* of Celyn John Lawson Jones and Gladys Irene Jones; *m* 1961, Susan Brenda (*née* McLeod); one *s* one *d*. *Educ:* Cranleigh School; University of Wales. BSc (Chemistry). With British Petroleum, 1957–61; Texaco Trinidad, 1961–68; Principal, Min. of Power, 1968–69; Min. of Technology, 1969–70; DTI, 1970–73; Asst Sec., Oil Emergency Group, 1973–74; Department Energy: Asst Sec., 1974–77; Under Sec., Gas Div., 1981–82; Counsellor (Energy), Washington, 1977–81; Dir for Energy Policy, EC, 1982–86; Dep. Dir Gen. for Energy, EC, 1987–94. Chm., European Consultative Cttees on Electricity and Gas Markets, 1990–91. *Recreation:* ephemera.

JONES, Clive William, CBE 2007; Chairman, since 2005 and Director, since 2001, GMTV; *b* 10 Jan. 1949; *s* of Kenneth David Llewellyn Jones and Joan Muriel Jones (*née* Withers); *m* 1st, 1971, Frances Mawer (marr. diss. 1988); two *s* one *d*; 2nd, 1988, Fern Britton (marr. diss. 2000); two *s* one *d*; 3rd, 2004, Victoria Mary Taylor Heywood, *qv*. *Educ:* Newbridge Grammar Sch.; LSE (BSc Econ.). Journalist, until 1978; with Yorks TV, 1978–82; Man. Editor, Editor, then Editor-in-Chief, TV-am Ltd, 1982–84; TVS: Controller, News, Current Affairs and Sport, 1984–87; Dep. Dir of Programmes, 1987–91; Dep. Man. Dir, 1991–92; Founding Man. Dir, London News Network, 1992–94; Man. Dir, Central Independent Television PLC, April–Dec. 1994; Man. Dir, Carlton UK Broadcasting Ltd, 1995; Chief Exec., Carlton Television, 1996–2004; Chairman: Westcountry Television, 1998–2001 (Dir, 1998–2007); HTV, 2000–07; Two Way TV, 2007– (Dir, 2007–); Jt Man. Dir, ITV, 2002–04; Chief Exec., ITV News and Regions, 2004–07; Dir, S4C, 2007–. Director: Runnymede Trust, 2004–; Skills Develt Agency, 2006–. Chairman: Skillset, 2002–; YCTV, 2002–; Wales IP Fund, 2005–; Creative Business Wales, 2006–; Mediabox, 2007–. Dir, Young Vic Th., 2003–. Governor, Nat. Film and Television Sch., 1998–. FRTS 2000; FRSA 2000. *Recreations:* Rugby, golf, films. *Address:* 48 Church Crescent, N10 3NE. *Club:* Reform.

JONES, Prof. Colin David Hugh, DPhil; FBA 2008; FRHistS; Professor of History, Queen Mary, University of London, since 2006; *b* Isleworth, 12 Dec. 1947; *s* of Lawrence and Frances Joyce Jones; *m* 1996, Josephine McDonagh; three *s* one *d* from previous marriage. *Educ:* St Mary's C of E Primary Sch., Twickenham; Hampton Grammar Sch.; Jesus Coll., Oxford (Edwin Jones Schol.; BA Modern Hist. and Modern Langs (French) 1971); St Antony's Coll., Oxford (DPhil 1978). Temp. Lectr in Hist., Univ. of Newcastle upon Tyne, 1972–73; University of Exeter: Lectr in Hist., 1974–87; Sen. Lectr, 1987–90; Prof. of Hist., 1991–95; Prof. of Hist., Univ. of Warwick, 1996–2006. Fellow, Columbia Univ. Inst. of Scholars at Reid Hall (Paris), 2001–02; Kratter Vis. Prof. in Eur. Hist., Stanford Univ., 1993–94, 2000, 2005; Vis. Prof., Coll. de France, Paris, 2003; Visiting Fellow: Shelby Cullom Davis Center for Histl Studies, Princeton Univ., 1986; Nat. Liby of Medicine, Washington, 2004. Member: Steering Cttee, Hist. at Univ. Defence Gp, 1995–2001; Hist. of Medicine Panel, Wellcome Trust, 1999–2003 (Vice-Chm., 2001–03); Res. Panel for Hist., AHRC, 2004–08 (Convenor, 2006–08). Royal Historical Society: Fellow 1984; Vice Pres., 2000–03; Pres., 2009–. Officier, Ordre des Palmes académiques (France), 2008. *Publications:* Charity and Bienfaisance: the treatment of the poor in the Montpellier Region, 1740–1815, 1982; The Longman Companion to the French Revolution, 1988; The Charitable Imperative: hospitals and nursing in Ancien Régime and Revolutionary France, 1989; (with J. Ardagh) Cultural Atlas of France, 1991; Cambridge Illustrated History of France, 1994; (with L. Brockliss) The Medical World of Early Modern France, 1997; The Great Nation: France from Louis XV to Napoleon (1715–99), 2002; Madame de Pompadour and her Image, 2002; Paris: biography of a city, 2004; edited books, articles and book chapters on French hist., esp. 17th–19th centuries, incl. French Revolution and hist. of medicine. *Recreations:* music, wine, cooking, cycling, Paris. *Address:* History Department, Queen Mary, University of London, Mile End Road, E1 4NS; *e-mail:* c.d.h.jones@qmul.ac.uk.

JONES, Courtney John Lyndhurst, OBE 1989 (MBE 1980); President, National Ice Skating Association, 1987–95; *b* 30 April 1933; *s* of Reginald Jones and Inez Jones (*née* Wilsher). *Educ:* Ringwood Grammar Sch.; Bournemouth Coll. of Art (NDD). NSA Gold Medals for Ice Dance and for Pair Skating, 1957; British Ice Dance Champion, with June Markham, 1956–57, with Doreen Denny, 1958–60; European Ice Dance Champion, with June Markham, 1957–58, with Doreen Denny, 1959–61; World Ice Dance Champion, with June Markham, 1957–58, with Doreen Denny, 1959–60. Free-lance fashion designer, 1977–. Mem., Internat. Skating Union Council, 2002–. Mem., US Figure Skating Hall of Fame, 1987; George Hasler Medal, Internat. Skating Union, 1991. *Recreations:* reading, music, the arts. *Address:* 31 Ruston Mews, St Mark's Road, W11 1RB. *T:* (020) 7727 5843.

JONES, Prof. David, OBE 1986; FRCN; Professor, School of Nursing and Midwifery, University of Sheffield, 1995–2000, now Emeritus (Foundation Dean, 1995–98); *b* 27 July 1940; *s* of John Evan Jones and Edith Catherine (*née* Edwards); *m* 1962, Janet Mary Ambler; two *s* two *d*. *Educ:* Boys' Grammar Sch., Bala, N Wales; Univ. of Wales (BEd). SRN; RMN; RNT; FRCN 1998. Divl Nursing Officer, Gwynedd, 1974–78; Chief Admin. Nursing Officer, Gwynedd HA, 1979–87; first Chm., Welsh Nat. Bd for Nursing, Midwifery and Health Visiting, 1979–86; Chief Exec., English Nat. Bd for Nursing, Midwifery and Health Visiting, 1987–89; Principal, Sheffield and N Trent Coll. of Nursing and Midwifery, 1990–95. Vis. Prof., NE Wales Inst., 2004–. Non-exec. Dir, Conwy and Denbighshire NHS Trust, 1999–2007. Board Mem., Clwyd Alyn Housing Assoc. Ltd, 2006–. Hon. DSc Sheffield, 2005. *Recreations:* public affairs, countryside, family. *Address:* Lawr-y-lôn, Carrog, Corwen, Denbighshire LL21 9AP. *T:* (01490) 430255.

JONES, Sir David A.; *see* Akers-Jones.

JONES, (David) Alan; HM Diplomatic Service, retired; High Commissioner to Belize, 2004–07; *b* 26 Oct. 1953; *m* 1st, 1975, Jennifer Anne Wright (marr. diss. 1992); 2nd, 1994, Daphne Patricia Foley; one *d*. Joined LCD, 1970; FCO, 1971–2007; served Tehran, 1975–78, Islamabad, 1978–81; MoD, 1981–83 (on loan); First Sec. (Commercial), Cairo, 1986–89; Dep. Head of Mission and Consul, Luanda, 1993–96; Dep. High Comr, Dar es Salaam, 1996–2000; High Comr, Sierra Leone, and non-resident Ambassador to Guinea, 2000–03. *Address:* c/o Foreign and Commonwealth Office, SW1A 2AH.

JONES, David Charles, CBE 1999; FCCA, FCIS; Chairman, CWM 2001 Ltd; *b* 2 Feb. 1943; *s* of Frederick Charles Thomas Jones and Annie Marcella Jones; *m* 1968, Jeanette Ann Crofts; two *s* one *d*. *Educ:* King's Sch., Worcester. FCIS 1974; FCCA 1975. Joined Kays Mail Order Co. (part of Great Universal Stores), 1960, Finance Dir, 1971–77; Man. Dir, BMOC, 1977–80; Chief Exec., Grattan Plc, 1980–86; Next Plc: Dep. Chief Exec., 1986–88; Chief Exec., 1988–2001; Dep. Chm., 2001–02; Chm., 2002–06. *Publication:* Next to Me (autobiog.), 2005. *Recreations:* golf, snooker. *Address:* Hepworth House, Claypit Lane, Leeds LS2 8DE. *T:* (0113) 244 0265.

JONES, David Evan Alun, CBE 1985; DL; Commissioner for Local Administration in Wales, 1980–85; *b* 9 Aug. 1925; *s* of David Jacob Jones, OBE, Master Mariner, and Margaret Jane Jones; *m* 1952, Joan Margaret Erica (*née* Davies); two *s*. *Educ:* Aberaeron County Sch.; University Coll. of Wales, Aberystwyth (LLB; Sir Samuel Evans Prize, 1949). Solicitor. Served War, RAF, 1943–47 (Flt Lieut). Articled service, Exeter, 1949–52; asst solicitor posts with Ilford Bor., Southampton County Bor., Berks County and Surrey County Councils, 1952–61; Dep. Clerk, Denbighshire CC, subseq. Clerk of CC and Clerk of the Peace, 1961–74; Chief Exec., Gwynedd CC, 1974–80. Chm., All Wales Adv. Panel on Develt of Services for Mentally Handicapped People, 1985–90; Member: Broadcasting Council for Wales, 1980–85; Local Govt Boundary Commn for Wales, 1985–89; Prince of Wales's Cttee, 1985–92 (Chm., Gwynedd County Gp, 1990–92); Gwynedd HA, 1986–88. Pres., Gwynedd Voluntary Services, 1994–96; Chm., N Wales Masonic Benevolent Assoc., 1996–99. Dir, Nat. Welsh-Amer. Foundn, 1992–2004. Treasurer, Univ. of Wales, Bangor (formerly UCNW), 1988–2000. Asst Provincial Grand Master, N Wales, 1987–94. DL Gwynedd, 1988. *Recreations:* gardening, travel, a little golf. *Address:* Min-y-Don, West End, Beaumaris, Anglesey LL58 8BG. *T:* (01248) 810225. *Club:* Baron Hill Golf (Beaumaris).

JONES, David George; Director General (formerly Assistant Under Secretary of State), Financial Management, Ministry of Defence, 1996–2001; *b* 31 May 1941; *s* of Frederick George Jones and Dorothy Jones (*née* Steele); *m* 1962, Leonie Usherwood Smith; three *s*. *Educ:* High Storrs Grammar Sch., Sheffield. Joined War Office as Exec. Officer, 1960; Asst Private Sec. to Army Minister, 1970–71; Principal, MoD Central Financial Planning Div., 1973–77; Private Sec. to Minister of State for Defence, 1977–80; Regl Marketing Dir, Defence Sales Organisation, 1980–84; Asst Sec., Air Systems Controllerate, 1984–85; Dep. Dir Gen., Al Yamamah Project Office, 1985–88; Dir Gen. Aircraft 2, Air Systems Controllerate, MoD (PE), 1988–89; Civil Sec., British Forces Germany, 1989–92; Dir Gen. Supplies and Transport (Naval), 1993–95, Dir Gen. Naval Bases and Supply, 1995–96, MoD. FCILT (FILog 1994). *Recreations:* gardening, travel.

JONES, David Hugh; Hon. Associate Director, Royal Shakespeare Company, since 1966; Masterclass Film Professor, Columbia University, since 2004; *b* 19 Feb. 1934; *s* of John David Jones and Gwendolen Agnes Langworthy (*née* Ricketts); *m* 1964, Sheila Allen (marr. diss.); two *s*. *Educ:* Taunton Sch.; Christ's Coll., Cambridge (MA 1st Cl. Hons English). 2nd Lieut RA, 1954–56. Production team of Monitor, BBC TV's 1st arts magazine, 1958–62, Editor, 1962–64; joined RSC, 1964; Aldwych Co. Dir, 1968–72; Artistic Dir, RSC (Aldwych), 1973–77; Producer, Play of the Month, BBC TV, 1977–78; Artistic Dir, Brooklyn Acad. of Music Theatre Co., 1979–81; Adjunct Prof. of Drama, Yale Univ., 1981. Productions for RSC incl. plays by Arden, Brecht, Gorky, Granville Barker, Günter Grass, Graham Greene, Mercer, O'Casey, Shakespeare, and Chekhov; dir. prodns for Chichester and Stratford, Ontario, Festival Theatres; other productions include: Old Times, Theatre Royal, Haymarket, and Los Angeles (LA Dramalogue Award for direction), 1985; No Man's Land, NY, 1994; The Hothouse, Chichester Fest., 1995; Taking Sides, NY, 1996; The Caretaker, NY, 2003; Triptych, NY, 2004; The Controversy of Valladolid, NY, 2005; On the Razzle, 2005, Sweet Bird of Youth, 2006, The Autumn Garden, 2007, Williamstown Fest.; The Last Confession, Chichester Fest.

and Theatre Royal, Haymarket, 2007. Dir, films for BBC TV, including: biography of poet, John Clare, 1969; adaptations of Hardy and Chekhov short stories, 1972 and 1973; Pinter's screenplay, Langrishe, Go Down, 1978; Merry Wives of Windsor, Pericles, 1982–83; The Devil's Disciple, 1987; Look Back in Anger, 1989 (ACE Award); directed for American TV: The Christmas Wife, 1988; Sensibility and Sense, 1990; The End of a Sentence, 1991; Fire in the Dark, 1991; And Then There Was One, 1994; Is There Life Out There?, 1994; Sophie and the Moonhanger, 1995; The Irvine Fertility Scandal, 1996; Time to Say Goodbye?, 1997; An Unexpected Life, 1998; A Christmas Carol, 1999; Custody of the Heart, 2000. Feature films directed: Pinter's Betrayal, 1982; 84 Charing Cross Road (royal film performance), 1987 (Christopher and Scriptor Awards, 1988); Jacknife, 1989; Kafka's The Trial, 1993; The Confession, 1998. Obie Awards, NY, for direction of RSC Summerfolk, 1975, for innovative programming at BAM Theatre Co., 1980. *Publication:* (with Richard Nelson) Making Plays, 1995. *Recreations:* restaurants, reading modern poetry, exploring mountains and islands. *Address:* 250 West 27th Street (# 6B), New York, NY 10001–5924, USA.

JONES, Rt Rev. David Huw; Bishop of St Davids, 1996–2001; *b* 1 July 1934; *s* of Joseph Elfed and Ethel Jones; *m* 1959, Gwyneth Jones; two *d*. *Educ:* Pontardawe Grammar Sch.; University Coll. of North Wales, Bangor (BA); University Coll., Oxford (MA). Curate: Aberdare, 1959–61; Neath, 1961–65; Vicar: Crynant, 1965–69; Michaelstone-super-Avon, 1969–73; Sub-Warden, St Michael's Coll., Llandaff, 1973–78; Lectr in Sch. of Theology, Univ. of Wales, Cardiff, 1973–78 (Asst Dean, 1977–78); Vicar of Prestatyn, 1978–82; Dean of Brecon, Vicar of Brecon, Battle and Llanddew, 1982–93; Asst Bishop, dio. of St Asaph, 1993–96. *Publications:* (ed jtly and contrib.) This Land and People, 1979; Guide to Brecon Cathedral, 1988. *Recreations:* reading, visiting historic gardens and homes, studying history of art, following Welsh Rugby. *Address:* 31 Cathedral Green, Llandaff, Cardiff CF5 2EB.

JONES, (David) Huw; Chief Executive, S4C (Welsh Fourth Channel), 1994–2005; *b* 5 May 1948; *s* of Idris Jones and Olwen Mair Lloyd Jones; *m* 1972, Sian Marylka Miarczynska; one *s* one *d*. *Educ:* Cardiff High Sch. for Boys; Jesus Coll., Oxford (BA, MA). Singer and TV presenter, 1968–76; Dir, Sain (Recordiau) Cyf, 1969–81; Man. Dir, Teledu'r Tir Glas, 1982–93; Director: Sgrin Cyf, 1996–2005; S4C Masnachol Cyf, 1999–2005; SDN Ltd, 1999–2005. Consultant, Bangor Univ. (formerly Univ. of Wales, Bangor), 2007–. Chairman: Barcud Cyf, 1981–93; TAC, 1984–86; Arianrhod Cyf, 1988–93; Celtic Film and TV Fest. Ltd, 2001–04; Portmeirion Ltd, 2007–; Cyfle Cyf, 2007–; Director: StrataMatrix Cyf, 2007–; Nant Gwrtheyrn Cyf, 2007–. Mem., FEFC for Wales, 1992–95; Dir, Skillset Ltd, 2001–05 (Patron, 2006–); Chair, Skillset Cymru Cyf, 2002–05. Member: Welsh Lang. Bd, 2007–; Adv. Cttee for Wales, RSPB, 2007–. FRTS 1999. Hon. Fellow, Univ. of Wales, Aberystwyth, 1997. *Recreations:* reading, cycling, walking. *Address:* 8 Heol Don, Whitchurch, Cardiff CF14 2AU.

JONES, Rev. Dr (David) Huw, FRCR, FRCP; Dean, Postgraduate Medical and Dental Education for East of England, since 2002; *b* 20 Feb. 1949; *s* of David and Nansi Jones; *m* 1984, Siân Davies; two *d*. *Educ:* Welsh Nat. Sch. of Medicine (MB BCh Hons 1972; MD 1979); MSc London 1978; MA Cantab 1987; E Anglian Ministerial Trng Course. FRCR 1983; FRCP 1996. Univ. Hosp. of Wales, Cardiff, 1972–75; MRC Fellow in Clin. Pharmacol., RPMS, Hammersmith Hosp., 1975–79; MRC Clin. Scientist, Clin. Oncology Unit, Cambridge, 1979–84; Consultant in Clinical Oncol., Addenbrooke's Hosp., Cambridge, 1984–2002; Associate Dean, Postgrad. Med. Educn, E Anglian Reg., 1998–2002. Vis. Prof. in Med. Educn, Anglia Ruskin Univ., 2003–. Ordained deacon 1998, priest 1999; NSM, Trumpington, 1998–2002; permission to officiate, dio Ely, 2002–; Dean's Vicar, Gonville and Caius Coll., Cambridge, 2006–. Hon. FFPM 2007. *Publications:* contribs on clinical pharmacol. and oncol. to peer-reviewed med. jls. *Recreations:* classical music, organ, gardening, carpentry. *Address:* East of England Deanery, Block 3, Ida Darwin, Fulbourn, Cambridge CB21 5EE. *T:* (01223) 884822, *Fax:* (01223) 884849.

JONES, David Ian; MP (C) Clwyd West, since 2005; *b* 22 March 1952; *s* of Bryn and Elspeth Savage Jones; *m* 1982, Sara Eluned Tudor; two *s*. *Educ:* Ruabon Grammar Sch.; University Coll. London (LLB); Coll. of Law. Admitted Solicitor, 1976; Sen. Partner, David Jones & Co., Llandudno, 1985–. Mem. (C) N Wales, Nat. Assembly for Wales, 2002–03. Contested (C): Conwy, 1997; City of Chester, 2001. *Recreation:* travel. *Address:* House of Commons, SW1A 0AA. *T:* (020) 7219 8070; *e-mail:* jonesdi@parliament.uk.

JONES, Rev. David Ian Stewart; Headmaster, Bryanston School, 1974–82; *b* 3 April 1934; *s* of Rev. John Milton Granville Jones and Evelyn Moyes Stewart Jones (formerly Chedburn); *m* 1967, Susan Rosemary Hardy Smith; twin *s* and *d*. *Educ:* St John's Sch., Leatherhead; Selwyn Coll., Cambridge (MA). Commnd Royal Signals, 1952–54. Curate at Oldham Parish Church, 1959–62; Vicar of All Saints, Elton, Bury, 1963–66; Asst Conduct and Chaplain of Eton Coll., 1966–70; Conduct and Sen. Chaplain of Eton Coll., 1970–74; Rector-designate of Bristol City, 1982–85; Dir, 1985–97, Consultant, 1997–99, Lambeth Endowed Charities. Chm., Inner Cities Young People's Proj., 1988–98. *Recreations:* reading, music, politics. *Address:* 3 Brackenwood, Pursell's Meadow, Naphill, High Wycombe, Bucks HP14 4TD. *T:* (01494) 564040. *Club:* East India, Devonshire, Sports and Public Schools.

JONES, Maj. Gen. David John R.; *see* Rutherford-Jones.

JONES, Sir David John Walter P.; *see* Prichard-Jones.

JONES, David le Brun, CB 1975; Director, Long Term Office, International Energy Agency, 1982–88; *b* 18 Nov. 1923; *s* of Thomas John Jones and Blanche le Brun. *Educ:* City of London Sch.; Trinity Coll., Oxford. Asst Principal, Min. of Power, 1947; Principal, MOP, 1952; Asst Sec., Office of the Minister for Science, 1962; Asst Sec., MOP, 1963; Under-Sec., MOP, later Min. of Technology and DTI, 1968–73; Dep. Sec., DTI, later DoI, 1973–76; Cabinet Office, 1976–77; Dept of Energy, 1978–82. Trustee, Nat. Energy Foundn, 1989–99. *Recreations:* walking, reading, chess. *Address:* 47 Grove End Road, NW8 9NB. *Club:* Oxford and Cambridge.

JONES, David Lewis, CBE 2005; FSA; Librarian, House of Lords, 1991–2006; *b* 4 Jan. 1945; *s* of late Gwilym Morgan Jones and of Joyce Jones (*née* Davies). *Educ:* Aberaeron County Sch.; Jesus Coll., Oxford (MA); Coll. of Librarianship, Wales. FSA 1998. Asst Librarian, Inst. of Histl Res., 1970–72; University of Wales, Aberystwyth: Asst Librarian, 1972–75; Law Librarian, 1975–77; Dep. Librarian, H of L, 1977–91. Hon. Sec., Honourable Soc. of Cymmrodorion, 1994–96. Trustee, Cross Inn, Llanon, Sch. and School-House, 1975–. Gorsedd y Beirdd (Aelod er Anrhydedd), 1996. Freeman, City of London, 1993; Liveryman, Stationers' and Newspapermakers' Co., 1994. FRHistS 2003; FRSA 2006. *Publications:* Books in English on the Soviet Union 1917–73, 1975; Paraguay: a bibliography, 1979; Debates and proceedings of the British Parliaments: a guide to printed sources, 1986; (ed jtly) Peers, politics and power: the House of Lords 1603–1911, 1986; A parliamentary history of the Glorious Revolution, 1988; Eirene: a tribute, 2001. *Address:* 10 Heathfield Court, Heathfield Terrace, W4 4LP. *T:* (020) 8995 6029. *Club:* Beefsteak.

JONES, Hon. Sir David Lloyd, Kt 2005; **Hon. Mr Justice Lloyd Jones;** a Judge of the High Court, Queen's Bench Division, since 2005; Presiding Judge, Wales Circuit, since 2008; *b* 13 Jan. 1952; *s* of William Elwyn Jones and Annie Blodwen Jones (*née* Lloyd-Jones); *m* 1983, Annmarie Harris; one *s* one *d*. *Educ:* Pontypridd Boys' Grammar Sch.; Downing Coll., Cambridge (MA, LLB, Whewell Scholar). Called to the Bar, Middle Temple, 1975, Bencher, 2005; Fellow, Downing Coll., Cambridge, 1975–91; Asst Recorder, 1989–94; a Recorder, 1994–2005; Junior Crown Counsel (Common Law), 1997–99; QC 1999; a Dep. High Court Judge, 2001–05. Asst Comr, 1996–2005, Dep. Chm., 2006–, Parly Boundary Commn for Wales; Mem., Lord Chancellor's Adv. Cttee on Private Internat. Law, 1997–. Mem., Council of Legal Educn, 1991–96; Governor, Inns of Court Sch. of Law, 1996–2002. Vis. Prof., City Univ., 1999–2005. *Publications:* articles in legal jls. *Recreations:* music, hill walking. *Address:* Royal Courts of Justice, Strand, WC2A 2LL.

JONES, David M.; *see* Mansel-Jones.

JONES, David Martin, FIBiol; Director, North Carolina Zoological Park, since 1994; *b* 14 Aug. 1944; *s* of John Trevor Jones and Mair Carno Jones; *m* 1969, Janet Marian Woosley; three *s*. *Educ:* St Paul's Cathedral Choir Sch.; St John's Sch., Leatherhead; Royal Veterinary Coll., London (BSc, BVetMed). MRCVS. Veterinary Officer, Whipsnade, 1969; Sen. Veterinary Officer, 1975, Asst Dir of Zoos, 1981, Dir of Zoos, 1984, Gen. Dir, 1991, Dir, Conservation and Consultancy Div., 1992, Zoological Soc. of London. Trustee, WWF UK, 1986–92, 1993–96 (Chm., Conservation Review Gp, subseq. Conservation Cttee, 1990–94); Member Council: WWF UK, 1994–2005; WWF US, 1996–2002; Chm., Fauna and Flora Internat., 1987–94. Chairman: Brooke Hosp. for Animals, 1990–98, 2000–02 (Vice-Chm., 1973–90); Yadkin Pee-Dee Lakes Project, 1998–; Board Member: Uwharrie Capital Corps, 1998–2004; Nat. Audubon (N Carolina), 2002–07; Environmental Defense (N Carolina), 2003–; Pfeiffer Univ., 2004–. *Publications:* over 100 papers on wildlife medicine, management and conservation, in veterinary, medical and zoological jls. *Recreations:* field conservation, travel, antiquarian books, driving, gardening. *Address:* North Carolina Zoological Park, 4401 Zoo Parkway, Asheboro, NC 27205, USA.

JONES, Dr (David) Timothy; Deputy Chairman, Education and Learning Wales (formerly Education and Training Wales), 2001–06; non-executive Director, Orpar SA, since 2002; *b* 21 Aug. 1944; *s* of David Percy Jones and Elvair (*née* Evans); *m* 1968, Jean Margaret Whitehead; four *d*. *Educ:* Leeds Univ. (PhD Physical Chem.); INSEAD, Fontainebleau (MBA with Dist.). MRSC 1967. Gen. Manager, Deutsche BP, 1985–88; Dir, BP France, 1988–89; Chief Exec., BP Oil Supply and Trading, 1990; Dir, BP Oil Europe, 1990–93; Dep. Chm., 1993–2000, Chief Exec., 1996–2000, Lloyd's Register. Chm., Marine Panel, Foresight Initiative, DTI, 1999–2002. *Recreations:* watching Rugby, walking, golf. *Address: e-mail:* tim.jones1@ntlworld.com.

JONES, Deborah Elizabeth Vavasseur B.; *see* Barnes Jones.

JONES, Deborah Mary; Editor, The Ark (Catholic Concern for Animals), since 1999; Deputy Editor, Priests & People, 1991–96 and 1999–2004; *b* 5 April 1948; *d* of Thomas Jones and Glenys Jones. *Educ:* W Kirby Grammar Sch. for Girls; University Coll. of S Wales, Cardiff (BA Gen. Hons); Leeds Univ. (PGCE); Regina Mundi Pontifical Inst., Rome; Margaret Beaufort Inst. of Theol.; Anglia Poly. Univ. (MA); Univ. of Wales, Lampeter (PhD). Teacher of English and Classical Studies, Clacton Co. High Sch., 1972–78; Dir, Adult Educn, dio. E Anglia, 1980–96 (pt-time, 1992–96); Lectr in Religious Studies, Suffolk Coll., 1987–92; Editor, Catholic Herald, 1996–98. *Publications:* Focus on Faith, 1987, 2nd edn 1996; This is My Body, 1989; contrib. articles to The Tablet, Priests & People, Ecotheology. *Recreations:* Baroque opera, golf, water-colouring.

JONES, Della Louise Gething; mezzo-soprano; *d* of Eileen Gething Jones and late Cyril Vincent Jones; *m* 1988, Paul Vigars; one *s*. *Educ:* Neath Girls' Grammar School; Royal College of Music. GRSM; LRAM (singing), ARCM (piano); Kathleen Ferrier Scholarship. Mem., ENO, 1977–82, leading roles; 1982–: guest artist, ENO and Royal Opera House; sings with major British opera companies; overseas concert and operatic appearances in all major European countries, also Russia, Japan and USA; radio and TV; prolific recordings with all major recording cos. Hon. FRWCMD (Hon. FWCMD 1995). Hon. Fellow, Univ. of Wales Swansea, 1999. *Recreations:* writing cadenzas, art galleries, animal welfare, reading, piano. *Address:* c/o Music International, 13 Ardilaun Road, Highbury, N5 2QR. *T:* (020) 7359 5183.

JONES, Denise Idris; Member (Lab) Conwy, National Assembly for Wales, 2003–07; *b* 7 Dec. 1950; *d* of James and Rhona Woodrow; *m* 1984, John Idris Jones; two *s*. Teacher in English and French, Grango Secondary Sch., Rhos, Wrexham, 1972–2003. Contested (Lab) Aberconwy, Nat. Assembly for Wales, 2007. *Recreations:* travelling, literature, arts, golf. *Address:* Borthwen, Llanfair Road, Ruthin, Denbs LL15 1DA.

JONES, Derek John Claremont, CMG 1979; Senior Fellow, Trade Policy Research Centre, 1986–90; retired; *b* 2 July 1927; *er s* of Albert Claremont Jones and Ethel Lilian Jones (*née* Hazell); *m* 1st, 1951, Jean Cynthia Withams; one *s* two *d*; 2nd, 1970, Kay Cecile Thewlis; one *s*. *Educ:* Colston Sch., Bristol; Bristol Univ.; London Sch. of Economics and Political Science. Economic Asst, Economic Section, Cabinet Office, 1950–53; Second Sec., UK Delegn to OEEC/NATO, Paris, 1953–55; Asst Principal, Colonial Office, 1955–57; Principal, Colonial Office, 1957–66; First Secretary, Commonwealth Office, 1966–67; Counsellor (Hong Kong Affairs), UK Mission, Geneva, 1967–71; Government of Hong Kong: Dep. Economic Sec., 1971–73; Sec. for Economic Services, 1973–76; Sec. for the Environment, 1976–81; Sec. for Transport, 1981–82; Minister for Hong Kong Relns with EC and Member States, 1982–86. *Recreations:* reading, travel, conversation. *Address:* Cliff House, Trevaunance Cove, St Agnes, Cornwall TR5 0RZ. *T:* (01872) 552334. *Clubs:* Hong Kong, Hong Kong Jockey.

JONES, Derek R.; *see* Rudd-Jones.

JONES, Derek William; Senior Director, Welsh Assembly Government, since 2003; *b* 8 Dec. 1952; *s* of William Jones and Patricia Mary Jones (*née* Gill); *m* 1976, Fiona Christine Anne Laidlaw; two *s*. *Educ:* UC Cardiff, Univ. of Wales (BA Hons). Worked on regional policy, company law and privatisation, DTI, 1977–82; HM Treasury: Public Expenditure Control, 1982–84; Head, Financial Instns and Markets Br., 1984–87; Head, Japan Desk and Overseas Trade Policy Div., DTI, 1987–89; Welsh Office: Asst Sec., 1989; Head, Industrial Policy Div., 1989–92; Head, Finance Progs Div., 1992–94; Under Sec., 1994; Dir, Industry and Trng Dept, 1994–99; Dir, Economic Affairs, Welsh Assembly Govt, 1999–2003. *Recreations:* family life, reading, blues guitar. *Address:* c/o Welsh Assembly Government, Cathays Park, Cardiff CF10 3NQ. *T:* (029) 2082 3325.

JONES, Diane C.; *see* Cellan-Jones.

JONES, Prof. Douglas Samuel, MBE 1945; FRS 1968; Ivory Professor of Mathematics, University of Dundee, 1965–92, now Emeritus Professor; *b* 10 Jan. 1922; *s* of late J. D. Jones and B. Jones (*née* Streather); *m* 1950, Ivy Styles; one *s* one *d*. *Educ:* Wolverhampton Grammar Sch.; Corpus Christi Coll., Oxford (MA 1947; Hon. Fellow, 1980); DSc Manchester 1957. FIMA 1964, CMath 1992; FRSE 1967; CEng, FIET (FIEE 1989); CSci 2005. Flt-Lt, RAFVR, 1941–45. Commonwealth Fund Fellow, MIT, 1947–48; Asst Lectr in Maths, University of Manchester, 1948–51; Lectr 1951–54, Research Prof. 1955, New York Univ.; Sen. Lectr in Maths, Univ. of Manchester, 1955–57; Prof. of Maths, Univ. of Keele, 1957–64. Vis. Prof., Courant Inst., 1962–63. Member: UGC, 1976–86 (Mem., 1971–86, Chm., 1976–86, Mathematical Scis Sub-Cttee); Computer Bd, 1977–82; Open Univ. Vis. Cttee, 1982–87. Member Council: Royal Soc., 1973–74; IMA, 1982–85, 1986–97 (Pres., 1988–89). Hon. DSc Strathclyde, 1975. Keith Prize, RSE, 1974; Marconi Prize, IEE, 1974; van der Pol Gold Medal, Internat. Union of Radio Sci., 1981; Naylor Prize, London Mathematical Soc., 1987. Trustee, Quarterly Jl of Mechanics and Applied Maths, 1980–92; Associate Editor: Jl IMA, 1964–2003; RSE, 1969–82; SIAM Jl on Applied Maths, 1975–92; Applicable Analysis, 1976–92; Mathematical Methods in the Applied Sciences, 1977–2002; Royal Soc., 1978–83; Methods and Applications of Analysis, 1992–; Jl of Engrg Maths, 1992–; Communications in Applied Analysis, 1997–. *Publications:* Electrical and Mechanical Oscillations, 1961; Theory of Electromagnetism, 1964; Generalised Functions, 1966; Introductory Analysis, vol. 1, 1969, vol 2, 1970; Methods in Electromagnetic Wave Propagation, 1979, 2nd edn 1994; Elementary Information Theory, 1979; The Theory of Generalised Functions, 1982; Differential Equations and Mathematical Biology, 1983, 2nd edn 2003; Acoustic and Electromagnetic Waves, 1986; Assembly Programming and the 8086 Microprocessor, 1988; 80×86 Assembly Programming, 1991; Introduction to Asymptotics, 1997; articles in mathematical and physical jls. *Recreations:* golf, walking, photography. *Address:* 1 The Nurseries, St Madoes, Glencarse, Perth PH2 7NX. *T:* (01738) 860544.

JONES, Dylan; Editor, GQ magazine, since 1999; Editor-in-Chief, GQ Style, since 2005; *b* 18 Jan. 1960; *s* of Michael and Audrey Jones; *m* 1997, Sarah Walter; two *d*. *Educ:* Chelsea Sch. of Art; St Martin's Sch. of Art (BA Hons Design and Photography). Ed., i-D mag., 1984–87; Contributing Ed., The Face, 1987–88; Ed., Arena, 1988–92; Associate Editor: Observer Mag., 1992–93; Sunday Times Mag., 1993–96; Gp Ed., The Face, Arena, Arena Homme Plus, 1996–97; Ed.-at-Large, Sunday Times, 1997–99. Chm., BSME, 2005. Chm., Fashion Rocks for Prince's Trust, 2005. Editor of Year Award, BSME, 1993, 2001, 2002, 2004, 2007. *Publications:* Dark Star, 1990; Sex, Power and Travel, 1996; Meaty, Beaty, Big and Bounty, 1997; iPod, Therefore I Am, 2005; Mr Jones' Rules, 2006; Cameron on Cameron: conversations with Dylan Jones, 2008. *Address:* GQ Magazine, Vogue House, Hanover Square, W1S 1JU. *T:* (020) 7499 9080; *e-mail:* dylan.jones@condenast.co.uk. *Clubs:* Chelsea Arts, Groucho, Soho House, Ivy, George.

JONES, Edward Bartley; QC 1997; a Recorder, since 2000; *b* Oswestry, 24 Dec. 1952; *o s* of Meurig Bartley Jones and late Ruby Jones (*née* Morris). *Educ:* Cardiff High Sch.; Balliol Coll., Oxford (BA Hons Modern Hist. 1973). Called to the Bar, Lincoln's Inn, 1975, Bencher, 2007; in practice as a Chancery/Commercial Barrister in Liverpool, 1976– (Hd, Commercial Dept, Exchange Chambers, Liverpool and Manchester, 1994–); Asst Recorder, 1996–2000. Part-time Lectr in Law, Liverpool Univ., 1977–81. Member: Northern Chancery Bar Assoc. (Chm.); Northern Circuit Commercial Bar Assoc.; Chancery Bar Assoc. *Recreations:* ski-ing, opera, travel, golf, shooting. *Address:* Exchange Chambers, Pearl Assurance House, Derby Square, Liverpool L2 9XX. *T:* (0151) 236 7747; 4 Ralli Courts, Manchester M3 5FT. *T:* (0161) 833 2722; Laurel Grove, Carden, Malpas, Cheshire SY14 7HP. *T:* (01829) 250257. *Clubs:* Oxford and Cambridge; Portal (Tarporley).

JONES, Edward David Brynmor, RIBA; architect in private practice, since 1973; Principal, Dixon Jones Ltd (formerly Jeremy Dixon·Edward Jones), since 1989; *b* 20 Oct. 1939; *s* of David Jones and Margot Derricourt; *m* 1st; one *s* two *d*; 2nd, Margot Griffin; one *s* two *d*. *Educ:* Haileybury and ISC; AA Sch. of Architecture (AADip Hons 1963); RIBA 1968; RAIC and Ont. Assoc. of Architects, Canada, 1983–89. Tutor, AA, PCL and UC Dublin, 1968–72; Sen. Tutor, Sch. of Environmental Design, RCA, 1973–83; Vis. Prof., 1973–82, Adjunct Prof., 1983–89, Univ. of Toronto; Visiting Professor: Cornell, Harvard, Princeton, Yale, Pennsylvania, Rice, Syracuse and Kent State (Florence) Univs, 1973–; Portsmouth Univ., 1994–98; Hon. Prof., Univ. of Wales, 2003–. RIBA External Examiner: AA 1985; Portsmouth Univ., Kingston Univ., Heriot-Watt Univ., 1990–93; Univ. of Wales, 1995–97; Univ. of Technol., Kingston, Jamaica, 1997–2000; Mackintosh Sch., Glasgow, 2007–. Member: RIBA President's Gold Medal Cttee, 1993, 1994; AA Council, 1993–99 (Vice Pres., 1995); RIBA Stirling Award Cttee, 2005–; Hon. Librarian, AA, 1994–95. Competitions, first prize: Northampton County Offices, 1973; Mississauga City Hall, Canada, 1982–87; Bus Stn, Venice, 1990; other projects include: Royal Opera House, Covent Garden, 1983–99; buildings for: Henry Moore Foundn at Leeds, 1989–93 and Perry Green, 1989–; Darwin Coll., Cambridge, 1989, 1994; Robert Gordon Univ., Aberdeen, 1991; superstores for J. Sainsbury at Plymouth; Portsmouth Univ. (Dept of Sci.), 1992–96; housing in New Delhi, 1994; Nat. Portrait Gall., 1994–2000; Saïd Business Sch., Oxford Univ., 1996–2001, Phase 2, Centre for Exec. Educn, 2007–; Somerset House, south terrace and central courtyard, 1998–2000; Student Centre, QUB, 2001; Panopticon Bldg, UCL, 2001–; Magna Carta Bldg, Salisbury Cathedral, 2001–; Portrait Gall. of Canada, 2003–; house in Bargemon, France, 2005; master plans for: Nat. Gall., 1998–2006; Somerset House, 1998–; Exhibition Road, 2003–; office developments: King's Cross for Parabola, 2001; Regent's Palace for Crown Estates, 2005; 5–6 St James's Square for Rio Tinto, 2006–; flats for Kensington and Chelsea Coll., 2000–; Manhattan lofts, 2003–. Rep. Britain at Biennale: Venice, 1980, 2002; Paris, 1981; Santiago, 1982. Chm. Jury, Laban Dance Sch. Competition, Deptford, 1987; Jury Member: Diana Princess of Wales Fountain Competition, London, 2002; new Parliament Bldg, Ottawa, 2003; Barbara Hepworth Gall. Competition, Wakefield, 2003; Univ. Boulevard Competition, UBC, 2005; Victoria Embankment Competition, 2005–; Nat. Theatre of Ireland, Dublin, 2008; Mem., Design Review Panel, 2012 Olympics. Trustee, Portsmouth Naval Base Property Trust, 2005–. FRSA. Hon. Fellow, Cardiff Univ., 2001; Hon. DLitt Portsmouth, 2001. Governor-General's Award for Architecture (Canada), 1988. *Publications:* A Guide to the Architecture of London (with C. Woodward), 1983, 4th edn 2008; (contrib.) Jeremy Dixon·Edward Jones Buildings and Projects, 1959–2002, 2002; contribs to arch. jls. *Recreations:* drawing, gardening, looking out of the window in France, Staffordshire bull terriers. *Address:* 41 Gloucester Crescent, NW1 7DL. *T:* (020) 7267 7015.

JONES, Edward W.; *see* Wilson Jones.

JONES, Edwina Currie; *see* Currie, E.

JONES, Eleri Wynne; Member, Independent Television Commission, with special responsibility for Wales, 1990–98; *b* 9 Aug. 1933; *d* of Ellis Edgar and Elen Mary Griffith; *m* 1960, Bedwyr Lewis Jones (*d* 1992); two *s* one *d*. *Educ:* Howell's Sch., Denbigh (Foundn Schol.); University Coll. of Wales, Aberystwyth; University Coll., Cardiff. BA (Wales); DipIPM. Journalist, Canada, 1956–57; Careers Officer, Gwynedd, 1957–64; Tutor, Marr. Guidance Council, 1978–87; Lectr, Gwynedd Technical Coll., 1980–84; Member: Welsh Fourth Channel Authy, 1984–91; Bd of Channel Four, 1987–90. Dir, Cais Ltd, 1993–. Member: Staff Commn for Local Govt Reorgn (Wales), 1994–97; HEFCW, 2000–; Rees Review into Devolution of Student Support System and Tuition Fees in Wales, 2004–05. Mem., Council, Univ. of Wales, Aberystwyth, 1995–98, Univ. of Wales, Bangor, 1998–2002 (Hon. Fellow, 2001). Formerly trainer and practitioner in psychotherapy and counselling. *Recreations:* walking, travel, television, films. *Address:* 3 Y Berllan, Lôn Las, Menai Bridge, Anglesey LL59 5BT. *T:* (01248) 717811.

JONES, Elin; Member (Plaid Cymru) Ceredigion, National Assembly for Wales, since 1999; Minister for Rural Affairs, since 2007; *b* 1 Sept. 1966; *d* of John and Avril Jones. *Educ:* Llanwnnen Primary Sch.; Lampeter Comprehensive; UC Cardiff (BScEcon); Univ. of Wales, Aberystwyth (MSc). Research Officer, Dept of Agric. Econs, UCW, Aberystwyth, 1988–91; Econ. Develt Officer, Develt Bd for Rural Wales, 1991–98; Regl Develt Manager, WDA, 1998–99. Mayor of Aberystwyth, 1997–98. Chm., Plaid Cymru, 2000–02. *Recreations:* music, Welsh culture. *Address:* (constituency office) Ty Goronwy, 32 Heol y Wig, Aberystwyth, Ceredigion SY23 2LN.

JONES, Elisabeth A.; *see* Arfon-Jones.

JONES, Elizabeth A.; *see* Blandino, E. A.

JONES, Elizabeth Sian; QC 2000; *b* 24 March 1960; *d* of John Oswald Jones and Margrette Rachel Jones; *m* 1997, John Clark; one *s* two *d*. *Educ:* Howell's Sch., Llandaf; Ryde Sch., IoW; King's Coll., Cambridge. Called to the Bar, Middle Temple, 1984; Bencher, Lincoln's Inn, 2007; in practice at the Bar, 1984–. *Recreations:* singing, opera, yoga, family. *Address:* Serle Court, 6 New Square, Lincoln's Inn, WC2A 3QS. *T:* (020) 7242 6105.

JONES, Prof. (Elphin) Wynne, PhD; FRAgS, FIAgrE; Principal, Harper Adams University College (formerly Harper Adams Agricultural College), since 1996; *b* 29 March 1949; *s* of Elphin and Eluned Jones; *m* 1977, Irfana Siddiqi; two *d*. *Educ:* University Coll. of N Wales, Bangor (BSc Hons); Univ. of Reading (PhD 1976). MIBiol 1978; FRAgS 1994; FIAgrE 2003. Lectr in Animal Prodn, 1975–78, Hd, Dept of Animal Prodn, 1978–88, Welsh Agricl Coll.; Vice Principal and Dir, Acad. Affairs, Harper Adams Agricl Coll., 1988–96. Mem., Bd of Mgt, BASIS, 2004–07. Chm., Trehane Trust, 2007–; Member, Board: of Trustees, Lantra, 2001–; of Mgt, AMTRA; of Mgt, Shrewsbury Sch. Vice Chm., Dairy Science Forum. Fellow, Inst. of Welsh Affairs, 2006. Hon. DSc Cranfield, 2006. Nat. Agricl Award, RASE, 2005. *Recreations:* travel, walking, reading. *Address:* Harper Adams University College, Newport, Shropshire TF10 8NB. *Club:* Farmers'.

JONES, Prof. Emrys Lloyd, FBA 1982; Goldsmiths' Professor of English Literature, Oxford University, and Fellow, New College, Oxford, 1984–98; *b* 30 March 1931; *s* of Peter Jones and Elizabeth Jane (*née* Evans); *m* 1965, Barbara Maud Everett; one *d*. *Educ:* Neath Grammar Sch.; Magdalen Coll., Oxford (BA, MA). Tutor in English, Magdalen Coll., 1955–77; Reader in Eng. Lit., Oxford Univ., 1977–84; Fellow, Magdalen Coll., Oxford, 1955–84. Hon. DPhil Lund, 1994. *Publications:* (ed) Poems of Henry Howard, Earl of Surrey, 1964; Pope and Dulness, 1972; Scenic Form in Shakespeare, 1971; The Origins of Shakespeare, 1977; (ed) Antony and Cleopatra, 1977; (ed) The New Oxford Book of Sixteenth Century Verse, 1991; contribs to jls and books. *Recreations:* looking at buildings, opera. *Address:* New College, Oxford OX1 3BN. *T:* (01865) 279555.

JONES, Ernest Edward; Member, Doncaster Metropolitan Borough Council, 1980–2000; *b* 15 Oct. 1931; *s* of William Edward Jones and Eileen Gasser; *m* 1955, Mary Armstrong; one *s* one *d*. *Educ:* Bentley Catholic Primary Sch., Doncaster; Sheffield De La Salle Coll.; Hopwood Hall Coll. of Educn, Middleton, Lancs; Manch. Univ. Sch. of Educn; Management Studies Unit, Sheffield Polytech. Min. of Educn Teaching Certif. (CertEd); Univ. Dipl. in Science Studies (DipSc); Dipl. in Educn Management (DEM). School Master, 1953–92. Doncaster County Borough: Councillor, 1962–74 (Chm. Health Cttee, 1971–74; Chm. Social Services Cttee, 1972–73; served on 15 other cttees at various times). South Yorkshire CC: Mem. 1973–77; Dep. Chm., 1973–75; Chm., 1975–76; Chm., Rec., Culture and Health Cttee, 1973–75; Doncaster Metropolitan Borough Council: Chairman: Libraries, Museums and Arts Cttee, 1982–91; Further Educn Cttee, 1983–85; Social Service Cttee, 1998–2000; Mem., Educn Services Cttee, 1980–2000 (Vice-Chm., 1982–95). Chairman: Trent Regional Assoc. of Community Health Councils, 1988–90; Doncaster CHC, 1981–90; Co. and Council of Management, Northern Coll., 1986–88, 1991– (Vice-Chm., 1982–86, 1990–91); Doncaster College (formerly Inst. of Further and Higher Educn), 1985–93; Mem., Doncaster Coll. Corp., 1993–2002. Member: Nat. Health Exec. Council, 1964–74; Doncaster and Dist Water Bd, 1972–74; AMC (Social Services), 1972–74; Peak Park Planning Bd, 1973–77; Yorks and Humberside Museum and Art Gall. Service, 1973–77, 1984–; Yorks and Humberside Jt Libraries Cttee, 1973–75, 1983–; Yorks and Humberside Assoc. of Further and High Educn, 1982–; Yorks and Humberside Assoc. of Educn Authorities, 1982– (Chm., 1988–89); Council, Museums Assoc., 1986; S Yorks Jt Archaeol Cttee, 1987–91 (Chm., 1987–88); S Yorks Jt Archives Cttee, 1987–91 (Chm., 1987–88); NEAB, 1992–; S Yorks Fire and Civil Defence Authy, 1997–; Cttee, Yorks Tourist Bd, 1999–; Exec. Mem., Nat. Field Studies Council, 1988–. Exec. Mem., Yorks Arts Assoc., 1983–85; former Member: Yorks Regional Land Drainage Cttee; Univ. of Hull Educn Delegacy; AMA; Yorks and Humberside Museums and Art Galleries Fedn; Yorks and Humberside Regional Sports Council; Yorks, Humberside and Cleveland Tourist Bd; Exec. Mem., Youth Assoc. of South Yorks. Member: Hull Univ. Ct, 1983–85; Sheffield Univ. Ct and Council, 1983–; Bradford Univ. Ct and Council, 1986–93; Governor: Sheffield Poly., 1982–90; Sheffield Hallam Univ., 1995–99. Fellow, Doncaster Coll., 2002. FRSH; FRSA 1980. *Recreations:* music and fine arts, general interest in sport, fell-walking, keen caravanner. *Address:* 11 Norborough Road, Doncaster, South Yorks DN2 4AR. *T:* (01302) 366122.

JONES, Eurfron Gwynne; Director of Education, BBC, 1992–94; *b* 24 Sept. 1934; *d* of William Gwynne Jones and Annie (*née* Harries); *m* 1968, Michael Coyle; one *s*. *Educ:* Aberdare Girls' Grammar Sch.; University Coll., Cardiff, Univ. of Wales (BSc (Zoology); PhD). Teaching Asst, Mount Holyoke Coll., Mass, 1955–56; joined BBC as gen. trainee, 1959; Producer, BBC Sch. Radio, Sch. Television and Continuing Educn, TV, 1959–75; freelance broadcaster, writer and cons., Media Cons. Internat. Children's Centre, Educn Commn of the States, 1975–83; Asst Hd, Sch. Radio, 1983–84; Hd of Sch. Television, 1984–87; Controller, Educnl Broadcasting, BBC, 1987–92. Member: Wyatt Commn on Violence, 1986; OU Council, 1987–94; Open Coll. Council, 1987–89; Council, Royal Instn, 1989–92, and 1994–97; COPUS, 1992–94; Educn Adv. Cttee, Nat. Museums and Galls of Wales, 1995–99; Res. Panel, Inst. of Welsh Affairs, 1996–2002; Chm., Digital Coll. for Wales, 1997–2001. Vis. Prof., Inst. of Educn, Univ. of London, 1994–97. Chm., Friends of Glynn Vivian Art Gall., 2006–. FRTS 1994 (Mem., 1984–94; Vice Pres., 1996–2002). Fellow, Univ. of Wales Cardiff, 1996. Hon. LLD Exeter, 1990; DUniv Open, 1996. *Publications:* Children Growing Up, 1973; The First Five Years, 1975; How

Did I Grow?, 1977; Television Magic, 1978; Lifetime I, Lifetime II, 1982; numerous articles on children and educn. *Recreations:* photography, swimming.

JONES, Fielding; *see* Jones, N. F.

JONES, Fred, CB 1978; CBE 1966; Deputy Secretary, HM Treasury, 1975–80, retired; *b* 5 May 1920; *s* of late Fred Jones and of Harriet (*née* Nuttall); *m* 1954, Joy (*née* Field); two *s*. *Educ:* Preston Grammar Sch.; St Catherine's Coll., Oxford. Economist, Trades Union Congress, 1951–59; Tutor in Economics and Industrial Relations, Ruskin Coll., Oxford, 1960–62; Economist, National Economic Development Office, 1962–64; Dept of Economic Affairs: Senior Economic Adviser, 1964–66; Asst Sec., 1966–68; Asst Under-Sec. of State, 1968–69; HM Treasury, Asst Under-Sec. of State, 1969–75. *Recreations:* walking, gardening, reading. *Address:* 16 Higher Greenfield, Ingol, Preston, Lancs PR2 3ZX.

JONES, Gareth; *see* Jones, J. G.

JONES, Gareth, OBE 1991; Member (Plaid Cymru) Aberconwy, National Assembly for Wales, since 2007; *b* 14 May 1939. *Educ:* UC, Swansea (BA Hons Geography). Former Headmaster; educnl consultant. Chm., Univ. of Wales Bd for Welsh Lang. Teaching, 2003–06. Mem. (Plaid Cymru) Conwy, Nat. Assembly for Wales, 1999–2003; contested same seat, 2003. Chm., Enterprise and Learning Cttee, Nat. Assembly for Wales, 2007–. Mem. (Plaid Cymru), Conwy CBC, 1997–2008. *Address:* Dolarfon, 21 Roumania Drive, Craig y Don, Llandudno LL30 1UY.

JONES, Gareth, OBE 2003; Registrar of Companies and Chief Executive, Companies House, since 2007; *b* 13 Aug. 1957; s of late Hubert John Jones and Audrey Margaret Jones; *m* 1979, Susan (*née* Brown); one *s* one *d*. *Educ:* Open Univ. (BA Hons Hist.). Civil Servant, 1979–; Private Sec. to Sec. of State for Trade and Ind., 1988–90; Welsh Assembly Government: Hd, CAP Mgt Div., Agric. and Rural Affairs Dept, 1999–2003; Dir, Dept for Envmt, Planning and Countryside, 2003–07. FRSA. *Address:* Cyncoed, Cardiff. *Club:* Cardiff and County.

JONES, Prof. Gareth (Hywel); QC 1986; FBA 1982; Fellow of Trinity College, Cambridge, since 1961; Downing Professor of the Laws of England, Cambridge University, 1975–98; *b* 10 Nov. 1930; *o c* of late B. T. Jones, FRICS, and late Mabel Jones, Tylorstown, Glam; *m* 1959, Vivienne Joy (*d* 2004), *o d* of late C. E. Puckridge, FIA, Debden Green, Loughton; two *s* one *d*. *Educ:* Porth County Sch.; University Coll. London (PhD; Fellow 1988); St Catharine's Coll., Cambridge (Scholar); Harvard Univ. (LLM). LLB London 1951; MA, LLB 1953, LLD 1972, Cantab. Choate Fellow, Harvard, 1953; Yorke Prize, 1960. Called to Bar, Lincoln's Inn, 1955 (Scholar); Hon. Bencher 1975. Lecturer: Oriel and Exeter Colls, Oxford, 1956–58; KCL, 1958–61; Trinity College, Cambridge: Lectr, 1961–75; Tutor, 1967; Sen. Tutor, 1972; Vice-Master, 1986–92 and 1996–99; Univ. Lectr, Cambridge, 1961–75; Chm., Faculty of Law, 1978–81; Chm., Fitzwilliam Mus. Syndicate, 1987–2001. Visiting Professor: Harvard, 1966 and 1975; Chicago, 1976–95; California at Berkeley, 1967 and 1971; Indiana, 1971, 1975; Michigan, 1983, 1997, 1999, 2001, 2002; Georgia, 1983; Texas, 1993. Lectures: Harris, Indiana, 1981; Wright, Toronto, 1984; Lionel Cohen, Hebrew Univ., 1985; Butterworth, QMC, 1987; Nambyar, India, 1991; Richard O'Sullivan, Thomas More Soc., 1991; Hochelaga, Hong Kong, 2000; Tory, Halifax, NS, 2001; Lansdowne, Victoria, BC, 2003. Mem., American Law Inst.; For. Mem., Royal Netherlands Acad. of Arts and Scis, 1991. Hon. LLD Glamorgan, 2008. *Publications:* (with Lord Goff of Chieveley) The Law of Restitution, 1966, 7th edn 2007; The History of the Law of Charity 1532–1827, 1969; The Sovereignty of the Law, 1973; (with Lord Goodhart) Specific Performance, 1986, 2nd edn 1996; various articles. *Address:* Trinity College, Cambridge CB2 1TQ; 9B Cranmer Road, Cambridge CB3 9BL. *T:* (01223) 363932; Clay Street, Thornham Magna, Eye, Suffolk IP23 8HE. *Club:* Beefsteak.

JONES, Dr Gareth L.; Director of Human Resources and Internal Communications, BBC, 1999–2001; *b* 21 Aug. 1951; *s* of Les and Gwen Jones; *m* 1990, Shirley Rose Neal; one *s* two *d*. *Educ:* BSc Econ, MA, PhD. Lecturer in Economic and Social Studies: UEA, 1974–85; London Business Sch., 1985–93; Sen. Vice Pres., Polygram Internat., 1993–96; BT Prof. of Orgnl Develt, Henley Mgt Coll., 1996–99. *Publications:* (with R. E. Goffee) The Character of a Corporation, 1998; contrib. articles to Eur. Jl Mgt, Human Relns, Harvard Business Rev. *Recreations:* soccer, squash, pub-visiting.

JONES, Gareth S.; *see* Stedman Jones.

JONES, Gemma; *see* Jones, Jennifer.

JONES, Geoffrey; *see* Jones, John G.

JONES, Geoffrey M.; *see* Melvill Jones.

JONES, George Quentin; Multi-media Political Correspondent, Press Association, since 2007; *b* 28 Feb. 1945; *s* of (John) Clement Jones, CBE; *m* 1st, 1972, Diana Chittenden (marr. diss. 1989); one *s* one *d*; 2nd, 1990, Teresa Grace Rolleston. *Educ:* Highfields Sch., Wolverhampton. Trainee journalist, Eastern Daily Press, 1963–67; journalist, S Wales Argus and Western Mail, 1967–69; Reuters, London, 1969; Parly Staff, The Times, 1969–73; Parly and Political Corresp., Scotsman, 1973–82; Political Correspondent: Sunday Telegraph, 1982–85; Sunday Times, 1985–86; Political Corresp., 1986–88, Political Ed., 1988–2007, Daily Telegraph. Regular broadcaster, BBC News and current affairs programmes, Sky News. Chairman: Parly Lobby Journalists, 1987–88; Parly Press Gallery, 1996–97. Judge, Spectator Parliamentarian of the Year Awards, 1993–2006. *Recreations:* walking (completing Offa's Dyke long distance path), cycling, travelling, time with family, escaping politics. *Address:* 92 Kyrle Road, SW11 6BA. *T:* (020) 7223 6646.

JONES, Prof. George William, OBE 1999; Professor of Government, University of London, 1976–2003, now Emeritus; *b* 4 Feb. 1938; *er s* of George William and Grace Annie Jones; *m* 1963, Diana Mary Bedwell; one *s* one *d*. *Educ:* Wolverhampton Grammar Sch.; Jesus Coll., Oxford (BA 1960, MA 1965); Nuffield Coll., Oxford; DPhil Oxon 1965. Univ. of Leeds: Asst Lectr in Govt, 1963; Lectr in Govt, 1965; London School of Economics and Political Science: Lectr in Political Science, 1966; Sen. Lectr in Polit. Sci., 1971; Reader in Polit. Sci., 1974; Chm., Graduate Sch., 1990–93; Vice-Chm., Appts Cttee, 1996–99. Sec., 1965–68, Mem. Exec. Cttee, 1969–75, Polit. Studies Assoc. of the UK; Mem., Exec. Council, Hansard Soc., 1968–70; Member, Editorial Committee: Local Government Studies, 1970–98, 2003–; The London Journal, 1973–80; Governance, 1987–92; Korean Jl of Public Policy, 1988–; Studies in Law and Politics, 1989–; Nonprofit Management and Leadership, 1989–; Hong Kong Jl of Public Admin, 1992–. Member: Layfield Cttee of Inquiry into Local Govt Finance, 1974–76; Exams Cttee, and Admin. Staff Qualifications Council, Local Govt Trng Bd, 1977–80; Political Science and Internat. Relns Cttee, SSRC, 1977–81; Jt Working Party on Internal Management of Local Authorities, 1992–93; Chm., Central-Local Govt Relations Panel, SSRC, 1978–81; Special Adviser, Select Cttee on Welsh Affairs, 1985–87. Vis. Prof., Queen Mary, London, 2004–; Hon. Prof., Birmingham Univ., 2003–; Vis. Res. Fellow, De Montfort Univ., 2007–. Member: Governing Council, Wolverhampton Polytechnic, 1978–83 (Hon. Fellow, 1986); Council, RIPA, 1984–90; Nat. Consumer Council, 1991–99 (Chm., Public Services Cttee, 1992–98); Beacon Councils Adv. Panel, 1999–2002; Vice-Pres., Assoc. of Councillors, 1980–. Hon. Member: CIPFA, 2003–; SOLACE, 2003–. FRHistS 1980. Hon. Fellow, Inst. of Local Govt Studies, Birmingham Univ., 1979. *Publications:* Borough Politics, 1969; (with B. Donoughue) Herbert Morrison: portrait of a politician, 1973, repr. 2001; (ed with A. Norton) Political Leadership in Local Authorities, 1978; (ed) New Approaches to the Study of Central-Local Government Relationships, 1980; (with J. Stewart) The Case for Local Government, 1983, 2nd edn 1985; (ed jtly) Between Centre and Locality, 1985; (ed) West European Prime Ministers, 1991; (with Tony Travers *et al*) The Government of London, 1991; Local Government and the Social Market, 1991; (with Tony Travers *et al*) The Impact of Population Size on Local Authority Costs and Effectiveness, 1993; Local Government: the management agenda, 1993; (with Tony Travers) Attitudes to Local Government in Westminster and Whitehall, 1994; (with Tony Travers *et al*) The Role of the Local Authority Chief Executive in Local Governance, 1997; The New Local Government Agenda, 1997; (jtly) At the Centre of Whitehall, 1998; (jtly) Regulation Inside Government, 1999; contribs to Political Studies, Public Admin., Political Qly, Parliamentary Affairs, Government and Opposition, Jl of Admin Overseas; Local Govt Chronicle; Internat. Jl Public Sector Mgt; Public Money and Mgt; Public Finance; The MJ; History and Policy. *Recreations:* cinema, politics. *Address:* Department of Government, London School of Economics, Houghton Street, WC2A 2AE. *T:* (020) 7955 7179; *e-mail:* g.w.jones@lse.ac.uk. *Club:* Beefsteak.

JONES, Geraint Anthony; QC 2001; *b* 5 April 1953; *s* of John and Lydia Jones; *m* 1976, Pauline Julia Gibson; two *d*. *Educ:* Christ Coll., Brecon; Jesus Coll., Cambridge (MA). MCIArb 2002. Called to the Bar, Middle Temple, 1976; in practice as barrister, specialising in chancery, commercial and professional negligence law, Cardiff, 1976–, and London, 2001–. Mem., Judicial Panel, Internat. Rugby Bd, 2002–. *Recreations:* hill walking, sailing. *Address:* Devonshire House, Fairbourne, Cobham, Surrey KT11 2BT.

JONES, Geraint Stanley, CBE 1993; international broadcasting consultant and producer, since 1994; Chief Executive, S4C, 1989–94; *b* 26 April 1936; *s* of Olwen and David Stanley Jones; *m* 1961, Rhiannon Williams; two *d*. *Educ:* Pontypridd Grammar Sch.; University Coll. of N Wales (BA Hons; DipEd; Hon. Fellow 1988). BBC-Wales: Studio Manager, 1960–62; Production Asst, Current Affairs (TV), 1962–65; TV Producer: Current Affairs, 1965–69; Features and Documentaries, 1969–73; Asst Head of Programmes, Wales, 1973–74; Head of Programmes, Wales, 1974–81; Controller, BBC Wales, 1981–85; Dir of Public Affairs, BBC, 1986–87; Man. Dir, Regl Broadcasting, BBC, 1987–89. Director: WNO, 1985–94; Welsh Film Council, 1992–97; Screen Wales, 1992–96; Wales Millennium Centre, 1999–2005; Chm., Sgrîn, Media Agency for Wales, 1999–2004. Mem., Arts Council of Wales, 1994–2000. Chm., EBU Television Commn, 1990–96. Chm., Ryan Davies Trust, 1977–; Member: UK Freedom from Hunger Campaign Cttee, 1978–97; BT Wales Adv. Forum, 1994–2001; British Council Film and TV Cttee, 1995–2002; UNA (Welsh Centre) Trust, 1999–2005; Bd, Clwyd Theatr Cymru, 2006–. Vice Pres., RWCMD (formerly WCMD), 2000– (Chm., Bd of Govs, 1990–2000); Mem., Court and Council, Univ. of Wales, Aberystwyth, 1990–96. Chm., Welsh Nat. Lang. Centre, 1994–97. Vis. Prof., Internat. Acad. of Broadcasting, Montreux, 1994–2001. Trustee: Pendyrus Trust, 2001–; Wales Video Gall., 2001–; Clwyd Theatr Cymru Develt Trust, 2004–. FRSA 1989; FRTS 1992. FRWCMD (FWCMD 2000). Hon. LLD Wales, 1998; Hon. DLitt Glamorgan, 1999. *Recreations:* music, painting, horse riding. *Address:* 12 Lady Mary Road, Roath Park, Cardiff CF23 5NS. *Clubs:* Royal Over-Seas League; Cardiff and County (Cardiff).

JONES, Dr Gerald, FRCP; Senior Principal Medical Officer, Department of Health (formerly of Health and Social Security), 1984–95; *b* 25 Jan. 1939; *s* of John Jones and Gladys Jones (*née* Roberts); *m* 1st, 1964, Anne Heatley (*née* Morris) (marr. diss. 1987); one *s* two *d*; 2nd, 1990, Jutta Friese. *Educ:* Swansea Grammar School; Merton College, Oxford; London Hosp. Med. Coll. (BA, BM, BCh, PhD, MSc). Appointments in hosp. medicine, 1965–69; research with MRC, 1969–73; pharmaceutical industry, 1974–75; medical staff, DHSS, later DoH, 1975–95. *Publications:* papers on cardiopulmonary physiology, respiratory medicine, cellular immunology and drug regulation. *Recreations:* music, gardening, mathematics. *Address:* 58 Palace Road, N8 8QP.

JONES, Gerald Kenneth; Chief Executive, Wandsworth Borough Council, since 1987; *b* 16 June 1943; *s* of Sir Kenneth Jones, CBE, QC and of Menna (*née* Jones); *m* 1976, Janet Norma Dymock; three *s* one *d*. *Educ:* Royal Grammar Sch., Guildford; St John's Coll., Cambridge (MA 1965); Brunel Univ. (MTech 1972). Operational Res. Scientist, NCB, 1966–69; Mgt Consultant, RTZ Corp., 1969–72; Corporate Planner, Haringey Council, 1972–74; Wandsworth Council: Asst Dir, Admin, 1974–81; Dir, Admin, 1981–83; Dep. Chief Exec., 1983–87. *Publications:* contrib. technical and professional jls. *Recreations:* collecting antiquarian books, triathlon. *Address:* The Town Hall, Wandsworth High Street, SW18 2PU.

JONES, Glyn Parry, FCA; Chairman: Towry Law Group, since 2006; Aspen Insurance Holdings Ltd, since 2007; Hermes, since 2008; *b* 17 March 1952; *m* 1976, Catherine Anne King; two *s* one *d*. *Educ:* Birkenhead Sch.; Gonville and Caius Coll., Cambridge (MA Econs and Social and Pol Scis). FCA 1976. Deloitte Haskins and Sells: Auditor, London, 1973–76; Consultant, Financial Mgt Consultancy, London, 1977–80; Man. Dir, Kenyan Consultancy, Nairobi, 1980–83; Partner, Midlands Consulting Practice, Birmingham, 1983–85; Partner in Charge, Financial Services Consulting, London, 1986–89; European Sector Leader, Financial Services, London, Coopers & Lybrand Mgt Consultants, 1989–91; Standard Chartered Bank: Divl Dir, Standard Chartered Equitor, Hong Kong, 1991–92; Gen. Manager, Internat. Private Banking, Hong Kong, 1993–97; Commercial Dir, NatWest Wealth Mgt, London, March–Oct. 1997; Chief Executive: Coutts Gp, 1997–2000; Gartmore Investment Mgt plc, 2000–04; Thames River Capital LLP, 2005–06. *Recreations:* tennis, squash, theatre.

JONES, Rev. Canon Glyndwr; Secretary General, Mission to Seafarers (formerly Missions to Seamen), 1990–2000; a Chaplain to the Queen, 1990–2005; *b* 25 Nov. 1935; *s* of late Bertie Samuel Jones and of Elizabeth Ellen Jones; *m* 1st, 1961, Cynthia Elaine Jenkins (*d* 1964); 2nd, 1966, (Marion) Anita Morris; one *s* one *d*. *Educ:* Dynefor Sch., Swansea; St Michael's Theol Coll., Llandaff, Univ. of Wales (DipTh); MA Wales 2005. Nat. Service, 1954–56: RAPC, attached 19 Field Regt RA; served Korea, Hong Kong; demobbed Sgt AER. Deacon 1962, priest 1963; Curate: Clydach, 1962–64; Llangyfelach with Morriston, 1964–67; Sketty, 1967–70; Rector, Bryngwyn with Newchurch and Llanbedr, Painscastle with Llanddewi Fach, 1970–72; The Missions to Seamen: Port Chaplain, Swansea and Port Talbot, 1972–76; Sen. Chaplain, Port of London, 1976–81; Auxiliary Ministries Sec., Central Office, 1981–85; Asst Gen. Sec., 1985–90. Hon. Chaplain, Royal Alfred Seafarers Soc., 1987–93; Chaplain to Lay Sheriff of London, 1993–94, 1999–2000; Hon. Canon, St Michael's Cathedral, Kobe, Japan, 1988–. Commissary to Bp of Cyprus in the Gulf, 1996–2000. Mem., Eddie Baird Meml Trust,

2003– (Treas., 2007–). Hon. Mem., Co. of Master Mariners, 1990–2000; Freeman, City of London, 1990; Chaplain: Co. of Information Technologists, 1989–2000; Co. of Innholders, 1990–2002; Co. of Farriers, 1990–2004 (Liveryman, 1999–); Co. of Carmen, 1990–2004 (Liveryman, 1995–). Sec. to Trustees, Orsett Churches Centre, 2003–07. President: Probus Club, Grays Thurrock, 2005–06; Batti-Wallahs' Soc., 2006–07. *Recreations:* sport, music, reading, theatre, travel. *Address:* 5 The Close, Grays, Essex RM16 2XU. *Clubs:* Little Ship (Hon. Chaplain, 1996–2000); Thurrock Rugby Football (Chaplain, 1999); Grays Thurrock Rotary (Pres., 2007–08).

JONES, Glynn, CBE 1992; Circuit Administrator, Western Circuit, Lord Chancellor's Department, 1987–93; *b* 5 March 1933; *s* of late Bertie Jones and Alice Maud Jones (*née* Griffiths); *m* 1957, Crystal Laura, *d* of late Edward William Kendall and Ivy Irene Kendall; one *s* one *d*. *Educ:* state schs in Monmouthshire; BA Open. Local Govt service, 1950–71; Lord Chancellor's Department: Crown Court, Newport, 1972, Winchester, 1973; Courts Administrator: Nottingham Group of Courts, 1976; South Wales Group of Courts, 1980. *Recreations:* Rugby Union football, golf. *Address:* 17 Rockfield Glade, Penhow, Newport, S Wales NP26 3JF. *T:* (01633) 400835. *Clubs:* Civil Service; St Pierre Golf and Country, Newport Golf.

JONES, Gordon Frederick; architect; *b* 25 Aug. 1929; *s* of Harold Frederick and Rose Isabel Jones; *m* 1954, Patricia Mary (*née* Rowley); one *s* one *d*. *Educ:* Saltley Grammar Sch.; The School of Architecture, Birmingham (DipArch 1950), and subseq. by BBC; Sch. of Planning, UCL (Cert. Landscape Design, 1963). RIBA 1950. FRSA. Architect: in local government, 1952; War Office, 1959; Asst City Architect, Sheffield, 1966; private practice, London, 1968; Property Services Agency, DoE: Architect, 1970; Head of Student Training Office, 1976; Head of Architectural Services, 1979–85; Res. Dir, 1985–90, Editor, 1990–93, Product Design Review. Dir, Building Centre, London, 1984–87. Chm. of Standards, BDB/–, BSI, 1984–87. *Recreations:* watching cats, listening to music, re-building houses. *Address:* Hilltop, Monkleigh, Bideford, Devon EX39 5JT.

JONES, Graham Edward, MA; Headmaster, Repton School, 1987–2003; *b* 22 Sept. 1944; *s* of late Edward Thomas Jones and of Dora Rachel Jones; *m* 1976, Vanessa Mary Heloise (*née* Smith). *Educ:* Birkenhead Sch.; Fitzwilliam Coll., Cambridge (schol.; 1st cl. Hons Econs Tripos 1966). Asst Master, Hd of Economics and Politics, Housemaster, Charterhouse, 1967–87; secondment to British Petroleum, 1981. Awarder in Economics, Oxford and Cambridge Schs Examination Bd, 1979–91; Reviser in Economics, JMB, 1981–91; Chm. Examrs, Oxford and Cambridge and RSA Examinations, 1996–2001; Chm., Ind. Schs Examinations Bd, 1998–2006. Governor: Birkenhead Sch., 2004–; Royal GS, Worcester, 2004–07; Malvern Coll., 2005. FRSA 1988. *Publications:* various articles on economics and teaching economics. *Recreations:* painting, walking, music, cooking, the classics. *Address:* Tilton House, Sutton St Nicholas, Hereford HR1 3BB. *T:* (01432) 882075.

JONES, His Honour Graham Julian; a Senior Circuit Judge, 2002–05 (a Circuit Judge, 1985–2005; authorised to sit as a Judge of the High Court, 1994–2005); a Judge of Technology and Construction Court (formerly a Circuit Official Referee), 1993–2005; Resident and Designated Judge, Cardiff County Court, 1994–98; Designated Civil Judge, Cardiff, 1998–2000, South and West Wales, 2000–05; Deputy High Court Judge, since 2005; acting Designated Civil Judge for Wales, 2008; *b* 17 July 1936; *s* of late David John Jones, CBE, and Edna Lillie Jones; *m* 1961, Dorothy, *o d* of late James Smith and Doris Irene Tickle, Abergavenny; two *s* one *d*. *Educ:* Porth County Grammar Sch. (state scholarship); St John's Coll., Cambridge. MA, LLM (Cantab). Admitted Solicitor, 1961; Partner, Morgan Bruce and Nicholas, 1961 (represented Parents and Residents Assoc., Aberfan Disaster, 1966). Dep. Circuit Judge, 1975–78; a Recorder, 1978–85. Pres., Pontypridd Rhondda and Dist Law Soc., 1973–75; Member Council: Cardiff Law Soc., 1975–78, 1984–85; Associated Law Socs of Wales, 1974–85 (Pres., 1982–84); Member: Lord Chancellor's Legal Aid Adv. Cttee, 1980–85; Adv. Bd, Centre for Professional Legal Studies, Cardiff Law Sch., 1995–; Civil Justice Council, 2004–; Judicial Estates Adv. Gp, 2004–. Mem. Court, UWCC, 1995–; Gov., Univ. of Glamorgan, 1999–2006. Council Mem., RNLI, 2002–05 (Vice Pres., 2005–). *Recreations:* golf, boats. *Clubs:* Cardiff and County (Cardiff), Radyr Golf, Royal Porthcawl Golf.

JONES, (Graham) Wyn, QPM 1987; Assistant Commissioner of Police of the Metropolis, 1989–93; *b* Ystradgynlais, Brecon, 12 Oct. 1943; *s* of Thomas James and Mary Elizabeth (*née* Almrott); *m* 1970, Joan Goodbrook. *Educ:* Thornbury Grammar Sch.; Univ. of Exeter (LLB). Joined Glos Police, 1963; Chief Inspector, Glos, 1971; Supt, 1976; Chief Supt, Oxford, 1979; Asst Chief Constable (Ops), Thames Valley Police, 1982; Dep. Asst Comr (CID), New Scotland Yard, 1984; Dep. Asst Comr, 2 Area (East), Metropolitan Police, 1985. Comd Police Ops, Greenham Common, 1983–84, Wapping, 1985–86. Vis. Lectr on policing and public disorder to Police Foundn, USA, and to Germany. *Publications:* articles and contribs to jls on public disorder, forensic investigation, police and media. *Recreations:* ballet, opera, tennis, golf, horse riding.

JONES, Gregory Dennis T.; *see* Treverton-Jones.

JONES, Griffith R.; *see* Rhys Jones.

JONES, Gwilym Haydn; *b* 19 Jan. 1947; *s* of late Evan Haydn Jonesand Mary Elizabeth Gwenhwyfar Jones (*née* Moseley); *m* 1974, Linda Margaret (*née* John); one *s* one *d*. Dir, Bowring Wales Ltd, 1980–93. Councillor, Cardiff CC, 1969–72 and 1973–83. MP (C) Cardiff North, 1983–97; contested (C) same seat, 1997. PPS to Minister of State, Dept of Transport, 1991–92; Parly Under-Sec. of State, Welsh Office, 1992–97. Secretary: Welsh Cons. Members Gp, 1984–93; All Party Gp for Fund for Replacement of Animals in Medical Experiments, 1987–92. Founder Chm., Friendship Force in Wales, 1978–81; Vice Pres., Kidney Res. Unit for Wales Foundn, 1986–93. Rowed for Wales in Speaker's Regatta, 1986. Liveryman, Welsh Livery Guild, 1993–. OStJ 1997. *Recreations:* golf, model railways, watching Wales win at Rugby. *Clubs:* County Conservative, Cardiff and County (Cardiff).

JONES, Gwyn; *see* Jones, Miah G.

JONES, Gwyn Idris M.; *see* Meirion-Jones.

JONES, Dame Gwyneth, DBE 1986 (CBE 1976); a Principal Dramatic Soprano: Royal Opera House, Covent Garden, since 1963; Vienna State Opera, since 1966 (Hon. Member, 1989); Deutsche Oper Berlin, since 1966; Bavarian State Opera, since 1967; *b* 7 Nov. 1936; *d* of late Edward George Jones and late Violet (*née* Webster); one *d*. *Educ:* Twmpath Sec. Mod. Sch., Pontypool, Mon; Royal College of Music, London; Accademia Chigiana, Siena; Zürich Internat. Opera Studio. Maria Carpi Prof., Geneva. Guest Artiste: La Scala, Milan; Berlin State Opera; Munich State Opera; Bayreuth Festival; Salzburg Festival; Verona; Tokyo; Zürich; Metropolitan Opera, New York; Paris; Geneva; Dallas; San Francisco; Los Angeles; Teatro Colon, Buenos Aires; Edinburgh Festival; Welsh National Opera; Rome; Hamburg; Cologne; Maggio Musicale, Florence; Chicago; Seoul; Peking; Hong Kong. Many opera roles including: Leonara in Il Trovatore; Desdemona in Otello; Aida; Leonore in Fidelio; Senta in The Flying Dutchman; Medea (Cherubini); Sieglinde in Die Walküre; Lady Macbeth; Elizabeth in Don Carlos; Madame Butterfly; Tosca; Donna Anna in Don Giovanni; Salome/Herodias; Kundry in Parsifal; Isolde; Helena in Die Ägyptische; Färberin in Die Frau ohne Schatten; Elektra/Klytaemnestra; Elizabeth/Venus in Tannhäuser; Octavian/Marschallin in Der Rosenkavalier; Brünnhilde in Der Ring des Nibelungen; Ortrud in Lohengrin; Minnie in Fanciulla del West; Norma; Erwartung (Schoenberg); La voix humaine (Poulenc); Esmeralda in Notre Dame (Schmidt); Leokadia Begwick in Aufsteig und Fall der Stadt Mahagonny (Brecht/Weil); Kusterin Buryja in Jenufa (Janáček); Kabanicha in Katia Kabanowa (Janáček); Queen of Hearts in Alice in Wonderland (Unsuk Chin); oratorio and recitals. Numerous recordings, radio and TV appearances. Début as Opera Dir, Der Fliegende Holländer, Deutsches Nat. Th., Weimar, 2003. Pres., Richard Wagner Soc., 1990–. FRCM. Kammersängerin, Austria and Bavaria. Hon. Member: RAM, 1980; Vienna State Opera, 1989; Hon. FRWCMD 1992. Hon. DMus: Wales; Glamorgan. Shakespeare Prize, FVS Hamburg, 1987; Golden Medal of Honour, Vienna, 1991; Ehrenkreuz für Wissenschaft und Kunst, I Klasse, Austria, 1992; Premio Puccini, 2003; Cymry for the World Honours, 2004. Bundesverdienstkreuz (FRG), 1988; Comdr, Ordre des Arts et des Lettres (France), 1992. *Address:* PO Box 2000, 8700 Küsnacht, Switzerland.

JONES, Gwynoro Glyndwr; External Assessor for European Foundation Quality Management, Investors in People, and Health Inspectorate; *b* 21 Nov. 1942; *s* of late J. E. and A. L. Jones, Minyrafon, Foelgastell, Cefneithin, Carms; *m* 1967, A. Laura Miles (marr. diss. 1991); two *s* one *d*. *Educ:* Gwendraeth Grammar Sch.; Cardiff Univ. BSc Econ (Hons) Politics and Economics. Market Research Officer, Ina Needle Bearings Ltd, Llanelli, 1966–67; Economist Section, Wales Gas Bd, 1967–69; Public Relations Officer, Labour Party in Wales, March 1969–June 1970; West Glamorgan County Council: Dir of Res., 1974–77; Asst Educn Officer, Develt Forward Planning, 1977–92; Lay Inspector of Schs, 1993–. Man. Dir, EPPC-Severn Crossing Ltd, 1999–. External Assessor, Performance Mgt of Headteachers, 2000–06. Vice-Pres., Dist Council Assoc., 1974; Mem., Council of European Municipalities, 1975–77; first Chm., Welsh Council of European Movt, 1995–97. Broadcaster and television interviewer, S4C, 1993–95. MP (Lab) Carmarthen, 1970–Oct. 1974; Member: House of Commons Expenditure Cttee, 1972–74; Council of Europe and WEU, 1974; PPS to Home Sec., 1974. Pres., Nat. Eisteddfod of Wales, 1974. Co-ordinator, Wales in Europe campaign, 1975; Sponsor, Wales Lab and TU Cttee for Europe, 1975; joined SDP, May 1981; contested: (SDP) Gower, Sept. 1982; (SDP/Alliance) Carmarthen, 1987; (Lib Dem) Hereford, 1992. Chairman: SDP Council for Wales, 1982–85, 1987–88; Alliance Cttee for Wales, 1983–88; Interim Chm., Welsh Soc & Lib Dem Exec., 1988; Member: Council for Social Democracy, 1982–88; SDP Nat. Cttee, 1982–85; SDP Orgn Cttee, 1987–88; Lib Dem Federal Exec., 1988–90; Vice Chm., Lib Dem Policy Cttee, 1988–89; rejoined Labour Party, 1997. *Publications:* booklets: The Record Put Straight, 1973; SDP and the Alliance in Wales 1981–1986, 1986; SLD Golden Opportunities, 1988; A Movement in Crisis, 1989. *Recreations:* sport (played Rugby for both 1st and 2nd class teams). *Address:* 180 West Street, Gorseinon, Swansea SA4 4AQ. *T:* (01792) 523260; *e-mail:* gwynoro@home.7xing.co.uk, gwynoro.jones@ntlworld.com.

JONES, Sir Harry (George), Kt 2000; CBE 1995; Member (Lab), Newport County Borough Council, since 1995 (Leader of Council, 1995–2003); *b* 29 April 1927; *s* of Edward and Alice Jones; *m* 1956, Hazel Kembrey; three *s*. *Educ:* St Woolos Sch.; Newport Tech. Coll. Officer, Merchant Navy, 1948. Apprentice engr, 1943; worked in aluminium ind., 1970s. Member (Lab), Newport DC, 1973–96 (Shadow Mem., 1973–74; Leader of Council, 1987–96; Mayor, 1990–91). Leader, Welsh LGA, 1986–; Vice-Chm., LGA, 1995–; Chm., Local Govt Mgt Bd, 1994. Mem., Welsh NEC, 1990–, and Nat. Policy Forum, 1997–, Labour Party. Hon. Mem. Council, NSPCC, 1993–; Patron, Prince's Trust, 1995–; Trustee, Firebrake Wales, 2005–. Freeman, Newport City and County, 2003. Hon. Mem., RSA, 2000. Hon. Fellow, UCW, Newport, 1999. *Recreations:* swimming, art, gardening. *Address:* 8 Beaufort Place, Newport, S Wales NP19 7NB. *T:* (01633) 769538, (office) (01633) 232121.

JONES, Helen Mary; MP (Lab) Warrington North, since 1997; an Assistant Government Whip, since 2008; *b* 24 Dec. 1954; *d* of late Robert Edward Jones and of Mary Scanlan; *m* 1988, Michael Vobe; one *s*. *Educ:* Ursuline Convent, Chester; UCL; Chester Coll.; Univ. of Liverpool; Manchester Metropolitan Univ. BA, PGCE, MEd, CPE, LSF. Teacher of English; Develt Officer, Mind; Justice and Peace Officer, Liverpool; Solicitor. Contested (Lab): Shropshire N, 1983; Lancashire Central, EP elecn, 1984; Ellesmere Port and Neston, 1987. *Address:* House of Commons, SW1A 0AA.

JONES, Helen Mary; Member (Plaid Cymru) Llanelli, National Assembly for Wales, 1999–2003 and since 2007 (Mid & West Wales, 2003–07); *b* 29 June 1960; *d* of John Mertyn Jones and late Daphne Stuart; one *d*. *Educ:* Colchester County High Sch. for Girls, Essex; Llanfair Caereinion High Sch.; UCW Aberystwyth (BA Hist.). Special Educn Teacher, Gwent, 1982–87; Orgnr for Wales, ActionAid, 1987–91; various positions in youth, community and social work, 1991–96; Sen. Develt Manager (Dep. Dir), EOC, Wales, 1996–99. Former Mem., Nat. Assembly Adv. Gp. Plaid Cymru spokesman, Nat. Assembly for Wales, on educn and equality, 2002–03, on the environment, planning and countryside, 2003–05, on educn, 2005–. Contested (Plaid Cymru): Islwyn, 1992; Montgomery, 1997. *Address:* National Assembly for Wales, Cardiff Bay, Cardiff CF99 1NA.

JONES, (Henry) John (Franklin); writer; *b* 6 May 1924; *s* of late Lt-Col James Walker Jones, DSO, IMS, and Doris Marjorie (*née* Franklin); *m* 1949, Jean Verity Robinson; one *s* one *d*. *Educ:* Blundell's Sch.; Colombo Public Library; Merton Coll., Oxford. Served War, Royal Navy: Ordinary Seaman, 1943; Intell. Staff, Eastern Fleet, 1944. Merton Coll., Oxford: Harmsworth Sen. Scholar, 1948; Fellow and Tutor in Jurisprudence, 1949; Univ. Sen. Lectr, 1956; Fellow and Tutor in Eng. Lit., 1962; Prof. of Poetry, Univ. of Oxford, 1979–84. Dill Meml Lectr, QUB, 1983. Football Correspondent, The Observer, 1956–59. TV appearances include The Modern World, 1988. *Publications:* The Egotistical Sublime, 1954, 5th edn 1978; (contrib.) The British Imagination, 1961; On Aristotle and Greek Tragedy, 1962, 5th edn 1980; (contrib.) Dickens and the Twentieth Century, 1962; (ed) H. W. Garrod, The Study of Good Letters, 1963; John Keats's Dream of Truth, 1969, 2nd edn 1980; (contrib.) The Morality of Art, 1969; The Same God, 1971; Dostoevsky, 1983, 3rd edn 2002; Shakespeare at Work, 1995, 3rd edn 2002. *Address:* Garden Flat, 41 Buckland Crescent, NW3 5DJ. *T:* (020) 7586 1808; Yellands, Brisworthy, Shaugh Prior, Plympton, Devon PL7 5EL. *T:* (01752) 839310.

JONES, Sir Hugh; *see* Hugh-Jones, Sir W. N.

JONES, His Honour Hugh Duncan Hitchings, DL; a Circuit Judge, 1991–2004; a Deputy Circuit Judge, since 2004; *b* 25 May 1937; *s* of Norman Everard Jones and Ann Jones (*née* Hitchings); *m* 1966, Helen Margaret Payne; three *d*. *Educ:* Mountain Ash Grammar School (State Scholarship); University College London (LLB). Admitted Solicitor, 1961; Registrar, Cardiff County Court and Dist Registrar of the High Court, Cardiff Dist Registry, 1978; a Recorder, 1988–91. Mem., County Court Rules Cttee,

1994–97. DL Mid Glamorgan, 2007. *Recreations:* cricket, gardening, golf, holidays in France. *Address:* The Cottage, Cwmpennar, Mountain Ash, Mid Glamorgan CF45 4DB. *Clubs:* MCC; Mountain Ash Golf.

JONES, Hugh Jarrett, (Hugo), H.; *see* Herbert-Jones.

JONES, Ven. Hughie; *see* Jones, Ven. T. H.

JONES, Huw; *see* Jones, D. H.

JONES, Rev. Huw; *see* Jones, Rev. D. H.

JONES, Hywel Ceri, CMG 1999; Director, Network of European Foundations, since 2004; *b* 22 April 1937; *m* 1967, Morwenna Armstrong; one *s* one *d. Educ:* UCW, Aberystwyth (BA French and Classics, DipEd; Hon. Fellow, 1990). Admin. appts, Sussex Univ., 1962–73; joined EC, 1973; Head, Dept for Educn and Youth Policies, 1973–79; Dir for Educn, Vocational Trng and Youth Policy, 1979–88; Dir, Task Force for Human Resources, Educn, Trng and Youth, 1989–93; Acting Dir-Gen., 1993–95, Dep. Dir-Gen., 1995–98, Employment, Social Policy and Indust. Relns. Vis. Fellow in Educn and Contemp. European Studies, Sussex Univ., 1973–80. Chm., Governing Bd, European Policy Centre, Brussels, 2000–07; Governor: Eur. Cultural Foundn, Amsterdam, 1999–2007; NE Wales Inst. of Higher Educn, 2003–06; Federal Trust for Educn and Research, 2004–. Board Member: Franco-British Council, 2004–; ECORYS Gp, 2006–. Hon. Fellow: Swansea, 1992; Aberystwyth, 1993; Glamorgan, 1994; Trinity Coll., Carmarthen, 2008. DUniv: Sussex, 1991; Leuven, 1992; Open, 2000; Hon. LLD NCEA, Ireland, 1992; DUniv Free Univ. Brussels, 2002. Gold Medal, Republic of Italy, 1987. *Recreations:* Rugby, cricket, snooker, theatre, travel. *Address:* 8 Queen's Mansions, Brook Green, W6 7EB. *Clubs:* Reform; Fondation Universitaire (Brussels).

JONES, Hywel Francis; Commissioner for Local Administration in Wales, 1985–91; *b* 28 Dec. 1928; *s* of late Brynmor and Beatrice Jones, Morriston, Swansea; *m* 1959, Marian Rosser Craven; one *d. Educ:* Bishop Gore Grammar School, Swansea; St John's College, Cambridge (BA 1949, MA 1953). IPFA 1953. Borough Treasurer's Dept, Swansea, 1949–56; Nat. Service, RAPC, 1953–55; Dep. County Treasurer, Breconshire, 1956–59; Asst County Treasurer, Carmarthenshire, 1959–66; Borough Treasurer, Port Talbot, 1966–75; Sec., Commn for Local Administration in Wales, 1975–85. Mem., Public Works Loan Board, 1971–75; Financial Adviser, AMC, 1972–74. Mem., Lord Chancellor's Adv. Cttee for West Glamorgan, 1990–97. Treasurer, Royal National Eisteddfod of Wales, 1975–95; Druid Mem., Gorsedd of Bards, 1977 (Treasurer, 1992–2007). *Recreations:* music, reading, gardening. *Address:* Godre'r Rhiw, 1 Lon Heulog, Baglan, Port Talbot, West Glam SA12 8SY. *T:* (01639) 813822.

JONES, Ian; *see* Jones, C. I. McM.

JONES, Ian Michael; Director, Office of Manpower Economics, since 2007; *b* 5 Sept. 1949; *s* of Derek and Jean Jones; *m* 1976, Vivien Hepworth; two *s. Educ:* St Bartholomew's Grammar Sch., Newbury; Fitzwilliam Coll., Cambridge (BA Econs and Politics 1972). Home Office, 1972–83; DTI, 1983–85, Grade 5, 1985; Dept of Employment, 1985–89; Sec., BOTB, 1989–90; Department of Trade and Industry, 1989–2000: Regl Dir, SE Reg., 1990–94; Leader, London City Action Team, 1992–94; Grade 3, 1994; Head, Textiles and Retail Div., 1994–96; Head, Posts, Retail and Textiles Directorate, 1996; Chief Exec., Employment Tribunals Service, 1997–2000; Dir, Regl Gp, British Trade Internat., 2000–01; Dep. Chief Exec., British Trade Internat., subseq. UK Trade and Investment, 2001–04; Dir, Efficiency Prog., 2004–05, Ops Directorate, 2005–07, DTI. FRSA. *Recreation:* cricket. *Address:* Office of Manpower Economics, 6th Floor, Kingsgate House, 66–74 Victoria Street, SW1E 6SW.

JONES, Most Rev. Idris; *see* Glasgow and Galloway, Bishop of.

JONES, Ieuan Wyn; Member (Plaid Cymru) Ynys Môn, since 1999, Leader, Plaid Cymru, since 2000, and Deputy First Minister and Minister for the Economy and Transport, since 2007, National Assembly for Wales; *b* 22 May 1949; *s* of late John Jones and of Mair Elizabeth Jones; *m* 1974, Eirian Llwyd; two *s* one *d. Educ:* Pontardawe Grammar School; Ysgol-y-Berwyn, Y Bala, Gwynedd; Liverpool Polytechnic. LLB Hons. Qualified Solicitor, 1973; Partner in practice, 1974–87. Plaid Cymru: National Vice-Chm., 1975–79; National Chm., 1980–82, 1990–92; Pres., 2000–03; Leader, Assembly Gp, 2003–. MP (Plaid Cymru) Ynys Môn, 1987–2001. Mem. Select Committee: on Welsh Affairs, 1990–92, 1997–2001; on Agriculture, 1992–97. Contested (Plaid Cymru) Ynys Môn (Anglesey), 1983. *Publications:* Europe: the challenge for Wales, 1996; Thomas Gee (biog.), 1998. *Recreations:* sport, local history. *Address:* Ty Elwyn Roberts, 45 Bridge Street, Llangefni, Ynys Môn, Gwynedd LL77 7PN. *T:* (01248) 723599.

JONES, Iona Elisabeth Lois; Chief Executive, S4C, since 2005; *b* 15 Jan. 1964; *d* of John Stuart Roberts and Verina Roberts (*née* Gravelle); *m* 1990, Wynford Jones; one *s* two *d. Educ:* Ysgol Gyfun Llanhari; Univ. of Exeter (BA Hons Econ. and Social Hist.); Cardiff Univ. (Postgrad. Dip. Journalism). Journalist, BBC Wales, 1986–95; Director, Corporate Affairs: S4C, 1995–2000; HTV Gp, 2000–03; Dir of Progs, S4C, 2003–05. *Address:* S4C, Parc Tŷ Glas, Llanishen, Cardiff CF14 5DU. *T:* (029) 2074 1400, *Fax:* (029) 2068 0864; *e-mail:* iona.jones@s4c.co.uk.

JONES, Jack L.; *see* Jones, James Larkin.

JONES, Jacqui; *see* Lait, J.

JONES, Prof. James Eirug Thomas, FRCPath; Courtauld Professor of Animal Health, Royal Veterinary College, University of London, 1984–93, now Emeritus Professor; *b* 14 June 1927; *s* of David John and Mary Elizabeth Jones; *m* 1953, Marion Roberts (*d* 2001); one *s* one *d. Educ:* Ystalyfera County Sch.; Royal Vet. Coll. MRCVS 1950, FRCVS 1994; PhD 1973. Gen. vet. practice, 1950–53; vet. officer, Birmingham Corp., 1953–54; Lectr in Path., RVC, 1954–58; Res. Officer, Animal Health Trust, 1958–63; Fulbright Scholar, Univ. of Pennsylvania, 1963–64; vis. worker, 1964, Sen. Lectr, 1967, Reader in Animal Health, 1975–84, RVC. J. T. Edwards Meml Medal, RCVS, 1985; Bledisloe Vet. Award, RASE, 1994. *Publications:* papers in sci. jls on infectious diseases of farm animals. *Recreations:* travel, Celtic history, National Portrait Gallery. *Address:* 19 West Park, SE9 4RZ. *T:* (020) 8299 7142.

JONES, James Larkin, (Jack), CH 1978; MBE 1950; FCILT (FCIT 1970); General Secretary, Transport and General Workers' Union, 1969–78; Member, TUC General Council, 1968–78; Chairman, TUC International, Transport and Nationalised Industries Committees, 1972–78; Deputy Chairman, National Ports Council, 1967–79; *b* 29 March 1913; *m* 1938, Evelyn Mary Taylor (*d* 1998); two *s. Educ:* elementary sch., Liverpool. Worked in engineering and docks industries, 1927–39. Liverpool City Councillor, 1936–39; served in Spanish Civil War; wounded Ebro battle, Aug. 1938; Coventry District Sec., Transport and General Workers' Union, also District Sec., Confedn of Shipbuilding and Engineering Unions, 1939–55; Midlands Regional Sec., Transport and General Workers' Union, 1955–63, Executive Officer, 1963–69. Mem., Midland Regional Bd for Industry, 1942–46, 1954–63; Chm., Midlands TUC Advisory Cttee, 1948–63. Coventry City Magistrate, 1950–63; Executive Chm., Birmingham Productivity Cttee, 1957–63; Member: Labour Party Nat. Exec. Cttee, 1964–67; Nat. Cttee for Commonwealth Immigrants, 1965–69; NEDC, 1969–78; Council, Advisory, Conciliation and Arbitration Service, 1974–78; British Overseas Trade Board, 1974–79; Cttee of Inquiry into Industrial Democracy, 1976–77 (Chm., Labour Party Wkg Party on Industrial Democracy, 1967); Bd, Crown Agents, 1978–80; Royal Commn on Criminal Procedure, 1978–80; Jt Chm. (with Lord Aldington), Special Cttee on the Ports, 1972. Pres., EFTA Trade Union Council, 1972–73; Founder Mem., European TUC, 1973. Vice-President: ITF, 1974–79; Anti-Apartheid Movement, 1976–; Age Concern, England, 1978–; European Fed of Retired and Elderly Persons, 1991–; Pres., Retired Members Assocs, TGWU, 1979–; Life President: Nat Pensioners' Convention, 2000; Internat. Bde Meml Trust, 2002–. Chm., Trustees, Nat. Museum of Labour History, 1988–2003. Vis. Fellow, Nuffield Coll., Oxford, 1970–78; Associate Fellow, LSE, 1978–82. Dimbleby Lecture, BBC, 1977. Hon. Fellow: Liverpool Poly. (later Liverpool John Moores Univ.), 1988; Central Lancs Univ., 1993. Hon. DLitt: Warwick, 1978; Coventry, 1996; DUniv Open, 2000. Freeman, City of London, 1979. Award of Merit, City of Coventry, 1978. *Publications:* (contrib.) The Incompatibles, 1967; (contrib.) Industry's Democratic Revolution, 1974; (with Max Morris) A–Z of Trade Unionism and Industrial Relations, 1982; Union Man (autobiog.), 1986, 2nd edn 2008. *Recreation:* walking. *Address:* 74 Ruskin Park House, Champion Hill, SE5 8TH. *T:* (020) 7274 7067.

JONES, (James) Roger; Head of Antiques Department, Sibyl Colefax & John Fowler (formerly Colefax and Fowler), since 1994; *b* 30 May 1952; *s* of late Albert James Jones and Hilda Vera Jones (*née* Evans). *Educ:* Shrewsbury; St Catharine's Coll., Cambridge (Sen. Schol.; MA). Called to the Bar, Middle Temple, 1974 (Lloyd Jacob Meml Exhibnr; Astbury Schol.); practised Oxford and Midland Circuit, 1975–83. Joined Office of Parly Counsel, 1983; with Law Commn, 1988–91; Dep. Parly Counsel, 1991–94. *Recreation:* walking the dog. *Address:* Sibyl Colefax & John Fowler, 39 Brook Street, W1K 4JE.

JONES, Rt Rev. James Stuart; *see* Liverpool, Bishop of.

JONES, Janet Ann L.; *see* Lewis-Jones.

JONES, Hon. Jeffrey Richard, CBE 1978; MA; Chief Justice and President of the Court of Appeal, Kiribati, 1980–85; Member, Appeal Courts of Solomon Islands and of Vanuatu, 1983; *b* 18 Nov. 1921; *s* of Rev. Thomas Jones and Winifred (*née* Williams); *m* 1955, Anna Rosaleen Carberry (*d* 2001); one *s* one *d. Educ:* Grove Park Sch., Wrexham; Denstone Coll., Staffs; Keble Coll., Oxford, 1940, 1946–49 (MA). Council of Legal Educn, 1950–52. Served RAFVR, Flt Lieut (Pilot), 1940–46. Schoolmaster, Mountgrace Comprehensive, Potters Bar, 1953–55. Called to the Bar, Middle Temple, 1954; private practice, Zaria, Nigeria, 1955–57; Magistrate, 1957, High Court Judge, 1965, Sen. Puisne Judge, 1970, Northern Nigeria; Chief Justice, Kano State, N Nigeria, 1975, Chief Judge (change of title, decree 41 of 1976), 1976–80. President, Rotary Club, Kano, 1977. Editor, Northern Nigeria Law Reports, 1966–74. *Publications:* Some Cases on Criminal Procedure and Evidence in Northern Nigeria, 1968; Some Cases on Criminal Procedure and Evidence in Northern Nigeria, 1969, 2nd edn combining 1968–69, 1970; Criminal Procedure in the Northern States of Nigeria (annotated), 1975, repr. 1978, 2nd edn 1979; Criminal Procedure in the Native Courts of Northern Nigeria, 1975. *Recreations:* painting, gardening, bridge, golf. *Address:* Bradley Cottage, Bradley Lane, Holt, near Trowbridge, Wilts BA14 6QE. *T:* (01225) 782004, *Fax:* (01225) 782361.

JONES, Jennifer, (Mrs Norton Simon); film actress (US); *b* Tulsa, Okla, 2 March 1919; *née* Phylis Isley; *d* of Philip R. Isley and Flora Mae (*née* Suber); *m* 1st, 1939, Robert Walker (marr. diss. 1945); two *s*; 2nd, 1949, David O. Selznick (*d* 1965); (one *d* decd); 3rd, 1971, Norton Simon (*d* 1993). *Educ:* schools in Okla and Tex; Northwestern Univ., Evanston, Illinois; American Academy of Dramatic Arts, New York City. Films include: Dick Tracy's G-Men, 1939; The New Frontier, 1939; The Song of Bernadette, 1943; Since You Went Away, 1944; Love Letters, 1945; The American Creed, 1946; Cluny Brown, 1946; Duel in the Sun, 1946; Portrait of Jenny, 1948; Madame Bovary, 1949; We Were Strangers, 1949; The Wild Heart, 1950; Ruby Gentry, 1952; Carrie, 1952; Indiscretion of an American Wife, 1953; Beat the Devil, 1954; Good Morning, Miss Dove, 1955; Love is a Many-Splendoured Thing, 1955; The Man in the Gray Flannel Suit, 1956; The Barretts of Wimpole Street, 1957; A Farewell to Arms, 1957; Tender is the Night, 1962; The Idol, 1966; Angel, Down We Go, 1969; The Towering Inferno, 1974. Awards include: American Academy of Motion Pictures, Arts and Sciences Award, 1943 (for Song of Bernadette); 4 other Academy nominations, etc. Pres., Norton Simon Mus., Pasadena, 1989–. Medal for Korean War Work.

JONES, Jennifer, (Gemma); actress; *b* 4 Dec. 1942; *d* of late Griffith Jones and Irene Jones (*née* Isaac); one *s* by Sebastian Graham Jones. *Educ:* Royal Acad. of Dramatic Art (Gold Medal). *Theatre* includes: Hamlet, Birmingham Rep., 1968; Getting On, Queen's, 1972; A Streetcar Named Desire, Nottingham Playhouse, 1978; Unfinished Business, 1994; The Master Builder, Haymarket, 1995; Cat on a Hot Tin Roof, Lyric, 2001; And Then There Were None, Gielgud, 2005; On Religion, Soho Th., 2006; Royal Shakespeare Co.: Julius Caesar, Twelfth Night, Henry VIII, The Winter's Tale; A Midsummer Night's Dream, 1970; *films* include: The Devils, 1971; Sense and Sensibility, 1995; Wilde, 1997; The Theory of Flight, 1998; The Winslow Boy, 1999; Captain Jack, 1999; Cotton Mary, 1999; Bridget Jones's Diary, 2001; Harry Potter and the Chamber of Secrets, 2002; Shanghai Knights, 2003; Kiss of Life, 2003; Bridget Jones: The Edge of Reason, 2004; *television* includes series: The Duchess of Duke Street, 1976; Chelworth, 1989; Devices and Desires, 1991; The Phoenix and the Carpet, 1997; Trial and Retribution, VII, 2003, VIII, 2004. *Recreation:* hill-walking. *Address:* c/o Conway van Gelder Grant Ltd, 18–21 Jermyn Street, SW1Y 6HP. *T:* (020) 7287 0077, *Fax:* (020) 7287 1940.

JONES, Jennifer, (Jenny); Member (Green), London Assembly, Greater London Authority, since 2000; London Mayor's Road Safety Ambassador, since 2002; *b* 23 Dec. 1949; *d* of Percy and Christine Jones; *m* (marr. diss.); two *d. Educ:* Westlain Grammar Sch., Brighton; Inst. of Archaeol., Univ. of London (BSc Envmtl Archaeol.). Archaeologist, 1990–99; Financial Controller, Metro Inspection Services, 1999–2000. Dep. Mayor of London, 2003–04; Greater London Authority: Chm., Standards Cttee, 2000–03; London Mayor's Green Transport Advr, 2006–; Mem., Metropolitan Police Authy, 2000–; Chair: London Food, 2004–; Mayor of London's Walking Adv. Panel (formerly Walking Forum), 2003–. *Recreations:* running, cinema, family and friends. *Address:* Greater London Authority, City Hall, Queen's Walk, SE1 2AA. *T:* (020) 7983 4358.

JONES, Jennifer Grace; international election adviser and observer, since 2003; *b* 8 Feb. 1948; *d* of Ernest Bew and Ivy Blake; *m* 1974, John Alun Charles Jones; one *s. Educ:* Bradford Univ. (BA Hons, CQSW 1972); Birmingham Univ. (MSocSc 1987); Wolverhampton Univ. (ITD). Legal Sec., ICI, 1968–69; Social Worker, Oxford CC, 1972–74; Housing Advr, Oxford Housing Aid Centre and Birmingham Housing Dept,

1974–77; Trng Officer, Birmingham Housing Co-op., 1980–85; Researcher, Wolverhampton Council, 1985–87; Business Advr, Black Country CDA, 1987–97. Trng Manager and Co. Dir, 1995–97. Mem. (Lab) Wolverhampton BC, 1991–97. MP (Lab) Wolverhampton SW, 1997–2001. Election advr, OSCE/UN Mission in Kosovo, 2002–03. *Recreations:* swimming, gardening, keeping cats, writing.

JONES, Joanne; *see* Elvin, J.

JONES, John; *see* Jones, H. J. F.

JONES, John Elfed, CBE 1987; CEng, FIET; DL; Chairman: International Greetings plc, 1996–2006; Eclectica Ltd, since 2007; *b* 19 March 1933; *s* of Urien Maelgwyn Jones and Mary Jones; *m* 1957, Mary Sheila (*née* Rosser); two *d. Educ:* Blaenau Ffestiniog Grammar Sch.; Denbighshire Technical Coll., Wrexham; Heriot Watts Coll., Edinburgh. Student apprentice, 1949–53, graduate trainee, 1953–55, CEGB; National Service, RAF, 1955–57 (FO); Rock Climbing Instr, Outward Bound Sch., Aberdyfi, 1957; Technical Engr with CEGB, 1957–59; Dep. Project Manager, Rheidol Hydro-Electric Project, 1959–61; Sen. Elec. Engr, Trawsfynydd Nuclear Power Station, 1961–63; Deputy Manager: Mid Wales Gp of Power Stations, 1963–67; Connah's Quay Power Station, 1967–69; Anglesey Aluminium Metal Ltd: Engrg Manager, 1969–73; Production Manager, 1973–76; Admin Director, 1976–77; Dep. Man. Dir, 1977–79; Industrial Dir, Welsh Office (Under Sec. rank), 1979–82. Chairman: Welsh Water Authy, later Welsh Water plc, 1982–93; British Water International Ltd, 1983–88. Dep. Chm., HTV Gp, 1991–96; Director: HTV Cymru/Wales Ltd, 1990–96 (Chm., 1992–96); W Midlands and Wales Regl Adv. Bd, National Westminster Bank, 1990–91; BMSS plc, 1993–96; Cwmni Rheilffordd Beddgelert Cyf., 1994–98; Cwmni Rheilffordd Caernarfon Cyf., 1994–99; Chm., Menter Mantis Cyf, 1999–2004. Chm. Adv. Gp, Nat. Assembly of Wales, 1997–99. Treasurer, Urdd Gobaith Cymru, 1964–67; Chm., Welsh Language Bd, 1988–93; Mem., Royal National Eisteddfod of Wales, 1981–90; Member: BBC Broadcasting Council for Wales, 1979–83; Council, Food from Britain, 1985–87; Prince of Wales Cttee, 1986–90. Mem., British/Irish Encounter, 2000–05. Pres., Univ. of Wales, Lampeter, 1992–98; Member: Court and Council: UCNW, Bangor, 1978–89; Nat. Lib. of Wales, 1983–88; Coleg Harlech, 1983–88; Court, Univ. Coll., Aberystwyth, 1984–93. Mem., Civic Trust for Wales, 1982–88; Pres., CPRW, 1995–2001. FRSA 1984; CCMI (CBIM 1990). DL Mid Glam, 1989. Hon. Fellow: Univ. of Wales, Aberystwyth, 1990; NE Wales Inst., 1996. Hon. Dr Glamorgan, 1997; Hon. LLD Wales, 2000. Hon. Col, Commonwealth of Kentucky, 1976. *Recreations:* fishing for salmon and trout, reading, attending Eisteddfodau, golf. *Address:* Ty Mawr, Coity, Bridgend, Mid Glamorgan CF35 6BN.

JONES, John Ernest P.; *see* Powell-Jones.

JONES, Sir John (Francis), Kt 2003; Educational Consultant and Managing Director, JFJ Training Ltd; *b* 20 Nov. 1950; *s* of late Thomas Jones and of Joan Jones (now Hogg); *m* 1990; two *s* one *d*; partner, Rachel Glazebrook. *Educ:* Univ. of Wales, Bangor (BA Hons French and Latin; PGCE); Liverpool Univ. (MEd). Teacher, 1974–89; Res. Fellow, Lancaster Univ., 1988–89; Headteacher: Rivington High Sch., St Helens, 1989–91; Ruffwood Sch., Knowsley, 1991–99; Maghull High Sch., Sefton, 1999–2004. Member: Policy Action Team, Social Exclusion Unit, 1998–99; Task Gp, Truancy and Exclusion in Cities, DFES, 1998–2002; Leadership Develt Unit, Manchester Univ., DFES and Nat. Coll. for Sch. Leadership, 2002–03. Non-exec. Dir, Aintree Hosps Trust, 1994–98. Dir, ALITE Ltd. *Recreations:* reading, keeping fit, golf, playing guitar, theatre, fell-walking. *Address:* 30 Douglas Road, Worsley, Manchester M28 2SG; *e-mail:* jfjtraining@hotmail.com.

JONES, John Francis A.; *see* Avery Jones.

JONES, Prof. (John) Gareth, MD; FRCP; FRCA; Professor of Anaesthesia, Cambridge University, 1990–99; *b* 20 Aug. 1936; *s* of late Dr John and Catherine Jones; *m* 1964, Susan Price; three *d. Educ:* Canton High Sch., Cardiff; Welsh Nat. Sch. of Medicine, Univ. of Wales (MB BCh 1960); MD Birmingham, 1967. MRCP 1963, FRCP 1983; FRCA (FFARCS 1970). Res. Fellow, Dept of Medicine, 1964–68, Lectr, Anaesthesia, 1968–70, Univ. of Birmingham; North Sen. Fellow, Cardiovascular Res. Inst., Univ. of California, San Francisco, 1970–74; Scientific Staff, MRC, Northwick Park, 1974–86; Prof. of Anaesthesia, Univ. of Leeds, 1986–91. Vis. Scientist, Chest Service, Univ. of California, San Francisco, 1977–78; Consultant, Baragwanath Hosp., Soweto, South Africa, 1986. Royal College of Anaesthetists: Mem. Council, 1996–99; Ed., Newsletter, 1997–99. Ed., Cardiff Med. Grads Jl, 1999–2001. Member: York Model Engrg Soc., 1999–; Crusoe Soc., 2003–; Yorks Philosophical Soc., 2005– (Mem. Council, 2006–). Hon. FANZCA 1992. *Publications:* Effects of Anaesthesia and Surgery on Pulmonary Mechanisms, 1984; (jtly) Aspects of Recovery from Anaesthesia, 1987; Depth of Anaesthesia, 1989, 2nd edn 1993; (jtly) The Upper Airway, 1995; res. papers on peri-operative hypoxaemia, oxygen delivery in neonates, the effect of gen. anaesthetics on cognitive function and the electroencephalogram, and the effect of sedation on eye movements. *Recreations:* writing, boats, model engineering, low flying. *Address:* Woodlands, Rufforth, York YO23 2QF. *Clubs:* Royal Society of Medicine; Sherburn Aero, York Gliding.

JONES, His Honour (John) Geoffrey; a Circuit Judge, 1975–96, a Deputy Circuit Judge, 1996–2001; *b* 14 Sept. 1928; *s* of Wyndham and Lilias Jones; *m* 1954, Sheila (*née* Gregory); three *s. Educ:* Brighton and Hove Grammar Sch.; St Michael's Sch., Llanelli; St David's Coll., Lampeter; University Coll., London. LLB London 1955; LLM London 1985. Army service, 1946–48, commnd into RASC, 1947. Electrical wholesale business, 1948–52. Called to Bar, Gray's Inn, 1956; practised Leicester, 1958–70 and London, 1970–75. Pres., Mental Health Review Tribunals, 1985–2000; Chm., Mental Health Rev. Tribunal for Wales, 1996–99. Hon. Sen. Academic Fellow, Leicester Polytechnic, 1989. Hon. LLD De Montfort, 1996. *Recreation:* golf. *Address:* 6 Llewellyn Court, Elmsleigh Avenue, Leicester LE2 2DH.

JONES, John Hubert E.; *see* Emlyn Jones.

JONES, John Knighton C.; *see* Chadwick-Jones.

JONES, John Lloyd, OBE 1995; farmer; Chairman, Countryside Council for Wales, since 2000; *b* 10 Nov. 1949; *s* of late Arthur Egryn Jones and of Elizabeth Jones (*née* Owen); *m* 1972, Anne Tudor Lewis; three *d. Educ:* Tywyn Primary Sch.; Llandovery Coll. Chairman: NFU Wales, 1993–98; NFU Parly Land Use and Envmt Cttee, England and Wales, 1998–2000. Chm., Welsh Adv. Cttee, Forestry Commn, 1994–2000; Member: Bd, Inst. of Grassland and Envmtl Res., 2002–08; Rural Economy and Land Use Prog. Adv. Cttee, 2004–. Lay Rep. for Disciplinary Hearings, Councils of Inns of Court, 2005–07. Mem., Gorsedd of Bards, 2002. FRSA 1995. Hon. Fellow, Univ. of Wales, Bangor, 2003. *Recreations:* woodland creation, gardening. *Address:* Hendy, Tywyn, Gwynedd LL36 9RU. *T:* (01654) 710457.

JONES, Air Vice-Marshal John Maurice, CB 1986; *b* 27 Jan. 1931; *s* of E. Morris Jones and Gladys Jones (*née* Foulkes); *m* 1962, Joan (*née* McCallum); one *s* one *d. Educ:* Liverpool Institute High Sch.; Univ. of Liverpool (BDS). LDSRCS, FDSRCS 1987. Hospital appt, Liverpool Dental Hosp., 1954; RAF Dental Branch: appts UK and abroad, incl. Christmas Island, Malta, Cyprus and Fontainebleau, 1955–73; Dep. Dir of RAF Dental Services, 1973; OC RAF Inst. of Dental Health and Training, 1976; Principal Dental Officer: HQ RAF Germany, 1979; HQ RAF Support Command, 1982; Dir, RAF Dental Services, 1982–88, and Dir, Defence Dental Services, MoD, 1985–88; QHDS, 1983–87. Sec., Ski Club of GB, 1988–91. Pres., RAF Squash Rackets Assoc., 1986–88. OBStJ 1978. *Recreations:* golf, fishing, ski-ing. *Address:* Wyckenhurst, St Michael's Close, Halton Village, Wendover, Bucks HP22 5NW. *T:* (01296) 624184. *Club:* Royal Air Force, Kandahar.

JONES, John Richard; QC 2002; a Recorder, since 1999; *b* 8 Feb. 1959; *s* of Harold Jones and Barbara Jones (*née* Jerstice); *m* 2000, Heather Billam; one *s. Educ:* Shevington High Sch.; Upholland Grammar Sch.; Liverpool Univ. (LLB Hons). Called to the Bar, Middle Temple (Winston Churchill Scholar), 1981. *Recreations:* golf, fell-walking, music. *Address:* Carmelite Chambers, 9 Carmelite Street, EC4Y 0DR. *T:* (020) 7936 6300, *Fax:* (020) 7936 6301; Exchange Chambers, Pearl Assurance House, Derby Square, Liverpool L2 9XX. *T:* (0151) 236 7741, *Fax:* (0151) 236 3433; *e-mail:* johnrjonesqc@exchangechambers.co.uk. *Clubs:* Royal Lytham and St Annes Golf; Formby Golf; Hindley Hall Golf; Phonecian Golf (Arizona, USA).

JONES, (John) Stanley, RCA 2005; Director, Curwen Studio, since 1959; *b* 10 June 1933; *s* of George White Jones and Elizabeth Jones; *m* 1961, Jennifer Frances Stone; one *s* one *d. Educ:* Wigan Grammar Sch.; Wigan Art Sch. (NDD); Slade Sch. of Fine Art, UCL (Dip. Fine Art). Lectr in Lithography, Slade Sch. of Fine Art, 1958–98. Pres., Printmakers' Council, 1981–96. Hon. RE 2004. Hon. DLitt Southampton, 1999. *Publications:* Lithography for Artists, 1967 (Italian edn 1981); (contrib.) Elizabeth Frink Original Prints, ed C. Wiseman, 1998; contribs to Printmaking Today, Graphion. *Recreations:* black and white photography (analogue), country walking, weather observation, appreciation of music (contemporary). *Address:* Curwen Studio, Chilford Hall, Linton, Cambs CB1 6LE. *T:* (01223) 893544, *Fax:* (01223) 893638; *e-mail:* info@thecurwenstudio.co.uk. *Club:* Double Crown.

JONES, Prof. (John) Stephen, PhD, DSc; Professor of Genetics, since 1992, and Head, Department of Genetics, Evolution and Environment, since 2008, University College London; *b* 24 March 1944; *s* of Thomas Gwilym Jones and Lydia Anne Jones; *m* 2004, Norma Percy. *Educ:* Wirral Grammar Sch.; Univ. of Edinburgh (BSc, PhD 1971, DSc 2005). Postdoctoral Fellow, Univ. of Chicago, 1969–71; Lectr in Genetics, Royal Free Hosp. Med. Sch., 1971–78; Lectr then Reader in Genetics, UCL, 1978–92; Head of Dept of Genetics and Biometry, 1989–94. Reith Lectr, 1991. Columnist, Daily Telegraph, 1992–. Faraday Medal, Royal Soc., 1996; Charter Medal, Inst. of Biology, 2002; Tercentenary Medal, Linnean Soc., 2007. *Publications:* (ed) Cambridge Encyclopedia of Human Evolution, 1992; The Language of the Genes, 1993 (Science Book Prize, 1994); In the Blood, 1996; Almost Like a Whale: the Origin of Species updated, 1999; Y: The Descent of Men, 2002; The Single Helix, 2005; Coral: a Pessimist in Paradise, 2007; scientific papers in learned jls. *Recreation:* not administrating. *Address:* Galton Laboratory, University College London, Gower Street, WC1E 6BT. *T:* (020) 7679 2000.

JONES, Jonathan Dallas George, PhD; FRS 2003; Senior Scientist, Sainsbury Laboratory, John Innes Centre, since 1988; *b* 14 July 1954; *s* of George Ronald Jones and Isabel Dallas Orr (*née* Pinkney); one *d*; *m* 1991, Caroline Dean, *qv*; one *s* one *d. Educ:* Univ. of Cambridge (BSc Nat. Scis 1976; PhD 1980). Post-doctoral Fellow, Harvard, 1981–82; Res. Scientist, Advanced Genetic Scis Inc., Oakland, Calif, 1983–88. Mem., EMBO, 1998. *Publications:* contribs to Cell, Science, Plant Cell, Plant Jl, Genetics, Plant Physiol., etc. *Recreations:* sailing, wind-surfing, children. *Address:* Sainsbury Laboratory, John Innes Centre, Colney Lane, Norwich NR4 7UH. *T:* (01603) 450327.

JONES, Jonathan Guy; Director General (formerly Legal Secretary to the Law Officers), Attorney General's Office, since 2004; *b* 21 May 1962; *s* of Leonard Martell Jones and Margaret Eleanor Jones (*née* Jones). *Educ:* Llandovery Coll.; Univ. of Durham (BA Law 1984). Called to the Bar: Middle Temple, 1985, Bencher, 2007; NI, 2006. Legal Advr, Motor Agents Assoc., 1986–89; Legal Div., OFT, 1989–93; Dept of Transport Adv. Div., Treasury Solicitor's Dept, 1993–94; Attorney General's Chambers, Legal Secretariat to the Law Officers, 1994–98; Dep. Legal Advr, HM Treasury, 1998–2002; Legal Dir, DFES and Dir, Treasury Solicitor's Dept, 2002–04. *Recreation:* music. *Address:* Attorney General's Office, 20 Victoria Street, SW1H 0NF.

JONES, Jonathan Owen; *b* 19 April 1954; *s* of Gwynfor Owen Jones and Dorothy Mary (*née* Davies); *m* 1989, Allison Clement; two *s* one *d. Educ:* Univ. of East Anglia (BSc Hons Ecology); Cardiff Univ. (PGCE). Science and biology teacher, 1977–92. MP (Lab and Co-op) Cardiff Central, 1992–2005; contested (Lab and Co-op) same seat, 2005. An Opposition Whip, 1993–97; a Lord Comr of HM Treasury (Govt Whip), 1997–98; Parly Under-Sec. of State, Welsh Office, 1998–99. A Forestry Comr, 2007–. *Recreations:* cooking, walking, watching Rugby, my family, caravanning. *Address:* 19 Ty Draw Road, Roath, Cardiff CF23 5HB. *Club:* Roath Labour.

JONES, Julia P.; *see* Peyton-Jones.

JONES, Julie, OBE 2003; Chief Executive, Social Care Institute for Excellence, since 2007; *b* 17 March 1948; *d* of Peter and Kitty Clark; *m* 1970, Alan Richard Watson Jones; two *d. Educ:* Benenden C of E Primary Sch.; Tunbridge Wells Grammar Sch. for Girls; University Coll., Cardiff (BSc Econ. Hons Sociology 1969); Brunel Univ. (MA Public and Soc. Admin 1980). Dep. Hd, Soc. Services Planning Unit, Camden, 1972–76; Westminster City Council: Principal Res. and Planning Officer for Soc. Services, 1982–85; Dep. Dir, 1992–96, Dir, 1996–2005, Soc. Services; Dep. Chief Exec., 2000–07; Dir, Children and Community Services, 2005–07. Pres., Assoc. of Dirs of Social Services, 2005–06 (Vice Pres., 2004–05; Chm., London Assoc., 2001–04). FRSA 2006. *Recreations:* reading, travel, opera, theatre, family and friends, Rugby Union. *Address:* Social Care Institute for Excellence, 1st Floor, Goldings House, 2 Hay's Lane, SE1 2HB. *T:* (020) 7089 6886, *Fax:* (020) 7089 6841; *e-mail:* julie.jones@scie.org.uk.

JONES, Prof. Kathleen; Professor of Social Policy, University of York, 1981–89 (Professor of Social Administration, 1965–81), now Emeritus Professor; *b* 7 April 1922; *d* of William Robert Savage and Kate Lilian Barnard; *m* 1944, Rev. David Gwyn Jones (*d* 1976); one *s. Educ:* North London Collegiate Sch.; Westfield Coll., Univ. of London (BA, PhD). Research Asst in Social Administration, Univ. of Manchester, 1951–53, Asst Lectr 1953–55; Sen. History Teacher, Victoria Instn, Kuala Lumpur, 1956–58, also Asst Lectr in History, Univ. of Malaya (part-time); Lectr in Social Administration, Univ. of Manchester, 1958–62, Sen. Lectr 1962–65. Chm., Social Scis Cttee, UK Commn for UNESCO, 1966–69. Mem., Gen. Synod of C of E, 1975–80; Member: Archbishops' Commn on Church and State, 1966–71; Lord Gardiner's Cttee on NI, 1974–75; Archbishops' Commn on Marriage, 1976–78; Mental Health Act Commn, 1983–86 (NE Chm., 1983–85). Chm., Assoc. of Psychiatric Social Workers, 1968–70; Chm., Social

Admin Assoc., 1980–83. Hon. FRCPsych, 1976. *Publications:* Lunacy, Law and Conscience, 1955; Mental Health and Social Policy, 1960; Mental Hospitals at Work, 1962; The Compassionate Society, 1965; The Teaching of Social Studies in British Universities, 1965; A History of the Mental Health Services, 1972; Opening the Door: a study of new policies for the mentally handicapped, 1975; Issues in Social Policy, 1978; (ed) Living the Faith: a call to the Church, 1980; Ideas on Institutions, 1984; Eileen Younghusband: a biography, 1985; Experience in Mental Health, 1988; The Making of Social Policy, 1991; Asylums and After, 1993; Poems of St John of the Cross, 1993; (ed) Butler's Lives of the Saints: June, 1997; December, 1999; Women Saints, 1999; Saints of the Anglican Calendar, 2000; A Basic Dictionary of Saints, 2001; Who are the Celtic Saints?, 2002; Songs of the Isles, 2004; Challenging Richard Dawkins, 2007; (series editor) International Library of Social Policy, 1968–85; (ed) Year Book of Social Policy in Britain, 1971–76. *Address:* 44 West Moor Lane, Heslington, York YO10 5ER. *T:* (01904) 411579.

JONES, Very Rev. Keith Brynmor; Dean of York, since 2004; *b* 27 June 1944; *s* of John Brynmor Jones and Mary Emily Jones; *m* 1973, Viola Mary, *d* of late Henry Leigh Jenkyns; three *d*. *Educ:* Selwyn Coll., Cambridge (BA 1965; MA 1969); Cuddesdon Coll., Oxford. Ordained deacon, 1969, priest, 1970; Asst Curate, Limpsfield with Titsey, Surrey, 1969–72; Dean's Vicar, Cathedral and Abbey Church of St Alban, 1972–76; Priest-in-charge, 1976–79, Team Vicar, 1979–82, St Michael's, Boreham Wood; Vicar of St Mary-le-Tower, Ipswich, 1982–95; Rural Dean of Ipswich, 1992–95; Hon. Canon, St Edmundsbury Cathedral, 1993–95; Dean of Exeter, 1996–2004. Mem., Gen. Synod of C of E, 1999–2005. Chm., Pilgrims Assoc., 2001–08. *Publications:* Adam's Dream, 2008; (with L. Hampson and R. Shephard) York Minster: a living legacy, 2008. *Recreations:* playing the piano, looking out of the window. *Address:* The Deanery, York YO1 7JQ. *T:* (01904) 557202. *Club:* Army and Navy.

JONES, Dr Keith Howard, CB 1997; FRCP, FRCPE; Chairman, European Medicines Evaluation Agency, 2000–03 (Member, 1995–2000); Chief Executive, Medicines Control Agency, Department of Health, 1989–2002; retired; *b* 14 Oct. 1937; *s* of Arthur Leslie Jones and Miriam Emily Jones; *m* 1962, Dr Lilian, (Lynne), Pearse; three *s*. *Educ:* Welsh Nat. Sch. of Medicine, Cardiff (MB, BCh 1960; MD 1966). FFPM 1989; FRCPE 1990; FRCP 1993. Posts in clinical and academic medicine, Cardiff, Edinburgh and Cambridge, 1960–67; Chief Toxicologist, Fisons Agrochemicals, 1967–70; Head, Safety Assessment, Beecham Res. Labs, 1970–79; Exec. Dir, Medical Affairs, Merck & Co., USA, 1979–89. Adjunct Prof. of Medicine, Thomas Jefferson Med. Sch., Philadelphia, 1985–89; Vis. Prof. of Pharmacology, Sch. of Pharmacy, Univ. of London, 1995–2002. UK Representative: EC Cttee for Pharmaceutical Medical Products, 1989–95; EC Pharmaceutical Cttee, 1989–2003; Chairman: EC Scientific Cttee for Medicinal Products and Med. Devices, 1997–2000; Expert Mem., EC Scientific Steering Cttee on Consumer Health and Food Safety, 1997–2003. *Publications:* contribs to learned jls on issues of metabolic medicine, toxicology, drug develt and regulatory matters. *Recreations:* sailing, tennis. *Address:* Shelford, Headley Road, Leatherhead, Surrey KT22 8PT. *T:* (01372) 376747.

JONES, Keith O.; *see* Orrell-Jones.

JONES, Sir Keith (Stephen), Kt 1980; FRCSE; FRACS; *b* 7 July 1911; *s* of Stephen William and Muriel Elsy Jones; *m* 1936, Kathleen Mary Abbott; three *s*. *Educ:* Newington Coll.; Univ. of Sydney (MB, BS). General practitioner, Army MO, Surgeon; President, Aust. Medical Assoc., 1973–76; Chief MO, NSW State Emergency Service, 1966–74; Mem., NSW Medical Bd, 1971–81. Mem., Newington Coll. Council, 1951–72; Mem., Nat. Specialist Recognition Appeals Cttee, 1970–83 (Chm., 1980–83; Chm., Nat. Spec. Qualifications Cttee, 1980–83). Chairman: Australasian Medical Publishing Co., 1976–82; Manly Art Gall., 1982–85; President: Medical Benefits Fund of Aust., 1983–85; Blue Cross Assoc. of Aust., 1983–85. Acting Editor, Medical Jl of Aust., 1981. Fellow, Australian Coll. of Emergency Medicine, 1984; Hon. FRACGP 1975. Gold Medal, AMA, 1976. *Publication:* One Man's Story (autobiog.), 2004. *Recreation:* swimming. *Address:* 123 Bayview Garden Village, Cabbage Tree Road, Bayview, NSW 2104, Australia. *T:* (2) 99972876.

JONES, Kevan David; MP (Lab) Durham North, since 2001; Parliamentary Under-Secretary of State, Ministry of Defence, since 2008; *b* 25 April 1964. *Educ:* Univ. of Southern Maine, USA; Newcastle upon Tyne Poly. (BA). Political Officer, 1989–2001, Regl Organiser, 1992–99, Sen. Organiser, 1999–2001, GMB. Newcastle upon Tyne City Council: Mem. (Lab), 1990–2001; Chair of Public Health, 1993–97; Chief Whip, 1994–2000; Chair and Cabinet Mem. for Develt and Transport, 1997–2001. Mem., Select Cttee on Defence, 2001–. Chair, 1998–2000, Vice-Chair, 2000–, Northern Regl Lab. Party. *Address:* c/o House of Commons, SW1A 0AA; (office) 9 Plawsworth Road, Sacriston, Co. Durham DH7 6HJ. *T:* (0191) 371 8834. *Club:* Sacriston Workmen's.

JONES, Kirsty Jackson; *see* Young, K. J.

JONES, Laura Anne; Member (C) South Wales East, National Assembly for Wales, 2003–07; *b* 21 Feb. 1979; *d* of John Dilwyn Jones and Penelope Anne Jones. *Educ:* Univ. of Plymouth (BSc Politics). Chm., SE Wales Cons. Future Area, 2000–02. Opposition spokesman on Sports, Nat. Assembly for Wales, 2003–07. Girl Guiding Ambassador, 2004–. Hon. Mem., Cardiff Business Club. *Recreations:* swimming, hockey, ski-ing, horse riding, cycling, Girl Guides. *Address:* Llanusk Cottage, Llanbadoc, Usk, Monmouthshire NP15 1TA; 105 Sovereign Quay, Cardiff Bay, Cardiff CF10 6SE. *Club:* Lord's Taverners.

JONES, Sir Lindsay Harwood O.; *see* Owen-Jones.

JONES, Sir Lyndon (Hugh), Kt 1999; Principal and Chief Executive, Harris City Technology College, 1990–99; *b* 2 Feb. 1943; *s* of late David Hugh Jones and Victoria Maud (*née* Elias); *m* 1st, 1965, Gillian Fortnum (marr. diss. 1981); two *s* one *d*; 2nd, 1990, Sandra Lees; two step *d*. *Educ:* Cardiff High Sch. for Boys; UC Cardiff (BA); Univ. of Reading (Postgrad. DipEd); Birmingham Univ. (MEd). Hd of Music Dept, Pool Hayes Comprehensive Sch., 1965–70; Sen. Lectr in Music and Educn, Bingley Teacher Trng Coll., 1970–76; Hd, Arts Faculty, Doncaster Inst. Higher Educn, 1976–78; Dir of Arts, Richmond Tertiary Coll., 1978–82; Dep. Principal, Westminster Further Educn Coll., 1982–85; Principal, S London Further Educn Coll., 1985–90. Chief Examr, GCE Music, London Univ., 1978–83. Tutor, Nat. Professional Qualification for Headship, 1998; Trainer, Leadership Prog. for Serving Head Teachers, 1999; Sch. Improvement Partner, Nat. Coll. for Sch. Leadership, 2006. Volunteer interviewer, Pecan jobs project. Mem., NAHT, 1990. FCMI (FIMgt 1976). Composer, The Prince and the Pauper, 1992. *Recreations:* playing the piano, composing, Rugby, mountaineering, opera, amateur chef and wine taster.

JONES, Dr Lynne Mary; MP (Lab) Birmingham, Selly Oak, since 1992; *b* 26 April 1951; two *s*. *Educ:* Birmingham Univ. (BSc, PhD Biochem.); Birmingham Polytechnic (Dip. Housing Studies). Joined Labour Party, 1974; ASTMS, then MSF, subseq. Amicus, 1972–. Mem. (Lab) Birmingham City Council, 1980–94 (Chair, Housing Cttee, 1984–87). Former Exec. Mem., Labour Housing Gp. Member: Select Cttee on science and technology, 1992–2001; Select Cttee on envmt, food and rural affairs, 2005–. *Address:* House of Commons, SW1A 0AA. *T:* (020) 7219 6971.

JONES, Prof. Malcolm Lang, PhD; FDSRCSE, FDSRCS; Professor of Child Dental Health and Orthodontics, since 1992 and Pro-Vice-Chancellor (Health and Estates), since 2006, Cardiff University (formerly University of Wales College of Medicine); Hon. Consultant in Orthodontics, Dental Hospital, Cardiff and Vale NHS Trust, since 1987; *b* Surbiton, 28 June 1950; *s* of Derek Lang Jones and Ellen Joan Jones; *m* 1976, Rhona Marie Logue; one *s* one *d*. *Educ:* King's Coll. Sch., Wimbledon; Welsh Nat. Sch. of Medicine (BDS 1973; PhD 1987); Univ. of London (MSc 1979). DOrthRCS 1979; FDSRCSE 1980; FDSRCS 2003. Community Dental Officer, Derbys, 1973–74; Resident Hse Officer, Oral and Maxillofacial Surgery, 1974–75; SHO, Chepstow Hosp., 1975; Registrar, Middlesex Hosp., 1976–77; Registrar, Orthodontics, 1977–79; Lectr, 1979–84, Sen. Lectr, 1984–92, in Orthodontics; Head, Child Dental Health, Univ. of Wales Coll. of Medicine, 1992–99; Dean and Hd of Sch. of Dentistry, Cardiff Univ., 1999–2006; Gen. Manager, Dental Services, Cardiff & Vale NHS Trust, 1999–2006. Non-exec. Dir, Swansea NHS Trust, 2004–08. Ed., British Jl Orthodontics, subseq. Jl Orthodontics, 1995–2000. Exec. Sec., UK Council of Deans and Heads of Dental Schs, 2005–08; Founder Chm., Forum of Eur. Heads and Deans of Dental Schs, 2007–08; Pres., Assoc. for Dental Educn in Europe, 2008–. Mem., Dental Council, RCSE, 2005–. Hon. Fellow, Hong Kong Coll. of Surgeons. Hon. MD Riga Stradins, Latvia; Hon. DDS Malmo. *Publications:* (with K. G. Isaacson) Orthodontic Radiography Guidelines, 1994; (with R. G. Oliver) Walther and Houston's Orthodontic Notes, 5th edn, 1995, 6th edn, 2000; (with J. Middleton and G. N. Pande) Computer Methods in Biomechanics and Biomedical Engineering, 1996; (with J. Middleton and N. G. Shrive) Computer Methods in Biomechanics and Biomedical Engineering: book 4, 2003; numerous contribs to scientific jls mostly in areas of clinical trials, applied computational biomechanics and dental education. *Recreations:* sailing, Morgan sports cars, reading as widely as time allows. *Address:* Vice Chancellor's Office, Cardiff University, Main Building, Park Place, Cardiff CF10 3AT. *T:* (029) 2074 2075, *Fax:* (029) 2074 5306; *e-mail:* JonesML@cf.ac.uk.

JONES, Dr Margaret Anne, OBE 2001; Chief Executive, Brook Advisory Centres, 1988–2001; *b* 30 Oct. 1940; *d* of Cecil Newton Collard and Rita Ross Collard (*née* White); *m* 1974, Hugh Vaughan Price Jones. *Educ:* Methodist Ladies' Coll., Burwood, Australia; Univ. of New South Wales (BSc, MSc); University College London (PhD); Dip. Mus. Open 2004. Postdoctoral Res. Fellow, Univ. of Cambridge, 1970–71; Res. Fellow, Univ. of Bath, 1971–74; Resources Officer, Health Education Council, 1974–88. Lay Mem., Chiltern and S Bucks Primary Care Gp, 1999–2002; non-exec. Dir, Chiltern and S Bucks Primary Care Trust, 2002–06. Mem., Indep. Adv. Gp, Teenage Pregnancy Unit, DoH, 2000–03. Hon. DSc Southampton, 2000. *Recreations:* music, cooking.

JONES, Mark Ellis Powell; Director, Victoria & Albert Museum, since 2001; *b* 5 Feb. 1951; *s* of John Ernest Powell-Jones, *qv* and Ann Paludan; *m* 1983, Ann Camilla, *d* of Stephen Edelston Toulmin, *qv*; two *s* two *d*. *Educ:* Eton College; Worcester College, Oxford (MA); Courtauld Inst. of Art. Asst Keeper, 1974–90, Keeper, 1990–92, Dept of Coins and Medals, BM; Dir, Nat. Mus of Scotland, 1992–2001. Co-Founder, 1994–96, Mem. Bd, 1996–2003, Chm., 2004–06, Scottish Cultural Resources Access Network. Director: Scottish Museums Council, 1992–2001; Edinburgh and Lothians Tourist Bd, 1998–2000. Member: Royal Mint Adv. Cttee, 1994–2006; Arts and Humanities Data Service Steering Cttee, 1997–99; Focus Gp, Nat. Cultural Strategy, 1999–2000; Bd, MLA, 2000–05; Council, RCA, 2001–; Chancellor's Forum, Univ. of the Arts, London, 2002–06; Council, Crafts Council, 2002–06; Chm., Nat. Mus Dirs' Conf., 2006–. President: Fédn Internat. de la Médaille, 1994–2000; British Art Medal Soc., 1998–2004 (Sec., 1982–94); Corresp. Mem., Amer. Numismatic Soc., 1990. Trustee: Gilbert Collection, 2001–; NT, 2005–; Pilgrim Trust, 2006–. Hon. Prof., Univ. of Edinburgh, 1997. Editor, The Medal, 1983–97. FSA 1992; FRSE 1999. Hon. DLit London, 2002. Chevalier, Ordre des Arts et des Lettres (France), 2005. *Publications:* The Art of the Medal, 1977; Impressionist Painting, 1979; Catalogue of French Medals in the British Museum, I, 1982, II, 1988; Contemporary British Medals, 1986; (ed) Fake?: the art of deception, 1990; (ed) Why Fakes Matter, 1992; (ed) Designs on Posterity, 1994; contrib. Sculpture Jl and Museums Jl. *Address:* Victoria & Albert Museum, Cromwell Road, SW7 2RL; *e-mail:* mark.jones@vam.ac.uk.

JONES, Prof. Martin Kenneth, DPhil; FSA; George Pitt-Rivers Professor of Archaeological Science, University of Cambridge, since 1990; *b* 29 June 1951; *s* of John Francis Jones and Margaret Olive (*née* Baldwin); *m* 1985, Lucy Walker; one *s* one *d*. *Educ:* Eltham Coll., Univ. of Cambridge (MA); Univ. of Oxford (DPhil 1985). FSA 1991. Oxford Archaeological Unit, 1973–79; Res. Asst, Oxford Univ., 1979–81; Lectr, 1981–89, Sen. Lectr, 1989–90, Durham Univ. DUniv Stirling, 1999. *Publications:* The Environment of Man: the Iron Age to the Anglo-Saxon period, 1981; Integrating the Subsistence Economy, 1983; England before Domesday, 1986; Archaeology and the Flora of the British Isles, 1988; Molecular Information and Prehistory, 1999; The Molecule Hunt: archaeology and the search for ancient DNA, 2001; Conflict, 2006; Feast: why humans share food, 2007. *Recreation:* dancing. *Address:* Department of Archaeology, Downing Street, Cambridge CB2 3DZ. *T:* (01223) 333520.

JONES, Martyn David; MP (Lab) Clwyd South, since 1997 (Clwyd South West, 1987–97); *b* 1 March 1947; *m* 1974, Rhona Bellis (marr. diss. 1991); one *s* one *d*. *Educ:* Liverpool and Trent Polytechnics. MIBiol. Microbiologist, Wrexham Lager Beer Co., 1968–87. Mem., Clwyd CC, 1981–89. An Opposition Whip, 1988–92; Opposition spokesman on food, agric. and rural affairs, 1994–95; Mem., Chairmen's Panel, 1992–94, 2005–. Member: Select Cttee on Agriculture, 1987–94 and 1996–97; Select Cttee on Welsh Affairs, 1997– (Chm., 1997–2005); Chm., Parly Labour Party Agriculture Cttee, 1987–94. *Address:* House of Commons, SW1A 0AA; Foundry Buildings, Gutter Hill, Johnstown, Wrexham, Clwyd LL14 1LU.

JONES, Maude Elizabeth, CBE 1973; Deputy Director-General, British Red Cross Society, 1970–77; *b* 14 Jan. 1921; 2nd *d* of late E. W. and M. E. H. Jones, Dolben, Ruthin, North Wales. *Educ:* Brynhyfryd Sch. for Girls, Ruthin. Joined Foreign Relations Dept, Jt War Organisation BRCS and OStJ, 1940; Dep. Dir, Jun. Red Cross, BRCS, 1949; Dir, Jun. Red Cross, 1960; Dep. Dir-Gen. for Branch Affairs, BRCS, 1966. Member: Jt Cttee (and Finance and Gen. Purposes Sub-Cttee) OStJ and BRCS, 1966–77; Council of Nat. Council of Social Service; Council of FANY, 1966–77. Governor, St David's Sch., Ashford, Middx. SSStJ 1959. *Recreations:* music, gardening, reading. *Address:* Dolben, Ruthin, Denbighshire, North Wales LL15 1RB. *T:* (01824) 702443. *Club:* New Cavendish.

JONES, Merfyn; *see* Jones, Richard M.

JONES, Mervyn; author; *b* 27 Feb. 1922; *s* of Ernest Jones and Katharine (*née* Jokl); *m* 1948, Jeanne Urquhart; one *s* two *d*. *Educ:* Abbotsholme School; New York University. Assistant Editor: Tribune, 1955–59; New Statesman, 1966–68; Drama Critic, Tribune,

1959–67. *Publications:* No Time to be Young, 1952; The New Town, 1953; The Last Barricade, 1953; Helen Blake, 1955; On the Last Day, 1958; Potbank, 1961; Big Two, 1962; A Set of Wives, 1965; Two Ears of Corn, 1965; John and Mary, 1966; A Survivor, 1968; Joseph, 1970; Mr Armitage Isn't Back Yet, 1971; Life on the Dole, 1972; Holding On, 1973; The Revolving Door, 1973; Strangers, 1974; Lord Richard's Passion, 1974; The Pursuit of Happiness, 1975; Scenes from Bourgeois Life, 1976; Nobody's Fault, 1977; Today The Struggle, 1978; The Beautiful Words, 1979; A Short Time to Live, 1980; Two Women and their Man, 1982; Joanna's Luck, 1985; Coming Home, 1986; Chances, 1987; That Year in Paris, 1988; A Radical Life, 1991; Michael Foot, 1994; The Amazing Victorian, 1999. *Address:* c/o 51 Upper Lewes Road, Brighton, E Sussex BN2 3FH.

JONES, Mervyn C.; *see* Colenso-Jones, G. M. B.

JONES, Mervyn Thomas; HM Diplomatic Service, retired; Partnership Development Officer, Diocese of Winchester, since 2004; *b* 23 Nov. 1942; *s* of William Clifford Jones and Winifred Mary Jones (*née* Jenkins); *m* 1965, Julia Mary Newcombe; two *s*. *Educ:* Bishop Gore Grammar Sch., Swansea; University Coll., Swansea (BA Hons Eng.). Entered HM Diplomatic Service, 1964: FCO, 1964–66; Calcutta, 1966; Bonn, 1966–70; Warsaw, 1970–73; FCO, 1973–77; Oslo, 1977–80; First Sec. (Mgt), then Hd of Chancery, Bangkok, 1981–85; jsdc, RNC Greenwich, 1985; on secondment to Commonwealth Secretariat as Asst Dir, Internat. Affairs Div., 1985–90; Dep. Consul Gen. and Consul (Commercial), LA, 1990–94; Asst Hd, Migration and Visa Dept, FCO, 1994–96; Counsellor (Commercial and Econ.), Brussels, and co-accredited to Luxembourg, 1996–99; Consul-Gen. and Dep. Head of Mission, Brussels, 1999–2000; Governor, Turks and Caicos Is, 2000–02. *Recreations:* reading, cinema, music, walking, Rugby (Welsh).

JONES, Miah Gwynfor, (Gwyn Jones), PhD; Director, Corporate Technologies, since 1989; *b* 2 Dec. 1948; *s* of Robert Jones and Jane Irene Jones (*née* Evans); *m* 1976, Maria Linda Johnson; two *d*. *Educ:* Ysgol Eifionydd, Porthmadog; Univ. of Manchester (BSc 1st Cl. Hons); Univ. of Essex (PhD). FBCS 1987. British Steel Corp., 1974–77; ICL, 1977–81; Chm., Business Micro Systems, 1981–85; Chm. and Chief Exec., Corporate Technology Gp plc, 1985–87; Chm., L. G. Software, 1985–87; Director: ACT Computers PLC, 1989–95; Welsh Water Enterprises Ltd, 1990–93; Tesco plc, 1992–98; Invesco English and Internat. Trust plc, 1993–; HBO (formerly HBOL) (UK) Ltd, 1996–97; Real Radio Ltd, 2000–02; RMR plc, 2001–02; Si Corporate Develt Ltd, 2004–07 (Chm., 2006–07); Unit Superheaters Ltd, 2005–; Dep. Chm., Agenda Television Ltd, 1997–2000; Partner, Quayside Properties, 1997–; Chairman: Agenda Multimedia Ltd, 2000–01; Press Red Ltd, 2003–05; Oxford English Trng Ltd, 2004–06; RogenSi, 2007–. Chm., Adv. Cttee, NW Equity Fund, 2005–. Chm., Welsh Develt Agency, 1988–93; BBC Nat. Gov. for Wales, 1992–96; Dir, S4C Authy, 1992–96; Pres., Royal Welsh Agric. Soc., 1993. Member: Council, Univ. of Wales, 1989–95; Court, UC of Swansea, 1989–95; Prince of Wales Cttee, 1989–92; Prince's Youth Business Trust, 1989–92. *Recreations:* boats, mountain walking.

JONES, Michael Abbott; communications consultant; *b* 3 May 1944; *s* of Ronald and Irene Jones; *m* 1973, Wendy (*née* Saward); twin *d*. *Educ:* Felsted; Magdalen Coll., Oxford (BA, DipEd). Joined Life Offices' Assoc., 1968, Jt Sec. 1982; transf. to Assoc. of British Insurers on its formation, as Manager, Legislation, 1985, Chief Exec., 1987–93; Hd of Corporate Affairs, Sun Alliance, 1993–96; Hd of Gp Corporate Affairs, Royal & Sun Alliance Insurance Gp plc, 1996–98. *Recreations:* reading, photography, sailing, theatre. *Address:* 10 Parkhill Road, E4 7ED.

JONES, Michael Frederick; Associate Editor (Politics), The Sunday Times, 1995–2002; *b* 3 July 1937; *s* of late Glyn Frederick Jones and of Elizabeth (*née* Coopey); *m* 1959, Sheila Joan Dawes; three *s*. *Educ:* Crypt Grammar Sch., Gloucester. Reporter: Maidenhead Advertiser, 1956–59; Northern Echo, Darlington, 1959–61; Manchester Evening News, 1961–64; Labour reporter, Financial Times, 1964–65; Industrial reporter, Daily Telegraph, 1965–67; News Editor, later Asst Editor, Times Business News, 1967–70; Managing Editor, The Asian, Hong Kong, 1971; Sunday Times: Associate News Editor, 1972–75; political correspondent, 1975–84; Political Editor, 1984–95; Associate Editor, 1990–2002. Chm., Parly Press Gallery, 1989–91. Vis. Fellow, Goldsmiths Coll., London, 2000–02. Exec. Mem., Meml to Women of World War 2 Fund, 2004–05. *Publication:* (with Betty Boothroyd) Betty Boothroyd: the autobiography, 2001. *Recreation:* exploring the London Library and National Archives. *Address:* 43 Hillview Road, Orpington, Kent BR6 0SE. *T:* (01689) 820796.

JONES, Rt Rev. Michael Hugh Harold B.; *see* Bedford-Jones.

JONES, Natascha; *see* Engel, N.

JONES, Dr Nevin Campbell H.; *see* Hughes Jones.

JONES, Nicholas Graham; His Honour Judge Nicholas Jones; a Circuit Judge, since 2001; *b* 13 Aug. 1948; *s* of Albert William Jones and Gwendolen Muriel Taylor-Jones; *m* 1976, Shelagh Ann Farror; one *s*. *Educ:* Latymer Upper Sch.; St Catherine's Coll., Oxford (MA). Film editing and prodn, BBC, 1969–73; called to the Bar, Inner Temple, 1975; S Eastern Circuit; a Recorder, 1994–2001. *Recreations:* sailing, walking, music. *Address:* Kingston Crown Court, 6–8 Penrhyn Road, Kingston-upon-Thames, Surrey KT1 2BB. *T:* (020) 8240 2500, *Fax:* (020) 8240 2675. *Clubs:* Royal London Yacht, Royal Ocean Racing, Bar Yacht (Cdre, 2008–).

JONES, Nicholas Keith Arthur; restaurateur; Managing Director, Soho House, since 1991; *b* 22 Sept. 1963; *s* of Keith and Anna Jones; *m* 1999, Kirsty Jackson Young, *qv*; two *d*, and one *s* one *d* from former marriage. *Educ:* Shiplake Coll. Opened: Café Bohème, London W1, 1992; Soho House, 1995; Babington House, Som, 1998; Bohème Kitchen Bar, London W1, 1999; Electric Cinema, House and Brasserie, London W11, 2002; Soho House New York, 2003; Balham Kitchen and Bar, 2003; Cecconi's, London W1, 2005; Cowshed, Clarendon Cross, 2005; High Road House, Chiswick, 2006; Shoreditch House, 2007. *Recreations:* cooking, eating, drinking, napping. *Address:* Soho House, 3–5 Bateman Street, W1D 4AG. *T:* (020) 7851 1171, *Fax:* (020) 7851 1198.

JONES, Nigel John I.; *see* Inglis-Jones.

JONES, Rt Rev. Noël Debroy, CB 1986; an Hon. Assistant Bishop, diocese of York, since 2003; *b* 25 Dec. 1932; *s* of Brinley and Gwendoline Jones; *m* 1969, Joyce Barbara Leelavathy Arulanandam; one *s* one *d*. *Educ:* Haberdashers' West Monmouth Sch.; St David's Coll., Lampeter (BA); Wells Theol Coll. Dio. of Monmouth, 1955–59; Vicar of Kano, N Nigeria, 1960–62; Chaplain, RN, 1962; GSM Brunei 1962, Borneo 1963; RM Commando Course prior to service in Aden with 42 Cdo, 1967; GSM S Arabia, 1967; Mid Service Clergy Course at St George's House, Windsor Castle, 1974; Staff Chaplain, MoD, 1974–77; Chaplain of the Fleet and Archdeacon for the Royal Navy, 1984–89; Bishop of Sodor and Man, 1989–2003. QHC 1983–89. OStJ 1995. *Recreations:* squash, swimming, music, family; formerly Rugby. *Club:* Army and Navy.

JONES, Norman Arthur W.; *see* Ward-Jones.

JONES, Dr (Norman) Fielding, FRCP; Consultant Physician, St Thomas' Hospital, London, 1967–93, now Emeritus; *b* 3 May 1931; *s* of William John and Winifred Jones; *m* 1958, Ann Pye Chavasse; three *s*. *Educ:* Christ Coll., Brecon; King's Coll., Cambridge (MA 1957; MD 1966); St Thomas' Hosp., London. FRCP 1970. Rockefeller Fellow, Univ. of N Carolina, 1963–64. Physician, King Edward VII's Hosp. for Officers, 1977–95; Consulting Physician, Metropolitan Police, 1980–92; Hon. Consulting Physician: to the Army, 1980–93; to Royal Hosp., Chelsea, 1987–93; CMO, Equitable Life Assurance Soc., 1985–97. Vice Chm., West Lambeth HA, 1989–90. Royal College of Physicians: Sen. Censor and Vice Pres., 1989–90; Treasurer, 1991–96; Chm., Cttee on Renal Disease, 1980–92; Chm., Cttee on Legal Aspects of Medicine, 1990–93. Special Trustee, St Thomas' Hosp., 1990–94; Treas., Royal Medical Benevolent Fund, 1996–2002. Member: Med. Res. Soc., 1962–; Assoc. of Physicians of GB and Ire., 1968–. *Publications:* (ed) Recent Advances in Renal Disease, 1975; (ed with Sir Douglas Black) Renal Disease, 1979; (ed with D. K. Peters) Recent Advances in Renal Medicine, 1982. *Recreations:* iconology, music. *Address:* The Old Coach House, Forest Park Road, Brockenhurst, Hants SO42 7SW.

JONES, His Honour Norman Henry; QC 1985; a Circuit Judge, 1992–2007 (a Senior Circuit Judge, 2000–07); *b* 12 Dec. 1941; *s* of late Henry Robert Jones and of Charlotte Isabel Scott Jones; *m* 1970, Trudy Helen Chamberlain; two *s* one *d*. *Educ:* Bideford Grammar School; North Devon Tech. Coll.; Univ. of Leeds (LLB, LLM). Called to the Bar, Middle Temple, 1968 (Harmsworth Schol.). A Recorder, 1987–92. Recorder of Leeds and Resident Judge at Leeds, 2001–07. *Recreations:* reading, walking, boating. *Address:* c/o The Crown Court, Oxford Road, Leeds LS1 3BG.

JONES, Sir (Owen) Trevor, Kt 1981; Member (Lib Dem), Liverpool City Council, since 2003; *b* 1927; *s* of Owen and Ada Jones, Dyserth; *m* Doreen. Mem., Liverpool City Council, 1968, Liverpool Metropolitan District Council, 1973–91 (Leader, 1981–83). Pres., Liberal Party, 1972–73; contested (L): Liverpool, Toxteth, Feb. 1974 and Gillingham, Oct. 1974. *Address:* 155 Waterloo Apartments, Liverpool L3 0BH.

JONES, Brig. Percival de Courcy, OBE 1953; Chief Secretary, The Royal Life Saving Society, 1965–75; *b* 9 Oct. 1913; *s* of P. de C. Jones, Barnsley; *m* 1st, 1947, Anne Hollins (marr. diss., 1951); one *s*; 2nd, 1962, Elaine Garnett. *Educ:* Oundle; RMC, Sandhurst. Commissioned KSLI 1933; Staff Coll., 1942; comd 1st Northamptons, Burma, 1945; Staff Coll. Instructor, 1949–50; AA & QMG, 11th Armoured Div., 1951–53; comd 1st KSLI, 1953–55; AQMG, War Office, 1955–58; NATO Defence Coll., 1958–59; Bde Comdr, 1959–62; retd 1962. Mem., Aylesbury Vale DC, 1976–79. Commonwealth Chief Sec., RLSS, 1965–75. Silver Medallion, Fedn Internat. de Sauvetage, 1976. *Recreation:* gardening. *Address:* Fairfield House, Ford, Shrewsbury, Shropshire SY5 9LG.

JONES, Peter; Chairman and Chief Executive Officer, Phones International Group, since 1998; *b* 18 March 1966; *s* of David and Eileen Jones; five *c*. *Educ:* Haileybury Jun. Sch.; Windsor Boys' Sch. Dir, Siemens Nixdorf, 1996–97. Founder and Chm., Peter Jones TV Ltd, 2006–. Appeared in BBC TV business series, Dragons' Den, 2005 and 2007; creator, presenter and judge, American Inventor, US, 2006, 2007; creator, presenter and mentor, Tycoon, 2007. Emerging Entrepreneur of Year, Ernst & Young/Times Nat. Awards, 2001. *Recreations:* tennis, golf, karate. *Address:* Phones International Group, Network House, Globe Park, Marlow, Bucks SL7 1LY; *e-mail:* info@pj.tv.

JONES, Peter Anthony; Group Chief Executive, Associated British Ports Holdings plc, since 2007; *b* 8 Jan. 1955. The Mersey Docks and Harbour Co.: Dir, 1993; Port Ops Dir, 1997–99; Dep. Chief Exec., 1999–2000; Chief Exec., 2000–05. Chm., Medway Ports, 2000–06. *Address:* Associated British Ports Holdings plc, 150 Holborn, EC1N 2LR.

JONES, Peter B.; *see* Bennett-Jones.

JONES, Peter Benjamin Gurner, CB 1991; Under Secretary; Director of Personnel, Board of Inland Revenue, 1984–92; *b* 25 Dec. 1932; *s* of Gurner Prince Jones and Irene Louise Jones (*née* Myall); *m* 1962, Diana Margaret Henly; one *s* one *d*. *Educ:* Bancroft's Sch.; St Catherine's Society, Oxford (BA (Hons) English Language and Literature). Inspector of Taxes, 1957; Inspector (Higher Grade), 1963; Sen. Inspector, 1969; Principal Inspector, 1975; Sen. Principal Inspector, 1980; Dir of Data Processing, Bd of Inland Revenue, 1981–84. Hon. Nat. Chm., CS Retirement Fellowship, 1994–2000 (Vice-Pres., 2001–). *Clubs:* Hampshire Rugby Union, Swanage and Wareham RFC.

JONES, Prof. Peter Brian, PhD; FRCPsych; Professor of Psychiatry and Head, Department of Psychiatry, University of Cambridge, since 2000; *b* 24 Jan. 1960; *s* of Owen Trevor Jones and Amy M. Anita Jones; *m* 1986, Caroline Lea-Cox; two *s*. *Educ:* Northampton Grammar Sch.; King's Coll., London (BSc Neuroanatomy); Westminster Med. Sch. (MB BS); London Sch. of Hygiene and Tropical Medicine (MSc Dist.); Inst. of Psychiatry (PhD 1997). MRCP 1987, FRCP 2002; MRCPsych 1990, FRCPsych 2007. House physician, Westminster Hosp., 1984; house surgeon, E Surrey Hosp., 1985; Casualty Officer, Westminster Hosp., 1985; SHO, Whittington Hosp., 1986–87; Med. Registrar, KCH, 1987; Registrar, Bethlem Royal and Maudsley Hosps, 1987–90; Sen. Registrar in Psychiatry, KCH, 1991; MRC Trng Fellow, 1991–93; Sen. Lectr, Inst. of Psychiatry, 1993–95 (Hon. Lectr, 1991–93); Hon. Consultant Psychiatrist, Bethlem Royal and Maudsley Hosps, 1993–95; University of Nottingham: Sen. Lectr in Psychiatric Epidemiol., 1995–96; Prof. of Psychiatry and Community Mental Health, 1997–2000; Head, Div. of Psychiatry, 1997–2000. SMO (part-time), R&D Div., DoH, 1994–96. Hon. Consultant Psychiatrist: and Dir, R&D, Nottingham Healthcare Trust, 1995–2000; Addenbrooke's NHS Trust, 2000–; Cambs and Peterborough Mental Health Partnership NHS Trust, 2002– (Dir, 2003–05). FMedSci 2003. Hon. MD Oulu, Finland, 2006. *Publications:* contribs to learned jls on causation, clinical features, epidemiology and treatment of adult mental illness and the psychoses, in particular. *Recreations:* playing the flute, walking high fells. *Address:* Department of Psychiatry, University of Cambridge, Box 189, Addenbrooke's Hospital, Cambridge CB2 0QQ. *T:* (01223) 336961.

JONES, Peter Derek; Deputy Chairman, Civil Service Appeal Board, 1992–2001; Secretary: Council of Civil Service Unions, 1980–92; Civil Service National Whitley Council (Trade Union Side), 1963–92; *b* 21 May 1932; *s* of Richard Morgan Jones and Phyllis Irene (*née* Lloyd); *m* 1st, 1962, Noreen Elizabeth (*née* Kemp) (*d* 2001); 2nd, 2006, Delwin Ann Kirkstone Hunter (*née* Wood); one step *d*. *Educ:* Wembley County Grammar School. National Service and TA, Green Jackets/Parachute Regt, 1950–56; Civil Service, Nat. Assistance Bd, 1952–59; Asst Sec., Civil Service Nat. Whitley Council, 1959–63. Chm., Civil Service Housing Assoc. Ltd, 1988–97 (Dir, 1963–81; Vice Chm., 1981–88, 1997–99); Dir, Civil Service Building Soc., 1963–87. Vice-Pres., RIPA, 1991–92 (Chm., 1987–90; Vice-Chm., 1986–87; Mem. Exec. Council, 1981–85); Member: Adv. Council, Civil Service Coll., 1982–92; Tourism and Leisure Industries EDC, 1987–92; Adv. Council, CS Occupational Health Service, 1988–92; Employment (formerly Industrial) Tribunals, 1992–2002; Security Vetting Appeals Panel, 1997–; Chm., CIPFA Disciplinary

Investigations Cttee, 2001–08. Trustee: Inst. of Contemporary Brit. History, 1985–; CS Benevolent Fund, 1992–99. Editor: Whitley Bulletin, 1963–83; CCSU Bulletin, 1984–92. *Publications:* articles in RIPA and personnel management jls. *Recreations:* relaxing, reading, painting. *Address:* Chaseview, Rowlands Hill, Wimborne, Dorset BH21 2QQ. *T:* (01202) 888824, *Fax:* (01202) 888831. *Clubs:* Belfry; Mansion House (Poole); Wimborne Cricket.

JONES, Peter Eldon, FRIBA, FRTPI; architect in private practice, since 1996; *b* 11 Oct. 1927; *s* of Wilfrid Eldon Jones and Jessie Meikle (*née* Buchanan); *m* 1st, 1954, Gisela Marie von Arnswaldt; two *s* one *d*; 2nd, 1985, Claudia Milner-Brown (*née* Laurence). *Educ:* Surbiton County Grammar Sch.; Kingston Polytechnic; University College London. DipTP. Private practice, 1950–54; joined LCC Architects Dept, 1954; Dep. Schools Architect, LCC, 1960–65; Town Development Architect/Planner, 1965–71; Technical Policy Architect, GLC, 1971–74; Education Architect, ILEA, 1974–82; Acting Director of Architecture, 1980–82, Dir of Architecture and Superintending Architect of Metrop. Bldgs, 1982–86, GLC. Consultant, DES, subseq. DFE, 1988–92. Dir, Assoc. of Small Historic Towns and Villages of the UK, 1993–95. Director: Interior Transformation Ltd, 1985–87; Watkins Gray Peter Jones, 1986–91. Part-time Lectr in Architectl Design, Kingston Poly., 1986–90. Mem., EC Adv. Cttee on Educn and Training in Architecture, 1987–92. Pres., Soc. of Chief Architects of Local Authorities, 1984–85; Mem. Council, Chm. Membership Cttee, and Vice-Pres., RIBA, 1985–87. *Publications:* articles and papers on town development, educn building, housing design and planning. *Recreations:* building, travel, golf. *Club:* Woking Golf.

JONES, Peter Ferry, MA, MChir, FRCS, FRCSE; Surgeon to the Queen in Scotland, 1977–85; Honorary Consulting Surgeon, Aberdeen Royal Infirmary and Royal Aberdeen Children's Hospital, Aberdeen (Consultant Surgeon, 1958–85); Clinical Professor of Surgery, University of Aberdeen, 1983–85, now Emeritus; *b* 29 Feb. 1920; *s* of Ernest and Winifred Jones; *m* 1950, Margaret Thomson; two *s* two *d*. *Educ:* Emmanuel Coll., Cambridge (MA); St Bartholomew's Hosp. Med. Sch., London (MB, MChir). FRCS 1948; FRCSE 1964. Served War, RAMC, 1944–46, Captain. House Surgeon, St Bartholomew's Hosp., 1943; Surg. Registrar, N Middlesex Hosp., 1948–51; Surg. Tutor, St Bartholomew's Hosp., 1951–53; Sen. Surg. Registrar, Central Middlesex Hosp. and the Middlesex Hosp., London, 1953–57; Reader in Surg. Paediatrics, Univ. of Aberdeen, 1965–83. *Publications:* Abdominal Access and Exposure (with H. A. F. Dudley), 1965; Emergency Abdominal Surgery in Infancy, Childhood and Adult Life, 1974, 2nd edn 1987, 3rd edn (jtly) 1998; (jtly) Integrated Clinical Science: Gastroenterology, 1984; A Colour Atlas of Colo-Rectal Surgery, 1985; A Surgical Revolution: surgery in Scotland 1837–1901, 2007; papers on paediatric and gen. surgery in Brit. Jl of Surg., BMJ, Lancet, etc. *Recreations:* gardening, surgical history. *Address:* 7 Park Road, Cults, Aberdeen AB15 9HR. *T:* (01224) 867702.

JONES, Peter George Edward Fitzgerald, CB 1985; Director, Atomic Weapons Research Establishment, 1982–87, retired; Consultant to the Ministry of Defence, 1987–2006; *b* 7 June 1925; *s* of John Christopher Jones and Isobel (*née* Howell); *m* 1st; two *s*; 2nd, Jacqueline Angela (*née* Gilbert); two *s* one *d*. *Educ:* various schs; Dulwich Coll.; London Univ. (BSc (Special) Physics 1st Cl. Hons 1951). FInstP. Served RAF, flying duties, 1943–47. GEC Res. Labs, 1951–54; AWRE and Pacific Test Site, 1955–63; Asst Dir of Res., London Communications Security, 1963; Atomic Weapons Research Establishment: Supt, Electronics Res., 1964; Head, Electronics Div., 1966; Head, Special Projs, 1971; Chief, Warhead Develt, 1974; Principal Dep. Dir, 1980. *Recreation:* motoring. *Address:* Yew Tree Cottage, Upper Llanover, Abergavenny, Gwent NP7 9ER. *T:* (01873) 880779.

JONES, Peter Henry Francis; His Honour Judge Peter Jones; a Circuit Judge, since 2001; *b* 25 Feb. 1952; *s* of late Eric Roberts Jones, MBE and Betty Irene Jones (*née* Longhurst); *m* 1978, Anne Elizabeth (*née* Jones); two *d*. *Educ:* Bishop Gore Grammar Sch., Swansea; Newport High Sch., Gwent; Balliol Coll., Oxford (MA (Hons) Lit.Hum.). Admitted Solicitor of Supreme Court, 1977. Partner: Darlington and Parkinson, Solicitors, London, 1978–87; J. Howell and Co., Solicitors, Sheffield, 1987–95; Asst Recorder, 1993–97; a Stipendiary Magistrate, then Dist Judge (Magistrates' Courts), S Yorks, 1995–2001; a Recorder, 1997–2001. Member: Lord Chancellor's Legal Aid Adv. Cttee, 1983–92; Legal Aid Bd, 1992–95; Sentencing Adv. Panel, 1999–2005; Magistrates' Cts Rules Cttee, 2001–04. *Recreations:* tennis, books, watching Rugby Union. *Address:* c/o Sheffield Combined Court Centre, 50 West Bar, Sheffield S3 8PH. *Clubs:* Dethreau Boat; Scorpions Cricket; Druidstone (Dyfed).

JONES, Prof. Peter (Howard), FRSE, FSAScot; Director and Trustee, Foundation for Advanced Studies in the Humanities, 1997–2002; Professor of Philosophy, 1984–98, now Emeritus, and Director, Institute for Advanced Studies in the Humanities, 1986–2000, University of Edinburgh; *b* 18 Dec. 1935; *s* of Thomas Leslie Jones and Hilda Croesora (*née* Parkinson); *m* 1960, (Elizabeth) Jean, *yr d* of R. J. Roberton, JP; two *d*. *Educ:* Highgate Sch.; Queens' Coll., Cambridge. With British Council, 1960–61; Asst Lectr in Philosophy, Univ. of Nottingham, 1963–64; Lectr, then Reader in Philosophy, Univ. of Edinburgh, 1964–84. Visiting Professor of Philosophy: Univ. of Rochester, NY, 1969–70; Dartmouth Coll., NH, 1973, 1983; Carleton Coll., Minn, 1974; Oklahoma Univ., 1978; Baylor Univ., 1978; Univ. of Malta, 1993; Belarusian State Univ., 1997; Jagiellonian Univ., Cracow, 2001, 2002, 2004–; Visiting Fellow: Humanities Res. Centre, ANU, 1984, 2002; Calgary Inst. for Humanities, 1992. Lothian Lectr, Edinburgh, 1993; Gifford Lectr, Univ. of Aberdeen, 1994–95; Loemker Lectr, Emory Univ., 1995–96. Mem., Spoliation Adv. Panel, 2000–. Trustee: Nat. Museums of Scotland, 1987–99 (Chm., Mus. of Scotland Client Cttee, 1991–99); Univ. of Edinburgh Develt Trust, 1990–98; Policy Inst., 1999–2008; Scots at War, 1999–; Morrison's Acad., 1984–98; Fettes Coll., 1995–2005; MBI Al Jaber Foundn, 2005–. Member: UNESCO forum on tolerance, Tbilisi, 1995–; UNESCO dialogue on Europe and Islam, 1997–. Member: Court, Univ. of Edinburgh, 1987–90; Council, RSE, 1992–95. Founder Mem., Hume Soc., 1974. FRSE 1989; FSAScot 1993. *Publications:* Philosophy and the Novel, 1975; Hume's Sentiments, 1982; A Hotbed of Genius, 1986, 2nd edn 1996; (ed) Philosophy and Science in the Scottish Enlightenment, 1988; (ed) The Science of Man in the Scottish Enlightenment, 1989; (ed) Adam Smith Reviewed, 1992; (ed) Investigation of the Principles of Knowledge, by James Hutton, 1999; (ed) The Enlightenment World, 2004; (ed) The Reception of David Hume in Europe, 2005; (ed) Elements of Criticism, by Henry Home, Lord Kames, 2005; Ove Arup Master Builder of the Twentieth Century, 2006; articles on philosophy, literature and culture. *Recreations:* opera, architecture, the arts, travel. *Address:* 6 Greenhill Terrace, Edinburgh EH10 4BS. *T:* (0131) 447 6344. *Club:* New (Edinburgh).

JONES, Peter Ivan, CBE 2008; Chairman, Horserace Totalisator Board, 1997–2007 (Director, 1995–97); *b* 14 Dec. 1942; *s* of Glyndwr and Edith Evelyn Jones; *m* 1st, 1964, Judith Watson (marr. diss. 1969); one *s* one *d*; 2nd, 1970, Elizabeth Gent; one *s* one *d*. *Educ:* Gravesend Grammar Sch.; London School of Economics (BSc Econs 1964). MIPA 1967. Chief Executive: Boase Massimi Pollitt, 1988–89; Omnicom UK plc, 1989–93 (Dir, Omnicom Inc., 1989–97); Pres., Diversified Agency Services, 1993–97. Dir, Sutton Gp Hldgs, 2005–. Dir, British Horseracing Bd, 1993–97; Mem., Horserace Betting Levy Bd, 1993–95. Chm., Dorset Police Authy, 1997–2003. Dir, Goodwood Racecourse, 2008–. Pres., Racehorse Owners Assoc., 1990–93. Gov., LSE, 2007–. *Publications:* Trainers Record, annually 1973 to 1987 (Editor, 1982–87); (ed) Ed Byrne's Racing Year, annually 1980 to 1983. *Recreations:* horse racing, computer programming, watching sport. *Address:* Melplash Farmhouse, Melplash, Bridport, Dorset DT6 3UH. *T:* (01308) 488383. *Club:* Sloane; Bridport and West Dorset Golf.

JONES, Maj.-Gen. (Peter) John R.; *see* Russell-Jones.

JONES, Peter Llewellyn G.; *see* Gwynn-Jones.

JONES, Peter Trevor S.; *see* Simpson-Jones.

JONES, Prof. Philip Alan; Vice-Chancellor, Sheffield Hallam University, since 2007; *b* 26 Nov. 1950; *s* of Jean Kier; partner, Hilary Bloor. *Educ:* Poly. of Central London (LLB Hons (ext.) 1972); London Sch. of Econs (LLM 1973); Univ. of Essex (MA Sociol. 1979); Univ. of Surrey (Postgrad. Dip. Practice of Higher Educn). Lectr, Manchester Poly., 1973–75; Polytechnic of Central London, later University of Westminster: Lectr, then Sen. Lectr, 1975–87; Principal Lectr, 1987–91; Dep. Hd and Actg Hd, 1991–92; University of Sheffield: Dir, Legal Practice Course, 1993–97; Dean, Faculty of Law, 1996–98; Pro Vice Chancellor, 1998–2004; Dep. Vice-Chancellor and Sub-Warden, Durham Univ., 2004–07. Vis. Lectr, Brunel Univ., 1988; Vis. Prof., DC Sch. of Law, Washington, 1991. Ed.-in-Chief, Legal Practice Guides, 1993–2000; Exec. Ed., Internat. Jl Legal Profession, 1993–; Mem., Editl Bd, Jl Professional Legal Educn, 1995–. Member: Bd of Studies and Consultant, Council of Legal Educn, 1993–96; NCVQ Policy Cttee, 1996–98; S Yorks Learning and Skills Council, 2001–04; Quality Assce Cttee, UK eUniv., 2001–04; Quality Assce, Learning and Teaching Cttee, HEFCE, 2003–; Advr to Higher Educn Quality Council, 1996–97; various QCA posts, 1998–2003, incl. Mem., Vocational Qualifications and Occupational Standards Cttee, 1998–2000 and Qualification Cttee, 2000–03. *Publications:* (ed jtly) Politics and Power, vol. 1 1980, vol. 2 1980, vol. 3 1981; (contrib.) Problems in Labour Politics, 1980; (contrib.) Law, Politics and Justice, 1982; Lawyers' Skills, 1993, 4th edn 1996, then reprints annually; (contrib.) Examining the Law Syllabus: beyond the core, 1993; Competences, Learning Outcomes and Legal Education, 1994; (contrib.) Teaching Lawyers' Skills, 1996; (contrib.) An Agenda for Comparative Legal Skills Research: the European Community and the Commonwealth, 1996; (contrib.) The Development of the NVQ Framework at the Higher Levels, 1997; (contrib.) NVQs and Higher Education, 1997; contribs to jls incl. Law Teacher, Modern Law Rev., Jl Law and Soc., New Law Jl, Internat. Jl Legal Profession; numerous conf. papers and res. reports. *Recreations:* rock climbing and biking, road and mountain. *Address:* Sheffield Hallam University, City Campus, Howard Street, Sheffield S1 1WB. *T:* (0114) 225 2050, *Fax:* (0114) 225 2042. *Club:* Dark Peak Fell Running.

JONES, Rear Adm. Philip Andrew; Commander UK Maritime Forces, since 2008; *b* 14 Feb. 1960; *s* of Edgar Jones and Edna Lilian Jones (*née* Peers); *m* 1987, Elizabeth Collins; one *s* two *d*. *Educ:* Birkenhead Sch.; Mansfield Coll., Oxford (BA Geog. 1981). HMS Fearless, Falklands War, 1982; Watchkeeping and Navigation Officer, Frigates and HMY Britannia, 1983–88; Prin. Warfare Officer, Frigates and Maritime Battle Staff, 1989–93; CO HMS Beaver, 1994–96; Directorate Navy Plans and Progs, MoD, 1997–99; CO HMS Coventry, 1999–2001; Chief of Defence Logistics Office, MoD, 2002–03; Dir, Jt Maritime Operational Trng Staff, 2003–04; ACOS C4ISTAR Fleet HQ, 2004–06; Comdr Amphibious Task Gp, 2006–08; FO Scotland, England, Wales and NI, and FO Reserves, 2008. Mem., Windsor Leadership Trust, 2008–. Vice Pres., RN Rugby Union, 2008–. *Recreations:* following most sports, reading, hill walking. *Address:* Fleet Battle Staff Headquarters, PP 301 Whale Island, Portsmouth, Hants PO2 8ER. *T:* (023) 9254 8171; *e-mail:* philip.jones586@mod.uk. *Clubs:* Caledonian, New, Royal Scots (Edinburgh).

JONES, Prof. Philip Douglas, PhD; FRMetS; Professor, since 1998, and Director, since 2003, Climatic Research Unit, School of Environmental Sciences, University of East Anglia; *b* 22 April 1952; *s* of late Douglas Idris Jones and Peggy Rita Yvonne Jones; *m* 1973, Ruth Anne Shackleton; one *s* one *d*. *Educ:* Univ. of Lancaster (BA Envmtl Scis 1973); Univ. of Newcastle upon Tyne (MSc Engrg Hydrol. 1974; PhD Hydrol. 1977). FRMetS 1992. Sen. Res. Associate, 1976–94, Reader, 1994–98, Co-Dir, 1998–2003, Climatic Res. Unit, Sch. of Envmtl Scis, UEA. Member, Editorial Board: Internat. Jl Climatol., 1989–94; Climatic Change, 1992–. Sec., Internat. Commn for Climatol., 1987–95. MAE 1998; Mem., Amer. Meteorol. Soc., 2001. Hugh Robert Mill Medal, 1995, Internat. Jl Climatol. Prize, 2002, RMetS; Hans Oeschger Medal, Eur. Geophysical Soc., 2002. *Publications:* (ed with R. S. Bradley) Climate since AD 1500, 1992, 2nd edn 1995; (ed Jtly) Climatic Variations and Forcing Mechanisms of the Last 2000 Years, 1996; (contrib.) Climate and Climate Impacts: the last 1000 years, 2001; (ed with D. Camuffo) Improved Understanding of Past Climatic Variability from Early Daily European Instrumental Sources, 2002; chapters in peer reviewed in books; contrib. Climate Change. *Recreation:* playing bridge for local club and for Norfolk. *Address:* Climatic Research Unit, University of East Anglia, Norwich NR4 7TJ. *T:* (01603) 592090, *Fax:* (01603) 507784; *e-mail:* p.jones@uea.ac.uk.

JONES, Philip Graham, CEng, FIChemE, FIExpE; occasional part-time safety adviser, since 1995; Deputy Director of Technology and Health Sciences Division, Health and Safety Executive, 1986–95; *b* 3 June 1937; *s* of Sydney and Olive Jones; *m* 1961, Janet Ann Collins; one *s* three *d*. *Educ:* Univ. of Aston in Birmingham (BSc). Eur Ing 1989. Professional positions in UK explosives industry, 1961–68 and 1972–76; service with Australian Public Service, 1969–71, with UK Civil Service, 1976–95; HM Chief Inspector of Explosives, 1981–86. Mem., Accreditation Bd, 1987–90, Professional Develt Cttee, 1988–91, IChemE. Chairman: Nat. Certification Scheme for Inservice Inspection Bodies, 1995–98; Engrg Inspection Technical Cttee, UK Accreditation Service, 1996–2001. Safety Advr, Severn Valley Rly, 1995–. Chm., Wenlock Olympian Soc., 2004–07. *Publications:* articles in The Chemical Engineer, Explosives Engineer, and railway jls. *Recreations:* walking, reading, curling.

JONES, Ven. Philip Hugh; Archdeacon of Lewes and Hastings, since 2005; *b* 13 May 1951; *m* 1979, Anne Atkinson; two *s* two *d*. *Educ:* Leys Sch., Cambridge; Chichester Theol Coll. Admitted solicitor, 1975. Ordained deacon, 1994, priest, 1995; Curate, Horsham, 1994–97; Vicar, Southwater, 1997–2005. RD Horsham, 2002–05. *Recreations:* ornithology, medieval history, music (esp. choral). *Address:* 27 The Avenue, Lewes, E Sussex BN7 1QT. *T:* (01273) 479530.

JONES, Philip John; QC 2006; *s* of Colin and Sally Jones; *m* 1990, Philippa Seal; one *s* one *d*. *Educ:* Ynysawdre Comprehensive Sch.; Hertford Coll., Oxford (BCL, MA); Dalhousie Univ., Canada (LLM). Called to the Bar, Lincoln's Inn, 1985; Jun. Counsel to the Crown, 1994–2006. Chm., Disciplinary Appeal Panel, LIFFE, 2000–. Mem., YMCA.

Address: 6 New Square, Lincoln's Inn, WC2A 3QS. *T:* (020) 7242 6105, *Fax:* (020) 7405 4004; *e-mail:* pjones@serlecourt.co.uk.

JONES, (Piers) Nicholas L.; *see* Legh-Jones.

JONES, Raymond Francis, OBE 1986; HM Diplomatic Service, retired; Chairman, Holywell Hook Heath Ltd, 2001–02 (Director, 1996–2002); *b* 15 Nov. 1935; *s* of late Hugh and Jessie Jones; *m* 1957, Maurag Annat (*d* 1994); two *d. Educ:* Liverpool Collegiate Sch. Nat. Service, RAF, 1954–56. Joined Foreign Office, 1953; served Amman, Tokyo, Cairo, Accra, 1956–70; Second Sec., FCO, 1970–73; Consul, Seattle, 1973–78; First Sec., 1978; on loan to DoI, 1978–82; New Delhi, 1982–86; Dep. Consul-Gen., Chicago, 1986–91; High Comr, Honiara, Solomon Is, 1991–95. *Recreations:* music, sport, reading. *Address:* Flat 5, Holywell, Hook Heath Road, Woking GU22 0LA.

JONES, Prof. Raymond Leonard, PhD; Professor of Social Work, Kingston University and St George's Medical School, since 2008; *b* 21 Oct. 1949; *s* of Leonard and Pauline Jones; *m* 1973, Mary Elaine Abbott; one *s* one *d. Educ:* Redruth Grammar Sch.; Univ. of Bath (BSc 1st Cl. Hons Sociol. 1972; MSc 1981; PhD 1983). CQSW 1972. Asst Warden, Mental Health Hostel, Cornwall CC, 1967–68; Social Worker, then Sen. Social Worker, Social Services, Berks CC, 1972–75; Lectr in Social Work, Univ. of Bath, 1975–80; Area Team Leader, Social Services, Wilts CC, 1981–84; Asst Divl Dir, Barnardo's, 1984–87; Divl Dir, Social Services, Surrey CC, 1987–89; Dep. Dir, Social Services, Berks CC, 1989–92; Chief Exec., Social Care Inst. for Excellence, 2001–02; Dir, Social Services, 1992–2001 and 2002–06, Adult and Community Services, 2002–06, Wiltshire CC. Chm., Marlborough Brandt Gp, 2003–07. Dep. Chm., then Chm., BASW, 2005–06. Vis. Prof. (formerly Vis. Fellow), Univ. of Bath, 1993–; Vis. Prof. (formerly Univ. Fellow), Univ. of Exeter, 1997–2004. Trustee, Quarriers, 2006–. FCMI (FIMgt 1992); AcSS 2002. Hon. Fellow, Univ. of Glos (formerly Cheltenham and Gloucester Coll.), 1995. *Publications:* Fun and Therapy, 1979; Intermediate Treatment and Social Work, 1979; Social Work with Adolescents, 1980; From Resident to Community Worker, 1983; Like Distant Relatives, 1987; chapters in books and papers on social work and social policy. *Recreations:* Rugby, fell walking. *Club:* Redruth Rugby Football.

JONES, Rhona Mary; Chief Nursing Officer, St Bartholomew's Hospital, 1969–74, retired; *b* 7 July 1921; *d* of late Thomas Henry Jones and late Margaret Evelyn King; single. *Educ:* Liverpool; Alder Hey Children's Hosp.; St Mary's Hosp., Paddington. RSCN 1943; SRN 1945; SCM 1948. Post-Registration Training, and Staff Nurse, Queen Charlotte's Hosp., 1946–48; Ward Sister, 1948–50, Departmental Sister, 1950–52, St Mary's Hosp., Paddington; General Duty Nurse, Canada, 1952–53; Asst Matron, Gen. Infirmary, Leeds, 1953–57; Dep. Matron, Royal Free Hosp., London, 1957–59; Matron, Bristol Royal Hosp., 1959–67; Matron and Superintendent of Nursing, St Bartholomew's Hosp., 1968–69. Chm., Bristol Branch, Royal Coll. of Nursing, 1962–65; Member: Standing Nursing Adv. Cttee, Central Health Services Council, 1963–74; Exec. Cttee, Assoc. Nurse Administrators (formerly Assoc. Hosp. Matrons for England and Wales), 1963–74; Area Nurse Trng Cttee, SW Region, 1965–67; NE Metropolitan Area Nurse Training Cttee, 1969–74; E London Group Hosp. Management Cttee, 1969–74. Vice-Pres., Bristol Royal Hosp. Nurses League. *Recreations:* reading, travel, listening to music. *Address:* Bedford Citizens Charter House, 1A Kimbolton Road, Bedford MK40 2PU. *T:* (01234) 365868.

JONES, Richard; operatic and theatrical director; *b* London. *Opera productions* include: English National Opera: The Love of Three Oranges, Die Fledermaus, 1993; Pelleas and Melisande (also for Opera North), 1995; From Morning to Midnight (David Sawer), 2001; Lulu, 2002; The Trojans, 2003 (Olivier Award); The Bitter Tears of Petra von Kant, 2005; Royal Opera: Der Ring des Nibelungen, 1994–95 (Evening Standard Award); Lady Macbeth of Mtsensk, 2004 (Olivier Award); L'Heure Espagnol, and Gianni Schicchi, 2007; Welsh National Opera: Hansel and Gretel, 1998 (Olivier Award); The Queen of Spades, 2000; Wozzeck, 2005; Glyndebourne: Flight (Jonathan Dove), 1998; Euryanthe, 2002; Macbeth, 2007; Der fliegende Holländer, 1993, Jenufa, 1997, The Cunning Little Vixen, 2006, Amsterdam; Julius Caesar (Opernwelt Prodn of Year), 1994, The Midsummer Marriage, 1998, The Cunning Little Vixen, 2006, Munich; L'enfant et les Sortilèges, and Der Zweig, Paris, 1998; Un ballo in maschera, 1999 ((jtly) Designer of the Year, 2000), La Bohème, 2001, Bregenz Fest.; The Fiery Angel, Brussels, 2007; Billy Budd, Frankfurt, 2007; Hansel and Gretel, Metropolitan Opera, 2007; Rusalka, Copenhagen, 2008; *theatre productions* include: Too Clever by Half (Olivier Award); The Illusion (Evening Standard Award), A Flea in Her Ear, 1989, Old Vic; Into the Woods, Phoenix, 1990 (Olivier and Evening Standard Awards); Le Bourgeois Gentilhomme, 1992, Tales from the Vienna Woods, 2003, NT; Holy Mothers, Royal Court, 1999; Six Characters Looking for an Author, 2001, Hobson's Choice, 2003, The Good Soul of Szechuan, 2008, Young Vic; A Midsummer Night's Dream, RSC, 2002; in New York: La Bête, 1991; Black Snow, 1992; All's Well That Ends Well; Titanic, 1997; Wrong Mountain, 1999. *Address:* c/o Judy Daish Associates, 2 St Charles Place, W10 6EG.

JONES, Prof. Richard Anthony Lewis, PhD; FRS 2006; Professor of Physics, University of Sheffield, since 1998; *b* 7 March 1961; *s* of Rev. Robert Cecil Jones and Sheila Howell Jones; *m* 1998, Dulcie Anne Jordan; one *s* one *d. Educ:* Denstone Coll.; St Catharine's Coll., Cambridge (BA Natural Scis 1983; PhD Physics 1987). Postdoctoral Res. Associate, Cornell Univ., 1987–89; Asst Lectr, 1989–94, Lectr, 1994–98, Univ. of Cambridge. *Publications:* Polymers at Surfaces and Interfaces (with R. W. Richards), 1999; Soft Condensed Matter, 2002; Soft Machines: nanotechnology and life, 2004; more than 100 papers in learned jls. *Recreations:* rock climbing, mountain walking. *Address:* Department of Physics and Astronomy, University of Sheffield, Hicks Building, Hounsfield Road, Sheffield S3 7RH. *T:* (0114) 222 4530; *e-mail:* r.a.l.jones@sheffield.ac.uk.

JONES, Rev. Richard Granville; Chairman of East Anglia District, Methodist Church, 1983–93; President of the Methodist Conference, 1988–89; *b* 26 July 1926; *s* of Henry William and Ida Grace Jones; *m* 1955, Kathleen Stone; three *d. Educ:* Truro School, Cornwall; St John's Coll., Cambridge (MA); Manchester Univ. (BD). Instructor Officer, RN, 1947–49. Methodist Minister in Plymouth East, 1949–50; Area Sec., SCM, 1953–55; Minister: Sheffield North Circuit, 1955–59; Sheffield Carver Street, 1959–64; Birkenhead, 1964–69; Tutor, Hartley Victoria Coll., Manchester, 1969–78, Principal 1978–82; Minister, Fakenham and Wells Circuit, 1982–83. Editor, Epworth Review, 1991–2005. Hon. DD Hull, 1988. *Publications:* (ed) Worship for Today, 1968; (with A. Wesson) Towards a Radical Church, 1972; How goes Christian Marriage?, 1978; Groundwork of Worship and Preaching, 1980; Groundwork of Christian Ethics, 1984; What to Do?: Christians and ethics, 1999. *Recreations:* walking, reading, writing. *Address:* 35 Davies Road, West Bridgford, Nottingham NG2 5JE. *T:* (0115) 914 2352.

JONES, Richard Henry; QC 1996; a Recorder, since 2000; *b* 6 April 1950; *s* of Henry Ingham Jones and Betty Marian Jones; *m* 1989, Sarah Jane Wildsmith; one *s* one *d. Educ:* Moseley Grammar Sch., Birmingham; St Peter's Coll., Oxford (MA Jurisp.). Called to the Bar, Inner Temple, 1972; in practice, 1973–80; Legal Adviser: Crown Life Insurance Gp, 1980–82; Financial Times Gp, 1982–86; in practice, 1986–. *Publication:* Investigations and Enforcement, 2001. *Recreations:* cricket and Rugby (spectating), sailing, ski-ing. *Address:* 5 Fountain Court, Steelhouse Lane, Birmingham B4 6DR. *T:* (0121) 606 0500. *Clubs:* Royal Automobile, MCC; London Scottish Football.

JONES, Richard Hugh Francis; HM Diplomatic Service; Consul-General, Basra, since 2006; *b* 28 Sept. 1962; *s* of late Lynn Jones and Audrey Comley. *Educ:* Dulwich Coll.; Merton Coll., Oxford (MA). Joined FCO, 1983; Arabic lang. trng, 1984–86; Third, later Second Sec., Abu Dhabi, 1986–89; FCO, 1989–94; First Sec., UK Perm. Rep. to EU, Brussels, 1994–98; Dep. Hd, Common Foreign and Security Policy Dept, FCO, 1998–2000; Counsellor, Dep. Hd, EU Dept (Internal), FCO, 2000–03; Ambassador to Albania, 2003–06. *Recreations:* music, places, words, the past, food. *Address:* c/o Foreign and Commonwealth Office, King Charles Street, SW1A 2AH.

JONES, Richard Mansell M.; *see* Mansell-Jones.

JONES, Prof. R(ichard) Merfyn, PhD; FRHistS; Professor of Welsh History, since 1994, Vice-Chancellor, since 2004, Bangor University (formerly University of Wales, Bangor); *b* 16 Jan. 1948; *s* of John Edwin Jones and Ellen Jones; *m* 1st, 1969, Dr Jill Lovecy (marr. diss. 2003); two *s*; 2nd, 2004, Dr Nerys Patterson (*née* Thomas). *Educ:* Univ. of Sussex (BA 1st cl. Hons 1968); Univ. of Warwick (MA; PhD 1976). Sen. Researcher, ESRC Coalfield Hist. Project, UC, Swansea, 1971–74; Lectr, then Sen. Lectr in Mod. Hist., Dept of Continuing Educn, Univ. of Liverpool, 1975–90; Sen. Lectr, Dept of Hist. and Welsh Hist., Univ. of Wales, Bangor, 1990–94. Chm., Higher Educn Wales, 2006–; Vice-Pres., UUK, 2006–. Writer and presenter of TV historical documentaries. Gov., BBC, 2002–06. Hon. Patron, Bevan Foundn, 2005–. FRHistS 1996. *Publications:* The North Wales Quarrymen 1874–1922, 1981; Cymru 2000: Hanes Cymru yn yr Ugeinfed Ganrif (History of Wales in the Twentieth Century), 1999; numerous articles in specialist jls. *Recreations:* mountaineering, cooking, Rugby. *Address:* Bangor University, Bangor, Gwynedd LL57 2DG; *e-mail:* merfyn.jones@bangor.ac.uk. *Club:* Athenæum.

JONES, (Robert) Alun; QC 1989; *b* 19 March 1949; *s* of late Owen Glyn Jones and Violet Marion Jones (*née* Luxton); *m* 1974, Elizabeth Clayton; one *s* three *d. Educ:* Oldershaw Grammar Sch., Wallasey, Cheshire; Bristol Univ. (BSc 1970). Called to the Bar, Gray's Inn, 1972. Asst Recorder, 1988–92; Recorder, 1992–96. *Publication:* Jones on Extradition, 1995, 2nd edn 2001, (jtly) 3rd edn, as Jones and Doobay on Extradition and Mutual Assistance, 2005. *Recreations:* bridge, cricket, gardening. *Address:* 37 Great James Street, WC1N 3HB. *T:* (020) 7440 4949.

JONES, Dr (Robert) Brinley, CBE 2000; FSA; President: National Library of Wales, 1996–2007 (Member, Court and Council, 1974–82); University of Wales, Lampeter, since 2007; *b* 27 Feb. 1929; *yr s* of John Elias Jones and Mary Ann Jones (*née* Williams); *m* 1971, Stephanie Avril Hall; one *s. Educ:* Tonypandy Grammar Sch.; University Coll. Cardiff (BA Wales 1st cl. Hons 1950; DipEd 1951; Fellow 1984); Jesus Coll., Oxford (DPhil 1960); Internat. Inst. for Advanced Studies, Clayton, Mo (MA 1984). FSA 1971. Commissioned RAF, 1955; Educn Officer, RAF Kidlington and Bicester, 1955–58. Asst Master, Penarth Grammar Sch., 1958–60; Lectr, UC Swansea, 1960–66; Asst Registrar, Univ. of Wales, 1966–69; Dir, Univ. of Wales Press, 1969–76; Warden, Llandovery Coll., 1976–88. Member: Literature Cttee, Welsh Arts Council, 1968–74, 1981–1987; Bd, British Council, 1987–96 (Chm., Welsh Cttee, 1987–96); Broadcasting Standards Council, 1988–91. Chairman: European Assoc. of Teachers, 1965; Dinefwr Tourism Gp, 1988–96; Carmarthenshire Tourist Forum, 1998–2007. Chm., Mgt Cttee, Univ. of Wales Centre for Advanced Welsh and Celtic Studies, 2002–07. Member: Council: St David's UC (later Univ. of Wales), Lampeter, 1977–95 (Hon. Fellow 1987); Trinity Coll., Carmarthen, 1984–2003 (Vice-Chm., 1998–2003; Hon. Fellow, 2003); Court: UC Swansea (later Univ. of Wales, Swansea), 1983–2007 (Hon. Fellow 2002); Univ. of Wales, 1997–2007; Univ. of Wales, Aberystwyth, 1997–2007; Univ. of Wales, Cardiff, 1997–2007; Governing Body, Church in Wales, 1981–2004 (Chairman: Provincial Validating Bd for Ministerial Educn, 1990–; Cathedrals and Churches Commn, 1994–2004; Church in Wales Publications, 1998–2001); Managing Trustee, St Michael's Theol Coll., 1982–94. Hon. Mem., Druidic Order, Gorsedd of Bards, 1979–; Mem., Welsh Acad., 1981–; Vice-Pres., Llangollen Internat. Musical Eisteddfod, 1989–. Fellow, Royal Commonwealth Soc., 1988–91. Editor, The European Teacher, 1964–69. Hon. DD Faraston Theol Seminary, Longview, WA, 1993; Hon. DLitt: Greenwich, 1997; Glamorgan, 2008; DUniv. Wales, 2006. *Publications:* The Old British Tongue, 1970; (ed and contrib.) Anatomy of Wales, 1972; (ed with M. Stephens) Writers of Wales, 1970– (100 titles published); (ed with R. Bromwich) Astudiaethau ar yr Hengerdd: studies in old Welsh poetry, 1978; Introducing Wales, 1978, 3rd edn 1988; Prifysgol Rhydychen a'i Chysylltiadau Cymreig, 1983; Certain Scholars of Wales, 1986; (ed with D. Ellis Evans) Cofio'r Dafydd, 1987; (contrib.) C. N. D. Cole, The New Wales, 1990; (introd.) Songs of Praises: the English hymns and elegies of William Williams Pantycelyn 1717–1791, 1991, 2nd edn 1995; Prize Days: a headmaster remembers his school 1976–1987, 1993; William Salesbury, 1994; A Lanterne to their Feete: remembering Rhys Prichard 1579–1644, 1994; Floreat Landubriense, 1998; The Particularity of Wales, 2001; World-Wide Wales, 2005; Sir John Williams *Bart*, MD, 1840–1926, 2007; articles and reviews in learned jls. *Recreations:* music, farming, walking. *Address:* Drovers Farm, Porthyrhyd, Llanwrda, Dyfed SA19 8DF. *T:* (01558) 650649.

JONES, Sir Robert (Edward), Kt 1989; author; sporting and political commentator; Founder, Robt Jones Holdings Ltd, 1961 (Chairman, 1982–92); *b* 24 Nov. 1939; *s* of Edward Llewyllan and Joyce Lillian Jones; three *s* five *d. Educ:* Victoria Univ. of Wellington. Leader, New Zealand Party, Gen. Elect., 1984. Chm., NZ Winter Olympics Cttee, 1988. New Zealand Commemoration Medal, 1990. *Publications:* New Zealand Boxing Yearbooks, 1972 and 1973; Jones on Property, 1977, 6th edn 1979; NZ The Way I Want It, 1978; Travelling, 1980; Letters, 1981; Wimp Walloping, 1989; Prancing Pavonine Charlatans, 1990; 80's Letters, 1990; Punchlines, 1991; A Year of It, 1992; Treading Water, 1993; Prosperity Denied—How the Reserve Bank Harms New Zealand, 1996; Memories of Muldoon, 1997; My Property World, 2005; Jones on Management, 2008; *novels:* The Permit, 1984; Full Circle, 2000; Ogg, 2002; True Facts, 2003; Degrees For Everyone, 2004. *Recreations:* reading, writing, gardening, trout-fishing, tennis, travel, golf, wind-surfing. *Address:* Melling, Lower Hutt, New Zealand; Darling Point, Sydney, Australia.

JONES, Prof. Robert Maynard, FBA 1993; Fellow, Yr Academi Gymreig, 1995; Professor of Welsh Language and Literature, University of Wales, 1980–89, now Professor Emeritus; *b* 20 May 1929; *s* of Sydney Valentine Jones and Mary Edith Jones; *m* 1952, Anne Elizabeth James; one *s* one *d. Educ:* Univ. of Wales (BA 1949; MA 1951; PhD 1965; DLitt 1979); Univ. of Ireland; Laval Univ., Québec. Teaching in Llanidloes and Llangefni, 1952–56; Lectr, Trinity Coll., Carmarthen, 1956–58; University of Wales, Aberystwyth: Lectr in Educn, 1958–66; Lectr, Sen. Lectr, Reader, Prof. and Head of Dept of Welsh Language and Literature, 1966–89. Chm., Yr Academi Gymreig (Welsh Acad. of Letters), 1975–79; Vice-President, UCCF, 1990–95. *Publications include:* Y Gân Gyntaf, 1957; Crwydro Môn, 1957; Nid yw Dŵr yn Plygu, 1958; I'r Arch, 1959; Y Tair Rhamant,

1960; Bod yn Wraig, 1960; Rhwng Taf a Thaf, 1960; Graddio Geirfa, 1962; Émile, 1963; Cyflwyno'r Gymraeg, 1964; Cymraeg i Oedolion, I & II, 1965–66; Y Dyn na Ddaeth Adref, 1966; Yr Ŵyl Ifori, 1967; Ci wrth y Drws, 1968; Highlights in Welsh Literature, 1969; Daw'r Pasg i Bawb, 1969; System in Child Language, 1970; Pedwar Emynydd, 1970; Sioc o'r Gofod, 1971; Allor Wydn, 1971; Traed Prydferth, 1973; Tafod y Llenor, 1974; (with M. E. Roberts) Cyfeiriadur i'r Athro Iaith I–III, 1974–79; Llenyddiaeth Gymraeg 1936–1972, 1975; Gwlad Llun, 1976; Llên Cymru a Chrefydd, 1977; Pwy laddodd Miss Wales, 1977; Seiliau Beirniadaeth, 4 vols, 1984–88; Hunllef Arthur, 1986; (with Gwyn Davies) The Christian Heritage of Welsh Education, 1986; (with Gwyn Thomas) The Dragon's Pen, 1986; Llenyddiaeth Gymraeg 1902–1936, 1987; Selected Poems (trans. Joseph P. Clancy), 1987; Blodeugerdd Barddas o'r 19 Ganrif, 1988; (with Rhiannon Ifans) Gloywi Iaith I–III, 1988; Casgliad o Gerddi, 1989; Crio Chwerthin, 1990; Dawn Gweddwon, 1991; Language Regained, 1993; Cyfriniaeth Gymraeg, 1994; Canu Arnaf, Vol. I, 1994, Vol. II, 1995; Crist a Chenedlaetholdeb, 1994; Epistol Serch a Selsig, 1997; Tair Rhamant Arthuraidd, 1998; Ysbryd y Cwlwm, 1998; Ynghylch Tawelwch, 1998; O'r Bedd i'r Crud, 2000; Mawl a'i Gyfeillion, 2000; Mawl a Gelynion ei Elynion, 2002; Ôl Troed, 2003; Dysgu Cyfansawdd, 2003; Beirniadaeth Gyfansawdd, 2003; Rhy Iach, 2004; Y Fadarchen Hudol, 2005; Meddwl y Gynghanedd, 2005. *Recreation:* walking. *Address:* Tandderwen, Ffordd Llanbadarn, Aberystwyth SY23 1HB. *T:* and *Fax:* (01970) 623603.

JONES, Robin Francis McN.; *see* McNab Jones.

JONES, Roger; *see* Jones, James R.

JONES, Rear-Adm. Roger Charles M.; *see* Moylan-Jones.

JONES, Prof. Roger Hugh, DM; FRCP, FRCGP, FRCPE, FMedSci; Wolfson Professor of General Practice, and Head, Department of General Practice and Primary Care, King's College London School of Medicine (formerly Guy's, King's and St Thomas's Medical School, King's College London), since 1993; *b* 11 Nov. 1948; *s* of (Sydney Elsom) Vernon Jones and Phyllis Marion Elsie Jones (*née* Yemm); *m* 1998, Prof. Janice Rymer; one *s* one *d* (and one *s* decd). *Educ:* Monmouth Sch.; St Peter's Coll., Oxford (MA 1973); St Thomas's Hosp. Med. Sch. (BM BCh 1973); Univ. of Southampton (DM 1990). MRCP 1976, FRCP 2000; FRCGP 1990; FRCPE 1992. House Surgeon and House Physician, St Richard's Hosp., Chichester, 1973–74; Registrar and Res. Fellow, Royal Sussex Co. Hosp., Brighton, and KCH, London, 1974–79; GP, Andover, 1979–84; Sen. Lectr in Primary Health Care, Univ. of Southampton, 1984–91; William Leech Prof. of Primary Health Care, Univ. of Newcastle upon Tyne, 1991–93; Dean for Ext. Affairs, 2001–07, Dean for Teaching, 2002–06, KCL. FMedSci 1998; FHEA 2007. FRSA 1996. Ed., Family Practice, 1990–2004. *Publication:* (Ed. in Chief) Oxford Textbook of Primary Medical Care, 2003. *Recreations:* literature, travel, golf, ski-ing, bridge. *Address:* 56 Scotts Sufferance Wharf, 5 Mill Street, SE1 2DE. *T:* (020) 7394 9586, *Fax:* (020) 7848 4102; *e-mail:* roger.jones@kcl.ac.uk. *Club:* Athenæum.

JONES, Roger Kenneth; Secretary, Co-operative Wholesale Society, 1996–98; *b* 10 Sept. 1947; *s* of George Ephraim Jones and Winifred Annie Jones; *m* 1972, Caroline Ruth Proctor; three *d*. *Educ:* Abbeydale Grammar Sch., Sheffield; Manchester Univ. (BA Hons Econs 1969). Called to the Bar, Gray's Inn, 1977; Asst Sec., Manchester Ship Canal Co., 1977–83; Dep. Sec., CWS Ltd, 1983–96; Secretary: Unity Trust Bank, PLC, 1984–92; Co-operative Bank PLC, 1992–96. Mem., UK Co-operative Council, 1991–98. Hon. Pres., Co-operative Law Assoc., 1999–. Hon. Chm., Manchester Cathedral Country Home, 2002–07.

JONES, Sir Roger (Spencer), Kt 2005; OBE 1996; Chairman, ZooBiotic Ltd, since 2005; *b* 2 July 1943; *s* of Richard David Jones and Gwladys Jones; *m* 1970, Ann Evans; one *s* one *d*. *Educ:* Bala Boys' Grammar Sch.; Univ. of Wales (BPharm); Univ. of Bradford (MSc). MRPharmS 1968. Area Manager, then Marketing Planning Manager, Wellcome Foundn Ltd, 1968–82; Man. Dir, Nigeria, Smith Kline & French Ltd, 1982–83; with Penn Pharmaceuticals Ltd, 1983–2000 (Chm., 1986–2000). Nat. Gov. for Wales, BBC, 1997–2003; Mem., S4C Broadcasting Authy, 2004–. Chairman: Gwent TEC, 1993–98; TEC SE Wales, 1998–2000; Council of Welsh TECs, 1995–2001; Welsh Develt Agency, 2002–06. Non-exec. Dir, Powys Healthcare NHS Trust, 1993–2000. Chm., Wales Inst. of Dirs, 1995–2002. Chairman: Children in Need, 1999–; Carmarthen Heritage Regeneration Trust, 2004–; Chm., Nat. Trust Wales Cttee, 2006– (Dep. Chm., 2005–06); Bd Mem., Botanic Gdns of Wales, 2005–. Pres., YMCA Wales, 2000–. Chm. Council, Univ. of Wales, Swansea, 2005–. DUniv Glamorgan, 1997; Hon. DSc Wales, 2000. *Recreations:* salmon and trout fishing, shooting, nature conservation. *Address:* Battle House, Battle, Brecon LD3 9RW. *T:* (01874) 611777. *Club:* Athenæum.

JONES, Prof. Ronald Mervyn, MD; FRCA; Director of Continuing Education and Professional Development, and Editor of Bulletin, Royal College of Anaesthetists, 1999–2002; *b* 24 April 1947; *s* of Comdr Glyn Owen Jones, RN and Doris Woodley Jones; *m* 1st, 1970, Angela Christine Parsonage (marr. diss.); one *s* one *d*; 2nd, 1989, Caroline Ann Marshall; two *d*. *Educ:* Devonport High Sch., Plymouth; Univ. of Liverpool (MB ChB 1971; MD 1990). FRCA 1978. Karolinska Inst., Stockholm, 1978; Univ. of Michigan, 1979–80; Consultant, Nottingham Hosps, 1981–82; Sen. Lectr and Hon. Consultant, Guy's Hosp. and Med. Sch., 1982–90; Foundn Prof. of Anaesthetics and Hd of Dept, ICSM at St Mary's, London, 1990–99. Mem. Council, Royal Coll. of Anaesthetists, 1997–2002. Academician, European Acad. Anaesthesiologists, 1984; Hon. Life Mem., Australian Soc. Anaesthetists, 1988. *Publications:* (ed jtly) Medicine for Anaesthetists, 3rd edn 1989; (ed jtly) Clinical Anaesthesia, 1996. *Recreations:* art history, sailing. *Address:* Kermolet, Treverec, 22290 Côtes d'Armor, France. *Club:* Royal Naval Sailing Assoc.

JONES, Prof. Ronald Samuel, OBE 1998; DVSc; FRCVS; FIBiol; JP; Professor of Veterinary Anaesthesia, 1991–2001, now Emeritus, and Head of Department of Anaesthesia, 1995–2000, University of Liverpool; *b* 29 Oct. 1937; *s* of Samuel and Gladys Jane Jones; *m* 1962, Pamela Evans; two *d*. *Educ:* High Sch. for Boys, Oswestry; Univ. of Liverpool (BVSc 1960; MVSc; DVA); DrMedVet Berne, 1980; DVSc Pretoria, 1991. FRCVS 1981; FIBiol 1987. University of Glasgow: house surgeon, 1960–61; Asst, 1961–62; University of Liverpool: Lectr, 1962–77; Sen. Lectr, 1977–86; Reader, 1986–90; Dean, Faculty of Vet. Sci., 1989–93. Visiting Professor: Univ. of Zurich, 1975; Cornell Univ., 1980, 1993; Univ. of Pretoria, 1994; Univ. of Valdivia, 2001, 2002, 2003; Univ. of Vienna, 2002, 2003. Member: Home Office Adv. Council on the Misuse of Drugs, 1994–2001; Medicines Commn, 1997–2005. Royal College of Veterinary Surgeons: Mem. Council, 1986–98; Treas., 1993–95; Jun. Vice-Pres., 1995–96; Pres., 1996–97; Sen. Vice-Pres., 1997–98. Mem., EC Adv. Cttee of Vet. Trng, 1990–93. FLS 2003; FRSA 1996. JP Liverpool City, 1981–2007. Hon. FRCA 2001. John Henry Steele Medal, RCVS, 1989; Coll. Medal, Royal Coll. Anaesthetists, 1996. *Publications:* (jtly) Principles of Veterinary Therapeutics, 1994; contrib. chapters to books and vet. and med. jls. *Recreations:* horse-racing, fly-fishing, vegetable gardening, philately. *Address:* 7 Birch Road, Prenton, Merseyside CH43 5UF. *T:* (0151) 653 9008. *Clubs:* Farmers', Royal Society of Medicine.

JONES, Samuel, CBE 1996; DL; Chairman, Heathrow Airport Consultative Committee, since 1997; *b* 27 Dec. 1939; *s* of late Samuel Jones and Sarah Johnston Jones (*née* McCulloch); *m* 1964, Jean Ann Broadhurst; two *d*. *Educ:* Morpeth Grammar Sch.; Manchester Univ. (LLB); Kent Univ. (MA). Admitted Solicitor, 1964. Asst Solicitor, Macclesfield Bor. Council, 1964–67; Asst Town Clerk, Bedford Bor. Council, 1967–71; Head of Legal Div., Coventry CBC, 1971–73; Head of Admin and Legal Dept, Sheffield Dist Council, 1973–76; Chief Exec. and County Clerk, Leics CC, and Clerk of Lieutenancy, 1976–91; Town Clerk, Corpn of London, 1991–96. Mem., Council on Tribunals, 1996–2002. Chairman: N Devon Marketing Bureau, 1996–98; Westcountry Ambulance Service NHS Trust, 1996–2004; N Devon NHS PCT, 2004–06; non-exec. Dir, Northern Devon Healthcare NHS Trust, 2006–. Mem., Adjudication Panel for England, 2002–. DL Leics, 1992. *Recreations:* dog and coastal walking. *Address:* Middleborough House, Baggy Point, Croyde, Devon EX33 1PA. *T:* (01271) 890210.

JONES, Sandy; *see* Jones, A. M.

JONES, Sarah Jane V.; *see* Vaughan Jones.

JONES, Sarah Louise R.; *see* Rowland-Jones.

JONES, Schuyler, CBE 1998; DPhil; Director (formerly Curator and Head of Department of Ethnology and Prehistory), Pitt Rivers Museum, 1985–97, and Fellow of Linacre College, 1970–97, now Emeritus Professor, Oxford University; *b* 7 Feb. 1930; *s* of Schuyler Jones, Jr and Ignace Mead Jones; *m* 1st, 1955, Lis Margit Søndergaard Rasmussen; one *s* one *d*; 2nd, 1998, Lorraine Christine Da'Luz Vieira. *Educ:* Edinburgh Univ. (MA Hons Anthropology); Oxford Univ. (DPhil Anthropology). Anthropological expeditions to: Atlas Mountains, Southern Algeria, French West Africa, Nigeria, 1951; French Equatorial Africa, Belgian Congo, 1952; East and Southern Africa, 1953; Morocco High Atlas, Algeria, Sahara, Niger River, 1954; Turkey, Iran, Afghanistan, Pakistan, India, Nepal, 1958–59; ten expeditions to Nuristan in the Hindu Kush, 1960–70; to Chinese Turkestan, 1985; Tibet and Gobi Desert, 1986; Southern China, Xinjiang, and Pakistan, 1988; Western Greenland, 1991; Greenland and E Africa, 1993. Asst Curator, Pitt Rivers Mus., 1970–71; Asst Curator and Univ. Lectr in Ethnology, 1971–85. Mem. Council, Royal Anthropological Inst., 1986–89. Trustee, Horniman Mus., 1989–94. *Publications:* Sous le Soleil Africain, 1955 (Under the African Sun, 1956); Annotated Bibliography of Nuristan (Kafiristan) and The Kalash Kafirs of Chitral, pt 1 1966, pt 2 1969; The Political Organization of the Kam Kafirs, 1967; Men of Influence in Nuristan, 1974; (jtly) Nuristan, 1979; Afghanistan, 1992; Tibetan Nomads: environment, pastoral economy and material culture, 1996; A Stranger Abroad: a memoir, 2007; numerous articles. *Recreation:* travel in remote places. *Address:* The Prairie House, 1570 N Ridgewood Drive, Wichita, KS 67208, USA.

JONES, Simon Alan, LVO 1998; Senior Partner, Gardiner & Theobald, since 2001; Managing Director, Gardiner & Theobald Management Services, since 1986; *b* 28 March 1956; *s* of Alan Reginald Walter Jones, MBE and Kathleen Jones; *m* 1998, Hon. Caroline Lucy, *d* of Baroness Billingham, *qv*; two *s*. *Educ:* King Edward VII Sch., Lytham; Reading Univ. (BSc Quantity Surveying). Joined Gardiner & Theobald, 1977: Project Dir on behalf of the Royal Household, Windsor Castle Fire Restoration, 1993–97. Trustee, Historic Royal Palaces, 1998–. Lt Col, Engrg and Logistics Staff Corp., 2001–. *Recreations:* tennis, golf, squash. *Address:* 32 Bedford Square, WC1B 3JT. *T:* (020) 7209 3333, *Fax:* (020) 7209 1850; *e-mail:* s.jones@gardiner.com. *Clubs:* All England Lawn Tennis; Cumberland Lawn Tennis (Chm.); Highgate Golf.

JONES, Simon Martin Dedman; Chair: Cardiff and Vale NHS Trust, since 2003; NHS Wales Confederation, since 2006; *b* 10 June 1958; *s* of Rev. Canon William David Jones and Sheila Mary Jones; *m* 2005, Lesley Ann Bird; one *s* two *d*. *Educ:* Mexborough Grammar Sch.; Durham Wearside Secondary Sch.; Exeter Univ. (BA Hons Politics). Business Manager, Rebecca, News Mag. of Wales, 1982–83; Research officer: TGWU, 1985–89; Wales TUC, 1989–93; Chief Exec., Wales Co-op. Centre, 1994–2004. Lead Chair, NHS Trusts in Wales, 2004–07. Mem. Bd, Charities Commn, 2007–. Member: S Glamorgan HA, 1989–96; Bro Taf HA, 1996–2003 (Chm., 2000–03). Chm., Welsh Assembly and Govt Commn to Review Voluntary Sector Scheme, 2003–04. Ind. Mem. Bd, RCT Homes, 2007–. Presenter, On the Fly, Radio Wales, 2005, 2006, 2007. Mem., Llandysul Angling Assoc. *Recreations:* surfing, ski-ing, fly fishing and fly tying. *Address:* Cardiff and Vale NHS Trust, Cardigan House, Heath Park, Cardiff CF14 4XN; *e-mail:* simon.jones57@ntlworld.com. *Club:* Cardiff and Vale NHS Sports and Social.

JONES, Sir Simon (Warley Frederick) Benton, 4th Bt *cr* 1919; JP; *b* 11 Sept. 1941; *o s* of Sir Peter Fawcett Benton Jones, 3rd Bt, OBE, and Nancy Benton Jones (*d* 1974); *S* father, 1972; *m* 1966, Margaret Fiona (OBE 1995, DL), *d* of David Rutherford Dickson; three *s* two *d*. *Educ:* Eton; Trinity College, Cambridge (MA). JP Lincolnshire, 1971 (Chm., Lincs Magistrates' Courts Cttee, 1996–2000); High Sheriff, Lincs, 1977. *Heir: s* James Peter Martin Benton Jones, *b* 1 Jan. 1973. *Address:* Irnham Hall, Grantham, Lincs NG33 4JD. *T:* (01476) 550212; 19 Sopley, Christchurch, Dorset BH23 7AX.

JONES, Stanley; *see* Jones, John S.

JONES, Stephen; *see* Jones, John S.

JONES, Stephen Morris, CBE 2005; Senior Partner, The In Practice Partnership, management consultants, since 2005; *b* 12 March 1948; *s* of late Owain Morus Jones and Sylvia Blanche Jones (*née* Moss); *m* 1970, Rosemary Diana Pilgrim; one *s* two *d*. *Educ:* Univ. of Manchester (BA Hons Town Planning, 1970). MRTPI 1972. Asst Chief Exec., Bolton MBC, 1978–85; Chief Executive: Blackburn BC, 1985–90; Wigan MBC, 1990–2005. Mem., Soc. of Local Govt Chief Execs, 1985–. *Recreations:* family, walking, sport, reading, S Africa. *Address:* The In Practice Partnership, 5 Lostock Park Drive, Bolton BL6 4AH.

JONES, Stephen O.; *see* Oliver-Jones.

JONES, Stephen Roger Curtis; Trustee, Employability Forum, since 2003; *b* 31 March 1944; *s* of Roger Henry Curtis Jones and Kate Alice Jones (*née* Pearson); *m* 1973, Janet Corkett; two *d*. *Educ:* Brentwood Sch., Essex; Univ. of Southampton (BA Hons French 1967; MA French 1968); Cambridge/RSA Cert. TEFLA, 1996. MoD, 1968–71; UK Delegn to NATO, 1971–73; DES, 1973–81 (Private Sec. to Sec. of State, Rt Hon. Shirley Williams, 1976–78); Asst Dir, City of London Poly., 1982–85; Department of Education and Science: Staff Inspector, HM Inspectorate, 1986–88; Head, Internat. Relations Div., 1988–92; Head of Internat. Relns, Youth and Gen. Br., DFE, 1992–94. Chm. Govs, Centre for Info. on Lang. Teaching and Res., 1996–2003. Comenius Fellow, CILT, 2004. *Recreations:* walking, choral singing. *Address:* Marne, Southdown Road, Woldingham, Surrey CR3 7DP. *T:* (01883) 653145; *e-mail:* jstjones@btinternet.com.

JONES, Stephen William, CB 2007; Director, Finance and Performance, Local Government Association, since 2007. *Educ:* King's Sch., Macclesfield; Balliol Coll., Oxford (BA 1976). FCMA 2006. Inland Revenue, subseq. HM Revenue & Customs, 1976–2006: Dir, Large Business Office, 2000–03; Finance Dir, 2003–06. *Address:* Local Government Association, Smith Square, SW1P 3HZ. *T:* (020) 7664 3171.

JONES, Stewart Elgan; QC 1994; a Recorder, since 1990; *b* 20 Jan. 1945; *s* of late Gwilym John Jones and of Elizabeth (*née* Davies); *m* 1979, Jennifer Anne (*née* Syddall); two *d*, and one step *s* one step *d*. *Educ:* Cheltenham Coll.; Queen's Coll., Oxford (MA Mod. Langs). Called to the Bar, Gray's Inn, 1972, Bencher, 2002; Mem., Western Circuit. *Recreations:* home, hearth, the great outdoors. *Address:* 3 Paper Buildings, Temple, EC4Y 7EU. *T:* (020) 7583 8055. *Club:* Athenæum.

JONES, Rev. Stewart William; Rector, St Martin-in-the Bullring, Birmingham, with St Andrew's, Bordesley, since 2005; *b* 17 March 1957; *s* of William Jones and Nettie Jean Jones; *m* 1st, 1982, Susan Kathleen Griffith (*d* 1990); one *d*; 2nd, 1992, Julie Marie Perkin; one *s* one *d*. *Educ:* Heriot-Watt Univ. (BA Hons Business Orgn); Bristol Univ. (Dip. Social Admin); Trinity Coll., Bristol (BA Hons Theol.). Grad. mgt trainee, National Westminster Bank, 1979–80; worker, Bristol Cyrenians, 1980–81; Supervisor, Bristol Churches Community Prog., 1983–85; ordained deacon 1988, priest 1989; Curate, St Mary's, Stoke Bishop, Bristol, 1988–92; Priest-in-charge, St Luke's, Brislington, Bristol, 1992–97; Archbp of Canterbury's Diocesan Chaplain and Tait Missioner, 1997–2003; Priest-in-charge, All Saints', Canterbury, 2001–05; Area Dean, Canterbury, 2002–05. Hon. Provincial Canon, Canterbury Cathedral, 2002–05. *Publications:* The Teaching of Jesus, 1994; The Touch of Jesus, 1995. *Recreations:* cooking, sport on TV, films, reading. *Address:* St Martin's Rectory, 37 Barlows Road, Edgbaston, Birmingham B15 2PN.

JONES, Dr (Sybil) Angela (Margaret), (Mrs Michael Pearson), FFPH; Consultant in Public Health Medicine, North (formerly North West) Thames Regional Health Authority, 1985–96; *b* 23 Aug. 1940; *d* of Cyril and Ida Jones; *m* 1964, Dr Michael Pearson; three *s* one *d*. *Educ:* Cranford House Sch.; King's College London (AKC); King's Coll. Hosp. (MB BS). Dist MO, Victoria Health Authy, 1982–85. Member: Tech. Sub-Gp of Achieving a Balance, 1988–92; Standing Cttee on Postgrad. Med. Educn, 1989–96 (Chm.), working gp on Health of the Nation); Jt Planning Adv. Cttee, 1988–92; Chm., Regl Med. Manpower and Personnel Gp, 1988–92. *Publications:* articles on med. manpower and public health issues in learned jls. *Recreations:* opera, dining with friends.

JONES, Tecwyn, CMG 2002; OBE 1974; FRES, CBiol, FIBiol; Chairman, BioNET-INTERNATIONAL Consultative Group, since 2000; Life President, BioNET-INTERNATIONAL, since 2002; consultant; *b* 7 Feb. 1929; *s* of Owen and Lily Jones; *m* 1952, Joan Peggy, (Joy), Edwards; three *s*. *Educ:* Aberaeron Co. Sch.; Imperial Coll., London (BSc Hons; ARCS). FRES 1952 (Hon. FRES 2001); FIBiol 1974; CBiol 1979. Entomologist i/c W African Timber Borer Res. Unit, Gold Coast/Ghana, 1952–59; Hd, Biol. and Forestry Divs, Dep. Dir, then interim Dir, E African Agric. and Forestry Res. Orgn, Kenya, 1959–74; Dep. Dir, Centre for Overseas Pest Res. and Natural Resources Inst., ODA, 1974–89; pest mgt and quarantine consultant, FAO, Africa and Asia, 1989–92; Dir, Internat. Inst. of Entomol., CAB Internat., UK, 1992–95; Founder 1993, and Dir, Technical Secretariat, BioNET-INTERNAT., 1993–2000. Ed., E African Agric. and Forestry Jl, 1963–74. Chm. Council, Internat. Bee Res. Assoc., 1977–90. Hon. Prof. of Entomol., Sch. of Pure and Applied Biol./Bioscis, Univ. of Cardiff (formerly UC, Cardiff), 1987–2002. Trustee, 2003–, Vice-Pres., 2004–07, Royal Entomol Soc. of London; Mem., Internat. Trust for Zool Nomenclature, 2006– (Mem., Mgt Cttee, 2006–). Chairman: Age Concern, Ceredigion, 2003–; Chairs and Vice-Chairs Cttee, Age Concern, All Wales, 2005–07; Age Concern Partnership, Wales, 2006– (Mem., 2004–06, Chm., 2006–, Exec. Cttee). Chairman: Senior Citizens' Club, Aberaeron, 2001–; Cross Inn and Maenygroes Retirement Assoc., 2004–. *Publications:* contrib. numerous scientific and technical papers, reports and bulletins on tropical pests of agric. and forestry, plant quarantine and R&D, incl. networking; conceptual papers on BioNET-INTERNAT., a global network for taxonomy to support sustainable devel t and implement the Convention on Biol Diversity. *Recreations:* amateur dramatics, the countryside, gardening, walking. *Address:* Perthygwenyn, New Quay, Ceredigion SA45 9TG. *T:* and *Fax:* (01545) 560662; Weston, South Road, Aberaeron, Ceredigion SA46 0DP. (01545) 571208. *Club:* Royal Commonwealth Society.

JONES, Prof. Terence Valentine, FREng; Donald Schultz Professor of Turbomachinery, 1988–2004, and Director, Technology Centre in Aerodynamics and Heat Transfer, 1993–2004, Oxford University; Professorial Fellow, St Catherine's College, Oxford, 1988–2004, now Emeritus Fellow; *b* 14 Feb. 1939; *s* of Albert Duncalf Jones and Frances Jones; *m* 1962, Lesley Lillian (*née* Hughes); one *s* one *d*. *Educ:* William Hulme's Grammar School, Manchester; Lincoln College, Oxford (MA, DPhil 1966). Lecturer: Keble College, Oxford, 1971–77; Lincoln College, Oxford, 1976–80; Jesus College, Oxford, 1977–86; Rolls Royce Tutorial Fellow, St Anne's College, Oxford, 1979–88. Senior Academic Visitor, NASA Lewis Research Center, Ohio, 1986. FREng 2000. Royal Soc. Esso Energy Award, 1996. *Publications:* articles on turbomachinery, heat transfer and fluid dynamics in NATO, ASME and ARC jls and conf. procs. *Recreations:* hiking, paragliding. *Address:* Department of Engineering Science, Parks Road, Oxford OX1 3PJ. *T:* (01865) 288734.

JONES, Terry, (Terence Graham Parry Jones); writer, film director and occasional performer; *b* 1 Feb. 1942; *s* of Alick George Parry Jones and Dilys Louisa Newnes; *m* Alison Telfer; one *s* one *d*. *Educ:* Esher C of E Primary Sch.; Royal Grammar Sch., Guildford; St Edmund Hall, Oxford. *Television and radio:* wrote for various TV shows, 1966–68; wrote and performed in series: Do Not Adjust Your Set, 1968–69; The Complete and Utter History of Britain, 1969; Monty Python's Flying Circus, 1969–75; wrote (with Michael Palin): Secrets (play), 1974; Ripping Yarns, 1976–79; presented: Paperbacks; Victorian Values, (radio); wrote and directed The Rupert Bear Story (documentary), 1981; wrote, directed and presented, So This Is Progress, 1991; co-wrote and presented: Crusades, 1995; Ancient Inventions, 1999; Gladiators, the Brutal Truth, 2000; Hidden History of Ancient Egypt/Ancient Rome, 2002/03; The Anti-Renaissance Show (radio), 2002; wrote and presented: Terry Jones's Medieval Lives, 2004; The Story of One, 2005; Terry Jones' Barbarians, 2006. *Films:* And Now For Something Completely Different, 1971; directed (with Terry Gilliam), co-wrote and performed, Monty Python and the Holy Grail, 1975; directed, co-wrote and performed Monty Python's Life of Brian, 1978; Monty Python's Meaning of Life, 1983 (Grand Prix Spécial du Jury, Cannes); directed Personal Services, 1986; wrote, directed and performed: Erik the Viking, 1989; The Wind in the Willows, 1996; Asterix and Obelix (English version), 2000. Wrote libretto and directed musical play, Evil Machines, São Luiz, Lisbon, 2008. *Publications:* Chaucer's Knight, 1980, 3rd edn 1984; Fairy Tales, 1981, 4th edn 1987; The Saga of Erik the Viking, 1983, 3rd edn 1986; Nicobobinus, 1985, 2nd edn 1987; Goblins of the Labyrinth, 1986; The Curse of the Vampire's Socks, 1988; Attacks of Opinion, 1988; Fantastic Stories, 1992; (with Brian Froud) Lady Cottington's Pressed Fairy Book, 1994; (with Alan Ereira) Crusades, 1994; The Knight and the Squire, 1997; (with Brian Froud) Lady Cottington's Pressed Fairy Journal, 1998; The Lady and the Squire, 2000; Who Murdered Chaucer?, 2003; (with Alan Ereira) Medieval Lives, 2004; Terry Jones' War on the War of Terror, 2005; (with Alan Ereira) Terry Jones' Barbarians, 2006; (with Michael Palin): Dr Fegg's Encyclopeadia (sic) of all World Knowledge, etc; Ripping Yarns, etc; contrib. to the various Monty Python books. *Recreation:* sleeping.

JONES, Thomas Glanville; barrister; a Recorder of the Crown Court, 1972–99; *b* 10 May 1931; *s* of late Evan James and Margaret Olive Jones; Welsh; *m* 1964, Valma Shirley Jones; three *s*. *Educ:* St Clement Dane's Grammar Sch.; University Coll., London (LLB). Called to Bar, 1956. Hd of Angel Chambers, 1972–. Chm., Jt Professional Cttees of Swansea Local Bar and Swansea Law Soc. and W Wales Law Soc., 1976–; Founder Mem. and Exec. Cttee Mem., Wales Medico-Legal Soc., 1990; Founder Mem. and Trustee, Swansea Legal Charitable Foundn, 1994. Exec. Mem., Swansea Festival of Music and the Arts, 1967; Pres., Guild for Promotion of Welsh Music, 1996– (Chm., 1970); Mem., Grand Theatre Trust, 1988–. *Recreations:* Welsh culture, Rugby, reading, music, poetry, gardening. *Address:* Gelligron, 12 Eastcliff, Southgate, Swansea SA3 2AS. *T:* (01792) 233118. *Club:* Ffynone (Swansea).

JONES, Ven. (Thomas) Hughie; Archdeacon of Loughborough, 1986–92, now Emeritus; *b* 15 Aug. 1927; *s* of Edward Teifi Jones and Ellen Jones; *m* 1949, Beryl Joan Henderson; two *d*. *Educ:* William Hulme's Grammar School, Manchester; Univ. of Wales (BA, LLM); Univ. of London (BD); Univ. of Leicester (MA; PhD 2002). Warden and Lectr, Bible Trng Inst., Glasgow, 1949–54; Minister, John Street Baptist Church, Glasgow, 1951–54; RE specialist, Leicester and Leics schs, 1955–63; Sen. Lectr in RE, Leicester Coll. of Educn, 1964–70; deacon 1966, priest 1967; Vice-Principal, Bosworth Coll., 1970–75; Principal, Hind Leys College, Leics, 1975–81; Rector, The Langtons and Stonton Wyville, 1981–86. Hon. Canon of Leicester Cathedral, 1983–86. Bishop's Officer, Clergy Widows and Retired Clergy, Ecclesiastical Law Soc., 1996–2003 (Vice-Chm., 1990; Hon. Exec. Officer, 1993–96); Member: Selden Soc., 1991; Canon Law Soc. of GB and Ireland, 1993. *Publications:* (contrib. OT articles) New Bible Dictionary, 1962, 2nd edn 1980; Old Testament, religious education and canon law articles in relevant jls. *Recreations:* entomology, genealogy, Welsh interests, canon law. *Address:* Four Trees, 68 Main Street, Thorpe Satchville, Melton Mowbray, Leics LE14 2DQ. *Clubs:* Carlton, Millbank; Leicestershire (Leicester).

JONES, Timothy; *see* Jones, D. T.

JONES, Timothy Aidan; *see* Marschall Jones, T. A.

JONES, Sir Tom; *see* Woodward, Sir T. J.

JONES, Sir Trevor; *see* Jones, Sir O. T.

JONES, Trevor; Chief Executive, Avon, Gloucestershire and Wiltshire Strategic Health Authority, 2004–06; *b* 23 Dec. 1950; *s* of John Jones and Florence Mary Jones (*née* Rogerson); *m* 1974, Hazel Oliver. Local Govt Finance, 1969–78; Sen. Asst Regl Treas., Northern RHA, 1978; Dep. Treas., S Manchester HA, 1983; Waltham Forest Health Authority: Dir of Finance, 1986; Dist Gen. Manager, 1989–92; Chief Exec., Forest Healthcare NHS Trust, 1992–95; Gen. Manager, then Chief Exec., Lothian Health Bd, 1995–2000; Chief Exec., NHS Scotland and Hd of Health Dept, Scottish Exec., 2000–04. Chm., Gen. Managers' Gp, Scottish Health Bd, 1998–2000. Director: Pinnacle Staffing Gp plc, 2006–; NHS Direct, 2007–; Patient Safety Agency, 2007–. Dir, Sport England SW, 2005–. CPFA, FCCA, CCMI. *Recreations:* golf, photography. *Address:* Cedar Lodge, 4 The Knoll, Malmesbury, Wilts SN16 9LJ. *Club:* Durham CC.

JONES, Trevor Charles B.; *see* Bish-Jones.

JONES, Trevor David K.; *see* Kent-Jones.

JONES, Trevor Mervyn, CBE 2003; PhD; FRSC, FPS; Director, Allergan Inc., since 2004; *b* 19 Aug. 1942; *s* of Samuel James Jones and Hilda May Jones (*née* Walley); *m* 1966, Verity Ann Bates; one *s* one *d*. *Educ:* Wolverhampton Grammar Sch.; King's Coll. London (BPharm Hons 1964; PhD 1967; FKC 1994). CChem 1975; FRSC 1978; FPS 1987; MCPP 1982. Lectr, Univ. of Nottingham, 1967–72; Hd of Pharmaceutical Develt, Boots Co. Ltd, 1972–76; Develt Dir, Wellcome Foundation Ltd, 1976–87; R&D Dir and Mem. Bd, Wellcome plc, 1987–94; Dir-Gen., Assoc. of British Pharmaceutical Industry, 1994–2004. Director: Wellcome Biotechnology Ltd, 1983–93; Wellgen Inc. USA, 1990–93; Merlin Partners, 1996– (Chm., Scientific Adv. Bd, 1996–); Sen. R&D Advr, Esteve SA, 2004–. Visiting Professor: KCL, 1984– (Vice Chm. Council, 2001–08); Univ. of Strathclyde, 1988–93; Adjunct Prof., Univ. of N Carolina, 1985–90. Non-executive Chairman: Health Reform Investment Trust plc, 1996–98; ReNeuron, 2000–; Chairman: Kinetique Biomedical Seed Fund, 2001–; Synexus Ltd, 2008–; Director: Next Pharma Ltd, 2004–; BAC bv, 2005–08; People in Health, 2006–; Verona Pharma plc, 2007–. Member: Expert Cttees, British Pharmacopoeia, 1976–89; Pharmacy Res. Bd, CNAA, 1978–83; UK Govt Medicines Commn, 1982–94; Adv. Bd on Human Genome, Cabinet Office, 1991–96; Expert Wkg Party on Use of Tissues, Nuffield Council for Bioethics, 1992–97; Exec. Cttee, Internat. Fedn of Pharmaceutical Manufrs, 1994–2004; Bd of Mgt, European Fedn of Pharmaceutical Industry Assoc., 1994–2004; Nat. Biological Standards Bd Review, 1995–97; Advisory Board: MRC, 2001–04; MRC Social, Genetic and Develtl Psychiatric Res. Centre, Inst. of Psych., 2002–; MRC Centre for Neurodegeneration Res.; Prime Minister's Task Force on Competitiveness of Pharmaceutical Industry, 2001; Chm., Adv. Gp on Genetics Res., 2003–07. Pres., Internat. Commn on Technology, 1979–83, Member: Pharmaceut. Scis Bd, 1980–84, 1996–, Fédn Internat. Pharmaceutique; Merk/WHO Commn on Intellectual Property Rights, Innovation and Public Health, 2004–06. Founder and Mem. Bd, Medicines for Malaria Venture, 1999–2007. Trustee: Epilepsy Res. Foundn, 1996–2004; Northwick Park Inst. of Med. Res., 1998–2004; British Urological Foundn, 2005–07. Life Sci. Advr, Fleming Family and Partners, 2006–. Liveryman, Co. of Apothecaries, 1989–. FR.SocMed 2007. Hon. FFPM 1995; Hon. FRCP 2005; Hon. Fellow: London Sch. of Pharmacy, 1998; British Pharmacol. Soc., 2005. For. Mem., Acad. Nat. de Pharmacie, 2005–. Hon. PhD Athens, 1993; Hon. DSc: Strathclyde, 1994; Nottingham, 1998; Bath, 2000; Bradford, 2003. Harrison Meml Medal, 1987, Charter Gold Medal, 1996, RPSGB; Gold Medal, Comenius Univ., 1992. *Publications:* Drug Delivery to the Respiratory Tract, 1987; Advances in Pharmaceutical Sciences, 1993. *Recreations:* golf, gardening, Wales RU. *Address:* Woodhyrst House, Friths Drive, Reigate, Surrey RH2 0DS. *Club:* Athenæum.

JONES, Ven. Trevor Pryce; Archdeacon of Hertford, since 1997; *b* 24 April 1948; *s* of John Pryce Jones and Annie (*née* Jepson); *m* 1976, Susan Diane Pengelley; one *s* one *d*. *Educ:* Dial Stone Sch., Stockport; St Luke's Coll., Exeter; Univ. of Southampton (BEd, BTh); Salisbury and Wells Theol Coll.; Univ. of Wales, Cardiff Law Sch. (LLM). Asst Teacher and Lay Chaplain, Shaftesbury Grammar Sch., 1969–73; ordained deacon, 1976, priest, 1977; Asst Curate, Gloucester St George, Lower Tuffley, 1976–79; Warden, Bishop Mascall Centre, Ludlow, and Mem., Hereford Diocesan Educn Team, 1979–84; Diocesan Communications Officer, Hereford, 1981–86; Team Rector, Hereford S Wye

Team Ministry, 1984–97. OCF, 1985–97. Prebendary, Hereford Cathedral, 1993–97; Hon. Canon, Cathedral and Abbey Church of St Alban, 1997. Chm., St Alban's and Oxford Ministry Course, 1998–2007; Vice-Chm., E Anglia Ministerial Trng Course, 2005–. Bishops' Selector, 2001–08. Mem., Legal Adv. Commn, Gen. Synod of C of E, 2006–. Chairman: Reach Out Projects, 1998–; Rural Strategy Gp, dio. St Albans, 2001–. Chm., Hockerill Educnl Foundn, 2005–. *Recreations:* country walks, vintage buses and trains. *Address:* St Mary's House, Church Lane, Stapleford, Hertford SG14 3NB. *T:* (01992) 581629, *Fax:* (01992) 558745; *e-mail:* archdhert@stalbans.anglican.org. *Club:* Royal Commonwealth Society.

JONES, Prof. Tudor Bowden, DSc; FInstP; CEng, FIET; Professor of Ionospheric Physics, 1980–98, Head of Department of Physics and Astronomy, 1993–98, University of Leicester, now Professor Emeritus; *b* 8 Nov. 1934; *s* of Idris Jones and Tydvil Ann Jones (*née* Bowden); *m* 1960, Patricia Brown; two *s*. *Educ:* County Grammar Sch., Ystradgynlais; University Coll. of Wales, Swansea (BSc Hons, PhD, DSc). FInstP 1975; CEng 1987; FIET (FIEE 1987). Res. Asst, UCW, Aberystwyth, 1959; University of Leicester: Lectr in Physics, 1960–69; Sen. Lectr, 1969–75; Reader, 1975–80. PPARC Nat. Co-ordinator for Solar Terrestrial Physics, 1998–2001. Guest Res. Scientist at various Govt estabts in UK and overseas, 1970–; Sen. Resident Associate, Nat. Oceanic and Atmospheric Admin Lab., Boulder, Colo, 1971–72. Leverhulme Emeritus Fellowship, 2001–02. Appleton Lectr, IEE, 1997. Appleton Prize, Internat. Union of Radio Sci. and Royal Soc., 1993; Charles Chree Prize and Medal, Inst. of Physics, 1995. *Publications:* (ed) Oblique Incidence Radio Wave Propagation, 1966; numerous papers in scientific jls on ionospheric physics and radio wave propagation. *Recreation:* classical music. *Address:* Department of Physics and Astronomy, University of Leicester, University Road, Leicester LE1 7RH. *T:* (0116) 252 3561.

JONES, Prof. Vaughan Frederick Randal, DCNZM 2002; FRS 1990; Professor of Mathematics, University of California, Berkeley, since 1985; *b* Gisborne, NZ, 31 Dec. 1952; *s* of J. H. Jones and J. A. Goodfellow (*née* Collins); *m* 1979, Martha Weare Jones (*née* Myers); one *s* two *d*. *Educ:* St Peter's Sch., Cambridge, NZ; Auckland Grammar Sch.; Univ. of Auckland (schol.; Gillies schol.; Phillips Industries Bursary; BSc, MSc 1st Cl. Hons); Ecole de Physique, Geneva (Swiss Govt schol.; F. W. W. Rhodes Meml schol.); Ecole de Mathématiques, Geneva (DèsSc Mathematics); Vacheron Constantin Prize, Univ. de Genève. Asst, Univ. de Genève, 1975–80; E. R. Hedrick Asst Prof., UCLA, 1980–81; University of Pennsylvania: Vis. Lectr, 1981–82; Asst Prof., 1981–84; Associate Prof., 1984–85. Alfred P. Sloan Res. Fellowship, 1983; Guggenheim Fellowship, 1986. Hon. Vice Pres., Internat. Guild of Knot-tyers, 1991. Fields Medal, 1990. *Publication:* Coxeter graphs and Towers of algebras, 1989. *Recreations:* music, tennis, squash, ski-ing. *Address:* Mathematics Department, University of California, Berkeley, Berkeley, CA 94720–3840, USA. *T:* (510) 6424196.

JONES, Vera June, (Mrs Ernest Jones); *see* Di Palma, V. J.

JONES, Victoria Mary Taylor; *see* Heywood, V. M. T.

JONES, Walter; *see* Jones, William W. A.

JONES, Wilfred, CMG 1982; HM Diplomatic Service, retired; *b* 29 Nov. 1926; *m* 1952, Millicent Beresford; two *s*. Joined Foreign Office, 1949; served in Tamsui, Jedda, Brussels, Athens and FCO, 1950–66; First Sec. (Admin), Canberra, 1966–68; FCO, 1968–71; Copenhagen, 1971–74, Blantyre, 1974–75; Lilongwe, 1975–77; FCO, 1977–81; High Comr to Botswana, 1981–86. *Recreations:* sailing, golf, tennis.

JONES, William George Tilston; independent telecommunications consultant, 1990–2004; *b* 7 Jan. 1942; *s* of late Thomas Tilston Jones and Amy Ethel Jones; *m* 1965, Fiona Mary; one *d*. *Educ:* Portsmouth Grammar School; Portsmouth Polytechnic (BSc; Hon. Fellow 1989). CEng, FIET. Post Office Engineering Dept, 1960; Head, Electronic Switching Gp, 1969; Head, System X Develt Div., 1978; Dir, System Evolution and Standards, 1983; Chief Exec., Technology, BT, 1984; seconded as Exec. in Residence, Internat. Management Inst., Geneva, 1987; Sen. Strategy Adviser, BT, 1988. Member: IEE Electronics Divl Bd, 1984–89; Parly IT Cttee, 1985–87; Chairman: IT Adv. Bd, Polytechnic of Central London, 1984–87; Adv. Gp, Centre of Communication and Information Studies, 1988–89; SE Centre, IEE, 1989–90; Dir, Technology Studies, British Telecom, 1988–90. Governor, Polytechnic of Central London, 1985–89. *Publications:* contribs on telecommunications to learned jls. *Recreations:* theatre, tennis, camping, making furniture.

JONES, William Pearce A.; *see* Andreae-Jones.

JONES, (William) Walter (Alexander); Principal, Kolej Tuanku Ja'afar, Malaysia, since 2005; *b* 11 Sept. 1949; *s* of Rev. Eric Jones and Elizabeth Jones; *m* 1974, Frances Linda Grant; one *s* two *d*. *Educ:* Campbell Coll., Belfast; Queens' Coll., Cambridge (MA; PGCE); Inst. of Education, Univ. of London (MA). Asst Teacher, St Edward's C of E Comprehensive, Romford, 1973–75; Head of Economics, King's Coll. Sch., Wimbledon, 1976–87; Second Master, King's Sch., Bruton, 1987–93; Headmaster, Royal Grammar Sch., Worcester, 1993–2005. *Publications:* contrib. to British Economic Survey. *Recreations:* Rugby, walking. *Address:* Kolej Tuanku Ja'afar, Mantin, 71700, Negeri Sembilan, Malaysia.

JONES, Wyn; *see* Jones, Graham W.

JONES, Sir Wynn Normington H.; *see* Hugh-Jones.

JONES, Wynne; *see* Jones, E. W.

JONES PARRY, Sir Emyr, GCMG 2007 (KCMG 2002; CMG 1992); PhD; HM Diplomatic Service, retired; UK Permanent Representative to the United Nations, 2003–07; *b* 21 Sept. 1947; *s* of Hugh Jones Parry and Eirwen Jones Parry (*née* Davies); *m* 1971, Lynn Noble; two *s*. *Educ:* Gwendraeth Grammar Sch.; University Coll. Cardiff (BSc, Dip Crystallography); St Catharine's Coll., Cambridge (PhD; Hon. Fellow, 2008). FO, 1973–74; First Sec., Ottawa, 1974–79; FO, 1979–82; First Sec., UK Rep. to EC, Brussels, 1982–86; Dep. Head, Office of Pres. of European Parlt, 1987–89; Head, EC Dept (External), FCO, 1989–93; Minister, British Embassy, Madrid, 1993–96; Dep. Pol Dir, FCO, 1996–97; Dir, EU, FCO, 1997–98; Political Dir, FCO, 1998–2001; UK Perm. Rep., UK Delegn to NATO, 2001–03. Pres., Aberystwyth Univ., 2008–. Hon. FInstP 2004; Hon. Fellow: Univ. of Cardiff, 2003; Univ. of Wales Aberystwyth, 2006; Trinity Coll., Carmarthen, 2007. Hon. Dr Laws Wales, 2005. *Publications:* various scientific articles. *Recreations:* gardening, theatre, reading, sport. *Address:* c/o Foreign and Commonwealth Office, King Charles Street, SW1A 2AH. *Club:* Glamorgan County Cricket.

JONES-PARRY, Tristram, MA; Head Master, Westminster School, 1998–2005; *b* 23 July 1947; *s* of Sir Ernest Jones-Parry and late Mary (*née* Powell). *Educ:* Westminster Sch.; Christ Church, Oxford (MA). Operational Researcher, NCB, 1968–70; Maths Teacher, Dulwich Coll., 1970–73; Head of Maths, Housemaster and Under Master, Westminster Sch., 1973–94; Headmaster, Emanuel Sch., 1994–98. *Recreations:* reading, walking, cycling, travelling. *Address:* 4 Bainton Road, Oxford OX2 7AF. *Club:* Athenæum.

JONKMAN, (Pieter Jan) Hans, Hon. GCVO 1982; Commander, Order of Orange Nassau; Cross of Honour, Order of House of Orange Nassau; Secretary-General of the Permanent Court of Arbitration, The Hague, 1990–99; *b* 2 June 1925; *s* of Jan A. Jonkman and Johanna L. M. de Bruïne; *m* 1959, Maria Elisabeth te Winkel; one *s* two *d*. *Educ:* Univ. of Leyden (law degree). Entered Min. of Foreign Affairs, 1955; served Paris, Pretoria, Leopoldville, Buenos Aires; Min. of Foreign Affairs, 1962–66; Brussels, Beirut, Jakarta; Min. of Foreign Affairs, 1975–80; Grand-Officer for Special Services of HM Queen of the Netherlands, 1980–82; Grand-Master, House of The Queen, 1982–87; Ambassador of the Netherlands to UK and concurrently to Iceland, 1987–90. Holds various foreign decorations.

JONSSON, Lars Ossian; artist, author, ornithologist; *b* 22 Oct. 1952; *s* of Sven and May Jonsson; *m* 1985, Ragnhild Erlandson; two *s* two *d*. *Educ:* autodidact. Wildlife artist, mainly specialising in birds; debut show at age 15, Nat. Mus. of Natural Hist., Stockholm, 1968. Hon. Dr Uppsala, 2002. Master Wildlife Artist, Leigh Yawkey Wordson Art Mus., Wis, USA, 1988. *Publications:* Birds of Sea and Coast, 1978; Birds of Lake, River, Marsh and Field, 1978; Birds of Wood, Park and Garden, 1978; Birds of Mountain Regions, 1980; Bird Island, 1984; Birds of Europe: with North Africa and the Middle East, 1992; Birds and Light: the art of Lars Jonsson, 2002. *Recreations:* guitar music, travelling, art. *Address:* Hamra, Norrgårde 311, 620 10 Burgsvik, Sweden.

JOPLING, family name of **Baron Jopling**.

JOPLING, Baron *cr* 1997 (Life Peer), of Ainderby Quernhow in the co. of N Yorkshire; **Thomas Michael Jopling;** PC 1979; farmer; *b* 10 Dec. 1930; *s* of Mark Bellerby Jopling, Masham, Yorks; *m* 1958, Gail, *d* of Ernest Dickinson, Harrogate; two *s*. *Educ:* Cheltenham Coll.; King's Coll., Newcastle upon Tyne (BSc Agric. Durham). Mem., Thirsk Rural District Council, 1958–64; Mem. National Council, National Farmers' Union, 1962–64. Contested (C) Wakefield, 1959. MP (C): Westmorland, 1964–83; Westmorland and Lonsdale, 1983–97. PPS to Minister of Agriculture, 1970–71; an Asst Govt Whip, 1971–73; a Lord Comr, HM Treasury, 1973–74; an Opposition Whip, March-June 1974; an Opposition spokesman on agriculture, 1974–79; Shadow Minister of Agriculture, 1975–76; Parly Sec. to HM Treasury, and Chief Whip, 1979–83; Minister of Agriculture, Fisheries and Food, 1983–87. Mem., Select Cttee on Foreign Affairs, 1987–97; Chm., Select Cttee on Sittings of the House (Jopling Report), 1991–92; Member: H of L Select Cttee on European Legislation, 2000–04, 2007– (Mem. Sub-Cttee (D) Agric., 1998–2000, (C) Defence and Foreign Policy, 2000–04 (Chm., 2001–04), (F) Home Office, 2006– (Chm., 2007–)); H of L Select Cttee on Merits of Statutory Instruments, 2003–07; Jt Sec., Cons. Parly Agric. Cttee, 1966–70. Hon. Sec., British Amer. Parly Gp, 1987–2001 (Vice Chm., 1983–86). Mem., UK Delegn to NATO Assembly, 1987–97, 2001–. Member, UK Executive: CPA, 1974–79, 1987–97 (Vice Chm., 1977–79); IPU, 1997–. Pres. Councils, EEC Agric. and Fishery Ministers, July–Dec. 1986; Leader, 1990–97, Mem., 2000–01, UK Delegn to OSCE Parly Assembly. Mem. Cttee, Assoc. of Cons. Peers, 1997–2000. Pres., Auto Cycle Union, 1989–2004. DL Cumbria, 1991–97, N Yorks, 1998–2005. Hon. DCL Newcastle, 1992. *Address:* Ainderby Hall, Thirsk, North Yorks YO7 4HZ. *T:* (01845) 567224. *Club:* Buck's (Hon.); Royal Automobile (Hon.).
See also J. Jopling.

JOPLING, Jeremy Michael Neal, (Jay); Founder, White Cube, art gallery, 1993; *s* of Lord Jopling, *qv*; *m* 1997, Samantha Taylor-Wood, *qv*; two *d*. *Educ:* Eton; Univ. of Edinburgh (MA Art Hist. 1984). *Address:* White Cube, 48 Hoxton Square, N1 6PB. *T:* (020) 7930 5373, *Fax:* (020) 7749 7480.

JORDAN, family name of **Baron Jordan**.

JORDAN, Baron *cr* 2000 (Life Peer), of Bournville in the co. of West Midlands; **William Brian Jordan,** CBE 1992; General Secretary, International Confederation of Free Trade Unions, 1995–2001; *b* 28 Jan. 1936; *s* of Walter and Alice Jordan; *m* 1958, Jean Ann Livesey; three *d*. *Educ:* Secondary Modern Sch., Birmingham. Convener of Shop Stewards, Guest Keen & Nettlefolds, 1966; full-time AUEW Divl Organiser, 1976; Pres., AEU, then AEEU, 1986–95. Mem., TUC General Council, 1986–95 (Chm., Cttee on European Strategy, 1988–95). A Gov., BBC, 1988–98. Member: NEDC, 1986–92; Engrg Industry Training Bd, 1986–91; Council, Industrial Soc., 1987–95; RIIA, 1987–; ACAS, 1987–95; Nat. Trng Task Force, 1989–92; Engrg Trng Authy, 1991–95; NACETT, 1993–95; English Partnerships, 1993–2002 (Chm., Pension Scheme, 2004–). President: European Metal-Workers Fedn, 1986–95; Exec., Internat. Metalworkers Fedn, 1986–95. Member: UN High Level Panel on Youth Employment; UN Global Compact Adv. Council; Victim Support Adv. Bd, 1990–2007; Steering Bd, Nat. Contact Point, 2007–. Fellow, World Econ. Forum. Governor: London School of Economics, 1987–2002; Manchester Business School, 1987–92; Ashridge Management Coll., 1992–; Mem. Ct of Govs, Henley Coll., 1991–. Hon. CGIA 1989. DUniv Central England, 1993; Hon. DSc Cranfield, 1995. *Recreations:* reading, keen supporter of Birmingham City FC. *Address:* 352 Heath Road South, Northfield, Birmingham B31 2BH.

JORDAN, Andrew; a Senior Immigration Judge, Asylum and Immigration Tribunal (formerly a Vice President, Immigration Appeal Tribunal), since 2003; *b* 30 Nov. 1949; *s* of Norman and Muriel Jordan; *m* 1978, Susan Jennifer Young; one *s* two *d*. *Educ:* Univ. of Warwick (LLB); Univ. of Wales, Cardiff (LLM Canon Law). Called to the Bar, Lincoln's Inn, 1973; in practice as barrister, 1973–2000 (specialized in gen. common law); Immigration Adjudicator, 2000–03. Dep. Chancellor, 2001–02, Chancellor, 2002–, Dio. Guildford. *Recreations:* music, London. *Address:* Asylum and Immigration Tribunal, Field House, 15 Breams Buildings, EC4A 1DZ.

JORDAN, Dame Carole, DBE 2006; PhD; FRS 1990; FInstP; Professor of Physics, University of Oxford, 1996–2008, now Emeritus; Wolfson Tutorial Fellow in Natural Science, Somerville College, Oxford, 1976–2008; *b* 19 July 1941; *d* of Reginald Sidney Jordan and Ethel May Jordan (*née* Waller). *Educ:* Harrow County Grammar School for Girls; University College London (BSc 1962; PhD 1965; Fellow 1991). FInstP 1973. Post-Doctoral Research Associate, Jt Inst. for Lab. Astrophysics, Boulder, Colorado, 1966; Asst Lectr, Dept of Astronomy, UCL, attached to Culham Lab., UKAEA, 1966–69; Astrophysics Research Unit, SRC, 1969–76; Oxford University: Lectr in Physics, 1976–94; Reader, Dept of Physics (Theoretical Physics), 1994–96. Member: SERC, 1985–90 (Chm., Solar System Cttee, 1983–86; Mem., Astronomy, Space and Radio Bd, 1979–86; Mem., Astronomy and Planetary Sci. Bd, 1986–90); PPARC, 1994–97. Pres., Royal Astronomical Soc., 1994–96 (Sec., 1981–90; Vice-Pres., 1990–91, 1996–97). DUniv Surrey, 1991; Hon. DSc QUB, 2008. *Publications:* scientific papers on astrophysical plasma spectroscopy and structure and energy balance in cool star coronae, in learned jls. *Address:* Department of Physics (Theoretical Physics), 1 Keble Road, Oxford OX1 3NP. *T:* (01865) 273980.

JORDAN, Edmund Patrick, (Eddie); Chief Executive Officer, Jordan Grand Prix, 1991–2004; *b* 30 March 1948; *s* of Patrick Jordan and Eileen Jordan; *m* 1979, Marie McCarthy; two *s* two *d*. *Educ:* Synge Street Sch., Dublin; Coll. of Commerce, Dublin. Winner, Irish Kart Championship, 1971; single seater racing in FF1600, 1974; winner, Irish Formula Atlantic Championship, 1978; teamed up with Stefan Johannson, Marlboro Team Ireland, for British Formula 3 Championship, 1978; Formula 2, 1979; test drove McLaren F1 car, 1979; retired from single seater racing, 1980; Founder: Eddie Jordan Racing, 1979; Jordan Grand Prix, 1991. Irish Sporting Ambassador, 1999. *Publication:* An Independent Man: the autobiography, 2007. *Recreations:* golf, music, ski-ing. *Clubs:* Sunningdale Golf, Oxfordshire Golf, Wentworth.

JORDAN, Gerard Michael, CEng; Site Director, AEA Technology Dounreay (formerly Director, Dounreay Nuclear Power Establishment, United Kingdom Atomic Energy Authority), 1987–92; *b* 25 Sept. 1929; *s* of Arthur Thomas and Ruby Eveline Jordan; *m* 1955, Vera Peers; one *s* one *d*. *Educ:* Grange Sch., Birkenhead; Univ. of Liverpool. BEng; CEng, MIMechE, 1974. Marine Engrg Officer, 1950–55; Gp Engr, Messrs Thomas Hedley Ltd, 1956–59; United Kingdom Atomic Energy Authority: Principal Professional and Technical Officer, 1959–73; Band Grade Officer, 1973–80; Asst Dir (Safety and Reliability Div.), 1980; Asst Dir (Engrg and Safety Dounreay), 1980–84; Dep. Dir (Engrg Northern Div.), 1984–85; Dir of Engrg (Northern Div.), 1985–87. *Publications:* Handbook on Criticality Data, 1974, 2nd edn 1979; various papers in Trans IMechE, Trans IChemE, Trans INucE. *Recreations:* hobby electronics, DIY, fishing. *Address:* 1 William Stumpe's Close, Malmesbury, Wilts SN16 9LD. *T:* (01666) 829380.

JORDAN, Graham Harold Ben, CB 2004; Science and Technology Director, Ministry of Defence, 2001–03; Senior Science and Technology Adviser, since 2004, and Associate Fellow, since 2007, Royal United Services Institute; *b* 1 April 1945; *s* of Harold Jordan and Violet Emily Jordan (*née* Wakefield); *m* 1977, Jean Anne Swale. *Educ:* Chislehurst and Sidcup Grammar Sch.; Downing Coll., Cambridge (Schol.; BA 1966 Nat. Scis and Chem. Eng; MA 1970); Brunel Univ. (MTech 1974 Op. Res.). DOAE, 1967–77; Dept of Chief Scientist, RAF, 1977–78; Supt, Land Air Studies Div., DOAE, 1978–82; Royal Aircraft Establishment: Supt, Air to Air Weapons Div., 1982–85; Head, Defensive Weapons Dept, 1985–87; Head, Civil Service Personnel Policy Div., HM Treasury, 1987–90; Scientific Advr (Command Inf. Systems), MoD, 1990–91; Asst Chief Scientific Advr (Capabilities), MoD, 1991–95; Dep. Chief Scientist (Scrutiny and Analysis), MoD, 1995; Dir of Central IT Unit, Cabinet Office (OPS), 1995–97; Dep. Under-Sec. of State (Science and Technol.), MoD, 1997–2001. Member: Technol. Bd, DSAC, 2004–07; European Security Res. Adv. Bd, 2005–07; NATO Sci. Cttee, 2006–. *Publication:* (with Lee and Cawsey) Learning from Experience (report), 1988. *Recreations:* riding, small scale farming, home maintenance, music.

JORDAN, Marc Lowis Aron, FSA; management consultant; *b* 12 July 1955; *s* of late Philip Jordan, MICE and Dr Louise Jordan (*née* Jackson); *m* 2000, Olivia, *d* of late Terence Kilmartin, CBE and Joanna Kilmartin; one *s*. *Educ:* William Ellis Sch.; Univ. of Exeter (BA Hons English Lit.); Courtauld Inst. of Art (MA Hist. of Art); London Business Sch. (MBA). Res. Assistant, Nat. Portrait Gallery, 1979–80; Cataloguer, Dept of Watercolours and Drawings, Phillips Auctioneers, 1981–82; Grove Dictionary of Art: Area Editor, 1985–88; Dep. Editor, 1988–92; Commissioning Editor, Phaidon Press, 1992–95; Publisher, Harvey Miller Publishers, 1998–99; Man. Dir, Acoustiguide Ltd, 1999–2003; Man. Consultant, AEA Consulting, 2003–06; Interim Dir, Contemporary Art Soc., 2006–07. Trustee, Hackney Historic Buildings Trust, 2000–04; Member: London Regl Cttee, Heritage Lottery Fund, 2001–07; Adv. Panel on European Capital of Culture 2008, 2002–03. Mem. Council, Univ. of Exeter, 2007–; Gov., Midhurst Rother Coll., 2008–. Jt author, Arts Council England Rev. of Presentation of Contemporary Visual Arts, 2005. FSA 2007. *Publications:* contribs to Apollo, Burlington Magazine, The Times, NY Times, TLS. *Recreations:* gardening, old houses, sailing. *Address:* 48 Cassland Road, E9 7AN. *Clubs:* Athenæum; Beaulieu River Sailing.

JORDAN, Michael Anthony; Chairman and Senior Partner, Cork Gully, Chartered Accountants, 1983–93; Partner, Coopers & Lybrand, Chartered Accountants, 1980–93; *b* 20 Aug. 1931; *s* of Charles Thomas Jordan and Florence Emily (*née* Golder); *m* 1st, 1956, Brenda Gee (marr. diss. 1989); one *s* one *d*; 2nd, 1990, Dorothea Rosine Estelle Coureau (*d* 2000). *Educ:* Haileybury. FCA 1956. Joined R. H. March Son & Co., 1958, Partner, 1959–68; Partner: Saker & Langdon Davis, 1963–93; W. H. Cork Gully & Co., 1968–80. Jt Inspector for High Court of IoM into the affairs of the Savings & Investment Bank Ltd, 1983. Gov., Royal Shakespeare Co., 1979–2001. Freeman, City of London; Liveryman, Bakers' Co. *Publication:* (jtly) Insolvency, 1986. *Recreations:* opera, DIY, gardening. *Address:* Ballinger Farm, Ballinger, near Great Missenden, Bucks. *T:* (01494) 863298.

JORDANOVA, Prof. Ludmilla Jane, PhD; FRHistS; Professor of Modern History, King's College London, since 2006; *b* 10 Oct. 1949; *d* of Ivan Nicholai Jordanov and Phyllis Elizabeth Jordanova (*née* Brown); *m* 1970, Simon Thomas Emmerson (marr. diss. 1974); two *d* by Karl Michael Figlio. *Educ:* Oxford High Sch. for Girls; New Hall, Cambridge (BA 1971; MA, PhD 1977); Univ. of Essex (MA 1987). FRHistS 1989. Res. Fellow, New Hall, Cambridge, 1975–78; Res. Officer, Wellcome Unit for History of Medicine, Univ. of Oxford, 1978–79; Lectr, 1980–88, Sen. Lectr, 1988–91, Prof., 1991–93, Dept of Hist., Univ. of Essex; Prof., Dept of Hist., Univ. of York, 1993–96; Prof. of Visual Arts, 1996–2005 and Dean, Schs of World Art Studies and Music, 1999–2002, UEA; Dir, Centre for Res. in the Arts, Social Scis and Humanities, Univ. of Cambridge and Fellow, Downing Coll., Cambridge, 2003–05 (on secondment). Mem., Educn Honours Cttee, 2005–07. President: British Soc. for Hist. of Sci., 1998–2000; Hist. of Sci. Sect., BAAS, 2006; Mem. Council, 1993–97, Vice-Pres., 2001–04, RHistS. FRSocMed 1999. Trustee, Nat. Portrait Gall., 2001–. *Publications:* Lamarck, 1984; Sexual Visions: images of gender in science and medicine between the Eighteenth and Twentieth Centuries, 1989; Nature Displayed: gender, science and medicine 1760–1820, 1999; Defining Features: scientific and medical portraits 1660–2000, 2000; History in Practice, 2000, 2nd edn 2006; several edited vols, book reviews, contribs to learned jls. *Recreations:* friendship, Edinburgh, travel, listening to music, art, museums, galleries. *Address:* 23 Cavendish Place, Cambridge CB1 3BH; 24 Lower Granton Road, Edinburgh EH5 3RT; *e-mail:* ludmilla.jordanova@kcl.ac.uk.

JORDON, William Eddy, CBE 2004; Headteacher, Dyke House School, Hartlepool, since 1993; *b* 17 Dec. 1947; *s* of John and Kathleen Jordon; *m* 1971, Doreen Thompson; one *s*. *Educ:* Newcastle upon Tyne Univ. (BPhil, MEd, DAES); Sunderland Polytech. (Teachers' Cert.). Hd, Phys. Educn, Marton Boarding Sch., Cheshire, 1969–73; Community Tutor and Dep. Hd (Community), Blyth Ridley High Sch., 1973–78; Hd, Referral Unit, 1978–81, Hd of House, 1981–83, Slatyford Comprehensive Sch., Newcastle upon Tyne; Sen. Teacher, Redewood Comprehensive Sch., 1983–89; Dep. Hd, Ralph Gardner High Sch., N Tyneside, 1989–93. FRSA 2004. *Recreations:* running, walking the dog, reading, fell-walking, listening to music. *Address:* Rosemount, Ovingham, Prudhoe, Northumberland NE42 6DE. *T:* (01661) 832431; Dyke House School, Mapleton Road, Hartlepool TS24 8NQ.

JOSCELYNE, Richard Patrick; British Council Director, Japan, 1991–94; *b* 19 June 1934; *s* of Dr Patrick C. Joscelyne and Rosalind Whitcombe; *m* 1st, 1961, Vera Lucia Mello (marr. diss. 1988); one *s* one *d*; 2nd, 1988, Irangani Dias. *Educ:* Bryanston; Queens' Coll., Cambridge. Teaching posts in France, Brazil and Britain, 1958–62. British Council: Montevideo, 1962; Moscow, 1967; Madrid, 1969; Director, North and Latin America Dept, 1973; Representative, Sri Lanka, 1977; Controller, Overseas Div. B (America, Pacific and Asia Div.), 1980; Controller, Finance Div., 1982; Representative, Spain, 1987. *Address:* 51385 Avenida Diaz, La Quinta, CA 92253, USA. *T:* (760) 5649588.

JOSEPH, David Philip; QC 2003; *b* 22 April 1961; *s* of late Dr Joe Joseph and of Judith Joseph (*née* Lobl); *m* 1990, Denise Bass; three *s*. *Educ:* St Paul's Sch., London; Pembroke Coll., Cambridge (BA 1982). Called to the Bar, Middle Temple, 1984; in practice specialising in internat. arbitration and commercial law. *Publication:* Jurisdiction and Arbitration Agreements and their Enforcement, 2005. *Recreations:* tennis, opera, singing, mountain walking. *Address:* Essex Court Chambers, 24 Lincoln's Inn Fields, WC2A 3ED; *e-mail:* djoseph@essexcourt.net.

JOSEPH, (Hon. Sir) James Samuel, (3rd Bt *cr* 1943, of Portsoken, City of London); *b* 27 Jan. 1955; *o s* of Baron Joseph, CH (Life Peer) and Hellen Louise (*née* Guggenheimer); *S* to baronetcy of father, 1994, but does not use the title and his name does not appear on the Official Roll of the Baronetage; *m* 1990, Sarah Jane Thwaites; two *s*. *Heir: s* Sam Nathan Joseph, *b* 7 Aug. 1991.

JOSEPH, Jenny, (Mrs C. A. Coles), FRSL; writer, lecturer and reader; *b* 7 May 1932; *d* of Louis Joseph and Florence Joseph (*née* Cotton); *m* 1961, Charles Anthony Coles (*d* 1985); one *s* two *d*. *Educ:* St Hilda's Coll., Oxford (BA Hons English). Newspaper reporter; part-time lectr for WEA and Cambridge Univ. Extra-Mural Dept, later for Bristol Univ. Extra-Mural Dept. *Publications:* The Unlooked-for Season, 1960; Rose in the Afternoon, 1974; The Thinking Heart, 1978; Beyond Descartes, 1983; Persephone, 1986; The Inland Sea, 1989; Beached Boats (with Robert Mitchell's photographs), 1991; Selected Poems, 1992; Ghosts and Other Company, 1995; Warning, 1997; Extended Similes, 1997; All the Things I See, 2000; Led by the Nose, 2002; Extreme of Things, 2006. *Address:* c/o Johnson & Alcock, Clerkenwell House, 45–47 Clerkenwell Green, EC1R 0HT. *T:* (020) 7251 0125, *Fax:* (020) 7251 2172; *e-mail:* info@johnsonandalcock.co.uk.

JOSEPH, Julian; jazz pianist and composer; *b* London, 11 May 1966. *Educ:* Berklee Sch. of Music, Boston, Mass (BA). Founder: own quartet, 1990; Julian Joseph Trio; Forum Project (8 piece); Electric Project; All Star Big Band; tours of Europe, USA, Canada, Asia, Australia and appearances at festivals. Presenter, TV series, Jazz with Julian Joseph, 1999, 2000; writer and presenter, Jazz Legends, Radio 3, 2000–. Composer, Bridgetower - A Fable of 1807 (jazz opera), UK tour, 2007. Patron, Jazz Develt Trust, 1998–. *Recordings:* The Language of Truth, 1991; Reality, 1993; Universal Traveller, 1996. *Address:* c/o James Joseph Music Management, 85 Cicada Road, SW18 2PA.

JOSEPH, Leslie; QC 1978; *b* 13 Aug. 1925; *s* of Benjamin Francis Joseph and Sarah Edelman; *m* 1st, 1964, Ursula Mary Hamilton (*d* 1988); one *s* two *d*; 2nd, 2001, Hedwig Erna Lydia Swan (*née* Pesendorfer). *Educ:* Haberdashers' Aske's, Hampstead; University Coll. London (LLB Hons). Served Army, 1943–47: Infantry, 1943–45 (Sgt); AEC, 1945–47. Called to the Bar, Middle Temple, 1953, Bencher, 1986; Master of the Revels, 1989–2000; Autumn Reader, 2003. Mem., Common Professional Examn Bd, 1989–2001 (Chm., 1996–98); Chairman: Bar Vocational Stage Sub-Cttee, 1996; Bar Vocational Course Validation Panel, 1996–97. Gov., Inns of Court Sch. of Law, 1994–96. *Recreations:* wine, water, cooking for friends. *Address:* 34 Upper Park Road, NW3 2UT. *T:* (020) 7722 3390; Church Cottage, Buckhorn Weston, Dorset SP8 5HS.

JOSEPH, Richard David; Chief Executive Officer, Arcadia Publishing International Ltd and Arcadia Publishing Inc., since 2002; *b* 6 June 1956; *s* of Philip and Pamela Joseph; *m* 1987, Nicole Beauchamp; three *s*. *Educ:* King Edward VII Sch., Johannesburg; Univ. of Witwatersrand (BCom). Higher Dip. in Accountancy, Public Accountants and Auditors Bd, SA. Articled clerk, Coopers & Lybrand, SA, 1978–80; Man. Dir, Books Etc Ltd, 1981–97; CEO, Borders (UK) Ltd, 1997–2000; Officer, Borders Gp Inc., 1997–2000. Member, Committee: Soc. of Bookmen, London, 1980–; Book Sellers' Assoc. of GB and Ireland, 1983–2000. *Recreations:* family, vacation, swimming, books, flying, boating. *Address:* 420 Wando Park Boulevard, Mount Pleasant, SC 29464, USA; *e-mail:* rjoseph@arcadiapublishing.com. *Club:* Groucho.

JOSEPH, Stephen Francis Waley, OBE 1996; Executive Director, Campaign for Better Transport (formerly Transport 2000), since 1988; *b* London, 20 April 1956; *s* of Peter and Margaret Joseph; *m* 1986, Dr Jill Bartlett; three *d*. *Educ:* University Coll. Sch., Hampstead; Queen's Coll., Oxford (BA Hons Modern Hist.). Co-ordinator, Youth Envmtl Action, 1977–78; Director: Youth Unit, Council for Envmtl Conservation, 1978–82; Youth Participation Unit, British Youth Council, 1982–85; Jt Co-ordinator, London Planning Aid Service, TCPA, 1986–88. Member: Standing Adv. Cttee on Trunk Rd Assessment, 1996–99; Commn for Integrated Transport, 1999–2005. FRSA. Lifetime Achievement Award, Nat. Transport Awards, 2005. *Publications:* Waking up Dormant Land, 1981; Urban Wasteland Now, 1989; contrib. articles and papers on aspects of transport to jls and newspapers. *Recreations:* family life, music, walking, exploring cities. *Address:* c/o Campaign for Better Transport, 12–18 Hoxton Street, N1 6NG. *T:* (020) 7613 0743, *Fax:* (020) 7613 5280; *e-mail:* stephen.joseph@bettertransport.org.

JOSEPH, His Honour Thomas John Cedric; a Circuit Judge, 1994–2008; *b* 25 Aug. 1938; *s* of Thomas Rees Joseph and Katherine Ann Joseph; *m* 1960 Mary Weston; three *d*. *Educ:* Cardigan GS; LSE (LLB). Called to the Bar, Gray's Inn, 1960; Crown Counsel, Nyasaland, 1962–64; practised at the Bar, 1964–94; Asst Recorder, 1987–92; Recorder, 1992–94; Resident Judge, Croydon Crown Court, 1998–2006. Mem., Adv. Council on Misuse of Drugs, 2001–07. *Recreations:* music, travel, collecting old wine glasses and using them. *Address:* c/o Lewes Crown Court, The Law Courts, High Street, Lewes, East Sussex BN17 1YB. *Club:* Travellers.

JOSEPH, Wendy Rose; QC 1998; **Her Honour Judge Wendy Joseph;** a Circuit Judge, since 2007; *b* 11 March 1952; *d* of late Norman Joseph and Carole Joseph (*née* Marks). *Educ:* Cathays High Sch., Cardiff; Westridge Sch. for Girls, Pasadena, Calif; New Hall, Cambridge (MA). Called to the Bar, Gray's Inn, 1975, Bencher, 2003; Asst Recorder, 1995–99; Recorder, 1999–2007. A Pres., Mental Health Review Tribunal, 2001–. *Recreation:* Mozart and the stars. *Address:* Snaresbrook Crown Court, 75 Hollybush Hill, E11 1QW.

JOSEPHSON, Prof. Brian David, FRS 1970; Professor of Physics, Cambridge University, 1974–2007, now Emeritus; Fellow of Trinity College, Cambridge, since 1962; *b* 4 Jan. 1940; *s* of Abraham Josephson and Mimi Josephson; *m* 1976, Carol Anne Olivier; one *d*. *Educ:* Cardiff High School; Cambridge Univ. BA 1960, MA, PhD 1964, Cantab. FInstP. Asst Dir of Res. in Physics, 1967–72, Reader in Physics, 1972–74, Univ. of

Cambridge. Res. Asst Prof., Illinois Univ., 1965–66; Vis., Fellow, Cornell Univ., 1971; Vis. Faculty Mem., Maharishi European Res. Univ., 1975; Visiting Professor: Wayne State Univ., 1983; Indian Inst. of Sci., Bangalore, 1984. Hon. MIEEE, 1982; For. Hon. Mem., Amer. Acad. of Arts and Scis, 1974. Hon. DSc: Wales, 1974; Exeter, 1984; Hon. PhD Bar-Ilan, 1999. Awards: New Scientist, 1969; Research Corp., 1969; Fritz London, 1970; Nobel Prize for Physics, 1973; Casys, 2000. Medals: Guthrie, 1972; van der Pol, 1972; Elliott Cresson, 1972; Hughes, 1972; Holweck, 1973; Faraday, 1982; Sir George Thomson, 1984. *Publications:* Consciousness and the Physical World, 1980 (ed jtly); The Paranormal and the Platonic Worlds (in Japanese), 1997; research papers on physics and theory of intelligence, paranormal phenomena, Platonism, the convergence of science and religion; musical composition, Sweet and Sour Harmony, 2005. *Recreations:* mountain walking, ice skating, music, astronomy. *Address:* Cavendish Laboratory, 19 J. J. Thomson Avenue, Cambridge CB3 0HE. *T:* (01223) 337260, *Fax:* (01223) 337356; *e-mail:* bdj10@cam.ac.uk; *web:* www.tcm.phy.cam.ac.uk/~bdj10.

JOSHI, Prof. Heather Evelyn, OBE 2002; FBA 2000; AcSS; Professor of Economic and Developmental Demography in Education, since 1998, and Director, Centre for Longitudinal Studies, since 2003, Institute of Education, London University; *b* 21 April 1946; *d* of Guy Malcolm Spooner, MBE and Molly Florence Spooner, MBE; *m* 1st, 1969, Vijay Ramchandra Joshi (marr. diss. 1977); 2nd, 1982, Gregory Hans David Martin; one *s* one *d*. *Educ:* St Hilda's Coll., Oxford (BA 1967, MA); St Antony's Coll., Oxford (MLitt 1970). Jun. Res. Officer, Oxford Inst. of Econs and Statistics, 1969–73; Econ. Advr, Govt Econ. Service, 1973–79; Res. Fellow, 1979–83, Sen. Res. Fellow, 1983–88, LSHTM; Sen. Res. Fellow, Birkbeck Coll., 1988–90; Sen. Lectr, LSHTM, 1990–93; Sen. Res. Fellow, subseq. Prof., City Univ., 1993–98. Dir (formerly Prin. Investigator), ESRC Millennium Cohort Study, 2000–. Pres., British Soc. for Population Studies, 1999–2001. *Publications:* (with V. R. Joshi) Surplus Labour and the City, 1976; (ed) The Changing Population of Britain, 1989; (with P. Paci) Unequal Pay for Women and Men, 1998; (ed with S. Dex) Children of the 21st Century: from birth to nine months, 2005; articles in economics, demography and social policy jls. *Recreations:* family life, listening to classical music. *Address:* Centre for Longitudinal Studies, Institute of Education, 20 Bedford Way, WC1H 0AL. *T:* (020) 7612 6874.

JOSIPOVICI, Prof. Gabriel David, FRSL; FBA 2001; Research Professor, School of Graduate Studies, University of Sussex, since 1998; *b* 8 Oct. 1940; *s* of Jean Josipovici and Sacha (*née* Rabinovitch) (*d* 1996). *Educ:* Victoria Coll., Cairo; Cheltenham Coll.; St Edmund Hall, Oxford (BA 1st Cl. Hons 1961). FRSL 1998. School of European Studies, University of Sussex: Asst Lectr in English, 1963–65; Lectr, 1965–74; Reader (part-time), 1974–84; Prof. of English, 1984–98. Lord Northcliffe Lectr, UCL, 1980–81; Weidenfeld Vis. Prof. in Eur. Comparative Lit., Univ. of Oxford, 1996–97. *Plays:* Dreams of Mrs Fraser, 1972; Evidence of Intimacy, 1973; Playback, 1973; A Life, 1974; Vergil Dying, 1976; A Moment, 1977; AG, 1977; Kin, 1982; Mr Vee, 1987; A Little Personal Pocket Requiem, 1989. *Publications: fiction:* The Inventory, 1968; Words, 1971; Mobius the Stripper, 1974; The Present, 1975; Migrations, 1977; The Air We Breathe, 1981; Conversations in Another Room, 1984; Contre-Jour, 1987; The Big Glass, 1989; In the Fertile Land, 1991; Steps, 1992; In a Hotel Garden, 1993; Moo Pak, 1994; Now, 1998; Goldberg: Variations, 2002; Everything Passes, 2006; *non-fiction:* The World and the Book, 1971, 3rd edn 1994; The Lessons of Modernism, 1977, 2nd edn 1986; Writing and the Body, 1982; The Mirror of Criticism, 1983; The Book of God, 1987, 2nd edn 1989; Text and Voice, 1992; Touch: an essay, 1996; On Trust, 1999; A Life, 2001; The Singer on the Shore, 2006. *Recreations:* walking, swimming. *Address:* 60 Prince Edward's Road, Lewes, Sussex BN7 1BH.

JOSLIN, Peter David, QPM 1983; DL; Chief Constable of Warwickshire, 1983–98; *b* 26 Oct. 1933; *s* of Frederick William Joslin and Emma Joslin; *m* 1960, Kathleen Josephine Monaghan; two *s* one *d*. *Educ:* King Edward VI Royal Grammar School, Chelmsford; Essex University. BA Hons. Joined Essex Police, 1954–74 (Police Constable to Superintendent); Chief Superintendent, Divl Comdr, Leicestershire Constabulary, 1974–76; Asst Chief Constable (Operations), Leics Constab., 1976–77; Dep. Chief Constable, Warwicks Constabulary, 1977–83. Chm., Traffic Cttee, ACPO, 1989–92. Pres., Warwickshire Assoc. for the Blind, 1993–. DL Warwickshire, 1999. *Recreations:* sport (now mainly as a spectator), house renovation, good wines, after dinner speaking. *Address:* Nash House, 41 High Street, Kenilworth, Warks CV8 1LY. *T:* (01926) 511517.

JOSPIN, Lionel Robert; Prime Minister of France, 1997–2002; *b* 12 July 1937; *s* of late Robert Jospin and Mireille Jospin (*née* Dandieu); *m*; one *s* one *d*; *m* 1994, Prof. Sylviane Agacinski; one step *s*. *Educ:* Institut d'Etudes Politiques, Paris; Ecole Nationale d'Administration. French Foreign Office, 1965–70; Prof. of Economics, Technical Univ. Inst., Paris-Sceaux, 1970–81; MP 1981–88; MEP 1984–88; French Socialist Party: Nat. Sec., various divs, 1973–81; First Sec., 1981–88 and 1995–97; Minister of State, Nat. Educn and Sports, 1988–92; Minister plenipotentiary, Foreign Office, 1992. Member: Conseil général, Haute-Garonne, 1988–2002; Conseil régional, Midi-Pyrénées, 1992–97. Grand-Croix, Ordre National du Mérite (France), 1997. *Publications:* L'invention du Possible, 1991; Propositions pour la France 1995–2000, 1995; Le Temps de Répondre, 2002; Le Monde comme je le vois, 2005. *Recreations:* basketball, tennis. *Address:* c/o Parti Socialiste, 10 Rue de Solferino, 75007 Paris, France.

JOST, H. Peter, CBE 1969; DSc; CEng; CSci; FIMechE; FIM; Hon. FIET; Chairman, Engineering & General Equipment Ltd, 1977–2006, Hon. Chairman, 2007; Director of overseas companies; Hon. Industrial Professor, Liverpool John Moores University (formerly Liverpool Polytechnic), since 1983; Hon. Professor of Mechanical Engineering, University of Wales, since 1986; *b* 25 Jan. 1921; *o s* of late Leo and Margot Jost; *m* 1948, Margaret Josephine, *o d* of late Michael and Sara Kadesh, Norfolk Is, S Pacific; two *d*. *Educ:* City of Liverpool Techn. Coll.; Manchester Coll. of Technology. Apprentice, Associated Metal Works, Glasgow and D. Napier & Son Ltd, Liverpool; Methods Engr, K & L Steelfounders and Engrs Ltd, 1943; Chief Planning Engr, Datim Machine Tool Co. Ltd, 1946; Gen. Man. 1949, Dir 1952, Trier Bros Ltd; Man. Dir, 1955–89, Chm., 1973–2000, K. S. Paul Products Ltd; Lubrication Consultant: Richard Thomas & Baldwins Ltd, 1960–65; August Thyssen Hütte AG 1963–66; Chairman: Bright Brazing Ltd, 1969–76; Peppermill Brass Foundry Ltd, 1970–76; Centralube Ltd, 1974–77 (Man. Dir, 1955–77); Associated Technology Gp Ltd, 1976–; Director: Williams Hudson Ltd, 1967–75; Stothert & Pitt, 1971–85; Fuchs Lubritech International, 2000–03. Chairman: Lubrication Educn and Res. Working Gp, DES, 1964–65; Cttee on Tribology, DTI, 1966–74; Industrial Technologies Management Bd, DTI, 1972–74; Dep. Chm., Cttee for Industrial Technologies, DTI, 1972–74; Member: Adv. Council on Technology, 1968–70; Cttee on Terotechnology, 1971–72; Consultative Gp on Sci. and Technol., FCO, 1994–99. Hon. Associate, Manchester Coll. of Science and Technology, 1962; University of Salford: Privy Council's Nominee to Ct, 1970–83; Mem. Council, 1974–84; Mem. Court, Middlesex Univ., 1996–. Mem. Council: IProdE, 1973–91 (Vice-Pres., 1975–77, Pres., 1977–78; Chm., Technical Policy Bd and Mem., Exec. Policy Cttee, 1974; Hon. Fellow, 1980); IMechE, 1974–92 (Member: Technical Bd, 1975; Finance Bd, 1979– (Chm., 1988–91); Disciplinary Bd, 1979–; Vice-Pres., 1987–92); Council of Engineering Institutions: Mem. Bd, 1977–83; Mem. Exec., 1979–83 (Mem. External Affairs Cttee, 1974–80; Chm. Home Affairs Cttee, 1980–83); Mem., Parly and Scientific Cttee, 1973– (Hon. Sec., 1990–93; Vice-Pres., 1993–95 and 1998–2001; Vice Chm., 1995–98; Mem., Gen. Purposes Cttee, 1991–; Mem. Council (formerly Steering Cttee), 1983–; Life Mem., 2002). President: Internat. Tribology Council, 1973–; Manchester Technology Assoc., 1984–85; Chm., Manchester Technology Assoc. in London, 1976–90. Chm. Trustees, Michael John Trust, 1986–. Rutherford Lectr, Manchester Technology Assoc., 1979; James Clayton Lectr, IMechE, 1981. Freeman, City of London, 1984; Liveryman, Engineers' Co., 1984. CCMI (CBIM 1984); Fellow, 1970, Life Fellow, 1986, ASME; FSME, USA, 1988 (Hon. Mem., 1977); Hon. MIPlantE, 1969; Hon. Member: Société Française de Tribologie, 1972; Gesellschaft für Tribologie, 1972; Chinese Mech. Engrg Soc., 1986; Russian (formerly USSR) Acad. of Engrg, 1991; Nat. Tribology Council of Bulgaria, 1991; Japanese Soc. of Tribologists, 1992; Slovak Tribology Soc., 1993; Ukrainian Acad. of Transport, 1994; Polish Tribolog. Soc., 1995; Belarus Acad. of Engrg and Technol., 1996; Hon. Life Mem., Soc. of Tribologists and Lubrication Engrs, USA, 1997 (Internat. Award, 1997); Hon. Fellow, Univ. of Central Lancs, 2003. Hon. DSc: Salford, 1970; Slovak Technical Univ., 1987; Bath, 1990; Technical Univ. of Budapest, 1993; Belarus Acad. of Scis, 2000; Hon. DTech CNAA, 1987; Hon. DEng: Leeds, 1989; UMIST 2004; San Fernando Valley Engineers Council (USA) Internat. Achievement Award, 1978; State of California State Legislature Commendation, 1978; Georg Vagelpohl Insignia, Germany, 1979. Sir John Larking Medal 1944, Derby Medal 1955, Liverpool Engrg Soc.; Hutchinson Meml Medal 1952, Silver Medal for Best Paper 1952–53, 1st Nuffield Award 1981, IProdE; Merit Medal, Hungarian Scientific Soc. of Mech. Engrs, 1983; Gold Medal, Slovak Tech. Univ., 1984; Colclough Medal and Prize, Inst. of Materials, 1992; Louwe Alberts Award, S African Inst. of Tribology, 1992. Gold Insignia, Order of Merit of Poland, 1986; Officer Cross, Order of Merit (Germany), 1992; Officier, Palmes Académiques (France), 1995; Decoration of Honour for Science and Art, 1st cl. (Austria), 2001. *Publications:* Lubrication (Tribology) Report of DES Cttee, 1966 (Jost Report); The Introduction of a New Technology, Report of DTI Cttee, 1973; Technology *vs* Unemployment, 1986; various papers in Proc. IMechE, Proc. IProdE, technical jls, etc. *Recreations:* music, opera, gardening. *Address:* Hill House, Wills Grove, Mill Hill, NW7 1QL. *T:* (020) 8959 3355. *Club:* Athenæum.

JOULWAN, Gen. George Alfred; Adjunct Professor, National Defense University, 2000–01; Olin Professor of National Security Studies, United States Military Academy, West Point, 1998–2000; Supreme Allied Commander, Europe, 1993–97; Commander-in-Chief, United States European Command, 1993–97; *b* 16 Nov. 1939; *m* Karen E. Jones; three *d*. *Educ:* US Mil. Acad., West Point (BS 1961); Loyola Univ. (Master of Pol Sci. 1968); US Army War Coll., Washington. Joined US Army, 1961; served Europe, US and Vietnam, 1962–73; Special Assistant: to the Pres., 1973–74; to Supreme Allied Comdr, SHAPE, 1974–75; Bn Comdr, Europe, 1975–77; US Army War College: student, 1977–78; Dir, Pol and Econ. Studies, 1978–79; Bde Comdr, Europe, 1979–81; COS, 3 Inf. Div., Europe, 1981–82; Exec. Officer to Chm., Jt Chiefs of Staff, Washington, 1982–86; US Army Europe and Seventh Army: DCS for Ops, 1986–88; Commanding General: 3rd Armoured Div., 1988–89; V Corps, 1989–90; C-in-C, US Southern Comd, Quarry Heights, Panama, 1990–93. Pres., One Team Inc. Defense Distinguished Service Medal, with two Oak Leaf Clusters (USA); Distinguished Service Medal (USA); Silver Star (with Oak Leaf Cluster) (USA). Foreign orders include: Grand Cross, Order of Merit, Hessian Order of Merit (Germany); Legion of Honour, Legion of Merit (France); Cross of Gallantry with three Gold Stars (Vietnam). *Address:* 2107 Arlington Ridge Road, Arlington, VA 22202, USA.

JOURDAN, Dr Martin Henry, FRCS; Consultant Surgeon, Guy's Hospital, since 1977, and St Thomas' Hospital, since 1982; Reader in Surgery, University of London, since 1982; *b* 7 Oct. 1941; *s* of Henry George Jourdan and Jocelyn Louise (*née* Courteney); *m* 1966, May McElwain; two *s* two *d*. *Educ:* Bishopshalt Sch., Hillingdon; Guy's Hosp. Med. Sch. (MB BS; PhD 1970; MS 1980). LRCP 1966; FRCS 1974. Lectr in Physiol., Guy's Hosp., 1967–70; MRC Travelling Fellow, Univ. of Calif, Berkeley, 1971–72; Registrar, then Sen. Registrar in Surgery, Guildford, Norwich and Guy's Hosp., 1974–77. Chm., Examrs in Surgery, Univ. of London, 1989–91; Mem., Court of Examrs, RCS, 1987–2000. Master, Soc. Apothecaries, 2001–02. *Publications:* (contrib.) The New Aird's Companion in Surgical Studies, 2000; papers on surgical nutrition and bowel disease. *Recreations:* tennis, theatre, gardening, opera. *Address:* 55 Shirlock Road, Hampstead, NW3 2HR. *T:* (020) 7267 1582. *Club:* Athenæum.

JOVINE, Nemat; *see* Shafik, N.

JOWELL, Prof. Jeffrey Lionel; barrister; Professor of Law (formerly Research Professor of Public Law), University College London, since 2006; Member, Royal Commission on Environmental Pollution, since 2003; *b* 4 Nov. 1938; *s* of Jack and Emily Jowell, Cape Town; *m* 1963, Frances Barbara, *d* of Helen Suzman, *qv*; one *s* one *d*. *Educ:* Cape Town Univ. (BA, LLB 1961); Hertford Coll., Oxford (BA 1963, MA 1969), Pres., Oxford Union Soc., 1963; Harvard Univ. Law Sch. (LLM 1966, SJD 1971). Called to Bar, Middle Temple, 1965 (Hon. Bencher, 1999). Research Asst, Harvard Law Sch., 1966–68; Fellow, Jt Center for Urban Studies of Harvard Univ. and MIT, 1967–68; Associate Prof. of Law and Admin. Studies, Osgoode Hall Law Sch., York Univ., Toronto, 1968–72; Leverhulme Fellow in Urban Legal Studies, 1972–74, and Lectr in Law, 1974–75, LSE; University College London: Prof. of Public Law, 1975–2006; Dean, Faculty of Laws, 1979–89 and 1998–2002; Head of Dept, 1982–89 and 1998–2002; Vice Provost, 1992–99; Hon. Fellow, 1997. Chairman, Social Sciences and The Law Cttee, 1981–84, and Vice-Chm., Govt and Law Cttee, 1982–84, Social Science Res. Council; Asst Boundary Comr, 1976–85; Chm., Cttee of Heads of University Law Schools, 1984–86; Member: Cttee of Management, Inst. of Advanced Legal Studies, 1978–89; Standing Cttee, Oxford Centre for Socio-Legal Studies, 1980–84; Gp for Study of Comparative European Admin., 1978–86; Nuffield Cttee on Town and Country Planning, 1983–86; Council, Justice, 1997–; Lord Chancellor's Review of Crown Office List, 1999–2000. UK deleg., Cttee of Experts, CSCE, Oslo, 1991; UK Mem., 2000–, Mem., Gov. Bd, 2001–, Venice Commn (Eur. Commn on Democracy through Law) (Vice Pres., 2003–05). Convenor of numerous internat. workshops and confs on constitutional law and human rights. Non-executive Director: UCL Press, 1993–95; Camden and Islington Community Health Services NHS Trust, 1994–97; Bd, Office of Rail Regulation, 2004–07; Chm., British Waterways Ombudsman Cttee, 2004–. Trustee: John Foster Meml Trust, 1986–; Internat. Centre for Public Law, 1992–98; Bd, Inst. of Commonwealth Studies, 1994–99; Prince of Wales's Foundn (formerly Inst. of Architecture), 1997–99; Chairman: Inst. of Philanthropy, 2000–04; Friends of S African Constitl Court Trust, 2003–. Lionel Cohen Lecture, Jerusalem, 1988; Visiting Professor: Univ. of Paris II, 1991; Univ. of Aix-Marseilles, 2002; Columbia Law Sch., NY, 2002; Hon. Prof., Univ. of Cape Town, 1999–2005. Hon. QC 1993. Hon. DJur Athens, 1987; Hon. LLD: Ritsumeikan, 1988; Cape Town, 2000. Member Editorial Bds: Public Law, 1977–93; Policy and Politics, 1976–83; Urban Law and Policy, 1978–83; Jl of Environmental Law, 1988–92; Public Law Review, 1995–; Judicial Review, 1996–; S African Law Jl, 2003–; Jt Editor, Current Legal Problems, 1984–89. *Publications:* Law and Bureaucracy, 1975; (ed jtly) Welfare Law and Policy, 1979; (ed jtly) Lord Denning: the Judge and the Law, 1984; (ed jtly) The Changing Constitution, 1985, 6th edn 2007; (ed jtly) New Directions in Judicial Review, 1988; (ed with H. Woolf) de Smith, Judicial Review of Administrative Action, 5th edn 1995, (with H. Woolf and A. P. Le Sueur) 6th edn as de Smith's Judicial Review, 2007; (ed jtly) Principles of Judicial Review, 1999; (ed jtly) Understanding Human Rights Principles, 2001; (ed jtly) Delivering Rights, 2003; articles and reviews on public law, human rights and planning law. *Recreations:* tennis, London, Exmoor. *Address:* Blackstone Chambers, Middle Temple, EC4Y 9BW. *T:* (020) 7583 1770.

JOWELL, Sir Roger Mark, Kt 2008; CBE 2001; AcSS; Director, European Social Survey, Centre for Comparative Social Surveys, City University, since 2003; *b* 26 March 1942; *s* of Jack and Emily Jowell, Cape Town, SA; *m* 1st, 1970, Tessa Jane Helen Douglas Palmer (*see* Rt Hon. T. J. H. D. Jowell) (marr. diss. 1977); 2nd, 1979, Nighat Gilani (marr. diss. 1995); two *s*; 3rd, 1996, Sharon Witherspoon. *Educ:* Cape Town Univ. (BA 1963). Researcher, Res. Services Ltd, 1964–68; Founder and Co-Dir, 1969–84, sole Dir, 1984–2001, Dir, European Social Survey, 2001–03, Social and Community Planning Res., later Nat. Centre for Social Res.; Co-dir, ESRC Centre for Res. into Elecns and Social Trends, 1994–2002; Fellow: Centre for Mgt and Policy Studies, Cabinet Office, 2001–03; Prime Minister's Strategy Unit, 2002–05. Mem., Commn on Taxation and Citizenship, 1999–2001; Chm., Cabinet Office Review of Govt 'Pilots', 2002–03. Visiting Professor: City Univ., 1980–88 and 2001–; LSE, 1993–2005. Founder Dir, British Social Attitudes Survey series, 1983–2001; Co-dir, British Election Studies, 1983–2000. Member, Editorial Boards: Jl Royal Statistical Soc., 1990–92; Electoral Studies, 1997–; Internat. Jl Mkt Res., 2001–. Formulated Internat. Code of Ethics for Statisticians, 1980–85. Founder Chm., Internat. Social Survey Prog., 1984–90; Chm., Assoc. Res. Centres in Social Scis, 1999–2001; Board Mem., Inf. Centre on Asylum and Refugees, 2001–06; Trustee, IPPR, 2001–. Alderman, Camden BC, 1970–77; Mem., Internat. Statistical Inst., 1985; FSS 1978. AcSS 1999. Hon. LLD Oxford Brookes, 1999; Hon. DSc: City, 2003; Umeå, Sweden, 2006. Descartes Prize Laureate, 2005; Helen Dinerman Award, 2005; Robert Kitchin Prize, 2006. *Publications:* (jtly) Britain into Europe, 1976; (jtly) Survey Research Practice, 1978; (jtly) How Britain Votes, 1985; (jtly) Understanding Political Change, 1991; (jtly) Labour's Last Chance?, 1994; (jtly) The Quality of Life in London, 1995; (jtly) The Rise of New Labour, 2001; (ed and contrib.) British Social Attitudes, annually 1984–2000; contribs to Jl Royal Stat. Soc., Public Opinion Qly, Amer. Behavioral Scientist, Parly Affairs, Eur. Sociol Rev., Jl Official Stats, British Jl of Pol Science, 21st Century. *Recreations:* tennis, cricket. *Address:* Centre for Comparative Social Surveys, School of Social Sciences, City University, Northampton Square, EC1V 0HB. *T:* (020) 7040 4904.

JOWELL, Rt Hon. Tessa Jane Helen Douglas; PC 1998; MP (Lab) Dulwich and West Norwood, since 1997 (Dulwich, 1992–97); Minister for the Olympics, since 2005; Paymaster General, since 2007; *b* 17 Sept. 1947; *d* of Kenneth and Rosemary Palmer; *m* 1st, 1970, Roger Mark Jowell (*see* Sir R. M. Jowell) (marr. diss. 1977); 2nd, 1979, David Mills; one *s* one *d*. *Educ:* St Margaret's Sch., Aberdeen; Aberdeen Univ. (MA); Edinburgh Univ. (DSA). Child Care Officer, Lambeth, 1969–71; psychiatric social worker training, Goldsmiths' Coll., London Univ., 1971–72; Psychiatric Social Worker, Maudsley Hosp., 1972–74; Asst Dir, Mind, 1974–86; Dir, Community Care Special Action Project, Birmingham, and Sen. Vis. Fellow, PSI, 1986–90; Dir, Community Care Prog., Joseph Rowntree Foundn, and Sen. Vis. Fellow, King's Fund Inst., 1990–92. Councillor, Camden, 1971–86. Chair, Social Services Cttee, AMA, 1984–86; Mem., Mental Health Act Commn, 1985–90. An Opposition Whip, 1994–95; frontbench Opposition spokesperson on health, and on women, 1995–97; Minister of State (Minister for Public Health), DoH, 1997–99; Minister for Women, 1998–2001, 2005–06; Minister of State (Minister for Employment, Welfare to Work and Equal Opportunities), DfEE, 1999–2001; Sec. of State for Culture, Media and Sport, 2001–07; Minister for London, 2007–08. Vis. Fellow, Nuffield Coll., Oxford, 1995. *Publications:* articles and contribs in social work and social policy jls. *Recreations:* hill walking, reading, music, Italy. *Address:* House of Commons, Westminster, SW1A 0AA.

JOWITT, Sir Edwin (Frank), Kt 1988; a Justice of the High Court, Queen's Bench Division, 1988–2000; *b* 1 Oct. 1929; *s* of Frank and Winifred Jowitt; *m* 1959, Anne Barbara Dyson (*d* 2008); three *s* two *d*. *Educ:* Swanwick Hall Grammar Sch.; London Sch. of Economics. LLB London 1950. Called to Bar, Middle Temple, 1951, Bencher 1977; Member Midland and Oxford Circuit, 1952–80. Dep. Chm. Quarter Sessions: Rutland, 1967–71; Derbyshire, 1970–71; QC 1969; a Recorder of the Crown Court, 1972–80; a Circuit Judge, 1980–88; a Sen. Circuit Judge, 1987–88; Hon. Recorder, Birmingham, 1987–88; Presiding Judge, Midland and Oxford Circuit, 1996–99. Chm., Robert Hamill Inquiry, 2004–. *Recreations:* walking, cycling. *Address:* Church House, Desborough, Northants NN14 2NP.

JOWITT, Juliet Diana Margaret, (Mrs Thomas Jowitt); DL; Director, Northern Ballet Theatre, since 2000; Member, Independent Broadcasting Authority, 1981–86; Director, Yorkshire Television, 1987–94; *b* 24 Aug. 1940; *yr d* of late Lt-Col Robert Henry Langton Brackenbury, OBE and Eleanor Trewlove (*née* Springman); *m* 1963, Frederick Thomas Benson Jowitt; one *s* one *d*. *Educ:* Hatherop Castle; Switzerland and Spain. Associate Shopping Editor, House and Garden and Vogue, 1966–69; Proprietor, Wood House Design (Interior Design) (formerly Colour Go Round), 1971–2002. Director: YTV Holdings PLC, 1988–92; Dancers Career Develt Trust Ltd, 2005–. Member: Domestic Coal Consumers' Council, 1985–95; Potato Marketing Bd, 1986–90. Fellow, IDDA, 1995 (Mem., 1985; Mem. Council, 1989). Gov., Barnardo's, Ripon, 2002–. JP North Yorks, 1973–89; DL N Yorks, 2004. *Address:* Thorpe Lodge, Littlethorpe, Ripon, N Yorkshire HG4 3LU.

JOXE, Pierre Daniel, Hon. KBE; Member, Constitutional Court, Paris, since 2001; *b* 28 Nov. 1934; *s* of Louis Joxe and Françoise-Hélène Joxe (*née* Halévy); *m* 3rd, 1981, Valérie Cayeux; two *s*, and two *d* from a previous marr. *Educ:* Lycée Henri-IV; Faculté de droit de Paris; Ecole Nat. d'Administration. Started career in Audit Office, 1962; elected Deputy for Saône-et-Loire, 1973, 1978, 1981, 1986, 1988; Mem., European Parlt, 1977–79; Minister of Industry, 1981; Minister of the Interior, 1984–86, 1988–91; Minister of Defence, 1991–93; Auditor General, Audit Office, Paris, 1993–2001. Mem. Exec., Socialist Party, 1971–. *Publications:* Parti socialiste, 1973; A propos de la France, 1997; L'Edit de Nantes: une histoire pour aujourd' hui, 1998; Pourquoi Mitterrand?, 2006. *Address:* (office) 2 rue de Montpensier, 75001 Paris, France.

JOY, David, CBE 1983; HM Diplomatic Service, retired; *b* 9 Dec. 1932; *s* of late Harold Oliver Joy and Doris Kate Buxton; *m* 1957, Montserrat Morancho Saumench, *o d* of late Angel Morancho Garreta and Josefa Saumench Castells, Zaragoza, Spain; one *s* one *d*. *Educ:* Hulme Grammar Sch., Oldham, Lancs; St Catharine's Coll., Cambridge (MA). HMOCS, Northern Rhodesia, 1956–64; Zambia, 1964–70: Cabinet Office, 1964; Under Sec. (Cabinet), 1968–70; joined HM Diplomatic Service, 1971; FCO, 1971–73; First Sec. (Inf.), Caracas, 1973–75; Head of Chancery, Caracas, 1975–77; Asst Head, Mexican and Caribbean Dept, FCO, 1977–78; Counsellor and Head of Chancery, Warsaw, 1978–82; Counsellor and Head of British Interests Section, Buenos Aires, 1982–84; Head of Mexico and Central America Dept, FCO, 1984–87; Ambassador to Honduras and El Salvador, 1987–89; Consul Gen. Barcelona, 1989–92. *Recreations:* golf, tennis, music, reading. *Address: e-mail:* dmmjoy@telefonica.net. *Clubs:* Oxford and Cambridge; Cercle del Liceu (Barcelona); Rotary, La Peñaza Golf (Zaragoza); Key Biscayne Yacht (Florida).

JOY, (Henry) Martin; His Honour Judge Joy; a Circuit Judge, since 2007; *b* Fleet, Hants, 18 April 1948; *s* of Henry and Margaret Joy; *m* 1977, Hilary Ann Smyth; one *s* one *d*. *Educ:* Bradfield Coll., Berks; Univ. of Southampton (LLB Hons). Called to the Bar, Lincoln's Inn, 1971; in practice as barrister, 1971–2007; Recorder, 1993–2007. *Recreations:* family, gardening, golf, Catholicism. *Address:* c/o Maidstone Combined Court Centre, Barker Road, Maidstone ME16 8EQ. *T:* (01622) 202000.

JOY, Peter, OBE 1969; HM Diplomatic Service, retired; *b* 16 Jan. 1926; *s* of late Neville Holt Joy and Marguerite Mary Duff Beith; *m* 1953, Rosemary Joan Hebden; two *s* two *d*. *Educ:* Downhouse Sch., Pembridge; New Coll., Oxford. Served with RAF, 1944–47. Entered Foreign (subseq. Diplomatic) Service, 1952; 1st Sec., Ankara, 1959; 1st Sec., New Delhi, 1962; FO, 1965; 1st Sec., Beirut, 1968; FCO, 1973; Counsellor, Kuala Lumpur, 1979–80; Counsellor, FCO, 1980–86. *Recreations:* gardening, fishing. *Address:* The Old Rectory, Stoke Bliss, near Tenbury, Worcs WR15 8QJ. *T:* (01885) 410342; Carrick House, Eday, Orkney KW17 2AB.

JOYCE, Prof. Bruce Arthur, DSc; FRS 2000; CPhys, FInstP; Professor of Semiconductor Materials, Department of Physics, Imperial College, London, 1988–2000, now Emeritus Professor of Physics and Senior Research Investigator; *b* 17 Oct. 1934; *s* of Frederick Charles James Joyce and Dorothy Joyce (*née* Crouch); *m* 1956, Beryl Ann Mead; three *s* one *d*. *Educ:* Birmingham Univ. (BSc 1956; DSc 1973). CPhys, FInstP 1973. Nat. Service Commn, RAF, 1956–58. Sen. Scientist, Allen Clark Res. Centre, Plessey Co., 1958–69; Sen. Principal Scientist, Philips Res. Labs, Redhill, 1969–88; Dir, Univ. of London IRC for Semiconductor Materials, ICSTM, 1988–99. *Publications:* contrib. numerous papers to learned jls. *Recreations:* hill-walking, athletics (track and road running), Rugby football, cricket, crosswords, gardening. *Address:* 15 Tennyson Rise, East Grinstead, W Sussex RH19 1SQ. *T:* (01342) 323059.

JOYCE, Eric Stuart; MP (Lab) Falkirk, since 2005 (Falkirk West, Dec. 2000–2005); *b* 13 Oct. 1960; *s* of Leslie Joyce and Sheila Joyce (*née* Christie); *m* 1991, Rosemary Jones; twin *d*. *Educ:* Univ. of Stirling (BA Hons 1986); W London Inst. (PGCE 1987); Univ. of Bath (MA 1994); Univ. of Keele (MBA 1995). Served Army, 1978–99: Black Watch, 1978–81; RMA Sandhurst, 1987; commnd RAEC, 1987; served AGC; Maj. 1992. Public Affairs Officer, CRE, 1999–2000. PPS to Minister for Trade, Investment and Foreign Affairs, 2003–05, to Minister of State for Work, 2005–07, to Sec. of State for Business, Enterprise and Regulatory Reform, 2007–. *Publications:* Arms and the Man: renewing the armed services, 1997; (ed) Now's the Hour!: new thinking for Holyrood, 1999. *Recreations:* climbing, judo, most sports. *Address:* House of Commons, SW1A 0AA; (constituency office) The Studio, Burnfoot Lane, Falkirk FK1 5BH. *T:* (01324) 638919; *e-mail:* ericjoycemp@parliament.uk. *Clubs:* Camelon Labour (Falkirk); Hallion (Glasgow).

JOYCE, Peter Robert, CB 2000; FCCA; Executive Director, International Association of Insolvency Regulators, since 2002; Director General, Insolvency Practitioners Association, since 2003; *b* 14 Jan. 1942; *s* of George Henry Joyce and Edith Doris Joyce; *m* 1st, 1965 (marr. diss. 1988); one *s* one *d*; 2nd, 1988, Marian Neal. *Educ:* Westwood's Grammar Sch., Northleach, Glos. FCCA 1970. Insolvency Service, Board of Trade, subseq. Department of Trade and Industry, 1960–2001: Examr, 1960–69; Sen. Examr, 1969–76; Asst Official Receiver and Chief Examr, 1976–82; Official Receiver and Principal Examr, 1982–85; Dep. Inspector General, 1985–89; Inspector General and Agency Chief Exec., 1989–2001. Consultant, World Bank, 2004–. Chairman: Internat. Assoc. of Insolvency Regulators, 1995–2001; World Bank Wkg Gp on Insolvency Regulatory Frameworks, 1999–2001. Mem. Council, Central Govt NTO, 1999–2001. Hon. FCIM 2000. *Recreations:* watching cricket, theatre, dining out. *Club:* Gloucestershire County Cricket.

JOYCE, Lt-Gen. Sir Robert John H.; *see* Hayman-Joyce.

JOYNSON-HICKS, family name of **Viscount Brentford**.

JOYNT, Rt Rev. Michael Charles S.; *see* Scott-Joynt.

JUCKES, Robert William Somerville; QC 1999; **His Honour Judge Juckes;** a Circuit Judge, since 2007; *b* 1 Aug. 1950; *s* of late Dr William Renwick Juckes and of Enid Osyth Juckes (*née* Hankinson); *m* 1974, Frances Anne MacDowel; three *s*. *Educ:* Marlborough Coll.; Exeter Univ. (BA Hons Sociol. and Law 1972). Called to the Bar, Inner Temple, 1974; in practice, Birmingham, 1975; Hd of Chambers, 2000–03. Asst Recorder, 1992–95; Recorder, 1995–2007. *Recreations:* golf, tennis, cricket, novels of Patrick O'Brian, culturing three sons. *Address:* Queen Elizabeth II Law Courts, 1 Newton Street, Birmingham B4 7NA.

JUDD, family name of **Baron Judd**.

JUDD, Baron *cr* 1991 (Life Peer), of Portsea in the County of Hampshire; **Frank Ashcroft Judd;** Professional Adviser to De Montfort University, since 1993 (Senior Fellow, since 1999); Trustee, Saferworld, since 2002 (Senior Fellow, 1994–2002); Member, Advisory Board, Centre for Human Rights, London School of Economics, since 2007; *b* 28 March 1935; *s* of late Charles Judd, CBE and Helen Judd, JP; *m* 1961, Christine Elizabeth Willington; two *d*. *Educ:* City of London Sch.; London Sch. of Economics. Sec.-Gen., IVS, 1960–66. Contested (Lab): Sutton and Cheam, 1959; Portsmouth West, 1964; MP (Lab) Portsmouth W, 1966–74, Portsmouth N, 1974–79; PPS: to Minister of Housing and Local Govt, 1967–70; to the Leader of the Opposition, 1970–72; Mem., Opposition's Front Bench Defence Team, 1972–74; Parliamentary Under-Secretary of State: for Defence (Navy), MoD, 1974–76; ODM 1976; Minister of State: for Overseas Develt, 1976–77; FCO, 1977–79; Mem., British Parly Delegn to Council of Europe and WEU, 1970–73, 1997–2005; Opposition front bench spokesperson, H of L, on for. affairs, 1991–92, on defence, 1995–97; principal spokesperson, on educn, 1992–94, on overseas develt co-operation, 1994–97; Member: Procedure Cttee, H of L, 2001–04; Ecclesiastical Cttee, H of C and H of L, 2001–; Human Rights Cttee, H of C and H of L, 2003–07. Indep. Advr to UK Delegn to UN Special Session on Disarmament, 1982. Associate Dir, Internat. Defence Aid Fund for Southern Africa, 1979–80; Director: VSO, 1980–85; Oxfam, 1985–91. Chairman: Centre for World Development Educn, 1980–85; Internat. Council of Voluntary Agencies, 1985–90; World Econ. Forum Conf., Geneva, on the future of S Africa, 1990 and 1991; Member: Steering Cttee, World Bank—NGO Cttee, 1989–91; Internat. Commn on Global Governance, 1992–2001; WHO Task Force on Health and Develt, 1994–98; Internat. Working Gp on Human Duties and Responsibilities in the New Millennium, 1997–99. Pres., European-Atlantic Gp, 1999–2001. Past Chm., Fabian Soc. Chm., Oxford Diocesan Bd for Social Responsibility, 1992–95; Convenor, Social Responsibility Forum, Churches Together in Cumbria,

1999–2005. Mem., NW Regl Cttee, Nat. Trust, 1996–2003; Dir (non-exec.), Portsmouth Harbour Renaissance Bd, 1998–2006; Vice-President: Council for Nat. Parks, 1998–; Lakeland Housing Trust, 2007–; UN Assoc.; Nat. Pres., YMCA England, 1996–2005; President: Friends of RN Mus., 2002–; Friends of the Lake Dist, 2005–. Trustee: Internat. Alert, 1994–2000 (Chm., 1997–2000); Selly Oak Colls, Birmingham, 1994–97 (Chm. Council, 1994–97); Ruskin Foundn, 2002–. Mem. Council, Univ. of Lancaster, 1996–2002, Mem. Court, 2002–; Mem. Court, Univ. of Newcastle upon Tyne, 2004–; Governor: LSE, 1982–; Westminster Coll., Oxford, 1991–98. Member: MSF; GMB. Freeman, City of Portsmouth, 1995. Hon. Fellow, Univ. of Portsmouth (formerly Portsmouth Poly.), 1978–. Hon. DLitt: Bradford Univ., 1987; Portsmouth, 1997; De Montfort, 2006; Hon. LLD Greenwich, 1999. FRSA 1988. *Publications:* (jtly) Radical Future, 1967; Fabian International Essays, 1970; Purpose in Socialism, 1973; (jtly) Our Global Neighbourhood, 1995; (jtly) Imagining Tomorrow: rethinking the global challenge, 2000; various papers and articles on current affairs. *Recreations:* relaxing in the countryside, family holidays, enjoying music. *Address:* House of Lords, SW1A 0PW. *Club:* Royal Commonwealth Society.

JUDD, Clifford Harold Alfred, CB 1987; Under Secretary, HM Treasury, 1981–87; *b* 27 June 1927; *s* of Alfred Ernest and Florence Louisa Judd; *m* 1951, Elizabeth Margaret Holmes; two *d.* *Educ:* Christ's Hospital; Keble Coll., Oxford. National Service, RA, 1946–48 (to 2/Lt). HM Treasury: Executive Officer, 1948, through ranks to Principal, 1964, Sen. Prin., 1969, Asst Sec., 1973. *Recreations:* cricket, golf, do-it-yourself. *Address:* 4 Colets Orchard, Otford, Kent TN14 5RA. *T:* (01959) 522398. *Clubs:* Forty; Sevenoaks Vine; Knole Park Golf.

JUDD, Lt-Gen. David Leslie, CB 2003; CEng, FIMechE; Deputy Commander Allied Joint Force Command Brunssum (formerly Deputy Commander-in-Chief, Allied Forces North), 2004–07; *b* 26 Jan. 1950; *s* of Leslie and Jean Judd; *m* 1973, Margot Hazell Patterson; one *s* one *d.* *Educ:* RMCS (BSc Hons Engrg). CEng 1976, MIMechE 1976, FIMechE 2006. Commnd 13th/18th Royal Hussars (Queen Mary's Own), 1970; 22 Air Defence Regt RA Workshop, REME, 1974; Life Guards, 1976; Adjt Comd, Maintenance Corps Troops, REME, 1978–81; Army Staff Coll., 1981–83; Dep. COS, 33 Armd Bde, 1983–85; OC, 5 Armd Workshop, REME, 1985–87; SO1 Directing Staff, Staff Coll., 1987–88; Comdr Maintenance, 1st Armd Div., 1988–90; Col QMG, 1990–92; Chief Maintenance, HQ ARRC, 1992–94; rcds 1994; Dep. COS, G1/G4 HQ ARRC, 1994–98; Dir, Equipt Support Change Mgt Prog., 1998–99; Dir Gen., Equipt Support (Land), 1999–2002, and QMG, 2000–02; GOC 4th Div., 2003–04. *Recreations:* anything mechanical, Rugby, furniture restoration. *Club:* Army and Navy.

JUDD, Prof. Denis, PhD; FRHistS; Professor of British and Imperial History, London Metropolitan University (formerly North London Polytechnic, then University of North London), 1990–2004, now Emeritus; *b* 28 Oct. 1938; *s* of Denis and Joan Judd; *m* 1964, Dorothy Woolf; three *s* one *d.* *Educ:* Magdalen Coll., Oxford (BA Hons Mod. Hist.); Birkbeck Coll., London (PhD; PGCE). Poly., then Univ., of N London, 1964–. Visiting Professor: Univ. of California, 2002–05; NY Univ., 2007–. Series Editor, Traveller's History Series, 1989–; Advr, BBC History Mag., 2000–; writer and presenter, BBC Radio. *Publications:* Balfour and the British Empire, 1968; The Victorian Empire, 1970; Posters of World War Two, 1972; Livingstone in Africa, 1973; George V, 1973, 5th edn 1993; The House of Windsor, 1973; Someone has Blundered: calamities of the British army in the Victorian age, 1973, 2nd edn 1999; Edward VII, 1975; Palmerston, 1975; The Crimean War, 1976; Eclipse of Kings, 1976; Radical Joe: a life of Joseph Chamberlain, 1977, 2nd edn 1993; The Adventures of Long John Silver, 1977; Return to Treasure Island, 1978; Prince Philip, 1980, 3rd edn 1991; (with Peter Slinn) The Evolution of the Modern Commonwealth 1902–80, 1982; Lord Reading, 1982; King George VI, 1982; Alison Uttley: the life of a country child, 1986, 2nd edn 2001; Jawaharlal Nehru, 1993; Empire: the British imperial experience from 1765 to the present, 1996, 3rd edn 2001; (with Keith Surridge) The Boer War, 2002, 2nd edn 2003; The Lion and the Tiger: the rise and fall of the British Raj, 2004, 2nd edn 2005; (ed) The Diaries of Alison Uttley, 2009; regular contribs and reviews for nat. press. *Recreations:* reading, writing, film, theatre, sport (supports QPR), gardening, talking, listening, food and wine, travel, the Suffolk coast, playing with grandchildren, fixing things. *Address:* 20 Mount Pleasant Road, Brondesbury Park, NW10 3EL. *T:* and *Fax:* (020) 8459 1118; *e-mail:* denisjudd@ntlworld.com.

JUDD, Frances Jean, (Mrs D. Pritchard); QC 2006; a Recorder, since 2002; *b* 13 Feb. 1961; *d* of Christopher and Jean Judd; *m* 1985, David Pritchard; two *s.* *Educ:* King's Sch., Canterbury; New Hall, Cambridge (BA Hons Hist. 1982). Called to the Bar, Middle Temple, 1984; in practice at the Bar, 1984–, specialising in family law. *Publication:* (jtly) Contact: The New Deal, 2006. *Recreations:* cycling, walking, swimming outdoors. *Address:* Harcourt Chambers, 3 St Aldates Courtyard, Oxford OX1 1BN. *T:* (01865) 791559, *Fax:* (01865) 791585; *e-mail:* fjudd@harcourtchambers.law.co.uk. *Club:* QI (Oxford).

JUDD, Judith Margaret; Editor-at-Large, Times Educational Supplement, since 2007 (Associate Editor, 2001–05; Editor, 2005–07); *b* 18 April 1949; *d* of John Berry and Joan Berry (*née* Edge); *m* 1973, Very Rev. Peter Somerset Margesson Judd, *qv*; one *s* one *d.* *Educ:* Bolton Sch.; St Anne's Coll., Oxford (BA Modern History). Reporter, 1972–74, Educn Reporter, 1974–75, Birmingham Post and Birmingham Mail; joined THES, 1975, News Editor, 1977–79; Reporter, 1979–82, Educn Correspondent, 1982–90, Observer; Education Correspondent: Independent on Sunday, 1990–93; Independent, 1991–93; Educn Ed., The Independent and The Independent on Sunday, 1993–2001. *Recreations:* gardening, reading, walking. *Address:* The Dean's House, 3 Harlings Grove, Chelmsford CM1 1YQ; Times Educational Supplement, 26 Red Lion Square, WC1R 4HQ.

JUDD, Nadine; *see* Nerina, Nadia.

JUDD, Very Rev. Peter Somerset Margesson; Dean (formerly Provost) of Chelmsford Cathedral, since 1997; *b* 20 Feb. 1949; *s* of William Frank Judd and Norah Margesson Judd (*née* Margesson); *m* 1973, Judith Margaret Berry (*see* J. M. Judd); one *s* one *d.* *Educ:* Charterhouse Sch.; Trinity Hall, Cambridge (MA Architecture); Cuddesdon Coll., Oxford (Cert. Theol.). Ordained deacon, 1974, priest, 1975; Asst Curate, St Philip with St Stephen, Salford, 1974–76; Chaplain, 1976–81, Fellow, 1980–81, Clare Coll., Cambridge; Team Vicar of Hitcham and Dropmore, Burnham Team Ministry, dio. of Oxford, 1981–88; Vicar, St Mary the Virgin, Iffley, 1988–97; Rural Dean of Cowley, 1995–97. *Recreations:* architecture, art, listening to music, literature, drawing, cooking, fell walking. *Address:* The Dean's House, 3 Harlings Grove, Chelmsford CM1 1YQ. *T:* (01245) 354318.

JUDGE, family name of Baron Judge.

JUDGE, Baron *cr* 2008 (Life Peer), of Draycote in the County of Warwickshire; **Igor Judge,** Kt 1988; PC 1996; Lord Chief Justice of England and Wales, since 2008; *b* 19 May 1941; *s* of Raymond and Rosa Judge; *m* 1965, Judith Mary Robinson; one *s* two *d.* *Educ:* Oratory Sch., Woodcote; Magdalene Coll., Cambridge (Exhbnr, MA). Harmsworth Exhibnr and Astbury Scholar, Middle Temple. Called to the Bar, Middle Temple, 1963, Bencher, 1987; a Recorder, 1976–88; Prosecuting Counsel to Inland Revenue, 1977–79; QC 1979; a Judge of the High Court, QBD, 1988–96; Leader, 1988, Presiding Judge, 1993–96, Midland and Oxford Circuit; a Lord Justice of Appeal, 1996–2005; Sen. Presiding Judge for England and Wales, 1998–2003; Dep. Chief Justice of England and Wales, 2003–05; Pres., QBD, High Ct of Justice, 2005–08. Member: Senate, Inns of Court and the Bar, 1980–83, 1984–86; Bar Council, 1987–88; Judicial Studies Bd, 1984–88, 1991–94 and 1996–98 (Chm. Criminal Cttee, 1991–93 and 1996–98). *Recreations:* history, music, cricket. *Address:* Royal Courts of Justice, Strand, WC2A 2LL.

JUDGE, Hon. Barbara Singer T.; *see* Thomas Judge.

JUDGE, Harry George, MA Oxon, PhD London; Fellow of Brasenose College, Oxford, since 1973; Senior Research Fellow, University of Oxford Department of Educational Studies, since 1988 (Director, 1973–88); *b* 1 Aug. 1928; *s* of George Arthur and Winifred Mary Judge; *m* 1956, Elizabeth Mary Patrick; one *s* two *d.* *Educ:* Cardiff High Sch.; Brasenose Coll., Oxford. Served RAF, 1946–48. Asst Master, Emanuel Sch. and Wallington County Grammar Sch., 1954–59; Dir of Studies, Cumberland Lodge, Windsor, 1959–62; Head Master, Banbury Grammar Sch., 1962–67; Principal, Banbury Sch., 1967–73. Visiting Professor: MIT, 1977 and 1980–82; Carnegie-Mellon Univ., 1984–86; Univ. of Virginia, 1987; Michigan State Univ., 1988–93; Pennsylvania State Univ., 1995–96; Visiting Scholar: Harvard Univ., 1985–87; Carnegie Foundn, 1998–2000; Sachs Lectr, Teachers' Coll., Columbia Univ., 1993; Read Distinguished Chair Lectr, Kent State Univ., 1996. Member: Public Schools Commission, 1966–70; James Cttee of Inquiry into Teacher Training, 1971–72; Educn Sub-Cttee, UGC, 1976–80; Oxon Educn Cttee, 1982–87. Chairman: School Broadcasting Council, 1977–81; RCN Commn on Education, 1984–85. Gen. Editor, Oxford Illus. Encyclopedia, 1985–93. *Publications:* Louis XIV, 1965; School Is Not Yet Dead, 1974; Graduate Schools of Education in the US, 1982; A Generation of Schooling: English secondary schools since 1944, 1984; The University and the Teachers: France, the United States, England, 1994; Faith-Based Schools and the State, 2002; (ed and contrib.) The University and Public Education: the contribution of Oxford, 2006; contribs on educational and historical subjects to collective works and learned jls. *Recreation:* canals. *Address:* Brasenose College, Oxford OX1 4AJ.
See also S. P. Judge.

JUDGE, Ian; stage director; *b* 21 July 1946; *s* of Jack and Marjorie Judge. *Educ:* King George V Grammar Sch., Southport; GSMD. Joined RSC as an asst dir, 1975; productions include: The Wizard of Oz, 1987; The Comedy of Errors, 1990; Love's Labour's Lost, 1993; Twelfth Night, 1994; A Christmas Carol, 1994; The Relapse, 1995; Troilus and Cressida, 1996; The Merry Wives of Windsor, 1996; *opera:* English National Opera: Faust, 1985; Cavalleria Rusticana and Pagliacci, 1987; Don Quichotte, 1994; La Belle Vivette, 1995; Mephistopheles, 1999; Sir John in Love, 2006; Opera North: Macbeth, 1987; Tosca, 1988; Boris Godunov, 1989; Attila, 1990; Show Boat, 1990 (also at London Palladium); Scottish Opera: Falstaff, 1991; Norma, 1993; Royal Opera House: The Flying Dutchman, 1992; Simon Boccanegra (1857), 1997; Simon Boccanegra (1881), 2008; Così Fan Tutte, Garsington, 1997; Eugene Onegin, Grange Park Opera, 2000; Los Angeles: Tosca, 1989; Madama Butterfly, 1991; Le Nozze di Figaro, 2004; Roméo et Juliette, 2005; Don Carlo, 2006; Tannhäuser, 2007; Melbourne and Sydney: Faust, 1990; Tales of Hoffman, 1992; Macbeth, Cologne, 1992; Kirov, St Petersburg: La Bohème, 2001; Der fliegende Holländer, 2008; Falstaff, Paris, 2001; Ernani, Holland, 2002; Salome, NY, 2002; *theatre:* Chichester: Oh! Kay, 1984; A Little Night Music, 1990 (also Piccadilly Theatre); Henry VIII, 1991; Love for Love, 1996; West Side Story (Sydney and Melbourne), 1994–96; Macbeth, Sydney Th. Co., 1999; The Mikado, Savoy Theatre, 2000. *Address:* *e-mail:* ijudge1@mac.com.

JUDGE, Sir Paul (Rupert), Kt 1996; Chairman, Schroder Income Growth Fund plc, since 2005 (Director, since 1995); *b* 25 April 1949; *s* of late Rupert Cyril Judge and Betty Rosa Muriel Judge (*née* Daniels), Forest Hill; *m*; two *s*; *m* 2002, Hon. Barbara Singer Thomas (*see* Hon. Barbara Thomas Judge). *Educ:* St Dunstan's Coll.; Trinity Coll., Cambridge (MA, Open Scholar); Wharton Business Sch., Univ. of Pennsylvania (MBA, Thouron Schol.). Cadbury Schweppes, 1973–86 (Group Planning Dir, 1984–86); Premier Brands: Man. Dir, 1986–87; Chm., 1987–89; Mem., Milk Marketing Bd, 1989–92; Chm., Food from Britain, 1990–92; Director: Grosvenor Development Capital plc, 1989–93; Boddington Group plc, 1989–93; WPP plc, 1991–97; Standard Bank Group Ltd (Johannesburg), 2003–; Tempur-Pedic Internat. Inc. (Kentucky), 2004–; ENRC plc, 2007–; Member Advisory Board: Barclays Private Bank Ltd, 2001–; Abraaj Capital, 2007–. Dir Gen., Cons. Party, 1992–95; Ministerial Advr, Cabinet Office, 1995–96. Chm., Adv. Bd, Judge Inst. of Management, Cambridge Univ., 1991–2002; Mem., Adv. Council, Inst. of Business Ethics, 2003–; Chairman: Wharton European Bd, 2000–; British-N American Cttee, 2001–; Digital Links Internat., 2003–. Chm. Trustees, Royal Soc. of Arts, 2003–06 (Dep. Chm., 2006–08); Trustee: Cambridge Foundn, 1991–2000 (Emeritus, 2000–); British Food Heritage Trust, 1997–2007; Imperial Soc. of Kts Bachelor, 1997–; Businessdynamics (formerly Understanding Industry) Trust, 1998– (Chm. Trustees, 1999–); Royal Instn, 1999–2005; Amer. Mgt Assoc., 2000– (Dep. Chm., 2004–). President: Assoc. of MBAs, 1997–; Chartered Mgt Inst., 2004–05 (Chm. Bd of Companions, 2001–04); Vice President: Mkting Council, 2001–07; CIM, 2008–. Chm., Mus. of Packaging and Advertising, 2003–; Member: Finance Cttee, Trinity Coll., Cambridge, 1992–; Shakespeare's Globe Develt Council, 1999–2007 (Dep. Chm., 2000–). Governor: Bromsgrove Sch., 1991–96; St Dunstan's Coll., 1997– (Chm., 2001–). FRSA 1971; FInstD; FCIM; Fellow, Marketing Soc. Alderman, City of London, 2007–; Freeman, City of London, 1971; Master, Marketors' Co., 2005–06 (Liveryman, 1993; Sen. Warden, 2004–05). Hon. LLD Cantab, 1995; LittD Westminster, 2006; ScD City, 2007. *Recreations:* family, travel. *Address:* 152 Grosvenor Road, SW1V 3JL. *Clubs:* Athenæum, Carlton; Mombasa (Kenya).

JUDGE, Richard, PhD; CEng, FIMechE; Chief Executive, Centre for Environment, Fisheries and Aquaculture Science, since 2007; *b* 2 Nov. 1962; *s* of Peter Judge and Elspeth Judge; *m* 1998, Susan Thompson; one *d.* *Educ:* Elizabeth Coll., Guernsey; Durham Univ. (BSc Hons Engrg Sci.; PhD 1987). CEng 1990, FIMechE 2006. Various roles, AEA Technology, 1987–2000; Man. Dir, AEA Technol. Rail BV, 2000–03; Gp Dir, AEA Envmt, 2003–05; an Interim Manager, 2005–07. *Address:* Centre for Environment, Fisheries and Aquaculture Science, Lowestoft Laboratory, Pakefield Road, Lowestoft, Suffolk NR33 0HT; *e-mail:* richard.judge@cefas.co.uk.

JUDGE, Simon Patrick; Director of Financial Strategy, Ministry of Justice (formerly Department for Constitutional Affairs), since 2005; *b* 10 Nov. 1959; *s* of Harry George Judge, *qv* and Elizabeth Mary Judge; *m* 1985, (Isobel) Jane Cox; three *s.* *Educ:* Banbury Sch.; Oxford Sch.; Clare Coll., Cambridge (BA 1981). Joined HM Treasury, 1985; Private Sec. to Paymaster Gen., 1987–88; Asst Sec., 1994; various posts, incl. Hd of Inf. Systems, 1995–97; on secondment to Planning and Finance Div., DSS, subseq. Welfare to Work

Directorate, DWP, 1999–2005. *Recreations:* canal boating, choral singing. *Address: e-mail:* simon.judge@justice.gsi.gov.uk.

JUGNAUTH, Rt Hon. Sir Anerood, GCSK 2003; KCMG 1988; PC 1987; QC (Mauritius) 1980; President of Mauritius, since 2003; *b* 29 March 1930; *m* Sarojni Devi Balla; one *s* one *d. Educ:* Church of England School, Palma, Mauritius; Regent Coll., Quatre Bornes. Called to the Bar, Lincoln's Inn, 1954. Teacher, New Eton Coll., 1948; worked in Civil Service, 1949. MLA Rivière du Rempart, 1963–67, Piton-Rivière du Rempart, 1976, 1982, 1983, 1987, 1991 and 2000; Town Councillor, Vacoas-Phoenix, 1964; Minister of State Develt, 1965–67; Minister of Labour, 1967; Leader of the Opposition, 1976–82; Prime Minister of Mauritius, 1982–95 and 2000–03; Minister of Finance, 1983–84 and 1990–91. Dist Magistrate, 1967–69; Crown Counsel, 1969; Sen. Crown Counsel, 1971. Attended London Constitutional Conf., 1965. Leader, Mouvement Socialiste Militant, 1983–2003. Dr *hc* Aix-en-Provence, 1985; Hon. DCL Mauritius, 1985; Dr of Law *hc* Madras, 2001. Order of Rising Sun (1st cl.) (Japan), 1988; Grand Officier, Ordre de la Légion d'Honneur (France), 1990. *Address:* State House, Le Réduit, Mauritius; *e-mail:* President@mail.gov.mu. (home) La Caverne No 1, Vacoas, Mauritius.

JUKES, Rt Rev. John, OFMConv; STL; Parish Priest, Huntly, RC Diocese of Aberdeen, since 2000; Retired Auxiliary Bishop of Southwark; Titular Bishop of Strathearn, since 1980; *b* 7 Aug. 1923; *s* of Francis Bernard Jukes and Florence Jukes (*née* Stampton). *Educ:* Blackheath; Rome. Professed in Order of Friars Minor Conventual, 1948; priest, 1952; Lectr in Canon Law, Franciscan Internat. Study Centre, Univ. of Kent at Canterbury, Rector, 1999–; Minister Provincial, English Province, 1979. Formerly: Episcopal Vicar for Religious, Southwark, Area Bishop with special responsibility for Deaneries of Canterbury, Chatham, Dover, Gravesend, Maidstone, Ramsgate and Tunbridge Wells, and an Auxiliary Bp in Southwark, 1980–2000. Mem., RC Bishops' Conf. of England and Wales (Chm., World of Work Cttee, 1983–2000; Mem., Internat. Bio-Ethics Cttee, 1996–); Vice Pres., Christian Council on Defence and Disarmament. Chm. Governors, St Mary's UC, Surrey Univ., 1991–99. DUniv Surrey. *Publications:* contribs to Misc. Francescana, Studia Canonica, New Life, Clergy Rev., etc. *Recreation:* mountain walking and climbing. *Address:* St Margaret, 30 Chapel Street, Huntly AB54 8BS.

JUKES, Very Rev. Keith Michael; Dean of Ripon, since 2007; *b* 18 Feb. 1954; *s* of George Jukes and Agnes Ethel Jukes (*née* Dobbs); *m* 1978, Susanne Weatherhogg, (Rev. Susanne Jukes); one *s* one *d. Educ:* Leeds Univ. (BA 1976); Lincoln Theol Coll. Ordained deacon, 1978, priest, 1979; Assistant Curate: Holy Trinity, Wordsley, 1978–81; St Chad's with St Peter's, Wolverhampton, 1981–83; Curate-in-charge, St Martin in the Delph, Stoneydelph, 1983–88; Team Rector, Glascote and Stoneydelph Team Ministry, 1988–91; Rural Dean, Tamworth, 1989–91; Team Rector, Cannock and Vicar, Hatherton, 1991–97; Priest-in-charge, 1997–99, Vicar, 1999–2007, Selby Abbey. Prebendary, Lichfield Cathedral, 1996–97. Vis. Lectr in Liturgy, W Midlands Ordination Trng Course, Queen's Coll., Birmingham, 1984–91. Non-exec. Dir, York Hosps NHS Trust, 1998–2006. Chaplain to Chm., N Yorks CC, 1999–2000, 2006–07. *Recreations:* photography, graphic design, architecture. *Address:* 17 High St Agnesgate, Ripon, N Yorks HG4 1QR.

JULIAN, Prof. Desmond Gareth, CBE 1993; MD, FRCP; Consultant Medical Director, British Heart Foundation, 1987–93; *b* 24 April 1926; *s* of Frederick Bennett Julian and Jane Frances Julian (*née* Galbraith); *m* 1st, 1956, Mary Ruth Jessup (decd); one *s* one *d*; 2nd, 1988, Claire Marley. *Educ:* Leighton Park Sch.; St John's Coll., Cambridge; Middlesex Hosp. MB BChir (Cantab) 1948; MA 1953; MD 1954; FRCPE 1967; FRCP 1970; FRACP 1970; FACC 1985. Surgeon Lieut, RNVR, 1949–51. Med. Registrar, Nat. Heart Hosp., 1955–56; Res. Fellow, Peter Bent Brigham Hosp., Boston, 1957–58; Sen. Reg., Royal Inf., Edinburgh, 1958–61; Cons. Cardiologist, Sydney Hosp., 1961–64, Royal Inf., Edinburgh, 1964–74; Prof. of Cardiology, Univ. of Newcastle upon Tyne, 1975–86. Mem., MRC Systems Bd, 1980–84. Pres., British Cardiac Soc., 1985–87; Second Vice-Pres., RCP, 1990–91. Hon. MD: Gothenburg, 1987; Edinburgh, 1997. Gold Medal, European Soc. of Cardiology, 1998; Mackenzie Medal, British Cardiac Soc., 2003; Internat. Service Award, Amer. Coll. of Cardiol., 2005. Editor, European Heart Jl, 1980–88. *Publications:* Cardiology, 1972, 8th edn 2004; (ed) Angina Pectoris, 1975, 2nd edn 1984; Acute Myocardial Infarction, 1967; (ed) Diseases of the Heart, 1989, 2nd edn 1995; Coronary Heart Disease: the facts, 1991; contribs to med. jls, particularly on coronary disease. *Recreations:* walking, writing. *Address:* Flat 1, 7 Netherhall Gardens, NW3 5RN. *T:* (020) 7435 8254. *Club:* Garrick.

JULIEN, Michael Frederick, FCA; FCT; Chairman, First Choice Holidays PLC (formerly Owners Abroad Group plc), 1993–97; *b* 22 March 1938; *s* of late Robert Auguste François and Olive Rita (*née* Evans); *m* 1963, Ellen Martinsen; one *s* two *d. Educ:* St Edward's Sch., Oxford. Price Waterhouse & Co., 1958–67; other commercial appts, 1967–76; Gp Finance Dir, BICC, 1976–83; Exec. Dir, Finance and Planning, Midland Bank, 1983–86; Man. Dir, Finance and Administration, Guinness PLC, 1987–88; Gp Chief Exec., Storehouse PLC, 1988–92. Director (non-executive): Littlewoods Orgn plc, 1981–86; Guinness PLC, 1988–97; Medeva PLC, 1993–98; Oxford English Online, subseq. Oxford Professional Training Ltd, 1999–2003. *Recreations:* family, travel. *Address: e-mail:* michael@julienco.com.

JULIUS, Dr Anthony Robert; Consultant, Mishcon de Reya, since 1998; *b* 16 July 1956; *s* of Morris and Myrna Julius; *m* 1st, 1979, Judith Bernie (marr. diss. 1998); two *s* two *d*; 2nd, 1999, Dina Rabinovitch (*d* 2007); one *s. Educ:* City of London Sch.; Jesus Coll., Cambridge (MA); University Coll. London (PhD 1992). Admitted Solicitor, 1981; Mishcon de Reya: Partner, 1984–98; Head of Litigation, 1988–98. Vis. Prof., Birkbeck Coll., Univ. of London, 2005–. Institute of Jewish Policy Research: Dir, 1996–2000; Mem. Council, 2000–; Chair, Law Cttee, 1998–2000; Mem., Appeals Cttee, Dermatrust, 1999–2004; foreword, report on holocaust denial and UK law, 2000. Chm., London Consortium, 2005–. Chair, Diana, Princess of Wales Meml Fund, 1997–99, Vice Pres., 2002–; Mem., Fest. Council, The Word. Chm. Mgt Bd, Centre for Cultural Analysis, Theory and History, Univ. of Leeds, 2001–05. Hon. PhD Haifa, 2005. *Publications:* T. S. Eliot, anti-Semitism, and literary form, 1995; (contrib.) Law and Literature, 1999; Idolizing Pictures, 2001; Transgressions: the offences of art, 2002. *Recreations:* cinema, cooking. *Address:* (office) Summit House, 12 Red Lion Square, WC1R 4QD. *T:* (020) 7440 7000.

JULIUS, DeAnne Shirley, CBE 2002; PhD; Chairman, Royal Institute of International Affairs, since 2003 (Member Council, 2000–03); *b* 14 April 1949; *d* of Marvin G. Julius and Maxine M. Julius; *m* 1976, Ian Harvey; one *s* one *d. Educ:* Iowa State Univ. (BSc Econs 1970); Univ. of Calif at Davis (MA 1974; PhD Econs 1975). Economic Analyst, US CS, 1970–71; Lectr, Univ. of Calif at Santa Barbara, 1975; project economist, then econ. advr, World Bank, 1975–82; Man. Dir, Logan Associates Inc., 1983–86; Prog. Dir for Econs, RIIA, 1986–89; Chief Economist: Shell Internat., 1989–93; British Airways, 1993–97; Chm., British Airways Pension Investment Mgt Ltd, 1995–97. Mem., Monetary Policy Cttee, 1997–2001, Mem. of Court, 2001–04, Bank of England. Chairman: Banking Code Review Gp, 2000–01; Public Services Industry Review, 2007–. Director: BP, 2001–; Lloyds TSB, 2001–07; Serco, 2001–07; Roche, 2002–. Vis. Prof., Univ. of Durham, 1998–. Vice Chm., Inst. Develt Studies, 2000–03. *Publications:* (jtly) Appropriate Sanitation Alternatives: a technical and economic appraisal, 1982; (jtly) The Monetary Implications of the 1992 Process, 1990; Global Companies and Public Policy: the growing challenge of foreign direct investment, 1990; (with A. Mashayekhi) Economics of Natural Gas: pricing, planning and policy, 1990. *Recreations:* ski-ing, sailing, tending bonsai. *Address:* Royal Institute of International Affairs, 10 St James's Square, SW1Y 4LE.

JUMA, Prof. Calestous, DPhil; FRS 2006; Professor of the Practice of International Development, and Director, Science, Technology and Globalization Project, Belfer Center for Science and International Affairs, John F. Kennedy School of Government, Harvard University; *b* Kenya; *m*; one *s. Educ:* Univ. of Sussex (DPhil). Sci. and envmt reporter, Daily Nation; Ed., Ecoforum mag., Envmt Liaison Centre Internat., Nairobi. Founding Director, African Centre for Technol. Studies, Nairobi, 1988; Exec. Sec., UN Convention on Biol Diversity, 1995. Co-Chm., African Panel on Biotechnol., African Union and New Partnership for Africa's Develt, 2005–; Co-ordinator, Task Force on Sci., Technol. and Innovation, UN Millennium Project; Mem., Nat. Econ. and Social Council, Kenya. Special Advr, Internat. Whaling Commn, 2008–. Dir, Internat. Diffusion of Biotechnol. Prog., Internat. Fedn of Insts of Advanced Studies. Chancellor, Univ. of Guyana, 2002. Mem., Kenya Nat. Acad. of Scis. Hon. FREng 2007. Order of the Elder of the Burning Spear (Kenya), 2006. *Publications:* articles in jls. *Address:* John F. Kennedy School of Government, Harvard University, 79 John F. Kennedy Street, Cambridge, MA 02138-5801, USA.

JUMAN, Curtis Mark; Director of Finance, UK Trade & Investment, since 2007; *b* London, 28 March 1968; *s* of Christopher and Nazina Juman; *m* 1990, Heather Revnell; one *s* two *d. Educ:* Kingsmead Comprehensive Sch.; Univ. of Birmingham (BSc Hons Chem.). CPFA 1994. Sen. Auditor, Nat. Audit Office, 1989–97; Sen. Manager, Deloitte, 1997–2000; Dep. Dir, Finance, Ofgem, 2000; Audit Dir, 2000–02, Dir, Finance Strategy, 2002–04, DTI; Change Dir, Finance, DWP, 2004–06; Dir, Finance Control, DTI, subseq. BERR, 2006–07. Mem. Bd and Chm., Gp Audit Cttee, LHA-ASRA Housing Gp, 2006–. Mem. Council, 2004–, Chm., Central Govt Panel, 2005–, CIPFA. *Recreations:* spending time with my young family, contributing to the life of Warlingham Methodist Church, watching sci-fi movies. *Address:* UK Trade & Investment, Kingsgate House, 66–74 Victoria Street, SW1E 6SW. *T:* (020) 7215 2425, *Fax:* (020) 7215 4070; *e-mail:* Curtis.Juman@ukti.gsi.gov.uk.

JUNCKER, Dr Jean-Claude; Prime Minister, Minister of State and Minister of Finance, Luxembourg, since 1995; *b* Redange-Attert, 9 Dec. 1954; *m* 1979, Christiane Frising. *Educ:* Secondary Sch., Clairefontaine, Belgium; Univ. of Strasbourg (Dr Public Law 1979). Parly Sec., Christian Social Party, 1979–82; State Sec. for Labour and Social Affairs, 1982–84; Minister of: Labour and Minister i/c Budget, 1984–89; Labour and of Finance, 1989–95; Labour and Employment, 1995–99. Pres., Christian Social Party, 1990–95. *Address:* Hôtel de Bourgogne, 4 rue de la Congrégation, 2910 Luxembourg. *T:* 4782101, *Fax:* 461720.

JUNG, Prof. Roland Tadeusz, MD; FRCP, FRCPE; Consultant Physician in Endocrinology and Diabetes, Ninewells Hospital, Dundee, since 1982; Chief Scientist, Scottish Government (formerly Executive) Health Department, 2001–07; *b* 8 Feb. 1948; *s* of Tadeusz Jung and Margaret (Pearl) Jung; *m* 1974, Felicity Helen King; one *d. Educ:* Pembroke Coll., Cambridge (BA 1969, MA 1972; MB, BChir 1972, MD 1980); St Thomas's Hosp. Med. Sch., London. FRCPE 1985; FRCP 1989. MRC Clinical Scientific Officer, Dunn Nutrition Unit, Cambridge, 1977–79; Sen. Registrar in Endocrinol. and Diabetes, RPMS, Hammersmith Hosp., 1980–82. Hon. Prof. of Medicine, Univ. of Dundee, 1998–. *Publications:* Colour Atlas of Obesity, 1990; chapters in books, original papers and reviews. *Recreations:* gardening, walking. *Address:* Diabetes Centre, Ninewells Hospital, Dundee DD1 9SY. *T:* (01382) 660111.

JUNGELS, Dr Pierre Jean Marie Henri, Hon. CBE 1989; Director, Baker Hughes Inc., since 2006; *b* 18 Feb. 1944; *s* of Henri and Jeanne Jungels; *m* 1988, Caroline Benc; one step *s* one step *d*; one *s* one *d* from former marriage. *Educ:* Univ. of Liège (Ing. Civ. 1967); California Inst. of Technology (PhD 1973). Petroleum Engr, Shell, 1973–74; Dist Manager, 1975–77, General Manager and Chief Exec., 1977–80, Petrangol (Angola); Man. Dir and Chief Exec., Petrofina UK, 1980–89; Exec. Dir, Downstream, Petrofina Gp, 1989–92; Exec. Dir, Exploration and Production, Petrofina Group, 1992–95; Man. Dir, Exploration and Production, British Gas, 1996; Chief Exec., Enterprise Oil plc, 1997–2001. Chairman: OHM plc, 2003–08; Rockhoffer Exploration plc, 2005–; Oxford Catalysts plc, 2006–; Director: Imperial Tobacco plc, 2002–; Woodside Petroleum Ltd, 2002–. Pres., Inst. of Petroleum, 1986–88 and 2002–03 (Jt Pres., Energy Inst., 2003). *Recreations:* tennis, shooting. *Address:* Enborne Chase, Enborne, Newbury, Berks RG20 0HD.

JUNGIUS, Vice-Adm. Sir James (George), KBE 1977; Supreme Allied Commander Atlantic's Representative in Europe, 1978–80, retired; Vice Lord-Lieutenant of Cornwall, 1995–98; *b* 15 Nov. 1923; *s* of Major E. J. T. Jungius, MC; *m* 1949, Rosemary Frances Turquand Matthey (*d* 2005); three *s. Educ:* RNC, Dartmouth. Served War of 1939–45 in Atlantic and Mediterranean; Commando Ops in Adriatic (despatches). Specialised in Navigation in 1946, followed by series of appts as Navigating Officer at sea and instructing ashore. Comdr, Dec. 1955; CO, HMS Wizard, 1956–57; Admlty, 1958–59; Exec. Officer, HMS Centaur, 1960–61; Captain, 1963; Naval Staff, 1964–65; CO, HMS Lynx, 1966–67; Asst Naval Attaché, Washington, DC, 1968–70; CO, HMS Albion, 1971–72; Rear-Adm., 1972; Asst Chief of Naval Staff (Operational Requirements), 1972–74; Vice-Adm., 1974; Dep. Supreme Allied Comdr Atlantic, 1975–77. County Pres., Cornwall, RBL, 1995–2004. Vice-Chm., SW War Pensions Cttee, 1996–2000. Fellow, Woodard Corp., 1988–95. Gov., Grenville Coll., 1981–96. CCMI. DL Cornwall, 1982. CStJ 1995 (Chm., St John Council for Cornwall, 1987–95). *Clubs:* Royal Navy Club of 1765 and 1785; Pilgrims.

JUNIPER, Anthony Thomas; Special Adviser, Prince of Wales' Rainforest Project, since 2008; Senior Associate, Cambridge University Programme for Industry, since 2008; *b* 24 Sept. 1960; *s* of late Austin Wilfred Juniper and Constance Margaret Juniper; *m* 1990, Susan Jane Sparkes; two *s* one *d. Educ:* Bristol Univ. (BSc Zool./Psychol. 1983); University Coll. London (MSc Conservation 1988). Worked with school children on nature conservation, S Oxon Countryside Educn Trust, 1984–85; Parrot Conservation Officer, Internat. Council for Bird Preservation, 1989–90; Friends of the Earth: Sen. Tropical Rainforest Campaigner, 1990–93; Sen. Biodiversity Campaigner, 1993–97; Campaign Dir, 1997–98; Policy and Campaigns Dir, 1998–2003; Exec. Dir, England, Wales and NI, 2003–08; Vice Chm., Friends of the Earth Internat., 2000–08. Mem., ACEVO, 2001–. Member, Advisory Board: BBC Wildlife magazine and Ecologist magazine, 1998–; NCC, 2002–; Founding Trustee and Bd Mem., Stop Climate Chaos, 2005–08. *Publications:* Parrots: a guide to the parrots of the world, 1998 (McColvin Medal, LA, 1999); Spix's Macaw, 2002; How many light bulbs does it take to change a planet?,

2007; Saving Planet Earth, 2007; contrib. to various scientific pubns. *Recreations:* natural history, fishing. *Address:* c/o Capel and Land, 29 Wardour Street, W1D 6PS. *T:* (020) 7734 2414; *e-mail:* Abi@capelland.co.uk.

JUNKIN, (William) Roy, CB 2008; Deputy Director of Public Prosecutions for Northern Ireland, 1998–2008 (Acting Director, Jan.–July 2007); *b* 29 May 1948; *o s* of William John Junkin and Elizabeth Margaret Junkin (*née* Parker); *m* 1972, Valerie Ann Elizabeth Barbour; two *s. Educ:* Rainey Endowed Sch.; Queen's Univ. Belfast (LLB); Univ. of Ulster (BA). Called to the Bar of NI, 1971 (Jt 1st, Bernard J. Fox Prize); called to the Bar, Gray's Inn, 1985, Bencher, 2006. Tutor in Law, QUB, 1970; Lectr in Law and Jurisp., QUB, and Asst Parly Draftsman, Parlt of NI, 1971–72; Lectr in Law, Ulster Coll. Univ. of Ulster, 1973; Government Legal Service, Northern Ireland, Department of Public Prosecutions: Professional Officer, 1974; Asst Sec., 1977; Under Sec., 1989. Part-time Vis. Lectr, Sch. of Public Admin., Univ. of Ulster, 1981–82. Mem., Exec. Bureau, Consultative Council of Prosecutors Gen. of Europe, Council of Europe, 2006–08. Member: Internat. Bar Assoc.; Human Rights Inst., Internat. Bar Assoc.; Review Group on Standards for Prosecutors, Internat. Assoc. of Prosecutors, 2006–08; FCMI. Gov., Castlereagh Coll. of Further Educn, 2002–07. *Publications:* (jtly) Budapest Guidelines: European guidelines on ethics and conduct for Public Prosecutors; contribs to Eurojustice and CCPE, notes and reviews in legal periodicals. *Recreations:* fly fishing, golf, cooking. *Address:* c/o Public Prosecution Service, 93 Chichester Street, Belfast BT1 3JR.

JUNOR, Penelope Jane, (Penny); journalist, writer and broadcaster; *b* 6 Oct. 1949; *d* of Sir John Junor and Pamela Mary (*née* Welsh); *m* 1970, James Stewart Leith; three *s* one *d. Educ:* Benenden Sch.; Univ. of St Andrews. Feature writer, 19 mag., 1970–71; reporter, Londoner's Diary, Evening Standard, 1971–74; freelance, 1974–; columnist, Private Eye, 1977–82; television: reporter, Collecting Now, 1981; Presenter: 4 What It's Worth, 1982–89; The Afternoon Show, 1984–85; The Travel Show, 1988–97. Gen. Ed., John Lewis Partnership, 1993–99. Patron: Women's Health Concern, 2002–; Cirencester beat Self-Help Gp, 2005–. Trustee: beat, 2006–; Central London, Samaritans, 2008–. *Publications:* Newspaper, 1979; Diana, Princess of Wales, 1982; Babyware, 1982; Margaret Thatcher: wife, mother, politician, 1983; Burton, the Man Behind the Myth, 1985; Charles, 1987; (ed) What Every Woman Needs to Know, 1988; Queen Elizabeth II: a pictorial celebration of her reign, 1991; Charles and Diana: portrait of a marriage, 1991; The Major Enigma, 1993; Charles: victim or villain?, 1998; Home Truths: life around my father, 2002; The Firm: the troubled life of the House of Windsor, 2005; Pattie Boyd: wonderful today, 2007; (with Sir Cliff Richard) My Life, My Way, 2008. *Recreation:* tennis. *Address:* c/o Jane Turnbull, Barn Cottage, Veryan, Truro, Cornwall TR2 5QA. *T:* (01872) 501317; *e-mail:* jane.turnbull@btinternet.com; Hilary Knight Management, Grange Farm, Church Lane, Old, Northants NN6 9QZ. *T:* (01604) 781818; *e-mail:* hilary@hkmanagement.co.uk. *Clubs:* Groucho, Century.

JUPE, George Percival; Under Secretary, Ministry of Agriculture, Fisheries and Food, 1979–90; *b* 6 April 1930; *s* of Frederick Stuart Jupe and Elizabeth (*née* Clayton); unmarried. *Educ:* Sandown Grammar Sch., IoW; Hertford Coll., Oxford. Ministry of Agriculture, Fisheries and Food: Asst Principal, 1955; Principal, 1960; Asst Sec., 1970–79:

Eggs and Poultry, and Potatoes Divs, 1970–74; Internat. Fisheries Div., 1975–78; Emergencies, Food Quality and Pest Controls Gp, 1979–85; Dir, ADAS Admin, 1985–88; Horticulture, Seeds, Plant Health and Flood Defence Gp, 1988–90. *Recreations:* hill walking, gardening, music. *Address:* Briar Cottages, Brook, Isle of Wight PO30 4EU.

JUPP, Elisabeth Anne; a Social Security and Child Support Commissioner, since 2001; *b* 4 April 1944; *d* of Alfred Barrett Tebb and Sarah Tebb (*née* Burnham); *m* 1968, Rev. Dr Peter Creffield Jupp; two *s. Educ:* Easingwold Sch.; King's Coll. London (LLB 1966). Admitted Solicitor, 1969; Partner, Alexanders, London, 1972–2001. Dep. Social Security and Child Support Comr, 1997–2001; Chm. (pt-time), Pensions Appeal Tribunal, 2001–. Chm., Ministerial Trng Cttee, URC, 1987–92. Mem. Council, Mansfield Coll., Oxford, 1984–88; Trustee, Homerton Coll., Cambridge, 1992–. *Recreations:* gardening, reading, theatre. *Address:* Commissioners' Office, Third Floor, Procession House, 55 Ludgate Hill, EC4M 7JW. *T:* (020) 7029 9850.

JUPPÉ, Alain Marie; Prime Minister of France, 1995–97; Mayor of Bordeaux, 1995–2004 and since 2006; *b* 15 Aug. 1945; *s* of Robert Juppé and Marie Darroze; *m* 1st, 1965, Christine Leblond (marr. diss.); one *s* one *d*; 2nd, 1993, Isabelle Bodin; one *d. Educ:* Lycées Victor-Duruy, Mont-de-Marsan and Louis-le-Grand, Paris; Ecole Normale Superieure (Dr in Classical Langs); Inst. of Political Studies; Nat. Sch. of Admin. Finance Inspector, 1972; Asst to Prime Minister Jacques Chirac, 1976; Advr to Minister for Co-operation, 1976–78; MEP, 1984–86; Deputy for Paris, 1988–93, for Bordeaux, 1997–2004, National Assembly; Dep. Minister of Finance, and Govt Spokesman, 1986–88; Minister of Foreign Affairs, France, 1993–95; Dep. Prime Minister and Minister of Environment, Energy and Transport, 2007. Rassemblement pour la République: Nat. Deleg., 1976–78; Nat. Sec., 1984–86; Gen. Sec., 1988–95; Pres., 1995–97. Adviser to Mayor of Paris, 1978; Dir of Finance and Economic Affairs, City of Paris, 1980–81; Mem., Paris City Council, 1983–95; Dep. Mayor of Paris, i/c Finance, 1983–95. Chm., Union for a Popular Movt, 2002–04. *Publications:* La Tentation de Venise, 1993; Entre Nous, 1996; Montesquieu le Moderne, 1999; Entre Quatre-Yeux, 2001; France mon pays: lettres d'un voyageur, 2006. *Address:* Mairie de Bordeaux, Place Pey-Berland, 33000 Bordeaux, France.

JURINAC, (Srebrenka) Sena; opera singer; Member of Vienna State Opera, 1944–82, now Honorary; retired from stage, 1982; *b* Travnik, Yugoslavia, 24 Oct. 1921; *d* of Ludwig Jurinac, MD, and Christine Cerv. *Educ:* High Sch.; Musical Academy. Made first appearance on stage as Mimi with Zagreb Opera, 1942. Frequent appearances at Glyndebourne Festivals, 1949–56, as well as at the Salzburg Festivals. Guest appearances at La Scala, Covent Garden, San Francisco, Teatro Colón. Principal parts include: Donna Anna and Donna Elvira in Don Giovanni; Elisabeth in Tannhauser; Tosca; Jenufa; Marie in Wozzeck; Marschallin in Der Rosenkavalier; Composer in Ariadne auf Naxos; Elisabeth in Don Carlos; Desdemona in Othello. *Film:* Der Rosenkavalier, 1962. Singing teacher; frequent appearances as mem. of jury in singing competitions. Kammersängerin award, 1951; Ehrenkreuz für Wissenschaft und Kunst, 1961; Grosses Ehrenzeichen für Verdienste um die Republik Oesterreich, 1967. *Address:* Lerchenweg 10, 86356 Neusäss-Hainhofen, Germany.

K

KABERRY, Hon. Sir Christopher Donald, (Hon. Sir Kit), 2nd Bt *cr* 1960, of Adel cum Eccup, City of Leeds; Finance Director: Union Railways (North) Ltd, since 2004; CTRL (UK) Ltd, since 2004; Channel Tunnel Rail Link Ltd, since 2005; *b* 14 March 1943; *s* of Lord Kaberry of Adel (Life Peer) and Lily Margaret (*d* 1992), *d* of Edmund Scott; *S* to baronetcy of father, 1991; *m* 1967, Gaenor Elizabeth Vowe, *d* of C. V. Peake; two *s* one *d*. *Educ:* Repton Sch. FCA 1967. Various overseas positions, Costain Group PLC, 1969–80; Financial Manager, United Buildings Factories, Bahrain, 1980–82; Resources Manager, Balfour Beatty Group, Indonesia and Bahamas, 1983–90; Hd of Finance, Union Railways, and CTRL Project, 1990–2007. Non-exec. Dir, Sage Bhartiya Infrastructure Fund IC Ltd, 2008. *Recreations:* walking, gardening, Land Rover driving. *Heir: s* James Christopher Kaberry [*b* 1 April 1970; *m* 1st, 1989, Juliet Clare Hill (marr. diss. 1995); two *s* one *d*; 2nd, 2001, Carole Gregory]. *Address:* Rock View, Chiddingstone Hoath, Kent TN8 7BT.

KADOORIE, Hon. Sir Michael (David), Kt 2005; GBS 2003; Chairman: CLP Holdings Ltd (formerly China Light & Power Co. Ltd), since 1996 (Director, 1967–96); Hongkong & Shanghai Hotels Ltd, since 1985 (Director, 1964–85); *b* Hong Kong, 19 July 1941; *s* of Baron Kadoorie, CBE and of Muriel Kadoorie (*née* Gubbay); *m* 1984, Betty Tamayo; one *s* two *d*. *Educ:* King George V Sch., Hong Kong; Le Rosey, Switzerland. Chairman: Heliservices (Hong Kong) Ltd, 1979–; Metrojet Ltd, 1996–; Dir, Sir Elly Kadoorie & Sons Ltd, 1988–; chairman, director and trustee of many other cos. Hon. LLD Hong Kong, 2004; Hon. DSc Imperial Coll. London, 2007. Commandeur: Ordre de Léopold II (Belgium), 1995; Ordre des Arts et des Lettres (France), 1998; Officier, Légion d'Honneur, 2003 (Chevalier, 1995). *Recreations:* world travel, flying, motor cars, photography. *Address:* 24th Floor, St George's Building, 2 Ice House Street, Central, Hong Kong SAR. *T:* 25249221, *Fax:* 28459133. *Clubs:* Hong Kong, Hong Kong Aviation, Hong Kong Jockey (Hong Kong).

KADRI, Sibghatullah; QC 1989; barrister-at-law; President, Standing Conference of Pakistani Organisations in UK, 1978–90 (Secretary General, 1975–78); *b* 23 April 1937; *s* of Haji Maulana Firasat Ullah Kadri and Begum Tanwir Fatima Kadri; *m* 1963, Carita Elisabeth Idman; one *s* one *d*. *Educ:* S. M. Coll., Karachi; Karachi Univ. Called to the Bar, Inner Temple, 1969, Bencher, 1997. Sec. Gen., Karachi Univ. Students Union, 1957–58; jailed without trial, for opposing military regime of Ayub Khan, 1958–59; triple winner, All Pakistan Students Debates, 1960; Gen. Sec., Pakistan Students' Fedn in Britain, 1961–62, Vice Pres., 1962–63; Pres., Inner Temple Students Assoc., 1969–70. Producer and broadcaster, BBC Ext. Urdu Service, 1965–68, and Presenter, BBC Home Service Asian Prog., 1968–70. In practice at the Bar, 1969– (Head of Chambers, 6 King's Bench Walk). Chm., Soc. of Afro-Asian and Caribbean Lawyers, UK, 1979–83. Vis. Lectr in Urdu, Holborn Coll., London, 1967–70. Org. Pakistani Def. Cttees during wave of 'Paki-bashing', 1970; active in immigrant and race-relations activities, 1970–; led Asian delegn to Prime Minister, June 1976; attended UN Conf., Migrant Workers in Europe, Geneva, 1975; led Pakistan delegn to 3rd Internat. Conf., Migrant Workers in Europe, Turin, 1977; Mem., Race Relations Cttee of the Bar, 1983–85, 1988, 1989; Chm., UK Lawyers Cttee of Human Rights and Justice, Pakistan. Gen. Sec., Pakistan Action Cttee, 1973; Convenor, Asian Action Cttee, 1976. Vice Chm., All Party Jt Cttee Against Racism, 1978–80. Publisher, Scopo News, London, until 1984. FRSA 1991. *Publications:* articles in ethnic minority press on immigration and race relations. *Recreations:* family and reading. *Address:* 6 King's Bench Walk, Temple, EC4Y 7DR. *T:* (020) 7353 4931/2.

KAFITY, Rt Rev. Samir; Presidential Consultant, Palestinian Presidency Office, since 1998; Anglican Bishop in Jerusalem, 1984–98; Bishop-in-Residence, St Bartholomew's Episcopal Church, Poway, since 1998; *b* 21 Sept. 1933; *s* of Hanna and Nazha Kafity; *m* 1963, Najat Abed; two *d*. *Educ:* American Univ., Beirut (BA); Near East Sch. of Theol. (DipTh). Ordained deacon, 1957, priest, 1958; Parish priest: to the Arab congregation at St George's Cathedral, Jerusalem, 1957–59; St Andrew's Ramallah, 1959–64; St Peter's, Beir Zeit, then All Saints, Beirut, 1964–77; Lectr, Beir Zeit Univ.; Archdeacon of Jerusalem, 1977–82; Coadjutor Bp in Jerusalem, 1982; Pres. Bishop, Episcopal Church in Jerusalem and the ME, 1986–96, Former Pres. Bishop, 1997–. Member: Standing Cttee, ACC, 1965; Bd of Managers and Exec. Cttee, Near East Sch. of Theol., 1965; Council of Evangelical Community in Syria and Lebanon, 1965–77. Hon. Life Pres., ME Council of Churches (Sec., 1974–94, Pres., 1985). Hon. Canon, Cathedral Church of St John the Divine, NY, 1988. Member: Royal Hashemite Commn on Jerusalem; Moslem-Christian Council, Palestine. President: Supreme Council, Jerusalem YMCA (Chm., Jerusalem); Jerusalem Crippled Children's Instn. Hon. STD Dickenson Coll., Pa, 1985; Hon. DD: Virginia Theol Seminary, 1986; Kent at Canterbury, 1998. KHS; KCLJ 1998; ChStJ. First recipient, Palestinian Jerusalem Medal, 1997. *Publications:* articles in Anglican and ecumenical jls. *Recreation:* travel. *Address:* 11964 Callado Road, San Diego, CA 92128, USA.

KAHAN, George; Director of Conciliation and Arbitration, Advisory, Conciliation and Arbitration Service, 1988–91; *b* 11 June 1931; *er s* of late Joseph Kahan and Xenia (*née* Kirschner); *m* 1959, Avril Pamela Cooper (*d* 2004); one *s*. *Educ:* St Paul's Sch. Nat. Service, RAF, 1950–51. Park Royal Woodworkers Ltd, 1951–74 (Dir, 1960–74); Principal: Dept. of Employment, 1975–76; Health and Safety Executive, Health and Safety Commn, 1976–80; Asst Sec., Dept of Employment, 1980–88. *Recreations:* lazing in the sun, reading, listening to music. *Address:* Half Timbers, The Thatchway, Rustington, Sussex BN16 2BN. *T:* (01903) 784070.

KAHN, (Jacob) Meyer; Group Chairman, SABMiller (formerly South African Breweries) plc, since 1999; *b* 29 June 1939; *s* of late Ben and Sarah Kahn; *m* 1968, Lynette Sandra Asher; two *d*. *Educ:* Univ. of Pretoria (BA, MBA). Joined South African Breweries Ltd, 1966; Man. Dir, Amrel, 1972–77; Man. Dir, 1977–80, Chm., 1980–83, OK Bazaars (1929) Ltd; Dir, 1981–, Man. Dir, 1983–90, Exec. Chm., 1990–97, South African Breweries plc; Chief Exec., South African Police Service, 1997–99 (on secondment). *Address:* SABMiller plc, PO Box 1099, Johannesburg 2000, South Africa.

KAHN, Paula; Chair: Equality Works, since 2000; Islington Primary Care Trust, since 2002; Camden Arts Centre, since 2008; *b* 15 Nov. 1940; *d* of Cyril Maurice Kahn and Stella Roscoe. *Educ:* Chiswick County High Sch.; Bristol Univ. (BA Hons). Teacher, administrator, 1962–66; Longman Group, 1966–94: editor, publisher, Publishing Director, Divl Man. Dir, 1966–79; Managing Director: ELT Div., Dictionaries Div. and Trade and Ref. Div., 1980–85; Internat. Sector, 1986–88; Chief Exec. (Publishing), 1988–89; Chief Exec. and Chm., 1990–94; Project Dir, World Learning Network, 1995–96; Man. Dir, Phaidon Press, 1996–97. Non-executive Director: Inst. of Internat. Visual Arts, 1994–; Focus Central London, TEC, 1998–2001; English Languages Services Internat. Ltd, 1998–; New Ways to Work, 1998–2001; ITDG Publishing, 1999–2004; Stonewall, 2000–06. Member: English Teaching Adv. Cttee, British Council, 1990–98; Educn and Training Sector Gp, DTI, 1993–98. Mem., Islington CHC, 1998–2001. Vice-Pres., Publishers Assoc., 1994–95. Mem., Governing Body, SOAS, 1993–95; Governor: Elizabeth Garrett Anderson Sch., Islington, 1997–2000; Cripplegate Foundn, 2000– (Chair, 2005–07). FRSA 1993; CCMI (CIMgt 1992). *Recreations:* cinema, theatre, France, books. *Address:* 4 Mica House, Barnsbury Square, N1 1RN.

KAHN-ACKERMANN, Georg; Secretary General, Council of Europe, 1974–79; *b* 4 Jan. 1918; *m* 1945, Rosmarie Müller-Diefenbach; one *s* three *d*. *Educ:* in Germany and Switzerland. Served in Armed Forces, 1939–45. Press Reporter and Editor from 1946; Commentator with Radio Bavaria and wrote for newspaper, Abendzeitung, 1950. Author of several books, a publisher's reader, and mem. Exec. Cttee of Bavarian Assoc. of Journalists. Dir, VG WORT, Munich, 1972–74; Vice-Chm., Bd of Deutschlandfunk (Cologne). Mem., Social Democratic Party (SDP), from 1946, and of the German Federal Parliament, 1953–57, 1962–69 and 1970–74. Previous appts include: Vice-Pres., Western European Union Assembly, 1967–70; Chm., Political Commn of Western European Union, 1971–74; Vice-Pres., Consultative Assembly of Council of Europe until elected Secretary General in 1974. Mem. Council, Deutsche Welthunger hilfe; Pres., VG WORT. *Recreation:* ski-ing. *Address:* Sterzenweg 3, 82541 Ammerland, Bayern, Germany.

KAHNEMAN, Anne Marie; *see* Treisman, A. M.

KAHNEMAN, Prof. Daniel, PhD; Eugene Higgins Professor of Psychology, and Professor of Public Affairs, Woodrow Wilson School, Princeton University, 1993–2007, now Emeritus and Senior Scholar; *b* 1934; *m* 1st, Irah; 2nd, 1978, Prof. Anne Marie Treisman, *qv*. *Educ:* Hebrew Univ. (BA 1954); Univ. of Calif, Berkeley (PhD 1961). Lectr, 1961–66, Sen. Lectr, 1966–70, Associate Prof., 1970–73, Prof. of Psychol., 1973–78, Hebrew Univ.; Professor of Psychology: Univ. of BC, 1978–86; Univ. of Calif, Berkeley, 1986–94. Corresp. FBA 2008. (Jtly) Nobel Prize in Econ. Scis, 2002. *Publications include:* Attention and Effort, 1973; (ed jtly) Well-Being: Foundations of Hedonic Psychology, 1999; (ed jtly) Choices, Values and Frames, 2000; (ed jtly) Heuristics and Biases: the psychology of intuitive judgement, 2002; contrib. learned jls. *Address:* 322 Wallace Hall, Woodrow Wilson School of Public and International Affairs, Princeton University, Princeton, NJ 08544–1013, USA.

KAIN, Prof. Roger James Peter, CBE 2005; PhD, DLit; FSA; FBA 1990; Montefiore Professor of Geography, since 1991, and Deputy Vice-Chancellor, since 2002, Exeter University; *b* 12 Nov. 1944; *s* of Peter Albert Kain and Ivy Kain; *m* 1970, Annmaree Wallington; two *s*. *Educ:* Harrow Weald County Grammar Sch.; University College London (BA; PhD 1973; DLit 1998; Fellow 2002). FSA 1992. Tutor, Bedford Coll., London, 1971–72; Exeter University: Lectr, 1972–88; Montefiore Reader in Geography, 1988–91; Hd, Sch. of Geog. and Archaeol., 1999–2001. British Academy: Vice-Pres., 1997–99; Chm. Grants Cttee, 1999–2002; Treas., 2002–. Gill Meml Medal, RGS, 1990; Kenneth Nebenzahl Prize, Newberry Liby, Chicago, 1991. *Publications:* Planning for Conservation: an international perspective, 1984; The Tithe Surveys of England and Wales, 1985, repr. 2006; An Atlas and Index of the Tithe Files of Mid-Nineteenth-Century England and Wales, 1986; (jtly) Cadastral Mapping in the Service of the State: a history of property mapping, 1992; (jtly) The Tithe Maps of England and Wales: a cartographic analysis and county-by-county catalogue, 1995 (McColvin Medal, LA, 1996); (jtly) English Cartography, 1997; (jtly) English Maps: a history, 1999; (ed) Historical Atlas of South-West England, 1999; (jtly) Tithe Surveys for Historians, 2000; Historic Parishes of England and Wales, 2001; (jtly) Enclosure Maps of England and Wales, 2004; (ed) England's Landscape: the South-West, 2006. *Recreations:* mountain walking, gardening. *Address:* University of Exeter, Northcote House, The Queen's Drive, Exeter, EX4 4QJ. *T:* (01392) 263333. *Club:* Athenæum.

KAISER, Michael Martin; President, John F. Kennedy Center for Performing Arts, Washington, since 2001; *b* 27 Oct. 1953; *s* of Harold and Marion Kaiser. *Educ:* Brandeis Univ. (BS); Sloan Sch., MIT (MSM). Pres., Kaiser Associates, 1981–85; Exec. Dir, Kansas City Ballet, 1985–87; Associate Dir, Pierpoint Morgan Library, 1987–91; Exec. Dir, Alvin Ailey American Dance Theatre, 1991–93; Pres., Kaiser-Engler Gp, 1994–95; Executive Director: American Ballet Theatre, 1995–98; Royal Opera House, 1998–2000. *Address:* c/o John F. Kennedy Center for Performing Arts, 2700 F Street NW, Washington, DC 20566–0001, USA.

KAJUMBA, Ven. Daniel Steven Kimbugwe; Archdeacon of Reigate, since 2001; *b* 20 Nov. 1952; *s* of Prince Adonia Kajumba, Buganda royal clan, and Lady Esther Kajumba; family exiled to UK, 1971; *m* 1974, Tina Carole Hewlett; one *s* one *d*. *Educ:* school in Uganda; Southwark Ordination Course; HND 1977; Dip. Inst Municipal Bldg Mgt,

1981; DipTh London 1985; BA (Open) 1987; Postgrad. Cert. Preaching (Univ. of Wales), 2007. Employment before ordination included: Auxiliary Nurse, Bournemouth; Youth Officer, West Cliff Baptist Ch; Dep. Warden, Christian Alliance Centre; Prop., Poole Parkside and Edward Russell Residential Homes for the Elderly. Ordained deacon, 1985, priest, 1986; Curate, Goldington, Dio. St Albans, 1985–87; employment in Uganda, 1987–98, included: Man. Dir, Transocean; Gen. Mgr, Rio Hldgs Internat.; Kingdom of Buganda: Sec. Gen.; Minister for Public Relns, Functions and Protocol, and Foreign Affairs; Team Vicar, Horley St Francis, Dio. Southwark, 1999–2001. *Address:* (home) 84 Higher Drive, Purley, Surrey CR8 2HJ. *T:* (020) 8660 9276; (office) St Matthew's House, 100 George Street, Croydon CR0 1PE. *T:* (020) 8681 5496, *Fax:* (020) 8686 2074; *e-mail:* daniel.kajumba@southwark.anglican.org.

KAKKAR, Prof. Vijay Vir, FRCS, FRCSE; Professor of Surgical Science, Guy's, King's and St Thomas' School of Medicine of King's College London (formerly King's College School of Medicine and Dentistry), 1975–97, and National Heart and Lung Institute, 1990–97, University of London, now Emeritus Professor, King's College London, and University of London; Director, Thrombosis Research Institute, since 1990; Founder, Chairman and Chief Executive, TRI India, since 2004; *b* 22 March 1937; *s* of Dr H. B. and Mrs L. W. Kakkar; *m* 1962, Dr Savitri Karnani; two *s. Educ:* Vikram Univ., Ujjain, India (MB, BS 1960). FRCS 1964; FRCSE 1964. Junior staff appts, 1960–64; Lectr, Nuffield Dept of Surgery, Univ. of Oxford, 1964–65; Dept of Surgery, King's College Hospital, London: Pfizer Res. Fellow and Hon. Sen. Registrar, 1965–68; Sen. Registrar, 1968–69; Lectr and Hon. Sen. Registrar, 1969–71; Sen. Lectr and Hon. Consultant Surgeon, 1972–76; Dir, Thrombosis Res. Unit, 1975–97; Hon. Consultant Surgeon: King's Coll. Hosp. Gp, 1972–97; Mayday Hosp., Croydon, 1984–97; Hon. Cons. Vascular Surgeon, Royal Brompton Nat. Heart and Lung Hosps, 1990–97. Vis. Prof., Harvard Univ. Med. Sch., Boston, 1972. Pres., British Soc. for Haemostasis and Thrombosis, 1984–85 (Founder Mem., 1980, Sec., 1982–83); Member: Eur. Thrombosis Res. Orgn; Concerted Action Cttee on Thrombosis, EEC; Internat. Soc. on Thrombosis and Haemostasis (Chm., Cttee on Venous Thromboembolism); Internat. Surg. Soc.; Assoc. of Surgeons of GB and NI; Vascular Surg. Soc. of GB; Pan-Pacific Surg. Assoc.; Internat. Soc. for Haematology; Internat. Soc. for Angiology; Surg. Res. Soc. of GB; Hon. Mem., Assoc. of Surgeons of India; Hon. Fellow: Acad. of Medicine of Singapore; Hellenic Surgical Soc. Hunterian Prof., RCS, 1969; Lectures: Gunnar Bauer Meml, Copenhagen, 1971; James Finlayson Meml, RCPGlas, 1975; Cross Meml, RCS, 1977; Wright-Schulte, Internat. Soc. on Thrombosis and Haemostasis, 1977; Freyer Meml, RCSI, 1981; Dos Santos, 1994. David Patey Prize, Surg. Soc. of GB and Ireland, 1971. Member Editorial Board: Haemostasis, 1982; Clinical Findings, 1982; Internat. Angiology, 1982; Thrombosis Research, 1990. *Publications:* (jtly) Vascular Disease, 1969; (jtly) Thromboembolism: diagnosis and treatment, 1972; (jtly) Heparin: chemistry and clinical usage, 1976; (jtly) Chromogenic Peptide Substrates: chemistry and clinical usage, 1979; Atheroma and Thrombosis, 1983; 500 pubns in jls on thromboembolism and vascular disease. *Recreations:* golf, ski-ing, cricket. *Address:* Thrombosis Research Institute, Emmanuel Kaye Building, Manresa Road, Chelsea, SW3 6LR. *T:* (020) 7351 8301. *Club:* Athenæum.

KALAM, Dr (Avul Pakir Jainulabdeen) Abdul; President of India, 2002–07; *b* 15 Oct. 1931. *Educ:* Madras Inst. of Technol. Joined Defence, R&D Orgn, India, 1958; Indian Space Res. Orgn, 1963 (posts incl. Project Dir, Satellite Launch Vehicle–III); rejoined Defence R&D Orgn, 1982 (conceived Integrated Guided Missile Devel Prog.); Scientific Advr to Minister of Defence and Sec., Dept of Defence R&D, 1992–99; Principal Scientific Advr, Indian govt, 1999–2001. Formerly Chm., Technol. Inf., Forecasting and Assessment Council. Prof. of Technol. and Societal Transformation, Anna Univ., Chennai. Indira Gandhi Award for Nat. Integration, 1997. Padma Bhushan, 1981; Padma Vibhushan, 1990; Bharat Ratna, 1997. *Address:* c/o Rashtrapati Bhavan, New Delhi 110004, India.

KALETSKY, Anatole; Associate Editor, since 1992, and columnist, The Times (Economics Editor, 1990–96); *b* Moscow, 1 June 1952; *s* of Jacob and Esther Kaletsky; *m* 1985, Fiona Murphy; two *s* one *d. Educ:* Melbourne High Sch., Australia; Westminster City Sch.; King's Coll., Cambridge (BA Maths); Harvard Univ. (MA Econs). Financial Writer, The Economist, 1976–79; Financial Times: Leader Writer, 1979–81; Washington Corresp., 1981–83; Internat. Econs Corresp., 1984–86; NY Bureau Chief, 1986–90; Moscow Assignment, 1990. Hon. Sen. Scholar, King's Coll., Cambridge, 1973–74; Kennedy Scholar, Harvard Univ., 1974–76. Mem., Adv. Bd, UK Know-How Fund for E Europe and former Soviet Union, 1991–; Dir, Kaletsky Economic Consulting, 1997–. Mem. Council, REconS, 1999–. Trustee, New Europe Res. Trust, 1999–. Specialist Writer of Year, British Press Awards, 1980, 1992; Commentator of the Year, What the Papers Say, 1996; Financial Journalist of the Year, Wincott Foundn Award, 1997. *Publications:* The Costs of Default, 1985; In the Shadow of Debt, 1992. *Recreations:* playing the violin, cinema, family life. *Address:* The Times, 1 Pennington Street, E98 1TT. *T:* (020) 7782 5000; Kaletsky Economic Consulting, 39 De Vere Gardens, W8 5AW. *T:* (020) 7589 6222.

KALLAS, Siim; Member, European Commission, since 2004; *b* 2 Oct. 1948; *s* of Udo Kallas and Rita Kallas; *m* 1972, Kristi Kartus; one *s* one *d. Educ:* Tartu State Univ. Chief Specialist, Min. of Finance, Estonia, 1975–79; Gen. Manager, Estonian Savings Bank, 1979–86; Dep. Ed., Rahva Hääl, 1986–89; Chm., Estonian Assoc. of Trade Unions, 1989–91; Pres., Bank of Estonia, 1991–95. MP, Estonia, 1995–2004; Minister: of Foreign Affairs, 1995–96; of Finance, 1999–2002; Prime Minister, 2002–03. Founder and Chm., Estonian Reform Party, 1994–2004. *Publications:* articles on econ. affairs, foreign policy and politics. *Address:* European Commission, Rue de la Loi 200, 1049 Brussels, Belgium.

KALLASVUO, Olli-Pekka; President and Chief Executive Officer, since 2006, Chairman of the Group Executive Board, since 2006 (Member, since 1990) and Member of the Board of Directors, since 2007, Nokia; *b* Lavia, Finland, 13 July 1953. *Educ:* Univ. of Helsinki (LLM). Various positions, Union Bank of Finland; Nokia: joined as Corporate Counsel, 1980; Asst Vice Pres., Legal Dept, 1987–88; Asst Vice Pres., 1988–90, Sen. Vice Pres., 1990–92, Finance; Exec. Vice Pres. and Chief Financial Officer, 1992–97; Corp. Exec. Vice Pres., Nokia Americas, 1997–98; Chief Financial Officer, 1999–2004; Exec. Vice Pres. and Gen. Manager, Mobile Phones, 2004–05; Pres. and Chief Operating Officer, 2005–06. Mem. Bd of Dirs, EMC Corp., 2004–. *Recreations:* golf, tennis, reading about political history. *Address:* Nokia, Keilalahdentie 2–4, PO Box 226, 00045 Helsinki, Finland.

KALLIPETIS, Michel Louis; QC 1989; a Recorder, since 1989; a Deputy High Court Judge; *b* 29 Aug. 1941; *s* of late Takis George Kallipetis and Sheila Gallally. *Educ:* Cardinal Vaughan Sch.; University Coll., London. FCIArb; Chartered Arbitrator, 2002. Exchequer and Audit Dept, 1960–66. Called to the Bar, Gray's Inn, 1968, Bencher, 1997. Registered and accredited mediator, 1996. *Recreations:* opera, cooking, travel. *Clubs:* Reform, Royal Automobile, Garrick.

KALMS, Baron *cr* 2004 (Life Peer), of Edgware in the London Borough of Barnet; **Harold Stanley Kalms,** Kt 1996; President, DSG International (formerly Dixons Group) plc, since 2002 (Chairman, 1972–2002); Treasurer, Conservative Party, 2001–03; *b* 21 Nov. 1931; *s* of Charles and Cissie Kalms; *m* 1954, Pamela Jimack (MBE 1995); three *s. Educ:* Christ's College, Finchley. Whole career with Dixons Group: started in 1948 in one store owned by father; went public, 1962; Man. Dir, 1962–72; Dir, British Gas, 1987–97. Chairman: Volvere plc, 2002–; NMT Gp plc, 2005–08; Acorn Brands, 2006–07. Chm., King's Healthcare NHS Trust, 1993–96. Director: Centre for Policy Studies, 1991–2001 (Treas., 1993–98); Business for Sterling, 1998–2001. Vis. Prof., Business Sch., Univ. (formerly Poly.) of N London, 1991–. Mem., Funding Agency for Schs, 1994–97. Governor: Dixons Bradford City Technol. Coll., 1988–2002; NIESR, 1995–2001. Trustee: Industry in Educn, 1993–2003; Economic Educn Trust, 1993–2002. Hon. FCGI 1991; Hon. Fellow, London Business Sch., 1995. Hon. DLitt: CNAA, 1991; Sheffield 2002; DUniv N London, 1994; Hon. DEcon Richmond, 1996; Hon. DSc Buckingham, 2002. *Recreations:* communal activities, opera, ballet. *Address:* DSG International plc, 84 Brook Street, W1K 5EH. *T:* (020) 7499 3494.

KALMUS, Prof. George Ernest, CBE 2000; FRS 1988; Associate Director, 1986–94, Director, 1994–97, Particle Physics, Rutherford Appleton Laboratory; Visiting Professor, Physics and Astronomy Department, 1984–2000, Fellow, 1998, University College London; *b* 21 April 1935; *s* of late Hans Kalmus and Anna Kalmus; *m* 1957, Ann Christine Harland; three *d. Educ:* St Albans County Grammar Sch.; University Coll. London (BSc Hons, PhD). Res. Asst, Bubble Chamber Gp, UCL, 1959–62; Research Associate, Powell-Birge Bubble Chamber Gp, Lawrence Radiation Lab., Univ. of California, Berkeley, 1962–63 and 1964–67; Lectr, Physics Dept, UCL, 1963–64; Sen. Physicist, Lawrence Rad. Lab., 1967–71; Gp Leader, Bubble Chamber and Delphi Gps, Rutherford Appleton Lab., 1971–86. Mem., various Programme Cttees at CERN, 1974–; Mem., CERN Scientific Policy Cttee, 1990–96 (Chm., 1999–2001). *Publications:* numerous articles on experimental particle physics in Phys. Rev., Phys. Rev. Letters, Nuclear Phys., etc. *Recreations:* ski-ing, reading. *Address:* 16 South Avenue, Abingdon, Oxon OX14 1QH. *T:* (01235) 523340.

See also P. I. P. Kalmus.

KALMUS, Prof. Peter Ignaz Paul, OBE 2001; PhD; CPhys, FInstP; Professor of Physics, 1978–98, and Head of Physics Department, 1992–97, Queen Mary and Westfield (formerly Queen Mary) College, University of London, now Emeritus Professor, Queen Mary, University of London (Hon. Fellow 2003); *b* 25 Jan. 1933; *s* of late Hans and Anna Kalmus; *m* 1957, Felicity (Trixie) Barker; one *s* one *d. Educ:* University Coll. London (BSc, PhD; Fellow 2001). CPhys, FInstP 1967. Res. Associate, University Coll. London, 1957–60; Lectr (part-time), Northern Poly. and Chelsea Poly., 1955–60; Physicist, Argonne Nat. Lab., USA, 1960–64; Queen Mary College, University of London: Lectr, 1964–66; Reader, 1966–78. Visiting Scientist: CERN, Geneva, 1961–62, 1970–71, 1981–82; Univ. of Chicago, 1965. Scientific Advr, UK Delegn to CERN, 1978–81; Member: SERC Nuclear Physics Bd, 1979–82, 1989–93; SERC Astronomy and Planetary Sci. Bd, 1990–93; PPARC Educn & Trng Cttee, 1994–98; PPARC Public Understanding of Sci. Panel, 1994–98. Member Council: Inst. of Physics, 1993–2000 (Vice-Pres., 1996–2000; Chairman: High Energy Physics Gp, 1989–93; London & SE Br., 2005–); Royal Instn, 1996–99 (MRI 1989; Vice-Pres., 1997–99; Chm., Davy Faraday Lab. Res. Cttee, 1998–99); Member: Amer. Phys. Soc., 1963 (Fellow, 1995); European Phys. Soc., 1970 (Mem., High Energy Particle Physics Bd, 1994–98); BAAS, 1986 (Pres., Physics Sect., 1990–91; Hon. Fellow, 2002); International Union of Pure and Applied Physics: Vice Pres., 1999–2002; Mem., 1993–2002, Hon. Sec., 1996–99, Chm., 1999–2002, Commn on Particles and Fields. Rutherford Medal and Prize, 1988, Kelvin Medal and Prize, 2002, Inst. Physics. Outreach Prize, Eur. Physical Soc., 2005. *Publications:* numerous papers in scientific jls. *Recreations:* photography, swimming, listening to jazz. *Address:* Department of Physics, Queen Mary, University of London, Mile End Road, E1 4NS. *T:* (020) 7882 5042; *e-mail:* p.i.p.kalmus@qmul.ac.uk.

See also G. E. Kalmus.

KALVĪTIS, Aigars; Prime Minister of the Republic of Latvia, since 2004; *b* Riga, 27 June 1966; *s* of Edmunds Kalvītis and Velta Kalvite; *m* Kristine Kalvite; three *s. Educ:* Riga Sec. Sch. No 41; Latvian Univ. of Agriculture (Bachelors degree 1992, Masters degree Agricl Economy 1995); University Coll. Cork (Masters course Food Ind. Bus. Admin, 1993). Milkman and tractor driver on farm, Sweden, 1990–91; Dir, Agro Biznesa Centrs, 1992–94; Chm. Bd, Zemgales Piens, jt stock co., 1994; Chm. Commn, Central Union of Latvian Dairying, 1994–98; in-service training, Holstein Assoc., Univ. of Wisconsin, 1995. Mem., 7th Saeima, 1998–99, Member: Budget and Finance (Taxation) Cttee; Public Expenditure and Audit Cttee; Minister: for Agriculture, 1999–2000; for Economics, 2000–02; Mem., 8th Saeima, 2002–04; Chm., parly gp of People's Party, 2002–04. *Address:* Ministru Kabinets, Brivibas Bulvaris 36, Riga 1520, Latvia. *T:* 7082800, *Fax:* 7286598; *e-mail:* vk@mk.gov.lv.

KAMALL, Syed Salah, PhD; Member (C) London Region, European Parliament, since 2005; *b* 15 Feb. 1967; *m* Sandira Beekoo; two *c. Educ:* Latymer Sch.; Univ. of Liverpool (BEng 1988); London Sch. of Econs and Pol Sci. (MSc 1989); City Univ. (PhD 2004). Business systems analyst, NatWest Bank Overseas Dept, 1989–91; Mgt Fellow, Sch. of Mgt, Univ. of Bath, 1994–96; Mgt Res. Fellow, Business Sch., Univ. of Leeds, 1996–97; Associate Dir and Consultant, Omega Partners, 1997–2001; Consultant, SSK Consulting, 2001–05. Co-founder, Prog. Dir, 2002–05, Chm., Global Business Monitor, 2005–, Global Business Res. Inst. Contested (C) West Ham, 2001. *Publication:* Telecommunications Policy, 1996. *Address:* (office) 200 Ewell Road, Surbiton, Surrey KT6 6HL; European Parliament, Rue Wiertz, 1047 Brussels, Belgium.

KAMBA, Prof. Walter Joseph; Herbert Chitepo/UNESCO Professor of Human Rights and Democracy, University of Zimbabwe, 2000; Distinguished Professor, Institute of Peace, Leadership and Governance, Africa University, Zimbabwe, since 2005; Founding Dean, and UNESCO Professor of Human Rights, Democracy and Law, Faculty of Law, University of Namibia, 1994–2000, now Emeritus Professor of Law; *b* 6 Sept. 1931; *s* of Joseph Mafara and Hilda Kamba; *m* 1960, Angeline Saziso Dube; three *s. Educ:* University of Cape Town (BA, LLB); Yale Law School (LLM). Attorney of the High Court of Rhodesia (now Zimbabwe), 1963–66; Research Fellow, Institute of Advanced Legal Studies, London Univ., 1967–68; Lecturer, then Sen. Lectr, in Comparative Law and Jurisprudence, 1969–80, Dean of the Faculty of Law, 1977–80, Univ. of Dundee; Prof. of Law, 1980–91, Vice-Prin., 1980–81, Vice-Chancellor, 1981–91, Univ. of Zimbabwe; Inaug. Dist. Knight Prof. of Law and Educn, Univ. of Manitoba, 1992; Inaug. UNESCO Africa Prof., Utrecht Univ., 1992–96. Chm., Kingstons (booksellers and distributors) (Zimbabwe), 1984–. Chm., Bd of Governors, Zimbabwe Broadcasting Corp., 1987 (Vice-Chm., 1980–87); Member: Public Service Professional Qualifications Panel, Harare, 1981–83; Council, ACU, 1981–83 (Member: Working Party on future policy, 1981; Budget Review Cttee, 1982–83); Commonwealth Standing Cttee on student mobility, 1981–88; Exec. Bd, Assoc. of African Univs, 1984 (Chm., Finance and Admin. Cttee, 1985); Nat. Commn, Law and Popn Studies Project, Zimbabwe, 1986–; Chairman:

Assoc. of Eastern and Southern African Univs, 1984–87; Bd, UNITWIN, 1992–; Vice-President: Internat. Assoc. of Univs, 1985–90; ACP-EEC Foundn for Cultural Co-op., Brussels, 1986–88; Mem., Zimbabwe Nat. Commn for UNESCO, 1987–. Mem., Univ. of Swaziland Commn on Planning, 1986. Legal Adviser, ZANU (Patriotic Front), until 1980; Chm., Electoral Supervisory Commn, 1984–94; Mem., S African Ind. Electoral Commn, 1994; Co-Chm., Malaŵi Nat. Constitutional Conf., 1995; Mem. Adv. Bd, Global Governance Review, 1994–. Trustee: Zimbabwe Mass Media Trust, 1981–; Conservation Trust of Zimbabwe, 1981–87; Legal Resources Foundn, Zimbabwe, 1984–90; African-American Inst., NY, 1985–; Zimbabwe Cambridge Trust, 1987–; Centre for Higher Educn Transformation, S Africa, 1995–; Internat. Trustee, Press Trust of Malaŵi, 1996–; Member: Bd of Trustees, Michael Gelfand Med. Res. Foundn, Zimbabwe, 1986–; Internat. Bd, United World Colls, 1985–87; Mem. Council: Univ. for Peace, Costa Rica, 1981–86; Univ. of Zambia, 1981–86; United Nations Univ., Tokyo, 1983–89 (Chm., Council, 1985–86; Mem., Cttee on Institutional and Programmatic Develt); Univ. of Lesotho, 1987–; Mem., Internat. Adv. Cttee, Synergos Inst., NY, 1987–; Patron, Commonwealth Legal Educn Assoc., 1986–; Governor, Ranche House Coll., Harare, 1980–; Member Board of Governors: Zimbabwe Inst. of Development Studies, 1981– (Chm. Bd, 1986–); Internat. Develt Res. Centre, Canada, 1986–; Commonwealth of Learning, 1988– (Vice-Chm., 1989–); Member: Nat. St John's Ambulance Council for Republic of Zimbabwe, 1982–87; Indep. Internat. Commn on Health Res. for Develt, 1987–; Bd, Internat. Cttee for Study of Educnl Exchange, 1988–; Exec. Cttee, Internat. Develt Res. Centre, Canada, 1989–. Hon. LLD: Dundee, 1982; Natal, 1995; Zimbabwe, 1998; Hon. DHL Rhode Is, 1991; Hon. DLett Charles Sturt, 1995. 50th anniv. Distinguished Service Award, Lesotho, 1995; Ten Years of Democracy Award, Ind. Electoral Commn, SA, 2004. Officier dans l'Ordre des Palmes Académiques (France). *Publications:* articles in Internat. and Comparative Law Quarterly, Juridical Review. *Recreation:* tennis. *Address:* Faculty of Law, University of Zimbabwe, PO Box MP 167, Mount Pleasant, Harare, Zimbabwe. *T:* (4) 333570, *Fax:* (4) 333563; *e-mail:* wkamba@yahoo.com.

KAMEN, Ruth H(ope), MBE 2007; Director, and Sir Banister Fletcher Librarian, British Architectural Library, Royal Institute of British Architects, 1988–2004; *b* NYC, 19 April 1944; *d* of Markus M. Epstein and Hilda W. Epstein (*née* Winner); *m* 1964, Dr Robert I. Kamen (marr. diss. 1985). *Educ:* Univ. of Wisconsin (BA 1964); Smith Coll., Northampton, Mass (MAT 1965); Simmons Coll., Boston (MSLS 1967). FCLIP (FLA 1993; ALA 1986). Ref. Librarian, Fine Arts Dept, Res. Div., Boston Public Liby, 1965–70; Royal Institute of British Architects, British Architectural Library: Cataloguer, Handley-Read Collection, 1973; Loans, Serials and Ref. Librarian, 1974; Sen. Inf. Librarian, 1974–76; Hd of Liby Inf. Services, 1976–88. Sec., British Architectural Liby Trust, 1988–2001, 2003–04. Chm., ARLIS UK and Ireland, 1982–86 (Hon. Mem., ARLIS, 2005). FRSA 1989. Hon. FRIBA 2002. *Publications:* British and Irish Architectural History: a bibliography and guide to sources of information, 1981 (Besterman Award, LA); contrib. to books, jls and websites on architecture and librarianship. *Recreations:* art and architecture, painting, theatre, riding, shopping (especially antiques). *Address:* 15 Bingham Place, W1U 5AZ. *T:* (020) 7935 8975. *Club:* Architecture.

KAMIL, Geoffrey Harvey; His Honour Judge Kamil; a Circuit Judge, since 1993; *b* 17 Aug. 1942; *s* of Peter and Sadie Kamil; *m* 1968, Andrea Pauline Kamil (*née* Ellis); two *d.* *Educ:* Leeds Grammar Sch.; Leeds University (LLB). Admitted as Solicitor of the Supreme Court, 1968; Partner with J. Levi & Co., solicitors, Leeds, 1968–87; Asst Stipendiary Magistrate, 1986–87; Stipendiary Magistrate, W Midlands, 1987–90, W Yorks, 1990–93; Asst Crown Court Recorder, 1986–91; Recorder, 1991–93; Ethnic Minority Liaison Judge, Leeds and Bradford, 1998–; Liaison Judge, Wakefield and Pontefract, 1998–; Chm., Immigration Appeals Tribunal, 1998–2000. Judicial Studies Board: Member: Magisterial Cttee, 1991–93; Equal Treatment Adv. Cttee, 2000–; Family Cttee, 2004–. Member: Centre for Criminal Justice Studies, Leeds Univ., 1992–; W Yorks Race Issues Adv. Gp, 1998–; Parole Bd, 2000–; Race Issues Adv. Cttee, NACRO, 2003–. Leeds Law Society: Mem. Cttee, 1983–87; Chm., Courts Cttee, 1983–87; Mem., Duty Solicitor Cttee, 1986–87; Mem., Leeds Bar/Law Soc. Liaison Cttee, 1983–87. Sec., Kirkstall Lodge Hostal for Ex-Offenders, 1976–87. *Recreations:* golf, swimming, pumping iron, the Dales, classic cars, TV soap addict. *Address:* Bradford Combined Court Centre, The Law Courts, Exchange Square, Drake Street, Bradford BD1 1JA. *Clubs:* Bradford (Bradford); Moor Allerton Golf (Leeds).

KAMPFNER, John Paul; Chief Executive, Index on Censorship, since 2008; *b* 27 Dec. 1962; *s* of Dr Fred Kampfner and Betty Kampfner (*née* Andrews); *m* 1992, Lucy Ash; two *d.* *Educ:* Westminster Sch.; Queen's Coll., Oxford (BA Hons Modern Hist. and Russian). Reuters, 1984–89 (Correspondent, Moscow, 1985–86, Bonn, 1987–89); Daily Telegraph: Berlin and Eastern Europe corresp., 1989–91; Moscow corresp., 1991–94; Chief Political Corresp., Financial Times, 1995–98; Political Corresp., Today prog., BBC Radio, 1998–2000; documentary maker, BBC, 2000–02; Political Ed., 2002–05, Ed., 2005–08, New Statesman. Columnist, Daily Telegraph, 2007–. Chm., Turner Contemporary, 2008–. FRSA 2003. Journalist of Year, For. Press Assoc., 2002. *Publications:* Inside Yeltsin's Russia, 1994; Robin Cook, 1998; Blair's Wars, 2003. *Recreations:* tennis, theatre, travel. *Address:* Index on Censorship, 6–8 Amwell Street, EC1R 1UQ. *T:* (020) 7278 2313; *e-mail:* john@jkampfner.net.

KAN Yuet-Keung, Sir, GBE 1979 (CBE 1967; OBE 1959); Kt 1972; JP; Chairman, Hong Kong Trade Development Council, 1979–83; Chairman, Bank of East Asia Ltd, 1963–83; *b* 26 July 1913; *s* of late Kan Tong Po, JP; *m* 1940, Ida; two *s* one *d.* *Educ:* Hong Kong Univ.; London Univ. BA Hong Kong 1934. Solicitor and Notary Public. Sen. Unofficial MLC 1968–72, Sen. Unofficial MEC 1974–80, Hong Kong. Pro-Chancellor, Chinese Univ. of Hong Kong, 1983–96 (Chm., Council, 1973–83). Hon. Fellow, LSE, 1980. Hon. LLD: Chinese Univ. of Hong Kong, 1968; Univ. of Hong Kong, 1973. Order of Sacred Treasure, 3rd Class, Japan; Officier de l'Ordre National du Mérite (France), 1978; Officer's Cross, Order of Merit 1st class (Germany), 1983; Grand Decoration of Honour in Gold with Star (Austria), 1983; Order of Sacred Treasure, 2nd class (Japan), 1983; Knight Grand Cross, Royal Order of Northern Pole Star (Sweden), 1983. *Recreations:* tennis, swimming, golf.

See also Yuet Wai Kan.

KAN, Prof. Yuet Wai, FRCP 1983; FRS 1981; Louis K. Diamond Professor of Hematology, University of California, San Francisco, since 1984; *b* 11 June 1936; *s* of Kan Tong Po and Kan Li Lai Wan; *m* 1964, Alvera L. Limauro; two *d.* *Educ:* Univ. of Hong Kong (MB, BS, DSc). Research Associate, Children's Hosp. Medical Center, Dept of Pediatrics, Harvard Medical Sch., Boston, Mass; Asst Prof. of Pediatrics, Harvard Medical Sch., 1970–72; Associate Prof. of Medicine, Depts of Medicine and Laboratory Medicine, Univ. of California, San Francisco, 1972–77; Chief, Hematology Service, San Francisco General Hospital, 1972–79; Investigator, Howard Hughes Med. Inst. Lab., 1976–2003; Prof. of Lab. Medicine and Medicine, Univ. of California, 1977–. Dir, Molecular Biology Inst., Univ. of Hong Kong, 1990–94 (Hon. Dir, 1988–90). Trustee, Croucher Foundn, 1992– (Chm., 1997–). Member: Nat. Acad. of Scis, USA, 1986; Academia Sinica, Taiwan, 1988; Foreign Mem., Chinese Acad. of Scis, 1996. Hon. MD Univ. of Cagliari, Sardinia, 1981; Hon. DSc: Chinese Univ. of Hong Kong, 1981; Univ. of Hong Kong, 1987; Open Univ. of Hong Kong, 1998. *Publications:* contribs to: Nature, Genetics, Proc. of Nat. Academy of Sciences, Jl of Clinical Investigation, Blood, British Jl of Haematology, and others. *Address:* HSW 901, University of California, 513 Parnassus Avenue, San Francisco, CA 94143–0793, USA. *T:* (415) 4765841, *Fax:* (415) 4762956.

See also Sir Kan Yuet-Keung.

KANDEL, Prof. Eric Richard, MD; University Professor, since 1983 and Senior Investigator, Howard Hughes Medical Institute, since 1984, Columbia University; *b* 7 Nov. 1929; *s* of Herman and Charlotte Kandel; *m* 1956, Denise Bystryn; one *s* one *d.* *Educ:* Harvard Coll. (BA 1952); New York Univ. Sch. of Medicine (MD 1956). Intern, Montefiore Hosp., NY, 1956–57; Associate in Res., Lab. of Neurophysiol., Nat. Inst. of Mental Health, Bethesda, 1957–60; Resident in Psychiatry, 1960–64, Staff Psychiatrist, 1964–65, Massachusetts Mental Health Center, Harvard Med. Sch., Boston (Milton Res. Fellow, 1961–62); Instructor, Dept of Psychiatry, Harvard Med. Sch., 1963–65; Associate Prof., then Prof., Depts of Physiol. and Psychiatry, NY Univ. Sch. of Medicine, 1965–74; Chief, Dept of Neurobiol. and Behavior, Public Health Res. Inst. of City of NY, 1968–74; College of Physicians and Surgeons, Columbia University: Prof., Depts of Physiol. and Psychiatry, 1974–, and Dept of Biochem. and Molecular Biophysics, 1992–; Dir, Center for Neurobiol. and Behavior, 1974–83. Associate Editor: Annual Rev. of Neurosci., 1977–82; Jl Neurophysiol., 1977–80; Jl Neurosci., 1981–83; Learning and Memory, 1993–; Reviews Ed., Neuron, 1988–; Mem., Editl Bd, Proc. NAS, 1991–97. Pres., Soc. for Neurosci., 1980–81. Member: Bd of Trustees, Cold Spring Harbor Labs, 1985–90; Bd of Dirs, McKnight Foundn, 1986–98; Bd of Scientific Advrs, Merck Foundn, 1991–94. Mem., numerous professional socs. Holds numerous hon. degrees, including: Hon. DSc: Edinburgh, 1999; (Medicine) UCL, 2001. Numerous prizes and awards, including: Internat. Award for Outstanding Achievement in Med. Sci., Gairdner Foundn, Canada, 1987; Nat. Medal of Sci., NAS, 1988; NY Acad. of Medicine Award, 1996; Gerard Prize, Soc. of Neurosci., 1997; Wolf Prize in Biol. and Medicine, Israel, 1999; (jtly) Nobel Prize for Physiol. or Medicine, 2000. *Publications:* Cellular Basis of Behavior: an introduction to behavioral neurobiology, 1976; (ed) Handbook of Physiology: The Nervous System, Vol. 1, Cellular Biology of Neurons, 1977; A Cell-Biological Approach to Learning, 1978; The Behavioral Biology of Aplysia: a contribution to the comparative study of opisthobranch molluscs, 1979; (ed jtly) Principles of Neural Science, 1981, 4th edn 2000; (ed jtly) Molecular Aspects of Neurobiology, 1986; (ed) Molecular Neurobiology in Neurology and Psychiatry, 1987; (ed jtly) Essentials of Neural Science and Behavior, 1995; (with L. Squire) From Mind to Molecules, 1999; In Search of Memory, 2006; contrib. numerous papers to learned jls incl. Jl Neurophysiol., Amer. Jl Physiol., Jl Physiol., Nature, Science, Brain Res., Scientific American. *Recreations:* tennis, opera. *Address:* Center for Neurobiology and Behavior, Columbia University College of Physicians and Surgeons, 1051 Riverside Drive, New York, NY 10032, USA. *T:* (212) 3054143, *Fax:* (212) 5435474; *e-mail:* erk5@Columbia.edu.

KANE, Archie Gerard, CA; Group Executive Director, Insurance and Investments, Lloyds TSB Group plc, and Chief Executive, Scottish Widows plc, since 2003; *b* 16 June 1952; *s* of Archie and Rose Kane; *m* 1986, Diana Muirhead; two *d.* *Educ:* Glasgow Univ. (BAcc); City Univ. (MBA); Harvard Business Sch. (AMP). CA 1977. FCIBS 2005. Student CA, Mann Judd, 1974–77; Asst Manager, Price Waterhouse, 1978–80; General Telephone & Electronics Corporation, 1980–85: Sen. Mgt Auditor, Sylvania, 1980–82; Asst Financial Controller, 1982–83, Finance Dir, 1983–85, Directories Corp.; Finance Dir, British Telecom Yellow Pages Sales Ltd, 1986; Gp Finance Controller, TSB Commercial Hldgs Ltd, 1986–89; TSB Bank plc: Financial Controller, then Dir, Financial Control, Retail Banking Div., 1989–91; Dir, Financial Control, 1991–92, Ops Dir, 1992–94, Retail Banking and Insce; Gp Strategic Develt Dir, 1994–96; Lloyds TSB Group plc: Project Dir, Post-Merger Integration, then Retail Financial Services Dir, 1996; Dir, Gp IT and Ops, 1997–99; Dir, 2000–; Gp Exec. Dir, IT and Ops, 2000–03; Dir of various cos in the Lloyds TSB and Scottish Widows Gp, 2000–. Chm., APACS (Admin) Ltd, 2001–03; Dir, Hill Samuel Asset Mgt Internat. Ltd, 2003–. Chm., ABI, 2007– (Mem. Bd, 2004–); Member: Takeover Panel, 2007–; Retail Financial Services Gp, 2007–. FCIBS 2005. *Recreations:* golf, tennis, ski-ing. *Address:* Lloyds TSB Group plc, 25 Gresham Street, EC2V 7HN. *T:* (020) 7356 1409; *e-mail:* archie.kane@lloydstsb.co.uk.

KANE, Prof. George, FBA 1968; Professor of English Language and Medieval Literature, 1965–76 and Head of English Department, 1968–76, King's College, London, Professor Emeritus, University of London, since 1976; *b* 4 July 1916; *o s* of George Michael and Clara Kane; *m* 1946, Katherine Bridget, *o d* of Lt-Col R. V. Montgomery, MC; one *d* (one *s* decd). *Educ:* St Peter's Coll.; British Columbia University; Toronto Univ.; University Coll., London. BA (University of BC), 1936; Research Fellow, University of Toronto, 1936–37; MA (Toronto), 1937; Research Fellow, Northwestern Univ., 1937–38; IODE Schol., for BC, 1938–39. Served War of 1939–45: Artists' Rifles, 1939–40; Rifle Bde, 1940–46 (despatches). PhD (London), 1946; Asst Lecturer in English, University Coll., London, 1946, Lecturer, 1948, Reader in English, 1953, Fellow, 1971; Prof. of English Language and Literature and Head of English Dept, Royal Holloway College, London Univ., 1955–65; William Rand Kenan Jr Prof. of English in Univ. of N Carolina at Chapel Hill, 1976–87, Chm. of Div. of Humanities, 1980–83, Prof. Emeritus, 1987–. Fellow, KCL, 1976. Vis. Prof., Medieval Acad. of America, 1970, 1982, Corresp. Fellow, 1975, Fellow, 1978; Fellow: Amer. Acad. of Arts and Scis, 1977–91 (resigned); Nat. Humanities Center, 1987–88; Sen. Fellow, Southeastern Inst. of Medieval and Renaissance Studies, 1978. Member: Council, Early English Text Soc., 1969–88; Governing Body, SOAS, 1970–76; Council, British Acad., 1974–76; Governing Body, Univ. of N Carolina Press, 1979–84. Sir Israel Gollancz Memorial Prize, British Acad., 1963, 1999; Haskins Medallist, Med. Acad. of Amer., 1978. Lectures: Chambers Meml, UCL, 1965; Accademia Nazionale dei Lincei, Rome, 1976; John Coffin Meml, Univ. of London, 1979; M. W. Bloomfield Meml, Harvard, 1989; Tucker-Cruse Meml, Bristol Univ., 1991; Public Orator, Univ. of London, 1962–66; Annual Chaucer Lectr, New Chaucer Soc., 1980. Gen. editor of London Edn of Piers Plowman. *Publications:* Middle English Literature, 1951; (ed) Piers Plowman, the A Version, 1960, the B Version, 1975, the C Version, 1997; Piers Plowman: The Evidence for Authorship, 1965; Geoffrey Chaucer, 1984; Chaucer and Langland, 1989; (ed) Chaucer, The Legend of Good Women, 1995; Piers Plowman Glossary, 2005; articles and reviews. *Recreation:* fishing. *Clubs:* Athenæum, Flyfishers'.

KANE, Peter Ronald, PhD; Director, Finance and Performance, Home Office, since 2006; *b* 24 Nov. 1956; *s* of Ronald Kane and Katherine Kane; *m* 1989, Jan Evans; two *d.* *Educ:* St Edmund Hall, Oxford (BA 1st Cl. Hons PPE); London Sch. of Econs (MSc Econs 1979; PhD Econs 1982). Economist, TUC, 1981–88; Chief Econ. Advr, London Bor. of Hackney, 1988–92; Principal, 1992–99, Team Leader, 1999–2001, HM Treasury; Dir, Office of Public Service Reform, Cabinet Office, 2002–05. *Recreations:* travelling the globe, ski-ing, tennis, cinema, reading, current affairs. *Address:* Home Office, 2 Marsham Street, SW1P 4DF. *T:* (020) 7035 1604; *e-mail:* Peter.Kane2@homeoffice.gsi.gov.uk.

KANE, Rosie; Member (Scot Socialist) Glasgow, Scottish Parliament, 2003–07. Scot Socialist spokesman for envmt and transport, Scottish Parlt, 2003–07. Contested: (Scot Socialist Alliance) Glasgow, Rutherglen, 1997; (Scot Socialist) Glasgow Shettleston, Scottish Parlt, 1999.

KAO, Charles Kuen, CBE 1993; PhD; FRS 1997; FREng, FIET, FIEEE; Chairman and Chief Executive Officer, ITx (formerly Transtech) Services Ltd, since 2000; Vice Chancellor, Chinese University of Hong Kong, 1987–96, Hon. Professor, since 1996; *b* Shanghai, 4 Nov. 1933; holds dual US/UK nationality; *s* of Chun-Hsian Kao and late Tisung-Fong Ming; *m* 1959, May-Wan Wong; one *s* two *d*. *Educ:* Woolwich Poly. (BSc London); UCL (PhD 1965). FIEEE 1978; FIET (FIEE 1979); FREng (FEng 1989). Engr, Standard Telephone & Cables Ltd, 1957–60; Res. Scientist, then Res. Manager, Standard Telecom Labs Ltd, ITT Central Europ. Lab., 1960–70; Hd, Electronics Dept, Chinese Univ. of Hong Kong, 1970–74; Chief Scientist, 1974–81, Vice-Pres. and Dir of Engrg, 1982–83, Electro-Optical Products Div., ITT, Va; Exec. Scientist and Corporate Dir of Res., ITT Advanced Tech. Centre, Conn, 1983–87. Fellow: Royal Swedish Acad. of Engrg Sci., 1989; US Nat. Acad. of Engrg, 1990; Europ. Acad. Scis and Art; Academia Sinica, Taiwan, 1994; Chinese Acad. of Sci., 1996. Hon. DSc: Chinese Univ. of Hong Kong, 1985; Sussex, 1990; Durham, 1994; Hull, 1998; Yale, 1999; Dr *hc* Soka, 1991; Hon. DEng Glasgow, 1992; Padova, 1996. Numerous awards and prizes including: Alexander Graham Bell Medal, IEEE, 1985; Marconi Internat. Fellowship, 1985; Faraday Medal, IEE, 1989; Japan Prize, 1996; Prince Philip Medal, Royal Acad. of Engrg, 1996; Charles Stark Draper Prize, Nat. Acad. of Engrg, USA, 1999. *Publications:* Optical Fiber Technology II, 1981; Optical Fiber Systems: technology, design and applications, 1982; Optical Fiber, 1988; A Choice Fulfilled: the business of high technology, 1991. *Recreations:* tennis, hiking, pottery-making. *Address:* c/o S. K. Yee Foundation, Unit 1708 Office Tower, Convention Plaza, 1 Harbour Road, Wanchai, HKSAR; *e-mail:* ckao@ie.cuhk.edu.hk.

KAPI, Hon. Sir Mari, KCMG 2008; Kt 1988; CBE 1983; Chief Justice of Papua New Guinea, since 2003 (Deputy Chief Justice, 1982–2003); a Justice of the Court of Appeal: Solomon Islands, since 1982; Fiji, since 1992; *b* 12 Dec. 1950; *s* of Kapi 'Ila and Mea Numa; *m* 1973, Tegana Kapi; three *s* three *d*. *Educ:* Univ. of Papua New Guinea (LLB); SOAS, Univ. of London (LLM). Admitted to practice in PNG and Australia, 1974. Dep. Public Solicitor, 1976; Associate Public Solicitor, 1977; Public Solicitor, 1978; a Judge of Nat. and Supreme Courts of PNG, 1979. Cross of Solomon Islands, 1994. *Recreations:* tennis, touch Rugby. *Address:* PO Box 7018, Boroko, Papua New Guinea. *T:* 3259273.

KAPLAN, Neil Trevor, CBE 2001; QC (Hong Kong) 1982; arbitrator, mediator; *b* 1 Sept. 1942; *s* of Leslie Henry Kaplan and Sybil Sylvia Kaplan (*née* Gasson); *m* 1st, 1971, Barbara Jane Spector (marr. diss. 1997); one *s* one *d*; 2nd, 1998, Paula White. *Educ:* St Paul's Sch.; King's College London (LLB). FCIArb. Called to the Bar, Inner Temple, 1965, Bencher 1991; practised London, 1965–80; Dep. Principal Crown Counsel, Hong Kong, 1980, Principal Crown Counsel, 1982; private practice, Hong Kong Bar, 1984–90; Solicitor-barrister, Victoria, NSW, 1983; NY Bar, 1986; High Court Judge, Hong Kong, 1990–94; Judge in charge of Construction and Arbitration List, 1990–94. Vis. Prof., City Univ. of Hong Kong, 1995–97 (Hon. Prof., 2001–). Pres., CIArb, 1999–2000 (Chm., Hong Kong Branch, 1984–87 and 1989–90); Chairman: Hong Kong Internat. Arbitration Centre, 1991–2004; Disputes Rev. Bd, new Hong Kong airport, 1995–99; Post-Release Supervision Bd, 1996–2006; WTO Rev. Body, Hong Kong, 2000–04; Hong Kong Telecommunications Appeal Tribunal, 2007– (Dep. Chm., 2001–07); Deputy Chairman: Justice, Hong Kong, 1988–90; Mem., Judicial Studies Bd, 1994–. Mem. Council, ICCA, 1995–. Liveryman, Arbitrators' Co., 1982–. JP Hong Kong, 1984. Silver Bauhinia Star (HKSAR), 2007. *Publications:* (jtly) Hong Kong Arbitration—Cases and Materials, 1991; (jtly) Arbitration in Hong Kong and China, 1994; (jtly) Model Law Decisions, 2002; articles on arbitration. *Recreations:* tennis, travel, food and wine, films, theatre, walking. *Address:* Pine House, The Square, Stow-on-the-Wold, Glos GL54 1AF. *T:* (01451) 833770; *e-mail:* neilkaplan@btconnect.com; 10th Floor, Bank of East Asia Building, 10 Des Voeux Road, Central, Hong Kong. *T:* 25263071; Essex Court Chambers, 24 Lincoln's Inn Fields, WC2A 3EG. *T:* (020) 7813 8000. *Clubs:* Athenæum, Oriental, Old Pauline; Hong Kong, Hong Kong Cricket.

KAPLICKY, Jan; Founder and Partner, Future Systems, since 1979; *b* Prague, 18 April 1937; *s* of Josef Kaplicky and Jirina Kaplicka (*née* Florova); *m* 1991; one *s*; *m* 2007. *Educ:* Coll. of Applied Arts and Architecture, Prague (DipArch 1962). Architect: private practice, Prague, 1964–68; Denys Lasdun & Partners, 1969–71; Piano & Rogers, 1971–73; Spencer & Webster, 1974–75 (Associate); Foster & Partners, 1977–83. *Projects* include: Space Station Wardroom Table (NASA Cert. of Recognition, 1989); MOMI Tent, 1991 (British Construction Industry Award, 1992); Stonehenge Visitor Centre (AJ/Bovis Royal Acad. Award), 1993; Hauer-King House, London, 1994 (Aluminium Imagination Award, Civic Trust, 1996); West India Quay Bridge, Canary Wharf, 1995 (Millennium Product Award, Civic Trust, and RIBA Award, 1998); Wild at Heart flower shop (RIBA Award), 1998; Comme des Garçons, NY and Tokyo, 1999; NatWest Media Centre, Lord's Cricket Ground (Millennium Product Award, and Aluminium Imagination Award, Civic Trust; Stirling Prize, RIBA), 1999; Marni shops, London, Milan, Tokyo, Paris, NY, 1999; Selfridges, Birmingham, 2003; Czech Nat. Liby, 2007. *Exhibitions* include: RIBA, 1982, 1991; Arch. Assoc., London, 1987; Storefront, NY, 1992; New Urban Environments, Tokyo, 1998; ICA, 1998, 2005; Nat. Gall., Prague, 1999; The Cube, Manchester, 1999; FS Originals, Faggionato Fine Arts, 2001. Broadcasts on TV and radio. *Publications:* For Inspiration Only, 1996; More for Inspiration Only, 1999; Confessions, 2002; Czech Inspiration, 2005; *relevant publications*: Future Systems, 1987; Future Systems: the story of tomorrow, 1993; Future Systems, ed M. Field, 1999; Unique Building, 2001; Sketches, 2005; Future Systems, by Deyan Sudjic, 2006; exhibn catalogues; articles in jls throughout the world. *Recreation:* history of modern architecture. *Address:* Future Systems, 20 Victoria Gardens, W11 3PE. *T:* (020) 7243 7670. *Club:* Architecture.

KAPOOR, Anish, CBE 2003; RA 1999; artist and sculptor; *b* Bombay, 12 March 1954; *s* of Rear Adm. D. C. Kapoor and Mrs H. Kapoor; *m* 1995, Susanne Spicale; one *s* one *d*. *Educ:* Hornsey Coll. Art; Chelsea Sch. Art. Lectr, Wolverhampton Polytechnic, 1979–83. Artist in Residence, Walker Art Gall., Liverpool, 1982–83. Mem., Arts Council England (formerly Arts Council of England), 1998–; Trustee, Tate Britain, 2006–. One-man exhibitions include: Lisson Gall., London, 1982, 1984, 1985, 1988, 1989–90, 1993, 1998, 2000, 2003, 2006; Walker Art Gall., Liverpool, 1982, 1983; Barbara Gladstone Gall., NY, 1984, 1986, 1989, 1990, 1998, 2001, 2004, 2007; Tate Gall., London, 1990–91, Tate Modern, 2002; San Diego Mus. Contemporary Art, 1992; Tel Aviv Mus. of Art, 1993; Nat. Gall. of Canada, Ottawa, 1993; Rockefeller Center, NY, 2006; retrospective exhibn, Hayward Gall., 1998; and others in Europe, USA, Australia and Japan; contrib. numerous group exhibns in Britain, Europe, USA, Canada, Australia and Japan, incl. Tate Gall., London, 1983, 1991, 1994; Art Inst., Chicago, 1990; Expo '92, Seville, 1992. Hon. Fellow, Univ. of Wolverhampton, 1999; Hon. FRIBA 2001. Hon. Dr: London Inst., 1997; Leeds, 1997. Premio Duemila, Venice Biennale, 1990; Turner Prize, 1991. *Address:* c/o Lisson Gallery, 67 Lisson Street, NW1 5DA.

KAPPLER, David John; Chairman, Premier Foods plc, since 2004; *b* Winchester, 24 March 1947; *s* of Alec and Hilary Kappler; *m* 1970, Maxine Lea; three *d*. *Educ:* Lincoln Sch. FCMA 1995. Finance Director: Jeyes Gp, 1977–85; Trebor Gp, 1985–89; Cadbury Ltd, 1989–91; Cadbury Confectionery, 1991–93; Cadbury Schweppes plc: Corporate Finance Dir, 1993–94; Chief Financial Officer, 1995–2004. Non-executive Director: Camelot plc, 1995–2001; HMV plc, 2001–06; Intercontinental Hotels plc, 2004–; Shire plc, 2004–. *Recreations:* playing golf, watching other sports, wine. *Address:* Willow House, 147 High Street, Old Amersham, Bucks HP7 0EB. *T:* 07785 714468, (office) (01727) 815897, *Fax:* (01727) 815979; *e-mail:* david.kappler@premierfoods.co.uk. *Clubs:* Royal Automobile, MCC (Associate); Harewood Downs Golf.

KARAMANLIS, Konstantinos A.; MP (NDP) Thessaloniki A, Greece, since 1989; Prime Minister of Greece, since 2004; President, New Democracy Party, since 1997; *b* 14 Sept. 1956; *s* of Alexandros and Ageliki Karamanlis; *m* 1998, Natasa Pazaiti; one *s* one *d* (twins). *Educ:* Sch. of Law, Univ. of Athens; Fletcher Sch. of Law and Diplomacy, Tufts Univ., Boston, USA. In practice as lawyer, 1984–89. Minister of Culture, 2004–06. Vice-President: EPP, 1999– (Hd, Western Balkan Democracy Initiative, 2001–03; Chm., SE European Forum, 2003–05); Internat. Democrat Union, 2002–; Co-Chm., Party Leaders Conf., European Democrat Union, 2003–. *Publications:* Eleftherios Venizelos and Greek Foreign Relations, 1986; (ed) Spirit and Era of Gorbachev, 1987. *Address:* (office) Maximos Mansion, Herodou Attikou 19, 10674 Athens, Greece.

KARAS, Jonathan Marcus; QC 2006; *b* 18 Sept. 1961; *s* of Arie Karas and Enid Novello Karas (*née* Owens); *m* 1989, Tracey Ann Elliott; three *d*. *Educ:* Brentwood Sch.; Trinity Coll., Oxford (Ford Student; MA Hons Lit.Hum.); City Univ. (Dip. Law). Called to the Bar, Middle Temple, 1986; Supplementary Panel, 1995–99, B Panel, 1999–2000, A Panel, 2000–06, of Jun. Counsel to the Crown. Subject Ed., Hill & Redman's Law of Landlord and Tenant, 1987–. *Publications:* (jtly) Elvin & Karas's Unlawful Interference with Land, 1995, 2nd edn 2002; (jtly) Commonhold and Leasehold Reform Act 2002, 2002; Halsbury's Laws of England, 4th edn: (jtly) Compulsory Purchase, 1996 (reissue); Distress, 2000 (reissue, consultant ed.), 2007 (reissue); Forestry, 2007 (reissue, consultant ed.). *Recreations:* writing, embarrassing my daughters. *Address:* Wilberforce Chambers, 8 New Square, Lincoln's Inn, WC2A 3QP. *T:* (020) 7306 0102, *Fax:* (020) 7306 0095. *Club:* Travellers.

KARASIN, Grigory Borisovich; State Secretary and Deputy Minister of Foreign Affairs, Russian Federation, since 2005; *b* 23 Aug. 1949; *m* 1971, Olga V. Karasina; two *d*. *Educ:* Coll. of Oriental Langs, Moscow State Univ. Joined USSR Diplomatic Service, 1972: served: Senegal, 1972–76; Australia, 1979–85; UK, 1988–92; Dir, Dept of Africa, 1992–93, Dept of Inf. and Press, 1993–96, Min. of Foreign Affairs; Dep. Minister of Foreign Affairs, Russian Fedn, 1996–2000; Ambassador to UK, 2000–05.

KARIM, Sajjad Haider; Member (Lib Dem) North West England, European Parliament, since 2004; Partner, Marsdens Solicitors, since 2001; *b* 11 July 1970; *s* of Fazal Karim and Shamshad Karim; *m* 1997, Zahida Chaudhary; one *s* one *d*. *Educ:* London Guildhall Univ. (LLB Hons Business Law); Coll. of Law, Chester. Admitted solicitor, 1997. Mem. (Lib Dem) Pendle BC, 1994–2002. *Address:* 8 Manchester Road, Nelson, Lancs BB9 7EG; *e-mail:* info@sajjadkarim.org.uk.

KARK, Nina Mary, (Mrs A. S. Kark); *see* Bawden, N. M.

KARLE, Jerome, PhD; Chief Scientist, Laboratory for the Structure of Matter, since 1968; *b* NY, 18 June 1918; *s* of Louis Karfunkle and Sadie Helen Kun; *m* 1942, Isabella, *d* of Zygmunt and Elizabeth Lugoski; three *d*. *Educ:* Abraham Lincoln High Sch.; City Coll. of NY (BS 1937); Harvard Univ. (AM 1938); Univ. of Michigan (MS 1942; PhD 1943). Research Associate, Manhattan Project, Chicago, 1943–44; US Navy Project, Michigan, 1944–46; Head, Electron Diffraction Section, Naval Res. Lab., 1946–58, Head of Diffraction Branch, 1958–68. Prof. (part-time), Univ. of Maryland, 1951–70. Pres., Amer. Crystallographic Assoc., 1972; Chm., US Nat. Cttee for Crystallography, NAS and Nat. Res. Council, 1973–75; Pres., Internat. Union of Crystallography, 1981–84. Fellow, Amer. Phys. Soc.; Mem., NAS. Nobel Prize for Chemistry, 1985 (jtly). *Publications:* articles in learned jls on study of atoms, molecules, crystals and solid surfaces by diffraction methods. *Recreations:* stereo-photography, swimming, ice skating. *Address:* Laboratory for the Structure of Matter, Code 6030, Naval Research Laboratory, Washington, DC 20375–5341, USA. *T:* (202) 7672665.

KARMEL, Emeritus Prof. Peter Henry, AC 1976; CBE 1967; Chairman, National Institute of the Arts, Australian National University, 1992–2003; *b* 9 May 1922; *s* of Simeon Karmel; *m* 1946, Lena Garrett; one *s* five *d*. *Educ:* Caulfield Grammar Sch.; Univ. of Melbourne (BA); Trinity Coll., Cambridge (PhD). Research Officer, Commonwealth Bureau of Census and Statistics, 1943–45; Lectr in Econs, Univ. of Melbourne, 1946; Rouse Ball Res. Student, Trinity Coll., Cambridge, 1947–48; Sen. Lectr in Econs, Univ. of Melbourne, 1949; Prof. of Econs, 1950–62, Emeritus, 1965, Univ. of Adelaide; Principal-designate, Univ. of Adelaide at Bedford Park (subseq. Flinders Univ. of SA), 1961–66; Vice-Chancellor, Flinders Univ. of SA, 1966–71; Chancellor, Univ. of Papua and New Guinea, 1969–70 (Chm., Interim Council, 1965–69); Chairman: Univs Commn, 1971–77; Commonwealth Tertiary Educn Commn, 1977–82; Vice-Chancellor, ANU, 1982–87. Chairman: Aust. Inst. of Health, 1987–92; Nat. Council on AIDS, 1988–92. Mem. Council, Univ. of Adelaide, 1955–69; Vis. Prof. of Econs, Queen's Univ., Belfast, 1957–58; Mem. Commonwealth Cttee: on Future of Tertiary Educn, 1961–65; of Economic Enquiry, 1963–65; Mem., Australian Council for Educn Research, 1968– (Pres., 1979–99); Chairman: Cttee of Enquiry into Educn in SA, 1969–70; Interim Cttee for Aust. Schools Commn, 1972–73; Cttee of Enquiry on Med. Schs, 1972–73; Cttee of Enquiry on Open Univ., 1973–74; Australia Council, 1974–77; Cttee on Post-Secondary Educn in Tasmania, 1975–76; Quality of Educn Review Cttee, 1984–85; Member: Commonwealth Govt Cttee to Review Efficiency and Effectiveness in Higher Educn, 1985–86; Adv. Cttee of Cities Commn, 1972–74; CSIRO Adv. Council, 1979–82; Australian Stats Adv. Council, 1988–97. Leader, OECD Review of US Educn Policy, 1978–79 and NZ Educn Policy, 1982. Chm., Canberra Inst. of the Arts, 1988–91. Mem. Council, Chinese Univ. of Hong Kong, 1990–94. FASSA 1952 (Pres., 1987–90); FACE 1969. Hon. LLD: Univ. of Papua and New Guinea, 1970; Univ. of Melbourne, 1975; Univ. of Queensland, 1985; ANU, 1996; Hon. LittD Flinders Univ. of SA, 1971; Hon. DLit Murdoch Univ., 1975; Hon. DLitt Macquarie, 1992; DU Newcastle, NSW, 1978. Mackie Medal, 1975; Aust. Coll. of Educn Medal, 1981. *Publications:* Applied Statistics for Economists, 1957, 1962 (1970 edn with M. Polasek, 4th edn 1977), Portuguese edn, 1972; (with M. Brunt) Structure of the Australian Economy, 1962, repr. 1963, 1966; (with G. C. Harcourt and R. H. Wallace) Economic Activity, 1967 (Italian edn 1969); articles in Economic Record, Population Studies, Jl Royal Statistical Assoc., Australian Jl of Education, and other learned jls. *Address:* 4/127 Hopetoun Circuit, Canberra, ACT 2600, Australia.

KARMILOFF-SMITH, Prof. Annette Dionne, CBE 2004; FBA 1993; Professorial Research Fellow, Developmental Neurocognition Laboratory, School of Psychology,

Birkbeck, University of London, since 2006; *b* 18 July 1938; *d* of late Jack Smith and Doris Ellen Ruth Smith (*née* Findlay); *m* 1st, 1966, Igor Alexander Karmiloff (marr. diss. 1991); two *d*; 2nd, 2001, Mark Henry Johnson. *Educ:* Edmonton County GS; Inst Français de Londres; Holborn Coll. of Law and Langs (Dip. Internat. Conf. Interpreting); Geneva Univ. (Dr of exptl and genetic psychol.). Internat. Conf. Interpreter, UN, 1966–70; Res. Consultant, UNWRA-UNESCO Inst. of Educn, Beirut, 1970–72; Res. Collaborator, Internat. Centre for Genetic Epistemiol., Geneva, 1972–76; Vis. Res. Associate, Max Planck Inst. for Psycholinguistics, Nijmegen, 1978–83; Sen. Res. Scientist (with Special Appt status), MRC Cognitive Development Unit, 1982–98; Hd, Neurocognitive Develt Unit, UCL Inst. Child Health, 1998–2006. Visiting Professor: Univs of Sussex, Brussels, Munich, Chicago, Tel-Aviv and Barcelona, 1979–88; of Psychol., UCL, 1982–2006. Sloan Fellow: Yale Univ., 1978; Univ. of Berkeley, 1981. MAE 1991; FMedSci 1999. FRSA 1997. Dr *hc* Louvain, 2002. BPsS Book Award, 1995; ESF Latsis Prize for Cognitive Science, 2002. *Publications:* A Functional Approach to Child Language, 1979, 2nd edn 1981; (jtly) Child Language Research in ESF Countries, 1981; Beyond Modularity: a developmental perspective on cognitive science, 1992; Baby It's You, 1994; (jtly) Rethinking Innateness: connectionism in a developmental framework, 1996; (jtly) Everything Your Baby Would Ask, 1999; (jtly) Pathways to Language: from foetus to adolescent, 2001; many chapters, and articles in learned jls. *Recreations:* writing/reading poetry, working out, going on multiple diets, writing a satire (Powerful Minds in Flabby Bodies). *Address:* River Quin Barn, Gravelly Lane, Braughing, Ware, Herts SG11 2RD. *T:* (01920) 821414; (work) (020) 7079 0767.

KARPINSKI, Marek Romuald K.; *see* Korab-Karpinski.

KARRAN, Graham, QFSM 1985; Managing Director, Blundell, Benson & Co. Ltd, planning and safety consultants, since 2004; *b* 28 Nov. 1939; *s* of Joseph Karran and Muriel Benson; *m* 1960, Thelma Gott; one *s* one *d*. *Educ:* Bootle Grammar Sch.; Liverpool College of Building. Estate Management, 1958–60; Southport Fire Bde, 1960–63; Lancashire County Fire Bde, 1963–74; Greater Manchester Fire Service, 1974–78; Cheshire County Fire Service, 1978–80; Chief Fire Officer, Derbyshire Fire Service, 1980–83; Chief Fire Officer, W Yorks Fire Service, and Chief Exec., W Yorks Fire and Civil Defence Authy, 1983–90; Man. Dir, Graham Karran & Associates Ltd, 1991–2003. *Publications:* articles in English and Amer. Fire jls. *Recreations:* music, beachcombing, sailing. *Address:* Princes Point, Torquay, Devon.

KARSTEN, Ian George Francis; QC 1990; **His Honour Judge Ian Karsten;** a Circuit Judge, since 1999; *b* 27 July 1944; *s* of late Dr Frederick Karsten and Edith Karsten; *m* 1984, Moira Elizabeth Ann O'Hara (marr. diss. 2002); one *s* two *d*. *Educ:* William Ellis School, Highgate; Magdalen College, Oxford (MA, BCL); Diplômé, Hague Acad. of Internat. Law. Called to the Bar, Gray's Inn, 1967; Midland and Oxford Circuit; commenced practice 1970; Lectr in Law, Southampton Univ., 1966–70, LSE, 1970–88; a Recorder, 1994–99. UK Deleg. to Hague Conf. on Private Internat. Law (Convention on the Law Applicable to Agency) (Rapporteur), 1973–77; Leader, UK Delegn to Unidroit Conf. on Agency in Internat. Sale of Goods, Bucharest, 1979, Geneva, 1983. *Recreations:* opera, travel, chess. *Address:* Blackfriars Crown Court, 1–15 Pocock Street, SE1 0BJ.

KARUNAIRETNAM, Usha; Her Honour Judge Karu; a Circuit Judge, since 2005; *b* 18 Dec. 1958; *d* of Dharamchandra Gupta and Saroj Gupta; *m* 1987, Nadesalingam, (Lee), Karunairetnam; two *s*. Called to the Bar, Middle Temple, 1984; specialist criminal practitioner, SE Circuit; Asst Recorder, 1998–2000; Recorder, 2000–05. *Recreations:* gardening, spending time with family, theatre. *Address:* Inner London Crown Court, Sessions House, Newington Causeway, SE1 6AZ. *T:* (020) 7234 3100, *Fax:* (020) 7234 3203.

KASER, Prof. Michael Charles, DLitt; Hon. Professor and Senior Research Fellow, Institute for German Studies, University of Birmingham, since 1994; Reader in Economics, University of Oxford, and Professorial Fellow of St Antony's College, 1972–93 (Sub-Warden, 1986–87), now Reader Emeritus and Emeritus Fellow; *b* 2 May 1926; *er s* of Charles Joseph Kaser and Mabel Blunden; *m* 1954, Elisabeth Anne Mary, *er d* of Cyril Gascoigne Piggford; four *s* one *d*. *Educ:* King's Coll., Cambridge (Exhibr); DLitt Oxon 1993. Economic Sect., Min. of Works, 1946–47; Foreign Service, London and Moscow, 1947–51; UN Secretariat, Econ. Commn for Europe, Geneva, 1951–63; Faculty Fellow, St Antony's Coll., Oxford, 1963–72; Institute of Slavonic Studies (formerly Institute of Russian, Soviet and East European Studies), University of Oxford: Dir, 1988–93; Sen. Res. Assoc., 1997–2004; Mem., Cttee on SE European Studies (formerly Prog. on Contemporary Turkey) in Oxford, 2000–. Associate Fellow, Green Templeton Coll. (formerly Templeton Coll.), Oxford, 1983–. Hon. Fellow, Divinity Faculty, Univ. of Edinburgh, 1993–96. Visiting Professor of Economics: Inst. Universitaire des Hautes Etudes Internats, Geneva, 1959–63; Univ. of Michigan, 1966; Vis. Faculty (formerly Fellow), Henley Management Coll., 1987–2002; Vis. Lectr, Cambridge Univ., 1967–68, 1977–78 and 1978–79; Vis. Lectr, INSEAD, Fontainebleau, 1959–82, 1988–92. Gen. Ed. Internat. Econ. Assoc., 1986–2007. Specialist Advr, Foreign Affairs Cttee, H of C, 1985–87. Oxford Univ. Latin Preacher, 1982. Convenor/Chm., Nat. Assoc. for Soviet and East European Studies, 1965–73, Chm., Jt Cttee with BUAS, 1980–84; Vice-Chm., Internat. Activities Cttee (Vice-Chm., Area Studies Panel, SSRC) ESRC, 1980–84; Chm., Co-ordinating Council, Area Studies Assocs, 1986–88 (Mem., 1980–93 and 1995; Sec., 1980–84, Vice-Chm., 1984–86); Governor, Plater Coll., Oxford, 1968–95, Emeritus Governor, 1995–2006; Chairman: Acad. Council, Wilton Park (FCO), 1986–92 (Mem., 1985–2001); Acad. Cttee, St Catharine's, Cumberland Lodge, 1991–2001 (Mem., 1973–2001); Sir Heinz Koeppler Trust, 1992–2001 (Mem., 1987–2001). President: British Assoc. for Slavonic and East European Studies, 1988–91 (Vice-Pres., 1991–93); British Assoc. of Former UN Civil Servants, 1994–2001; Chairman: Standing Cttee on E European Affairs, European Econ. Assoc., 1990–93; Keston Inst., 1994–2002. Member: Council, Royal Econ. Soc., 1976–86, 1987–90; Council, RIIA, 1979–85, 1986–92; Internat. Soc. Sci. Council, UNESCO, 1980–91; Council, SSEES, 1981–87; E Europe Cttee, CAFOD, 2001–05; Project Evaluation Gp, Univ. of Halle, 2002–05. Sec., British Acad. Cttee for SE European Studies, 1988–93 (Mem., 1970–75, 1983–93). Steering Cttee, Königswinter Anglo-German Confs, 1969–90 (Chm., Oxford Organizing Cttee, 1975–78). Hon. Mem., Eur. Assoc. Comparative Econs, 2006. Pres., Albania Soc. of Britain, 1992–95; Trustee, King George VI and Queen Elizabeth Foundn, 1987–2006. Missions for various internat. agencies, 1955–, incl. EC to Moscow, 1991, UNICEF to Albania, 1991, Turkmenistan and Uzbekistan, 1992, and IMF to Kyrgyzstan, 1998. Editorial Boards: Member: Central Asian Survey; Slavonic and East European Rev.; former Member: Econ. Jl; Jl of Industrial Econs; Soviet Studies; Oxford Rev. of Educn; CUP E European Monograph Series; World Develt; European Econ. Rev.; Energy Econs. Hon. DSocSc Birmingham, 1994. KSG 1990. Knight's Cross, Order of Merit (Poland), 1999; Order of Naim Frashëri (Albania), 1999. *Publications:* Comecon: Integration Problems of the Planned Economies, 1965, 2nd edn 1967; (ed) Economic Development for Eastern Europe, 1968; (with J. Zieliński) Planning in East Europe, 1970; Soviet Economics, 1970; (ed, with R. Portes) Planning and Market Relations, 1971; (ed, with H. Höhmann and K. Thalheim) The New Economic Systems of Eastern Europe, 1975; (ed, with A. Brown) The Soviet Union since the Fall of Khrushchev, 1975, 2nd edn 1978; Health Care in the Soviet Union and Eastern Europe, 1976; (ed with A. Brown) Soviet Policy for the 1980s, 1982; (ed jtly) The Cambridge Encyclopaedia of Russia and the Soviet Union, 1982, revd edn as The Cambridge Encyclopaedia of Russia and the Former Soviet Union, 1994; Gen. Ed., The Economic History of Eastern Europe 1919–1975, vols I and II (1919–49), vol. III (1949–75), 1985–86; (ed with E. A. G. Robinson) Early Steps in Comparing East-West Economies, 1992; (ed with D. Phillips) Education and Economic Change in Eastern Europe and the Former Soviet Union, 1992; (with S. Mehrotra) The Central Asian Economies after Independence, 1992; Privatization in the CIS, 1995; The Economies of Kazakhstan and Uzbekistan, 1997; papers in economic jls and symposia. *Address:* 31 Capel Close, Oxford OX2 7LA. *T:* (01865) 515581; *e-mail:* michael.kaser@economics.ox.ac.uk. *Club:* Reform.

KASMIN, John; art dealer, since 1960; *b* 24 Sept. 1934; *s* of Vera D'Olzewski and David Kosminsky (known as Kaye); *m* 1959, Jane Nicholson (marr. diss.); two *s*. *Educ:* Magdalen College School, Oxford. Adventurous and varied jobs in New Zealand, 1952–56; art gallery assistant, London, 1956–60; Founder Director: Kasmin Ltd, 1961– (in partnership with late Marquess of Dufferin and Ava); Knoedler Kasmin Ltd, 1977–92. *Recreations:* reading, walking in landscapes, museums, cities, collecting old postcards. *Address:* c/o Kasmin Ltd, 34 Warwick Avenue, W9 2PT.

KASPAROV, Garry Kimovich; chess player, retired; *b* Baku, Azerbaijan, 13 April 1963; *né* Harry Weinstein; *s* of Kim Moiseyevich Weinstein and Klara Kasparova; *m* 1st, 1989, Maria Arapova (marr. diss. 1994); one *d*; 2nd, 1996, Yulia Vovk; one *s*; 3rd, Dasha; one *d*. Youngest world chess champion, 1985; retained title, 1986, 1987, 1990, 1993, 1995; lost title, 2000. Resigned from FIDE and formed Professional Chess Assoc. (with Nigel Short); introduced (with Nigel Short) Rapid Chess, 1987; won first title, 1993; rejoined FIDE, 1994; won PCA World Championship, NY, 1995. Played supercomputer Deep Blue, Philadelphia, 1996 and NY, 1997, series drawn; played first Advanced chess against Topolov, Spain, 1998; played The World, 1999. Founded Kasparov Chess Acad., 1997. *Publications:* New World Chess Champion, 1985; The Test of Time, 1986; London-Leningrad Championship Games, 1987; (with Donald Trelford) Child of Change, 1987; Unlimited Challenge, 1990; (with Daniel King) Kasparov Against the World, 2000; Garry Kasparov on My Great Predecessors: Part I and Part II, 2003, Part III and Part IV, 2004, Part V, 2006; How Life Imitates Chess, 2007; Garry Kasparov on Modern Chess: Part I, 2007. *Address:* c/o SMSI, 249 Peruvian Avenue, F-2, Palm Beach, FL 33480, USA.

KATCHALSKI-KATZIR, Prof. Ephraim; *see* Katzir.

KATENGA-KAUNDA, Reid Willie; Malaŵi Independence Medal, 1964; Malaŵi Republic Medal, 1966; Political Adviser to State President, Malaŵi, since 1994; *b* 20 Aug. 1929; *s* of Gibson Amon Katenga Kaunda and Maggie Talengeske Nyabanda; *m* 1951, Elsie Nyabanda; one *s* three *d* (and one *s* one *d* decd). *Educ:* Ndola Govt Sch., Zambia; Inst. of Public Administration, Malaŵi; Trinity Coll., Oxford Univ.; Administrative Staff Coll., Henley; LSE. Sec., Nkhota Kota Rice Co-op. Soc. Ltd, 1952–62; Dist. Comr, Karonga, Malaŵi, 1964–65; Sen. Asst Sec., Min. of External Affairs, Zomba, Malaŵi, 1966; MP and Parly Sec., Office of the President and Cabinet, Malaŵi, 1966–68; Dep. Regional Chm., MCP, Northern Region, 1967–68; Under Sec., Office of the President and Cabinet, 1968–69; High Comr in London, 1969–70; Perm. Sec., Min. of Trade, Industry and Tourism, 1971–72; High Comr in London, 1972–73, and concurrently to the Holy See, Portugal, Belgium, Holland and France; business exec., 1975–94. Dep. Sec. Gen., 1992–99, Sec. Gen., 1999–, United Democratic Front, Malaŵi. Chm., Interparty Technical Cttee on Peace and Unity, 1999–. Dep. Chm., Ncheu and Mchinji Inquiry Commn, 1967. *Recreations:* reading, walking, cinema, Association football. *Address:* c/o PO Box 511, Blantyre, Malaŵi.

KATIN, Peter Roy; concert pianist; Professor, London College of Music and Media, Thames Valley University, since 2001; *b* 14 Nov. 1930; *m* 1954, Eva Zweig; two *s*. *Educ:* Henry Thornton Sch.; Westminster Abbey; Royal Academy of Music. First London appearance at Wigmore Hall, 1948. A leading Chopin interpreter. Performances abroad include most European countries, West and East, S and E Africa, Japan, Canada, USA, Hong Kong, India, New Zealand, Singapore, Malaysia. Many recordings, incl. complete sonatas of Mozart, complete nocturnes and impromptus of Chopin, complete preludes of Rachmaninov, complete lyric pieces of Grieg, fortepiano works of Clementi, Chopin and Schubert, and major works by Brahms, Mendelssohn, Scarlatti, Schubert, Schumann and Tchaikovsky. Professor: Royal Acad. of Music, 1956–59; RCM, 1992–2001. Vis. Prof. in piano, Univ. of Western Ontario, 1978–84. Founder: Katin Centre for Advanced Piano Studies, 1991; Katin Trio, 1997. Mem. Incorporated Soc. of Musicians (ISM). FRAM, ARCM. Hon. DMus De Montfort, 1994. Chopin Arts Award, NY, 1977. *Recreations:* reading, writing, theatre, tape recording, photography. *Address:* 41 First Avenue, Bexhill-on-Sea, E Sussex TN40 2PL. *T:* (01424) 211167; *e-mail:* peter.katin@btinternet.com.

KATKHUDA, Samih Suleiman; His Honour Judge Katkhuda; a Circuit Judge, since 1995; *b* 15 Dec. 1941; *s* of Dr S. M. Katkhuda and U. Katkhuda (*née* Ciĉiĉ); *m* 1968, Suzanne Gundred de Warrenne Crews; two *s*. *Educ:* King's Sch., Bruton, Som; Inns of Court Sch. of Law. Court Admin, CCC, Old Bailey, 1964–73; called to the Bar, Gray's Inn, 1974; in practice as barrister, 1974–95; a Recorder, 1994–95. *Publications:* Forms of Indictment, 1990; Crown Court Index, 2006. *Recreations:* music, travel, reading. *Address:* Snaresbrook Crown Court, 75 Hollybush Hill, Snaresbrook, E11 1QW. *Club:* Savage.

KATKOWSKI, Christopher Andrew Mark; QC 1999; *b* 16 Jan. 1957; *s* of Edward and Maria Katkowski; *m* 1976, Anna Thérèse Louise Gunstone. *Educ:* Fitzwilliam Coll., Cambridge (BA Law 1978; LLB 1979). Lectr in Law, City of London Poly., 1979–83; called to the Bar, Gray's Inn, 1982, Bencher, 2007; in practice at the Bar, 1984–; Jun. Counsel to the Crown (Common Law), 1992–99; Hd of Chambers, 2006–. Mem., Attorney-Gen.'s Supplementary Panel, 1988–92. *Recreation:* time with Anna and our dogs on our farm on Exmoor. *Address:* Landmark Chambers, 180 Fleet Street, EC4A 2HG. *T:* (020) 7430 1221.

KATRITZKY, Prof. Alan Roy, DPhil, PhD, ScD; FRS 1980; FRSC; Kenan Professor of Chemistry, since 1980, and Director, Center for Heterocyclic Compounds, since 1986, University of Florida; *b* 18 Aug. 1928; *s* of Frederick Charles Katritzky and Emily Catherine (*née* Lane); *m* 1952, Agnes Juliane Dietlinde Kilian; one *s* three *d*. *Educ:* St Catherine's Coll., Oxford (BA, BSc 1953, MA; DPhil 1954; Hon. Fellow, 2005); Trinity Hall, Cambridge (PhD 1963); Churchill Coll., Cambridge (ScD 1963). FRIC 1963. Sen. Demy, Magdalen Coll., Oxford, 1954–57; Lecturer: Pembroke Coll., Oxford, 1956–58; Trinity Hall, Cambridge, 1958–63; Founder Fellow of Churchill Coll., Cambridge, 1960–63; Prof. of Chemistry, Univ. of E Anglia, 1963–80, Dean, Sch. of Chem. Sciences, UEA, 1963–70 and 1976–80. Foreign Member: Polish Acad. of Sci., 1991; Real Acad. Catalonia, Barcelona, 1995; Slovenian Acad., 2001; Russian Acad. of Sci., Siberian Section, 2003; Indian Nat. Acad. of Sci., 2003; Eur. Acad. of Arts and Scis, Salzburg, 2008. Foreign Fellow, RACI, 1983; FAAAS 2000; Fellow, World Innovation Foundn, 2003; Hon. Fellow: Italian Chem. Soc., 1978; Polish Chem. Soc., 1985; Internat. Soc. of

Heterocyclic Chem., 1995; Chem. Res. Foundn of India, 2003. Hon. Prof., Beijing Inst. of Tech., China, 1995. Dr *hc*: Univ. Nacional, Madrid, 1986; Univ. Poznan, Poland, 1990; Medical Acad., Gdansk, 1994; Univ. of E Anglia, 1995; Univ. of Toulouse, 1996; Univ. of St Petersburg, 1997; Technical Univ., Bucharest, 1998; Rostov Univ., 2000; Univ. Ghent, 2001; Bundelkhand Univ., 2001; Univ. of Timişoara, Romania, 2003; Univ. of Wrotzlaw, Poland, 2005; Univ. of Jena, Germany, 2006. Tilden Medal, Chem. Soc., 1975–76. Heterocyclic Award, RSC, 1983; Medals of Tartu State Univ., subseq. Univ. of Tartu, Estonia, 1986, 1992; Golden Tiger award, Exxon Corp., 1989; Internat. Soc. of Heterocyclic Chemistry Award, 1993; Medal of Univ. of Thessaloniki, 1993; Florida Award, 1995, Cope Sen. Scholar Award, 2001, ACS; Heyrovski Medal, Czech Acad., 1997; Kametani Prize, Japan, 1999; Gold Medal, Scientific Partnership Foundn, Moscow, 2001; Curie Medal, Polish Chem. Soc., 2003; Globe Award, Scientific Partnership Foundn, Moscow, 2003; Lifetime Achievement Award, Indian Chem. Soc., 2003. Cavaliere ufficiale, Order Al Merito Della Repubblica Italiana, 1975. *Publications:* (ed) Advances in Heterocyclic Chemistry, Vols 1–95, 1963–; (ed) Physical Methods in Heterocyclic Chemistry, Vols 1–6, 1963–72; Principles of Heterocyclic Chemistry, 1968 (trans. into French, German, Italian, Japanese, Russian, Polish and Spanish); Chemistry of Heterocyclic N-Oxides (monograph), 1970; Heteroaromatic Tautomerism (monograph), 1975; Handbook of Heterocyclic Chemistry, 1985, 2nd edn 2000; Heterocycles in Life and Society, 1998; Chm. Editorial Bd, Comprehensive Heterocyclic Chemistry (8 vols), 1985, 2nd edn (10 vols) 1996; 3rd edn (17 vols) 2008; Chm. Editorial Bd, Comprehensive Organic Functional Group Transformations (7 vols), 1995, 2nd edn (7 vols) 2003; scientific papers in Heterocyclic Chem. *Recreations:* walking, travel, windsurfing. *Address:* Department of Chemistry, University of Florida, Gainesville, FL 32611, USA. *T:* (352) 3920554, *Fax:* (352) 3929199. *Club:* Oxford and Cambridge.

KATSAV, Moshe; President of the State of Israel, 2000–07; *b* Iran, 5 Dec. 1945; emigrated to Israel, 1951; *m* Gila; four *s* one *d. Educ:* Hebrew Univ. of Jerusalem. Newspaper reporter, Yediot Aharonot, 1966–68; Member of Knesset, 1977–2000; Mem., Interior and Educn Cttees, Knesset, 1977–81; Dep. Minister of Housing and Construction, 1981–84; Minister: of Labour and Social Affairs, 1984–88; of Transportation, and Mem., Ministerial Cttee on Defence, 1988–92; Chm., Parly Cttee of Chinese-Israeli Friendship League, 1992–96; Dep. Prime Minister, Minister of Tourism, and Minister for Israeli-Arab Affairs, 1996–99; Chm., Ministerial Cttee for Nat. Events and Mem., Ministerial Cttee on Defence, 1996–99; Mem., Foreign Affairs and Defence Cttee, 1999–2000. Mem., Commn on adoptive children, 1978; Chm., Commn to determine higher educn tuition, 1982. Chairman, Likud Party: at Hebrew Univ., Jerusalem, 1969; in Knesset, 1992–96. Pres., B'nai B'rith Youth, 1968. Mayor, Kiryat Malachi, 1969 and 1974–81. Mem., Bd of Trustees, Ben-Gurion Univ., 1978. Hon. Dr: Nebraska, 1998; George Washington, 2001; Hartford, Connecticut, 2001; Yeshiva, 2002; Bar Ilan, 2003; China Agricl Univ., Beijing, 2003; Sorbonne, 2004; ELTE Univ. of Budapest, 2004. Bene Merito Medal, Acad. of Sci., Australia, 2004. *Publications:* contrib. articles in newspapers, Maariv and Yediot Aharonot. *Address:* c/o Office of the President, 3 Hanassi Street, Jerusalem, 92188 Israel.

KATZ, Ian Alexander; Executive Editor, The Guardian, since 2006; *b* 9 Feb. 1968; *s* of John Katz and Adrienne (*née* Karnovsky); *m* 1997, Justine Roberts; two *s* two *d. Educ:* University College Sch., London; New Coll., Oxford (BA PPE 1989). Reporter, Sunday Correspondent, 1989–90; The Guardian: reporter, 1991–94; NY Corresp., 1994–97; Internet Editor, 1997–98; Features Ed., 1998–2006. *Recreations:* sailing, tree-house construction. *Address:* The Guardian, Kings Place, 90 York Way, N1 9AG.

KATZ, Philip Alec Jackson; QC 2000; a Recorder, since 2000; *b* 8 May 1953; *s* of Stanley Zeb Jackson (*née* Katz) and Anita Jackson; adopted patronymic Katz, 1976. *Educ:* Roundhay Grammar Sch., Leeds; University Coll., Oxford (MA). Called to the Bar, Middle Temple, 1976. *Address:* 9–12 Bell Yard, WC2A 2JR. *T:* (020) 7400 1800.

KATZIR, Prof. Ephraim (Katchalski), PhD; Institute Professor, Weizmann Institute of Science, since 1978; President, State of Israel, 1973–78; *b* Kiev, Ukraine, 16 May 1916; *s* of Yehuda and Tsila Katchalski; *m* 1938, Nina Gotlieb (decd); one *s* (two *d* decd). *Educ:* Rehavia High Sch., Jerusalem; Hebrew Univ., Jerusalem (chemistry, botany, zool., bacteriol.; MSc *summa cum laude* 1937; PhD 1941). Settled in Israel with parents, 1922; involved in Labour youth movement; Inf. Comdr, Jewish Self-Defence Forces (Hagana). Asst, Dept of Theoretical and Macromolecular Chem., Hebrew Univ., 1941–45; Res. Fellow, Polytechnic Inst., and Columbia Univ., NY, 1946–48; Actg Head, Dept of Biophys., Weizmann Inst. of Science, Rehovot, Israel, 1949–51, Head 1951–73 (mem. founding faculty of Inst.); Chief Scientist, Israel Def. Min., 1966–68; Head, Dept of Biotechnology, Tel Aviv Univ., 1980–88. Vis. Prof. of Biophys., Hebrew Univ., 1953–61; Guest Scientist, Harvard Univ., 1957–59; Vis. Prof., Rockefeller Univ., NY, and Univ. of Mich, Ann Arbor, 1961–65; Sen. Foreign Scientist Fellowship, UCLA, 1964; Battelle Seattle Res. Center, Washington, 1971; Regents Prof., Univ. of Calif., San Diego, 1979; First Herman F. Mark Chair in Polymer Sci., Poly. Inst., NY, 1979. President: World ORT Union, 1986–90; Cobiotech, 1989–95. Member: Biochem. Soc. of Israel; Israel Acad. of Sciences and Humanities; Israel Chem. Soc.; Council, Internat. Union of Biochem.; AAAS; Assoc. of Harvard Chemists; Leopoldina Acad. of Science, Germany; World Acad. of Art and Science; New York Acad. of Science (Life Mem.). Centennial Foreign Fellow, Amer. Chem. Soc.; For. Associate, Nat. Acad. of Sciences of USA. For. Member: The Royal Soc.; Amer. Philosoph. Soc.; Acad. des Scis, France, 1989. Hon. Fellow, Scientific Acad. of Argentina, 1986; Hon. Member: Amer. Acad. of Arts and Sciences; Amer. Soc. of Biol Chemists; Harvey Soc.; Romanian Acad. of Scis, 1991; Hon. MRI 1989. Hon. PhD: Hebrew Univ., 1973; Poly. Inst. of NY, 1975; Brandeis Univ., Univ. of Mich, and Hebrew Union Coll., 1975; Weizmann Inst. of Science, 1976; Northwestern Univ., Evanston, 1978; Harvard, 1978; McGill, 1980; ETH Zurich, 1980; Thomas Jefferson, 1981; Oxford, 1981; Miami, 1983; Technion, Israel Inst. of Technology, 1983; Univ. of Buenos Aires, 1986. Tchernikhovski Prize, 1948; Weizmann Prize, 1950; Israel Prize in Nat. Sciences, 1959; Rothschild Prize in Nat. Sciences, 1961; Linderstrøm Lang Gold Medal, 1969; Hans Krebs Medal, 1972; Alpha Omega Achievement Medal, 1979; Underwood Prescott Award, MIT, 1982; first Japan Prize, Science and Technol. Foundn of Japan, 1985; Internat. Enzyme Engineering Award, 1987. Hon. Founding Editor, Biopolymers, 1986– (Mem., Editorial Bd, 1963–86). Comdr, Legion of Honour (France), 1990. *Address:* Weizmann Institute of Science, Rehovot 76100, Israel.

KAUFFMANN, Prof. C. Michael, MA, PhD; FBA 1987; FMA; FSA; Professor of History of Art and Director, Courtauld Institute of Art, University of London, 1985–95, now Professor Emeritus; *b* 5 Feb. 1931; *s* of late Arthur and late Tamara Kauffmann; *m* 1954, Dorothea (*née* Hill); two *s. Educ:* St Paul's Sch.; Merton Coll., Oxford (Postmaster); Warburg Inst., London Univ. (Jun. Research Fellow). Asst Curator, Photographic Collection, Warburg Inst., 1957–58; Keeper, Manchester City Art Gall., 1958–60; Victoria and Albert Museum: Asst Keeper, 1960–75, Keeper, 1975–85, Dept of Prints & Drawings and Paintings; Asst to the Director, 1963–66; Visiting Associate Prof., Univ. of Chicago, 1969. Mem. Exec. Cttee, NACF, 1987–2005; Trustee, Nat. Museums and Galls on Merseyside, 1986–99. *Publications:* The Baths of Pozzuoli: medieval illuminations of

Peter of Eboli's poem, 1959; An Altar-piece of the Apocalypse, 1968; Victoria & Albert Museum: Catalogue of Foreign Paintings, 1973; British Romanesque Manuscripts 1066–1190, 1975; Catalogue of Paintings in the Wellington Museum, 1982; John Varley, 1984; Studies in Medieval Art, 1992; Biblical Imagery in Medieval England 700–1550, 2003.

KAUFMAN, Rt Hon. Sir Gerald (Bernard), Kt 2004; PC 1978; MP (Lab) Manchester, Gorton, since 1983 (Manchester, Ardwick, 1970–83); *b* 21 June 1930; *s* of Louis and Jane Kaufman. *Educ:* Leeds Grammar Sch.; The Queen's Coll., Oxford. Asst Gen.-Sec., Fabian Soc., 1954–55; Political Staff, Daily Mirror, 1955–64; Political Correspondent, New Statesman, 1964–65; Parly Press Liaison Officer, Labour Party, 1965–70. Parly Under-Sec. of State, DoE, 1974–75, Dept of Industry, 1975; Minister of State, Dept of Industry, 1975–79; Shadow Envmt Sec., 1980–83; Shadow Home Sec., 1983–87; Shadow Foreign Sec., 1987–92. Chm., Select Cttee on Nat. Heritage, 1992–97, on Culture, Media and Sport, 1997–2005. Chm., All-Party Dance Gp, 2006–; Mem., Parly Cttee of PLP, 1980–92. Mem., Labour Party NEC, 1991–92. Mem., Royal Commn on H of L reform, 1999. Chm., Booker Prize Judges, 1999. HPk (Pakistan), 1999. *Publications:* (jtly) How to Live Under Labour, 1964; (ed) The Left, 1966; To Build the Promised Land, 1973; How to be a Minister, 1980, 2nd edn 1997; (ed) Renewal: Labour's Britain in the 1980s, 1983; My Life in the Silver Screen, 1985; Inside the Promised Land, 1986; Meet Me in St Louis, 1994. *Recreations:* travel, going to the pictures. *Address:* 87 Charlbert Court, Eamont Street, NW8 7DA. *T:* (office) (020) 7219 3000.

KAUFMAN, Prof. Matthew Howard, PhD, DSc; FRCPE, FRCSE, FRSE; Professor of Anatomy, University of Edinburgh, 1985–2008, now Emeritus (Head of Department of Anatomy, 1985–95); *b* 29 Sept. 1942; *s* of Benjamin and Dora Kaufman; *m* 1973, Claire Lesley Kaufman (*née* Farrow); two *s. Educ:* Westminster City Sch.; Univ. of Edinburgh (MB ChB 1967; DSc 1984); Univ. of Cambridge (PhD 1973; MA 1975; ScD 1993). FRCPE 1996; FRCSE 2000; FRSE 2008. Pre- and post-registration clinical posts, 1967–69; Research Associate, Inst. of Animal Genetics, Edinburgh, 1970; MRC Jun. Research Fellow, Physiol Lab., Cambridge, 1970–73; Royal Soc./Israel Acad. of Scis Research Fellow, and MRC Travelling Fellow, Weizmann Inst. of Science, 1973–75; University of Cambridge: Univ. Demonstrator, 1975–77; Lectr in Anatomy, 1977–85; Fellow and College Lectr in Anatomy, King's Coll., 1980–85. Chm., W. R. Henderson Trust, 1988–2007. Symington Meml Prize in Anatomy, Anatomical Soc., 1979; Evian Health Award, 1988. *Publications:* Early Mammalian Development: parthenogenetic studies, 1983; The Atlas of Mouse Development, 1992; (with J. B. L. Bard) The Anatomical Basis of Mouse Development, 1999; Surgeons at War, 2000; The Regius Chair of Military Surgery in the University of Edinburgh, 2003; Musket-ball and Sabre Injuries, 2003; Medical Teaching in Edinburgh during the 18th and 19th centuries, 2003; Edinburgh Phrenological Society: a history, 2005; Dr John Barclay (1758–1826): extra-mural teacher of anatomy in Edinburgh, 2007; research papers in the fields of experimental and descriptive embryology (co-author, first paper pub. on embryonic stem cells, 1981), cytogenetics, developmental biology and teratology, medical history. *Recreations:* history of medicine, particularly of anatomy; the artefacts of phrenology, military surgery. *Address:* e-mail: professor.kaufman@yahoo.co.uk.

KAUFMANN, Julia Ruth, OBE 1997; freelance consultant for voluntary sector, since 2000; *b* 29 March 1941; *d* of Prof. Felix Kaufmann and Ruth (*née* Arnold); marr. diss.; two *s* one *d. Educ:* St George's Hosp., London (SRN); Sidney Webb Coll. (BEd London); Brunel Univ. (Dip. Social Policy and Admin). Advisory teacher, ILEA, 1974–76; Dir, Centre for Social Educn, 1976–78; Press Officer, 1978–79, Dir, 1979–87, Gingerbread; Dir, BBC Children in Need Appeal, 1987–2000. Mem., Employment Relns Adv. Panel on Public Appts, 2001–04; Comr, Postcomm, 2000–05. Chairman: Nat. Assoc. of Toy and Leisure Libraries, 2000–04; Whizz Kidz, 2006–; Bd Mem., Capacity Builders, 2006–; Vice-Pres., DEAFAX, 2000–; Trustee, Community Network, 2000–. *Address:* 2 Carberry Road, SE19 3RU. *T:* (020) 8653 3877.

KAUL, Mahendra Nath, OBE 1975; Chairman, India's Restaurants Ltd, since 1997; *b* 28 July 1922; *s* of Dina Nath Kaul and Gauri Kaul; *m* 1955, Rajni Kapur, MA, MLS; one *d. Educ:* Univ. of the Punjab, India (BA). Joined Radio Kashmir of All India Radio, as news reader, actor and producer of dramas, 1949; appeared in two feature films and assisted in producing several documentaries, 1950–52; news reader and actor in three languages, also drama producer, All India Radio, New Delhi, 1952–55; joined Indian service of Voice of America, Washington DC, 1955, later becoming Editor of the service; joined external service of BBC, as newscaster, producer and dir of radio plays; producer/presenter, BBC TV prog. for Asian Viewers in UK, 1966–82. OBE awarded for services to race relations in Gt Britain. Received The Green Pennant from HRH The Duke of Edinburgh, awarded by Commonwealth Expedition (COMEX 10), 1980. *Recreations:* golf, cooking, boating, classical and light classical music, reading political works. *Address:* 109 Clive Court, Maida Vale, W9 1SF. *T:* (020) 7286 8131.

KAUNDA, Kenneth David; President of Zambia, Oct. 1964–1991 (Prime Minister, N Rhodesia, Jan.–Oct. 1964); Chancellor of the University of Zambia, 1966–91; *b* 28 April 1924; *s* of late David Julizgia and Hellen Kaunda, Missionaries; *m* 1946, Betty Banda; five *s* two *d* one adopted *s* (and two *s* decd). *Educ:* Lubwa Training Sch.; Munali Secondary Sch. Teacher, Lubwa Training Sch., 1943–44, Headmaster, 1944–47; Boarding Master, Mufulira Upper Sch., 1948–49. African National Congress: District Sec., 1950–52; Provincial Organising Sec., 1952–53; Sec.-Gen., 1953–58; Nat. Pres., Zambia African Nat. Congress, 1958–59; founded United Nat. Independence Party, 1958, Nat. Pres., 1960–91, re-elected, 1995–2000; Chm., Pan-African Freedom Movement for East, Central and South Africa, 1962; Minister of Local Government and Social Welfare, N Rhodesia, 1962–63. Chairman: Organization of African Unity, 1970, 1987; Non-aligned Countries, 1970. Hon. Doctor of Laws: Fordham Univ., USA, 1963; Dublin Univ., 1964; University of Sussex, 1965; Windsor Univ., Canada, 1966; University of Chile, 1966; Univ. of Zambia, 1974; Univ. of Humboldt, 1980; DUniv York, 1966. *Publications:* Black Government, 1961; Zambia Shall Be Free, 1962; Humanist in Africa, 1966; Humanism in Zambia and its implementation, 1967; Letter to My Children; Kaunda on Violence, 1980. *Recreations:* golf, music, table tennis, football, draughts, gardening and reading. *Address:* c/o UNIP, POB 30302, 10101 Lusaka, Zambia.

KAUNDA, Reid Willie K.; *see* Katenga-Kaunda.

KAVANAGH, Prof. Dennis Anthony; Professor of Politics, 1996–2006, Emeritus Professor and Research Fellow in Politics and Communications, since 2007, University of Liverpool; *b* 27 March 1941; *s* of Patrick Kavanagh and Agnes Kavanagh; *m* 1966, Monica Anne Taylor; one *s* three *d. Educ:* St Anselm's Coll., Birkenhead; Univ. of Manchester (BA, MA Econ). Asst Lectr, Univ. of Hull, 1965–67; Lectr, then Sen. Lectr, Univ. of Manchester, 1967–81; Prof. of Politics, Univ. of Nottingham, 1982–95. Ford Foundn Fellow, Univ. of Stanford, Calif, 1969–70; Visiting Professor: European Univ. Inst., Florence, 1977; Univ. of Calif, San Diego, La Jolla, 1979; Hoover Instn, Stanford Univ., 1985. Member Council, ESRC, 1991–94; Aurora, 1999. Mem. Editl Bd, political jls. FRSA. *Publications:* Constituency Electioneering in Britain, 1970; Political Culture, 1972;

(with R. Rose) New Trends in British Politics: contemporary issues for research and discussions, 1977; The Politics of the Labour Party, 1982; Political Science and Political Behaviour, 1983; (ed) Comparative Politics and Government: essays in honour of S. E. Finer, 1984; British Politics, continuities and change, 1985, 4th edn 2000; Thatcherism and British Politics: the end of consensus?, 1987, 2nd edn 1990; Consensus Politics from Attlee to Thatcher, 1989, 2nd edn 1994; The Thatcher Effect, 1989; Personalities and Politics, 1990; Electoral Politics, 1992; (ed with A. Seldon) The Major Effect, 1995; Election Campaigning: the new marketing of politics, 1995; The Reordering of British Politics, 1997; (ed) Oxford Dictionary of Political Leadership, 1998; (with A. Seldon) The Powers Behind the Prime Minister, 1999; (ed with A. Seldon) The Blair Effect, 2005; with David Butler: The British General Election of October 1974, 1975; The British General Election of 1979, 1980; The British General Election of 1983, 1984; The British General Election of 1987, 1988; The British General Election of 1992, 1992; The British General Election of 1997, 1997; The British General Election of 2001, 2002; The British General Election of 2005, 2006; over 100 contribs to jls and books. *Recreations:* running, tennis, music, obituaries. *Address:* Lynton, Belgrave Road, Bowdon, Altrincham, Cheshire WA14 2NZ; *e-mail:* dennis.kavanagh@talktalk.net. *Club:* Bowdon Lawn Tennis.

KAVANAGH, George Collins; Sheriff of North Strathclyde at Paisley, since 1999; *b* 29 May 1940; *s* of George and Mary Kavanagh (*née* Donagher); *m* 1967, Rosaleen Anne-Marie McCrudden or Kavanagh; two *s* two *d*. *Educ:* St John's Sch., Cumnock; St Joseph's High Sch., Kilmarnock; Univ. of Glasgow. Home Office, 1961–71; Hughes Dowdall, Solicitors, 1971–99, Sen. Partner, 1991–99. Examr, Soc. of Apothecaries, 2000–. KCHS 2000 (KHS 1995). *Recreations:* reading, cricket, sailing. *Address:* Sheriff's Chambers, Sheriff Court House, St James Street, Paisley PA3 2HW.

KAVANAGH, Patrick Bernard, CBE 1977; QPM 1974; Deputy Commissioner, Metropolitan Police, 1977–83; *b* 18 March 1923; *s* of late Michael Kavanagh and late Violet Kavanagh (*née* Duncan); *m* Beryl (*d* 1984), *er d* of late Lt-Comdr Richard Owen Williams, RNR and Annie (*née* McShiells); one *s* two *d*. *Educ:* St Aloysius Coll., Glasgow. Rifle Bde, 1941–43; Para. Regt, 1943–46 (Lieut). Manchester City Police (Constable to Supt), 1946–64; Asst Chief Constable, Cardiff City Police, 1964–69; Asst and Dep. Chief Constable, S Wales Constabulary, 1969–73; Asst Comr (Traffic), Metropolitan Police, 1974–77. Attended Administrative Staff Coll., Henley-on-Thames, 1961. Mem., Gaming Bd for GB, 1983–91. *Recreations:* walking, bird watching, music, crosswords. *Address:* c/o Metropolitan Police, 2 Bessborough Street, SW1V 2JF. *Club:* Royal Automobile.

KAVANAGH, P. J., (Patrick Joseph Gregory Kavanagh), FRSL; writer; columnist: Times Literary Supplement, 1997–2002; The Spectator, 1983–97; *b* 6 Jan. 1931; *s* of H. E. (Ted) Kavanagh and Agnes O'Keefe; *m* 1st, 1956, Sally Philipps (*d* 1958); 2nd, 1965, Catherine Ward; two *s*. *Educ:* Douai Sch.; Lycee Jaccard, Lausanne; Merton Coll., Oxford (MA). British Council, 1957–59. Actor, 1959–70. Mem., Kingman Cttee of Inquiry into English Lang., 1986–88. *Publications: poems:* One and One, 1960; On the Way to the Depot, 1967; About Time, 1970; Edward Thomas in Heaven, 1974; Life before Death, 1979; Selected Poems, 1982; Presences (new and selected poems), 1987; An Enchantment, 1991; Collected Poems, 1992 (Cholmondely Prize, 1992); Something About, 2004; *novels:* A Song and Dance, 1968 (Guardian Fiction Prize, 1968); A Happy Man, 1972; People and Weather, 1979; Only by Mistake, 1986; *essays:* People and Places, 1988; A Kind of Journal, 2003; *autobiography:* The Perfect Stranger, 1966 (Richard Hillary Prize, 1966); *travel autobiography:* Finding Connections, 1990; *for children:* Scarf Jack, 1978; Rebel for Good, 1980; *edited:* Collected Poems of Ivor Gurney, 1982; (with James Michie) Oxford Book of Short Poems, 1985; The Bodley Head G. K. Chesterton, 1985; Selected Poems of Ivor Gurney, 1990; A Book of Consolations, 1992; Voices in Ireland: a traveller's literary companion, 1994. *Recreation:* walking. *Address:* c/o Peters, Fraser, Dunlop, Drury House, 34–43 Russell Street, WC2B 5HA.

KAVANAGH, Trevor Michael Thomas; Associate Editor, The Sun, since 2006; *b* 19 Jan. 1943; *s* of Bernard George Kavanagh and Alice Rose (*née* Thompson); *m* 1967, Jacqueline Gai Swindells; two *s*. *Educ:* Reigate Grammar Sch. The Sun, 1978–: Industrial Corresp., 1981–83; Political Ed., 1983–2006. Chairman: Parly Lobby Journalists, 1990; Parly Press Gall., 2000. Journalist of the Year, Specialist Reporter of the Year, 1997, Reporter of the Year, 2005, British Press Awards; Scoop of the Year, What the Papers Say, 2000, 2004; Print Story of the Year, For. Press Assoc., 2004; Political Journalist of the Year, Pol Studies Assoc., 2004. *Recreations:* golf, swimming, travel. *Address:* Press Gallery, House of Commons, SW1A 0AA. *Club:* Royal Automobile.

KAWCZYNSKI, Daniel; MP (C) Shrewsbury and Atcham, since 2005; *b* 24 Jan. 1972; *s* of Leonard and Halina Kawczynski; *m* 2000, Kate Lumb. *Educ:* Univ. of Stirling (BA Hons Business Studies with French 1994). Sales account manager with BT and Cable and Wireless, in Europe, Middle East and Africa, 1994–2004. Contested (C) Ealing Southall, 2001. Mem., Internat. Develt Select Cttee, 2008–; Chm., All Party Gp for Dairy Farmers, 2006–. *Address:* House of Commons, SW1A 0AA; *e-mail:* kawczynskid@parliament.uk.

KAY, Sir Andrew Watt, Kt 1973; retired; Regius Professor of Surgery, University of Glasgow, 1964–81; part-time Chief Scientist, Scottish Home and Health Department, 1973–81; *b* 14 Aug. 1916; of Scottish parentage; *m* 1st, 1943, Janetta M. Roxburgh (*d* 1990); two *s* two *d*; 2nd, 1992, Phyllis Gillies. *Educ:* Ayr Academy; Glasgow Univ. MB, ChB (Hons) with Brunton Memorial Prize, 1939; FRCSEd 1942; FRFPSG 1956 (Pres. 1972–); FRCS 1960; FRCSGlas 1967; FRSE 1971; MD (Hons) with Bellahouston Gold Medal, 1944. Major Royal Army Medical Corps i/c Surgical Div., Millbank Military Hospital, 1946–48; ChM (Hons) 1949; Consultant Surgeon in charge of Wards, Western Infirmary, Glasgow, 1956–58; Asst to Regius Prof. of Surgery, Glasgow Univ., 1942–56; Prof. of Surgery, University of Sheffield, 1958–64. Sims Travelling Prof., Australasia, 1969; McLaughlin Foundn Edward Gallie Vis. Prof., Canada, 1970. Rock Carling Fellowship, 1977. Pres., Surgical Research Soc., 1969–71. Member: Royal Commission on Medical Education, 1965–68; MRC, 1967–71; Chm., Scottish Hosps Endowment Research Trust, 1983–89; Hon. Mem., The N Pacific Surgical Assoc. FRACS 1970; FRCSCan 1972; FCS(SoAf) 1972; Hon. Fellow: Norwegian Surgical Assoc., Belgian Surgical Soc.; Amer. Surg. Assoc., 1972; Hon. FACS, 1973; Hon. FRCSI, 1979. Hon. DSc: Leicester, 1973; Sheffield, 1975; Manchester, 1981; Nebraska, 1981; Hon. MD Edinburgh, 1981. Cecil Joll Prize, RCS, 1969; Gordon-Taylor Lectureship and Medal, 1970. *Publications:* (with R. A. Jamieson, FRCS) Textbook of Surgical Physiology, 1959 (2nd edn 1964); Research in Medicine: problems and prospects, 1977; several papers in medical and surgical jls on gastroenterological subjects. *Recreation:* gardening. *Address:* 5 Loch Road, Milngavie, Glasgow G62 8BB.

KAY, Prof. Anthony Barrington, (Barry), PhD, DSc; FRCPE, FRCP, FRCPath, FMedSci; FRSE; Professor of Clinical Immunology and Head, Department of Allergy and Clinical Immunology, Imperial College, London University, 1980–2004, now Professor Emeritus; Senior Research Investigator, National Heart and Lung Institute Division, Imperial College London, since 2004; Hon. Consultant Physician, Royal Brompton Hospital, since 1980; Consultant Physician (Allergy), The London Clinic, since 2005; *b* 23 June 1939; *s* of Anthony Chambers and Eva Gertrude (*née* Pearcey; she *m* 2nd H. Kay; now Mrs E. G. Reuben); *m* 1966, Rosemary Margaret Johnstone; three *d*. *Educ:* King's Sch., Peterborough; Edinburgh Univ. (MB, ChB 1963; DSc 1976); Jesus Coll., Cambridge (MA 1966; PhD 1970); Harvard Med. Sch. FRCPE 1975; FRCP 1980; FRCPath 1989. T. K. Stubbins Res. Fellow, RCP, 1969; Res. Fellow, Harvard Med. Sch., 1970–71; Lectr in Respiratory Diseases, Univ. of Edinburgh, 1972–74; Dep. Dir and Consultant, Immunology Div., Blood Transfusion Service, Royal Infirmary, Edinburgh, 1974–76; Sen. Lectr, then Reader, in Exptl Pathology, Dept of Pathology, Univ. of Edinburgh, 1977–79. Specialist Advr, H of L Select Cttee Enquiry into Allergy, 2006–07. Co-founder and Consultant, Circassia Ltd. President: European Acad. of Allergology and Clinical Immunology, 1989–92; Brit. Soc. of Allergy and Clinical Immunology, 1993–. Jt Editor, Clinical and Exptl Allergy, 1984–. FRSE 1993; FMedSci 1999. Hon. Fellow: Amer. Coll. of Allergy, 1986; Amer. Acad. of Allergy, Asthma and Immunology, 2004; Hon. Member: Amer. Assoc. of Physicians, 1988; Hungarian Soc. of Allergology and Clinical Immunology, 1990; Swiss Soc. of Allergology and Clinical Immunology, 1991; Belgian Soc. for Allergol. and Clin. Immunol., 1999. Hon. Dr Medicine and Surgery, Ferrara, 2000. Scientific Achievement Award, Internat. Assoc. of Allergology and Clinical Immunology, 1991; Paul Ehrlich Medal, Eur. Acad. of Allergology and Clin. Immunol., 2005. *Publications:* edited: Asthma: clinical pharmacology and therapeutic progress, 1986; Allergy and Inflammation, 1987; Allergic Basis of Asthma, 1988; Allergy and Asthma: new trends and approaches to therapy, 1989; Eosinophils, Allergy and Asthma, 1990; Eosinophils in Allergy and Inflammation, 1993; Allergy and Allergic Diseases, 1997, 2nd edn 2008; numerous scientific articles on allergy and asthma. *Recreations:* Baroque and modern bassoon, tennis, country walks. *Address:* Stamford Brook House, 12 Stamford Brook Avenue, W6 0YD. *T:* (020) 8741 5899. *Clubs:* Chelsea Arts, Hurlingham.

KAY, Brian Christopher; broadcaster and musician; *b* 12 May 1944; *s* of Noel Bancroft Kay and Gwendoline Mary (*née* Sutton); *m* 1st, 1970, Sally Lyne; one *s* one *d*; 2nd, 1983, Gillian Fisher. *Educ:* Rydal Sch.; King's Coll., Cambridge (MA 1966); New Coll., Oxford (DipEd 1967). Bass Singer: Westminster Abbey Choir, 1968–71; King's Singers, 1968–82; Chorus Master, Huddersfield Choral Soc., 1983–93; Conductor: Cecilian Singers of Leicester, 1984–92; Cheltenham Bach Choir, 1989–97; Leith Hill Musical Fest., 1996–; Mary Wakefield Westmorland Fest., 1996–2003; Burford Singers, 2002–; Musical Dir, Bradford Fest. Choral Soc., 1998–2002. Presenter: Music in Mind, Radio 4, 1989–98; Brian Kay's Sunday Morning, Radio 3, 1992–2001; Comparing Notes, Radio 4, 1996–98; Brian Kay's Light Programme, Radio 3, 2001–07. Friday Night is Music Night, Radio 2, 1998–. President: Nottingham Choral Trust; Harrogate Choral Soc.; Market Harborough Singers; Derbys Singers; Bristol Bach Choir. Vice-Pres., Assoc. of British Choral Dirs; Patron, Stars Orgn for Scope. Vice-Pres., RSCM, 2005–. Hon. FTCL 2004. Music Presenter of the Year, Sony Gold Award, 1996. *Recreations:* gardening, reading. *Address:* Bell Cottage, Church Lane, Fulbrook, Burford, Oxon OX18 4BA.

KAY, Prof. Elizabeth Jane, PhD; FDSRCPSGlas; Professor of Oral Health and Dean, Peninsula Dental School, since 2006; *b* 10 March 1959; *d* of late Robert Brian Kay and of Cynthia Kay (*née* Bianchi); partner, Stella Ruth Tinsley. *Educ:* Univ. of Edinburgh (BDS 1982); Univ. of Glasgow (MPH 1984; PhD 1991). FDSRCPSGlas 1988; FDSRCS *ad eundem* 2002. Res. Fellow in Dental Epidemiology, Univ. of Edinburgh, 1982–86; Lectr in Community Dental Health, Univ. of Glasgow, 1986–90; Sen. Lectr in Dental Public Health, Univ. of Dundee, 1990–92; Sen. Registrar in Dental Public Health, South Glamorgan HA, 1992–94; University of Manchester: Sen. Lectr in Dental Health Services Res., 1994–98; Prof. of Dental Health Services Res., 1998–2006. *Publications:* (jtly) Communication for the Dental Team, 1996, 2nd edn 2004; (jtly) Clinical Decision Making: an art or a science, 1997; (jtly) A Review of Effectiveness of Oral Health Promotion, 1997; (ed) A Guide to Prevention in Dentistry, 2004; Oral Health Promotion Toolkit, 2004; (jtly) Integrated Dental Treatment Planning, 2005; 120 learned papers in acad. and professional jls. *Recreations:* all things equine, rural or historical. *Address:* Peninsula Dental School, The John Bull Building, Tamar Science Park, Research Way, Plymouth PL6 8BU. *T:* (01752) 437333.

KAY, Prof. Helen Sheppard, (Sarah), DPhil, LittD; FBA 2004; Professor, Department of French and Italian, Princeton University, since 2006; *b* 12 Nov. 1948; *d* of Brian Wilfrid Kay and Dorothea Sheppard Kay; *m* John Williamson (marr. diss.); one *s* two *d*. *Educ:* Somerville Coll., Oxford (BA 1st cl. (Mod. Langs (French)) 1971; DPhil 1976); Univ. of Reading (MA (Linguistics) 1972); LittD Cantab 2005. Kathleen Bourne Res. Fellow, St Anne's Coll., Oxford, 1973–75; Lectr in French, Univ. of Liverpool, 1975–84; University of Cambridge: Lectr, Dept of French, 1984–95; Reader, 1995–2001; Prof. of French and Occitan Lit., 2001–05; Fellow, 1984–2005, Life Fellow, 2005, Girton Coll. Visiting Professor: Dept of Romance Langs, Univ. of Pennsylvania, 1993; Centre for Medieval and Renaissance Studies, QMW, 1996–99; Center for Medieval and Renaissance Studies, UCLA, 1999; Dept of Comparative Lit., Stanford Univ., 2004; Prof. invité, Univ. d'Artois, 1999. Chevalier, Ordre des Palmes Académiques (France). *Publications:* Subjectivity in Troubadour Poetry, 1990; (ed) Raoul de Cambrai, 1992; (ed with Miri Rubin) Framing Medieval Bodies, 1994; The Chanson de geste in the Age of Romance: political fictions, 1995; The Romance of the Rose, 1995; (ed with S. Gaunt) The Troubadours: an introduction, 1999; Courtly Contradictions: the emergence of the literary object in the twelfth century, 2001; Zizek: a critical introduction, 2003; (jtly) A Short History of French Literature, 2003; The Place of Thought: the complexity of one in late Medieval French didactic poetry, 2007; numerous articles and chapters in books. *Recreations:* eating, drinking, walking, reading difficult books. *Address:* Department of French and Italian, Princeton University, East Pyne 303, Princeton, NJ 08544, USA; *e-mail:* sarahkay@princeton.edu; 33 Richard Court, Princeton, NJ 08540, USA.

KAY, Prof. Humphrey Edward Melville, MD, FRCP, FRCPath; Haematologist, Royal Marsden Hospital, 1956–84; Professor of Haematology, University of London, 1982–84 (Professor Emeritus, since 1984); *b* 10 Oct. 1923; *s* of late Rev. Arnold Innes and Winifred Julia Kay; *m* 1st, 1950, April Grace Lavinia Powlett (*d* 1990); one *s* two *d*; 2nd, 1996, Sallie Diana (*née* Charlton), *widow* of Roy Perry, RI. *Educ:* Bryanston Sch.; St Thomas's Hospital. MB, BS 1945. RAFVR, 1947–49; junior appts at St Thomas's Hosp., 1950–56. Sec., MRC Cttee on Leukaemia, 1968–84; Dean, Inst. of Cancer Research, 1970–72. Editor, Jl Clinical Pathology, 1972–80. Member: Council, Wiltshire Wildlife Trust (formerly Wiltshire Trust for Nature Conservation), 1983–96; Nat. Badger Adv. Panel, 1988–98. Christopher Cadbury Medal, Wildlife Trusts, 1996. *Publications:* Poems Polymorphic, 2002; Survey of Wiltshire Hedgehogs, 2002; papers and chapters on blood diseases, etc. *Recreation:* natural history including gardening. *Address:* New Mill Cottage, Pewsey, Wilts SN9 5LD.

KAY, Jervis; *see* Kay, R. J.

KAY, Prof. John Anderson, FBA 1997; FRSE; economist; *b* 3 Aug. 1948; *s* of late James Scobie Kay and of Allison (*née* Anderson); *m* 1986, Deborah Freeman (marr. diss. 1995). *Educ:* Royal High Sch., Edinburgh; Univ. of Edinburgh (MA); Nuffield Coll., Oxford. Fellow of St John's Coll., 1970–, and Lectr in Econs, 1971–79, Univ. of Oxford; Res. Dir, 1979–81, Dir, 1981–86, Inst. for Fiscal Studies; London Business School: Prof., 1986–96;

Dir, Centre for Business Strategy, 1986–91; Prof. of Mgt and Dir, Saïd Business Sch., Univ. of Oxford, 1997–99. Vis. Prof. LSE, 2000–. Chairman: Undervalued Assets Trust, then SVM UK Active Fund, 1994–2005; Clear Capital Ltd, 2004–; Director: London Econs Ltd, 1986–2000 (Chm., 1986–96); Halifax plc (formerly Halifax Building Soc.), 1991–2000; Foreign & Colonial Special Utilities Investment Trust Plc, 1993–2003; Value and Income Trust plc, 1994–; Law Debenture Corp. plc, 2004–. Member: Council and Exec. Cttee, NIESR, 1989–97; Council of Econ. Advrs, Scottish Govt, 2007–. Vice-Pres., Econs & Business Educn Assoc., 1996–. FRSE 2007. *Publications:* (with L. Hannah) Concentration in Modern Industry, 1977; (with M. A. King) The British Tax System, 1978, 5th edn 1997; (jtly) The Reform of Social Security, 1984; (jtly) The Economic Analysis of Accounting Profitability, 1987; Foundations of Corporate Success, 1993; Why Firms Succeed, 1995; The Business of Economics, 1996; The Truth about Markets, 2003; Culture and Prosperity, 2004; Everlasting Light Bulbs, 2004; The Hare and the Tortoise, 2006; contrib. articles in learned jls and columns in Financial Times. *Recreation:* walking, especially in France. *Address:* Erasmus Press Ltd, PO Box 4026, W1A 6NZ. *T:* (020) 7224 8797, *Fax:* (020) 7402 1368.

KAY, Jolyon Christopher; HM Diplomatic Service, retired; *b* 19 Sept. 1930; *s* of Colin Mardall Kay and Gertrude Fanny Kay; *m* 1956, Shirley Mary Clarke; two *s* two *d. Educ:* Charterhouse; St John's Coll., Cambridge (BA). MEng 1993. Chemical Engr, Albright and Wilson, 1954; UKAEA, Harwell, 1958; Battelle Inst., Geneva, 1961; Foreign Office, London, 1964; MECAS, 1965; British Interests Section, Swiss Embassy, Algiers, 1967; Head of Chancery and Information Adviser, Political Residency, Bahrain, 1968; FCO, 1970; Economic Counsellor, Jedda, 1974–77; Consul-Gen., Casablanca, 1977–80; Science, later Commercial, Counsellor, Paris, 1980–84; Counsellor and Consul-Gen., Dubai, 1985–90. Editl Dir, London Insurance Insider, 1996–98. Convenor, Transport Gp, Oxfordshire CPRE, 1995–97. Chm., Southern Croquet Fedn, 1999–2003; Mem. Council, Croquet Assoc., 2001–04. *Recreations:* theatre, croquet. *Address:* 1 Anexartisias Street, 4603 Anogyra, Limassol District, Cyprus.

KAY, Rt Hon. Sir Maurice (Ralph), Kt 1995; PC 2004; **Rt Hon. Lord Justice Maurice Kay;** a Lord Justice of Appeal, since 2004; *b* 6 Dec. 1942; *s* of Ralph and Hylda Kay; *m* 1968, Margaret Angela Alcock; four *s. Educ:* William Hulme's Grammar Sch., Manchester; Sheffield Univ. (LLB, PhD). Called to the Bar, Gray's Inn, 1975; Bencher, 1995. Lecturer in Law: Hull Univ., 1967–72; Manchester Univ., 1972–73; Prof. of Law, Keele Univ., 1973–82. Practising barrister, 1975–95; an Asst Recorder, 1987–88; a Recorder, 1988–95; QC 1988; a Judge of the High Ct of Justice, QBD, 1995–2003; Lead Judge, Administrative Ct, 2002–03. Chm., Judicial Studies Bd, 2007–. Judicial Visitor, UCL, 2006–. Hon. Fellow, Robinson Coll., Cambridge, 2007. Hon. LLD: Sheffield; Keele. *Publications:* (author, contributor) numerous legal books and jls. *Recreations:* music, theatre, sport. *Address:* Royal Courts of Justice, Strand, WC2A 2LL. *Club:* Reform.

KAY, Michael Jack David; QC 2002; **His Honour Judge Kay;** a Circuit Judge, since 2004; a Deputy High Court Judge, since 2007; *b* 13 Oct. 1959; *m* 1984, Victoria Reuben; two *s* one *d. Educ:* Manchester Grammar Sch.; Christ's Coll., Cambridge. Called to the Bar, Lincoln's Inn, 1981; an Assistant Recorder, 1998–2000, Recorder, 2000–04; pt-time Chm., Employment Tribunals, 2001–04. *Recreations:* service to the community, football, theatre, praying.

KAY, Neil Vincent; Director of Social Services, Sheffield, 1979–90 (Deputy Director, 1971–79); *b* 24 May 1936; *s* of Charles Vincent Kay and Emma Kay; *m* 1961, Maureen (*née* Flemons); one *s* two *d. Educ:* Woodhouse Grammar Sch.; Downing Coll., Cambridge (MA); Birmingham Univ. (Prof. Social Work Qual.). Social Worker (Child Care), Oxford CC, and Sheffield CC, 1960–66; Lectr and Tutor in Social Work, Extramural Dept, Sheffield Univ., 1966–71. *Address:* 22 Westwood Road, Sheffield S11 7EY. *T:* (0114) 230 1934.

KAY, Nicholas Peter, CMG 2007; HM Diplomatic Service; Ambassador to the Democratic Republic of the Congo and to the Republic of Congo, since 2007; *b* 8 March 1958; *s* of Ralph Peter Kay and Josephine Alice Kay (*née* Poyner); *m* 1986, Susan Ruth Wallace; one *s* two *d. Educ:* Abingdon Sch., Oxon; St Edmund Hall, Oxford (BA Hons English Lang. and Lit.); Univ. of Reading (MA Applied Linguistics). English lang. teacher, Spain, Peru, Brazil, Saudi Arabia, Cyprus and UK, 1980–94; entered FCO, 1994; Hd, Pakistan and Afghanistan Section, FCO, 1994–96; 1st Sec. and Dep. Hd of Mission, Havana, 1997–2000; Dep. Hd, Policy Planning Staff (later Directorate for Strategy and Innovation), FCO, 2000–02; Counsellor and Dep. Hd of Mission, Madrid, 2002–06; UK Regl Co-ordinator, Southern Afghanistan, 2006–07. *Recreations:* sailing, vegetarian cookery, travel. *Address:* c/o Foreign and Commonwealth Office, King Charles Street, SW1A 2AH; *e-mail:* nick.kay@fco.gov.uk.

KAY, Maj.-Gen. Patrick Richard, CB 1972; MBE 1945; RM retired; *b* 1 Aug. 1921; *y s* of late Dr and Mrs A. R. Kay, Blakeney, Norfolk; *m* 1944, Muriel Austen Smith; three *s* one *d. Educ:* Eastbourne Coll. Commissioned in Royal Marines, 1940; HMS Renown, 1941–43; 4 Commando Bde, 1944–45; Combined Ops HQ, 1945–48; Staff of Commandant-Gen., Royal Marines, 1948–50 and 1952–54; Staff Coll., Camberley, 1951; 40 Commando, RM, 1954–57; Joint Services Amphibious Warfare Centre, 1957–59; Plans Div., Naval Staff, 1959–62; CO, 43 Commando, RM, 1963–65; CO, Amphibious Training Unit, RM, 1965–66; Asst Dir (Jt Warfare) Naval Staff, 1966–67; Asst Chief of Staff to Comdt-Gen. RM, 1968; IDC, 1969; C of S to Comdt-Gen., RM, 1970–74, retired 1974. Dir of Naval Security, 1974–81. Sec., Defence, Press and Broadcasting Cttee, 1984–86. *Recreations:* gardening, golf. *Address:* c/o Barclays Bank, Fleet, Hants GU13 8BS.

KAY, (Robert) Jervis; QC 1996; *b* 25 Feb. 1949; *s* of late Philip Jervis Kay, VRD and Pamela Kay; *m* 1988, Henrietta Kathleen Ward; one *s* three *d. Educ:* Wellington Coll.; Nottingham Univ. (LLB Hons). Called to the Bar, Lincoln's Inn, 1972 (Bencher 2005); in practice at the Bar, 1973–. *Publications:* (Ed.) Atkins Court Forms, Vol. 3 Admiralty, 1979, 1990, 1994, 2000, 2004, 2008. *Recreation:* sailing. *Address:* Stone Chambers, 4 Field Court, Gray's Inn, WC1R 5EF. *Clubs:* Turf, MCC, Royal Ocean Racing.

KAY, Sarah; *see* Kay, H. S.

KAY, Steven Walton; QC 1997; a Recorder, since 2000; *b* 4 Aug. 1954; *s* of late John Walton Kay and Eunice May Kay; *m* 1st (marr. diss.); one *s*; 2nd, 2000, Valerie (*née* Logan); one *d. Educ:* Epsom Coll.; Leeds Univ. (LLB). Called to the Bar, Inner Temple, 1977. Defence Counsel, first trial, Internat. Criminal Tribunal for former Yugoslavia, 1996; *Amicus Curiae,* 2001–04, Assigned Defence Counsel, 2004–06, trial of ex-Pres. Milosevic. Sec., Criminal Bar Assoc., 1993–96. Dir, perfect-nutrition Ltd, 2007–. *Publication:* (contrib.) The Rome Statute of the International Criminal Court, ed Casese, Gaeta and Jones, 2002. *Recreations:* ski-ing, golf. *Address:* 9 Bedford Row, WC1A 4AZ. *T:* (020) 7489 2727. *Club:* Hurtwood Park Polo.

KAY, William John; Money columnist, Sunday Times, since 2006 (Money Editor, 2005–06); *b* 12 Sept. 1946; *s* of William Jarvie Kay and Agnes Sutherland Walker; *m* 1968

(marr. diss. 1986); two *s*; partner, 1987, Lynne Bateson. *Educ:* Westminster City Sch.; The Queen's Coll., Oxford (MA). London Evening News, 1968; London Evening Standard, 1972; Daily Telegraph, 1977; Features Editor, Financial Weekly, 1979; Dep. Business Editor, Now!, 1979; Sen. Writer, Sunday Times Business News, 1981; City Editor, The Times, 1984; freelance, 1986–95; Financial Editor, Independent on Sunday, 1995; City Editor, Mail on Sunday, 1995–99; freelance, 1999–2001; Personal Finance Ed., Independent, 2001–05. Wincott Foundn Personal Finance Journalist of the Year, 2002; Headlinemoney Columnist of the Year, 2005; Lifetime Achievement Award, ABI, 2005. *Publications:* A–Z Guide to Money, 1983; Tycoons, 1985; Big Bang, 1986; (ed) The Stock Exchange: a market place for tomorrow, 1986; Battle for the High Street, 1987; (ed) Modern Merchant Banking, 1988; The Bosses, 1994; Lord of the Dance: the story of Gerry Robinson, 1999. *Recreations:* cricket, travel, cheese, ice cream, Chelsea FC. *Address:* e-mail: william.kay@sunday-times.co.uk. *Club:* MCC.

KAY-SHUTTLEWORTH, family name of **Baron Shuttleworth**.

KAYE, Rev. Dr Bruce Norman, AM 2005; General Secretary, The Anglican Church of Australia General Synod, 1994–2004; *b* 30 June 1939; *s* of John Harold Kaye and Elsie Evelyn Kaye; *m* 1st, 1965, Rosemary Jeanette Hutchison (*d* 1979); one *s* one *d*; 2nd, 1983, Margaret Louise Mathieson. *Educ:* Sydney Boys' High Sch.; Moore Theol Coll. (ThL 1963); Univ. of London (BD 1964); Univ. of Sydney (BA 1966); Univ. of Basel (Dr Theol 1976). Professional Officer, Sydney Water Bd, NSW, 1955–60. Deacon 1964, priest 1965; Curate, St Jude's, Dural, NSW, 1964–66; St John's College, University of Durham: Asst Tutor, 1968; Tutor, 1969; Tutor-Librarian, 1970–75; Sen. Tutor, 1975–82; Vice-Principal, 1979–82; Lectr, Faculty of Divinity, Univ. of Durham, 1970–82; Master, New Coll., Univ. of NSW, 1983–94; Founding Dir, New Coll. Inst. for Values Research, 1987–92. Visiting Fellow: Deutsche Akademische Austauschdienst, Freiberg, 1974; Sch. of Sci. and Technol. Studies, 1984–94, Sch. of Hist., 2005–, Univ. of NSW; Fellow Commoner, Churchill Coll., and Vis. Schol., Faculty of Divinity, Univ. of Cambridge, 1991–92; Professorial Associate, Charles Sturt Univ., 2007–. Founding Ed., Jl of Anglican Studies, 2002–. Hon. ThD Australian Coll. of Theol., 2006. *Publications:* Using the Bible in Ethics, 1976; The Supernatural in the New Testament, 1977; (ed) Obeying Christ in a Changing World, 1977; (ed) Law, Morality and the Bible, 1978; The Argument of Romans with Special Reference to Chapter 6, 1979; (ed) Immigration: what kind of Australia do we want?, 1989; A Church Without Walls: being Anglican in Australia, 1995; (ed) Authority and the Shaping of Tradition, 1997; Godly Citizens, 1999; Web of Meaning, 2000; (Gen. Ed.) Anglicanism in Australia, 2002; Reinventing Anglicanism, 2003; Introduction to World Anglicanism, 2008; contrib. numerous articles to theological and other learned jls. *Recreations:* theatre, golf, walking, reading. *Address:* 217 Hopetown Avenue, Watson's Bay, NSW 2030, Australia. *Club:* Australian (Sydney).

KAYE, Dr Elaine Hilda, FRHistS; Headmistress, Oxford High School, GPDST, 1972–81; *b* 21 Jan. 1930; *d* of late Rev. Harold Sutcliffe Kaye and Kathleen Mary (*née* White). *Educ:* Bradford Girls' Grammar Sch.; Milton Mount Coll.; St Anne's Coll., Oxford; Sheffield Univ. (PhD 1995). Assistant Mistress: Leyton County High Sch., 1952–54; Queen's Coll., Harley Street, 1954–59; South Hampstead High Sch., GPDST, 1959–65; Part-time Tutor, Westminster Tutors, 1965–67; Dep. Warden, Missenden Abbey Adult Coll., 1967–72. Project Dir, Oxford Project for Peace Studies, 1989–92 (Vice-Chair and Editor, 1984–89); (non-stipendiary) Lectr in Theology (Church History), Mansfield Coll., Oxford, 1996–99 (College Historian, 1990–95). Pres., URC History Soc., 1997–2002. FRHistS 2004. *Publications:* History of the King's Weigh House Church, 1968; History of Queen's College, Harley St, 1972; Short History of Missenden Abbey, 1973, 2nd edn 1992; (contrib.) Biographical Dictionary of Modern Peace Leaders, 1985; (ed) Peace Studies: the hard questions, 1987; C. J. Cadoux: theologian, scholar and pacifist, 1988; (with Ross Mackenzie) W. E. Orchard: a study in Christian exploration, 1990; Mansfield College, Oxford: its origin, history and significance, 1996; (contrib.) Oxford Dictionary of the Christian Church, 3rd edn 1997; For the Work of Ministry: Northern College and its predecessors, 1999; (contrib) Christian Thinking and Social Order, 1999; (contrib.) Modern Christianity and Cultural Aspiration, 2003; (with Janet Lees and Kirsty Thorpe) Daughters of Dissent, 2004. *Recreations:* music, walking, conversation. *Address:* 4 Fairlawn Flats, First Turn, Oxford OX2 8AP.

KAYE, Geoffrey John; President, Animal Shelter AC, Mexico; *b* 14 Aug. 1935; *s* of Michael and Golda Kaye; two *d. Educ:* Christ's College, Finchley. Started with Pricerite Ltd when business was a small private company controlling six shops, 1951; apptd Manager (aged 18) of one of Pricerite Ltd stores, 1953; Supervisor, Pricerite Ltd, 1955; Controller of all stores in Pricerite Ltd Gp, 1958; Director, 1963; Chairman and Man. Dir, 1966–73. Pres., Allied Automotive Inc., 1992. *Recreations:* tennis, golf.

KAYE, Sir John Phillip Lister L.; *see* Lister-Kaye.

KAYE, Lindsey Joy, (Mrs D. N. Kaye); *see* Kushner, L. J.

KAYE, Maj. Sir Paul (Henry Gordon), 5th Bt *cr* 1923, of Huddersfield, Co. York; Australian Army, retired 2001; *b* 19 Feb. 1958; *s* of Sir David Alexander Gordon Kaye, 4th Bt and of Adelle Francis Kaye (*née* Thomas); *S* father, 1994; *m* 1st, 1984, Sally Ann Louise Grützner (marr. diss. 2000); 2nd, 2005, Bonita Bonife Yang. *Educ:* Downlands Coll., Toowoomba; Univ. of Queensland (Dip. Applied Science (Rural Technol.) 1978). Lieut, Australian Regular Army, 1982; Captain, 1986; Major, 1991. Australian Service Medal, 1995; Multi-National Force and Observers Medal, 1995; Defence Force Service Medal, 1998. *Recreations:* horse riding, Rugby Union. *Heir:* *b* John Egidio Gordon Kaye, *b* 9 Sept. 1967.

KAYE, Roger Godfrey, TD 1980 and Bar 1985; QC 1989; **His Honour Judge Kaye;** a Circuit Judge, since 2005; Specialist Chancery/Mercantile Judge, North Eastern Circuit, since 2005; *b* 21 Sept. 1946; *s* of late Anthony Harmsworth Kaye and Heidi Alice (*née* Jordy); *m* 1974, Melloney Rose, *d* of late Rev. H. M. Westall. *Educ:* King's Sch., Canterbury; Birmingham Univ. (LLB 1968). FCIArb 2001. Lectr in Law, Kingston Poly., 1968–73. Called to the Bar, Lincoln's Inn, 1970, Bencher, 1997; Jun. Treasury Counsel in Insolvency Matters, 1978–89; Dep. High Court Registrar in Bankruptcy, 1985–2001; Dep. High Court Judge, Chancery Div., QBD and Family Div., 1990–2005; a Recorder, 1994–2005. Dep. Chancellor, dio. of Southwark, 1995–99; Chancellor: dio. of Hereford, 2000– (Dep. Chancellor, 1997–2000); dio. of St Albans, 2002– (Dep. Chancellor, 1995–2002). Chairman: Fees Collection Cttee, Bar Council, 1991–93 (Dep. Chm., 1990–91); Bristol & Cardiff Chancery Bar Assoc., 1990–95. Member: Professional Conduct Cttee, Bar Council, 1995–97; Panel of Chairmen, City Disputes Panel, 1997–2005. Varied TA service in Europe, 1967–97; Hon. Colonel: Intelligence and Security Gp (Volunteers), 1998–99; 3rd (Volunteer) Mil. Intelligence Bn, 1999–. FRSA 1995. *Recreation:* going home. *Address:* Leeds Combined Court Centre, 1 Oxford Row, Leeds LS1 3BG. *Clubs:* Athenæum, Army and Navy, Royal Automobile, Special Forces.

KAYE, Rosalind Anne, (Mrs J. A. Kaye); *see* Plowright, R. A.

KAYE, Prof. Stanley Bernard, MD; FRCP; FRSE; FMedSci; Head of Section of Medicine and Drug Development Unit, Institute of Cancer Research, London and Cancer Research UK (formerly Cancer Research Campaign) Professor of Medical Oncology, Institute of Cancer Research and Royal Marsden NHS Foundation Trust (formerly Hospital), since 2000; *b* 5 Sept. 1948; *s* of Peter Kaye and Dora Kaye (*née* Thomas); *m* 1975, Anna Catherine Lister; two *s* one *d*. *Educ:* Charing Cross Hosp. Med. Sch., London (BSc Biochem. 1969); Univ. of London (MB BS 1972; MD 1980). FRCP 1990. University of Glasgow: Sen. Lectr in Med. Oncology, 1980–85; Prof. of Med. Oncology, 1985–2000. FRSE 2001; FMedSci 2004. *Publication:* (ed jtly) Textbook of Medical Oncology, 1997, 3rd edn 2004. *Recreations:* playing squash, tennis and golf to varying degrees of indifference. *Address:* Royal Marsden Hospital, Downs Road, Sutton, Surrey SM2 5PT. *T:* (020) 8661 3539, *Fax:* (020) 8661 3541; *e-mail:* stan.kaye@rmh.nhs.uk; (home) 44 Burdon Lane, Sutton, Surrey SM2 7PT. *Club:* Royal Automobile.

KAYSEN, Prof. Carl; David W. Skinner Professor of Political Economy, Massachusetts Institute of Technology, 1977–90, now Emeritus (Director, Program in Science, Technology, and Society, 1981–87); *b* 5 March 1920; *s* of Samuel and Elizabeth Kaysen; *m* 1st, 1940, Annette Neutra (*d* 1990); two *d*; 2nd, 1994, Ruth Butler. *Educ:* Philadelphia Public Schs; Overbrook High Sch., Philadelphia; Pennsylvania, Columbia and Harvard Univs. AB Pa 1940; MA 1947, PhD 1954, Harvard. Nat. Bureau of Economic Research, 1940–42; Office of Strategic Services, Washington, 1942–43; Intelligence Officer, US Army Air Force, 1943–45; State Dept, Washington, 1945. Dep. Special Asst to President, 1961–63. Harvard University, 1947–66: Teaching Fellow in Econs, 1947; Asst Prof. of Economics, 1950–55; Assoc. Prof. of Economics 1955–57; Prof. of Economics, 1957–66; Assoc. Dean, Graduate Sch. of Public Administration, 1960–66; Lucius N. Littauer Prof. of Political Economy, 1964–66; Jr Fellow, Soc. of Fellows, 1947–50, Actg Sen. Fellow, 1957–58, 1964–65; Syndic, Harvard Univ. Press, 1964–66; Dir, Inst. for Advanced Study, Princeton, NJ, 1966–76, Dir Emeritus, 1976; Vice Chm., and Dir of Research, Sloan Commn on Govt and Higher Educn, 1977–79. Sen. Fulbright Res. Schol., LSE, 1955–56. Trustee: Pennsylvania Univ., 1967–; Russell Sage Foundn, 1979–89. *Publications:* United States *v* United Shoe Machinery Corporation, an Economic Analysis of an Anti-Trust Case, 1956; The American Business Creed (with others), 1956; Anti-Trust Policy (with D. F. Turner), 1959; The Demand for Electricity in the United States (with F. M. Fisher), 1962; The Higher Learning, The Universities, and The Public, 1969; (contrib.) Nuclear Energy Issues and Choices, 1979; A Program for Renewed Partnership (Sloan Commn on Govt and Higher Educn Report), 1980; (ed jtly and contrib.) Emerging Norms of Justified Intervention, 1995; (ed) The American Corporation Today, 1996; numerous articles on economic theory, applied economics, higher education, military strategy and arms control. *Address:* E38–614, Massachusetts Institute of Technology, Cambridge, MA 02139, USA.

KEABLE-ELLIOTT, Dr (Robert) Anthony, OBE 1988; FRCGP; general practitioner, 1948–87; *b* 14 Nov. 1924; *s* of Robert Keable and Jolie Buck; *m* 1953, Gilian Mary Hutchison; four *s*. *Educ:* Sherborne Sch., Dorset; Guy's Hosp., London, 1943–48 (MB BS London). Founder Mem., Chiltern Medical Soc., 1956, Vice-Pres. 1958, Pres. 1964; Member, Faculty Board of Thames Valley, Faculty of Royal Coll. of General Practitioners, 1960; Upjohn Travelling Fellowship, 1962; Member: Bucks Local Med. Cttee, 1958–75 (Chm., 1964–68; Hon. Life Mem., 1975–); GMC, 1989–94. British Medical Association: Mem., 1948–; Mem. Council, 1974–94; Treasurer, 1981–87; Chm., Journal Cttee, 1987–93; Chm., Gen. Med. Services Cttee, 1966–72. Mem., Finance Corp. of General Practice, 1974–79. Mem., Soc. of Apothecaries, 1985–; Freeman, City of London, 1986. Asst Editor, Guy's Hospital Gazette, 1947–48. BMA Gold Medal, 1994. *Recreations:* sailing, golf, gardening. *Address:* Peels, Ibstone, near High Wycombe, Bucks HP14 3XX. *T:* (01491) 638385.

KEAL, Anthony Charles; Partner, Simpson Thatcher & Bartlett LLP, since 2005; *b* Aldershot, 12 July 1951; *s* of Kitchener Keal and Joan Marjorie Keal; *m* 1979, Janet Michele King; four *s*. *Educ:* New Coll., Oxford (BA Juris.). Admitted solicitor, 1976; Partner, Allen & Overy, 1982–2005. *Recreations:* sailing, ski-ing, walking, opera, theatre. *Address:* Simpson Thatcher & Bartlett LLP, One Ropemaker Street, EC2Y 9HU. *T:* (020) 7275 6500, *Fax:* (020) 7275 6502.

KEAL, Dr Edwin Ernest Frederick, FRCP; Honorary Consulting Physician, St Mary's and Brompton Hospitals, London; *b* 21 Aug. 1921; *s* of Frederick Archibald Keal and Mabel Orange Keal; *m* 1945, Constance Mary Gilliams (*d* 2008); one *s*. *Educ:* Kingston High Sch., Hull; London Hospital Med. Coll. MB BS London 1952, DCH 1954, MD London 1971; FRCP 1973 (MRCP 1957). Service in RNVR (Exec. Lieut), 1939–46. Junior hosp. posts, London Hosp., 1952–59; Sen. Medical Registrar, Brompton Hosp., 1959–63; Consultant Physician: St Charles Hosp., London, 1963–77; Kensington Chest Clinic, 1963–86; Brompton Hosp., 1966–86; St Mary's Hosp., London, 1977–86; Cardiothoracic Institute: Sen. Lectr, 1972–77; Hon. Sen. Lectr, 1978–86; Dean, 1979–84. Hon. Consultant in Chest Diseases to the Army, 1979–86. Member: Bd of Governors, National Heart and Chest Hosps, 1975–85; Cttee of Management, Cardiothoracic Inst., 1978–84. *Publications:* chapters in various books, and articles, mainly related to diseases of the chest. *Recreations:* gardening, travel. *Address:* Blackberry Cottage, 2 Huntsmans Drive, Oakham, Rutland LE15 6RP. *T:* (01572) 755603.

KEALEY, Gavin Sean James; QC 1994; a Recorder of the Crown Court, since 2000; a Deputy High Court Judge, Queen's Bench Division (Commercial Court), since 2002; *b* 2 Sept. 1953; *m* 1981, Karen Elizabeth Nowak; three *d*. *Educ:* Charterhouse; University Coll., Oxford (BA Jurisp.). Lectr in Law, King's Coll. London, 1976–77; called to the Bar, Inner Temple, 1977, Bencher, 2002; Commercial Barrister, 1978; Head of Chambers, 2003–. *Address:* 7 King's Bench Walk, Temple, EC4Y 7DS. *T:* (020) 7910 8300.

KEALEY, Dr (George) Terence (Evelyn); Vice-Chancellor, University of Buckingham, since 2001; *b* 16 Feb. 1952; *s* of Paul and Evelyn Kealey; *m* 1989, Sally Harwood Gritten, *d* of late Donald Meredith Gritten and of Stella Harwood Gritten (now Huber); one *s* one *d*. *Educ:* Charterhouse Sch.; St Bartholomew's Hosp. Med. Sch. (MB BS 1975; BSc Biochem. 1976); Balliol Coll., Oxford (DPhil 1982); MA Cantab 1995. House physician, St Bartholomew's Hosp., 1976–77; MRC Trng Fellow, Nuffield Dept of Clinical Biochem., Oxford, 1977–82; Jun. Dean, Balliol Coll., Oxford, 1980–81; Sen. Registrar in Clinical Biochem. and Metabolic Medicine, Royal Victoria Infirmary, Newcastle upon Tyne, 1982–86; Wellcome Sen. Res. Fellow in Clinical Sci., Nuffield Dept of Clinical Biochem., Univ. of Oxford, 1986–88; Lectr, Dept of Clinical Biochem., Univ. of Cambridge, 1988–2001. Mem., Academic Adv. Council, Globalization Inst., 2005–; Sen. Fellow in Educn, Adam Smith Inst., 2008–. Trustee, Buckingham Centre for the Arts, 2005–. Hon. Consultant Chemical Pathologist: Oxford HA, 1986–88; Cambridge HA, 1988–2001. Lectures incl. 16th Annual IEA Hayek Meml Lect., 2007. Caldwell Prize, Pope Center for Higher Educn Policy, USA, 2001; Free Enterprise Award, IEA, 2004. *Publications:* The Economic Laws of Scientific Research, 1996; Sex, Science and Profits, 2008; contrib. papers in the molecular cell biol. of human skin develt. *Recreation:* playing with our *d* Helena, our *s* Teddy and their dog Rusty. *Address:* University of Buckingham, Hunter Street, Buckingham MK18 1EG. *T:* (01280) 820207. *Club:* Athenæum.

KEALY, Robin Andrew, CMG 1991; HM Diplomatic Service, retired; Director, Sir Harold Hillier Gardens, Romsey, since 2006; *b* 7 Oct. 1944; *s* of Lt-Col H. L. B. Kealy, Royal Signals and Mrs B. E. Kealy; *m* 1987, Annabel Jane Hood; two *s*. *Educ:* Harrow Sch.; Oriel Coll., Oxford (Open Scholar; BA Lit. Hum. (1st Cl. Hons Mods); MA). Joined HM Diplomatic Service, 1967; FO, 1967; MECAS, 1968; Tripoli, 1970; Kuwait, 1972; ME Dept, FCO, 1975; Port of Spain, 1978; Commercial Sec., Prague, 1982; Asst, Aid Policy Dept, FCO, 1985; Counsellor and Consul Gen., Baghdad, 1987–90; Dir of Trade Promotion and Investment, Paris, 1990–95; Head, Aviation and Maritime Dept, FCO, 1995–97; Consul-Gen., Jerusalem, 1997–2001; Ambassador to Tunisia, 2002–04. Chm., Welfare Assoc. (UK), 2006–; Vice-Chm., Med. Aid to Palestinians, 2006–. Trustee, Arab-British Chamber Charitable Foundn, 2007–. *Recreations:* music, theatre, ski-ing, cooking, gardening. *Address:* Sir Harold Hillier Gardens, Jermyns House, Jermyns Lane, Ampfield, Romsey, Hants SO51 0QA. *T:* (01794) 369304. *Club:* Travellers.

KEANE, Fergal Patrick, OBE 1997; BBC Special Correspondent, since 1997; *b* 6 Jan. 1961; *s* of Eamon Patrick Keane and Maura Theresa (*née* Hassett); *m* 1986, Anne Frances Flaherty; one *s*. *Educ:* Terenure Coll., Dublin; Presentation Coll., Cork. Reporter: Limerick Leader, 1979–82; Irish Press, 1982–84; RTE, 1984–88; joined BBC, 1988: Ireland Corresp., 1988–90; Southern Africa Corresp., 1990–94; Asia Corresp., 1994–97. Radio Journalist of Year, Sony, 1994; Journalist of Year, RTS, 1994. BAFTA award, TV documentary, 1997. *Publications:* The Bondage of Fear, 1994; Season of Blood, 1995; Letter to Daniel, 1996; Letters Home, 1999; A Stranger's Eye, 2000; All of These People, 2005. *Recreations:* fishing, sailing, reading. *Address:* c/o BBC Television, Wood Lane, W12 7RJ. *T:* (020) 8743 8000. *Clubs:* Foreign Correspondents' (Hong Kong); Royal Cork Yacht (Cork).

KEANE, Francis Joseph; Sheriff of Tayside, Central and Fife at Kirkcaldy, 1998–2004; *b* 5 Jan. 1936; *s* of Thomas and Helen Keane; *m* 1960, Lucia Corio Morrison; two *s* one *d*. *Educ:* Blairs Coll., Aberdeen; Gregorian Univ., Rome (PhL); Univ. of Edinburgh (LLB). Solicitor; Partner, McCluskey, Keane & Co., 1959; Depute Procurator Fiscal, Perth, 1961, Edinburgh, 1963; Senior Depute PF, Edinburgh, 1971; Senior Legal Asst, Crown Office, Edinburgh, 1972; PF, Airdrie, 1976; Regional PF, S Strathclyde, Dumfries and Galloway, 1980; Sheriff: of Glasgow and Strathkelvin, 1984–93; of Lothian and Borders at Edinburgh, 1993–98. Pres., PF Soc., 1982–84. *Recreations:* music, painting, tennis.

KEANE, John Granville Colpoys; artist; *b* 12 Sept. 1954; *s* of Granville Keane and Elaine Violet Meredith Keane (*née* Doubble); *m* 1996, Rosemary Anne McGowan; one *s* one *d*. *Educ:* Hardenwick Sch., Harpenden; Cheam Sch., Berks; Wellington Coll.; Camberwell Sch. of Art, London (BA Fine Art). 55 solo exhibns in UK, Europe and USA, 1980–; official British War Artist, Gulf War, 1991; Artist in Residence, Independent on Sunday, 2000–01. Vis. Prof., London Inst., 2000; Vis. Res. Fellow, Camberwell Coll. of Arts, 2000–. FRSA 2005. *Publications:* Gulf, 1992; (with Duncan Green) Guatemala: burden of paradise, 1992; (with Mark Lawson) Conflicts of Interest, 1995. *Recreation:* tennis. *Address:* c/o Flowers East, 82 Kingsland Road, E2 8DP. *T:* (020) 7920 7777, *Fax:* (020) 7920 7770; *e-mail:* gallery@flowerseast.com. *Clubs:* Groucho, Chelsea Arts.

KEANE, Major Sir Richard (Michael), 6th Bt *cr* 1801; farmer; *b* 29 Jan. 1909; *s* of Sir John Keane, 5th Bart, DSO, and Lady Eleanor Hicks-Beach (*d* 1960), *e d* of 1st Earl St Aldwyn; *S* father, 1956; *m* 1939, Olivia Dorothy Hawkshaw (*d* 2002); two *s* one *d*. *Educ:* Sherborne Sch.; Christ Church, Oxford. Diplomatic Correspondent to Reuters 1935–37; Diplomatic Corresp. and Asst to Editor, Sunday Times, 1937–39. Served with County of London Yeomanry and 10th Royal Hussars, 1939–44; Liaison Officer (Major) with HQ Vojvodina, Yugoslav Partisans, 1944; attached British Military Mission, Belgrade, 1944–45. Publicity Consultant to Imperial Chemical Industries Ltd, 1950–62. *Publications:* Germany: What Next?, (Penguin Special), 1939; Modern Marvels of Science (editor), 1961. *Recreation:* fishing. *Heir: s* John Charles Keane [*b* 16 Sept. 1941; *m* 1977, Corinne, *d* of Jean Everard de Harzir; two *s* one *d*]. *Address:* Cappoquin House, Cappoquin, County Waterford, Ireland. *T:* (58) 54004. *Club:* Kildare Street and University (Dublin).

KEANE, Ronan; Chief Justice of Ireland, 2000–04; *b* 20 July 1932; *s* of John Patrick Keane and Katherine Gertrude Keane (*née* Boylan); *m* 1962, Ann Therese O'Donnell; one *s* two *d*. *Educ:* Blackrock Coll., Co. Dublin; University Coll., Dublin (BA 1953). Called to the Irish Bar, King's Inns, Dublin, 1954 (Bencher, 1979); in practice at the Bar, 1954–79; Jun. Counsel, 1954–70; Sen. Counsel, 1970–79; Judge: High Court of Ireland, 1979–96; Supreme Court of Ireland, 1996–2000. Chm., Irish Bar Council, 1974–75; Pres., Law Reform Commn, 1987–92. Hon. Bencher: Lincoln's Inn, 2000; NI Inn of Court, 2000. *Publications:* The Law of Local Government in the Republic of Ireland, 1982; Company Law in the Republic of Ireland, 1985, 3rd edn 2001; Equity and the Law of Trusts in the Republic of Ireland, 1988. *Recreations:* music, theatre, reading. *Address:* 39 Richmond Park, Monkstown, Co. Dublin, Ireland. *T:* (1) 2843618.

KEAR, Graham Francis; Under-Secretary, Department of Energy, 1974–80; *b* 9 Oct. 1928; *s* of Richard Walter Kear and Eva Davies; *m* 1978, Joyce Eileen Parks (*d* 2006). *Educ:* Newport (St Julian's) High Sch., Mon; Balliol Coll., Oxford (BA). Min. of Supply, 1951–52 and 1954–57; UK Delegn to ECSC, 1953–54; Min. of Aviation, 1957–59 and 1960–63; NATO Maintenance Supply Agency, Paris, 1959–60; MoD, 1963–65; Cabinet Office, 1968–71; Min. of Aviation Supply/DTI, 1971–72; Fellow, Harvard Univ. Center for Internat. Affairs, 1972–73. Asst Sec., 1984–92, volunteer mem., 1992–2001, Abbeyfield Richmond Soc. *Recreation:* music.

KEARL, Guy Alexander; QC 2002; a Recorder, since 2001; *b* 29 Sept. 1959; *s* of Ian Alexander Kearl and Sheila Kearl; *m* 1985, Anea Jayne Ellison; two *s*. *Educ:* Millfield Sch.; Univ. of Central Lancashire (BA Hons Law); Inns of Court Sch. of Law. Called to the Bar, Middle Temple, 1982; in practice, specialising in serious crime law. *Recreations:* ski-ing, marathon running, tennis, cycling. *Address:* St Paul's Chambers, St Paul's House, 23 Park Square, Leeds LS1 2ND. *T:* (0113) 245 5866.

KEARLEY, family name of **Viscount Devonport**.

KEARNEY, Brian; Sheriff of Glasgow and Strathkelvin, 1977–2007; Temporary Sheriff Principal, South Strathclyde, Dumfries and Galloway, 2007–08; *b* 25 Aug. 1935; *s* of late James Samuel and Agnes Olive Kearney; *m* 1965, Elizabeth Mary Chambers; three *s* one *d*. *Educ:* Largs Higher Grade; Greenock Academy; Glasgow Univ. (MA, LLB). Qualified solicitor, 1960; Partner, Biggart, Lumsden & Co., Solicitors, Glasgow, 1965–74. Sheriff of N Strathclyde at Dumbarton (floating sheriff), 1974–77. Sometime tutor in Jurisprudence, and external examnr in legal subjects, Glasgow Univ.; Hon. Lectr, Social Work Dept, Dundee Univ., 1995–. Chm., Inquiry into Child Care Policies in Fife, 1989–92 (report published, 1992). Mem., Judicial Studies Cttee (Scotland), 1997–2005. Pres., Glasgow Juridical Soc., 1964–65; Chm., Glasgow Marriage Guidance Council, 1977–90; Hon. President: Glasgow Marriage Counselling Service, 1990–; Family Law Assoc., Scotland,

1999–. *Publications:* An Introduction to Ordinary Civil Procedure in the Sheriff Court, 1982; Children's Hearings and the Sheriff Court, 1987, 2nd edn 2000; (ed jtly) Butterworths' Scottish Family Law Service, 1995; The Scottish Children's Hearings System in Action, 2007; articles in legal jls. *Recreations:* cutting sandwiches for family picnics, listening to music, reading, writing and resting. *Address:* c/o Sheriff's Chambers, Sheriff Court House, 1 Carlton Place, Glasgow G5 9DA. *Club:* Glasgow Art.

KEARNEY, Martha Catherine; BBC broadcaster; presenter: Newsnight Review, since 2005; The World at One, BBC Radio 4, since 2007; *b* 8 Oct. 1957; *d* of Hugh and Catherine Kearney; *m* 2001, Christopher Thomas Shaw, *qv*. *Educ:* George Watson's Ladies' Coll., Edinburgh; St Anne's Coll., Oxford. LBC Radio, 1981–87; A Week in Politics, Channel Four, 1987–88; BBC, 1988–: reporter, On the Record, 1988–94; Panorama, 1993; reporter, 1994–2000, Political Ed., 2000–07, Newsnight; presenter, Woman's Hour, Radio 4, 1999–2007. Year back packing, 1989–90. Hon. DLit Keele, 2007. *Recreations:* reading, cooking, travel, beekeeping. *Address:* c/o BBC, TV Centre, Wood Lane, W12 7RJ. *T:* (020) 8624 9800; *e-mail:* martha.kearney@bbc.co.uk. *Clubs:* Royal Over-Seas League, Soho House; Wortham Tennis.

KEARNEY, Hon. Sir William (John Francis), Kt 1982; CBE 1976; Judge of the Supreme Court of the Northern Territory, 1982–99; *b* 8 Jan. 1935; *s* of William John Kilbeg Kearney and Gertrude Ivylene Kearney; *m* 1959, Jessie Alice Elizabeth Yung; three *d*. *Educ:* Univ. of Sydney (BA, LLB); University Coll. London (LLM). Legal Service of Papua New Guinea, 1963–75; Sec. for Law, 1972–75; dormant Commn as Administrator, 1972–73, and as High Comr, 1973–75; Judge, Supreme Ct of PNG, 1976–82; Dep. Chief Justice, 1980–82. Aboriginal Land Comr, 1982–86. *Recreations:* travelling, literature.

KEARNS, David Todd; Deputy Secretary of Education, US Department of Education, 1991–93; *b* 11 Aug. 1930; *m* 1954, Shirley Cox; two *s* four *d*. *Educ:* Univ. of Rochester (BS). Served US Navy; IBM, 1954–71; Xerox Corp.: Corporate Vice Pres., 1971; Group Vice Pres. and Board of Dirs, 1976; Pres. and Chief Operating Officer, 1977; Chief Exec., 1982–90; Chm., 1985–91. Mem. Boards of Directors: Chase Manhattan Corp.; Time Inc.; Dayton Hudson Corp; Ryder System. Member: Council on Foreign Relations; Business Roundtable; Business Council; President's Commn on Executive Exchange. Trustee, Cttee for Economic Develt; Chairman: Nat. Urban League; New American Sch.; Univ. of Rochester (Mem. Exec. Adv. Commn, William E. Simon Sch. of Business); Member: Bd of Dirs, Junior Achievement; Bd of Visitors, Fuqua Sch. of Business Administration, Duke Univ. *Publications:* (with D. P. Doyle) Winning the Brain Race, 1988; (with David Nadler) Profits in the Dark, 1992; (with James Harvey) A Legacy of Learning, 2000.

KEARNS, Dr William Edward, FFPH; consultancy in health policy and public health, 1993–2000; *b* 10 July 1934; *s* of William Edward Kearns and Kathleen Wolfenden; *m* 1954, Beryl Cross; four *s* one *d* (and one *s* decd). *Educ:* Liverpool Coll.; Univ. of Liverpool (MB ChB); Univ. of London (MSc; DipTh 1995). MRCS, LRCP. Hosp. posts in cardiorespiratory physiology, gen. medicine and pathology, United Liverpool Hosps, 1958–70; NW Metropolitan Regional Hospital Board: Asst SMO, 1970–73; Regional Sci. Officer, 1973–74; Dist Community Physician, Kensington and Chelsea and Westminster AHA (Teaching), 1974–82; Hon. Sen. Lectr in Community Medicine, St Mary's Hosp. Med. Sch., 1975–86; Dist MO, Paddington and N Kensington HA, 1982–86; Regional MO and Dir of Health Care Policy, 1986–90, Dir of Public Health, 1990–92, CMO, 1990–93, NE Thames RHA. Reader, Neasden Parish Church (S Catherine); Sec. for Readers, dio. of London, 1996–2003; Oblate Novice, Monastery of Our Lady and St Benedict, Elmore Abbey, 1996–98; Oblate, Monastery of St Mary at the Cross, Edgware Abbey, 1998–. FRSA 1997. *Publications:* The Health Report, North East Thames Health Region, 1990, 1991; contribs to med. jls. *Recreations:* gardening for wild life conservation, grandparenting. *Address:* Five Midholm, Barn Hill, Wembley Park, Middx HA9 9LJ. *T:* (020) 8908 1511, *Fax:* (020) 8904 3884; *e-mail:* williamkearns@compuserve.com. *Club:* Royal Society of Medicine.

KEARON, Rev. Canon Kenneth Arthur; Secretary General, Anglican Communion, since 2005; *b* 4 Oct. 1953; *s* of Hubert Kenneth Maurice Kearon and Ethel Maria Kearon (*née* Shattock); *m* 1978, Jennifer Poyntz; three *d*. *Educ:* Trinity Coll., Dublin (BA Mod. 1976, MA 1979); Irish Sch. of Ecumenics (MPhil Ecum. 1991); Jesus Coll., Cambridge. Ordained deacon, 1981, priest, 1982; Curate, All Saints Raheny and St John's Coolock, Dublin, 1981–84; pt-time Lectr, 1981–99, Dean of Residence, 1984–91, Trinity Coll., Dublin; Rector, Tullow Parish, Dublin, 1991–99; Dir, Irish Sch. of Ecumenics, Trinity Coll., Dublin, 1999–2004. Canon, 1996–, Chancellor, 2002–04, Christ Church Cathedral, Dublin. Hon. Canon: St Paul's Cathedral, London, 2005; St George's Cathedral, Jerusalem, 2005; Christ Church Cathedral, Canterbury, 2005–. Hon. DD General Theological Seminary, NY, 2006. *Publications:* Medical Ethics: an introduction, 1995, 2nd edn 1999; (ed with F. O'Ferrall) Medical Ethics and the Future of Healthcare, 2000; *contributions to:* A Parish Adult Education Handbook, 1987; Ethics and the Christian, 1991; Family: fading embers, kindling flames, 1994; Minorities—the right to be different, 1995; Relationships and Sexuality Education in Primary Schools, 1996; Bioethics Research: policy methods and strategy, 1997; A Time to Build, 1999; A New Dictionary of Christian Spirituality, 2006; The Irish School of Ecumenics (1970–2007), 2008; jls, inc. Search, Medico-Legal Jl of Ireland. *Address:* Anglican Communion Office, St Andrew's House, 16 Tavistock Crescent, W11 1AP. *Clubs:* Kildare Street and University (Dublin); Blainroe Golf (Wicklow).

KEATES, Jonathan Basil; writer; Assistant English Master, City of London School, since 1974; *b* 7 Nov. 1946; *s* of Richard Herbert Basil Keates and Evangeline Sonia Wilcox. *Educ:* Bryanston Sch., Dorset (Schol.); Magdalen Coll., Oxford (MA); Exeter Univ. (PGCE). FRSL 1993. *Publications:* The Companion Guide to the Shakespeare Country, 1979; Allegro Postillions (James Tait Black Prize; Hawthornden Prize), 1984; Handel: the man and his music, 1985; The Strangers' Gallery, 1987; Italian Journeys, 1991; Stendhal, 1994 (Enid McLeod Prize, 1995); Henry Purcell, 1995; Soon To Be a Major Motion Picture, 1997; Smile Please, 2000; The Siege of Venice, 2005. *Recreations:* Venice, libraries, music, friendship. *Address:* 23 Hightrees House, Nightingale Lane, SW12 8AQ. *T:* (020) 8675 6783. *Club:* Athenæum.

KEATING, Frank; Sports Columnist, The Guardian, since 1976; *b* 4 Oct. 1937; *s* of Bryan Keating and Monica Marsh; *m* 1987, Jane Sinclair; one *s* one *d*. *Educ:* Belmont Abbey; Douai. Local newspapers, Stroud, Hereford, Guildford, Bristol, Southern Rhodesia, Gloucester and Slough, 1956–63; Editor, Outside Broadcasts, Rediffusion Television, 1963–67; Editor, Features, and Head of Special Projs, Thames Television, 1968–72; columnist: The Guardian, 1972–; Punch, 1979–90; The Spectator, 1990–96, 2004–08; The Oldie, 1997–. Astroturf Sportswriter of the Year, 1978; 'What the Papers Say' Sportswriter of the Year, 1979; Sports Council Magazine Writer of the Year, 1987; Specialist Writer of Year, Magazine Publishers Awards, 1988; Sports Journalist of the Year, British Press Awards, 1988. *Television series:* Maestro, BBC, 1981–85. *Publications:* Caught by Keating, 1979; Bowled Over, 1980; Another Bloody Day in Paradise, 1981; Up and Under, 1983; Long Days, Late Nights, 1984; High, Wide and Handsome, 1986; Gents and Players, 1986; Passing Shots, 1988; Sportswriter's Eye, 1989; Half-Time Whistle (autobiog.), 1992; The Great Number Tens, 1994; (with Graham Gooch) Gooch: My Autobiography, 1995; Band of Brothers, 1996; Frank Keating's Sporting Century, 1998; contrib. New Statesman, BBC. *Recreation:* roses. *Address:* Church House, Marden, near Hereford HR1 3EN. *T:* (01432) 880213. *Club:* Chelsea Arts.

KEATING, Henry Reymond Fitzwalter; author; *b* 31 Oct. 1926; *s* of John Hervey Keating and Muriel Marguerita Keating (*née* Clews); *m* 1953, Sheila Mary Mitchell; three *s* one *d*. *Educ:* Merchant Taylors' Sch.; Trinity Coll., Dublin. Journalism, 1952–60; Crime Reviewer for The Times, 1967–83. Chairman: Crime Writers' Assoc., 1970–71; Society of Authors, 1983–84; Pres., Detection Club, 1985–2001. FRSL 1990. *Publications:* Death and the Visiting Firemen, 1959; Zen there was Murder, 1960; A Rush on the Ultimate, 1961; The Dog it was that Died, 1962; Death of a Fat God, 1963; The Perfect Murder, 1964 (filmed 1988); Is Skin-Deep, Is Fatal, 1965; Inspector Ghote's Good Crusade, 1966; Inspector Ghote Caught in Meshes, 1967; Inspector Ghote Hunts the Peacock, 1968; Inspector Ghote Plays a Joker, 1969; Inspector Ghote Breaks an Egg, 1970; Inspector Ghote goes by Train, 1971; The Strong Man, 1971; (ed) Blood on My Mind, 1972; Inspector Ghote Trusts the Heart, 1972; The Underside, 1974; Bats Fly Up for Inspector Ghote, 1974; A Remarkable Case of Burglary, 1975; Filmi, Filmi, Inspector Ghote, 1976; Murder Must Appetize, 1976; (ed) Agatha Christie: First Lady of Crime, 1977; A Long Walk to Wimbledon, 1978; Inspector Ghote Draws a Line, 1979; Sherlock Holmes: the man and his world, 1979; The Murder of the Maharajah, 1980; Go West, Inspector Ghote, 1981; (ed) Whodunit, 1982; The Lucky Alphonse, 1982; The Sheriff of Bombay, 1984; Mrs Craggs, Crimes Cleaned Up, 1985; Under a Monsoon Cloud, 1986; Writing Crime Fiction, 1986; The Body in the Billiard Room, 1987; Crime and Mystery: the 100 best books, 1987; Dead on Time, 1988; Inspector Ghote, His Life and Crimes, 1989; (ed) Bedside Companion to Crime, 1989; The Iciest Sin, 1990; (ed) Crime Wave 1, 1991; Cheating Death, 1992; (ed) The Man Who, 1992; The Rich Detective, 1993; Doing Wrong, 1994; The Good Detective, 1995; The Bad Detective, 1996; Asking Questions, 1996; The Soft Detective, 1997; In Kensington Gardens Once, 1997; Bribery, Corruption Also, 1999; Jack, the Lady Killer (verse), 1999; The Hard Detective, 2000; Breaking and Entering, 2000; A Detective in Love, 2001; A Detective Under Fire, 2002; The Dreaming Detective, 2003; Detective at Death's Door, 2004; One Man and his Bomb, 2006; Rules, Regs and Rotten Eggs, 2007; Inspector Ghote's First Case, 2008. *Recreation:* popping round to the post. *Address:* 35 Northumberland Place, W2 5AS. *T:* (020) 7229 1100.

KEATING, Kay Rosamond Blundell; a District Judge (Magistrates' Courts) (formerly Metropolitan Stipendiary Magistrate), 1987–2004; *b* 3 Oct. 1943; *d* of Geoffrey Blundell Jones and Avis Blundell Jones; *m* 1st, 1965, Edmund Deighton (decd); one *d* decd; 2nd, 1978, Donald Norman Keating, QC (*d* 1995); one *s*. *Educ:* St Hugh's College, Oxford (BA Jurisp. 1965; MA 1968). Called to the Bar, Gray's Inn, 1966. *Recreations:* travel, walking, tennis, riding, opera.

KEATING, Michael Ray; Director, Education and Lifelong Learning, Rhondda Cynon Taff County Borough Council, since 2005; *b* 31 Aug. 1946; *s* of Raymond and Marion Keating; *m* 1967, Jacqueline Ann Pope; two *s*. *Educ:* Ifield Grammar Sch., Crawley; Nottingham Coll. of Educn (Teachers Cert. 1967); Univ. of Newcastle upon Tyne (BEd Hons 1976); Univ. of Warwick (Advanced Dip. Educn 1987). Primary sch. teacher, Breaston, Derbys, then St Albans, and Newcastle upon Tyne, 1967–78; Headteacher, S Benwell Jun. Sch., 1978–80, S Benwell Primary Sch., 1980–88, Newcastle upon Tyne; Primary Advr, 1988–91, Sen. Advr, 1991–96, Mid Glamorgan CC; Asst Dir, Educn, Rhondda Cynon Taff CBC, 1996–2005. Lectr (pt-time), Univ. of Newcastle upon Tyne, 1984–86; External Examnr, Manchester Metropolitan Univ., 1990–94. *Recreations:* football, supporting Newcastle United, Alfa Romeo cars, steam trains, modern jazz and blues music, food and wine, caravanning. *Address:* Channel View, Heol Las, Coity, Bridgend CF35 6BS. *T:* (01656) 657105; *e-mail:* mike.keating@rhondda-cynon-taff.gov.uk.

KEATING, Dr Michael Stockton, AC 1996 (AO 1990); Chairman, Independent Pricing and Regulatory Tribunal, New South Wales, since 2004; *b* 25 Jan. 1940; *s* of Russell James Keating and Alice (*née* Skinner); *m* 1962, Rosemary Gardner; four *s*. *Educ:* Geelong Coll.; Univ. of Melbourne (BCom Hons); ANU (PhD). Hd, Growth Studies and Resource Allocation Div., OECD, 1976–78; First Asst Sec., Econ. Div., Dept of Prime Minister and Cabinet, Australia, 1979–82; Dep. Sec., Dept of Finance, 1982–83; Secretary: Dept of Employment and Industrial Relns, 1983–86; Dept of Finance, 1986–91; Dept of the PM and Cabinet, 1991–96. Adjunct Prof., Griffith Univ., 1997–; Fellow, Econs Dept, Res. Sch. of Soc. Scis, ANU, 1997. Mem., Econ. Develt Bd, SA, 2005–. Board Mem., Australia Post, 1996–2001. Mem. Council, ANU, 1996–2004. DUniv Griffith, 2000. *Publications:* The Australian Workforce 1910–1911 to 1960–61, 1973; (jtly) The Making of Australian Economic Policy: 1983–88, 1989; (jtly) The Future of Governance, 2000; (jtly) Institutions on the Edge, 2000; Who Rules?: how government retains control of a privatised economy, 2004. *Recreations:* bushwalking, reading, golf. *Address:* 11/7 Bowen Drive, Barton, ACT 2600, Australia. *T:* (2) 62739405.

KEATING, Hon. Paul John; Prime Minister of Australia, 1991–96; *b* 18 Jan. 1944; *s* of Matthew and Minnie Keating; *m* 1975, Annita Johanna Maria Van Iersel; one *s* three *d*. *Educ:* De La Salle College, Bankstown, NSW. Research Officer, Federated Municipal and Shire Council Employees Union of Australia, 1967. MP (ALP) Blaxland, NSW, 1969–96; Minister for Northern Australia, Oct.–Nov. 1975; Shadow Minister for Agriculture, Jan.–March 1976, for Minerals and Energy, 1976–80, for Resources and Energy, 1980–83; Shadow Treasurer, Jan.–March 1983; Federal Treas. of Australia, 1983–91; Dep. Prime Minister, 1990–91. Member: Cabinet Expenditure Review Cttee (Dep. Chm.), 1987–91; Parly Structural Adjustment Cttee, 1987; Parly Social and Family Policy Cttee, 1983. Chm., Australian Loan Council, 1983–91. Mem., Bd of Architects of NSW, 2000–04. Dir, Brain Resource Co. Ltd, 2001–. Hon. LLD: Keio, Tokyo, 1995; Nat. Univ. of Singapore, 1999; NSW, 2003. *Publication:* Engagement: Australia faces the Asia Pacific, 2000. *Recreations:* classical music, architecture, fine arts, swimming. *Address:* PO Box 1265, Potts Point, NSW 1335, Australia.

KEATING, Roland Francis Kester, (Roly); Director, Archive Content, BBC, since 2008; *b* 5 Aug. 1961; *s* of Donald Norman Keating and Betty Katharine Keating (*née* Wells); *m* 1989, Caroline Marguerite Cumine Russell; one *s* two *d*. *Educ:* Westminster Sch.; Balliol Coll., Oxford (BA Hons). Joined BBC as gen. trainee, 1983: attachments to Radio Ulster, Kaleidoscope, Everyman, Newsnight progs; producer and dir, Music and Arts Dept, 1985–89; Editor: The Late Show, 1990–92; Bookmark, 1992–97; Executive Producer: (also devised and launched) One Foot in the Past, 1992; A History of British Art, 1996; The House Detectives, 1997; How Buildings Learn, 1997; Hd of Develt, Music and Arts, with special resp. for New Services, 1995; on secondment (part-time) to BBC Broadcast to develop new channel propositions for BBC Worldwide/Flextech jt venture, UKTV, 1996; Hd of Programming, UKTV, 1997–99; Controller, Digital Channels, 1999–2000, Controller of Arts Commissioning and Digital Channels, 2000–01, BBC TV; Controller, BBC4, 2001–04, on secondment as Jt Leader, BBC Charter Review, 2003; Controller, BBC2, 2004–08; Actg Controller, BBC1, 2007–08. *Recreations:* children, reading, walking, being by the seaside. *Address:* BBC Television Centre, Wood Lane, W12 7RJ. *Club:* Soho House.

KEATLEY, Robert Leland; Editor, The Hong Kong Journal, since 2005; *b* 14 Feb. 1935; *s* of Robert L. Keatley and Eva S. Keatley; *m* 1st, 1970, Anne Greene (marr. diss.); one *s*; 2nd, 1982, Catharine Williams; two *d*. *Educ:* Univ. of Washington (BA); Stanford Univ. (MA). Diplomatic Corresp., Wall St Jl, Washington, 1969–77; Foreign Ed., Wall St Jl, NY, 1978; Editor: Asian Wall St Jl, Hong Kong, 1979–84; Wall St Jl Europe, Brussels, 1984–92; columnist and feature editor, Wall St Jl, Washington, 1992–98; South China Morning Post: Sen. Associate Editor, 1998–99; Editor, 1999–2001. Mem. Bd, Washington Inst. Foreign Affairs, 2006–. *Publication:* China: behind the mask, 1974. *Recreations:* hiking, golf. *Address:* 3109 Cathedral Avenue NW, Washington, DC 20008, USA. *Clubs:* Hong Kong, China, Ladies Recreation (Hong Kong); Cosmos (Washington).

KEAY, John Stanley Melville; author and history writer, since 1971; *b* 18 Sept. 1941; *s* of Capt. Stanley Walter Keay and Florence Jessie Keay (*née* Keeping); *m* 1972, Julia Margaret Atkins; two *s* two *d*. *Educ:* Ampleforth Coll.; Magdalen Coll., Oxford (BA Hons Modern Hist.). Various jobs in advertising, printing, journalism (freelance, mostly as special corresp. on India for The Economist), 1963–71; writer and presenter of radio documentaries, mainly on Asia, 1981–95. *Publications:* Into India, 1973, 3rd edn 1999; When Men and Mountains Meet, 1977, The Gilgit Game, 1979, combined as The Explorers of the Western Himalayas, 1996; India Discovered, 1981, 3rd edn 2001; Eccentric Travellers, 1983, 2nd edn 2001; Highland Drove, 1984; Explorers Extraordinary, 1985, 2nd edn 2001; (Gen. Ed.) The Royal Geographical Society History of World Exploration, 1991; The Honourable Company: a history of the East India Company, 1991; (ed with Julia Keay) Collins Encyclopaedia of Scotland, 1994, 2nd edn 2000; Indonesia: from Sabang to Merauke, 1995; Last Post: the end of Empire in the Far East, 1997, 2nd edn 2000; India: a history, 2000; The Great Arc, 2000; Sowing the Wind: the seeds of conflict in the Middle East, 2003; Mad About the Mekong: exploration and empire in South East Asia, 2005; The Spice Route: a history, 2005; (ed with Julia Keay) The London Encyclopaedia, 3rd edn 2008; China: a history, 2008. *Recreations:* weeding, walking, the warmer parts of Asia. *Address:* Succoth, Dalmally, Argyll PA33 1BB. *T:* (01838) 200250.

KEDDIE, Dr Alistair William Carnegie, CB 2003; FRAS; Deputy Director General, Innovation Group, Department of Trade and Industry, 2002–03 (Acting Director General, 2002); part-time Principal Fellow, Warwick Manufacturing Group, University of Warwick, since 2003; *b* 1 Jan. 1943; *s* of late Stuart Keddie and Ethel Carnegie Keddie; *m* 1966, Marjorie Scott Masterton; one *s* one *d*. *Educ:* Breadalbane Acad., Aberfeldy; Univ. of Glasgow (BSc Hons; PhD 1970). FRAS 1969. Res. Asst, then Asst Lectr, Dept of Astronomy, Univ. of Glasgow, 1967–70; res. mgt posts, 1970–77; Hd, Air Pollution Div., Warren Spring Lab., Stevenage, 1977–84; Department of Trade and Industry: Mem., Policy Planning Unit, 1984–85; Dir, Sci. and Technol. Policy, 1985–89; Dir, Single Market Unit, 1989–91; Hd, Innovation Unit, 1991–99; Dir, Envmt, Innovation, 1999–2002. Member: EPSRC, 2001–03; Bd, Carbon Trust, 2001–04. Trustee, Green Alliance, 2003–. *Recreations:* walking, bird watching, music. *Address:* Pitully, Dull, Aberfeldy, Perthshire PH15 2JQ. *T:* (01887) 820367.

KEE, Robert, CBE 1998; author and broadcaster; *b* 5 Oct. 1919; *s* of late Robert and Dorothy Kee; *m* 1st, 1948, Janetta (marr. diss. 1950), *d* of Rev. G. H. Woolley, VC; one *d*; 2nd, 1960, Cynthia (marr. diss. 1989), *d* of Edward Judah; one *s* one *d* (and one *s* decd); 3rd, 1990, Catherine Mary, *yr d* of Humphrey and Violet Margaret Trevelyan. *Educ:* Stowe Sch. (Schol.); Magdalen Coll., Oxford (Exhibr, MA). RAF, 1940–46. Atlantic Award for Literature, 1946. Picture Post, 1948–51; Picture Editor, WHO, 1953; Special Corresp., Observer, 1956–57; Literary Editor, Spectator, 1957; Special Corresp., Sunday Times, 1957–58; BBC TV (Panorama, etc), 1958–62; Television Reporters International, 1963–64; ITV (Rediffusion, Thames, London Week-End, ITN, Yorkshire (documentary series, Faces of Communism)), 1964–78, Presenter, First Report, ITN's first lunch-time news prog., 1972–74; BBC, 1978–82; Presenter: Ireland: a television history (13 part television series), 1980; Panorama, BBC1, 1982; TV-am, 1983; Channel 4's Seven Days, 1984–88; miscellaneous BBC radio broadcasts, 1946–. Alistair Horne Research Fellow, St Antony's Coll., Oxford, 1972–73. Hon. DLitt London Metropolitan, 2003. BAFTA Richard Dimbleby Award, 1976. *Publications:* A Crowd Is Not Company, 1947, repr. 2000; The Impossible Shore, 1949; A Sign of the Times, 1955; Broadstrop In Season, 1959; Refugee World, 1961; The Green Flag, 1972, repr. 2000; Ireland: a history, 1980, new edn 2003; The World We Left Behind, 1984; The World We Fought For, 1985; Trial and Error, 1986; Munich: the eleventh hour, 1988; The Picture Post Album, 1989; The Laurel and the Ivy: Parnell and Irish nationalism, 1993; many translations from German. *Recreations:* swimming, listening to music. *Address:* c/o Rogers, Coleridge and White, 20 Powis Mews, W11 1JN. *Club:* Reform.

KEEBLE, Sir (Herbert Ben) Curtis, GCMG 1982 (KCMG 1978; CMG 1970); HM Diplomatic Service, retired; Ambassador at Moscow, 1978–82; *b* 18 Sept. 1922; *s* of Herbert Keeble and Gertrude Keeble, BEM; *m* 1947, Margaret Fraser; two *d* (and one *d* decd). *Educ:* Clacton County High Sch.; London University. Served HM Forces, 1942–47. Entered HM Foreign (subsequently Diplomatic) Service, 1947; served in Jakarta, 1947–49; Foreign Office, 1949–51; Berlin, 1951–54; Washington, 1954–58; Foreign Office, 1958–63; Counsellor and Head of European Economic Organisations Dept, 1963–65; Counsellor (Commercial), Berne, 1965–68; Minister, Canberra, 1968–71; Asst Under-Sec. of State, FCO, 1971–73; HM Ambassador, German Democratic Republic, 1974–76; Dep. Under Sec. of State (Chief Clerk), FCO, 1976–78. Special Adviser, H of C Foreign Affairs Cttee, 1985–86; A Governor, BBC, 1985–90. Chairman: Britain-Russia Centre (formerly GB-USSR Assoc.), 1985–95 (Vice Pres., 1995–2000); Foundn for Accountancy and Financial Management, 1993–2000; Thames Ditton Hosp. Foundn, 1996–2000; Member Council: RIIA, 1985–90; SSEES, 1985–90. *Publications:* (ed) The Soviet State, 1985; Britain and The Soviet Union, 1917–1989, 1990; (contrib.) Harold Macmillan: aspects of a political life, 1999; Britain, Russia and the Soviet Union, 2000. *Recreations:* sailing, painting. *Address:* Dormers, St Leonards Road, Thames Ditton, Surrey KT7 0RR. *T:* (020) 8398 7778. *Club:* Royal Over-Seas League.

See also S. C. Keeble.

KEEBLE, Sally Curtis; MP (Lab) Northampton North, since 1997; *b* 13 Oct. 1951; *d* of Sir Curtis Keeble, *qv* and Margaret Keeble; *m* 1990, Andrew Porter; one *s* one *d*. *Educ:* St Hugh's Coll., Oxford (BA Hons); Univ. of S Africa (BA Hons). Journalist, Daily News, Durban, SA, 1974–79; Reporter, Birmingham Post, 1979–83; Press Officer, Labour Party, 1983–84; Asst Dir, Ext. Relns, ILEA, 1984–86; Hd of Communications, GMB, 1986–90; Public Affairs Consultant, 1994–97. Parly Under-Sec. of State, DTLR, 2001–02, DFID, 2002–03. Mem. (Lab) Southwark BC, 1986–94 (Leader, 1990–93). Hon. Fellow, S Bank Univ. *Publications:* Collectors' Corner, 1984; Conceiving Your Baby: how medicine can help, 1995. *Recreations:* walking, antiques, reading. *Address:* House of Commons, SW1A 0AA; 8 Oakpark Close, Northampton NN3 5JG. *T:* (01604) 646310.

KEEFE, Denis Edward Peter Paul; HM Diplomatic Service; Ambassador to Georgia, since 2007; *b* 29 June 1958; *s* of late Dr John Victor Keefe and of Dr Oonagh Rose Keefe (*née* McAleer); *m* 1983, Catherine Ann Mary Wooding; three *s* three *d*. *Educ:* Campion Sch., Hornchurch; Churchill Coll., Cambridge (MA Classics); Hertford Coll., Oxford; Malmö Univ. Joined HM Diplomatic Service, 1982; FCO, 1982–84; Second Sec., Prague, 1984–88; First Secretary: FCO, 1988–92; Nairobi, 1992–95; Dep. Hd, S Asian Dept, FCO, 1996–97; Hd, Asia-Europe Meeting Unit, 1997–98; Dep. Hd of Mission, Prague, 1998–2002; on secondment as Counter Terrorism Strategy Team Leader, Cabinet Office, 2002–03; Head, China Hong Kong Dept, 2003–04, Far Eastern Gp, 2004–06, FCO. *Recreations:* singing, sailing, walking, learning languages. *Address:* c/o Foreign and Commonwealth Office, King Charles Street, SW1A 2AH; *e-mail:* denis.keefe@fco.gov.uk.

KEEFFE, Barrie Colin; dramatist; *b* 31 Oct. 1945; *s* of late Edward Thomas Keeffe and Constance Beatrice Keeffe (*née* Marsh); *m* 1st, 1969, Dee Sarah Truman (marr. diss. 1979); 2nd, 1981, Verity Eileen Proud (*née* Bargate) (*d* 1981); Guardian of her two *s*; 3rd, 1983, Julia Lindsay (marr. diss. 1993). *Educ:* East Ham Grammar School. Formerly actor with Nat. Youth Theatre; began writing career as journalist; Thames Television Award writer-in-residence, Shaw Theatre, 1977; Resident playwright, Royal Shakespeare Co., 1978; Associate Writer, Theatre Royal, Stratford East, 1986–91. Member: Board of Directors: Soho Theatre Co., 1978–; Theatre Royal, Stratford E, 1988–91; Tutor, City Univ., London, 2002–05. Edith J. Wilson Fellow, Christ's Coll., Cambridge, 2003–04. UN Ambassador, 1995. French Critics Prix Revelation, 1978; Giles Cooper Best Radio Plays, 1980; Mystery Writers of America Edgar Allan Poe Award, 1982. *Theatre plays:* Only a Game, 1973; A Sight of Glory, 1975; Scribes, 1975; Here Comes the Sun, 1976; Gimme Shelter, 1977; A Mad World My Masters, 1977, 1984; Barbarians, 1977; Frozen Assets, 1978; Sus, 1979; Bastard Angel, 1980; She's So Modern, 1980; Black Lear, 1980; Chorus Girls, 1981; Better Times, 1985; King of England, 1988; My Girl, 1989; Not Fade Away, 1990; Wild Justice, 1990; I Only Want to Be With You, 1995; The Long Good Friday, 1997; Shadows on the Sun, 2001; Still Killing Time, 2006; *television plays:* Substitute, 1972; Not Quite Cricket, 1977; Gotcha, 1977; Nipper, 1977; Champions, 1978; Hanging Around, 1978; Waterloo Sunset, 1979; King, 1984; *television series:* No Excuses, 1983; *film:* The Long Good Friday, 1981; also radio plays. *Publications: novels:* Gadabout, 1969; No Excuses, 1983; *plays:* Gimme Shelter, 1977; A Mad World My Masters, 1977; Barbarians, 1977; Here Comes the Sun, 1978; Frozen Assets, 1978; Sus, 1979; Bastard Angel, 1980; The Long Good Friday, 1984, new edn 1998; Better Times, 1985; King of England, 1988; My Girl, 1989; Wild Justice, Not Fade Away, Gimme Shelter, 1990; Barrie Keeffe Plays 1, 2001. *Recreation:* origami. *Address:* 110 Annandale Road, SE10 0JZ.

KEEGAN, Donal Arthur John, OBE 1999; FRCP, FRCPE, FRCPI; Lord-Lieutenant of Londonderry, since 2002; *b* 8 Oct. 1938; *s* of Daniel McManus Keegan and Geraldine Keegan (*née* Halpin); *m* 1973, Doreen Elizabeth Nelson; one *d*. *Educ:* St Columb's Coll., Londonderry; Queen's Univ., Belfast (BSc Hons, MB BCh, BAO); DPhysMed. FRCPI 1973; FRCPE 1989; FRCP 1990. Consultant Physician: Highland and Westen Isles Health Bd Areas, 1970–75; Altnagelvin Hosp., Londonderry, 1975–2003, Emeritus, 2004. Chairman: Regl Adv. Cttee on Cancer, 1997–; NI Council for Postgrad. Med. and Dental Educn, 1998–2004; Central Med. Adv. Cttee, NI, 1999–2003; Mem., Cttee on Higher Med. Trng, RCPI, 2004–. Med. Dir, Distinction and Meritorious Service Awards Cttee, NI, 2001–04. Hon. Col, 204 (N Irish) Field Hosp. (V), 2004–. *Publications:* articles on cardiology and musculoskeletal disease. *Recreations:* fishing, shooting, bird migration. *Address:* Auskaird, 5 Greenwood, Culmore, Londonderry BT48 8NP. *T:* (028) 7135 1292. *Club:* Royal Society of Medicine.

KEEGAN, Dame (Elizabeth) Mary, DBE 2007; FCA; Head, Government Finance Profession and Board Member, HM Treasury, 2004–08; *b* 21 Jan. 1953; *d* of Michael Keegan and Elizabeth Keegan (*née* Sarginson). *Educ:* Brentwood County High Sch. for Girls; Somerville Coll., Oxford (Caroline Haslett Meml Scholar, Coombs Exhibitioner; rowing blue; BA Natural Sci. 1974; MA 1977). ACA 1977, FCA 1983. Price Waterhouse, subseq. PricewaterhouseCoopers: articled London, 1974; Paris, 1979; Chicago, 1982; Partner, 1985–2001; Nat. Technical Partner, 1991–96; Dir Professional Standards Europe, 1994–98; Hd Global Corporate Reporting Gp, 1998–2001; Mem. Supervisory Bd, European Financial Reporting Adv. Gp, 2001–04; Man. Dir, Govt Financial Mgt and Finance Dir, HM Treasury, 2004–07. Chm., Accounting Standards Bd, 2001–04. Member: Urgent Issues Task Force, Accounting Standards Bd, 1993–99; Standing Interpretations Cttee, Internat. Accounting Standards Cttee, 1997–2001; Internat. Forum on Accountancy Develt, 1999–2001; Chm., Financial Reporting Cttee, 1994–97, Mem. Council, 1994–97, ICAEW; Vice-Pres. and Mem. Council, Chm. Auditing Working Party, FEE, 1997–2001; Mem., Financial Reporting Rev. Panel, Financial Reporting Council, 2007–. Gov., University Coll. Falmouth, 2007–. FRSA. *Publications:* (jtly) The ValueReporting Revolution: moving beyond the earnings game, 2001; frequent contrib. to professional jls. *Recreations:* gardening, classical music, sailing. *Address:* Old Matthews Farm, Kerswell, Cullompton, Devon EX15 2EL.

KEEGAN, Dame Geraldine (Mary Marcella), DBE 2000 (OBE 1995); Headmistress, St Mary's College, Londonderry, 1987–2006; *b* 17 Jan. 1941; *d* of Daniel Anthony McManus Keegan and Geraldine Catherine Veronica (*née* Halpin). *Educ:* St Mary's UC, Belfast (Cert Ed 1963); Univ. of Ulster (DipEd 1972); Univ. of Manchester (MEd 1975). Secondary sch. teacher of music, history and English, 1963–75; Sen. Lectr in Educnl Psychology, St Mary's UC, Belfast, 1975–85; Dep. Dir, NI Centre for Educn Mgt, 1985–87. Pro-Chancellor, 1997–2001, Vis. Prof., 2001–, Univ. of Ulster. Mem. Cttee, European Foundn for Quality Mgt, 2001–; Board Member: Community of Practice (Educn) SENTINUS, 1996–2007; Centre for Migration Studies, 1997–; Museums and Art Galls of NI, 2002–; Optimus Approvals Cttee, Failte Ireland, 2005–; NW Regional Coll., 2007–. NI representative: UK Bd, Investors in People, 2002–08; Leadership and Mgt Adv. Panel, 2007–. Member: Bd, President's Award, Ireland, 2002–; RUC George Cross Foundn, 2002–; Bd, Spirit of Enniskillen Trust, 2005–; Trustee, Scotch Irish Trust, 1994–. FRSA 1995. *Recreations:* classical music, travel, fishing. *Address:* 7 Locarden, Culmore Point Road, Londonderry BT48 8RP.

KEEGAN, Sir John (Desmond Patrick), Kt 2000; OBE 1991; FRSL; FRHistS; military historian; Defence Editor, The Daily Telegraph, since 1986; *b* 15 May 1934; *e s* of Francis Joseph Keegan and Eileen Mary Keegan (*née* Bridgman); *m* 1960, Susanne Ingeborg Everett; two *s* two *d*. *Educ:* King's Coll., Taunton; Wimbledon Coll.; Balliol Coll., Oxford (BA 1957; MA 1962; Hon. Fellow, 1999). Political Analyst, US Embassy, London, 1958–60; Sen. Lectr in Mil. Hist., RMA Sandhurst, 1960–86; corresp. from numerous countries, incl. Gulf, 1991. Delmas Vis. Dist. Prof. of Hist., Vassar Coll., 1997–98; Vis. Fellow, Princeton, 1984; Lectures: Lees Knowles, Cambridge, 1986; Eisenhower Meml, Kansas State, 1986; Brown Meml, Brown Univ., 1989; Whidden Meml, McMaster, 1990; Frum Meml, Toronto, 1994; Reith, BBC, 1998. Visitor, Hugh Sexey's Hosp., 1986–; Dir, E Somerset NHS Trust, 1991–97. Trustee: Nat. Heritage Meml Fund, 1994–2000; Heritage Lottery Fund, 1994–2000; Comr, Commonwealth War Graves Commn, 2001–06. Contributing Editor: The New Republic, 1980–90; US News and World

Report, 1986–. Hon. LLD New Brunswick, 1997; Hon. DLit QUB, 2000; Hon. DLitt Bath, 2002. Samuel Eliot Morison Prize, US Soc. for Mil. Hist., 1996. KM 1999. *Publications:* The Face of Battle, 1976; World Armies, 1978; Six Armies in Normandy, 1982; The Mask of Command, 1987; The Price of Admiralty, 1988, reissued as Battle at Sea, 1993; The Second World War, 1989; (ed) The Times Atlas of the Second World War, 1989; (ed) Churchill's Generals, 1991; A History of Warfare, 1993 (Duff Cooper Prize, 1994); Warpaths: travels of a military historian in North America, 1995; The Battle for History, 1996; The First World War, 1998 (Westminster Medal, 1999); War and Our World: the Reith Lectures, 1998; (ed) The Penguin Book of War: great military writings, 1999; Churchill, 2002; Intelligence in War, 2003; The Iraq War, 2004; contribs to DNB, Encyclopaedia Britannica. *Address:* The Manor House, Kilmington, near Warminster, Wilts BA12 6RD. *T:* (01985) 844856. *Clubs:* Garrick, Beefsteak, Pratt's; Brook (NY).

KEEGAN, (Joseph) Kevin, OBE 1982; professional footballer, 1966–84; Manager, Newcastle United Football Club, 2008; *b* 14 Feb. 1951; *s* of late Joseph Keegan; *m* 1974, Jean Woodhouse; two *d*. Professional footballer with: Scunthorpe Utd, 1966–71; Liverpool, 1971–77; Hamburg, 1977–80; Southampton, 1980–82; Newcastle Utd, 1982–84. Internat. appearances for England, 1973–82, Captain, 1976–82. Manager, Newcastle Utd FC, 1992–97; Chief Operating Officer, Fulham FC, 1997–99; Coach, England Football Team, 1999–2000; Manager, Manchester City FC, 2001–05. Formerly football expert, Thames TV. Winners' medals: League Championships, 1973, 1976; UEFA Cup, 1973, 1976; FA Cup, 1974; European Cup, 1977. European Footballer of the Year, 1978, 1979. *Publications:* Kevin Keegan, 1978; Against the World: playing for England, 1979; Kevin Keegan: my autobiography, 1997.

KEEGAN, Dame Mary; *see* Keegan, Dame E. M.

KEEGAN, William James Gregory; Senior Economics Commentator, The Observer, since 2003 (Economics Editor, 1977–2003); *b* 3 July 1938; *s* of William Patrick Keegan and Sheila Julia Keegan (*née* Buckley); *m* 1st, 1967, Tessa (*née* Young, *widow* of John Ashton) (marr. diss. 1982); two *s* two *d*; 2nd, 1992, Hilary, *d* of Maurice Stonefrost, *qv*; one *s* two *d*. *Educ:* Wimbledon Coll.; Trinity Coll., Cambridge (MA). National Service (Army), 1957–59 (commissioned). Journalist, Financial Times, Daily Mail and News Chronicle, 1963–67; Economics Correspondent, Financial Times, 1967–76; Economic Intell. Dept, Bank of England, 1976–77; The Observer: Asst Editor and Business Editor, 1981–83; Associate Editor, 1983–2003. Member: BBC Adv. Cttee on Business and Indust. Affairs, 1981–88; Council, Employment Inst., 1987–92; Adv. Bd, Dept of Applied Economics, Cambridge, 1988–92; Cttee for Soc. Scis., CNAA, 1991–92; Nat. Council, The Catalyst Forum, 1998–. Gov., NIESR, 1998–. Vis. Prof. of Journalism, 1989–, Hon. Res. Fellow, 1990–, Sheffield Univ. Hon. LittD Sheffield, 1995; Hon. DLitt City, 1998. *Publications:* Consulting Father Wintergreen, 1974; A Real Killing, 1976; (jtly) Who Runs the Economy?, 1978; Mrs Thatcher's Economic Experiment, 1984; Britain Without Oil, 1985; Mr Lawson's Gamble, 1989; The Spectre of Capitalism, 1992; 2066 and All That, 2000; The Prudence of Mr Gordon Brown, 2003; contribs to The Tablet. *Address:* 76 Lofting Road, Islington, N1 1JB. *T:* (020) 7607 3590; The Observer, 3–7 Herbal Hill, EC1R 5EJ. *T:* (020) 7278 2332. *Clubs:* Garrick, MCC.

KEEHAN, Michael Joseph; QC 2001; a Recorder, since 2000; *b* 31 March 1960; *s* of Michael and Alice Keehan; *m* 1988, Sarah Elizabeth Monk; two *d*. *Educ:* Birmingham Univ. (LLB). Called to the Bar, Middle Temple, 1982. *Recreations:* family life, gardening, walking. *Address:* St Ives Chambers, Whittall Street, Birmingham B4 6DH.

KEEL, Aileen Margaret, (Mrs Paul Dwyer), CBE 2008; FRCPath; FRCPGlas, FRCPE; Deputy Chief Medical Officer, Scottish Government (formerly Scottish Executive), since 1999; *b* Glasgow, 23 Aug. 1952; *d* of Walter and Everina Keel; *m* 1995, Paul Dwyer; one *s*. *Educ:* Univ. of Glasgow (MB ChB 1976). MRCP 1979; MRCPath 1986, FRCPath 1995; FRCPGlas 1992; FRCPE 2005; MFPH 2004. Trng in gen. medicine and haematol., Glasgow and Aberdeen, 1976–84; Consultant Haematologist and Dir of Pathol., Cromwell Hosp., London, 1987–89; Hon. Consultant Haematologist and Hon. Res. Fellow, Central Middx and Middx Hosp., London, 1988–92; SMO, 1992–98, PMO, 1998–99, Scottish Office. Founding Fellow, Inst. for Contemp. Scotland, 2000. *Recreations:* the arts in general, music, particularly opera, current affairs, good food and wine, evidence based arguing! *Address:* Scottish Government Health Department, St Andrew's House, Regent Road, Edinburgh EH1 3DG. *T:* (0131) 244 2799, *Fax:* (0131) 244 3477; *e-mail:* aileen.keel@scotland.gsi.gov.uk.

KEELER, Walter Charles John; self-employed potter, since 1965; *b* 22 April 1942; *s* of Walter Stanley Keeler and Iris Eileen Keeler (*née* Callaghan); *m* 1964, Madoline; two *s* one *d*. *Educ:* Harrow Sch. of Art (Intermediate NDD); Hornsey Coll. of Art (Art Teachers Cert). Sen. Lectr in Studio Pottery, Harrow Sch. of Art, 1964–78; Bristol Polytechnic, subseq. University of West of England: Sen. Lectr in Ceramics, 1978–94; Reader, 1994–98; Prof. of Ceramics, 1998–2002. Pottery Studio: Bledlow Ridge, Bucks, 1965–76; Moorcroft Cottage, Penallt, Mons, 1976–. Associate Dir, Nat. Electronic and Video Archive of the Crafts, 1992–2002. Exhibitions include: Craft Potters Assoc., London, 1982; Contemp. Applied Arts, London, 1989, 1999; Leeds City Art Gall., 1993; Contemp. Ceramics, London, 2002; work in public collections including: V&A Mus.; Crafts Council Collection; Nat. Mus. of Wales, Cardiff; Fitzwilliam Mus., Cambridge, and worldwide. Fellow, Craft Potters Assoc., 1967; Mem., Contemp. Applied Arts (formerly British Crafts Centre), 1969–. *Relevant publication:* Walter Keeler, by E. Cooper and A. Fielding, 2004. *Recreations:* gardening, music, travel, cooking and eating. *Address:* Moorcroft Cottage, Penallt, Monmouthshire NP25 4AH. *T:* (01600) 713946, *Fax:* (01600) 712530; *e-mail:* Penalltpottery@hotmail.com.

KEELEY, Barbara Mary; MP (Lab) Worsley, since 2005; an Assistant Government Whip, since 2008; *b* 26 March 1952; *d* of late Edward and Joan Keeley; *m* Colin Huggett. *Educ:* Univ. of Salford (BA 1st Cl. Hons Pols and Contemp. Hist.). Field Systems Engr and Systems Engrg Manager, IBM UK, until 1989; community regeneration advr, 1989–94; Area Manager, BITC, 1994–95; local govt and voluntary sector, 1995–2001; Consultant, researching policy issues, Princess Royal Trust for Carers, 2001–05. PPS to Parly Sec., Cabinet Office, then Minister of State, DWP, 2006–07, to Minister of State for Women and Equality, 2007–08. Chm., PLP Women's Cttee, 2007–. Mem., Trafford MBC, 1995–2004 (Cabinet Mem., 1999–2004). Dir, Pathfinder Children's Trust, 2002–04. *Recreations:* listening to live music and opera, running and swimming (quite slowly). *Address:* c/o House of Commons, SW1A 0AA. *T:* (020) 7219 2303; *e-mail:* keeleyb@parliament.uk.

KEELING, Maj.-Gen. Andrew Myles, CB 1994; CBE 1992 (OBE 1988); freelance consultant, since 1996; UK Representative, Saab Microwave Systems (formerly Ericsson Microwave Systems AB), since 1997; *b* 4 July 1943; *s* of late Richard George Maynard Keeling, OBE and Audrey Stuart Baxter (*née* Frederick); *m* 1st, 1965, Ann Margaret Grey Dudley (*d* 2001); one *s* two *d*; 2nd, 2003, Woppy (*née* Brittan). *Educ:* Rugby School. Commissioned 2nd Lieut RM, 1961; served 41, 42 and 45 Commandos, and training jobs at BRNC, Dartmouth and RMA, Sandhurst, 1963–75; student, Canadian Forces Command and Staff Coll., 1975–76; HQ 3 Cdo Bde RM, 1976–78; 41 Cdo, 1978–80; Bde Major, HQ 3 Cdo Bde, 1980–81; Directing Staff, NDC and JSDC, 1982–83; Jt Force HQ, 1984–85; CO 45 Cdo, 1985–87; MoD, 1987–89; Comd, 3 Cdo Bde, 1990–92; COS to Comdt-Gen. RM, 1992–93; Maj.-Gen., RM, 1992–94; retired RM, 1995. Rep. Col Comdt, RM, 1998–2002. Sec., Salisbury Dio. Sudan Link, 2001–05; Lay Canon, Salisbury Cathedral, 2003–. Specialist Advr, Defence Select Cttee, H of C, 1997–98. Dir of Humanitarian Affairs, AMAR Internat. Charitable Foundn, 1995–96. Freeman, City of London, 1993. President: City of Winchester Br., RMA, 1996–2004; SBS Assoc., 2001–; Devon County RBL, 2005–08; Naval Vice-Pres., CCF Assoc., 1995–2001; Mem. Council, St Dunstan's, 1995– (Vice-Chm., 2004–); Vice-Pres., St George's Day Club, 2006–. *Recreations:* sailing, walking. *Clubs:* Special Forces; Royal Marines Sailing (Hon. Life Vice-Commodore), Hornet Sailing.

KEEMER, Peter John Charles; Assistant Auditor General, National Audit Office, 1989–93; *b* 27 Jan. 1932; *s* of late Frederick and Queenie Keemer; *m* 1954, Yvonne Griffin (*d* 2002); one *s* one *d* (and one *s* decd). *Educ:* Price's Sch., Fareham; Univ. of Bath (MPhil). Exchequer and Audit Department: Asst Auditor and Auditor, 1950–62; Private Sec. to Comptroller and Auditor Gen., 1962–65; seconded to Parly Comr for Administration as Chief Exec. Officer, 1966–70; Chief Auditor, 1970; Dep. Dir, 1973; Dir, 1978–89 (seconded to European Court of Auditors as Director, 1978–86). External Auditor, European Univ. Inst., Florence, 1994–97. Mem., Conciliation Cttee, EC, 2001–06. Mem., CIPFA, 1982. Chm., 1995–2001, Trustee, 1995–, Dir, 1997–, Breakthrough Breast Cancer; Mem. Council, Inst. of Cancer Res., 1994–2000 (Hon. Treas., 1996–2000). *Address:* How Green Cottage, How Lane, Chipstead, Coulsdon CR5 3LL. *T:* (01737) 553711; *e-mail:* keemer@globalnet.co.uk. *Club:* Royal Anglo-Belgian.

KEEN, Alan; *see* Keen, D. A.

KEEN, Ann Lloyd; MP (Lab) Brentford and Isleworth, since 1997; Parliamentary Under-Secretary of State, Department of Health, since 2007; *b* 26 Nov. 1948; *d* of late John Fox and Ruby Fox; one *s*; *m* 1980, (David) Alan Keen, *qv*; one step *s* one step *d*. *Educ:* Elfed Secondary Modern Sch., Clwyd; Univ. of Surrey (PGCE). Formerly: Hd, Faculty of Advanced Nursing, Queen Charlotte's Coll., Hammersmith; Gen. Sec., Community and District Nursing Assoc. Contested (Lab) Brentford and Isleworth, 1987, 1992. Hon. Prof. of Nursing, Thames Valley Univ. *Address:* House of Commons, SW1A 0AA.

KEEN, (David) Alan; MP (Lab and Co-op) Feltham and Heston, since 1992; *b* 25 Nov. 1937; one *s* one *d*; *m* 1980, Ann Lloyd (*see* Ann Keen); one step *s*. *Educ:* Sir William Turner's Sch., Redcar. Various posts as systems analyst, accountant and manager, 1963–92. Mem. (Lab) Hounslow BC, 1986–90. Mem., Select Cttee on Culture, Media and Sport, 1997–; Chm., All Party Football Gp, 2001–. *Address:* House of Commons, SW1A 0AA.

KEEN, Kenneth Roger; QC 1991; **His Honour Judge Keen;** a Circuit Judge, since 2001; *b* 13 May 1946; *s* of Kenneth Henry Keen and Joan Megan Keen (*née* Weetman); *m* Mary Lorraine Raeburn; one *s* one *d* by previous marriage. *Educ:* Doncaster Grammar School. Qualified Solicitor, 1968; called to the Bar, Gray's Inn, 1976; practice on NE circuit; a Recorder, 1989. *Recreations:* tennis, travel, golf. *Address:* Sheffield Crown Court, 50 West Bar, Sheffield S3 8PH.

KEEN, Laurence John, OBE 2000; FSA, FRHistS; President, British Archaeological Association, 1989–2004; County Archaeological Officer, Dorset County Council, 1975–99; Consultant, John Stark & Crickmay Partnership, architects, 1999–2003; *b* 11 July 1943; *er s* of late John William Frederick Keen and Dorothy Ethel Keen (*née* French). *Educ:* Kilburn GS; St John's Coll., York (Cert Ed (Music) 1966); Inst. of Archaeology, Univ. of London (Postgrad. Dip. in European Archaeol. 1969; Gordon Childe Meml Prize); UCL (MPhil 1978). FRHistS 1974; FSA 1979; MIFA 1985; FSAScot 1995. Répétiteur, Lycée Mohammed V, Marrakech, 1962–63; Asst Master, Cundall Manor Sch., York, 1966–67; Dir, Southampton Archaeol Res. Cttee, 1972–75. Archaeol Cons., MPBW, then DoE, then English Heritage, 1964–. Dir, Census of Medieval Tiles in Britain, 2004–. Director of excavations: Wardour Castle, Wilts; Blackfriars, Gloucester; Kingswood Abbey, Glos; Tattershall Coll., Lincs; Mountgrace Priory, Yorks; Beeston Castle, Cheshire; Prudhoe Castle, Northumberland; Sherborne Abbey, Dorset. Vis. Lectr in Archaeology, Univ. of Southampton, 1973–75. Winston Churchill Fellow, 1970; Hon. Research Fellow: Centre for South-Western Hist. Studies, Univ. of Exeter, 1995–98; York St John Univ. (formerly UC of Ripon and York St John, then York St John Coll.), 1995–. Member: DAC for Faculties, 1977–97, Diocesan Redundant Churches Cttee, 1985–97, 2005–, Salisbury; Paintings Cttee, Council for the Care of Churches, 1979–96; Fabric Advisory Committee: Gloucester Cath., 1991–; St George's Chapel, Windsor Castle, 1998– (Chm., 1999–); Exeter Cath., 2006–. Chairman: Dorset Local Hist. Gp, 1985–99; Dorset Archaeol Cttee, Dorset Nat. Hist. and Archaeol Soc., 2002–; Member, Council: Soc. for Medieval Archaeology, 1973–76; British Archaeol Assoc., 1973–76, 1978–81, 1984–87 (Vice-Pres., 1988, 2004–; Reginald Taylor Essay Prize, 1969); Royal Archaeol Inst., 1982–85. Trustee, Oxford Archaeol., 2004–. Foreign Corresp. Associate Mem., Société Nat. des Antiquaires de France, 1990. Freeman, City of London, 1991; Freeman and Liveryman, Co. of Painter-Stainers, 1991. *Publications:* (jtly) William Barnes: the Dorset engravings, 1986 ((jtly) Mansel-Pleydell Essay Prize, Dorset Nat. Hist. & Archaeol. Soc., 1985), 2nd edn 1989; William Barnes: the Somerset engravings, 1989; (ed jtly) Historic Landscape of the Weld Estate, 1987; Dorset Domesday: an introduction, 1991; (ed jtly) Medieval Art and Architecture at Salisbury Cathedral, 1996; (ed) Almost the Richest City: Bristol in the Middle Ages, 1997; (jtly) Dorset from the Air, 1998; (ed) Studies in the Early History of Shaftesbury Abbey, 1999; (ed jtly) Windsor Castle: medieval archaeology, art and architecture of the Thames Valley, 2002; (jtly) Sherborne Abbey and School: excavations 1972–76 and 1990, 2005; (jtly) Mount Grace Priory: excavations of 1957–92, 2008; articles and reviews in nat. and county jls. *Recreations:* making music, entertaining, perfecting bread and butter pudding. *Address:* Hardye Chambers, 7 Church Street, Dorchester, Dorset DT1 1JN. *T:* (01305) 265460. *Club:* Royal Over-Seas League.

KEEN, Lady Mary; *see* Keen, Lady P. M. R.

KEEN, Maurice Hugh, OBE 2004; FSA; FBA 1990; Fellow of Balliol College, Oxford, 1961–2000, now Emeritus; *b* 30 Oct. 1933; *e s* of Harold Hugh Keen and Catherine Eleanor Lyle Keen (*née* Cummins); *m* 1968, Mary Agnes Keegan; three *d*. *Educ:* Winchester College; Balliol College, Oxford (BA 1st Cl. Mod. Hist. 1957). FSA 1987. Nat. Service 1952–54, commissioned Royal Ulster Rifles. Oxford University: Junior Res. Fellow, The Queen's Coll., 1957–61; Tutor in Medieval History, Balliol Coll., 1961–2000; Clerk of the Market, 2002–06. External examr, Nat. Univ. of Ireland, 1971–78. Fellow, Winchester Coll., 1989–2002. Alexander Prize, RHistS, 1962. *Publications:* The Outlaws of Medieval Legend, 1961; The Laws of War in the Later Middle Ages, 1965; A History of Medieval Europe, 1968; England in the Later Middle Ages, 1973; Chivalry, 1984 (Wolfson Lit. Award for History, 1985); English Society in the later Middle Ages, 1990; Origins of the English Gentleman, 2002. *Recreations:* fishing,

shooting. *Address:* 4 Walton Street, Oxford OX1 2HG. *Club:* Oxford and Cambridge.
See also G. L. Norman.

KEEN, Nigel John, FCA; Chairman, The Laird Group plc, since 2000; *b* 21 Jan. 1947; *s* of Peter and Margaret Keen; *m* 1972, Caroline Jane Cumming; two *s*. *Educ:* Charterhouse; Peterhouse, Cambridge (MA). FCA 1979. Auditor, Touche Ross & Co., 1968–74; Dir, Eur. Banking Co. Ltd, 1974–83; Chm., Cygnus gp of cos, 1983–2001; Dep. Chm., Laird Gp, 1999–2000; Chairman: Oxford Instruments plc, 1999–; Axis-Shield plc, 1999–; Deltex Med. Gp plc, 2000–. Director: Channel Is Develt Corp., 1996–2007; Bioquell plc, 2008–. Trustee, David Shepherd Wildlife Foundn, 1999–. *Recreations:* opera, golf. *Address:* 19 Pembroke Square, W8 6PA. *T:* (020) 7937 6008. *Club:* HAC.

KEEN, Prof. Peter Marley, PhD; Professor of Pre-Clinical Veterinary Studies, Department of Pharmacology, University of Bristol, 1988–95, now Professor Emeritus; *b* 14 May 1930; *s* of Ernest Keen and Kathleen (*née* Marley); *m* 1956, Pauline Helen Franklin; four *d*. *Educ:* Wellington Sch., Somerset; Univ. of Bristol (BVSc); PhD London Univ. 1964. MRCVS 1955. Nat. Service, RAF, 1948–50. Veterinary practice, 1955–59; Lectr in Vet. Pharmacol., RVC, London, 1959–64; University of Bristol: Lectr, then Reader, in Vet. Pharmacol., 1964–88; Head of Vet. Sch., 1988–93; Dean of Medicine, 1993–95. *Publications:* articles in learned jls. *Recreations:* oil painting, pub walks, local architecture. *Address:* Old Orchard, Winscombe Hill, Winscombe BS25 1DF. *T:* (01934) 842026.

KEEN, Lady (Priscilla) Mary (Rose); garden designer, writer and lecturer; *b* 12 Feb. 1940; *d* of 6th Earl Howe and of Priscilla (*née* Weigall, who *m* 2nd, Harold Coriat); *m* 1962, Charles Keen; one *s* three *d*. *Educ:* Lawnside, Malvern; Lady Margaret Hall, Oxford. Gardening Columnist: Evening Standard, 1980–88; Perspectives, 1988–98; Independent on Sunday, 1988–98; freelance journalist: Gardening; Daily Telegraph; designed Glyndebourne Opera House new gardens, 1992–93, and many large private commissions, as Mary Keen and Pip Morrison, Designed Landscapes. National Trust: Member: Gardens Panel, 1982–2006; Thames and Chilterns Regl Cttee, 1982–92; Severn Regl Cttee, 1996–2002. Inspirational Garden Journalist of the Year, Garden Writer's Guild Awards, 1999. *Publications:* The Garden Border Book, 1987; The Glory of the English Garden, 1989; Colour Your Garden, 1991; Decorate Your Garden, 1993; Creating a Garden, 1996. *Recreation:* gardening. *Address:* The Old Rectory, Duntisbourne Rous, Cirencester, Glos GL7 7AP.

KEEN, Richard Sanderson; QC (Scot.) 1993; *b* 29 March 1954; *s* of Derek Michael Keen and Jean Sanderson Keen; *m* 1978, Jane Carolyn Anderson; one *s* one *d*. *Educ:* King's Sch., Rochester; Dollar Acad.; Edinburgh Univ. (LLB Hons 1976; Beckman Schol.). Admitted Faculty of Advocates, 1980 (Treas., 2006–07; Dean, 2007–); Standing Jun. Counsel in Scotland to DTI, 1986–93. Chairman: Appeals Cttee, ICAS, 1996–2001; Police Appeals Tribunal, 2004–. *Recreations:* golf, ski-ing, shooting, opera. *Address:* The Castle, Elie, Fife KY9 1DN. *T:* (01333) 330010; 39 Ann Street, Edinburgh EH4 1PL. *T:* (0131) 343 1935; Advocate's Library, Parliament House, Edinburgh EH1 1RF. *T:* (0131) 226 5071. *Clubs:* New (Edinburgh); Bruntsfield Links Golfing Society (Edinburgh); Golf House (Elie).

KEENE, Rt Hon. Sir David (Wolfe), Kt 1994; PC 2000; **Rt Hon. Lord Justice Keene;** a Lord Justice of Appeal, since 2000; *b* 15 April 1941; *s* of Edward Henry Wolfe Keene and Lilian Marjorie Keene; *m* 1965, Gillian Margaret Lawrance; one *s* one *d*. *Educ:* Hampton Grammar Sch.; Balliol Coll., Oxford (Winter Williams Prizewinner, 1962; BA 1st Cl. Hons Law, 1962; BCL 1963; Hon. Fellow, 2004). Called to the Bar, Inner Temple, 1964 (Eldon Law Scholar, 1965; Bencher, 1987; Treas., 2006); QC 1980; a Recorder, 1989–94; a Dep. High Court Judge, 1993–94; a Judge of High Court of Justice, QBD, 1994–2000; a Judge, Employment Appeal Tribunal, 1995–2000. Chm. of Panel, Cumbria Structure Plan Examination in Public, 1980; conducted County Hall, London, Inquiry, 1987; Chairman: Planning and Envmtl Law Reform Working Gp, 1997–; Judicial Studies Bd, 2003–07 (Chm., Adv. Cttee on Equal Treatment, 1998–2003). Chm., Planning Bar Assoc., 1994 (Vice-Chm., 1990–94). Visitor, Brunel Univ., 1995–2000. Hon. Fellow, Soc. of Advanced Legal Studies, 1998. Hon. LLD Brunel, 2001. *Recreations:* walking, opera, jazz, gardening. *Address:* Royal Courts of Justice, Strand, WC2A 2LL. *Club:* Athenæum.

KEENE, Prof. Derek John, DPhil; Leverhulme Professor of Comparative Metropolitan History, Institute of Historical Research, 2001–08; *b* 27 Dec. 1942; *s* of Charles Henry Keene and Edith Anne Keene (*née* Swanston); *m* 1969, Suzanne Victoria Forbes (*see* S. V. Keene); one *s* one *d*. *Educ:* Ealing Grammar Sch.; Oriel Coll., Oxford (MA, DPhil). FRHistS. Researcher, 1968–74, Asst Dir, 1974–78, Winchester Research Unit; Institute of Historical Research: Dir, Social and Economic Study of Medieval London, 1987–99; Dir, Centre for Metropolitan History, 1987–2002; Actg Dir, 2008. Member: RCHM, 1987–99; Commn internat. pour l'histoire de villes, 1990–; Fabric Adv. Cttee, St Paul's Cathedral, 1991–; London Adv. Cttee, 1998–2004, Urban Panel, 2000–, English Heritage. *Publications:* Winchester in the Early Middle Ages (jtly), 1976; Survey of Medieval Winchester, 1985; Cheapside Before the Great Fire, 1985; (with V. Harding) A survey of documentary sources for property holding in London before the Great Fire, 1985; (with V. Harding) Historical Gazetteer of London before the Great Fire, 1987; (ed with P. J. Corfield) Work in Towns 850–1850, 1990; (jtly) A Medieval Capital and its Grain Supply: agrarian production and distribution in the London region *c* 1300, 1993; (ed jtly) St Paul's: the cathedral church of London 604–2004, 2004; contribs to learned jls and to collections of essays. *Recreations:* metropolises, walking uphill, making and repairing things. *Address:* 162 Erlanger Road, SE14 5TJ. *T:* (020) 7639 5371.

KEENE, John Robert R.; *see* Ruck-Keene.

KEENE, Dr Suzanne Victoria, FIIC; Course Director, Museum Studies, Institute of Archaeology, University College London, since 2001; *b* 21 July 1944; *d* of late Lt-Comdr Lachlan Andrew Forbes, RN and Adelaide Talbot Suzanne Forbes; *m* 1969, Derek John Keene, *qv*; one *s* one *d*. *Educ:* various schools; University Coll. London (Dip. Archaeol Conservation; Gordon Childe Prize, Inst. of Archaeol., 1969; PhD 1993). FIIC 1985. Archaeol Asst, British Sch. at Rome, 1964–66; Winchester Research Unit: Archaeol Conservator, 1969–75; Ed., Medieval Finds pubn, 1975–77; Museum of London: Hd of Section, Archaeol Conservation, 1979–86; Hd of Conservation, 1986–92; Hd of Collections Mgt, Science Mus., 1992–2000. Member: Exec. Cttee, 1970–74, Gen. Sec., 1972–76, UK Inst. for Conservation; Panel on Archaeol Collections, Area Mus. for S Eastern England, 1976–90; UK Nat. Cttee, ICOM, 1993–99; Bd, Textile Conservation Centre, 1993–2000. Member: Working Parties, English Heritage and Mus and Galls Commn, 1988–90 and 1992; Working Gp on Mus and Nat. Grid for Learning, DCMS, 1998–99; Bd, London Museums Agency, 2001–04; Bd, Collections Trust (formerly Mus Documentation Assoc.), 2006–. Trustee, Tank Mus., 1998–2005. *Publications:* Managing Conservation in Museums, 1996, 2nd edn 2002; Digital Collections: museums in the information age, 1998; Fragments of the World, 2005; contrib. numerous articles on museum digitisation and conservation. *Recreations:* beautiful country-side, reading novels, films, the internet. *Address:* Institute of Archaeology, 31–34 Gordon Square, WC1H 0PY.

KEENLYSIDE, Simon John, CBE 2003; baritone; *b* London, 3 Aug. 1959; *s* of Raymond Keenlyside and Ann Leonie Hirsch; *m* 2006, Zenaida Yanowsky, ballerina. *Educ:* St John's Coll., Cambridge (BA Zoology 1983); Royal Northern Coll. of Music. With Scottish Opera, 1989–94 (rôles incl. Marcello, Danilo, Guglielmo, Figaro in Barber of Seville, Billy Budd, Papageno and Belcore); *débuts:* Royal Opera, Covent Garden, 1989 (Silvio in Pagliacci); ENO, 1990 (Guglielmo in Così fan tutte); WNO, 1991 (Falke); San Francisco, 1993 (Olivier in Capriccio); Geneva, 1993 (Papageno in Die Zauberflote); Paris Opéra (Papageno), Australian Opera (Figaro) and La Scala, Milan, 1995; Glyndebourne, 1996 (Guglielmo); Metropolitan Opera, NY (Belcore in L'elisir d'amore); other rôles incl. Count Almaviva, Don Giovanni, Orfeo, Pelléas, Dandini in La Cenerentola, Wolfram in Tannhäuser, Yeletski in Queen of Spades, Oreste in Iphigénie en Tauride, Ubalde in Armide, Ford in Falstaff, title rôle in Hamlet, Prospero in The Tempest, Valentin in Gounod's Faust, Winston in 1984. Frequent concerts and recitals; recordings incl. operas, recitals of Schubert, Strauss and Mahler, and Schumann lieder. *Recreations:* a passion for all things zoological, diving, walking, painting, fly fishing. *Address:* c/o Askonas Holt, Lincoln House, 300 High Holborn, WC1V 7JH. *T:* (020) 7400 1700.

KEEP, Charles Reuben; Chairman and Managing Director, Resource Management Associates Ltd, since 1992; Chairman and Chief Executive, Bellair Holdings Ltd (formerly Bellair Cosmetics plc), since 1984; *b* 1932; *m*; one *d*. *Educ:* HCS, Hampstead. Joined Lloyds & Scottish Finance Ltd, 1956, Director, 1969; Man. Dir, International Factors Ltd, 1970; Group Man. Dir, Tozer Kemsley & Millbourn (Holdings) Ltd, 1973–77; Chm., Tozer Kemsley & Millbourn Trading Ltd, 1978–80; Director: Tozer Standard & Chartered Ltd, 1973–77; Barclays Tozer Ltd, 1974–77; Manufacturers Hanover Credit Corp., 1977–80; Chm., Export Leasing Ltd, Bermuda 1974–77; Pres., France Motors sa Paris, 1974–81. *Address:* The Oaks, 20 Forest Lane, Chigwell, Essex IG7 5AE. *T:* (020) 8504 3897. *Club:* Chigwell Golf.

KEETCH, Paul Stuart; MP (Lib Dem) Hereford, since 1997; *b* 21 May 1961; *s* of late John Norton Keetch and Agnes, (Peggy), Keetch; *m* 1991, Claire Elizabeth Baker; one *s*. *Educ:* Boys' High Sch., Hereford; Hereford Sixth Form Coll. With Midland Bank, 1978, then various water hygiene cos, 1979–95; Dir, MarketNet, 1996. Political and media advr to Lithuanian and Bosnian political parties, 1995–96. OSCE monitor to Albanian elections, 1996. Joined Liberal Party, 1975; Mem. (Lib Dem) Hereford CC, 1983–86. Lib Dem spokesman on: health, 1997; employment and training, 1997–99; defence, 1999–2005. Member: Educn and Employment Select Cttee, 1997–99; Armed Forces Bill Select Cttee, 2001; Envmtl Audit Select Cttee, 1999–2001; Foreign Affairs Select Cttee, 2005–; Quadripartite (Strategic Arms Export Control) Cttee, 2005–. All Party Groups: Pres., Cider Gp (Founder 1997); Founder and Co-Chm., British Lithuanian Gp; Vice-Chairman: Overseas Territories; Trinidad and Tobago; Childcare; Treasurer: Botswana; Serbia and Montenegro; Secretary: Albanian, 1997–; RN; Member: RM; Macedonia; Iraq; Bermuda; Bosnia; Czech and Slovak; Hungary; Madagascar; Netherlands; Montserrat; Channel Is; Turks and Caicos Is; Somaliland; Shipbuilding and Ship Repair; Racing and Bloodstock Issues. Dir, and Mem. Council, Electoral Reform Soc., 1997–. Member: CPA, 1997–; IPU. Patron, St Michael's Hospice, Hereford, 1997; President: Hereford Hosp. Radio, 1998–; Pegasus Juniors FC; Ross Sea Cadets; Vice-President: Nat. Childminding Assoc., 1998; Westfields FC, Hereford, 1997–; Hereford Young Europeans Gp; Ross-on-Wye Horticl Soc.; Hereford Amateur Operatic Soc.; Barrs Ct Sch., Hereford. Member: IISS; IPMS, 1998–; RUSI, 1999–. Hon. Mem., Falkland Is Assoc. *Recreations:* swimming, entertaining, building model warships. *Address:* House of Commons, SW1A 0AA. *T:* (020) 7219 2419, *Fax:* (020) 7219 1184; *e-mail:* keetchp@parliament.uk. *Clubs:* National Liberal; Herefordshire Farmers; Herefordshire County Cricket (Life Mem.), Surrey County Cricket.

KEIGHLEY, Prof. Michael Robert Burch, FRCS, FRCSE; Barling Professor of Surgery, University of Birmingham, 1988–2004, now Professor Emeritus; *b* 12 Oct. 1943; *s* of late Dr Robert Arthur Spink Keighley and of Dr Jacqueline Vivian Keighley; *m* Dr Dorothy Margaret; one *s* one *d*. *Educ:* Monkton Combe Sch.; St Bartholomew's Hosp., Univ. of London (MB BS 1967; MS 1976). FRCS 1970; FRCSE 1970. Prof. of Surgery, General and Dental Hosps, Univ. of Birmingham, 1984–88. Boerhaave Prof. of Surgery, Univ. of Leiden, 1985; Eyber's Vis. Prof., Univ. of OFS, 1987; Vis. Prof., Harvard Univ., 1990; Penman Vis. Prof., Univ. of Cape Town, 1992; Vis. Prof., St Mark's Hosp., London, 1995; Rupert Turnbull Prof., Washington Univ., 1996; Vis. Prof., Karolinska Inst., 2000; Hon. Prof., Christian Med. Coll., Vellore, India, 2004–. Chairman: Public Affairs, United European Gastroenterol Fedn, 2000–05; Public Relns and Ethics, 2002–, Res. Foundn, 2005–, Assoc. of Coloproctol. of GB and Ire. Mem., Christian Med. Fellowship, 1967–. Hon. Fellow, Brazilian Coll. of Surgeons, 1991; Hon. FRACS 1992; Hon. Mem., Portuguese Soc. of Surgery, 2004. Jacksonian Prize, RCS, 1979; Hunterian Prof., RCS, 1979. *Publications:* Antimicrobial Prophylaxis in Surgery, 1979; Inflammatory Bowel Diseases, 1981, 3rd edn 1995; Gastrointestinal Haemorrhage, 1983; Textbook of Gastroenterology, 1985, 2nd edn 1994; Surgery of the Anus, Rectum and Colon, 1994, 3rd edn 2008; Atlas of Colorectal Surgery, 1996. *Recreations:* painting, music, sailing, climbing. *Address:* Whalebone Cottage, Vicarage Hill, Tanworth in Arden, Warwicks B94 4AN. *T:* (01564) 742903, *Fax:* (01564) 742705; *e-mail:* Keighleycolo@btinternet.com. *Clubs:* Athenæum, Royal Society of Medicine; Aston Martin Owners.

KEIGHLEY, Rev. Thomas Christopher, TSSF; FRCN; independent health care consultant, since 2001; Assistant Priest, Christchurch and St John with St Luke, Isle of Dogs, since 2007; *b* 4 May 1951; *s* of late John Charles Keighley and of Frances Louise Keighley (*née* Leary); *m* 1st, 1974, Anne Gibson (marr. diss. 1978); 2nd, 1979, Elizabeth Redfern (marr. diss. 1989); 3rd, 1990, Amanda Gunner; one step *s* one step *d*. *Educ:* St Michael's Coll., Kirkby Lonsdale; Preston Sch. of Nursing (SRN 1974; RMN 1976); Charles Frear Sch. of Nursing (NDN Cert. 1976); Huddersfield Polytechnic (RCNT 1979); Dip. Nursing, London Univ., 1981; BA Hons Open Univ. 1985; NE Oecumenical Course, Ushaw Coll., Durham (DipHE (Theol)). FRCN 2004. Aux. Nurse, Deepdale Hosp., Preston, 1970; Staff Nurse, Preston Royal Infirmary, 1974; Community Charge Nurse, NW Leics, 1976; Clinical Teacher: Maidstone, 1977; Cambridge HA, 1979; RCN Adviser, Research, 1982; Dist Dir of Nursing, 1986, of Nursing and Quality, 1988, Waltham Forest; Regl Dir of Nursing, Yorkshire Health, 1990–95; Dir, Inst. of Nursing, Univ. of Leeds, 1993–96; Dir of Internat. Develt, Sch. of Healthcare Studies, Univ. of Leeds, 1997–2001. Associate Researcher, Lincoln Theol Inst., Sheffield Univ., 1998–2002. Mem., EU Adv. Cttee on Training for Nursing, 1990–2000. Ordained deacon, C of E, 2003, priest, 2004; Curate, Upper Nidderdale, 2003–06; Asst Priest, Dacre with Hartwith and Darley with Thornthwaite, dio. Ripon and Leeds, 2006–07. Winifred Raphael Meml Lecture, RCN Res. Soc., 1988; Ven. Catherine McAuley Meml Lecture, Mater Misericordiae Hosp., Dublin, 2002. TSSF, 2001–. Editor, Nursing Management, 1997–2004. *Publications:* articles on nursing and health care. *Recreations:* opera, art, walking, rug making. *Address:* 86 Saunders Ness Road, E14 3EA. *T:* (020) 7517 9628.

KEIGHTLEY, Maj.-Gen. Richard Charles, CB 1987; Chairman, Southampton University Hospitals NHS Trust, 2002–08; *b* 2 July 1933; *s* of General Sir Charles Keightley, GCB, GBE, DSO, and late Lady (Joan) Keightley (*née* Smyth-Osbourne); *m*

1958, Caroline Rosemary Butler, *er d* of Sir Thomas Butler, 12th Bt, CVO, DSO, OBE; three *d. Educ:* Marlborough Coll.; RMA, Sandhurst. Commissioned into 5th Royal Inniskilling Dragoon Guards, 1953; served Canal Zone, BAOR, N Africa, Singapore, Cyprus; sc Camberley, 1963; comd 5th Royal Inniskilling Dragoon Guards, 1972–75; Task Force Comdr, 3 Armd Div., 1978–79; RCDS 1980; Brigadier General Staff HQ UKLF, 1981; GOC Western Dist, 1982–83; Comdt, RMA Sandhurst, 1983–87. Col, 5th Royal Inniskilling Dragoon Guards, 1986–91. Defence Consultant, Portescap (UK), 1987–92. Chairman: W Dorset, subseq. Dorset, HA, 1988–95, 1998–2002; Dorset Healthcare NHS Trust, 1996–98. President: Dorset Br., Royal British Legion, 1990–; Dorset Relate, 2001–; St John Ambulance Dorset, 2008–. Chm., Combined Services Polo Assoc., 1982–86. *Recreations:* field sports, cricket, farming. *Address:* Kennels Farmhouse, Tarrant Gunville, Blandford, Dorset DT11 8JQ. *Club:* Cavalry and Guards.

KEIR, James Dewar; QC 1980; Director, Open University Educational Enterprises Ltd, 1983–88; Chairman, City and East London Family Practitioner Committee, 1985–89; part-time Member, Monopolies and Mergers Commission, 1987–92; *b* 30 Nov. 1921; *s* of David Robert Keir and Elizabeth Lunan (*née* Ross); *m* 1948, Jean Mary, *e d* of Rev. and Mrs E. P. Orr; two *s* two *d. Educ:* Edinburgh Acad.; Christ Church, Oxford (MA 1948). Served War, 1941–46: ME, Italy; Captain, The Black Watch (RHR). Called to the Bar, Inner Temple, 1949; Yarborough-Anderson Scholar, Inner Temple, 1950. Legal Adviser, United Africa Co. Ltd, 1954–66, Sec., 1966; Dep. Head of Legal Services, Unilever Ltd, 1973; Jt Sec., Unilever PLC and Unilever NV, 1976–84; Dir, UAC Internat. Ltd, 1973–77. Chm., 1969–72, Pres., 1980–82, Bar Assoc. for Commerce, Finance and Industry; Member: Bar Council, 1971–73; Senate of Inns of Ct and Bar, 1973–78. Chairman: Pharmacists Rev. Panel, 1986–97; Professional Cttee, Royal Coll. of Speech and Language Therapists, 1993–2001. *Recreations:* watching Rugby and ski-ing, active in opera, reading. *Address:* 15 Clays Close, East Grinstead, West Sussex RH19 4DJ. *T:* (01342) 323189. *Club:* Caledonian.

KEITH, family name of **Earl of Kintore**.

KEITH, Hon. Sir Brian (Richard), Kt 2001; **Hon. Mr Justice Keith;** a Judge of the High Court, Queen's Bench Division, since 2001; *b* 14 April 1944; *s* of late Alan Keith, OBE, broadcaster, and of Pearl Keith (*née* Rebuck); *m* 1978, Gilly, *d* of late Air Cdre Ivan de la Plain, CBE; one *s* one *d. Educ:* University College School, Hampstead; Lincoln College, Oxford (MA). John F. Kennedy Fellow, Harvard Law School, 1966–67; called to the Bar, Inner Temple, 1968, Bencher, 1996; in practice, 1969–91; Assistant Recorder, 1988; QC 1989; a Recorder, 1993–2001. A Judge of the Supreme Court of Hong Kong, 1991–97; a Judge of the Court of First Instance, High Court of Hong Kong, 1997–99; Presiding Judge, Admin. Law List, High Court of Hong Kong, 1997–99; a Judge of the Court of Appeal, Hong Kong, 1999–2001. Hon. Lectr, Univ. of Hong Kong, 1994–2001. Mem., Judicial Studies Bd, Hong Kong, 1994–2001. Chm., Zahid Mubarek Inquiry, 2004–06. *Recreations:* travel, tennis, cinema. *Address:* Royal Courts of Justice, Strand, WC2A 2LL. *Club:* Hong Kong.

KEITH, Rt Hon. Sir Kenneth (James), ONZ 2007; KBE 1988; PC 1998; a Judge of the International Court of Justice, since 2006; a Judge of the Supreme Court of Fiji, since 2003; a Judge of the Court of Appeal: Western Samoa, since 1982; Cook Islands, since 1982; Niue, since 1995; *b* 19 Nov. 1937; *s* of Patrick James Keith and Amy Irene Keith (*née* Witheridge); *m* 1961, Jocelyn Margaret Buckett; two *s* two *d. Educ:* Auckland Grammar Sch.; Auckland Univ.; Victoria Univ. of Wellington (LLM); Harvard Law Sch. Barrister and Solicitor, High Court of New Zealand; QC (NZ) 1994. NZ Dept of External Affairs, 1960–62; Victoria Univ. of Wellington, 1962–64, 1966–91, Prof. of Law, 1974–91, now Emeritus; UN Secretariat, NY, 1968–70; NZ Inst. of Internat. Affairs, 1972–74; Pres., NZ Law Commn, 1991–96; a Judge of NZ Court of Appeal, 1996–2003; a Judge of Supreme Ct, NZ, 2004–05. Permanent Ct of Arbitration, 1985–2008. Mem., 1991–2006, Pres., 2002–06, Internat. Fact Finding Commn (Geneva Conventions). Mem., Inst de Droit Internat., 2003– (Assoc. Mem., 1997–2003). Hon. LLD: Auckland, 2001; Victoria, Wellington, 2004. *Publications:* (ed) Human Rights in New Zealand, 1968; The Extent of the Advisory Jurisdiction of the International Court, 1971; contrib. to Amer. Jl of Internat. Law, Internat. and Comparative Law Qly, NZ Univs Law Rev., etc. *Recreations:* walking, reading, music. *Address:* International Court of Justice, The Peace Palace, 2517 KJ The Hague, Netherlands. *T:* (70) 302 2483.

KEITH, Penelope Anne Constance, (Mrs Rodney Timson), CBE 2007 (OBE 1989); DL; actress; *b* 2 April; *d* of Frederick A. W. Hatfield and Constance Mary Keith; *m* 1978, Rodney Timson. *Educ:* Annecy Convent, Seaford, Sussex; Webber Douglas Sch., London. First prof. appearance, Civic Theatre, Chesterfield, 1959; repertory, Lincoln, Salisbury and Manchester, 1960–63; RSC, Stratford, 1963, and Aldwych, 1965; rep., Cheltenham, 1967; Maggie Howard in Suddenly at Home, Fortune Theatre, 1971; Sarah in The Norman Conquests, Greenwich, then Globe Theatre, 1974; Lady Driver in Donkey's Years, 1976; Orinthia in The Apple Cart, Chichester, then Phoenix Theatre, 1977; Epifania in The Millionairess, Haymarket, 1978; Sarah in Moving, Queen's Theatre, 1981; Maggie in Hobson's Choice, Haymarket, 1982; Lady Cicely Waynflete in Captain Brassbound's Conversion, Haymarket, 1982; Judith Bliss in Hay Fever, Queen's, 1983; The Dragon's Tail, Apollo, 1985; Miranda, Chichester, 1987; The Deep Blue Sea, Haymarket, 1988; Dear Charles, Yvonne Arnaud, Guildford, 1990; The Merry Wives of Windsor, Chichester, 1990; Lady Bracknell in The Importance of Being Earnest, UK tour, 1991; On Approval, UK tour, 1992; Glyn and It, Richmond, 1994; Monsieur Amilcar, Chichester, 1995; Mrs Warren's Profession, Richmond, 1997; Good Grief, nat. tour, 1998; Star Quality, Apollo, 2001; Time and the Conways, nat. tour, 2003; Madame Arcati in Blithe Spirit, Th. Royal, Bath, transf. Savoy Th., 2004; Entertaining Angels, Chichester, 2006; The Importance of Being Earnest, Vaudeville, 2008; directed: Relatively Speaking, nat. tour, 1992; How the Other Half Loves, nat. tour, 1994; *film:* The Priest of Love, 1980. Television plays and series include: The Good Life, 1974–77; The Norman Conquests, 1977; To the Manor Born, 1979, 1980 and 1981; Sweet Sixteen, 1983; Moving, 1985; Executive Stress, 1986–88; No Job for a Lady, 1990–92; Next of Kin, 1995–97; Margery and Gladys, 2003; presenter: What's My Line?, 1988; Growing Places, 1989. Mem., HFEA, 1990–96. Pres., The Actors' Benevolent Fund, 1990–. Gov., Queen Elizabeth's Foundn for the Disabled, 1989–. Patron, Yvonne Arnaud Theatre, 1992–. High Sheriff, Surrey, 2002–03; DL Surrey, 2004. Awards: BAFTA, 1976 and 1977; SWET, 1976; Variety Club of GB, 1976 and 1979. *Recreation:* gardening. *Address:* c/o The Actors' Benevolent Fund, 6 Adam Street, WC2N 6AA. *T:* (020) 7439 1456.

KEITH, Shona; *see* McIsaac, S.

KELBURN, Viscount of; courtesy title of heir of Earl of Glasgow, not used by current heir.

KELL, Prof. Douglas Bruce, DPhil; FIBiol; Chief Executive and Deputy Chairman, Biotechnology and Biological Sciences Research Council, since 2008; Professor of Bioanalytical Science, University of Manchester (formerly University of Manchester Institute of Science and Technology), since 2002 (on secondment); *b* 7 April 1953; *s* of William Howard Kell and Nancy Kell (*née* Finniston); *m* 1989, Dr Antje Wagner; one *s* two *d. Educ:* Bradfield Coll., Berks (Top Schol.); St John's Coll., Oxford (BA Hons Biochem. Upper 2nd Cl. with Dist. in Chem. Pharmacol.; Sen. Schol., 1975–76; MA, DPhil 1978). FIBiol 1999. UCW, Aberystwyth, then University of Wales, Aberystwyth: SRC Postdoctoral Res. Fellow, 1978–80; SERC Advanced Fellow, 1981–83; New Blood Lectr, 1983–88; Reader, 1988–92; Prof. of Microbiology, 1992–2002, Dir of Res., 1997–2002, Inst. of Biol Scis; Dir, Manchester Centre for Integrative Systems Biology, 2005–08. Fleming Lectr, Soc. for Gen. Microbiol., 1986. Founding Director: Aber Instruments, 1988–2008 (Queen's Award for Export Achievement 1998); Predictive Solutions Ltd (formerly Aber Genomic Computing), 2000–08. Member: Council, 2000–06, Strategy Bd, 2001–06, BBSRC; numerous scientific cttees of SRC, SERC and BBSRC, incl.: Plant Scis and Microbiol., 1985–88, Biotech. Directorate, 1992–94, Chemicals and Pharmaceuticals Directorate, 1994–96, Engrg and Biol Systems, 1999–2000; Biosci. for Industry Panel, 2007–; DTI LINK Prog. Mgt Cttees for Technol. for Analytical and Physical Measurement, 1992–94, Biochem. Engrg, 1994–98, Analytical Biotech. (Chm., 1995–99); Basic Technol. Strategic Adv. Cttee, Res. Councils UK, 2001–04; Sci. Bd, STFC, 2007–08; Adv. Bd, UK PubMed Central, 2007–08. Interdisciplinary Award, 2004, Chem. Biol. Award, 2005, SAC Gold Medal, 2006, RSC; Theodor Bücher Medal, FEBS-IUBMB, 2005; Royal Soc./Wolfson Merit Award, 2005. *Publications:* numerous scientific pubns. *Recreation:* family. *Address:* Biotechnology and Biological Sciences Research Council, Polaris House, North Star Avenue, Swindon SN2 1UH.

KELL, Michael Stuart; Director, Economic Consulting, Deloitte and Touche LLP, since 2008; *b* 27 Jan. 1965; *s* of Malcolm Kell and Jill Kell (*née* Wood); *m* 1995, Jane Morris; three *d. Educ:* St Edmund Hall, Oxford (BA Hons PPE 1986); Nuffield Coll., Oxford (MPhil Econs 1991). Res. Officer, Inst. for Fiscal Studies, 1986–89; Econ. Advr, HM Treasury, 1991–96; Advr to UK Exec. Dir, IMF and World Bank, 1996–98; Sen. Economist, Fiscal Affairs Dept, IMF, 1998–2002; Hd, Central Econ. Analysis, 2002–03, Chief Economist, 2003–08, ODPM, subseq. DCLG. *Recreations:* spending time with Ruby, Alice and Josie. *T:* (office) (020) 7007 7295; *e-mail:* mikell@deloitte.co.uk.

KELLAND, John William, LVO 1977; QPM 1975; Overseas Police Adviser and Inspector General of Dependent Territories' Police, Foreign and Commonwealth Office, 1985–91; *b* 18 Aug. 1929; *s* of William John Kelland and Violet Ethel (*née* Olsen); *m* 1st, 1960, Brenda Nancy (*née* Foulsham) (decd); 2nd, 1986, Frances Elizabeth (*née* Byrne); one step *d. Educ:* Sutton High Sch.; Plymouth Polytechnic. FIMgt. RAF, 1947–49. Constable, later Insp., Plymouth City Police, 1950–67; Insp., later Supt, Devon & Cornwall Constabulary, 1968–72; Asst Chief Constable, Cumbria Constabulary, 1972–74; Dir, Sen. Comd Courses, Nat. Police Coll., Bramshill, 1974–75 and 1978–80; Comr, Royal Fiji Police, 1975–78; 1981–85: Management Consultant and Chm., CSSBs; Sen. Consultant, RIPA; Sen. Lectr, Cornwall Coll.; Facilitator, Interpersonal Skills, Cornwall CC Seminars. Mem., Cornwall & Isles of Scilly FHSA, 1992–93. Chm., Old Suttonian Assoc. *Publications:* various articles in learned jls. *Recreations:* Rugby football, choral singing, wildlife. *Club:* Civil Service.

KELLAWAY, (Charles) William; Secretary and Librarian, Institute of Historical Research, University of London, 1971–84; *b* 9 March 1926; *s* of late Charles Halliley Kellaway, FRS; *m* 1952, Deborah (*d* 2006), *d* of late Sir Hibbert Alan Stephen Newton; one *s* two *d. Educ:* Geelong Grammar Sch.; Lincoln Coll., Oxford. BA Modern History, 1949, MA 1955. FCLIP, FRHistS. Asst Librarian, Guildhall Library, 1950–60; Sub-Librarian, Inst. of Historical Research, 1960–71. Hon. General Editor, London Record Society, 1964–83. *Publications:* The New England Company, 1649–1776, 1961; (ed jtly) Studies in London History, 1969; Bibliography of Historical Works Issued in UK, 1957–70, 3 vols, 1962, 1967, 1972; (ed jtly) The London Assize of Nuisance 1301–1431, 1973. *Address:* 18 Canonbury Square, N1 2AL. *T:* (020) 7354 0349.

KELLAWAY, Richard Edward, CBE 2005; Director General, Commonwealth War Graves Commission, since 2000; *b* 13 Aug. 1946; *s* of late Edward John Kellaway and Elsie May Kellaway (*née* Judd); *m* 1968, Ann Clarke; two *d. Educ:* Poole Grammar Sch. Commnd as Officer of Customs and Excise, 1966: Sen. Investigation Officer, 1975–79; Principal, VAT Admin, 1979–80; Asst Chief Investigation Officer, 1980–84; Chief Staff Inspector, 1984–87; Head: Customs Dept, Bermuda, 1987–90; Estates and Security, 1990–94; Chief Investigation Officer, 1994–99; on secondment as Drugs and Serious Crime Advr, FCO, 1999–2000. *Recreations:* industrial archaeology, cooking, gardening. *Address:* c/o Commonwealth War Graves Commission, 2 Marlow Road, Maidenhead, Berks SL6 7DX. *T:* (01628) 507152. *Clubs:* Royal Air Force; Automobile de l'Ouest (France).

KELLEHER, Dame Joan, (Joanna), DBE 1965; Hon. ADC to the Queen, 1964–67; Director, Women's Royal Army Corps, 1964–67; *b* 24 Dec. 1915; *d* of late Kenneth George Henderson, barrister-at-law, Stonehaven; *m* 1970, Brig. Mortimer Francis Howlett Kelleher (*d* 2006), OBE, MC, late RAMC. *Educ:* privately at home and abroad. Joined ATS, 1941; commissioned ATS, 1941; WRAC, 1949. *Recreation:* gardening.

KELLEHER, Patricia Mary; Principal, Perse School for Girls and Stephen Perse Sixth Form College (Headmistress, Perse School for Girls, Cambridge, 2001); *b* 17 March 1962; *d* of Liam and Margaret Kelleher. *Educ:* Lady Margaret Hall, Oxford (MA Modern Hist. 1984); Univ. of Sussex (MA Renaissance Theory and Culture 1995); Univ. of Nottingham (PGCE 1985). History Teacher, Haberdashers' Aske's Sch. for Girls, Elstree, 1985–88; Hd of History and Hd of Year 7, Brighton and Hove High Sch. (GDST), 1988–97; Dep. Headmistress, Brentwood Sch., Essex, 1997–2001. *Recreations:* walking, travel, reading. *Address:* Perse School for Girls, Union Road, Cambridge CB2 1HF. *T:* (01223) 454700, *Fax:* (01223) 467420; *e-mail:* headmistress@admin.perse.cambs.sch.uk.

KELLENBERGER, Dr Jakob; President, International Committee of the Red Cross, since 2000; *b* 19 Oct. 1944; *s* of Jakob and Klara Kellenberger; *m* 1973, Elisabeth Kellenberger-Jossi; two *d. Educ:* Univ. of Zurich (DPhil 1975). Joined Swiss Diplomatic Service, 1974: served Madrid, EU (Brussels), London, 1974–84; Hd, Dept for European Integration, Berne, 1984–92 (Minister, 1984–88; Ambassador, 1988–92); State Sec. for Foreign Affairs, Switzerland, 1992–99. Hon. Councillor, Swiss Fed. Inst. of Technology, Zurich, 2007. Dr *hc*: Basle, 2003; Catania, 2006. *Publications:* Calderón de la Barca und das Komische, 1975; numerous articles, particularly on Swiss–EU relations. *Recreations:* reading (literature, philosophy), cross country ski-ing, jogging, tennis.

KELLER, Prof. Rudolf Ernst, MA Manchester; DrPhil Zürich; Professor of German Language and Medieval German Literature, University of Manchester, 1960–82, now Emeritus; *b* 3 Feb. 1920; *m* 1947, Ivy Sparrow; two *d. Educ:* Kantonsschule Winterthur, Switzerland; University of Zürich. Teacher at Kantonsschule Winterthur, 1944–46; Asst, 1946–47, Asst Lecturer, 1947–49, University of Manchester; Lecturer in German, Royal Holloway College, University of London, 1949–52; Sen. Lecturer, 1952–59, Reader in German, 1959–60, Dean of Faculty of Arts, 1968–70, Pro-Vice-Chancellor, 1976–79, University of Manchester. Corresp. Mem., Inst. für deutsche Sprache, 1969; Goethe

Medal, 1981. *Publications:* Die Ellipse in der neuenglischen Sprache als semantisch-syntaktisches Problem, 1944; Die Sprachen der Welt, 1955 (trans. Bodmer: The Loom of Language); German Dialects, Phonology and Morphology with Selected Texts, 1961; The German Language, 1978; articles in learned periodicals. *Recreations:* reading, travel. *Address:* 8 Wadham Way, Hale, Altrincham, Cheshire WA15 9LJ. *T:* (0161) 980 5237.

KELLETT, Sir Stanley Charles, 7th Bt *cr* 1801; *b* 5 March 1940; *s* of Sir Stanley Everard Kellett, 6th Bt, and of Audrey Margaret Phillips; *S* father, 1983, but his name does not appear on the Official Roll of the Baronetage; *m* 1st, 1962, Lorraine May (marr. diss. 1968), *d* of F. Winspear; 2nd, 1968, Margaret Ann (marr. diss. 1974), *d* of James W. Bofinger; 3rd, 1982, Catherine Lorna (marr. diss. 1991), *d* of W. J. C. Orr; two *d*; 4th, 1991, Yvonne Patricia (*d* 2001), *d* of Alan Blogg. *Heir: cousin* Maxwell Rex Kellett [*b* 1947; *m* 1968, Jennifer Maher; one *d*]. *Address:* 21 Debussy Place, Cranebrook, NSW 2749, Australia.

KELLETT-BOWMAN, Edward Thomas; JP; business and management consultant in private practice, since 1974; *b* 25 Feb. 1931; *s* of late R. E. Bowman and M. Bowman (*née* Mathers); *m* 1st, 1960, Margaret Patricia Blakemore (*d* 1970); three *s* one *d*; 2nd, 1971, (Mary) Elaine Kellett (*see* Dame Elaine Kellett-Bowman). *Educ:* Reed's Sch.; Cranfield Inst. of Technol. MBA, DMS. Technical and management trng in textiles, 1951–53; textile management, 1953–55; pharmaceutical man., 1955–72. Mem. (C) Lancs East, European Parlt, 1979–84; contested same seat, 1984; MEP (C) Hampshire Central, Dec. 1988–1994, Itchen, Test and Avon, 1994–99; contested (C) SE Region, 1999. Freeman: City of London, 1978; Wheelwrights' Co., 1979. Hon. Citizen, New Orleans, 1960. FCMI. JP Middx, 1966. *Recreations:* shooting, tennis, swimming. *Address:* Endymion, Ampfield, Romsey, Hants SO51 9BD.

KELLETT-BOWMAN, Dame (Mary) Elaine, DBE 1988; MA; *b* 8 July 1924; *d* of late Walter Kay; *m* 1st, 1945, Charles Norman Kellett (decd); three *s* one *d*; 2nd, 1971, Edward Thomas Kellett-Bowman, *qv*. *Educ:* Queen Mary Sch., Lytham; The Mount, York; St Anne's Coll., Oxford; Barnett House, Oxford (post-graduate distinction in welfare diploma). Called to Bar, Middle Temple, 1964. Mem., Denbigh BC, 1952–55; Camden Borough Council: Alderman, 1968–74; Vice-Chm., Housing Cttee, 1968; Chm., Welfare Cttee, 1969. Contested (C): Nelson and Colne, 1955; South-West Norfolk, March and Oct. 1959; Buckingham, 1964, 1966. MP (C) Lancaster, 1970–97. Mem. (C) European Parlt, 1975–84 (Mem. for Cumbria, 1979–84); Mem. Social Affairs, Regional Policy and Development Cttees, Europ. Parlt, 1975–84. Lay Mem., Press Council, 1964–68. Pres., Nat. Assoc. of Widows, 1999–2001. Governor, Culford Sch., 1963–2003; Mem. Union European Women, 1956; Delegate to Luxemburg, 1958. No 1 Country Housewife, 1960; Christal MacMillan Law Prize, 1963. *Recreation:* gardening. *Address:* Endymion, Ampfield, Romsey, Hants SO51 9BD.

KELLEY, Joan, CB 1987; Member, Official Side Panel, Civil Service Appeal Board, 1987–96; *b* 8 Dec. 1926; *er d* of late George William Kelley and Dora Kelley. *Educ:* Whalley Range High Sch. for Girls, Manchester; London Sch. of Econs and Polit. Science (BScEcon 1947). Europa Publications Ltd, 1948; Pritchard, Wood & Partners Ltd, 1949; joined Civil Service as Econ. Asst in Cabinet Office, 1949; admin. work in Treasury, 1954; Principal, 1956; Asst Sec., 1968; Under Sec., 1979; on secondment to NI Office, 1979–81; Under Sec., 1979–86, Principal Estabt Officer and Principal Finance Officer, 1984–86, HM Treasury. Mem. Council, Univ. of London Inst. of Educn, 1992–98. *Recreations:* gardening, map reading, drinking wine, foreign travel. *Address:* 21 Langland Gardens, NW3 6QE.

KELLNER, family name of **Baroness Ashton of Upholland**.

KELLNER, Peter Jon; President, YouGov, online polling and market research company, since 2007 (Chairman, 2001–07); *b* 2 Oct. 1946; *s* of Michael Kellner and Lily Agnes Samson Kellner (*née* McVail); *m* 1st, 1972, Sally Collard (marr. diss. 1988); one *s* two *d*; 2nd, 1988, Catherine Margaret Ashton (*see* Baroness Ashton of Upholland); one *s* one *d*. *Educ:* Minchenden Grammar Sch., Southgate, London; Royal Grammar Sch., Newcastle upon Tyne; King's Coll., Cambridge (BA 1st Cl. Hons 1969). Journalist, Sunday Times, 1969–80; Political Ed., New Statesman, 1980–87; political columnist: Independent, 1986–92; Sunday Times, 1992–96; Observer, 1996–97; Evening Standard, 1997–2003. TV political analyst and commentator: A Week in Politics, 1982–88; Newsnight and election progs, 1990–97; Powerhouse, 1999–2003; radio presenter, Analysis, 1995–98. Journalist of Year, BPA, 1978; Chairman of the Year, Quoted Company Awards, 2007. *Publications:* (with C. Hitchens) Callaghan: the road to Number Ten, 1976; (with Lord Crowther-Hunt) The Civil Servants, 1980; contribs to various jls, incl. Parly Affairs, Political Qly, British Journalism Rev., Internat. Jl Mkt Res. *Recreations:* reading, arguing, travel. *Address:* YouGov, 50 Featherstone Street, EC1Y 8RT. *T:* (020) 7012 6000. *Club:* Royal Commonwealth Society (Trustee).

KELLOCK, Jane Ursula; JP; Member, Council on Tribunals, 1987–93; *b* 21 Oct. 1925; *d* of late Arthur George Symonds and late Gertrude Frances Symonds; *m* 1967, His Honour Thomas Oslaf Kellock (*d* 1993). *Educ:* Priors Field Sch., Godalming. WRNS, 1943–45. Sec., Africa Bureau, London, 1957–67; Editor, Africa Digest, 1957–75; Member: Bd, Commonwealth Development Corporation, 1965–73; Police Complaints Board, 1977–85. Former Mem., S Metropolitan Conciliation Cttee, Race Relations Bd. JP: Inner London, 1968–77; Nottingham City Bench, 1977–91; Inner London (N Westminster), 1992–95. Editor, Commonwealth Judicial Jl, 1985–89. *Recreation:* travel. *Address:* 4 Pound Lane, Dorchester DT1 1LP.

KELLS, Ronald David, OBE 1999; DL; Group Chief Executive, Ulster Bank Ltd, 1994–98; *b* 14 May 1938; *s* of Robert Kells and Frances Elizabeth Kells; *m* 1964, Elizabeth Anne Kells; one *s* one *d*. *Educ:* Bushmills Grammar Sch.; Sullivan Upper Sch.; Queen's Univ., Belfast (BSc Econ). FCIS 1979; FIB 1985. Joined Ulster Bank, 1964; Investments Manager, 1969–76; Dep. Head, Related Banking Services, 1976–79; Head of Planning and Marketing, 1972–82; seconded to National Westminster Bank, 1982–84; Dir and Head, Retail Services (formerly Branch Banking Div.), 1984–94. Chm., Cunningham Coates Ltd, stockbrokers, 1998–2002; Non-exec. Director: United Drug Plc, 1999– (Chm., 2005–); Readymix PLC, 1999–. Pres., Confedn of Ulster Socs, 1999–2004. Gov., BFI, 1998–2003. DL Belfast, 1998. *Recreations:* golf, ski-ing. *Address:* The Moyle, 10 Upper Knockbreda Road, Belfast BT6 9QA. *T:* (028) 9079 7912. *Clubs:* Ulster Reform (Belfast); Royal County Down Golf, Royal Belfast Golf, Portmarnock Golf.

KELLY, Andrew; *see* Kelly, T. A.

KELLY, Prof. Anthony, CBE 1988; DL; FRS 1973; FREng; Life Fellow, Churchill College, Cambridge, 1985; *b* 25 Jan. 1929; *s* of late Group Captain Vincent Gerald French and Mrs Violet Kelly; *m* 1956, Christina Margaret Dunleavie, BA (*d* 1997); three *s* one *d*. *Educ:* Presentation Coll., Reading; Univ. of Reading (Schol.; BSc 1949); Trinity Coll., Cambridge (PhD 1953, ScD 1968). Research Assoc., Univ. of Illinois, 1953–55; ICI Fellow, Univ. of Birmingham, 1955; Asst, Associate Prof., Northwestern Univ., 1956–59; Univ. Lectr, Cambridge, 1959–67; Founding Fellow, Churchill Coll., 1960; Dir of Studies, Churchill Coll., 1960–67; Supt, Div. of Inorganic and Metallic Structure, 1967–69, Dep. Dir, 1969–75, Nat. Physical Lab. (seconded to ICI, 1973–75); Vice-Chancellor, Univ. of Surrey, 1975–94. Univ. Prof., Univ. of Surrey, 1987. Director: Johnson Wax Ltd, 1981–96; QUO-TEC Ltd, 1984–2000; NPL Management Ltd, 1995–2001; Chm., Surrey Satellite Technology, 1985–95. Vis. Fellow, Univ. of Göttingen, 1960; Vis. Prof., Carnegie Inst. of Technol., 1967; Prof. invité, Ecole Polytechnique Fédérale de Lausanne, 1977. Chm., Jt Standing Cttee on Structural Safety, Instns of Civil and Structural Engrs, 1988–98; Member: SRC Cttee, 1967–72; Council, Inst. of Metals, 1969–74; Council, British Non-Ferrous Metals Res. Assoc., 1970–73; Engrg Materials Requirements Bd, DoI, 1973–75 (Chm., 1976–80); Adv. Cttee, Community Ref. Bureau of EEC, 1973–75. Pres., Inst. of Materials, 1996–97. Mem., Academia Europaea, 1990; Foreign Associate, Nat. Acad. of Engrg of USA, 1986. Lee Kuan Yew Dist. Visitor to Commonwealth of Singapore, 1999. Eminent Speaker, Engineers Australia, 2008. FRSA 1992. DL Surrey, 1993. Hon. FIL 1988; Hon. FIStructE 1996; Hon. FICE 1997. DUniv Surrey, 1994; Hon. DSc: Birmingham, 1997; Reading, 2002; Hon. DEng Hanyang, S Korea, 2001; Dr *hc* Navarra, Spain, 2003. William Hopkins Prize, Cambridge Philosophical Soc., 1967; Beilby Medal, RIC, 1967; A. A. Griffith Medal, 1974, Platinum Medal, 1992, Inst. of Materials; Medal of Excellence, Univ. of Delaware, 1984; Internat. Gold Medal, Amer. Soc. for Materials, 1991; Acta Metallurgica Gold Medal, 2000; Alfred Ewing Medal, ICE, 2003. KSG 1992. *Publications:* Strong Solids, 1966, 3rd edn (with N. H. Macmillan) 1986; (with G. W. Groves) Crystallography and Crystal Defects, 1970, rev. edn (with P. Kidd) 1999; many papers in jls of physical sciences. *Recreations:* science of materials, sailing. *Address:* 29 Madingley Road, Cambridge CB3 0EG. *Clubs:* Oxford and Cambridge, Royal Over-Seas League; Island Sailing (Cowes).

KELLY, Dame Barbara (Mary), DBE 2007 (CBE 1992); DL; Convenor, Crichton Foundation, since 2003; *b* 27 Feb. 1940; *d* of John Maxwell Prentice and Barbara Bain Adam; *m* 1960, Kenneth Archibald Kelly; one *s* two *d* (and two *s* decd). *Educ:* Dalbeattie High Sch.; Kirkcudbright Academy; Moray House Coll., Edinburgh. DipEd. Partner in mixed farming enterprise. Dir, Clydesdale Bank, 1994–98; Member: Scottish Adv. Bd, BP plc, 1990–2003; Scottish PO Bd, 1997–2003. Chairman: Area Manpower Bd, MSC, 1987–88; Scottish Consumer Council, 1985–90; Rural Forum, 1988–92 (Hon. Pres., 1992–99); Training 2000, 1991–97; Architects Registration Bd, 1997–2002; Member: Nat. Consumer Council, 1985–90; Scottish Enterprise Bd, 1990–95; Priorities Bd, MAFF, 1990–95; BBC Rural Affairs and Agric. Adv. Cttee, 1991–97; Scottish Econ. Council, 1991–98; Scottish Tourist Bd, 1993–97; Rathbone Community Industry Bd, 1993–98; Scottish Nat. Heritage Bd, 1995–2001; BBC Broadcasting Council for Scotland, 1997–2002; Comr, EOC, 1991–95. Convener, Millennium Forest for Scotland Trust, 1995–. Nat. Vice-Chm., Scottish Women's Rural Insts, 1983–86. Hon. Pres., Scottish Conservation Projects Trust. Chm., Scottish Adv. Cttee, and Mem., Nat. Adv. Cttee, Duke of Edinburgh's Award Scheme, 1980–85. Trustee: Scottish Community (formerly Caledonian) Foundn, 1995–2002; Strathclyde Foundn, 1997–2002; Robertson Trust, 2002–; Royal Botanic Gdn, Edinburgh, 2002–. Freeman, City of London, 2002. DL Dumfries, 1998. Fellow, Bell Coll., 2006; Hon. Fellow, Queen Margaret UC, 2005. Hon. LLD: Strathclyde, 1995; Aberdeen, 1997; Glasgow, 2002; DUniv Glasgow, 2002. *Recreations:* home and family, music, painting, the pursuit of real food, gardening of necessity. *Address:* Barncleugh, Irongray, Dumfries DG2 9SE. *T:* (01387) 730210.

KELLY, Rt Hon. Sir Basil; *see* Kelly, Rt Hon. Sir J. W. B.

KELLY, Ben, RDI 2007; interior designer; Principal, Ben Kelly Design, since 1976; *b* Welwyn Garden City, 1 April 1949; *s* of Herbert and Doreen Kelly; two *s*; *m* 2008, Clare Cumberlidge. *Educ:* Appletreewick Prim. Sch., N Yorks; Ermysteds Grammar Sch., Skipton; Lancaster Coll. of Art; Royal Coll. of Art (MA 1974). Notable projects include: Howie Shop, Covent Garden, 1977; Seditionaries, King's Rd, London, 1977; Sex Pistols rehearsal studio, Denmark St, London, 1978; The Haçienda, Manchester, 1982; Smile, King's Rd, London, 1983; DRY 201, Manchester, 1989; BAR TEN, Glasgow, 1991; The Basement, Sci. Mus., London, 1995; Design Council offices, Bow St, London, 1997; Borough Hotel, Edinburgh, 2001; Gymbox, St Martin's Lane, London, 2006; The Public, West Bromwich, 2008; Stubbs Mill conversion, New Islington, Manchester, 2008. Hon. DDes Kingston, 2000. *Publication:* (contrib.) Plans and Elevations: Ben Kelly Design, 1990. *Recreations:* walking, looking at art, making art, studying the work of Marcel Duchamp, watching Finbar (my younger son) grow up, Pop culture, looking at the colour orange, looking out of my window at the sea, looking out of my window at the stars. *Address:* c/o Ben Kelly Design, 10 Stoney Street, SE1 9AD. *T:* (020) 7378 8116; *e-mail:* ben@bkduk.co.uk.

KELLY, Bernadette Mary; Executive Director, Planning, Department for Communities and Local Government, since 2007; *b* 10 March 1964; *d* of Edward Kelly and Teresa Bridget Kelly (*née* Garvey); *m* 1998, Howard Ewing; one *s*. *Educ:* King Edward VI Camp Hill Sch. for Girls, Birmingham; Hull Univ. (BA Hons); Imperial Coll., London (MBA 1997). Department of Trade and Industry: Admin trainee, 1987–91; Grade 7, 1991–97; Sen. Civil Servant, HM Treasury, 1998–2000 (on secondment); Principal Private Sec. to Sec. of State for Trade and Industry, 2000–02; on secondment to ICI, 2002–03; Dir, Corporate Law and Governance, DTI, 2003–05; Sen. Policy Advr, Policy Directorate, Prime Minister's Office, 2005–06; Dir, Planning Reform, Cabinet Office, 2006–07. *Address:* Department for Communities and Local Government, Eland House, Bressenden Place, SW1E 5DU. *Club:* Goodwood (Sussex).

KELLY, Brendan Damien; QC 2008; barrister; a Recorder, since 2002; *b* Manchester, 14 Oct. 1965; *s* of John Bosco Kelly and Maureen Olive Kelly; *m* 1992, Sallie Ann Bennett-Jenkins, QC; six *c*. *Educ:* Leeds Poly. Called to the Bar, Gray's Inn, 1988. *Recreations:* Rugby, golf, fishing. *Address:* 2 Hare Court, Temple, EC4Y 7BH. *T:* (020) 7353 5324; *e-mail:* brendankelly@2harecourt.com.

KELLY, Brian; *see* Kelly, H. B.

KELLY, Prof. Catriona Helen Moncrieff, DPhil; FBA 2007; Professor of Russian, and Co-Director, European Humanities Research Centre, University of Oxford, since 2002; Fellow, New College, Oxford, since 1996; *b* 6 Oct. 1959; *d* of late Alexander Kelly and of (Helen) Margaret Kelly (*née* Moncrieff); *m* 1993, Prof. Ian Thompson. *Educ:* St Hilda's Coll., Oxford (BA 1st cl. Hons Mod. Langs (German and Russian)); DPhil Oxon 1986. Christ Church, Oxford: Sen. Schol., 1983–87; Jun. Res. Fellow, 1987–90; British Acad. Post-Doctoral Fellow, 1990–93; Lectr, SSEES, Univ. of London, 1993–96; Lectr in Russian, Univ. of Oxford, 1996–2002. Gen. Ed., Cambridge Studies in Russian Lit., 1995–2000; Mem., Editl Bd, Antropologicheskii forum (Forum for Anthropol. and Culture) (St Petersburg). *Publications:* (ed jtly) Discontinuous Discourses in Modern Russian Literature, 1989; Petrushka, the Russian Carnival Puppet Theatre, 1990; A History of Russian Women's Writing 1820–1992, 1994; (ed) An Anthology of Russian Women's Writing 1777–1992, 1994; (ed with D. Shepherd) Constructing Russian Culture in the Age of Revolution, 1998; (ed with D. Shepherd) Russian Cultural Studies:

an introduction, 1998; (ed) Utopias: Russian modernist texts 1905–1940, 1999; (ed with S. Lovell) Russian Literature, Modernism and the Visual Arts, 2000; Refining Russia: advice literature, polite culture and gender from Catherine to Yeltsin, 2001; Russian Literature: a very short introduction, 2001; Comrade Pavlik: the rise and fall of a Soviet boy hero, 2005; Children's World: growing up in Russia 1890–1991, 2007; *translations:* Leonid Borodin, The Third Truth, 1989; (contrib.) New Russian Fiction, ed O. Chukhontsev, 1989; Sergei Kaledin, The Humble Cemetery, 1990; (contrib.) Paradise, 1993; (contrib.) The Silk of Time, 1994; contrib. numerous articles to professional jls and edited books, and reviews in TLS, Guardian, Evening Standard, etc. *Recreations:* freezing in the Atlantic, walking in St Petersburg. *Address:* New College, Oxford OX1 3BN. *T:* (01865) 271978; *e-mail:* catriona.kelly@new.ox.ac.uk.

KELLY, Charles Henry, CBE 1986; QPM 1978; DL; Chief Constable of Staffordshire, 1977–96; *b* 15 July 1930; *s* of Charles Henry Kelly and Phoebe Jane Kelly; *m* 1952, Doris (*née* Kewley) (*d* 1999); one *s* one *d. Educ:* Douglas High Sch. for Boys, IOM; London Univ. LLB (Hons). Asst Chief Constable of Essex, 1972; Dep. Chief Constable of Staffordshire, 1976. Associate Prof., Criminal Justice Dept, Michigan State Univ., 1990–2000. Pres., Staffordshire Small Bore Rifle Assoc., 1977–96; Chairman: Staffordshire Police St John Special Centre, 1978–96; ACPO Communications Cttee, 1982–92; No 3 Region, ACPO Cttee, 1985–93. Pres., Staffordshire Soc., 1997–99. Mem. Court, Keele Univ., 1990–. MUniv Keele, 1991; Hon. LLD Staffordshire Univ., 1996. DL Stafford, 1979. KStJ 1991 (County Pres., Staffordshire, 1996–). *Recreations:* cricket, reading, walking. *Address:* c/o Chief Constable's Office, Cannock Road, Stafford ST17 0QG. *T:* (01785) 257717. *Club:* Special Forces.

KELLY, Sir Christopher (William), KCB 2001; Chairman: National Society for the Prevention of Cruelty to Children, since 2002; Financial Ombudsman Service, since 2005 (non-executive Director, since 2002); Committee on Standards in Public Life, since 2008; *b* 18 Aug. 1946; *s* of late Reginald and of Peggy Kelly; *m* 1970, Alison Mary Collens Durant; two *s* one *d. Educ:* Beaumont College; Trinity College, Cambridge (MA); Manchester University (MA (Econ)). HM Treasury, 1970; Private Sec. to Financial Sec., 1971–73; Sec. to Wilson Cttee of Inquiry into Financial Instns, 1978–80; Under Sec., 1987–97; Dir of Fiscal and Monetary Policy, 1994–95; Dir of Budget and Public Finances, 1995; Hd of Policy Gp, DSS, 1995–97; Permanent Sec., DoH, 1997–2000. Mem. Bd, NCC, 2001–08. Gov., Acland Burghley Sch., 1991–98. *Recreations:* narrow-boating, walking.

KELLY, Daniel; QC (Scot.) 2007; *b* Dunfermline, 22 Jan. 1958; *s* of Daniel and Madeline Kelly; *m* 1985, Christine Marie MacLeod; three *s* one *d. Educ:* Univ. of Edinburgh (LLB Hons); Coll. of Europe, Bruges (Cert. de Hautes Études Européennes). Solicitor, 1981–90; lawyer, Brussels, 1983–84; Procurator Fiscal Depute, 1984–90; Advocate, 1991–; Temp. Sheriff, 1997–99; Pt-time Sheriff, 2005–. Chair, Scottish Child Law Centre, 2007–. Ed., Scots Law Times Sheriff Court Reports, 1992–. *Publications:* Criminal Sentences, 1993; (contrib.) Green's Litigation Styles, 1994; various legal articles. *Recreations:* literature, travel, cycling, golf. *Address:* Advocates Library, Parliament House, Edinburgh EH1 1RF. *T:* (0131) 226 5071, *Fax:* (0131) 225 3642; *e-mail:* daniel.kelly@advocates.org.uk.

KELLY, Sir David (Robert Corbett), Kt 1996; CBE 1991; Chairman, Kelly Packaging Limited, 1962–99 (Managing Director, 1962–85); Chairman, Conservative Party Committee on Candidates, 1995–2000; *b* 10 Dec. 1936; *s* of late Col Robert Cecil Kelly, TD, DL, JP and Jean Haswell Kelly (*née* Bowran), JP; *m* 1969, Angela Frances Taylor; four *d. Educ:* Sedbergh; St John's Coll., Cambridge (Lamor Award; MA). Farm labourer, 1955–56; Nat. Service, Stick of Honour, Mons OCS; 2nd Lt, 2nd Bn, 7th DEO Gurkha Rifles, 1960–61; 17th (later 4th) Bn, Parachute Regt (9 DLI), TA, 1962–69 (Major); Mil. Mem., TA&VRA for N of England, 1969–75. Board Member: Regl Bd, Brit. Technol. Gp, 1980–84; Northumbrian Water Authy, 1983–89; Washington Develt Corp., 1984–88; NE Industrial Develt Bd, 1989–97. Chm., NE Reg., 1966–67, Industrial Relns Cttee, 1968–71, British Box and Packaging Assoc. Confederation of British Industry: Member: Smaller Firms Council, 1977–83; Regl Council, 1979–86; Council, 1981–83; Industrial Policy Cttee, 1981–83; Mem., Lord Chancellor's Adv. Cttee on Tax Comrs, Tyne and Wear, 1981–93. Contested (C) Gateshead W, 1979. Chm., Northern Area Conservatives, 1990–93; Vice Pres., 1992–95, Pres., 1995–96, Nat. Union of Cons. and Unionist Assocs; Chm., Cons. Pty Conf., 1995; Chm. Trustees, Cons. Agents Benevolent Fund, 2000–; Trustee, Cons. Agents Superannuation Fund, 2000–. Mem., Gateshead CHC, 1975–77. President: Gateshead Dispensary Housing Assoc., 1992– (Chm., 1982–92 and 1993–); Craigielea Community Nursing Home, 1992– (Chm., 1988–92, and 1993–); Chm., Gateshead Dispensary Trust, 1999– (Trustee, 1965–); Trustee, Northumbrian Educnl Trust, 1981– (Chm., 1983–93). Vice Pres., Cancer Bridge, 1999–. Exec. Vice Chm., SCF Newcastle City Appeal, 1996–98; Patron, Spirit of Enterprise Appeal, 1997–2000. Chm. Govs, Westfield Sch., 1983–93. *Recreations:* family, country pursuits, theatre, light adventure (Mount Kilimanjaro, 1994). *Address:* Stanton Fence, Morpeth, Northumberland NE65 8PP. *T:* (01670) 772236; *e-mail:* stantonfence@hotmail.com. *Club:* Northern Counties (Newcastle upon Tyne).

KELLY, Prof. Deirdre Anne, (Lady Byatt), DL; MD; FRCP, FRCPI, FRCPCH; Director, Liver Unit, Birmingham Children's Hospital, since 1989 (Medical Director, 2000–07); Hon. Professor of Paediatric Hepatology, University of Birmingham, since 2001; *b* 1 Feb. 1950; *d* of Frank Kelly and Kathleen Kelly (*née* Scannell); *m* 1st, 1973, Miles Parker (marr. diss. 1990); two *s*; 2nd, 1997, Sir Ian (Charles Rayner) Byatt, *qv. Educ:* Convent of Holy Child, Killiney, Dublin; TCD (MB BCh BAO 1973; MD 1979). FRCPI 1990; FRCP 1995; FRCPCH 1997. Lectr in Medicine, TCD, 1980–82; Wellcome Res. Fellow, Royal Free Hosp., London, 1982–84; Lectr in Child Health, St Bartholomew's Hosp., 1987; Asst Prof. in Pediatrics, Univ. of Nebraska, 1987–89. Chm., Nat. Adv. Commn (formerly Panel) for Enquiry into Child Health, 2004–; Mem., Healthcare Commn, 2007–. President: Internat. Pediatric Transplant Assoc., 2002–05; British Soc. of Paediatric Gastroenterol., Hepatol. and Nutrition, 2004–07; Eur. Soc. of Paediatric Gastroenterol., Hepatol. and Nutrition, 2007–; Eur. Fedn of Biliary Atresia Res., 2004–. Chairman: Cttee of Hepatol., Eur. Soc. of Paediatric Gastroenterol., Hepatol. and Nutrition, 2001–04; Coll. Specialty Adv. Cttee, RCPCH, 2004–07; Lunar Soc., 2007–. Gov., Health Foundn, 2008–. Gov., St Martin's Sch., Solihull, 2004–05. DL W Midlands, 2008. Hosp. Dr of the Year, 1991. *Publications:* Pediatric Gastroenterology and Hepatology, 1996; Diseases of the Liver and Biliary System in Children, 1999, 3rd edn 2008; Paediatric Solid Organ Transplantation, 2000, 2nd edn 2007; contribs on clinical and basic sci. related to paediatric liver disease. *Recreations:* gardening, hill-walking, opera, entertaining friends and family. *Address:* Liver Unit, Birmingham Children's Hospital, Steelhouse Lane, Birmingham B4 6NH. *T:* (0121) 333 8253, *Fax:* (0121) 333 8251; *e-mail:* d.a.kelly@bham.ac.uk.

KELLY, Edward Ronald; journalist and trout farmer; *b* 14 Oct. 1928; *s* of late William Walter Kelly and of Millicent Kelly; *m* 1954, Storm Massada. *Educ:* Honiton Sch. Journalist: Bath Evening Chronicle, 1952; East African Standard, 1953; Sunday Post, Kenya, 1954; Reuters, 1956; Central Office of Information, 1958–84: Editor in Chief, Overseas Press Services Div., 1964; Asst Overseas Controller, 1968; Dir, Publications and Design Services Div., 1970; Home Controller, 1976; Overseas Controller, 1978–84. Chm., Assoc. of Stillwater Game Fishery Managers, 1993–96. *Recreations:* fishing, fly-tying, carpentry. *Address:* Windover House, Runcton Lane, Runcton, near Chichester, West Sussex PO20 1PT. *T:* (01243) 783069. *Club:* Flyfishers'.

KELLY, Prof. Francis Patrick, (Frank), FRS 1989; Professor of the Mathematics of Systems, University of Cambridge, since 1990; Master of Christ's College, Cambridge, since 2006 (Fellow, since 1976); *b* 28 Dec. 1950; *s* of Francis Kelly and Margaret Kelly (*née* McFadden); *m* 1972, Jacqueline Pullin; two *s. Educ:* Cardinal Vaughan Sch.; Van Mildert Coll., Durham (BSc 1971); Emmanuel Coll., Cambridge (Knight Prize 1975; PhD 1976; Hon. Fellow, 2007). Operational Research Analyst, Scicon, 1971–72; Cambridge University: Asst Lectr in Op. Res., Faculty of Engineering, 1976–78; Lectr in Statistical Lab., 1978–86; Reader in Faculty of Maths, 1986–90; Dir, Statistical Lab., 1991–93; variously Research Fellow, Dir of Studies, Tutor, Mem. College Council and Investments Cttee, Christ's Coll., 1976–. Chm., Lyndewode Research Ltd, 1987–. Chief Scientific Advr, DfT, 2003–06. Clifford Paterson Lectr, Royal Soc., 1995; Blackett Lectr, ORS, 1996. CompOR 2006. Hon. DSc Heriot-Watt, 2001. Rollo Davidson Prize, Cambridge Univ., 1979; Guy Medal in Silver, Royal Statistical Soc., 1989; Lanchester Prize, ORS of Amer., 1992; Naylor Prize, London Math. Soc., 1996; Koji Kobayashi Award, IEEE, 2005. *Publications:* Reversibility and Stochastic Networks, 1979; (ed) Probability, Statistics and Optimization, 1994; (ed jtly) Stochastic Networks, 1995; Mathematical Models in Finance, 1995; Stochastic Networks: theory and application, 1996; articles in math. and stat. jls. *Recreations:* golf, ski-ing. *Address:* Statistical Laboratory, Centre for Mathematical Sciences, Wilberforce Road, Cambridge CB3 0WB. *T:* (01223) 337963.

KELLY, Graham; *see* Kelly, R. H. G.

KELLY, Air Vice-Marshal (Herbert) Brian, CB 1983; LVO 1960; MD, FRCP; RAF, retired; *b* 12 Aug. 1921; *s* of late Surg. Captain James Cecil Kelly and of Meta Matheson (*née* Fraser). *Educ:* Epsom Coll.; St Thomas' Hosp. (MB, BS 1943, MD 1948). MRCP 1945, FRCP 1968; DCH 1966; MFOM 1982. House appts, St Thomas' Hosp., and St Luke's Hosp., Guildford, 1943–45; RNVR, Med. Specialist, RNH Hong Kong, 1945–48; Med. Registrar and Lectr in Medicine, St Thomas' Hosp., 1948–53; joined RAF Medical Br., 1953; Consultant in Medicine at RAF Hosps, Aden, Ely, Nocton Hall, Singapore, Cyprus, Germany, 1953–83; Consultant Adviser in Medicine to RAF, 1974, Senior Consultant, 1979–83. QHS 1978–83. Consultant, CAA, 1974–93. FRSocMed. Liveryman, Worshipful Soc. of Apothecaries, 1978; Freeman, City of London, 1978. *Publications:* papers in BMJ, Lancet, Brit. Heart Jl, and Internat. Jl of Epidemiology. *Recreation:* choir singing. *Address:* 32 Chiswick Quay, Hartington Road, W4 3UR. *T:* (020) 8995 5042; *e-mail:* brian@b-kelly.org.uk. *Club:* Royal Air Force.

KELLY, Iain Charles MacDonald; HM Diplomatic Service; Ambassador to Uzbekistan, since 2007; *b* 5 March 1949; *s* of Walter John Kelly and Doreen Sylvia Wilkins; *m* 1981, Linda Clare McGovern; two *s* (and one *s* decd). *Educ:* Cathays High Sch. for Boys; UCW, Aberystwyth (BSc Econs); Univ. of London (DipLib 1974). Joined HM Diplomatic Service, 1974; Russian Wing, Army Sch. of Languages, 1975–76; Moscow, 1976–79; Kuala Lumpur, 1979–82; Istanbul, 1986–88; Los Angeles, 1990–92; Moscow, 1992–95; Amsterdam, 1995–98; Sen. Mem., Jesus Coll., Oxford, 1998–99; Ambassador and Consul General, Belarus, 1999–2003; FCO, 2003–07; Sen. Mem., St Antony's Coll., Oxford, 2007. RGS 1999. *Recreations:* early music, privacy. *Address:* c/o Foreign and Commonwealth Office, SW1A 2AH. *Clubs:* Oriental, Highland Soc. of London.

KELLY, James Anthony; Member (Lab) Glasgow Rutherglen, Scottish Parliament, since 2007; *b* 23 Oct. 1963; *s* of Frank and Lilian Kelly; *m* 1992, Alexandra Mullan; two *d. Educ:* Trinity High Sch., Cambuslang; Glasgow Coll. of Technol. (BSc Computer Information Systems 1985). CIMA 1994. Analyst/programmer, Argyll and Clyde Health Bd, 1985–88; Scottish Power: Analyst/Programmer, 1988–90; Computer Auditor, 1990–92; Analyst Programmer, 1992–93; Asset Mgt Proj., 1993–95; Finance Officer, 1995–99; Scottish Electricity Settlements, 1999–2004; Business Analyst, SAIC, 2004–07. *Recreations:* running, five-a-side football, golf. *Address:* Constituency Office, 51 Stonelaw Road, Rutherglen G73 3TN. *T:* (0141) 647 0707, *Fax:* (0141) 643 1491; *e-mail:* james.kelly.msp@scottish.parliament.uk.

KELLY, Jane Maureen, (Mrs M. Blanckenhagen); Chairman, Mulberry Centre, West Middlesex University Hospital, since 2005 (Founder Patron, 2000; Trustee, since 2005); *b* 20 Sept. 1948; *d* of late Captain Adrian Morgan Kelly and of Monica Dallas Kelly (*née* Edwards); *m* 1994, Michael Blanckenhagen; three step *d. Educ:* Notre Dame High Sch., Sheffield; Univ. of Birmingham (LLB). Admitted solicitor, 1971; solicitor in private practice, England, Hong Kong and Brunei, 1971–79; AMI Healthcare Group plc, 1979–90: legal advr, 1979–83; Co. Sec., 1983–88; Dir, Corporate Health Services, 1988–90; Dir, 1987–90; independent mgt consultant, 1990–. Chairman: W Middx Univ. Hosp. NHS Trust, 1992–2002; NW London Strategic HA, 2002–03; NHS Bd Leadership Prog., 2001–04; London Regl Comr, NHS Appts Commn, 2003–05. Associate, Centre for Leadership and Mgt, Univ. of York, 1996–2006. Lay Mem., Gen. Council and Register of Osteopaths, 1990–95. Chm., Women in Mgt, 1987–89. Mem. Council, English Nature, 1992–2000. Mem. Council, Brunel Univ., 2006–. *Recreations:* family life, wildlife holidays, walking in Italy, theatrical biographies. *Address:* Mulberry Centre, West Middlesex University Hospital, Twickenham Road, Isleworth, TW7 6AF.

See also S. C. Hollins.

KELLY, John Philip, CMG 2000; LVO 1994; MBE 1984; HM Diplomatic Service, retired; Vice-President, Victoria League for Commonwealth Friendship, since 2007 (Chairman, 2002–07); *b* 25 June 1941; *s* of William Kelly and Norah Kelly (*née* Roche); *m* 1964, Jennifer Anne Buckler; one *s. Educ:* Oatlands Coll., Stillorgan, Dublin. Joined Foreign Office, 1959; Leopoldville, 1962–65; Cairo, 1965–68; Bonn, 1968–70; FCO, 1970–73; Canberra, 1973–77; Antwerp, 1977–78; FCO, 1978–81; seconded to Dept of Trade, 1981; Grenada, 1982–86; FCO, 1986–89; Dep. Gov., Bermuda, 1989–94; FCO, 1994–96; Gov., Turks and Caicos Islands, 1996–2000. *Recreations:* cruise lecturing, golf, walking, reading. *Address:* The Laurels, 56 Garden Lane, Royston, Herts SG8 9EH. *Club:* Royston Golf (Captain, 2003–04).

KELLY, Rt Hon. Sir (John William) Basil, Kt 1984; PC 1984; PC (NI) 1969; a Lord Justice of Appeal, Supreme Court of Judicature, Northern Ireland, 1984–95; a Judge of the High Court of Justice in Northern Ireland, 1973–84; *b* 10 May 1920; *o s* of late Thomas William Kelly and late Emily Frances (*née* Donaldson); *m* 1957, Pamela, *o d* of late Thomas Colmer and Marjorie Colthurst; one step *d. Educ:* Methodist Coll., Belfast; Trinity Coll., Dublin. BA (Mod.) Legal Science, 1943; LLB (Hons) 1944. Called to Bar: Inn of Court of N Ireland, 1944 (Bencher, 1968); Middle Temple, 1970 (Bencher, 2002). QC (N Ireland) 1958. MP (U) Mid-Down, Parliament of Northern Ireland, 1964–72; Attorney-Gen. for Northern Ireland, 1968–72. Chairman: Council of Legal Educn, NI,

1989–93; Judicial Studies Bd, NI, 1993–95; Mem., Law Adv. Cttee, British Council, 1982–92. *Recreations:* golf, music.

KELLY, Joseph Anthony; Editorial Director, Gabriel Communications, since 1998; Editor, The Universe, since 1995; *b* 10 Aug. 1958; *s* of Terence Christopher Kelly and Catherine Ethel Kelly (*née* Walsh); *m* 1999, Catherine Jane, *d* of William and Margaret Brownlie; one *s*. *Educ:* Presentation Coll., Reading; Ruskin Coll., Oxford; Univ. of Manchester (MA Theol. 2004). Associate, Instn of Buyers, 1980. Sen. Buyer, Church & Co., Reading, 1979–81; Buyer, J. Sainsbury, Reading, 1981–82; freelance photo-journalist, 1984–91; Editor: Welsh Arts Council Lit. Rev., 1991–94; Deeside Midweek Leader, 1991–92; Dep. Editor, Wrexham Leader, 1992–93; Ed., Country Quest (mag. for Wales), 1993; Dep. Ed., The Universe, 1994; Editor: Catholic Life mag., 1995, 1998–2006; School Building mag., 2004–; Urban Building mag., 2006–; Church Building mag., 2006–. Chm., NW Region, Soc. of Editors, 1999; Vice Chm., Catholic Writers' Guild (North), 2002–03. Mem., Historic Bldgs Adv. Council for Wales, 2008. Gov., RNLI, 1997–; Foundn Gov., St Richard Gwyn RC High Sch., Flint, 2002–. Photo-journalism Award, Irish Post, 1981. *Publications:* From Sulham Head, Collected Poems, 1980; The Pendulum, 1982. *Recreations:* hill-walking, ecclesiastical history, photography. *Address:* c/o Gabriel Communications Ltd, Landmark House, Station Road, Cheadle Hulme, Stockport SK8 7JH. *T:* (office) (0161) 488 1700. *Club:* Frontline.

KELLY, Judith Pamela, (Jude), OBE 1997; Artistic Director, South Bank Centre, since 2005; Chair, Metal, since 2005 (Artistic Director, 2002–05); *b* 24 March 1954; *d* of John Kelly and Ida Kelly; *m* 1993, Michael Bird (known professionally as Michael Birch); one *s* one *d*. *Educ:* Calder High Sch.; Birmingham Univ. (BA 2nd Cl. Hons). Freelance singer (folk and jazz), 1970–75; actress, Leicester Phoenix Theatre, 1975–76; Founder Dir, Solent People's Theatre, 1976–80; Artistic Dir, Battersea Arts Centre, 1980–85; Dir of Plays, Nat. Theatre of Brent, 1982–85; freelance dir, 1986–88; Festival Dir, York Fest. and Mystery Plays, 1986–88; Artistic Dir, 1988–2002, Chief Exec., 1993–2002, West Yorkshire Playhouse. Major productions include: West Yorkshire Playhouse: Merchant of Venice, 1994; Beatification of Area Boy, 1996 (also NY and Eur. tour); The Seagull, The Tempest, 1998; Singin' in the Rain, 1999, 2001 (also RNT, 2000; Olivier Award, 2001); Half a Sixpence, 2000; Sarcophagus, RSC, 1986; When We Are Married, Chichester Fest. Th., transf. Savoy, 1996; Othello, Shakespeare Th., Washington, 1997; English National Opera: The Elixir of Love, 1997; On the Town, 2005; The Wizard of Oz, RFH, 2008. British Rep. on culture for UNESCO, 1997–. Visiting Professor of Drama: Leeds Univ.; Kingston Univ. Chair: Common Purpose Charitable Trust, 1997–; QCA, 2001–03. Chm., London 2012 Olympic Cttee for Culture, Educn and Ceremonies, 2004–; Vice-Chm., Nat. Adv. Cttee on Creative and Cultural Educn, 1998; Member: Council, RSA, 1998–; ITC, 1999–; Bd, British Council. Mem. Bd, Liverpool Biennale, 2004–. Hon. Fellow, Dartington Coll. of Arts, 1999. Hon. Prof., York Univ., 2000. Hon. DLitt: Leeds Metropolitan, 1995; Bradford, 1996; Hon. LitD Leeds, 2000; DUniv Open, 2001. *Recreation:* wind-surfing. *Address:* South Bank Centre, SE1 8XX; *e-mail:* jude.kelly@southbankcentre.co.uk.

KELLY, Kathryn Mary; *see* Thirlwall, K. M.

KELLY, Laurence Charles Kevin, FRSL; FRGS; non-executive Director, 1972–93, and Vice-Chairman, 1988–93, Helical Bar PLC (Deputy Chairman, 1981–84; Chairman, 1984–88); *b* 11 April 1933; *s* of late Sir David Kelly, GCMG, MC, and Lady Kelly (*née* Jourda de Vaux); *m* 1963, (Alison) Linda McNair Scott; one *s* two *d*. *Educ:* Downside Sch.; New Coll., Oxford (Beresford Hope Schol.; MA Hons); Harvard Business Sch. Lieut, The Life Guards, 1949–52; served (temp.) Foreign Office, 1955–56; Guest, Keen and Nettlefolds, 1956–72; Director: GKN International Trading Ltd, 1972–77; Morganite International Ltd, 1984–91; KAE, subseq. Mintel, Ltd, 1980–2003; Chm., Queenborough Steel Co., 1980–89. Member: Northern Ireland Development Agency, 1972–78; Monopolies and Mergers Commn, 1982–89. Chairman, Opera da Camera Ltd (charity), 1981–87; Trustee, Choir of Carmelite Priory, Kensington (charity), 1997–. Vice-Chm., British Iron and Steel Consumers' Council, 1976–85. Sen. Associate Mem., St Antony's Coll., Oxford, 1985–91. FRGS 1972; FRSL 2003. Gen. Ed., Travellers' Companion series, 2004–. *Publications:* Lermontov, Tragedy in the Caucasus, 1978 (Cheltenham Literary Prize, 1979); (ed) St Petersburg, a Travellers' Anthology, 1981; (ed) Moscow, a Travellers' Anthology, 1983; Istanbul, a Travellers' Anthology, 1987; (with Linda Kelly) Proposals, 1989; Diplomacy and Murder in Teheran: Alexander Griboyedov and Imperial Russia's mission to the Shah of Persia, 2001; reviews, TLS, etc. *Recreation:* opera-going. *Address:* 44 Ladbroke Grove, W11 2PA. *T:* (020) 7727 4663; Lorton Hall, Low Lorton, near Cockermouth, Cumbria CA13 9UP. *T:* (01900) 85252. *Clubs:* Beefsteak, Brooks's, Turf; Kildare Street and University (Dublin).

KELLY, Linda Mary; Chief Executive, Lloyds TSB Foundation for England and Wales, since 2006; *b* 2 Jan. 1955; *d* of John Nicholl Millar and Vicenta Amy Gibson Millar (*née* Smith); *m* 1987, Brian James Kelly; two *d*. *Educ:* Nottingham Univ. (BPharm Hons). MRPharmS. Basic grade pharmacist, 1977–78; various appts in med. information, clin. trials, mkt res. and product mgt, Merck Sharpe & Dohme Ltd, 1978–87; New Product Planning Manager, 1987–88, Mktg Dir, 1988–91, Smith Kline Beecham; Man. Dir, Bristol Myers Squibb (UK and Ireland), 1991–95; Pres., Astra Pharmaceuticals Ltd (UK), 1995–99; Chief Exec., Parkinson's Disease Soc., 2001–05. FRSA 2003. *Recreations:* the arts, walking. *Address:* (office) 3rd Floor, 4 St Dunstan's Hill, EC3R 8UL. *T:* (020) 7398 1701; *e-mail:* linda.kelly@lloydstsbfoundations.org.uk. *Club:* Riverside.

KELLY, Dame Lorna (May) B.; *see* Boreland-Kelly.

KELLY, Mandi N.; *see* Norwood, M.

KELLY, Matthias John; QC 1999; SC (Ire.) 2005; a Recorder, since 2002; *b* 21 April 1954; *s* of Ambrose and Annie Kelly; *m* 1979, Helen Holmes; one *s* one *d*. *Educ:* St Patrick's Secondary Modern; St Patrick's Acad., Dungannon; Trinity Coll., Dublin (BA Mod., LLB). Called to the Bar, Gray's Inn, 1979, Bencher, 2002; in practice as Barrister, 1979–; called to Irish Bar, Belfast and Dublin, 1983; admitted Attorney: NY Bar, 1986; US Federal Bar, 1987; Consultant to EU Commn on UK Health and Safety Law, 1994–96. Mem., Inter-Disciplinary Wkg Pty on Actuarial Tables (Ogden Tables), 1997–2003. Chairman: Personal Injuries Bar Assoc., 2001–02; Bar Council (England and Wales), 2003 (Mem., 1998–2003; Vice Chm., 2002; Chm., Public Affairs Gp, 2001; Chm., Policy Gp, 2000). Non-exec. Dir, Allied Irish Bank, 2004–. Chairman: End the Vagrancy Act Campaign, 1989–93; Alcohol Recovery Project, 1993–96. FRSA 2003. *Publications:* (ed jtly) Personal Injury Manual, 1997, 2nd edn 2001; (contrib.) Munkman Employer's Liability, 13th edn 2001. *Recreations:* walking, reading, cycling, theatre, travel, life. *Address:* 39 Essex Street, WC2R 3AT. *T:* (020) 7832 1111.

KELLY, Dr Michael, CBE 1983; JP; DL; Managing Director, Michael Kelly Associates, since 1984; Chairman, Children 1st (formerly Royal Scottish Society for the Prevention of Cruelty to Children), 1987–96; *b* 1 Nov. 1940; *s* of David and Marguerite Kelly; *m* 1965, Zita Harkins; one *s* two *d*. *Educ:* Univ. of Strathclyde (BSc(Econ), PhD). FCIM (FInstM 1988). Asst Lectr in Economics, Univ. of Aberdeen, 1965–67; Lectr in Economics, Univ. of Strathclyde, 1967–84. Councillor: Anderston Ward Corp. of Glasgow, 1971–75 (Convener, Schools and Sch. Welfare; Vice-Convener, Transport); Hillington Ward, Glasgow Dist, 1977–84 (Chairman: General Purposes Cttee; Buildings and Property Cttee); Lord Provost of Glasgow, 1980–84 (masterminded "Glasgow's Miles Better" Campaign); Campaign Dir, Edinburgh—Count Me In, 1987–89. Rector, Univ. of Glasgow, 1984–87. Dir, Celtic Football Club, 1990–94. Member: Scottish Cttee, NACF, 1990–93; ESRC External Relns Adv. Gp (formerly Media Relns Cttee), 2000–. Founding Editor, Jl Economic Studies, 1965. Columnist, Scotsman, 1996–2001. BBC Radio Scotland News Quiz Champion, 1986, 1987. Presenter, Clyde 2 Talk-In, 1997–2000. Hon. Mem., Clan Donald, USA; Hon. Mayor, Tombstone, Ariz; Hon. Citizen: Illinois; San José; St Petersburg; Kansas City; Dallas; Fort Worth; Winnipeg. JP Glasgow 1973; DL Glasgow 1984. Hon. LLD Glasgow, 1984. Glasgow Herald Scot of the Year, 1983. OStJ 1983. Knight's Star, Order of Merit (Poland), 1998. *Publications:* Studies in the British Coal Industry, 1970; Paradise Lost: the struggle for Celtic's soul, 1994; London Lines, 1996. *Recreations:* photography, ski-ing, golf. *Address:* 50 Aytoun Road, Glasgow G41 5HE. *T:* (0141) 427 1627.

KELLY, Prof. Michael Joseph, FRS 1993; FREng; FInstP, FIET; Prince Philip Professor of Technology, University of Cambridge, since 2002; Fellow of Trinity Hall, Cambridge, 1974–81, 1989–92 and since 2002; Chief Scientific Adviser, Department for Communities and Local Government, since 2006; *b* New Plymouth, NZ, 14 May 1949; *s* of late Steve and Mary Constance Kelly; *m* 1991, Ann Elizabeth Taylor, BA, *d* of late Dr Daniel Brumhall Cochrane Taylor; one *d*. *Educ:* Francis Douglas Meml Coll., New Plymouth, NZ; Victoria Univ. of Wellington (BSc Hons 1970; MSc 1971); Gonville and Caius Coll., Univ. of Cambridge (PhD 1974); Trinity Hall, Cambridge (MA 1975; ScD 1994). FInstP 1988; FIET (FIEE 1989); FREng (FEng 1998). IBM Res. Fellow, Univ. of Calif., Berkeley, 1975–76; SRC Advanced Fellow, Cavendish Lab., 1977–81; Mem., Research Staff, GEC Hirst Res. Centre, 1981–92, Co-ordinator, GEC Superlattice Res., 1984–92; University of Surrey: Prof. of Physics and Electronics, 1992–96; Hd of Dept of Electronic and Electrical Engrg, 1996; Hd of Sch. of Electronic Engrg, Inf. Technol. and Maths, then Sch. of Electronics, Computing and Maths, 1997–2001; Hd of Advanced Technol. Inst. and Dir, Centre for Solid State Electronics, 2001–02; Exec. Dir, Cambridge-MIT Inst., 2003–05. Vis. Scientist, Cavendish Lab., 1988–92; Royal Soc./SERC Industrial Fellow, 1989–91; Erskine Fellow, Univ. of Canterbury, NZ, 1999. Non-executive Director: Surrey Satellite Technol. Ltd, 1997–2002; Laird Gp, 2006–. Mem. Council, Royal Soc., 2001–02. Mem. Council, Univ. of Surrey, 1996–2002; Mem. Council, 1997–2001, Vice-Pres., 2001–05, Inst. of Physics. Hon. FRSNZ 1999. Hon. ScD Victoria Univ. of Wellington, 2002. Royal Soc. Rutherford Meml Lectr, NZ, 2000. Paterson Medal and Prize, Inst. of Physics, 1989; GEC Nelson Gold Medal, 1991; Silver Medal, Royal Acad. Engrg, 1999; Hughes Medal, Royal Soc., 2006. *Publications:* (ed jtly) The Physics and Fabrication of Microstructures and Microdevices, 1986; Low Dimensional Semiconductors, 1995; numerous papers and review articles on semiconductor physics-for-devices in scientific jls. *Recreations:* music, literature. *Address:* Department of Engineering, University of Cambridge, Electronic Engineering Division, CAPE Building, J. J. Thomson Avenue, Cambridge CB3 0FA. *T:* (01223) 748303, *Fax:* (01223) 748348; *e-mail:* mjk1@cam.ac.uk.

KELLY, Owen, QPM 1987; Director, Webb Estate Ltd, since 2004; Commissioner of Police for City of London, 1985–93; *b* 10 April 1932; *s* of Owen Kelly and Anna Maria (*née* Hamill); *m* 1957, Sheila Ann (*née* McCarthy); five *s*. *Educ:* St Modan's High School, St Ninians, Stirlingshire. National Service, RAF, 1950–52; Metropolitan Police in all ranks from Police Constable to Commander, 1953–82; Asst and Dep. to Comr of Police for City of London, 1982–85; created secure zone in City of London (Ring of Steel) for prevention of terrorist activity, July 1993, and scheme continues. 18th Senior Command Course, Nat. Police Coll., 1981; Graduate, 14th Session of Nat. Exec. Inst., FBI, USA, 1991. Mem., Police Disciplinary Appeals Bd, Home Office, 1994–2000. Hon. Sec., Chief Constables' Club, 1989–93. Chm., City of London Br., Leukaemia Res. Fund, 1985–93. Freeman, City of London, 1984. CStJ 1987 (OStJ 1986). Commendation, Order of Civil Merit, Spain, 1986; Ordre du Wissam Alouite Class III, Morocco, 1987; Ordre du Mérite, Senegal, 1988; Ordem do Merito, Class III (Portugal), 1993. *Publications:* contrib. Police Review and Policing. *Recreations:* enjoying the society of a large family, do-it-yourself house maintenance, reading, cycling, hill walking. *Address:* c/o City of London Police HQ, 37 Wood Street, EC2P 2NQ.

KELLY, Most Rev. Patrick Altham; *see* Liverpool, Archbishop of, (RC).

KELLY, Peter (John); Under-Secretary for Atomic Energy, United Kingdom Department of Energy, 1980–82; *b* 26 Nov. 1922; *s* of Thomas and Lucy Kelly; *m* 1949, Gudrun Kelly (*née* Falck); two *s* three *d* (and one *s* decd). *Educ:* Downside; Oxford Univ. (BA). RNVR, 1942–46. 3rd Secretary, Moscow Embassy, 1948–49; journalism, 1950; rejoined public service, 1956; posts in Foreign Office, Defence Dept, Dept of Trade and Industry; Asst Secretary for Internat. Atomic Affairs, 1969–71; Counsellor, Office of UK Permanent Representative to the European Communities, Brussels, 1972–75; Director, Internat. Energy Agency, 1976–79. *Publication:* Safeguards in Europe, 1985. *Recreations:* walking, music. *Address:* 2 The Crouch, Seaford, Sussex BN25 1PX. *T:* (01323) 896881.

KELLY, Philip Charles; City Treasurer, then Director of Resources and Chief Finance Officer, Liverpool City Council, 1986–2000; *b* 23 Aug. 1948; *s* of late Charles and Irene May Kelly; *m* 1971, Pamela (*née* Fagan); one *s* two *d*. *Educ:* Inst. of Science and Technology, Univ. of Wales (BSc Econ). DipM; CIPFA. Market Research, British Steel Corp., 1970–72; Economist, Coventry City Council, 1972–74; Technical Officer, 1974–78, Asst Dir of Finance, 1978–82, Kirklees MDC; Dep. City Treasurer, Liverpool City Council, 1982–86; Treas., Merseyside Fire and Civil Defence Authy, 1986–2003. *Recreations:* family, Institute of Advanced Motoring.

KELLY, Philip John; journalist and political consultant; Director, Butler Kelly Ltd, since 1998; *b* 18 Sept. 1946; *s* of late William Kelly and Mary Winifred Kelly; *m* 1988, Dorothy Margaret Jones; two *s*. *Educ:* St Mary's Coll., Crosby; Leeds Univ. (BA Hons Politics). Freelance journalist and PR consultant, 1970–87; Editor, Tribune, 1987–91; Press Officer to Michael Meacher, MP, 1991–92. Dir, Grandfield Public Affairs, 1995–98. Co-Founder: Leveller, 1976; State Research, 1977; Chair, London Freelance Br., NUJ, 1983. Councillor (Lab) London Borough of Islington, 1984–86, 1990–98 (Chm., Educn Cttee, 1993–97; Dep. Leader, 1997–98), 2006–. Contested (Lab) Surrey SW, 1992. *Recreations:* railways, model railways, Arsenal FC. *Address:* 56 Windsor Road, N7 6JL. *T:* (020) 3008 8525; *e-mail:* philk@butlerkellyltd.co.uk. *Club:* Red Rose.

KELLY, (Robert Henry) Graham, FCIS; freelance writer and broadcaster; Chief Executive/General Secretary of the Football Association, 1989–98; *b* 23 Dec. 1945; *s* of Thomas John Kelly and Emmie Kelly; *m* 1st, 1970, Elizabeth Anne Wilkinson (marr. diss. 1996); one *s* one *d*; 2nd, 1999, Romayne Armstrong (marr. diss. 2003); 3rd, 2004, Jeanette Bailey. *Educ:* Baines Grammar Sch., Poulton-le-Fylde. FCIS 1973. Barclays Bank, 1964–68; Football League, 1968–88, Sec., 1979–88. Trustee, Football Grounds

Improvement Trust, 1985–88. Chm., Fylde and Wyre Older People's Strategic Partnership Bd, 2007–.

KELLY, Rosaline; publishing and industrial relations consultant; Visiting Lecturer in Journalism, London College of Printing, 1981–1985; *b* 27 Nov. 1922; *d* of Laurence Kelly and Ellen (*née* Fogarty), Drogheda, Co. Louth, Eire. *Educ:* St Louis Convent, Carrickmacross; University Coll., Dublin, NUI. Journalist with Woman magazine, 1958–77; local management, IPC Magazines Ltd, 1977–80. Active in NUJ, 1958–: Mem., National Exec. Council, 1972–78; first woman Pres., 1975–77; Membership of Honour, 1979; Member: NUJ Appeals Tribunal, 1978–; NUJ Standing Orders Cttee, 1978–2000; Trustee, NUJ Provident Fund Management Cttee, 1977– (Chairperson, 1980–82). Mem., Press Council, 1977–80 (first woman to represent Press side). Has been rejected as a catalogue holder by Empire Stores. *Recreations:* language and languages, music, compulsive reader. *Address:* c/o Royal Bank of Scotland, 127 High Holborn, WC1V 6PQ; Arash Areesh, 7 Lakeview Road, Wicklow, Eire. *T:* (404) 69596.

KELLY, Rt Hon. Ruth (Maria); PC 2004; MP (Lab) Bolton West, since 1997; *b* 9 May 1968; *d* of late Bernard James Kelly and of Gertrude Anne Kelly (*née* Murphy); *m* 1996, Derek John Gadd; one *s* three *d*. *Educ:* Queen's Coll., Oxford (BA PPE); London School of Economics (MSc Econs). Economics Writer, The Guardian, 1990–94; Bank of England: Dep. Head, Inflation Report Div., 1994–96; Manager, Special Projects Div., 1997. PPS to Minister of Agric., Fisheries and Food, 1998–2001; Economic Sec., 2001–02, Financial Sec., 2002–04, HM Treasury; Minister of State, Cabinet Office, 2004; Secretary of State: for Educn and Skills, 2004–06; for Communities and Local Govt, 2006–07; Minister for Women, 2006–07; Sec. of State for Transport, 2007–08. Mem., Treasury Select Cttee, 1997–98. *Recreations:* walking, family. *Address:* House of Commons, SW1A 0AA.

KELLY, Samuel Thomas, (Tom), CB 2008; Director, Corporate Affairs, BAA Ltd, since 2008; *b* Belfast, 8 July 1955; *s* of late Monty Kelly and of Mary Kelly; *m* 2003, Linda; two *s* two *d*. *Educ:* Royal Belfast Academical Instn; Univ. of Birmingham. Trainee journalist, Belfast Telegraph, 1979–81; Press Officer, NI Housing Exec., 1981–82; joined BBC, 1982: reporter, producer, asst ed., Radio and Current Affairs, NI, 1982–87; Producer, Newsnight, 1987–88; Political Ed., NI, 1988–91; Ed., NI News, 1992–95; Asst Ed., World at One, 1995–96; Actg Ed., Talkback prog., Radio Ulster, 1996–97; Dir of Communications, NI Office, 1998–2001; Prime Minister's Official Spokesman, 2001–07. *Recreations:* spending time with my family, gardening, beach walking, reading, music, watching Rugby when I can.

KELLY, Susan; *see* Hamilton, S.

KELLY, (Thomas) Andrew; QC 2000; *b* Oakville, Ontario, 18 July 1955; *s* of John Kelly and Mary Rea Kelly (*née* McKelvey). *Educ:* Bangor Grammar Sch., NI; Christ Church, Oxford (MA). Called to the Bar: Lincoln's Inn, 1978; NI, 1982; in practice at the Bar, 1981–; res. asst, H of C, 1981–84. *Recreations:* sports, arts, travel, gardening. *Address:* Francis Taylor Building, Temple, EC4Y 7BY. *T:* (020) 7353 8415. *Clubs:* Royal Automobile; Royal Ulster Yacht; Clandeboye Golf.

KELLY, Tom; *see* Kelly, S. T.

KELMAN, James; novelist, short story writer, occasional essayist and dramatist; *b* Glasgow, 9 June 1946. *Publications:* An Old Pub Near the Angel (short stories), 1973; (jtly) Three Glasgow Writers, 1975; Short Tales from the Nightshift, 1978; Not, Not While the Giro (short stories), 1983; The Busconductor Hines, 1984; A Chancer, 1985; (jtly) Lean Tales, 1985; Greyhound for Breakfast (Cheltenham Prize), 1987; A Disaffection (James Tait Black Meml Prize), 1989; The Burn (short stories), 1991; Hardie and Baird and Other Plays, 1991; Some Recent Attacks: essays cultural and political, 1992; How Late it Was, How Late (Booker Prize), 1994; The Good Times (short stories), 1998; Translated Accounts, 2001; Selected Stories, 2001; And the Judges Said… (essays), 2002; You have to be careful in the Land of the Free, 2004; Kieron Smith, Boy, 2008. *Address:* c/o Rodgers, Coleridge and White, 20 Powis Mews, W11 1JN.

KELNER, Simon; Managing Director and Editor-in-Chief, The Independent and The Independent on Sunday, since 2008 (Editor-in-Chief, The Independent, 1998–2008); *b* 9 Dec. 1957; *m* 1st, 1988, Karen Bowden (marr. diss. 2001); one *d*; 2nd, 2001, Sally Ann Lasson. *Educ:* Bury Grammar Sch.; Preston Poly. Trainee reporter, Neath Guardian, 1976–79; sports reporter, Extel, 1979–80; Sports Ed., Kent Evening Post, 1980–83; Asst Sports Ed., Observer, 1983–86; Dep. Sports Ed., Independent, 1986–89; Sports Editor: Sunday Correspondent, 1989–90; Observer, 1990–91; Ed., Observer Mag., 1991–93; Sports Ed., Independent on Sunday, 1993–95; Night Ed., 1995, Features Ed., 1995–96, Independent; Ed., Night & Day mag., Mail on Sunday, 1996–98. Hon. Fellow, Univ. of Central Lancashire, 1999. Ed. of the Year, What the Papers Say Awards, 1999 and 2003; Edgar Wallace Award, London Press Club, 2000; Ed. of the Year, GQ Awards, 2004; Media Achiever of the Year, Campaign Media Awards, 2004; Marketeer of the Year, Marketing Week Effectiveness Awards, 2004. *Publication:* To Jerusalem and Back, 1996. *Address:* The Independent, Independent House, 191 Marsh Wall, E14 9RS. *Clubs:* Groucho; Swinton Rugby League Supporters; Kirtlington Golf.

KELSALL, Ian Maxwell, OBE 1982; DL; Chairman, Informing Healthcare, since 2004; Principal, Ian Kelsall Development, since 2006; Member, Electoral Commission, since 2008; *s* of Harry Kelsall and Elsie Kelsall (*née* Hansard); *m* 1983, Julia Ann Harding. *Educ:* Carre's Grammar Sch., Sleaford, Lincs; Nottingham Univ. (BA Hons Hist.). Dir, CBI Wales, 1966–94; Director: Merthyr Tydfil Business Forum Ltd, 1994–98; Business for Merthyr, 1998–2001. Chairman: TSW Mgt Solutions Ltd, 1995–2006; TSW Ltd, 1995–2006; Welsh Risk Pool, 1998–2003; @teb, 2001–06; non-exec. Dir, Sedgewick Wales, 1994–97. Non-exec. Dir, Llandough NHS Trust, 1993–94; Chairman: E Glamorgan NHS Trust, 1994–99; Pontypridd and Rhondda NHS Trust, 1999–2004; Velindre NHS Trust, 2008–. Chm., Welsh NHS Confedn, 1998–2001. DL Mid Glamorgan, 1991. *Recreations:* music (playing the organ), reading, current affairs, watching football, Rugby, cricket, my two German Shepherds. *Address:* c/o Electoral Commission, Trevelyan House, Great Peter Street, SW1P 2HW. *T:* (020) 7271 0692, *Fax:* (020) 7271 0505; *e-mail:* ikelsall@electoralcommission.org.uk.

KELSALL, John Arthur Brooks, MA; Headmaster, Brentwood School, Essex, 1993–2004; *b* 18 June 1943; *o s* of Joseph Brooks Kelsall and Dorothy Kelsall (*née* Bee); *m* 1965, Dianne Scott Woodward, *o d* of Rev. William James Vaughan Woodward and Jean Ewart Woodward; one *s* one *d*. *Educ:* Royal Grammar Sch., Lancaster; Emmanuel Coll., Cambridge (BA 1965; MA 1969). Head of Economics, King Edward VII Sch., Lytham St Annes, 1965–68; Head of Geography, Whitgift Sch., Croydon, 1968–78; Dep. Headmaster, 1978–81, Headmaster, 1981–87, Bournemouth Sch.; Headmaster, Arnold Sch., Blackpool, 1987–93. *Recreations:* golf, fell-walking, opera, ornithology. *Clubs:* Royal Lytham St Annes Golf, Cretingham Golf.

KELSEY, Maj.-Gen. John, CBE 1968; Director, Wild Heerbrugg (UK) Ltd, 1978–87; Director of Military Survey, 1972–77; *b* 1 Nov. 1920; *s* of Benjamin Richard Kelsey and Daisy (*née* Powell); *m* 1944, Phyllis Margaret (*d* 1995), *d* of Henry Ernest Smith, Chingford; one *s* one *d*. *Educ:* Royal Masonic Sch.; Emmanuel Coll., Cambridge; Royal Mil. Coll. of Science. BSc. Commnd in RE, 1940; war service in N Africa and Europe; Lt-Col 1961; Col 1965; Dep. Dir Mil. Survey; Brig. Dir Field Survey, Ordnance Survey, 1968; Dir of Mil. Survey, Brig. 1972; Maj.-Gen. 1974. *Recreations:* Rugby football (played for Cambridge Univ., Richmond, Dorset, Wilts; Mem. RFU, 1965–66); sailing.

KELSEY, Linda; journalist and author; *b* 15 April 1952; *d* of Samuel Cohen and Rhona (*née* Fox); *m* 1st, 1972 (marr. diss. 1980); 2nd, 1999, Christian Testorf; one *s*. *Educ:* Woodhouse Grammar Sch., N12. Sub-editor, Good Housekeeping, 1970–72; Features Editor, Cosmopolitan, 1975–78; Deputy Editor: Company, 1978–81; Options, 1981–82; Cosmopolitan, 1983–85, Editor, 1985–89; Editor, She magazine, 1989–95; Editor at Large, Nat. Magazine Co., 1996–98; Consultant Ed., Parkhill Publishing, and freelance writer, 1999–2007; Exec. Ed., In Style, 2000–02. Editor of the Year Award: PPA, 1989, for Cosmopolitan; Brit. Soc. Mag. Editors, 1990, for She. *Publications:* Was it Good for You, Too?, 2003; Fifty is Not a Four-letter Word (novel), 2007; The Secret Lives of Sisters (novel), 2008. *Recreations:* reading, walking, theatre, film, family.

KELSON, Peter John; QC 2001; a Recorder, since 1997; *b* 7 March 1959; *s* of Gordon Charles and Patricia Sylvia Kelson; *m* 1982, Rosalind Margaret Clark; two *s*. *Educ:* Sheffield Univ. (LLB Hons). Called to the Bar, Middle Temple, 1981; Hd of Chambers, 2004–. *Recreation:* golf, piano, chess, travel, music. *Address:* Bank House Chambers, Old Bank House, 3 Hartshead, Sheffield S1 2EL. *T:* (0114) 275 1223. *Club:* Sickleholme Golf (Derbys).

KELTZ, Jennie, (Mrs James Keltz); *see* Bond, J.

KEMAKEZA, Hon. Sir Allan, Kt 2001; MP (People's Alliance) Savo/Russel, Solomon Islands, since 1989; Minister of Forestry, since 2007; *b* 11 Oct. 1950; *m* Joycelyn; two *s* three *d*. *Educ:* Police Acad.; CID Course, W Yorks Metropolitan Police; VIP Protection Course, Fed. Police Coll., Canberra. Royal Solomon Is Police Force, 1972–88: Constable; Asst Superintendent of Police; ADC to Governor-Gen.; Hd of CID; Sen. SO to Comr of Police; Asst to Comr of Police Admin. Minister: for Police and Justice, 1989–90; for Housing and Govt Services, 1991–93; for Forests, Envmt and Conservation, 1995–96; for Nat. Unity, Reconciliation and Peace, and Dep. Prime Minister, 2000–01; Prime Minister, 2001–06; Dep. Speaker of Parlt, 2006–07. Dep. Leader of Opposition, 1993–94, Leader, 1997–99. *Recreations:* reading, fishing, farming. *Address:* Parliament House, PO Box G19, Vavaya Ridge, Honiara, Solomon Islands.

KEMBALL, Brig. Humphrey Gurdon, CBE 1971 (OBE 1966); MC 1940; *b* 6 Nov. 1919; *s* of late Brig.-Gen. Alick Gurdon Kemball (late IA) and late Evelyn Mary (*née* Synge); *m* 1945, Ella Margery Emmeline (*née* Bickham) (*d* 1997); no *c*. *Educ:* Trinity Coll., Glenalmond; RMC, Sandhurst. Commissioned 1939, 1st Bn The Prince of Wales's Volunteers. Served War of 1939–45 (MC); Staff Coll., 1943. JSSC, 1956; commanded 1st Bn The Lancashire Regt (PWV), 1961–63; i/c Administration, HQ Federal Regular Army, Aden, 1964–66; Asst Dir, MoD, 1966–68; Mil. Attaché, Moscow, 1968–71; HQ British Forces, Near East, 1971–73; Dep. Comdr, SW District, 1973–74, retired. *Recreations:* fishing, travelling. *Address:* 28 Windsor End, Beaconsfield, Bucks HP9 2JW. *T:* (01494) 671698. *Club:* Naval and Military.

KEMBALL, Air Marshal Sir (Richard) John, KCB 1990; CBE 1981; FRAeS; DL; Co-ordinator of British-American Community Relations, Ministry of Defence, 1994–2004; Chief Executive, Racing Welfare, 1995–2004; *b* 31 Jan. 1939; *s* of Richard and Margaret Kemball; *m* 1962, Valerie Geraldine Webster; two *d*. *Educ:* Uppingham; Open Univ. (BA 1990). Commissioned RAF, 1957; OC No 54 Squadron, 1977; OC RAF Laarbruch, 1979; Commandant, CFS, 1983–85; Comdr, British Forces, Falkland Islands, 1985–86; COS and Dep. C-in-C, Strike Command and UK Air Forces, 1989–93. ADC to HM The Queen, 1984–85. Chm., Essex Rivers Healthcare NHS Trust, 1993–95. Hon. Col, 77 Engr Regt (V), 1993–96. President: RAFA, 1995–98 (Vice-Pres., 1993–95; Life Vice-Pres., 1998); Corps of Commissionaires, 2002–08 (Gov., 1993–08). Pres., Southend Br., RAeS, 1999–April 2009. Freeman, City of London, 1995. DL 1999, High Sheriff, 2007–08, Suffolk. FRAeS 2003. *Recreations:* country pursuits, tennis, cricket, gardening. *Address:* c/o HSBC, 46 Market Hill, Sudbury, Suffolk CO10 6ES. *Club:* Royal Air Force.

KEMBER, Anthony Joseph, MA; Communications Adviser, Department of Health, 1989–92; *b* 1 Nov. 1931; *s* of Thomas Kingsley Kember and May Lena (*née* Pryor); *m* 1957, Drusilla Mary (*née* Boyce); one *s* two *d*. *Educ:* St Edmund Hall, Oxford (MA). MHSM, DipHSM. Deputy House Governor and Secretary to Bd of Governors, Westminster Hospital, 1961–69; Gp Secretary, Hillingdon Gp Hospital Management Cttee, 1969–73; Area Administrator, Kensington and Chelsea and Westminster AHA(T), 1973–78; Administrator, 1978–84, Gen. Man., 1984–89, SW Thames RHA. Mem., Lord Chancellor's Adv. Cttee on JPs for SW London (formerly SW London Area Adv. Cttee on Appointment of JPs), 1994–2002. Trustee, Disabled Living Foundn, 1981–2000 (Chm., 1993–2000); Founder Trustee, Charity Trust Networks, 1998–2000 (Vice-Chm., 1998–99). Chm., Richmond Art Soc., 1995–97 (Sec., 1992–95); Mem., Richmond upon Thames Arts Council, 2001–02. CCMI (CBIM 1988). *Publications:* The NHS—a Kaleidoscope of Care, 1994; various articles for professional jls. *Recreations:* painting, inside and out; tennis, royal and common-or-garden. *Address:* 16 Orchard Rise, Richmond, Surrey TW10 5BX. *Clubs:* Roehampton; Royal Tennis Court, Hamsters Real Tennis (Hampton Court).

KEMBER, William Percy, FCA; FCT; Group Financial Controller, British Telecommunications, 1981–92; *b* 12 May 1932; *s* of late Percy Kember and Mrs Q. A. Kember, Purley, Surrey; *m* 1982, Lynn Kirkham. *Educ:* Uppingham. Chartered Accountant; Corporate Treasurer. Various posts with Royal Dutch/Shell Group in Venezuela, 1958–63; British Oxygen Co., 1963–67; Coopers & Lybrand, 1967–72; Post Office (Telecommunications), 1972–81. Director: Centel Financial Systems Inc., 1983–86; Marshalls Finance, 1991–98. Visitor, Royal Institution, 1977–79, Chm., 1979. *Recreation:* golf. *Address:* 83 Hillway, N6 6AB. *Clubs:* Royal Automobile; Highgate Golf, Royal Dornoch Golf.

KEMP, family name of **Viscount Rochdale**.

KEMP, Prof. Barry John, FBA 1992; Professor of Egyptology, 2005–07, now Emeritus, and Fellow, McDonald Institute of Archaeological Research, since 2008, University of Cambridge; Fellow of Wolfson College, Cambridge, 1990–2007, now Emeritus; *b* 14 May 1940. *Educ:* Liverpool Univ. (MA); MA Cantab 1965. Lectr, 1969–90, Reader in Egyptology, 1990–2005, Univ. of Cambridge. Project Dir, Amarna Project, 2006–; Chm., Amarna Trust, 2006–. *Publications:* Amarna Reports, Vols. 1–6, 1984–95; Ancient Egypt: anatomy of a civilisation, 1989, 2nd edn 2005; (jtly) Survey of the Ancient City of El-

Amarna, 1993. *Address:* 4 Abu Hureiba Street, Darb el-Ahmar, Cairo, Egypt; *e-mail:* bjk2@cam.ac.uk.

KEMP, Prof. Bruce Ernest, PhD; FRS 2002; FAA; Federation Fellow, Commonwealth Scientific and Industrial Research Organisation, since 2003; Hon. NHMRC Fellow, St Vincent's Institute of Medical Research, since 2003 (NHMRC Senior Principal Research Fellow and Deputy Director, 1989–2003); *b* 15 Dec. 1946; *s* of Norman Beck Kemp and Mary Frances Kemp (*née* Officer); *m* 1970, Alison Virginia Sanders; three *s*. *Educ:* Adelaide Univ. (BAgrSc Hons); Flinders Univ., SA (PhD 1975). Postdoctoral Fellow, Edwin G. Krebs Lab., Univ. of Calif, Davis, 1974–76; Nat. Heart Foundn Fellow, Flinders Med. Centre, 1977–78; Queen Elizabeth II Sen. Res. Fellow, Howard Florey Inst., Univ. of Melbourne, 1979–84; Sen. Res. Fellow, Dept of Medicine, Repatriation Gen. Hosp., Heidelberg, Vic, 1984–88. FAA 2000. *Publications:* (ed and contrib.) Peptides and Protein Phosphorylation, 1990; chapters in books; contrib. conf. procs and learned jls incl. Nature, Science. *Recreations:* tennis, walking, bicycle riding. *Address:* St Vincent's Institute of Medical Research, 41 Victoria Parade, Fitzroy, Vic 3065, Australia. *T:* (3) 92882480, *Fax:* (3) 94162676. *Club:* University House (Melbourne).

KEMP, Charles James Bowring; His Honour Judge Kemp; a Circuit Judge, since 1998; *b* 27 April 1951; *s* of late Michael John Barnett Kemp and of Brigid Ann (*née* Bowring; now Vernon-Smith); *m* 1974, Fenella Anne Herring; one *s* one *d*. *Educ:* Shrewsbury Sch.; University Coll. London (LLB). Called to the Bar, Gray's Inn, 1973; in practice at the Bar, 1974–98; Asst Recorder, 1987–91; a Recorder, 1991–98; South Eastern Circuit. Member: Sussex Probation Bd, 2001–07; Sussex Courts Bd, 2004–07; Surrey and Sussex Courts Bd, 2007–. *Recreations:* music, tennis, swimming, golf, country pursuits. *Address:* Law Courts, High Street, Lewes, E Sussex BN7 1YB. *T:* (01273) 480400; *e-mail:* CKemp@lix.compulink.co.uk; CharlesKemp@tiscali.co.uk. *Club:* Piltdown Golf.

KEMP, Prof. David Thomas, PhD; FRS 2004; Professor of Auditory Biophysics, University College London, since 1990; Director, Otodynamics Ltd, since 1989; *b* 24 Feb. 1945; *s* of Rev. Thomas Kemp and Alice Kemp (*née* Holliday); *m* 1970, Gillian Barbara Langford; one *s* one *d* (and one *s* one *d* decd). *Educ:* Southport Technical Coll.; KCL (BSc Hons (Physics) 1966; AKC; PhD (Radiophysics) 1970). Res. Scientist, CEGB, 1970; PSO, RNTNEH, London, 1971; Sen. Lectr, Inst. of Laryngol. and Otol., London, 1980–86; Reader in Auditory Biophysics, UCL, 1986–90. Patented invention of otoacoustic emission hearing screening device, in widespread use (Queen's Award for Export Achievement, 1993, for Technol Achievement, 1998, Otodynamics Ltd; Queen's Award for Technol Achievement, Inst. of Laryngol. and Otol., UCL, 1998). *Publications:* articles in Jl of Acoustical Soc. of America and in jls concerned with hearing and geophysics; book chapters. *Recreations:* history of radio, astronomy, family history and genealogy, walking. *Address:* UCL Centre for Auditory Research, The Ear Institute, 332 Gray's Inn Road, WC1X 8EE; Otodynamics Ltd, 30–38 Beaconsfield Road, Hatfield, Herts AL10 8BB. *T:* (01707) 267540, *Fax:* (01707) 262327; *e-mail:* d.kemp@ucl.ac.uk.

KEMP, Rt Rev. Eric Waldram, DD; Bishop of Chichester, 1974–2001; *b* 27 April 1915; *o c* of Tom Kemp and Florence Lilian Kemp (*née* Waldram), Grove House, Waltham, Grimsby, Lincs; *m* 1953, Leslie Patricia, 3rd *d* of late Rt Rev. K. E. Kirk, sometime Bishop of Oxford; one *s* four *d*. *Educ:* Brigg Grammar Sch., Lincs; Exeter Coll., Oxford (MA); St Stephen's House, Oxford (Hon. Fellow 2005). Deacon 1939; Priest 1940; Curate of St Luke, Southampton, 1939–41; Librarian of Pusey House, Oxford, 1941–46; Chaplain of Christ Church Oxford, 1943–46; Actg Chap., St John's Coll., Oxford, 1943–45; Fellow, Chaplain, Tutor, and Lectr in Theology and Medieval History, Exeter Coll., Oxford, 1946–69, Emeritus Fellow, 1969; Dean of Worcester, 1969–74. Exam. Chaplain: to Bp of Mon, 1942–45; to Bp of Southwark, 1946–50; to Bp of St Albans, 1946–69; to Bp of Exeter, 1949–69; to Bp of Lincoln, 1950–69. Proctor in Convocation for University of Oxford, 1949–69. Bp of Oxford's Commissary for Religious Communities, 1952–69; Chaplain to the Queen, 1967–69. Canon and Prebendary of Caistor in Lincoln Cathedral, 1952–2001; Hon. Provincial Canon of Cape Town, 1960–; Canon of Honour, Chartres Cathedral, 1998. Bampton Lecturer, 1959–60. FRHistS 1951. Hon. Fellow, University Coll., Chichester, 2002. Hon. DLitt Sussex, 1986; Hon. DD Berne, 1987. *Publications:* (contributions to) Thy Household the Church, 1943; Canonization and Authority in the Western Church, 1948; Norman Powell Williams, 1954; Twenty-five Papal Decretals relating to the Diocese of Lincoln (with W. Holtzmann), 1954; An Introduction to Canon Law in the Church of England, 1957; Life and Letters of Kenneth Escott Kirk, 1959; Counsel and Consent, 1961; The Anglican-Methodist conversations: A Comment from within, 1964; (ed) Man: Fallen and Free, 1969; Square Words in a Round World, 1980; Shy But Not Retiring (memoirs), 2006; contrib. to English Historical Review, Jl of Ecclesiastical History. *Recreations:* music, travel. *Address:* 5 Alexandra Road, Chichester PO19 7LX. *Club:* National Liberal (Pres., 1994–).

KEMP, Fraser; MP (Lab) Houghton and Washington East, since 1997; *b* 1 Sept. 1958; *s* of William and Mary Kemp; *m* 1989, Patricia Mary (marr. diss. 2002), *d* of Patrick and Patricia Byrne; two *s* one *d*. *Educ:* Washington Comp. Sch. Civil Servant (clerical asst/officer), 1975–81; Labour Party: Agent, Leicester, 1981–84; Asst Regl Organiser, E Midlands, 1984–86; Regl Sec., W Midlands, 1986–94; Nat. Gen. Election Co-ordinator, 1994–96. An Asst Govt Whip, 2001–05. Mem., Select Cttee on Public Admin, 1997–99. Chm., PLP Cabinet Office Cttee, 1997–2001; Vice-Chm., Labour Election Planning Gp, 2004–05. *Recreation:* people. *Address:* House of Commons, SW1A 0AA. *T:* (020) 7219 5181, (constituency) (0191) 584 9266. *Club:* Usworth and District Working Men's (Washington).

KEMP, Air Vice-Marshal George John, CB 1976; *b* 14 July 1921; *m* 1943, Elspeth Beatrice Peacock; one *s* two *d*. Commnd RAF, 1941; served in night fighter sqdns with spell on ferrying aircraft to Middle East; RAF Staff Coll., 1952; AHQ Iraq, 1953–54; Air Secretary's Dept, Air Ministry, 1955–57; jssc, 1958; MoD Secretariat, 1959; Far East Planning Staff, 1960–61; RAF Staff Coll. Directing Staff, 1962–63; UNISON Planning Staff, MoD, 1964; Dir of Personnel (Policy and Plans), RAF, 1965–67; Stn Comdr RAF Upwood, 1968–69; Dir of Manning (RAF), 1970–72; Dir-Gen. of Personnel Management, RAF, 1973–75. *Recreations:* working with wood, 20th century history, reading The Times. *Address:* Myatts, White Horse Square, Steyning, W Sussex BN44 3GQ. *T:* (01903) 813804. *Club:* Royal Air Force.

KEMP, Kenneth Reginald; Hon. Life President, Smith & Nephew plc, 1990 (Chairman, 1976–90); *b* 13 Nov. 1921; *s* of Philip R. Kemp and Siew Pukalanan of Thailand; *m* 1949, Florence M. Hetherington (marr. diss.); *m* 1996, Frances M. Kemp-Bell; one *s* one *d*. *Educ:* Bradfield College, Berks. FCA. Joined Leeds Rifles, 1939; commissioned Royal Artillery, 1940–46; served in France, Germany, India, Far East (Captain). Peat, Marwick Mitchell & Co., 1947; qualified CA, 1950; Smith & Nephew: Company Sec., 1953, later Finance Dir; Dir, 1962; Chief Exec., 1968–76. Mem., Ct of Patrons, RCS, 1984–. *Recreations:* unlimited. *Address:* Smith & Nephew, Heron House, 15 Adam Street, WC2N 6LA. *T:* (020) 7401 7646.

KEMP, Leslie Charles, CBE 1982; Chairman, Griffiths McGee Ltd, Demolition Contractors, 1982–87; Proprietor, Leslie Kemp Associates, 1976–97; *b* 10 Oct. 1920; *s* of Thomas and Violet Kemp. *Educ:* Hawkhurst Moor Boys' School. Apprentice blacksmith, 1934–39; served War, 1939–46: Infantry, N Africa and Italy. Civil Engrg Equipment Operator, 1947–51; served in Korea, 1951; District Organiser, 1951–57, Regional Organiser, 1958–63, Nat. Sec. (Construction), TGWU, 1963–76. Jt Registrar, 1975–76, Dep. Chm., 1976–81, Demolition and Dismantling Industry Registration Council. Member, Nat. Jt Council for Building Industry, 1957–76; Operatives Sec., Civil Engrg Construction Conciliation Bd for GB, 1963–76; Mem., 1964–73, Dep. Chm., 1973–76, Chm., 1976–85, Construction Industry Trng Bd (Chm., Civil Engrg Cttee, 1964–76); Member: EDC for Civil Engrg, 1964–76; Construction Ind. Liaison Gp, 1974–76; Construction Ind. Manpower Bd, 1976; Bragg Adv. Cttee on Falsework, 1973–75; Vice-Pres., Construction Health and Safety Gp. Chm., Corby Develt Corp., 1976–80; Dep. Chm., Peterborough Develt Corp., 1974–82. Member, Outward Bound Trust, 1977–88; Pres., W Norfolk Outward Bound Assoc., 1983–88. Chm., Syderstone Parish Council, 1983–87. Construction News Man of the Year Award, 1973; in recognition of services to trng, Leslie Kemp Europ. Prize for Civil Engrg trainees to study in France, instituted 1973. CompICE; FCMI. *Recreations:* travel, bird-watching, fishing. *Address:* Lamberts Yard, Syderstone, King's Lynn, Norfolk PE31 8SF. *Clubs:* Lighthouse; Fakenham Golf (Pres., 1985–88).

KEMP, Lindsay; Founder, Artistic Director and Principal Performer, Lindsay Kemp Co., since 1962; painter, designer, teacher; *b* 3 May 1938; *s* of Norman Kemp and Marie (*née* Gilmour). *Educ:* Sunshine Sch. of Dancing, Bradford; Royal Merchant Navy Sch., Bearwood; Bradford Coll. of Art; Sigurd Leeder Sch. of Modern Dance; Ballet Rambert Sch.; studied with Marcel Marceau. Lindsay Kemp Co. productions include: Illuminations, Lyric, Hammersmith, 1965; Turquoise Pantomime; Woyzeck; Salomé; Legends; Flowers, West End, 1974, later Broadway and world tour, 1974–94; Mr Punch's Pantomime; A Midsummer Night's Dream; Duende; Nijinsky; Façade; The Big Parade; Alice; Onnagata; Cinderella: a gothic operetta; Dreamdances, Peacock Th., 2002; Hoffman Tales, Santander, 2007. Dir, David Bowie's Ziggy Stardust concerts, 1972; created for Ballet Rambert: The Parade's Gone By, 1975; Cruel Garden, 1978; film appearances include: Savage Messiah, 1971; The Lindsay Kemp Circus, 1971; Wicker Man, 1972; Sebastian, 1974; Jubilee, 1977; Italian Postcards, 1986; Travelling Light, 1993. *Publication:* (with D. Haughton) Drawing and Dancing, 1988; *relevant publications:* Lindsay Kemp, by David Haughton, 1982; Flowers, 1987. *Recreation:* interior decorating.

KEMP, Prof. Martin John, FBA 1991; Professor of the History of Art, Oxford University, 1995–2008; Fellow of Trinity College, Oxford, 1995–2008; British Academy Wolfson Research Professor, 1993–98; *b* 5 March 1942; *s* of Frederick Maurice Kemp and Violet Anne Tull; *m* 1966, Jill Lightfoot (marr. diss. 2005), *d* of Dennis William Lightfoot and Joan Betteridge; one *s* one *d*. *Educ:* Windsor Grammar Sch.; Downing Coll., Cambridge (MA Nat. Scis and Art History; Hon. Fellow, 1999); Courtauld Inst. of Art, London Univ. (Academic Dip.). Lectr in History of Art, Dalhousie Univ., Halifax, NS, Canada, 1965–66; Lectr in History of Fine Art, Univ. of Glasgow, 1966–81; Fellow, Inst. for Advanced Study, Princeton, 1984–85; University of St Andrews: Prof. of Fine Arts, subseq. of Hist. and Theory of Art, 1981–95; Associate Dean of Graduate Studies, Faculty of Arts, 1983–87; Mem. Court, 1988–91; Provost of St Leonard's Coll., 1991–95. Prof. of History and Hon. Mem., Royal Scottish Acad., 1985–; Slade Prof. of Fine Art, Cambridge Univ., 1987–88; Visiting Professor: Benjamin Sonnenberg, Inst. of Fine Arts, New York Univ., 1988; Wiley, Univ. of N Carolina, Chapel Hill, 1993; Vis. Scholar, Getty Res. Inst., LA, 2002; Mellon Sen. Fellow, Canadian Centre for Architecture, 2004. Co-Founder, Wallace Kemp/Artakt, 2001; Res. Dir, Universal Leonardo, 2001–07. Chair, Assoc. of Art Historians, 1989–92; Member: Board, Scottish Museums Council, 1990–95; Res. Awards Adv. Cttee, Leverhulme Trust, 1991–98; Board, Mus. Trng Inst., 1993–99; Board, Interalia, 1993–; Council, British Soc. for History of Sci., 1994–97. Pres., Leonardo da Vinci Soc., 1987–96. Trustee: National Gall. of Scotland, 1982–87; V&A Museum, 1985–89; BM, 1995–2005. Broadcasts, Radio 3 and TV. For. Mem., American Acad. of Arts and Scis, 1996. FRSA 1983–98; FRSE 1992. Hon. FRIAS 1988. Hon. DLitt Heriot-Watt, 1995. Mitchell Prize for best first book in English on Art History, 1981; Armand Hammer Prize for Leonardo Studies, 1992; President's Prize, Italian Assoc. of America, 1998. *Publications:* Leonardo da Vinci, The Marvellous Works of Nature and Man, 1981; (jtly) Leonardo da Vinci, 1989; (jtly) Leonardo on Painting, 1989; The Science of Art, 1990; Behind the Picture, 1997; (ed) The Oxford History of Western Art, 2000; Visualizations, 2000; (with Marina Wallace) Spectacular Bodies, 2000; Leonardo, 2004; Seen/Unseen, 2006; Leonardo da Vinci: experience, experiment, design, 2006; The Human Animal, 2007; articles in Jl of Warburg and Courtauld Insts, Burlington Magazine, Art History, Art Bull., Connoisseur, Procs of British Acad., Jl of RSA, L'Arte, Bibliothèque d'Humanisme et Renaissance, Med. History, TLS, London Rev. of Books, Guardian, Nature, Sunday Times, etc. *Recreations:* keeping fit, avoiding academics.

KEMP, Neil Reginald, OBE 1990 (MBE 1980); PhD; Senior Adviser (International), Institute of Education, University of London, since 2005; *b* 18 March 1945; *s* of Harry Reginald Kemp and Ada Mary Kemp (*née* Roberts); *m* 1982, Elizabeth Jacob; two *s*. *Educ:* University College of Wales, Swansea (BSc; PhD Analytical Chem. 1971). Laboratory technician, 1961–63; VSO as Lectr, Gordon Coll., Rawalpindi, Pakistan, 1967–68; joined British Council, 1971: Jakarta, 1971–74; Calcutta, 1976–79; Res. Associate, Univ. of London Inst. of Educn, 1979–80; Head, Sci. and Technol. Dept, London, 1981–85; New Delhi, 1985–89; Colombo, 1990–91; Develt and Trng Services, Manchester, 1991–95; Director: Indonesia, 1995–2001; Educn UK Div., 2001–05. Board Member: Assoc. of Ind. Higher Educn, 2005–; Open Univ. Worldwide Ltd, 2005–. *Recreations:* athletics, cycling, cricket and basketball, travelling, jazz and blues. *Address:* 37 Houndean Rise, Lewes, E Sussex BN7 1EQ.

KEMP, Prof. Peter Anthony, DPhil; Barnett Professor of Social Policy, University of Oxford, since 2006; Fellow, St Cross College, Oxford, since 2006; *b* 25 Dec. 1955; *s* of Ronald Percy James Kemp and Emilie Kemp; partner, Prof. Jo Neale; two *d*. *Educ:* Univ. of Southampton (BSc 1977); Univ. of Glasgow (MPhil 1979); Univ. of Sussex (DPhil 1984). Researcher, SHAC, 1983–85; Res. Fellow, Univ. of Glasgow, 1985–87; Lectr, Univ. of Salford, 1987–90; Joseph Rowntree Prof. of Housing Policy and Founder Dir, Centre for Housing Policy, Univ. of York, 1990–95; Prof. of Housing and Social Policy, Univ. of Glasgow, 1996–2002; Prof. of Social Policy and Dir, Social Policy Research Unit, Univ. of York, 2002–06. *Publications:* The Private Provision of Rented Housing, 1988; Housing and Social Policy, 1990; Tax Incentives and the Revival of Private Renting, 1991; A Comparative Study of Housing Allowances, 1997; Private Renting in Transition, 2004; Sick Societies?: trends in disability benefits in post-industrial welfare states, 2006; Cash and Care: challenges in the welfare state, 2006; Housing Allowances in Comparative Perspective, 2007. *Recreations:* cycling, going to the gym, reading. *Address:* c/o Barnett House, University of Oxford, 32 Wellington Square, Oxford OX1 2ER; *e-mail:* peter.kemp@socres.ox.ac.uk.

KEMP, Richard Geoffrey Horsford, MA; Director, Langford Educational Ltd, since 2006; Head Master, Pate's Grammar School, Cheltenham, 2000–06; *b* 27 Oct. 1948; *s* of Athole Stephen Horsford Kemp and Alison Kemp (*née* Bostock); *m* 1st, 1970 (marr. diss. 1990); 2nd, 1996, Denise (*née* Fraser); one step *s* one step *d*. *Educ:* Westminster Sch.; Christ Church, Oxford (MA). Marketing and Advertising Manager, Unilever, 1970–73; Teacher: Eton Coll., 1973–74; Henry Box Sch., Witney, 1974–78; Lord Williams's Sch., Thame, 1978–84; res., Dept of Educn, Oxford Univ., 1984–85; Buckinghamshire LEA, 1985–92 (Sen. Educn Advr, 1989–92); Sen. Dep. Head, Actg Headmaster, Aylesbury Grammar Sch., 1992–99. *Publications:* various geography textbooks and atlases. *Recreations:* gardening, wine, travel, military history. *Address:* Kemp's Yard, Langford, Lechlade, Glos GL7 3LF. *T:* (01367) 860176.

KEMP, Robert Thayer; export credit consultant; *b* 18 June 1928; *s* of Robert Kemp and Ada Kemp (*née* Thayer); *m* 1951, Gwendolyn Mabel Minty; three *s*. *Educ:* Bromley Grammar Sch.; London Univ. (BA (Hons) Medieval and Mod. History). Export Credits Guarantee Department: Asst Sec., 1970; Under-Sec., 1975; Head of Project Underwriting Gp, 1981–85; Director: Internat. Gp, 1985–88; Sedgwick Credit, 1989–95. *Publication:* Review of Future Status Options (ECGD), 1989. *Recreations:* cricket, music, theatre. *Address:* 18 Stowell Crescent, Wareham, Dorset BH20 4PY. *T:* (01929) 551919.

KEMP-GEE, Mark Norman; non-executive Director: Murgitroyd Group plc, since 2001; Moncreiffe & Co. plc, since 1986; *b* 19 Dec. 1945; *s* of late Bernard Kemp-Gee and of Ann Kemp-Gee (*née* Mackilligin); *m* 1980, Hon. Lucy Lyttelton, *d* of 10th Viscount Cobham, KG, GCMG, GCVO, TD, PC; three *s*. *Educ:* Marlborough Coll.; Pembroke Coll., Oxford (MA). Chm., Greig Middleton & Co. Ltd, 1978–99; Chief Exec., Exeter Investment Gp plc, 1999–2004. Director: King & Shaxson Hldgs plc, 1993–96; Gerrard Gp plc, 1996–99. Member (C): Lambeth BC, 1982–86; Hampshire CC, 2005–. *Recreation:* point-to-pointing. *Address:* Park House, Upper Wield, Alresford, Hants SO24 9RU. *Clubs:* City of London; Oxford Union.

KEMP-WELCH, Sir John, Kt 1999; Director, HSBC Holdings, 2000–06; Chairman, London Stock Exchange, 1994–2000 (Director, 1991–2000); *b* 31 March 1936; *s* of late Peter Wellesbourne Kemp-Welch, OBE and Peggy Penelope Kemp-Welch; *m* 1964, Diana Elisabeth Leishman; one *s* three *d*. *Educ:* Abberley Hall, Worcs; Winchester Coll. Hoare & Co., 1954–58; Cazenove & Co., 1959–94 (Jt Sen. Partner, 1980–94). Chairman: Scottish Eastern Investment Trust, 1994–99 (Dir, 1993–99); Lowland Investment Co., 1993–97 (Dir, 1963–97); Claridge's Hotel, 1995–97; Martin Currie Portfolio Investment Trust plc, 1999–2000; Director: Savoy Hotel PLC, 1985–98; Royal & Sun Alliance Insurance Gp (formerly Sun Alliance Gp), 1994–99; British Invisibles, 1994–98; Pro Share, 1995–97. Dep. Chm., Financial Reporting Council, 1994–2000; Director: SFA, 1994–97; Accountancy Foundn, 2000–01. Member: City Capital Markets Cttee, 1989–94; Panel on Takeovers and Mergers, 1994–2000. Mem., Stock Exchange, 1959–86. Vice Pres., Fedn of European Stock Exchanges, 1996–98; Mem. Exec. Cttee, Federation Internationale des Bourses de Valeurs, 1994–98; President: Investor Relations Soc., 1994–2000; Securities Industry Mgt Assoc., 1994–2000. Member: (Lord Mayor of London's) City No 1 Consultancy, 1994–2000; Council, London First, 1994–96. Pres., Reed's Sch. Foundn Appeal, 2003–04; Vice-Pres., Reed's Sch., 2005–; Governor: Ditchley Foundn, 1980–; North Foreland Lodge Sch., 1980–92; Chm., King's Med. Res. Trust, 1991–2006 (Trustee, 1984–2006); Trustee: KCH Special Trustees, 1997–99; KCH Charitable Trust, 1998–99; Trustee and Mem. Council, Game Conservancy Trust, 1990–94 (Hon. Res. Fellow, 1998–); Mem. Adv. Council, PYBT, 1996–2000; Pres., Cazenove Assoc., 2005–; Trustee: Stock Exchange Benevolent Fund, 1980–2000; Sandford St Martin Trust, 1994–99; Dulverton Trust, 1994– (Dep. Chm., 2001–); Farmington Trust, 2002–; St Paul's Knightsbridge Foundn, 2002–; Chm., Lucy Kemp-Welch Meml Trust, 1965–. Mem., Highland Soc. of London, 1992–. Mem., Guild of Internat. Bankers, 2004–. Hon. FSI (MSI 1992; FSI 1996). CCMI (CBIM 1984); FRSA 1989. Hon. DBA London Guildhall Univ., 1998. Joseph Nickerson Heather Award, Joseph Nickerson Heather Improvement Foundn, 1988. *Recreations:* the hills of Perthshire, country life, City of London history, cricket nostalgia, champagne and claret, Lucy Kemp-Welch paintings, heather moorland management. *Address:* 4 Park Place, St James's, SW1A 1LP. *Clubs:* White's, City of London, Pilgrims, MCC; Essex.

KEMPE, John William Rolfe, CVO 1980; Headmaster of Gordonstoun, 1968–78; *b* 29 Oct. 1917; *s* of late William Alfred Kempe and Kunigunda Neville-Rolfe; *m* 1957, Barbara Nan Stephen, *d* of late Dr C. R. Huxtable, MC, FRCS and of Mrs Huxtable, OAM, Sydney, Australia; two *s* one *d*. *Educ:* Stowe; Clare Coll., Cambridge (Exhibitioner in Mathematics). Served war of 1939–45, RAFVR Training and Fighter Command; CO 153 and 255 Night Fighter Squadrons. Board of Trade, 1945; Firth-Brown (Overseas) Ltd, 1946–47; Head of Maths Dept, Gordonstoun, 1948–51; Principal, Hyderabad Public Sch., Deccan, India, 1951–54; Headmaster, Corby Grammar School, Northants, 1955–67. Chm., Round Square Internat. Service Cttee, 1979–87; Vice-Chm., The European Atlantic Movement, 1982–92 (Vice-Pres., 1992–). Exploration and mountaineering, Himalayas, Peru, 1952–56; Member: Cttee, Mount Everest Foundation, 1956–62; Cttee, Brathay Exploration Group, 1964–73; Foundn Trustee, Univ. of Cambridge Kurt Hahn Trust, 1986–89; Trustee: Thornton Smith Trust, 1981–96; Plevins Charity, 1987–96. *Publications:* A Family History of the Kempes, 1991; articles in Alpine Jl, Geographical Jl, Sociological Review. *Address:* 6 Marlpit Gardens, Ticehurst, E Sussex TN5 7BB. *T:* (01580) 201445. *Clubs:* Royal Air Force, Alpine.

KEMPNER, Prof. Thomas; Principal and Professor of Management Studies, Henley Management College (formerly Administrative Staff College), 1972–90, now Emeritus Professor; Director of Business Studies, Brunel University, 1972–90, now Emeritus Professor; Director, Henley Centre for Forecasting, 1974–2001 (Chairman, 1974–95); *b* 28 Feb. 1930; *s* of late Martin and Rosa Kempner; *m* 1st, 1958, June Maton (*d* 1980); two *d* (and one *d* decd); 2nd, 1981, Mrs Veronica Ann Vere-Sharp; one step *s* two step *d*. *Educ:* Denstone Coll.; University Coll. London (BSc (Econ)). Asst Administrator, Hyelm Youth Hostels, 1948–49, and part-time, 1951–55; Research Officer, Administrative Staff Coll., Henley, 1954–59; Lectr (later Sen. Tutor) in Business Studies, Sheffield Univ., 1959–63; Prof. of Management Studies, Founder, and Dir of Management Centre, Univ. of Bradford, 1963–72. Chm., Henley Distance Learning Ltd, 1980–95. Member of various cttees, including: Social Studies and Business Management Cttees of University Grants Cttee, 1966–76; Management, Education and Training Cttee of NEDO, 1969–72 (Chm. of its Student Grants Sub-Cttee); Chm., Food Industry Manpower Cttee of NEDO, 1968–71; Jt Chm., Conf. of Univ. Management Schools, 1973–75. Chm. Council, Brunel Univ., 1997–99 (Vice-Chm., 1992–97). Trustee, Greenwich Foundn for RNC, 1997–2002. CCMI (FBIM 1971). Hon. DSc Cranfield, 1976; Hon. LLD Birmingham, 1983; DUniv Brunel, 1990. Burnham Gold Medal, 1970. *Publications:* editor, author, and contributor to several books, including: Bradford Exercises in Management (with G. Wills), 1966; Is Corporate Planning Necessary? (with J. Hewkin), 1968; A Guide to the Study of Management, 1969; Management Thinkers (with J. Tillet and G. Wills), 1970; Handbook of Management, 1971, 4th edn 1987; (with K. Macmillan and K. H. Hawkins) Business and Society, 1974; Models for Participation, 1976; numerous articles in management jls. *Recreation:* travel. *Address:* Garden House, Maidensgrove, Henley-on-Thames, Oxon RG9 6EZ. *T:* (01491) 638597.

KEMPSELL, Rosemary Ann; Worldwide President, Mothers' Union, since 2007 (Trustee, 2001–06); *b* 29 Sept. 1943; *d* of Laurence and Ada Harriet Jackson; *m* 1967, John Baron Kempsell; two *d*. *Educ:* Collingwood Sch., Wallington; Willows Co. Sch., Morden; Open Univ. (BA 1992; DipEurHum 1993). Examnr, Estate Duty Office, 1963–71. Mem., Mgt Bd, S London Industrial Mission, 1993–2002. Pres., Southwark Dio., Mothers' Union, 1998–2000. *Recreations:* listening to opera, participating in choral singing, reading, swimming. *Address:* c/o Mothers' Union, Mary Sumner House, 24 Tufton Street, SW1P 3RB. *T:* (020) 7222 5533; *e-mail:* rosemary.kempsell@themothersunion.org. *Clubs:* Oriental; Purley Downs Golf.

KEMPSON, Martyn Rex; Principal Advisor to John Lyon's Charity, since 2002; *b* 31 July 1947; *s* of Horace and Winifred May Kempson; *m* 1986, Carole J. Kendall; two *s*. *Educ:* Luton Grammar Sch.; North-Western Poly. MCLIP (ALA 1968). Librarian: Luton Public Libraries, 1963–68; Buckinghamshire CC Libraries, 1968–71; London Borough of Sutton Libraries, 1971–91: Borough Librarian, 1987–88; Asst Dir of Leisure, 1988–91; Barnet London Borough Council, 1991–2002: Controller: Libraries and Arts, 1991–94; Recreation, Leisure and Arts, and Dep. Dir, Educn Services, 1995–98; Dir, Educnl Services, 1998–99; Strategic Dir of Educn and Children, 1999–2002. FRSA. *Publication:* I-Spy Football, 1991. *Recreations:* supporting Luton Town FC, tennis, Barnet Judo Club.

KEMPSON, Prof. Ruth Margaret, (Mrs M. J. Pinner), FBA 1989; Leverhulme Personal Research Professor, King's College London, 1999–2004; *b* 26 June 1944; *d* of Edwin Garnett Hone Kempson and Margaret Cecilia Kempson; *m* 1973, Michael John Pinner; two *s*. *Educ:* Univ. of Birmingham (BA (2 ii) Music and English); Univ. of London (MA (with dist.) Mod. English Language 1969; PhD Linguistics 1972). Res. Asst to Survey of English Usage, UCL, 1969–70; School of Oriental and African Studies: Lectr in Linguistics, 1971–85; Reader in Gen. Linguistics, 1985–87, Prof. of Gen. Linguistics, 1987–99, Univ. of London; Head of Linguistics Dept, 1992–96. Vis. Prof. in Semantics, Univ. of Massachusetts, 1982–83. Pres., Linguistics Assoc. of GB, 1986–91. *Publications:* Presupposition and the Delimitation of Semantics, 1975; Semantic Theory, 1977; Mental Representations: the interface between language and reality, 1988; (jtly) Dynamic Syntax: the flow of language understanding, 2000; articles in Linguistics and Philosophy, Jl of Linguistics and edited collections. *Address:* Philosophy Department, King's College London, Strand, WC2R 2LS.

KEMSLEY, 3rd Viscount *cr* 1945, of Dropmore, co. Bucks; **Richard Gomer Berry;** Bt 1928; Baron Kemsley 1936; *b* 17 April 1951; *o s* of Hon. Denis Gomer Berry, 2nd *s* of 1st Viscount Kemsley, GBE and Pamela Berry (*née* Wellesley); *S* uncle, 1999; *m* 1994, Elizabeth Jane Barker; two *s*. *Educ:* Eton. *Heir: s* Hon. Luke Gomer Berry, *b* 2 Feb. 1998. *Address:* Church Hill Farm, Church Lane, Brockenhurst, Hants SO42 7UB.

KENDAL, Felicity Ann, CBE 1995; actress; *d* of late Geoffrey and Laura Kendal; *m* (marr. diss.); one *s*; *m* 1983, Michael Rudman, *qv* (marr. diss. 1994); one *s*. *Educ:* six convents in India. First appeared on stage at age of 9 months, when carried on as the Changeling boy in A Midsummer Night's Dream; grew up touring India and Far East with parents' theatre co., playing pageboys at age of eight and graduating through Puck, at nine, to parts such as Viola in Twelfth Night, Jessica in The Merchant of Venice, and Ophelia in Hamlet; returned to England, 1965; made London debut, Carla in Minor Murder, Savoy, 1967; Katherine in Henry V, and Lika in The Promise, Leicester, 1968; Amaryllis in Back to Methuselah, Nat. Theatre, 1969; Hermia in A Midsummer Night's Dream, and Hero in Much Ado About Nothing, Regent's Park, 1970; Anne Danby in Kean, Oxford, 1970, London, 1971; Romeo and Juliet, 'Tis Pity She's A Whore, and The Three Arrows, 1972; The Norman Conquests, Globe, 1974; Viktosha in Once Upon a Time, Bristol, 1976; Arms and The Man, Greenwich, 1978; Mara in Clouds, Duke of York's, 1978; Constance Mozart in Amadeus, NT, 1979; Desdemona in Othello, NT, 1980; Christopher in On the Razzle, NT, 1981; Paula in The Second Mrs Tanqueray, NT, 1981; The Real Thing, Strand, 1982; Jumpers, Aldwych, 1985; Made in Bangkok, Aldwych, 1986; Hapgood, Aldwych, 1988; Ivanov, and Much Ado About Nothing, Strand, 1989 (Best Actress Award, Evening Standard); Hidden Laughter, Vaudeville, 1990; Tartuffe, Playhouse, 1991; Heartbreak House, Haymarket, 1992; Arcadia, NT, 1993; An Absolute Turkey, Globe, 1994; Indian Ink, Aldwych, 1995; Mind Millie for Me, Haymarket, 1996; Waste, and The Seagull, Old Vic, 1997; Alarms and Excursions, Gielgud, 1998; Fallen Angels, Apollo, 2000; Humble Boy, Gielgud, 2002; Happy Days, Arts Th., 2003; Amy's View, Garrick, 2006; The Vortex, Apollo, 2008. *Television:* four series of The Good Life, 1975–77; Viola in Twelfth Night, 1979; Solo, 1980, 2nd series 1982; The Mistress, 1985, 2nd series 1986; The Camomile Lawn, 1992; Honey for Tea, 1994; How Proust Can Save Your Life, 1999; Rosemary and Thyme, 3 series 2003–05; plays and serials. *Films:* Shakespeare Wallah, 1965; Valentino, 1976. Variety Club Most Promising Newcomer, 1974, Best Actress, 1979, 2001; Clarence Derwent Award, 1980; Variety Club Woman of the Year Best Actress Award, 1984. *Publication:* White Cargo (memoirs), 1998. *Recreations:* reading, working. *Address:* c/o Chatto & Linnit, 123A King's Road, SW3 4PL. *T:* (020) 7352 7722.

KENDALL, Bridget, MBE 1994; Diplomatic Correspondent, BBC News, since 1998; *b* 27 April 1956; *d* of Prof. David George Kendall, FRS. *Educ:* Lady Margaret Hall, Oxford (BA Hons); Harvard Univ. (Harkness Fellow); Moscow State Univ.; St Antony's Coll., Oxford (Hon. Fellow, 2005). Joined BBC, 1983: trainee, World Service, 1983; presenter, Newsnight, 1983–84; producer/reporter, World Service, 1984–89; Moscow Corresp., 1989–93; Washington Corresp., 1994–98. Jubilee Lectr, St Antony's Coll., Oxford, 2000; Roskill Lectr, Churchill Coll., Cambridge, 2003. Member, Advisory Boards: Russia and Eurasia Prog., Chatham House, 2000–; RUSI Council, 2001–05. DUniv UCE, 1999; Hon. LLD: St Andrews, 2001; Exeter, 2002. *Publications:* (jtly) David the Invincible, 1980; (contrib.) The Day that Shook the World, 2001; (contrib.) The Battle for Iraq, 2003. *Recreations:* literature, cinema, tennis, hiking, square-dancing. *Address:* Room 2505, BBC TV Centre, Wood Lane, W12 7RJ. *T:* (020) 8743 8000, *Fax:* (020) 8743 7591.

See also W. S. Kendall.

KENDALL, David William; Chairman, G-T-P Group Ltd, since 2006; *b* 8 May 1935; *s* of William Jack Kendall and Alma May Kendall; *m* 1st, 1960, Delphine Hitchcock (marr. diss.); one *s* one *d*; 2nd, 1973, Elisabeth Rollison; one *s* one *d*. *Educ:* Enfield Grammar School; Southend High School. FCA. Elles Reeve, Shell-Mex & BP, Irish Shell & BP, 1955–70; British Petroleum Co.: Crude Oil Sales Manager, 1971–72; Manager, Bulk Trading Div., 1973–74; Organisation Planning Cttee, 1975; BP New Zealand: Gen. Manager, 1976–79; Man. Dir and Chief Exec., 1979–82; Chm., BP SW Pacific, 1979–82; BP Oil: Finance and Planning Dir, 1982–85; Man. Dir and Chief Exec., 1985–88; Director: BP Chemicals Internat., 1985–88; BP Oil Internat., 1985–88; Associated Octel Co., 1985–88. Chairman: Bunzl, 1990–93 (Dir, 1988–93); Ruberoid plc, 1993–2000; Whitecroft plc, 1993–2000; Blagden Industries plc, 1994–2000; Meyer Internat., 1994–95; Celtic Energy Ltd, 1994–2003; Wagon Industrial Hldgs, subseq. Wagon plc, 1997–2005; Danka Business Systems plc, 1998–2001 (Dir, 1993–2001); Dep. Chm.,

British Coal Corp., 1989–91; Director: STC plc, 1988–90; Gowrings plc, 1993–2005; South Wales Electricity plc, 1993–96; BSI, 2000–05. President: UK Petroleum Industries Assoc., 1987–88; Oil Industries Club, 1988. *Recreations:* golf, music, France and its history. *Address:* 41 Albion Street, W2 2AU. *T:* (020) 7258 1955. *Clubs:* Rye Golf, Royal Mid Surrey Golf.

KENDALL, Rev. Frank; Member, Northern Rent Assessment Panel, since 1997; Non-stipendiary Priest, since 2002, and Chairman, World Development Group, since 2007, diocese of Blackburn; *b* 15 Dec. 1940; *s* of Norman and Violet Kendall; *m* 1965, Brenda Pickin; one *s* one *d. Educ:* Bradford Grammar School; Corpus Christi College, Cambridge (MA Classics); Southwark Ordination Course (London Univ. Dip. in Religious Studies). MPBW, 1962; DEA, 1967–68; MPBW, DoE and Dept of Transport, 1969–89; Under Secretary 1984; Chief Exec., St Helens MBC, 1989–91; Venue Develt Manager, British Olympic Bid, 1992; Inspector of Schs, 1993–2000. Ordained deacon, 1974, priest, 1975; Hon. Curate: Lingfield, dio. Southwark, 1974–75 and 1978–82; Sketty, dio. Swansea and Brecon, 1975–78; Limpsfield, dio. Southwark, 1982–84; Licensed Preacher, dio. of Manchester, 1984–89; Non-stipendiary Priest, 1989–2001 and Chm., Bd for Social Responsibility, 1996–2001, dio. of Liverpool. FRSA 1990. *Recreations:* painting: (i) pictures, (ii) decorating. *Address:* 52 Kingsway, Penwortham, Preston PR1 0ED. *T:* (01772) 748021.

KENDALL, Graham; *b* 24 Sept. 1943; *s* of Robert David Kendall and Phillis Margaret Moreton; *m* 1968, Helen Sheila Blackburn; two *s* two *d. Educ:* Helsby Grammar Sch.; Leicester Univ. (BSc); Liverpool Univ. (Post-grad. CertEd). Entered Civil Service as Asst Principal, 1966; DTI; joined Dept of Employment, subseq. DFEE, 1981; Grade 3, 1990; Chief Exec., Sheffield Develt Corp. (on secondment), 1990–97. *Recreations:* running, gardening, family. *Address:* 56 Blackamoor Road, Dore, Sheffield S17 3GJ. *T:* (0114) 236 4533.

KENDALL, Prof. Kevin, FRS 1993; Professor of Formulation Engineering, University of Birmingham, since 2000; *b* 2 Dec. 1943; *s* of Cyril Kendall and Margaret (*née* Swarbrick); *m* 1969, Patricia Jennifer Heyes; one *s* one *d. Educ:* London Univ. (BSc Physics External); PhD Cantab. Joseph Lucas, 1961–66; Cavendish Lab., 1966–69; British Rail Research, 1969–71; Monash Univ., 1972–74 (QEII fellowship); Akron Univ., 1974; ICI Runcorn, 1974–93; Prof. of Materials Science, Keele Univ., 1993–2000. *Publications:* Molecular Adhesion and its Applications, 2001; (with S. C. Singhal) High Temperature Solid Oxide Fuel Cells, 2003; papers in learned jls on adhesion, fracture, ceramics, material properties. *Recreation:* squash. *Address:* Wycherley, Tower Road, Ashley Heath, Market Drayton, Shropshire TF9 4PY. *T:* (01630) 672665.

KENDALL, Peter Ashley; President, National Farmers' Union, since 2006; *b* Bedford, 8 May 1960; *s* of John and Jasmine Kendall; *m* 1999, Emma McAlley; two *s* one *d. Educ:* Nottingham Univ. (BA Agricl Econs). Farmer, family business, farming and contracting. Chm., Cereals, 2003, Dep. Pres., 2004–06, NFU. Mem., Rural Climate Change Panel, DEFRA, 2006–. Vice Pres., COPA, 2007–. Mem., Policy Issues Council, IGD, 2006–. *Recreations:* countryside, shooting, occasional veteran's Rugby, ski-ing. *Address:* Church Farm, Eyeworth, Sandy, Beds SG19 2HH. *T:* (01767) 631262, *Fax:* (01767) 631278; *e-mail:* peter.kendall@nfu.org.uk.

KENDALL, Raymond Edward, QPM 1984; Secretary General, International Criminal Police Organization (Interpol), 1985–2000, now Hon. Secretary General; *b* 5 Oct. 1933; *m. Educ:* Simon Langton School, Canterbury; Exeter College, Oxford (MA Hons). RAF, 1951–53 (principally Malaya). Asst Supt of Police, Uganda Police, 1956–62; Metropolitan Police, New Scotland Yard, 1962–86 (principally Special Branch). Mem., Supervisory Cttee, Eur. Anti-Fraud Office. Mem., Forensic Sci. Soc. Editor-in-Chief: Counterfeits and Forgeries; Internat. Criminal Police Review. *Recreations:* shooting, golf. *Address:* BP 202, 69657 Villefranche-Cedex, France. *Clubs:* Special Forces; Chief Constables.

KENDALL, Prof. Wilfrid Stephen, DPhil; Professor of Statistics, University of Warwick, since 1994; *b* 5 Nov. 1954; *s* of Prof. David George Kendall, FRS; *m* 1984, Catherine Mary Usher; two *s* two *d. Educ:* Perse Sch., Cambridge; Queen's Coll., Oxford (BA 1975; MA 1986); Linacre Coll., Oxford (MSc 1976; DPhil 1979). Lectr, in Mathematical Stats, Univ. of Hull, 1978–84; Sen. Lectr in Stats, Univ. of Strathclyde, 1984–88; University of Warwick: Lectr in Stats, 1988–91; Reader, 1991–94; Chm., Dept of Stats, 1999–2002. Co-Dir, Acad. for PhD Trng in Statistics, 2006–. Scientific Sec., Bernoulli Soc., 1996–2000. *Publications:* (jtly) Stochastic Geometry and its Applications, 1985, 2nd edn 1995; (jtly) New Directions in Dirichlet Forms, 1998; (ed jtly) Markov chain Monte Carlo: innovations and applications, 2005; contrib. numerous papers to learned jls. *Recreations:* family, hill-walking. *Address:* Department of Statistics, University of Warwick, Coventry CV4 7AL. *T:* (024) 7652 3082, *Fax:* (024) 7652 4532; *e-mail:* wsk@wilfridkendall.co.uk.
See also B. Kendall.

KENDRICK, Dominic John; QC 1997; *b* 23 Feb. 1955; *s* of late Anthony Kendrick and Joan Kendrick; *m* 1984, Marice Chantal; one *s* two *d. Educ:* St Ambrose Coll.; Trinity Coll., Cambridge (BA Hons, MA); City Univ. (Dip. Law); Inns of Court Sch. of Law. Called to the Bar, Middle Temple, 1981. *Recreations:* old books, restoration of old houses, theatre. *Address:* 7 King's Bench Walk, Temple, EC4Y 7DS. *T:* (020) 7583 0404.

KENDRICK, Graham Andrew; song and hymn writer; *b* 2 Aug. 1950; *s* of Maurice and Olive Kendrick; *m* 1976, Jill Gibson; four *d. Educ:* Avery Hill Coll. of Educn (Cert Ed 1972). Music Dir, British Youth for Christ, 1976–80; Kendrick & Stevenson (music and mime duo), 1981–84; Mem., Leadership Team, Ichthus Christian Fellowship, 1984–2004; Co-founder, March for Jesus, 1987. Songs and hymns sung in many languages worldwide; has recorded numerous albums, 1971–. Hon. DD Brunel, 2000. *Publications:* Worship, 1984; Ten Worshipping Churches, 1987; March for Jesus, 1992; Shine Jesus Shine, 1992; Awakening our Cities for God, 1993. *Recreations:* family, walking, music. *Address:* c/o Make Way Music, PO Box 320, Tunbridge Wells, Kent TN2 9DE; *e-mail:* info@makewaymusic.com.

KENEALLY, Thomas Michael, AO 1983; FRSL; FAAAS; author; *b* 7 Oct. 1935; *s* of Edmond Thomas Keneally; *m* 1965, Judith Mary Martin; two *d.* Studied for NSW Bar. Schoolteacher until 1965; Commonwealth Literary Fellowship, 1966, 1968, 1972; Lectr in Drama, Univ. of New England, 1968–69. Vis. Prof., Dept of English, Univ. of California, Irvine, 1985; Berg Prof., Dept of English, New York Univ., 1988; Distinguished Prof., Dept of English and Comparative Lit., Univ. of Calif, Irvine, 1991–95. Chm., Australian Republican Movement, 1991–94. Member: (inaugural) Australia-China Council, 1978–83; Adv. Panel, Australian Constitutional Commn, 1985–88; Literary Arts Bd, Australia, 1985–88; Chm., Aust. Soc. Authors, 1987–90 (Mem. Council, 1985–); Pres., Nat. Book Council Australia, 1985–89. FRSL 1973. Silver City (screenplay, with Sophia Turkiewicz), 1985. Hon. DLitt: Queensland, 1993; NUI, 1994; Fairleigh Dickinson, NJ, 1994; Western Sydney, 1997. *Publications:* The Place at Whitton, 1964; The Fear, 1965, 2nd edn 1973; Bring Larks and Heroes, 1967, 2nd edn 1973; Three Cheers for the Paraclete, 1968; The Survivor, 1969; A Dutiful Daughter, 1971; The Chant of Jimmie Blacksmith, 1972 (filmed 1978); Blood Red, Sister Rose, 1974; Gossip from the Forest, 1975 (TV film, 1979); The Lawgiver, 1975; Season in Purgatory, 1976; A Victim of the Aurora, 1977; Ned Kelly and the City of the Bees, 1978; Passenger, 1979; Confederates, 1979; Schindler's Ark, 1982, reissued as Schindler's List, 1994 (Booker Prize; LA Times Fiction Prize; filmed as Schindler's List, 1994); Outback, 1983; The Cut-Rate Kingdom, 1984; A Family Madness, 1985; The Playmaker, 1987 (stage adaptation, perf. Royal Court, 1988); Towards Asmara, 1989; Flying Hero Class, 1991 (also screenplay); The Place where Souls are born, 1992; Now and in Time to be, 1992; Woman of the Inner Sea, 1992 (also screenplay); Memoirs from a Young Republic, 1993; Jacko, 1993; The Utility Player (biog.), 1994; A River Town, 1995; Homebush Boy: a memoir, 1995; The Great Shame, 1998; Bettany's Book, 2000; American Scoundrel: the life of the notorious Civil War General Dan Sickles, 2002; The Office of Innocence, 2002; The Tyrant's Novel, 2003; Lincoln, 2003; The Widow and Her Hero, 2007. *Recreations:* swimming, crosswords, hiking, cross-country ski-ing. *Address:* c/o Deborah Rogers, 20 Powis Mews, W11 1JN.

KENILOREA, Rt Hon. Sir Peter (Kauona Keninaraiso'ona), KBE 1982; PC 1979; Speaker, Solomon Islands Parliament, since 2001; Ombudsman of the Solomon Islands, 1996–2001; Prime Minister of the Solomon Islands, 1978–81 and 1984–86; *b* Takataka, Malaita, 23 May 1943; *m* 1971, Margaret Kwanairara; two *s* two *d. Educ:* Univ. and Teachers' Coll., NZ (Dip. Ed.). Teacher, King George VI Secondary Sch., 1968–70. Asst Sec., Finance, 1971; Admin. Officer, Dist Admin, 1971–73; Lands Officer, 1973–74; Dep. Sec. to Cabinet and to Chief Minister, 1974–75; Dist Comr, Eastern Solomon Is, 1975–76; MLA, subseq. MP, East Are-Are, 1976–91; Chief Minister, Solomon Is, 1976–78; Leader of the Opposition, 1981–84; Dep. Prime Minister, 1987–89; Minister of Foreign Affairs, 1987–89, for Foreign Affairs and Trade Relations, 1990. Dir, Forum Fisheries Agency, 1991–94. Silver Jubilee Medal, 1977; Solomon Is Indep. Medal, 1978. *Publications:* political and scientific, numerous articles. *Address:* (office) Kalala House, PO Box 535, Honiara, Guadalcanal, Solomon Islands.

KENILWORTH, 4th Baron *cr* 1937, of Kenilworth; **(John) Randle Siddeley;** Managing Director, Siddeley Landscapes, since 1976; Director, John Siddeley International Ltd; *b* 16 June 1954; *s* of John Tennant Davenport Siddeley (3rd Baron Kenilworth) and of Jacqueline Paulette, *d* of late Robert Gelpi; *S* father, 1981; *m* 1st, 1983, Kim (marr. diss. 1989), *o d* of Danie Serfontein, Newcastle upon Tyne; 2nd, 1991, Mrs Kiki McDonough; two *s. Educ:* Northease Manor, near Lewes, Sussex; West Dean College (studied Restoration of Antique Furniture); London College of Furniture. Worked at John Siddeley International as interior designer/draughtsman, 1975; formed own company, Siddeley Landscapes, as landscape gardener, 1976; formed Randle Siddeley Associates, as landscape designer, 1994. *Recreation:* ski-ing. *Heir: s* Hon. William Randle John Siddeley, *b* 24 Jan. 1992. *Address:* Randle Siddeley Associates, 3 Palmerston Court, Palmerston Way, SW8 4AJ. *Clubs:* St James's, Annabel's.

KENNARD, Prof. Christopher, PhD; FRCP, FMedSci; Professor of Clinical Neurology, and Head, Department of Clinical Neurology, University of Oxford, since 2008; *b* 5 Jan. 1946; *s* of late Keith and Enid Kennard; *m* 1973, Cherry Fay Mortimer; two *d. Educ:* St Marylebone Grammar Sch., London; Charing Cross Hosp. Med. Sch., Univ. of London (MB BS Hons 1970; PhD 1978). FRCP 1988. Research Fellow: NIMR, 1973–76; Neuro-ophthalmology Unit, Univ. of Calif, San Francisco, 1980; Jun. hosp. appts, Charing Cross Hosp. and London Hosp., 1976–81; Consultant Neurologist, Royal London Hosp., 1981–91; Prof. of Clinical Neurology, Charing Cross and Westminster Med. Sch., 1991–97; Imperial College London: Prof. of Clinical Neurology, 1997–2008; Hd, Div. of Neurosci. and Psychol Medicine, 1997–2003; Dean, Charing Cross Campus, 2001–08; Dep. Principal, Faculty of Medicine, and Hd, Dept of Visual Neurosci., subseq. Dept of Clinical Neurosci., 2003–08; Clinical Dir, Neuroscis, Hammersmith Hosp. NHS Trust, 1998–2004 (Chief of Service, 1995–98). Non-exec. Mem., W London Mental Health NHS Trust, 2001–07. Chm., Cttee on Neurology, RCP, 1997–2005. Mem., MRC, 2006–08 (Mem., 2000–04, Chm., 2006–, Neuroscience and Mental Health Bd). Pres., Assoc. of British Neurologists, 2003–05 (Asst Sec., 1990–92; Hon. Sec., 1992–95). Sec.-Gen., World Congress of Neurol., 2001. Trustee: Migraine Trust, 1991–2008; Brain and Spine Foundn, 1993–2005. Ed., Jl Neurology, Neurosurgery and Psychiatry, 1997–2003. FMedSci 2001 (Mem. Council, 2004–07). *Publications:* editor, several books on clinical neurology; papers on cognitive neuroscience and neuro-ophthalmology. *Recreation:* music. *Address:* Department of Clinical Neurology, Level 6, West Wing, John Radcliffe Hospital, Headley Way, Headington, Oxford OX3 9DU. *Club:* Athenæum.

KENNARD, Dr Olga, (Lady Burgen), OBE 1988; ScD; FRS 1987; Director, Cambridge Crystallographic Data Centre, 1965–97; *b* 23 March 1924; *d* of Joir and Catherina Weisz; *m* 1st, 1948, David William Kennard (marr. diss. 1961); two *d*; 2nd, 1993, Sir Arnold Burgen, *qv. Educ:* Newnham Coll., Cambridge (BA 1945, MA 1948); Lucy Cavendish Coll., Cambridge (ScD 1973). Res. Asst, Cavendish Laboratory, Cambridge, 1944–48; MRC Scientific Staff: Inst. of Ophthalmology, London, 1948–51; Nat. Inst. for Med. Res., London, 1951–61; seconded to University Chemical Laboratory, Cambridge, 1961–71; MRC special appt, 1974–89. Mem. Council, Royal Soc., 1995–97. Trustee, British Mus., 2004–. Hon. LLD Cantab, 2003. *Publications:* about 200 pubns in field of X-ray structure determination of organic and bioactive molecules and correlation between structure, chemical properties and biological activity, and technical innovations in X-ray crystallography; ed 20 standard reference books. *Recreations:* music, swimming, architecture. *Address:* Keelson, 8A Hills Avenue, Cambridge CB1 7XA. *T:* (01223) 415381.

KENNAWAY, Sir John (Lawrence), 5th Bt *cr* 1791; *b* 7 Sept. 1933; *s* of Sir John Kennaway, 4th Bt and Mary Felicity (*d* 1991), *yr d* of late Rev. Chancellor Ponsonby; *S* father, 1956; *m* 1961, Christina Veronica Urszenyi, MB, ChB (Cape Town) (marr. diss. 1976); one *s* two *d. Educ:* Harrow; Trinity Coll., Cambridge. *Heir: s* John Michael Kennaway [*b* 17 Feb. 1962; *m* 1988, Lucy Frances, *yr d* of Dr Jeremy Houlton Bradshaw-Smith; two *d*]. *Address:* Escot, Ottery St Mary, Devon EX11 1LU.

KENNEDY, family name of **Marquess of Ailsa**.

KENNEDY OF THE SHAWS, Baroness *cr* 1997 (Life Peer), of Cathcart in the City of Glasgow; **Helena Ann Kennedy;** QC 1991; *b* 12 May 1950; *d* of Joshua Patrick Kennedy and Mary Veronica (*née* Jones); partner, 1978–84, (Roger) Iain Mitchell; one *s*; *m* 1986, Dr Iain Louis Hutchison; one *s* one *d. Educ:* Holyrood Secondary Sch., Glasgow; Council of Legal Educn. Called to the Bar, Gray's Inn, 1972, Bencher, 1999; established chambers at: Garden Court, 1974; Tooks Court, 1984; Doughty St, 1990. Member: Bar Council, 1990–93; Cttee, Assoc. of Women Barristers, 1991–92; Nat. Bd, Women's Legal Defence Fund, 1989–91; Council, Howard League for Penal Reform, 1989– (Chm., commn of inquiry into violence in penal instns for children, report, 1995); CIBA Commn into Child Sexual Abuse, 1981–83; Exec. Cttee, NCCL, 1983–85; Bd, Minority Access to Legal Profession Project, Poly. of South Bank, 1984–85; British Council Law Adv. Cttee, 1995–98; Chairman: British Council, 1998–2004; Human Genetics Commn, 2000–.

Chancellor, Oxford Brookes Univ., 1994–2001. Chairman: Haldane Soc., 1983–86 (Vice-Pres., 1986–); Charter '88, 1992–97; Standing Cttee for Youth Justice, NACRO, 1993–; Cttee on widening participation of FEFC, 1995–97 (report, Learning Works); Leader of inquiry into health, envmtl and safety aspects of Atomic Weapons Establishment, Aldermaston (report, 1993). Member: Adv. Council, World Bank Inst.; Internat. Task Force On Terrorism, IBA, 2001–02. Commissioner: BAFTA inquiry into future of BBC, 1990; Hamlyn Nat. Commn on Educn, 1991–. Chm., London Internat. Fest. of Theatre, 1993–2002. Member Board: City Limits Magazine, 1982–84; Counsel Magazine, 1990–; Hampstead Theatre, 1989–98; Chm., Arts and Business, 2006–. Broadcaster: first female moderator, Hypotheticals (Granada) on surrogate motherhood and artificial insemination; presenter: Heart of the Matter, BBC, 1987; Putting Women in the Picture, BBC2, 1987; The Trial of Lady Chatterley's Lover, Radio 4, 1990; Raw Deal, series of progs on med. negligence, BBC2, 1990; co-producer, Women Behind Bars, Channel 4, 1990; presenter, The Maguires: forensic evidence on trial, BBC2, 1991; creator, drama series, Blind Justice, BBC, 1988; host, After Dark, Channel 4, 1988; presenter, Time Gentlemen Please, BBC Scotland, 1994. FRSA; FCGI. Hon. Fellow, Inst. of Advanced Legal Studies, Univ. of London, 1997; Hon. Mem., Acad. Universelle des Cultures, Paris. Holds 18 hon. degrees. UK Woman of Europe Award, 1995. *Publications:* (jtly) The Bar on Trial, 1978; (jtly) Child Abuse Within the Family, 1984; (jtly) Balancing Acts, 1989; Eve was Framed, 1992; Just Law, 2004; lectures; contribs on issues connected with law, civil liberties and women. *Recreations:* theatre, spending time with family and friends. *Address:* House of Lords, SW1A 0PW. *T:* and *Fax:* (01708) 379482; *e-mail:* hilary.hard@btinternet.com.

KENNEDY, Maj.-Gen. Alasdair Ian Gordon, CB 1996; CBE 1991 (OBE); Secretary, Royal Automobile Club, since 1998 (Assistant General Secretary, 1997); *b* 6 Oct. 1945; *m* 1980, Meade Funsten; one *s* one *d*. *Educ:* RMCS. psc. Commnd Gordon Highlanders, 1966; Brig. 1988, Maj.-Gen. 1991. Comdr, HQ 24 Airmobile Bde, 1988–90; Dir Gen., Territorial Army, 1992–95; Sen. Army Mem., RCDS, 1995–96, retired 1997. Hon. Col, Tayforth Univs OTC, 1991–97. *Address:* Royal Automobile Club, 89 Pall Mall, SW1Y 5HS.

KENNEDY, (Alastair) James; Director, International Office, University of Warwick, since 2008; *b* 6 May 1954; *s* of David Kennedy and Janet Farquahar Kennedy; *m* 1982, Kathryn Patricia Lawry; two *s* two *d*. *Educ:* Univ. of Exeter (BA Modern Langs); Inst. of Educn, Univ. of London (PGCE); Edinburgh Univ. (MSc Applied Linguistics). VSO, Laos, then Tanzania, 1978; British Council: Kuwait, 1982–84; Malaysia, 1984–86; London, 1986–90; Swaziland, 1990–94; Malaŵi, 1994–98; Manchester, 1998–2001; Kazakhstan, 2001–04; Regional Dir, Russia, 2004–08. *Address:* University of Warwick, Coventry CV4 7AL.

KENNEDY, A(lfred) James, CBE 1979; DSc (London), PhD (London); FREng, MIET, FIMMM, FInstP; physicist; *b* 6 Nov. 1921; *m* 1950, Anna Jordan (*d* 1986); no *c*. *Educ:* Haberdashers' Aske's Hatcham Sch.; University Coll., London (BSc (Physics) 1943; Fellow 1976). Commissioned R Signals, 1944; Staff Major (Telecommunications) Central Comd, Agra, India, 1945–46 and at Northern Comd, Rawalpindi, 1946–47; Asst Lectr in Physics, UCL 1947–50; Res. Fellow, Davy-Faraday Lab. of Royal Institution, London, 1950–51; Royal Society, Armourers' and Brasiers' Research Fellow in Metallurgy (at Royal Institution), 1951–54; Head of Metal Physics Sect., BISRA, 1954–57; Prof. of Materials and Head of Dept. of Materials, Coll. of Aeronautics, Cranfield, 1957–66; Dir, British Non-Ferrous Metals Res. Assoc., later BNF Metals Technol. Centre, Wantage, 1966–78; Dir of Research, Delta Metal Co., and Man. Dir, Delta Materials Research Ltd, 1978–81; Dep. Dir, Technical Change Centre, 1981–86; Dir, BL Technology Ltd, 1979–83. Vis. Prof. in Metallurgy, Imperial Coll. of Science and Technol., London, 1981–86. Institution of Metallurgists: Pres., 1976–77; a Vice Pres., 1971–74, 1975–76; Mem. Council, 1968–76. President: Inst. of Metals, 1970–71 (Mem. Council, 1968–73; Fellow, 1973); Engrg Section, BAAS, 1983; Member: Metallurgy Cttee, CNAA, 1965–71; ARC, 1967–70, 1971–74, 1977–80 (also Mem., ARC cttees); Adv. Council on Materials, 1970–71; Council, The Metals Soc., 1974–84 (Platinum Medallist, 1977); Inst. of Physics, 1968–71; SRC, 1974–78; Metall. and Mat. Cttee, SRC, 1970–75 (Chm. 1973–74); Engrg Bd, 1973–78; Council of Env. Sci. and Eng., 1973–78; Adv. Council for Applied R&D, 1976–80; Mat. and Chem. Res. Requirements Bd, DoI, 1981–83 (Chm., Non-Ferrous Metals Cttee); Chm., Council of Sci. and Tech. Insts, 1983–84. Fellow, Amer. Soc. Met., 1972. Pres., Brit. Soc. of Rheology, 1964–66; a Governor, Nat. Inst. for Agric. Engrg, 1966–74. Hon. DSc Aston, 1980. *Publications:* Processes of Creep and Fatigue in Metals, 1962; The Materials Background to Space Technology, 1964; Creep and Stress Relaxation in Metals (English edn), 1965; (ed) High Temperature Materials, 1968; research papers and articles, mainly on physical aspects of deformation and fracture in crystalline materials, particularly metals. *Recreations:* music, painting. *Address:* Woodhill, Milton under Wychwood, Chipping Norton, Oxford OX7 6EP. *T:* (01993) 830334. *Club:* Athenæum.

KENNEDY, Alison Louise; writer; *b* 22 Oct. 1965; *d* of Robert Alan Kennedy and Edwardine Mildred Kennedy. *Educ:* Warwick Univ. (BA Hons Theatre Studies and Dramatic Arts). Community arts worker, Clydebank and Dist, 1980–89; Writer-in-Residence: Hamilton and E Kilbride Social Work Dept, 1989–91; Project Ability, 1989–95; Copenhagen Univ., 1995; Lectr (pt-time), Creative Writing Prog., St Andrews Univ., 2003–07; Associate Prof., Creative Writing Prog., Warwick Univ., 2007–. *Publications:* Night Geometry and the Garscadden Trains, 1990; Looking for the Possible Dance, 1993; Now That You're Back, 1994; So I Am Glad, 1995; The Life and Death of Colonel Blimp, 1997; Original Bliss, 1997; On Bullfighting, 1999; Everything You Need, 1999; Indelible Acts, 2002; Paradise, 2004; Day, 2007. *Recreations:* few. *Address:* c/o Antony Harwood, Antony Harwood Ltd, 103 Walton Street, Oxford OX2 6EB. *T:* (01865) 559615, *Fax:* (01865) 310660; *e-mail:* ant@antonyharwood.com.

KENNEDY, Anthony McLeod; Associate Justice of the Supreme Court of the United States, since 1988; *b* 23 July 1936; *s* of Anthony J. Kennedy and Gladys Kennedy; *m* Mary Davis; two *s* one *d*. *Educ:* Stanford Univ. (AB 1958); LSE; Harvard Univ. (LLB 1961). Mem., Calif. Bar, 1962, US Tax Court Bar, 1971. Associate, Thelen Marrin Johnson & Bridges, San Francisco, 1961–63; sole practice, 1963–67; partner Evans, Jackson & Kennedy, 1967–75. Prof. of Constitutional Law, McGeorge Sch. of Law, Univ. of Pacific, 1965–88; Judge, US Court of Appeals, 9th Circuit, Sacramento, 1976–88. Hon. Fellow: Amer. Bar Assoc.; Amer. Coll. of Trial Lawyers. Hon. Bencher, Inner Temple. *Address:* Supreme Court Building, 1 First Street NE, Washington, DC 20543, USA.

KENNEDY, Prof. Arthur Colville, CBE 1992; FRCPE, FRCPGlas, FRCP; FRSE 1984; Muirhead Professor of Medicine, Glasgow University, 1978–88; *b* 23 Oct. 1922; *s* of Thomas and Johanna Kennedy; *m* 1947, Agnes White Taylor; two *d* (one *s* decd). *Educ:* Whitehill Sch., Glasgow; Univ. of Glasgow. MB ChB 1945; MD 1956. FRCPE 1960; FRCPGlas 1964; FRCP 1977; FRCPI 1988. Hon. Consultant in Medicine, Royal Infirmary, Glasgow, 1959–88; Titular Professor, Univ. of Glasgow, 1969–78. Former External Examiner to Univs of Edinburgh, Dundee, Manchester, Dublin, West Indies, Hong Kong, Kuwait, Malaysia. Member: Greater Glasgow Health Bd, 1985–89; GMC, 1989–92 (Chm., Professional and Linguistic Bd, 1987–89). President: RCPSG, 1986–88; BMA, 1991–92; Royal Medico-Chirurgical Soc. of Glasgow, 1971–72; Europ. Dialysis and Transplant Assoc., 1972–75; Scottish Soc. of Physicians, 1983–84; Harveian Soc. of Edinburgh, 1985. Hon. FACP 1987; Hon. FRACP 1988. *Publications:* various papers on renal disease. *Recreations:* gardening, walking, reading, photography. *Address:* 16 Boclair Crescent, Bearsden, Glasgow G61 2AG. *T:* (0141) 942 5326. *Club:* Royal Over-Seas League.

KENNEDY, Rt Hon. Charles (Peter); PC 1999; MP (Lib Dem) Ross, Skye and Lochaber, since 2005 (Ross, Cromarty and Skye, 1983–97, Ross, Skye and Inverness West, 1997–2005; SDP, 1983–88, Lib Dem, 1988–2005); Leader of the Liberal Democrats, 1999–2006; *b* Inverness, 25 Nov. 1959; *yr s* of Ian Kennedy, crofter, and Mary McVarish MacEachen; *m* 2002, Sarah Gurling; one *s*. *Educ:* Lochaber High Sch., Fort William; Univ. of Glasgow (joint MA Hons Philosophy and Politics). President, Glasgow Univ. Union, 1980–81; winner, British Observer Mace for Univ. Debating, 1982. Journalist, BBC Highland, Inverness, 1982; Fulbright Schol. and Associate Instructor in Dept of Speech Communication, Indiana Univ., Bloomington Campus, 1982–83. SDP spokesman on health, social services, social security and Scottish issues, 1983–87; SDP-Liberal Alliance spokesman on social security, 1987; Lib Dem spokesman on trade and industry, 1988–89, on health, 1989–92, on Europe and East-West relations, 1992–97, on agriculture and rural affairs, 1997–99. Member, Select Committee: on Social Services, 1986–87; on Televising of H of C, 1988–90; on Standards and Privileges, 1997–99. Chm., SDP Council for Scotland, 1986–88; Pres., Lib Dems, 1990–94. Occasional journalist, broadcaster and lecturer. *Publication:* The Future of Politics, 2000. *Address:* House of Commons, SW1A 0AA. *T:* (020) 7219 0356. *Club:* National Liberal.

KENNEDY, Danny; *see* Kennedy, T. D.

KENNEDY, David, CMG 1997; Director-General, Commonwealth War Graves Commission, 1993–2000; *b* 7 Nov. 1940; *s* of Lilian Alice Kennedy; *m* 1964, Peta Jennifer Hatton; two *d*. *Educ:* Ryhope Robert Richardson Grammar Sch., Co. Durham; City of London Coll. Exchequer and Audit Dept, 1959–69; Commonwealth War Graves Commission: Higher Exec. Officer, 1969–71; Sen. Exec. Officer, 1971–74; Principal: Dir of Management Services, 1975–79; Dir, Outer Area, 1979–84; Senior Principal: Dir, France Area, 1984–86; Dir of Personnel, 1986–87; Dep. Dir-Gen., Admin, 1987–92; rcds 1992. Mem., MENSA, 2002–; Licentiate, British Professional Photographers Assoc., 2004–. *Recreations:* golf, ski-ing, photography, hill-walking, travel. *Address:* March House, Blands Close, Burghfield Common, Berks RG7 3JY. *T:* (0118) 983 2941.

KENNEDY, David Patrick Leslie; Chief Executive, Northampton Borough Council, since 2007; *b* Cork, 21 Oct. 1959; *s* of Prof. Patrick Brendan Kennedy and Pamela Mary Kennedy; *m* 1998, Sarah Jacqueline Mela Sheehan. *Educ:* York Minster Song Sch.; Lord Wandsworth Coll.; Nunthorpe Grammar Sch., York; Newcastle Poly. (BA Hons Govt 1983); Univ. of Bristol (Masters Public Policy Studies 1987). Res. and Intelligence Asst, 1984–86, Res. and Analysis Officer, 1986–87, Arun DC; Performance Mgt Officer, 1987–89, Hd, Policy and Performance Services, 1989–90, City of York Council; Hd, Strategic Develt, Watford BC, 1990–96; Chief Exec., Gedling BC, 1996–2000; Dir, Envmt and Develt, 2001–03, Dir of Develt and Dep. Chief Exec., 2003–07, Barnsley MBC. *Recreations:* travels with wife and camera, French wine, cricket spectating, relaxing with friends, the world of music and art, envying architects. *Address:* c/o Northampton Borough Council, The Guildhall, St Giles Square, Northampton NN1 1DE. *T:* (01604) 837726; *e-mail:* mail@dkennedy.co.uk.

KENNEDY, Denise Margaret; Her Honour Judge Kennedy; a County Court Judge, Northern Ireland, since 2000; *b* 13 April 1942; *d* of late David L. R. Halliday and Doris Halliday (*née* Molyneaux); *m* 1966, John Andrew Dunn Kennedy; two *s* one *d*. *Educ:* Cheltenham Ladies' Coll.; Exeter Univ. (BA Hons); Queen's Univ. of Belfast. Called to the Bar: NI, 1977; Ireland, 1985; in practice at the Bar, 1977–90; Legal Sec. to Lord Chief Justice of NI, 1990–93; Master, High Court, Supreme Court of Judicature of NI, 1993–2000; Dep. County Court Judge, 1993–2000; Dep. Clerk of Crown for NI, 1993–2000. Part-time Chm., Industrial Tribunals, NI, 1985–90; Mem., Independent Commn for Police Complaints, NI, 1988–90. Mem., Civil Justice Reform Gp for NI, 1998–2000. *Recreations:* travel, gardening, cinema. *Address:* c/o Northern Ireland Court Service, Windsor House, Bedford Street, Belfast BT2 7LT. *Clubs:* Royal Over-Seas League; Royal North of Ireland Yacht.

KENNEDY, Edward Moore; US Senator (Democrat) from Massachusetts, since 1962; *b* Boston, Mass, 22 Feb. 1932; *y s* of late Joseph Patrick Kennedy and Rose Kennedy (*née* Fitzgerald); *m*; two *s* one *d*; *m* 1992, Victoria Anne Reggie. *Educ:* Milton Acad.; Harvard Univ. (BA 1956); Internat. Law Inst., The Hague; Univ. of Virginia Law Sch. (LLB 1959). Served US Army, 1951–53. Called to Massachusetts Bar, 1959; Asst Dist Attorney, Suffolk County, Mass, 1961–62. Senate majority whip, 1969–71; Chairman: Judiciary Cttee, 1979–81; Labor and Human Resources Cttee, now Health, Educn, Labor and Pensions Cttee, 1987– (Ranking Democrat, 1981–86 and 1995–2006); Member: Senate Armed Forces Cttee; Senate Jt Economic Cttee. Pres., Joseph P. Kennedy Jr Foundn, 1961–; Trustee: John F. Kennedy Lib.; John F. Kennedy Center for the Performing Arts; Robert F. Kennedy Meml Foundn. Holds numerous hon. degrees, foreign decorations and awards. *Publications:* Decisions for a Decade, 1968; In Critical Condition, 1972; Our Day and Generation, 1979; (with Senator Mark Hatfield) Freeze: how you can help prevent nuclear war, 1982; America Back on Track, 2006; My Senator and Me, 2006. *Address:* United States Senate, Washington, DC 20510–2101, USA.

KENNEDY, Sir Francis, KCMG 1986; CBE 1977 (MBE 1958); DL; HM Diplomatic Service, retired; Chancellor, University of Central Lancashire, 1995–2002; *b* 9 May 1926; *s* of late James Kennedy and Alice (*née* Bentham); *m* 1957, Anne O'Malley; two *s* two *d*. *Educ:* Univs of Manchester and London. RN, 1944–46. Min. of Supply, 1951–52; HM Colonial Service, Nigeria, 1953–63; Asst Dist Officer, 1953–56; Dist Officer, 1956–59; Principal Asst Sec. to Premier E Nigeria, 1961–62; Provincial Sec., Port Harcourt, 1962–63; HM Diplomatic Service, 1964; First Sec., Commercial and Economic, Dar-es-Salaam, 1965; First Sec. and Head of Post, Kuching, 1967–69; Consul, Commercial, Istanbul, 1970–73; Consul-Gen., Atlanta, 1973–78; Counsellor later Minister Lagos, 1978–81; Ambassador to Angola, 1981–83; Dir-Gen., British Trade and Investment, and Consul-Gen., NY, 1983–86. Special Advr to Chm. and Bd, 1986–96, Dir, 1987–96, British Airways; Chairman: British Airways Regl, 1993–96 (Dir, 1993–); Fluor Daniel Ltd, 1989–96 (Dir, 1986–96); Director: Leslie & Godwin Ltd, 1986–91; Global Analysis Systems, 1986–88; Hambourne Development Co., 1987–94; Smith & Nephew, 1988–96; Fleming Overseas Investment Trust, 1988–96; Brunner Mond Hldgs, 1992–99; Magadi Soda Co., 1994–2001; Mem. Bd and Council, Inward, 1986–90; Advr, Brook Lowe Internat., 1999–2000. Chm., Africa Centre, 1999–2000; Mem., Nigeria British Consultative Process, 2002–04; Dir, Pan African Health Foundn, 2004–. Mem. Bd, Univ. of Central Lancs (formerly Lancashire Polytechnic), 1989–96. Governor, British Liver Foundn, 1990–93. Pres., Assoc. of Lancastrians in London, 2004–05. DL Lancs 1995.

Clubs: Brooks's; Shaw Hill Golf and Country.
See also Rt Rev. Mgr J. Kennedy.

KENNEDY, Hon. Geoffrey Alexander, AO 1994; Judge of the Supreme Court of Western Australia, 1981–2001; *b* 6 Sept. 1931; *s* of Alexander Patrick Kennedy and Dorothy Kennedy (*née* Everington); *m* 1964, Alison King; one *s* two *d*. *Educ:* Scotch College, WA; Univ. of Western Australia (BA, LLB); Wadham Coll., Oxford (Rhodes Scholar, 1955; BCL). Partner, Robinson Cox & Co., Solicitors, 1958–75; Mem., Independent Bar, 1976–80; QC (WA) 1977. Mem., Judicial System Adv. Cttee, Constitutional Commn, Australia, 1986–88; Chm., Royal Commn on Commercial Activities of WA Govt, 1991–92; Royal Comr into WA Police Service, 2001–04. Member: Bd, Princess Margaret Hosp. for Children, 1970–88; WA Medical Bd, 1976–81. Chancellor, Univ. of Western Australia, 1990–98; Chairman: Council, Scotch Coll., WA, 1974–83; Nat. Council of Indep. Schs, 1979–81; WA Mus., 1984–91. Hon. LLD Univ. of WA, 1999. *Address:* 32 Keane Street, Peppermint Grove, WA 6011, Australia. *T:* (8) 93845635. *Club:* Weld (Perth).

KENNEDY, (George) Michael (Sinclair), CBE 1997 (OBE 1981); Music Critic, The Sunday Telegraph, 1989–2005; Staff Music Critic, The Daily Telegraph, 1950–89 (Joint Chief Critic, 1987–89); *b* 19 Feb. 1926; *s* of Hew Gilbert Kennedy and Marian Florence Sinclair; *m* 1st, 1947, Eslyn Durdle (*d* 1999); no *c*; 2nd, 1999, Dr Joyce Bourne. *Educ:* Berkhamsted School. Joined Daily Telegraph, Manchester, 1941; served Royal Navy (BPF), 1943–46; rejoined Daily Telegraph, Manchester, serving in various capacities on editorial staff; Asst Northern Editor, 1958; Northern Ed., 1960–86. Mem. Cttee, Vaughan Williams Trust, 1965– (Chm., 1977–); Vice-Pres., Elgar Foundn and Elgar Soc. Hon. Mem., Royal Manchester Coll. of Music, 1971. Hon. Mem., Royal Philharmonic Soc., 2005. FJI 1967; FRNCM 1981; CRNCM 1999. Hon. MA 1975, Hon. DMus 2003, Manchester. *Publications:* The Hallé Tradition, 1960; The Works of Ralph Vaughan Williams, 1964, 2nd edn 1980; Portrait of Elgar, 1968, 4th edn 1993; Portrait of Manchester, 1970; Elgar Orchestral Works, 1970; History of Royal Manchester College of Music, 1971; Barbirolli: Conductor Laureate, 1971, revd edn 2003; (ed) The Autobiography of Charles Hallé, 1973; Mahler, 1974, 3rd edn 2000 (Japanese edn 1978); Richard Strauss, 1976, 2nd edn 1995; (ed) Concise Oxford Dictionary of Music, 3rd edn, 1980, 5th edn 2006; Britten, 1981, 3rd edn 2000; The Hallé, 1858–1983, 1983; Strauss Tone Poems, 1984; Oxford Dictionary of Music, 1985, 3rd edn 2006; Adrian Boult, 1987; Portrait of Walton, 1989, 2nd edn 1997; Music Enriches All: 21 years of the Royal Northern College of Music, 1994; Richard Strauss: man, musician, enigma, 1999; The Life of Elgar, 2004; Buxton: an English festival, 2004; scripts for BBC, contrib. musical jls. *Recreations:* listening to music, watching cricket. *Address:* The Bungalow, 62 Edilom Road, Manchester M8 4HZ. *T:* (0161) 740 4528; *e-mail:* majkennedy@bungalow62.fsnet.co.uk. *Clubs:* Athenæum; Lancashire CC, Middlesex CC.

KENNEDY, Heather Claire; *see* Lloyd, H. C.

KENNEDY, Sir Ian (Alexander), Kt 1986; Judge of the High Court of Justice, Queen's Bench Division, 1986–2000; *b* 7 Sept. 1930; *s* of late Gerald Donald Kennedy, OBE, and Elizabeth Jane (*née* McBeth); *m* 1962, Susan Margaret, *d* of late Lt-Col Edward John Hatfield, OBE, DL, and of Eileen (*née* Menneer); three *s* one *d*. *Educ:* Wellington Coll., Berks; Pembroke Coll., Cambridge (BA). Called to the Bar, Middle Temple, 1953; Treas., 1999. Dep. Chm., IoW QS, 1971; a Recorder of the Crown Court, 1972; QC 1974. Judge, Employment Appeal Tribunal, 1990–2000. Mem., Parole Bd, 1991–94 (Vice-Chm., 1992–93). *Recreations:* sailing, theatre, walking, gardening. *Address:* c/o Messrs C. Hoare & Co., 37 Fleet Street, EC4P 4DQ.

KENNEDY, Sir Ian (McColl), Kt 2002; FBA 2002; Chairman, Commission for Healthcare Audit and Inspection, since 2004 (Shadow Chairman, 2002–04); Professor of Health Law, Ethics and Policy, School of Public Policy, University College London, 1997–2001, now Emeritus; *b* 14 Sept. 1941; *s* of late Robert Charles Kennedy and Dorothy Elizabeth Kennedy; *m* 1980, Andrea, *d* of late Frederick and of Barbara Gage, Ventura, Calif; two *s*. *Educ:* King Edward VI Sch., Stourbridge; University Coll. London (1st Cl. Hons LLB; Fellow, 1999); Univ. of Calif, Berkeley (LLM); LLD London. Called to the Bar, Inner Temple, 1974 (Hon. Bencher, 1996). Fulbright Fellow, 1963–65; Lectr in Law, UCL, 1965–71; Ford Foundn Fellow, Yale Univ. and Univ. of Mexico, 1966–67; Vis. Prof., Univ. of Calif, LA, 1971–72; King's College, London: Lectr in Law, 1973–78; Reader in English Law 1978–83; British Acad. Res. Fellow, 1978; Dir, Centre of Law, Medicine and Ethics, subseq. Centre of Med. Law and Ethics, 1978–93; Prof. of Med. Law and Ethics, 1983–97; Hd, Dept of Laws, 1986–89; Hd and Dean of Sch. of Law, 1989–92 and 1993–96; Pres., Centre of Med. Law and Ethics, 1993–97. FKC 1988. Vis. Prof., LSE, 2003–. Chairman: Sec. of State for Health's Adv. Gp on Ethics of Xeno-transplantation, 1996–97; Minister of Agriculture's Adv. Gp on Quarantine, 1997–98; Public Inquiry into paediatric cardiac surgical services at Bristol Royal Infirmary, 1998–2001; UK Panel for Res. Integrity in Health and Biomed. Sci., 2006–; Member: Medicines Commn, 1984–91; GMC, 1984–93; Expert Adv. Gp on AIDS, DHSS, later Dept of Health, 1987–94; Gen. Adv. Council, BBC, 1987–91; Med. Ethics Cttee, BMA, 1990–98; Nuffield Council on Bioethics, 1991–2002 (Chm., 1998–2002); Archbishop of Canterbury's Adv. Gp on Med. Ethics, 1994–2003; Register of Ind. Mems, Defence Scientific Adv. Council, MoD, 1997–; Genetics Cttee, ABI, 1997–2001; Science in Society Cttee, Royal Soc., 2000–04; Adv. Gp on Human Remains, Natural Hist. Mus., 2006–. Mem., Council, Open Section, RSM, 1978–88 (Vice-Pres., 1981–86; FRSocMed 1985); Regent, RCSE, 2006. Reith Lectr, 1980. Editor, Medical Law Review, 1993–98. Hon. FRCGP 2002; Hon. FRCP 2003; Hon. FRCPCH 2004; Hon. FRCA 2004; Hon. FRCSE 2005. Hon. DSc Glasgow, 2003; Hon. DM Birmingham, 2006. *Publications:* The Unmasking of Medicine, 1981, rev. edn 1983; Treat Me Right, 1988; (with A. Grubb) Medical Law: cases and materials, 1989, 2nd edn as Medical Law: text with materials, 1994, 3rd edn 2000; (with A. Grubb) Principles of Medical Law, 1998. *Club:* Garrick.

KENNEDY, James; *see* Kennedy, Alastair J. and Kennedy, Alfred J.

KENNEDY, Rt Hon. Jane (Elizabeth); PC 2003; MP (Lab) Liverpool, Wavertree, since 1997 (Liverpool Broadgreen, 1992–97); Minister of State, Department for Environment, Food and Rural Affairs, since 2008; *b* 4 May 1958; *d* of Clifford and Barbara Hodgson; *m* 1977, Robert Malcolm Kennedy (marr. diss. 1998); two *s*. *Educ:* Haughton Comprehensive Sch.; Darlington; Queen Elizabeth Sixth Form Coll.; Liverpool Univ. Child care residential worker 1979–84, Care Assistant 1984–88, Liverpool Social Services; Area Organiser, NUPE, 1988–92. An Asst Govt Whip, 1997–98; a Lord Comr of HM Treasury (Govt Whip), 1998–99; Parly Sec., LCD, 1999–2001; Minister of State: NI Office, 2001–04; DWP, 2004–05; DoH, 2005–06; Financial Sec., HM Treasury, 2007–08. Mem., Social Security Select Cttee, 1992–94. *Recreation:* dogs. *Address:* House of Commons, SW1A 0AA. *T:* (020) 7219 4523; First Floor, Threlfall Building, Trueman Street, Liverpool L3 2EX. *T:* (0151) 236 1117.

KENNEDY, Jane Hope, (Mrs J. Maddison), RIBA; Principal (formerly Partner), Purcell Miller Tritton (Architects), since 1992; *b* 28 Feb. 1953; *d* of Thomas Brian Kennedy and Emily Hope Kennedy (*née* Bailey); *m* 1975, John Maddison; two *s*. *Educ:* Manchester Polytech. (DipArch). RIBA 1990; IHBC 1997; AABC 2000. Assistant: British Waterways Bd, 1978–80; David Jeffcoate, 1980–81; self-employed architect, 1981–86; Historic Bldgs Architect, Norwich CC, 1986–88; architect, 1988–90, Associate, 1990–92, Purcell Miller Tritton. Major projects include: repairs to Mansion House, Stowe House, Bucks, 1999–; repairs, 1997–2000, Processional Way, 2001, Ely Cathedral; restoration of Ballyfin, Central Eire, 2002–; re-presentation of Kew Palace, 2004–. Surveyor to Fabric of Ely Cathedral, 1994–; Architect to Newcastle Cathedral, 2006–; Architect to Foundn, Christ Church, Oxford, 2008–. Comr, English Heritage, 2006–. Sec., Cathedral Architects' Assoc., 2000–06. FRSA 1994. *Publications:* articles in conservation jls. *Recreations:* old buildings, walking, re-learning the violin. *Address:* Purcell Miller Tritton, 46 St Mary's Street, Ely, Cambs CB7 4EY. *T:* (01223) 278700, *Fax:* (01353) 658725; *e-mail:* janekennedy@pmt.co.uk.

KENNEDY, Joanna Alicia Gore, OBE 1995; FREng, FICE; Director, Ove Arup and Partners, since 1996; *b* 22 July 1950; *d* of late Captain G. A. G. Ormsby, DSO, DSC, RN and Susan Ormsby; *m* 1979, Richard Paul Kennedy, *qv*; two *s*. *Educ:* Queen Anne's School, Caversham; Lady Margaret Hall, Oxford (Scholar, 1969; BA 1st cl. Hons Eng. Sci. 1972; MA 1976). MICE 1979, FICE 1992; FREng (FEng 1997); MCIArb 2000. Ove Arup and Partners, consulting engineers: Design Engineer, 1972; Sen. Engr, 1979; Arup Associates, 1987; Arup Project Management, 1990; Associate, 1992; Associate Dir, 1994; Leader, Arup Project Management Europe, 2006–. Member: Engineering Council, 1984–86 and 1987–90; Council, ICE, 1984–87; Adv. Council, RNEC Manadon, 1988–94; Engrg, later Engrg and Technol. Bd, SERC, 1990–94; EPSRC, 2002–06 (Mem., Tech. Opportunities Panel, 1994–97); Dir, Engrg and Technol. Bd, 2002–05. Mem. Bd, PLA, 2000–; Dir, Port of London Properties Ltd, 2001–05. Comr, Royal Commn for Exhibn of 1851, 2003–. Trustee, Nat. Mus. of Science and Industry, 1992–2002; Member, Council: Univ. of Southampton, 1996–99; RCA, 2001–. Hon. DSc Salford, 1994. FRSA 1986. *Address:* Ove Arup and Partners, 13 Fitzroy Street, W1T 4BQ. *T:* (020) 7636 1531; *e-mail:* joanna.kennedy@arup.com.

KENNEDY, Sir Jock; *see* Kennedy, Sir T. L.

KENNEDY, Rt Rev. Mgr John; Parish Priest, Holy Family, Southport, since 1991; *b* 31 Dec. 1930; *s* of James Kennedy and Alice Kennedy (*née* Bentham). *Educ:* St Joseph's College, Upholland; Gregorian University, Rome (STL); Oxford University (MPhil). Curate: St John's, Wigan, 1956–63; St Austin's, St Helens, 1963–65; St Edmund's, Liverpool, 1965–68; Lectr in Theology, Christ's College, Liverpool, 1968–84 (Head of Dept, 1976–84); Rector, Ven. English Coll., Rome, 1984–91; Asst Lectr in Theol., Gregorian Univ., Rome, 1984–91. *Recreations:* golf, squash. *Address:* Holy Family Presbytery, 1 Brompton Road, Southport, Merseyside PR8 6AS.
See also Sir Francis Kennedy.

KENNEDY, John Maxwell; Senior Partner, Allen & Overy, 1986–94; *b* 9 July 1934; *s* of George and Betty Gertrude Kennedy; *m* 1958, Margaret Joan (*née* Davies); four *s*. *Educ:* University Coll., London (LLB). Admitted Solicitor, 1957; Partner, Allen & Overy, 1962. Chm., Law Debenture Corp., 1994–2000; Dir, Amlin (formerly Angerstein Underwriting Trust) plc, 1993–2004 (Chm., 1996–98). Mem., FSA (formerly SIB), 1993–98. Dir, Nuclear Liabilities (formerly Nuclear Generation Decommissioning) Fund Ltd, 1996–2008. Chm., Lloyd's Corporate Capital Assoc., 1995–97. *Recreations:* sport, music, reading. *Address:* 16 Kensington Park Road, W11 3BU. *T:* (020) 7727 6929. *Clubs:* City of London, City Law, Hurlingham; Royal Wimbledon Golf.

KENNEDY, Rev. Dr Joseph; Principal, College of the Resurrection, Mirfield, since 2008; *b* Edinburgh, 1 Jan. 1969; *s* of late Andrew Kennedy and of Margaret Anne Kennedy (*née* Lawson); *m* 2001, Emily Elizabeth Lyons Connell. *Educ:* Edinburgh Univ. (BSc 1991; BD 1994); Moray House Inst. of Educn (PGCE 1997); St Stephen's House, Oxford; St Hugh's Coll., Oxford (MSt 2000); Keble Coll., Oxford (Gosden Scholar; DPhil 2006). Ordained deacon, 2002, priest, 2003; Assistant Curate: Mortimer, 2002–03; Abingdon, 2003–05; Dean of Chapel, Chaplain and Fellow, Selwyn Coll., Cambridge, 2005–08; Chaplain, Newnham Coll., Cambridge, 2005–08. *Recreations:* walking, reading, travel. *Address:* College of the Resurrection, Stocks Bank Road, Mirfield, W Yorks WF14 0BW. *T:* (01924) 490441, *Fax:* (01924) 492738; *e-mail:* jkennedy@mirfield.org.uk.

KENNEDY, Sir Ludovic (Henry Coverley), Kt 1994; FRSL; writer and broadcaster; *b* Edinburgh, 3 Nov. 1919; *o s* of Captain E. C. Kennedy, RN (killed in action, 1939, while commanding HMS Rawalpindi against German battle-cruisers Scharnhorst and Gneisenau), and Rosalind, *d* of Sir Ludovic Grant, 11th Bt of Dalvey; *m* 1950, Moira Shearer King, ballerina (*d* 2006); one *s* three *d*. *Educ:* Eton; Christ Church, Oxford (MA; Hon. Student, 2003). Served War, 1939–46, RNVR. Priv. Sec. and ADC to Gov. of Newfoundland, 1943–44. Librarian, Ashridge (Adult Education) Coll., 1949; Rockefeller Foundation Atlantic Award in Literature, 1950; Winner, Open Finals Contest, English Festival of Spoken Poetry, 1953; Editor, feature, First Reading (BBC Third Prog.), 1953–54; Lecturer for British Council, Sweden, Finland and Denmark, 1955; Belgium and Luxembourg, 1956. Lectures: Voltaire Meml, 1985; Stevens, RSocMed, 1993. Mem. Council, Navy Records Soc., 1957–60. Contested (L) Rochdale, by-elec., 1958 and Gen. elec., 1959; Pres., Nat. League of Young Liberals, 1959–61; Mem., Lib. Party Council, 1965–67. Pres., Sir Walter Scott Club, Edinburgh, 1968–69; Patron, Russian Convoy Club, 1989–. Pres., Dignity in Dying (formerly Voluntary Euthanasia Soc.), 1995–. Columnist: Newsweek International, 1974–75; Sunday Standard, 1981–82. Chm., Royal Lyceum Theatre Co. of Edinburgh, 1977–84. Dir, The Spectator, 1988–90. Chm. of Judges, NCR Book Award, 1990–91. FRSA 1974–76; FRSL 1998. Hon. LLD: Strathclyde, 1985; Southampton, 1993; Dr *hc* Edinburgh, 1990; DUniv Stirling, 1991. Richard Dimbleby BAFTA Award, 1988. Cross, First Class, Order of Merit, Fed. Repub. of Germany, 1979. *TV and radio:* Introd. Profile, ATV, 1955–56; Newscaster, Independent Television News, 1956–58; Introducer of AR's feature On Stage, 1957; Introducer of AR's, This Week, 1958–59; Chm. BBC features: Your Verdict, 1962; Your Witness, 1967–70; Commentator: BBC's Panorama, 1960–63; Television Reporters Internat., 1963–64 (also Prod.); Introducer, BBC's Time Out, 1964–65, World at One, 1965–66; Presenter: Lib. Party's Gen. Election Television Broadcasts, 1966; The Middle Years, ABC, 1967; The Nature of Prejudice, ATV, 1968; Face the Press, Tyne-Tees, 1968–69, 1970–72; Against the Tide, Yorkshire TV, 1969; Living and Growing, Grampian TV, 1969–70; 24 Hours, BBC, 1969–72; Ad Lib, BBC, 1970–72; Midweek, BBC, 1973–75; Newsday, BBC, 1975–76; Tonight, BBC, 1976–78; A Life with Crime, BBC, 1979; Change of Direction, BBC, 1979; Lord Mountbatten Remembers, 1980; Did You See?, 1980–88; Timewatch, 1984; Indelible Evidence, 1987 and 1990; A Gift of the Gab, 1989; Portrait, 1989. *Television films include:* The Sleeping Ballerina; The Singers and the Songs; Scapa Flow; Battleship Bismarck; Life and Death of the Scharnhorst; U-Boat War; Target Tirpitz; The Rise of the Red Navy; Lord Haw-Haw; Coast to Coast; Who Killed the Lindbergh Baby; Elizabeth: the first thirty years; Happy Birthday, dear Ma'am; Consider The End; From Princess to Queen. *Publications:* Sub-Lieutenant, 1942; Nelson's Band of Brothers, 1951; One Man's Meat, 1953; Murder Story (play, with essay on Capital

Punishment), 1956; play: Murder Story (Cambridge Theatre), 1954; Ten Rillington Place, 1961; The Trial of Stephen Ward, 1964; Very Lovely People, 1969; Pursuit: the chase and sinking of the Bismarck, 1974; A Presumption of Innocence: the Amazing Case of Patrick Meehan, 1975; Menace: the life and death of the Tirpitz, 1979; The Portland Spy Case, 1979; Wicked Beyond Belief, 1980; (ed) A Book of Railway Journeys, 1980; (ed) A Book of Sea Journeys, 1981; (ed) A Book of Air Journeys, 1982; The Airman and the Carpenter, 1985 (republished in USA as Crime of the Century, 1996; filmed as Crime of the Century, 1996); On My Way to the Club (autobiog.), 1989; Euthanasia: the good death, 1990; Truth to Tell (collected writings), 1991; In Bed with an Elephant: a journey through Scotland's past and present, 1995; All In The Mind: a farewell to God, 1999; Thirty-Six Murders and Two Immoral Earnings, 2002; Gen. Editor, The British at War, 1973–77. *Address:* c/o Rogers, Coleridge and White, 20 Powis Mews, W11 1JN. *Clubs:* Brooks's, Army and Navy.

KENNEDY, Dr Malcolm William, CBE 2000; FRSE; FREng, FIET; Chairman: PB Power (incorporating Merz and McLellan), 1999–2002 (Executive Chairman, Merz and McLellan, 1995–98); National Energy Action, since 2001; *b* 13 March 1935; *s* of William and Lily Kennedy; *m* 1962, Patricia Ann Forster; one *d*. *Educ:* Durham Univ. (BSc 1961); Univ. of Newcastle upon Tyne (PhD 1964). FIET (FIEE 1974); FREng (FEng 1985); FRSE 2002. Apprentice, C. A. Parsons, 1951–56; Merz and McLellan, 1964–2002: Power Systems Design Engr, 1964; Head, Electrical Div., 1976; Sen. Partner, 1988–91; Chm. and Man. Dir, 1991–95. Mem. Electricity Panel, 1993–98, Water and Telecommunications Panel, 1998–2001, Monopolies and Mergers Commn. Non-exec. Director: Port of Tyne Authority, 1994–2001; New and Renewable Energy Centre, 2003–; Renewable Energy Generation Ltd, 2007–. Pres., IEE, 1999–2000 (Henry Nimmo Premium, 1961; Chm., Power Div., 1986–87; Vice-Pres., 1994–96; Dep. Pres., 1996–99). CCMI (CIMgt 1992). Methodist local preacher. *Publications:* papers on electricity industry, UK and overseas. *Recreations:* cricket, railways. *Address:* 39 Princess Mary Court, Jesmond, Newcastle upon Tyne NE2 3BG. *Club:* National.

KENNEDY, Michael; *see* Kennedy, G. M. S.

KENNEDY, His Honour Michael Denis; QC 1979; a Circuit Judge, 1984–2004; *b* 29 April 1937; *s* of Denis George and Clementina Catherine (*née* MacGregor); *m* 1964, Elizabeth June Curtiss; two *s* two *d*. *Educ:* Downside School; Gonville and Caius College, Cambridge (open Schol., Mod. Langs; MA). 15/19 King's Royal Hussars, 1955–57. Called to the Bar, Inner Temple, 1961; a Recorder, 1979–84; Designated Civil Judge for Sussex, 1999–2004. *Address:* Iford Court, Iford, Lewes, E Sussex BN7 3EU. *T:* (01273) 476432, *Fax:* (01273) 486092.

KENNEDY, Sir Michael Edward, 8th Bt *cr* 1836, of Johnstown Kennedy, Co. Dublin; *b* 12 April 1956; *s* of Sir (George) Ronald Derrick Kennedy, 7th Bt and of Noelle Mona, *d* of Charles Henry Green; *S* father, 1988, but his name does not appear on the Official Roll of the Baronetage; *m* 1984, Helen Christine Jennifer (marr. diss. 2005), *d* of Patrick Lancelot Rae; one *s* three *d*. *Heir: s* George Mathew Rae Kennedy, *b* 9 Dec. 1993.

KENNEDY, Nigel Paul; solo concert violinist; Artistic Director, Polish Chamber Orchestra, since 2002; *b* 28 Dec. 1956; *s* of John Kennedy and Scylla Stoner; one *s*; *m* Agnieszka Chowaniec. *Educ:* Yehudi Menuhin School; Juilliard School of Performing Arts, NY. ARCM. Début at Festival Hall with Philharmonia Orch., 1977; regular appearances with London and major orchestras throughout the world, 1978–; Berlin début with Berlin Philharmonic, 1980; Henry Wood Promenade début, 1981; New York début with BBC SO, 1987; tour of Hong Kong and Australia, with Hallé Orch., 1981; foreign tours, 1978–: India, Japan, S Korea, Turkey, USA, Europe, Scandinavia; many appearances as jazz violinist with Stephane Grappelli, incl. Edinburgh Fest., 1974 and Carnegie Hall, 1976; many TV and radio appearances, incl. Vivaldi's Four Seasons with ECO (Golden Rose of Montreux, 1990), and two documentaries. Pop, jazz and classical recordings, incl. Vivaldi's Four Seasons (best-selling album of a complete classical work; No 1 in UK Classical Chart for over one year (Guinness Book of Records, 1990)); Best Classical Record, British Record Industry Awards: for Elgar Violin Concerto, 1985; for Beethoven Violin Concerto, 1991; Best Recording, Gramophone mag., for Elgar Violin Concerto, 1985. Variety Club Showbusiness Personality of the Year, 1991. Sen. Vice-Pres., Aston Villa FC, 1990–. Hon. DLitt Bath, 1991. *Publication:* Always Playing, 1991. *Recreations:* golf, football (watching and playing), cricket. *Address:* Russells, solicitors, Regency House, 1–4 Warwick Street, W1R 5WB.

KENNEDY, Rt Hon. Sir Paul (Joseph Morrow), Kt 1983; PC 1992; a Lord Justice of Appeal, 1992–2005; Interception of Communications Commissioner, since 2006; Member, Court of Appeal of Gibraltar, since 2006; *b* 12 June 1935; *o s* of late Dr J. M. Kennedy, Sheffield; *m* 1965, Virginia, twin *d* of Baron Devlin, FBA and of Madeleine, *yr d* of Sir Bernard Oppenheimer, 1st Bt; two *s* two *d*. *Educ:* Ampleforth Coll.; Gonville and Caius Coll., Cambridge (MA, LLB; Hon. Fellow, 1998). Called to Bar, Gray's Inn, 1960, Bencher, 1982 (Vice Treas., 2001; Treas., 2002); a Recorder, 1972–83; QC 1973; Judge, High Court of Justice, QBD, 1983–92; Presiding Judge, N Eastern Circuit, 1985–89; Vice-Pres., QBD, High Ct of Justice, 1997–2002. Mem., Judicial Studies Bd, 1993–96 (Chm., Criminal Cttee, 1993–96). Hon. LLD Sheffield, 2000.

KENNEDY, Prof. Peter Graham Edward, MD, PhD, DSc; FRCP, FRCPath, FMedSci; FRSE; Burton Professor of Neurology, since 1987, and Head, Division of Clinical Neurosciences, University of Glasgow; Consultant Neurologist, Institute of Neurological Sciences, Southern General Hospital, Glasgow, since 1987; *b* 28 March 1951; *s* of Philip Kennedy and Trudy Sylvia Kennedy (*née* Summer); *m* 1983, Catherine Ann King; one *s* one *d*. *Educ:* University Coll. Sch.; University College London and UCH Med. Sch. (MB BS, MD, PhD, DSc); Univ. of Glasgow (MLitt, MPhil). FRCP 1988; FRCPath 1997. FRSE 1992. Med. Registrar, UCH and Whittington Hosps, 1977–78; Hon. Res. Asst, MRC Neuroimmunology Project, UCL, 1978–80; Registrar and Res. Fellow, Univ. of Glasgow, 1981; Registrar then Sen. Registrar, Nat. Hosp. for Nervous Diseases, 1982–84; Asst Prof. of Neurology, Johns Hopkins Univ. Hosp., USA, 1985; New Blood Sen. Lectr in Neurology and Virology, Univ. of Glasgow, 1986–87. Chm., Scientist Panel on Infections incl. AIDS, European Fedn of Neurol Socs, 2000–07. Vis. Fellow in Medicine, Jesus Coll., Cambridge, 1992; Fogarty Internat. Scholar-in-Residence, NIH, 1993–94. Lectures: Fleming, 1990, Livingstone, 2004, RCPSG; Stevens, Univ. of Colorado, 1994; Brain Bursary, KCH, London, 1999. Founder FMedSci 1998; FRAS 2004. Member: Assoc. of Physicians of GB and Ire.; Assoc. of British Neurologists; Corresp. Mem., Amer. Neurol Assoc., 1989–. Pres., Internat. Soc. for Neurovirology, 2004– (Sec., 2000–03; Pres.-elect, 2003). Member Editorial Board: Jl of Neuroimmunology, 1988–; Jl of Neurovirology, 1994– (Sen. Associate Editor, 1996–); Jl of Neurological Scis, 1997–; Brain, 1998–2004; Neurocritical Care, 2004–; Scottish Med. Jl, 2004–. BUPA Med. Foundn Doctor of the Year Res. Award, 1990; Linacre Medal and Lectr, RCP, 1991; T. S. Srinivasan Gold Medal and Endowment Lectr, 1993. *Publications:* (with R. T. Johnson) Infections of the Nervous System, 1987; (with L. E. Davis) Infectious Diseases of the Nervous System, 2000; The Fatal Sleep, 2007; numerous papers on neurology, neurobiology, neurovirology and sleeping sickness. *Recreations:* philosophy, tennis, music, astronomy, walking in the country. *Address:* Glasgow University Department of Neurology, Institute of Neurological Sciences, Southern General Hospital, Glasgow G51 4TF. *T:* (0141) 201 2474, *Fax:* (0141) 201 2993; *e-mail:* p.g.kennedy@clinmed.gla.ac.uk.

KENNEDY, Richard Paul, MA; Head Master of Highgate School, 1989–2006; *b* 17 Feb. 1949; *e s* of David Clifton Kennedy and Evelyn Mary Hall (*née* Tindale); *m* 1979, Joanna Alicia Gore Ormsby (*see* J. A. G. Kennedy); two *s*. *Educ:* Charterhouse; New College, Oxford (BA Maths and Phil. 1970; MA 1977). Assistant Master, Shrewsbury Sch., 1971–77, Westminster Sch., 1977–84; Dep. Headmaster, Bishop's Stortford Coll., 1984–89 (Acting Headmaster 1989). Headmasters' Conference: Mem., Sports Cttee, 1992–95; Mem., Cttee, 1995–96; Chm., London Div., 1996; Mem., Finance Steering Gp, 2001–04. Mem. Council, ISCO, 1995–2000. Governor: The Hall Sch., Hampstead, 1989–2006; Wycombe Abbey Sch., 1992–2002. GB internat. athlete (sprints), 1973–76. Mem., Acad. of St Martin-in-the-Fields Chorus, 1977–2000. *Recreations:* choral music, walking in Dorset. *Address:* Luscombe Hall, 9 Luscombe Road, Poole, Dorset BH14 8ST. *T:* (01202) 466810.

KENNEDY, Rosemary; *see* Foot, R. J.

KENNEDY, Thomas Alexander; economist; *b* 11 July 1920; *s* of late Rt Hon. Thomas Kennedy, PC, and Annie S. Kennedy (*née* Michie); *m* 1947, Audrey (*née* Plunkett) (*d* 1991); one *s* two *d*. *Educ:* Alleyn's Sch., Dulwich; Durham Univ. (BA). Economist: Bd of Trade, 1950–52; Colonial Office, 1952–55; Lectr in Econs, Makerere Coll., Uganda, 1955–61; Economist: HM Treasury, Foreign Office, DEA, 1961–67; Economic Dir, NEDO, 1967–70; Under-Secretary: DTI, 1970–74; Dept of Energy, 1974–80, resigned. Chief Tech. Adviser (Economist Planner), Min. of Petroleum and Mineral Resources, Bangladesh, 1980–81. Vis. Fellow, Clare Hall, Cambridge, 1981–82. Consultant, World Bank: Uganda, Zambia, Swaziland, 1983–86, retired 1987. *Publication:* Harry Hyndman: an uncommon socialist, 1995. *Address:* 1 Beckside Mews, Staindrop, Darlington, Co. Durham DL2 3PG. *T:* (01833) 660616.

KENNEDY, Thomas Daniel, (Danny); Member (UU) Newry and Armagh, Northern Ireland Assembly, since 1998; *b* 6 July 1959; *s* of John Trevor Kennedy and Mary Ida Kennedy (*née* Black); *m* 1988, Karen Susan McCrum; two *s* one *d*. *Educ:* Bessbrook Primary Sch.; Newry High Sch. With BTNI, 1978–98. Mem., UU Party, 1974–; Mem., Newry and Mourne DC, 1985– (Chm., 1994–95). Northern Ireland Assembly: Chm., Educn Cttee, 1999–2002, Cttee of the Centre, 2007–; Mem., Exec. Rev. Cttee, 2007–; Dep. Leader, Parly UU Party, 2005–. Mem., NI Tourist Bd, 1996–98. Contested (UU) Newry and Armagh, 1997, 2005. Clerk of Kirk Session and Sabbath Sch. Superintendent, Bessbrook Presbyterian Church. *Recreations:* family, Church activities, sport (purely spectating), reading. *Address:* Parliament Buildings, Stormont, Belfast BT4 3XX. *T:* (028) 9052 1336; Ulster Unionist Advice Centre, 107 Main Street, Markethill, Co. Armagh BT60 1PH. *T:* (028) 3755 2831, *Fax:* (028) 3755 2832.

KENNEDY, Thomas John, LVO 2004; HM Diplomatic Service; Ambassador to Costa Rica, since 2006; *b* 3 Feb. 1957; *m* 1985, Clare Marie Ritchie; one *s*. Entered FCO, 1992; Second Sec. (Aid/Information), Buenos Aires, 1994–97; First Sec., FCO, 1997–2002; Consul Gen., Bordeaux, 2002–06. *Address:* c/o Foreign and Commonwealth Office, King Charles Street, SW1A 2AH.

KENNEDY, Air Chief Marshal Sir Thomas Lawrie, (Sir Jock), GCB 1985 (KCB 1980 CB 1978); AFC 1953 and Bar 1960; Lord-Lieutenant of Rutland, 1997–2003; Royal Air Force, retired; Controller, RAF Benevolent Fund, 1988–93; *b* 19 May 1928; *s* of James Domoné Kennedy and Margaret Henderson Lawrie; *m* 1959, Margaret Ann Parker; one *s* two *d*. *Educ:* Hawick High Sch. RAF Coll., Cranwell, 1946–49; commissioned, 1949. Sqdn service, 1949–53; exchange service, RAAF, 1953–55; returned to UK, 1955; 27 Sqdn (Canberra), 1955–57; Radar Research Estabt, 1957–60; RAF Coll. Selection Bd, 1960–62; RN Staff Coll., Greenwich, 1962; HQ Middle East, 1962–64; CO, No 99 (Britannia) Sqdn, 1965–67; HQ Air Support Comd, 1967–69; CO, RAF Brize Norton, 1970–71; Dep. Comdt, RAF Staff Coll., 1971–73; Dir of Ops (AS) MoD, 1973–75; Royal Coll. of Defence Studies, 1976; Comdr, Northern Maritime Air Region, 1977–79; Deputy C-in-C, RAF Strike Command, 1979–81; C-in-C, RAF Germany, and Comdr, 2nd Allied Tactical Air Force, 1981–83; Air Mem. for Personnel, 1983–86; Air ADC to the Queen, 1983–86. Dir, Dowty Group, 1987–92. Freeman, City of London, 1987; Hon. Liveryman, Fruiterers' Co., 1987. DL Leics, 1989. *Recreations:* golf, sailing. *Address:* c/o Lloyds TSB, Cox's & King's Branch, PO Box 1190, SW1Y 5NA. *Club:* Royal Air Force.

KENNEDY, William Andrew; His Honour Judge William Kennedy; a Circuit Judge, since 2001; *b* 13 Feb. 1948; *s* of late Sidney Herbert and Kathleen Blanche Kennedy; *m* 1st, 1974, Alice Steen Wilkie (*d* 1987); 2nd, 1988, Lindsey Jane Sheridan; one *s* one *d*. *Educ:* Buckhurst Hill County High Sch.; College of Law, Lancaster Gate. Articled Clerk, Trotter Chapman & Whisker, Epping, Essex, 1966–72; admitted Solicitor, 1972; Partner 1972–75, Jt Sen. Partner 1975–91, Trotter Chapman & Whisker, later Whiskers; Notary Public, 1981; Metropolitan Stipendiary Magistrate, then Dist Judge (Magistrates' Courts), 1991–2001; Chm., Youth Courts, 1992–2001; an Asst Recorder, 1995–99; a Recorder, 1999–2001; part-time (Plate) Judge Advocate, 1995–2001. Mem., London Probation Bd, 2005–. Pres., W Essex Law Soc., 1983–84. *Recreations:* golf, gentle domestic pursuits. *Address:* c/o Snaresbrook Crown Court, Snaresbrook, E11 1QW. *Club:* Chigwell Golf.

KENNEDY MARTIN, (Francis) Troy; writer; *b* 15 Feb. 1932; *s* of Frank Martin and Kathleen Flanagan; *m* 1967, Diana Aubrey; one *s* one *d*. *Educ:* Finchley Catholic Grammar Sch.; Trinity Coll., Dublin (BA (Hons) History). Following nat. service with Gordon Highlanders in Cyprus, wrote Incident at Echo Six, a TV play, 1959; *television:* The Interrogator, 1961; Z Cars, 1962; Diary of a Young Man, 1964; Man Without Papers, 1965; Reilly, Ace of Spies, 1983; Edge of Darkness, 1985; Hostile Waters, 1998; Race Dust, 2005; *films:* The Italian Job, 1969; Kelly's Heroes, 1970. Jt Screenwriters' Guild Award, 1962; BAFTA Scriptwriter's Award, 1962. *Publication:* Beat on a Damask Drum, 1961. *Recreation:* collecting marine models. *Address:* 6 Ladbroke Gardens, W11 2PT.

KENNERLEY, Prof. (James) Anthony (Machell), CEng, CMath; Complaints Commissioner, Channel Tunnel Rail Link, 1997–2007; Infrastructure Information Referee, Crossrail, 2002–08; *b* 24 Oct. 1933; *s* of late William James Kennerley and Vida May (*née* Machell); *m* 1978, Dorothy Mary (*née* Simpson); one *s* one *d* (twins). *Educ:* Universities of Manchester (BSc; Silver Medallist, 1955) and London (MSc 1967; IMechE James Clayton Fellow). AFIMA, AFRAeS; MIMechE. Fourth Engr, Blue Funnel Line, Alfred Holt, 1954; Engineer, A. V. Roe, Manchester, 1955–58; Aerodynamicist, Pratt & Whitney, Montreal, Canada, 1958–59; Jet Pilot, RCAF, 1959–62; Asst Professor of Mathematics, Univ. of New Brunswick, Canada, 1962–67; Director of Graduate Studies, Manchester Business Sch., 1967–69; Associate Professor of Business Studies, Columbia Univ., New York, 1969–70; Director, Executive Programme, London Business Sch.,

1970–73; Prof. of Business Admin, and Dir, Strathclyde Business Sch., 1973–83; Dir, InterMatrix Ltd, Management Consultants, 1984–92; Vis. Prof. of Management, City Univ., 1984–93; Prof. of Health Care Mgt, Univ. of Surrey, 1993–97. Chm., Council for Professions Supplementary to Medicine, 1990–96. Tutor to sen. management courses in the public sector, Sunningdale, 1985–2000. Chairman: W Surrey and NE Hants, then NW Surrey, HA, 1986–95; W Surrey Health Commn, 1995–96. Chairman: Management Res. Gp, Scotland, 1981–82; Scottish Milk Marketing Scheme Arbitration Panel, 1981–83. Member: South of Scotland Electricity Bd, 1977–84; Management Studies Bd, CNAA, 1977–84; BIM Educn Cttee, 1982–92; Competition (formerly Monopolies and Mergers) Commn, 1992–2001; Adv. Bd, Meta Generics, Cambridge, 1992–95; Council, Inst. of Mgt, 1995–98. Ind. Comr, Stanstead Airport Develt, 2005–. Chm., Conf. of Univ. Management Schs, 1981–83; Director: Business Graduates Assoc., 1983–86; First Step Housing Co., Waverley BC, 1990–94. Arbitrator, ACAS, 1976–. Mem., Trans-Turkey Highway World Bank Mission, 1982–83. Founder Mem., Bridgegate Trust, Glasgow, 1982–85. *Publications:* Guide to Business Schools, 1985; Arbitration: cases in industrial relations, 1994; articles, papers on business studies, on Public Sector management, and on applied mathematics. *Recreations:* flying, travelling. *Address:* 15 Stone Lodge Lane, Ipswich, Suffolk IP2 9PF. *T:* (01473) 603127. *Clubs:* Reform, Caledonian.

KENNET, 2nd Baron *cr* 1935; **Wayland Hilton Young;** author and politician; *b* 2 Aug. 1923; *s* of 1st Baron Kennet, PC, GBE, DSO, DSC, and of Kathleen Bruce (who *m* 1st, Captain Robert Falcon Scott, CVO, RN, and died 1947); *S* father, 1960; *m* 1948, Elizabeth Ann, *d* of late Captain Bryan Fullerton Adams, DSO, RN; one *s* five *d*. *Educ:* Stowe; Trinity Coll., Cambridge. Served in RN, 1942–45. Foreign Office, 1946–47, and 1949–51. Correspondent in Rome and N Africa, Observer, 1953–54; theatre critic, Tribune, 1957–58; founding Sec., campaign to abolish theatre censorship, 1958; columnist, The Guardian, 1959–64. Deleg., Parly Assemblies, WEU and Council of Europe, 1962–65; Parly Sec., Min. of Housing and Local Govt, 1966–70; Opposition Spokesman on Foreign Affairs and Science Policy, 1971–74; SDP Chief Whip in H of L, 1981–83; SDP spokesman in H of L on foreign affairs and defence, 1981–90. Co-founder, POST, 1988. Chairman: Adv. Cttee on Oil Pollution of the Sea, 1970–74; Commonwealth Human Ecology Council, 1970–72; CPRE, 1971–72; Internat. Parly Confs on the Environment, 1972–78; Dir, Europe Plus Thirty, 1974–75; Member: Polar Cttee, NERC; Internat. Bioethics Cttee, UNESCO, 1994–98. Member: European Parlt, 1978–79; North Atlantic Assembly, 1997–99; Vice Pres., Parly and Scientific Cttee, 1989–98. Pres., Architecture Club, 1983–93; Mem., Redundant Churches Fund, 1978–84. Former Chairman, now President: Avebury Soc., 1990–; Stonehenge Alliance, 1995–; Pres., then Patron, Action for River Kennet, 1995–. Hon. FRIBA 1970. Editor of Disarmament and Arms Control, 1962–65. *Publications:* (as Wayland Young): The Italian Left, 1949; The Deadweight, 1952; Now or Never, 1953; Old London Churches (with Elizabeth Young), 1956; The Montesi Scandal, 1957; Still Alive Tomorrow, 1958; Strategy for Survival, 1959; The Profumo Affair, 1963; Eros Denied, 1965; Thirty-Four Articles, 1965; (ed) Existing Mechanisms of Arms Control, 1965; (as Wayland Kennet) Preservation, 1972; The Futures of Europe, 1976; The Rebirth of Britain, 1982; (with Elizabeth Young) London's Churches, 1986; (with Elizabeth Young) Northern Lazio, 1990 (trans. Italian 1993); Parliaments and Screening, 1995; (contrib.) Enciclopedia Treccani (The Italian Encyclopedia), 1998; Fabian and SDP pamphlets on defence, disarmament, environment, multinational companies, etc. *Heir: s* Hon. William Aldus Thoby Young [*b* 24 May 1957; *m* 1987, Hon. Josephine, *yr d* of 2nd Baron Keyes; two *s* one *d*]. *Address:* 100 Bayswater Road, W2 3HJ.

KENNETT, Prof. Brian Leslie Norman, PhD, ScD; FRS 2005; FAA; Professor of Seismology, since 1984, Director, since 2006, Research School of Earth Sciences, Australian National University; *b* 7 May 1948; *s* of Norman and Audrey Kennett; *m* 1971, Heather Margaret Duncan; one *s* one *d*. *Educ:* Dulwich Coll.; Emmanuel Coll., Cambridge (BA 1969; PhD 1973; ScD 1992). Fellow, Emmanuel Coll., Cambridge, 1972–84; Lectr, Univ. of Cambridge, 1976–84; Pro Vice Chancellor, 1994–97, Chm. Bd, Inst. of Advanced Studies, 1994–97 and 2001–03, ANU. Editor: Geophysical Jl Internat., 1979–99; Physics of the Earth and Planetary Interiors, 2003–06. Fellow, Amer. Geophysical Union, 1988; FAA 1994; Associate, RAS, 1996. Humboldt Foundn Res. Award, 2004; Jaeger Medal, Australian Acad. Scis, 2005; Murchison Medal, Geol Soc., 2006; Gutenberg Medal, Eur. Geoscis Union, 2007; Gold Medal for Geophysics, Royal Astronomical Soc., 2008. Centenary Medal (Australia), 2003. *Publications:* Seismic Wave Propagation in Stratified Media, 1983; IASPEI Seismological Tables, 1991; The Seismic Wavefield, Vol. I 2001, Vol. II 2002; numerous scientific contribs. *Recreations:* walking, photography. *Address:* Research School of Earth Sciences, Australian National University, Canberra, ACT 0200, Australia. *T:* (2) 61254621, *Fax:* (2) 62572737; *e-mail:* Brian.Kennett@anu.edu.au.

KENNETT, Hon. Jeffrey (Gibb), AC 2005; Chairman: Australian Seniors Finance Ltd; Open Windows Australia Pty Ltd; Beyondblue, the National Depression Initiative, since 2000; *b* 2 March 1948; *m* 1972, Felicity; three *s* one *d*. Government of Victoria: MLA (L) Burwood, 1976–99; Minister for Aboriginal Affairs, Immigration, Ethnic Affairs and Housing, 1981–82; Leader of the Opposition, 1982–89, 1991–92; Minister for Multicultural Affairs and the Arts, 1996–99; Premier of Victoria, 1992–99. Director: Q Ltd, 2003–; Jumbuck Entertainment Ltd, 2004–. Pres., Hawthorn Football Club, 2005–. Chm., Enterprize Ship Trust, 2005–. *Address:* (office) 484 Swan Street, Richmond, Vic 3121, Australia.

KENNETT, Ronald John, FRAeS; Director, Royal Aeronautical Society, 1988–98; *b* 25 March 1935; *s* of William John and Phyllis Gertrude Kennett; *m* 1957, Sylvia Barstow; one *s* three *d*. *Educ:* Bradford Technical College. Lucas Aerospace: joined 1956; Chief Engineer, 1978–86; Quality Assurance Manager, 1986–88. Non-exec. Dir, Beds and Herts Ambulance and Paramedic Service NHS Trust, 2000–06. *Recreations:* reading, photography, music, country recreation, golf. *Address:* Greenbanks, Toms Hill Road, Aldbury, Herts HP23 5SA. *Club:* Stocks Golf.

KENNEY, Anthony, FRCS; FRCOG; Consultant Obstetrician and Gynaecologist, St Thomas' Hospital, 1980–2002; *b* 17 Jan. 1942; *s* of late Eric Alfred Allen Kenney and Doris Winifred Kenney; *m* 1973, Patricia Clare Newbery (*d* 2007); four *s* one *d*. *Educ:* Brentwood School; Gonville and Caius College, Cambridge (MA 1967); London Hosp. Med. Coll. MB BChir 1966; FRCS 1970; MRCOG 1972, FRCOG 1987. House appts, London Hosp., Queen Charlotte's Hosp. and Chelsea Hosp. for Women, 1966–72; Registrar and Sen. Registrar, Westminster and Kingston Hosps, 1972–79. Past Examiner: in Obstetrics and Gynaecology, RCOG; Univs of London, Liverpool and Cambridge. Mem., Higher Trng Cttee, RCOG, 1997–2000. Co-founder and Trustee, Tommy's The Baby Charity (formerly Tommy's Campaign), 1989–; Trustee, Quit, 1995–. Fellow, Med. Soc. of London, 2002– (Treas., 2002–07; Pres., 2007–08). *Publications:* contribs to med. jls. *Recreations:* canal cruising, foreign travel. *Address:* Perching Sands Farmhouse, Edburton Road, Fulking, W Sussex BN5 9LS. *T:* (01273) 857171. *Club:* Royal Society of Medicine.

KENNEY, Prof. Edward John, FBA 1968; Kennedy Professor of Latin, University of Cambridge, 1974–82; Fellow of Peterhouse, Cambridge, 1953–91; *b* 29 Feb. 1924; *s* of George Kenney and Emmie Carlina Elfrida Schwenke; *m* 1955, Gwyneth Anne, *d* of late Prof. Henry Albert Harris. *Educ:* Christ's Hospital; Trinity Coll., Cambridge. BA 1949, MA 1953. Served War of 1939–45: Royal Signals, UK and India, 1943–46; commissioned 1944, Lieut 1945. Porson Schol., 1948; Craven Schol., 1949; Craven Student, 1949; Chancellor's Medallist, 1950. Asst Lectr, Univ. of Leeds, 1951–52; University of Cambridge: Research Fellow, Trinity Coll., 1952–53; Asst Lectr, 1955–60, Lectr, 1966–70; Reader in Latin Literature and Textual Criticism, 1970–74; Peterhouse: Director of Studies in Classics, 1953–74; Librarian, 1953–82, Perne Librarian, 1987–91; Tutor, 1956–62; Senior Tutor, 1962–65; Domestic Bursar, 1987–88. James C. Loeb Fellow in Classical Philology, Harvard Univ., 1967–68; Sather Prof. of Classical Literature, Univ. of California, Berkeley, 1968; Carl Newell Jackson Lectr, Harvard Univ., 1980. President: Jt Assoc. of Classical Teachers, 1977–79; Classical Assoc., 1982–83; Horatian Soc., 2002–07. For. Mem., Royal Netherlands Acad. of Arts and Scis, 1976. Treasurer and Chm., Council of Almoners, Christ's Hosp., 1984–86. Jt Editor, Classical Qly, 1959–65; Jt Gen. Ed., Cambridge Greek and Latin Classics, 1966–. *Publications:* P. Ouidi Nasonis Amores etc (ed), 1961, 2nd edn 1995; (with Mrs P. E. Easterling) Ovidiana Graeca (ed), 1965; (with W. V. Clausen, F. R. D. Goodyear, J. A. Richmond) Appendix Vergiliana (ed), 1966; Lucretius, De Rerum Natura III (ed), 1971; The Classical Text, 1974 (trans. Italian, 1995); (with W. V. Clausen) Latin Literature (ed and contrib.) (Cambridge History of Classical Literature II), 1982; The Ploughman's Lunch (*Moretum*), 1984; introd. and notes to Ovid, Metamorphoses, trans. A. D. Melville, 1986; Ovid, The Love Poems, 1990; Apuleius, Cupid & Psyche (ed), 1990; introd. and notes to Ovid, Sorrows of an Exile (*Tristia*), trans. A. D. Melville, 1992; Ovid, Heroides XVI-XXI (ed), 1996; (trans., with introd. and notes) Apuleius, The Golden Ass, 1998, 2nd edn 2004; articles and reviews in classical jls. *Recreations:* cats and books. *Address:* Peterhouse, Cambridge CB2 1RD.

KENNEY, Rt Rev. William, CP; Auxiliary Bishop of Birmingham, (RC), and Titular Bishop of Midica, since 2006; *b* 7 May 1946; *s* of Leonard Kenney and Christine (*née* Farrell). *Educ:* Heythrop Coll., Oxon (STL 1969); Univ. of Gothenburg (Fil. Kand. 1973). Entered novitiate of Passionist Congregation, Broadway, Worcs, 1963; ordained priest, 1969; Researcher, Inst. for Sociology of Religion, Stockholm, 1973–77; Institute for Scientific Study of Religions, University of Gothenburg: Lectr, 1979–82; Dean of Studies, 1980–82; Lectr and Dean of Studies, 1984–87; Gen. Counsellor, Passionist Congregation, Rome, 1982–84; Superior, Passionists, Sweden, 1985–87; ordained bishop, 1987; Aux. Bishop of Stockholm, 1987–2006. Chair: Caritas Sweden, 1987–2006; Commn for Financing Religious Bodies, Swedish Govt, 1990–98 (Mem., 1988–98); Caritas Europe, 1991–99; Justice & Peace Commn, Stockholm, 1999–2006; Gothenburg Process, 2000– (Internat. Chair, 2007–); Vice-Chair, Caritas Internationalis, 1991–99 (Mem., Legal Affairs Commn, 1999–); Member: Bd for Religious Affairs, Swedish Govt, 1998–2006; Commn of the Bishops' Confs of the EC, Brussels, 2000–; Passionists Internat., NY, 2004; Governing Bd, Life and Peace Inst., Uppsala, Sweden, 2008–. Spokesperson on European questions, Cath. Bishops' Conf. of England and Wales, 2006–. Hon. PhD Gothenburg, 1988. KCHS 2003. *Publications:* various articles on European, social and religious affairs. *Recreations:* listening to music, walking, reading (professionally but also history, biography and politics). *Address:* St Hugh's House, 27 Hensington Road, Woodstock, Oxon OX20 1JH. *T:* (01993) 812234; *e-mail:* wk@beeb.net.

KENNICUTT, Prof. Robert Charles, Jr, PhD; Plumian Professor of Astronomy and Experimental Philosophy, since 2005, and Director, Institute of Astronomy, since 2008, University of Cambridge; Fellow, Churchill College, Cambridge, since 2006; *b* 4 Sept. 1951; *s* of Robert Charles Kennicutt and Joyce Ann Kennicutt; one *d*. *Educ:* Rensselaer Polytechnic Inst. (BS Phys 1973); Univ. of Washington (MS 1976, PhD Astronomy 1978). Carnegie Postdoctoral Fellow, Hale Observatories, 1978–80; Associate, then Asst Prof., Dept of Astronomy, Univ. of Minnesota, 1985–88; Prof. and Astronomer, Steward Observatory, Univ. of Arizona, 1988–2005. Beatrice M. Tinsley Centennial Prof., Univ. of Texas, 1994; Adriaan Blaauw Prof., Univ. of Groningen, 2001. Editor-in-Chief, Astrophysical Jl, 1999–2006. *Publications:* Galaxies: interactions and induced star formation, 1998; Hubble's Science Legacy in Future Optical/Ultraviolet Astronomy from Space, 2003. *Recreations:* book collecting, lapidary arts. *Address:* Institute of Astronomy, University of Cambridge, Madingley Road, Cambridge CB3 0HA. *T:* (01223) 765844, *Fax:* (01223) 766658; *e-mail:* robk@ast.cam.ac.uk.

KENNON, Andrew Rowland; Clerk of the Journals, House of Commons, since 2008; *b* 15 July 1955; *y s* of Vice-Adm. Sir James Edward Campbell Kennon, KCB, CBE and Anne Kennon; *m* 1983, Mary Gamblin; one *s* two *d*. *Educ:* Stowe Sch.; Jesus Coll., Cambridge (exhibitioner; BA Law 1977). Called to the Bar, Gray's Inn, 1979. House of Commons: Asst Clerk, 1977; various procedural, cttee and internat. posts, 1977–87; Clerk of Select Committees: on Trade and Ind., 1987–92; on Procedure, 1992–95; on Defence, 1995–97; on Home Affairs, 1999–2002; seconded to Cabinet Office to advise on parly and constitutional reform, 1997–99; Hd, Scrutiny Unit, 2002–04; Prin. Clerk of Select Cttees, 2004–06; a Prin. Clerk and Sec., H of C Commn, 2006–08. Hon. Res. Fellow, Dept of Politics, Univ. of Exeter, 2003–. *Publication:* (with R. Blackburn) Griffith and Ryle, Parliament: functions, practice and procedures, 2nd edn 2002. *Recreation:* sailing. *Address:* Journal Office, House of Commons, SW1A 0AA.

KENNY, Sir Anthony (John Patrick), Kt 1992; FBA 1974; Pro-Vice-Chancellor, Oxford University, 1984–2001 (Pro-Vice-Chancellor for Development, 1999–2001); Warden, Rhodes House, 1989–99; Professorial Fellow, St John's College, Oxford, 1989–99, now Emeritus Fellow; Master of Balliol College, Oxford, 1978–89; *b* Liverpool, 16 March 1931; *s* of John Kenny and Margaret Jones; *m* 1966, Nancy Caroline, *d* of Henry T. Gayley, Jr, Swarthmore, Pa; two *s*. *Educ:* Gregorian Univ., Rome (STL); St Benet's Hall, Oxford; DPhil 1961, DLitt 1980. Ordained priest, Rome, 1955; Curate in Liverpool, 1959–63; returned to lay state, 1963. Asst Lectr, Univ. of Liverpool, 1961–63; University of Oxford: Fellow, 1964–78, Sen. Tutor, 1971–72 and 1976–78, Balliol Coll.; Lectr in Philosophy, Exeter and Trinity Colls, 1963–64; University Lectr, 1965–78; Wilde Lectr in Natural and Comparative Religion, 1969–72; Speaker's Lectureship in Biblical Studies, 1980–83; Mem., Hebdomadal Council, 1981–93; Vice-Chm., Libraries Bd, 1985–88; Curator, Bodleian Library, 1985–88; Deleg., and Mem., Finance Cttee, OUP, 1986–93. Jt Gifford Lectr, Univ. of Edinburgh, 1972–73; Stanton Lectr, Univ. of Cambridge, 1980–83; Bampton Lectr, Columbia Univ., 1983. Visiting Professor: Univs of Chicago, Washington, Michigan, Minnesota and Cornell, Stanford and Rockefeller Univs. Chairman: British Liby Bd, 1993–96 (Mem., 1991–96); Soc. for Protection of Science and Learning, 1989–93; British Nat. Corpus Adv. Bd, 1990–95; British Irish Assoc., 1990–94; Bd, Warburg Inst., Univ. of London, 1996–2000. Pres., British Acad., 1989–93 (Mem. Council, 1985–88; Vice-Pres., 1986–88). MAE 1991; Member: Amer. Phil Soc., 1993; Norwegian Acad. of Scis, 1993; Amer. Acad. of Arts and Scis, 2003. Hon. Fellow, Harris Manchester Coll., Oxford, 1996. Hon. DLitt: Bristol, 1982; Liverpool, 1988; Glasgow, 1990; TCD, 1992; Hull, 1993; Sheffield, Warwick, 1995; Hon. DHumLitt: Denison Univ., Ohio, 1986; Lafayette Univ., Penn, 1990; Hon. DCL: Oxon,

1987; QUB, 1994; Hon. DLit London, 2002. Hon. Bencher, Lincoln's Inn, 1999. Aquinas Medal, Amer. Catholic Philos. Assoc., 2006. Editor, The Oxford Magazine, 1972–73. *Publications:* Action, Emotion and Will, 1963, 2nd edn 2003; Responsa Alumnorum of English College, Rome, 2 vols, 1963; Descartes, 1968; The Five Ways, 1969; Wittgenstein, 1973, 2nd edn 2005; The Anatomy of the Soul, 1974; Will, Freedom and Power, 1975; The Aristotelian Ethics, 1978; Freewill and Responsibility, 1978; Aristotle's Theory of the Will, 1979; The God of the Philosophers, 1979; Aquinas, 1980; The Computation of Style, 1982; Faith and Reason, 1983; Thomas More, 1983; The Legacy of Wittgenstein, 1984; A Path from Rome (autobiog.), 1985; Wyclif, 1985; The Logic of Deterrence, 1985; The Ivory Tower, 1985; A Stylometric Study of the New Testament, 1986; The Road to Hillsborough, 1987; Reason and Religion, 1987; The Heritage of Wisdom, 1987; God and Two Poets, 1988; The Metaphysics of Mind, 1989; The Oxford Diaries of Arthur Hugh Clough, 1990; Mountains: an anthology, 1991; Aristotle on the Perfect Life, 1992; What is Faith?, 1992; Aquinas on Mind, 1993; (ed) Oxford Illustrated History of Western Philosophy, 1994; Frege, 1995; A Life in Oxford (autobiog.), 1997; A Brief History of Western Philosophy, 1998, 2nd illus. edn 2006; Essays on the Aristotelian Tradition, 2001; (ed) The History of the Rhodes Trust, 2001; Aquinas on Being, 2002; The Unknown God, 2004; A New History of Western Philosophy, vol. 1, 2004, vol. 2, 2005, vol. 3, 2006, vol. 4, 2007; Arthur Hugh Clough: the life of a poet, 2005; What I Believe, 2006; (with C. Kenny) Life, Liberty and the Pursuit of Utility, 2006; (with R. Kenny) Can Oxford be Improved?, 2007; From Empedocles to Wittgenstein, 2008. *Address:* The Old Bakery, 1A Larkins Lane, Oxford OX3 9DW. *Club:* Athenæum.

KENNY, Bernadette Joan; Director General, Personal Taxes (formerly Customer Contact and Processing), since 2006, Commissioner, since 2008, HM Revenue and Customs, (Acting Director General, 2005–06); *b* 10 Dec. 1956; *d* of James Francis Kenny and Mary Lourdes Kenny (*née* Carroll); *m* 1981, Jonathan Appleby; three *s* (incl. twins) (and twin *s* decd). *Educ:* Chichester High Sch. for Girls; Univ. of Manchester (LLB Hons 1978). Called to the Bar, Lincoln's Inn, 1979; LCD, 1980–91 and 1993–95; Court Service: Dep. Circuit Administrator, 1991–93; Dir of Personnel and Training, 1995–98; Dir of Operational Policy, 1999–2002; Change Dir, LCD, subseq. DCA, 2002–05; Chief Exec., Royal Parks Agency, 2005; Dir of Distributed Processes, HMRC, 2005. *Recreations:* twins (Mem., Twins and Multiple Births Assoc.), gardening, ski-ing. *Address:* HM Revenue and Customs, 1 Parliament Street, SW1A 2BQ. *Club:* Ski Club of GB.

KENNY, Gen. Sir Brian (Leslie Graham), GCB 1991 (KCB 1985); CBE 1979; Bath King of Arms, since 1999; *b* 18 June 1934; *s* of late Brig. James Wolfenden Kenny, CBE, and of Aileen Anne Georgina Kenny (*née* Swan); *m* 1958, Diana Catherine Jane Mathew; two *s. Educ:* Canford School. Commissioned into 4th Hussars (later Queen's Royal Irish Hussars), 1954; served BAOR, Aden, Malaya and Borneo; Pilot's course, 1961; Comd 16 Recce Flt QRIH; psc 1965; MA/VCGS, MoD, 1966–68; Instructor, Staff Coll., 1971–73; CO QRIH, BAOR and UN Cyprus, 1974–76; Col GS 4 Armd Div., 1977–78; Comd 12 Armd Bde (Task Force D), 1979–80; RCDS 1981; Comdr 1st Armoured Div., 1982–83; Dir, Army Staff Duties, MoD, 1983–85; Comdr 1st (British) Corps, BAOR, 1985–87; Comdr, Northern Army Gp, and C-in-C, BAOR, 1987–89; Dep. SACEUR, 1990–93. Gov., Royal Hosp., Chelsea, 1993–99. Col QRIH, 1985–93; Colonel Commandant: RAVC, 1983–95; RAC, 1988–93. Chm., Army Benevolent Fund, 1993–99. Non-exec. Dir, Dorset Ambulance Trust, 2000–; Trustee, Dorset and Somerset Air Ambulance Trust, 2000–. Governor, Canford Sch., 1983–. *Recreations:* ski-ing, golf, shooting, racing. *Address:* c/o Lloyds TSB, Camberley, Surrey GU15 3SE. *Clubs:* Sloane, MCC, I Zingari, Free Foresters.

KENNY, David John, CBE 1991; Regional General Manager, North West Thames Regional Health Authority, 1984–91 (Regional Administrator, 1982–84); *b* 2 Dec. 1940; *s* of late Gerald Henry Kenny and Ellen Veronica (*née* Crosse); *m* 1964, Elisabeth Ann, *d* of late Robert and of Jean Ferris; three *s. Educ:* Royal Belfast Academical Instn; Queen's Univ., Belfast (LLB). FHSM. Dep. House Governor, Bd of Governors, London Hosp., 1972; Dist Administrator, Tower Hamlets Health Dist, 1974; Area Administrator, Kensington and Chelsea and Westminster AHA, 1978. Mem. Nat. Council, Inst. of Health Service Managers, 1975–86 and 1988–91 (Pres. 1981–82); Chm., Gen. Managers of RHAs, 1989–91. Chm., Data Protection Working Gp, Internat. Med. Informatics Assoc., 1979–87. *Publications:* (jtly) Data Protection in Health Information Systems, 1980; articles on management topics, data protection and ethics. *Recreations:* cinema, theatre, athletics, rugby football. *Address:* 131 Maze Hill, SE3 7UB. *T:* (020) 8858 1545.

KENNY, Mary Cecilia, (Mrs R. West); journalist and writer; *b* 4 April 1944; *d* of Patrick and Ita Kenny; *m* 1974, Richard West; two *s. Educ:* Loreto Coll., Dublin; Birkbeck Coll., Univ. of London (BA Hons French Studies 1997). Journalist and broadcaster, 1966–: feature writer and European Corresp., London Evening Standard, 1966–69; Woman's Ed., Irish Press, Dublin, 1969–71; Features Ed. and writer, Evening Standard, 1971–73; freelance journalist, subseq. Columnist, Sunday Telegraph, 1976–96; TV Critic, Daily Mail, 1981–86; contributor: Daily Mail, The Tablet, Daily Telegraph, The Times, Guardian, Spectator, Listener, New Statesman, TLS, The Oldie, Irish Independent (also columnist), Sunday Independent, Irish Times, Studies (Dublin), Catholic Herald, Irish Catholic, and others; *TV and radio* including: panellist, Late, Late Show, RTE; Question Time, BBC; Any Questions, Radio 4; The Panel, RTE; presenter, and contrib. to, various documentaries in UK and Ireland. *Publications:* Abortion: the whole story, 1986; A Mood for Love (short stories), 1989; Goodbye to Catholic Ireland: a social history, 1997; Death by Heroin, Recovery by Hope, 2001; Germany Calling: a personal biography of William Joyce, Lord Haw-Haw, 2003; Allegiance: Michael Collins and Winston Churchill 1921–1922, 2005; Crown and Shamrock: British royalty and Irish values from the reign of Queen Victoria, 2008. *Recreations:* cinema, theatre, reading in French, running away from the kitchen sink. *Address:* 26 St Georges Road, Deal, Kent CT14 6BA; *e-mail:* mary@mary-kenny.com; 15 Kildare Street, Dublin 2, Ireland. *Club:* Reform.

KENNY, Siobhan Mary, (Mrs P. Pearson); Director, Communications, HarperCollins Publishers, since 2007; *b* 15 Oct. 1959; *d* of late Patrick Kenny and of Della Kenny (*née* Raftery); *m* 1996, Pat Pearson. *Educ:* St Michael's Convent Grammar Sch., Finchley, London; Univ. of Manchester (BA English, French, German 1982); Birkbeck Coll., London (MA French 1988). Press Officer: TV-am, 1986–89; Govt Inf. Service, 1989–93; Attachée de Presse, Council of Europe, Strasbourg, 1993–94; Press Officer, then Strategy Advr, No 10 Downing Street, 1994–99; Dir of Communications, National Magazine Co., 1999–2002; Dir of Strategic Communication, DCMS, 2002–05; Vice Pres., Communications, Europe, Middle E and Africa, Walt Disney TV, 2005–07. *Recreations:* sailing, ski-ing, film. *Address: e-mail:* siobhan.kenny@harpercollins.co.uk. *T:* (020) 8307 4507.

KENNY, Stephen Charles Wilfrid; QC 2006; *b* 12 Aug. 1964; *s* of late Charles John Michael Kenny and Gillian Beatrice Maud Kenny (*née* Shelford); *m* 1998, Anna Aida, *d* of Dr John Vincent Cable, *qv*; one *s. Educ:* Farleigh House Sch.; Ampleforth Coll. (scholar); Worcester Coll., Oxford (Exhibnr; MA; BCL 1st Cl. Hons). Called to the Bar, Inner

Temple, 1987; in practice as a barrister, 1987–, specialising in commercial law. *Recreations:* family and friends, music, literature, early medieval history, ski-ing, kickboxing. *Address:* 7 King's Bench Walk, Temple, EC4Y 7DS. *T:* (020) 7910 8300, *Fax:* (020) 7910 8400; *e-mail:* skenny@7kbw.co.uk.

KENNY, Yvonne Denise, AM 1989; international opera singer; *b* Australia, 25 Nov. 1950; *d* of late Arthur Raymond Kenny and of Doris Jean (*née* Campbell). *Educ:* Sydney Univ. (BSc). Operatic début in Donizetti's Rosmonda d'Inghilterra, Queen Elizabeth Hall, 1975; joined Royal Opera House, Covent Garden as a principal soprano, 1976; roles include: Pamina in Die Zauberflöte; Ilia in Idomeneo; Marzelline in Fidelio; Susanna, and Countess, in Le Nozze di Figaro; Adina in L'Elisir d'Amore; Liu in Turandot; Aspasia in Mitridate; Alcina; Semele; Cleopatra in Giulio Cesare; Donna Anna in Don Giovanni; Fairy Queen; Countess in Capriccio; Die Feldmarshallin in Der Rosenkavalier; Alice Ford in Falstaff; international appearances include: ENO; Glyndebourne; Berlin Staatsoper; Vienna State Opera; La Scala, Milan; La Fenice, Venice; Paris; Munich; Zurich; Australian Opera, Sydney, etc; regular concert appearances with major orchs and conductors in Europe and USA. Has made numerous recordings. Hon. DMus Sydney, 2000. *Recreations:* swimming, walking, gardening. *Address:* c/o Askonas Holt Ltd, Lincoln House, 300 High Holborn, WC1V 7JH.

KENSINGTON, 8th Baron *cr* 1776 (Ire.); **Hugh Ivor Edwardes;** Baron Kensington (UK) 1886; *b* 24 Nov. 1933; *s* of Hon. Hugh Owen Edwardes (*d* 1937) (2nd *s* of 6th Baron) and of Angela Dorothea (who *m* 1951, Lt Comdr John Hamilton, RN retd), *d* of late Lt-Col Eustace Shearman, 10th Hussars; *S* uncle, 1981; *m* 1961, Juliet Elizabeth Massy Anderson; two *s* one d. *Educ:* Eton. *Heir: s* Hon. William Owen Alexander Edwardes [*b* 21 July 1964; *m* 1991, Marie Hélène Anne Véronique, *d* of Jean-Alain Lalouette; one *s* two d]. *Address:* Friar Tuck, PO Box 549, Mooi River, Natal 3300, Republic of S Africa. *Clubs:* Boodle's; Victoria Country (Pietermaritzburg).

KENSINGTON, Area Bishop of; *no new appointment at time of going to press.*

KENSWOOD, 2nd Baron *cr* 1951; **John Michael Howard Whitfield;** *b* 6 April 1930; *o s* of 1st Baron Kenswood; *S* father, 1963; *m* 1951, Deirdre Anna Louise, *d* of Colin Malcolm Methven, Errol, Perthshire; four *s* one d. *Educ:* Trinity Coll. Sch., Ontario; Harrow; Grenoble Univ.; Emmanuel Coll., Cambridge (BA). FRSA. *Heir: s* Hon. Michael Christopher Whitfield, *b* 3 July 1955.

KENT, Brian Hamilton, FREng, FIET, FIMechE; Deputy Chairman, Industrial Acoustics Corp. Ltd, since 2000; Chairman, Wellington Holdings plc, 1993–2005; President, Institution of Mechanical Engineers, 1994–95; *b* 29 Sept. 1931; *s* of Clarence Kent and Edyth (*née* Mitchell); *m* 1954, Margery Foulds; one *s* two d. *Educ:* Hyde Grammar Sch.; Salford Coll. of Technology (BSc Eng). FREng (FEng 1995). Instructor Lieut, RN Short Service Commn, 1954–57. Mather & Platt Ltd: graduate apprentice, 1952–54; Asst Technical Manager, Electrical Gp, then Gen. Manager, Mather & Platt Contracting Ltd, 1957–65; Morgan Crucible Co. Ltd, London, 1965–69; Man. Dir and Chief Exec., Alfa-Laval Ltd, 1969–78; Dir, Staveley Industries Ltd, 1978–80; Staveley Industries plc: Chief Exec., 1980–87; Chm., 1987–93; non-exec. Chm., 1993–94. Chm., British Printing Co. Ltd, 1996–98. Senator, Engrg Council, 1996–99. Chm., Management Cttee, Industry and Parlt Trust, 1988–90. Gov., Kingston Univ., 1996–2003 (Chm., Finance Bd). FInstD; FRSA. Hon. DSc Salford, 1995. *Recreation:* sailing. *Address:* Industrial Acoustics Corp. Ltd, IAC House, Moorside Road, Winchester SO23 7US. *T:* (01962) 873000. *Club:* Royal Automobile.

KENT, Bruce; campaigner for nuclear disarmament; Chairman, Campaign for Nuclear Disarmament, 1987–90 (General Secretary, 1980–85; Vice-Chairman, 1985–87; Hon. Vice President, 1985); *b* 22 June 1929; *s* of Kenneth Kent and Rosemary Kent (*née* Marion); *m* 1988, Valerie Flessati. *Educ:* Lower Canada Coll., Montreal; Stonyhurst Coll.; Brasenose Coll., Univ. of Oxford. LLB. Ordination, Westminster, 1958; Curate, Kensington, North and South, 1958–63; Sec., Archbishop's House, Westminster, 1963–64; Chm., Diocesan Schools Commn, 1964–66; Catholic Chaplain to Univ. of London, 1966–74; Chaplain, Pax Christi, 1974–77; Parish Priest, Somers Town, NW1, 1977–80; retired from active Ministry, Feb. 1987. President: Internat. Peace Bureau, 1985–92; Nat. Peace Council, 1999–2000. Mem., Nat. Exec., UNA, 1993–97. Contested (Lab) Oxford West and Abingdon, 1992. Hon. LLD Manchester, 1987; DUniv Middx, 2002. *Publications:* Undiscovered Ends (autobiog.), 1992; essays and pamphlets on disarmament, Christians and peace. *Recreations:* friends, walking. *Address:* 11 Venetia Road, N4 1EJ.

KENT, Mark Andrew Geoffrey; HM Diplomatic Service; Ambassador to the Socialist Republic of Vietnam, since 2008; *b* Spilsby, 14 Jan. 1966; *s* of Geoffrey Kent and Patricia June Kent; *m* 1991, Martine Delogne; one *s* one d. *Educ:* Horncastle Grammar Sch.; Lincoln Coll., Oxford (BA Law 1986); Univ. Libre de Bruxelles (Licence Speciale en Droit Européen 1987); Open Univ. (Postgrad. Cert. in Business Admin 2007). Joined HM Diplomatic Service, 1987; Nr East and N Africa Dept, FCO, 1987–89; Third Sec., later Second Sec., Brasilia, 1989–93; Second, later First Sec., UK Perm. Repn to EU, 1993–98; First Sec., News Dept, FCO, 1998–2000; First Sec., later Counsellor (Commercial) and Consul-Gen., Mexico City, 2000–04; on secondment to SHAPE, 2004–05; Hd, Migration Gp, FCO, 2005–07. *Recreations:* running, football (especially Arsenal), Michael Caine films, foreign languages. *Address:* c/o Foreign and Commonwealth Office, King Charles Street, SW1A 2AH; *e-mail:* mark.kent@fco.gov.uk.

KENT, Michael Harcourt; QC 1996; a Recorder, since 2000; *b* 5 March 1952; *s* of late Captain Barrie Harcourt Kent, RN and of Margaret Harcourt Kent; *m* 1977, Sarah Ann Ling; two *s. Educ:* Nautical Coll., Pangbourne; Sussex Univ. (BA Hons). Called to the Bar, Middle Temple, 1975; SE Circuit; Supplementary Panel, Junior Counsel to the Crown, Common Law, 1988–96. Member: London Common Law and Commercial Bar Assoc.; Admin. Law Bar Assoc. An Asst Recorder, 1999–2000. *Recreation:* sailing. *Address:* Crown Office Chambers, 2 Crown Office Row, Temple, EC4Y 7HJ. *T:* (020) 7797 8100.

KENT, Nicolas; *see* Kent, R. N.

KENT, Paul Welberry; JP; DSc; FRSC; Student Emeritus of Christ Church, Oxford; *b* Doncaster, 19 April 1923; *s* of Thomas William Kent and Marion (*née* Cox); *m* 1952, Rosemary Elizabeth Boutflower, *y d* of Major C. H. B. Shepherd, MC; three *s* one d. *Educ:* Doncaster Grammar Sch.; Birmingham Univ. (BSc 1944, PhD 1947); Jesus Coll., Oxford (MA 1951, DPhil 1953, DSc 1966). Asst Lectr, subseq. ICI Fellow, Birmingham Univ., 1946–50; Vis. Fellow, Princeton Univ., 1948–49; Univ. Demonstrator in Biochem., Oxford, 1950–72; Lectr, subseq. Student, Tutor and Dr Lees Reader in Chem., 1955–72, Censor of Degrees, 2000–, Christ Church, Oxford; Durham University: Master of Van Mildert Coll. and Dir, Glycoprotein Res. Unit, 1972–82; Mem. of Senate, 1972–82; Mem. of Council, 1976–80. Research Assoc., Harvard, 1967; Vis. Prof., Windsor Univ., Ont, 1971, 1980. Bodleian Orator, 1959. Mem., Oxford City Council, 1964–72; Governor: Oxford Coll. of Technology, subseq. Oxford Polytechnic, 1964–72,

1983–89 (Vice-Chm. 1966–69, Chm. 1969–70); Oxford Polytechnic Higher Educn Corp., 1988–92 (Dep. Chm., 1988–92); Oxford Brookes Univ., 1992–97 (Vice-Chm., 1992–94). Member: Cttee, Biochemical Soc., 1963–67; Chemical Council, 1965–70; Res. Adv. Cttee, Cystic Fibrosis Res. Trust, 1977–82; Commn on Religious Educn in School. Sec., Foster and Wills Scholarships Bd, 1960–72; Pres., Soc. for Maintenance of the Faith, 1974–99 (Vice-Pres., 2000–); Governor, Pusey House, 1983–2000 (Vice-Pres., 2003–); Chm., Patrons Consultative Gp, 1994–. JP Oxford, 1972. Hon. Fellow, Canterbury Coll., Ont, 1976. Hon. DLitt Drury, 1973; Hon. DSc CNAA, 1991. Rolleston Prize, 1952; Medal of Société de Chemie Biologique, 1969; Verdienstkreuz (Germany), 1970. *Publications:* Biochemistry of Amino-sugars, 1955; (ed) Membrane-Mediated Information, Vols I and II, 1972; (ed) International Aspects of the Provision of Medical Care, 1976; (ed) New Approaches to Genetics, 1978; (ed with W. B. Fisher) Resources, Environment and the Future, 1982; Some Scientists in the life of Christ Church, Oxford, 2001; (ed with A. Chapman) Robert Hooke and The English Renaissance, 2005; articles in sci. and other jls. *Recreations:* music, travel. *Address:* 18 Arnolds Way, Cumnor Hill, Oxford OX2 9JB. *T:* (01865) 862087. *Club:* Athenæum.

KENT, Pendarell Hugh, CBE 1997; Executive Director, Bank of England, 1994–97; *b* 18 Aug. 1937; *s* of Hugh and Ann Kent; *m* 1960, Jill George; one *s* one *d. Educ:* University College Sch.; Jesus Coll., Oxford (MA Hons). Intelligence Corps, 2nd Lieut, 1959–61. Bank of England, 1961–97: UK Alternate Exec. Dir, IMF, 1976–79; Head: of Inf. Div., 1984–85; of Internat. Div. (Internat. Financial Instns and Developing Countries), 1985–88; Associate Dir, Finance and Industry, 1988–94. Dir, Private Finance Panel, 1993–97. Chm., CRESTCo, 1994–96; Exec. Chm., European Securities Forum, 2000–02; Chm., Euroclear UK Mkt Adv. Cttee, 2002–; non-executive Director: BR Southern Region, 1986–92 (Chm., 1989–92); NatWest Gp, 1997–2000; Strategic Rail Authy, 1999–2006 (Chm., 2006); Schroder & Co. Ltd, 2001–; F & C Capital and Income Investment Trust, 2003– (Chm., 2005–); CDC (Mem., Commonwealth Develt Corp., 1995–2001); Punjab Nat. Bank Internat., 2007–. Dir, City of London Fest., 1996–2002 (Chm., 1997–2001); Dep. Chm., Heart of the City, 2000–. Gov., NYO, 2000–. Patron, Blind in Business, 2003– (Trustee, 1992–2002; Chm., 1996–2001). Property Award, Coll. of Estate Mgt, 1997. *Publication:* Nursery Schools for All (with Jill Kent), 1970. *Recreations:* art, jazz, ski-ing.

KENT, Peter Humphreys, CMG 2001; President, European Intelligent Building Group, since 2002; private sector government trade adviser; *b* 21 April 1937; *s* of Cosmo Weatherley Kent and Beatrice Humphreys Tordoff; *m* 1964, Noel Mary Curwen; one *s. Educ:* Denehurst Prep. Sch.; Royal Grammar Sch., Guildford. Commnd Queen's Royal W Surrey Regt, 1956; seconded RWAFF, 1956; served: 5 Bn Queen's Own Nigeria Regt, 1956–57; 1st Bn Queen's Royal Regt, TA, 1957–60. Union Internat. Co. Ltd, London and Nigeria, 1958–61; I. H. S. Lotinga Ltd, Nigeria, 1961–64; Newton Chambers & Co. Ltd, 1964–73 (Man. Dir, Izal Overseas Ltd, and Dir, Izal Ltd); Mktg Dir, Europe, Sterling Winthrop Ltd, 1973–76; Arthur Guinness & Sons, 1975–78 (Internat. Mktg Dir, Jackel Ltd); Man. Dir, Steinerco (UK) Ltd, 1978–83; Dir, More O'Ferrall Plc, 1983–97. Chairman: Starlite Media LLC, NY, 2000–02; Starlite Media Internat. Ltd, UK, 2000–02; non-exec. Dir, GruppeM Investments plc, 2007–. Dir, Taiwan Trade Centre (TAITRA (formerly CETRA)) Ltd, 1993–; Chm., Taiwan Advrs Gp, 1997–; Vice-Chm., Taiwan Britain Business Council, 1998–; Member: Singapore Britain Business Council, 2003–; Malaysia Britain Business Council, 2005–. Asia Pacific Advr, DTI/BTI/UK Trade & Investment (formerly Trade Partners UK), 1985–. Mem., CBI Internat. Cttee, 1998–2000. Dir, 1993–2003, Mem. Council, 2005–, Internat. Shakespeare Globe Centre; Dir, Shakespeare's Globe Centre (USA) Ltd, 2007–. Trustee, 1992–2005, Vice-Chm., 2004–05, Colchester and Dist Visual Arts Trust. Freeman, City of London, 1980; Liveryman, Co. of Launderers, 1980–. Member: RSAA, 2001; European-Atlantic Gp, 1993. FInstD 1968; Fellow, Inst. of Export, 1967. Friend of the Foreign Service Medal (Taiwan), 2000; Economic Medal (Taiwan), 2003. *Recreations:* film and theatre, travelling, socialising. *Address:* Cherry Ground, Holbrook, Suffolk IP9 2PS. *T:* (01473) 328203, *Fax:* (01473) 328472; 202 Marlyn Lodge, Portsoken Street, E1 8RB; *e-mail:* phkent1937@ aol.com. *Clubs:* Naval and Military, Academy; Jockey Club Rooms (Newmarket); Hintlesham Golf.

KENT, (Robert) Nicolas; director and producer, theatre, television and radio; Artistic Director, Tricycle Theatre, since 1984; *b* London, 26 Jan. 1945; *s* of Henry and Mary Kent. *Educ:* Stowe Sch.; St Catharine's Coll., Cambridge (BA Hons English 1967). ABC TV trainee dir, Liverpool Playhouse, 1967–68; Artistic Dir, Watermill Th., 1970; Associate Dir, Traverse Th., Edinburgh, 1970–72; Admin. Dir, Oxford Playhouse Co., 1976–82; freelance prodns at Royal Court Th., Young Vic, National Th., RSC and West End include: Ain't Misbehavin', Lyric, 1995; Colour of Justice, Victoria Palace, 1999; Guantanamo, New Ambassadors and NY, 2004; Co-Producer: Before the Party, Queens, 1979; The Price, Apollo, 2003; 39 Steps, Criterion, 2006–; director of plays for TV including: Playboy of the West Indies, 1984; Pentecost, 1990; Justifying War, 2003. Member: Council, AA, 1998–2000; Mayor of London's Cultural Strategy Gp, 1998–2000; Council, Arts Council, London, 2002–06. Dir, Soc. of London Theatres, 2000–07. Hon. DLitt Westminster, 2007. *Publications:* Srebrenica, 2005 (broadcast on BBC World Service); (contrib.) Verbatim Verbatim, 2008. *Recreations:* country walks, tennis, African-American literature, art, architecture, politics, French films on winter afternoons, dead-heading roses in the sun. *Address:* Tricycle Theatre, 269 Kilburn High Road, NW6 7JR. *T:* (020) 7372 6611, *Fax:* (020) 7328 0795; *e-mail:* nicolas@ nicolaskent.com.

KENT, Roderick David; Chairman, Bradford & Bingley Group plc, since 2002; *b* 14 Aug. 1947; *s* of Dr Basil Stanley Kent, MB, BS, FFARCS and Vivien Margaret Kent (*née* Baker); *m* 1972, Belinda Jane Mitchell; three *d. Educ:* King's Sch., Canterbury; Corpus Christi Coll., Oxford (MA); INSEAD (MBA 1972). MSI. Investment Div., J. Henry Schroder Wagg, 1969–71; Triumph Investment Trust, 1972–74; Dir, 1974–2002, Chm., 1990–2002, Close Brothers Ltd; Man. Dir, 1975–2002, non-exec. Dir, 2002–06, Chm., 2006–08, Close Brothers Gp plc. Chm., Grosvenor Ltd, 2000–. Non-executive Director: Wessex Water plc, 1988–98; English and Scottish Investors plc, 1988–98; M & G Gp plc, 1995–99 (non-exec. Chm., 1998–99); Grosvenor Group Ltd, 2000–; Whitbread plc, 2002–08. Chm., BT Pension Scheme, 2008–. Trustee, Esmée Fairbairn Foundn, 2001–08; Gov., Wellcome Trust Foundn, 2008–. Liveryman, Co. of Pewterers, 1976–. *Recreations:* dairy farming, antique furniture restoration, sports. *Address:* Bradford & Bingley Group plc, 21-27 Lamb's Conduit Street, WC1N 3BD.

KENT, Thomas George, CBE 1979; CEng, MIMechE, FRAeS; aerospace and defence consultant; Director: Third Grosvenor Ltd, since 1987; Grosvenor General Partner, since 1995; *b* 13 Aug. 1925. *Educ:* Borden Grammar School; Medway College of Technology. Joined English Electric Co., 1951; Special Director, British Aircraft Corp., 1967; Dep. Man. Dir, 1974; Man. Dir, 1977; Director, Hatfield/Lostock Division and Stevenage/ Bristol Div. of Dynamics Group, British Aerospace, 1977–79; Gp Dep. Chief Exec., BAe Dynamics Gp, 1980–85; Bd Mem., BAe, 1981–85; Director: BAe Australia Ltd, 1980–86 (Chm., 1984–86); Arab British Dynamics, 1980–85; BAJ Vickers Ltd, 1982–87 (non-

exec.); Grosvenor Technol. Ltd, 1984–95; Grosvenor Develt Capital, 1993–95; Mercury Grosvenor Trust PLC, 1995–97. *Address:* Weeamara, Grove Park, Hampton on the Hill, Warwick CV35 8QR.

KENT-JONES, His Honour Trevor David, TD; a Circuit Judge, 1991–2006; *b* 31 July 1940; *s* of late David Sandford Kent-Jones and Madeline Mary Kent-Jones (*née* Russell-Pavier); one *s* one *d. Educ:* Bedford Sch.; Liverpool Univ. (LLB; DipIntLaw). Called to the Bar, Gray's Inn, 1962; Mem., NE Circuit, 1963–91; Junior, 1969; a Recorder, 1985–91. Commnd KOYLI TA, 1959; served 4th Bn KOYLI, 5th Bn Light Infantry, HQ NE Dist, 1959–85; Lt-Col 1977. *Recreations:* cricket, Rugby, travel, fell-walking. *Address:* Harrogate, N Yorks. *Club:* Naval and Military.

KENTFIELD, Graham Edward Alfred; Deputy Director, 1994–98, and Chief Cashier, 1991–98, Bank of England; *b* 3 Sept. 1940; *s* of late E. L. H. Kentfield and F. E. M. Kentfield (*née* Tucker); *m* 1965, Ann Dwelley Hewetson; two *d. Educ:* Bancroft's Sch., Woodford Green, Essex; St Edmund Hall, Oxford (BA 1st cl. Lit.Hum.). Entered Bank of England, 1963; seconded to Dept of Applied Econs, Cambridge, 1966–67; Editor, Bank of England Qly Bull., 1977–80; Adviser: Financial Stats Div., 1980–84; Banking Dept, 1984–85; Dep. Chief of Banking Dept and Dep. Chief Cashier, 1985–91; Chief of Banking Dept, 1991–94. Member: Bldg Socs Investment Protection Bd, 1991–2001; Financial Law Panel, 1994–98; Chm., Insolvency Practices Council, 2000–04. Trustee: CIB Pension Fund, 1994–2006 (Chm., 2000–06); Overseas Bishoprics Fund, 1999– (Chm., 2005–). Vice-Pres., CIB, 2000–. Chm., Building Socs Trust Ltd, 2002–. Hon. Treas., Soc. for Promotion of Roman Studies, 1991–. Mem. Council, Univ. of London, 2000–. *Recreations:* Roman history, genealogy, philately.

KENTRIDGE, Sir Sydney (Woolf), KCMG 1999; QC 1984; *b* Johannesburg, 5 Nov. 1922; *s* of Morris and May Kentridge; *m* 1952, Felicia Geffen; two *s* two *d. Educ:* King Edward VII Sch., Johannesburg; Univ. of the Witwatersrand (BA); Exeter Coll., Oxford Univ. (MA; Hon. Fellow, 1986). War service with S African forces, 1942–46. Advocate 1949, Senior Counsel 1965, South Africa; called to the English Bar, Lincoln's Inn, 1977, Bencher, 1986. Mem., Ct of Appeal, Botswana, 1981–88; Judge, Cts of Appeal, Jersey and Guernsey, 1988–92; acting Justice, Constitutional Court of S Africa, 1995–96. Roberts Lectr, Univ. of Pennsylvania, 1979. Hon. Mem., Bar Assoc., NY, 2001. Hon. Fellow, American Coll. of Trial Lawyers, 1999. Hon. LLD: Seton Hall Univ., NJ, 1978; Leicester, 1985; Cape Town, 1987; Natal, 1989; London, 1995; Sussex, 1997; Witwatersrand, 2000. Granville Clark Prize, USA, 1978. *Recreation:* opera-going. *Address:* Brick Court Chambers, 7–8 Essex Street, WC2R 3LD. *T:* (020) 7379 3550. *Club:* Athenæum.

KENWARD, Michael Ronald John, OBE 1990; science writer and editorial consultant; *b* 12 July 1945; *s* of late Ronald Kenward and of Phyllis Kenward; *m* 1969, Elizabeth Rice. *Educ:* Wolverstone Hall; Sussex Univ. Res. scientist, UKAEA, Culham Laboratory, 1966–68; Technical editor, Scientific Instrument Res. Assoc., 1969; various editorial posts, New Scientist, 1969–79, Editor, 1979–90; Science Consultant, The Sunday Times, 1990. Member: Royal Soc. COPUS, 1986–90; Public Affairs Cttee, 1989–93, Sci. and Industry Cttee, 1994–99, BAAS; Bd, Assoc. of British Editors, 1986–90; Royal Instn Task Force, 1995–96; Centre Cttee, Wellcome Centre for Med. Sci., 1997–98; Medicine in Society Panel, Wellcome Trust, 1998–2000; Adv. Cttee, AlphaGalileo electronic news service, 1999–. Writer in residence, OST Foresight Projects on Cognitive Systems, 2002–04, on Intelligent Infrastructure Systems, 2005. Internat. Rep., Assoc. of British Sci. Writers, 1993–97. Member: Editl Cttee, Science and Public Affairs, 1994–97; Editl Bd, Ingenia, Royal Acad. of Engrg, 2004–. *Publications:* Potential Energy, 1976; articles on science, technology, and business. *Recreations:* walking, photography, collecting 'middle-aged' books, listening to baroque opera and Texas rock-and-roll, reconfiguring my operating system. *Address:* Grange Cottage, Staplefield, W Sussex RH17 6EL.

KENWAY-SMITH, Wendy Alison, FCA; Assistant Auditor General, National Audit Office, since 2000; *b* 21 Feb. 1959; *d* of Derek Peter Kenway-Smith and Muriel Anne Kenway-Smith (*née* Stevens). *Educ:* Marist Sch., Ascot; Guildford Tech. Coll.; City of London Poly. (BA Hons Accountancy). ACA 1983, FCA 1993. Joined BDO Stoy Hayward, 1980, Partner, 1990–95; Dir, Nat. Audit Office, 1995–99. Freeman, City of London, 1993. *Recreations:* travel, gardening, good food, theatre, classical music. *Address:* National Audit Office, 157-197 Buckingham Palace Road, SW1W 9SP. *T:* (020) 7798 7391.

KENWORTHY, family name of **Baron Strabolgi.**

KENWORTHY, Duncan Hamish, OBE 1999; film producer; Managing Director, Toledo Productions Ltd, since 1995; Director, DNA Films Ltd, since 1997; *b* 9 Sept. 1949; *s* of Bernard Ian Kenworthy and Edna Muriel Kenworthy (*née* Calligan). *Educ:* Rydal Sch.; Christ's Coll., Cambridge (MA English 1975); Annenberg Sch., Univ. of Pennsylvania (MA Communications 1973). Children's Television Workshop, NY, 1973–76; Consulting Producer, Arabic Sesame Street, Kuwait, 1977–79; Prod. and Exec., Jim Henson Productions, London, 1979–95. Associate Prod., The Dark Crystal (film), 1980; Producer: *television:* Fraggle Rock, 1982 (Outstanding Children's Programming, Emmy Award, 1983); The Storyteller, 1986–88 (Best Children's Prog., BAFTA, 1989); Living with Dinosaurs, 1988 (Best Children's Prog., Emmy Award, 1990); Monster Maker, 1988; Greek Myths, 1990 (Best Children's Fictional Prog., BAFTA, 1991); Gulliver's Travels, 1996 (Outstanding Mini-series, Emmy Award, 1996); *films:* Four Weddings and a Funeral, 1994 (Best Film, and Lloyd's Bank Peoples' Choice Award, BAFTA, 1994; Best Foreign Film, Cesar Award, 1994); Lawn Dogs, 1997; Notting Hill, 1999 (Orange Audience Award, BAFTA, 2000); The Parole Officer, 2001; Love Actually, 2003. Chm., BAFTA, 2004–06 (Chm., Film, 2002–04); Mem., Film Policy Review Gp, 1997–99; Dir, Film Council, 1999–2003; Chm., Film Adv. Cttee, British Council, 1999–; Gov., Nat. Film and TV Sch., 2001–. British Producer of the Year, London Film Critics, 1994. FRSA 2000. *Address:* Toledo Productions, 1st Floor, 15 Greek Street, W1D 4DP. *Club:* Garrick.

KENWORTHY, (Frederick) John; Adviser, Information Strategy, University of Cambridge, since 2002; Managing Director, Aktus (formerly Align) Consulting (UK) Ltd, since 1997; *b* 6 Dec. 1943; *s* of late Rev. Fred Kenworthy and of Mrs Ethel Kenworthy; *m* 1968, Diana Flintham; one *d. Educ:* William Hulme's Grammar Sch., Manchester; Manchester Univ. (BA Econ Hons Politics). Entered Admin. Class, Home Civil Service, as Asst Principal, MoD (Navy), 1966; Treasury Centre for Admin. Studies, 1968–69; joined BSC, Sheffield, 1969; Principal, MoD, 1972; Royal Commn on the Press Secretariat, 1974; Asst Sec., Dir, Weapons Resources and Progs (Naval), MoD, 1979–83; Head of Resources and Progs (Navy) (formerly DS4), RN Size and Shape Policy, and Sec. to Navy Bd, MoD, 1983–86; Dir of Ops, Disablement Services Authy (formerly Div.), DHSS, 1986–88; Dir, IT Systems Directorate (Under Sec.), 1989–90, Chief Exec., IT Services Agency, 1990–93, Dept of Social Security; Management Consultant, ICL (Internat.), 1993–95; Prin. Consultant, Independent Management Consultants, 1996. Interim Dir of Mgt Inf. Services, Univ. of Cambridge, 2001. Sen. Associate Mem., Hughes Hall, Cambridge, 2007. MInstD. Freeman, Co. of Information Technologists, 1992. *Publications:* contribs on Hungarian revenue collection and on pensions. *Recreations:*

music, history, photography. *Address:* PO Box 20031, NW2 4ZN. *T:* (020) 8208 1043; *e-mail:* jk304@cam.ac.uk.

KENWORTHY, Joan Margaret, BLitt, MA; Principal, St Mary's College, University of Durham, 1977–99; *b* Oldham, Lancs, 10 Dec. 1933; *o d* of late Albert Kenworthy and Amy (*née* Cobbold). *Educ:* Girls Grammar Sch., Barrow-in-Furness; St Hilda's Coll., Oxford (BLitt, MA). Henry Oliver Beckit Prize, Oxford, 1955; Leverhulme Overseas Res. Scholar, Makerere Coll., Uganda, and E African Agriculture and Forestry Res. Org., Kenya, 1956–58; Actg Tutor, St Hugh's Coll., Oxford, 1958–59; Tutorial Res. Fellow, Bedford Coll., London, 1959–60; Univ. of Liverpool: Asst Lectr in Geography, 1960–63; Lectr, 1963–73; Sen. Lectr, 1973–77; Warden of Salisbury Hall, 1966–77 and of Morton House, 1974–77. IUC short-term Vis. Lectr, Univ. of Sierra Leone, 1975; Vis. Lectr, Univ. of Fort Hare, Ciskei, 1983. Mem., NE England, Churches Regl Broadcasting Council, 1978–82; Bishop's Selector for ACCM, 1982–87. Member: Council, African Studies Assoc. of UK, 1969–71, 1994–97; Standing Cttee on Univ. Studies of Africa, 1994–98; Council, Inst. of Brit. Geographers, 1976–78; Cttee, Merseyside Conf. for Overseas Students Ltd, 1976–77; Council, RMetS, 1980–83 (Mem., Cttee, History Gp, 2001–); Treasurer, Assoc. of Brit. Climatologists, 1976–79. Northern Chm., Durham Univ. Soc., 1979–82. Gov., St Anne's Sch., Windermere, 1992–95. Member: Satley PCC, 2000–05 (Treas., 2002–05); Stanhope Deanery Synod, 2001–04. A Dir (formerly Trustee), Wear Valley CAB, 2001–04. *Publications:* (contrib.) Geographers and the Tropics, ed R. W. Steel and R. M. Prothero, 1964; (contrib.) Oxford Regional Economic Atlas for Africa, 1965; (contrib.) Studies in East African Geography and Development, ed S. Ominde, 1971; (contrib.) An Advanced Geography of Africa, ed J. I. Clarke, 1975; (contrib.) Rangeland Management and Ecology in East Africa, ed D. J. Pratt and M. D. Gwynne, 1977; (contrib.) The Climatic Scene: essays in honour of Emeritus Prof. Gordon Manley, ed M. J. Tooley and G. Sheail, 1985; (ed with B. D. Giles) Observatories and Climatological Research, 1994; (ed with J. M. Walker) Colonial Observatories and Observations, 1997; articles in jls, encycs and reports of symposia. *Address:* 3 Satley Plough, Satley, Bishop Auckland, Co. Durham DL13 4JX. *T:* (01388) 730848. *Clubs:* Royal Commonwealth Society, Penn, Oxford and Cambridge.

KENWORTHY, John; *see* Kenworthy, F. J.

KENWORTHY-BROWNE, (Bernard) Peter (Francis); a District Judge (formerly Registrar) of the High Court (Family Division), 1982–2002; *b* 11 May 1930; *s* of late Bernard Evelyn Kenworthy-Browne and Margaret Sibylla Kenworthy-Browne; *m* 1975, Jane Elizabeth Arthur (marr. diss. 1982); *m* 1989, Elizabeth, *o d* of late Dr J. A. Bowen-Jones. *Educ:* Ampleforth; Oriel Coll., Oxford. MA. 2nd Lieut, Irish Guards, 1949–50. Called to the Bar, Lincoln's Inn, 1955; Oxford, and Midland and Oxford Circuit, 1957–82; a Recorder of the Crown Court, 1981–82. *Recreations:* music, field sports, gardening. *Address:* The Old Vicarage, Staverton, Northants NN11 6JJ. *T:* (01327) 704667. *Club:* Cavalry and Guards.

KENWRIGHT, Prof. John, MD; FRCS; FRCSE; Nuffield Professor of Orthopaedic Surgery, Oxford University, 1992–2001; Professorial Fellow, Worcester College, Oxford, 1992–2001, now Emeritus; *b* 2 May 1936; *s* of Cecil Kenwright and Norah (*née* Langley); *m* 1960, Vivien Mary Curtis; two *s. Educ:* University College Sch.; Nottingham High Sch.; St John's Coll., Oxford; University College Hosp. MA Oxon; BM, BCh; MD Stockholm 1972. FRCS 1966; FRCSE (*ad hominem*) 1998. Nuffield Surgical Res. Fellow, Oxford, 1968; Res. Fellow, Karolinska Inst., Stockholm, 1971; Consultant Orthopaedic Surgeon, Nuffield Orthopaedic Centre and John Radcliffe Hosp., Oxford, 1973–2001. Royal College of Surgeons of England: Hunterian Prof., 1991–92; Robert Jones Lectr, 1998; Res. Dir, Wishbone Trust, British Orthopaedic Assoc., 2002–03. President: Girdlestone Orthopaedic Soc., 1993–2002; Oxford Medico-legal Soc., 1998–; British Limb Reconstruction Soc., 1998–2000; British Orthopaedic Res. Soc., 1999–; Internat. Soc. for Fracture Repair, 2002–04. *Publications:* articles in scientific jls on factors which control fracture and soft tissue healing; also on leg lengthening and correction of post traumatic deformity. *Recreation:* sailing. *Address:* Nuffield Orthopaedic Centre, Headington, Oxford OX3 7LD. *T:* (01865) 862695, *Fax:* (01865) 862695; *e-mail:* john.kenwright@virgin.net. *Club:* Oxford and Cambridge Sailing Society.

KENWRIGHT, William, (Bill), CBE 2001; theatre producer, since 1970; *b* 4 Sept. 1945; *s* of Albert Kenwright and Hope Kenwright (*née* Jones); partner, Jennifer Ann Seagrove, *qv. Educ:* Liverpool Inst. Actor, 1964–70; has produced more than 500 plays and musicals, including: Joseph and The Amazing Technicolor Dreamcoat; A Streetcar Named Desire; Stepping Out; Blood Brothers, 1988, transf. NY; Shirley Valentine; Travels with My Aunt; Piaf; Medea; A Doll's House; An Ideal Husband; Passion; Long Day's Journey into Night; Cat on a Hot Tin Roof, etc; *films:* Stepping Out; Don't Go Breaking My Heart, 1999. Dir, Everton FC (Dep. Chm., 1998). Hon. Prof., Tameside Univ. Hon. Dr Liverpool John Moores, 1994. Has won Tony, Olivier and Evening Standard awards. *Address:* Bill Kenwright Ltd, BKL House, 106 Harrow Road, W2 1RR. *T:* (020) 7446 6200.

KENYA, Archbishop of, since 2002; **Most Rev. Benjamin Mwanzia Nzimbi;** Bishop of All Saints Cathedral Diocese, since 2002; *b* 17 Oct. 1945; *s* of Paul Nzimbi Munuve and Martha Nditi Nzimbi; *m* 1974, Alice Kavula Nzimbi; three *s* two *d. Educ:* Univ. of Nairobi (BA Religious Studies and Philos. 1974); Trinity Coll., Nairobi; Hamline Univ., St Paul, USA (MA Mgt for Non-Profit 1999). Taught in secondary sch. and teachers' colls, 1974–84. Ordained, deacon, 1978, priest, 1979; Curate, All Souls Parish, Machakos, and Chaplain, Machakos Teachers' Coll., 1978–84; Vicar, St Francis Parish, Karen, Nairobi, 1984–85; Bishop: Machakos Dio., 1985–95; Kitui Dio., 1995–2002. *Address:* Anglican Church of Kenya, PO Box 40502, 00100 Nairobi, Kenya. *T:* (20) 2714755, *Fax:* (20) 2718442; *e-mail:* archoffice@swiftkenya.com.

KENYON, family name of **Baron Kenyon**.

KENYON, 6th Baron *cr* 1788; **Lloyd Tyrell-Kenyon;** Bt 1784; Baron of Gredington, 1788; *b* 13 July 1947; *s* of 5th Baron Kenyon, CBE and of Leila Mary, *d* of Comdr John Wyndham Cookson, RN and *widow* of Hugh William Jardine Ethelston Peel; *S* father, 1993; *m* 1971, Sally Carolyn, *e d* of J. F. P. Matthews; two *s. Educ:* Eton; Magdalene Coll., Cambridge (BA). Mem. (C), Wrexham County (formerly Wrexham Maelor) BC, 1991–. Mem., EU Cttee of the Regions, 1994–97. High Sheriff, Clwyd, 1986. *Heir: s* Hon. Lloyd Nicholas Tyrell-Kenyon, *b* 9 April 1972. *Address:* Gredington, Whitchurch, Shropshire SY13 3DH.

KENYON, Ian Roy; HM Diplomatic Service, retired; Executive Secretary, Preparatory Commission for Organisation for Prohibition of Chemical Weapons, The Hague, 1993–97; *b* 13 June 1939; *s* of late S. R. Kenyon and Mrs E. M. Kenyon; *m* 1962, Griselda Rintoul; one *s* one *d. Educ:* Lancaster Royal Grammar School; Edinburgh University (BSc Hons). Lever Bros, 1962–68; Birds Eye Foods, 1968–74; First Secretary, FCO, 1974–76; Geneva, 1976–78; Head of Chancery, Bogota, 1979–81; FCO, 1982–83; Head of Nuclear Energy Dept, FCO, 1983–85; Overseas Inspectorate, 1986–88; Dep. Leader, UK Delegn

to Conf. on Disarmament, Geneva, 1988–92. Visiting Senior Research Fellow: Mountbatten Centre for Internat. Studies, Southampton Univ., 1997–; Sci. and Technol. Policy Res. Unit, Sussex Univ., 2003–. *Recreation:* carriage driving.

KENYON, Margaret; DL; Headmistress, Withington Girls' School, Manchester, 1986–2000; *b* 19 June 1940; *d* of Hugh Richard Parry and Aileen Cole (*née* Morgan); *m* 1962, Christopher George Kenyon; two *s. Educ:* Merchant Taylors' Sch. for Girls, Crosby; Somerville Coll., Oxford (MA; Hon. Fellow, 1999). Asst French Mistress, Cheadle Hulme Sch., 1962–63 and 1974–83; Hd of French, Withington Girls Sch., 1983–85. Girls' School Association: Chm., NW Region, 1989–91; Pres., 1993–94. Mem. Adv. Council, Granada Foundn, 1986–. Trustee, Mus. of Science and Industry, Manchester, 1998–2004. Mem. Court, Univ. of Manchester, 1991–2004 (Chair, Press Bd, 2001–). Governor: Bolton Sch., 2001–; Cheadle Hulme Sch., 2001–; Haberdashers' Aske's Schs, Elstree, 2002–. DL Greater Manchester, 1998. *Recreations:* reading, talking, family. *Address:* Westow Lodge, Macclesfield Road, Alderley Edge, Cheshire SK9 7BW.

KENYON, Sir Nicholas (Roger), Kt 2008; CBE 2001; Managing Director, Barbican Centre, since 2007; *b* 23 Feb. 1951; *s* of Thomas Kenyon and Kathleen Holmes; *m* 1976, Marie-Ghislaine Latham-Koenig; three *s* one *d. Educ:* Balliol College, Oxford (BA Hons 1972). Music critic: The New Yorker, 1979–82; The Times, 1982–85; The Observer, 1985–92; Music Editor, The Listener, 1982–87; Editor, Early Music, 1983–92; Controller, BBC Radio 3, 1992–98; Dir, BBC Promenade Concerts, 1996–2007; Controller, BBC Proms, Live Events and TV Classical Music, 2000–07. Mem., AHRB, subseq. AHRC, 2004–08. Mem. Bd, ENO. Trustee, Dartington Hall Trust. Gov., Wellington Coll. *Publications:* The BBC Symphony Orchestra 1930–80, 1981; Simon Rattle, 1987, 2nd edn 2001; The Faber Pocket Guide to Mozart, 2005; *edited:* Authenticity and Early Music, 1988; (jtly) The Viking Opera Guide, 1993; (jtly) The Penguin Opera Guide, 1995; BBC Proms Guide to Great Symphonies, 2003; BBC Proms Guide to Great Concertos, 2003; Musical Lives, 2003; BBC Proms Guide to Great Choral Works, 2004; BBC Proms Guide to Great Orchestral Works, 2004. *Recreation:* family. *Address:* Barbican Centre, Silk Street, EC2Y 8DW. *T:* (020) 7382 7005.

KENYON-SLANEY, (William) Simon (Rodolph), OBE 2004; JP; Vice Lord-Lieutenant of Shropshire, 1996–2007; *b* 31 Jan. 1932; *s* of Major R. O. R. Kenyon-Slaney, Grenadier Guards, and Nesta, *d* of Sir George Ferdinand Forestier-Walker, 3rd Bt; *m* 1960, Mary Helena, *e d* of Lt-Col Hon. H. G. O. Bridgeman, DSO, MC, RA, and Joan, *d* of Hon. Bernard Constable Maxwell; three *s. Educ:* Eton. FLAS 1964; FRICS 1970. Grenadier Guards, 1950–52; formerly: Chartered Land Agent and Surveyor; farmer. Non-exec. Dir, South Staffs Gp PLC, 1988–02. Chm., Ludlow Cons. Assoc., 1989–91. Trustee, Ironbridge Gorge Museum, 1995–. Former school governor. Shropshire: JP 1969 (Chm., Shropshire Magistrates' Courts Cttee, 1994–97); CC, 1977–85; High Sheriff, 1979; DL 1986. Mem. Council, Shropshire, SJAB, 1969– (Chm., 1974–02). KStJ 1993 (Mem., Chapter-General, 1990–99, Priory Chapter, 1999–02). *Recreations:* gardening, travel, theatre, fishing. *Address:* Chyknell, Bridgnorth, Shropshire WV15 5PP. *T:* (01746) 710210.

KEOGH, Prof. Sir Bruce (Edward), KBE 2003; MD; FRCS, FRCSE; NHS Medical Director, Department of Health, since 2007; *b* 24 Nov. 1954; *s* of Gerald Keogh and Marjorie Beatrice Keogh (*née* Craig); naturalised British citizen, 2004; *m* 1979, Ann Katherine (*née* Westmore); four *s. Educ:* St George's Coll., Zimbabwe; Charing Cross Hosp. Med. Sch., Univ. of London (BSc Hons 1977; MB BS 1980; MD 1989). MRCS 1980, FRCS *ad eundem* 2000; LRCP 1980; FRCSE 1985. Demonstrator in Anatomy, Charing Cross Hosp. Med. Sch., 1981–82; Registrar training: Northern Gen. Hosp., Sheffield, 1984–85; Hammersmith Hosp., 1985–89 (BHF Jun. Res. Fellow, 1987–88); Sen. Registrar in Cardiothoracic Surgery, St George's and Harefield Hosps, 1989–91; BHF Sen. Lectr in Cardiac Surgery, RPMS Hammersmith Hosp., 1991–95; Consultant in Cardiothoracic Surgery, 1995–2004, and Associate Med. Dir for Clinical Governance, 1998–2003, University Hosp. Birmingham NHS Trust; Prof. of Cardiac Surgery, 2004–07, Hon. Prof., 2008, UCL; Dir of Surgery, 2004–08, Consultant Cardiothoracic Surgeon, 2004–, The Heart Hosp., UCL Hosps NHS Trust. Vis. Prof. of Surgery, Chinese Univ. of HK, 2007; King James IV Prof., RCSE, 2005; RCS Tudor Edwards Lectr, 2007. Member: Commn for Health Improvement, 2002–04; Commn for Healthcare Audit and Inspection, 2004– (Chm., Clinical Adv. Gp, 2004–06); Chairman: Jt Commn for Health Improvement and Audit Commn Nat. Service Framework Prog. Bd, 2002–04; Jt DoH, Healthcare Commn and Soc. for Cardio Thoracic Surgery Central Cardiac Audit Database Oversight Cttee, 2004–07. Member: NHS Nat. Taskforce for Coronary Heart Disease, 2000–06; NHS Standing Med. Adv. Cttee, 2002–04; Chairman: W Midlands NHS Regl Coronary Heart Disease and Tobacco Modernisation Gp, 2000–02; DoH Inf. Taskforce on Clinical Outcomes, 2006–07. Founder and Co-ordinator, Nat. Adult Cardiac Surgical Database, 1995–2007. Member: Intercollegiate Specialist Adv. Cttee on higher surgical trng in cardiothoracic surgery, 1999–2004; Intercollegiate Exam. Bd in Cardiothoracic Surgery, 1999–2003 (Examr, 1999–2004). Mem. Council, RCS, 2002–04, 2006–08; Cardiothoracic section, Royal Society of Medicine: Mem. Council, 1992–99; Hon. Sec., 1993–99; Pres., 2005–07; Society for Cardio Thoracic Surgery in GB and Ireland: Ronald Edwards Medal, 1991; Hon. Sec., 1999–2003; Pres., 2006–08; Sec.-Gen., European Assoc. for Cardio-Thoracic Surgery, 2004–08. Fellow: European Soc. of Cardiology, 1992; European Bd of Thoracic and Cardiovascular Surgery, 1999. Member, Editorial Board: Jl RSocMed, 1994–99; CTSNet, 1999–2007; Heart, 2000–. Hon. FRCP 2005. *Publications:* Normal Surface Anatomy, 1984; National Adult Cardiac Surgical Database Report, 1999, 5th edn 2004; articles in jls on cardiac surgery and measurement of health outcomes. *Recreation:* diving. *Address:* Claremont House, 68 Oakfield Road, Selly Park, Birmingham B29 7EG.

KEOHANE, Desmond John, OBE 1991; consultant in education and training, retired; *b* 5 July 1928; *s* of William Patrick Keohane and Mabel Margaret Keohane; *m* 1960, Mary Kelliher; two *s* two *d. Educ:* Borden Grammar Sch., Sittingbourne; Univ. of Birmingham (BA and Baxter Prize in History, 1949); London Univ. (Postgrad. Cert in Educn). Postgrad. res., 1949–50; Nat. Service, Educn Officer, RAF, 1950–52; sch. teacher and coll. lectr, 1953–64; Head, Dept of Social and Academic Studies, 1964–68, and Vice-Principal, 1969–71, Havering Technical Coll.; Principal, Northampton Coll. of Further Educn, 1971–76; Principal, Oxford Coll. of Further Educn, 1976–90. Part-time Lectr in Educnl Management, Univ. of Leicester, 1990–93; Vis. Fellow (Educn), 1991–94, Hon. Fellow, 1991, Oxford Brookes Univ. (formerly Oxford Polytechnic). Member: Council, Southern Regional Council for Further Educn, 1977–90; Secondary Exams Council, 1983–86; Berks and Oxon Area Manpower Board, 1985–88; Special Employment Measures Adv. Gp, MSC, 1986–89; Northampton RC Diocesan Educn Commn, 1991–2002; E Midlands Panel, Nat. Lottery Charities Bd, 1995–98; Co-opted Mem. Educn Cttee, Northants CC, 1996–2002. Chm. Trustees, Stress at Work, 1987–2002. Formerly governor of various educnl instns; Chm. of Govs, Thomas Becket Sch., Northampton, 1983–98. Gen. Ed., series Managing Colleges Effectively, 1994–99. FCMI (FBIM 1981). *Recreations:* enjoying family and friends, watching cricket. *Address:* 14

Abington Park Crescent, Northampton NN3 3AD. *T:* (01604) 638829; *e-mail:* desmond.keohane@btinternet.com.

KEPPEL, family name of **Earl of Albemarle**.

KER; *see* Innes-Ker, family name of Duke of Roxburghe.

KERBY, John Vyvyan; Chief Executive, National Talking Newspapers and Magazines, since 2007; *b* 14 Dec. 1942; *s* of Theo Rosser Fred Kerby and Constance Mary (*née* Newell); *m* 1978, Shirley Elizabeth Pope; one step *s* one step *d. Educ:* Eton Coll.; Christ Church, Oxford (MA). Temp. Asst Principal, CO, 1965; Asst Principal, ODM, 1967; Pvte Sec. to Parly Under-Sec. of State, FCO, 1970; Principal, ODA, 1971–74, 1975–77; CSSB, 1974–75; Asst Sec., ODA, 1977; Head of British Develt Div. in Southern Africa, 1983; Under Sec. and Prin. Establishment Officer, ODA, 1986–93; Hd, Asia and Pacific Div., ODA, subseq. Dir, Asia and Pacific, DFID, 1993–97; Dir, Eastern Europe and Western Hemisphere Div., DFID, 1997–2001; UK Dir, EBRD, 2001–03. Gov., subseq. Mem. Adv. Council, Centre for Internat. Briefing, 1986–2004. Mem., Heathfield and Waldron Parish Council, 2005–. *Recreations:* gardening, cricket, music, entomology. *Address:* Yulden Farm, Sandy Cross Lane, Heathfield, E Sussex TN21 8QR. *T:* (01435) 864253.

KERDEL-VEGAS, Francisco, Hon. CBE 1973; MD; Venezuelan Ambassador to UNESCO, 1994–99, and to France, 1995–99; *b* 3 Jan. 1928; *s* of Oswaldo F. Kerdel y Sofia Vegas de Kerdel; *m* 1977, Martha Ramos de Kerdel; two *s* four *d. Educ:* Liceo Andrés Bello, Caracas (BSc); Univ. Central de Venezuela (MD); Harvard; New York Univ. (MSc). Prof. of Dermatology, Central Univ. of Venezuela, 1954–77; Vis. Scientist, Dept of Experimental Pathology, ARC Inst. of Animal Physiology, Cambridge, 1966–67; Mem., Trinity Coll., Cambridge, 1966–67; Scientific Attaché, Venezuelan Embassy, London, 1966–67; Vice-Chancellor, Simón Bolívar Univ., 1969–70; Venezuelan Ambassador to UK, 1987–92. Mem. Board, Univ. Metropolitana, Caracas, 1970–. Visiting Professor: of Dermatol., UMDS of Guy's and St Thomas' Hosps, 1990; of Dermatol. and Cutaneous Biol., Jefferson Med. Coll., 2003–04. Prosser White Oration, RCP, 1972. A Dir, Internat. Foundn of Dermatol., 1987–. Fellow, Venezuelan Acads of Medicine, 1967–, of Sciences, 1971–; Mem., Nat. Res. Council, Venezuela, 1969–79; President: FUDENA (Nat. chapter of WWF), 1974; Internat. Soc. of Dermatol., 1985–90. Fellow: Amer. Coll. of Physicians; Philadelphia Coll. of Physicians; Amer. Acad. of Dermatology. Foreign Mem., Nat. Academies of Medicine of Brazil, Chile and Paraguay; Hon. Member: RSM; British Assoc. of Dermatologists; German Assoc. of Dermatologists; Socs of Dermatology of France, Austria, Spain, Portugal, Brazil, Argentina, Mexico, Colombia, Ecuador, Peru, Central America, Cuba, Israel, S Africa. Hon. DSc: California Coll. of Podiatric Medicine, 1975; Cranfield, 1991. Venezuelan Orders of: Andrés Bello, 1970; Cecilio Acosta, 1976; Francisco de Miranda, 1978; Diego de Losada, 1985; El Libertador, 1986; Chevalier de la Legion d'Honneur (France), 1972. *Publications:* Tratado de Dermatologia, 1959, 4th edn 1986; chapters of textbooks of Dermatology, UK, USA, Canada, Spain, Mexico. *Recreations:* travelling, swimming, photography. *Address:* c/o Ministry of Foreign Affairs, Torre MRE, Conde a Carmelitas, Caracas 1010, Venezuela. *Clubs:* Oxford and Cambridge, White's; Caracas Country, Camurí Grande (Venezuela).

KERIN, Hon. John Charles, AM 2001; Chairman, Australian Meat and Livestock Corporation, 1994–97; Forestry Commissioner, New South Wales, 1998–2003; *b* 21 Nov. 1937; *s* of Joseph Sydney Kerin and Mary Louise Fuller; *m* 1st, Barbara Elizabeth Large (marr. diss.); one *d*; 2nd, 1983, Dr June Raye Verrier. *Educ:* Univ. of New England (BA); ANU (BEc). Axeman and bricksetter, then farmer and businessman, 1952–71; Res. Economist, 1971–72, Principal Res. Economist, 1976–78, Bureau of Agricl Econs. MP (ALP) for Macarthur, NSW, 1972–75, for Werrina, 1978–93; Minister: for Primary Industry, 1983–87; for Primary Industries and Energy, 1987–91; Treas., 1991; Minister: for Transport and Communications, 1991; for Trade and Overseas Develt, 1991–93. Statutory office holder and businessman, 1993–. Chairman: Corporate Investment Australia Funds Management Ltd, 1994–99; John Kerin and Associates, 1994–; Spire Technologies, 1998–2001; Chm., Coal Mines Australia Ltd, subseq. Mem. Bd, Billiton, 1995–2001. Chairman: NSW Water Adv. Council, 1995–2003; Reef Fisheries Management Adv. Cttee, 1995–2003; Stored Grain Res. Lab., 2002–05; Co-operative Research Centres: Sustainable Plantation Forestry (formerly Temperate Hardwood Forests), 1994–; Tropical Savannas, 1995–; Australian Weed Mgt (formerly Weed Mgt Systems), 1995–; Sensor Signals and Information Processing, 1995–. Chm., Qld Fisheries Mgt Authy, 1999–2000; Bd Mem., Southern Rivers Catchment Mgt Authy, 2002–. Chm. Adv. Cttee, Nat. Ovine Johne's Prog., 2000–; Mem., Safe Food Prodn Adv. Cttee, NSW, 2000–03. Dep. Pres., UNICEF (Australia), 1994–; Mem., Birds Australia Council, 2002–05. NSW Chm., Crawford Fund, 2000–. Mem. Bd of Trustees, Univ. of Western Sydney, 1996–; Trustee, Clunies Ross Foundn, 2004–. Fellow, Aust. Inst. of Agricl Sci., 1995; FTSE 2001. Hon. Dr Rural Sci., New England, 1993; Hon. DLitt Western Sydney, 1995; Hon. Dr Sci. Tasmania, 2001. *Recreations:* live arts, music, reading, walking. *Address:* 26 Harpur Place, Garran, ACT 2605, Australia. *T:* (2) 62852480.

KERMACK, Stuart Ogilvy; Sheriff of Tayside, Central and Fife: at Forfar, 1971–93; at Perth, 1971–75; at Arbroath, 1975–91; at Dundee, 1991–93; *b* 9 July 1934; *s* of late Stuart Grace Kermack, CBE and of Nell P., *y d* of Thomas White, SSC; *m* 1961, Barbara Mackenzie, BSc; three *s* one *d. Educ:* Glasgow Academy; Jesus Coll., Oxford; Glasgow Univ.; Edinburgh Univ. BA Oxon (Jurisprudence), 1956; LLB Glasgow, 1959. Called to Scots Bar, 1959. Sheriff Substitute of Inverness, Moray, Nairn and Ross, at Elgin and Nairn, 1965–71. *Publications:* contrib. Pictish Arts Soc. Jl; articles in legal journals. *Address:* 23 South Learmonth Gardens, Edinburgh EH4 1EZ. *T:* (0131) 332 1898; 1 Linshader, Uig, Isle of Lewis HS2 9DR. *T:* (01851) 621201.

KERMAN, Prof. Joseph Wilfred; Professor of Music, University of California at Berkeley, 1974–94, now Emeritus (Chambers Professor of Music, 1986–89); *b* 3 April 1924; *m* 1945, Vivian Shaviro; two *s* one *d. Educ:* New York Univ. (AB); Princeton Univ. (PhD). Dir of Graduate Studies, Westminster Choir Coll., Princeton, NJ, USA, 1949–51; Music Faculty, Univ. of California at Berkeley, 1951–72, 1974– (Dep. Chm., 1960–63, 1991–93); Heather Prof. of Music, Oxford Univ., and Fellow of Wadham Coll., Oxford, 1972–74. Co-editor, 19th Century Music, 1977–88. Guggenheim, Fulbright and NEH Fellowships; Visiting Fellow: All Souls Coll., Oxford, 1966; Society for the Humanities, Cornell Univ., USA, 1970; Clare Hall, Cambridge, 1971; Walker-Ames Vis. Prof., Univ. of Washington, 1986; Valentine Vis. Prof., Amherst Coll., 1988; Gauss Lectr, Princeton Univ., 1988; Phi Beta Kappa Scholar, 1993; Charles Eliot Norton Prof. of Poetry, Harvard Univ., 1997–98. Fellow: American Academy of Arts and Sciences; Amer. Philos. Soc.; Corresp. FBA 1984. Hon. Mem., Amer. Musicol Soc., 1995. Hon. FRAM. Hon. DHL Fairfield Univ., 1970. *Publications:* Opera as Drama, 1956, rev. edn 1988; The Elizabethan Madrigal, 1962; The Beethoven Quartets, 1967; A History of Art and Music (with H. W. Janson), 1968; (ed) Ludwig van Beethoven: Autograph Miscellany, 1786–99 (Kafka Sketchbook), 2 vols, 1970 (Kinkeldey Award); Listen, 1972; The Masses and Motets of William Byrd, 1981 (Kinkeldey Award; Deems Taylor Award); The New Grove Beethoven (with A. Tyson), 1983; (co-ed) Beethoven Studies, vol. 1 1973, vol. 2 1977, vol. 3 1982; Musicology, 1985; (ed) Music at the Turn of the Century, 1990; Write All These Down, 1994 (Deems Taylor Award); Concerto Conversations, 1999; The Art of Fugue, 2005; essays, in music criticism and musicology, in: Hudson Review, New York Review, San Francisco Chronicle, etc. *Address:* Music Department, University of California, Berkeley, CA 94720, USA; 107 Southampton Avenue, Berkeley, CA 94707–2036, USA.

KERMODE, Sir (John) Frank, Kt 1991; MA; FBA 1973; *b* 29 Nov. 1919; *s* of late John Pritchard Kermode and late Doris Pearl Kermode; *m* 1947, Maureen Eccles (marr. diss. 1970; she *d* 2004); twin *s* and *d. Educ:* Douglas High Sch.; Liverpool Univ. (BA 1940; MA 1947). War Service (Navy), 1940–46. Lectr, King's Coll., Newcastle, in the University of Durham, 1947–49; Lectr, Univ. of Reading, 1949–58; John Edward Taylor Prof. of English Literature, Univ. of Manchester, 1958–65; Winterstoke Prof. of English, Univ. of Bristol, 1965–67; Lord Northcliffe Prof. of Modern English Lit., UCL, 1967–74, Hon. Fellow, 1996; King Edward VII Prof. of English Literature, Cambridge Univ., 1974–82; Fellow, King's Coll., Cambridge, 1974–87, Hon. Fellow, 1988. Charles Eliot Norton Prof. of Poetry at Harvard, 1977–78. Co-editor, Encounter, 1966–67. Editor: Fontana Masterguides and Modern Masters series; Oxford Authors. FRSL 1958. Mem. Arts Council, 1968–71; Chm., Poetry Book Soc., 1968–76. For. Hon. Mem., Amer. Acad. of Arts and Scis; For. Mem., Accademia dei Lincei, 2002; Hon. Mem. AAAL. Hon. DHL Chicago, 1975; Hon. DLitt: Liverpool, 1981; Newcastle, 1993; London, 1997; Hon. Dr: Amsterdam, 1988; Yale, 1995; Wesleyan, 1997; Sewanee, 1999; Columbia, 2003; Harvard, 2004. Officier de l'Ordre des Arts et des Sciences. *Publications:* (ed) Shakespeare, The Tempest (Arden Edition), 1954; Romantic Image, 1957; John Donne, 1957; The Living Milton, 1960; Wallace Stevens, 1960; Puzzles & Epiphanies, 1962; The Sense of an Ending, 1967; Continuities, 1968; Shakespeare, Spenser, Donne, 1971; Modern Essays, 1971; Lawrence, 1973; (ed, with John Hollander) Oxford Anthology of English Literature, 1973; The Classic, 1975; (ed) Selected Prose of T. S. Eliot, 1975; The Genesis of Secrecy, 1979; Essays on Fiction, 1971–82, 1983; Forms of Attention, 1985; (ed jtly) The Literary Guide to the Bible, 1987; History and Value, 1988; An Appetite for Poetry, 1989; Poetry, Narrative, History, 1990; (ed with Keith Walker) Andrew Marvell, 1990; Uses of Error, 1991; (ed with Anita Kermode) The Oxford Book of Letters, 1995; Not Entitled (memoirs), 1996; Shakespeare's Language, 2000; Pleasing Myself, 2001; Pieces of My Mind, 2003; The Age of Shakespeare, 2004; Pleasure and Change, 2004; contrib. New Republic, Partisan Review, New York Review, New York Times, New Statesman, London Rev. of Books, etc. *Address:* 9 The Oast House, Grange Road, Cambridge CB3 9AP. *T:* (01223) 357931.

KERN, Karl-Heinz; Head of Arms Control Department, Ministry of Foreign Affairs, German Democratic Republic, 1987–90; research in international affairs, since 1990; *b* 18 Feb. 1930; *m* 1952, Ursula Bennmann; one *s. Educ:* King George Gymnasium, Dresden; Techn. Coll., Dresden (chem. engrg); Acad. for Polit. Science and Law (Dipl. jur., post-grad. History. Leading posts in diff. regional authorities of GDR until 1959; foreign policy, GDR, 1959–62; Head of GDR Mission in Ghana, 1962–66; Head of African Dept, Min. of For. Affairs, 1966–71; Minister and Chargé d'Affaires, Gt Britain, 1973; Ambassador to UK, 1973–80; Dep. Head of Western European Dept, Min. of Foreign Affairs, 1980–82; Ambassador to N Korea, 1982–86. Holds Order of Merit of the Fatherland, etc. *Recreations:* sport, reading, music. *Address:* Karl-Marx-Allee 70a, 10243 Berlin, Germany.

KERNAGHAN, Paul Robert, CBE 2005; QPM 1998; Chief Constable, Hampshire Constabulary, 1999–2008; *b* 27 Dec. 1955; *s* of Hugh Kernaghan and Diane Kernaghan (*née* Herdman); *m* 1983, Mary McCleery; one *d. Educ:* Methodist Coll., Belfast; Queen's Univ., Belfast (LLB Hons); Univ. of Ulster (DPM); Univ. of Leicester (MA Public Order). MIPD 1991. Served UDR (part-time), 1974–77; commnd 1976, Second Lieut; served RUC, 1978–91: grad. entrant, Constable, 1978; served Belfast, Londonderry, Strabane and Warrenpoint, operational and staff appts; Superintendent, 1991–92, Detective Superintendent, 1992–95, W Midlands Police; Asst Chief Constable, 1995; Asst Chief Constable (Designated), 1996–99, N Yorks Police; rcds 1997. Internat. affairs portfolio holder, ACPO, 2000–08. Mem., UN Internat. Policing Adv. Council, 2006–. *Recreations:* family, international security. *Address: e-mail:* p.kernaghan@btinternet.com.

KERR, family name of **Marquess of Lothian** and **Barons Kerr of Kinlochard** and **Teviot**.

KERR OF KINLOCHARD, Baron *cr* 2004 (Life Peer), of Kinlochard in Perth and Kinross; **John Olav Kerr,** GCMG 2001 (KCMG 1991; CMG 1987); Deputy Chairman, Royal Dutch Shell plc, since 2005; Director: Scottish American Investment Trust, since 2002; Rio Tinto plc, since 2003; *b* 22 Feb. 1942; *s* of late Dr J. D. O. Kerr; *m* 1965, Elizabeth, *d* of late W. G. Kalaugher; two *s* three *d. Educ:* Glasgow Academy; Pembroke Coll., Oxford (Hon. Fellow, 1991). HM Diplomatic Service, 1966–2002; HM Treasury, 1979–84: Principal Private Sec. to Chancellor of the Exchequer, 1981–84; Asst Under-Sec. of State, FCO, 1987–90; Ambassador and UK Perm. Rep. to the EU, Brussels, 1990–95; Ambassador to USA, 1995–97; Perm. Under-Sec. of State, FCO, and Hd, Diplomatic Service, 1997–2002; Sec.-Gen., European Convention, 2002–03. Dir, Shell Transport and Trading, 2002–05. Mem., EU Select Cttee, H of L, 2006–. Mem. Adv. Bd, Scottish Power, 2007–. Member Council: Centre for Eur. Reform, 2004–; Business for New Europe, 2006–; Hon. Pres., UK/Korea Forum for the Future, 2007–; Vice-Pres., Eur. Policy Centre, 2007–. Trustee: Rhodes Trust, Oxford, 1997–; Nat. Gall., 2002–; Fulbright Commn, 2004–; Carnegie Trust, 2005–. Chm., Ct and Council, Imperial Coll. London, 2005–. Hon. LLD: St Andrews, 1996; Glasgow, 1999. *Address:* House of Lords, SW1A 0PW. *Club:* Garrick.

KERR, Alan Grainger, OBE 2000; FRCS, FRCSE; Consultant Otolaryngologist, Royal Victoria and Belfast City Hospitals, since 1968; *b* 15 April 1935; *s* of Joseph William and Eileen Kerr; *m* 1962, Patricia Margaret M'Neill (*d* 1999); two *s* one *d. Educ:* Methodist College, Belfast; Queen's Univ., Belfast (MB). DObst RCOG. Clinical and Res. Fellow, Harvard Med. Sch., 1967; Prof. of Otorhinolaryngology, QUB, 1979–81. Otolaryngology Mem. Council, RCS, 1987–92; President: Otorhinolaryngological Res. Soc., 1985–87; Internat. Otopathology Soc., 1985–88; Otology Sect., RSM, 1989–90; British Assoc. of Otorhinolaryngologists—Head and Neck Surgeons, 1993–96; Irish Otolaryngological Soc., 1997–99; Politzer Soc., 1998–2002. Master, British Academic Conf. in Otolaryngology, 2006. Lectures, UK, Europe and USA. Prizes: Jobson Horne, BMA; Harrison, RSocMed; Howells, Univ. of London. Gen. Editor, Scott-Brown's Otolaryngology, 1987–. *Publications:* papers on ear surgery. *Recreations:* tennis, ski-ing, hill walking, bowls. *Address:* 6 Cranmore Gardens, Belfast BT9 6JL. *T:* (028) 9066 9181. *Club:* Royal Society of Medicine.

KERR, Prof. Allen, AO 1992; FRS 1986; FAA; Professor of Plant Pathology, University of Adelaide, 1980–91, Professor Emeritus, since 1992; *b* 21 May 1926; *s* of A. B. Kerr and J. T. Kerr (*née* White); *m* 1951, Rosemary Sheila Strachan; two *s* one *d. Educ:* George Heriot's Sch., Edinburgh; Univ. of Edinburgh. North of Scotland Coll. of Agric., 1947–51; University of Adelaide: Lectr, 1951–59; Sen. Lectr, 1959–67 (seconded to Tea

Research Inst., Ceylon, 1963–66); Reader, 1968–80. For. Associate, Nat. Acad. of Scis, USA, 1991. *Recreation:* golf. *Address:* 419 Carrington Street, Adelaide, SA 5000, Australia. *T:* (8) 82322325.

KERR, Andrew Mark; Partner, Bell & Scott, WS, Edinburgh, 1969–99 (Senior Partner, 1987–96); Clerk to Society of Writers to HM Signet, 1983–2003; *b* Edinburgh 17 Jan. 1940; *s* of William Mark Kerr and Katharine Marjorie Anne Stevenson; *m* 1967, Jane Susanna Robertson; one *d*. *Educ:* Edinburgh Acad.; Cambridge Univ. (BA); Edinburgh Univ. (LLB). Served RNR, 1961–76. British Petroleum, 1961–62; apprenticeship with Davidson & Syme, WS, Edinburgh, 1964–67; with Bell & Scott, Bruce & Kerr, WS, now Bell & Scott, WS, 1967–99. Vice-Chm., Edinburgh New Town Conservation Cttee, 1972–76; Chm., Edinburgh Solicitors' Property Centre, 1976–81. Chairman: Penicuik House Preservation Trust, 1985–2001; Arts Trust of Scotland, 1996–; Dunedin Concerts Trust, 1996–; Member: Council, Edinburgh Internat. Fest., 1978–82; Scottish Arts Council, 1988–94 (Chm., Drama Cttee, 1988–91, and 1993–94); Director: Edinburgh Fest. and King's Theatres, 1997–2003; Edinburgh World Heritage Trust, 1999–; Historic Scotland Foundn, 2001–06; Sec., Edinburgh Fest. Fringe Soc. Ltd, 1969–2002. Trustee, Usher Hall Conservation Trust, 1999–. Mem. Council, St George's Sch. for Girls, Edinburgh, 1985–93; Gov., New Sch., Butterstone, 1995–2007. *Recreations:* architecture, hill walking, music, ships, ski-ing, theatre. *Address:* 16 Ann Street, Edinburgh EH4 1PJ. *T:* (home) (0131) 332 9857. *Club:* New (Edinburgh).

KERR, Andrew Palmer; Member (Lab) East Kilbride, Scottish Parliament, since 1999; *b* 17 March 1962; *s* of William and May Kerr; *m* 1992, Susan Kealy; three *d* (incl. twins). *Educ:* Glasgow Coll. (BA Social Scis). Dep. Pres., Glasgow Coll. Students' Assoc., 1983–85; Convenor, Glasgow Area, NUS, 1985–86; Dep. Pres., NUS (Scotland), 1986–87; R&D Officer, Strathkelvin DC, 1987–90; Man. Dir, Achieving Quality, QA Consultancy, 1990–93; Strategy and Develt Manager, Cleansing Dept, Glasgow CC, 1993–99. Scottish Executive: Minister: for Finance and Public Services, 2001–04; for Health and Community Care, 2004–07. *Recreations:* family, half marathon and 10K running, football, reading. *Address:* 6 Muirkirk Gardens, Strathaven ML10 6FS.

KERR, Rt Hon. Sir Brian (Francis), Kt 1993; PC 2004; Lord Chief Justice of Northern Ireland, since 2004; *b* 22 Feb. 1948; *s* of late James William Kerr and Kathleen Rose Kerr; *m* 1970, Gillian Rosemary Owen Widdowson; two *s*. *Educ:* St Colman's College, Newry, Co. Down; Queen's Univ., Belfast (LLB 1969). Called to NI Bar, 1970, to the Bar of England and Wales, Gray's Inn, 1974 (Hon. Bencher, 1997); QC (NI) 1983; Bencher, Inn of Court of NI, 1990; Junior Crown Counsel (Common Law), 1978–83; Sen. Crown Counsel, 1988–93; Judge of the High Ct of Justice, NI, 1993–2004. Chm., Mental Health Commn for NI, 1988. Member: Judicial Studies Bd, NI, 1995–2004; Franco British Judicial Co-operation Cttee, 1995–2001. Chm., Distinction and Meritorious Service Awards Cttee, NI, 1997–2001. Eisenhower Exchange Fellow, 1999. Hon. Bencher, King's Inns, 2004. Hon. Fellow, American Bd of Trial Advocates 2004. *Recreations:* France, accepting defeat by sons at tennis. *Address:* Royal Courts of Justice, Belfast BT1 3JY.

KERR, Caroline, (Mrs G. Harvey); Media Consultant and Company Secretary, Millbank Media, since 2006; *b* 27 May 1962; *d* of John and Maureen Kerr; *m* 1994, Gerard Harvey; one *s* one *d*. *Educ:* Newnham Coll., Cambridge (MA English). Joined ITN, 1984: trainee, 1984–91; gen. reporter, 1991–94; Asia Corresp., 1994–98; Consumer Affairs Corresp., 1998–99; Business and Economics Ed., 1999–2004. *Address:* Millbank Media, 4 Millbank, SW1 3JA.

KERR, Prof. David James, CBE 2002; MD; DSc; FRCP, FMedSci; Rhodes Professor of Therapeutics, University of Oxford, since 2001; Fellow, Corpus Christi College, Oxford, since 2001; *b* 14 June 1956; *s* of Robert James Andrew Kerr and Sarah Pettigrew Kerr (*née* Hogg); *m* 1980, Anne Miller Young; one *s* two *d*. *Educ:* Univ. of Glasgow (BSc 1st Cl. Hons 1977; MB ChB 1980; MSc 1985; MD 1987; PhD 1990; DSc 1997). FRCPGlas 1995; MRCP 1983, FRCP 1996. Sen. Registrar (Med. Oncol.), Western Infirmary, Glasgow, 1985–89; Sen. Lectr, Glasgow Univ., 1989–92; Prof. of Clinical Oncol., and Clinical Dir, CRC Inst. For Cancer Studies, Univ. of Birmingham, 1992–2001. Visiting Professor: Univ. of Strathclyde, 1991–; Univ. of Nils, Yugoslavia, 1999–. FMedSci 2000. *Publications include:* (ed jtly) Regional Chemotherapy, 1999; contrib. numerous articles to peer reviewed med. and scientific jls. *Recreations:* football, busking. *Address:* Corpus Christi College, Oxford OX1 4JF; Department of Clinical Pharmacology, University of Oxford, Old Road Campus Research Building, Old Road Campus, off Roosevelt Drive, Headington, Oxford OX3 7DQ. *Clubs:* Reform; Partick Thistle Supporters' (Glasgow).

KERR, Dr David Leigh; *b* 25 March 1923; *s* of Myer Woolf Kerr and Paula (*née* Horowitz); *m* 1st, 1944, Aileen Saddington (marr. diss. 1969); two *s* one *d*; 2nd, 1970, Margaret Dunlop; one *s* two *d*. *Educ:* Whitgift Sch., Croydon; Middlesex Hosp. Med. Sch., London. Hon. Sec., Socialist Medical Assoc., 1957–63; Hon. Vice-Pres., 1963–72. LCC (Wandsworth, Central), 1958–65, and Coun., London Borough of Wandsworth, 1964–68; Mem., Herts CC (Welwyn Garden City S), 1989–2001. Contested (Lab) Wandsworth, Streatham (for Parlt), 1959; MP (Lab) Wandsworth Central, 1964–70; PPS to Minister of State, FCO, 1967–69. Vis. Lectr in Medicine, Chelsea Coll., 1972–82. War on Want: Dir, 1970–77; Vice-Chm., 1973–74; Chm., 1974–77. Family Doctor, Tooting, 1946–82; Chief Exec., Manor House Hosp., London, 1982–87. Member: Inter-departmental Cttee on Death Certification and Coroners; E Herts CHC, 1992–2000 (Vice-Chm., 1998–2000); Med. Assessor, Registered Homes Tribunals, 1986–93. Hon. Vice Pres., Community Practitioners & Health Visitors' Assoc. (formerly Health Visitors' Assoc.), 1969–2005; Trustee, CPHVA Charitable Trust, 1996–2005. FRSocMed. Governor, British Film Inst., 1966–71. *Recreations:* reading other people's biographies, refusing to write own. *Address:* 19 Homewood Avenue, Cuffley, Herts EN6 4QG. *T:* (01707) 872150.

KERR, Prof. David Nicol Sharp, CBE 1992; MSc; FRCP, FRCPE; Professor of Renal Medicine, 1987–91, Dean, 1984–91, Royal Postgraduate Medical School, University of London; Professor Emeritus of Renal Medicine, Imperial College London; *b* 27 Dec. 1927; *s* of William Kerr and Elsie (Ransted) Kerr; *m* 1960, Eleanor Jones; two *s* one *d*. *Educ:* George Watson's Boys' College; Edinburgh University (MB ChB); University of Wisconsin (MSc). FRCPE 1966; FRCP 1967. House Physician and Surgeon, Royal Infirmary, Edinburgh, 1951–52; Exchange scholar, Univ. of Wisconsin, 1952–53; Surgeon Lieut, RNVR, 1953–55; Asst Lectr, Univ. of Edinburgh, 1956–57; Registrar, Hammersmith Hosp., 1957–59; Lectr, Univ. of Durham, 1959–63; Consultant Physician, Royal Victoria Infirmary, Newcastle upon Tyne, 1962–83; Senior Lectr, 1963–68, Prof. of Medicine, 1968–83, Univ. of Newcastle upon Tyne. Postgrad. Med. Advr, NW Thames RHA, later N Thames Regl Office, NHS Executive, 1991–97. Med. Awards Administrator, Commonwealth Scholarships Commn, 1993–98. Member: Council, Internat. Soc. of Nephrology, 1984–93; Council, British Heart Foundn, 1989–97; NW Thames RHA, 1989–91; Hammersmith and Queen Charlotte's SHA, 1984–91; Ealing Hosp. NHS Trust, 1991–95; Standing Med. Adv. Cttee, DHSS, 1979–90. Sen. Censor and First Vice Pres., RCP, 1990–91. Eur. Dialysis Transplant Assoc., subseq. ERA EDTA: Founder Mem., 1964; Ed., 1964–70; Pres., 1983; Hon. Mem., 1987. Hon. Fellow, SA Coll. of Medicine, 1992; Hon. Mem., Spanish Soc. of Nephrology, 1992. Vice-Pres., Nat. Kidney Res. Fund, 2003– (Trustee, 1999–, Chm. Trustees, 2000–02). Hon. DSc Khartoum, 2005. Editor, Jl of RCP, 1994–98. *Publications:* Short Textbook of Renal Disease, 1968; (ed) Oxford Textbook of Clinical Nephrology, 1992, 2nd edn 1997; chapters in numerous books incl. Cecil-Loeb Textbook of Medicine and Oxford Textbook of Medicine; articles on renal disease in med. jls. *Recreations:* church, walking, theatre, opera. *Address:* 22 Carbery Avenue, W3 9AL. *T:* and *Fax:* (020) 8992 3231.

KERR, Dr Edwin, CBE 1986; Chairman, Student Employment Services Ltd, since 1995; *b* 1 July 1926; *e s* of late Robert John Kerr and Mary Elizabeth Kerr (*née* Ferguson); *m* 1949, Gertrude Elizabeth (*née* Turbitt); one *s* two *d*. *Educ:* Royal Belfast Academical Instn; Queen's Univ., Belfast (BSc, PhD). FIMA, FBCS. Asst Lectr in Maths, QUB, 1948–52; Lectr in Maths, Coll. of Technology, Birmingham (now Univ. of Aston in Birmingham), 1952–55; Lectr in Maths, Coll. of Science and Technology, Manchester (now Univ. of Manchester Inst. of Science and Technology), 1956–58; Head of Maths Dept, Royal Coll. of Advanced Technology, Salford (now Univ. of Salford), 1958–66; Principal, Paisley Coll. of Technology, 1966–72; Chief Officer, CNAA, 1972–86; Chm. and Chief Exec., Exam. Bd for Financial Planning, 1987–89; Chief Exec., Coll. for Financial Planning, 1988–96; Chm., Vocational and Academic Bd, Inst. of Health and Care Develts, 1996–99; Academic Dir, Regent's Business Sch., Regent's Coll., London, 1997–2001. Member: Adv. Cttee on Supply and Training of Teachers, 1973–78; Adv. Cttee on Supply and Educn of Teachers, 1980–85; Bd for Local Authority Higher Educn, 1982–85; Bd for Public Sector Higher Educn, 1985–86; Mem. and Vice-Chm., Continuing Educn Standing Cttee, 1985–88. President: Soc. for Res. into Higher Educn, 1974–77; The Mathematical Assoc., 1976–77. Hon. FCP 1984; Hon. Fellow: Coventry Lanchester, Newcastle upon Tyne, Portsmouth and Sheffield Polytechnics, 1986; Huddersfield Polytechnic, and Paisley Coll. of Technol., 1987; Goldsmiths' Coll., London, 1991. DUniv: Open, 1977; Paisley, 1993; Hon. DSc Ulster, 1986; Hon. DEd CNAA, 1989. *Publications:* (with R. Butler) An Introduction to Numerical Methods, 1962; various mathematical and educational. *Recreation:* gardening. *Address:* 17 Old Galgorm Manor, Ballymena, Co. Antrim BT42 1RY. *Club:* Travellers.

KERR, Frith Zelda; graphic designer; Partner, Kerr/Noble, since 1997; *b* 3 Oct. 1973; *d* of Peter and Jenny Kerr. *Educ:* Surbiton High Sch.; Kingston Poly.; Camberwell Coll. of Art (BA Hons); Royal Coll. of Art (MA). Vis. Lectr, Camberwell Coll. of Art, 1998–2003. Clients include Liberty, V&A Mus., British Council, Design Mus., David Chipperfield Architects, and Tate Modern. *Recreation:* reading in the bath. *Address:* Kerr/Noble, 3–4 Hardwick Street, EC1R 4RB. *T:* (020) 7833 7277; *e-mail:* frith@kernoble.com.

KERR, Hugh; Brussels correspondent, The Scotsman, 2004; *b* 9 July 1944; *m*; one *s*. Former Sen. Lectr, Univ. of North London. Former Mem. (Lab) Harlow DC. MEP (Lab 1994–98, Ind. Lab 1998–99), Essex W and Herts E. Press officer for Scottish Socialist Party, 2000–04.

KERR, James, QPM 1979; Chief Constable, Lincolnshire Police, 1977–83; *b* 19 Nov. 1928; *s* of William and Margaret Jane Kerr; *m* 1952, Jean Coupland; one *d*. *Educ:* Carlisle Grammar School. Cadet and Navigating Officer, Merchant Navy, 1945–52 (Union Castle Line, 1949–52). Carlisle City Police and Cumbria Constabulary, 1952–74; Asst Director of Command Courses, Police Staff Coll., Bramshill, 1974; Asst Chief Constable (Operations), North Yorkshire Police, 1975; Deputy Chief Constable, Lincs, 1976. Officer Brother, OStJ, 1980. *Recreations:* music, squash. *Address:* 21 Strathfield Parade, Croydon, Vic 3136, Australia. *Club:* Yarra Valley Country, Royal Automobile Club of Victoria (Victoria).

KERR, John, MBE 1986; DL; Vice Lord-Lieutenant of Suffolk, since 2003; *b* 19 Nov. 1939; *s* of William Kerr and Mary Laurie Kerr; *m* 1967, Gillian Hayward; two *s* two *d*. *Educ:* Framlingham Coll.; Writtle Coll. Farmer and company dir. Director: Wm Kerr (Farms) Ltd, 1971–; Grosvenor Farms Ltd, 1992–2005; Easton Events Ltd, 1994–; Suffolk Top Attractions Gp, 1997–; Grosvenor Farms Hldgs Ltd, 1999–2005; Anglian Pea Growers, 1999–; Cogent Breeding Ltd, 2002–05; Forum for Sustainable Farming, 2004–; Chm., Rural East, Clydesdale Bank. Dir, Suffolk Agricl Assoc. Ltd, 1983– (Chm., 1999–2002; Pres., 2006; Hon. Dir, Suffolk Show, 1982–84). Director: Ipswich Town FC, 1983–2008 (Chm., 1991–95); Ipswich Town plc, 2004–. Chm., Farmers' Club Charitable Trust, 1995– (Trustee, 1995). Governor: Seckford Foundn., 1986–2002 (Chm., Finance, 1993–2000); Framlingham Coll., 1987–. Liveryman, Farmers' Co., 1985. JP 1972–93, DL 1988, High Sheriff 1997, Suffolk. DUniv Essex, 2002. *Address:* Blaxhall, Suffolk. *Club:* Farmers' (Chm., 1994).

KERR, John Andrew Sinclair; Director of Development, Edge Foundation, since 2005; *b* 29 May 1958; *s* of Andrew Kerr and Frances Kerr; *m* 1979, Beverly Johnston; one *s* one *d*. *Educ:* Hutchesons' Grammar Sch., Glasgow; Univ. of Glasgow (LLB Hons). Contracts Lawyer, British Steel, 1979–83; film industry, 1983–88; Sen. Manager, Regulatory Affairs, Stock Exchange, 1988–98; Corporate Affairs Dir, 1998–2001, Chief Exec., 2001–05, Edexcel Ltd. FRSA. *Recreations:* gardening, running smallholding, film. *Address:* Manor Barn, The Common, Sissinghurst, Cranbrook, Kent TN17 2AE.

KERR, Adm. Sir John (Beverley), GCB 1993 (KCB 1989); DL; Commander-in-Chief, Naval Home Command, 1991–94; Flag Aide-de-Camp to the Queen, 1991–94; *b* 27 Oct. 1937; *s* late Wilfred Kerr and Vera Kerr (*née* Sproule); *m* 1964, Elizabeth Anne, *d* of late Dr and Mrs C. R. G. Howard, Burley, Hants; three *s*. *Educ:* Moseley Hall County Grammar Sch., Cheadle; Britannia Royal Naval Coll., Dartmouth. Served in various ships, 1958–65 (specialized in navigation, 1964); Staff, BRNC, Dartmouth, 1965–67; HMS Cleopatra, 1967–69; Staff, US Naval Acad., Annapolis, 1969–71; NDC, Latimer, 1971–72; i/c HMS Achilles, 1972–74; Naval Plans, MoD, 1974–75; Defence Policy Staff, MoD, 1975–77; RCDS, 1978; i/c HMS Birmingham, 1979–81; Dir of Naval Plans, MoD, 1981–83; i/c HMS Illustrious, 1983–84; ACNS (Op. Requirements), 1984; ACDS (Op. Requirements) (Sea Systems), 1985–86; Flag Officer First Flotilla/Flotilla One, 1986–88; MoD, 1988–91. Member, Independent Review: of Armed Forces' Manpower, Career and Remuneration Structures, 1994–95; of Higher Educn Pay and Conditions, 1998–99. Mem., Museums and Galls Commn, 1994–2000. Mem., CWGC, 1994–2001 (Vice-Chm., 1998–2001). Cdre, RNSA, 1992–95; Member: Cttee of Management, RNLI, 1993–98; Cttee, Manchester Mus., 1994–2004 (Chm., 1996–2004); Central Council, Royal Over-Seas League, 2001–04. Member: Audit Cttee, 1994–98 (Chm., 1995–98), Council, 1995–98, Lancaster Univ.; Court and Council, Manchester Univ., 1998–2004; Court, UMIST, 2000–04; Pro-Chancellor, Univ. of Manchester, 2004–. Mem., Lake District Nat. Park Authy, 2007–. CCMI (CIMgt 1993); Associate FRIN 2006. DL Lancs 1995. *Recreations:* music, sailing, hill walking, history.

KERR, Judith; writer and illustrator, since 1968; *b* Berlin, 14 June 1923; *d* of Alfred and Julia Kerr; *m* 1954, Nigel Kneale; one *s* one *d*. *Educ:* Ten different schs in four different countries; Central Sch. of Arts and Crafts, London (Schol.; failed Dip. in Book Illustration

1948). Painter, textile designer and art teacher, 1948–52; script reader, script ed., then script writer for BBC Television, 1952–57; full-time mum, 1958–65. Peter Pan Award, Action for Children's Arts, 2006. *Publications: for children:* The Tiger Who Came to Tea, 1968; Mog the Forgetful Cat, 1970; When Hitler Stole Pink Rabbit, 1971; When Willy Went to the Wedding, 1972; The Other Way Round, 1975, re-issued as Bombs on Aunt Dainty, 2002; Mog's Christmas, 1976; A Small Person Far Away, 1978; Mog and the Baby, 1980; Mog in the Dark, 1983; Mog and Me, 1984; Mog's Family of Cats, 1985; Mog's Amazing Birthday Caper, 1986; Mog and Bunny, 1988; Mog and Barnaby, 1991; How Mrs Monkey Missed the Ark, 1992; Mog on Fox Night, 1993; The Adventures of Mog, 1993; Mog in the Garden, 1994; Mog's Kittens, 1994; Out of the Hitler Time (trilogy: When Hitler Stole Pink Rabbit, The Other Way Round, A Small Person Far Away), 1994; Mog and the Granny, 1995; Mog and the Vee Ee Tee, 1996; The Big Mog Book, 1997; Birdie Halleluyah!, 1998; Mog's Bad Thing 2000; The Other Goose, 2001; Goodbye Mog, 2002; Mog Time, 2004; Goose in a Hole, 2005; Twinkles, Arthur and Puss, 2007. *Recreations:* walking across the river in the early morning, talking to cats, watching old films, remembering, staying alive. *Address:* c/o Society of Authors, 84 Drayton Gardens, SW10 9SB.

KERR, Malcolm James; Partner, DP9, planning consultants, since 2004; *b* Glasgow, 20 Oct. 1959; *s* of Michael and Evelyn Kerr; *m* 1989, Lorraine Mary Keating; one *s* two *d*. *Educ:* Jordanhill College Sch., Glasgow; Univ. of Strathclyde (LLB 1980; Dip. Legal Studies 1981). ARICS 1986. Trainee solicitor, Shepherd and Wedderburn, WS, 1981–83; NP, 1983; Montagu Evans, Chartered Surveyors, 1983–2004. *Recreations:* countryside, walking, cycling, Roman history, architecture, Charlton Athletic. *Address:* DP9, 100 Pall Mall, SW1Y 5NQ. *T:* (020) 7004 1729; *e-mail:* malcolm.kerr@dp9.co.uk. *Club:* Royal Automobile.

KERR, Rear-Adm. Mark William Graham; Chief Executive, Powys County Council, since 2004; *b* 18 Feb. 1949; *s* of Captain M. W. B. Kerr, DSC, RN and Pat Kerr; *m* 1978, Louisa Edwards; two *s* one *d*. *Educ:* Marlborough Coll.; New Coll., Oxford (BA). FCIPD 2002. Joined RN, 1967; i/c HMS Alert, 1976; Principal Warfare Officer, HMS Charybdis, 1978–79; Staff Navigation Officer, Captain MinecounterMeasures, 1979–81; i/c HMS Beachampton, 1982–84; Officer i/c RN Schs Presentation Team, 1984–85; First Lieut, HMS Ariadne, 1985–88; i/c HMS Broadsword, 1988–90; MoD, 1990–94; i/c HMS Cumberland, 1994–95; Captain, RN Presentation Team, 1995–96; Dep. Flag Officer, Sea Trng, 1996–99; Commodore, BRNC, Dartmouth, 1999–2002; Naval Sec., 2002–04. Hon. Col, Powys ACF, 2006–. Vice Chm., Soc. of Local Authy Chief Execs (Wales), 2008–. *Recreations:* sailing, ski-ing, history. *Address:* County Hall, Llandrindod Wells, Powys LD1 5LG.

KERR, Ronald James, CBE 1998; Chief Executive, Guy's and St Thomas' NHS Foundation Trust, since 2007; *b* 2 Feb. 1950; *s* of James Boe Kerr and Margaret Catherine Kerr (*née* Robson); *m* 2005, Nicola Jane Martin; one *d* from a previous marriage. *Educ:* Sandbach Sch., Cheshire; Cambridgeshire Coll. of Arts and Technol.; London Univ. (BSc Hons Geog. with Econs); London Business Sch. (MSc Business Studies). Sec., S Manchester CHC, 1974–77; Asst Sec., NE Thames RHA, 1977–79; Dep. House Gov., Moorfields Eye Hosp., 1979–80; Hosp. Sec., London Hosp., 1980–85; Dist Gen. Manager, N Herts HA, 1985–88; Dep. Dir of Financial Mgt, NHS Exec., 1988–90; Dist Gen. Manager, Lewisham and N Southwark HA and Chief Exec., SE London Commng Agency, 1990–93; Regl Gen. Manager, NW Thames RHA, 1993–94; Regl Dir, N Thames Regl Office, NHS Exec., 1994–98; Dir of Ops, NHS Exec., DoH, 1998–2001; Chief Executive: Nat. Care Standards Commn, 2001–04; United Bristol Healthcare NHS Trust, 2004–07. *Recreations:* travel, reading, restaurants, music, Manchester City FC. *Address:* 17 Julian Road, Sneyd Park, Bristol BS9 1JZ.

KERR, Rose; Deputy Keeper, Asian Department (formerly Curator, then Chief Curator, Far Eastern Collections, subseq. Far Eastern Department), Victoria and Albert Museum, 1990–2003; *b* 23 Feb. 1953; *d* of William Antony Kerr and Elizabeth Rendell; *m* 1990. *Educ:* SOAS, Univ. of London (BA Hons 1st Cl., Art and Archaeology of China); Languages Inst., Beijing. Fellow, Percival David Foundn of Chinese Art, 1976–78; joined Far Eastern Dept, V&A, 1978, Keeper, 1987–90. Hon. Associate, Needham Res. Inst., Cambridge, 2003. Member: Council, Oriental Ceramic Soc., 1987– (Pres., 2000–); GB–China Educnl Trust, 1995– (Chm., 2005–). Hon. Fellow, Univ. of Glasgow, 2004. *Publications:* (with P. Hughes-Stanton) Kiln Sites of Ancient China, 1980; (with John Larson) Guanyin: a masterpiece revealed, 1985; Chinese Ceramics: porcelain of the Qing Dynasty 1644–1911, 1986; Later Chinese Bronzes, 1990; (ed and contrib.) Chinese Art and Design: the T. T. Tsui Gallery of Chinese Art, 1991; (with Rosemary Scott) Ceramic Evolution in the Middle Ming Period, 1994; England's Victoria and Albert Museum: Chinese Qing Dynasty Ceramics (in Chinese), 1995; (with John Ayers *et al*) Blanc de Chine: porcelain from Dehua, 2002; Song Dynasty Ceramics, 2004; (with Nigel Wood) Science & Civilisation in China, vol. V, pt 12: Ceramic Technology, 2004; articles in Oriental Art, Orientations, Apollo, Craft Magazine, V&A Album. *Recreation:* gardening. *Address:* Garrison House, Church Street, Presteigne, Powys LD8 2BU.

KERR, Timothy Julian; QC 2001; *b* 15 Feb. 1958; *s* of Rt Hon. Sir Michael Robert Emanuel Kerr, PC and of Julia Kerr; one *s*; *m* 1990, Nicola Mary Croucher; two *s*. *Educ:* Westminster Sch.; Magdalen Coll., Oxford (BA 1st Cl. Hons Juris.). Called to the Bar, Gray's Inn, 1983; in practice as barrister, specialising in public law, sport and education law, 1983–. Pt-time Chm., Employment Tribunals, 2001–06. Member: Sport Resolution UK Arbitrators' Panel, 2000–; FA Premier League Arbitrators' Panel, 2007–. *Publications:* (jtly) Sports Law, 1999; contrib. various articles to learned jls. *Recreations:* music, travel, reading, friends, family, marathon running, supporting Chelsea Football Club. *Address:* (chambers) 11 King's Bench Walk, Temple, EC4Y 7EQ. *T:* (020) 7632 8500.

KERR, William Francis Kennedy, OBE 1984; PhD, CEng, FIMechE; Principal, Belfast College of Technology, 1969–84; *b* 1 Aug. 1923; *m* 1953, H. Adams; two *s*. *Educ:* Portadown Technical Coll. and Queen's Univ., Belfast. BSc (Hons) in Mech. Engineering, MSc, PhD. Teacher of Mathematics, Portadown Techn. Coll., 1947–48; Teacher and Sen. Lectr in Mech. Engrg, Coll. of Techn., Belfast, 1948–55; Lectr and Adviser of Studies in Mech. Engrg, Queen's Univ. of Belfast, 1955–62; Head of Dept of Mech., Civil, and Prod. Engrg, Dundee Coll. of Techn., 1962–67; Vice-Principal, Coll. of Techn., Belfast, 1967–69. Chm., NI Cttee for Educnl Technology, 1973–79; Member: Mech. and Prodn Engrg Subject Panel, CNAA, 1964–67; Council for Educnl Technology, 1973–79; Belfast Educn and Library Bd, 1977–81; NI Council for Educnl Develt, 1980–84; NI Manpower Council, 1981–84; Chm., Assoc. of Principals of Colleges (NI Branch), 1982; Governor, Royal Belfast Academical Instn, 1969–84; Mem. Court, Ulster Univ., 1985–92. *Publications:* contribs on environmental testing of metals, etc. *Recreations:* golf, motoring, reading. *Address:* Apt 1, Avoca House, 83 Princetown Road, Bangor, Co. Down, Northern Ireland BT20 3TD.

KERR-DINEEN, Peter Brodrick; Joint Chairman: Howe Robinson and Co. Ltd, since 1994; Howe Robinson Group (formerly Investments) Ltd, since 1996; Chairman, Baltic Exchange, 2003–05 (Member, since 1976; Director, 1998–2005); *b* 26 Nov. 1953; *s* of late Canon F. G. Kerr-Dineen and of Hermione Kerr-Dineen; *m* 1996, Dr Susan Dodd, FRCPath; one *s* one *d*. *Educ:* Marlborough Coll.; Gonville and Caius Coll., Cambridge (BA 1975, MA (Arch. and Anthropol.) 1978). Mgt trainee, Ocean Transport and Trading, 1975–76; joined Howe Robinson, 1976; Dir, Great Eastern Shipping Co. London Ltd, 1989–. Liveryman, Shipwrights' Co., 2007–. *Recreations:* riding, fishing, drama, anthropology, painting. *Address:* Baltic Exchange Ltd, St Mary Axe, EC3A 8BH. *T:* (020) 7369 1621; *e-mail:* kerrdineen@hotmail.com. *Clubs:* Hurlingham, Oxford and Cambridge.

KERRIGAN, Greer Sandra, CB 2006; Director of Legal Services, Department for Work and Pensions; *b* Port of Spain, Trinidad, 7 Aug. 1948; *d* of Wilfred M. Robinson and Rosina Robinson (*née* Ali); *m* 1974, Donal Brian Mathew Kerrigan; one *s* one *d*. *Educ:* Bishop Anstey High Sch., Trinidad; Coll. of Law, Inns of Court. Called to the Bar, Middle Temple, 1971. Legal Advr, Public Utilities Commn, Trinidad, 1972–74; Department of Health and Social Security, subseq. Department of Social Security, then Department for Work and Pensions, 1974–: Legal Assistant, 1974–77; Sen. Legal Assistant, 1977–85; Asst Solicitor, 1985–91; Principal Asst Solicitor, subseq. Legal Dir (Health), then Legal Director (Work and Pensions), later Dir of Legal Services (Work and Pensions), 1991–; Principal Asst Solicitor, then Legal Dir (Health), DoH, 1991–2004. *Recreations:* reading, music, bridge. *Address:* Department for Work and Pensions, New Court, 48 Carey Street, WC2A 2LS. *T:* (020) 7412 1465.

KERRIGAN, Herbert Aird; QC (Scot.) 1992; *b* 2 Aug. 1945; *s* of Herbert Kerrigan and Mary Agnes Wallace Hamilton or Kerrigan; one adopted *s*. *Educ:* Whitehill, Glasgow; Univ. of Aberdeen (LLB Hons 1968); Hague Acad. of Internat. Law; Keele Univ. (MA 1970). Admitted Faculty of Advocates, 1970; Lectr in Criminal Law and Criminology, 1969–73, in Scots Law, 1973–74, Edinburgh Univ.; called to the Bar, Middle Temple, 1990; in practice, 1991–. Vis. Prof., Univ. of Southern Calif., 1979–. Mem., Longford Commn, 1972. Church of Scotland: Elder, 1967– (now at Greyfriars Tolbooth and Highland Kirk, Edinburgh); Reader, 1969; Mem., Assembly Council, 1981–85; Sen. Chaplain to Moderator, Gen. Assembly of Church of Scotland, 1999–2000; Convener, Cttee on Chaplains to HM's Forces, 2001– (Vice Convener, 1998–2001). Pres., Edinburgh Royal Infirmary Samaritan Soc., 1992– (Vice-Pres., 1989–92). *Publications:* An Introduction to Criminal Procedure in Scotland, 1970; (contrib.) Ministers for the 1980s, 1979; (contributing ed.) The Law of Contempt, 1982; (contrib.) Sport and the Law, 2nd edn 1995. *Recreation:* travel. *Address:* c/o Advocates' Library, Parliament House, Edinburgh EH1 4RF. *T:* (0131) 226 5071; 9–12 Bell Yard, WC2A 2JR. *T:* (020) 7400 1800, *Fax:* (020) 7400 1405; (home) 20 Edinburgh Road, Dalkeith, Midlothian EH22 1JY. *T:* (0131) 660 3007.

KERRIGAN, Prof. John Francis; Professor of English 2000, University of Cambridge, since 2001; Fellow, St John's College, Cambridge, since 1982; *b* 16 June 1956; *s* of late Stephen Francis Kerrigan and of Patricia Kerrigan (*née* Baker); one *d*. *Educ:* St Edward's Coll., Liverpool (Christian Brothers); Keble Coll., Oxford (BA). Domus Sen. Schol., 1977–79, Jun. Res. Fellow, 1979–82, Merton Coll., Oxford; University of Cambridge: Asst Lectr in English, 1982–86; Lectr in English, 1986–98; Reader in English Lit., 1998–2001; Dir of Studies in English, St John's Coll., 1987–97; Chm., English Faculty Bd, 2003–06. Vis. Prof., Meiji Univ., Tokyo, 1986. Visiting Fellow: Jadavpur Univ., Calcutta, 2008; Univ. of Delhi, 2008. Res. Reader, British Acad., 1998–2000; J. A. W. Bennett Meml Lectr, Perugia, 1998. Lectures: Chatterton, British Acad., 1988; Acad. for Irish Cultural Heritages, 2003; F. W. Bateson, Oxford, 2004; Gareth Roberts, Exeter, 2007; Nicholson and Poetics, Chicago, 2007; Shakespeare, British Acad., 2009. Foundn Fellow, English Assoc., 1999; Fellow, Wordsworth Trust, 2001. Trustee, Dove Cottage, Wordsworth Trust, 1984–2001. Charles Oldham Shakespeare Prize, 1976, Matthew Arnold Meml Prize, 1981, Oxford Univ.; Truman Capote Award for Literary Criticism, 1998. *Publications:* (ed) Love's Labour's Lost, 1982; (ed) Shakespeare's Sonnets and A Lover's Complaint, 1986, 2nd edn 1995; (ed with J. Wordsworth) Wordsworth and the Worth of Words, by Hugh Sykes Davies, 1987; Motives of Woe: Shakespeare and Female Complaint, 1991; (ed jtly) English Comedy, 1994; Revenge Tragedy: Aeschylus to Armageddon, 1996; (ed with P. Robinson) The Thing about Roy Fisher: critical studies, 2000; On Shakespeare and Early Modern Literature: essays, 2001; Archipelagic English: literature, history and politics 1603–1707, 2008; contrib. numerous articles in essay collections and learned jls; reviews in Irish Rev., London Rev. of Books, TLS and poetry mags. *Recreation:* music. *Address:* St John's College, Cambridge CB2 1TP. *T:* (01223) 338620; *e-mail:* jk10023@cam.ac.uk.

KERRY, Earl of; Simon Henry George Petty-Fitzmaurice; *b* 24 Nov. 1970; *s* and heir of Marquess of Lansdowne, *qv*. *Educ:* Eton; Jesus Coll., Cambridge.

KERRY, Knight of; see FitzGerald, Sir A. J. A. D.

KERRY, John Forbes, JD; US Senator from Massachusetts, since 1985; *b* 11 Dec. 1943; *s* of Richard John Kerry and Rosemary Kerry (*née* Forbes); *m* 1st, 1970, Julia S. Thorne (marr. diss. 1985); two *d*; 2nd, 1995, (Maria) Teresa (Thierstein) Heinz (*née* Simoes-Ferreira). *Educ:* Yale Univ. (BA 1966); Boston Coll. (MA; JD 1976). Served US Navy, 1966–70; Nat. Co-ordinator, Vietnam Veterans Against the War, 1969–71. Called to the Bar, Mass, 1976; Asst Dist Attorney, Middx Co., Mass, 1976–79; Partner, Kerry & Sragow, Boston, 1979–82; Lt Gov., Mass, 1982–84. Presidential cand. (Democrat), US elections, 2004. *Publications:* The New Soldier, 1971; The New War: the web of crime that threatens America's security, 1997. *Address:* US Senate, 304 Russell Senate Office Building, Washington, DC 20510–0001, USA.

KERRY, Sir Michael (James), KCB 1983 (CB 1976); QC 1984; *b* 5 Aug. 1923; *s* of Russell Kerry and Marjorie (*née* Kensington); *m* 1951, Sidney Rosetta Elizabeth (*née* Foster) (*d* 2003); one *s* two *d*. *Educ:* Rugby Sch.; St John's Coll., Oxford (MA; Hon. Fellow 1986). Served with RAF, 1942–46. Called to Bar, Lincoln's Inn, 1949, Bencher 1984. Joined BoT as Legal Asst, 1951; Sen. Legal Asst, 1959; Asst Solicitor, 1964; Principal Asst Solicitor, Dept of Trade and Industry, 1972, Solicitor, 1973–80; HM Procurator Gen. and Treasury Solicitor, 1980–84. Dep. Chm., LAUTRO, 1988–91. *Recreations:* golf, gardening. *Address:* South Bedales, Lewes Road, Haywards Heath, W Sussex RH17 7TE. *T:* (01444) 831303. *Club:* Piltdown Golf.

KERSE, Prof. Christopher Stephen, CB 2003; PhD; Professor of Law, University of Surrey, since 2007; *b* 12 Dec. 1946; *s* of late William Harold Kerse and Maude Kerse; *m* 1971, Gillian Hanks (*d* 2007); one *s* one *d*. *Educ:* King George V Sch., Southport; Univ. of Hull (LLB; PhD 1995). Admitted Solicitor, 1972. Lecturer in Law: Univ. of Bristol, 1968–72; Univ. of Manchester, 1972–76; Asst Prof., Faculty of Law, Univ. of British Columbia, 1974–75; Sen. Legal Asst, OFT, 1976–81; Department of Trade and Industry: Sen. Legal Asst, 1981–82; Asst Solicitor, 1982–88; Head, Consumer Affairs Div., 1991–93; Under-Sec. (Legal), 1988–95; Second Counsel to Chm. of Cttees and Legal Advr to EU Cttee, H of L, 1995–2007. Vis. Prof., KCL, 1992–. *Publications:* The Law Relating to Noise, 1975; EC Antitrust Procedure, 1981, 5th edn 2005 (with N. Khan); (with J. C.

Cook) EC Merger Control, 1991, 4th edn 2005; articles in various legal jls. *Recreations:* the double bass, travel.

KERSFELT, Anita Ingegerd; *see* Gradin, A. I.

KERSHAW, family name of **Baron Kershaw**.

KERSHAW, 4th Baron *cr* 1947; **Edward John Kershaw;** Chartered Accountant; business consultant; Partner, Bartlett Kershaw Trott, Chartered Accountants, 1996–2001; *b* 12 May 1936; *s* of 3rd Baron and Katharine Dorothea Kershaw (*née* Staines); *S* father, 1962; *m* 1963, Rosalind Lilian Rutherford; one *s* two *d*. *Educ:* Selhurst Grammar Sch., Surrey. Entered RAF Nov. 1955, demobilised Nov. 1957. Admitted to Inst. of Chartered Accountants in England and Wales, Oct. 1964. Mem., Acad. of Experts, 1995. Lay Governor, The King's Sch., Gloucester, 1986–95. JP Gloucester, 1982–95. *Heir: s* Hon. John Charles Edward Kershaw, *b* 23 Dec. 1971. *Address:* 38 High View, Hempsted, Gloucester GL2 5LN.

KERSHAW, Andrew; broadcaster and journalist, since 1984; *b* 9 Nov. 1959; *s* of John (Jack) Kershaw and Eileen Kershaw (*née* Acton); one *s* one *d* by Juliette Banner. *Educ:* Hulme Grammar Sch., Oldham; Leeds Univ. Joined BBC, 1984: presenter: Whistle Test, 1984–87 (Live Aid, 1985); Andy Kershaw Prog., Radio 1, 1985–2000, Radio 3, 2001–; Andy Kershaw's World of Music, World Service, 1987–2000; occasional foreign news reports for Radio 4, 1990– (incl. reports from Haiti, Angola, Rwanda, N Korea, Iraq); Travelog, Channel 4, 1991–97 (incl. first ever film made inside N Korea, 1995); freelance journalist, 1988–; Radio Critic, Independent, 1999. Hon. MusD: UEA, 2003; Leeds, 2005. Sony Radio Awards, 1987, 1989 (two), 1996, 2002 (three). *Recreations:* music, motorcycle racing, travels to extreme countries, boxing, fishing. *Address:* c/o Sincere Management, 35 Bravington Road, W9 3AH. *T:* (020) 8960 4438. *Clubs:* Academy; Peel Sailing and Cruising.

KERSHAW, Dame Betty; *see* Kershaw, Dame J. E. M.

KERSHAW, David Andrew; Chief Executive, M&C Saatchi plc, since 2004 (Founding Partner, 1995–2004); *b* 26 Feb. 1954; *s* of Lawrence Kershaw and Rona Kershaw (now Lucas); *m* 1993, Clare Whitley; one *s* one *d*. *Educ:* Bedales Sch.; Univ. of Durham (BA Hons Pols 1977); London Business Sch. (MBA 1982). Account Exec., Wasey Campbell-Ewald, 1977–80; Saatchi & Saatchi UK: Account Dir, 1982–90; Man. Dir, 1990–94; Chief Exec., 1994–95. Trustee, Creative and Cultural Skills, 2005–; Chm., Cultural Leadership Prog., 2006–. *Recreations:* Arsenal, golf, opera, clarinet. *Address:* M&C Saatchi plc, 36 Golden Square, W1F 9EE. *T:* (020) 7543 4500; *e-mail:* davidk@mcsaatchi.com. *Clubs:* Groucho; Coombe Hill Golf.

KERSHAW, Helen Elizabeth, (Mrs W. J. S. Kershaw); *see* Paling, H. E.

KERSHAW, Sir Ian, Kt 2002; DPhil; FBA 1991; Professor of Modern History, University of Sheffield, since 1989; *b* Oldham, 29 April 1943; *s* of late Joseph Kershaw and of Alice (*née* Robinson); *m* 1966, Janet Elizabeth Murray Gammie (*see* Dame J. E. M. Kershaw); two *s*. *Educ:* St Bede's Coll., Manchester; Univ. of Liverpool (BA 1965); Merton Coll., Oxford (DPhil 1969; Hon. Fellow, 2005). FRHistS, 1972–74, 1991. University of Manchester: Asst Lectr in Medieval Hist., 1968–70, Lectr, 1970–74; Lectr in Modern Hist., 1974–79, Sen. Lectr, 1979–87, Reader elect, 1987; Prof. of Modern History, Univ. of Nottingham, 1987–89. Vis. Prof. of Contemporary Hist., Ruhr-Univ., Bochum, 1983–84. Fellow: Alexander von Humboldt-Stiftung, 1976; Wissenschaftskolleg zu Berlin, 1989–90. Bundesverdienstkreuz (Germany), 1994. Hon. DLitt: Manchester, 2004; QUB, 2007; DUniv Stirling, 2006. *Publications:* (ed) Rentals and Ministers' Accounts of Bolton Priory 1473–1539, 1969; Bolton Priory: the economy of a Northern monastery, 1973; Der Hitler-Mythos: Volksmeinung und Propaganda im Dritten Reich, 1980, Eng. trans. 1987; Popular Opinion and Political Dissent in the Third Reich: Bavaria 1933–1945, 1983; The Nazi Dictatorship: problems and perspectives of interpretation, 1985, 4th edn 2000; (ed) Weimar: why did German democracy fail?, 1990; Hitler: a profile in power, 1991, 2nd edn 2000; (ed with M. Lewin) Stalinism and Nazism, 1997; Hitler 1889–1936: hubris, 1998; Hitler 1936–1945: nemesis, 2000 (Bruno Kreisky Prize (Austria), 2000; Wolfson Prize for History, 2000; British Acad. Prize, 2001); (ed with David M. Smith) The Bolton Priory Compotus 1286–1325, 2001; Making Friends with Hitler: Lord Londonderry and Britain's road to war, 2004 (Elizabeth Longford Historical Biog. Prize, 2005); Fateful Choices: ten decisions that changed the world 1940–1941, 2007; articles in learned jls. *Recreations:* Rugby League, cricket, music, real ale, outings in the Yorkshire dales. *Address:* Department of History, University of Sheffield, Sheffield S10 2TN. *T:* (0114) 222 2550.

KERSHAW, Dame Janet Elizabeth Murray, (Dame Betty), DBE 1998; FRCN; Professor and Dean of the School of Nursing and Midwifery, University of Sheffield, 1999–2006, now Dean Emeritus; *b* 11 Dec. 1943; *d* of Ian U. Gammie and Janet Gammie; *m* 1966, Ian Kershaw (*see* Sir Ian Kershaw); two *s*. *Educ:* Crossley and Porter Grammar Sch., Halifax; United Manchester Hosps (SRN; OND); Manchester Univ. (MSc Nursing; RNT). Dir of Educn, Royal Marsden Hosp., 1984–87; Principal, Stockport, Tameside and Glossop Coll. of Nursing, 1987–94; Dir of Nurse Educn, Coll. of Midwifery and Nursing, Manchester, 1994–97; Dir, Centre for Professional Policy Develt, Sch. of Nursing, Midwifery and Health Visiting, Univ. of Manchester, 1997–98. Visiting Professor: Manchester Metropolitan Univ., 2006; Birmingham City Univ., 2007–. Pres., RCN, 1994–98 (FRCN 2001). Chm., GNC Trust, 2007–. Chief Officer, Nursing and Social Care, St John Ambulance, 1998–2005. Hon. LLD Manchester, 1995. *Publications:* (with J. Salvage) Models For Nursing, 1986; (with J. Salvage) Models for Nursing 2, 1990; (with Bob Price) The Riehl Model of Care, 1993; (with J. Marr) Caring for Older People, 1998. *Recreations:* theatre, music, travel. *Address:* School of Nursing and Midwifery, University of Sheffield, Winter Street, Sheffield S3 7ND.

KERSHAW, Jann Peta Olwen; *see* Parry, J. P. O.

KERSHAW, Jennifer Christine; QC 1998; **Her Honour Judge Kershaw;** a Circuit Judge, since 2005; *b* 1 May 1951. *Educ:* King's Coll., London (LLB 1973). Called to the Bar, Lincoln's Inn, 1974; a Recorder, 2000–05. *Recreations:* horses, gardening.

KERSHAW, Joseph Anthony; *b* 26 Nov. 1935; *s* of Henry and Catherine Kershaw, Preston; *m* 1959, Ann Whittle; three *s* two *d*. *Educ:* Ushaw Coll., Durham; Preston Catholic Coll., SJ. Short service commn, RAOC, 1955–58; Unilever Ltd, 1958–67; Gp Marketing Manager, CWS, 1967–69; Managing Director: Underline Ltd, 1969–71; Merchant Div., Reed International Ltd, 1971–73; Head of Marketing, Non-Foods, CWS, 1973–74; (first) Director, Nat. Consumer Council, 1975; independent management consultant, 1975–91. Chairman: Antonian Investments Ltd, 1985–87; Organised Business Data Ltd, 1987–89; Director: John Stork & Partners Ltd, 1980–85; Allia (Holdings) Ltd, 1984–88; Associate Director: Foote, Cone & Belding Ltd, 1979–84; Phoenix Advertising, 1984–86. *Recreations:* turning, woodcarving, water colour painting, fishing, cooking, gardening, RHS, NACF. *Address:* Westmead, Meins Road, Blackburn, Lancs BB2 6QF. *T:* (01254) 55915.

KERSHAW, Michael; *see* Kershaw, P. M.

KERSHAW, (Philip) Michael; QC 1980; DL; *b* 23 April 1941; *m* 1980, Anne (*née* Williams); one *s*. *Educ:* Ampleforth Coll.; St John's Coll., Oxford (MA). FCIArb 1991. Called to the Bar, Gray's Inn, 1963; in practice, 1963–90; a Recorder, 1980–90. Consulting Ed., Atkin's Court Forms, 1997. Fellow, Soc. for Advanced Legal Studies, 1999. DL Lancs, 2007. *Publications:* Fraud and Misrepresentation, Injunctions, Bills of Sale, Bonds and Banking and Bills of Exchange, in Atkin's Court Forms; (contrib.) Interests in Goods, 1993. *Recreation:* choral singing.

KERSHAW, Stephen Edward; Director, Police Reform and Resources, Home Office, since 2007; *b* 20 Sept. 1959; *s* of Barry Kershaw, railway signal engr, and Audrey Kathleen (*née* Breadmore). *Educ:* St Peter's C of E Primary Sch., Rickmansworth; William Penn Comprehensive Sch., Rickmansworth, Herts; Wadham Coll., Oxford (Open Schol.; BA 1st Cl. Hons Mod. Hist. 1981; MA; res., 1981–84). Lectr in Mod. Hist., Wadham Coll., Oxford, 1984–85; Cabinet Office, 1985–87 (Private Sec. to Second Perm. Sec., 1986–87); DES, 1987–89; Next Steps Team, Cabinet Office, 1989–92; DFE, later DfEE, 1992–99; on secondment as Hd, Strategic Planning, Manchester LEA, 1999–2000; Actg Dir, Pupil Support and Inclusion Gp, DfEE, 2000–01; Dir, Teachers' Gp, subseq. Sch. Workforce Unit, DfEE, later DfES, 2001–03; Finance Dir, DfES, 2003–06; Dir, Prime Minister's Delivery Unit, Cabinet Office, 2006–07. *Publications:* (contrib.) The Tudor Nobility, ed G. W. Bernard, 1992; contrib. reviews in various jls. *Recreations:* family history, Spain, Laurel and Hardy, indulging my niece and nephews. *Address:* Home Office, 2 Marsham Street, SW1P 4DF.

KERSLAKE, Sir Robert (Walter), Kt 2005; Chief Executive, Homes and Communities Agency, since 2008; *b* 28 Feb. 1955; *m* Anne; one *s* one *d*. *Educ:* Univ. of Warwick (BSc Hons Maths). CPFA. Greater London Council, 1979–85: CIPFA trainee, 1979–82; Transport Finance, 1982–85; with ILEA, 1985–89; Dir of Finance, 1989–90, Chief Executive: London Borough of Hounslow, 1990–97; Sheffield CC, 1997–2008. *Recreations:* music, walking. *Address:* Homes and Communities Agency, Ashdown House, 123 Victoria Street, SW1E 6DE.

KERTÉSZ, Imre; writer and translator, since 1953; *b* Budapest, 9 Nov. 1929; *m* Magda. With Világosság newspaper, Budapest, 1948–51; mil. service, 1951–53. Nobel Prize in Literature, 2002. Books translated into numerous languages, incl. English, German, Spanish, French, Czech, Russian, Swedish and Hebrew. *Publications include:* novels: Sorstalanság, 1975 (Fateless, 1992); A nyomkeresö (The Pathfinder), 1977; A kudarc (Fiasco), 1988; Kaddis a meg nem született gyermekért, 1990 (Kaddish for a Child not Born, 1997); Az angol labogó (The English Flag), 1991; Gályanapló (Galley Diary), 1992; Jegyzökönyv, 1993; Valaki más: a változás krónikája (I, Another: chronicle of a metamorphosis), 1997; Felszámolás (Liquidation), 2003; essays: A holocaust mint kultúra (The Holocaust as Culture), 1993; A gondolatnyi csend, amíg kivégzöosztag újratölt (Moments of Silence while the Execution Squad Reloads), 1998; A száműzött nyelv (The Exiled Language), 2001. *Address:* c/o Magvetö Press, Balassi BU 7, 1055 Budapest, Hungary.

KESSLER, Dinah Gwen Lison; *see* Rose, D. G. L.

KESSLER, Edward David, PhD; Founder and Executive Director: Centre for the Study of Jewish-Christian Relations, Cambridge, since 1998; Centre for the Study of Muslim-Jewish Relations, Cambridge, since 2006; Fellow, St Edmund's College, Cambridge, since 2002; *b* 3 May 1963; *s* of William and Joanna Kessler; *m* 1989, Patricia Josephine Oakley; one *s* two *d*. *Educ:* Univ. of Leeds (BA Jt Hons 1985); Harvard Univ. (MTS 1987); Univ. of Stirling (MBA 1989); Univ. of Cambridge (PhD 1999). W. H. Smith, 1987–89; Kesslers Internat. Ltd, 1989–95. Sternberg Interfaith Award, 2006. *Publications:* An English Jew: the life and writings of Claude Montefiore, 1989, 2nd edn 2002; (ed with J. Pawlikowski) Jews and Christians in Conversation: crossing cultures and generations, 2002; Bound by the Bible: Jews, Christians and the Sacrifice of Isaac, 2004; The Founders of Liberal Judaism: Israel Abrahams, Claude Montefiore, Israel Mattuck and Lily Montagu, 2004; (ed with D. Goldberg) Aspects of Liberal Judaism: essays in honour of Rabbi John D. Rayner, 2004; (ed with M. Wright) Themes in Jewish-Christian Relations, 2005; (ed with N. Wenborn) A Dictionary of Jewish-Christian Relations, 2005; (ed with J. Aitken) Challenges in Jewish-Christian Relations, 2006; What do Jews Believe?, 2006. *Recreations:* family, supporting Arsenal, Mediterranean cycling. *Address:* Wesley House, Jesus Lane, Cambridge CB5 8BJ. *T:* (01223) 741048, *Fax:* (01223) 741049; *e-mail:* edk21@cjcr.cam.ac.uk. *Club:* Athenæum.

See also J. R. Kessler.

KESSLER, James Richard; QC 2003; *b* 6 Sept. 1959; *s* of William and Joanna Kessler; *m* 1983, Jane Marie Pinto; two *s* one *d*. *Educ:* Brasenose Coll., Oxford (MA). FTII 1990. Called to the Bar: Gray's Inn, 1984; Northern Ireland, 2003; in practice at Revenue Bar. Founder, Trusts Discussion Forum, 1999. *Publications:* Tax Planning for the Foreign Domiciliary, 1987; Tax Planning and Fundraising for Charities, 1989, 6th edn as Taxation of Charities, 2007; Drafting Trusts and Will Trusts, 1992, 9th edn 2008; Taxation of Foreign Domiciliaries, 2001, 7th edn 2008; Drafting Trusts and Will Trusts in Canada, 2003, 2nd edn 2007; Drafting Trusts and Will Trusts in Northern Ireland, 2004, 2nd edn 2007; Drafting Cayman Island Trusts, 2007; Drafting Trusts and Will Trusts in the Channel Islands, 2007; Drafting Trusts and Will Trusts in Singapore, 2007; Drafting Trusts and Will Trusts in Australia, 2008. *Recreations:* cinema, jogging. *Address:* 15 Old Square, Lincoln's Inn, WC2A 3UE. *T:* (020) 7242 2744; *e-mail:* kessler@kessler.co.uk.

See also E. D. Kessler.

KESTELMAN, Sara; actress and writer; *d* of late Morris Kestelman, RA and Dorothy Mary (*née* Creagh). *Educ:* Hampstead Parochial Sch.; Camden Sch. for Girls; Cecchetti ballet trng; Central Sch. of Speech and Drama. Royal Shakespeare Co. includes: A Midsummer Night's Dream (dir. Peter Brooks), 1970–72, Broadway, 1971; Macbeth, 1982–83; King Lear, 1983; Lear (by Edward Bond), 1983; Moscow Gold, 1990–91; Misha's Party, 1994; National Theatre, subseq. Royal National Theatre, includes: As You Like It, 1979; Love for Love; 3D Opera; American Clock, 1986; Bedroom Farce; Square Rounds, 1992; Copenhagen, 1998, transf. Duchess, 1999; Hamlet, 2000; other productions: The Way of the World, Chichester Festival, 1984; Waste, Lyric, 1985; Three Sisters, Greenwich, transf. Albery, 1987; Lettice and Lovage, Globe, 1989; Another Time, Wyndham's, 1990; The Cabinet Minister, Albery, 1991; The Cherry Orchard, Gate, Dublin, 1992; Cabaret, Donmar, 1993–94 (Olivier and Derwent Awards, for best supporting performance in a musical); Fiddler on the Roof, London Palladium, 1994; Three Tall Women, Wyndham's, 1995; A Two Hander (songwriter, jt writer, performer), Hampstead, 1996; Nine, Donmar, 1996–97; The Shape of Metal, Abbey Th., Dublin, 2003; Flower Drum Song (musical), Lilian Baylis Th., 2006; My Child, Royal Court, 2007; one woman cabaret show, All About Me! (tour), 1998–2003; *films:* Zardoz, 1973;

Lisztomania, 1975; Break of Day, 1976; Lady Jane, 1984; Ex Memoria, 2006; *television* includes: Caucasian Chalk Circle, 1973; The Cafeteria, 1975; Crown Court; The Last Romantics, 1991; Casualty, 1996, 2003; Tom Jones, 1997; Kavanagh QC, 1997; Invasion Earth, 1998; Anna Karenina, 2000; Trial and Retribution, 2003, 2004; Midsomer Murders, 2004; Ultimate Force, 2004; Instinct, 2006; Rome, 2006; narrations for documentaries; numerous radio plays, incl. Hitler in Therapy (Actress of the Year, World Air Awards, BBC World Service, 2005), and book readings; adapted Molly Keane's Full House for Book at Bedtime, 1991. Pt-time Lectr, Central Sch. of Speech and Drama, 2007–. Life Coach certificates, 2006 and 2007; Master practitioner in Neuro-linguistic programming, 2007. *Publication:* (with Susan Penhaligon) A Two Hander (poems), 1996. *Recreations:* writing - song writer and poet, tapestry, drawing, photography, dance. *Address:* c/o Jonathan Altaras Associates, 11 Garrick Street, WC2E 9AR.

KESTENBAUM, Jonathan Andrew; Chief Executive, National Endowment for Science, Technology and the Arts, since 2005; *b* 5 Aug. 1961; *s* of late Ralph Kestenbaum and of Gaby Kestenbaum; *m* 1984, Deborah Zackon; three *s* one *d*. *Educ:* London Sch. of Econs (BA Hons 1982); Wolfson Coll., Cambridge; Cass Business Sch. (MBA 1994). Chief Executive: Office of Chief Rabbi, 1991–96; UJIA, 1996–2002; Portland Trust, 2002–06; COS to Sir Ronald Cohen, Chm. of Apax Partners, 2002–06. Non-exec. Chm., Quest Ltd, 2002–06. Board Member: Enterprise Insight, 2005–08; Design Council, 2006–; Mem., Technology Strategy Bd, 2007–. Tutor, Cass Business Sch., 1999–. Trustee, London Community Centre, 2003–; Gov. and Mem. Bd, RSC, 2007–. CCMI. *Recreations:* tennis, ski-ing. *Address:* NESTA, 1 Plough Place, EC4A 1DE. *T:* (020) 7438 2525, *Fax:* (020) 7438 2524. *Club:* MCC.

KESTER, David Martin Albert; Chief Executive, Design Council, since 2003; *b* 23 May 1964; *s* of Simon and Stephanie Kester; *m* 1992, Sophia Adamou; two *s*. *Educ:* Bristol Univ. (BA Hons). Friends of the Earth, 1990–93; Chartered Soc. of Designers, 1993–94; Chief Exec., British Design and Art Direction, 1994–2003. Member: Bd, Design Business Assoc., 2003–; Council, RCA, 2003–; Adv. Council, RSA, 2004–; Bd, Kingston Rose Th., 2007–; Bd, Home Office Design and Technol. Alliance, 2007–.

KESTING, Very Rev. Sheilagh Margaret; Secretary, Committee on Ecumenical Relations, Church of Scotland, 1993–2007 and since 2008; Moderator of the General Assembly of the Church of Scotland, 2007–08; *b* 10 June 1953; *d* of Douglas Norman Kesting and Joan Robertson Kesting (*née* Blair). *Educ:* Nicolson Inst., Stornoway; Edinburgh Univ. (BA 1974; BD Hons 1977). Ordained, C of S, 1980; Parish Minister: Overtown, Lanarkshire, 1980–86; St Andrew's High, Musselburgh, 1986–93. Hon DD Edinburgh, 2008. *Recreations:* gardening, photography, embroidery. *Address:* Church of Scotland Offices, 121 George Street, Edinburgh EH2 4YN. *T:* (0131) 225 5722, *Fax:* (0131) 240 2239; *e-mail:* skesting@cofscotland.org.uk.

KESWICK, Hon. Annabel Thérèse, (Tessa); Deputy Chairman, Centre for Policy Studies, since 2004 (Director, 1995–2004); *b* 15 Oct. 1942; *d* of 17th Baron Lovat, DSO, MC and of Rosamond, *o d* of Sir Delves Broughton, 11th Bt; *m* 1st, 1964, 14th Lord Reay, *qv* (marr. diss. 1978); two *s* one *d*; 2nd, 1985, Henry Neville Lindley Keswick, *qv*. *Educ:* Convent of the Sacred Heart, Woldingham. Trainee, J. W. Thompson, 1960–62; Dir, Cluff Investments, 1980–95. Special Advr to Rt Hon. Kenneth Clarke, 1989–95. Mem. (C), Kensington Council, 1982–86 (Member: Housing Cttee; Special Services Cttee). Contested (C), Inverness, Nairn and Lochaber, 1987. Gov., St James' Norland Colville Nursery Sch., and Colville Primary Sch., N Kensington, 1981–86. London Editor, B and E International, 1975–78. Hon. FKC 2007. *Recreations:* travelling, breeding horses. *Address:* 6 Smith Square, SW1P 3HT.

KESWICK, Sir Chippendale; *see* Keswick, Sir J. C. L.

KESWICK, Henry Neville Lindley; Chairman: Matheson & Co. Ltd, since 1975; Jardine, Matheson Holdings Ltd, Hong Kong, 1972–75 and since 1989 (Director, since 1967); Jardine Strategic Holdings, since 1989 (Director, since 1988); *b* 29 Sept. 1938; *e s* of Sir William Keswick and of Mary, *d* of Rt Hon. Sir Francis Lindley, PC, GCMG; *m* 1985, Tessa, Lady Reay (*see* A. T. Keswick). *Educ:* Eton Coll.; Trinity Coll., Cambridge. BA Hons Econs and Law; MA. Commnd Scots Guards, Nat. Service, 1956–58. Director: Sun Alliance and London Insurance, 1975–96; Robert Fleming Holdings Ltd, 1975–2000; Rothmans Internat., 1988–94; Hongkong Land Co., 1988–; Mandarin Oriental Internat., 1988–; Dairy Farm Internat. Hldgs, 1988–; Royal & Sun Alliance (formerly Sun Alliance) Gp, 1989–2000; The Telegraph, 1990–2001; Mem., Adv. Bd, Telegraph Gp Ltd, 2002–04; Rothschilds Continuation Hldgs AG, 2006–. Member: London Adv. Cttee, Hongkong and Shanghai Banking Corp., 1975–92; 21st Century Trust, 1987–97. Proprietor, The Spectator, 1975–81. Trustee, Nat. Portrait Gall., 1982–2001 (Chm., 1994–2001). Pres., RHASS, 2003–04; Mem. Council, NT, 2005–07. Chm., Hong Kong Assoc., 1988–2001. *Recreation:* country pursuits. *Address:* Matheson & Co. Ltd, 3 Lombard Street, EC3V 9AQ. *Clubs:* White's, Turf; Third Guards.

See also Sir J. C. L. Keswick, S. L. Keswick.

KESWICK, Sir (John) Chippendale (Lindley), Kt 1993; Director, De Beers SA, since 2001; *b* 2 Feb.1940; 2nd *s* of Sir William Keswick and of Mary, *d* of Rt Hon. Sir Francis Lindley, PC, GCMG; *m* 1966, Lady Sarah Ramsay, *d* of 16th Earl of Dalhousie, KT, GCVO, GBE, MC; three *s*. *Educ:* Eton; Univ. of Aix/Marseilles. Glyn Mills & Co., 1961–65; Jt Vice Chm., 1986, Jt Dep. Chm., 1990–97, Gp Chief Exec., 1995–97, Chm., 1997–98, Hambros PLC; Chief Exec., 1985–95, Chm., 1986–98, Hambros Bank. A Dir, Bank of England, 1993–2001. Sen. Banking and Capital Mkts Advr, Société Générale, 1998–2000. Director: Persimmon Plc, 1984–2006; Edinburgh Investment Trust, 1992–2001; De Beers Consolidated Mines, 1993–2006; De Beers Centenary AG, 1994–2005; IMI plc, 1994–2003; Anglo Amer. plc, 1995–2001; Investec Bank (UK) Ltd, 2000–; Investec plc, 2002–; Arsenal Hldgs plc, 2005–; Arsenal FC, 2005–. Mem., Queen's Body Guard for Scotland, Royal Company of Archers, 1976. Chm., Test & Itchen Assoc., 1992–. *Recreations:* bridge, country pursuits. *Address:* E. Oppenheimer & Son Holdings Ltd, 1 Charterhouse Street, EC1N 6SA. *T:* (020) 7421 9823. *Clubs:* White's, Portland.

See also H. N. L. Keswick, S. L. Keswick.

KESWICK, Simon Lindley; Director: Jardine Matheson Holdings Ltd, since 1972 (Chairman, 1983–89); Jardine Lloyd Thompson Group plc, since 2001; *b* 20 May 1942; *s* of Sir William Keswick and of Mary, *d* of Rt Hon. Sir Francis Lindley, PC, GCMG; *m* 1971, Emma, *d* of Major David Chetwode; two *s* two *d*. *Educ:* Eton Coll. Director: Hong Kong and Shanghai Banking Corp., 1983–88; Matheson & Co. Ltd, 1982–; Jardine Strategic Hldgs Ltd, 1987– (Chm., 1987–89); Hanson plc, 1991–2005; Wellcome plc, 1995–96; Fleming Mercantile Investment Trust, 1988–2007 (Chm., 1990–2003); Chairman: Hongkong Land Hldgs Ltd, 1983–; Mandarin Oriental Internat. Ltd, 1984–; Dairy Farm Internat. Hldgs Ltd, 1984–; Trafalgar House plc, 1993–96. Dir, Cheltenham Town FC, 2004–. Trustee: British Museum, 1989–99; Henry Moore Foundn, 2003–. Patron, RCS, 1998–. *Recreations:* country pursuits, bridge, soccer. *Address:* May Tower 1, 5–7 May Road, Hong Kong; 7 Ennismore Gardens, SW7 1NL. *Clubs:* White's, Portland; Shek O (Hong Kong).

See also H. N. L. Keswick, Sir J. C. L. Keswick.

KESWICK, Hon. Tessa; *see* Keswick, Hon. A. T.

KETTERLE, Prof. Wolfgang, PhD; John D. MacArthur Professor of Physics, Massachusetts Institute of Technology, since 1998; *b* Heidelberg, 21 Oct. 1957; German citizen with permanent residency in US; *m* (marr. diss.); two *s* one *d*. *Educ:* Univ. of Heidelberg (Vordiplom Physics 1978); Tech. Univ. Munich (Diplom Physics 1982); Ludwig Maximilians Univ. of Munich and Max-Planck Inst. for Quantum Optics (PhD 1986). Intern, Volkswagen Co., Puebla, Mexico, 1980; res. asst, 1982–85, staff scientist, 1985–88, Max-Planck Inst. for Quantum Optics, Germany; res. scientist, Dept of Physical Chem., Univ. of Heidelberg, 1989–90; Department of Physics, Massachusetts Institute of Technology: Res. Associate, 1990–93; Asst Prof. of Physics, 1993–97; Prof. of Physics, 1997–98. NATO/Deutscher Akademischer Austauschdienst Postdoctoral Fellow, 1990–91; David and Lucile Packard Fellow, 1996–2001; Dist. Traveling Lectr, Div. of Laser Sci., APS, 1998–99. Member: German Physical Soc.; Optical Soc. of America, 1997; Eur. Acad. of Scis and Arts, 2002; Acad. of Scis in Heidelberg, 2002; Eur. Acad. of Arts, Scis and Humanities, 2002; Bavarian Acad. of Scis, 2003; For. Associate, NAS, 2002; Fellow: APS, 1997; Amer. Acad. Arts and Scis, 1999; FInstP 2002. Michael and Philip Platzman Award, MIT, 1994; I. I. Rabi Prize, APS, 1997; Gustav-Hertz Prize, German Physical Soc., 1997; Award for Technological Innovation, Discover Mag., 1998; Fritz London Prize in Low Temp. Physics, 1999; Dannie-Heineman Prize, Acad. of Scis, Göttingen, 1999; Benjamin Franklin Medal in Physics, 2000; (jtly) Nobel Prize in Physics, 2001. Kt Comdr's Cross (Badge and Star), Order of Merit (Germany), 2002; Medal of Merit, State of Baden-Wurtemberg (Germany), 2002; Officer, Legion of Honour (France), 2002. *Address:* Massachusetts Institute of Technology, 77 Massachusetts Avenue, Cambridge, MA 02139, USA. *T:* (617) 2536815, *Fax:* (617) 2534876; *e-mail:* ketterle@mit.edu; 24 Grassmere Road, Brookline, MA 02467, USA.

KETTLE, Captain Alan Stafford Howard, CB 1984; Royal Navy (retired); General Manager, HM Dockyard, Chatham, 1977–84; *b* 6 Aug. 1925; *s* of Arthur Stafford Kettle and Marjorie Constance (*née* Clough); *m* 1952, Patricia Rosemary (*née* Gander); two *s*. *Educ:* Rugby School. Joined RN, 1943; Comdr, Dec. 1959; Captain, Dec. 1968; retired, Sept. 1977. Entered Civil Service as Asst Under-Sec., Sept. 1977. *Address:* Woodside, 9 Roland Bailey Gardens, Tavistock, Devon PL19 0RB. *T:* (01822) 618721.

KETTLEWELL, Comdt Dame Marion M., DBE 1970 (CBE 1964); Director, Women's Royal Naval Service, 1967–70; *b* 20 Feb. 1914; *d* of late George Wildman Kettlewell, Bramling, Virginia Water, Surrey, and of Mildred Frances (*née* Atkinson), Belford, Northumberland. *Educ:* Godolphin Sch., Salisbury; St Christopher's Coll., Blackheath. Worked for Fellowship of Maple Leaf, Alta, Canada, 1935–38; worked for Local Council, 1939–41; joined WRNS as MT driver, 1941; commnd as Third Officer WRNS, 1942; Supt WRNS on Staff of Flag Officer Air (Home), 1961–64; Supt WRNS Training and Drafting, 1964–67; Gen. Sec., GFS, 1971–78. Pres., Assoc. of Wrens, 1981–92. *Recreations:* needlework, walking, and country life. *Address:* Flat 2, 9 John Islip Street, SW1P 4PU.

KEVERNE, Prof. Eric Barrington, (Barry), DSc; FRS 1997; Professor of Behavioural Neuroscience, since 1998, and Fellow of King's College, since 1985, University of Cambridge. *Educ:* London Univ. (BSc, PhD); MA 1975, DSc 1993, Cantab. University of Cambridge: Lectr, Dept of Anatomy, then of Zoology, until 1990; Reader in Behavioural Neurosci., 1990–98. Chm., Healthy Organism Strategy Panel, BBSRC, 2005–07; Member: Royal Soc. Res. Fellowships Cttee, 1998–2003; Animals Res. Cttee, Royal Soc., 2004–; MRC Cross Bds Cttee, 2000–03. FMedSci 2005. Foreign Hon. Fellow, American Acad. of Arts and Scis, 1998. *Address:* Sub-Department of Animal Behaviour, University of Cambridge, Madingley, Cambridge CB3 8AA. *T:* (01954) 210301; King's College, Cambridge CB2 1ST.

KEVILL, Siân Louise; Editorial Director, BBC World Ltd, since 2004; *b* Enfield, 29 Jan. 1961; *d* of David Courtney Kevill and Frances Morfydd Kevill; *m* 1987 (marr. diss. 1999); one *s* one *d*. *Educ:* Newnham Coll., Cambridge (BA 1st Cl. Hons Hist. 1982). Staff writer, Keesing's Contemp. Archives, Longman Publishing, 1983–84; BBC: Talks writer, BBC World Service, 1984–85; News Trainee, 1986–88; Asst Producer, 1988–90, Producer, 1990–92, Asst Ed., 1992–94, Newsnight; Dep. Ed., On the Record, 1994–95; Ed., Foreign Progs, BBC Radio, 1995–97; Dep. Hd, Political Progs, 1997–98; Ed., Newsnight, 1998–2003; Hd, Political Progs Rev., 2003–04. *Publications:* Sino-Soviet Relations, 1984; Aquino and the Philippines, 1985. *Recreations:* sport, swimming, running, cinema, reading, socialising. *Address:* BBC World Ltd, Woodlands, Wood Lane, W12 0TT. *T:* (020) 8433 2000; *e-mail:* sian.kevill@bbc.co.uk.

KEY, Brian Michael; Member (Lab) Yorkshire South, European Parliament, 1979–84; *b* 20 Sept. 1947; *s* of Leslie Granville Key and Nora Alice (*née* Haylett); *m* 1974, Lynn Joyce Ambler. *Educ:* Darfield County Primary Sch.; Wath upon Dearne Grammar Sch.; Liverpool Univ. (BA Hons). Careers Officer, West Riding County Council, 1970–73; Sen. Administrative Officer, South Yorkshire CC, 1973–79. *Address:* 25 Cliff Road, Darfield, Barnsley S73 9HR. *Clubs:* Darfield Working Men's; Trades and Labour (Doncaster).

KEY, John Phillip; MP (Nat.) Helensville, New Zealand, since 2002; Leader, National Party, since 2006; Leader of the Opposition, since 2006; *b* 9 Aug. 1961; *s* of George Key and Ruth (*née* Lazar); *m* 1984, Bronagh Dougan; one *s* one *d*. *Educ:* Canterbury Univ. (BCom Accounting 1981). Hd, Treasury, Bankers Trust of NZ, 1988–95; Merrill Lynch, 1995–2001: Asian Hd, Foreign Exchange, Singapore; Global Hd, Foreign Exchange, London; Europ. Hd, Bonds and Derivatives, London; Hd, Fixed Income, Australia. *Recreations:* spending time with family, cooking, watching Rugby. *Address:* Parliament of New Zealand, PO Box 18–888, Wellington, New Zealand. *T:* (4) 4719307, *Fax:* (4) 4733689; *e-mail:* john.key@parliament.govt.nz.

KEY, Matthew David; Chairman and Chief Executive Officer, Telefónica Europe plc, since 2008; Member, Executive Committee, Telefónica SA, since 2008; *b* 3 March 1963; *s* of Kenneth Charles Key and Christina Mary Key; *m* 1990, Karen Lorraine Cook; two *s* one *d*. *Educ:* Sir Joseph Williamson's Mathematical Sch., Rochester; Univ. of Birmingham (BSocSc 1st cl. Hons Econs; 2nd Yr Undergraduate Prize). ACA 1987. Arthur Young, 1984–89; Grand Metropolitan Foods Europe, 1989–91; Coca-Cola & Schweppes Beverages Ltd, 1991–95; Woolworths, Kingfisher plc, 1995–99; appts in retail and network divs, 1999–2001, Finance Dir, 2001–02, Vodafone UK; Chief Financial Officer, 2002–05, CEO, 2005–07, O_2 UK Ltd, subseq. Telefónica O_2 UK Ltd. *Address:* Telefónica Europe plc, Wellington Street, Slough SL1 1YP.

KEY, Very Rev. Robert Frederick; Dean of Jersey, since 2005; *b* 29 Aug. 1952; *s* of Frederick and Winifred Key; *m* 1974, Daphne Mary Manning; one *s* two *d*. *Educ:* Bristol Univ. (BA 1973); Oak Hill Coll. (DPS 1976). Ordained deacon, 1976, priest, 1977;

Curate, St Ebbe's, Oxford, 1976–80; Minister, St Patrick's, Wallington, 1980–85; Vicar: Eynsham and Cassington, 1985–91; St Andrew's, Oxford, 1991–2001; Gen. Dir, CPAS, 2001–05. Canon Preacher, Dio. Rio Grande, 2004–. *Recreations:* civil aviation, detective fiction. *Address:* The Deanery, David Place, St Helier, Jersey JE2 4TE; *e-mail:* robert_f_key@yahoo.com.

KEY, (Simon) Robert; MP (C) Salisbury, since 1983; *b* 22 April 1945; *s* of late Rt Rev. J. M. Key; *m* 1968, Susan Priscilla Bright Irvine, 2nd *d* of late Rev. T. T. Irvine; one *s* two *d* (and one *s* decd). *Educ:* Salisbury Cathedral Sch.; Forres Sch., Swanage; Sherborne Sch.; Clare Coll., Cambridge. MA; CertEd. Assistant Master: Loretto Sch., Edinburgh, 1967; Harrow Sch., 1969–83. Warden, Nanoose Field Studies Centre, Wool, Dorset, 1972–78; Governor: Sir William Collins Sch., NW1, 1976–81; Special Sch. at Gt Ormond Street Hosp. for Sick Children, 1976–81; Roxeth Sch., Harrow, 1979–82. Founder Chm., ALICE Trust for Autistic Children, 1977–82; Council Mem., GAP Activity Projects, 1975–84. Vice-Chm., Wembley Br., ASTMS, 1976–80. Contested (C) Camden, Holborn and St Pancras South, 1979. Political Sec. to Rt Hon. Edward Heath, 1984–85; PPS: to Minister of State for Energy, 1985–87; to Minister for Overseas Develt, 1987–89; to Sec. of State for the Envmt, 1989–90; Parly Under-Sec. of State, DoE, 1990–92, Dept of Nat. Heritage, 1992–93, Dept of Transport, 1993–94; Opposition front bench spokesman on defence, 1997–2001, on trade and industry, 2001–02, on internat. develt, 2002–03. Mem., Select Cttee on Educn, Science and the Arts, 1983–86, on Health, 1994–95, on Defence, 1995–97, on Science and Technology, 2003–05, on Defence, 2005–; Chm., Select Cttee on Information, 2004–05; Sec., Cons. Parly Backbench Cttee on Arts and Heritage, 1983–84; Jt Parly Chm., Council for Educn in the Commonwealth, 1984–87; Vice-Chm., 1988–90, Chm., 1996–97, All-Party Gp on AIDS. Chm., Harrow Central Cons. Assoc., 1980–82; Vice-Chm., Central London Cons. Euro-Constit., 1980–82; Mem., Cons. Party Nat. Union Exec., 1981–83. Member: UK Nat. Commn for UNESCO, 1984–85; MRC, 1989–90 (Mem., AIDS Cttee, 1988–90). Dir and Trustee, Wessex Archaeology, 2004–; Mem. Council, Winston Churchill Meml Trust, 2004–07. Mem., Gen. Synod, C of E, 2005–. Vice-Pres., Haemophilia Soc., 1988–90. Hon. FCollP, 1989. FSA 2007. *Recreations:* singing, cooking, country life. *Address:* House of Commons, SW1A 0AA. *T:* (020) 7219 3000.

KEYES, family name of **Baron Keyes**.

KEYES, 3rd Baron *cr* 1943, of Zeebrugge and of Dover, co. Kent; **Charles William Packe Keyes;** Bt 1919; *b* 8 Dec. 1951; *s* of 2nd Baron Keyes and Grizelda Mary Keyes (*née* Packe); *S* father, 2005, but does not use the title; *m* 1984, Sally Jackson; one *d*. *Educ:* Camberwell Sch. of Arts and Crafts (OND Conservation of Paper). Retained Firefighter, Suffolk Fire and Rescue Service, 1990–2006. Operational Postal Grade, Royal Mail, 2000–. Warden, Aldham Roadside Nature Reserve. Queen's Golden Jubilee Medal, 2002. *Recreations:* bird watching, drawing, auctions, drinking coffee, Scotland, botany, gardening. *Heir: b* Hon. (Leopold Roger) John Keyes [*b* 8 June 1956; *m* 1988, Jane Owen (marr. diss. 1997); two *d*]. *Club:* Deben Lounge.

KEYES, Timothy Harold, MA; Headmaster, King's School, Worcester, since 1998; *b* 15 Dec. 1954; *s* of Alfred Edward Keyes and Mary Irene Keyes (*née* Mylchreest); *m* 1979, Mary Anne Lucas; two *s*. *Educ:* Christ's Hospital, Horsham; Wadham Coll., Oxford (BA 1st cl. Classics, MA, PGCE). Teacher: of classics and rowing, Tiffin Sch., Kingston upon Thames, 1979–83; of classics and hockey, Whitgift Sch., Croydon, 1983–88; Head of Classics, Perse Sch., Cambridge, 1988–93; Dep. Head, Royal Grammar Sch., Guildford, 1993–98. *Recreations:* choral singing, bell-ringing, walking, Yorkshire cricket. *Address:* The King's School, Worcester WR1 2LL. *T:* (01905) 721700.

KEYNES, Prof. Richard Darwin, CBE 1984; MA, PhD, ScD Cantab; FRS 1959; Professor of Physiology, University of Cambridge, 1973–87; Fellow of Churchill College, since 1961; *b* 14 Aug. 1919; *e s* of Sir Geoffrey Keynes, MD, FRCP, FRCS, FRCOG, and late Margaret Elizabeth, *d* of Sir George Darwin, KCB; *m* 1945, Anne Pinsent Adrian, *e d* of 1st Baron Adrian, OM, FRS, and Dame Hester Agnes Adrian, DBE, *o d* of Hume C. and Dame Ellen Pinsent, DBE; three *s* (and one *s* decd). *Educ:* Oundle Sch. (Scholar); Trinity Coll., Cambridge (Scholar). Temporary experimental officer, HM Anti-Submarine Establishment and Admiralty Signals Establishment, 1940–45. 1st Class, Nat. Sci. Tripos Part II, 1946; Michael Foster and G. H. Lewes Studentships, 1946; Research Fellow of Trinity Coll., 1948–52; Gedge Prize, 1948; Rolleston Memorial Prize, 1950. Demonstrator in Physiology, University of Cambridge, 1949–53; Lecturer, 1953–60; Fellow of Peterhouse, 1952–60 (Hon. Fellow, 1989); Head of Physiology Dept and Dep. Dir, 1960–64, Dir, 1965–73, ARC Inst. of Animal Physiology. Sec.-Gen., Internat. Union for Pure and Applied Biophysics, 1972–78, Vice-Pres., 1978–81, Pres., 1981–84; Chairman: Internat. Cell Research Orgn, 1981–83; ICSU/Unesco Internat. Biosciences Networks, 1982–93; Pres., Eur. Fedn of Physiol Socs, 1991–94; a Vice-Pres., Royal Society, 1965–68, Croonian Lectr, 1983. Fellow of Eton, 1963–78. Foreign Member: Royal Danish Acad., 1971; American Philosophical Soc., 1977; Amer. Acad. of Arts and Scis, 1978; Amer. Physiolog. Soc., 1994; Acad. Brasileira de Ciencias, 1994. Dr *hc* Brazil, 1968; Rouen, 1996; Nairobi, 1999. Order of Scientific Merit (Brazil), 1997. *Publications:* The Beagle Record, 1979; (with D. J. Aidley) Nerve and Muscle, 1981, 3rd edn 2001; (ed) Charles Darwin's Beagle Diary, 1988; (ed jtly) Lydia and Maynard: the letters of Lydia Lopokova and John Maynard Keynes, 1989; (ed) Charles Darwin's Zoology Notes and Specimen Lists from HMS Beagle, 2000; Fossils, Finches and Fuegians: Charles Darwin's adventures and discoveries on the Beagle 1832–1836, 2002; papers in Journal of Physiology, Proceedings of Royal Soc., etc. *Recreations:* writing, pre-Columbian antiquities. *Address:* 4 Herschel Road, Cambridge CB3 9AG. *T:* (01223) 353107.

See also S. D. Keynes, S. J. Keynes.

KEYNES, Prof. Simon Douglas, PhD, LittD; FBA 2000; FSA, FRHistS; Elrington and Bosworth Professor of Anglo-Saxon, University of Cambridge, since 1999; Fellow, Trinity College, Cambridge, since 1976; *b* Cambridge, 23 Sept. 1952; *y s* of Prof. Richard Darwin Keynes, *qv*; one *s* with Tethys Lucy Carpenter. *Educ:* King's Coll. Choir Sch., Cambridge; Leys Sch., Cambridge; Trinity Coll., Cambridge (BA Hons 1973; MA 1977; PhD 1978; LittD 1992). FRHistS 1982; FSA 1985. University of Cambridge: Asst Lectr, Dept of Anglo-Saxon, Norse and Celtic, 1978–82; Lectr, 1982–92; Reader in Anglo-Saxon Hist., 1992–99; Head, Dept of Anglo-Saxon, Norse and Celtic, 1999–2006. British Acad. Res. Reader in Humanities, 1991–93. Member: British Acad./RHistS Jt Cttee on Anglo-Saxon Charters, 1982– (Sec., 1983–); British Acad. Cttee for Sylloge of Coins of British Isles, 1995– (Chm., 2003–); Chm., Sect. H8 (Medieval Studies: Hist. and Lit.), British Acad., 2005–08. Member, Editorial Board: Anglo-Saxon England, 1979–; Cambridge Studies in Anglo-Saxon England, 1986–; Early English MSS in Facsimile, 1996–2002; Associate Ed., Oxford DNB, 1993–2004. Liveryman, Goldsmiths' Co., 1991–. *Publications:* The Diplomas of King Æthelred 'the Unready' 978–1016, 1980; (with M. Lapidge) Alfred the Great: Asser's Life of King Alfred and other contemporary sources, 1983; Anglo-Saxon History: a select bibliography, 1987, 8th edn, as Anglo Saxon England: a bibliographical handbook, 2007; Facsimiles of Anglo-Saxon Charters, 1991; The Liber Vitae of the New Minster and Hyde Abbey, Winchester, 1996; (ed jtly and contrib.) The Blackwell Encyclopaedia of Anglo-Saxon England, 1999; Quentin Keynes: explorer, film-maker, lecturer and book collector 1921–2003, 2004; (ed and contrib.) Ethiopian Encounters: Sir William Cornwallis Harris and the British mission to the Kingdom of Sheba (1841–3), 2007; contrib. articles in books and learned jls, incl. Anglo-Saxon England, Anglo-Norman Studies, English Hist. Rev. and Early Medieval Europe. *Recreation:* research. *Address:* Trinity College, Cambridge CB2 1TQ. *T:* (01223) 338421; Primrose Farm, Wiveton, Norfolk NR25 7TQ. *T:* (01263) 740317. *Club:* Roxburghe.

KEYNES, Stephen John, OBE 1993; Founder, 1999, and Chairman, since 2003, Charles Darwin Trust; *b* 19 Oct. 1927; 4th *s* of Sir Geoffrey Keynes, MD, FRCP, FRCS, FRCOG, and late Margaret Elizabeth, *d* of Sir George Darwin, KCB; *m* 1955, Mary, *o d* of late Senator the Hon. Adrian Knatchbull-Hugessen, QC (Canada), and late Margaret, *o d* of G. H. Duggan; three *s* two *d*. *Educ:* Oundle Sch.; King's Coll., Cambridge (Foundn Scholar; MA). Royal Artillery, 1949–51. Partner, J. F. Thomasson & Co., Private Bankers, 1961–65; Director: Charterhouse Japhet Ltd and Charterhouse Finance Corp., 1965–72; Arbuthnot Latham Holdings Ltd, 1973–80; Sun Life Assce Soc. plc, 1965–89; English Trust Co. Ltd, 1980–90; Hawkshead Ltd, 1987–91. Member: IBA (formerly ITA), 1969–74; Cttee and Treas., Islington and North London Family Service Unit, 1956–68; Adv. Cttee, Geffrye Museum, 1964–78; Trustee: Centerprise Community Project, 1971–75; Needham Research Inst. (formerly E Asian Hist. of Science Trust), 1984–; Chm., English Chamber Theatre, 1986–92; Chairman of Trustees: Whitechapel Art Gallery, 1979–96; William Blake Trust, 1981–; Mark Baldwin Dance Co., 1997–2001. Associate Producer, The Heart of the Dragon, 1981–84. FLS 1999. *Recreations:* medieval manuscripts, gardening, travelling. *Address:* 14 Canonbury Park South, Islington, N1 2JJ. *T:* and *Fax:* (020) 7226 8170; Lammas House, Brinkley, Newmarket, Suffolk CB8 0SB. *T:* (01638) 507268. *Clubs:* Cranium, Roxburghe, Ad Eundem.

See also R. D. Keynes.

KEYSER, Andrew John; QC 2006; a Recorder, since 2002; *b* 19 Dec. 1963; *s* of James William Keyser and Elizabeth Jane Keyser (*née* Hall); *m* 1985, Kathryn Goldsmith (marr. diss. 1998); two *s*. *Educ:* Cardiff High Sch.; Balliol Coll., Oxford (BA 1985, MA 1989); Inns of Court Sch. of Law. Called to the Bar, Middle Temple, 1986. An Asst Boundary Comr for Wales, 2003–. Dep. Chancellor, Dio. of Llandaff, 2007–; Mem., Disciplinary Tribunal of the Church in Wales, 2007–. *Recreations:* reading, music. *Address:* 9 Park Place, Cardiff CF10 3DP. *T:* (029) 2038 2731, *Fax:* (029) 2022 2542; *e-mail:* andrewkeyser@9parkplace.co.uk.

KHALIDI, Prof. Tarif, PhD; Sheikh Zayed Professor of Islamic and Arabic Studies, Beirut's Centre for Arab and Middle Eastern Studies, American University of Beirut, since 2002; *b* 24 Jan. 1938; *s* of Ahmad Samih Khalidi, MBE and Anbara Salam; *m* 1st, 1960, Amal Saidi (decd); one *s* one *d*; 2nd, 2001, Magda Moussallem. *Educ:* Haileybury Coll., Hertford; University Coll., Oxford (BA; MA); Univ. of Chicago (PhD). Prof. of History, American Univ. of Beirut, 1970–96; Sir Thomas Adams's Prof. of Arabic, and Fellow of King's Coll., Cambridge Univ., 1996–2002. *Publications:* Islamic Historiography, 1975; (ed) Land Tenure and Social Transformation in the Middle East, 1983; Classical Arab Islam, 1984; Arabic Historical Thought in the Classical Period, 1994; The Muslim Jesus: sayings and stories in Islamic literature, 2001. *Recreations:* gliding, admiring trees. *Address:* American University of Beirut, PO Box 11–0236, Beirut, Lebanon.

KHALIL, Karim; QC 2003; a Recorder, since 2000; *b* 7 Jan. 1962; *s* of Dr Hassan and Anna Shakir-Khalil; *m* 1986, Sally Ann Boyle; two *s*. *Educ:* Cheadle Hulme Sch., Manchester; Queens' Coll., Cambridge (MA Hons Law). Called to the Bar, Lincoln's Inn, 1984; in practice, specialising in criminal law and health and safety; an Asst Recorder, 1997–2000. Chairman: S Eastern Circuit Liaison Cttee; Cambridge and Peterborough Bar Mess. *Publication:* (contrib. chapter) Fraud: law, practice and procedure, 2005. *Recreations:* tennis, golf, alto sax in The Eye, food and wine. *Address:* 1 Paper Buildings, Temple, EC4Y 7EP. *T:* (020) 7353 3728, *Fax:* (020) 7353 2911; *e-mail:* karimkhalil@onepaper.co.uk. *Clubs:* Hawks, Gog Magog Golf, Next Generation Sports (Cambridge); Okeford Duck Golf.

KHAMENEI, Ayatollah Sayyed Ali; religious and political leader of the Islamic Republic of Iran, since 1989; *b* Mashhad, Khorasan, 1940; *m* 1964; four *s* two *d*. *Educ:* Qom; studied under Imam Khomeini, 1956–64. Imprisoned six times, 1964–78; once exiled, 1978; Mem., Revolutionary Council, 1978 until its dissolution, 1979 (Rep. in Iranian Army and Assistant of Revolutionary Affairs in Min. of Defence); Rep. of First Islamic Consultative Assembly, and of Imam Khomeini in the Supreme Council of Defence, 1980; Comdr, Revolutionary Guards, 1980; Friday Prayer Leader, Teheran, 1980; Sec. Gen., and Pres. of Central Cttee, Islamic Republic Party, 1980–87; survived assassination attempt, June 1981; Pres., Islamic Republic of Iran, 1981–89. *Recreations:* reading, art, literature. *Address:* Office of Religious Leader, Tehran, Islamic Republic of Iran.

KHAMISA, Mohammed Jaffer; QC 2006; a Recorder, since 2003; *b* 16 Feb. 1962; *s* of Isak Ismail and Sugra Khamisa; *m* 1992, Roumana; two *s* one *d*. *Educ:* City of London Poly. (BA Hons Law). Called to the Bar, Middle Temple, 1985. Pres., Mental Health Rev. Tribunals, 2002–; Standing Counsel, DTI, 2005–; Special Advocate, Special Immigration Appeals Commn, 2005–. Legal Assessor, GMC. *Recreations:* reading, cricket, Rugby, jazz and blues. *Address:* 9–12 Bell Yard, WC2A 2JR. *T:* (020) 7400 1800.

KHAN, Akram Hossain, MBE 2005; dancer and choreographer; Artistic Director, Akram Khan Dance Company, since 2000; *b* 29 July 1974; *s* of Mosharaf Hossain Khan and Anwara Khan; *m* 2005, Shanell Winlock. *Educ:* De Montfort Univ. (BA); Northern Sch. of Contemporary Dance (BPA Hons (Dance)). The Mahabharata, RSC, 1987–89; Associate Artist: RFH, 2003–05; Sadler's Wells Th., 2005–. *Recreations:* cinema, world music, Rugby. *Address:* Unit 232a, 35 Britannia Row, N1 8NU. *T:* (020) 7354 4333, *Fax:* (020) 7354 5554; *e-mail:* office@akramkhancompany.net.

KHAN, Prof. Geoffrey Allan, PhD; FBA 1998; Professor of Semitic Philology, University of Cambridge, since 2002; *b* 1 Feb. 1958; *s* of Clive and Diana Khan; *m* 1984, Colette Alcock; one *s* one *d*. *Educ:* Acklam Sixth Form Coll.; SOAS, London Univ. (BA Semitic Langs 1980; PhD 1984). Res. Asst, 1983–87, Res. Associate, 1987–93, Taylor-Schechter Genizah Res. Unit, Cambridge Univ. Liby; Cambridge University: Lectr in Hebrew and Aramaic, 1993–99; Reader in Semitic Philology, 1999–2002. Fellow, Inst. for Advanced Studies, Jerusalem, 1990–91. Lidzbarski Gold Medal for Semitic Philology, Deutsche Morgenländische Ges., 2004. *Publications:* Studies in Semitic Syntax, 1988; Karaite Bible manuscripts from the Cairo Genizah, 1990; Arabic Papyri: selected material from the Khalili collection, 1992; Arabic Legal and Administrative Documents in the Cambridge Genizah collections, 1993; Bills, Letters and Deeds: Arabic papyri of the 7th–11th centuries, 1993; A Grammar of Neo-Aramaic, 1999; The Early Karaite Tradition of Hebrew Grammatical Thought, 2000; Early Karaite Grammatical Texts, 2000; Exegesis and Grammar in Medieval Karaite Texts, 2001; The Neo-Aramaic Dialect of Qaraqosh, 2002; The Karaite Tradition of Hebrew Grammatical Thought in its Classical Form, 2003; The Jewish Neo-Aramaic Dialect of Sulemaniyya and Halabja,

2004; Arabic Documents from Early Islamic Khurasan, 2007; The Neo-Aramaic Dialect of Barwar, 2008; Neo-Aramaic Dialect Studies, 2008. *Recreations:* mountain-walking, miniature carpentry. *Address:* The Faculty of Oriental Studies, Sidgwick Avenue, Cambridge CB3 9DA. *T:* (01223) 335114.

KHAN, Humayun; Director, Commonwealth Foundation, 1993–99; *b* 31 Aug. 1932; *s* of K. B. Safdar Khan and Mumtaz Safdar; *m* 1961, Munawar; three *d. Educ:* Bishop Cotton Sch., Simla; Trinity College, Cambridge (MA); Univ. of Southern California (MPA, Dr PA). Called to the Bar, Lincoln's Inn, 1954; joined Pakistan CS, 1955; Sec. to Govt of NWFP, 1970–73; Jt Sec., Pakistan Govt, 1973–74; Minister, Pakistan Embassy, Moscow, 1974–77; Dep. Perm. Rep., UNO, Geneva, 1977–79; Ambassador to Bangladesh, 1979–82; Additional Sec., Min. of Foreign Affairs, Pakistan, 1982–84; Ambassador to India, 1984–88; Foreign Sec. of Pakistan, 1988–89; High Comr in UK, 1990–92. *Publication:* Cross-Border Talks: Diplomatic Divide, 2004. *Recreations:* golf, cricket, shooting, fishing. *Club:* Islamabad.

KHAN, Imran, (Imran Ahmad Khan Niazi); Hilal-e-Imtiaz, Pakistan, 1993; MP (PTI) Mainwali, Pakistan, 2002–07; *b* Lahore, 25 Oct. 1952; *m* 1995, Jemima (marr. diss. 2004), *d* of Sir James Goldsmith; two *s. Educ:* Aitchison Coll.; Keble Coll., Oxford (BA Hons; cricket blue, 1973, 1974, 1975; Captain, Oxford XI, 1974; Hon. Fellow, 1988). Début for Lahore A, 1969; played first Test for Pakistan, 1970, Captain, 1982–84, 1985–87, 1988–89, 1992; with Worcs CCC, 1971–76 (capped, 1976); with Sussex CCC, 1977–88 (capped, 1978; Hon. Life Mem., 1988). Editor-in-Chief, Cricket Life Internat., 1989–90. Mem., Internat. Cricket Council, 1993–. Founder, Pakistan Teehreek-e-Insaf Party (PTI), 1997 (Chm.). Chancellor, Bradford Univ., 2005–. Special Sports Rep., UNICEF; Founder, Imran Khan Cancer Hosp. Appeal, 1991–. Pride of Performance Award, Pakistan. *Publications:* Imran, 1983; All-Round View (autobiog.), 1988; Indus Journey, 1990; Warrior Race, 1993. *Recreations:* shooting, films, music.

KHAN, Imran; Partner, Imran Khan and Partners, Solicitors, since 2000; *b* 19 Nov. 1964; *s* of Habib Shah and Khursheed Shah. *Educ:* Univ. of East London (LLB Hons). Trainee Solicitor, Birnberg Pierce, 1989–91; Asst Solicitor, then Partner, J. R. Jones Solicitors, 1991–2000. Council Mem., Law Soc., 2002–03. Vis. Lectr, South Bank Univ., 2002. Vice Chm., Nat. Civil Rights Movement, 1999–. Trustee, Anne Frank Trust, 2002–. Hon. Dr: East London; Staffordshire; DUniv Oxford Brookes, 2000. Lawyer of the Year, Lawyer Mag., 1999. *Address:* Imran Khan and Partners, 47 Theobald's Road, WC1X 8SP. *T:* (020) 7404 3004, *Fax:* (020) 7404 3005.

KHAN, Sadiq Aman; MP (Lab) Tooting, since 2005; Parliamentary Under-Secretary of State, Department for Communities and Local Government, since 2008; *b* 8 Oct. 1970; *s* of late Amanullah Ahmad Khan and of Sehrun Nisa Khan; *m* 1994, Saadiya Ahmad; two *d. Educ:* Ernest Bevin Secondary Comprehensive Sch.; Univ. of N London (LLB Hons 1992); Coll. of Law, Guildford. Christian Fisher Solicitors: trainee solicitor, 1993–95; Solicitor, 1995–98; Partner, 1998–2000; Equity Partner: Christian Fisher Khan Solicitors, 2000–02; and Co-founder, Christian Khan Solicitors, 2002–04. Vis. Lectr, Univ. of N London and London Metropolitan Univ., 1998–2004. Mem. (Lab), Wandsworth BC, 1994–2006; Dep. Leader of Labour Gp, 1996–2001; Hon. Alderman, 2006. PPS to Lord Privy Seal and Leader of H of C, 2007; an Asst Govt Whip, 2007–08. Chm., All-Party Parly Gp for Citizens Advice, 2006–. Chair, Liberty, 2001–04; Founding Mem., Human Rights Lawyers Assoc., 2003. Exec. Mem., 2006–, Vice Chair, 2007–, Fabian Soc. Vice Chair, Legal Action Gp, 1999–2004; Patron, Progress, 2005–. *Publications:* Challenging Racism, 2003; Police Misconduct: Legal Remedies, 2005. *Recreations:* playing and watching sport, cinema, family, friends, local community. *Address:* House of Commons, SW1A 0AA. *T:* (020) 7219 6967, *Fax:* (020) 7219 6477; *e-mail:* sadiqkhanmp@parliament.uk.

KHANBHAI, Bashir Yusufali Simba; Member (C) Eastern Region, England, European Parliament, 1999–2004; *b* 22 Sept. 1945; *s* of Yusufali Simba Khanbhai and Jenambai Khanbhai; *m* 1981, Maria Bashir Khanbhai (*née* Da Silva); one *s. Educ:* Sch. of Pharmacy, Univ. of London (BPharm Hons 1966); Balliol Coll., Oxford (MA Hons PPE 1969). Manufg industry, export and finance, 1970–97; Chief Executive Officer: Headlands Chemicals Ltd, 1970–76; Khanbhai Industries Ltd, 1977–84; Teqny Ltd, 1984–99. *Publication:* (ed) The Jowett Papers, 1970. *Recreations:* tennis, travel, theatre, music, food. *Address:* 20 Burntwood Road, Sevenoaks, Kent TN13 1PT; *e-mail:* euaccess@yahoo.com.

KHARCHENKO, Ihor, PhD; Ambassador of Ukraine to the Court of St James's, since 2005; Permanent Representative of Ukraine to the International Maritime Organization, since 2006; *b* 15 May 1962; *s* of Yuri and Raiisa; *m* 1986, Maria Rozhytsina; two *d. Educ:* Taras Shevchenko Kyiv State Univ. (Internat. Relns; PhD History). Lectr, then Asst Prof., Taras Shevchenko Kyiv State Univ., 1988–92; Ministry of Foreign Affairs, Ukraine: Policy Planning Staff, 1992–93; Dir, Policy Planning Staff, 1993–97; Ambassador-at-Large, Hd of Secretariat of Pres. of UN Gen. Assembly and Dep. Perm. Rep. of Ukraine to the UN, NY, 1997–98; Ambassador of Ukraine to Romania, 1998–2000; Dep. Foreign Minister of Ukraine, 2000–03, Special Rep. of Pres. of Ukraine to the Balkans, 2001–03; Ambassador of Ukraine to Poland, 2003–05. Order of Merit (Ukraine), 2002. *Recreations:* literature, music. *Address:* Embassy of Ukraine, 60 Holland Park, W11 3SJ. *T:* (020) 7727 6312, *Fax:* (020) 7792 1708; *e-mail:* office@ukremb.org.uk.

KHATAMI, Hojjatoleslam Seyed Mohammad; President of the Islamic Republic of Iran, 1997–2005; *b* 29 Sept. 1943; *s* of Ayatollah Sayyid Ruhollah Khatami, religious scholar; *m* 1974, Zohreh Sadeghi; one *s* two *d. Educ:* High Sch.; Qom Theol. Sch.; Isfahan Univ. (BA Philosophy); Tehran Univ. (MA); Qom Seminary. Head, Hamburg Islamic Centre, Germany, 1979; Mem. for Ardakan and Maybod, first Islamic Consultative Assembly, 1980–82; Dep. Hd of Jt Comd of Armed Forces, and Chm., War Propaganda HQ, Iran-Iraq War, 1980–88; Dir, Keyhan Newspaper Inst., 1981; Minister of Culture and Islamic Guidance, 1982–92; Advr to Pres. Rafsanjani, 1992–96. Mem., High Council for Cultural Revolution, 1996. Chm., 8th Session, Islamic Summit Conf., 1997–2000. *Publications:* From the World of the City to the City of the World, 1994; Fear of Wave, 1997; Faith and Thought Trapped by Despotism; contrib. articles to Arabic mags and newspapers.

KHAW, Prof. Kay-Tee, (Mrs Kay-Tee Fawcett), CBE 2003; FRCP; Professor of Clinical Gerontology, University of Cambridge, since 1989; Fellow, Gonville and Caius College, Cambridge, since 1991; *b* 14 Oct. 1950; *d* of Khaw Kai Boh and Tan Chwee Geok; *m* 1980, Prof. James William Fawcett, *qv*; one *s* one *d. Educ:* Girton Coll., Cambridge (BA, MA; MB BChir); St Mary's Hosp. Med. Sch., London; London Sch. of Hygiene and Tropical Med. (MSc). MRCP 1977, FRCP 1993; DCH 1978; MFPHM 1993. LTCL 1969. Wellcome Trust Research Fellow, LSHTM, St Mary's Hosp. and Univ. of California San Diego, 1979–84; Asst Adjunct Prof., Univ. of California Sch. of Med., San Diego, 1985; Sen. Registrar in Community Medicine, Univ. of Cambridge Sch. of Clinical Medicine, 1986–89. Member: NHS Central R&D Cttee, 1991–97; HEFCE, 1992–97; MRC Health Services and Public Health Res. Bd, 1999–2003; MRC Cross Bd Gp, 2001–05. Vice-Chair, World Heart Fedn Council on Epidemiology and Prevention, 2002–; Chair, Nutrition Forum, Food Standards Agency, 2002–. FMedSci 1999. Daland Fellow, Amer. Philosophical Soc., 1984. Trustee, Help the Aged, 1993–98. *Publications:* contribs to scientific jls on chronic disease epidemiology. *Address:* Clinical Gerontology Unit, University of Cambridge School of Clinical Medicine, Addenbrooke's Hospital, Cambridge CB2 2QQ.

KHAYAT, Georges Mario; QC 1992; **His Honour Judge Khayat;** a Circuit Judge, since 2002; *b* 15 Aug. 1941; *s* of Fred Khayat and Julie Germain. *Educ:* Terra Sancta Coll., Nazareth; Prior Park Coll., Bath. Called to the Bar, Lincoln's Inn, 1967. A Recorder, 1987–2002. Head of Chambers, 1999–2002. Chm., Surrey and S London Bar Mess, 1995–98. *Recreations:* horse riding, reading, boating, music. *Address:* Snaresbrook Crown Court, 75 Hollybush Hill, Snaresbrook, E11 1QW.

KHIYAMI, Dr Sami Madani; Ambassador of the Syrian Arab Republic to the Court of St James's, since 2004; *b* Damascus, 28 Aug. 1948; *s* of Dr Madani and Jamila Khiyami; *m* 1978, Yamina Farhan; one *s* two *d. Educ:* American Univ. of Beirut (BE 1972); Univ. of Claude Bernard, Lyons, France (Dip. Electronics 1974; PhD 1979). Asst, Faculty of Mech. and Electrical Engrg, Damascus Univ., 1972–73; with Siemens-Karlsruhe, Germany, 1972–74; Asst Prof., Univ. of Damascus, and researcher and gp leader, Scientific Studies and Res. Centre, Damascus, 1979–85; Prof. of Computer Engrg and Electronic Measurements, Univ. of Damascus, 1985–94; Higher Institute of Applied Sciences and Technology, Damascus: Hd, Electronics Dept, Chief Researcher, then Dir of Res., 1986–95; Actg Dir, 1993; Vice-Dir for Res., 1993–95. Consultant, Systems Internat., Syria, 1993–94; Nat. Telecom and Technol. Consultant, 1999–2002. Board Member: Syrian Arab Airlines, 2004; Spacetel, 2004. Co-founder and Dir, Syrian Computer Soc., 1989. *Publications:* Electronic Measurements and Measuring Devices, 1982; Microprocessors and Microprocessor Based Systems, 1982; Algorithms and Data Structures, 1983; numerous contribs to scientific reviews on technol. and related econ. policies, IT and telecom strategies. *Recreations:* philately, gardening, music. *Address:* Syrian Embassy, 8 Belgrave Square, SW1X 8PH. *T:* (020) 7245 9012, *Fax:* (020) 7235 4621.

KHOKHAR, Mushtaq Ahmed; His Honour Judge Khokhar; a Circuit Judge, since 2006; *b* 2 Feb. 1956; *s* of Yousaf and Sakina Khokhar; *m* 1991, Dr Ramla Mumtaz; two *s. Educ:* Leeds Poly. (BA Hons Law 1980); Queen Mary Coll., London (LLM 1981). Called to the Bar, Lincoln's Inn, 1982; Asst Recorder, 1998–2000; a Recorder, 2000–06. Standing Counsel to HM Customs and Excise, then HMRC, 2001–06. *Recreations:* watching cricket and football, su doku, walking, theatre, eating out, reading biographies, playing snooker and squash. *Address:* Manchester Crown Court, Minshull Street, Manchester M1 3FS.

KHOO, Francis Kah Siang; writer; solicitor and advocate; *b* 23 Oct. 1947; *s* of late Teng Eng Khoo and Swee Neo Chew; *m* 1977, Dr Swee Chai Ang, MB BS, MSc, FRCS. *Educ:* Univ. of Singapore (LLB (Hons) 1970); Univ. of London (MA 1980). Advocate and Solicitor, Singapore, 1971. Lawyer, Singapore, 1971–77; journalist and political cartoonist, South magazine, and Mem., NUJ (UK), 1980–87; Gen. Sec. (Dir), War on Want, 1988–89; Solicitor, England and Wales, 1998–. Founding Mem. and Trustee of British charity, Medical Aid for Palestinians, 1984–; Sec., RADICLE charity, 2000– (Chm., Trustees, 2004–); Trustee, Living Stones charity, 2004–. *Publications:* And Bungaraya Blooms All Day: collection of songs, poems and cartoons in exile, UK, 1978; Hang On Tight, No Surrender: tape of songs, 1984; Rebel and the Revolutionary (poems), 1995. *Recreations:* photography, hill-walking, singing and song-writing, camera designing and inventions, swimming. *Address:* 285 Cambridge Heath Road, Bethnal Green, E2 0EL. *T:* and *Fax:* (020) 7729 3994.

KHORANA, Prof. Har Gobind; Sloan Professor of Chemistry and Biology, Massachusetts Institute of Technology, 1970–97, now Emeritus; *b* Raipur, India, 9 Jan. 1922; *s* of Shri Ganpat Rai and Shrimata Krishna (Devi); *m* 1952, Esther Elizabeth Sibler; one *s* two *d. Educ:* Punjab Univ. (BSc 1943; MSc 1945); Liverpool Univ. (PhD 1948; Govt of India Student). Post-doctoral Fellow of Govt of India, Federal Inst. of Techn., Zurich, 1948–49; Nuffield Fellow, Cambridge Univ., 1950–52; Head, Organic Chemistry Group, BC Research Council, 1952–60. Univ. of Wisconsin: Prof. and Co-Dir, Inst. for Enzyme Research, 1960–70; Prof., Dept of Biochemistry, 1962–70; Conrad A. Elvehjem Prof. in the Life Sciences, 1964–70. Visiting Professor: Rockefeller Inst., NY, 1958–60; Stanford Univ., 1964; Harvard Med. Sch., 1966; Andrew D. White Prof.-at-large, Cornell Univ., 1974–80. Has given special or memorial lectures in USA, Poland, Canada, Switzerland, UK and Japan. Fellow: Chem. Inst. of Canada, 1959; Amer. Assoc. for Advancement of Science, 1966; Amer. Acad. of Arts and Sciences, 1967. Overseas Fellow, Churchill Coll., Cambridge, 1967. Member: Nat. Acad. of Sciences, 1966; Deutsche Akademie der Naturforscher Leopoldina, 1968; Pontifical Acad. of Scis, Rome, 1978; Foreign Member: Indian Acad. of Scis, 1976; Royal Society, 1978; RSE, 1982. Various hon. degrees. Merck Award, Chem. Inst. Canada, 1958; Gold Medal for 1960, Professional Inst. of Public Service of Canada; Dannie-Heineman Preis, Germany, 1967; Remsen Award, Johns Hopkins Univ., ACS Award for Creative Work in Synthetic Organic Chemistry, Louisa Gross Horwitz Award, Lasker Foundn Award for Basic Med. Research, Nobel Prize for Physiology or Medicine (jtly), 1968; Gairdner Foundn Award, 1980; US Nat. Medal of Science, 1987. Order of San Carlos (Columbia), 1986. *Publications:* Some Recent Developments in the Chemistry of Phosphate Esters of Biological Interest, 1961; numerous papers in Biochemistry, Jl Amer. Chem. Soc., Proc. Nat. Acad. Scis, etc. *Recreations:* hiking, swimming. *Address:* Department of Biology, Massachusetts Institute of Technology, Cambridge, MA 02139, USA.

KHUSH, Dr Gurdev Singh, FRS 1995; consultant to Director General, International Rice Research Institute, Philippines, 2001–04 (Principal Plant Breeder, and Head, Division of Plant Breeding, Genetics and Biochemistry, 1989–2001); *b* 22 Aug. 1935; *s* of Kartar Singh and Pritam Kaur; *m* 1961, Harwant Kaur Grewal; one *s* three *d. Educ:* Punjab Univ., Chandigarh, India (BScAgr); Univ. of Calif, Davis (PhD Genetics 1960). University of California, Davis: Research Asst, 1957–60; Asst Geneticist, 1960–67; International Rice Research Institute, Philippines: Plant Breeder, 1967–72; Head, Dept of Plant Breeding, 1972–89. Adjunct Prof., Dept of Vegetable Crops, Univ. of Calif., Davis, 2003–. Hon. DSc: Punjab Agricl, 1987; Tamil Nadu Agricl, 1995; C. S. Azad Univ. of Agric. and Technol., 1995; G. B. Pant Univ. of Agric. and Technol., 1996; De Montfort, 1998; Cambridge, 2000; ND Univ. of Agric. and Technol., 2003. Borlaug Award in Plant Breeding, Coromandel Fertilizers Ltd, India, 1977; Japan Prize, Japan Sci. and Technol. Foundn, 1987; Fellows Award 1989, Internat. Agronomy Award 1990, Amer. Soc. of Agronomy; Emil M. Mrak Internat. Award, Univ. of California, Davis, 1990; World Food Prize, World Food Prize Foundn, 1996; Rank Prize, Rank Prize Funds, 1998; Wolf Prize, Wolf Foundn, Israel, 2000. *Publications:* Cytogenetics of Aneuploids, 1973; Host Plant Resistance to Insects, 1995; *edited:* Rice Biotechnology, 1991; Nodulation and Nitrogen Fixation in Rice, 1992; Apomix: exploiting hybrid vigor in rice, 1994; Rice Genetics III, 1996; Rice Genetics IV, 2001; contrib. chapters in books; numerous papers in jls. *Recreation:* reading world history. *Address:* 39399 Blackhawk Place, Davis, CA 95616–7008, USA.

KIBAKI, Mwai; President (Nat. Rainbow Coalition, 2002–07, Party of National Unity, since 2007), and Commander in Chief of the Armed Forces, Kenya, since 2002; *b* Othaya, Kenya, 1931; *m* Lucy Muthoni; three *s* one *d*. *Educ:* Makerere UC (BA); London Sch. of Econs (BSc Econs). Lectr in Econs, Makerere UC, 1959–60; Nat. Exec. Officer, Kenya African Nat. Union (KANU), 1960–64; Kenyan Rep. to E African Legislative Assembly of E African Common Services Orgn, 1962; Mem. (KANU) Nairobi Doonholm, House of Reps, 1963–74; Parly Sec. to Treasury, 1963–64; Asst Minister of Econ. Planning and Develt, 1964–66; Minister: for Commerce and Industry, 1966–69; of Finance, 1969–70; of Finance and Econ. Planning, 1970–78; of Finance, 1978–82; of Home Affairs, 1978–88; of Health, 1988–91; Vice Pres. of Kenya, 1978–88; Leader, Official Opposition, 1998–2002. Vice-Pres., KANU, 1978–91; Leader: Democratic Party, 1991–2002; Party of Nat. Unity, 2008. Chief of the Golden Heart (Kenya), 2002. *Recreations:* reading, golf. *Address:* Office of the President, PO Box 30510, Nairobi, Kenya; State House Nairobi, PO Box 40530, Nairobi, Kenya. *Fax:* (2) 250264; *e-mail:* contact@statehousekenya.go.ke.

KIBBEY, Sidney Basil; Under-Secretary, Department of Health and Social Security, 1971–76; *b* 3 Dec. 1916; *y s* of late Percy Edwin Kibbey and Winifred Kibbey, Mickleover, Derby; *m* 1939, Violet Gertrude, (Jane), Eyre; (twin) *s* and *d*. *Educ:* Derby Sch. Executive Officer, Min. of Health, 1936; Principal, Min. of National Insurance, 1951; Sec., Nat. Insurance Adv. Cttee, 1960–62; Asst Sec., Min. of Pensions and Nat. Insurance, 1962. *Address:* 29 Beaulieu Close, Datchet, Berks SL3 9DD. *T:* (01753) 549101.

KIBBLE, Prof. Thomas Walter Bannerman, CBE 1998; PhD; FRS 1980; Emeritus Professor of Theoretical Physics, and Senior Research Fellow, Imperial College, London, since 1998; *b* 1932; *s* of Walter Frederick Kibble and Janet Cowan Watson (*née* Bannerman); *m* 1957, Anne Richmond Allan; one *s* two *d*. *Educ:* Doveton-Corrie Sch., Madras; Melville Coll., Edinburgh; Univ. of Edinburgh (MA, BSc, PhD). Commonwealth Fund Fellow, California Inst. of Technology, 1958–59; Imperial College, London: NATO Fellow, 1959–60; Lecturer, 1961; Sen. Lectr, 1965; Reader in Theoretical Physics, 1966; Prof. of Theoretical Physics, 1970–98; Hd, Dept of Physics, 1983–91. Sen. Visiting Research Associate, Univ. of Rochester, New York, 1967–68; Lorentz Prof., Univ. of Leiden, 2007. Member: Nuclear Physics Bd, SERC, 1982–86; Astronomy, Space and Radio Bd, 1984–86; Physical Sciences Sub-cttee, UGC, 1985–89. Chairman: Scientists Against Nuclear Arms, 1985–91 (Vice-Chm., 1981–85); Martin Ryle Trust, 1985–96. Mem. Council, Royal Soc., 1987–89 (Vice-Pres., 1988–89). (Jtly) Hughes Medal, Royal Soc., 1981; (jtly) Rutherford Medal, 1984, Guthrie Medal, 1993, Inst. of Physics. *Publications:* Classical Mechanics, 1966, 5th edn 2004; papers in Phys. Rev., Proc. Royal Soc., Nuclear Physics, Nuovo Cimento, Jl Physics, and others. *Recreations:* cycling, walking, destructive gardening. *Address:* Blackett Laboratory, Imperial College, Prince Consort Road, SW7 2AZ. *T:* (020) 7594 7845.

KIDD, Prof. Cecil; Regius Professor of Physiology, 1984–97, part-time Professor of Physiology, 1997–2000, now Emeritus, Marischal College, University of Aberdeen; *b* 28 April 1933; *s* of Herbert Cecil and Elizabeth Kidd; *m* 1956, Margaret Winifred Goodwill; three *s*. *Educ:* Queen Elizabeth Grammar School, Darlington; King's College, Newcastle upon Tyne, Univ. of Durham (BSc, PhD). FIBiol; FRSA. Research Fellow then Demonstrator in Physiology, King's Coll., Univ. of Durham, 1954–58; Asst Lectr then Lectr in Physiol., Univ. of Leeds, 1958–68; Res. Fellow in Physiol., Johns Hopkins Univ., 1962–63; Sen. Lectr then Reader in Physiol., 1968–84, Sen. Res. Associate in Cardiovascular Studies, 1973–84, Univ. of Leeds. *Publications:* scientific papers in physiological jls. *Recreations:* opera, walking, food, alpines, gardening. *Address:* c/o School of Medical Sciences, College of Life Sciences and Medicine, University of Aberdeen, Aberdeen AB25 2ZD. *T:* (01224) 273005.

KIDD, Charles William; Editor of Debrett's Peerage and Baronetage, since 1980; *b* 23 May 1952; *yr s* of late Charles Vincent Kidd and of Marian Kidd, BEM (*née* Foster), Kirkbymoorside. *Educ:* St Peter's Sch., York; Bede Coll., Durham. Assistant Editor: Burke's Peerage, 1972–77; Debrett's Peerage and Baronetage, 1977–80. FSG 2000. *Publications:* Debrett's Book of Royal Children (jtly), 1982; Debrett Goes to Hollywood, 1986. *Recreations:* cinema, researching film and theatre dynasties, tennis.

KIDD, Hon. Douglas Lorimer, DCNZM 2000; Member, Waitangi Tribunal, since 2004; Speaker, House of Representatives, New Zealand, 1996–99; *b* 12 Sept. 1941; *s* of Lorimer Edward Revington Kidd and Jessie Jean Kidd (*née* Mottershead); *m* 1964, Jane Stafford Richardson; one *s* two *d*. *Educ:* Ohau Primary Sch.; Horowhenua Coll.; Victoria Univ., Wellington (LLB 1964). Mil. service, Territorial Service, Royal Regt of NZ Artillery, 1960–64. Admitted Barrister and Solicitor, 1964; Partner, Wisheart Macnab & Partners, 1964–78. MP (N) Marlborough, 1978–96, Kaikoura, 1996–99; List MP (N), 1999–2002. Minister of Fisheries, 1990–93, and of State-Owned Enterprises, 1990–91; Associate Minister of Finance, 1990–94; Minister of Maori Affairs, 1991–94; Minister of Energy, Fisheries, Labour, Accident Rehabilitation and Compensation Insce, 1994–96. Chair, Cabinet Revenue and Expenditure Cttee; Chm., Regulations Rev. Select Cttee, 1999–2002; Mem., Privileges and Maori Affairs Select Cttee, 1999–2002. Dir and Partner, plantation forestry, marine farming and wine co. ventures, Marlborough, 1968–94. Hon. Mem., Canterbury/Nelson/Marlborough/W Coast Regt, 1980–97 (Hon. Col, 1997–2003). CGS's Commendation for outstanding service to NZ Army, 1999. NZ Commemoration Medal, 1990. *Recreations:* fishing, reading, travel. *Club:* Marlborough (Blenheim).

KIDD, Prof. Ian Gray, FBA 1993; Emeritus Professor of Greek, since 1987, Chancellor's Assessor, 1989–98, University of St Andrews; *b* 6 March 1922; *s* of A. H. Kidd and I. Gray; *m* 1949, Sheila Elizabeth Dow (*d* 2007); three *s*. *Educ:* Dundee High Sch.; Univ. of St Andrews (MA, Miller Prize 1947); Queen's Coll., Oxford (BA Greats, MA). Served War of 1939–45: commnd Argyll and Sutherland Highlanders; Sicily, Italy, 1943–44; POW, 1944–45. St Andrews University: Lectr in Greek, 1949–65; Sen. Lectr, 1965–73; Professor: of Ancient Philosophy, 1973–76; of Greek, 1976–87; Vice-Pres., Univ. Court, 1997–98; Provost, St Leonard's Coll., 1978–83 (Hon. Fellow, 1987). Vis. Prof. of Classics, Univ. of Texas at Austin, 1965–66; Mem., Inst. for Advanced Study, Princeton, 1971–72 and 1979–80. General Comr of Inland Revenue, 1982–97. Chm., E Fife Educnl Trust, 1977–89. Gov., Dollar Acad., 1982–91. Hon. Fellow, Inst. for Res. in Classical Philosophy and Sci., Princeton, 1989–. Hon. DLitt St Andrews, 2001. *Publications:* (ed) Posidonius, Works: vol. I, (with L. Edelstein) The Fragments, 1972, 2nd edn 1989; vol. II(i) and (ii), The Commentary, 1988; vol. III, The Translation of the Fragments, 1999; (with R. Waterfield) Plutarch, Essays, 1992; contributions to: Concise Encyclopedia of Western Philosophy and Philosophers, 1960; The Encyclopedia of Philosophy, ed P. Edwards, 1967; Problems in Stoicism, 1971; The Stoics, 1978; Les Stoiciens et leur Logique, 1978; Stoic and Peripatetic Ethics, 1983; Aspects de la Philosophie Hellénistique, 1986; The Criterion of Truth, 1989; Philosophia Togata, 1989; Owls to Athens, 1990; Handbook of Metaphysics and Ontology, 1991; Theophrastus, 1992; Socratic Questions, 1992; Philosophen der Antike, 1996; The Oxford Classical Dictionary, 1996; Polyhistor: studies in the history of ancient philosophy, 1996; Collecting Fragments, 1997; Fragmentsammlungen philosophischer Texte der Antike, 1998; The Philosophy of Zeno, 2002; articles in learned jls. *Recreations:* music, reading, thinking, looking at pictures. *Address:* Ladebury, Lade Braes Lane, St Andrews, Fife KY16 9EP. *T:* (01334) 474367.

KIDD, Paul Ashley; Chief Finance Officer, Royal Borough of Kensington and Chelsea, since 2008; *b* Gravesend, 6 Sept. 1951; *s* of Ronald William and Marion Kidd; *m* 1975, Jennifer Davies; one *s*. *Educ:* York Univ. (BA Hons Social Sci.). CPFA 1976. London Borough of Croydon: Finance trainee, 1973–75; Sen. Accountant, 1976–78; Royal Borough of Kensington and Chelsea: Sen. Accountant, 1978–81; Principal Accountant, 1981–82; Asst Chief Accountant, 1982–88; Chief Accountant, 1988–91; Hd, Accountancy Services, 1991–95; Hd, Financial Services, 1995–2008. *Recreations:* walking, gardening, DIY, digital photography, compiling quizzes, visiting France, sport (watching not playing), music (listening and playing badly).

KIDGELL, John Earle, CB 2003; consultant in economic statistics; Director of Economic Statistics, Office for National Statistics (formerly Head of Economic Accounts Division, Central Statistical Office), 1994–2002 (Grade 3, 1988–2002); *b* 18 Nov. 1943; *s* of Gilbert James Kidgell and Cicely Alice (*née* Earle); *m* 1968, Penelope Jane Tarry; one *s* two *d*. *Educ:* Eton House Sch., Southend-on-Sea; Univ. of St Andrews (MA); London School of Economics and Political Science (MSc). NIESR, 1967–70; Gallup Poll, 1970–72; Statistician, CSO and Treasury, 1972–79; Chief Statistician, DoE, 1979–86; Hd of Finance Div., PSA, 1986–88; Head of Directorate D, Central Statistical Office, 1989–91. *Publications:* articles in Nat. Inst. Econ. Rev., Econ. Trends, etc. *Recreations:* hill walking, tennis, golf, reading.

KIDMAN, Nicole Mary, AC 2006; actress; *b* Hawaii, 20 June 1967; *d* of Dr Antony David Kidman, AM and Janelle Ann Kidman (*née* Glenny); *m* 1990, Tom Cruise (*see* T. Cruise Mapother) (marr. diss. 2001); one adopted *s* one adopted *d*; *m* 2006, Keith Urban; one *d*. *Educ:* N Sydney High Sch. Worked at Phillip Street Th., Sydney. *TV mini-series:* Vietnam, 1986; Bangkok Hilton, 1989; *theatre:* The Blue Room, Donmar Warehouse, 1998, NY 1999; *films include:* Bush Christmas, 1983; Dead Calm, 1989; Days of Thunder, 1990; Billy Bathgate, 1991; Far and Away, Flirting, 1992; Malice, My Life, 1993; Batman Forever, To Die For, 1995; The Portrait of a Lady, 1996; The Peacemaker, 1997; Practical Magic, Eyes Wide Shut, 1999; Moulin Rouge, The Others, 2001; Birthday Girl, 2002; The Hours (Academy and BAFTA Awards for best actress, 2003), The Human Stain, Cold Mountain, 2003; Dogville, The Stepford Wives, Birth, 2004; The Interpreter, Bewitched, 2005; Fur: An Imaginary Portrait of Diane Arbus, The Invasion, The Golden Compass, 2007; Margot at the Wedding 2008; prod., In the Cut 2003. *Address:* Shanahan Management Pty Ltd, PO Box 1509, Darlinghurst, NSW 1300, Australia.

KIDNER, Rear-Adm. Peter Jonathan, CEng, FRAeS; Proprietor, TrimTrees, tree and hedge specialist, since 2005; *b* 21 July 1949; *s* of Col Peter Kidner and Patricia (*née* Bunyard); *m* 1973, Jean Caley; one *s* one *d*. *Educ:* Sherborne Sch.; RNEC (BSc). CEng 1992; FRAeS 1995. Air Engineer Officer: 849 B Flight, HMS Ark Royal, 1975–76; 899 Sqn, 1981; Dir, Helicopter Support, 1997–2000; CO, HMS Sultan, 2000–02; Chief Exec., Defence Med. Trng Org., subseq. Defence Med. Educn and Trng Agency, 2002–04. Mem., Ramblers' Assoc. *Recreations:* walking, Dolomites.

KIDNEY, David Neil; MP (Lab) Stafford, since 1997; *b* 21 March 1955; *s* of Neil Bernard Kidney and Doris Kidney; *m* 1978, Elaine Dickinson; one *s* one *d*. *Educ:* Bristol Univ. (LLB). Solicitor in private practice, Kenneth Wainwright & Co., then Wainwrights, subseq. Jewels & Kidney, 1977–97, Partner, 1983–97. Mem. (Lab) Stafford BC, 1987–97. Team PPS, DEFRA, 2002–03. Contested (Lab) Stafford, 1992. *Recreations:* bridge, chess. *Address:* 6 Beechcroft Avenue, Stafford ST16 1BJ.

KIELY, Dr David George; Chief Naval Weapons Systems Engineer (Under Secretary), Ministry of Defence, Procurement Executive, 1983–84; consultant engineer; *b* 23 July 1925; *o s* of late George Thomas and Susan Kiely, Ballynahinch, Co. Down; *m* 1956, Dr Ann Wilhelmina (*née* Kilpatrick), MB, BCh, BAO, DCH, DPH, MFCM, Hillsborough, Co. Down; one *s* one *d*. *Educ:* Down High Sch., Downpatrick; Queen's Univ., Belfast (BSc, MSc); Sorbonne (DSci). CEng, FIET; CPhys, FInstP; psc 1961. Appts in RN Scientific Service from 1944; Naval Staff Coll., 1961–62; Head of Electronic Warfare Div., ASWE, 1965–68; Head of Communications and Sensor Dept, ASWE, 1968–72; Dir-Gen., Telecommunications, 1972–74, Dir-Gen., Strategic Electronic Systems, 1974–76, Dir-Gen., Electronics Res., 1976–78, Exec. Officer, Electronics Research Council, 1976–78, Dir, Naval Surface Weapons, ASWE, 1978–83, MoD, PE. Gp Chief Exec. and Dir, Chemring PLC, 1984–85. Chm., R&D Policy Cttee, Gen. Lights Authorities of UK and Eire, 1974–89. Governor: Portsmouth Coll. of Technology, 1965–69; Springfield Sch., Portsmouth, 1993–97. Mem., 1982–89, Chm., 1985–89, Council, Chichester Cathedral. *Publications:* Dielectric Aerials, 1953; Marine Navigational Aids for Coastal Waters of the British Isles, 1987; Naval Electronic Warfare, 1988; Naval Surface Weapons, 1988; Defence Procurement, 1990; The Future for the Defence Industry, 1990; chapter: in Progress in Dielectrics, 1961; in Fundamentals of Microwave Electronics, 1963; in Naval Command and Control, 1989; papers in Proc. IEE and other learned jls, etc. *Recreations:* fly fishing, gardening. *Address:* Cranleigh, 107 Havant Road, Emsworth, Hants PO10 7LF. *T:* (01243) 372250. *Club:* Naval and Military.

KIERNAN, Prof. Christopher Charles; Professor of Behavioural Studies in Mental Handicap, University of Manchester, 1984 (Director, Hester Adrian Research Centre, 1984–2000); *b* 3 June 1936; *s* of Christopher J. and Mary L. Kiernan; *m* 1962, Diana Elizabeth Maynard; two *s* one *d*. *Educ:* Nottingham Univ. (BA); London Univ. (PhD); ABPsS. Lecturer in Psychology, Birkbeck Coll., London Univ., 1961–70; Sen. Lectr, Child Development, Univ. of London Inst. of Education, 1970–74; Dep. Director, Thomas Coram Research Unit, Univ. of London Inst. of Education, 1975–84. *Publications:* Behaviour Assessment Battery, 1977, 2nd edn 1982; Starting Off, 1978; Behaviour Modification with the Severely Retarded, 1975; Analysis of Programmes for Teaching, 1981; Signs and Symbols, 1982; Research to Practice, 1993. *Recreation:* survival.

KILBRACKEN, 4th Baron *cr* 1909, of Killegar, co. Leitrim; **Christopher John Godley;** *b* 1 Jan. 1945; *s* of 3rd Baron Kilbracken, DSC and Penelope Anne, *y d* of Rear-Adm. Sir Cecil Nugent Reyne, KBE; *S* father, 2006; *m* 1969, Gillian Christine, *yr d* of Lt-Comdr Stuart Wilson Birse, OBE, DSC, RN retd; one *s* one *d*. *Educ:* Rugby; Reading Univ. (BSc Agric 1967). ICI: Agriculturalist, 1968–78; Gp Buyer, Hd Office, 1978–81; Countertrade Mgr, 1982–2000. Chm., London Countertrade Roundtable, 1997–2002. Patron, John Robert Godley Meml Trust, NZ; Vice Patron, Canterbury Assoc., NZ. *Recreations:* yachting, gardening. *Heir:* *s* Hon. James John Godley [*b* 3 Jan. 1972; *m* 2002, Anna Charlotte Weld-Forester; two *d*]. *Address:* Four Firs, Marley Lane, Haslemere, Surrey GU27 3PZ.

KILCLOONEY, Baron *cr* 2001 (Life Peer), of Armagh in the County of Armagh; **John David Taylor;** PC (NI) 1970; Member (UU) Strangford, Northern Ireland Assembly, 1998–2007; *b* 24 Dec. 1937; *er s* of George D. Taylor and Georgina Baird; *m* 1970, Mary Frances Todd; one *s* five *d*. *Educ:* Royal Sch., Armagh; Queen's Univ. of Belfast (BSc).

AMInstHE, AMICEI. MP (UU) S Tyrone, NI Parlt, 1965–73; Mem. (UU), Fermanagh and S Tyrone, NI Assembly, 1973–75; Mem. (UU), North Down, NI Constitutional Convention, 1975–76; Parly Sec. to Min. of Home Affairs, 1969–70; Minister of State, Min. of Home Affairs, 1970–72; Mem. (UU), North Down, NI Assembly, 1982–86. Mem., Strangford, NI Forum, 1996–98. Mem. (UU) NI, Europ. Parlt, 1979–89. MP (UU) Strangford, 1983–2001 (resigned seat Dec. 1985 in protest against Anglo-Irish Agreement; re-elected Jan. 1986). Mem. Assembly, Council of Europe, 1997–2004. Partner, G. D. Taylor and Associates, Architects and Civil Engineers, 1966–74; Director: West Ulster Estates Ltd, 1968–; Bramley Apple Restaurant Ltd, 1974–; West Ulster Hotels Co. Ltd, 1976–86; Gosford Housing Assoc. Ltd, 1977–; Tontine Rooms Ltd, 1978–; Ulster Gazette (Armagh) Ltd, 1983–; Cerdac (Belfast) Ltd, 1986–; Tyrone Printing Co. Ltd, 1986–; Tyrone Courier Ltd, 1986–; Sovereign Properties (NI) Ltd, 1989–; Carrickfergus Advertiser Ltd, 1992–; Tyrone Constitution Ltd, 1999–; Outlook Press Ltd, 1999–; Coleraine Chronicle Ltd, 2003–; Northern Constitution Ltd, 2003–; East Antrim Newspapers Ltd, 2003–; Northern Newspapers Ltd, 2003–; Midland Tribune Ltd, 2003–; Alpha Newspapers Ltd, 2003–; Veldtstar Ltd, 2004–; Seven FM Ltd, 2005–; Athlone Voice Ltd, 2005–; BoL Pubs Ltd, 2006–; Six FM Ltd, 2006–; Five FM Ltd, 2006–; Q 101 FM Ltd, 2006–; Q 97 FM Ltd, 2006–; Q 102 FM Ltd, 2006–; Northern Media Gp Ltd, 2007–. *Publication:* (jtly) Ulster—the facts, 1982. *Recreation:* foreign travel. *Address:* Mullinure, Portadown Road, Armagh, Northern Ireland BT61 9EL. *T:* (028) 3752 2409, (020) 7931 7211. *Clubs:* Farmers'; Armagh County (Armagh).

KILFOIL, His Honour Geoffrey Everard; a Circuit Judge, 1987–2004; *b* 15 March 1939; *s* of Thomas Albert and Hilda Alice Kilfoil; *m* 1962, Llinos Mai Morris; one *s* one *d.* *Educ:* Acrefair Jun. Bd Sch.; Ruabon Grammar Sch.; Jesus Coll., Oxford (BA Hons Jurisprudence; MA; Sankey Bar Schol., 1960). NCB underground worker, Gresford and Hafod Collieries, 1960–62; Lectr, English and Liberal Studies Dept, Denbs Tech. Coll. and Hd, English Dept, Gwersyllt Secondary Sch., 1962–66. Called to the Bar, Gray's Inn, 1966 (Holker Sen. Schol.); practised Wales & Chester Circuit; Dep. Circuit Judge, Asst Recorder then Recorder, 1976–87; pt-time *ad hoc* local Chm., Med. Appeals Tribunal (Wales) and Police Appeals Tribunals, 1976–87. Member (Lab), 1962–67: Cefn Mawr Parish Council (Chm., 1965–67); Wrexham RDC; Denbs CC; prospective parly cand. (Lab) Ludlow, 1965. Pres. and Trustee Mem., Mgt Bd, Miners' Welfare Inst., Rhosllanerchrugog and Neuadd Coffa Ceiriog, Glynceiriog; Vice-Pres., Llangollen Internat. Musical Eisteddfod; Life Vice-Pres. and Mem. Council, Denbs Hist. Soc.

KILFOYLE, Peter; MP (Lab) Liverpool, Walton, since July 1991; *b* 9 June 1946; *s* of Edward and Ellen Kilfoyle; *m* 1968, Bernadette (*née* Slater); two *s* three *d.* *Educ:* St Edward's Coll., Liverpool; Durham Univ.; Christ's Coll., Liverpool. Building labourer, 1965–70; student, 1970–73; building labourer, 1973–75; teacher/youth worker, 1975–85; Labour Party Organiser, 1985–91. Parly Sec., Cabinet Office, 1997–99 (OPS, 1997–98); Parly Under Sec. of State, MoD, 1999–2000. *Publication:* Left Behind: lessons from Labour's heartlands, 2000. *Recreations:* reading, music, spectator sport, bonsai. *Address:* 69–71 County Road, Walton, Liverpool L4 3QD; House of Commons, SW1A 0AA. *T:* (020) 7219 3000.

KILGALLON, William, OBE 1992; Chief Executive, St Gemma's Hospice, Leeds, since 2007; *b* 29 Aug. 1946; *s* of William and Bridget Agnes Kilgallon (*née* Early); *m* 1978, Stephanie Martin; two *s.* *Educ:* Gregorian Univ., Rome (STL); London Sch. of Econs (Dip. Social Admin); Univ. of Warwick (MA); Univ. of Lancaster (MSc). RC Priest, Dio. Leeds, 1970–77; Asst Priest, St Anne's Cathedral, Leeds, 1970–74; Founder, and Chm., St Anne's Shelter & Housing Action, 1971–74; social work trng, 1974–76; Social Worker, Leeds Catholic Children's Soc., 1976–77; returned to lay state, 1977; Manager, St Anne's Centre, 1977–78; Chief Executive: St Anne's Shelter & Housing Action, 1978–2002; Social Care Inst. for Excellence, 2003–07. Leeds City Council: Mem. (Lab), 1979–92; Chairman: Housing Cttee, 1984–88; Social Services Cttee, 1988–90; Envmt Cttee, 1991–92; Lord Mayor, 1990–91. Member: Leeds FPC, 1978–80; Leeds AHA (T), 1980–82; Leeds E DHA, 1982–86; Yorks RHA, 1986–90 (non-exec. Dir and Vice Chm., 1990–92); Chairman: Leeds Community and Mental Health Services NHS Trust, 1992–98; Leeds Teaching Hosps NHS Trust, 1998–2002. Mem., W Yorks Police Authy, 2007–. Member: Council, NHS Confedn, 1996–2002; CCETSW, 1998–2001. Leader: Indep. Inquiry into Abuse Allegations, Northumberland, 1994–95; Ext. Rev., Earls House Hosp., Durham, 1997–98; Member: Cumberlege Commn reviewing protection of children and vulnerable adults in Catholic Ch in England and Wales, 2006–07; Joseph Rowntree Charitable Trust Commn of Inquiry into destitution among asylum seekers, 2006–07. Chair, Nat. Catholic Safeguarding Commn. Member: Indep. Ref. Gp on Mental Health, NSF, 1998–99; Nat. Task Force on Learning Disability, 2001–04. Non-exec. Dir, Places for People Gp, 2004–05. Mem. Council, Univ. of Leeds, 1992–2000; Gov., Park Lane FE Coll., 2000–02. Mem., Leeds & Dist Rugby League Referees Soc., 1992–. Hon. LLD Leeds, 1997; DUniv Leeds Metropolitan, 2000. *Recreations:* reading, travel, cricket, Rugby League. *Address:* St Gemma's Hospice, 329 Harrogate Road, Leeds LS17 6QD. *T:* (0113) 218 5500, *Fax:* (0113) 218 5502. *Club:* Yorkshire County Cricket.

KILGOUR, Dr John Lowell, CB 1987; Occupational Health consultant, 1994–2002; *b* 26 July 1924; *s* of Ormonde John Lowell Kilgour and Catherine (*née* MacInnes); *m* 1955, Daphne (*née* Tully); two *s.* *Educ:* St Christopher's Prep. Sch., Hove; Aberdeen Grammar Sch.; Aberdeen Univ. MB, ChB 1947, MRCGP, FFCM. Joined RAMC, 1948; served in: Korea, 1950–52; Cyprus, 1956; Suez, 1956; Singapore, 1961–64 (Brunei, Sarawak); comd 23 Para. Field Amb., 1954–57; psc 1959; ADMS GHQ FARELF, 1961–64; jssc 1964; Comdt, Field Trng Sch., RAMC, 1965–66. Joined Min. of Health, 1968, Med. Manpower and Postgrad. Educn Divs; Head of Internat. Health Div., DHSS, 1971–78; Under-Sec. and Chief Med. Advr, Min. of Overseas Develt, 1973–78; Dir of Co-ordination, WHO, 1978–83; Dir, Prison Medical Services, Home Office, 1983–89; Chairman: CS Commn Recruitment Bds, 1989–91; Industrial Injuries and War Pensions Med. Bds, 1989–94; Med. Examnr, Benefits Agency, DSS, 1989–94. UK Deleg. to WHO and to Council of Europe Public Health Cttees; Chm., European Public Health Cttee, 1976; Mem. WHO Expert Panel on Communicable Diseases, 1972–78, 1983; Chm., Cttee for Internat. Surveillance of Communicable Diseases, 1976; Consultant, WHO Special Programme on AIDS, 1987. Vis. Lectr, 1976–89, Governor, 1987–89, LSHTM; Mem. Governing Council, Liverpool Sch. of Tropical Medicine, 1973–87; Mem. Council, 1983–89, Mem. Exec. Cttee, 1987–90, Royal Commonwealth Society for the Blind. Winner, Cons. Constituency Speakers' Competition for London and the SE, 1968. Cantacucino Medal, for services to internat. health, Medical Inst. of Bucharest, Romania, 1980. *Publications:* chapter in, Migration of Medical Manpower, 1971; chapter in, The Global Impact of AIDS, 1988; contrib. The Lancet, BMJ, Hospital Medicine, Health Trends and other med. jls. *Recreations:* horse racing, reading, gardening, travel. *Address:* Stoke House, 22 Amersham Road, Chesham Bois, Bucks HP6 5PE.

KILGOUR, Rear Adm. Niall Stuart Roderick, CB 2005; Secretary and Chief Executive, Hurlingham Club, since 2005; *b* 4 March 1950; *s* of Leonard and Kathleen Kilgour; *m* 1974, Jane Birtwistle; one *s* two *d.* *Educ:* Pangbourne Coll. Commanding Officer: HMS Porpoise, 1980–82; HMS Courageous, 1986–88; Captain, 6th Frigate Sqdn, 1994–96; Commanding Officer: HMS Norfolk, 1994–95; HMS Montrose, 1995–96; Asst COS Ops C-in-C Fleet, 1996–98; Comdr, Amphibious Task Gp, 1998–2001; Comdr Ops to C-in-C Fleet and Rear Adm. Submarines, 2001–04. Younger Brother, Trinity House. QCVS 2000. *Recreations:* shooting, walking, history, sport. *Address:* The Cottage, Beercrocombe, Taunton TA3 6AG. *T:* (01823) 480251.

KILGOUR, Very Rev. Richard Eifl; Rector and Provost, Cathedral Church of St Andrew, Aberdeen, since 2003; *b* 26 Oct. 1957; *s* of Owen Frederick George Kilgour and Barbara Kilgour; *m* 1981, Janet Katharine Williams; three *d.* *Educ:* Eirias High Sch., Colwyn Bay; Hull Nautical Coll.; Edinburgh Univ. (BD Hons 1985). Apprentice Navigation Officer, 1977–80, Serving Deck Officer, to 1981, Anchor Line, Glasgow; Jun. Officer, Trinity House Corp., 1981; 1st Officer, Fishery Protection Fleet, Dept of Agriculture and Fisheries, Scotland, 1981. Ordained deacon, 1985, priest, 1986, Church in Wales; Curate, Rectorial Benefice of Wrexham, 1985–88; Vicar, Whitford, and Industrial Chaplain, NE Wales, Industrial Mission for Council of Churches for Wales, 1988–97; Vicar/Rector, Newtown, Llanllwchaiarn, Aberhafesp, 1998–2003; Priest-in-charge, St Ninian, Aberdeen, 2003–06. RD, Cedewain, dio. St Asaph, 2001–03. Hon. Canon, Christchurch Cathedral, Hartford, Conn, 2004. *Recreations:* sailing, foreign travel, dry-stone walling. *Address:* Cathedral Office, St Andrew's Cathedral, 28 King Street, Aberdeen AB24 5AX. *T:* (01224) 640119; *e-mail:* provost@aberdeen.anglican.org.

KILLALEA, Stephen Joseph; QC 2006; barrister; *b* 25 Jan. 1959; *s* of Edward James Killalea and (Isabelle) Marie-Louise Killalea (*née* Elliott); *m* 1991, Catherine Marie Stanley; two *d.* *Educ:* Bishopshalt Sch., Hillingdon; Univ. of Sheffield (LLB Hons). Called to the Bar, Middle Temple, 1981; barrister in private practice specialising in catastrophic brain and spinal injuries and health and safety prosecutions. *Publications:* (jtly) Health and Safety: the modern legal framework, 2nd edn 2001. *Recreations:* my girls, pubs, grey squirrels. *Address:* Devereux Chambers, Devereux Court, Temple, WC2R 3JH. *T:* (020) 7353 7534.

KILLALOE, Bishop of, (RC), since 1994; **Most Rev. William Walsh;** *b* 16 Jan. 1935; *s* of Bill Walsh and Ellen Maher. *Educ:* St Flannan's Coll., Ennis; St Patrick's Coll., Maynooth (BSc); Irish Coll., Rome; Lateran Univ., Rome (LTh, DCL); Univ. Coll., Galway (HDipEd). Ordained priest, 1959; postgrad. studies, 1959–63; Teacher of mathematics and physics, St Flannan's Coll., Ennis, 1963–88; Curate at Ennis Cathedral, 1988–94; Priest Dir, 1969–94, Pres., Nat. Exec., 1995–, ACCORD (formerly Catholic Marriage Adv. Council); Mem., Episcopal Educn and Pastoral Commns, 2003–. *Publications:* contrib. Furrow Magazine and other theol jls. *Recreations:* hurling (sometime coach/selector of many teams), golf, walking. *Address:* Bishop's House, Westbourne, Ennis. *T:* (065) 28638. *Clubs:* Eire Og Hurling (Ennis); Ennis, Lahinch and Woodstock Golf.

KILLANIN, 4th Baron *cr* 1900, of Galway, co. Galway; **George Redmond Fitzpatrick Morris;** Bt 1885; film producer; *b* 26 Jan. 1947; *e s* of 3rd Baron Killanin, MBE, TD and Mary Sheila Cathcart Morris (*née* Dunlop), MBE; *S* father, 1999; *m* 1st, 1972, Pauline Horton (marr. diss. 1999); one *s* one *d*; 2nd, 2000, Sheila Lynch; one *d.* *Educ:* Ampleforth Coll., York; Trinity Coll., Dublin. Films produced: The Miracle, 1991; Splitting Heirs, 1993; The Butcher Boy, 1998; co-producer: Interview with the Vampire, 1994; Michael Collins, 1996; In Dreams, 1999. *Recreations:* film, theatre, music, Ireland. *Heir:* *s* Hon. Luke Michael Geoffrey Morris, *b* 22 July 1975. *Address:* 9 Lower Mount Pleasant Avenue, Dublin 6, Ireland. *Club:* Groucho.

KILLEARN, 3rd Baron *cr* 1943, of Killearn, co. Stirling; **Victor Miles George Aldous Lampson;** Bt 1866; Director, AMP Ltd, 1999–2003; Chairman (non-executive), Henderson Global Investors (Holdings) Ltd, 2001–05; *b* 9 Sept. 1941; *s* of 1st Baron Killearn, GCMG, CB, MVO, PC and of his 2nd wife, Jacqueline Aldine Leslie, *o d* of Marchese Count Aldo Castellani; *S* half-brother, 1996; *m* 1971, Melita Amaryllis Pamela Astrid, *d* of Rear Adm. Sir Morgan Morgan-Giles, *qv*; two *s* two *d.* *Educ:* Eton. Late Captain, Scots Guards. Partner, 1979–2001, Man. Dir, Corporate Finance, 2001–02, Cazenove & Co. Ltd. Non-executive Director: Maxis Communications Bhd, Malaysia, 2002–06; Shanghai Real Estate Ltd, 2002–07; Ton Poh Emerging Thailand Fund, 2005; Vietnam Dragon Fund, 2006. *Heir:* *s* Hon. Miles Henry Morgan Lampson, *b* 10 Dec. 1977. *Clubs:* White's, Pratt's; Hong Kong.

KILLEN, Prof. John Tyrrell, PhD; FBA 1995; Professor of Mycenaean Greek, Cambridge University, 1997–99, now Emeritus; Fellow, Jesus College, Cambridge, since 1969; *b* 19 July 1937; *e s* of John Killen and Muriel Caroline Elliott Killen (*née* Bolton); *m* 1964, Elizabeth Ann Ross; one *s* two *d.* *Educ:* High Sch., Dublin; Trinity Coll., Dublin (1st Foundn Schol. in Classics 1957; 1st Vice-Chancellor's Latin Medallist 1959; BA 1st Cl. 1960); St John's Coll., Cambridge (Gardiner Meml Schol. 1959; PhD 1964). Cambridge University: Asst Lectr in Classics, 1967–70; Lectr, 1970–90; Reader in Mycenaean Greek, 1990–97; Chm., Faculty Bd of Classics, 1984–86; Churchill College: Gulbenkian Res. Fellow, 1961–62; Fellow and Librarian, 1962–69; Jesus College: Lectr, 1965–97; acting Bursar, 1973; Sen. Bursar, 1979–89; Dir, Quincentenary Develt Appeal, 1987–90. *Publications:* (jtly) Corpus of Mycenaean Inscriptions from Knossos, 1986–98; (ed jtly) Studies in Mycenaean and Classical Greek, festschrift for John Chadwick, 1987; (with J.-P. Olivier) The Knossos Tablets, 1989; (ed with S. Voutsaki) Economy and Politics in the Mycenaean Palace States, 2001; articles in learned jls. *Recreations:* golf, watching sport on television, reading the FT, music. *Address:* Jesus College, Cambridge CB5 8BL. *T:* (01223) 339424. *Club:* Gog Magog Golf.

KILLICK, Angela Margaret; Deputy Chairman, Children and Families Court Advisory and Support Service, 2001–03; *b* 18 May 1943; *o d* of late Tom Killick and Dora (*née* Jeffries); *m* 1983, Alec Grezo; one *s.* *Educ:* Watford Grammar Sch. for Girls. Various posts, incl. voluntary sector and abroad, until 1970; civil servant, incl. Hd, Res. Grants and Council Secretariat, SERC and AFRC; Hd, Radioactive Waste Policy Unit, DoE, 1970–91. Chairman: Hampstead HA, 1990–92; Enfield Community Care NHS Trust, 1992–98; Mt Vernon and Watford Hosps NHS Trust, 1998–2000. Member: Radioactive Waste Mgt Adv. Cttee, 1991–98; Lay Associate Mem., GMC, 2001–06. Lay Chm., NHS Ind. Review Panels, 2000–05; Lay Reviewer, Healthcare Commn, 2004–06. Mem. (C) Westminster CC, 1974–90. Trustee: Tennant Housing Assoc., 1976–85; Westminster Children's Soc., 1988–95 (Chm., 1993–95). Lay Visitor, Postgrad. Med. Educn Trng Bd, 2005–. Ind. Custody Visitor, 2008–. Governor: St Clement Danes Sch., Covent Gdn, 1976–82; St Mary's Sch., Bryanston Sq., 1990–96; Russell Sch., Chorleywood, 1997– (Chm. of Govs, 1998–2002). Binney Award Certificate for Bravery, Binney Meml Trust, 1985. JP Camberwell, 1983–86. *Publication:* Council House Blues, 1976. *Recreations:* reading, gardening, family history, Private Pilot's licence, 1972.

KILLICK, Anthony John, (Tony), OBE 2007; consultant on economic development and aid policies; Senior Research Associate, Overseas Development Institute, since 1999 (Director, 1982–87; Senior Research Fellow, 1987–99); *b* 25 June 1934; *s* of William and Edith Killick; *m* 1958, Ingeborg Nitzsche; two *d.* *Educ:* Ruskin and Wadham Colls, Oxford (BA Hons PPE). Lectr in Econs, Univ. of Ghana, 1961–65; Tutor in Econs,

Ruskin Coll., Oxford, 1965–67; Sen. Econ. Adviser, Min. of Overseas Develt, 1967–69; Econ. Adviser to Govt of Ghana, 1969–72; Res. Fellow, Harvard Univ., 1972–73; Ford Foundn Vis. Prof., Econs Dept, Univ. of Nairobi, 1973–79; Res. Officer, Overseas Develt Inst., 1979–82. Vis. Fellow, Wolfson Coll., and Vis. Scholar, Dept of Applied Economics, Cambridge Univ., 1987–88. Vis. Prof., Dept of Economics, Univ. of Surrey, 1988–. Member: Commn of Inquiry into Fiscal System of Zimbabwe, 1984–86; Council, Royal Africa Soc. Chm. Bd of Dirs, African Econ. Res. Consortium, 1995–2001. Former consultant to various internat. orgns, and to Government of: Sierra Leone; Kenya; Republic of Dominica; Nepal; Ethiopia; Mozambique; Rwanda; Pakistan; Tanzania. Associate, Inst. of Develt Studies, Univ. of Sussex, 1986–94. Pres., Develt Studies Assoc., 1986–88. Hon. Res. Fellow, Dept of Political Economy, UCL, 1985–98. Editorial adviser: Journal of Economic Studies; Develt Policy Review; World Develt. *Publications:* The Economies of East Africa, 1976; Development Economics in Action: a study of economic policies in Ghana, 1978; Policy Economics: a textbook of applied economics on developing countries, 1981; (ed) Papers on the Kenyan Economy: structure, problems and policies, 1981; (ed) Adjustment and Financing in the Developing World: the role of the IMF, 1982; The Quest for Economic Stabilisation: the IMF and the Third World, 1984; The IMF and Stabilisation: developing country experiences, 1984; The Economies of East Africa: a bibliography 1974–80, 1984; A Reaction Too Far: the role of the state in developing countries, 1989; The Adaptive Economy: adjustment policies in low income countries, 1993; The Flexible Economy: causes and consequences of the adaptability of national economies, 1995; IMF Programmes in Developing Countries, 1995; Aid and the Political Economy of Policy Change, 1998; learned articles and contribs to books on Third World develt and economics. *Recreations:* gardening, music. *Address:* Karibu, Millers Mews, Standard Hill, Ninfield, Battle, East Sussex TN33 9JU. *T:* (01424) 892184; *e-mail:* t.killick@odi.org.uk.

KILLIK, Paul Geoffrey; Senior Partner, Killik & Co., since 1989; *b* 24 Dec. 1947; *s* of Guy Frederick Killik and Rita Mildred (*née* Brewer); *m* 1981, Karen Virginia Mayhew; one *s* one *d*. *Educ:* Clayesmore Sch., Dorset. MSI (Dip.) 1969. Hedderwick Borthwick, 1969–71; Killik Haley, 1971–74; Partner, Killik Cassel Haley, 1974–75; joined Quilter Goodison, 1975: Partner, 1977–85, Dir, 1985–88; Head, Private Client Dept, 1983–88. Mem., Stock Exchange, 1973. *Address:* (office) 46 Grosvenor Street, W1K 3HN. *T:* (020) 7337 0400. *Club:* Hurlingham.

KILMAINE, 7th Baron *cr* 1789; **John David Henry Browne;** Bt 1636; Director: Whale Tankers Ltd, 1974–2001; Fusion (Bickenhill) Ltd, 1969–96; *b* 2 April 1948; *s* of 6th Baron Kilmaine, CBE, and Wilhelmina Phyllis, *o d* of Scott Arnott, Brasted, Kent; *S* father, 1978; *m* 1982, Linda, *yr d* of Dennis Robinson; one *s* one *d*. *Educ:* Eton. *Heir:* *s* Hon. John Francis Sandford Browne, *b* 4 April 1983.

KILMARNOCK, 7th Baron *cr* 1831; **Alastair Ivor Gilbert Boyd;** Chief of the Clan Boyd; *b* 11 May 1927; *s* of 6th Baron Kilmarnock, MBE, TD, and Hon. Rosemary Guest (*d* 1971), *er d* of 1st Viscount Wimborne; *S* father, 1975; *m* 1st, 1954, Diana Mary (marr. diss. 1970, she *d* 1975), *o d* of D. Grant Gibson; 2nd, 1977, Hilary Ann, *yr d* of Leonard Sidney and Margery Bardwell; one *s*. *Educ:* Bradfield; King's Coll., Cambridge. Lieutenant, Irish Guards, 1946; served Palestine, 1947–48. Mem. SDP, 1981–92; Chief SDP Whip, House of Lords, 1983–86; Dep. Leader, SDP Peers, 1986–87. Chm., All-Party Parly Gp on AIDS, 1987–96. *Publications:* Sabbatical Year, 1958; The Road from Ronda, 1969; The Companion Guide to Madrid and Central Spain, 1974, revised edn 2002; (ed) The Radical Challenge: the response of social democracy, 1987; The Essence of Catalonia, 1988; The Sierras of the South, 1992; The Social Market and the State, 1999; Rosemary: a memoir, 2005. *Heir:* *b* Dr the Hon. Robin Jordan Boyd, MB BS, MRCP, MRCPEd, DCH, *b* 6 June 1941. *Address:* Apartado 445, 29400 Ronda (Málaga), Spain.

KILMARTIN, Dr John Vincent, FRS 2002; Staff Scientist, Medical Research Council Laboratory of Molecular Biology, Cambridge, since 1969; *b* 22 July 1943; *s* of Vincent Kilmartin and Sadie (*née* Blake); *m* 1985, Margaret Scott Robinson; one *d*. *Educ:* Mt St Mary's Coll., Spinkhill, Sheffield; St John's Coll., Cambridge (MA, PhD 1969). Visitor, Yale Univ., 1976–77. Mem., EMBO, 1995. *Publications:* contrib. papers to scientific jls on hemoglobin and yeast mitosis. *Recreations:* reading, wine, cooking, opera, walking. *Address:* MRC Laboratory of Molecular Biology, Hills Road, Cambridge CB2 0QH. *T:* (01223) 248011.

KILMISTER, (Claude Alaric) Anthony, OBE 2005; Founder, 1994, and President, since 2004, Prostate Research Campaign UK; *b* 22 July 1931; *s* of late Dr Claude E. Kilmister and Margaret E. Mogford, *d* of Ernest Gee; *m* 1958, Sheila Harwood (*d* 2006). *Educ:* Shrewsbury Sch. National Service (army officer), 1950–52. NCB, 1952–54; Conservative Party Org., 1954–60; Asst Sec. 1960–61, Gen. Sec. 1962–72, Cinema & Television Benevolent Fund; Sec., Royal Film Performance Exec. Cttee, 1961–72; Exec. Dir, Parkinson's Disease Soc. of UK, 1972–91. Founding Cttee Mem., Action for Neurological Diseases, 1987–91. Founding Mem. and Dep. Chm., Prayer Book Soc. (and its forerunner, BCP Action Gp), 1972–89, Chm., 1989–2001, Vice-Pres., 2001–; Pres., Anglican Assoc., 2007–; Member: Internat. Council for Apostolic Faith, 1987–93; Steering Cttee, Assoc. for Apostolic Ministry, 1989–96; St Alban's Diocesan Synod, 2006–. Observer, Council, Forward in Faith, 1997–. Freeman, City of London, 2002. MA Lambeth, 2002. *Publications:* The Good Church Guide, 1982; When Will Ye be Wise?, 1983; My Favourite Betjeman, 1985; The Prayer Book and Ordination: a Prayer Book view of women bishops, 2006; contribs to jls, etc. *Recreations:* walking, writing. *Address:* 36 The Drive, Northwood, Middlesex HA6 1HP. *T:* (01923) 824278.

KILMISTER, Prof. Clive William; Professor of Mathematics, King's College, London, 1966–84; *b* 3 Jan. 1924; *s* of William and Doris Kilmister; *m* 1955, Peggy Joyce Hutchins; one *s* two *d*. *Educ:* Queen Mary Coll., Univ. of London. BSc 1944, MSc 1948, PhD 1950. King's Coll. London: Asst Lectr, 1950; Lectr, 1953; Reader, 1959; FKC 1983. Gresham Prof. of Geometry, 1972–88. President: British Soc. for History of Mathematics, 1973–76; Mathematical Assoc., 1979–80; British Soc. for Philos. of Science, 1981–83. *Publications:* (with G. Stephenson) Special Relativity for Physicists, 1958; (with B. O. J. Tupper) Eddington's Statistical Theory, 1962; Hamiltonian Dynamics, 1964; The Environment in Modern Physics, 1965; (with J. E. Reeve) Rational Mechanics, 1966; Men of Physics: Sir Arthur Eddington, 1966; Language, Logic and Mathematics, 1967; Lagrangian Dynamics, 1967; Special Theory of Relativity, 1970; The Nature of the Universe, 1972; General Theory of Relativity, 1973; Philosophers in Context: Russell, 1984; (ed) Schrödinger: centenary celebration of a polymath, 1987; Eddington's search for a fundamental theory, 1995; (with Ted Bastin) Combinatorial Physics, 1995. *Recreation:* opera going. *Address:* Red Tiles Cottage, High Street, Barcombe, Lewes, East Sussex BN8 5DH.

KILMORE, Bishop of, (RC), since 1998; **Most Rev. Leo O'Reilly,** STD; *b* 10 April 1944; *s* of Terence O'Reilly and Maureen (*née* Smith). *Educ:* St Patrick's Coll., Maynooth (BSc, BD, HDipEd); Gregorian Univ., Rome (STD 1982). Ordained priest, 1969; on staff: St Patrick's Coll., Cavan, 1969–76; Irish Coll., Rome, 1978–81; Chaplain, Bailieborough Community Sch., 1981–88; missionary work, Nigeria: diocese of Minna, 1988–90; staff, St Paul's Seminary, Abuja, 1990–95; Parish Priest, Castletara, Cavan, 1995–97; Coadjutor Bishop of Kilmore, 1997–98. *Publication:* Word and Sign in the Acts of the Apostles: a study in Lucan theology, 1987. *Recreations:* walking, reading, golf. *Address:* Bishop's House, Cullies, Cavan, Co. Cavan, Ireland.

KILMORE, ELPHIN AND ARDAGH, Bishop of, since 2001; **Rt Rev. Kenneth Herbert Clarke;** *b* 23 May 1949; *s* of Herbert Clarke and Anne Clarke (*née* Gage); *m* 1971, Helen Good; four *d*. *Educ:* Holywood Primary Sch.; Sullivan Upper Sch., Holywood, Co. Down; TCD (BA 1971; Div. Testimonium 1972). Ordained deacon, 1972, priest, 1973; Curate: Magheralin, 1972–75; Dundonald, 1975–78; served in Chile with S Amer. Mission Soc., 1978–81; Incumbent: Crinken Ch, Dublin, 1982–86; Coleraine Parish, 1986–2001; Archdeacon of Dalriada, 1998–2001. *Publication:* Called to Minister?, 1990. *Recreations:* walking, reading, golf. *Address:* 48 Carrickfern, Cavan, Co. Cavan, Republic of Ireland. *T:* (49) 437 2759; *e-mail:* bishop@kilmore.anglican.org.

KILMOREY, 6th Earl of, *cr* 1822; **Richard Francis Needham, (Rt Hon. Sir Richard Needham),** Kt 1997; PC 1994; Viscount Kilmorey 1625; Viscount Newry and Mourne 1822; Chairman: Biocompatibles plc, 2000–06; Avon Rubber plc, since 2007; Vice Chairman, NEC Europe Ltd, since 1997; *b* 29 Jan. 1942; *e s* of 5th Earl of Kilmorey and of Helen, *y d* of Sir Lionel Faudel-Phillips, 3rd Bt; *S* father, 1977; *m* 1965, Sigrid Juliane Thiessen-Gairdner; two *s* one *d*. *Educ:* Eton College. Chm., R. G. M. Print Holdings Ltd, 1967–85. CC Somerset, 1967–74. Contested (C): Pontefract and Castleford, Feb. 1974; Gravesend, Oct. 1974; MP (C): Chippenham, 1979–83; Wilts N, 1983–97. PPS to Sec. of State for NI, 1983–84, to Sec. of State for the Environment, 1984–85; Parly Under-Sec. of State, NI Office, 1985–92 (Minister for Health and Social Security, 1988–89, for Envmt, and for Economy, 1989–92); Minister of State (Minister for Trade), DTI, 1992–95. Mem., Public Accts Cttee, 1982–83. Chairman: GPT Ltd, 1996–97; Quantum Imaging Ltd, 1999–2003; Newfield IT Ltd, 2003–08; Dir, GEC plc, 1995–97; Independent Director: Dyson Ltd, 1995– (Dep. Chm., 2000–04); Mivan Ltd, 1995–99; Meggitt PLC, 1997–2002; Tough Glass Ltd, 1997–2001; MICE plc, 1998–2003; Hansard Gp plc, 2003–04; deltaDOT Ltd, 2006–07; Disenco plc, 2006–07; Advr, Amec plc, 1998–. Chm., Gleneagles (UK) Ltd (formerly Nat. Heart Hosp.), 1995–2001. Patron, Mencap (NI), 1996–. Pres., British Exporters Assoc., 1998–. Founder Member: Anglo-Japanese 21st Century (formerly 2000) Gp, 1984–; Anglo-Korean Forum for the Future, 1993–2000; Mem., British Indonesian Business Council, 2005–. Governor, British Inst. of Florence, 1983–85. Hon. Life Mem., British-Singapore Business Council, 2002. Gold and Silver Star, Order of the Rising Sun (Japan), 2004. *Publications:* Honourable Member, 1983; Battling for Peace, 1999. *Heir:* *s* Viscount Newry and Morne, *qv*. *Address:* Dyson Ltd, Tetbury Hill, Malmesbury, Wilts SN16 0RP. *Club:* Pratt's.

KILNER, Prof. John Anthony, PhD; CPhys, FInstP; FIMMM; B. C. H. Steele Professor of Energy Materials, Imperial College of Science, Technology and Medicine, London University, since 2006; *b* 15 Dec. 1946; *s* of Arnold and Edith Kilner; *m* 1973, Ana Maria del Carmen Sánchez; one *s* one *d*. *Educ:* Univ. of Birmingham (BSc Hons 1968; MSc 1971; PhD 1975). MInstP, CPhys 1987; FIMMM (FIM 2000); FInstP 2002; CSci 2005; CEng 2007. Res. Fellow and SERC Postdoctoral Res. Fellow, Univ. of Leeds, 1975–79; Department of Materials, Imperial College: Wolfson Res. Fellow, 1979–83; SERC Advanced Res. Fellow, IT, 1983–87; Lectr, 1987–91; Reader in Materials, 1991–95; Prof. of Materials Sci., 1995–2006; Head of Dept, 2000–06; Dean, RSM, 1998–2000. Member: Polar Solids Discussion Gp, RSC, 1981–; European Materials Res. Soc., 1991–. An Associate Ed., Materials Letters, 1992–; European Ed., Solid State Ionics, 2004. FCGI 2007. *Publications:* contribs to sci. jls. *Recreations:* travel, walking, food, drink. *Address:* 34 Castle Avenue, Ewell, Surrey KT17 2PQ. *T:* (020) 8224 7959. *Club:* Athenæum.

KILPATRICK, family name of **Baron Kilpatrick of Kincraig**.

KILPATRICK OF KINCRAIG, Baron *cr* 1996 (Life Peer), of Dysart in the district of Kirkcaldy; **Robert Kilpatrick,** Kt 1986; CBE 1979; President, General Medical Council, 1989–95 (Member, 1972–76 and 1979–95); *b* 29 July 1926; *s* of Robert Kilpatrick and Catherine Sharp Glover; *m* 1950, Elizabeth Gibson Page Forbes; two *s* one *d*. *Educ:* Buckhaven High Sch.; Edinburgh Univ. MB, ChB (Hons) 1949; Ettles Schol.; Leslie Gold Medallist; MD 1960; FRCP(Ed) 1963; FRCP 1975; FRCPSGlas 1991; FRSE 1998. Med. Registrar, Edinburgh, 1951–54; Lectr, Univ. of Sheffield, 1955–66; Rockefeller Trav. Fellowship, MRC, Harvard Univ., 1961–62; Commonwealth Trav. Fellowship, 1962; Prof. of Clin. Pharmacology and Therapeutics, Univ. of Sheffield, 1966–75; Dean, Faculty of Medicine, Univ. of Sheffield, 1970–73; Univ. of Leicester: Prof. and Head of Dept of Clinical Pharmacology and Therapeutics, 1975–83; Dean, Faculty of Medicine, 1975–89; Prof. of Medicine, 1984–89. Chairman: Adv. Cttee on Pesticides, 1975–87; Soc. of Endocrinology, 1975–78; Scottish Hosp. Endowment Res. Trust, 1996–2000. Pres., BMA, 1997–98. Hon. FRCS 1995; Hon. FRCPI 1995; Hon. FRCPath 1996; Hon. FRCSE 1996; Hon. FRCPE 1996. Dr *hc* Edinburgh, 1987; Hon. LLD: Dundee, 1992; Sheffield, 1995; Hon. DSc: Hull, 1994; Leicester, 1994. *Publications:* articles in med. and sci. jls. *Recreation:* golf. *Address:* 12 Wester Coates Gardens, Edinburgh EH12 5LT. *Clubs:* New (Edinburgh); Royal and Ancient (St Andrews).

KILPATRICK, Francesca; *see* Greenoak, F.

KILPATRICK, Prof. (George) Stewart, OBE 1986; MD; FRCP, FRCPE; retired; David Davies Chair of Tuberculosis and Chest Diseases and Head of Department, 1968–92, Vice-Provost, 1987–90, University of Wales College of Medicine, Cardiff; Senior Hon. Consultant Physician to South Glamorgan Health Authority, 1963–90; *b* 26 June 1925; *s* of Hugh Kilpatrick and Annie Merricks Johnstone Stewart; *m* 1954, Joan Askew. *Educ:* George Watson's Coll., Edinburgh; Edinburgh Univ. Med. Sch. (MB ChB 1947, MD 1954). MRCPE 1952, FRCPE 1966; MRCP 1971, FRCP 1975. Medical posts in Edinburgh; Captain RAMC, 1949–51; Mem., Scientific Staff, MRC Pneumoconiosis Research Unit, 1952–54; med. and res. posts, London, Edinburgh and Cardiff; Dean of Clin. Studies, Univ. of Wales Coll. of Medicine, 1970–87. Formerly Chm., Sci. Cttees, Internat. Union Against Tuberculosis (formerly Chm., Treatment Cttee); Chm. Council, Assoc. for Study of Med. Educn, 1981–86; Chm., Assoc. of Medical Deans in Europe, 1982–85. Ext. Examr in Medicine, Queen's Univ. Belfast, 1986–88. Marc Daniels Lectr, RCP 1987. Pres., Cardiff Medical Soc., 1990–91. FRSocMed. Silver Jubilee Medal, 1977. *Publications:* numerous papers to med. and sci. jls; chapters in books on chest diseases, tuberculosis, heart disease, anaemia and med. educn. *Recreations:* travel, reading, photography. *Address:* Millfield, 14 Millbrook Road, Dinas Powys, Vale of Glamorgan CF64 4DA. *T:* (029) 2051 3149.

KILPATRICK, Helen Marjorie; Director General, Financial and Commercial, Home Office, since 2005; *b* 9 Oct. 1958; *d* of Henry Ball and Nan Dixon Ball; one *s* one *d*. *Educ:* King's Coll., Cambridge (BA 1981). Mem. CIPFA 1986. Finance posts at GLC, London Bor. of Tower Hamlets and London Bor. of Southwark, 1982–89; Controller of Financial Services, London Bor. of Greenwich, 1989–95; Dir for Resources, Co. Treas. and Dep. Chief Exec., West Sussex CC, 1995–2005; Treas., Sussex Police Authy, 1995–2005. *Address:* Home Office, 2 Marsham Street, SW1P 4DF. *T:* (020) 7035 0988, *Fax:* 0870 336 9102; *e-mail:* helen.kilpatrick@homeoffice.gsi.gov.uk.

KILPATRICK, Stewart; *see* Kilpatrick, G. S.

KILROY-SILK, Robert; Member (UK Ind, then Veritas) East Midlands, European Parliament, since 2004; Chairman, The Kilroy Television Co., since 1989; *b* 19 May 1942; *s* of William Silk (RN, killed in action, 1943) and Rose O'Rooke; *m* 1963, Jan Beech; one *s* one *d*. *Educ:* Saltley Grammar Sch., Birmingham; LSE (BScEcon). Lectr, Dept of Political Theory and Institutions, Liverpool Univ., 1966–74; television presenter: Day to Day, 1986–87; Kilroy, 1987–2004; Shafted, 2001. Contested (Lab) Ormskirk, 1970; MP (Lab): Ormskirk, Feb. 1974–1983; Knowsley N, 1983–86; PPS to Minister for the Arts, 1974–75; opposition frontbench spokesman on Home Office, 1984–85. Mem., Home Affairs Select Cttee, 1979–84; Vice-Chairman: Merseyside Gp of MPs, 1974–75; PLP Home Affairs Gp, 1976–86; Chairman: Parly All-Party Penal Affairs Gp, 1979–86; PLP Civil Liberties Gp, 1979–84; Parly Alcohol Policy and Services Group, 1982–83. Contested (Veritas) Erewash, 2005. Member: Council, Howard League for Penal Reform, 1979–; Adv. Council, Inst. of Criminology, Cambridge Univ., 1984–; Sponsor, Radical Alternatives to Prison, 1977–; Patron, APEX Trust; Chm., FARE, 1981–84. Governor, National Heart and Chest Hospital, 1974–77. Political columnist: Time Out, 1985–86; Police Review, 1983–; columnist: The Times, 1987–90; Today, 1988–90; Daily Express, 1990–96; Sunday Express, 2001–04. *Publications:* Socialism since Marx, 1972; (contrib.) The Role of Commissions in Policy Making, 1973; The Ceremony of Innocence: a novel of 1984, 1984; Hard Labour: the political diary of Robert Kilroy-Silk, 1986; articles in Political Studies, Manchester School of Economic and Social Science, Political Quarterly, Industrial and Labor Relations Review, Parliamentary Affairs, etc. *Recreation:* gardening. *Address:* European Parliament, Rue Wiertz, 1047 Brussels, Belgium.

KILVINGTON, Frank Ian; Headmaster of St Albans School, 1964–84; *b* West Hartlepool, 26 June 1924; *e s* of H. H. Kilvington; *m* 1949, Jane Mary, *d* of late Very Rev. Michael Clarke and of Katharine Beryl (*née* Girling); one *s* one *d*. *Educ:* Repton (entrance and foundn scholar); Corpus Christi, Oxford (open class. scholar). 2nd cl. Lit Hum, 1948; MA 1950. Served War of 1939–45: RNVR, 1943–46 (Lt); West Africa Station, 1943–45; RN Intelligence, Germany, 1945–46. Westminster School: Asst Master, 1949–64; Housemaster of Rigaud's House, 1957–64. Chairman: St Albans Marriage Guidance Council, 1968–74; St Albans CAB, 1981–86; Herts Record Soc., 1985–90; St Albans Hospice Care Team, 1988–93. Pres., St Albans and Herts Architectural and Archæological Soc., 1974–77. *Publication:* A Short History of St Albans School, 1970. *Recreations:* music, local history. *Address:* 122 Marshalswick Lane, St Albans, Herts AL1 4XD.

KIM DAE-JUNG; President of Republic of Korea, 1998–2003; *b* 3 Dec. 1925; *m* Lee Lee Ho; three *s*. *Educ:* Mokpo Commercial High Sch.; Korea Univ.; Kyung-hee Univ.; Diplomatic Acad. of Foreign Ministry, Russia. Pres., Mokpo Merchant Shipping Co., 1948; arrested by N Korean Communists, escaped from jail, 1950; Pres., Mokpo Daily News, 1950; Dep. Comdr, S Cholla Region, Maritime Defence Force, 1950; Pres., Heungkuk Merchant Shipping Co., 1951; Pres., Dae-yang Shipbldg Co., 1951. Mem., Nat. Assembly of Republic of Korea (S Korea), 1961–72, 1988–97; held posts with Democratic Party, People's Party and New Democratic Party; periods of house-arrest, imprisonment and exile; returned from exile in USA to co-lead New Korea Democratic Party, 1985; Pres., Peace and Democracy Party, 1987; Pres., New Democratic Party, later Democratic Party, 1991; Founder, Nat. Congress for New Politics, 1995, which formed alliance with United Liberal Democrats, 1997. Founder and Chm., Kim Dae-Jung Peace Foundn for Asia-Pacific Region, 1994. Nobel Peace Prize, 2000. *Publications include:* Conscience in Action, 1985; Prison Writings, 1987; Building Peace and Democracy, 1987; Kim Dae-Jung's Views on International Affairs, 1990; In the Name of Justice and Peace, 1991; Korea and Asia, 1994; The Korean Problem: nuclear crisis, democracy and reunification, 1994; Unification, Democracy and Peace, 1994; Mass Participatory Economy: Korea's road to world economic power, 1996. *Address:* c/o Chong Wa Dae, 1 Sejong-no, Chongno-ku, Seoul, Republic of Korea.

KIM, Young Sam; President, Republic of Korea, 1993–98; *b* 20 Dec. 1927; *m* 1951, Sohn Myoung Soon; two *s* three *d*. *Educ:* Coll. of Liberal Arts and Science, Seoul Nat. Univ. (BA). Mem., Nat. Assembly, 1954–93; Member: Liberal Party, 1954–60; Democratic Party, 1960–63; Civil Rule Party, 1963–65; Minjung Party, 1965–67 (also spokesman and floor leader); New Democratic Party, 1967–86 (floor leader, 1967–71, Pres., 1974–76 and 1979); Advr to New Korea Democratic Party, 1986–87; Pres., Reunification Democratic Party, 1987–90; Exec. Chm., 1990–92, Pres., 1992–96, Democratic Liberal Party; Pres., New Korea Party, 1996–97. Candidate for Pres., Republic of Korea, 1987. Chm., Council for the Promotion of Democracy, 1984–86. Averell Harriman Democracy Award, Nat. Democratic Inst. for Internat. Affairs, USA, 1993; Global Leadership Award, UNA, USA, 1995. Grand Order of Mugunghwa (Republic of Korea). *Publications:* We Can Depend on No One but Ourselves, 1964; Why our Country needs Standard-Bearers who are in their 40s, 1971; Government Power is Short, Politics is Long; Hoisting the Flag of Democracy; The True Reality of My Fatherland, 1984; My Resolution, 1987; Democratization, the Way of Salvation of My Country, 1987; Society which wins Honesty and Truth, 1987; New Korea 2000, 1992. *Address:* 7–6 Sangdo 1-dong, Dongjak-ku, Seoul, Korea 156–031.

KIMBALL, family name of **Baron Kimball**.

KIMBALL, Baron *cr* 1985 (Life Peer), of Easton in the County of Leicestershire; **Marcus Richard Kimball,** Kt 1981; DL; *b* 18 Oct. 1928; *s* of late Major Lawrence Kimball; *m* 1956, June Mary Fenwick; two *d*. *Educ:* Eton; Trinity Coll., Cambridge. Dir, Royal Trust Co. of Canada, subseq. Royal Trust Bank, 1970–94. External Mem. Council, Lloyd's, 1982–90. Contested (C) Derby South, 1955; MP (C) Lincs, Gainsborough, Feb. 1956–1983. Privy Council Rep., Council of RCVS, 1969–82, Hon. ARCVS 1982. Jt Master and Huntsman: Fitzwilliam Hounds, 1950–51 and 1951–52; Cottesmore Hounds, 1952–53, 1953–54, 1955–56 (Jt Master, 1956–58). Chm., 1966–82, Pres., 1995–98, British Field Sports Soc.; Dep. Pres., Countryside Alliance, 1999–. Chairman: River Naver Fishing Bd, 1964–92; Firearms Consultative Cttee, 1989–94; British Greyhound Racing Fund, 1993–96. President: Hunters Improvement Soc., 1990; Olympia Internat. Showjumping, 1991–99; British Inst. of Innkeeping, 1992–97; Chm., Cambridge Univ. Vet. Sch. Trust, 1989–98. Lt Leics Yeo. (TA), 1947; Capt., 1951. Mem. Rutland CC, 1955. DL Leics, 1984. *Address:* Great Easton Manor, Market Harborough, Leics LE16 8TB. *T:* (01536) 770333. *Clubs:* White's, Pratt's.

KIMBER, Herbert Frederick Sidney; Director, Southern Newspapers Ltd, 1975–82 (Chief Executive, 1980–81); *b* 3 April 1917; *s* of H. G. Kimber; *m* Patricia Boulton (*née* Forfar); one *s*. *Educ:* elementary sch., Southampton. Southern Newspapers Ltd, office boy, 1931. Served War, Royal Navy, 1939–46: commissioned Lieut RNVR, 1941. Manager, Dorset Evening Echo, 1960; Advertisement Manager-in-Chief, Southern Newspapers Ltd, 1961; then Dep. Gen. and Advertisement Manager, 1972; Gen. Manager, 1974. Chairman: Bird Bros, Basingstoke, 1976–81; W. H. Hallett, 1981–82; Southtel, 1981–82. Dir, Regl Newspaper Advertising Bureau, 1980–81. Member: Press Council, 1977–81; Council, Newspaper Soc., 1974–81 (Mem., Industrial Relations Cttee, 1975–81). *Recreations:* reading, travel, gardening under protest.

KIMBER, Sir Timothy (Roy Henry), 4th Bt *cr* 1904, of Lansdowne Lodge, co. London; DL; Chairman, Border Asset Management, since 2005 (Director, since 1988); *b* 3 June 1936; *s* of Sir Charles Dixon Kimber, 3rd Bt and Ursula Roy Nettie Kimber (*née* Bird); *S* father, 2008; *m* 1st, 1960, Antonia Kathleen Brenda Williams (marr. diss. 1974); two *s*; 2nd, 1979, Susan Hare (*née* Brooks), *widow* of Richard North. *Educ:* Eton Coll. Sub.-Lt 2nd Submarine Sqdn, RNVR, 1955–57. English Electric Co., 1958–64; Dir, Algrey Holdings, 1965; Trainee, then Exec. Dir, Lazard Bros, 1966–89; Director: Lazard Securities, 1974–89; Romney Trust, 1982–88; Development Capital Group, 1983–86; Raeburn Investment Trust, 1983–88; Japan Ventures Ltd, 1984–91; Noble & Co., 1989–2006; Adam Investment Management, 1989–2005; Martin Currie Pacific Trust, 1988– (Chm., 1992–2005); Jardine Fleming India Fund (Saffron Trust), 1995–2004; Cumberland Building Soc., 1995–2004; Invesco Japan Discovery Investment Trust, 1994– (Chm., 2003–07); Dep. Chm., New Zealand Investment Trust, 1988–2008; Chairman: Dartmoor Investment Trust, 1990–2005; Exeter Selective Investment Trust, 1991–2004; Taiwan Opportunities Fund, 1995–; Taiwan Catalyst Partnership, 2006–. Chairman: Lancs Assoc. of Clubs for Young People, 1999–2004; Friends of Eden, Lakeland and Lunesdale Scenery, 2003–. Pres., Wildlife Trust of Lancs, Greater Manchester and N Merseyside, 2005–. Mem. Council (Dep. Treas.), Lancaster Univ., 1990–96. High Sheriff, 1996–97, DL 1997, Lancs. *Recreations:* country activities, golf, football, travel, military history. *Heir: s* Rupert Edward Watkin Kimber [*b* 20 June 1962; *m* 1997, Lisa Cave; three *d*]. *Address:* Newton Hall, near Carnforth, Lancs LA6 2NZ. *T:* (015242) 71232, *Fax:* (015242) 71552; *e-mail:* TK@TimothyKimber.com. *Clubs:* Boodles; Royal Lytham & St Anne's Golf.

KIMBERLEY, 5th Earl of, *cr* 1866; **John Armine Wodehouse,** CEng; Bt 1611; Baron Wodehouse 1797; Senior Internet Analyst, GlaxoSmithKline, since 2003; *b* 15 Jan. 1951; *s* of 4th Earl of Kimberley and his 2nd wife, Carmel June (*née* Maguire); *S* father, 2002; *m* 1973, Hon. Carol Palmer, (Rev. Lady Kimberley), MA (Oxon), PGCE, *er d* of 3rd Baron Palmer, OBE; one *s* one *d*. *Educ:* Eton; Univ. of East Anglia (BSc (Chemistry) 1973; MSc (Physical Organic Chemistry) 1974). CEng 1993; MBCS 1988; CITP 2004. Glaxo, subseq. Glaxo Wellcome: Research Chemist, 1974–79; Systems Programmer, 1979–86, Prin. Systems Programmer, 1987–95; Advanced Informatics and Tech. Specialist, Glaxo Wellcome, subseq. GlaxoSmithKline, 1996–2003. Chm., UK Info Users Gp, 1981–83. Fellow, British Interplanetary Soc., 1984 (Associate Fellow, 1981–83). Reader, C of E, 2008–. FRSA. *Recreations:* interest in spaceflight, photography, computing, fantasy role playing games. *Heir:* *s* Lord Wodehouse, *qv*. *Address:* The Vicarage, Great Hormead, Buntingford, Herts SG9 0NT.

KIMBLE, Dr David (Bryant), OBE 1962; Editor, Journal of Modern African Studies, 1972–97; *b* 12 May 1921; *s* of John H. and Minnie Jane Kimble; *m* 1st, 1949, Helen Rankin (marr. diss.); three *d* (and one *d* decd); 2nd, 1977, Margareta Westin. *Educ:* Eastbourne Grammar Sch.; Reading Univ. (BA 1942, DipEd 1943, Pres. Students Union, 1942–43); London Univ. (PhD 1961). Lieut RNVR, 1943–46. Oxford Univ. Staff Tutor in Berks, 1946–48, and Resident Tutor in the Gold Coast, 1948–49; Dir, Inst. of Extra-Mural Studies, Univ. of Ghana, 1949–62, and Master of Akuafo Hall, 1960–62; Prof. of Political Science, Univ. Coll., Dar es Salaam, Univ. of E Africa, and Dir, Inst. of Public Admin, Tanzania, 1962–68; Research Advr in Public Admin and Social Sciences, Centre africain de formation et de recherche administratives pour le développement, Tanger, Morocco, 1968–70, and Dir of Research, 1970–71; Prof. of Govt and Admin, Univ. of Botswana, Lesotho, and Swaziland, 1971–75, and Nat. Univ. of Lesotho, 1975–77, Prof. Emeritus, 1978; Tutor in Politics to King Moshoeshoe II, 1975, and Queen 'MaMohato, 1977; Vice-Chancellor, Univ. of Malaŵi, and Chm., Malaŵi Certificate Exam. and Testing Bd, 1977–86. Trustee, Malaŵi Against Polio, and Gov., Kamuzu Acad., 1977–86. Chm., Malaŵi/German/UK Study for Estabt of Med. Sch. in Stages, 1986. Founder and Joint Editor (with Helen Kimble), West African Affairs, 1949–51, Penguin African Series, 1953–61, and Jl of Modern African Studies, 1963–71. Officier, Ordre des Palmes Académiques, 1982. *Publications:* Public Opinion and Government, 1950; The Machinery of Self-Government, 1953; (with Helen Kimble) Adult Education in a Changing Africa, 1955; A Political History of Ghana, Vol. I, The Rise of Nationalism in the Gold Coast, 1850–1928, 1963; nine University Congregation Addresses, 1978–86; (with Margareta Kimble) Jl of Modern African Studies: indexed bibliography of contents 1963–97, vols 1–35, 1999. *Recreations:* cricket, photography, editing. *Address:* Huish, Chagford, Devon TQ13 8AR.

KIMMANCE, Peter Frederick, CB 1981; Chief Inspector of Audit, Department of the Environment, 1979–82; Member, Audit Commission for Local Authorities in England and Wales, 1983–87; *b* 14 Dec. 1922; *s* of Frederick Edward Kimmance, BEM, and Louisa Kimmance; *m* 1944, Helen Mary Mercer Cooke. *Educ:* Raines Foundation, Stepney; University of London. Post Office Engineering Dept, 1939; served Royal Signals, 1943; District Audit Service, 1949; District Auditor, 1973; Controller (Finance), British Council, 1973–75; Dep. Chief Inspector of Audit, DoE, 1978. Mem. Council, CIPFA, 1979–83; Hon. Mem., British Council, 1975. *Recreations:* sailing, books, music. *Address:* 6 Laurel Court, Stanley Road, Folkestone, Kent CT19 4RL. *T:* (01303) 273773. *Clubs:* Royal Over-Seas League; Medway Yacht (Lower Upnor).

KIMMINS, Simon Edward Anthony, VRD 1967; Lt-Comdr RNR; *b* 26 May 1930; *s* of late Captain Anthony Kimmins, OBE, RN, and Elizabeth Kimmins; three *s* three *d*; *m* 2007, Ingrid Jeanne Aleida Sickler. *Educ:* Horris Hill; Charterhouse. Man. Dir, London American Finance Corp. Ltd (originally BOECC Ltd), 1957–73; Dir, Balfour Williamson, 1971–74; Chief Exec., Thomas Cook Gp, 1973–75; Dir, Debenhams Ltd, 1972–85; Chief Exec., Delfinance SA Geneva, 1984–98; Chm., Associated Retail Develts Internat., 1980–85; Pres., Piguet Internat., 1986–91; Chief Exec., then Chm., Interoute Telecommunications (Switzerland) SA, 1996–99; Chief Exec., YoStream Holdings BV, Holland, 2000–05; Strategic Investment Dir, Ron Winter Gp, 2005–. Vice-Pres., British Export Houses Assoc., 1974–80 (Chm., 1970–72); Chm., Protelecom Carriers Cttee, 1998–2000. Governor, RSC, 1975–2007. *Recreations:* cricket (played for Kent), golf, writing. *Address:* 3 Westbourne House, Mount Park Road, Harrow on the Hill, Middx HA1 3JT. *Club:* Garrick.

KIMMONS, Rear Adm. Michael, CB 2008; Chief Executive, St Philips Chambers Ltd, Birmingham, since 2008; *b* 24 Dec. 1953; *s* of Robert Edward Kimmons and Patricia Kimmons (*née* Wyn); *m* 1979, Christine Joy Spittle; one *s* one *d*. *Educ:* Stamford Sch.; Heriot-Watt Univ. (BA Hons Modern Langs). Joined RN, 1972; served in HM Ships, Intrepid, Jupiter, Hermes, Active, Illustrious, Royal Yacht Britannia; Sec. to First Sea Lord, 1999–2001; rcds 2002; Director: Naval Personnel Corporate Programming, 2002–03; Naval Staff, 2003–05; COS to Second Sea Lord and COS (Support) to C-in-C Fleet, 2005–07; Chief Naval Logistics Officer, 2005–08; Sen. Directing Staff (Navy), RCDS, 2007–08. ADC to the Queen, 2004–05. NATO Medal 1995. *Publication:* (contrib.) Seaford House Papers, 2002. *Recreations:* golf, mountain biking, jogging, international relations, developing coping strategies for a close relative with Asperger's Syndrome. *Club:* Porters Park Golf (Radlett).

KINAHAN, Maj.-Gen. Oliver John, CB 1981; Paymaster-in-Chief and Inspector of Army Pay Services, 1979–83; *b* 17 Nov. 1923; *m* 1950, Margery Ellis Fisher (*née* Hill) (*d* 2007); one *s* two *d*. Commissioned Royal Irish Fusiliers, 1942; served with Nigeria Regt, RWAFF, Sierra Leone, Nigeria, India, Burma, 1943–46; Instr, Sch. of Signals, 1947–49, Sch. of Infantry, 1950–51; transf. to RAPC, 1951; Japan and Korea, 1952–53; psc 1957; Comdt, RAPC Trng Centre, 1974–75; Chief Paymaster, HQ UKLF, 1975–76; Dep. Paymaster-in-Chief (Army), 1977–78. Col Comdt RAPC, 1984–87. FIMgt. *Recreations:* country pursuits. *Address:* c/o Drummonds Branch, Royal Bank of Scotland, 49 Charing Cross, SW1A 2DX.

KINCADE, James, CBE 1988; MA, PhD; Headmaster, Methodist College, Belfast, 1974–88; *b* 4 Jan. 1925; *s* of George and Rebecca Jane Kincade; *m* 1952, Elizabeth Fay, 2nd *d* of J. Anderson Piggot, OBE, DL, JP; one *s* one *d*. *Educ:* Foyle Coll.; Magee University Coll.; Trinity Coll. Dublin (Schol. and Gold Medallist, MA, Stein Research Prize); Oriel Coll., Oxford (MA, BLitt); Edinburgh Univ. (PhD). Served RAF, India and Burma, 1943–47 (commnd, 1944). Senior English Master, Merchiston Castle Sch., 1952–61; Vis. Professor of Philosophy, Indiana Univ., 1959; Headmaster, Royal Sch., Dungannon, 1961–74. Dir, Design Council, NI, 1990–93; Mem., Design Council, UK, 1993–94 (Chm., NI Cttee, 1993–94); Chairman: Fashion Business Centre, NI, 1992–94; NI Fashion & Design Centre, 1992–94. Nat. Gov. for NI, BBC, 1985–91. President, Ulster Headmasters' Assoc., 1975–77; Vice Pres., Assoc. for Art and Design Educn, 1991–; Mem., Council for Catholic Maintained Schools, 1987–90. Mem. of Senate, and Mem. Standing Cttee, QUB, 1982–98. Pres., Belfast Literary Soc., 2002–03. Trustee, Save the Homeless Fund, 1990–2007. Hon. LLD QUB, 2000. *Publications:* articles in Mind, Hermathena, Jl of Religion. *Recreations:* reading, writing and arithmetic. *Address:* 10A Harry's Road, Hillsborough BT26 6HJ. *T:* (028) 9268 3865.

KINCH, Carol Lesley; *see* Atkinson, C. L.

KINCH, Christopher Anthony; QC 1999; a Recorder, since 1998; *b* 27 May 1953; *s* of late Anthony Alec Kinch, CBE and Barbara Patricia Kinch; *m* 1994, Carol Lesley Atkinson, *qv*; one *s* two *d*. *Educ:* Bishop Challoner Sch., Shortlands, Bromley; Christ Church, Oxford (MA Modern Hist.). Called to the Bar, Lincoln's Inn, 1976, Bencher, 2007; Stagiaire, EC Commn, 1976–77; in practice at the Bar, 1977–; Asst Recorder, 1994–98. Mem., SE Circuit Cttee, 1992–95 and 1996–99. Dir of Educn, Criminal Bar Assoc., 2005–08. Chairman: Kent Bar Mess, 2001–04; Nat. Mock Trial for Schs Competition Working Party, 1999–. *Recreations:* travel, wine, cricket, Rugby. *Address:* 23 Essex Street, WC2R 3AA. *T:* (020) 7413 0353; *e-mail:* christopherkinch@23es.com. *Club:* Beckenham Rugby Football.

KINCHEN, Richard, MVO 1976; HM Diplomatic Service, retired; Ambassador to Belgium, 2003–07; *b* 12 Feb. 1948; *s* of Victor and Margaret Kinchen; *m* 1972, Cheryl Vivienne Abayasekera; one *s* two *d* (and one *d* decd). *Educ:* King Edward VI Sch., Southampton; Trinity Hall, Cambridge (BA). Entered FCO, 1970; attached British Commn on Rhodesian Opinion, 1972; MECAS, 1972; Kuwait, 1973; FCO, 1974; Luxembourg, 1975; Paris, 1977; FCO, 1980; Pvte Sec. to Parly Under-Sec. of State, 1982; Rabat, 1984; Counsellor, UK Mission to UN, 1988–93; Head: Regl Secretariat for British Dependent Territories in Caribbean, 1993–96; Resource Planning Dept, FCO, 1997–2000; Ambassador to Lebanon, 2000–03. Member: UN Adv. Cttee on Admin. and Budgetary Questions, 1991–93; UN Jt Staff Pension Bd, 1992–93. *Address:* 26 Pottery Court, Farnham, Surrey GU10 4QW.

KINCLAVEN, Hon. Lord; Alexander Featherstonhaugh Wylie; a Senator of the College of Justice in Scotland, since 2005; *b* 2 June 1951; *s* of Ian Hamilton Wylie and Helen Jane Mearns or Wylie; *m* 1975, Gail Elizabeth Watson Duncan; two *d*. *Educ:* Edinburgh Univ. (LLB Hons). ACIArb 1977, FCIArb 1991. Qualified Solicitor in Scotland, 1976; called to the Scottish Bar, 1978; called to the Bar, Lincoln's Inn, 1990. Standing Junior Counsel in Scotland to Accountant of Court, 1986–89; Advocate Depute, 1989–92; QC (Scot.) 1991; part-time Sheriff, 2000–05. Chm. (part-time), Police Appeals Tribunal, 2001–05. Jt Chm., Discipline Cttee, Inst. of Chartered Accountants of Scotland, 1994–2005; Member: (part-time), Scottish Legal Aid Bd, 1994–2002; Scottish Council of Law Reporting, 2001–05. *Address:* Court of Session, Parliament House, Parliament Square, Edinburgh EH1 1RQ.

KINDER, Eric; Chairman: Smith & Nephew, 1990–97; Brunner Mond plc, 1992–98; *b* 26 Dec. 1927; *s* of William and Amy Kinder; *m* 1954, Isobel Margaret Barnes; one *s* one *d*. *Educ:* Ashton-under-Lyne and Accrington Grammar Schs. ATI. Joined Textile Div., Smith & Nephew plc, 1957: Divisional Man. Dir, 1969–72; Dir, 1972–97; Chief Exec., 1982–90. Chm., Merchant Retail plc, 1991–94; non-exec. Dir, Intermediate Capital Group plc, 1994–98. Non-exec. Dir, Christie Hosp. NHS Trust, Manchester, 1994–97. *Recreations:* tennis, angling, golf, music.

KINDERSLEY, family name of **Baron Kindersley.**

KINDERSLEY, 3rd Baron *cr* 1941; **Robert Hugh Molesworth Kindersley;** DL; Chairman, Commonwealth Development Corporation, 1980–89; a Vice-Chairman, Lazard Brothers & Co. Ltd, 1981–85 (Director, 1960–90); *b* 18 Aug. 1929; *s* of 2nd Baron Kindersley, CBE, MC, and Nancy Farnsworth (*d* 1977), *d* of Dr Geoffrey Boyd, Toronto; *S* father, 1976; *m* 1st, 1954, Venice Marigold (Rosie) (marr. diss. 1989), *d* of late Captain Lord (Arthur) Francis Henry Hill; two *s* one *d* (and one *s* decd); 2nd, 1989, Patricia Margaret Crichton-Stuart, *d* of late Hugh Norman. *Educ:* Eton; Trinity Coll., Oxford; Harvard Business Sch., USA. Lt Scots Guards; served Malaya, 1948–49. Chairman: Siam Selective Growth Fund, 1990–2000; Brent Walker Gp, 1991–92; Director: London Assurance, 1957–96; Witan Investment Co. Ltd, 1958–85; Steel Company of Wales, 1959–67; Marconi Co. Ltd, 1963–68; Sun Alliance & London Insurance Gp, 1965–96; English Electric Co. Ltd, 1966–68; Gen. Electric Co. Ltd, 1968–70; British Match Corp. Ltd, 1969–73; Swedish Match Co., 1973–85; Maersk Co. Ltd, 1986–2001; Maersk India, 1988–2001. Financial Adviser to Export Gp for the Constructional Industries, 1961–86; Mem., Adv. Panel, Overseas Projects Gp, 1975–77; Dep. Chm., ECGD Adv. Council, 1975–80; Chm., Exec. Cttee, BBA, 1976–78; Pres., Anglo-Taiwan Trade Cttee, 1976–86. Hon. Treasurer, YWCA, 1965–76. Mem., Institut International d'Etudes Bancaires, 1971–85. Chm., Smith's Charity, 1990–97. Mem. Ct, Fishmongers' Co., 1973–, Prime Warden, 1989–90. DL Kent, 1986. *Recreations:* all country pursuits, including tennis and ski-ing. *Heir:* *s* Hon. Rupert John Molesworth Kindersley [*b* 11 March 1955; *m* 1975, Sarah, *d* of late John D. Warde; one *s* one *d*]. *Address:* West Green Farm, Shipbourne, Kent TN11 9PU. *T:* (01732) 810293. *Clubs:* Pratt's, MCC, All England Lawn Tennis and Croquet, Queen's; Vincent's (Oxford).

KINDERSLEY, Lydia Helena L. C.; *see* Lopes Cardozo Kindersley.

KINDERSLEY, Peter David; Chairman, Dorling Kindersley, publishers, 1974–2000; *b* 13 July 1941; *s* of late David Kindersley, MBE and of Christine Kindersley; *m* 1965, Juliet Elizabeth Martyn; one *s* one *d*. *Educ:* King Edward VI School, Norwich; Camberwell

School of Arts and Crafts. Founding Art Director, Mitchell Beazley, 1969–74. Owner, Sheepdrove Organic Farm. Chm., Neal's Yard Remedies; Mem. Council, Soil Assoc. Fellow, Univ. of the Arts London (formerly London Inst.), 2001; FRSA 2000. DUniv Open 2002. *Recreations:* environment, biodiversity, interesting work.

KING, family name of **Baron King of Bridgwater** and **Earl of Lovelace.**

KING OF BRIDGWATER, Baron *cr* 2001 (Life Peer), of Bridgwater in the County of Somerset; **Thomas Jeremy King,** CH 1992; PC 1979; *b* 13 June 1933; *s* of late J. H. King, JP; *m* 1960, Jane, *d* of late Brig. Robert Tilney, CBE, DSO, TD; one *s* one *d*. *Educ:* Rugby; Emmanuel Coll., Cambridge (MA). National service, 1951–53: commnd Somerset Light Inf., 1952; seconded to KAR; served Tanganyika and Kenya; Actg Captain 1953. Cambridge, 1953–56. Joined E.S. & A. Robinson Ltd, Bristol, 1956; various positions up to Divisional Gen. Man., 1964–69; Chairman: Sale, Tilney Co. Ltd, 1971–79 (Dir 1965–79); London Internat. Exhibition Centre Ltd, 1994–; Dir, Electra Investment Trust, 1992–2008. MP (C) Bridgwater, March 1970–2001. PPS to: Minister for Posts and Telecommunications, 1970–72; Minister for Industrial Develt, 1972–74; Front Bench spokesman for: Industry, 1975–76; Energy, 1976–79; Minister for Local Govt and Environmental Services, DoE, 1979–83; Sec. of State for the Environment, Jan.–June 1983, for Transport, June–Oct. 1983, for Employment, 1983–85, for NI, 1985–89, for Defence, 1989–92. Chm., Parly Intelligence and Security Cttee, 1994–2001; Mem., Cttee on Standards in Public Life, 1994–97. *Recreations:* cricket, ski-ing. *Address:* House of Lords, SW1A 0PW.
See also S. R. Clarke.

KING OF WEST BROMWICH, Baron *cr* 1999 (Life Peer), of West Bromwich in the county of West Midlands; **Tarsem King;** JP; Managing Director, Sandwell Polybags Ltd, since 1990; *b* Kultham, Punjab, 24 April 1937; *s* of Ujagar Singh and Dalip Kaur; *m* 1957, Mohinder Kaur; one *s*. *Educ:* Punjab Univ. (BA); Nat. Foundry Coll., Wolverhampton (Dip. Foundry Technol. and Mgt); Aston Univ. (Dip. Mgt Studies); Teacher Trng Coll., Wolverhampton (CertEd); Essex Univ. (MSc Stats and Operational Res.). Lab. Asst, 1960–62; Foundry Trainee, 1964–65; Teacher, Churchfield Sch., W Bromwich, 1968–74; Dep. Hd, Maths Dept, Great Barr Sch., Birmingham, 1974–90. Formerly non-exec. Dir, Sandwell TEC; non-exec. Dir, Sandwell HA, 1990–. Member: (Lab) Sandwell MBC, 1979– (Leader, 1997–); Sandwell CHC, 1982–83; Sandwell DHA, 1983–89. JP West Bromwich, 1987. *Recreations:* reading, music. *Address:* (office) Unit 3, Thomas Street, West Bromwich B70 6LY; 27 Roebuck Lane, West Bromwich B70 6QP.

KING, (Albert) Norman, CMG 2002; OBE 1997; LVO 1983; HM Diplomatic Service, retired; *b* 29 March 1943; *s* of late Albert King and Muriel Elizabeth King (*née* McBrien); *m* 1969, Dympna Mary Farren; one *s* two *d*. *Educ:* Strabane Grammar Sch., Co. Tyrone. Trng posts, Customs and Excise, then Govt Actuary's Dept, 1963; entered HM Diplomatic Service, 1964; CRO, 1964–67; Ibadan, 1967–70; BMG, Berlin, 1971–72; Second Secretary (Commercial): Singapore, 1972–76; Muscat, 1976–80; First Secretary: Dhaka, 1980–84; S Asia Dept, FCO, 1984–86; Personnel Services Dept, 1986–88; Vienna, 1988–93; Inf. Services Dept, FCO, 1993–94; Lagos, 1994–97; Resources Dept, FCO, 1997–99; Counsellor, New Delhi, 1999–2003. *Recreations:* Rugby, music, photography, reading. *Address:* Raj Bhavan, Glenevish Hill, Strabane, Co. Tyrone BT82 8LZ.

KING, Andrew; *b* 14 Sept. 1948; *s* of late Charles King and Mary King; *m* 1975, Semma Ahmet; one *d*. *Educ:* St John the Baptist Sch., Uddingston; Coatbridge Tech. Coll.; Missionary Inst., London; Hatfield Poly.; Stevenage Coll. (CQSW); Nene Coll., Northants (CMS). Labourer; Postal Officer; apprentice motor vehicle mechanic; Social Work Manager, Northants CC, 1989–97. Member: Warwickshire CC, 1989–98 (Chm., Social Services, 1993–96); Rugby BC, 1995–98. MP (Lab) Rugby and Kenilworth, 1997–2005; contested (Lab) same seat, 2005. Member: Social Security Select Cttee, 1999–2001; Deregulation Select Cttee, 1999–2005. Member: Unison (formerly NALGO), 1978–; Co-op. Party, 1995–. *Recreations:* golf, dominoes. *Clubs:* Hillmorton Ex-Servicemen's; Bilton Social; Rugby Golf, Rugby Labour.

KING, Angela Audrey Mary; Founder Director and Joint Co-ordinator, Common Ground, since 1983; *b* 27 June 1944; *d* of Dr George John Graham King and Audrey Thora Dorothee King. *Educ:* Queensmount Sch.; St Christopher Sch., Letchworth; Millfield Sch., Som; Mayer Sch. of Fashion Design, NY. Fashion designer and buyer, NY, 1965–70; Friends of the Earth: wildlife campaigner, 1971–75; campaigned for ban on imports of leopard, cheetah and tiger skins, implemented 1972; (jtly) drafted Wild Creatures and Wild Plants Bill (enacted 1975), and Endangered Species (Import and Export) Act (enacted 1976); Initiator: Save the Whale Campaign, 1972 (campaigned for import ban on baleen whale products, introduced 1973, and Internat. Whaling Commn's 10 year ban on commercial whaling, introduced 1982); (jtly) Otter Project, 1976 (campaigned for ban on otter hunting in England and Wales, introduced 1978); Jt Co-ordinator, Otter Haven Project, 1977–80; Consultant, Earth Resources Res., 1979–80; author of NCC report on wildlife habitat loss, 1981; initiator with Sue Clifford of several projects, including: New Milestones, 1985; Trees, Woods and the Green Man, 1986; Parish Maps Project, 1987; Campaign for Local Distinctiveness, 1990; Confluence, 1998; Orgnr, exhibns which link the arts and the envmt. *Publications:* (ed jtly) Second Nature, 1984; (jtly) Holding Your Ground: an action guide to local conservation, 1987; (ed jtly) Trees Be Company (poetry anthology), 1989, 2nd edn 2001; (jtly) The Apple Source Book, 1991, enlarged edn 2007; (ed jtly) Local Distinctiveness: place particularity and identity, 1993; (jtly) Celebrating Local Distinctiveness, 1994; (ed jtly) from place to PLACE: maps and Parish Maps, 1996; (ed jtly) Field Days: an anthology of poetry, 1998; (ed jtly) The River's Voice: an anthology of poetry, 2000; (ed jtly) The Common Ground Book of Orchards, 2000; (with Sue Clifford) England in Particular: a celebration of the commonplace, the local, the vernacular and the distinctive, 2006; (with Sue Clifford) Community Orchards Handbook, 2008; conservation guides, and pamphlets, for Friends of the Earth, Common Ground, etc. *Recreations:* gardening, walking, watching wildlife, reading. *Address:* Common Ground, Gold Hill House, 21 High Street, Shaftesbury, Dorset SP7 8JE. *T:* (01747) 840820, *Fax:* (01747) 850821.

KING, Anthony James Langdale; Pensions Ombudsman, since 2007; *b* Birmingham, 20 Feb. 1953; *s* of late Norman Edward King and of Florence Elizabeth King; partner, Alvine Elizabeth Baltzars. *Educ:* St David's University Coll., Univ. of Wales (BA Hons 1976). Casework Dir for Pensions Ombudsman, 1994; Financial Ombudsman Service: Ombudsman, 2003; Lead Ombudsman, Pensions and Securities, 2005–07. *Recreations:* music (listening and playing badly), walking, reading, beer. *Address:* Pensions Ombudsman, 11 Belgrave Road, SW1V 1RB.

KING, Prof. Anthony Stephen; Professor of Government, University of Essex, since 1969; *b* 17 Nov. 1934; *o s* of late Harold and Marjorie King; *m* 1st, 1965, Vera Korte (*d* 1971); 2nd, 1980, Jan Reece. *Educ:* Queen's Univ., Kingston Ont. (1st Cl. Hons, Hist. 1956); Magdalen Coll., Oxford (Rhodes Schol.; 1st Cl. Hons, PPE, 1958). Student, Nuffield Coll., Oxford, 1958–61; DPhil (Oxon) 1962. Fellow of Magdalen Coll., Oxford,

1961–65; Sen. Lectr, 1966–68, Reader, 1968–69, Essex Univ. ACLS Fellow, Columbia Univ., NY, 1962–63; Fellow, Center for Advanced Study in the Behavioral Scis, Stanford, Calif., 1977–78; Visiting Professor: Wisconsin Univ., 1967; Princeton Univ., 1984. Elections Commentator: BBC; Daily Telegraph. Member: Cttee on Standards in Public Life, 1994–98; Royal Commn on H of L Reform, 1999. Chm., RSA Commn on Illegal Drugs, Communities and Public Policy, 2005–07. Hon. Foreign Mem., Amer. Acad. of Arts and Scis, 1993; Hon. Life FRSA 2006. *Publications:* (with D. E. Butler) The British General Election of 1964, 1965; (with D. E. Butler) The British General Election of 1966, 1966; (ed) British Politics: People, Parties and Parliament, 1966; (ed) The British Prime Minister, 1969, 2nd edn 1985; (with Anne Sloman) Westminster and Beyond, 1973; British Members of Parliament: a self-portrait, 1974; (ed) Why is Britain Becoming Harder to Govern?, 1976; Britain Says Yes: the 1975 referendum on the Common Market, 1977; (ed) The New American Political System, 1978, 2nd edn 1990; (ed) Both Ends of the Avenue: the Presidency, the Executive Branch and Congress in the 1980s, 1983; (ed) Britain at the Polls 1992, 1992; (with Ivor Crewe) SDP: the birth, life and death of the British Social Democratic Party, 1995; Running Scared: why America's politicians campaign too much and govern too little, 1997; (ed) New Labour Triumphs: Britain at the polls, 1997; (ed) British Political Opinion 1937–2000: the Gallup polls, 2001; Does the United Kingdom still have a Constitution?, 2001; (ed) Britain at the Polls 2001, 2001; (ed) Leaders' Personalities and the Outcomes of Democratic Elections, 2002; (ed) Britain at the Polls 2005, 2005; The British Constitution, 2007; frequent contributor to British and American jls and periodicals. *Recreations:* music, theatre, holidays, walking. *Address:* Department of Government, University of Essex, Wivenhoe Park, Colchester, Essex CO4 3SQ. *T:* (01206) 873393; The Mill House, Lane Road, Wakes Colne, Colchester, Essex CO6 2BP. *T:* (01787) 222497.

KING, Anthony William Poole; His Honour Judge Anthony King; a Circuit Judge, since 1993; *b* 18 Aug. 1942; *s* of late Edmund Poole King and Pamela Midelton King (*née* Baker); *m* 1971, Camilla Anne Alexandra Brandreth; two *s* one *d*. *Educ:* Winchester Coll.; Worcester Coll., Oxford (MA Jur.). Called to the Bar, Inner Temple, 1966; a Recorder, 1987–93; Midland and Oxford Circuit. *Recreations:* fishing, other people's gardens. *Address:* Oxford Crown and County Court, St Aldate's, Oxford OX1 1TL. *T:* (01865) 264200.

KING, Prof. Bernard, Hon. CBE 2003; PhD; FIWSc; CBiol, FIBiol; Vice-Chancellor, University of Abertay Dundee, since 1994 (Principal, Dundee Institute of Technology, 1992–94); *b* 4 May 1946; *s* of Bernard and Cathleen King; *m* 1970, Maura Antoinette Collinge; two *d*. *Educ:* Synge St Christian Brothers Sch., Dublin; Coll. of Technology, Dublin; Univ. of Aston in Birmingham (MSc 1972; PhD 1975). FIWSc 1975; CBiol, FBiol 1987. Research Fellow, Univ. of Aston in Birmingham, 1972–76; Dundee Institute of Technology: Lectr, 1976–79; Sen. Lectr, 1979–83; Head, Dept of Molecular Life Scis, 1983–91; Dean, Faculty of Sci., 1987–89; Asst Principal, Robert Gordon Inst. of Technol., 1991–92. Chairman: Scottish Crop Res. Inst., 2003–08; Mylnefield Res. Services Ltd, 2003–08. Board Member: Scottish Leadership Foundn, 2004–; Higher Educn Acad., 2005–. Gov., Unicorn Preservation Soc., 1993–. CCMI (CIMgt 1999). *Publications:* numerous scientific and tech. papers on biodeterioration with particular ref. to biodeterioration and preservation of wood. *Recreations:* reading, music, sailing. *Address:* 11 Dalhousie Place, Arbroath, Angus DD11 2BT.

KING, Billie Jean; tennis player; Chief Executive Officer, Team Tennis, 1981–91; Founder, WTT Charities Inc., 1987; *b* 22 Nov. 1943; *d* of Willard J. Moffitt; *m* 1965, Larry King. *Educ:* Los Cerritos Sch.; Long Beach High Sch.; Los Angeles State Coll. Played first tennis match at age of eleven; won first championship, Southern California, 1958; coached by Clyde Walker, Alice Marble, Frank Brennan and Mervyn Rose; won first All England Championship, 1966, and five times subseq., and in 1979 achieved record of 20 Wimbledon titles (six Singles, ten Doubles, four Mixed Doubles); has won all other major titles inc. US Singles and Doubles Championships on all four surfaces, and 24 US national titles in all. Pres., Women's Tennis Assoc., 1980–81. *Publications:* Tennis to Win, 1970; Billie Jean, 1974; (with Joe Hyams) Secrets of Winning Tennis, 1975; Tennis Love (illus. Charles Schulz), 1978; (with Frank Deford) Billie Jean King, 1982; (with Cynthia Starr) We Have Come a Long Way: the story of women's tennis, 1989. *Address:* (office) 960 Harlem Avenue, Suite 983, Glenview, IL 60025, USA; WTT Charities Inc., World TeamTennis, 1776 Broadway, Suite 600, New York, NY 10019, USA.

KING, Bradley Maurice; Director, HMS Belfast, Imperial War Museum, since 2002; *b* 10 June 1955; *s* of Maurice Wilfrid King and June King (*née* Wright); *m* 1977, Linda Ann (*née* Baker); one *s*. *Educ:* Chigwell Sch.; Polytech. of North London (BA Hons 1988); Univ. of Greenwich (MA 1999). Imperial War Museum: joined as Clerical Officer, 1980; Public Services Officer, Film Archive, 1987–2000; on secondment as Mus. Project Officer, Bridport Mus., Dorset, 2000; Keeper, Photograph Archive, 2001–02. Bd Mem., 2006–, Internat. Co-ordinator, 2007–, Historic Naval Ships Assoc. (Internat. Leadership Award, 2006). Freeman: Shipwrights' Co., 2006; City of London, 2007. Trustee, Bridport Mus. Trust, 2003–. *Publication:* Royal Naval Air Service 1912–1918, 1997. *Recreations:* history, genealogy, woodworking, cooking, flying, motoring. *Address:* c/o HMS Belfast, Morgan's Lane, Tooley Street, SE1 2JH. *T:* (020) 7940 6333; *e-mail:* bking@iwm.org.uk.

KING, Dr Brian Edmund; owner manager, King Innovations, since 1994; *b* 25 May 1928; *s* of Albert Theodore King and Gladys Johnson; *m* 1952 (marr. diss.); two *s*; *m* 1972, Eunice Wolstenholme; one *d*. *Educ:* Pocklington Sch.; Leeds Univ. TMM (Research) Ltd, 1952–57; British Oxygen, 1957–67; Dir, 1967–87, and Chief Exec., 1977–87, Wira Technology Group Ltd (formerly Wool Industries Research Assoc.); Dir and Chief Exec., Barnsley Business and Innovation Centre, 1987–93. *Recreations:* bridge, swimming, travel.

KING, Caradoc; literary agent; Managing Director, 1991–95, Joint Managing Director, since 1996, and Chairman, since 1992, A. P. Watt Ltd; *b* 19 Dec. 1946; *s* of late Joan Bartlett (*née* Richardson); *m* 1975, Jane Grant Morris (marr. diss. 2001); one *s* one *d*; partner, Ingrid Boeck; one *d*. *Educ:* Belmont Abbey; Exeter Coll., Oxford (MA). With Associated Book Publishers, 1968–70; Senior Editor: Allen Lane, Penguin Press, 1970–72; Penguin Books, 1970–75; joined A. P. Watt, 1976: Associate, A. P. Watt & Son, 1976–81; Dir, A. P. Watt Ltd, 1981–. *Recreations:* ski-ing, lunch, collecting wine, motor-biking. *Address:* c/o A. P. Watt Ltd, 20 John Street, WC1N 2DR. *T:* (020) 7405 6774. *Club:* Soho House.

KING, (Catherine) Mary; mezzo soprano; Director of Voicelab, Southbank Centre, since 2006. *Educ:* Univ. of Birmingham (BA English); St Anne's Coll., Oxford (PGCE); Guildhall Sch. of Music and Drama. Vocal career encompasses music theatre, opera and recital, with specialism in contemporary repertoire. Dir, The Knack, 1995–2006, Artistic Associate, Baylis Prog., 2004–06, ENO. Mem., Music Council, Royal Philharmonic Soc. Trustee, Orpheus Centre, 1999–2004. Hon. ARAM; Hon. Fellow, Rose Bruford Coll. *Publications:* (with A. Legge) The Singer's Handbook, 2007; Boosey Voice Coach, vol. 1: singing in English, 2007. *Recreation:* gardening.

KING, Prof. Christine Elizabeth, CBE 2007; DL; PhD; FRHistS; Vice-Chancellor and Chief Executive, since 1995, and Professor of History, Staffordshire University; *b* 31 Aug. 1944; *d* of William Edwin King and Elizabeth Violet May King (*née* Coates). *Educ:* Birmingham Univ. (BA Hons Hist. and Theol. 1966; MA Theol. 1973; PhD Religious Hist. 1980). FRHistS 1994. Teaching, research and management posts in sch., further and higher educn sectors; Head, Sch. of Histl and Critical Studies, 1985–87, Dean, Faculty of Arts, 1987–90, Lancs Poly.; Staffordshire Polytechnic, subseq. Staffordshire University, 1990–: Prof. of History, 1991–; Dean of Business, Humanities and Social Scis, 1990–92; Pro Vice-Chancellor, 1992–95. Pres., NIACE, 2001–06. FRSA; CCMI (CIMgt 1995; FIMgt 1993). DL Staffs, 1999. Hon. Fellow, Univ. of Central Lancs, 2001; Hon. DLitt: Birmingham, 1998; Portsmouth, 2001; DUniv Derby, 2001; Dr *hc* Edinburgh, 2005. *Publications:* The Nazi State and the New Religions, 1983; (ed) Through the Glass Ceiling: effective management development for women, 1993; articles and chapters on history of religion in Nazi Germany, women in management, higher educn and on Elvis Presley and his fans. *Address:* Staffordshire University, Beaconside, Stafford ST18 0AD. *T:* (01785) 353202.

KING, Colin Sainthill W.; *see* Wallis-King.

KING, Sir David (Anthony), Kt 2003; FRS 1991; FRSC, FInstP; Director of Research, Department of Chemistry, University of Cambridge, since 2005; Fellow, Queens' College, Cambridge, since 2001; Director, Smith School of Enterprise and the Environment, University of Oxford, since 2008; *b* 12 Aug. 1939; *s* of Arnold King and Patricia (*née* Vardy), Durban; *m* Jane Lichtenstein; one *s* one *d*, and two *s* by previous marriage. *Educ:* St John's Coll., Johannesburg; Univ. of the Witwatersrand, Johannesburg (BSc; PhD 1963); ScD E Anglia, 1974; ScD Cantab, 1999. Shell Scholar, Imperial Coll., 1963–66; Lectr in Chemical Physics, Univ. of E Anglia, Norwich, 1966–74; Brunner Prof. of Physical Chemistry, Univ. of Liverpool, 1974–88; Cambridge University: 1920 Prof. of Physical Chemistry, 1988–2005; Head, Dept of Chemistry, 1993–2000; Fellow, St John's College, 1988–95; Master, Downing Coll., 1995–2000, Hon. Fellow, 2001. Chief Scientific Advr to the Govt, and Hd, Office of Sci. and Technol., then of Sci. and Innovation, subseq. Govt Office for Sci., 2000–07. Member: Comité de Direction of Centre de Cinétique Physique et Chimique, Nancy, 1974–81; Nat. Exec., Assoc. of Univ. Teachers, 1970–78 (Nat. Pres., 1976–77); British Vacuum Council, 1978–87 (Chm., 1982–85); Internat. Union for Vacuum Science and Technology, 1978–86; Faraday Div., Council, Chem. Soc., 1979–82; Scientific Adv. Panel, Daresbury Lab., 1980–82; Res. Adv. Cttee, Leverhulme Trust, 1980–92 (Chm., 1995–2001); Beirat, Fritz Haber Inst., West Berlin, 1981–93. Pres., BAAS, 2007–08. Chairman: Gallery Cttee, Bluecoat Soc. of Arts, 1986–88; Kettle's Yard Gall., Cambridge, 1989–2000. Miller Vis. Res. Prof., Univ. of Calif, Berkeley, 1996. Lectures: Tilden, Chem. Soc., 1989; Frontiers, Texas A & M Univ., 1993; Dupont Distinguished, Indianapolis Univ., 1993; Dow Chemical Canada, Univ. W Ont, 1994; Zuckerman, Foundn for Sci. and Technol., 2002; Plenary, AAAS, Seattle, 2003; Annual British Ecol Soc., 2004; Greenpeace Business, 2004; Pimentel, Berkeley, 2005; Magna Carta, Australian Parlt, 2005. Member Editorial Board: Jl of Physics C, 1977–80; Surface Science Reports, 1983–98; Surface Science, 2000–; Editor, Chemical Physics Letters, 1989–2001. Hon. FREng 2006; Hon. Fellow: Indian Acad. of Scis, 1998; Third World Acad. of Scis, 2000; Amer. Acad. of Arts and Scis, 2002; Hon. FRSSAf 2001; Hon. Life FRSA 2006. Hon. Fellow, Cardiff Univ., 2001. Hon. DSc: UEA, Liverpool, Cardiff, 2001; Leicester, Milan, Stockholm, 2002; Witwatersand, York, St Andrews, 2003; La Trobe, QUB, 2005; Newcastle, Goldsmiths Coll. London, Turin, 2006. Chem. Soc. Award for surface and colloid chemistry, 1978; British Vacuum Council medal and prize for research, 1991; Liversidge Lect. and Medal, RSC, 1997; Rumford Medal and Prize, Royal Soc., 2002; WWF Awareness Award, 2004; Linnaeus Medal, Royal Swedish Acad. of Scis, 2007. *Publications:* (with Gabrielle Walker) The Hot Topic, 2008; papers on the physics and chemistry of solid surfaces in Proc. Royal Soc., Surface Science, Science, Jl Chemical Physics, Physical Rev. Letters etc, and on science in govt, global warming etc in Nature and Science. *Recreations:* photography, art. *Address:* Department of Chemistry, Lensfield Road, Cambridge CB2 1EW; 20 Glisson Road, Cambridge CB1 2HD; Smith School of Enterprise and the Environment, 71–79 George Street, Oxford OX1 2BQ.

KING, David E., FCCA; Deputy Chief Executive Officer, Global Banking, Middle East and North Africa, since 2007, and Managing Director, Business Development, Global Banking and Markets, since 2005, HSBC Middle East; *b* 18 Aug. 1945; *m* 1972, Jenny Hall; four *s*. *Educ:* Manchester Poly.; Cranfield Sch. of Mgt (MBA 1984). FCCA 1976. Qualified as Certified Accountant, 1976; sen. financial positions both overseas and in UK, 1976–; joined London Metal Exchange, 1987, Chief Exec., 1989–2001; Man. Dir, Supervision, later Acting CEO, Dubai Internat. Financial Centre, Dubai Financial Services Authy, 2003–05. *Address:* HSBC Bank Middle East Ltd, Level 4, Building 4, Gate District, PO Box 506553, Dubai, United Arab Emirates.

KING, (Denys) Michael (Gwilym), CVO 1989; FICE, MIMechE; Director, 1986–91, Assistant Chief Executive, 1991, BAA plc, retired (Member, British Airports Authority, 1980–86); *b* 29 May 1929; *s* of William James King, FCIS, and Hilda May King; *m* 1st, 1956, Monica Helen (marr. diss. 1973); three *d*; 2nd, 1985, Ann Elizabeth. *Educ:* St Edmund's Sch., Canterbury; Simon Langton Sch., Canterbury; Battersea Polytechnic, London (BScEng Hons London, 1949). MIMechE 1966; FICE 1977. Engr, J. Laing Construction Ltd, 1961–71, Dir, 1971–74; Engrg Dir, BAA, 1974–77; Dir, 1977–86, Man. Dir, 1986–88, Heathrow Airport; Man. Dir, Airports Div., BAA, 1988–91. *Recreations:* yachting, preserved railways.

KING, Deryk Irving; Managing Director, North America, Centrica plc, since 2000; Chairman and Chief Executive Officer, Direct Energy Marketing Ltd, since 2000; *b* 20 Dec. 1947; *s* of Cyril Montford King and Irene Muriel King (*née* Irving); *m* 1971, Janet Lorraine Amos; one *d*. *Educ:* Arnold Sch., Blackpool; University Coll., Oxford (MA Chem.). Joined Air Products Ltd as sales engr, 1970; with Imperial Chemical Industries PLC, 1973–96: Product Manager, 1973–77; Asst Gen. Manager, Chemicals, ICI Japan Ltd, 1977–79; Sen. Product Manager, 1979–83; Export Sales Manager, Mond Div., 1983–84; Commercial Manager, ICI Soda Ash Products, and Dir, Magadi Soda Co., 1984–88; Dir, Ellis & Everard (Chemicals) Ltd, 1987–88; Commercial Manager, 1988–91, Gen. Manager, 1991–92, ICI Fertilizers; Chm., Scottish Agricl Industries and BritAg Industries, and Dir, Irish Fertilizer Industries, 1991–92; Man. Dir, ICI Polyester, 1992–96; Chm., ICI Far Eastern, 1995–96; Gp Man. Dir, PowerGen plc, 1996–98; Dir, Ellis & Everard plc, 1999–2001; Projects Dir, Centrica plc, 1999–2000. Director: Kvaerner ASA, 1997–2001; Consumers' Waterheater Income Fund, 2002–; Allstream (formerly AT&T Canada) Inc., 2003–04; Trustee, Coventry 2000, 1997–2000. Chm., W Midlands Regl Awards Cttee, and Mem., England Cttee, Nat. Lottery Charities Bd, 1998–2000. FCIM 1992. *Recreations:* travel, wine and food, watching sport. *Address:* Centrica North America, Suite 1500, 25 Sheppard Avenue West, Toronto, ON M2N 6S6, Canada.

KING, Prof. Desmond Stephen, PhD; FBA 2003; Andrew W. Mellon Professor of American Government, University of Oxford, and Fellow, Nuffield College, Oxford, since 2002; *b* 23 Oct. 1957; *s* of Desmond and Margaret King; *m* 1995, Dr Carolyn Cowey; one *s*. *Educ:* Trinity Coll., Dublin (BA 1st cl. 1979); Northwestern Univ., Illinois (MA 1981; PhD 1985). Lectr in Politics, Univ. of Edinburgh, 1984–88; Lectr in Govt, LSE, 1988–91; University of Oxford: Lectr in Politics, 1991–2002; titular Prof., 1996–; Official Fellow and Tutor in Politics, St John's Coll., 1991–2002, Emeritus Fellow, 2002–. *Publications:* (jtly) the State and the City, 1987; The New Right: politics, markets and citizenship, 1987; (ed jtly and contrib.) Challenges to Local Government, 1990; Separate and Unequal: Black Americans and the US Federal Government, 1995; Actively Seeking Work?: the politics of unemployment and welfare policy in the US and Britain, 1995; (ed jtly and contrib.) Preferences, Institutions and Rational Choice, 1995; (ed jtly and contrib.) Rethinking Local Democracy, 1996; In the Name of Liberalism: illiberal social policy in the USA and Britain, 1999; Making Americans: immigration, race and the origins of the diverse democracy, 2000; The Liberty of Strangers: making the American nation, 2005; articles in British Jl of Pol Sci., Cambridge Jl of Econs, Comparative Pol Studies, Comp. Studies in Soc. and Hist., Ethnic and Racial Studies, Governance, Government and Opposition, Jl of Historical Sociol., Minerva, Pol Qly, Pol Studies, Pouvoirs, Public Admin, Theory and Society, Urban Affairs Rev., West European Politics, World Politics, American Pol Sci. Rev. *Address:* Nuffield College, Oxford OX1 1NF. *T:* (01865) 278500.

KING, Edmund Valerian; President, Automobile Association, since 2008; *b* Aldershot, 6 March 1958; *s* of Michael Dominic King and Mary Angela King; *m* 2000, Deirdre Elizabeth Lavelle; two *s* one *d*. *Educ:* St Hugh's Coll., Tollerton; Chipping Norton Sch.; Santa Monica Coll.; Newcastle upon Tyne Univ. (BA Hons Politics). Wine taster and PR, Bouchard Aîné et fils, Beaune, 1976–77; Cttee Sec., SSRC, 1981–82; grad. trainee, Dept of Employment, 1982–84; Job Centre Manager, Hackney, 1983–84; proprietor, English antiques business, Los Angeles, 1984–86; reporter, KRTH radio, LA, 1985–87; Dir, Marathon Rent a Car, LA, 1985–88; Campaign Dir, British Rd Fedn, 1988–92; Hd of Campaigns, RAC, 1992–99; Exec. Dir, RAC Foundn, 1999–2007. *Recreations:* mountain biking, running, football (with sons), cooking, fine wines, antiques auctions, driving. *Address:* Automobile Association, Fanum House, Basing View, Basingstoke, Hants RG21 4EA. *T:* (01256) 491538, *Fax:* (01256) 492090; *e-mail:* edmund.king@theAA.com. *Club:* 2 Brydges Place.

KING, Hon. Dame Eleanor (Warwick), DBE 2008; **Hon. Mrs Justice Eleanor King;** a Judge of the High Court of Justice, Family Division, since 2008; *b* 13 Sept. 1957; *d* of Selby William Guy Hamilton and Dr Margaret Hamilton; *m* 1981, (David) Thomas King; four *d*. *Educ:* Queen Margaret's Sch., Escrick; Hull Univ. (LLB). Called to the Bar, Inner Temple, 1979; QC 1999; Asst Recorder, 1996–2000; Recorder, 2000–08; a Dep. High Court Judge, 2000–08. Chm. Governors, Queen Margaret's Sch., 1992–; Mem. Chapter, York Univ. Fellow, Internat. Acad. of Matrimonial Lawyers, 2004. *Recreations:* walking, cycling, running. *Address:* Royal Courts of Justice, Strand, WC2A 2LL.

KING, Frances; Headmistress, Roedean School, since 2008; *b* 26 Sept. 1960; *d* of Sir Colin Henry Imray, *qv*; *m* 1982, Timothy King; one *s* one *d*. *Educ:* Ashford Sch., Kent; St Hilda's Coll., Oxford (BA Theology); Heythrop Coll., London Univ. (MA); Hull Univ. (MBA). Actg Hd of RE, Lady Eleanor Holles Sch., Hampton, 1984–85; Head of Religious Education: Francis Holland Sch., London, 1985–90; Guildford Co. Sch., 1990–93; Tormead Sch., Guildford, 1993–2000; Dep. Headmistress, St Mary's Sch., Ascot, 2000–03; Headmistress, Heathfield St Mary's Sch., Ascot, 2003–07. *Recreation:* walking. *Address:* Roedean School, Roedean Way, Brighton BN2 5RQ. *T:* (01273) 667500. *Club:* Royal Over-Seas League.

KING, Francis Henry, CBE 1985 (OBE 1979); FRSL 1948; author; Drama Critic, Sunday Telegraph, 1978–88; *b* 4 March 1923; *o s* of late Eustace Arthur Cecil King and Faith Mina Read. *Educ:* Shrewsbury; Balliol Coll., Oxford. British Council, 1950–63 (Asst Rep., Helsinki, 1957–58; Regl Dir, Kyoto, 1958–63). Chm., Soc. of Authors, 1975–77; Internat. Vice-Pres., PEN, 1989– (Pres., English PEN, 1978–86; Vice-Pres., 1977; Internat. Pres., 1986–89). *Publications: novels:* To the Dark Tower, 1946; Never Again, 1947; An Air That Kills, 1948; The Dividing Stream, 1951 (Somerset Maugham Award, 1952); The Dark Glasses, 1954; The Widow, 1957; The Man on the Rock, 1957; The Custom House, 1961; The Last of the Pleasure Gardens, 1965; The Waves Behind the Boat, 1967; A Domestic Animal, 1970; Flights (two short novels), 1973; A Game of Patience, 1974; The Needle, 1975; Danny Hill, 1977; The Action, 1978; Act of Darkness, 1983; Voices in an Empty Room, 1984; Frozen Music, 1987; The Woman Who Was God, 1988; Punishments, 1989; Visiting Cards, 1990; The Ant Colony, 1991; (with Tom Wakefield and Patrick Gale) Secret Lives, 1991; The One and Only, 1994; Ash on an Old Man's Sleeve, 1996; Dead Letters, 1997; Prodigies, 2001; The Nick of Time, 2003; With My Little Eye, 2007; *short stories:* So Hurt and Humiliated, 1959; The Japanese Umbrella, 1964 (Katherine Mansfield Short Story Prize, 1965); The Brighton Belle, 1968; Hard Feelings, 1976; Indirect Method, 1980; One is a Wanderer, 1985; A Hand at the Shutter, 1996; The Sunlight on the Garden, 2006; *poetry:* Rod of Incantation, 1952; *biography:* E. M. Forster and His World, 1978; (ed) My Sister and Myself: the diaries of J. R. Ackerley, 1982; Yesterday Came Suddenly (autobiog.), 1993; *general:* (ed) Introducing Greece, 1956; Japan, 1970; Florence, 1982; (ed) Lafcadio Hearn: Writings from Japan, 1984; Florence: A Literary Companion, 1991. *Address:* 19 Gordon Place, W8 4JE. *T:* (020) 7937 5715; *e-mail:* fhk@dircon.co.uk. *Club:* PEN.

KING, Graeme Crockatt; Company Director and Board Consultant, Rank Foundation, since 2006; *b* 8 Sept. 1948; *s* of late William Ramsay Morrison King and Margaret Lowe Robertson (*née* Crockatt); *m* 1975, Dr Susan Margaret Hobbins; one *s* one *d*. *Educ:* High Sch. of Dundee; St Andrews Univ. (MA Science 1970). Member: ICAS, 1974; Inst. of Chartered Accts of Canada, 1976. Arthur Andersen, 1970–79; Finance Dir, Aurora Gp, 1979–81; Mintz and Partners, Toronto, 1982–84; Chief Acct, then Gen. Manager, Lloyd's of London, 1984–94; Principal, Binder Hamlyn/Arthur Andersen, 1994–96; Man. Dir, Insurance Captives, P & O, 1997–2000; Gen. Sec., SPCK, 2001–06. Chm., Hydro Hotel Eastbourne PLC, 2004–. Chm., Rochester Dio. Bd of Finance, 2000–; Trustee: All Saints Educnl Trust, 2001–06; NCVO, 2002–08; Hon. Treas., Farnborough Hosp. Special Care Baby Fund, 1985–. Master, Insurers' Co., Oct. 2009– (Hon. Treas., 2002). *Recreations:* golf, climbing, ski-ing, outdoors. *Address:* Strath Darent House, Shoreham Road, Otford, Kent TN14 5RW. *T:* (01959) 522118; *e-mail:* hobbinsking@btinternet.com. *Clubs:* Lloyds, Nikaean, Caledonian; Grampian; Wildernesse Golf (Sevenoaks), Rye Golf.

KING, Harold Samuel; dancer and choreographer; Artistic Director, Ballet de Zaragoza, Spain, since 2001; Artistic Co-ordinator, Cape Town City Ballet, since 2005; *b* Durban, 13 May 1949. *Educ:* University Ballet Sch., Cape Town. Soloist, Cape Performing Arts Bd Ballet Co., 1968–70; joined Western Th. Ballet, in GB, as dancer and choreographer, 1970; with Opera Ballet, Covent Gdn, 1976–77, incl. seasons with Nat. Ballet of Zimbabwe, as Guest Artist with Cape Performing Arts Bd, and Guest Teacher, Royal Acad. of Dance Summer Sch.; Artistic Co-ordinator, Victor Hochhauser Gala Ballet Season, RFH, 1978; asst, Rudolf Nureyev seasons at London Coliseum, 1978; Dir and toured with, newly-formed London City Ballet, 1978–96; founder, and Artistic Dir, City Ballet of London, 1996–2001, produced Dances from Napoli and choreographed Prince Igor, Nutcracker Suite and Carmen; guest artist, Cape Town City Ballet (performed Madge, the witch, in La Sylphide), Cape Town, 2003; choreographed: The Little Princess, 1995 and created Flowers for Mrs Harris, 1998, for London Children's Ballet; The Lion, the Witch and the Wardrobe for London Studio Centre, 1996; Requiem de Fauré for Ballet de Zaragoza, 2001; Shostakovich Suites for Univ. of Cape Town Sch. of Ballet, 2004; Habanera for Dance for All, township dance co., S Africa, 2005. Chief Trustee, David Blair Meml Trust, 2000–. Fundraising Consultant: Union Dance Co., 2003; Mavin Khoo Dance, 2003.

KING, Isobel Wilson; *see* Buchanan, I. W.

KING, Jean Mary; Under Secretary, Chief Executive, Employment Division of the Manpower Services Commission, 1979–82, retired; Member, Civil Service Appeal Board, 1984–93; *b* 9 March 1923; *d* of Edgar and Elsie Bishop; *m* 1st, 1951, Albert Robert Collingridge (*d* 1994); one *d*; 2nd, 1996, John Ernest Agar King (*d* 2000). *Educ:* County High School, Loughton, Essex; University College London (BSc Econ); LSE (Social Science Course). Asst Personnel Officer, C. and J. Clark, 1945–49; Personnel Manager, Pet Foods Ltd, 1949–50; Ministry of Labour/Department of Employment: Personnel Management Adviser and Industrial Relations Officer, 1950–65; Regl Industrial Relations Officer/Sen. Manpower Adviser, 1965–71; Assistant Secretary, Office of Manpower Economics 1971–73, Pay Board 1973–74, Dept of Employment HQ 1974–76; Dep. Chief Exec., Employment Service Div. of Manpower Services Commn, 1976–79. Chm., Kent Area Manpower Bd, 1983–88. Chm., Fareham Good Neighbours, 1999–2003. *Publication:* (jtly) Personnel Management in the Small Firm, 1953. *Recreations:* voluntary work at local hospice, with the bereaved and the elderly, travel, the arts. *Address:* 16 Faregrove Court, Grove Road, Fareham, Hants PO16 7AS. *T:* (01329) 236340.

KING, Jeremy Richard Bruce; restaurateur; *b* 21 June 1954; *s* of late Charles Henry King and of Molly King (*née* Chinn); *m* 1982, Debra Hauer (marr. diss.); one *s* two *d*. *Educ:* Christ's Hosp., Horsham. Co-founder (with Christopher Corbin) and Director: Caprice Hldgs Ltd, 1982–2003; restaurants: Le Caprice, 1981–2003; The Ivy, 1990–2003; J. Sheekey, 1998–2003; The Wolseley, 2003–; St Alban, 2007–. Chm., Tate Gall. Restaurants, 1999–; Dir, Tate Enterprises Ltd, 2006–. Mem. Council, Tate Gall. of Modern Art, 1999–. Trustee: Artangel Trust, 1994–2005; Soho Th. *Recreations:* contemporary art, theatre, solitude. *Clubs:* Garrick, Royal Automobile.

KING, John Arthur Charles; Chairman, Superscape plc (formerly Superscape VR), 1998–2003; *b* 7 April 1933; *s* of late Charles William King and Doris Frances King; *m* 1958, Ina Solavici; two *s*. *Educ:* Univ. of Bristol (BSc). IBM UK, 1956–70; Managing Director, Telex Computer Products UK Ltd, 1970–73; Dir, DP Div., Metra Consulting Gp, 1974–75; Marketing Dir, UK, later Europe (Brussels), ITT Business Systems, 1976–81; Commercial Dir, Business Communications Systems, Philips (Hilversum), 1981–83; Dir, Marketing and Corporate Strategy, subseq. Corporate Dir and Man. Dir, Overseas Div., BT plc, 1984–88; Man. Dir, Citicorp Information Business Internat., 1988–91; Chairman: Quotron Internat., 1988–91; Analysys Ltd, 1991–2001. Non-executive Director: olsy (formerly Olivetti) UK Ltd, 1991–98 (Chm., 1995–98); Leeds Permanent Building Society, 1991–95 (Vice-Chm., 1994–95); Knowledge Support Systems Ltd, 1997–2001 (non-exec. Chm., 1998–2001); TTP Capital Partners Ltd, 1999–2003. Non-exec. Dir, CSA, 1996–98; Mem. Supervisory Bd, FUGRO NV, 1997–2003; Advr, Enterprise First (formerly Surrey Business Advice), 2004–08. Sec. Gen., Eur. Foundn for Quality Management, 1993–94. Mem., Restrictive Practices Ct, 1995–2000. Freeman, City of London, 1987; Liveryman, Co. of Information Technologists, 1992. FBCS 1968; CCMI (CBIM 1986); FInstD 1986; FRSA 1993. *Recreations:* golf, bridge, music. *Address: e-mail:* jacking33@btinternet.com. *Club:* Wisley.

KING, Sir John (Christopher), 4th Bt *cr* 1888, of Campsie, Stirlingshire; *b* 31 March 1933; *s* of Sir James Granville Le Neve King, 3rd Bt, TD and of Penelope Charlotte, *d* of late Capt. E. Cooper-Key, CB, MVO, RN; *S* father, 1989; *m* 1st, 1958, Patricia Foster (marr. diss. 1972); one *s* one *d*; 2nd, 1984, Aline Jane Holley (marr. diss. 2000), *d* of Col D. A. Brett, GC, OBE, MC. *Educ:* Eton. Sub Lt, RNVR, 1952–54; Lt, Berks Yeomanry, 1955–60. Mem., Stock Exchange, 1961–73. *Recreations:* sailing, travelling. *Heir:* *s* James Henry Rupert King [*b* 24 May 1961; *m* 1995, Elizabeth, *y d* of Richard Ellingworth, *qv*]. *Club:* Brooks's.

KING, John Edward; Principal Establishment Officer and Under Secretary, Welsh Office, 1977–82; Chairman, 1990–92, President, 1992–2002, Friends of the Welsh College of Music and Drama; *b* 30 May 1922; *s* of late Albert Edward and Margaret King; *m* 1st, 1948, Pamela White (marr. diss.); one *d*; 2nd, 1956, Mary Margaret Beaton; two *d*. *Educ:* Penarth County Grammar Sch.; Sch. of Oriental and African Studies, London Univ. Served with Rifle Bde, RWF and Nigeria Regt, 1941–47; Captain, Chindit campaign, Burma (despatches). Cadet, Colonial Admin. Service, N Nigeria, 1947; Permanent Sec., Fed. Govt of Nigeria, 1960; retired from HMOCS, 1963. Principal, CRO, 1963; Navy Dept, MoD, 1966–69; Private Sec. to Sec. of State for Wales, 1969–71; Asst Sec., Welsh Office, 1971–77. CS Mem., 1977–82, External Mem., 1982–86, Final Selection Bd, CS Commn. Consultant, Dept of Educn and Dir, China Studies Centre, UC, Cardiff, 1984–87. *Recreations:* books, swimming, watercolour painting. *Address:* Old Pavilion Place, 86 Glenburnie Road, SW17 7NF. *Clubs:* Civil Service; Outer Hebrides Tennis.

See also E. J. I. Stourton.

KING, Jonathan Colin Harmsworth; anthropologist and museum curator; Keeper, Department of Africa, Oceania and the Americas, British Museum, since 2005; *b* 5 Jan. 1952; *s* of Michael King and Elizabeth King (*née* Hobhouse); *m* 1976, Fionn O'Beirne; one *s* one *d*. *Educ:* Eton; St John's Coll., Cambridge (MA 1975). Curator, Native N American Collections, Dept of Ethnography, BM, 1975–2005. *Publications:* Artificial Curiosities from the Northwest Coast of America, 1981; (ed with H. Lidchi) Imaging the Arctic, 1998; First Peoples First Contacts, 1999; (ed jtly) Arctic Clothing, 2005; (with H. Waterfield) Provenance, 2006; (with C. Feest) Woodlands Art, 2007. *Recreations:* ephemera, reading, collecting, swimming. *Address:* Department of Africa, Oceania and the Americas, British Museum, Great Russell Street, WC1B 3DG.

KING, Prof. Julia Elizabeth, CBE 1999; PhD; FREng, FIMMM, FRAeS, FIMarEST; CSci, FInstP; Vice Chancellor, Aston University, Birmingham, since 2006; Fellow, Churchill College, Cambridge, 1987–94 and since 2002; *b* 11 July 1954; *d* of Derrick Arthur King and Joan (*née* Brewer); *m* 1984, Dr Colin William Brown. *Educ:* Godolphin and Latymer Girls' Sch.; New Hall, Cambridge (BA 1975; MA 1978; PhD 1979; Hon. Fellow, 2003). Rolls-Royce Res. Fellow, Girton Coll., Cambridge, 1978–80; Univ. Lectr, Nottingham Univ., 1980–87; Cambridge University: British Gas/FEng Sen. Res. Fellow, 1987–92; Univ. Lectr, 1992–94; Asst Dir, Univ. Technology Centre for Ni-Base Superalloys, 1993–94; Hd of Materials, Rolls-Royce Aerospace Gp, 1994–96; Dir of Advanced Engrg, Rolls-Royce Industrial Power Gp, 1997–98; Man. Dir, Fan Systems, Rolls-Royce plc, 1998–2000; Dir, Engrg and Technology-Marine, Rolls-Royce plc, 2000–02; Chief Exec., Inst. of Physics, 2002–04; Principal, Faculty of Engrg, Imperial Coll. London, 2004–06. Dir, Birmingham Technology Ltd and Aston Sci. Park, 2007–.

Chm., DSAC, 2003–07; Member: Technology Strategy Bd, 2004–; BERR Ministerial Adv. Gp on Manufacturing, 2007–; Higher Educn Statistics Agency Bd, 2007–; Innovation and Technol. Council, RDA Advantage W Midlands, 2007–; DIUS Strategic Bd, 2008–; DEFRA Cttee on Climate Change, 2008–; Global Agenda Council on Future of Mobility, World Economic Forum, 2008–; Low Carbon Vehicle Partnership Bd, 2008–. Council Mem. and Hon. Sec. for Educn and Trng, Royal Acad. of Engrg, 2003–06. Member: Internat. Sci. Cttee, L'Oréal-UNESCO For Women in Science Awards, 2007; Selection Cttee, Royal Soc. Res. Fellowships (Physical Scis), 2007–. Mem., Governing Body, European Inst. of Innovation and Technol., 2008–. Member, Editorial Board: Internat. Jl of Fatigue, 1989–96; Fatigue and Fracture of Engrg Materials and Structures, 1990–97. Hon. Fellow, Cardiff Univ., 2003. FIMMM (FIM 1993); FREng (FEng 1997); FRAeS 1998; FIMarEST (FIMarE 2001); FInstP 2002; FCGI 2002; FRSA. Freeman, City of London, 1998; Liveryman, Co. of Goldsmiths, 2005–. Hon. DSc QMUL, 2008. Grunfeld Medal, 1992, (jtly) Bengough Medal, 1995, Inst. of Materials; Kelvin Medal, ICE, 2001. *Publications:* (ed) Aerospace Materials and Structures, 1997; Educating Engineers for the 21st Century, 2007; King Review of Low Carbon Cars: part I, the potential for CO_2 reduction, 2007; part 2, recommendations for action, 2008; over 150 papers on fatigue and fracture in structural materials, aeroengine materials and marine propulsion technology. *Recreations:* people, growing orchids, collecting modern prints, gardening, walking. *Address:* Aston University, Aston Triangle, Birmingham B4 7ET. *T:* (0121) 204 4884.

KING, Julian Beresford, CMG 2006; HM Diplomatic Service; Chef de Cabinet to Rt Hon. Peter Mandelson, Member of the European Commission, since 2008 (on loan); *b* 22 Aug. 1964; *s* of Brian Harold King and Barbara Mary King (*née* Beresford); *m* 1992, Lotte Vindelev Knudsen. *Educ:* Bishop Vesey's Grammar Sch.; St Peter's Coll., Oxford (BA). FCO, 1985; Ecole Nat. d'Admin, Paris, 1987–88; Paris, 1988–90; Luxembourg and The Hague, 1991; Second, later First, Sec., FCO, 1992; Private Sec. to Perm. Under-Sec. of State, FCO, 1995–98; UK Perm. Repn to EU, Brussels, 1998–2003; Counsellor and Hd of Chancery, UK Mission to UN, NY, 2003–04; UK Rep. to EU Pol and Security Cttee and UK Perm. Rep. to WEU, Brussels, 2004–07. *Address:* European Commission, 200 rue de la Loi, 1049 Brussels, Belgium.

KING, Justin Matthew; Chief Executive, J. Sainsbury plc, since 2004; *b* 17 May 1961; *s* of Alan and Elaine King; *m* 1990, Claire Andrea Simmons; one *s* one *d*. *Educ:* Tudor Grange Sch.; Solihull Sixth Form Coll.; Bath Univ. (BSc Business Admin). Nat. Account Manager, Mars Confectionery, 1983–89; Sales and Mktg Dir, Egypt, Pepsi Internat., 1989–90; Man. Dir, UK, Haagen-Dazs, 1990–93; Man. Dir, Hypermkts, Asda Stores, 1993–2000; Exec. Dir, Food, Marks and Spencer plc, 2000–04. *Address:* J. Sainsbury plc, 33 Holborn, EC1N 2HT. *T:* (020) 7695 3444; *e-mail:* justin.king@sainsburys.co.uk. *Club:* Hayling Island Sailing.

KING, Kanya, MBE 1999; Founder and Chief Executive Officer, Mobo Organisation, since 1996; *b* London; *d* of Christian Ocloo and Mary Folan; one *s*. *Educ:* Goldsmith's Coll., Univ. of London (BA English Lit.). TV researcher, Carlton TV. Patron, Horniman Mus., 2000–. Hon. Fellow, Goldsmith's Coll., Univ. of London, 2004. Hon. DBA London Metropolitan, 2006. *Recreations:* walking, travelling, reading. *Address:* Mobo Organisation, 22 Stephenson Way, NW1 2HD. *T:* (020) 7419 1200, *Fax:* (020) 7419 1600; *e-mail:* cristel@mobo.com. *Club:* Home House.

KING, Hon. Leonard James, AC 1987; Chief Justice of South Australia, 1978–95; *b* 1 May 1925; *s* of Michael Owen and Mary Ann King; *m* 1953, Sheila Therese (*née* Keane); two *s* three *d*. *Educ:* Marist Brothers Sch., Norwood, S Aust; Univ. of Adelaide, S Aust (LLB). Admitted to Bar, 1950; QC 1967. Member, House of Assembly, Parlt of S Australia, 1970; Attorney-General and Minister of Community Welfare, 1970; additionally, Minister of Prices and Consumer Affairs, 1972. Judge of Supreme Court of S Aust, 1975. *Address:* 19 Wall Street, Norwood, SA 5067, Australia. *T:* (8) 83317220.

KING, Mary; *see* King, C. M.

KING, Mary Elizabeth; three-day event rider; *b* 8 June 1961; *d* of late Lt Comdr Michael Dillon Harding Thomson and of Patricia Gillian Thomson; *m* 1995, Alan David Henry King; one *s* one *d*. *Educ:* Manor House Sch., Honiton; King's Sch., Ottery St Mary; Evendine Court, Malvern (Distinction, Cordon Bleu, 1980). British Open Champion, 1990, 1991, 1997, 2007; Winner: Windsor Horse Trials, 1988, 1989, 1992; Badminton Horse Trials, 1992, 2000; Mem., Olympic Team, Barcelona, 1992, Atlanta, 1996, Sydney, 2000, Athens, 2004 (Team Silver Medal); European Championships: Team Gold Medal, 1991, 1994, 1997, 2007; World Equestrian Games: Team Gold Medal, 1995; Team Silver Medal, 2006. *Publications:* Mary Thomson's Eventing Year, 1993; All the King's Horses, 1997; William and Mary, 1998. *Recreations:* tennis, snow and water ski-ing. *Address:* Old Barn Cottage, Salcombe Regis, Sidmouth, Devon EX10 0JQ. *T:* (01395) 514882.

KING, Prof. Mervyn Allister, FBA 1992; Governor, Bank of England, since 2003; *b* 30 March 1948; *s* of Eric Frank King and Kathleen Alice Passingham. *Educ:* Wolverhampton Grammar School; King's College, Cambridge (BA 1st cl. hons 1969, MA 1973; Hon. Fellow, 2004). Research Officer, Dept of Applied Economics, Cambridge, 1969–76; Kennedy Schol., Harvard Univ., 1971–72; Fellow, St John's Coll., Cambridge, 1972–77 (Hon. Fellow, 1997); Lectr, Faculty of Economics, Cambridge, 1976–77; Esmée Fairbairn Prof. of Investment, Univ. of Birmingham, 1977–84; Prof. of Economics, LSE, 1984–95; Bank of England: non-exec. Dir, 1990–91; Chief Economist and Exec. Dir, 1991–98; Founder Mem., Monetary Policy Cttee, 1997, Chm., 2003–; Dep. Gov., 1998–2003. Vis. Professor of Economics: Harvard Univ., 1982, 1990; MIT, 1983–84; LSE, 1996–; Vis. Fellow, Nuffield Coll., Oxford, 2002–. Co-Dir, LSE Financial Markets Gp, 1987–91. Member: City Capital Markets Cttee, 1989–91; Group of Thirty, 1997–. President: Eur. Econ. Assoc., 1993; Inst. for Fiscal Studies, 1999–2003. Member: Meade Cttee, 1975–78; Council and Exec., Royal Economic Soc., 1981–86, 1992–97; Bd, The Securities Assoc., 1987–89. Fellow, Econometric Soc., 1982. Managing Editor, Review of Economic Studies, 1978–83; Associate Editor: Jl of Public Economics, 1982–98; Amer. Economic Review, 1985–88. Trustee: Kennedy Meml Trust, 1990–2000; Nat. Gall., 2005–. Mem., Adv. Council, LSO, 2001–. Sen. Vice-Pres., Aston Villa FC, 1995–99; Patron, Worcs CCC, 2004–. Hon. Foreign Mem., Amer. Acad. of Arts and Scis, 2000. Hon. Dr: London Guildhall, 2001; City, Birmingham, 2002; Wolverhampton, LSE, 2003; Dr *hc* Edinburgh, 2005; Helsinki, 2006; Hon. LLD Cantab, 2006. Helsinki Univ. Medal, 1982. *Publications:* Public Policy and the Corporation, 1977; (with J. A. Kay) The British Tax System, 1978, 5th edn 1990; (with D. Fullerton) The Taxation of Income from Capital, 1984; numerous articles in economics jls. *Address:* Bank of England, Threadneedle Street, EC2R 8AH. *Clubs:* Athenæum, Brooks's, Garrick; All England Lawn Tennis and Croquet.

KING, Michael; *see* King, D. M. G.

KING, His Honour Michael Gardner; a Circuit Judge, 1972–87; *b* 4 Dec. 1920; *s* of late David Thomson King and late Winifred Mary King, Bournemouth; *m* 1951, Yvonne Mary Lilian, *d* of late Lt-Col M. J. Ambler; two *s* one *d*. *Educ:* Sherborne Sch.; Wadham Coll., Oxford (MA). Served in RN, Lieut RNVR, 1940–46. Called to Bar, Gray's Inn, 1949. Dep. Chm., IoW QS, 1966–72; Dep. Chm., Hants QS, 1968–72. *Recreations:* sailing, shooting, golf. *Clubs:* Royal Naval Sailing Association, Royal Lymington Yacht (Cdre, 1986–88).

KING, Neil Gerald Alexander; QC 2000; *b* 14 Nov. 1956; *s* of late Joseph and of Leila King; *m* 1978, Matilda Magdalen Grenville (*née* Oppenheimer); four *d*. *Educ:* Harrow Sch.; New Coll., Oxford (MA). Called to the Bar, Inner Temple, 1980. Director: White Lodge Properties Ltd, 1985–; Scarista House Ltd, 2000–; Garsington Opera Ltd, 2002–; Harrison Housing Ltd, 2004–. *Publication:* (ed jtly) Ryde on Rating and the Council Tax, 1990–2004. *Recreations:* classical music, golf, walking, Real tennis. *Address:* The White House, High Street, Whitchurch-on-Thames, Oxon RG8 7HA. *T:* (0118) 984 2915. *Clubs:* Royal Automobile; Huntercombe Golf; Isle of Harris Golf; Royal Jersey Golf; Royal St George's Golf.

KING, Norman; *see* King, A. N.

KING, Vice-Adm. Sir Norman (Ross Dutton), KBE 1989; Chairman, Buckinghamshire Health Authority, 1993–96; President, Safety Centre (Milton Keynes) Ltd, since 1997 (Chairman, 1992–96); *b* 19 March 1933; *s* of Sir Norman King, KCMG and Lady (Mona) King (*née* Dutton); *m* 1967, Patricia Rosemary, *d* of Dr L. B. Furber; two *d*. *Educ:* Fonthill School; RNC Dartmouth; graduate, Naval Command College, Newport, USA, 1969; RCDS 1978. RN Cadet, 1946; served HM Ships Indefatigable, Tintagel Castle, Ceylon, Wild Goose, Hickleton, 1951–57, and Corunna, 1957–59; long TAS course, 1960; BRNC Dartmouth, 1961–63; CO HMS Fiskerton, 1963–64; Jun. Seaman Appointer, Naval Sec's Dept, 1965–66; CO HMS Leopard, 1967–68; Staff Officer (TAS) to CBNS (Washington), 1969–71; XO HMS Intrepid, 1972–73; Staff Warfare TAS Officer, to Dir Naval Warfare, 1974–75; Naval Asst to Second Sea Lord, 1975–77; CO HMS Newcastle and Capt. 3rd Destroyer Sqn, 1979–80; CSO to CBNS (Washington), 1981–82; Dir of Naval Officer Appts (Seaman Officers), 1983–84; Comdr, British Navy Staff and British Naval Attaché, Washington, and UK Nat. Liaison Rep. to SACLANT, 1984–86; Naval Sec., 1987–88; COS to Comdr Allied Naval Forces Southern Europe, 1988–91. Mem., Lord Chancellor's Panel of Independent Inspectors, 1992–2001. *Publications:* (jointly) All The Queen's Men, 1967, paperback edn as Strictly Personal, 1972. *Recreations:* tennis, golf, music, chess. *Address:* c/o Lloyd's Bank, Secklow Gate West, Milton Keynes MK9 3EH. *Club:* Royal Navy Club of 1765 and 1785.

KING, Oona Tamsyn; broadcaster and political campaigner; Associate Fellow, Chatham House; *b* 22 Oct. 1967; *d* of Prof. Preston King and Hazel King; *m* 1994, Tiberio Santomarco; one adopted *s*. *Educ:* Haverstock Comprehensive Secondary Sch.; York Univ. (BA 1st cl. Hons Politics); Univ. of Calif, Berkeley (Scholar). Political Asst to Glyn Ford, MEP, 1991–93; Mem., John Smith's Campaign Team for leadership of Labour Party, 1992; Political Asst to Glenys Kinnock, MEP, 1994–95; Trade Union Organiser, Equality Officer, GMB Southern Region, 1995–97. MP (Lab) Bethnal Green and Bow, 1997–2005; contested (Lab) same seat, 2005. PPS to Sec. of State for Trade and Industry, 2003–05. Member, Select Committee: on Internat. Develt, 1997–2001; on Urban Affairs, 2001–03; founding Chair, All-Party Gp on Great Lakes Reg. of Africa, 1998–. Chair, Tower Hamlets Advocacy Network and Community Support, 1995–. *Publication:* House Music, 2007. *Recreations:* cinema, music. *Address:* 129 Antill Road, E3 5BW.

KING, Dr Paul Frederick; Transport Consultant, KPMG Passenger Transport Group, 1997–2004; *b* 4 Jan. 1946; *s* of Cedric Marcus King and Theresa Mary King; *m* 1980, Bertha Ines Avila de King; two *s*. *Educ:* Charterhouse Sch.; Queens' Coll., Cambridge (MA); Univ. of London (MSc, PhD). Lectr, Management Studies, Cambridge Univ., 1970–75; Dir, Special Assignments, TI Group, 1975–79; Sales and Marketing Dir, TI Raleigh, 1979–87; Planning and Marketing Dir, British Shoe Corp., 1987–90; Regional Railways, BR: Planning and Marketing Dir, 1990–93; Man. Dir, 1993–94; Gp Man. Dir, North and West, BRB, 1994–97. Non-executive Director: British Waterways, 1998–2001; Connex Rail Ltd, 1999–2003. *Recreation:* boat building. *Address:* 8 Steeple Close, SW6 3LE. *T:* (020) 7013 0818.

KING, Paul William; Agent General for British Columbia in the United Kingdom and Europe, 1995–2002; *b* Srinagar, Kashmir, 6 Sept. 1943; *s* of late Rev. Canon Roderick King and of Kathleen King; *m* 1969, Susan Jane Glenny (*d* 2000); two *s*. *Educ:* Exeter Sch.; Univ. of Alberta (BA). With E. I. du Pont de Nemours, USA, 1964; Kodak Canada Ltd, 1965–77; Dir responsible for trade with Pacific Rim countries, Govt of Alberta, 1977–81; Director: European Ops, Alberta House, London, 1982–90; Trade and Investment, BC House, London, 1990–95. MInstD. Freeman, City of London, 1996. *Recreations:* gardening, travel, motor-racing. *Address:* 1 West Common Close, Gerrards Cross, Bucks SL9 7QR. *T:* (01753) 891195. *Club:* East India.

KING, Rev. Peter Duncan, TD 1986; a Senior Immigration Judge, Asylum and Immigration Tribunal (formerly a Vice-President, Immigration Appeal Tribunal), since 2004; *b* 13 Feb. 1948; *s* of Clifford Norman King and Margaret Fraser King; *m* 1982, Maureen Diane Williams; one *s* one *d*. *Educ:* King's Coll., London (LLB 1970; AKC); Fitzwilliam Coll., Cambridge (MA); Westcott House, Cambridge. ACIArb 2004. Called to the Bar, Gray's Inn, 1970; Legal Officer, Army Legal Services, 1972–77; barrister in private practice, specialising in common law and crime, in London and Cambridge, 1977–2000; Plate Judge Advocate, 1995–; Special Immigration Adjudicator, 1995; Acting Stipendiary Magistrate, 1998–2000; Legal Mem., Immigration Appeals Tribunal, 1999; Dep. Dist Judge (Magistrates' Courts), 2000–; Immigration Adjudicator, 2000–04. Pres., Council of Immigration Judges, 2007–08; Member: Internat. Assoc. of Refugee Law Judges, 2000–; Commonwealth Magistrates' and Judges' Assoc., 2005–. Ordained Minister in Secular Employment, C of E, 1980; Hon. Priest, Mortlake with E Sheen, 1982–; Dean for MSE, Kingston Episcopal Area, 1999–. Mem. Exec. and Moderator, CHRISM. Liveryman, Co. of Arbitrators, 2004. RCT (TA) (Movt Control/Liaison), 1967–72 and 1977–97. *Recreations:* golf, bowls, Rotary International (Dist Gov., 2002–03). *Address:* Asylum and Immigration Tribunal, Field House, 15 Bream's Buildings, EC4A 1DZ. *Club:* Royal Commonwealth Society.

KING, Air Vice-Marshal Peter Francis, CB 1987; OBE (mil.) 1964; FRCSE; The Senior Consultant, RAF, 1985–87; Air Vice-Marshal, Princess Mary's RAF Hospital, Halton, 1983–87; Consultant Otorhinolaryngologist, King Edward VII Hospital, Midhurst, 1988–96; *b* 17 Sept. 1922; *s* of Sqn Ldr William George King, MBE, RAF, and Florence Margaret King (*née* Sell); *m* 1945, Doreen Maxwell Aaröe (*d* 2006), 2nd *d* of Jorgen Hansen-Aaröe; one *s* one *d*. *Educ:* Framlingham Coll.; King's Coll. London, 1940–42; Charing Cross Hosp., 1942–45; Univ. of Edinburgh, 1947. DLO; MRCS, LRCP; MFOM. Kitchener Med. Services Schol. for RAF, 1941; Ho. Phys., Ho. Surg., Charing Cross Hosp., 1945; commnd RAF, 1945; specialist in Otorhinolaryngology, employed Cosford, Ely, Fayid, Halton, CME; Cons. in Otorhinolaryngology, 1955; Hunterian Prof., RCS, 1964; Cons. Adviser in Otorhinolaryngology, 1966; Air Cdre 1976; Reader in Aviation Med., Inst. of Aviation Med., 1977; Whittingham Prof. in Aviation Med., IAM and RCP, 1979; QHS 1979–87; Dean of Air Force Medicine, 1983.

Cons. to Herts HA, 1963, and CAA, 1973; Examiner for Dip. in Aviation Med., RCP, 1980. Littler Meml Lectr, British Soc. of Audiology, 2001. Pres., Sect. of Otology, RSocMed, 1977–78 (Sec., 1972–74); Chm., Brit. Soc. of Audiology, 1979–81 (Hon. Life Mem., 1998); Vice-Pres., RNID, 1990–2004 (Vice-Chm., 1980–88); Member: BMA, 1945– (Life Mem., 1996); Scottish Otological Soc., 1955–90; Royal Aeronaut. Soc., 1976– (FRAeS 1998); Council, Brit. Assoc. of Otorhinolaryngologists, 1960–89 (Hon. Life Mem., 1996); Editorial Bd, British Jl of Audiology, 1980–88. Fellow, Inst. of Acoustics, 1977. FRSocMed. CStJ 1987. Lady Cade Medal, RCS, 1967; (jtly) Howells Meml Prize, Univ. of London, 1992; recognised as co-descriptor of King-Kopetzky Syndrome, 1992. *Publications:* Noise and Vibration in Aviation (with J. C. Guignard), 1972; (with John Ernsting) Aviation Medicine, 1988; (jtly) Assessment of Hearing Disability, 1992; numerous articles, chapters, lectures and papers, in books and relevant jls on aviation otolaryngology, noise deafness, hearing conservation, tympanoplasty, facial paralysis, otic barotrauma, etc. *Recreations:* sculpture, looking at prints. *Address:* 5 Churchill Gate, Oxford Road, Woodstock, Oxon OX20 1QW. *T:* (01993) 813115. *Club:* Royal Air Force.

KING, Philip Henry Russell; QC 2002; *b* 15 Feb. 1949; *s* of Percy Sydney King and Patricia Maude (*née* Ball); *m* 2005, Jacqueline Riley (*née* Green). *Educ:* Clifton Coll.; Univ. of East Anglia (BA Hons). Called to the Bar, Inner Temple, 1974; in practice as barrister, 1976–. *Recreations:* history, food, the countryside, travel. *Address:* (chambers) 187 Fleet Street, EC4A 2AT.

KING, Phillip, CBE 1975; RA 1991 (ARA 1977); sculptor; President, Royal Academy of Arts, 1999–2004; Professor of Sculpture: Royal College of Art, 1980–90, Emeritus since 1991; Royal Academy Schools, 1990–99; *b* 1 May 1934; *s* of Thomas John King and of Gabrielle (*née* Liautard); *m* 1st, 1957, Lilian Odelle (marr. diss. 1987); (one *s* decd); 2nd, 1988, Judith Corballis. *Educ:* Mill Hill Sch.; Christ's Coll., Cambridge Univ. (languages; Hon. Fellow, 2002); St Martin's Sch. of Art (sculpture). Teacher at St Martin's Sch. of Art, 1959–78; Asst to Henry Moore, 1959–60. Trustee: Tate Gallery, 1967–69; NPG, 1999–; Mem. Art Panel, Arts Council, 1977–79. Vis. Prof., Berlin Sch. of Art, 1979–81. *One-man exhibitions include:* British Pavilion, Venice Biennale, 1968; European Mus. Tour, 1974–75 (Kroller-Muller Nat. Mus., Holland; Kunsthalle, Düsseldorf; Kunsthalle, Bern; Musée Galliera, Paris; Ulster Mus., Belfast); UK Touring Exhibn, 1975–76 (Sheffield, Cumbria, Aberdeen, Glasgow, Newcastle, Portsmouth); Hayward Gall. (retrospective), 1981; Forte di Belvedere, Florence, 1997. Commissions include: Cross Bend, European Patent Office, Munich, 1978; Hiroshima Mus. of Art, 1989. First Prize, Socha Piestanskych Parkov, Piestany, Czechoslovakia, 1969. *Address:* c/o Bernard Jacobson Gallery, 14a Clifford Street, W1X 1RF.

KING, Reyahn; Director of Art Galleries, National Museums Liverpool, since 2007; *b* Edinburgh, 1965; *d* of Robert Bruce King and Jamela King (*née* Abrams); *m* 2008, Garry Morris; one step *s* one step *d*. *Educ:* Balliol Coll., Oxford (BA Hons Modern Hist.); Boston Univ. (MA Hist. of Art). AMA 1997. Archive Asst, NPG, 1990–91; Curatorial Asst, Boston Univ. Art Gall., Mass, 1991–93; Grad. Fellow, Photographic Resource Center, Boston (pt-time), 1992–93; Periodicals Librarian, National Gall., London, 1994–97; Guest Curator, Ignatius Sancho exhibn, NPG (pt-time), 1996–97; Curator, Prints and Drawings, Birmingham Mus and Art Gall., 1997–2001; Art Gall. and Mus. Develt Manager, Coventry Arts and Heritage, 2001–03; Hd, Interpretation and Exhibns, Birmingham Mus and Art Gall., 2003–07. FRSA. *Publications:* Ignatius Sancho: an African man of letters (1729–1780), 1997; Anwar Shenza, 1997; Varvara Shavrova: inscriptions, 2001. *Recreations:* Tai Chi, seeing friends and family, enjoying food. *Address:* Walker Art Gallery, William Brown Street, Liverpool L3 8EL. *T:* (0151) 478 4101.

KING, Robert George Cecil; Chairman, Social Security Appeal Tribunals, 1987–98; Under Secretary (Legal), HM Customs and Excise, 1985–87; *b* 21 Jan. 1927; *s* of Stanley Cecil and Kathleen Mary King; *m* 1952, Mary Marshall. *Educ:* Nunthorpe Grammar School, York. Called to the Bar, Lincolns Inn, 1965. Army, 1945–48; British Rail, 1948–53; Judicial Dept, Kenya, 1954–61; East African Common Services Organisation, 1962–64; Solicitor's Office, HM Customs and Excise, 1965–87. *Recreations:* golf, bowls, gardening, watching cricket, watching television. *Address:* 181 Greenshaw Drive, Wigginton, York YO32 2SD. *T:* (01904) 765039. *Clubs:* York Golf, Royal Nairobi Golf.

KING, Robert John Stephen; conductor; harpsichordist; Artistic Director, The King's Consort, 1980–2007; *b* 27 June 1960; *s* of Stephen King and Margaret Digby. *Educ:* Radley Coll.; St John's Coll., Cambridge (MA). Writer; editor of much music *pre* 1750; broadcaster; conductor, orchestras and choirs, incl. Nat. SO Washington, Stavanger SO, Aarhus SO, Danish Radio SO, Malmö SO, Zurich Chamber Orch., Seattle SO, Orq. Sinfonica Euskadi, Orq. Ciudad de Madrid, Orebro Chamber Orch., Netherlands Chamber Orch. and Chamber Choir, RTL Symphony Orch., Orch. d'Auvergne, English Chamber Orch., Norrköping SO, Atlanta SO, Houston SO, Minnesota SO, Detroit SO, Westdeutscher Rundfunk SO, Il Giardino Armonico, Orquesta de Cadaqués, Granada SO, Tölzer Knabenchor, Collegium Vocale Ghent, BBC Singers. Artistic Director: Aldeburgh Easter Fest., 1998–2000; Nordic Baroque Music Fest., 2001–04; Internat. Organ Week Nuremberg, 2003. *Publications:* Henry Purcell, 1994; numerous musical edns. *Recreations:* ski-ing, cricket, lupin growing.

KING, Robert Shirley; Under Secretary, Department of Health and Social Security, 1976–80; *b* 12 July 1920; *s* of late Rev. William Henry King, MC, TD, MA, and Dorothy King (*née* Sharpe); *m* 1st, 1947, Margaret Siddall (*d* 1956); two *d*; 2nd, 1958, Mary Rowell (*d* 1996); one *s* two *d*; 3rd, 1998, Daphne Shercliff. *Educ:* Alexandra Road Sch., Oldham; Manchester Grammar Sch.; Trinity Coll., Cambridge (Schol., MA). Served War, RAF, 1940–45. Colonial Service, Tanganyika, 1949–62 (Dist Comr, Bukoba, 1956–58, Geita, 1959–62); Home Office: Principal, 1962–69 (seconded to Civil Service Dept, 1968–69); Asst Sec., 1969–70; transf., with Children's Dept, to DHSS, 1971; Asst Sec., DHSS, 1971–76; Sec., Wkg Party on Role and Tasks of Social Workers, Nat. Inst. for Social Work, 1980–82; part-time Asst Sec., Home Office, 1985–86. Sec., Health Promotion Res. Trust, 1984–89. Member Council: British and Foreign Sch. Soc., 1982–89; Shape, 1982–89. Governor: Cheshunt Foundn, 1976–83; Bell Educnl Trust, 1984–89. *Recreations:* walking, cycling, African affairs. *Address:* 12 Merton Street, Cambridge CB3 9JD.

KING, Roger Douglas; Chief Executive, Road Haulage Association, since 2000; *b* 26 Oct. 1943; *s* of Douglas and Cecilie King; *m* 1976, Jennifer Susan (*née* Sharpe); twin *s* one *d*. *Educ:* Solihull Sch. Served automobile engrg apprenticeship with British Motor Corp., 1960–66; sales rep., 1966–74; own manufg business, 1974–81; self-employed car product distributor, 1982–83; Dir of Public Affairs, 1992–99, Dep. Chief Exec., 1999–2000, SMMT. Director: Prince Michael Road Safety Awards Scheme, 1992–; Roadsafe, 2000–. Non-executive Director: Nat. Express Hldgs, 1988–91; Coventry Bldg Soc., 1995–2007. Vice Chm., Internat. Road Transport Union Goods Transport Council, 2006–. MP (C) Birmingham, Northfield, 1983–92. PPS to Minister for Local Govt, 1987–88, for Water and Planning, 1988, DoE, to Sec. of State for Employment, 1989–92. Mem., H of C Transport Select Cttee, 1984–87; Vice-Chm., All Party Motor Industry Gp, 1985–92; Jt Sec., Cons. Tourism Cttee, 1985–87. FIMI 1986. Mem., Co. of Carmen, 2001–. *Recreation:* classic car motoring. *Address:* 241 Tessall Lane, Northfield, Birmingham B31 5EQ. *T:* (0121) 476 6649.

KING, Prof. Roger Patrick; Vice-Chancellor, University of Lincolnshire and Humberside (formerly Humberside), 1992–2000; *b* 31 May 1945; *s* of Timothy Francis King and Vera May King; *m* 1966, Susan Winifred Ashworth; one *d*. *Educ:* Wimbledon Coll.; Univ. of London (BSc Hons Econ.); Univ. of Birmingham (MSocSci). HM Civil Service, 1963; Sales Management Trainee, United Glass, 1964; Sales Manager, Marley Tiles, 1965; Lectr and Sen. Lectr in Social Scis, Manchester Polytechnic, 1970–75; Principal Lectr, later Head of Dept of Behavioural Scis, Huddersfield Poly., 1976–85; Dep. Dir, 1985–89, Dir and Chief Exec., 1989–92, Humberside Poly. Vis. Fellow, ACU, 2003–05; Vis. Prof., OU, 2003–; Res. Associate, LSE, 2007–. *Publications:* (with N. Nugent) The British Right, 1977; (with N. Nugent) Respectable Rebels, 1979; The Middle Class, 1981; Capital and Politics, 1983; The State in Modern Society, 1986; (with J. Simmie) The State in Action, 1990; (with G. Kendall) The State, Democracy and Globalization, 2004; The University in the Global Age, 2004; The Regulatory State in an Age of Governance, 2007. *Recreations:* reading, running, music. *Address:* Telham Lodge, Telham Lane, Battle, E Sussex TN33 0SN. *T:* (01424) 830056.

KING, Stephen Edwin; author; *b* Portland, Maine, 21 Sept. 1947; *s* of Donald King and Nellie Ruth King (*née* Pillsbury); *m* 1971, Tabitha Jane Spruce; two *s* one *d*. *Educ:* Lisbon Falls High Sch.; Univ. of Maine at Orono (BS 1970). Laundry worker, 1970; English Teacher, Hampden Acad., 1971–73; writer in residence, Univ. of Maine at Orono, 1978–79. *Screenplay,* Sleepwalkers, 1991; many of his stories have been filmed; writer, TV series, Kingdom Hospital, 2004; dir, Maximum Overdrive, 1986. *Publications:* Carrie, 1974; 'Salem's Lot, 1975; The Shining, 1976; The Stand, 1978; Night Shift (short stories), 1978; Firestarter, 1980; Danse Macabre, 1981; Cujo, 1981; Different Seasons, 1982; The Dark Tower: vol. 1, The Gunslinger, 1982, vol. 2, The Drawing of the Three, 1987, vol. 3, Waste Lands, 1991, vol. 4, Wizard and Glass, 1997, vol. 5, Wolves of the Calla, 2003, vol. 6, Song of Susannah, 2004, vol. 7, The Dark Tower, 2004; Christine, 1983; Pet Sematary, 1983; (jtly) The Talisman, 1984; Cycle of the Werewolf, 1985; It, 1986; Skeleton Crew (short stories), 1986; The Eyes of the Dragon, 1987; Misery, 1987; The Tommyknockers, 1987; The Dark Half, 1989; The Stand (unabridged edn), 1990; Four Past Midnight, 1990; (jtly) Dark Visions, 1990; Needful Things, 1991; Gerald's Game, 1992; Dolores Claiborne, 1992; Nightmares and Dreamscapes (short stories), 1993; Insomnia, 1994; Desperation, 1996; The Green Mile, 1996; Bag of Bones, 1998; The Girl Who Loved Tom Gordon, 1999; Hearts In Atlantis, 1999; On Writing: a memoir of the craft, 2000; Dreamcatcher, 2001; Everything's Eventual (short stories), 2002; From a Buick 8, 2002; (with Stewart O'Nan) Faithful: two diehard Boston Red Sox fans chronicle the historic 2004 season, 2004; Cell, 2006; Lisey's Story, 2006; Duma Key, 2008; (as Richard Bachman): Rage, 1977; The Long Walk, 1979; Roadwork, 1981; The Running Man, 1982; Thinner, 1984; The Regulators, 1996; Blaze, 2007. *Address:* c/o Hachette Livre UK, 338 Euston Road, NW1 3BH.

KING, Hon. Sir Timothy (Roger Alan), Kt 2007; **Hon. Mr Justice King;** a Judge of the High Court of Justice, Queen's Bench Division, since 2007; *b* 5 April 1949; *s* of late Harold Bonsall King and Dorothy King; *m* 1986, Bernadette Goodman. *Educ:* Booker Avenue County Primary Sch., Liverpool; Liverpool Inst. High Sch.; Lincoln Coll., Oxford (MA, BCL). Called to the Bar, Lincoln's Inn, 1973 (Bencher, 2000); Mem., Northern Circuit, 1973; QC 1991; a Recorder, 1991–2007. *Recreations:* travel, Association football. *Address:* Royal Courts of Justice, Strand, WC2A 2LL. *Clubs:* Athenæum (Liverpool); Liverpool Cricket.

KING, Timothy Russell; His Honour Judge King; a Circuit Judge, since 1995; *b* 4 June 1946; *s* of late Charles Albert King and Elizabeth Lily King (*née* Alexander); *m* 1st, 1973, Christine Morison (marr. diss. 1979); two *s*; 2nd, 1989, Rotraud Jane (*née* Oppermann). *Educ:* St Mary's Coll., Bitterne Park, Southampton; Inns of Court Sch. of Law. HM Diplomatic Service (Colonial Office), 1966–67; called to the Bar, Gray's Inn, 1970; in practice, SE Circuit, 1970–86; Dep. Judge Advocate, 1986; AJAG, 1990–95; Asst Recorder, 1989–93; Recorder, 1993–95. Legal Mem., Restricted Patients Panel, Mental Health Review Tribunal, 2002–. Pres., St Leonard's Soc., 1998–2006. *Recreations:* sailing, ski-ing, classical music, reading, walking, cooking, golf. *Address:* Crown Court at Snaresbrook, Hollybush Hill, E11 1QW. *T:* (020) 8530 0000. *Clubs:* Royal London Yacht, Island Sailing, Osborne Golf (Cowes).

KING, Prof. Ursula, PhD; freelance lecturer and writer; Professor Emerita of Theology and Religious Studies, and Senior Research Fellow at Institute for Advanced Studies, University of Bristol, since 2002; Professorial Research Associate, Centre for Gender and Religions Research, School of Oriental and African Studies, University of London, since 2002; *b* 22 Sept. 1938; *d* of Hedwig and Adolf Brenke; *m* 1963, Prof. Anthony Douglas King; four *d*. *Educ:* Univs of Bonn, Munich, Paris (STL), Delhi (MA; Indian Philosophical Congress Gold Medal, 1969) and London (PhD). Lectr in Divinity, Coloma Coll. of Educn, 1963–65; Visiting Lecturer, 1965–70: Dept of Philosophy, Univ. of Delhi; Indian Inst. of Technology; Indian Social Inst.; Lectr and Sen. Lectr, Dept of Theology and Religious Studies, Univ. of Leeds, 1971–89; S. A. Cook Bye-Fellow, Newnham Coll. and Gonville and Caius Coll., Cambridge, 1976–77; Bristol University: Prof. of Theology and Religious Studies, 1989–2002; Head of Dept, 1989–97; Dir, Centre for Comparative Studies in Religion and Gender, 1996–2002. Visiting Professor: in Feminist Theology, Univ. of Oslo, 1999–2001; in Ecumenical Theology and Interreligious Dialogue, Xavier Univ., Cincinnati, 1999; Dist. Bingham Prof. of Humanities, Univ. of Louisville, Ky, 2005. Lectures include: Hibbert, London, 1984; Lambeth Interfaith, Lambeth Palace, 1985; Teape, Delhi, Calcutta, Santiniketan, 1986; Bampton, 1996, Whyte, 2000, Sir Alister Hardy, 2002, Oxford; Sir George Trevelyan, London, 2002; Anne Spencer, Bristol, 2002; Julian of Norwich, Norwich, 2007; wide internat. lecturing in Europe, America, Asia, Australasia, and S Africa. Past mem. of many editorial and adv. bds of jls; consultant to numerous internat. publishers. President: British Assoc. for the Study of Religions, 1991–94; European Soc. of Women in Theological Research, 1993–95; Vice-Pres., World Congress of Faiths, 1972–; Mem., Shap Working Party on World Religions in Educn, 1975–. Fellow, Heythrop Coll., Univ. of London, 2004; Life FRSA. Hon. DD: Edinburgh, 1996; Dayton, 2003; Hon. Dr Theol Oslo, 2000. Student awards from Germany and France. *Publications:* Towards a New Mysticism, 1980; The Spirit of One Earth, 1989; Women and Spirituality, 1989; (ed) Turning Points in Religious Studies, 1990; (ed) Feminist Theology from the Third World, 1994; (ed) Religion and Gender, 1995; Spirit of Fire, 1996; Christ in All Things: exploring spirituality with Teilhard de Chardin, 1997; (ed) Pierre Teilhard de Chardin: writings selected with an introduction, 1999; (ed) Spirituality and Society in the New Millennium, 2001; Christian Mystics: their lives and legacies throughout the ages, 2001; (ed with Tina Beattie) Gender, Religion and Diversity: crosscultural approaches, 2004; contribs to acad. jls. *Recreations:* walking, reading, travelling, meeting old friends.

KING, Sir Wayne Alexander, 8th Bt *cr* 1815; Business Development Co-ordinator, The Canadian Hearing Society, Toronto; *b* 2 Feb. 1962; *s* of Sir Peter Alexander King, 7th Bt, and of Jean Margaret (who *m* 2nd, 1978, Rev. Richard Graham Mackenzie), *d* of Christopher Thomas Cavell, Deal; *S* father, 1973; *m* 1984 (marr. diss. 1990); one *s*; *m* 2003, Deborah Lynn, *d* of Douglas Arthur MacDougall, Sydney, NS. *Educ:* Sir Roger Manwood's Sch., Sandwich, Kent; Algonquin Coll., Ottawa, Ont (majored in Accounting and Retail Management). *Recreations:* all sports. *Heir:* *s* Peter Richard Donald King, *b* 4 May 1988. *Address:* 5142 Plantation Place, Mississauga, ON L5M 7H5, Canada.

KING-HAMILTON, His Honour (Myer) Alan (Barry); QC 1954; an additional Judge of the Central Criminal Court, 1964–79; a Deputy Circuit Judge, 1979–83; *b* 9 Dec. 1904; *o s* of Alfred King-Hamilton; *m* 1935, Rosalind Irene Ellis (*d* 1991); two *d*. *Educ:* York House Prep. Sch.; Bishop's Stortford Grammar Sch.; Trinity Hall, Cambridge (BA 1927, MA 1929; Hon. Fellow, 2003). President: Cambridge Univ. Law Soc., 1926–27; Cambridge Union Soc., 1927. Called to Bar, Middle Temple, 1929 (Bencher, 1961); served War of 1939–45, RAF, finishing with rank of Squadron Leader; served on Finchley Borough Council, 1938–39 and 1945–50. Recorder of Hereford, 1955–56; Recorder of Gloucester, 1956–61; Recorder of Wolverhampton, 1961–64; Dep. Chm. Oxford County Quarter Sessions, 1955–64, 1966–71; Leader of Oxford Circuit, 1961–64. Elected to General Council of Bar, 1958. Pres., West London Reform Synagogue, 1967–75, 1977–83 (Hon. Life Pres., 1995); Vice-Pres., World Congress of Faiths, 1967–. Legal Member: Med. Practices Cttee, Min. of Health, 1961–64; ABTA Appeal Bd, 1980–95; Mem., Arts and Library Cttee, MCC, 1985–89; first Chm., Pornography and Violence Res. Trust (formerly Mary Whitehouse Res. and Educn Trust), 1986–96 (Mem. Cttee, 1996–2003). President: Westlon Housing Assoc., 1995–97 (Founder Mem. and first Chm., 1975–95; Hon. Life Pres., 1998); Birnbeck Housing Assoc., 1995–98 (Founder Mem. and Mem. Cttee, 1982–95; Hon. Life Pres., 1998). Trustee, Barnet Community Trust, 1986–89. Co-founder, Refreshers CC, 1935. Freeman of City of London; Master, Needlemakers' Co., 1969. *Publication:* And Nothing But the Truth (autobiog.), 1982. *Recreations:* cricket, gardening, the theatre. *Clubs:* Royal Air Force, MCC.

KING-HELE, Desmond George, FRS 1966; author; Deputy Chief Scientific Officer, Space Department, Royal Aircraft Establishment, Farnborough, 1968–88, retired; *b* 3 Nov. 1927; *s* of late S. G. and of B. King-Hele, Seaford, Sussex; *m* 1954, Marie Thérèse Newman (separated 1992); two *d*. *Educ:* Epsom Coll.; Trinity Coll., Cambridge. BA (1st cl. hons Mathematics) 1948; MA 1952. At RAE, Farnborough, 1948–88, working on space research from 1955. Mem., International Academy of Astronautics, 1961. Chairman: Satellite Optical Tracking Cttee, Royal Soc., 1972–97; History of Science Grants Cttee, Royal Soc., 1990–93; British Nat. Cttee for History of Science, Medicine and Technol., 1985–89; Adv. Panel for Culture of Sci., Technol. and Medicine, BL, 1992–2002. Pres., Birmingham and Midland Inst., 2002. Lectures: Symons, RMetS, 1961; Duke of Edinburgh's, Royal Inst. of Navigation, 1964; Jeffreys, RAS, 1971; Halley, Oxford, 1974; Bakerian, Royal Soc., 1974; Sydenham, Soc. of Apothecaries, 1981; H. L. Welsh, Univ. of Toronto, 1982; Milne, Oxford, 1984; Wilkins, Royal Soc., 1997. FIMA; FRAS. Hon. DSc Aston, 1979; DUniv Surrey, 1986. Eddington Medal, RAS, 1971; Charles Chree Medal, Inst. of Physics, 1971; Lagrange Prize, Acad. Royale de Belgique, 1972; Nordberg Medal, Internat. Cttee on Space Res., 1990. Editor, Notes and Records of Royal Soc., 1989–96. *Publications:* Shelley: His Thought and Work, 1960, 3rd edn 1984; Satellites and Scientific Research, 1960; Erasmus Darwin, 1963; Theory of Satellite Orbits in an Atmosphere, 1964; (ed) Space Research V, 1965; Observing Earth Satellites, 1966, 2nd edn 1983; (ed) Essential Writings of Erasmus Darwin, 1968; The End of the Twentieth Century?, 1970; Poems and Trixies, 1972; Doctor of Revolution, 1977; (ed) The Letters of Erasmus Darwin, 1981; (ed) The RAE Table of Earth Satellites, 1981, 4th edn 1990; Animal Spirits, 1983; Erasmus Darwin and the Romantic Poets, 1986; Satellite Orbits in an Atmosphere: theory and applications, 1987; A Tapestry of Orbits, 1992; (ed) John Herschel, 1992; (ed) A Concordance to the Botanic Garden, 1994; Erasmus Darwin: a life of unequalled achievement (Society of Authors' Medical History Prize), 1999; Antic and Romantic (poems), 2000; (ed) Charles Darwin's The Life of Erasmus Darwin, 2002; (ed) The Collected Letters of Erasmus Darwin, 2007; *radio drama scripts:* A Mind of Universal Sympathy, 1973; The Lunaticks, 1978; 300 papers in Proc. Royal Society, Nature, Keats-Shelley Memor. Bull., New Scientist, Planetary and Space Science, and other scientific and literary jls. *Recreations:* tennis, reading, cross-country running. *Address:* 7 Hilltops Court, 65 North Lane, Buriton, Hants GU31 5RS. *T:* (01730) 261646.

KING MURRAY, Ronald; *see* Murray.

KING-REYNOLDS, Guy Edwin; Head Master, Dauntsey's School, West Lavington, 1969–85; *b* 9 July 1923; *er s* of late Dr H. E. King Reynolds, York; *m* 1st, 1947, Norma Lansdowne Russell (*d* 1949); 2nd, 1950, Jeanne Nancy Perris Rhodes; one *d*. *Educ:* St Peter's Sch., York; Emmanuel Coll., Cambridge (1944–47). LRAM (speech and drama) 1968. Served RAF, 1942–44. BA 1946, MA 1951. Asst Master, Glenhow Prep. Sch., 1947–48; Head of Geography Dept, Solihull Sch., Warwickshire, 1948–54; family business, 1954–55; Head of Geography, Portsmouth Grammar Sch., 1955–57; Solihull School: Housemaster, 1957–63, Second Master, 1963–69. Part-time Lecturer in International Affairs, Extra-Mural Dept, Birmingham Univ., 1951–55, 1957–62; Chm., Solihull WEA, 1957–62. Mem., BBC Regl Adv. Council, 1970–73. Headmasters' Conference: Mem., 1969–85; Mem. Cttee, 1977–78, Chm., SW Div., 1978; Member: Political and PR Cttee, 1971–79; Governing Council, ISIS, 1977–83; Editl Bd, Conference and Common Room, 1977–84. Mem., DES Assisted Places Cttee, 1980–93. Vice-Chm., Boarding Schs Assoc., 1975–76; Mem. Cttee, GBA, 1986–89, 1990–97. Governor: St Peter's Sch., York, 1984–97; Dean Close Sch., Cheltenham, 1985–94 (Vice Pres., 1994–99, and Life Gov., 1994); La Retraite, Salisbury, 1985–88. Mem., Bp of Salisbury's DAC, 1983–86. JP: Solihull, 1965–69; Wiltshire, 1970–91 (Chm., 1982–85, Vice-Chm., 1985–91, Devizes Bench); Avon (Bath), 1991–93. Freeman, City of London, 1988. *Recreations:* drama (director and actor); travel. *Address:* 14 Pulteney Mews, Great Pulteney Street, Bath, Avon BA2 4DS.

KING-SMITH, Ronald Gordon, (Dick); author; *b* 27 March 1922; *s* of Ronald King-Smith and Grace King-Smith; *m* 1943, Myrle England (*d* 2000); one *s* two *d*; *m* 2001, Zona Bedding. *Educ:* Marlborough; Bristol Univ. (BEd 1975). Served Grenadier Guards, 1941–46. Farmer, 1947–67; teacher, Farmborough Primary Sch., 1975–82. *Publications:* over 110 titles include: The Fox Busters, 1978; Daggie Dogfoot, 1980; The Mouse Butcher, 1982; Magnus Powermouse, 1982; The Queen's Nose, 1983; The Sheep Pig, 1984 (filmed as Babe, 1995); Harry's Mad, 1984; Saddlebottom, 1985; Noah's Brother, 1986; The Hedgehog, 1987; George Speaks, 1988; Martin's Mice, 1988; Sophie's Snail, 1988; The Toby Man, 1989; Dodos are Forever, 1989; Ace, 1990; Paddy's Pot of Gold, 1990; The Water Horse, 1990; The Cuckoo Child, 1991; Sophie's Tom, 1991; Sophie Hits Six, 1991; The Guard Dog, 1991; Find the White Horse, 1991; Lady Daisy, 1992; Pretty Polly, 1992; Dragon Boy, 1993; The Merrythought, 1993; Sophie in the Saddle, 1993; The Schoolmouse, 1994; Harriet's Hare, 1994; Sophie is Seven, 1994; Bobby the Bad, 1994; King Max the Last, 1995; Sophie's Lucky, 1995; The Terrible Trins, 1995; Clever Duck, 1996; Godhanger, 1996; Dick King-Smith's Animal Friends, 1996; Treasure Trove, 1997; Puppy Love, 1997; What Sadie Saw, 1997; The Stray, 1997; The Merman, 1998; How Green Was My Mouse, 1998; A Mouse Called Wolf, 1998; The Crowstarver, 1998; Mr Ape, 1998; Poppet, 1999; The Magic Carpet Slippers, 2000; The Roundhill, 2000; Funny Frank, 2001; Chewing the Cud (autobiog.), 2001. *Recreations:* reading, enjoying the countryside, washing-up.

KING-TENISON, family name of **Earl of Kingston**.

KINGARTH, Rt Hon. Lord; Hon. Derek Robert Alexander Emslie; PC 2006; a Senator of the College of Justice in Scotland, since 1997; *b* 21 June 1949; *s* of Baron Emslie, PC, MBE; *m* 1974, Elizabeth Jane Cameron Carstairs, *d* of Andrew McLaren Carstairs; one *s* two *d*. *Educ:* Edinburgh Acad.; Trinity Coll., Glenalmond; Gonville and Caius Coll., Cambridge (Hist. Schol.; BA); Edinburgh Univ. (LLB). Advocate 1974; Standing Jun. Counsel, DHSS, 1979–87; Advocate Depute, 1985–88; QC (Scot.) 1987; part time Chairman: Pension Appeal Tribunal (Scotland), 1988–95; Medical Appeal Tribunal (Scotland), 1990–95. Vice-Dean, Faculty of Advocates, 1995–97. *Recreations:* golf, cinema, football. *Address:* 35 Ann Street, Edinburgh EH4 1PL. *T:* (0131) 332 6648.
See also Hon. Lord Emslie.

KINGDON, Roger Taylor, CBE 1990; FIMechE, FIMMM; Chief Executive, Davy Corporation, 1987–90; *b* 27 June 1930; *s* of late Fletcher Munroe Kingdon and Laetitia May Kingdon (*née* Wissler); *m* 1956, Gaynor Mary Downs; two *s* one *d*. *Educ:* Christ's Hospital; Pembroke College, Cambridge (MA). CEng. Graduate trainee, Woodall Duckham Construction Co., 1954–58; Ashmore Benson Pease & Co., 1958–68 (Dir, 1964–68); Managing Director: Newell Dunford Group, 1968–80; Herbert Morris (Davy Group), 1980–83; Chm., Davy McKee (Stockton), 1983–87; Director: Dunford & Elliot, 1971–80; Peugeot Talbot Motor Co., 1979–92; Davy Corp., 1986–90; Teesside Develt Corp., 1987–98; Carbo plc (formerly Hopkinson Group), 1992–2002. President: Process Plant Assoc., 1979–80; NE Engineering Employers' Assoc., 1986–89; Chairman: British Metallurgical Plant Constructors' Assoc., 1985–87; Latin American Trade Adv. Group, 1989–90. Vice Chm., South Tees Acute NHS Trust, 1992–95. Mem. Council, Durham Univ., 1995–2000. CCMI. *Recreations:* fell walking, sailing. *Address:* Borrowby Hill, The Green, Borrowby, Thirsk, North Yorks Y07 4QL. *T:* (01845) 537663. *Club:* Army and Navy.

KINGHAM, Teresa Jane, (Tess); Consultant, Coe and Kingham; *b* 4 May 1963; *d* of Roy Thomas Kingham and Patricia Ribian Kingham (*née* Murphy); *m* 1991, Mark Luetchford; one *s* two *d* (of whom one *s* one *d* are twins). *Educ:* Dartford Girls' Grammar Sch.; Royal Holloway Coll., Univ. of London (BA Hons German 1984); Univ. of East Anglia (PGCE Mod. Langs 1985). Appeals Dir, War on Want, 1986–90; Mktg and Communications Dir, Blue Cross (animal welfare), 1990–92; Editor, Youth Express, Daily Express, 1992–94; Communications Exec., Oxfam, 1994–96. Contested (Lab) Cotswolds, EP elecn, 1994. MP (Lab) Gloucester, 1997–2001. Chair, All Party Gp on Western Sahara, 1997–2001. Mem., Egypt Exploration Soc. *Publication:* (with Jim Coe) The Good Campaigns Guide, 2nd edn 2005. *Recreations:* international travel/affairs, archaeology, walking with family.

KINGHAN, Neil, CB 2005; consultant to Essex County Council, since 2007; Adviser to Dignity Management Consultancy; Chairman, Policy Commission on Primary School Organisation in Shropshire, 2008–09; *b* 20 Aug. 1951; *s* of late Derek Kinghan and of Esme Kinghan; *m* 1994, Dr Lilian Pusavat. *Educ:* Hertford Coll., Oxford (MA, MPhil). Department of the Environment: admin trainee, 1975; Private Sec. to Parly Under-Sec. of State, 1978–80; Principal, 1980; Private Sec. to Minister of State, 1984–87; Asst Sec., 1987; Head: Sport and Recreation Div., 1987–89; Homelessness Policy Div., 1989–92; Director: Housing Policy, 1992–94; DoE Mgt Review, 1994–96; Local Govt Finance, 1996–97; Local Government Association: Dir, Local Govt Finance, 1997–2002; Econ and Envmtl Policy, 2002–03; Dir Gen., Local and Regl Govt, then Local Govt and Fire, ODPM, subseq. Local and Regl Governance, then Fire and Resilience, DCLG, 2003–07. *Recreations:* ski-ing, cricket, watching ballet, trying to run a marathon in less than five hours. *Address:* *e-mail:* neil.kinghan@btinternet.com. *Club:* Surrey County Cricket.

KINGHORN, Prof. George Robert, MD; FRCP, FRCPGlas; Consultant Physician in Genitourinary Medicine, Sheffield, since 1979; Clinical Director for Communicable Diseases, Sheffield Teaching Hospitals NHS Foundation Trust, since 1991; *b* 17 Aug. 1949; *s* of Alan Douglas Kinghorn and Lilian Isabel Kinghorn; *m* 1973, Sheila Anne Littlewood; one *s* one *d*. *Educ:* Newburn Manor Sch.; Royal Grammar Sch., Newcastle upon Tyne; Univ. of Sheffield (MB ChB; MD 1972). FRCP 1988; FRCPGlas 2003. Sen. Registrar, Royal Infirmary, Sheffield, 1976–79; Cons. Physician in Genitourinary Medicine, Leeds Gen. Infirmary, 1979. Mem., Ind. Adv. Gp on Sexual Health and HIV, 2003–. Mem., MRC Coll. of Experts. Pres., Med. Soc. for Study of Venereal Diseases, 1991–2001; Mem., BASHH (formerly Med. Soc. for Study of Venereal Diseases), 1976– (Trustee, 2001–05); Trustee, Med. Foundn for Aids and Sexual Health, 2003–. FRSocMed 1998. Freeman, Soc. of Apothecaries, 2007. *Publications:* scientific papers and book chapters on genital tract infections, sexual health and HIV. *Recreations:* gardening, golf, travel. *Address:* 3 Serlby Drive, Harthill, Sheffield, S Yorks S26 7UJ. *T:* (01909) 772610; *e-mail:* george.kinghorn@sth.nhs.uk, g.r.kinghorn@virgin.net.
See also M. A. Kinghorn.

KINGHORN, Myra Anne; Chair, Scheme Management Committee, European Payments Council, since 2007; *b* 24 Jan. 1951; *d* of Alan Douglas Kinghorn and Lilian Isabel Kinghorn; *m* 1986, Richard John Haycocks; two *s*. *Educ:* La Sagesse High Sch., Newcastle upon Tyne; Univ. of Wales, Aberystwyth (BLib Jt Hons (Hist. and Librarianship) 1973). FCA (ACA 1977); CDir 2000. Exec. Manager, Ernst & Young, 1984–88; Chief Exec. and Company Sec., Investors Compensation Scheme, 1988–2001; non-exec. Dir, Serious Fraud Office, 2001–04; Chief Exec., Pension Protection Fund, 2004–06. Non-exec. Mem., OPRA, 2003–04. Mem., Architects Registration Council, 2008–. Gov., Morley Coll., 2007–. *Recreations:* theatre visits, music, photography, French, cooking. *Address:* 10 Courtenay Drive, Beckenham, Kent BR3 6YE. *Club:* Institute of Directors.
See also G. R. Kinghorn.

KINGHORN, William Oliver; Chief Agricultural Officer, Department of Agriculture and Fisheries for Scotland, 1971–75; *b* 17 May 1913; *s* of Thomas Kinghorn, Duns, and Elizabeth Oliver; *m* 1943, Edith Johnstone; one *s* two *d*. *Educ:* Berwickshire High Sch.; Edinburgh Univ. BSc (Agr) Hons, BSc Hons. Senior Inspector, 1946; Technical Develt Officer, 1959; Chief Inspector, 1970. SBStJ. *Publication:* contrib. Annals of Applied Biology, 1936. *Address:* Strachan House, 93 Craigcrook Road, Edinburgh EH4 3PE. *T:* (0131) 336 0050.

KINGMAN, Sir John (Frank Charles), Kt 1985; FRS 1971; mathematician; Vice-Chancellor, University of Bristol, 1985–2001; *b* 28 Aug. 1939; *er s* of late Dr F. E. T. Kingman, FRSC and Maud (*née* Harley); *m* 1964, Valerie Cromwell, FSA, FRHistS (Dir, History of Parlt, 1991–2001; High Sheriff of Bristol, 2004–05), *d* of late F. Cromwell,

OBE, ISO; one *s* one *d*. *Educ:* Christ's Coll., Finchley; Pembroke Coll., Cambridge (MA, ScD; Smith's Prize, 1962; Hon. Fellow, 1988). CStat 1993. Fellow of Pembroke Coll., 1961–65, and Asst Lectr in Mathematics, 1962–64, Lectr, 1964–65, Univ. of Cambridge; Reader in Maths and Stats, 1965–66, Prof. 1966–69, Univ. of Sussex; Prof. of Maths, Univ. of Oxford, 1969–85; Fellow, St Anne's Coll., Oxford, 1978–85, Hon. Fellow, 1985; N. M. Rothschild & Sons Prof. of Mathematical Scis, Dir of Isaac Newton Inst. for Mathematical Scis, and Fellow of Pembroke Coll., Univ. of Cambridge, 2001–06. Visiting appointments: Univ. of Western Australia, 1963, 1974; Stanford Univ., USA, 1968; ANU, 1978. Chairman: Science Bd, SRC, 1979–81; SERC, 1981–85; founding Chm., Statistics Commn, 2000–03; Vice-Pres., Parly and Scientific Cttee, 1986–89, 2002–05 (Vice-Chm., 1983–86); Mem. Bd, British Council, 1986–91. Chm., Cttee of Inquiry into the Teaching of English Language, 1987–88. Director: IBM UK Holdings Ltd, 1985–95; Beecham Group plc, 1986–89; SmithKline Beecham plc, 1989–90; British Technology Group plc, 1992 (Mem. Council, British Technol. Gp, 1984–92); SW RHA, 1990–94; Avon HA, 1996–99. Chm., 1973–76, Vice-Pres., 1976–92, Inst. of Statisticians; President: Royal Statistical Soc., 1987–89 (Vice-Pres., 1977–79; Guy Medal in Silver, 1981; Hon. Fellow, 1993); London Math. Soc., 1990–92; European Math. Soc., 2003–06. Mem., Brighton Co. Borough Council, 1968–71; Chm., Regency Soc. of Brighton and Hove, 1975–81. MAE 1995; AcSS 2000. For. Associate, US Nat. Acad. of Scis, 2007. Hon. Senator, Univ. of Hannover, 1991. Hon. DSc: Sussex, 1983; Southampton, 1985; West of England, 1993; Brunel, 2004; Hon. LLD: Bristol, 1989; Queen's Univ., Kingston, Ontario, 1999; Hon. DPhil Cheltenham and Gloucester, 1998; Dr *hc* St Petersburg Univ. of Humanities and Social Scis, 1994. Royal Medal, Royal Soc., 1983. Officier des Palmes Académiques, 1989. *Publications:* Introduction to Measure and Probability (with S. J. Taylor), 1966; The Algebra of Queues, 1966; Regenerative Phenomena, 1972; Mathematics of Genetic Diversity, 1980; Poisson Processes, 1993; papers in mathematical and statistical jls. *Address:* Harley Lodge, Clifton Down, Bristol BS8 3BP. *Clubs:* Lansdowne; Clifton (Bristol).

See also J. O. F. Kingman.

KINGMAN, John Oliver Frank; Managing Director, Public Services and Growth, since 2006, Second Permanent Secretary, since 2007, HM Treasury; *b* 24 April 1969; *s* of Sir John Frank Charles Kingman, *qv*. *Educ:* Dragon Sch., Oxford; Westminster Sch. (Queen's Schol.); St John's Coll., Oxford (Casberd Schol.; BA 1st Cl. Hons). HM Treasury, 1991–94, Private Sec. to Financial Sec., 1993–94; Prin. Private Sec. to Sec. of State, DNH, 1994–95; Lex Columnist, FT, 1995–97; Gp Chief Exec.'s Office, BP, 1997–98; Press Sec. to Chancellor of the Exchequer, 1999–2000; Hd, Productivity and Structural Reform, 2000–02, Dir, Enterprise and Growth Unit, 2003–06, Man. Dir, Finance and Industry, 2006, HM Treasury. Dir, EIB, 2003–06; non-exec. Dir, Framestore CFC Ltd, 2004–06. Vis. Fellow, Inst. of Political and Econ. Governance, Univ. of Manchester, 2003–06; World Fellow, Yale Univ., 2004. Mem., Develt Trust Bd, St Martin-in-the-Fields, 2006–. *Address:* HM Treasury, 1 Horse Guards Road, SW1A 2HQ. *T:* (020) 7270 6325, *Fax:* (020) 7451 7559; *e-mail:* john.kingman@hm-treasury.gsi.gov.uk.

KINGSALE, 36th Baron *cr* 1223 (by some reckonings 31st Baron); **Nevinson Mark de Courcy;** Baron Courcy and Baron of Ringrone; Premier Baron of Ireland; *b* 11 May 1958; *s* of late Nevinson Russell de Courcy, and Nora Lydia de Courcy (*née* Plint); *S* cousin, 2005. *Educ:* Auckland Grammar Sch.; Univ. of Auckland; Emmanuel Coll., Cambridge. *Recreations:* reading, conservation, jigsaws. *Address:* 22 Armadale Road, Remuera, Auckland 1050, New Zealand. *T:* (9) 5248875; *e-mail:* nmdecourcy@clear.net.nz.

KINGSBOROUGH, Viscount; Charles Avery Edward King-Tenison; *b* 18 Nov. 2000; *s* and *heir* of Earl of Kingston, *qv*.

KINGSBURY, Derek John, CBE 1988; FREng, FIET; Chairman: Fairey Group plc, 1987–96 (Group Chief Executive, 1982–91); David Brown Group plc, 1992–96; Goode Durrant plc, 1992–96; *b* 10 July 1926; *s* of late Major Arthur Kingsbury, BEM, Virginia Water and Gwendoline Mary Kingsbury; *m* 1st, 1959, Muriel June Drake; one *s* (and one *s* decd); 2nd, 1980, Sarah Muriel Morgan (*d* 2006); one *s*; 3rd, 2007, Wendy Christine Jacobs. *Educ:* Strode's Secondary Sch., City and Guilds Coll. BScEng Hons; DIC. FIET (FIEE 1968); FCGI 1977; FREng (FEng 1991). 2nd Lieut, REME, 1947–49. Apprentice, Metropolitan Vickers, 1949–51; Exch. Schol., Univ. of Pennsylvania, 1952–53; Associated Electrical Industries: Manager, E Canada, 1954–61; PA to Chm., 1961–63; Gen. Manager, AEI Distribution Transformers, 1963–66; Gen. Manager, Overseas Manufacturing Develt, 1966–69; Thorn Electrical Industries: Man. Dir, Foster Transformers, 1969–76; Man. Dir, Elect. & Hydr. Div., 1972–76, Exec. Dir, 1973–76; Dowty Group: Dep. Chief Exec., 1976–82. Chm., Ultra Electronics, 1977–82; non-executive Director: Vickers, 1981–91; ACAL plc, 1991–94. Institution of Electrical Engineers: Dir Peter Peregrinus, 1976–81; Mem., Finance Cttee, 1978–80; Confederation of British Industry: Mem. Council, 1980–86; Chm., Overseas Cttee, 1980–84; missions to Japan 1981, 1983, 1985; Defence Manufacturers Association: Mem. Council, 1985–92; Chm., 1987–90; Chm., F and GP Cttee, 1990–92; Vice-Pres., 1993–2002. Member: Review Bd for Govt Contracts, 1986–94; Engineering Council, 1990–93 (Chm., CET Pilot Scheme Steering Cttee, 1988–90); Council, BEAMA, 1973–75. Freeman, City of London, 1994; Liveryman, Scientific Instrument Makers' Co., 1994. CCMI; FRSA 1994. President: BHF Horse Show, 1977–98; Aircraft Golfing Soc., 1995–. *Recreations:* golf, swimming, walking. *Address:* Trecaven, Rock, Cornwall PL27 6LB. *T:* (01208) 863608. *Clubs:* Royal Automobile, MCC, Lord's Taverners; Beaconsfield Golf, Isle of Harris Golf, St Enodoc Golf (Vice-Captain, 1997–99; Captain, 1999–2001); Rock Sailing.

KINGSBURY, Sally Jane; *see* O'Neill, S. J.

KINGSDOWN, Baron *cr* 1993 (Life Peer), of Pemberton in the County of Lancashire; **Robert Leigh-Pemberton, (Robin),** KG 1994; PC 1987; Governor, Bank of England, 1983–93; Lord-Lieutenant of Kent, 1982–2002 (Vice Lord-Lieutenant, 1972–82); *b* 5 Jan. 1927; *e s* of late Robert Douglas Leigh-Pemberton, MBE, MC, Sittingbourne, Kent; *m* 1953, Rosemary Davina, OBE, *d* of late Lt-Col D. W. A. W. Forbes, MC, and late Dowager Marchioness of Exeter; four *s* (and one *s* decd). *Educ:* St Peter's Court, Broadstairs; Eton; Trinity Coll., Oxford (MA; Hon. Fellow, 1984). Grenadier Guards, 1945–48. Called to Bar, Inner Temple, 1954 (Hon. Bencher, 1983); practised in London and SE Circuit until 1960. National Westminster Bank: Dir, 1972–83; Dep. Chm., 1974; Chm., 1977–83. Director: Birmid Qualcast, 1966–83 (Dep. Chm., 1970; Chm., 1975–77); University Life Assce Soc., 1967–78; Redland Ltd, 1972–83, 1993–98; Equitable Life Assce Soc., 1979–83 (Vice-Pres., 1982–83); Glaxo-Wellcome (formerly Glaxo Holdings), 1993–96; Foreign and Colonial Investment Trust, 1993–98; Hambros, 1993–98. County Councillor (Chm. Council, 1972–75), 1961–77, CA 1965, Kent. Member: SE Econ. Planning Council, 1972–74; Medway Ports Authority, 1974–76; NEDC, 1982–92; Prime Minister's Cttee on Local Govt Rules of Conduct, 1973–74; Cttee of Enquiry into Teachers' Pay, 1974; Cttee on Police Pay, 1977–79. Chm., Cttee of London Clearing Bankers, 1982–83. Trustee: Glyndebourne Arts Trust, 1978–83; RA Trust, 1982–88 (Hon. Trustee Emeritus, 1988–). Pro-Chancellor, Univ. of Kent at Canterbury, 1977–83; Seneschal, Canterbury Cathedral, 1983–. Hon. Colonel: Kent and Sharpshooters Yeomanry Sqn, 1979–92; 265 (Kent and Co. of London Yeo.) Signal Sqn (V), 1979–92; 5th (Volunteer) Bn, The Queen's Regt, 1987–92. Gov., Ditchley Foundn, 1987–2002. Hon. DCL Kent, 1983; Hon. DLitt: City, 1988; Loughborough, 1990. FRSA 1977; FCMI (FBIM 1977). JP 1961–75, DL 1970, Kent. KStJ 1983. *Recreation:* country life. *Address:* Torry Hill, Sittingbourne, Kent ME9 0SP. *Clubs:* Brooks's, Cavalry and Guards.

KINGSHOTT, (Albert) Leonard; Director: International Banking Division, Lloyds Bank Plc, 1985–89; Mutual Management Services, since 1993; Member, Monopolies and Mergers Commission, 1990–96; *b* 16 Sept. 1930; *s* of A. L. Kingshott and Mrs K. Kingshott; *m* 1958, Valerie Simpson; two *s* one *d*. *Educ:* London Sch. of Economics (BSc); ACIS 1958, FCIS 1983. Flying Officer, RAF, 1952–55; Economist, British Petroleum, 1955–60; Economist, British Nylon Spinners, 1960–62; Financial Manager, Iraq Petroleum Co., 1963–65; Chief Economist, Ford of Britain, 1965; Treas., Ford of Britain, 1966–67; Treas., Ford of Europe, 1968–70; Finance Dir, Whitbread & Co., 1972; Man. Dir, Finance, BSC, 1972–77; Dir, Lloyds Bank International, responsible for Merchant Banking activities, 1977–80, for European Div., 1980–82, for Marketing and Planning Div., 1983–84; Dep. Chief Exec., Lloyds Bank International, 1985. Exec. Dir, The Private Bank & Trust Co., 1989–91; Director: Bank of London and South America Ltd, 1977–89; Lloyds Bank International, 1977–89; Lloyds Bank (France) Ltd, 1980–89; Lloyd's Bank California, 1985–88; Rosehaugh plc, 1991–92 (Chm.); Shandwick plc, 1993–2000; Newmarket Foods Ltd, 1994–97; Man. Dir, Cypher Science Ltd, 1996–. Mem. Bd, Crown Agents for Oversea Govts and Admin, and Crown Agents Hldg and Realisation Bd, 1989–92. Associate Mem. of Faculty, 1978, Governor, 1980–91, Ashridge Management Coll. Chm., Oakbridge Counselling, 1990–. FCIS. *Publication:* Investment Appraisal, 1967. *Recreations:* golf, chess. *Address:* 4 Delamas, Beggar Hill, Fryerning, Ingatestone, Essex CM4 0PW. *T:* (01277) 352077.

KINGSHOTT, Air Vice-Marshal Kenneth, CBE 1972; DFC 1953; Royal Air Force, retired 1980; *b* 8 July 1924; *s* of Walter James Kingshott and Eliza Ann Kingshott; *m* 1st, 1948, Dorrie Marie (*née* Dent) (*d* 1978); two *s*; 2nd, 1990, Valerie Rosemary Brigden. Joined RAF, 1943; served: Singapore and Korea, 1950; Aden, 1960; Malta, 1965; MoD, London, 1968; OC RAF Cottesmore, 1971; HQ 2 Allied Tactical Air Force, 1973; HQ Strike Command, 1975; Dep. Chief of Staff Operations and Intelligence, HQ Allied Air Forces Central Europe, 1977–79. *Recreations:* golf, fishing, music. *Club:* Royal Air Force.

KINGSHOTT, Leonard; *see* Kingshott, A. L.

KINGSLAND, Baron *cr* 1994 (Life Peer), of Shrewsbury in the County of Shropshire; **Christopher James Prout,** Kt 1990; TD 1987; PC 1994; QC 1988; DL; barrister-at-law; a Recorder, since 2000; a Deputy High Court Judge, since 2005; *b* 1 Jan. 1942; *s* of late Frank Yabsley Prout, MC and bar, and Doris Lucy Prout (*née* Osborne). *Educ:* Sevenoaks Sch.; Manchester Univ. (BA); The Queen's Coll., Oxford (Scholar; BPhil, DPhil; Hon. Fellow 2006). TA Officer (Major): OU OTC, 1966–74; 16/5 The Queen's Royal Lancers, 1974–82; 3rd Armoured Div., 1982–88; RARO, 1988–97. Called to the Bar, Middle Temple, 1972 (Bencher, 1996; Master of the Garden, 1999–); an Asst Recorder, Wales and Chester Circuit, 1997–99. English-Speaking Union Fellow, Columbia Univ., NYC, 1963–64; Staff Mem., IBRD (UN), Washington DC, 1966–69; Leverhulme Fellow and Lectr in Law, Sussex Univ., 1969–79. MEP (C) Shropshire and Stafford, 1979–94; contested (C) Herefordshire and Shropshire, Eur. parly elecns, 1994. Leader, British Cons. MEPs, 1987–94; Dep. Whip, 1979–82, Chief Whip, 1983–87, Chairman and Leader, 1987–92, EDG; Vice Chm., Eur. People's Party Parly Gp, 1992–94; Chm., Parlt Cttee on Legal Affairs, 1987. Rapporteur, Revision of Europ. Parlt's Rules of Procedure, 1987 and 1993. Shadow Lord Chancellor, 1997–. Chm. Sub-Cttee F, H of L Select Cttee on EC, 1996–97. Chm., Jersey Competition Regulatory Authy, 2004–. Vice Chm., Justice, 2006–. Chm., Plymouth Marine Lab., 2002–. Pres., Shropshire and W Midlands Agricl Soc., 1993. Master, Shrewsbury Drapers' Co., 1995. DL Shropshire, 1997. Grande Médaille de la Ville de Paris, 1988; Schuman Medal, EPP, 1995. *Publications:* Market Socialism in Yugoslavia, 1985; (contrib.) vols 8, 51 and 52, Halsbury's Laws of England, 4th edn; various lectures, pamphlets, chapters and articles. *Recreations:* boating, gardening, musical comedy, the turf. *Address:* c/o House of Lords, SW1A 0PW. *Clubs:* White's, Pratt's, Beefsteak, Buck's (Hon. Mem.), Royal Ocean Racing; Royal Yacht Squadron.

KINGSLAND, Sir Richard, Kt 1978; AO 1989; CBE 1967; DFC 1940; idc; psa; President, Barnardos Canberra, 1995–2003; *b* Moree, NSW, 19 Oct. 1916; *m* 1943, Kathleen Jewel, *d* of late R. B. Adams; one *s* two *d*. Served War: No 10 Sqdn, Eng., 1939–41; commanded: No 11 Sqdn, New Guinea, 1941–42; RAAF Stn, Rathmines, NSW, 1942–43; Gp Captain 1943; Dir, Intell., RAAF, 1944–45. Dir, Org. RAAF HQ, 1946–48; Manager, Sydney Airport, 1948–49; Airline Pilot, 1949–50; SA Reg. 1950–51, NT Reg. 1951–52, Dept of Civil Aviation; Chief Admin. Asst to CAS, RAAF, 1952–53; IDC 1955; Asst Sec., Dept of Air, Melb., 1954–58; First Asst Sec., Dept of Defence, 1958–63; Secretary: Dept of Interior, 1963–70; Dept of Repatriation, 1970–74; Repatriation and Compensation, 1974–76; Dept of Veterans' Affairs, Canberra, 1976–81. Chairman: Repatriation Commn, 1970–81; ACT Arts Develt Bd (first Chm.), 1981–83; Commonwealth Films Bd of Review, 1982–86; Uranium Adv. Council, 1982–84. Member-at-Large, Nat. Heart Foundn, 1990– (Hon. Nat. Sec., 1976–90); Chm., ACT Health Promotion Fund, 1990–94; a Dir, Sir Edward Dunlop Med. Res. Foundn, 1995–. A Dir, Arts Council of Aust., 1970–72; first Chairman Council: Canberra Sch. of Music, 1970–74; Canberra Sch. of Art, 1976–83; Mem. Original Council, Australian Conservation Foundn, 1967–69; Member: Canberra Theatre Trust, 1965–75; Aust. Opera Nat. Council, 1983–96; Canberra Festival Cttee, 1988–92; Mem. Bd of Trustees, Aust. War Meml, Canberra, 1966–76; Mem. Council, E. V. Llewellyn Meml Trust, 1982–; a Dir, Aust. Bicentennial Authority, 1983–89. Pres., Bd of Management, Goodwin Retirement Villages, 1984–88; Vice Pres., Australia Day in the Nat. Capital Cttee, 1987–91. Life Governor: Sir Moses Montefiore Homes, NSW, 1975; Nat. Gall. of Aust., 1982. *Address:* 36 Vasey Crescent, Campbell, ACT 2612, Australia. *Clubs:* Commonwealth, National Press (Canberra).

KINGSLEY, Sir Ben, Kt 2002; actor; *b* 31 Dec. 1943; *s* of Rahimtulla Harji Bhanji and Anna Leina Mary Bhanji; surname changed to Kingsley by Deed Poll, 1982; *m* 2003, Alexandra Christmann; *m* 2007, Daniela Barbosa de Carneiro; three *s* one *d* from former marriages. *Educ:* Manchester Grammar Sch. Associate artist, Royal Shakespeare Co.; work with RSC includes, 1970–80; 1985–86: Peter Brook's Midsummer Night's Dream, Stratford, London, Broadway, NY; Gramsci in Occupations; Ariel in The Tempest; title role, Hamlet; Ford in Merry Wives of Windsor; title role, Baal; Squeers and Mr Wagstaff in Nicholas Nickleby; title rôle, Othello, Melons; National Theatre, 1977–78: Mosca in Volponë; Trofimov in The Cherry Orchard; Sparkish in The Country Wife; Vukhov in Judgement; additional theatre work includes: Johnny in Hello and Goodbye (Fugard), King's Head, 1973; Errol Philander in Statements After An Arrest (Fugard), Royal Court, 1974; Edmund Kean, Harrogate, 1981, Haymarket, 1983 (also televised); title role, Dr

Faustus, Manchester Royal Exchange, 1981; Waiting for Godot, Old Vic, 1997; *television* 1974–, includes The Love School (series), 1974, Silas Marner (film), 1985, Murderers Amongst Us (mini-series), 1989, Anne Frank - the full story (Best Actor award, Screen Actors' Guild), 2001, and several plays; *films:* title role, Gandhi, 1980 (2 Hollywood Golden Globe awards, 1982; NY Film Critics' Award, 2 BAFTA awards, Oscar, LA Film Critics Award, 1983, Variety Club of GB Best Film Actor award, 1983); Betrayal, 1982; Turtle Diary, 1985; Harem, 1986; Testimony, Maurice, 1987; Pascali's Island, The Train, 1988; Without a Clue, 1989; Bugsy, Sneakers, Dave, 1992; Schindler's List, 1993; Innocent Moves, 1994; Death and the Maiden, Species, 1995; Twelfth Night, 1996; Photographing Fairies, 1997; The Assignment, Weapons of Mass Distraction, Sweeney Todd, Alice in Wonderland, Crime and Punishment, Spookey House, 1998; The Confession, Rules of Engagement, What Planet are you from?, 1999; Sexy Beast, 2001; Tuck Everlasting, 2002; Suspect Zero, Sound of Thunder, House of Sand and Fog, 2003; Thunderbirds, Triumph of Love, 2004; Oliver Twist, 2005; Lucky Number Slevin, 2006; You Kill Me, 2007; Elegy, The Wackness, 2008. Best Film Actor, London Standard Award, 1983; Best Actor: European Film Acad., 2001; British Ind. Film Award, 2001; Screen Actors Guild, 2002; Broadcast Critics Award, 2002. Medici Soc. Award, 1989; Simon Wiesenthal Humanitarian Award, 1989; Berlin Golden Camera Award, 1990. Hon. MA Salford, 1984. Padma Shri (India), 1984. *Address:* c/o Independent Talent Group Ltd, Oxford House, 76 Oxford Street, W1D 1BS.

KINGSLEY, David John, OBE 2006; consultant in management, marketing and communications, since 1975; Chairman, Kingsley and Kingsley, since 1974; Director, Francis Kyle Gallery Ltd, since 1978; *b* 10 July 1929; *s* of Walter John Kingsley and Margery Kingsley; *m* 1st, 1954, Enid Sophia Jones; two *d*; 2nd, 1968, Gillian Leech; two *s*; 3rd, 1988, Gisela Reichardt. *Educ:* Southend High Sch.; London School of Economics (BScEcon; Hon. Fellow, 1992). Pres., Students' Union, LSE, 1952; Vice-Pres., Nat. Union of Students, 1953. Served RAF, Personnel Selection, commnd 1948. Prospective Parly Candidate (Lab) E Grinstead, 1952–54; founded Kingsley, Manton and Palmer, advertising agency, 1964; Publicity Advisor to Labour Party and Govt, 1962–70; Publicity and Election advisor to President of Republic of Zambia, 1974–82; Election and Broadcasting advisor to Govt of Mauritius, 1976–81; Publicity advisor to SDP, 1981–87. Mem. Boards, CNAA, 1970–82; Mem., Central Religious Adv. Cttee for BBC and IBA, 1974–82; Governor, LSE, 1965–2005 (Gov. Emeritus, 2006). Chair, Worldaware, 1992–96; Dir, At-Bristol (formerly Bristol 2000), 1993–2002; Chairman: Children 2000, 1994–; Abracadabra Children's Radio for London, 2000–05; Children's Discovery Centre, 2003–06; Dir, Fun Radio UK (formerly Children's Radio UK), 2005–. Chairman: Inter-Action Trust, 1981–90; Design and Industries Assoc., 1994–96. Trustee, Royal Philharmonic Orch., 1993–99 (Vice-Chm., 1972–77); Dir, Wren Orch., 1990–98; Mem., Develt Cttee, RCM, 1985–2000. Vice-Pres., Schumacher Soc., 1999–2004 (Trustee, 1980–); Vice-Chm., Media Soc., 2001–04. Hon. Pres., LSE Envmtl Network, 2000–; Founder Chm., 2005–07, Chair Emeritus, 2008, LSE Alumni Assoc. Chairman: Cartoon Arts Trust, 1994–2001; Creative Summit, 1999; Member: Bd, Mediawise, 2003–06; Adv. Bd, Inst. for Global Ethics, 2003–; Advr, Greenhouse Project, 2003–06. FIPA; FRSA; MCSD. Hon. RCM. Hon. Fellow, Soka Univ., Tokyo, 1990. *Publications:* Albion in China, 1979; How World War II Was Won on the Playing Fields of LSE, 2003; contribs to learned jls; various articles. *Recreations:* politics, creating happy national events, music, travel, art and books. *Address:* 81 Mortimer Road, N1 5AR. *Club:* Reform.

KINGSLEY, Joy, (Mrs Michael Blackburn); Senior Partner, Pannone LLP, since 2008; *b* Manchester, 16 Jan. 1956; *d* of late Roger James Kingsley, OBE and of Valerie Marguerite Mary Kingsley (*née* Hanna); *m* 1991, Michael Blackburn; two *s*. *Educ:* Manchester High Sch.; Nottingham Univ. (LLB). Admitted Solicitor, 1980; with Pannone LLP (formerly: Goldberg Blackburn, Goldberg Blackburn and Howards, Pannone and Partners, Pannone Marsh Pearson, Pannone Pritchard Englefield, Pannone and Partners), 1978–: Partner, 1983; Hd, Private Client Dept, 1989–95; Man. Partner, 1993–2008. Gov., Manchester GS, 1999–. *Recreations:* travel, reading, ski-ing, cinema and theatre, music. *Address:* Pannone LLP, 123 Deansgate, Manchester M3 2BU. *T:* (home) (0161) 941 1258, 07788 970020; *e-mail:* joy.kingsley@pannone.co.uk.

KINGSLEY, Nicholas William, FSA; Head, National Advisory Services, and Secretary, Historical Manuscripts Commission, National Archives, since 2005; *b* 14 Sept. 1957; *s* of Philip Francis Kingsley and Joan Rosamond Kingsley (*née* Holliday); *m* 1980, (Susan) Mary Summerhayes. *Educ:* St Paul's Sch., London; Keble Coll., Oxford (BA 1978, MA 1982). Archive trainee, Bodleian Liby, Oxford, 1978–79; Asst Archivist, 1979–82, Modern Records Archivist, 1982–89, Glos Record Office; City Archivist, Birmingham City Archives, 1989–96; Central Liby Manager, Birmingham Central Liby, 1996–2000; Co. and Diocesan Archivist, Glos Record Office, 2000–05. Member: Nat. Council on Archives, 1991– (Sec., 1993–99; Vice-Chm., 2000–01; Chm., 2001–05); Govt Archives Taskforce, 2002–04; MLA, 2004–06. Dir and Trustee, Media Archive of Central England, 1994–2004; Chairman: Nat. Cttee, Victoria County History, 2005–; EU Document Lifecycle Mgt Forum, 2006. Gen. Ed., Phillimore & Co. English Country Houses series, 1994–2004. FSA 2003. Hon. DLitt Birmingham, 2006. *Publications:* Handlist of the Contents of the Gloucestershire Record Office, 1988, 4th edn 1998, Supplement, 2002; The Country Houses of Gloucestershire: 1500–1660, 1989, 2nd edn 2001, 1660–1830, 1992, 1830–2000 (with M. Hill), 2001; Archives Online, 1998; (jtly) Full Disclosure, 1999; Changing the Future of our Past, 2002; Gloucestershire Country Houses, 2008; contribs and reviews for Country Life and professional jls. *Recreations:* architectural and historical research, photography, food. *Address:* Tor Bank, 38 Dial Hill Road, Clevedon, N Somerset BS21 7HN. *T:* (01275) 542263; *e-mail:* nick.kingsley@blueyonder.co.uk; 45 Grosvenor Road, Brentford, Middx TW8 0NW; *e-mail:* nickk2@globalnet.co.uk. *T:* (020) 8560 5392.

KINGSMILL, family name of **Baroness Kingsmill**.

KINGSMILL, Baroness *cr* 2006 (Life Peer), of Holland Park, in the Royal Borough of Kensington and Chelsea; **Denise Patricia Byrne Kingsmill,** CBE 2000; a Deputy Chairman, Competition (formerly Monopolies and Mergers) Commission, 1997–2003; *b* 24 April 1947; *d* of Patrick Henry Byrne and Hester Jean Byrne; *m* 1st, 1970, David Gordon Kingsmill (marr. diss. 2002); one *s* one *d*; 2nd, 2006, Richard Wheatly. *Educ:* Girton Coll., Cambridge. Admitted Solicitor, 1980. With ICI Fibres, then Internat. Wool Secretariat, 1968–75; Robin Thompson & Partners, 1979–82; Russell Jones and Walker, 1982–85; Denise Kingsmill & Co., 1985–90; Partner, D. J. Freeman, 1990–93; Consultant, Denton Hall, 1994–2000. Chm., Optimum Health Services NHS Trust, 1992–99. Non-executive Director: Rainbow UK, 1993–94; MFI Furniture Gp, 1997–2001 (Dep. Chm., 1999–2001); Norwich and Peterborough Bldg Soc., 1997–2001; Telewest Communications, 2001–03; Manpower UK, 2001–03; British Airways, 2004–; Chm. Adv. Forum, Laing O'Rourke, 2003–04; Sen. Advr, RBS, 2005–08. Chairman: Women's Employment and Pay Review, 2001; Accounting for People Taskforce, DTI, 2003–; Model Health Inquiry, 2007. Trustee, Design Mus., 2000–. Chm., Sadler's Wells Foundn, 2003–04. Mem., Develt Cttee, Judge Business Sch. (formerly Judge Inst.), Cambridge Univ., 2000–; Pro-Chancellor, Brunel Univ., 2002–06. Gov., Coll. of Law, 1992–2001. Hon. Fellow, Univ. of Wales, Cardiff, 2000. Hon. LLD Brunel, 2001; Hon Dr: Stirling, 2003; Cranfield, 2007. *Recreation:* trying to stay fit. *Address:* House of Lords, SW1A 0PW.

KINGSTON, 12th Earl of, *cr* 1768 (Ire.); **Robert Charles Henry King-Tenison;** Bt 1682; Baron Kingston 1764; Viscount Kingston of Kingsborough 1766; Baron Erris 1800; Viscount Lorton 1806; *b* 20 March 1969; *o s* of 11th Earl of Kingston and his 1st wife, Patricia Mary (*née* Killip); *S* father, 2002; *m* 1994, Ruth Margaret Buckner; one *s* one *d*. *Heir: s* Viscount Kingsborough, *qv*.

KINGSTON (Ontario), Archbishop of, (RC), since 2007; **Most Rev. Brendan O'Brien;** *b* Ottawa, 28 Sept. 1943; *s* of Redmond and Margaret O'Brien (*née* Foran). *Educ:* Univ. of Ottawa (BA); St Paul Univ., Ottawa (BTh); Lateran Univ., Rome (Dr Moral Theology). Ordained priest, 1968; Pastor in several Ottawa parishes; ordained bishop, 1987; Auxiliary Bishop of Ottawa, 1987–93; Bishop of Pembroke, 1993–2000; Archbishop of St John's, 2000–07. *Address:* 390 Palace Road, Kingston, ON K7L 4T3, Canada. *T:* (613) 5484461, *Fax:* (613) 5484744; *e-mail:* archbishop@romancatholic.kingston.on.ca.

KINGSTON, (William) Martin; QC 1992; a Recorder, 1991–99; *b* 9 July 1949; *s* of William Robin Kingston and Iris Edith Kingston; *m* 1972, Jill Mary Bache; one *s* two *d*. *Educ:* Middlewich Secondary Modern Sch.; Hartford Coll. of Further Educn; Liverpool Univ. (LLB). Called to the Bar, Middle Temple, 1972, Bencher, 2002; Asst Recorder, 1987. Dep. Chm., Agricl Lands Tribunal, 1985–. Asst Comr, Parly Boundary Commn for England, 1992–. *Recreations:* ski-ing, fishing, reading, going on holiday. *Address:* (chambers) 5 Fountain Court, Steelhouse Lane, Birmingham B4 6DR; Bevere Green, Bevere, Worcester WR3 7RG; 25–27 Old Queen Street, SW1H 9JA.

KINGSTON-upon-THAMES, Area Bishop of, since 2002; **Rt Rev. Richard Ian Cheetham,** PhD; *b* 18 Aug. 1955; *s* of John Brian Margrave Cheetham and Mollie Louise Cheetham; *m* 1977, Felicity Mary Loving; one *s* one *d*. *Educ:* Kingston Grammar Sch.; Corpus Christi Coll., Oxford (MA, PGCE); Ripon Coll., Cuddesdon (Cert. Theol. 1987); King's Coll., London (PhD 1999). Science Teacher, Richmond Sch., N Yorks, 1978–80; Physics Master, Eton Coll., 1980–83; Investment Analyst, Legal & General, London, 1983–85; ordained deacon, 1987, priest 1988; Asst Curate, Holy Cross, Fenham, Newcastle upon Tyne, 1987–90; Vicar, St Augustine of Canterbury, Luton, 1990–99; RD of Luton, 1995–98; Archdeacon of St Albans, 1999–2002. *Publication:* Collective Worship: issues and opportunities, 2004. *Recreations:* hockey, squash, tennis, walking, theatre, cinema. *Address:* Kingston Episcopal Area Office, 620 Kingston Road, Raynes Park, SW20 8DN.

KINKEAD-WEEKES, Prof. Mark, FBA 1992; Professor of English and American Literature, University of Kent at Canterbury, 1974–84, now Professor Emeritus; *b* 26 April 1931; *s* of Lt-Col Alfred Bernard Kinkead-Weekes, MC and Vida May Kinkead-Weekes; *m* 1959, Margaret Joan Irvine; two *s*. *Educ:* Potchefstroom Boys' High Sch.; Univ. of Cape Town (BA); Brasenose Coll., Oxford (BA, MA). University of Edinburgh: Asst Lectr in English, 1956–58; Lectr, 1958–65; University of Kent at Canterbury: Lectr, 1965–66; Sen. Lectr, 1966–74; Pro-Vice-Chancellor, 1974–77. Rhodes Scholarship (Cape Province), 1951; Woodrow Wilson Fellow, Smithsonian Instn, 1993–94. Former Governor: Christ Church Coll., Canterbury; King's Coll., Rochester; Contemp. Dance Trust. Chm., Friends of St George, Ramsgate. *Publications:* William Golding, a Critical Study (with Ian Gregor), 1967, 2nd edn 1984; Samuel Richardson: dramatic novelist, 1973; (ed) D. H. Lawrence: The Rainbow, 1989; D. H. Lawrence: triumph to exile 1912–1922, 1996; William Golding: a critical study of the novels, 2002; articles, mainly on fiction. *Recreations:* walking, music, travel. *Address:* 189c Ramsgate Road, Broadstairs, Kent CT10 2EW. *T:* (01843) 872582.

KINKEL, Dr Klaus; Senior Adviser, Lehman Brothers Europe, 2003–08; Minister of Foreign Affairs, Germany, 1992–98; *b* 17 Dec. 1936; *m* 1961, Ursula Vogel; one *s* three *d*. *Educ:* Bonn, Cologne and Tubingen univs. LLD. State Sec., Ministry of Justice, 1982–83, and 1987–91; Head of External Intelligence Service, 1983–87; Minister of Justice, 1991–92; Mem. (FDP) Bundestag, 1994–2002. Leader, FDP, 1993–95.

KINLOCH, Prof. Anthony James, PhD, DSc; FRS 2007; FREng, CEng; CChem, FRSC; FIMMM; FCGI; Professor of Adhesion, since 1990, and Head, Department of Mechanical Engineering, since 2007, Imperial College, London; *b* 7 Oct. 1946; *s* of Nathan and Hilda May Kinloch; *m* 1969, Gillian Patricia Birch; two *s* one *d*. *Educ:* London Nautical Sch.; Queen Mary Coll., London (PhD 1972); DSc London 1989. CChem 1982; FRSC 1982; FIMMM (FIM 1982); FREng (FEng 1997). RARDE, MoD, 1972–84; Reader, Imperial Coll., London, 1984–89. Visiting Professor: EPFL, Lausanne, 1986; Univ. of Utah, 1988. Lectures: C&G Centenary, 1995; Thomas Hawksley, IMechE, 1996. Mem. Council, Inst. Materials, 1997–2002; Chm., Soc. for Adhesion and Adhesives, 2000–02. Fellow, US Adhesion Soc., 1995 (Pres., 2002–04); FCGI 2001. Adhesion Soc. of Japan Award, 1994; Griffith Medal and Prize, 1996, Wake Meml Medal, 2002, Inst. of Materials; Thomas Hawksley Gold Medal, IMechE, 1997. *Publications:* Adhesion and Adhesives: science and technology, 1987; (with R. J. Young) Fracture Behaviour of Polymers, 1983; (ed) Durability of Structural Adhesives, 1983; (ed jtly) Toughened Plastics: I 1993, II 1996; over 200 papers in learned jls. *Recreations:* opera, tennis, walking. *Address:* Imperial College, London, Department of Mechanical Engineering, Exhibition Road, SW7 2BX.

KINLOCH, Sir David, 13th Bt *cr* 1686, of Gilmerton; *b* 5 Aug. 1951; *s* of Sir Alexander Davenport Kinloch, 12th Bt and of Anna, *d* of late Thomas Walker, Edinburgh; *S* father, 1982; *m* 1st, 1976, Susan Middlewood (marr. diss. 1986); one *s* one *d*; 2nd, 1987, Maureen Carswell; two *s*. *Educ:* Gordonstoun. Career in research into, and recovery and replacement of, underground services. *Recreation:* treasure hunting. *Heir: s* Alexander Kinloch, *b* 31 May 1978. *Address:* Gilmerton House, North Berwick, East Lothian EH39 5LQ. *T:* (01620) 880207.

KINLOCH, Sir David Oliphant, 5th Bt *cr* 1873, of Kinloch, co. Perth; CA; Director, Caledonia Investments PLC, 1988–2004; *b* 15 Jan. 1942; *s* of Sir John Kinloch, 4th Bt and Doris Ellaline (*d* 1997), *e d* of C. J. Head; *S* father, 1992; *m* 1st, 1968, Susan Minette Urquhart (marr. diss. 1979), *y d* of Maj.-Gen. R. E. Urquhart, CB, DSO; three *d*; 2nd, 1983, Sabine Irene, *o d* of Philippe de Loës; one *s* one *d*. *Educ:* Charterhouse. *Heir: s* Alexander Peter Kinloch, *b* 30 June 1986. *Address:* House of Aldie, Kinross KY13 0QH; 29 Walpole Street, SW3 4QS.

KINLOCH, Henry, (Harry); Chairman, Quartermaine & Co., since 1989; *b* 7 June 1937; *s* of William Shearer Kinloch and Alexina Alice Quartermaine Kinloch; *m* 1st, 1966, Gillian Anne Ashley (marr. diss. 1979); one *s* one *d*; 2nd, 1987, Catherine Elizabeth Hossack. *Educ:* Queen's Park Sch., Glasgow; Univs of Strathclyde, Birmingham and Glasgow. MSc, PhD, ARCST, CEng, FIMechE. Lecturer in Engineering: Univ. of Strathclyde, 1962–65; Univ. of Liverpool, 1966; Vis. Associate Prof. of Engrg, MIT, 1967;

Sen. Design Engr, CEGB, 1968–70; PA Management Consultants, 1970–73; Chief Exec., Antony Gibbs (PFP) Ltd, 1973–74; Chm. and Chief Exec., Antony Gibbs Financial Services Ltd, 1975–77; Man. Dir, British Shipbuilders, 1978–80; Dep. Man. Dir and Chief Exec., Liberty Life Assce Co., 1980–83; Associate, Lazard Brothers, 1980–84; Chm. and Chief Exec., Ætna Internat. (UK), 1984–89. Chm., Helm Investments Ltd, 1995–98; Gp Man. Dir, Ultraseal Internat. Ltd, 1997–98. Dir, Barfoots of Botley Ltd, 2005–. *Publications:* many publications on theoretical and applied mechanics, financial and business studies. *Recreations:* reading book reviews, opera, political biography, walking, sometimes with others! *Address:* Oasis Europe Ltd, 211 Regent Street, W1B 4NF. *Clubs:* Athenæum (Mem., Gen. and Exec. Cttees, 2003–08; Dep. Chm., 2005–08); Worplesdon Golf, Tydd St Giles Golf.

KINLOSS, Lady (12th in line, of the Lordship *cr* 1602); **Beatrice Mary Grenville Freeman-Grenville;** (surname changed by Lord Lyon King of Arms, 1950); *b* 18 Aug. 1922; *e d* of late Rev. Hon. Luis Chandos Francis Temple Morgan-Grenville, Master of Kinloss; *S* grandmother, 1944; *m* 1950, Dr Greville Stewart Parker Freeman-Grenville (*d* 2005), FSA, FRAS (name changed from Freeman by Lord Lyon King of Arms, 1950), Capt. late Royal Berks Regt, *er s* of late Rev. E. C. Freeman; one *s* two *d*. Cross-bencher; Mem., EC Sub-Cttee C (Social and Consumer Affairs), H of L, 1993–95; has served on numerous select cttees. FRAS 1997. *Heir: s* Master of Kinloss, *qv*. *Address:* North View House, Sheriff Hutton, York YO60 6ST. *T:* (01347) 878447.

KINLOSS, Master of; Hon. Bevil David Stewart Chandos Freeman-Grenville; *b* 20 June 1953; *s* of late Dr Greville Stewart Parker Freeman-Grenville, FSA, Capt. late Royal Berks Regt, and of Lady Kinloss, *qv*; *m* 2001, Marie-Thérèse, d of late William Driscoll, and *widow* of Stuart Sturrock. *Educ:* Redrice Sch. *Address:* Orchard House, 6 Warwick Close, Sheriff Hutton, York YO60 6QW. *T:* (01347) 878346; *e-mail:* bevilkinloss@aol.com.

KINMONTH, Prof. Ann-Louise, (Mrs Ann-Louise Davis), CBE 2002; MD; FRCP, FRCPCH, FRCGP, FMedSci; Professor of General Practice, and Fellow of St John's College, University of Cambridge, since 1997; *b* 8 Jan. 1951; *d* of Maurice Henry Kinmonth and Gwendolyn Stella (*née* Phillipps); *m* 2005, Prof. John Allen Davis, *qv*. *Educ:* New Hall, Cambridge (MA); St Thomas' Hosp. Med. Sch. (MB, BChir, MSc, MD 1984). FRCGP 1992; FRCP 1994; FRCPCH 1997. House Officer, Lambeth and Salisbury Hosps, 1975–76; SHO, Oxford Hosps, 1976–78; Res. Fellow in Paediatrics, Oxford Univ., 1978–80; Oxfam MO, Somalia, 1981; general practice trng, Oxford, 1981–82; Principal, Aldermoor Health Centre, Southampton, 1983–96; University of Southampton: Lectr, 1983–84; Sen. Lectr, 1984–91; Reader, 1991–92; Prof., 1992–96. Advr in Primary Care to MRC/DoH, 2004–05; Associate Dir (Primary Care), UK Clinical Res. Network, 2005–07; Ext. Associate, Inst of Medicine (USA), 2007. FounderFMedSci 1998. *Publications:* (ed with J. D. Baum) Care of the Child with Diabetes Mellitus, 1986; (ed with R. Jones) Critical Reading for Primary Care, 1995; (ed jtly) Evidence Base for Diabetes Care, 2002; contrib. papers on diabetes care and prevention of cardio-vascular disease in peer reviewed jls. *Address:* 1 Cambridge Road, Great Shelford, Cambridge CB2 5JE.

KINNAIR, Dame Donna, DBE 2008; Director of Nursing and Head of Integrated Children's Commissioning, Southwark Primary Care Trust, since 2002; *b* London, 17 Feb. 1961; *d* of Victor and Dolores Nesbitt; *m* 1981, Stephen Kinnair; two *s* one *d*. *Educ:* Rushmore Prim. Sch.; Skinners' Company's Sch. for Girls; Princess Alexandra Sch. of Nursing; Univ. of E London (LLB); King's Coll. London (Dip. Healthcare Ethics); Univ. of Greenwich (PGCE); Univ. of Manchester (MA Ethics and Law). Nurse: London Hosp., 1983–87; Antigua, WI, 1987; Health Visitor, London Boroughs of Newham, Tower Hamlets and Hackney, 1988–96; Child Protection Nurse Specialist, Optimum Health Services, Lewisham and Southwark, 1996–99; Strategic Comr, Children's Services, Lambeth, Southwark and Lewisham HA, 1999–2002. Nurse Advr, Victoria Climbié Inquiry, 2001. Vis. Prof. of Primary Care, London Southbank Univ., 2008–. Consultant Ed., Nursing Management, 2006–. *Recreations:* cycling, walking, theatre, cinema. *Address:* Southwark Primary Care Trust, Mabel Goldwin House, 49 Grange Walk, SE1 3DY.

KINNAIRD, Alison Margaret, (Mrs R. Morton), MBE 1997; free-lance musician and artist, since 1970; *b* 30 April 1949; *d* of John and Margaret Kinnaird; *m* 1974, Robin Morton; one *s* one *d*. *Educ:* George Watson's Ladies' Coll.; Edinburgh Univ. (MA 1970). Artworks in public and private collections incl. V&A Mus., Scottish Nat. Portrait Gall., Corning Mus. of Glass, NY and Scottish Parlt; specialises in engraved glass. Has performed, playing Scottish harp, nationally and internationally; has made recordings. *Publications:* (with Keith Sanger) Tree of Strings: a history of the harp in Scotland, 1992; The Small Harp, 1989; The Lothian Collection, 1995. *Address:* Shillinghill, Temple, Midlothian EH23 4SH. *T:* (01875) 830328, *Fax:* (01875) 830392; *e-mail:* alisonk@templerecords.co.uk.

KINNEAR, Ian Albert Clark, (Tim), CMG 1974; HM Diplomatic Service, retired; *b* 23 Dec. 1924; *s* of late George Kinnear, CBE and Georgina Lilian (*née* Stephenson), Nairobi; *m* 1966, Rosemary, *d* of late Dr K. W. D. Hartley, Cobham; two *d*. *Educ:* Pembroke House, Gilgil, Kenya; Marlborough Coll.; Lincoln Coll., Oxford (MA). HM Forces, 1943–46 (1st E Africa Reconnaissance Regt). Colonial Service (later HMOCS): Malayan Civil Service, 1951–56: District Officer, Bentong, then Alor Gajah, Asst Sec. Econ. Planning Unit; Kenya, 1956–63: Asst Sec., then Sen. Asst Sec., Min. of Commerce and Industry; 1st Sec., CRO, later Commonwealth Office, 1963–66; 1st Sec. (Commercial), British Embassy, Djakarta, 1966–68; 1st Sec. and Head of Chancery, British High Commn, Dar-es-Salaam, 1969–71; Chief Sec., later Dep. Governor, Bermuda, 1971–74; Senior British Trade Comr, Hong Kong, 1974–77; Consul-Gen., San Francisco, 1977–82. *Recreation:* painting. *Address:* Castle Hill Cottage, Crook Road, Brenchley, Tonbridge, Kent TN12 7BN. *T:* (01892) 723782.

KINNEAR, Tim; *see* Kinnear, I. A. C.

KINNELL, Ian; QC 1987; professional arbitrator; *b* 23 May 1943; *o s* of Brian Kinnell and Grace Madeline Kinnell; *m* 1970, Elizabeth Jane Ritchie; one *s* one *d*. *Educ:* Sevenoaks Sch., Kent. Called to the Bar, Gray's Inn, 1967. A Recorder, 1987–89; Immigration Appeal Adjudicator, 1990–91; part-time Chm., Immigration Appeal Tribunal, 1991–97. Mem., London Maritime Arbitrator's Assoc., 1991. *Recreations:* rural pursuits. *Address:* The Vineyard, Heyope, Knighton, Powys LD7 1RE. *T:* (01547) 520990.

KINNOCK, family name of **Baron Kinnock**.

KINNOCK, Baron *cr* 2005 (Life Peer), of Bedwellty in the County of Gwent; **Neil Gordon Kinnock;** PC 1983; Chairman, British Council, since 2004; *b* 28 March 1942; *s* of Gordon Kinnock, labourer, and Mary Kinnock (*née* Howells), nurse; *m* 1967, Glenys Elizabeth Parry (*see* Lady Kinnock); one *s* one *d*. *Educ:* Lewis Sch., Pengam; University Coll., Cardiff. BA in Industrial Relations and History, UC, Cardiff (Chm. Socialist Soc., 1963–66; Pres. Students' Union, 1965–66; Hon. Fellow, 1982). Tutor Organiser in Industrial and Trade Union Studies, WEA, 1966–70; Mem., Welsh Hosp. Bd, 1969–71. MP (Lab) Bedwellty, 1970–83, Islwyn, 1983–95. PPS to Sec. of State for Employment, 1974–75; Chief Opposition spokesman on educn, 1979–83; Leader of the Labour Party, and Leader of the Opposition, 1983–92. Mem., 1995–2004, and a Vice Pres., 1999–2004, EC. Non-exec. Dir, Data & Research Services plc, 2005–. Member: Nat. Exec. Cttee, Labour Party, 1978–94 (Chm., 1987–88); Parly Cttee of PLP, 1980–92. Chm. Internat. Cttee, Labour Party, 1993–94; Vice-Pres., Socialist Internat., 1984–. Trustee, IPPR, 2002–. Hon. Prof., Thames Valley Univ., 1993–; Pres., Univ. of Cardiff, 1998–. Hon. FIHT 1997. Hon. LLD: Wales, 1992; Glamorgan, 1996; Robert Gordon, 2002; Queen Margaret, 2007. Alexis de Tocqueville Prize, European Inst. of Public Admin, 2003; Danish Shipowners' Assoc. Maritime Award, 2004. *Publications:* Making Our Way, 1986; Thorns and Roses, 1992; contribs to various jls. *Recreations:* music esp. opera and male choral, Rugby and Association football, cricket, theatre, being with family. *Address:* British Council, 10 Spring Gardens, SW1A 2BN.

KINNOCK, Lady; Glenys Elizabeth Kinnock; Member (Lab) Wales, European Parliament, since 1999 (South Wales East, 1994–99); *b* 7 July 1944; *m* 1967, Neil Gordon Kinnock (*see* Baron Kinnock); one *s* one *d*. *Educ:* Holyhead Comprehensive Sch.; University College of Wales, Cardiff. Teacher in secondary and primary schools, and special sch., 1966–93. Vice-Pres., Univ. of Wales, Cardiff, 1988–95; Pres., Coleg Harlech, 1998–. Member: Bd, Internat. AIDS Vaccine Initiative; Council, VSO; Council, Britain in Europe; Adv. Bd, Internat. Res. Network on Children and Armed Conflict; Bd, World Parliamentarian Mag. Pres., One World Action; Vice President: Parliamentarians for Global Action; SE Wales Racial Equality Council; St David's Foundn; Special Needs Adv. Project Cymru; UK Nat. Breast Cancer Coalition Wales; Community Enterprise Wales; Charter Housing. Patron: Saferworld; Drop the Debt Campaign; Burma Campaign UK; Crusaid; Elizabeth Hardie Ferguson Trust; Med. Foundn for Victims of Torture; Nat. Deaf Children's Soc. Hon. Fellow, Univ. of Wales Coll., Newport, 1998. Hon. LLD Thames Valley, 1994; Hon. Dr: Brunel, 1997; Kingston, 2001. *Publications:* Eritrea: images of war and peace, 1988; (ed) Voices for One World, 1988; Namibia: birth of a nation, 1990; By Faith and Daring, 1993; Zimbabwe on the Brink, 2003. *Address:* (office) 1 Cathedral Road, Cardiff CF11 9SD. *T:* (029) 2022 7654, *Fax:* (029) 2022 4725; *e-mail:* gkinnock@welshlabourmeps.org.uk.

KINNOULL, 15th Earl of, *cr* 1633; **Arthur William George Patrick Hay;** Viscount Dupplin and Lord Hay, 1627, 1633, 1697; Baron Hay (Great Britain), 1711; *b* 26 March 1935; *o* surv. *s* of 14th Earl and Mary Ethel Isobel Meyrick (*d* 1938); *S* father, 1938; *m* 1961, Gay Ann, *er d* of Sir Denys Lowson, 1st Bt; one *s* three *d*. *Educ:* Eton. Chartered Land Agent, 1960; Mem., Agricultural Valuers' Assoc., 1962; Fellow, Chartered Land Agents' Soc., 1964; FRICS 1970. Pres., National Council on Inland Transport, 1964–76. Mem. of Queen's Body Guard for Scotland (Royal Company of Archers), 1965. Junior Cons. Whip, House of Lords, 1966–68; Cons. Opposition Spokesman on Aviation, House of Lords, 1968–70. Mem., British Delegn, Council of Europe, 1985–95. Chairman: Property Owners' Building Soc., 1976–87 (Dir, 1971–87); Woolwich Homes, 1994–97; Dir, Woolwich Equitable Building Soc., 1987–97. Mem., Air League Council, 1972; Council Mem., Deep Sea Fishermen's Mission, 1977 (Chm., 1997–2001). Vice-Pres., Nat. Assoc. of Local Councils (formerly Nat. Assoc. of Parish Councils), 1970–80. Vice-Chm., Bd of Regents, Harris Manchester Coll., Oxford, 2002–. Gov., St John's Sch., Leatherhead, 1978–2005. *Heir: s* Viscount Dupplin, *qv*. *Address:* 15 Carlyle Square, SW3 6EX; Pier House, Seaview, Isle of Wight PO34 5BN. *Clubs:* Turf, Pratt's, Lansdowne, MCC.

KINROSS, 5th Baron *cr* 1902; **Christopher Patrick Balfour;** Partner in HBJ Gateley Wareing, since 2005; *b* 1 Oct. 1949; *s* of 4th Baron Kinross, OBE, TD, and Helen Anne (*d* 1969), *d* of A. W. Hog; *S* father, 1985; *m* 1st, 1974, Susan Jane (marr. diss. 2004), *d* of I. R. Pitman, WS; two *s*; 2nd, 2004, Catherine Ierenka, *d* of Stanislav Ostrycharz. *Educ:* Belhaven Hill School, Dunbar; Eton College; Edinburgh Univ. (LLB). Mem., Law Soc. of Scotland, 1975; WS 1975. Partner: Shepherd & Wedderburn, WS, Solicitors, 1977–97; Taylor Kinross Legal Partnership, 1997–2005. UK Treas., James IV Assoc. of Surgeons, 1981– (Hon. Mem., 1985–). Member, Queen's Body Guard for Scotland, Royal Company of Archers, 1980–. Member: Mil. Vehicle Trust; Scottish Land Rover Owners' Club. Golden Jubilee Medal, 2002. Grand Baili, Grand Bailiwick of Scotland, Order of St Lazarus of Jerusalem, 2002. *Recreations:* rifle and shotgun shooting, stalking, motorsport. *Heir: s* Hon. Alan Ian Balfour [*b* 4 April 1978; *m* 2006, Lindsay Fiona Gourlay]. *Address:* 27 Walker Street, Edinburgh EH3 7HX. *T:* (0131) 225 3476. *Club:* New (Edinburgh).

KINSELLA, (Jonathan) Neil; Chief Executive and Managing Partner, Russell Jones and Walker Solicitors, since 2003; *b* Leigh, Lancs, 17 May 1958; *s* of Donald John and Irene Kinsella; *m* 1982, Susan Elizabeth Cotterell; one *s* one *d*. *Educ:* Manchester Univ. (LLB Hons Law); Coll. of Law, Chester. Admitted Solicitor, 1983; trained at Goldberg Blackburn, 1981–83; Partner, Pannone Napier, 1986–91, specialising in conduct of disaster litigation, incl. Manchester Air Crash, Chinook Helicopter Disaster, Piper Alpha Disaster; joined Russell Jones and Walker, 1991. Retained Lawyer to PFA. Law Soc. apptd rep. on Lord Chancellor's Adv. Gp on awards of damages in serious injury cases. Founder Mem., Claims Standards Council. Medal for work on internat. transport, Assoc. of Young Internat. Lawyers, 1988. *Publications:* contrib. articles on legal issues with particular interest in access to justice and alternative business structures in legal profession. *Recreations:* painting, wild swimming, tennis, history of early rock and roll and punk music. *Address:* Russell Jones and Walker, 80–86 Gray's Inn Road, WC1X 8NH.

KINSELLA, Thomas; poet; *b* 4 May 1928; *m* 1955, Eleanor Walsh; one *s* two *d*. Entered Irish Civil Service, 1946; resigned from Dept of Finance, 1965. Artist-in-residence, 1965–67, Prof. of English, 1967–70, Southern Illinois Univ.; Prof. of English, Temple Univ., Philadelphia, 1970–90. Elected to Irish Academy of Letters, 1965; Mem., Amer. Acad. of Arts and Scis, 2000. J. S. Guggenheim Meml Fellow, 1968–69, 1971–72; Hon. Sen. Fellow, Sch. of English, University Coll., Dublin, 2003–. Freeman, City of Dublin, 2007. Hon. PhD: NUI, 1984; Turin Univ., 2005. *Publications: poetry:* Poems, 1956; Another September, 1958; Downstream, 1962; Nightwalker and other poems, 1968; Notes from the Land of the Dead, 1972; Butcher's Dozen, 1972; A Selected Life, 1972; Finistère, 1972; New Poems, 1973; Selected Poems 1956 to 1968, 1973; Vertical Man and The Good Fight, 1973; One, 1974; A Technical Supplement, 1976; Song of the Night and Other Poems, 1978; The Messenger, 1978; Fifteen Dead, 1979; One and Other Poems, 1979; Poems 1956–73, 1980; Peppercanister Poems 1972–78, 1980; One Fond Embrace, 1981; Songs of the Psyche, 1985; Her Vertical Smile, 1985; St Catherine's Clock, 1987; Out of Ireland, 1987; Blood and Family, 1988; Personal Places, 1990; Poems from Centre City, 1990; Madonna, 1991; Open Court, 1991; From Centre City, 1994; Collected Poems 1956–1994, 1996; The Pen Shop, 1997; The Familiar, 1999; Godhead, 1999; Citizen of the World, 2000; Littlebody, 2000; Collected Poems 1956–2001, 2001; Marginal Economy, 2005; Man of War, 2007; Belief and Unbelief, 2007; Selected Poems, 2007; *translations and general:* (trans.) The Táin, 1969; contrib. essay in Davis, Mangan, Ferguson, 1970; (ed) Selected Poems of Austin Clarke, 1976; An Duanaire—Poems of the Dispossessed (trans. Gaelic poetry, 1600–1900), 1981; (ed) Our Musical Heritage: lectures on Irish traditional music by Seán Ó Riada, 1982; (ed, with translations) The New Oxford Book of Irish Verse, 1986; The Dual Tradition: an essay on poetry and politics in Ireland, 1995; Readings in Poetry, 2005; The Divided Mind - collected occasional prose, 2008.

KINSEY, Thomas Richard Moseley, FREng; Chairman, Delcam International (formerly Deltacam Systems), since 1989; *b* 13 Oct. 1929; *s* of late Richard Moseley Kinsey and Dorothy Elizabeth Kinsey; *m* 1953, Ruth (*née* Owen-Jones); two *s*. *Educ:* Newtown Sch.; Trinity Hall, Cambridge (MA). FIMechE; FREng (FEng 1982). ICI Ltd, 1952–57; Tube Investments, 1957–65; joined Delta plc, 1965: Director, 1973–77; Jt Man. Dir, 1977–82; Dir, 1980, Dep. Chief Exec., 1982–87, Mitchell Cotts plc, 1980–87. Chm., Birmingham Battery & Metal Co., 1984–89; Director: Gower Internat., 1984–89; Telcon, 1984–89; Unistrut Europe, 1989–92. CCMI. *Recreations:* golf, travel. *Address:* 6 Sutton Lodge, Blossomfield Road, Solihull, W Midlands B91 1NB. *T:* (0121) 704 2592. *Clubs:* Athenæum; Edgbaston Golf.

KINSMAN, Jeremy Kenneth Bell; Canadian Ambassador to the European Union, 2002–06; *b* Montreal, 28 Jan. 1942; *s* of Ronald Kinsman and Katharine Nixon Bell; *m* 1992, Hana Tallichova; two *d*. *Educ:* Princeton Univ.; Institut d'Etudes Politiques, Paris. Aluminium Co. of Canada, 1965–66; entered Foreign Service of Canada, 1966; Econ. Div., Ext. Affairs, 1966–68; Third, then Second, Sec. and Vice-Consul, Brussels/EEC, 1968–70; Central Secretariat, Ottawa, 1970–72; Commercial Div., 1972–73; First Sec., Algiers, 1973–75; Counsellor, then Minister and Dep. Perm. Rep., Perm. Mission of Canada to UN, NY, 1975–80; Chm., Policy Planning Secretariat, Ottawa, 1980–81; Minister, Pol Affairs, Washington, 1981–85; Assistant Deputy Minister: Cultural Affairs and Broadcasting, Ottawa, 1985–89; Pol and Internat. Security Affairs, and Pol Dir, Ext. Affairs, 1990–92; Ambassador: to Russia, 1993–96; to Italy, 1996–2000 (concurrently Ambassador to San Marino and High Comr to Malta); High Comr in UK, 2000–02. *Publications:* contribs to jls, incl. Internat. Jl, Internat. Perspectives, Behind the Headlines, McGill Law Rev., Racquet mag. *Recreations:* tennis, running, ski-ing, hiking, books, theatre, music.

KINSMAN, Prof. Rodney William, RDI 1990; FCSD; Chairman and Managing Director, OMK Design, since 1966; *b* 9 April 1943; *s* of John Thomas Kinsman and Lilian Kinsman (*née* Bradshaw); *m* 1966, Lisa Sai Yuk; one *s* two *d*. *Educ:* Mellow Lane Grammar Sch.; Central Sch. of Art (NDD 1965). FCSD 1983. Founded: OMK Design Ltd, 1966; Kinsman Associates, 1981. Mem., British Furniture Council, 1995 (Exec. Mem., RDI Cttee). Numerous internat. exhibns; work in permanent collections incl. Omstak Chair and other designs, in V&A, museums in USA, Spain, Germany. Broadcasts on TV and radio. Vis. Prof., 1985–86 and Ext. Examr, 1986–88, RCA; Vis. Prof., Univ. of the Arts (formerly London Inst.), 1996–. Hon. FRCA 1988; FRSA. Many internat. awards. *Recreations:* polo, ski-ing. *Address:* OMK Design, Stephen Building, 30 Stephen Street, W1T 1QR. *T:* (020) 7631 1335. *Clubs:* Reform, Groucho, Chelsea Arts.

KINTORE, 14th Earl of, *cr* 1677 (Scot.); **James William Falconer Keith;** Lord Keith of Inverurie and Keith Hall, 1677 (Scot.); Bt 1897; Baron 1925; Viscount Stonehaven, 1938; *b* 15 April 1976; *s* of 13th Earl of Kintore and Mary Keith (*née* Plum); *S* father, 2004; *m* 2006, Carrie Fiona, *d* of Ian and Dr Fiona Paxton, Edinburgh. *Heir: sister* Lady Iona Delia Mary Gaddis Keith, *b* 1 Jan. 1978. *Address:* The Stables, Keith Hall, Inverurie, Aberdeenshire AB51 0LD.

KINVIG, Maj.-Gen. Clifford Arthur; Director, Educational and Training Services (Army) (formerly Director of Army Education, Ministry of Defence), 1990–93, retired; *b* 22 Nov. 1934; *s* of Frank Arthur Kinvig and Dorothy Maud (*née* Hankinson); *m* 1956, Shirley Acklam; two *s* one *d*. *Educ:* Waterloo Grammar Sch., Liverpool; Durham Univ. (BA 1956); King's Coll., London (MA War Studies 1969). Commnd, RAEC, 1957; educnl and staff appts in Lichfield, Beaconsfield and York, 1957–65; served FE, 1965–68; Sen. Lectr, RMA, Sandhurst, 1969–73; SO2 Educn, UKLF, 1973–75; Chief Educn Officer, W Midland Dist, 1976–79; SO1 Educn, MoD, 1979–82; Sen. Lectr and Head of Econs, Politics and Social Studies Br., RMCS, Shrivenham, 1982–86; Col AEd1, MoD, 1986; Comdt, RAEC Centre, 1986–90. Dep. Col Comdt, AGC, 1997–2000. Mem., Management Bd, NFER, 1990–93. Trustee and Sec., Gallipoli Meml Lect. Trust, 1990–92. *Publications:* Death Railway, 1973; River Kwai Railway, 1992; (contrib.) The Forgotten War, 1992; Scapegoat: General Percival of Singapore, 1996; (contrib.) Japanese Prisoners of War, 2000; Sixty Years On, 2002; Churchill's Crusade, 2006; contribs to books and jls on mil. hist. topics. *Recreations:* writing, gardening, reading, walking. *Address:* c/o Lloyds TSB, Castle Street, Cirencester, Glos GL7 1QJ.

KIPKULEI, Benjamin Kipkech; Chairman, Kenya Commercial Bank, 2001–03; *b* 5 Jan. 1946; *s* of Mr and Mrs Kipkulei Chesoro; *m* 1972, Miriam; three *s* two *d*. *Educ:* BAEd Nairobi; DipEd Scotland; MEd London. Local Government, 1964 and 1965; Teacher, 1970; Education Officer, 1974; Under Secretary, 1982; High Comr for Kenya in UK, and Ambassador to Italy and Switzerland, 1984–86; Permanent Secretary: Min. of Educn, 1987–92; Min. of Finance, 1993–97; Chm., Harmonisation Commn, Office of the Pres., Kenya, 1998–2001. Alternate Gov. for Kenya, World Bank, 1993; Alternate Dir, IMF, 1993; Director: Central Bank of Kenya; Kenya Commercial Bank, 1993–2003. *Recreations:* swimming, photography.

KIRBY, Prof. Anthony John, PhD; FRS 1987; CChem, FRSC; Professor of Bioorganic Chemistry, University of Cambridge, 1995–2002, now Emeritus; Fellow, Gonville and Caius College, Cambridge, since 1962; *b* 18 Aug. 1935; *s* of Samuel Arthur Kirby and Gladys Rosina Kirby (*née* Welch); *m* 1962, Sara Sophia Benjamina Nieweg; one *s* two *d*. *Educ:* Eton College; Gonville and Caius College, Cambridge (MA, PhD 1962). NATO postdoctoral Fellow: Cambridge, 1962–63; Brandeis Univ., 1963–64; Cambridge University: Demonstrator, 1964–68, Lectr, 1968–85, Reader, 1985–95, in Organic Chemistry; Gonville and Caius College: Dir of Studies in Natural Scis and Coll. Lectr, 1968–2002; Tutor, 1966–74. Visiting Professor/Scholar: Paris (Orsay), 1970; Groningen, 1973 (Backer Lectr, 2003); Cape Town, 1987; Paris VI, 1987; Haifa, 1991; Queen's, Kingston, Ont, 1996; Toronto, 1997; Western Ontario, 1997. Co-ordinator, European Network on Catalytic Antibodies, 1993–96, on Gemini Surfactants, 1997–2001, on Artificial Nucleases, 2000–04. Fellow, Japan Soc. for Promotion of Science, 1986; Royal Society of Chemistry: Fellow, 1980; Award in Organic Reaction Mechanisms, 1983; Tilden Lectr, 1987; Chm., Organic Reaction Mechanisms Gp, 1986–90; Ingold Lectr, 1996–97. Hon. DPhil Univ. of Turku, 2006. *Publications:* The Organic Chemistry of Phosphorus (with S. G. Warren), 1967; The Anomeric Effect and Related Stereoelectronic Effects at Oxygen, 1983; Stereoelectronic effects, 1996; papers in Jls of RSC and Amer. Chem. Soc. *Recreations:* chamber music, walking. *Address:* University Chemical Laboratory, Cambridge CB2 1EW. *T:* (01223) 336370; 14 Tenison Avenue, Cambridge CB1 2DY. *T:* (01223) 359343.

KIRBY, Carolyn; solicitor; President, Law Society of England and Wales, 2002–03; Chairman, Mental Health Review Tribunal for Wales, since 1999; *b* 24 May 1953; *d* of Cyril Treharne-Jones and Elaine Margaret Sanders; *m* 1977, Anthony Robert Kirby. *Educ:* Cheltenham Ladies' Coll.; University Coll., Cardiff (LLB Hons). Admitted solicitor, 1979; Partner, Kirby & Partners, Solicitors, Swansea, 1985–97. Legal Registrar to Archdeacon of Gower, 1997–. Chm., Cancer Information and Support Services, 1995–. Chm., Council of Govs, Cheltenham Ladies Coll., 2004–. *Recreations:* walking, dogs, gardening, long distance running. *Address:* Admirals Wood, Vennaway Lane, Parkmill, Swansea SA3 2EA. *T:* and *Fax:* (01792) 234494; *e-mail:* sxlawsoc@aol.com.

KIRBY, Dennis, MVO 1961; MBE 1955; Hon. Manager, European Investment Bank, Luxembourg; *b* 5 April 1923; *s* of William Ewart Kirby and Hannah Kirby; *m* 1st, 1943, Mary Elizabeth Kilby (*d* 1994); 2nd, 1994, Ava Robertson. *Educ:* Hull Grammar Sch.; Queens' Coll., Cambridge. Lt (A) RNVR (fighter pilot), 1940–46. Colonial Service, Sierra Leone, 1946–62 (District Comr, 1950; Perm. Sec., 1961–62); 1st Sec., UK Diplomatic Service, 1962; Managing Director: East Kilbride Development Corp., 1963–68; Irvine Development Corp., 1967–72; Industrial Dir, Scotland, DTI, 1972–74; European Investment Bank, 1974–87: Conseiller Principal, 1974; Dir Adjoint, 1976; Dir Associé, 1984; Dir, NM UK Ltd, 1988–93. *Recreations:* shooting, golf, bridge. *Address:* Bottle Cottage, Almodington, Chichester, W Sussex PO20 7LD. *Clubs:* Oxford and Cambridge, Royal Commonwealth Society; Wisley Golf (Dir, 1991–95).

KIRBY, Dame Georgina (Kamiria), DBE 1994; QSO 1981; JP; Executive Director, Maori Women's Development Inc. (formerly Maori Women's Development Fund), since 1978; *b* 31 Jan. 1936; *d* of William Tawhiri Matea Smith and Tuhe Nga Tukemata Christie (*née* Thompson); *m* 1961, Brian Ian Kirby; two *s* one *d*. *Educ:* Horohoro Sch., Rotorua; Rotorua High Sch.; Auckland Univ. Cert. Book-keeping; Cert. Practical Accounting. Jun. Asst Teacher, Rotorua, 1953–55; NZ PO Trng Officer, 1955–63; managed and partnered husband in service businesses, 1966–70; Personnel Officer, Stock & Station, 1971–76. Estabd Te Taumata Art Gall., 1991; Foundn Trustee, Maori Arts NZ (Toi Maori Aotearoa). Mem., Maori Women's Welfare League Inc., 1976– (Nat. Pres., 1983–87); formed Matatau Maori In Business (Maori Business and Professional Assoc.), 2006. NZ Vice Pres., Commonwealth Countries League, London, 1988–. JP NZ, 1987. Commemoration Medal (NZ), 1988; Women's Suffrage Medal (NZ), 1993. *Publications:* Liberated Learning, 1993; Vision Aotearoa Kaupapa New Zealand, 1994; contrib. NZ Maori Artists and Writers Mag., Koru. *Recreations:* reading, badminton, horse-riding. *Address:* 11A Northland Street, Grey Lynn, Auckland 1, New Zealand. *T:* (9) 3767032, *T:* and *Fax:* (9) 3077014. *Club:* Zonta International (Auckland).

KIRBY, Prof. Gordon William, ScD, PhD; FRSC; FRSE; FRAS; Regius Professor of Chemistry, 1972–96, Professor of Chemistry, 1997, now Emeritus, University of Glasgow; *b* 20 June 1934; *s* of William Admiral Kirby and Frances Teresa Kirby (*née* Townson); *m* 1964, Audrey Jean Rusbridge (marr. diss. 1983; remarried 2004), *d* of Col C. E. Rusbridge; two *s*. *Educ:* Liverpool Inst. High Sch.; Gonville and Caius Coll., Cambridge (Schuldham Plate 1956; MA, PhD, ScD); FRIC 1970; FRSE 1975; FRAS 2004. 1851 Exhibn Senior Student, 1958–60, Asst Lectr, 1960–61, Lectr, 1961–67, Imperial Coll. of Science and Technology; Prof. of Organic Chemistry, Univ. of Technology, Loughborough, 1967–72; Mem., Chem. Cttee, SRC, 1971–75. Chm., Jls Cttee, Royal Soc. of Chemistry, 1981–84. Corday-Morgan Medal, Chem. Soc., 1969; Tilden Lectr, Chem. Soc., 1974–75. *Publications:* Co-editor: Elucidation of Organic Structures by Physical and Chemical Methods, vol. IV, parts I, II, and III, 1972; Fortschritte der Chemie organischer Naturstoffe, subseq. entitled Progress in the Chemistry of Organic Natural Products, 1971–2003; (ed) Comprehensive Organic Functional Group Transformations, vol. IV, 1995; contributor to Jl Chem. Soc., etc. *Address:* Tugwell Farm, Halse, Taunton, Somerset TA4 3JL.

KIRBY, Michael Donald, AC 1991; CMG 1983; **Hon. Justice Kirby;** Justice of the High Court of Australia, since 1996; Acting Chief Justice of Australia, 2007–08; *b* 18 March 1939; *s* of Donald Kirby and late Jean Langmore Kirby; partner, since 1969, Johan van Vloten. *Educ:* Fort Street Boys' High Sch.; Univ. of Sydney (BA, LLM, BEc). Admitted Solicitor, 1962; admitted to the Bar of NSW, 1967; Mem., NSW Bar Council, 1974; Judge, Federal Court of Australia, 1983–84; President, Court of Appeal: NSW, 1984–96; Solomon Is, 1995–96; Actg Chief Justice of NSW, 1988, 1990, 1993. Dep. Pres., Aust. Conciliation and Arbitration Commn, 1975–83; Chairman: Australian Law Reform Commn, 1975–84; OECD Inter-govtl Gp on Privacy and Internat. Data Flows, 1978–80; OECD Inter-govtl Gp on Security of Information Systems, 1991–92; Member: Admin. Review Council of Australia, 1976–84; Council of Aust. Acad. of Forensic Scis, 1978–89 (Pres., 1987–89); Aust. National Commn for Unesco, 1980–83, 1996–2007; Aust. Inst. of Multi-cultural Affairs, 1981–84; Exec., CSIRO, 1983–86. Deleg., Unesco Gen. Conf., Paris, 1983; Chm., Unesco Expert Gp on Rights of Peoples, 1989 (Rapporteur, Budapest, 1991); Member: Unesco Expert Gps on Self-Determination and Rights of Peoples, 1984; Perm. Tribunal of Peoples, Rome, 1992; ILO Fact Finding and Conciliation Commn on S Africa, 1991–92; Ethics Cttee, Human Genome Orgn 1995–2004; Internat. Bioethics Cttee, UNESCO, 1996–2005; Internat. Jury, UNESCO Prize for Teaching of Human Rights, 1994–96; Judicial Ref. Gp, UN High Comr for Human Rights, 2007–; Special Rep. of UN Sec.-Gen., for Human Rights in Cambodia, 1993–96; Ind. Chm., Malaŵi Constitl Conf., 1994, Chm. Constitl Seminar, 1997; Hon. Advr on bioethics to UN High Comr for Human Rights, 2001–03. International Commission of Jurists: Comr, 1984–2001; Mem. Exec. Cttee, 1989–95, Chm., 1992–95; Pres., 1995–98; Pres., Aust. Section, 1989–96. Internat. Consultant, Commn for Transborder Data Flow Develt, Intergovtl Bureau of Informatics, Rome, 1985–86; Mem., Bd, Internat. Trustees, Internat. Inst. for Inf. and Communication, Montreal, 1986–2000; President: Criminology Sect., ANZAAS, 1981–82; Law Sect., ANZAAS, 1984–85. Granada Guildhall Lectr, 1984; Acting Prof., Fac. of Salzburg Seminar, Salzburg, 1985, 2000; Hon. Prof., Nat. Law Sch. of India Univ., Bangalore, 1995–; Sen. Anzac Fellow, NZ Govt, 1981; Fellow, NZ Legal Res. Foundn, 1985. Pres., Nat. Book Council of Australia, 1980–83; Member: Library Council of NSW, 1976–85; NSW Ministerial Adv. Cttee on AIDS, 1987; Trustee, AIDS Trust of Australia, 1987–93; Comr, Global Commn on AIDS, WHO, Geneva, 1989–91; Chm., UN AIDS expert gp on HIV testing of UN peacekeepers, 2001–02, on human rights and access to treatment, 2002; Member: UN AIDS gp on AIDS and human rights, 2003–; UNODC Judicial Integrity Gp, 2002–. Mem. Council, Australian Opera, 1983–89; Patron, RSPCA, Australia. Fellow, Senate, Sydney Univ., 1964–69; Dep. Chancellor, Univ. of Newcastle, NSW, 1978–83; Chancellor, Macquarie Univ., Sydney, 1984–93. Mem. Bd of Governors, Internat. Council for Computer Communications, Washington, 1984–; Bd Mem., Kinsey Inst. for Res. in Sex, Gender and Reprodn, Indiana Univ., 2001–; Adv. Bd Mem., Internat. Human Rights Law Inst., De Paul Univ., Chicago, 2002–. Hon. Member: Amer. Law Inst., 2000; Soc. of Legal Scholars, 2006; Hon. FASSA 1997; Hon. Fellow, Australian Acad. of Humanities, 2006; Hon. Bencher, Inner Temple, 2006. Hon. DLitt: Newcastle, NSW, 1987; Ulster, 1998; James Cook, 2003; Hon. LLD: Macquarie, 1994; Sydney, 1996; Nat. Law Sch. of India Univ., 1997; Buckingham, 2000; ANU, 2004; DUniv: S Australia, 2001; Southern Cross, 2007. Australian Human Rights Medal, 1991; UNESCO Prize for Human Rights Educn, 1998. *Publications:* Industrial Index to Australian Labour Law, 1978, 2nd edn 1983; Reform the Law, 1983; The Judges (Boyer Lectures), 1983; (ed jtly) A Touch of Healing, 1986; Through the World's Eye, 2000; Judicial Activism (Hamlyn Lectures), 2004; essays and articles in legal and other jls. *Recreation:* work. *Address:*

High Court of Australia, Canberra, ACT 2600, Australia. *T:* (2) 92308202, *Fax:* (2) 92308626; *e-mail:* kirbyj@hcourt.gov.au.

KIRBY, Maj.-Gen. Norman George, OBE 1971; FRCS; Consultant Accident and Emergency Surgeon, Guy's Nuffield House, since 1994; Consultant Accident and Emergency Surgeon, 1982–93, Director, Clinical Services, Accidents and Emergencies, 1985–93, Guy's Hospital; *b* 19 Dec. 1926; *s* of George William Kirby and Laura Kirby; *m* 1949, Cynthia Bradley; one *s* one *d. Educ:* King Henry VIII Sch., Coventry; Univ. of Birmingham (MB, ChB). FRCS 1964, FRCSE 1980; FICS 1980; FCEM (FFAEM 1993); DMCC 1997; FIFEM 2000. Surgical Registrar: Plastic Surg. Unit, Stoke Mandeville Hosp., 1950–51; Birmingham Accident Hosp., 1953–55; Postgraduate Med. Sch., Hammersmith, 1964. Regt MO 10 Parachute Regt, 1950–51; OC 5 Parachute Surgical Team, 1956–59 (Suez Landing, 5 Nov. 1956); Officer i/c Surg. Div., BMH Rinteln, 1959–60; OC and Surg. Specialist, BMH Tripoli, 1960–62; OC and Consultant Surgeon, BMH Dhekelia, 1967–70; Chief Cons. Surgeon, Cambridge Mil. Hosp., 1970–72; Cons. Surg. HQ BAOR, 1973–78; Dir of Army Surgery, Cons. Surg. to the Army and Hon. Surgeon to the Queen, 1978–82; Hon. Cons. Surgeon, Westminster Hosp., 1979–. Examnr in Anatomy, RCSE, 1982–90; Mem., Court of Examiners, RCS, 1988–94. Chm., Army Med. Dept Working Party Surgical Support for BAOR, 1978–80; Member: MoD Med. Bds, 1978–82; Med. Cttee, Defence Scientific Adv. Council, 1979–82. Hon. Colonel: 308 (Co. of London) Gen. Hosp. RAMC, TA, 1982–87; 144 Para Field Sqdn (formerly Field Ambulance) RAMC (Volunteers), TA, 1985–96; Col Comdt, RAMC, 1987–92. Member: Council, Internat. Coll. of Surgeons; Airborne Med. Soc.; British Assoc. for Accident and Emergency Medicine (formerly Casualty Surgeons Assoc.), 1981–94 (Vice-Pres., 1988; Pres., 1990–93); Pres., Med. Soc. of London, 1992–93 (FMS 1981; Hon. Editor, 2003–); Vice-Pres., British Assoc. of Trauma in Sport, 1982–88; Chm., Accidents & Emergencies Cttee, SE Thames RHA, 1984–88. Mem. Council, TAVRA, Gtr London, 1990–97. Liveryman, Soc. of Apothecaries of London, 1983–; Mem., HAC, 1988. Fellow, British Orthopaedic Assoc., 1967. Hon. Mem., Amer. Coll. of Emergency Physicians, 1993. McCombe Lectr, RCSE, 1979. Mem., Editl Bd, Brit. Jl Surg. and Injury, 1979–82. Mem., Surgical Travellers Club, 1979–. OStJ 1977 (Mem. Council, London, 1990–2005). Mitchener Medal, RCS, 1982. *Publications:* (ed) Field Surgery Pocket Book, 1981; Pocket Reference, Accidents and Emergencies, 1988, 2nd edn 1991; contrib. Brit. Jl Surg., Proc. RSocMed, etc. *Recreations:* travel, motoring, reading, archaeology. *Address:* 12 Woodsyre, Sydenham Hill, Dulwich, SE26 6SS. *T:* (020) 8670 5327.

KIRBY-HARRIS, Robert, PhD; Chief Executive, Institute of Physics, since 2005; *b* 12 June 1952; *s* of Lionel George Harris and Enid Josephine Harris; adopted surname Kirby-Harris; *m* 1979, Abigail Anne Mee; two *s. Educ:* Ashford Grammar Sch.; Univ. of Kent at Canterbury (BSc 1st Cl. Hons Theoretical Phys 1973); Clare Coll., Cambridge (MA (III) Applied Maths and Theoretical Phys 1974); Univ. of Sussex (PGCE Secondary Sci. 1975); Plymouth Poly. (DMS 1985); Lancaster Univ. (PhD Educnl Res. 2003). CPhys 1985, FInstP 2005; MIMA 1985, CMath 1999; CSci 2006. Secondary Sci. Teacher, Wakeford Sch., Havant, 1975–77; RN Instructor Officer, Lt RN, 1977–82, Lt Comdr RN, 1982–85: Lectr in Electronics and Maths, RN Weapons Engrg Sch., Fareham, 1977–79; Sen. Instructor Officer, RN Supply and Secretariat Sch., Chatham, 1980–83; Sen. Lectr in Maths, RNEC Manadon, Plymouth, 1983–85; Exec. Dir, Poly Enterprise Plymouth, 1985–90; Dep. Vice-Chancellor (Resources), Middlesex Univ., 1991–95; Pro Vice-Chancellor (Admin and Finance), Univ. of Namibia, S Africa, 1996–2002; Corp. Dir, Ops and Finance, Royal Botanic Gardens, Kew, 2003–05. Vice Pres., Science Council, 2006–. MCMI (MBIM 1986); Mem., SRHE, 1997. *Publication:* contrib. Higher Educn jl. *Recreations:* hill walking, ski-ing, gardens, arts, family life. *Address:* Institute of Physics, 76 Portland Place, W1B 1NT. *T:* (020) 7470 4804, *Fax:* (020) 7470 4937; *e-mail:* robert.kirby-harris@iop.org. *Club:* Naval.

KIRCHNER, Prof. Emil Joseph, PhD; Professor of European Studies, Department of Government, University of Essex, since 1992; *b* 19 March 1942; *m* 1975, Joanna Bartlett; two *s. Educ:* Case Western Reserve Univ. (BA Econ 1970; MA 1971; PhD 1976, Pol. Sci.). Essex University: Lectr and Sen. Lectr, Dept of Govt, 1974–92; Hon. Jean Monnet Prof. of European Integration, 1997–. Visiting Professor: Dept of Pol. Sci., Univ. of Connecticut, 1986–87; Centre for Econ. Res. and Grad. Educn, Charles Univ., Prague, 1997–2000; Hon. Guest Prof., Renmin Univ. of China, 2001–; NATO Fellowship, 2001. Chm., Assoc. for Study of German Politics, 2002– (Mem., 1989–90). Gen. Series Editor, Europe in Change (Manchester Univ. Press), 1993; Exec. Ed., Jl of European Integration, 1997–2007. Cross, Order of Merit (Germany), 2002. *Publications:* Decision Making in the European Community, 1992; (jtly) The Federal Republic of Germany and NATO: 40 years after, 1992; (jtly) The Future of European Security, 1994; (jtly) The Recasting of the European Order: security architectures and economic co-operation, 1996; (jtly) The New Europe: east, west, centre, 1997; Decentralization and Transition in the Visegrad, 1999; (jtly) Committee Governance in the EU, 2000; (jtly) Studies on Policies and Policy Processes of the European Union, 2003–; (ed with James Sperling) Global Security Governance, 2007; (with James Sperling) EU Security Governance, 2008. *Recreations:* music, sports, travel.

KIRCHNER, Peter James, MBE 1970; HM Diplomatic Service, retired; Consul General, Berlin, 1978–80; *b* 17 Sept. 1920; *s* of late William John Kirchner and Winifred Emily Homer (*née* Adams); *m* 1952, Barbro Sarah Margareta (*née* Klockhoff); one *s* two *d. Educ:* St Brendan's Coll., Clifton, Bristol; BA Open, 1991, BA Hons 1996. Served War, RA, 1939–41. Timber production, UK and Germany, 1941–48; FO, Germany, 1948; Home Office Immigration Dept, 1952–64; Head of UK Refugee Missions in Europe, 1960–63; FCO (formerly FO): Barbados, 1965; Nairobi, 1968; Ankara, 1970; Vienna, 1973; Jerusalem, 1976. Mem., Bd of Trustees, Retirement Trust (Chm., 1995–2001). Freeman, City of London, 1963. *Recreations:* golf, croquet, modern European history, northern baroque architecture, travel in Europe. *Address:* 86 York Mansions, Prince of Wales Drive, SW11 4BN. *T:* (020) 7622 7068.

KIRK, Anthony James Nigel; QC 2001; *b* 3 May 1958; *s* of late James Brian Kirk and of Lavinia Mary Kirk (*née* Kellow). *Educ:* Ipswich Sch.; King Edward VII Sch., Lytham St Anne's; King's Coll., London (LLB Hons; AKC). Called to the Bar, Gray's Inn, 1981 (Stuart Cunningham Macaskie and Lord Justice Holker Schol.; Bencher, 2006); in practice as barrister, 1982–. Chm., Family Law Bar Assoc., 2006– (Vice-Chm., 2003–05; Nat. Sec., 1999–2002); Member: Bar Council, 1996–99 (Mem., Professional Conduct and Complaints Cttee, 1999–2002); Bd, Family Mediators' Assoc., 1999–2002; ADR Cttee, 2002–; Internat. Family Law Cttee, 2002–. Mem., RCO. *Publications:* (contrib.) Jackson & Davies Matrimonial Finance and Taxation, 6th edn 1996; (contrib.) Rayden & Jackson on Divorce, 19th edn. *Recreation:* classical music. *Address:* (chambers) 1 King's Bench Walk, Temple, EC4Y 7DB. *T:* (020) 7936 1500.

KIRK, Geoffrey Eric, RDI 2001; FREng, FIMechE; FRAeS; FIED; Chief Design Engineer, Civil Aerospace, Rolls-Royce, since 1994; *b* 24 Feb. 1945; *s* of Eric and Lily Kirk (*née* Melbourne); *m* 1966, Linda Jean Butcher. *Educ:* Bramcote Hills Tech. Grammar Sch.; Loughborough Tech. Coll.; Loughborough Univ. (Associateship). CEng 1973, FREng 2005; FIMechE 1993; FRAeS 1993; FIED 2002. Drawing office student apprentice, 1961–66, Design Draughtsman, 1966–68, Brush Electrical Engrg Co.; design engr, Rolls-Royce, 1968–73; adult trainee, Rolls-Royce/Loughborough Univ., 1971–72; Chief Design Engr, Ariel Pressings, 1973–75; Rolls-Royce: Sen. Tech. Designer, 1975–82; Chief Design Engr, RB211-535E4, 1982–85; Chief Engineer: V2500, 1985–87; Res. and Mfg Technol., 1987–89; Chief Design Engineer, Civil Engineers, 1989–92; Head of Powerplant Engineering, 1992–94. Visiting Professor: Queen Mary, Univ. of London (formerly QMW), 1996– (Hon. Fellow, 2005); Nottingham Univ., 2003–; Cambridge Univ., 2006–. Mem., Design Council, 2005–. FRSA 2002. Hon. Pres., IED, 2006– (Gerald Frewer Meml Trophy, 2002). British Bronze Medal, RAeS, 1998; Prince Philip Designers' Prize, 2002; Sir Misha Black Medal, RCA, 2006. *Publications:* contribs to various confs and seminars, predominantly on design. *Recreations:* sport, photography, private flying. *Address:* Rolls-Royce plc, PO Box 31, Derby DE24 8BJ. *T:* (01332) 249680; *e-mail:* geoff.kirk@rolls-royce.com.

KIRK, Rt Hon. Herbert Victor; PC (N Ireland) 1962; Member (U) for South Belfast, Northern Ireland Assembly, 1973–75; *b* 5 June 1912; *s* of Alexander and Mary A. Kirk; *m* 1944, Gladys A. Dunn; three *s. Educ:* Queen's Univ., Belfast (BComSc). FCA 1940. MP Windsor Div. of Belfast, NI Parlt, 1956–72; Minister of Labour and Nat. Insce, Govt of N Ireland, 1962–64; Minister of Education, 1964–65; Minister of Finance, 1965–72, Jan.–May 1974, resigned. *Recreation:* golf. *Clubs:* Royal Portrush Golf, Belvoir Park Golf.

KIRK, Matthew John Lushington; Director, External Relationships, Vodafone Group Plc, since 2006; *b* 10 Oct. 1960; *s* of Sir Peter Michael Kirk, MP and Elizabeth Mary Kirk (*née* Graham); *m* 1989, Anna Thérèse Macey, *d* of Rear-Adm. David Edward Macey, *qv*; two *d. Educ:* Vinehall Sch.; Coll. Joseph d'Arbaud; Felsted Sch.; St John's Coll., Oxford (MA Phil. and Theol.); Ecole Nat. d'Admin, Paris (Dip. Internat. d'Admin Public). Entered HM Diplomatic Service, 1982; UK Mission to UN, NY, 1982, Vienna, 1983; FCO, 1983–84; 3rd, later 2nd, Sec., Belgrade, 1984–87; FCO, 1987–88; Office of Governor of Gibraltar, 1988; FCO, 1989–92; 1st Secretary: Paris, 1993–97; FCO, 1997–98; Cabinet Secretariat (on secondment), 1998–99; FCO, 1999–2002; Ambassador to Finland, 2002–06. Alternate Dir, Vodafone Essar Ltd (India). Mem., Koenigswinter Cttee. FRGS 1989. *Recreations:* music, wine, walking, travel. *Address:* Vodafone Group Plc, Vodafone House, The Connection, Newbury, Berks RG14 2FN. *T:* (01635) 664086; *e-mail:* matthew.kirk@vodafone.com. *Clubs:* Brooks's, Beefsteak.

KIRK, Prof. Raymond Maurice, FRCS; Honorary Professor of Surgery, Royal Free and University College London School of Medical Sciences (formerly Royal Free Hospital School of Medicine), since 2004 (part time Lecturer in Anatomy, since 1989); Hon. Consulting Surgeon, Royal Free Hospital (Consulting Surgeon, 1989); *b* 31 Oct. 1923; *m* 1952, Margaret Schafran; one *s* two *d. Educ:* Mundella Sch., Nottingham; County Secondary Sch., West Bridgford; King's College London; Charing Cross Hosp. MB BS, MS, London; LRCP. RN 1942–46; Lieut RNVR. Charing Cross Hosp., 1952–53; Lectr in Anatomy, King's Coll. London, 1953–54; Hammersmith Hosp., 1954–56; Charing Cross Hosp., 1956–60; Senior Surgical Registrar, Royal Free Hosp., 1961; Consultant Surgeon: Willesden Gen. Hosp., 1962–74; Royal Free Hosp. Group, 1964–89. Dir, Overseas Doctors' Trng Scheme, RCS, 1990–95; formerly Mem. Court of Examrs, RCS; formerly Examr to RCPSG, Univs of London, Liverpool, Bristol, Khartoum, Colombo, Kuwait; Mem. Council, RCS, 1983–91; FRSocMed (Pres., Surgical Section, 1986–87). Member: British Soc. of Gastroenterol.; Soc. of Academic and Res. Surgery; Med. Soc. of London (Pres., 1988–89); Hunterian Soc. (Pres., 1995–96); Soc. of Authors. Hon. Fellow: Assoc. of Surgeons of Poland; Coll. of Surgeons of Sri Lanka. Hon. Editor, Annals of RCS, 1983–92. *Publications:* Manual of Abdominal Operations, 1967; Basic Surgical Techniques, 1973, 5th edn 2002; (jtly) Surgery, 1974; General Surgical Operations, 1978, 5th edn 2006; Complications of Upper Gastrointestinal Tract Surgery, 1987; (jtly) Clinical Surgery in General, 1993, 4th edn 2004; A Career in Medicine, 1998; (jtly) Essential General Surgical Operations, 2001, 2nd edn 2007; papers in sci. jls and chapters in books on peptic ulcer, oesophageal, gastric and general abdominal surgery and surgical trng. *Recreations:* opera, theatre, squash, cycling. *Address:* 10 Southwood Lane, Highgate Village, N6 5EE. *T:* (020) 8340 8575, *Fax:* (020) 7472 6444; *e-mail:* r.kirk@medsch.ucl.ac.uk. *Club:* Royal Society of Medicine.

KIRK, Richard Stanley, CBE 2006; Chief Executive, Peacock's Stores, since 1996; *b* 16 Nov. 1945; *s* of Charles Kirk and Margaret (*née* Green); *m* 1st, 1969 (marr. diss. 1988); two *s*; 2nd, 1995, Barbara Mount. *Educ:* Chesterfield Grammar Sch. Store Manager, then Area Manager, F. W. Woolworth, 1966–77; Iceland Frozen Foods, subseq. Iceland Gp, PLC, 1977–96: Stores Dir, 1982–86; Man. Dir, 1986–96. *Recreations:* ski-ing, shooting, travel.

KIRK-GREENE, Anthony Hamilton Millard, CMG 2001; MBE 1963; FRHistS; Emeritus Fellow, St Antony's College, Oxford, since 1992; *b* 16 May 1925; *e s* of late Leslie and Helen Kirk-Greene; *m* 1967, Helen Margaret Martyn Sellar. *Educ:* Rugby Sch. (Open Schol.); Clare Coll., Cambridge (Open Schol.; MA); Edinburgh Univ. Served Indian Army, 8th Punjab Regt, 1943–47. Colonial Admin. Service, Northern Nigeria, 1950–66; Supervisor, Admin. Service Trng, 1957–60; Sen. Dist Officer, 1960–66; Reader in Govt, Ahmadu Bello Univ., 1962–66; Vis. Fellow, Clare Coll., Cambridge, 1967; Sen. Res. Fellow in African Studies, St Antony's Coll., Oxford, 1967–80; Special Lectr in Modern Hist. of Africa, Oxford Univ., 1981–92; Director: Oxford Colonial Records Project, 1980–84; Oxford Univ. Foreign Service Prog., 1986–90. Chm., Bd of Mgt, Beit Fund, 1987–92. ODA Consultant, E African Staff Coll., 1972; UK Election Supervisor, Rhodesia/Zimbabwe, 1980. Harkness Fellow, Northwestern Univ. and UCLA, 1958–59; Hans Wolff Lectr, Indiana Univ., 1973. Killam Vis. Prof., Calgary Univ., 1985; Leverhulme Emeritus Fellow, 1993; Adjunct Prof., Stanford Univ. in Oxford, 1992–99. Mem. Council, Britain-Nigeria Assoc., 1984–; Pres., African Studies Assoc., UK, 1988–90 (Distinguished Africanist Award, 2005); Vice-Pres., Royal African Soc., 1990–2006. Mem., Oral History Cttee, British Empire and Commonwealth Mus., 1998–. Gen. Ed., Methuen Studies in African History, 1970–80; Academic Consultant: Holmes and Meier African Series, 1980–85; Radcliffe Press, 1992–; Jt Ed., Hoover Colonial Series, 1985–90; Series Ed., Modern Revivals in Africa, Gregg Press, 1990–95; Reviews Editor: Corona Club Jl, 1990–2000; Britain-Nigeria Assoc. Newsletter, 2002–07; Associate Ed., Oxford DNB, 1996–2002. *Publications:* Adamawa Past and Present, 1958; Barth's Travels in Nigeria, 1962; Principles of Native Administration in Nigeria, 1965; (with S. J. Hogben) Emirates of Northern Nigeria, 1966; Hausa Proverbs, 1967; Crisis and Conflict in Nigeria 1966–1970, 1971; (with C. Kraft) Teach Yourself Hausa, 1975; A Biographical Dictionary of the British Colonial Governor, 1980; 'Stay by Your Radios': the military in Africa, 1981; (with D. Rimmer) Nigeria since 1970, 1981; A Biographical Dictionary of the British Colonial Service, 1991; Diplomatic Initiative: a Jubilee history, 1994; (with J. H. Vaughan) Hamman Yaji: diary of a Nigerian Chief, 1995 (Best Text Award, African Studies Assoc., USA, 1996); On Crown Service, 1999; (with D. Rimmer) Britain's Intellectual Engagement with Africa, 2000; Britain's Imperial Administrators, 2000; Glimpses of Empire, 2001; Symbol of Authority, 2005; numerous monographs, chapters and articles on African and Imperial history. *Recreations:* reading, travel, controlled walking, wine tasting; played hockey for Cambridge Univ. 1948–50 (Capt., CU Wanderers, 1949–50). *Address:* c/o St Antony's College, Oxford OX2 6JF. *T:* (01865) 284700. *Clubs:* Royal Commonwealth Society; Hawks (Cambridge).

KIRKBRIDE, Julie; MP (C) Bromsgrove, since 1997; *b* 5 June 1960; *d* of late Henry Raymond Kirkbride and of Barbara (*née* Bancroft); *m* 1997, A. J. MacKay, *qv*; one *s*. *Educ:* Highlands Sch., Halifax; Girton Coll., Cambridge. Researcher, Yorkshire TV, 1983–86; Producer: BBC news and current affairs, 1986–89; ITN, 1989–92; Political Correspondent: Daily Telegraph, 1992–96; also Social Affairs Ed., Sunday Telegraph, 1996. Shadow Sec. of State for Culture, Media and Sport, 2003–04. Rotary Foundn Scholar, Yorkshire Area, 1982–83. *Recreations:* walking, travelling, opera. *Address:* House of Commons, SW1A 0AA.

KIRKBY, Dame (Carolyn) Emma, DBE 2007 (OBE 2000); freelance classical concert singer; soprano; *b* 26 Feb. 1949; *d* of late Capt. Geoffrey Kirkby, CBE, DSC, RN and of Daphne Kirkby; one *s* by Anthony Rooley, *qv*. *Educ:* Hanford School; Sherborne School for Girls; Somerville College, Oxford (BA Classics). FGSM 1991. Private singing lessons with Jessica Cash. Regular appearances with Taverner Choir and Players, 1972–; Member: Consort of Musicke, 1973–; Academy of Ancient Music, 1975–; numerous radio broadcasts, gramophone recordings, appearances at the Proms, 1977–. Hon. DLitt Salford, 1985; Hon. DMus: Bath, 1994; Sheffield, 2000. *T:* (Consort of Musicke) (020) 8444 6565; *e-mail:* consort@easynet.co.uk.

KIRKHAM, family name of **Baroness Berners**.

KIRKHAM, Baron *cr* 1999 (Life Peer), of Old Cantley in the county of South Yorkshire; **Graham Kirkham,** Kt 1996; CVO 2001; Chairman, DFS Furniture Company Ltd, since 1983. Sen. Party Treas., Conservative Party, 1997–98. *Address:* (office) Redhouse Interchange, Adwick-le-Street, Doncaster, S Yorkshire DN6 7NA.

KIRKHAM, Donald Herbert, CBE 1996; FCIS; Group Chief Executive, Woolwich Building Society, 1991–95 (Chief Executive, 1986–90); *b* 1 Jan. 1936; *s* of Herbert and Hettie Kirkham; *m* 1960, Kathleen Mary Lond; one *s* one *d*. *Educ:* Grimsby Technical Sch. Woolwich Equitable Building Society, later Woolwich Building Society: Representative, 1959; Branch Manager, 1963; Gen. Manager's Asst, 1967; Business Planning Manager, 1970; Asst Gen. Manager, 1972; Gen. Manager, 1976; Mem. Local Board, 1979; Dep. Chief Gen. Manager, 1981; Mem. Board, 1982; non-exec. Dir, 1996–97; Dir, Gresham Insurance Co. Ltd, 1995–96. President: Banque Woolwich SA, 1995–2001; Banca Woolwich SpA, 1995–2002. Director: Horniman Museum and Public Park Trust, 1989–2004 (Chm., 1996–2004); Building Socs Investor Protection Bd, 1995–97; Bexley and Greenwich HA, 1996–98 and 1999–2001; Oxleas NHS Foundn Trust, 2006–. Chartered Building Societies Institute: Mem. Council, 1976; Dep. Pres., 1980; Pres., 1981; Vice-Pres., 1986–93; then Vice-Pres., CIB, 1993–98; Institute of Chartered Secretaries and Administrators: Mem. Council, 1979; Vice-Pres., 1985; Sen. Vice-Pres., 1990; Pres., 1991; Building Societies Association: Mem. Council, 1991–95; Dep. Chm., 1993–94; Chm., 1994–95. Trustee, Ranyard Meml Charitable Trust, 2001–. Hon. DBA Thames Poly., 1991. *Recreations:* boating, sea fishing. *Address:* 2 Chaundrye Close, The Court Yard, Eltham, SE9 5QB. *T:* (020) 8859 4295. *Club:* Christchurch Sailing.

KIRKHAM, Elizabeth Anne, (Libby); see Wiener, E. A.

KIRKHAM, Frances Margaret, FCIArb; **Her Honour Judge Kirkham;** a Circuit Judge, Technology and Construction Court, Birmingham, since 2000; Chartered Arbitrator; *b* 29 Oct. 1947; *d* of Brian Llewellyn Morgan Davies and Natalie May Davies (*née* Stephens); *m* 1971, Barry Charles Kirkham. *Educ:* King's Coll. London (BA Hons 1969; AKC 1969). FCIArb 1991. Bank of England, 1969–73; Lloyds Bank Internat., 1973–74; admitted solicitor, 1978; Pinsent & Co., 1976–84; Bettinsons, 1984–87; Edge & Ellison, 1987–95; Dibb Lupton Alsop, 1995–2000. Parly Boundary Comr, 2000; Mem., Judicial Appts Commn, 2006–. Member: Wkg Party on Civil Justice Reform, Law Soc. and Bar Council, 1992–93; Civil Litigation Cttee, 1988–92, Litigation Casework Cttee, 1990–92, Law Soc.; Civil Litigation Cttee, Birmingham Law Soc., 1992–93; Council, CIArb, 1992–97, 2000 (Chm., W Midlands Br., 1994–97). Founder Chm., W Midlands Assoc. Women Solicitors; Sec., UK Assoc. of Women Judges, 2003–06. Hon. Member: Arbrix, 2002–; Technol. and Construction Ct Solicitors' Assoc., 2005– (formerly Founder Cttee Mem.). Mem., Adv. Bd, Centre for Advanced Litigation, Nottingham Law Sch., 1992–97. Hon. Bencher, Inner Temple, 2008. Gov., Heathfield Sch., Harrow, 1981–91 (Chm., 1984–91). *Recreations:* time with friends, sailing, ski-ing, walking, music, theatre, gardening. *Address:* Priory Courts, 33 Bull Street, Birmingham B4 6DW. *T:* (0121) 681 3181. *Clubs:* University Women's; Bank of England Sailing.

KIRKHAM, Rt Rev. John Dudley Galtrey; Assistant Bishop, Diocese of Salisbury, since 2001; *b* 20 Sept. 1935; *s* of late Rev. Canon Charles Dudley Kirkham and Doreen Betty Galtrey; *m* 1986, Mrs Hester Gregory. *Educ:* Lancing Coll.; Trinity Coll., Cambridge (BA 1959, MA 1963). Commnd, Royal Hampshire Regt, seconded to 23 (K) Bn, King's African Rifles, 1954–56. Trinity Coll., Cambridge, 1956–59; Westcott House, 1960–62; Curate, St Mary-le-Tower, Ipswich, 1962–65; Chaplain to Bishop of Norwich, 1965–69; Priest in Charge, Rockland St Mary w. Hellington, 1967–69; Chaplain to Bishop of New Guinea, 1969; Asst Priest, St Martin-in-the-Fields and St Margaret's, Westminster, 1970–72; Domestic Chaplain to Archbishop of Canterbury, and Canterbury Diocesan Director of Ordinands, 1972–76; Bp Suffragan, later Area Bp, of Sherborne, 1976–2001; Canon and Preb., Salisbury Cath., 1977–2001, and 2002–; Bp to the Forces, 1992–2001. Archbishop of Canterbury's Advr to HMC, 1990–92. Commissary to Bp of Polynesia and Archbp of PNG. Hon. Chaplain: Princess of Wales Royal Regt, 1992–; KAR and EAF Assoc., 2001–. Provost, Western Region, Woodard Schs, 2002–. ChStJ 1991; Chaplain to the Guild of the Nineteen Lubricators. Croix d'Argent de Saint-Rombaut, 1973. *Recreations:* walking, bicycling, gardening, woodwork. *Address:* Flamston House, Flamstone Street, Bishopstone, Salisbury, Wilts SP5 4BZ. *Clubs:* Army and Navy, Kandahar.

KIRKHAM, Keith Edwin, OBE 1987; PhD; Administrative Director, Clinical Research Centre, Medical Research Council, 1988–94; *b* 20 Oct. 1929; *s* of Thomas Kirkham and Clara Prestwich Willacy; *m* 1953, Dorothea Mary Fisher; two *s*. *Educ:* Kirkham Grammar Sch.; Birmingham Univ. (BSc); Fitzwilliam House, Cambridge (DipAgSci; T. H. Middleton Prize); MA, PhD Cantab. National Service, 2nd Lieut RA, 1955–57. Asst in Res., Cambridge, 1951–54; Univ. Demonstr, Cambridge, 1954–60; Sci. Staff, Clin. Endocrinology Res. Unit, MRC, 1960–73; Asst Dir (Admin), Clin. Res. Centre, MRC, 1973–88. Sec., Soc. for Endocrinology, 1975–79. Governor: Harrow Coll. of Higher Educn, 1983–90 (Chm. of Govs, 1986–90); Univ. of Westminster (formerly Poly. of Central London), 1990–2000. Hon. DSc Westminster, 1999. *Publications:* contribs to sci. jls on endocrinology. *Recreations:* cruising, sport (watching).

KIRKHILL, Baron *cr* 1975 (Life Peer), of Kirkhill, Aberdeen; **John Farquharson Smith;** *b* 7 May 1930; *s* of Alexander F. Smith and Ann T. Farquharson; *m* 1965, Frances Mary

Walker Reid; one step *d*. Lord Provost of the City and Royal Burgh of Aberdeen, 1971–75. Minister of State, Scottish Office, 1975–78. Chm., N of Scotland Hydro-Electric Bd, 1979–82. Deleg. to Parly Assembly of Council of Europe and WEU, 1987–2001 (Chm., Cttee on Legal Affairs and Human Rights, 1991–95). Hon. LLD Aberdeen, 1974. *Address:* 3 Rubislaw Den North, Aberdeen AB15 4AL. *T:* (01224) 314167.

KIRKHOPE, Timothy John Robert; Member (C) Yorkshire and the Humber Region, European Parliament, since 1999; solicitor; *b* 29 April 1945; *s* of late John Thomas Kirkhope and Dorothy Buemann Kirkhope (*née* Bolt); *m* 1969, Caroline (*née* Maling); four *s*. *Educ:* Royal Grammar School, Newcastle upon Tyne; College of Law, Guildford. Conservative Party: joined 1961 (N Area Vice-Chm. of YC and Mem., Nat. Cttee); Hexham Treasurer, 1982–85; Exec., N Area, 1975–87; Mem., Nat. Exec., 1985–87; Mem. Bd, 2005–07; Mem., Northern Bd, 2007–. County Councillor, Northumberland, 1981–85. Mem., Newcastle Airport Bd, 1982–85; Mem., Northern RHA, 1982–86; Founder Lawyer Mem., Mental Health Act Commn, 1983–86. Contested (C): Durham, Feb. 1974; Darlington, 1979. MP (C) Leeds North East, 1987–97; contested (C) same seat, 1997. PPS to Minister of State for the Envmt and Countryside, 1989–90; an Asst Govt Whip, 1990–92; a Lord Comr of HM Treasury (Govt Whip), 1992–95; Vice Chamberlain, HM Household, 1995; Parly Under-Sec. of State, Home Office, 1995–97. Mem., Select Cttee on Statutory Instruments, 1987–90; Vice Chm., Backbench Legal Cttee, 1988–89; Jt Hon. Sec., Cons. Backbench Envmt Cttee, 1988–89. European Parliament: Chief Whip, 1999–2001, Leader, 2004–07, UK Conservatives; Cons. spokesman: on justice and home affairs, 1999–2007; on transport and tourism, 2007–; Mem., Culture, Media, Arts, Youth and Educn Cttee, 1999–2002; Cons. Mem., Future of Europe Convention, 2002–04; Vice-Chm., EPP-ED, 2004–05; Vice-Pres., EP Const. Affairs Cttee, 2007–; Dir, Movt for European Reform, 2007–; Chm., EP Delegn to Australia and NZ, 2008–. Chm., Kirkhope Commn on Asylum, 2003, on Immigration, 2004, Cons Party. Dir, Bournemouth and W Hampshire Water Co., 1999–. Dep. Chm., GBA, 1990–98. Gov., Royal Grammar Sch., Newcastle upon Tyne, 1989–99. MInstD 1998. *Recreations:* flying (holds private pilot's licence), tennis, golf, swimming, watching TV quiz shows. *Address:* Beechwood Farm, Scotton, Knaresborough, N Yorks HG5 9HY; European Parliament, Rue Wiertz, Brussels 1047, Belgium. *Clubs:* Northern Counties (Newcastle upon Tyne); Dunstanburgh Castle Golf (Northumberland).

KIRKMAN, William Patrick, MBE 1993; Secretary: University of Cambridge Careers Service, 1968–92; Cambridge Society, 1992–2003; Administrator, American Friends of Cambridge University, 2000–01; Fellow, Wolfson College, (formerly University College), Cambridge, 1968–2000, now Emeritus; *b* 23 Oct. 1932; *s* of late Geoffrey Charles Aylward Kirkman and Bertha Winifred Kirkman; *m* 1959, Anne Teasdale Fawcett; two *s* one *d*. *Educ:* Churcher's Coll., Petersfield, Hants; Oriel Coll., Oxford. 2nd cl. hons, mod. langs, 1955; MA 1959; MA (Cantab) by incorporation, 1968. National Service, 1950–52, RASC (L/Cpl); TA, 1952–59, Intell. Corps (Lieut). Editorial staff: Express & Star, Wolverhampton, 1955–57; The Times, 1957–64 (Commonwealth staff, 1960–64, Africa Correspondent, 1962–64). Asst Sec., Oxford Univ. Appointments Cttee, 1964–68. Chm., Standing Conf. of University Appointments Services, 1971–73; Member: Management Cttee, Central Services Unit for Univ. Careers and Appointments Services, 1971–74, 1985–87; British Cttee, Journalists in Europe, 1985–97; Cambridge Univ. PR Co-ordinating Cttee, 1987–96; Trng Bd, ESRC, 1990–93; Non-service Mem., Home Office Extended Interview Bds, 1993–2002. Member: BBC South and East Regl Adv. Council, 1990–92, Midlands and E Regl Adv. Council, 1992–93, E Regl Adv. Council, 1994–96; Chm., BBC Radio Cambridgeshire Adv. Council, 1992–96. Wolfson College: Vice-Pres., 1980–84; Mem. Council, 1969–73, 1976–80, 1988–92, 1994–95; Dir, Press Fellowship Programme, 1982–96. Churchwarden, St Mary and All Saints Willingham, 1978–85, 1996–97. Vice-Chm., Assoc. of Charitable Foundns, 1994–97; Mem. Regl Cttee, RSA, 1997–2003; Mem. Council, U3A, Cambridge, 2007–. Trustee: Sir Halley Stewart Trust, 1969– (Hon. Sec., 1978–82; Vice-Chm., 1998–2002); Willingham British Sch. Trust, 1974–91; Homerton Coll., 1980–89; Lucy Cavendish Coll., 1989–97; Mem. Cttee, Cambridge Soc., 1979–83. Editor: Cambridge, 1992–2003; CRAC Newsletter, 1997–98; Chm., CAMREAD, 2004–. *Publications:* Unscrambling an Empire, 1966; contrib.: Policing and Social Policy, 1984; Models of Police/Public Consultation in Europe, 1985; Managing Recruitment, 4th edn 1988; Graduate Recruitment: a 25-year retrospective, 1993; Reflections on Change, 2007; contributor to journals incl.: Africa Contemporary Record, Cambridge Rev., The Hindu (Chennai), The Round Table and to BBC. *Recreations:* local and international politics, church activities, writing. *Address:* 14 George Street, Willingham, Cambridge CB24 5LJ. *T:* (01954) 260393; *e-mail:* wpk1000@cam.ac.uk. *Club:* Royal Commonwealth Society.

KIRKNESS, Donald James, CB 1980; Deputy Secretary, Overseas Development Administration, 1977–80; *b* 29 Sept. 1919; *s* of Charles Stephen and Elsie Winifred Kirkness; *m* 1947, Monica Mary Douch; one *d*. *Educ:* Harvey Grammar Sch., Folkestone. Exchequer and Audit Dept, 1938. Served War: RA and Royal Berkshire Regt, 1939–46. Colonial Office, 1947 (Asst Principal); Financial and Economic Adviser, Windward I, 1955–57; Dept of Economic Affairs, 1966; Civil Service Dept, 1970–73; ODA/ODM, 1973. UK Governor, Internat. Fund for Agricultural Develt, 1977–81; Mem., Exec. Bd, UNESCO, 1978–83.

KIRKPATRICK, Sir Ivone Elliott, 11th Bt *cr* 1685; *b* 1 Oct. 1942; *s* of Sir James Alexander Kirkpatrick, 10th Bt and Ellen Gertrude, *o d* of Captain R. P. Elliott, late RNR; *S* father, 1954. *Educ:* Wellington Coll., Berks; St Mark's Coll., University of Adelaide. *Heir:* *b* Robin Alexander Kirkpatrick, *b* 19 March 1944.

KIRKPATRICK, Janice Mary; Designer and Creative Director, Graven Images, since 1985; Chairman, Lighthouse Trust, since 2004 (Director, since 1999); *b* 16 April 1962; *d* of James Burns Kirkpatrick and Jane Henry Coupland Kirkpatrick (*née* Borthwick); partner, 1984, Ross Buchanan Hunter. *Educ:* Glasgow Sch. of Art (BA 1st Cl Hons Glass Graphic Design 1984; MA Design 1985). Vis. Prof., Glasgow Sch. of Art, 2000– (Gov., 1999–). Trustee, NESTA, 1999–2005. *Recreations:* motorcycling, trying to be a gardener, breeding British Saddleback pigs. *Address:* Graven Images, 175 Albion Street, Glasgow G1 1RU. *T:* (0141) 522 6626, *Fax:* (0141) 552 0433; *e-mail:* janice@graven.co.uk.

KIRKPATRICK, William Brown, OBE 1998; Member: Gaming Board for Great Britain, 1990–99; National Lottery Charities Board, 1994–98; *b* 27 April 1934; *s* of late Joseph and Mary Kirkpatrick, Thornhill, Dumfriesshire; *m* 1990, Joan L. Millar. *Educ:* Morton Acad., Thornhill; George Watson's Coll., Edinburgh; Univ. of Strathclyde (BScEcon); Columbia Business Sch., NY (MS and McKinsey Scholar); Stanford Executive Program. After three years in manufacturing industry in Glasgow, Dundee and London, served 3i, 1960–85, latterly at director level, and worked in London, Scotland and Australia in investment capital, corporate finance, fixed interest capital markets, on secondment as Industrial Director of Industry Department for Scotland, in shipping finance and as a nominee director; company dir and corporate advr with various cos, 1985–95 (incl. appt within DoE on water privatisation). JP Inner London, 1985–92.

Recreations: Scottish paintings, porcelain pigs, current affairs. *Address:* Roughhills, Sandyhills, Dalbeattie, Kirkcudbrightshire DG5 4NZ. *T:* (01387) 780239. *Club:* Caledonian.

KIRKUP, James; travel writer, poet, novelist, playwright, translator, broadcaster; *b* 23 April 1918; *o s* of James Harold Kirkup and Mary Johnson. *Educ:* South Shields High Sch.; Durham Univ. (BA; Hon. Fellow, Grey Coll., 1992). FRSL 1964. Gregory Fellow in Poetry, University of Leeds, 1950–52; Visiting Poet and Head of English Dept, Bath Academy of Art, Corsham Court, Wilts, 1953–56; Lectr in English, Swedish Ministry of Education, Stockholm, 1956–57; Prof. of Eng. Lang. and Lit., University of Salamanca, 1957–58, of English, Tohoku Univ., Sendai, Japan, 1958–61; Lecturer in English Literature, University of Malaya in Kuala Lumpur, 1961–62; Literary Editor, Orient/West Magazine, Tokyo, 1963–64; Prof., Japan Women's Univ., 1964–; Poet in Residence and Visiting Prof., Amherst Coll., Mass, 1968–; Prof. of English Literature, Nagoya Univ., 1969–72; Arts Council Fellowship in Creative Writing, Univ. of Sheffield, 1974–75; Morton Vis. Prof. of Internat. Literature, Ohio Univ., 1975–76; Playwright in Residence, Sherman Theatre, University Coll., Cardiff, 1976–77; Prof. of English Lit., Kyoto Univ. of Foreign Studies, Kyoto, Japan, 1977–89. President: Poets' Soc. of Japan, 1969; British Haiku Soc., 1990; Sponsor, Inst. of Psychophysical Res., 1970. Atlantic Award in Literature (Rockefeller Foundn), 1950; Mabel Batchelder Award, 1968; Keats Prize for Poetry, 1974; Scott-Moncrieff Prize for Translation, 1997. *Plays performed:* Upon this Rock (perf. Peterborough Cathedral), 1955; Masque, The Triumph of Harmony (perf. Albert Hall), 1955; The True Mistery of the Nativity, 1957; Dürrenmatt, The Physicists (Eng. trans.), 1963; Dürrenmatt, The Meteor (Eng. trans.); Dürrenmatt, Play Strindberg (Eng. trans.), 1972; The Magic Drum, children's play, 1972, children's musical, 1977; Dürrenmatt, Portrait of a Planet, 1972; Dürrenmatt, The Conformer, 1974; Schiller, Don Carlos, 1975; Cyrano de Bergerac, 1975; *operas:* An Actor's Revenge, 1979; Friends in Arms, 1980; The Damask Drum, 1982; *television plays performed:* The Peach Garden, Two Pigeons Flying High, The Prince of Homburg, etc. Contributor to BBC, The Listener, The Spectator, Times Literary Supplement, The Independent, Modern Poetry in Translation, Time and Tide, New Yorker, Botteghe Oscure, London Magazine, Japan Qly, English Teachers' Magazine (Tokyo), etc. *Publications:* The Drowned Sailor, 1948; The Cosmic Shape, 1947; The Creation, 1950; The Submerged Village, 1951; A Correct Compassion, 1952; A Spring Journey, 1954; Upon This Rock, 1955; The True Mistery of the Nativity, 1957; The Descent into the Cave, 1957; Sorrows, Passions and Alarms, 1959; These Horned Islands, A Journal of Japan, 1962; frères Gréban, The True Mistery of the Passion, 1962; Refusal to Conform, 1963; Tropic Temper: a Memoir of Malaya, 1963; Japan Industrial, 1964–65 (2 vols); Daily Life in the French Revolution, 1964; Tokyo, 1965; England, Now, 1965; Japan, Now, 1966; Frankly Speaking, I-II, 1968; Bangkok, 1968; One Man's Russia, 1968; Filipinescas, 1968; Streets of Asia, 1969; Japan Physical, 1969; Aspects of the Short Story, 1969; Hong Kong, 1970; Japan Behind the Fan, 1970; Heaven, Hell and Hara-Kiri, 1974; (with Birgit Skiöld) Zen Gardens, 1974; Scenes from Sesshu, 1977; Zen Contemplations, 1979; (with Birgit Skiöld) The Tao of Water, 1980; Folktales Japanesque, 1982; Modern American Myths, 1982; I Am Count Dracula, 1982; I Am Frankenstein's Monster, 1983; Miniature Masterpieces of Kawabata Yasunari, 1983; When I was a Child: a study of nursery-rhymes, 1983; My Way-USA, 1984; The Glory that was Greece, 1984; The Mystery & Magic of Symbols, 1987; The Cry of the Owl: Native Folktales & Legends, 1987; (ed) A Certain State of Mind: an anthology of modern and contemporary Japanese haiku poets, 1995; (ed) Burning Giraffes: modern and contemporary Japanese poets, 1995; *poems:* The Prodigal Son, 1959; Paper Windows: Poems from Japan, 1968; Shepherding Winds (anthol.), 1969; Songs and Dreams (anthol.), 1970; White Shadows, Black Shadows: Poems of Peace and War, 1970; The Body Servant; poems of exile, 1971; A Bewick Bestiary, 1971; Modern Japanese Poetry (anthol.), 1978; Dengonban Messages (one-line poems), 1980; To the Ancestral North: poems for an autobiography, 1983; The Sense of the Visit: new poems, 1984; The Guitar-Player of Zuiganji, 1985; Fellow Feelings, 1986; Shooting Stars (haiku), 1992; First Fireworks (haiku), 1992; Short Takes (one-line poems), 1993; Words for Contemplation, 1993; Look at it this way! (for children), 1993; Blue Bamboo: haiku, senryu and tanka, 1994; Formulas for Chaos, 1994; Strange Attractors, 1995; An Extended Breath: collected longer poems, 1995; Selected Shorter Poems, vol. 1 Omens of Disaster, vol. 2 Once and for All, 1995; Noems, Koans and a Navel Display, 1995; Counting to 9,999: haiku and tanka, 1995; Utsusemi: tanka, 1996; The Patient Obituarist: new poems, 1996; A Book of Tanka (Japan Fest. Foundn Award), 1997; Figures in a Setting, 1997; He Dreamed he was a Butterfly: tanka, 1997; One-Man Band: poems without words, 1999; A Crack in the Wall: an anthology of modern Arab poetry, 2000; Tokonoma, 2000; TankAlphabet, 2001; A Tiger in your Tanka, 2001; Shields Sketches, 2002; An Island in the Sky: poems for Andorra, 2004; The Authentic Touch, 2007; Marsden Rock, 2008; *poems and translations:* Ecce Homo: My Pasolini, 1982; No More Hiroshimas, 1982, new edn 2004; *autobiography:* vol. 1, The Only Child, 1957 (trans. Japanese, 1986, reprinted with vol. 2 as A Child of the Tyne, 1997); vol. 2, Sorrows, Passions and Alarms, 1987 (trans. Japanese); vol. 3, I, of All People: an Autobiography of Youth, 1990; vol. 4, A Poet could not But be Gay: some Legends of my Lost Youth, 1991; vol. 5, Me All Over: memoirs of a misfit, 1993; Throwback: poems towards an autobiography, 1992; *novels:* The Love of Others, 1962; Insect Summer (for children), 1971; The Magic Drum (for children), 1973; Gaijin on the Ginza, 1991; Queens have Died Young and Fair, 1993; *essays:* Eibungaku Saiken, 1980; The Joys of Japan, 1985; Lafcadio Hearn (biog.), 1985; James Kirkup's International Movie Theatre, 1985; Trends and Traditions, 1986; Portraits & Souvenirs (biog.), 1987; *opera:* The Damask Drum, 1982; An Actor's Revenge, 1989 (also complete music score of adaptation); The Genius of Haiku: essays on R. H. Blyth, 1994; *translations:* Camara Laye, The Dark Child, 1955; Ancestral Voices, 1956; Camara Laye, The Radiance of the King, 1956; Simone de Beauvoir, Memoirs of a Dutiful Daughter, 1958; The Girl from Nowhere, 1958; It Began in Babel, 1961; The Captive, 1962; Sins of the Fathers, 1962; The Gates of Paradise, 1962; The Heavenly Mandate, 1964; Daily Life of the Etruscans, 1964; Erich Kästner, The Little Man, 1966; Erich Kästner, The Little Man and The Little Miss, 1969; Heinrich von Kleist, Michael Kohlhaas, 1966; E. T. A. Hoffmann, Tales of Hoffmann, 1966; Camara Laye, A Dream of Africa, 1967; The Eternal Virgin (Eng. trans. of Valéry's La Jeune Parque), 1970; (with C. Fry) The Oxford Ibsen, vol III, Brand and Peer Gynt, 1972; Selected Poems of Kyozo Takagi, 1973, rev. edn as How to Cook Women, 1997; Camara Laye, The Guardian of the Word, 1980; Cold Mountain Poems (trans. Han Shan), 1980; Petru Dimitriu, To the Unknown God, 1982; Michel Kpomassié, An African in Greenland, 1982; Tierno Monénembo, The Bush Toads, 1982; Margherita Guidacci, This Little Measure, 1990; Patrick Drevet, A Room in the Woods, 1991; Marc Rigaudis, Ito-san, 1991; Jean-Baptiste Niel, Painted Shadows, 1991; Jean-Noël Pancrazi, Vagabond Winter, 1992; Pascal Quignard, All the World's Mornings, 1992; Patrick Drevet, My Micheline, 1993; Hervé Guibert, The Man in the Red Hat, The Compassion Protocol, 1993; Georges-Arthur Goldschmidt, Worlds of Difference, 1993; Hervé Guibert, Blindsight, Paradise, 1995; Tahar Ben Jelloun, State of Absence, 1995; Marcelle Lagesse, Isabelle, 1995; Patrick Drevet, Auvers-sur-Oise, 1997; Saito Fumi, In Thickets of Memory (700 tanka poems), 2002; Fumiko Miura, Pages from the Seasons, 2002; Takahashi Mutsuo, Myself as an Anatomical Love-making Chart and other poems, 2004; We of Zipangu: poems of Takahashi Mutsuo (trans. with Makoto Tamaki), 2007; A Pilgrimage in Hell: poems by Iwan Gilkin, 2007; *translation and adaptation:* The Best Way to Travel, from The Works of Zhuangzi, 2004; *festschrift:* Diversions: Festschrift for James Kirkup's 80th Birthday, 1998. *Recreation:* living.

KIRKUP, William, CBE 2008; FRCP, FRCOG, FFPH; Associate NHS Medical Director, Department of Health, since 2008 (Director General, Clinical Programmes, and Associate Chief Medical Officer, 2005–08); *b* 29 April 1949; *s* of late William Kirkup and Patience Kirkup (*née* Wilford); *m* 1972 (marr. diss. 1983); three *d*; *m* 2004, Denise Lambert; one *d*. *Educ:* Newcastle Royal Grammar Sch.; Worcester Coll., Oxford (MA, BM BCh 1974). MRCOG 1979, FRCOG 1993; MFPHM 1986, FFPH (FFPHM 1994); FRCP 2006. Obstetrics and gynaecology posts, Oxford, Sheffield and Newcastle, 1975–82; public health trng, 1982–86; Consultant, Newcastle, 1986–87; Sen. Lectr, Newcastle Univ., 1986–91; Dir of Public Health, N Tyneside, 1987–91; Dir posts, (Performance Review, Healthcare Develt, NHS Trusts Div.), Northern Reg. and NHS Exec., 1991–99; Regl Dir of Public Health and Healthcare, Northern and Yorks, NHS Exec., DoH, 1999–2002; Regl Dir of Public Health, NE, DoH, 2002–05. *Publications:* contribs to learned jls. *Recreations:* Newcastle United FC, music, playing with computers. *Address:* Department of Health, Richmond House, 79 Whitehall, SW1A 2NS. *T:* (020) 7210 5017.

KIRKWOOD, family name of **Barons Kirkwood** and **Kirkwood of Kirkhope**.

KIRKWOOD, 3rd Baron *cr* 1951, of Bearsden; **David Harvie Kirkwood;** Senior Lecturer in Metallurgy, 1976–87, Hon. Senior Lecturer and Metallurgical Consultant, since 1987, Sheffield University; *b* 24 Nov. 1931; *s* of 2nd Baron Kirkwood and Eileen Grace (*d* 1999), *d* of Thomas Henry Boalch; *S* father, 1970; *m* 1965, Judith Rosalie, *d* of late John Hunt; three *d*. *Educ:* Rugby; Trinity Hall, Cambridge (MA, PhD); CEng. Lectr in Metallurgy, Sheffield Univ., 1962; Warden of Stephenson Hall, Sheffield Univ., 1974–80. Mem., Select Cttee on Sci. and Technology, H of L, 1987–92, 1996–99. *Heir:* *b* Hon. James Stuart Kirkwood [*b* 19 June 1937; *m* 1965, Alexandra Mary, *d* of late Alec Dyson; two *d*]. *Address:* 56 Endcliffe Hall Avenue, Sheffield S10 3EL. *T:* (0114) 266 3107.

KIRKWOOD OF KIRKHOPE, Baron *cr* 2005 (Life Peer), of Kirkhope in Scottish Borders; **Archibald Johnstone Kirkwood,** Kt 2003; *b* 22 April 1946; *s* of David Kirkwood and Jessie Barclay Kirkwood; *m* 1972, Rosemary Chester; one *d* one *s*. *Educ:* Cranhill School; Heriot-Watt Univ. (BSc Pharmacy). Notary Public; Solicitor. MP Roxburgh and Berwickshire, 1983–2005 (L/Alliance 1983–88, Lib Dem 1988–2005). Lib Dem convenor and spokesman on welfare, 1988–92, on social security, 1992–94 and 1997–2001, on community care, 1994–97; Chief Whip, 1992–97. Chairman: Social Security Select Cttee, 1997–2001; Work and Pensions Select Cttee, 2001–05. Trustee, Joseph Rowntree Reform Trust, 1985–2007 (Chm., 1999–2006). *Address:* House of Lords, SW1A 0PW.

KIRKWOOD, Rt Hon. Lord; Ian Candlish Kirkwood; PC 2000; a Senator of the College of Justice in Scotland, 1987–2005; *b* 8 June 1932; *o s* of late John Brown Kirkwood, OBE, and Mrs Constance Kirkwood, Edinburgh; *m* 1970, Jill Ingram Scott; two *s*. *Educ:* George Watson's Boys' Coll., Edinburgh; Edinburgh Univ.; Univ. of Michigan, USA. MA (Edin) 1952; LLB (Edin) 1954; LLM (Mich) 1956. Called to Scottish Bar, 1957; apptd Standing Junior Counsel to Scottish Home and Health Dept, 1963; QC (Scot.) 1970. Mem., Parole Bd for Scotland, 1994–97. Formerly Pres., Wireless Telegraphy Appeal Tribunal in Scotland. Chm., Med. Appeal Tribunal in Scotland. *Recreations:* fishing, golf, chess, tennis. *Address:* 58 Murrayfield Avenue, Edinburgh EH12 6AY. *T:* (0131) 477 1994; Knockbrex House, near Borgue, Kirkcudbrightshire. *Club:* New (Edinburgh).

KIRKWOOD, Hon. Sir Andrew (Tristram Hammett), Kt 1993; a Judge of the High Court of Justice, Family Division, 1993–2008; a Deputy High Court Judge, since 2008; *b* 5 June 1944; *s* of Maj. T. G. H. Kirkwood, RE (killed in action, 1944) and late Lady Faulks; *m* 1968, Penelope Jane (*née* Eaton); two *s* one *d*. *Educ:* Radley Coll., Abingdon, Oxon; Christ Church, Oxford (MA). Called to the Bar, Inner Temple, 1966, Bencher, 1993; QC 1989; a Recorder, 1987–93; a Judge, Employment Appeal Tribunal, 1996–98; Liaison Judge, Family Div., Midland and Oxford Circuit, 1999–2001, Midland Circuit, 2001–06. Chm., Leics Inquiry, 1992. Mem., Judicial Studies Bd, 1994–99 (Co-Chm., Civil and Family Cttee, 1994–98; Chm., Family Cttee, 1998–99). *Address:* c/o Royal Courts of Justice, Strand, WC2A 2LL. *Club:* MCC.

KIRKWOOD, Ian Candlish; *see* Kirkwood, Rt Hon. Lord.

KIRKWOOD, Dr James Kerr; Chief Executive and Scientific Director: Universities Federation for Animal Welfare, since 2000; Humane Slaughter Association, since 2000; *b* 8 Nov. 1951; *s* of late Andrew Kerr Kirkwood and of Patricia Mary Kirkwood (*née* Brown); *m* 1983, Julia Mary Christine Brittain; two *s* one *d*. *Educ:* Bradfield Coll., Berks; Bristol Univ. (BVSc 1975; PhD 1982). CBiol, FIBiol 1997; MRCVS. Research Associate, later Res. Fellow, Dept of Pathology, Bristol Univ., 1981–84; Sen. Vet. Officer, Zoological Soc. of London, and Head of Vet. Sci. Gp, Inst. of Zoology, 1984–96; specialist in zoo and wildlife medicine, RCVS, 1992–2000; Scientific Dir, UFAW, and Hon. Dir, Humane Slaughter Assoc., 1996–2000. Ed.-in-Chief, Animal Welfare, 1996–. Dir, Master's Course in Wild Animal Health, RVC/Inst. of Zoology, 1994–96; Vis. Prof., Dept of Pathology and Infectious Diseases, RVC, 1997–; Hon. Res. Fellow, Inst. of Zoology, 1997–2003. Chm., Zoos Forum, 2005– (Mem., 1999–); Dep. Chm., Companion Animal Welfare Council, 2003– (Mem., 2000–); Chm., DEFRA Ind. Wkg Gp on Snares, 2004–05; Member: IUCN Vet. Specialist Gp, 1990–; Council, Zool Soc. of London, 2004–07; TB Adv. Gp, 2006–, Wildlife Health and Welfare Strategy Bd, 2006–, DEFRA; Head of UK Delegn at Internat. Whaling Commn Workshop on Welfare, St Kitts, 2006. Trustee, Zebra Foundn for Vet. Zool Educn, 1990–; Pres., British Vet. Zool Soc., 1994–96. *Publications:* (with K. Stathatos) Biology, Rearing and Care of Young Primates, 1992; (ed jtly) Science in the Service of Animal Welfare, 2004; sundry publications in the scientific literature on aspects of the biology, diseases, conservation and welfare of animals. *Recreations:* wind surfing, music, literature, natural history. *Address:* Universities Federation for Animal Welfare and Humane Slaughter Association, The Old School, Wheathampstead, Herts AL4 8AN. *T:* (01582) 831818.

KIRKWOOD, Michael James, CMG 2003; FCIB; Chief Country Officer, Citigroup Inc., United Kingdom, since 1999; *b* Glasgow, 7 June 1947; *s* of James Kirkwood and June Alexandra Scott Kirkwood (*née* Peters); *m* 1969, Karen Marie Wolf; one *s* one *d*. *Educ:* Trinity Coll., Glenalmond; Stanford Univ., Calif. (BA Hons). FCIB 2001. Hongkong and Shanghai Banking Corp., 1965–68; Alt. Dir, Temenggong Securities Ltd, Singapore, 1973–76; Chief Exec., Temenggong Merchant Bankers Ltd, Singapore, 1974–76; Dir, Scotland, Ansbacher & Co. Ltd, 1976–77; Citigroup, 1977–: Country Senior Officer: Scotland, 1977–80; Denmark, 1981–83; CEO, Citicorp Investment Bank Switzerland SA, 1985–88; Gp COS, NY, 1988–91; Div. Hd, Continental Europe, 1991–92; Hd, UK Corporate Banking, 1993–. Chm., British American Business Inc., 2001–03; non-exec. Dir, Kidde plc, 2001–05. Chairman: American Banks Assoc., 2000–02; Assoc. of Foreign

Banks, 2004; Pres., Chartered Inst. of Bankers, 2003–04 (Dep. Pres., 2002–03); Vice Chm. (formerly Vice Pres.), British Bankers' Assoc., 2001–. Chm., Habitat for Humanity GB, 2004–; Dir and Trustee, Stone Foundn, 1996–2004. MInstD; FRSA. HM Lieut for the City of London, 2004. Freeman, City of London, 2002; Mem. Ct, Co. of Internat. Bankers, 2001– (Master, 2005–06). *Recreations:* Mediterranean horticulture, golf, Rugby, country pursuits (field sports). *Address:* Citigroup Inc., 33 Canada Square, Canary Wharf, E14 5LB. *T:* (020) 7986 5959. *Club:* Boodle's.

KIRKWOOD, Prof. Thomas Burton Loram, PhD; Professor of Medicine, Head of Gerontology, since 1999, Director, Institute for Ageing and Health, since 2006 (Co-Director, 2004–06), and Director, Centre for Integrated Systems Biology of Ageing and Nutrition, since 2005, University of Newcastle upon Tyne; *b* 6 July 1951; *s* of late Kenneth Kirkwood; *m* 1973, Betty Rosamund Bartlett (marr. diss. 1995); one *s* one *d*; *m* 1995, Jane Louise Bottomley. *Educ:* Dragon Sch., Oxford; Magdalen Coll. Sch., Oxford; St Catharine's Coll., Cambridge (MA; PhD 1983); Worcester Coll., Oxford (MSc). Scientist, Nat. Inst. for Biol Standards and Control, 1973–81; National Institute for Medical Research: Sen. Scientist, 1981–88; Head, Lab. of Mathematical Biol., 1988–93; Prof. of Biol Gerontology, Univ. of Manchester, 1993–99. Various distinguished lectures incl. Reith Lectures, 2001. Chm., Brit. Soc. for Research on Ageing, 1992–99; Dir, Jt Centre on Ageing, Univs of Manchester and Newcastle upon Tyne, 1996–99; Gov., 1998–2001, and Chm., Res. Adv. Council, 1999–2000, Research into Ageing; Chm., Foresight Task Force on Health Care of Older People, 1999–2001; Member: WHO Expert Adv. Panel on Biol Standardization, 1985–2004; UK Human Genome Mapping Project Cttee, 1991–93; Basic Scis Interest Gp., Wellcome Trust, 1992–97; BBSRC, 2001–04; Science and Industry Council, NE England, 2007–. Specialist Advr, Inquiry into Scientific Aspects of Ageing, H of Lords Select Cttee on Sci. and Technol., 2004–06. Trustee, Cumberland Lodge, 2007–. Co-Ed., Mechanisms of Ageing and Develt, 2000–06. President: Internat. Biometric Soc. (British Reg.), 1998–2000; (Biol.), Eur. Section, Internat. Assoc. of Gerontology, 2003–07. Fellow, Inst. for Advanced Study, Budapest, 1997; Tower Fellow, NZ Inst. for Res. on Ageing, 2004. FMedSci 2001 (Mem. Council, 2002–06). Hon. FFA 2002. Hon. DSc Hull, 2003. Heinz Karger Prize, 1983; Fritz Verzár Medal, 1996; Dhole-Eddlestone Prize, British Geriatrics Soc., 2001; Henry Dale Prize, Royal Instn, 2002; Cohen Medal, British Soc. for Res. on Ageing, 2006. *Publications:* (jtly) Accuracy in Molecular Processes: its control and relevance to living systems, 1986; Time of Our Lives: the science of human ageing, 1999; (with C. E. Finch) Chance, Development and Aging, 2000; The End of Age, 2001; (jtly) Sex and Longevity: sexuality, gender, reproduction, parenthood, 2001; many scientific articles. *Recreations:* hill-walking, pottery, gardening. *Address:* Institute for Ageing and Health, Henry Wellcome Laboratory for Biogerontology Research, Campus for Ageing and Vitality, Newcastle upon Tyne NE4 5PL. *T:* (0191) 248 1103, *Fax:* (0191) 248 1101; *e-mail:* Tom.Kirkwood@newcastle.ac.uk.

KIRNER, Hon. Joan Elizabeth, AM 1980; Chairman, Australian Centre for Equity through Education, 1996–2001; Co-Convenor, 1996–2006, Ambassador, since 2006, EMILY's List, Australia; *b* 20 June 1938; *d* of J. K. and B. E. Hood; *m* 1960, Ronald Kirner; two *s* one *d*. *Educ:* University High Sch.; Melbourne Univ. (BA, Dip. Educn). English and Social Studies Teacher, Ballarat Tech. Sch., 1959–60; positions with Vic. Fedn of State Schs Parents' Clubs, Aust. Council of State Schs Orgns, to 1982. Joined ALP 1976; MLC Melbourne West, 1982–88; MLA (ALP) Williamstown, Victoria, 1988–94; Minister for: Conservation, Forests and Lands, 1985–88; Education, 1988–90; Ethnic Affairs, 1990–91; Women's Affairs, 1990–92; Dep. Premier, 1989–90; Premier of Victoria, 1990–92; Leader of the Opposition, 1992–94; Shadow Minister for Ethnic Affairs, and for Women's Affairs, 1992–93. Chairman: Employment Services Regulatory Authy, 1994–97; Adv. Cttee, Centenary of Federation, 1994–96; Victorian Cttee on Federation, 2000–02; Ministerial Adv. Cttee on Social Inclusion and Social Inclusion Report, 2004–07. Board Member: Playbox Th., 1995–97; Aust. Children's Television Foundn, 2001–06; Mus. of Vic, 2003–; Member: Victorian Women's Trust, 1983–; Australian Conservation Foundn. Patron: Women's Circus, 1985–; Living Mus. of the West, 1985–; Positive Women, 1993–2003; Victorian Women's Refuges and Domestic Violence Services, 2002–; Royal Dist Nursing Service, 2002–; Victorian Community Amb., 2006–. Participant, 2020 Summit, Australian Govt. Fellow, Aust. Coll. of Educn, 1983. *Publications:* (with Moira Rayner) Women's Power Handbook, 1999; (with Moira Rayner) Women's Power Pocket Book, 2001. *Recreations:* films, walking, music. *Address:* Old Treasury Building, Spring Street, Melbourne, Vic 3000, Australia. *T:* (3) 96516510.

KIRSHBAUM, Ralph; cellist; *b* Texas, 4 March 1946; *m* 1982, Antoinette Reynolds; one *s*. Founder and Artistic Dir, RNCM Manchester Internat. Cello Fest., 1988–. Has performed with major orchestras including: BBC Symphony; Boston Symphony; Cleveland Orch.; London Symphony; Orchestre de Paris; Pittsburgh Symphony; San Francisco Symphony; Chicago Symphony; Tonhalle; Berlin Radio Symphony; Royal Danish; Stockholm Philharmonic. Festival appearances at Aspen, Bath, Edinburgh, Lucerne, New York and Ravinia. Chamber music collaboration with Gyorgy Pauk, Peter Frankl and Pinchas Zukerman. Recordings include: concertos: Barber; Elgar; Haydn D major; Tippett Triple; Walton; Beethoven Triple; Brahms Double; Ravel, Shostakovich and Brahms Trios, complete Bach suites. *Address:* c/o Ingpen & Williams, 7 St George's Court, 131 Putney Bridge Road, SW15 2PA.

KIRTON, Muriel Elizabeth; international consultant and teacher of Daoist healing arts, management training and lifestyle, since 2002; *b* 4 July 1950; *d* of William Waddell Kirton and Belle Jane Kirton (*née* Barnett). *Educ:* Glasgow Univ. (MA Hons Eng. and French 1974); Kent Univ. (MA TEFL 1979); Edinburgh Univ. (DipEd 1975); Moray House Coll. of Educn (PGCE 1975). Teacher of French and English, Cornwall Coll., Montego Bay, Jamaica, 1975–77; teacher of French, Dane Court Tech. High Sch., Broadstairs, 1977–78; Lectr in ELT, Hilderstone Coll., Kent, 1978–79; Sen. Lectr in ELT, Nonington Coll., Kent, 1979–82; joined British Council, 1982: Project Manager, ELT, China, 1982–85; Projects Dir, Hong Kong, 1985–89; Educn Officer, Egypt, 1990–93; Director: Vietnam, 1993–96; Commonwealth Relations, 1996–2000; Cyprus, 2000–01; Yugoslavia, 2001–02. *Recreations:* scuba diving, alternative/complementary healing therapies, reading, cinema, theatre. *Address:* 8 Elmbank Mansions, The Terrace, Barnes, SW13 0NS. *T:* (020) 8878 5693; *e-mail:* muriel.kirton@btinternet.com, muriel@river-of-jade.com.

KIRUI, Nancy Chepkemoi; Permanent Secretary, Office of the Vice-President and Ministry of Home Affairs, Kenya, since 2006; *b* 4 June 1957; *d* of Isaiah Cheluget and Rael Cheluget; *m* 1993, Nicholas Kirui; two *d*, and three step *s* one step *d*. *Educ:* Alliance Girls' Sch., Kikuyu, Kenya; Univ. of Nairobi (LLB); Kenya Sch. of Law (Postgrad. Dip. Law). Legal Officer: Min. of Foreign Affairs, Nairobi, 1985–88; Perm. Mission of Kenya to UN, Geneva, 1988–91; Min. of Foreign Affairs, 1991–94; Kenya High Commn, London, 1994–98; Hd of Legal Div., then Hd, Americas Div., Min. of Foreign Affairs, 1998–2000; High Comr in London, 2000–03; Permanent Secretary: Min. of Gender, Sports, Culture and Social Services, Nairobi, 2003–04; Min. of Labour and Human Resource Develt, Nairobi, 2004–06. *Recreations:* sketching, painting, cooking. *Address:* Jogoo House, A Taifa Road, PO Box 30520, Nairobi, Kenya.

KIRYA, Prof. George Barnabas; High Commissioner for Uganda in the United Kingdom, 1990–2003, and Ambassador to Ireland, 1995–2003 (Senior High Commissioner at the Court of St James's, 1997); Dean of the Diplomatic Corps, 1999–2003; *b* 9 Feb. 1939; *m*; five *s* one *d*. *Educ:* Univ. of E Africa (MB ChB 1966); Birmingham Univ. (MSc Gen. Virology 1971); Manchester Univ. (Dip. Bacteriology 1974). Med. House Officer, Mulago Hosp., Uganda, 1966–67; Sen. House Officer, Dept of Paediatrics and Child Health, Makerere Fac. of Medicine, 1967; East Africa Virus Res. Inst., Entebbe: Virologist, 1967; Sen. Med. Res. Officer, 1968; Principal Med. Res. Officer and Head, Dept of Arbovirology, 1969; Hon. Lectr, Dept of Med. Microbiol., Makerere Univ., 1970; Consultant on Yellow Fever Epidemics, WHO, 1970; Department of Microbiology, Faculty of Medicine, Makerere University: Sen. Lectr, 1973–75; Associate Prof. and Hd of Dept, 1975–78; Prof. and Hd of Dept, 1978; Makerere University: Mem. Senate, 1977–90; Mem. Univ. Council, 1981–90; Vice Chancellor, 1986–90. Chairman: Commonwealth Finance Cttee, 1993–2003; African Union (formerly OAU) Heads of Mission Gp, London, 1997–2003; Commonwealth Heads of Mission Gp, 1997–; Commonwealth Africa Gp, 1997–; Commonwealth People's Assoc. of Uganda, 2006–. Mem., WHO Scientific and Technical Adv. Gp, serving as WHO Temp. Advr, 1990–93. Dir, Central Public Health Labs in Uganda supported by WHO, UNICEF and Min. of Health; Chairman: Disease Surveillance Sub-Cttee, Min. of Health; Exec. Bd, Uganda Nat. Health Consumers' Orgn, 2006–; Member: Nat. Cttee for Prevention of Blindness in Uganda; Adv. Cttee for Res. of Viruses in Uganda; E and Central African Physicians Assoc.; Uganda Health Service Commn, 2004–; Founder Mem., Uganda Health Mktg Gp, 2006–; Uganda Medical Association: Treas., 1978–82; Pres., 1982–86; Chm., Continuing Professional Develt, 2005–08. Chancellor, Lugazi Univ., 2007–; Mem. Gov. Council, Ernest Cook Ultrasound Research and Educn Inst., 2005–. Teaching and supervising undergrad. and post-grad. med. students, med. lab. technologists, nurses and midwives and health visitors. Internal examnr and external examnr for several univs incl. Univ. of Ibadan, Lagos Univ. and Univ. of Nairobi. Member, Editorial Bd: E African Jl for Med. Res.; Uganda Med. Jl. Hon. LLD Birmingham, 2001. *Address:* PO Box 5406, Kampala, Uganda. *Club:* Africa Cricket (Kampala).

KISSIN, Evgeny Igorevich; concert pianist; *b* 10 Oct. 1971; *s* of Igor Kissin and Emilia Kissina. *Educ:* Gnessin Special Sch. of Music, Moscow; Gnessin Russian Acad. of Music, Moscow. Début, Moscow State Philharmonic Orch., conducted by Dmitry Kitaenko, Great Hall, Moscow Conservatoire, 1984; toured Japan, 1986; European début with Berlin Radio Orch., 1987; UK début with BBC Manchester Orch., Lichfield Fest., 1987; USA début with NY Philharmonic Orch., 1990. Has made numerous recordings. Hon. RAM 2005. Hon. DMus Manhattan Sch. of Music, 2001. Musician of the Year, Chigiana Music Acad., Italy, 1991; Instrumentalist of the Year, Musical America mag., 1994; Triumph Award for outstanding contrib. to Russian culture, Triumph Ind. Charity Foundn, 1997; various awards for recordings in UK, France, Holland, incl. Grammy Award, 2006. *Recreations:* reading, long and fast walks, getting together with friends. *Address:* c/o Askonas Holt Ltd, Lincoln House, 300 High Holborn, WC1V 7JH. *T:* (020) 7400 1700.

KISSINGER, Henry Alfred, Hon. KCMG 1995; Bronze Star (US); Chairman, Kissinger Associates Inc., since 1982; Counselor to Center for Strategic and International Studies, since 1977 and Trustee, since 1987; *b* Germany, 27 May 1923; *s* of late Louis Kissinger and Paula (*née* Stern); *m* 1st, 1949, Anne Fleischer (marr. diss. 1964); one *s* one *d*; 2nd, 1974, Nancy Maginnes. *Educ:* George Washington High Sch., NYC; Harvard Univ., Cambridge, Mass (BA 1950, MA 1952, PhD 1954). Emigrated to United States, 1938; naturalised, 1943. Served Army, 1943–46. Teaching Fellow, Harvard Univ., 1950–54; Study Director: Council on Foreign Relations, 1955–56: Rockefeller Bros Fund, 1956–58; Associate Professor of Govt, Harvard Univ., 1958–62, Prof. of Govt, 1962–71, and Faculty Mem., Center for Internat. Affairs, Harvard; Director: Harvard Internat. Seminar, 1951–69; Harvard Defense Studies Program, 1958–69; Asst to US President for Nat. Security Affairs, 1969–75; Secretary of State, USA, 1973–77. Chm., Nat. Bipartisan Commn on Central America, 1983–84; Member: President's Foreign Intelligence Adv. Bd, 1984–90; Commn on Integrated Long-Term Strategy of the National Security Council and Defense Dept, 1986–88; Dir, Internat. Rescue Cttee, 1987–; Hon. Gov., Foreign Policy Assoc., 1985–. Chm., Internat. Adv. Bd, American Internat. Group, Inc., 1988–; Counselor and Mem., Internat. Adv. Cttee, Chase Manhattan Corp. (formerly Chase Manhattan Bank), 1977–; Advr to Bd of Dirs, American Express Co.; Director: Continental Grain Co.; Freeport-McMoRan; formerly Dir, Hollinger Internat. Inc. Trustee, Metropolitan Mus. of Art, 1977–. Syndicated writer, Los Angeles Times, 1984–. (Jtly) Nobel Peace Prize, 1973; Presidential Medal of Freedom, 1977; Medal of Liberty, 1986. *Publications:* A World Restored: Castlereagh, Metternich and the Restoration of Peace, 1957; Nuclear Weapons and Foreign Policy, 1957 (Woodrow Wilson Prize, 1958; citation, Overseas Press Club, 1958); The Necessity for Choice: Prospects of American Foreign Policy, 1961; The Troubled Partnership: a reappraisal of the Atlantic Alliance, 1965; Problems of National Strategy: A Book of Readings (ed), 1965; American Foreign Policy: three essays, 1969, 3rd edn 1977; White House Years (memoirs), 1979; For the Record: selected statements 1977–1980, 1981; Years of Upheaval (memoirs), 1982; Observations: selected speeches and essays 1982–1984, 1985; Diplomacy, 1994; Years of Renewal, 1999; Does America Need a Foreign Policy?, 2001. *Address:* Suite 400, 1800 K Street, NW, Washington, DC 20006, USA; 350 Park Avenue, New York, NY 10022, USA. *Clubs:* Century, River, Brook (New York); Metropolitan (Washington); Bohemian (San Francisco).

KISZELY, Lt-Gen. Sir John (Panton), KCB 2004; MC 1982; Director, Defence Academy of the UK, 2005–08; *b* 2 April 1948; *s* of Dr John Kiszely and Maude Kiszely; *m* 1984, Hon. Arabella Jane, *d* of Baron Herschell, *qv*; three *s*. *Educ:* Marlborough Coll.; RMA Sandhurst. Commnd into Scots Guards, 1969; Co. Comdr, 2nd Bn Scots Guards, 1981–82; Bde Major, 7 Armd Bde, 1982–85; CO 1st Bn Scots Guards, 1986–88 (mentioned in dispatches); Comdr, 22 Armd Bde, 1991–92; Comdr, 7 Armd Bde, 1993; Dep. Comdt, Staff Coll., Camberley, 1993–96; GOC 1st (UK) Armd Div., 1996–98; ACDS (Progs), MOD, 1998–2001; Dep. Comdr, NATO Force, Bosnia, 2001–02; Comdr Regl Forces, Land Comd, 2002–04; Dep. Comdr, Multinat. Force, Iraq, 2004–05. Regtl Lt-Col, Scots Guards, 1995–2001; Col Comdt, Intelligence Corps, 2000–08. CRAeS 2006. Hon. Col, Univ. of London OTC, 2003–. Hon. Liveryman, Painter-Stainers' Co. QCVS 2002. Officer, Legion of Merit (USA), 2005. *Publications:* (contrib.) The Science of War: back to first principles, 1993; Military Power: land warfare in theory and practice, 1997; The Falklands Conflict Twenty Years On, 2004; (contrib.) The Past as Prologue: history and the military profession, 2006; (contrib.) The Impenetrable Fog of War, 2008; numerous articles in military jls. *Recreations:* sailing, fishing, music, chess. *Address:* c/o Headquarters Scots Guards, Wellington Barracks, Birdcage Walk, SW1E 6HQ. *Clubs:* Cavalry and Guards; Royal Yacht Squadron, Royal Solent Yacht.

KITAMURA, Hiroshi, Hon. KBE 2003; Corporate Advisor to Mitsubishi Corporation, 1994–99; President, Shumei University, 1998–2001; *b* 20 Jan. 1929; *s* of Teiji and Fusako Kitamura; *m* 1953, Sachiko Ito; two *d*. *Educ:* Univ. of Tokyo (LLB 1951); Fletcher School of Law and Diplomacy, Medford, USA, 1952. Joined Min. of Foreign Affairs, Tokyo, 1953; postings to Washington DC, New York, New Delhi, London; Dir, Policy Planning Div., Res. and Planning Dept, Tokyo, 1974; Private Sec. to Prime Minister, 1974–76; Dep. Dir-Gen., Amer. Affairs Bureau, 1977–79; Consul-Gen., San Francisco, 1979–82; Dir-Gen., American Affairs Bureau, 1982–84; Dep. Vice Minister for Foreign Affairs, 1984–87; Dep. Minister, 1987–88; Ambassador: to Canada, 1988–90; to UK, 1991–94. *Publication:* Psychological Dimensions of US-Japanese Relations, 1971. *Recreations:* traditional Japanese music, culinary arts, golf. *Address:* 1–15–6 Jingumae, Shibuya-ku, Tokyo 150–0001, Japan.

KITCHEN, Very Rev. Dr Martin; Priest-in-Charge, South Rodings, since 2008; Theological Consultant, Ministry Division, Archbishop's Council, since 2008; *b* 18 May 1947; *s* of Reginald Thomas Kitchen and Alice Kitchen (*née* Johnson); *m* 1971, Sheila Solveig Pettersen; one *s*. *Educ:* Sir Walter St John's Sch., Battersea; Poly. of N London (BA 1971); King's Coll. London (BD 1976; AKC 1977); Univ. of Manchester (PhD 1988). Ordained deacon, 1979, priest, 1980; Lectr, Church Army Trng Coll., and Curate, St James, Kidbrooke, 1979–83; Chaplain, Manchester Poly., 1983–88; Team Vicar, 1983–86, Team Rector, 1986–88, Whitworth, Manchester; Diocese of Southwark: Advr, In-Service Trng, 1988–95; Co-ordinator of Trng, 1995–97; Residentiary Canon, Southwark Cathedral, 1988–97; Durham Cathedral: Residentiary Canon, 1997–2005; Sub-Dean, 1998–99; Vice Dean, 1999–2004; Dean of Derby, 2005–07. Sec., 1996–2001, Dir, 2001–, Archbishop's Exam. in Theol.; Sec., Anglo-Nordic-Baltic Theol Conf., 1997–; Consultant, C of E Doctrine Commn, 1999–2005. *Publications:* Ephesians, 1971; Guide to Durham Cathedral, 2000; A Talent for Living, 2003; editor and co-author: Word of Life, 1997; Word of Promise, 1998; Word of Truth, 1999; Word in Our Time, 2000; Word Among Us, 2001; various articles and translations in bks and jls. *Recreations:* piano, classical guitar, German poetry, learning Italian, good food, wine and malt whisky, golf, astronomy, needlepoint. *Address:* The Rectory, Stortford Road, Leaden Roding, Dunmow CM6 1GY. *T:* (01279) 876147.

KITCHEN, Michael; actor; *b* 31 Oct. 1948; *s* of Arthur and Betty Kitchen; partner, Rowena Miller; two *s*. *Educ:* City of Leicester Boys' Grammar School. Entered acting profession, 1970; *stage includes:* seasons at Belgrade Theatre, Coventry, National Youth Theatre; Royal Court, 1971–73; Big Wolf, Magnificence, Skyvers; Young Vic, 1975: Othello, Macbeth, As You Like It, Charley's Aunt; National Theatre: Spring Awakening, 1974; Romeo and Juliet, 1974; State of Revolution, 1977; Bedroom Farce, 1977; No Man's Land, 1977; The Homecoming, 1978; Family Voices, 1981; On the Razzle, 1981; The Provok'd Wife, 1981; Rough Crossing, 1984; Royal Shakespeare Co: Romeo and Juliet, Richard II, 1986; The Art of Success, 1987; *films include:* The Bunker; Breaking Glass; Towards the Morning; Out of Africa; Home Run; The Russia House; Fools of Fortune; The Dive; Goldeneye; Mrs Dalloway; The Last Contract; The World is not Enough; *television series:* Steven Hind; Divorce; Freud, 1983; The Justice Game, 1989; The Guilty, 1992; To Play the King, 1993; Dandelion Dead, 1994; The Hanging Gale, 1995 (Best Actor Award, Internat. Fest. of Audiovisual Progs, Biarritz, 1996); Reckless, 1997; Oliver Twist (serial), 1999; Foyle's War, 2002, 2004; Alibi, 2003; *television films and plays include:* Caught on a Train; Benefactors; Ball-Trap; Pied Piper; The Enchanted April; Hostage; Falling; Mobile; numerous other TV and radio performances. *Recreations:* piano, guitar, flying, writing, tennis, riding. *Address:* c/o Independent Talent Group Ltd, Oxford House, 76 Oxford Street, W1D 1BS.

KITCHENER OF KHARTOUM, 3rd Earl *cr* 1914, and of Broome, in the county of Kent; **Henry Herbert Kitchener,** TD; DL; Viscount Kitchener of Khartoum; and of the Vaal, Transvaal, and of Aspall, Suffolk, 1902; Viscount Broome, 1914; Baron Denton, 1914; late Major, Royal Corps of Signals; *b* 24 Feb. 1919; *er s* of Viscount Broome (*d* 1928) and Adela Mary Evelyn (*d* 1986), *e d* of late J. H. Monins, Ringwould House, near Dover; *S* grandfather, 1937. *Educ:* Sandroyd Sch.; Winchester Coll.; Trinity Coll., Cambridge. President: Lord Kitchener Nat. Meml Fund, 1950–; Henry Doubleday Res. Assoc. DL Cheshire, 1972. *Heir:* none. *Address:* Westergate Wood, Eastergate, Chichester, W Sussex PO20 3SB. *T:* (01243) 545797. *Club:* Brooks's.

KITCHENER-FELLOWES, Julian Alexander, (Julian Fellowes); DL; screenwriter, actor, producer, director and lecturer; *b* 17 Aug. 1949; *s* of late Peregrine Edward Launcelot Fellowes and Olwen Mary (*née* Stuart-Jones); *m* 1990, Emma Kitchener, LVO (Lady-in-Waiting to HRH Princess Michael of Kent), *d* of Hon. Charles Kitchener; one *s*. *Educ:* Ampleforth Coll., Yorkshire; Magdalene Coll., Cambridge (BA, MA); Webber Douglas Acad. As actor: *theatre includes:* Joking Apart, Queen's, 1978; Present Laughter, Vaudeville, 1981; Futurists, RNT; *television includes:* For the Greater Good, 1991; Our Friends in the North, 1996; Aristocrats, 1999; Monarch of the Glen, 1999–2005; *films include:* Shadowlands, 1993; Damage, 1993; Tomorrow Never Dies, 1997; Place Vendôme, 1998; (co-prod.) A Married Man, 1982. As writer: *television:* Little Lord Fauntleroy, 1994 (Internat. Emmy, 1995); The Prince and the Pauper (also co-prod.), 1997; *films:* Gosford Park, 2001 (NY Film Critics' Circle Award, Best Screenplay, 2001; Nat. Soc. of Film Critics of America Award, Best Screenplay, 2001; Screenwriter of Year, ShoWest, 2002; Writer's Guild Award, Best Orig. Screenplay, 2002); Academy Award, Best Orig. Screenplay, 2002); Vanity Fair, 2005; *theatre:* Mary Poppins, Prince Edward Th., 2004, New Amsterdam, NY, 2006. As writer/director: *film:* Separate Lies, 2005 (Best Directorial Debut, Nat. Bd of Review, 2006). Chm., RNIB Talking Books Appeal, 2005–; Vice-Pres., Weldmar Hospicecare Trust, 2006–; Pres., Thomas Hardy Soc., 2007–; Patron, Help the Aged, Dorset. Paul Harris Fellowship, Rotary Club, 2007. DL Dorset, 2008. Hon. DLitt Bournemouth, 2007. *Publication:* Snobs (novel), 2004. *Recreations:* too little sport and too much eating. *Address:* c/o Independent Talent Group Ltd, Oxford House, 76 Oxford Street, W1D 1BS. *Clubs:* Boodle's, Annabel's.

KITCHIN, Hon. Sir David (James Tyson), Kt 2005; **Hon. Mr Justice Kitchin;** a Judge of the High Court, Chancery Division, since 2005; *b* 30 April 1955; *s* of late Norman Tyson Kitchin and Shirley Boyd Kitchin (*née* Simpson); *m* 1989, Charlotte Anne Cadbury, *d* of Comdr David Jones; one *s* one *d*. *Educ:* Oundle Sch. (schol.); Fitzwilliam Coll., Cambridge (MA). Called to the Bar, Gray's Inn, 1977, Bencher, 2003; pupilled to Robin Jacob, 1978; entered chambers of Thomas Blanco White, 1979; QC 1994; a Dep. High Ct Judge, 2001–05; apptd to hear Trade Mark Appeals, 2001–05. Chm., Vet. Code of Practice Cttee, Nat. Office of Animal Health, 1995–2001. Chm., Intellectual Property Bar Assoc., 2004–05; Mem., Bar Council, 2004–05 (Mem., European Cttee, 2004–05). Mem. Council, Queen Mary, Univ. of London, 2006–. *Publications:* (ed jtly) Patent Law of Europe and the United Kingdom, 1979; (ed jtly) Kerly's Law of Trade Marks and Trade Names, Supplement to 12th edn 1994, 13th edn, 2001, 14th edn 2005; (jtly) The Trade Marks Act 1994 (text and commentary), 1995. *Recreations:* golf, tennis. *Address:* Royal Courts of Justice, Strand, WC2A 2LL. *Clubs:* Hawks (Cambridge); Leander (Henley); Walton Heath Golf.

KITCHING, Alan, RDI 1994; Typographer and Proprietor, The Typography Workshop, since 1989; *b* 29 Dec. 1940; *s* of Walter Kitching and Kathleen (*née* Davies); *m* 1962, Rita Haylett (*d* 1984); two *s*; *m* 2007, Celia Stothard. Apprentice compositor, 1955–61; Asst, Exptl Printing Workshop, Watford Coll. of Technol. Sch. of Art, 1963–68; Vis. Tutor in Typography, Central Sch. of Art and Design, 1968–72; Established freelance design practice, working in magazine, book and exhibition design, 1971; Partner, Omnific Studios (Graphic Design), 1977–88; established Typography Workshop, Printroom and Studio (with Celia Stothard), 2005; Vis. Tutor in Typography, RCA, 1988–2006; Vis. Prof., Univ. of the Arts London (formerly London Inst.), 2001–. AGI 1994. Hon. FRCA 2006 (FRCA 1998). *Publication:* Typography Manual, 1970. *Recreations:* accordion, snooker. *Address:* 19 Cleaver Street, SE11 4DP. *Club:* Chelsea Arts.

KITCHING, Christopher John, CBE 2004; PhD; FSA, FRHistS; Secretary, Historical Manuscripts Commission, National Archives (formerly Royal Commission on Historical Manuscripts), 1992–2004; *b* 5 Aug. 1945; *s* of Donald Walton Kitching and Vera (*née* Mosley); *m* 1976, Hilary Mary Ruth Horwood; two *s*. *Educ:* Durham Univ. (BA Mod. Hist. 1967; PhD 1970). Registered Mem., Soc. of Archivists, 1987. Asst Keeper, PRO, 1970–82; Asst Sec., Royal Commn on Historical MSS, 1982–92. Asst Editor, Archivum, 1984–92. Hon. Treasurer, 1980–85, Vice-Pres., 2002–05, RHistS; Mem., Archives Task Force, MLA, 2002–04. Council Mem., Canterbury and York Soc., 1974–2004. Chm., Trustees, St Mary-the-Virgin, Primrose Hill, 1998–; Trustee, Miss E. M. Johnson's Charitable Trust, 1997–2005. Mem. Editl Bd, Jl of Soc. of Archivists, 1992–2004. Alexander Prize, RHistS, 1973. *Publications:* The Royal Visitation of 1559, 1975; Survey of the Central Records of the Church of England, 1976; London and Middlesex Chantry Certificate 1548, 1980; Surveys of historical manuscripts in the United Kingdom: a select bibliography, 1989, 3rd edn 1997; The impact of computerisation on archival finding aids, 1990; Archive Buildings in the United Kingdom 1977–1992, 1993; Archives: the very essence of our heritage, 1996; Archive Buildings in the United Kingdom 1992–2005, 2007; articles and reviews. *Recreations:* singing, Freedom-pass exploration. *Address:* 11 Creighton Road, NW6 6EE. *T:* (020) 8969 6408.

KITCHING, Peter Marshall; Chairman, Baltic Exchange, 2000–03 (Member, 1961–2003); *b* 24 June 1938; *s* of Horace and Clare Kitching; *m* 1961, Anna; one *s* one *d*. *Educ:* Stowe Sch. Sen. Partner, Simpson Spence & Young, 1992–2001. *Recreations:* golf, travel, music. *Address:* 59 Crown Lodge, Elystan Street, Chelsea, SW3 3PR. *Club:* Effingham Golf.

KITNEY, Prof. Richard Ian, OBE 2001; PhD, DSc(Eng); FRCPE; FREng; Professor of Biomedical Systems Engineering, since 1997, and Senior Dean, Faculty of Engineering, since 2007, Imperial College of Science, Technology and Medicine; *b* 13 Feb. 1945; *s* of Leonard Walter Richard Kitney and Gladys Simpson Kitney; *m* 1977, Vera Baraniecka; two *s*. *Educ:* Enfield Grammar Sch.; Univ. of Surrey (DipEE, MSc); Imperial Coll., London Univ. (PhD, DIC 1972; DSc(Eng) 1993). FRCPE 1996; FREng 1999. Electronics Engr, Thorn Electrical Industries, 1963–72; Lectr in Biophysics, Chelsea Coll., London Univ., 1972–78; Imperial College, London: Lectr, 1975–85; Reader, 1985–89; Dir, Centre for Biol and Med. Systems, 1991–97; Hd, Dept of Biol and Med. Systems, 1997–2001; Dean, Faculty of Engrg, 2003–06; Dir, Graduate Sch. of Engrg and Physical Scis, 2006–; Chm., Inst. of Systems & Synthetic Biology; Gov., 1995–98, 2006–; Gov., RPMS, 1995–98. Visiting Professor: Georgia Inst. of Technology, 1981–90; MIT, 1991–. Tech. Dir, Intravascular Res. Ltd, 1987–94; Dir, St Mary's Imaging plc, 1991–96; Dep. Chm. and Tech. Dir, comMedica Ltd, 1999–2006; Chm., Visbion Ltd, 2006–; Trustee, Smith and Nephew Foundn, 1996–. Mem., Adv. Cttee on Technology in Medicine, DTI, 1995. FIAMBE 2003; FAIMBE 2005. FRSocMed 1994; FRSA 2001; FCGI 2005; Hon. FRCS 2006; Hon. FRCP 2006. Freeman, City of London, 1996; Liveryman, Co. of Engineers, 1995. Regular contributor, BBC Radio. Nightingale Prize, Internat. Fedn of Biol Engrg Socs, 1975. *Publications:* (jtly) Recent Advances in the Study of Heart Rate Variability, 1980; (jtly) The Beat-by-Beat Investigation of Cardiac Function, 1987; (jtly) The Coming of the Global Healthcare Industry, 1998; conf. proceedings, papers in learned jls. *Recreations:* history, cooking, France. *Address:* Department of Bioengineering, Imperial College London, Exhibition Road, SW7 2BX. *T:* (020) 7594 6226. *Club:* Athenæum.

KITSON, Gen. Sir Frank (Edward), GBE 1985; (CBE 1972; OBE 1968; MBE 1959); KCB 1980; MC 1955 and Bar 1958; DL; *b* 15 Dec. 1926; *s* of late Vice-Adm. Sir Henry Kitson, KBE, CB and Lady (Marjorie) Kitson (*née* de Pass); *m* 1962, Elizabeth Janet, DL, *d* of late Col C. R. Spencer, OBE, DL; three *d*. *Educ:* Stowe. 2nd Lt Rifle Bde, 1946; served BAOR, 1946–53; Kenya, 1953–55; Malaya, 1957; Cyprus, 1962–64; CO 1st Bn, Royal Green Jackets, 1967–69; Defence Fellow, University Coll., Oxford, 1969–70; Comdr, 39 Inf. Bde, NI, 1970–72 (CBE for gallantry); Comdt, Sch. of Infantry, 1972–74; RCDS, 1975; GOC 2nd Division, later 2nd Armoured Division, 1976–78; Comdt, Staff College, 1978–80; Dep. C-in-C, UKLF, and Inspector-Gen., TA, 1980–82; C-in-C, UKLF, 1982–85. ADC Gen. to the Queen, 1983–85. 2nd Bn, The Royal Green Jackets: Col Comdt, 1979–87; Rep. Col Comdt, 1982–85; Hon. Col, Oxford Univ. OTC, 1982–87. DL 1989. *Publications:* Gangs and Counter Gangs, 1960; Low Intensity Operations, 1971; Bunch of Five, 1977; Warfare as a Whole, 1987; Directing Operations, 1989; Prince Rupert: portrait of a soldier, 1994; Prince Rupert: Admiral and General-at-sea, 1998; Old Ironsides: the military biography of Oliver Cromwell, 2004; When Britannia Ruled the Waves, 2007. *Address:* c/o Lloyds TSB, Farnham, Surrey GU9 7LT. *Club:* Boodle's.

KITSON, George McCullough; Principal, Central School of Speech and Drama, London, 1978–87; *b* Castlegore, Ireland, 18 May 1922; *s* of George Kitson and Anna May McCullough-Kitson; *m* 1951, Jean Evelyn Tyte; four *s*. *Educ:* early educn in Ireland; London Univ. (Dip. in Child Develt, 1947); Trent Park Coll. (Teachers' Cert., 1949). Associate, Cambridge Inst. of Educn, 1956; MEd Leicester, 1960. Served War, RAF, 1940–45; Navigator, Coastal Comd. Asst Master, schs in Herts, 1949–54; Dep. Headmaster, Broadfield Sch., Hemel Hempstead, Herts, 1954–56; Lectr in Educn, Leicester Coll. of Educn, 1956–66; Tutor i/c Annexe for Mature Teachers, Northampton, 1966–71; Dep. Principal, Furzedown Coll., London, 1971–76; Vice-Principal, Philippa Fawcett and Furzedown Coll., 1976–78. Member: Nat. Council for Drama Trng, 1978–88; Conference of Drama Schs, 1980– (Chm., 1980–87; Pres., 1999–); Hon. Mem., GSMD, 1998. *Publications:* (contrib.) Map of Educational Research, 1969; articles on educn, social psychol., and interprofessionalism in Forum, New Era, Educn for Teaching, and Brit. Jl of Educnl Psychol. *Recreations:* book collecting (first editions), sailing, walking, music, theatre. *Address:* 11 Bates Close, Burnmill Grange, Market Harborough, Leics LE16 7NT. *Club:* Arts.

KITSON, Richard David; a District Judge (Magistrates' Courts), since 2002; *b* 30 Dec. 1954; *s* of Stanley Kitson and Maisie Kitson; *m* 1980, Barbara Ann Kitching; one *s* one *d*. *Educ:* Doncaster Grammar Sch.; Newcastle upon Tyne Poly. (BA Hons 1976; Maxwell Prize). Admitted solicitor, 1979; Partner, Ward Bracewell & Co., then Taylor Bracewell, Solicitors, Doncaster, 1981–2002. Chairman: Doncaster FHSA, 1994–96 (non-exec. Mem., 1985–94); Doncaster Royal and Montagu Hosp. NHS Trust, 1996–2001; Doncaster Central Primary Care Trust, 2001–02. *Recreations:* hill walking, running, tennis, gardening, Rugby Union. *Address:* Leeds District Magistrates' Court, PO Box No 97, Westgate, Leeds LS1 3JP. *T:* (0113) 245 9653.

KITSON, Sir Timothy (Peter Geoffrey), Kt 1974; Director, Hamilton Insurance, since 1995; *b* 28 Jan. 1931; *s* of late Geoffrey H. and of Kathleen Kitson; *m* 1959, Diana Mary Fattorini; one *s* two *d*. *Educ:* Charterhouse; Royal Agricultural College, Cirencester. Farmed in Australia, 1949–51. Chairman: Provident Financial Gp, later Provident Financial plc, 1983–95; London Clubs Internat. plc, 1995–2002; Vice Chm., Halifax Bldg Soc., 1995–98; Director: Leeds Permanent Bldg Soc., 1983–95; Alfred McAlpine plc, 1983–94; SIG plc, 1995–2002. Member: Thirsk RDC, 1954–57; N Riding CC, 1957–61. MP (C) Richmond, Yorks, 1959–83; PPS to Parly Sec. to Minister of Agriculture, 1960–64; an Opposition Whip, 1967–70; PPS to the Prime Minister, 1970–74, to the Leader of the Opposition, 1974–75. Chm., Defence Select Cttee, 1982–83. *Recreations:* shooting, hunting, racing. *Address:* Ulshaw Farm, Middleham, Leyburn, N Yorks DL8 4PU.

KITZINGER, Sheila Helena Elizabeth, MBE 1982; author, social anthropologist, lecturer and birth educator; *b* 29 March 1929; *d* of Alec and Clare Webster; *m* 1952, Uwe Kitzinger, *qv*; five *d*. *Educ:* Bishop Fox's Girls' Sch., Taunton; Ruskin Coll., Oxford; St Hugh's Coll., Oxford; motherhood; educn continuing. Res. Asst, Dept of Anthropology, Univ. of Edinburgh, 1952–53 (MLitt 1954; thesis on race relations in Britain). Course Team Chm., Open Univ., 1981–83. Mem. Editl Bd, Midwives Information and Resource Service; Chairperson, Foundation for Women's Health Res. and Develt, 1985–87; Consultant, Internat. Childbirth Educn Assoc.; Adviser: Baby Milk Coalition; Maternity Alliance. Founder and Dir, Birth Crisis Network, 1996–. Hon. Pres., Birth Companions, 1996–; Patron: Seattle Sch. of Midwifery; Doula UK. Co-founder (with Uwe Kitzinger), Lentils for Dubrovnik, 1991 (relief agency sending aid to women and children in Croatia). MRSocMed. Hon. Prof., Thames Valley Univ., 1994. Joost de Blank Award, to do research on problems facing West Indian mothers in Britain, 1971–73. *Publications:* The Experience of Childbirth, 1962, 6th edn 1987, updated and expanded edn as The New Experience of Childbirth, 2004; Giving Birth, 1971, rev. and expanded edn 1987; Education and Counselling for Childbirth, 1977; Women as Mothers, 1978; (ed with John Davis) The Place of Birth, 1978; Birth at Home, 1979; The Good Birth Guide, 1979; The Experience of Breastfeeding, 1979, 2nd edn 1987; Pregnancy and Childbirth, 1980; Sheila Kitzinger's Birth Book, 1981; (with Rhiannon Walters) Some Women's Experiences of Episiotomy, 1981; Episiotomy: physical and emotional aspects, 1981; Birth over Thirty, 1982; The New Good Birth Guide, 1983; Woman's Experience of Sex, 1983; (ed with Penny Simkin) Episiotomy and the Second Stage of Labor, 1984; Being Born, 1986; Celebration of Birth, 1987; Freedom and Choice in Childbirth (US edn Your Baby Your Way), 1987; Giving Birth: how it really feels, 1987; Some Women's Experiences of Epidurals, 1987; (ed) The Midwife Challenge, 1988; The Crying Baby, 1989; Breastfeeding Your Baby, 1989; (with Celia Kitzinger) Talking With Children About Things That Matter, 1989; (contrib.) Ethnography of Fertility and Birth, 1982; (contrib.) The Management of Labour, 1985; (contrib.) Effective Care in Pregnancy and Childbirth, 1989; (with Vicky Bailey) Pregnancy Day by Day, 1990; Homebirth, 1991; (contrib.) Women's Health Matters, 1991; Ourselves as Mothers, 1992; The Year After Childbirth, 1994; Birth Over Thirty-Five, 1994; The New Pregnancy and Childbirth, 1997; Becoming a Grandmother, 1997; (contrib.) Childbirth and Authoritative Knowledge, 1997; Breastfeeding, 1998; Rediscovering Birth, 2000; Birth Your Way, 2002; Pregnancy and Childbirth: choices and challenges, 2003; The Politics of Birth, 2005; Understanding Your Crying Baby, 2005; Birth Crisis, 2006. *Recreations:* painting, talking. *Address:* The Manor, Standlake, Oxfordshire OX29 7RH. *T:* (01865) 300266, *Fax:* (01865) 300438; *web:* www.sheilakitzinger.com.

KITZINGER, Uwe, CBE 1980; Affiliate, Lowell House and Centre for European Studies, Harvard University, since 2003 (Visiting Scholar, 1993–2003); Senior Research Fellow, Atlantic Council, since 1993; *b* 12 April 1928; *o s* of late Dr G. and Mrs L. Kitzinger, Abbots Langley, Herts; *m* 1952, Sheila Helena Elizabeth Webster (*see* S. H. E. Kitzinger); five *d*. *Educ:* Watford Grammar Sch.; Balliol Coll. and New Coll. (Foundn Schol.), Oxford. 1st in Philosophy, Politics and Economics, MA, MLitt; Pres., Oxford Union, 1950. Economic Section, Council of Europe, Strasbourg, 1951–58; Nuffield College, Oxford: Research Fellow, 1956–62, Official Fellow, 1962–76, Emeritus Fellow, 1976; Acting Investment Bursar, 1962–64; Investment Bursar, 1964–76; Mem., Investment Cttee, 1962–88; Assessor of Oxford University, 1967–68; leave of absence as Adviser to Sir Christopher (later Lord) Soames, Vice-Pres. of the Commn of the European Communities, Brussels, 1973–75; Dean, INSEAD (European Inst. of Business Admin), Fontainebleau, 1976–80 (Mem. Board, 1976–83); Dir, Oxford Centre for Management Studies, 1980–84; Founding Pres., Templeton Coll. (now Green Templeton Coll.), Oxford, 1984–91 (sabbatical, 1991–93; Hon. Fellow, 2001–). Visiting Professor: of Internat. Relations, Univ. of the West Indies, 1964–65; of Government, at Harvard, 1969–70; at Univ. of Paris 1970–73. Member: ODM Cttee for University Secondment, 1966–68; British Universities Cttee of Encyclopædia Britannica, 1967–98; Nat. Council of European Movement, 1974–76; Council, RIIA, 1973–85; Court, Cranfield Inst. of Technology, 1984–85. Founding Chm., Cttee on Atlantic Studies, 1967–70. Co-Founder, Lentils for Dubrovnik, 1991–. Founding Pres., 1987–92, Pres., 1996–, Internat. Assoc. of Macro-Engrg Socs. Member: Oxfam Council, 1981–84; Major Projects Assoc., 1981–91 (Founding Chm., 1981–86); Adv. Bd, Pace Univ., NY, 1982–92; Berlin Science Centre, 1983–90; Acad. Adv. Bd, World Management Council, 1989–; Bd, Jean Monnet Foundn, Lausanne, 1990–; Adv. Bd, Asian Disaster Preparedness Center, Bangkok, 2000–; Tufts Inst. for Global Leadership, 2006–. Pres., Féd. Britannique des Alliances Françaises, 1999–2004. Trustee: European Foundn for Management Educn, Brussels, 1978–80; Oxford Trust for Music and the Arts, 1986–91. Patron, Asylum Welcome, 2005–. Chm., Oxford Radio Consortium, 1988. Founding Editor, Jl of Common Market Studies, 1962–. Hon. LLD Buena Vista, 1986. Order of the Morning Star (Croatia), 1997. *Publications:* German Electoral Politics, 1960 (German edn, 1960); The Challenge of the Common Market, 1961 (Amer. edn, The Politics and Economics of European Integration, 1963, et al); Britain, Europe and Beyond, 1964; The Background to Jamaica's Foreign Policy, 1965; The European Common Market and Community, 1967; Commitment and Identity, 1968; The Second Try, 1968; Diplomacy and Persuasion, 1973 (French edn, 1974); Europe's Wider Horizons, 1975; (with D. E. Butler) The 1975 Referendum, 1976, 2nd edn 1996; (ed with E. Frankel) Macro-Engineering and the Earth, 1998. *Recreations:* sailing, travel, old buildings. *Address:* Standlake Manor, near Witney, Oxon OX29 7RH. *T:* (01865) 300266, 300438, *Fax:* (01865) 300702; La Rivière, 11100 Bages, France. *T:* and *Fax:* (4) 68417013; *e-mail:* uwe_kitzinger@yahoo.com. *Clubs:* Royal Thames Yacht, Oxford and Cambridge.

KIYOTAKI, Prof. Nobuhiro, PhD; FBA 2003; Professor, Department of Economics, Princeton University, since 2006; *b* 24 June 1955. *Educ:* Univ. of Tokyo (BA 1978); Harvard Univ. (PhD 1985). Asst Prof., Dept of Econs, Univ. of Wisconsin-Madison, 1985–91; Lectr, Dept of Econs, LSE, 1989–91; Associate Prof., Dept of Econs, Univ. of Minnesota, 1991–97; Cassel Prof. of Econs, LSE, 1997–2006; Sen. Economist and Resident Schol., Fed. Reserve Bank of NY, 2005–06. Visiting Professor: LSE, 1995–96; Dept of Econs, MIT, 2000–01. *Address:* Department of Economics, Princeton University, Fisher Hall, Princeton, NJ 08544–1021, USA.

KLARE, Hugh John, CBE 1967; *b* Berndorf, Austria, 22 June 1916; *yr s* of F. A. Klare; *m* 1946, Eveline Alice Maria, *d* of Lieut-Col J. D. Rankin, MBE. *Educ:* privately. Came to England, 1932. Served war in Middle East and Europe; Major. Dep. Dir, Economic Organisation Br., Brit. Control Commn for Germany, 1946–48; Sec., Howard League for Penal Reform, 1950–71; seconded to Coun. of Europe as Dep. Head, Div. of Crime Problems, 1959–61; Head of Div., 1971–72; Member of Council: Internat. Soc. of Criminology, 1960–66; Inst. for Study and Treatment of Delinquency, 1964–66; Nat. Assoc. for Care and Resettlement of Offenders, 1966–71. Chm. Planning Cttee, Brit. Congress on Crime, 1966. Member: Bd of Visitors, Long Lartin Prison, 1972–76; Gloucestershire Probation and Aftercare Cttee, 1972–85; Parole Board, 1972–74. Founder and Trustee, Cheltenham and N Cotswold Eye Therapy Trust, 1976–; Chm. of Trustees, Gloucestershire Arthritis Trust, 1987–95 (Trustee, 1984). A Governor, British Inst. of Human Rights, 1974–80. *Publications:* Anatomy of Prison, 1960; (ed and introd) Changing Concepts of Crime and its Treatment, 1966; (ed jtly) Frontiers of Criminology, 1967; People in Prison, 1972; contribs on crime and penology to Justice of the Peace. *Address:* 34 Herriots Court, St George's Crescent, Droitwich, Worcs WR9 8HJ. *T:* (01905) 773332.

KLAUS, Prof. Václav; President of Czech Republic, since 2003; *b* 19 June 1941; *s* of Václav Klaus and Marie Klausová; *m* 1968, Livia Klausová; two *s*. *Educ:* Prague Sch. of Economics (Hon. Dr 1994); Cornell Univ. Researcher, Inst. of Econs, Czechoslovak Acad. of Scis, to 1970; Czechoslovak State Bank, 1971–86 (Head, Dept of Macroeconomic Policy); Inst. of Forecasting, Czechoslovak Acad. of Scis, 1987; founder, Civic Forum Movt (Chm., 1990–91); Minister of Finance, Czech Republic, 1989–92; Dep. Prime Minister, 1991–92; Prime Minister, 1992–97; Pres., Chamber of Deputies, 1998–2003. Chm., Civic Democratic Party, Czech Republic, 1991–2002. Vice-Chm., European Democratic Union, 1996–. Prof. of Finance, Prague Sch. of Economics, 1994–. Hon. doctorates from Univs in USA, Canada, Guatemala, Mexico, Argentina, France, UK, Czech Republic, Germany; numerous awards from USA, Germany, France, Denmark, Austria, Switzerland, Czech Republic. *Publications:* A Road to Market Economy, 1991; Tomorrow's Challenge, 1991; Economic Theory and Economic Reform, 1991; Signale aus dem Herzen Europas, 1991; I Do Not Like Catastrophic Scenarios, 1991; Dismantling Socialism, 1992; Why Am I a Conservative?, 1992; The Year: how much is it in the history of the country?, 1993; The Czech Way, 1994; Rebirth of a Country, 1994; Summing Up to One, 1995; Tschechische Transformation & Europäische Integration, 1995; Economic Theory and Reality of Transformation Processes, 1995; Between the Past and the Future, 1996; Renaissance, 1997; The Defence of Forgotten Ideas, 1997; Thus Spoke Václav Klaus, 1998; Why I Am not a Social Democrat, 1998; The Country without Governing, 1999; The Way out of the Trap, 1999; From the Opposition Treaty to the Tolerance Patent, 2000; Europe from the Point of View of a Politician and an Economist, 2001; Conversations with Václav Klaus, 2001; The First Year, 2004; Europe of Václav Klaus, 2004; The Second Year, 2005; On the Road to Democracy, 2005. *Recreations:* tennis, ski-ing. *Address:* Office of the President, Pražský hrad, 11908 Prague 1, Czech Republic.

KLEIN, Anita, RE 1995 (ARE 1992); artist; President, Royal Society of Painter Printmakers, 2003–06; *b* Sydney, 14 Feb. 1960; *d* of Prof. Anthony George Klein and Mavis Klein; *m* 1984, Nigel Swift; two *d*. *Educ:* Chelsea Sch. of Art (Foundn Cert. 1979); Slade Sch. of Fine Art (Henrique Schol. 1982 and 1983; BA Hons Painting 1983; Higher Dip. Fine Art (Printmaking) 1985). *Solo exhibitions* include: paintings and prints: Creaser Gall., London, 1986; Printworks, Colchester, 1990; Wilson Hale, London, 1991; Royal Pavilion Contemp. Gall., Brighton, 1992; Woodlands Art Gall., 1993; Cambridge Contemp. Art, 1996, 1998, 2000; prints: Leigh Gall., London, 1987; Tall House Gall., London, 1990; Victorian Artists Soc., Melbourne, 1992; Brighton Fest., Brighton Marina Arts Index, 1993; two person show (with Paula Rego), Gateway Arts Centre, Shrewsbury, 1995; CCA, Oxford, 1996; Leeds City Art Gall., 1997; New Ashgate Gall., Farnham, 1998; Old Town Gall., Tustin, Calif, 1999; Port Jackson Press, Melbourne, 1999, 2000; Pyramid Gall., York (and ceramics), 1999); Advanced Graphics, London, 2002 (retrospective exhibn, 20 Years of Printmaking), 2004; paintings: Royal Exchange Th., Manchester, 1994; Europ. Art Fair, Ghent, 1995; Beaux Arts, Bath, 1996, 1998; Helen Gory Gall., Melbourne, 2003; paintings, drawings and watercolours: Boundary Gall., London, 2001 (and ceramics), 2002, 2004, 2006; Advanced Graphics, London, 2006, 2008; Bankside Gall., London, 2006; Royal Commonwealth Club, 2007; Chelsea and Westminster Hosp., 2008; *group exhibitions* include: Hayward Gall.; RA; ICA; Blond Fine Art; Contemp. Arts Soc.; Christies; Discerning Eye Exhibn, Mall Galls, London; Hunting Art Prizes, RCA; Cleveland Drawing Biennale; Glasgow Print Studio; London Art Fair; Barbican Concourse Gall. Trustee, Paintings in Hosps. Joseph Webb Award, Royal Soc. of Painter Printmakers, 1984; John Purcell Award: for an outstanding print, Bankside Open, 1991; Nat. Print Exhibn, London, 1995; Univ. of Wales Purchase Prize, Nat. Print Exhibn, London, 2003. *Publication:* Anita Klein, Painter Printmaker, 2006. *Recreations:* walking, gardening, visiting Italy, laughing, drinking red wine. *Address: e-mail:* anita@anitaklein.com. *T:* (020) 8691 2374. *Club:* Chelsea Arts.

KLEIN, Bernat, CBE 1973; FCSD (FSIAD 1974); Chairman and Managing Director, Bernat Klein Ltd, 1973–93; *b* 6 Nov. 1922; *s* of Lipot Klein and Serena Weiner; *m* 1951, Margaret Soper; one *s* two *d*. *Educ:* Senta, Yugoslavia; Bezalel Sch. of Arts and Crafts, Jerusalem; Leeds Univ. Designer to: Tootal, Broadhurst, Lee, 1948–49; Munrospun, Edinburgh, 1949–51; Chm. and Man. Dir, Colourcraft, 1952–62; Man. Dir of Bernat Klein Ltd, 1962–66; Chm. and Man. Dir, Bernat Klein Design Ltd, 1966–81. Member: Council of Industrial Design, Scottish Cttee, 1965–71; Royal Fine Art Commn for Scotland, 1980–87. Exhibitions of paintings: E-SU, 1965; Alwyn Gall., 1967; O'Hana Gall., 1969; Assoc. of Arts Gall., Capetown, Goodman Gall., Johannesburg, and O'Hana Gall., 1972; Laing Art Gall., Newcastle upon Tyne, 1977; Manchester Polytechnic, 1977; Scott Gall., Hawick, 2005; Heriot-Watt Univ., 2006. Hon. FRIAS 1990. Hon. DLitt Heriot-Watt, 2003. *Publications:* Eye for Colour, 1965; Design Matters, 1976. *Recreations:* reading, tennis, walking. *Address:* High Sunderland, Galashiels, Selkirkshire TD1 3PL. *T:* (01750) 20730.

KLEIN, Calvin Richard; fashion designer; *b* 19 Nov. 1942; *s* of Leo Klein and Flore (*née* Stern); *m* 1st, 1964, Jayne Centre (marr. diss. 1974); one *d*; 2nd, 1986, Kelly Rector. *Educ:* Fashion Inst. of Technology, NY; High Sch. of Art and Design. Started own fashion business, 1968; Vice Chm., 1969, Consulting Creative Dir, 2003, Calvin Klein Inc. Dir, Fashion Inst. of Technology, 1975–. Numerous awards.

KLEIN, Prof. Dan Victor; Director, Dan Klein Associates, consultants in contemporary glass, since 1994; Research Professor in Glass, University of Sunderland, since 1996; *b* 4 Nov. 1938; *s* of Frederick Klein and Bianka Breitmann. *Educ:* Westminster Sch.; Wadham Coll., Oxford (BA Hons Greats). Guest soloist, Sadler's Wells Opera, 1966; Member, English Opera Group, 1968–73; freelance singer performing in operas and recitals, also founded and perf. with own ensemble, 1973–77; owner, 20th Century Decorative Arts Gall., Belgravia, 1978–84; Dir, 20th Century Decorative Arts, Christie's, London, 1985–95; Vice-Pres., Christie's, Switzerland, 1990–95; Chm., Adv. Bd, North Lands

Creative Glass, 1995–; Internat. Exec. Dir, Phillips Internat. Auctioneers, 1998–2001. Regular lectr in Britain, USA, Switzerland, Sweden and Australia; orgnr, Venezia Aperto Vetro, first Internat. Biennale of Contemporary Glass, Venice, 1996. Trustee, Nat. Glass Centre, Sunderland, 2002–; Patron, Guild of Glass Engravers, 2006–. Mem. Bd, Pilchuck Glass Sch., USA, 1985–. *Publications:* All Colour Book of Art Deco, 1974; (ed jtly) The History of Glass, 1985; (jtly) Decorative Arts from 1880 to the Present Day, 1986, 2nd edn, 1998; (jtly) In the Deco Style, 1986; Glass: a contemporary art, 1989; (contrib.) L'Art Décoratif en Europe, vol. III, 1994; (ed jtly) Venezio Aperto Vetro (catalogue), 1996; Artists in Glass: late twentieth century masters in glass, 2001; 21st Century British Glass, 2005; articles in jls. *Recreations:* collecting 20th Century Decorative Arts, contemporary British glass. *Address:* Dan Klein Associates, 43 Hugh Street, SW1V 1QJ. *T:* (020) 7821 6040.

KLEIN, Deborah; Joint Chief Executive, Engine Group, since 2008; Chairman, WCRS, since 2008; *b* Zimbabwe, 10 Aug. 1968; *d* of Len and Audrey Klein; *m* 2002, Max Cantor; one *s* one *d*. *Educ:* Brooklyn Primary Sch.; Pretoria High Sch. for Girls; Univ. of Cape Town (BBus Sci. (Econs and Mktg)). AC Nielson, 1990–92; strategic planner, Saatchi & Saatchi, 1993–97 (Dir, 1996–97); WRCS: Hd of Planning, 1997–2003; Chief Exec., 2004–08. Member: WACL; Mktg Gp of GB. *Publication:* Women in Advertising, 2000. *Recreations:* yoga, cooking, walking, my children. *Address:* Engine, 60 Great Portland Street, W1W 7RT; *e-mail:* debbie.klein@theenginegroup.com.

KLEIN, Prof. Jacob, PhD; Professorial Research Fellow, University of Oxford, since 2008; Professor, Weizmann Institute of Science, Israel, since 1987; *b* 20 Aug. 1949; *s* of Moshe Klein and Edna Klein (*née* Lipper); *m* 1974, Michele Castle; two *s* two *d*. *Educ:* in Israel; Whittingehame Coll., Brighton; St Catharine's Coll., Cambridge (BA 1st Cl. Hons Physics 1973; MA, PhD 1977). Mil. Service, Israel, 1967–70; Post-doctoral res., Weizmann Inst., Israel, 1977–80; Demonstrator, Cavendish Lab., and Fellow of St Catharine's Coll., Cambridge, 1980–84; Weizmann Institute, Israel: Sen. Scientist, 1980–84; Associate Prof., 1984–87; Chairman: Polymer Res. Dept, 1989–91; Scientific Council, 1998–2000; University of Oxford: Dr Lee's Prof. of Physical Chemistry, 2000–07; Hd, Dept of Chemistry, 2000–05. FAPS 2003; FInstP 2004. Somach Sacks Prize, Weizmann Inst., 1983; Charles Vernon Boys Prize, Inst. Physics (GB), 1984; Jeanett and Samuel Lubel Prize, 1989; Internat. Kao Fellow (Japan), 1994; Ford Prize for Polymer Physics, APS, 1995; Kolthoff Prize, Technion Israel Inst. of Technology, 2007. *Publications:* contrib. numerous papers to scientific jls, etc. *Recreations:* reading, family holidays, hiking. *Address:* 10 Norham End, Norham Road, Oxford OX2 6SG; 1 Ruppin Street, Rehovot 76353, Israel; Materials & Interfaces Department, Weizmann Institute of Science, Rehovot 76100, Israel; Physical and Theoretical Chemistry Laboratory, South Parks Road, Oxford OX1 3QZ.

KLEIN, Jonathan David; Co-Founder and Chief Executive Officer, Getty Images Inc., since 1995; *b* 13 May 1960; *s* of Louis and Hilda Klein; *m* 1988, Deborah Ann Hunter; three *s*. *Educ:* Trinity Hall, Cambridge (MA). Hambros Bank Ltd, 1983–98: Dir, 1989–93; non-exec. Dir, 1993–98. *Recreations:* all sports, travel, the environment, movies. *Address:* 3815 East John Street, Seattle, WA 98112–5007, USA. *T:* (206) 268 1900.

KLEIN, Prof. Lawrence Robert; economist; Benjamin Franklin Professor, University of Pennsylvania, 1968–91, Emeritus 1991; *b* Omaha, 14 Sept. 1920; *s* of Leo Byron Klein and Blanche Monheit; *m* 1947, Sonia Adelson; one *s* three *d*. *Educ:* Univ. of Calif at Berkeley (BA); MIT (PhD 1944); Lincoln Coll., Oxford (MA 1957; Hon. Fellow, 2005). Chicago Univ., 1944–47; Nat. Bureau of Econ. Res., NY, 1948–50; Michigan Univ., 1949–54; Oxford Inst. of Stats, 1954–58; Prof., 1958, University Prof., 1964, Univ. of Pennsylvania. Consultant: UNCTAD, 1966, 1967, 1975; UNIDO, 1973–75; Congressional Budget Office, 1977–; Council of Econ. Advisers, 1977–80. Mem., Commn on Prices, Fed. Res. Bd, 1968–70. Member: Adv. Bd, Strategic Studies Center, Stanford Res. Inst., 1974–76; Adv. Council, Inst. for Advanced Studies, Vienna, 1977–; Director: Nat. Bureau of Econ. Res., Inc., 1989–; Inst. for East-West Security Studies, 1989–; W. P. Carey & Co., 1984–. Corresp. FBA, 1991; Fellow: Econometric Soc. (past Pres.); Amer. Acad. of Arts and Scis; Member: Nat. Acad. of Scis; Amer. Philosophical Soc.; Amer. Economic Assoc. (Past Pres.; J. B. Clark Medal, 1959). Hon. DSc Pennsylvania, 2006. William F. Butler Award, NY Assoc. of Business Economists, 1975; Nobel Prize for Economics, 1980. *Publications:* The Keynesian Revolution, 1947; Textbook of Econometrics, 1953; An Econometric Model of the United States 1929–52, 1955; Wharton Econometric Forecasting Model, 1967; Essay on the Theory of Economic Prediction, 1968; (ed) Econometric Model Performance, 1976; (ed) Comparative Performance of US Econometric Models, 1991. *Address:* 101 Cheswold Lane 4C, Haverford, PA 19041, USA.

KLEIN, Prof. Michael Lawrence, PhD; FRS 2003; Earle Hepburn Professor of Physical Science, and Director, Laboratory for Research on the Structure of Matter, University of Pennsylvania, Philadelphia, since 1993; *b* 13 March 1940; *s* of Jack Klein and Bessie Klein (*née* Bloomberg); *m* 1962, Brenda Woodman; two *d*. *Educ:* Bristol Univ. (BSc Hons 1961; PhD Chemistry 1964). Assoc. Res. Officer, 1968–74, Sen. Res. Officer, 1974–85, Prin. Res. Officer, 1985–87, Chemistry Div., NRCC, Ottawa; University of Pennsylvania, Philadelphia: Prof. of Chemistry, 1987–91; William Smith Prof. of Chemistry, 1991–93. Fellow Commoner, Trinity Coll., Cambridge, 1985–86; Louis Néel Prof., Ecole Normale Supérieure, Lyon, 1988; Guggenheim Fellow, 1989–90; Sen. Humboldt Fellow, Max Planck Inst., Stuttgart, 1995; Miller Prof., Univ. of Calif., Berkeley, 1997; Linnett Vis. Prof., Univ. of Cambridge, 1998; Schlumberger Prof., Oxford and Cambridge, 2003. Associate Fellow, Acad. of Scis for the Developing World, 2004–. FInstP 2003; FRSCan 1984; FCIC 1979; Fellow, American Acad. of Arts and Scis, 2003. Hon. Fellow, Indian Acad. of Scis, 2006. Computational Physics Prize, APS, 1999; CECAM Prize, 2004; Physical Chemistry Prize, ACS, 2008. *Publications:* over 550 articles in scientific jls and books. *Address:* Laboratory for Reseach on the Structure of Matter Building, University of Pennsylvania, 3231 Walnut Street, Philadelphia, PA 19104–6202, USA; *e-mail:* klein@lrsm.upenn.edu.

KLEIN, Ralph Phillip; Premier of Alberta, Canada, 1992–2006; Senior Business Adviser, Borden, Ladner, Gervais, LLP, since 2007; *b* Calgary, 1 Nov. 1942; *m* Colleen; one *d*. *Educ:* Calgary Business Coll. Teacher, later Principal, Calgary Business Coll.; PR with Alberta Div. of Red Cross and United Way of Calgary and Dist, 1963–69; Sen. Civic Affairs reporter, CFCN TV and Radio, 1969–80. Mayor of Calgary, 1980–89; Government of Alberta: MLA (Progressive C) for Calgary-Elbow, 1989–2007; Minister of Envmt, 1989–92; Leader, Progressive Cons. Party, 1992–2006. OStJ 1986. *Address:* Borden, Ladner, Gervais, LLP, 1000 Canterra Tower, 400 Third Avenue SW, Calgary, AB T2P 4H2, Canada.

KLEIN, Prof. Rudolf Ewald, CBE 2001; FBA 2006; Professor of Social Policy, University of Bath, 1978–98, now Emeritus; *b* 26 Aug. 1930; *o s* of Robert and Martha Klein; *m* 1957, Josephine Parfitt (*d* 1996); one *d*. *Educ:* Bristol Grammar Sch.; Merton Coll., Oxford (Postmaster) (Gibbs Schol. 1950; MA). Leader Writer, London Evening Standard, 1952–62; Editor, 'The Week', Leader Writer, Home Affairs Editor, The Observer, 1962–72; Research Associate, Organisation of Medical Care Unit, London Sch. of Hygiene and Tropical Medicine, 1972–73; Sen. Fellow, Centre for Studies in Social Policy, 1973–78; Professorial Fellow, then Sen. Associate, King's Fund, 1995–2001. Visiting Professor: LSE, 1996–; LSHTM, 2001–. Member: Wiltshire AHA, 1980–82; Bath DHA, 1982–84. Jt Editor, Political Quarterly, 1981–87. Foreign Associate, Inst. of Medicine, NAS, USA, 2001. FMedSci 2006. Hon. DArts Oxford Brookes, 1998. Margaret E. Mahoney Award, Commonwealth Fund, NY, 1999. *Publications:* Complaints Against Doctors, 1973; (ed) Social Policy and Public Expenditure, 1974; (ed) Inflation and Priorities, 1975; (with Janet Lewis) The Politics of Consumer Representation, 1976; The Politics of the NHS, 1983; (ed with Michael O'Higgins) The Future of Welfare, 1985; (with Patricia Day) Accountabilities, 1987; (with Linda Challis *et al*) Joint Approaches to Social Policy, 1988; (with Patricia Day) Inspecting the Inspectorates, 1990; (with Neil Carter and Patricia Day) How organisations measure success, 1991; (with Patricia Day and David Henderson) Home Rules, 1993; The New Politics of the NHS, 1995; (with Patricia Day and Sharon Redmayne) Managing Scarcity, 1996; papers on public policy, health policy and public expenditure in various jls. *Recreations:* opera, cooking, football. *Address:* 12A Laurier Road, NW5 1SG. *T:* (020) 7428 9767.

KLEINPOPPEN, Prof. Hans Johann Willi, FRSE; Professor of Experimental Physics, 1968–96, now Emeritus, and Head, Unit of Atomic and Molecular Physics, 1982–96, University of Stirling; *b* Duisburg, Germany, 30 Sept. 1928. *Educ:* Univ. of Giessen (Dipl. Physics 1955); Univ. of Tübingen; Dr re.nat. 1961. Habilitation, Tübingen, 1967. Head, Physics Dept, 1971–73, Dir, Inst. of Atomic Physics, 1975–81, Univ. of Stirling. Vis. Fellow, Univ. Colorado, 1967–68; Vis. Associate Prof., Columbia Univ., 1968; Fellow, Center for Theoretical Studies, Univ. of Miami, 1972–73; Bielefeld University: Guest Prof., 1978–79; Vis. Fellow, Zentrum für interdisziplinäre Forschung, 1979–80; Sen. Res. Fellow, 1980–98; Res. Visitor, Fritz Haber Inst., Berlin, 1991–; Leverhulme Emeritus Fellow, 1998–2000. Chairman: Internat. Symposium on Physics of One- and Two-Electron Atoms (Arnold Sommerfeld Centennial Meml Meeting, Munich 1968); Internat. Symposium on Electron and Photon Interactions with Atoms, in honour of Ugo Fano, Stirling, 1974; Internat. Workshop on Coherence and Correlation in Atomic Collisions, dedicated to Sir Harrie Massey, UCL, 1978; Internat. Symp. on Amplitudes and State Parameters in Atomic Collisions, Kyoto, 1979; Orgng Cttee on Workshops on Polarized Electron and Polarized Photon Physics, SERC, 1993, 1994; Co-Chm. (with D. M. Campbell), Peter Farago Symposium on Electron Physics, RSE, 1995; Co-Dir, Advanced Study Inst. on Fundamental Processes in Energetic Atomic Collisions, Maratea, Italy, 1982; Dir, Advanced Study Inst. on Fundamental Processes in Atomic Collision Physics, S Flavia, Sicily, 1984; Co-Dir, Advanced Study Inst. on Fundamental Processes on Atomic Dynamics, Maratea, Italy, 1987. FInstP 1969; Fellow Amer. Physical Soc. 1969; FRAS 1974; FRSE 1987; FRSA 1990. *Publications:* edited: (with F. Bopp) Physics of the One- and Two-Electron Atoms (A. Sommerfeld centennial meml conf.), 1969; (with M. R. C. McDowell) Electron and Photon Interactions with Atoms, 1976; Progress in Atomic Spectroscopy, (with W. Hanle) Vol. A 1978, Vol. B 1979, (with H. J. Beyer) Vol. C 1984, Vol. D 1987; (with J. F. Williams) Coherence and Correlations in Atomic Collisions, 1980; (with D. J. Fabian and L. H. Watson) Inner-Shell and X-Ray Physics of Atoms and Solids, 1981; (with J. S. Briggs and H. O. Lutz): Fundamental Processes in Energetic Atomic Collisions, 1983; Fundamental Processes in Atomic Collision Physics, 1985; Fundamental Processes in Atomic Dynamics, 1988; (with W. R. Newell) Polarized Electron/Polarized Photon Physics, 1995; (with D. M. Campbell) Selected Topics on Electron Physics, 1996; series editor (with P. G. Burke), Physics of Atoms and Molecules (about 50 monographs and conf. proceedings); (contrib.) McGraw-Hill Yearbook of Science/Technology, 2005; about 200 papers in Zeitschr. f. Physik, Z. f. Naturf., Z. f. Angew Physik, Physikalische Blätter, Physical Review, Physical Review Letters, Jl of Physics, Physics Letters, Internat. Jl of Quantum Chemistry, Physics Reports, Advances of Atomic, Molecular and Optical Physics, Applied Physics, Physica, Philosophical Trans of Royal Soc.; *festschriften:* (for 60th birthday) (ed H.-J. Beyer, K. Blum and R. Hippler) Coherence in Atomic Collision Physics, 1988; (for 70th birthday) (ed U. Becker and A. Crowe) Hans Kleinpoppen Symposium on Complete Scattering Experiments, 1998. *Address:* Orberstrasse 12, 14193 Berlin, Germany.

KLEINWORT, Sir Richard (Drake), 4th Bt *cr* 1909, of Bolnore, Cuckfield, Sussex; DL; Chairman, Richard Kleinwort Consultancy Group, since 2001; *b* 4 Nov. 1960; *s* of Sir Kenneth Drake Kleinwort, 3rd Bt and his 1st wife, Lady Davina Pepys (*d* 1973), *d* of 7th Earl of Cottenham; *S* father, 1994; *m* 1989, Lucinda, *d* of William Shand Kydd; three *s* one *d*. *Educ:* Stowe; Exeter Univ. (BA). Kleinwort Benson, Geneva, 1979; Banco General de Negocios, Buenos Aires, 1984; Deutsche Bank AG, Hamburg and Frankfurt, 1985–88; Biss Lancaster plc, 1988–89; Grandfield Rork Collins Financial, 1989–91; Partner, 1991–2000, Dir, 1994–2000, Cardew & Co.; Head of Financial PR, Ogilvy PR Worldwide, 2000–01. Non-exec. Dir, RDF Gp plc; Amb. for Kleinwort Benson Private Bank. President: Haywards Heath Hospital, 1991–97; The Little Black Bag Housing Assoc., 1991–. Dir, Steppes East Gp, 1998–. Life Mem., British Field Sports Soc., 1981; Member: WWF (1001) Club, 1979– (Mem., Council of Ambassadors, WWF, 2005–); S of England Agricl Soc., 1988–; RHS, 1991–. Chm., Knepp Castle Polo Club, 1997–2006. Fellow, World Scout Foundn, Geneva, 1989. Mem., Instn of King Edward VII Hosp., Midhurst, 1992–; Patron: Cuckfield Soc., 1995–; Ackroyd Trust, 1995–; Vice Pres., Chichester Cathedral Millennium Endowment Trust, 1998–2005. Ambassador, The Prince's Trust, 1998–. Gov., Stowe Sch. (Chm., Foundn Appeal), 1999–2004. DL 2005, High Sheriff 2008, W Sussex. *Recreations:* travel, my family, laughter, shooting, gardening, farming, watching England winning any sport. *Heir:* *s* Rufus Drake Kleinwort, *b* 16 Aug. 1994. *Clubs:* White's, MCC, Turf.

KLEMPERER, Prof. Paul David, PhD; FBA 1999; Edgeworth Professor of Economics, University of Oxford, since 1995; Fellow, Nuffield College, Oxford, since 1995; *b* 15 Aug. 1956; *s* of late Hugh G. Klemperer and Ruth M. M. Klemperer (*née* Jordan); *m* 1989, Margaret Meyer; two *s* one *d*. *Educ:* King Edward's Sch., Birmingham; Peterhouse, Cambridge (BA Engrg, 1st Cl. Hons with Dist., 1978); Stanford Univ. (MBA 1982 (Top Student Award); PhD Econs 1986). Consultant, Andersen Consulting, 1978–80; Harkness Fellow, Commonwealth Fund, 1980–82; Oxford University: Univ. Lectr in Operations Res. and Mathematical Econs, 1985–90; Reader in Econs, 1990–95; John Thomson Fellow and Tutor, St Catherine's Coll., 1985–95. Visiting positions: MIT, 1987; Berkeley, 1991, 1993; Stanford, 1991, 1993; Yale, 1994; Princeton, 1998. Mem., UK Competition Commn, 2001–05. Consultant: UK Radiocommunications Agency (principal auction theorist for UK 3G auction, 2000), 1997–2000; US Federal Trade Commn, 1999–2001; Advr to EU, US, UK, and other govts and private firms. Mem., Council, Royal Econ. Soc., 2001–05. Foreign Hon. Mem., Amer. Acad. of Arts and Scis, 2005; Hon. Mem., Argentine Economic Assoc., 2006. Fellow: Econometric Soc., 1994 (Mem. Council, 2001–06); European Economic Assoc., 2004 (Mem. Council, 2002–07). Hon. Fellow, ESRC Centre for Econ. Learning and Social Evolution, 2001. Editor, RAND Jl of Econs, 1993–99; Associate Editor or Member, Editorial Board: Rev. of Econ. Studies, 1989–97; Jl of Industrial Econs, 1989–96; Oxford Econ. Papers, 1986–2000; Internat. Jl of Industrial Orgn, 1993–2000; Eur. Econ. Rev., 1997–2001; Rev. of Econ. Design, 1997–2000;

Econ. Policy, 1998–99; Econ. Jl, 2000–04; Frontiers in Econs, 2000–; BE Jl of Econ. Analysis and Policy, 2001–; Jl of Competition Law and Econs, 2004–. *Publications:* The Economic Theory of Auctions, 2000; Auctions: theory and practice, 2004; articles in econs jls on industrial organization, auction theory, and other econ. theory. *Address:* Nuffield College, Oxford OX1 1NF. *T:* (01865) 278588; *e-mail:* paulklemperer@economics.ox.ac.uk.

KLEOPAS, Myrna Y.; High Commissioner for Cyprus in the United Kingdom, 2000–04; *b* Nicosia, 23 Aug. 1944; *m* Yiangos P. Kleopas; one *s* one *d.* Called to the Bar; practised law in Cyprus, 1971–77; Legal Advr, Min. of Foreign Affairs, Cyprus, 1977–79; entered Cyprus Foreign Service, 1979; Pol Affairs Div., Min. of Foreign Affairs, 1979–80; Counsellor, 1980–86, Consul-Gen., 1981–86, London; Pol Affairs Div., 1986–90; Rep. of Min. of Foreign Affairs to Central Agency for Women's Rights, Cyprus, 1988; Rep. of Cyprus to UN Commn on Status of Women, 1989; Dir, Office of Perm. Sec., Min. of Foreign Affairs, 1990–93; Ambassador to China, and also to Japan, Pakistan, Mongolia and the Philippines, 1993–96; Dir, Pol Affairs Div. (Cyprus Question), Min. of Foreign Affairs, 1996–97; Ambassador to Italy, and also to Switzerland, Malta and San Marino, 1997–2000. *Recreations:* reading, the arts, swimming, walking. *Address:* c/o Cyprus High Commission, 93 Park Street, W1Y 4ET.

KLEPSCH, Dr Egon Alfred; President, European Parliament, 1992–94; *b* 30 Jan. 1930; *m* 1952, Anita Wegehaupt; three *s* three *d. Educ:* Marburg Univ. (DPhil 1954). Mem., CDU, 1951– (Mem. of Bureau, 1977–94); Fed. Chm., Young Christian Democrats, 1963–69; Chm., European Young Christian Democrats, 1964–70; Mem. for Koblenz-St Goar, Bundestag, 1965–80; European Parliament: Member, 1973–79, elected Mem. (EPP/CDU), 1979–94; Vice-Pres., 1982–84; Mem., Political Affairs and other Cttees, 1989–92; Vice-Pres., EPP, 1977–92; Chm., EPP Gp, 1977–82, 1984–92; Mem. Bureau, EPP, 1992–94. Chm., Europa-Union Deutschland, 1989–97 (Hon. Chm., 1997–); Vice-Chm., German Council of Eur. Movement, 1990–99 (Hon. Mem., 1999–). Hon. LLD Sunderland; Dr *hc* Buenos Aires. Grosses Verdienstkreuz mit Stern und Schulterband (Germany), 1986; orders from Italy, Luxembourg, Argentina and Chile. *Publications:* Die Deutsche Russlandpolitik unter dem Reichsminister des Auswärtigen Dr Gustav Stresemann, 1955; Der Kommunismus in Deutschland, 1964; Der Europäische Abgeordnete, 1978; Programme für Europa, 1978; Die Abgeordneten Europas, 1984.

KLOOTWIJK, Jaap; Managing Director, Shell UK Oil, and Joint Managing Director, Shell UK, 1983–88; *b* 16 Nov. 1932; *s* of J. L. Klootwijk and W. J. Boer. *Educ:* Rotterdam Grammar Sch.; Technological Univ., Delft (MSc Mech. Eng, 1956). Lieut Royal Netherlands Navy, 1956–58. Joined Royal Dutch/Shell Gp, 1958; worked in various capacities in Holland, UK, France, Switzerland, Sweden, Algeria, Kenya; Area Co-ordinator, SE Asia, 1976–79; Man. Dir, Shell Internat. Gas Ltd, 1979–82; Chm., UK Oil Pipelines, 1983–88. Director: The Flyfishers' Co. Ltd, 1985–94; Grove Hldgs Ltd, 1991–2001. Pres., UK Petroleum Industry Assoc., 1985–87. *Recreations:* shooting, fishing, reading. *Address:* 46 Oak Lodge, Chantry Square, W8 5UL. *T:* (020) 7937 6099. *Club:* Flyfishers' (Pres., 1985–87).

KLOSE, Hans-Ulrich; Member (SPD), Bundestag, Germany, since 1983; *b* 14 June 1937; *m* 1992, Dr Anne Steinbeck-Klose; two *s* two *d* by former marriages. *Educ:* Bielefeld; Clinton, Iowa; Freiburg Univ. (Law graduate 1965). Joined SPD 1964; Dep. Chm., Young Socialists, 1966; Dep. Chm., SPD, 1968; Mayor of Hamburg, 1974–81; Treasurer, SPD, 1987–91. Bundestag: Leader of the Opposition, 1991–94; Vice-Pres., 1994–98; Chm., 1998–2002, Vice-Chm., 2002–, Cttee on Foreign Affairs; Chm., German-American Parly Gp, 2003–. *Publications:* Altern der Gesellschaft, 1993; Altern hat Zukunft, 1993. *Address:* c/o Bundeshaus, 11011 Berlin, Germany.

KLUG, Sir Aaron, OM 1995; Kt 1988; ScD (Cantab); FRS 1969; Director, Medical Research Council Laboratory of Molecular Biology, Cambridge, 1986–96 (member of staff, since 1962, Joint Head, Division of Structural Studies, 1978–86); President, Royal Society, 1995–2000; Hon. Fellow of Peterhouse, since 1993 (Fellow, 1962–93); *b* 11 Aug. 1926; *s* of Lazar Klug and Bella Klug (*née* Silin); *m* 1948, Liebe, *o d* of Alexander and Annie Bobrow, Cape Town, SA; one *s* (and one *s* decd). *Educ:* Durban High Sch.; Univ. of the Witwatersrand (BSc); Univ. of Cape Town (MSc). Junior Lecturer, Cape Town, 1947–48; 1851 Exhibn Overseas Fellow from SA to Cambridge; Research Student, Cavendish Laboratory, Cambridge, 1949–52; Rouse-Ball Research Studentship, Trinity Coll., Cambridge, 1949–52; Colloid Science Dept, Cambridge, 1953; Nuffield Research Fellow, Birkbeck Coll., London, 1954–57; Head, Virus Structure Research Group, Birkbeck Coll., 1958–61. Mem., Council for Sci. and Technology, 1993–2000. Hon. Prof., Univ. of Cambridge, 1989. Lectures: Carter-Wallace, Princeton, 1972; Leeuwenhoek, Royal Soc., 1973; Dunham, Harvard Medical Sch., 1975; Harvey, NY, 1979; Lane, Stanford Univ., 1983; Silliman, Yale Univ., 1985; Nishina Meml, Tokyo, 1986; Pauli, ETH Zürich, 1986; Cetus, Univ. of California, Berkeley, 1987; Konrad Bloch, Harvard, 1988; Steenbock, Univ. of Wisconsin, 1989; National, US Biophysical Soc., Washington, 1993; William and Mary, Leiden, 1996. Founder FMedSci 1998. For. Associate, Nat. Acad. of Scis, USA, 1984; Foreign Member: Max Planck Soc., Germany, 1984; Japan Acad., 1996; For. Hon. Mem., Amer. Acad. of Arts and Scis, 1969; For. Associate, Acad. des Scis, Paris, 1989. Hon. FRCP 1987; Hon. FRCPath 1991. Hon. Fellow: Trinity Coll., Cambridge, 1983; Amer. Phil Soc., 1996. Hon. DSc: Chicago, 1978; Columbia Univ., 1978; Witwatersrand, 1984; Hull, 1985; St Andrews, 1987; Western Ontario, 1991; Warwick, 1994; Cape Town, 1997; Weizmann Inst., 1997; Stirling, 1998; London, 2000; Oxford, 2001; Dr *hc* Strasbourg, 1978; Hon. PhD Jerusalem, 1984; Hon. Dr Fil. Stockholm, 1980; Hon. LittD Cantab, 1998. Heineken Prize, Royal Netherlands Acad. of Science, 1979; Louisa Gross Horwitz Prize, Columbia Univ., 1981; Nobel Prize in Chemistry, 1982; Gold Medal of Merit, Univ. of Cape Town, 1983; Copley Medal, Royal Soc., 1985; Harden Medal, Biochem. Soc., 1985; Baly Medal, RCP, 1987; William Bate Hardy Prize, Cambridge Phil. Soc., 1996; Croonian Prize Lect., Royal Soc., 2007. Order of Mapungubwe (Gold) (S Africa), 2005. *Publications:* papers in scientific jls. *Recreations:* reading, ancient history. *Address:* MRC Laboratory of Molecular Biology, Hills Road, Cambridge CB2 0QH. *T:* (01223) 248011.

KLUG, Francesca Marilyn Simone, OBE 2002; Professorial Research Fellow, London School of Economics, since 2001; *b* 16 Dec. 1953; *d* of Isaac and Bertha Klug; *m* 1993, Michael Shew; one *d. Educ:* London Sch. of Econs (BSc Sociol.). Res. and Information Officer, Runnymede Trust, 1980–84; Policy Advr, Hackney Council, 1984–89; Dir, Civil Liberties Trust, 1989–92; Res. Fellow, Human Rights Centre, Essex Univ., 1992–96; Sen. Res. Fellow, Law Sch., KCL, 1996–2001. Mem., Commn for Equality and Human Rights, 2007–. *Publications:* (jtly) The Three Pillars of Liberty, Political Rights and Freedoms in the UK, 1996; Values for a Godless Age: the history of the Human Rights Act and its political and legal consequences, 2000; contribs to national press, various anthologies and jls incl. Public Law, Eur. Human Rights Law Rev., Policy and Politics. *Recreations:* reading, walking our dog Ruby with my daughter Tania, having fun with friends. *Address:* London School of Economics, Houghton Street, WC2A 2AE. *T:* (020) 7955 6429; *e-mail:* f.m.klug@lse.ac.uk.

KLYBERG, Rt Rev. Mgr Charles John; *b* 29 July 1931; *s* of late Captain Charles Augustine Klyberg, MN and Ivy Lilian Waddington, LRAM; unmarried. *Educ:* Eastbourne College. Eaton Hall OCS, 1953; 2nd Lieut, 1st Bn The Buffs, Kenya Emergency, 1953–54; Lieut 1955. MRICS. Asst Estates Manager, Cluttons, 1954–57. Lincoln Theological Coll., 1957–60. Curate, S John's, East Dulwich, 1960–63; Rector of Fort Jameson, Zambia, 1963–67; Vicar, Christ Church and S Stephen, Battersea, 1967–77; Dean of Lusaka Cathedral, Zambia, and Rector of the parish, 1977–85, Dean Emeritus, 1985; Vicar General, 1978–85; Bishop Suffragan of Fulham, 1985–96; first Archdeacon of Charing Cross, 1989–96. Received into RC Ch and ordained priest, 1996; Prelate of Honour, 2000. UK Commissary for Anglican Church in Zambia, 1985–89. Chairman: Church Property Development Gp, 1978–85; Fulham Palace Museum Trust, 1991–96. Pres., Guild of All Souls, 1988–95. Guardian, Shrine of Our Lady of Walsingham, 1991–96. Warden, Quainton Hall Sch., Harrow, 1992–96. *Recreations:* reading, music, travel. *Club:* Athenæum.

KLYNE, Dame Barbara Evelyn; *see* Clayton, Dame B. E.

KNAPMAN, Dr Paul Anthony, FRCP, FRCS; DL; HM Coroner for Westminster, since 1980 (Jurisdiction of Inner West London); *b* 5 Nov. 1944; *s* of Frederick Ethelbert and Myra Knapman; *m* 1970, Penelope Jane Cox; one *s* three *d. Educ:* Epsom Coll.; King's Coll., London; St George's Hosp. Med. Sch. (MB, BS 1968). MRCS, LRCP 1968; DMJ 1975; FRCP 1998; FRCS 1999. Called to the Bar, Gray's Inn, 1972. Dep. Coroner for Inner W London, 1975–80. Hon. Lectr in Med. Jurisprudence, St George's Hosp. Med. Sch., 1978–2004; Hon. Clinical Teacher (Forensic Medicine), Royal Free and UC (formerly Middlesex and UCH) Med. Sch., 1981–2004; Hon. Clinical Sen. Lectr, ICSTM (formerly Westminster and Charing Cross Med. Sch.), 1987–2006. Langdon-Brown Lectr, RCP, 1998; Christmas Lectr, ICSTM, 1999. President: S Eastern England Coroners' Soc., 1980; Sect. of Clinical Forensic Medicine, RSocMed, 1995–97; Vice-Pres., Coroners' Soc. of England and Wales, 2000. Gov., London Nautical Sch., 1981–99 (Chm., 1995–99); Pres., Old Epsomian Club, 1999–2000. Liveryman, 1982–, and Mem., Ct of Assistants, 1993–, Soc. of Apothecaries (Master, 2006–07). Mem., Lodge of Friendship (No 6). DL Greater London, 2007. Specialist Editor (Coroners Law), JP Reports, 1990–. *Publications:* (jtly) Coronership: the law and practice on coroners, 1985; Medicine and the Law, 1989; Casebook on Coroners, 1989; Sources of Coroners' Law, 1999; contributor to: Medical Negligence, 1990, 3rd edn 2000; Atkin's Court Forms, vol. 13, 1992, 3rd edn 2000; papers on medico-legal subjects. *Recreations:* boating, beagling. *Address:* Westminster Coroner's Court, Horseferry Road, SW1P 2ED. *T:* (020) 7834 6515. *Clubs:* Athenæum, Garrick; Royal Dart Yacht; RNVR Yacht.

KNAPMAN, Roger Maurice; Member (UK Ind) South West Region, European Parliament, since 2004; Leader, UK Independence Party, 2002–06 (Political Adviser, 2000–02); *b* 20 Feb. 1944; *m* 1967, Carolyn Trebell (*née* Eastman); one *s* one *d. Educ:* Royal Agricl Coll., Cirencester. FRICS 1967. MP (C) Stroud, 1987–97; contested (C) same seat, 1997; contested (UK Ind): N Devon, 2001; Totnes, 2005. PPS to Minister of State for Armed Forces, 1991–93; an Asst Govt Whip, 1995–96; a Lord Comr of HM Treasury (Govt Whip), 1996–97. Vice-Chm., Cons. backbench European Affairs Cttee, 1989–90; Mem., Select Cttee on Agric., 1994–95. Mem., AFRC, 1991–94. *Address:* Coryton House, Coryton, Okehampton, Devon EX20 4PA.

KNAPP, David; *see* Knapp, J. D.

KNAPP, (John) David, OBE 1986; Director of Conservative Political Centre, 1975–88; an Assistant Director, Conservative Research Department, 1979–88; *b* 27 Oct. 1926; *s* of late Eldred Arthur Knapp and Elizabeth Jane Knapp; *m* 1st, 1954, Dorothy Ellen May (*née* Squires) (marr. diss.); one *s*; 2nd, 1980, Daphne Monard, OBE, *widow* of Major S. H. Monard. *Educ:* Dauntsey's Sch., Wilts; King's Coll., London (BA Hons). Dir, Knapp and Bates Ltd, 1950–54. Vice-Chm., Fedn of University Conservative and Unionist Assoc., 1948–49; Conservative Publicity and Political Educn Officer, Northern Area, 1952–56; Political Educn Officer, NW Area, 1956–61, and Home Counties N Area, 1961; Dep. Dir, Conservative Political Centre, 1962–75. Member (C), Hampshire CC, 1989–93. *Recreations:* philately, walking cavalier spaniels. *Address:* Greenway, Yaverland Road, Yaverland, Isle of Wight PO36 8QP. *T:* (01983) 401045.

KNAPP, Trevor Frederick William Beresford; Director, KADE, since 1997; *b* 26 May 1937; *s* of Frederick William Knapp and Linda Knapp (*née* Poffley); *m* 1964, Margaret Fry; one *s* one *d. Educ:* Christ's Hospital; King's College London (BSc 1958). ARIC 1960. Ministry of Aviation, 1961; Sec., Downey Cttee, 1965–66; Sec., British Defence Research and Supply Staff, Canberra, 1968–72; Asst Sec., MoD, 1974; GEC Turbine Generators Ltd, 1976; Central Policy Review Staff, 1977–79; Ministry of Defence: Under-Sec., 1983; Dir Gen. (Marketing), 1983–88; Asst Under Sec. of State (Supply and Organisation) (Air), 1988–91; Asst Under-Sec. of State (Infrastructure and Logistics), 1992–96. Member Board: Waltham Abbey Royal Gunpowder Mills Co., 1997– (Chm., 1998–); Waltham Abbey Trust, 1997–; Trustee: Bromley Voluntary Sector Trust, 1999– (Chm., 2003–); Bromley MIND, 2006–. *Address:* c/o National Westminster Bank, Charing Cross, WC2H 0PD.

KNARESBOROUGH, Bishop Suffragan of, since 2004; **Rt Rev. James Harold Bell;** *b* 20 Nov. 1950; *s* of James and Melita Jane Bell. *Educ:* St John's Coll., Durham Univ. (BA (Mod. Hist.) 1972); Wycliffe Hall, Oxford (BA (Theol.) 1974, MA 1978). Ordained deacon, 1975, priest, 1976; Chaplain and Lectr, 1976–82, Official Fellow, 1979–82, Brasenose Coll., Oxford; Pro-proctor, Oxford Univ., 1982; Rector, St Mary, Northolt, 1982–93; Area Dean, Ealing, 1991–93; Willesden Area Advr for Ministry, and Dir, Willesden Ministry Trng Prog., 1993–97; Dir of Ministry and Trng, Dio. Ripon, and Res. Canon, Ripon Cathedral, 1997–99; Dir of Mission, Dio. Ripon and Leeds, 1999–2004. Hon. Canon, Ripon Cathedral, 1999–2004. *Recreations:* entertaining (and being entertained), collecting, gardening (as required). *Address:* Thistledown, Main Street, Exelby, Bedale, N Yorks DL8 2HD. *T:* (01677) 423525, *Fax:* (01677) 423525; *e-mail:* bishop.knaresb@btinternet.com.

KNATCHBULL, family name of **Baron Brabourne** and **Countess Mountbatten of Burma**.

KNEALE, Byran; *see* Kneale, R. B. C.

KNEALE, Judith; *see* Kerr, J.

KNEALE, (Robert) Bryan (Charles), RA 1974 (ARA 1970); sculptor; Professor of Drawing, Royal College of Art, 1990–95; *b* 19 June 1930; *m* 1956, Doreen Lister (*d* 1998); one *d* (one *s* decd). *Educ:* Douglas High Sch.; Douglas Sch. of Art, IOM; Royal Academy Schools: Rome prize, 1949–51; RA diploma. Tutor, RCA Sculpture Sch., 1964–; Head of Sculpture Sch., Hornsey, 1967; Assoc. Lectr, Chelsea Sch. of Art, 1970. Fellow RCA, 1972, Sen. Fellow, 1995; Head of Sculpture Dept, RCA, 1985–90 (Sen. Tutor, 1980–85); Royal Academy: Master of Sculpture, 1982–85; Prof. of Sculpture, 1985–90; Trustee, 1995–2007. Member: Fine Art Panels, NCAD, 1964–71, Arts Council, 1971–73, CNAA,

1974–82; Chm., Air and Space, 1972–73. *Organised:* Sculpture '72, RA, 1972; Battersea Park Silver Jubilee Sculpture, 1977 (also exhibited); Sade Exhbn, Cork, 1982. *Exhibitions:* Redfern Gallery, 1954, 1956, 1958, 1960, 1962, 1964, 1967, 1970, 1976, 1978, 1981; 1983; John Moores, 1961; Sixth Congress of Internat. Union of Architects, 1961; Art Aujourd'hui, Paris, 1963; Battersea Park Sculpture, 1963, 1966; Profile III Bochum, 1964; British Sculpture in the Sixties, Tate Gall., 1965; Whitechapel Gall. 1966 (retrospective), 1981; Structure, Cardiff Metamorphis Coventry, 1966; New British Painting and Sculpture, 1967–68; City of London Festival, 1968; Holland Park, Sculpture in the Cities, Southampton, and British Sculptors, RA, 1972; Holland Park, 1973, 2000; Royal Exchange Sculpture Exhibition, 1974; New Art, Hayward Gallery, 1975; Sculpture at Worksop, 1976; Taranman Gall., 1977, 1981; Serpentine Gall., 1978; Compass Gall., Glasgow, 1981; 51 Gall., Edinburgh, 1981; Bath Art Fair, 1981; Henry Moore Gall., RCA (retrospective), 1986; Fitzwilliam Mus., 1987; Sala Uno, Rome, 1988; Chichester Fest., 1988; New Art Centre, 1990; Nat. History Mus., 1991; Manx Mus., 1992; RWA (retrospective), 1995; Angela Flowers Gall., 1998; 70th Birthday Exhibn, Roche Court, 2000; Eye of the Storm, Turin, 2000; Hart Gall., 2002, 2004; Cass Sculpture Foundn, London, 2005; *commissions:* LCC, Fenwick Place, 1961; Loughborough campus, 1962; Camberwell Beauty Liby, Old Kent Rd, 1964; Hall Caine Meml, Douglas, 1971; King Edward Sch., Totnes, 1972; Woodside Sculpture, Gloversville, NY, 1972–73; Monumental Sculpture for Manx Millennium, Ronaldsway, IOM, 1979; Wall Sculpture for Govt Bldgs, Douglas, IOM, 1996; Sculpture at Goodwood Sculpture Park, 1996; Bronze doors, Portsmouth Cathedral, 1997; Relief Sculpture for Westminster Cath., 1999; Sculpture for Villa Marina, Douglas, IOM, 2003; Sculpture for New Nobles Hosp., IOM, 2004; Trafalgar Meml Sculpture, Castletown, IOM, 2005; Meml to Illiam Dhone, Malew Ch, IOM, 2006; Sculpture for Rio Tinto Zinc HQ, Paddington, 2008. Arts Council Tours, 1966–71. *Collections:* Arts Council of GB; Contemp. Art Soc.; Manx Museum; Leics Educn Authority; Nat. Galls of Victoria, S Australia and New Zealand; City Art Galls, York, Nottingham, Manchester, Bradford and Leicester; Tate Gall.; Beaverbrook Foundn, Fredericton; Museum of Modern Art, São Paulo, Brazil; Bahia Museum, Brazil; Oriel Coll., Oxford; Museum of Modern Art, New York; City Galleries, Middlesbrough, Birmingham, Wakefield; Fitzwilliam Museum, Cambridge; W Riding Educn Authority; Unilever House Collection; Walker Art Gallery; Nat. History Mus., Taiwan; Nat. History Mus., London. Marsh Award for Public Sculpture, Public Monuments and Sculpture Assoc., 2007. *Address:* 10A Muswell Road, N10 2BG. *T:* (020) 8444 7617; New Art Centre, Roche Court, East Winterslow, Wilts. *T:* (01980) 862447; Hart Gallery, 113 Upper Street, N1 1QN.

KNEBWORTH, Viscount; Philip Anthony Scawen Lytton; *b* 7 March 1989; *s* and *heir* of Earl of Lytton, *qv.*

KNIBB, Prof. Michael Anthony, PhD; FBA 1989; Samuel Davidson Professor of Old Testament Studies, 1997–2001, now Emeritus, and Head, School of Humanities, 2000–01, King's College London; *b* 14 Dec. 1938; third *s* of Leslie Charles Knibb and Christian Vera Knibb (*née* Hoggar); *m* 1972, Christine Mary Burrell. *Educ:* Wyggeston Sch., Leicester; King's Coll. London (BD, PhD; FKC 1991); Union Theol Seminary, NY (STM); Corpus Christi Coll., Oxford. King's College London: Lectr in OT Studies, 1964–82; Reader, 1982–86; Prof. of OT Studies, 1986–97; Head, Dept of Theology and Religious Studies, 1989–93, 1998–2000; Dep. Head, Sch. of Humanities, 1992–97. British Academy: Res. Reader, 1986–88; Mem. Council, 1992–95; Schweich Lectr, 1995; Mem., Humanities Res. Bd, 1995–98 (Chm., Postgrad. Cttee, 1996–98). Editor: Book List of SOTS, 1980–86; Guides to the Apocrypha and Pseudepigrapha, 1995–2004. Hon. Sec., Palestine Exploration Fund, 1969–76. Member, Governing Body: Watford GS for Girls, 1993–2002; SOAS, 2000– (Vice-Chm., 2006–). FRAS 1993. *Publications:* The Ethiopic Book of Enoch: a new edition in the light of the Aramaic Dead Sea Fragments, 2 vols, 1978; Het Boek Henoch, 1983; Cambridge Bible Commentary on 2 Esdras, 1979; (ed jtly) Israel's Prophetic Tradition: essays in honour of P. R. Ackroyd, 1982; The Qumran Community, 1987; (ed with P. W. van der Horst) Studies on the Testament of Job, 1989; Translating the Bible: the Ethiopic version of the Old Testament, 1999; (ed) The Septuagint and Messianism, 2006; reviews and articles in books and learned jls. *Recreation:* hill walking. *Address:* 6 Shootersway Park, Berkhamsted, Herts HP4 3NX. *T:* (01442) 871459. *Club:* Athenæum.

KNIGHT, family name of **Baroness Knight of Collingtree.**

KNIGHT OF COLLINGTREE, Baroness *cr* 1997 (Life Peer), of Collingtree in the co. of Northamptonshire; **Joan Christabel Jill Knight,** DBE 1985 (MBE 1964); *m* 1947, Montague Knight (*d* 1986); two *s. Educ:* Fairfield Sch., Bristol; King Edward Grammar Sch., Birmingham. Mem., Northampton County Borough Council, 1956–66. MP (C) Birmingham, Edgbaston, 1966–97. Member: Select Cttee on Race Relations and Immigration, 1969–72; Select Cttee for Home Affairs, 1980–83, 1992–97; Chairman: Lords and Commons All-Party Child and Family Protection Gp, 1978–97; Cons. Back Bench Health and Social Services Cttee, 1982–97; Member: Exec. Cttee, 1922 Cttee, 1979–97 (Sec., 1983–87; Vice-Chm., 1987–88, 1992–97); Council of Europe, 1977–88, 1999–; WEU, 1977–88, 1999– (Chm., Cttee for Parly and Public Relations, 1984–88); Exec. Cttee, IPU, 1991–97 (Chm., 1994–97). Mem., Select Cttee on EU, 1999–2001. Vice-Chm., Assoc. of Cons. Peers, 2002–. Pres., West Midlands Conservative Political Centre, 1980–83. Vice-Pres., Townswomen's Guilds, 1986–95. Director: Computeach International plc, 1991–2006; Heckett Multiserv, 1999–2006. Chm., Sulgrave Manor Trust, 2007–. Hon. DSc Aston, 1999. Kentucky Colonel, USA, 1973; Nebraska Admiral, USA, 1980. *Publication:* About the House, 1995. *Recreations:* music, reading, tapestry work, theatre-going, antique-hunting. *Address:* c/o House of Lords, SW1A 0PW.

KNIGHT, Prof. Alan Sydney, DPhil; Professor of the History of Latin America, and Fellow of St Antony's College, Oxford, since 1992; *b* 6 Nov. 1946; *s* of William Henry Knight and Eva Maud Crandon; *m* 1st, 1969, Carole Jones (marr. diss. 1979); one *d*; 2nd, 1985, Lidia Lozano; two *s. Educ:* Balliol Coll., Oxford (BA Modern Hist. 1968); Nuffield Coll., Oxford (DPhil 1974). Research Fellow, Nuffield Coll., Oxford, 1971–73; Lectr in Hist., Essex Univ., 1973–85; Worsham Centennial Prof. of History, Univ. of Texas at Austin, 1986–92. *Publications:* The Mexican Revolution (2 vols), 1986; US-Mexican Relations 1910–40, 1987; contrib. Jl of Latin American Studies, Bull. of Latin American Res., etc. *Recreation:* kayaking. *Address:* St Antony's College, Oxford OX2 6JF. *T:* (01865) 274486.

KNIGHT, Very Rev. Alexander Francis, OBE 2006; Dean of Lincoln, 1998–2006, now Emeritus; *b* 24 July 1939; *s* of late Rev. Benjamin Edward Knight and of Dorothy Mary Knight; *m* 1962, Sheelagh Elizabeth (*née* Faris); one *s* three *d. Educ:* Taunton Sch.; St Catharine's Coll., Cambridge (MA). Curate, Hemel Hempstead, 1963–68; Chaplain, Taunton Sch., 1968–74; Dir, Bloxham Project, 1975–81; Dir of Studies, Aston Training Scheme, 1981–83; Priest-in-charge, Easton and Martyr Worthy, 1983–90; Archdeacon of Basingstoke and Canon Residentiary of Winchester Cathedral, 1990–98. Hon. DLitt Lincoln, 2004. *Publications:* contrib. SPCK Taleteller series. *Recreations:* hill walking, theatre, reading, gardening. *Address:* Shalom, Clay Street, Whiteparish, Salisbury SP5 2ST.

KNIGHT, Andrew Stephen Bower; farmer in Warwickshire and Dannevirke; *b* 1 Nov. 1939; *s* of late M. W. B. Knight and S. E. F. Knight; *m* 1st, 1966, Victoria Catherine Brittain (marr. diss.); one *s*; 2nd, 1975, Sabiha Rumani Malik (marr. diss. 1991); two *d*; 3rd, 2006, Marita Georgina Phillips Crawley. Editor, The Economist, 1974–86; Chief Exec., 1986–89, Editor-in-Chief, 1987–89, Daily Telegraph plc; Chairman: News Internat. plc, 1990–94; Times Newspapers Hldgs, 1990–94 (Dir, 1990–). Director: The News Corporation Ltd, 1991–; Rothschild Investment Trust CP, 1996–; Dep. Chm., Home Counties Newspapers Hldgs, 1996–98. Member: Steering Cttee, Bilderberg Meetings, 1980–98; Adv. Bd, Center for Economic Policy Research, Stanford Univ., 1981–; Adv. Council, Inst. of Internat. Studies, Stanford Univ., 1990–. Chm., Harlech Scholars' Trust, 2001– (Trustee, 1986–). Governor and Mem. Council of Management, Ditchley Foundn, 1982–. Chm., Shipston Home Nursing, 1997–2004; Trustee, Spinal Muscular Atrophy Trust, 2003–. *Address:* Compton Scorpion, Warwicks. *Clubs:* Beefsteak, Brooks's, Royal Automobile; Tadmarton Heath Golf.

KNIGHT, Angela Ann, CBE 2007; Chief Executive, British Bankers' Association, since 2007; *b* 31 Oct. 1950; *d* of Andrew McTurk Cook and late Barbara Jean (*née* Gale); *m* 1981, David George Knight (marr. diss.); two *s. Educ:* Penrhos Coll., N Wales; Sheffield Girls' High Sch.; Bristol Univ. (BSc Hons Chem. 1972). Management posts with Air Products Ltd, 1972–77; Man. Dir and Chm., Cook & Knight (Metallurgical Processors) Ltd, 1977–84; Chm., Cook & Knight (Process Plant), 1984–91. Chief Exec., Assoc. of Private Client Investment Managers and Stockbrokers, 1997–2006. Non-executive Director: PEP and ISA (formerly PEP) Managers Assoc., 1997–99; Scottish Widows, 1997–2006; Saur Water Services and South East Water plc (formerly Saur Water Services), 1997–2004; Mott MacDonald, 1998–2001; Logica, 1999–2003; Logica CMG, 2003–; Lloyds TSB, 2003–06. Mem. Bd, PLA, 2002–. MP (C) Erewash, 1992–97; contested (C) same seat, 1997. PPS to Minister for Industry, 1993–94, to Chancellor of the Exchequer, 1994–95; Econ. Sec. to HM Treasury, 1995–97. Governor: Gayhurst Sch., 2000–02; Bradfield Coll., 2001–. *Recreations:* walking, ski-ing, music, books. *Address:* British Bankers' Association, Pinners Hall, 105–108 Old Broad Street, EC2N 1EX. *Club:* Capital.

KNIGHT, Prof. Bernard Henry, CBE 1993; MD, FRCPath; novelist; consultant in forensic medicine; Consultant Pathologist to Home Office, 1965–96; Professor of Forensic Pathology, University of Wales College of Medicine, 1980–96, now Emeritus; *b* 3 May 1931; *s* of Harold Ivor Knight and Doris (*née* Lawes); *m* 1955, Jean Gwenllian Ogborne; one *s. Educ:* Univ. of Wales (BCh, MD); MRCPath 1964, FRCPath 1966; DMJ (Path) 1967; MRCP 1983. Called to the Bar, Gray's Inn, 1967. Captain RAMC, Malaya, 1956–59. Lecturer in Forensic Medicine: Univ. of London, 1959–61; Univ. of Wales, 1961–65; Sen. Lectr, Forensic Med., Univ. of Newcastle, 1965–68; Sen. Lectr, then Reader of Forensic Pathology, Univ. of Wales Coll. Med., 1968–80. Hon. Consultant Pathologist, Cardiff Royal Infirmary, 1968–96. Vis. Prof., Univs of Hong Kong, Kuwait, Malaya and Guangzhou (China). Mem., Home Office Policy Adv. Cttee in Forensic Pathology; Chm., Forensic Sub-Cttee and Bd Examnrs, RCPath, 1990–93; Mem., GMC, 1979–94. President: Brit. Assoc. Forensic Med., 1991–93; Forensic Science Soc., 1988–90; Vice-Pres., Internat. Acad. Legal Med., 1980–. Hon. FRSocMed 1994; Hon. FRCP 2007. Hon. Mem., German, Finnish and Hungarian Socs of Forensic Med. Hon. DSc Glamorgan, 1995; Hon. LLD Wales, 1998; Hon. MD Turku, Finland, 2000; Hon. PhD Tokyo, 2000. GSM Malaya, 1956. *Publications: fiction:* The Lately Deceased, 1961; The Thread of Evidence, 1963; Russian Roulette, 1968; Policeman's Progress, 1969; Tiger at Bay, 1970; Deg y Dragwyddoldeb (Welsh), 1972; Edyfyn Brau (Welsh), 1973; Lion Rampant, 1973; The Expert, 1975; Prince of America, 1977; The Sanctuary Seeker, 1998; The Poisoned Chalice, 1998; Crowner's Quest, 1999; The Awful Secret, 2000; The Tinner's Corpse, 2000; The Grim Reaper, 2001; Fear in the Forest, 2003; Brennan, 2003; The Witch Hunter, 2004; Figure of Hate, 2005; The Tainted Relic, 2005; The Elixir of Death, 2006; The Sword of Shame, 2006; The Noble Outlaw, 2007; The House of Shadows, 2007; The Manor of Death, 2008; The Lost Prophesies, 2008; *biography:* Autopsy: the memoirs of Milton Helpern, 1977; *non-fiction:* Murder, Suicide or Accident, 1965; Discovering the Human Body, 1980; *medical textbooks:* Legal Aspects of Medical Practice, 1972, 5th edn 1992; Forensic Radiology, 1982; Sudden Infant Death, 1982; Post-mortem Technician's Handbook, 1983; Forensic Medicine for Lawyers, 1984, 2nd edn 1998; Forensic Medicine, 1985; (ed) Simpson's Forensic Medicine, 9th edn 1985, 11th edn 1996; Coroner's Autopsy, 1985; Forensic Pathology, 1991, 3rd edn 2004; Estimation of the Time of Death, 1995, 2nd edn 2002. *Recreation:* writing. *Address:* 26 Millwood, Llysfaen, Cardiff CF14 0TL. *T:* (029) 2075 2798.

KNIGHT, Brian Joseph; QC 1981; **His Honour Judge Knight;** a Senior Circuit Judge, since 1998; Mercantile Judge, London Mercantile Court, and Judge in charge of the Technology and Construction Court List at Central London Civil Justice Centre (formerly Business List Judge, Central London County Court), since 1998; *b* 5 May 1941; *s* of Joseph Knight and Vera Lorraine Knight (*née* Docksey); *m* 1967, Cristina Karen Wang Nobrega de Lima (*d* 2003). *Educ:* Colbayns High Sch., Clacton; University Coll. London. LLB 1962, LLM 1963. FCIArb 1995. Called to the Bar, Gray's Inn, 1964, *ad eundem* Lincoln's Inn, 1979; called to the Bar of Hong Kong, 1978, of Northern Ireland, 1979; a Recorder, 1991–98. Asst Parly Boundary Comr, 1992. *Address:* Central London Civil Justice Centre, 26–29 Park Crescent, W1N 4HT. *T:* (020) 7917 7889. *Clubs:* Garrick, MCC.

KNIGHT, Brigid Agnes; a District Judge (Magistrates' Courts), since 2002; *m*; one *s* two *d. Educ:* Liverpool Univ. (LLB Hons); Coll. of Law, Guildford. Solicitor in private practice, 1975–2002. *Recreations:* family, theatre, ballet, contemporary dance, drawing and sketching. *Address:* Cheshire Magistrates' Courts, Justices' Clerks' Office, Winmarleigh Street, Warrington WA1 1PB. *T:* (01925) 236250.

KNIGHT, Rt Hon. Gregory; PC 1995; MP (C) Yorkshire East, since 2001; writer, consultant solicitor; *b* 4 April 1949; *s* of late George Knight and Isabella Knight (*née* Bell). *Educ:* Alderman Newton's Grammar School, Leicester; College of Law, Guildford. Self employed solicitor, 1973–83. Member: Leicester City Council, 1976–79; Leicestershire County Council, 1977–83 (Chm., Public Protection Cttee). MP (C) Derby North, 1983–97; contested (C) same seat, 1997. PPS to the Minister of State: Home Office, 1987; Foreign Office, 1988–89; an Asst Govt Whip, 1989–90; a Lord Comr of HM Treasury, 1990–93; Dep. Govt Chief Whip and Treas. of HM Household, 1993–96; Minister of State, DTI, 1996–97; Shadow Dep. Leader, H of C, 2001–03; Opposition front bench spokesman: on transport and envmt, 2003–05; on transport, 2005–06. Chm., H of C Procedure Select Cttee, 2006–. Vice Chm., Cons. Candidates' Assoc., 1998–2001. Dir, Leicester Theatre Trust, 1979–85 (Chm., Finance Cttee, 1982–83). *Publications:* (jtly) Westminster Words, 1988; Honourable Insults: a century of political insult, 1990; Parliamentary Sauce: more political insults, 1992; Right Honourable Insults, 1998; Naughty Graffiti, 2005; pamphlets and articles for law, motoring and entertainment publications. *Recreations:* driving cars and making music. *Address:* House of Commons, SW1A 0AA. *Club:* Bridlington Conservative.

KNIGHT, Sir Harold (Murray), KBE 1980; DSC 1945; *b* 13 Aug. 1919; *s* of W. H. P. Knight, Melbourne; *m* 1951, Gwenyth Catherine Pennington; four *s* one *d. Educ:* Scotch Coll., Melbourne; Melbourne Univ. Commonwealth Bank of Australia, 1936–40. AIF (Lieut), 1940–43; RANVR (Lieut), 1943–45. Commonwealth Bank of Australia, 1946–55; Asst Chief, Statistics Div., Internat. Monetary Fund, 1957–59; Reserve Bank of Australia: Research Economist, 1960–62; Asst Manager, Investment Dept, 1962–64, Manager, 1964–68; Dep. Governor and Dep. Chm. of Board, 1968–75; Governor and Chm. of Bd, 1975–82. Chairman: Mercantile Mutual Hldgs, 1985–89; IBJ Australia Bank Ltd, 1985–92; Dir, Western Mining Corp., 1982–91. Mem., Police Bd of NSW, 1988–89, 1991–93. Mem. Council, Macquarie Univ., 1990–92. Pres., Scripture Union, NSW, 1983–2002. *Publication:* Introducción al Analisis Monetario (Spanish), 1959.

KNIGHT, Henrietta Catherine, (Mrs T. W. Biddlecombe); licensed racehorse trainer, since 1989; *b* 15 Dec. 1946; *d* of late Maj. Guy Knight, MC and Hester Knight; *m* 1995, Terence Walter Biddlecombe. *Educ:* Didcot Girls' Grammar Sch.; Westminster Coll. of Educn, Oxford (BEd Oxon); Berkshire Coll. of Agric. (Advanced NCA). Schoolteacher, hist. and biol., St Mary's Sch., Wantage, 1970–74; ran private livery Point to Point yard, 1974–84 (trained over 100 Point to Point winners). Chm., Sen. Selection Cttee, British Horse Soc. (Three Day Eventing), 1984–88. National Hunt winners include: Stompin, Glenlivet Hurdle, Aintree, 1995; Karshi, Stayers Hurdle, Cheltenham, 1997; Edredon Bleu, Grand Annual Chase, Cheltenham, 1998; Lord Noelie, Sun Alliance Chase, Edredon Bleu, Queen Mother Champion Chase, Cheltenham, 2000; Best Mate, 2002, Edredon Bleu, 2003, King George VI Steeplechase, Kempton; Best Mate, 3 Cheltenham Gold Cups, 2002, 2003, 2004. *Publications:* Best Mate: Chasing Gold, 2003; Best Mate: Triple Gold, 2004. *Recreations:* farming, breeding Connemara ponies, judging at major horse shows each summer. *Address:* West Lockinge Farm, Wantage, Oxon OX12 8QF. *T:* (01235) 833535, *Fax:* (01235) 820110; *e-mail:* hen@westlockinge.co.uk.

KNIGHT, Rt Hon. James Philip, (Jim); PC 2008; MP (Lab) Dorset South, since 2001; Minister of State, Department for Children, Schools and Families (formerly Department for Education and Skills), since 2006; *b* 6 March 1965; *s* of Philip Knight and Hilary Howlett; *m* 1989, Anna Wheatley; one *s* one *d. Educ:* Eltham Coll., London; Fitzwilliam Coll., Cambridge (BA Hons Geog. and Social and Pol Sci.). Worker, Works Theatre Co-operative Ltd, 1986–88; Manager, Central Studio Arts Centre, 1988–90; Dir, W Wilts Arts Centre Ltd, 1990–91; Dentons Directories Ltd: Sales Exec., 1991–96; Gen. Manager, 1997–98; Dir, 1998–2000; Prodn Manager, 2000–01. PPS to Minister of State, DoH, 2003–04; Parly Under-Sec. of State, DEFRA, 2005–06. *Recreations:* cooking, tennis, watching Arsenal and Weymouth Football Clubs, literature. *Address:* (office) 42 Southview Road, Weymouth, Dorset DT4 0JD.

KNIGHT, Jeffrey Russell, FCA; Chief Executive, The Stock Exchange, 1982–89; *b* 1 Oct. 1936; *s* of Thomas Edgar Knight and Ivy Cissie Knight (*née* Russell); *m* 1959, Judith Marion Delver Podger; four *d. Educ:* Bristol Cathedral Sch.; St Peter's Hall, Oxford (MA). Chartered Accountant, 1966; The Stock Exchange, subseq. Internat. Stock Exchange, 1967–90: Head of Quotations Dept, 1973; Dep. Chief Executive, 1975. Member: City Company Law Cttee, 1974–80; Dept of Trade Panel on Company Law Revision, 1980–84; Accounting Standards Cttee, 1982–89; Special Adviser to Dept of Trade, 1975–81; Adviser to Council for the Securities Industry, 1978–85; UK Delegate: to EEC Working Parties; to Internat. Fedn of Stock Exchanges, 1973–90 (Chm., Task Force on Transnational Settlement, 1987–91); to Fedn of Stock Exchanges in EEC, 1974–90 (Chm., Wking Cttee, 1980–90); to Internat. Orgn of Securities Commns, 1987–91 (Chm. Wkg Party on Capital Adequacy). *Recreations:* cricket, music. *Address:* Lordsmeade, Hurtmore Road, Godalming, Surrey GU7 2DY. *T:* (01483) 424399. *Clubs:* Brooks's, MCC; Woking Golf.

KNIGHT, Sir Kenneth John, (Sir Ken), Kt 2006; CBE 2001; QFSM 1992; DL; Chief Fire and Rescue Adviser, Department for Communities and Local Government, since 2007; *b* 3 Jan. 1947; *s* of Dennis and Nancy Knight; *m* 1999, Sandra Louise Peach. MIFireE 1970. Westminster Bank, Reigate, 1964–66; joined Surrey Fire Bde, 1966; Home Office, 1985–87; Asst Chief Officer, London Fire Bde, 1987–92; Dep. Chief Officer, Devon Fire Bde, 1992–94; Chief Fire Officer: Dorset, 1994–98; W Midlands, 1998–2003; Comr for Fire and Emergency Planning, London Fire Bde, 2003–07. Chair, European Tech. Cttee; Principal Advr on fire matters, LGA; Bd, Chief Fire Officers' Assoc. Master, Worshipful Co. of Firefighters, 1998. DL Greater London, 2006. CCMI 2005. OStJ 2005. *Recreations:* theatre, horse riding. *Address:* Department for Communities and Local Government, Eland House, Bressenden Place, SW1E 5DU.

KNIGHT, Malcolm Donald; General Manager and Chief Executive Officer, Bank for International Settlements, since 2003; *b* 11 April 1944; *s* of Gordon James Knight and Muriel Edith Knight (*née* McGregor); *m* 1972, Amy W. Crumpacker; three *d. Educ:* Gen. Amherst High Sch.; Univ. of Toronto (BA Hons Pol Sci. and Econs 1967); London Sch. of Econs (MSc Econ. 1968; PhD 1972). Asst Prof. of Econs, Univ. of Toronto, 1971–72; Lectr in Econs, LSE, 1972–75; International Monetary Fund: economist, 1975–83, Chief, Ext. Adjustment Div., 1983–87, Res. Dept; Div. Chief, 1987–89, Asst Dir, 1989–91, ME Dept; Asst Dir, Res. Dept, 1991–93; Sen. Advr, 1993–96, and Dep. Dir, 1995–96, ME Dept; Dep. Dir, Monetary and Exchange Affairs Dept, 1996–98; Dep. Dir, European I Dept, 1998–99; Sen. Dep. Gov., Bank of Canada, 1999–2003. Adjunct Professor: Virginia Poly. and State Univ. Grad. Prog., Northern Virginia, 1978–85; Sch. of Advanced Internat. Studies, Johns Hopkins Univ., 1980–96. Trustee: Internat. Accounting Standards Cttee Foundn, 2003–; Per Jacobsson Foundn, 2003–; European Assoc. of Banking and Financial History; Member: IMF Capital Markets Consultation Gp, 2003–; Financial Stability Forum, 2005–. Mem., Soc. of Scholars, Johns Hopkins Univ., 2006. Woodrow Wilson Nat. Fellow, 1967; Canada Council Doctoral Fellow, 1968–70. Hon. Dr Toronto, 2006. *Publications:* (ed jtly) Transforming Financial Systems in the Baltics, Russia and Other Countries of the Former Soviet Union, 1999; The Canadian Economy, 1989, rev. edn 1996; contrib. numerous articles to learned jls on internat. finance, stabilization progs in developing countries, monetary policy and empirical aspects of growth theory. *Recreations:* tennis, ski-ing, bicycling, hiking, swimming, jogging, watercolour. *Address:* Bank for International Settlements, Centralbahnplatz 2, 4002 Basel, Switzerland. *T:* (61) 2808750, *Fax:* (61) 2809100; *e-mail:* malcolm.knight@bis.org.

KNIGHT, Maureen R.; *see* Rice-Knight.

KNIGHT, Sir Michael (William Patrick), KCB 1983 (CB 1980); AFC 1964; Chairman, Exmoor Calvert Trust, since 2000; *b* 23 Nov. 1932; *s* of William and Dorothy Knight; *m* 1967, Patricia Ann (*née* Davies) (decd); one *s* two *d. Educ:* Leek High Sch.; Univ. of Liverpool (BA Hons 1954; Hon. DLitt 1985). FRAeS 1985. Univ. of Liverpool Air Sqn, RAFVR, 1951–54; commnd RAF, 1954; served in Transport and Bomber Comds, and in Middle and Near East Air Forces, 1956–63; Comd No 32 Sqn, RAF Akrotiri, 1961–63; RAF Staff Coll., 1964; Min. of Aviation, 1965–66; Comd Far East Strike Wing, RAF Tengah, 1966–69; Head of Secretariat, HQ Strike Comd, 1969–70; Mil. Asst to Chm., NATO Mil. Cttee, 1970–73; Comd RAF Laarbruch, 1973–74; RCDS, 1975; Dir of Ops (Air Support), MoD, 1975–77; SASO, HQ Strike Command/DCS (Ops & Intelligence) HQ UK Air Forces, 1977–80; AOC No 1 Gp, 1980–82; Air Mem. for Supply and Organisation, 1983–86; UK Military Rep. to NATO, 1986–89; Air ADC to the Queen, 1986–89 (ADC, 1973–74); retd in rank of Air Chief Marshal, 1989; commnd Flying Officer, RAFVR (Trng Br.), 1989–2004. Adjunct Prof., Internat. Peace and Security, Carnegie Mellon Univ., Pittsburgh, 1989–95. Dep. Chm., 1994–95, Chm., 1995–2001, Cobham plc; Chairman: Page Gp Hldgs Ltd, 1996–2000; Cranfield Aerospace Ltd, 2000–03; Director: Craigwell Research, 1990–97; RAFC Co. Ltd, 1993–2003; SBAC (Farnborough) Ltd, 1996–98; non-executive Director: FR Group plc, 1990–94; Page Aerospace Gp, 1991–96; Smiths Industries Aerospace and Defence Systems Group, 1992–95; Associate, JGW Associates Ltd, 1989–; Chm., Northern Devon Healthcare NHS Trust, 1991–94. Mem., Internat. Adv. Bd, British/Amer. Business Council, 1995–2001. Mem., IISS, 1968–2002; Member Council: RUSI, 1984–87; The Air League, 1990–2004 (Chm., 1992–98; Pres., 1998–2004; Life Vice-Pres., 2004; Founders' Medal, 2005); SBAC, 1995–99; Calvert Trust, 2000–; Pres., Council, NAAFI, 1984–86; Vice-Pres., Atlantic Council of UK, 1994–2008. Chm., N Devon Family Support Service, Leonard Cheshire Foundn, 1989–91; Devon County Rep., RAF Benev. Fund, 1990–; RAF Pres., 1991–97, Sen. Pres., 1997–2000, Officers' Assoc.; President: Aircrew Assoc., 1992–97; Buccaneer Aircrew Assoc., 1994–; No 32 (The Royal) Sqn Assoc., 1997–; Royal Internat. Air Tattoo, 2005–08 (Vice-Pres., 1991–2002; Vice-Patron, 2003–04); Vice-Pres., The Youth Trust, 1994–98; Chm., 2003–07, Life Pres., 2007–, Vulcan to the Sky Trust (Patron, Vulcan Restoration Appeal, 2000–03); Chm., RAF Charitable Trust, 2005–08. Trustee: RAF Central Fund, 1983–86; RAF Mus., 1983–86. Patron, Guild of Aviation Artists, 2005– (Vice-Pres., 1997–2005); Vice-Patron, Yorks Air Mus., 1997–. Gov. and Council Mem., Taunton Sch., 1987–2000; Mem., Univ. of Liverpool Develt Team, 1986–. Rugby Football Union: Mem. Cttee, 1977–92; Mem. Exec. Cttee, 1989–92; Chm., Internat. Sub Cttee, 1987–90; Chm., Forward Planning Sub Cttee, 1990–92; Privilege Mem., 1992–. President: RAF Rugby Union, 1985–89 (Chm., 1975–78); Combined Services RFC, 1987–89 (Chm., 1977–79); RAF Lawn Tennis Assoc., 1984–86; Vice-President: Leek RUFC, 1959–; Crawshay's Welsh RFC, 1997–; Penguin Internat. RFC, 2001–. Hon. Air Cdre, No 7630 (VR) Intelligence Sqn, RAuxAF, 2001–07. FRGS 1994 (Mem. Council, 1995–97); FRSA 1994. Freeman, City of London, 1989; Liveryman, GAPAN, 1993– (Upper Freeman, 1990–93; Guild Award of Honour, 2007). *Publications:* (contrib.) War in the Third Dimension, 1986; Strategic Offensive Air Power and Technology, 1989; articles in prof. pubns, 1975–. *Recreations:* Rugby football, lesser sports, music, writing, travel, public speaking. *Address:* c/o National Westminster Bank, Leek, Staffs. *Clubs:* Royal Air Force (Vice-Pres., 1983–2003), Colonels (founder).

KNIGHT, Nicholas David Gordon; photographer; Director: N. K. Image Ltd, since 1998; Showstudio Ltd, since 2000; *b* 24 Nov. 1958; *s* of Michael A. G. Knight and Beryl Rose Knight; *m* 1995, Charlotte Esme Wheeler; one *s* two *d. Educ:* Hinchingbrooke Comprehensive Sch., Huntingdon; Chelsea Coll., London Univ.; Bournemouth and Poole Coll. of Art (PQE Dip. in Art and Design (Distinction) 1982; Hon. Fellow, 1998). Commissioning Picture Editor, ID magazine, 1990; Photographer, Vogue, 1995–. Hon. MA Anglia Poly. Univ., 2000. *Publications:* Skinhead, 1982; Nicknight, 1994; Flora, 1997. *Recreations:* architecture, natural history. *T:* (020) 8940 1086.

KNIGHT, Dr Peter Clayton, CBE 1995; DL; Vice-Chancellor, University of Central England in Birmingham, 1992–2006 (Director, Birmingham Polytechnic, 1985–92); *b* 8 July 1947; *s* of Norman Clayton Knight and Vera Catherine Knight; *m* 1977, Catherine Mary (*née* Ward); one *s* one *d. Educ:* Bishop Vesey's Grammar Sch., Sutton Coldfield; Univ. of York (BA 1st cl. Hons Physics; DPhil). SRC Studentship, 1968; Asst Teacher, Plymstock Comprehensive Sch., 1971; Plymouth Polytechnic: Lectr, 1972; Sen. Lectr, 1974; Head of Combined Studies, 1981; Dep. Dir, Lancashire Polytechnic, 1982–85. Nat. Pres., NATFHE, 1977; Chm., SRHE, 1987–89; Member: Burnham Cttee of Further Educn, 1976–81; Working Party on Management of Higher Educn, 1977; Nat. Adv. Body on Public Sector Higher Educn, 1982–85; PCFC, 1989–93; Polytechnic and Colleges Employers Forum, 1989–94; Teacher Training Agency, 1994–2000. Mem., Armed Forces Pay Review Bd, 2004–. Mem., Focus Housing Assoc., 1991–; Chm., Prime Focus Regeneration Gp (formerly Focus Housing Gp), 1996–2006. DL W Midlands, 2008. DUniv York, 1991; Hon. DSc Aston, 1997. *Publications:* articles, chapters and reviews in learned jls on educnl policy, with particular ref. to higher educn. *Recreation:* flying and building light aircraft. *Address:* Sandy Lodge, Sandy Lane, Brewood, Staffs ST19 9ET. *T:* (01902) 851339.

KNIGHT, Prof. Sir Peter Leonard, Kt 2005; DPhil; FRS 1999; FInstP; Professor of Quantum Optics, since 1988, and Principal, Faculty of Natural Sciences, since 2006, Imperial College of Science, Technology and Medicine, University of London; *b* 12 Aug. 1947; *s* of Joseph and Eva Knight; *m* 1965, Christine Huckle; two *s* one *d. Educ:* Bedford Modern Sch.; Sussex Univ. (BSc, DPhil). FInstP 1991. Research Associate, Univ. of Rochester, NY, 1972–74; SRC Res. Fellow, Sussex Univ., 1974–76; Jubilee Res. Fellow, 1976–78, SERC Advanced Fellow, 1978–79, RHC; Imperial College, London: SERC Advanced Fellow, 1979–83; Lectr, 1983–87; Reader, 1987–88; Head, Laser Optics and Spectroscopy, then Quantum Optics and Laser Sci., Physics Dept, 1992–2001; Head, Physics Dept, 2001–05; Acting Principal of Physical Scis, 2004–05. Chief Scientific Advr, NPL, 2002–05. Mem., SERC Atomic and Molecular Physics Sub Cttee, 1987–90; Co-ordinator, SERC Nonlinear Optics Initiative, 1989–92 (Chm., Prog. Adv. Gp, 1992–95). Mem. Council, Royal Soc., 2005–07. Chairman: Quantum Electronics Div., European Physical Soc., 1988–92; Sci. Bd, STFC, 2007–; President: Physics Sect., BAAS, 1994–95; Optical Soc. of America, 2004 (Fellow 1996; Dir, 1999–2001). Corresp. Mem., Mexican Acad. of Scis, 2000. Hon. DSc: Nat. Inst. for Astronomy, Optics and Electronics, Mexico, 1998; Slovak Acad. of Scis, 2000. Parsons Meml Lectr, Royal Soc. and Inst. of Physics, 1991; Humboldt Res. Award, Alexander von Humboldt Foundn, 1993; Einstein Medal and Prize for Laser Science, Soc. of Optical and Quantum Electronics and Eastman Kodak Co., 1996; Thomas Young Medal and Prize, Inst. of Physics, 1999. Editor: Jl of Modern Optics, 1987–2006; Contemporary Physics, 1993–. *Publications:* Concepts of Quantum Optics, 1983; (with Chris Gerry) Introductory Quantum Optics, 2004; papers in Phys. Rev., Phys. Rev. Letters and other jls. *Recreations:* traditional music, walking. *Address:* Faculty of Natural Sciences, Imperial College of Science, Technology and Medicine, SW7 2AZ. *T:* (020) 7594 5477.

KNIGHT, Roger David Verdon, OBE 2007; Secretary & Chief Executive, Marylebone Cricket Club, 2000–06 (Secretary, 1994–2000); *b* 6 Sept. 1946; *s* of late David Verdon Knight and Thelma Patricia Knight; *m* 1971, Christine Ann McNab (*née* Miln); one *s* one *d. Educ:* Dulwich Coll.; St Catharine's Coll., Cambridge (BA Modern and Medieval Langs 1969; MA 1972; DipEd 1970). Assistant Master: Eastbourne Coll., 1970–78; Dulwich Coll., 1978–83; Housemaster, Cranleigh Sch., 1983–90; Headmaster, Worksop Coll., 1990–93. Professional cricketer (summers only): Gloucestershire, 1971–75; Sussex, 1976–77; Surrey, 1978–84 (Captain, 1978–83). Vice-Chm., SE Region, Sports Council, 1985–90; Chm. Management Cttee, SE Region, Centres of Excellence, 1987–90; Member: Cricket Cttee, Surrey CCC, 1987–90 (Pres., 2008–March 2009); MCC Cttee, 1989–92; HMC Sports Sub-Cttee, 1991–93; ICC Develt Cttee, 1996–2006, 2007–; Mgt

Bd, ECB, 1997–2006; Council, London Playing Fields Soc., 1998–2002; European Cricket Council, 1998– (Chm., 2006–); Chm., Interim Bd, ECB Assoc. of Cricket Officials, 2008–; Pres., European Cricket Fedn, 1994–97. Governor: TVS Trust, 1987–92; Rendcomb Coll., 1995–99; King's Sch., Taunton, 1998– (Chm., Educn Cttee, 2005–); Dulwich Coll., 2004–. *Recreations:* cricket, tennis, bridge, piano music, 17th Century French literature.

KNIGHT, Prof. Roger John Beckett, PhD; FRHistS; Professor of Naval History, University of Greenwich, since 2006 (Visiting Professor, 2001–06); *b* 11 April 1944; *s* of John Beckett Knight and Alyson Knight (*née* Nunn); *m* 1st, 1968, Elizabeth Magowan (marr. diss. 1980); two *s*; 2nd, 1998, Jane Hamilton-Eddy. *Educ:* Tonbridge Sch.; Trinity Coll., Dublin (MA); Sussex Univ. (PGCE); University Coll. London (PhD). FRHistS 1988. Asst Master, Haberdashers' Aske's Sch., Elstree, 1972–73; National Maritime Museum: Dep. Custodian of Manuscripts, 1974–77, Custodian, 1977–80; Dep. Head, Printed Books and Manuscripts Dept, 1980–84; Head, Inf. Project Gp, 1984–86; Head, Documentation Div., 1986–88; Chief Curator, 1988–93; Dep. Dir, 1993–2000. Trustee, Nat. Maritime Mus., Cornwall, 1998–2002. Member Council: Soc. for Nautical Research, 1977–81 (Vice-Pres., 1993–2006); Navy Records Soc., 1974– (Vice-Pres., 1980–84, 2003–). *Publications:* Guide to the Manuscripts in the National Maritime Museum, vol. 1, 1977, vol. 2, 1980; (with Alan Frost) The Journal of Daniel Paine 1794–1797, 1983; Portsmouth Dockyard Papers 1774–1783: the American War, 1987; (ed jtly) British Naval Documents 1204–1960, 1993; The Pursuit of Victory: the life and achievement of Horatio Nelson, 2005 (Mountbatten Maritime Prize, British Maritime Charitable Foundn, 2005; Duke of Westminster's Medal, RUSI, 2006); articles, reviews in jls. *Recreations:* sailing, cricket, music. *Address:* Greenwich Maritime Institute, University of Greenwich, Old Royal Naval College, Greenwich, SE10 9LS. *T:* (020) 8331 7688. *Clubs:* Athenæum; West Wittering Sailing.

KNIGHT, Steven; writer, since 1989; *b* 5 Aug. 1959; *s* of George and Ida Knight. *Educ:* University Coll. London (BA Hons English). Writer, producer, Capital Radio, 1983–87; writer for television, 1990–: Detectives; Canned Carrott; Ruby Wax Show; Commercial Breakdown; All About Me; Co-creator, Who Wants To Be a Millionaire?, 1998; screenwriter: Gypsy Woman, 2000; Dirty Pretty Things, 2003 (awards include: Best British Screenwriter, London Film Critics' Circle Awards, 2003; Humanitas Award, 2004; Edgar Award for Best Motion Picture Screenplay, 2004); Amazing Grace, 2007 (Epiphany Prize, John Templeton Foundn, 2008); Eastern Promises, 2007 (Cadillac People's Choice Award, Tribeca Film Fest., 2007; Genie Award, Acad. of Canadian Cinema and TV, 2008); writer for theatre: The President of an Empty Room, NT, 2005. *Publications:* The Movie House, 1994; Alphabet City, 1998; Out of the Blue, 1999. *Recreation:* writing. *Address:* c/o United Agents, 12–26 Lexington Street, W1F 0LE.

KNIGHT, Terence Gordon, FRICS; Consultant, Atisreal Ltd (formerly ATIS Real Weatheralls), since 2002; *b* 1 June 1944; *s* of Albert Henry and Eileen Doris Knight; *m* 1968, Gillian Susan West; two *s*. *Educ:* St Paul's Sch. FRICS 1976. Joined Weatherall Green & Smith, Chartered Surveyors, 1962; Partner, 1976–2001; Sen. Partner, 1992–98. Liveryman, Chartered Surveyors' Co., 1988 (Master, 2004–05). *Recreations:* golf, walking. *Address:* Atisreal Ltd, Norfolk House, 31 St James's Square, SW1Y 4JR. *T:* (020) 7338 4280. *Clubs:* Naval and Military; Worplesdon Golf.

KNIGHT, Veronica Lesley; *see* Hammerton, V. L.

KNIGHT, Warburton Richard, CBE 1987; Director of Educational Services, Bradford Metropolitan District Council, 1974–91; *b* 2 July 1932; *s* of late Warburton Henry Johnston and Alice Gweneth Knight; *m* 1961, Pamela Ann (*née* Hearmon); two *s* one *d*. *Educ:* Trinity Coll., Cambridge (MA). Teaching in Secondary Modern and Grammar Schs in Middlesex and Huddersfield, 1956–62; joined West Riding Educn Authority, 1962; Asst Dir for Secondary Schs, Leics, 1967; Asst Educn Officer for Sec. Schs and later for Special and Social Educn in WR, 1970. Hon. DLitt Bradford, 1992. *Recreations:* walking, choral music, travel. *Address:* Thorner Grange, Sandhills, Thorner, Leeds LS14 3DE. *T:* (0113) 289 2356. *Club:* Royal Over-Seas League.

KNIGHT, William John Langford; Chairman, Financial Reporting Review Panel, since 2004; Senior Partner, Simmons & Simmons, 1996–2001; *b* 11 Sept. 1945; *s* of William Knight and Gertrude Alice Knight; *m* 1973, Stephanie Irina Williams; one *s* one *d*. *Educ:* Sir Roger Manwood's Sch., Sandwich; Bristol Univ. (LLB). Admitted solicitor, 1969; joined Simmons & Simmons, 1967; Partner, 1973; i/c Hong Kong Office, 1979–82; Head, Corporate Dept, 1994–96. Chairman: London Weighting Adv. Panel, GLA, 2002; Enforcement Cttee, Gen. Insce Standards Council, 2002–05; Member: Financial Reporting Council, 2004–07 (Dir, 2008–); Gaming Bd for GB, 2004–05; Gambling Commn, 2005–. Trustee, Common Purpose Internat., 2008–. Mem. Council, Lloyd's, 2000– (Dep. Chm., 2003–). Liveryman, Solicitors' Co., 1983 (Master, 2007–08). FRSA. *Publication:* The Acquisition of Private Companies and Business Assets, 1975, 7th edn 1997. *Recreations:* tennis, photography, Arsenal FC. *Clubs:* Travellers; Hong Kong (Hong Kong).

KNIGHT SMITH, Ian; *see* Smith.

KNIGHTLEY; *see* Finch-Knightley, family name of Earl of Aylesford.

KNIGHTLEY, Sharman; *see* Macdonald, S.

KNIGHTON, Dr Tessa Wendy; writer; Editor, Early Music, since 1992 (Assistant Editor, 1988–91); Fellow, Clare College, Cambridge, since 1996; *b* 31 March 1957; *d* of Geoffrey Morris Knighton and (Margaret) Wendy Knighton; *m* 1984, Ivor Bolton, *qv*; one *s*. *Educ:* Felixstowe Coll., Suffolk; Clare Coll., Cambridge (MA 1980; PhD 1984). Jun. Res. Fellow, Lady Margaret Hall, Oxford, 1982–84; freelance writer and editor, 1984–; Lectr, Faculty of Music, Cambridge Univ., 1991–93; Res. Associate, RHBNC, Univ. of London, 1993–99; Leverhulme Res. Asst, Faculty of Music, Univ. of Cambridge, 2000–03. Artistic Dir, Lufthansa Fest. of Baroque Music, 1986–97; Early Music Critic: Gramophone, 1988–; The Times, 1995–; radio broadcasts. *Publications:* (ed jtly) Companion to Medieval and Renaissance Music, 1992; Música y Músicos en la Corte de Fernando de Aragón 1474–1516, 2000; (jtly) Felipe II y la Música, 2001; articles in Early Music History, Early Music, Plainsong and Medieval Music, Revista de Musicología, Renaissance Studies, Artigrama, etc. *Recreations:* wine, walking, whippets, song. *Address:* Clare College, Cambridge CB2 1TL. *T:* (01223) 333243.

KNIGHTON, William Myles, CB 1981; Principal Establishment and Finance Officer, Department of Trade and Industry, 1986–91; *b* 8 Sept. 1931; *s* of late George Harry Knighton, OBE, and Ella Knighton (*née* Stroud); *m* 1957, Brigid Helen Carrothers; one *s* one *d*. *Educ:* Bedford School; Peterhouse, Cambridge (MA). Asst Principal, Min. of Supply, 1954; Principal, Min. of Aviation, 1959; Cabinet Office, 1962–64; Principal Private Sec. to Minister of Technology, 1966–68; Asst Sec., Min. of Technology, subseq. DTI and Dept of Trade, 1967–74; Under Sec., 1974–78, Dep. Sec., 1978–83, Dept of Trade; Dep. Sec., Dept of Transport, 1983–86. *Publication:* (with D. E. Rosenthal)

National Laws and International Commerce, 1982. *Recreations:* gardening, hill-walking, music, painting, reading. *Address:* Court Green, St Anne's Hill, Midhurst, W Sussex GU29 9NN. *T:* (01730) 817860. *Club:* Oxford and Cambridge.

KNIGHTS, family name of **Baron Knights**.

KNIGHTS, Baron *cr* 1987 (Life Peer), of Edgbaston in the County of West Midlands; **Philip Douglas Knights,** Kt 1980; CBE 1976 (OBE 1971); QPM (Dist. Service) 1964; DL; Chief Constable, West Midlands Police, 1975–85; *b* 3 Oct. 1920; *s* of Thomas James Knights and Ethel Knights; *m* 1945, Jean Burman. *Educ:* King's Sch., Grantham. Lincolnshire Constabulary: Police Cadet, 1938–40; Constable, 1940. Served War, RAF, 1943–45. Sergeant, Lincs Constab., 1946; seconded to Home Office, 1946–50; Inspector, Lincs Constab., 1953, Supt 1955, Chief Supt 1957. Asst Chief Constable, Birmingham City Police, 1959; seconded to Home Office, Dep. Comdt, Police Coll., 1962–66; Dep. Chief Constable, Birmingham City Police, 1970; Chief Constable, Sheffield and Rotherham Constab., 1972–74; Chief Constable, South Yorks Police, 1974–75. Winner of Queen's Police Gold Medal Essay Competition, 1965. Mem., Lord Devlin's Cttee on Identification Procedures, 1974–75. Pres., Assoc. of Chief Police Officers, 1978–79. Member: Council, Univ. of Aston, 1985–98; Adv. Council, Cambridge Univ. Inst. of Criminology, 1986–2002. CCMI. DL W Midlands, 1985. Hon. DSc Aston, 1996. *Recreations:* sport, gardening. *Address:* House of Lords, SW1A 0PW. *Club:* Royal Over-Seas League.

KNIGHTS, Laurence James W.; *see* West-Knights.

KNIGHTS, Rosemary Margaret; Chief Executive, Warrington Hospital NHS Trust, 1993–98; *b* 2 Nov. 1945; *d* of Donald and Margaret Robson; *m* 1983, Michael A. Knights. *Educ:* Houghton-le-Spring Grammar School; Coll. of Nursing, Sunderland AHA. RGN, OND. Clinical nursing career, 1962–75 (Ward Sister posts, Sunderland and Harrogate); Nursing Officer, Harrogate, 1975–78; Sen. Nursing Officer, North Tees, Stockton, 1978–80; Dir of Nursing, Central Manchester HA, 1981–85; Unit Gen. Manager and Dist Nursing Officer, Manchester Royal Eye Hosp., 1985–88; Regl Nursing Officer, 1988–90, Dep. Chief Exec., 1989–91, Mersey RHA; Exec. Dir, NHS Mgt Exec. Trust Monitoring Unit (NW), 1991–93. Mem., S Manchester HA, 1983–88; Sec. and Chief Exec., Ophthalmic Nursing Bd, 1983–88. *Publications:* articles in nursing and health service papers. *Recreations:* music (piano; Friends of Hallé), fashion. *Address:* 21 Crossfield Drive, Worsley, Manchester M28 1GP. *Club:* Soroptomist International (Manchester).

KNILL, Sir Thomas (John Pugin Bartholomew), 5th Bt *cr* 1893, of The Grove, Blackheath, Kent; *b* 23 Aug. 1952; *er s* of Sir John Kenelm Stuart Knill, 4th Bt and Violette Maud Florence Martin (*née* Barnes; *d* 1983); *S* father, 1998; *m* 1977, Kathleen Muszynski (marr. diss. 1996); three *d*. *Heir:* *b* Jenkyn Martin Benedict Stuart Knill [*b* 19 Jan. 1954; *m* 1978, Helen Marguerite Gulliver; two *s* one *d*].

KNOLLYS, family name of **Viscount Knollys**.

KNOLLYS, 3rd Viscount *cr* 1911, of Caversham; **David Francis Dudley Knollys;** Baron *cr* 1902; *b* 12 June 1931; *s* of 2nd Viscount Knollys, GCMG, MBE, DFC, and Margaret (*d* 1987), *o d* of Sir Stuart Coats, 2nd Bt; *S* father, 1966; *m* 1959, Hon. Sheelin Virginia Maxwell (*see* Viscountess Knollys); three *s* one *d*. *Educ:* Eton. Lt, Scots Guards, 1951. *Heir:* *s* Hon. Patrick Nicholas Mark Knollys [*b* 11 March 1962; *m* 1998, Mrs Sarah Wright, *o d* of Michael Petch; one *s* one *d*]. *Address:* The Bailiff's House, Bramerton Hall Farm, Norwich, Norfolk NR14 7DN.

KNOLLYS, Viscountess; Sheelin Virginia Knollys, OBE 2005; Vice Lord-Lieutenant, Norfolk, since 2005; *b* 5 Dec. 1937; *d* of late Hon. Somerset Maxwell, MP and Susan Maxwell (*née* Roberts); *m* 1959, Hon. David Francis Dudley Knollys (*see* Viscount Knollys); three *s* one *d*. *Educ:* Hatherop Castle Sch.; Sorbonne. Partner in dried flower business, 1975–97. Mem., E Anglian Tourist Bd, 1988–91; Chairman: Norwich Area Tourism Agency, 1993–2005; English Rural Housing Assoc., 1996–; Inland Waterways Amenity Adv. Council, 1997–2006; Norfolk and Suffolk Broads Authy, 1997–2003 (Mem., 1987–2003). Non-exec. Dir, E Norfolk HA, 1990–99; Dir, VisitNorwich Ltd, 2005–. Vice Pres., Inland Waterways Assoc., 2004–. Branch Pres., Arthritis Care, 1965–2005. Trustee, How Hill Trust, 2000–; Chm., S Norfolk Buildings Preservation Trust, 2000–. Mem. (C) S Norfolk DC, 1983–2003 (Chm., 1996–97). DL 1996, High Sheriff 2008, Norfolk. Gov., Wymondham Coll., 1989–97; Lay Mem., Council, UEA, 1997–. *Recreations:* gardening, golf. *Address:* The Bailiff's House, Bramerton Hall Farm, Norwich, Norfolk NR14 7DN.

See also Baron Farnham.

KNOPF, Elliot Michael; His Honour Judge Knopf; a Circuit Judge, since 2002; *b* 23 Dec. 1950; *s* of Harry and Clara Knopf; *m* 1976, Elizabeth Carol Lieberman; one *s* one *d*. *Educ:* Bury Grammar Sch.; University Coll. London (LLB Hons); Coll. of Law, Chester. Admitted solicitor, 1976; Partner, Pannone and Partners, Manchester, 1979–91; a District Judge, 1991–2002; Asst Recorder, 1996–2000; a Recorder of the Crown Court, 2000–02. *Recreations:* foreign travel, reading, entertaining friends and being entertained by them, the family. *Address:* Bolton Combined Courts, Blackhorse Street, Bolton BL1 1SU. *T:* (01204) 392881.

KNORPEL, Henry, CB 1982; QC 1988; Counsel to the Speaker, House of Commons, 1985–95; *b* 18 Aug. 1924; 2nd *s* of late Hyman and Dora Knorpel; *m* 1953, Brenda Sterling; two *d*. *Educ:* City of London Sch.; Magdalen Coll., Oxford. BA 1945, BCL 1946, MA 1949. Called to Bar, Inner Temple, 1947, Entrance Scholar, 1947–50, Bencher, 1990; practised 1947–52; entered Legal Civil Service as Legal Asst, Min. of Nat. Insce, 1952; Sen. Legal Asst, Min. of Pensions and Nat. Insce, 1958; Law Commn, 1965; Min. of Social Security, 1967; Dept of Health and Social Security: Asst Solicitor, 1968; Principal Asst Solicitor (Under-Sec.), 1971; Solicitor (also to OPCS and Gen. Register Office), 1978–85. Vis. Lecturer: Kennington Coll. of Commerce and Law, 1950–58; Holborn Coll. of Law, Languages and Commerce, 1958–70; Univ. of Westminster (formerly Polytechnic of Central London), 1970–. *Publications:* articles on community law. *Recreation:* relaxing. *Address:* Conway, 32 Sunnybank, Epsom, Surrey KT18 7DX. *T:* (01372) 721394.

KNOTT, (Graeme) Jonathan; HM Diplomatic Service; Deputy Head of Mission and Minister Counsellor, Seoul, South Korea, since 2008; *b* 2 Nov. 1966; *s* of Daniel Wilfred Knott and Anne Lesley Knott; *m* 2005, Angela Susan Jepson. *Educ:* Portsmouth Grammar Sch.; Mansfield Coll., Oxford (MA Law); MSP. ACMA 2007. Entered FCO, 1988; Dep. Eur. Corresp. to EU, 1995–96; Hd, Political/Econ. Section, Mexico City, 1996–2000; UK Trade and Finance negotiator, OECD, 2000–04; Prog. Dir, FCO Services Trading Fund, 2005–06; Hd, Financial Planning and Perf., FCO, 2006–08. *Recreations:* tennis, golf, travel. *Address:* c/o Foreign and Commonwealth Office, King Charles Street, SW1A 2AH.

KNOTT, Prof. John Frederick, OBE 2004; ScD; FRS 1990; FREng; Feeney Professor of Metallurgy and Materials, University of Birmingham, since 1990 (Head, School of Metallurgy and Materials, 1990–96, and Dean of Engineering, 1995–98); *b* Bristol, 9 Dec. 1938; *s* of Fred Knott and Margaret (*née* Chesney); *m* 1st, 1963, Christine Mary Roberts (marr. diss. 1986); two *s*; 2nd, 1990, Susan Marilyn Cooke (*née* Jones); two step *s*. *Educ:* Queen Elizabeth's Hosp., Bristol; Sheffield Univ. (BMet 1st cl. Hons 1959); Cambridge Univ. (PhD 1963; ScD 1991). FIMMM (FIM 1974); FWeldI 1985; FREng (FEng 1988); FIMechE 1994. Res. Officer, Central Electricity Res. Labs, Leatherhead, 1962–67; Cambridge University: Lectr, Dept of Metallurgy, 1967–81; Reader in Mechanical Metallurgy, 1981–90; Churchill College: Goldsmiths' Fellow, Coll. Lectr and Dir of Studies in Metallurgy and Materials Sci., 1967–90; Tutor, 1969–79; Tutor for Advanced Students, 1979–81; Vice-Master, 1988–90; Extra-Ordinary Fellow, 1991–2006. Member: Materials, Manufacturing and Structures Adv. Bd (formerly Materials and Processing Adv. Bd), Rolls-Royce plc, 1987– (Chm., 2000–); Technical Adv. Gp on Structural Integrity, Nuclear Power Industries, 1988–; Res. Bd, Welding Inst., 1989–; Nuclear Safety Adv. Cttee (formerly Adv. Cttee on the Safety of Nuclear Installations), HSE, 1990–2005 (Acting Chm., 2004); Graphite Technical Adv. Cttee, 2004–; Defence Nuclear Safety Cttee, 2006–. Pres., Internat. Congress on Fracture, 1993–97. Editor, Materials Sci. and Technology, 2003–. Hon. Professor: Beijing Univ. of Aeronautics and Astronautics, 1992; Xian Jiaotong Univ., 1995; Hatfield Lecture, IMMM, 2006. Mem. Governing Body, Shrewsbury Sch., 1996–2001. FRSA. Foreign Member: Acad. of Scis of the Ukraine, 1993; Japan Inst. of Metals, 2005; Foreign Associate, NAE, USA, 2003; Foreign Fellow, Indian NAE, 2006. Hon. DEng Glasgow, 2004. L.B. Pfeil Prize, 1973, Rosenhain Medal, 1978, Metals Soc.; Leslie Holliday Prize, Materials Sci. Club, 1978; Griffith Medal, 1999; Robert Franklin Mehl Award, Metals, Materials and Minerals Soc., USA, 2005; Leverhulme Medal, Royal Soc., 2005. *Publications:* Fundamentals of Fracture Mechanics, 1973, 2nd edn 1979; (with P. A. Withey) Fracture Mechanics: worked examples, 1993; many scientific papers in Acta Met., Metal Sci., Materials Sci. and Technology, Met. Trans, Engrg Fracture Mechanics, etc. *Recreations:* bridge, cryptic crosswords, traditional jazz, playing the tenor recorder with enthusiasm rather than skill. *Address:* 43 West Street, Stratford-upon-Avon, Warwickshire CV37 6DN.

KNOTT, Jonathan; *see* Knott, G. J.

KNOWLAND, Raymond Reginald, CBE 1992; Managing Director, British Petroleum, 1990–92; *b* 18 Aug. 1930; *s* of Reginald George Knowland and Marjorie Doris Knowland (*née* Alvis); *m* 1956, Valerie Mary Higgs; three *s*. *Educ:* Bristol Grammar Sch.; Sir John Cass College London. CChem, FRSC 1972. BP Chemicals: specialty plastics and PVC Plant Management, Barry Works, 1957–69; Works Gen. Manager, Barry Works, 1969–75, Baglan Bay Works, 1975–78; Man. Dir, Belgium, 1978–80; Dir, London, 1980–90; Chief Exec. Officer, London, 1983–90. Non-exec. Dir, BSI plc, 1992–99. President: British Plastics Fedn, 1983–84; Assoc. of Petrochemical Producers in Europe, 1985–88; CIA, 1990–92; Vice Pres., SCI, 1993–96. Chm., European Chemical Industry Ecology and Toxicology Centre, 1986–90. Liveryman, Horners' Co., 1987 (Master, 2000, Dep. Master, 2001). *Recreations:* sailing, photography, Rugby football (spectator). *Address:* Heron's Wake, Flowers Hill, Pangbourne, Reading RG8 7BD. *T:* (0118) 984 4576. *Clubs:* Athenæum, Savage.

KNOWLES, Ann; *see* Knowles, P. A.

KNOWLES, Ben; Director, War Child, since 2008; *b* 29 Aug. 1973; *s* of John and Pat Knowles. *Educ:* Beverley Grammar Sch.; Hertford Coll., Oxford (BA Hons Hist.). Writer: Daily Mirror, 1994–95; Smash Hits, 1995–97; Melody Maker, 1998–2000; Ed., New Musical Express, 2000–02; Dep. Ed., Zoo mag., 2003–06; Jt Dep. Ed., Daily Star, 2006–08. Mem., Cultural Strategy Gp for London, GLA, 2000–04. Dir, War Child Music, 2004–. *Recreations:* Fulham FC, pubs, rock 'n' roll. *Address:* War Child, 5–7 Anglers Lane, NW5 3DG.

KNOWLES, Sir Charles (Francis), 7th Bt *cr* 1765; architect in private practice, since 1984; *b* 20 Dec. 1951; *s* of Sir Francis Gerald William Knowles, 6th Bt, FRS, and of Ruth Jessie, *d* of late Rev. Arthur Brooke-Smith; *S* father, 1974; *m* 1979, Amanda Louise Margaret, *d* of Lance Lee Bromley, *qv*; two *s*. *Educ:* Marlborough Coll.; Oxford Sch. of Architecture (DipArch 1977; RIBA 1979). Director: Charles Knowles Design Ltd (architects); Richmond Knowles Architects; works include: new Battersea Dogs Home, London and Old Windsor; refurbishment of Bank of England, historic country houses and listed London properties. FRSA. *Recreations:* shooting, travel, piloting light aircraft. *Heir:* *s* (Charles) William (Frederick Lance) Knowles, *b* 27 Aug. 1985. *Address:* c/o Charles Knowles Design Ltd, 5 The Powerhouse, 70 Chiswick High Road, W4 1SY.

KNOWLES, Colin George, PhD; feudal title, Lord Knowles of Houghton and Burnett, 2006; Director of Development and Public Relations, University of Bophuthatswana, 1985–95; Secretary and Trustee, University of Bophuthatswana Foundation, 1985–95; *b* 11 April 1939; *s* of late George William Knowles, Tarleton, Lancs; *m* 1998, Dr Rosalie Marion Lander (*née* Turner); three *d* by former marriages. *Educ:* King George V Grammar Sch., Southport; CEDEP, Fontainebleau, France; Trinity Coll., Delaware, USA (MA 1991; PhD 1994). MInstM 1966; MCIPR (MIPR 1970); Mem. BAIE 1972; FPRISA 1993 (MPRISA 1983); APR 1987; AAArb 1991; MSAAIE 1993. Appointed Comr of Oaths, 1991. Joined John Player & Sons, 1960; sales and marketing management appts; Head of Public Relations, 1971–73; joined Imperial Tobacco Ltd, 1973; Hd of Public Affairs, 1973–80; Company Sec., 1979–80. Chairman: Griffin Associates Ltd, 1980–83; Concept Communications (Pty) Ltd (S Africa), 1983–84; Dir, TWS Public Relations (Pty) Ltd (S Africa), 1984–85. Mem. Council, Tobacco Trade Benevolent Assoc., 1975–80; Chm., Bophuthatswana Reg., PRISA, 1988–91. Dir, Bophuthatswana Council for Consumer Affairs, 1991–94. Director: Nottingham Festival Assoc. Ltd, 1969–71; English Sinfonia Orchestra, 1972–80; Midland Sinfonia Concert Soc. Ltd, 1972–80; (also co-Founder) Assoc. for Business Sponsorship of The Arts Ltd, 1975–84 (Chm., 1975–80); Bristol Hippodrome Trust Ltd, 1977–81; Bath Archaeological Trust Ltd, 1978–81; The Palladian Trust Ltd, 1979–82; Mem., Chancellor of Duchy of Lancaster's Cttee of Honour on Business and the Arts, 1980–81. Arts sponsorship initiatives include responsibility for: Internat. Cello Competition (with Tortelier), Bristol, 1975 and 1977; Internat. Conductors Awards, 1978; Pompeii Exhibn, RA, 1976–77; new prodns at Royal Opera House, Covent Garden, at Glyndebourne, and at National Theatre. Governor: Manning Grammar Sch., Nottingham, 1972–73; Clayesmore Sch., Dorset, 1975–85. Chm., St John Ambulance Foundn in Bophuthatswana, 1989–94; Mem. Chapter, Priory of St John, S Africa, 1992–99. Liveryman, Worshipful Co. of Tobacco Pipe Makers and Tobacco Blenders, 1973; Freeman, City of London, 1974. FCMI (FBIM 1972); FRSA 1975; FRCSoc 1976. KStJ 1995 (CStJ 1991; OStJ 1977). *Recreations:* reading, travel, country pursuits. *Address:* 15 Standen Park House, Lancaster LA1 3FF; *e-mail:* lkhb@talktalk.net. *Clubs:* Carlton, MCC.

KNOWLES, Sir Durward (Randolph), Kt 1996; OBE 1964; OM (Bahamas) 1996; President, Caribbean Towing Company, since 1982; *b* 2 Nov. 1917; *s* of late Harry Knowles and Charlotte Knowles; *m* 1947, Holly; one *s* two *d*. *Educ:* Queen's Coll., Nassau, Bahamas. Captain of freighters plying in Caribbean, 1942–46; various Captain appts, 1946–52; Harbour Pilot, Nassau, 1952–96. Pres., Island Sand; Vice-Pres., Island Shipping. Bronze Medal for Yachting, 1956 Olympics, Gold Medal, 1964 Olympics. *Relevant publication:* Driven by the Stars: the story of Durward Knowles, by Douglas Hanks, Jr, 1992. *Recreation:* yachting. *Address:* Winton Highway, PO Box N–1216, Nassau, Bahamas. *Clubs:* Nassau Yacht; Coral Reef Yacht (Coconut Grove, Florida).

KNOWLES, George Peter; Registrar of the Province and Diocese of York, and Archbishop of York's Legal Secretary, 1968–87; *b* 30 Dec. 1919; *s* of Geoffrey Knowles and Mabel Bowman; *m* 1948, Elizabeth Margaret Scott; one *s* two *d*. *Educ:* Clifton Coll., Bristol; Queens' Coll., Cambridge. MA, LLM. Served war, Royal Artillery, 1939–46 (Lieut). Admitted a solicitor, 1948; Chm., York Area Rent Tribunal, 1959; Mem., Mental Health Review Tribunal for Yorkshire Regional Health Authority Area, 1960. *Recreations:* gardening, fishing, wildlife. *Address:* 11 Lang Road, Bishopthorpe, York YO23 2QJ. *T:* (01904) 706443. *Club:* Yorkshire (York).

KNOWLES, Rt Rev. Graeme Paul; Dean of St Paul's, since 2007; *b* 25 Sept. 1951; *s* of Grace and Stanley Knowles; *m* 1973, Susan Gail Knowles. *Educ:* Dunstable Grammar Sch., 1963–70; King's Coll. London, 1970–73 (AKC). Ordained deacon, 1974, priest, 1975; Asst Curate, St Peter in Thanet, 1974–79; Precentor and Sen. Curate, Leeds Parish Church, 1979–81; Chaplain and Precentor, 1981–87, Chapter Clerk, 1985–87, Portsmouth Cathedral; Vicar of Leigh Park, 1987–93; Rural Dean of Havant, 1990–93; Archdeacon of Portsmouth, 1993–99; Dean of Carlisle, 1999–2003; Bishop of Sodor and Man, 2003–07. Member: Council for the Care of Churches, 1991–2000 (Chm., 2003–08); Church Buildings Council (Chm., 2008–); Gen. Synod of C of E, 2002–07. *Recreations:* Victorian and Edwardian songs, the books of E. F. Benson, wine and food. *Address:* The Deanery, 9 Amen Court, EC4M 7BU. *T:* (020) 7236 2827, *Fax:* (020) 7332 0298.

KNOWLES, Rev. John Geoffrey; Warden of Readers, Diocese of Chester and Priest-in-charge, Woodford, since 2005; *b* 12 June 1948; *s* of Geoffrey and Jean Knowles; *m* 1974, Roey Wills; three *d*. *Educ:* St Bees Sch.; Univ. of Manchester (BSc Physics); Worcester Coll., Oxford (CertEd); Univ. of London (MSc Nuclear Physics); W Midlands Ministerial Trng Course. Assistant Master: Mill Hill Sch., 1970–75; Wellington Coll., 1975–76; Head of Physics, Watford GS, 1976–84; Vice Master, Queen Elizabeth's GS, Blackburn, 1984–90; Headmaster, King Edward VI Five Ways Sch., Birmingham, 1990–99; Rector, Hutchesons' GS, 1999–2004. Ordained deacon 1998, priest 1999; Non-Stipendiary Curate, Holy Trinity, The Lickey, 1998–99. Chief Examr, A-Level Physics (Nuffield), 1990–99. Vice-Chm., 1996–98, Chm., 1998–99, Assoc. Heads of Grant Maintained Schools. Chm. Governors, Kingsmead Sch., 1986–92; Mem., Gen. Convocation, Univ. of Strathclyde, 2003–04. Treas., 1976–84, Vice-Chm., 1991–95, Elgar Soc. *Publications:* Elgar's Interpreters on Record, 1978, 2nd edn 1985; (contrib.) Elgar Studies, 1988; (contrib.) This is the Best of Me, 1999. *Recreation:* music. *Address:* The Vicarage, 531 Chester Road, Woodford, Stockport SK7 1PR. *T:* (0161) 439 2286.

KNOWLES, Michael; independent political consultant, since 1992; *b* 21 May 1942; *s* of Martin Christopher and Anne Knowles; *m* 1965, Margaret Isabel Thorburn; three *d*. *Educ:* Clapham Coll. RC Grammar Sch. Sales Manager, Export & Home Sales. Mem. (C), 1971–83, Leader, 1974–83, Kingston upon Thames Borough Council. MP (C) Nottingham East, 1983–92; PPS to Minister for Planning and Regional Affairs, 1986, to Minister for Housing and Planning, 1987–88, DoE; Member: Select Cttee on European Legislation, 1984; Select Cttee on Defence, 1990. *Recreations:* walking, history. *Address:* 2 Ditton Reach, Portsmouth Road, Thames Ditton, Surrey KT7 0XB.

KNOWLES, Michael Ernest, PhD; CChem, FRSC; FIFST; Director, Scientific and Regulatory Affairs, Greater Europe, Coca-Cola, Brussels, since 1997 (Director, Scientific and Regulatory Affairs (Europe, Middle East and Africa), Coca-Cola International, Brussels, 1992–97); *b* 6 May 1942; *s* of late Ernest Frederick Walter Knowles and Lesley (*née* Lambert); *m* 1st, 1965, Rosalind Mary Griffiths (marr. diss. 1975); two *s*; 2nd, 1994, Alexandra Knowles (*née* Hadjiyianni). *Educ:* Nottingham Univ. (BPharm 1st cl. Hons; PhD). CChem 1969; FRSC 1982; FIFST 1983. ICI Postdoctoral Fellow, Nottingham Univ., 1967–69; Ministry of Agriculture, Fisheries and Food: Food Sci. Unit, Norwich, 1969–74; Scientific Advr, Food Sci. Div., 1974–79; Head, Food Sci. Lab., 1979–85; Head, Food Sci. Div., 1985–89; Chief Scientist (Fisheries and Food), 1989–91. FRSA. *Publications:* series of papers on chemical aspects of food safety in learned jls. *Recreations:* target shooting, walking. *Address:* Avenue d'Italie, 12–B6, 1050 Brussels, Belgium. *T:* (2) 497052452. *Clubs:* Strangers (Norwich); Château St Ann (Brussels).

KNOWLES, (Patricia) Ann, (Mrs P. A. Knowles-Foster); Director, Emirates Project, Marriage Care, since 2006; *b* 31 Oct. 1944; *d* of John and Margaret Miller; *m* 1st, 1964, Leslie John Knowles (*d* 1996); two *s* one *d*; 2nd, 2000, Malcolm Foster. *Educ:* Our Lady's Prep. Sch., Barrow-in-Furness; Our Lady's Convent Sch.; Open Univ. (BA); CENTRA (Dip. Therapeutic Counselling, 1999); St John's Coll., Leeds Univ. (Cert. Couple Counselling, 2000). Reporter: North Western Evening Mail, Barrow, 1962–68; North Somerset Mercury, Clevedon, 1969–70; Western Daily Press, Bristol, 1970–72; Theatre Critic, Evening Star, Burnley, 1973–77; Sub-Editor, Dep. Chief Sub-Editor, News Editor, Burnley Express, 1977–84; Asst Editor, Citizen Publications, Blackburn, 1985–87; Sub-Editor, Keighley News, 1987–89; Group Editor, Herald and Post, Burnley, 1989–90; Editor, The Universe, 1990–95. NW Regl Develt Worker, 1997–2001, Dir, Marriage Support, 2001–05, Marriage Care. Member: Nat. Assoc. of Tangent Clubs, 1984–; Soroptimists International, Burnley, 1990–92; Catholic Union of GB, 1991–99; Nat. Bd of Catholic Women, 1994–98. *Publication:* (with Mgr John Furnival) Archbishop Derek Worlock—His Personal Journey, 1997. *Recreations:* gardening, interior decoration, family interests, travel. *Address:* 2 Horton Lodge, Horton in Craven, Skipton, N Yorks BD23 3JX.

KNOWLES, Peter Francis Arnold, CB 1996; Parliamentary Counsel, 1991–2008; *b* 10 July 1949; *s* of Sidney Francis Knowles and Patricia Anette Knowles; *m* 1972, Patricia Katharine Clifford; two *s*. *Educ:* Whitgift School, Croydon; University College, Oxford (MA). Called to the Bar, Gray's Inn, 1971. In practice at Chancery Bar, 1973–75; joined Parliamentary Counsel Office, 1975; with Law Commission, 1979–81, 1993–96; with Tax Law Rewrite Project, 2001–03. *Publications:* (contrib.) Halsbury's Laws of England; The Giulia Coupés 1963–1976, 1998. *Recreations:* music, walking, ski-ing, surfing, classic car restoration.

KNOWLES, Robin St John, CBE 2006; QC 1999; a Recorder, since 2000; *b* 7 April 1960; *s* of Norman Richard Knowles and Margaret Mary Knowles (*née* Robinson); *m* 1987, Gill Adams; one *d*. *Educ:* Sir Roger Manwood's Grammar Sch.; Trinity Coll., Cambridge (MA). Called to the Bar: Middle Temple, 1982, Bencher 2004; Gray's Inn (*ad eundem*); in practice at the Bar, 1983–; Asst Recorder, 1998–2000. Member: Exec., Commercial Bar Assoc., 1999– (Chm., N American Cttee, 2000–); various Bar Council and Commercial Bar Assoc. and Inn cttees and working parties; and Trustee, Mgt Cttee, Bar Pro Bono Unit, 1996–; Trustee: Solicitors Pro Bono Gp, 2001–; Bar in the

Community, 2001–; Advice Bureau, RCJ, 1999–. *Recreations:* the East End of London, and being with friends and family. *Address:* 3–4 South Square, Gray's Inn, WC1R 5HP. *T:* (020) 7696 9900.

KNOWLES, Timothy; Director, Welsh Water, then Hyder, plc, 1989–99; *b* 17 May 1938; *s* of Cyril William Knowles and Winifred Alice Knowles (*née* Hood); *m* 1967, Gaynor Hallett; one *d. Educ:* Bishop Gore Grammar Sch., Swansea. Chartered Accountant. Company Sec./Accountant, Louis Marx & Co. Ltd, 1960–68; Controller, Modco Valenite, 1968–69; HTV Ltd: Company Sec., 1969–78; Financial Dir, 1975–81; Asst Man. Dir, 1981–86; HTV Group plc: Financial Dir, 1976–86; Gp Man. Dir, 1986–88; Finance Dir, Insurance Services Gp, ECGD (for privatisation), 1990–91; Dir, Frost & Reed (Holdings) Ltd, 1985–88. Member: S Wales Electricity Bd, 1981–82; Welsh Water Authority, 1982–89; Disciplinary Cttee, 1993–2002 (Chm. Tribunals, 1996–2002); Appeal Cttee, 2002–, ICAEW. Dir, University Hosp. of Wales Healthcare NHS Trust, 1995–99. Chm., CG90, 1994–97 (Treas., 2000–). Contested (C) Swansea East, 1966. Mem., Welsh Livery Guild, 1994– (Treas., 2001–05; Emeritus Treas., 2006–). *Recreations:* travel, watching cricket, golf. *Address:* Cae Ffynnon, 12 Ger-y-Llan, St Nicholas, Cardiff CF5 6SY. *T:* (01446) 760726. *Clubs:* Cardiff and County (Cardiff); Glamorgan CC; Cottrell Park Golf.

KNOWLES, Wyn; Editor, Woman's Hour, BBC, 1971–83; *b* 30 July 1923; *d* of Frederick Knowles and Dorothy Ellen Knowles (*née* Harrison). *Educ:* St Teresa's Convent, Effingham; Convents of FCJ in Ware and Switzerland; Polytechnic Sch. of Art, London. Cypher Clerk, War Office, 1941–45. Secretarial work, 1948–57; joined BBC, 1951; Asst Producer, Drama Dept, 1957–60; Woman's Hour: Producer, Talks Dept, 1960–65; Asst Editor, 1965–67; Dep. Editor, 1967–71. *Publication:* (ed with Kay Evans) The Woman's Hour Book, 1981. *Recreations:* travel, cooking, writing, painting.

KNOWLES-FOSTER, (Patricia) Ann; *see* Knowles, P. A.

KNOWLTON, Richard James, CBE 1983; QFSM 1977; HM Chief Inspector of Fire Services (Scotland), 1984–89; *b* 2 Jan. 1928; *s* of Richard John Knowlton and Florence May Humby; *m* 1949, Pamela Vera Horne; one *s. Educ:* Bishop Wordsworth's Sch., Salisbury. FIFE. Served 42 Commando RM, 1945. Southampton Fire Bde, 1948; Station Officer, Worcester City and County Fire Bde, 1959; London Fire Brigade: Asst Divl Officer, 1963; Divl Officer, 1965; Divl Comdr, 1967; Winston Churchill Travelling Fellowship, 1969; Firemaster: SW Area (Scotland) Fire Bde, 1971; Strathclyde Fire Bde, 1975–84. Mem., later Chm., Bds, Fire Service Coll. Extended Interview, 1970–81; Mem., Fire Service Coll. Bd, 1978–82; Mem., later Chm., Scottish Fire Services Examinations Panel, 1971–75; Mem., Scottish Fire Service Examinations Bd, 1974–75; Fire Adviser: to Scottish Assoc. of CCs, 1974; to Convention of Scottish Local Authorities, 1975–81; Sec. to Appliances and Equipment Cttee of Chief and Asst Chief Fire Officers Assoc., 1974–81, Pres. of the Assoc., 1980; Chm., Scottish Dist Chief and Asst Chief Fire Officers Assoc., 1977–81; Zone Fire Comdr (Designate), CD for Scotland, 1975–84; Member: Scottish Central Fire Bdes Adv. Council, 1977–81 (Uniform and Personal Equipment Cttee, 1974–82); Jt Cttee on Design and Develt, 1978–82; England and Wales Central Fire Bdes Adv. Council, 1979–81; Chairman: London Branch, Instn of Fire Engineers, 1969; Scottish Assoc., Winston Churchill Fellows, 1979–81; Hazfile Cttee, 1979–81; Vice-Pres., Fire Services Nat. Benevolent Fund, 1981– (Chm. 1980). Mem., Nat. Jt Council for Chief Fire Officers, 1980–82; Mem., later Chm., Management Structures Working Gp of Nat. Jt Council for Local Authority Fire Bdes, 1980–83; British Mem., Admin. Council of European Assoc. of Professional Fire Bde Officers, 1981–85 (Vice Pres., 1984–85).

KNOX, family name of **Earl of Ranfurly**.

KNOX, (Alexander) David, CMG 1988; Vice President, International Bank for Reconstruction and Development, 1980–87, retired; *b* 15 Jan. 1925; *s* of James Knox and Elizabeth Maxwell Knox; *m* 1950, Beatrice Lily (*née* Dunell); one *s* two *d. Educ:* Univ. of Toronto (BA); London School of Economics and Political Science (Hon. Fellow, 1982). LSE, 1949–63, Reader in Economics, 1955–63; International Bank for Reconstruction and Development (World Bank), 1963–87: Vice President: W Africa, 1980–84; Latin America, 1984–87. Chm., Task Force on Project Quality, African Develt Bank, 1993–94. Member: Bd of Dirs, Liverpool Associates in Tropical Health, 1990–99; Prog. Adv. Panel, SCF, 1993–99; Council, Worldaware, 1994–2002. *Publications:* Latin American Debt: facing facts, 1990; articles in Economica, OECF Res. Qly (Japan), etc. *Recreations:* opera, walking. *Address:* Knights Barn, Manor Farm Lane, East Hagbourne, Oxon OX11 9ND. *T:* (01235) 817792.

KNOX, Bryce Harry, CB 1986; a Deputy Chairman, and Director General, Internal Taxation Group, Board of Customs and Excise, 1983–88, retired; *b* 21 Feb. 1929; *e s* of late Brice Henry Knox and Rose Hetty Knox; *m* Norma, *d* of late George and Rose Thomas; one *s. Educ:* Stratford Grammar Sch.; Nottingham Univ. BA(Econ). Asst Principal, HM Customs and Excise, 1953; Principal, 1958; on loan to HM Treasury, 1963–65; Asst Sec., HM Customs and Excise, 1966; seconded to HM Diplomatic Service, Counsellor, Office of UK Perm. Rep. to European Communities, 1972–74; Under-Sec., 1974, Comr, 1975, HM Customs and Excise. *Address:* 9 Manor Way, Blackheath, SE3 9EF. *T:* (020) 8852 9404. *Clubs:* Reform, MCC.

KNOX, David; *see* Knox, A. D.

KNOX, Sir David (Laidlaw), Kt 1993; *b* 30 May 1933; *s* of late J. M. Knox, Lockerbie and Mrs C. H. C. Knox (*née* Laidlaw); *m* 1980, Mrs Margaret Eva Maxwell, *d* of late A. McKenzie. *Educ:* Lockerbie Academy; Dumfries Academy; London Univ. (BSc (Econ) Hons). Management Trainee, 1953–56; Printing Executive, 1956–62; O&M Consultant, 1962–70. Contested (C): Stechford, Birmingham, 1964 and 1966; Nuneaton, March 1967. MP (C) Leek Div. of Staffs, 1970–83, Staffordshire Moorlands, 1983–97. PPS to Ian Gilmour, Minister of State for Defence, 1973, Sec. of State for Defence, 1974. Member: Select Cttee on European Legislation, 1976–97; House of Commons Chairmen's Panel, 1983–97; Secretary: Cons. Finance Cttee, 1972–73; Cons. Trade Cttee, 1974; Vice-Chm., Cons. Employment Cttee, 1979–80; Chairman: W Midlands Area Young Conservatives, 1963–64; W Midlands Area Cons. Political Centre, 1966–69; a Vice Chairman: Cons. Party Organisation, 1974–75; Cons. Gp for Europe, 1984–87. Editor, Young Conservatives National Policy Group, 1963–64. Chm., London Union of Youth Clubs, 1998–99; Dep. Chm., Fedn of London Youth Clubs, 1999–2008. Vice President: Commercial Travellers' Benevolent Instn, 1998–; One World Trust, 2004–. *Recreations:* watching association football and cricket, reading, theatre, walking. *Address:* The Mount, Alstonefield, Ashbourne, Derbys DE6 2FS.

KNOX, James Richard Dunsmuir, FSAScot; Managing Director, The Art Newspaper, since 2005; *b* Kilwinning, Ayrshire, 18 Oct. 1952; *s* of Sir Bryce Muir Knox, KCVO, MC, TD and Patricia Mary Knox (*née* Dunsmuir); *m* 1983, Caroline Angela Owen; one *s* one *d. Educ:* Eton Coll.; Trinity Coll., Cambridge (BA 1974); INSEAD (MBA). FSAScot 1975. Writer, Antique Collector, and Associate Publisher, Ebury Press, 1975–78;

Illustrated London News Gp, 1980–82; Publisher, The Spectator, 1983–92; Founder, Art for Work Consultancy, 1992–2005. Trustee: National Galls of Scotland, 2007–; Great Steward of Scotland's Dumfries House Trust, 2007–. *Publication:* The Trinity Foot Beagles, 1978; Robert Byron, 2003; Cartoons and Coronets: the genius of Osbert Lancaster, 2008. *Recreations:* architecture, the visual arts. *Address:* Martnaham Lodge, by Ayr, Ayrshire KA6 6ES. *T:* (01292) 560204. *Club:* Glasgow Arts.

KNOX, John, (Jack), RSA 1979 (ARSA 1972); RGI 1980; RSW 1987; Head of Painting Studios, Glasgow School of Art, 1981–92; *b* 16 Dec. 1936; *s* of Alexander and Jean Knox; *m* 1960, Margaret Kyle Sutherland; one *s* one *d. Educ:* Lenzie Acad.; Glasgow Sch. of Art (DA). On the Drawing and Painting Staff at Duncan of Jordanstone Coll. of Art, Dundee, 1965–81. Work in permanent collections: Scottish Nat. Gallery of Modern Art; Arts Council; Contemporary Arts Soc.; Scottish Arts Council; Otis Art Inst., Los Angeles; Olinda Museum, São Paulo; Aberdeen, Dundee and Manchester art galleries; Hunterian Museum, Glasgow; Scottish Nat. Portrait Gall.; Kelvingrove Art Galls and Mus. Retrospective exhibn, Knox 1960–83, Scottish Arts Council, 1983. Member: Scottish Arts Council, 1974–79; Trustees Cttee, Scottish Nat. Gall. of Modern Art, 1975–81; Bd of Trustees, Nat. Galls of Scotland, 1982–87. Sec., Royal Scottish Acad., 1990–91. Member: Bd of Governors, Duncan of Jordanstone Coll. of Art, Dundee, 1980–82; Bd of Governors, Glasgow Sch. of Art, 1985–88. Hon. FRIAS 1997. Hon. DLitt Glasgow, 2005. *Address:* 66 Seafield Road, Broughty Ferry, Dundee DD5 3AQ.

KNOX, John Andrew; Director of Finance, Mental Health Act Commission, since 2008 (non-executive Board Member, since 2006); *b* 22 July 1937; *s* of late James Telford Knox and Mary Knox; *m* 1964, Patricia Mary Martin; one *s* one *d. Educ:* Dame Allan's Sch., Newcastle upon Tyne; Merton Coll., Oxford (MA). ACA 1964, FCA 1974. Cooper Brothers & Co. Chartered Accountants, 1961–65; Vickers Ltd, 1966–72; entered CS as a Sen. Accountant, 1972; Chief Accountant, 1973; Asst Sec., 1976; Head of Accountancy Services Div., 1977–85; Grade 3, 1979–96; Hd of Industrial Financial Appraisal Div., DTI, 1985–87; Chief Accountant, 1987–90, and Dep. Dir, 1990–96, Serious Fraud Office. Bd Mem., Criminal Cases Review Commn, 1997–2003; Member: Registration and Conduct Cttees, Gen. Social Care Council, 2003–; Disciplinary Panel, Actuarial Profession, 2004–; Audit Cttee, Criminal Injuries Compensation Authy, 2004–. Leonard Shaw Award for Management Accountancy, Leonard Shaw Meml Fund, 1973.

KNOX, Prof. John Henderson, FRS 1984; FRSE 1971; University Fellow and Emeritus Professor of Physical Chemistry, University of Edinburgh, since 1984; *b* 21 Oct. 1927; *s* of John Knox and Elizabeth May Knox (*née* Henderson); *m* 1957, Josephine Anne Wissler; four *s. Educ:* George Watson's Boys' Coll.; Univ. of Edinburgh (BSc 1949, DSc 1963); Univ. of Cambridge (PhD 1953). University of Edinburgh: Lectr in Chemistry, 1953–66; Reader in Physical Chemistry, 1966–74; Director of Wolfson Liquid Chromatography Unit, 1972–92; Personal Prof. of Phys. Chem., 1974–84. Sen. Vis. Research Scientist Fellow, Univ. of Utah, 1964. *Publications:* Gas Chromatography, 1962; Molecular Thermodynamics, 1971, 2nd edn 1978; Applications of High Speed Liquid Chromatography, 1974; High Performance Liquid Chromatography, 1978, 3rd edn 1983. *Recreations:* ski-ing, sailing, hill walking. *Address:* 67 Morningside Park, Edinburgh EH10 5EZ. *T:* (0131) 447 5057.

KNOX, Sir John (Leonard), Kt 1985; a Judge of the High Court of Justice, Chancery Division, 1985–96; *b* 6 April 1925; *s* of Leonard Needham Knox and Berthe Hélène Knox; *m* 1st, 1953, Anne Jacqueline Mackintosh (*d* 1991); one *s* three *d;* 2nd, 1993, Benedicta Eugenie Cooksey. *Educ:* Radley Coll.; Worcester Coll., Oxford (Hon. Mods, 1st Cl.; Jurisprudence, 1st Cl.). Called to the Bar, Lincoln's Inn, 1953, Bencher, 1977; Member, Senate of the Inns of Court, 1975–78. QC 1979; Junior Treasury Counsel: in *bona vacantia,* 1971–79; in probate, 1978–79; Attorney-Gen., Duchy of Lancaster, 1984–85. Mem., Council of Legal Educn, 1975–79; Chm., Chancery Bar Assoc., 1985. Dep. Chm., Parly Boundary Commn, 1987–95.

KNOX, (John) Robert, FSA; Keeper, Department of Asia (formerly of Oriental Antiquities), British Museum, 1994–2006; *b* Port Alberni, BC, Canada, 4 June 1946; *s* of John Arthur Knox and Rosalind Knox (*née* Kingscote); *m* 1981, Helen Elizabeth Irène Zarb; three *d. Educ:* Univ. of Victoria, BC (BA Hons); Emmanuel Coll., Cambridge (MA). Asst Keeper, 1978, Dep. Keeper, 1992, Dept of Oriental Antiquities, British Museum. Mem. Council, Britain-Nepal Academic Council, 2000–. Trustee, Gurkha Mus., 2000–. FSA 1991 (Vice Pres., 1994–97). *Publications:* Ancient China, 1978; (jtly) India: past into present, 1982; (jtly) Explorations and Excavations in Bannu District, North-West Frontier Province, Pakistan 1985–88, 1991; Amaravati, Buddhist Sculpture from the Great Stupa, 1992; (jtly) Akra, the First Capital of Bannu (NWFP Pakistan), 2000; articles in learned jls on archaeol. of India and Pakistan. *Recreations:* walking, music, theatre, 78s, France. *Address: e-mail:* jrknox57@googlemail.com.

KNOX, Peter; *see* Knox, S. C. P.

KNOX, Robert; *see* Knox, J. R.

KNOX, Prof. Selby Albert Richard, PhD, DSc; CChem, FRSC; Pro-Vice-Chancellor, University of Bristol, 2004–08; *b* 24 Sept. 1944; *s* of George Henry Knox and Elsie (*née* Stobbart); *m* 1979, Julie Dawn Edwards; one *s* two *d. Educ:* Univ. of Bristol (BSc; PhD 1967; DSc 1985). CChem 1990, FRSC 1990. University of Bristol: Prof. of Inorganic Chem., 1990–96, Alfred Capper Pass Prof. of Chem., 1996–2004; Hd, Sch. of Chem., 1992–2001; Hd of Inorganic and Materials Chem., 2001–04. *Publications:* numerous contribs on organometallic chemistry to learned jls. *Recreations:* fly fishing, sailing, hill-walking/trekking.

KNOX, (Simon Christopher) Peter; QC 2006; *b* London, 21 Jan. 1957; *s* of Oliver Arbuthnot and Patricia Knox; *m* 1987, Teresa (separated 2003); one *s* two *d. Educ:* Westminster Sch., London; Wadham Coll., Oxford (BA Hons). Called to the Bar, Middle Temple, 1983. *Recreations:* music, wine. *Address:* 3 Hare Court, Temple, EC4Y 7BJ. *T:* (020) 7415 7800, *Fax:* (020) 7415 7811; *e-mail:* peterknox@3harecourt.com.

KNOX, Timothy Aidan John, FSA; Director, Sir John Soane's Museum, since 2005; *b* 9 Aug. 1962; *s* of Andrew Knox and Margaret Barbara Knox (*née* Allen); civil partnership 2006, Robert Todd Longstaffe-Gowan. *Educ:* Ratcliffe Coll., Leics; Courtauld Inst. of Art, Univ. of London (BA Hons). Liby Asst, King's Fund Inst. Liby, 1987–88; Photographic Librarian, Press Assoc., 1988–89; Res. Asst, 1989–91, Asst Curator, 1991–95, RIBA Drawings Collection; Architectural Historian, 1995–2002, Head Curator, 2002–05, NT. Mem. Editl Bd, 2002–04, Mem. Consultative Cttee, 2005–, Sculpture Jl: Jl of Public Monuments and Sculpture Assoc. Historic Bldgs Advr to FCO, 2005–. Member: Reviewing Cttee on Export of Works of Art, 2002–; Conseil scientifique de l'Etablissement public du musée et du domaine nat. de Versailles, 2005–; Adv. Cttee on Design of Coins, Medals, Seals and Decorations, Royal Mint, 2008–. Chm. and Trustee, Mausolea and Monuments Trust, 1997–2004 (Patron, 2008–). Trustee: Monument 85 Trust, 1996–2005; Hall Bequest (Stowe Sch.), 1998–; Spitalfields Historic

Bldgs Trust, 1999–2005; Pilgrim Trust, 2006–; Stowe House Preservation Trust, 2006–; Member, Advisory Committee: for Moggerhanger House Preservation Trust, 1998–; Strawberry Hill, 2007–; Mem. Council, Attingham Trust, 2006–. Curator of exhibn, The Return of the Gods: Neoclassical Sculpture in Britain, Tate Britain, 2008. FSA 2006. *Publications:* (contrib.) Artifici d'Aque e Giardini: la cultura delle grotte e dei ninfei in Italiae in Europa, 1999; (contrib.) Enlightenment: discovering the world in the eighteenth century, 2003; (contrib.) Collecting Sculptures in Early Modern Europe, 2008; (contrib.) Follies of Europe: architectural extravaganzas, 2008; numerous country house guidebooks; contribs to Apollo, Country Life, Sculpture Jl, Architectural Hist., Georgian Gp Jl, London Gardener. *Recreations:* art and architecture, collecting, dachshunds. *Address:* Malplaquet House, 137–9 Mile End Road, Stepney, E1 4AQ.

KNOX-JOHNSTON, Sir William Robert Patrick, (Sir Robin), Kt 1995; CBE 1969; RD (and bar) 1983; Marina Consultant since 1974; *b* 17 March 1939; *s* of late David Robert Knox-Johnston and Elizabeth Mary Knox-Johnston (*née* Cree); *m* 1962, Suzanne (*née* Singer) (*d* 2003); one *d. Educ:* Berkhamsted School. Master Mariner; FRIN. Merchant Navy, 1957–69. First person to sail single-handed non-stop Around the World, 14 June 1968 to 22 April 1969, in yacht Suhaili; won Sunday Times Golden Globe, 1969; won Round Britain Race, Ocean Spirit, 1970; won round Britain Race, British Oxygen, 1974; set British transatlantic sailing record, from NY to the Lizard, 11 days 7 hours 45 mins, 1981; established new record of 10 days 14 hours 9 mins, 1986; set world sailing record for around Ireland, 76 hours 5 mins 34 secs, May 1986; World Class II Multihull Champion, 1985; completed Guardian Columbus voyage, 1989; with Peter Blake, set non-stop around the world sailing record, 74 days, 22 hours, 17 mins 22 secs, 1994; Velux 5-Oceans Race, 2006–07. Man. Dir, St Katharine's Yacht Haven Ltd, 1975–76; Director: Mercury Yacht Harbours Ltd, 1970–73; Rank Marine International, 1973–75; Troon Marina Ltd, 1976–83; National Yacht Racing Centre Ltd, 1979–86; Knox-Johnston Insurance Brokers Ltd, 1983–92; St Katherine's Dock, 1975–93 (Man. Dir, 1991–93); Caversham Lake Trust Ltd, 2001–03; Chm., Clipper Ventures plc, 1997–. Pres., British Olympic Yachting Appeal, 1972–77; Pres. (formerly Chm.), STA, 1993–2001; Pres., Cruising Assoc., 2008. Member: Cttee of Management, RNLI, 1973–; Sports Council Lottery Panel, 1995–99; Sport England Council, 1999–2002. Trustee: Nat. Maritime Mus., Greenwich, 1993–2002; Nat. Maritime Mus., Cornwall, 1997–2006. Younger Brother, Trinity House, 1973. Freeman: Borough of Bromley, Kent, 1969; City of London, 1992. Liveryman, Co. of Master Mariners, 1975. Lt-Comdr RNR 1971, retired. Hon. Life Rear Cdre, RNSA. Fellow, Liverpool John Moores Univ., 2006. Hon. DSc Maine Maritime Acad., 1989; Hon. DTech Nottingham, 1993. Yachtsman of the Year, Yachting Journalists' Assoc., 1969, 1994, 2008; Silk Cut Seamanship Award, 1990; Seamanship Foundn Trophy, RYA, 1991; Gold Medal, RIN, 1992; ISAF Sailor of the Year, 1994. *Publications:* A World of my Own, 1969; Sailing, 1975; Twilight of Sail, 1978; Last but not Least, 1978; Bunkside Companion, 1982; Seamanship, 1986; The BOC Challenge 1986–1987, 1988; The Cape of Good Hope, 1989; History of Yachting, 1990; The Columbus Venture, 1991 (Book of the Sea Award); Sea, Ice and Rock, 1992; Cape Horn, 1994; Beyond Jules Verne, 1995; Force of Nature, 2007. *Recreation:* sailing. *Address:* Curdridge Cottage, Wickham Road, Curdridge, Southampton SO32 2HG. *Clubs:* Little Ship (Pres.); Royal Yacht Squadron (Hon. Mem.) (Cowes); Royal Harwich Yacht (Hon. Mem.); Royal Western Yacht (Hon. Mem.); Royal Southampton Yacht (Hon. Mem.); Benfleet Yacht (Hon. Mem.); Liverpool Yacht (Hon. Mem.); Brixham Yacht (Hon. Mem.); Royal Irish Yacht (Hon. Life Mem., 1969) (Dublin); Howth Yacht (Hon. Mem.) (Eire); Royal Bombay Yacht (Hon. Mem.); Fremantle Sailing (Hon. Mem.) (Perth); Point Yacht (Hon. Mem.) (Durban); Nat. Yacht (Hon. Mem.) (Dublin).

KNOX-LECKY, Maj.-Gen. Samuel, CB 1979; OBE 1967; BSc(Eng); CEng, FIMechE; Director-General, Agricultural Engineers Association, 1980–88; *b* 10 Feb. 1926; *s* of late J. D. Lecky, Coleraine; *m* 1947, Sheila Jones; one *s* two *d. Educ:* Coleraine Acad.; Queen's Univ., Belfast (BSc). Commnd REME, 1946; served Egypt, 1951–52; Kenya, 1953–54; jssc 1964; AA&QMG HQ 1(BR) Corps, 1965–66; CREME 4 Div., 1966–68; Sec., Principal Personnel Officers, MoD, 1968–70; RCDS, 1971; Comdt, SEME, 1972–74; DEME, BAOR, 1975; Dir, Military Assistance Office, MoD, 1976–77; Minister (DS), British Embassy, Tehran, 1977–79. Hon. Col, QUB OTC, 1978–83; Col Comdt, REME, 1980–86. *Recreations:* fishing, sailing.

KNOX-MAWER, Ronald; retired; *b* 3 Aug. 1925; *s* of George Robert Knox-Mawer and Clara Roberts; *m* 1951, June Ellis (*d* 2006), writer and broadcaster; one *s* one *d. Educ:* Grove Park Sch. (Denbighshire County Exhibnr); Emmanuel Coll., Cambridge (Exhibitioner; MA). Royal Artillery, 1943–47. Called to Bar, Middle Temple; Wales and Chester Circuit, 1947–52; Chief Magistrate and Actg Chief Justice, Aden, 1952–58; Sen. Magistrate, Puisne Judge, Justice of Appeal, Actg Chief Justice, Fiji, and conjointly Chief Justice, Nauru and Tonga, 1958–71; Northern Circuit, 1971–75; Metropolitan Stipendiary Magistrate, 1975–84; Dep. Circuit Judge, London, 1979–84. Various series of humorous reminiscences broadcast on BBC Radio: Tales from a Palm Court, 1984; Islands of Hope and Glory, 1985; Wretchedness in Wrexham, 1986; More Tales from a Palm Court, 1987–88; Tales of a Man called Father, 1989; The Queen Goes West, 1990; A Case of Bananas, 1992; Family Failings, 1994; Tales from Land of My Father, 1998; A Man Called Father (new series), 1999. *Publications:* Palm Court, 1979 (as Robert Overton); Tales from a Palm Court, 1986; Tales of a Man Called Father, 1989; A Case of Bananas and other South Sea Trials, 1992; Land of My Father, 1994; Are You Coming or Going?, 1999; (contrib.) Wales: a celebration, 2000; (contrib.) Young and Easy: childhood in Wales, 2004; short stories and features (under different pseudonyms) in Punch, Cornhill, Argosy, The Times, Sunday Express, Blackwoods, Listener, Weekend Telegraph, Times Saturday Review, Sunday Telegraph; various contribs to legal jls. *Recreation:* countryside. *Address:* c/o HSBC, Ruabon, N Wales LL14.

KNUSSEN, (Stuart) Oliver, CBE 1994; composer and conductor; Music Director, London Sinfonietta, 1998–2002, now Conductor Laureate; *b* Glasgow, 12 June 1952; *s* of Stuart Knussen and Ethelyn Jane Alexander; *m* 1972, Susan Freedman (*d* 2003); one *d. Educ:* Watford Field Sch.; Watford Boys Grammar Sch.; Purcell Sch. Private composition study with John Lambert, 1963–68; Countess of Munster Awards, 1964, 1965, 1967; Peter Stuyvesant Foundn Award, 1965; début conducting Symph. no 1 with LSO, 1968; Watney-Sargent award for Young Conductors, 1969; Fellowships to Berkshire Music Center, Tanglewood, 1970, 1971, 1973; Caird Trav. Schol., 1971; Margaret Grant Composition Prize (Symph. no 2), Tanglewood, 1971; study with Gunther Schuller in USA, 1970–73; Koussevitzky Centennial Commn, 1974; Composer-in-residence: Aspen Fest., 1976; Arnolfini Gall., 1978; Instr in composition, RCM Jun. Dept, 1977–82; BBC commn for Proms 1979 (Symph. no 3); Co-Artistic Dir, Aldeburgh Fest., 1983–98; Berkshire Music Center, Tanglewood: Guest Teacher, 1981; Composer-in-residence, 1986; Co-ordinator of Contemporary Music Activities, 1986–90. Arts Council Bursaries, 1979, 1981; winner, first Park Lane Gp Composer award (suite from Where the Wild Things Are), 1982; BBC commn for Glyndebourne Opera, 1983. Frequent guest conductor, Philharmonia Orch., many other ensembles, UK and abroad, 1981–; Associate Guest Conductor, BBC SO, 1989–; Dir, Almeida Ensemble, 1986. Mem. Exec. Cttee, SPNM, 1978–85; Member: Leopold Stokowski Soc.; International Alban Berg Soc., New York; Hon. Mem., AAAL, 1994. *Publications* include: Symphony no 1 op. 1, 1966–67; Symphony no 2 op. 7, 1970–71; Symphony no 3 op. 18, 1973–79; Where the Wild Things Are—opera (Maurice Sendak), op. 20, 1979–83 (staged, Glyndebourne at NT, 1984); Higglety Pigglety Pop!—opera (Sendak), op. 21, 1983–85 (staged Glyndebourne, 1984 and 1985); Horn Concerto, 1994 (commnd for Barry Tuckwell); numerous orchestral, chamber, vocal works; articles in Tempo, The Listener, etc. *Recreations:* cinema, record collecting, record producing, visual arts. *Address:* c/o Faber Music Ltd, 3 Queen Square, WC1N 3AR; c/o HarrisonParrott Ltd, 12 Penzance Place, W11 4PA.

KNUTSFORD, 6th Viscount *cr* 1895; **Michael Holland-Hibbert;** DL; Bt 1853; Baron 1888; *b* 27 Dec. 1926; *s* of Hon. Wilfrid Holland-Hibbert (*d* 1961) (2nd *s* of 3rd Viscount) and of Audrey, *d* of late Mark Fenwick; *S* cousin, 1986; *m* 1951, Hon. Sheila, *d* of 5th Viscount Portman; two *s* one *d. Educ:* Eton College; Trinity Coll., Cambridge (BA). Welsh Guards, 1945–48. SW Regional Director, Barclays Bank, 1956–86. National Trust: Chm. Cttee for Devon and Cornwall, 1973–86; Mem. Exec. Cttee, 1973–86; Mem. Council, 1979–85; Mem. Finance Cttee, 1986–99. DL 1977, High Sheriff 1977–78, Devon. *Heir: er s* Hon. Henry Thurstan Holland-Hibbert [*b* 6 April 1959; *m* 1988, Katherine, *d* of Sir John Ropner, Bt, *qv*; two *s* two *d*]. *Address:* Munden, Watford, Herts WD25 8PZ. *Club:* Brooks's.

KOBBORG, Johan; ballet dancer; Principal, Royal Ballet, since 1999; *b* Odense, Denmark; *s* of Martinus Vedel Kobborg and Käthe Kobborg. *Educ:* Royal Danish Ballet Sch. Joined Royal Danish Ballet, 1991, Principal, 1994–99. Guest dancer with Mariinsky Ballet, Bolshoi Ballet, La Scala Ballet, Nat. Ballet of Canada, Stuttgart Ballet, Hamburg Ballet and Teatro San Carlo, Naples. Performances include main rôles in La Sylphide, Swan Lake, The Nutcracker, Coppélia, Romeo and Juliet, Giselle, Sleeping Beauty, Don Quixote, Onegin, Cinderella, Anastasia, The Dream, Masquerade and Manon. *Address:* c/o Royal Ballet, Royal Opera House, Covent Garden, WC2E 9DD.

KOCH, Edward Irving; Partner, Bryan Cave LLP (formerly Robinson, Silverman, Pearce, Aronsohn & Berman), New York, since 1990; Mayor, City of New York, 1978–89; *b* 12 Dec. 1924; *s* of Louis Koch and Joyce Silpe. *Educ:* Southside High School, Newark, NJ; City Coll. of NY; NY Univ. Law Sch. Served US Army, 1943–46, USA, France, Rhineland. Mem., NY State Bar, 1949; private law practice, 1949–64; Senior Partner, Koch, Lankenau, Schwartz & Kovner, 1965–69. Democratic dist. leader, Greenwich Village, 1963–65; Mem., NY City Council, 1967–68; NY Congressman, 1969–77. *Publications:* Mayor, 1983; Politics, 1985; (jtly) His Eminence and Hizzoner, 1989; All the Best, 1990; Citizen Koch (autobiog.), 1992; Ed Koch on Everything, 1994; Murder at City Hall, 1995; Murder on Broadway, 1996; Murder on 34th Street, 1997; The Senator Must Die, 1998; Giuliani: nasty man, 1999; I'm not done yet, 1999. *Address:* (office) 1290 6th Avenue, New York, NY 10104, USA.

KOCIENSKI, Prof. Philip Joseph, PhD; FRS 1997; FRSE; FRSC; Professor and Head of Department of Organic Chemistry, University of Leeds, since 2000; *b* 23 Dec. 1946; *s* of Philip Joseph Kocienski and Marian Edyth (*née* Peters); *m* 1st, 1967, Anna Petruso (marr. diss. 1987); one *s* one *d*; 2nd, 1987, Joanna Davie. *Educ:* Brown Univ., Providence, RI (PhD 1973). FRSC 1995; FRSE 1998. Lectr, Leeds Univ., 1979–85; Prof. of Chemistry, Southampton Univ., 1985–97. Regius Prof. of Chemistry, Glasgow Univ., 1997–2000. Mem., EPSRC, 1999–. Marie Sklodowska Curie Medal, Polish Chem. Soc., 1997. *Publications:* Protecting Groups, 1994; numerous res. papers in learned jls. *Recreations:* Russian and Eastern European music, violin. *Address:* Department of Chemistry, Leeds University, Leeds LS2 9JT. *T:* (0113) 343 6555.

KOENIGSBERGER, Prof. Helmut Georg, MA, PhD; FBA 1989; Professor of History, King's College London, 1973–84, now Emeritus; *b* 24 Oct. 1918; *s* of late Georg Felix Koenigsberger, chief architect, borough of Treptow, Berlin, Germany, and of late Käthe Koenigsberger (*née* Born); *m* 1961, Dorothy M. Romano; two *d* (twins). *Educ:* Adams' Grammar Sch., Newport, Shropshire; Gonville and Caius Coll., Cambridge. Asst Master: Brentwood Sch., Essex, 1941–42; Bedford Sch., 1942–44. Served War of 1939–45, Royal Navy, 1944–45. Lectr in Economic History, QUB, 1948–51; Sen. Lectr in Economic History, Univ. of Manchester, 1951–60; Prof. of Modern History, Univ. of Nottingham, 1960–66; Prof. of Early Modern European History, Cornell, 1966–73. Visiting Lecturer: Brooklyn Coll., New York, 1957; Univ. of Wisconsin, 1958; Columbia Univ., 1962; Cambridge Univ., 1963; Washington Univ., St Louis, 1964; Fellow, Historisches Kolleg, Munich, 1984–85. Sec., 1955–75, Vice-Pres., 1975–80, Pres., 1980–85, Internat. Commn for the History of Representative and Parliamentary Institutions; Vice-Pres., RHistS, 1982–85. Hon. FKC 1999. Encomienda, Order of Isabel the Catholic (Spain), 1997. *Publications:* The Government of Sicily under Philip II of Spain, 1951, new edn, as The Practice of Empire, 1969; The Empire of Charles V in Europe (in New Cambridge Modern History II), 1958; Western Europe and the Power of Spain (in New Cambridge Modern History III), 1968; Europe in the Sixteenth Century (with G. L. Mosse), 1968, 2nd edn (with G. L. Mosse and G. Q. Bowler) 1989; Estates and Revolutions, 1971; The Habsburgs and Europe, 1516–1660, 1971; (ed) Luther: a profile, 1972; Politicians and Virtuosi, 1986; Medieval Europe, 1987; Early Modern Europe, 1987; (ed) Republiken und Republikanismus im Europa der frühen Neuzeit, 1988; Monarchies, States Generals and Parliaments, 2001; contrib. to historical journals. *Recreations:* playing chamber music, sailing, travel. *Address:* 116 Waterfall Road, N14 7JN. *T:* (020) 8886 6416.

KOFFMANN, Pierre; chef; Proprietor, La Tante Claire, 1977; *b* 21 Aug. 1948; *s* of Albert and Germaine Koffmann; *m* 1972, Annie Barrau; one *d. Educ:* Ecole Jean Jacques Rousseau, Tarbes. Mil. Service, 1967–69. Commis: L'Aubette, Strasbourg, 1966; Grand Hôtel Palais, Juan les Pins, 1967; Le Provençal, La Ciotat, 1969–70; La Voile d'Or, Lausanne, 1970; Le Gavroche, 1970–71; Chef: Brasserie Benoist, London, 1971; Waterside Inn, Bray, 1971–77. *Publications:* Memories of Gascony, 1990; La Tante Claire: recipes from a master chef, 1992.

KOHL, Dr Helmut; Grosskreuz Verdienstorden, 1979; Member, Bundestag, 1976–2002; Chancellor, Federal Republic of Germany, 1982–98 (re-elected, 1991, as Chancellor of reunited Germany); *b* 3 April 1930; *s* of Hans and Cäcilie Kohl; *m* 1960, Hannelore Renner (*d* 2001); two *s*; *m* 2008, Maike Richter. *Educ:* Frankfurt Univ.; Heidelberg Univ. (Dr phil 1958 Heidelberg). On staff of a Trade Assoc., 1958–59; Mem., Parlt of Rhineland Palatinate, 1959–76; Leader, CDU Parly Party in Rhineland Palatinate Parlt, 1963–69; Mem., Federal Exec. Cttee of CDU at federal level, 1964–98; Chairman: CDU, Rhineland Palatinate, 1966–74; CDU, 1973–98; Minister-President, Rhineland Palatinate, 1969–76; Leader of the Opposition, Bundestag, 1976–82. Numerous foreign decorations. *Publications:* Die politische Entscheidung in der Pfalz und das Wiedererstehen der Parteien nach 1945, 1958; Hausputz hinter den Fassaden, 1971; Zwischen Ideologie und Pragmatismus, 1973; Die CDU: Porträt einer Volkspartei, 1981; Der Weg zur Wende, 1983; Reden 1982–1984, 1984; Die Deutsche Einheit, 1992; Der Kurs der CDU, 1993; Mein Tagebuch 1998–2000, 2000. *Address:* Marbacher Strasse 11, 67071 Ludwigshafen (Rhein), Germany.

KÖHLER, Dr Horst; President, Federal Republic of Germany, since 2004; *b* 22 Feb. 1943; *s* of Eduard and Elisa Köhler; *m* 1969, Eva Luise Bohnet; one *s* one *d. Educ:* Tübingen Univ. (PhD Econs and Pol Sci. 1977). Inst. for Applied Econ. Res., 1969–76; economist, German Federal Min. of Econs, 1976–80; Advr to Ministerpräsident, Chancellery, Schleswig-Holstein, 1981–82; German Federal Min. of Finance, 1982–93 (Permanent Under Sec., 1990–93); Pres., German Savings Banks Assoc., 1993–98; Pres., EBRD, 1998–2000; Man. Dir, IMF, 2000–04. *Address:* Bundespräsidialamt, Spreeweg 1, 10557 Berlin, Germany.

KOHLHAUSSEN, Martin; Chairman, Supervisory Board, Commerzbank AG, since 2001; *b* 6 Nov. 1935; *m*; three *c. Educ:* Univs of Frankfurt (Main), Freiburg, Marburg (Law). Worked domestically in banking, Frankfurt and Hanau (Br. Manager), 1965–76; worked internationally in banking (Br. Manager), Tokyo and New York, 1976–81. Mem., 1982–2001, Chm., 1991–2001, Bd of Man. Dirs, Commerzbank AG. *Address:* Commerzbank AG, 60261 Frankfurt, Germany. *T:* (69) 13620.

KOHLI, Jitinder; Chief Executive, Better Regulation Executive, Department for Business, Enterprise and Regulatory Reform (formerly at Cabinet Office), since 2005; *b* 2 Feb. 1973; *s* of Inder Pal and Swarn Kohli. *Educ:* Univ. of Oxford (BA Hons PPE 1995); Southampton Univ. (BSc Sociol. and Soc. Policy 1996). Co-ordinator, Oxford Access Scheme, 1992–93; DTI, 1996–98; Cabinet Office: Econ. and Domestic Secretariat, 1998–99; Prime Minister's Strategy Unit, 1999–2000; Productivity and Structural Reform Team, HM Treasury, 2000–02; Hd, Community Cohesion Unit, Home Office, 2002–03; Hd, Productivity and Structural Reform Team, HM Treasury, 2003–04; Dir, Active Communities, Home Office, 2004–05. Non-exec. Dir, Circle Anglia Housing Gp, 2003–; Chm. of Trustees, EPIC Trust, 2005–. *Address:* Better Regulation Executive, 1Victoria Street, SW1H 0ET. *T:* (020) 7215 0358.

KOHN, Dr Ralph, FRPharmS; Chairman, Harley Street Holdings Ltd, since 1998; baritone; *b* Leipzig, 9 Dec. 1927; *s* of Marcus Kohn and Lena Kohn (*née* Aschheim); *m* 1963, Zahava Kanarek; three *d. Educ:* primary sch., Amsterdam; Manchester Univ. (BSc, MSc; Wilde Prize for Pharmacol., 1953; PhD 1954). FRPharmS (FPS 1952). Charter Travelling Fellow, 1954–56, Paterno Fellow, 1956–57, Inst. of Health, Rome; Riker Fellow, Albert Einstein Coll. of Medicine, NY, 1957–58; Head, exploratory pharmacology, Smith Kline & French Labs, UK, 1958–65; Man. Dir, UK subsid. of Robapharm AG, 1965–71; estabd Adv. Services (Clinical and Gen.) Ltd, first co. in Adv. Services Hldgs Gp, 1971; Man. Dir, Adv. Services Hldgs Gp, 1971–98 (Queen's Award for Export Achievement, to Gp, 1990). Bynum Tudor Lectr and Vis. Fellow, Kellogg Coll., Oxford, 2008. Med. Advr, Nat. Osteoporosis Soc., 1986– (Founder Mem., 1986; Mem., Med. Adv. Gp, 1994–); Mem. Exec. Cttee, Brit. Digestive Foundn, 1997–. Chm. Cttee, Sir John Eliot Gardiner's Millennium Bach Cantata Pilgrimage. Curator, Bach Archive, Leipzig, 2001–. Member: President's Circle, Royal Soc., 1997– (Mem., Royal Soc. 350th Anniv. Campaign Bd, 2007); RSocMed; RPSGB; Brit. Pharmacol Soc.; RSH; CRUK, 2004–. Has given numerous recitals and performances with orchestras in UK and abroad, incl. concerts at Wigmore Hall, Purcell Room, St John's, Smith Sq., Queen Elizabeth Hall and Royal Albert Hall; orchestral broadcasts for radio; has made numerous recordings; lectures on medical, scientific and musical topics. Chairman: Cttee, Wigmore Hall Internat. Song Comp., 1997–2004; Wigmore Hall/Kohn Foundn Internat. Song Comp., 2006–. Founder Mem., Jewish Music Inst., 2000–; Member: Curatorium Bach Archiv, Leipzig, 2003; Cttee, RAM Annual Bach Prize, 2006; Cttee, Imperial Coll. Annual Sir Ernst Chain Prize, 2003; Cttee, Royal Soc. Kohn Award for Excellence in Engaging the Public with Science, 2006. Chm. Trustees, Kohn Foundn, 1991–; Trustee, Rudolf Kempe Soc., 1998–; Hon. Trustee, Monteverdi Choir and Orch., 2001–. Hon. FRAM 2003; Hon. FMedSci 2003; Hon. FRS 2006; Hon. FBPharmacolS 2008. Hon. Fellow, Chorherren Foundn, St Thomas's, Leipzig, 2003. Hon. MAE 2008. Hon. MusD, Manchester, 2009. *Recreations:* music, chess, literature. *Address:* 50 West Heath Road, NW3 7UR. *T:* (020) 8458 2037, (office) (020) 7436 6001. *Club:* Athenæum.

KOHN, Prof. Walter, PhD; Professor of Physics, 1984–91, now Emeritus, and Research Professor, since 1991, University of California at Santa Barbara; *b* Vienna, 9 March 1923; *s* of Salomon and Gittel Kohn; *m* 1st, 1948, Lois Mary Adams; three *d*; 2nd, 1978, Maia Schiff. *Educ:* Univ. of Toronto (BA Math. and Physics 1945; MA Applied Math. 1946); Harvard Univ. (PhD Physics 1948; Lehman Fellow). Indust. Physicist (pt-time), Sutton Horsley Co., 1941–43; Geophysicist (pt-time), Koulomzine, Quebec, 1944–46; Instr, Dept of Physics, Harvard Univ., 1948–50; Asst Prof., 1950–53, Associate Prof., 1953–56, Prof., 1956–60, Dept of Physics, Carnegie Mellon Univ.; Prof., 1960–79, and Chm., 1961–63, Dept of Physics, UCSD; Dir, Inst. of Theoretical Physics, UCSB, 1979–84. Consultant: Westinghouse Res. Lab., 1953–57; Bell Telephone Labs, 1953–66; Gen. Atomic, 1960–72; IBM, 1978. Oersted Fellow, Copenhagen, 1951–52; Sen. NSF Fellow, Imperial Coll., London, 1958; Guggenheim Fellow, Paris, 1963. Member: Amer. Acad. of Arts and Scis, 1963–; NAS, 1969–; Reactor Div., Nat. Inst. of Sci. and Technol., 1946–98; Bd of Govs, Tel Aviv Univ.; Bd of Govs, Weizmann Inst., 1996–. Numerous hon. doctorates. Buckley Medal, 1960, Davisson-Germer Prize, 1977, APS; Feenberg Medal, 1991; Nobel Prize for Physics, 1998; Niels Bohr Medal, UNESCO, 1998. *Publications:* more than 200 articles and reviews in Phys. Review, Phys. Review Letters, Review of Modern Phys., etc. *Recreations:* listening to classical music, reading, going for walks, roller blading. *Address:* Department of Physics, University of California at Santa Barbara, Santa Barbara, CA 93106, USA. *T:* (805) 8933061.

KOHNSTAMM, Max, Groot Officier, Order of Orange-Nassau, 1988; Comdr of the Order of House of Orange, 1949; Hon. Secretary-General, Action Committee for Europe, since 1989 (Sec.-Gen., 1985–88); Senior Fellow, European Policy Centre, Brussels, since 1991; *b* 22 May 1914; *s* of Dr Philip Abraham Kohnstamm and Johanna Hermana Kessler; *m* 1944, Kathleen Sillem; two *s* three *d. Educ:* Univ. of Amsterdam (Hist. Drs); American Univ., Washington. Private Sec. to Queen Wilhelmina, 1945–48; subseq. Head of German Bureau, then Dir of European Affairs, Netherlands FO; Sec. of High Authority, 1952–56; 1st Rep. of High Authority, London, 1956; Sec.-Gen. (later Vice-Pres.), Action Cttee for United States of Europe, 1956–75; Pres., European Community Inst. for Univ. Studies, 1958–75; Principal, Eur. Univ. Inst. of Florence, 1975–81. Co-Chm., Cttee on Soc. Develt and Peace, World Council of Churches and Pontifical Commn for Justice and Peace, 1967–75; European Pres., Trilateral Commn, 1973–75. Grande Ufficiale dell' Ordine Al Merito della Repubblica Italiana, 1981; Grosse Verdienstkreuz, 1982, mit Stern, 1989, Bundesrepublik Deutschland. *Publications:* The European Community and its Role in the World, 1963; (ed jtly) A Nation Writ Large?, 1972; (jtly) Europe: l'impossible statu quo, 1996. *Recreation:* walking. *Address:* 24 Fenffe, 5560 Houyet, Belgium. *T:* (84) 377183, *Fax:* (84) 377113.

KOK, William, (Wim); Prime Minister and Minister for General Affairs, the Netherlands, 1994–2002; *b* 29 Sept. 1938. *Educ:* Nijenrode Business Sch. Mil. Service, 1959–60. Netherlands Federation of Trade Unions: Asst Internat. Officer, Construction Div., 1961–65; Mem. for Econ. Affairs, 1965–67; Union Sec., 1967–69; Sec., 1969–72; Dep. Chm., 1972–73; Chm., 1973–85. Leader, Parly Labour Party, and Mem., Lower House, Netherlands, 1986–89, re-elected 1994, and 1998; Dep. Prime Minister and Minister of Finance, 1989–94. Vice Chm. of Bd, Netherlands Bank. Member, Supervisory Board: ING Gp, 2003–; TNT NV, 2003–; Royal Dutch Shell plc, 2005–; KLM Royal Dutch Airlines, 2003–. Chm., ETUC, 1979–82.

KOLADE, Christopher Olusola, CON 2000; High Commissioner for Nigeria in the United Kingdom, 2002–07; *b* 28 Dec. 1932; *s* of Abraham and Lydia Kolade; *m* Beatrice; two *d. Educ:* Fourah Bay Coll., Sierra Leone (BA, DipEd). Educn Officer, 1955–60; Controller, 1960–72, Dir-Gen., 1972–78, Nigerian Broadcasting Corp.; Dir, 1978–89, CEO, 1989–93, Chm., 1993–2002, Cadbury Nigeria. Lectr, Lagos Business Sch., 1995. Hon. DCL 1976. *Recreations:* church music, lawn tennis, walking. *Address:* c/o Nigeria High Commission, 9 Northumberland Avenue, WC2N 5BX. *Clubs:* Royal Commonwealth Society, Travellers.

KOLAKOWSKI, Leszek, PhD; FBA 1980; Senior Research Fellow, All Souls College, Oxford, 1970–95; *b* 23 Oct. 1927; *s* of Jerzy and Lucyna (*née* Pietrusiewicz); *m* 1949, Dr Tamara Kołakowska (*née* Dynenson); one *d. Educ:* Łódź Univ., Poland 1945–50; Warsaw Univ. (PhD 1953). Asst in Philosophy: Łódź Univ., 1947–49; Warsaw Univ., 1950–59; Prof. and Chm., Section of History of Philosophy, Warsaw Univ., 1959–68, expelled by authorities for political reasons; Visiting Professor: McGill Univ., 1968–69; Univ. of California, Berkeley, 1969–70; Yale Univ., Conn, 1975; Univ. of Chicago, 1981–94. McArthur Fellowship, 1983. MAE; Member: Internat. Inst. of Philosophy, 1969; Académie Universelle des Cultures, 1993; Polish Acad. of Scis, 1997; Foreign Mem., Amer. Academy of Arts and Science, 1997; Mem.-correspondent, Bayerische Akademie der Künste, 1977. Hon. Dr Lit. Hum. Bard Coll., 1984; Hon. LLD Reed Coll., 1985; Hon. DHum: Adelphi, and NY State, USA; Hon. DPhil: Wrocław, 2001; Łódź, Gdansk, and Szczecin, Poland. Friedenpreis des Deutschen Buchhandels, 1977; Jurzykowski Foundn award, 1968; Charles Veillou Prix Européen d'Essai, 1980; (jtly) Erasmus Prize, 1984; Jefferson Award, 1986; Prix Tocqueville, Assoc. Alexis de Tocqueville, 1993; Kluge Prize, Library of Congress, 2003. *Publications:* about 30 books, some of them only in Polish; trans. of various books in 21 languages; *in English:* Marxism and Beyond, 1968; Conversations with the Devil, 1972; Positivist Philosophy, 1972; Husserl and the Search for Certitude, 1975; Main Currents of Marxism, 3 vols, 1978 (trans. from Polish); Religion, 1982; Bergson, 1985; Metaphysical Horror, 1988; Modernity on Endless Trial, 1990; God Owes Us Nothing: a brief remark on Pascal's religion and the spirit of Jansenism, 1995; Freedom, Fame, Lying and Betrayal (essays), 1999; The Two Eyes of Spinoza, 2004; My Correct Views on Everything, 2005; *in French:* Chrétiens sans Eglise, 1969; *in German:* Traktat über die Sterblichkeit der Vernunft, 1967; Geist und Ungeist christlicher Traditionen, 1971; Die Gegenwärtigkeit des Mythos, 1973; Der revolutionäre Geist, 1972; Leben trotz Geschichte Lesebuch, 1977; Zweifel um die Methode, 1977.

KOLANKIEWICZ, Prof. Jerzy, (George), PhD; Professor of Sociology with special reference to Central Europe, since 1999, and Director, 2001–06, School of Slavonic and East European Studies, University College London; Managing Director, ESRC/AHRC/HEFCE Centre for East European Language Based Area Studies, since 2006; *b* 10 April 1946; *s* of late Józef and of Janina Kolankiewicz; *m* 1977, Danuta Elzbieta Manthey; one *s* one *d. Educ:* Salesian Coll., Farnborough; Univ. of Leeds (BA 1st cl. Hons 1968); Univ. of Essex (PhD 1984). Res. Officer, Univ. of Essex, 1969–71; Lecturer in Sociology: UC, Swansea, 1971–72; Univ. of Essex, 1972–99. Fellow, Woodrow Wilson Internat. Center for Scholars, Smithsonian Instn, Washington, DC, 1986–87. Dir, E-W Prog., ESRC, 1990–96; Member: Econ. and Social Cttee on Overseas Res., DFID, 1994–2000; HEFCE Chief Executive's Strategically Important Subjects Adv. Gp, 2005. Mem. Governing Body, British Assoc. for Central and Eastern Europe, 2002–08. Dep. Pres., Polish Educnl Soc., 2002–. Diploma of Polish Min. of Foreign Affairs, 2007. Comdr's Cross and Star, Order of Merit (Poland), 2004; Officer's Cross, Order of Merit (Hungary), 2006. *Publications:* (with D. Lane) Social Groups in Polish Society, 1973; (with P. Lewis) Poland: politics, economics and society, 1988; Towards a Sociology of the Transition: rights, resources and social integration in Poland, 2000; (ed with T. Zarycki) Regional Issues in Polish Politics, 2003; contribs to British Jl Sociol., Internat. Affairs, Daedalus, E European Politics and Societies, Sociologia Ruralis. *Recreations:* walking (Lake District, Tatras), swimming. *Address:* c/o School of Slavonic and East European Studies, University College London, 16 Taviton Street, WC1H 0BW; *e-mail:* g.kolankiewicz@ssees.ucl.ac.uk.

KOLBERT, His Honour Colin Francis; Assistant Surveillance Commissioner, since 2001; Deputy Chairman, Regulatory Decisions Committee, Financial Services Authority, 2001–06; *b* 3 June 1936; *s* of late Arthur Richard Alexander Kolbert and Dorothy Elizabeth Kolbert (*née* Fletcher); *m* 1959, Jean Fairgrieve Abson; two *d. Educ:* Queen Elizabeth's, Barnet; St Catharine's Coll., Cambridge (Harold Samuel Schol., 1959; BA 1959; PhD 1962; MA 1963). FCIArb 1997. RA, 1954–56. Called to the Bar, Lincoln's Inn, 1961, Bencher, 2005; a Recorder, SE Circuit, 1985–88; a Circuit Judge, 1988–95. Oxford University: Fellow and Tutor in Jurisprudence, St Peter's Coll., 1964–68 (MA, DPhil (Oxon) by incorp., 1964); CUF Lectr, Faculty of Law, 1965–68; Cambridge University: Fellow, Magdalene Coll., 1968– (Tutor, 1969–88); Univ. Lectr in Law, Dept of Land Economy, 1969–88; Sec., Faculty of Music, 1969–75; Coll. Rugby Administrator, CURUFC, 1982–88 (Trustee, 1989–); Mem. CUCC Cttee, 1996–. Vis. Prof. and Moderator, Univs of Ife, Lagos, Enugu, and Ahmadu Bello, Nigeria, 1970–80. Ind. Bd Mem., 1995–2000, Chm., Disciplinary Tribunal, 1995–2001, SFA. Mem., Cambridge City Council, 1970–74. Member: Istituto di Diritto Agrario Internazionale e Comparato, Florence, 1964–; Secretariat, World Conf. on Agrarian Reform and Rural Develt, FAO Rome, 1978–79 (Customary Land Tenure Consultant, 1974–80). Freeman, City of London, 1998; Liveryman, Wax Chandlers' Co., 1999–. Governor: Wellingborough Sch., 1970–80; Cranleigh Sch., 1970–88; Glenalmond Coll., 1978–89; Hurstpierpoint Coll., 1978–89; Wisbech GS, 2001–; Feoffee, Chetham's Hosp. and Library, 1993–. Violin music critic, Records and Recording, 1972–78. *Publications:* (trans. and ed) The Digest of Justinian, 1979, 4th edn 1993; various legal and musical. *Recreations:* music (especially playing the violin), cricket, Rugby, military history, cooking, walking in London and Yorkshire. *Address:* Magdalene College, Cambridge CB3 0AG; Outer Temple Chambers, 222 Strand, Temple WC2R 1BA. *Clubs:* MCC, Farmers'; Leeds; Hawks (Cambridge); Cambridge University Rugby Union Football; Colonsay Golf.

KOLTAI, Ralph, CBE 1983; RDI 1984; freelance stage designer; designer for Drama, Opera and Dance, since 1950; Associate Designer, Royal Shakespeare Company, 1963–66 and since 1976; *b* 31 July 1924; Hungarian-German; *s* of Dr(med) Alfred Koltai and Charlotte Koltai (*née* Weinstein); *m* 1956, Annena Stubbs. *Educ:* Central Sch. of Art and Design (Dip. with Dist.). Early work entirely in field of opera. First production, Angelique, for London Opera Club, Fortune Theatre, 1950. Designs for The Royal Opera House, Sadler's Wells, Scottish Opera, National Welsh Opera, The English Opera Group. First of 7 ballets for Ballet Rambert, Two Brothers, 1958. Head, Sch. of Theatre Design, Central Sch. of Art & Design, 1965–72. *Productions:* RSC: The Caucasian Chalk Circle, 1962; The Representative, 1963; The Birthday Party, Endgame, The Jew of Malta, 1964; The Merchant of Venice, Timon of Athens, 1965; Little Murders, 1967; Major Barbara, 1970; Too True To Be Good, 1975; Old World, 1976; Wild Oats, 1977; The

Tempest, Love's Labour's Lost, 1978; Hippolytus, Baal, 1979; Romeo and Juliet, Hamlet, 1980; The Love Girl and the Innocent, 1981 (London Drama Critics Award); Much Ado About Nothing, Molière, 1982; Custom of the Country, Cyrano de Bergerac (SWET Award), 1983; Troilus and Cressida, Othello, 1985; They Shoot Horses, Don't They?, 1987; for National Theatre: an "all male" As You Like It, 1967; Back to Methuselah, 1969; State of Revolution, 1977; Brand (SWET Award), The Guardsman, 1978; Richard III, The Wild Duck, 1979; Man and Superman, 1981; *other notable productions include: opera:* for Sadler's Wells/English National Opera: The Rise and Fall of the City of Mahagonny, 1963; From the House of the Dead, 1965; Bluebeard's Castle, 1972; Wagner's (complete) Ring Cycle, 1973; Seven Deadly Sins, 1978; Anna Karenina, 1981; Pacific Overtures, 1987; for The Royal Opera House: Taverner, 1972; The Ice Break, 1977; Tannhäuser, Sydney, 1973; Wozzeck, Netherlands Opera, 1973; Fidelio, Munich, 1974; Verdi's Macbeth, Edinburgh Festival, 1976; Les Soldats, Lyon Opera, 1983; Italian Girl in Algiers, 1984, Tannhäuser, 1986, Geneva; (also dir.) Flying Dutchman, Hong Kong, 1987; La Traviata, Hong Kong, 1990, Stockholm, 1993; The Makropulos Affair, Oslo, 1991; Otello, Essen, 1994; Madam Butterfly, Tokyo, 1995; Simon Boccanegra, WNO, and Carmen, Royal Albert Hall, 1997; Dalibor, Scottish Opera and Nabucco, Chorégie Orange, 1998; Don Giovanni, Kirov, 1999; Genoveva, Opera North, 2000; Katya Kabanova, Venice, 2003; Simon Boccanegra, Tel Aviv, 2003; *theatre:* Pack of Lies, Lyric, 1983; Across from the Garden of Allah, Comedy, 1986; Twelfth Night, Theatre Royal, Copenhagen, 1996; Midsummer Night's Dream, and Macbeth, Teater Gladsaxe, Copenhagen, 1998; (also dir.) Suddenly Last Summer, Nottingham Playhouse, 1998; The Romans in Britain, Crucible Th., Sheffield, 2006; for Aalborg Theatre, Denmark: Threepenny Opera, 1979; The Love Girl and the Innocent, 1980; Terra Nova, 1981; The Carmelites, 1981; Mahagonny, 1984; *musicals:* Billy, Drury Lane, 1974; Bugsy Malone, Her Majesty's, 1983; Dear Anyone, Cambridge Theatre, 1983; Carrie, Stratford, NY, 1988; Metropolis, Piccadilly, 1989; My Fair Lady, NY, 1993; *ballet:* The Planets, Royal Ballet, 1990; Cruel Garden, 1992; has worked in most countries in Western Europe, also Bulgaria, Argentine, USA, Canada, Australia, Japan. Retrospective exhibition, London, Beijing, HK, Taipei, Prague, 1997–99; exhibitions: Landscapes of the Theatre, Tokyo, 2003; Designer for the Stage, NT, 2004. Fellow: Acad. of Performing Art, Hong Kong, 1994; London Inst., 1996; Rose Bruford Coll.; FRSA. London Drama Critics Award, Designer of the Year, 1967 (for Little Murders and As You Like It); (jtly) Gold Medal, Internat. Exhibn of Stage Design, Prague Quadriennale, 1975, 1979; Individual Silver Medal, Prague Quadriennale, 1987; Special Award for Dist. Service to the Theater, USA, 1993. *Publication:* Ralph Koltai: designer for the stage, 1997. *Recreation:* wildlife photography. *Address:* c/o Marc Berlin Associates, 14 Floral Street, WC2E 9DH. *T:* (020) 7836 1112.

KOMANSKY, David H.; Chief Executive Officer, 1996–2002, Chairman, 1997–2003, Merrill Lynch & Co. Inc.; *b* 27 April 1939; *m* Phyllis; two *d. Educ:* Univ. of Miami; Harvard Univ. (AMP 1990). Joined Merrill Lynch & Co. Inc., 1968: Financial Consultant, 1968–75, Sales Manager, 1975, Forest Hills, NY office; Sales Manager, Garden City, NY office, 1975–77; Office Manager, Manhasset, NY office, 1977–81; Private Client Group: Regional Director: Mideast Reg., 1981–83; Metropolitan Reg., 1983–85; Pres. and CEO, Merrill Lynch Realty Inc., 1985–88; Dir, Nat. Sales, 1988–93; Executive Vice President: Global Equity Mkts Gp, 1990–92; Debt Mkts Gp, 1992–93; Debt and Equity Mkts Gp, 1993–95. Member, Board of Directors: NY Stock Exchange; Business Council of NY State Inc.; NYC Investment Fund; Associates of Harvard Business Sch.

KOMISARENKO, Prof. Sergiy Vassiliovych, MD; PhD; Director, Palladin Institute of Biochemistry, since 1998; President: Ukrainian Institute for Peace and Democracy, since 1999; Special Olympics, Ukraine, since 2002; *b* 9 July 1943; *s* of late Prof. Vassiliy Komisarenko and Lubov Drosovska-Komisarenko; *m* 1970, Natalia Ignatiuk; one *d. Educ:* Ukrainian-English Sch., Kiev; Kiev Med, Inst. (MD with dist. 1966); Kiev Univ.; Inst. of Biochem., Kiev (PhD 1970); Inst. of Molecular Biology, Kiev (DSc 1989). Palladin Institute of Biochemistry, Ukrainian Academy of Sciences, Kiev: Jun., then Sen. Scientific Researcher, 1969–75; Scientific Sec., 1972–74; Hd of Dept, 1975–92; Prof. of Biochem., 1989; Dir, 1989–92; Dep. Prime Minister, Ukraine, 1990–92; Ambassador of Ukraine to UK, 1992–98, and to Ireland, 1995–98. Visiting Scientist: Pasteur Inst., Paris, 1974–75; Sloan-Kettering Cancer Inst., NY, 1981. Chairman: Nat. Commn on Biosafety, 2007–; Bd, Internat. Foundn of the Ukrainian Nat. Heritage, 2007–. Pres., Ukrainian Biochem. Soc., 1999–. Member: Ukrainian Nat. Acad. of Scis, 1991 (Academician-Sec., 2004–); Ukrainian Acad. of Med. Scis, 1993. Hon. DSc: Kingston, 1997; London Metropolitan, 1997. Ukrainian State Award, 1979; Ukrainian State Order of Merit, 1996. *Publications:* Radiation and Human Immunity, 1994; numerous articles on biochem. and immunology; also articles on Ukrainian culture and politics. *Recreations:* music, ski-ing, clay pigeon shooting, lawn tennis, wind-surfing. *Address:* Palladin Institute of Biochemistry, 9 Leontovicha Street, Kiev, 01601, Ukraine. *T:* (44) 2345974; *e-mail:* svk@biochem.kiev.ua.

KOMOROWSKI, Dr Stanislaw Jerzy, Hon. KCVO 2004; Ambassador, Asia and Pacific Department, Ministry of Foreign Affairs, Poland, since 2007; *b* 18 Dec. 1953; *s* of Henryk Komorowski and Helena Komorowska (*née* Krokowska); *m* 1st, 1976, Irena Kwiatkowska (marr. diss. 1987); two *s*; 2nd, 1989, Maria Wegrzecka (marr. diss. 1997); one *s*; 3rd, 2001, Ewa Minkowska. *Educ:* Inst. of Physics, Univ. of Warsaw (MSc 1978); Inst. of Physical Chem., Polish Acad. of Scis (PhD 1985). Research Fellow, Physical Chem. Inst., Polish Acad. of Scis, 1978–90; Post-doctoral Fellow, Univ. of Utah, Salt Lake City, 1986–87; Adjunct, Physical Chem. Inst., 1987–89; Asst Prof., Univ. of Utah, 1989–90; Ministry for Foreign Affairs, Poland: Head of Section and Asst Head, Personnel Dept, 1991; Asst Head, 1991–92, Head, 1992–94, Eur. Dept; Ambassador to the Netherlands, 1994–98; Head, Office of Minister for Foreign Affairs, 1998–99; Ambassador to UK, 1999–2004; Dir, Asia and Pacific Dept, 2004–05, Under-Sec. of State for European Affairs, 2005–06, Ministry of Foreign Affairs, Warsaw. Grand Cross, Order of Orange Nassau (Netherlands), 1998. *Publications:* articles in American, French and Dutch physical chemistry jls. *Recreations:* tennis, ski-ing, photography. *Address:* Ministry of Foreign Affairs, Al. J. Ch. Szucha 23, 00–580 Warsaw, Poland.

KONG, Janis Carol, OBE 2002; Chairman, Heathrow Airport Ltd, 2001–06; Director, BAA plc, 2002–06. *Educ:* Univ. of Edinburgh (BSc Psychol.); Harvard Business Sch. Joined BAA, Edinburgh Airport, 1973; Mktg Manager, Scottish Airports; Gen. Manager, Terminal 4, Heathrow Airport; Ops Dir, 1994–97, Man. Dir, 1997–2001, Gatwick Airport Ltd. Non-exec. Dir, Portmeirion Hldgs plc. Former Mem., SE England Develt Agency; Mem. Bd, VisitBritain, 2006–. DUniv Open. *Address:* c/o VisitBritain, Thames Tower, Blacks Road, W6 9EL.

KONIGSBERG, Allen Stewart; *see* Allen, Woody.

KONSTANT, Rt Rev. David Every; Bishop of Leeds, (RC), 1985–2004, now Emeritus; *b* 16 June 1930; *s* of Antoine Konstant and Dulcie Marion Beresford Konstant (*née* Leggatt). *Educ:* St Edmund's College, Old Hall Green, Ware; Christ's College, Cambridge (MA); Univ. of London Inst. of Education (PGCE). Priest, dio. Westminster, 1954; Cardinal Vaughan School, Kensington, 1959; Diocesan Adviser on Religious Educn, 1966; St Michael's School, Stevenage, 1968; Dir, Westminster Religious Educn Centre, 1970; Auxiliary Bishop of Westminster (Bishop in Central London) and Titular Bishop of Betagbara, 1977–85. Chm., Dept for Catholic Educn and Formation (formerly Dept for Christian Doctrine and Formation), 1984–99, Dept for Internat. Affairs, 1999–2004, Bishops' Conf. of Eng. and Wales; Chm., Catholic Educn Service, 1991–99. FRSA 1996. Freeman, City of London, 1984. Hon. DLaws Leeds Metropolitan, 2004; DUniv Bradford, 2006. *Publications:* various books on religious education and liturgy. *Recreation:* music. *Address:* Ashlea, 62 Headingley Lane, Leeds LS6 2BU.

KOOLHAAS, Prof. Remment; Joint Founder and Partner, Office for Metropolitan Architecture, since 1975; Professor in Practice of Architecture and Urban Design, Graduate School of Design, Harvard University, since 1995; *b* Rotterdam, 17 Nov. 1944. *Educ:* Architectural Assoc. Sch. of Architecture (DipArch 1972). Journalist and script writer, 1962–72; taught at: Sch. of Architecture, UCLA, 1975; AA, 1976; Professor of Architecture: Technical Univ., Delft, 1988–89; Rice Univ., Houston, 1991–92; Arthur Rotch Adjunct Prof. of Architecture, Graduate Sch. of Design, Harvard Univ., 1990–95. Projects include: Netherlands Dance Theatre, The Hague, 1987; Nexus World Housing, Fukuoka, 1991; Kunsthal, Rotterdam, 1992; Grand Palais and city centre masterplan, Lille, 1994; Educatorium, Univ. of Utrecht, 1997; house in Bordeaux, 1998; Second Stage Theatre, NY, 1999; Prada stores, NY, 2001, LA, 2004; McCormick Tribune Campus, Illinois Inst. of Technol., Chicago, 2003; Seattle Central Library, 2004; Casa da Musica, Porto, 2005; Netherlands Embassy, Berlin, 2005 (Mies van der Rohe Award, EU, 2005); China Central Television, Beijing, 2008. Pritzker Prize, 2000; Praemium Imperiale, Japan Art Assoc., 2003; Royal Gold Medal, RIBA, 2004. Co-founder, Volume Magazine, 2005. *Publications include:* Delirious New York: a retroactive manifesto for Manhattan, 1978; (jtly) S,M,L,XL, 1997; OMA Rem Koolhaas Living, Vivre, Leben, 1999; OMA 30: 30 Colours, 1999; Content, 2004; Lagos: how it works, 2007. *Address:* Office for Metropolitan Architecture, Heer Bokelweg 149, 3032 AD Rotterdam, Netherlands; Department of Architecture, Harvard Design School, 48 Quincy Street, Cambridge, MA 02138, USA.

KOOMPIROCHANA, Dr Vikrom; Ambassador of Thailand to the Court of St James's, and concurrently to Republic of Ireland, 2003–06; *b* 23 Jan. 1946; *m* Sasin Monvosin; one *d. Educ:* Chulalongkorn Univ., Bangkok (BA (Hist.) 1967); Michigan State Univ. (MA (Hist.) 1968; PhD (Hist.) 1972). Lectr in Hist., Chulalongkorn Univ., 1972; Ministry of Foreign Affairs: Second Sec., Southeast Asia Div., Dept of Pol Affairs, 1973; Second Sec., later First Sec., Kuala Lumpur, 1976–80; Director: News Div., Dept of Inf., 1981; Americas Div., Dept of Pol Affairs, 1982–84; Counsellor, later Minister Counsellor, London, 1985–88; Ambassador attached to Ministry, Office of Perm. Sec., 1989–90; Ambassador of Thailand: to Singapore, 1991–95; to Malaysia, 1996; to NZ, and concurrently to Samoa and Tonga, 1997–99; Dep. Perm. Sec., Office of Perm. Sec., 2000–01; Ambassador to Italy, and concurrently to Albania and Cyprus, 2002. Chakrabarti Mala Medal (Thailand), 1997. Special Grand Cordon: Most Noble Order of Crown of Thailand, 1995; Most Exalted Order of White Elephant (Thailand), 2000. *Address:* c/o Royal Thai Embassy, 29–30 Queen's Gate, SW7 5JB; *e-mail:* vikrom@mfa.go.th.

KOOPMAN, Prof. Antonius Gerhardus Michael, (Ton); harpsichordist, organist and conductor; Founder and Conductor, Amsterdam Baroque Orchestra, since 1978, and Choir, since 1992; Professor: of Harpsichord, Royal Conservatory, The Hague, since 1989; for Musicology, Leiden University, since 2003; *b* 10 Oct. 1944; *m* 1975, Tini Mathot; three *d. Educ:* Amsterdam Conservatory; Univ. of Amsterdam (degree in musicology 1968). Professor: of Harpsichord and Performance Practice, Early Music, Conservatory of Zwolle, 1968–73; of Harpsichord, Conservatory of Groningen, 1973–79; of Harpsichord, Conservatory of Amsterdam, 1979–89. Principal Conductor, Netherlands Radio Chamber Orch., 1994–2001; Principal Guest Conductor, Lausanne Chamber Orch., 1999–; guest conductor with orchestras in USA, Europe and Japan. Established: chamber ensemble, Musica da Camera, 1966; baroque orch., Musica Antiqua Amsterdam, 1968. Hon. RAM, 1985. Hon. Dr Utrecht, 2000. Prix de l'Académie du Disque Lyrique, 1994; Prix Hector Berlioz, Paris, 1995; Deutsche Schallplattenpreis Echo Klassik, 1997. *Publications:* Barokmuzick: theorie en praktijk, 1985; (contrib.) The World of the Bach Cantatas, ed Christopher Wolff, 1997; contrib. Early Music, Mens en Melodie, etc. *Address:* Postbus 1163, 1400 BD Bussum, The Netherlands. *T:* (35) 6913676, *Fax:* (35) 6939752; *e-mail:* info@tonkoopman.nl.

KOOPS, Hon. Dame Mary Claire; *see* Hogg, Hon. Dame M. C.

KOPELMAN, Prof. Peter Graham, MD; FRCP, FFPH; Principal, St George's, University of London, since 2008; Hon. Consultant Physician, St George's Hospital NHS Trust, since 2008; *b* London, 23 June 1951; *s* of Dr Harry Kopelman and Joan Kopelman (*née* Knowlman); *m* 1981, Susan Mary Sarah Lewis; one *s* two *d. Educ:* Felsted Sch.; St George's Hosp. Med. Sch., London (MB BS 1974; MD 1982). FRCP 1992; FFPH 2005. Sen. Lectr in Medicine, 1986–97, Reader in Medicine, 1997–99, Prof. of Clinical Medicine, 1999–2006, London Hosp. Med. Coll., subseq. St Bartholomew's and Royal London Sch. of Medicine and Dentistry, then Barts and The London Sch. of Medicine and Dentistry, QMUL; Deputy Warden and Vice Principal, QMUL, 2001–06; Consultant Physician, Newham Gen. Hosp., 1986–95; Hon. Consultant Physician, Barts and The London NHS Trust, 1999–2006; Dean, Fac. of Health, UEA, 2006–08; Hon. Prof. of Medicine, Norfolk and Norwich Hosp., Norwich, 2006–08. Non-exec. Dir, NE London Strategic HA, 2003–06. Member: Scientific Adv. Cttee on Nutrition, DoH/Food Standards Agency, 2001–; HEFCE Res. Strategy Cttee, 2007–; Chairman: MRCP(UK) Clin. Examining Bd, RCP, 2004–08; NIHR Clin. Acad. Careers Panel, DoH, 2005–. Pres., Eur. Assoc. for the Study of Obesity, 2003–06. *Publications:* (ed jtly) Clinical Obesity, 1998, 3rd edn; scientific articles and book chapters on obesity, its causes, complications, treatment and prevention. *Recreations:* all sports, music, drawing, modern literature, political biographies. *Address:* Principal's Office, St George's, University of London, Cranmer Terrace, SW17 0RE. *T:* (020) 8725 5008, *Fax:* (020) 8672 6940; *e-mail:* pkopelman@sgul.ac.uk. *Club:* Athenæum.

KOPELOWITZ, Dr (Jacob) Lionel (Garstein); JP; General Medical Practitioner, since 1953; *b* 9 Dec. 1926; *s* of Maurice and Mabel Kopelowitz; *m* 1980, Sylvia Waksman (*née* Galler). *Educ:* Clifton Coll., Bristol; Trinity Coll., Cambridge (MA 1947); University Coll. Hosp. London. MRCS, LRCP 1951; MRCGP 1964. Resident MO, London Jewish Hosp., 1951–52; Flying Officer, RAF Med. Branch, 1952–53. Member: General Medical Council, 1984–94; General Optical Council, 1979–93; Standing Med. Adv. Cttee, DHSS, 1974–78; British Medical Association: Fellow, 1980; Mem. Council, 1982–94; Chm., Newcastle Div., 1968–69; Pres., Northern Regional Council, 1984–88; Mem., Gen. Med. Services Cttee, 1971–90 (Past Chm., Maternity Services Sub-Cttee); Chm., Central Adv. Cttee, Deputising Services, 1980–90; Dep. Chm., Private Practice Cttee, 1972–89; Chairman: St Marylebone and Bloomsbury Div., 1992–; London Regl Council, 2001–04. Chm., Newcastle upon Tyne FPC, 1979–85; Pres., Soc. of FPCs of England and Wales, 1978–79; Mem. Council, RCGP, 1995–. Vice-Pres., Trades Adv.

Council, 1988–. President: Board of Deputies of British Jews, 1985–91; Nat. Council for Soviet Jewry, 1985–91; European Jewish Congress, 1986–91; Vice President: Conf. on Jewish Material Claims Against Germany, 1988–; Conf. on Jewish Material Claims Against Austria, 1988–. Member: Exec. Cttee, Meml Foundn for Jewish Culture, 1988–; United Synagogue, 1991–96. Vice-Pres., Assoc. of Baltic Jews, 1995–; Mem., Chm., Pres., numerous med. bodies and Jewish organisations, UK and overseas. Vice-Pres., British Council, Share Zedek Med. Centre, 1990–. Mem. Bd of Govs, Clifton Coll., Bristol, 1988–; Pres., Old Cliftonian Soc., 1991–93; Mem., Cambridge Union Soc. Liveryman, Apothecaries' Co., 1969. JP Northumberland, 1964. Grand Cross, Order of Merit (Germany), 1993. *Publications:* articles in med. jls; contrib. to Med. Annual. *Recreations:* foreign travel, contract bridge. *Address:* 10 Cumberland House, Clifton Gardens, W9 1DX. *T:* (020) 7289 6375; Little Jesmond, 145 Barrack Lane, Aldwick, W Sussex PO21 4ED. *T:* (01243) 268134. *Club:* Athenæum.

KORAB-KARPINSKI, Marek Romuald, FRCS, FRCSE; Consultant Orthopaedic and Spinal Surgeon, East Yorkshire Hospitals NHS Trust, since 1987; *b* 29 Jan. 1950; *s* of Lt Col Marian Korab-Karpinski, MC, VM and Zofia Korab-Karpinska; *m* 1999, Dr Malgorzata Szymanska, orthopaedic surgeon; two *s* one *d* by previous marriage. *Educ:* Univ. of Nottingham (BMedSci 1977; BM BS); Univ. of Liverpool (MChOrth 1985). FRCS 1981; FRCSE 1981 (FRCSE (Orth) 1985). Higher surgical orthopaedic trng, Birmingham, 1981–83, Nottingham, 1983–87. Hon. Vis. Prof., Poznan Acad. of Orthopaedics, Poland, 1997. Fellow, Brit. Orthopaedic Assoc., 1985. Patron, PPA Internat., 1997. Hon. Fellow, Univ. of Hull, 1996. Computer Assisted Operative Surgery Prize, BCS, 1996. Designated co-inventor, Computer Assisted Robotic Surgery Technique, 1997. *Publications:* Posterior Lumbar Interbody Fusion and Cages, 1977; (contrib.) Current Concepts in Lumbar Spine Disorders, Vol. 2, 1997; various articles related to orthopaedics and computers, incl. robotic surgery; res. papers. *Recreations:* tennis, snow ski-ing, travel, charity work of a surgical nature. *Address:* 10 Harley Street, W1N 1AA. *T:* (020) 7436 5252. *Club:* Kandahar.

KORALEK, Paul George, CBE 1984; RA 1991 (ARA 1986); RIBA; FRIAI; Founding Partner, 1961 and Director, Ahrends Burton and Koralek, architects; *b* 7 April 1933; *s* of late Ernest and Alice Koralek; *m* 1958, Jennifer Chadwick; two *d* (one *s* decd). *Educ:* Aldenham School; Architectural Assoc. School of Architecture. RIBA 1957; AA Dip. Hons. FRIAI 2001. Architect: with Powell & Moya, London, 1956–57; with Marcel Breuer, New York, 1959–60. Part-time teaching, Sch. of Arch., Leicester Polytechnic, 1982–84. *Major projects include: public buildings:* Maidenhead Libr., 1972; Roman Catholic Chaplaincy, Oxford, 1972; Nucleus Low Energy Hosp., IoW, 1982; winning entry, Nat. Gall. Extension Hampton Site Comp., 1982; Dover Heritage Centre, 1988–90 (Civic Trust Award, 1992); British Embassy, Moscow, 1993–99; Dublin Dental Hosp., Trinity Coll., 1994–98 (RIBA Arch. Award; RIAI Award); Techniquest Science Centre, Cardiff, 1995 (RIBA Arch. Award); Offaly County Council offices, 2002–; County Offices, Neneagh, Tipperary, 2004; *educational buildings:* Chichester Theol Coll., 1965; Berkeley Liby, TCD, 1967 (1st Prize, Internat. Comp., 1961); Templeton Coll., Oxford, 1967; Arts Faculty Bldg, TCD, 1975–79; Portsmouth Poly. Liby, 1975–79; Residential bldg, Keble Coll., Oxford, 1976 (RIBA Arch. Award, 1978); Selly Oak Colls Learning Resources Centre, 1997; Insts of Technol. at Tralee, Waterford and Blanchardstown, 1997–2002; Loughborough Univ. Business Sch., 1998; Innovation Centre, TCD, 2001; John Wheatley Coll., Glasgow, 2007–; *residential buildings:* houses, Dunstan Rd, Oxford, 1969; Nebenzahl House, Jerusalem, 1972; Chalvedon Housing, 1975–77; Whitmore Court Housing, Basildon, 1975 (RIBA Good Design in Housing Award, 1977); Felmore Housing, 1975–80; *commercial/industrial buildings:* Habitat Warehouse, Showroom and Offices, Wallingford, 1974 (Financial Times Indust. Arch. Award, and Structl Steel Design Award (Warehouse), 1976); factory bldgs and refurbishment, Cummins Engine Co., Shotts, Scotland, 1975–83 (Structl Steel Design Award, 1980); J. Sainsbury supermarket, Canterbury, 1984 (Structl Steel Design Award, 1985; FT Arch. at Work Award Commendation, 1986); W. H. Smith Offices, Greenbridge, 1985 and 1996 (FT Arch. at Work Award Commendation, 1987); John Lewis Dept Store, Kingston-upon-Thames, 1987 (Civic Trust Commendation, 1991). *Exhibitions of drawings and works:* RIBA Heinz Gall., 1980; Douglas Hyde Gall. Dublin, 1981; Technical Univ. of Braunschweig and Tech. Univ. of Hanover, Germany, Mus. of Finnish Arch., Helsinki, Univ. of Oulu, and Alvar Aalto Mus., Jvasklya, Finland, 1982; HQ of AA, Oslo, 1983. Chm., SE Regl Design Panel, 2002–. Member: Develt Adv. (formerly Design and Architectural Rev.) Panel, Cardiff Bay Develt Corp., 1988; ARCUK Bd of Architectural Educn, 1987–93; Trustee, Bldg Industry Youth Trust, 1981–95. External Examiner: Sch. of Arch., Univ. of Manchester, 1981–85; Plymouth Poly., 1988; Assessor: RIBA competitions, incl. Toyota UK HQ, 1997; Irish Dept of Educn Schs competition; Civic Trust Awards; Advr, Cardiff Bay Opera House, 1994–95. Papers and lectures, UK and abroad, 1964–. *Publications:* paper and articles in RIBA and other prof. jls. *Recreations:* drawing, walking, gardening. *Address:* Unit 1, 7 Chalcot Road, NW1 8LH. *T:* (020) 7586 3311, *Fax:* (020) 7722 5445; *e-mail:* abk@abklondon.com.

See also C. L. Ricks.

KORNBERG, Prof. Sir Hans (Leo), Kt 1978; MA, DSc, ScD, PhD; FRS 1965; FIBiol; University Professor and Professor of Biology, Boston University, since 1995 (Director, 2002–05 and 2007–Aug. 2009); Sir William Dunn Professor of Biochemistry, University of Cambridge, 1975–95, and Fellow of Christ's College, Cambridge, since 1975 (Master, 1982–95); *b* 14 Jan. 1928; *o s* of Max Kornberg and Margarete Kornberg (*née* Silberbach); *m* 1st, 1956, Monica Mary King (*d* 1989); twin *s* two *d*; 2nd, 1991, Donna, *d* of William B. Haber and Ruth Haber. *Educ:* Queen Elizabeth Grammar Sch., Wakefield; Univ. of Sheffield (BSc, PhD); MA 1958, DSc 1961, Oxon; ScD Cantab 1975. FIBiol 1965 (Hon. Fellow, 2004). Commonwealth Fund Fellow of Harkness Foundation, at Yale University and Public Health Research Inst., New York, 1953–55; Mem. of scientific staff, MRC Cell Metabolism Res. Unit, University of Oxford, 1955–60; Lectr, Worcester Coll., Oxford, 1958–61 (Hon. Fellow 1980); Prof. of Biochemistry, Univ. of Leicester, 1960–75. Visiting Instructor, Marine Biological Lab., Woods Hole, Mass, 1964–66, 1981–85, Trustee, 1982–93. Dir, UK Nirex Ltd, 1986–95. Member: SRC, 1967–72 (Chm., Science Bd, 1969–72); UGC Biol. Sci. Cttee, 1967–77; NATO Adv. Study Inst. Panel, 1970–76 (Chm., 1974–75); Kuratorium, Max-Planck Inst., Dortmund, 1979–90 (Chm., Sci. Adv. Cttee); AFRC (formerly ARC), 1980–84; Priorities Bd for R & D in Agriculture, 1984–90; BP Venture Res. Council, 1981–91; ACARD, 1982–85; Adv. Council on Public Records, 1984–86; UK Cttee on Eur. Year of the Environment, 1986–88; Vice-Chm., EMBO, 1978–81; Chairman: Royal Commn on Environmental Pollution, 1976–81; Adv. Cttee on Genetic Modification, 1986–95; Co-ordinating Cttee on Environmental Res., Res. Councils, 1986–88; Sci. Adv. Cttee, Inst. for Mol. Biol. and Medicine, Monash Univ., 1987–; President: BAAS, 1984–85 (Hon. Mem., 2003); Biochemical Soc., 1990–95; IUBMB, 1991–94 (Dist. Service Award, 2003); Assoc. for Science Educn, 1991–92; Vice-Pres., Inst. of Biol., 1971–73. A Managing Trustee, Nuffield Foundn, 1973–93; Trustee, 1990–92, Gov., 1992–95, Wellcome Trust; Academic Governor, Hebrew Univ. of Jerusalem, 1976–97 (Hon. Gov., 1997–); Governor: Weizmann Inst., 1980–97 (Hon. Gov., 1997–); Lister Inst., 1990–95. Hon. Fellow: Brasenose Coll., Oxford, 1983; Wolfson Coll., Cambridge, 1990. FRSA 1972. Fellow, Amer. Acad. of Microbiol., 1992. For. Associate, Nat. Acad. of Sciences, USA, 1986; Foreign Member: Amer. Philosoph. Soc., 1993; Accademia Nazionale dei Lincei, 1997; Hon. For. Mem., Amer. Acad. of Arts & Scis, 1987; Member: Leopoldina German Acad. of Scis, 1982; Acad. Europaea, 1989; Hon. Member: Amer. Soc. Biol Chem., 1972; Biochem. Soc., FRG, 1973; Japanese Biochem. Soc., 1981; Biochem. Soc. (UK), 2001; Phi Beta Kappa, 1996; Hon. FRCP 1989. Hon. ScD Cincinnati, 1974; Hon. DSc: Warwick, 1975; Leicester, 1979; Sheffield, 1979; Bath, 1980; Strathclyde, 1985; South Bank, 1994; Leeds, 1995; La Trobe, 1997; DUniv Essex, 1979; Hon. Dr med Leipzig, 1984; Hon. LLD Dundee, 1999. Colworth Medal of Biochemical Soc., 1965; Otto Warburg Medal, Biochem. Soc. of Federal Republic of Germany, 1973. *Publications:* (with Sir Hans Krebs) Energy Transformations in Living Matter, 1957; articles in scientific jls. *Recreations:* cooking and conversation. *Address:* The University Professors, 745 Commonwealth Avenue, Boston, MA 02215, USA; (home) 134 Sewall Avenue, # 2, Brookline, MA 02446, USA.

KORNER, Joanna Christian Mary, CMG 2004; QC 1993; a Recorder, since 1995; *b* 1 July 1951; *d* of John Hugh George Korner and Martha (*née* Tupay von Isertingen). *Educ:* Queensgate Sch.; Inns of Court Sch. of Law. Called to the Bar, Inner Temple, 1974, Bencher, 1996. Member: Bar Council, 1994–97; Crown Court Rules Cttee, 1994–2000. Sen. Prosecuting Counsel, Internat. Criminal Tribunal (formerly Internat. War Crimes Tribunal) for former Yugoslavia, 1999–2004. *Recreations:* collecting books and porcelain, cinema, tennis. *Address:* 9 Bedford Row, WC1R 4AZ. *T:* (020) 7489 2727.

KORNICKI, Prof. Peter Francis, DPhil; FBA 2000; Professor of East Asian Studies, since 2007, and Fellow of Robinson College, since 1986, University of Cambridge; *b* 1 May 1950; *er s* of Sqn Leader Franciszek Kornicki and Patience Ceridwen Kornicka (*née* Williams); *m* 1st, 1975, Catharine Olga Mikolaski (*d* 1995); one *s* one *d*; 2nd, 1998, Francesca Orsini. *Educ:* St George's Coll., Weybridge; Lincoln Coll., Oxford (BA 1972; MSc 1975; Hon. Fellow, 2004); St Antony's Coll., Oxford (DPhil 1979). Lectr, Univ. of Tasmania, 1978–82; Associate Prof., Kyoto Univ., 1982–84; Cambridge University: Lectr, 1985–95; Reader in Japanese History and Bibliography, 1995–2001; Prof. of Japanese History and Bibliography, 2001–07; Sandars Reader in Bibliography, 2007–08; Chm., Faculty Bd of Oriental Studies, 1993–95, 2004–05; Dep. Warden, Robinson Coll., 2008–. Pres., European Assoc. for Japanese Studies, 1997–2000. Special Prize, Japan Foundn, 1992. *Publications:* The Reform of Fiction in Meiji Japan, 1982; Early Japanese Books in Cambridge University Library, 1991; (jtly) Cambridge Encyclopedia of Japan, 1993; The Book in Japan: a cultural history, 1998; Early Japanese Books in the Russian State Library, 1999; The Iwakura Embassy, vol. 4, 2002; numerous articles and reviews in jls. *Recreations:* travel, cooking, languages. *Address:* Faculty of Asian and Middle Eastern Studies, Sidgwick Avenue, Cambridge CB3 9DA. *T:* (01223) 335106.

KOSCIUSZKO, Stefan Henry; Chief Executive, Asia House, since 2002; *b* 2 June 1959; *s* of late Konstanty Kosciuszko and of Elisabeth Kerr Kosciuszko (*née* Havelock); *m* 1985, Takako Yamaguchi; two *d*. *Educ:* Gordonstoun Sch.; Divine Mercy Coll., Henley-on-Thames; Keele Univ. (Josiah Wedgwood Meml Award for Hist.; BA Hons (Internat. Relns) 1980). National Westminster Bank, 1980–82; Sumitomo Bank, London/Tokyo, 1982–85; Chemical Bank, London/Tokyo, 1985–88; Schroders: Gen. Manager, Tokyo, 1988–91; Asst Dir, Internat. Finance Dept, London, 1992–95; Director, 1995–98; Hd, Asia-Pacific Equity Capital Markets Regl Investment Banking Cttee and Asian Securities Mgt Cttee, 1995–97; Hd, Corporate Finance, Indonesia, 1997–98; Man. Dir, Gavin Anderson & Co., 1999–2000; Dir, Credit Suisse First Boston, 2000–02. Executive Director: Pakistan Britain Trade and Investment Forum, 2003–; Korea Forum for the Future, 2007–; Sec., Indo-British Partnership Network, 2005–07. Gov., Gainsborough House Mus., 2002–06. Sec., Sudbury Soc., 2002–06; Pres., Sudbury Girls' Football Club, 2003–07. FRSA 2006. *Recreations:* sports, chess, fine wine, antiques, Asian culture, history, hard work and my two daughters—living life to fullest extent possible. *Address:* Abbas Hall, Cornard Tye, Great Cornard, Suffolk CO10 0QD; *e-mail:* stefan@kosciuszko.com; Asia House, 63 New Cavendish Street, W1G 7LP. *Club:* Naval and Military.

KOSHIBA, Prof. Masatoshi, PhD; Professor, Department of Physics, 1970–87, now Emeritus, and Director, International Centre for Elementary Particle Physics, 1984–87, now Senior Counsellor, University of Tokyo; *b* 19 Sept. 1926; *m* 1959, Kyoko Kato. *Educ:* Univ. of Tokyo; Univ. of Rochester, NY (PhD 1955). Res. Associate, Dept of Physics, Univ. of Chicago, 1955–58; Associate Prof., Inst. of Nuclear Study, Univ. of Tokyo, 1958–63; Sen. Res. Associate, Dept of Physics, Univ. of Chicago, 1959–62 (on secondment); Associate Prof., Dept of Physics, Univ. of Tokyo, 1963–70. (Jtly) Nobel Prize in Physics, 2002. *Address:* International Centre for Elementary Particle Physics, University of Tokyo, 7–3–1 Hongo, Bunkyo-ku, Tokyo 113–0033, Japan.

KOSMINSKY, Peter; freelance film director and writer, since 1995; *b* London, 21 April 1956; *s* of Leon and Erika Kosminsky; partner, Helen Marriage; two *d*. *Educ:* Haberdashers' Aske's Sch., Herts; Worcester Coll., Oxford (BA Hons Chem. 1978; MA 1980). Gen. trainee, 1980–82, Asst Producer, 1982–85, BBC; producer and dir, Documentaries Dept, Yorkshire TV, 1985–95; programmes include: The Falklands War: the untold story (UK Broadcast Press Guild Award, BFI Special Award, 1987); Cambodia: children of the killing fields (One World Broadcasting Trust Award, 1988); director: Shoot to Kill, 1990 (UK Broadcast Press and RTS Awards); (film) Wuthering Heights, 1992; dir and producer, The Dying of the Light, 1994; freelance, 1995–: *film:* White Oleander, 2002; *television:* producer and director: No Child of Mine, 1997 (BAFTA Award); Walking on the Moon, 1999; Innocents, 2000; director: Warriors, 1999 (BAFTA and RTS Awards); The Project, 2002; writer and director: The Government Inspector, 2005 (BAFTA and RTS Awards); Britz, 2007 (BAFTA and RTS Awards). Mem. Council, Liberty, 2008–. FRSA 2005; FRTS 2006. Special Award for TV Achievement, BFI, 1989; Alan Clarke Award, BAFTA, 1999. *Recreations:* photography, cinema, being a daddy. *Address:* c/o United Agents, 12–26 Lexington Street, W1F 0LE; *e-mail:* ajones@unitedagents.co.uk. *Clubs:* Groucho, Century.

KOTCH, Laurie, (Mrs J. K. Kotch); *see* Purden, R. L.

KOTSOKOANE, Hon. Joseph Riffat Larry; Commander, Order of Ramatseatsana, 1982; development consultant (agriculture and rural development, formerly human and natural resources), since 1986; Minister of Education, Sports and Culture, Lesotho, 1984–86; *b* 19 Oct. 1922; *s* of Basotho parents, living in Johannesburg, South Africa; *m* 1947, Elizabeth (*née* Molise); two *s* three *d*. *Educ:* BSc (SA); BSc Hons (Witwatersrand); Cert. Agric. (London). Development Officer, Dept of Agric., Basutoland, 1951–54; Agric. Educn Officer i/c of Agric. Sch. for junior field staff, 1955–62; Agric. Extension Officer i/c of all field staff of Min. of Agric., 1962–63; Prin. Agric. Off. (Dep. Dir), Min. of Agric., 1964–66; High Comr for Lesotho, in London, 1966–69; Ambassador to Germany, Holy See, Rome, France, and Austria, 1968–69; Permanent Sec. and Hd of Diplomatic Service, Lesotho, 1969–70; Permanent Sec. for Health, Educn and Social Welfare, Lesotho, 1970–71; High Comr for Lesotho in East Africa, Nigeria and Ghana, 1972–74; Minister: of Foreign Affairs, Lesotho, 1974–75; of Education, 1975–76; of Agriculture, 1976–78;

Perm. Rep. to UN, 1978; Sec. to the Cabinet and Head of CS (Sen. Perm. Sec.), 1978–84. Guest of Min. of Agric., Netherlands, 1955; studied agric. educn, USA (financed by Carnegie Corp. of NY and Ford Foundn), 1960–61; FAO confs in Tunisia, Tanganyika and Uganda, 1962 and 1963; Mem. Lesotho delegn to 24th World Health Assembly, 1971; travelled extensively to study and observe methods of agric. administration, 1964; meetings on nutrition, Berlin and Hamburg, 1966; diplomatic trainee, Brit. Embassy, Bonn, 1966. Hon. PhD Fort Hare, S Africa, 2001. Gold Medal, Fertilizer Soc. of SA, 1998; Merit Award, Nat. African Farmers' Union of SA, 1998; Medal, ARC of SA, 1999. *Recreations:* swimming, amateur dramatics, photography, debating, reading, travelling. *Address:* PO Box 1015, Maseru 100, Lesotho, Southern Africa. *T:* 22312913, *Fax:* 22311769.

KOUCHNER, Bernard Jean, Hon. KBE 2005; Minister of Foreign and European Affairs, France, since 2007; *b* Avignon, 1 Nov. 1939; *s* of Georges Kouchner and Léone Mauric; *m* Evelyne Pisier (marr. diss.); three *c*; one *s* with Christine Ockrent. *Educ:* Faculté de Médicine de Paris (Cert. d'études spéciales in gastroenterology); Dip. digestive endoscopy. Co-founder, Evènement, 1965–69; Mem., Red Cross med. mission to Biafra, 1968–69; humanitarian missions to help victims in most of major natural and industrial disasters and political crises, 1968–; Co-founder, Actuel jl, 1970; Co-founder and Pres., Médecins Sans Frontières, 1971–79; Gastroenterologist, Cochin Hosp., Paris, 1975–87. Minister of State: with resp. for Social Integration, 1988; with resp. for Humanitarian Action, 1988–92; Minister: for Health and Humanitarian Action, 1992–93; MEP (Réunir/Socialiste), 1994–97; Pres., Commn for Develt and Co-operation, Eur. Parlt, 1994–96; Minister of State for Health, 1997–98, for Health and Social Action, 1998–99; UN Sec. Gen.'s Special Rep. for Kosovo, 1999–2001; Minister Delegate for Health, 2001–02. Mem., Socialist Party, 1997–2007. Prof. of Health and Develt, Conservatoire national des arts et métiers, 2002–07. Lectr, Harvard Sch. of Public Health, 2003. Founder Chm., BK Consultants. Mem., Bd of Dirs, PlaNet Finance. Founder, 1980, Pres., 1980–84, Hon. Pres., 1984–88, Médecins du Monde; Founder, Volontaires européens du développement, 1988. Chm., ESTHER public interest gp, 2001–07. Pres., then Hon. Pres., Réunir, 1993–2007. Member: Hon. Cttee, Children Action; Bd of Dirs, Internat. Women's Coalition. Founder Mem., La chaîne de l'espoir. Writer, TV series, under pseudonym Bernard Gridaine: Médecins de nuit, 1978; Hôtel de police, 1985. Prix Dag Hammarskjöld, 1979; Prix Athinai de la fondation Alexandre Onassis, 1981; Prix Europa, 1984; Prix européen des Droits de l'homme, 2005. *Publications:* (jtly) La France sauvage, 1970; (jtly) Les Voraces, 1974; L'Ile de lumière, 1979 (Prix Louise Weiss, Eur. Parlt); Charité business, 1986; (jtly) Le Devoir d'ingérence, 1988; Les Nouvelles solidarités, 1989; Le Malheur des autres, 1991; (jtly) Dieu et les hommes, 1993; Ce que je crois, 1995; Vingt idées pour l'an 2000, 1995; La Dictature médicale, 1996; Le Premier qui dit la vérité, 2002; Les Guerriers de la paix: du Kosovo à l'Irak, 2004; (jtly) Quand tu seras président, 2004; Deux ou trois choses que je sais de nous, 2006; La Fabrique démocratique, 2006; articles. *Address:* Ministère des Affaires Etrangères, 37 quai d'Orsay, 75007 Paris, France.

KOUMI, Margaret, (Maggie); freelance editorial consultant, since 2001; *b* 15 July 1942; *d* of Yiasoumi Koumi and Melexidia Paraskeva; *m* 1980, Ramon Sola. *Educ:* Buckingham Gate Sch., London. Sec., Thomas Cook Travel, 1957–60; Sub-Editor and writer, Boyfriend and Trend magazines, 1960–66; Sub-Editor, TV World, 1967–68; Production Editor, 1968–70, Editor, 1970–86, 19 magazine; Man. Editor, Practical Parenting and Practical Health, 1986–87; Jt Ed., 1988–93, Ed., 1993–2001, Hello! mag. (the magazine has won several awards). *Recreation:* reading.

KOUZARIDES, Prof. Tony; Royal Society Napier Research Professor of Cancer Biology, since 2002, and Deputy Director, Wellcome Trust/Cancer Research UK Gurdon Institute, since 2004, University of Cambridge; *b* 17 Jan. 1958; *s* of Takis and Annie Kouzarides; *m* 1984, Penny Hall; one *s* one *d*. *Educ:* Univ. of Leeds (BSc Genetics 1981); Univ. of Cambridge (PhD Virology 1984). Postdoctoral Fellow: MRC Lab. of Molecular Biology, Cambridge, 1984–86; New York Univ. Med. Center, 1986–89; Res. Associate, Dept of Pathology, Univ. of Cambridge, 1989–91; Wellcome Trust/Cancer Research UK (formerly Cancer Research Campaign) Institute, University of Cambridge: Sen. Res. Associate, 1991–96; Reader, 1996–99; Prof. of Molecular Cancer Biology, 1999–2001; Hd of CRUK Labs, 2002–04. Co-founder and Director: Abcom Ltd, 1998–; Chroma Therapeutics, 2001–. *Publications:* various articles in many scientific jls. *Recreations:* films, music. *Address:* The Wellcome Trust/Cancer Research UK Gurdon Institute, University of Cambridge, Tennis Court Road, Cambridge CB2 1QR. *T:* (01223) 334112, *Fax:* (01223) 334089; *e-mail:* tk106@mole.bio.cam.ac.uk.

KOVACEVICH, Stephen; pianist and conductor; *b* 17 Oct. 1940; *s* of Nicholas Kovacevich and Loreta (*née* Zuban, later Bishop). *Educ:* studied under Lev Shorr and Myra Hess. Solo and orchestral debut, San Francisco, USA 1951; London debut, Nov. 1961. First known professionally as Stephen Bishop, then as Stephen Bishop-Kovacevich, and since 1991 as Stephen Kovacevich. Concert tours: in England, Europe and USA, with many of the world's leading orchestras, incl. New York Philharmonic, Los Angeles Philharmonic, Israel Philharmonic, Amsterdam Concertgebouw, London Symphony, London Philharmonic, and BBC Symphony. Has appeared at Edinburgh, Bath, Berlin and San Sebastian Festivals. Gave 1st performance of Richard Rodney Bennett's Piano Concerto, 1969 (this work is dedicated to and has been recorded by him, under Alexander Gibson). Performed all Mozart Piano concertos, 1969–71; recorded all Beethoven sonatas, 2003. Principal Guest Conductor: Australian Chamber Orch., 1987–91; Zagreb Philharmonic Orch.; Music Dir, Irish Chamber Orch., 1990–93. Edison Award for his recording of Bartok's 2nd Piano Concerto and Stravinsky's Piano Concerto, with BBC Symphony Orch., under Colin Davis; Gramophone Award, 1993 and Stereo Review Record of the Year for Brahms' Piano Concerto No 1 with LPO, under Wolfgang Sawallisch. *Recreations:* snooker, chess, films, tennis. *Address:* c/o Van Walsum Management, The Tower Building, 11 York Road, SE1 7NX. *T:* (020) 7902 0520.

KOVÁCS, László; Member, European Commission, since 2004; *b* 3 July 1939; *m*; one *d*. *Educ:* Petrik Lajos Tech. Sch. for Chem. Industry, Budapest; Univ. of Econ. Scis, Budapest; Coll. of Politics. Chem. Technician, Medicolor, and Kőbánya Pharmaceutical Works, 1957–66; Consultant and Dep. Hd, Dept for Internat. Relns, Hungarian Socialist Workers' Party, 1975–86; Dep. Foreign Minister, Hungary, 1986–89; Sec. of State, Min. of Foreign Affairs, 1989–90; MP, 1990–2004; Minister for Foreign Affairs, 1994–98, 2002–04. Leader, Hungarian Socialist Party, 1998–2004. *Address:* European Commission, Rue de la Loi 200, 1049 Brussels, Belgium.

KOVOOR, Rev. George Iype; Principal, Trinity College, Bristol, since 2005; Chaplain to the Queen, since 2003; *b* 6 June 1957. *Educ:* Delhi Univ. (BA 1977); Serampore Univ. (BD 1980); Christian Medical Assoc. of India (Dip. Counselling and Hosp. Chaplaincy 1985); Union Biblical Seminary, Yavatmal. Ordained deacon and priest, 1980, Ch of N India; Curate, Shanti Niwas Ch, Faridabad, 1980–82; Presbyter: Santokh Majra Ch, 1982–83; St Paul's Cathedral, Ambala, 1984–88; Nat. Youth Dir, Ch of N India, 1987–90; Principal Chaplain, St Stephen's Hosp., Delhi, 1988–90; Curate, St Augustine's, Derby, and Minister, Derby Asian Christian Ministry Project, 1990–94; Tutor, 1994–97, Principal, 1997–2004, Crowther Hall CMS Trng Coll.; Mission Educn Dir, CMS, 1997–2005; Dir, Centre for Anglican Communion Studies, Selly Oak. Hon. Canon, Worcester Cathedral, 2001–. *Address:* Trinity College, Stoke Hill, Bristol BS9 1JP.

KOWALSKI, Gregor; Parliamentary Counsel, since 2005; *b* 7 Oct. 1949; *s* of Mieczyslaw Kowalski and Jeanie Hutcheson Kowalski (*née* MacDonald); *m* 1974, Janet McFarlane Pillatt; two *s*. *Educ:* Airdrie Academy; Strathclyde Univ. (LLB 1971). Apprentice, then Asst Solicitor, Levy & McRae, Glasgow, 1971–74; Procurator Fiscal Depute, Glasgow, 1974–78; Asst, later Deputy Parly Draftsman for Scotland and Asst Legal Sec. to Lord Advocate, 1978–87; seconded to Govt of Seychelles as Legal Draftsman, 1982–83; Scottish Parly Counsel and Asst Legal Sec. to Lord Advocate, 1987–99; Scottish Parly Counsel to UK Govt, 1999–2000; Dep. Parly Counsel, 2000–05. *Recreations:* choral singing, opera. *Address:* 36 Whitehall, SW1A 2AY. *T:* (020) 7210 6622.

KRAEMER, (Thomas Whilhelm) Nicholas; conductor; *b* 7 March 1945; *s* of William Paul Kraemer and Helen Bartrum; *m* 1984, Elizabeth Mary Anderson; two *s* two *d* (and one *s* decd). *Educ:* Edinburgh Acad.; Lancing Coll.; Dartington Coll. of Arts; Nottingham Univ. (BMus 1967). ARCM. Harpsichordist with Acad. of St Martin in the Fields, 1972–80, with Monteverdi Choir and Orchestra, 1970–80; Musical Director: Unicorn Opera, Abingdon, 1971–75; West Eleven Children's Opera, 1971–88; Founder and Dir, Raglan Baroque Players, 1978–2003; Principal Conductor, Divertimenti, 1979–89; Permanent Guest Conductor: Manchester Camerata, 1995– (Principal Conductor, 1992–95); Music of the Baroque, Chicago, 2002–; Guest Conductor, English Chamber Orch., 1975–84; Conductor, Glyndebourne, 1980–82; Musical Dir, Opera 80, 1980–83; Associate Conductor, BBC Scottish SO, 1983–85; Artistic Director: London Bach Orch., 1985–93; Irish Chamber Orch., 1985–90; Guest Conductor: Scottish Chamber Orch.; Orch. of Age of Enlightenment; Northern Sinfonia; Israel Chamber Orch.; BBC Nat. Orch. of Wales; City of London Sinfonia; Hallé Orch.; St Paul Chamber Orch. (USA); Berlin Philharmonic; ENO; Philharmonia Baroque (USA); Bergen Philharmonic; Chicago SO; Detroit SO; Toronto SO. Prog. Dir, Bath Fest., 1994. Recordings include works by Vivaldi, Locatelli, Mozart, Handel. *Recreation:* keeping fit. *Address:* c/o Caroline Phillips Management, The Old Brushworks, 56 Pickwick Road, Corsham, Wilts SN13 9BX.

KRAMER, Prof. Ivor Robert Horton, OBE 1984; MDS; DSc (Med); FDSRCS, FFDRCSI, Hon. FRACDS, FRCPath; Emeritus Professor of Oral Pathology, University of London; *b* 20 June 1923; *yr s* of late Alfred Bertie and Agnes Maud Kramer; *m* 1st, 1946, Elisabeth Dalley (*d* 1978); one *s*; 2nd, 1979, Mrs Dorothy Toller (*d* 1985); 3rd, 1991, Mrs Virginia Webster. *Educ:* Royal Dental Hosp. of London Sch. of Dental Surgery; MDS 1955; DSc (Med) London 1993. FDSRCS 1960 (LDSRCS 1944); FRCPath 1970 (MRCPath 1964); FFDRCSI 1973. Asst to Pathologist, Princess Louise (Kensington) Hosp. for Children, 1944–48; Wright Fleming Inst. of Microbiol., 1948–49; Instr in Dental Histology, Royal Dental Hosp. Sch. of Dental Surgery, 1944–50; Asst Pathologist, Royal Dental Hosp., 1950–56; Institute of Dental Surgery: Lectr in Dental Path., 1949–50, Sen. Lectr, 1950–57; Reader in Oral Path., 1957–62; Prof. of Oral Path., 1962–83; Sub-dean, 1950–70; Dean and Dir of Studies, 1970–83; Head, Dept of Path., Eastman Dental Hosp., 1950–83. Civilian Cons. in Dental Path., RN, 1967–83. Member: WHO Expert Adv. Panel on Dental Health, 1975–97; Bd of Faculty of Dental Surgery, RCS, 1964–80, Council, RCS, 1977–80; GDC, 1973–84; Mem., Council for Postgrad. Med. Educn in Eng. and Wales, 1972–77 (Chm., Dental Cttee, 1972–77); Pres., Odontological Section, RSocMed, 1973–74; Pres., British Div., Internat. Assoc. for Dental Res., 1974–77. Hon. Pres. of the Assoc., 1974–75. Editor, Archives of Oral Biology, 1959–69. Lectures: Wilkinson, Manchester, 1962; Charles Tomes, 1969, Webb Johnson, 1981, RCS; Holme, UCH, 1969; Elwood Meml, QUB, 1970; Hutchinson, Edinburgh, 1971; Wilkinson, IDS, 1987. Hon. FRACDS 1978. Howard Mummery Prize, BDA, 1966; Maurice Down Award, Brit. Assoc. of Oral Surgeons, 1974; Colyer Gold Medal, FDS, RCS, 1985. Dr *hc* Helsinki, 2000. *Publications:* (with R. B. Lucas) Bacteriology for Students of Dental Surgery, 1954, 3rd edn 1966; (with J. J. Pindborg and H. Torloni) World Health Organization International Histological Classification of Tumours: Odontogenic Tumours, Jaw Cysts and Allied Lesions, 1972 (2nd edn, with J. J. Pindborg and M. Shear, as World Health Organisation Histological Typing of Odontogenic Tumours, 1992); (with B. Cohen) Scientific Foundations of Dentistry, 1976; numerous papers in med. and dental jls. *Address:* 11 Sheepcote Close, Beaconsfield, Bucks HP9 1SX. *T:* (01494) 680306.

KRAMER, Prof. Jeffrey, PhD; CEng, FIET; Professor of Distributed Computing, Imperial College of Science, Technology and Medicine, University of London, since 1995; *b* 7 Jan. 1949; *s* of Dr Bobby Kramer and Joyce Kramer (*née* Feitelberg); *m* 1981, Nitza Omer; one *s* one *d*. *Educ:* Univ. of Natal (BSc Eng Electrical Engrg 1971); Imperial College, London (MSc Computing 1972; PhD Computing 1979). CEng 1986; FIET (FIEE 1992). Department of Computing, Imperial College, London: programmer, 1973–75; Res. Asst, 1975–76; Lectr, 1976–87; Sen. Lectr, 1987–90; Reader in Distributed Computing, 1990–95; Head of Dept, 1999–2004; Dean, Faculty of Engineering, 2006–. Ernest Oppenheimer Meml Trust/W. D. Wilson Vis. Fellow, S Africa, 1995. Computing Expert, World Bank Project for Provincial Univs, Peoples Republic of China, 1991. Founding Mem., Wkg Gp on Requirements Engrg, IFIP, 1995; Chm., Steering Cttee, Internat. Conf. on Software Engrg, 2000–02. Ed.-in-Chief, IEEE Trans on Software Engrng, 2006. FACM 2000; FCGI 2007. (Jtly) Outstanding Res. Award, ACM Special Interest Gp on Software Engrng, 2005. *Publications:* (with M. S. Sloman) Distributed Systems and Computer Networks, 1986 (trans. Japanese and German); (ed jtly) Software Process Modelling and Technology, 1994; (with J. Magee) Concurrency: state models & Java programs, 1999; contrib. over 200 papers to learned internat. jls on software engrg, distributed computing, requirements engrg, software architectures and model checking. *Recreations:* fanatical about films and music, travel, tennis, ski-ing, mountain walking, diving and surfing, whenever the opportunity arises. *Address:* Department of Computing, Imperial College London, SW7 2AZ. *T:* (020) 7594 8271, *Fax:* (020) 7594 8282.

KRAMER, Prof. Dame Leonie (Judith), AC 1993; DBE 1983 (OBE 1976); DPhil; Professor of Australian Literature, University of Sydney, 1968–89, now Professor Emeritus; Chancellor, University of Sydney Senate, 1991–2001 (Deputy Chancellor, 1989–91); *b* 1 Oct. 1924; *d* of Alfred and Gertrude Gibson; *m* 1952, Harold Kramer (*d* 1988); two *d*. *Educ:* Presbyterian Ladies Coll., Melbourne; Univ. of Melbourne (BA 1945); St Hugh's Coll., Oxford Univ. (DPhil 1953; Hon. Fellow, 1994); MA Sydney, 1989. FAHA; FACE. Tutor and Lectr, Univ. of Melb., 1945–49; Tutor and Postgrad. Student, St Hugh's Coll., Oxford, 1949–52; Lectr, Canberra University Coll., 1954–56; Lectr, subseq. Sen. Lectr and Associate Prof., Univ. of NSW, 1958–68. Chm., Quadrant Mag., 1986–99. Member: Univs Council, 1974–86; NSW Bd of Studies, 1990–; Adv. Bd, World Book Encyclopaedia, 1989–99; Internat. Adv. Cttee, Encyc. Brit., 1991–98; Council, Sci. Foundn for Physics, Univ. of Sydney, 2002–. Director: Australia and NZ Banking Gp, 1983–94; Western Mining Corp., 1984–96. Mem., NSW Council, Aust. Inst. of Co. Dirs, 1992–2001. Comr, Electricity Commn, NSW, 1988–95. Chairman: ABC, 1982–83; Operation Rainbow Aust. Ltd, 1996–2001; Chm., 1987–91, Dep. Chm.,

1991–95, Bd of Dirs, Nat. Inst. of Dramatic Art. Dir, St Vincent's Hosp., Sydney, 1988–93. Mem. Council, Nat. Roads & Motorists Assoc., 1984–95; National President: Australia-Britain Soc., 1984–93; Order of Australia Assoc., 2001–04; Member Council: Asia Soc., 1991–2000; Foundn for Young Australians, 1989–. Sen. Fellow, Inst. of Public Affairs, 1988–96. Hon. Fellow: St Andrew's Coll., Univ. of Sydney, 2002; Janet Clarke Hall, Univ. of Melbourne, 2005. Hon. DLitt: Tasmania, 1977; Queensland, 1991; New South Wales, 1992; Hon. LLD: Melbourne, 1983; ANU, 1984. Britannica Award, 1986. *Publications:* as L. J. Gibson: Henry Handel Richardson and Some of Her Sources, 1954; as Leonie Kramer: A Companion to Australia Felix, 1962; Myself when Laura: fact and fiction in Henry Handel Richardson's school career, 1966; Henry Handel Richardson, 1967, repr. as contrib. to Six Australian Writers, 1971; (with Robert D. Eagleson) Language and Literature: a synthesis, 1976; (with Robert D. Eagleson) A Guide to Language and Literature, 1977; A. D. Hope, 1979; (ed and introd) The Oxford History of Australian Literature, 1981; (ed with Adrian Mitchell) The Oxford Anthology of Australian Literature, 1985; (ed and introd) My Country: Australian poetry and short stories—two hundred years, 1985; (ed and introd) James McAuley, 1988; (ed) Collected Poems of David Campbell, 1989; (ed) Collected Poems of James McAuley, 1995. *Recreations:* gardening, music. *Address:* 12 Vaucluse Road, Vaucluse, NSW 2030, Australia. *T:* (2) 93514164.

KRAMER, Stephen Ernest; QC 1995; **His Honour Judge Kramer;** a Circuit Judge, since 2003, at the Central Criminal Court, since 2005; *b* 12 Sept. 1947; *s* of Frederic Kramer and Lotte Karoline Kramer (*née* Wertheimer); *m* 1978, Miriam Leopold; one *s* one *d*. *Educ:* Hampton Grammar Sch.; Keble Coll., Oxford (BA 1969; MA 1987); Université de Nancy. Called to the Bar, Gray's Inn, 1970, Bencher, 2002; Standing Counsel to HM Customs and Excise (Crime), S Eastern Circuit, 1989–95; a Recorder, 1991–2003; Hd of Chambers, 2 Hare Court, 1996–2003. Chm., Liaison Cttee, Bar Council/Inst. of Barristers' Clerks, 1996–99; Criminal Bar Association: Chm., 2000–01; Vice-Chm., 1999–2000; acting Vice-Chm., 1998–99. Contested (L), Twickenham, Feb. and Oct. 1974. *Recreations:* swimming, walking, theatre, watching Rugby Union. *Address:* Central Criminal Court, Old Bailey, EC4M 7EH.

KRAMER, Susan Veronica; MP (Lib Dem) Richmond Park, since 2005; *b* 21 July 1950; *m* 1972, John Davis Kramer; one *s* one *d*. *Educ:* St Hilda's Coll., Oxford (BA PPE, MA 1972); Illinois Univ. (MBA Business/Finance 1982). Staff Associate, Nat. Acad. of Engrg, 1972–73; Second Vice-Pres., Continental Bank, USA, 1982–88; Vice-Pres., Corporate Finance, Citibank/Citicorp, USA, 1988–92; Chief Operating Officer, Future Water Internat., 1992–95; Partner, Kramer & Associates, 1995–99. Board Mem., CAIB Infrastructure Project Advrs, 1997–99; Director: Infrastructure Capital Partners Ltd, 1999–; Speciality Scanners plc, 2001–. Mem. Bd, Transport for London, 2000–05. London Mayoral candidate, 2000. *Publication:* (contrib.) Harnessing the Markets to Achieve Environmental Goals, 2004. *Recreations:* dog walking, opera, theatre, reading, rowing. *Address:* House of Commons, SW1A 0AA. *T:* (020) 7219 2859, *Fax:* (020) 7219 5946; *e-mail:* info@susankramer.org.uk; (constituency office) Parkway House, Suite 302, Sheen Lane, East Sheen SW14 8LS. *T:* and *Fax:* (020) 8876 8914. *Clubs:* National Liberal, Capital.

KRAYE, Prof. Jill Adrian; Professor of the History of Renaissance Philosophy, since 2004, Librarian, since 2002, Warburg Institute; *b* 27 Aug. 1947; *d* of Philip M. and Frances B. Kraye; *m* 1986, Martin Charles Davies. *Educ:* Univ. of Calif, Berkeley (BA Hist. 1969); Columbia Univ. (MA Hist. 1970; PhD 1991). Warburg Institute: Asst Librarian (Acad.), 1974–86; Lectr in Hist. of Philos., 1987–96; Sen. Lectr, 1996–98; Reader in Hist. of Renaissance Philos., 1999–2004. Vis. Prof., Seminar für Geistesgeschichte und Philosophie der Renaissance, Ludwig-Maximilians Univ., Munich, 2002. Vice-Pres., European Soc. for Early Modern Philosophy, 2007–. Jt-Ed., Jl Warburg and Courtauld Insts, 1997–. *Publications:* (ed) The Cambridge Companion to Renaissance Humanism, 1996 (trans. Spanish 1998); (ed) Cambridge Translations of Renaissance Philosophical Texts, 2 vols, 1997; Classical Traditions in Renaissance Philosophy, 2002; contrib. articles to Jl Hist. of Philosophy, Renaissance Studies, Rinascimento and other jls. *Recreations:* reading, cinema, feeding squirrels, avoiding writing book reviews. *Address:* Warburg Institute, Woburn Square, WC1H 0AB. *T:* (020) 7862 8916, *Fax:* (020) 7862 8939; *e-mail:* Jill.Kraye@sas.ac.uk.

KREBS, Baron *cr* 2007 (Life Peer), of Wytham in the county of Oxfordshire; **John Richard Krebs,** Kt 1999; DPhil; FRS 1984; Principal, Jesus College, Oxford, since 2005; *b* 11 April 1945; *s* of Sir Hans Adolf Krebs, FRCP, FRS and Margaret Cicely Krebs; *m* 1968, Katharine Anne Fullerton; two *d*. *Educ:* City of Oxford High School; Pembroke College, Oxford (BA 1966; MA 1970; DPhil 1970). Asst Prof., Univ. of British Columbia, 1970–73; Lectr in Zoology, UCNW, 1973–75; University of Oxford: Univ. Lectr in Zoology, 1976–88; Royal Soc. Res. Prof., Dept of Zoology, 1988–2005 (on leave of absence, 1994–99); Fellow, Pembroke Coll., 1981–2005 (E. P. Abraham Fellow, 1981–88; Hon. Fellow, 2005). Dir, AFRC Unit of Ecology and Behaviour, NERC Unit of Behavioural Ecology, 1989–94; Chief Exec., NERC, 1994–99; Chm., Food Standards Agency, 2000–05. Storer Lectr, Univ. of Calif, 1985; Croonian Lectr, Royal Soc., 2004. Mem., AFRC, 1988–94 (Animals Res. Cttee, 1990–94; sen. scientific consultant, 1991–94). President: Internat. Soc. for Behavioral Ecology, 1988–90; Assoc. for the Study of Animal Behaviour, 1993–94. Scientific Member: Max Planck Soc., 1985–; Council, Zoological Soc. of London, 1991–92; Academia Europæa, 1995. FMedSci 2004. Hon. Mem., British Ecol Soc., 1999; Foreign Mem., Amer. Philosophical Soc., 2000; Hon. Foreign Mem., Amer. Acad. Arts and Scis, 2000; Hon. Fellow, German Ornithologists' Union, 2003; Foreign Associate, US Nat. Acad. of Scis, 2004. Hon. Fellow: Cardiff Univ., 1999; UWIC, 2006; Univ. of Wales, Bangor, 2006; Hon. FZS 2006. Hon. DSc: Sheffield, 1993; Wales, Birmingham, 1997; Exeter, 1998; Warwick, 2000; Cranfield, Kent, Plymouth, 2001; QUB, Heriot-Watt, 2002; South Bank, 2003; Lancaster, 2005; Guelph, 2006; DUniv Stirling, 2000. Scientific Medal, Zool Soc., 1981; Bicentenary Medal, Linnaean Soc., 1983; Frink Medal, Zool Soc., 1997; Elliot Coues Award, Amer. Ornithol Union, 1999; Medal, Assoc. for Study of Animal Behaviour, 2000; Benjamin Ward Richardson Gold Medal, RSH, 2002; Wooldridge Medal, BVA, 2003; Lord Rayner Medal, RCP, 2005; Outstanding Achievement Award, Soc. for Food Hygiene Technology, 2005; Harben Gold Medal, RIPH, 2006. *Publications:* Behavioural Ecology, 1978, 4th edn 1997; Introduction to Behavioural Ecology, 1981, 3rd edn 1993; Foraging Theory, 1986; Behavioural and Neural Aspects of Learning and Memory, 1991; articles in Animal Behaviour, Jl of Animal Ecology. *Recreations:* gardening, violin, running, walking, cooking. *Address:* Jesus College, Oxford OX1 3DW; *e-mail:* principal@jesus.ox.ac.uk.

KREBS, Prof. Edwin Gerhard, MD; Professor, Departments of Pharmacology and Biochemistry, University of Washington, Seattle, 1983–88, now Professor Emeritus (Professor and Chairman, Department of Pharmacology, 1977–83); *b* Iowa, 6 June 1918; *m* 1945, Virginia French; one *s* two *d*. *Educ:* Univ. of Illinois (AB Chem. 1940); Washington Univ. Sch. of Med., St Louis, Mo (MD 1943). Intern and Asst Resident in Internal Med., Barnes Hosp., St Louis, Mo, 1944–45; Res. Fellow, Washington Univ. Sch. of Med., St Louis, 1946–48; University of Washington, Seattle: Asst Prof. of Biochem., 1948–52; Associate Prof., 1952–57; Prof., 1957–68; Asst Dean for Planning, Sch. of Med., 1966–68; Prof. and Chm., Dept of Biol Chem., Sch. of Med., Univ. of Calif, Davis, 1968–76; Howard Hughes Medical Institute: Investigator, 1977–80; Sen. Investigator, 1980–90, Emeritus, 1991–. Member: Editl Bd, Jl Biol Chem., 1965–70 (Associate Ed., 1972–93); Editl Adv. Bd, Biochem., 1971–76; Editl and Adv. Bd, Molecular Pharmacol., 1972–77; Editl Advr, Molecular and Cellular Biochem., 1987–. Member: Amer. Soc. for Biochem. and Molecular Biol., 1951–; Amer. Acad. Arts and Scis, 1971–; Nat. Acad. Scis, 1973–; Amer. Soc. Pharmacology and Exptl Therapeutics, 1980–. Hon. DSc Geneva, 1979. Numerous awards; (jtly) Nobel Prize in Physiology or Medicine, 1992. *Address:* Department of Pharmacology and Biochemistry, Box 357370, University of Washington, Seattle, WA 98195–7370, USA.

KREISEL, Prof. Georg, FRS 1966; Professor Emeritus of Logic and the Foundations of Mathematics, Stanford University, Stanford, California, USA; *b* 15 Sept. 1923. *Address:* Institut für Wissenschaftstheorie, Internationales Forschungszentrum, Mönchsberg 2, 5020 Salzburg, Austria.

KREMER, Gidon; violinist; founder and Artistic Director, Kremerata Baltica, since 1997; *b* 27 Feb. 1947. *Educ:* Riga Sch. of Music; Moscow Conservatory. First Prize, Internat. Tchaikovsky Competition, Moscow, 1970. Has played with most major internat. orchestras including: Berlin Philharmonic; Boston Symphony; Concertgebouw; London Philharmonic; LA Philharmonic; NY Philharmonic; Philadelphia; Royal Philharmonic; Vienna Philharmonic. Founded Lockenhaus Fest., Austria, 1981. *Address:* c/o ICM Artists, 40 West 57th Street, New York, NY 10019, USA.

KREMER, Lorraine; *see* Sutherland, L.

KRETZMER, Herbert; journalist and lyricist; *b* Kroonstad, S Africa, 5 Oct. 1925; *s* of William and Tilly Kretzmer; *m* 1st, 1961, Elisabeth Margaret Wilson (marr. diss., 1973); one *s* one *d*; 2nd, 1988, Sybil Sever. *Educ:* Kroonstad High Sch.; Rhodes Univ., Grahamstown. Entered journalism, 1946, writing weekly cinema newsreel commentaries and documentary films for African Film Productions, Johannesburg. Reporter and entertainment columnist, Sunday Express, Johannesburg, 1951–54; feature writer and columnist, Daily Sketch, London, 1954–59; Columnist, Sunday Dispatch, London, 1959–61; feature writer and theatre critic, Daily Express, 1962–78; TV critic, Daily Mail, 1979–87. TV Critic of the Year, Philips Industries Award, 1980; commended in British Press Awards, 1981. As lyric writer, contributed weekly songs to: That Was The Week…, Not So Much A Programme…, BBC 3, That's Life. Wrote lyrics of Goodness Gracious Me, 1960 (Ivor Novello Award) and Yesterday When I was Young, 1969 (ASCAP award); Gold record for She, 1974; Our Man Crichton, Shaftesbury Theatre, 1964 (book and lyrics); The Four Musketeers, Drury Lane, 1967 (lyrics); Les Misérables, RSC, 1985 (lyrics (Tony Award, 1987; Grammy Award, 1988)); Marguerite, Haymarket Th., 2008 (lyrics); *film:* Can Heironymus Merkin Ever Forget Mercy Humppe And Find True Happiness?, 1969 (lyrics); has also written lyrics for other films, and for TV programmes. Hon. Dr of Letters, Richmond Coll., Amer. Internat. Univ. in London, 1996. Jimmy Kennedy Award, British Acad. of Songwriters, Composers and Authors, 1989. Chevalier de l'Ordre des Arts et des Lettres, 1988. *Publications:* Our Man Crichton, 1965; (jointly) Every Home Should Have One, 1970. *Address:* c/o Berlin Associates, 14 Floral Street, WC2E 9DH. *Clubs:* Garrick, Royal Automobile.

KRIER, Léon; architect; *b* Luxembourg, 7 April 1946. *Educ:* Univ. of Stuttgart. Asst to James Stirling, London, 1968–70, 1973–74; Project Partner, J. P. Kleihues, Berlin, 1971–72; private architectl practice, London, 1974–. Lecturer: Architectl Assoc. Sch., 1973–76; Princeton Univ., 1974–77; RCA, 1977; Jefferson Prof. of Architecture, Univ. of Virginia, 1982; Davenport Prof., Yale Univ., 1990–91, 2002, 2004–05. *Projects* include: Spitalfields Market, 1987; Poundbury Farm develt, 1989; Justice Palace, Luxembourg, 1994; Village Hall, Windsor, Fla, 1997; Archaeol Mus., Sintra, Portugal, 1999; Heulebrug Urban Develt, Knokke, Belgium, 1998; Urban Centre Alessandria, Italy, 1999; Masterplans: Hardelot, France, 2000; Noordwijk, Holland, 2002; Newquay Growth Area, for Duchy of Cornwall, 2002–06; Cayala, Guatemala City, 2003; Meriam Park, Chico, Calif, 2003; New Educnl Campus and Urban Centre, Osio Sotto, Bergamo, Italy, 2005–; Sch. of Architecture Auditorium, Miami Univ., 2002; Brasserie Val d'Europe, Eurodisney, 2000–03; Market Tower, Seaside, Fla, 2004–06; furniture designs for Giorgetti, Italy, 1991–; garden furniture for the Prince of Wales, Duchy Originals, 1995–2003. *Exhibitions* include: Triennale, Milan, 1973; Inst. for Architecture and Urban Studies, NY, 1978; Walker Art Center, Minn and US tour, 1980; Verona, 1980; Drawings, Max Protetch Gall., NY, 1981; ICA, 1983; Max Protetch Gall., NY, 1984; solo exhibn, MOMA, NY, 1985. Jefferson Meml Medal, 1985; Chicago AIA Award, 1987; City of Berlin Architecture Prize, 1987; Eur. Culture Prize, 1995; Silver Medal, Acad. Française, 1997; Richard Driehaus Prize, 2003; Lifetime Achievement Award, Congress of New Urbanism, 2006. *Publications* include: (ed) James Stirling: Buildings and Projects, 1974; (ed) Cities Within the City, 1977; Rational Architecture, 1978; Houses, Palaces, Cities, 1984; Albert Speer: architecture 1932–42, 1985; The Completion of Washington DC, 1986; Atlantis, 1987; New Classicism, 1990; Architecture and Urban Design 1967–1992, 1992; Architecture: choice or fate, 1997; articles in jls.

KRIKLER, Dennis Michael, MD; FRCP; Consultant Cardiologist, Hammersmith Hospital, and Senior Lecturer in Cardiology, Royal Postgraduate Medical School, 1973–94, now Emeritus; *b* 10 Dec. 1928; *s* of late Barnet and Eva Krikler; *m* 1955, Anne (*née* Winterstein); one *s* one *d*. *Educ:* Muizenberg High Sch.; Univ. of Cape Town, S Africa. Ho. Phys. and Registrar, Groote Schuur Hosp., 1952–55; Fellow, Lahey Clinic, Boston, 1956; C. J. Adams Meml Travelling Fellowship, 1956; Sen. Registrar, Groote Schuur Hosp., 1957–58; Consultant Physician: Salisbury Central Hosp., Rhodesia, 1958–66; Prince of Wales's Hosp., London, 1966–73; Consultant Cardiologist, Ealing Hosp., 1973–89. Expert Clinicien en Cardiologie, Ministère des Affaires Sociales, Santé, France, 1983. Visiting Professor: Baylor, Indiana and Birmingham Univs, 1985; Boston, Los Angeles and Kentucky, 1988; Lectures: Internat., Amer. Heart Assoc., 1984 (Paul Dudley White Citation for internat. achievement); George Burch Meml, Assoc. of Univ. Cardiologists, 1989; Joseph Welker Meml, Univ. of Kansas, 1989; Denolin, Eur. Soc. of Cardiology, 1990; Hideo Ueda, Japanese Soc. of Electrocardiology, 1990; Howard Burchell, Univ. of Minnesota, 1991. Member, British Cardiac Soc., 1971– (Treasurer, 1976–81); Hon. Member: Soc. Française de Cardiologie, 1981–; Soc. di Cultura Medica Vercellese, Italy; Soc. de Cardiologia de Levante, Spain. Editor, British Heart Journal, 1981–91 (Editor Emeritus, 1992–); Member, Editorial Committee: Cardiovascular Res., 1975–91; Archives des Maladies du Coeur et des Vaisseaux, 1980–; Revista Latina de Cardiologia, 1980–; ACCEL Audiotape Jl, 1987–2000. Mem. Scientific Council, Revista Portuguesa de Cardiologia, 1982–. FACC 1971; Fellow, Eur. Soc. of Cardiology, 1988 (Medal of Honour, 1990). Hon. Fellow, Council on Clin. Cardiol., Amer. Heart Assoc., 1984. Freeman: Soc. of Apothecaries, 1989; City of London, 1990. McCullough Prize, 1949; Sir William Osler Award, Miami Univ., 1981; Silver Medal, British Cardiac Soc., 1992. Chevalier, Legion of Honour (France), 1999. *Publications:* Cardiac Arrhythmias (with J. F. Goodwin), 1975; (with A. Zanchetti) Calcium antagonism in cardiovascular therapy, 1981; (with D. A. Chamberlain and W. J. McKenna) Amiodarone and arrhythmias, 1983; (jtly) 20th Century British Cardiology, 2000; papers on cardiology in British, American and French jls. *Recreations:* reading (and also writing), especially history (contemporary and cardiological); photography. *Address:* 2 Garden Court, Grove End Road, NW8 9PP.

KRIKLER, His Honour Leonard Gideon; a Circuit Judge, 1984–2001; *b* 23 May 1929; *s* of late Major James Harold Krikler, OBE, ED, and Tilly Krikler; *m* 1st, 1955, Dr Thilla Krikler (*d* 1973); four *s*; 2nd, 1975, Lily Shub; one *s*, and one step *s* two step *d*. *Educ:* Milton Sch., Bulawayo, S Rhodesia (Zimbabwe). Called to Bar, Middle Temple, 1953. Crown Counsel, Court Martial Appeals Court, 1968; Dep. Circuit Judge, 1974; a Recorder, 1980–84; Dep. Circuit Judge, SE and Midland Circuits, 2001–04. Head of Chambers, London and Cambridge, 1975–84. *Recreations:* cartooning, carpentry, painting. *Club:* Cressbrook.

KRIKORIAN, Gregory, CB 1973; Solicitor for the Customs and Excise, 1971–78; *b* 23 Sept. 1913; *s* of late Kevork and late Christine Krikorian; *m* 1943, Seta Mary (*d* 1995), *d* of Souren Djirdjirian; one *d*. *Educ:* Polytechnic Secondary Sch.; Lincoln Coll., Oxford (BA). Called to Bar, Middle Temple, 1939; practised at Bar, 1939; BBC Overseas Intell. Dept, 1940; served in RAF as Intell. Officer, Fighter Comd, 1940–45 (despatches); practised at Bar, 1945–51, Junior Oxford Circuit, 1947; joined Solicitor's Office, HM Customs and Excise, 1951. *Publications:* (jtly) Customs and Excise, in Halsbury's Laws of England, 1975; Through the Eye of an Armenian Needle, 2002. *Recreations:* gardening, bird-watching. *Address:* The Coach House, Hawkchurch, Axminster, Devon EX13 5TX. *T:* (01297) 678414. *Clubs:* Reform, Civil Service.

KRIWET, Dr Heinz; Member, Supervisory Board, ThyssenKrupp (formerly Thyssen) AG, Düsseldorf (Chairman: Executive Board, 1991–96; Supervisory Board, 1996–2001); *b* Bochum, 2 Nov. 1931. *Educ:* Univs of Köln and Freiburg (Masters degree 1957; Dr rer. pol. 1959). Trainee, German Iron and Steel Fedn, 1960–61; Hüttenwerk Rheinhausen (Krupp), 1962–67; Gen. Manager, Sales, 1968, Mem. Exec. Bd i/c Sales, Friedrich Krupp Hüttenwerke AG, Bochum, 1969–72; Mem. Exec. Bd i/c Sales, Thyssen AG, Düsseldorf, 1973–83; Chm. Exec. Bd, Thyssen Stahl AG, Duisburg, 1983–91. *Address:* c/o ThyssenKrupp AG, August Thyssen-Strasse 1, 40211 Düsseldorf, Germany. *T:* (211) 8241.

KROEMER, Prof. Herbert, PhD; Professor of Electrical and Computer Engineering, University of California at Santa Barbara, since 1985; *b* Weimar, Germany, 25 Aug. 1928. *Educ:* Univ. of Göttingen (PhD 1952). Semiconductor research: Central Telecommunications Laboratory, Germany, 1952; RCA Labs, Princeton, NJ, 1954; Varian Associates, Palo Alto, Calif, 1963–66; Univ. of Colorado, 1968; UCSB. (Jtly) Nobel Prize for Physics, 2000. *Publications:* Quantum Mechanics: for engineering, materials science and applied physics; (jtly) Thermal Physics; articles in jls. *Address:* Electrical and Computer Engineering Department, University of California, Santa Barbara, CA 93106–9560, USA.

KROES, Neelie; Member, European Commission, since 2004; *b* 19 July 1941; *m*; one *s*. *Educ:* Erasmus Univ., Rotterdam (MSc 1965). Asst Prof. of Transport Econs, Erasmus Univ., Rotterdam, 1965–71; Mem., Rotterdam Municipal Council, 1969–71; MP (VVD), Netherlands, 1971–77; Dep. Minister of Transport, Public Works and Telecommunications, 1977–81; Minister of Transport and Public Works, then of Transport and Waterways, 1982–89; Advr, European Transport Comr, Brussels, 1989–91; Pres., Nijenrode Univ., 1991–2000; Chm., Supervisory Bd, MeyerMonitor, until 2004. Non-executive Director: Ballast Nedam, 1990–2004; New Skies Satellites, 1999–2004; mmO_2, 2001–04; Volvo Gp, 2003–04; Royal P&O Nedlloyd, 2004. Trustee, Prologis, 2002–04. *Address:* European Commission, Rue de la Loi 200, 1049 Brussels, Belgium.

KROHN, Dr Peter Leslie, FRS 1963; Professor of Endocrinology, University of Birmingham, 1962–66; *b* 8 Jan. 1916; *s* of Eric Leslie Krohn and Doris Ellen Krohn (*née* Wade); *m* 1941, Joanna Mary French; two *s*. *Educ:* Sedbergh; Balliol Coll., Oxford (BA 1st Cl. Hons Animal Physiol, 1937; BM, BCh Oxon, 1940). Wartime Research work for Min. of Home Security, 1940–45; Lectr, then Reader in Endocrinology, University of Birmingham, 1946–53; Nuffield Sen. Gerontological Research Fellow and Hon. Prof. in University, 1953–62. *Publications:* contrib. to scientific jls on physiology of reproduction, transplantation immunity and ageing. *Recreations:* scuba diving, mountain walking. *Address:* Coburg House, New St John's Road, St Helier, Jersey, Channel Islands JE2 3LD. *T:* (01534) 874870.

KROLL, Nicholas James, CB 2002; Director, BBC Trust, since 2007; *b* 23 June 1954; *s* of Alexander Kroll and Maria Kroll (*née* Wolff); *m* 1981, Catherine Askew; one *s* one *d* (and one *d* decd). *Educ:* St Paul's Sch.; Corpus Christi Coll., Oxford. Entered Civil Service, 1977: DoE/Dept of Transport, 1977–86; HM Treasury, 1986–93; Department of National Heritage, then Department for Culture, Media and Sport, 1993–2004: Dir, Creative Industries Media and Broadcasting Gp, 1996–2000; Corporate Services Dir, 2000–02 (acting Perm. Sec., 2001); Chief Operating Officer and Dep. to Perm. Sec., 2002–04; Dir of Governance, BBC, 2004–06. Mem. Bd, NYO, 2005–. *Recreation:* music. *Address:* BBC, 35 Marylebone High Street, W1U 4AA.

KROLL, Rev. Dr Una (Margaret Patricia), CJC; writer and broadcaster, since 1970; *b* 15 Dec. 1925; *d* of George Hill, CBE, DSO, MC, and Hilda Hill; *m* 1957, Leopold Kroll (*d* 1987); one *s* three *d*. *Educ:* St Paul's Girls' Sch.; Malvern Girls' Coll.; Girton Coll., Cambridge; The London Hosp. MB, BChir (Cantab) 1951; MA 1969. MRCGP 1967. House Officer, 1951–53; Overseas service (Africa), 1953–60; General Practice, 1960–81; Clinical MO, 1981–85, Sen. Clinical MO, 1985–88, Hastings Health Dist. Theological trng, 1967–70; worker deaconess, 1970–88; ordained deacon, 1988, priest, 1997, Church in Wales; Sister, Soc. of the Sacred Cross, 1991–94; political work as a feminist, with particular ref. to status of women in the churches in England and internationally, 1970–89. *Publications:* Transcendental Meditation: a signpost to the world, 1974; Flesh of My Flesh: a Christian view on sexism, 1975; Lament for a Lost Enemy: study of reconciliation, 1976; Sexual Counselling, 1980; The Spiritual Exercise Book, 1985; Growing Older, 1988; In Touch with Healing, 1991; Vocation to Resistance, 1995; Trees of Life, 1997; Forgive and Live, 2000; Anatomy of Survival, 2001; Living Life to the Full, 2006; contrib. Cervical Cytology (BMJ), 1969. *Recreation:* doing nothing. *Address:* 6 Hamilton House, 57 Hanson Street, Bury, Lancs BL9 6LR.

KROOK, (Elizabeth) Jane; *see* Maher, E. J.

KROTO, Sir Harold (Walter), Kt 1996; FRS 1990; Frances Eppes Professor, Department of Chemistry and Biochemistry, Florida State University, since 2004; *b* 7 Oct. 1939; *s* of Heinz and Edith Kroto; *m* 1963, Margaret Henrietta Hunter; two *s*. *Educ:* Bolton Sch.; Univ. of Sheffield (BSc, PhD). Res. in fullerenes, spectroscopy, radioastronomy, clusters and nanotechnology; Res. student, Sheffield Univ., 1961–64; Postdoctoral Fellow, NRCC, 1964–66; Res. scientist, Bell Telephone Labs, NJ, 1966–67; University of Sussex: Tutorial Fellow, 1967–68; Lectr, 1968–77; Reader, 1977–85; Prof. of Chemistry, 1985–91 and 2001–04; Royal Soc. Res. Prof., 1991–2001. Visiting Professor: UBC 1973; USC 1981; UCLA, 1988–92; Univ. of Calif, Santa Barbara, 1996–. Chm., Vega Sci. Trust, 1995–. Pres., RSC, 2002–04. Longstaff Medal, RSC, 1993; (jtly) Nobel Prize for Chemistry, 1996; Erasmus Medal, Acad. Europaea, 2002; Michael Faraday Prize, 2001, Copley Medal, 2004, Royal Soc. *Publications:* Molecular Rotation Spectra, 1975, 2nd edn 1983; 300 papers in chemistry, chem. physics and astronomy jls. *Recreations:* graphic design, tennis. *Address:* Department of Chemistry and Biochemistry, Florida State University, Tallahassee, FL 32306–4390, USA; School of Chemistry, Physics and Environmental Science, University of Sussex, Brighton BN1 9QJ.

KRUGER, Prudence Margaret, (Mrs Rayne Kruger); *see* Leith, P. M.

KUBEKOV, Susannah Kate; *see* Simon, S. K.

KUBIŠ, Ján; Minister of Foreign Affairs, Slovak Republic, since 2006; *b* Bratislava, 12 Nov. 1952; *m*; one *d*. *Educ:* Jura Hronca High Sch., Bratislava; Moscow State Inst. for Internat. Affairs. Internat. Econ. Orgns Dept, Min. of Foreign Affairs, Prague, 1976–77; Office of the Minister, 1978–80; Attaché and Third Sec., Addis Ababa, 1980–85; Second Sec., 1985–87, Hd of Section, Security and Arms Control, 1987–88, Main Political Questions Dept, Min. of Foreign Affairs, Prague; First Sec. and Counsellor, Moscow, 1989–90; Dep. Hd of Embassy and Hd of Political Section, Moscow, 1990–91; Dir-Gen., Euro-Atlantic Section, Min. of Foreign Affairs, Prague, and Ambassador-at-large, 1991–92; Chm., Cttee of Sen. Officials, CSCE, 1992; Perm. Rep. of Czechoslovakia, 1992, of Slovak Republic, 1993–94, to UN and GATT, Geneva; Special Ministerial Envoy and Slovak Chief Negotiator on Pact for Stability in Europe, 1994; Dir, Conflict Prevention Centre, OSCE, 1994–98; Special Rep. of UN Sec.-Gen. for Tajikistan and Head, UN Mission of Observers to Tajikistan, 1998–99; Sec. Gen., OSCE, 1999–2005; EU Special Rep. for Central Asia, 2005–06. OSCE Medal, 1998. *Publications:* contrib. learned jls. *Address:* Ministry of Foreign Affairs of the Slovak Republic, Hlbok cesta 2, 833 36 Bratislava, Slovak Republic.

KUCHMA, Leonid Danylovych; President of Ukraine, 1994–2004; *b* 1938. *Educ:* Dnipropetrovsk State Univ. Constructor, Research-Production Union, Pirdenny Machine-Bldg Plant, 1960–75; Sec., Party Cttee, 1975–82; Dep. Dir Gen., 1982–86; Dir Gen., 1986–92; Chm., Ukrainian Union of Industrialists and Entrepreneurs, 1993–94. Deputy, Ukraine Parlt, 1991–94; Prime Minister, Ukraine, 1992–93. Mem., Central Cttee, Ukraine Communist Party, 1981–91; Mem., CPSU, 1960–91. *Address:* c/o Office of the President, Bankova Street 11, 01220 Kyiv, Ukraine.

KUENSSBERG, Nicholas Christopher, OBE 2004; Principal, Horizon Co-Invest, since 1995; *b* 28 Oct. 1942; *s* of late Ekkehard von Kuenssberg, CBE; *m* 1965, Sally Robertson (CBE 2000); one *s* two *d*. *Educ:* Edinburgh Acad.; Wadham Coll., Oxford (BA Hons). FCIS. Worked overseas, 1965–78; Dir, J. & P. Coats Ltd, 1978–91; Chm., Dynacast International Ltd, 1978–91; Director: Coats Patons Plc, 1985–91; Coats Viyella plc, 1986–91; Dawson International PLC, 1991–95. Chairman: David A. Hall Ltd, 1996–98; GAP Gp Ltd, 1996–2005; Stoddard Internat. PLC, 1997–2000; Canmore Partnership Ltd, 1999–; Iomart Gp Plc, 2000–08; Keronite PLC, 2005–07; eTourism Ltd, 2007–; Director: Scottish Power plc (formerly S of Scotland Electricity Bd), 1984–97; W of Scotland Bd, Bank of Scotland, 1984–88; Standard Life Assce Co., 1988–97; Baxi Partnership, 1996–99; Chamberlin & Hill plc, 1999–2006; Citizens Theatre Glasgow Ltd, 2000–03; RingProp plc, 2002–06; Amino Technols plc, 2004–07. Member: Scottish Legal Aid Bd, 1996–2004; SEPA, 1999– (Dep. Chm., 2003–07); Scottish Cttee, British Council, 1999–2008; QAA Scotland, 2004– (Chm., 2007–); Dir, QAA, 2007–. Chm., Assoc. of Mgt Educn & Trng in Scotland, 1996–98. Strathclyde Business School: Hon. Res. Fellow, 1986–88; Vis. Prof., 1988–91; Ext. Examr, Aberdeen Business Sch., 1998–2003; Hon. Prof., Univ. of Glasgow, 2008–. Chairman: Scottish Networks Internat., 2001–08; ScotlandIS, 2001–03; Scotland the Brand, 2002–04; Glasgow Sch. of Art, 2003–. Gov., Queen's Coll., Glasgow, 1989–91. Trustee, David Hume Inst., 1994–. CCMI; FInstD (Chm., Scotland, 1997–99); FRSA. *Publication:* (ed) The First Decade: the first ten years of the David Hume Institute, 1996. *Recreations:* sport, travel, opera, languages. *Address:* 6 Cleveden Drive, Glasgow G12 0SE. *T:* (0141) 339 8345.

KUFUOR, John Agyekum, Hon. GCB 2007; President, Republic of Ghana, 2001–09; *b* 8 Dec. 1938; *m* Theresa Mensah; five *c*. *Educ:* Prempeh Coll., Kumasi; Univ. of Oxford (BA 1964). Called to the Bar, Lincoln's Inn, 1961. Chief Legal Officer and Town Clerk of Kumasi, 1967; Mem., Constituent Assembly, Ghana, 1968–69, 1979; formerly MP and a Dep. Foreign Minister; imprisoned after mil. coup, 1972–73; returned to law practice; Sec. for Local Govt, 1982. Founding Member: Progress Party, 1969; Popular Front Party, 1979; New Patriotic Party, 1992 (Leader, 1996–2007). Hon. Fellow, Exeter Coll., Oxford, 2002. *Address:* (office) PO Box 1627, Osu, Accra, Ghana.

KUH, Prof. Diana Jane Lewin, PhD; Professor of Life Course Epidemiology, since 2003, Director, MRC National Survey of Health and Development, since 2006, and Director MRC Unit for Lifelong Health and Ageing, since 2007, University College London; *b* Chichester, 23 Feb. 1953; *d* of Allan and Doris Lewin; *m* 1974, Peter Michael Kuh; one *s* one *d*. *Educ:* King Edward VI Camp Hill Sch. for Girls, Birmingham; New Hall Coll., Cambridge (BA Econs 1974); London Sch. of Econs (PhD 1993). Res. scientist, Inst. of Biometry and Community Medicine, 1975–81, Res. Fellow, Paediatric Res. Unit, 1982–87, Univ. of Exeter; Scientist, 1987–93, Sen. Scientist, 1994–2006, MRC Nat. Survey of Health and Develt, UCL. FFPH 2007. *Publications:* (with Prof. Y. Ben-Shlomo) A Life Course Approach to Chronic Disease Epidemiology, 1997, 2nd edn 2004; (with Dr R. Hardy) A Life Course Approach to Women's Health, 2002; contrib. articles to learned jls. *Recreations:* country walking, relaxing and having fun with my grandchildren, family and friends. *Address:* MRC Unit for Lifelong Health and Ageing, Department of Epidemiology and Public Health, University College London Medical School, 33 Bedford Place, WC1B 5JU. *T:* (020) 7679 1720, *Fax:* (020) 7679 5963; *e-mail:* d.kuh@nshd.mrc.ac.uk.

KUHN, Prof. Annette Frieda, PhD; FBA 2004; Professor of Film Studies, Queen Mary, University of London, since 2006; *b* 29 Sept. 1945; *d* of Henry Philip Kuhn and Minnie Alice, (Betty), Cowley; *m* 1967, Peter Robert Brodnax Moore (marr. diss. 1982). *Educ:* Twickenham County Grammar Sch.; Univ. of Sheffield (BA (Econ.) 1969; MA 1975); Inst. of Educn, Univ. of London (PhD 1986). Adult Educn Tutor, Open Univ. and Univ. of London, 1971–88; pt-time Lectr in Film Studies, Polytech. of Central London, 1977–88; Lectr, 1989–91, Reader, 1991–98, in Film and TV Studies, Univ. of Glasgow; Reader in Cultural Res., 1998–2000, Prof. of Film Studies, 2000–06, Lancaster Univ. *Publications:* (ed with AnnMarie Wolpe) Feminism and Materialism, 1978; (ed jtly) Ideology and Cultural Production, 1979; Women's Pictures: feminism and cinema, 1982, 2nd edn 1994; The Power of the Image, 1985; Cinema, Censorship and Sexuality 1909 to 1925, 1988; (ed) The Women's Companion to International Film, 1990; (ed) Alien Zone: cultural theory and contemporary science fiction cinema, 1990; Family Secrets, 1995, rev. edn 2002; (ed) Queen of the Bs: Ida Lupino behind the camera, 1995; (ed with

Jackie Stacey) Screen Histories, 1998; (ed) Alien Zone II: the spaces of science fiction cinema, 1999; An Everyday Magic: cinema and cultural memory, 2002; (ed with Catherine Grant) Screening World Cinema, 2006; (ed with Kirsten Emiko McAllister) Locating Memory: photographic acts, 2006; Ratcatcher, 2008. *Recreations:* arboriculture, housekeeping, rail travel. *Address:* School of Languages, Linguistics and Film, Queen Mary, University of London, Mile End Road, E1 4NS. *T:* (020) 7882 3335.

KUHN, Prof. Karl Heinz, FBA 1987; Professor of Coptic, Durham University, 1982–84, now Emeritus Professor; *b* 2 Aug. 1919; *s* of Max Kuhn and Gertrud Kuhn (*née* Hiller); *m* 1949, Rachel Mary Wilkinson; one *s* one *d*. *Educ:* school in Germany; St John's Coll., Univ. of Durham (BA 1949, PhD 1952). Scarbrough Research Studentship, Durham Univ. and abroad, 1949–53; Univ. of Durham: Research Fellow in Arts, 1953–55; Lectr, later Sen. Lectr in Hebrew and Aramaic, 1955–77; Reader in Coptic, 1977–82; Prof. of Coptic, 1982–84. Mem., editl bd, Corpus Scriptorum Christianorum Orientalium, Louvain, 1970–2000. *Publications:* Letters and Sermons of Besa, 1956; Pseudo-Shenoute: on Christian behaviour, 1960; A Panegyric on John the Baptist attributed to Theodosius, Archbishop of Alexandria, 1966; A Panegyric on Apollo, Archimandrite of the Monastery of Isaac by Stephen, Bishop of Heracleopolis Magna, 1978; (contrib.) Sparks, The Apocryphal Old Testament, 1984; (with W. J. Tait) Thirteen Coptic Acrostic Hymns from Manuscript M574 of the Pierpont Morgan Library, 1996; (contrib.) English trans. of Foerster, Gnosis, 1974, and Rudolph, Gnosis, 1983; articles in Jl of Theol Studies, Le Muséon and other learned jls. *Recreations:* music. *Address:* 28 Nevilledale Terrace, Durham DH1 4QG. *T:* (0191) 384 2993.

KUHN, Michael Ashton; Chairman, Qwerty Films, since 1999; *b* 7 May 1949; *s* of George and Bea Kuhn; *m* 1995, Caroline Burton; two *s*. *Educ:* Dover Coll.; Clare Coll., Cambridge (BA 1971); Coll. of Law. Admitted Solicitor, 1974. Denton, Hall & Burgin, 1971–72; Legal Advr, Polygram UK, 1972–74; Asst Solicitor, Field, Fisher & Martineau, 1974–75; Polygram Internat., 1975–98 (Gen. Counsel, 1975, subseq. Bd Mem. and Pres., Polygram Filmed Entertainment, 1990–98). Chairman: Nat. Film and TV Sch., 2002–; Ind. Cinema Office, 2004–. Mem. Council, BAFTA, 2006–. Producer, The Duchess, 2008. Michael Balcon Award, BAFTA, 1998. *Publication:* 100 Films and a Funeral, 2001. *Recreation:* playwriting. *Address:* Qwerty Films, 7–12 Noel Street, W1F 8GQ. *T:* (020) 7440 5920, *Fax:* (020) 7440 5959; *e-mail:* info@qwertyfilms.com. *Club:* Groucho.

KÜHNL, Karel; Minister of Defence, Czech Republic, 2004–06; *b* 12 Sept. 1954; *s* of Karel Kühnl and Marie Kühnlova (*née* Větrovcová); *m* 1983, Daniela Kusin; one *s* one *d*. *Educ:* Charles Univ., Prague (BA Law 1978); Univ. of Vienna (BA Econs 1983). Left Czechoslovakia in 1980 for political reasons; free-lance journalist, Vienna and Munich, 1983–87; editor and analyst, Radio Free Europe, Munich (Czech and Slovak broadcasting), 1987–91; returned to Czechoslovakia, 1991, after fall of communism in 1989; Sen. Lectr, Law Faculty, Charles Univ., Prague, 1991–93; Chief Advr to Prime Minister of Czech Republic, 1991–93; Ambassador to UK, 1993–97; Minister of Industry and Trade, 1997–98; Mem. (Civic Democratic Alliance, 1997–98, Freedom Union, 1998–2004), Chamber of Deputies, Czech Republic. Chm., Freedom Union Party, 1999–2001. Hd of Bd, Czech TV, 1992–93. *Publications:* numerous articles in Czech, German and Austrian newspapers and jls. *Recreations:* family, history, archaeology, architecture.

KUHRT, Prof. Amélie Thekla Luise, FBA 2001; Professor of Ancient Near Eastern History, University College London, since 1997; *b* 23 Sept. 1944; *d* of Edith Woodger and Ernest Woodger (adoptive father); *m* 1965, David Alan Kuhrt (marr. diss. 1977); two *d*. *Educ:* King's Coll., London; University Coll. London; Sch. of Oriental and African Studies (BA Hons Ancient Hist.). Lectr in Near Eastern Hist., 1979–89, Reader, 1989–97, UCL. James Henry Breasted Prize, Amer. Historical Assoc., 1997. *Publications:* (with A. Cameron) Images of Women in Antiquity, 1983, 2nd edn 1993; (with H. Sancisi-Weerdenburg) Achaemenid History II–IV, 1987–90, VI, 1991, VIII, 1994; (with S. Sherwin-White) Hellenism in the East, 1987; From Samarkhand to Sardis, 1992; The Ancient Near East, 2 vols, 1995 (trans. Spanish, Persian, Hungarian, Croat); The Persian Empire: a corpus of sources for the Achaemenid period, 2 vols, 2007. *Recreations:* music, literature. *Address:* Department of History, University College London, Gower Street, WC1E 6BT. *T:* (020) 7679 3634.

KUHRT, Ven. Dr Gordon Wilfred; Associate Minister, Tredington and Darlingscott with Ilmington with Stretton-on-Fosse, and Ditchford with Preston-on-Stour with Whitchurch and Atherstone-on-Stour, since 2006; Archdeacon Emeritus, diocese of Southwark, since 1996; *b* 15 Feb. 1941; *s* of Wilfred and Doris Kuhrt; *m* 1963, Olive Margaret Powell; three *s*. *Educ:* Colfe's Grammar School; London Univ. (BD Hons); Oak Hill Theol Coll.; Middx Univ. (Dr Professional Studies 2001). Religious Education teacher, 1963–65; Curate: Illogan, Cornwall, 1967–70; Wallington, Surrey, 1970–74; Vicar: Shenstone, Staffs, 1974–79; Emmanuel, South Croydon, Surrey, 1979–89; RD, Croydon Central, 1981–86; Hon. Canon, Southwark Cathedral, 1987–89; Archdeacon of Lewisham, 1989–96; Chief Sec., ABM, Gen. Synod of C of E, 1996–98; Dir of Ministry, Archbishops' Council, C of E, 1999–2006. Mem., C of E Gen. Synod, 1986–96 (Mem., Bd of Ministry, 1991–96). Fellow, Coll. of Preachers (Mem. Council, 1992–97). Theological Lectr, London Univ. Extra-Mural Dept, 1984–89. *Publications:* A Handbook for Council and Committee Members, 1985; Believing in Baptism, 1987; (contrib.) The Church and its Unity, 1992; (ed and contrib.) Doctrine Matters, 1993; (contrib.) Growing in Newness of Life: Christian initiation in Anglicanism today, 1993; (ed) To Proclaim Afresh, 1995; (contrib.) Church Leadership, 1997; Issues in Theological Education and Training, 1997; Clergy Security, 1998; An Introduction to Christian Ministry, 2000; Ministry Issues for the Church of England: mapping the trends, 2001; (ed) Bridging the Gap: Reader ministry today, 2002. *Address:* The Rectory, Tredington, Shipston on Stour, Warwicks CV36 4NG. *T:* (01608) 661264.

KULKARNI, Prof. Shrinivas Ramachandra, PhD; FRS 2001; Professor of Astronomy and Planetary Science, California Institute of Technology, Pasadena, since 1996; Director, Caltech Optical Observatories, since 2006; *b* 4 Oct. 1956; *s* of Dr Ramachandra H. Kulkarni and Vimala Kulkarni; *m* 1985, Dr Hiromi Komiya; two *d*. *Educ:* Indian Inst. of Technology, New Delhi (MS Physics 1978); Univ. of California at Berkeley (PhD Astronomy 1983). Post-doctoral Fellow, Radio Astronomy Lab., Univ. of California at Berkeley, 1983–85; California Institute of Technology: Robert A. Millikan Fellow in Radio Astronomy, 1985–87; Asst Prof. of Astronomy, 1987–90; Associate Prof. of Astronomy, 1990–92; Prof. of Astronomy, 1992–95; Exec. Officer, Astronomy, 1997–2000; Sen. Fellow, Mount Wilson Inst., Pasadena, 1998–. John D. and Catherine T. MacArthur Prof. of Astronomy and Planetary Sci., 2001. Helen B. Warner Prize, 1991, Alan T. Waterman Prize, 1992, NSF. *Publications:* (contrib.) Interstellar Processes, 1987; contrib. Nature in fields of pulsers, brown dwarfs and gamma-ray bursters. *Address:* Department of Astronomy, California Institute of Technology, 1200 East California Boulevard, Pasadena, CA 91125, USA. *T:* (626) 395 4010; *e-mail:* srk@astro.caltech.edu.

KULUKUNDIS, Sir Eddie, Kt 1993; OBE 1988; Chairman, Ambassadors Theatre Group, since 1992; Director, Rethymnis & Kulukundis Ltd, since 1964; Member of Lloyd's, 1964–95 (Member Council, 1983–89); *b* 20 April 1932; *s* of late George Elias Kulukundis and Eugénie (*née* Diacakis); *m* 1981, Susan Hampshire, *qv*. *Educ:* Collegiate Sch., New York; Salisbury Sch., Connecticut; Yale Univ. Mem., Baltic Exchange, 1959–2001. Chairman: Sports Aid Foundn Ltd, 1988–93 (Gov., 1977–2006); London Coaching Foundn, 1990–; British Athletics Charitable Trust (formerly British Athletics Field Events Charitable Trust), 1996–; Vice-Pres., UK Athletics, 1998–2003. Governor: Royal Shakespeare Theatre, 1976–2003; The Raymond Mander and Joe Mitchenson Theatre Collection Ltd, 1981–2001; Vice-Pres., Traverse Theatre, 1988–; Director: Hampstead Theatre Ltd, 1969–2004; Hampstead Theatre Trust, 1980–2003. Mem., Richmond Theatre Trust, 2001–. Mem. Bd, SOLT, 1973–2003 (Hon. Vice-Pres., 2003). Trustee: Theatres Trust, 1976–95; Salisbury Sch., Connecticut, 1983–. FRSA. Theatrical Producer, 1969–96; London productions include (some jtly): Enemy, 1969; The Happy Apple, Poor Horace, The Friends, How the Other Half Loves, Tea Party and The Basement (double bill), The Wild Duck, 1970; After Haggerty, Hamlet, Charley's Aunt, Straight Up, 1971; London Assurance, Journey's End, 1972; Small Craft Warnings, A Private Matter, Dandy Dick, 1973; The Waltz of the Toreadors, Life Class, Pygmalion, Play Mas, The Gentle Hook, 1974; A Little Night Music, Entertaining Mr Sloane, The Gay Lord Quex, What the Butler Saw, Travesties, Lies, The Sea Gull, A Month in the Country, A Room With a View, Too True to Be Good, The Bed Before Yesterday, 1975; Dimetos, Banana Ridge, Wild Oats, 1976; Candida, Man and Superman, Once A Catholic, 1977; Privates on Parade, Gloo Joo, 1978; Bent, Outside Edge, Last of the Red Hot Lovers, 1979; Beecham, Born in the Gardens, 1980; Tonight At 8.30, Steaming, Arms and the Man, 1981; Steafel's Variations, 1982; Messiah, Pack of Lies, 1983; Of Mice and Men, The Secret Diary of Adrian Mole Aged 13¾, 1984; Camille, 1985; The Cocktail Party, 1986; Curtains, 1987; Separation, South Pacific, Married Love, 1988; Over My Dead Body, 1989; Never the Sinner, 1990; The King and I, Carmen Jones, 1991; Noël and Gertie, A Slip of the Tongue, Shades, Making it Better, 1992; The Prime of Miss Jean Brodie, 1994; New York productions (jtly): How the Other Half Loves, 1971; Sherlock Holmes, London Assurance, 1974; Travesties, 1975; The Merchant, 1977; Players, 1978; Once a Catholic, 1979. *Address:* c/o Ambassadors Theatre Group, 39–41 Charing Cross Road, WC2R 0AR. *T:* (020) 7534 6100. *Club:* Garrick.

KUMAR, Dr Ashok; MP (Lab) Middlesbrough South and Cleveland East, since 1997; *b* 28 May 1956; *s* of Jagat Ram Saini and late Santosh Kumari. *Educ:* Univ. of Aston in Birmingham (BSc ChemEng 1978; MSc Process Control 1980; PhD Fluid Mechanics 1982). Res. Officer, British Steel Research, 1978–79; Res. Fellow, Imperial Coll. of Science and Technology, 1982–85; Sen. Res. Investigator, Teesside Labs, British Steel, 1985–91; Res. Officer, British Steel Technical, 1992–97. Mem., Middlesbrough BC, 1987–97: Chair, Equal Opportunities Sub-Cttee, 1995–97; Vice Chair, Educn Cttee, 1995–97. MP (Lab) Langbaurgh, Nov. 1991–1992; contested (Lab) Langbaurgh, 1992. PPS to Sec. of State for Internat. Devlt, 2003–07. Member: Sci. and Technol Select Cttee, 1997–2001; Trade and Industry Select Cttee, 2001–03. Chairman: Parly Gp for Energy Studies, 1999–2002 (Vice-Chm., 2002–); All Party Parly British-Bahrain Gp, 1999–; All Party Parly Gp for Chemical Industry, 2000–03 (Jt Sec., 1997–2000); All Party British-Indo Parly Gp, 2006–. Chairman: Chem. Eng. Soc., 1981–82; Labour Club, Univ. of Aston, 1980–81. *Publications:* articles in scientific and mathematical jls. *Recreations:* reading, listening to music, cricket, badminton. *Address:* House of Commons, SW1A 0AA. *Clubs:* Reform; Easterside and Beechwood Social; Marton Cricket.

KUMAR, Harpal Singh; Chief Executive, Cancer Research UK, since 2007 (Chief Operating Officer, 2004–07); *b* London, 13 Jan. 1965; *s* of Mohinder Singh and Prem Kaur Kumar; *m* 1998, Benita Sokhey; one *s* one *d*. *Educ:* St John's Coll., Cambridge (BA Chem. Engrg 1986; MEng 1987); Harvard Grad. Sch. of Business Admin (MBA 1991). Associate Engagement Manager, McKinsey & Co. Inc., 1987–89, 1991–93; Chief Executive: Papworth Trust, 1993–97; Nexan Gp plc, 1997–2002; Cancer Research Technology, 2002–07. *Recreations:* theatre, opera, football. *Address:* Cancer Research UK, 61 Lincoln's Inn Fields, WC2A 3PX. *T:* (020) 7061 8469, *Fax:* (020) 7061 8428; *e-mail:* harpal.kumar@cancer.org.uk.

KUMAR, Prof. Parveen June, (Mrs D. Leaver), CBE 2001; MD; FRCP, FRCPE; Professor of Medicine and Education, Barts and the London School of Medicine and Dentistry, Queen Mary, University of London, since 2004; Hon. Consultant Physician and Gastroenterologist, Barts and the London NHS Trust (formerly St Bartholomew's Hospital) and Homerton University Hospital Foundation NHS Trust (formerly Homerton Hospital), since 1983; *b* 1 June 1942; *d* of Cyril Proshuno Fazal Kumar and Grace Nazira Kumar; *m* 1970, Dr David Leaver (*d* 2003); two *d*. *Educ:* Lawrence Sch., Sanawer, India; Maida Vale High Sch., London; St Bartholomew's Hosp. Med. Coll., London (BSc Hons 1963; MB BS; MD 1976). FRCP 1987; FRCPE 1998. Dir of Postgrad. Med. Educn, Royal Hospital NHS Trust, 1994–96; Hd, Acad. Unit of Gastroenterolology, Homerton Hosp., 1998–2002; Associate Med. Dir, 1998–2000, non-exec. Dir, 1999–2003, Barts and the London NHS Trust; Prof. of Clin. Med. Educn, Barts and the London, Queen Mary Sch. of Medicine and Dentistry, Univ. of London, 1999–2004. Mem., 1994–2005, Chm., 2002–05, Medicines Commn; non-exec. Dir, NICE, 1999–2002. Royal College of Physicians: Dep. Regl Advr, Coll. and Clinical Tutor, 1989–96; Sub Dean for Undergrad. Educn, 1995–98; Censor, 1996–98; Dir, Continual Professional Develt, 1998–2002; Vice-Pres. (Acad.), 2003–05. Pres., BMA, 2006–07; Mem. Council, British Soc. of Gastroenterology, 2001–04. Erasmus Vis. Prof., Univ. Sapienza, Rome, 1992. Trustee: St Bartholomew's Hosp. Med. Coll. Trust, 2002–; CancerBackup, 2003–08. FCGI 2007; Hon. FAPI. Hon. DM Nottingham, 2006. *Publications:* Kumar and Clark, Clinical Medicine (with Michael Clark), 1987, 7th edn 2007; Acute Clinical Medicine, 2000, 2nd edn 2006; series co-editor, 6 pocket essentials; other books; res. articles mainly on coeliac disease and small bowel disorders in med. jls. *Recreations:* opera, ski-ing, walking, reading. *Address:* Centre for Gastroenterology, Institute of Cell and Molecular Sciences, Barts and the London School of Medicine, 4 Newark Street, E1 2AD. *T:* (020) 7882 7191; *e-mail:* p.j.kumar@qmul.ac.uk. *Clubs:* Royal Automobile, Forum.

KUMAR, Surendra, FRCGP; general medical practitioner, since 1971; *b* 15 Sept. 1945; *m* 1971, Dr Santosh Kumar; two *d*. *Educ:* Univ. of Delhi (MB BS). Mem., 1999–2003, Assoc. Mem., and Chair, Fitness to Practice Panel, 2003–, GMC; Mem., GPs' Cttee, BMA, 1993–; Pres., British Internat. (formerly Overseas) Doctors Assoc., 2003– (Nat. Chm., 1993–99). SBStJ 1991. *Recreation:* medical politics. *Address:* Kumar and Kumar, Upton Medical Centre, Bechers, Hough Green, Widnes WA8 4TE. *T:* (0151) 424 9518.

KUMARATUNGA, Chandrika Bandaranaike; President of Sri Lanka, 1994–2005; *b* 29 June 1945; *d* of late Solomon W. R. D. Bandaranaike and Sirimavo R. D. Bandaranaike, former Prime Minister of Sri Lanka; *m* 1978, Wijaya Kumaratunga (*d* 1988); one *s* one *d*. *Educ:* St Bridget's Convent, Colombo; Inst. of Pol Studies, Paris; Ecole Pratique des Hautes Etudes, Paris. Chm. and Man. Dir, Dinakara Sinhala, 1975–85; Chief Minister, W Province Council, 1993–94; Prime Minister of Sri Lanka, Aug.–Nov. 1994; Minister of Finance and Planning, of Ethnic Affairs and Nat. Integration, of Defence, and of Buddha Sasana, 1994. Sri Lanka Freedom Party: Member: Exec. Cttee, and Women's League, 1974; Exec. Cttee and Wkg Cttee, 1980; Central Cttee, 1992; Dep. Leader, 1992; Vice-

Pres., 1984, Pres., 1986, Sri Lanka Mahajana Party; Leader, People's Alliance, 1988. *Publications:* research papers on agrarian and land reforms and food policies. *Address:* c/o President's Secretariat, Republic Square, Colombo 1, Sri Lanka. *T:* (1) 24801.

KUME, Yutaka; President, 1985–92, Chairman, 1992, Nissan Motor Co.; *b* 20 May 1921; *s* of Kinzaburo Kume and Chiyo Kume; *m* 1947, Aya Yamamoto; one *s* one *d*. *Educ:* Univ. of Tokyo (BE aircraft engineering). Joined Nissan Motor Co., 1946; General Manager: Production control and Engineering Dept, Zama Plant, 1964; Yoshiwara Plant, 1971; Tochigi Plant, 1973–78; Dir and Mem. Bd, 1973; Managing Dir, 1977; Exec. Managing Dir, 1982; Exec. Vice-Pres. and Gen. Manager, Quality Admin Div., 1983. Blue Ribbon Medal from Emperor of Japan, 1986; Commander, Order of Orange Nassau (Holland), 1986; Order of Cruz de San Jordi (Catalonia, Spain), 1990; Commander, Order of the Crown (Belgium), 1991. *Recreations:* photography, haiku (Japanese short poems), reading.

KUNCEWICZ, Eileen, (Mrs Witold Kuncewicz); *see* Herlie, E.

KUNDERA, Milan; writer; *b* Brno, 1 April 1929; *s* of Dr Ludvik Kundera and Milada Kunderova-Janosikova; *m* 1967, Věra Hrabánková. *Educ:* Film Faculty, Acad. of Music and Dramatic Arts, Prague, later Asst Prof. and Prof. there, 1958–69; Prof., Univ. of Rennes, 1975–80; Prof., Ecole des hautes études en sciences sociales, Paris, 1980. Mem., Union of Czechoslovak Writers, 1963–69. Member: Editl Bd, Literární noviny, 1963–67, 1968; Editl Bd, Listy, 1968–69. Czechoslovak Writers' Publishing House Prize, 1969; Commonwealth Award, 1981; Prix Europa-Littérature, 1982; Jerusalem Prize, 1985; Nelly Sachs Preis, 1987; Österreichische Staatspreis, 1988; London Independent Prize, 1991; State Prize for Literature (Czech Republic), 2007. *Publications:* The Joke, 1967; Laughable Loves (short stories), 1970; Jacques et son maître (drama), 1971–81; Life is Elsewhere, 1973 (Prix Médicis); The Farewell Waltz, 1976 (Prem. lett. Mondello); The Book of Laughter and Forgetting, 1979; The Unbearable Lightness of Being, 1984 (LA Times Prize); The Art of the Novel, 1987; Immortality, 1990; Les testaments trahis, 1993; Slowness, 1996; Francis Bacon, 1996; Identity, 1998; La Ignorancia, 2000; Le Rideau (essays), 2005 (English trans., The Curtain: an essay in seven parts, 2007).

KUNEVA, Meglena Shtilianova, PhD; Member, European Commission, since 2007; *b* Sofia, 22 June 1957. *Educ:* Sofia Univ. St Kliment Ohridski (MA Law 1981; PhD Envmtl Law 1984); Georgetown Univ., Washington, DC (Postgrad. PEW Econ. Prog. 1995; Postgrad. Prog. Law Sch. 2000). Ed. and Radio Anchor, Bulgarian Nat. Radio, 1987–90; Asst Prof., Sofia Univ. St Kliment Ohridski, 1987–89; Prof., Bourgas Free Univ., 1992–94. Sen. Legal Advr, Council of Ministers, 1990–2001; legal consultant, 1992–98. Member: Supervisory Bd, Privatization Agency, 1994–95; Bulgarian Delegn, 4th Session Commn for Sustainable Develt, UN, 1995. Founder Mem. and Mem. Pol Council, Nat. Movement Simeon II. MP (Nat. Movement Simeon II), 2001, 2005. Dep. Minister of For. Affairs and Chief Negotiator with EU, 2001–02; Minister for Eur. Affairs, 2002–06, and Chief Negotiator with EU, 2002–05; Special Rep. of Bulgaria to Convention on Future of EU, 2002–03. Member: Bd Trustees, Berlin Conf. 'A Soul for Europe'; Internat. Council of Envmtl Law, UN; Access to Information Prog. Foundn; Adv. Bd and Steering Cttee, TIME Eco-projects Foundn; Atlantic Club, Bulgaria (Gold distinction, 2005); Union of Bulgarian Jurists. Writer of screenplay, Stories of Murders (documentary film), 1993. Order of Civil Merit (Spain), 2002; Legion d'Honneur (France), 2003; Order of Prince Enrique (Portugal), 2004; Order of Star of Italian Solidarity (Italy), 2005. *Publications:* articles in jls and newspapers. *Address:* European Commission, Rue de la Loi 200, 1049 Brussels, Belgium. *T:* (2) 2993384, *Fax:* (2) 2995372.

KÜNG, Prof. Dr Hans; Ordinary Professor of Ecumenical Theology, 1980–96 and Director of Institute for Ecumenical Research, 1963–96, University of Tübingen, now Professor Emeritus; *b* Sursee, Lucerne, 19 March 1928. *Educ:* schools in Sursee and Lucerne; Papal Gregorian Univ., Rome (LPhil, LTh); Sorbonne; Inst. Catholique, Paris. DTheol 1957. Further studies in Amsterdam, Berlin, Madrid, London. Ordained priest, 1954. Pastoral work, Hofkirche, Lucerne, 1957–59; Asst for dogmatic theol., Univ. of Münster, 1959–60; Ord. Prof. of fundamental theol., 1960–63, Ord. Prof. of dogmatic and ecumenical theol., 1963–80, Univ. of Tübingen. Official theol. consultant (peritus) to 2nd Vatican Council, 1962–65; Guest Professor: Union Theol. Seminary, NYC, 1968; Univ. of Basle, 1969; Univ. of Chicago Divinity Sch., 1981; Univ. of Michigan, 1983; Toronto Univ., 1985; Rice Univ., Texas, 1987, 1989; guest lectures at univs in Europe, America, Asia and Australia; Hon. Pres., Edinburgh Univ. Theol Soc., 1982–83. President: Foundn Global Ethic, Germany, 1995, Switzerland, 1997. Editor series, Theologische Meditationen; co-Editor series, Ökumenische Forschungen and Ökumenische Theologie; Associate Editor, Jl of Ecum. Studies. Mem., Amer. and German Pen Clubs. Holds hon. doctorates. *Publications:* (first publication in German) The Council and Reunion, 1961; That the World may Believe, 1963; The Living Church, The Changing Church, 1963, 2nd edn 1965; Justification: the doctrine of Karl Barth and a Catholic reflection, 1965; Structures of the Church, 1965; (contrib.) Theologische Meditationen, 1965 (Amer. edn as Freedom Today, 1966); The Church, 1967; (contrib.) Christian Revelation and World Religions, ed J. Neuner, 1967; Truthfulness: the future of the Church, 1968; Infallible? an inquiry, 1971 (paperback 1972); Why Priests?, 1972; 20 Thesen zum Christsein, 1975; On Being a Christian, 1977 (abridged as The Christian Challenge, 1979); Was ist Firmung?, 1976; Jesus im Widerstreit: ein jüdisch-christlicher Dialog (with Pinchas Lapide), 1976; Brother or Lord?, 1977; Signposts for the Future, 1978; Freud and the Problem of God, 1979; The Church—Maintained in Truth?, 1980; Does God Exist?, 1980; Art and the Question of Meaning, 1981; Eternal Life?, 1984; (jtly) Christianity and World Religions, 1986; The Incarnation of God, 1986; Church and Change: the Irish experience, 1986; Why I am still a Christian, 1987; Theology for the Third Millennium: an ecumenical view, 1988; (with Julia Ching) Christianity and Chinese Religions, 1989; Reforming the Church Today: keeping hope alive, 1990; Global Responsibility: in search of a new world ethic, 1991; Judaism: the religious situation of our time, 1992; Mozart: traces of transcendence, 1992; Credo: the Apostles' Creed explained for today, 1993; Great Christian Thinkers, 1994; Christianity: essence and history, 1995; (jtly) A Dignified Dying: a plea for personal responsibility, 1995; Yes to a Global Ethic, 1996; A Global Ethic for Global Politics and Economics, 1997; (ed with Helmut Schmidt) A Global Ethic and Global Responsibilities: two declarations, 1998; The Catholic Church: a short history, 2001; Tracing the Way, 2002; Women in Christianity, 2002; My Struggle for Freedom (memoirs), 2003; Islam: History, Present, Future, 2007. *Address:* Waldhäuserstrasse 23, 72076 Tübingen, Germany.

KUNKEL, Edward Thomas; Director, President and Chief Executive Officer, Foster's Group Ltd, 1992–2004; Chairman, Billabong International Ltd, since 2005; *b* 22 May 1943; *s* of Francis James Kunkel and Doris Kunkel (*née* Baulcombe). *Educ:* Auckland Univ. (BSc Chem. and Zool.). Joined Carlton & United Breweries, Melbourne, 1968 as Asst Brewer; sen. positions throughout Group, 1968–84; Gen. Manager, NSW, 1985–87; Pres. and Chief Exec. Officer, Carling O'Keefe Breweries of Canada Ltd, 1987–89; Exec. Chm., Molson Breweries, N America, 1989–92; Chm., Molson Breweries, Canada, 1996–98. *Recreations:* golf, fitness. *Address:* Billabong International Ltd, 1 Billabong Place, Burleigh Heads, Qld 4220, Australia. *Clubs:* Huntingdale Golf, National Golf (Victoria); Sanctuary Cove Country (Qld).

KUPER, Prof. Adam Jonathan, PhD; FBA 2000; Professor of Social Anthropology, Brunel University, since 1985; *b* 29 Dec. 1941; *s* of Simon Meyer Kuper and Gertrude (*née* Hesselson); *m* 1966, Jessica Sue Cohen; two *s* one *d*. *Educ:* Univ. of Witwatersrand (BA 1961); King's Coll., Cambridge (PhD 1966). Lecturer: in Social Anthropol., Makerere Univ., Kampala, 1967–70; in Anthropol., UCL, 1970–76; Prof. of African Anthropol. and Sociol., Univ. of Leiden, 1976–85. Vice-Pres., British Acad., 2006–07. MAE 1993. Hon. DFil Gothenburg, 1978. Rivers Meml Medal, 2000, Huxley Medal, 2007, RAI. *Publications:* Kalahari Village Politics: an African democracy, 1970; (ed with A. Richards) Councils in Action, 1971; Anthropologists and Anthropology: the British School 1922–1972, 1973, 3rd edn 1996; Changing Jamaica, 1976; (ed) The Social Anthropology of Radcliffe-Brown, 1977; Wives for Cattle: bridewealth and marriage in Southern Africa, 1982; (ed with J. Kuper) The Social Science Encyclopedia, 1985, 3rd edn 2004; South Africa and the Anthropologist, 1987; The Invention of Primitive Society: transformations of an illusion, 1988; (ed) Conceptualising Society, 1992; The Chosen Primate: human nature and cultural diversity, 1994; Culture: the anthropologists' account, 1999; Among the Anthropologists: history and context in anthropology, 1999. *Address:* 16 Muswell Road, N10 2BG. *T:* (020) 8883 0400. *Club:* Hampstead Golf.

KUREISHI, Hanif, CBE 2008; writer; *b* 5 Dec. 1954; *s* of Rafiushan Kureishi and Audrey Buss. *Educ:* King's College London. *Filmscripts:* My Beautiful Laundrette, 1984; Sammy and Rosie Get Laid, 1987; (also dir.) London Kills Me, 1991; My Son the Fanatic, 1998; The Mother, 2003; Venus, 2007; Weddings and Beheadings, 2007. *Publications: plays:* Outskirts, 1981; Borderline, 1981; Birds of Passage, 1983; Outskirts and Other Plays, 1992; Sleep With Me, 1999; When the Night Begins, 2004; *novels:* The Buddha of Suburbia, 1990 (televised 1993); The Black Album, 1995; Intimacy, 1998 (adapted as a film, 2000); Gabriel's Gift, 2001; Something to Tell You, 2008; *short stories:* Love in a Blue Time, 1997; Midnight All Day, 1999; *novella and short stories:* The Body, 2002; *non-fiction:* (ed jtly) The Faber Book of Pop, 1995; Dreaming and Scheming: reflections on writing and politics, 2002; My Ear at his Heart (memoir), 2004; The Word and The Bomb (essays), 2005. *Recreations:* pop music, cricket, sitting in pubs. *Address:* c/o Deborah Rogers, Rogers, Coleridge & White Ltd, 20 Powis Mews, W11 1SN.

KURTH, Air Vice-Marshal Nicholas Julian Eugene, CBE 2006 (OBE 1996; MBE 1990); Chief of Staff Support Air Command, since 2007; *b* 13 Sept. 1955; *s* of Heinz Kurth and Renate Kurth; *m* 1983, Sandra Johnson; two *s* one *d*. *Educ:* Archbishop Tenison's Grammar Sch.; Open Univ. Business Sch. (MBA 1991); King's Coll. London (MA Internat. Studies 2001). CEng 1999. Joined RAF as apprentice, RAF Halton, 1972; commnd 1978; Jun. Engrg Officer 3(F) Sqdn, 1980–83; Sen. Engrg Officer XI(F) Sqdn, 1988–90; RAF advanced staff course, 1991; Support Mgt Develt, 1991–95; OC Engrg and Supply Wing, RAF Leuchars, 1995–97; Aircraft Logistics Policy, 1997–2000, Dep. Dir Support Mgt Airworthiness, 2000–01, HQ Logistics Comd; rcds, 2001; Ministry of Defence: Jt Warfare, 2002–03; Dir of Progs, Defence Estates, 2003–06; Dir Logistics (Strike) Plans/Future, Defence Logistics Orgn, 2006–07. FRGS 1997; FRAeS 1999. *Recreations:* rock climbing, mountaineering (Pres., RAF Mountaineering Assoc., 2005–), fencing (Pres., RAF Fencing Union, 2002–), painting, enjoying the odd glass of wine (but not while fencing or rock climbing!). *Address:* Headquarters Air Command, Spitfire Block, Room 3E05, RAF High Wycombe, Bucks HP14 4UE. *Club:* Royal Air Force.

KUSHNER, Lindsey Joy; QC 1992; **Her Honour Judge Kushner;** a Circuit Judge, since 2000; *b* 16 April 1952; *d* of Harry Kushner and Rita Kushner (*née* Alexander); *m* 1976, David Norman Kaye; one *s* one *d*. *Educ:* Manchester High Sch. for Girls; Liverpool Univ. (LLB). Called to the Bar, Middle Temple, 1974; part time Chm., Medical Appeal Tribunal, 1989–2000, Disablement Appeal Tribunal, 1992–99; Asst Recorder, 1989–93; a Recorder, 1993–2000. Mem., Ethnic Adv. Cttee, Lord Chancellor's Dept, 1994–99. *Recreations:* cooking, cinema. *Address:* c/o Northern Circuit Administrator, Young Street Chambers, 76 Quay Street, Manchester M3 4PR.

KUSTOW, Michael David; writer, producer and director; *b* 18 Nov. 1939; *m* 1973, Orna (marr. diss. 1998), *d* of Jacob and Rivka Spector, Haifa, Israel. *Educ:* Haberdashers' Aske's; Wadham Coll., Oxford (BA Hons English). Festivals Organiser, Centre 42, 1962–63; Royal Shakespeare Theatre Company: Dir, RSC Club, Founder of Theatregoround, Editor of Flourish, 1963–67; Dir, Inst. of Contemporary Arts, 1967–70; Associate Dir, National Theatre, 1973–81; Commissioning Ed. for Arts progs, Channel Four TV, 1981–89; Dir, Michael Kustow Productions, 1990–; Co-Dir, The Greek Collection, 1990–. Lectr in Dramatic Arts, Harvard Univ., 1980–82; Vis. Prof., Royal Holloway, London Univ., 2000–. Chevalier de l'Ordre des Arts et des Lettres, République Française, 1980. *Productions:* Punch and Judas, Trafalgar Square, 1963; I Wonder, ICA, 1968; Nicholas Tomalin Reporting, 1975; Brecht Poetry and Songs, 1976; Larkinland, Groucho Letters, Robert Lowell, Audience, 1977–78; Miss South Africa, Catullus, A Nosegay of Light Verse, The Voice of Babel, Anatol, 1979; Iris Murdoch's Art and Eros, Shakespeare's Sonnets, Stravinsky's Soldier's Tale, 1980; Charles Wood's Has Washington Legs, Harold Pinter's Family Voices, 1981; The Mahabharata, 1989; The War that Never Ends, 1991; The Last Bolshevik, 1993; ABC of Democracy, 1994; A Maybe Day in Kazakhstan, 1994; Fireworks, 1994; Shakespeare Workshops, 1994; Everybody's Shakespeare Festival, 1994; Hiroshima, 1995; Jerusalem, Between Heaven and Hell, 1996; Dionysus and the Mighty Mouse, 1998; *films:* Prometheus, 1998; Pandaemonium, 1999; Tantalus, 2000. *Exhibitions:* Tout Terriblement Guillaume Apollinaire, ICA, 1968; AAARGH! A Celebration of Comics, ICA, 1971. *Publications:* Punch and Judas, 1964; The Book of US, 1968; Tank: an autobiographical fiction, 1975; One in Four, 1987; theatre@risk, 2000; Peter Brook: and the way of theatre, 2005. *Recreations:* painting, jazz. *Address:* 17 Haslemere Road, N8 9QP. *T:* (020) 8347 6423.

KVERNDAL, Simon Richard; QC 2002; *b* 22 April 1958; *s* of late Ole Sigvard and of Brenda Kverndal; *m* 1997, Sophie Rowsell; two *s*. *Educ:* Haileybury; Sidney Sussex Coll., Cambridge (MA). Called to the Bar, Middle Temple, 1982; barrister, specialising in maritime and commercial law, 1983–. Lloyd's Open Form Salvage Arbitrator, 2006–. Mem., Ct of Assts, Co. of Shipwrights, 1999–. Comdr d'Honneur, Commanderie du Bontemps de Medoc et Graves, 1994. *Recreations:* Real tennis, rackets, wine-tasting. *Address:* Quadrant Chambers, Quadrant House, 10 Fleet Street, EC4Y 1AU. *T:* (020) 7583 4444, *Fax:* (020) 7583 4455; *e-mail:* info@quadrantchambers.com. *Clubs:* Garrick, Queen's, MCC, Jesters; Hawks (Cambridge).

KWAPONG, Alexander Adum, MA, PhD Cantab; Director, African Programmes, Teacher Education, Research and Evaluation, The Commonwealth of Learning, Vancouver, 1991–93; *b* Akropong, Akwapim, 8 March 1927; *s* of E. A. Kwapong and Theophilia Kwapong; *m* 1956, Evelyn Teiko Caesar, Ada; six *d*. *Educ:* Presbyterian junior and middle schools, Akropong; Achimota Coll.; King's Coll., Cambridge (Exhibr, Minor Schol. and Foundn Schol.). BA 1951, MA 1954, PhD 1957, Cantab. 1st cl. prelims, Pts I and II, Classical Tripos, 1951; Sandys Res. Student, Cambridge Univ.; Richards Prize, Rann Kennedy Travel Fellowship, King's Coll., Cambridge. Lectr in Classics, UC Gold

Coast, 1953, Sen. Lectr in Classics 1960; Vis. Prof., Princeton Univ., 1961–62; Prof. of Classics, Univ. of Ghana, 1962; Dean of Arts, Pro-Vice-Chancellor, Univ. of Ghana, 1962–65, Vice-Chancellor 1966–75; Vice-Rector for Instl Planning and Resource Develt, UN Univ., 1976–88 (Sen. Advr to Rector, 1988–); Lester B. Pearson Prof. in Develt Studies, Dalhousie Univ., Halifax, Canada, 1988–91. Chairman: Educn Review Cttee, Ghana Govt, 1966–67; Smithsonian Instn 3rd Internat. Symposium, 1969; Assoc. of Commonwealth Univs, 1971. Sir Samuel Manuwa Meml Lectr, W African Coll. of Surgeons, 1990. Member: Admin. Bd, Internat. Assoc. Univs, Paris, 1970–80; Exec. Bd, Assoc. African Univs, 1967–74; Bd of Trustees, Internat. Council for Educnl Develt, NY; Aspen Inst. for Humanistic Studies, 1972–85; Board of Directors: Internat. Assoc. for Cultural Freedom, Paris, 1967–75; Internat. Cttee for the Study of Educnl Exchange; Aspen Berlin Inst., 1975–; IDRC; Harold Macmillan Trust, 1986–; Internat. Foundn for Educn and Self Help, Phoenix, Arizona, 1988–; African Leadership Forum. Consultant, World Bank, 1988–89. Fellow, Ghana Academy of Arts and Sciences. Hon. DLitt: Warwick; Ife; Ghana; Hon. LLD Princeton. Order of Volta, Ghana. *Publications:* The Role of Classical Studies in Africa Today, 1969; Higher Education and Development in Africa Today: a reappraisal, 1979; Underdevelopment and the Challenges of the 1980's: the role of knowledge, 1980; The Relevance of the African Universities to the Development Needs of Africa, 1980; What Kind of Human Beings for the 21st Century—a second look, 1981; The Humanities and National Development: a second look, 1984; The Crisis of Development: education and identity, 1985; Medical Education and National Development, 1987; Culture, Development and African Unity, 1988; African Scientific and Technical Institution—Building and the Role of International Co-operation, 1988; The Challenge of Education in Africa, 1988; (ed with B. Lesser) Capacity Building and Human Resource Development in Africa, 1990; (ed with B. Lesser) Meeting the Challenge: the African Capacity Building Initiative, 1992; *contribs to:* Grecs et Barbars, 1962; Dawn of African History (ed R. Oliver); Man and Beast: Comparative Social Behaviour (ed J. F. Eisenberg and W. S. Dillon), 1971; Pearson Notes, 1988–89; The Role of Service-Learning in International Education (procs of Wingspread conf.) (ed S. W. Showalter), 1989; Culture, Development and Democracy: role of intellectuals in Africa, 1991; Recent Trends in Governance in African Universities: the challenge of scientific and intellectual leadership, 1992; various articles in classical jls, especially on Ancient and Greco-Roman Africa; various addresses and lectures on internat. higher educn in ICED pubns. *Recreations:* tennis, billiards, music and piano-playing, learning Japanese. *Address:* 19 Highfield Avenue, Golders Green, NW11 9EU. *T:* (020) 8209 0878. *Club:* Athenæum.

KYDD, Ian Douglas; HM Diplomatic Service, retired; *b* 1 Nov. 1947; *s* of late Alexander Henry John Kydd and Sheila Doreen Riley Kydd (*née* Kinnear); *m* 1968, Elizabeth Louise Pontius; one *s* one *d. Educ:* Melville Coll., Edinburgh. DSAO, later FCO, 1966; Attaché, New Delhi, 1970–74; Dep. Dir, later Dir, Radio and TV Div., British Inf. Services, NY, 1974–79; FCO, 1979; Press Officer to Prime Minister, 1981–83; First Sec., Lagos, 1984–88, Ottawa, 1988–92; Dep. Head, News Dept and Head of Newsroom, FCO, 1993–95; Consul-Gen. and Counsellor (Mgt), Moscow, 1995–98; Consul-Gen., Vancouver, 1998–2002; Counsellor (Mgt), New Delhi, 2003–06; Counsellor: Beirut, 2006; Kabul, 2006–07. *Recreations:* all sport, esp. downhill ski-ing, golf. *Address:* e-mail: ian@kydd.com. *Clubs:* Gog Magog Golf (Cambridge); Tuesday Lunch (New Delhi).

KYDLAND, Prof. Finn Erling, PhD; Jeffrey Henley Professor, University of California, Santa Barbara, since 2004; Richard P. Simmons Distinguished Professor, Tepper School of Business, Carnegie Mellon University, since 2007; *b* 1943; *s* of Martin Kydland and Johanna Kydland; *m* 1968, Liv Kjellevold (marr. diss.); two *s* two *d; m* Tonya Schooler. *Educ:* Norwegian Sch. of Econs and Business Admin (BS 1968); Carnegie Mellon Univ. (PhD 1973). Norwegian Sch. of Econs and Business Admin, 1973–76; Associate Prof., then Prof. of Econs, Carnegie Mellon Univ., 1977–2004. (Jtly) Nobel Prize in Economics, 2004. *Publications:* contrib. learned jls. *Address:* Department of Economics, 2127 North Hall, University of California, Santa Barbara, CA 93106, USA.

KYLE, Barry Albert; freelance director, since 1991; Hon. Associate Director, Royal Shakespeare Company, since 1991 (Associate Director, 1978–91); *b* 25 March 1947; *s* of Albert Ernest Kyle and Edith Ivy Bessie Gaskin; *m* 1st, 1971, Christine Susan Iddon (marr. diss. 1988); two *s* one *d;* 2nd, 1990, Lucy Joy Maycock (marr. diss. 2003); one *d. Educ:* Birmingham Univ. (BA, MA). Associate Dir, Liverpool Playhouse, 1970–72; joined RSC as Asst Dir, 1973; first Artistic Dir, Swan Theatre, Stratford-upon-Avon, 1987; numerous RSC productions and directing abroad, incl. Australia, Israel, USA, Czechoslovakia, Japan, Italy and Asia; founding Artistic Dir, Swine Palace Productions, La, USA; Dir, Theatre for a New Audience, NYC, 1995–96; Shakespeare's Globe, London: Master of Play, 2001; Dir, Women's Co., 2003. Dir, The Coventry Mysteries, 2006 (Daily Mail Dir of the Year). Vis. Dir, Czechoslovak Nat. Theatre, Prague (first Briton to direct there). Prof., Univ. of Missouri, 2003. *Publications:* Sylvia Plath: a dramatic portrait, 1976; contribs to Literary Review. *Recreation:* foreign travel. *Address:* Flat 5, 20 Charing Cross Road, WC2H 0HU. *T:* (020) 7836 5911.

KYLE, David William, CBE 2006; Member, Criminal Cases Review Commission, 1997–2005; *b* 30 March 1951; *s* of William and Judy Kyle; *m* 1st, 1975, Rosemary Elizabeth Bazire (marr. diss. 2006); two *d;* 2nd, 2007, Glenys Stacey. *Educ:* Monkton Combe Sch.; Queens' Coll., Cambridge (BA). Called to the Bar, Inner Temple, 1973; Office of Director of Public Prosecutions: Legal Asst, 1975–79; Sen. Legal Asst, 1979–86; Crown Prosecution Service: Branch Crown Prosecutor, 1986–89; Head of Div., HQ Casework, 1989–93; Head of HQ Casework, then Chief Crown Prosecutor, Central Casework, 1993–97. Member: Fitness to Practise Panel, GMC, 2006–; Disciplinary Cttee, RICS; Professional Conduct Bd, BPsS. *Recreations:* music, walking, cycling.

KYLE, Francis Ferdinand; Founder and Director, Francis Kyle Gallery, since 1978; *b* 20 Jan. 1944; *s* of Ferdinand and Dilys Kyle; *m* 1996, Christine Ann Caddick. *Educ:* Harrow; Jesus Coll., Oxford (Schol.; MA). Foreign Rights: George Rainbird Publishers, 1968–71; William Heinemann Publishers, 1972–73; Dir, Thumb Gall., 1974–78. *Publications:* (with R. Ingrams) The Ridgeway, Europe's Oldest Road: paintings from Francis Kyle Gallery, 1988; Lair of the Leopard: twenty artists go in search of Lampedusa's Sicily, 2006; numerous exhibn catalogues. *Recreations:* reading, walking. *Address:* Francis Kyle Gallery, 9 Maddox Street, W1S 2QE. *T:* (020) 7499 6870, *Fax:* (020) 7495 0180; *e-mail:* info@ franciskylegallery.com. *Clubs:* Garrick, Arts.

KYLE, James, CBE 1989; FRCSE; FRCSI; FRCS; Chairman, Raigmore Hospital NHS Trust, 1993–97; *b* 26 March 1925; *s* of John Kyle and Dorothy Frances Kyle; *m* 1950, Dorothy Elizabeth Galbraith; two *d. Educ:* Queen's Univ., Belfast. MB BCh BAO 1947 (Gold Medal in Surgery); MCh 1956 (Gold Medal); DSc 1972. FRCSI 1954; FRCS 1954; FRCSEd 1964. Mayo Clinic, USA, 1950; Tutor in Surgery, QUB, 1952; Lectr in Surgery, Univ. of Liverpool, 1957; Aberdeen University: Sen. Lectr, Surgery, 1959; Mem., Univ. Senatus, 1970; Consultant Surgeon, Aberdeen Royal Infirmary, 1959–89; Chm., Grampian Health Bd, 1989–93 (Mem., 1973). Mem., GMC, 1979–94; Chairman: Scottish Cttee for Hosp. Med. Services, 1977–81; Rep. Body, BMA, 1984–87; Scottish Jt Consultants' Cttee, 1984–89. British Council lectr, SE Asia, S America, 1963–74. Ext.

Examr, Belfast, Dublin, Dundee, Edinburgh, Sydney, West Indies. Pres., Aberdeen Medico-Surgical Soc. Bicentenary, 1989–90; Member: Council, Surgical Res. Soc., 1972–74; Internat. Soc. of Surgery, 1971–84; Cons. Med. Soc., 1988–93. Regl Rep., War Memls Trust, 2004–. Patron, Royal Scottish Nat. Orch. MInstD. FRPSL; FRAS. Burgess of Aberdeen, 1990. *Publications:* Peptic Ulceration, 1960; Pye's Surgical Handicraft, 21st edn, 1962; Scientific Foundations of Surgery, 4th edn, 1989; Crohn's Disease, 1973; papers on surgery, history, philately. *Recreations:* astronomy, amateur radio (callsign GM4 CHX), philately. *Address:* Grianan, 7 Fasaich, Gairloch, Ross-shire IV21 2DH. *T:* (01445) 712398. *Club:* Royal Northern (Aberdeen).

KYLE, (James) Terence; General Counsel, Nomura International plc, 2004–07; *b* 9 May 1946; *s* of James Kyle and Elizabeth Kyle (*née* Cinnamond); *m* 1975, Diana Jackson; one *s* two *d. Educ:* Royal Belfast Academical Instn; Christ's Coll., Cambridge (MA). Linklaters & Paines, later Linklaters & Alliance, subseq. Linklaters: Articled Clerk, 1970–72; Solicitor, 1972–79; Partner, 1979–89; Head, Internat. Finance, 1989–95; Managing Partner, 1995–98; Chief Exec., 1998–2001; Managing Partner, Americas, 2001–03. *Recreations:* cricket, tennis, golf.

KYLE, Peter William; Chief Executive, The Shakespeare Globe Trust (formerly General Director, International Shakespeare Globe Centre), since 1998; *b* 21 Nov. 1948; *s* of late Robert Kyle and Evelyn Kyle (*née* Palliser-Bosomworth); *m* Kathryn Anna Grundy; two *d. Educ:* Rambert Sch. of Ballet; Bretton Hall Coll., Yorks; Inst. fur Buhnentanz, Cologne. Former ballet dancer; soloist: Northern Ballet Theatre, 1971–73; Royal New Zealand Ballet, 1973–75; Dance Advr, Leics Educn Authy, 1975–81; Dance Officer, Arts Council of GB, 1981–83; Artistic Dir, Queen's Hall Arts Centre, Hexham, 1983–88; Chief Exec., Scottish Ballet, 1988–95; arts consultant and choreographer, 1995–97; Dean, Arts Educational Sch., London, 1997–98. CCMI 2002. Hon. Fellow, London South Bank Univ., 2005. *Address:* The Shakespeare Globe Trust, 21 New Globe Walk, SE1 9DT.

KYLE, Air Vice-Marshal Richard Henry, CB 1997; MBE 1977; a Gentleman Usher to the Queen, since 2002; *b* 4 Jan. 1943; *s* of Air Chief Marshal Sir Wallace Hart Kyle, GCB, KCVO, CBE, DSO, DFC and Lady (Molly) Kyle; *m* 1971, Anne Weatherup; two *s* two *d. Educ:* Cranbrook Sch., Kent; RAF Tech. College, Henlow; Southampton Univ. (BSc Eng 1964). CEng 1971. FRAeS 1993. Served RAF stations: Syerston, 1965–67; Acklington, 1967–68; Ternhill, 1968–69; Changi, 1969–71; MoD, 1971–73; No 1 (F) Sqn, RAF Wittering, 1973–76; MoD, 1976–78; RAF Staff Coll., 1978; RAF Gütersloh, 1979–81; MoD, 1982–84; RAF Halton, 1984–86; RCDS, 1987; MoD, 1988–89; RAF St Athan, 1990–92; Dir Gen. Support Services (RAF), 1992–93; AOC Maintenance Units, RAF Logistics Comd, 1993–97. *Recreations:* squash, orienteering, golf, offshore sailing, hill walking. *Club:* Royal Air Force.

KYLE, Terence; *see* Kyle, J. T.

KYLES, Raymond William; HM Diplomatic Service; Deputy High Commissioner, Islamabad, Pakistan, since 2008; *b* 10 March 1956; *s* of William and Elizabeth Kyles; *m* 2007, Kate Short; two *s. Educ:* Glasgow Acad.; Univ. of Strathclyde (BA Business Admin 1980). Joined HM Diplomatic Service, 1980: FCO, 1980–82; UKMIS Geneva, 1982–85; UKREP Brussels, 1985–87; FCO, 1987–91; First Sec., Pretoria, 1991–95; Dep. Press Sec. to Sec. of State, 1996–98 and 2000–01; Dep. Perm. Rep. to OECD, 1998–2000; Pol Advr, Unilever UK, 2001–03 (on secondment); Dep. High Comr, Kenya, 2003–07. *Recreations:* indie music, football, golf, Rugby, films, travel. *Address:* c/o Foreign and Commonwealth Office, King Charles Street, SW1A 2AH; *e-mail:* ray.kyles@fco.gov.uk.

KYLIÁN, Jirí; Resident Choreographer and Adviser, Nederlands Dans Theater, since 1999 (Artistic Director, 1975–99); *b* Prague, 21 March 1947; *s* of Vaclav Kylián and Marketá Pestová. *Educ:* Ballet Sch., Nat. Theatre, Prague; Prague Conservatory; Royal Ballet Sch., London. Stuttgarter Ballett, Germany; Guest Choreographer, Nederlands Dans Theater, 1973–75; *works choreographed* include: Viewers, 1973; Stoolgame, 1974; La cathédrale engloutie, 1975; Return to a Strange Land, 1975; Sinfonietta, 1978; Symphony of Psalms, 1978; Forgotten Land, 1981; Svadebka, 1982; Stamping Ground, 1983; L'Enfant et les Sortilèges, 1984; No More Play, 1988; Falling Angels, 1989; Sweet Dreams, 1990; Sarabande, 1990; Petite Mort, 1991; As If Never Been, 1992; No Sleep Till Dawn of Day, 1992; Whereabouts Unknown, 1993; Double You, 1994; Arcimboldo, 1995; Tears of Laughter, 1996; Wings of Wax, 1997; A Way a Lone, 1998; Indigo Rose, 1998; Half Past, 1999; Doux Mensonges, 1999; Study from Blackbird, 2002. Has worked with numerous cos, incl. Royal Swedish Ballet, Royal Danish Ballet, Royal Ballet, London, Finnish Nat. Ballet, Aust. Ballet, Nat. Ballet of Canada, Amer. Ballet Theatre, Wiener Staatsoper, Tokyo Ballet, Opéra de Paris, Rambert Dance Co. Hon. Dr, Juilliard Sch., NY, 1997. Critics' Award for Dance, Edinburgh Fest., 1996, 1997; Joost van den Vondel Preis, 1997. Officier: Ordre des arts et des lettres (France); Order of Oranje Nassau (Netherlands), 1995; Golden Medal for Outstanding Merits (Czech Republic); Chevalier de la Légion d'Honneur (France), 2004. *Address:* c/o Nederlands Dans Theater, Schedeldoekshaven 60, 2511 En Den Haag, Netherlands. *T:* (70) 3609931; Kylián Foundation, Antonie Duyckstr. 115, 2582 TG Den Haag, Netherlands.

KYME, Rt Rev. Brian Robert; Director, Institute of Anglican Studies at St George's Cathedral, Perth, WA, since 2006; *b* 22 June 1935; *s* of John Robert Kyme and Ida Eileen Benson; *m* 1961, Doreen Muriel Williams; one *s* one *d. Educ:* Melbourne High School; Ridley Theological Coll., Melbourne; Aust. Coll. of Theology (ThL 1956); Melbourne Coll. of Divinity (Dip RE 1958); WA Coll. of Advanced Educn (BA 1989); Edith Cowan Univ. (MA 2005). MACE 1991. Ordained deacon, 1958, priest, 1960; Curate: St John's, E Malvern, 1958–60; Glenroy and Broadmeadows, 1960–61; Morwell, 1961–63; Vicar, St Matthew's, Ashburton, 1963–69; Dean, Holy Cross Cathedral, Geraldton, WA, 1969–74; Rector, Christ Church, Claremont, Perth, 1974–82; Archdeacon of Stirling, 1977–82; Asst Bishop of Perth, 1982–93; Nat. Dir, Australian Bd of Missions, later Anglican Bd of Mission-Australia, 1993–2000; Episcopal Asst to Primate of Australia, 2000–05. ChLJ, WA, 1985–93; ChLJ, NSW, 1998–99. *Recreations:* reading, music. *Address:* 153 Carr Street, West Perth, WA 6005, Australia. *T:* (home) (8) 93286065, (office) (8) 9325 5766, *Fax:* (8) 93256741.

KYNASTON, Nicolas; freelance organist, since 1971; Organist, Athens Concert Hall, since 1995; *b* 10 Dec. 1941; *s* of late Roger Tewkesbury Kynaston and Jessie Dearn Caecilia Kynaston (*née* Parkes); *m* 1st, 1961, Judith Felicity Heron (marr. diss. 1989); two *s* two *d;* 2nd, 1989, Susan Harwood Styles. *Educ:* Westminster Cathedral Choir Sch.; Downside; Accademia Musicale Chigiana, Siena; Conservatorio Santa Cecilia, Rome; Royal Coll. of Music. Organist of Westminster Cathedral, 1961–71; concert career, 1971–, travelling throughout Europe, North America, Asia and Africa. Début recital, Royal Festival Hall, 1966; Recording début, 1968. Artistic Dir, Athens Organ Fest., 1997, 1999. Organ professor, Royal Acad. of Music, 2002–. Consultant, J. W. Walker & Sons Ltd, 1982–83 (Artistic Dir, 1978–82); Organ Consultant: Bristol Cathedral, 1986–91; St Chad's Cathedral, Birmingham, 1989–94; Bath Abbey, 1989–97; Tewkesbury Abbey, 1993–97; City of Halle, Germany, 1997–2000; Rugby Sch., 1998–2001. Mem., Westminster Abbey Fabric Commn, 2000–04. Jury member: Grand Prix de Chartres,

1971; St Albans Internat. Organ Festival, 1975. Pres., Incorp. Assoc. of Organists, 1983–85; Chm., Assoc. of Ind. Organ Advrs, 1997–2000. Chm., Nat. Organ Teachers' Encouragement Scheme, 1993–95. Hon. FRCO 1976. Records incl. 6 nominated Critic's Choice; EMI/CFP Sales Award, 1974; MTA nomination Best Solo Instrumental Record of the Year, 1977; Deutscher Schallplattenpreis, 1978; Preis der Deutschen Schallplattenkritik, 1988. *Publication:* Transcriptions for Organ, 1997. *Recreations:* walking, church architecture. *Address:* 28 High Park Road, Kew Gardens, Richmond-upon-Thames, Surrey TW9 4BH. *T:* (020) 8878 4455, *Fax:* (020) 8392 9314.

KYNOCH, George Alexander Bryson; Drumduan Associates, since 1997; *b* 7 Oct. 1946; *s* of late Lt Col Gordon Bryson Kynoch, CBE and Nesta Alicia Janet Thora (*née* Lyon); *m* 1971, Dr Rosslyn Margaret McDevitt (*d* 2002); one *s* one *d. Educ:* Cargilfield Sch., Edinburgh; Glenalmond Coll., Perthshire; Univ. of Bristol (BSc Hons Mech. Engrg). Plant Engr Silicones Plant, ICI Ltd, Nobel Div., 1968–71; G. and G. Kynoch, subseq. Kynoch Group, 1971–92; Finance Dir, then Jt Man. Dir; Chief Exec., 1981–90; Gp Exec. Dir, 1990–92; non-exec. Dir, 1992–95. Non-executive Director: Aardvark Holdings Ltd, 1992–95; PSL Holdings, 1998; Premisys Technologies (formerly WML Gp, then Premisys Gp) plc, 1998–2001; Talent Gp plc, 2003–; tecc-IS plc, 2003–04; non-executive Chairman: Silvertech Internat., 1997–2000; London Marine Gp, 1998–2004; Muir Matheson, 1998–2007; Benson Gp, 1998–2005; Jetcam Internat. Hldgs, 1999–2003; TEP Exchange Gp plc, 2001–; RDF Gp plc (formerly Eurolink Managed Services plc), 2003–06; Toluna plc, 2005–; OCZ Technology Inc., 2006–; Madwaves (UK) Ltd, 2006–; Mercury Group plc, 2007–. Chm., Scottish Woollen Publicity Council, 1983–90; Pres., Scottish Woollen Industry, 1990–91; Mem., Aberdeen and Dist MMB, 1988–92; Dir, Moray Badenoch and Strathspey Local Enterprise Co. Ltd, 1991–92. MP (C) Kincardine and Deeside, 1992–97; contested (C) Aberdeenshire West and Kincardine, 1997. Parliamentary Private Secretary: to Minister of State, FCO, 1992–94; to Sec. of State for Educn, 1994–95; Parly Under Sec. of State, Scottish Office (Minister for Industry and Local Govt), 1995–97. Mem., Scottish Affairs Select Cttee, 1992–95. Chm., Moray and Banff Cons. and Unionist Assoc., 1990–92; Vice-Chm., Northern Area, Scottish Cons.

and Unionist Assoc., 1991–92. *Recreations:* golf, travel. *Address:* Newton of Drumduan, Dess, Aboyne, Aberdeenshire AB34 5BD. *Club:* Carlton.

KYPRIANOU, Markos; Minister of Foreign Affairs, Cyprus, since 2008; *b* 22 Jan. 1960. *Educ:* Univ. of Athens; Trinity Coll., Cambridge (LLM 1983); Harvard Law Sch. Associate, Antis Triantafyllides & Sons, law firm, 1985–91; Partner, Kyprianou & Boyiadjis, subseq. George L. Savvides & Co., 1991–2003. Mem., Nicosia Municipal Council, 1986–91. MP (Democratic) Nicosia, Cyprus, 1991–2003; Minister of Finance, 2003–04. Mem., EC, 2004–08. *Address:* Ministry of Foreign Affairs, Presidential Palace Avenue, 1447 Nicosia, Cyprus.

KYRIAZIDES, Nikos Panayis; Comdr, Order of George I of Greece; Deputy Minister, Ministry of Finance, Greece, 1994–96; *b* 3 Sept. 1927; *m* 1960, Ellie Kyrou; one *s* one *d. Educ:* Exeter Coll., Oxford Univ. (MA); Chicago Univ. Min. of Co-ordination, 1949; Head, Monetary Policy Div., 1950–51; Dir, External Payments and Trade, 1951–54; Alternate Economic Advr, Bank of Greece, 1956–60; Mem., Greek Delegn, negotiations for EFTA and assoc. of Greece to EEC, 1957–61; seconded to Min. of Co-ordination as Dir Gen., relations with EEC, 1962–64; Economic Advr, Nat. Bank of Greece, 1964–67; Sen. Economist, IMF, 1968–70; Advr to Cyprus Govt, negotiations for assoc. of Cyprus to EEC, 1971–72; Dep. Governor, Bank of Greece, 1974–77; Head of Greek delegn to Accession negotiations to the EEC, 1974–77; Advr to Cyprus Govt on relations with EEC, 1979–82; Ambassador to UK, and to Republic of Iceland, 1982–85; Alternate Exec. Dir, IMF, 1986–92. Knight Commander: Order of Merit (Italy); Order of Leopold II (Belgium); Comdr, Order of Merit (FRG). *Address:* 28 Loukianou Street, Athens 10675, Greece. *Club:* Athens (Athens).

KYTE, Peter Eric; QC 1996; a Recorder, since 1991; *b* 8 May 1945; *s* of Eric Frank Kyte and Cicely Evelyn Leslie Kyte; *m* 1969, Virginia Cameron Cornish-Bowden; one *s* one *d. Educ:* Wellington Coll.; Trinity Hall, Cambridge (MA Law). Called to the Bar, Gray's Inn, 1970; in business, 1970–74; Asst Recorder, 1988. *Recreations:* tennis, motorcycling, scuba diving, watching England perform on the sports field. *Address:* Queen Elizabeth Building, Temple, EC4Y 9BS. *T:* (020) 7583 5766. *Club:* Aula (Cambridge).

L

LAAJAVA, Jaakko, Commander First Class, Order of the Lion of Finland, 2004; Hon. CMG 1995; Ambassador of Finland to the Court of St James's, since 2005; *b* Joensuu, Finland, 23 June 1947; *s* of Erkki Laajava and Aune Laajava; *m* 1971, Pirjoriitta, (Rita), Väyrynen; one *s* two *d. Educ:* Stockholm Univ. (BA 1972); Helsinki Univ. (MA 1972). Entered Finnish Foreign Service, 1972; assignments in Geneva, Paris, Warsaw, Belgrade, Madrid and Washington, DC, 1973–90; Dir-Gen. for Political Affairs, 1992; Ambassador to the US, 1996–2001; Under-Sec., 2001–05. Fellow, Harvard Univ., 1985. *Publications:* several articles on foreign and security policy. *Recreations:* music, golf. *Address:* Embassy of Finland, 38 Chesham Place, SW1X 8HW. *T:* (020) 7838 6200; *e-mail:* jaakko.laajava@formin.fi. *Clubs:* Travellers, Royal Automobile; Harvard Club of Finland.

LABANYI, Prof. Jo(sephine), FBA 2005; Professor of Spanish, New York University, since 2006; *b* 28 March 1946; *d* of Cyril and Louisa Wood; *m* 1969, Peter Labanyi (marr. diss. 1975). *Educ:* Lady Margaret Hall, Oxford (BA Hons 1st cl. Spanish 1967). Birkbeck Coll., London, 1971–2000: Lectr, 1971–85, Sen. Lectr, 1985–92, Reader, 1992–95, in Spanish; Prof. in Spanish Cultural Studies, 1995–2000; Dir, Inst. of Romance Studies, Sch. of Advanced Study, London, 1997–2002; Prof. of Spanish and Cultural Studies, Univ. of Southampton, 2001–06. Vis. King Juan Carlos I Prof. of Spanish Culture and Civilization, NY Univ., 2002. An Ed., Jl of Spanish Cultural Studies, 2000– (Founding Ed., 2000); Mem. Adv. Bd, Jl of Romance Studies, 2003– (Founding Ed., 2001). *Publications:* Ironía e historia en 'Tiempo de silencio', 1985; Myth and History in the Contemporary Spanish Novel, 1989; (ed) Galdós, 1992; (ed and trans) Benito Pérez Galdós, Nazarín, 1993; (ed jtly) Spanish Cultural Studies: an introduction, 1995; (ed jtly) Culture and Gender in Nineteenth-century Spain, 1995; Gender and Modernization in the Spanish Realist Novel, 2000; (ed) Constructing Identity in Contemporary Spain, 2002. *Recreations:* classical music, walking round cities. *Address:* Department of Spanish and Portuguese, New York University, 13–19 University Place, New York, NY 10003–4556, USA. *T:* (212) 9987570, *Fax:* (212) 9954149; *e-mail:* jo.labanyi@nyu.edu.

LACEY, George William Brian; Keeper, Department of Transport, Science Museum, London, 1971–86; *b* 15 Nov. 1926; *m* 1956, Lynette (*née* Hogg); two *s. Educ:* Brighton, Hove and Sussex Grammar Sch., 1938–44; Brighton Technical Coll., 1944–47; BSc(Eng) 2nd Cl. Hons (External, London). National Service, REME, 1947–49. Rolls-Royce Ltd, Derby: Grad. Apprentice, Tech. Asst, Mechanical Develt and Performance Analysis, 1949–54; Asst Keeper, Science Museum, London, SW7, 1954–71. Chm., Historical Gp, Royal Aeronautical Soc., 1971–78; Vice-Pres., Assoc. British Transport Museums, 1990– (Chm., 1973–83); Mem. Council, Transport Trust, 1978–89. *Recreations:* golf, genealogy. *Address:* Hurst Grange Cottage, Albourne Road, Hurstpierpoint, W Sussex BN6 9ES. *T:* (01273) 833914.

LACEY, Prof. (John) Hubert, MD; FRCPsych; Professor of Psychiatry, St George's, University of London, since 1991; *b* 4 Nov. 1944; *s* of Percy Hubert Lacey and Sheila Margaret Lacey (*née* Neal); *m* 1976, Susan Millicent Liddiard; two *s* one *d. Educ:* Loughborough Grammar Sch.; Univ. of St Andrews (MB ChB 1969); Univ. of London (MPhil 1974); Univ. of Dundee (MD 1988); DRCOG 1972. MRCPsych 1974, FRCPsych 1985. Jun. hosp. appts, Dundee, St Thomas' and St George's Hosps, London, 1969–78; Sen. Lectr, Middlesex Hosp. Med. Sch., London, 1978–80; Sen. Lectr, 1980–87, Reader, 1987–91, Chm., 1991–2003, St George's, Univ. of London. Clinical Director and Consultant: St George's Eating Disorders Service, 1980–; Yorkshire Centre for Eating Disorders, Leeds, 2003–07; Peninsula Eating Disorder Service, Exeter, 2004–; Medical Adviser: BUPA, 1994–99; Priory Hosp. Gp, 1990–; Surrey NHS Trust; Consultant, Eating Disorder Unit, Priory Hosp., 1989–; Clin. Dir, Capio Nightingale Hosp., London, 2007–. Dir, Newbridge Healthcare Systems, 2006–. Non-exec. Dir, various NHS Trusts, 1991–99. Mem., Court of Electors, 1991–2006, Council, 2002–06, RCPsych. Chm., Europ. Council on Eating Disorders; Past Pres., Internat. Coll. of Psychosomatic Medicine. Patron, Eating Disorders Assoc. Freeman, City of London, 1986; Liveryman, Co. of Plaisterers, 1986– (Mem. Ct of Assts, 2007–). *Publications:* Psychological Management of the Physically Ill, 1989; Overcoming Anorexia Nervosa, 2007; over 140 contribs in books and learned jls on anorexia nervosa, bulmic nervosa, obesity, psychosomatic illnesses. *Recreations:* using the running-machine, interior decoration, hill walking. *Address:* 5 Atherton Drive, Wimbledon, SW19 5LB. *T:* (020) 8947 5976; *e-mail:* jhubertlacey@hotmail.com; Department of Psychiatry, Level 6, St George's, University of London, SW17 0RE. *T:* (020) 8725 5528/5529; *e-mail:* hlacey@sgul.ac.uk. *Club:* Athenæum.

LACEY, Prof. Nicola Mary, FBA 2001; Professor of Criminal Law and Legal Theory, London School of Economics, since 1998; *b* 3 Feb. 1958; *d* of John McAndrew and Gillian Wroth; *m* 1991, David Soskice. *Educ:* University Coll. London (LLB 1979); University Coll., Oxford (BCL 1981). Lectr in Law, UCL, 1981–84; Fellow in Law, New Coll., Oxford, and CUF Lectr, Univ. of Oxford, 1984–95; Prof. of Law, Birkbeck Coll., Univ. of London, 1995–97. Guest Prof., Humboldt Univ., 1995; Adjunct Prof., Res. Sch. of Social Scis, ANU, 1998–; Fellow, Wissenschaftskolleg zu Berlin, 1999–2000; Vis. Prof., Global Law Sch., New York Univ., 2001–. Hon. Fellow, New Coll., Oxford, 2007–. *Publications:* State Punishment: political principles and community values, 1988; (with Celia Wells and Oliver Quick) Reconstructing Criminal Law, 1990, 3rd edn, 2003; (with Elizabeth Frazer) The Politics of Community, 1993; Criminal Justice: a reader, 1994; Unspeakable Subjects: feminist essays in legal and social theory, 1998; A Life of H. L. A. Hart: the nightmare and the noble dream, 2004: *Address:* Law Department, London School of Economics, Houghton Street, WC2A 2AE. *T:* (020) 7955 7254, *Fax:* (020) 7955 7366; *e-mail:* n.lacey@lse.ac.uk.

LACEY, Air Vice-Marshal Richard Howard, CBE 2004; Commander British Forces and Administrator of the Sovereign Base Areas, Cyprus, 2006–08; *b* 11 Dec. 1953; *s* of Henry Howard Lacey and Mary Elliot Lacey; *m* 1980, Catherine Helen Brown; one *s* one *d. Educ:* John Ruskin Grammar Sch.; Peterhouse, Cambridge (BA 1975). RAF Coll., Cranwell, 1975–77; Flying Instr, 1984–85; Flight Comdr, 72 Sqn, 1985–87; RAF Staff Coll., 1988; PSO to Dep. C-in-C, later C-in-C, HQ STC, 1989–91; OC 33 Sqn, 1992–94; Station Comdr, RAF Benson, 1997–99; Dir NATO Policy, MoD, 2000–03; Comdr British Forces Falkland Is, 2003–05; UK Nat. Mil. Rep. to SHAPE, 2005–06. *Recreations:* photography, model engineering, industrial archaeology. *Address: e-mail:* cateandrichlacey@gmail.com. *Club:* Royal Air Force.

LACEY, Prof. Richard Westgarth, MD, PhD; FRCPath; Professor of Medical Microbiology, University of Leeds, 1983–98, now Emeritus; Consultant to Leeds Health Authority, 1983–98; *b* 11 Oct. 1940; *s* of Jack and Sybil Lacey; *m* 1972, Fionna Margaret Stone; two *d. Educ:* Felsted Sch., Essex; Cambridge Univ. (BA, MB, BChir; MD 1969); London Hosp.; Univ. of Bristol (PhD 1974). FRCPath 1985; DCH 1966. House Officer, London and Eastbourne, 1964–66; Sen. House Officer, 1966–67, Registrar, 1967–68, Bristol Royal Infirmary; Lectr, 1968–73, Reader in Clinical Microbiology, 1973–74, Univ. of Bristol; Consultant in Microbiology, 1974–83, and Consultant in Chemical Pathology, 1975–83, Queen Elizabeth Hosp., King's Lynn; Consultant in Chem. Path., E Anglian RHA, 1974–83. Consultant, WHO, 1983–. Evian Health Award, 1989; Caroline Walker Award, 1989; Freedom of Information Award, 1990. *Publications:* Safe Shopping, Safe Cooking, Safe Eating, 1989; Unfit for Human Consumption, 1991; Hard to Swallow, 1994; Mad Cow Disease: a history of BSE in Britain, 1994; Poison on a Plate, 1998; 210 contribs to learned scientific jls. *Recreations:* antique furniture, gardening, chess, sleeping, walking, eating (not recently).

LACEY, Robert (David Weston); author and broadcaster; *b* 3 Jan. 1944; *s* of late Leonard John Lacey and Vida Ivy Pamela (*née* Winch); *m* 1971, Alexandra Jane Avrach (separated 2005); two *s* one *d. Educ:* Clifton Nat. Infants' Sch.; Bristol Grammar Sch.; Selwyn Coll., Cambridge (MA, DipEd). Reporter and columnist, Johannesburg Sunday Times, 1967; ed. and compiler, Jackdaw collections of historical documents for children, 1967–74; writer, Illustrated London News, 1968; writer and Asst Ed., Sunday Times mag., 1969–73; Ed., Look! pages, Sunday Times, 1973–74; Guest Ed., The Court Historian, 2003, 2004; book reviewer, Oxford Jl of Islamic Studies; royal commentator, ITN, CNN, Good Morning America, ABC; writer and presenter: Aristocrats, BBC2 series, 1983; BBC Radio 4 series: The Year 1000, 2000; The Year 1901, 2001; Crown and People, 2002; The Year 1953, 2003; 1914: The Diaries of King George V, 2004. Mem., Cttee, Soc. for Court Studies, 2001–. Sec., Careers Cttee, Old Bristolians Soc., 2002–06. *Publications:* Robert, Earl of Essex, 1971; The Life and Times of Henry VIII, 1972; The Queens of the North Atlantic, 1973; Sir Walter Ralegh, 1973; Majesty: Elizabeth II and the House of Windsor, 1977; The Kingdom: Arabia and the House of Saud, 1981; (with M. Rand) Princess, 1982; Aristocrats, 1983; Ford: the men and the machine, 1986; God Bless Her!, 1987; Little Man: Meyer Lansky and the gangster life, 1991; Grace, 1994; Sotheby's: bidding for class, 1998; (with D. Danziger) The Year 1000, 1999; (with M. Rand) The Queen Mother's Century, 1999; Royal: Her Majesty Queen Elizabeth II, 2002 (US edn as Monarch: the life and reign of Elizabeth II); series Great Tales from English History: vol. 1, Cheddar Man to the Peasants' Revolt, 2003; vol. 2, Chaucer to the Glorious Revolution, 2004; vol. 3, Battle of the Boyne to DNA, 2006; 3 vol. omnibus edn, Great Tales from English History, 2007. *Recreations:* swimming, yoga, meditating, telephoning friends. *Address:* c/o Curtis Brown, 28/29 Haymarket, SW1Y 4SP; *e-mail:* robert@robertlacey.com. *Clubs:* Chelsea Arts, Frontline.

LACEY, Stephen Charles David Lloyd; gardener, author, journalist and broadcaster; *b* 6 May 1957; *s* of late Charles Leslie Lacey and Myra Lloyd Lacey (*née* Lloyd Williams). *Educ:* Trearddur House Prep. Sch.; Shrewsbury Sch.; Trinity Coll., Oxford (MA Mod. Langs). Early career in property investment; gardening columnist and feature writer, Daily Telegraph, 1989–; a presenter, Gardeners' World, BBC TV, 1992–2002; freelance horticultural lectr in UK, USA and Canada. FLS 2005. *Publications:* The Startling Jungle, 1986; Scent in Your Garden, 1991; Lawns and Ground Cover, 1991; Gardens of the National Trust, 1996, 2nd edn 2005; Real Gardening, 2002. *Recreations:* adventurous travel, tropical birdwatching, collecting, ski-ing. *Address:* 2 Queen's Gate Place, SW7 5NS. *T:* (020) 7584 8410.

LACHMANN, Sir Peter (Julius), Kt 2002; FRCP, FRCPath; FRS 1982; FMedSci; Sheila Joan Smith Professor of Immunology (formerly Tumour Immunology), University of Cambridge, 1977–99, now Emeritus Professor; Fellow of Christ's College, Cambridge, 1962–71 and since 1976; Head, Microbial Immunology Group, Centre for Veterinary Science, Cambridge, 1997–2006; *b* 23 Dec. 1931; *s* of late Heinz Lachmann and Thea (*née* Heller); *m* 1962, Sylvia Mary, *d* of Alan Stephenson; two *s* one *d. Educ:* Christ's Coll., Finchley; Trinity Coll., Cambridge (Hon. Fellow, 2007); University College Hosp. MA, MB BChir, PhD, ScD (Cantab). FRCP 1973; FRCPath 1981. John Lucas Walker Student, Dept of Pathology, Cambridge, 1958–60; Vis. Investigator, Rockefeller Univ., New York, 1960–61; Empire Rheumatism Council Res. Fellow, Dept of Pathology, Cambridge, 1962–64; Asst Dir of Res. in Pathology, Univ. of Cambridge, 1964–71; Prof. of Immunology, Royal Postgraduate Med. Sch., 1971–75; Hd, 1976–77, Hon. Hd, 1977–80, MRC Gp on Mechanisms in Tumour Immunity; Hon. Dir, MRC Mechanisms in Tumour Immunity Unit, later MRC Molecular Immunopathology Unit, 1980–97; Hon. Clin. Immunologist, Cambridge HA, 1976–99. Member: Systems Bd, MRC, 1982–86; Med. Adv. Cttee, British Council, 1983–97; Council, RCPath, 1982–85, 1989–93 (Pres., 1990–93); Gene Therapy Adv. Cttee, 1993–96; UNESCO Internat. Bioethics Cttee, 1993–98; Med. Educn Res. Co-ordinating Cttee, 1994–98; Scientific Adv. Bd, SmithKline Beecham, 1995–2000; Chm. Scientific Adv. Bd, Adprotech plc, 1997–2004; non-exec. Dir, Synovis plc, 2001–05. Chairman: Med. Res. Cttee, Muscular

Dystrophy Gp, 1987–91; Sci. Cttee, Assoc. Medical Res. Charities, 1988–92; Res. Adv. Cttee, CORE, 2003–. Trustee: Darwin Trust, 1991–2001; Arthritis Res. Campaign, 2000–06. President: Henry Kunkel Soc., 2003–05; European Fedn of Academies of Medicine, 2004–05. Vis. Investigator, Scripps Clinic and Research Foundn, La Jolla, 1966, 1975, 1980, 1986, 1989; Vis. Scientist, Basel Inst. of Immunology, 1971; RSM Vis. Prof. in USA (various centres), 1983; Smith Kline & French Vis. Prof. in Australia (various centres), 1987; Vis. Prof., Dept of Medicine, RPMS, London, 1986–89 (Fellow, 1995; FIC 2001). Meyerhoff Vis. Prof., Weizmann Inst., Rehovoth, 1989; Prof., Collège de France, 1993; RCS Sir Arthur Sims Travelling Prof., India, 1994; Lectures: Foundn, RCPath, 1983; Langdon-Brown, RCP, 1986; first R. R. Porter Meml, 1986; Heberden Oration, 1986; Prathap Meml, Malaysia, 1991; Charnock Bradley Meml, Royal (Dick) Vet. Sch., Edinburgh, 1994; Frank May Med. Scis, Univ. of Leicester, 1994; Vanguard Medica, Univ. of Surrey, 1998; Lloyd Roberts, Med. Soc. of London, 1999; first Jean Shanks, Acad. Med. Scis, 2001. Biological Sec., and a Vice-Pres., Royal Soc., 1993–98; Founder FMedSci 1998 (Pres., 1998–2002). Foreign Fellow, Indian Nat. Sci. Acad., 1997; Foreign Member: Norwegian Acad. of Science and Letters, 1991; Academia Europea, 1992. Hon. Fellow, Faculty of Pathology, RCPI, 1993; Hon. Mem., Assoc. of Physicians, 1998. Hon. DSc Leicester, 2005. Gold Medal, Eur. Complement Network, 1997; Medicine and Europe Sen. Prize, Acad. des Scis de la Santé, 2003. Associate Editor, Clinical and Experimental Immunology, 1989–2001. *Publications:* co-ed, Clinical Aspects of Immunology, 3rd edn 1975, 4th edn 1982, 5th edn 1993; papers in sci. jls on complement, microbial immunology and immunopathology. *Recreations:* walking in mountains, keeping bees. *Address:* Conduit Head, 36 Conduit Head Road, Cambridge CB3 0EY. *T:* (01223) 354433. *Club:* Athenæum.

LACKEY, Mary Josephine, CB 1985; OBE 1966; former Under Secretary, Department of Trade and Industry; *b* 11 Aug. 1925; *d* of William and Winifred Lackey. *Educ:* King Edward VI High Sch., Birmingham; Lady Margaret Hall, Oxford (MA). Board of Trade, 1946; Asst Principal, Central Land Bd, 1947–50; BoT, 1950–61; UK Delegn to EFTA and GATT, 1961–66; BoT, subseq. DTI and Dept of Trade, 1966–85; Asst Sec., 1968; Under Sec., 1974. *Club:* Oxford and Cambridge.

LACLOTTE, Michel René; Commandeur de la Légion d'honneur; Commandeur de l'ordre national du Mérite; Hon. CBE 1994; Director, The Louvre Museum, Paris, 1987–94; *b* 27 Oct. 1929; *s* of Pierre Laclotte, advocate, and Huguette (*née* de Kermabon). *Educ:* Lycée Pasteur, Neuilly; Institut d'art et d'archéologie, l'Université de Paris; Ecole du Louvre. Inspector, Inspectorate General of provincial museums, 1955–66; Chief Conservator: Dept of Paintings, Louvre Mus., 1966–87; Collections of Musée d'Orsay, 1978–86. *Publications:* works on history of art, catalogues, articles in art reviews, esp. on Italian paintings of 14th and 15th centuries and French primitives. *Address:* 10 bis rue du Pré-aux-Clercs, 75007 Paris, France.

LACOME, Myer; professional artist/designer; Principal, Duncan of Jordanstone College of Art, Dundee, 1978–87; *b* 13 Nov. 1927; *s* of Colman Lacome and Sara (*née* Sholl); *m* 1954, Jacci Edgar (*d* 2008); one *s* two *d. Educ:* Regional Coll. of Art, Liverpool. MSIAD, MSTD; FRSA. National Service, RAF, 1946–48. Post-grad. course, 1948–49; designer, New York, 1949–51; consultant designer, London, 1951–59; Head of Sch. of Design, Duncan of Jordanstone Coll. of Art, Dundee, 1962–77. Vis. Fellow, Royal Melbourne Inst. of Technol., 1979. Chm., Visual Art Cttee, Scottish Arts Council, 1986–93; Member: Council, CNAA, 1979–84; Higher Educn Cttee, Scottish Design Council, 1984–86; Governor, Scottish Film Council, 1982–. One-man exhibitions include: Paris: paintings and collages, French Cultural Inst., Edin., Paperpoint Gall., Covent Gdn, and Univ. of Dundee, 1992; Holocaust and After?, Chessel Gall., Edinburgh, 1995, Mackintosh Mus. Sch., Glasgow, 1996, Manchester Jewish Mus., 1997; Scottish Exec., 2000, 2001, 2003; works in permanent collections of nat. museums and galls in Europe and USA. *Publications:* papers on crafts in Scotland and on Scandinavian design and crafts. *Recreations:* enjoying: no longer sitting on committees or quangos, not wearing a tie, painting in my studio, listening to Bach, Glenn Gould, Miles Davis and Thelonius Monk. *Address:* 4 Campbells Close, off Royal Mile, Edinburgh EH8 8JJ.

LACON, Sir Edmund (Vere), 8th Bt *cr* 1818; *b* 3 May 1936; *s* of Sir George Vere Francis Lacon, 7th Bt, and of Hilary Blanche, *d* of late C. J. Scott, Adyar, Walberswick; *S* father, 1980; *m* 1963, Gillian, *d* of J. H. Middleditch, Wrentham, Suffolk; one *s* one *d. Educ:* Taverham Hall, Norfolk; Woodbridge School, Suffolk. RAF Regiment, 1955–59. *Recreations:* golf, water ski-ing, being politically incorrect. *Heir: s* (Edmund) Richard (Vere) Lacon [*b* 2 Oct. 1967; *m* 1997, Natalie, *o d* of Joginder Shinh].

LACOSTE, Prof. Paul, OC 1977; DUP; Rector, Université de Montréal, 1975–85, Professor Emeritus since 1987; Chairman, Federal Environmental Assessment Review of the Great Whale Project, 1991–98; *b* 24 April 1923; *s* of Emile Lacoste and Juliette Boucher Lacoste; *m* 1973 (marr. diss.); one *s* two *d. Educ:* Univ. de Montréal (BA, MA, LPh, LLL). DUP 1948. Fellow, Univ. of Chicago, 1946–47; Univ. de Montréal: Prof., Faculty of Philosophy, 1948; Full Prof., 1958; Vice-Rector, 1968–75; Vis. Prof., Faculty of Law, 1962–70 and 1985–87. Practising lawyer, 1964–66. Pres., Assoc. des universités partiellement ou entièrement de langue française, 1978–81. Hon. LLD: McGill, 1975; Toronto, 1978; Hon. DU Laval, 1986. Chevalier de la Légion d'Honneur, 1985. *Publications:* (jtly) Justice et paix scolaire, 1962; A Place of Liberty, 1964; Le Canada au seuil du siècle de l'abondance, 1969; Principes de gestion universitaire, 1970; (jtly) Education permanente et potentiel universitaire, 1977. *Address:* Université de Montréal, PO Box 6128, succursale Centre-Ville, Pavillon 2910, Montréal, QC H3C 3J7, Canada. *T:* (514) 3437727.

LACROIX, Christian Marie Marc; Commandeur de l'Ordre des Arts et des Lettres, 1998; Chevalier de la Légion d'Honneur, 2002; designer; *b* 16 May 1951; *s* of Maxime Lacroix and Jeannette Bergier; *m* 1989, Françoise Roesenstiehl. *Educ:* Paul Valéry Univ., Montpellier; Sorbonne. History of Art degree. Assistant at Hermès, 1978; Asst for Guy Paulin, 1980; designer for Patou, 1981–86; Creative Dir, Pucci, 2002–05. Pres., Centre National du Costume de Scène, 2006–. Golden Thimble Award, 1986 and 1988; CFDA Award, NY, 1987; Prix Balzac, 1989; Goldene Spinnrad, Krefeld, Germany, 1990; Molière Theatre Award, 1996, 2007. *Publications:* Pieces of a Pattern (autobiog.), 1992; The Diary of a Collection, 1996; Qui est là?, 2004; illustrator of albums, Styles d'aujourd'hui, 1995; Christian Lacroix on Fashion, 2006. *Address:* 73 Faubourg St Honoré, 75008 Paris, France. *T:* (1) 42687900.

LACROIX, Prof. Robert, OC; OQ; PhD; Fellow, Centre for Interuniversity Research and Analysis on Organisations, Montreal; Rector, University of Montreal, 1998–2005; *b* 15 April 1940; *s* of Léo Lacroix and Léonne Galarneau; *m* 1962, Ginette Teasdale; three *d. Educ:* Univ. of Montreal (BA, BSc, MA Econs); Univ. of Louvain, Belgium (PhD Econs 1970). University of Montreal: Asst Prof., 1970, Prof., 1979, Dept of Econs; Chm., Dept of Econs, 1977–83; Dir, Centre for R&D in Econs, 1985–87; Dean, Faculty of Arts and Scis, 1987–93; Pres. and CEO, Centre for Interuniv. Res. and Analysis on Orgns, 1994–98. Project Dir, Econ. Council of Canada, 1976–. Member, Board of Directors: Assoc. of Univs and Colls of Canada, 1998– (Pres., 2001–); Conf. of Rectors and Principals of Quebec Univs, 1998–; Ecole Polytechnique de Montréal, 1998–; Ecole des Hautes Etudes Commerciales, 1998–; Bd of Trade, Metropolitan Montreal, 2001–. Mem., Academic Adv. Cttee, Inst. of Canadian Bankers, 1999–; Mem. Bd of Govs, Montreal Conf. and Foundn for Educnl Exchange between Canada and USA. *Publications:* (with J. M. Cousineau) Wage Determination in Major Collective Agreements in the Private and Public Sectors, 1977; (with Y. Rabeau) Politiques nationales, Conjonctures régionales: la stabilisation économique, 1981; (with F. Martin) Les conséquences de la décentralisation régionale des activités de R&D, 1987; (with M. Huberman) Le partage de l'Emploi: solution au chômage ou frein à l'emploi, 1996. *Address:* CIRANO, 2020 Rue University, Montreal, QC H3A 2A5, Canada. *Clubs:* Mount Royal, Saint-Denis (Montreal).

LACY, Very Rev. David William; Moderator of the General Assembly of the Church of Scotland, 2005–06; Minister, Henderson, Kilmarnock, since 1989; *b* 26 April 1952; *s* of Peter and Nan Lacy; *m* 1974, Joan Stewart Robertson; one *s* one *d. Educ:* Univ. of Strathclyde (BA 1972); Univ. of Glasgow (BD 1975). Asst Minister, St George's West Church, Edinburgh, 1975–77; Minister, St Margaret's, Knightswood, Glasgow, 1977–89. Convener: Bd of Practice and Procedure, 2000–04; Gen. Assembly Business Cttee, 2000–04. Hon. DLitt Strathclyde, 2006. *Recreations:* sailing, choral singing. *Address:* 52 London Road, Kilmarnock, Ayrshire KA3 7AJ. *T:* and *Fax:* (01563) 523113; *e-mail:* thelacys@tinyworld.co.uk. *Club:* Kilmarnock.

LACY, Sir John (Trend), Kt 1992; CBE 1983; General Director of Party Campaigning, Conservative Central Office, 1989–92; *b* 15 March 1928; *s* of Rev. Hubert Lacy and Mrs Gertrude Lacy (*née* Markham); *m* 1956, Pamela Guerin; one *s. Educ:* King's Sch., Ely, Cambs. Served RN, 1945–48. Harvey & Clark (Manufrs), 1948–50; Conservative Party: London, 1950–56; Aylesbury, 1956–61; W Midlands area, 1961–64; Northern area, 1964–71; S Eastern area, 1971–85; Dir of Campaigning, 1985–89. *Recreations:* racing, fishing, philately. *Address:* 18 Windmill Close, Milford-on-Sea, Hants SO41 0SX. *T:* (01590) 643984. *Clubs:* Carlton, St Stephen's (Vice Chm., 1988–93).

LACY, Sir Patrick Bryan Finucane, 4th Bt *cr* 1921, of Ampton, co. Suffolk; *b* 18 April 1948; *s* of Sir Maurice John Pierce Lacy, 2nd Bt and of his 2nd wife, Nansi Jean (*née* Evans); *S* brother, 1998; *m* 1971, Phyllis Victoria James; one *s* one *d. Educ:* Downside. *Heir: s* Finian James Pierce Lacy, *b* 24 Sept. 1972.

LADDIE, Prof. Sir Hugh (Ian Lang), Kt 1995; Professor of Intellectual Property Law, University College London, since 2005; consultant to Rouse & Co. International, solicitors, since 2005; *b* 15 April 1946; *s* of late Bertie Daniel Laddie and of Rachel Laddie; *m* 1970, Stecia Elizabeth (*née* Zamet); two *s* one *d. Educ:* Aldenham Sch.; St Catharine's Coll., Cambridge (MA). Called to the Bar, Middle Temple, 1969 (Blackstone Pupillage Award; Bencher, 1993); Jun. Counsel to HM Treasury in Patent Matters, 1981–86; QC 1986; Judge of the High Ct of Justice, Chancery Div., 1995–2005. Jun. Bar Rep., Patents Procedure Cttee, 1976. Sec., 1971–75, Chm., 1993–94, Patent Bar Assoc.; Mem. Cttee, Chancery Bar Assoc., 1991–92. Chm., Vet. Code of Practice Cttee, Nat. Office of Animal Health; Dep. Chm., Copyright Tribunal, 1993–95; Dep. Ind. Chm., London Theatre Council and Provincial Theatre Council, 1993–95. Vice-Pres., Intellectual Property Inst., 1997–. Vis. Prof., Queen Mary, Univ. of London, 2005– (Mem. Council, 2000–05; Vice-Chm., 2005). Asst Ed.-in-Chief, Annual of Industrial Property Law, 1975–79; UK Correspondent, European Law Rev., 1978–83; Editor, Supreme Court Practice, 1995–2000; Ed.-in-Chief, In Context, 1998. *Publications:* (jtly) Patent Law of Europe and the United Kingdom, 1978; (jtly) The Modern Law of Copyright, 1980, 3rd edn 2000. *Recreations:* music, fishing, grandchildren.

LADDS, Rt Rev. Robert Sidney; *see* Whitby, Bishop Suffragan of.

LADE, Hilary Jane; Director, since 2003 and Vice Chairman, since 2006, Oxford Inspires; *b* 11 June 1957; *d* of Herbert Alfred Lade and Margaret (*née* Clark); *m* 2002, Mark Wilson. *Educ:* Selwyn Coll., Cambridge (MA Oriental Studies (Chinese)); Harvard Univ. (MA E Asian Langs and Civilisations); Univ. of Calif, Berkeley (MA Internat. Relns). Oil trader, Shell Internat., 1984–87; Man. Dir, Shell Gas Ltd, Shell UK, 1987–91; Estate Manager, Fountains Abbey and Studley Royal, NT, 1991–93; Dir of Historic Properties, English Heritage, 1993–97; Hd of Business Improvement, Shell, 1997–99. Chm., Royal Parks Adv. Bd, 1999–2002. Director: Nat. Forest Co., 1998–2002; Southern Arts Bd, 1998–2002; YHA, 1999–2001; BTA, 2000–03; Trustee: Nat. Trust, 2001–06; Heritage Lottery Fund, 2008–. Winston Churchill Travelling Fellow, 1978; Harkness Fellow, 1980. *Recreations:* music (violin player), travel, ski-ing, mountaineering. *Address: e-mail:* hilary.lade@virgin.net.

LADENIS, Nicholas Peter; Chef Patron, Chez Nico Restaurants, 1973–2003; *b* 22 April 1934; *s* of Peter and Constandia Ladenis; *m* 1963, Dinah-Jane Zissu; two *d. Educ:* Prince of Wales Sch., Nairobi; Regent Street Poly.; LSE; Hull Univ. (BSc Econs 1958). Appts with various cos, incl. Caltex, Ford Motor Co., Sunday Times, up to 1970; entered catering trade, 1971; opened restaurants (with wife and business partner): Chez Nico, 1973; Simply Nico, 1986; Nico Central, 1989; Incognico, 2000; Deca, 2002. Hon. DSc(Econ) Hull, 1997. *Publications:* My Gastronomy, 1987; Nico, 1996. *Recreations:* food, family, home, travel, expensive cars. *Address:* 23 Conduit Street, W1S 2XS.

LADER, Prof. Malcolm Harold, OBE 1996; MD, PhD, DSc; FRCPsych, FMedSci; Professor of Clinical Psychopharmacology, Institute of Psychiatry, University of London, 1978–2001, now Emeritus; *b* 27 Feb. 1936; *s* of Abe and Minnie Lader; *m* 1961, Susan Ruth Packer; three *d. Educ:* Univ. of Liverpool (BSc 1956; MB ChB 1959; MD 1964); University Coll. London (PhD 1963; DSc 1976); DPM 1966; Open Univ. (LLB 2006). FRCPsych 1976. Res. Asst, UCL, 1960–63; Registrar in Psychiatry, 1963–66, Hon. Consultant, 1970–2001, Maudsley Hosp.; Mem., MRC External Staff, 1966–2001. Trustee, Psychiatry Res. Trust, 2002–. FRSocMed 1963; FMedSci 1999. Hon. Fellow: Amer. Coll. of Psychiatrists, 1993; Soc. for Study of Addiction, 1998; British Assoc. for Psychopharmacology, 1994. *Publications:* Psychiatry on Trial, 1978; (ed jtly) Psychiatry and General Practice, 1982; (jtly) Role of Neurotransmitter Systems in Anxiety Modulation, 1984; (contrib.) Patterns of Improvement in Depressed In-patients, 1987; (ed) Psychopharmacology of Addiction, 1988; Biological Treatments in Psychiatry, 1990, 2nd edn 1996; (ed jtly) Nature of Alcohol and Drug-related Problems, 1992; (jtly) Anxiety, Panic and Phobias, 1997; 670 articles in scientific jls. *Recreations:* antiques, eating too much. *Address:* 16 Kelsey Park Mansion, 78 Wickham Road, Beckenham, Kent BR3 6QH. *T:* (020) 8650 0366.

LADER, Philip, JD; Chairman, WPP Group, since 2001; Senior Adviser, Morgan Stanley International, since 2001; *b* 17 March 1946; *s* of Phil and Mary Tripoli Lader; *m* 1980, Linda LeSourd; two *d. Educ:* Duke Univ. (BA 1966); Univ. of Michigan (MA History 1967); Pembroke Coll., Oxford (Hon. Fellow, 1994); Harvard Law Sch. (JD). Admitted to Bar: Florida, 1972; District of Columbia, 1973; S Carolina, 1979; Associate, Sullivan & Cromwell, 1972; Law Clerk to US Circuit Judge, 1973; President: Sea Pines Co., 1979–83; Winthrop Univ., 1983–86; GOSL Land Assets Mgt, 1986–88; Business Execs for Nat. Security, 1990; Exec. Vice-Pres., Sir James Goldsmith's US Hldgs, 1986–89; Pres.

and Vice Chancellor, Bond Univ., Australia, 1991–92; Dep. Dir for Mgt, Office of Mgt and Budget, US Govt, 1993; White House Dep. Chief of Staff and Asst to the Pres., 1993–94; Adminr, Small Business Admin, and Mem., President's Cabinet, 1994–97; Ambassador of the USA to the UK, 1997–2001. West Prof. of Internat. Studies, The Citadel, 2001–. Partner, Nelson Mullins Law Firm, 2001–; Director: American Red Cross, 1995–96; RAND Corp., 2001–; AES Corp., 2001–; Marathon Oil, 2001–; UC RUSAL, 2006–; Songbird Estates, 2006–. Mem. Council, Lloyd's, 2004–. Trustee: British Museum, 2001–06; St Paul's Cathedral Trust, 2002–; Windsor Leadership Trust, 2002–06; Salzburg Global Seminar, 2004–; Smithsonian Mus. of American Hist., 2006–. Chm., Amer. Assoc., Royal Acad. of Arts Trust, 2001–04; Founder, Renaissance Inst., 1981. Mem., Council on Foreign Relns, Chief Execs' Orgn; Member, Advisory Board: British-American Business Council, 2000–; The Prince's Trust, 2001–. John C. Whitehead Lecture, RIIA, 1998. Hon. Bencher, Middle Temple, 1998. Hon. Fellow: Liverpool John Moores Univ., 1998; London Business Sch., 2000. Fourteen hon. doctorates. Benjamin Franklin Medal, RSA, 2001; Global Service to Humanity Award, Rotary Internat. Foundn, 2007. *Recreations:* walking, tennis. *Address:* (office) 20 Bank Street, Canary Wharf, E14 4AD. *Clubs:* Harvard (New York); Metropolitan (Washington).

LADYMAN, Dr Stephen John; MP (Lab) South Thanet, since 1997; *b* 6 Nov. 1952; *s* of Frank Ladyman and Winifred Ladyman; *m* 1st, 1975 (marr. diss. 1994); 2nd, 1995, Janet Ann Baker; one *d*, and two step *s* one step *d*. *Educ:* Liverpool Poly. (BSc Hons Applied Biol. 1975); Strathclyde Univ. (PhD 1982). Res. scientist, MRC Radiobiol. Unit, 1979–84; Head: of Computing, Mathilda and Terence Kennedy Inst. of Rheumatology, 1984–90; of Computer-User Support, Pfizer Central Res., 1990–97. Mem. (Lab) Thanet DC, 1995–99 (Chm., Finance and Monitoring, 1995–97). Contested (Lab) Wantage, 1987. PPS to Minister for the Armed Forces, 2001–03; Parly Under-Sec. of State, DoH, 2003–05; Minister of State, DfT, 2005–07. Mem., Select Cttee on Envmt, Transport and the Regs, 1999–2001 (Mem., Transport Sub-Cttee, 1999–2001). Chairman: All Party Parly Gp on Autism, 2000–03; All-Party British-Netherlands Parly Gp, 2001–03. Vice Chm. with responsibility for SE England, Labour Party. *Publications:* Natural Isotopic Abundances in Soil Studies, 1982; various learned articles. *Recreations:* occasional golf, walking the dog, watching soccer, house renovations. *Address:* House of Commons, SW1A 0AA; *e-mail:* stephenladymanMP@souththanetlabour.org.uk; *web:* www.stephenladyman.info; 28 Newington Road, Ramsgate, Kent CT12 6EE. *T:* (01843) 852696.

LAFFERTY, John; His Honour Judge Lafferty; a Circuit Judge, since 2007; *b* Baillieston, 26 Dec. 1949; *s* of James and Susannah Lafferty. *Educ:* Univ. of Strathclyde (BA Hons English and Hist.); Nottingham Trent Univ. (LLM); Univ. of Glasgow (MPhil); Jordan Hill Coll. of Educn (Cert Ed); Leeds Poly. (CPE and Solicitors' Finals). Adminr/instructor, W Africa, 1974–76; English teacher, Our Lady's High Sch., Motherwell, 1976–80; Edward Fail, Bradshaw and Waterson: Articled clerk, 1983–85; Solicitor, 1985–87; Partner, 1987–90; Man. Partner, 1990–2005; Consultant, 2005–07; Recorder, 2000–07. Trustee: Disability Law Service, 2004–; Sightsavers Internat., 2005–. *Recreations:* walking, reading history, literature, theatre, music, travel. *Address:* Snaresbrook Crown Court, 75 Hollybush Hill, E11 1QW.

LAFONTAINE, Oskar; Member of Bundestag, 1990–94 and 1998–99; Minister of Finance, Germany, 1998–99; *b* 16 Sept. 1943; *m* 1993, Christa Müller; one *s*, and one *s* from a former marriage. *Educ:* Bonn Univ.; Saarbrücken Univ. Social Democratic Party (SPD), Germany: joined, 1966; officer, Saarland, 1970–75; Chm., Saarland Reg., 1977–96; Mem., Nat. Exec., 1994–2005; Chm., SPD, 1995–99. Mem., 1970–75 and 1985–98, Premier, 1985–98, Saarland Regl Parlt; Mayor, 1974–76, Lord Mayor, 1976–85, Saarbrücken; Pres., Bundesrat, 1995–96; Chm., Jt Cttee of Bundesrat and Bundestag, 1995–96. *Publications:* Angst vor den Freunden: die Atomwaffen-Strategie der Supermächte Zerstört die Bündnisse, 1983; Der andere Fortschritt: Verantwortung statt Verweigerung, 1985; Die Gesellschaft der Zukunft, 1988; Das Lied vom Teilen, 1989; Deutsche Wahrheiten, 1990; Das Herz schlägt links (autobiog.), 1999; Die Wut wächst, 2002.

LA FRENAIS, Ian, OBE 2007; writer, screenwriter and producer; *b* 7 Jan. 1937; *s* of Cyril and Gladys La Frenais; *m* 1984, Doris Vartan; one step *s*. *Educ:* Dame Allan's School, Northumberland. *Television:* writer or co-writer (with Dick Clement): The Likely Lads, 1965–68; The Adventures of Lucky Jim, 1968; Whatever Happened to the Likely Lads, 1971–73; Seven of One, 1973; Thick as Thieves, 1974; Comedy Playhouse, 1975; Porridge, 1974–77; Going Straight, 1978; Further Adventures of Lucky Jim, 1983; Auf Wiedersehen Pet, 1983–84, 2002–04; Mog, 1985; Lovejoy, 1986; Spender, 1990; Freddie and Max, 1990; Old Boy Network, 1991; Full Stretch, 1993; Over the Rainbow, 1993; The Rotters' Club (adaptation), 2005; Archangel, 2005; *US television:* On The Rocks, 1976–77; Billy, 1979; Sunset Limousine, 1983; Tracy Ullman Special, 1993; Tracy Takes On, 1995–99; *films:* writer or co-writer (with Dick Clement): The Jokers, 1967; The Touchables, 1968; Otley, 1968; Hannibal Brooks, 1969; The Virgin Soldiers, 1969; Villain, 1970; Catch Me a Spy, 1971; The Likely Lads, 1975; Porridge, 1979; To Russia with Elton, 1979; Prisoner of Zenda, 1981; Water, 1984; writer-producer, Vice Versa, 1987; co-writer (with Dick Clement): The Commitments, 1991; Excess Baggage, 1997; Still Crazy, 1998 (also Exec. Prod.); Honest, 2000; Goal!, 2005; Flushed Away, 2006; Across the Universe, 2007; The Bank Job, 2008; *stage:* writer, Billy, 1974; co-producer, Anyone for Denis?, 1982; writer, Gwen, 2001. Partner (with Dick Clement and Allan McKeown), Witzend Productions; producer, co-producer, director, numerous productions. Hon. DCL. Awards from BAFTA, Broadcasting Guild, Evening News, Pye, Screen Writers' Guild, Soc. of TV Critics, Writers' Guild of America, London Film Critics' Circle, Acad. of Television Arts and Scis, Nat. Television Awards, British Comedy Awards.

LAGACOS, Eustace P.; *b* 4 June 1921; one *d*. *Educ:* Univ. of Athens (Graduate of Law). Embassy Attaché, 1949; served Athens, Paris, Istanbul, Nicosia, London; Minister, 1969; Foreign Ministry, Athens, 1970; Ambassador to Nicosia, 1972; Dir Gen., Economic Affairs, Foreign Ministry, Athens, 1974; Permanent Representative to NATO, Brussels, 1976; Ambassador to UK, 1979–82. Mem., Eur. Parlt, 1989–94. Grand Officer of Order of the Phoenix, Greece; Commander of Order of George I, Greece; Grand Cordon of Order of Manuel Amadoi Guerrero, Panama; Commander of Legion of Honour, France; Kt Commander of Order of Queen Isabella I, Spain; Grand Officer of Order of the Republic, Egypt. *Publications:* The Cyprus Question, 1987; Populism in Foreign Affairs Issues, 1996. *Address:* 7 Kapsali Street, Athens 10674, Greece.

LAGARDÈRE, Arnaud Georges André; General Partner and Chief Executive Officer, Lagardère SCA, since 2003 (Co-Managing Director, 1998–2003); Chairman and Chief Executive Officer: Hachette SA, since 1999; Arjil Commanditée Arco, since 2004; Chairman, Board of Directors, European Aeronautic Defence and Space Company (EADS NV), since 2003; *b* Boulogne-Billancourt, 18 March 1961; *s* of late Jean-Luc Lagardère. *Educ:* Univ. of Paris-Dauphine (DEA Econs). CEO, Multi Média Beaujon, 1986; Vice-Chm., Supervisory Bd, Arjil & Cie, 1987–2005; CEO and Mem. Bd, 1988–2003, Chm., 2003–, Lagardère Capital and Mgt (formerly Arjil Gp); manager of emerging activities and media, Mem. Mgt and Strategic Cttee, Lagardère Gp, 1989–92; Dep. Chm. and Chief Operating Officer, Arjil Commanditée Arco, 1992–2004; Chairman: Grolier Inc., USA, 1994–98; Lagardère Active Broadband (formerly Grolier Interactive Europe), 1994–; Actg Chm., Europe 1 Communication, subseq. Lagardère Active Broadcast, 1999–2007; Chm. and CEO, 1999–2001, Man. Dir, 2001–03, Europe Régies, subseq. Lagardère Publicité; Chairman, Supervisory Board: Hachette Filipacchi Medias; Lagardère Active (Chm., 2001–06). Man. Dir, Nouvelles Messageries de la Presse Parisienne, 1999–2003; Member Board: Société d'Agences et de Diffusion, 2000–03; CanalSatellite, 2001–03; Lagardère-Sociétés, 2002–03; France Telecom, 2003–; Moët Hennessy Louis Vuitton, 2003–; Fimalac, 2003–06; Hachette Livre; Hachette Distribution Services; Lagardère Ressources; Member Supervisory Board: Aerospatiale Matra, 1999–2000; DaimlerChrysler AG, 2005–; Le Monde, 2005–; Virgin Stores; Lagardère Sports. Member: France Galop Cttee, 2003–06; Conseil Stratégie des Technologies de l'Information, 2004–. Chm., Jean-Luc Lagardère (formerly Hachette) Foundn, 2003– (Pres.). President: Club des Entreprises Paris 2012, 2004–06; Assoc. des Amis de Paris Jean-Bouin, 2004–; Nouvel Elan Croix Catelan Assoc., 2006–; Lagardère Paris Racing Assoc. *Address:* Lagardère SCA, 4 Rue de Presbourg, 75116 Paris, France. *T:* (1) 40691600, *Fax:* (1) 40691835.

LAGOS, Archbishop of, (RC), since 1973 (and Metropolitan); **His Eminence Cardinal Anthony Olubunmi Okogie,** CON 1999; DD; *b* Lagos, 16 June 1936. *Educ:* St Gregory's Coll., Lagos; St Theresa's Minor Seminary, Ibadan; St Peter and St Paul's Seminary, Ibadan; Urban Univ., Rome. Priest, 1966; appointments include: Acting Parish Priest, St Patrick's Church, Idumagbo, 1967–71; Asst Priest, and Master of Ceremonies, Holy Cross Cathedral, Lagos, 1967–71; Religious Instructor, King's Coll., Lagos, 1967–71; Director of Vocations, Archdiocese of Lagos, 1968–71; Manager, Holy Cross Group of Schools, Lagos, 1969–71; Auxiliary Bishop of Oyo, 1971–72; Auxiliary Bishop to Apostolic Administrator, Archdiocese of Lagos, 1972–73. Cardinal, 2003. Vice-Pres., 1983–88, Pres., 1988–94, Catholic Bishops Conf. of Nigeria; Roman Catholic Trustee of Christian Assoc. of Nigeria, 1974–; Member: State Community Relns Cttee, 1984–; Prerogative of Mercy, 1986–; Adv. Council on Religious Affairs, 1987–; Pontifical Council for Social Communications, 2003–; Congregation for the Evangelization of Peoples, 2003–; Council of Cardinals for Study of Organizational and Econ. Questions of Holy See, 2006–. Special Envoy of HH Pope Benedict XVI, Nat. Eucharistic Congress, Ghana, 2005. Chm., Christian Assoc. of Nigeria, 1989–97. *Address:* Holy Cross Cathedral, PO Box 8, Lagos, Nigeria. *T:* (1) 2635729 and (1) 2633841, *Fax:* (1) 2633841.

LAGOS ESCOBAR, Ricardo, PhD; United Nations Special Envoy on Climate Change, since 2007; President of Chile, 2000–06; *b* 2 March 1938; *s* of Froilán Lagos and Emma Escobar; *m* 1971, Luisa Durán; five *c*. *Educ:* Sch. of Law, Univ. of Chile; Duke Univ., N Carolina (PhD 1962). University of Chile, 1963–72: Prof., and Hd, Sch. of Pol and Admin. Scis; Dir, Inst. of Econs; Sec. Gen., 1969–72; Sec. Gen., Latin American Faculty of Social Scis (UNESCO initiative), 1972–74; Vis. Prof., Univ. of N Carolina, 1974–75; Econ. Hd, Regl Prog. for Latin America and the Caribbean, UN, 1978–84. Chairman: Alianza Democrática, 1983–84; Partido por la Democracia, 1987–90; Minister of Educn, 1990–92, of Public Works, 1994–98. *Publications:* Población, Pobreza y Mercado de Trabajo en América Latina, 1997; books and articles on econs and politics. *Address:* c/o Palacio de la Moneda, Santiago, Chile.

LAHNSTEIN, Prof. Manfred; Chairman, Zeit Foundation, since 1995; Professor of Culture- and Media-Management, Hochschule für Musik und Theater, Hamburg, since 1989; *b* 20 Dec. 1937; *s* of Walter and Hertha Lahnstein; *m*; one *s* one *d*. *Educ:* Cologne Univ. (Dipl. Kfm). German Trade Union Fedn, Dusseldorf, 1962–64; European Trade Union Office, Brussels, 1965–67; European Commn, 1967–73; German Govt service, 1973–82: served in Finance Min. and as Head of Chancellor's Office; Minister of Finance, April–Oct. 1982. Bertelsmann Corporation: Mem., Exec. Bd, 1983–94; Mem., Supervisory Bd, 1994–98; Pres., Bertelsmann printing and manufacturing gp, 1983–85; Pres., Electronic-Media Div., 1985. Chm. Bd of Governors, Univ. of Haifa, 2001–04. Pres., German-Israel Soc., 1994–. *Publications:* various articles. *Recreation:* classical music. *Address:* Zeit Stiftung, Feldbrunnenstrasse 56, 20148 Hamburg, Germany.

LAÏDI, Ahmed; Algerian Ambassador to Mexico, 1988–89; *b* 20 April 1934; *m* 1964, Aicha Chabbi-Lemsine; one *s* one *d* (and one *s* decd). *Educ:* Algiers Univ. (BA); Oran Univ. (LLB). Counsellor to Presidency of Council of Algerian Republic, 1963; Head of Cabinet of Presidency, 1963–64; Dir Gen. of Political and Economic Affairs, Min. of Foreign Affairs, 1964–66; Chm., Prep. Cttee, second Afro-Asian Conf., 1964–65; Special Envoy to Heads of States, Senegal, Mali, Ivory Coast and Nigeria, 1966; Ambassador to Spain, 1966–70; Head, Delegn to Geneva Conf. of non-nuclear countries, 1968; Wali (Governor): province Médea, 1970–74; province Tlemcen, 1975–78; Ambassador to Jordan, 1978–84; Special Envoy to Heads of States and govts, Zambia, Malaŵi, Botswana, Zimbabwe, 1985; Ambassador to UK, 1984–88, and to Ireland, 1985–88. Member: Algerian Football Fedn, 1964–66; Algerian Nat. Olympic Cttee, 1965–72. Foreign Orders: Liberia, 1963; Bulgaria, 1964; Yugoslavia, 1964; Spain, 1970; Jordan, 1984. *Recreations:* theatre, cinema, football.

LAIDLAW, Baron *cr* 2004 (Life Peer), of Rothiemay in Banffshire; **Irvine Alan Stewart Laidlaw;** founder Chairman, IIR Holdings Ltd, 1974–2005; *b* 22 Dec. 1942; *s* of Roy Alan and Margaret Laidlaw; *m* 1987, (Marie) Christine Laidlaw. *Educ:* Merchiston Castle Sch.; Univ. of Leeds (BA Hons); Columbia Univ. (MBA). Chm., Abbey Business Centres Ltd, 1998–. Chm., Laidlaw Youth Trust, 2003–. Sponsor, Excelsior Acad., Newcastle upon Tyne, 2004–. Hon. LLD St Andrews, 2003; Hon. DHC Aberdeen. *Recreations:* historic motor racing, sailing, opera, piloting helicopters. *Address:* 95 Eaton Square, SW1W 9AQ; 11 Avenue President Kennedy, MC 98000, Monaco; *e-mail:* irvine.laidlaw@rothiemay.net. *Clubs:* Royal Thames Yacht; New York Yacht.

LAIDLAW, Sir Christophor (Charles Fraser), Kt 1982; Chairman: BP Oil, 1977–81; BP Oil International, 1981; *b* 9 Aug. 1922; *m* 1952, Nina Mary Prichard; one *s* three *d*. *Educ:* Rugby Sch.; St John's Coll., Cambridge (MA; Hon. Fellow, 1996). Served War of 1939–45: Europe and Far East, Major on Gen. Staff; Intelligence Corps, 1941–46. Joined British Petroleum, 1948: BP Rep. in Hamburg, 1959–61; Gen. Manager, Marketing Dept, 1963–67; Dir, BP Trading, 1967; Dir (Ops), 1971–72; a Man. Dir, 1972–81, and Dep. Chm., BP, 1980–81; Dir, Soc. Française BP, 1964–85; President, BP: Belgium, 1967–71; Italiana, 1972–73; Deutsche BP, 1972–83; Chm., Boving & Co. Ltd, 1984–86. Chm., ICL plc, 1981–84; Pres., ICL France, 1983; Chm., Bridon, 1985–90. Director: Commercial Union Assurance, 1978–83; Barclays Bank International, 1980–87; Barclays Bank plc, 1981–88; Barclays Merchant Bank Ltd, 1984–86; Equity Capital for Industry Ltd, 1983–86; Amerada Hess Corp., 1983–94; Amerada Hess Ltd, 1986–99; Dalgety, 1984–92; Redland, 1984–92; TWIL Ltd, 1985–89; Mercedes-Benz (UK) Ltd, 1986–93; Daimler-Benz (UK) Ltd, 1994–99; Daimler-Chrysler (UK) Hldgs Ltd, 1999–2001. Pres., German Chamber of Industry and Commerce, 1983–86; Vice Pres., British-German

Assoc., 1996–2002. Institut Européen d'Administration des Affaires: Mem., Internat. Council, 1980–96; Chm. UK Adv. Bd, 1984–91; Dir, 1987–94. Trustee, Internat. Spinal Res. Trust, 1991–2002 (Patron, 2002–). FRSA 1996. Master, Tallow Chandlers' Co., 1988–89. *Address:* 49 Chelsea Square, SW3 6LH. *Clubs:* Buck's, Garrick.

See also W. S. H. Laidlaw.

LAIDLAW, (Henry) Renton; golf correspondent, Evening Standard, 1973–98; *b* 6 July 1939; *s* of late Henry Renton Laidlaw and Margaret McBeath Laidlaw (*née* Raiker). *Educ:* James Gillespie's Boys' School, Edinburgh; Daniel Stewart's College, Edinburgh. Golf corresp., Edinburgh Evening News, 1957–67; news presenter and reporter, Grampian Television, Aberdeen, 1968–69; BBC news presenter, Edinburgh, 1970–72; BBC Radio golf reporter, 1976–90; presenter: BBC Radio Sport on 2, 1986, 1987; ITV Eurosport, 1988; golf presenter: BSB, 1989–91; Golf Channel, US, 1995–; Chief Commentator, PGA European Tour Prodns, 1988–. Jack Nicklaus Meml Journalism Award, 2000; PGA of America Lifetime Achievement Award in Journalism, 2003. *Publications:* Play Golf (with Peter Alliss), 1977; Jacklin—the first 40 years, 1984; (ed) Johnnie Walker Ryder Cup '85, 1985; Play Better Golf, 1986; (ed) Johnnie Walker Ryder Cup '87, 1987; Ten Years—the history of the European Open, 1988; Golf Heroes, 1989; (ed) Johnnie Walker Ryder Cup '89, 1989; (with Bernard Gallacher) Captain at Kiawah, 1991; Wentworth: a host of happy memories, 1993; (ed) The Royal and Ancient Golfer's Handbook, annually, 1998–; (ed) The Golfers' Guide to Scotland, 2000–01. *Recreations:* theatre, golf. *Address:* c/o Mrs Kay Clarkson, 10 Buckingham Place, Victoria, SW1E 6HX. *T:* (020) 7233 9055, *Fax:* (020) 7233 9155. *Clubs:* Caledonian; Royal & Ancient (St Andrews); Sunningdale Golf, Wentworth, Royal Burgess Golf, Ballybunion Golf.

LAIDLAW, Jonathan James; QC 2008; Senior Treasury Counsel to the Crown, Central Criminal Court, since 2001; a Recorder, since 1998; *b* 28 Feb. 1960. *Educ:* Univ. of Hull (LLB). Called to the Bar, Inner Temple, 1982. Jun. Treasury Counsel, 1995–2001. *Address:* 2 Hare Court, Temple, EC4Y 7BH.

LAIDLAW, Renton; *see* Laidlaw, H. R.

LAIDLAW, William Samuel Hugh, (Sam); Chief Executive, Centrica plc, since 2006; *b* 3 Jan. 1956; *s* of Sir Christophor Charles Fraser Laidlaw, *qv*; *m* 1989, Deborah Margaret Morris-Adams; three *s* one *d*. *Educ:* Eton College; Gonville and Caius College, Cambridge (MA); MBA. Admitted Solicitor, 1980; Insead, Fontainebleau, 1981. Soc. Françaises Petroles BP, 1980; Amerada Hess: Manager, corporate planning, NY, 1981–83; Vice-Pres., London, 1983–85, Sen. Vice-Pres., 1986–90, Man. Dir, 1986–95, London; Exec. Vice-Pres., NY, 1990–95; Pres. and CEO, NY, 1995–2001; Chm., London, 1995–2001; Chief Exec., Enterprise Oil plc, 2001–02; Exec. Vice-Pres., ChevronTexaco Corp., 2003–06. Non-executive Director: Premier Oil, 1995; Yes Television plc, 2000–03; Hanson plc, 2003–07; HSBC Hldgs plc, 2008–; Chm., Sponsorship Consulting Ltd, 2002–07. Dir, Business Council of Internat. Understanding, 1998–. Mem., Govt Energy Adv. Panel, 1994–98. Chm., Petroleum Sci. and Tech. Inst., 1993–94; NEL, 1993–95. Pres., UKOOA, 1991. FInstPet (Vice-Pres., 1994–95); FRSA 1990. *Address:* (office) Centrica plc, Millstream, Maidenhead Road, Windsor, Berks SL4 5GD. *Clubs:* Buck's; Royal Thames Yacht, Royal Yacht Squadron.

LAIGHT, Barry Pemberton, OBE 1970; Eur Ing; FREng, FIMechE, FRAeS; Consultant to: Design Council, since 1983; VAWT Ltd, since 1983; RES Ltd, since 1983; Production Engineering Research Association, since 1986; Department of Trade and Industry, 1988–90; *s* of Donald Norman Laight and Nora (*née* Pemberton); *m* 1951, Ruth Murton; one *s* one *d*. *Educ:* Johnston Sch., Durham; Birmingham Central Tech. Coll.; Merchant Venturers' Tech. Coll., Bristol; Bristol Univ. (MSc). FREng (FEng 1981). SBAC Scholar, apprentice, Bristol Aeroplane Co., 1937; Chief Designer, 1952, Technical Dir, 1960, Blackburn & General Aircraft (develt of Beverley and design of Buccaneer, 1953, for RN service, 1960); Chief Engineer Kingston, 1963, Dir for Military Projects, 1968, Hawker Siddeley Aviation (Harrier develt to RAF service; introd. Hawk Trainer); Exec. Dir Engineering, Short Brothers, 1977–82 (develt SD360 and Blowpipe); Sec., RAeS, 1983–85. Mem. Council, RAeS, 1955–90 (Pres., 1974–75; British Silver Medal in Aeronautics, 1963); Chairman: Educn Cttee, SBAC, 1962–67; Tech. Board, SBAC, 1967–82; Member: Aircraft Res. Assoc. Board, 1972–77 (Chm., Tech. Cttee); ARC, 1973–76; Air Educn and Recreational Organisation Council, 1969–72; CBI: Mem., Res. and Tech. Cttee; Educn Cttee; Chm., Transport Technology Panel, SRC, 1969–73; Hon. Treasurer, Internat. Council of Aero. Scis, 1978–84; AGARD Nat. Delegate, 1968–73; Sec., Bristol Gliding Club, 1949–52. Mem., Mensa, 1945. AFAIAA; FInstD. *Publications:* papers in RAeS jls. *Recreations:* reading on any subject, house and car maintenance, music. *Address:* 5 Littlemead, Esher, Surrey KT10 9PE. *T:* (01372) 463216.

LAINÉ, Christopher Norman; Chairman, Allied Textile Companies plc, 1999–2000 (Director, 1998–2000); Partner, Coopers & Lybrand, 1971–98; President, Institute of Chartered Accountants in England and Wales, 1997–98; *b* 12 Oct. 1936; *s* of James Norman Balliol Lainé and Sybil Mary Lainé (*née* Fuge); *m* 1967, Sally Outhwaite; one *s* one *d*. *Educ:* King's Sch., Canterbury (Scholar); Trinity Coll., Oxford (Exhibnr; MA). FCA. Nat. Service, RA, 1955–57; commnd 1956. Cooper Brothers & Co., later Coopers & Lybrand: joined 1960; Partner i/c S Coast, 1971–90; Sen. Partner, S Coast, 1990–98. Pres., Southern Soc. of Chartered Accountants, 1986–87; Institute of Chartered Accountants in England and Wales: Mem. Council, 1990–2000; Chm., 1999–2000; Chm., Dist Socs Cttee, 1991–95; Exec., 1993–98; Vice-Pres., 1995–96; Dep. Pres., 1996–97; Dir, Accountancy Investigation and Discipline Bd, 2001–. Gov., Canford Sch., 1990–2004. *Recreations:* cricket, golf, classical music, painting. *Clubs:* Hampshire CC; Stoneham Golf; Hampshire Hogs Cricket, Forty.

LAINE, Dame Clementine Dinah, (Dame Cleo), (Lady Dankworth), DBE 1997 (OBE 1979); vocalist, actress; *b* 28 Oct. 1927; British; *m* 1st, 1947, George Langridge (marr. diss. 1957); one *s*; 2nd, 1958, John Philip William Dankworth (*see* Sir John Dankworth); one *s* one *d*. Joined Dankworth Orchestra, 1953; with John Dankworth estabd Performing Arts Centre, Wavendon Stables, 1969. Melody Maker and New Musical Express Top Girl Singer Award, 1956; Moscow Arts Theatre Award for acting role in Flesh to a Tiger, 1958; Top place in Internat. Critics Poll by Amer. Jazz magazine, Downbeat, 1965. Lead, in Seven Deadly Sins, Edinburgh Festival and Sadler's Wells, 1961; acting roles in Edin. Fest., 1966, 1967, Cindy-Ella, Garrick, 1968; film, Last of the Blonde Bombshells, 2000. Many appearances with symphony orchestras performing Façade (Walton), Pierrot Lunaire and other compositions; played Julie in Show Boat, Adelphi, 1971; title role in Colette, Comedy, 1980; Hedda Gabler; Valmouth; A Time to Laugh; The Women of Troy; The Mystery of Edwin Drood, 1986; Into the Woods (US nat. tour), 1989; Noyes Fludde (Proms), 1990. Frequent TV appearances. Hon. Freeman, Musicians' Co., 2002. Hon. MA Open, 1975; Hon. DMus: Berklee Sch. of Music, 1982; York, 1993; Cambridge, 2004; Brunel, 2007. Woman of the Year, 9th annual Golden Feather Awards, 1973; Edison Award, 1974; Variety Club of GB Show Business Personality Award (with John Dankworth), 1977; TV Times Viewers Award for Most Exciting Female Singer on TV, 1978; Grammy Award for Best Female Jazz Vocalist, 1985; Theatre World Award, 1986; NARM Presidential Lifetime Achievement Award, 1990; British Jazz Awards Vocalist of the Year, 1990; Distinguished Artists Award, Internat. Soc. for the Performing Arts, 1999; Bob Harrington Lifetime Achievement Award (with John Dankworth), Back Stage, 2001; Lifetime Achievement Award, BBC Radio Jazz Awards (with John Dankworth), 2002. Gold Discs: Feel the Warm; I'm a Song; Live at Melbourne; Platinum Discs: Best Friends; Sometimes When We Touch. *Publications:* Cleo (autobiog.), 1994; You Can Sing If You Want To, 1997. *Recreation:* painting. *Fax:* (01908) 584414.

LAING, family name of **Baron Laing of Dunphail**.

LAING OF DUNPHAIL, Baron *cr* 1991 (Life Peer), of Dunphail in the District of Moray; **Hector Laing,** Kt 1978; Life President, United Biscuits (Holdings) plc, 1990 (Director, 1953; Managing Director, 1964; Chairman, 1972–90); *b* 12 May 1923; *s* of Hector Laing and Margaret Norris Grant; *m* 1950, Marian Clare, *d* of Maj.-Gen. Sir John Laurie, 6th Bt, CBE, DSO; three *s*. *Educ:* Loretto Sch., Musselburgh, Scotland; Jesus Coll., Cambridge (Hon. Fellow, 1988). Served War, Scots Guards, 1942–47 (American Bronze Star, despatches, 1944); final rank, Captain. McVitie & Price: Dir, 1947; Chm., 1963. Mem. Bd, Royal Insurance Co., 1970–78; Director: Allied-Lyons, 1979–82; Exxon Corp. (USA), 1984–94. A Dir, Bank of England, 1973–91. Chairman: Food and Drink Industries Council, 1977–79; Scottish Business in the Community, 1982–91; Business in the Community, 1987–91; Dir, Grocery Manufrs of America, 1984–90; President: Eur. Catering Assoc., 1990–93; Inst. of Business Ethics, 1991–94. Treas., Cons. Party, 1988–93. Chm. Trustees, Lambeth Fund, 1983–97; Trustee: The Duke of Edinburgh's Commonwealth Study Conf., 1986–93; Royal Botanic Gardens Kew Foundn, 1990–94. Mem., St George's Council, Windsor, 1989–93 and 1995–2002; Gov., Wycombe Abbey Sch., 1981–94. FRSE 1989. DUniv Stirling, 1985; Hon. DLitt Heriot-Watt, 1986. Businessman of the Year Award, 1979; National Free Enterprise Award, 1980. *Recreations:* gardening, walking. *Address:* High Meadows, Windsor Road, Gerrards Cross, Bucks SL9 8ST. *T:* (01753) 882437. *Club:* White's.

LAING, Alastair David, FSA; Curator of (formerly Adviser on) Pictures and Sculpture, National Trust, since 1986; *b* 5 Aug. 1944; *s* of late Malcolm Strickland Laing and Margaret Clare Laing (*née* Briscoe); *m* 1979, Hana Novotná; one *s*. *Educ:* Chafyn Grove Sch.; Bradfield Coll.; Corpus Christi Coll., Oxford (BA Hons 1966; Dip. Hist. Art 1967); Courtauld Inst. of Art, Univ. of London. FCO, 1967–68; translator, 1969–76; Night Operator, Internat. Telephone Exchange, 1973–76; Researcher, Heim Gall., 1976–83; Researcher and Jt Curator, François Boucher exhibn, NY, Detroit and Paris, 1983–85; Area Editor, Macmillan Dictionary of Art, 1985–86. Member: Adv. Council, Hamilton Kerr Inst., 1986–; Paintings Panel, Council for the Care of Churches, 1993–2006; Acceptance in Lieu Panel, 1994–2005; Export Reviewing Cttee, 1996–2002; Sci. Cttee for restoration of The Apotheosis of Hercules, Versailles, 1999–2001; Sci. Cttee, Arthéna, 1999–; Adv. Panel, Apsley House, 2005–; Conservation Cttee, Chatsworth House, 2008–. Trustee, Holburne Mus., Bath, 1998–2007; Trustee and Dir, Burlington Mag., 2001–. Chevalier, l'Ordre des Arts et des Lettres (France), 1988. *Publications:* (with Anthony Blunt) Baroque & Rococo, 1978; Lighting, 1982; (with Richard Walker) Portrait Miniatures in National Trust Houses: vol. 1, Northern Ireland, 2003; vol. II, Cornwall, Devon and Somerset, 2005; (jtly) The James A. de Rothschild Bequest at Waddesdon Manor: drawings for architecture, design and ornament, 2006; exhibition catalogues include: François Boucher, 1986; In Trust for the Nation, 1995; The Drawings of François Boucher, 2003; articles in Country Life, Apollo, Burlington Mag., Umění, etc. *Recreation:* church- and tomb-crawling. *Address:* 24 Aberdeen Road, N5 2UH. *Club:* Travellers.

LAING, Christine Katherine; QC 2006; a Recorder, since 2004; *b* 4 Nov. 1961; *d* of Ludovic Baillie Laing and Christina (*née* Easton). *Educ:* St Thomas of Aquinas RC High Sch., Edinburgh; Univ. of Newcastle-upon-Tyne (LLB Hons 1983). Called to the Bar, Lincoln's Inn, 1984; criminal practitioner, 1984–. *Recreations:* travel, music, arts, rich friends, inexpensive wine. *Address:* 9–12 Bell Yard, WC2A 2JR. *T:* (020) 7400 1800, *Fax:* (020) 7404 1405; *e-mail:* ck.laing@tinyonline.co.uk.

LAING, Dr Douglas Rees; consultant on agricultural and environmental issues in the American tropics, since 1995; Director General, CAB International, 1993–94; *b* 31 Aug. 1936; *s* of Douglas Harvey Laing and Jessie Hilda Laing; *m* 1st, 1966, Rosemary Isabel Whiting; one *s* one *d*; 2nd, 1992, Olga Lucia Villa. *Educ:* Univ. of Queensland (BAgrSc Hons); Iowa State Univ. (PhD 1966). Fulbright Scholar, 1962. Lectr, then Sen. Lectr, Dept of Agronomy, Univ. of Sydney, 1966–73; International Center for Tropical Agriculture, Colombia: Physiologist, 1974–79; Dir, Crop Research, 1979–84; Dep. Dir General, 1984–92. FAIAS 1993. *Publications:* Ornamental Gardening in the American Tropics, 2001; contrib. chaps in books; numerous pubns and workshop and conference contribs on crop physiology, and internat. agriculture. *Recreations:* natural history, scuba diving, reading. *Address:* Apartado Aereo 25470, Cali, Colombia; *e-mail:* drlaing99@hotmail.com.

LAING, Eleanor Fulton; MP (C) Epping Forest, since 1997; *b* 1 Feb. 1958; *d* of late Matthew and Betty Pritchard; *m* 1983, Alan Laing (marr. diss. 2003); one *s*. *Educ:* St Columba's Sch., Kilmacolm; Edinburgh Univ. (Pres., Union, 1980–81; BA, LLB 1982). Solicitor, Edinburgh and London, 1983–89; Special Advr to Rt Hon. John MacGregor, MP, 1989–94. Contested (C) Paisley N, 1987. An Opposition Whip, 1999–2000; frontbench opposition spokesman on constitutional affairs, 2000–01, on educn, 2001–03, on women and equality, 2004–07; Shadow Sec. of State for Scotland, 2005; Shadow Minister for Justice, 2007–. *Recreations:* theatre, music, golf, Agatha Christie Society. *Address:* House of Commons, SW1A 0AA.

LAING, Gerald O.; *see* Ogilvie-Laing.

LAING, Ian Michael, CBE 2004; DL; Chairman, MEPC Milton Park Ltd, 1993–2006; *b* 24 Dec. 1946; *s* of Anthony and Ruth Laing; *m* 1973, Caroline Pender Cudlip; two *s* one *d*. *Educ:* Bedford Sch.; St Edmund Hall, Oxford (MA); London Business Sch. (MSc). Dir, English Property Corp. plc, 1972–85; Man. Dir, Lansdown Estates Gp Ltd, subseq. MEPC Milton Park Ltd, 1984–93. Non-executive Director: Oxford Radcliffe NHS Trust, 1992–99; Stanhope plc, 2006–. Governor: London Business Sch., 1996–2005; Royal Shakespeare Co., 1998–2005 and 2006–. Hon. Bencher, Inner Temple, 2004. DL 1998, High Sheriff, 2005–06, Oxon. *Recreations:* sailing, ski-ing, opera, theatre. *T:* (01865) 559092; *e-mail:* ianlaing@cix.co.uk. *Clubs:* Boodles; Royal Yacht Squadron; Kandahar Ski.

LAING, James Findlay; Under Secretary, Scottish Office Environment Department (formerly Scottish Development Department), 1988–93; *b* 7 Nov. 1933; *s* of Alexander Findlay Laing and Jessie Ross; *m* 1969, Christine Joy Canaway; one *s*. *Educ:* Nairn Academy; Edinburgh Univ. MA (Hons History). Nat. Service, Seaforth Highlanders, 1955–57. Asst Principal and Principal, Scottish Office, 1957–68; Principal, HM Treasury, 1968–71; Asst Sec., Scottish Office, 1972–79; Under Sec., Scottish Econ. Planning Dept, later Industry Dept for Scotland, 1979–88. *Recreations:* squash, chess. *Address:* 6 Barnton Park Place, Edinburgh EH4 6ET. *T:* (0131) 336 5951. *Club:* Edinburgh Sports.

LAING, Jennifer Charlina Ellsworth; Associate Dean, External Relations, London Business School, 2002–07; Chairman and Chief Executive Officer, North American Operations, Saatchi & Saatchi, 1997–2000; *b* 1947; *d* of late James Ellsworth Laing, FRCS, and Mary McKane (*née* Taylor); *m* John Henderson (marr. diss.). Joined Garland-Compton, 1969; Dir, Saatchi & Saatchi Garland-Compton, 1977; Dep. Chm., 1983, Jt Chm., 1987, Saatchi & Saatchi Advertising UK; Chm. and CEO, Aspect Hill Holiday (later Laing Henry Ltd), 1988, which merged with Saatchi & Saatchi Advertising UK, 1995; Chm., Saatchi & Saatchi Advertising UK, 1995–96. Mem. Exec. Bd, Saatchi & Saatchi Worldwide, 1996–2000. Non-executive Director: Hudson Highland Inc., 2003–; InterContinental Hotels, 2005–. Former non-executive Director: Remploy; Great Ormond Street Hosp. for Children NHS Trust.

LAING, Prof. John Archibald, PhD; Professor Emeritus, University of London, since 1984 (Courtauld Professor of Animal Husbandry and Hygiene, at Royal Veterinary College, University of London, 1959–84); *b* 27 April 1919; *s* of late John and Alexandra Laing; *m* 1946, June Margaret Lindsay Smith, *d* of Hugh Lindsay Smith, Downham Market; one *s* two *d*. *Educ:* Johnston Sch., Durham; Royal (Dick) School of Veterinary Studies, Edinburgh University (BSc); Christ's Coll., Cambridge. (PhD). CBiol, FIBiol; MRCVS 1941. Aleen Cust Scholar, Royal Coll. of Veterinary Surgeons. Research Officer, 1943–46, Asst Veterinary Investigation Officer, 1946–49, Ministry of Agriculture; Univ. of Bristol, 1949–59 (Reader in Veterinary Science, 1957–59). Anglo-Danish Churchill Fellowship, Univ. of Copenhagen, 1954; Visiting Professor, Univs of: Munich, 1967; Mexico, 1967; Queensland, 1970 (and John Thompson Memorial Lectr); Ankara, 1977; Assiut, 1980; Consultant to FAO, UN, 1955–57; Representative of FAO in Dominican Republic, 1957–58; Consultant to UNESCO in Central America, 1963–65; Mem., British Agricultural Mission to Peru, 1970. Member: EEC Veterinary Scientific Cttee, 1981–84; Dairy Product Quota Tribunal for England and Wales, 1984. Hon. Mem., Internat. Congress on Animal Reproduction, 1988 (Sec., 1961–80; Pres., 1980–84). Chm., Melrose Meml Trust, 1984–91; Member: Governing Body, Houghton Poultry Research Station, 1968–74; Council, Royal Veterinary Coll., 1975–84; Vice-Pres., University Fedn for Animal Welfare, 1977–84 (Treasurer, 1969–75; Chm., 1975–77). Pres., World Assoc. for Transport Animal Welfare Studies, 1996–98. Hon. Fellow Veterinary Acad., Madrid. Editor, British Veterinary Journal, 1960–84. *Publications:* Fertility and Infertility in the Domestic Animals, 1955, 4th edn 1988; papers on animal breeding and husbandry in various scientific journals. *Address:* Lower Meadows, Ayot St Lawrence, Herts AL6 9BW. *T:* (01438) 820413. *Club:* Athenæum.

LAING, Sir (John) Martin (Kirby), Kt 1997; CBE 1991; DL; Chairman, 1985–2001, non-executive Director, 2001–04, Hon. President, 2004–06, John Laing plc; non-executive Chairman, NHP plc, 1999–2005; *b* 18 Jan. 1942; *s* of Sir (William) Kirby Laing, *qv*; *m* 1965, Stephanie Stearn Worsdell; one *s* one *d*. *Educ:* St Lawrence College, Ramsgate; Emmanuel College, Cambridge (MA). FRICS. Joined Laing Group 1966; Dir, John Laing, 1980. Chairman: BOTB, 1995–99; Construction Industry Employers Council, 1995–2000; Vice-Chm., British Trade Internat., 1999; Member: Major Contractors Gp, 1985 (Chm., 1991–92); CBI Council, 1986–2002; CBI Overseas Cttee, 1983–96 (Chm., 1989–96); CBI Task Force on Business and Urban Regeneration, 1987–88; Cttee for Middle East Trade, 1982–86; SE Asia Trade Adv. Group, 1985–89; UK Adv. Cttee, British American Chamber of Commerce, 1985–2002; Council, World Economic Forum, 1986–2002; NEDO Construction Industry Sector Gp, 1988–93; Business in the Community, 1986–2002 (Mem. Bd, 1995–2000); World Business Council for Sustainable Develt, 1991–2002; UK-Japan 2000 Gp, 1988–2002; British Council, 1997–; Council, BESO, 1999–2003; Corporate Finance Adv. Bd, PriceWaterhouseCoopers, 2003–05; Chm., British Urban Develt, 1988–90; Dep. Chm., Building Experience Trust, 1992–95. Chm., Americas Advrs, Trade Partners UK, 2000–03. Mem. Council, London First, 1992–2002. Non-executive Director: Parsons Brinckerhoff Inc., USA, 2003–06; Eskmuir Properties Ltd, 2003–. Member: Home Office Parole Review Cttee, 1987–88; Archbishop's Council, Church Urban Fund, 1987–94; Trilateral Commn, 1993–99. President: Construction Confedn, 1997–2000; Inst. of Export, 2001–. Dir, City of London Sinfonia, 1988–95. Dir, Herts Groundwork Trust, 1986–91; Trustee: Nat. Energy Foundn, 1988–99; WWF Internat., 1991–97; Marine Stewardship Council, 1998–2006; Trustee Emeritus, WWF (UK), 1998– (Trustee, 1988–97; Chm., 1990–97). Adv., RP&C Internat. Ltd, 2006–07. Crown Mem., Court of Univ. of London, 1987–95; Member: Council, United World Coll. of the Atlantic, 1996–; Board of Governors, Papplewick School, Ascot, 1983–93; Governor: St Lawrence Coll., Ramsgate, 1988–95; NIESR, 1999–. Trustee, RICS Foundn, 2001–04. Master, Paviors' Co., 1995–96. CIEx 1987; FICE 1993; FCIOB 1995. DL Hertford, 1987. Hon. DSc: City, 1996; Birmingham, 2002; Kingston, 2004. Hon. DEng UWE, 1997. *Recreations:* gardening, music, travel. *Address:* 2 Balluta Building, Apt 9, Triq-il-Karmelitani, St Julians, Malta.

LAING, (John) Stuart; Master, Corpus Christi College, Cambridge, since 2008; *b* 22 July 1948; *s* of late Dr Denys Laing and Dr Judy Laing (*née* Dods); *m* 1972, Sibella Dorman, *d* of Sir Maurice Dorman, GCMG, GCVO; one *s* two *d*. *Educ:* Rugby Sch.; Corpus Christi Coll., Cambridge. Joined HM Diplomatic Service, 1970; FCO, 1970–71; MECAS, Lebanon, 1971–72; 2nd Sec., Jedda, 1973–75; First Secretary: UK Perm. Rep. to EC, 1975–78; FCO, 1978–83; Cairo, 1983–87; FCO, 1987–89; Counsellor, Prague, 1989–92; Dep. Hd of Mission and HM Consul-Gen., British Embassy, Riyadh, 1992–95; Hd, Know How Fund for Central Europe, FCO, later DFID, 1995–98; High Comr to Brunei, 1998–2002; Ambassador: to Oman, 2002–05; to Kuwait, 2005–08. *Recreations:* music, hill-walking, desert travel. *Address:* Corpus Christi College, Cambridge CB2 1RH.

LAING, Sir Kirby; *see* Laing, Sir W. K.

LAING, Sir Martin; *see* Laing, Sir J. M. K.

LAING, Richard George, FCA; Chief Executive, CDC Group plc (formerly Commonwealth Development Corporation), since 2004; *b* 24 Feb. 1954; *s* of George Denys Laing, MB BChir and Julian (Judy) Ursula Laing (*née* Dods), MB ChB; *m* 1979, Susan Pamela Mills, MA, PhD; four *s*. *Educ:* Rugby Sch.; Corpus Christi Coll., Cambridge (BA 1975). MA. FCA 1980. Marks & Spencer, 1975–76; Price Waterhouse, 1976–81; Booker Agric. Internat., 1981–84; De la Rue Plc, 1984–96; De la Rue Brazil: Finance Dir, 1986–89; Gp Financial Controller, 1989–96; Gp Finance Dir, 1996–99; Finance Dir, CDC Gp Plc, 2000–04. Trustee, ODI. *Recreations:* classical music, gardening, Munro bagging, and much else that involves being outside. *Address:* CDC Group plc, Cardinal Place, 80 Victoria Street, SW1E 5JL. *T:* (020) 7963 4700, *Fax:* (020) 7963 4750; *e-mail:* rlaing@cdcgroup.com.

LAING, Sophie Henrietta T.; *see* Turner Laing.

LAING, Stuart; *see* Laing, J. S.

LAING, Sir (William) Kirby, Kt 1968; JP; DL; MA; FREng, FICE; Chairman, Laing Properties plc, 1978–87, President, 1987–90; *b* 21 July 1916; *s* of Sir John Laing, CBE, and Lady Laing (*née* Beatrice Harland); *m* 1st, 1939, Joan Dorothy Bratt (*d* 1981); three *s*; 2nd, 1986, Dr (Mary) Isobel Lewis, *yr d* of late Edward C. Wray. *Educ:* St Lawrence Coll., Ramsgate; Emmanuel Coll., Cambridge (Hon. Fellow, 1983). FREng (FEng 1977). Served with Royal Engineers, 1943–45. Dir, John Laing plc (formerly John Laing & Son Ltd), 1939–80 (Chm., 1957–76). President: London Master Builders Assoc., 1957; Reinforced Concrete Assoc., 1960; Nat. Fedn of Building Trades Employers (later Building Employers' Confedn) 1965, 1967 (Hon. Mem., 1975); ICE, 1973–74 (a Vice-Pres., 1970–73); Construction Industry Res. and Inf. Assoc., 1984–87 (Chm., 1978–81); Chm., Nat. Jt Council for Building Industry, 1968–74. Member, Board of Governors: St Lawrence Coll. (Chm., 1977–89, Life Pres., 1979); Princess Helena Coll., 1984–87; Member: Court of Governors, The Polytechnic of Central London, 1963–82; Council, Royal Albert Hall, 1970–92 (Pres., 1979–92; Life Vice-Pres., 2000); RAEng, 1977; Royal Instn of GB, 1989; Ct of Benefactors, Oxford Univ.; Ct of Benefactors, RSM, 2008. Dist. Mem., Amer. Assoc. of Civil Engineers, 2008. Mem., Smetonian Soc., 1969 (Pres., 1988). Master, Paviors' Co., 1987–88. DL Greater London, 1978–91. Hon. Fellow, UCNW, 1988. Hon. DTech, Poly. of Central London, 1990; Dr *hc* Edinburgh, 1991. *Publications:* papers in Proc. ICE and other jls concerned with construction. *Recreations:* flyfishing, travelling, listening to music. *Clubs:* Piscatorial Society; Royal Fowey Yacht.
See also Sir J. M. K. Laing.

LAINSON, Prof. Ralph, OBE 1996; FRS 1982; Director, Wellcome Parasitology Unit, Instituto Evandro Chagas, Belém, Pará, Brazil, 1965–92; *b* 21 Feb. 1927; *s* of Charles Harry Lainson and Anne (*née* Denyer); *m* 1st, 1957, Anne Patricia Russell; one *s* two *d*; 2nd, 1974, Zeá Constante Lins. *Educ:* Steyning Grammar Sch., Sussex; London Univ. (BSc, PhD, DSc). Lecturer in Medical Protozoology, London Sch. of Hygiene and Tropical Medicine, London Univ., 1955–59; Officer-in-Charge, Dermal Leishmaniasis Unit, Baking-Pot, Cayo Dist, Belize, 1959–62; Attached Investigator, Dept of Medical Protozoology, London Sch. of Hygiene and Tropical Medicine, 1962–65. Career devoted to research in Medical Protozoology in the Tropics. Hon. Fellow, LSHTM, 1982; Hon. Professor, Federal Univ. of Pará, Brazil, 1982; Associate Fellow, Third World Acad. of Scis, 1989; Hon. FRSTM&H 1997; Hon. Member: British Soc. of Parasitology, 1984; Soc. of Protozoologists, 1997. Chalmer's Medal, Royal Soc. of Tropical Medicine and Hygiene, 1971; Oswaldo Cruz Medal, Conselho Estadual de Cultura do Pará, 1973; Manson Medal, Royal Soc. of Tropical Medicine and Hygiene, 1983; Commemorative medals: 10th anniv., Health Council for State of Pará, Brazil, 1983; 30th anniv., Fed. Univ. of Pará, Brazil, 1988. *Publications:* author, or co-author, of approximately 300 pubns in current scientific jls and text-books, on protozoal parasites of man and animals. *Recreations:* fishing, swimming, collecting South American Lepidoptera, music, philately. *Address:* Avenida Visconde de Souza Franco, 1237 (Edificio 'Visconti'), Apartamento 902, 66053–000 Belém, Pará, Brazil. *T:* (91) 32232382.

LAIRD, family name of **Baron Laird**.

LAIRD, Baron *cr* 1999 (Life Peer), of Artigarvan in the county of Tyrone; **John Dunn Laird;** Chairman, John Laird Public Relations Ltd, 1976–2001; *b* Belfast, 23 April 1944; *s* of late Dr Norman Davidson Laird, OBE, sometime NI MP, and Margaret Laird; *m* 1971, Caroline Ethel Ferguson; one *s* one *d*. *Educ:* Royal Belfast Academical Institution. Bank Official, 1963–67; Bank Inspector, 1967–68; Computer Programmer, 1968–73. MP (UU) St Anne's, Belfast, NI Parlt, 1970–73; Member (UU) West Belfast: NI Assembly, 1973–75; NI Constitutional Convention, 1975–76. Vis. Prof. of Public Relns, Univ. of Ulster, 1993–. Chm., Ulster Scots Agency, 1999–2004. Mem. Bd Govs, Royal Belfast Academical Instn, 1993–2004. FCIPR (FIPR 1991). *Recreations:* history, railways, travel. *Address:* House of Lords, SW1A 0PW. *T:* (020) 7219 8626.

LAIRD, David Logan, OBE 2000; JP, DL; WS; FRICS; solicitor; Partner, Thorntons WS, since 1985; chartered surveyor; *b* 13 April 1937; *s* of William Twaddle Laird and Janet Nicolson (*née* MacDonald); *m*; two *s* one *d*. *Educ:* Bell Baxter Sch., Cupar. Chartered surveyor and land agent, 1963; Partner, Clark Oliver Dewar & Webster, SSC, 1971–85. Mem., and Chm. NE Region, NCC Scotland, now Scottish Natural Heritage, 1990– (Chm., E Area Bd, 1997–2000); Chm. Bd, Cairngorms Partnership, 1994–97. JP 1968, DL 1989, Angus. *Recreations:* stalking, gardening, shooting, fishing. *Address:* West Memus, Forfar, Angus DD8 3TY. *T:* (01307) 860251. *Club:* New (Edinburgh).

LAIRD, Endell Johnston; Director and Editor in Chief, Scottish Daily Record and Sunday Mail, 1988–94; Editor in Chief, The Glaswegian, 1988–94; *m* 1958, June Keenan; one *s* two *d*. *Educ:* Forfar Academy. Served RAF, 1952–54. Journalist: Dundee Courier, 1954–56; Scottish Daily Express, 1956–58; Evening Times, 1958–60; Sunday Mail, 1960–71; Daily Record, 1971–81; Editor, Sunday Mail, 1981–88. Editl Dir (SDR), Mirror Gp Newspapers, 1991–94. Chm., Scottish Editors Cttee, 1986–88; Mem., D-Notice Cttee, 1986–94. Mem. Bd, Children's Hospice Assoc. Scotland, 1994–. *Recreations:* walking, golf, bridge. *Clubs:* Bishopbriggs Golf; Bishopbriggs Bridge.

LAIRD, Sir Gavin (Harry), Kt 1995; CBE 1988; General Secretary, AEU Section, Amalgamated Engineering and Electrical Union, 1992–95; Chairman, Greater Manchester Buses North, 1994–97; *b* 14 March 1933; *s* of James and Frances Laird; *m* 1956, Catherine Gillies Campbell; one *d*. *Educ:* Clydebank High School. Full-time Trade Union Official, 1972–95; Mem. Exec. Council, 1975–95, Gen. Sec., 1982–94, AUEW, subseq. AEU, then AEEU. Mem., TUC Gen. Council, 1979–82; Mem. Exec., CSEU, 1975–95. Director: BNOC, 1976–86; Bank of England, 1986–94; non-exec. Director: Scottish Media Group plc (formerly Scottish TV), 1986–99; FS Assurance, then Britannia Life, 1988–99; GEC Scotland, 1991–99; Edinburgh Investment Trust, 1994–2003; Britannia, then Britannic, Investment Managers, 1996–2001; Chm., Murray VCT 4, 2000–03; Mem. Adv. Cttee, Murray Johnstone Pvte Equity Partnerships 1 & 2, 1995–. Pt-time Mem., SDA, 1987–92. Member: Arts Council of GB, 1983–86; London Cttee, Scottish Council for Develt and Industry, 1984–95; President's Cttee, Business in the Community, 1988–90; Forestry Commn, 1991–94; Envmtl Council, BNFL, 1993–96; Adv. Bd, Know How Fund, 1988–95; Armed Forces Pay Review Body, 1995–98; Employment Appeal Tribunal, 1996–2003. Chm., Trade Union Friends of Israel, 1980–96. Dir, Westminster Foundn for Democracy, 1992–96. Mem. Governing Council, 1987–91, Gov., 1991–97, Atlantic Coll.; Trustee, Anglo-German Foundn, 1994–2002. Pres., Kent Active Retirement Assoc., 1996–2003. Fellow, Paisley Coll. of Technol., 1991. Hon. DLitt: Keele, 1994; Heriot-Watt, 1994. *Recreations:* hill walking, reading, music. *Address:* 9 Clevedon House, Holmbury Park, Bromley BR1 2WG. *T:* and *Fax:* (020) 8460 8998.

LAIRD, Margaret Heather, OBE 1999; Third Church Estates Commissioner, 1989–99; *b* 29 Jan. 1933; *d* of William Henry Polmear and Edith Polmear; *m* 1961, Rev. Canon John Charles Laird; two *s*. *Educ:* High Sch., Truro; Westfield College, London (BA Hons Mediaeval History, 1954); King's College London (Cert. in Religious Knowledge, 1955). Divinity Mistress: Grey Coat Hospital, SW1, 1955–59; Newquay Grammar Sch., 1959–60; St Albans High Sch., 1960–62; Head of Religious Studies, Dame Alice Harpur Sch., Bedford, 1969–89. Member: Gen. Synod of C of E, repr. Dio. St Albans, 1980–90, ex officio, 1990–99 (Mem., Standing Cttee, 1989–98); Panel of Assessors, Dio. St Albans, 1988–2000; C of E Pensions Bd, 1989–98. Dep. Chm., English Clergy Assoc., 2001–. Vice-Pres., Soc. for Maintenance of the Faith, 1995–. Trustee: Lambeth Palace Library,

1993–99; Oxford Movt Anniv. Appeal Trust, 1996–; Kentish's Educnl Foundn, 2001–06; Cleaver Ordination Candidates Foundn, 2001–; Member: Allchurches Trust Ltd, 1994–; Exec., Open Churches Trust, 1995–2007. Mem., Royal Instn of Cornwall, 1997–. Governor, Pusey House, Oxford, 1993–. FRSA 1996. *Publications:* Through A Glass Darkly (contrib.), 1993; From Now to Eternity, 2001. *Recreations:* mediaeval art, architecture, pilgrims' routes. *Address:* The Chaplaincy, Fore Street Lodge, Hatfield Park, Hatfield, Herts AL9 5NQ. *Club:* Oxford and Cambridge.

LAIRD, Hon. Melvin R.; Consultant, Reader's Digest Association, since 1999 (Senior Counsellor for National and International Affairs, 1974–99); *b* 1 Sept. 1922; *s* of Melvin R. Laird and Helen Laird (*née* Connor); *m* 1945, Barbara Masters (*d* 1992); two *s* one *d*. *Educ:* Carleton Coll., Northfield, Minn (BA 1944). Enlisted, US Navy, 1942, commissioned, 1944; served in Third Fleet and Task Force 58 (Purple Heart and other decorations). Elected: to Wisconsin State Senate, 1946 (re-elected, 1948); to US Congress, Nov. 1952 (83rd through 90th); Chm., House Republican Conf., 89th and 90th); Sec. of Defense, 1969–73; Counsellor to President of the US, 1973–74. Chm., Communications Satellite Corp., 1992–96 (Dir, 1974–96); Director: Metropolitan Life Insurance Co., 1974–; Northwest Airlines, 1974–93; IDS Mutual Fund Gp Inc., 1974–97; Phillips Petroleum Co., 1976–93; Science Applications Internat. Corp., 1979–97; Martin Marietta Corp., 1981–95; Public Oversight Bd, 1984– (SEC Practice Sect., AICPA); DeWitt Wallace, and Lila Wallace, Reader's Digest Funds (for the promotion of the arts and humanities), 1990–98; Reader's Digest Assoc. Inc., 1990–98. Member Board of Trustees: George Washington Univ.; Kennedy Center. Various awards from Assocs, etc (for med. research, polit. science, public health, nat. educn); many hon. memberships and hon. degrees. *Publications:* A House Divided: America's Strategy Gap, 1962; Editor: The Conservative Papers, 1964; Republican Papers, 1968. *Recreations:* golf, fishing. *Address:* Suite 212, 1730 Rhode Island Avenue NW, Washington, DC 20036, USA. *Clubs:* Burning Tree (Washington, DC); Augusta National Golf.

LAIT, Jacqui; MP (C) Beckenham, since Nov. 1997; *b* 16 Dec. 1947; *d* of Graham Harkness Lait and Margaret Stewart (*née* Knight); *m* 1974, Peter Jones. *Educ:* Paisley Grammar Sch.; Univ. of Strathclyde. Public relations posts: jute trade, Dundee; Visnews, internat. TV news agency; with Govt Inf. Service, in Scottish Office, Privy Council Office and Dept of Employment, 1974–80; Parly Advr, Chemical Inds Assoc., 1980–84; Parly Consultancy, 1984–92. Contested (C): Strathclyde W, Euro-election, 1984; Tyne Bridge, Dec. 1985. MP (C) Hastings and Rye, 1992–97; contested (C) same seat, 1997. An Asst Govt Whip, 1996–97; Opposition Whip, 1999–2000; Opposition spokesman on pensions, 2000–01; Shadow Scottish Sec., 2001–03; Shadow Minister for Home, Constitutional and Legal Affairs, 2003–05, for London, 2005–07, for Planning, 2007–. Chm., City and E London FHSA, 1988–91. Chm., British Section, European Union of Women, 1990–92; Vice-Chm., Cons. Women's Nat. Cttee, 1990–92. *Recreations:* walking, theatre, food and wine. *Address:* House of Commons, SW1A 0AA.

LAIT, His Honour Leonard Hugh Cecil, (Josh); a Circuit Judge, 1987–2003; *b* 15 Nov. 1930; *m* 1967, Cheah Phaik Teen; one *d*. *Educ:* John Lyon School, Harrow; Trinity Hall, Cambridge (BA). Called to the Bar, Inner Temple, 1959; Mem., SE circuit; a Recorder, 1985–87. *Recreations:* music, gardening.

LAITHWAITE, Anthony Hugh Gordon; Founder, Bordeaux Direct, subsequently Laithwaites, 1969; Chairman, Direct Wines Ltd, since 1972; *b* 22 Dec. 1945; *s* of Eric and Winneth Laithwaite; *m* 1975, Barbara Anne Hynds; three *s*. *Educ:* Windsor Boys' Grammar Sch.; Bishop Vesey's Grammar Sch., Sutton Coldfield; Univ. of Durham (BA Hons (Geog.) 1968. Founded first shop, Windsor, 1969; Co-founder, Sunday Times Wine Club, 1973. *Publication:* Laithwaite's Great Wine Trek, 1984. *Recreation:* wine. *Address:* The Old Brewery House, 86 New Street, Henley-on-Thames, Oxon RG9 2BT. *T:* (01491) 844780, *Fax:* (01491) 410562; *e-mail:* tonylaithwaite@directwines.co.uk. *Club:* Royal Automobile.

LAITHWAITE, John, FIMechE, FInstPet; engineering consultant; Director, Capper Neill Ltd, 1965–83 (Vice-Chairman, 1972–82); *b* 29 Nov. 1920; *s* of Tom Prescott Laithwaite and Mary Anne Laithwaite; *m* 1943, Jean Chateris; one *s* two *d*. *Educ:* Manchester Univ. (BSc Hons Mech. Eng.) FIMechE 1974; FInstPet 1960; MInstW 1950. Wm Neill & Son (St Helens) Ltd, 1942–43; Dartford Shipbuilding & Engineering Co., 1943–44; Dir, Wm Neill & Son (St Helens) Ltd, 1955–58, Man. Dir, 1958–64; Man. Dir, Capper Neill Ltd, 1968–72. Mem. Council, NW Regional Management Centre. Chm., Process Plant Assoc., 1975–77, Hon. Vice-Pres., 1980–. *Publications:* articles on process plant industry and pressure vessel standardisation. *Recreations:* shooting, golf. *Address:* 44 Deganwy Beach, Deganwy, Conwy LL31 9YR. *T:* (01492) 582214.

LAITTAN, James S.; *see* Smith-Laittan.

LAITY, Mark Franklyn; Chief Strategic Communications, Supreme Headquarters Allied Powers Europe, since 2007; *b* 18 Dec. 1955; *s* of Frank and Pamela Laity; *m* 1990, Lisa Parker-Gomm. *Educ:* Redruth Co. Grammar Sch.; Univ. of York (BA Hons Hist./Politics; MA Southern African Studies). Reporter, Western Mail, 1978–81; BBC Radio: Producer: Radio Wales, 1981–82; Today prog., 1982–86; Sen. Producer, Analysis prog., 1986–88; Dep. Ed., The World This Weekend, 1988–89; Defence Corresp., BBC, 1989–2000; Dep. Spokesman and Personal Advr, subseq. Special Advr to NATO Sec.-Gen., 2000–03; Special Advr, later Chief of Public Inf., SACEUR, 2004–06; NATO spokesman in Kabul, Afghanistan, 2006–07. *Recreation:* sailing. *Address:* Rue Fetis 17, Bte C1, Mons 7000, Belgium; *e-mail:* markflaity@hotmail.com. *Clubs:* Royal Air Force; Thames Sailing.

LAKE, Sir (Atwell) Graham, 10th Bt *cr* 1711; Senior Technical Adviser, Ministry of Defence, retired 1983; *b* 6 Oct. 1923; *s* of Captain Sir Atwell Henry Lake, 9th Bt, CB, OBE, RN, and Kathleen Marion, *d* of late Alfred Morrison Turner; *S* father, 1972; *m* 1983, Mrs Katharine Margaret Lister, *d* of late D. W. Last and M. M. Last. *Educ:* Eton. British High Commission, Wellington, NZ, 1942; Gilbert and Ellice Military Forces, 1944; Colonial Administrative Service, 1945 (Secretary to Govt of Tonga, 1950–53); Norris Oakley Bros, 1957; Min. of Defence, 1959; British High Commission, New Delhi, 1966; attached Foreign and Commonwealth Office, 1969–72. Chm., Abbeyfield Epping Soc., 1995–97 (Hon. Sec., 1987–96). *Recreations:* golf, bridge, chess. *Heir:* *b* Edward Geoffrey Lake [*b* 17 July 1928; *m* 1965, Judith Ann, *d* of John Fox; one *s* one *d*]. *Club:* Lansdowne.

LAKE, (Charles) Michael, CBE 1996; Director General, Help the Aged, since 1996; *b* 17 May 1944; *s* of Stanley Giddy and late Beryl Giddy (*née* Heath); step *s* of late Percival Redvers Lake; *m* 1970, Christine Warner; three *d*. *Educ:* Humphry Davy Grammar Sch., Penzance; RMA, Sandhurst. FILog 1995. SCLI 1963; commnd RCT, 1965; Regtl appts, Germany, Hong Kong, NI, Oman; attached Commandant-Gen., RM, 1977–78; Directing Staff, Staff Coll., 1982–83; Comd, 1st Div. Transport Regt, 1983–86; Comdr Transport, HQ British Forces Riyadh, Gulf War, 1990–91; Regtl Col., RLC, 1992–96; retired 1997. Member: Bd, HelpAge Internat., 1996–2004; Benevolent and Strategy

Cttee, RBL, 1997– (External Advr, RBL, 1999); Council, Occupational Pensions Adv. Service, 1997–2001; Bd, Network Housing Assoc., 1999–2001; Council, Oxford Inst. of Ageing, 2000–; Bd, CAF, 2006–; Lay Mem., Lord Chancellor's Adv. Cttee on Conscientious Objectors, 2002–. Vice-Chm., Air Ambulance Foundn, 2003–04; Trustee: Disasters Emergency Cttee, 1999–; Pensions Policy Inst., 2001–. Mem. Bd, Chelsea Arts Club, 1997–. Freeman: City of London, 1995; Carmen's Co., 1995. *Recreations:* sports, avid golfer, cricketer, Rugby; Post Impressionism, Penzance and Newlyn school. *Address:* Help the Aged, 207–221 Pentonville Road, N1 9UZ; c/o Holt's Bank, Royal Bank of Scotland, Farnborough, Hants GU14 7NR. *Clubs:* MCC; Penguin International Rugby; W Cornwall Golf, North Hants Golf.

LAKE, Robert Andrew; Director of Social Care Information Delivery, NHS Information Centre, since 2007; *b* 14 April 1948; *s* of Rev. William Henry Lake and Ruth Lake (*née* Hammond); *m* 1975, Celia Helen Probert; one *s* two *d*. *Educ:* Hull Grammar Sch.; Univ. of Coventry (CQSW). Welfare Asst, Bolton Welfare Dept, 1968–70; various posts, Coventry Social Services Dept, 1972–80; Area Manager, 1980–82, Principal Asst, 1982–84, Newcastle upon Tyne Social Services; Asst Dir, 1984–91, Dir, 1991–96, Humberside Social Services Dept; Dir of Social Services, Staffs CC, 1996–2005; Chm., Staffordshire Ambulance Service, 2005–07. FRSocMed 2006. Vis. Fellow, Keele Univ., 1997. *Recreations:* music, D-I-Y, the family. *Address: e-mail:* ralake1@btinternet.com.

LAKEY, Prof. John Richard Angwin, PhD; CEng, FEI; CPhys, FInstP, CRadP; radiological protection consultant; founder, 1989, independent consultant, 1989–2000, John Lakey Associates; *b* 28 June 1929; *s* of late William Richard Lakey and Edith Lakey (*née* Hartley); *m* 1955, Dr Pamela Janet, *d* of late Eric Clifford Lancey and Florence Elsie Lancey; three *d*. *Educ:* Morley Grammar Sch.; Sheffield Univ. BSc (Physics) 1950, PhD (Fuel Technology) 1953. R&D posts with Simon Carves Ltd, secondment to AERE Harwell and GEC, 1953–60; Royal Naval College, Greenwich: Asst Prof., 1960–80; Prof. of Nuclear Sci. and Technol., 1980–89; Dean, 1984–86, 1988–89. Reactor Shielding Consultant, DG Ships, 1967–89; Radiation Consultant, WHO, 1973–74; Mem. and Vice-Chm., CNAA Physics Board, 1973–82; Mem., Medway Health Authy, 1981–90; Chm., UK Liaison Cttee for Scis Allied to Medicine and Biology, 1984–87. University of Surrey: External Examr, 1980–86; Hon. Vis. Prof., 1987–94; Vis. Lectr, Harvard Univ., 1984–2004; Vis. Prof., Univ. of Greenwich, 1998–2004. Mem. Editl Bd, Physics in Medicine and Biology, 1980–83; News Editor, Health Physics, 1980–88. President: Internat. Radiation Protection Assoc., 1988–92 (Publications Dir, 1979–88); Instn of Nuclear Engrs, 1988–90 (Vice-Pres., 1983–87); Vice-President: London Internat. Youth Science Forum, 1988–; European Nuclear Soc., 1989–95. Liveryman, Engineers' Co., 1988–. Eur Ing 1989; CSci 2004; CRadP 2008. Hon. FSRP 1992. G. William Morgan Award, US Health Physics Soc., 1997. *Publications:* Protection Against Radiation, 1961; Radiation Protection Measurement: philosophy and implementation, 1975; (ed) ALARA principles and practices, 1987; (ed) IRPA Guidelines on Protection Against Non-Ionizing Radiation, 1991; (ed) Off-site Emergency Response to Nuclear Accidents, 1993; (jtly) Radiation and Radiation Protection: a course for primary and secondary schools, 1995; Radiation Protection for Emergency Workers, 1997; papers on nuclear safety, radiological protection and management of emergencies. *Recreations:* photography, conversation. *Address:* 5 Pine Rise, Meopham, Gravesend, Kent DA13 0JA. *T:* (01474) 812551. *Clubs:* Athenæum; Royal Naval Sailing Association.

LAKHA, (Gulam) Abbas; QC 2003; *b* 2 Oct. 1962; *s* of Hassan Lakha and Leila (*née* Alibhai); *m* 1992, Shamira Fazal; one *s* two *d*. *Educ:* Stowe Sch.; Leeds Poly. (BA Hons Law). Called to the Bar, Inner Temple, 1984, Bencher, 2007; *ad eundem* Mem., Gray's Inn, 2002; in practice as barrister, specialising in criminal law, 1984–. Inspector, DTI, 1997–99. Mem. N London Bar Mess Cttee, 1998–. *Recreations:* travel, fast cars, modern architecture, work. *Address:* 9 Bedford Row, WC1R 4AZ. *T:* (020) 7489 2727, *Fax:* (020) 7489 2828; *e-mail:* abbaslakha@9bedfordrow.co.uk.

LAKHANI, Kamlesh, (Mrs N. Lakhani); *see* Bahl, K.

LAKHANI, Mayur Keshavji, CBE 2007; FRCP, FRCPE, FRCGP; Principal in General Practice, Highgate Medical Centre, Sileby, Loughborough, since 1991; *b* 20 April 1960; *s* of Keshavji Vithaldas. Lakhani and Shantaben Keshavji Lakhani; *m* 1988, Mayuri Jobanputra; one *s* two *d*. *Educ:* Univ. of Dundee (MB ChB 1983). DFFP 1997; FRCGP 1998; FRCPE 2002; FRCP 2006. Vis. Prof., Dept of Health Scis, Leicester Univ. Sch. of Medicine, 2006–. Editor in Chief, Quality in Primary Care, 2005–. Chm., RCGP, 2004–07. *Publications:* (ed jtly) Evidence Based Audit in General Practice, 1998; (ed) A Celebration of General Practice, 2003; (ed jtly) Recent Advances in Primary Care, 2005; various articles on quality in health care and health policy. *Recreation:* tennis (Mem., Rothley Ivanhoe Tennis Club). *Address:* Royal College of General Practioners, 14 Prince's Gate, Hyde Park, SW7 1PU; *e-mail:* mlakhani@aol.com.

LAKIN, Sir Michael, 4th Bt *cr* 1909; *b* 28 Oct. 1934; *s* of Sir Henry Lakin, 3rd Bt, and Bessie (*d* 1965), *d* of J. D. Anderson, Durban; *S* father, 1979; *m* 1st, 1956, Margaret Wallace (marr. diss. 1963); 2nd, 1965, Felicity Ann Murphy; one *s* one *d*. *Educ:* Stowe. *Heir:* *s* Richard Anthony Lakin [*b* 26 Nov. 1968; *m* 1997, Lara Maryanne Rose; one *s* one *d*]. *Address:* Little Sherwood, Tunley, near Cirencester, Glos GL7 6LW.

LAKIN, Peter Maurice; His Honour Judge Lakin; a Circuit Judge, since 1995; Resident Judge, Manchester Crown Court, since 2006; *b* 21 Oct. 1949; *s* of late Ronald Maurice Lakin and of Dorothy Kathleen Lakin (*née* Cowlishaw); *m* 1971, Jacqueline Jubb; one *s* one *d*. *Educ:* King Henry VIII Sch., Coventry; Manchester Univ. (LLB). Articled Clerk, Conn Goldberg, solicitors, Manchester, 1971–74; Goldberg Blackburn, solicitors, Manchester (later Pannone & Partners): Asst Solicitor, 1974–76; Partner i/c of Corporate Defence and Forensic Unit, 1976–95; Asst Recorder, 1989–93; Recorder, 1993–95. Hon. Sec., Manchester and Dist Medico-Legal Soc., 1989–95. *Recreations:* fell-walking, opera, gardening, local history. *Address:* Manchester Crown Court, Minshull Street, Manchester M1 3FS.

LAL, Prof. Devendra, PhD; FRS 1979; Professor, Geological Research Division, Scripps Institution of Oceanography, University of California, La Jolla, since 1967; Fellow: Physical Research Laboratory, Ahmedabad, since 1990 (Director, 1972–83; Senior Professor, 1983–89); Tata Institute of Fundamental Research, Bombay, since 1996; *b* 14 Feb. 1929; *s* of Radhekrishna Lal and Sita Devi; *m* 1955, Aruna L. Damany (*d* 1993). *Educ:* Banaras Hindu Univ. (BSc; MSc); Univ. of Bombay (PhD). Fellow, Indian Acad. of Sciences, 1964. Tata Inst. of Fundamental Research, Bombay: Res. Student, 1949–50; Res. Asst, 1950–53; Res. Fellow, 1953–57; Fellow, 1957–60; Associate Prof., 1960–63; Prof., 1963–70; Sen. Prof., 1970–72. Res. Geophysicist, UCLA-IGPP, 1965–66. Vis. Prof., UCLA, 1983–84. K. S. Krishnan Meml Lect., INSA, 1981. Foreign Sec., Indian Nat. Sci. Acad., 1981–84 (Fellow, 1971); Founder Mem., Third World Acad. of Scis, Trieste, 1983; President: Internat. Assoc. of Physical Scis of the Ocean, 1979–83; Internat. Union of Geodesy & Geophysics, 1983–87. Fellow: Nat. Acad. of Scis, Allahabad, 1988; Physical Res. Lab., Ahmedabad, 1996; Tata Inst. of Fundamental Res., Bombay, 1996; Amer. Geophysical Union, 2005; FAAAS 1997; Foreign Associate, Nat. Acad. of

Sciences, USA, 1975; For. Mem., Amer. Acad. of Arts and Scis, 1989; Associate, RAS, 1984; Mem., Internat. Acad. Astronautics, 1985. Mem., Sigma Xi, USA, 1984. Hon. Fellow, Geol Soc. of India, 1992. Hon. DSc Banaras Hindu Univ., 1981. Krishnan Medal for Geochemistry and Geophysics, Indian Geophysical Union, Hyderabad, 1965; Shanti Swarup Bhatnagar Award for Physical Sciences, CSIR, 1967; Outstanding Scientist Award, Fedn of Indian Chambers of Commerce and Industry, 1974; Pandit Jawaharlal Nehru Award for Scis, Madhya Pradesh Govt, 1986; C. V. Raman Birth Centenary Award, Indian Sci. Congress Assoc., 1996–97; V. M. Goldschmidt Medal, and Fellow, Geochem. Soc., USA, 1997. Padma Shri, 1971. *Publications:* (ed) Early Solar System Processes and the Present Solar System, 1980; (ed) Biogeochemistry of the Arabian Sea, 1994; *contributed:* Earth Science and Meteoritics, 1963; International Dictionary of Geophysics, 1968; The Encyclopedia of Earth Sciences: vol. IV, Geochemistry and Environmental Sciences, 1972; Further Advances in Lunar Research: Luna 16 and 20 samples, 1974; McGraw Hill Encyclopedia of Science and Technology, 1992; jt author of chapters in books; scientific papers to learned jls; proc. confs. *Recreations:* music, puzzles, painting, photography. *Address:* Scripps Institution of Oceanography, University of California at San Diego, La Jolla, CA 92093–0244, USA. *T:* (office) (858) 5342134, (home) (858) 5871535; *e-mail:* dlal@ucsd.edu.

LALANDI-EMERY, Lina, (Mrs Ralph Emery), OBE 1975; Director, English Bach Festival, since 1962; *b* Athens; *d* of late Nikolas Kaloyeropoulos (former Dir of Byzantine Museum, Athens, and Dir of Beaux Arts, Min. of Educn, Athens) and Toula Gelekis. *Educ:* Athens Conservatoire (grad. with Hons in Music); privately, in England (harpsichord and singing studies). International career as harpsichordist in Concert, Radio and TV. Founded English Bach Festival Trust, 1962; later specialised in presentation of baroque opera perfs at Royal Opera House, Covent Gdn and numerous music fests. Officier, l'Ordre des Arts et des Lettres (France), 1978; Gold Cross of the Phoenix (Greece), 2004. *Recreations:* astrophysics, reading, knitting. *Address:* 15 South Eaton Place, SW1W 9ER. *T:* (020) 7730 5925, *Fax:* (020) 7730 1456; *e-mail:* info@ebf.org.uk.

LALANNE, Bernard Michel L.; *see* Loustau-Lalanne.

LALL, Vikram, CBE 2005; Director, Heriot Services Ltd, since 1996; *b* 5 Dec. 1946; *s* of late Jag Mohan Lall and Dr Shuki Lall; *m* 1981, Carol Anne Ask; one *s* one *d*. *Educ:* Doon Sch., Dehra Dun; St Stephen's Coll., Delhi (BA Hons Econs 1966). CA 1972. Executive Director: Noble Grossart Ltd, 1975–77; Vikram Lall & Co. Ltd, 1977–82; McNeill Pearson Ltd, 1982–85; Heriot & Co. Ltd, 1985–87; Bell Lawrie White & Co., 1987–2003; Brewin Dolphin Hldgs plc, 1989–2003 (non-exec. Dir, 2003–08). Non-executive Director: Isis Property Trust, 2003–; Crown Place VCT, 2006–; Ramco Hldgs Ltd, 2005–; Corsie Gp plc, 2006–; non-exec. Chm., Ryden LLP, 2005–. Chm., Scottish Industrial Develt Adv. Bd, 2002–07 (Mem., 2000–07). Member: Bd, Royal Lyceum Th. Co., 2002–07; Governing Body, Queen Margaret UC, Edinburgh, 2003–; Finance and Develt Cttee, RCSE, 2005–. *Recreations:* golf, travel, mind exercise. *Address:* Newmains House, Drem, East Lothian EH39 5BL. *T:* (01620) 825130, *Fax:* (01620) 825098; *e-mail:* vikramlall@macace.net. *Club:* Luffness New Golf.

LALLY, Patrick James; DL; Lord Provost and Lord-Lieutenant of Glasgow, 1995–99; Chairman, Scottish Senior Citizens Unity Party; *s* of Patrick James Lally and Sarah Joyce Lally; *m* 1967, Margaret Beckett McGuire (*d* 2007); two *s*. Former Dir, Retail Clothing Co. Member: Glasgow Corp., 1966–75 (Dep. Leader, 1972–75); Glasgow DC, 1975–77, 1980–96 (Treas., 1984–86; Leader, 1986–92, 1994–96). Contested (Ind.) Glasgow Cathcart, Scottish Parly elecns, 2003, 2005. Chairman: Gtr Glasgow Tourist Bd, 1989–96; Gtr Glasgow and Clyde Valley Tourist Bd, 1996–99; Director: Glasgow Internat. Jazz Fest. (Chm., 1989–99); Glasgow Develt Agency, 1990–92; Scottish Exhibn Centre Ltd, 1994–99; Glasgow 1999 Co. Ltd, 1996–99; Castlemilk Pensioners' Action Centre. Mem., RGI. Hon. Mem., Royal Faculty of Procurators in Glasgow. Member: Merchants House of Glasgow; Incorporation of Tailors, Glasgow; Incorporation of Gardiners, Glasgow. JP Glasgow, 1970–2007, DL Glasgow, 1986. Hon. Citizen, Dalian, China, 1995. OStJ 1997. Hon. LLD Strathclyde. Silver Thistle Award, Scottish Tourist Bd, 1999. Comdr, Ordre Nat. du Mérite (France), 1996. *Publication:* Lazarus Only Done it Once (autobiog.), 1999. *Recreations:* enjoying the arts, reading, watching TV, football. *Address:* 2 Tanera Avenue, Simshill, Glasgow G44 5BU. *Club:* Glasgow Art.

LALONDE, Hon. Marc; PC (Can.) 1972; OC 1989; QC 1971; sole law practioner, since 2006; *b* 26 July 1929; *s* of late J. Albert Lalonde and Nora (*née* St Aubin); *m* 1955, Claire Tétreau; two *s* two *d*. *Educ:* St Laurent Coll., Montreal (BA 1950); Univ. of Montreal (LLL 1954; MA Law 1955); Oxford Univ. (Econ. and Pol. Science; MA 1957); Ottawa Univ. (Dip. of Superior Studies in Law, 1960). Prof. of Commercial Law and Econs, Univ. of Montreal, 1957–59; Special Asst to Minister of Justice, Ottawa, 1959–60; Partner, Gelinas, Bourque Lalonde & Benoit, Montreal, 1960–68; Lectr in Admin. Law for Doctorate Students, Univ. of Ottawa and Univ. of Montreal, 1961–62; Policy Advisor to Prime Minister, 1967; Principal Sec. to Prime Minister, 1968–72; MP (L) Montreal-Outremont, 1972–84; Minister of National Health and Welfare, 1972–77; Minister of State for Federal-Provincial Relations, 1977–78; Minister resp. for Status of Women, 1975–78; Minister of Justice and Attorney-Gen., 1978–79; Minister of Energy, Mines and Resources, 1980–82; Minister of Finance, 1982–84. Law Partner, 1984–2003, Sen. Counsel, 2003–06, Stikeman Elliott, Montreal. *Ad hoc* Judge, Internat. Court of Justice, 1985–. Counsel before several Royal Commns inc. Royal Commn on Great Lakes Shipping and Royal Commn on Pilotage. Mem., Cttee on Broadcasting, 1964; Dir, Canadian Citizenship Council, 1960–65; Member, Bd of Directors: Inst. of Public Law, Univ. of Montréal, 1960–64; Citibank Canada, 1985–; O&Y Properties, 1993–2005; Sherritt Power, subseq. Sherritt International, Inc., 1998–; Oxbow Equities Corp., 2000–. Dr *hc* Univ. of Limburg, Maastricht, 1992. Dana Award, Amer. Public Health Assoc., 1978. *Publications:* The Changing Role of the Prime Minister's Office, 1971; New Perspectives on the Health of Canadians (working document), 1974. *Recreations:* ski-ing, jogging, sailing, reading. *Address:* 1155 René-Lévesque Boulevard West, 33rd Floor, Montreal, QC H3B 3V2, Canada.

LALUMIÈRE, Catherine; French politician; President, Maison de l'Europe, Paris; Vice-President, European Movement International; *b* Rennes, 3 Aug. 1935. Dr in Public Law; degree in Pol Scis and History of Law. Asst, Univ. of Bordeaux I, and Bordeaux Inst. of Pol Studies, 1960–71; Sen. Lectr, Univ. of Paris I, 1971–81. Mem., National Assembly for Gironde, 1981, and 1986–89: Vice-Pres., Cttee of For. Affairs; Vice-Pres., Delegn to EC. Sec. of State i/c Public Service, 1981; Minister of Consumer Affairs, 1981–84; Sec. of State, resp. for Eur. Affairs, Min. of For. Affairs, 1984–86; Mem., Parly Assembly, Council of Europe, 1987–89; Sec. Gen., Council of Europe, 1989–94; Mem., 1994–2004, a Vice-Pres., 2001–04, Eur. Parlt; Pres., Eur. Radical Alliance Gp, 1994–2004. Mem. and Vice-Pres., Parti Radical de Gauche; Vice-Pres., Eur. Movement, France; Pres., Relais-Culture Europe. Regl Councillor, Ile de France, 1998–2004. *Recreation:* walking. *Address:* Maison de l'Europe de Paris, 35–37 rue des Francs-Bourgeois, 75004 Paris, France.

LAM, Martin Philip; *b* 10 March 1920; *m* 1953, Lisa Lorenz; one *s* one *d*. *Educ:* University College Sch.; Gonville and Caius Coll., Cambridge (Scholar). Served War of 1939–45, Royal Signals and Special Ops Mediterranean. Asst Principal, Board of Trade, 1947; Nuffield Fellowship (Latin America), 1952–53; Asst Sec., 1960; Counsellor, UK Delegn to OECD, 1963–65, Advr, Commercial Policy, 1970–74, Leader UNCTAD Delegn, 1972; Under-Sec. (Computer Systems and Electronics), DoI, 1974–78; Associate of BIS Mackintosh, and of General Technology Systems, 1979–90; on contract to Directorate-Gen. XIII, European Commn, 1986–88; consultant: Scaneurope, 1989–90; KCL, 1991–92. *Publications:* (jtly) Kanji from the Start, 1995; contrib. Jl of World Trade, Knowledge Engrg Review. *Address:* 44 York Lodge, Pegasus Court, Park Lane, Tilehurst, Reading RG31 5DB.

LAMB, family name of **Baron Rochester**.

LAMB, Sir Albert Thomas, (Sir Archie), KBE 1979 (MBE 1953); CMG 1974; DFC 1945; HM Diplomatic Service, retired; *b* 23 Oct. 1921; *s* of R. S. Lamb and Violet Lamb (*née* Haynes); *m* 1944, Christina Betty Wilkinson; one *s* two *d*. *Educ:* Swansea Grammar Sch. Served RAF 1941–46. FO 1938–41; Embassy, Rome, 1947–50; Consulate-General, Genoa, 1950; Embassy, Bucharest, 1950–53; FO 1953–55; Middle East Centre for Arabic Studies, 1955–57; Political Residency, Bahrain, 1957–61; FO 1961–65; Embassy, Kuwait, 1965; Political Agent in Abu Dhabi, 1965–68; Inspector, 1968–70, Sen. Inspector, 1970–73, Asst Under-Sec. of State and Chief Inspector, FCO, 1973–74; Ambassador to Kuwait, 1974–77; Ambassador to Norway, 1978–80. Mem., BNOC, 1981–82; Dir, Britoil plc, 1982–88; Member Board: British Shipbuilders, 1985–87; Nat. Bank of Kuwait (Internat.), 1994–2008; Sen. Associate, Conant and Associates Ltd, Washington DC, 1985–93; Adviser, Samuel Montagu and Co. Ltd, 1986–88. Clerk to Parish Councils of Zeals and Stourton with Gasper, 1991–97. Hon. Fellow: Swansea Inst. of Higher Educn, 2004; Univ. of Wales Swansea, 2005. *Publications:* A Long Way from Swansea, 2003; Abu Dhabi 1965–1968, 2003; The Last Voyage of SS Oronsay, 2004. *Address:* White Cross Lodge, Zeals, Wilts BA12 6PF. *T:* (01747) 840321. *Club:* Royal Air Force.
See also R. D. Lamb.

LAMB, Prof. Christopher John, PhD; FRS 2008; Director, John Innes Centre, and John Innes Professor of Biology, University of East Anglia, since 1999; *b* 19 March 1950; *s* of late John Mungall Lamb and Eileen Blanche Lamb (*née* Marley); *m* 1970, Jane Susan Wright; two *s* one *d*. *Educ:* Fitzwilliam Coll., Cambridge (BA 1972, PhD 1976, in Biochemistry). Oxford University: ICI Postdoctoral Fellow, Sch. of Botany, 1975–77; Deptl Demonstr., Dept of Biochemistry, 1977–82; Browne Res. Fellow, Queen's Coll., 1977–82; Dir and Prof., Plant Biology Lab., Salk Inst. for Biol Studies, Calif, 1982–98; Adjunct Prof., UCSD, 1988–98; Regius Prof. of Plant Sci., Univ. of Edinburgh, 1999. Founder, Akkadix Inc., 1998; Dir, Plant Bioscience Ltd, 1999–. Mem., EMBO, 2001. FAAAS 1992. McKnight Schol., 1983, Herman Frasch Award, 1986, ACS. *Publications:* numerous articles in Nature, Science, Cell and other learned jls. *Recreations:* fell walking, swimming, wine, sushi. *Address:* John Innes Centre, Norwich Research Park, Colney, Norwich NR4 7UH. *T:* (01603) 450000.

LAMB, (Emma) Harriet, CBE 2006; Executive Director, Fairtrade Foundation, since 2001; *b* 3 June 1961; *d* of Gilbert and Sarah Lamb; partner, Steve Percy; one *s* one *d*. *Educ:* Trinity Hall, Cambridge (BA Social and Pol Sci. 1982); Inst. of Develt Studies Univ. of Sussex (MPhil Develt Studies 1986). Volunteer, village co-operatives, India, 1982–84; researcher, Northern Reg. Low Pay Unit, 1987–90; Co-ordinator, NE Refugee Service, 1990–92; Campaigns Co-ordinator, World Develt Movt, 1992–99; Interim Dir/Banana Co-ordinator, Fairtrade Labelling Orgns Internat., Germany, 1999–2001. *Publications:* Working for Big Mac, 1987; Fighting the Banana Wars and Other Fairtrade Battles: how we took on the corporate giants to change the world, 2008. *Recreations:* cycling slowly, gardening badly, chatting loudly, playing with my kids, walking Northumbrian hills, swimming. *Address:* Fairtrade Foundation, Room 204, 16 Baldwin's Gardens, EC1N 7RJ. *T:* (020) 7440 7673, *Fax:* (020) 7405 5943; *e-mail:* harriet.lamb@fairtrade.org.uk.

LAMB, Air Vice-Marshal George Colin, CB 1977; CBE 1966; AFC 1947; Chairman, Yonex (UK) Ltd, 1995–97 (Managing Director, 1990–95); *b* 23 July 1923; *s* of late George and Bessie Lamb, Hornby, Lancaster; *m* 1st, 1945, Nancy Mary Godsmark; two *s*; 2nd, 1981, Mrs Maureen Margaret Mepham. *Educ:* Lancaster Royal Grammar School. War of 1939–45: commissioned, RAF, 1942; flying duties, 1942–53; Staff Coll., 1953; Air Ministry, special duties, 1954–58; OC No 87 Sqdn, 1958–61; Dir Admin. Plans, MoD, 1961–64; Asst Comdt, RAF Coll., 1964–65; Dep. Comdr, Air Forces Borneo, 1965–66; Fighter Command, 1966; MoD (Dep. Command Structure Project Officer), 1967; HQ, Strike Command, 1967–69; OC, RAF Lyneham, 1969–71; RCDS, 1971–72; Dir of Control (Operations), NATS, 1972–74; Comdr, Southern Maritime Air Region, RAF Mount Batten, 1974–75; C of S, No 18 Gp Strike Comd, RAF, 1975–78. RAF Vice-Pres., Combined Cadet Forces Assoc., 1978–94. Chief Exec., Badminton Assoc. of England, 1978–89; Gen. Sec., London Inst. of Sports Medicine, 1989–90. Consultant, Television, Sport and Leisure Ltd, 1989–90. Chairman: Lilleshall Nat. Sports Centre, 1984–2005; British Internat. Sports Develt Aid Trust, 1995–2005; Member: Sports Council, 1983–88 (Mem., Drug Abuse Adv. Gp, 1988–92); Sports Cttee, Prince's Trust, 1985–88; British Internat. Sports Cttee, 1989–2005; Privilege Mem. of RFU, 1985– (Mem., RFU Cttee, 1973–85). Dir (non-exec.), Castle Care-Tech. Security, 1993–2005. President: St George's Day Club, 1994–; Assoc. of Lancastrians in London, 1999. Vice-Pres., British Berlin Airlift Assoc., 1998–. Internat. Rugby referee, 1966–71. FCMI. *Recreations:* Rugby football, cricket (former Pres., Adastrian Cricket Club), gardening, walking. *Address:* Hambledon, 17 Meadway, Berkhamsted HP4 2PN. *T:* (01442) 862583. *Club:* Royal Air Force.

LAMB, Lt-Gen. Graeme Cameron Maxwell, CMG 2003; DSO 2004; OBE 1991 (MBE 1988); Commander, Field Army, since 2007; *b* 21 Oct. 1953. *Educ:* Rannoch Sch.; Royal Mil. Acad. Sandhurst. Commnd Queen's Own Highlanders, 1973; Comdr, 81 Army Youth Team, Inverness, 1975–77; Northern Ireland (despatches, 1981); Staff Coll., Camberley, 1985; Comdr, B Co., 1st Bn, 1988–90; jsdc, 1989–90; Comdr, 1st Bn, 1991–93; Mil. Ops, MoD, 1993–94; HCSC, 1996; Comdr, 5th Airborne Bde, 1996–97; rcds, 1998; Asst Comdt (Land), JSCSC, 1999–2001; MoD, 2001–03; GOC 3rd (UK) Div., 2003–05; Dir Gen., Trng Support, MoD, 2005–06; Dep. Comdg Gen., Multinat. Force, Iraq, 2006–07. Chm., Army Snowboarding Assoc., 2001–. QCVS 1994. *Address:* c/o Army Personnel Centre, Kentigern House, 65 Brown Street, Glasgow G2 8EX.

LAMB, Harriet; *see* Lamb, E. H.

LAMB, Prof. Joseph Fairweather, PhD; FRCPE; FRSE; Chandos Professor of Physiology, St Leonard's College, University of St Andrews, 1969–93, now Professor Emeritus; *b* 18 July 1928; *s* of Joseph and Agnes May Lamb; *m* 1st, 1955, Olivia Janet Horne (marr. diss. 1989); three *s* one *d*; 2nd, 1989, Bridget Cecilia Cook; two *s*. *Educ:* Auldbar Public Sch.; Brechin High School (Dux, 1947); Edinburgh Univ. (MB ChB, BSc, PhD). FRCPE 1985. National Service, RAF, 1947–49. House Officer, Dumfries and Edinburgh, 1955–56; Hons Physiology Course, 1956–57; Univ. Junior Res. Fellow, 1957; Lectr in Physiology, Royal (Dick) Vet. Sch., 1958–61; Lectr, Sen. Lectr in Physiol., Glasgow, 1961–69. Sec., Physiol. Soc., 1982–85; Chm., Save British Science Soc.,

1986–97; Chm./Organiser, Gas Greed Campaign, 1994–95. Gov., Rowett Res. Inst., Aberdeen, 1998–2004. Editor: Jl of Physiol., 1968–74; Amer. Jl of Physiol., 1985–88. FRSA; FRSE 1985. Mem., RYA. *Publications:* Essentials of Physiology, 1980, 3rd edn 1991; articles in learned jls. *Recreations:* sailing, boatbuilding, reading. *Address:* 53 Darnell Road, Trinity, Edinburgh EH5 3PH. *T:* (0131) 476 2537.

LAMB, Juliet; *see* Warkentin, J.

LAMB, Martin James; Chief Executive, IMI plc, since 2001; *b* 7 Jan. 1960; *s* of Dr Trevor Lamb and Shirley Lamb; *m* 1983, Jayne Louise Bodenham; four *d. Educ:* Bradford Grammar Sch.; Solihull Sixth Form Coll.; Imperial Coll., London (BSc Mech. Eng. 1982); Cranfield Business Sch. (MBA 1990). Grad. Trainee, IMI Cornelius Inc., USA, 1982–83; Project Engr, IMI Air Conditioning, UK, 1983–85; R&D Manager, Coldflow Ltd, 1985–87; Mktg Dir, 1987–91, Man. Dir, 1991–96, IMI Cornelius (UK) Ltd; Exec. Dir, IMI plc, 1996–2000. Non-exec. Dir, Spectris plc, 1999–2006. Trustee, City Technol. Coll., Birmingham, 1997–. *Recreations:* family, tennis, golf. *Address:* IMI plc, Lakeside, Solihull Parkway, Birmingham Business Park, Birmingham B37 7XZ. *T:* (0121) 717 3700, *Fax:* (0121) 717 3801; *e-mail:* information@imiplc.com.

LAMB, Prof. Michael Ernest, PhD; Professor of Psychology in the Social Sciences, University of Cambridge, since 2004; *b* Lusaka, N Rhodesia, 22 Oct. 1953; *s* of Frank Lamb and Michelle Lamb (*née* de Lestang); *m* 2005, Hilary S. Clark; four step *d*, and three *s* one *d* from previous marriage. *Educ:* Univ. of Natal, S Africa (BA Psychol. and Econs); Johns Hopkins Univ. (MA Psychol.); Yale Univ. (MS, MPhil; PhD 1976). Assistant Professor of Psychology: Univ. of Wisconsin, 1976–78; Univ. of Michigan, 1978–80; Prof. of Psychol., Psychiatry and Pediatrics, Univ. of Utah, 1980–87 (Dist. Res. Award, 1986); Sen. Scientist and Section Chief, Nat. Inst. of Child Health and Human Develt, USA, 1987–2004. Mem., ESRC, 2006–. Hon. PhD Goteborg, 1995; Hon. DCL UEA, 2006. Cattell Award for Lifetime Contribn to Psychol., Amer. Psychol. Soc., 2004. *Publications:* (ed) The Role of the Father in Child Development, 1976, trans. Japanese 1981, 4th edn 2004; (ed) Social and Personality Development, 1978; (ed jtly) Social Interaction Analysis, 1979; (jtly) Child Psychology Today, 1982, 2nd edn 1986; (ed jtly) Advances in Developmental Psychology, 1981, 1986; (ed jtly) Infant Social Cognition, 1982; (jtly) Development in Infancy: an introduction, 1982, 4th edn 2002; (jtly) Socialization and Personality Development, 1982; (ed) Nontraditional Families, 1982, trans. Japanese 1998; (jtly) Infant-Mother Attachment, 1985; (ed) The Father's Role: applied perspectives, 1986; (ed jtly) Adolescent Fatherhood, 1986; (ed) The Father's Role: cross-cultural perspectives, 1987; (ed jtly) Adolescent Problem Behaviours, 1994; (ed jtly) Images of Childhood, 1996; (jtly) Investigative Interviews of Children, 1998; (ed) Parenting and Child Development in Nontraditional Families, 1999; (ed jtly) Developmental Science: an advanced textbook, 5th edn 2005; (ed jtly) Hunter-gatherer Childhoods, 2005; (ed jtly) Child Sexual Abuse, 2007; (jtly) Tell Me What Happened: structured investigative interviews of child victims and witnesses, 2008. *Recreations:* travel, family, performing arts, literature. *Address:* Faculty of Social and Political Science, Free School Lane, Cambridge University, Cambridge CB2 3RQ. *T:* (01223) 334523, *Fax:* (01223) 334550; *e-mail:* mel37@cam.ac.uk.

LAMB, Norman Peter; MP (Lib Dem) Norfolk North, since 2001; *b* 16 Sept. 1957; *s* of late Hubert Horace Lamb and of Beatrice Moira Lamb; *m* 1984, Mary Elizabeth Green; two *s. Educ:* Wymondham Coll., Norfolk; Leicester Univ. (LLB). Sen. Asst Solicitor, Norwich CC, 1984–86; Solicitor, 1986–87, Partner, 1987–2001, Steele & Co. *Publication:* Remedies in the Employment Tribunal, 1998. *Recreations:* football, walking. *Address:* House of Commons, SW1A 0AA. *T:* (020) 7219 8480; (office) 15 Market Place, North Walsham NR28 9BP.

LAMB, Robin David; HM Diplomatic Service, retired; Head of Business Development, Arab-British Chamber of Commerce, since 2007; *b* 25 Nov. 1948; *s* of Sir Albert Thomas Lamb, *qv*; *m* 1977, Susan Jane Moxon; two *s* one *d. Educ:* St John's, Leatherhead; Brasenose Coll., Oxford (MA Oriental Studies). Mgt asst, Abu Dhabi Cement Mktg Assoc., 1966–67; Mgt Develt Prog., Barclays Bank, 1970–71; joined FCO, 1971: lang. trng, MECAS, 1974–75; Res. Officer, FCO, 1975–79; Second Sec., Jedda, 1979–82; Principal Res. Officer, FCO, 1982–85; First Secretary: Riyadh, 1985–87; FCO, 1988–93; Hd, Pol Section, Cairo, 1993–96; FCO, 1996–99; British Trade Internat., 1999–2001; Counsellor and Dep. Hd of Mission, Kuwait, 2001–03; Ambassador, Bahrain, 2003–06; Consul-Gen., Basra, April–Aug. 2006. Dir, BESO, 1999–2001. Fellow, British Soc. for ME Studies, 1992. Bahrain Medal (1st cl.) (Bahrain), 2006; Iraq Reconstruction Service Medal, 2007. *Recreations:* family, swimming, reading. *Address:* (office) 43 Upper Grosvenor Street, W1K 2NJ.

LAMB, Hon. Timothy Michael; Chief Executive, Central Council of Physical Recreation, since 2005; *b* 24 March 1953; *s* of Baron Rochester, *qv*; *m* 1978, Denise Ann Buckley; one *s* one *d. Educ:* Shrewsbury Sch.; Queen's Coll., Oxford (MA Modern Hist.). Professional cricketer: with Middx CCC, 1974–77; with Northants CCC, 1978–83; Sec. and Gen. Manager, Middx CCC, 1984–88; Cricket Sec., 1988–96, Dep. Chief Exec., May–Oct. 1996, TCCB; Chief Exec., TCCB, then ECB, 1996–2004. *Recreations:* golf, travel, walking, photography. *Address:* (office) Burwood House, 14–16 Caxton Street, SW1H 0QT.

LAMB, Timothy Robert; QC 1995; **His Honour Judge Lamb;** a Circuit Judge, since 2008; *b* 27 Nov. 1951; *s* of Stephen Falcon Lamb and Pamela Elizabeth Lamb (*née* Coombes); *m* 1978, Judith Anne Ryan; one *s* one *d. Educ:* Brentwood Sch.; Lincoln Coll., Oxford (MA Jurisp.). Called to the Bar, Gray's Inn, 1974, Bencher, 2003. Asst Recorder, 1998–2000; Recorder, 2000–08. Jt Head of Chambers, 3 Paper Buildings, Temple, 2004–08. Bar Council: Western Circuit Rep., 2005–08; Circuits Rep., Law Reform Cttee, 2005–08. Legal Assessor, GDC, 2002–08; Legal Adviser: Royal Pharmaceutical Soc., 2006–08; General Optical Council, 2006–08. Accredited mediator and adjudicator. FCIArb. *Recreations:* family, travel, water sports, gliding. *Address:* Snaresbrook Crown Court, 75 Hollybush Hill, Snaresbrook, E11 1QW.

LAMB, Prof. Trevor David, FRS 1993; FAA; Distinguished Professor and Research Director, ARC Centre of Excellence in Vision Science, John Curtin School of Medical Research, Australian National University, since 2006 (ARC Federation Fellow, 2003–07); *b* 20 Sept. 1948; *s* of Arthur and Margaret Lamb; *m* 1979, (Janet) Clare Conway; two *s* one *d. Educ:* Melbourne Grammar Sch.; Univ. of Melbourne (BE 1st Cl. Hons 1969); Univ. of Cambridge (PhD 1975; ScD 1988). FAA 2005. University of Cambridge: Wellcome Sen. Res. Fellow, 1978–80, Royal Soc. Locke Res. Fellow, 1980–84, Physiological Lab.; Univ. Lectr in Physiol., 1984–91; Reader in Neuroscience, 1991–94; Prof. of Neurosci., 1994–2002; Fellow, Darwin Coll., 1985–2002. *Publications:* articles on photoreceptors and sensory transduction in Jl Physiol. and other learned jls. *Address:* Division of Neuroscience, John Curtin School of Medical Research, Australian National University, Canberra, ACT 2601, Australia. *T:* (2) 61258929, *Fax:* (2) 61252687; *e-mail:* trevor.lamb@anu.edu.au.

LAMBART, family name of **Earl of Cavan**.

LAMBECK, Prof. Kurt, DPhil, DSc; FRS 1994; FAA; Professor of Geophysics, Australian National University, since 1977; *b* 20 Sept. 1941; *s* of Jacob and Johanna Lambeck; *m* 1967, Bridget Marguerite Nicholls; one *s* one *d. Educ:* Univ. of NSW (BSurv. Hons); Hertford Coll., Oxford (DPhil, DSc). Geodesist, Smithsonian Astrophysical Observatory and Harvard Coll. Observatory, Cambridge, Mass, 1967–70; Directeur Scientifique, Observatoire de Paris, 1970–73; Prof. of Geophysics, Univ. of Paris, 1973–77; Dir, Res. Sch. of Earth Scis, ANU, 1984–93. Tage Erlander Prof., Swedish Res. Council, 2001–02. Pres., Aust. Acad. Sci., 2006– (Vice Pres., 1998–2000; Foreign Sec., 2000–04). Fellow, Amer. Geophysical Union, 1976; FAA 1984. Foreign Member: Royal Netherlands Acad. of Arts and Scis, 1993; Norwegian Acad. of Science and Letters, 1994; Foreign MAE, 1999; Associé étranger, Institut de France, Académie des Sciences, 2005; Hon. Mem., European Geophysical Soc., 1987. Hon. DEng Nat. Tech. Univ., Athens, 1994; Hon. DSc NSW, 1999. Macelwane Medal, 1976, Whitten Medal, 1993, Amer. Geophysical Union; Jaeger Medal, Aust. Acad. of Sci., 1995; Alfred Wegener Medal, Eur. Union of Geoscis, 1997; Georges Lemâitre Prize, Catholic Univ. of Louvain, 2001; Federation Medal, 2003. *Publications:* The Earth's Variable Rotation, 1980; Geophysical Geodesy: the slow deformations of the earth, 1988; numerous articles in fields of geodesy, geophysics and geology. *Address:* Research School of Earth Sciences, Australian National University, Canberra, ACT 0200, Australia; 31 Brand Street, Hughes, ACT 2605, Australia.

LAMBERT, Anne; *see* Lambert, G. M. A.

LAMBERT, David Arthur Charles; General President, National Union of Knitwear, Footwear and Apparel Trades, 1991–94 (General Secretary, 1975–82, General President, 1982–90, National Union of Hosiery and Knitwear Workers); President, International Textile, Garment and Leather Workers' Federation, Brussels, 1992–96 (Vice-President, 1984–92); *b* 2 Sept. 1933; *m* Beryl Ann (*née* Smith); two *s* one *d. Educ:* Hitchin Boys' Grammar Sch., Herts. Employed as production worker for major hosiery manufr; active as lay official within NUHKW; full-time official, NUHKW, 1964–90. Member: Employment Appeal Tribunal, 1978–2004; TUC Gen. Council, 1984–94; CRE, 1987–93. Gov., Welbeck Coll., 2001–.

LAMBERT, David George; Registrar of Diocese of Llandaff, since 1986; Provincial Registrar, Church in Wales, since 2002; *b* 7 Aug. 1940; *s* of George and Elsie Lambert; *m* 1966, Diana Mary Ware; one *s* one *d. Educ:* Barry Grammar Sch.; UCW, Aberystwyth (LLB). Notary Public; Solicitor in private practice, 1965; Welsh Office: Legal Officer, 1966–74; Asst Legal Adviser, 1974–91; Solicitor and Legal Advr, 1991–99; Legal Advr, Presiding Office, Nat. Assembly for Wales, 2000–04. Mem., Wales Cttee, Law Soc., 2004–. Res. Fellow, Cardiff Univ., 2000–. Dep. Chapter Clerk, Llandaff Cath., 1980–. *Recreations:* ecclesiastical law, Baroque music. *Address:* 9 The Chantry, Llandaff, Cardiff CF5 2NN. *T:* (029) 2056 8154.

LAMBERT, (Gillian Mary) Anne, CMG 2006; UK Deputy Permanent Representative to the European Union, Brussels, since 2003; *b* 11 July 1956; *d* of late Roy and of Joyce Lambert. *Educ:* St Anne's Coll., Oxford (BA Hons Exptl Psychol. 1977). Joined Department of Trade and Industry, 1977: Telecommunications Div., 1982–84; Industrial Policy Div. (Grade 7), 1984–86; Insce Div., 1986–88; Personnel Div. (Grade 6), 1989–90; Insce Div. (Grade 5), 1990–93; on secondment to FCO as Counsellor (Industry), UK Perm. Repn to EU, Brussels, 1994–98; Dep. Dir Gen., Oftel, 1998–2002; Hd of Nuclear Liabilities, DTI, 2002–03. *Recreations:* theatre, squash, tennis, walking. *Address:* c/o Foreign and Commonwealth Office, King Charles Street, SW1A 2AH.

LAMBERT, Henry Uvedale Antrobus; Chairman: Sun Alliance Insurance Group, 1985–93; Agricultural Mortgage Corporation PLC, 1985–93; *b* 9 Oct. 1925; *o s* of late Roger Uvedale Lambert and Muriel, *d* of Sir Reginald Antrobus, KCMG, CB; *m* 1951, Diana, *y d* of Captain H. E. Dumbell, Royal Fusiliers; two *s* one *d. Educ:* Winchester College (Scholar); New College, Oxford (Exhibitioner; MA). Served War of 1939–45, Royal Navy, in HM Ships Stockham and St Austell Bay in Western Approaches and Mediterranean, subseq. RNR; Lt-Comdr (retired). Entered Barclays Bank 1948; a Local Dir at Lombard Street, 1957, Southampton, 1959, Birmingham, 1969; Vice-Chm., Barclays Bank UK Ltd, 1972; Vice-Chm., Barclays Bank Ltd, 1973; Chm., Barclays Bank Internat., 1979–83; Dep. Chm., 1979–85, Dir, 1966–91, Barclays Bank PLC; Agricultural Mortgage Corporation: Dir, 1966; Dep. Chm., 1977–85; Sun Alliance Insurance Group: Dir, 1972; Vice-Chm., 1978–83; Dep. Chm., 1983–85. Dir, British Airways, 1985–89. Mem. Council, RASE, 1985–2000 (Vice Pres., 1994–96; Hon. Vice Pres., 1996–2000). Trustee: Imperial War Graves Endowment Fund, 1987–94 (Chm., 1989–94); Nat. Maritime Mus., 1990–95. Vice-Pres., Navy Records Soc., 1985–89, 1992–96, 2001– (Hon. Treas., 1974–85); Mem. Council, White Ensign Assoc., 1982–2002 (Chm., 1992–96). Fellow, Winchester Coll., 1979–91. Hon. Mem., RICS, 1993. *Recreations:* fishing, gardening, golf, naval history. *Address:* Lowton Manor, Taunton, Somerset TA3 7SX. *Clubs:* Brooks's, MCC.

LAMBERT, Jean Denise; Member (Green) London Region, European Parliament, since 1999; *b* 1 June 1950; *d* of Frederick John and Margaret Archer; *m* 1977, Stephen Lambert; one *s* one *d. Educ:* Palmers Grammar Sch. for Girls, Grays, Essex; University Coll., Cardiff (BA Modern Langs); St Paul's Coll., Cheltenham (PGCE). ADB(Ed). Secondary sch. teacher, Waltham Forest, 1972–89 (exmnr in spoken and written English, 1983–88). Green Party: joined 1977 (then Ecology Party); London Area Co-ordinator, 1977–81; Co-Chm. Council, 1982–85, 1986–87; Rep. to European Green Parties, 1985–86, 1988–89; UK rep. to Green Gp in European Parlt, 1989–94; Green Party Speaker, 1988–, Jt Principal Speaker, 1992–93; Chair of Executive, 1993–94. Vice-Pres., Green/EFA Gp, 2002–. Contested (Green Party): GLC, 1981; local Council, 1986; London NE, European Parlt, 1984, 1989, 1994; Walthamstow, gen. elec., 1992. Founder Member: Ecology Building Soc., 1981 (Bd, 1981–84; Chm., 1982–83; now Patron); Play for Life, 1984; Member: Council, Charter 88, 1990–; Cttee, Voting Reform Gp, 1995–. Trustee, London Ecology Centre, 1995–97. Radio and TV broadcaster. *Publications:* (contrib.) Into the 21st Century, 1988; No Change? No Chance!, 1996; Refugees and the Environment, 2002; articles to magazines. *Recreations:* reading (esp. detective fiction), cooking, dance. *Address:* Suite 58, The Hop Exchange, 24 Southwark Street, SE1 1TY. *T:* (020) 7407 6269; *e-mail:* jeanlambert@greenmeps.org.uk.

LAMBERT, Sir John (Henry), KCVO 1980; CMG 1975; HM Diplomatic Service, retired; President, Heritage of London Trust, since 2005 (Director, 1981–96; Vice-President, 1996–2005); *b* 8 Jan. 1921; *s* of Col R. S. Lambert, MC, and Mrs H. J. F. Mills; *m* 1950, Jennifer Ann (*née* Urquhart); one *s* two *d. Educ:* Eton Coll.; Sorbonne; Trinity Coll., Cambridge. Grenadier Guards, 1940–45 (Captain). Appointed 3rd Secretary, HM Embassy, The Hague, 1945; Member of HM Foreign Service, 1947; FO, 1948; 2nd Secretary, Damascus, 1951; 1st Secretary, 1953; FO, 1954; Dep. to UK Representative on International Commn for Saar Referendum, 1955; Belgrade, 1956; Head of Chancery, Manila, 1958; UK Delegation to Disarmament Conference, Geneva, 1962; FO, 1963; Counsellor, Head of Chancery, Stockholm, 1964–67; Head of UN (Political) Dept, FCO, 1967–70; Commercial Counsellor and Consul-Gen. Vienna, 1971–74; Minister and Dep.

Comdt, Berlin, 1974–77; Ambassador to Tunisia, 1977–81. Chm., Channel Tunnel Investments plc, 1986–92. *Recreations:* the arts, music, tennis, golf. *Address:* 103 Rivermead Court, SW6 3SB. *T:* (020) 7731 5007. *Clubs:* MCC; Hurlingham, Royal St George's Golf.

LAMBERT, John Sinclair; Partner, John Lambert Associates, since 2000; Director: Aim4Growth Ltd, since 2001; executive coach and mentor; *b* 8 April 1948; *s* of late Norman Lambert and of Doris Lambert; *m* 1971, Ann Dowzell; two *s*. *Educ:* Denstone Coll.; Selwyn Coll., Cambridge (MA); Sheffield Hallam Univ. (MSc 2005). Department of Employment, subseq. Department for Education and Employment, 1970–2000: Private Sec. to Perm. Sec., 1973–74; on secondment to Marconi Space and Defence Systems, 1977–78; Dep. Chief Conciliation Officer, ACAS, 1982–83; Head of European Communities Branch, 1983–85; Dir of Field Ops, MSC, 1987–90; Dir of Ops (N and W), 1990–92; Dir, Adult Learning Div., 1992–93; Dir, Sheffield First Partnership, 1993–97 (on secondment); Regl Dir, Govt Office for Eastern Reg., 1997–98; Dir, Learning Ops, Univ. for Industry, 1998–99. Dep. Chm., Govs, Sheffield Hallam Univ. *Recreations:* birdwatching, music, mountain walking. *Address:* The Corner House, Hydro Close, Baslow, Derbys DE45 1SH.

LAMBERT, Nigel Robert Woolf; QC 1999; a Recorder, since 1996; *b* 5 Aug. 1949; *s* of Dr E. Vivian Lambert, MB BS, MRCS, LRCP, and Sadie Lambert (*née* Woolf); *m* 1975, Roamie Elisabeth Sado; one *s* one *d*. *Educ:* Cokethorpe Sch., Oxford; Coll. of Law, London. Called to the Bar, Gray's Inn, 1974, Bencher, 2004; *ad eundem* Mem., Inner Temple, 1986. Asst Recorder, 1992–96; Dep. Hd of Chambers, 2004–. Member: Bar Council, 1993–2000 (Member: Professional Standards Cttee, 1993–95, 1997–99; Public Affairs Cttee, 1994; Finance Cttee, 1994; Legal Aid and Fees Cttee, 1996); S Eastern Circuit Cttee, 1992–2007 (Mem. Exec. Cttee, 2001–07; Chm., S Eastern Circuit/Inst. of Barristers' Clerks Cttee, 2001–07); Inner Temple Bar Liaison Cttee, 2002–03; Inner Temple Circuit Cttee, 2002–03. Member: Criminal Bar Assoc. (Mem., Cttee, 1993–2000); Justice. Chm., N London Bar Mess, 2001–07. Gov., Cokethorpe Sch., 1971–78 (Life Vice Pres., Cokethorpe Old Boys' Assoc.). *Recreations:* supervising, organising, gossiping. *Address:* (chambers) Carmelite Chambers, 9 Carmelite Street, EC4Y 0DR. *T:* (020) 7936 6300; *e-mail:* nlambert@carmelitechambers.co.uk. *Clubs:* Garrick, MCC.

LAMBERT, Rear Adm. Paul, CB 2008; Capability Manager (Precision Attack), 2006–May 2009; Controller of the Navy, 2007–May 2009; Deputy Chief of Defence Staff (Equipment Capability) (in rank of Vice Adm.), from May 2009; *b* 17 Nov. 1954; *s* of Ernest Harry Lambert and Lillian Lambert (*née* Rutter); *m* 1979, Patricia Ann Smith; three *s* one *d*. *Educ:* City Univ., London (BSc 1978); Darwin Coll., Cambridge (MPhil 1989); DipFM, ACA 2002. Joined RN, 1974; Commanding Officer: HMS Onyx, 1989–91; HMS Tireless, 1991–92; submarine comd course, 1992–94; CO, HMS Coventry, 1996–98; Capt. Submarine Sea Trng, 1998–99; rcds 2000; hcsc 2001; Dir, Equipment Capability (Underwater Battlespace), MoD, 2001–04; Comdr Ops to C-in-C Fleet, Comdr Submarines and Allied Naval Force N and Rear Adm. Submarines, 2004–06. *Recreations:* walking, modern history, politics. *Address:* Ministry of Defence, Main Building, Whitehall, SW1A 2HB. *Club:* Royal Navy of 1765 and 1785.

LAMBERT, Paul Julian Lay; His Honour Judge Lambert; a Circuit Judge, since 2004; *b* 24 Aug. 1961; *s* of Arnold Michael Lay Lambert and late Rowena Lambert; *m* 2003, Sharon Dawn Curzon; two *s*. *Educ:* LSE (LLB). Called to the Bar, Middle Temple, 1983; in practice as barrister, 1983–2004, specialising in fraud and corporate crime. Mem., Professional Conduct Cttee, 1998–2001. *Recreations:* urbane pursuits. *Address:* Bristol Crown Court, Small Street, Bristol BS1 1DA. *Club:* Clifton (Bristol).

LAMBERT, Sir Peter John Biddulph, 10th Bt *cr* 1711, of London; teacher; *b* 5 April 1952; *s* of John Hugh Lambert (*d* 1977) (*g s* of 5th Bt) and of Edith May, *d* of late James Bance; *S* kinsman, Sir Greville Foley Lambert, 9th Bt, 1988, but his name does not appear on the Official Roll of the Baronetage; *m* 1989, Leslie Anne, *d* of R. W. Lyne; one *s* one *d*. *Educ:* Upper Canada Coll., Toronto; Trent Univ. (BSc 1975); Univ. of Manitoba (MA 1980); Univ. of Toronto (BEd). *Heir: s* Thomas Hugh John Lambert, *b* 14 March 1999.

LAMBERT, Captain Richard Edgar, CBE 1982; RN; Vice Lord-Lieutenant, County of Powys, 1997–2004; *b* 24 Oct. 1929; *s* of Joseph Edgar Hugo Lambert and Mildred Lambert (*née* Mason); *m* 1954, Eleanor Ruth Owen; two *s* one *d*. *Educ:* RNC, Dartmouth; BA Hons Open 1994. RN 1943–82; RCDS 1977; CO, HMS Raleigh, 1978–79. Marconi Underwater Systems, 1982–88. Non-exec. Dir, S and E Wales Ambulance NHS Trust, 1993–97. Dir, Machynlleth Tabernacle Trust, 1986–. President: Côr Meibion Powys, 1989–2008; Montgomeryshire Area Scout Council, 1997–2004. DL Powys, 1993. *Recreations:* gardening, music, art, ornithology. *Address:* Felin Rhisglog, Glaspwll, Machynlleth, Powys SY20 8TU. *T:* (01654) 702046. *Club:* Army and Navy.

LAMBERT, Richard Peter; Director General, Confederation of British Industry, since 2006; *b* 23 Sept. 1944; *s* of Peter and late Mary Lambert; *m* 1973, Harriet Murray-Browne; one *s* one *d*. *Educ:* Fettes Coll.; Balliol Coll., Oxford (BA). Staff of Financial Times, 1966–2001: Lex Column, 1972; Financial Editor, 1978; New York Correspondent, 1982; Dep. Editor, 1983; Editor, 1991–2001. Mem., Monetary Policy Cttee, Bank of England, 2003–06. Chancellor, Univ. of Warwick, 2008–. Trustee, BM, 2003–. Hon. DLitt City, 2000; Hon. LLD: Warwick, 2004; Brighton, 2005; DUniv York, 2007; Hon. DSc Cranfield, 2008. *Address:* CBI, Centre Point, 103 New Oxford Street, WC1A 1DU.

LAMBERT, Sophia Jane, CB 2004; *b* 15 May 1943; *d* of Michael Lambert and Florence Lambert (*née* Macaskie). *Educ:* Univ. of Paris; LSE (BSc). Entered FCO, 1966; Second Secretary: Bonn, 1968–72; FCO, 1972–76; First Secretary: Pretoria, 1976–80; FCO, 1980–82; Counsellor, Cabinet Office, 1982–85; Department of Transport: Head: Internat. Div., 1985–87; Public Transport (Metropolitan) Div., 1987–91; Channel Port Link Div., 1991–92; Director: Road and Vehicle Safety, 1992–98; Wildlife and Countryside, DETR, then DEFRA, 1998–2003 (also Dir, Flood Mgt, 2001–03). Chair, Standards Cttee, RBKC, 2006–. Lay Mem., Gen. Council of the Inns of Court, 2005–. *Address: e-mail:* sophia.lambert@ukonline.co.uk.

LAMBERT, Stephen; Chief Executive, Studio Lambert Ltd, since 2008; *b* 22 March 1959; *s* of Roger Lambert and Monika Lambert (*née* Wagner); *m* 1988, Jenni Russell; one *s* one *d*. *Educ:* Univ. of East Anglia; Nuffield Coll., Oxford. Joined BBC Television, 1983; Producer and Dir, BBC Documentary Features Dept, 1986–94, prog. series incl. 40 Minutes (East Side Story, Dolebusters, Greenfinches, Who'll win Jeanette?, Crack Doctors, Hilary's in Hiding, Malika's Hotel), Inside Story (Children of God, The Missing, Suicide Killers, Dogs of War), and True Brits; Exec. Producer, BBC Documentaries Dept, 1994–99, progs incl. The System (Best Factual Series, RTS, 1996), 42 Up (Best Documentary, BAFTA, 1998), The Mayfair Set (Best Factual Series, BAFTA, 1999), Mersey Blues, The Clampers, Lakesiders, Premier Passions, The Day the Guns Fell Silent; Editor: Modern Times, BBC TV, 1994–98; Real Life, ITV, 1998–2001; Dir of Progs, 1998–2005, Exec. Producer, 1999–2007, RDF Television; Chief Creative Officer, RDF Media Gp, 2005–07; progs incl. Faking It (Best Popular Arts Prog., Internat. Emmy Awards, 2002; Best Features Prog., BAFTA, 2002 and 2003; Best Primetime Features Prog., RTS, 2002; Golden Rose, Montreux, 2003), Perfect Match (Silver Rose, Montreux, 2002), The Century of the Self (Best Documentary Series, Broadcast Awards, 2003), Wife Swap (Best Features Prog., BAFTA, 2004; Golden Rose, Lucerne, 2004; Golden Nymph, Monte Carlo, 2004), The Power of Nightmares (Best Factual Series, BAFTA, 2005; Best Documentary Series, RTS, 2005), The Secret Millionaire (Best Reality Prog., Golden Rose, Lucerne, 2007), The Hip Hop Years, Shipwrecked, Going Native. Mem. Exec. Cttee, Edinburgh Internat. TV Fest., 2002–; Dir, Sheffield Internat. Documentary Fest., 2003–05. Mem. Council, BAFTA, 1996–98. FRSA. Best Commissioning Editor, Broadcast Awards, 1996. *Publication:* Channel Four: television with a difference?, 1982. *Recreations:* ski-ing, sailing, walking, cinema, my children. *Address:* Studio Lambert Ltd, 42 Beak Street, S1F 9RH. *T:* (020) 7432 3141; *e-mail:* stephen.lambert@studiolambert.com.

LAMBERT, Susan Barbara, (Mrs J. D. W. Murdoch); Hon. Head, Museum of Design in Plastics, Arts Institute, Bournemouth, since 2007; *b* 24 Jan. 1944; *d* of Alan Percival Lambert and Barbara May Lambert (*née* Herbert); *m* 1990, John Derek Walter Murdoch, *qv* (marr. diss. 2007). *Educ:* Downe House; Courtauld Inst. of Art, London Univ. (BA). Victoria and Albert Museum: Department of Prints and Drawings, subseq. Prints, Drawings and Paintings: Res. Asst, 1968–75; Asst Keeper, 1975–79; Dep. Keeper, 1979–89; Chief Curator, 1989–2002; Keeper, Word & Image Dept, 2002–05. *Publications:* Printmaking, 1983; Drawing, Technique and Purpose, 1984; The Image Multiplied, 1987; Form Follows Function?, 1993; Prints, Art and Technique, 2001. *Address:* Brick Hill, Burghclere, Berks RG20 9HJ. *T:* (01635) 278295.

LAMBETH, Archdeacon of; *see* Skilton, Ven. C. J.

LAMBIE, David; *b* 13 July 1925; *m* 1954, Netta May Merrie; one *s* four *d*. *Educ:* Kyleshill Primary Sch.; Ardrossan Academy; Glasgow University; Geneva University. BSc, DipEd. Teacher, Glasgow Corp., 1950–70. Chm., Glasgow Local Assoc., Educnl Inst. for Scotland, 1958–59; Chm., Scottish Labour Party, 1964; Chief Negotiator on behalf of Scottish Teachers in STSC, 1969–70; Sec., Westminster Branch, Educnl Inst. for Scotland, 1985–88, 1991–92. MP (Lab) Ayrshire Central, 1970–83, Cunninghame South, 1983–92. Chm., Select Cttee on Scottish Affairs, 1981–87; Sec., Parly All-Party Cttee for Energy Studies, 1980–92; Chm., PLP Aviation Cttee, 1990–92. Chm., Saltcoats Labour Party, 1993–95, 2000–03; Member: Cunninghame N Constituency Labour Party, 1993–2004; N Ayrshire and Arran Constituency Labour Party, 2004–. Chm. Develt Cttee, Cunninghame Housing Assoc., 1992–. Dir, Galloway Training Ltd, 1997–. Member: Council of Europe, 1987–92; WEU, 1987–92. FEIS 1970. *Recreation:* watching football. *Address:* 11 Ivanhoe Drive, Saltcoats, Ayrshire KA21 6LS. *T:* (01294) 464843. *Club:* North Ayrshire and Arran Constituency Labour Social (Saltcoats).

LAMBIE-NAIRN, Martin John, RDI 1987; FCSD; Founder and Partner, M-LN Branding Consultancy, since 2008; *b* 5 Aug. 1945; *s* of Stephen John and Joan Lois Lambie-Nairn; *m* 1970, Cordelia Margot Summers; one *s* two *d*. *Educ:* King Ethelbert Sch., Birchington, Kent; Canterbury Coll. of Art. NDD. Asst Designer, Graphic Design Dept, BBC, 1965; Designer, Rediffusion, 1966; freelance graphic designer, 1967; Art Dir, Conran Associates, 1968; Dep. to Sen. Designer, ITN, overseeing changeover from black and white to colour TV, 1968; Designer, LWT, working on light entertainment, drama and current affairs progs, 1970; Founder and Creative Director, Robinson Lambie-Nairn Ltd, later Lambie-Nairn, design consultancy producing film and TV graphics, corporate identity, packaging and financial lit., 1976–2008 (Chm., 1976–97); work included Channel 4 TV corporate identity, 1982, develt of original idea for Spitting Image, 1984, Anglia TV corporate identity, 1988, TFI (France) corporate identity, 1989, BBC1 and BBC2 channel identities, 1991, Carlton Television corporate identity, 1993, Orange (Sky NZ) channel identity, and ARTE corporate identity, 1995, BBC corporate identity, 1997–, New Millennium Experience corporate identity, 1998, BAE SYSTEMS corporate identity, 1999. Creative Dir, NTL, 2001–03. Mem. Cttee, D & AD, 1985– (Pres., 1990–91; Chm., Corporate Identity Jury, 2000); Chm., Graphics Jury, BBC Design Awards, 1987. Visiting Prof., Lincoln Univ., 2006–. FCSD (FSIAD 1982); FRTS 2004. Hon. Fellow, Kent Inst. of Art and Design, 1994. Hon. DArts Lincoln, 2004. Jt winner, BAFTA Craft Awards (for excellence in craft of graphics), 1991; RTS Judges' Award, 1996; President's Award, D&AD, 1997; Prince Philip Designers' Prize, 1998. *Publication:* Brand Identity for Television with Knobs On, 1997. *Recreations:* opera, family, France.

LAMBIRTH, Mark Nicholas; Director of Planning and Performance, Department for Transport, since 2007; *b* 30 May 1953; *s* of late Peter Mabson Lambirth and of Jean Margaret Lambirth; *m* 1986, Anne Catherine Wood. *Educ:* St Albans Sch.; Queens' Coll., Cambridge. Price Commn, 1975; entered Civil Service, 1977; Department of Transport, 1983–95: Ministerial speechwriter and Dep. Head, Inf. Div., 1988–89; Asst. Sec., 1989; Head, Public Transport in London Div., 1989–92; Head, Central Finance Div., 1992–95; Under-Sec., 1995; Dir of Planning and Transport, Govt Office for London, 1995–98; Dir of Local Govt Finance Policy, DETR, then of Local Govt Finance, DTLR, 1998–2002; Dir of Railways, then of Rail Strategy and Resources, DTLR, then DfT, 2002–05; Dir of Rail Strategy and Finance, subseq. of Rail Strategy, DfT, 2005–07. *Recreations:* poetry, cooking, wine. *Address:* Planning and Performance Directorate, Department for Transport, Great Minster House, 76 Marsham Street, SW1P 4DR. *Club:* MCC.

LAMBTON, family name of **Earl of Durham**.

LAMBTON, Viscount; Frederick Lambton; environmental campaigner; *b* 23 Feb. 1985; *s* and *heir* of Earl of Durham, *qv*.

LAMBTON, Lucinda; photographer and writer, since 1960; broadcaster, since 1983; *b* 10 May 1943; *e d* of Viscount Lambton (disclaimed Earldom, 1970; *d* 2006), *s* of 5th Earl of Durham, and Belinda, *d* of Major D. H. Blew-Jones; *m* 1st, 1965, Henry Mark Harrod (marr. diss. 1973); two *s*; 2nd, 1986, Sir Edmund Fairfax-Lucy, *qv* (marr. diss. 1989); 3rd, 1991, Sir Peregrine Worsthorne, *qv*. *Educ:* Queensgate Sch., London. Television series include: Hurray for Today, 1989; Hurray for Today, USA, 1990; Lucinda Lambton's Alphabet of Britain (3 series), 1990; Old New World, 2001; Lucinda Lambton's Jamaican Adventure, 2004. Lectures throughout Britain on subjects researched for broadcasts and publications. Hon. FRIBA 1997. *Publications:* Vanishing Victoriana, 1976; Temples of Convenience, 1978, 2nd edn 1995; Chambers of Delight, 1983; Beastly Buildings, 1985; An Album of Curious Houses, 1988; (ed) Magnificent Menagerie (anthology), 1992; Lucinda Lambton's Alphabet of Britain, 1996; Old New World, 2000. *Recreations:* talking to dogs and taking them for walks, pre-1960s movies. *Address:* The Old Rectory, Hedgerley, Bucks SL2 3UY. *T:* (01753) 646167. *Clubs:* Chelsea Arts, City University.

LAMEY, Steven; Chief Operating Officer and Director General, since 2007, Commissioner, since 2008, HM Revenue and Customs; *b* 26 Dec. 1955; *s* of Kenneth Gordon Lamey and Sylvia Patricia Lamey; *m* 1981, Ann Williams; one *s* one *d*. *Educ:* UC Cardiff (BSc Mining and Mineral 1978). BOC Group, 1978–99: Proj. Manager; Sen. Ops

Manager; European Infrastructure Manager; Inf. Mgt Dir, Global User Service; British Gas Gp, 1999–2004: Vice Pres., Inf. Mgt; Chief Inf. Officer; Chief Inf. Officer and Dir Gen., HMRC, 2004–07. *Recreations:* music—Bruce Springsteen/Marillion through to classical/opera, Rugby. *Address:* HM Revenue and Customs, 100 Parliament Street, SW1A 2BQ. *T:* (020) 7147 3174, *Fax:* (020) 7147 2124; *e-mail:* steve.lamey@hmrc.gsi.gov.uk.

LAMFALUSSY, Baron Alexandre; President, European Monetary Institute, 1994–97; Professor, Institute of European Studies, Catholic University of Louvain, since 1997; *b* 26 April 1929; *cr* Baron, 1993; *m* 1957, Anne-Marie Cochard; two *s* two *d*. *Educ:* Catholic Univ., Louvain (economics degree); Nuffield Coll., Oxford (PhD). Banque de Bruxelles: economist, 1955–61; Economic Advr, 1962; Exec. Dir, later Chm., Exec. Bd, 1965–76; Bank for International Settlements, Basle: Economic Advr, 1976–80; Asst Gen. Manager, 1981; Gen. Manager, 1985–93. Dir, Assoc. for the Monetary Union of Europe, 2000–. Vis Lectr, Yale, 1961–62. Hon. doctorates: Univ. Lumière-Lyon, 1987; Inst. d'Etudes Politiques, Paris, 1993. *Publications:* Investment and Growth in Mature Economies, 1961; The UK and the Six, 1963; Les marchés financiers en Europe, 1968; The Restructuring of the Financial Industry, 1992; The Per Jacobsson Lecture, 1994; Financial Crises in Emerging Markets: an essay on financial globalisation and fragility, 2000. *Recreations:* hiking, sailing. *Address:* c/o European Monetary Institute, Eurotower, Kaiserstrasse 29, 60311 Frankfurt, Germany. *T:* (69) 272270.

LAMFORD, (Thomas) Gerald, OBE 1979; ASVU Representative, Cyprus, 1985–88; Commandant, Police Staff College, 1976–79; *b* Carmarthen, 3 April 1928; *s* of late Albert and Sarah Lamford; *m* 1952, Eira Hale (decd); one *s* one *d*. *Educ:* Technical Coll., Swansea; London Univ. (LLB 1969); Police Coll. (Intermed. Comd Course, 1969; Sen. Comd Course, 1973). Radio Officer, Merchant Navy, 1945; Wireless Operator, RAF, 1946–48, Aden. Carmarthenshire Constab. (now Dyfed Powys Police), 1949; reached rank of Chief Inspector, CID, Crime Squad; Force Trng Officer, 1965–69; Supt, Haverfordwest, 1970; Chief Supt, Llanelli, 1971–74; Asst Chief Constable, Greater Manchester Police, 1974–79; Investigating Officer, FCO, 1981–84. Vis. Prof. of Police Science, John Jay Coll. of Criminal Justice, City Univ. of New York, 1972; sometime Vis. Lecturer: Southern Police Inst., Univ. of Louisville, Ky; N Eastern Univ., Boston; NY Univ. Sch. of Law; Rutgers Univ., NJ; Mercy Coll., Detroit. County Comr, St John Amb. Bde, Pembrokeshire, 1970; SBStJ. Mem., Probus Club, Ammanford (Pres., 1996). *Publications:* The Defence of Lucy Walter, 2001; articles in Police Studies, Internat. Rev. of Police Devélt, Police Rev., Bramshill Jl, World Police. *Recreations:* photography, genealogy. *Address:* 2A Walter Road, Ammanford SA18 2NH.

LAMING, Baron *cr* 1998 (Life Peer), of Tewin in the co. of Hertfordshire; **William Herbert Laming,** Kt 1996; CBE 1985; DL; Chief Inspector, Social Services Inspectorate, Department of Health, 1991–98; *b* 19 July 1936; *s* of William Angus Laming and Lillian Laming (*née* Robson); *m* 1962, Aileen Margaret Pollard. *Educ:* Univ. of Durham (Applied Social Scis); Rainer House (Home Office Probation Trng, 1960–61); LSE (Mental Health Course, 1965–66). Notts Probation Service: Probation Officer, 1961–66; Sen. Probation Officer, 1966–68; Asst Chief Probation Officer, Nottingham City and Co. Probation Service, 1968–71; Dep. Dir, 1971–75, Dir, 1975–91, Social Services, Herts CC. Pres., Assoc. of Dirs Social Services, 1982–83. Chairman: Ind. Inquiry into care and treatment of Ms Justine Cummings, 2000; Modernising the Management of the Prison Service, 2000; Victoria Climbié Inquiry, 2001–03. DL Hertford, 1999. *Publication:* Lessons from America: the balance of services on social care, 1985. *Address:* House of Lords, SW1A 0PW.

LAMMER, Dr Peter; non-executive Director, Sophos Plc, since 2006 (Joint Chief Executive Officer, 2000–05); *b* 18 Dec. 1958; *s* of Alfred Ritter von Lammer and Benedicta (*née* Countess Wengersky). *Educ:* Alleyn's Sch.; Univ. of Warwick (BSc (Eng) 1981); St John's Coll., Oxford (DPhil 1986). Co-founder, 1985, Man. Dir, 1985–2000, Sophos Plc. KM 2004. *Recreations:* stalking, ski-ing, bridge, forestry, old sports cars. *Address:* c/o Sophos Plc, The Pentagon, Abingdon, Oxon OX14 3YP. *T:* (01235) 559933. *Club:* Travellers'.

LAMMIMAN, Surg. Rear Adm. David Askey, CB 1993; LVO 1978; FFARCS; Medical Director General (Naval), 1990–93; Deputy Surgeon General: Health Services, 1990–91; Operations and Plans, 1991–93; Consultant Anaesthetist, London Fertility Centre, since 1992; *b* 30 June 1932; *s* of Herbert Askey Lammiman and Lilian Elsie (*née* Park); *m* 1st, 1957, Sheila Mary Graham (marr. diss. 1984); three *s* one *d*; 2nd, 1984, Caroline Dale Brooks. *Educ:* Wyggeston Sch., Leicester; St Bartholomew's Hosp. (MB, BS 1957). DA 1962; DObstRCOG 1962; FFARCS 1969. Resident House Officer, Redhill County Hosp. and St Bartholomew's Hosp., 1957–58; joined RN, 1959; gen. service and hosp. appts at home and abroad; Clinical Asst, Southampton Gp of Hosps, Alder Hey Children's Hosp., Liverpool, and Radcliffe Infirmary, Oxford, 1966–69; served in: HMS Chaplet, 1959; HMS Eagle, 1967–68; HMY Britannia, 1976–78; Consultant Anaesthetist, RN Hospital: Malta, 1969–71; Haslar, 1971–73; Gibraltar, 1973–75; Plymouth, 1975–76; Haslar, 1978–82; Dir of Med. Personnel, MoD, 1982–84; Medical Officer i/c RN Hospital: Plymouth, 1984–86; Haslar, 1986–88; Surg. Rear Adm. (Support Med. Services), 1989–90. QHS 1987–93. *Recreations:* fly fishing, golf, tennis. *Club:* Flyfishers'.

LAMMY, Rt Hon. David (Lindon); PC 2008; MP (Lab) Tottenham, since June 2000; Minister of State, Department for Innovation, Universities and Skills, since 2008; *b* 19 July 1972; *s* of David and Rosalind Lammy; *m* 2005, Nicola Green; one *s*. *Educ:* King's Sch., Peterborough; SOAS, London Univ. (LLB Hons 1993); Harvard Law Sch. (LLM 1997). Called to the Bar, Lincoln's Inn; Attorney, Howard Rice, Calif, 1997–98; with D. J. Freeman, 1998–2000. Mem. (Lab), London Assembly, GLA, May–June 2000. PPS to Sec. of State for Educn and Skills, 2001–02; Parliamentary Under-Secretary of State: DoH, 2002–03; DCA, 2003–05; DCMS, 2005–07; DIUS, 2007–08. Member: Procedure Cttee, 2001; Public Admin Cttee, 2001. Member: Gen. Synod, C of E, 1999–2002; Archbishops' Council, 1999–2002. Trustee, Actionaid, 2001–. *Recreations:* film, live music, Spurs FC. *Address:* c/o House of Commons, SW1A 0AA. *T:* (020) 7219 0767.

LAMOND, Jilly; *see* Forster, J.

LAMONT, family name of **Baron Lamont of Lerwick**.

LAMONT OF LERWICK, Baron *cr* 1998 (Life Peer), of Lerwick in the Shetland Islands; **Norman Stewart Hughson Lamont;** PC 1986; politician, writer and company director; *b* Lerwick, Shetland, 8 May 1942; *s* of late Daniel Lamont and of Helen Irene; *m* 1971, Alice Rosemary White; one *s* one *d*. *Educ:* Loretto Sch. (scholar); Fitzwilliam Coll., Cambridge (BA). Chm., Cambridge Univ. Conservative Assoc., 1963; Pres., Cambridge Union, 1964. PA to Rt Hon. Duncan Sandys, MP, 1965; Conservative Research Dept, 1966–68; Merchant Banker, N. M. Rothschild & Sons, 1968–79; Dir, Rothschild Asset Mgt, 1978. Non-exec. Dir, N. M. Rothschild & Sons, 1993–95; Director: Balli Gp Plc, 1995–; RAB Capital 2004–; Jupiter Second Split Trust, 2005–; Chm., Jupiter Adria plc, 2006–. Chm., British-Iranian Chamber of Commerce, 2004–; Adviser to: Romanian Govt, on privatisation, 1995–97; Consensus Business Gp, 2002–; Western Union Corp., 2007–08; Hermitage Capital, 2007–. Contested (C) East Hull, Gen. Election, 1970. MP (C) Kingston-upon-Thames, May 1972–97; contested (C) Harrogate and Knaresborough, 1997. PPS to Norman St John-Stevas, MP, Minister for the Arts, 1974; an Opposition Spokesman on: Prices and Consumer Affairs, 1975–76; Industry, 1976–79; Parly Under Sec. of State, Dept of Energy, 1979–81; Minister of State, DTI (formerly DoI), 1981–85; Minister of State for Defence Procurement, 1985–86; Financial Sec. to HM Treasury, 1986–89; Chief Sec. to HM Treasury, 1989–90; Chancellor of the Exchequer, 1990–93. Chairman: G7 Gp of Finance Ministers, 1991; EU Finance Ministers, 1992; Mem., H of L Select Cttee on EU, 1999–2003, on Economic Affairs, 2005–. Chairman: Coningsby Club, 1970–71; Bow Group, 1971–72; Vice Pres., Bruges Gp; Pres., Economic Res. Council, 2008–. Pres., Clan Lamont Soc., 2006–. *Publications:* Sovereign Britain, 1995; In Office, 1999. *Recreations:* books, ornithology, music, theatre. *Address:* c/o Balli Group Plc, 5 Stanhope Gate, W1K 1AH. *T:* (020) 7306 2000. *Clubs:* Garrick, Beefsteak, White's.

LAMONT, Donald Alexander; HM Diplomatic Service, retired; Chief Executive, Wilton Park, since 2007; *b* 13 Jan. 1947; *s* of Alexander Lamont and Alexa Lee Lamont (*née* Will); *m* 1981, Lynda Margaret Campbell; one *s* one *d*. *Educ:* Aberdeen Grammar Sch.; Aberdeen Univ. (MA Russian Studies). British Leyland Motor Corp., 1970; Second Sec., subseq. First Sec., FCO, 1974; First Sec., UNIDO/IAEA, Vienna, 1977; First Sec. (Commercial), Moscow, 1980; First Sec., FCO, 1982; Counsellor on secondment to IISS, 1988; Political Advr and Head of Chancery, British Mil. Govt, Berlin, 1988–91; Ambassador to Uruguay, 1991–94; Hd of Republic of Ireland Dept, FCO, 1994–97; COS and Dep. High Rep., Sarajevo, 1997–99; Gov., Falkland Is, and Comr for S Georgia and S Sandwich Is, 1999–2002; Ambassador to Venezuela, 2003–06. *Address:* Wilton Park, Wiston House, Steyning, W Sussex BN44 3DZ. *Clubs:* Caledonian, Royal Commonwealth Society.

LAMONT, Johann MacDougall; Member (Lab) Glasgow Pollok, Scottish Parliament, since 1999; *b* 11 July 1957; *y d* of Archie Lamont and Effie Lamont (*née* Macleod); *m* Archie Graham; one *s* one *d*. *Educ:* Univ. of Glasgow (MA Hons); Jordanhill Coll. of Educn (postgrad. secondary teaching qualification). Secondary School teacher, 1979–99. Dep. Minister for Communities, Scottish Exec., 2004–06, for Justice, 2006–07. Mem., EIS, 1979–. *Recreations:* running, watching football, doing crosswords, enjoying time with my children. *Address:* Scottish Parliament, Edinburgh EH99 1SP.

LAMONT, John; Member (C) Roxburgh and Berwickshire, Scottish Parliament, since 2007; *b* 15 April 1976; *s* of Robert Lamont and Elizabeth Lamont. *Educ:* Kilwinning Acad.; Univ. of Glasgow. Solicitor: Freshfields, 2000–04; Bristows, 2004–05; Brodies, 2005–07. *Recreations:* cooking, travel. *Address:* Scottish Parliament, Edinburgh EH99 1SP. *T:* (0131) 348 6532, *Fax:* (0131) 348 6534; 25 High Street, Hawick, Roxburghshire TD9 9BU. *e-mail:* john.lamont.msp@scottish.parliament.uk.

LAMONTAGNE, Hon. (J.) Gilles; PC (Can.) 1978; OC 1991; CQ 2000; CD 1980; Lieutenant-Governor of Quebec, 1984–90; *b* 17 April 1919; *s* of Trefflé Lamontagne and Anna Kieffer; *m* 1949, Mary Katherine Schaefer; three *s* one *d*. *Educ:* Collège Jean-de-Bréboeuf, Montréal, Québec (BA). Served RCAF, 1941–45 (despatches, 1945). Businessman in Québec City, 1946–66. Alderman, Québec City, 1962–64, Mayor, 1965–77. MP (L) Langelier, 1977–84; Parly Sec. to Minister of Energy, Mines and Resources, 1977; Minister without Portfolio, Jan. 1978; Postmaster Gen., Feb. 1978–1979; Actg Minister of Veterans Affairs, 1980–81; Minister of National Defence, 1980–83. Dir, Québec City Chamber of Commerce and Industry; Member: Econ. Council of Canada; Br. 260, Royal Canadian Legion (Grand Pres., 1991–94). Special Counsel, GPC Internat. (formerly GPC Consilium, then GPC Relations gouvernementales), 2002 (Consultant, 1992; Sen. Counsel, 1995). Mem. Bd, Canadian Centre of Substance Abuse, 1991–95. Chm. Bd of Govs, Royal Mil. Coll., Kingston, Canada, 1995–2002. Hon. Col, Tactical Aviation Wing (Montreal), 1987. KStJ 1985. Hon. LLD Kingston Royal Mil. Coll., 1986; Hon. DAdmin St Jean Royal Mil. Coll., 1989. UN Medal 1987. Croix du Combattant de l'Europe; Chevalier, Légion d'honneur (France), 2006. *Address:* 8 Jardins Mérici # 1405, QC G1S 4N9, Canada. *Clubs:* Cercle de la Garrison de Québec, Royal Québec Golf.

LAMPERT, Catherine Emily; independent curator; Director, Whitechapel Art Gallery, 1988–2001; *b* 15 Oct. 1946; *d* of Emily F. Schubach and Chester G. Lampert; *m* 1971, Robert Keith Mason (marr. diss. 1994); one adopted *d*. *Educ:* Brown Univ. (BA); Temple Univ. (MFA). UCL, 1966–67; Asst Curator, RI Sch. of Design, Mus. of Art, 1968–69; Studio Internat., 1971–72; Sen. Exhibn Organiser, Hayward Gall., 1973–88. Vis. Prof., Univ. of the Arts, 2007–. Curator: Frank Auerbach: painting and drawing 1954–2001, RA, Paris and tour, 2001–02; Nan Goldin, Centre Pompidou and tour, 2001; Lucian Freud, Dublin, Humleback, The Hague, 2007–08; Co-curator, Rodin, RA, 2006. *Publications:* Rodin: sculpture and drawings, 1986; Lucian Freud: recent work, 1993; The Prophet and the Fly: Francis Alÿs, 2003; Euan Uglow: the complete paintings, 2007; numerous catalogue essays on Frank Auerbach, Barry Flanagan, Tony Cragg, Francisco Toledo and other subjects of Twentieth Century art. *Address:* 92 Lenthall Road, E8 3JN. *T:* (020) 7249 7650.

LAMPL, Sir Frank (William), Kt 1990; President, Bovis Lend Lease Holding, since 2000 (Chairman, 1999–2000); Director, Mills Corporation, Washington, 2004–07; *b* Czechoslovakia, 6 April 1926; adopted British nationality, 1974; *s* of Dr Otto Lampl and Olga (*née* Jelinek); *m* 1st, 1948, Blanka (*née* Kratochvílová) (*d* 2001); one *s*; 2nd, 2002, Wenda (*née* Scarborough). *Educ:* Univ. of Brno, Czechoslovakia (Dip Eng, Faculty of Architecture and Engineering). Emigrated from Czechoslovakia to UK, 1968, after Russian invasion; Exec. Dir, Bovis Construction, 1974; Man. Dir, Bovis International, 1978; Dir, Bovis, 1979; Chm., Bovis Construction and Bovis International, 1985; Dep. Chm., Lehrer MacGovern-Bovis, NY, 1987; Chm., Bovis Construction Gp, 1989–2000; Exec. Dir, P&OSN Co., 1985–99. Mem., Adv. Bd, Intelligent Engrg, 2007–. First Chancellor, Kingston Univ., 1994–2000. FCIOB 1973 (Pres.'s Gold Medal, 1993); FAPM 1973; CCMI. Hon. DEng Technical Univ., Brno, 1993; Dr *hc* Kingston, 1994; Hon. DSc: Reading, 1995; Middlesex, 1998. Building Lifetime Achievement Award, Building Magazine, 2002. *Recreation:* reading. *Address:* Bovis Lend Lease, 142 Northolt Road, Harrow, Middx HA2 0EE. *Club:* Royal Automobile.

LAMPL, Sir Peter, Kt 2003; OBE 2000; Chairman, Sutton Trust, since 1997; *b* 21 May 1947; *s* of Frederick and Margaret Lampl; *m* 1st, 1976, Janet Clowes (marr. diss. 1980); 2nd, 1994, Karen Gordon; one *s* two *d*. *Educ:* Reigate Grammar Sch.; Cheltenham Grammar Sch.; Corpus Christi Coll., Oxford (BA, MA; Hon. Fellow, 1998); London Business Sch. (MBA). Mktg Exec., Beecham Gp, London, 1970–71; Mgt Consultant, Boston Consulting Gp, Boston, Paris, Munich, 1973–77; Dir, Planning and Business Develt, Internat. Paper, NY, then Pres., Internat. Paper Realty, 1977–83; Founder, Pres., then Chm., Sutton Co. (private equity firm), NY, London, Munich, 1983–97; Founder, Sutton Trust, 1997 (provides educnl opportunities for young people from non-privileged backgrounds). Ind. Advr to Sec. of State for Educn, 2000–. Member: Bd, Specialist Schs Trust, 1999–; Council for Industry and Higher Educn, 2002–; Social Mkt Foundn, 2002–;

Teach First, 2002–05. Mem. Council, KCL, 2001–04; Chm., Develt Bd, Corpus Christi Coll., Oxford, 2002–06. Fellow, Birkbeck Coll., London, 2007. Hon. DSc: Nottingham, 1999; Imperial Coll. London, 2004; City, 2007; Hon. Dr jur Bristol, 2001; DUniv: Birmingham, 2003; Brunel, 2004. *Recreations:* golf, tennis, ski-ing, swimming, body surfing, opera. *Address:* The Sutton Trust, 111 Upper Richmond Road, SW15 2TJ. *T:* (020) 8788 3223. *Clubs:* Athenæum, Queen's, Hurlingham, Royal Automobile, Roehampton; Wisley Golf (Surrey); Westchester Country (NY); Pine Tree Golf (Palm Beach).

LAMPORT, Sir Stephen (Mark Jeffrey), KCVO 2002 (CVO 1999); DL; Chapter Clerk and Receiver General, Westminster Abbey, since 2008; *b* 27 Nov. 1951; *s* of Eric and Jeanne Lamport; *m* 1979, Angela Vivien Paula Hervey; two *s* one *d*. *Educ:* Dorking Co. Grammar Sch.; Corpus Christi Coll., Cambridge (Schol., MA); Sussex Univ. (MA). HM Diplomatic Service, 1974–2002: UK Mission to UN, 1974; Tehran, 1975–79; FCO, 1979–84; Private Secretary to Minister of State, 1981–84; First Sec., Rome, 1984–88; FCO, 1988–93; Dep. Private Sec. to the Prince of Wales, 1993–96; Private Sec. and Treas. to the Prince of Wales, 1996–2002; Gp Dir, RBS, 2002–07. Non-exec. Dir, Brewin Dolphin Holdings plc, 2007–. Member: Exec. Cttee, British Red Cross Queen Mother Meml Fund, 2003–06; Court, Royal Foundn of St Katharine, 2004–; Council of Mgt, Arvon Foundn, 2004–; Council, Guildford Cathedral, 2006–; Chm., British Red Cross Flood Relief Adv. Panel, 2007–08. Trustee, Surrey Community Foundn, 2006–. DL Surrey, 2006. *Publication:* (with D. Hurd) The Palace of Enchantments, 1985. *Address:* Westminster Abbey, SW1P 3PA. *Clubs:* Royal Automobile, Grillion's.

LAMPSON, family name of **Baron Killearn**.

LAMY, Pascal Lucien Fernand; Director General, World Trade Organisation, since 2005; *b* 8 April 1947; *s* of Jacques Lamy and Denise (*née* Dujardin); *m* 1972, Geneviève Luchaire; three *s*. *Educ:* Ecole des Hautes Etudes Commerciales; Inst d'Etudes Politiques, Paris; Ecole Nat. d'Admin. Inspector-Gen. of Finances, 1975–79; French Treasury, 1979–81; Advr to Minister for Econ. Affairs and Finance, 1981–83; Dep. Hd, Prime Minister's Pvte Office, 1983–84; Head, Pvte Office of Pres. of EC, 1985–94; with Crédit Lyonnais, 1994–99, Dir Gen., 1997; Mem., European Commn, 1999–2004. Mem. Steering Cttee, Socialist Party of France, 1985–94. Officier, Légion d'Honneur, 1999; Grosses Verdienstkreuz (Germany), 1991; Commandeur de l'Ordre Nat. du Mérite (Luxembourg), 1995; Officer, Order of Merit (Gabon), 2000; Order of Aztec Eagle (Mexico), 2003. *Publications:* (jtly) L'Europe de nos Volontes, 2000; L'Europe en Première Ligne, 2000; La démocratie-monde, 2004. *Address:* World Trade Organisation, Centre William Rappard, 154 Rue de Lausanne, 1211 Geneva 21, Switzerland.

LAN, David Mark, PhD; playwright, director and social anthropologist; Artistic Director, Young Vic Theatre, since 2000; *b* 1 June 1952; *s* of Joseph Lan and Lois Lan (*née* Carklin). *Educ:* Univ. of Cape Town (BA); London Sch. of Econs (BSc; PhD 1984). Writer in Residence, Royal Court Th., 1995–97. *Plays:* Painting a Wall, Almost Free Th., 1974; Bird Child, 1974, Homage to Been Soup, Paradise, The Winter Dancers, 1975, Royal Ct Th. Upstairs; Red Earth, ICA, 1976; Not in Norwich, Royal Ct Young People's Th. Scheme, 1977; Sergeant Ola and His Followers, Royal Ct, 1979; (with C. Churchill) A Mouthful of Birds, Jt Stock Th. Gp, 1986; Flight, RSC, 1986; Ghetto (English trans. of play by Joshua Sobol), NT, 1989; Desire, 1990, Hippolytos (version of Euripides' play), 1991, Almeida; Ion (version of Euripides' play), RSC, 1994; The Ends of the Earth, NT, 1996; Uncle Vanya (new version), RSC at Young Vic, 1998; La Lupa (English version of play by Giovanni Verga), RSC, 2000; Cherry Orchard (new version), NT, 2000; The Magic Flute, 2007; *television:* BBC 2: The Sunday Judge, 1985; The Crossing, 1988; Welcome Home Comrades, Dark City, 1989; *film:* (jtly) Streets of Yesterday, 1988; *radio:* Charley Tango, Radio 4 and World Service, 1995; *libretti:* Tobias and the Angel, 1999, Ion, 2000, Almeida Opera; *director:* Artist Unknown, 1995, Royal Court Diaries, 1996, BBC 1; The Glass Menagerie, Palace Th., Watford, 1998; for Young Vic: Tis Pity She's a Whore, 1999; Julius Caesar, 2000; A Raisin in the Sun, 2001, tour 2005; Dr Faustus, The Daughter-in-Law, 2002; The Skin of Our Teeth, 2004; As You Like It, Wyndham's, 2005; The Soldier's Fortune, 2007. John Whiting Award, Arts Council, 1975; George Orwell Award, 1980; Zurich Internat. TV Award, 1989; Laurence Olivier Award, 2004. *Publications:* Guns and Rain: guerillas and spirit mediums in Zimbabwe, 1985; all plays published. *Address:* c/o Judy Daish Associates, 2 St Charles Place, W10 6EG. *T:* (020) 8964 8811.

LANCASHIRE, Sarah Jane Abigail, (Mrs P. Salmon); actress; *b* 10 Oct. 1964; *d* of late Geoffrey Lancashire and of Hilda Lancashire (*née* McCormack); *m* 1st, 1987, Gary Hargreaves (marr. diss. 1997); two *s*; 2nd, 2001, Peter Salmon, *qv*; one *s*. *Educ:* Werneth Private Prep. Sch., Oldham; Hulme Grammar Sch. for Girls, Oldham; Oldham Coll. of Technol.; Guildhall Sch. of Music and Drama. Lectr (pt-time), Salford Univ. Coll., 1987–90. *Theatre:* professional début, The Beauty Game and Pacific Overtures, Manchester Liby Th., 1986; Educating Rita, Hornchurch, 1991; The Little Shop of Horrors, Oldham, 1993; West End début, Blood Brothers, Albery, 1990; *television:* Coronation Street, 1991–96 (Best Actress Award, RTS (NW), 1996); Where the Heart Is, 1996–99; Blooming Marvellous, 1997; Clocking Off, 1999; Seeing Red, 1999 (Best Actress, Nat. TV Awards, 2000; Drama TV Performer of Year, TV and Radio Industry Awards, 2001); Chambers, 2000; Gentleman's Relish, 2000; My Fragile Heart, 2000; The Cry, 2000 (Best Actress, Monte Carlo TV Fest., 2002); The Glass, 2000; The Birthday Girl, 2001; Sons and Lovers, 2002; Rose & Maloney, 2002–; Rotters' Club, 2004; Cherished, 2004; Dir, Viva las Blackpool, 2003 (Best New Talent, RTS (Midlands), 2004). Hon. MA Salford, 2002. *Recreations:* gardening, family, cinema. *Address:* c/o Independent Talent Group Ltd, Oxford House, 76 Oxford Street, W1D 1BS.

LANCASTER, Bishop of, (RC), since 2001; **Rt Rev. Patrick O'Donoghue;** *b* 4 May 1934; *s* of Daniel O'Donoghue and Sheila O'Donoghue (*née* Twomey). *Educ:* St Edmund's Coll., Ware, Herts. Ordained priest, 1967; Asst priest, Willesden, 1967–70; Mem., Diocesan Mission Team, Westminster, 1970–73; Pastoral Dir, Allen Hall, 1973–78; Asst Administrator, Westminster Cathedral, 1978–85; Rector, Allen Hall, 1985–91; Administrator, Westminster Cathedral, 1991–93; Auxiliary Bishop of Westminster (Bishop in W London), 1993–2001. *Recreations:* football, theatre, country walking, the Arts. *Address:* Bishop's Apartment, Cathedral House, Balmoral Road, Lancaster LA1 3BT. *T:* (01524) 596050, *Fax:* (01524) 596053.

LANCASTER, Bishop Suffragan of, since 2006; **Rt Rev. Geoffrey Seagrave Pearson;** *b* 18 July 1951; *m* 1973, Jean Richardson; one *s* two *d*. *Educ:* St John's Coll., Durham (BA 1972); Cranmer Hall, Durham. Ordained deacon, 1974, priest, 1975; Asst Curate, Kirkheaton, 1974–77; Curate-in-charge, 1977–82, Incumbent, 1982–85, Ch of the Redeemer, Blackburn; Asst Home Sec., Gen. Synod Bd for Mission and Unity, and Hon. Curate, Forty Hill, 1985–89; Vicar, Roby, 1989–2006. Exec. Sec., BCC Evangelism Cttee, 1986–89; Area Dean, Huyton, 2002–06; Hon. Canon, Liverpool Cathedral, 2003–06. *Address:* The Vicarage, Shireshead, Forton, Preston PR3 0AE.

LANCASTER, Archdeacon of; *see* Ballard, Ven. P. J.

LANCASTER, Anthony Trevor; His Honour Judge Lancaster; a Circuit Judge, since 2001; *b* 26 June 1948; *s* of late Thomas William Lancaster and of Jean Margaret Lancaster (*née* Grainger); *m* 1997, Beverley Anne Conlon; four *s* two *d*. *Educ:* Austin Friars Sch., Carlisle; Univ. of Leeds (LLB Hons 1970). Admitted solicitor, 1973; in private practice, 1973–88; County Court Registrar, 1988–91; a Dist Judge, 1991–2001; Asst Recorder, 1995–99; a Recorder, 1999–2001. Pt-time Chm., Social Security Appeals Tribunal, 1985–88. Pres., Assoc. of Dist Judges, 2000–01. *Recreations:* family activities, cooking, music, opera. *Address:* Law Courts, Quayside, Newcastle upon Tyne NE1 3LA. *T:* (0191) 201 2000, *Fax:* (0191) 201 2001.

LANCASTER, (Charles) Roy, OBE 1999; freelance author, lecturer, plant explorer and dendrologist, since 1980; *b* 5 Dec. 1937; *s* of Charles and Nora Lancaster; *m* 1977, Susan Lloyd; one *s* one *d*. *Educ:* Castle Hill Co. Secondary Sch., Bolton; Cambridge Univ. Botanic Garden. Curator, Hillier Arboretum, 1970–80. Member: Mgt Cttee, Sir Harold Hillier Gardens and Arboretum, 1990–2007 (Patron, 2007–); Arboreta Adv. Cttee, Nat. Arboreta (formerly Consultative Cttee, Westonbirt Nat. Arboretum), 1990–; Gardens Panel, NT, 2000–; Vice Chm., Woody Plant Cttee (formerly Floral Cttee B), RHS, 1998–. Vice Pres., RHS, 2005–; Pres., The Hardy Plant Soc., 2007–. Trustee, Tree Register of British Isles, 2001–. Veitch Meml Medal, RHS, 1972; VMH 1989; Inst. of Horticulture Award, 1996; TV Gardening Presenter of the Year, 1993, Lifetime Achievement Award, 2002, Garden Writers' Guild. *Publications:* Trees for your Garden, 1974; (with Vicomte Noailles) Mediterranean Gardens and Plants, 1977; A Plantsman in Nepal, 1981; In Search of the Wild Asparagus, 1983; Garden Plants for Connoisseurs, 1987; Travels in China: a plantsman's paradise, 1989; Garden Shrubs Through the Seasons, 1991; What Plant Where, 1995; What Perennial Where, 1997; (with Matthew Biggs) What House Plant Where, 1998; Perfect Plant Perfect Place, 2001; contribs to Gdn Jl of RHS. *Recreations:* bird watching, walking, travel, gardening, music. *Address:* 58 Brownhill Road, Chandlers Ford, Hants SO53 2EG. *Club:* Sloane.

LANCASTER, (John) Mark, TD 2002; PhD; MP (C) Milton Keynes North East, since 2005; *b* 12 May 1970; *s* of Rev. Ronald Lancaster, *qv*; *m* 1996, Katie; one foster *s*. *Educ:* Kimbolton Sch., Cambs; Buckingham Univ. (BSc 1992; PhD 2007); Exeter Univ. (MBA 1993). Served Army, RE, 1988–90; Officer, TA, RE, 1990–. Dir, Kimbolton Fireworks Ltd, 1993–2005. Mem. (C) Huntingdon DC, 1995–99. *Publication:* (contrib.) Fireworks Principles and Practice, 3rd edn 1998. *Recreations:* collector and restorer of classic British motorcycles, avid football supporter. *Address:* House of Commons, SW1A 0AA; *e-mail:* lancasterm@parliament.uk.

LANCASTER, Rev. Ronald, MBE 1993; Founder, 1964, Managing Director, 1986, Director and Chairman, since 2007, Kimbolton Fireworks Limited; *b* 9 March 1931; *s* of Jack and Kathleen Lancaster; *m* 1966, Kathleen Smith; one *s* one *d*. *Educ:* Durham Univ. (BA 1953; MA 1956); Cuddesdon Coll., Oxford. Ordained deacon, 1957, priest, 1958; Curate: St Peter, Morley, Yorks, 1957–60; St Peter, Harrogate, 1960–63; Chaplain, Kimbolton Sch., Huntingdon, 1963–88. Hon. CChem, FRSC 1983. *Publication:* Fireworks Principles and Practice, 1972, 4th edn 2006. *Recreations:* gardening, organist. *Address:* 7 High Street, Kimbolton, Huntingdon, Cambs PE28 0HB. *T:* (01480) 860498, *Fax:* (01480) 861277; *e-mail:* ron@kimboltonfireworks.co.uk.

See also J. M. Lancaster.

LANCASTER, Roy; *see* Lancaster, C. R.

LANCE, Seán Patrick; Chairman, African Leadership Institute, since 2003; *b* 4 Aug. 1947; *s* of James Lance and Kathleen (*née* Carmody); *m* 1st, 1969, Pamela Joan Gray (marr. diss. 1990); two *s* two *d*; 2nd, 1990, Patricia Anne (*née* Bungay). *Educ:* Christian Brothers Coll., Pretoria. Noristan Gp, S Africa, 1967–82; Chm., Boots Co., S Africa, 1982–85; Man. Dir, Glaxo, S Africa, 1985–87; Regl Dir (London), Glaxo Hldgs plc, 1987–89; Man. Dir, Glaxo Pharms UK Ltd, 1989–93; Dir, Glaxo Hldgs plc, 1993–97; Chief Operating Officer, Glaxo Wellcome plc, 1997; Chief Exec. and Pres., 1998–2003, Chm., Bd of Dirs, 1998–2004, Chiron Corp. Mem., Supervisory Bd, Crucell, 2004–. President: Proprietary Assoc. of S Africa, 1983–84; Pharmaceutical Manufacturers Assoc. of S Africa, 1987–88; Internat. Fedn of Pharmaceut. Manufacturers Assoc., 1996–2000; Vice-Pres., Assoc. of British Pharmaceutical Industry, 1993–94. Special Forces, S Africa, 1965–75. *Recreations:* hockey, golf, football, cricket, Kyukoshin karate (2nd Dan). *Clubs:* Special Forces; Harlequins, Pretoria Country (Pretoria); Richmond Hockey.

LANCELOT, James Bennett, FRCO; Master of the Choristers and Organist, Durham Cathedral, since 1985; *b* 2 Dec. 1952; *s* of late Rev. Roland Lancelot; *m* 1982, Sylvia Jane (*née* Hoare); two *d*. *Educ:* St Paul's Cathedral Choir Sch.; Ardingly Coll., Royal College of Music (ARCM); King's Coll., Cambridge (Dr Mann Organ Student; MA; BMus). Asst Organist, St Clement Danes and Hampstead Parish Ch., 1974–75; Sub-Organist, Winchester Cath., 1975–85; Asst Conductor, Winchester Music Club, 1983–85; Conductor, Durham Univ. Choral Soc., 1987–; Organist, Durham Univ., 2002–. Member: Council, RCO, 1988–99, 2002–; Cathedrals Liturgy Gp, 1993–2003. President: Cathedral Organists' Assoc., 2001–03; Darlington and Dist Organists' and Choirmasters' Assoc., 2004–05. Lay Canon, Durham Cathedral, 2002–07. Hon. FGCM 2002; Hon. Fellow, St Chad's Coll., Durham, 2006; FRSCM 2008. Has played or conducted premières, incl. Mathias' Berceuse, Tavener's Ikon of St Cuthbert, Josephs' Mass for St Cuthbert. Organ recitals and broadcasts in UK; concerts in Germany, Denmark, France, Norway, Sweden, Poland, Belgium, Russia, Brazil, Canada, USA, NZ. Recordings with choirs of King's Coll., Cambridge, Winchester Cath., Durham Cath., and as soloist. *Publications:* (with R. Hird) Durham Cathedral Organs, 1991; (contrib.) The Sense of the Sacramental, 1993. *Recreations:* railways, the works of John Buchan. *Address:* 6 The College, Durham DH1 3EQ. *T:* (0191) 3864766.

LANCHESTER, John Henry, FRSL; writer; *b* Hamburg, 25 Feb. 1962; *s* of G. W., (Bill), Lanchester and Julie Lanchester; *m* 1994, Miranda Carter; two *s*. *Educ:* Gresham's Sch., Holt; St John's Coll., Oxford (BA 1st cl. Hons; Violet Vaughan Morgan Award, Charles Oldham Shakespeare Prize). Asst Ed., London Review of Books, 1987–91; Ed., Penguin Books, 1991–92; Dep. Ed., London Review of Books, 1993–96. FRSL 2003. *Publications:* The Debt to Pleasure, 1996 (Whitbread First Novel Award, Betty Trask Prize, 1996; Hawthornden Prize, Julia Child Award, 1997); Mr Phillips, 2000; Fragrant Harbour, 2002 (Premi Llibreter, 2005); Family Romance, 2007 (E. M. Forster Award, AAAL, 2008). *Recreation:* watching television. *Address:* c/o A. P. Watt Ltd, 20 John Street, WC1N 2DR. *T:* (020) 7405 6774, *Fax:* (020) 7831 2154; *e-mail:* apw@apwatt.co.uk.

LANCHIN, Gerald, OBE 2001; consultant; *b* 17 Oct. 1922; *o s* of late Samuel Lanchin, Kensington; *m* 1951, Valerie Sonia Lyons; one *s* two *d*. *Educ:* St Marylebone Grammar Sch.; London Sch. of Economics. BCom 1st cl. hons 1951; Leverhulme Schol. 1950–51. Min. of Labour, 1939–51; served with Army, RAOC and REME, 1942–46; Board of Trade (subseq. DTI and Dept of Trade): Asst Principal, 1952; Principal 1953; 1st Sec., UK Delegn to OEEC, Paris, 1955–59; Principal, Estabt and Commercial Relations and Exports Divs, 1959–66; Asst Sec., Finance and Civil Aviation Divs, 1966–71; Under-Sec., Tariff, Commercial Relations and Export, Shipping Policy, General and Consumer Affairs

Divs, 1971–82. Chairman: Packaging Council, 1983–84; Direct Mail Services Standards Bd, 1983–89; Member: Council, Consumers' Assoc., 1983–88; Data Protection Tribunal 1985–98; Consumer Panel, PIA, 1994–98; Financial Services Consumer Panel, 1998–2000. A Vice-Pres., Nat. Fedn of Consumer Gps, 1984–2002. Mem., Berkhamsted Town Council, 1997–2007. FRSA. *Publication:* Government and the Consumer, 1985. *Recreations:* photography, reading, music. *Address:* 28 Priory Gardens, Berkhamsted, Herts HP4 2DS. *T:* (01442) 875283.

LAND, Gillian; *see* Lynne, Gillian.

LAND, Prof. Michael Francis, FRS 1982; PhD; Professor of Neurobiology, University of Sussex, since 1984; *b* 12 April 1942; *s* of late Prof. Frank William Land and of Nora Beatrice Channon; *m* 1980, Rosemary (*née* Clarke); one *s* two *d*. *Educ:* Birkenhead Sch., Cheshire; Jesus Coll., Cambridge (MA); University Coll. London (PhD). Asst Lectr in Physiology, UCL, 1966–67; Miller Fellow, 1967–79, and Asst Prof. of Physiology-Anatomy, 1979–81, Univ. of Calif, Berkeley; Lectr in Biol Sciences, 1971–77, Reader, 1977–84, Univ. of Sussex. Vis. Prof., Univ. of Oregon, 1980; Sen. Res. Fellow, ANU, 1982–84. Frink Medal, Zool Soc. of London, 1994; Rank Prize for Optoelectronics, 1998. *Publications:* (with D. E. Nilsson) Animal Eyes, 2002; numerous papers on animal and human vision in learned jls. *Recreations:* photography, music. *Address:* White House, Cuilfail, Lewes, East Sussex BN7 2BE. *T:* (01273) 476780.

LAND, Nicholas Charles Edward, FCA; Chairman, Ernst & Young, 1995–2006; *b* 6 Feb. 1948; *s* of Charles and Norma Land; *m* 1975, Sonia Tan; one *s*. *Educ:* Steyning Grammar Sch. FCA 1971. Articled Spain Brothers Dalling & Co., 1967–71; joined Turquand Young, later Ernst & Young, 1971: Partner, 1978–2006; Managing Partner, London Office, 1986–92; Managing Partner, 1992–95. Non-executive Director: Royal Dutch Shell plc, 2006–; BBA Aviation plc (formerly BBA Gp plc), 2006–; Ashmore Gp Ltd, 2006–; Vodafone, 2006–; Adv. Bd Mem., Three Delta LLP, 2006–. Chm., Practice Adv. Bd, ICAEW, 2006–08. Member: Adv. Bd, Cambridge Judge Business Sch., 2005–; Finance and Audit Cttees, Nat. Gall., 2005–. Chm., Bd of Trustees, Farnham Castle, 2007–; Trustee, Vodafone Gp Foundn, 2007–. CCMI 1992; FRSA 1995. *Recreations:* carpentry, ballet. *Address:* (office) Three Delta LLP, 25 Hanover Square, W1S 1JE. *T:* (020) 7788 8000.

LANDALE, Sir David (William Neil), KCVO 1993; DL; company director; *b* 27 May 1934; *s* of David Fortune Landale and Louisa (*née* Forbes); *m* 1961, Melanie Roper; three *s*. *Educ:* Eton Coll.; Balliol Coll., Oxford (MA Hist. 1958). Served Black Watch, RHR, 1952–54. Joined Jardine Matheson & Co. Ltd, Hong Kong, 1958; served in Thailand, Hong Kong, Taiwan and Japan, 1960–71; Director: Jardine Matheson and Co. Ltd, 1976–75; Matheson & Co. Ltd, 1975–96; Pinneys of Scotland, Annan, 1982–87; Duchy Originals Ltd, 1992–95. Chm., T. C. Farries & Co. Ltd, 1982–97. Regl Chm., Timber Growers, Scotland, 1983–85; Chm., Timber Growers UK Ltd, 1985–87. Chairman: Scottish Forestry Trust, 1995–2001; Ingliston Develt Trust, 1996–; Nith Dist Fisheries Bd, 2000–. Member: Exec. Cttee and Council, NT for Scotland, 1980–85; Exec. Cttee, Scottish Landowners Fedn, 1980–87. Sec. and Keeper of Records, Duchy of Cornwall, 1987–93. Chairman: Sargent Cancer Care, Scotland (formerly Cttee for Scotland, Malcolm Sargent Cancer Fund for Children), 1994–96; Crichton Foundn (formerly Crichton Coll. Endowment Trust), 1998–2000, Convenor, 2001. Mem., Royal Co. of Archers, Queen's Body Guard for Scotland, 1966–. FRSA 1990. DL Nithsdale/Annandale Dumfries, 1988. *Recreations:* all countryside pursuits, theatre, reading, history. *Address:* Bankhead, Dalswinton, Dumfries DG2 0XZ. *T:* (01387) 740208. *Clubs:* Boodle's, Pratt's; New (Edinburgh).

LANDAU, Dr David, Hon. CBE 2007; Chairman, Saffron Hill Ventures, since 2000; *b* 22 April 1950; *s* of Aharon Landau and Evelyne Conti; *m* 2001, Marie-Rose Kahane; one *s* one *d* (twins). *Educ:* Univ. of Pavia, Italy (MD 1978); Wolfson Coll., Oxford (MA 1979). Print Curator, The Genius of Venice, RA, 1983; Chm., Steering Cttee, Andrea Mantegna exhibn, RA and Metropolitan Mus. of Art, NY, 1992. Founder and Jt Man. Dir, Loot, 1985–95; Chm., Loot Gp of Cos, 1995–2000. Founder and Editor, Print Qly, 1984–; Founder, FAPIA (Free-ad Papers Internat. Assoc.), 1986, Chm., 1990–91; Dir, Nat. Gall. Co. (formerly Nat. Gall. Pubns), 1995–2003 (Chm., 1998–2003). Trustee: British Friends of Art Museums of Israel, 1995–2007; Nat. Gall. Trust, 1996–; NACF (The Art Fund), 1996–; Nat. Gall., 1996–2003; Venice in Peril Fund, 1996– (Treas., 1997–); NGT Foundn, 1997–; Rothschild Foundn Europe, 2001–; Warburg Charitable Trust, 2001–; Borletti-Buitoni Charitable Trust, 2002–; Courtauld Inst., 2002–. Supernumerary Fellow, Worcester Coll., Oxford, 1980–. Commendatore dell'Ordine al Merito della Repubblica Italiana, 2007. *Publications:* Georg Pencz, 1978; Federica Galli, 1982; (with Prof. P. Parshall) The Renaissance Print, 1994; articles in Print Qly, Master Drawings, Burlington Mag., etc. *Recreations:* looking at and collecting art, opera, Venice. *Address:* 51 Kelso Place, W8 5QQ. *T:* (020) 7795 4989.

LANDAU, Sir Dennis (Marcus), Kt 1987; Chief Executive, Co-operative Wholesale Society Ltd, 1980–92 (Deputy Chief Executive Officer, 1974–80); *b* 18 June 1927; *s* of late Michael Landau, metallurgist; *m* 1992, Mrs Pamela Garlick; two step *s*. *Educ:* Haberdashers' Aske's Hampstead Sch. Schweppes Ltd, 1952; Man. Dir, Schweppes (East Africa) Ltd, 1958–62; Chivers-Hartley: Prodn Dir, 1963; Man. Dir, 1966–69; Chm., Schweppes Foods Div., 1969; Dep. Chm. and Man. Dir, Cadbury Schweppes Foods, 1970; Controller, Food Div., Co-operative Wholesale Society Ltd, 1971. Chairman: CWS (India) Ltd, 1980–92; Unity Trust Bank plc, 1992–2000 (Dir, 1984–2000); Dep. Chm., Co-operative Bank plc, 1989–92; Vice-Chm., Lancashire Enterprises plc, 1989–97; Director: Co-operative Retail Services Ltd, 1980–91; CWS (NZ Hldgs) Ltd, 1980–91; Co-operative Insce Soc. Ltd, 1980–92. Chm., Social Economy Forum, 1993–2001; Member: Metrication Bd, 1972–80; Exec. Cttee, Food & Drink Fedn (formerly Food Manufacturers' Fedn Inc.), 1972–92. Member: Council, Manchester Business Sch., 1982–93 (Chm., 1991–93); Court, Manchester Univ., 1992–2000. FIGD 1977 (Pres. 1982–85); CCMI (CBIM 1980). FRSA 1992. *Recreations:* Rugby, cricket, music. *Clubs:* Royal Over-Seas League; Lancashire CC (Hon. Treas., 1997–2003; Pres., 2003–07).

LANDAU, Toby Thomas; QC 2008; FCIArb; *b* London, 9 Oct. 1967; *s* of late Dr Thomas L. Landau and of Marianne Landau; *m* 1998, Nudrat B. Majeed; one *d*. *Educ:* University Coll., Sch., Hampstead; Merton Coll., Oxford (BA 1st Cl. Hons Juris; BCL 1st Cl.); Harvard Law Sch. (LLM); Inns of Court Sch. of Law. FCIArb 2000; Chartered Arbitrator, 2000. Called to the Bar, Middle Temple, 1993; Member: NY State Bar, 1994; NI Bar, 2000; in private practice as barrister and arbitrator, 1993–. Vis. Sen. Lectr, KCL, 2005–. Dir, London Court of Internat. Arbitration, 2000–. Trustee, CIArb, 2004–. Advr and Asst on drafting of English Arbitration Act, 1996. Member, Editorial Board: Global Arbitration Rev., 2005–; Jl Internat. Arbitration, 2007–. *Publications:* contrib. articles to ICCA Congress series and other law jls. *Address:* c/o Essex Court Chambers, 24 Lincoln's Inn Fields, WC2A 3EG. *Club:* Harvard (New York).

LANDEG, Frederick John, CBE 2008; Deputy Chief Veterinary Officer, 2004–07, Interim Chief Veterinary Officer, 2007–08, Department for Environment, Food and Rural Affairs; *b* 16 Jan. 1948; *s* of Frederick Henry Landeg and Ivy May Landeg; *m* 1973, Sandra Stagg; three *s*. *Educ:* Sir Walter St John's Sch., Battersea; Royal Veterinary Coll., London (BVetMed; MSc). MRCVS. Gen. veterinary practice, 1971–75; Ministry of Agriculture, Fisheries and Food: Vet. Officer, 1975–83; Sen. Vet. Officer, 1983–87; Div. Vet. Officer, Preston, 1987–90; Dep. Regl Vet. Officer, Reading, 1990–93; Hd, Vet. Resources Div., 1993–2000; Hd, Vet. Exotic Diseases Div., 2000–04, MAFF, subseq. DEFRA. *Recreations:* reading, walking. *Address:* 6 Oak Tree Copse, Tilehurst, Reading RG31 6PX.

LANDELS, William, (Willie); painter, typographer; *b* Venice, 14 June 1928; *s* of late Reynold Landels and Carla Manfredi; *m* 1st, 1958, Angela Ogden (marr. diss. 1986); two *d*; 2nd, 2002, Josephine Grever. *Educ:* privately. Apprentice stage designer at La Scala, Milan, 1947; Art Director: J. Walter Thompson, 1950; Queen Magazine, 1965; Editor, Harpers & Queen, 1970–86; Editor, Departures, 1989–90. One-man Exhibitions: Hamburg, 1992; Rebecca Hossack Gall., London, 1993, 1995, 1998; Olsen-Carr Gall., Sydney, 1994; Gallery 482, Brisbane, 1997; Pasricha Fine Arts, London, 2002. Designer, carpets and tapestries, 2003–. *Publication:* (with Alistair Burnet) The Best Years of Our Lives, 1981. *Recreation:* cooking. *Address:* 292 South Lambeth Road, SW8 1UJ.

LANDER, Nicholas Laurence; Restaurant Correspondent, The Financial Times, since 1989; foodservice consultant; *b* 8 April 1952; *s* of Israel Lennard and Pauline Lander; *m* 1981, Jancis Mary Robinson, *qv*; one *s* two *d*. *Educ:* Manchester Grammar Sch.; Jesus Coll., Cambridge (MA); Manchester Business Sch. (DipBA). Restaurateur, 1980–88; Foodservice Consultant: South Bank Centre, 1993–; Glyndebourne Opera, 1998–2005; Royal Opera House, Covent Garden, 1999–; V&A Mus., 2001–; BM, 2004–; Somerset House; Royal Albert Hall. *Publications:* Dinner for a Fiver, 1994; Harry's Bar London, 2005. *Recreations:* cooking, reading, sitting round a table with friends. *Address:* *e-mail:* nick@jancisrobinson.com. *Club:* Manchester United.

LANDER, Sir Stephen (James), KCB 2000 (CB 1995); Member, Solicitors Regulation Authority (formerly Regulation Board, Law Society), since 2006 (Independent Commissioner, 2002–05); Chairman, Serious Organised Crime Agency, since 2004; *b* 1947; *s* of John N. B. Lander and (Eleanor) Tessa Lander (*née* Heanley); *m* 1972, Felicity Mary Brayley; one *d* (one *s* decd). *Educ:* Bishops Stortford Coll.; Queens' Coll., Cambridge (BA, MA, PhD). Inst. of Historical Research, Univ. of London, 1972–75; Security Service, 1975–2002, Dir Gen., 1996–2002; non-exec. Dir, HM Customs and Excise, 2002–05. Non-executive Director: Northgate Information Solutions, 2004–08; Streamshield Networks, 2004–07. Panel Chm., Judicial Appts Commn, 2008–. Hon. LLD Hertfordshire, 2005; Hon. DSc Cranfield, 2007. *Address:* PO Box 12378, SW1P 1XU.

LANDERER, John, CBE 1997; AM 1990; lawyer; Senior Partner, Landerer & Co., since 1979; *b* 3 May 1947; *s* of William and Felicia Landerer; *m* 1986, Michelle H. Sugar; one *s* one *d*. *Educ:* Sydney Univ. (LLB 1969). Chairman: FAI Insurances Ltd, 1989–99 (Actg Chm., 1988); Tiger Investment Co. Ltd, 1994–99; Goldsearch Ltd, 1995–; Nat. Hire Gp Ltd, 1997–2004; Terrace Tower Gp, 1997–2007; Director: TNT Ltd, 1985–93; Internat. Distillers Hldgs Ltd, 1986–99; Advance Bank Aust. Ltd, 1989–97; Goodman Fielder Ltd, 1989–94; Aust. Nat. Industries Ltd, 1989–96; Bridge Oil Ltd, 1991–94; Gandel Gp Pty Ltd, 1995–98; D. W. Gp of Cos, 1996–. Chm., NSW Govt Home Purchase Assistance Authy, 1994–2001. University of Sydney: Hon. Fellow, 1990; Hon. Gov., Law Sch. Foundn, 1990–; Mem. Bd, Asia Pacific Law Centre, 1994; Chm., Endocrinol. and Diabetes Res. Foundn, 2008– (Councillor, 2006–08); Macquarie University: Chm., Adv. Bd, Business Law Dept, 1994–; Vis. Prof., 1998–. Trustee, WWF Australia, 1992–99. Councillor, Sydney Conservatorium of Music Foundn, 1994–96. Vice Pres., Temora Aviation Mus., 1998–; Board Member: Sydney Jewish Mus., 2004 (Pres., 2005–); Life Educn Aust., 2004–; JewishCare Foundn, 2004–; Garvan Res. Foundn, 2007–. Dir, Royal Inst. of Deaf and Blind Children, 2005–. Member: Fundraising Cttee, 1989–93, Victor Chang Cardiac Centre Appeal Cttee, 1993–96, St Vincent's Hosp.; Red Shield Appeal Cttee, Salvation Army, 1991–98. Vice Chm., Bd of Govs, Tel Aviv Univ., 2000– (Hon. Fellow, 2008). Hon. LLD Macquarie, 1999. B'nai B'rith Internat. Award, 2001. Commendatore dell'Ordine della Stella della Solidarieta Italiana, 2008. *Recreations:* reading, walking, swimming. *Address:* (office) Level 31, 133 Castlereagh Street, Sydney, NSW 2000, Australia. *T:* (612) 92614242, *Fax:* (612) 92618523. *Clubs:* Carlton; American, Tattersalls (Sydney).

LANDERS, Brian James; Finance and Operations Director, Penguin Group, since 2003; *b* 21 April 1949; *s* of James Jocelyn Landers, OBE and Beatrice Edith Landers (*née* Western); *m* 1st, 1975, Elsa Louise Dawson (marr. diss.); 2nd, 1986, Thérèse Doumit (marr. diss.); one *s*; 3rd, 1993, Sarah Catherine Cuthbert; two *d*. *Educ:* Univ. of Exeter (BA); London Business Sch. (MSc). With Commercial Union, 1973–79; Internat. Planned Parenthood Fedn, 1979–82; Tenneco Automotive, 1982–83; Chief Internal Auditor, then Retail Financial Controller, J. Sainsbury plc, 1985–88; Price Waterhouse, 1988–90; UK Finance Dir, then Gp Finance Dir, Habitat, 1990–93; Finance Director: HM Prison Service, 1993–96; W. H. Smith Retail, 1996–97; with Waterstones Ltd, 1997–98; Gp Finance Dir, 2000, Chief Operating Officer, 2000–03, Pearson Education. Dep. Chm., Financial Ombudsman Service, 1999–2005. Trustee, Royal Armouries, 1999–2002. *Address:* Penguin Group, 80 Strand, WC2R 0RL.

LANDERS, Dr John Maxwell; Principal, Hertford College, Oxford, since 2005; *b* 25 Jan. 1952; *s* of William Maxwell Landers and Muriel Landers; *m* 1991, Diana Parker. *Educ:* Southgate Tech. Coll.; Hertford Coll., Oxford (MA; LittD 2006); Churchill Coll., Cambridge (PhD 1984). Oil demand analyst, Shell UK Ltd, 1979–80; Lectr in Biol Anthropol., UCL, 1980–90; Lectr in Histl Demography, and Fellow, All Souls Coll., Oxford, 1991–2005. *Publications:* Death and the Metropolis: studies in the historical demography of London 1670–1830, 1993; The Field and the Forge: population, production and power in the pre-industrial West, 2003. *Address:* The Principal's Lodgings, Hertford College, Oxford OX1 3BW. *Clubs:* Athenæum, Oxford and Cambridge.

LANDON, Prof. David Neil; Professor of Neurocytology, University of London, 1991–2001, now Emeritus Professor; Dean, and Member Committee of Management, Institute of Neurology, London, 1987–95; *b* 15 May 1936; *er s* of late Christopher Guy Landon and Isabella Catherine (*née* Campbell); *m* 1960, Karen Elizabeth, *yr d* of late John Copeland and Else Margrethe Poole, Bolney, Sussex; two *s* one *d*. *Educ:* Lancing Coll.; Guy's Hospital Med. Sch. (BSc Hons Anat. 1957, MB BS 1960). LRCP, MRCS 1959. Ho. Officer, Guy's Hosp., 1959–60; Lectr in Anatomy, Guy's Hosp. Med. Sch., 1961–64; Lectr, later Sen. Lectr, in Neurobiology, MRC Res. Gp in Applied Neurobiology, 1964–77; Reader in Neurocytology, Inst. of Neurology, 1977–91. Hon. Cons. in Morbid Anatomy, National Hosps, Queen Square, 1974–2001. University of London: Member: Senate and Academic Council, 1992–94; Univ. Council, 1996–2001; Mem., Med. Cttee, 1996–98; Convenor, Subject Panel in Anatomy, 1996–2001. Vis. Prof., Coll. of Medicine, Lagos, 1975. Gov., National Hosps for Nervous Diseases SHA, 1988–95; Appointed Mem., GMC, 1988–94. Member: Res. Cttee, World Fedn of Neurology, 1987–2001; Cttees of Management, Inst. of Child Health, 1987–96, Inst. of Dental Surgery, 1993–95; Chm., Med. Res. Ethics Cttee, 1987–93, Chm., Med. Cttee,

1998–2000, Nat. Hosp. for Neurology and Neurosurgery. Mem. Grants Council, 1999–2001, Mem. Adv. Council, 2001–05, Charities Aid Foundn; Trustee, Brain Res. Trust, 2004–. Hon. Fellow, Inst. of Child Health, London Univ., 1996. Freeman, Pewterers' Co., 2001. Editorial Cttee, Jl of Anatomy, 1981–94; Associated Editor: Jl of Neurocytol., 1980–83; Neuromuscular Disorders, 1990–94; Muscle and Nerve, 1997–2001. *Publications:* The Peripheral Nerve, 1976; contribs to learned jls on the fine structure, develt and pathology of nerve and muscle. *Recreations:* gardening, travel. *Address:* Woodmans, Wallcrouch, Wadhurst, East Sussex TN5 7JG. *T:* (01580) 200833.

LANDON, Howard Chandler Robbins; author and music historian; *b* 6 March 1926; *s* of late William Grinnell Landon and Dorothea LeBaron Robbins; *m* 1977, Else Radant. *Educ:* Aiken Preparatory Sch.; Lenox Sch.; Swarthmore Coll.; Boston Univ., USA (BMus). European rep. of Intercollegiate Broadcasting System, 1947; founded Haydn Soc. (which recorded and printed music of Joseph Haydn), 1949; became a Special Correspondent of The Times, 1957 and contrib. to that newspaper until 1961. Visiting Prof., Queen's Coll., NYC, 1969; Regents Prof. of Music, Univ. of California (Davis), 1970, 1975, 1979; John Bird Prof. of Music, UC Cardiff, 1978–; Christian Johnson Prof. of Music, Middlebury Coll., Vermont, USA, 1980–. Advr, Prague Mozart Foundn, 1992–. Hon. Professorial Fellow, University Coll., Cardiff, 1971–79; Hon. Fellow, Lady Margaret Hall, Oxford, 1979–. Hon. DMus: Boston Univ., 1969; Queen's Univ., Belfast, 1974; Bristol, 1982. Verdienstkreuz für Kunst und Wissenschaft from Austrian Govt, 1972; Gold Medal, City of Vienna, 1987; Haydn Prize, Govt of Burgenland, Austria, 1990. Co-editor, The Haydn Yearbook, 1962–. *Publications:* The Symphonies of Joseph Haydn, 1955; The Mozart Companion (co-ed with Donald Mitchell), 1956; The Collected Correspondence and London Notebooks of Joseph Haydn, 1959; Essays on Eighteenth-Century Music, 1969; Ludwig van Beethoven: a documentary study, 1970; critical edn of the 107 Haydn Symphonies, (completed) 1968; five-vol. biog. of Haydn: vol. 3, Haydn in England, 1976; vol. 4, Haydn: The Years of The Creation, 1977; vol. 5, Haydn: The Late Years, 1977; vol. 1, Haydn: The Early Years, and vol. 2, Haydn in Eszterhaza, 1978–80; Haydn: a documentary study, 1981; Mozart and the Masons, 1982; Handel and his World, 1984; 1791: Mozart's Last Year, 1988; (with David Wyn Jones) Haydn: his life and music, 1988; Mozart: the golden years, 1989; (ed) The Mozart Compendium, 1990; Mozart and Vienna, 1991; Five Centuries of Music in Venice, 1991; Vivaldi: voice of the Baroque, 1993; The Mozart Essays, 1995; Horns in High C: a memoir of musical discoveries and adventures, 1999; scholarly edns of eighteenth-century music (various European publishing houses). *Recreations:* swimming, cooking, walking. *Address:* Château de Foncoussières, 81800 Rabastens, Tarn, France. *T:* 563406145.

LANDRY, Prof. (Jean-) Bernard; Professor of Business Studies, University of Quebec at Montreal, since 2005; *b* 9 March 1937; *s* of Bernard Landry and Thérèse Landry (*née* Granger); *m* 1963, Lorraine Jacquemin (*d* 1999); one *s* two *d*; *m* Chantal Renaud. *Educ:* Acad. Saint Louis, Saint-Jacques, Québec; Séminaire de Joliette; Univ. de Montréal; Inst. d'études politiques, Paris. Tech. Advr, Min. of Natural Resources, Quebec, Co-ordinator for Quebec, Canadian Council of Resource Ministers and chargé de mission, Min. of Educn, 1964–68; called to the Bar, Quebec, 1965; Min. of Finance and Econ. Affairs, Paris, 1965–67; in practice as lawyer, Joliette and Montréal, 1969–76. Associate Prof., Dept of Admin, Univ. du Québec à Montréal, 1986–94. National Assembly of Quebec: contested Joliette, 1970, Joliette-Montcalm, 1973; Mem. (Parti Québécois) for Fabre, 1976–81, for Laval-des-Rapides, 1981–85, for Verchères, 1994–2005; Minister of State for Econ. Develt, 1977–82; Minister: for External Trade, 1982–84; of Internat. Relations, 1984–85; of Finance, 1985; Dep. Prime Minister, 1994–2001; Prime Minister, 2001–03; Leader of the Opposition, 2003–05. Mem. Nat. Exec., Parti Québécois, 1974–2005 (Vice-Chm., 1989–94; Chm., 2001–05).

LANDSHOFF, Prof. Peter Vincent, PhD; Professor of Mathematical Physics, University of Cambridge, 1994–2004; Fellow, Christ's College, Cambridge, since 1963 (Vice-Master, 1999–2002); Consultant, Cambridge-MIT Institute, 2004–07; *b* 22 March 1937; *m* 1962, Pamela Carmichael; three *s*. *Educ:* City of London Sch.; St John's Coll., Cambridge (MA, PhD). FInstP 1999. Cambridge University: Fellow, St John's Coll., 1961–63; Reader in Mathematical Physics, 1974–94. Instructor, Princeton Univ., 1961–62; Scientific Associate, CERN, Geneva, 1975–76, 1984–85, 1991–92. Chairman, Management Committee: Isaac Newton Inst. for Mathematical Scis, 1990–94 and 2001–06; Cambridge eScience Centre, 2001–04; Nat. Inst. for Envmtl eScience, 2002–04; Cambridge Computational Biol. Inst., 2003–04; Council, Sch. of Physical Scis, Cambridge Univ., 2004. Editor, Physics Letters B (Elsevier Science), 1982–2005. FRSA. *Publications:* (jtly) The Analytic S-matrix, 1966; (jtly) Simple Quantum Physics, 1979, 2nd edn 1997; research papers on theoretical high-energy physics. *Address:* Department of Applied Mathematics and Theoretical Physics, Centre for Mathematical Sciences, Wilberforce Road, Cambridge CB3 0WA. *T:* (01223) 337880; *e-mail:* pvl@damtp.cam.ac.uk.

LANDSMAN, David Maurice, OBE 2000; PhD; HM Diplomatic Service; Ambassador to Greece, since 2009; *b* 23 Aug. 1963; *s* of Sidney Landsman and Miriam Landsman (*née* Cober); *m* 1990, Catherine Louise Holden; one *s*. *Educ:* Chigwell Sch.; Oriel Coll., Oxford (BA Lit. Hum. 1985; MA 1988); Clare Coll., Cambridge (MPhil 1986; PhD 1989). Univ. of Cambridge Local Exams Syndicate, 1988–89; entered FCO, 1989; Second Secretary: (Econ.) Athens, 1991–94; FCO, 1994–97; Dep. Hd of Mission, Belgrade, 1997–99; FCO, 1999; Hd of Office, Banja Luka, and concurrently First Sec., Budapest, 1999–2000; Hd, British Interests Section, Embassy of Brazil, and subseq. Chargé d'Affaires, British Embassy Belgrade, 2000–01; Ambassador to Albania, 2001–03; Hd, Counter-Proliferation Dept, FCO, 2003–06; on secondment as Internat. Affairs Advr, De La Rue Identity Systems, 2006–08; Balkans Dir, FCO, 2008. *Publications:* contrib. occasional articles on the Greek lang. *Recreations:* travel, languages, music, food, visiting zoos. *Address:* c/o Foreign and Commonwealth Office, King Charles Street, SW1A 2AH. *Clubs:* Athenæum, Commonwealth.

LANDY, John Michael, AC 2001; CVO 2005; MBE 1955; Governor of Victoria, Australia, 2001–06; *b* 12 April 1930; *s* of Clarence Gordon Landy and Elva Katherine Ashton; *m* 1971, Lynne (*née* Fisher); one *s* one *d*. *Educ:* Malvern Grammar Sch.; Geelong Grammar; Univ. of Melbourne (BAgSc). Holder: 1500m World Record, 1954–55; one mile World Record, 1954–57; Olympic and Commonwealth Games medals; second man to run the mile in under 4 mins. ICI Australia, 1962–82, R&D Manager, Biological Gp, 1971–82. Chairman: Wool R&D Corp., 1989–94; Clean-up Australia, 1990–94; Australia Day Cttee (Victoria), 1990–93; Coode Is. (major chemical spill) Review Panel, 1991–92; Athletics Task Force, 1992–93; Meat Res. Corp., 1995–98; Dir, Australian Sports Drug Agency, 1998–2000. Chairman: Bd Governors, Australian Nat. Insect Collection, 1995–2000; Aust. Wool Testing Authy Ltd Wool Educn Trust, 1997–2000; Athletics Internat. Trust, 1997–2000; Pres., Greening Australia (Victoria), 1998–2000; Member: Land Conservation Council of Victoria, 1971–79; Reference Areas Cttee, Victoria's system of Scientific Reference Areas, 1979–86; Bd Dirs, Australian Inst. of Sport, 1985–87; External Earnings Review Working Party, Aust. Sci. and Technol. Council, 1993–94. Hon. LLD: Victoria, BC, 1994; Melbourne, 2003; Deakin, 2004; Hon. D Rural Sci. New England, 1997. *Publications:* Close to Nature, 1985 (C. J. Dennis Award); A Coastal Diary, 1993.

LANE, family name of **Baron Lane of Horsell**.

LANE OF HORSELL, Baron *cr* 1990 (Life Peer), of Woking in the County of Surrey; **Peter Stewart Lane,** Kt 1984; JP; FCA; Senior Partner, Binder Hamlyn, Chartered Accountants, 1979–92; *b* 29 Jan. 1925; *s* of Leonard George Lane; *m* Doris Florence (*née* Botsford) (*d* 1969); two *d*. *Educ:* Sherborne Sch., Dorset. Served RNVR (Sub-Lieut), 1943–46. Qualified as chartered accountant, 1948; Partner, Binder Hamlyn or predecessor firms, 1950–92. Chairman: Brent Internat., 1985–95; Elswick, 1993–94; Attwoods, 1994; Automated Security (Hldgs), 1994–96; Dep. Chm., More O'Ferrall, later More Gp, 1985–97. National Union of Conservative Associations: Vice Chm., 1981–83; Chm., 1983–84; Chm., Exec. Cttee, 1986–91. Chm., Nuffield Hosps, 1993–96 (Dep. Chm., 1990–93). Chm., Action on Addiction, 1991–94. JP Surrey, 1976–; Freeman, City of London. *Address:* c/o House of Lords, SW1A 0PW. *Clubs:* Boodle's, Beefsteak, MCC.
See also Baron Trefgarne.

LANE, Dr Anthony John, FRCP, FFPH; Regional Medical Officer, North Western Regional Health Authority, 1974–86, retired; *b* 6 Feb. 1926; *s* of John Gill Lane and Marian (*née* Brumfield); *m* 1948, Hannah Holečková; one *s* two *d*. *Educ:* St Christopher's Sch., Letchworth; Emmanuel Coll., Cambridge. MA, MB, BChir. House posts in surgery, medicine, obstetrics, and paediatrics, London area, 1949–51; MO with Methodist Missionary Soc., Andhra State, India, 1951–57; Registrar: Tropical Diseases, UCH, 1958; Gen. Med., St James' Hosp., Balham, 1958–61; Infectious Diseases, Western Hosp., Fulham, 1961–63; MO (Trainee), Leeds RHB, 1963–64; Asst Sen. MO, Leeds RHB, 1964–66; Principal Asst Sen. MO, Leeds RHB, 1966–70; Dep. Sen. Admin. MO, SW Metrop. RHB, 1970–71; Sen. Admin. MO, Manchester RHB, 1971–74. Hon. MD Manchester, 1986. *Publications:* contrib. Positions, Movements and Directions in Health Services Research, 1974; contrib. Proc. Royal Soc. Med. *Recreations:* music, competitive indoor games, walking, gardening. *Address:* 5A Chapel Lane, Wilmslow, Cheshire SK9 5HZ. *T:* (01625) 532572.

LANE, Anthony John, CB 1990; consultant on public policy issues; Deputy Secretary, Department of Trade and Industry, 1987–96; *b* 30 May 1939; *s* of late Eric Marshall Lane and Phyllis Mary Lane; *m* 1967, Judith Sheila (*née* Dodson); two *s* one *d*. *Educ:* Caterham Sch.; Balliol Coll., Oxford (BA PPE, MA). Investment Analyst, Joseph Sebag & Co., 1964–65; joined Civil Service as Asst Principal, 1965; various appts in DTI, Dept of Transport, DoE and OFT; Prin. Pvte Sec. to several Ministers; Asst Sec., 1975; Under Sec., 1980; Head of Internat Trade Policy, DTI, 1984–87; Dep. Dir Gen., OFT, 1987–90; Dir Gen. for Industry, DTI, 1990–94; Chief Exec., PSA, 1994–96. Brighton University: Mem., Bd of Govs, 1997– (Dep. Chm., 1999–2002); Chm., Univ. Property Cttee, 1998–99. *Recreations:* music, gardens, travel. *Address:* Foxbury, East Grinstead, W Sussex RH19 3SS.

LANE, Dr Anthony Milner, FRS 1975; Deputy Chief Scientific Officer, Atomic Energy Research Establishment, Harwell, 1976–89; *b* 27 July 1928; *s* of Herbert William Lane and Doris Ruby Lane (*née* Milner); *m* 1st, 1952, Anne Sophie Zissman (*d* 1980); two *s* one *d*; 2nd, 1983, Jill Valerie Parvin (*d* 2002); five step *d*. *Educ:* Trowbridge Boys' High Sch.; Selwyn Coll., Cambridge. BA Maths, PhD Theoretical Physics. Joined Harwell, 1953. *Publications:* Nuclear Theory, 1963; numerous research articles in Review of Modern Physics, Phys. Review, Nuclear Physics, etc. *Recreations:* gardening, bird-watching. *Address:* 21 Squitchey Lane, Oxford OX2 7LD. *T:* (01865) 556565.

LANE, Maj.-Gen. Barry Michael, CB 1984; OBE 1974 (MBE 1965); Chief Executive, Cardiff Bay Development Corporation, 1987–92; *b* 10 Aug. 1932; *m* 1st, 1956, Eveline Jean (*d* 1986), *d* of Vice-Adm. Sir Harry Koelle, KCB and Enid (*née* Corbould-Ellis); one *s* one *d*; 2nd, 1987, Shirley Ann, *d* of E. V. Hawtin. *Educ:* Dover Coll. Commissioned, 1954; served Somerset LI, 1954–59, Somerset and Cornwall LI, 1959–68, LI, 1968–75; Instructor, Staff Coll. Camberley, 1970–72; CO, 1st Bn, LI, 1972–75; Comd, 11 Armoured Bde, 1977–78; RCDS, 1979; Dep. Dir, Army Staff Duties, MoD, 1980–81; Dir, Army Quartering, 1981–82; VQMG, 1982–83; GOC SW Dist, 1984–87. Col, The LI, 1982–87. Hon. Colonel: 6th Bn, LI, 1987–97; Bristol Univ., OTC, 1988–99. Pres. of Council, and Chm. of Govs, Taunton Sch., 1997–2001; Vice Pres., St Margaret's Somerset Hospice, 2003–. *Club:* Army and Navy.

LANE, David Goodwin; QC 1991; a Recorder of the Crown Court, since 1987; *b* 8 Oct. 1945; *s* of James Cooper Lane and Joyce Lilian Lane; *m* 1991, Jacqueline Elizabeth Cocks. *Educ:* Crypt Sch., Gloucester; King's College London (LLB, AKC). Lord Justice Holker Junior Exhibnr; Lee Essay Prizeman, H. C. Richard Ecclesiastical Law Prizeman; Albion Richardson Scholar. Called to the Bar, Gray's Inn, 1968; Asst Recorder, 1982. Freeman, City of London. *Address:* Peel Court Chambers, Sunlight House, Quay Street, Manchester M3 3JZ. *T:* (0161) 832 3791.

LANE, David Ian, (David Ian); theatre producer, since 1991; Chairman of Global Theatre, Live Nation, 2005–07; *b* 15 Feb. 1961; *s* of Reg and Jean Lane; *m* 1994, Tracy Carter; one *s* one *d*. *Educ:* Ilford County High Grammar Sch. Joined Live Nation (formerly Clear Channel Entertainment), 2000. Actor: title rôle, Joseph and the Amazing Technicolor Dreamcoat; Pirates of Penzance, London Palladium; Time, Dominion. Producer, 1991–: Ain't Misbehavin', Lyric, 1995; Saturday Night Fever, London Palladium, 1998; Defending the Caveman, Apollo, 1999; The King and I, London Palladium, 2000; Grease (revival), Dominion, 2001, transf. Cambridge Th. and Victoria Palace; Daisy Pulls It Off, Lyric, 2002; Anything Goes, 2003, The Producers, 2004, Drury Lane Th. Royal; Guys and Dolls, Piccadilly, 2005; The Sound of Music, London Palladium, 2006; Grease, Piccadilly, 2007; also many UK tours and productions in USA and Australia. *Recreations:* sport, marathon running, theatre. *Address:* (office) David Ian Productions Ltd, 33 Henrietta Street, WC2E 8NA. *Club:* Garrick.

LANE, David Neil, CMG 1983; HM Diplomatic Service, retired; *b* 16 April 1928; *er s* of late Clive and Hilda Lane, Bath; *m* 1968, Sara, *d* of late Cecil Nurcombe, MC; two *d*. *Educ:* Abbotsholme Sch.; Merton Coll., Oxford. Army, 1946–48; Foreign (later Foreign and Commonwealth) Office: 1951–53, 1955–58, 1963–68, 1972–74; British Embassy, Oslo, 1953–55; Ankara, 1959–61, 1975–78; Conakry, 1961–63; UK Mission to the United Nations, New York, 1968–72, 1979; NI Office, 1978–79; High Comr in Trinidad and Tobago, 1980–85; Ambassador to the Holy See, 1985–88. Pres., UN Trusteeship Council, 1971–72; UK Delegate, Internat. Exhibns Bureau, 1973–74. Asst Sec.-Gen., 1989–92, Sec., 1990–92, Order of St John; OStJ 1990. Chm., Anglo-Turkish Soc., 1995–2001. *Publication:* Three Carols for chorus and orchestra, 2000. *Address:* 6 Montagu Square, W1H 2LB. *T:* (020) 7486 1673.

LANE, Sir David (Philip), Kt 2000; PhD; FRCPath, FMedSci; FRS 1996; FRSE; Professor of Molecular Oncology, University of Dundee, since 1990; Chairman, Biomedical Research Council, Agency for Science, Technology and Research, Singapore, since 2007; Chief Executive Officer, Experimental Therapeutic Centre, Singapore, since 2007; Chief Scientist, Cancer Research-UK, since 2008; *b* 1 July 1952; *s* of John Wallace Lane and Cecelia Frances Evelyn Lane (*née* Wright); *m* 1975, Ellen Birgitte Muldal; one *s* one *d*. *Educ:* John Fisher Sch., Purley; University College London (BSc 1973, PhD 1976; Fellow). FRCPath 1996. FRSE 1992. Res. Fellow, ICRF, 1976–77; Lectr, Imperial Coll., 1977–85; Staff Scientist, ICRF, 1985–90; Exec. Dir, Inst. of Molecular and Cell Biology, Proteos, Singapore, 2004–07 (on sabbatical). Vis. Fellow, Cold Spring Harbor Labs, NY, 1978–80; Gibb Fellow, Cancer Res. UK (formerly CRC), 1990–. Mem., EMBO, 1990. Founder FMedSci 1998. Hon. DSc: Abertay Dundee, 1999; Stirling, 2000; Aberdeen, 2002; Birmingham, 2002; Hon. MD Nottingham, 2006; Dr *hc* Univ. Paul Sabatier, Toulouse, 2007. Prize, Charles Rodolphe Brupbacher Foundn, 1993; Prize, Joseph Steiner Foundn, 1993; Howard Hughes Internat. Scholar, Howard Hughes Med. Inst., 1993; Yvette Mayent Prize, Inst. Curie, 1994; Medal, Swedish Soc. of Oncology, 1994; Prize, Meyenburg Foundn, 1995; Black Prize, Jefferson Hosp., 1995; Silvanus Thompson Medal, British Inst. of Radiol., 1996; Henry Dryerre Prize, 1996; Paul Ehrlich Prize, 1998; Tom Connors Prize, 1998; Bruce-Preller Prize, 1998; SCI Medal, 2003; Anthony Dipple Carcinogenesis Award, 2004; Buchanan Medal, Royal Soc., 2004; Biochem. Soc. Award, 2004; Internat. Agency for Res. on Cancer Medal, 2005; Sergio Lombroso Award for Cancer Research Work, 2005; INSERM Medal d'Etranger, 2006; Gregor Mendel Medal, Masaryk Cancer Inst., Czech Republic, 2006; Colin Thomson Medal, Beatson Inst., Glasgow, 2007; David Hungerford Medal, Bangalore, 2007; Royal Medal, RSE, 2008. *Publications:* Antibodies: a laboratory manual, 1988; numerous papers in learned jls. *Recreations:* tennis, motor cycles, walking. *Address:* Cancer Research UK Laboratories, Department of Molecular Medicine, Dundee University, Dundee DD1 9SY. *T:* (01382) 381046.

LANE, David Stuart, PhD, DPhil; Reader in Sociology, 1992–2000, and Official Fellow of Emmanuel College, 1974–80 and 1990–2000, Senior Research Associate, since 2001, University of Cambridge; *b* Monmouthshire (now Gwent), 24 April 1933; *s* of Reginald and Mary Lane; *m* 1962, Christel Noritzsch; one *s* one *d*. *Educ:* Univ. of Birmingham (BSocSc); Univ. of Oxford (DPhil); PhD Cantab. Graduate student, Nuffield Coll., Oxford, 1961–62, 1964–65. Formerly engrg trainee, local authority employee, sch. teacher; univ. teacher, Birmingham, Essex (Reader in Sociology) and Cambridge Univs; Prof. of Sociology, Univ. of Birmingham, 1981–90; Lectr in Sociology, Cambridge Univ., 1990–92. Visiting Professor: Lund Univ., 1985; Cornell Univ., 1987; Univ. of Graz, 1991, 1996; Harvard Univ., 1993, 2001; Kennan Inst., Washington, 1986, 1996; Sabanci Univ., 2000–02. Member: Exec. Cttee, British Sociol Assoc., 1987–92; Exec. Cttee, European Social Assoc., 1999–2001; Co-Chair, first European Conf. of Sociology, 1992. Vice-Chm., Birmingham Rathbone, 1986–90; Vice-Chm., Down's Children's Assoc., 1981–82; Chm., W Midlands Council for Disabled People, 1983–86. ESRC res. award to study Soviet and Russian political elites, 1991–95, econ. elites, 1996–98, and financial business elite, 1999–2002; Leverhulme Trust res. award to study transformation of state socialism, 2004–07; British Acad. network award for study of strategic elites and European enlargement, 2004–; Mem., EU Inter-Univs Consortium to study new modes of governance within the EU, 2004–. Member, Editorial Boards: Sociology, 1985–88; Disability, Handicap and Society, 1987–90; Mir Rossii, 2006–. *Publications:* Roots of Russian Communism, 1969, 2nd edn 1975; Politics and Society in the USSR, 1970, 2nd edn 1978; The End of Inequality?, 1971; (with G. Kolankiewicz) Social Groups in Polish Society, 1973; The Socialist Industrial State, 1976; (with F. O'Dell) The Soviet Industrial Worker, 1978; The Work Needs of Mentally Handicapped Adults, 1980; Leninism: a sociological interpretation, 1981; The End of Social Inequality?: class status and power under state socialism, 1982; State and Politics in the USSR, 1985; Soviet Economy and Society, 1985; (ed jtly and contrib.) Current Approaches to Down's Syndrome, 1985; (ed) Employment and Labour in the USSR, 1986; Soviet Labour and the Ethic of Communism, 1987; (ed and contrib.) Political Power and Elites in the USSR, 1988; Soviet Society under Perestroika, 1990, 2nd edn 1992; (ed and contrib.) Russia in Flux, 1992; (ed and contrib.) Russia in Transition, 1995; The Rise and Fall of State Socialism, 1996, trans. Russian, 2006, Japanese, 2007; (with C. Ross) The Transition from Communism to Capitalism: ruling elites from Gorbachev to Eltsin, 1998; (ed and contrib.) Political Economy of Russian Oil, 1999; (ed and contrib.) The Legacy of State Socialism and the Future of Transformation, 2002; (ed and contrib.) Russian Banking: evolution, problems and prospects, 2002; (ed with M. Myant and contrib.) Varieties of Capitalism in Post-Communist Countries, 2007; (ed and contrib.) The Transformation of State Socialism: system change, capitalism or something else?, 2007; (ed jtly and contrib.) Revolution in the Making of the Modern World, 2007; (ed jtly) Restructuring of Economic Elites after State Socialism: recruitment, institutions and attitudes, 2007; contribs to jls incl. Perspectives on European Politics and Society, Pol Studies, Europe-Asia Studies, Sociology, Jl of Communist Studies and Transition Politics, Comparative Econ. Studies, Eur. Societies, Mir Rossii, Sotsiologicheski Zhurnal, Sotsiologicheskie Issledovaniya, Revue Française de Sci. Politique. *Recreations:* soccer, squash, films, TV. *Address:* Emmanuel College, Cambridge CB2 3AP. *T:* (01223) 359113, *Fax:* (01223) 334426; *e-mail:* dsl10@cam.ac.uk.

LANE, Denis Joseph; Editor in Chief, The Universe, 1994–97; Managing Director and Editor in Chief, Gabriel Communications, 1994–97; *b* 20 Nov. 1960; *s* of Richard and Annie Lane; *m* 1991, Fiona Fahey; one *s* one *d*. *Educ:* University Coll., Cork (BComm). Sen. Auditor, Peat Marwick Mitchell, 1981–83; Gp Accountant, James A. Barry, 1983–87; Manager of Finance, Princeton Gp, 1987–91; Financial Controller, 1991–93, Chief Exec., 1993–94, Gabriel Communications. Member: Grouse Shooting Ground Club, 1994–; British Assoc. for Shooting and Conservation, 1993–. *Recreations:* shooting, fell walking, chess.

LANE, Ian Francis, DM; FRCS, FRCSE; Consultant Vascular Surgeon, University Hospital of Wales, since 1988; Medical Director, Cardiff and Vale NHS Trust, since 1999; *b* 14 May 1952; *s* of Frank Ernest Lane and Teresa Ellen Lane (*née* Wallace); *m* 1980, Carol Myhill Morris; one *s* one *d*. *Educ:* Downside Sch.; Lincoln Coll., Oxford (BA (Physiol.) 1973; BM BCh 1976; MA 1979; DM 1987; MCh 1988); St Thomas' Hosp. Med. Sch. MRCS 1976, FRCS 1981; FRCSE 1981. Lectr in Surgery, Charing Cross and Westminster Med. Sch., 1981–88; Hon. Teacher in Vascular Surgery, Univ. of Wales Coll. of Medicine, 1988–. Mem. Council, Vascular Surgical Soc. of GB and Ireland, 1999–2002; Sec., Venous Forum, RSocMed, 2000–. Mem., Ct of Examrs, RCS, 1995–2001. *Publications:* res. and teaching articles in peer-reviewed jls on aspects of arterial and venous disease. *Recreations:* fine arts, travel to remote areas, exotic cars, wine. *Address:* University Hospital of Wales, Heath Park, Cardiff CF14 4XW. *T:* (029) 2074 4463, *Fax:* (029) 2074 5148; *e-mail:* ian.lane@cardiffandvale.wales.nhs.uk. *Club:* Royal Society of Medicine.

LANE, Jane; *see* Tewson, J.

LANE, John Bristowe; Partner, Linklaters, since 2000; *b* Johannesburg, 18 May 1965; *s* of William and Elizabeth Lane; *m* 1990, Karen Ann Maher; three *s*. *Educ:* St John's Coll., Johannesburg; Univ. of Cape Town (BA 1985; LLB 1987); Trinity Hall, Cambridge (LLM 1991). Qualified as Attorney, Webber Wentzel, Johannesburg, 1989; Linklaters: trainee, 1991–93; admitted Solicitor, 1993; Asst Solicitor, Corporate Dept, London, 1993–99. *Recreations:* walking, cycling, tennis, the Listing Rules. *Address:* Linklaters LLP, One Silk Street, EC2V 8HQ. *T:* (020) 7456 3542, *Fax:* (020) 7456 2222; *e-mail:* john.lane@linklaters.com.

LANE, Rev. John Ernest, OBE 1994; charity consultant; Associate: Craigmyle & Co., 2001–05; Bill Bruty Associates and Fundraising Training Co., since 2001; Director, Corporate Affairs, St Mungo Community Housing Association Ltd, 1996–2001; *b* 16 June 1939; *s* of Ernest William Lane and Winifred (*née* Lloyd); *m* 1st, 1962, Eileen Williams (marr. diss. 1988); three *d*; 2nd, 2001, Ishbel Margaret, *d* of William Curr and Jean (*née* Payne). *Educ:* Burnley Grammar Sch.; Handsworth Coll., Birmingham; City of London Polytechnic (DMS); Cranfield Inst. of Technol. (MSc). Methodist Minister: Llanharan, 1962–64; Great Harwood, 1964–67; Lewisham and Peckham, 1967–72; Dir, Peckham Settlement, 1972–77; Nat. Public Relns Officer, YWCA of GB, 1977–80; Dir and Sec., St Mungo Community Housing Assoc. Ltd, 1980–96; Sec., 1980–96, Dir, 1994–96, St Mungo Assoc. Charitable Trust. Ordained deacon and priest, 1980; Hon. Curate, St John and St Andrew, Peckham, 1980–95; permission to officiate: dio. of Southwark, 1995–98; Lichfield Cathedral, 2002–; NSM, St Alfege with St Peter, Greenwich, 1998–2000. Administrateur, European Fedn of Nat. Orgns Working with the Homeless, 1991–95. Dir, Nat. Sleep Out Week, 1990–94. Trustee, Newton's Trust, 2006. *Publication:* (ed) Homelessness in Industrialised Countries, 1987. *Recreations:* politics, social affairs, cooking, washing up, cricket, travel, arts, persuading Yvonne not to support Arsenal, vetting Vanessa's boyfriends, following Alison around the world, doting on Sophie. *Address:* 2 Tregony Rise, Lichfield, Staffs WS14 9SN. *T:* (01543) 415078.

LANE, Kenneth Frederick; former mining consultant; Director, RTZ Consultants, 1988–97; *b* 22 March 1928; British; *m* 1950, Kathleen Richards; one *s* two *d*. *Educ:* Emmanuel Coll., Cambridge. Degree in Maths. Steel Industry in Sheffield, 1951–59; North America, 1959–61; Rio Tinto-Zinc Corp., 1961–65; Man. Dir, RTZ Consultants Ltd, 1965–70; Dir, RTZ Corp., 1970–75. Vis. Prof., RSM, 1979–85. *Publication:* The Economic Definition of Ore, 1988. *Recreations:* bridge, boat building, sailing. *Address:* 4 Towerdene, 16 Tower Road, Poole, Dorset BH13 6HZ. *T:* (01202) 751958.

LANE, Dr Nancy Jane, OBE 1994; CBiol, FIBiol; FZS; Senior Research Associate, Zoology Department, University of Cambridge, since 1990; Lecturer, since 1970, Fellow, 1970–2006, now Life Fellow, Girton College, Cambridge; *d* of Temple Haviland Lane and Frances de Forest Gilbert Lane; *m* 1969, Prof. Richard Nelson Perham, *qv*; one *s* one *d*. *Educ:* Dalhousie Univ., Nova Scotia (BSc, MSc); Lady Margaret Hall, Oxford (DPhil 1963); Girton Coll., Cambridge (PhD 1968; ScD 1981). CBiol 1991, FIBiol 1991; FZS 1986. Res. Asst Prof., Albert Einstein Coll. of Medicine, NY, 1964–65; Res. Staff Biologist, Yale Univ., 1965–68; University of Cambridge: SSO, 1968–73, PSO, 1973–82, SPSO, 1982–90, AFRC Unit, Zoology Dept; Tutor, Girton Coll., 1975–98; Project Dir, Women in Science, Engrg and Technology Initiative, 1999–2006. Editor-in-Chief, Cell Biol. Internat., 1995–98; Chm., Editl Cttee, Science and Public Affairs, 2001–. Vis. Lectr, British Council, 1999–2004. Non-executive Director: Smith & Nephew plc, 1991–2000; Peptide Therapeutics plc, 1995–98. Mem., PM's Adv. Panel for Citizen's Charter, 1991–93; Chairman: BTEC's Adv. Bd for Sci. and Caring, 1991–94; Wkg Party for Women in Sci. and Engrg (OST), Cabinet Office, 1993–94. Member: Forum UK, 1994–; All Souls Gp, Oxford, 1994–2005; CVCP's Commn on Univ. Career Opportunities (CUCO), 1996–2000; UNESCO's Sci. Cttee for Women, Sci. and Technol., 1997–; Scientific, Engrg and Envmt Adv. Cttee, British Council, 2003–07; Dep. Chm., Steering Cttee for CUCO/OST/HEFCE Athena Project, 1998–2003; UNESCO Cttee for Natural Scis, 2005–. Chm., Athena Project, 2003–07. Dir, Women of the Year Lunch and Assembly, 1997–2004; Partner, UK Resource Centre for Women in Sci., DTI, 2004–; Chm., UK Resource Centre Experts Database, 2005–07. Pres., Inst. of Biology, 2002–04; Member: Council, Zool Soc. of London, 1998–2001 (Vice-Pres., 1999–2001); Brit. Soc. Cell Biol., 1980– (Sec., 1982–90); Exec. Council, Biosciences Fedn, 2002–06. Co-author, SET Fair, Greenfield Report, 2002. FRSA 1992; MInstD 1991. Hon. Fellow, BAAS, 2005. Hon. LLD Dalhousie, 1985; Hon. ScD: Salford, 1994; Sheffield Hallam, 2002; Oxford Brookes, 2003; Surrey, 2005. Elected to Nova Scotia Hall of Fame for Sci. and Technology, 2006. *Publications:* contrib. numerous scientific papers and chapters on cell-cell junctions, cellular structures and interactions, in field of cell biology, in a range of learned scientific jls. *Recreations:* theatre and opera, 20th century art, travelling. *Address:* Department of Zoology, University of Cambridge, Downing Street, Cambridge CB2 3EJ. *T:* (01223) 330116/336600/363710, *Fax:* (01223) 330116/336676; *e-mail:* njl1@cam.ac.uk. *Club:* Oxford and Cambridge.

LANE, Peter Alfred; artist potter and author; *b* 26 April 1932; *s* of late Alfred John Lane and Freda Margaret Lane; *m* 1958, Margaret Jean Edwards; two *d*. *Educ:* Bath Acad. of Art (Art Teacher's Cert.); Cert Ed Bristol 1956. Art teacher: Botley Co. (All-Age) Sch., Berks, 1956–58; Head, Art Department: Matthew Arnold Secondary Sch., Cumnor, Berks, 1958–60; Andover GS, 1961–64; Lectr/Organiser, Somerset Coll. of Art, Taunton, 1964–66; Keswick Hall College of Education, Norwich: Lectr in Art Educn and Ceramics, 1966–70; Sen. Lectr, 1970–80; Hd, Art Dept, 1980–81; University of E Anglia: Sen. Lectr and Hd, Dept of Art Educn and Ceramics, 1981–84; Sen. Fellow in Art Educn, 1984–87. Examr/Assessor at various art colls, 1980–88. Judge, international ceramics exhibitions: 2nd Biennale Canadian Ceramics, 1986; Fletcher Challenge Ceramics Award, NZ, 1989; 1st Taiwan Ceramics Biennale, 2004; Zelli Porcelain Award, 2005. Has exhibited, lectured and demonstrated ceramics widely throughout the world; individual ceramics in many public collections in UK, Australia, Canada, Europe, Korea, USA. Co-founder, Norfolk Contemporary Crafts Soc., 1971. Fellow: Craft Potters' Assoc. of GB, 1962 (Hon. Fellow 2004); Soc. of Designer Craftsmen, 1976. Mem., Internat. Acad. Ceramics, Geneva, 1997. Centennial Silver Medal, Soc. Designer Craftsmen, 1981. *Publications:* Studio Porcelain, 1980; Studio Ceramics, 1983; Ceramic Form, 1988, new enlarged edn 1998; (consultant ed and contrib.) Ceramics Manual, 1990; Contemporary Porcelain, 1995; Contemporary Studio Porcelain, 2003; contrib. numerous mag. articles on ceramics. *Recreations:* fell-walking, painting, photography, foreign travel, theatre. *Address:* Ivy House, Jacklyns Lane, Alresford, Hants SO24 9LG; *e-mail:* peter@studio-porcelain.co.uk.

LANE, Peter Richard; a Senior Immigration Judge, Asylum and Immigration Tribunal (formerly a Vice President, Immigration Appeal Tribunal), since 2003; Legal Member, Special Immigration Appeals Commission, since 2005; *b* 26 April 1953; *s* of Frank and June Lane; *m* 1980, Shelley Munjack; one *s* one *d*. *Educ:* St Stephen's Primary Sch., Worcester; Worcester Royal Grammar Sch.; Hertford Coll., Oxford (BA 1st cl. (Jurisprudence) 1974); Univ. of Calif, Berkeley (LLM 1975). Called to the Bar, Middle Temple, 1976; re-qualified as Solicitor, 1985. In practice at Bar, 1977–80; Lectr in Laws, QMC, 1978–80; Asst Parly Counsel, 1980–85; Solicitor and Parly Agent, 1985–2001, Partner, 1987–2001, Rees & Freres; Immigration Adjudicator, pt-time, 1996–2001, full-time, 2001–03. *Publications:* (jtly) Blackstone's Guide to the Transport and Works Act 1992, 1992; (jtly) Blackstone's Guide to the Environment Act 1995, 1995; (contrib.)

Douglas & Geen on the Law of Harbours, Coasts and Pilotage, 5th edn 1997; articles on, and reviews of, film music. *Recreations:* hill-walking, opera, American and British film music 1930–1975. *Address:* Asylum and Immigration Tribunal, Field House, 15 Bream's Buildings, EC4A 1DZ. *T:* (020) 7073 4085; *e-mail:* peter.lane@judiciary.gsi.gov.uk.

LANE, Dr Richard Paul; Director of Science, Natural History Museum, since 2003; *b* 16 May 1951; *s* of Alfred George Lane and Patricia Ann Lane (*née* Trotter); *m* 1972, Maureen Anne Grogan; two *s* one *d. Educ:* Imperial Coll., Univ. of London (BSc, ARCS, DIC, PhD). Dept of Entomology, British Museum (Natural History), 1974–85, Head of Med. Insects Sect., 1983–85; Sen. Lectr, LSHTM, Univ. of London, 1985–92, Head of Vector Biology and Transmission Dynamics Unit, 1989–92; Keeper of Entomology, Natural History Mus., 1992–97; Internat. Prog. Dir, Wellcome Trust, 1997–2004. Vis. Prof., Imperial Coll., London, 2005–. Member: Council, RSTM&H, 1985–89, 1999–; Biological Council, 1985–89; Wellcome Trust Panels, 1986–97; Expert Adv. Panel on Parasitic Diseases, WHO, 1988–; Steering Cttee on Leishmaniasis, WHO, 1988–93; Bd of Trustees, Biosis, Philadelphia, 1993–98; Exec. Cttee, Consortium for Barcode of Life, 2005–. Royal Entomological Society: Mem. Council, 1980–83, 1989–92; Vice-Pres., 1991–92; Pres., 1994–96. Mem. Council, Internat. Congress of Entomology, 1992–2008. Trustee, Against Malaria Foundn, 2004–. *Publications:* (ed jtly) Medical Insects and Arachnids, 1993; papers on insects of medical importance in sci. jls, esp. on sandflies and transmission of leishmaniasis. *Recreation:* sailing. *Address:* Natural History Museum, Cromwell Road, SW7 5BD.

LANE, Maj.-Gen. Roger Guy Tyson, CBE 2003 (OBE 1994); Managing Director, Roger Lane Consulting Ltd, since 2007; Deputy Commander Operations, Headquarters International Security Assistance Force, Kabul, 2005–06; *b* 23 Feb. 1954; *s* of Capt. and Mrs M. E. Lane; *m* 1981, Nichola J. Redrobe; one *s* one *d. Educ:* Christ's Hospital, Horsham. Joined RM, 1972; OC, HMS Zulu, 1977–79; Intelligence Security Gp, NI, 1979–80 (despatches); Adjutant, 1982–84; Canadian Comd and Staff Coll., 1985–86; Co. Comdr 42 Commando, 1988–90 (despatches 1990); SO G2 NI Ops Policy, MoD, 1991–94; RM Rep., US Marine Corps Combat and Develt Comd, USA, 1994–96; CO 42 Commando, 1996–98; CSO Ops HQ RM, 1998–99; rcds, 2000; HCSC, 2001; Comdr 3 Commando Bde, 2001–02; Dir, HCSC, 2002–03; Dep. Comdr, HQ NATO Rapid Deployable Corps, Italy, 2003–06. FCMI. Bronze Star, USA, 2002; Commendatore, Order of Merit (Italy), 2006; Baryal Medal, 1st Grade (Afghanistan), 2007. *Publications:* articles on NATO, leadership and stabilisation. *Recreations:* ski-ing, sailing, gardening, fly fishing, genealogy, writing.

LANE FOX, Robin James, FRSL; Fellow, since 1977, and Garden Master, since 1981, New College, Oxford; Reader in Ancient History, Oxford, since 1990; *b* 5 Oct. 1946; *s* of James Henry Lane Fox and Anne (*née* Loyd); *m* 1970, Louisa Caroline Mary (marr. diss. 1993), *d* of Charles and Lady Katherine Farrell; one *s* one *d. Educ:* Eton; Magdalen Coll., Oxford (Craven and de Paravicini scholarships, 1966; Passmore Edwards and Chancellors' Latin Verse Prize, 1968). FRSL 1974. Fellow by examination, Magdalen Coll., Oxford, 1970–73; Lectr in Classical Lang. and Lit., 1973–76, Res. Fellow, Classical and Islamic Studies, 1976–77, Worcester Coll., Oxford; Lectr in Ancient Hist., Oxford Univ., 1977–90. Weekly gardening correspondent, Financial Times, 1970–. *Publications:* Alexander the Great, 1973, 3rd edn 1978 (James Tait Black, Duff Cooper, W. H. Heinemann Awards, 1973–74); Variations on a Garden, 1974, rev. edn 1986; Search for Alexander, 1980; Better Gardening, 1982; Pagans and Christians, 1986; The Unauthorized Version, 1991; The Making of 'Alexander', 2004; (ed and contrib.) The Long March: Xenophon and the Ten Thousand, 2004; The Classical World: an epic history from Homer to Hadrian, 2005 (Runciman prize, 2006); Travelling Heroes: Greeks and their myths in the epic age of Homer, 2008. *Recreations:* gardening, remembering fox-hunting. *Address:* New College, Oxford OX1 3BN. *Club:* Beefsteak.

LANE-FOX-PITT-RIVERS, Valerie; *see* Pitt-Rivers, V.

LANE-NOTT, Rear Adm. Roger Charles, CB 1996; Director General and Chief Executive Officer, Agricultural Engineers Association, since 2007; *b* 3 June 1945; *s* of John Henry Lane-Nott, MBE and Kathleen Mary Lane-Nott; *m* 1968, Roisin MacQuillan; one *s* two *d. Educ:* Pangbourne Coll.; BRNC, Dartmouth. Joined RN, 1963: qualified submarines, 1966; served in HM Submarines: Andrew, Opossum, Otus, Revenge (Starboard), Conqueror, Aeneas, 1966–74; commanded HM Submarines: Walrus, 1974–76; Swiftsure, 1979; Splendid, 1979–82 (mentioned in despatches, Falklands, 1982); US Naval War Coll., 1983; Captain SM, Third Submarine Sqdn, 1985–86; Asst Dir, Defence Concepts, MoD, 1986–89; RCDS 1989; Captain First Frigate Sqdn and in comd HMS Coventry, 1990–91; Sen. Naval Officer, ME, 1991; Chief of Staff to Flag Officer Submarines, 1992–93; Flag Officer Submarines, and Comdr Submarines (NATO), Eastern Atlantic and Northwest, 1993–96; COS (Ops) to C-in-C Fleet, 1994–96; RN retd, 1996. Formula One Race Dir and Safety Delegate, Fédn Internat. de l'Automobile, 1996–97; Chief Exec., Centre for Marine and Petroleum Technol., 1997–99; Sec., British Racing Drivers' Club, 1999–2007. MRIN 1976; MNI 1991; FCMI (FIMgt 1983); MInstPet 1997. *Recreations:* watching sport (Rugby, cricket, motor racing), unusual stationery. *Address:* AEA, Samuelson House, Paxton Road, Peterborough PE2 5LT.

LANE-SMITH, Roger; Senior Partner, DLA (formerly Dibb Lupton Alsop), Solicitors, 1998–2005; Senior Consultant, DLA Piper, since 2005; *b* 19 Oct. 1945; *s* of Harry Lane-Smith and Dorothy Lane-Smith; *m* 1969, Pamela; one *s* one *d. Educ:* Stockport Grammar Sch.; Guildford Coll. of Law. Admitted Solicitor, 1969; founded Lee Lane-Smith, 1977; Lee Lane-Smith merged with Alsop Stevens, 1983; Alsop Stevens merged with Wilkinson Kimbers to form Alsop Wilkinson, 1988; Chm. and Sen. Partner, Alsop Wilkinson, 1993–96; Alsop Wilkinson merged with Dibb Lupton to form Dibb Lupton Alsop, 1996; Dep. Sen. Partner, Dibb Lupton Alsop, 1996–98. Non-exec. Dir, JJB Sports, 1998– (Chm., 2005–). *Recreations:* golf, tennis, shooting. *Address:* (office) 3 Noble Street, EC2V 7EE. *T:* (020) 7796 6090. *Clubs:* Mark's; St James' (Manchester).

LANG, family name of **Baron Lang of Monkton**.

LANG OF MONKTON, Baron *cr* 1997 (Life Peer), of Merrick and the Rhinns of Kells in Dumfries and Galloway; **Ian Bruce Lang;** PC 1990; DL; company chairman and director; *b* 27 June 1940; *y s* of late James Fulton Lang, DSC, and of Maude Margaret (*née* Stewart); *m* 1971, Sandra Caroline *e d* of late John Alastair Montgomerie, DSC; two *d. Educ:* Lathallan Sch., Kincardineshire; Rugby Sch.; Sidney Sussex Coll., Cambridge (BA 1962). Insurance Broker, 1962–79. Chairman: Thistle Mining Inc. (Can.), 1998–; China Internet Ventures Ltd, 2000–; US Special Opportunities (formerly BFS US Special Opportunities) Trust plc, 2001–08; Second Scottish Nat. Trust plc, 2002–04 (Dir, 1997–2002); Director: CGU (formerly General Accident) plc, 1997–2000; Marsh & McLennan Cos Inc., 1997–; Lithgows Ltd, 1997–; Automobile Assoc., 1998–99; Charlemagne Capital Ltd, 2006–. Trustee: Savings Bank of Glasgow, 1969–74; West of Scotland Trustee Savings Bank, 1974–83. Member, Queen's Body Guard for Scotland (Royal Company of Archers), 1974–. Contested (C): Central Ayrshire, 1970; Glasgow Pollok, Feb. 1974; MP (C) Galloway, 1979–83, Galloway and Upper Nithsdale, 1983–97;

contested (C) Galloway and Upper Nithsdale, 1997. An Asst Govt Whip, 1981–83; a Lord Comr of HM Treasury, 1983–86; Parliamentary Under Secretary of State: Dept of Employment, 1986; Scottish Office, 1986–87; Minister of State, Scottish Office, 1987–90; Sec. of State for Scotland and Lord Keeper of the Great Seal of Scotland, 1990–95; Pres., Board of Trade, and Sec. of State for Trade and Industry, 1995–97. Mem., Constitution Cttee, H of L, 2001–05. Chm., Patrons of Nat. Galls of Scotland, 1999–2007. Gov., Rugby Sch., 1997–2007. DL Ayrshire and Arran, 1998. OStJ 1974. *Publication:* Blue Remembered Years, 2002. *Address:* House of Lords, SW1A 0PW. *Clubs:* Athenæum, Pratt's; Prestwick Golf.

LANG, Alistair Laurie, MBE 1970; Chief Executive, Drugs Abuse Resistance Education (DARE) UK Ltd, 2002–05; *b* 9 Sept. 1943; *s* of late Comdr John Robert Lang, RN (retd) and Jennifer Douglas Lang; *m* 1979, Ilona Augusta Avery; one *s* one *d. Educ:* Hurstpierpoint Coll.; BRNC; University Coll., Oxford (BA 1979); Internat. Management Inst., Geneva (MBA 1989). Served Royal Navy, 1962–75: in HM Ships Wizard, Salisbury, Devonshire, Malcolm, Plymouth and Kent; loan service to: Kenya Navy (Kenya Navy Ship Chui), 1966; Royal Malaysian Navy (i/c Kapel di-Raja Sri Sarawak and Fleet Ops Officer), 1968–70; Imperial Iranian Navy, 1974. Hong Kong Civil Service, 1979–90: Asst Sec. for Security, 1980–82; City Dist Officer, Kowloon City, 1982–83; support to Governor during negotiation with China on future of Hong Kong, 1983–85; Clerk of Councils (Sec. to Exec. and Legislative Councils), 1985–88; attached British Embassy, Beijing (on secondment), 1989; UK Rep., Hong Kong Exec. and Legislative Councils, 1990–92. Clerk to Drapers' Co., 1993–2000; Chief Exec., Canine Partners for Independence, 2000–02. *Recreations:* swimming, walking, reading, theatre. *Address:* Little Mead, Home Lane, Sparsholt, Winchester, Hants SO21 2NN. *T:* (01962) 776204.
See also Rear-Adm. J. S. Lang.

LANG, Beverley Ann Macnaughton; QC 2000; a Recorder, since 2006; *b* 13 Oct. 1955; *d* of William Macnaughton Lang and Joan Margaret Mantua Lang (*née* Utting); one *d. Educ:* Wycombe Abbey Sch., Bucks; Lady Margaret Hall, Oxford (BA Hons Jurisprudence 1977). Called to the Bar, Inner Temple, 1978, Bencher, 2006; Lectr, UEA, 1978–81; in practice at the Bar, 1981–; Chairman (part-time): Employment Tribunals, 1995–2001; Special Educnl Needs and Disability Tribunal, 2004–. *Address:* Blackstone Chambers, Blackstone House, Temple, EC4Y 9BW. *T:* (020) 7583 1770.

LANG, Dr Brian Andrew; Principal and Vice-Chancellor, University of St Andrews, 2001–08; *b* 2 Dec. 1945; *s* of Andrew Ballantyne Lang and Mary Bain Lang (*née* Smith); *m* 1st, 1975 (marr. diss. 1982); one *s*; 2nd, 1983 (marr. diss. 2000); one *s* one *d*; 3rd, 2002, Tari Hibbitt, *d* of late Suwondo and of Carmel Budiardjo. *Educ:* Royal High Sch., Edinburgh; Univ. of Edinburgh (MA, PhD). Social anthropological field research, Kenya, 1969–70; Lectr in social anthropology, Aarhus Univ., 1971–75; Scientific Staff, SSRC, 1976–79; Scottish Office (Sec., Historic Buildings Council for Scotland), 1979–80; Sec., Nat. Heritage Meml Fund, 1980–87; Dir of Public Affairs, Nat. Trust, 1987–91; Chief Exec. and Dep. Chm., British Library, 1991–2000; Chairman: Eur. Nat. Libraries Forum, 1993–2000; Heritage Image Partnership (formerly Nat. Heritage Image Liby), 2000–02. Member: Bd, Scottish Enterprise, Fife, 2003–08; Scottish Exec. Cultural Commn, 2004–05; Cttee for Scotland, Heritage Lottery Fund, 2004– (Chair, 2005–). Member: Liby and Inf. Services Council (England), 1991–94; Liby and Inf. Commn, 1995–2000. Vis. Prof., Napier Univ., Edin., 1999–; Vis. Scholar, Getty Inst., Calif, 2000. Pforzheimer Lecture, Univ. of Texas, 1998. Trustee: 21st Century Learning Initiative, 1995–99; Hopetoun House Preservation Trust, 2001–05; Nat. Heritage Meml Fund, 2005–. Chm. Trustees, Newbattle Abbey Coll., 2004–08. Member, Council: Nat. Trust for Scotland, 2001–04; St Leonard's Sch., 2001–08. Pres., Inst. of Information Scientists, 1993–94 (Hon. Fellow, 1994). FRSE 2006. Hon. FCLIP (Hon. FLA 1997). Dr *hc* Edinburgh, 2008. *Publications:* numerous articles, contribs etc to professional jls. *Recreations:* music, museums and galleries, pottering. *Address:* 10 Carlton Terrace, Edinburgh EH7 5DD. *Clubs:* Caledonian; New (Edinburgh); Royal & Ancient (St Andrews).

LANG, David Geoffrey, CMG 2007; CBE 1992; QC (Turks and Caicos) 1985; Attorney General, Falkland Islands, 1987–2006; *b* Scarborough, 4 Nov. 1941; *s* of Alexander and Nora Lang; *m* 1975, Theresa Margaret Hurt; one *s* three *d. Educ:* St Edmund's Sch., Canterbury; College of Law, London. Admitted solicitor, 1965; Asst Solicitor, Bognor Regis UDC, 1965–68; Partner, Wintle & Co. Solicitors, Bognor Regis, 1968–69; Asst Solicitor, 1969–71, Partner, 1971–76, Hedges & Mercer Solicitors, Oxon. Sec. for Justice, Rep. of Nauru, 1977–82; Attorney General, Turks and Caicos Is, 1982–87. *Recreations:* bridge, computer strategy games, science fiction, amateur dramatics. *Address:* 28 Goss Road, Stanley, Falkland Islands FIQQ 1ZZ.

LANG, Rt Rev. Declan; *see* Clifton, Bishop of, (RC).

LANG, Hugh Montgomerie, CBE 1978; Chairman, Acertec Holdings Ltd, 1999–2006; *b* Glasgow, 7 Nov. 1932; *s* of John Montgomerie Lang and Janet Allan (*née* Smillie); *m* 1st, 1959, Marjorie Jean Armour (marr. diss. 1981); one *s* one *d*; 2nd, 1981, Susan Lynn Hartley (*née* Russell). *Educ:* Shawlands Acad., Glasgow; Glasgow Univ. (BSc). ARCST 1953; CEng 1967; FIET (FIProdE 1976); FIMC 1970. Officer, REME, 1953–55 (National Service). Colvilles Ltd, 1955–56; Glacier Metal Co. Ltd, 1956–60; L. Sterne & Co. Ltd, 1960–61; P-E Consulting Group, 1961–92: Manager for ME, 1965–68; Scottish Reg. Manager, 1968–72; Man. Dir, 1974–77; Chm., P-E Internat., 1980–92 (Dir, 1972–92); Chief Exec., 1977–92). Chairman: Brammer plc, 1990–98; Manganese Bronze Hldgs, 1992–2000; Victaulic, 1995; Albion Automotive, 1997–98; Director: Redman Heenan Internat., 1981–86 (Chm., 1982–86); Fairey Holdings Ltd, 1978–82; UKO International, 1985–86; B. Elliott, 1986–88; Siebe, 1987–91; Strong & Fisher (Hldgs), 1988–90; Co-ordinated Land and Estates, 1988–93; OGC International, 1993–94; Ericsson Ltd, 1993–99. Chairman: Food, Drink and Packaging Machinery Sector Working Party, 1976–81; Technology Transfer Services Adv. Cttee, 1982–85 (Mem., 1978–85); Member: Business Educn Council, 1980–81; CBI Industrial Policy Cttee, 1980–83; Design Council, 1983–90 (Dep. Chm., 1986–90); Engrg Council, 1984–86. *Recreations:* fishing, gardening, golf, reading, walking. *Address:* Welders Wood, Chalfont St Peter, Bucks SL9 8TT. *Club:* Denham Golf.

LANG, Jack Mathieu Emile, Chevalier de la Légion d'Honneur; Hon. GCVO 1992; Deputy (Soc.) for Pas de Calais, National Assembly, France, since 2002; *b* 2 Sept. 1939; *s* of Roger Lang and Marie-Luce Lang (*née* Bouchet); *m* 1961, Monique Buczynski; two *d. Educ:* Inst. d'Etudes Politiques; Dr of Public Law. Founder and Producer, World Fest. Univ. Theatre, Nancy, 1963–72; Dir, Nancy Univ. Theatre, 1963–72; Dir, Palais de Chaillot Théâtre, 1972–74; Prof. of Internat. Law, 1971–81; Dir, teaching and research unit in legal and econ. scis, Nancy, 1977–80; Prof., Univ. of Paris X, 1986–88. Paris councillor, 1977–89; nat. deleg. for cultural affairs, Socialist Party, 1979–81; Minister of Culture, 1981–83 and 1984–86; Deputy, Loir-et-Cher, 1986–88 and 1997–2000; Minister of Culture and Communication, 1988–92; Govt Spokesman, 1991–92; Minister of State, and Minister of Nat. Educn and Culture, 1992–93; Minister for Educn, 2000–02. Pres., Foreign Affairs Cttee, French Nat. Assembly, 1997–2000. Mayor of Blois, 1989–2001; Conseiller Général de Blois, 1992–93. Order of Orange Nassau

(Netherlands), 1991; Order of the Crown of Belgium, 1992. *Publications:* L'Etat et le Théâtre, 1968; Le plâteau continental de la mer du nord, 1970; Les politiques culturelles comparée en Europe; La jonction au fond des exceptions préliminaires devant la cour, 1971; Demain les femmes, 1995; Lettre à Malraux, 1996; François 1er ou le rêve italien, 1997; contribs to newspapers. *Address:* Assemblée Nationale, 126 rue de l'Université, 75355 Paris Cedex 07 SP, France.

LANG, Jacqueline Shelagh; Headmistress, Walthamstow Hall, Sevenoaks, 1984–2002; *b* 17 June 1944; *d* of James Wicks and Mary Mills Wicks (*née* Green); *m* 1965, Andrew Lang; two *d*. *Educ:* Walthamstow Hall; St Anne's Coll., Oxford (Schol.; MA). Res., mediaeval French literature, KCL, 1964–66; Ursuline Convent School, Wimbledon: Asst Mistress, 1970–76; Head of Langs, 1976–83; Foundn Gov., 1984–93. Chairman: London and SE Region, ISIS, 1991–95; Assisted Places Cttee, ISC, 1998–2002; Pres., GSA, 1997. *Recreations:* history of architecture, gardens, visiting archaeological sites. *Address:* 82 Richmond Road, SW20 0PD.

LANG, Very Rev. John Harley; Dean of Lichfield, 1980–93, now Emeritus; Chaplain to HM the Queen, 1976–80; Member, Broadcasting Standards Commission, 1997–98 (Broadcasting Standards Council, 1994–97); *b* 27 Oct. 1927; *e s* of Frederick Henry Lang and Eileen Annie Lang (*née* Harley); *m* 1972, Frances Rosemary Widdowson; three *d*. *Educ:* Merchant Taylors' Sch.; King's Coll., London (BD); MA Cantab; MST Oxon 1999; LRAM. Subaltern, XII Royal Lancers, 1951–52; Asst Curate, St Mary's Portsea, 1952–57; Priest Vicar, Southwark Cathedral, 1957–60; Chaplain, Emmanuel Coll., Cambridge, 1960–64; Asst Head of Religious Broadcasting, BBC, 1964–67; Head of Religious Programmes, Radio, 1967–71; Head of Religious Broadcasting, BBC, 1971–80. Mem., English Heritage Cathedrals and Churches Adv. Cttee, 1994–99. Trustee, Historic Churches Preservation Trust, 1994–2000. President: Staffordshire Soc., 1993–95; Lichfield Festival, 1994–2006. Mem., Kellogg Coll., Oxford, 1997–. Freeman, Goldsmiths' Co., 1994. Hon. DLitt Keele, 1988. *Recreations:* books, music.

LANG, Rear-Adm. John Stewart, FNI, FRIN; DL; Royal Navy, retired; Chief Inspector of Marine Accidents, Marine Accident Investigation Branch, Department for Transport, Local Government and the Regions (formerly Department of Transport, then Department of the Environment, Transport and the Regions), 1997–2002; *b* 18 July 1941; *s* of late Comdr John Robert Lang, RN and Jennifer Douglas Lang; *m* 1971, Joanna Judith Pegler; two *d*. *Educ:* Cheltenham Coll. Jun. Sch.; Nautical Coll., Pangbourne. FNI 1986; FRIN 1997. Navigating Officer Apprentice, P&OSN Co., 1959–62; RN 1962; served HM Ships Chilcompton, Totem, Auriga, Oberon, Revenge, Opossum, 1964–71; qualified Submarine Command, 1971; commanded: HMS Walrus, 1971–72; HMS Renown, 1976–78; HMS Beaver, 1983–85; Captain, Royal Naval Presentation Team, 1986–87; ACOS (Ops) to C-in-C Fleet, 1987–89; Dir, Naval Ops and Trade, 1989–91; Dep. Chief of Defence Intelligence, 1992–95. Chm., EC Marine Accident Investigation Wkg Gp, 2004–06. President: Inst. of Seamanship, 2001–; Assoc. of Sea Trng Orgns, 2003–; Winchester Sea Cadets TS Itchen, 2003–. Mem. Council, RNLI, 2006–; Patron, Sea Safety Gp, 2002–04; Trustee: Shipwrecked Mariners Soc., 2003– (Chm., 2008–); Royal Nat. Mission to Deep Sea Fishermen, 2003–; Trustee Dir, Nautilus UK (formerly NUMAST), 2003–. Younger Brother, Trinity House, 1982–. Gov., Southampton Solent Univ. (formerly Southampton Inst.), 2004–. DL Hants, 2008. Hon. DTech Nottingham Trent, 2002. *Recreations:* sailing, photography, oil painting, pharology, writing. *Address:* Wangfield House, Martyr Worthy, Winchester, Hants SO21 1AT.

See also A. L. Lang.

LANGAN, Peter St John Hevey; QC 1983; **His Honour Judge Langan;** a Circuit Judge, since 1991; Specialist Mercantile Circuit Judge, North Eastern Circuit, since 2004; *b* 1 May 1942; *s* of late Frederick Hevey Langan and Myrrha Langan (*née* Jephson), Mount Hevey, Hill of Down, Co. Meath; *m* 1st, 1976, Oonagh May Winifred McCarthy (marr. diss.); 2nd, 2003, Alison Felicity Tuffnell; one step *d*. *Educ:* Downside School; Trinity College, Dublin (MA, LLB); Christ's College, Cambridge (PhD). Lectr in Law, Durham Univ., 1966–69. In practice at the Bar, 1970–91; a Recorder, 1989–91; Designated Civil Judge, Norwich and Cambridge, 1998–2001; Mercantile and Chancery Judge, NE Circuit, 2001–04. Legal Assessor: GMC, 1990–91; GDC, 1990–91. Mem., Legal Commn, Caritas Internationalis, Rome, 1991–93; Trustee, CAFOD, 1993–99 (Mem., Management Cttee, 1984–91). *Publications:* Maxwell on Interpretation of Statutes, 12th edn 1969; Civil Procedure and Evidence, 1st edn 1970, 3rd edn (with L. D. J. Henderson) as Civil Procedure, 1983; (with P. V. Baker) Snell's Principles of Equity, 28th edn 1982, 29th edn 1990. *Address:* The Court House, 1 Oxford Row, Leeds LS1 3BG. *T:* (0113) 283 0040.

LANGDALE, Simon John Bartholomew; Director of Grants and Special Projects (formerly Educational and General Grants), The Rank Foundation, 1988–2002; *b* 26 Jan. 1937; *s* of late Geoffrey Ronald Langdale and Hilda Joan Langdale (*née* Bartholomew); *m* 1962, Diana Marjory Hall; two *s* one *d*. *Educ:* Tonbridge Sch.; St Catharine's Coll., Cambridge. Taught at Radley Coll., 1959–73 (Housemaster, 1968–73); Headmaster: Eastbourne Coll., 1973–80; Shrewsbury Sch., 1981–88. *Recreations:* reading, gardening, golf. *Address:* Park House, Culworth, Banbury, Oxon OX17 2AP. *T:* (01295) 760222. *Clubs:* Hawks (Cambridge); Free Foresters, Jesters.

See also T. J. Langdale.

LANGDALE, Timothy James; QC 1992; a Recorder, 1996–99; *b* 3 Jan. 1940; *m* twice; two *d*; *m* 3rd, 2001, Susan Smith (*née* Hare). *Educ:* Sevenoaks Sch.; St Andrews Univ. (MA). Called to the Bar, Lincoln's Inn, 1966. Res. Assistant, Community Justice Center, Watts, Los Angeles, 1969–70; Jun. Prosecuting Counsel to the Crown, 1979–87, Sen. Prosecuting Counsel, 1987–92, CCC. Appeal Steward, BBB of C. *Recreations:* reading, the arts. *Address:* Cloth Fair Chambers, 39–40 Cloth Fair, EC1A 7NT. *T:* (020) 7710 6444.

See also S. J. B. Langdale.

LANGDON, Andrew Dominic; QC 2006; a Recorder, since 2002; *b* 23 July 1963; *s* of Michael and Phillipa Langdon; *m* 1989, Caroline; one *s* three *d*. *Educ:* Bristol Univ. (LLB). Called to the Bar, Middle Temple, 1986. *Recreations:* music, tennis, water-sports. *Address:* Guildhall Chambers, Broad Street, Bristol BS1 2HG. *T:* (0117) 927 3366; *e-mail:* andrew.langdon@guildhallchambers.co.uk.

LANGDON, Anthony James; Deputy Under Secretary of State, Home Office, 1989–95; *b* 5 June 1935; *s* of Dr James Norman Langdon and Maud Winifred Langdon; *m* 1969, Helen Josephine Drabble, *y d* of His Honour J. F. Drabble, QC; one *s* one *d*. *Educ:* Kingswood Sch., Bath; Christ's Coll., Cambridge. Entered Home Office, 1958; Office of Minister for Science, 1961–63; Treasury, 1967–69; Under Sec., Cabinet Office, 1985–89. *Publication:* (with Ian Dunbar) Tough Justice, 1998.

LANGDON, David, OBE 1988; FRSA; cartoonist, illustrator and caricaturist; contributor to Punch, since 1937, The New Yorker, since 1952, and The Spectator, since 1997; *b* 24 Feb. 1914; *er s* of late Bennett and Bess Langdon; *m* 1955, April Sadler-Phillips; two *s* one *d*. *Educ:* Davenant Gram. Sch., London. Architect's Dept, LCC, 1931–39; Executive Officer, London Rescue Service, 1939–41; served in Royal Air Force, 1941–46; Squadron Leader, 1945. Editor, Royal Air Force Jl, 1945–46. Creator of Billy Brown of London Town for LPTB. Official Artist to Centre International Audio-Visuel d'Etudes et de Recherches, St Ghislain, Belgium, 1970–75. Cartoonist to Sunday Mirror, 1948–93. Caricatures: of High Court Judges for Sweet and Maxwell, 1956; of racing celebrities for Ladbrokes Racing Calendar, 1959–94. Exhibitions: Ottawa, Oxford, New York, Lille, London. Lifetime Achievement Award, Cartoon Art Trust, 2001. *Publications:* Home Front Lines, 1941; All Buttoned Up, 1944; Meet Me Inside, 1946; Slipstream (with R. B. Raymond), 1946; The Way I See It, 1947; Hold Tight There!, 1949; Let's Face It, 1951; Wake Up and Die (with David Clayton), 1952; Look at You, 1952; All in Fun, 1953; Laugh with Me, 1954; More in Fun, 1955; Funnier Still, 1956; A Banger for a Monkey, 1957; Langdon At Large, 1958; I'm Only Joking, 1960; Punch with Wings, 1961; How to Play Golf and Stay Happy, 1964; David Langdon's Casebook, 1969; How To Talk Golf, 1975; Punch in the Air, 1983; Soccer—It's a Funny Old Game, 1998. *Recreation:* golf. *Address:* 4 Oaklands Court, Chesham Road, Amersham, Bucks HP6 5ES. *T:* (01494) 432545. *Club:* Royal Air Force.

LANGDON, Janet Mary; Director and Secretary, Water Services Association of England and Wales, 1992–98; *b* 5 March 1940; *d* of late Geoffrey Harry Langdon and Iris Sarah Langdon. *Educ:* St Hilda's Coll., Oxford (BSc, MA). Asst Lectr, Wellesley Coll., Mass, 1962–63; Distillers' Co. Ltd, 1963–68; NEDO, 1968–71; Shell Chemicals UK Ltd and Shell Internat. Chemical Co. Ltd, 1971–82; Projects and Export Policy Div., DTI, 1982–85; Director: Asia, Gp Exports, GEC PLC, 1985–89; Export Div., GEC ALSTHOM Ltd, 1989–92. Member: Sch. Teachers' Rev. Body, 1996–2002; POUNC, 1998–2000. *Recreations:* walking, tennis, travel, theatre. *Address:* 43 Fairfax Place, NW6 4EJ. *T:* (020) 7624 3857.

LANGDON, Prof. John Dudley, FDSRCS, FRCSE, FMedSci; Professor of Oral and Maxillofacial Surgery, King's College London, 1992–2004; *b* 24 March 1942; *s* of Jack Langdon and Daphne Irene Heloise Liebsch. *Educ:* London Hosp. Med. Coll., Univ. of London (BDS, MB BS, MDS). LDSRCS 1965, FDSRCS 1971; FRCSE 1985. Sen. Lectr in Oral and Maxillofacial Surgery, KCL, 1983–92; Consultant Oral and Maxillofacial Surgeon, Queen Mary's Hosp., Roehampton and Ashford Gen. Hosp., Middx, 1977–83; Hon. Consultant: St George's Hosp., 1984–2000; Royal Surrey Co. Hosp., Guildford, 1993–2003; Epsom Gen. Hosp., 1994–2004. FMedSci 1998; FKC 2002. *Publications:* Malignant Tumours of the Mouth, Jaws and Salivary Glands, 1985, 2nd edn 1995; Surgical Pathology of the Mouth and Jaws, 1996; Operative Maxillofacial Surgery, 1998; The Infratemporal Fossa, 2002. *Recreations:* opera, ballet, gardening, antiques. *Address:* The Old Rectory, Limington, Somerset BA22 8EQ.

LANGDON-DOWN, Antony Turnbull; Volunteer Consultant, Sevenoaks Citizens' Advice Bureau, 1995–2003; Clerk to Merchant Taylors Company, 1980–85; *b* 31 Dec. 1922; *s* of Dr Reginald Langdon-Down and Ruth Langdon-Down (*née* Turnbull); *m* 1954, Jill Elizabeth Style (*née* Caruth) (*d* 2001); one *s* one *d*. *Educ:* Harrow School. Member of Lincoln's Inn, 1940–60, called to the Bar, 1948; enrolled as a solicitor, 1960; practised as solicitor, 1961–80. Pt-time Chm., Social Security Appeals Tribunal, 1985–95. Pilot, Royal Air Force, 1942–47 (finally Flt Lieut). Master of Merchant Taylors Company, 1979–80. *Recreations:* sailing, tennis, bridge, music, art. *Address:* Drumard, The Street, Plaxtol, Sevenoaks, Kent TN15 0QP. *T:* (01732) 810720. *Clubs:* Savile, MCC; Bough Beech Sailing.

LANGER, Bernhard; golfer; *b* Germany, 27 Aug. 1957; *m* 1984, Vikki Lopez; two *s* two *d*. Major championships include: US Masters, 1985, 1993; German Open 5 times; 10 Ryder Cup appearances for Europe, 1981–97, and 2002, Europe Captain, 2004. *Publications:* (with Bill Elliott) While the Iron is Hot (autobiog.), 1988; (with Stuart Weir) Bernhard Langer: the autobiography, 2002. *Address:* c/o IMG, McCormack House, Hogarth Business Park, W4 2TH.

LANGFORD, 9th Baron *cr* 1800; **Colonel Geoffrey Alexander Rowley-Conwy,** OBE (mil.) 1943; DL; RA, retired; Constable of Rhuddlan Castle and Lord of the Manor of Rhuddlan; *b* 8 March 1912; *s* of late Major Geoffrey Seymour Rowley-Conwy (killed in action, Gallipoli, 1915), Bodrhyddan, Flints, and Bertha Gabrielle Rowley-Conwy, JP (*d* 1984), *d* of late Lieutenant Alexander Cochran, Royal Navy, Ashkirk, Selkirkshire; *S* kinsman, 1953; *m* 1st, 1939, Ruth St John (marr. diss. 1956; she *d* 1991), *d* of late Albert St John Murphy, The Island House, Little Island, County Cork; 2nd, 1957, Grete (*d* 1973), *d* of late Col E. T. C. von Freiesleben, formerly Chief of the King's Adjutants Staff to the King of Denmark; three *s*; 3rd, 1975, Susan Winifred Denham, *d* of C. C. H. Denham, Chester; one *s* one *d*. *Educ:* Marlborough; RMA Woolwich. Served War of 1939–45, with RA (2nd Lieut, 1932; Lieut, 1935; Captain, 1939; Major 1941); Singapore, 1942 (POW escaped) and with Indian Mountain Artillery in Burma (Arakan, Kohima), 1941–45 (despatches, OBE); Staff Coll., Quetta, 1945; Berlin Airlift, Fassberg, 1948–49; GSOI 42 Inf. Div., TA, 1949–52; Lt-Col 1945; retired 1957; Colonel (Hon.), 1967. Freeman, City of London, 1986–. DL Clwyd, 1977. *Heir: s* Hon. Owain Grenville Rowley-Conwy [*b* 27 Dec. 1958; *m* 1986, Joanna (marr. diss. 1993), *d* of Jack Featherstone; one *s* one *d*]. *Address:* Bodrhyddan, Rhuddlan, Denbighshire LL18 5SB. *Club:* Army and Navy.

LANGFORD, Anthony John, CB 1996; FRICS; Chief Executive, Valuation Office Agency, 1994–96; *b* 25 June 1936; *s* of Freeman and Ethel Langford; *m* 1958, Joan Winifred Barber; one *s* one *d*. *Educ:* Soham Grammar School. FRICS 1978. Joined Valuation Office, Inland Revenue, 1957; District Valuer, Camden, 1976; Superintending Valuer, Northern Region, 1981; Asst Chief Valuer, 1983; Dep. Chief Valuer, then Dep. Chief Exec., Valuation Office Agency, 1988–94. *Recreations:* walking, gardening, bowls.

LANGFORD, Prof. Paul, DPhil; FRHistS; FBA 1993; Professor of Modern History, University of Oxford, since 1996; Fellow, and Tutor in Modern History, since 1970, and Rector, since 2000, Lincoln College, Oxford; *b* 20 Nov. 1945; *s* of Frederick Wade Langford and Olive Myrtle Langford (*née* Walters); *m* 1970, Margaret Veronica Edwards; one *s*. *Educ:* Monmouth Sch.; Hertford Coll., Oxford (MA, DPhil; Hon. Fellow, 2000). FRHistS 1979. Jun. Res. Fellow, Lincoln Coll., Oxford, 1969–70; Reader in Modern History, Oxford Univ., 1994–96. Ford's Lectr in English History, Oxford Univ., 1990; Raleigh Lectr, British Acad., 1996. Mem., Humanities Res. Bd, British Acad., 1995–98. Chm. and Chief Exec., AHRB, 1998–2000. Sen. Fellow, RCA, 2001. General Editor: The Writings and Speeches of Edmund Burke, 1974–; Oxford History of the British Isles, 1996–. Hon. DLitt Sheffield, 2002. *Publications:* The First Rockingham Administration 1765–66, 1973; The Excise Crisis: society and politics in the age of Walpole, 1975; (ed) Writings and Speeches of Edmund Burke, vol. II: Party, Parliament and The American Crisis 1766–74, 1981; A Polite and Commercial People 1727–83, 1989 (New Oxford History of England series); Public Life and the Propertied Englishman 1689–1789, 1991; Englishness Identified: manners and character 1650–1850, 2000. *Recreation:* gardening. *Address:* Lincoln College, Oxford OX1 3DR. *Club:* Athenæum.

LANGHAM, Sir John (Stephen), 16th Bt *cr* 1660, of Cottesbrooke, Northampton; *b* 14 Dec. 1960; *s* of Sir James Michael Langham, 15th Bt, TD and of Marion Audrey Eleanor Langham (*née* Barratt); *S* father, 2002; *m* 1991, Sarah Jane Verschoyle-Greene; one *s* two *d*. Farmer and landowner. Web media and internet consultant. *Heir: s* Tyrone Denis James Langham, *b* 13 Aug. 1994. *Address:* Tempo Manor, Demesne, Tempo, Co. Fermanagh BT94 3PA. *T:* (028) 8954 1953.

LANGHAM, Patricia Anne; Principal, Wakefield Grammar School Foundation, since 2000; Headmistress, Wakefield Girls' High School, since 1987; *b* Carlisle, 1 Jan. 1951; *d* of Andrew and Mary Lowrie; *m* 2008, Nev Hanley; one step *s* two step *d*. *Educ:* Carlisle and County High Sch. for Girls; Univ. of Leeds (BA English and Russian; MEd). Ilkley Grammar Sch., 1973–78; Brigshaw Comp. Sch., 1978–82; Dep. Head, Woodkirk High Sch., 1982–87. *Recreations:* literature, gardening, travel, dog walking, collecting flying ducks. *Address: e-mail:* headmistress@wghsss.org.uk.

LANGHORNE, Prof. Richard Tristan Bailey, FRHistS; Professor of Political Science, and Director, Division of Global Affairs (formerly Center for Global Change and Governance), Rutgers University, New Jersey, since 1996; *b* 6 May 1940; *s* of late Eadward John Bailey Langhorne and of Rosemary Scott-Foster; *m* 1971, Helen Logue (*d* 2005), *o d* of William Donaldson, CB and Mary Donaldson; one *s* one *d*. *Educ:* St Edward's Sch., Oxford; St John's Coll., Cambridge (Exhibr). BA Hist. Tripos, 1962; Certif. in Hist. Studies, 1963; MA 1965. Tutor in History, Univ. of Exeter, 1963–64; Research Student, St John's Coll., Cambridge, 1964–66; Lectr in History, 1966–74 and Master of Rutherford Coll., 1971–74, Univ. of Kent at Canterbury; St John's College, Cambridge: Steward, 1974–79; Junior Bursar, 1974–87; Fellow, 1974–93; Dir, Centre of Internat. Studies, Univ. of Cambridge, 1987–93; Dir and Chief Exec., Wilton Park, FCO, 1993–96. Vis. Prof., Univ. of Southern Calif, 1986; Hon. Prof. of Internat. Relns, Univ. of Kent at Canterbury, 1994–97; Vis. Prof., Canterbury Christchurch Univ., 2006. Freeland K. Abbott Meml Lectr, Tufts Univ., 1990; Queen Beatrix Lectr, Royal Foundn, Amsterdam, 1998. *Publications:* The Collapse of the Concert of Europe, 1890–1914, 1980; (ed) Diplomacy and Intelligence during the Second World War, 1985; (with K. Hamilton) The Practice of Diplomacy, 1994; The Coming of Globalization, 2000; (ed) Guide to International Relations and Diplomacy, 2002; (with C. Jönsson) Diplomacy (3 vols), 2004; The Essentials of Global Politics, 2006; chapter in British Foreign Policy under Sir Edward Grey, 1977; reviews and articles in Historical Jl, History, Review of International Studies, and Diplomacy and Statecraft. *Recreations:* music, railways. *Address:* Rutgers University, 123 Washington Street, Suite 510, Newark, NJ 07102–1895, USA; 7 The Pines, Puckle Lane, Canterbury, Kent CT1 3HE. *Club:* Athenæum.

LANGLANDS, Sir Alan; *see* Langlands, Sir R. A.

LANGLANDS, Allister Gordon; Chief Executive, John Wood Group PLC, since 2007; *b* 31 March 1958; *s* of John and Diana Langlands; *m* 1993, Helen Shoreman; four *s* one *d*. *Educ:* Forfar Acad.; Univ. of Edinburgh (MA Hons Econs 1980); Harvard Univ. (AMP 1999). CA. Deloitte Haskins & Sells: Trainee Chartered Accountant, 1980–83; Manager Corporate Finance/Audit, 1984–89; Partner, 1989–91; John Wood Group PLC: Gp Finance Dir, 1991–99; Dep. Chief Exec., 1999–2006. *Recreations:* family, golf, racquet sports, gardening. *Address:* John Wood Group PLC, John Wood House, Greenwell Road, Aberdeen AB12 3AX. *T:* (01224) 851229; *e-mail:* allister.langlands@woodgroup.com.

LANGLANDS, Sir (Robert) Alan, Kt 1998; Principal and Vice-Chancellor, Dundee University, since 2000; *b* 29 May 1952; *s* of James Langlands and May Langlands (*née* Rankin); *m* 1977, Elizabeth McDonald; one *s* one *d*. *Educ:* Allan Glen's Sch.; Univ. of Glasgow (BSc Pure Sci). FRSE 2002. Grad. Trainee, NHS Scotland, 1974–76; Argyll and Clyde Health Bd, 1976–78; Simpson Meml Maternity Pavilion, Elsie Inglis Hosp., 1978–81; Unit Administrator, Middx and University Coll. Hosps and Hosp. for Women, Soho, 1981–85; Dist Gen. Manager, Harrow HA, 1985–89; Practice Leader, Health Care, Towers Perrin, 1989–91; Gen. Manager, NW Thames RHA, 1991–92; Dep. Chief Exec., 1993–94, Chief Exec., 1994–2000, NHS Executive. Member: Central R&D Cttee, NHS, 1991–92; Nat. Forum R&D, 1994–99; Health Sector Gp, BOTB, 1998–2000. Chairman: UK Biobank, 2004–; Commn on Good Governance, 2004–05. Non-executive Director: Office for Strategic Coordination of Health Research, 2007–; UK Statistics Authy, 2008–. Trustee, Nuffield Trust, 2007–. Hon. Prof., 1996, and Mem. Bd, Univ. of Warwick Business Sch., 1999–2000; Member: Council and Court, Univ. of York, 1998–2000; Adv. Bd, INSEAD, 1999–2003; US Nat. Adv. Bd, Johns Hopkins Univ. Bioethics Inst., 2000–04. Hon. FFPH (Hon. FFPHM 1994); FIA 1999; FCGI 2000; CCMI (CIMgt 2000); Hon. FRCP 2001; Hon. FRCGP 2001; Hon. FRCSE 2001; Hon. FRCPSGlas 2002. DUniv Glasgow, 2001. *Recreation:* living and walking in Scotland and Yorkshire. *Address:* University of Dundee, Dundee DD1 4HN.

LANGLANDS, Prof. Robert Phelan, FRS 1981; Professor of Mathematics, Institute for Advanced Study, Princeton, New Jersey, since 1972; *b* 6 Oct. 1936; *s* of Robert Langlands and Kathleen Johanna (*née* Phelan); *m* 1956, Charlotte Lorraine Cheverie; two *s* two *d*. *Educ:* Univ. of British Columbia (BA 1957, MA 1958); Yale Univ. (PhD 1960). FRSC 1972. Princeton University: Instructor, 1960–61; Lectr, 1961–62; Asst Prof., 1962–64; Associate Prof., 1964–67; Prof., Yale Univ., 1967–72. Associate Prof., Ortadoğu Teknik Universitesi, 1967–68; Gast Prof., Universität Bonn, 1980–81. Mem., Nat. Acad. of Scis, USA, 1993. Hon. DSc: British Columbia, 1985; McMaster, 1985; CUNY, 1985; Paris VII, 1989; McGill, 1991; Toronto, 1993; Montreal, 1997; Laval, 2002; Madras, 2005; Hon. DMath Waterloo, 1988. Wilbur L. Cross Medal, Yale Univ., 1975; Cole Prize, 1982, Steele Prize, 2005, Amer. Math. Soc.; Common Wealth Award, Sigma Xi, 1984; Maths Award, Nat. Acad. of Scis, 1988; Wolf Prize in Maths, Wolf Foundn of Israel, 1996; Grande Médaille d'Or, Acad. des Scis, Paris, 2000; Frederic Esser Nemmers Prize, Northwestern Univ., 2006; Shaw Prize, 2007. *Publications:* Automorphic Forms on GL(2) (with H. Jacquet), 1970; Euler Products, 1971; On the Functional Equations satisfied by Eisenstein Series, 1976; Base Change for GL(2), 1980; Les débuts d'une formule des traces stable, 1983; contrib. Canadian Jl Maths, Proc. Amer. Math. Soc. Symposia, Springer Lecture Notes. *Address:* Institute for Advanced Study, School of Mathematics, Princeton, NJ 08540, USA. *T:* (609) 7348106.

LANGLEY, Hon. Sir Gordon; *see* Langley, Hon. Sir J. H. G.

LANGLEY, Hon. Sir (Julian Hugh) Gordon, Kt 1995; a Judge of the High Court, Queen's Bench Division, 1995–2007; *b* 11 May 1943; *s* of late Gordon Thompson Langley and of Marjorie Langley; *m* 1968, Beatrice Jayanthi Langley; two *d*. *Educ:* Westminster School; Balliol College, Oxford (MA, BCL). Called to the Bar, Inner Temple, 1966, Bencher, 1996; QC 1983; a Recorder, 1986–95. *Recreations:* music, sport. *Address:* c/o Fountain Court Chambers, Temple, EC4Y 9DH.

LANGLEY, Ven. Robert; Archdeacon of Lindisfarne, 2001–07; *b* 25 Oct. 1937; *s* of Maurice and Kathleen Langley; *m* 1961, Elisabeth Hart; one *s* two *d*. *Educ:* Worksop Coll.; St Catherine's Coll., Oxford (BA Maths 1961). Ordained deacon, 1963, priest, 1964; Asst Curate, Aston cum Aughton, Sheffield, 1963–68; Midlands and HQ Sec., Christian Educn

Movt, 1968–74; Principal: Ian Ramsay Coll., Brasted, 1974–77; St Albans Dio. Ministerial Trng Scheme, 1977–85; Canon Missioner, Newcastle Dio., 1985–98; Dir, Ministry and Trng, Newcastle Dio., 1998–2001. Chm., Northumberland Strategic Partnership, 2008–. Chairman: William Temple Foundn, 1994–2006; Community Action Northumberland, 2005–; Vice Chm., SE Northumberland and N Tyneside Regeneration Initiative, 2006–. *Recreations:* cycling, walking, music. *Address:* 109 Goldspink Lane, Newcastle upon Tyne NE2 1NR.

LANGLEY, Prof. Robin Stewart, PhD; Professor of Mechanical Engineering, since 1998, and Deputy Head (Graduate Studies), Department of Engineering, 1999–2002, Cambridge University; Fellow of Fitzwilliam College, Cambridge, since 1998; *b* 5 April 1957; *s* of Robert Langley and Marie Langley (*née* Lewins); *m* 1st, 1982, Pamela Heath (marr. diss. 1997); 2nd, 2007, Elizabeth Napchapkina. *Educ:* Univ. of Leicester (BSc 1978); Cranfield Univ. (MSc 1981; PhD 1983). CMath, FIMA 1989; CEng, MRAeS 1990. Accountant, Armitage and Norton, 1978–79; Teaching Associate, 1983–84, Lectr in Structural Dynamics, 1984–91, Cranfield Univ.; Sen. Lectr in Aerospace Structures, 1991–95, Prof. of Structural Dynamics, 1995–98, Southampton Univ. Fellow, Acoustical Soc. of Amer., 2000. *Publications:* articles in academic jls, mainly on random vibration, structural dynamics, and acoustics. *Recreations:* walking, literature, family and friends. *Address:* Department of Engineering, University of Cambridge, Trumpington Street, Cambridge CB2 1PZ. *T:* (01223) 766385.

LANGMAN, Prof. Michael John Stratton, MD; FRCP; Hon. Professor, University of Warwick, since 2005; William Withering Professor of Medicine, University of Birmingham, 1987–2000, now Emeritus (Dean, Faculty of Medicine and Dentistry, 1992–97); *b* 30 Jan. 1935; *s* of John A. H. and E. Margaret Langman; *m* 1960, Rosemary A. Hempton; two *s* two *d*. *Educ:* St Paul's Sch.; Guy's Hosp. Med. Sch., Univ. of London (BSc, MB (Hons), MD). FRCP 1973; FFPM (by distinction) 1989. House Physician and Surg., Guy's Hosp., 1958–59; House Physician, Brompton, Hammersmith and Queen Square Hosps, 1959–61; Registrar, Central Middlesex Hosp., 1961–63; Lectr in Medicine, Guy's Hosp., 1963–68; Mem., Scientific Staff, MRC Statistical Res. Unit, UCH, 1963–68; Consultant Physician and Sen. Lectr, 1968–70, Reader, 1970–74, in Medicine, Nottingham Hosps and Univ.; Boots Prof. of Therapeutics, Univ. of Nottingham, 1974–87. Non-exec. Dir, Birmingham HA, 1992–98. Hon. Sen. Res. Fellow, European Inst. of Oncology, Milan, 1996–2003; Hon. Consultant, WHO, 1996–99. Lectures: Avery Jones, Central Middx Hosp., 1977; Melrose, Caledonian Soc. of Gastroenterology, 1987; William Withering Prize, RCP, 1988; Honeyman Gillespie, Edinburgh Univ., 1989; Barany, Swedish Soc. of Gastroenterology, 1992. Chairman: Adv. Expert Gp on Vitamins and Minerals, Food Standards Authy (formerly MAFF), 1999–2003; Jt Cttee on Vaccination and Immunization UK, 2000–05; Member: Cttee on Review of Medicines, 1980–87; Cttee on Safety of Medicines, 1987–2005 (Chm., Subcttee on Pharmacovigilance, 1992–95). Chm., Coventry and Warwicks Ambulance NHS Trust, 2000–06. Pres., British Soc. of Gastroenterology, 1997–99. Gov., St Martin's Sch., Solihull, 1997–2003. Founder FMedSci 1998. *Publications:* Concise Textbook of Gastroenterology, 1973; various papers on chronic digestive disease. *Recreations:* tennis, music, cricket. *Address:* Department of Medicine, Queen Elizabeth Hospital, Birmingham B15 2TH. *T:* (0121) 627 2380. *Clubs:* Athenæum, MCC.

LANGRIDGE, Philip Gordon, CBE 1994; FRAM, FRCM; concert and opera singer (tenor), since 1964; *b* 16 Dec. 1939; *m* 1981, Ann Murray, *qv*; one *s* (and one *s* two *d* by former marriage). *Educ:* Maidstone Grammar Sch.; Royal Academy of Music, London. ARAM 1977; FRAM 1985; FRCM 1997. Glyndebourne Festival début, 1964; BBC Promenade Concerts, 1970–; Edinburgh Fest., 1970–; Netherlands Opera, Scottish Opera, Handel Opera etc. Covent Garden: L'Enfant et les Sortilèges, Rossignol, Boris, Jenufa, Idomeneo, Peter Grimes, Death in Venice, Rheingold, Palestrina, The Tempest, Le Nozze di Figaro; ENO: Turn of the Screw, Osud (Olivier Award, Outstanding Individual Performer in a New Opera Production, 1984), The Mask of Orpheus, Billy Budd, Beatrice and Benedict, Makropoulos Case; Peter Grimes; Oedipus Rex; Glyndebourne, 1977–: Don Giovanni, Idomeneo, Fidelio, Jenufa, La Clemenza di Tito; The Second Mrs Kong; La Scala, 1979–: Rake's Progress, Wozzeck, Boris Godunov, Il Sosia, Idomeneo, Oberon, Peter Grimes; Frankfurt Opera: Castor and Pollux, Rigoletto, Die Entführung; Bavarian State Opera: Peter Grimes, Midsummer Marriage, La Clemenza di Tito, Rheingold; Zurich Opera: Poppea, Lucio Silla; Don Giovanni; La Fenice: Janacek's Diary; Palermo: Otello (Rossini); Pesaro: La Donna del Lago; Maggio Musicale: Peter Grimes; Boris Godunov; Aix en Provence: Alcina, Les Boriades; Metropolitan Opera, NY: Così fan Tutte, Boris Godunov, Das Rheingold, Billy Budd, Peter Grimes, Moses und Aron; Vienna State Opera: Wozzeck; Salzburg Festival: Moses und Aron, Idomeneo, From the House of the Dead, Poppea, Boris Godunov; Amsterdam: Poppea, Idomeneo, Il Barbieri di Seviglia, Dorian Gray, Pelléas et Mélisande; Los Angeles: Peter Grimes; Barcelona: Billy Budd; Boris Godunov. Concerts with major, international orchestras and conductors including: Berlin Phil. (Abbado, Ozawa), Boston (Previn), Chicago (Solti, Abbado), Los Angeles (Christopher Hogwood), Sydney (Mackerras), Vienna Phil. (Previn), Orchestre de Paris (Barenboim, Mehta), and all major British orchestras; recitals with Pollini, Schiff, Donohoe, Norris. Many first performances of works, some dedicated to and written for him. Master classes on communication through singing. Has made over 100 records of early, baroque, classical, romantic and modern music (Grammy Awards: for Schönberg's Moses und Aron, 1985; for Peter Grimes, 1996). Mem., Music Panel, Arts Council of GB, 1983–86. Singer of the Year, RPS/Heidsieck Award, 1989; Santay Award, Co. of Musicians; Making Music/Sir Charles Groves Award, 2001. *Recreation:* collecting water colour paintings and Victorian postcards. *Address:* c/o Allied Artists Agency, 42 Montpelier Square, SW7 1JZ. *T:* (020) 7589 6243.

LANGRIDGE, Richard James, CVO 1992; HM Diplomatic Service, retired; Consul-General, Bordeaux, 1990–92; *b* 29 Oct. 1932; *m* 1965, Jeannine Louise Joosen; one *d*. HM Forces, 1951–53; joined FO 1953; served NY, Leopoldville, Athens, Dakar, Paris and FCO; Ambassador to Madagascar, 1979–84; FCO, 1985; Dep. High Comr, Colombo, 1985–89.

LANGRISH, Rt Rev. Michael Laurence; *see* Exeter, Bishop of.

LANGRISHE, Sir James Hercules, 8th Bt *cr* 1777, of Knocktopher Abbey, Kilkenny; *b* 3 March 1957; *o s* of Sir Hercules Ralph Hume Langrishe, 7th Bt and of Hon. Grania Sybil Enid Wingfield, *o d* of 9th Viscount Powerscourt; *S* father, 1998; *m* 1985, Gemma Mary Philomena, *e d* of Patrick O'Daly; one *s* one *d*. *Heir: s* Richard James Hercules Langrishe, *b* 8 April 1988. *Address:* Arlonstown, Dunsany, Co. Meath, Ireland.

LANGSDALE, Philip Richard, FIET; Chief Executive, Langsdale Crook LLP (formerly Langsdale Associates), since 2002; *b* 23 Dec. 1955; *s* of Reginald Eric Langsdale and Dorothy May Langsdale; *m* 1984, Vanessa Gabrielle Marsland; two *d*. *Educ:* King's Coll., Cambridge (MA Maths); London Busines Sch. (MSc 2004). CEng 1993; FIET (FIEE 2002). Systems Engr, IBM UK, 1979–82; IT Consultant, Nolan Norton & Co., 1982–85; Associate Dir, Coopers & Lybrand, 1985–88; Dir, IT Planning, Midland Bank, 1988–92; IT Director: Asda Gp, 1992–97; Cable & Wireless Communications, 1997–98; BBC: Dir,

Technology, subseq. Distribution and Technology, 1998–2001; Chief Exec., BBC Technology, 2001–02; Mem., Exec. Cttee, 2000–02. *Recreations:* opera, sailing, music, mountain-climbing. *Address:* 25 Highbury Place, N5 1QP.

LANGSHAW, George Henry; Managing Director, UK Regions, British Gas, 1992; *b* 6 Dec. 1939; *s* of George Henry and Florence Evelyn Langshaw; *m* 1962, Maureen Cosgrove; one *s* two *d*. *Educ:* Liverpool Inst. High Sch. FCMA; ACIS. Various accountancy appts, Wm Crawford & Sons, 1957–63, Littlewoods Orgn, 1963–67; British Gas: Accountant, NW, 1967–70; Develt Accountant, Southern, 1970–73; Prin. Financial Analyst, HQ, 1973–76; Chief Accountant, Wales, 1976–78; Dir of Finance, Southern, 1978–82; Dep. Chm., NW, 1982–87; Regional Chm., British Gas (Wales), 1987–89; Gp Dir of Personnel, 1989–90; Man. Dir, Global Gas, 1990–92. Chm., BG Corporate Ventures, 1990. Director: British Gas Deutschland GmbH, 1991; British Gas Holdings (Canada), 1992; BG Holdings Inc., 1992. Dir, Bd of Gas Consumers, Canada, 1990. CIGEM (CIGasE 1988); CCMI (CBIM 1991). *Recreations:* soccer, reading, golf.

LANGSLOW, Derek Robert, CBE 2000; PhD; Chairman, East of England Tourism, since 2006; *b* 7 Feb. 1945; *s* of Alexander Frederick Langslow and Beatrice Bibby Langslow (*née* Wright); *m* 1969, Helen Katherine (*née* Addison); one *s* one *d*. *Educ:* Ashville College, Harrogate; Queens' College, Cambridge (MA, PhD). Post-Doctoral Fellow, Cambridge and Univ. of Kansas; Lectr, Univ. of Edinburgh, 1972–78; Nature Conservancy Council: Senior Ornithologist, 1978–84; Asst Chief Scientist, 1984–87; Dir, Policy and Planning, 1987–90; Chief Scientist, 1990; Chief Exec., English Nature, 1990–2000; Chm., Rail Passenger Cttee for Eastern England, 2000–05. Director: British Waterways, 2000–06; Harwich Haven Authy, 2001– (Dep. Chm., 2007–). Member: Agriculture and Envmt Biotechnol. Commn, 2000–05; Passenger Focus, 2005–. Trustee, Heritage Lottery Fund, 2002–08. *Publications:* numerous papers in learned jls. *Recreations:* badminton, walking, sheep, bird watching, music. *Address:* 4 Engaine, Orton Longueville, Peterborough PE2 7QA. *T:* (01733) 232153.

LANGSTAFF, Hon. Sir Brian (Frederick James), Kt 2005; **Hon. Mr Justice Langstaff;** a Judge of the High Court, Queen's Bench Division, since 2005; *b* 30 April 1948; *s* of Frederick Sidney Langstaff and Muriel Amy Maude Langstaff (*née* Griffin); *m* 1975, Deborah Elizabeth Weatherup; one *s* one *d*. *Educ:* George Heriot's Sch.; St Catharine's Coll., Cambridge (BA); Inns of Court Sch. of Law. VSO, Sri Lanka, 1966–67. Called to the Bar, Middle Temple, 1971 (Harmsworth Schol., 1975), Bencher, 2001. Called to the Bar of NI, 1999. Lectr and Sen. Lectr in Law, Mid-Essex Technical Coll. and Sch. of Art, Chelmsford, 1971–75; Asst Recorder, SE Circuit, 1991–95; QC 1994; a Recorder, 1995–2005; Judge, Employment Appeal Tribunal, 2000–03. Hd of Cloisters Chambers, 2002–05. Leading Counsel, Bristol Royal Infirmary Inquiry, 1998–2000. Chairman: Personal Injury Bar Assoc., 1999–2001; Exec. Cttee, Industrial Law Soc., 1997–2005 (Hon. Vice-Pres., 2005–); Law Reform Cttee, Bar Council, 2001–03 (Vice-Chm., 1999–2001); Master of Rolls' working party on structured settlements, 2001–02; Serious Injury and Clinical Negligence Cttee, Civil Justice Council, 2003–06. Gov., local primary sch., 1986– (Chm. Govs, 1991–98). Adv. Editor, Occupational Health, Safety & Environment, 1997–2000. *Publications:* Concise College Casenotes: equity and trusts, 1975; Health and Safety at Work: Halsbury's Laws vol. 20, 4th edn 1994; (ed and contrib.) Personal Injury Handbook, 2000, 3rd edn 2007; Bullen, Leake and Jacobs, Precedents of Pleading, (adv. ed.) 14th edn 2001, and 15th edn 2003, (gen. ed.) 16th edn 2007; (contrib.) Munkman's Employers' Liability, 13th edn 2001, 14th edn 2006; Personal Injury Schedules: calculating damages, 2001, 2nd edn 2005; (contrib.) Butterworths Personal Injury Litigation Service, part 1, 2004; legal articles. *Recreations:* sport, politics, mowing the lawn, bell-ringing, travel. *Address:* Royal Courts of Justice, Strand, WC2A 2LL.

LANGSTAFF, Rt Rev. James Henry; *see* Lynn, Bishop Suffragan of.

LANGSTON, Group Captain John Antony S.; *see* Steff-Langston.

LANGTON; *see* Temple-Gore-Langton, family name of Earl Temple of Stowe.

LANGTON, Lord; James Grenville Temple-Gore-Langton; *b* 11 Sept. 1955; *er s* and *heir* of Earl Temple of Stowe, *qv*.

LANGTON, Bryan David, CBE 1988; Director, Bass plc, 1985–96; Chairman and Chief Executive Officer, Holiday Inn Worldwide, 1990–96; *b* 6 Dec. 1936; *s* of Thomas Langton and Doris (*née* Brown); *m* 1960, Sylva Degenhardt; two *d*. *Educ:* Accrington Grammar Sch.; Westminster Tech. Coll. (Hotel Operation Dip.); Ecole Hotelière de la SSA, Lausanne (Operations Dip.). Dep. Manager, Russell Hotel, London, 1959–63; General Manager: Victoria Hotel, Nottingham, 1964–66; Grand Hotel, Manchester, 1966–71; Crest Hotels: Divl Manager, 1971–73; Ops Dir UK, 1973–75; Ops Dir Europe, 1975–77; Divl Managing Dir, Europe, 1977–81; Managing Dir, Ops, 1981–82; Man. Dir, 1982–88; Chairman, 1985–90. Chairman: Holiday Inns International, 1988–90; Toby Restaurants, 1988–90; Fairfield Communities Inc., 1999–2002 (non-exec. Dir, 1996–99); Dir, Caribiner Internat. Inc., 1996–2001; Vice Chm., E Suites LLC, 2007–; Member: Adv. Bd, Mote Marine Sarasota, 1997–2001; Bd, Florida West Coast Symphony, 1997–2008 (Pres., 2005–06). Vice Pres., Internat. Hotel Assoc., 1990. Trustee, Educnl Inst., Amer. Hotel and Motel Assoc., 1990–97. Member, Board of Trustees: Woodruff Arts Center, Atlanta, 1990–97; Northside Hosp. Foundn Bd, 1990–97; YMCA, Sarasota, Fla, 1999–2002. Trustee, Bd of Visitors, Emory Univ., 1990–97. Hon. Fellow, Manchester Poly., later Manchester Metropolitan Univ., 1990–99. *Recreations:* golf, cricket, reading, theatre. *Address:* 3632 Fair Oaks Place, Longboat Key, FL 34228–4151, USA. *T:* (941) 3835046, *Fax:* (941) 3834862; *e-mail:* bryanlangton@comcast.net.

LANGTRY, (James) Ian; Education Officer, Association of County Councils, 1988–96; *b* 2 Jan. 1939; *s* of late Rev. H. J. Langtry and I. M. Langtry (*née* Eagleson); *m* 1959, Eileen Roberta Beatrice (*née* Nesbitt) (*d* 1999); one *s* one *d*. *Educ:* Coleraine Academical Instn; Queen's Univ., Belfast (Sullivan Schol.; BSc 1st Cl., Physics). Assistant Master, Bangor Grammar Sch., 1960–61; Lectr, Belfast College of Technology, 1961–66; Asst Director of Examinations/Recruitment, Civil Service Commission, 1966–70; Principal, Dept of Educn and Science, 1970–76, Asst Sec., 1976–82, Under Sec., 1982–87; Under Sec., DHSS, 1987–88. *Address:* 7 Bucklerburn Drive, Peterculter, Aberdeen AB14 0XJ.

LANIGAN, Audrey Cecelia; *see* Slaughter, A. C.

LANKESTER, Patricia; consultant in arts, voluntary sector and education; *b* 28 July 1946; *d* of Leo Cockcroft and Jennie Cockcroft; *m* 1968, Sir Timothy Patrick Lankester, *qv*; three *d*. *Educ:* King's Coll., London (BA 1967); Inst. of Educn, London (PGCE 1976). Hd of Hist., Barnsbury Sch., Islington, 1980–83; Hd of Humanities, Islington VI Form Centre, 1983–85; Hd of Educn, Nat. Trust, 1988–96; Dir, Paul Hamlyn Foundn, 1998–2004. Trustee: Heritage Lottery Fund, 1998–2003; Tate, 2005–; Nat. Gall., 2007–. Trustee: Open Coll. of the Arts, 1988–96; Farms for City Children, 1996–99; Villiers Park Educnl Trust, 2000–07; Eureka!, Halifax, 2004–; Foundling Mus., 2005–; The Hanover Foundn, 2006–; Sage Music Centre, Gateshead, 2007–. Mem. RSA. *Recreations:* art, theatre, historic buildings, fiction, walking. *Address:* c/o Corpus Christi College, Oxford OX1 4JF; *e-mail:* patricia.lankester@btinternet.com. *Club:* Academy.

LANKESTER, Richard Shermer; Clerk of Select Committees, House of Commons, 1979–87; Registrar of Members' Interests, 1976–87; *b* 8 Feb. 1922; *s* of late Richard Ward Lankester; *m* 1950, Dorothy, *d* of late Raymond Jackson, Worsley; two *s* one *d* (and one *s* decd). *Educ:* Haberdashers' Aske's Hampstead Sch.; Jesus Coll., Oxford (MA). Served Royal Artillery, 1942–45. Entered Dept of Clerk of House of Commons, 1947; Clerk of Standing Cttees, 1973–75; Clerk of Expenditure Cttee, 1975–79. Co-Editor, The Table, 1962–67. *Address:* The Old Farmhouse, The Green, Boughton Monchelsea, Maidstone, Kent ME17 4LT. *T:* (01622) 743749.

LANKESTER, Sir Timothy Patrick, (Sir Tim), KCB 1994; President, Corpus Christi College, Oxford, since 2001; *b* 15 April 1942; *s* of late Preb. Robin Prior Archibald Lankester and of Jean Dorothy (*née* Gilliat); *m* 1968, Patricia Cockcroft (*see* P. Lankester); three *d*. *Educ:* Monkton Combe Sch.; St John's Coll., Cambridge (BA; Hon. Fellow, 1995); Jonathan Edwards Coll., Yale (Henry Fellow, MA). Teacher (VSO), St Michael's Coll., Belize, 1960–61; Fereday Fellow, St John's Coll., Oxford, 1965–66; Economist, World Bank, Washington DC, 1966–69; New Delhi, 1970–73; Principal 1973, Asst Sec. 1977, HM Treasury; Private Secretary to Rt Hon. James Callaghan, 1978–79; to Rt Hon. Margaret Thatcher, 1979–81; seconded to S. G. Warburg and Co. Ltd, 1981–83; Under Sec., HM Treasury, 1983–85; Economic Minister, Washington and Exec. Dir, IMF and World Bank, 1985–88; Dep. Sec., HM Treasury, 1988–89; Perm. Sec., ODA, FCO, 1989–94; Perm. Sec., Dept for Educn, 1994–95; Dir, SOAS, London Univ., 1996–2000. Dep. Chm., British Council, 1997–2003. Non-executive Director: CGU plc, 1997–2002; London Metal Exchange, 1997–2002; Smith and Nephew plc, 1997–2003; Mitchells and Butler plc, 2003–; Actis Capital LLP, 2004–. Chm., Bd of Mgt, LSHTM, 2006–. Gov., Asia-Europe Foundn, 1997–; Member: UK-India Round Table, 1997–; UK Nat. Cttee, Aga Khan Foundn, 2000–. Chm., Contemporary Dance Trust, 2007–. *Address:* Corpus Christi College, Oxford OX1 4JF. *T:* (01865) 276740, *Fax:* (01865) 276769; *e-mail:* tim.lankester@ccc.ox.ac.uk.

LANNON, Frances, DPhil; FRHistS; Principal, Lady Margaret Hall, University of Oxford, since 2002; *b* 22 Dec. 1945; *d* of Martin Lannon and Margaret (*née* O'Hare). *Educ:* Sacred Heart Grammar Sch., Newcastle upon Tyne; Lady Margaret Hall, Oxford (BA 1st Cl. Hons Mod. Hist., MA 1972); St Antony's Coll., Oxford (DPhil Mod. Spanish Hist. 1976). FRHistS 1986. Lectr in Hist., QMC, London, 1975–77; Fellow and Tutor in Mod. Hist., LMH, Oxford, 1977–2002. Vis. Prof., Univ. of South Carolina, 1986. Mem., Commonwealth Scholarship Commn, 1982–91; Fellow, Woodrow Wilson Center, Washington, 1992. *Publications:* Privilege, Persecution and Prophecy: the Catholic Church in Spain 1875–1975, 1987; (ed with Paul Preston) Elites and Power in Twentieth-Century Spain, 1990; The Spanish Civil War, 2002; contrib. Oxford DNB, TLS, Jl of Contemporary Hist., other learned jls. *Recreations:* Spain, visual arts, contemporary fiction. *Address:* Lady Margaret Hall, Oxford OX2 6QA. *T:* (01865) 274300, *Fax:* (01865) 274294; *e-mail:* frances.lannon@lmh.ox.ac.uk.

LANSBURY, Angela Brigid, CBE 1994; actress; *b* London, England, 16 Oct. 1925; *d* of Edgar Lansbury and late Moyna Macgill (who *m* 1st, Reginald Denham); *m* 1st, Richard Cromwell; 2nd, 1949, Peter Shaw; one *s* one *d* and one step *s*. *Educ:* South Hampstead High Sch. for Girls; Webber Douglas Sch. of Singing and Dramatic Art, Kensington; Feagin Sch. of Drama and Radio, New York. With Metro-Goldwyn-Mayer, 1943–50; *films:* Gaslight, 1944; National Velvet, 1944; The Picture of Dorian Gray, 1945; The Harvey Girls, 1946; The Hoodlum Saint, 1946; Till the Clouds Roll By, 1946; The Private Affairs of Bel-Ami, 1947; If Winter Comes, 1948; Tenth Avenue Angel, 1948; State of the Union, 1948; The Three Musketeers, 1948; The Red Danube, or Storm over Vienna, or Vespers in Vienna, 1949; Samson and Delilah, 1949; Kind Lady, 1951; Mutiny, 1952; Remains to be Seen, 1953; A Life at Stake, or Key Man, 1955; The Purple Mask, 1956; The Court Jester, 1956; A Lawless Street, 1956; Please Murder Me, 1956; The Long Hot Summer, 1958; The Reluctant Debutante, 1958; Breath of Scandal, 1960; The Dark at the Top of the Stairs, 1960; Season of Passion, 1961; Blue Hawaii, 1961; All Fall Down, 1962; The Manchurian Candidate, 1962; In the Cool of the Day, 1963; The World of Henry Orient, 1964; Dear Heart, 1964; The Greatest Story Ever Told, 1965; Harlow, 1965; The Amorous Adventures of Moll Flanders, 1965; Mister Buddwing, or Woman Without a Face, 1966; Something for Everyone, or Black Flowers for the Bride, 1970; Bedknobs and Broomsticks, 1971; Death on the Nile, or Murder on the Nile, 1978; The Lady Vanishes, 1980; The Mirror Crack'd, 1980; The Pirates of Penzance, 1982; The Company of Wolves, 1983; Beauty and the Beast, 1991; Nanny McPhee, 2005; *plays:* appearances include: Hotel Paradiso (Broadway debut), 1957; Helen, in A Taste of Honey, Lyceum Theatre, New York, 1960; Anyone Can Whistle (Broadway musical), 1964; Mame (Tony Award for best actress in a Broadway musical), Winter Garden, NYC, 1966–68; Dear World (Broadway), 1969 (Tony Award); Pretty Belle, 1971; All Over, RSC, 1971; Gypsy (Broadway Musical), Piccadilly, 1973, US tour, 1974 (Tony Award; Chicago, Sarah Siddons Award, 1974); Gertrude, in Hamlet, Nat. Theatre, 1975; Anna, in The King and I (Broadway), 1978; Mrs Lovett, in Sweeney Todd (Broadway), 1979 (Tony Award); A Little Family Business, 1983; Deuce, NY, 2007; *television includes:* series, Murder She Wrote, 1984–95 (Golden Globe Award, 1984, 1986, 1991, 1992); Little Gloria, Happy At Last, 1982; The Gift of Love: a Christmas Story, 1983; A Talent for Murder (with Laurence Olivier), 1984; Lace, 1984; The First Olympico-Athens 1896, 1984; Rage of Angels II, 1986; Shootdown, 1988; The Shell Seekers, 1989; The Love She Sought, 1990; Mrs Arris Goes to Paris, 1992; Mrs Santa Claus, 1996; South by Southwest, 1997; The Unexpected Mrs Pollifax, 1998; A Story to Die for, 2000. NY Drama Desk Award, 1979; Sarah Siddons Award, 1980 and 1983; inducted Theatre Hall of Fame, 1982; Silver Mask for Lifetime Achievement, BAFTA, 1991; Lifetime Achievement Award, Screen Actors' Guild, 1997; Nat. Medal of the Arts, USA, 1997.

LANSDOWN, Gillian Elizabeth, (Mrs Richard Lansdown); *see* Tindall, G. E.

LANSDOWNE, 9th Marquess of, *cr* 1784 (GB); **Charles Maurice Petty-Fitzmaurice,** LVO 2002; DL; 30th Baron of Kerry and Lixnaw, 1181; Viscount Clanmaurice and Earl of Kerry, 1722; Baron Dunkeron and Viscount Fitzmaurice, 1751; Earl of Shelburne, 1753; Baron Wycombe (GB), 1760; Viscount Calne and Calston and Earl of Wycombe (GB), 1784; *b* 21 Feb. 1941; *s* of 8th Marquess of Lansdowne, PC and Barbara, *d* of Harold Stuart Chase; *S* father, 1999; *m* 1st, 1965, Lady Frances Eliot, *o d* of 9th Earl of St Germans; two *s* two *d*; 2nd, 1987, Fiona Merritt, *d* of Lady Davies and Donald Merritt. *Educ:* Eton. Page of Honour to The Queen, 1956–57. Served with Kenya Regt, 1960–61; with Wiltshire Yeomanry (TA), amalgamated with Royal Yeomanry Regt, 1963–73. Pres., Wiltshire Playing Fields Assoc., 1965–74; Wiltshire County Councillor, 1970–85; Mem., South West Economic Planning Council, 1972–77; Chairman: Working Committee Population & Settlement Pattern (SWEPC), 1972–77; North Wiltshire DC, 1973–76; Mem., Calne and Chippenham RDC, 1964–73. Mem., Historic Bldgs and Monuments Commn, 1983–89; President: HHA, 1988–93 (Dep. Pres., 1986–88); South West Tourism, 1989–2006; Wiltshire Historic Bldgs Trust, 1994–; Wilts & Berks Canal

Partnership, 2001–. Mem., Prince's Council, Duchy of Cornwall, 1990–2001; President: Wiltshire Assocs Boys Clubs and Youth Clubs, 1976–2003; North-West Wiltshire District Scout Council, 1977–88; N Wilts Cons. Assoc., 1986–89. Contested (C) Coventry North East, 1979. DL Wilts, 1990. *Heir:* s Earl of Kerry, *qv*. *Address:* Bowood House, Calne, Wiltshire SN11 0LZ. *T:* (01249) 813343. *Clubs:* Turf, Brooks's.

LANSLEY, Andrew David, CBE 1996; MP (C) Cambridgeshire South, since 1997; *b* 11 Dec. 1956; *s* of Thomas and Irene Lansley; *m* 1st, 1985, Marilyn Jane Biggs (marr. diss. 2001); three *d*; 2nd, 2001, Sally Anne Low; one *s* one *d*. *Educ:* Univ. of Exeter (BA). Administration trainee, Dept of Industry, 1979; Private Sec. to Sec. of State for Trade and Industry, 1984–85; Principal Private Sec. to Chancellor of Duchy of Lancaster, 1985–87; Dir, Policy, 1987–89, Dep. Dir-Gen., 1989–90, ABCC; Director: Cons. Res. Dept, 1990–95; Public Policy Unit, 1995–97. Shadow Minister for the Cabinet and Shadow Chancellor of the Duchy of Lancaster, 1999–2001; Shadow Sec. of State for Health, 2003–. Member: Select Cttee on Health, 1997–98; Trade and Industry Select Cttee, 2001–04. A Vice-Chm., Cons. Party, 1998–99. *Publications:* A Private Route?, 1988; Conservatives and the Constitution, 1997. *Recreations:* travel, cricket, films, history. *Address:* House of Commons, SW1A 0AA. *T:* (020) 7219 3000.

LANTOS, Prof. Peter Laszlo, PhD, DSc; FRCPath, FMedSci; Professor of Neuropathology, Institute of Psychiatry, King's College, London, 1979–2001, now Professor Emeritus; *b* 22 Oct. 1939; *s* of late Sandor Leipniker and Ilona Leipniker (*née* Somlo); name changed by deed poll to Lantos, 1961. *Educ:* Medical Univ. Szeged, Hungary (MD 1964); Middlesex Hosp. Sch. of Medicine, Univ. of London (PhD 1973, DSc 1992). FRCPath. Wellcome Res. Fellow, 1968–69; Lectr, 1969–75, Sen. Lectr and Hon. Consultant, 1976–79, in Neuropathol., Middx Hosp. Sch. of Medicine; Hon. Consultant in Neuropathology: Bethlem Royal and Maudsley Hosp., 1979–2001; KCH, 1984–2002; St Thomas' Hosp., 1992–2002; Dir, Neuropathol. Service, King's Neurosci. Centre, 1995–2001. Advr, German Fed. Ministry for Educn and Res., 2000–02. Chairman: Bd of Examrs in Neuropathol., RCPath, 1983–89; Scientific Adv. Panel, Brain Res. Trust, 1985–91; Samantha Dickson Res. Trust, 2003–; Trustee: Psychiatry Res. Trust, 1996–; Alzheimer Res. Trust, 2001–. FMedSci 2001. *Publications:* (ed) Greenfield's Neuropathology, 6th edn 1997, 7th edn 2002; Parallel Lines, 2006; contrib. numerous book chapters and scientific and med. papers and rev. articles to jls incl. Lancet and Nature. *Recreations:* travel, languages, theatres, fine arts. *T:* (020) 7487 5275, *Fax:* (020) 7487 2572; *e-mail:* peter.lantos@btinternet.com. *Club:* Athenæum.

LANYON, (Harry) Mark, CEng; Regional Director, Government Office for East Midlands, 1994–98; *b* 15 July 1939; *s* of late Henry Lanyon and Heather Gordon (*née* Tyrrell); *m* 1970, Elizabeth Mary Morton; one *s* one *d*. *Educ:* Ardingly Coll.; St Andrews Univ. (BSc Hons 1962). CEng 1965; MIMechE 1965. Ministry of Aviation: Engr Cadet, 1963–65; Aeronautical Inspectorate, 1965–68; Concorde Div., Min. of Technol., 1968–75; Department of Trade and Industry: Shipbuilding Policy Div., 1975–77; Dep. Dir, SW Region, 1977–82; Regl Dir, W Midlands, 1982–85; Hd of Br., Mechanical and Electrical Engrg Div., 1985–90; Asst Dir, Consumer Affairs, OFT, 1990–93; Regl Dir, Yorks and Humberside, DTI, 1993–94.

See also L. E. Lanyon.

LANYON, Prof. Lance Edward, CBE 2001; Principal, Royal Veterinary College, 1989–2004; Pro-Vice-Chancellor, University of London, 1997–99; *b* 4 Jan. 1944; *s* of late Henry Lanyon and Heather Gordon (*née* Tyrrell); *m* 1st, 1972, Mary Kear (marr. diss. 1997); one *s* one *d*; 2nd, 2003, Joanna Price. *Educ:* Christ's Hospital; Univ. of Bristol (BVSC, PhD, DSc). MRCVS. Lectr, 1967, Reader in Vet. Anatomy, 1967–79, Univ. of Bristol; Associate Prof., 1980–83, Prof., 1983–84, Tufts Sch. of Vet. Medicine, Boston, Mass; Prof. of Vet. Anatomy, Royal Vet. Coll., Univ. of London, 1984–89, personal title, 1989–2004, now Prof. Emeritus (Head, Dept of Vet. Anatomy, 1984–87, of Vet. Basic Scis, 1987–88). Almoner, Christ's Hosp., 1998–. Chm., Governing Body, Christ's Hosp. Sch., 2007–. Founder FMedSci 1998; FRVC 2005. Hon. DSc Bristol, 2004. *Publications:* chapters in books on orthopaedics, osteoporosis, and athletic training; articles in professional jls. *Recreations:* building, home improvements, sailing. *Address:* Royal Veterinary College, Royal College Street, NW1 0TU. *T:* (020) 7468 5000.

See also H. M. Lanyon.

LANYON, Mark; *see* Lanyon, H. M.

LAPIDGE, Prof. Michael, PhD, LittD; FBA 1994; Fellow of Clare College, Cambridge, since 1990; *b* 8 Feb. 1942; *s* of Rae H. Lapidge and Catherine Mary Lapidge (*née* Carruthers). *Educ:* Univ. of Calgary (BA 1962); Univ. of Alberta (MA 1965); Univ. of Toronto (PhD 1971); LittD Cantab 1988. Cambridge University: Lectr, 1974–88; Reader in Insular Latin Literature, 1988–91; Elrington and Bosworth Prof. of Anglo-Saxon, 1991–98; Notre Dame Prof. of English, Univ. of Notre Dame, Indiana, 1999–2004. Corresponding Fellow: Bayerische Akademie der Wissenschaften, 1997; Accad. dei Lincei, 2001. *Publications:* Aldhelm: the prose works, 1979; Alfred the Great, 1983; Aldhelm: the poetic works, 1985; A Bibliography of Celtic Latin Literature 400–1200, 1985; Wulfstan of Winchester: the life of St Ethelwold, 1991; Anglo-Saxon Litanies of the Saints, 1991; Anglo-Latin Literature 900–1066, 1993; Biblical Commentaries from the Canterbury School of Theodore and Hadrian, 1994; Archbishop Theodore, 1995; Byrhtferth's Enchiridion, 1995; Anglo-Latin Literature 600–899, 1996; The Cult of St Swithun, 2003; The Anglo-Saxon Library, 2006; articles in learned jls. *Recreation:* mountaineering. *Address:* 143 Sturton Street, Cambridge CB1 2QH. *T:* (01223) 363768.

LA PLANTE, Lynda, CBE 2008; writer and producer; Founder and Chairman, La Plante Productions, since 1994; *m* Richard La Plante (marr. diss.). *Educ:* RADA (schol.). Former actress. Writer: *television: series:* Widows, 1983; Prime Suspect, 1991, series 3, 1993; Civvies, 1992; Seekers, 1993; The Lifeboat, 1994; The Governor, 1995, series 2, 1996; The Prosecutors (US); Supply and Demand, 1996, series 2, 1998; Trial and Retribution, annual series, 1997–; Killer Net, 1998; Mind Games, 2000; The Commander, 2003, 2005; *play:* Seconds Out. *Publications:* The Legacy, 1988; The Talisman, 1989; Bella Mafia, 1991 (televised, US); Entwined, 1992; Framed, 1993; Seekers, 1993; Widows, 1994; Cold Shoulder, 1994; Prime Suspect, 1995; Prime Suspect 3, 1995; She's Out, 1995; The Governor, 1995; Cold Blood, 1986; Cold Heart, 1998; Trial and Retribution, no 1, 1997, no 2, 1998, no 3, 1999, no 4, 2000; Sleeping Cruelty, 2000; Royal Flush, 2002; Above Suspicion, 2004; The Red Dahlia, 2006; Clean Cut, 2007. *Address:* La Plante Productions Ltd, Paramount House, 162–170 Wardour Street, W1V 3AT.

LAPLI, Sir John Ini, GCMG 1999; Governor General, Solomon Islands, 1999–2004; baptized 24 June 1955; *s* of Christian Mekope and Ellen Lauai; *m* 1985, Helen; three *s* one *d*. *Educ:* Nabakaenga Jun. Primary Sch., Solomon Is; Lueslemba Sen. Primary Sch., Solomon Is; Selwyn Coll., Guadalcanal; Bp Patterson Theol Coll., Guadalcanal (Cert. Theol.); St John's Theol Coll., Auckland (LTh, Dip. and Licentiate in Theol.). Tutor, Theol Coll., 1982–83; teacher, Catechist Sch., Rural Trng Centre, 1985; parish priest, 1986; Bible translator, 1987–88; Premier, Temotu Province, Solomon Is, 1988–99. *Recreation:* gardening, before taking up public office. *Address:* c/o Government House, PO Box 252, Honiara, Solomon Islands.

LAPOINTE, Paul André; Ambassador for Fisheries Conservation, Canada, 1994–96, retired; *b* 1 Nov. 1934; *s* of Henri and Regina Lapointe; *m* 1965, Iris Donati; one *d*. *Educ:* Université Laval. BA, LLL. Called to the Bar, Québec, 1958. Journalist, Le Soleil, 1959–60; joined Canadian Foreign Service, 1960; served Vietnam and Laos, 1961–62, NATO, Paris, 1962–64, Geneva, 1968–72, New Delhi, 1975–76, New York, 1976–79; Dep. Perm. Rep. to UN Security Council, 1977–78; Dep. High Comr in UK, 1981–85; Consul Gen., Marseille, France, 1985–87; Sen. Negotiator, Canada-France Maritime Affairs, Dept of External Affairs, Canada, 1987–90; Canadian Ambassador to Turkey, 1990–93. *Address:* 2837 Hank Rivers Drive, Ottawa, ON K1T 4A2, Canada. *Club:* Travellers.

LAPOTAIRE, Jane Elizabeth Marie; actress; *b* 26 Dec. 1944; *d* of unknown father and Louise Elise Lapotaire; *m* 1st, 1965, Oliver Wood (marr. diss. 1967); 2nd, 1974, Roland Joffé (marr. diss. 1982); one *s*. *Educ:* Northgate Grammar Sch., Ipswich; Old Vic Theatre Sch., Bristol. Bristol Old Vic Co., 1965–67; Nat. Theatre Co., 1967–71, incl. Measure for Measure, Flea in Her Ear, Dance of Death, Way of the World, Merchant of Venice, Oedipus, The Taming of the Shrew; freelance films and TV, 1971–74; RSC, 1974–75 (roles included Viola in Twelfth Night, and Sonya in Uncle Vanya); Prospect Theatre Co., West End, 1975–76 (Vera in A Month in the Country, Lucy Honeychurch in A Room with a View); freelance films and TV, 1976–78; Rosalind in As You Like It, Edin. Fest., 1977; RSC, 1978–81: Rosaline in Love's Labours Lost, 1978–79; title role in Piaf, The Other Place 1978, Aldwych 1979, Wyndhams 1980, Broadway 1981 (SWET Award 1979, London Critics Award and Variety Club Award 1980, and Broadway Tony Award 1981); National Theatre: Eileen, Kick for Touch, 1983; Belvidera, Venice Preserv'd, Antigone, 1984; Saint Joan (title rôle), Compass Co., 1985; Double Double, Fortune Theatre, 1986; RSC, 1986–87: Misalliance, 1986; Archbishop's Ceiling, 1986; Greenland, Royal Court, 1988; Shadowlands, Queen's, 1989–90 (Variety Club Best Actress Award); RSC, 1992–94: Gertrude in Hamlet, 1992; Mrs Alving in Ghosts, 1993; Katharine of Aragon in Henry VIII, RSC, UK and USA tour, 1996–98 (Helen Hayes Award, USA, 1998); one-woman show, Shakespeare as I knew her, Bristol, 1996, Stratford and USA, 1997; *television:* Marie Curie (serial), 1977; Antony and Cleopatra, 1981; Macbeth, 1983; Seal Morning (series), 1985; Napoleon and Josephine, 1987; Blind Justice (serial), 1988 (British Press Guild Best Actress Award); The Dark Angel, 1989; Love Hurts (series), 1992, 1993; The Big Battalions (series), 1992; Johnny and the Dead (series), 1994; He Knew He Was Right, 2004; Trial and Retribution, 2008; *films* include: Eureka, 1983; Lady Jane, 1986; Surviving Picasso, 1996; There's Only One Jimmy Grimble, 2000. Vis. Fellow, Sussex Univ., 1986–2002. Mem., Marie Curie Meml Foundn Appeals Cttee, 1986–88. Pres., Bristol Old Vic Theatre Club, 1985–; Hon. Pres., Friends of Shakespeare's Globe, 1986–. Hon. Associate Artist, RSC, 1992. Hon. Fellow, Exeter Univ., 2007. Hon. DLitt: Bristol, 1997; East Anglia, 1998; Warwick, 2000; Exeter, 2005. *Publications:* Grace and Favour (autobiog.), 1989 (repubd as Everybody's Daughter, Nobody's Child, 2007); Out of Order: a haphazard journey through one woman's year, 1999; Time Out of Mind: recovering from a brain haemorrhage, 2003. *Recreation:* walking. *Address:* Gardner Herrity, 24 Conway Street, W1 6BG. *T:* (020) 7388 0088.

LAPPER, Maj.-Gen. John; Medical Director, International Hospitals Group, 1984–1988; *b* 24 July 1921; *s* of late Col Wilfred Mark Lapper, OBE, Legion of Merit (USA), late RE, and Agnes Lapper (*née* Powner); *m* 1948, Dorothy, *d* of late Roland John and Margaret Simpson (*née* Critchlow); three *s*. *Educ:* Wolverhampton Grammar Sch.; King Edward VI Sch., Birmingham; Birmingham Univ. MB, ChB 1946; DLO 1952. House appts, Queen Elizabeth and Children's Hosp., Birmingham, and Ronkswood Hosp. and Royal Infirm., Worcester; Registrar, Royal Berks Hosp., Reading. Commnd RAMC, 1950; ENT specialist, Mil. Hosps in UK, Libya, Egypt, Germany, Singapore, Malaya; CO 14 Field Amb., BAOR, 1958; CO BMH Rinteln, BAOR, 1964; Asst Comdt, Royal Army Med. Coll., 1965–68; ADMS Hong Kong, 1969–71; CO Queen Alexandra's Mil. Hosp., Millbank, 1971–73; ADMS 3 Div., 1973; DDMS HQ UKLF, 1974–77; Dir, Med. Supply, MoD, 1977; Dir, Med. Policy and Plans, MoD, 1978–80, retired; QHS 1977–80. Hospital and Medical Dir, Nat. Guard Saudi Arabia, 1981–83. Hudson-Evans Lectr, W Kent Medico-Chirurgical Soc., 1980; Mem. Sands Cox Med. Soc., Birmingham Univ. FFPH (FFCM 1980); FCMI (FBIM 1980); FRSocMed; FMedSoc London; Mem. BMA; Pres. Med. Soc., Hong Kong, 1970–71; Mem., RUSI; Chm. Council, Yateley Industries for the Disabled, 1983–95. OStJ 1959. *Publications:* articles in professional jls. *Recreations:* travel, militaria. *Address:* The Chimes, 4 Manor Fields, Alrewas, Burton-upon-Trent, Staffs DE13 7DA. *T:* (01283) 791628.

LAPPERT, Prof. Michael Franz, FRS 1979; Research Professor of Chemistry, University of Sussex, since 1997 (Professor of Chemistry, 1969–97); *b* 31 Dec. 1928; *s* of Julius Lappert and Kornelie Lappert (*née* Beran); *m* 1980, Lorna McKenzie. *Educ:* Wilson's Grammar School; Northern Polytechnic, London. BSc, PhD, DSc (London). FRSC. Northern Polytechnic, London: Asst Lecturer, 1952–53; Lecturer, 1953–55; Sen. Lectr, 1955–59. UMIST: Lectr, 1959–61; Sen. Lectr, 1961–64; Reader, Univ. of Sussex, 1964–69. SERC Sen. Res. Fellow, 1980–85. Pres., Dalton Div., RSC, 1989–91. Tilden Lectr, Chem. Soc., 1972–73; Nyholm Lectr, 1994, Frankland Lectr, 1999, RSC. Hon. Dr rer. nat. München, 1989. First recipient of (London) Chemical Soc. Award in Main Group Metal Chemistry, 1970; Award in Organometallic Chemistry, 1978; F. S. Kipping Award of American Chem. Soc., 1976; Alfred Stock Meml Award, German Chem. Soc., 2008. *Publications:* (ed jtly) Developments in Inorganic Polymer Chemistry, 1962; (jtly) Metal and Metalloid Amides, 1980; (jtly) Organo-zirconium and -hafnium Compounds, 1986; more than 750 papers in Jl Chem. Soc., etc. *Recreations:* theatre, opera, tennis, walking. *Address:* Department of Chemistry, School of Life Sciences, University of Sussex, Brighton BN1 9QJ; 4 Varndean Gardens, Brighton BN1 6WL; John Dalton Cottage, Eaglesfield, Cockermouth, Cumbria CA13 0SD.

LAPPING, Anne Shirley Lucas, CBE 2005; independent television producer; Director, Brook Lapping Productions (formerly Brook Associates), 1982–2008; *b* 10 June 1941; *d* of late Frederick Stone and of Dr Freda Lucas Stone; *m* 1963, Brian Michael Lapping, *qv*; three *d*. *Educ:* City of London Sch. for Girls; London Sch. of Econs. New Society, 1964–68; London Weekend TV, 1970–73; writer on The Economist, 1974–82. Other writing and broadcasting. Director: Channel Four, 1989–94; NW London Mental Health NHS Trust, 1992–99; Scott Trust, 1994–2004; Interights, 2006–; Vice-Chm., Central and NW London Mental Health Trust, 1999–2004. Member: SSRC, 1977–79; Nat. Gas Consumers' Council, 1978–79. Trustee, Open Media, 2006–. Gov., LSE, 1994– (Mem. Council, 2004–; Vice Chm., 2008–). *Recreations:* reading, cooking, arguing. *Address:* 61 Eton Avenue, NW3 3ET. *T:* (020) 7586 1047.

LAPPING, Brian Michael, CBE 2005; television producer; Chairman: Teachers' TV; Brook Lapping Productions Ltd; *b* 13 Sept. 1937; *s* of Max and Doris Lapping; *m* 1963, Anne Shirley Lucas Stone (*see* A. S. L. Lapping); three *d*. *Educ:* Pembroke Coll., Cambridge (BA). Reporter, Daily Mirror, 1959–61; reporter and Dep. Commonwealth

Corresp., The Guardian, 1961–67; Ed., Venture (Fabian Soc. monthly jl), 1963–68; feature writer, Financial Times, 1967–68; Dep. Ed., New Society, 1968–70; Granada TV, 1970–88: Producer: What the Papers Say; Party confs; This is Your Right; Executive Producer: World in Action; Hypotheticals; End of Empire; Apartheid; Breakthrough at Reykjavik, etc; Dir, Brian Lapping Associates, subseq. Brook Lapping Productions, 1988–: executive producer: Countdown to War, 1989; The Second Russian Revolution, 1991; Question Time, 1991–94; Watergate, 1993; The Death of Yugoslavia, 1995; Fall of the Wall, Death of Apartheid, 1996; The 50 Years' War—Israel and the Arabs, 1998; Hostage, Playing the China Card, Finest Hour, 1999; Endgame in Ireland, 2001; Tackling Terror, 2002; The Fall of Milosevic, 2003; Elusive Peace, Israel and the Arabs, 2005. Awards include: RTS Awards, 1978, 1991, 1995, 2006; Emmy Award, 1994; BPG Awards, 1986, 1991, 1995, 2003; Gold Medal, NY Internat. Film and TV Fest., 1986, 1990, 1995; Silver/Gold Batons, du Pont/Columbia Awards, 1994, 1996 and 2007; The Indie, Producers Alliance for Cinema and Television, 1996; BAFTA Lifetime Achievement Award, 2003. *Publications:* (with G. Radice) More Power to the People, 1962; The Labour Government 1964–70, 1970; End of Empire, 1985; Apartheid: a history, 1987. *Recreation:* tending vines. *Address:* 61 Eton Avenue, NW3 3ET. *T:* (020) 7586 1047.

LAPPING, Peter Herbert; Headmaster of Sherborne, 1988–2000; *b* 8 Aug. 1941; *s* of late Dr Douglas James Lapping, MBE and Dorothy Lapping (*née* Horrocks) of Nhlangano, Swaziland; *m* 1967, Diana Dillworth, *d* of late Lt-Col E. S. G. Howard, MC, RA; one *s* one *d. Educ:* St John's College, Johannesburg; Univ. of Natal, Pietermaritzburg (BA Hons *cum laude*); Lincoln College, Oxford (MA). Asst Master, Reed's Sch., Cobham, 1966–67; Head of History, Loretto Sch., 1967–79 (Housemaster, Pinkie House, 1972–79); Headmaster, Shiplake Coll., Oxon, 1979–88. Governor: Sherborne Prep. Sch., 1998–; King's Sch., Gloucester, 2008–. Chm., Governors, Pinewood Sch., Bourton, 2001–. *Recreations:* cricket and other games, cooking, walking, basking in the beauty of the Cotswolds. *Address:* Lower Bubblewell, Minchinhampton, Glos GL6 9DL. *Clubs:* MCC; Vincent's (Oxford); Glos County Cricket.

LAPSLEY, Peter Michael; Patient Editor, British Medical Journal, since 2005; *b* 19 June 1943; *s* of Air Marshal Sir John Hugh Lapsley, KBE, CB, DFC, AFC and Jean Margaret (*née* McIvor); *m* 1st, 1970, Jennifer Mary Blockley (marr. diss. 1985); one *s* one *d*; 2nd, 1986, Elizabeth Ann Wyatt. *Educ:* Aldenham Sch., Elstree; RMA, Sandhurst. Served Army, King's Own Royal Border Regt, 1962–73: served Germany, UK, British Guyana, Aden, Trucial States (UAE), NI; Principal, then Sen. Principal, MoD, 1973–80; Co-owner/Manager, Rockbourne Trout Fishery, 1980–84; Sen. Principal, MoD, 1984–87; Chief Exec., Nat. Back Pain Assoc., 1987–90; Dept of Transport, 1990–96 (HM Chief Inspector of Aviation Security, 1991–96); Chief Executive: Nat. Eczema Soc., 1997–2001; Skin Care Campaign, 2001–07. Mem. Exec. Cttee, Falkland Is Assoc., 1996–2005. *Publications:* The Bankside Book of Stillwater Trout Flies, 1978, 2nd edn 1983; Trout From Stillwaters, 1981; River Trout Flyfishing, 1988; (ed) The Complete Fly Fisher, 1990; (jtly) Fly Fishing by J. R. Hartley, 1991; Fly Fishing for Trout, 1992; (jtly) J. R. Hartley Casts Again, 1992; Fishing for Falklands Sea Trout, 2000; River Fly-Fishing, 2003. *Recreations:* fly fishing, writing, photography, travel. *Address:* 27 Lillian Avenue, W3 9AN. *T:* (020) 8993 7453. *Club:* Flyfishers'.

LAPTHORNE, Richard Douglas, CBE 1997; Chairman, Cable and Wireless plc, since 2003; *b* 25 April 1943; *s* of Eric Joseph Lapthorne and Irene Ethel Lapthorne; *m* 1967, Valerie Waring; two *s* two *d. Educ:* Calday Grange GS, West Kirby; Liverpool Univ. (BCom). FCMA, FCCA, FCT. Unilever plc: Audit, 1965–67; Lever Brothers, Zambia, 1967–69; Central Pensions Dept, 1969–71; Food Industries, 1971–75; Synthetic Resins, 1975–77; Sheby, Paris, 1978–80; Crosfield Chemicals, 1980–83; Gp Financial Controller, 1983–86, Gp Finance Dir, 1986–92, Courtaulds plc; Gp Finance Dir, 1992–98, Vice Chm., 1998–99, British Aerospace plc; Chm., 1996–97, 1999–2003, Dep. Chm., 1997–99, Nycomed Amersham, subseq. Amersham plc; Chairman: Morse Hldgs plc, 1998–2008; Avecia Ltd, 1999–2005; Tunstall Ltd, 2000–04; TI Automotive Systems plc, 2001–03; Arlington Securities Ltd, 2005; New Look Retailers Ltd, 2005–07; Vice-Chm., JP Morgan Investment Bank, 2001–05. Director: Oasis Internat. Leasing (Abu Dhabi), 1998–2006; Orange plc, 2001–03. Dir, Working Age Project, HM Treasury, 2000; Ext. Advr, Navy Bd, 2000–03. Trustee: Royal Botanic Gdns, Kew, 1998– (Chm., Foundn and Friends, 1997–2004); HM the Queen's Trustee, 2004–); Calibre, 1999–2008; Tommy's Campaign, 2003–. CCMI. Hon. CRAeS 1997. *Recreations:* gardening, opera, travel.

LAQUEUR, Walter; historian, political commentator and writer; Chairman, Research Council, Center for Strategic and International Studies, Washington, 1978–2001; Academic Adviser, Institute of Contemporary History and Wiener Library, London, 1964–92; *b* 26 May 1921; *s* of late Fritz Laqueur and late Else Laqueur; *m* 1st, 1941, Barbara (*d* 1995), *d* of Prof. Richard Koch and Maria Koch (*née* Rosenthal); two *d*; 2nd, 1996, Christa Susi Wichmann (*née* Genzen). Agricultural labourer during War, 1939–44. Journalist, free lance author, 1944–55; Editor of Survey, 1955–65; Co-editor of Journal of Contemporary History, 1966–2005. Prof., History of Ideas, Brandeis Univ., 1967–71; Prof. of Contemporary History, Tel Aviv Univ., 1970–; Vis. Professor: Chicago Univ.; Johns Hopkins Univ.; Harvard Univ. Hon. Dr: Hebrew Union Coll., NY, 1988; Adelphi Univ., 1990; Brandeis Univ., 1991. Grand Cross of Merit, FRG, 1986. *Publications:* Communism and Nationalism in the Middle East, 1956; Young Germany, 1961; Russia and Germany, 1965; The Road to War, 1968; Europe Since Hitler, 1970; Out of the Ruins of Europe, 1971; Zionism, a History, 1972; Confrontation: the Middle East War and World Politics, 1974; Weimar: a Cultural History, 1918–33, 1974; Guerrilla, 1976; Terrorism, 1977; The Missing Years, 1980; (ed jtly) A Reader's Guide to Contemporary History, 1972; (ed) Fascism: a reader's guide, 1978; The Terrible Secret, 1980; Farewell to Europe, 1981; Germany Today: a personal report, 1985; World of Secrets: the uses and limits of intelligence, 1986; The Long Road to Freedom, 1989; Stalin: the glasnost revelations, 1991; Europe in Our Time, 1992; Thursday's Child Has Far to Go, 1994; Generation Exodus, 2001; The Last Days of Europe, 2007. *Recreations:* swimming, motor-boating. *Address:* e-mail: walter@laqueur.net.

LARA, Brian Charles; cricketer; *b* Trinidad, 2 May 1969; *s* of Banty and Pearl Lara. *Educ:* San Juan Secondary Sch.; Fatima Coll., Port of Spain. Started playing cricket aged 6; left-handed batsman; played for: WI Under-19s (Captain, WI Youth XI against India); Trinidad and Tobago, 1987– (Captain, 1993); Warwickshire, 1994, 1998 (Captain) (world record 1st cl. score of 501 not out, *v* Durham at Edgbaston, 1994); West Indies, 1990–2007 (Captain, 1997, 1998–99, 2000, 2003–04, 2007; world record score of 400 in a Test Match, St John's, Antigua, 2004); 34 Test, 64 1st class, centuries. *Publication:* Beating the Field (autobiog.), 1995. *Recreations:* golf, horse-racing. *Address:* c/o West Indies Cricket Board, PO Box 616, St John's, Antigua.

LARCOMBE, Brian Paul; Chief Executive, 3i Group plc, 1997–2004; *b* 27 Aug. 1953; *s* of John George Larcombe and Joyce Lucille Larcombe (*née* Westwood); *m* 1983, Dr Catherine Bullen. *Educ:* Bromley Grammar Sch.; Univ. of Birmingham (BCom). Joined 3i Gp, 1974: Local Dir, 1982; Regl Dir, 1988; Finance Dir, 1992–97. Non-executive Director: Smith and Nephew plc, 2002–; F&C Asset Management, 2005–; Party Gaming

plc, 2005–06; Gallaher Gp plc, 2006–07; Chm., Bramdean Alternatives Ltd, 2007–. Member: Council, British Venture Capital Assoc., 1989–96 (Chm., 1994–95); UK Council, INSEAD, 1997–2006; Singapore British Business Council, 1997–2004; Exchange Markets Gp, London Stock Exchange, 2001–03. *Recreations:* golf, biographies, modern paintings. *Address:* 32 Fife Road, East Sheen, SW14 7EL.

LARGE, Sir Andrew (McLeod Brooks), Kt 1996; Deputy Governor, Bank of England, 2002–06; *b* 7 Aug. 1942; *s* of late Maj.-Gen. Stanley Eyre Large, MBE and of Janet Mary Large (*née* Brooks); *m* 1967, Susan Mary Melville; two *s* one *d. Educ:* Winchester Coll.; Corpus Christi Coll., Cambridge (BA Hons Econ; MA); INSEAD, Fontainebleau (MBA). BP, 1964–71; Man. Dir, Orion Bank, 1971–79; Exec. Bd Mem., Swiss Bank Corp., 1980–89; Large, Smith & Walter, 1990–92; Chairman: SIB, 1992–97; IOSCO, 1992; a Dep. Chm., Barclays Bank, 1998–2002. Chm., Euroclear, 1998–2000; non-executive Director: Nuclear Electric, 1990–94; Rank Hovis McDougall, 1990–92; Phoenix Securities, 1990–92; Dowty Gp, 1991–92; English China Clays, 1991–96; London Fox, 1991–92 (Chm.); Luthy Baillie Dowsett Pethick, 1990–92 (Chm.); Axis Capital, Bermuda, 2006–; MW Tops Ltd, 2006– (Chm.). Chm., Securities Assoc., 1986–87; Member: Council, Stock Exchange, 1986–87; Panel on Takeovers and Mergers, 1987–88; Lloyds Council, 1992–93; Bd of Banking Supervision, 1996–97; Chm., Hedge Funding Wkg Gp, 2007–08. Member Board: Inst. of Internat. Finance, Washington, 1998–2001; INSEAD, 1998– (Chm. UK Council, 1997–2002). Governor: Abingdon Sch., 1991–98; Winchester Coll., 1998– (Warden, 2003–08); Christ Coll., Brecon, 1998–. *Recreations:* ski-ing, walking, photography, music, old apple trees. *Club:* Brooks's.

LARKEN, Comdt Anthea, CBE 1991; Director and Company Secretary, Operational Command Training Organisation Ltd, 1991–96; *b* 23 Aug. 1938; *d* of Frederick William Savill and Nance (*née* Williams); *m* 1987 (marr. diss. 1997). *Educ:* Stafford Girls' High Sch. Joined WRNS as Range Assessor, 1956; commnd, 1960; qualified: as Photographic Interpreter, 1961; as WRNS Secretarial Officer, 1967; Staff Officer in Singapore, 1964–66; i/c WRNS Officers' Training, BRNC Dartmouth, 1976–78; NATO Military Agency for Standardisation, Brussels, 1981–84; CSO (Admin) to Flag Officer Plymouth, 1985–86; RCDS, 1987; Dir, WRNS, 1988–91. ADC to the Queen, 1988–91. Hon. LLD Greenwich, 2000. *Recreations:* theatre, music, reading, home, family and friends. *Club:* Army and Navy.

LARKEN, Rear Adm. (Edmund Shackleton) Jeremy, DSO 1982; Managing Director, OCTO, since 1991; advisory consultant in corporate crisis and emergency management and leadership; *b* 14 Jan. 1939; *s* of Rear Adm. Edmund Thomas Larken, CB, OBE and Eileen Margaret (*née* Shackleton); *m* 1st, 1963, Wendy Nigella Hallett (marr. diss. 1987); two *d*; 2nd, 1987, Anthea Savill (*see* Comdt Anthea Larken) (marr. diss. 1997); 3rd, 1997, Helen Shannon; one *s* one *d. Educ:* Bryanston Sch.; BRNC, Dartmouth. Joined RN as Cadet, 1957; qualified: in Submarines, 1960; in Navigation, 1965; in Submarine Comd, 1960; served HMS Tenby, Finwhale, Tudor, Ambush and Narwhal; Navigation Officer, HMS Valiant; First Lieut, HMS Otus; commanded HMS Osiris, Glamorgan and Valiant, Third Submarine Sqn, and HMS Fearless (including Falklands Campaign, 1982); exchange with USN (Submarines), 1971–73; Naval Plans; Dir, Naval Staff Duties, 1985; Cdre Amphibious Warfare, 1985–87; ACDS (Overseas), 1988–90. Mem., RUSI, 1970–2006. Governor, Bryanston Sch., 1988–99. FInstD 2003 (MInstD 1996). *Publications:* papers and articles in professional books and periodicals. *Recreations:* maritime and aviation interests, strategy, theatre, reading, home, family and friends. *Address:* OCTO, Caerlleon House, 142 Boughton, Chester CH3 5BP; e-mail: Jeremy.Larken@octo.uk.com. *Club:* Reform.

LARKINS, Prof. Richard Graeme, AO 2002; MD, PhD; Vice-Chancellor and President, Monash University, since 2003; Chair, Universities Australia, 2008; *b* 17 May 1943; *s* of Graeme Larkins and Margaret Larkins (*née* Rosanove, now Lusink); *m* 1966, Caroline Cust; three *d. Educ:* Univ. of Melbourne (MB BS 1966; MD 1972); RPMS London (PhD 1974). FRACP 1975; FRCP 1990; FRCPI 2000. Resident, Sen. Resident, then Med. Registrar, 1967–69; Asst Endocrinologist, 1970–72, Royal Melbourne Hosp.; Res. Fellow (Churchill Fellow and MRC Fellow), Endocrine Unit, RPMS, Hammersmith Hosp., London, 1972–74; Physician to Endocrine Lab., and to Outpatients, Royal Melbourne Hosp., 1974–77; University of Melbourne: First Asst, 1978–83, Reader in Medicine, 1983, Dept of Medicine, and Dir, Endocrine and Metabolic Unit, 1979–83, Repatriation Gen. Hosp., Heidelberg, Vic; James Stewart Prof. of Medicine, and Hd, Dept of Medicine, Royal Melbourne Hosp./Western Hosp., 1984–97; Associate Dean, Planning, 1996–97, Dean, 1998–2003, Fac. of Medicine, Dentistry and Health Scis; Royal Melbourne Hospital: Endocrinologist, 1984; Dir, Dept of Diabetes and Endocrinology, 1989–93; Chm., Div. of Medicine, 1991–94; Med. Dir, Clinical Business Unit, Internal Medicine, 1994–96. Chairman: Accreditation Cttee, Australian Med. Council, 1991–95; NH&MRC, Australia, 1997–2000; Member: Prime Minister's Sci., Engrg and Innovation Council, 1997–2000; Nat. Aboriginal and Torres Strait Islander Health Council, 1997–2000. President: Endocrine Soc. of Aust., 1982–84; RACP, 2000–02. Honorary Fellow: Academy of Medicine: Malaysia; Singapore; Royal Coll. of Physicians of Thailand; Ceylon Coll. of Physicians; Hon. FACP. Hon. LLD Melbourne. Eric Susman Prize for Med. Res., RACP, 1982; Sir William Upjohn Medal, Univ. of Melbourne, 2002. *Publications:* (jtly) A Textbook of Clinical Medicine: an approach to patients' major problems, 1983; A Practical Approach to Endocrine Disorders, 1985; (jtly) Problems in Clinical Medicine, 1989; (ed jtly) Diabetes 1988, 1989; (with R. A. Smallwood) Clinical Skills, 1993; author or co-author of over 180 refereed jl articles. *Recreations:* golf, reading. *Address:* 10 Hawthorn Grove, Hawthorn, Vic 3122, Australia. *T:* (3) 99052046, *Fax:* (3) 99052096; e-mail: Richard.Larkins@adm.monash.edu.au. *Clubs:* Melbourne; Royal Melbourne Golf; Barwon Heads Golf.

LARMINIE, (Ferdinand) Geoffrey, OBE 1971; Director, British Geological Survey, 1987–90; *b* 23 June 1929; *s* of late Ferdinand Samuel Larminie and of Mary Larminie (*née* Willis); *m* 1956, Helena Elizabeth Woodside Carson; one *s* one *d. Educ:* St Andrews Coll., Dublin; Trinity Coll., Dublin (BA 1954, MA 1972; Hon. Fellow, 1989). Asst Lectr in Geology, Univ. of Glasgow, 1954–56; Lectr in Geology, Univ. of Sydney, 1956–60; joined British Petroleum Co. Ltd, 1960: Exploration Dept in Sudan, Greece, Canada, Libya, Kuwait, California, New York, Thailand and Alaska, 1960–74; Scientific Advr, Inf. Dept, London, 1974–75; Gen. Manager, Public Affairs and Inf. Dept, London, 1975–76; Gen. Manager, Environmental Control Centre, London, 1976–84; External Affairs Co-ordinator, Health, Safety and Environmental Services, BP plc, 1984–87. Chm., Cambridge Arctic Shelf Prog., 1996–98 (Vice-Chm., 1993–96). Member: Royal Commn on Environmental Pollution, 1979–83; NERC, 1983–87. Council Mem., RGS, 1984–90, Vice-Pres., 1987–90. President: Alaska Geol Soc., 1969; Soc. of Underwater Technol., 1987–89 (Hon. Fellow, 1992). Trustee, Bermuda Biological Station 1978–91, Life Trustee, 1991; Member: Bd of Management, Inst. of Offshore Engrg, Heriot-Watt Univ., 1981–90; Polar Res. Bd, Nat. Res. Council, Washington, DC, 1984–88. Mem., IBA Gen. Adv. Council, 1980–85. Mem. of numerous scientific and professional socs. *Publications:* papers in scientific and technical jls on oil ind., and occasional reviews. *Recreations:*

archaeology, natural history, reading, shooting. *Address:* Lane End, Lanes End, Tring, Herts HP23 6LF. *T:* (01296) 624907.

LaROCQUE, Judith Anne, CVO 1992; Deputy Minister of Canadian Heritage, since 2002 (Associate Deputy Minister, 2000–02); Secretary to the Governor General of Canada, since 1990; Secretary General, Order of Canada and Order of Military Merit, and Herald Chancellor of Canada, since 1990; *b* Hawkesbury, Ontario, 27 Sept. 1956; *d* of Olier LaRocque and Elizabeth (*née* Murray); *m* 1991, André Roland Lavoie. *Educ:* Carleton Univ. (BA Pol Sci. 1979; MA Public Admin 1992). Admin. Asst, Internal Audit Directorate, Public Service Commn, 1979; writer/researcher, Prime Minister's Office, 1979; Special Asst, Office of Leader of Opposition, 1980–82; Cttee Clerk, Cttees and Private Legislation Br., H of C, 1982–84; Legislative Asst to Govt House Leader, 1984–85; Head of House Business, Office of Govt House Leader, Pres. Queen's Privy Council for Canada and Minister Responsible for Regulatory Affairs, 1985–86; Exec. Asst to Minister of Justice and Attorney Gen. of Canada, 1986–89; COS to Govt Leader in Senate and Minister of State for Federal-Provincial Relns, 1989–90. OStJ 1990. *Recreations:* gardening, cross-country ski-ing. *Address:* (office) Room 12A14, 25 Eddy Street, Gatineau, QC K1A 0M5, Canada.

LAROSIÈRE de CHAMPFEU, Jacques Martin Henri Marie de; *see* de Larosière de Champfeu.

LARPENT, Andrew Lionel Dudley de H.; *see* de Hochepied Larpent.

LARSEN, Prof. Henning; architect; founder and owner, Henning Larsen Architects A/S, architectural practice; Professor of Architecture, Royal Academy of Fine Arts, Copenhagen, since 1968; *b* 20 Aug. 1925; *s* of Erik Peter Larsen and Johanne Mary Gøbel; *m* Lone Backe. *Educ:* Royal Acad. of Fine Arts, Copenhagen (Dip. 1952); Sch. of Architecture, London; MIT, USA. Major projects include: Trondheim Univ., 1978; Min. of Foreign Affairs, Riyadh, 1984; Copenhagen Business Sch., 1989; Nation Centre, Nairobi, 1992; Roskilde Univ. Centre, 1996–; NeuroSearch Co. HQ, 1999; Physics Res. Centre, Stockholm, 2001; Ferring Co. HQ, 2002; Copenhagen Opera House, 2004; housing and commercial develts in Denmark and Sweden. Founder: architectural magazine Skala; Gallery Skala, 1985–94. Guest Professor: Yale, 1964, Princeton, 1965. Member: Royal Danish Acad. of Fine Arts; Royal Swedish Acad. of Fine Arts, Hon. mem. of Arch. Insts in England, Scotland, Germany, USA. Awards in competitions include: Kammergericht, Berlin, 1979; Compton Verney Opera House, 1989; Conf. Centre, Cambridge, 1989; Extension of Ny Carlsberg Glyptotek, Copenhagen, 1992; New Concert Hall, Copenhagen, 1993; City Library, Malmö, 1993; Danish Design Centre, Copenhagen, 1994; Max Planck Inst., Rostock, 1996; Terminal 2, Copenhagen Airport, 1997; Kunsthalle Adolf Würth, Germany, 1997; Faculty of Arts, Univ. of Plymouth, 2004. Hon. Dr Royal Inst. of Technol., Stockholm, 2001. Architectural prizes include: Internat. Design Award, UK, 1987; Domino's 30 Architects, USA, 1988; Aga Khan Award, 1989; Marble Architectural Award, Carrara, 1990 and 1999; Europa Nostra Diploma of EC, 1998. *Address:* (office) Vesterbrogade 76, 1620 Copenhagen V, Denmark. *T:* 8233 3000.

LARSON, Gary; cartoonist; *b* 14 Aug. 1950; *s* of Vern and Doris Larson; *m* 1988. *Educ:* Washington State Univ. (BA Communications). Cartoonist: The Far Side syndicated panel (1900 newspapers worldwide), 1980–95 (Best Syndicated Panel Award, 1985); The Far Side syndicated panel (syndicated internationally in 40 countries), 1995–. *Films:* Gary Larson's Tales From The Far Side, 1994; Gary Larson's Tales From The Far Side II, 1998. Reuben Award for Outstanding Cartoonist of Year, 1991 and 1994; Max and Moritz Prize, Best Internat. Cartoon, 1993; Grand Prix, Annecy Film Fest., 1995; Internat. Comics Fest. Award, for French lang. edn of Hound of The Far Side, 1997. *Publications:* The Far Side, 1982; Beyond The Far Side, 1983; In Search of The Far Side, 1984; Valley of The Far Side, 1985; Bride of The Far Side, 1985; It Came From The Far Side, 1986; Hound of The Far Side, 1987; The Far Side Observer, 1987; Night of The Crash-Test Dummies, 1988; Wildlife Preserves, 1989; Wiener Dog Art, 1990 (Wheatley Medals Award, Liby Assoc., 1991); Unnatural Selections, 1991; Cows of Our Planet, 1992; The Chickens are Restless, 1993; The Curse of Madame C, 1994; Last Chapter and Worse, 1996; There's a Hair in My Dirt! A Worm's Story, 1998; *anthologies:* The Far Side Gallery, 1, 2, 3, 4, 5; The PreHistory of The Far Side, 1989; The Complete Far Side, 2 vols, 2003. *Recreations:* jazz guitar, pick-up basketball. *Address:* c/o Creators Syndicate, Suite 700, 5777 W Century Boulevard, Los Angeles, CA 90045, USA. *T:* (310) 3377003; c/o Andrews McMeel Publishers, 4520 Main Street, Kansas City, MO 64111–7701, USA. *T:* (816) 9326700.

LARSSON, Gen. John; General of The Salvation Army, 2002–06; *b* 2 April 1938; *s* of Sture and Flora Larsson; *m* 1969, Freda Turner; two *s*. *Educ:* London Univ. (BD). Commnd as Salvation Army Officer, 1957, in corps, youth and trng work; Chief Sec., S America West, 1980–84; Principal, William Booth Meml Trng Coll., 1984–88; Admin. Planning, 1988–90; Territorial Commander: UK and Republic of Ireland, 1990–93; NZ and Fiji, 1993–96; Sweden and Latvia, 1996–99; CoS, Salvation Army Internat. HQ, 1999–2002. *Publications:* Doctrine Without Tears, 1974; Spiritual Breakthrough, 1983; The Man Perfectly Filled with the Spirit, 1986; How Your Corps can Grow, 1988. *Recreations:* music, walking. *Address:* 3 Oakbrook, 8 Court Downs Road, Beckenham, Kent BR3 6LR.

LASCELLES, family name of **Earl of Harewood**.

LASCELLES, Viscount; David Henry George Lascelles; freelance film and television producer; *b* 21 Oct. 1950; *s* and *heir* of 7th Earl of Harewood, *qv*; *m* 1979, Margaret Rosalind Messenger; three *s* one *d*; *m* 1990, Diane Jane Howse. *Educ:* The Hall Sch.; Westminster; Bristol Univ. Productions include: *films:* Tibet - a Buddhist Trilogy, 1977; Richard III, 1995; The Wisdom of Crocodiles, 1998; *television:* Inspector Morse IV and V, 1990 (BAFTA Best TV Series award); Wide-Eyed & Legless, 1992; Moll Flanders, 1996; Second Sight, 1999. Chm., Harewood House Trust Ltd, 1993–; Trustee: Orient Foundn, 1983–; Yorkshire Film Archive, 1994–; Kala Sangam, 2004–. *Address:* Harewood House, Harewood, Leeds, West Yorks LS17 9LG.

LASH, Prof. Nicholas Langrishe Alleyne, DD; Norris-Hulse Professor of Divinity, University of Cambridge, 1978–99, now Emeritus; Fellow, Clare Hall, Cambridge, since 1988; *b* 6 April 1934; *s* of late Henry Alleyne Lash and Joan Mary Lash (*née* Moore); *m* 1976, Janet Angela Chalmers; one *s*. *Educ:* Downside Sch.; Oscott Coll.; St Edmund's House, Cambridge. MA, PhD, BD, DD. Served RE, 1952–57. Oscott Coll., 1957–63; Asst Priest, Slough, 1963–68; Fellow, 1969–85, Dean, 1971–75, St Edmund's House, Cambridge; Univ. Asst Lectr, Cambridge, 1974–78. Hon. DD London, 2002. *Publications:* His Presence in the World, 1968; Change in Focus, 1973; Newman on Development, 1975; Voices of Authority, 1976; Theology on Dover Beach, 1979; A Matter of Hope, 1982; Theology on the Way to Emmaus, 1986; Easter in Ordinary, 1988; Believing three ways in one God, 1992; The Beginning and the End of 'Religion', 1996; Holiness, Speech and Silence, 2004; Seeing in the Dark: university sermons, 2005; Theology for Pilgrims, 2008. *Address:* 4 Hertford Street, Cambridge CB4 3AG.

LASKEY, Prof. Ronald Alfred, FRS 1984; FMedSci; Charles Darwin Professor, since 1983, Fellow of Darwin College, since 1982, and Hon. Joint Director, MRC Cancer Cell Unit, since 1999, University of Cambridge; *b* 26 Jan. 1945; *s* of Thomas Leslie and Bessie Laskey; *m* 1971, Margaret Ann Page; one *s* one *d*. *Educ:* High Wycombe Royal Grammar Sch.; Queen's Coll., Oxford. MA, DPhil 1970. Scientific Staff: Imperial Cancer Research Fund, 1970–73; MRC Lab. of Molecular Biology, 1973–83; Co-Dir, Molecular Embryology Group, Cancer Research Campaign, 1983–91; CRC Dir, Wellcome Cancer Res. UK (formerly CRC) Inst., 1991–2001. Mem. Bd, UK Panel for Res. Integrity, 2007–. Member, Scientific Advisory Committee: EMBL, 1999–; Max-Planck Inst. for Biochem., 2000– (Chm., 2002–); CRUK London Res. Inst.; Louis Jeantet Foundn, 2008–. Pres., British Soc. of Cell Biology, 1996–99. Vice-Pres., Acad. of Med. Scis, 2007–. Mem., Academia Europaea, 1989; Founder FMedSci 1998. Trustee: Strangeways Res. Lab., 1993–; Inst. of Cancer Res., 2007–. Croonian Lect., Royal Soc., 2001. Colworth Medal, Biochem. Soc., 1979; CIBA Medal, Biochem. Soc., 1997; Feldberg Foundn Prize, 1998; Louis Jeantet Prize for Medicine, Jeantet Foundn, Geneva, 1998; Medical Futures Health Innovation Award, 2007. *Publications:* articles on cell biology in scientific jls; Songs for Cynical Scientists and Selected Songs for Cynical Scientists. *Recreations:* music, mountains. *Address:* Hutchison/MRC Research Centre, Hills Road, Cambridge CB2 0XZ. *T:* (01223) 334106, 334107.

LASOK, (Karol) Paul (Edward); QC 1994; PhD; a Recorder, since 2000; *b* 16 July 1953; *s* of Prof. Dominik Lasok, QC; *m* 1991, Karen Bridget Morgan Griffith; two *d*. *Educ:* St Mary's Sch., Clyst St Mary; Jesus Coll., Cambridge (MA); Exeter Univ. (LLM, PhD). Called to the Bar, Middle Temple, 1977, Bencher, 2002; Legal Sec., Court of Justice of the EC, 1980–84 and (*locum tenens*) 1985; private practice, 1985–. Chm., Bar European Gp, 2007–. Consultant Editor, Butterworths European Court Practice; Jt Editor, Common Market Law Reports, 1996–. *Publications:* The European Court of Justice: practice and procedure, 1984, 2nd edn 1994; contribs to: Halsbury's Laws of England, 4th edn, vols 51 and 52; Law of European Communities (ed D. Vaughan); Law and Institutions of the European Union, 7th edn 2001; Weinberg and Blank on Takeovers and Mergers; legal periodicals. *Recreation:* amusing daughters. *Address:* 1 & 2 Raymond Buildings, Gray's Inn, WC1R 5NR. *T:* (020) 7405 7211.

LAST, Maj.-Gen. Christopher Neville, CB 1990; OBE 1976; health management consultant, 1998–2000; *b* 2 Sept. 1935; *s* of late Jack Neville Last, MPS, FSMC, FBOA and Lorna (*née* Goodman), MPS; *m* 1961, Pauline Mary Lawton, BA; two *d*. *Educ:* Culford Sch.; Brighton Tech. Coll. psc†, ndc. Commnd Royal Signals, 1956; Germany, Parachute Bde, Borneo, Singapore, 1956–67; OC 216 Para. Signal Sqdn, 1967; RMCS and Staff Coll., Logistics Staff 1 (BR) Corps, 1968–71; NDC, 1972; Lt-Col, Signal Staff HQ, BAOR, 1973; CO Royal Signals NI, 1974; Staff, MoD Combat Develt, 1976, Mil. Ops, 1977; Col, Project Manager MoD (PE) for Army ADP Comd and Control, 1977; CO (Col) 8 Signal Regt Trng, Royal Signals, 1980; Brig., Comd 1 Signal Bde 1 (BR) Corps, 1981; Dir, Mil. Comd and Control Projects, MoD (PE), 1984; Head of Defence Procurement Policy (Studies Team), on Chief of Defence Procurement Personal Staff, MoD (PE), 1985; Maj.-Gen. 1986; Vice Master Gen. of the Ordnance, 1986–88; Mil. Dep. to Head of Defence Export Services, 1988–90; Chief Exec., Clwyd FHSA, 1990–96; Dir of Business Management, Clwyd and Oswestry Tissue Bank, 1996–97; Advr and Chm. (designate), 2002–05, UK Human Tissue Bank. Col Comdt, RCS, 1990–96. Chairman: Royal Signals Instn, 1994–98; Bd of Trustees, Royal Signals Mus., 1994–2004. Mem., RFCA for Wales, 1996–. Pres., BRCS N Wales, 1996–2004, 2007– (Chm., 2004–07); Vice-Pres., BRCS Wales, 2000–04. Chm., Kigezi Foundn, 2001–02; Trustee, The Community Foundn in Wales, 2002–. Liveryman, Co. of Information Technologists, 1988 (Chm., Med. and Health Panel, 1998–2002); Freeman, City of London, 1988. *Recreations:* travel, theatre, ballet, sailing, ski-ing, shooting and country pursuits. *Address:* c/o National Westminster Bank, 34 North Street, Lancing, Sussex BN15 9AB. *Clubs:* Special Forces, Fadeaways.

LAST, John William, CBE 1989; Director, Public Affairs, United Utilities plc (formerly North West Water Group), 1993–98; Chairman, Museums Training Institute, 1990–97; *b* 22 Jan. 1940; *s* of late Jack Last (sometime Dir of Finance, Metrop. Police) and Freda Last (*née* Evans); *m* 1967, Susan Josephine, *er d* of late John and Josephine Farmer; three *s*. *Educ:* Sutton Grammar Sch., Surrey; Trinity Coll., Oxford (MA 1965). Littlewoods Organisation, Liverpool, 1969–93. Chairman: Dernier Properties Ltd, 1996–; Bute Communications Ltd, 2004–; Director: Boom, 1990–93; Inward, investment agency for NW, 1992–96; sparesFinder.com Ltd, 1999–2002. Mem., Merseyside CC, 1973–86 (Chm., Arts Cttee, 1977–81). Prospective Parly Cand. (L), Ilkeston, 1963; contested (C) Liverpool, West Derby, Feb. and Oct. 1974, Stockport N, 1979. Hon. Treas., 2002–03, Chm., 2008–, Welsh Lib Dem Party; Dep. Treas., 2003–05, Welsh Mem., UK Exec., 2007–, UK Lib Dem Party. Vis. Prof., City Univ., London, 1987–. Bd Mem., Royal Liverpool Philharmonic Soc., 1973–93 (Chm., 1977–81, 1986–92); Founder Chairman: Merseyside Maritime Museum, 1977; Empire Theatre (Merseyside) Trust, 1979–81 (Bd Mem., 1986–); Chairman: Walker Art Gall., Liverpool, 1977–81; Library Assoc./Arts Council Wkg Party on Art in Libraries, 1982–84; Wkg Party to form Merseyside TEC, 1989–90; Enquiry into Local Authorities and Museums, 1989–91; Develt Bd, Nat. Mus. of Wales, 2006–; Nat. Chm., Area Museums Councils of GB, 1979–82; Vice-Pres., NW Museum and Art Gall. Service, 1992– (Chm., 1977–82, 1987–92); Vice-Chm., Merseyside Arts, 1985–88; Member: Museums Assoc. Council, 1978–86 (Vice-Pres., 1983); Arts Council of GB, 1980–84 (Chm., Housing the Arts Cttee, 1981–84; Chm., Regional Cttee, 1981–84); Museums and Galleries Commn, 1983–95 (Mem., Scottish Wkg Pty, 1984–85); Enquiry into Tyne and Wear Service, 1988–89; Bd, Northern Ballet Theatre, 1986–98 (Vice Chm., 1986–88); Merseyside Tourism Bd, 1986–92; NW Industrial Council, 1985–98; Calcutt Cttee on Privacy and Intrusion by the Press, 1989–90; Video Appeals Cttee, BBFC, 2002–; Lay Member: Press Council, 1980–86; Bar Standards Bd, 2008–. Advr on Local Govt to Arts Council, 1984–91; Chm., Arts, Initiative and Money Cttee, Gulbenkian Foundn, 1980–83. Mem. Bd, Charities Trust, 1990–94; Trustee: Norton Priory Museum, 1983–87; V&A Museum, 1984–86 (Mem., Adv. Council, 1978–84; Mem., Theatre Museum Cttee, 1983–86); Nat. Museums and Galls on Merseyside, 1986–99; Community Foundn in Wales, 2004–06; Governor: NYO, 1985–93; Nat. Mus. of Wales, 1994–97 and 2003–. Member Court: Liverpool Univ., 1973–96 (Mem., Council, 1977–81, 1986–96); Univ. of Wales, 2005–08; Vice-Chm. Council, NE Wales Inst., 2002–08 (Mem., 1999–2008). Mem., Peel Gp, 2002–. Patron, N Wales Music Festival, 1994–. Chm., Centenary Develt Trust, Sutton Grammar Sch., 1998–2005. FRSA 1988. Hon. FMA, 1987. Hon. Fellow, Liverpool John Moores Univ. (formerly Liverpool Polytechnic), 1989. Freedom of City of London, 1985; Barber Surgeons' Co.: Freeman, 1985; Liveryman, 1987–; Mem., Ct of Assts, 1999–; Master, 2005–06; Freeman, Guild of Educators, 2006–08. Hon. DLitt City, 1995. Hon. Mem., Amer. Chapter, Order of King Charles the Martyr, 1996. Merseyside Gold Medal for Achievement, 1991. *Publications:* A Brief History of Museums and Galleries, 1986; The Last Report on Local Authorities and Museums, 1991; reports: (jtly) Arts: the way forward, 1978; (jtly) A Future for the Arts, 1987. *Recreations:* swimming, music, memorabilia of Edward VIII. *Address:* Llannerch Hall, near St Asaph, Denbighshire LL17 0BD. *Club:* Garrick.

LATASI, Rt Hon. Sir Kamuta, KCMG 2007; OBE 1982; PC 1996; MP for Funafuti, Tuvalu, since 2000; Speaker of Parliament of Tuvalu, since 2006; *b* 4 Sept. 1936; *s* of Latasi and Malili; *m* 1966, Naama; two *s* two *d* (and one *d* decd). *Educ:* South Devon Tech. Coll., Torquay (Dip. Public and Soc. Admin). Gilbert and Ellice Islands Colony: Admin. Officer (Cadet), 1960–64; Lands Officer, 1965–66; Secretary: Min. of Natural Resources, 1967; Min. of Works and Utilities, 1968–70; Dist Officer, Funafuti, Ellice Is, 1972; Dist Comr, Ocean Is., 1972–75; Magistrate, Criminal and Civil Courts, 1965–75; Tuvalu Government: Asst Sec. to Chief Minister's Office, 1975; Sec., Min. of Natural Resources, 1976–77; First High Comr of Tuvalu to Fiji, also accredited to PNG and Perm. Rep. to S Pacific Commn, Noumea, New Caledonia and S Pacific Forum, Suva, 1978–83; Dean, Diplomatic Corp, Fiji, 1981–83; Manager, SW Pacific, British Petroleum Co., Tuvalu, 1983–93. MP, Tuvalu, 1983–97; Prime Minister of Tuvalu, 1993–96. *Recreations:* fishing, gardening. *Address:* Parliament of Tuvalu, Funafuti, Tuvalu. *T:* 20252, 20254.

LATCHMAN, Prof. David Seymour; Professor of Genetics, and Master of Birkbeck College, University of London, since 2003; Professor of Human Genetics, University College London, since 1999; *b* 22 Jan. 1956; *s* of Emanuel Latchman and Ella Latchman (*née* Wohl); *m* 2002, Hannah Garson. *Educ:* Haberdashers' Aske's Sch.; Queens' Coll., Cambridge (BA 1978; MA 1981; PhD 1981); DSc London 1994. FRCPath 1999. Lectr in Molecular Genetics, Dept of Biology, UCL, 1984–88; Dir, Med. Molecular Biology Unit and Reader in Molecular Biology, Dept of Biochemistry, UCL and Middlesex Sch. of Medicine, 1988–91; University College London: Prof. of Molecular Pathology, 1991–99; Head, Div. of Pathol., 1995–99; Dir, Windeyer Inst. of Med. Scis, 1996–99; Dep. Hd, UCL Graduate Sch., 1998–99; Dean, Inst. of Child Health, UCL and Great Ormond Street Hosp. for Children, 1999–2002. Chm., Sci. Expert Adv. Cttee, Univ. of London, 1988–97. External Examiner: Brunel Univ., 1993–97; Nottingham Univ., 1999–2002; Mem., Examng Panel in Genetics, RCPath, 1999–. Member: Med. Adv. Panel, Parkinson's Disease Soc., 1995–2008 (Dep. Chm., 1997–2008); MRC Adv. Bd, 1997–2004; Project Grants Cttee, BHF, 1998–2002; Sci. Policy Adv. Cttee, 1998– (Chm., 2003–); Nat. Biol Standards Bd, 2002–; Nat. Inst. for Biol Standards and Control; DoH Genetics and Insurance Cttee, 2002–; Health Protection Agency Bd, 2003–07; HEFCE Res. Strategy Cttee, 2003–06; MRC Coll. of Experts, 2004–; UUK Res. Strategy Cttee, 2004–; UUK England and NI Council, 2007–. Non-exec. Dir, Gt Ormond St Hosp. for Children NHS Trust, 2001–02; Chairman: London 'Ideas' Genetic Knowledge Park, 2002–; London Higher, 2006–. Mem. Council, Lifelong Learning UK, 2005–; Bd Observer, LDA, 2006–; Gov., SOAS, 2004–; Gov., and Mem. Bd of Mgt, LSHTM, 2004–. Pres., The Maccabaeans, 2007–. FRSA 2003. Haldane Lectr, 1994, Crabtree Orator, 1997 (Pres., 2008), Sainer Lectr, 2007, UCL. Dep. Chm., Editl Bd, Biochemical Jl, 1995–97. *Publications:* Gene Regulation, 1990, 5th edn 2005; Eukaryotic Transcription Factors, 1991, 5th edn 2008; (ed) Transcription Factors: a practical approach, 1993, 2nd edn 1999; (ed) From Genetics to Gene Therapy, 1994; (ed) PCR applications in Pathology, 1995; (ed) Genetic Manipulation of the Nervous System, 1995; (ed) Basic Molecular and Cell Biology, 1997; (ed) Landmarks in Gene Regulation, 1997; (ed) Stress Proteins, 1999; (ed) Viral Vectors for Treating Diseases of the Nervous System, 2003. *Recreations:* book collecting, opera. *Address:* Birkbeck College, Malet Street, WC1E 7HX. *Club:* Athenæum.

LATHAM, family name of **Baron Latham**.

LATHAM, 2nd Baron *cr* 1942, of Hendon; **Dominic Charles Latham**; Senior Structural Engineer with Gerard Barry Associates, since 1992; *b* 20 Sept. 1954; *s* of Hon. Francis Charles Allman Latham (*d* 1959) and Gabrielle Monica (*d* 1987), *d* of Dr S. M. O'Riordan; *S* grandfather, 1970. *Educ:* Univ. of New South Wales, Australia (BEng (civil), 1977, Hons I; MEngSc 1981). Civil Engr, Electricity Commn, NSW, 1979–88; Structl Engr, Rankine & Hill, Consulting Engrs, 1988–91. Teacher, Rock around the Clock Dancing, 1993–. *Recreations:* rock-'n'-roll/ballroom dancing, electronics, personal computing, sailboarding. *Heir:* yr twin *b* Anthony Michael Latham [*b* 20 Sept. 1954; *m* Margot].

LATHAM, Alison Mary; editor and writer; *b* 13 July 1948; *d* of John Llewellyn Goodall and Patricia Anne Goodall (*née* Tapper); *m* 1972, Richard Brunton Latham, *qv*; three *s*. *Educ:* Univ. of Birmingham (BMus Hons). Associate Editor, The Musical Times, 1977–88; Publications Editor, Royal Opera House, Covent Garden, 1989–2000; ed., Edinburgh Fest. progs, 2003–. FRSA 1999. *Publications:* (ed with S. Sadie) The Cambridge Music Guide, 1985; (ed with R. Parker) Verdi in Performance, 2001; The Oxford Companion to Music, 2002; (ed) Sing, Ariel: essays and thoughts for Alexander Goehr's seventieth birthday, 2003. *Recreations:* sailing, glass collecting, walking. *Address:* c/o The Oxford Companion to Music, Oxford University Press, Great Clarendon Street, Oxford OX2 6DP; *e-mail:* Alison.Latham@btinternet.com.

LATHAM, Arthur Charles; Member (Lab), Havering Council (formerly Romford Borough Council), 1952–78 and 1986–98; *b* Leyton, 14 Aug. 1930; *m* 1st, 1951, Margaret Green (*d* 2000); one *s* one *d*; 2nd, 2001, Caroline Warren. *Educ:* Romford Royal Liberty Sch.; Garnett Coll. of Educn; LSE. Further Educn Coll. Lectr, 1967–. Havering Council (formerly Romford Borough Council): Leader, Labour Gp, 1962–70 and 1986–98; Leader of the Opposition, 1986–90; Leader of Council, 1990–96; Alderman, 1962–78. Mem., NE Regional Metropolitan Hosp. Bd, 1966–72; part-time Mem., July-Nov. 1983, Mem., 1983–84, LTE. MP (Lab) Paddington N, Oct. 1969–1974, City of Westminster, Paddington, 1974–79; Founder, and Jt Chm., All Party Gp for Pensioners, 1971–79; Chm., Tribune Gp, 1975–76 (Treasurer, 1977–79). Contested (Lab): Woodford, 1959; Rushcliffe, Notts, 1964; City of Westminster, Paddington, 1979; Westminster N, 1983. Chm., Greater London Lab. Party, 1977–86; Vice-Chm., Nat. Cttee, Labour League of Youth, 1949–53; Vice-President: Labour Action for Peace; AMA; Treasurer, Liberation (Movement for Colonial Freedom), 1969–79; Member: British Campaign for Peace in Vietnam; Campaign for Nuclear Disarmament. Vegetarian. Resigned from Labour Party, May 2003 over Iraq War and other issues. *Recreations:* bridge, chess, cricket, country music, walking. *Address:* 9 Cotleigh Road, Romford, Essex RM7 9AS.

LATHAM, Christopher George Arnot; Chairman, James Latham PLC, 1988–95; *b* 4 June 1933; *s* of late Edward Bryan Latham and Anne Arnot Duncan; *m* 1963, Jacqueline Cabourdin; three *s*. *Educ:* Stowe Sch.; Clare Coll., Cambridge (MA). FCA. Articled Fitzpatrick Graham, chartered accountants, 1955; joined James Latham Ltd, timber importers, 1959, Dir 1963. A Forestry Comr, 1973–78. Dir, CILNTEC, 1991–97. Pres., Inst. of Wood Sci., 1977–79; Chairman: Timber Res. and Develt Assoc., 1972–74; Commonwealth Forestry Assoc., 1975–77; Psychiatric Rehabilitation Assoc., 1983–91. Mem., Co. of Builders Merchants, 1985– (Master, 1999–2000); Almoner, 2002–07; Trustee, 2008). *Recreations:* forestry, classic cars. *Address:* Quarry Court, Quarry Wood, Marlow.

LATHAM, David John; Regional Employment Judge (formerly Regional Chairman, Employment Tribunals), London Central Region, since 2001; *b* 21 April 1946; *s* of William and Edna Latham; *m* 1969, Cherill Disley; one *s* one *d*. *Educ:* Quarry Bank Sch., Liverpool; Hull Univ. (LLB Hons). Admitted solicitor, 1971; Partner, Chambers Thomas, Solicitors, Hull, 1972–85; Principal, D. J. Latham & Co., Solicitors, Hull, 1986–87; Partner, Sandersons, Solicitors, Hull, 1988–96. Chm., Employment Tribunals (pt-time), 1992–96, (full-time), 1996–2001; Dir, Nat. Trng Employment Tribunals Judiciary, 1998–. Chm., Hull FC, 1993–95. *Recreations:* sport, particularly basketball and Rugby, walking, gardening, theatre, opera, Rotary member. *Address:* Employment Tribunals, Victory House, 30–34 Kingsway, WC2B 6EX. *T:* (020) 7273 8579; *e-mail:* djl.jroburn@ yahoo.co.uk. *Club:* Reform.

LATHAM, Rt Hon. Sir David (Nicholas Ramsay), Kt 1992; PC 2000; **Rt Hon. Lord Justice Latham**; a Lord Justice of Appeal, since 2000; Vice-President, Court of Appeal (Criminal Division), since 2006; *b* 18 Sept. 1942; *s* of late Robert Clifford Latham, CBE, FBA and Eileen (*née* Ramsay); *m* 1967, Margaret Elizabeth (*née* Forrest); three *d*. *Educ:* Bryanston; Queens' Coll., Cambridge (MA). Called to the Bar, Middle Temple, 1964, Bencher, 1989; QC 1985; one of the Junior Counsel to the Crown, Common Law, 1979–85; Junior Counsel to Dept of Trade in export credit matters, 1981–85; a Recorder, 1983–92; a Judge of the High Court, QBD, 1992–2000; Presiding Judge, Midland and Oxford Circuit, 1995–99. Vice-Chm., Council of Legal Educn, 1992–97 (Mem., 1988–97); Member: Gen. Council of the Bar, 1987–92; Judicial Studies Bd, 1988–91. *Recreations:* reading, music, travel. *Address:* Royal Courts of Justice, Strand WC2A 2LL. *Clubs:* Travellers; Leander.

LATHAM, Derek James, RIBA; Chairman [...] Co., (Lathams), since 1989; *b* 12 July 1946; [...] Managing Director, Derek Latham & Pauline Latham (*née* Turner); *m* 1968, Pauline [...] late James Horace Latham and Mary King Edward VI Grammar Sch., Retford; Leices[...] beth Tuxworth; two *s* one *d*. *Educ:* Nottingham Trent Poly. (DipTP 1974, DipLD 19[...]h. of Architecture (DipArch 1970); 2003. Clifford Wearden & Associates (architect[...]RIBA 1972; MRTPI 1975; AABC Housing Architect and Planner, Derby CC, 1970–[...]planners), London, 1968–70; Derbys CC, 1974–78; Principal, Derek Latham a[...]sign and Conservation Officer, Michael Saint Develts Ltd, 1984–96; Dir, Acanthus A[...]ciates, 1980–89; Man. Dir, 1984–98 (Chm., 1987–89). RIBA Client Design [...]d Architectural Practices Ltd, Converts Ltd, 1996–; Opun (Architecture and Built [...]005–. Chairman: Church Historic Bldgs Trust, 1978–98; Member: Exec. Cttee, [...]–). Tech. Advr, Derbys 1985–91; Cttee, SPAB, 1993–2001. Regl Ambassador, [...]for Care of Churches, CABE. Chm., RSA at Dean Clough, 1995–98. Mem., [...]ducn Enabler, 2002–; Fund, 2001–06. MLI 1979; IHBC 1999; Member: AHI[...]ee, Heritage Lottery FRSA. Hon. Dr Derby, 2008. *Publications:* Creative Re-use[...]IEMA, 1991–2006. tech. articles on urban design and conservation. *Recreations:* [...]ngs, 2000; various rambling, cycling, swimming, painting. *Address:* Lathams, St M[...] sailing, ski-ing, *T:* (01332) 365777, *Fax:* (01332) 290314; *e-mail:* d.latham@lath[...]rby DE21 5EA. Duffield Squash and Lawn Tennis, Little Eaton Lawn Tennis (P[...]s.co.uk. *Clubs:*

LATHAM, Sir Michael (Anthony), Kt 1993; DL; Deputy Cha[...]2003). Ltd, since 2002 (Chairman, 1999–2002); *b* 20 Nov. 1942; *m* 19[...]Dixon 2006); two *s*. *Educ:* Marlborough Coll.; King's Coll., Cambridge [...]Terry (*d* BA Cantab 1964, MA Cantab 1968, CertEd Oxon 1965. Housing and [...] Officer, Conservative Research Dept, 1965–67; Parly Liaison Officer, Nat.[...]lding Trades Employers, 1967–73; Dir, House-builders Fedn, 1971–73. [...]City Councillor, 1968–71. Contested (C) Liverpool, West Derby, 1970; MP[...]eb. 1974–1983, Rutland and Melton, 1983–92. Deputy Chairman: J. R. Kno[...] 1997–2003; BIW Technols (formerly Building Information Warehouse)[...] Chairman: Partnership Sourcing, 2000–05; Construction Skills, 2003–; CW[...] E. C. Harris Public Sector Exec., 2004–07; Consultant on partnering and Inspace plc, 2005–. Chairman: Construction Industry Bd, 1995–96; Jt Major Gp, 1996–; Jt Industry Bd for Electrical Contracting Industry, 1998–; CITB-C Skills (formerly CITB), 2002–; ConstructionSkills, 2003–; Roofing Industr 2003– (Dep. Chm., 1997–2003); Major Projects Agreement Forum, 2003–; British Flat Roofing Council, 1996–99; Flat Roofing Alliance, 1999–; Construction Inst., 2002–08. Chairman: Jt Govt/Industry Rev. of Procurem Contractual Problems in Construction Industry, 1993–94; Govt Review of Construction Act, 2004. Mem., Adv. Council on Public Records, 1985–91. Vice-Pre Building Socs Assoc., 1981–91. Mem. Exec. Cttee, 1987–2000, Dir, 1992, Jt Hon. Treas., 1996–2000, Vice-Pres., 2000–, CCJ. Visiting Professor: Northumbria Univ., 1995–2000; Bartlett Sch. of Architecture, UCL, 1997–2001; UCE, 2001–08. C of E Lay Reader, 1988–. Trustee, Oakham Sch., 1987–2001. FRSA 1992. Hon. Mem. RICS, 1996; Hon. FCIPS 1994; Hon. FCIOB 1995; Hon. FICE 1995; Hon. FASI 1995; Hon. Fellow, Inst. of Building Control, 1995; Hon. FREng (Hon. FEng 1997); Hon. FLI 1997; Hon. FRIAS 1998; Hon. FRIBA 2000; Hon. CIBSE 2003. DL Leics, 1994. Hon. LLD Nottingham Trent, 1995; Hon. DEng Birmingham, 1998; Hon. DCL Northumbria, 1999; Hon. DTech Loughborough, 2004. *Publications:* Trust and Money, 1993; Constructing the Team, 1994; articles on housing, land, town planning and building. *Recreations:* gardening, fencing, listening to classical music, cricket. *Address:* 508 Hood House, Dolphin Square, SW1V 3NH. *Club:* Carlton.

LATHAM, Air Vice-Marshal Peter Anthony, CB 1980; AFC 1960; *b* 18 June 1925; *s* of late Oscar Frederick Latham and Rhoda Latham; *m* 1953, Barbara Mary; two *s* six *d*. *Educ:* St Phillip's Grammar Sch., Birmingham; St Catharine's Coll., Cambridge. psa 1961. Joined RAF, 1944; 1946–69: served No 26, 263, 614, and 247 Sqdns; CFE; Air Min.; Comd No 111 Sqdn; RAF Formation Aerobatic Team (Leader of Black Arrows, 1959–60); MoD Jt Planning Staff; Comd NEAF Strike and PR Wing; Coll. of Air Warfare; Ops No 38 Gp; Comd RAF Tengah, 1969–71; MoD Central Staff, 1971–73; Comd Officer and AOC, Aircrew Selection Centre, Biggin Hill, 1973–74; SASO No 38 Gp, 1974–76; Dir Def. Ops, MoD Central Staff, 1976–77; AOC No 11 Group, 1977–81. Principal, Oxford Air Trng Sch., and Dir, CSE Aviation Ltd, 1982–85; Sen. Air Advr, Short Bros, 1985–90. Cdre, RAF Sailing Assoc., 1974–80; Pres., Assoc. of Service Yacht Clubs, 1978–81. Pres., British Horological Inst., 1996. Liveryman, Clockmakers' Co., 1987 (Mem., Ct of Assts, 1990–; Master, 1996). *Recreations:* sailing, horology. *Address:* c/o Lloyds TSB, 134 New Street, Birmingham B2 4QZ. *Club:* Royal Air Force.

LATHAM, His Honour Peter Heaton; a Circuit Judge, 1997–2008; *b* 3 June 1938; *s* of Tom Heaton Latham and Dorothy Latham (*née* Williams). *Educ:* The Grammar Sch., Ashton-in-Makerfield, Lancs; Pembroke Coll., Oxford (BA Juris 1962). Nat. Service, 2nd Lieut, RA, 1957–59. Instructor, Univ. of Pennsylvania Law Sch., 1962–64; called to the Bar Gray's Inn, 1965 (James Mould Schol., 1965; Lee Essay Prize, 1965); in practice, 1965–97. *Address:* c/o Willesden County Court, 9 Acton Lane, NW10 8SB. *T:* (020) 8963 8200.

LATHAM, Richard Brunton; QC 1991; a Recorder, since 1987; *b* 16 March 1947; *s* of Frederick and Joan Catherine Latham; *m* 1972, Alison Mary Goodall (see A. M. Latham);

three *s.* *Educ:* Farnborough Grammar School; Univ. of Birmingham (LLB 1969). Called to the Bar, Gray's Inn, 1971; Bencher, 2000; practice on Midland Circuit; Standing Prosecuting Counsel to Inland Revenue, Midland and Oxford Circuit, 1987–91. *Recreations:* sailing, opera. *Address:* 7 Bedford Row, WC1R 4BS. *T:* (020) 7242 3555.

LATHAM, Sir Richard Thomas Paul, 3rd Bt *cr* 1919, of Crow Clump; *b* 15 April 1934; *s* of Sir (Herbert) Paul Latham, 2nd Bt, and Lady Patricia Doreen Moore (*d* 1947), *o d* of 10th Earl of Drogheda; *S* father, 1955; *m* 1958, Marie-Louise Patricia, *d* of Frederick H. Russell, Vancouver, BC; two *d.* *Educ:* Eton; Trinity Coll., Cambridge. *Address:* 2125 Birnam Wood Drive, Santa Barbara, CA 93108, USA.

LATHAM, Roger Alan; Chief Executive, Nottinghamshire County Council, 2002–08; *b* 3 May 1950; *s* of Edward and Florrie Latham; *m* 1973, Angela Judith Warwick (*née* Pearce); one *s.* *Educ:* Bristol Univ. (BSc Econs with Stats); Birmingham Univ. (MSocSc); Liverpool Polytechnic. CPFA; CStat. Economic Assistant, National Westminster Bank, 1972–76; Economist, 1976–85, Asst Chief Finance Officer, 1985–90, Dudley MBC; Dep. County Treasurer, 1990–91, County Treasurer, 1991–2002, Notts CC. Pres., CIPFA, June 2009– (Vice Pres., 2008–June 2009). Methodist Local Preacher. *Recreations:* photography, gardening, computers, reading, dinosaurs, Japanese films, t'ai chi. *Address:* 25 Potters Lane, East Leake, Loughborough, Leics LE12 6NQ. *T:* (01509) 856562.

LATHE, Dr Richard Frank; Director, Piea Research, since 2002; *b* 23 April 1952; *s* of late Prof. Grant Henry Lathe; one *s* fou... *Educ:* Univ. of Edinburgh (BSc Molecular Biol. ...1976). Research Scientist: Univ. of Heidelberg, 1973); Free Univ. of Brussels (DS... ...9–81; Asst Sci. Dir, Transgene SA, Strasbourg, 1977–79; Univ. of Cambridge, ...nal Breeding Res. Orgn, 1984–85; Prof. of Genetics 1981–84; Principal Sci. Officer, A... ...ic Molecular Genetics, and Co-Dir, Ecole Supérieure and Genetic Engrg, Lab. of Euk... ...ourg, 1985–89; University of Edinburgh: Dir, Centre de Biotechnologie, Univ. of S... ...s. Prof., 1989–2002. *Publication:* Autism, Brain, and for Genome Res., 1989–9... ...a Research, PO Box 27069, Edinburgh EH10 5YW. *T:* Environment, 2006. *Addres*... (0131) 466 8311.

LATIMER, Sir (Court... **Robert,** Kt 1966; CBE 1958 (OBE 1948); *b* 13 July 1911; *er s* of late Sir Court... ...imer, KCIE, CSI; *m* 1st, 1944, Elizabeth Jane Gordon (*née* Smail) (*d* 1989); one... 2nd, 1990, Frederieka Jacoba Blankert (*née* Witteween). *Educ:* Rugby; Christ Ch... ...xford. ICS, 1934 (Punjab); IPS, 1939; Vice-Consul, Bushire, 1940–41; Sec. F... ...ublicity Office, Delhi, 1941–42; Sec. Indian Agency Gen., Chungking, 19... ...W Frontier Prov., as Asst Political Agent N Waziristan, Dir of Civil Supplies... ...Governor and District Comr, Bannu, 1942–43 and 1945–47. HM Overseas S... ...48; served in Swaziland, 1948–49; Bechuanaland Protectorate, 1951–54; ...High Comr for Basutoland, the Bechuanaland Protectorate and Swazilan... ...Sec., 1949–51; Sec. for Finance, 1954–60; Chief Sec., 1960–64; Ministe... ...mbassy, Pretoria, 1965–66; Registrar, Kingston Polytechnic, 1967–76. *Recrea*... ...hotography. *Address:* Benedicts, Old Avenue, Weybridge, Surrey KT13 0PS.

LA... **Graham (Stanley),** KBE 1980; President, New Zealand Maori Council, ...elegate, 1964; Vice-President, 1969–72); *b* Waiharara, N Auckland, 7 Feb. ...raham Latimer and Lillian Edith Latimer (*née* Kenworthy); *m* 1948, Emily ...ore; two *s* two *d.* *Educ:* Pukenui and Kaitaia District High School. Dairy ...61–. Chairman: Aotearoa Fisheries, 1991; Crown Forestry Rental Trust, 1991–; ...acific, 1991–98; Dep. Chm., Maori Fisheries Commn, 1989–90; Negotiator, NZ ...isheries. Member: Tai Tokerau Dist Maori Council, 1962– (Sec. 1966–75; Chm., ...; Otamatea Maori Exec., 1959– (Sec. Treas. 1962–72, Chm. 1975–); Otamatea ... Cttee, 1955–62; Arapaoa Maori Cttee, 1962– (Chm. 1962–69 and 1972–); N ...kland Power Bd, 1977–; Waitangi Tribunal, 1976–. Chairman: (since inception) ...hland Community Coll.; Tai Tokerau Maori Trust Bd, 1979– (Mem., 1975–); ...ific Foundn, 1990–; Trustee: Kohanga Reo Nat. Trust, 1979–; Maori Education ...oundn; Member: Ngatikahu Trust Bd, 1976–; Cttee, Nat. Art Gall. Museum and War ...Memorial; NZ Maori Arts and Crafts Inst., 1980–; Tourist Adv. Council; Northland Regional Develt Council, 1980–; Alcoholic Liquor Adv. Council, 1980–. Lay Canon, Auckland Anglican Cathedral, 1978; Mem. Gen. Synod. JP. *Relevant publication:* Graham Latimer: a biography, 2002. *Recreations:* Rugby football, tennis. *Address:* PO Box 661, Kaitaia, New Zealand.

LATIMER, Sir Robert; *see* Latimer, Sir C. R.

LATNER, Stephen; Managing Director, Warburg Dillon Read, 1998–99; *b* 23 July 1946; *s* of late Julius Latner and of Anita Latner; *m* 1971, Jennifer Keidan; three *s.* *Educ:* Grocers' Sch.; Queen Mary Coll., London (BSc); Manchester Business Sch. (MBA). With ICL, 1968–71; joined S. G. Warburg, 1973: Dir, 1983–96; Dep. Chm., 1993–96; UK Country Hd, SBC Warburg, then Warburg Dillon Read, 1996–98. Chm. Council, Bobath Centre for Children with Cerebral Palsy, 2002– (Mem. Council, 1999–). *Recreations:* music, cinema, theatre, reading, sport.

LATOUR-ADRIEN, Hon. Sir (Jean François) Maurice, Kt 1971; Chief Justice of Mauritius, 1970–77; Chairman, Mauritius Union Assurance Co. Ltd, 1982–2005 (Director, 1978–82); *b* 4 March 1915; 2nd *s* of late Louis Constant Emile Adrien and late Maria Ella Latour. *Educ:* Royal Coll., Mauritius; Univ. Coll., London; Middle Temple, London. LLB 1940. Called to the Bar, Middle Temple, 1940. Mauritius: Dist Magistrate, 1947; Crown Counsel, 1950; Additl Subst. Procureur and Advocate-Gen., 1954; Sen. Crown Counsel, 1958; Asst Attorney-Gen., 1960; Solicitor-Gen., 1961; Dir of Public Prosecutions, 1964; Puisne Judge, 1966–70; Acting Governor-Gen., Feb. 1973, July–Aug. 1974, Jan.–Feb. and June–Aug. 1975, July–Sept. 1976. Pres., Mauritius Red Cross Soc., 1978–; Vice-Pres., Inst. Internat. de Droit d'Expression Française (IDEF). Pres., Mauritius Commercial Bank Ltd, 1993–94 (Dir, 1980–83, 1984–87, 1988–91, 1992–95, 1996–99, 2000–02; Vice-Pres., 1992–93, 1996–97); Legal Consultant: Mauritius Commercial Bank Ltd, 1983–; Promotion and Development Ltd, 1985–; Mauritius Commercial Bank Finance Corp., 1991–94; Mauritius Commercial Bank Registry and Securities, 1991–; Caudan Development Co. Ltd, 1991–; Fincorp Investment Ltd, 1994–. President: Mental Health Assoc., 1985– (Vice-Pres., 1978–84); Mauritius Red Cross, 1978–. Mem., War Meml Bd of Trustees, 1978–84 (Vice Pres., 1985–). KLJ 1969. *Address:* Vacoas, Mauritius.

LA TROBE-BATEMAN, Richard George Saumarez; structures designer/maker; *b* 17 Oct. 1938; *s* of late John La Trobe-Bateman and of Margaret (*née* Schmid); *m* 1969, Mary Elizabeth Jolly (OBE 2000); one *s* two *d.* *Educ:* Westminster Sch.; St Martin's Sch. of Art; Royal Coll. of Art (MDesRCA). Set up workshop, 1968. Member: Council of Management, British Crafts Centre, 1975–86; Council, Contemporary Applied Arts, 1987–94; Crafts Council: Mem., 1984–86; Index Selector, 1972–73; Chm., Index Selection Cttee, 1980–82. Work in: V&A Collection, 1979; Crafts Council Collection, 1981 and 1984; Keble Coll., Oxon, 1981; Temple Newsam Collection, 1983; Southern Arts Collection, 1983; Pembroke Coll., Oxon, 1984; Crafts Study Centre Collection, Bath, 1985; Northern Arts Collection, 1988; Royal Soc. of Arts, 1994; work presented by Crafts Council to the Prince of Wales, 1982; Longlands footbridge, Cumbria, 1995; Nat. Pinetum footbridge, Kent, 1999; swing-lift opening bridge, Glos (Wood Award), 2003; Langport footbridge, Somerset, 2005–06; Tassajara Footbridge, Calif, 2005–06. Vis. Prof., San Diego State Univ., 1986–87. *Publications:* articles in Crafts, American Crafts. *Recreations:* listening to music, hill-walking. *Address:* Elm House, Batcombe, Shepton Mallet, Somerset BA4 6AB. *T:* (01749) 850442. *Club:* Contemporary Applied Arts.

LATTER, (Henry) James (Edward); Senior Immigration Judge, Asylum and Immigration Tribunal (formerly a Vice President, Immigration Appeal Tribunal), since 2001; *b* 19 April 1950; *s* of Henry Edward Latter and Hilda Bessie Latter; *m* 1978, Penelope Jane Morris; one *s* one *d.* *Educ:* Reigate Grammar Sch.; Trinity Hall, Cambridge (BA 1971; MA 1974). Called to the Bar, Middle Temple, 1972; in practice as Barrister, 1972–95; full-time Immigration Adjudicator, 1995–96; Regl Adjudicator, Hatton Cross, 1996–98; Dep. Chief Adjudicator, 1998–2001. *Address:* Asylum and Immigration Tribunal, Field House, Bream's Buildings, Chancery Lane, EC4A 1DZ.

LATTO, Prof. Jennifer Elizabeth; Chairman, North West Heritage Lottery Fund, since 2005; *b* 3 Aug. 1944; *d* of Prof. Sir Henry Clifford Darby, CBE, FBA, and Eva Constance Darby (*née* Thomson); *m* 1967, Richard Matheson Latto; one *s.* *Educ:* Berkhamsted Sch. for Girls; Newnham Coll., Cambridge (BA Exptl Psychol. 1966); Homerton Coll., Cambridge (PGCE 1967); University Coll. London (Dip. Educnl Psychol. 1969). Educnl Psychologist, Essex CC, 1968–72; Lectr in Educnl Psychol., Homerton Coll., Cambridge, 1970–73; SSRC Studentship, Dept of Education, Univ. of Cambridge, 1972–75; Educnl Psychologist, Cheshire CC, 1978–79; Sen. Lectr, then Hd, Educn Dept, Liverpool Poly., 1979–92; Liverpool John Moores University: Prof. of Educnl Psychol., 1992–2002; Dir, Sch. of Educn and Community Studies, 1992–94; Provost, 1994–2002; Adviser: on Higher Educn, Govt Office NW, 2002–05; on Higher Educn Strategy, NW Develt Agency, 2003–07. Dir, Liverpool City of Learning, 2000–02. Chm., Univs Council for Educn of Teachers, 1993–95. Trustee, Tate, and Chm. Council, Tate Liverpool, 1998–2007. Mem., Adv. Cttee, Granada Foundn, 2004–. *Recreations:* modern design, opera. *Address:* Monksferry House, Grassendale Park, Liverpool L19 0LS.

LATYMER, 9th Baron *cr* 1431; **Crispin James Alan Nevill Money-Coutts;** *b* 8 March 1955; *s* of 8th Baron Latymer and Hon. Penelope Ann Clare (*née* Emmet); *S* father, 2003; *m* 1st, 1978, Hon. Lucy Rose (marr. diss. 1995), *y d* of Baron Deedes, KBE, MC, PC; one *s* two *d*; 2nd, 1995, Mrs Shaunagh Heneage. *Educ:* Eton Coll.; Keble Coll., Oxford. E. F. Hutton & Co., 1977–81; Bankers Trust, 1981–84; European Banking Co., 1984–86; Coutts & Co., 1986–99; Cazenove & Co., 2000–. Director: Manek Investment Mgt, 1994–; Throgmorton Trust, 2007–. Trustee: Astor Foundn, 1993–; UCLH Charities, 2005– (Chm., Investment Cttee, 2005–). *Recreation:* travelling. *Heir:* *s* Hon. Drummond William Thomas Money-Coutts, *b* 11 May 1986. *Address:* 28 Chelsham Road, SW4 6NP; *e-mail:* crispinlatymer@aol.com. *Clubs:* City of London, Beefsteak, Mark's; House of Lords Yacht, Ocean Cruising.

LAUDER, Desmond Michael Frank Scott; Head, Contracts and Projects Delivery, British Council, since 2008; *b* 28 July 1947; *s* of late Col Philip Lauder and Frances Lauder; *m* 1975, Xanthe Aristidou Theodosiadou; one *s* one *d.* *Educ:* Magdalene Coll., Cambridge (BA, MA); Inst. of Education, Univ. of London (PGCE). Teacher: Royal Grammar School, Guildford, 1970–72; Saint Ignatius Coll., Enfield, 1972–73; British Council: Asst Dir, Salonika, Greece, 1973–76; Asst Dir, Rio de Janeiro, Brazil, 1976–79; Asst Sec., CNAA, 1979–83; British Council: service in Czechoslovakia and Singapore, 1983–87; Corporate Planning Dept, 1987–91; Dir, Ecuador, 1991–93; Regl Dir, Asia Pacific, 1994–97; Director: Hong Kong, 1997–2003; Greece, 2003–07; Acting Dir, Marketing and Customer Services, 2007–08. *Recreations:* tennis, walking, music. *Address:* c/o British Council, 10 Spring Gardens, SW1A 2BN.

LAUDER, Prof. Ian, FRCPath; FMedSci; Dean of Medicine, 2000–08, and Dean, Faculty of Medicine and Biological Sciences, 2003–08, University of Leicester; *b* 17 June 1946; *s* of late Thomas William Lauder and of Joan Lauder; *m* 1969, Patricia Christine Purvis; one *s* one *d.* *Educ:* King James Ist Grammar Sch., Bishop Auckland; Univ. of Newcastle upon Tyne (MB BS 1969). FRCPath 1985. Lectr in Pathol., Univ. of Newcastle upon Tyne, 1970–78; Sen. Lectr, Pathol., Univ. of Leeds, 1978–84; Prof. of Pathol., Univ. of Leicester, 1984–2000; Dean: Leicester Warwick Med. Schs, 2000–07; Faculty of Medicine, Univ. of Warwick, 2002–04. Chairman: Adv. Cttee on Assessment of Lab. Standards, DoH, 1990–95; Armed Services Consultants Appts Bd Pathology, 2003–08. Non-exec. Dir, Univ. Hosps of Leicester NHS Trust, 2000–08; Mem., GMC, 2002–03. Treas., Council of Hds of Med. Schs, 2000–05. Sec., British Lymphoma Pathol. Gp, 1980–90; Royal College of Pathologists: Chm., Speciality Adv. Cttee, 1990–93; Vice-Pres., 1996–99. FMedSci 1998 (Treas., 2005–). Chancellor's Medal, Univ. of Warwick, 2007. *Publications:* Lymphomas other than Hodgkin's Disease, 1981; Malignant Lymphomas, 1988; contrib. numerous papers on malignant lymphomas, cancer pathol. and quality assurance in pathol. *Recreations:* fly-fishing, hill-walking, marathon running, ballroom dancing. *Address:* Paddock House, Illston on the Hill, Leicester LE7 9EG. *T:* (0116) 259 6511; *e-mail:* prof_lauder@hotmail.com. *Club:* Reform.

LAUDER, Sir Piers Robert Dick-, 13th Bt *cr* 1688; *S* father, 1981.

LAUDERDALE, 17th Earl of, *cr* 1624; **Patrick Francis Maitland;** Baron Maitland, 1590; Viscount Lauderdale, 1616; Viscount Maitland, Baron Thirlestane and Boltoun, 1624; Bt of Nova Scotia, 1680; Hereditary Bearer of the National Flag of Scotland, 1790 and 1952; Chief of the Clan Maitland; *b* 17 March 1911; *s* of Rev. Hon. Sydney G. W. Maitland and Ella Frances (*née* Richards); *S* brother, 1968; *m* 1936, Stanka (*d* 2003), *d* of Professor Milivoje Lozanitch, Belgrade Univ.; two *s* two *d.* *Educ:* Lancing Coll., Sussex; Brasenose Coll., Oxford. BA Hons Oxon, 1933. Journalist 1933–59. Appts include: Balkans and Danubian Corresp., The Times, 1939–41; Special Corresp. Washington, News Chronicle, 1941; War Corresp., Pacific, Australia, New Zealand, News Chronicle, 1941–43. Foreign Office, 1943–45. MP (U) for Lanark Div. of Lanarks, 1951–Sept. 1959 (except for period May–Dec. 1957 when Ind. C). Founder and Chairman, Expanding Commonwealth Group, House of Commons, 1955–59; re-elected Chairman, Nov. 1959. Chm., Sub-Cttee on Energy, Transport and Res., House of Lords Select Cttee on EEC Affairs, 1974–79; Vice Chm. and Co-founder, Parly Gp for Energy Studies, 1980–99. Dir, Elf Petroleum (UK). Editor of The Fleet Street Letter Service, and of The Whitehall Letter, 1945–58. Mem., Coll. of Guardians of National Shrine of Our Lady of Walsingham, Norfolk, 1955–82 (Guardian Emeritus, 1982–). President, The Church Union, 1956–61. FRGS. *Publications:* European Dateline, 1945; Task for Giants, 1957. *Heir:* *s* The Master of Lauderdale, Viscount Maitland, *qv.* *Address:* 10 Ovington Square, SW3 1LH. *T:* (020) 7589 7451; 12 St Vincent Street, Edinburgh EH3 6SH. *T:* (0131) 556 5692. *Club:* New (Edinburgh).

See also R. W. P. H. Hay, Lady H. O. Maitland.

LAUDERDALE, Master of; *see* Maitland, Viscount.

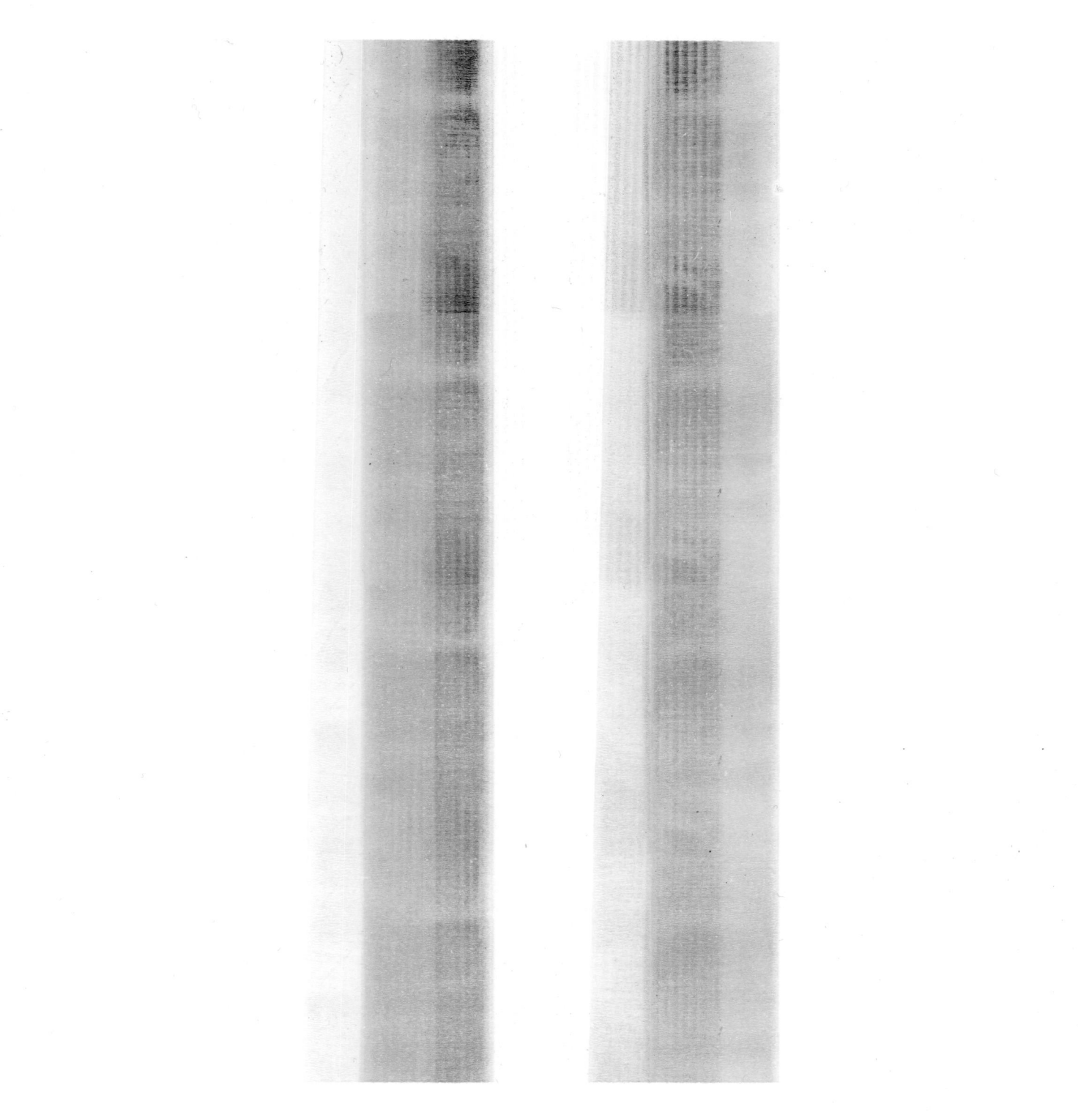

LAUENER, Peter Rene, CB 2004; Director of Local Transformation, Department for Children, Schools and Families (formerly Department for Education and Skills), since 2006; *b* 29 Sept. 1954; *s* of Rene George Lauener and Anne McLean Lauener (*née* Ross); *m* 1976, Angela Margaret Mulliner; one *s* two *d*. *Educ:* George Watson's Coll., Edinburgh; Univ. of Durham (BA Hons Econs 1975). Economic Assistant, Scottish Office, 1975–82; Manpower Services Commission: Economic Advr, 1982–85; Hd of Strategy, Evaluation and Res., 1986–87; Area Manager, Manchester, 1987–89; Dept of Employment, 1989–92, 1995–96; Dir, Skills & Enterprise, Govt Office for E Midlands, 1992–95; Head of Resources & Budget Mgt, DfEE, 1996–2000; Dir, Learning, Delivery and Standards Gp, DfEE, subseq. DfES, 2000–04; Dir, Qualifications and Young People's Gp, 2004–05, Acting Dir Gen. for Lifelong Learning, 2005, DfES. Treas., Holy Trinity C of E, Millhouses, Sheffield. *Recreations:* reading, walking, wine. *Address:* 82 Pingle Road, Sheffield S7 2LL. *T:* (0114) 236 2188, *T:* (office) (0114) 259 3735.

LAUGHARNE, Albert, CBE 1983; QPM 1978; Deputy Commissioner, Metropolitan Police, 1983–85; *b* 20 Oct. 1931; *s* of Reginald Stanley Laugharne and Jessica Simpson Laugharne; *m* 1st, 1954, Barbara Thirlwall (*d* 1994); two *d*; 2nd, 1999, Margaret Ann Blackmore; four step *s*. *Educ:* Baines' Grammar Sch., Poulton-le-Fylde; Manchester Univ. Detective Inspector, Manchester City Police, 1952–66; Supt, Cumbria Constab., 1966–70; Chief Supt, W Yorks Constab., 1970–73; Asst Chief Constable, Cheshire Constab., 1973–76; Chief Constable: Warwicks, 1977–78; Lancashire, 1978–83. RCDS, 1975. *Publication:* Seaford House Papers, 1975. *Recreations:* gardening, painting.

LAUGHLIN, Prof. Robert Betts, PhD; Anne T. and Robert M. Bass Professor of Physics, School of Humanities and Sciences, Stanford University, since 1992; *b* 1 Nov. 1950; *s* of David H. and Margaret B. Laughlin; *m* 1979, Anita R. Perry; two *s*. *Educ:* Univ. of Calif, Berkeley (AB Maths 1972); Massachusetts Inst. of Technol. (PhD Physics 1979). Post-doctoral res., Bell Telephone Labs, 1979–81; post-doctoral res., then Res. Physicist, Lawrence Livermore Nat. Lab., 1981–84; Associate Prof. of Physics, 1984–89, Prof., 1989–92, Stanford Univ. Member: Amer. Acad. Arts and Scis, 1990–; NAS, 1994–. E. O. Lawrence Award for Physics, US Dept of Energy, 1985; Oliver E. Buckley Prize, APS, 1986; Franklin Medal for Physics, 1998; (jtly) Nobel Prize for Physics, 1998. *Publications:* contrib. numerous articles in Physical Rev. Letters, Physical Rev., Advances in Physics, etc. *Recreations:* hiking, ski-ing, computers, music. *Address:* Department of Physics, Stanford University, Stanford, CA 94305, USA. *T:* (650) 7234563, *Fax:* (650) 72565411; *e-mail:* rbl@large.stanford.edu.

LAUGHLIN, Prof. Simon Barry, PhD; FRS 2000; Professor of Neurobiology, Department of Zoology, University of Cambridge, since 2004; Fellow, Churchill College, Cambridge, since 1991; *b* 19 Dec. 1947; *s* of Peter and Margaret Laughlin; *m* 1980, Barbara Frances Howard; two *s* one *d*. *Educ:* Clare Coll., Cambridge (BA, MA); Australian Nat. Univ. (PhD Neurobiol. 1974). Fellow, Res. Sch. of Biol Scis, ANU, 1976–84; Cambridge University: Lectr in Zool., 1984–96; Reader in Sensory Neuroscience, 1996–99; Rank Res. Prof. in Opto-electronics, 1999–2004. *Publications:* contribs on vision, neural processing and insects to learned jls. *Recreations:* classical bassoon, sailing. *Address:* Department of Zoology, Downing Street, Cambridge CB2 3EJ. *T:* (01223) 336608.

LAUGHTON, Sir Anthony Seymour, Kt 1987; FRS 1980; oceanographic consultant; Director, Institute of Oceanographic Sciences, 1978–88; *b* 29 April 1927; *s* of Sydney Thomas Laughton and Dorothy Laughton (*née* Chamberlain); *m* 1st, 1957, Juliet Ann Chapman (marr. diss. 1962); one *s*; 2nd, 1973, Barbara Clare Bosanquet; two *d*. *Educ:* Marlborough Coll.; King's Coll., Cambridge (MA, PhD). RNVR, 1945–48. John Murray Student, Columbia Univ., NY, 1954–55; Nat. Inst. of Oceanography, later Inst. of Oceanographic Sciences, 1955–88: research in marine geophysics in Atlantic and Indian Oceans, esp. in underwater photography, submarine morphology, ocean basin evolution, midocean ridge tectonics; Principal Scientist of deep sea expedns. Member: Co-ordinating Cttee for Marine Sci. and Technol., 1987–91; nat. and internat. cttees on oceanography and geophysics. President: Challenger Soc. for Marine Sci., 1988–90; Soc. for Underwater Technol., 1995–97 (Mem. Council, 1986–92; President's Award, 1998); Hydrographic Soc., 1997–99. Member Council: Royal Soc., 1986–87; Marine Biology Assoc., 1980–83, 1988–92. Mem. Cttee, 1966–2003, Chm., 1987–2003, Gen. Bathymetric Chart of the Oceans. Member: Governing Body, Charterhouse Sch., 1981–2000 (Chm., 1995–2000); Council, University Coll. London, 1983–93; Adv. Council, Ocean Policy Inst., Hawaii, 1991–93. Trustee, Natural Hist. Mus., 1990–94. Pres., Haslemere Musical Soc., 1997–. Silver Medal, RSA, 1958; Cuthbert Peek grant, RGS, 1967; Prince Albert 1er Monaco Gold Medal for Oceanography, 1980; Founders Medal, RGS, 1987; Murchison Medal, Geol. Soc., 1989. *Publications:* papers on marine geophysics and oceanography. *Recreations:* music, gardening, sailing. *Address:* Okelands, Pickhurst Road, Chiddingfold, Surrey GU8 4TS. *T:* (01428) 683941.

LAUGHTON, Prof. Michael Arthur, PhD, DSc (Eng); FREng, FIET; Professor of Electrical Engineering, Queen Mary and Westfield (formerly Queen Mary) College, University of London, 1977–2000, now Emeritus; *b* 18 Dec. 1934; *s* of William Arthur Laughton and Laura (*née* Heap); *m* 1960, Margaret Mary Coleman (marr. diss. 1994); two *s* two *d*. *Educ:* King Edward's Five Ways Sch., Birmingham; Etobicoke Collegiate Inst., Toronto; Toronto Univ. (BASc 1957); Univ. of London (PhD 1965; DSc(Eng) 1976). CEng, FREng (FEng 1989); FIET (FIEE 1977). GEC, Witton, 1957–61; Queen Mary, later Queen Mary and Westfield, College, London University: Res. Student, Dept of Elect. Engrg, 1961–64; Lectr, 1964–72; Reader, 1972–77; Dean, Faculty of Engrg, 1983–85; Pro-Principal, 1985–89; Dean of Engrg, London Univ., 1990–94. Visiting Professor: Purdue Univ., USA, 1966; Tokyo Univ., 1977; ICSTM, 2002–. Sec. and Dir, Unicom Ltd, 1971–74; Dir, QMC Industrial Res. Ltd, 1979–91 (Chm., 1988–91); Chm., Tower Shakespeare Co. Ltd, 1985–93. Organising Sec., 1963–81, Chm., 1981–, Power Systems Computation Confs; Science and Engineering Research Council: Chm., Machines and Power Educn and Trng Cttee, 1983–86; Member: Elect. Engrg Cttee, 1982–84; Wind Energy Panel, 1985–86; Institution of Electrical Engineers: Chm., Wkg Gp on New Electronic Technol. in Publishing, 1983–87; Member: Council, 1990–94; Governing Cttee, Benevolent Fund, 1990–93; Mem. Exec., Watt Cttee on Energy, 1986– (Chm., Wkg Gp on Renewable Energy Sources, 1986–88); Mem., Inf. Cttee, 1988–92, Mem., Energy Policy Adv. Gp, 2001–, Royal Soc.; Mem., Internat. Cttee, Royal Acad. of Engrg, 2002–. Specialist Adviser: Sub-Cttee B (Energy, Transport and Technol.), H of L Select Cttee on Eur. Communities, 1987–89; H of C Select Cttee on Welsh Affairs, 1993–94. Member: Fulbright Commn Scholarships Cttee, 1991–; Council, Cranfield Inst of Technol., 1991–96. Freeman: City of London, 1990; Barbers' Co., 1990 (Liveryman, 1995). Founder and Jt Ed., Internat. Jl of Electrical Power and Energy Systems, 1978–; Ed., Procs of Power System Computation Confs 5–8, 1975–84. Career Achievement Medal, IEE, 2002. *Publications:* edited: Energy Policy Planning, 1979; Electrical Engineers Reference Book, 14th edn 1985, 15th edn 1993, 16th edn 2002; Renewable Energy Sources, 1990; Expert System Applications in Power Systems, 1990; numerous papers and contribs in the fields of control systems, electrical power systems, energy economics, electrical machines, computational techniques and modelling theory. *Recreations:* music, cricket, Rugby. *Address:* 28 Langford Green, Champion Hill, SE5 8BX. *T:* (020) 7326 0081; *e-mail:* m.a.laughton@elec.qmul.ac.uk. *Club:* Athenæum.

LAUGHTON, Roger Froome, CBE 2000; Director, Laughton Media Associates, since 2003; *b* 19 May 1942; *s* of late Eric Laughton and Elizabeth Laughton (*née* Gibbons); *m* 1967, Suzanne Elizabeth Taylor; one *d*. *Educ:* King Edward VII Sch., Sheffield; Merton Coll., Oxford (Postmaster; BA 1st Cl. Hons Modern Hist.); Inst. of Educn, Oxford Univ. (DipEd (Dist)). Royal Insce Co. Fellow, Stanford Univ., USA, 1964–65; BBC, 1965–90: Producer, 1965–77; Editor, Features, Manchester, 1977–80; Head: Network Features, 1980–85 (Jt Series Producer, River Journeys (BAFTA Award for best documentary series), 1984); Daytime Programmes, 1985–87; Dir, Co-prodns and BBC Enterprises, 1987–90; Man. Dir, MAI Media, 1990–96; Chief Executive: Meridian Broadcasting, 1991–96; United Broadcasting and Entertainment, 1996–99; Hd, Media Sch., Bournemouth Univ., 1999–2005. Chm., ITV Broadcast Bd, 1995–97; Director: ITV, 1992–99; United News and Media, 1996–2000; ITN, 1997–99; Chm., South West Screen, 2004–09; Mem. Bd, Services Sound and Vision Corp., 2007–. Chm., DCMS/Skillset Audio-Visual Industries Trng Gp, 1999–2001. Chm., Screen Heritage Prog. Bd, 2008–. Governor: BFI, 2002–08 (Dep. Chair, 2006–08); Arts Inst. of Bournemouth, 2006–. Mem., Internat. TV Acad., 1994; FRTS 1994 (Gold Award, 1999). *Recreations:* walking, cricket, reading. *Address:* 6 Lawn Crescent, Richmond, Surrey TW9 3NR. *T:* (020) 8948 0231. *Club:* Royal Automobile.

LAUNDER, Prof. Brian Edward, FRS 1994; FREng, FIMechE, FRAeS; Research Professor, School of Mechanical, Aerospace and Civil Engineering, University of Manchester (formerly Department of Mechanical, Aerospace and Manufacturing Engineering, UMIST), since 1998; *b* 20 July 1939; *s* of Harry Edward Launder and Elizabeth Ann Launder (*née* Ayers); *m* 1967, Dagny Simonsen; one *s* one *d*. *Educ:* Enfield Grammar Sch.; Imperial Coll., London (BScEng Mech Engrg 1961); MIT (SM 1963; ScD 1965 Mech Engrg). Res. Asst, MIT, 1961–64; Lectr, 1964–71, Reader in Fluid Mechanics, 1971–76, Imperial Coll.; Prof. of Mech. Engrg, Univ. of California, Davis, 1976–80; University of Manchester Institute of Science and Technology: Prof. of Mech. Engrg, 1980–98; Head, Thermo-Fluids Div., 1980–90; Head, Dept of Mech. Engrg, 1983–85 and 1993–95; Regl Dir (North), Tyndall Centre for Climate Change Res., 2000–06; Dir, Mason Centre for Envmtl Flows, 2003–06. Hon. Prof., Nanjing Aeronautics Inst., 1993. FREng (FEng 1994); FASME. Dr *hc*: Inst Nat. Polytechnique de Toulouse, 1999; Thessaloniki, 2005. *Publications:* (with D. B. Spalding) Mathematical Models of Turbulence, 1972; (ed) Turbulent Shear Flows, vol. 1, 1978–vol. 9, 1994; numerous articles on turbulent flow in learned jls. *Recreations:* vacationing in France, photography, country walking, gentle bicycling. *Address:* School of Mechanical, Aerospace and Civil Engineering, University of Manchester, PO Box 88, Manchester M60 1QD. *T:* (0161) 200 3801.

LAURANCE, Anthony John, CBE 2005; Adviser, Public Administration Development Programme, Libya, since 2006; *b* 11 Nov. 1950; *s* of Dr Bernard Laurance and Margaret Audrey Laurance (*née* Kidner); *m* 1981, Judith Allen; two *d*. *Educ:* Bryanston Sch.; Clare Coll., Cambridge (MA). Drum Publications, Zambia, 1973–74; News Training Scheme, BBC, 1975; joined DHSS, 1975; Admin. Trainee, subseq. HEO(D), 1975–80; Mgt Services, 1980–81; Policy Strategy Unit, 1981–83; Finance Div., 1983–85; Prin. Private Sec. to Sec. of State for Social Services, 1985–87; Newcastle Central Office, 1987–90; Territorial Dir, Benefits Agency, 1990–95; Regl Gen. Manager/Regl Dir, South and West RHA, 1995; Regl Dir, SW, NHS Exec., DoH, 1995–2002; Prog. Dir, NHSU, DoH, 2002–04; Iraq: Health Team Leader, Coalition Provisional Authy, 2004; Sen. Advr to Minister of Health, 2004–05; Adviser to Centre of Govt, 2005–06. *Recreations:* modern fiction, poker, tennis. *Address:* 54 Stane Grove, SW9 9AL.

LAUREN, Ralph; fashion designer; Chairman, Polo Ralph Lauren Corporation; *b* 14 Oct. 1939; *s* of Frank and Frieda Lifschitz; changed name to Lauren, 1955; *m* 1964, Ricky Beer; three *s*. Salesman, New York: Bloomingdale's; Brooks Bros; Asst Buyer, Allied Stores; Rep., Rivetz Necktie Manufrs; Neckwear Designer, Polo Div., Beau Brummel, 1967–69; creator of designer and ready-to-wear clothing, accessories, fragrances, home furnishings, etc; Founder: Polo Menswear Co., 1968; Ralph Lauren's Women's Wear, 1971; Polo Leathergoods, 1978; Polo Ralph Lauren Luggage, 1982; Ralph Lauren Home Collection, 1983. Numerous fashion awards. *Address:* Polo Ralph Lauren Corporation, 650 Madison Avenue, New York, NY 10022, USA.

LAURENCE, Ven. Christopher; *see* Laurence, Ven. J. H. C.

LAURENCE, George Frederick; QC 1991; *b* 15 Jan. 1947; *s* of Dr George Bester Laurence and Anna Margaretha Laurence; *m* 1st, 1976, (Ann) Jessica Chenevix Trench (*d* 1999); one *s* one *d*, and one step *s*; 2nd, 2000, (Anne) Jacqueline Baker; one *s* one *d*. *Educ:* Pretoria High Sch. for Boys; Univ. of Cape Town (Smuts Meml Scholarship; BA); University College, Oxford (Rhodes Scholar; MA). Called to the Bar, Middle Temple, 1972 (Harmsworth Law Scholar; Bencher, 1999); Asst Recorder, 1993–2000; Dep. High Court Judge, 1997–2004; a Recorder, 2000–04. Mem. Council, S African Inst. of Race Relns, 1998–. Fellow, Soc. for Advanced Legal Studies, 1998. Patron, Sir John Soane's Mus., 2007–. *Publications:* articles in Jl of Planning and Envmt Law and Rights of Way Law Review. *Recreations:* theatre, access to the countryside, cricket, tennis. *Address:* 12 New Square, Lincoln's Inn, WC2A 3SW. *T:* (020) 7419 8000.

LAURENCE, Ven. (John Harvard) Christopher; Archdeacon of Lindsey, Diocese of Lincoln, 1985–94, now Archdeacon Emeritus; *b* 15 April 1929; *s* of Canon H. P. Laurence and Mrs E. Laurence; *m* 1952, E. Margaret E. Chappell; one *s* one *d*. *Educ:* Christ's Hospital; Trinity Hall, Cambridge (MA); Westcott House, Cambridge. Nat. service commn, Royal Lincolnshire Regt, 1948–50. Asst Curate, St Nicholas, Lincoln, 1955–59; Vicar, Crosby St George, Scunthorpe, 1959–73; St Hugh's Missioner, Lincoln Diocese, 1974–79; Bishops' Director of Clergy Training, London Diocese, 1979–85. *Recreation:* sculpture. *Address:* 5 Haffenden Road, Lincoln LN2 1RP. *T:* (01522) 531444.

LAURENCE, Vice Adm. Timothy James Hamilton, CB 2007; MVO 1989; Chief Executive, Defence Estates, since 2007; Personal Aide-de-Camp to the Queen, since 2004; *b* 1 March 1955; *s* of Guy Stewart Laurence and Barbara Alison Laurence (*née* Symons); *m* 1992, HRH The Princess Royal. *Educ:* Sevenoaks Sch.; Durham Univ. (BSc Geog.). Joined RN, 1973; in command: HMS Cygnet, 1979–80; HMS Boxer, 1989–91; MoD, 1992–95; in command: HMS Cumberland, 1995–96; HMS Montrose and 6th Frigate Sqdn, 1996–97; MoD, 1997–98; Hudson Vis. Fellow, St Antony's Coll., Oxford, 1999; Asst Comdt (Maritime), JSCSC, Shrivenham, 1999–2001; Dir, Navy Resources & Plans, MoD, 2001–04; ACDS (Resources and Plans), MoD, 2004–07. *Recreations:* most sporting and outdoor activities. *Address:* c/o Buckingham Palace, SW1A 1AA.
See also under Royal Family.

LAURENCE SMYTH, Liam Cledwyn; Clerk of Overseas Office, House of Commons, since 2005; *b* 2 Sept. 1955; *s* of Wing Comdr William Laurence Smyth, MBE, RAF, retired, and late Joan Laurence Smyth (*née* Davies); *m* 1st, 1983, Helen Susan Elizabeth

Kingham (marr. diss. 1988); one step *d*; 2nd, 1990, Sally Anne de Ste Croix (*née* Coussins); one *s*, and one step *s* one step *d*. *Educ:* Plymouth Coll.; New Coll., Oxford (Scholar; MA PPE). A Clerk, House of Commons, 1977–: Clerk: Social Security Cttee, 1994–99; Educn and Employment Cttee, 1999–2001; Educn and Skills Cttee, 2001–02; Delegated Legislation, 2003–05. *Recreation:* Gascony in August. *Address:* Overseas Office, House of Commons, SW1A 0AA. *T:* (020) 7219 3314, *Fax:* (020) 7219 2402.

LAURENS, André Antoine; Editor-in-Chief of Le Monde, 1982–84; *b* 7 Dec. 1934; married. Journalist: L'Eclaireur méridional, Montpellier, 1953–55; l'Agence centrale de la presse, Paris, 1958–62; joined Le Monde, 1963; Home Affairs reporter, 1969; Associate Editor, Home Affairs, 1979; Dir, 1982–85; Médiateur, 1992–96; Vice-Pres Dir Gen. L'Independent du Midi, 2000–07; Vice-Pres., Directoire des Journaux du Midi (Midi-Libre, L'Independent, Centre Presse), 2004–07. Vice-Pres., Société des Rédacteurs. *Publications:* Les nouveaux communistes, 1972; D'une France à l'autre, 1974; Le métier politique, 1980.

LAURENSON, James Tait; Managing Director, Adam & Company Group, 1984–93 (founder Director and Deputy Chairman, 1983); Chairman, Adam & Company plc, 1985–1993; *b* 15 March 1941; *s* of James Tait Laurenson, FRCS and Vera Dorothy Kidd; *m* 1969, Hilary Josephine Thompson; one *s* three *d*. *Educ:* Eton; Magdalene College, Cambridge (MA). FCA. Ivory & Sime, investment managers, 1968–83, Partner 1970, Dir 1975; Tayburn Design Group: Man. Dir, 1983–84; Chm., 1984–89; Man. Dir, Hillhouse Investments Ltd, 1993–2005. Director: Alvis, 1971–95; ISIS (formerly I & S UK) Smaller Companies Trust, 1983–2005; The Life Association of Scotland, 1991–93; Fidelity Special Values, 1994–2005. Chairman: Hopetoun House Preservation Trust, 1999–2004; Governing Council, Erskine Stewart's Melville, 1994–99. *Recreations:* family, golf, gardening, travel. *Address:* PO Box 69, Helensville, New Zealand. *T:* (9) 4207195. *Clubs:* Boodle's; Hon. Company of Edinburgh Golfers.

LAURIE, Sir Bayley; *see* Laurie, Sir R. B. E.

LAURIE, (James) Hugh (Calum), OBE 2007; actor, comedian, writer; *b* 11 June 1959; *s* of late Dr (William George) Ranald (Mundell) Laurie; *m* 1989, Jo Green; two *s* one *d*. *Educ:* Dragon Sch., Oxford; Eton Coll.; Selwyn Coll., Cambridge (Rowing Blue; Pres., Footlights). *Television series:* Alfresco, 1982–84; Blackadder II, 1985; Blackadder the Third, 1987; Blackadder Goes Forth, 1989; A Bit of Fry and Laurie, 1989–95; Jeeves and Wooster, 1990–92; All or Nothing at All; Fortysomething, 2003; House, 2005– (Best Actor, Golden Globes, 2006, 2007); *television film* The Young Visiters, 2003; *films:* Plenty, 1985; Peter's Friends, 1992; Sense and Sensibility, 1996; 101 Dalmatians, 1996; Cousin Bette, 1998; Maybe Baby, 2000; Stuart Little, 2000; That Girl from Rio, 2001; Stuart Little 2, 2002; Flight of the Phoenix, 2003; *theatre* Gasping, Theatre Royal, Haymarket, 1990. *Publication:* The Gun Seller, 1996. *Address:* Hamilton Hodell Ltd, 5th Floor, 66–68 Margaret Street, W1W 8SR. *T:* (020) 7636 1221.

LAURIE, Sir (Robert) Bayley (Emilius), 7th Bt *cr* 1834; *b* 8 March 1931; *s* of Maj.-Gen. Sir John Emilius Laurie, 6th Bt, CBE, DSO, and Evelyn Clare, (*d* 1987), *d* of late Lt-Col Lionel James Richardson-Gardner; *S* father, 1983; *m* 1968, Laurelie, *d* of Sir Reginald Lawrence William Williams, 7th Bt, MBE, ED; two *d*. *Educ:* Eton. National Service, 1st Bn Seaforth Highlanders, 1949–51; Captain, 11th Bn Seaforth Highlanders (TA), 1951–67. Lloyd's, 1951–92, Mem., 1955–; with C. T. Bowring & Co. Ltd, 1958–89; Chief Exec., C. T. Bowring (Underwriting Agencies) Ltd, 1974–83; Chm., Bowring Members' Agency, 1983–89; Dir, Murray Lawrence Members' Agency, 1989–92. *Heir: cousin* Andrew Ronald Emilius Laurie [*b* 20 Oct. 1944; *m* 1970, Sarah Anne, *e d* of C. D. Patterson; two *s*]. *Address:* The Old Rectory, Little Tey, Colchester, Essex CO6 1JA. *T:* (01206) 210410.

LAURIE, His Honour Robin; a Circuit Judge, 1986–2003; a Deputy Circuit Judge, since 2003; *b* 26 Jan. 1938; *s* of J. R. Laurie and Dr W. Metzner; *m* 1965, Susan Jane (*neé* Snelling); two *d*. *Educ:* Fettes Coll.; Geneva Univ.; Jesus Coll., Oxford (MA). Called to the Bar, Inner Temple, 1961; practice at the Bar (South Eastern Circuit), 1961–86. *Recreations:* mountaineering, mycology. *Club:* Alpine.

LAURISTON, Richard Basil; a Permanent Chairman of Industrial Tribunals, 1976–89; formerly Senior Partner, Alex Lauriston & Son, Solicitors, Middlesbrough; *b* 26 Jan. 1917; *s* of Alexander Lauriston, MBE, and Nellie Lauriston; *m* 1944, Monica, *d* of Wilfred Leslie Deacon, BA, Tonbridge, and Dorothy Louise Deacon; three *s*. *Educ:* Sir William Turner's Sch., Redcar; St John's Coll., Cambridge (MA, LLM). Solicitor, 1948; a Recorder of the Crown Court, 1974–82. Commnd and served in War of 1939–45, Royal Corps of Signals. *Recreations:* fishing, travelling. *Address:* Auchlochan House, 19 The Courtyard, New Trows Road, Lesmahagow, Lanarks ML11 0JS.

LAUTENBERG, Alexis Peter; Ambassador of Switzerland to the Court of St James's, since 2004; *b* Zürich, 28 Oct. 1945; *s* of Anatole Lautenberg and Nelly Schnapper-Lautenberg; *m* 1972, Gabrielle Feik; one *s* two *d*. *Educ:* Univ. of Lausanne (BA Pol Sci.). Entered Swiss Diplomatic Service, 1974; Attaché, CSCE, Geneva and Stockholm, 1974–75; Dep. Hd of Mission, Warsaw, 1976; Mem., Swiss Delegn to EFTA and GATT, Geneva, 1977–81; Econ. Counsellor, Bonn, 1981–85; Dep. Dir of Internat. Orgns, Berne, 1985–86; Hd, Econ. and Finance Div., Fed. Dept of Foreign Affairs, Berne, 1986–93; Ambassador and Hd, Mission to EC, Brussels, 1993–99; Ambassador to Italy and Malta, in Rome, 1999–2004. Chairman: Gp for negotiations on financial services during Uruguay Round, GATT, 1990–91; Financial Action Task Force on Money Laundering, OECD, 1991–92. Mem. Bd, Foundn for Res. in Internat. Banking and Finance, at Calif Univ., Riverside, 1987–94. Mem. Bd, Coll. of Europe, Bruges, 1994–99. *Recreations:* golf, ski-ing. *Address:* Embassy of Switzerland, 16–18 Montagu Place, W1H 2BQ. *T:* (020) 7616 6000. *Clubs:* Athenæum, Travellers, London Capital.

LAUTERPACHT, Sir Elihu, Kt 1998; CBE 1989; QC 1970; Fellow of Trinity College, Cambridge, since 1953; Director, Research Centre for International Law, 1983–95, now Director Emeritus, and Hon. Professor of International Law, since 1994, University of Cambridge; practising international lawyer and arbitrator; *b* 13 July 1928; *o s* of late Sir Hersch Lauterpacht, QC and Rachel Steinberg; *m* 1955, Judith Maria (*d* 1970), *er d* of Harold Hettinger; one *s* two *d*; *m* 1973, Catherine Daly; one *s*. *Educ:* Phillips Acad., Andover, Mass; Harrow; Trinity Coll., Cambridge (Entrance Schol.). 1st cl. Pt II of Law Tripos and LLB; Whewell Schol. in Internat. Law, 1950; Holt Schol. 1948 and Birkenhead Schol. 1950. Gray's Inn; called to Bar, 1950, Bencher, 1983. Joint Sec., Interdepartmental Cttee on State Immunity, 1950–52; Cambridge University: Asst Lectr in Law, 1953; Lecturer, 1958–81; Reader in Internat. Law, 1981–88. Founding Sec., Internat. Law Fund, 1955–85; Dir of Research, 1959–60, Lectr 1976 and 1996, Hague Academy of Internat. Law; Vis. Prof. of Internat. Law, Univ. of Delhi, 1960. Chm., East African Common Market Tribunal, 1972–75; Consultant to Central Policy Review Staff, 1972–74, 1978–81; Legal Adviser, Australian Dept of Foreign Affairs, 1975–77; Consultant on Internat. Law, UN Inst. for Training and Res., 1978–79; mem. arbitration panel, Internat. Centre for Settlement of Investment Disputes; Chm., North Atlantic Free Trade Area Dispute Settlement Panels, 1996 and 1997; Panel Chm., UN Compensation Commn, 1998–99; Pres., Eritrea-Ethiopia Boundary Commn, 2001–; Deputy Leader: Australian Delegn to UN Law of the Sea Conf., 1975–77; Australian Delegn to UN Gen. Assembly, 1975–77. Judge *ad hoc*, Internat. Court of Justice (Bosnia *v* Yugoslavia), 1993–2002. Pres., Eastern Reg., UNA, 1991–2001; Pres., World Bank Admin. Tribunal, 1996–98 (Mem., 1980–98; Vice-Pres., 1995–96); Chm., Asian Develt Bank Admin. Tribunal, 1991–95; Member: Social Sciences Adv. Cttee, UK Nat. Commn for Unesco, 1980–84; Panel of Arbitrators, Internat. Energy Agency Dispute Settlement Centre; Panel of Arbitrators, UN Law of the Sea Convention, 1998–; Inst. of Internat. Law, 1983– (Associate, 1979); Trustee, Internat. Law Fund, 1983. Editor: British Practice in International Law, 1955–68; International Law Reports, 1960–. Hon. Fellow, Hebrew Univ. of Jerusalem, 1989. Hon. Mem., Amer. Soc. of Internat. Law, 1993 (Annual Cert. of Merit, 1972; Hudson Medal, 2005). Comdr, Order of Merit (Chile), 1969; Order of Bahrain, 2001; Datuk (Malaysia), 2005. *Publications:* Jerusalem and the Holy Places, 1968; (ed) International Law: the collected papers of Sir Hersch Lauterpacht, vol I, 1970, vol. II, 1975, vol. III, 1977, vol. IV, 1978, vol. V, 2004; The Development of the Law of International Organization, 1976; (ed) Individual Rights and the State in Foreign Affairs, 1977; Aspects of the Administration of International Justice, 1991; various articles on international law. *Address:* Lauterpacht Centre for International Law, 5 Cranmer Road, Cambridge CB3 9BL. *T:* (01223) 335358; 20 Essex Street, WC2R 3AL. *T:* (020) 7583 9294, *Fax:* (020) 7583 1341. *Club:* Garrick.

LAUTI, Rt Hon. Sir Toaripi, GCMG 1990; PC 1979; Governor-General of Tuvalu, 1990–93; *b* Papua New Guinea, 28 Nov. 1928; *m*; three *s* two *d*. *Educ:* Tuvalu; Fiji; Wesley Coll., Paerata, NZ; St Andrew's Coll., Christchurch, NZ; Christchurch Teachers' Coll., NZ. Taught in KGV, Tarawa, Kiribati, 1953–62; Labour Relations and Trng Officer, Nauru and Ocean Islands, engaged by British Phosphate Comrs; returned to Tuvalu, 1974, and entered politics; MP, elected unopposed to House of Assembly, May 1975; elected Chief Minister, Tuvalu, upon separation of Ellice Islands (Tuvalu) from Kiribati, Oct. 1975, re-elected Chief Minister in Sept. 1977; First Prime Minister, Tuvalu, 1978–81; Leader of the Opposition, 1981–90. Chm., 18th South Pacific Conference, Noumea, Oct. 1978. *Address:* PO Box 84, Funafuti, Tuvalu, Central Pacific.

LAVELLE, Roger Garnett, CB 1989; financial executive; Hon. Vice-President, European Investment Bank, since 1993 (Vice-President, 1989–93); *b* 23 Aug. 1932; *s* of Henry Allman Lavelle and Evelyn Alice Garnett; *m* 1956, Elsa Gunilla Odeberg; three *s* one *d*. *Educ:* Leighton Park; Trinity Hall, Cambridge (BA, LLB). Asst Principal, Min. of Health, 1955; Principal, HM Treasury, 1961; Special Assistant (Common Market) to Lord Privy Seal, 1961–63; Private Sec. to Chancellor of the Exchequer, 1965–68; Asst Secretary, 1968, Under Sec., 1975, Dep. Sec., 1985, HM Treasury; Dep. Sec., Cabinet Office, 1987. Dir, EBRD, 1993–2000. *Recreations:* music and gardening. *Address:* 36 Cholmeley Crescent, Highgate, N6 5HA. *T:* (020) 8340 4845.

LAVENDER, Rt Rev. Mgr Gerard; Parish Priest, Holy Family, Darlington, since 1993; Diocesan Episcopal Vicar, since 2005; *b* 20 Sept. 1943; *s* of Joseph and Mary Lavender. *Educ:* Ushaw Coll., Durham. Ordained, 1969; Asst Priest, St Mary Cath., Newcastle upon Tyne, 1969–75; loaned to Royal Navy as Chaplain, 1975; completed All Arms Commando Course, 1976; served with RM, 1976–79; sea going, 1979–80, 1987–89; Exchange Chaplain to San Diego, with US Navy, 1981–83; Chaplain in: Scotland (Rosyth), 1983–85; Portsmouth, 1985–87; Plymouth, 1989–90. GSM, NI, 4 visits 1977–79; Prin. RC Chaplain (Navy), MoD, 1990–93, retired. *Recreations:* golf, tennis, hill walking. *Address:* Holy Family Presbytery, 60 Cockerton Green, Darlington, Co. Durham DL3 9EU.

LAVENDER, Nicholas; QC 2008; *b* Barnsley, 7 Aug. 1964; *s* of Brian and Betty Lavender; *m* 2002, Anuja Ravindra Dhir; two *s* one *d*. *Educ:* Queen Elizabeth Grammar Sch., Wakefield; Corpus Christi Coll., Cambridge (BA 1987); Oriel Coll., Oxford (BCL). Called to the Bar, Inner Temple, 1989. *Publication:* (ed jtly) Barristers, Vol. 3(1) of Halsbury's Laws of England, 2005. *Address:* Serle Court, 6 New Square, Lincoln's Inn, WC2A 3QS. *Clubs:* MCC; Yorkshire County Cricket.

LAVER, Frederick John Murray, CBE 1971; Member, Post Office Corporation, 1969–73, retired; *b* 11 March 1915; *er s* of late Clifton F. Laver and Elsie Elizabeth Palmer, Bridgwater; *m* 1948, Kathleen Amy Blythe; one *s* two *d*. *Educ:* Plymouth Coll. BSc London. Entered PO Engrg Dept, 1935; PO Research Stn, 1935–51; Radio Planning, 1951–57; Organization and Efficiency, 1957–63; Asst Sec., HM Treasury, 1963–65; Chief Scientific Officer, Min. of Technology, 1965–68; Director, National Data Processing Service, 1968–70; Mem., NRDC, 1974–80. Vis. Prof., Computing Lab., Univ. of Newcastle upon Tyne, 1975–79. Mem. Council: IEE, 1966–69, 1972–73; British Computer Soc., 1969–72; Nat. Computing Centre, 1966–68, 1970–73; IEE Electronic Divl Bd, 1966–69, 1970–73. Mem. Council, 1979–87, Chm., 1985–87, Pro-Chancellor, 1981–87, Exeter Univ. Pres., Devonshire Assoc., 1990–91. CEng, FIET; Hon. FBCS. Hon. DSc Exeter, 1988. *Publications:* nine introductory books on physics and computing; several scientific papers. *Recreations:* reading, writing, and watching the sea. *Address:* The Old Vicarage, Otterton, Devon EX9 7JF.

LAVER, Gillian Margaret; non-executive Director and Chairman of Audit Committee, West Midlands Strategic Health Authority, since 2006; *b* 10 Jan. 1949; *d* of Alfred Robert Mansbridge and Doris Edna Mansbridge; *m* 1999, Barry Charles Laver. *Educ:* Horsham High Sch. for Girls; Univ. of Keele (BA Hons 1971). CA 1977. Sen. Consultant, Strategy Div., PA Management Consultants, 1986–89; Finance Dir, Wedgwood Div., Waterford Wedgwood plc, 1989–94; Gp Finance and IT Dir, GEC Avery Ltd, 1994–98; Nat. Dir of Finance, Eversheds, 1998–2000; Cogenza Consulting Ltd, 2001–05; Dir of Finance and Central Services, Archbishops' Council, 2005–06. Member: Auditing Practices Bd, 2001–06; Audit Cttee, Arts Council England, 2004–; Audit Cttee, Univ. of Keele, 2007–. Trustee and Hon. Treas., Diabetes UK, 2001–05. FRSA. *Recreations:* tennis, golf, ski-ing, gardening.

LAVER, Graeme; *see* Laver, W. G.

LAVER, Prof. John David Michael Henry, CBE 1999; FBA 1990; FRSE; Emeritus Professor of Speech Sciences, Queen Margaret University (formerly Queen Margaret University College) (Research Professor, 2001–04, Vice-Principal, 2002–03, Deputy Principal, 2003–04); *b* 20 Jan. 1938; *s* of Harry Frank Laver and Mary Laver (*née* Brearley); *m* 1st, 1961, Avril Morna Anel Macqueen Gibson; two *s* one *d*; 2nd, 1974, Sandra Traill; one *s*. *Educ:* Churcher's Coll., Petersfield; Univ. of Edinburgh (MA Hons; Postgrad. Dip. in Phonetics; PhD; DLitt). Asst Lectr and Lectr in Phonetics, Univ. of Ibadan, 1963–66; University of Edinburgh: Lectr, Sen. Lectr, Reader in Phonetics, 1966–85; Prof. of Phonetics, 1985–2000; Dir, 1984–89, Chm., 1989–94, Centre for Speech Technology Research; Associate Dean, Faculty of Arts, 1989–92; Vice-Principal, 1994–97. Pres., Internat. Phonetic Assoc., 1991–95 (Mem. Council, 1986–); Member: Board, European Speech Communication Assoc., 1988–92; Council, Philological Soc., 1994–97; Council, British Acad., 1998–2001 (Chm., Humanities Res. Bd, 1994–98); Board of Governors:

Edinburgh Univ. Press, 1999–2000; Caledonian Res. Foundn, 1999–2006. FRSE 1994 (Vice-Pres., 1996–99; Fellowship Sec., 1999–2002; Bicentenary Medal, 2004; Royal Medal, 2007); FRSA 1995–2006; Fellow, Inst. of Acoustics, 1988–2001. Hon. FRCSLT 2003. Hon. DLitt: Sheffield, 1999; De Montfort, 1999; Queen Margaret UC, 2006. *Publications:* Communication in Face to Face Interaction, 1972; Phonetics in Linguistics, 1973; The Phonetic Description of Voice Quality, 1980; The Cognitive Representation of Speech, 1981; Aspects of Speech Technology, 1988; The Gift of Speech, 1991; Principles of Phonetics, 1994; The Handbook of Phonetic Sciences, 1997, 2nd edn 2009. *Recreations:* reading, birdwatching, lexicography. *Address:* Queen Margaret University, Queen Margaret University Drive, Musselburgh EH21 6UU.

LAVER, (William) Graeme, PhD; FRS 1987; Head, Influenza Research Unit, Australian National University, 1983–2001; *b* 3 June 1929; *s* of Lawrence and Madge Laver; *m* 1954, Judith Garrard Cahn; one *s* two *d*. *Educ:* Ivanhoe Grammar Sch., Melbourne; Univ. of Melbourne (BSc, MSc); Univ. of London (PhD). Technical Asst, Walter & Eliza Hall Inst. of Med. Res., Melbourne, 1947–52; Res. Asst, Dept of Biochemistry, Melbourne Univ., 1954–55; Res. Fellow, 1958–62, Fellow, 1962–64, Senior Fellow, 1964–90, Special Prof., 1990–2002, John Curtin Sch. of Med. Res., ANU. International Meetings: Rougemont, Switzerland, 1976; Baden, Vienna, 1977; Thredbo, Australia, 1979; Beijing, China, 1982; Banbury Center, Cold Spring Harbor, NY, 1985; Kona, Hawaii, 1989. (Jtly) Australia Prize, 1996. *Publications:* papers on structure of influenza virus antigens, molecular mechanisms of antigenic shift and drift in type A influenza viruses and develt of anti-influenza drugs; numerous research articles. *Recreations:* raising beef cattle, viticulture, wine-making, ski-ing, climbing volcanoes. *Address:* 3047 Barton Highway, Murrumbateman, NSW 2582, Australia. *T:* (2) 62270061.

LAVERCOMBE, Dr Brian James; Honorary Member, British Council, since 1997 (Regional Director for the Americas, 1994–96); *b* 17 Dec. 1938; *s* of Ralph Lavercombe and Doris (*née* Hawkins); *m* 1966, Margaret Jane Chambers; one *s* one *d*. *Educ:* Barnstaple Grammar Sch.; Imperial Coll., London (BSc Hons Physics, ARCS, MSc, DIC; PhD 1966); Reading Univ. (MA Medieval Studies 2001). Post-doctoral Fellow and Asst Prof. in Residence, UCLA, 1966–68; British Council: Science Officer: Chile, 1968–72; Spain, 1972–77; Israel, 1977–80; Projects Officer, Science and Technol. Div., 1980–81; Dir, Science Dept, 1981–84; Rep., Colombia, 1984–87; Dep. Controller, Sci., Technol. and Educn Div., 1987–90; Dir, Mexico, 1990–94. Advr, Earthwatch, 1997–2002. *Publications:* papers on scientific co-operation and technology transfer; research papers in Nature and Accoustica; articles on ornithology. *Recreations:* cricket, ornithology, painting, mediaeval history. *Address:* 37 Playfield Road, Kennington, Oxford OX1 5RS. *T:* (01865) 739659. *Clubs:* Whiteditch Wanderers Cricket (Basingstoke); Isis Probus.

LAVERICK, David John; Pensions Ombudsman, 2001–07; President, Adjudication Panel for England, since 2001; *b* 3 Aug. 1945; *s* of Wilfred Henry Laverick and I. M. Doreen Laverick (*née* Lockhart); *m* 1968, Margaret Elizabeth Myatt; three *s*. *Educ:* Sir William Turner's Sch., Redcar; King's Coll. London (LLB Hons 1967); Coll. of Law. Admitted solicitor, 1970; Asst Solicitor, Beds and Lincs CC, 1970–73; Dir of Admin, E Lindsey DC, 1973–75; Dir, Local Govt Ombudsman Service, 1975–95; Chief Exec., Family Health Services Appeal Authy, 1995–2001. Legal Mem., Mental Health Rev. Tribunals, 1999–2002. *Recreation:* Scottish country dancing.

LAVERICK, Elizabeth, OBE 1993; PhD, CEng, FIET; CPhys, FInstP, FIEEE (US); Project Director, Advanced Manufacturing in Electronics, 1985–88; *b* 25 Nov. 1925; *d* of William Rayner and Alice Garland; *m* 1st, 1946 (marr. diss. 1960); no *c*; 2nd, 2004, Peter Ogden (*d* 2004). *Educ:* Dr Challoner's Grammar Sch., Amersham; Durham Univ. Research at Durham Univ., 1946–50; Section Leader at GEC, 1950–53; Microwave Engineer at Elliott Bros, 1954; Head of Radar Research Laboratory of Elliott-Automation Radar Systems Ltd, 1959; Jt Gen. Manager, Elliott-Automation Radar Systems Ltd, 1968–69, Technical Dir, 1969–71; Dep. Sec., IEE, 1971–85; Electronics CADMAT (Computer Aided Design, Manufacture and Test) Project Dir, 1982–85. Mem. Electronics Divisional Bd, 1967–70, Mem. Council, 1969–70, IEE. Chm., Engrg Careers Co-ordinating Cttee, 1983–85; Member: DE Adv. Cttee on Women's Employment, 1970–82; Adv. Cttee for Electronic and Electrical Engrg, Sheffield Univ., 1984–87; Nat. Electronics Council, 1986–98; Chm., Ninth Internat. Conf. of Women Engrs and Scientists, 1989–91; Hon. Sec., Women's Engrg Soc., 1991–95 (Pres., 1967–69). Member Council: Inst. of Physics, 1970–73 (Chm., Women in Physics Cttee, 1985–90); City and Guilds of London Inst., 1984–87 (Hon. Mem., 1991; Fellow, 1998); Member Court: Brunel Univ., 1985–88; City Univ., 1991–95. Mem. Ct of Govs, IEE Benevolent Fund, 1991–99. Liveryman, Co. of Engrs, 1985–88. FRSA 1991. Hon. FUMIST, 1969. Editor, Woman Engr (Jl of Women's Engrg Soc.), 1984–90. *Publications:* contribs to IEE and IEEE Jls. *Recreations:* music, tapestry.

LAVERS, Richard Douglas; HM Diplomatic Service, retired; Ambassador to Guatemala, 2001–06, and concurrently non-resident Ambassador to El Salvador, 2003–06 and to Honduras, 2004–06; *b* Nairobi, 10 May 1947; *s* of Douglas Arthur Lavers and Edyth Agnes (*née* Williams); *m* 1986, Brigitte Anne Julia Maria Moers, *e d* of late Robert Moers, Turnhout, Belgium; two *s*. *Educ:* Hurstpierpoint Coll.; Exeter Coll., Oxford (MA). Joined HM Diplomatic Service, 1969; Third Sec., Buenos Aires, 1970–72; Second, later First Sec., Wellington, 1973–76; FCO, 1976–81; First Sec., Pol and Econ., Brussels, 1981–85; on secondment to Guinness Mahon, 1985–87; FCO, 1987–89; NATO Defence Coll., Rome, 1989; Dep. Hd of Mission and HM Consul General, Santiago, 1990–93; Ambassador to Ecuador, 1993–97; FCO, 1997–99; Hd of Research Analysts, FCO, 1999–2001. Non-exec. Dir, PetroLatina, 2006–07. Chairman: Anglo-Ecuadorian Soc., 2007–; Anglo-Central American Soc., 2008. Vis. Res. Fellow, Inst. of Latin American Studies, 2001. *Recreations:* books, pictures, travel, fishing, golf. *Club:* Oxford and Cambridge.

LAVERTY, Ashley; *see* Page, A.

LAVERY, (Charles) Michael; QC (NI) 1971; Chairman, Standing Advisory Commission on Human Rights, 1995–99; *b* 10 June 1934; *s* of Charles Lavery and Winifred (*née* McCaffrey); *m* 1962, Anneliese Gisela Lehmann; three *s* two *d*. *Educ:* Queen's Univ., Belfast (LLB 1954); Trinity Coll., Dublin (BA 1956). Member of the Bar: NI, 1956– (Bencher, 1974, Treas., 1987, Inn of Court); Ireland, 1974–. Chm., Gen. Council of Bar, NI, 1987–89. *Recreations:* walking, reading, cooking. *Address:* The Bar Library, Royal Courts of Justice, Belfast.

LAVERY, Gerald; Senior Finance Director, Department of Agriculture and Rural Development, Northern Ireland, since 2003; *b* 9 April 1952; *s* of David and Mary Lavery; *m* 2002, Kathy McClurg; one *s* two *d*. *Educ:* Christian Brothers' Grammar Sch., Belfast; Queen's Univ., Belfast (BA Hons Italian Lang. and Lit. 1974). Joined NI Civil Service, 1974; Dept of Manpower Services, 1974–81; Dept of Econ. Develt, 1982–89; Trng and Employment Agency, 1990; NI Office, 1991–94; Sen. Civil Service, 1995; Department of Agriculture and Rural Development, 1995–: Fisheries Sec., 1996–2000; Finance Dir, 2000–03. *Recreations:* prayer and Christian life, choral singing, keeping fit, enjoyment of all arts. *Address:* Department of Agriculture and Rural Development, Dundonald House, Upper Newtownards Road, Belfast BT4 3SB. *T:* (028) 9052 4638, *Fax:* (028) 9052 4813.

LAVIGNE, Marc T.; *see* Tessier-Lavigne.

LAVIN, Deborah Margaret; Principal-elect of new college, and Co-Director, Research Institute for the Study of Change, University of Durham, 1995–97; Hon. Fellow, Department of History, University of Durham, since 1998; *b* 22 Sept. 1939. *Educ:* Roedean Sch., Johannesburg, SA; Rhodes Univ., Grahamstown, SA; Lady Margaret Hall, Oxford (MA, DipEd). Asst Lectr, Dept of History, Univ. of the Witwatersrand, 1962–64; Lectr, 1965–78, Sen. Lectr, 1978–80, Dept of Mod. Hist., The Queen's Univ. of Belfast; Principal, Trevelyan College, Durham Univ., 1980–95 (Hon. Fellow, 1997); Pres., Howlands Trust, Univ. of Durham, 1993–97. Sen. Associate, St Antony's Coll., Oxford, 2001–. Trustee, Westlakes Research Ltd, 1995–2001. Chm., East Hendred Heritage Trust, 2005–. Member: Council, Benenden Sch., 1998–; Ct of Govs, Truro Coll., 2005–. Hon. Life Mem., Nat. Maritime Mus. Cornwall, 2003–. Assoc. Fellow, RIIA, 1997–2000. *Publications:* South African Memories, 1979; The Making of the Sudanese State, 1990; The Transformation of the Old Order in the Sudan, 1993; From Empire to International Commonwealth: a biography of Lionel Curtis, 1995; articles in learned jls. *Recreations:* the arts, gardening, some sport. *Address:* Hickmans Cottages, Cat Street, East Hendred, Oxon OX12 8JT. *T:* (01235) 833408. *Club:* Reform.

LAVOIE, Judith Anne, (Mrs A. R. Lavoie); *see* LaRocque, J. A.

LAW, family name of **Barons Coleraine** and **Ellenborough**.

LAW, Prof. Colin Nigel, PhD; Head of Laboratory, Cambridge Laboratory, Institute of Plant Science Research, John Innes Centre, Norwich, 1989–92; *b* 18 Nov. 1932; *s* of Joseph and Dorothy Mildred Law; *m* 1964, Angela Patricia Williams; three *d*. *Educ:* Queen Elizabeth's Grammar Sch., Blackburn; Univ. of Birmingham (BSc Hons Genetics); UCW, Aberystwyth (PhD). Nat. Service, RA, 1955–57. Res. worker, Plant Breeding Inst., Cambridge, 1960–87, Head of Cytogenetics Dept, 1972–87; Divl Head, Plant Genetics and Breeding, Inst. of Plant Sci. Res., 1987–89. Sen. Foreign Res. Fellow, Nat. Sci. Foundn, N Dakota State Univ., 1969. Hon. Prof., Univ. of East Anglia, 1990–. Prix Assinsel, Assoc. Internationale des Sélectionneurs, 1982. *Publications:* papers and articles on chromosome manipulation techniques to identify genes of agric. importance in crop plants, esp. wheat; genetic control of cereal plant responses to envmtl stress, particularly salinity. *Recreations:* fishing, painting. *Address:* 41 Thornton Close, Girton, Cambridge CB3 0NF. *T:* (01223) 276554.

LAW, (David) Jude; actor; *b* 29 Dec. 1972; *s* of Peter Law and Maggie Law; *m* 1997, Sadie Frost (marr. diss. 2003); two *s* one *d*. *Educ:* Alleyn's Sch., Dulwich. Co-founder and Dir, Natural Nylon, prodn co., 2000–03. *Theatre includes:* Les Parents Terribles, NT, 1994; Death of a Salesman, W Yorks Playhouse; Ion, Royal Court, 1995; 'Tis a Pity She's a Whore, 1999, Doctor Faustus, 2002, Young Vic. *Films include:* Shopping, 1994; Gattaca, Wilde, Midnight in the Garden of Good and Evil, Bent, 1997; Music From Another Room, Final Cut, The Wisdom of Crocodiles, 1998; eXistenz, The Talented Mr Ripley (Best Supporting Actor, BAFTA, 2000), 1999; Love, Honour and Obey, 2000; Enemy at the Gates, A. I. Artificial Intelligence, 2001; Road to Perdition, 2002; Cold Mountain, 2003; I Heart Huckabees, (also prod.) Sky Captain and the World of Tomorrow, Alfie, 2004; Closer, The Aviator, 2005; All The King's Men, Breaking and Entering, The Holiday, 2006; Sleuth, 2007; My Blueberry Nights, 2008. Chevalier des Arts et des Lettres (France), 2007. *Address:* c/o Premier PR, 91 Berwick Street, W1F 0NE.

LAW, Francis Stephen, (Frank Law), CBE 1981; *b* 31 Dec. 1916; *s* of Henry and Ann Law-Lowensberg; *m* 1959, Nicole Vigne (*née* Fesch); one *s*, and one *d* from previous marriage. *Educ:* on the Continent. War service, 1939–45. Wills Law & Co., 1947; Truvox Engrg, 1960, subseq. Dir of Controls and Communications; Dep. Chm., NFC, 1982–85 (Dir, Consortium and its predecessors, 1969–87). Chairman: Varta Gp UK, 1971–2001; Rubis Investment & Cie, 1990–2001 (Pres., 2001–); Aegis (formerly WRCS) Gp plc, 1992–2000 (Dir, 1982–92); Director: B. Elliott Plc, 1968–86; BMW (GB) Ltd, 1978–88; Siemens, 1984–98; NFC Internat. Hldgs, 1985–92; Celab Ltd, 1991–2001; Mem. Adv. Bd, Berliner Bank, 1988–92. Chm., Social Responsibilities Council, NFC, 1988–92; Member: Org. Cttee, NFC, 1968; Economic and Social Cttee, EEC, 1978–86. Life Governor, RSC, 1985–. *Recreations:* music, theatre, swimming. *Address:* La Clergie, St Sulpice de Roumagnac, 24600 Riberac, France. *Clubs:* Boodle's; Pilgrims.

LAW, George Llewellyn; Vice Chairman, Morgan Grenfell Group plc, 1987–89; *b* 8 July 1929; *s* of late George Edward Law and Margaret Dorothy Law, OBE (*née* Evans); *m* 1960, Anne Stewart, *d* of late Arthur Wilkinson and Ness Wilkinson (*née* Muir); one *d*. *Educ:* Westminster Sch. (Schol.); Clare Coll., Cambridge (Schol.; BA). ACIArb. Solicitor. Slaughter and May, Solicitors, 1952–67, Partner 1961–67; Dir, Morgan Grenfell & Co. Ltd, 1968–91; Dir, Morgan Grenfell Gp plc, 1971–89. Deputy Chairman: Baker Perkins plc, 1986–87 (Dir, 1981–87); Blackwood Hodge plc, 1988–90 (Dir, 1968–90); Director: Bernard Sunley Investment Trust, 1968–75; Sidlaw Group, 1974–82; APV, 1987–90. Mem., Arbitration Panel, SFA Consumer Arbitration Scheme, 1988–2001. Member of Council: Furniture Hist. Soc., 1978–85; Ancient Monuments Soc., 1992– (Actg Hon. Treas., 2008); British-Italian Soc., 1994–97. Chm., Council of Mgt, Spitalfields Fest., 2002–06 (Mem., Trustee, and Chm., Fest. Patrons' Cttee, 1995–2006; Hon. Life Patron, 2001; Hon. Advr, 2006). Trustee and Hon. Treas., Nat. Assoc. for Gambling Care, Educnl Resources and Trng, 1998–2004. Trustee, Opera Holland Park Friends, 2003. FRSA. *Recreations:* history of furniture and decorative arts, architectural history, music, reading, swimming, cricket. *Address:* 6 Phillimore Gardens Close, W8 7QA. *T:* (020) 7937 3061. *Clubs:* Brooks's, MCC, Surrey County Cricket.

LAW, Jude; *see* Law, D. J.

LAW, Prof. Malcolm Ross, FRCP, FFPH, FMedSci; Professor of Epidemiology and Preventive Medicine, Wolfson Institute of Preventive Medicine, Barts and The London, Queen Mary's School of Medicine and Dentistry, since 2001; *b* 9 May 1946; *s* of Harold Palmer Law and Jessie Maud Law; *m* 1976, Amelia Anne McRedmond; one *s*. *Educ:* Adelaide High Sch.; Univ. of Adelaide (MB BS 1970; MSc 1984). MRCP, FRCP 1995; FFPH 2002. Jun. med. posts, Adelaide, London and Cardiff, 1971–78; Lectr and Sen. Registrar, Royal Brompton Hosp., London, 1979–83; Lectr, 1984–87, Sen. Lectr, 1987–94, Reader, 1994–2001, in Epidemiology and Preventive Medicine, Wolfson Inst. of Preventive Medicine, Barts and The London, Queen Mary's Sch. of Medicine and Dentistry. FMedSci 2006. *Publications:* contrib. learned jls. *Address:* Wolfson Institute of Preventive Medicine, Barts and The London, Queen Mary's School of Medicine and Dentistry, Charterhouse Square, EC1M 6BQ. *T:* (020) 7882 6268.

LAW, Patricia; Member (Ind) Blaenau Gwent, National Assembly for Wales, since June 2006; *m* 1976, Peter John Law, MP (*d* 2006); two *s* three *d*. *Educ:* Glanyravon Secondary Modern Sch.; Ebbw Vale Coll. Former Nursing Asst, Gwent Healthcare NHS Trust.

Address: (office) 24 James Street, Ebbw Vale, Blaenau Gwent NP23 6JG; National Assembly for Wales, Cardiff Bay, Cardiff CF99 1NA.

LAW, Phillip Garth, AC 1995 (AO 1975); CBE 1961; MSc, FAIP, FTSE, FAA, FRSV; scientist, Antarctic explorer, educationist; *b* 21 April 1912; *s* of Arthur James Law and Lillie Lena Chapman; *m* 1941, Nellie Isabel Allan; no *c. Educ:* Hamilton High Sch.; Ballarat Teachers' Coll.; Melbourne Univ. FAIP 1948; FTSE 1976; FAA 1978. Science master, State secondary schs, Vic., 1933–38; Tutor in Physics, Newman Coll., Melbourne Univ., 1940–47; Lectr in Physics, 1943–48. Research Physicist and Asst Sec. of Scientific Instrument and Optical Panel of Austr. Min. of Munitions, 1940–45. Sen. Scientific Officer, ANARE, 1947–48; cosmic ray measurements in Antarctica and Japan, 1948; Dir, Antarctic Div., Dept of External Affairs, Aust., and Leader, ANARE, 1949–66; Expedition relief voyages to Heard I. and Macquarie I., 1949, 1951, 1952, 1954. Australian observer with Norwegian-British-Swedish Antarctic Exped., 1950; Leader of expedition: to establish first permanent Australian station in Antarctica at Mawson, MacRobertson Land, 1954; which established second continental station at Davis, Princess Elizabeth Land, 1957; which took over Wilkes station from USA, 1959; to relieve ANARE stations and to explore coast of Australian Antarctic Territory, annually, 1955–66. Chm., Australian Nat. Cttee for Antarctic Research, 1966–80. Exec. Vice-Pres., Victoria Inst. of Colls, 1966–77; Pres., Victorian Inst. of Marine Scis, 1978–80. Member: Council of Melbourne Univ., 1959–78; Council, La Trobe Univ., 1964–74; Chm., RMIT Foundn, 1995–98; President: Royal Soc. of Victoria, 1967, 1968; Aust. and NZ Schs Exploring Soc., 1977–82. Dep. Pres., Science Museum of Victoria, Melbourne, 1979–82 (Trustee, 1968–83). Pres., Grad. Union, Melbourne Univ., 1972–77. Patron, British Schs Exploring Soc. Fellow, Aust. Inst. of Physics; ANZAAS; Foundn FRSV 1995. Hon. Fellow, Royal Melbourne Inst. of Technology. Hon. DAppSc Melbourne, 1962; Hon. DEd Victoria Inst. of Colls, 1978; Hon. DSc La Trobe, 1995. Founder's Gold Medal, RGS, 1960; Gold Medal, Aust. Geographic Soc., 1988; Clunies Ross Nat. Sci. and Technol. Award, 2001. *Publications:* (with John Béchervaise) ANARE, 1957; Antarctic Odyssey, 1983; The Antarctic Voyage of HMAS Wyatt Earp, 1995; You Have to be Lucky, 1995; chapters in: It's People that Matter, ed Donald McLean, 1969; Search for Human Understanding, ed M. Merbaum and G. Stricker, 1971; Australian Antarctic Science, ed Marchant, Lugg and Quilty, 2003; ed series of ANARE scientific reports; numerous papers on Antarctica and education. *Recreations:* tennis, ski-ing, music, photography. *Address:* Unit 3 Balwyn Manor, 23 Maleela Avenue, Balwyn, Vic 3103, Australia. *Clubs:* Melbourne, Kelvin, Melbourne Cricket, Royal South Yarra Lawn Tennis (Melbourne).

LAW, Prof. Robin Christopher Charles, PhD; FBA 2000; FRSE; FRHistS; Professor of African History, Stirling University, since 1993; *b* 7 Aug. 1944. *Educ:* Balliol Coll., Oxford (BA 1st cl. Hons Lit.Hum. 1966); PhD (Hist. and African Studies) Birmingham 1971. Res. Asst to Dir of African Studies, Lagos Univ., 1966–69; Res. Fellow, Centre of W African Studies, Birmingham Univ., 1970–72; Stirling University: Lectr in Hist., 1972–78; Sen. Lectr, 1978–83; Reader, 1983–93. Visiting posts: Ilorin Univ., Nigeria, 1978; Leiden Univ., Netherlands, 1993–94; York Univ., Canada, 1996–97; Hebrew Univ. of Jerusalem, 2000–01. FRHistS 1997; FRSE 2002. *Publications:* The Oyo Empire *c*1600–*c*1836, 1977; The Horse in West African History, 1980; The Slave Coast of West Africa 1550–1750, 1991; (ed) From Slave Trade to Legitimate Commerce: the commercial transition in 19th century West Africa, 1995; (with Paul Lovejoy) The Biography of Mahommah Gardo Baquaqua, 2001; Ouidah: the social history of a West African slaving 'port' 1727–1892, 2004. *Address:* Department of History, Stirling University, Stirling FK9 4LA. *T:* (01786) 467583.

LAW, Roger, RDI 2000; artist and caricaturist; *b* 6 Sept. 1941; *m* 1960, Deirdre Amsden; one *s* one *d. Educ:* Littleport Secondary Mod. Sch.; Cambridge Sch. of Art (expelled 1960). Acquitted of malicious damage, 1959; fined £5 for rioting, 1960; cartoonist and illustrator, The Observer, 1962–65; voluntary probation for assault, 1963; illustrator, Sunday Times, 1965–67; probation for theft, 1967; Artist in Residence, Reed Coll., Oregon, and first puppet film, 1967; freelance illustrator, Pushpin Studios, NY, 1968–69; deported voluntarily from USA, 1969; caricaturist and features editor, Sunday Times, 1971–75; with Peter Fluck: formed Luck & Flaw, 1976; founder, Spitting Image, 1982 (first series televised, 1984, 18th series, 1996); Creative Dir, Spitting Image Productions Ltd, 1983–97; first American show for NBC TV, 1986; TV series, The Winjin' Pom, 1991; deported from China, 1998; Artist in residence, Nat. Art Sch., Sydney, 1998; film, Potshots, 1999. Major installation for Barbican art gall., 1992; ceramic exhibitions with Janice Tchalenko: V&A, 1993; Richard Dennis Gall., 1996; puppet installation, RA, 1997; one-man exhibitions: Aussie Stuff, Hossack Gall., 2000; The Land of Oz, Fine Art Soc., 2005; retrospective exhibn, Still Spitting at Sixty, Newsroom Archive and Visitor Centre, 2005. Mem., AGI, 1993; Fellow, Internat. Specialised Skills, Melbourne, 1997. Hon. FRCA 2004. Hon. DLitt Loughborough, 1999. DAAD Award, 1967; Assoc. of Illustrators Award (to Luck & Flaw), 1984; BPG TV Award for Best Light Entertainment Prog., 1984; DAAD Award (to Luck and Flaw), 1984; Internat. Emmy Award (for Spitting Image), 1986; Grammy Award, 1987; Emmy Award (for Peter and the Wolf), 1994; Lifetime Achievement Award, Cartoon Art Trust, 1998. *Publications:* The Appallingly Disrespectful Spitting Image Book, 1985; Spitting Images, 1987; The Spitting Image Giant Komic Book, 1988; (with L. Chester) A Nasty Piece of Work, 1992; Goodbye, 1992; Thatcha: the real Maggie memoirs, 1993; Still Spitting at Sixty (autobiog.), 2005; illustrator with Peter Fluck: A Christmas Carol, 1979; Treasure Island, 1986. *Recreations:* making mischief, over-age sex.

LAWES, Glenville Richard; Chairman: West Midlands Museums, Libraries and Archives Council, since 2006; Darwin Birthplace Society, since 2005; *b* 28 May 1945; *s* of Eric Lawes and Phyllis (*née* Witchalls); *m* 1969, Isobel Prescott Thomas; one *s* two *d. Educ:* Univ. of Birmingham (BSc Eng). Technol. Editor, New Scientist, 1967–70; HM Diplomatic Service, 1970–80: served Moscow, Geneva and Paris; First Sec., FCO, 1976; with British Petroleum Co. plc, 1980–91; Sen. Analyst, BP Internat., 1980–86; Gen. Manager, BP Middle East, 1986–90; Regl Manager, BP Oil Internat., 1990–91. Chief Exec., Ironbridge Gorge Mus. Trust, 1991–2006. FRSA 1999. *Recreations:* music, reading, theatre, renovating old houses. *Address:* MLA West Midlands, Floor 2, Grosvenor House, 14 Bennetts Hill, Birmingham B2 5RS. *T:* (01743) 363429; *e-mail:* glenlawes@btopenworld.com.

LAWES, William Patrick Lagan; Partner, Freshfields Bruckhaus Deringer (formerly Freshfields), since 1994; *b* Swanage, Dorset, 2 Jan. 1964; *s* of Colin Lawes and Paddy Lawes (*née* Lagan); *m* 1995, Rebecca Yongman; three *s* one *d. Educ:* Victoria Univ., Wellington (LLB Hons); Gonville and Caius Coll., Cambridge (LLM 1986). Law Clerk, NZ Court of Appeal and the High Court, Wellington, 1984–85; joined Freshfields, 1986. Vis. Fellow, Centre for Corporate Reputation, Univ. of Oxford, 2008–. Mem., Soc. of Merchants Trading to the Continent. *Recreations:* golf, sailing, ski-ing, Real tennis. *Address:* c/o Freshfields Bruckhaus Deringer, 65 Fleet Street, EC4Y 1HS. *T:* (020) 7832 7029, *Fax:* (020) 7832 7645; *e-mail:* william.lawes@freshfields.com. *Clubs:* Hurlingham, City Law; Brancaster Golf, Berkshire, Royal North Devon Golf.

LAWLER, Geoffrey John; Managing Director, The Public Affairs Company (GB) Ltd (formerly Lawler Associates), since 1987; Vice-President, International Access Inc., since 1987; *b* 30 Oct. 1954; *s* of late Major Ernest Lawler, RAEC and Enid Lawler; *m* 1989, Christine (marr. diss. 1998), *d* of Carl Roth, Cheyenne, Wyoming. *Educ:* Richmond Sch., N Yorks; Hull Univ. (BSc (Econ); Pres., Students' Union, 1976–77). Trainee chartered accountant, 1977–78. Community Affairs Dept, 1978–80, Research Dept, 1980–82, Cons. Central Office; Public Relations Exec., 1982–83; Dir, publicity co., 1983. Contested (C) Bradford N, 1987. MP (C) Bradford N, 1983–87. EC Observer for Russian elections, 1993, 1995, 1996, for Liberian election, 1997; UN Observer for S African elections, 1994. Dir, Democracy Internat. Ltd, 1995–. Mem. Council, UKIAS, 1987–93. Hon. Pres., British Youth Council, 1983–87; Pres., W Yorks Youth Assoc., 1995–2004 (Vice-Pres., 1986–95). *Recreations:* cricket, music, travel. *Address:* 1 Moorland Leys, Leeds LS17 5BD. *T:* (0113) 266 0583; *e-mail:* geoff@glawler.com.

LAWLER, Sir Peter (James), Kt 1981; OBE 1965; retired 1987; Australian Ambassador to Ireland and the Holy See, 1983–86; *b* 23 March 1921; *m*; six *s* two *d. Educ:* Univ. of Sydney (BEc). Prime Minister's Dept, Canberra, 1949–68 (British Cabinet Office, London, 1952–53); Dep. Secretary: Dept of the Cabinet Office, 1968–71; Dept of the Prime Minister and Cabinet, 1972–73; Secretary: Dept of the Special Minister of State, 1973–75; Dept of Admin. Services, Canberra, 1975–83. *Recreation:* writing. *Clubs:* Melbourne (Melbourne); University House, Wine & Food (Canberra).

LAWLER, Simon William; QC 1993; **His Honour Judge Lawler;** a Circuit Judge, since 2002; *b* 26 March 1949; *s* of Maurice Rupert Lawler and Daphne Lawler (*née* Elkins); *m* 1985, Josephine Sallie Day; two *s. Educ:* Winchester County Secondary Sch.; Peter Symonds, Winchester; Univ. of Hull (LLB Hons). Called to the Bar, Inner Temple, 1971; in practice at the Bar, 1972–2002; Asst Recorder, 1983–89; a Recorder, 1989–2002. A Pres., Mental Health Rev. Tribunal, 2002–07. *Recreations:* cricket, gardening, opera, wine. *Address:* The Crown Court, 50 West Bar, Sheffield S3 8PH. *T:* (0114) 281 2400.

LAWLEY, Dr Leonard Edward; Director of Kingston Polytechnic, 1969–82; *b* 13 March 1922; *yr s* of late Albert Lawley; *m* 1944, Dorothy Beryl Round; one *s* two *d. Educ:* King Edward VI Sch., Stourbridge; Univs of Wales and Newcastle upon Tyne. BSc, PhD; FInstP. Served with RAF, 1941–46; Lectr, Univ. of Newcastle upon Tyne, 1947–53; Sen. Lectr, The Polytechnic, Regent Street, 1953–57; Kingston Coll. of Technology: Head of Dept of Physics and Maths, 1957–64; Vice-Principal, 1960–64; Principal, 1964–69. *Publications:* various papers in scientific jls on transmission ultrasonic sound waves through gases and liquids and on acoustic methods for gas analysis.

LAWLEY, Susan, (Sue), OBE 2001; broadcaster, since 1970; *b* 14 July 1946; *d* of Thomas Clifford and Margaret Jane Lawley; *m* 1st, 1975, David Ashby (marr. diss. 1985); one *s* one *d*; 2nd, 1987, Hugh Williams. *Educ:* Dudley Girls' High Sch., Worcs; Bristol Univ. (BA Hons Modern Languages). Thomson Newspapers' graduate trainee, Western Mail and South Wales Echo, Cardiff, 1967–70; BBC Plymouth: sub-editor/reporter/presenter, 1970–72; presenter, BBC Television: Nationwide, 1972–75; Tonight, 1975–76; Nationwide, 1977–83; Nine O'Clock News, 1983–84; Six O'Clock News, 1984–88; Here and Now, 1995–97; Presenter, Desert Island Discs, BBC Radio Four, 1988–2006. Board Member: English Tourism Council, 2000–03; ENO, 2001–05. Hon. LLD Bristol, 1989; Hon. MA Birmingham, 1989; Hon. DLitt CNAA, 1991. *Publication:* Desert Island Discussions, 1989. *Recreations:* family, walking, golf, bridge. *Address:* c/o BBC, Broadcasting House, W1A 1AA.

LAWRANCE, Cynthia; *see* Lawrance, J. C.

LAWRANCE, John Ernest; Under Secretary, Director, Technical Division 1, Inland Revenue, 1982–88, retired; *b* 25 Jan. 1928; *s* of Ernest William and Emily Lewa Lawrance; *m* 1956, Margaret Elsie Ann Dodwell; two *s* one *d. Educ:* High School for Boys, Worthing; Southampton Univ. (BA Hons Modern History). Entered Inland Revenue as Inspector of Taxes, 1951; Principal Inspector, 1968; Senior Principal Inspector on specialist technical duties, 1974. *Address:* 71A Alderton Hill, Loughton, Essex IG10 3JD. *T:* (020) 8508 7562.

LAWRANCE, Mrs (June) Cynthia; Headmistress of Harrogate Ladies' College, 1974–93; *b* 3 June 1933; *d* of late Albert Isherwood and Ida Emmett; *m* 1957, Rev. David Lawrance, MA, BD (*d* 1999); three *d. Educ:* St Anne's Coll., Oxford (MA). Teaching appts: Univ. of Paris, 1954–57; Cyprus, 1957–58; Jordan, 1958–61; Oldham, Lancs, 1962–70; Headmistress, Broughton High Sch., Salford, 1971–73. *Recreations:* music, French literature, chess. *Address:* Kinver House, The Green, Kirklington, Bedale DL8 2NQ.

LAWRANCE, Keith Cantwell; Deputy Chairman, Civil Service Appeal Board, 1981–89 (Member 1980–89); Vice-President, Civil Service Retirement Fellowship, since 1988 (Chairman, 1982–88); *b* 1 Feb. 1923; *s* of P. J. Lawrance; *m* 1952, Margaret Joan (*née* Scott); no *c. Educ:* Latymer Sch., N9. Clerical Officer, Admiralty, 1939. Served War, RNVR, 1942–46; Sub-Lt (A), 1945. Exec. Officer, Treasury, 1947; Asst Principal, Post Office, 1954; Principal, Post Office, 1959; Asst Sec., Dept of Economic Affairs, Dec. 1966; Under-Sec., Civil Service Dept, 1971–79. Vice-Chm., Inst. of Cancer Research, 1989–95. *Recreations:* model engineering, music. *Address:* White Gables, 35 Fairmile Avenue, Cobham, Surrey KT11 2JA. *T:* (01932) 863689.

LAWRENCE, family name of **Baron Lawrence** and of **Baron Trevethin and Oaksey**.

LAWRENCE, 5th Baron *cr* 1869; **David John Downer Lawrence;** Bt 1858; *b* 4 Sept. 1937; *s* of 4th Baron Lawrence and Margaret Jean (*d* 1977), *d* of Arthur Downer, Kirdford, Sussex; *S* father, 1968. *Educ:* Bradfield College. *Address:* c/o Bird & Bird, 15 Fetter Lane, EC4A 1JP.

LAWRENCE, Prof. Andrew, PhD; FRAS; Regius Professor of Astronomy, since 1994, and Head, School of Physics, since 2003, University of Edinburgh (Head, Institute for Astronomy, 1994–2004); *b* 23 April 1954; *s* of Jack Lawrence and Louisa Minnie (*née* Sandison); partner, Debbie Ann Capel; three *s* one *d. Educ:* Chatham House Grammar Sch., Ramsgate; Univ. of Edinburgh (BSc Hons 1976); Univ. of Leicester ((PhD 1980). FRAS 1983. Exchange scientist, MIT, 1980–81; Sen. Res. Fellow, Royal Greenwich Observatory, 1981–84; PDRA, QMC, 1984–87; Queen Mary and Westfield College, London: SERC Advanced Fellow, 1987–89; Lectr, 1989–94. Mem., various res. councils and internat. cttees, panels, etc, 1983–99; Mem., PPARC, 2000–03. FRSE 1997. *Publications:* (ed) Comets to Cosmology, 1987; numerous contribs to professional astronomy jls. *Recreations:* acting, painting electrons, teasing publishers. *Address:* Edinburgh Institute for Astronomy, University of Edinburgh, Royal Observatory Edinburgh, Blackford Hill, Edinburgh EH9 3HJ. *T:* (0131) 668 8346.

LAWRENCE, Andrew Steven; Director, Delivery Transformation, Department for Environment, Food and Rural Affairs, since 2007; *b* Epsom, 26 Jan. 1973; *s* of Keith Lawrence and Val Long; *m* 2001, Nicolette Sanders; two *d. Educ:* Corpus Christi Coll., Cambridge (BA Modern Langs 1995); Tanaka Business Sch., Imperial Coll. London

(MBA 2002). Ministry of Agriculture, Fisheries and Food, subseq. Department for Environment, Food and Rural Affairs: EU Policy Team, Veterinary Medicines Directorate, 1995–96; Envmt, Fisheries and Internat. Sci. Div., 1996–97; Stagiaire DG XIV (Fisheries), EC, Brussels, 1997–98 (on secondment); Pvte Sec. to Perm. Sec., 1998–99; Hd, EU Enlargement Unit, 1999–2001; Manager, Waste Implementation Prog., 2002–03; Dep. Dir, CAP Reform and EU Strategy, 2003–07. *Recreations:* spending time with family, enjoying the great outdoors, armchair sports expert - cricket and Rugby in particular, admiring others' gardens and beautiful buildings, travelling, very amateur ornithology. *Address:* c/o Department for Environment, Food and Rural Affairs, Nobel House, 17 Smith Square, SW1P 3JR.

LAWRENCE, Most Rev. Caleb James; *see* Moosonee, Archbishop of.

LAWRENCE, Hon. Carmen (Mary), PhD; MP (ALP) Fremantle, since 1994; *b* 2 March 1948; *d* of Ern and Mary Lawrence; *m* (marr. diss.); one *s*. *Educ:* Univ. of Western Australia (BPsych 1st cl. Hons 1968; PhD 1983). Univ. lectr, tutor, researcher, consultant, 1968–83; Research Psychologist, Psychiatric Services Unit, Health Dept, 1983–86. MLA (ALP): Subiaco, WA, 1986–89; Glendalough, WA, 1989–94; Minister for Education, 1988–90; Premier of WA, 1990–93; Leader of the Opposition, WA, 1993–94; Minister for Human Services and Health, and Minister assisting the Prime Minister for the Status of Women, Australia, 1994–96; Shadow Minister: for the Envmt, for the Arts, and assisting the Leader of the Opposition on the Status of Women, Australia, 1996–97; for Industry, Innovation and Technol., 2000–01; for the Arts and Status of Women, 2000–02; for Reconciliation, Aboriginal and Torres Strait Islander Affairs, 2001–02. *Publications:* psychological papers. *Recreations:* literature, theatre, music. *Address:* Parliament House, Canberra, ACT 2600, Australia.

LAWRENCE, Christopher Nigel, NDD, FTC; FIPG; goldsmith, silversmith; modeller, medallist, industrial and graphic designer; *b* 23 Dec. 1936; *s* of late Rev. William W. Lawrence and Millicent Lawrence; *m* 1958, Valerie Betty Bergman; two *s* two *d*. *Educ:* Westborough High Sch.; Central School of Arts and Crafts. Apprenticed, C. J. Vander Ltd; started own workshops, 1968. *One man exhibitions:* Galerie Jean Renet, 1970, 1971; Hamburg, 1972; Goldsmiths' Hall, 1973; Ghent, 1975; Hasselt, 1977. Major commissions from Royalty, British Govt, City Livery cos, banks, manufacturing cos; official silversmith to Bank of England. Judge and external assessor for leading art colleges; specialist in symbolic presentation pieces and limited edns of decorative pieces, *eg* silver mushrooms. Chm., Goldsmiths, Craft and Design Council, 1976–77; Liveryman, Goldsmiths' Co., 1978–; television and radio broadcaster. Jacques Cartier Meml award for Craftsman of the Year, 1960, 1963, 1967 (unique achievement). *Recreations:* badminton, tennis, bowls, carpentry, painting. *Address:* 20 St Vincent's Road, Westcliff-on-Sea, Essex SS0 7PR. *T:* (01702) 338443, (workshop) (01702) 344897.

LAWRENCE, Prof. Clifford Hugh, FRHistS; Professor of Medieval History, 1970–87, now Emeritus (Head of the Department of History, Bedford College, Royal Holloway and Bedford New College (formerly at Bedford College), University of London, 1981–85); *b* 28 Dec. 1921; *s* of Ernest William Lawrence and Dorothy Estelle; *m* 1953, Helen Maud Curran; one *s* five *d*. *Educ:* Stationers' Co.'s Sch.; Lincoln Coll., Oxford (BA 1st Cl. Hons Mod. Hist. 1948; MA 1953; DPhil 1956). FRHistS 1960; FSA 1984. War service in RA and Beds and Herts: 2nd Lieut 1942, Captain 1944, Major 1945. Asst Archivist to Co. of Gloucester, 1949. Bedford Coll., London: Asst Lectr in History, 1951; Lectr, 1953–63; Reader in Med. History, 1963–70. External Examr, Univ. of Newcastle upon Tyne, 1972–74, Univ. of Bristol, 1975–77, Univ. of Reading, 1977–79; Chm., Bd of Examnrs in History, London Univ., 1981–83. Mem., Press Council, 1976–80; Vice-Chm. of Govs, Governing Body, Heythrop Coll., Univ. of London; Mem. Council, Westfield Coll., Univ. of London, 1981–86. *Publications:* St Edmund of Abingdon, History and Hagiography, 1960; The English Church and the Papacy in the Middle Ages, 1965, 2nd edn 1999; Medieval Monasticism, 1984, 3rd edn 2000; The Friars: the impact of the early mendicant movement on western society, 1994; (trans. with biog.) Matthew Paris, The Life of St Edmund, 1996; (trans. and ed) The Letters of Adam Marsh, 2 vols, 2006–08; contribs to: Pre-Reformation English Spirituality, 1967; The Christian Community, 1971; The History of the University of Oxford, Vol. I, 1984; The Oxford Companion to Christian Thought, 2000; The Medieval World, 2001; articles and reviews in Eng. Hist. Review, History, Jl Eccles. Hist., Oxoniensia, Encycl. Brit., Lexicon für Theol u Kirche, etc. *Recreations:* gardening, painting. *Address:* 11 Durham Road, SW20 0QH. *T:* (020) 8946 3820.

LAWRENCE, Sir Clive Wyndham, 4th Bt *cr* 1906, of Sloane Gardens, Chelsea; *b* 6 Oct. 1939; *yr s* of Sir Roland Lawrence, 2nd Bt, MC and Susan, 3rd *d* of Sir Charles Addis, KCMG; *S* brother, 2002; *m* 1966, Sophia Annabel Stuart (marr. diss. 2003), *d* of (Ian) Hervey Stuart Black, TD; three *s*. *Heir:* *s* James Wyndham Stuart Lawrence, *b* 25 Dec. 1970.

LAWRENCE, David Kenneth, DPhil; Head, Research and Development, Syngenta AG, since 2003 (Head, Research, 2000–03); *b* 9 March 1949; s of Ken and Dorothy Lawrence; *m* 1971, Elizabeth Ann Robertson; two *d*. *Educ:* Highbury Avenue Jun. Sch., Salisbury; Bishop Wordsworth Grammar Sch., Salisbury; Keble Coll., Oxford (BA Hons Chem. 1971; DPhil 1974). ICI: Scientist, 1974–86; Manager, Biochemistry, 1986–90; Proj. Leader, 1990–95; Hd, Plant Scis, Zeneca, 1995–2000; Hd, Projects, Syngenta, 2000–02. Member: BBSRC, 2008–; BBSRC Biomolecular Scis Panel, 1991–94. Mem. Adv. Bd, Krebs Inst., 1990–95. Dir and Trustee, Rothamsted Research Ltd, 2007–. *Recreations:* trying to understand how things work, photography, music including choral singing as a tenor, travel, gadgets, anything else which stimulates the mind and avoids boredom but is suitable for an introvert. *Address:* Syngenta, Jealott's Hill International Research Station, Bracknell RG42 6EY; *e-mail:* david.lawrence@syngenta.com.

LAWRENCE, Dennis George Charles, OBE 1963; Director, 1978–82, Board Member, 1981–84, Cooperative Development Agency; retired; *b* 15 Aug. 1918; *s* of George Herbert and Amy Frances Lawrence; *m* 1946, Alida Jantine, *d* of Willem van den Berg, The Netherlands. *Educ:* Haberdashers' Aske's Hatcham School. Entered Civil Service as Clerical Officer, Min. of Transport, 1936; served RA, 1939–46; Exec. Officer 1946; Asst Principal, Central Land Board, 1947; Principal, 1949; GPO, 1953; Asst Sec. 1960; Sec., Cttee on Broadcasting, 1960–62; Asst Sec., GPO, 1962; Under-Secretary: GPO, 1969; Min. of Posts and Telecommunications, 1969–74; Dept of Industry, 1974–78. Chm., Working Group on a Cooperative Develt Agency, 1977. *Publications:* Democracy and Broadcasting (pamphlet), 1986; The Third Way, 1988. *Recreations:* reading, gardening, remembrance of things past. *Address:* Little London Farmhouse, Cann, Shaftesbury, Dorset SP7 0PZ.

LAWRENCE, Sir Henry (Peter), 7th Bt *cr* 1858, of Lucknow; Head of Radiation Metrology (formerly Dosimetry), Bristol Haematology and Oncology Centre (formerly Bristol Oncology Centre), since 1991; *b* 2 April 1952; *s* of late George Alexander Waldemar Lawrence and Olga Lawrence (*née* Schilovsky); *S* uncle, 1999; *m* 1st, 1979, Penny Maureen Nunan (marr. diss. 1993); one *s* one *d*; 2nd, 2001, Elena Jennie Norman, theatre designer. *Educ:* Eton Coll.; Hackney Coll. BSc Physics with Astronomy, MSc Radiation Physics, London Univ. Builder and scaffolder, 1970–79; Physicist, Royal London Hosp., 1981–86; Sen. Physicist, Cheltenham Gen. Hosp., 1986–90. Author of Europlan radiotherapy treatment planning system. Mem., Inst. of Physics and Engineering in Medicine. Hon. Mem., Romanian Assoc. of Medical Physics. *Publication:* Physics in Medicine and Biology, 1990. *Recreations:* music (folk), juggling, cycling, football. *Heir:* *s* Christopher Cosmo Lawrence, *b* 10 Dec. 1979.

LAWRENCE, (Henry) Richard (George); writer and lecturer on music; *b* 16 April 1946; *s* of late George Napier Lawrence, OBE, and Peggy Neave (*née* Breay). *Educ:* Westminster Abbey Choir Sch.; Haileybury (music schol.); Worcester Coll., Oxford (Hadow Schol.; BA 1967). Overseas Dept, Ginn & Co., educational publishers, 1968–73; Music Officer, 1973–83, Music Dir, 1983–88, Arts Council of GB; Chief Exec., RSCM, 1990–94; Acting Ed., 1994–95, Ed., 1995–96, Early Music News; Ed., Leading Notes, 1997–99. Tutor at various adult educn colls and for WEA, 1997–; lectr abroad on opera, 2000–. Qualif. London Registered Blue Badge Guide, 2001. Occasional broadcaster, 1989–. Chm., Arts Council Staff Assoc., 1974–76. Voluntary work, Friends of the Earth Trust, 1989–90. *Publications:* (contrib.) Collins Classical Music Encyclopedia, 2000; revs and articles in TLS, Church Times, Opera Now, BBC Music Mag, Jl of RAS, Early Music Today, The Gramophone, Amadeus (Milan). *Recreations:* travelling in Asia, pre-1914 Baedekers. *Address:* 1 Claverton Street, SW1V 3AY. *T:* (020) 7834 9846.

LAWRENCE, Sir Ivan (John), Kt 1992; QC 1981; barrister-at-law; broadcaster, lecturer and after-dinner speaker; *b* 24 Dec. 1936; *o s* of late Leslie Lawrence and Sadie Lawrence, Brighton; *m* 1966, Gloria Hélène; one *d*. *Educ:* Brighton, Hove and Sussex Grammar Sch.; Christ Church, Oxford (MA). Nat. Service with RAF, 1955–57. Called to Bar, Inner Temple, 1962 (Yarborough-Anderson Schol.; Bencher, 1991); S Eastern Circuit; Asst Recorder, 1983–87; a Recorder, 1987–2002; Hd of Chambers, 1 Essex Ct, 1997–2000. Contested (C) Peckham (Camberwell), 1966 and 1970. MP (C) Burton, Feb. 1974–1997; contested (C) same seat, 1997. Mem., Select Cttee on Foreign Affairs, 1983–92; Chm., Select Cttee on Home Affairs, 1992–97; Chairman: Cons. Parly Legal Cttee, 1987–97; Cons. Parly Home Affairs Cttee, 1988–97; All-Party Parly Anti-Fluoridation Cttee; All-Party Parly Barristers Gp, 1987–97; Member: Parly Expenditure Select Sub-Cttee, 1974–79; Jt Parly Cttee on Consolidation of Statutes, 1974–87. Mem. Exec., 1922 Cttee, 1988–89, 1992–97. Chm., Exec. Cttee, UK CPA, 1994–97 (Mem., 1989–97). Member: Council of Justice, 1989–95; Council, Statute Law Soc., 1985–95; Exec., Soc. of Conservative Lawyers, 1989–97 and 1999– (Chm., Criminal Justice Cttee, 1997–); Bar Council, 2005–. Fellow, Soc. of Advanced Legal Studies, 2002–. Vis. Prof. of Law, Univ. of Buckingham, 2004. Vice-Pres., Fed. of Cons. Students, 1980–82; Mem., W Midlands Cons. Council, 1985–97. Vice Chm., Cons. Friends of Israel, 1994–97; Mem. Bd of Deputies of British Jews, 1979–. Chm., Burton Breweries Charitable Trust, 1979–97. Pres., Past and Present Assoc., Brighton, Hove and Sussex Grammar Sch., 1999–. Freeman, City of London, 1993. *Publications:* pamphlets (jointly): Correcting the Scales; The Conviction of the Guilty; Towards a New Nationality; Financing Strikes; Trial by Jury under attack; nat. newspaper articles on law and order topics and foreign affairs. *Recreations:* piano, squash, travel, friends. *Address:* Clarendon Chambers, 1 Plowden Buildings, Temple, EC4Y 9BU. *T:* (020) 7353 0003. *Clubs:* Carlton, Pratt's; Burton (Burton-on-Trent).

LAWRENCE, Jacqueline Rita, (Jackie); *b* 9 Aug. 1948; *d* of Sidney and Rita Beale; *m* 1968, David Lawrence; two *s* one *d*. *Educ:* Upperthorpe Sch., Darlington, Co. Durham; Upperthorpe Coll.; Open Univ. With TSB Bank plc, until 1992. Member (Lab): Dyfed CC, 1993–96; Pembs CC, 1995–97 (Leader, Lab Gp). MP (Lab) Preseli Pembrokeshire, 1997–2005. PPS to Dep. Minister for Women and Equality, DTI, 2003–05. Member, Select Committee: on Welsh Affairs, 1997–99; on Trade and Industry, 2001–03; Chm., All Pty Parly Gp on Nat. Parks, 2001–05. Hon. Sec., Welsh Gp of Labour MPs, 2000–05.

LAWRENCE, Sir (John) Patrick (Grosvenor), Kt 1988; CBE 1983; DL; Chairman: Enterprise Venture Capital Trust plc, 1996–2004; The VCT Charitable Trust, since 2005; *b* 29 March 1928; *s* of Ernest Victor Lawrence and Norah Grosvenor Lawrence (*née* Hill); *m* 1954, Anne Patricia (*née* Auld); one *d* (one *s* decd). *Educ:* Denstone Coll., Staffs. Served RNVR, 1945–48. Admitted Solicitor 1954; Partner, Wragge & Co., Solicitors, Birmingham 1959–93 (Sen. Partner, 1982–93). Chm., Midland Rent Assessment Panels, 1971–98. Chm., Kidderminster Healthcare NHS Trust, 1993–96. Mem., Bromsgrove RDC, 1967–74. Chm., Nat. Union of Conservative and Unionist Assocs, 1986–87; Pres., W Midlands Conservative Council, 1988–91 (Chm., 1979–82). Pres., British Shooting Sports Council, 2005–08 (Vice-Chm., 1985–96; Chm., 1996–2002; Vice-Pres., 2002–05). Member of Council: Denstone Coll., Staffs, 1989–98; Birmingham Chamber of Industry and Commerce, 1989–93; ABCC, 1990–93; Aston Univ., 1990–2001 (Vice-Chm. Council, 1999–2001); White Ensign Assoc. Ltd, 1996–2005 (Vice Pres., 2005–). Chm., Birmingham Cathedral in Need Appeal, 1990; Mem., Admin. Chapter, Birmingham Cathedral, 1995–2002. Freeman, City of London, 1991; Liveryman, Gunmakers' Co., 1991. DL West Midlands, 1993. Hon. DSc Aston, 1996. *Address:* 8 Malvern Priors, Malvern Place, Cheltenham, Glos GL50 2JL. *Clubs:* Bean (Birmingham); Law Society's Yacht.

LAWRENCE, Air Vice-Marshal John Thornett, CB 1975; CBE (mil.) 1967 (OBE (mil.) 1961); AFC 1945; *b* 16 April 1920; *s* of late T. L. Lawrence, JP, and Mrs B. M. Lawrence; *m* 1951, Hilary Jean (*née* Owen); three *s* one *d*. *Educ:* The Crypt School, Gloucester. RAFVR 1938. Served War of 1939–45 in Coastal Command (235, 202 and 86 Squadrons); Directing staff, RAF Flying Coll., 1949–53; CO 14 Squadron, 1953–55; Group Captain Operations, HQ AFME, 1962–64; CO RAF Wittering, 1964–66; AOC, 3 Group, Bomber Command, 1967; Student, IDC, 1968; Dir of Organisation and Admin Plans (RAF), 1969–71; Dir-Gen. Personnel Management (RAF), 1971–73; Comdr N Maritime Air Region and AOC Scotland and NI, 1973–75, retired 1975. Vice-Pres., Glos County SSAFA, 1990– (Chm., 1980–90); Mem., Nat. Council, SSAFA, 1987–90. Order of Leopold II, Belgium, 1945; Croix de Guerre, Belgium, 1945. *Recreations:* golf, bridge. *Address:* The Coach House, Wightfield Manor, Apperley, Glos GL19 4DP. *Club:* Royal Air Force.

LAWRENCE, John Wilfred, RE 1987; book illustrator and wood engraver; *b* 15 Sept. 1933; *s* of Wilfred James Lawrence and Audrey Constance (*née* Thomas); *m* 1957, Myra Gillian Bell; two *d*. *Educ:* Salesian Coll., Cowley, Oxford; Hastings Sch. of Art; Central Sch. of Art. Visiting Lecturer in Illustration: Brighton Polytech., 1960–68; Camberwell Sch. of Art, 1960–94; Visiting Professor in Illustration: London Inst., 1994–2000; Anglia Ruskin Univ., 2006–; External Assessor in Illustration: Bristol Polytech., 1978–81; Brighton Polytech., 1982–85; Duncan of Jordanstone Coll. of Art, 1986–89; Exeter Coll. of Art, 1986–89; Kingston Polytechnic, 1989–93; Edinburgh Coll. of Art, 1991–94. Member: Art Workers Guild, 1972 (Master, 1990); Soc. of Wood Engravers, 1984. Work represented in Ashmolean Mus., V&A Mus., Nat. Mus. of Wales, and collections abroad. *Publications:* The Giant of Grabbist, 1968; Pope Leo's Elephant, 1969; Rabbit and Pork Rhyming Talk, 1975 (Francis Williams Book Illustration Award, 1977); Tongue Twisters,

1976; George, His Elephant and Castle, 1983; A Selection of Wood Engravings, 1986; Good Babies, Bad Babies, 1987; *illustrated:* more than 150 books, incl.: Colonel Jack, 1967 (Francis Williams Book Illustration Award, 1971); Diary of a Nobody, 1969; The Blue Fairy Book, 1975; The Illustrated Watership Down, 1976; Everyman's Book of English Folk Tales, 1981; The Magic Apple Tree, 1982; Mabel's Story, 1984; Entertaining with Cranks, 1985; Emily's Own Elephant, 1987; Christmas in Exeter Street, 1989; A New Treasury of Poetry, 1990; The Sword of Honour trilogy, 1990; Treasure Island, 1990; Shades of Green, 1991 (Signal Prize for Poetry); Poems for the Young, 1992; King of King's, 1993; The Twelve Days of Christmas, 1994; The Christmas Collection, 1994; Memoirs of a Georgian Rake, 1995; Robin Hood, 1995; Poems for Christmas, 1995; Collected Poems for Children by Charles Causley, 1996; (with Allan Ahlberg) The Mysteries of Zigomar, 1997; A Year and a Day, 1999; This Little Chick, 2002 (NY Times Cert. of Excellence); The Once and Future King, 2003; Tiny's Big Adventure, 2004; Sea Horse: the shyest fish in the sea, 2006. *Address:* 6 Worts Causeway, Cambridge CB1 8RL.

LAWRENCE, Josie; actress; *b* 6 June 1959; *d* of Bert and Kathleen Lawrence. *Educ:* Dartington Coll. of Arts (BA Hons Theatre). Professional acting début, 1983; joined Comedy Store Players, 1986; *theatre* includes: Painting Churches, 1988; Tatyana, 1992, Eliza in Pygmalion, 1994, Nottingham Playhouse; Moll Flanders, Lyric Hammersmith, 1993; The Cherry Orchard, Faust and Kate in The Taming of the Shrew, RSC, 1995; The Alchemist, NT, 1996; Alarms and Excursions, Gielgud, 1998; Anna in The King and I, Palladium, 2001; Frozen, NT, 2002; Much Ado About Nothing, Globe, 2004; Acorn Antiques - The Musical, Th. Royal, Haymarket, 2005; Hapgood, Birmingham Rep., 2008; *films* include: Enchanted April, 1992; The Sin Eater, 1999; *television* includes: Friday Night Live, 1988; Whose Line Is It Anyway?, 1988–97; Not With a Bang, 1990; Josie, 1991; Downwardly Mobile, 1994; Maggie in Outside Edge, 3 series, 1994–96; A Many Splintered Thing, 2000; Fat Friends, 2000; Easy Peasy, 2006. Hon. Dr Plymouth; Hon. DLitt Wolverhampton; Hon. DA Aston. Best Actress Award, Manchester Evening News; Globe Award for Best Actress; Dame Peggy Ashcroft Prize, Shakespeare Golden Globe Awards, 1997. Charity walks for breast cancer research in Cuba, Peru, Africa and China; climbed Kilimanjaro for Sunfield Sch., 2005 (Patron, 1995–). *Recreations:* painting, walking. *Address:* c/o International Artistes, Holborn Hall, 193–197 High Holborn, WC1V 7BD. *T:* (020) 7025 0600.

LAWRENCE, Michael John, PhD; FCA; Chief Executive, London Stock Exchange, 1994–96; *b* 25 Oct. 1943; *s* of Geoffrey Frederick Lawrence and Kathleen (*née* Bridge); *m* 1967, Maureen Joy Blennerhassett; two *s* one *d*. *Educ:* Exeter Univ. (BSc 1st Cl. Hons Physics); Bristol Univ. (PhD Mathematical Physics). FCA 1972. With Price Waterhouse, 1969–87, Partner 1978; Finance Dir, Prudential Corp., 1988–93. Non-executive Director: PLA, 1983–89; London Transport, 1994–99; Yattendon Investment Trust, 1998–. Chm., 100 Gp of Finance Dirs, 1991–93. Mem. (C), Royal Borough of Windsor and Maidenhead Unitary Council, 1996–2004 (Leader, 2000–04). Freeman, City of London, 1974; Liveryman, Tin Plate Workers' Co., 1974– (Master, 2000–01). *Recreations:* sailing, bridge, tennis, opera. *Address:* Springmead, Bradcutts Lane, Cookham Dean, Berks SL6 9AA.

LAWRENCE, Murray; *see* Lawrence, W. N. M.

LAWRENCE, Sir Patrick; *see* Lawrence, Sir J. P. G.

LAWRENCE, Hon. Patrick John Tristram; QC 2002; *b* 29 June 1960; *s* and *heir* of Lord Oaksey, *qv*; *m* 1987, Lucinda, *e d* of Demetri Marchessini and Mrs Nicholas Peto; one *s* two *d*. *Educ:* Christ Church Coll., Oxford. Called to the Bar, Inner Temple, 1985. *Address:* 4 New Square, Lincoln's Inn, WC2A 3RJ. *T:* (020) 7822 2000.

LAWRENCE, Peter Anthony, PhD; FRS 1983; Staff Scientist, Medical Research Council Laboratory of Molecular Biology, Cambridge, 1969–2006; *b* 23 June 1941; *s* of Ivor Douglas Lawrence and Joy Lawrence (*née* Liebert); *m* 1971, Birgitta Haraldson. *Educ:* Wennington Sch., Wetherby, Yorks; Cambridge Univ. (MA, PhD). Harkness Fellowship, 1965–67; Dept of Genetics, Univ. of Cambridge, 1967–69. *Publications:* Insect Development (ed), 1976; The Making of a Fly, 1992; scientific papers. *Recreations:* Ascalaphidae, fungi, gardening, golf, theatre, trees. *Address:* Zoology Department, University of Cambridge, Cambridge CB2 3EJ; MRC Laboratory of Molecular Biology, Hills Road, Cambridge CB2 2QH.

LAWRENCE, Richard; *see* Lawrence, H. R. G.

LAWRENCE, His Honour Timothy; a Circuit Judge, 1986–2006; *b* 29 April 1942; *s* of late A. Whiteman Lawrence, MBE, and Phyllis G. Lawrence (*née* Lloyd-Jones). *Educ:* Bedford School; Coll. of Law. Admitted Solicitor, 1967; with Solicitor's Dept, New Scotland Yard, 1967–70; Partner with Claude Hornby & Cox, Solicitors, 1970–86 (Sen. Partner, 1977–86). An Asst Recorder, 1980; a Recorder, 1983–86; Pres., Industrial Tribunals for Eng. and Wales (as Sen. Circuit Judge), 1991–97. Legal Mem., Mental Health Review Tribunals, 1989–; Mem., Parole Bd, 1998–2004, 2005–; Chm., No 14 Area, Regional Duty Solicitor Cttee, 1984–86; Mem., No 13 Area, Legal Aid Cttee, 1983–86. Pres., London Criminal Courts Solicitors' Assoc., 1984–86 (Sec., 1974–84); Member: Law Society's Criminal Law Cttee, 1980–86; Council, Westminster Law Soc., 1979–82; Judicial Studies Bd, 1984–88, 1991–96; British Academy of Forensic Sciences, 1972– (Pres., 1992–93); Dep. Chm., Adv. Cttee on Conscientious Objectors, 2003–. Legal Assessor: Professions Supplementary to Medicine, 1976–86; Insurance Brokers Registration Council, 1983–86. Jt Editor, Medicine, Science and the Law, 1996–2002. FRSA 1991. *Publications:* various articles in legal jls. *Recreations:* walking, wine, travel. *Address:* 8 Slaidburn Street, SW10 0JP; Hill Cottage, Great Walsingham, Norfolk NR22 6DR. *Clubs:* Reform, Hurlingham.

LAWRENCE, Vanessa Vivienne, CB 2008; FRICS; Director General and Chief Executive, Ordnance Survey, since 2000; *b* 14 July 1962; *d* of Leonard Walter Sydney Lawrence and Margaret Elizabeth Lawrence. *Educ:* St Helen's Sch., Northwood, Middx; Sheffield Univ. (BA (Soc. Sci.) Hons Geography); Dundee Univ. (MSc Remote Sensing, Image Processing and Applications). CGeog 2002; FRICS 2003. Longman Group UK Ltd: Publisher, 1985–89; Sen. Publisher, 1989–91; Publishing Manager, 1991–92; Tech. Dir, GeoInformation Internat. (Pearson Gp), 1993–96; Regl Business Develt Manager, UK, ME, Africa, GIS Solutions Div., Autodesk Ltd, 1996–2000; Global Manager, Strategic Mktg and Communications, GIS Solutions Div., Autodesk Inc., 2000. Non-exec. Dir, DCLG (formerly ODPM), 2002–06. Hon. Res. Associate, Manchester Univ., 1990–; Visiting Professor: Southampton Univ., 2000–; Kingston Univ., 2003–. Mem. Court, Southampton Univ., 2001– (Mem. Council, 2002–). Member: RGS, 1987– (Mem. Council, 2002–); Assoc. for Geographic Inf., 1992– (Mem. Council, 1995–2000; Chm., 1999); Bd, Open Geospatial Consortium, 2005–; Hon. Vice-Pres., Geographical Assoc., 2006–. Chm., ACE, 2003–; Patron: MapAction, 2006–; Cure Parkinson's Trust, 2007–. CCMI 2003. Hon. FInstCES 2001. Hon. Fellow, UCL, 2003. Hon. DSc: Sheffield, 2001; Southampton Inst., 2002; Kingston, 2002; Glasgow, 2005; DUniv Oxford Brookes, 2001; Hon. LLD Dundee, 2003. Scottish Geographical Medal, RSGS, 2006. *Publications:* contrib. many books and jls on Geographical Inf. Systems. *Recreations:* scuba diving, sailing, tennis, collecting antique maps. *Address:* Ordnance Survey, Romsey Road, Southampton SO16 4GU. *Club:* Rickmansworth Sailing.

LAWRENCE, Vernon John; freelance television producer; *b* 30 April 1940; *m* 1960, Jennifer Mary Drewe; two *s* one *d*. *Educ:* Dulwich Coll.; Kelham Coll. BBC Studio Manager, 1958; BBC Radio Producer, 1964; BBC TV Producer and Dir, 1967; Yorkshire Television: Exec. Producer, 1973; Controller, Entertainment, 1985; Controller, Network Drama and Entertainment, ITV, 1993–95; Man. Dir, 1995–97, Chm., 1997–2000, MAI Prodns, subseq. United Film & TV Prodns, then United Prodns. FRTS 1995. *Recreations:* oil painting, fishing, walking, gardening.

LAWRENCE, (Walter Nicholas) Murray; Chairman of Lloyd's, 1988–90 (a Deputy Chairman 1982, 1984–87; Member: Committee of Lloyd's, 1979–82; Council of Lloyd's, 1984–91); Chairman, Murray Lawrence Holdings Ltd, 1988–94; *b* 8 Feb. 1935; *s* of Henry Walter Neville Lawrence and Sarah Schuyler Lawrence (*née* Butler); *m* 1961, Sally Louise O'Dwyer (*d* 2008); two *d*. *Educ:* Winchester Coll.; Trinity Coll., Oxford (BA, MA). C. T. Bowring & Co. (Ins.) Ltd, 1957–62; Asst Underwriter, H. Bowring & Others, 1962–70, Underwriter, 1970–84; Director: C. T. Bowring (Underwriting Agencies) Ltd, 1973–84; C. T. Bowring & Co. Ltd, 1976–84; Murray Lawrence Members Agency Ltd, 1988–94 (Chm., 1988–93); Murray Lawrence & Partners Ltd, 1989–95 (Sen. Partner, 1985–89; Chm., 1989–92); Chm., Fairway (Underwriting Agencies) Ltd, 1979–85. Mem., Lloyd's Underwriters Non-Marine Assoc., 1970–84 (Dep. Chm., 1977; Chm., 1978). *Recreations:* golf, opera, travelling. *Clubs:* Boodle's, MCC; Royal & Ancient (St Andrews), Swinley, Royal St George's (Sandwich), Rye, New Zealand.

LAWRENCE, Sir William (Fettiplace), 5th Bt *cr* 1867, of Ealing Park, Middlesex; OBE 2003; General Manager, Newdawn & Sun Ltd, 1981–98; *b* 23 Aug. 1954; *s* of Sir William Lawrence, 4th Bt and of Pamela, *yr d* of J. E. Gordon; *S* father, 1986. *Educ:* King Edward VI School, Stratford-upon-Avon. Assistant Accountant, Wilmot Breeden Ltd/W. B. Bumpers Ltd, 1973–81. Member: Stratford-on-Avon District Council, 1982– (Chm., 1990–91); S Warwickshire CHC, 1983–84; S Warwickshire HA, 1984–92; S Warwickshire Gen. Hosps NHS Trust, 1993–; Cttee, Employment of People with Disabilities, Coventry and Warwickshire, 1994–97; Rural Develt Commn, Warwickshire, 1995–; Dir, S Warwickshire Business Partnership, 1995–. Chm., Heart of England Tourist Bd, 1991– (Mem. Bd, 1989–); Mem., W Midlands Arts, 1989–91 (Mem., Management Council, 1984–89); Director: Unicorn Tourism Ltd, 1994–98; Stratford-upon-Avon and Dist Marketing Ltd, 1995–97; Midland Music Fests, 1996–98; Stratford-upon-Avon Crossroads Care Attendant Scheme Ltd, 1996–. President: Stratford and District Mencap, 1990–; Stratford-upon-Avon Chamber Music Soc., 1991–; Stratford Town FC, 1992–94; Pres., and Chm. of Trustees, Action Unlimited Trust, 1991– (Trustee, 1988–). Consultant Trainer, Insite Consultancy, Edinburgh, 1995–. Mem. Court, Univ. of Birmingham, 1990–. Mem., Corp. of Stratford-upon-Avon Coll., 1996–; Gov., King Edward VI GS, Stratford-upon-Avon, 1987–. Gov., Royal Shakespeare Theatre, 1991–. *Heir: cousin* Aubrey Lyttelton Simon Lawrence [*b* 22 Sept. 1942; *m* 1984, Danielle de Froidmont; one *s*]. *Address:* The Knoll, Walcote, near Alcester, Warwickshire B49 6LZ. *T:* (01789) 488303.

LAWRENCE-JONES, Sir Christopher, 6th Bt *cr* 1831; *S* uncle, 1969; *m* 1967, Gail Pittar, Auckland, NZ; two *s*. *Educ:* Sherborne; Gonville and Caius Coll., Cambridge; St Thomas' Hospital. MA Cantab 1964; MB, BChir Cantab 1964; DIH Eng. 1968. MFOM 1979, FFOM 1987; FRCP 1991. Medical adviser to various orgns, 1967–94; CMO, Imperial Chemical Industries PLC, 1985–93; Chm., Medichem, 1986–92. Pres., Section of Occupational Medicine, RSM, 1990–91. *Heir: s* Mark Christopher Lawrence-Jones, *b* 28 Dec. 1968. *Club:* Royal Cruising.

LAWRENSON, Mark Thomas; football pundit, BBC Television, since 1997; *b* Preston, 2 June 1957; *s* of Thomas and Theresa Lawrenson; *m* 2001, Suzanne; one *s* one *d*. *Educ:* Preston Catholic Coll. Professional footballer: Preston N End, 1974–77; Brighton & Hove Albion, 1977–81; Republic of Ireland, 1977–87 (39 Caps); Liverpool, 1981–88; Barnet, 1988–89; Tampa Bay Rowdies, 1989; Corby Town, 1990–91; Manager: Oxford United, 1988; Peterborough United, 1989–90. Hon. Citizen of Preston, 2002. *Recreations:* cricket, golf. *Address:* c/o BBC Sport, Television Centre, Wood Lane, W12 7RJ; *e-mail:* claire.donohoe@bbc.co.uk.

LAWRENSON, Prof. Peter John, DSc; FRS 1982; FREng, FIET, FIEEE; Founder Chairman, Switched Reluctance Drives Ltd, 1981–97 (Managing Director, 1986–94; Director, 1997–2002); Professor of Electrical Engineering, Leeds University, 1966–91, now Emeritus; *b* 12 March 1933; *s* of John Lawrenson and Emily (*née* Houghton); *m* 1958, Shirley Hannah Foster; one *s* three *d*. *Educ:* Prescot Grammar Sch.; Manchester Univ. (BSc, MSc; DSc 1971). FIET (FIEE 1974); FIEEE 1975; FREng (FEng 1980). Duddell Scholar, IEE, 1951–54; Res. Engr, Associated Electrical Industries, 1956–61; University of Leeds: Lectr, 1961–65; Reader, 1965–66; Head, Dept of Electrical and Electronic Engrg, 1974–84; Chm., Faculty of Science and Applied Science, 1978–80; Chm., Faculty of Engrg, 1981. Science and Engineering Research Council: Mem., Electrical and Systems Cttee, 1971–77; Chm., Electrical Engrg Sub-Cttee, 1981–84; Mem., Machines and Power Cttee, 1981–84; Mem., Engrg Bd, 1984–87; Organiser, National Initiative, Integrated Drive Systems, 1984–86. Tech. Dir, Internat. Drives, Motors, Controls Conf. and Exhibn, 1981–88. Director: Allenwest Ltd, 1988–91; Dale Electric Internat., 1988–94; Consultant: Emerson Electric Co., 1994–97; Rolls-Royce, 2000–02. Institution of Electrical Engineers: Mem. Council, 1966–69 and 1981–98; Chm., Accreditation Cttee, 1979–83; Chm., Power Divisional Bd, 1985–86; Dep. Pres., 1990–92; Pres., 1992–93. Mem. of cttees, Engrg Council, 1983–89 and 1997–2000; Mem. Council, Buckingham Univ., 1987–93. IEE Awards: Premia-Crompton, 1957 and 1967; John Hopkinson, 1965; The Instn, 1981; Faraday Medal, 1990; James Alfred Ewing Medal, ICE and Royal Soc., 1983; Royal Soc. Esso Energy Award, 1985; Edison Medal, IEEE, 2005; Sir Frank Whittle Medal, Royal Acad. of Engrg, 2005. *Publications:* (with K. J. Binns) Analysis and Computation of Electromagnetic Field Problems, 1963, 2nd edn 1973; (with M. R. Harris and J. M. Stephenson) Per Unit Systems, 1970; (with K. J. Binns and C. W. Trowbridge) The Analytical and Numerical Solution of Electric and Magnetic Fields, 1992; papers and patents in areas of electromagnetism, electromechanics and control. *Recreations:* lawn tennis, chess, bridge, jewellery design, gardening, music. *Address:* Hard Gap, Linton, Wetherby LS22 4HT.

LAWREY, Keith; JP; Learned Societies' Liaison Officer, Foundation for Science and Technology, since 1997; *b* 21 Aug. 1940; *s* of George William Bishop Lawrey and Edna Muriel (*née* Gass); *m* 1969, Helen Jane Marriott, BA; two *s* two *d*. *Educ:* Colfe's Sch.; Birkbeck Coll., Univ. of London (MSc Econ; LLB); Heythrop Coll., Univ. of London (MA). Barrister-at-Law; called to Bar, Gray's Inn, 1972. Education Officer, Plastics and Rubber Inst., 1960–68; Lectr and Sen. Lectr, Bucks Coll. of Higher Educn, 1968–74; Head of Dept of Business Studies, Mid-Kent Coll. of Higher and Further Educn, 1974–78; Sec.-Gen., Library Assoc., 1978–84; Dean, Faculty of Business and Management, Harrow Coll. of Higher Educn, subseq. Head, Sch. of Business and Management, Polytechnic of

Central London/Harrow Coll., 1984–90; Sec. and Registrar, RCVS, 1990–91; Headmaster, Cannock Sch., 1992–95; Clerk to Corp. of S Kent Coll., 1996–99. Member: Social Security Appeal Tribunal, 1996–99; Registration Authy, Sci. Council, 2004–; Privy Council Panel, Engrg Council. FCollP (Hon. Treas., Coll. of Preceptors, then Coll. of Teachers, 1987–); FCIS. Gov., Cannock Sch., 1976–92; Mem. Court, City Univ., 2004–. Mem., Orpington Rotary Club, 1993–2007 (Pres., 1999–2000); Trustee, Carers Bromley (formerly Carers Support and Information Service), 2001–05; Sec., Alice Shepherd Foundn, 2002–05; Trustee: and Hon. Treas., Trust for Educn and Care of Child Workers in Ecuador, 2003–06; and a Dir, Hosp. Saturday Fund, 2007–. Hon. FRIN 2007. Mem., Worshipful Co. of Chartered Secretaries and Administrators; Hon. Clerk, Guild of Educators, 1997–. JP Inner London, 1974–. Hon. Mem., RPS, 2004 (Fenton Medallist, 2004); Hon. MCIL 2005. Mem. Editl Bd, Graya, 1976–. *Publications:* papers in Law Soc. Gazette, Educn Today, Jl Assoc. of Law Teachers, Trans and Jl of Plastics Inst. *Recreations:* preaching, sailing, swimming, theatre, gardening. *Address:* c/o Guild of Educators, Bakers' Hall, Harp Lane, EC3R 6DP. *Clubs:* Old Colfeians; Dell Quay Sailing.

LAWS, David Anthony; MP (Lib Dem) Yeovil, since 2001; *b* 30 Nov. 1965; *s* of David Anthony, (Tony), Laws and Maureen Teresa Laws. *Educ:* St George's Coll., Weybridge (Observer Mace Schs Debating Champion 1984); King's Coll., Cambridge (schol.) Double 1st Cl. Hons Econs 1987). Vice Pres., Treasury Dept, J. P. Morgan and Co., 1987–92; Man. Dir, Hd of Sterling and US Dollar Treasury, Barclays de Zoete Wedd, 1992–94; Econs Advr, Lib Dem Parly Party, 1994–97; Dir of Policy and Res., Lib Dems, 1997–99; drafted first Partnership Agreement for Lib Dem–Lab Coalition in Scottish Parlt, 1999. Lib Dem Dep. Treasury spokesman, 2002–05; Lib Dem spokesman for work and pensions, 2005–07, for children, schools and families, 2007–. Mem., Treasury Select Cttee, 2001–03. Contested (Lib Dem) Folkestone and Hythe, 1997. *Recreations:* running, watching Rugby, visiting desert regions. *Address:* House of Commons, SW1A 0AA; (constituency office) 5 Church Street, Yeovil, Som BA20 1HB.

LAWS, Frederick Geoffrey; Vice-Chairman, Commission for Local Administration in England, 1984–94; *b* Blackpool, 1 Aug. 1928; *s* of Frederick and Annetta Laws. *Educ:* Arnold School; Manchester Univ.; London Univ. (LLB); solicitor 1952. Asst Solicitor, Blackpool Corp., 1952–54; Bournemouth Corp., 1954–59; Southend-on-Sea Corporation: Asst Sol., 1959–62; Dep. Town Clerk and Clerk of the Peace, 1962–71; Town Clerk, 1971–74; Chief Exec., Southend-on-Sea Borough Council, 1974–84. Pres., Southend-on-Sea Law Soc., 1981. Hon. Freeman, Southend-on-Sea Borough Council, 1985.

LAWS, Rt Hon. Sir John (Grant McKenzie), Kt 1992; PC 1999; **Rt Hon. Lord Justice Laws;** a Lord Justice of Appeal, since 1999; *b* 10 May 1945; *s* of late Dr Frederic Laws and Dr Margaret Ross Laws, *d* of Prof. John Grant McKenzie; *m* 1973, Sophie Susan Sydenham Cole Marshall, BLitt, MA; one *d. Educ:* Durham Cathedral Choir Sch.; Durham Sch. (King's Scholar); Exeter Coll., Oxford (Sen. Open Classical Scholar; BA 1967, Hon. Sch. of Lit. Hum. 1st Cl.; MA 1976; Hon. Fellow, 2000). Called to the Bar, Inner Temple, 1970, Bencher, 1985; practice at Common Law Bar, 1971–92; First Junior Treasury Counsel, Common Law, 1984–92; Asst Recorder, 1983–85; Recorder, 1985–92; a Judge of the High Court of Justice, QBD, 1992–98; admitted to Bar: New South Wales, 1987; Gibraltar, 1988. Pres., Bar European Gp, 1994–. An Hon. Vice-Pres., Administrative Law Bar Assoc., 1992. Judicial Visitor, UCL, 1997–; Visitor, Cumberland Lodge, 2004–. Hon. Fellow, Robinson Coll., Cambridge, 1992. *Publications:* contributor to: Halsbury's Laws of England, 4th edn 1973; Dict. of Medical Ethics, 1977; Supperstone and Goudie, Judicial Review, 1992, 2nd edn 1997; Importing the First Amendment, 1998; The Golden Metwand and the Crooked Cord, 1998; Cicero the Advocate, 2004; reviews for Theology, Law & Justice; contribs to legal jls. *Recreations:* Greece, living in London, philosophy. *Address:* Royal Courts of Justice, WC2A 2LL. *Club:* Garrick.

LAWS, Richard Maitland, CBE 1983; PhD, ScD; FRS 1980; Director, British Antarctic Survey, 1973–87; Master, St Edmund's College, Cambridge, 1985–96; *b* 23 April 1926; *s* of Percy Malcolm Laws and Florence May (*née* Heslop); *m* 1954, Maureen Isobel Winifred (*née* Holmes); three *s. Educ:* Dame Allan's Sch., Newcastle-on-Tyne; St Catharine's Coll., Cambridge (Open Scholar, 1944–47; BA 1st Cl. Hons 1947, MA 1952; Res. Scholar, 1952–53; PhD 1953; ScD 1994; Hon. Fellow, 1982). FIBiol 1973. Biologist, Base Leader, Magistrate and Postmaster, Falkland Is Dependencies Survey, 1947–53; Biologist and Whaling Inspector, F/F Balaena, 1953–54; Sen. and Principal Sci. Officer, Nat. Inst. of Oceanography, 1954–61; Dir, Nuffield Unit of Tropical Animal Ecology, Uganda, 1961–67; Dir, Tsavo Research Project, Kenya, 1967–68; University of Cambridge: Smuts Meml Fund Fellowship, 1968–69; Leverhulme Research Fellowship, 1969; Head, Life Sciences Div., British Antarctic Survey, 1969–73; Dir, NERC Sea Mammal Res. Unit, 1977–87; ICSU Scientific Committee for Antarctic Research: Member: Biology Working Gp, 1972–90 (Chm., 1980–86); Logistics Working Gp, 1974–80; Member Group of Specialists: on Seals, 1972–98 (Convener, 1972–88); on Marine Living Resources, 1972–90; on Envmtl Impact Assessment of Mineral Resource Exploitation and Exploitation in Antarctica, 1976–78; UK Delegate, 1984–93 and 1998; Pres., 1990–94; Hon. Mem., 1996; Member: UK Nat. Cttee on Antarctic Res., 1973–2005 (Chm., 1988–94); UK Nat. Cttee on Ocean Res., 1973–79. Food and Agriculture Organization: Mem., 1974–77, Chm., 1976–77, Working Party on Marine Mammals; Chm., Scientific Consultation on Conservation and Management of Marine Mammals and their Environment, 1976. Zoological Society of London: Mem. Council, 1982–84; Vice-Pres., 1983–84; Sec., 1984–88; Zoo Mgt Cttee, 1984–88; Zoology Liaison Gp, 1985–88. University of Cambridge: Mem., Financial Bd, 1988–91; Mem., Council of Senate, 1989–92; Chm., Local Examinations Syndicate, 1990–94. Vice-Pres., Inst. Biol., 1984–85. Mem., NERC Polar Scis Cttee, 1986–93; Chm. Ditchley Foundn Conf. on Antarctica, 1988; Trustee, UK Antarctic Heritage Trust, 1992–2000. Chm., Antarctic Science Ltd, 2001–06. Mem., Soc. of Wildlife Artists, 1963–75. Mem. Editl Bd, Applied Biology, 1976–84. Hon. Mem., Soc. for Marine Mammalogy, 1994. Foreign Mem., Norwegian Acad. of Sci. and Letters, 1998. Hon. Lectr, Makerere Univ., 1962–66. Lectures: 22nd annual, Univ. of Saskatchewan, 1969; 36th annual, CIBA Foundn, 1984; 2nd Cranbrook Meml, Mammal Soc., 1986; 4th DICE (Durrell Inst. Conservation and Ecol.), Univ. of Kent, 1997. Hon. Warden, Uganda Nat. Parks, 1996. Hon. Fellow, St Edmund's Coll., Cambridge, 1996. Hon. DSc Bath, 1991. Bruce Medal, RSE, 1954; Scientific Medal, Zool. Soc. London, 1965; Polar Medal, 1976, and clasp, 2001; Jubilee Medal, 1977. *Publications:* (with I. S. C. Parker and R. C. B. Johnstone) Elephants and their Habitats, 1975; (ed) Scientific Research in Antarctica, 1977; (ed) Antarctic Ecology, 1984; (ed jtly) Antarctic Nutrient Cycles and Food Webs, 1985; Antarctica: the last frontier, 1989; (ed jtly) Life at Low Temperatures, 1990; (ed jtly) Antarctica and Environmental Change, 1992; (ed) Antarctic Seals: research methods and techniques, 1993; (ed jtly) Elephant Seals: aspects of population, ecology, behaviour and physiology, 1994; papers mainly on large mammals in their envmts in biol and other jls. *Recreations:* gardening, photography, painting. *Address:* 3 The Footpath, Coton, Cambridge CB3 7PX. *T:* (01954) 210567.

LAWS, Stephen Charles, CB 1996; First Parliamentary Counsel, since 2006; *b* 28 Jan. 1950; *s* of late Dennis Arthur Laws and Beryl Elizabeth Laws (*née* Roe); *m* 1st, 1972, Angela Mary Deardon (*d* 1998); two *s* three *d*; 2nd, 2001, Elizabeth Ann Owen (*née* Williams). *Educ:* St Dunstan's College, Catford; Bristol Univ. (LLB Hons 1972). Called to the Bar, Middle Temple, 1973. Asst Lectr, Univ. of Bristol, 1972; Legal Asst, Home Office, 1975; Asst, Sen. Asst, then Dep. Parly Counsel, 1976–91; Parly Counsel, 1991–2006. *Publications:* (with Peter Knowles) Statutes title in Halsbury's Laws of England, 4th edn, 1983. *Address:* Office of the Parliamentary Counsel, 36 Whitehall, SW1A 2AY. *T:* (020) 7210 6619.

LAWSON, family name of **Barons Burnham** and **Lawson of Blaby**.

LAWSON OF BLABY, Baron *cr* 1992 (Life Peer), of Newnham in the County of Northamptonshire; **Nigel Lawson;** PC 1981; *b* 11 March 1932; *o s* of Ralph Lawson and Joan Elisabeth Lawson (*née* Davis); *m* 1st, 1955, Vanessa Salmon (marr. diss. 1980; she *d* 1985); one *s* two *d* (and one *d* decd); 2nd, 1980, Thérèse Mary Maclear; one *s* one *d. Educ:* Westminster; Christ Church, Oxford (Scholar; 1st class hons PPE, 1954). Served with Royal Navy (Sub-Lt RNVR), 1954–56. Mem. Editorial Staff, Financial Times, 1956–60; City Editor, Sunday Telegraph, 1961–63; Special Assistant to Prime Minister (Sir Alec Douglas-Home), 1963–64; Financial Times columnist and BBC broadcaster, 1965; Editor of the Spectator, 1966–70; regular contributor to: Sunday Times and Evening Standard, 1970–71; The Times, 1971–72; Fellow, Nuffield Coll., Oxford, 1972–73; Special Pol Advr, Cons. Party HQ, 1973–74. Contested (C) Eton and Slough, 1970; MP (C) Blaby, Leics, Feb. 1974–1992. An Opposition Whip, 1976–77; an Opposition Spokesman on Treasury and Economic Affairs, 1977–79; Financial Sec. to the Treasury, 1979–81; Sec. of State for Energy, 1981–83; Chancellor of the Exchequer, 1983–89. Chairman: Central Europe Trust Co., 1990–; OXIP, 2006–; Dir, Barclays Bank, 1990–98. Pres., British Inst. of Energy Econs, 1995–2003. Mem., Governing Body, Westminster Sch., 1999–2005. Hon. Student, Christ Church, Oxford, 1996. *Publications:* (with Jock Bruce-Gardyne) The Power Game, 1976; The View from No 11: memoirs of a Tory radical, 1992; (with Thérèse Lawson) The Nigel Lawson Diet Book, 1996; An Appeal to Reason: a cool look at global warming, 2008. *Address:* House of Lords, SW1A 0PW. *Clubs:* Garrick, Pratt's, Beefsteak.

See also Hon. D. R. C. Lawson, N. L. Lawson.

LAWSON, Sir Charles (John Patrick), 4th Bt *cr* 1900, of Weetwood Grange, West Riding of Yorks; *b* 19 May 1959; *o s* of Sir John Charles Arthur Digby Lawson, 3rd Bt, DSO, MC and Tresilla Anne Elinor (*née* Buller-Leyborne-Popham); *S* father, 2001; *m* 1987, Lady Caroline Lowther, *d* of 7th Earl of Lonsdale; three *s* one *d. Educ:* Harrow; Univ. of Leeds; RAC Cirencester. MRICS. Partner, Jackson-Stops & Staff, Exeter, 1992–; Truro, 2000–05, Barnstaple, 2004–. *Heir: s* Jack William Tremayne Lawson, *b* 6 Dec. 1989. *Address:* Heckwood, Sampford Spiney, Yelverton, Devon PL20 6LG. *T:* (office) (01392) 214222; *e-mail:* lawson@brandan.co.uk.

LAWSON, Christopher John; Chief Executive, Meat Hygiene Service, Food Standards Agency, 2001–07; *b* 16 March 1947; *s* of late John Hedley Lawson and of Joyce Patricia Lawson (*née* Robson); *m* 1969, Janice Ray Langley; two *s* one *d* (and one *d* decd). *Educ:* Ascham House Sch.; Rossall Sch.; Univ. of Newcastle upon Tyne (BSc Hons Agric). Livestock Husbandry Advr, NAAS, 1970–72; ADAS, 1972–73; MAFF, 1973–2000: Dir of Policy, Vet. Medicines Directorate, 1991–96; Hd, Meat Hygiene Div., 1996–2000; Food Standards Agency, 2000–07. Member: NE Rly Assoc.; NE Locomotive Preservation Gp; Vintage Carriage Trust. *Recreations:* steam railway preservation, fell walking, photography, DIY, industrial archaeology, supporting Newcastle United, sport generally, the North East. *Address:* Autumn, Wych Hill, Woking, Surrey GU22 0EX. *Club:* Gateshead RU.

LAWSON, Prof. Colin James, PhD, DMus; FRCM, FLCM; international clarinet soloist; Director, Royal College of Music, since 2005; *b* 24 July 1949; *s* of Eric William and Edith Mary Lawson; *m* 1982, Aileen Hilary Birch; one *s. Educ:* Keble Coll., Oxford (MA); Univ. of Birmingham (MA); Univ. of Aberdeen (PhD 1976); Univ. of London (DMus 2000). ARCM 1967, FRCM 2005; FLCM 2005. Lectr in Music, Aberdeen Univ., 1973–77; Sheffield University: Lectr, 1978–90; Sen. Lectr, 1991–96; Reader, 1996–97; Prof. of Performance Studies, Goldsmiths Coll., Univ. of London, 1998–2001; Pro-Vice Chancellor, Thames Valley Univ., 2001–05. Concert appearances as clarinet soloist include: Carnegie Hall; Lincoln Center, NY; Principal Clarinet: Hanover Band, 1987–; English Concert, 1991–. *Publications:* The Chalumeau in Eighteenth-Century Music, 1981; (ed) Cambridge Companion to the Clarinet, 1995; Mozart Clarinet Concerto, 1996; Brahms' Clarinet Quintet, 1998; (with R. Stowell) The Historical Performance of Music, 1999; The Early Clarinet, 2000; (ed) Cambridge Companion to the Orchestra, 2003. *Recreations:* travel, acquisition of early clarinets. *Address:* Royal College of Music, Prince Consort Road, SW7 2BS. *T:* (020) 7591 4363, *Fax:* (020) 7591 4356; *e-mail:* clawson@rcm.ac.uk. *Club:* Athenæum.

LAWSON, Prof. David Hamilton, CBE 1993; Hon. Consultant Physician, Glasgow Royal Infirmary, since 2003 (Consultant Physician, 1973–2003); *b* 27 May 1939; *s* of David Lawson and Margaret Harvey Lawson (*née* White); *m* 1963, Alison Diamond (*d* 1996); three *s. Educ:* High Sch. of Glasgow; Univ. of Glasgow. MB, ChB 1962; MD 1973. FRCPE 1975; FRCPGlas 1986; FFPM 1989; FRCP 2001; FFPH (FFPHM 2001). Junior medical posts in Royal Infirmary and Western Infirmary, Glasgow; Boston Collaborative Drug Surveillance Prog., Boston, Mass, 1970–72; Attending Physician, Lemuel Shattuck Hosp., Boston, 1971; Adviser on Adverse Drug Reactions, Wellcome Foundn, 1975–87; Vis. Prof., Faculty of Sci., Univ. of Strathclyde, 1976–2005; Hon. Prof. of Medicine, Univ. of Glasgow, 1993–. Chairman: Medicines Commn, 1994–2001; Scottish Medicines Consortium, 2000–04; Member: Health Services Res. Cttee of Chief Scientist Office, SHHD, 1984–88; Cttee on Safety of Medicines, Dept of Health (formerly DHSS), 1987–93; Mem., 1979–91, Chm., 1987–91, Cttee on Review of Medicines, Dept of Health (formerly DHSS). Mem. Council, RCPE, 1992–99 (Vice-Pres., 1997–99; Trustee, 2005–). Examiner, Final MB, Univs of Glasgow, Dundee, Birmingham, London, Kota Bharu, Malaysia. Hon. DSc Hertfordshire, 2000; Strathclyde, 2001. *Publications:* Clinical Pharmacy and Hospital Drug Management (ed with R. M. E. Richards), 1982; Current Medicine 2, 1990; (ed jtly) Risk Factors for Adverse Drug Reactions: epidemiological approaches, 1990; Current Medicine 3, 1991; Current Medicine 4, 1994; papers on clinical pharmacol, haematol and renal topics. *Recreations:* hill-walking, photography, bird-watching. *Address:* 25 Kirkland Avenue, Blanefield, Glasgow G63 9BY. *T:* (01360) 770081. *Club:* Royal Commonwealth Society.

LAWSON, Denis; actor and director; *b* 27 Sept. 1947; *s* of Laurence and Phyllis Lawson; *m* 2004, Sheila Gish (*d* 2005); one *s*, and two step *d. Educ:* Crieff Primary Sch.; Morrison's Acad., Crieff; Royal Scottish Acad. of Music and Drama, Glasgow. *Productions:* as *actor: theatre* includes: Pal Joey, Albery, 1980 (Most Promising New Actor, Drama Critics' Award); Mr Cinders, Fortune, 1983 (Best Actor in a Musical Award, SWET, 1984); Lend Me a Tenor, Globe, 1986; The Importance of Being Earnest, Royalty, 1987; Volpone, Almeida, 1990; Lust, Haymarket, 1993; *films* include: Providence, The Man in the Iron

Mask, 1977; Star Wars, 1977, 1980, 1983, 2001; Local Hero, 1983; The Chain, 1984; *television* includes: The Kit Curran Radio Show, 1984; That Uncertain Feeling, Dead Head, 1986; The Justice Game, 1989; Natural Lies, 1992; Hornblower, The Ambassador, 1998; Bob Martin, Other People's Children, 2000; The Fabulous Bagel Boys, 2001; Holby City, 2002–04; Lucky Jim, 2003; Sensitive Skin, Bleak House, 2005; Jekyll, 2006; as *director. theatre*: Little Malcolm and His Struggle Against the Eunuchs, Comedy, 1998; The Anniversary, Garrick, 2004; *films*: The Bass Player, 1998; Solid Geometry, 2002. *Recreations:* vodka martinis, jazz. *Address:* c/o Harriet Robinson, Independent Talent Group Ltd, Oxford House, 76 Oxford Street, W1N 0AX. *T:* (020) 7636 6565, *Fax:* (020) 7323 0101.

LAWSON, Hon. Dominic Ralph Campden; journalist and broadcaster; *b* 17 Dec. 1956; *s* of Baron Lawson of Blaby, *qv* and late Vanessa Mary Addison Lawson (*née* Salmon); *m* 1st, 1982, Jane Whytehead (marr. diss.); 2nd, 1991, Hon. Rosamond Mary Monckton, *qv*; two *d*. *Educ:* Westminster Sch.; Christ Church, Oxford (exhibnr; Hons PPE). Researcher, BBC TV and radio, 1979–81; Financial Times: joined 1981; energy corresp., 1983–86; columnist (Lex), 1986–87; The Spectator: Dep. Editor, 1987–90; Editor, 1990–95; Editor, Sunday Telegraph, 1995–2005; columnist: Sunday Correspondent, 1990; Financial Times, 1991–94; Daily Telegraph, 1994–95; Independent, 2006–. Mem., Press Complaints Commn, 1998–2002. Vis. Schol., Green Templeton (formerly Green) Coll., Oxford, 2007–. FRSA 1993. Harold Wincott Prize for financial journalism, 1987. *Publications:* (with Raymond Keene) Kasparov-Korchnoi, the London Contest, 1983; (jtly) Britain in the Eighties, 1989; The Inner Game, 1993. *Recreation:* chess. *Address:* Cox's Mill, Dallington, Heathfield, East Sussex TN21 9JG. *Club:* MCC.

See also N. L. Lawson.

LAWSON, Prof. Donald Douglas; Professor of Veterinary Surgery, University of Glasgow, 1974–86; *b* 25 May 1924; *s* of Alexander Lawson and Jessie Macnaughton; *m* 1949, Barbara Ness (*d* 1998); one *s* one *d* (and one *s* one *d* decd). *Educ:* Whitehill Sch., Glasgow; Glasgow Veterinary Coll. MRCVS, BSc, DVR. Asst in Veterinary Practice, 1946–47; Asst, Surgery Dept, Glasgow Vet. Coll., 1947–49; Glasgow Univ.: Lectr, Vet. Surgery, 1949–57; Sen. Lectr, 1957–66; Reader, 1966–71; Titular Prof., 1971–74. *Publications:* many articles in Veterinary Record and Jl of Small Animal Practice. *Recreations:* gardening, motoring. *Address:* 5 Hewlings Place, Temuka 8752, New Zealand.

LAWSON, Edmund James; QC 1988; *b* 17 April 1948; *s* of late Donald Lawson and of Veronica Lawson; *m* 1st, 1973, Jennifer Cleary (marr. diss. 2002); three *s*; 2nd, 2003, Christina Russell; two *s* one *d*, and one step *s*. *Educ:* City of Norwich Sch.; Trinity Hall, Cambridge (BA Hons Law). Called to the Bar, Gray's Inn, 1971, Bencher, 1998; in chambers of: Dr F. Hallis, 1971–76; Sir Arthur Irvine, QC, subseq. Gilbert Gray, QC, 1976–2006; Head of Chambers, 1990–98; Founder Mem., Cloth Fair Chambers, 2006. *Recreations:* music, Rugby. *Address:* 39–40 Cloth Fair, EC1A 7NT.

LAWSON, Elizabeth Ann; QC 1989; a Recorder, since 1998; *b* 29 April 1947; *d* of Alexander Edward Lawson, FCA, and Helen Jane Lawson (*née* Currie). *Educ:* Croydon High School for Girls (GPDST); Nottingham Univ. (LLB). Called to Bar, Gray's Inn, 1969, Bencher, 1999. Chm., Family Law Bar Assoc., 1995–97. Chm., Leeways Enquiry for London Borough of Lewisham, 1985; Chm., Liam Johnson Review for Islington Area Child Protection Cttee, 1989. *Recreations:* knitting, reading, cake decoration. *Address:* 1 Pump Court, Temple, EC4Y 7AB.

LAWSON, Rear-Adm. Frederick Charles William, CB 1971; DSC 1942 and Bar, 1945; Chief Executive, Royal Dockyards, Ministry of Defence, 1972–75; *b* 20 April 1917; *s* of M. L. Lawson, formerly of Public Works Dept, Punjab, India; *m* 1945, Dorothy (*née* Norman) (*d* 1986), Eastbourne; one *s* three *d*. *Educ:* Eastbourne Coll.; RNEC. Joined RN, 1935; specialised in engrg; Cmdr 1949; Captain 1960; Cdre Supt Singapore, 1965–69; Rear-Adm. 1969; Flag Officer, Medway and Adm. Supt, HM Dockyard, Chatham, 1969–71, retired. *Address:* 17 Kingfisher Court, Avon Park, Limpley Stoke, Bath BA2 7JS.

See also Vice-Adm. Sir M. A. C. Moore.

LAWSON, Prof. Gerald Hartley; Professor of Business Finance, Manchester Business School, University of Manchester, 1969–88, now Emeritus; financial and economic consultant; *b* 6 July 1933; of English parents; *m* 1957, Helga Elisabeth Anna Heine; three *s*. *Educ:* King's Coll., Univ. of Durham. BA (Econ), MA (Econ); MBA, PhD Manchester; FCCA. Accountant in industry, 1957–59; Lectr in Accountancy and Applied Economics, Univ. of Sheffield, 1959–66; Prof. of Business Studies, Univ. of Liverpool, 1966–69. British Council Scholar, Hochschule für Welthandel, Vienna, 1967, and Univ. of Louvain, 1978. Visiting Professor: Univ. of Augsburg, Germany, 1971–72; Univ. of Texas, 1977, 1981; Ruhr Univ., Bochum, 1980; Southern Methodist Univ., Dallas, 1989–93; Nanyang Technological Univ., Singapore, 1989; Martin Luther Univ., Halle-Wittenberg, 1993–96; Otto-von-Guericke-Univ. of Magdeburg, 1998–2001; Vis. Erskine Fellow, Univ. of Canterbury, NZ, 1997. Dir, Dietsmann (UK), 1984–89. Lifetime Achievement Award, BAA, 2008. *Publications:* (with D. W. Windle): Tables for Discounted Cash Flow, etc, Calculations, 1965 (6th repr. 1979); Capital Budgeting in the Corporation Tax Regime, 1967; (with M. Schweitzer and E. Trossman) Break-Even Analyses: basic model, variants, extensions, 1991; Studies in Cash Flow Accounting, 1992; Aspects of the Economic Implications of Accounting, 1997; many articles and translations. *Recreations:* cricket, ski-ing, opera. *Address:* 1702 Woodcreek Drive, Richardson, TX 75082, USA. *Club:* Manchester Business School.

LAWSON, James Robert; Regional Nursing Officer, Mersey, 1985–89, retired; *b* 29 Dec. 1939; *s* of James and Grace Lawson; *m* 1962, Jean; two *d*. *Educ:* Keswick High School; Royal Albert Hosp. (Registered Nurse of Mentally Handicapped); Cumberland Infirmary (Registered Gen. Nurse). Chief Nurse, 1972; Area Nurse, Personnel, 1974; Divl Nursing Officer, 1976; District Nursing Officer, 1982–85. *Recreations:* fellwalking, caravanning, active sports. *Address:* 11 Hazelgarth, Church Road, Allithwaite, Grange-over-Sands, Cumbria LA11 7RS.

LAWSON, John David, ScD; FRS 1983; Deputy Chief Scientific Officer, Rutherford Appleton Laboratory, Science and Engineering Research Council, Chilton, Oxon, 1978–87, retired, now Hon. Scientist; *b* 4 April 1923; *s* of Ronald L. Lawson and Ruth (*née* Houseman); *m* 1949, Kathleen (*née* Wyllie); two *s* one *d*. *Educ:* Wolverhampton Grammar Sch.; St John's Coll., Cambridge (BA, ScD). FInstP. TRE Malvern, Aerials group, 1943; AERE Malvern Br., Accelerator gp, 1947; AERE Harwell, Gen. Physics Div., 1951–62; Microwave Laboratory, Stanford, USA, 1959–60; Rutherford Laboratory (later Rutherford Appleton Laboratory), Applied Phys. Div., and later Technology Div., 1962–87, except, Vis. Prof., Dept of Physics and Astronomy, Univ. of Maryland, USA, 1971; Culham Lab., Technology Div., 1975–76. *Publications:* The Physics of Charged Particle Beams, 1977, 2nd edn 1988; papers on various topics in applied physics in several jls. *Recreations:* travel, walking, collecting old books. *Address:* 7 Clifton Drive, Abingdon, Oxon OX14 1ET. *T:* (01235) 521516.

LAWSON, Sir John Philip H; *see* Howard-Lawson.

LAWSON, Lesley, (Twiggy); actress, singer and model; *b* 19 Sept. 1949; *y d* of late (William) Norman Hornby and of Nell (Helen) Hornby (*née* Reeman); *m* 1st, 1977, Michael Whitney Armstrong (*d* 1983); one *d*; 2nd, 1988, Leigh Lawson. Started modelling in London, 1966; toured USA and Canada, 1967; world's most famous model, 1966–71. *Films:* The Boy Friend, 1971 (most promising newcomer and best actress in a musical or comedy, Golden Globe Awards); W, 1973; There Goes the Bride, 1979; Blues Brothers, 1981; The Doctor and the Devils, 1986; Club Paradise, 1986; Madame Sousatzka, 1989; Harem Hotel, Istanbul, 1989; Woundings, 1998; *stage:* Cinderella, 1976; Captain Beaky, 1982; My One and Only, 1983, 1984; Blithe Spirit, Chichester, 1997; Noel and Gertie, NY, 1998; If Love Were All, NY, 1999; Blithe Spirit, NY, 2002; Mrs Warren's Profession (UK tour), 2003; *television:* numerous appearances and series, UK and USA, incl. The Taming of the Shrew, 2005; judge on America's Next Top Model, 2005–08; numerous recordings. Many awards and honours including Hon. Col, Tennessee Army, 1977. *Publications:* Twiggy, 1975; An Open Look, 1985; Twiggy in Black and White (autobiog.), 1997. *Recreations:* daughter Carly, music, dressmaking. *Address:* c/o Peters, Fraser & Dunlop, Drury House, 34–43 Russell Street, WC2B 5HA. *T:* (020) 7344 1010, *Fax:* (020) 7836 9544.

LAWSON, Mark Gerard; journalist, broadcaster and author; *b* 11 April 1962; *s* of Francis Lawson and Teresa Lawson (*née* Kane); *m* 1990, Sarah Bull; two *s* one *d*. *Educ:* St Columba's Coll., St Albans; University College London (BA Hons English). Junior reporter and TV critic, The Universe, 1984–85; TV previewer, Sunday Times, 1985–86; TV critic and parly sketchwriter, The Independent, 1986–89; feature writer, Independent Magazine, 1988–95; columnist, The Guardian, 1995–; presenter for radio and TV, 1990–, including: Late Review, later Review, subseq. Newsnight Review (BBC2), 1994–2005; Front Row (Radio 4), 1998–; Mark Lawson Talks To... (BBC4); Never Ending Stories (BBC2); scriptwriter for radio and TV, including: The Vision Thing (BBC2), 1993; The Man Who Had 10,000 Women (Radio 4), 2002; St Graham and St Evelyn, Pray for Us (Radio 4), 2003; Absolute Power (BBC2), 2003–05; The Third Soldier Holds His Thighs (Radio 4), 2005; London, this is Washington (Radio 4), 2006; Expand This (Radio 4), Sex After Death (Radio 4), 2007. British Press Award, 1987; TV critic of the Year, 1989, 1990. *Publications:* Bloody Margaret, 1991; The Battle for Room Service, 1993; Idlewild, 1995; John Keane, 1995; Going Out Live, 2001; Enough Is Enough, 2005. *Recreations:* theatre, cricket, tennis, wine, reading. *Address:* c/o The Guardian, Kings Place, 90 York Way, N1 9AG.

LAWSON, Ven. Michael Charles; Archdeacon of Hampstead, since 1999; *b* 23 May 1952; *s* of Gerald Simon Lawson and Myrtle Helena Lawson; *m* 1978, Claire Mary MacClelland; three *d*. *Educ:* Hove Grammar Sch.; Guildhall Sch. of Music; Ecoles d'Art Américaines, Fontainebleau; Univ. of Sussex (BA); Trinity Coll., Bristol (BCTS). Composer and pianist, 1970–75. Deacon 1978, priest 1979; Curate, St Mary the Virgin, Horsham, 1978–81; Dir of Pastoring, All Souls, Langham Place, W1, 1981–86; Vicar, Christ Church, Bromley, 1987–99. *Publications:* Sex and That, 1985, 2nd edn 1992; Facing Anxiety and Stress, 1986, 2nd edn 1995; The Unfolding Kingdom, 1987; Facing Depression, 1989, 2nd edn 1997; Facing Conflict, 1990; The Better Marriage Guide, 1998; Conflict, 1999; Living by God's Master Plan, 2000; D is for Depression, 2006. *Recreations:* my wife and children, friends, music, writing, video production, photography, computers, theatre, cookery, lots of things. *Address:* London Diocesan House, 36 Causton Street, SW1P 4AU.

LAWSON, Michael Henry; QC 1991; **His Honour Judge Lawson;** a Circuit Judge, since 2004; *b* 3 Feb. 1946; *s* of late Dr Richard Pike Lawson, MC and Margaret Haines (*née* Knight); *m* 1969, Ann Pleasance Symons Brisker; two *d*. *Educ:* Monkton Combe School, Bath; London Univ. (LLB). Called to the Bar, Inner Temple, 1969, Bencher, 1993; a Recorder, 1987–2004. Leader, SE Circuit, 1997–2000. Mem., Bar Council, 1997–2003. Master, Curriers' Co., 2007–08. *Publications:* (jtly) Professional Conduct (Inns of Court School of Law Manual), annually, 1989–2000; (contrib.) Refocus on Child Abuse, 1994. *Recreations:* opera, music, wine, walking. *Address:* Crown Court, Maidstone, Kent ME16 8EQ.

LAWSON, Nigella Lucy; freelance journalist and broadcaster, since 1982; *b* 6 Jan. 1960; *d* of Baron Lawson of Blaby, *qv* and late Vanessa (*née* Salmon); *m* 1st, 1992, John Diamond (*d* 2001); one *s* one *d*; 2nd, 2003, Charles Saatchi, *qv*. *Educ:* Lady Margaret Hall, Oxford (BA (Hons) Medieval and Mod. Langs). Presenter, television series: Nigella Bites, 2000; Nigella Bites II, 2001; Forever Summer with Nigella, 2002; Nigella's Christmas Kitchen, 2006; Nigella Express, 2007. *Publications:* How to Eat, 1998; How to be a Domestic Goddess, 2000; Nigella Bites, 2001; Forever Summer, 2002; Feast, 2004; Nigella Express, 2007. *Address:* c/o Ed Victor Ltd, 6 Bayley Street, Bedford Square, WC1B 3HB. *T:* (020) 7304 4100.

See also Hon. D. R. C. Lawson.

LAWSON, Gen. Sir Richard (George), KCB 1980; DSO 1962; OBE 1968; Commander-in-Chief, Allied Forces Northern Europe, 1982–86; *b* 24 Nov. 1927; *s* of John Lawson and Florence Rebecca Lawson; *m* 1956, Ingrid Lawson (*d* 2006); one *s*. *Educ:* St Alban's Sch.; Birmingham Univ. CO, Independent Squadron, RTR (Berlin), 1963–64; GSO2 MoD, 1965–66; CofS, South Arabian Army, 1967; CO, 5th RTR, 1968–69; Comdr, 20th Armoured Bde, 1972–73; Asst Military Deputy to Head of Defence Sales, 1975–77; GOC 1st Armoured Div., 1977–79; GOC Northern Ireland, 1980–82. Col Comdt, RTR, 1980–82. Leopold Cross (Belgium), 1963; Knight Commander, Order of St Sylvester (Vatican), 1964. *Publications:* Strange Soldiering, 1963; All the Queen's Men, 1967; Strictly Personal, 1972. *Address:* c/o Drummonds, 49 Charing Cross, SW1A 2DX.

LAWSON, Richard Henry, CBE 1994; Chairman: Greenwell Montagu, Stockbrokers, 1987–91; Securities and Futures Authority, 1991; *b* 16 Feb. 1932; *s* of Sir Henry Brailsford Lawson, MC, and Lady (Mona) Lawson; *m* 1958, Janet Elizabeth Govier; three *s* (one *d* decd). *Educ:* Lancing College. ICI, 1952–54; W. Greenwell & Co. (now Greenwell Montagu & Co.), 1954–91; Jt Sen. Partner, 1980–86. Deputy Chairman: Stock Exchange, 1985–86; Securities Assoc., 1986–91. Chm., Investors Compensation Scheme, 1993–96 (Dir, 1989–96); Dir, Securities Institute, 1992–93. *Recreations:* golf, tennis, walking, birdwatching, ski-ing.

LAWSON, Roger Hardman; Director, Zotefoams plc, since 2002; *b* 3 Sept. 1945; *s* of Harold Hardman Lawson and Mary Doreen Lawson; *m* 1974, Jenniferjane Grey; three *d*. *Educ:* Bedford School. CA 1967; FCA. Articled Wilson de Zouche & Mackenzie, 1963–67; joined ICFC, subseq. 3i, 1968; Manager, Regions, 1968–84; Dir, 3i International (USA, Asia and Pacific), 1984–92; Dir Resource (handling substantial investments), 3i plc, 1993–2002; Dir of several unquoted trading cos. Mem., Takeover Panel, 1994–95. Chairman: London Soc. of Chartered Accountants, 1985–86; CCAB Ltd, 1994–95; Pres., ICAEW, 1994–95 (Vice-Pres., 1992–93; Dep.-Pres., 1993–94). Trustee: Thalidomide Trust, 2001–; St Paul's Cathedral Staff Pension Fund, 2003–. *Recreations:* food, family, golf. *Address:* 62 Thurleigh Road, SW12 8UD. *T:* (020) 8675 0386. *Clubs:* Royal Wimbledon Golf; Rye Golf.

LAWSON, Hon. Rosa(mond) Mary; see Monckton, Hon. R. M.

LAWSON, Sonia, RA 1991 (ARA 1982); RWS 1988 (ARWS 1985); artist; Visiting Lecturer, Royal Academy Schools; *b* 2 June 1934; *d* of Frederick Lawson and Muriel (*née* Metcalfe), artists; *m* 1969, C. W. Congo; one *d. Educ:* Leyburn; Southwick Girls' Sch.; Doncaster Sch. of Art; Royal Coll. of Art (ARCA 1st cl. 1959). Postgraduate year, RCA; Travelling Scholarship, France, 1960. *Annual exhibitions:* RA, 1961–; RWS, 1983–. *Solo exhibitions:* Zwemmer, London, 1960; New Arts Centre, London, 1963; Queen's Sq. Gall., Leeds, 1964; Trafford Gall., London, 1967; Bradford New Liby, 1972; Middlesbrough and Billingham, 1977; Open Univ., Darlington and Harrogate Art Galls, 1979; Harrogate Northern Artists, 1980; Manchester City Art Gall., 1987; Wakefield City Art Gall., 1988, 2008; Cartwright Hall, Bradford, 1989; Boundary Gall., London, 1989, 1995, 1998, 2000, 2003, 2005; Univ. of Birmingham, 1994, 2006; Shire Hall, Stafford, 1999; RWA, Bristol, 2000; Carlow Arts Fest., Ireland, 2001; Vertigo Gall., London, 2002; *retrospectives:* Shrines of Life, toured 1982–83, Sheffield (Mappin), Hull (Ferens), Bradford (Cartwright), Leicester Poly., Milton Keynes (Exhibn Gall); Dean Clough Gall., Halifax, 1996; Aylesbury Art Gall. and Mus., 2006; *mixed exhibitions:* Arts Council of GB Touring Exhibns (Fragments against Ruin, The Subjective Eye); Tolly Cobbold National Exhibns; Moira Kelly Fine Art; Hayward Annual; Soho, New York (8 in the 80s); Fruitmarket Gall., Edinburgh; London Gp; RCA (Exhibition Road, to celebrate 150 years of RCA), 1988; Smith Gall., London, 1988, 1989; Faces of Britain, China (British Council Touring Exhibn), 1989–90; Glasgow Royal Inst. of Fine Art, 1990; Galerie zur alten deutschen Schule, Thun, Switzerland, 1990; Royal Academy (The Infernal Method, etchings by Academicians), 1991; John Moores, Liverpool, 1991; Bonnington Gall., Nottingham Trent Univ. (Representing Lives), 1997. Works in public collections: Arts Council of GB; Graves Art Gall., Sheffield; Huddersfield, Bolton, Carlisle, Belfast, Middlesbrough, Bradford, Dewsbury, Rochdale, Wakefield, and Harrogate Art Galls; Imperial War Mus.; Min. of Educn; Min. of Works; Leeds Univ.; Open Univ.; Cranfield Univ.; RCA; St Peter's Coll., Oxford; Nuffield Foundn; Royal Acad.; Augustine (commissioned), presented by Archbishop of Canterbury to Pope John Paul II, Vatican Collection, Rome, 1989; private collections in UK, Germany, Australia, USA. BBC TV, Monitor, 1960, John Schlesinger's doc. "Private View". Visual records of preparations for Exercise Lionheart, BAOR, 1984 (Imperial War Mus. commn). Hon. RWA 2005. Rowney Prize, Royal Acad., 1984; Gainsborough House Drawing Prize, Eastern Arts, 1984; Lorne Scholarship, Slade Sch. of Fine Art, 1986; Lady Evershed Drawing Prize, Eastern Arts Open, 1990. *Address:* c/o Royal Academy of Arts, Burlington House, Piccadilly, W1V 0DS. *T:* (020) 7300 5680; *e-mail:* art@sonialawson.co.uk. *Clubs:* Royal Over-Seas League; Arts.

LAWSON JOHNSTON, family name of **Baron Luke.**

LAWSON-ROGERS, (George) Stuart; QC 1994; a Recorder, since 1990; *b* 23 March 1946; *s* of late George Henry Roland Rogers, CBE, sometime MP and Mary Lawson; *m* 1969, Rosalind Denise Leach; one *s* one *d. Educ:* LSE (LLB Hons). Called to the Bar, Gray's Inn, 1969; Asst Recorder, 1987–89. Asst Comr, Parly and Local Govt Boundary Commns, 1981, 1983; Chm., Structure Plan Exams in Public, DoE, 1984; Legal Assessor, GMC and GDC, 1988–2005; Standing Counsel (Crime, SE Circuit) to HM Customs and Excise, 1989–94; DTI Inspector, Insider Dealing, 1989; Dept of Transport Inspector, Merchant Shipping Act 1988, 1989–90. Dir, Watford AFC Ltd, 1990–96. *Recreations:* theatre, music, opera, reading, gardening. *Address:* 7 Harrington Street, Liverpool L2 9YH. *T:* (0151) 242 0707, *Fax:* (0151) 236 2800; *e-mail:* clerks@harringtonstreet.co.uk; 23 Essex Street, WC2R 3AS. *T:* (020) 7413 0353, *Fax:* (020) 7413 0374.

LAWSON-TANCRED, Sir Henry, 10th Bt *cr* 1662; JP; *b* 12 Feb. 1924; *e surv. s* of Major Sir Thomas Lawson-Tancred, 9th Bt, and Margery Elinor (*d* 1961), *d* of late A. S. Lawson, Aldborough Manor; *S* father, 1945; *m* 1st, 1950, Jean Veronica (*d* 1970), 4th and *y d* of late G. R. Foster, Stockeld Park, Wetherby, Yorks; five *s* one *d*; 2nd, 1978, Mrs Susan Drummond, *d* of Sir Kenelm Cayley, 10th Bt. *Educ:* Stowe; Jesus Coll., Cambridge. Served as Pilot in RAFVR, 1942–46. JP West Riding, 1967. *Heir:* s Andrew Peter Lawson-Tancred [*b* 18 Feb. 1952; *m* 2004, Julia, *d* of John Murray; one *s* one *d*]. *Address:* Flat 1, Aldborough Manor, Boroughbridge, York YO51 9EP.

LAWTON, Prof. Denis; Professor of Education, University of London Institute of Education, 1974–2003, now Emeritus; *b* 5 April 1931; *s* of William Benedict Lawton and Ruby (*née* Evans); *m* 1953, Joan Weston; two *s. Educ:* St Ignatius Coll.; Univ. of London Goldsmiths' Coll. (BA); Univ. of London Inst. of Education (PhD). Asst Master, Erith Grammar Sch., 1958–61; Head of English/Housemaster, Bacon's Sch., SE1, 1961–63; University of London Institute of Education: Research Officer, 1963–64; Lectr in Sociology, 1964–67; Sen. Lectr in Curriculum Studies, 1967–72; Reader in Education, 1972–74; Dep. Dir, 1978–83; Dir, 1983–89. Chairman: Univ. of London Sch. Exams Bd, subseq. Sch. Exams and Assessment Council, 1984–96; Consortium for Assessment and Testing in Schools, 1989–91; Jt Council for GCSE, 1996–99; Acad. Sec., UCET, 2000–02. Hon. Fellow, College of Preceptors, 1983. *Publications:* Social Class, Language and Education, 1968; Social Change, Education Theory and Curriculum Planning, 1973; Class, Culture and the Curriculum, 1975; Social Justice and Education, 1977; The Politics of the School Curriculum, 1980; An Introduction to Teaching and Learning, 1981; Curriculum Studies and Educational Planning, 1983; (with P. Gordon) HMI, 1987; Education, Culture and the National Curriculum, 1989; Education and Politics in the 1990s, 1992; The Tory Mind on Education, 1994; Beyond the National Curriculum, 1996; Royal Education Past, Present and Future, 1999; (with P. Gordon) A History of Western Educational Ideas, 2002; Education and Labour Party Ideologies 1900–2001 and Beyond, 2004. *Recreations:* walking German Shepherd dogs, photographing bench-ends, sampling real ale, music. *Address:* Laun House, Laundry Lane, Nazeing, Essex EN9 2DY.

LAWTON, Sir John (Hartley), Kt 2005; CBE 1997; FRS 1989; Chairman, Royal Commission on Environmental Pollution, since 2005 (Member, 1989–96); Chief Executive, Natural Environment Research Council, 1999–2005; *b* 24 Sept. 1943; *s* of Frank Hartley Lawton and Mary Lawton; *m* 1966, Dorothy (*née* Grimshaw); one *s* one *d. Educ:* Balshaw's Grammar Sch., Leyland, Lancs; University Coll. and Dept of Zoology, Univ. of Durham (BSc, PhD). Res. Student, Univ. of Durham, 1965–68; Deptl Demonstrator in Animal Ecology, Oxford Univ., 1968–71; College Lectr in Zoology, St Anne's and Lincoln Colls, Oxford, 1970–71; University of York: Lectr, 1971–78; Sen. Lectr, 1978–82; Reader, 1982–85; Personal Chair, 1985–89; Dir, NERC Centre for Population Biology, ICSTM, 1989–99. Mem., NERC, 1995–99. Hon. Vis. Res. Fellow, Nat. Hist. Mus., 1990–2005; Adjunct Scientist, Inst. of Ecosystem Studies, NY Botanic Garden, 1991–2000. Vice-President: RSPB, 1999– (Chm. Council, 1993–98); British Trust for Ornithology, 1999–2008. FIC 2006. Hon. DSc: Lancaster, 1993; Birmingham, York, 2005; East Anglia, Aberdeen, 2006. *Publications:* Insects on Plants: community patterns and mechanisms (with D. R. Strong and T. R. E. Southwood), 1984; (ed jtly) The Evolutionary Interactions of Animals and Plants, 1991; (ed jtly) Extinction Rates, 1996; (ed jtly) Linking Species and Ecosystems, 1996; Community Ecology in a Changing World, 2000; over 300 sci. papers in specialist jls. *Recreations:* bird watching, natural history

photography, travel, gardening, walking. *Address:* The Hayloft, Holburns Croft, Heslington, York YO10 5DP.

LAWTON, Julie Grace; Headmistress, Wolverhampton Girls' High School, since 2004; *b* 2 April 1958; *d* of Arthur and Audrey Barber; *m* 1979, Mark Lawton. *Educ:* Univ. of Hull (BA; PGCE); Univ. of Birmingham (MEd); NPQH 2002. Teacher of French and German, Newland High Sch. for Girls, Hull, 1980–83; i/c German, Parkfield Sch., Wolverhampton, 1983–86; Hd, Modern Langs, Kingswinford Sch., Dudley, 1987–94; Vice Principal and Dir, Sixth Form Studies, St Peter's Collegiate Sch., Wolverhampton, 1995–2003. *Recreations:* walking, travelling abroad, foreign languages. *Address:* Wolverhampton Girls' High School, Tettenhall Road, Wolverhampton WV6 0BY. *T:* (01902) 312186, *Fax:* (01902) 312187; *e-mail:* jglawton@girlshigh.biblio.net.

LAXTON, Robert; MP (Lab) Derby North, since 1997; *b* 7 Sept. 1944; *s* of Alan and Elsie Laxton; *m*; one *s. Educ:* Woodlands Secondary Sch.; Derby Coll. of Art and Technology. Branch Officer, CWU, 1974–97; Telecommunications Engr, BT plc, 1961–97. Mem., Derby CC, 1979–97 (Leader, 1986–88, 1994–97). PPS to Minister of State: DTI, 2001–03; DFES, 2003–04; PPS to Secretary of State: DWP, 2004–05; DTI, 2005. Mem., Trade and Industry Select Cttee, 1997–2001. Vice Chairman: Trade Union Gp of Lab. MPs; PLP DTI Deptl Cttee. Chm., E Midlands Local Govt Assoc., 1995–97; Vice Pres., LGA. *Address:* House of Commons, SW1A 0AA.

LAY, Richard Neville, CBE 2001; Chairman, DTZ (formerly Debenham Tewson & Chinnocks) Holdings plc, 1987–2000; President, Royal Institution of Chartered Surveyors, 1998–99; *b* 18 Oct. 1938; *s* of late Edward John Lay; *m* 1st, 1964; one *s* one *d*; 2nd, 1991; 3rd, 2003, Veronica Anne Jones (*née* Hamilton-Russell). *Educ:* Whitgift School. FRICS. Partner, Debenham Tewson & Chinnocks, 1965–87. Vice Chm., 1992–2001, Chm., 2001–, Central London Board, Royal and Sun Alliance (formerly Sun Alliance and London) Insurance Group. Dir, Nat. House Building Council, 2001–07. Chairman: cttee advising RICS on market requirements of the profession, 1991; Commercial Property Panel, RICS, 1992–95; Member: Council, British Property Fedn, 1992–99; General Council, RICS, 1994–2000; Bank of England Property Forum, 1994–99; Chm., Commercial Property Gp, DCLG (formerly Wkg Party on Commercial Property Issues, ODPM), 2004–; Mem., Adv. Panel on Standards in Planning Inspectorate, 1993–2000. Chm. and Trustee, Portman Estate, 1999–. Co-Chm., Corby Regeneration Co. Ltd, 2003–06; Chm., N Northants Develt Co. Ltd, 2006–08. Chm., London Underwriting Centre, 2005–. Trustee, Tate Gall. Foundn, 1989–94. Master, Armourers' and Brasiers' Co., 2003–04 (Surveyor, 1983–98; Mem., Ct of Assts, 1998–). Governor, Belmont Sch., Surrey, 1983–88; Mem. Bd, Coll. of Estate Mgt, 2000–05. Property Person of the Year, Property Week, 1999. *Recreations:* gardening, walking. *Address:* 12 Paultons Street, SW3 5DR. *T:* (01608) 685458. *Club:* Royal Automobile.

LAYARD, Baron *cr* 2000 (Life Peer), of Highgate in the London Borough of Haringey; **Peter Richard Grenville Layard,** FBA 2003; Director, Well-Being Programme, Centre for Economic Performance, London School of Economics, since 2003 (Professor of Economics, 1980–99, now Emeritus); *b* 15 March 1934; *s* of Dr John Layard and Doris Layard; *m* 1991, Molly Meacher (*see* Baroness Meacher). *Educ:* Eton Coll.; King's Coll., Cambridge (BA); London School of Economics (MScEcon; Hon. Fellow, 2004). History Master: Woodberry Down Sch., 1959–60; Forest Hill Sch., 1960–61; Senior Research Officer, Robbins Cttee on Higher Educn, 1961–63; London School of Economics: Dep. Director, Higher Educn Research Unit, 1964–74 (part-time from 1968); Lectr in Economics, 1968–75; Reader in the Economics of Labour, 1975–80; Hd, Centre for Labour Econs, 1974–90; Dir, Centre for Econ. Performance, 1990–2003. Chm., Employment Inst., 1987–92. Mem., UGC, 1985–89. Econ. Consultant to Russian Govt, 1991–97; Consultant: DfEE, 1997–2001; Cabinet Office, 2001; DoH, 2006–. Fellow, Econometric Soc., 1986. Leontief Medal, Russian Acad. of Natural Scis, 2005. *Publications:* (jtly) The Causes of Graduate Unemployment in India, 1969; (jtly) The Impact of Robbins: Expansion in Higher Education, 1969; (jtly) Qualified Manpower and Economic Performance: An Inter-Plant Study in the Electrical Engineering Industry, 1971; (ed) Cost-Benefit Analysis, 1973, 2nd edn 1994; (jtly) Microeconomic Theory, 1978; (jtly) The Causes of Poverty, 1978; More Jobs, Less Inflation, 1982; How to Beat Unemployment, 1986; (jtly) Handbook of Labour Economics, 1986; (jtly) The Performance of the British Economy, 1988; (jtly) Unemployment: Macroeconomic Performance and the Labour Market, 1991; (jtly) Reform in Eastern Europe, 1991; (jtly) East-West Migration: the alternatives, 1992; (jtly) Post-Communist Reform: pain and progress, 1993; Macroeconomics: a text for Russia, 1994; (jtly) The Coming Russian Boom, 1996; What Labour Can Do, 1997; Tackling Unemployment, 1999; Tackling Inequality, 1999; (ed) What the Future Holds, 2002; Happiness: lessons from a new science, 2005. *Recreations:* tennis, the clarinet. *Address:* London School of Economics, Houghton Street, WC2A 2AE. *T:* (020) 7955 7281.

LAYARD, Adm. Sir Michael (Henry Gordon), KCB 1993; CBE 1982; Second Sea Lord, and Chief of Naval Personnel (Member of Admiralty Board, Defence Council), 1993–95; Commander-in-Chief Naval Home Command, 1994–95; Flag Aide-de-Camp to the Queen, 1994–95; *b* Sri Lanka, 3 Jan. 1936; *s* of late Edwin Henry Frederick and Doris Christian Gordon (*née* Spence); *m* 1966, Elspeth Horsley Fisher; two *s. Educ:* Pangbourne Coll.; RN Coll., Dartmouth. Joined RN, 1954; specialised in aviation, 1958; Fighter Pilot, 1960–72; Air Warfare Instructor, 1964; Commanded: 899 Naval Air Sqn, in HMS Eagle, 1970–71; HMS Lincoln, 1971–72; ndc, 1974–75; Directorate, Naval Air Warfare, MoD, 1975–77; Comdr (Air), HMS Ark Royal, 1977–78; CSO (Air), FONAC, 1979–82; Sen. Naval Officer, SS Atlantic Conveyor, Falklands conflict, 1982 (CBE); Commanded: RNAS Culdrose, 1982–84; HMS Cardiff, 1984–85; Task Gp Comdr, Persian Gulf, 1984; Dep. Dir, Naval Warfare (Air), MoD, 1985–88; Flag Officer Naval Aviation (formerly Air Comd), 1988–90; Dir Gen., Naval Manpower and Trng, 1990–92; Leader of RN Officers Study Gp, MoD, 1992–93; Adm. Pres., RNC, Greenwich, 1993–94. Gentleman Usher to the Sword of State, 1997–2005. Non-exec. Dir, Taunton & Somerset NHS Trust, 1996–2000. Trustee, FAA Mus., 1995–2006. Mem., FAA Officers' Assoc., 1964–; Member Council: White Ensign Assoc., 1996–2006 (Chm., 1996–99); Royal Patriotic Fund, 1995–. Governor: Pangbourne Coll., 1995–; King's Coll., Taunton, 1997–2005; King's Hall, Taunton, 1997–2005. Chevalier Bretvin, 1984. Freeman, City of London, 1994. *Recreations:* painting, sailing, music, history, collecting experiences. *Address:* Harwood House, Aller, Somerset TA10 0QN. *Clubs:* Army and Navy; Royal Navy of 1765 and 1785; Royal Naval Sailing Association; Royal Navy Golfing Society (Pres, 1988–94).

LAYCRAFT, Hon. James Herbert, OC 2002; Chief Justice of Alberta, 1985–92; *b* 5 Jan. 1924; *s* of George Edward Laycraft and Hattie Cogswell Laycraft; *m* 1948, Helen Elizabeth Bradley; one *s* one *d. Educ:* University of Alberta (BA, LLB 1951). Admitted to Bar, 1952; law practice, 1952–75; Trial Div. Judge, Supreme Court of Alberta, 1975; Judge, Court of Appeal, Alberta, 1979–85. Hon. LLD Calgary, 1986. *Publications:* articles in Canadian Bar Review and Alberta Law Review. *Recreations:* outdoor activities. *Address:*

200 Lincoln Way SW, Apt 419, Calgary, AB T3E 7G7, Canada. *Club:* Ranchman's (Calgary).

LAYDEN, Anthony Michael; HM Diplomatic Service, retired; Special Representative for Deportation with Assurances, Foreign and Commonwealth Office, since 2006; *b* 27 July 1946; *s* of Sheriff Michael Layden, SSC, TD and Eileen Mary Layden; *m* 1969, Josephine Mary McGhee; three *s* one *d. Educ:* Holy Cross Academy, Edinburgh; Edinburgh Univ. (LLB Hons Law and Econ. 1968). Lieut, 15th (Scottish Volunteer) Bn, Parachute Regt, 1966–69. Foreign Office, 1968; MECAS, Lebanon, 1969; Jedda, 1971; Rome, 1973; FCO, Middle East, Rhodesia, Personnel Ops Depts, 1977–82; Head of Chancery, Jedda, 1982–85; Hong Kong Dept, FCO, 1985–87; Counsellor and Head of Chancery, Muscat, 1987–91; Counsellor (Economic and Commercial), 1991–95, and Dep. Hd of Mission, 1994–95, Copenhagen; Head of Western European Dept, FCO, 1995–98; Ambassador to Morocco and (non-resident) to Mauritania, 1999–2002; Ambassador to Libya, 2002–06. *Recreations:* sailing, walking, music, bridge. *Club:* Travellers.
See also P. J. Layden.

LAYDEN, Patrick John, TD 1981; QC (Scot.) 2000; Deputy Solicitor, Office of the Solicitor to the Scottish Government (formerly Scottish Executive), since 2003; Commissioner, Scottish Law Commission, since 2008; *b* 27 June 1949; *s* of Sheriff Michael Layden, SSC, TD and Eileen Mary Layden; *m* 1984, Patricia Mary Bonnar; three *s* one *d. Educ:* Holy Cross Acad., Edinburgh; Edinburgh Univ. (LLB Hons). Called to the Scottish Bar, 1973; Lord Advocate's Department: Dep. Scottish Parly Counsel and Asst Legal Sec., 1977–87; Scottish Parly Counsel and Sen. Asst Legal Sec., 1987–99; Legal Sec. to Lord Advocate, 1999–2003. Univ. of Edinburgh OTC, 1967–71; 2/52 Lowland Vol., TA, 1971–77; 1/51 Highland Vol., 1977–81 (OC London Scottish, 1978–81); OC 73 Ord. Co. (V), 1981–84. *Recreations:* reading, walking. *Address:* Office of the Solicitor to the Scottish Government, Victoria Quay, Edinburgh EH6 6QQ.
See also A. M. Layden.

LAYMAN, Rear-Adm. Christopher Hope, CB 1991; DSO 1982; LVO 1977; Commander, British Forces, Falkland Islands, 1986–87; *b* 9 March 1938; *s* of late Captain H. F. H. Layman, DSO, RN and Elizabeth Hughes; *m* 1964, Katharine Romer Ascherson (*d* 2008); one *s* one *d. Educ:* Winchester. Joined Royal Navy, 1956; specialised Communications and Electronic Warfare, 1966; commanded HM Ships: Hubberston, 1968–70; Lynx, 1972–74; Exec. Officer, HM Yacht Britannia, 1976–78; Captain, 7th Frigate Sqn, 1981–83; commanded HM Ships: Argonaut, 1981–82; Cleopatra, 1982–83; Invincible, 1984–86; Asst Dir (Communications and Information Systems), IMS, NATO HQ, Brussels, 1988–91, retd. Consultant in communications and inf. systems and maritime affairs, 1991–2001. Gentleman Usher of the Green Rod, Order of the Thistle, 1997–. *Publications:* Man of Letters, 1990; The Falklands and the Dwarf, 1995. *Recreations:* fishing, archaeology. *Club:* New (Edinburgh).

LAYTON, family name of **Baron Layton.**

LAYTON, 3rd Baron *cr* 1947, of Danehill; **Geoffrey Michael Layton;** Director: Imperial Aviation Group, since 1992; Historical Aviation Group, since 1992; Wellington International Ltd, since 1992; Historical Aviation Mail Order Ltd, since 1996; *b* 18 July 1947; *s* of 2nd Baron Layton and Dorothy Rose (*d* 1994), *d* of Albert Luther Cross; *S* father, 1989; *m* 1st, 1969, Viviane Cracco (marr. diss. 1971); 2nd, 1989, Caroline Jane Soulis (marr. diss. 1999). *Educ:* St Paul's School; Stanford Univ., California; Univ. of Southern California. Director: The Toxbox Co. Ltd, 1986–93; Westminster and Whitehall Environmental Consultants Ltd, 1990–92. Trustee, Historical Aviation Foundn, 1995–. *Recreation:* riding. *Heir: uncle* Hon. David Layton, MBE [*b* 5 July 1914; *m* 1st, 1939, Elizabeth (marr. diss. 1972; she *d* 2000), *d* of Robert Gray; two *s* one *d*; 2nd, 1972, Joy Parkinson].
See also Hon. C. W. Layton.

LAYTON, Alexander William; QC 1995; barrister; a Recorder, since 2000; a Deputy High Court Judge, since 2007; *b* 23 Feb. 1952; *s* of Paul Henry Layton and Frances Evelyn Layton (*née* Weekes); *m* 1988, Sandy Forshaw (*née* Matheson); two *d. Educ:* Marlborough Coll.; Brasenose Coll., Oxford (MA); Ludwig-Maximilian Univ., Munich. Called to the Bar, Middle Temple, 1976 (Astbury Law Scholar), Bencher, 2004; Asst Recorder, 1998–2000. Chairman: British-German Jurists Assoc., 1988–93; Bar European Gp, 2005–07; Bd of Trustees, Brit. Inst. of Internat. and Comparative Law, 2005–. Trustee: Allachy Trust, 1979–; Rivendell Trust, 1979–2004; Lincoln Clinic and Centre for Psychotherapy, 2003–06; Frensham Heights Sch., 2008–. FCIArb 2000. *Publications:* (contrib.) The Bar on Trial, 1977; (jtly) European Civil Practice, 1989, 2nd edn 2004; (contrib.) Practitioners' Handbook of EC Law, 1998; (contrib.) Forum Shopping in the European Judicial Area, 2007. *Recreation:* family. *Address:* 20 Essex Street, WC2R 3AL. *T:* (020) 7842 1200, *Fax:* (020) 7842 1270; *e-mail:* alayton@20essexst.com.

LAYTON, Hon. Christopher Walter; Chairman: Action for a Global Climate Community, since 2003; Peace Building UK, since 2006; *b* 31 Dec. 1929; *s* of 1st Baron Layton, CH, CBE; *m* 1st, 1952, Anneliese Margaret, *d* of Joachim von Thadden, Hanover (marr. diss. 1957); one *s* one *d*; 2nd, 1961, Margaret Ann, *d* of Leslie Moon, Molesey, Surrey (marr. diss. 1995); two *d* (and one *d* decd); 3rd, 1995, Wendy Daniels, *d* of Kenneth Bartlett, Hemel Hempstead; one *d. Educ:* Oundle; King's Coll., Cambridge. Intelligence Corps, 1948–49; ICI Ltd, 1952; The Economist Intelligence Unit, 1953–54; Editorial writer, European affairs, The Economist, 1954–62; Economic Adviser to Liberal Party, 1962–69; Dir, Centre for European Industrial Studies, Bath Univ., 1968–71; Commission of European Communities: Chef de Cabinet to Commissioner Spinelli, 1971–73; Dir, Computer Electronics, Telecomms and Air Transp. Equipment Manufg, Directorate-Gen. of Internal Market and Industrial Affairs, 1973–81, now Hon. Dir-Gen.; Editor, Alliance, 1982–83, Associate Editor, New Democrat, 1983–85. Dir, World Order Project, Federal Trust, 1987–90; Trustee, One World Trust, 1986–; Founder Mem., Grimstone Community, 1990–2007; Vice Chm., Moor Trees, 2002–06. Contested: (L) Chippenham, Nov. 1962, 1964, 1966; (SDP) London W, European Parly Elecn, 1984. *Publications:* Transatlantic Investment, 1966; European Advanced Technology, 1968; Cross-frontier Mergers in Europe 1970; (jtly) Industry and Europe, 1971; (jtly) Ten Innovations: International Study on Development Technology and the Use of Qualified Scientists and Engineers in Ten Industries, 1972; Europe and the Global Crisis, 1987; A Step Beyond Fear, 1989; The Healing of Europe, 1990; A Climate Community: a European initiative with the South, 2001. *Recreations:* painting, sculpture, healing. *Address:* Monkswell House, Jordan Lane, Horrabridge, Yelverton, Devon PL20 7QY.

LAYTON, Peter Stephen; Founder and Managing Director: London Glassblowing, since 1976; Peter Layton & Associates Ltd, since 1992; *b* 21 June 1937; *s* of Freddie Layton (*né* Löwe) and Edith Beatrice Layton (*née* Hecht); *m* 1st, 1966, Tessa Schneideman (marr. diss. 1982; she *d* 2001); one *s*; 2nd, 1984, Ann Ashmore; one *s* one *d. Educ:* Bellevue Grammar Sch. for Boys, Bradford; Bradford Coll. of Art; Central Sch. of Art and Design (Dip.). Various lectureships and professorships including: Univ. of Iowa, Sacramento State Univ.,

Univ. of Calif, Davis and Art Inst. of Chicago, 1966–68; Stoke on Trent Coll. of Art, Hornsey Coll. of Art, Camberwell Coll. of Art, Croydon Coll. of Art and Sir John Cass Coll. of Art, 1968–78. Chairman: British Artists in Glass, 1983–85; Contemp. Glass Soc., 1997–99 (Hon. Life Mem.); Member: Glass Circle; Glass Assoc.; Glass Art Soc. Freeman: City of London; Glass Sellers' Co. Hon. DLitt Bradford, 2003. *Publications:* Glass Art, 1996; Neues Glas, 2003; Peter Layton and Friends, 2006. *Recreations:* art, travel, beachcombing, theatre, film, food, country living. *Address:* London Glassblowing, 7 The Leathermarket, Weston Street, SE1 3ER. *T:* (020) 7403 2800, *Fax:* (020) 7403 7778; *e-mail:* info@londonglassblowing.co.uk.

LAYTON, Stephen David, FRCO; conductor; Fellow and Director of Music, Trinity College, Cambridge, since 2006; *b* 23 Dec. 1966; *s* of David Layton and Hazel Layton (*née* Bestwick). *Educ:* Pilgrim's Sch., Winchester; Eton Coll. (Music Schol.); King's Coll., Cambridge (A. H. Mann Organ Schol.; BA 1988; MA 1991). FRCO 1985. Asst Organist, Southwark Cathedral, 1988–97; Dir of Music, 1997–2006, Organist, 1997–2004, Temple Church, London; Founder and Music Dir, Polyphony, 1986–; Music Dir, Holst Singers, 1993–. Conductor, BBC Promenade Concerts, 1995–; Chief Guest Conductor, Danish Nat. Choir, 1999–; Chief Conductor, Netherlands Kammerchor, 2001–05 (Guest Conductor, 1998–2001); conducted: Orch. of the Age of Enlightenment, 1999–; ENO, 2000, 2002; Australian Chamber Orch., 2000–; Irish Chamber Orch., 2001; Britten Sinfonia, 2001–; City of London Sinfonia, 2001–; Acad. of Ancient Music, 2002–; Scottish Chamber Orch., 2002–; English Chamber Orch., 2003–; London Sinfonietta, 2004–; Philadelphia Orch., 2005; *tours* as conductor include: USA, 1989, 1994, 1996, 2004; Brazil, 1995, 1998; Estonia, 1993, 1995; Australia, 2000, 2001. Recordings incl. premières of Pärt, Tavener and Adès. *Recreations:* food, cyberspace, kite flying, gadgets. *Address:* Trinity College, Cambridge CB2 1TQ. *Club:* Athenaeum.

LAZARE, Philippe Henri; Director-General, Sofipost, since 2004; *b* Neuilly-sur-Seine, 30 Oct. 1956; *s* of Robert Lazare and Suzanne (*née* Legallo); *m* 1995, Sophie Muth; two *s*, and two *s* from previous marriage. *Educ:* Lycée Marcel Roby, Saint-Germain-en-Laye; École Supérieure d'architecture, Paris-la-Défense (Architect Govt Dip.). Industrial buyer, 1983–87; Project Manager for 605 Peugeot, 1987–89; Peugeot Planning Manager, Soc. Gén. d'achats PSA gp, 1989–90; Groupe Sextant Avionique: Industrial sub-contracting Manager, 1990–91; Site Industrial Manager, 1991–93; Site Dir at Chatellerault, 1993–94; Manager, Peat Marwick Consultants, 1994–95; Air France: Dir, Maintenance Result Centre, 1995–96; Man. Dir, Industries Profit Centre, and Dep. Manager i/c industrial logistics, 1996; Chm., Servair Gp and Cie de réparation de moteurs d'avion (CRMA), 1997–98; Man. Dir, Lucien Barrière Gp, 1998–2000; Man. Dir, 2000–01, CEO, 2001, Eurotunnel; Dir of Buying and Cost-Reduction, Groupe La Poste, 2003–04. *Recreations:* sports: Rugby, show jumping.

LAZAREV, Alexander Nikolaevich; Principal Conductor, Japan Philharmonic Orchestra, 2008; *b* 5 July 1945; *m* Tamara Lazareva; one *d. Educ:* St Petersburg Conservatory; Moscow Conservatory. Bolshoi Theatre: Founder, Ensemble of Soloists, 1978; Chief Conductor and Artistic Dir, 1987–95; UK début with Liverpool Philharmonic Orch., 1987; Principal Guest Conductor: BBC SO, 1992–95; Royal Scottish Nat. Orch., 1994–97; Principal Conductor, Royal Scottish Nat. Orch., 1997–2005. Hon. Prof., Univ. of Glasgow, 2005. 1st Prize and Gold Medal, Karajan Comp., Berlin, 1972; People's Artist of Russia, 1982; Glinka Prize, 1986. *Address:* c/o Tennant Artists, Unit 2, 39 Tadema Road, SW10 0PZ.

LAZARIDIS, Stefanos, RDI 2003; freelance opera, ballet and theatre designer and director in UK and abroad, since 1967; Artistic Director and General Manager, Greek National Opera, 2006–07; *b* Ethiopia, 28 July 1942; *s* of Nicholas Lazaridis and Alexandra Cardovillis. *Educ:* Greek Sch., Addis Ababa; Ecole Internationale, Geneva; Byam Shaw Sch. of Art; Central Sch. of Speech and Drama. Professional début, Eccentricities of a Nightingale, Yvonne Arnaud Theatre, Guildford, 1967; *ballet:* El Amor Brujo, 1969, Knight Errant, 1975, Royal Ballet, Covent Garden; *theatre:* London (Almeida, Barbican and West End), Stratford-upon-Avon, Chichester Fest., Oxford, Guildford, Watford, Milan, Bologna, Paris, Athens, 1967–95; *opera:* prodns for ENO incl. Doctor Faust, The Mikado (SWET Award, for Doctor Faust and The Mikado, 1986), Hansel and Gretel, Lady Macbeth of Mtsensk, Italian season (Laurence Olivier Award, 2000); prodns for Royal Opera incl. The Greek Passion (Laurence Olivier Award, 2001), Wozzeck (Laurence Olivier Award, 2002), Wagner's Ring cycle, 2004–06; directed and designed: Oedipus Rex, Opera North; Duke Bluebeard's Castle, Oedipus Rex, Maria Stuarda, Scottish Opera; Orphée et Eurydice, Australian Opera, 1994; The Ark of Life, by Dimitriadis, world première, Athens, 1995; *arena prodn:* Carmen, Earl's Court, 1988, also internat. tour; *rock show:* Duran Duran, US tour, 1993; designs for opera houses of Paris, Berlin, Frankfurt, Munich, Stuttgart, Brussels, Zurich, La Scala Milan, Florence, Bologna, Venice, Tel Aviv, Amsterdam, Moscow, St Petersburg, Tokyo, Vancouver, Sydney, Melbourne, Houston, Los Angeles, NY and San Francisco; also Bregenz, Pesaro, and Bayreuth Festivals. Laurence Olivier and Evening Standard Awards for Most Outstanding Achievement in Opera, 1987; German Critics' Award, Designer of the Year, 1998; Diploma of Honour, Internat. Exhibn of Stage Design, Prague Quadrennial, 1999; Martinu Foundn Medal, for outstanding services to Martinu's operas, 2000. *Recreations:* reading, travel. *Address:* Kydathinaion 9, 10558 Athens, Greece.

LAZAROWICZ, Marek Jerzy, (Mark); MP (Lab) Edinburgh North and Leith, since 2001; *b* 8 Aug. 1953. *Educ:* Univ. of St Andrews (MA); Univ. of Edinburgh (LLB; Dip. Legal Practice). Member (Lab): City of Edinburgh DC, 1980–96; City of Edinburgh Council, 1999–2001. Special Rep. of the Prime Minister on carbon trading, 2008–. Mem., H of C Modernisation and Envtl Audit Cttees. *Publications:* (jtly) The Scottish Parliament: an introduction, 1999, 3rd edn 2003; various articles and papers on legal and political matters. *Address:* c/o House of Commons, SW1A 0AA; (constituency office) 86–88 Brunswick Street, Edinburgh EH7 5HV. *T:* (0131) 557 0577.

LAZENBY, Prof. Alec, AO 1988; FTSE, FIBiol, FAIAST; consultant on agricultural research and development and higher education, since 1991; *b* 4 March 1927; *s* of G. and E. Lazenby; *m* 1957, Ann Jennifer, *d* of R. A. Hayward; one *s* two *d. Educ:* Wath on Dearne Grammar Sch.; University Coll. of Wales, Aberystwyth. BSc 1949, MSc 1952, Wales; MA 1954, PhD 1959, ScD 1985, Cantab. Scientific Officer, Welsh Plant Breeding Station, 1949–53; Demonstr in Agricultural Botany, 1953–58, Lectr in Agricultural Botany, 1958–65, Univ. of Cambridge; Fellow and Asst Tutor, Fitzwilliam Coll., Cambridge, 1962–65; Foundation Prof. of Agronomy, Univ. of New England, NSW, 1965–70, now Professor Emeritus; Vice-Chancellor, Univ. of New England, Armidale, NSW, 1970–77; Dir, Grassland Res. Inst., 1977–82; Vice-Chancellor, Univ. of Tasmania, 1982–91. Principal Consultant, Internat. Develt Prog., Aust. Univs, 1985–99. Vis. Prof., Reading Univ., 1978. Hon. Professorial Fellow, Univ. of Wales, 1979; Hon. Prof., Victoria Univ. of Technol., 1992–97. Hon. DRurSci New England, NSW, 1981; Hon. LLD Tasmania, 1992. Centenary Medal, Australia, 2003. *Publications:* (ed jtly) Intensive Pasture Production, 1972; (ed jtly) Australian Field Crops, vol. I, 1975, vol. II, 1979; Australia's Plant Breeding Needs, 1986; (ed jtly) The Grass Crop, 1988; (jtly) The Story of IDP, 1999; (ed jtly) Competition and Succession in Pastures, 2001; papers on: pasture plant breeding; agronomy; weed ecology, in various scientific jls. *Recreation:* golf. *Address:* 16/99 Groom Street, Hughes, ACT 2605, Australia.

LEA OF CRONDALL, Baron *cr* 1999 (Life Peer), of Crondall in the county of Hampshire; **David Edward Lea**, OBE 1978; Assistant General Secretary of the Trades Union Congress, 1977–99; *b* Tyldesley, Lancs, 2 Nov. 1937; *s* of Edward Cunliffe Lea and Lilian May Lea. *Educ:* Farnham Grammar Sch.; Christ's Coll., Cambridge (MA). Pres., CU Liberal Club, 1960; Nat. Pres., Union of Liberal Students, 1961; Inaugural Chair, Cambridge Univ. Students' Representative Council, 1961. Nat. Service, RHA, 1955–57. Economist Intelligence Unit, 1961; Economic Dept, TUC, 1964, Asst Sec., 1967, Sec. 1970. Jt Sec., TUC-Labour Party Liaison Cttee, 1972–86; Secretary: TUC Cttee on European Strategy, 1989–99; Envmt Action Gp, 1989–99; Task Force on Representation at Work, 1994–99; Chm., Econ. Cttee, 1980–91, Mem. Steering Cttee, 1991–99, Vice Pres., 1997–98, ETUC; Member: Royal Commn on the Distribution of Income and Wealth, 1974–79; Adv. Gp on Channel Tunnel and Cross-Channel Services, 1974–75; Cttee of Inquiry on Industrial Democracy, 1975–77; Energy Commn, 1977–79; Retail Prices Index Adv. Cttee, 1977–99; Delors Cttee on Economic and Social Concepts in the Community, 1977–79; NEDC Cttee on Finance for Investment, 1978–92; Kreisky Commn on Unemployment in Europe, 1986–89; Franco-British Council, 1982–99; EU Steering Cttee on Social Dialogue, 1992–99; Central Arbitration Cttee, 2000–; UK Round Table on Sustainable Develt, 1995–99; Chm., Round Table Gp on Greening Business, 1997–98; Expert Adviser, UN Commn on Transnational Corporations, 1977–81; Hon. Mem., UK Delegn, Earth Summit on Envmt and Develt, Rio, 1992. Mem., Sub Cttee A, EU Cttee, 1999–, Sub Cttee C, Foreign Affairs, Defence and Develt, 2003–, H of L; Chm., All Party Parly Gp on Bolivia, 2005–; Vice-Chairman: All Party Gp on Africa, 2003–; PLP Gp on Transport, 2003–; Anglo-Swiss Parly Gp, 2003–; Franco-British Parly Gp, 2004–; Vice-Pres., All Party Gp on Arts and Heritage, 2003–; Sec., All Party Parly Gp on Algeria; Treas., All Party Parly Gps on Serbia and Macedonia. Governor, NIESR, 1981–; Trustee, Employment Policy Inst., 1992–99. Chm., Farnham Roads Action, 1986–; Mem. Cttee, Tilford Bach Soc., 1995–99; Patron, Third Age Trust, 1991–97. Joined Labour Party, 1963. FRSA 1993. Mem. Editl Bd, New Economy (IPPR review), 1993–2000. *Publications:* Trade Unionism, 1966; (contrib.) The Multinational Enterprise, 1971; Industrial Democracy (TUC), 1974; Keynes Plus: a participatory economy (ETUC), 1979; (jtly) Europe and Your Rights at Work, 2006. *Address:* South Court, Crondall, Hants GU10 5QF. *T:* (01252) 850711; 17 Ormonde Mansions, 106 Southampton Row, WC1B 4BP. *T:* (020) 7405 6237. *Club:* Bourne (Farnham).

LEA, Jeremy Hugh Chaloner; His Honour Judge Lea; a Circuit Judge, since 2005; Designated Family Judge, Leicester County Court, since 2008; *b* 29 March 1954; *s* of Henry Hugh Edgar Lea and Teresa Lea (*née* Baker). *m* 1992, Jane Elizabeth Turrill; one *s* one *d*. *Educ:* John Fisher Sch., Purley; Univ. of Sussex (BA 1976; LLB 1977); Univ. de Strasbourg. Called to the Bar, Middle Temple, 1978; a barrister, Midland Circuit, 1979–2005; a Recorder, 2001–05. *Recreations:* coarse ski-ing, real ale, watching cricket. *Address:* c/o Leicester County Court, 90 Wellington Street, Leicester LE1 6ZZ. *T:* (0116) 222 2323.

LEA, Vice-Adm. Sir John (Stuart Crosbie), KBE 1979; retired; Director General, Naval Manpower and Training, 1977–80; *b* 4 June 1923; *m* 1947, Patricia Anne Thoseby; one *s* two *d*. *Educ:* Boxgrove Sch., Guildford; Shrewsbury Sch.; RNEC, Keyham. Entered RN, 1941; Cruisers Sheffield and Glasgow, 1943; RNEC, 1942–45; HMS Birmingham, 1945; entered Submarines, 1946; HMS/Ms Talent, Tireless, Aurochs, Explorer; Sen. Engr, HMS Forth (Depot Ship), 1952–53; on Staff, RNEC, 1954–57; psc 1958; Sqdn Engr Officer, 2nd Destroyer Sqdn and HMS Daring, 1959–61; Staff of CinC Portsmouth, 1961–62; Naval Staff in Ops Div., 1963–65; Engr Officer, HMS Centaur, 1966; Staff of Flag Officer Submarines; Dep. Supt, Clyde Submarine Base, 1967–68; idc 1969; Dir of Naval Admin. Planning, 1970–71; Cdre HMS Nelson, 1972–75; Asst Chief of Fleet Support, 1976–77. Comdr 1957; Captain 1966; Rear-Adm. 1976; Vice-Adm. 1978. Chm., 1980–86, Dir, 1986–88, GEC Marine & Industrial Gears Ltd. Chairman: Portsmouth Naval Heritage Trust, 1983–87; Regular Forces Employment Assoc., 1986–89; RN and RM Br. and Special Duties Officers Benevolent Fund, 1993–98. Chm., RN Athletics Assoc., 1972–80; Pres., RN Boxing Assoc., 1975–80. President: Hayling Island Horticultural Soc., 1994–2006 (Chm., 1980–94); Hants Autistic Soc., 1988–95. Trustee, Hayling Island Community Centre, 1981–2001; Plumbers Museum and Workshop, Singleton, 1993–2001. Master, Worshipful Co. of Plumbers, 1988–89. *Recreations:* walking, woodwork, gardening.

LEA, Judith Elizabeth; *see* Hackitt, J. E.

LEA, Ruth Jane; Director, Global Vision, since 2007; Economic Adviser, Arbuthnot Banking Group, since 2007 (non-executive Director, since 2005); *b* 22 Sept. 1947; *d* of Thomas Lea and late Jane (*née* Brown). *Educ:* Lymm Grammar Sch.; York Univ. (BA); Bristol Univ. (MSc). FSS 1996. Asst Statistician, later Sen. Economic Assistant, HM Treasury, 1970–73; Lectr in Econs, Thames Poly., 1973–74; Statistician: CS Coll., 1974–77; HM Treasury, 1977–78; CSO, 1978–84; Statistician, 1984–87, Dep. Dir, Invest in Britain Bureau, 1987–88, DTI; Sen. Economist, 1988–90, Chief Economist, 1990–93, Mitsubishi Bank; Chief UK Economist, Lehman Bros, 1993–94; Econs Ed., ITN, 1994–95; Hd of Policy Unit, Inst. of Dirs, 1995–2003; Dir, Centre for Policy Studies, 2004–07. Member: Retail Prices Adv. Cttee, 1992–94; NCC, 1993–96; Nurses' Pay Rev. Body, 1994–98; Bd, ESRC Res. Priorities (formerly ESRC Res. Centres), 1996–97. ONS Stats Adv. Cttee, 1996–97. Member Council: REconS, 1995–2000; Univ. of London, 2001–06. Gov., LSE, 2003–08. FRSA 1993. Hon. DBA Greenwich, 1997. *Publications:* numerous research papers and articles on economic issues. *Recreations:* music, natural history and countryside, heritage, philately. *Address:* 25 Redbourne Avenue, N3 2BP. *T:* (020) 8346 3482. *Club:* Reform.

LEA, Sir Thomas (William), 5th Bt *cr* 1892, of The Larches, Kidderminster and Sea Grove, Dawlish; *b* 6 Sept. 1973; *s* of Sir Julian Lea, 4th Bt and of Gerry Valerie, *d* of late Captain Gibson C. Fahnestock; *S* father, 1990. *Educ:* Uppingham Sch. *Heir: b* Alexander Julian Lea, *b* 28 Oct. 1978.

LEACH, family name of **Baron Leach of Fairford**.

LEACH OF FAIRFORD, Baron *cr* 2006 (Life Peer), of Fairford in the County of Gloucestershire; **(Charles Guy) Rodney Leach**, MA; Director, Jardine Matheson Holdings Ltd, since 1984; Deputy Chairman, Jardine Lloyd Thompson Group plc, since 1997; *b* 1 June 1934; *s* of late Charles Harold Leach and Nora Eunice Ashworth; *m* 1st, 1963, Felicity Ballantyne (marr. diss. 1989); two *s* three *d*; 2nd, 1993, Mrs Jessica Violet Douglas-Home, *qv. Educ:* Harrow; Balliol Coll., Oxford (1st Cl. Hon. Mods, 1st Cl. Lit. Hum.). N. M. Rothschild & Sons, 1963–76: Partner, 1968; Dir, 1970; Director: Trade Development Bank, 1976–83; Matheson & Co., 1983–; Hongkong Land, 1985–; Dairy Farm, 1987–; Mandarin Oriental, 1987–; Robert Fleming Hldgs Ltd, 1999–2000; Rothschild Continuation AG, 2006–. Chairman: Business for Sterling, 1999–; Open

Europe, 2005–. Mem. Bd, British Library, 1996–2004. *Publication:* Europe: a concise encyclopedia of the European Union, 1998, 4th edn 2004. *Recreations:* the humanities, sport, bridge. *Address:* 3 Lombard Street, EC3V 9AQ. *T:* (020) 7816 8100; House of Lords, SW1A 0PW. *Clubs:* White's, Portland.

LEACH OF FAIRFORD, Lady; *see* Douglas-Home, J. V.

LEACH, Allan William, FCLIP; Director-General and Librarian, National Library for the Blind, 1982–95; *b* 9 May 1931; *yr s* of Frank Leach, MBE and Margaret Ann Bennett; *m* 1962, Betty (*d* 2004), *e d* of William George Gadsby and Doris Cree; one *s* one *d. Educ:* Watford Grammar Sch.; Loughborough Coll. BA Open; DPA London. Various posts with Hertfordshire County Library, 1948–59; Librarian, RAF Sch. of Educn, 1949–51; Regional Librarian, Warwickshire County Libr., 1959–65; County Librarian, Bute County Libr., 1965–71; Librarian and Curator, Ayr Burgh, 1971–74; Dir of Library Services, Kyle and Carrick District, 1974–82. Vice-Chm., UK Assoc. of Braille Producers, 1994–96 (Chm., 1991–94); Member: Standing Cttee, Section of Libraries for the Blind, IFLA, 1983–95 (Chm., 1985–87; Ed., Newsletter, 1985–92); Nat. Steering Cttee, Share the Vision, 1992–95. Chm., Ulverscroft Foundn, 1999– (Trustee, 1993–). Editor: Rickmansworth Historian, 1961–66; Ayrshire Collections, 1973–82. *Publications:* Begin Here, 1966; Rothesay Tramways, a brief history, 1969; Round old Ayr (with R. Brash and G. S. Copeland), 1972; Libraries in Ayr, 1975; Looking Ahead, 1987; articles on libraries, local history, literature, braille and educn. *Recreations:* music, the countryside, books, people. *Address:* 4 Windsor Road, Hazel Grove, Stockport, Cheshire SK7 4SW. *T:* (0161) 285 1287.

LEACH, Clive William, CBE 2000; Chairman: YFM (formerly Yorkshire Enterprise) Group Ltd, since 1995; Gabriel Communications Ltd, since 1997; *b* 4 Dec. 1934; *s* of Stanley and Laura Leach; *m* 1st, 1958, Audrey (*née* Parker) (*d* 1978); three *s*; 2nd, 1980, Stephanie (*née* McGinn); one *s. Educ:* Sir John Leman Grammar Sch., Beccles, Suffolk. Gen. Sales Manager, Tyne Tees Television, 1968–74; Sales Dir, 1974–79, Dir of Sales and Marketing, 1979–82, Trident Television; Man. Dir, Link Television, 1982–85; Dir of Sales and Marketing, 1985–88, Man. Dir, 1988–93, Yorkshire Television; Man. Dir, 1985–88, Chm., 1988–93, Yorkshire Television Enterprises. Chairman: Yorkshire Television Internat., 1988–93; Yorkshire-Tyne Tees Television Holdings, 1993 (Gp Chief Exec., 1992–93); Dir, ITN, 1988–93. Chm., Yorkshire Fund Managers Ltd, 1996–; Dir, British Small Cos Venture Capital Trust plc, 1996–2004; Durham CCC (Hldgs) Ltd, 2005–. Dep. Chm., Regl Chamber, subseq. Regl Assembly, for Yorks and Humber, 2001–. Chairman: Leeds TEC, 1991–2000; Leeds HA, 1996–2000; W Yorks Learning and Skills Council, 2000–; Yorks Cultural Consortium, 2001–; Dir, Opera North Ltd, 1992–2003. FRSA; MCIM 1994. *Recreations:* golf, cricket, travel. *Address:* The White House, Barkston Ash, Tadcaster, N Yorks LS24 9TT. *Clubs:* Reform, MCC; Alwoodley Golf.

LEACH, Prof. Donald Frederick, CBE 1996; Principal, 1985–96, and Vice Patron, 1993–96, Queen Margaret College, Edinburgh; *b* 24 June 1931; *s* of Frederick John Mansell Leach and Annie Ivy Foster; *m* 1st, 1952, June Valentine Reid (*d* 1997); two *s* one *d*; 2nd, 1999, Marilyn Annette Jeffcoat. *Educ:* John Ruskin Grammar Sch., Croydon; Norwood Tech. Coll.; Dundee Tech. Coll.; Univ. of London (Ext. Student, BSc); Jordanhill Coll. of Educn, MInstP, CPhys, 1960; FIMA, CMath, 1969; MBCS, CEng, 1968. Pilot Officer, RAF, 1951–53. Physicist, British Jute Trade Res. Assoc., Dundee, 1954–65; Tech. Dir, A. R. Bolton & Co., 1965–66; Napier College: Lectr and Sen. Lectr in Maths, 1966–68; Head, Dept of Maths and Computing, 1968–74; Asst Principal/Dean, Faculty of Science, 1974–85. Interim Chief Exec., Edinburgh's Lifelong Learning Partnership, 1998. Chairman: Creative Edge Software Ltd, 1999–2002; D. M. Vaughan & Co. Ltd, 1999–2004. Member: Council for Professions Supplementary to Medicine, 1985–97; Exec. Cttee, Scottish Council Develt and Indust., 1987–96; Boards of: Edinburgh Chamber of Commerce and Manufactures, 1991–98 (Sen. Vice-Pres., 1996; Pres., 1996–98); Leith Chamber of Commerce, 1991–96 (Pres., 1994–96); British Chambers of Commerce, 1997–99; Higher Educn Quality Council, 1992–96; The Capital Enterprise Trust, 1993–98. Director: Businessweb Ltd, 1999–; Mull Theatre Ltd, 2004–. Trustee, Mendelssohn on Mull Trust, 2005–. Vice Convenor, One Parent Families Scotland, 1998–99. Contested: (L) W Edinburgh, 1959; (L) E Fife by-election, 1961; (Lab) Kinross and W Perthshire, 1970. Hon. Prof., Queen Margaret Coll., 1993. Hon. Fellow, Soc. of Chiropodists and Podiatrists, 1994. FRSA. Hon. DEd Queen Margaret UC, 2003. *Publications:* Future Employment and Technological Change (jtly), 1986; papers in sci., tech. and eductl jls on textile physics, electronic instrumentation, maths and statistics, higher educn. *Recreations:* music, Scrabble, walking, cooking. *Address:* 18 Rothesay Terrace, Edinburgh EH3 7RY. *T:* (0131) 226 7166. *Clubs:* New, Scottish Arts (Edinburgh).

LEACH, Admiral of the Fleet Sir Henry (Conyers), GCB 1978 (KCB 1977); DL; *b* 18 Nov. 1923; 3rd *s* of Captain John Catterall Leach, MVO, DSO, RN and Evelyn Burrell Leach (*née* Lee), Yarner, Bovey Tracey, Devon; *m* 1958, Mary Jean (*d* 1991), *yr d* of Adm. Sir Henry McCall, KCVO, KBE, CB, DSO; two *d. Educ:* St Peter's Court, Broadstairs; RNC Dartmouth. Cadet 1937; served in: cruiser Mauritius, S Atlantic and Indian Ocean, 1941–42; battleship Duke of York, incl. Scharnhorst action, 1943–45; destroyers in Mediterranean, 1945–46; spec. Gunnery, 1947; various gunnery appts, 1948–51; Gunnery Officer, cruiser Newcastle, Far East, 1953–55; staff appts, 1955–59; comd destroyer Dunkirk, 1959–61; comd frigate Galatea as Captain (D) 27th Sqdn and Mediterranean, 1965–67; Dir of Naval Plans, 1968–70; comd Commando Ship Albion, 1970; Asst Chief of Naval Staff (Policy), 1971–73; Flag Officer First Flotilla, 1974–75; Vice-Chief of Defence Staff, 1976–77; C-in-C, Fleet, and Allied C-in-C, Channel and Eastern Atlantic, 1977–79; Chief of Naval Staff and First Sea Lord, 1979–82. First and Principal Naval ADC to the Queen, 1979–82. psc 1952; jssc 1961. Chm., St Dunstan's, 1983–98 (Hon. Vice Pres., 1999–); President: RN Benevolent Soc., 1983–95; Sea Cadet Assoc., 1984–93; Royal Bath and West of England Soc., 1993 (Vice-Pres., 1994–); Patron, Hampshire RBL, 1994–. Chm. Council, King Edward VII Hosp., 1987–98. Gov., Cranleigh Sch., 1983–93. Freeman: City of London; Shipwrights' Co.; Hon. Freeman, Merchant Taylors' Co. DL Hampshire, 1992. *Publications:* Endure no Makeshifts (autobiog.), 1993; Anecdotage, 1996. *Recreations:* fishing, shooting, gardening, antique furniture repair. *Address:* Wonston Lea, Wonston, Winchester, Hants SO21 3LS.

LEACH, Jennifer Irene, CBE 2006; Chief Guide, Girlguiding UK (Guide Association), 2001–06; Chief Commissioner, Commonwealth Girl Guides Associations, 2001–06; *b* 11 Oct. 1944; *d* of Arthur and Beatrice Garner; *m* 1966, Arthur John Leach; one *s* one *d*. Guide Association: Unit Guider, 1974–87; Dist Comr, 1980–86; Co. Comr, W Yorks, 1987–92; Chief Comr, NE England, 1994–99. FRSA 2002. *Recreations:* learning about Norman church architecture, cooking, France. *Address:* Laithe Croft, Rastrick, Brighouse, W Yorks HD6 3HL. *T: and Fax:* (01484) 714950.

LEACH, Penelope, PhD; psychologist and writer on childcare; *b* 19 Nov. 1937; *d* of late Nigel Marlin Balchin and Elisabeth Balchin; *m* 1963, Gerald Leach (*d* 2004); one *s* one *d*. *Educ:* Newnham Coll., Cambridge (BA Hons 1959); LSE (Dip. in Soc. Sci. Admin 1960;

MA Psychol. 1962; PhD Psychol. 1964). Home Office, 1960–61; Lectr in Psychol., LSE, 1965–67; Res. Officer and Res. Fellow, MRC, 1967–76; Ext Med. Ed., Penguin Books, 1970–78; Founder and Dir, Lifetime Productions (childcare videos), 1985–87; Res. Consultant, Internat. Centre for Child Studies, 1984–90. Dir, Families, Children and Child Care Project, 1997–2005, and Hon. Sen. Res. Fellow, 1997–2002, Royal Free and UCL Med. Sch., Univ. of London. Hon. Senior Research Fellow: Tavistock Centre, 2000–; Inst. for the Study of Children, Families and Social Issues, Birkbeck Coll., Univ. of London, 2002–. Mem., Voluntary Licensing Authy on IVF, 1985–89; Comr, Commn on Social Justice, 1993–95; Mem., Commn on Children and Violence, 1993–95. Founder and Parent-Educn Co-ordinator, End Physical Punishment for Children, 1989–; Chm., Child Develt Soc., 1993–95 (Pres., 1992–93); Pres., Nat. Child Minders' Assoc., 1999–; Vice-President: Pre-School Playgroups Assoc., 1977; Health Visitors Assoc., 1982–99. Mem. Adv. Council, Amer. Inst. for Child, Adolescent and Family Studies, 1993–. Mem., professional socs and assocs; FBPsS 1988; Hon. Fellow, Dept of Mental Health, Bristol Univ., 1988. Hon. DEd Kingston, 1996. *Publications:* Babyhood, 1974; Baby and Child, 1977, 2nd edn 1989; Who Cares?, 1979; The Parents' A–Z, 1984; The First Six Months, 1987; The Babypack, 1990; Children First, 1994; Your Baby and Child, 1997, 3rd edn 2003; Child Care: what we know and what we need to know, 2009. *Recreations:* cooking, family and friends, gardening, travel. *Address:* 2 Bull Lane, Lewes, E Sussex BN7 1UA. *T:* (01273) 474702.

LEACH, Philippa Mary; *see* McAtasney, P. M.

LEACH, Rodney, PhD; CEng; FRINA; FCIM; company director; Chief Executive and Managing Director, VSEL Consortium plc, 1986–88; Chief Executive, 1985–88, and Chairman, 1986–88, Vickers Shipbuilding and Engineering Ltd; Chairman, Cammell Laird Shipbuilders Ltd, 1985–88; *b* 3 March 1932; *s* of Edward and Alice Leach; *m* 1958, Eira Mary (*née* Tuck); three *s* one *d. Educ:* Baines Grammar Sch., Poulton Le Fylde, Lancs; Birmingham Univ. (BSc, PhD). CEng, FRINA 1987; FCIM (FInstM 1972); FCMI(FIIM 1987). Radiation Physicist, Nuclear Power Plant Co. Ltd, 1957; Physicist, UKAEA, 1960; Sen. Physicist, South of Scotland Electricity Board, 1963; Associate, McKinsey & Co. Inc., 1965, Partner, 1970; Peninsular & Oriental Steam Navigation Co.: Hd of European and Air Transport Div., 1974; Dir, 1978–85; Chairman: P&O European Transport Services Ltd, 1979–83; P&O Cruises Ltd, 1980–85. Director: Jasmin plc, 1989–97; United Utilities (formerly North West Water Group) plc, 1989–99; Mem., NW Water Authority, 1989; Vice-Chm. and Dir, S Cumbria Community and Mental Health NHS Trust, 1993–97. Member: Gen. Council, Cumbria Tourist Bd, 1986–92; Northern Council for Sport and Recreation, 1991–95. Dir, 1989–93, Vice-Chm., 1991–94, Renaissance Arts Theatre Trust Ltd. Pres., Lakeland Sinfonia Concert Soc., 1998–2004. Conseiller Spécial, Chambre de Commerce et d'Industrie de Boulogne-sur-Mer et de Montreuil, 1989–94. Mem., RYA, 1977–. Gov., St Anne's Sch., Windermere, 1991–97. Liveryman: Worshipful Company of Carmen, 1976; Worshipful Company of Shipwrights, 1988–; Freeman, City of London, 1976. FRSA 1989. *Publications:* (jtly) Containerization: the key to low cost transport, 1965; frequent papers in scientific and technical jls, 1965–72. *Recreations:* fell-walking, sailing, gardening, literature. *Address:* April Cottage, Loughrigg Meadow, Ambleside, Cumbria LA22 0DZ. *T:* (01539) 431800. *Club:* Royal Automobile.

LEACH, Stephen James, CB 2007; Director of Criminal Justice, Northern Ireland Office, and Chairman, Criminal Justice Board, since 2000; *b* 12 Feb. 1951; *s* of late Edward Stephen Leach and Mollie Leach (*née* O'Hara); *m* 1982, Jane Williams; one *s* two *d. Educ:* De La Salle Coll., Jersey; Peterhouse, Cambridge (1st cl. Hons English Tripos). NI Office, 1975–84; Dept of Energy, 1984–87; Prin. Private Sec. to Sec. of State for NI, 1988–90; Humphrey Fulbright Fellow, Univ. of Minnesota, 1990–91; Northern Ireland Office: responsibilities in security, personnel policy and political development, 1991–96; Associate Political Dir, then Associate Policing and Security Dir, 1996–2000. *Recreations:* reading, tennis, watching Rugby. *Address:* Northern Ireland Office, Stormont, Belfast BT4 3SX. *T:* (028) 9052 7500; *e-mail:* stephen.leach@nio.x.gsi.gov.uk.

LEADBETTER, Alan James, CBE 1994; DSc; Directeur Adjoint, Institut Laue Langevin, Grenoble, France, 1994–99; *b* 28 March 1934; *s* of Robert and Edna Leadbetter; *m* 1957, Jean Brenda Williams; one *s* one *d. Educ:* Liverpool Univ. (BSc 1954; PhD 1957); Bristol Univ. (DSc 1971). CPhys 1972; FInstP 1972; CChem 1980; FRSC 1980. Fellow, NRCC, 1957–59; Res. Asst, Lectr and Reader, Univ. of Bristol, 1959–74; Prof. of Phys. Chem., Univ. of Exeter, 1975–82; Associate Dir, Science, Rutherford Appleton Lab., SERC, 1982–88; Dir, Daresbury Lab., SERC, 1988–94. Chairman: Internat. Scientific Adv. Bd, Vestale project, French Atomic Energy Commn, 2002–06; Evaluation Panels for EC Sixth Framework Programme: Res. Infrastructures action, 2002–06; Marie-Curie actions, 2004–07; Member: Divl Review Cttee, Los Alamos Nat. Lab., 1999–2003; Technical Adv. Cttee, Australian Nuclear Sci. and Technol. Orgn, 2000–06. Hon. Professor: Univ. of Manchester, 1989–94; Univ. of Hull, 1992–2005; Vis. Prof., De Montfort Univ., 1994–2001; Hon. Vis. Prof., Univ. of Exeter, 2002–05. Hon. DSc De Montfort, 2000. *Publications:* res. papers in chem. and phys in learned jls. *Recreations:* gardening, walking, cooking. *Address:* 23 Hillcrest Park, Exeter EX4 4SH.

See also M. Leadbetter.

LEADBETTER, Michael; consultant in children's and adult care services; Founder and Managing Director, Leadbetter Ltd, since 2003; Chairman, Children's Workforce Development Council, since 2007; *b* 25 July 1946; *s* of Robert Leadbetter and Edna (*née* Garlic); *m* Pamela Corti; two *s. Educ:* Ladybarn Secondary Mod. Sch.; Manchester Coll. of Sci. and Technol.; Manchester Coll., of Art and Design (DA); Manchester Univ. Extra Mural Dept (CQSW); MA (Econ) Manchester Univ. 1982. Works and prodn manager, 1971–72; Manchester Social Services: Social Worker, then Sen. Social Worker, 1972–82; Residential and Day Care Services Manager, 1982–86; Director of Social Services: Tameside, 1986–92; Essex, 1993–2003. Pres., Assoc. of Dirs of Social Services, 2001–02. Mem. Bd, General Social Care Council, 2007–. Chairman: Voice; Parentline Plus; Founder Mem., British Inst. of Transactional Analysis, 1974. England International, Rugby Union, 1970; 35 appearances for Lancs, 1968–74; Rugby League professional, Rochdale Hornets, 1974–76. *Recreations:* weight training, ski-ing, food, wine, opera. *Club:* England Internationals.

See also A. J. Leadbetter.

LEADLAY, Prof. Peter Francis, DPhil, PhD; FRS 2000; FRSC; Herchel Smith Professor of Biochemistry, University of Cambridge, since 2006; Fellow of Clare College, Cambridge, since 1979; Co-Founder and Director, BIOTICA Technology Ltd, since 1996; *b* 13 Dec. 1949; *s* of late Kenneth Rupert Simpson Leadlay, RN and Ellen Theresa Leadlay (*née* Coleman); *m* 1974, Christina Maria Peake; three *d. Educ:* St Joseph's Coll., London; New Coll., Oxford (Gibbs Schol.; BA 1971); Corpus Christi Coll., Oxford (Sen. Schol.; DPhil 1974; MA 1974); Clare Coll., Cambridge (PhD 1979). FRSC 2006. Royal Soc. European Res. Fellow, ETH, Zürich, 1974–76; Demonstr, Dept of Biochemistry, and Jun. Res. Fellow, Wolfson Coll., Univ. of Oxford, 1976–79; University of Cambridge: Demonstr in Biochemistry, 1979–84; Lectr, 1984–95; Reader, 1995–99; Prof. of Molecular Enzymology, 1999–2006; Sen. Res. Fellow, BBSRC, 1999–2004. Blaise Pascal Res. Prof., Institut Pasteur, Paris, 2002–03. Remsen Award, Amer. Chem. Soc., 2007. *Publications:* Enzyme Chemistry, 1969; articles in scientific jls, particularly on enzymes and antibiotic biosynthesis. *Recreations:* reading, walking, sailing. *Address:* Department of Biochemistry, University of Cambridge, 80 Tennis Court Road, Cambridge CB2 1GA. *T:* (01223) 766041.

LEAHY, Helen Blodwen R.; *see* Rees Leahy.

LEAHY, Sir John (Henry Gladstone), KCMG 1981 (CMG 1973); HM Diplomatic Service, retired; *b* 7 Feb. 1928; *s* of late William Henry Gladstone and late Ethel Leahy; *m* 1954, Elizabeth Anne, *d* of late J. H. Pitchford, CBE; two *s* two *d. Educ:* Tonbridge Sch.; Clare Coll., Cambridge; Yale University. RAF, 1950–52; FO, 1952–54 (Asst Private Sec. to Minister of State, 1953–54); 3rd, later 2nd Sec., Singapore, 1955–57; FO, 1957–58; 2nd, later 1st Sec., Paris, 1958–62; FO, 1962–65; Head of Chancery, Tehran, 1965–68; Counsellor, FCO, 1969; Head of Personnel Services Dept, 1969–70; Head of News Dept, FCO, 1971–73; Counsellor and Head of Chancery, Paris, 1973–75; seconded as Under Sec., NI Office, 1975–76; Asst Under-Sec. of State, FCO, 1977–79; Ambassador to South Africa, 1979–82; Dep. Under-Sec. of State, FCO, 1982–84; High Comr, Australia, 1984–88. Chm., Lonrho, 1994–97 (Dir, 1993–98; Vice-Chm., 1994); Dir, The Observer, 1989–93. Chm., Urban Foundn (London), 1991–94 (Exec. Dir, 1989–91). Pro-Chancellor, City Univ., 1991–97. Chm., British-Australia Soc., 1994–97. Mem., Franco-British Council (Chm., 1989–93). Master, Skinners' Co., 1993–94. Hon. DCL City, 1997. Officier, Légion d'Honneur (France), 1996. *Publication:* A Life of Spice, 2006. *Recreation:* golf. *Address:* 16 Ripley Chase, The Goffs, Eastbourne, East Sussex BN21 1HB. *T:* (01323) 725368.

LEAHY, Michael James, OBE 2004; General Secretary, Community (formerly Iron and Steel Trades Confederation), since 1999; *b* 7 Jan. 1949; *s* of Michael James Cyril Leahy, ISM, and Iris Jarrett Leahy; *m* 1974, Irene Powell; two *s. Educ:* Twmpath Secondary Modern Sch., Pontypool. Chargehand, Cold Rolling Dept, Panteg Works, Richard Thompson & Baldwins Ltd, 1965–77; Iron and Steel Trades Confederation, later Community: Mem., 1965–; Organiser, 1977–86; Sen. Organiser, 1986–92; Asst Gen. Sec. Elect, 1992–93; Asst Gen. Sec., 1993–98; Gen. Sec. Elect, 1998–99. Various posts, British Steel/Corus Gp plc, 1995– (Employees' Sec., Eur. Works Council, 1998–). Chm., Steel Partnership Trng Ltd, subseq. Knowledge Skills Partnership, 2000–; Member Board: Unions Today Ltd, 1999–2002; UK Steel Enterprise Ltd, 2003–. Mem., 1992–, Chm., 1998–, Steel Co-ordinating Cttee, Nat. Trades Union; Mem. Exec. Council, CSEU, 1994–99; Mem., 1995–2002, Mem., Sub-cttee for Mkts and Forward Studies, 1995–2002, Consultative Cttee, ECSC; General Federation of Trade Unions: Mem., Exec. Council, 1996–2003; Mem., Educnl Trust, 1996–2003 (Trustee, 1999–); Vice Pres., 1999–2001; Pres., 2001–03; Mem. Gen. Council, 1999–, Mem., Exec. Cttee, 2000–, TUC; Mem., Consultative Commn on Industrial Change, Eur. Econ. and Social Cttee, 2002–. Hon. Sec., British Section, 1999–, Pres., Iron, Steel and Non-Ferrous Metals Dept, 1999–, Internat. Metalworkers Fedn; European Metalworkers' Federation: Member: Exec. Cttee, 1999– (Steering Gp, 2003–); Industrial Policy Cttee, 1999–; Steel Cttee, 1999–. Mem., Central Arbitration Cttee, 2002–. Labour Party: Mem., 1966–; Member: NEC, 1996; Nat. Policy Forum, 1996–99; Auditor, 2002–. Chm., Bevan Foundn, 2000–02 (Mem., Bd of Dirs, 2002–; Chm. Trustees, 2002–); Pres., Welsh Trust for Prevention of Abuse, 2005–. FRSA. *Recreations:* golf, Rugby. *Address:* Community, 324 Gray's Inn Road, WC1X 8DD. *T:* (020) 7239 1200.

LEAHY, Sir Terence Patrick, (Sir Terry), Kt 2002; Chief Executive, Tesco plc, since 1997; *s* of Terence and Elizabeth Leahy; *m* Alison; two *s* one *d. Educ:* St Edward's Coll., Liverpool; UMIST (Bsc Hons Mgt Scis). Joined Tesco, 1979, as Mktg Exec.; Marketing Dir, 1984–86; Dir, 1992–; Dep. Man. Dir, 1995–97. *Recreations:* sport, reading, theatre, architecture. *Address:* Tesco plc, Tesco House, PO Box 18, Delamare Road, Cheshunt, Waltham Cross, Herts EN8 9SL. *T:* (01992) 632222.

LEAKE, Prof. Bernard Elgey, PhD, DSc, FRSE, FGS; Hon. Research Fellow, School of Earth and Ocean Sciences (formerly School of Earth, then Earth, Ocean and Planetary Sciences), Cardiff University, since 1998; Leverhulme Emeritus Fellow, 2000–02; Professor of Geology, Department of Geology and Applied Geology (formerly Department of Geology), and Keeper of Geological Collections in Hunterian Museum, University of Glasgow, 1974–97, now Professor Emeritus (Head, Department of Geology and Applied Geology (formerly Department of Geology), 1974–92); *b* 29 July 1932; *s* of late Norman Sidney Leake and Clare Evelyn (*née* Walgate); *m* 1955, Gillian Dorothy Dobinson; five *s. Educ:* Wirral Grammar Sch., Bebington, Cheshire; Liverpool Univ. (1st Cl. Hons BSc, PhD); Bristol Univ. (DSc 1974); Glasgow Univ. (DSc 1998). Leverhulme post-doctoral Res. Fellow, Liverpool Univ., 1955–57; Asst Lectr, subseq. Lectr in Geology, Bristol Univ., 1957–68, Reader in Geol., 1968–74. Res. Associate, Berkeley, Calif, 1966; Gledden Sen. Vis. Fellow, Univ. of W Australia, 1986; Erskine Vis. Res. Fellow, Univ. of Canterbury, NZ, 1999. Chm., Cttee on amphibole nomenclature, Internat. Mineral Assoc., 1982–2006 (Sec., 1968–79); Member: NERC, 1978–84 (Chm., Vis. Gp to Brit. Geol Survey, formerly Inst. of Geological Sciences, 1982–84; Chm., Isotope Facilities Prog. Cttee, 1981–85, 1987–91); Council, Mineral Soc., 1965–68, 1978–80, 1996–99 (Vice-Pres., 1979–80, 1996–97; Pres., 1998–99; Managing Trustee, 1997–98, 2000–04; Hon. Life Mem., 2004); Council, Geol Soc., 1971–74, 1979–85, 1989–96, 2002–05 (Vice-Pres., 1980; Treasurer, 1981–85, 1989–96; Pres., 1986–88; Lyell Medal, 1977); Council, RSE, 1988–90; publication cttees, Mineral Soc., 1970–85, Geol Soc., 1970–85, and 1986–96; Geol Soc. Publication Bd, 1987–2005 (Chm., 1987–96); Treas., Geologists' Assoc., 1997–2009. FRSE 1978. Hon. Life Mem., Liverpool Geol Soc., 2007. Sodic amphibole mineral, leakeite, named by Internat. Mineral Assoc., 1992. Editor: Mineralogical Magazine, 1970–83; Jl of Geol Soc., 1973 and 1974. *Publications:* A Catalogue of analysed calciferous and sub-calciferous amphiboles, 1968; The Geology of South Mayo, 1989; The Geology of the Dalradian and associated rocks of Connemara, W Ireland, 1994; The Life of Frank Coles Phillips (1902–82) and the Structural Geology of the Moine Petrofabric Controversy, 2002; over 150 papers in geol, mineral and geochem. jls on geol. of Connemara, study of amphiboles, X-ray fluorescence anal. of rocks and use of geochem. in identifying origins of highly metamorphosed rocks; geological maps: Connemara, 1982; South Mayo, 1985; Slyne Head, 1985; Errismore, 1990; Clifden, 1997; Central Galway granite and its northern margin, Oughterard, 2006. *Recreations:* walking, reading, theatre, museums, genealogy, study of railway and agricultural development. *Address:* School of Earth and Ocean Sciences, Cardiff University, Main Building, Park Place, Cardiff CF10 3YE. *T:* (029) 2087 6421; The Chippings, Bridge Road, Llanblethian, Cowbridge, Vale of Glamorgan CF71 7JG. *Club:* Geological Society.

LEAKE, Rt Rev. David, CBE 2003; Bishop of Argentina, 1990–2002; Hon. Assistant Bishop, Diocese of Norwich, since 2003; *b* 26 June 1935; *s* of Rev. Canon William Alfred Leake and Dorothy Violet Leake; *m* 1961, Rachel Yarham; two *s* one *d. Educ:* St Alban's Coll., Buenos Aires; London Coll. of Divinity. ALCD 1959 (LTh). Deacon 1959, priest 1960; Assistant Bishop: Paraguay and N Argentina, 1969–73; N Argentina, 1973–79; Bishop of Northern Argentina, 1979–89; Presiding Bishop, Province of Anglican Ch of

Southern Cone of America, 1982–89. *Recreation:* observing people's behaviour at airports, railway stations and bus terminals. *Address:* The Anchorage, Lower Common, East Runton, Cromer, Norfolk NR27 9PG. *T:* (01263) 513536.

LEAKEY, Lt Gen. (Arundell) David, CMG 2006; CBE 1997; Director General, European Union Military Staff, since 2007; *b* 18 May 1952; *s* of Maj.-Gen. (Arundell) Rea Leakey, CB, DSO, MC and Muriel Irene Le Poer Trench; *m* 1983, Shelagh Jane Lawson; two *s*. *Educ:* Sherborne Sch.; Fitzwilliam Coll., Cambridge (MA Law); RMA Sandhurst. CO 2nd RTR, 1991; Comdr 20 Armoured Bde, 1996; Dir Mil. Ops, MoD, 1997–99; COS HQ NI, 1999–2001; Dir Gen., Army Trng and Recruiting, and Chief Exec., Army Trng and Recruiting Agency, 2001–04; Comdr, EU Force in Bosnia and Herzegovina, 2004–05; MoD, 2006–07. Col Comdt, RTR, 2006– (Dep. Col Comdt, 1999–2006); Col, Dorset Yeomanry, 2008–. Hon. Col, ACF Music, 2004–. Chm., Wyke Hall (Management) Ltd, 1996–. Gov., Nat. Children's Orch., 2001–. Pres., Army Squash Rackets Assoc., 1997–. *Recreations:* music, field sports, squash, hockey, tennis, sailing, skiing, golf, chain-sawing. *Address:* *e-mail:* davidleakey@aol.com. *Clubs:* Hawks (Cambridge); Jesters; Escorts; GB Veterans Squash.

LEAKEY, Dr David Martin, FREng; Group Technical Adviser, British Telecom, 1990–92; independent consultant, David Leakey Consultancy in telecommunication services, systems and networks, since 1992; *b* 23 July 1932; *s* of Reginald Edward and Edith Doris Leakey; *m* 1st, 1957, Shirley May Webster (*d* 2003); one *s* one *d*; 2nd, 2006, Betty Ethel, *widow* of Cedric Walter Garland. *Educ:* Imperial College, Univ. of London (BScEng, PhD, DIC). FCGI 1976; FIET (FIEE 1969); FREng (FEng 1979). GEC Coventry, 1953–57; GEC Hirst Research Centre, 1957–63; Tech. Manager, Public Exchange Div., GEC Coventry, 1963–66; Head, Elect. Eng. Dept, Lanchester Polytechnic, 1966–67; Advanced Product Planning Manager, 1967–69, Technical Dir, 1969–84, GEC Coventry; Dep. E-in-C, 1984–86, Chief Scientist, 1986–90, British Telecom. Director: Fulcrum Ltd, 1985–92; Mitel Corp., 1986–92. Vis. Prof., Univ. of Bristol, 1987–. Vice-Pres., IEE, 1984–87. Freeman, City of London, 1985; Liveryman, Worshipful Co. of Engineers, 1985–. Hon. DEng Bristol, 1995. *Publications:* papers to professional journals. *Recreations:* horticulture, wine. *Address:* 33 MacDonald Close, Chesham Bois, Amersham, Bucks HP6 5LZ.

LEAKEY, Richard Erskine Frere, FRS 2007; Permanent Secretary, Secretary to the Cabinet and Head of the Public Service, Kenya, 1999–2001; *b* 19 Dec. 1944; *s* of late Louis Seymour Bazett Leakey, FBA, and Mary Douglas Leakey, FBA; *m* 1970, Dr Meave (*née* Epps); three *d*. *Educ:* Nairobi Primary Sch.; Lenana (formerly Duke of York) Sch., Nairobi. Self employed tour guide and animal trapper, 1961–65; Dir, Photographic Safaris in E Africa, 1965–68; Administrative Dir, 1968–74, Dir, 1974–89, Nat. Museums of Kenya; Dir, Wildlife and Conservation Management Service, Kenya, 1989–90; Chm., 1989–93, Dir, 1993–94 and 1998–99, Kenya Wildlife Service; Man. Dir, Richard Leakey and Associates, wildlife consultancy, 1994–98; Sec. Gen. SAFINA, 1995–98. MP Kenya, 1998. Co-leader, palaeontol expedn to Lake Natron, Tanzania, 1963–64; expedn to Lake Baringo, Kenya, in search of early man, 1966; Co-leader, Internation Omo River Expedn, Ethiopia, in search of early man, 1967; Leader, E Turkana (formerly E Rudolf) Res. Proj. (multi-nat., interdisciplinary sci. consortium investigation of Plio/Pleistocene, Kenya's northern Rift Valley), 1968–. Chairman: Foundn for Res. into Origin of Man (FROM), 1974–81; E African Wild Life Soc., 1984–89 (Vice-Chm., 1978–84); Kenya Cttee, United World Colls, 1987; Bd of Governors and Council, Regent's Coll., London, 1985–90; Nat. Museums of Kenya, 1999–; Trustee: Nat. Fund for the Disabled; Wildlife Clubs of Kenya, 1980–; Rockford Coll., Illinois, 1983–85. Presenter: The Making of Mankind, BBC TV series, 1981; Earth Journal, US TV series, 1991. Mem., Selection Cttee, Beyond War Award, 1985–; Juror: Kalinga Prize, Unesco, 1986–88; Rolex Awards, 1990. Hon. Mem., Bd of Dirs, Thunderbird Res. Corp., USA, 1988–. Hon. degrees from Wooster Coll., Rockford Coll., SUNY, Univs of Kent, Ohio, Aberdeen, Washington and Bristol. Golden Ark Medal for Conservation, 1989. *Publications:* (contrib.) General History of Africa, vol. 1, 1976; (with R. Lewin) Origins, 1978; (with R. Lewin) People of the Lake, 1979; (with M. G. Leakey) Koobi Fora Research Project, vol. I, 1979; The Making of Mankind, 1981; Human Origins, 1982; One Life, 1984; (with R. Lewin) Origins Reconsidered, 1992; (with R. Lewin) The Origins of Humankind, 1995; (with R. Lewin) The Sixth Extinction: biodiversity and its survival, 1996; articles on palaeontol. in Nature, Jl of World Hist., Science, Amer. Jl of Phys. and Anthropol. *Address:* PO Box 24926, Nairobi, Kenya.

LEAN, Geoffrey; Environment Editor, Independent on Sunday, since 2000; *b* 21 April 1947; *s* of late Garth Dickinson Lean and Margaret Mary Lean (*née* Appleyard); *m* 1972, Judith Eveline Wolfe; one *s* one *d*. *Educ:* Sherborne Sch.; St Edmund Hall, Oxford (BA (Hons) Mod. Hist). Grad. Trainee, Yorkshire Post Newspapers, 1969–72; reporter, Goole Times, 1969; Yorkshire Post: reporter, 1969–72; Feature Writer, 1972–77; Envmt Correspondent, 1973–77; Reporter, 1977–79, Envmt Correspondent, 1979–93, The Observer; Dir, Central Observer, 1990–93; Envmt Correspondent, Independent on Sunday, 1993–2000. Editor, Our Planet, 1994–, Tunza, 2003–, UNEP; Mem., Exec. Cttee, Stakeholder Forum for Our Common Future (formerly UNED Forum), 1989–. Trustee, European Sect., Internat. Inst. of Energy Conservation, 1995–98; UK rep. to Commn IV, Gen. Conf. of UNESCO, 1997; Mem. Bd, Leadership in Envmt and Develt Internat., 1998–2003; Trustee, LEAD UK, 2000–06. Consultancies for UNEP, UNDP, UNICEF, World Bank, FAO and WMO. Clerk, Yorkshire Post and Yorkshire Evening Post jt chapels, NUJ, 1975–77; Vice Chm., Leeds Branch, NUJ, 1977. Chair of Judges, Andrew Lees Meml Award, 1994–; Juror, Goldman Envmtl Prize, 1996–. Yorkshire Council for Social Services Press Award, 1972; Glaxo Science Fellowship, 1972; World Envmt Fest. Rose Award, 1986; Communication Arts Award of Excellence, 1986; UN Global 500, 1987; Awareness Award, 1991, Journalist of the Year, 1993, 2002, British Envmt and Media Awards; Schumacher Award, 1994; Foundn Award to launch IUCN/Reuters press awards, 1998; Scoop of the Year, London Press Club Awards, 2000, British Press Awards, 2001; Martha Gellhorn Prize, Martha Gellhorn Trust Cttee, 2002. *Publications:* Rich World, Poor World, 1978; (jtly) The Worst Accident in the World, 1986; (jtly) Chernobyl: the end of the nuclear dream, 1987; (gen. ed.) Atlas of the Environment, 1990, revd edn 1994; (ed) Radiation: doses, effects, risks, 1985; (ed) Action on Ozone, 1988, revd edn 1990; (contrib. ed.) Dimensions of Need: a world atlas of food and agriculture, 1995; (ed) Down to Earth, 1995; (ed) Human Development Report, 1998; (ed) Progress of Nations Report, 1999; (ed) A Sea of Troubles, 2001; (ed) Protecting the Oceans from Land-Based Activities, 2001. *Recreations:* family, garden, West Cork, bad puns. *Address:* c/o Independent on Sunday, 191 Marsh Wall, E14 9RS. *T:* (020) 7005 2000.

LEANING, Very Rev. David; Dean (formerly Provost) and Rector of Southwell, 1991–2006, now Dean Emeritus; Priest-in-charge, Edingley with Halam, 2003–06; *b* 18 Aug. 1936. *Educ:* Keble Coll., Oxford, 1957–58; Lichfield Theological Coll. Deacon 1960, priest 1961, dio. Lincoln; Curate of Gainsborough, 1960–65; Rector of Warsop with Sookholme, 1965–76; Vicar of Kington and Rector of Huntington, Diocese of Hereford, 1976–80; RD of Kington and Weobley, 1976–80; Archdeacon of Newark, 1980–91; Warden, Community of St Laurence, Belper, then Southwell, 1984–96 and 2002–. Mem., Bd of Selectors, ABM (formerly ACCM), 1988–96, 2000–06. MA Lambeth, 2001; Hon. MA Nottingham Trent, 2003. *Address:* 52 Greetwell Road, Lincoln LN2 4AX. *T:* (01522) 531361.

LEAPER, Prof. Robert Anthony Bernard, CBE 1975; Professor of Social Administration, University of Exeter, 1970–86, Professor Emeritus 1987; *b* 7 June 1921; *s* of William Bambrick Leaper and Gertrude Elizabeth (*née* Taylor); *m* 1950, Elizabeth Arno; two *s* one *d*. *Educ:* Ratcliffe Coll., Leicester; St John's Coll., Cambridge (MA); Balliol Coll., Oxford (MA). Dipl. Public and Social Admin. (Oxon). Coal miner, 1942–45. Warden, St John Bosco Youth Centre, Stepney, 1945–47; Cadet officer, Civil Service, 1949–50; Co-operative Coll., Stanford Hall, 1950–56; Principal, Social Welfare Trng Centre, Zambia, 1956–59; Lectr, then Sen. Lectr, then Acting Dir, Social Admin., UC, Swansea, 1960–70. Vis. Lectr, Roehampton Inst., Univ. of Surrey, 1986–98; Vis. Prof., Post-grad. Med. Sch., Univ. of Exeter, 1996–2001. Exec., later Vice-Chm., Nat. Council of Social Service, 1964–80; Pres., European Region, Internat. Council on Social Welfare, 1971–79; Chm., Area Bd, MSC, 1975–86; Governor, Centre for Policy on Ageing, 1982–88; Trustee, Age Concern England, 1993–98; Chm., AGILE (Devon Action Gp on Later Life), 2000–03. Editor, Social Policy and Administration, 1973–93. DUniv Surrey, 1992; Dr *hc* Univ. de Rennes, 1987. Médaille de l'Ecole Nationale de la Santé, France, 1975; Certificat d'Honneur Marcinelle, Inst. Européen Interuniversitaire de l'Action Sociale, 2006. *Publications:* Communities and Social Change, 1966; Community Work, 1969, 2nd edn 1972; Health, Wealth and Housing, 1980; Change and Continuity, 1984, 2nd enlarged edn 2005; At Home in Devon, 1986; Age Speaks for Itself, 1988; Age Speaks for Itself in Europe, 1993; Employment Post 50, 1998. *Recreations:* walking, railways, wine. *Address:* Birchcote, New North Road, Exeter EX4 4AD. *T:* (01392) 272565.

LEAR, Joyce, (Mrs W. J. Lear); *see* Hopkirk, J.

LEAR, Peter; *see* Lovesey, P. H.

LEARMONT, Gen. Sir John (Hartley), KCB 1989; CBE 1980 (OBE 1975); Quarter Master General, Ministry of Defence, 1991–94, retired; *b* 10 March 1934; *s* of Captain Percy Hewitt Learmont, CIE, RIN and Doris Orynthia Learmont; *m* 1957, Susan (*née* Thornborrow); three *s*. *Educ:* Fettes College; RMA Sandhurst. Commissioned RA, 1954; Instructor, RMA, 1960–63; student, Staff Coll., 1964; served 14 Field Regt, Staff Coll. and 3 RHA, 1965–70; MA to C-in-C BAOR, 1971–73; CO 1 RHA, 1974–75 (despatches 1974); HQ BAOR, 1976–78; Comdr, 8 Field Force, 1979–81; Dep. Comdr, Commonwealth Monitoring Force, Rhodesia, Nov. 1979–March 1980; student RCDS, 1981; Chief of Mission, British Cs-in-C Mission to Soviet Forces in Germany, 1982–84; Comdr Artillery, 1 (British) Corps, 1985–87; COS, HQ UKLF, 1987–88; Comdt, Staff Coll. Camberley, 1988–89; Mil. Sec., MoD, 1989–91. Conducted review (Learmont Inquiry) of Prison Service security in Eng. and Wales, 1995. Colonel Commandant: Army Air Corps, 1988–94; RA, 1989–99; RHA, 1990–99; Hon. Colonel: 2nd Bn Wessex Regt (Vols), 1990–95; 2nd (Vol.) Bn, Royal Gloucestershire, Berkshire and Wiltshire Regt, 1995–97. Patron: Glider Pilot Regtl Assoc., 1996–; Air OP Officers' Assoc., 2000–. *Recreations:* fell walking, golf, theatre.

LEARY, Brian Leonard; QC 1978; FCIArb; *b* 1 Jan. 1929; *o s* of late A. T. Leary; *m* 1965, Myriam Ann Bannister, *d* of Kenneth Bannister, CBE, Mexico City. *Educ:* King's Sch., Canterbury; Wadham Coll., Oxford (MA). Called to the Bar, Middle Temple, 1953; Harmsworth Scholar; Bencher, 1986. Senior Prosecuting Counsel to the Crown at Central Criminal Court, 1971–78. Chm., British-Mexican Soc., 1989–92. *Recreations:* travel, sailing, growing herbs. *Address:* Calle Reforma, 13 San Angel, Mexico DF 01000, Mexico. *T:* (55) 55508270.

LEASK, Maj.-Gen. Anthony de Camborne Lowther, CB 1996; CBE 1990 (OBE 1984; MBE 1979); *b* 4 Jan. 1943; *s* of Lt-Gen. Sir Henry Leask, KCB, DSO, OBE, and of Zoë Leask (*née* Paynter); *m* 1974, Heather Catherine Moir; one *s* two *d*. *Educ:* Wellington Coll.; RMA, Sandhurst. Comnd Scots Guards, 1963; mentioned in despatches, 1974; CO Bn, 1981–83; attached US Army, 1983–85; Col Mil. Ops 2, MoD, 1986–89; in Comd, 15 Inf. Bde, 1989–91; rcds 1992; Dir, Defence Commitments, Far East and Western Hemisphere, 1993–94; Maj.-Gen. 1994; retd 1996. Director: Nat. Assoc. of Almshouses, 1996–2004; Corps of Commissionaires Mgt Ltd, 1999– (Chm., 2001–). Mem., Queen's Bodyguard for Scotland, Royal Co. of Archers, 1976–. *Publication:* Sword of Scotland, 2006. *Recreations:* wildlife, country pursuits. *Address:* c/o Bank of Scotland, Aberfoyle, by Stirling.

See also Lord Hyde.

LEASK, Derek William; High Commissioner for New Zealand in the United Kingdom, since 2008; *b* Wellington, NZ, 29 Feb. 1948; *s* of Lloyd Samuel Leask and Judith Leask (*née* Poynter); *m* 1972, Annabel E. Murray (marr. diss.); one *s* one *d*; partner, Patricia D. Stevenson. *Educ:* Victoria Univ. of Wellington (BCA); Univ. of Canterbury, NZ (MComm Hons). Entered NZ Diplomatic Service, 1969; Counsellor, London, 1985–89; Ambassador to EC, 1995–99; Dep. Sec., NZ Ministry of Foreign Affairs and Trade, 2005–08. *Recreations:* golf, NZ history (19th century wars in NZ). *Address:* New Zealand High Commission, Haymarket, SW1Y 4TQ. *T:* (020) 7316 8962; *e-mail:* derek.leask@mfat-govt.nz. *Clubs:* Athenæum, Royal Over-Seas League, Commonwealth; Royal Wellington Golf.

LEATES, Margaret; freelance parliamentary draftsman, since 1990; *b* 30 March 1951; *d* of Henry Arthur Sargent Rayner and Alice (*née* Baker); *m* 1973, Timothy Philip Leates; one *s* one *d*. *Educ:* Lilley and Stone Girls' High Sch., Newark; King's Coll., London (LLB 1st cl. hons, LLM distinction; undergrad. and postgrad. schol.; AKC); MA (Theol) distinction, Univ. of Kent. Admitted Solicitor, 1975; joined Office of Parliamentary Counsel, 1976; with Law Commn, 1981–83 and 1987–89; Dep. Parly Counsel, 1987–90. FRSA. *Publications:* When I'm 64: a guide to pensions law; Review of Planning Law of States of Guernsey. *Recreations:* hermeneutics, junk, other people's gardens. *Address:* Crofton Farm, 161 Crofton Lane, Orpington, Kent BR6 0BP. *T:* (01689) 820192; Nyanza, 87 Bennell's Avenue, Whitstable, Kent CT5 2HR. *T:* (01227) 272335; Mumford House, Church Hill, Kingsnorth, Ashford, Kent TN23 3EG. *T:* (01223) 610269; *e-mail:* ml@leates.org.uk.

LEATHAM, Dr Aubrey (Gerald), FRCP; cardiologist; Hon. Consulting Physician: St George's Hospital, London; National Heart Hospital; King Edward VII Hospital, London; *b* 23 Aug. 1920; *s* of Dr H. W. Leatham (*d* 1973), Godalming and Kathleen Pelham Burn (*d* 1971), Nosely Hall, Leicester; *m* 1954, Judith Augustine Savile Freer; one *s* three *d*. *Educ:* Charterhouse; Trinity Hall, Cambridge; St Thomas' Hospital. BA Cambridge 1941; MB, BChir 1944; MRCP 1945; FRCP 1957. House Phys., St Thomas' Hosp., 1944; RMO, Nat. Heart Hosp., 1945; Phys., RAMC, 1946–47; Sherbrook Research Fellow, Cardiac Dept, and Sen. Registrar, London Hosp., 1948–50; Asst Dir, Inst. of Cardiology, 1951–54, Dean, 1962–69. Goulstonian Lectr, RCP, 1958. R. T. Hall Travelling Prof., Australia and NZ, 1963. Member: Brit. Cardiac Soc.; Sociedad Peruana de Cardiologia, 1966; Sociedad Colombiana de Cardiologia, 1966. Hon. FACC 1986. Royal Order of

Bhutan, 1966. *Publications:* Auscultation of the Heart and Phonocardiography, 1970; (jtly) Lecture Notes in Cardiology, 1990; articles in Lancet, British Heart Jl, etc, on auscultation of the heart and phonocardiography, artificial pacemakers, coronary artery disease, etc. *Recreations:* ski-ing and ski-touring, mountain walking, tennis, racquets, gardening, photography. *Address:* 22 Upper Wimpole Street, W1G 6NB. *T:* 0845 612 1213; Rookwood Farmhouse, West Wittering, Sussex PO20 8QH. *T:* (01243) 514649; *e-mail:* aubreyleatham@sagainternet.co.uk.

LEATHAM, Dorian; Chief Executive, London Borough of Hillingdon, since 1998; *b* 2 Aug. 1949; *s* of Robert Clement Leatham and Anna Ismay Leatham; partner, Janet Patrick; one *s* one *d*. *Educ:* High Wycombe Coll. of Technol. (BSc Sociol. (ext.) London); Brunel Univ. (MA Public and Social Admin). Various posts, 1970–75; Allocations Manager, Lambeth, 1975–77; District Housing Manager: City of Westminster, 1977–83; Camden, 1983–87; Dep. Dir of Housing, Brent, 1987–92; Dir, Housing Mgt, Circle 33 Housing Trust, 1992–93; Asst Dir of Housing, Hounslow, 1993–95; Dir of Housing, Croydon, 1995–98. *Recreations:* watching cricket, going to cinema and theatre, cooking, reading, supporting voluntary groups. *Address:* London Borough of Hillingdon, Civic Centre, Uxbridge UB8 1UW. *T:* (01895) 250569.

LEATHER, Dame Susan Catherine, (Dame Suzi), DBE 2006 (MBE 1994); Chair, Charity Commission for England and Wales, since 2006; *b* 5 April 1956; *d* of Dr Hugh Moffat Leather and Dr Catherine Margaret Leather (*née* Stephen); *m* 1986, Prof. Iain Hampsher-Monk; one *s* two *d*. *Educ:* Exeter Univ. (BA Hons Politics 1977; BPhil Dist. Social Work 1986); Leicester Univ. (MA Eur. Politics 1978). CQSW 1986. Mkt res. exec., 1978–79; Res. Officer, then Sen. Res. Officer, Consumers in Europe Gp, 1979–84; trainee Probation Officer, 1984–86; freelance consumer consultant, 1988–97; Chair: Exeter and Dist Community NHS Trust, 1997–2001; Human Fertilisation and Embryology Authy, 2002–06. Chair, Sch. Food Trust, 2005–06; Dep. Chair, Food Standards Agency, 2000–02. FRCOG *ad eund* 2004. Hon. FRSH 2006. Hon. DLitt Exeter, 2003; Hon. DCL Huddersfield, 2005; DLaws Leicester, 2007; DUniv Aberdeen, 2007. *Publications:* The Making of Modern Malnutrition, 1996; contrib. articles on consumer, food and health policy. *Recreations:* keeping fit, walking, running, cinema, family discussions. *Address:* Charity Commission for England and Wales, Harmsworth House, 13–15 Bouverie Street, EC4Y 8DP. *T:* (020) 7674 2321; *e-mail:* suzi.leather@charitycommission.gsi.gov.uk.

LEATHERBARROW, Prof. Robin John, DPhil; FRSC; Professor and Head of Biological and Biophysical Chemistry, Department of Chemistry, since 2002, and Director, Chemical Biology Centre, since 2001, Imperial College London; *b* Farnworth, 14 Jan. 1959; *s* of John and Dorothy Leatherbarrow; *m* 1988, Marcella Mary Beale; two *d*. *Educ:* St John's C of E Primary Sch., Mosley Common; Leigh Grammar Sch.; Eccles Sixth Form Coll.; Liverpool Univ. (BSc Hons Biochem.); Exeter Coll., Oxford (DPhil 1983). FRSC 2004. Res. Lectr, Christ Church, Oxford, 1982–84; Imperial College London: MRC Postdoctoral Fellow, 1984; Royal Soc. Pickering Res. Fellow, 1984; Lectr, 1984–99; Reader, 1999–2002. Man. Dir, Erithacus Software Ltd, 1989–. Hon. Treas., British Biophysical Soc., 1993–99. *Publications:* scientific contribs to learned jls; computer progs. *Recreations:* playing cricket and squash, watching Manchester United on TV, programming computers, refurbishing old houses. *Address:* Department of Chemistry, Imperial College London, South Kensington Campus, SW7 2AZ. *T:* (020) 7594 5752.

LEATHERBARROW, Prof. William John; Professor of Russian, University of Sheffield, 1994–2007, now Emeritus; *b* 18 Oct. 1947; *s* of William and Lily Leatherbarrow; *m* 1968, Vivien Jean Burton; one *s* one *d*. *Educ:* Univ. of Exeter (BA Hons 1969; MA 1972). University of Sheffield: Lectr, 1970–90; Sen. Lectr, 1990–92; Reader in Russian, 1992–94; Dean, Faculty of Arts, 1997–99; Chm., Sch. of Modern Langs, 2001–04, 2005–06. *Publications:* Fedor Dostoevsky, 1981; (with D. C. Offord) A Documentary History of Russian Thought, 1987; Fedor Dostoevsky: a reference guide, 1990; Dostoyevsky: The Brothers Karamazov, 1992; Dostoevsky and Britain, 1995; Dostoevsky's "The Devils", 1999; The Cambridge Companion to Dostoevskii, 2002; A Devil's Vaudeville: the demonic in Dostoevsky's major fiction, 2005; many edns and articles in scholarly jls. *Recreations:* wine collecting, hiking, cricket, astronomy. *Address:* Department of Russian and Slavonic Studies, University of Sheffield, Sheffield S10 2TN. *T:* (0114) 222 7404, *Fax:* (0114) 222 7416; *e-mail:* w.leatherbarrow@sheffield.ac.uk.

LEATHERS, family name of **Viscount Leathers**.

LEATHERS, 3rd Viscount *cr* 1954, of Purfleet, Co. Essex; **Christopher Graeme Leathers;** Baron Leathers, 1941; *b* 31 Aug. 1941; *er s* of 2nd Viscount Leathers and his 1st wife, Elspeth Graeme Stewart (*d* 1985); *S* father, 1996; *m* 1964, Maria Philomena, *yr d* of Michael Merriman, Charlestown, Co. Mayo; one *s* one *d*. *Educ:* Rugby Sch.; Open Univ. (BA Hons). New Zealand Shipping Co. Ltd, 1961–63; Wm Cory & Son Ltd, 1963–84; Mostyn Docks Ltd, 1984–88; with Dept of Transport, then DETR, subseq. DTLR, then DfT, 1988–2003. MICS 1965; MCMI (MIMgt 1987). Liveryman, Shipwrights' Co., 1969–. JP Clwyd, 1993. *Heir: s* Hon. James Frederick Leathers, *b* 27 May 1969. *Address:* 53 Daisy Avenue, Bury St Edmunds, Suffolk IP32 7PG.

LEATHWOOD, Barry, OBE 1998; National Secretary, Rural, Agricultural and Allied Workers National Trade Group, Transport and General Workers' Union, 1987–2002; *b* 11 April 1941; *s* of Charles and Dorothy Leathwood; *m* 1963, Veronica Ann Clarke; one *d*. Apprentice Toolmaker, 1956–62; Toolmaker/Fitter, 1962–73; District Organiser, Nat. Union of Agric. and Allied Workers, 1973–83; Regional Officer, TGWU Agric. Group, 1983–87. Member: British Potato Council, 2002–; Nat. Access Forum, 1999–. UK Delegate/Expert to ISO Wkg Gp on Social Responsibility, 2005. Patron, Community Council for Somerset, 2001–; CAB Voluntary Advr, 2004–. FRSA 1996. *Recreations:* socialist politics, reading, photography. *Address:* 32 Nursery Close, Comwich, Bridgwater, Som TA5 2JB.

LEAVER, Sir Christopher, GBE 1981; JP; director of private and public companies; Vice Chairman, Thames Water Plc, 1994–2000 (Deputy Chairman, 1989–93; Chairman, 1993–94); *b* 3 Nov. 1937; *s* of Dr Robert Leaver and Mrs Audrey Kerpen; *m* 1975, Helen Mireille Molyneux Benton; one *s* two *d*. *Educ:* Eastbourne Coll. Commissioned (Army), RAOC, 1956–58. Member, Retail Foods Trades Wages Council, 1963–64. JP Inner London, 1970–83, City, 1974–92; Member: Council, Royal Borough of Kensington and Chelsea, 1970–73; Court of Common Council (Ward of Dowgate), City of London, 1973; Alderman (Ward of Dowgate), City of London, 1974–2002; Sheriff of the City of London, 1979–80; Lord Mayor of London, 1981–82; one of HM Lieutenants, City of London, 1982–2002. Chm., London Tourist Bd, 1983–89; Dep. Chm., Thames Water Authority, 1983–89; Chm., Thames Line Plc, 1987–89; Director: Bath & Portland Gp, 1983–85; Thermal Scientific plc, 1986–88; Unionamerica Holdings Plc, 1994–97. Advr on Royal Parks to Sec. of State for Nat. Heritage, 1993–96. Member: Bd of Brixton Prison, 1975–78; Court, City Univ., 1978–2002 (Chancellor, 1981–82); Council of the Missions to Seamen, 1983–95; Council, Wine and Spirit Benevolent Soc., 1983–88; Finance Cttee, London Diocesan Fund, 1983–86; Transitional Council, St Paul's Cathedral, 1999; Trustee: Chichester Festival Theatre, 1982–97; LSO, 1983–91; Vice-President: Bridewell Royal Hosp., 1982–89; NPFA, 1983–99; Governor: Christ's Hospital Sch., 1975–2002; City of London Girls' Sch., 1975–78; City of London Freemen's Sch., 1980–81; Chm., Council, Eastbourne Coll., 1989–2005 (Mem., 1988–2005); Almoner Trustee, St Paul's Cathedral Choir Sch. Foundn, 1986–90. Trustee, Music Therapy Trust, 1981–89; Chairman, Young Musicians' Symphony Orch. Trust, 1979–81; Hon. Mem., Guildhall Sch. of Music and Drama, 1982–. Church Warden, St Olave's, Hart Street, 1975–90 (Patronage Trust, 1990–96); Church Comr, 1982–93, 1996–99. Mem., Ct of Assistants, Carmen's Co., 1973 (Master, 1987–88); Hon. Liveryman: Farmers' Company, 1980; Water Conservators' Co., 2000 (Hon. Freeman, 1995); Freeman, Co. of Watermen and Lightermen, 1988; Hon. Freeman, Co. of Environmental Cleaners, 1983; Hon. Col, 151 (Greater London) Tpt Regt RCT (V), 1983–88; Hon. Col Comdt, RCT, 1988–91. Hon. DMus City, 1981. KStJ 1982. Order of Oman Class II. *Recreations:* gardening, music.

LEAVER, Prof. Christopher John, CBE 2000; FRS 1986; FRSE; Sibthorpian Professor of Plant Sciences, 1990–2007, now Professor Emeritus, and Head, Department of Plant Sciences, 1991–2007, University of Oxford; Fellow, St John's College, 1989–2007, now Emeritus; *b* 31 May 1942; *s* of Douglas Percy Leaver and Elizabeth Constance Leaver; *m* 1971, Anne (*née* Huggins); one *s* one *d*. *Educ:* Imperial College, University of London (BSc, ARCS, DIC, PhD); MA (Oxon) 1990. Fulbright Scholar, Purdue Univ., 1966–68; Scientific Officer, ARC Plant Physiology Unit, Imperial Coll., 1968–69; University of Edinburgh: Lectr, Dept of Botany, 1969–80; Reader, 1980–86; SERC Sen. Res. Fellow, 1985–89; Prof. of Plant Molecular Biol., 1986–89. Vis. Prof., Univ. of WA, Perth, 2002–. Member: AFRC, 1990–94; Priorities Bd for R&D to advise MAFF, 1990–94 (Chm., Arable Crops Adv. Sectoral Gp, 1990–94); Council, EMBO, 1991–97 (Chm., 1996–97); ACOST, 1992–93; Council, Royal Soc., 1992–94; BBSRC, 2000–03 (Mem., Individual Merit Promotion Panel, 1996–2005); Chairman: Adv. Bd, IACR, Rothamsted, 1995–2000; Exec. Cttee, Biochemical Soc., 2005–07 (Vice-Chm., 2002–05; Chm., 2005–07). Chm., Scientific Adv. Bd, Inst. for Molecular and Cell Biology, Porto, 2000–; Mem., Cttee of Scientific Planning and Rev., ICSU, Paris, 2006–. Curator, Oxford Botanic Garden, 1991–98. Mem. Gov. Council, John Innes, 1984–; Trustee: John Innes Foundn, 1987–; Nat. History Mus., 1997–2006; Sense About Sci., 2002–. Deleg., OUP, 2002–07. Corresp. Mem., Amer. Soc. of Plant Biologists, 2003, Fellow, 2007. FRSE 1987; MAE 1988. T. H. Huxley Gold Medal, Imperial Coll., 1970; Tate & Lyle Award, Phytochem. Soc. of Europe, 1984; Humboldt Prize, Alexander von Humboldt Foundn, Bonn, 1997. *Publications:* numerous papers in internat. sci. jls. *Recreations:* walking and talking in Upper Coquetdale. *Address:* St John's College, Oxford OX1 3JP; *e-mail:* chris.leaver@plants.ox.ac.uk.

LEAVER, David; *see* Leaver, J. D.

LEAVER, Elaine Kildare; *see* Murray, E. K.

LEAVER, Prof. (John) David, PhD; CBiol, FIBiol; FRAgS, FIAgrE; Principal, Royal Agricultural College, Cirencester, 2002–07, now Professor Emeritus; *b* 5 Jan. 1942; *s* of John and Elsie Leaver; *m* 1969, Sally Ann Posgate; two *s* one *d*. *Educ:* Univ. of Durham (BSc Agric.); Wye Coll., Univ. of London (PhD 1967). CBiol, FIBiol 1988; FRAgS 1986; FIAgrE 2003. PSO, Nat. Inst. for Res. in Dairying, 1967–76; Hd, Dept of Animal Prodn and Farm Dir, Crichton Royal W of Scotland Agricl Coll., 1976–87; Prof. of Agriculture and Vice Principal, Wye Coll., Univ. of London, 1987–2000; Vice Provost, Wye, Imperial Coll., 2000–02. Dir, UCAS, 2006–. Dir, NMR plc, 1994–97. Member: Adv. Cttee, BSE, the Cost of a Crisis, Nat. Audit Office, 1997; Prog. Mgt Cttee, DEFRA Sustainable Livestock Prog., 2002– (Chm., 2007–). Mem., Wilson Cttee, Nat. Cattle Genetic Database, 1989–90; Scientific Advr, Internat. Foundn for Science, 1994–. President: British Soc. of Animal Sci., 1995–96; British Grassland Soc., 2000–01. Chairman: Frank Parkinson Agricl Trust, 1999–; Frank Parkinson Yorks Trust, 2008–. *Publications:* Herbage Intake Handbook, 1982; Milk Production, Science and Practice, 1983; contribs to numerous peer-reviewed jls and conf. papers on dairy systems res. *Recreations:* sport, music, poetry, countryside. *Address:* Sole Street Farm, Crundale, Canterbury, Kent CT4 7ET; *e-mail:* jdleaver@gmail.com. *Club:* Farmers.

LEAVER, Marcus Edward; President, Sterling Publishing Co. Inc., since 2008 (Executive Vice-President and Chief Operating Officer, 2005–08); *b* 1 April 1970; *s* of Peter Lawrence Oppenheim Leaver, *qv*; *m* 1997, Anna Gwendoline Morgan; one *s* one *d*. *Educ:* Eton Coll.; UEA (BA Hons (Hist. of Art and Architecture) 1992); London Business Sch. (MBA 1999). Corporate Devel Dir, Chrysalis Gp plc, 2001–03; Chief Exec., Chrysalis Books Gp plc, 2003–05. *Recreations:* wine, Tottenham Hotspur, reading, cricket, baseball, life coaching. *Address:* 575 West End Avenue, New York, NY 10024, USA. *T:* (212) 7990252; *e-mail:* marcuseleaver@aol.com; Sterling Publishing Co. Inc., 387 Park Avenue South, New York, NY 10016, USA. *T:* (212) 5327160, *Fax:* (212) 5324238; *e-mail:* mleaver@sterlingpub.com. *Clubs:* MCC, Groucho, Soho House.

LEAVER, Parveen June; *see* Kumar, P. J.

LEAVER, Peter Lawrence Oppenheim; QC 1987; a Recorder, since 1994; *b* 28 Nov. 1944; *er s* of Marcus Isaac Leaver and Lena Leaver (*née* Oppenheim); *m* 1969, Jane Rachel, *o d* of Leonard and Rivka Pearl; three *s* one *d*. *Educ:* Aldenham Sch., Elstree; Trinity Coll., Dublin. Called to the Bar, Lincoln's Inn, 1967, Bencher, 1995. Chairman: Bar Cttee, 1989; Internat. Practice Cttee, 1990; Member: Gen. Council of the Bar, 1987–90; Cttee on the Future of the Legal Profession, 1986–88; Council of Legal Educn, 1986–91. Chief Exec., FA Premier League, 1997–99. Dir, IMRO Ltd, 1994–2000. Chm., London Court of Internat. Arbitration, 2008–. Pres., UK Nat. Anti-Doping Panel, 2008–. *Recreations:* sport, theatre, wine. *Address:* 1 Essex Court, Temple, EC4Y 9AR. *T:* (020) 7583 2000. *Clubs:* Garrick, MCC.

See also M. E. Leaver.

LEAVETT, Alan; Chairman, Long Ashton Parish Council, 1997–99; *b* 4 May 1924; *s* of George and Mabel Dorothy Leavett; *m* 1948, Jean Mary Wanford; three *d*. *Educ:* Gosport County Sch.; UC, Southampton. BA Hons 1943. MAP (RAE), 1943; HM Customs and Excise, 1947; HM Foreign Service, 1949; Rio de Janeiro, 1950–53; Bangkok, 1955–59; UK Perm. Delegate to ECAFE, 1958; Cabinet Office, 1961; Min. of Housing and Local Govt, 1963; Sec., Noise Adv. Council, 1970; Under-Sec., Civil Service Selection Bd, 1973, Dept of Environment, 1974–81. Gen. Sec., Avon Wildlife Trust, 1981–84; Member: Rural Devel Commn, 1982–91; Council, World Wildlife Fund UK, 1983–86; Clifton Suspension Bridge Trust, 1991–95; Vice-Pres., ACRE, 1987–92; Vice-Chm., Avon Community Council, 1981–89. Mem., Woodspring DC, 1986–95. *Publication:* Historic Sevenoaks, 1969. *Recreations:* book-collecting, music. *Address:* Elm View Nursing Home, Moor Lane, Clevedon N Som BS21 6EU. *T:* (01275) 878670.

LEAVEY, Thomas Edward, PhD; Director General, International Bureau of Universal Postal Union, 1995–2005; *b* Kansas City, 10 Nov. 1934; *s* of Leonard J. Leavey and Mary (*née* Horgan); *m* 1968, Anne Roland. *Educ:* Josephinium Coll., Columbus, Ohio (BA

1957); Institut Catholique, Paris; Princeton Univ. (MA 1967; PhD 1968). Sch. administrator and teacher, Kansas City, Mo, 1957–63; Prof., Fairleigh Dickinson Univ., NJ and George Washington Univ., Washington, 1968–70; United States Postal Service: Prof., Trng and Develt Inst., Bethesda, Md, 1970–72; Dir, Postal Service Trng and Develt Mgt Trng Center, LA, 1973–75; Gen. Manager, Employment and Placement Div., HQ, 1976–78; Dir, Postal Career Exec. Service, HQ, 1979; Postmaster/Sectional Manager, Charlottesville, Va, 1980; Regl Dir of Human Resources, Central Reg., Chicago, 1981; Controller, HQ, 1982; Gen. Manager, Internat. Mail Processing Div., HQ, 1982–87; Asst PMG and Sen. Dir, Internat. Postal Affairs, HQ, 1987–94. Universal Postal Union: Chairman: Customs Co-operation Council Contact Cttee, 1987–89; Private Operators Contact Cttee, 1991–94; Postal Develt Action Gp, 1991–94; Provident Scheme Mgt Bd, Internat. Bureau, 1989–94; Exec. Council, 1989–94. USPS Special Achievement Awards for Distinguished Service, 1970–90; John Wanamaker Award, USPS, 1991. *Publications:* numerous articles on business and postal matters in postal and trade jls. *Recreations:* golf, tennis, ski-ing. *Address:* 13978 Siena Loop, Bradenton, FL 34202, USA.

LE BAILLY, Vice-Adm. Sir Louis (Edward Stewart Holland), KBE 1972 (OBE 1952); CB 1969; DL; Director-General of Intelligence, Ministry of Defence, 1972–75; *b* 18 July 1915; *s* of Robert Francis Le Bailly and Ida Gaskell Le Bailly (*née* Holland); *m* 1946, Pamela Ruth Berthon; three *d*. *Educ:* RNC Dartmouth. HMS Hood, 1932; RNEC, 1933–37; HMS Hood, 1937–40; HMS Naiad, 1940–42; RNEC, 1942–44; HMS Duke of York, 1944–46; Admiralty, 1946–52 (Schs Liaison Officer, 1946–47; Birmingham Univ., 1947–48; Sec. to Lord Geddes' Admiralty Oil Cttee and Chm., NATO Fuels and Lubricants Standardisation Cttee, 1948–52); HMS Bermuda, 1952–53; Dept of Second Sea Lord, 1953–55; RNEC, 1955–58; Admiralty: Staff Officer to Dartmouth Review Cttee, 1958; Asst Engineer-in-Chief, 1958–60; Naval Asst to Controller of the Navy, 1960–63; IDC, 1963; Dep. Dir of Marine Engineering, 1963–67; Naval Attaché, Washington, DC, and Comdr, British Navy Staff, 1967–69; Min. of Defence, 1970–72; Vice-Adm. 1970, retired 1972. Chm., civil service, police and fire service selection bds, 1976–82. Mem. Council, Research Inst. for Study of Conflict and Terrorism, 1976–85. Chm. of Govs, Rendcomb Coll., 1979–85. DL Cornwall, 1982. FIMechE; FInstPet; FIMarEST. Hon. DSc Plymouth, 1994. *Publications:* The Man Around the Engine, 1990; From Fisher to the Falklands, 1991; Old Loves Return, 1993; We Should Look to Our Moat, 2007. *Address:* Garlands House, St Tudy, Bodmin, Cornwall PL30 3NN.

LeBLANC, Rt Hon. Roméo; PC (Can.) 1974; CC 1995; CMM 1995; CD 1995; Governor General and Commander-in-Chief of Canada, 1995–99; *b* 18 Dec. 1927; *s* of Philias and Lucie LeBlanc; *m* Diana Fowler. *Educ:* Université St-Joseph, Memramcook (BA 1948; BEd 1951); Paris Univ. Teacher, New Brunswick, 1951–59; corresp. for Radio-Canada, in Ottawa, UK and US, 1960–67; Press Sec. to Prime Minister of Canada, 1967–71; Asst to Pres. and Dir of Public Relns, Moncton Univ., 1971–72. MP (L) Westmorland-Kent, 1972–84; Minister of State, Fisheries, 1974–76; Minister of: Fisheries and the Envmt, 1976–79; Fisheries and Oceans, 1980–82; Public Works, 1982–84; served on various Cabinet cttees; Mem., Senate, 1984–94; served on various Senate cttees; Speaker, 1993–94. Hon. DCL Mt Allison, 1977; Hon. Dr in Public Admin Moncton, 1979; Hon. LLD: Sainte-Anne, 1995; St Thomas, 1997; Meml, 1997; McGill, 1997; Hon. DLitt Ryerson, 1996; DUniv Ottawa, 1996. *Address:* PO Box 5254, Shediac, NB E4P 8T9, Canada.

LEBRECHT, Andrew John, CB 2006; Deputy Permanent Representative, UK Permanent Representation to the European Union, since 2008; *b* 13 Dec. 1951; *s* of late Heinz Martin Lebrecht and of Margaret (*née* Cardis); *m* 1976, Judit Catan; two *d*. *Educ:* De La Salle Coll., Hove; Leeds Univ. (BA Econs); Reading Univ. (MSc Agricl Econs). Ministry of Agriculture, Fisheries and Food, 1977–2001: Private Sec. to Parly Sec., 1980–82; on secondment to HM Diplomatic Service as First Sec. (Fisheries and Food), UK Rep. Brussels, 1985–89; Principal Private Sec. to Minister of Agriculture, 1989–91; Head: Sheep and Livestock Subsidies Div., 1991–93; Review of Animal Health and Veterinary Gp, 1993–94; EU Div., 1994–98; EU and Internat. Policy, 1998–2001; Dir Gen., Food, Farming and Fisheries, then Sustainable Farming, Food and Fisheries, then Sustainable Farming and Food, subseq. Food and Farming, DEFRA, 2001–07. *Recreations:* family life, the countryside, reading.

LEBRECHT, Norman; Assistant Editor and Arts Columnist, Evening Standard, since 2002; *b* 11 July 1948; *s* of late Solomon and Marguerite Lebrecht; *m* 1977, Elbie Spivack; three *d*. *Educ:* Hasmonean Grammar Sch. Radio and TV producer, 1970–79; specialist contributor: Sunday Times, 1982–91; Independent mag., 1991–92; Music Columnist, Daily Telegraph, 1993–2002. Contributor, The Late Show, BBC TV, 1994–95; Presenter, Lebrecht Live, BBC Radio 3, 2000–. *Publications:* Discord, 1982; Hush, Handel's in a Passion, 1985; The Book of Musical Anecdotes, 1985; Mahler Remembered, 1987; The Book of Musical Days, 1987; The Maestro Myth, 1991; The Companion to 20th Century Music, 1992; When the Music Stops, 1996; The Complete Companion to 20th Century Music, 2000; Covent Garden: the untold story, 2000; Maestros, Masterpieces and Madness, 2007; *novel:* The Song of Names (Whitbread First Novel Award), 2002. *Recreations:* reading, prayer, listening to music, watching cricket, vigorous disputation, deltiology. *Address:* c/o Evening Standard, Derry Street, W8 5EE; *e-mail:* norman@normanlebrecht.com.

LE BRETON, David Francis Battye, CBE 1978; HM Diplomatic Service, retired; Secretary, Overseas Service Pensioners Association and Benevolent Society, since 1992; *b* 2 March 1931; *e s* of late Lt-Col F. H. Le Breton, MC, and Elisabeth, (Peter), Le Breton (*née* Trevor-Battye), Endebess, Kenya; *m* 1961, Patricia June Byrne; one *s* two *d*. *Educ:* Winchester; New Coll., Oxford. Colonial Administrative Service, Tanganyika, 1954; Private Sec. to Governor, 1959–60; Magistrate, 1962; Principal, CRO, 1963; HM Diplomatic Service, 1965; First Sec., Zanzibar, 1964; Lusaka, 1964–68; FCO, 1968–71; Head of Chancery, Budapest, 1971–74; HM Comr in Anguilla, 1974–78; Counsellor and Head of Chancery, Nairobi, 1978–81; High Comr in The Gambia, 1981–84; Head of Commonwealth Co-ordination Dept, FCO, 1984–86; Head of Nationality and Treaty Dept, FCO, 1986–87. Financial Advr/Sales Associate, Allied Dunbar Assurance, 1987–91. *Recreations:* country living, garden-clearing, African and colonial affairs. *Address:* Brackenwood, French Street, near Westerham, Kent TN16 1PN.

le BROCQUY, Louis, FCSD (FSIAD 1960); HRHA 1983; painter since 1939; *b* Dublin, 10 Nov. 1916; *s* of late Albert le Brocquy, MA, and late Sybil Staunton; *m* 1st, 1938, Jean Stoney (marr. diss., 1948); one *d*; 2nd, 1958, Anne Madden Simpson; two *s*. *Educ:* St Gerard's Sch., Wicklow, Ireland. Self-taught. Founder-mem. of Irish Exhibn of Living Art, 1943; Visiting Instructor, Central Sch. of Arts and Crafts, London, 1947–54; Visiting Tutor, Royal Coll. of Art, London, 1955–58. Member: Irish Council of Design, 1963–65; Adv. Council, Guinness Peat Awards, 1980–85. Dir, Kilkenny Design Workshops, 1965–77; Founding Bd Mem., Irish Mus. of Modern Art, 1989–94. Represented Ireland, Venice Biennale (awarded internat. prize), 1956. Work exhibited in: "50 Ans d'Art Moderne", Brussels, 1958; Painting since World War II, Guggenheim Mus., New York, 1987–88; Olympiad of Art, Seoul, 1988; L'Europe des Grands Maîtres 1870–1970, Inst. de France, 1989; Internat. Art Fest., Seoul, 1991; Premiers Chefs d'Oeuvres des Grands Maîtres, Museums of Art, Tokyo, Osaka, Kyoto, 1992. One Man Shows: Leicester Galleries, London, 1948; Gimpel Fils, London, 1947, 1949, 1951, 1955, 1956, 1957, 1959, 1961, 1966, 1968, 1971, 1974, 1978, 1983, 1988, 1991, 1993, 1997, 2001, 2006; Waddington, Dublin, 1951; Robles Gallery, Los Angeles, 1960; Gallery Lienhard, Zürich, 1961; Dawson/Taylor Gallery, Dublin, 1962, 1966, 1969, 1971, 1973, 1974, 1975, 1981, 1985, 1986, 1988, 1991, 1992, 1993, 1994, 1995, 1996, 1998, 1999, 2000, 2006; Municipal Gallery of Modern Art, Dublin, 1966, 1978, 1992; Ulster Mus., Belfast, (retrospective) 1967, 1987, 1993; Gimpel-Hanover, Emmerich Zürich, 1969, 1978, 1983; Gimpel, NY, 1971, 1978, 1983; Fondation Maeght, 1973; Bussola, Turin, 1974; Arts Council, Belfast, 1975, 1978; Musée d'Art Moderne, Paris, 1976; Giustiniani, Genoa, 1977; Waddington, Montreal, Toronto, 1978; Maeght, Barcelona, Madrid, Granada, 1978–79; Jeanne Bucher, Paris, 1979, 1982, 2006; NY State Mus., 1981; Boston Coll. 1982; Westfield Coll., Mass, 1982; Palais des Beaux Arts, Charleroi, 1982; Art 13, Internat. Basel (Börjeson), 1982; Chicago Internat. Expo (Brownstone Gall.), 1986; Arts Council, Dublin, 1987; Nat. Gall. of Vic, Melbourne, Festival Centre, Adelaide, and Mus. of Contemp. Art, Brisbane, 1988; Musée Picasso, Antibes, 1989; Kerlin, Dublin, 1991; Mus. of Modern Art, Kamakura, 1991; Itami City Mus. of Art, Osaka, 1991; City Mus. of Contemp. Art, Hiroshima, 1991; Carré Davidson, Tours, 1995; Irish Mus. of Modern Art, 1996, 2006; Espace Ricard, Paris, 1996; Galerie Maeght, Paris, 1996; Château Musée de Tours, 1997; Municipal Gall. of Modern Art, Ljubljana, 1998; Museo de Arte Contemporaneo, Instituto de Artes Gráficas, Oaxaca, 2000; Agnew's, 2001; Hunt Mus., Limerick, 2006; Nat. Gall. of Ireland, 2007; Dublin City Gall. The Hugh Lane, 2007. Public Collections possessing work include: Albright Museum, Buffalo; Arts Council of Ireland; Arts Council, London; Carnegie Inst., Pittsburgh; Centre Georges Pompidou, Paris; Chicago Arts Club; l'Etat Français; Columbus Mus., Ohio; Detroit Inst. of Art; Dublin Municipal Gallery; Fort Worth Center, Texas; Foundation of Brazil Museum, Bahia; Gulbenkian Mus., Lisbon; Guggenheim Museum, NY; J. H. Hirshhorn Foundation, Washington; Ho-Am Mus., Seoul; Hugh Lane Municipal Gall. of Modern Art, Dublin; Irish Mus. of Modern Art, Dublin; Itami Mus., Osaka; Kunsthaus, Zürich; Fondation Maeght, St Paul; Leeds City Art Gallery; Musée d'Art Moderne, Paris; Musée Picasso, Antibes; Mus. of Contemp. Art, Hiroshima; Mus. of Modern Art, Kamakura; NY State Mus.; Nat. Gall. of Ireland; San Diego Mus., Calif.; Tate Gallery; Uffizi, Florence; Ulster Museum, Belfast; Vatican Mus.; V&A Museum. RHA 1950–69. *Films:* An Other Way of Knowing, RTE, 1986; The Inner Human Reality, RTE, 2006. Freeman, City of Dublin, 2007. Hon. Associate, Nat. Coll. of Art and Design, Dublin, 2006. Hon. DLitt Dublin, 1962; Hon. LLD NUI, 1988; Hon. DPh: Dublin City, 1999; Dublin Inst. of Technol., 2004; DUniv QUB, 2002. Saoi, Aosdána, Irish Arts Council, 1993. Commandeur du Bontemps de Médoc et des Graves, 1969. Chevalier de la Légion d'Honneur, 1975; Officier: Ordre des Arts et des Lettres (France), 1996; Ordre de la Couronne (Belgium), 2001. *Illustrated work:* The Táin, trans. Thomas Kinsella, 1969; The Playboy of the Western World, Synge, 1970; The Gododdin O'Grady, 1978; Dubliners, Joyce, 1986; Stirrings Still, Samuel Beckett, 1988. *Relevant publications:* Louis le Brocquy by D. Walker, introd. John Russell, Ireland 1981, UK 1982; The Irish Landscape, by G. Morgan, 1992; Seeing his Way, by A. Madden le Brocquy, 1994; Procession, by G. Morgan, 1994; The Head Image: interviews by G. Morgan and M. Peppiatt, 1996. *Address:* c/o Gimpel Fils, 30 Davies Street, W1Y 1LG.

LE BRUN, Christopher Mark, RA 1997; artist; Professor of Drawing, Royal Academy, 2000–02; *b* 20 Dec. 1951; *s* of late John Le Brun, BEM and of Eileen Betty (*née* Miles); *m* 1979, Charlotte Eleanor Verity; two *s* one *d*. *Educ:* Portsmouth Southern Grammar Sch.; Slade Sch. of Fine Art (DFA); Chelsea Sch. of Art (MA). Lecturer: Brighton Coll. of Art, 1975–82; Wimbledon Coll. of Art, 1982–84; Vis. Lectr, Slade Sch. of Fine Art, 1984–90. Deutsche Akademische Austauschdienste Fellowship, Berlin, 1987–88. Designer, Ballet Imperial, Royal Opera Hse, Covent Gdn, 1984. One man exhibitions include: Nigel Greenwood Gall., London, 1980, 1982, 1985, 1989; Gillespie-Laage-Salomon, Paris, 1981; Sperone Westwater, NY, 1983, 1986, 1988; Fruitmarket Gall., Edinburgh, 1985; Arnolfini Gall., Bristol, 1985; Kunsthalle, Basel, 1986; Daadgalerie, Berlin, 1988; Galerie Rudolf Zwirner, Cologne, 1988; Art Center, Pasadena, Calif, 1992; LA Louver Gall., Venice, Calif, 1992; Marlborough Fine Art, 1994, 1998, 2001, 2003; Galerie Fortlaan 17, Ghent, 1994, 2002; Astrup Fearnley Mus. of Modern Art, Oslo, 1995; Fitzwilliam Mus., Cambridge, 1995; Marlborough Chelsea, NY, 2004; New Art Gall., Walsall, 2008; group exhibitions include: Milan, 1980; Berlin, 1982; Tate Gall., 1983; Mus. Modern Art, NY, 1984, 2005; The British Show, toured Australia and NZ, 1985; Oxford, Budapest, Prague, Warsaw, 1987; LA County Mus., 1987; Cincinatti Mus. and American tour, 1988–89; Setagaya Art Mus. and Japanese tour, 1990–91; Scottish Nat. Gall. Modern Art, 1995; Yale Center for British Art, New Haven, 1995; Nat. Gall., 2000; work in public collections includes: Arts Council of GB, British Council, BM, NY Mus. Modern Art, Scottish Nat. Gall. Modern Art, Tate Gall., Walker Art Gall., Liverpool, Whitworth Art Gall., Manchester and Fitzwilliam Mus., Cambridge. Trustee: Tate Gall., 1990–95; Nat. Gall., 1996–2003; Dulwich Picture Gall., 2000–05; Member: Slade Cttee, 1992–95; Develt Cttee, Tate Gall. of British Art, 1995–97. Advr, Prince of Wales's Drawing Studio, Shoreditch, 2000–03; Trustee, Prince's Drawing Sch., 2004–. Prizewinner, John Moores Liverpool Exhibns, 1978 and 1980; Gulbenkian Foundn Printmakers Award, 1983. *Relevant publication:* Christopher Le Brun, by Charles Saumarez Smith and Bryan Robertson, 2001. *Address:* c/o Royal Academy of Arts, Piccadilly, W1J 0BD.

LECAROS DE COSSÍO, (Luis) Armando (José); Ambassador of Peru to Spain; *b* 12 Feb. 1943; *s* of late Armando Lecaros and of María Dolores de Cossío de Lecaros; *m* 1986, Véronique Gauthier; three *s* two *d*. *Educ:* Markham Coll., Lima; Pontificia Univ. Católica, Peru (BA 1961, LLB 1966); Peruvian Diplomatic Acad. (Bach. Internat. Relns). Joined Diplomatic Service of Peru, 1967; Third Sec., America Dept, 1967–68; Third, later Second, Sec., Mexico, 1968–72; Second, later First, Sec., London, 1972–75; First Secretary: Under Secretariat of Foreign Policy, 1975–76; Hd, Eur. Dept, Directorate for Pol and Diplomatic Affairs, 1976–77; Counsellor, 1977–80 (Chargé d'Affaires *ai*, Nicaragua, 1979–80); Minister-Counsellor, Chargé d'Affaires *ai*, Cuba, 1980–81; Chargé d'Affaires *ai*, then Minister, London, 1981–84; Minister, then Ambassador, Australia, 1984–86; Ambassador, Nicaragua, 1986–88; Under Sec. for Special Policy, for Planning, and subseq. for Bilateral Policy, 1988–90; Ambassador: USSR, then Russian Fedn, 1990–95 (concurrently to Ukraine, 1993–95); Spain, 1998–2000 (concurrently to Andorra, 2000); Mexico, 2000–01; UK, concurrently to Ireland, and Permt Rep. to IMO, 2001–03; Dep. Minister and Sec. Gen. of Foreign Affairs, 2004. Holds numerous decorations, including: Grand Officer, Order of Merit (Peru); Grand Cross, El Sol (Peru); Comdr, Order of Civil Merit (Spain); Grand Cross, Order of Isabel la Católica (Spain); Grand Cross, Order of Simon Bolivar (Bolivia). *Recreations:* horse racing, tennis, music. *Address:* c/o Ministry of Foreign Affairs, Jirón Lampa 535, Lima, Peru. *Clubs:* Athenæum, Travellers, Carlton, Naval and Military, Canning, Mosimann's.

LE CARRÉ, John; *see* Cornwell, David John Moore.

LE CHEMINANT, Air Chief Marshal Sir Peter (de Lacey), GBE 1978; KCB 1972 (CB 1968); DFC 1943, and Bar, 1951; Lieutenant-Governor and Commander-in-Chief of Guernsey, 1980–85; *b* 17 June 1920; *s* of Lieut-Colonel Keith Le Cheminant and Blanche Etheldred Wake Le Cheminant (*née* Clark); *m* 1st, 1940, Sylvia (*d* 1998), *d* of J. van Bodegom; one *s* two *d*; 2nd, 2007, Norma Gardiner, MVO. *Educ:* Elizabeth Coll., Guernsey; RAF Coll., Cranwell. Flying posts in France, UK, N Africa, Malta, Sicily and Italy, 1940–44; comd No 223 Squadron, 1943–44; Staff and Staff Coll. Instructor, 1945–48; Far East, 1949–53; comd No 209 Sqn, 1949–51; Jt Planning Staff, 1953–55; Wing Comdr, Flying, Kuala Lumpur, 1955–57; jssc 1958; Dep. Dir of Air Staff Plans, 1958–61; comd RAF Geilenkirchen, 1961–63; Dir of Air Staff Briefing, 1964–66; SASO, HQ FEAF, 1966–67, C of S, 1967–68; Comdt Joint Warfare Estabt, MoD, 1968–70; Asst Chief of Air Staff (Policy), MoD, 1971–72; UK Mem., Perm. Mil. Deputies Gp, CENTO, Ankara, 1972–73; Vice-Chief of Defence Staff, 1974–76; Dep. C-in-C, Allied Forces, Central Europe, 1976–79. FRUSI 2001. KStJ 1980. *Publications:* The Royal Air Force - A Personal Experience, 2001; Ridiculous Rhymes, 2005; *as Desmond Walker:* Bedlam in the Bailiwicks, 1987; Task Force Channel Islands, 1989. *Recreations:* golf, writing, reading. *Address:* La Madeleine De Bas, Ruette de la Madeleine, St Pierre du Bois, Guernsey, CI. *Club:* Royal Air Force.

LECHÍN-SUÁREZ, General Juan; Condor de los Andes (Bolivia), 1966; *b* 8 March 1921; *s* of Juan Alfredo Lechín and Julia Suárez; *m* 1947, Ruth Varela; one *s* three *d*. *Educ:* Bolivian Military College. Chief of Ops, Bolivian Army HQ, 1960–61; Military and Air Attaché, Bolivian Embassy, Bonn, 1962–63; Comdr, Bolivian Army Fifth Inf. Div., 1964; Pres., Bolivian State Mining Corp. (with rank of Minister of State), 1964–68; Comdr, Bolivian Army Third Inf. Div., 1969; Bolivian Ambassador to the UK and to the Netherlands, 1970–74; Minister for Planning and Co-ordination, 1974–78; Chm., Nat. Adv. and Legislation Council, 1980–81. Guerrillero José Miguel Lanza, Mérito Aeronautico, and Mérito Naval, 1966, Bolivia. Das Grosse Verdienstkreuz (FRG), 1975. *Publications:* La Estrategia del Altiplano Boliviano, 1975; La Batalla de Villa Montes, 1989; Historia Trágica de un Camino Inexistente, 2000. *Recreations:* tennis, swimming. *Address:* Casilla 4405, La Paz, Bolivia.

LECHLER, Prof. Robert Ian, PhD; FRCP, FRCPath; FMedSci; Professor of Immunology, since 2004, Vice-Principal for Health, since 2005 and Dean, School of Medicine and Dental Institute, Guy's, King's College and St Thomas' Hospitals (formerly Guy's, King's and St Thomas' Schools of Medicine and Dentistry), since 2005, King's College London; Hon. Consultant, Department of Renal Medicine and Transplantation, Guy's Hospital, since 2004; *b* 24 Dec. 1951; *s* of Ian Lechler and Audrey Lechler (*née* Wilson); *m* 1975, Valerie Susan Johnston (marr. diss. 1990); two *s* one *d*; partner, Giovanna Lombardi; one *s* one *d*. *Educ:* Monkton Combe Sch.; Victoria Univ. of Manchester (MB ChB 1975); Royal Postgrad. Med. Sch., Univ. of London (PhD 1983). FRCP 1990; FRCPath 1996. Postgrad. med. trng in internal medicine and renal medicine, Manchester Royal Infirmary, Wythenshawe Hosp. and St Bartholomew's Hosp., London, 1975–79; Med. Res. Trng Fellow, Dept of Immunol., RPMS, 1979–82; Renal Registrar, 1982–83, Sen. Renal Registrar, 1983–84, Professorial Med. Unit, Hammersmith Hosp.; Wellcome Trust Travelling Fellow, Lab. of Immunol., NIH, Bethesda, USA, 1984–86; Royal Postgraduate Medical School: Sen. Lectr in Immunol., 1986–98; Reader in Immunol., 1989–92; Prof. of Molecular Immunol., 1992–94; Hon. Consultant in Medicine, 1986–94; Consultant Transplant Physician, Hammersmith Hosps NHS Trust, 1986–2004; Imperial College, University of London: Prof. of Immunol., 1994–2004; Dean of Hammersmith Campus, 2001–04; Hd, Div. of Medicine, 2003–04; Dean, GKT Sch. of Medicine, KCL, 2004–05. Internat. Advr to NIH Immune Tolerance Network, 2000–. Chairman: Scientific Adv. Bd, Embryonic Stem Cell Internat., 2003–; Expert Adv. Gp, Cttee for Safety of Medicines, 2007–. Councillor, Internat. Xenotransplantation Assoc., 2001–05; Mem. Exec., Council of Hds of Med. Schs, 2006–. Mem., Scientific Cttee, Inst de transplantation et de recherche en transplantation, Nantes, 2000–06; Dir, Ruggero Ceppellini Sch. of Immunol., Naples, 2001–; Chm., Chairs and Prog. Grants Cttee, BHF, 2003–07. FMedSci 2000 (Council Mem., 2006–). *Publications:* HLA in Health and Disease, 1994, 2nd edn 2000; numerous contribs to leading jls on transplantation and immune tolerance. *Recreations:* theatre, music. *Address:* (home) 78 Woodstock Road, W4 1EQ; King's College London School of Medicine, First Floor, Hodgkin Building, Guy's Campus, SE1 9RT; *e-mail:* robert.lechler@kcl.ac.uk.

LECHMERE, Sir Reginald Anthony Hungerford, 7th Bt *cr* 1818, of The Rhydd, Worcestershire; *b* 24 Dec. 1920; *s* of Anthony Hungerford Lechmere, 3rd *s* of 3rd Bt, and Cicely Mary Lechmere; *S* cousin, 2001; *m* 1956, Anne Jennifer Dind; three *s* one *d*. *Educ:* Charterhouse; Trinity Hall, Cambridge. Served Army, 1940–47, 5th Royal Inniskilling Dragoon Guards, HQ6 Armoured Div. Publicity Manager, Penguin Books, 1950–51; journalist, 1952–56; antiquarian bookseller, 1955–87. *Heir:* *s* Nicholas Anthony Hungerford Lechmere [*b* 24 April 1960; *m* 1991, Caroline Gahan; three *s* one *d*].

LECKIE, Carolyn; Member (Scot Socialist) Scotland Central, Scottish Parliament, 2003–07; *b* 5 March 1965. Midwife. Contested (Scot Socialist), Springburn, 2001. Scot Socialist spokesperson for Health and Community Care, Scottish Parlt, 2003–07.

LECKY, (Arthur) Terence, CMG 1968; HM Diplomatic Service, retired; *b* 10 June 1919; *s* of late Lieut-Colonel M. D. Lecky, DSO, late RA, and Bertha Lecky (*née* Goss); *m* 1946, Jacqualine (*d* 1974), *d* of late Dr A. G. Element; three *s*. *Educ:* Winchester Coll.; Clare Coll., Cambridge (1938–39). Served RA, 1939–46. FO (Control Commission for Germany), 1946–49; FO, 1950–54; Vice-Consul, Zürich, 1954–56; FO, 1957–61; First Secretary, The Hague, 1962–64, FCO (formerly FO), 1964–70, retired. Mem., Hants CC, 1981–89. Vice-Chm., Hants Police Authority, 1988–89. *Address:* 1 Old Blackmore Museum, St Ann Place, Salisbury, Wilts SP1 2SU. *T:* (01722) 338937.

LECKY, Maj.-Gen. Samuel K.; *see* Knox-Lecky.

LECKY, Terence; *see* Lecky, A. T.

LE COCQ, Timothy John; QC (Jersey) 2008; HM Solicitor General for Jersey, since 2008; *b* Jersey, 9 Dec. 1956; *s* of Bernard Reginald Le Cocq and Janet Le Cocq (*née* Gibbs); *m* 1994, Ruth Iona Leighton; three *s* one *d*. *Educ:* De La Salle Coll., Jersey; Univ. of Keele (BA Hons Law and Psychol. 1980). Called to the Bar, Inner Temple, 1981; called to Jersey Bar, 1985; in practice as Jersey Advocate, 1985–2008; Crown Advocate, Jersey, 1996–2008. *Recreations:* choral singing, reading, Western martial arts, horse-riding, Medieval re-enactment. *Address:* c/o Law Officers' Department, Morier House, St Helier, Jersey JE1 1DD. *T:* (01534) 441233, *Fax:* (01534) 441299; *e-mail:* tj.lecocq@gov.je. *Club:* United (Jersey).

LECONFIELD, Baron; *see* Egremont.

LEDERER, Peter Julian, CBE 2005 (OBE 1994); Chairman, Gleneagles Hotels Ltd, since 2007 (Managing Director, 1984–2007); Chairman, VisitScotland (formerly Scottish Tourist Board), since 2001; *b* 30 Nov. 1950; *s* of Thomas F. Lederer and Phoebe J. Lederer; *m* 1981, Marilyn R. MacPhail; two *s*. *Educ:* City of London Sch.; Middlesex Poly. (Nat. Dip. Hotelkeeping and Catering). Manager, Four Seasons Hotels, 1972–79; Partner and Vice Pres., Wood Wilkings Ltd, 1979–81; Gen. Manager, Plaza Hotels Ltd, 1981–83. Hon. Prof., Univ. of Dundee, 1994. Director: Guinness Enterprises Ltd, 1987–; Leading Hotels of the World, 1998–. Dir, Springboard Charitable Trust, 2000–; Patron: Hospitality Industry Trust Scotland, 2004– (Chm., 1992–2003); Queen Margaret UC Foundn, 1998. FIH (FHCIMA 1987; Pres., Inst. of Hospitality, 2007); CCMI 2002. Liveryman, Co. of Innholders, 1999–. Hon. DBA Queen Margaret UC, 1997. Master Innholder, 1988. *Recreations:* motor racing, current affairs, travel. *Address:* The Gleneagles Hotel, Auchterarder, Perthshire PH3 1NF. *T:* (01764) 662231, *Fax:* (01764) 664444; *e-mail:* peter.lederer@gleneagles.com.

LEDERMAN, David; QC 1990; a Recorder, since 1987; *b* 8 Feb. 1942; *s* of late Eric Kurt Lederman and Marjorie Alice Lederman; *m* 2003, Jennifer Oldland; one *s* two *d* from a previous marriage. *Educ:* Clayesmore School, Dorset; Gonville and Caius College, Cambridge. Called to the Bar, Inner Temple, 1966; criminal practice, fraud, murder, etc. *Recreations:* tennis, horses, France, family.

LEDERMAN, Dr Leon Max, FInstP; Director, Fermi National Accelerator Laboratory, 1979–89, Director Emeritus, since 1989; Pritzker Professor of Science, Illinois Institute of Technology, since 1992; *b* 15 July 1922; *s* of Minnie Rosenberg and Morris Lederman; *m* 1st, Florence Gordon; one *s* two *d*; 2nd, 1981, Ellen. *Educ:* City College of New York (BS 1943); Columbia Univ. (AM 1948; PhD 1951). FInstP 1998. US Army, 1943–46. Columbia University: Research Associate, Asst Prof., Associate Prof., 1951–58; Prof. of Physics, 1958–89; Associate Dir, Nevis Labs, 1953, Director, 1962–79. Resident Scholar, Ill Maths and Sci. Acad., 1998–. Ford Foundn Fellow, 1958–59; John Simon Guggenheim Foundn Fellow, 1958–59; Ernest Kempton Adams Fellow, 1961. Fellow, Amer. Physical Soc.; Mem., Nat. Acad. of Scis, 1965. Numerous hon. degrees. Nat. Medal of Science, 1965; (jtly) Nobel Prize in Physics, 1988; Enrico Fermi Prize, DOE, US, 1992. *Publications:* From Quarks to the Cosmos, 1989; The God Particle, 1992; Symmetry and the Beautiful Universe, 2004; papers and contribs to learned jls on high energy physics. *Recreations:* mountain hiking, ski-ing, jogging, piano, riding, gardening. *Address:* Fermi National Accelerator Laboratory, PO Box 500, Batavia, IL 60510, USA. *T:* (630) 8402856, (312) 5678920.

LEDGER, Frank, CBE 1992 (OBE 1985); FREng; Deputy Chairman, Nuclear Electric plc, 1990–92, retired; *b* 16 June 1929; *s* of Harry and Doris Ledger; *m* 1953, Alma Moverley; two *s*. *Educ:* Leeds College of Technology (BSc Eng). FREng (FEng 1990); FIMechE; FIET. Student Apprentice, Leeds Corp. Elect. Dept, 1947; appts in power station construction and generation operation in CEA then CEGB, 1955–65; Station Manager, Cottam Power Station, 1965; Central Electricity Generating Board: Group Manager, Midlands Region, 1968; System Operation Engineer, 1971; Dir, Resource Planning, Midlands Region, 1975; Dir of Computing, 1980; Dir of Operations, 1981; Exec. Bd Mem. for Prodn, 1986. Sen. Associate, Nichols Associates Ltd, 1992–98. Member: Council, IEE, 1987–92; British Nat. Cttee, UNIPEDE, 1981–90; Council, British Energy Assoc., 1990–92; Vice-Pres., Energy Industries Club, 1988–92. *Publication:* (jtly) Crisis Management in the Power Industry: an inside story, 1994. *Recreations:* music, photography, gardening, walking. *Address:* 3 Barns Dene, Harpenden, Herts AL5 2HH. *T:* (01582) 762188.

LEDGER, Sir Philip (Stevens), Kt 1999; CBE 1985; Principal, Royal Scottish Academy of Music and Drama, 1982–2001; *b* 12 Dec. 1937; *s* of Walter Stephen Ledger and Winifred Kathleen (*née* Stevens); *m* 1963, Mary Erryl (*née* Wells); one *s* one *d*. *Educ:* Bexhill Grammar Sch.; King's Coll., Cambridge (Maj. Schol.); John Stewart of Rannoch Schol. in Sacred Music; 1st Cl. Hons in Pt I and Pt II, of Music Tripos; MA, MusB. FRCO (Limpus and Read prizes); FRCM 1983; FRNCM 1989. Master of the Music, Chelmsford Cathedral, 1962–65; Dir of Music, Univ. of East Anglia, 1965–73 (Dean of Sch. of Fine Arts and Music, 1968–71); Dir of Music and Organist, King's Coll., Cambridge, 1974–82; Conductor, CU Musical Soc., 1973–82. Artistic Dir, 1968–89, Vice-Pres., 1989–, Aldeburgh Festival of Music and the Arts. Hon. Prof., Univ. of Glasgow, 1993–98. President: RCO, 1992–94; ISM, 1994–95; Chm., Cttee of Principals of Conservatoires, 1994–98. Composer, Requiem (A Thanksgiving for Life), 2007. Hon. RAM 1984; Hon. GSM 1989. Hon. LLD Strathclyde, 1987; DUniv UCE, 1998; Hon. DMus: Glasgow, 2001; RSAMD, 2001; St Andrews, 2001. *Publications:* (ed) Anthems for Choirs 2 and 3, 1973; (ed) The Oxford Book of English Madrigals, 1978; other edns, compositions, arrangements. *Recreations:* swimming, theatre, membership of Sette of Odd Volumes. *Address:* 2 Lancaster Drive, Upper Rissington, Cheltenham, Glos GL54 2QZ; *web:* www.sirphilipledger.com.

LEDINGHAM, Prof. John Gerard Garvin, DM; FRCP; May Reader in Medicine, 1974–95, Professor of Clinical Medicine, 1989–95, and Director of Clinical Studies, 1977–82 and 1991–95, University of Oxford; Fellow of New College, Oxford, 1974–95, Emeritus, 1995–2000, Hon. Fellow, since 2000; Hon. Clinical Director, Biochemical and Clinical NMR Unit, Medical Research Council, Oxford, 1988–95; *b* 1929; *s* of late John Ledingham, MB BCh, DPH, and late Una Ledingham, MD, FRCP, *d* of J. L. Garvin, CH, Editor of The Observer; *m* 1961, Elaine Mary, *d* of late R. G. Maliphant, MD, FRCOG, and of Dilys Maliphant, Cardiff; four *d*. *Educ:* Rugby Sch.; New Coll., Oxford; Middlesex Hosp. Med. Sch. (1st Cl. Physiol.; BM BCh; DM 1966). FRCP 1971 (MRCP 1959). Junior appts, Middlesex, London Chest, Whittington, and Westminster Hospitals, London, 1957–64; Travelling Fellow, British Postgraduate Med. Fedn, Columbia Univ., New York, 1965–66; Consultant Physician, Oxford AHA(T), 1966–82, Hon. Consultant Physician, Oxfordshire HA, 1982–. Chm., Medical Staff Council, United Oxford Hosps, 1970–72. Chm., Medical Res. Soc., 1988–92; Hon. Sec., Assoc. of Physicians of Gt Britain and Ireland 1977–82, Hon. Treas., 1982–88; Pro-Censor, RCP, 1983–84, Censor, 1984–85. Member: Commonwealth Scholarship Commn, ACU, 1993–98; Nuffield Council on Bioethics, 2000–03. Governing Trustee, Nuffield Trust (formerly Nuffield Provincial Hosps Trust), 1978–2002; Trustee, Beit Trust, 1989–2008. Osler Meml Medal, Oxford Univ., 2000. *Publications:* (ed jtly) Oxford Textbook of Medicine, 1982, 3rd edn 1995; contribs to med. books and scientific jls in the field of hypertension and renal diseases. *Recreations:* music, golf. *Address:* 124 Oxford Road, Cumnor, Oxford OX2 9PQ. *T:* and *Fax:* (01865) 865806; *e-mail:* jeled@btopenworld.com. *Club:* Vincent's (Oxford).

LEDLIE, John Kenneth, CB 1994; OBE 1977; Director, Peter Harrison Foundation, since 2002; *b* 19 March 1942; *s* of late Reginald Cyril Bell Ledlie and Elspeth Mary Kaye; *m* 1965, Rosemary Julia Allan (marr. diss. 2006); three *d*. *Educ:* Westminster School (Hon. Schol.); Brasenose Coll., Oxford (Triplett Exbnr; MA Lit Hum). Solicitor of the High Court; articles with Coward Chance, 1964–67; Min. of Defence, 1967; Asst Private Sec. to Minister of State for Equipment and Sec. of State for Defence, 1969–70; First Sec., UK Delegn to NATO, Brussels, 1973–76; Dep. Chief, Public Relations, 1977–79; NI Office and Cabinet Office, 1979–81; Procurement Exec., MoD, 1981–83; Head, Defence Secretariat 19, MoD, 1983; Regional Marketing Dir, Defence Sales Orgn, 1983–85; Chief of PR, MoD, 1985–87; Fellow, Center for Internat. Affairs, Harvard Univ., 1987–88; Asst Under-Sec. of State, MoD, 1988–90; Dep. Sec., NI Office, 1990–93; Dep. Under Sec. of State (Personnel and Logistics), MoD, 1993–95; Partnership Sec., Linklaters & Paines, subseq. Linklaters, 1995–2002. *Recreations:* ornithology, cricket, tennis, theatre, opera. *Address:* c/o Peter Harrison Foundation, 42/48 London Road, Reigate, Surrey RH2 9QQ. *T:* (01737) 228013. *Club:* Oxford and Cambridge.

LEDSOME, Neville Frank, CB 1988; Deputy Chairman, Civil Service Appeal Board, 1994–99; Under Secretary, Personnel Management Division, Department of Trade and Industry, 1983–89, retired; *b* 29 Nov. 1929; *s* of late Charles Percy Ledsome and Florence Ledsome; *m* 1953, Isabel Mary Lindsay; three *s*. *Educ:* Birkenhead Sch. Exec. Officer, BoT, 1948; Monopolies Commn, 1957; Higher Exec. Officer, BoT, 1961; Principal, 1964; DEA, 1967; HM Treasury, 1969; DTI, 1970; Asst Sec., 1973; Under Sec., 1980. *Recreations:* gardening, theatre.

LEDWITH, Prof. Anthony, CBE 1995; FRS 1995; Professor and Head of Department of Chemistry, University of Sheffield, 1996–99, now Emeritus Professor; Chairman, Engineering and Physical Sciences Research Council, 1999–2003 (Member, 1994–97); *b* 14 Aug. 1933; *s* of Thomas Ledwith and Mary (*née* Coghlan); *m* 1960, Mary Clare Ryan; one *s* three *d*. *Educ:* BSc (external) London 1954; PhD 1957, DSc 1970, Liverpool Univ. FRSC 1986. Liverpool University: Lectr, 1959, Prof., 1976, Campbell Brown Prof. of Industrial Chem., 1980, Dept of Inorganic Physical and Industrial Chem.; Dean, Faculty of Sci., 1980–83; Dep. Dir, Group R&D, 1984–88, Dir, Group Res., 1988–96, Pilkington plc. Chm., DSAC, 2001– (Mem., 1988–91); Mem., SERC, 1990–94. Pres., RSC, 1998–2000. *Publications:* (with A. D. Jenkins) Reactivity, Mechanism and Structure in Polymer Chemistry, 1974; (with A. M. North) Molecular Behaviour and the Development of Polymeric Materials, 1975; (with S. J. Moss) The Chemistry of the Semiconductor Industry, 1987; (ed jtly) Comprehensive Polymer Science, 7 vols, 1989. *Recreations:* squash, tennis, golf. *Address:* 193 Wigan Road, Standish, Wigan WN6 0AE.

LEE, family name of **Baron Lee of Trafford**.

LEE OF TRAFFORD, Baron *cr* 2006 (Life Peer), of Bowdon in the County of Cheshire; **John Robert Louis Lee;** DL; FCA; company director, investor and financial journalist; *b* 21 June 1942; *s* of late Basil and Miriam Lee; *m* 1975, Anne Monique Bakirgian; two *d*. *Educ:* William Hulme's Grammar Sch., Manchester. Accountancy Articles, 1959–64; Henry Cooke, Lumsden & Co., Manchester, Stockbrokers, 1964–66; Founding Dir, Chancery Consolidated Ltd, Investment Bankers; non-executive Director: Paterson Zochonis (UK) Ltd, 1974–75; Paterson Zochonis PLC, 1990–99; Emerson Developments (Hldgs), 2000–; Chm., Wellington Market plc, 2006–. Contested (C) Manchester, Moss Side, Oct. 1974; MP (C) Nelson and Colne, 1979–83, Pendle, 1983–92; contested (C) Pendle, 1992. PPS to Minister of State for Industry, 1981–83, to Sec. of State for Trade and Industry, 1983; Parly Under Sec. of State, MoD, 1983–86, Dept of Employment, 1986–89 (Minister for Tourism, 1987–89). Chm., All-Party Tourism Cttee, 1991–92. Jt Sec., Conservative Back Benchers' Industry Cttee, 1979–80. Lib Dem spokesman on Defence, H of L, 2007–. Chm., Christie Hosp. NHS Trust, 1992–98. Chairman: ALVA, 1990–; Mus. of Sci. and Industry in Manchester, 1990–2001; Mem., English Tourist Bd, 1992–99. Vice-Chm., NW Conciliation Cttee, Race Relations Bd, 1976–77; Chm. Council, Nat. Youth Bureau, 1980–83. DL 1995, High Sheriff 1998, Greater Manchester. *Recreations:* golf, fly fishing, collecting. *Address:* House of Lords, SW1A 0PW.

LEE, Alan John; book illustrator, since 1972; film conceptual designer, since 1983; *b* 20 Aug. 1947; *s* of George James Lee and Margaret Lee (*née* Cook); *m* 1979, Marja Kruyt (separated); one *s* one *d*. *Educ:* Manor Secondary Modern Sch., Ruislip; Ealing Sch. of Art. Conceptual designer of films: Legend, 1985; Erik the Viking, 1989; conceptual designer and set decorator of films: The Fellowship of the Ring, 2001; The Two Towers, 2002; The Return of the King, 2003. *Publications: illustrator:* The Importance of Being Ernest, 1972; Faeries, 1978, 2nd edn 2003; The Mabinogion, 1982, 2nd edn 2002; Castles, 1984; Michael Palin, The Mirrorstone, 1986; Joan Aiken, The Moon's Revenge, 1987; Peter Dickinson, Merlin Dreams, 1988; J. R. R. Tolkien, The Lord of the Rings, 1992; Rosemary Sutcliff, Black Ships Before Troy (Kate Greenaway Medal), 1993; Rosemary Sutcliff, The Wanderings of Odysseus, 1995; J. R. R. Tolkien, The Hobbit, 1997; J. R. R. Tolkien, The Children of Hurin, 2007; J. R. R. Tolkien, Tales from the Perilous Realm, 2008; *written and illustrated:* The Lord of the Rings Sketchbook, 2005. *Recreation:* tango dancing. *Address: e-mail:* alanlee@dircon.co.uk. *Club:* Pudding (Chagford).

LEE, Alan Peter; racing correspondent, The Times, since 1999; *b* 13 June 1954; *s* of Peter Alexander Lee and Christina Carmichael; *m* 1980, Patricia Drury; one *s* one *d*. *Educ:* Cavendish Grammar Sch., Hemel Hempstead. With Watford Observer, 1970–74; Hayters Agency, 1974–78; freelance, 1978–82; cricket correspondent: Mail on Sunday, 1982–87; The Times, 1988–99. *Publications:* A Pitch in Both Camps, 1979; Diary of a Cricket Season, 1980; Lambourn, Village of Racing, 1983; *biographies:* (with Tony Greig) My Story, 1978; (with David Gower) With Time to Spare, 1980; (with Graham Gooch) Out of the Wilderness, 1985; Fred (biog. of Fred Winter), 1991; (with Pat Eddery) To Be A Champion, 1992; Lord Ted, 1995; Raising the Stakes, 1996. *Recreations:* National Hunt racing (has owned or part-owned ten horses), tennis, wine. *Address:* 8 The Courtyard, Montpellier Street, Cheltenham, Glos GL50 1SR. *T:* (01242) 572637. *Club:* Cricketers'.

LEE, Hon. Allen; *see* Lee Peng-Fei, A.

LEE, Dr Anne Mary Linda; educational and business adviser; Academic Development Adviser, University of Surrey, since 2005; *b* 14 Oct. 1953; *d* of Cecil and Eugenie Covell; *m* 1973, Anthony Mervyn Lee, *qv*; one *s* one *d*. *Educ:* Shenfield High Sch.; Open Univ. (BA); Univ. of Surrey (PhD). FCIPD; GMBPS. Inf. Officer, Unilever, 1972–74; Trng Officer, G. D. Searle & Co., 1974–76; Management and Trng Advr, Industrial Soc., 1976–78; Head of Trng, Morgan Guaranty Trust Co., 1978–81; Dir, Anne M. Lee (Training) Ltd, 1983–94; Headmistress, Malvern Girls' Coll., 1994–96. Dir, Next Chapter Ltd, 1998–2006. Mem., Huhne Commn on Future of Public Services, 2001–02. Mem. (Lib Dem), Guildford BC, 1997–2001. Contested (Lib Dem): Norfolk S, 2001; Woking, 2005. Past Member Board/Trustee: Guildford and Waverly PCT; Guildford CAB; Merrow Sunset Homes. Gov., Queenswood Sch., 1996–2005. *Publications:* contribs to educnl, personnel and management jls and The Times. *Recreations:* singing, walking, friendship, words and music. *Address:* The Post House, West Clandon, Guildford, Surrey GU4 7ST. *T:* (01483) 222610.

LEE, Anthony Mervyn; Chief Executive (formerly Director), Age Concern Surrey, since 2001; *b* 21 Feb. 1949; *s* of Sydney Ernest Lee and Evelyn May Lee; *m* 1973, Anne Mary Linda Lee, *qv*; one *s* one *d*. *Educ:* Romford Sch.; Cranfield Sch. of Mgt (MBA). FCCA 1971; FCMA 1975. Financial trng, Eastern Electricity Bd, 1967–72; Finance Manager, ITT SemiConductors, 1972–74; Financial Controller, Mars Confectionery, 1974–77; Managing Director: Am Bruning Ltd, 1978–82; Citibank Trust, 1982–86; Chief Exec., Access (JCCC Ltd), 1987–91; Ops Dir, Natwest Card Services, 1991–97; Exec. Dir, Muscular Dystrophy Campaign, 1998–2001. *Recreations:* keep fit, gardening, politics. *Address:* The Post House, The Street, West Clandon, Surrey GU4 7ST. *T:* (01483) 222610.

LEE, Christopher Frank Carandini, CBE 2001; actor; entered film industry, 1947; *b* 27 May 1922; *s* of Geoffrey Trollope Lee (Lt-Col 60th KRRC) and Estelle Marie Carandini; *m* 1961, Birgit, *d* of Richard Emil Kroencke; one *d*. *Educ:* Wellington Coll. RAFVR, 1941–46 (Flt Lieut; mentioned in despatches, 1944). Films include: Moulin Rouge, 1952; Tale of Two Cities, Dracula, 1958; Rasputin, 1966; The Devil Rides Out, 1968; Private Life of Sherlock Holmes, 1970; The Wicker Man, The Three Musketeers, 1973; The Four Musketeers, The Man with the Golden Gun, 1974; To the Devil, a Daughter, 1976; Airport '77, 1977; The Passage, Bear Island, 1941, 1979; The Serial, 1980; An Eye for An Eye, The Salamander, 1981; The Last Unicorn, Safari 3000, 1982; The Return of Captain Invincible, The House of the Long Shadows, 1983; Mio Min Mio, 1987; The Return of the Musketeers, The French Revolution, 1989; Gremlins II, The Rainbow Thief, 1990; A Feast at Midnight, 1994; The Stupids, 1996; Jinnah, 1998; Sleepy Hollow, 1999; The Fellowship of the Ring, 2001; Star Wars, Episode II: Attack of the Clones, The Two Towers, 2002; The Return of the King, 2003; Star Wars, Episode III: Revenge of the Sith, Charlie and the Chocolate Factory, The Corpse Bride, 2005; The Adventures of Greyfriars Bobby, 2006; The Golden Compass, 2007; television includes: Charles and Diana: a royal love story, 1982; The Far Pavilions, 1984; The Disputation, 1986; Treasure Island, 1990; Sherlock Holmes - The Golden Years, 1991; Young Indy, 1992; Death Train, 1993; Tales of Mystery and Imagination, 1994; Moses 1995; Gormenghast, 2000. CStJ 1997 (OStJ 1986). Officier de l'Ordre des Arts et des Lettres (France), 2002. *Publications:* Christopher Lee's 'X' Certificate, 1975 (2nd edn 1976); Christopher Lee's Archives of Evil, USA 1975 (2nd edn 1976); Tall, Dark and Gruesome (autobiog.), 1977, new edn 1997; Lord of Misrule, 2005. *Recreations:* opera, golf. *Address:* c/o Independent Talent Group Ltd, Oxford House, Oxford Street, W1D 1BS. *Clubs:* Buck's; Honourable Company of Edinburgh Golfers; Travellers (Paris).

LEE, Christopher Robin James, RD 1981 (Bar 1991); historian, writer and broadcaster; *b* 13 Oct. 1941; *s* of James Thomas Lee and Winifred Lee (*née* Robertson); *m* 1969, Christine Elisabeth Adams; two *d*. *Educ:* Dartford Tech. Sch.; Wilmington Grammar Sch.; Goldsmiths' Coll., London; MA Cantab. Deck apprentice, 1958–59; freelance writer, 1962–67; journalist, Daily Express, 1967–76 (Asst Ed., 1975–76); Defence and Foreign Affairs Corresp., BBC radio, 1976–86; Quatercentenary Fellow in Contemporary Hist., Emmanuel Coll., Cambridge, 1986–91; lecturer, author and scriptwriter, 1991–; various BBC radio drama and comedy series incl. The Archers, The House, Colvil and Soames, The Trial of Walter Ralegh, Our Brave Boys, 1987–2005; Kicking the Habit, 2007–; This Sceptred Isle, hist. of Britain, 1995–96, This Sceptred Isle, 90-pt hist. series, 2005–06, Radio 4. Dir, This Sceptred Isle Publishing Ltd, 2006–; Editl Adv. Bd, BBC History Mag., 2001–; Historical Advr to NT production of Saint Joan, 2007. Vis. Lectr, Univ. of Utah, 1986; Gomes Lectr, Emmanuel Coll., Cambridge, 2001. Royal Naval Reserve: Services Intelligence Wing, 1966–82; OC Public Affairs Br., 1982–86; CO, HMS Wildfire, 1988–90. Trustee, Sail Trng Assoc., 1994–2001. Younger Brother, Trinity House, 2002–. *Publications:* Seychelles: political castaways, 1976; Final Decade, 1981; (with Bhupendra Jasani) Countdown to Space War, 1984; War in Space, 1987; (ed) Nicely Nurdled Sir, 1988; From the Sea End, 1989; The Madrigal, 1993; The House, 1994; The Bath Detective, 1995; (ed) Through the Covers, 1996; Killing of Sally Keemer, 1997; This Sceptred Isle 55 BC–1901, 1997; (ed) History of the English-speaking Peoples, 1998; The Killing of Cinderella, 1998; The 20th Century, 1999; Eight Bells and Topmasts, 2001; Dynasties, 2002; 1603: a turning point in English history, 2003; This Sceptred Isle: Empire, 2005; Nelson & Napoleon: the long haul to Trafalgar, 2005. *Recreation:* sailing. *Address:* Virginia House, Sissinghurst, Kent TN17 2JJ. *Clubs:* Athenæum; Royal Naval Sailing Association.

LEE, Ven. David John, PhD; Archdeacon of Bradford, since 2004; *b* 31 Jan. 1946; *s* of John and Sheila Lee; *m* 1989, Janet Mary Strong; two *s*. *Educ:* Bristol Univ. (BSc Mech. Eng 1967); London Univ. (DipTh 1973); Fitzwilliam Coll., Cambridge (BA (Theol.) 1976, MA 1979); Birmingham Univ. (PhD (NT Studies) 1996). Schoolmaster: Lesotho, Southern Africa, 1967; Walsall, 1968. Ordained deacon, 1977, priest, 1978; Curate, St Margaret's, Putney, 1977–80; Lecturer: in Theol., Bp Tucker Coll., Mukono, Uganda, 1980–86; in Missiology, Selly Oak Colls, Birmingham, 1986–91; Rector, Middleton and Wishaw, Birmingham, 1991–96; Dir of Mission, Dio. Birmingham, and Canon Residentiary, Birmingham Cathedral, 1996–2004. *Publications:* Discovering Science (jtly), 1970; Jesus in the Stories of Luke, 1999; (ed) Ministry and Mission in a Multifaith Context, 2001. *Recreations:* conversation, music, walking, motoring, multi-media, DIY in its better manifestations, redeeming the vocation of property landlords. *Address:* 14 Park Cliffe Road, Undercliffe, Bradford BD2 4NS. *T:* (01274) 200698; *e-mail:* davidandjanet@leefamily.uk.net.

LEE, Prof. David Morris, FInstP; James Gilbert White Distinguished Professor of Physical Sciences, Cornell University, since 1997; *b* 20 Jan. 1931; *s* of Marvin and Annette Lee; *m* 1960, Dana Thorangkul; two *s*. *Educ:* Harvard Univ. (AB 1952); Connecticut Univ. (MS 1955); Yale Univ. (PhD Physics 1959). FInstP 1998. US Army, 1952–54. Cornell University: Instructor in Physics, 1959–60; Asst Prof., 1960–63; Associate Prof., 1963–68; Prof. of Physics, 1968–. Guggenheim Fellow, 1966, 1974; Fellow, Japan Soc. for Promotion of Science, 1977. Member: Amer. Acad. Arts and Scis, 1987; Nat. Acad. of Scis, 1991. Sir Francis Simon Meml Prize, British Inst. of Physics, 1976; Oliver Buckley Prize, APS, 1981; (jtly) Nobel Prize for Physics, 1996. *Publications:* articles in learned jls. *Recreations:* hiking in the mountains, fishing, boating, running. *Address:* Cornell University Physics Department, Clark Hall, Ithaca, NY 14853–2501, USA. *T:* (607) 2555286.

LEE, Derek William, FCIB; Chairman, Friendly Societies Commission, 1992–98; *b* 11 April 1935; *s* of Richard William Lee and Ivy Elizabeth Lee; *m* 1960, Dorothy Joan Preece; one *d*. *Educ:* St Dunstan's Coll.; London Univ. (LLB Hons external). FCIB 1973. Nat. Service, REME, Malaya, 1953–55. Lloyds Bank, 1955–73, Manager, Threadneedle St Br., 1970–73; Asst Gen. Manager, 1973–77, Gen. Manager, 1977–87, Mercantile Credit Co. Ltd; Man. Dir, H & H Factors, 1988–89; Registrar, Friendly Societies, 1989–95. Gov., Guy's and St Thomas' Hosp. Foundn Trust, 2004–07; Mem. Cttee, Samaritan Fund, Hosp. Authy Charitable Foundn, 2007–. Freeman, City of London, 1999. *Recreations:* tennis, clarinet, art, golf, bowls. *Clubs:* Sundridge Park Lawn Tennis; High Elms Golf; Bromley Town Bowling.

LEE, Brig. Sir Henry; *see* Lee, Brig. Sir L. H.

LEE, Prof. Hermione, CBE 2003; FRSL; FBA 2001; President, Wolfson College, Oxford, since 2008; *b* 29 Feb. 1948; *d* of Dr Benjamin Lee and Josephine Lee (*née* Anderson); *m* 1991, Prof. John Michael Barnard, *qv*. *Educ:* St Hilda's Coll., Oxford (MA; Hon. Fellow, 1998); St Cross Coll., Oxford (MPhil; Hon. Fellow, 1998). Instructor, Coll. of William and Mary, Williamsburg, Va, 1970–71; Lectr, Dept of English, Univ. of Liverpool, 1971–77; Department of English and Related Literature, University of York: Lectr. 1977–87; Sen. Lectr, 1987–90; Reader, 1990–93; Prof., 1993–98; Goldsmiths' Prof. of English Literature, Univ. of Oxford, 1998–2008; Fellow, New Coll., Oxford, 1998–2008. Presenter, Book Four, Channel 4, 1982–86. Chair of Judges, Man Booker Prize, 2006. FRSL 1992. For. Hon. Mem., Amer. Acad. of Arts and Scis, 2003.

Publications: The Novels of Virginia Woolf, 1977; Elizabeth Bowen, 1981, 2nd edn 1999; Philip Roth, 1982; (ed) The Mulberry Tree: writings of Elizabeth Bowen, 1986; Willa Cather: a life saved up, 1989, US edn as Willa Cather: double lives, 1991; (ed) The Selected Stories of Willa Cather, 1989; Virginia Woolf, 1996; Body Parts: essays on life-writing, 2005; Edith Wharton, 2007. *Recreations:* reading, music, countryside. *Address:* Wolfson College, Oxford OX2 6UD. *Club:* Athenæum.

LEE, James Giles; Principal, Lee & Company, since 1992; *b* 23 Dec. 1942; *s* of John Lee, CBE and Muriel Giles; *m* 1966, Linn Macdonald; one *s* two *d*. *Educ:* Trinity Coll., Glenalmond; Glasgow Univ.; Harvard Univ., USA. Consultant, McKinsey & Co., 1969–80; Mem., Central Policy Review Staff, 1972. Dep. Chm. and Chief Exec., Pearson Longman, 1980–83; Chairman: Penguin Publishing Co., 1980–84; Direct Broadcasting by Satellite Consortium, 1986–87; Deputy Chairman: Westminster Press, 1980–84; Financial Times, 1980–84; Yorkshire TV, 1982–85; Dir, S. Pearson & Son, 1981–84; Chm., 1981–85, Chief Exec., 1983–85, Goldcrest Films and Television; Dir, Boston Consulting Gp, 1987–92. Non-executive Director: Pearson Television, 1993–2001; Phoenix Pictures Inc., 1996–2004; Nation Media Gp, Kenya, 2001–. Chairman: Performing Arts Labs Trust, 1989–99; Scottish Screen, 1998–2002; Dir, Film Council, 1999–2004. Chm., Maidstone and Tunbridge Wells NHS Trust, 2003–07. *Publications:* Planning for the Social Services, 1978; The Investment Challenge, 1979. *Recreations:* photography, travelling, sailing. *Address:* Meadow Wood, Penshurst, Kent TN11 8AD. *T:* (01892) 870309. *Clubs:* Reform; Harvard (New York, USA).

LEE, Hon. James Matthew; PC (Can.) 1982; Chairman, PEI Workers Compensation Board, since 1998; Leader, Progressive Conservative Party, Prince Edward Island, 1981–96; *b* Charlottetown, 26 March 1937; *s* of late James Matthew Lee and of Catherine Blanchard Lee; *m* 1960, Patricia, *d* of late Ivan Laurie; one *s* two *d*. *Educ:* Queen's Square Sch.; St Dunstan's Univ. Architectural draftsman. Elected MLA (PC) for 5th Queens Riding, by-election, 1975; former Minister: of Health and Social Services; of Tourism, Parks and Conservation; Premier and Pres. Exec. Council, PEI, 1981–86. Comr, Canadian Pension Commn, 1986–97. Jaycee Internat. Senator, 1983. *Address:* 2906 Bayshore Road, Stanhope, PE C0A IP0, Canada. *T:* (902) 6722870.

LEE, Maj.-Gen. (James) Stuart, CB 1990; MBE 1970; Director of Army Education, 1987–90; *b* 26 Dec. 1934; *s* of George Lee and Elizabeth (*née* Hawkins); *m* 1960, Alice Lorna (*d* 2007); one *s*. *Educ:* Normanton Grammar Sch.; Leeds Univ. (BA Hons); King's Coll., London (MA War Studies, 1976). Pres., Leeds Univ. Union, 1958–59. Educn Officer in UK Trng Units, Catterick, Taunton, Bovington, 1959–64; Mil. Trng Officer, Beaconsfield, 1964; RMCS and Staff Coll., 1964–65; DAQMG HQ Cyprus Dist, 1966 and HQ NEARELF, 1967; SO2 MoD (Army Educn 1), 1968–70; DAA&QMG HQ FARELF, 1970 and GSO2 HQ FARELF, 1970–71; OC Officer Wing, Beaconsfield, 1971–74; Gp Educn Officer, 34 AEC, Rheindahlen, 1974–75; Chief Educn Officer, HQ NE Dist, 1976–78; Hd, Officer Educn Br., 1978–79; SO1 Trng HQ UKLF, 1979; Chief Inspector of Army Educn and Col Res., 1980–82; Res. Associate, IISS, 1982–83; Comdr Educn, HQ BAOR, 1983–87. Dep. Col Comdt, AGC, 1993–97. Pres., RAEC Assoc., 1993–97. Dep. Comr, British Scouts Western Europe, 1983–87; Mem., Management Bd, NFER, 1987–90. Non-exec. Dir, Exhibition Consultants Ltd, 1990–99. Dir and Trustee, Assessment and Qualifications Alliance, 1998–2002; Member: Nat Adv. Bd, Duke of Edinburgh Award Scheme, 1987–90; Council, Scout Assoc., 1988–98. City and Guilds of London Institute: Mem. Council, 1989–2007; Jt Hon. Sec., 1993–2004; Chm., Sen. Awards Cttee, 1990–99; Chm., Inst. Affairs and Awards Cttee, 1999–2002; Chm., Strategy and Advancement Cttee, 2002–04. Trustee and Sec., Gallipoli Meml Lecture Trust, 1987–90. Gov., 1991–99, Mem. Court, 1999, Imperial Coll.; Mem. Court, Univ. of Leeds, 1994–2004. FRSA 1987; FIPD (FITD 1991); Hon. FCGI 1996. *Publication:* contrib. Arms Transfers in Third World Development, 1984. *Recreations:* theatre, boats.

LEE, John Michael Hubert; Barrister-at-Law; *b* 13 Aug. 1927; *s* of late Victor Lee, Wentworth, Surrey, and late Renee Lee; *m* 1960, Margaret Ann, *d* of late James Russell, ICS, retired, and late Kathleen Russell; one *s* one *d*. *Educ:* Reading Sch.; Christ's Coll., Cambridge (Open Exhibnr Modern Hist.; 2nd Cl. Hons Pts I and II of Hist. Tripos; MA). Colonial Service: Administrative Officer, Ghana, 1951–58; Principal Assistant Secretary, Min. of Communications, Ghana, 1958. On staff of BBC, 1959–65. Called to the Bar, Middle Temple, 1960; practising, Midland and Oxford Circuit, 1966–; Dep. Circuit Judge, 1978–81; Assistant Recorder, 1981–87. MP (Lab) Reading, 1966–70; MP (Lab) Birmingham, Handsworth, Feb. 1974–1979; Chm., W Midland Gp of Labour MPs, 1974–75. *Recreations:* watching tennis, watching cricket, walking, studying philosophy, studying green issues. *Address:* Bell Yard Chambers, 116–118 Chancery Lane, WC2A 1PP. *Club:* Royal Over-Seas League.

LEE KUAN YEW; Prime Minister, Singapore, 1959–90; Minister Mentor, Prime Minister's Office, since 2004; *b* 16 Sept. 1923; *s* of Lee Chin Koon and Chua Jim Neo; *m* 1950, Kwa Geok Choo; two *s* one *d*. *Educ:* Raffles Coll., Singapore; Fitzwilliam Coll., Cambridge (class 1 both parts of Law Tripos). Called to Bar, Middle Temple, 1950, Hon. Bencher, 1969. Advocate and Solicitor, Singapore, 1951. Formed People's Action Party, 1954, Sec.-Gen., 1954–92; People's Action Party won elections, 1959; became PM, 1959, re-elected 1963, 1968, 1972, 1976, 1980, 1984, 1988; MP Fed. Parlt of Malaysia, 1963–65; Sen. Minister, Prime Minister's Office, 1990–2004. Hon. Freeman, City of London, 1982. Hon. CH 1970; Hon. GCMG 1972. *Publications:* The Singapore Story (memoirs), 1998; From Third World to First: the Singapore Story 1965–2000 (memoirs), 2000. *Recreation:* swimming. *Address:* Prime Minister's Office, Orchard Road, Istana, Singapore 238823.

LEE, Brig. Sir (Leonard) Henry, Kt 1983; CBE 1964 (OBE 1960); Deputy Director, Conservative Board of Finance, 1970–92; *b* 21 April 1914; *s* of late Henry Robert Lee and Nellie Lee; *m* 1949, Peggy Metham (*d* 2000). *Educ:* Portsmouth Grammar Sch.; Southampton Univ. (Law). Served War, 1939–45; with BEF in France, ME and NW Europe (despatches, 1945); Royal Scots Greys, Major; Staff Lt-Col 1954: Chief of Intelligence to Dir of Ops, Malaya, 1957–60; Mil. and Naval Attaché, Saigon, S Vietnam, 1961–64; Chief of Personnel and Admin, Allied Land Forces Central Europe, France, 1964–66; Chief of Intelligence, Allied Forces Central Europe, Netherlands, 1966–69; retd 1969. *Recreation:* gardening. *Address:* Fairways, Sandy Lane, Kingswood, Surrey KT20 6ND. *T:* (01737) 832577.

LEE, Martin; *see* Lee Chu-Ming, M.

LEE, Dr Melanie Georgina, FMedSci; Executive Vice-President, Research and Development, UCB Group, since 2004; *d* of William and Pamela Brown; *m* 1981; two *s*. *Educ:* York Univ. (BSc Hons 1979); NIMR (PhD 1982). Postdoctoral Research Fellow: CRC, London, at Imperial Coll., 1982–85; ICRF, London, at Lincoln's Inn Fields, 1985–88; R&D, Glaxo Gp Res. and Glaxo Wellcome, 1988–98; Bd Dir, Celltech Gp plc, 1998–2004. Chairman: Applied Genomics Link Scheme, 2000–; Cancer Res. Technol., 2003–. Trustee, CRUK, 2004–. FMedSci 2003. *Recreations:* gym, keeping fit, gardening in containers, flowers. *Address:* UCB Group, 208 Bath Road, Slough, Berks SL1 3WE. *T:* (01753) 777142, *Fax:* (01753) 447590; *e-mail:* Melanie.Lee@ucb-group.com.

LEE, Michael Charles M.; *see* Malone-Lee.

LEE, Maj.-Gen. Patrick Herbert, CB 1982; MBE 1964; CEng, FIMechE; Director: Road Haulage Association, 1988–98 (Chairman, 1994–96; Vice-Chairman, 1990–94); Wincanton Ltd (formerly Wincanton Transport, subseq. Wincanton Distribution Services, Ltd), 1983–98; *b* 15 March 1929; *s* of Percy Herbert and Mary Dorothea Lee; *m* 1952, Peggy Eveline Chapman; one *s* one *d*. *Educ:* King's Sch., Canterbury; London Univ. (BSc (Gen.), BSc (Special Physics)). Commnd RMA Sandhurst, 1948; Staff Coll., 1960; WO Staff Duties, 1961–63; CO, Parachute Workshop, 1964–65; JSSC, 1966; Military Asst to Master General of Ordnance, 1966–67; Directing Staff, Staff Coll., 1968–69; Commander, REME 2nd Div., 1970–71; Col AQ 1 British Corps, 1972–75; Dep. Comdt, Sch. of Electrical and Mechanical Engrg, 1975–77; Comdt, REME Trng Centre, 1977–79; Dir Gen., Electrical and Mechanical Engrg (Army), 1979–83. Col Comdt, REME, 1983–89. Mem., Wessex Water Authy, 1983–88. Confederation of British Industry: Mem. Council, 1991–98; Vice-Chm., 1992–94, Chm., 1994–96, SW Region. Gov., Wellington Sch., Som, 1992–2002 (Chm., 2000–02). FCMI; MIEMA. *Recreations:* gardening, railways, Roman history, industrial archaeology. *Club:* Army and Navy.

LEE, Rt Rev. Patrick Vaughan, DD; Bishop of Rupert's Land, 1994–99; *b* 20 June 1931; *s* of William Samuel Lee and Elizabeth Miriam (*née* Struthers); *m* 1958, Mary Thornton; four *d*. *Educ:* Univ. of Manitoba (BA 1953); St John's Coll., Winnipeg (LTh 1957; DD 1978). Missioner, Interlake/Eriksdale, Manitoba, 1956–59; Rector: St Bartholomew, Winnipeg, 1959–67; St Mary la Prairie, Portage la Prairie, Manitoba, 1967–75; District Dean, Portage and Pembina Deaneries, 1970–75; Dean of Cariboo and Rector, St Paul's Cathedral, Kamloops, BC, 1975–84; Dean of Training and Educn Sec., Dio. of W Buganda, 1984–90; Exec. Archdeacon of Rupert's Land, 1990–94. *Recreations:* cross country ski-ing, cycling, woodworking, reading, stamp collecting. *Address:* 137 Mile Point Road, RR 5, Perth, ON K7H 3C7, Canada. *T:* (613) 2670174.

LEE, Rt Rev. Paul Chun Hwan, Hon. CBE 1974; Bishop of Seoul, 1965–83; *b* 5 April 1922; unmarried. *Educ:* St Michael's Theological Seminary, Seoul; St Augustine's College, Canterbury. Deacon, 1952 (Pusan Parish); Priest, 1953 (Sangju and Choungju Parish). Director of Yonsei University, Seoul, 1960–, Chm., Bd of Trustees, 1972–, Hon. DD 1971. Chairman: Christian Council of Korea, 1966–67; Christian Literature Soc. of Korea, 1968–83; Korean Bible Soc., 1972–83 (Vice-Pres., 1969–72); Nat. Council of Churches in Korea, 1976–78. Hon. LLD Korea, 1978. *Recreation:* reading. *Address:* 104–401 Dae Woo Apt, Bang Bae 3 Dong, 981, So'cho-Ku, Seoul 137–063, Korea.

LEE, Sir Paul (Joseph) S.; *see* Scott-Lee.

LEE, Paul Winston Michael B.; *see* Boyd-Lee.

LEE, Peter Gavin; DL; FRICS; Senior Partner, Strutt & Parker, 1979–96; *b* 4 July 1934; *s* of late Mr and Mrs J. G. Lee; *m* 1963, Caroline Green; two *s* one *d*. *Educ:* Midhurst Grammar School; College of Estate Management; Wye College. FRICS 1966. Joined Strutt & Parker, 1957. Chm., Prince's Trust for Essex, 1998–2005. High Sheriff, 1990, DL 1991, Essex. *Recreations:* the restoration and enjoyment of vintage cars and aircraft, flying, country pursuits. *Address:* Fanners, Great Waltham, Chelmsford, Essex CM3 1EA. *T:* (01245) 360470.

LEE, Peter Wilton, CBE 1994; Vice Lord-Lieutenant of South Yorkshire, since 1997; Director, since 1987, Chairman, 1994–2005, Edward Pryor & Son Ltd; *b* 15 May 1935; *s* of Sir (George) Wilton Lee, TD and late Bettina Stanley Lee (*née* Haywood); *m* 1962, Gillian Wendy Oates; three *s* one *d*. *Educ:* Uppingham Sch.; Queens' Coll., Cambridge (MA). Lieut, RE, 1956. Grad. Engr, Davy & United Engrg Co. Ltd, 1958–62; Arthur Lee & Sons plc: Engr, Works Manager, 1962–67; Works Dir, 1967–70; Jt Man. Dir, 1970–72; Man. Dir, 1972–79; Chm. and Man. Dir, 1979–92; Chm., 1992–93; Dep. Chm., 1993–95, Dir, 1995–2003, Carclo Engrg Gp PLC. Dir, Sanderson Gp (formerly Sanderson Electronics) PLC, 1994–2000. Dir, Sheffield Enterprise Agency Ltd, 1987–2002. President: Brit. Independent Steel Producers' Assoc., 1981–83; Engrg Employers' Sheffield Assoc., 1994–96. Confederation of British Industry: Member: Nat. Council, 1992–95; Nat. Mfg Council, 1992–94; Chm., Yorks and Humberside Regl Council, 1993–95. University of Sheffield: Mem. Council, 1965–2005 (Chm., 1996–2005); Pro Chancellor, 1987–2005. Trustee: Sheffield Church Burgesses Trust, 1977–; S Yorks Community Foundn, 1986–99 (Vice-Pres., 1999–); Dir, Sheffield Royal Soc. for Blind, 1997– (Chm., 1998–). Chm. Council, Sheffield & Dist YMCA, 1972–81. CCMI (CIMgt 1976). Chm. Govs, Monkton Combe Sch., 1996–2001 (Gov., 1982–2001). Master, Co. of Cutlers in Hallamshire, 1985–86. DL 1978, High Sheriff, 1995–96, S Yorks. Hon. DEng Sheffield, 2005. *Recreations:* family, music and the arts, walking. *Address:* Mayfield House, 48 Canterbury Avenue, Sheffield S10 3RU. *T:* (0114) 230 5555. *Club:* Royal Automobile.

LEE, Seng Tee; Director: Singapore Investments (Pte) Ltd, since 1951; Lee Rubber Co. (Pte) Ltd, since 1951; Lee Pineapple Co. (Pte) Ltd, since 1951; Lee Foundation, since 1952; *b* April 1923; *s* of Lee Kong Chian and Alice Lee; *m* 1950, Betty Wu; two *s* one *d*. *Educ:* Anglo-Chinese Sch., Singapore; Wharton Business Sch., Univ. of Pennsylvania. Member: Singapore Preservation of Monuments Bd, 1971–88; Bd, Singapore Art Mus., 1995– (Mem., Adv. Cttee, 1992–94). Member Council: Univ. of Malaya in Singapore, 1959–61; Univ. of Singapore, 1962–63; Hon. Advr, Xiamen Univ., China, 1993–; Member: Bd of Advrs, Nat. Univ. of Singapore Endowment Fund, 1997–; Adv. Cttee, E Asia Inst., Cambridge Univ., 1998–. Mem., Chancellor's Court of Benefactors, Oxford, 1996–. Hon. Trustee, Royal Botanic Gardens, Kew, 1996. Hon. Foreign Mem., American Acad. of Arts and Scis, 2001. Hon. FBA 1998; Hon. Fellow: Wolfson Coll., Cambridge, 1986; Needham Res. Inst., Cambridge, 1992; Oriel Coll., Oxford, 1992; SOAS, London Univ., 2001. Hon. DTech Asian Inst. of Technol., Thailand, 1998; Hon. LitD Victoria Univ. of Wellington, NZ, 2006. Distinguished Service Award, Wharton Sch., Univ. of Penn., 1995. *Recreations:* reading, natural history. *Address:* GPO Box 1892, Singapore 903742, Republic of Singapore. *Club:* Executive (Singapore).

LEE, Prof. Simon Francis; Vice-Chancellor, Leeds Metropolitan University, since 2003; *b* 29 March 1957; *s* of Norman John Lee and Mary Teresa Lee (*née* Moran); *m* 1982, Patricia Mary, *d* of Bernard Anthony McNulty and Maud Catherine McNulty (*née* Kenny); one *s* two *d*. *Educ:* Balliol Coll., Oxford (Scholar, BA 1st Cl. Jurisp); Yale Law Sch. (Harkness Fellow, LLM). Lecturer in Law: Trinity Coll., Oxford, 1981–82; KCL, 1982–88; Queen's University, Belfast: Prof. of Jurisprudence, 1989–95; Dean, Faculty of Law, 1992–94; Prof. Emeritus, 1995; Rector and Chief Exec., Liverpool Hope UC, 1995–2003. Gresham Prof. of Law, 1995–98; Hon. Prof., Univ. of Liverpool, 1995–2003. Mem., Standing Adv. Commn on Human Rights, 1992–96. Mem., Nat. Standards Task Force, DFEE, 1997–2001. Non-exec. Dir, S & E Belfast Health and Social Services NHS Trust, 1994–95. Chairman: Merseyside Rapid Transit Project Bd, 1997–99; Netherley-

Valley Partnership, 1998–2002; Liverpool & Merseyside Theatres Trust (Everyman & Playhouse), 1998–2002; Ind. Monitoring Bd, Liverpool Educn Authy, 1999–2001. Co-founder, Initiative '92, 1992. Mem. Bd, The Tablet, 2002–. *Publications:* Law and Morals, 1986; Judging Judges, 1988; (with Peter Stanford) Believing Bishops, 1990; The Cost of Free Speech, 1990; (with Marie Fox) Learning Legal Skills, 1991; (ed) Freedom from Fear, 1992; Uneasy Ethics, 2003. *Recreations:* family, sport. *Address:* Leeds Metropolitan University, Beckett Park, Leeds LS6 3QS. *T:* (0113) 283 3100, *Fax:* (0113) 283 3109; *e-mail:* s.lee@leedsmet.ac.uk.

LEE, Maj.-Gen. Stuart; *see* Lee, Maj.-Gen. J. S.

LEE, Prof. Tak Hong, MD, ScD; FRCP, FRCPath, FHKCP; Asthma UK Professor of Allergy and Respiratory Medicine, King's College London, since 1988; Director, MRC and Asthma UK Centre in Allergic Mechanisms of Asthma at King's College London and Imperial College, since 2005; *b* 26 Jan. 1951; *s* of Ming and Maria Lee; *m* 1980, Andrée Ma; one *s* one *d. Educ:* Clare Coll., Cambridge (BA 1972; MB BChir 1976; MD 1985; ScD 1996). FHKCP 1987; FRCP 1989; FRCPath 1997. House Physician, House Surgeon, then Jun. Registrar, Guy's Hosp., 1975–77; SHO, Brompton Hosp., 1977–78, Nat. Hosp., Queen Square, 1978; Registrar, Guy's Hosp., 1978–89; Clin. Lectr, Cardiothoracic Inst., Brompton Hosp., 1980–82; Res., Fellow, Harvard Univ., USA, 1982–84; Lectr, 1984–85, Sen. Lectr, 1985–88, Guy's Hosp. Hon. Consultant Physician, Guy's and St Thomas' NHS Foundn Trust, 1988–. FMedSci 2000; FKC 2007. *Recreations:* golf, wining and dining, travelling to exotic places. *Address:* 5th Floor, Tower Wing, Guy's Hospital, SE1 9RT. *T:* (020) 7188 1943, *Fax:* (020) 7403 8640; *e-mail:* tak.lee@kcl.ac.uk. *Clubs:* Athenæum, Royal Automobile; Wentworth Golf.

LEE, Sir Timothy John B.; *see* Berners-Lee.

LEE, Tsung-Dao; Enrico Fermi Professor of Physics, since 1964, and University Professor, since 1984, Columbia University, USA; *b* 25 Nov. 1926; 3rd *s* of C. K. and M. C. Lee; *m* 1950, Jeannette H. C. Chin; two *s. Educ:* National Chekiang Univ., Kweichow, China; National Southwest Associated Univ., Kunming, China; University of Chicago, USA. Research Associate: University of Chicago, 1950; University of California, 1950–51; Member, Inst. for Advanced Study, Princeton, 1951–53. Columbia University: Asst Professor, 1953–55; Associate Professor, 1955–56; Professor, 1956–60; Member, Institute for Advanced Study, Princeton, 1960–63; Columbia Univ.: Adjunct Professor, 1960–62; Visiting Professor, 1962–63; Professor, 1963–. Hon. Professor: Univ. of Sci and Technol. of China, 1981; Jinan Univ., China, 1982; Fudan Univ., China, 1982; Qinghua Univ., 1984; Peking Univ., 1985; Nanjing Univ., 1985; Nankai Univ., 1986; Shanghai Jiao Tong and Suzhou Univs, 1987; Zhejiang Univ., 1988; Northwest Univ., Xian, 1993. Member: Acad. Sinica, 1957; Amer. Acad. of Arts and Scis, 1959; Nat. Acad. of Scis, 1964; Amer. Philosophical Soc., 1972; Acad. Nazionale dei Lincei, Rome, 1982; Chinese Acad. of Scis, Beijing, 1994. Hon. DSc: Princeton, 1958; City Coll., City Univ. of NY, 1978; Bard Coll., 1984; Peking, 1985; Bologna, 1988; Columbia, 1990; Adelphi, 1991; Tsukuba, 1992; Rockefeller, 1994; Hon. LLD Chinese Univ. of Hong Kong, 1969; Hon. LittD Drexel Univ., 1986; Dip. di Perfezionamento in Physics, Scuola Normale Superiore, Pisa, 1982. Nobel Prize for the non-conservation of parity (with C. N. Yang), 1957; Albert Einstein Award in Science, 1957; Ettore Majorana-Erice Sci. for Peace Prize, 1990. Grand'Ufficiale, Order of Merit (Italy), 1986. *Publications:* Particle Physics: an introduction to field theory, 1981; papers mostly in Physical Review, and Nuclear Physics. *Address:* Department of Physics, Columbia University, New York, NY 10027, USA.

LEE, Most Rev. William; *see* Waterford and Lismore, Bishop of, (RC).

LEE YONG LENG, Dr; Professor of Geography, National University of Singapore, 1977–90, retired; *b* 26 March 1930; *m* Wong Loon Meng; one *d. Educ:* Univs of Oxford, Malaya and Singapore. BLitt (Oxon), MA (Malaya), PhD (Singapore). Research Asst, Univ. of Malaya, 1954–56; University Lectr/Sen. Lectr, Univ. of Singapore, 1956–70; Associate Prof., Univ. of Singapore, 1970–71; High Comr for Singapore in London, 1971–75; Ambassador to Denmark, 1974–75, and Ireland, 1975; Min. of Foreign Affairs, Singapore, 1975–76. Mem., Govt Parly Cttee on Defence and For. Affairs, 1987–90. Chm., Singapore Nat. Library Bd, 1978–80. Dir, Centre for Advanced Studies, National Univ. of Singapore, 1983–85. *Publications:* North Borneo, 1965; Sarawak, 1970; Southeast Asia and the Law of the Sea, 1978; The Razor's Edge: boundaries and boundary disputes in Southeast Asia, 1980; Southeast Asia: essays in political geography, 1982; articles in: Population Studies; Geog. Jl; Erdkunde; Jl Trop. Geog., etc. *Recreations:* swimming, tennis, travelling, reading.

LEE, Prof. Yuan Tseh; President, Academia Sinica, Taiwan, since 1994; *b* 29 Nov. 1936; *s* of Tse Fan Lee and Pei Tsai; *m* 1963, Bernice Chinli Wu; two *s* one *d. Educ:* Nat. Taiwan Univ. (BSc 1959); Nat. Tsinghua Univ., Taiwan (MSc 1961); Univ. of California (PhD 1965). Military service, 1961–62. University of California, Berkeley: Postdoctoral Fellow, 1965–67; Research Fellow, 1967–68; James Franck Inst. and Dept of Chemistry, Univ. of Chicago: Asst Prof. of Chemistry, 1968–71; Associate Prof. of Chemistry, 1971–72; Prof. of Chemistry, 1973–74; University of California, Berkeley: Prof. of Chemistry, 1974–91; Univ. Prof. of Chemistry, 1991–94; Principal Investigator, Materials and Molecular Research Div., Lawrence Berkeley Lab., 1974–94. Vis. Lectr, US and overseas univs. Mem., editl boards, chem. and sci. jls. Mem., Nat. Acad. of Sciences, 1979, and other learned bodies. Nobel Prize in Chemistry (jtly), 1986; numerous awards from US and foreign instns. *Publications:* papers on molecular chemistry and related subjects. *Recreations:* sports (baseball, ping pong, tennis), classical music. *Address:* Academia Sinica, Nankang, Taipei 11529, Taiwan.

LEE CHU-MING, Martin, (Martin Lee); QC (Hong Kong) 1979; JP; Chairman, Democratic Party, Hong Kong, 1994–2002; Member, Hong Kong Legislative Council, 1985–97 and since 1998; *b* 8 June 1938; *m* 1969, Amelia Lee; one *s. Educ:* Wah Yan College, Kowloon; Univ. of Hong Kong (BA 1960). Called to the Bar, Lincoln's Inn, 1966. Member: Hong Kong Law Reform Commn, 1985–91; Hong Kong Fight Crime Cttee, 1986–92; Basic Law Drafting Cttee, 1985–89; numerous groups and cttees advising on Govt, law, nationality and community matters. Chm., United Democrats of Hong Kong, 1990–94. JP Hong Kong, 1980. *Publication:* The Basic Law: some basic flaws (with Szeto Wah), 1988. *Address:* Admiralty Centre, Room 704A, Tower I, 18 Harcourt Road, Hong Kong. *T:* 25290864. *Clubs:* Hong Kong; Hong Kong Golf, Hong Kong Jockey.

LEE-EMERY, Louise Wendy; *see* Tulett, L. W.

LEE-JONES, Christine, MA; JP; DL; Head Mistress, Manchester High School for Girls, 1998–2008; *b* 13 June 1948; *d* of George and Marion Pickup; *m* 1972, Denys Lee-Jones; one *d. Educ:* Lawnswood High Sch. for Girls, Leeds; St Mary's Coll., Bangor; University Coll. of N Wales (BEd Biblical Studies and Far Eastern Religions); Univ. of London Inst. of Educn (MA 1982); Open Univ. (Advanced Dip. Educnl Mgt 1990). Primary teacher, Bethnal Green, 1970–71; Head, Religious Education: Archbp Temple Sch., London, 1971–74; Archbp Michael Ramsey Sch., London, 1974–82; Sen. Lectr, Woolwich Coll. of Further Educn, 1983–86; Vice-Principal, Leyton Sixth Form Coll., 1986–91; Principal, Eccles Sixth Form Coll., Salford, 1991–98. Teacher/Tutor, Univ. of London Inst. of Educn, 1978–79. Mem., Gen. Assembly, Univ. of Manchester, 2005–. Jt Chair, Professional Develt Cttee, HMC/GSA, 2005–. Mem., Network Club, 1998–. Mem., RSC, 2003–. FRSA 1999. DL Greater Manchester, 2007; JP Trafford, 2008. *Recreations:* literature, theatre, the arts, travel, tennis, fine wines. *Address:* *e-mail:* cleejones@tiscali.co.uk. *Club:* University Women's.

LEE PENG-FEI, Allen, (Allen Lee), CBE 1988 (OBE 1982); JP; Chairman, Pacific Dimensions Consultants Ltd, since 1998; *b* 24 April 1940; *m* Maria Lee; two *s* one *d. Educ:* Univ. of Michigan (BSc Engineering Maths). Test Engineer Supervisor, Lockheed Aircraft International, 1966–67; Engineering Ops Manager, Fabri-teck, 1967; Test Engineer Manager, Lockheed Aircraft International, 1968–70; Test Manager, Ampex Ferrotec, 1970–72; Gen. Manager, Dataproducts HK, 1972–74; Managing Dir, Ampex Ferrotec, 1974–79; Gen. Manager, Ampex World Operations, 1979–83; Managing Dir, Ampex Far East Operations, 1983–84; Pres., Meadville, 1984–95. Appointed Mem., Hong Kong Legislative Council, 1978–98; MEC, Hong Kong, 1985–92; Dep. for HKSAR, 9th Nat. People's Congress, China, 1997–2004; Chm., HK Liberal Party, 1993. Mem., Commn on Strategic Develt, HKSAR, 1998. Chm., Bd of Overseers, Hong Kong Inst. of Biotechnol., 1990–. JP Hong Kong, 1980. FHKIE, 1985. Hon. DEng Hong Kong Poly., 1990; Hon. LLD Chinese Univ. of Hong Kong, 1990. Nat. Award, Asian Productivity Organization, 1986; Outstanding Young Persons Award, Hong Kong, 1977. *Recreations:* swimming, tennis. *Clubs:* Hong Kong Jockey, Hong Kong Country, Dynasty (Hong Kong).

LEE-POTTER, Jeremy Patrick, FRCPath; Life Vice-President, British Medical Association, 1998; Consultant Haematologist, Poole General Hospital, 1969–95; *b* 30 Aug. 1934; *s* of Air Marshal Sir Patrick Lee Potter, KBE, MD, QHS and Audrey Mary (*née* Pollock); *m* 1957, Lynda Higginson (OBE 1998) (*d* 2004); one *s* two *d. Educ:* Epsom Coll.; Guy's Hosp. Med. Sch. (MB BS 1958). MRCS, LRCP 1958; DTM&H 1963; DCP 1965; FRCPath 1979. Specialist in Pathology, 1960, Sen. Specialist, 1965, RAF (Sqn Ldr); in charge of Haematology Dept, RAF Inst. of Pathology and Tropical Medicine; Lectr in Haematology, St George's Hosp. Med. Sch., 1968–69. British Medical Association: Chm. Council, 1990–93 (Mem. Council, 1988–95); Dep. Chm., Central Consultants and Specialists Cttee, 1988–90 (Chm., Negotiating Cttee); Chm., Audit Cttee, 1999–2002. Member: Standing Med. Adv. Cttee, 1990–93; GMC, 1994–99 (Dep. Chm., Professional Conduct Cttee, 1996–99); Clinical Disputes Forum, 1999. Consultant Surveyor, King's Fund Orgnl Audit, 1993–95. Engineering Council: Mem. Senate, 2000–02; Mem., Bd for Engrs' Regulation, 2001–02. Pres., Old Epsomian Club, 2004–05. *Publication:* A Damn Bad Business: the NHS deformed, 1997. *Recreations:* printing, printmaking, visual arts. *Address:* Icen House, Stoborough, Wareham, Dorset BH20 5AN. *T:* (01929) 556307. *Clubs:* Athenæum; Parkstone Golf.

LEE-STEERE, Sir Ernest (Henry), KBE 1977 (CBE 1963); JP; Lord Mayor of Perth, Western Australia, 1972–78; company director, pastoralist and grazier; *b* Perth, 22 Dec. 1912; *s* of Sir Ernest Lee-Steere, JP, KStJ; *m* 1942, Jessica Margaret, *d* of Frank Venn; two *s* three *d. Educ:* Hale Sch., Perth; St Peter's Coll., Adelaide. Served War: Captain Army/Air Liaison Group, AIF; SW Pacific Area, 1944–45 (Philippine Liberation Medal, 1996). President (for WA): Pastoralists and Graziers Assoc., 1959–72; Boy Scout Assoc., 1957–64; National Trust, 1969–72. Vice-Pres., Council of Royal Flying Doctor Service of WA, 1954–59 and 1962–74. Chairman: State Adv. Cttee, CSIRO, 1962–71 (Councillor, Fed. Adv. Council, 1960–71); WA Soil Conservation Adv. Cttee, 1955–72; Aust. Capital Cities Secretariat, 1975–76; WA Turf Club, 1963–84 (Vice-Chm., 1959–63). Member: Nat. Council of Aust. Boy Scouts Assoc., 1959–64; Exec. Cttee of WA State Cttee, Freedom from Hunger Campaign; WA State Adv. Cttee, Aust. Broadcasting Commn, 1961–64; Aust. Jubilee Cttee for the Queen's Silver Jubilee Appeal for Young Australians, 1977; Aust. Wool Industry Conf., 1971–74 (also Mem. Exec. Cttee). Councillor: Aust. Wool Growers and Graziers Council (Pres., 1972–73); St George's Coll., Univ. of WA, 1945–81. Chm. and dir of several cos. Leader, Trade Mission to India, 1962. JP Perth, 1965. *Publication:* Be Fair & Fear Not (autobiog.), 1995. *Recreation:* polo (played in WA Polo Team in Australasian Gold Cup). *Address:* Dardanup, 26 Odern Crescent, Swanbourne, WA 6010, Australia. *T:* (9) 3842929. *Club:* Weld (Perth).

LEE-STEERE, Gordon Ernest; Vice Lord-Lieutenant of Surrey, since 1996; *b* 26 Dec. 1939; *s* of Charles Augustus Lee-Steere and Patience Hargreaves Lee-Steere; *m* 1966, Mary Katharine Stuart; one *s* three *d. Educ:* Eton; Trinity Coll., Cambridge (MA). Computer consultant, 1966–74; self-employed farmer, 1960–. Pres., CLA, 1987–89. *Recreations:* shooting, walking. *Address:* Jayes Park, Ockley, Surrey RH5 5RR. *T:* (01306) 621223. *Club:* Boodle's.

LEECH, Prof. Geoffrey Neil, FBA 1987; Research Professor of English Linguistics, University of Lancaster, 1996–2002, now Professor Emeritus; *b* 16 Jan. 1936; *s* of Charles Richard Leech and Dorothy Eileen Leech; *m* 1961, Frances Anne Berman; one *s* one *d. Educ:* Tewkesbury Grammar School; University College London (BA 1959; MA 1963; PhD 1968). Asst Lectr, UCL, 1962–64; Harkness Fellow, MIT, 1964–65; Lectr, UCL, 1965–69; University of Lancaster: Reader, 1969–74; Prof. of Linguistics and Modern English Lang., 1974–96. Visiting Professor: Brown Univ., 1972; Kobe Univ., 1984; Kyoto Univ., 1991; Meikai Univ., 1999, 2000. Hon. Fil Dr Lund, 1987; Hon. DLitt: Wolverhampton, 2002; Lancaster, 2002. *Publications:* English in Advertising, 1966; A Linguistic Guide to English Poetry, 1969; Towards a Semantic Description of English, 1969; Meaning and the English Verb, 1971, 3rd edn 2004; (with R. Quirk, S. Greenbaum and J. Svartvik) A Grammar of Contemporary English, 1972; Semantics, 1974, 2nd edn 1981; (with J. Svartvik) A Communicative Grammar of English, 1975, 3rd edn 2002; Explorations in Semantics and Pragmatics, 1980; (ed with S. Greenbaum and J. Svartvik) Studies in English Linguistics: for Randolph Quirk, 1980; (with M. Short) Style in Fiction, 1981, 2nd edn 2007; (with R. Hoogenraad and M. Deuchar) English Grammar for Today, 1982, 2nd edn 2005; Principles of Pragmatics, 1983; (with R. Quirk, S. Greenbaum, and J. Svartvik) A Comprehensive Grammar of the English Language, 1985; (ed with C. N. Candlin) Computers in English Language Teaching and Research, 1986; (ed with R. Garside and G. Sampson) The Computational Analysis of English: a corpus-based approach, 1987; An A–Z of English Grammar and Usage, 1989, 2nd edn (with B. Cruickshank and R. Ivanič) 2001; Introducing English Grammar, 1992; (ed with E. Black and R. Garside) Statistically-driven Computer Grammars of English, 1993; (ed with G. Myers and J. Thomas) Spoken English on Computer, 1995; (ed with R. Garside and T. McEnery) Corpus Annotation: linguistic information from computer text corpora, 1997; (jtly) Longman Grammar of Spoken and Written English, 1999; (with P. Rayson and A. Wilson) Word Frequencies in Written and Spoken English, 2001; (with D. Biber and S. Conrad) Student Grammar of Spoken and Written English, 2002; (with J. Svartvik) English: One Tongue - Many Voices, 2006; A Glossary of English Grammar, 2006; Language in Literature, 2008. *Recreations:* music, esp. playing the piano in chamber music groups and playing the church organ, walking. *Address:* Department of Linguistics and English Language, University of Lancaster, Bailrigg, Lancaster LA1 4YT.

LEECH, John; MP (Lib Dem) Manchester Withington, since 2005; *b* 11 April 1971; *s* of Rev. John Leech and Jean Leech; partner, Catherine Kilday. *Educ:* Manchester Grammar Sch.; Loretto Coll.; Brunel Univ. (BA Hons Pols and Hist.). Mem. (Lib Dem), Manchester CC, 1998– (Dep. Leader, Lib Dem Gp, 2002–). *Recreations:* sport, amateur dramatics, season ticket holder Manchester City. *Address:* 53b Manley Road, Manchester M16 8HP; *e-mail:* leechj@parliament.uk.

LEECH, John, (Hans-Joachim Freiherr von Reitzenstein); Head of External Relations and Member of Management Board, Commonwealth Development Corporation, 1981–85; Chairman, Farm Services Co. BV, 1988–2000; Deputy Chairman, Rural Investment Overseas Ltd, 1990–2000 (Chairman, 1985–90); *b* 21 April 1925; *s* of Hans-Joachim and Josefine von Reitzenstein; *m* 1st, 1949, Mair Eiluned Davies (marr. diss. 1958); one *d*; 2nd, 1963, Noretta Conci, concert pianist. *Educ:* Bismarck Gymnasium, Berlin; Whitgift, Croydon. L. G. Mouchel & Partners, Consulting Civil Engineers, 1942–52; Bird & Co. Ltd, Calcutta, 1953–57; Dir, Europe House, London, and Exec. Mem. Council, Britain in Europe Ltd, 1958–63; Pres., Internat. Fedn of Europe Houses, 1961–65; Dir, Joint Industrial Exports Ltd, 1963–65; with Commonwealth Develt Corp., London and overseas, 1965–85; Co-ordinator, Interact Gp of European develt finance instns, 1973–85; Europ. Co-ordinator, West-West Agenda, 1987–. Asst Dir, NATO Parliamentarians' Conf., 1959–60. Vice-Chm., Indian Concrete Soc., 1953–57; Member: Council, Federal Trust for Educn and Research, 1985–; Adv. Council (formerly Exec. Cttee), London Symphony Orch., 1979–96; Council, Royal Commonwealth Soc. for the Blind, 1983–99; Internat. Council, Duke of Edinburgh's Award Internat. Assoc., 1993–98. Chm., Keyboard Charitable Trust for Young Professional Performers, 1991–. Liveryman, Worshipful Co. of Paviors, 1968– (Mem. Court of Assts, 1992–2002, now Emeritus). FRSA. *Publications:* The NATO Parliamentarians' Conference 1955–59, 1960; Europe and the Commonwealth, 1961; Aid and the Community, 1972; Halt! Who Goes Where?: the future of NATO in the new Europe, 1991; Asymmetries of Conflict: war without death, 2002; (ed) Whole and Free: EU enlargement and transatlantic relations, 2002; contrib. to jls on aspects of overseas develt, European matters and arts subjects. *Recreations:* music, travel, Italy. *Address:* 8 Chester Square Mews, SW1W 9DS. *T:* (020) 7730 2307. *Club:* Travellers.

LEECH, Rev. Kenneth; M. B. Reckitt Urban Fellow, St Botolph's Church, Aldgate, 1991–2004; *b* 15 June 1939; *s* of late John and Annie Leech; *m* 1970, Rheta Wall (marr. diss. 1993); one *s*. *Educ:* King's College London (BA Hons Mod. History, AKC 1961); Trinity Coll., Oxford (BA Hons Theol. 1961, MA 1968); St Stephen's House, Oxford. Deacon 1964, priest 1965; Curate: Holy Trinity, Hoxton, N1, 1964–67; St Anne, Soho, W1, 1967–71; Sec., Soho Drugs Group, 1967–71; Dir, Centrepoint, Soho, 1969–71; Chaplain and Tutor, St Augustine's Coll., Canterbury, 1971–74; Rector of St Matthew, Bethnal Green, 1974–80; Field Work Sec., BCC, 1980; Race Relations Field Officer, C of E Bd for Social Responsibility, 1981–87; Dir, Runnymede Trust, 1987–90. Visiting Lecturer: St Stephen's House, Chicago, 1978–90; Brent House, Chicago, 1990–2003. DD Lambeth, 1998. *Publications:* Pastoral Care and the Drug Scene, 1970; A Practical Guide to the Drug Scene, 1972; Keep the Faith, Baby, 1972; Youthquake, 1973; Soul Friend, 1977; True Prayer, 1980; The Social God, 1981; True God, 1984; Spirituality and Pastoral Care, 1986; Struggle in Babylon: Racism in the Cities and Churches of Britain, 1988; Care and Conflict, 1990; Subversive Orthodoxy, 1992; The Eye of the Storm, 1992 (HarperCollins Religious Book Award, 1993); We Preach Christ Crucified, 1994; The Sky is Red, 1997; Drugs and Pastoral Care, 1998; Through Our Long Exile, 2001; Race, 2005; Doing Theology in Altab Ali Park, 2006. *Recreations:* cartoon drawing, Lancashire dialect poetry, pubs. *Address:* 89 Manchester Road, Mossley, Ashton-under-Lyne OL5 9LZ. *T:* (01457) 835119; *e-mail:* kenleech@aol.com.

LEECH, Kevin Ronald; Founder and Chairman, ML Laboratories plc, 1987–2000; non-executive Director, Accura Animal Health, since 2008 (Chairman, 2007–08); *b* 18 Aug. 1943; two *s* one *d* from former marriage. *Educ:* St Bede's Coll., Manchester. Accountancy, until 1964; built up family business, R. T. Leech & Sons Ltd, into UK's largest private funeral dir, 1964–82; entrepreneur, business manager, and venture capitalist, 1982–; non-executive Chairman: Queensborough Holdings plc, 1994–2000; Top Jobs on the Net, 1999; CI4Net.Com Ltd, 1999–. FCMI (FIMgt 1983); FInstD 1984; FRSA 1997. Hon. LLD Manchester, 1998. *Recreations:* Manchester United, football generally, ski-ing, sailing, fishing. *Address:* La Vignette, Rue de la Vignette, St Saviour, Jersey JE2 7NY.

LEECH, Melanie Jane; Director General, Food and Drink Federation, since 2005; *b* 28 May 1962; *d* of Michael and Margaret Leech; two *s*. *Educ:* Brighton and Hove High Sch. for Girls GDST; St Hugh's Coll., Oxford (BA Hons Maths). Principal Private Sec. to Cabinet Sec. and Hd of Home Civil Service, 1992–95; Hd of Arts Policy, 1995–98, Hd of Broadcasting Policy, 1998–99, DCMS; Dir, Office of the Rail Regulator, 1999–2001; Exec. Dir, Assoc. of Police Authorities, 2001–04; Dir of Communications, Cabinet Office, 2004–05. Trustee, Carnegie UK Trust, 2005–. MInstD. FRSA. *Address:* Food and Drink Federation, 6 Catherine Street, WC2B 5JJ. *T:* (020) 7420 7101, *Fax:* (020) 7836 9757; *e-mail:* melanie.leech@fdf.org.uk.

LEECH, Prof. Rachel Mary, DPhil; Professor of Biology, University of York, 1978–99, now Emeritus; *b* 3 June 1936; *d* of Alfred Jack Leech and Frances Mary Ruth Leech (*née* Cowley). *Educ:* Prince Henry's Grammar Sch., Otley, W Yorks; St Hilda's Coll., Oxford (MA, DPhil 1961; Christopher Welch Scholar). Naples Biol Scholar, Stazione Zoologica, Naples, 1957–60; Professorial Res. Fellow, 1960–63, Lectr in Analytical Cytology, 1963–66, Imperial Coll., London; University of York: Lectr in Biology, 1966–69; Sen. Lectr, 1969–75; Reader, 1975–78. Leverhulme Emeritus Fellow, 2001–02. Mem., BBSRC, 1994–96. *Publications:* (with R. A. Reid) The Biochemistry and Structure of Subcellular Organelles, 1980; articles in Plant Physiology, Nature, The Biochemical Jl, The Plant Jl, Proc. of NAS, NY. *Recreations:* gardening, walking, enjoying the company of friends. *Address:* Department of Biology, University of York, Heslington, York YO10 5DD. *T:* (01904) 430000.

LEEDER, Prof. Michael Robert, PhD; Professor of Environmental Sciences, University of East Anglia, since 1999; *b* 22 Nov. 1947; *s* of Norman George Leeder and Evelyn (*née* Patterson). *Educ:* Univ. of Durham (BSc 1st Cl. Hons Geology); Univ. of Reading (PhD 1972). University of Leeds: Lectr in Earth Scis, 1972–85; Reader, 1985–91; Prof., 1991–99. Lyell Medal, Geol Soc., 1992; Phillips Medal, Geol Soc. of Yorks, 1990. *Publications:* Dynamic Stratigraphy of the British Isles, 1979; Sedimentology, 1982; Sedimentology and Sedimentary Basins, 1999; Fire Over East Anglia, 1999; Physical Processes in the Earth and Environmental Sciences, 2006; contrib. various scientific papers. *Recreation:* living generally. *Address:* School of Environmental Sciences, University of East Anglia, Norwich NR4 7TJ.

LEEDHAM, Carol Jean; *see* Mountford, C. J.

LEEDS, Bishop of, (RC), since 2004; **Rt Rev. Arthur Roche;** *b* 6 March 1950; *s* of Arthur Francis Roche and Frances Roche (*née* Day). *Educ:* Christleton Hall, Chester; English Coll., Valladolid; Pontifical Gregorian Univ., Rome (STL). Ordained priest, 1975; Asst Priest, Holy Rood, Barnsley, 1975–77; Sec. to Rt Rev. Gordon Wheeler, Bishop of Leeds, 1977–82; Vice-Chancellor, 1979–89, Financial Administrator, 1986–90, dio. of Leeds; Asst Priest, Leeds Cathedral, 1982–89; Parish Priest, St Wilfrids's, Leeds, 1989–91; Spiritual Dir, Venerable English Coll., Rome, 1992–96; Gen. Sec. to Catholic Bps' Conf. of England and Wales, 1996–2001; Auxiliary Bishop of Westminster, 2001–02; Coadjutor Bishop of Leeds, 2002–04. Hon. Ecumenical Canon: Wakefield Cath., 2006–; Bradford Cath., 2008–. Titular Bishop of Rusticiana, 2001–02. Chm., Dept of Christian Life and Worship, Catholic Bps' Conf. of England and Wales, 2004–. Chm., Internat. Commn for English in the Liturgy, 2002–. Co-ordinator of the Papal Visit to York, 1982. Prelate of Honour to Pope John Paul II. *Recreations:* gardening, walking, travel. *Address:* Bishop's House, 13 North Grange Road, Leeds LS6 2BR. *T:* (0113) 230 4533, *Fax:* (0113) 278 9890.

LEEDS, Archdeacon of; *see* Burrows, Ven. P.

LEEDS, Sir Christopher (Anthony), 8th Bt *cr* 1812; researcher; *b* 31 Aug. 1935; *s* of Geoffrey Hugh Anthony Leeds (*d* 1962) (*b* of 6th Bt) and Yoland Thérèse Barré (*d* 1944), *d* of James Alexander Mitchell; *S* cousin, 1983; *m* 1974, Elaine Joyce (marr. diss. 1981), *d* of late Sqdn Ldr C. H. A. Mullins. *Educ:* King's School, Bruton; LSE, Univ. of London (BSc Econ. 1958); Univ. of Southern California (Fulbright Travel Award; Sen. Herman Fellow in Internat. Relations, MA 1966). Assistant Master: Merchant Taylors' School, Northwood, 1966–68; Christ's Hospital, 1972–75; Stowe School, 1978–81. Publisher, 1975–78. University of Nancy 2: Sen. Lectr, 1982; Assoc. Prof., 1988–2000; Researcher, 2002–; Vis. Lectr, Univ. of Strasbourg I, 1983–87; Vis. Res. Fellow, Univ. of Kent at Canterbury, 2000–01. *Publications:* Political Studies, 1968, 3rd edn 1981; European History 1789–1914, 1971, 2nd edn 1980; Italy under Mussolini, 1972; Unification of Italy, 1974; Historical Guide to England, 1976; (with R. S. Stainton and C. Jones) Management and Business Studies, 1974, 3rd edn 1983; Basic Economics Revision, 1982; Politics in Action, 1986; World History—1900 to the present day, 1987; Peace and War, 1987; English Humour, 1989; contrib to learned jls incl. Peacekeeping, Internat. Business Rev., Internat. Jl of Peace Studies. *Recreations:* hill-walking, modern art, travel. *Heir: cousin* John Charles Leeds [*b* 25 Dec. 1941; *m* 1965, Eileen Rose, *d* of Joseph Francis Shalka; one *s* two *d*]. *Address:* 6 Hurlingham Lodge, 14 Manor Road, Eastcliff, Bournemouth BH1 3EY; 7 rue de Turique, 54000 Nancy, France.

LEEMING, Cheryl Elise Kendall, (Mrs J. C. Leeming); *see* Gillan, C. E. K.

LEEMING, Geraldine Margaret; *see* Coleridge, G. M.

LEEMING, Ian; QC 1988; **His Honour Judge Leeming;** a Circuit Judge, since 2006; *b* Preston, Lancs, 10 April 1948; *s* of late Thomas Leeming (Bombing Leader, RAF), and of Lilian (*née* Male); *m* 1973, Linda Barbara Cook; one *s* two *d*. *Educ:* The Catholic Coll., Preston; Manchester Univ. (LLB 1970). Called to the Bar: Gray's Inn, 1970; Lincoln's Inn (*ad eundem*), 1981; in practice at Chancery and Commercial Bars, 1971–2006; a Recorder, 1989–2006. Dep. Deemster, Manx High Court, 1998; Mem., Court of Appeal, IOM, 1998. Legal Assessor: GMC, 2002–06; GDC, 2003–06. Lectr in Law (part-time), Manchester Univ., 1971–75. Formerly Counsel to Attorneys, Malcolm A. Hoffmann & Co., NY. Dir of limited cos. Vice-Chm., Northern Soc. of Cons. Lawyers, 1985–88. Fellow, Soc. for Advanced Legal Studies, 1998. Member: Chancery Bar Assoc.; Professional Negligence Bar Assoc.; Technol. and Construction Court Bar Assoc. FCIArb, Chartered Arbitrator, 2005–. *Publications:* (with James Bonney) Observations upon the Insolvency Bill, 1985; (ed) Equity and Trusts sect., Butterworth's Law of Limitation, 2000; articles, notes and reviews in legal jls and specialist periodicals. *Recreations:* squash, real tennis. *Address:* Plymouth Combined Court Centre, Armada Way, Plymouth, Devon PL1 2ER.

LEEMING, John Coates; retired space consultant; Director General, British National Space Centre, 1987–88 (Director, Policy and Programmes, 1985–87); *b* 3 May 1927; *s* of late James Arthur Leeming and Harriet Leeming; *m* 1st, 1949 (marr. diss. 1974); two *s*; 2nd, 1985, Cheryl Elise Kendall Gillan, *qv*. *Educ:* Chadderton Grammar Sch., Lancs; St John's Coll., Cambridge (Schol.). Teaching, Hyde Grammar Sch., Cheshire, 1948. Asst Principal, HM Customs and Excise, 1950 (Private Sec. to Chm.); Principal: HM Customs and Excise, 1954; HM Treasury, 1956; HM Customs and Excise, 1958; Asst Sec., HM Customs and Excise, 1965; IBRD (World Bank), Washington, DC, 1967; Asst Sec., 1970, Under Sec., 1972, CSD; a Comr of Customs and Excise, 1975–79; Dept of Industry (later DTI), 1979–85. *Recreation:* golf. *Club:* Royal Automobile.

LEES, Prof. Andrew John, MD; FRCP; Francis and Renee Hock Professor of Neurology, Institute of Neurology, and Director, Reta Lila Weston Institute of Neurological Studies, University College London, since 1998; Consultant Neurologist, National Hospital for Neurology and Neurosurgery (now part of University College London Hospitals NHS Trust), since 1982; *b* 27 Sept. 1947; *s* of Lewis Lees and Muriel Lees (*née* Wadsworth); *m* 1973, Juana Luisa Pulin Perez Lopez; one *s* one *d*. *Educ:* Roundhay Sch., Leeds; Royal London Hosp. Med. Sch., Univ. of London (MD 1978). FRCP 1982. Co-Ed.-in-Chief, Movement Disorders Jl, 1994–2004. Chm., Med. Adv. Panel, Progressive Supranuclear Palsy (PSP Europe) Assoc., 1995–; Dir, Sara Koe PSP Res. Centre, Inst. of Neurol., 2002–. Pres., Movt Disorder Soc., 2005–06 (Pres., Eur. Sect., 1998–2000). Appeal Steward, BBB of C, 1998–. Visiting Professor: Univ. Federal de Ceara Fortaleza, Brazil, 1988–; Univ. of Liverpool, 2002–. *Publications:* Parkinson's Disease, The Facts, 1980; Tics and Related Disorders, 1984; Ray of Hope: authorised biography of Ray Kennedy, 1992. *Recreations:* Brazilianist, Liverpool FC supporter. *Address:* National Hospital for Neurology and Neurosurgery, Queen Square, WC1N 3BG. *T:* (020) 7837 3611; *e-mail:* alees@ion.ucl.ac.uk. *Club:* Royal Society of Medicine.

LEES, Sir Antony; *see* Lees, Sir W. A. C.

LEES, His Honour C(harles) Norman; a Circuit Judge, 1980–96; Designated Family Judge, Greater Manchester, 1991–96; *b* 4 Oct. 1929; *s* of late Charles Lees, Bramhall, Cheshire; *m* 1961, Stella (*d* 1987), *d* of late Hubert Swann, Stockport; one *d*. *Educ:* Stockport Sch.; Univ. of Leeds. LLB 1950. Called to Bar, Lincoln's Inn, 1951. Dep. Chm., Cumberland County QS, 1969–71; a Recorder of the Crown Court, 1972–80; Chm., Mental Health Review Tribunal, Manchester Region, 1977–80 (Mem., 1971–80; Pres. (restricted patients), 1983–98). *Recreations:* tennis, music, history. *Address:* 24 St John Street, Manchester M3 4ES. *T:* (0161) 214 6000. *Clubs:* Lansdowne; Northern Lawn Tennis.

LEES, Sir David (Bryan), Kt 1991; DL; FCA; Chairman, Tate & Lyle plc, since 1998; Deputy Chairman, QinetiQ Group plc, since 2005; a Director, Bank of England, 1991–99; *b* 23 Nov. 1936; *s* of late Rear-Adm. D. M. Lees, CB, DSO, and C. D. M. Lees; *m* 1961, Edith Mary Bernard; two *s* one *d*. *Educ:* Charterhouse. Qualified as a chartered accountant, 1962. Chief Accountant, Handley Page Ltd, 1964–68; GKN Sankey Ltd: Chief Accountant, 1970–72; Dep. Controller, 1972–73; Director, Secretary and Controller, 1973–76; Guest Keen and Nettlefolds, later GKN plc: Group Finance

Executive, 1976–77; General Manager Finance, 1977–82; Dir, 1982–2004; Finance Dir, 1982–87; Man. Dir, 1987–88; Chief Exec., 1988–96; Chm., 1988–2004. Chm., Courtaulds plc, 1996–98 (Dir, 1991–98); Dep. Chm., Brambles Industries Ltd, and Brambles Industries plc, 2001–06. Mem. Council, CBI, 1988– (Chm., Economic Affairs (formerly Economic and Financial Policy) Cttee, 1988–94); Pres., EEF, 1990–92; Member: Audit Commission, 1983–90; Listed Cos Adv. Cttee, 1990–97; European Round Table, 1995–2001; Nat. Defence Industries Council, 1995–2004; Panel on Takeovers and Mergers, 2001–. Dir, Inst. for Manufacturing, 1998–2001. Pres., Soc. of Business Economists, 1994–99. Dir, Royal Opera House, 1998–. Mem. Governing Body, Shrewsbury Sch., 1986–2007 (Chm., 2004–07); Gov., Suttons Hosp., Charterhouse, 1995–2005. DL Shropshire, 2007. Hon. Fellow, Wolverhampton Poly., 1990. ICAEW Award for outstanding achievement, 1999. Officer's Cross, Order of Merit (Germany), 1996. *Recreations:* walking, golf, opera, music. *Address:* Tate & Lyle plc, Sugar Quay, Lower Thames Street, EC3R 6DQ. *Club:* MCC.

See also Rear-Adm. R. B. Lees.

LEES, Diane Elizabeth; Director-General, Imperial War Museum, since 2008; *b* 28 March 1964; *d* of late William Lees and of Brenda Lees (*née* Gilman); *m* 2007, Michael Hague. *Educ:* Oriel Bank High Sch.; Stockport Coll. of Technol. Exhibns Asst, Mary Rose Project, 1982–84; Registrar: Royal Naval Mus., 1984–89; Nottingham City Museums, 1989–91; Nat. Outreach Manager, Museums Documentation Assoc., 1991–94; Chief Exec., Galls of Justice, 1994–2000; Dir, Mus. of Childhood, 2000–08. Vice Chair, Assoc. of Indep. Museums, 2005– (Sec., 1998–2002); Instnl Vice Pres., Museums Assoc., 2002–04. FMA 1996; FRSA 2004. *Publications:* (ed) Museums and Interactive Multimedia, 1993; Computers in Museums, 1994, 3rd edn 1996; contribs to Museums Jl, IBBY Procs, Library and Inf. Scis. *Recreations:* walking, tennis, cooking, collecting ceramics. *Address:* Imperial War Museum, Lambeth Road, SE1 6HZ. *T:* (020) 7416 5320, *Fax:* (020) 7416 5374; *e-mail:* dlees@iwm.org.uk.

LEES, Geoffrey William; Headmaster, St Bees School, 1963–80; *b* 1 July 1920; *o s* of late Mr and Mrs F. T. Lees, Manchester; *m* 1949, Joan Needham, *yr d* of late Mr and Mrs J. Needham, Moseley, Birmingham. *Educ:* King's Sch., Rochester; Downing Coll., Cambridge. Royal Signals, 1940–46 (despatches): commissioned 1941; served in NW Europe and Middle East, Captain. 2nd Class Hons English Tripos, Pt I, 1947; History Tripos, Part II, 1948; Asst Master, Brighton Coll., 1948–63. Leave of absence in Australia, Asst Master, Melbourne Church of England Gram. Sch., 1961–62. *Recreations:* reading, lepidoptera, walking. *Address:* 10 Merlin Close, Upper Drive, Hove, Sussex BN3 6NU. *Clubs:* Hawks, Union (Cambridge).

LEES, Captain Nicholas Ernest Samuel; Chairman, Leicester Racecourse, since 2006 (Assistant Manager, 1970–71; Clerk of the Course, 1972–2004; Managing Director, 1972–2005); Chairman, Stratford-on-Avon Racecourse Co. Ltd, since 2001 (Director, since 1990); *b* 3 May 1939; *s* of Ernest William Lees and Marjorie May Lees; *m* 1st, 1969, Elizabeth Helen Spink (marr. diss. 1985); one *d*; 2nd, 1985, Jocelyn Kosina; one *d*. *Educ:* Abbotsholme Sch., Rocester, Staffs. Shell Oil, 1956–59; commnd 17/21 Lancers, 1959; retd from Army, 1967; studied for Chartered Surveyors exams, 1967–69 (passed final exams but never practised); auctioneer, Warner, Sheppard & Wade Ltd, Leicester, 1969–73; Clerk of the Course: Teesside Park, 1972–73; Great Yarmouth, 1977–91; Chief Exec., 1974–97, Clerk of the Course, 1974–2000, and Dir of Racing, 1998–2000, Newmarket. Dir, Racecourse Assoc. Ltd, 1988–93, 2004–05. *Recreations:* horse racing, point to pointing, antique furniture, silver, sporting art. *Address:* Capers End, Bradfield St George, Bury St Edmunds, Suffolk IP30 0AY. *T:* (01284) 386651.

LEES, Norman; *see* Lees, C. N.

LEES, Robert Ferguson, CBE 1999; Regional Procurator Fiscal for Lothian and Borders, 1991–98; *b* 15 Sept. 1938; *s* of William Lees and Martha Lees (*née* McAlpine); *m* 1966, Elizabeth (Elsie) Loughridge. *Educ:* Bellshill Acad.; Strathclyde Univ. (LLB). Joined Procurator Fiscal Service, 1972; Legal Asst, Paisley, 1972–75; Legal Asst, 1975–76, Sen. Legal Asst, 1976–78, and Sen. Depute Fiscal, 1978–81, Glasgow; Asst Procurator Fiscal, Dundee, 1982–88; Regl Procurator Fiscal for N Strathclyde, 1989–91. Vis. Scholar, Valdosta State Univ., Ga, 1999–2000. *Publication:* (jtly) Criminal Procedure, 1990. *Recreations:* music, travel, languages, photography.

LEES, Air Vice-Marshal Robin Lowther, CB 1985; MBE 1962; Air Officer in charge of Administration, RAF Support Command, 1982–85, and Head of Administration Branch, RAF, 1983–85, retired; *b* 27 Feb. 1931; *e s* of late Air Marshal Sir Alan Lees, KCB, CBE, DSO, AFC, and Norah Elizabeth (*née* Thompson); *m* 1966, Alison Mary Benson, *o d* of late Col C. B. Carrick, MC, TD, JP; three *s*. *Educ:* Wellington Coll.; RAF Coll., Cranwell. Commissioned RAF, 1952; served AAFCE Fontainebleau, 1953–56; Waterbeach, 1956–58; UKSLS Ottawa, 1958–61; DGPS(RAF) Staff MoD, 1962–66; Wyton, 1966–68; HQ Far East Comd, 1968–70; Directing Staff RAF Staff Coll., 1971–74; RAF PMC, 1974–76; Dir of Personnel (Ground) MoD, 1976; Dir of Personal Services (2) (RAF) MoD, 1976–80; RCDS 1980; Dir of Personnel Management (Policy and Plans) (RAF) MoD, 1981–82. Chief Exec., BHA, 1986–96. Mem. Council, CBI, 1990–93. Vice-Pres., HOTREC, 1991–93; Mem. Bd, Internat. Hotel and Restaurant Assoc., 1994–95. Gov., Wellington Coll., 1990–2001. Protocol Dir, Wentworth Golf Club, 1996–2006. FBIM, 1974–94; FIPM, 1976–94. *Recreations:* real tennis, lawn tennis, golf. *Address:* c/o Barclays Bank, 6 Market Place, Newbury, Berks RG14 5AY. *Clubs:* Royal Air Force (Chairman, 1977–82); Jesters', All England Lawn Tennis and Croquet.

LEES, Rear-Adm. Rodney Burnett, CVO 2001; Defence Services Secretary to the Queen, and Director General of Reserve Forces and Cadets, 1998–2001; Chief Naval Supply Officer, 1998–2000; *b* 31 Dec. 1944; *s* of Rear-Adm. Dennis Maresceaux Lees, CB, DSO and Daphne Lees; *m* 1st, 1969, Rosemary Elizabeth Blake (marr. diss. 1978); two *s*; 2nd, 1982, Molly McEwen. *Educ:* Charterhouse. Called to Bar, Gray's Inn, 1976. Joined RN 1962; HMS Devonshire, 1966–68; Captain SM10, 1968–70; HMS Apollo, 1972–74; legal training, 1974–77; Staff Legal Adviser to FO Portsmouth and Command Legal Adviser to C-in-C Naval Home Comd, 1977–79; Dep. Supply Officer, HM Yacht Britannia, 1980; DCSO (Pay), MoD 1980–82; Supply Officer, HMS Illustrious, 1982–83; Fleet Legal and Admin Officer, 1984–86; Sec. to Chief of Fleet Support, 1986–88; Dep. Comd Sec. to C-in-C Fleet, 1988–90; Sec. to First Sea Lord, 1990–92; Dir, Defence Personnel, 1992–95; Dir Gen., Naval Personnel Strategy and Plans, COS to Second Sea Lord and C-in-C Naval Home Comd, 1995–98. *Recreations:* horse racing, soccer, golf, country and folk music. *Address:* Langham House, Langham, Norfolk NR25 7BX. *Club:* Army and Navy.

See also Sir D. B. Lees.

LEES, Sir Thomas (Edward), 4th Bt *cr* 1897; landowner; *b* 31 Jan. 1925; 2nd *s* of Sir John Victor Elliott Lees, 3rd Bt, DSO, MC, and Madeline A. P. (*d* 1967), *d* of Sir Harold Pelly, 4th Bt; *S* father, 1955; *m* 1st, 1949, Faith Justin (*d* 1996), *d* of G. G. Jessiman, OBE, Great Durnford, Wilts; one *s* three *d*; 2nd, 1998, Ann Christine, *d* of Major Cyril Thomas Kelleway, Auckland, NZ. *Educ:* Eton; Magdalene Coll., Cambridge. Served War in RAF; discharged 1945, after losing eye. Magdalene, Cambridge, 1945–47; BA Cantab 1947 (Agriculture). Since then has farmed at and managed South Lytchett estate. Chm., Post Green Community Trust Ltd. Mem., General Synod of C of E, 1970–90. JP 1951, CC 1952–74, High Sheriff 1960, Dorset. Hon. DLitt Bournemouth, 1992. *Recreation:* sailing. *Heir: s* Christopher James Lees [*b* 4 Nov. 1952; *m* 1st, 1977, Jennifer (marr. diss. 1987), *d* of John Wyllie; 2nd, 1989, Clare, *d* of Austen Young, FRCS, Aberystwyth; two *s* three *d*]. *Address:* Little Chimney, Post Green Road, Lytchett Minster, Poole, Dorset BH16 6AP. *T:* (01202) 622048. *Club:* Royal Cruising.

LEES, Sir Thomas Harcourt Ivor, 8th Bt *cr* 1804 (UK), of Black Rock, County Dublin; *b* 6 Nov. 1941; *s* of Sir Charles Archibald Edward Ivor Lees, 7th Bt, and Lily, *d* of Arthur Williams, Manchester; *S* father, 1963. *Heir: kinsman* John Cathcart d'Olier-Lees [*b* 12 Nov. 1927; *m* 1957, Wendy Garrold, *yr d* of late Brian Garrold Groom; two *s*]. *Address:* c/o Mrs Janet Chisholm, Fosseys, The Street, Slinfold, Horsham, W Sussex RH13 0RS.

LEES, Dr William, CBE 1970; TD 1962; FRCOG; Medical Manpower Consultant to South West Thames Regional Health Authority, 1981–87, retired; *b* 18 May 1924; *s* of William Lees and Elizabeth Lees (*née* Massey); *m* 1947, Winifred Elizabeth (*née* Hanford); three *s*. *Educ:* Queen Elizabeth's, Blackburn; Victoria Univ., Manchester. MB ChB; LRCP; MRCS; MRCOG, FRCOG; DPH; MFCM. Obstetrics and Gynaecology, St Mary's Hosps, Manchester, 1947–58; Min. of Health, later DHSS, 1959–81; Under Sec., (SPMO) 1977–81. QHP, 1969–72. Col, 10th, later no 257, Gen. Hosp., TAVR RAMC, 1966–71; Col Comdt, NW London Sector, ACF, 1971–76; Mem. for Greater London, TA&VRA, 1966–. OStJ 1967. *Publications:* numerous contribs on: intensive therapy, progressive patient care, perinatal mortality, day surgery, district general hospital. *Recreations:* music, golf, travel. *Address:* 13 Hall Park Hill, Berkhamsted, Herts HP4 2NH. *T:* (01442) 863010. *Clubs:* Athenæum, St John's.

LEES, Sir (William) Antony Clare, 3rd Bt *cr* 1937; *b* 14 June 1935; *s* of Sir (William) Hereward Clare Lees, 2nd Bt, and of Lady (Dorothy Gertrude) Lees, *d* of F. A. Lauder; *S* father, 1976; *m* 1986, Joanna Olive Crane. *Educ:* Eton; Magdalene Coll., Cambridge (MA). *Heir:* none.

LEESE, Sir Richard Charles, Kt 2006; CBE 2001; Member (Lab), since 1984, and Leader, since 1996, Manchester City Council; *b* 21 April 1951; *s* of Samuel and Hilda Leese; *m* 1st, 1982, Michal Evans (marr. diss. 2000); one *s* one *d*; 2nd, 2003, Joanne Green. *Educ:* Warwick Univ. (BSc Maths). Teacher of Maths, Sidney Stringer Sch. and Community Coll., Coventry, 1974–78, with one year at Washington Jun. High School, Duluth, Minn; youth worker, 1979–82; researcher, 1983–84; community worker, 1984–88. Manchester City Council: Chair: Educn Cttee, 1986–90; Finance Cttee, 1990–95; Dep. Leader, 1990–96. *Recreations:* swimming, football (Manchester City), cricket, political campaigning, the Labour Party, travel, friends, family, music. *Address:* Manchester City Council, Town Hall, Albert Square, Manchester M60 2LA. *T:* (0161) 234 3004.

LEESON, Air Vice-Marshal Kevin James, CBE 2003; CEng, FIET; Assistant Chief of the Defence Staff (Resources and Plans), since 2007; *b* 11 June 1956; *s* of Albert V. Leeson and Joan Leeson (*née* Teale). *Educ:* Univ. of Manchester Inst. of Sci. and Technol. (BSc). CEng 1983; FIET (FIEE 1997). MoD PE, 1988–93; OC Engrg and Supply Wing, RAF Marham, 1994–96; Gp Capt. Logistics 3, HQ Strike Comd, 1996–99; rcds 1999; Dir, Air Resources and Plans, MoD, 2000–04; ACDS (Logistics Ops), 2005–07. Vice Pres., Organising Cttee, Royal Internat. Air Tattoo, 2005– (Mem., 1996–). Pres., Combined Services Winter Sports Assoc., 2006–. *Recreations:* snow ski-ing, water ski-ing, squash, tennis. *Address:* Ministry of Defence, Main Building, Whitehall, SW1A 2HB. *T:* (020) 7218 2188; *e-mail:* Kevin.leeson383@mod.uk. *Clubs:* Royal Air Force, Royal Commonwealth Society.

LE FANU, Mark, OBE 1994; General Secretary, The Society of Authors, since 1982; *b* 14 Nov. 1946; *s* of Admiral of the Fleet Sir Michael Le Fanu, GCB, DSC and Prudence, *d* of Admiral Sir Vaughan Morgan, KBE, CB, MVO, DSC; *m* 1976, Lucy Cowen; three *s* one *d*. *Educ:* Winchester; Univ. of Sussex. Admitted Solicitor, 1976. Served RN, 1964–73; McKenna & Co., 1973–78; The Society of Authors, 1979–. Vice Chm., British Copyright Council, 1992–98; Council Mem., Book Aid Internat., 2004–. Chairman: Strachey Trust, 1995–; W11 Opera, 1997–2000. *Recreations:* sailing, travel, golf, singing. *Address:* 25 St James's Gardens, W11 4RE. *T:* (020) 7603 4119; The Society of Authors, 84 Drayton Gardens, SW10 9SB. *T:* (020) 7373 6642. *Clubs:* Arts, Chelsea Arts; Thorney Island Sailing.

LeFANU, Prof. Nicola Frances; composer; Professor of Music, University of York, 1994–2008 (Head of Department of Music, 1994–2001); *b* 28 April 1947; *d* of late William Richard LeFanu and Dame Elizabeth Violet Maconchy, DBE; *m* 1979, David Newton Lumsdaine; one *s*. *Educ:* St Mary's Sch., Calne; St Hilda's Coll., Oxford (BA Hons 1968, MA 1972; Hon. Fellow, 1993); Royal Coll. of Music; DMus London, 1988. Cobbett Prize for chamber music, 1968; BBC Composers' Competition, 1st Prize, 1971; Mendelssohn Scholarship, 1972; Harkness Fellowship for composition study, Harvard, 1973–74. Dir of Music, St Paul's Girls' Sch., 1975–77; Composer in Residence (jtly with David Lumsdaine), NSW Conservatorium of Music, Sydney, 1979; Sen Lectr in Music, 1977–93, Prof. of Musical Composition, KCL, 1993–94. Deleg. to Moscow Internat. New Music Festival, 1984. FRCM 1995. FTCL 2002. Hon. DMus Durham, 1995; DUniv: Open, 2004; Aberdeen, 2006. Leverhulme Res. Award, 1989. *Publications:* numerous compositions, incl. opera, orchestral works, chamber music with and without voice, choral music and solo pieces; *major works include:* The Same Day Dawns (for soprano and ensemble), 1974; Columbia Falls (for symphony orch.), 1975; Dawnpath (chamber opera), 1977; The Old Woman of Beare (for soprano and ensemble), 1981; The Story of Mary O'Neill (radio opera), 1986; The Green Children (children's opera), 1990; Blood Wedding (opera), 1992; The Wildman (opera), 1995; Duo Concertante (for violin, viola and orch.), 1999; Amores (for solo horn and strings), 2004; Light Passing (chamber opera), 2004. *Recreations:* natural history, and therefore conservation; peace movement, women's movement. *Address:* 5 Holly Terrace, York YO10 4DS. *T:* (01904) 651759. *Club:* Athenæum.

LEFF, Prof. Gordon; Professor of History, University of York, 1969–88, now Emeritus; *b* 9 May 1926; *m* 1953, Rosemary Kathleen (*née* Fox) (marr. diss 1980); one *s*. *Educ:* Summerhill Sch.; King's Coll., Cambridge. BA 1st Cl. Hons, PhD, LittD. Fellow, King's Coll., Cambridge, 1955–59; Asst Lectr, Lectr, Sen. Lectr, in History, Manchester Univ., 1956–65; Reader in History, Univ. of York, 1965–69. Carlyle Vis. Lectr, Univ. of Oxford, 1983. *Publications:* Bradwardine and the Pelagians, 1957; Medieval Thought, 1958; Gregory of Rimini, 1961; The Tyranny of Concepts, 1961; Richard Fitzralph, 1963; Heresy in the Later Middle Ages, 2 vols, 1967; Paris and Oxford Universities in 13th and 14th Centuries, 1968; History and Social Theory, 1969; William of Ockham: the metamorphosis of scholastic discourse, 1975; The Dissolution of the Medieval Outlook, 1976; Heresey, Philosophy and Religion in the Medieval West, 2002. *Recreations:* walking, gardening, watching cricket, listening to music. *Address:* The Sycamores, 12 The Village, Strensall, York YO32 5XS. *T:* (01904) 490358.

LEFF, Prof. Julian Paul, MD; FRCPsych; Director, Team for Assessment of Psychiatric Services, 1985–2005; *b* 4 July 1938; *s* of Samuel Leff and Vera Miriam (*née* Levy); *m* 1975, Joan Lilian Raphael; three *s* one *d. Educ:* University Coll. London (BSc, MB BS); MD London 1972. FRCPsych 1979; MRCP. House Officer: University Coll. Hosp., 1961–62; Whittington Hosp., 1962–63; career scientist, MRC, 1972–2002; Prof. of Social and Cultural Psychiatry, inst. of Psychiatry, Univ. of London, 1987–2002, now Emeritus; Dir, MRC Social and Community Psychiatry Unit, 1989–95. FMedSci 2000. Starkey Prize, Royal Coll. of Health, 1976; Burghölzli Award, Univ. of Zürich, 1999. *Publications:* Psychiatric Examination in Clinical Practice, 1978, 3rd edn 1990; Expressed Emotion in Families, 1985; Psychiatry around the Globe, 1981, 2nd edn 1988; Family Work for Schizophrenia, 1992, 2nd edn 2002; Principles of Social Psychiatry, 1993; Care in the Community: illusion or reality?, 1997; The Unbalanced Mind, 2001; Advanced Family Work for Schizophrenia, 2005; Social Inclusion of People with Mental Illness, 2006. *Recreations:* piano, swimming, silversmithing.

le FLEMING, Sir David (Kelland), 13th Bt *cr* 1705, of Rydal, Westmorland; freelance designer-artist; *b* 12 Jan. 1976; *s* of Sir Quentin John le Fleming, 12th Bt and of Judith Ann le Fleming (*née* Peck); *S* father, 1995. *Educ:* Queen Elizabeth Coll., Palmerston North; Wairarapa Polytech. Coll.; Wellington Polytech. Coll. (BA Visual Communications Design 1997). *Heir: b* Andrew John le Fleming, *b* 4 Oct. 1979. *Address:* 250 Colyton Road, RD5, Feilding, Manawatu, New Zealand. *T:* (6) 3287719.

le FLEMING, Morris John; DL; Chief Executive, Hertfordshire County Council, and Clerk to the Lieutenancy, Hertfordshire, 1979–90; *b* 19 Aug. 1932; *s* of late Morris Ralph le Fleming and Mabel le Fleming; *m* 1960, Jenny Rose Weeks; one *s* three *d. Educ:* Tonbridge Sch.; Magdalene Coll., Cambridge (BA). Admitted Solicitor, 1958. Junior Solicitor, Worcester CC, 1958–59; Asst Solicitor: Middlesex CC, 1959; Nottinghamshire CC, 1959–63; Asst Clerk, Lindsey (Lincolnshire) CC, 1963–69; Hertfordshire CC: Second Dep. Clerk, 1969–74; County Secretary, 1974–79; Clerk, Magistrates' Courts Cttee, 1979–90; Sec., Probation Care Cttee, 1979–90. Dir, Herts TEC, 1989–90. Chm., Stansted Airport Consultative Cttee, 1991–2007; Mem., N Wales Child Abuse Tribunal of Enquiry, 1996–99. Dir, Herts Groundwork Trust, 1990–98; Trustee, Herts Community Trust, 1991–96. Pres., Herts Scouts, 1997–2002 (Chm., 1991–97). DL Herts, 1991. Hon. LLD Hertfordshire, 1994. *Address:* Holt, Wilts BA14 6TB. *T:* and *Fax:* (01225) 783514. *Clubs:* Royal Over-Seas League; Worcestershire Cricket.

LE FLEMING, Peter Henry John; health management consultant, since 1988; Regional General Manager, South East Thames Regional Health Authority, 1984–88; *b* 25 Oct. 1923; *s* of late Edward Ralph Le Fleming and Irene Louise Le Fleming (*née* Adams); *m* 1st, 1949, Gudrun Svendsen (marr. diss. 1981); two *s*; 2nd, 1987, Jean, *yr d* of Edgar and Alice Price, Llangenny, Wales. *Educ:* Addison Gardens Sch., Hammersmith; Pembroke Coll., Cambridge. MA; FHSM. Served 1942–47, RTR and Parachute Regt, MEF, CMF, Palestine; commnd 1943. Sudan Political Service, Equatoria, Kassala, Blue Nile Provinces, 1949–55; National Health Service: Redevelt Sec., St Thomas's Hosp., London, 1955–57; Hosp. Sec., The London Hosp., 1957–61; Dep. Clerk to the Governors, Guy's Hosp., 1961–69; Gp Sec., Exeter and Mid Devon Hosp. Management Cttee, 1969–74; Area Administrator, Kent AHA, 1974–81; Regional Administrator, SE Thames RHA, 1981–84. Mem., Health Service Supply Council, 1982–86. Clerk to Special Trustees, Guy's Hosp., 1988–97; Chm., Evelina Family Trust, 1996–98. Freeman, City of London, 1992. *Recreations:* long distance fell walking, horse riding, trad jazz and serious music. *Address:* Lilacs, Leys Road, Tostock, near Bury St Edmunds, Suffolk IP30 9PN. *T:* (01359) 271015.

LEGARD, Sir Charles Thomas, 15th Bt *cr* 1660; *S* father, 1984. *Heir: s* Christopher John Charles Legard [*b* 19 April 1964; *m* 1986, Miranda, *d* of Maj. Fane Gaffney; one *s* one *d*].

LÉGER, Most Rev. Ernest Raymond; Archbishop of Moncton, (RC), 1996–2002, now Emeritus; *b* 27 Feb. 1944; *s* of Sifroid Léger and Imelda Johnson. *Educ:* Univ. du Sacré Coeur, Bathurst, NB (BA); Univ. de Moncton (BEd); Univ. Laval, Quebec (MTh); Univ. St Paul, Ottawa (LCL). Ordained, 1968; Parish priest, 1968–96: Moncton, 1968–70, 1972–73; St Louis de Kent, 1970–72, 1974–75; St Charles de Kent, 1975–80; Rogersville, 1980–83; Irishtown, 1985–87; St Paul de Kent, 1988–92, 1995–96; Sackville and Dorchester, 1993–95; Judicial Vicar of Marriage Tribunal, Halifax Region, 1985–96; Vicar General, 1992–94, Administrator, 1995–96, Archdio. of Moncton. *Address:* c/o 452 rue Amirault, Dieppe, NB E1A 1G3, Canada. *T:* (506) 8579531.

LEGG, Barry Charles, FCCA; investor and company director; *b* 30 May 1949; *s* of Henry and Elfreda Legg; *m* 1974, Margaret Rose; one *s* two *d. Educ:* Sir Thomas Rich's Grammar Sch., Gloucester; Manchester Univ. (BA Hons Hist.). ATII. Courtaulds Ltd, 1971–76; Coopers & Lybrand, 1976–78; Hillsdown Holdings plc, 1978–92. MP (C) Milton Keynes South West, 1992–97; contested (C) same seat, 1997. Member: Treasury and Civil Service Select Cttee, 1992–96; Treasury Select Cttee, 1996–97 (Chm.). Chief Exec., Conservative Party, 2003. Co-Chm., Bruges Gp, 2005–. *Publications:* Maintaining Momentum: a radical tax agenda for the 1990s, 1992; Who Benefits?—Reinventing Social Security, 1993; Civil Service Reform, a Case for More Radicalism, 1994. *Recreation:* watching cricket. *Address:* 22 Chapel Street, SW1X 7BY. *Club:* Gloucestershire CC.

LEGG, Prof. Brian James, FIBiol; FREng; Director, NIAB (formerly National Institute of Agricultural Botany), 1999–2005; *b* 20 July 1945; *s* of Walter and Mary Legg; *m* 1972, Philippa Whitehead; one *s* one *d. Educ:* Balliol Coll., Oxford (BA Physics 1966); Imperial Coll. London (PhD 1972). FIBiol, FREng (FEng 1994). Voluntary Service Overseas, The Gambia, 1966–67; Res. Scientist, Rothamsted Exptl Station, 1967–83; Head, Res. Divs, Silsoe Res. Inst., 1983–90; Dir, Silsoe Res. Inst., BBSRC (formerly AFRC), 1990–99. Vis. Scientist, CSIRO Div. of Envtl Mechanics, Canberra, 1980–82; Vis. Prof., Silsoe Coll., Cranfield Univ. (formerly Inst. of Technology), 1990–. *Publications:* contribs to learned jls. *Recreations:* sailing, golf, music.

LEGG, Cyrus Julian Edmund; Blue Arrow Personnel Services, 1997–2001; *b* 5 Sept. 1946; *s* of Cyrus and Eileen Legg; *m* 1967, Maureen Jean (*née* Lodge); two *s. Educ:* Tiffin School. Agricultural and Food Research Council, 1967–83; HM Treasury, 1983–87; Sec., BM (Natural Hist.) subseq. Natural History Mus., 1987–97. *Recreation:* gardening. *Address:* 34 Colchester Way, Bedford MK41 8BG. *T:* (01234) 364198.

LEGG, Sir Thomas (Stuart), KCB 1993 (CB 1985); QC 1990; Permanent Secretary, Lord Chancellor's Department, and Clerk of the Crown in Chancery, 1989–98; *b* 13 Aug. 1935; *e s* of late Stuart Legg and Margaret Legg (*née* Amos); *m* 1st, 1961, Patricia Irene Dowie (marr. diss.); two *d*; 2nd, 1983, Marie-Louise, *e d* of late Humphrey Jennings. *Educ:* Horace Mann-Lincoln Sch., New York; Frensham Heights Sch., Surrey; St John's Coll., Cambridge (MA, LLM). 2nd Lieut, Royal Marines (45 Commando), 1953–55. Called to the Bar, Inner Temple, 1960, Bencher, 1984; joined Lord Chancellor's Dept, 1962;

Private Secretary to Lord Chancellor, 1965–68; Asst Solicitor, 1975; Under Sec., 1977–82; SE Circuit Administrator, 1980–82; Dep. Sec., 1982–89; Dep. Clerk of the Crown in Chancery, 1986–89; Sec. of Commns, 1989–98. Conducted Sierra Leone Arms Investigation, 1998. Consultant, Clifford Chance, 1998–. Ext. Mem., Audit Cttee, H of C, 2004–; Mem., Audit Commn, 2005–. Chm., Hammersmith Hosps NHS Trust, 2000–07; Dir, Imperial Coll. Healthcare Trust, 2007–. Trustee, Civil Service Benevolent Fund, 1998–2000 (Chm., 1993–98). Chm., London Library, 2004– (Trustee, 2001–). Visitor, Brunel Univ., 2001–06 (Mem. Council, 1993–2000); Vis. Fellow, Univ. of Essex, 2008–. Hon. LLD Brunel, 2006. *Address:* The Blue House, Ginsberg Yard, Back Lane, Hampstead, NW3 1EW. *Club:* Garrick.

LEGGATT, Rt Hon. Sir Andrew (Peter), Kt 1982; PC 1990; Chief Surveillance Commissioner, 1998–2006; a Lord Justice of Appeal, 1990–97; *b* 8 Nov. 1930; *er s* of late Captain William Ronald Christopher Leggatt, DSO, RN and Dorothea Joy Leggatt (*née* Dreyer); *m* 1953, Gillian Barbara Newton; one *s* one *d. Educ:* Eton; King's Coll., Cambridge (Exhibr). MA 1957. Commn in Rifle Bde, 1949–50; TA, 1950–59. Called to the Bar, Inner Temple, 1954, Bencher, 1976. QC 1972; a Recorder of the Crown Court, 1974–82; Judge, High Court of Justice, QBD, 1982–90. Mem., Top Salaries Review Body, 1979–82; conducted review, Tribunals for Users, 2000–01; Chm. Appeals Cttee, Takeover Panel, 2001–06. Mem., Judges' Council, 1988–97. Pres., Council of Inns of Court, 1995–97; Member: Bar Council, 1971–82; Senate, 1974–83; Chm. of the Bar, 1981–82. Hon. Member: American Bar Assoc.; Canadian Bar Assoc.; non-resident mem., American Law Inst.; Hon. Fellow, Amer. Coll. of Trial Lawyers, 1996. *Recreations:* listening to music, personal computers. *Clubs:* MCC, Pilgrims.

See also G. A. M. Leggatt.

LEGGATT, George Andrew Midsomer; QC 1997; a Recorder, since 2002; a Deputy High Court Judge, since 2008; *b* 12 Nov. 1957; *s* of Rt Hon. Sir Andrew Peter Leggatt, *qv* and Gillian Barbara Leggatt (*née* Newton); *m* 1987, Dr Stavia Brigitte Blunt; one *s* one *d. Educ:* Eton (King's Schol.); King's Coll., Cambridge (MA); Harvard (Harkness Fellow); City Univ. (Dip. Law). Bigelow Teaching Fellow, Univ. of Chicago Law Sch., 1982–83; called to the Bar, Middle Temple, 1983, Bencher, 2004; Associate, Sullivan & Cromwell, New York, 1983–84. Vice-Chm., Bar Standards Bd, 2006–08. Sec., Commercial Bar Assoc., 2004–07. *Publication:* (contrib.) Halsbury's Laws of England, 4th edn (reissues) 1989 and 2005. *Recreations:* wine, philosophy. *Address:* Brick Court Chambers, 7–8 Essex Street, WC2R 3LD.

LEGGATT, Sir Hugh (Frank John), Kt 1988; art dealer, retired; *b* 27 Feb. 1925; 2nd *s* of late Henry and Beatrice Leggatt; *m* 1st, 1953, Jennifer Hepworth (marr. diss. 1990); two *s*; 2nd, 1991, Gaynor, *yr d* of late W. L. Tregoning, CBE and D. M. E. Tregoning. *Educ:* Eton; New Coll., Oxford. RAF, 1943–46. Joined Leggatt Bros, 1946; Partner, 1952; Sen. Partner, 1962–92. Hon. Rep., Nat. Portrait Galls of London and Edinburgh, 1946–92. Pres., Fine Art Provident Instn, 1960–63; Chm., Soc. of London Art Dealers, 1966–70; Mem., Museums and Galleries Commn, 1983–92. Hon. Sec., Heritage in Danger, 1974–. *Address:* 21 Rue du Lac, 1800 Vevey, Switzerland. *T:* and *Fax:* (21) 9236810. *Club:* White's.

LEGGE, family name of **Earl of Dartmouth**.

LEGGE, Anthony; Director of Opera, Royal Academy of Music, since 2003; Music Director, Clonter Opera, since 2004; *b* 12 March 1948; *s* of Harry and Nancy, (Judy), Legge; *m* 1980, Christine Elizabeth Anderson Tyrer; one *d. Educ:* Dean Close Sch., Cheltenham; Queen's Coll., Oxford (MA). Member, Music Staff: London Opera Centre, 1971–72; Scottish Opera, 1972–77; Visiting Guest Coach: Australian Opera, 1978–88; Bayreuth, 1988–93; Nederlandsche Oper, 1995–; Opera Australia, 2005–; Hd of Music, ENO, 1989–2003; Music Advr, Grange Park Opera, 2006–. Chm., The Rehearsal Orch., 2004–. Reader for the Queen's Anniversary Prize, 1999–. Judge, Operatunity, Channel 4, 2003. Has made numerous recordings. Hon. RAM 2007. *Publications:* The Art of Auditioning, 1988, 2nd edn 1993, updated and re-issued 2001; The Singer's Handbook, 2007. *Recreation:* walking the dog. *Club:* Garrick.

LEGGE, (John) Michael, CB 2001; CMG 1994; Chairman, Civil Service Healthcare, since 2001; *b* 14 March 1944; *s* of late Alfred John Legge and Marion Frances Legge (*née* James); *m* 1971, Linda (*née* Bagley); two *s. Educ:* Royal Grammar Sch., Guildford; Christ Church Oxford (BA, MA). Ministry of Defence: Asst Principal, 1966; Asst Private Sec. to Sec. of State for Defence, 1970; Principal, 1971; 1st Sec., UK Delegn to NATO, 1974–77; Asst Sec., MoD, 1979–87; Rand Corp., Santa Monica, California, 1982; Asst Under Sec. of State (Policy), MoD, 1987–88; Asst Sec. Gen. for Defence Planning and Policy, NATO, 1988–93; Deputy Under-Secretary of State: NI Office, 1993–96; MoD, 1996–2001. Sec. and Dir of admin, Royal Hosp. Chelsea, 2001–07. *Publication:* Theatre Nuclear Weapons and the NATO Strategy of Flexible Response, 1983. *Recreations:* golf, gardening, travel. *Address:* 53 St Mary's Road, Leatherhead, Surrey KT22 8HB.

LEGGE-BOURKE, Hon. (Elizabeth) Shân (Josephine), LVO 1988; Lord-Lieutenant of Powys, since 1998; *b* 10 Sept. 1943; *o c* of 3rd Baron Glanusk, DSO and Margaret (*née* Shoubridge, later Dowager Viscountess De L'Isle); *m* 1964, William Legge-Bourke, DL; one *s* two *d.* Lady-in-waiting to HRH Princess Anne, now HRH Princess Royal, 1978–. President: Royal Welsh Agricl Soc., 1997; Nat. Fedn of Young Farmers Clubs of England and Wales, 1998–2000; Save the Children Fund (Wales), 1989–. High Sheriff of Powys, 1991–92. *Address:* Gliffaes-Fach, Crickhowell, Powys NP8 1LP.

LEGGETT, Sir Anthony (James), KBE 2004; DPhil; FRS 1980; John D. and Catherine T. MacArthur Professor of Physics, and Center for Advanced Study Professor of Physics, University of Illinois, since 1983; Mike and Ophelia Lazaridis Distinguished Research Professor, Institute for Quantum Computing, University of Waterloo, since 2007; *b* 26 March 1938. *Educ:* Balliol Coll., Oxford (BA 1959; Hon. Fellow 1994); Merton Coll., Oxford (BA 1961; Hon. Fellow 2004); Magdalen Coll., Oxford (DPhil 1964). Res. Associate, Univ. of Illinois, 1964–65; Fellow, Magdalen Coll., Oxford, 1963–67; Lectr, 1967–71, Reader, 1971–78, Prof. of Physics, 1978–83, Univ. of Sussex. Hon. FInstP 1999. (Jtly) Nobel Prize for Physics, 2003. *Publications:* The Problems of Physics, 1987; (jtly) Quantum Tunnelling in Condensed Media, 1992; (jtly) Quantum Computing and Quantum Bits in Mesoscopic Systems, 2003; articles in learned jls. *Address:* Department of Physics, University of Illinois at Urbana-Champaign, 1110 West Green Street, Urbana, IL 61801–3080, USA; 607 West Pennsylvania Avenue, Urbana, IL 61801, USA.

LEGGETT, Dr Jeremy Kendal; Founder and Chairman, Solarcentury, since 1997; *b* 16 March 1954; *s* of Dennis and Audrey Leggett; *m* (marr. diss.); one *d. Educ:* Univ. of Wales, Aberystwyth (BSc Hons 1975); Wolfson Coll., Oxford (DPhil (Earth Scis) 1978). Lectr in Earth Scis, 1978–87, Reader, 1987–89, Royal Sch. of Mines, ICSTM; Founder and Dir, Verification Technol. Inf. Centre (VERTIC), 1985–89; Scientific Dir, Climate Campaign, Greenpeace Internat., 1989–96. Oxford University: Vis. Fellow, Centre for Envmtl Policy and Understanding, 1996; Associate Fellow, Envmtl Change Inst., 1997–. Dir, New Energies Invest AG, 2000–; Mem., Renewables Adv. Bd, 2002–06. Award for advancing understanding, US Climate Inst., 1996; Sustainable Leadership Award, SAM, 2006; CNN Principal Voice, 2007. *Publications:* Global Warming: the Greenpeace report, 1990 (ed and contrib.); The Carbon War, 1999; Half Gone, 2005. *Recreation:* salsa dancing. *Address:* Solarcentury, 91–94 Lower Marsh, SE1 7AB. *T:* (020) 7803 0100; *e-mail:* jeremy.leggett@solarcentury.com.

LEGH; *see* Cornwall-Legh, family name of Baron Grey of Codnor.

LEGH, family name of **Baron Newton**.

LEGH-JONES, (Piers) Nicholas; QC 1987; *b* 2 Feb. 1943; *s* of late John Herbert Legh-Jones and Elizabeth Anne (*née* Halford). *Educ:* Winchester College; New College, Oxford (MA Hist. 1964, Jurisp. 1966). Legal Instructor, Univ. of Pennsylvania, 1966–67; Lectr in Law, New College, Oxford, 1967–71; Eldon Law Scholar, Univ. of Oxford, 1968. Called to the Bar, Lincoln's Inn, 1968. Vis. Prof., King's Coll., London, 1998–2005. *Publications:* (ed) MacGillivray and Parkington on Insurance Law, 6th edn to 8th edn 1988; (gen. ed.) MacGillivray on Insurance Law, 9th edn, 1997, 10th edn 2002; contribs to Modern Law Review and Cambridge Law Jl. *Recreations:* vintage motorcars, modern history.

LEGHARI, Farooq Ahmed Khan; President of Pakistan, 1993–97; *b* 2 May 1940; *s* of Nawab Sardar Muhammad Khan Leghari; *m;* two *s* two *d. Educ:* Aitchison Coll., Lahore; Punjab Univ. (BA Hons); St Catherine's Coll., Oxford (BA Hons PPE, MA). Civil Servant, 1964–73; Mem., Pakistan People's Party, 1973–93; Senate of Pakistan, 1975; Mem. for Dera Ghazi Khan, Nat. Assembly, 1977; Minister for Production, 1977; jailed on numerous occasions, 1977–88; Sec.-Gen. and Mem. Exec. Cttee, Pakistan People's Party, 1978–83; Mem., Nat. Assembly, and Minister for Water and Power, 1989–90; re-elected 1990 and 1993; Dep. Leader of Opposition, 1990–93; Finance Minister, later Minister for Foreign Affairs, 1993. Chief, Baluchi Leghari Tribe.

LEGON, Prof. Anthony Charles, PhD, DSc; FRS 2000; Professor of Physical Chemistry, 2005–08, University Senior Research Fellow, since 2008, University of Bristol; *b* 28 Sept. 1941; *s* of George Charles Legon and late Emily Louisa Florence Legon (*née* Conner); *m* 1963, Deirdre Anne Rivers; two *s* one *d. Educ:* Coopers' Co. Sch., London (Gibson Exhibnr); UCL (BSc 1963; PhD 1967; DSc 1981). FRSC 1978. Turner & Newall Fellow, Univ. of London, 1968–70; University College London: Lectr, 1970–83, Reader, 1983–84, in Chemistry; Thomas Graham Prof. of Chemistry, 1989–90; Prof. of Physical Chemistry, 1984–89 and 1990–2005, and EPSRC Sen. Fellow, 1997–2002, Univ. of Exeter. Vis. Res. Associate Prof., Univ. of Illinois, 1980; Hassel Lectr, Univ. of Oslo, 1997. Mem., Physical Chemistry Sub Cttee, 1984–87; NATO Postdoctoral Fellowships (Chemistry) Cttee, 1987, 1988, 1991–93, Advanced Fellowships (Chemistry) Cttee, 1991–92 (Chm., 1991), SERC; Royal Society of Chemistry: Chairman: Peninsula Section, 1988–89, 2002–03; High Resolution Spectroscopy Gp, 1998–2000; Tilden Lectr and Medallist, 1990; Mem. Council, 1996–99, Vice-Pres., 2001–04, Faraday Div.; Associate Ed., Chem. Communications, 1996–98; Spectroscopy Award, 1999. Member Editorial Board: Chemical Physics Letters, 1988–; Spectrochimica Acta, 1989–97; Jl of Molecular Structure, 1990–2005; Jl Chem. Soc. Faraday Trans, 1994–98. *Publications:* Principles of Molecular Recognition, 1993; numerous res. papers in learned jls. *Recreations:* watching soccer (Exeter City AFC), and cricket. *Address:* School of Chemistry, University of Bristol, Bristol BS8 1TS; *e-mail:* A.C.Legon@bristol.ac.uk.

LE GOY, Raymond Edgar Michel, FCILT; a Director General, Commission of the European Communities, now European Union, 1981, now Emeritus; *b* 1919; *e s* of J. A. S. M. N. and May Le Goy; *m* 1960, Ernestine Burnett, Trelawny, Jamaica; one *s* (and one *s* decd). *Educ:* William Ellis Sch.; Gonville and Caius Coll., Cambridge (BA 1st cl. hons Hist. Tripos, 1939, 1940; MA). Sec. Cambridge Union; Chm., Union Univ. Liberal Socs. Served Army, 1940–46: Staff Captain, HQ E Africa, 1944; Actg Major, 1945. LPTB, 1947; Min. of Transport, 1947; UK Shipping Adviser, Japan, 1949–51; Far East and SE Asia, 1951; Dir, Goeland Co., 1952; Asst Secretary: MoT, 1958; Min. of Aviation, 1959; BoT and DEA, 1966; Under-Sec., 1968, BoT, later DTI; Dir Gen. for Transport, EEC, 1973–81. FCILT (FCIT 1974; FILT 1999). *Publication:* The Victorian Burletta, 1953. *Recreations:* theatre, music, race relations. *Address:* c/o Fortis Banque, Agence Schuman, Rond Point Schuman 10, 1040 Brussels, Belgium.

LE GRAND, Julian Ernest Michael, PhD; Richard Titmuss Professor of Social Policy, London School of Economics, since 1993 (on secondment as Senior Policy Adviser, Prime Minister's Office, 2003–05); *b* 29 May 1945; *s* of late Roland John Le Grand and Eileen Joan Le Grand; *m* 1971, Damaris May Robertson-Glasgow; two *d. Educ:* Eton; Univ. of Sussex (BA); Univ. of Pennsylvania (PhD 1972). Lectr in Econs, Univ. of Sussex, 1971–78; Lectr in Econs, 1978–85, Sen. Res. Fellow, 1985–87, LSE; Prof. of Public Policy, Univ. of Bristol, 1987–93. Mem., ESRC Bds, 1982–86 and 1988–92. Mem., Commn for Health Improvement, 1999–2003; Chairman: Social Care Practices Wkg Gp, DFES, 2006–07; Health England, DoH, 2007–. Sen. Associate, 2005–07, Trustee, 2007–, King's Fund. Non-executive Director: Avon FHSA, 1990–94; Avon HA, 1994–95; Vice-Chm., Frenchay NHS Trust, 1996–99. Gov., LSE, 1999–2003. Founding AcSS 1999. Hon. FPH (Hon. FPHM 1997). Hon. DLitt Sussex, 2006. *Publications:* (with R. Robinson) The Economics of Social Problems, 1976, 3rd edn 1992; The Strategy of Equality, 1982; (ed with R. Robinson) Privatisation and the Welfare State, 1984; (with R. Goodin) Not Only the Poor, 1987; (ed with S. Estrin) Market Socialism, 1989; Equity and Choice, 1991; (ed with W. Bartlett) Quasi-markets and Social Policy, 1993; (ed with R. Robinson) Evaluating the NHS Reforms, 1994; (with B. New) Rationing in the NHS, 1996; (ed jtly) A Revolution in Social Policy, 1998; (ed jtly) Learning from the NHS Internal Market, 1998; (ed with E. Mossialos) Health Care and Cost Containment in the European Union, 1999; (ed jtly) Understanding Social Exclusion, 2002; Motivation, Agency and Public Policy: of knights and knaves, pawns and queens, 2004, 2nd edn 2006; The Other Invisible Hand, 2007; contrib. articles to Econ. Jl, Jl Public Econs, Economica, Jl Social Policy, Jl Human Resources, Eur. Econ. Review, British Jl Pol Sci., Jl Health Econs, BMJ, Health Affairs, Social Sci. and Medicine, The Lancet. *Recreations:* reading, drawing, supporting daughters. *Address:* 31 Sydenham Hill, Bristol BS6 5SL. *T:* (0117) 942 5253; *e-mail:* J.Legrand@lse.ac.uk.

LE GREW, Daryl John; Vice-Chancellor and President, University of Tasmania, since 2003; *b* Melbourne, 17 Sept. 1945; *s* of A. J. and N. M. R. Le Grew; *m* 1971, Josephine de Tarczynska; one *s* two *d. Educ:* Trinity Grammar Sch., Kew; Univ. of Melbourne (BArch, MArch). University of Melbourne: Lectr, Dept of Town and Regl Planning, 1969–73; Lectr, then Sen. Lectr, Dept of Architecture and Bldg, 1973–85; Deakin University: Prof. of Architecture, 1986–98; Dean, Faculty of Design and Technol., 1992–93; Chm., Acad. Bd, 1992–98; Pro-Vice-Chancellor (Acad.), 1993–94; Dep. Vice-Chancellor and Vice-Pres. (Acad.), 1994–98; Vice-Chancellor, Univ. of Canterbury, NZ, 1998–2002. Life Fellow, Mus. of Victoria, 1997. *Recreations:* swimming, music, poetry, philosophy. *Address:* University of Tasmania, Private Bag 51, Hobart, Tas 7001, Australia.

LE GRICE, (Andrew) Valentine; QC 2002; barrister; *b* 26 June 1953; *s* of late Charles Le Grice and Wilmay Le Grice (*née* Ward); *m* 1st, 1977, Anne Elizabeth Moss (marr. diss.

2001); two *s* one *d;* 2nd, 2001, Jayne Elizabeth Sandford-Hill; one *d. Educ:* Shrewsbury Sch.; Univ. of Durham (BA Hons). Called to the Bar, Middle Temple, 1977. *Recreations:* watching sport (particularly football), throwing things away. *Address:* 1 Hare Court, Temple, EC4Y 7BE. *Club:* Travellers.

LE GUIN, Ursula Kroeber; writer; *b* Berkeley, California, 21 Oct. 1929; *d* of Alfred L. Kroeber and Theodora Kroeber; *m* 1953, Charles A. Le Guin; one *s* two *d. Educ:* Radcliffe Coll. (BA 1951); Columbia Univ. (MA 1952; Fellow, 1953). Instructor in French, Mercer Coll. and Univ. of Idaho, 1956–57; Lectr, Guest Lectr or Writer in Residence, 1971–, at univs, colls, confs and workshops in USA, Australia and UK, incl. Portland State Univ., Indiana Univ., Kenyon Coll., Stanford Univ., Clarion West, Revelle Coll. of UCSD, Tulane, Bennington, Beloit, Haystack, Flight of the Mind. Arbuthnot Lectr, Amer. Lib. Assoc., 2004. Grand Master, Sci. Fiction and Fantasy Writers of America, 2003. Holds hon. degrees from 9 US univs. Gandalf Award, 1979; Harold Vursell Award, AAIL, 1991; Bumbershoot Arts Award, Seattle, 1998; Robert Kirsch Lifetime Achievement Award, LA Times, 2000; Lifetime Achievement Award, Pacific NW Booksellers' Assoc., 2001; PEN/Malamud Award, World Fantasy Award, 2002; Margaret A. Edwards Award for lifetime achievement, Young Adult Liby Services Assoc., 2004; Maxine Cushing Gray Award for literary achievement, 2006. *Publications: novels:* Planet of Exile, 1966; Rocannon's World, 1966; City of Illusion, 1967; A Wizard of Earthsea, 1968 (Boston Globe – Horn Bk Award, 1968; Lewis Carroll Shelf Award, 1979); The Left Hand of Darkness, 1969 (Nebula and Hugo Awards, 1969); Tiptree Retrospective Award, 1996); The Tombs of Atuan, 1970 (Newbery Silver Medal, 1972); The Lathe of Heaven, 1971 (Locus Award, 1973; filmed 1979); The Farthest Shore, 1972 (Nat. Book Award for Children's Books); The Dispossessed: an ambiguous Utopia, 1974 (Hugo and Nebula Awards, 1975); The Word for World is Forest, 1976 (Hugo Award); Very Far Away From Anywhere Else, 1976 (Prix Lectures-Jeunesse, 1987); Malafrena, 1979; The Beginning Place, 1980; The Eye of the Heron, 1983; Always Coming Home, 1985 (Janet Heidinger Kafka Prize for Fiction, 1986); Tehanu (Nebula Award), 1990; The Telling, 2000 (Locus Readers Award, Endeavour Award, 2001); Tales from Earthsea, 2001 (Locus Readers Award, 2002, Endeavour Award, 2003); The Other Wind, 2001; Gifts, 2004 (Literary Award, PEN Center USA); Voices, 2006; Powers, 2007; Lavinia, 2008; *short story collections:* The Wind's Twelve Quarters, 1975; Orsinian Tales, 1976; The Compass Rose, 1982 (Locus Award, 1984); Buffalo Gals, 1987 (Internat. Fantasy Award, Hugo Award, 1988); Searoad, 1991 (H. L. Davis Fiction Award, 1992); A Fisherman of the Inland Sea, 1994; Four Ways to Forgiveness, 1995 (Locus Readers Award, 1996); Unlocking the Air, 1996; The Birthday of the World, 2002; Changing Planes, 2003; *poetry:* Wild Angels, 1974; Walking in Cornwall, 1976; (with T. Kroeber) Tillai and Tylissos, 1979; Hard Words, 1981; (with H. Pander) In the Red Zone, 1983; Wild Oats and Fireweed, 1988; No Boats, 1992; (with R. Dorband) Blue Moon over Thurman Street, 1993; Going out with Peacocks, 1994; Sixty Odd, 1999; *translation:* Lao Tzu: Tao Te Ching: a book about the way and the power of the way, 1997; (with D. Bellessi) The Twins, The Dream/Las Gemelas, El Sueno, 1997; Kalpa Imperial, stories by Angelica Gorodischer, 2003; Selected Poems of Gabriela Mistral, 2003; *criticism:* The Language of the Night, 1979, rev. edn 1992; Dancing at the Edge of the World, 1989; Steering the Craft, 1998; The Wave in the Mind, 2004; *for children:* Leese Webster, 1979; Cobbler's Rune, 1983; Solomon Leviathan, 1988; A Visit from Dr Katz, 1988; Fire and Stone, 1989; Fish Soup, 1992; A Ride on the Red Mare's Back, 1992; Tom Mouse, 2002; *Catwings books:* Catwings, 1988; Catwings Return, 1989; Wonderful Alexander and the Catwings, 1994; Jane on her Own, 1999; *screenplay:* King Dog, 1985. *Address:* c/o Virginia Kidd Agency, PO Box 278, Milford, PA 18337, USA.

LEHANE, Maureen, (Mrs Peter Wishart); concert and opera singer, retired; now teaching privately; *d* of Christopher Lehane and Honor Millar; *m* 1966, Peter Wishart (*d* 1984), composer. *Educ:* Queen Elizabeth's Girls' Grammar Sch., Barnet; Guildhall Sch. of Music and Drama. Studied under Hermann Weissenborn, Berlin (teacher of Fischer Dieskau); also under John and Aida Dickens (Australian teachers of Joan Sutherland); gained Arts Council award to study in Berlin. Speciality is Handel; has sung numerous leading roles (operas inc. Ezio, Ariadne and Pharamondo) with Handel opera societies of England and America, in London, and in Carnegie Hall, New York, also in Poland, Sweden and Germany; gave a number of master classes on the interpretation of Handel's vocal music (notably at s'Hertogenbosch Festival, Holland, July 1972; invited to repeat them in 1973); masterclasses on Handel and Purcell, The Hague and Maastricht, 1991; has taught at GSMD, Reading Univ. and WCMD. Debut at Glyndebourne, 1967. Festival appearances include: Stravinsky Festival, Cologne; City of London; Aldeburgh; Cheltenham; Three Choirs; Bath; Oxford Bach; Göttingen Handel Festival, etc; has toured N America; also 3-month tour of Australia at invitation of ABC and 2-month tour of Far East and ME, 1971; sang in Holland, and for Belgian TV, 1978; visits also to Berlin, Lisbon, Poland and Rome, 1979–80, to Warsaw, 1981. Title and lead rôles in: Purcell's Dido and Aeneas, Netherlands Opera, 1976; Peter Wishart's operas, Clytemnestra and The Lady of the Inn; Mozart's Marriage of Figaro, Cologne Opera; Rossini's La Cenerentola; 13 of Handel's operas. Cyrus in first complete recording of Handel's Belshazzar. Appeared regularly on BBC; also in promenade concerts. Has made numerous recordings (Bach, Haydn, Mozart, Handel, etc). Mem. Jury, Internat. Singing Comp., s'Hertogenbosch Fest., Holland, 1982–; Adjudicator, Llangollen Internat. Eisteddfod 1991–93 and 1997. Founder and Music Dir, Great Elm Music Festival, 1987–98; Founder and Artistic Dir, Jackdaws Educnl Trust, 1993–. *Publication:* (ed with Peter Wishart) Songs of Purcell. *Recreations:* cooking, gardening, reading. *Address:* Ironstone Cottage, Great Elm, Frome, Somerset BA11 3NY. *T:* (01373) 812383.

LEHMAN, Prof. Meir, (Manny), DSc, PhD; FREng, FBCS, FIET, FIEEE, FACM; Professor of Computer Science, Jerusalem College of Technology, 2002 and since 2006; Professor, School of Computer Science, and Consultant, Middlesex University, 2002–07, now Professor Emeritus; *b* 24 Jan. 1925; *s* of late Benno and Theresa Lehman; *m* 1953, Chava Robinson; three *s* two *d. Educ:* Letchworth Grammar Sch.; Imperial Coll. of Science and Technol. (BSc Hons 1953, PhD 1956, ARCS, DIC); DSc (London) 1987. FIET (FIEE 1972; StuIEE 1947); FIEEE 1985 (MIEEE 1974); FBCS 1986 (MBCS 1956); FREng (FEng 1989); FACM 1994 (MACM 1953). Murphy Radio, 1941–50; Imperial Coll., 1950–56; London Labs, Ferranti, 1956–57; Scientific Dept, Israeli Defence Min., 1957–64; Res. Div., IBM, 1964–72; Department of Computing, Imperial College: 1972–84 (part-time 1984–87); Prof. of Computing Sci., 1972–84, now Emeritus; Hd of Dept, 1979–84; Sen. Res. Fellow, 1989–2002; Sen. Res. Investigator, 1998–2002; Principal Investigator, Feedback Evolution and Software Technology, EPSRC Project, 1996–98 and 1999–2001; Imperial Software Technology Ltd: Founder, 1982; Chm., 1982–84; Dir, 1984–87; Exec. Dir, 1987–88; Man. and Tech. Dir, Lehman Software Technology Associates Ltd, 1985–2003. Vice-Chm. of Exec., Kisharon Day Sch. for Special Educn and Vice-Chm. of Trustees and Gov., 1976–2000. *Publications:* Software Evolution—Processes of Program Change, 1985; over 250 refereed pubns and 20 book chapters. *Recreations:* family, Talmudic studies, classical orchestral music, DIY. *Address:* 17 R'Binjamin Mitudela, Rediavia, Jerusalem, Israel; Department of Computing, Machon Lev, Jerusalem College of Technology, Jerusalem, Israel; *e-mail:* mml@onetel.com, mannyml@netvision.net.il.

LEHN, Prof. Jean-Marie, Officier, Ordre National du Mérite, 1993 (Chevalier, 1976); Commandeur, Légion d'Honneur, 1996 (Chevalier, 1983; Officier, 1988); Professor of Chemistry, Collège de France, Paris, since 1979; *b* Rosheim, Bas-Rhin, 30 Sept. 1939; *s* of Pierre Lehn and Marie Lehn (*née* Salomon); *m* 1965, Sylvie Lederer; two *s*. *Educ:* Univ. of Strasbourg (PhD); Research Fellow, Harvard, 1964. CNRS, 1960–66; Asst Prof., Univ. of Strasbourg, 1966–69; University Louis Pasteur, Strasbourg: Associate Prof., 1970; Prof. of Chemistry, 1970–79. Visiting Professor, 1972–: Harvard, Zürich, Cambridge, Barcelona, Frankfurt. Mem. or Associate, and hon. degrees from professional bodies in Europe, Asia and USA; Hon. FRSC 1987; For. Mem., Royal Soc., 1993. Nobel Prize for Chemistry (jtly), 1987, and numerous awards from sci. instns. Orden pour le mérite für Wissenschaften und Künste (FRG), 1990. *Publications:* many chapters in books and contribs to learned jls on supramolecular chemistry, physical organic chemistry and photochemistry. *Recreation:* music. *Address:* Institut de Science d'Ingénierie Supramoléculaires, Université Louis Pasteur, 8 Allée Gaspard Monge, BP 70028, 67083 Strasbourg, France. *T:* (3) 90245145, *Fax:* (3) 90245140; *e-mail:* lehn@isis.u-strasbg.fr; Collège de France, 11 place Marcelin Berthelot, 75005 Paris, France. *T:* (1) 44271360, *Fax:* (1) 44271356.

LEHRER, Thomas Andrew; writer of songs since 1943; *b* 9 April 1928; *s* of James Lehrer and Anna Lehrer (*née* Waller). *Educ:* Harvard Univ. (AB 1946, MA 1947); Columbia Univ.; Harvard Univ. Student (mathematics, especially probability and statistics) till 1953. Part-time teaching at Harvard, 1946–53. Theoretical physicist at Baird-Atomic, Inc., Cambridge, Massachusetts, 1953–54. Entertainer, 1953–55, 1957–60. US Army, 1955–57. Lecturer in Business Administration, Harvard Business Sch., 1961; Lecturer: in Education, Harvard Univ., 1963–66; in Psychology, Wellesley Coll., 1966; in Political Science, MIT, 1962–71; Lectr, Univ. of Calif, Santa Cruz, 1972–2002. *Publications:* Tom Lehrer Song Book, 1954; Tom Lehrer's Second Song Book, 1968; Too Many Songs by Tom Lehrer, 1981; contrib. to Annals of Mathematical Statistics, Journal of Soc. of Industrial and Applied Maths. *Recreation:* piano. *Address:* 11 Sparks Street, Cambridge, MA 02138–4711, USA. *T:* (617) 3547708.

LEICESTER, 7th Earl of, *cr* 1837; **Edward Douglas Coke,** CBE 2005; DL; Viscount Coke 1837; *b* 6 May 1936; *er s* of 6th Earl of Leicester and his 1st wife, Moyra Joan (*d* 1987), *d* of Douglas Crossley; *S* father, 1994; *m* 1st, 1962, Valeria Phyllis (marr. diss. 1985), *e d* of late L. A. Potter; two *s* one *d*; 2nd, 1986, Mrs Sarah de Chair. *Educ:* St Andrew's, Grahamstown, CP, S Africa. Mem., King's Lynn and W Norfolk BC, 1973–91 (Leader, 1980–85; Chm. Planning Cttee, 1987–91). Comr, English Heritage, 2002–. Pres., HHA, 1998–2003. President: Wells, Norfolk Br., RNLI; League of Friends, Wells Cottage Hosp.; Royal Norfolk Show, 1995. Mem. Council, Royal Norfolk Agricl Assoc. DL Norfolk, 1981–85, 2005. *Recreations:* history, conservation of the built heritage, wildlife matters, reading, shooting. *Heir:* *s* Viscount Coke, *qv*. *Address:* Model Farm, Holkham, Wells-next-the-Sea, Norfolk NR23 1RP. *Clubs:* Brooks's, White's, Farmers'.

LEICESTER, Bishop of, since 1999; **Rt Rev. Timothy John Stevens;** *b* 31 Dec. 1946; *s* of late Ralph and Jean Ursula Stevens; *m* 1973, Wendi Kathleen; one *s* one *d*. *Educ:* Chigwell Sch.; Selwyn Coll., Cambridge (BA 1968; MA 1972); Ripon Hall, Oxford (Dip Th). BOAC, 1968–72; FCO, 1972–73. Ordained priest, 1976; Curate, East Ham, 1976–79; Team Vicar, Upton Park, 1979–80; Team Rector, Canvey Island, 1980–88; Bp of Chelmsford's Urban Officer, 1988–91; Archdeacon of West Ham, 1991–95; Bishop Suffragan of Dunwich, 1995–99. Hon. Canon of Chelmsford, 1987–95. Chm., Urban Bishops' Panel, Gen. Synod of C of E, 2001–06; Member: Archbps' Council, 2006–; Standing Cttee, House of Bishops, 2006–. Chm., Council, Children's Soc., 2004–. Mem. Bd of Govs, De Montfort Univ., 2006–; Chm. Bd of Govs, Westcott House Theol Coll., 2006–. Took seat in H of L, 2004. Hon. DCL De Montfort, 2002; Hon. DLitt Leicester, 2003. *Recreations:* golf, cricket. *Address:* Bishop's Lodge, 10 Springfield Road, Leicester LE2 3BD. *T:* (0116) 270 8985, *Fax:* (0116) 270 3288.

LEICESTER, Dean of; *see* Faull, Very Rev. V. F.

LEICESTER, Archdeacon of; *see* Atkinson, Ven. R. W. B.

LEIFLAND, Leif, Hon. GCVO 1983; Ambassador of Sweden to the Court of St James's, 1982–91; *b* 30 Dec. 1925; *s* of Sigfrid and Elna Leifland; *m* 1954, Karin Abard; one *s* two *d*. *Educ:* Univ. of Lund (LLB 1950). Joined Ministry of Foreign Affairs, 1952; served: Athens, 1953; Bonn, 1955; Stockholm, 1958; Washington, 1961; Stockholm, 1964; Washington, 1970; Stockholm, 1975. Secretary, Foreign Relations Cttee, Swedish Parliament, 1966–70; Under Secretary for Political Affairs, 1975–77; Permanent Under-Secretary of State for Foreign Affairs, 1977–82; Chm. Bd, Swedish Inst. of Internat. Affairs, 1991–. *Publications:* books and articles on foreign policy and national security questions. *Address:* Nybrogatan 77, 11440 Stockholm, Sweden.

LEIGH, family name of **Baron Leigh**.

LEIGH, 6th Baron *cr* 1839, of Stoneleigh, co. Warwick; **Christopher Dudley Piers Leigh;** *b* 20 Oct. 1960; *s* of 5th Baron Leigh and his 1st wife, Cecilia Poppy, *y d* of Robert Cecil Jackson; *S* father, 2003; *m* 1990, Sophy-Ann, *d* of Richard Burrows, MBE; one *s* one *d*. *Educ:* Eton; RAC Cirencester. *Heir:* *s* Hon. Rupert Dudley Leigh, *b* 21 Feb. 1994.

LEIGH, His Honour Christopher Humphrey de Verd; QC 1989; a Circuit Judge, 2001–08; *b* 12 July 1943; *s* of late Wing Commander Humphrey de Verd Leigh and of Johanna Leigh; *m* 1970, Frances Powell. *Educ:* Harrow. Called to the Bar, Lincoln's Inn, 1967, Bencher, 1999. A Recorder, 1985–2001. *Recreations:* ski-ing, photography. *Address:* 1 Paper Buildings, Temple, EC4Y 7ZP. *T:* (020) 7353 3728.

LEIGH, David, PhD; Secretary-General, International Institute for Conservation, since 2006; *b* 11 Jan. 1943; *s* of Jacques Leigh and Gwendoline (*née* Bright); *m* 1969, Judith Mary Latham; one *s* two *d*. *Educ:* Univ. of Durham (BSc Physics 1966); Inst. of Archaeology, Univ. of London (Dip. Archaeol Conservation 1968); UC, Cardiff (PhD 1980). Experimental Officer (Conservation), Dept of Archaeology, Univ. of Southampton, 1968–74; Lectr in Archaeol Conservation, UC, Cardiff, 1975–87; Head of Conservation Unit, Museums and Galls Commn, 1987–93; Dir, Mus. Training Inst., 1993–95; Principal, West Dean Coll., 1995–2000; Exec. Dir, 2001–05, Sen. Policy Advr and Communications Manager, 2005–07, UK Inst. for Conservation, subseq. Inst. of Conservation. Member: Internat. Inst. for Conservation, 1970–75 (Mem. Council, 1990–94; Treas., 2001–06); Sci. and Conservation Panel, 1984–94, Ancient Monuments Adv. Cttee, 1988–90, English Heritage; Arts Panel, 2004–, Council, 2007–, NT; Rescue. Trustee: Conf. on Trng in Architectural Conservation, 2000–08; Anna Plowden Trust, 2007–. FSA; FIIC; ACR. Plowden Medal, Royal Warrant Holders' Assoc., 2002. *Publications:* (ed) First Aid for Finds, 1976; articles on Anglo-Saxon artefacts, especially early Anglo-Saxon jewellery, conservation and restoration, training and educn. *Recreations:* family, music, walking.

LEIGH, Edward Julian Egerton; MP (C) Gainsborough, since 1997 (Gainsborough and Horncastle, 1983–97); *b* 20 July 1950; *s* of Sir Neville Egerton Leigh, KCVO; *m* 1984, Mary Goodman; three *s* three *d*. *Educ:* St Philip's Sch., Kensington; Oratory Sch., Berks; French Lycée, London; UC, Durham Univ. (BA Hons). Called to the Bar, Inner Temple, 1977. Mem., Cons. Res. Dept, seconded to office of Leader of Opposition, GLC, 1973–75; Prin. Correspondence Sec. to Rt Hon. Margaret Thatcher, MP, 1975–76. Member (C): Richmond Borough Council, 1974–78; GLC, 1977–81. Contested (C) Teesside, Middlesbrough, Oct. 1974. PPS to Minister of State, Home Office, 1990; Parly Under-Sec. of State, DTI, 1990–93. Chm., Public Accounts Cttee, H of C, 2001–; Sec., Conservative backbench Cttees on agric., defence and employment, 1983–90; Vice Chm., Conservative Back bench Cttees on foreign affairs and social security, 1997–2001. Chm., Nat. Council for Civil Defence, 1980–82; Dir, Coalition for Peace Through Security, 1982–83. Kt of Honour and Devotion, SMO Malta, 1994. *Publications:* Right Thinking, 1979; Responsible Individualism, 1994. *Recreations:* walking, reading. *Address:* House of Commons, SW1A 0AA.

LEIGH, Sir Geoffrey (Norman), Kt 1990; Chairman, Allied London Properties, 1987–98 (Managing Director, 1970–87); Director, Arrow Property Investments Ltd, 2000–06; *b* 23 March 1933; *s* of late Rose Leigh and Morris Leigh; *m* 1st, 1955, Valerie Lennard (marr. diss. 1975; she *d* 1976); one *s* two *d*; 2nd, 1976, Sylvia Pell; one *s* one *d*. *Educ:* Haberdashers' Aske's Hampstead Sch.; Univ. of Michigan. Man. Dir, 1965, Chm., 1980–98, Sterling Homes. Founder and First Pres., Westminster Junior Chamber of Commerce, 1959–63; Underwriting Mem., Lloyd's, 1973–97. Special Advisor, Land Agency Bd, Commn for the New Towns, 1994–96; Member: Cttee, Good Design in Housing for Disabled, 1977; Cttee, Good Design in Housing, 1978–79; British ORT Council, 1979–80; Internat. Adv. Bd, American Univ., Washington, 1983–97; Adv. Council, Prince's Youth Business Trust, 1985–; Main Finance Bd, NSPCC, 1985–2003 (Hon. Mem. Council, 1995–); Governing Council, Business in the Community, 1987–; Somerville Coll. Appeal, 1987–; Royal Fine Art Commn Art and Arch. Educn Trust, 1988–99; Per Cent Club, 1988–2000; Council, City Technology Colls Trust, 1988–; City Appeal Cttee, Royal Marsden Hosp., 1990–93; Review Body on Doctors' and Dentists' Remuneration, 1990–93; Wellbeing Council, 1994–; Chancellor's Ct of Benefactors, Oxford Univ., 1991–; Emmanuel Coll., Cambridge, Develt Campaign, 1994–96; Chm., St Mary's Hosp. 150th Anniversary Appeal, 1995–. Comr and Trustee, Fulbright Commn, 1991–99 (Chm., Fulbright US-UK. Adv. Bd, 1995–); Mem., Duke of Edinburgh's Award World Fellowship, 1992–; Sponsor, Leigh City Technology Coll., subseq. Leigh Technology Acad., Dartford (Chm. of Govs, 1988–2006; Chm. of Trustees, 2006–); Founder/Sponsor, Friends of British Liby, 1987– (Vice-Pres., 2000–); Founder, Margaret Thatcher Centre, Somerville Coll., Oxford, 1991; Treasurer: Commonwealth Jewish Council, 1983–89; Commonwealth Jewish Trust, 1983–89; a Treas., Cons. Party, 1995–97; Vice President: Hampstead and Highgate Cons. Assoc., 1997–2005 (Patron, 1991–94; Pres., 1994–97); Conservatives Abroad, 1995–; Treas. and Trustee, Action on Addiction, 1991–2003; Trustee: Margaret Thatcher Foundn, 1991–; Industry in Educn, 1993–98; Philharmonia, 1992–99. Governor: Royal Sch., Hampstead, 1991–2003; City Lit. Inst., 1991–98. Hon. Mem., Emmanuel Coll., Cambridge, 1995; Foundn Fellow, Somerville Coll., Oxford, 1998; Univ. of Greenwich Assembly, 2003. Hon. Life Mem., Cons. Med. Soc., 1998. Freeman, City of London, 1976; Liveryman: Haberdashers' Co., 1992–; Furniture Makers' Co., 1987– (Chm., Premises Cttee, 2003–06; Asst *hc*, 2006). Mem., Soc. of the Four Arts. FRSA. Hon. FICPD. Presidential Citation, The American Univ., 1987. *Recreations:* photography, reading, golf. *Address:* 42 Berkeley Square, W1J 5AW. *T:* (020) 7409 5054. *Clubs:* Carlton (Hon. Mem., Political Cttee, 2004), United and Cecil, Pilgrims, Royal Automobile; Wentworth; Palm Beach Country, Palm Beach Yacht, Palm Beach Ocean.

LEIGH, Prof. Irene May, OBE 2006; MD; DSc; FRCP, FMedSci; Head, College of Medicine, Dentistry and Nursing, University of Dundee, since 2006; Director, CR-UK Skin Tumour Laboratory, since 1989; *b* 25 April 1947; *d* of Archibald and May Lilian Allen; *m* 1st, 1969, (Peter) Nigel Leigh, *qv* (marr. diss. 1999); one *s* three *d*; 2nd, 2000, John E. Kernthaler. *Educ:* London Hosp. Med. Coll. (BSc 1968; MB BS 1971; MD 1992; DSc 1999). FRCP 1987. Consultant Dermatologist and Sen. Lectr, 1983–92, Prof. of Dermatol., 1992–97, Royal London Hosp. and London Hosp. Med. Coll.; St Bartholomew's and Royal London School of Medicine and Dentistry, QMW, then Barts and the London, Queen Mary's School of Medicine and Dentistry, London University: Prof. of Cellular and Molecular Medicine, 1999–2006; Research Dean, 1997–2002; Jt Res. Dir, 2002–05. FMedSci 1999. *Publications:* contrib. numerous articles on keratinocyte biol., genodermatoses and skin carcinogenesis to peer-reviewed jls. *Recreations:* music, film, opera, theatre. *Address:* College of Medicine, Dentistry and Nursing, University of Dundee, Level 10, Ninewells Hospital and Medical School, Dundee DD1 9SY. *T:* (01382) 632763.

LEIGH, Jonathan; Headmaster, Ridley College, Ontario, since 2005; *b* 17 June 1952; *s* of Rupert M. Leigh and Isabel A. Leigh (*née* Villiers); *m* 1976, Emma Mary, *d* of Rear-Adm. Michael Donald Kyrle Pope, CB, MBE; one *s* one *d*. *Educ:* Eton Coll.; Corpus Christi Coll., Cambridge (MA History). Cranleigh School: Asst Master, 1976–82; Housemaster, 1982–88; Head of History, 1987; Second Master, 1988–92; Head Master, Blundell's Sch., 1992–2004. Mem., Devon County Residential Care Standards Adv. Cttee, 1993–2002 (Chm., 1994–98); Vice Pres., Devon Playing Fields Assoc., 1998–2004. Member: Council, ISIS South-West, 1995–2001; Cttee, Belgian Sect., Assoc. Européene des Enseignants, 1994–2004; Admiralty Interview Bd, 1994–2004; Interviewing Panel, ESU, 1996–; Sec., SW Div., HMC, 2000 (Chm., 2001). Member: Adv. Bd, Vimy Foundn, 2005–; Evaluation Gp, Canadian Educnl Standards Inst., 2008. Trustee: Tiverton Adventure Playground Assoc., 1992–2004; Inner Cities Young People's Project, 1996–2004. FRSA 1994. Governor: St Petroc's Sch., Bude, 1993–2004; Wolborough Hill Sch., Newton Abbot, 1998–2000; Abbey Sch., Tewkesbury, 2000–03 (Chm., 2002); Dir, Highfield Sch., Liphook, 2000–. Dir, 2000–, Vice Chm., 2002–04, Devon and Exeter Steeplechases. *Recreations:* singing, horse racing, opera, labradors, late 19th century African history, the Charente. *Address:* Ridley College, PO Box 3013, St Catharine's, ON L2R 7C3, Canada. *T:* (905) 6841889. *Clubs:* East India, Lansdowne.

LEIGH, Prof. Leonard Herschel; freelance author and lecturer; Professor of Criminal Law in the University of London, at the London School of Economics and Political Science, 1982–97; *b* 19 Sept. 1935; *s* of Leonard William and Lillian Mavis Leigh; *m* 1960, Jill Diane Gale; one *s* one *d*. *Educ:* Univ. of Alberta (BA, LLB); Univ. of London (PhD 1966). Admitted to Bar: Alberta, 1959; NW Territories, 1961; Inner Temple, 1993. Private practice, Province of Alberta, 1958–60; Dept of Justice, Canada, 1960–62; London School of Economics: Asst Lectr in Law, 1964–65; Lectr, 1965–71; Reader, 1971–82. Vis. Prof., Queen's Univ., Kingston, Ont, 1973–74; Bowker Vis. Prof., Univ. of Alberta, 1999. British Council Lecturer: Univ. of Strasbourg, 1978; National Univ. of Mexico, 1980; UN Asia and Far East Inst., Tokyo, 1986; South India, 1989, 1991. Mem., Canadian Govt Securities Regulation Task Force, 1974–78. Bd Mem., Criminal Cases Review Commn, 1997–2005. UK Convenor, Université de l'Europe Steering Cttee, 1987–90; Chm., English Nat. Section, 1988–, Mem., Conseil de Direction, 1989–, Internat. Assoc. of Penal Law. Mem., Exec. Cttee, Canada-UK Colloquia, 1993–. Member, Council of Europe Training Missions: Hungary, 1990; Poland, 1991; Albania, 1992; Mem., Council of Europe Wkg Party on Reform of Russian Penal Law, 1994–95. UK Rep., Internat. Penal and Penitentiary Foundn, 1994–2005. Chm., Awards Cttee, Canada Meml Fellowships, 2002–. Hon. Fellow, Faculty of Law, Birmingham Univ., 1997–. *Publications:* The Criminal Liability of Corporations in English Law, 1969; (jtly) Northey and Leigh's Introduction to Company Law, 1970, 4th edn 1987; Police Powers in England and Wales, 1975, 2nd edn 1986; Economic Crime in Europe, 1980; (jtly) The Companies Act 1981, 1981; (jtly) The Management of the Prosecution Process in Denmark, Sweden and the Netherlands, 1981; The Control of Commercial Fraud, 1982; Strict and Vicarious Liability, 1982; (jtly) A Guide to the Financial Services Act, 1986; (contrib.) Blackstone's Criminal Practice, 1991–2007; (ed) Criminal Procedure in English Public Law, 2005; articles in British, European, Amer. and Canadian jls. *Recreations:* music, walking. *Address:* (chambers) 2 Pump Court, Temple, EC4Y 7AH. *T:* (020) 7353 5597.

LEIGH, Mike, OBE 1993; dramatist; theatre and film director; *b* 20 Feb. 1943; *s* of late Alfred Abraham Leigh, MRCS, LRCP and Phyllis Pauline Leigh (*née* Cousin); *m* 1973, Alison Steadman, *qv* (marr. diss. 2001); two *s*. *Educ:* North Grecian Street County Primary Sch.; Salford Grammar Sch.; RADA; Camberwell Sch. of Arts and Crafts; Central Sch. of Art and Design (Theatre Design Dept); London Film Sch. Sometime actor, incl. Victoria Theatre, Stoke-on-Trent, 1966; Assoc. Dir, Midlands Arts Centre for Young People, 1965–66; Asst Dir, RSC, 1967–68; Drama Lectr, Sedgley Park and De La Salle Colls, Manchester, 1968–69; Lectr, London Film Sch., 1970–73. Arts Council of GB: Member: Drama Panel, 1975–77; Dirs' Working Party and Specialist Allocations Bd, 1976–84; Member: Accreditation Panel, Nat. Council for Drama Trng, 1978–91; Gen. Adv. Council, IBA, 1980–82. Chm., Bd of Govs, London Film Sch., 2001–. NFT Retrospective, 1979; BBC TV Retrospective (incl. Arena: Mike Leigh Making Plays), 1982. Hon. MA: Salford, 1991; Northampton, 2000; Hon. DLitt Staffordshire, 2000; DU Essex, 2002. George Devine Award, 1973; Michael Balcon Award, 1995; Alexander Korda Award, 1996. Productions of own plays and films; *stage plays:* The Box Play, 1965, My Parents Have Gone To Carlisle, The Last Crusade Of The Five Little Nuns, 1966, Midlands Arts Centre; Nenaa, RSC Studio, Stratford-upon-Avon, 1967; Individual Fruit Pies, E15 Acting Sch., 1968; Down Here And Up There, Royal Ct Th. Upstairs, 1968; Big Basil, 1968, Glum Victoria And The Lad With Specs, Manchester Youth Theatre, 1969; Epilogue, Manchester, 1969; Bleak Moments, Open Space, 1970; A Rancid Pong, Basement, 1971; Wholesome Glory, Dick Whittington and his Cat, Royal Ct Th. Upstairs, 1973; The Jaws of Death, Traverse, Edinburgh Fest., 1973; Babies Grow Old, Other Place, 1974, ICA, 1975; The Silent Majority, Bush, 1974; Abigail's Party, Hampstead, 1977; Ecstasy, Hampstead, 1979; Goose-Pimples, Hampstead, Garrick, 1981 (Standard Best Comedy Award); Smelling a Rat, Hampstead, 1988; Greek Tragedy, Sydney, 1989, Edinburgh Fest. and Theatre Royal, Stratford East, 1990; It's A Great Big Shame!, Theatre Royal, Stratford East, 1993; Two Thousand Years, NT, 2005. *BBC radio play:* Too Much Of A Good Thing, 1979; *feature films:* Bleak Moments, 1971 (Golden Hugo, Chicago Film Fest., 1972; Golden Leopard, Locarno Film Fest., 1972); High Hopes, 1989 (Critics' Award, Venice Film Fest., 1988; Evening Standard Peter Sellers Comedy Award, 1989); Life is Sweet, 1991; Naked, 1993 (Best Dir, Cannes Film Fest., 1993); Secrets and Lies, 1996 (Palme d'Or, Cannes Film Fest., 1996); Career Girls, 1997; Topsy-Turvy, 1999 (Evening Standard Best Film Award, 2001); All or Nothing, 2002; Vera Drake, 2004; Happy-Go-Lucky, 2008; *BBC TV plays and films:* A Mug's Game, 1972; Hard Labour, 1973; The Permissive Society, Afternoon, A Light Snack, Probation, Old Chums, The Birth Of The 2001 FA Cup Final Goalie, 1975; Nuts in May, Knock For Knock, 1976; The Kiss Of Death, Abigail's Party, 1977; Who's Who, 1978; Grown-Ups, 1980; Home Sweet Home, 1982; Four Days In July, 1984; *Channel Four films:* Meantime, 1983 (People's Prize, Berlin Film Fest., 1984); The Short and Curlies, 1987. *Relevant publications:* The Improvised Play: the work of Mike Leigh, by Paul Clements, 1983; The World According to Mike Leigh, by Michael Coveney, 1996; The Films of Mike Leigh: embracing the world, by Ray Carney and Leonard Quart, 2000. *Address:* c/o United Agents, 12–26 Lexington Street, W1F 0LE.

LEIGH, Prof. (Peter) Nigel, PhD; FRCP, FMedSci; Professor of Clinical Neurology, Institute of Psychiatry and King's College London School of Medicine, since 1989 (Head, Department of Clinical Neuroscience, King's College London, 1989–2007); Hon. Consultant Neurologist, King's College Hospital, since 1989; *b* 26 Sept. 1946; *s* of Dr A. Denis Leigh and Pamela Leigh (*née* Parish); *m* 1st, 1969, Irene May Allen (*see* Irene May Leigh) (marr. diss. 1999); one *s* three *d*; 2nd, 2000, Catherine Margaret Lloyd; one *d*. *Educ:* Sevenoaks Sch., Kent; London Hosp. Med. Sch., Univ. of London (BSc 1st Cl. Hons; MB BS Dist.); PhD London 1986. FRCP 1988. House Physician and House Surgeon, 1970–71, SHO, 1971–72, The London Hosp.; SHO, Hammersmith Hosp., 1972–73; Registrar, UCH, 1974, Hammersmith Hosp., 1974–75; Specialist in Neurology, Muhimbili Hosp., and Lectr in Neurology, Univ. of Dar es Salaam, 1975–77; Sen. Registrar, St George's Hosp., 1977–82; Wellcome Trust Res. Fellow, Inst. of Psychiatry, 1980–81; Consultant Neurologist, Wessex Neurol Centre, Southampton, 1982–86, and Sen. Lectr in Neurology, Southampton Univ., 1984–86; Sen. Lectr in Neurology and Hon. Cons. Neurologist, St George's Hosp. Med. Sch., 1986–89. Forbes Norris Award, Internat. Alliance of ALS/MND Assocs, 1997; Erb-Duchenne Prize, German Neuro-Muscular Soc., 2003; Sheila Essey Prize, Amer. Acad. of Neurology, 2004. FMedSci 2003. *Publications:* (ed with M. Swash) Motor Neurone Disease: biology and management, 1995; articles on motor neurone disease, Parkinson's disease and related disorders and other medical topics. *Recreations:* attempts at fly-fishing, travel. *Address:* PO41, Academic Neurosciences Building, Institute of Psychiatry, De Crespigny Park, SE5 8AF. *T:* (020) 7848 5187; *e-mail:* n.leigh@iop.kcl.ac.uk.

LEIGH, Peter William John, FRICS; chartered surveyor and property consultant; *b* 29 June 1929; *s* of John Charles Leigh and Dorothy Grace Leigh; *m* 1956, Mary Frances (*née* Smith); two *s* one *d*. *Educ:* Harrow Weald County Grammar Sch.; Coll. of Estate Management (ext.). National Service, Royal Signals, 1947–49. Private surveying practice, 1949–53; Valuation Asst, Middx CC, 1953–60; Commercial Estates Officer, Bracknell Develt Corp., 1960–66; sen. appts, Valuation and Estates Dept, GLC, 1966–81; Dir of Valuation and Estates, GLC, 1981–84; Dir of Property Services, Royal County of Berks, 1984–88. Member: Gen. Council, RICS, 1984–86; RICS Gen. Practice Divl Council, 1993–96; Govt Property Adv. Gp, 1984–88. Exec. Mem., Local Authority Valuers Assoc., 1981–88. Editor, Old Wealden Newsletter, 1978–. *Recreations:* exploring Cornwall, drawing, gardening (therapy). *Address:* 41 Sandy Lane, Wokingham, Berks RG41 4SS. *T:* (0118) 978 2732.

LEIGH, Sir Richard (Henry), 3rd Bt *cr* 1918, of Altrincham, Cheshire; *b* 11 Nov. 1936; *s* of Eric Leigh (*d* 1982), 2nd *s* of Sir John Leigh, 1st Bt, and his 1st wife, Joan Lane Fitzgerald (*d* 1973), *e d* of M. C. L. Freer, South Africa; *S* uncle, 1992; *m* 1st, 1962, Barbro Anna Elizabeth (marr. diss. 1977), *e d* of late Stig Carl Sebastian Tham, Sweden; 2nd, 1977, Cherie Rosalind, *e d* D. D. Dale, Cherval, France and *widow* of Alan Reece, RMS. *Educ:* England and Switzerland. *Recreations:* fishing, gardening. *Heir:* half *b* Christopher John Leigh [*b* 6 April 1941; *m* 1963, Gillian Ismay, *o d* of W. K. Lowe; one *s* one *d*]. *Address:* PO Box 48621, NW8 9WN. *T:* (020) 7266 5512.

LEIGH, Prof. Roger Allen, PhD; FIBiol; Head, School of Agriculture, Food and Wine, University of Adelaide, since 2006; *b* 7 Feb. 1949; *s* of Harry Leigh and Catherine Leigh (*née* O'Neill); *m* 1974, Beatrice Katherine Halton (marr. diss. 1999). *Educ:* Ellesmere Port Boys' GS; UCNW, Bangor (BSc 1970; PhD 1974). FIBiol 1991. Maria Moors Cabot Fellow in Botanical Res., Harvard Univ., 1974–76; Royal Society Pickering Res. Fellow, Botany Sch., Univ. of Cambridge, 1976–79; Scientist, Rothamsted Experimental Station, Harpenden, 1979–98; Head of Crop Production Dept, 1987–89; Head of Biochemistry and Physiology Dept, 1989–98; Head of Soils and Crop Scis Div., 1989–94; Dep. Dir, 1994–98; Prof. of Botany, Univ. of Cambridge, 1998–2006; Professorial Fellow, Girton Coll., Cambridge, 1998–2006. Pres., Soc. for Experimental Biology, 2005–07 (Vice-Pres., 2003–05). *Publications:* (jtly) Long-Term Experiments in Agricultural and Ecological Sciences, 1994; (jtly) Membrane Transport in Plants and Fungi: molecular mechanisms and control, 1994; scientific papers in learned jls, incl. Plant Physiology, Planta, Jl of Exptl Botany. *Recreations:* sports of all kinds, bird watching, photography. *Address:* School of Agriculture, Food and Wine, University of Adelaide, PMB 1, Glen Osmond, SA 5064, Australia. *T:* (8) 83037136; *e-mail:* roger.leigh@adelaide.edu.au.

LEIGH FERMOR, Sir Patrick; *see* Fermor.

LEIGH-HUNT, Barbara; actress; *b* 14 Dec. 1935; *d* of Chandos A. Leigh-Hunt and Elizabeth Leigh-Hunt; *m* 1967, Richard Edward Pasco, *qv*. *Educ:* Bath, Som; Kensington High Sch.; Bristol Old Vic Theatre Sch. (Most Promising Student, Bristol Evening Post Award, 1953). Began broadcasting for BBC at age 12 in Children's Hour, and has continued to do so regularly on Radios 3 and 4. *Theatre:* début in Midsummer Night's Dream, London Old Vic tour to USA and Canada, 1954–55; subseq. also Twelfth Night and Merchant of Venice, Old Vic and tours, 1957–60; seasons at Nottingham and Guildford, 1960–62; Bristol Old Vic and tours to Europe, Middle East, US and Canada, 1961–68; The Seagull, Hedda Gabler, She Stoops to Conquer, Much Ado About Nothing, Blithe Spirit, Love's Labour's Lost, Hamlet, and Macbeth; A Severed Head, Criterion, 1963; Mrs Mouse, are you within?, Duke of York's, 1968; Venice Preserv'd, Prospect Th. Co. tour, 1970; Royal Shakespeare Company: Sherlock Holmes, Travesties, 1974; A Winter's Tale, Richard III, 1975; King Lear, Troilus and Cressida, 1976; That Good Between Us, Every Good Boy Deserves Favour, 1977; Richard III, Hamlet, 1980; The Forest, La Ronde, 1981; Pack of Lies, Lyric 1983; Barnaby and the Old Boys, Theatr Clwyd, 1987; Royal National Theatre: Cat on a Hot Tin Roof, 1988; Bartholomew Fair, The Voysey Inheritance, 1989; Racing Demon, 1990 and Los Angeles, 1995; An Inspector Calls, 1992 (Best Supporting Actress, Olivier Award, 1993); Absence of War, 1993; A Woman of No Importance, RSC, and Haymarket, 1992; The Importance of Being Earnest, Old Vic, 1995; frequent appearances in poetry and prose anthology progs in UK and abroad; works as speaker with Medici String Quartet. *Films:* Frenzy, 1972, Henry VIII and his Six Wives, 1972; A Bequest to the Nation, 1973; Oh, Heavenly Dog, 1978; Paper Mask, 1990; Keep the Aspidistra Flying, 1997; Billy Elliott, 2000; The Martins, 2000; Iris, 2001; Vanity Fair, 2003. *Television* includes: Search for the Nile, 1971; Loves Lies Bleeding; The Voysey Inheritance; Macbeth; Wagner, 1984; The Siegfried Idyll; All for Love; Tumbledown, 1988; A Perfect Hero; Cold Feet; Pride and Prejudice, 1995; The Echo, 1998; Sunburn, Wives and Daughters, 1999; Longitude, 2000; Kavanagh QC, 1998, 2000; Midsummer Murders, 2001; George Eliot, 2002. Gov. and Associate Actor, RSC; Pres., Friends of the Other Place, 1993–97; Vice-President: Theatrical Guild of Charity (formerly Theatrical Ladies Guild of Charity), 1983–; Royal Theatrical Fund, 1995; J. B. Priestley Soc.; Patron: Soc. of Teachers of Speech and Drama, 1995; Orch. of The Swan, 1997. Tutor, Samling Foundn. *Recreation:* book collecting. *Address:* c/o Conway Van Gelder Grant Ltd, 18–21 Jermyn Street, SW1Y 6HP. *T:* (020) 7287 0077, *Fax:* (020) 7287 1940.

LEIGH-PEMBERTON, family name of **Baron Kingsdown**.

LEIGH-SMITH, Alfred Nicholas Hardstaff; a District Judge (Magistrates' Courts), since 2004; *b* 21 Dec. 1953; *s* of late Dr Alfred Leigh Hardstaff Leigh-Smith, TD, DL and Marguerite Calvert Leigh-Smith; *m* 1996, Samantha Sian Morgan; two *s*. *Educ:* Epsom Coll.; Leeds Univ. (LLB 1975). Called to the Bar, Lincoln's Inn, 1976; in practice as barrister, Lincoln's Inn, 1976–80; Court Clerk, then Sen. Court Clerk, then Princ. Asst, Willesden Magistrates' Court, 1980–85; Deputy Clerk: to Bromley Justices, 1985–89; to Brent Justices, 1989–94; Clerk to Justices, Cambridge and E Cambs, 1995–2001; in practice as barrister, Leicester, 2001–04. Asst Stipendiary Magistrate, then Dep. Dist Judge (Magistrates' Courts), 1999–2004. *Recreations:* walking, clay-pigeon shooting, church bell ringing, Rugby Union (watching now), reading history and biographies, vegetable gardening. *Address:* Luton Magistrates' Court, Stuart Street, Luton LU1 5BL. *T:* (01532) 524232, *Fax:* (01582) 524259; *e-mail:* a.leighsmith@btinternet.com.

LEIGHFIELD, John Percival, CBE 1998; FBCS; Chairman, RM plc, since 1994; *b* 5 April 1938; *s* of Henry Tom Dainton Leighfield and Patricia Zilpha Maud Leighfield (*née* Baker); *m* 1963, Margaret Ann Mealin; one *s* one *d*. *Educ:* Magdalen Coll. Sch., Oxford (State Scholarship); Exeter Coll., Oxford (MA Lit.Hum.). FIDPM 1990; FBCS 1991. Mgt trainee, Ford Motor Co., 1962–65; Systems Manager, EDP Exec., Plessey Telecomms, 1965–69; Systems Planning, EDP Exec., Plessey Co. Ltd, 1969–72; British Leyland: Systems Planning Manager, 1972–75; Systems Dir, 1975–79; Man. Dir, BL Systems Ltd, 1979–84; Man. Dir and Chm. ISTEL Ltd, 1984–89; AT&T ISTEL: Chm., 1989–93; Dir, 1993–97; Officer and Sen. Vice-Pres., AT&T, 1989–93; Chairman: Synstar plc, 1998–2004; Minerva Computer Systems, 2001–03; Director: Birmingham Midshires Bldg Soc., 1993–99 (Chm., 1996–99); RM Ltd, 1993–94; ICom Solutions Ltd, 1997–98; Halifax plc, 1999–2001; KnowledgePool Ltd, 2000–01; Getmapping, 2005–. Dir, Central England TEC, 1991–97. Mem., Alvey Prog. Steering Cttee, 1983–87. President: BCS, 1993–94; Computing Services and Software Assoc., 1995–96; Inst. Data Processing Mgt, 2000–06. Hon. Prof., 1992, Chm., Adv. Bd, 1997–2002, Warwick Business Sch.; Mem. Council, Warwick Univ., 1991–96, 1997– (Pro-Chancellor, 2002–); Gov., Magdalen Coll. Sch., Oxford, 1993–2001 (Chm. 1996–2001). Liveryman, Co. of Information Technologists, 1992– (Master, 2005–06). FInstD 1989; FRSA 1996. DUniv Central England, 1993; Hon. DTech: De Montfort, 1994; Wolverhampton, 2001. *Publications:* various papers on information technology. *Recreations:* historical cartography, music, walking, computing. *Address:* 91 Victoria Road, Oxford OX2 7QG. *T:* (01865) 559055. *Clubs:* Royal Automobile; Royal Fowey Yacht.

LEIGHTON OF ST MELLONS, 3rd Baron *cr* 1962, of St Mellons, co. Monmouth; **Robert William Henry Leighton Seager;** Bt 1952; *b* 28 Sept. 1955; *er s* of 2nd Baron Leighton of St Mellons and Elizabeth Rosita (*née* Hopgood; *d* 1979); *S* father, 1998; *m* 1978, Wendy Elizabeth Hopwood; one *d*. *Heir:* *b* Hon. Simon John Leighton Seager [*b* 25 Jan. 1957; *m* 1982, Gillian Rawlinson; three *d*].

LEIGHTON, Prof. Angela, FBA 2000; Senior Research Fellow, Trinity College, Cambridge, since 2006; *b* 23 Feb. 1954; *d* of Kenneth Leighton and Lydia Leighton (*née* Vignapiano). *Educ:* St Hugh's Coll., Oxford (BA Hons 1976; MLitt 1981). University of Hull: Lectr in English, 1979–93; Sen. Lectr, 1993–95; Reader, 1995–97; Prof. of English, 1997–2006. *Publications:* Shelley and the Sublime, 1984; Elizabeth Barrett Browning,

1986; Victorian Women Poets: writing against the heart, 1992; Victorian Women Poets: a critical anthology, 1995; A Cold Spell, 2000; On Form: poetry, aestheticism and the legacy of a word, 2007; Sea Level, 2007. *Address:* Trinity College, Cambridge CB2 1TQ.

LEIGHTON, Jane; Chair, Waveney Primary Care NHS Trust, 2003–06; Deputy Chair, Broadcasting Standards Commission, 1997–2001; *b* 17 March 1944. Administrator, British Pregnancy Adv. Service, 1971–74; Sec., Liverpool CHC, 1974–79; reporter, World in Action, Granada TV, 1979–85; Producer, Channel 4, 1985–88; Independent Consultancy, Littlewoods Orgn, 1985–88; Exec. Dir, Mersey TV, 1988–90; Hd of Public Affairs, Granada TV Ltd, 1990–92; Industrial Relns Consultant, Liverpool HAT, 1992–96; Hd of Organisational Develt, Tate Gall., 1995–97; Dir, London Mental Health Learning Partnership, subseq. Virtuall, 2000–05. Chair: Mental Health Services, Salford NHS Trust, 1993–95; Camden and Islington Area Mental Health Cttee, 1998–2000; non-exec. Dir, Camden and Islington NHS Community Trust, 1998–2001. Mem., Broadcasting Complaints Commn, 1993–96 (Chm., 1996–97). Non-executive Director: City of London Sinfonia, 1992–97; Hallé Concerts Soc., 1992–95; Royal Liverpool Philharmonic Orch., 1990–92. Mem., NW Arts Bd. Gov., UC, Salford, 1992–95. FRSA 1997. RTS Award for best internat. current affairs programme, 1981; BMA Award for medical progs, 1983; Equal Opportunities Award, Women in Mgt Award, 1987. *Address:* 94 London Road, Halesworth, Suffolk IP19 8LS; *e-mail:* leightonjane@btinternet.com.

LEIGHTON, Leonard Horace; Under Secretary, Department of Energy, 1974–80; *b* 7 Oct. 1920; *e s* of Leonard and Pearl Leighton, Bermuda; *m* 1945, Mary Burrowes; two *s*. *Educ:* Rossall Sch.; Magdalen Coll., Oxford (MA). FInstF. Royal Engrs, 1940–46; Nat. Coal Bd, 1950–62; Min. of Power, 1962–67; Min. of Technology, 1967–70; Dept of Trade and Industry, 1970–74. *Publications:* papers in various technical jls. *Address:* 18 River Park Drive, Marlborough, Wilts SN8 1NH.

LEIGHTON, Sir Michael (John Bryan), 11th Bt *cr* 1693; *b* 8 March 1935; *o s* of Colonel Sir Richard Tihel Leighton, 10th Bt, and Kathleen Irene Linda (*d* 1993), *o d* of Major A. E. Lees, Rowton Castle, Shrewsbury; *S* father, 1957; *m* 1st, 1974 (marr. diss. 1980); 2nd, 1988 (marr.diss. 1990); 3rd, 1991, Diana Mary Gamble (marr. diss. 1998); one *d*. *Educ:* Stowe; Tabley House Agricultural Sch.; Cirencester Coll. *Address:* Loton Park, Shrewsbury, Salop SY5 9AJ.

LEIGHTON WILLIAMS, John; *see* Williams.

LEINSTER, 9th Duke of, *cr* 1766; **Maurice FitzGerald;** Baron of Offaly, 1205; Earl of Kildare, 1316; Viscount Leinster (GB), 1747; Marquess of Kildare, 1761; Earl of Offaly, 1761; Baron Kildare, 1870; Premier Duke, Marquess, and Earl, of Ireland; landscape and contract gardener; *b* 7 April 1948; *s* of 8th Duke of Leinster, and Anne, *d* of Lt-Col Philip Eustace Smith, MC; *S* father, 2004; *m* 1972, Fiona Mary Francesca, *d* of Harry Hollick; two *d* (only *s* Thomas FitzGerald (Earl of Offaly) *d* 1997). *Educ:* Millfield School. Pres., Oxfordshire Dyslexia Assoc. Chm., Thomas Offaly Meml Fund. *Address:* Courtyard House, Oakley Park, Frilford Heath, Oxon OX13 6QW.

LEINSTER, Dr Paul, CBE 2008; CChem; Director of Operations, Environment Agency, since 2004; *b* 20 Feb. 1953; *s* of Victor and Eva Leinster; *m* 1976, Felicity Lawrence; two *s* one *d*. *Educ:* Imperial Coll., London (BSc Chemistry 1974; PhD Envmtl Engrg 1977); Cranfield Sch. of Management (MBA 1991). FIOH 1991; CChem, FRSC 1998; FIEMA 2004; CEnv 2005. BP International plc: Analytical Support and Res. Div., Res. Centre, 1977–79; Health, Safety and Envmt Directorate, 1979–85; Schering Agrochemicals, 1985–88; Thomson-MTS Ltd: Head of Res. and Consultancy, 1988–90; Man. Dir, 1990–94; Dir, Envmtl Services, SmithKline Beecham, 1994–98; Dir of Envmtl Protection, Envmt Agency, 1998–2004. *Recreations:* golf, local church, reading, walking.
See also S. J. Leinster.

LEINSTER, Prof. Samuel John, MD; FRCS, FRCSE; Dean, School of Medicine, Health Policy and Practice, University of East Anglia, since 2001; *b* 29 Oct. 1946; *s* of Victor and Eva Leinster; *m* 1971, Jennifer Woodward; three *s* one *d*. *Educ:* Univ. of Edinburgh (BSc 1968; MB ChB 1971); Univ. of Liverpool (MD 1990). FRCSE 1976; FRCS 1998. MO, RAF, 1971–77; Lectr in Surgery, Welsh Nat. Sch. of Medicine, 1978–81; University of Liverpool: Sen. Lectr in Surgery, 1982–92; Reader in Surgery, 1992–95; Prof. of Surgery, 1995–2000. FHEA 2007. *Publications:* Systemic Diseases for Dental Students, 1984; Shared Care in Breast Cancer, 1999; articles on breast cancer care, psychological impact of cancer and med. educn in learned jls. *Recreations:* family, gardening, DIY, wood turning, active committed Christian. *Address:* School of Medicine, Health Policy and Practice, University of East Anglia, Norwich NR4 7TJ. *T:* (01603) 593939; *e-mail:* s.leinster@uea.ac.uk. *Clubs:* Royal Air Force; Royal Society of Medicine.
See also P. Leinster.

LEIPER, Quentin John, FICE; Director for Engineering and the Environment, Carillion plc, since 2000; President, Institution of Civil Engineers, 2006–07; *b* 7 Oct. 1951; *s* of John W. G. Leiper and Betty Leiper; *m* 1980, Dorothy Ellen East; two *s* one *d*. *Educ:* King's Sch., Ely; Univ. of Glasgow (BSc 1975); Univ. of Surrey (MSc 1984). CCE 1985; CEng 1985; MICE 1985, FICE 1994; CEnv 2005. Nuttall Geotechnical Services, 1975–77; Geotechnical Engr, Soil Mechanics, 1977–78; Manager: Nuttall Geotechnical Services, 1978–80; Terresearch, 1982–86; Contracts Manager, GKN Keller Foundns, 1986–89; Chief Engr, Westpile, 1989–91; Piling Ops Manager, Lilley Construction, 1990–91; Chief Geotech. Engr, Tarmac plc, 1991–96; Co. Chief Engr, Carillion plc, 1996–2000. Initiated and developed the Carillion sustainability strategy model and "sun" impacts diagram. Vis. Prof., Sch. of Civil Engrg, Univ. of Edinburgh, 1998–. Mem., Vice-Chm., 1997–99, Chm., 1999–2001, British Geotechnical Assoc. (formerly British Geotechnical Soc.); Vice Pres., ICE, 2003–06. Founding Chm. and Hon. Ed., Engineering Sustainability, 2002–04. *Publications:* over 50 jl articles and conf. papers. *Recreations:* hockey, kites (including fighting and traction), sailing, saxophone and clarinet (member, Alveley Village Band). *Address:* Institution of Civil Engineers, One Great George Street, SW1P 3AA; *e-mail:* qleiper@carillionplc.com. *Clubs:* Bridgnorth Cricket and Hockey.

LEISER, Helen; JP; consultant, US Department of Energy, then French Commissariat à l'énergie atomique, as Chairs to Generation IV International Forum (inter-governmental nuclear energy research collaboration), 2005–07; *b* 3 July 1947; *d* of George and Audrey Leiser. *Educ:* Twickenham County Grammar Sch.; LSE (BScEcon). Economic Dept, TUC, 1968–73; Employment Dept, 1974–83; seconded to Cabinet Office, Machinery of Govt Div., 1983–85; Asst Sec., gen. policy, then resources and planning, later offshore reforms, HSE, 1986–93; Dir of Business Develt, Employment Service, 1993; Head, Industrial Relations Div., Dept of Employment, 1994; Dir, Employment Relns Policy, DTI, 1995–98; Dir, Nuclear Industries, DTI, and non-exec. Dir, UKAEA, 1998–2003; on secondment from DTI to US Dept of Energy, 2003–05; consultant, report for Nuclear Decommissioning Authy on feasibility of a Nat. Nuclear Archive, 2005–06. Mem., Grants Cttee, Hampstead Garden Suburb Trust, 2007–. Trustee, Dame Henrietta Barnett Fund, 2007–. FRSA 2003. JP Barnet and Hendon, 2006. *Recreations:* travel, learning bridge, aunt-ing. *Address:* 11 Asmuns Place, NW11 7XE; *e-mail:* helen.leiser@btinternet.com. *Club:* Lansdowne.

LEITCH, family name of **Baron Leitch**.

LEITCH, Baron *cr* 2004 (Life Peer), of Oakley in Fife; **Alexander Park Leitch;** Chairman: Intrinsic Financial Services Ltd, since 2005; BUPA, since 2005; Chief Executive, Zurich Financial Services (UKISA Asia Pacific) Ltd, 1998–2004; *b* 20 Oct. 1947; *s* of late Donald Leitch, Blairhall, Dunfermline, and Agnes Smith (*née* Park); *m* 1st (marr. diss.); three *d*; 2nd, 2003, Noelle Dowd, Dallas, Texas; one *d*. *Educ:* Dunfermline High Sch. MBCS 1966. Chief Systems Designer, Nat. Mutual Life, then Hambro Life, 1969–88; Allied Dunbar Plc, 1988–96 (Dep. Chm., 1990; Chief Exec., 1993–96); Chm., Allied Dunbar Assce Plc, 1996–2001; Chief Exec., British American Financial Services (UK and Internat.) Ltd, 1996–98; Chairman: Dunbar Bank, 1994–2001; Eagle Star Hldgs Plc, 1996–2004; Threadneedle Asset Mgt, 1996–; Dir, BAT Industries Plc, 1997–98; non-executive Director: United Business Media plc, 2005–; Lloyds TSB plc, 2005–; Paternoster, 2006–; Scottish Widows, 2007– (Chm., 2007–). Chairman: Pensions Protection and Investment Accreditation Bd, 2001–02; Balance Charitable Foundn for Unclaimed Assets, 2004–05; Leitch Rev. of UK Skills, 2005. Mem. Bd, 1996–98, Dep. Chm., 1997–98, Chm., 1998–2000, ABI. Dep. Chm., BITC, 1996–2004; Chm., Nat. Employment Panel, 2001–; Dep. Chair, Commonwealth Educn Fund, 2003–. Chm., SANE, 1999–2000; Vice-Pres., UK Cares, 2004. Trustee: Nat. Galls Scotland, 1999–2003; Philharmonia Orch., 2000–04. Freeman, City of London, 2002; Mem., Co. of Insurers, 2002. Prince of Wales Ambassador's Award for charitable work, 2001. *Recreations:* football, antiques, poetry, antiquarian books. *Address:* House of Lords, SW1A 0PW.

LEITCH, David Alexander; Under Secretary, Social Work Services Group, Scottish Education Department, 1983–89; *b* 4 April 1931; *s* of Alexander and Eileen Leitch; *m* 1954, Marie (*née* Tain); two *s* one *d*. *Educ:* St Mungo's Acad., Glasgow. Min. of Supply, 1948–58; Dept of Agriculture and Fisheries for Scotland: Asst Principal, 1959; Principal, 1963; Asst Sec., 1971; Asst Sec., Local Govt Finance, Scottish Office (Central Services), 1976–81, Under Sec., 1981–83. Part-time Mem., Scottish Legal Aid Bd, 1989–97. *Recreation:* hill-walking.

LEITCH, Sir George, KCB 1975 (CB 1963); OBE 1945; retired; *b* 5 June 1915; *er s* of late James Simpson and Margaret Leitch; *m* 1942, Edith Marjorie Maughan (*d* 2003); one *d*. *Educ:* Wallsend Grammar Sch.; King's Coll., University of Durham. Research and teaching in mathematics, 1937–39. War Service in Army (from TA), 1939–46 (despatches, OBE): Lieut-Colonel in charge of Operational Research in Eastern, then Fourteenth Army, 1943–45; Brigadier (Dep. Scientific Adviser, War Office), 1945–46; entered Civil Service, as Principal, 1947; Ministry of Supply, 1947–59 (Under-Secretary, 1959); War Office, 1959–64; Ministry of Defence: Asst Under-Secretary of State, 1964–65; Dep. Under-Sec. of State, 1965–71; Procurement Executive, MoD: Controller (Policy), 1971–72; 2nd Permanent Sec., 1972–74; Chief Exec. (Permanent Sec.), 1974–75; Chm., Short Brothers Ltd, 1976–83. Chm., Adv. Cttee on Trunk Rd Assessment, 1977–80. Commonwealth Fund Fellow, 1953–54. Hon. DSc Durham, 1946. *Address:* 5 West Avenue, Gosforth, Newcastle upon Tyne NE3 4ES. *T:* (0191) 285 2619.

LEITH, family name of **Baron Burgh**.

LEITH, Sir George Ian David F.; *see* Forbes-Leith.

LEITH, Prudence Margaret, (Mrs Rayne Kruger), OBE 1989; DL; Chairman, Leith's Ltd, 1992–96; Deputy Chairman, Royal Society of Arts, since 1998 (Council Member, since 1992; Chairman, 1995–97); *b* 18 Feb. 1940; *d* of late Sam Leith and of Margaret Inglis; *m* Rayne Kruger (*d* 2002); one *s* one *d*. *Educ:* Cape Town Univ.; Sorbonne, Paris; Cordon Bleu, London. French studies at Sorbonne, and preliminary cooking apprenticeship with French families; Cordon Bleu sch. course; small outside catering service from bedsitter in London, 1960–65; started Leith's Good Food (commercial catering co.), 1965, and Leith's (restaurant), 1969 (Michelin star, 1994); Man. Dir, Prudence Leith Ltd, 1972; Cookery Corresp., Daily Mail, 1969–73; opened Leith's Sch. of Food and Wine, 1975; added Leith's Farm, 1976; Cookery Corresp., Sunday Express, 1976–80; Cookery Editor, 1980–85, Columnist, 1986–90, The Guardian. Board Member: British Transport Hotels, 1977–83; Halifax plc (formerly Leeds Permanent, then Halifax, Bldg Soc.), 1992–99; Whitbread plc, 1995–2005; Triven VCT, 1999–2003; Woolworths plc, 2002–06; Omega Internat. plc, 2004–; Nations Healthcare, 2006–07; Orient Express Hotels Ltd, 2006–; pt-time Mem., BRB, 1980–85. Member: Food from Britain Council, 1983–86; Leisure Industries EDC, NEDO, 1986–90; Nat. Trng Task Force, 1989–90; NCVQ, 1992–96; Bd, UK Skills, 1993–; Chm., 3E's Enterprises, 1997–2007. Chm., Restaurateurs' Assoc. of GB, 1990–94; Mem. Council, Museum of Modern Art, Oxford, 1984–90. Governor, City Technology Coll., 1994–2007; Chairman of Governors: Kings Coll., Guildford, 1999–2007; Ashridge Mgt Coll., 2002–07 (Gov., 1992–2007). Trustee, Food Foundn, 1996–; Chairman: British Food Trust, 1997–2006; Forum for the Future, 2000–03; School Food Trust, 2007–. FRSA 1984–90; FCGI 1992. DL Greater London, 1998. Business Woman of the Year, 1990. *Publications:* Leith's All-Party Cook Book, 1969; Parkinson's Pie (in aid of World Wild Life Fund), 1972; Cooking For Friends, 1978; The Best of Prue Leith, 1979; (with J. B. Reynaud) Leith's Cookery Course (3-part paperback), 1979–80, (comp. hardback with C. Waldegrave), 1980; The Cook's Handbook, 1981; Prue Leith's Pocket Book of Dinner Parties, 1983; Dinner Parties, 1984; (with Polly Tyrer) Entertaining with Style, 1986; Confident Cooking (52 issue part-work), 1989–90; (with Caroline Waldegrave): Leith's Cookery School, 1985; Leith's Cookery Bible, 1991; Leith's Complete Christmas, 1992; Leith's Book of Baking, 1993; Leith's Vegetarian Cookery, 1993; *novels:* Leaving Patrick, 1999; Sisters, 2001; A Lovesome Thing, 2004; The Gardener, 2007. *Recreations:* tennis, walking. *Address:* (office) Chastleton Glebe, Chastleton, Moreton-in-Marsh, Glos GL56 0SZ. *T:* (01608) 674908; *e-mail:* pmleith@dsl.pipex.com.

LEITH-BUCHANAN, Sir Gordon Kelly McNicol, 8th Bt *cr* 1775, of Burgh St Peter, Norfolk; *b* 18 Oct. 1974; *s* of Sir Charles Alexander James Leith-Buchanan, 7th Bt and Marianne (*née* Kelly); *S* father, 1998, but his name does not appear on the Official Roll of the Baronetage.

le JEUNE d'ALLEGEERSHECQUE, Susan Jane; HM Diplomatic Service; Consul-General and Counsellor (Change Management), Washington, since 2005; *b* 29 April 1963; *d* of Gerald Miller, FCA, and Judith Anne Miller (*née* Rolfe); *m* 1991, Stéphane Hervé Marie le Jeune d'Allegeershecque; two *s*. *Educ:* Ipswich High Sch. for Girls, GPDST; Univ. of Bristol (BA Hons 1985). Licentiate, CIPD 1999. Joined HM Diplomatic Service, 1985: FCO, 1985–87; Third, later Second Sec., UK Perm. Representation to EC, 1987–90; FCO, 1990–92; Second Sec. (Press/Econ.), Singapore, 1992–95; FCO, 1995–99; Dep. Hd of Mission, Caracas, 1999–2002; Dep. Hd of Mission, Colombia, 2002–05. *Recreations:* art, music, France. *Address:* Management Group, BFPO 2; c/o Foreign and Commonwealth Office, King Charles Street, SW1A 2AH.

LELLO, Walter Barrington, (Barry); Deputy Director, North-West Region, Department of Trade and Industry, 1988–91; *b* 29 Sept. 1931; *o s* of Walter Joseph Lello and Louisa (*née* McGarrigle); *m* 1959, Margaret, *o d* of Alexander and Alice McGregor. *Educ:* Liverpool Institute High School. Nat. Service, RN, 1950–52. Open Exec. Comp. to Civil Service, 1949; Min. of Supply, later Aviation, 1952–64; Asst British Civil Aviation Rep., Far East, Hong Kong, 1964–67; BoT, later Dept of Trade, 1967–71; Civil Air Attaché, Middle East, Beirut, 1971–76; DTI, 1976–78; Dir Gen., Saudi–British Economic Co-operation Office, Riyadh, 1978–81; seconded to British Electricity International as Dir, Middle East Ops, 1981–83; DTI, 1983; Commercial Counsellor, Cairo, 1984–88. *Recreations:* walking, public rights of way and Wirral Green Belt protection, reading. *Address:* 15 Long Meadow, Gayton, Wirral CH60 8QQ.

LE MARCHANT, Sir Francis (Arthur), 6th Bt *cr* 1841, of Chobham Place, Surrey; artist and farmer; *b* 6 Oct. 1939; *s* of Sir Denis Le Marchant, 5th Bt and of Elizabeth Rowena, *y d* of late Arthur Hovenden Worth; *S* father, 1987. *Educ:* Gordonstoun; Royal Academy Schools. Principal one-man shows include: Agnews; Sally Hunter Fine Art; Roy Miles; Mus. of Arts and Sci., Evansville, USA; ING Bank, sponsored by Barings; group shows include: Leicester Galls; RA Summer Exhibns; Spink; work in public collections includes: Govt Art Collection; FT; Mus. of Arts and Sci., Evansville, USA; Univ. of Evansville, In, collection of late Mrs Anne Kessler. *Recreations:* landscape conservation, garden design, music. *Heir: cousin* Michael Le Marchant [*b* 28 July 1937; *m* 1st, 1963, Philippa Nancy (marr. diss.), *er d* of late R. B. Denby; two *s* two *d*; 2nd, 1981, Sandra Elisabeth Champion (*née* Kirby) (marr. diss.)]. *Address:* c/o HSBC, 88 Westgate, Grantham, Lincs NG31 6LF. *Club:* Savile.

LE MARECHAL, Robert Norford, CB 1994; Deputy Comptroller and Auditor General, National Audit Office, 1989–2000; *b* 29 May 1939; *s* of late Reginald Le Marechal and of Margaret Le Marechal; *m* 1963, Linda Mary (*née* Williams); two *d*. *Educ:* Taunton's School, Southampton. CIPFA 1983. Joined Exchequer and Audit Dept, 1957; Nat. Service, RAEC, 1958–60; Senior Auditor, Exchequer and Audit Dept, 1971; Chief Auditor, 1976; Dep. Dir of Audit, 1980; Dir of Audit, 1983; Dir of Policy and Planning, 1984–86, Asst Auditor General, 1986–89, Nat. Audit Office. FRSA 1997. *Recreations:* reading, gardening. *Address:* 62 Woodcote Hurst, Epsom, Surrey KT18 7DT. *T:* (01372) 721291.

LEMLEY, Jack Kenneth; Principal, Lemley International, Inc. (formerly Lemley & Associates), Boise, Idaho, since 1988; *b* 2 Jan. 1935; *s* of Kenneth Clyde Lemley and Dorothy Whitsitte; *m* 1st, 1961, Georgia Marshall (marr. diss. 1978); two *s* one *d*; 2nd, 1983, Pamela (*née* Hroza). *Educ:* Coeur d'Alene High Sch., Idaho; Univ. of Idaho (BA Architecture 1960). Asst Project Engineer, Guy F. Atkinson Co., 1960–69; Pres., Healthcare, 1969–70; Manager, Indust. and Power Construction Div., Guy F. Atkinson Co., 1971–77; Sen. Vice-Pres., Constr. Div., Morrison-Knudsen Co., 1977–87; Pres. and Chief Exec., Blount Construction Gp, 1987–88; Management Consultant, Lemley & Associates, 1988–89; Chief Exec. Officer, Transmanche-Link, Channel tunnel contractors, 1989–93; Chm. and CEO, American Ecology Corp., 1995–2001. Chm., Olympic Delivery Authy, London, 2006. *Publications:* numerous papers on underground construction projects and international tunnelling. *Recreations:* snow ski-ing, sailing, white water rafting, reading. *Address:* Lemley International, Inc., 604 N 16th Street, Boise, ID 83702, USA. *T:* (208) 3455253; (home) 2045 Table Rock Road, Boise, ID 83712, USA. *T:* (208) 3839253. *Club:* Arid (Boise, Idaho).

LEMMON, Rt Rev. George Colborne; Bishop of Fredericton, 1989–2000; *b* 20 March 1932; *m* 1957, Lois Jean Foster; two *s* one *d*. *Educ:* Univ. of New Brunswick (BA 1959); Wycliffe Coll., Toronto (LTh 1962; BD 1965). Linotype operator, Globe Print, Telegraph Jl, Toronto Telegram, 1949–62. Deacon 1962, priest 1963; Incumbent, Canterbury with Benton, 1962; Rector of: Wilmot with Wicklow and Peel, 1965; Renforth, 1969; Sackville with Dorchester, dio. of Fredericton, 1972–84; Christ Church, Fredericton, 1984–89; Canon of Fredericton, 1983–89. Hon. DD: King's Coll., Halifax, 1990; Wycliffe Coll., Toronto, 1991. *Recreation:* golfing. *Address:* 16 Riverside Court, Fredericton, NB E3B 5P1, Canada.

LE MOIGNAN, Rev. Christina; Chair, Birmingham Methodist District, 1996–2004; President, Methodist Conference, 2001–02; *b* 12 Oct. 1942; *d* of Edward Frank Le Moignan and (Winifred) Muriel Le Moignan. *Educ:* Somerville Coll., Oxford (MA; Dip. Public and Social Admin); Univ. of Ibadan, Nigeria (PhD 1970); Wesley House, Cambridge (MA). Ordained, 1976; Methodist minister, Huntingdon, Southampton, Portchester, 1976–89; Tutor, Queen's Coll., Birmingham, 1989–94; Principal, W Midlands Ministerial Trng Course (Queen's Coll., Birmingham), 1994–96. Hon. DD Birmingham, 2002. *Publication:* Following the Lamb: a reading of Revelation for the new millennium, 2000. *Recreation:* music. *Address:* 29 Hound Street, Sherborne, Dorset DT9 3AB.

LEMOINE, Prof. Nicholas Robert, MD, PhD; FRCPath, FMedSci; Professor of Molecular Oncology, and Director, Institute of Cancer, Queen Mary, University of London, since 2003; Director, Cancer Research UK Clinical Centre, Barts and the London NHS Trust, since 2003; *b* 11 Dec. 1957; *s* of Robert and Janet Lemoine; *m* 1980, Louise Nunley; one *s* one *d*. *Educ:* Abingdon Sch.; St Bartholomew's Med. Coll., Univ. of London (BSc 1980; MB BS 1983; MD 1992); PhD Wales 1989. FRCPath 1992. Lectr, University Hosp. of Wales, 1985–88; Lectr, 1989–92, Sen. Lectr, 1992–96, Prof., 1996–2003, RPMS, London; Dir, Cancer Res. Molecular Oncol. Unit, Imperial Coll., London, 1997–2003. FMedSci 2006. *Publications:* Understanding Gene Therapy, 1999; Progress in Pathology, 2001; numerous scientific articles on molecular pathology of cancer and gene therapy. *Recreations:* motorcycles, Rugby football, the fruit of serendipity. *Address:* Institute of Cancer, Barts and the London School of Medicine, Charterhouse Square, EC1M 6BQ. *T:* (020) 7014 0420, *Fax:* (020) 7014 0461; *e-mail:* nick.lemoine@cancer.org.uk.

LEMON, Prof. Roger Nicholas, PhD; FMedSci; Sobell Professor of Neurophysiology, since 1994 and Director, since 2002, Institute of Neurology, University College London; *b* 6 March 1946; *s* of late Charles Lemon, MBE and Rosaleen Lemon (*née* Morrissey); *m* 1971, Judith Christine (*née* Kirby); two *s* one *d*. *Educ:* Sheffield Univ. (BSc, PhD 1971); MA Cantab. Lectr, Dept of Physiol., Univ. of Sheffield, 1971–77; Res. Fellow, Dept of Physiol., Monash Univ., Australia, 1974–75; Sen. Lectr, Dept of Anatomy, 1977–84, Reader, 1984–85, Erasmus Univ., Rotterdam; Lectr, Dept of Anatomy, 1985–94, and Fellow, New Hall, 1987–94, Univ. of Cambridge; Hd, Sobell Dept, Inst. of Neurol., UCL, 1994–2002. FMedSci 2002. *Publications:* (with R. Porter) Corticospinal Function and Voluntary Movement, 1993; contrib. papers and articles in general area of motor neurosci. *Recreations:* walking, naval history, Samuel Pepys. *Address:* Institute of Neurology, University College London, Sobell Department of Motor Neurosciences and Movement Disorders (Box 28), Queen Square, WC1N 3BG.

LEMOS, Gerard Anthony, CMG 2001; writer, social researcher; Partner, Lemos & Crane, since 1990; *b* 26 Feb. 1958; *s* of late Ronald Lemos and Cynthia (*née* Mitchell). *Educ:* Dulwich Coll.; Univ. of York. Dir, ASRA Housing Assoc., 1982–85; Area Manager and Dir of Develt, Circle 33 Housing Trust, 1985–90; Dir of Studies, Sch. for Social Entrepreneurs, 1997–99. Director: Mortgage Code Compliance Bd, 2000–01; Banking Code Standards Bd, 2000– (Dep. Chm., 2001–05, Chm., 2005–); Chm., Notting Hill Housing Gp, 2004–06. Mem., Audit Commn, 2000–04; Civil Service Comr, 2001–06. Non-exec. Dir, CPS, 2006–. Vis. Prof., Chongqing Business and Technology Univ., 2006–. Member of Board: London Internat. Fest. of Theatre, 1993–2001; British Council, 1999– (Dep. Chm., 2003–); The Place Theatre, 2002–03; Chm., Bd of Dirs, Akram Khan Dance Co., 2003–08; Trustee, Dartington Hall Trust, 2008–. *Publications:* Interviewing Perpetrators of Racial Harassment, 1994; Fair Recruitment and Selection, 1995; Safe as Houses: supporting people experiencing racial harassment, 1996; (jtly) The Communities We Have Lost and Can Regain, 1997; Urban Village, Global City: the regeneration of Colville, 1998; A Future Foretold: new approaches to meeting the long-term needs of single homeless people, 1999; Racial Harassment: action on the ground, 2000; (jtly) Dreams Deferred: the families and friends of homeless and vulnerable people, 2002; The Search for Tolerance: challenging and changing racist attitudes and behaviour among young people, 2005; Military History: the experiences of people who become homeless after military service, 2005; Steadying the Ladder: social and emotional aspirations of homeless and vulnerable people, 2006; (jtly) Different World: how young people can work together on human rights and citizenship. *Recreations:* literature, cricket. *Address:* (office) 64 Highgate High Street, N6 5HX. *T:* (020) 8348 8263.

LENDRUM, Christopher John, CBE 2005; Group Vice Chairman, 2004, and Executive Director, 1998–2004, Barclays plc; *b* 15 Jan. 1947; *s* of late Herbert Colin Lendrum and of Anne Margaret (*née* Macdonell); *m* 1970, Margaret Patricia Parker; one *s* one *d*. *Educ:* Felsted Sch., Essex; Durham Univ. (BA Econs 1968). FCIB 1992. Joined Barclays Bank plc, 1969: Regl Dir, 1991–93; Dep. Man. Dir of Banking Div., 1993–95; Man. Dir of UK Business Banking, 1995–98; Chief Exec., Corporate Banking, 1998–2003. Chm., Barclays Pension Fund Trustees Ltd, 2005–. Trustee, CAB, 2005–06 (Mem. Adv. Bd, 2001–04); Gov., Motability, 2005–. Freeman, City of London, 1999; Liveryman, Woolmen's Co., 1999–. CCMI 2002. Gov., Kent Coll., Pembury, 2000–08. Chm., Aston Martin Heritage Trust, 2006– (Trustee, 2003–). Hon. DLitt Durham, 2008. *Recreations:* gardening, travel, restoring neglected motor cars. *Address:* Hazon House, Guyzance, Northumberland NE65 9AT; *e-mail:* christopher.lendrum@barclays.com. *Club:* Royal Automobile.

LENG, James William; Chairman, Corus Group Ltd (formerly Corus Group plc), 2003–07 and since 2007; Deputy Chairman, Tata Steel, since 2007; *b* 19 Nov. 1945; *m* 1974, Carole Ann Guyll. John Waddington, 1967–84; Low & Bonar: Man. Dir, Bonar & Flotex, 1984–86; Chief Exec., Plastics Div., 1986–88; Chief Exec., European Ops, 1988–92; Dir, 1989–95; Group Chief Exec., 1992–95; Chief Exec., Laporte plc, 1995–2001; Chm., Doncasters Gp Ltd, 2001–03; Dep. Chm., 2001–03, Corus Gp plc (non-exec. Dir, 2001–07). Non-executive Director: Pilkington plc, 1998–2006; IMI plc, 2002–05; Alstom SA, 2003–; Hanson plc, 2004–07. Vice-Pres., CIA, 1999–2001. Mem. Court, Univ. of Newcastle-upon-Tyne, 2005–. Gov., NIESR, 1999. FRSA 2005. *Recreations:* sport, music. *Address:* (office) 30 Millbank, SW1P 4WY. *Club:* Royal Automobile.

LENG, Gen. Sir Peter (John Hall), KCB 1978 (CB 1975); MBE 1962; MC 1945; Master-General of the Ordnance, 1981–83, retired; *b* 9 May 1925; *s* of J. Leng; *m* 1st, Virginia Rosemary Pearson (marr. diss. 1981); three *s* two *d*; 2nd, 1981, Mrs Flavia Tower, *d* of late Gen. Sir Frederick Browning and Lady Browning (Dame Daphne du Maurier, DBE). *Educ:* Bradfield Coll. Served War of 1939–45: commissioned in Scots Guards, 1944; Guards Armoured Div., Germany (MC). Various post-war appts; Guards Independent Parachute Company, 1949–51; commanded: 3rd Bn Royal Anglian Regt, in Berlin, United Kingdom and Aden, 1964–66; 24th Airportable Bde, 1968–70; Dep. Military Sec., Min. of Defence, 1971–73; Comdr Land Forces, N Ireland, 1973–75; Dir, Mil. Operations, MoD, 1975–78; Comdr 1 (Br) Corps, 1978–80. Colonel Commandant: RAVC, 1976–83; RMP, 1976–83. Fund Raising Dir, Jubilee Sailing Trust, 1984–85. Chm., Racecourse Assoc., 1985–89. *Recreations:* fishing, gardening. *Address:* c/o Barclays Bank, 1 Brompton Road, SW3 1EB.

See also V. H. A. Elliot.

LENG, Virginia Helen Antoinette; *see* Elliot, V. H. A.

LENNAN, David John; Chief Executive, Business HR Solutions Ltd, since 2004; *b* 15 Dec. 1948; *s* of John D. Lennan and Mair E. Lennan; *m* 1975, Diane Griffiths. *Educ:* Northampton Town and Co. Grammar Sch. ACIB 1971. Joined District Bank, 1966; NatWest Group PLC: Dep. Regl Dir, SE Reg., 1992–93; Dep. Dir, Human Resources, and Hd, UK Develt, 1993–95; Dir, Retail Insce Services, 1995–98; Dir, Corporate Develt, Surrey CC, 1998–2001; Dir Gen., British Chambers of Commerce, 2001–02; Chief Exec., Agricultural Industries Confedn, 2003–04. Non-executive Chairman: Workwise UK, 2006–; Pilotlight, 2006–; non-exec. Dir, IT Forum Foundn, 2004–. Tuck Exec. Prog., Dartmouth Univ., USA, 1996. *Recreations:* sailing, theatre, healthy sport. *Address:* 513 Butlers Wharf, 36 Shad Thames, SE1 2YE.

LENNARD, Sir Peter John B.; *see* Barrett-Lennard.

LENNON, Hon. Paul Anthony; Premier of Tasmania, Australia, 2004–08; *b* 8 Oct. 1955; *s* of Charles and Marg Lennon; *m* 1978, Margaret Gaff; two *d*. Storeman/clerk, 1974–78; Tasmanian Branch, Storemen and Packers Union: Organiser, 1978–80; Sec., 1980–84; Sen. Vice-Pres., Federated Storemen and Packers Union of Australia, 1982–84; Sec., Tasmanian Trades and Labor Council, 1984–89; Asst Gen. Manager, Develt, Tasmanian Develt Authy, 1989–90. MHA (ALP) Franklin, Tasmania, 1990–2008; Opposition Whip and Shadow Minister for Police and Emergency Services, 1992; Shadow Minister for: Racing and Gaming, 1992–98; Industrial Relns, 1993–98; Employment and Trng, 1993–95; Forestry, 1995–96; Opposition Leader of Business in the House, 1995–96; Dep. Leader of Opposition, 1996–98; Minister for Workplace Standards and Workers' Compensation, Forests and Mines, 1997–98; Dep. Premier, 1998–2004; Minister for Infrastructure, Energy and Resources and for Racing and Gaming, 1998–2002; Minister for Econ. Develt, Energy and Resources, and for Racing and Sport and Recreation, 2002–04; Treas., 2004–06; Minister for Local Govt, 2004–08, for Econ. Develt and Resources, 2006–08. Mem., Parly Public Accounts Cttee, 1990–96. *Address:* c/o Office of the Premier, Level 11, Executive Building, 15 Murray Street, Hobart, Tas 7000, Australia.

LENNOX; *see* Gordon-Lennox and Gordon Lennox.

LENNOX, Annie; singer and songwriter; *b* 25 Dec. 1954; *d* of late Thomas A. Lennox and Dorothy Lennox (*née* Ferguson); *m* 1st, 1984, Radha Raman (marr. diss.); 2nd, 1988, Uri Fruchtmann; two *d* (and one *s* decd). *Educ:* Aberdeen High Sch. for Girls; Royal Acad. of Music. Singer with: The Catch, subseq. The Tourists, 1977–81; Eurythmics, 1981–89, 1999; solo singer, 1988–. *Albums include:* with The Tourists: The Tourists, 1979; Reality Affect, 1980; Luminous Basement, 1980; with Eurythmics: In the Garden, 1981; Sweet

Dreams (Are Made of This), 1983; Touch, 1984; 1984 (For the Love of Big Brother), 1984; Be Yourself Tonight, 1985; Revenge, 1986; Savage, 1987; We Too Are One, 1989; Peace, 1999; solo: Diva, 1992; Medusa, 1995; Train in Vain, 1995; Bare, 2003; Songs of Mass Destruction, 2007. *Address:* c/o 19 Management Ltd, 33 Ransomes Dock, 35–37 Parkgate Road, SW11 4NP.

LENNOX, Lionel Patrick Madill; Registrar of the Province and Diocese of York, Legal Secretary to the Archbishop of York, and Registrar of the Convocation of York, since 1987; Partner, Denison Till, Solicitors, York, since 1987; *b* 5 April 1949; *s* of Rev. James Lennox and late May Lennox; *m* 1979, Barbara Helen Firth; two *s* one *d. Educ:* St John's Sch., Leatherhead; Univ. of Birmingham (LLB). Admitted Solicitor, 1973; Ecclesiastical Notary, 1987; Notary Public, 1992. Solicitor in private practice, 1973–81; Asst Legal Advr to Gen. Synod, 1981–87. Secretary: Archbishop of Canterbury's Gp on Affinity, 1982–84; Legal Adv. Commn, Gen. Synod of C of E, 1986–; Registrar of Tribunals, Province of York, 2006–. Pres., Yorks Law Soc., 2007–08. Sec., Yorks Mus. of Farming, 1991–94. Trustee: Yorks Historic Churches Trust, 1988–; St Leonard's Hospice, York, 2000–. Under Sheriff, City of York, 2006–07. *Address:* Stamford House, Piccadilly, York YO1 9PP. *T:* (01904) 623487.

LENNOX-BOYD, family name of **Viscount Boyd of Merton.**

LENNOX-BOYD, Arabella, (Lady Lennox-Boyd); garden designer; Principal, Arabella Lennox-Boyd Landscape Design, since 1984; *b* 15 Jan. 1938; *d* of Piero Parisi and Irene Diaz della Vittoria; *m* 1974, Hon. Sir Mark Alexander Lennox-Boyd, *qv;* one *d,* and one *d* from former marriage. *Educ:* privately in Italy. Commissioned designs in UK, Europe and USA, range from small town gdns to country landscapes; major projects incl. roof gdn at No 1 Poultry, gdns at Ascott House and Eaton Hall. Trustee: Kew Gdns, 1989–98; Castle Howard Arboretum Trust, 1997–; former Mem., Historic Parks and Gdns Cttee, English Heritage. Hon. DDes Greenwich, 2003. Premio Firenze Donna, 2005. *Publications:* Traditional English Gardens, 1987; Private Gardens of London, 1990; (jtly) Designing Gardens, 2002. *Recreations:* gardening, embroidery, listening to music. *Address:* 4–5 Dells Mews, Churton Place, SW1V 2LW. *T:* (020) 7931 9995, *Fax:* (020) 7821 6585; *e-mail:* office@arabellalennoxboyd.com.

LENNOX-BOYD, Hon. Sir Mark (Alexander), Kt 1994; *b* 4 May 1943; 3rd *s* of 1st Viscount Boyd of Merton, CH, PC and of Lady Patricia Guinness, 2nd *d* of 2nd Earl of Iveagh, KG, CB, CMG, FRS; *m* 1974, Arabella Lacloche (*see* A. Lennox-Boyd); one *d. Educ:* Eton Coll.; Christ Church, Oxford. Called to the Bar, Inner Temple, 1968. MP (C) Morecambe and Lonsdale, 1979–83, Morecambe and Lunesdale, 1983–97; contested (C) Morecambe and Lunesdale, 1997. Parliamentary Private Secretary: to Sec. of State for Energy, 1981–83; to the Chancellor of the Exchequer, 1983–84; Asst Govt Whip, 1984–86; a Lord Comr of HM Treasury (Govt Whip), 1986–88; PPS to Prime Minister, 1988–90; Parly Under-Sec. of State, FCO, 1990–94. *Recreation:* travel. *Address:* Gresgarth Hall, Caton, Lancashire LA2 9NB. *Clubs:* Brooks's, Pratt's, Beefsteak.

LENON, Andrew Ralph Fitzmaurice; QC 2006; *b* 7 April 1957; *s* of late Rev. Philip John Fitzmaurice Lenon and of Jane Alethea Lenon (*née* Brooke); *m* 1987, Sheila Cook; one *s* three *d. Educ:* St John's Sch., Leatherhead; Lincoln Coll., Oxford (BA); City Univ. (Dip. Law). Called to the Bar, Lincoln's Inn, 1981; in practice specialising in commercial law. *Publications:* contribs to legal jls. *Recreations:* music, languages. *Address:* Chambers of Lord Grabiner, QC, One Essex Court, Temple, EC4Y 9AR. *T:* (020) 7583 2000.

    See also B. J. Lenon.

LENON, Barnaby John, MA, CGeog; Head Master, Harrow School, since 1999; *b* 10 May 1954; *s* of late Rev. Philip John Fitzmaurice Lenon and of Jane Alethea Lenon (*née* Brooke); *m* 1983, Penelope Anne Thain, BA; two *d. Educ:* Eltham Coll.; Keble Coll., Oxford (schol.; BA 1st Cl. Hons 1976; MA); St John's, Cambridge (PGCE; Univ. Prize for Educn 1978). Assistant Master: Eton Coll., 1977; Sherborne Sch., 1978–79; Eton Coll., 1979–90; Teacher, Holland Park Sch., 1988; Dep. Head Master, Highgate Sch., 1990–95; Headmaster, Trinity Sch. of John Whitgift, 1995–99. Governor: John Lyon Sch., 1999–; Swanbourne Sch., 1999–2005; Orley Farm Sch., 1999–; Wellesley House Sch., 1999–; Beacon Sch., 2000–05; Papplewick Sch., 2001–; Francis Holland Schs, 2002–; Aysgarth Sch., 2006–. FRGS 1987 (Mem. Council, 1987–90 and 1998–2000; Chm., Educn Sub-Cttee, 1996–99). CGeog 2000. *Publications:* Techniques and Fieldwork in Geography, 1983; London, 1988; London in the 1990s, 1993; Fieldwork Techniques and Projects in Geography, 1994; The United Kingdom: geographical case studies, 1995; (ed jtly) Directory of University Geography Courses, 1995, 2nd edn 1997; contribs to geographical jls. *Recreations:* oil painting, athletics, deserts. *Address:* Harrow School, Harrow-on-the-Hill, Middlesex HA1 3HT. *T:* (020) 8872 8000. *Clubs:* East India, Lansdowne.

    See also A. R. F. Lenon.

LEON, Sir John (Ronald), 4th Bt *cr* 1911; actor (stage name, **John Standing**); *b* 16 Aug. 1934; *er s* of 3rd Bt and late (Dorothy) Katharine (stage name Kay Hammond), *d* of Sir Guy Standing, KBE; *S* father, 1964; *m* 1961, Jill (marr. diss. 1972), *d* of Jack Melford; one *s; m* 1984, Sarah, *d* of Bryan Forbes, *qv;* one *s* two *d. Educ:* Eton. Late 2nd Lt, KRRC. *Plays include:* Darling Buds of May, Saville, 1959; leading man, season, Bristol Old Vic, 1960; The Irregular Verb to Love, Criterion, 1961; Norman, Duchess, 1963; So Much to Remember, Vaudeville, 1963; The Three Sisters, Oxford Playhouse, 1964; See How They Run, Vaudeville, 1964; Seasons at Chichester Theatre, 1966, 1967; The Importance of Being Earnest, Ring Round the Moon, Haymarket, 1968; The Alchemist, and Arms and the Man, Chichester, 1970; Popkiss, Globe, 1972; A Sense of Detachment, Royal Court, 1972; Private Lives, Queen's and Globe, 1973, NY and tour of USA, 1974; Jingo, RSC, 1975; Plunder, The Philanderer, NT, 1978; Close of Play, NT, 1979; Tonight at 8.30, Lyric, 1981; The Biko Inquest, Riverside, 1984; Rough Crossing, National, 1984; Hay Fever, Albery, 1992; A Month in the Country, Albery, 1994; Son of Man, RSC, 1995; A Delicate Balance, Haymarket, 1997; Shadowlands, Wyndham's, 2007. *Films:* The Wild and the Willing, 1962; Iron Maiden, 1962; King Rat, 1964; Walk, Don't Run, 1965; Zee and Co., 1973; The Eagle has Landed, 1976; The Class of Miss MacMichael, 1977; The Legacy, 1977; The Elephant Man, 1979; The Sea Wolves, 1980; (TV film) The Young Visiters, 1984; Nightflyers; 8½ Women, Rogue Trader, 1999; The Good Woman, 2003; V for Vendetta, 2005; I Want Candy, Shooter, Before the Rains, 2007. *Television* appearances incl.: for British TV: Arms and the Man; The First Churchills; Charley's Aunt; Rogue Male; The Sinking of HMS Victoria; Home and Beauty; Tinker, Tailor, Soldier, Spy; The Other 'Arf; Old Boy Network; Tonight at 8.30; Count of Solar; Gulliver's Travels; Shadow in the North; for American TV: Lime Street; Hotel; Flap Jack Floozie; Visitors; Murphy's Law; The Endless Game; Murder She Wrote; LA Law; Windmills of the Gods; Drovers' Gold; A Dance to The Music of Time; Longitude; King Solomon's Mines. *Recreation:* painting. *Heir: s* Alexander John Leon, *b* 3 May 1965. *Address:* c/o Independent Talent Group Ltd, Oxford House, 76 Oxford Street, W1D 1BS.

LEONARD, Anthony James; QC 1999; a Recorder, since 2000; *b* 21 April 1956; *s* of late Sir (Hamilton) John Leonard and Doreen Enid Leonard (*née* Parker); *m* 1983, Shara

Jane Cormack; two *d. Educ:* Hurstpierpoint Coll., Sussex; Council of Legal Educn. Short Service Limited Commn, Queen's Regt, 1975–76; Major, 6/7 Queen's (TA), 1976–85. Called to the Bar, Inner Temple, 1978, Bencher, 2002; Standing Counsel to Inland Revenue, S Eastern Circuit, 1993–99. Vice-Chm., Professional Conduct Cttee, 2001–04, 2006–. Liveryman, Plaisterers' Co. *Recreations:* opera, wine, reading. *Address:* 6 King's Bench Walk, Temple, EC4Y 7DR. *Club:* Garrick.

LEONARD, Brian Henry, CBE 2008; consultant; Director, Industry, Department for Culture, Media and Sport, 2005–08; *b* 6 Jan. 1948; *s* of William Henry Leonard and Bertha Florence Leonard (*née* Thomas); *m* 1975, Margaret Meade-King; two *s. Educ:* Dr Challoner's Grammar Sch., Amersham; LSE (BSc Econ 1969). Heal & Son, 1969–73; Price Commn, 1973–74; joined DoE, 1974; Circle 33 Housing Trust, 1982–83; Fellow, Hubert H. Humphrey Inst., Minneapolis, 1987–88; Regl Dir, N Reg., DoE and Dept of Transport, 1993–94; Regl Dir, Govt Office for SW, 1994–97; Dir, Envmt Protection Strategy, DETR, 1997–98; Dir, Regions, Tourism, Millennium and Internat., then Tourism, Lottery and Regions, subseq. Tourism, Libraries and Communities, DCMS, 1998–2005. *Recreations:* friends, games, pottering about. *Address:* 46 Defoe House, Barbican, EC2Y 8DN. *Club:* MCC.

LEONARD, David Charles; Chairman, Kingfieldheath Ltd, 2001–04; Group Chief Executive, BPB plc, 1999–2000; *b* 26 June 1938; *s* of Charles and Audrey Leonard; *m* 1961, Jennifer Capes; two *s* one *d. Educ:* Hellesdon Secondary Sch., Norwich. FCMA, ACIS. Managing Dir, food and other manufacturing industries; BPB plc: Man. Dir, British Gypsum, 1990–94; Dir, New Business Develt, 1993–97; Mem. Main Bd, 1995; Dep. Chm., Gypsum, 1996; Chm., British Gypsum, 1996; Chief Operating Officer, all building products, 1997; Dir, BMP, 1999. FRSA. *Recreations:* reading, music, opera, an interest in most sports, tennis, walking, golf.

LEONARD, David John, TD 1974; Judge, Supreme Court of Hong Kong, 1991–97; *b* 18 Sept. 1937; *s* of Jeremiah Leonard and Rosaleen Oonagh Leonard (*née* Mellett); *m* 1966, Frances Helen Good; two *s. Educ:* Hendon Grammar Sch.; Magdalene Coll., Cambridge (MA); Bath Spa Univ. Coll. (MA 2005). Admitted solicitor, 1967; admitted solicitor and barrister, Victoria, Australia, 1982. Solicitors' Dept, New Scotland Yard, 1966–71; Batten & Co., Solicitors, Yeovil, 1971–77; Hong Kong: Permanent Magistrate, 1977–81; Dist Judge, 1981–91; Judicial Comr, High Court, Brunei Darussalam, 2001–07. Chm., Judicial Studies Bd, Hong Kong, 1994–97. Served in TA: HAC, RA, Intelligence Corps, 1960–77, Maj. (retd) Intelligence Corps; Royal Hong Kong Regt (Volunteers), 1977–91, Maj. (retd). Part-time Immigration Adjudicator, 1997–98. Member: Acad. of Experts, 1995– (Vice-Chm., 1997–98); Arbitration Panel: Hong Kong Internat. Arbitration Centre, 1996–; China Internat. Economic and Trade Arbitration Commn, 1997–; Professional Conduct Cttee, Chartered Inst. of Arbitrators, 2000–06; Qingdao Arbitration Commn, 2001–; Internat. Commn for Holocaust Era Ins. Claims, 2002–06; Beijing Arbitration Commn, 2003–. Mem. Cttee, Wilts RFCA (formerly TAVRA), 1997–2007. FCIArb 1995. Fellow, Hong Kong Inst. of Arbitrators, 1997–2007. Freeman and Liveryman, Painter-Stainers' Co., 1996–. *Recreations:* travel, reading, walking. *Address: e-mail:* dleo1937@aol.com. *Clubs:* Cavalry and Guards; Bath & County (Bath); Hong Kong (Hong Kong).

LEONARD, Dick; *see* Leonard, Richard Lawrence.

LEONARD, (Fergus) Miles; Managing Director, Parlophone Records, since 2003; *b* 17 June 1967; *s* of Eric and Yvonne Leonard; *m* 2005, Luca Smit; one *s* one *d. Educ:* Great Marlow Sch. A&R Scout, Virgin Records, 1991–93; A&R Manager, Roadrunner Records, 1993–95; Parlophone Records: A&R Manager, 1995–96; Sen. A&R Manager, 1996–99; Dir of A&R, 1999–2003. *Recreations:* Glastonbury, Secrets, arguing, Christmas. *Address:* Parlophone Records, EMI House, 43 Brook Green, W6 7EF. *T:* (020) 7605 5000. *Clubs:* Electric; Bowls (Marrakech).

LEONARD, Rt Rev. Mgr and Rt Hon. Graham Douglas, KCVO 1991; PC 1981; *b* 8 May 1921; *s* of late Rev. Douglas Leonard, MA; *m* 1943, Vivien Priscilla, *d* of late M. B. R. Swann, MD, Fellow of Gonville and Caius Coll., Cambridge; two *s. Educ:* Monkton Combe Sch.; Balliol Coll., Oxford (Hon. Fellow, 1986). Hon. Sch. Nat. Science, shortened course. BA 1943, MA 1947. Served War, 1941–45; Captain, Oxford and Bucks Light Infantry; Army Operational Research Group (Ministry of Supply), 1944–45. Westcott House, Cambridge, 1946–47. Deacon 1947, Priest 1948; Vicar of Ardleigh, Essex, 1952–55; Director of Religious Education, Diocese of St Albans, 1955–58; Hon. Canon of St Albans, 1955–57; Canon Residentiary, 1957–58; Canon Emeritus, 1958; General Secretary, Nat. Society, and Secretary, C of E Schools Council, 1958–62; Archdeacon of Hampstead, Exam. Chaplain to Bishop of London, and Rector of St Andrew Undershaft with St Mary Axe, City of London, 1962–64; Bishop Suffragan of Willesden, 1964–73; Bishop of Truro, 1973–81; Bishop of London, 1981–91; received into RC Ch and ordained priest *sub conditione,* 1994. Prelate of Honour to HH the Pope, 2000. Dean of the Chapels Royal, 1981–91; Prelate of the Order of the British Empire, 1981–91; Prelate of the Imperial Soc. of Knights Bachelor, 1986–91. Chairman: C of E Cttee for Social Work and the Social Services, 1967–76; C of E Board for Social Responsibility, 1976–83; Churches Main Cttee, 1981–91; C of E Board of Education, 1983–88; BBC and IBA Central Religious Adv. Cttee, 1984–89. Member: Churches Unity Commn, 1977–78, Consultant 1978; Churches Council for Covenanting, 1978–82; PCFC, 1989–93. An Anglican Mem., Commn for Anglican Orthodox Jt Doctrinal Discussions, 1974–81; one of Archbp of Canterbury's Counsellors on Foreign Relations, 1974–81. Pres., Path to Rome Internat. Convention (Miles Jesu), 1997–2001. Elected delegate, 5th Assembly WCC, Nairobi, 1975. House of Lords, 1977–91. Select Preacher to University of Oxford, 1968, 1984 and 1989; Hensley Henson Lectr, Univ. of Oxford, 1991–92. Lectures: John Findley Green Foundn, Fulton, Missouri, 1987; Earl Mountbatten Meml, Cambridge Union, 1990. Freeman, City of London, 1970. President: Middlesex Assoc., 1970–73; Corporation of SS Mary and Nicholas (Woodard Schools), 1973–78, Hon. Fellow, 1978. Fellow, Sion Coll., 1991–. Member Court of City Univ., 1981–91. Hon. Bencher, Middle Temple, 1982. Hon. DD: Episcopal Seminary, Kentucky, 1974; Westminster Coll., Fulton, Missouri, 1987; Hon. DCnL Nashotah, USA, 1983; STD Siena Coll., USA, 1984; Hon. LLD, Simon Greenleaf Sch. of Law, USA, 1987; Hon. DLitt CNAA, 1989. Episcopal Canon of Jerusalem, 1982–91. *Publications:* Growing into Union (Jt author), 1970; The Gospel is for Everyone, 1971; God Alive: Priorities in Pastoral Theology, 1981; Firmly I Believe and Truly, 1985; Life in Christ, 1986; (jtly) Let God be God, 1990; contrib. to: The Christian Religion Explained, 1960; Retreats Today, 1962; Communicating the Faith, 1969; A Critique of Eucharistic Agreement, 1975; Is Christianity Credible?, 1981; The Price of Peace, 1983; The Cross and the Bomb, 1983; Unholy Warfare, 1983; Synod of Westminster, 1986; After the Deluge, 1987; (ed) Faith and the Future, 1988; Tradition and Unity, 1991; Families for the Future, 1991; Challenge: spreading the faith, 1997; The Path to Rome, 1999. *Recreations:* reading, especially biographies; music. *Address:* 25 Woodlands Road, Witney, Oxon OX28 2DR.

    See also J. V. Leonard.

LEONARD, Hugh, (John Keyes Byrne); playwright since 1959; Programme Director, Dublin Theatre Festival, since 1978; Literary Editor, Abbey Theatre, 1976–77; *b* 9 Nov. 1926; *m* 1955, Paule Jacquet (decd); one *d*; *m* Kathy Hayes. *Educ:* Presentation College, Dun Laoghaire. Hon. DHL Rhode Island, 1980; Hon. DLitt TCD, 1988. *Stage plays:* The Big Birthday, 1956; A Leap in the Dark, 1957; Madigan's Lock, 1958; A Walk on the Water, 1960; The Passion of Peter Ginty, 1961; Stephen D, 1962; The Poker Session, and Dublin 1, 1963; The Saints Go Cycling In, 1965; Mick and Mick, 1966; The Quick and the Dead, 1967; The Au Pair Man, 1968; The Barracks, 1969; The Patrick Pearse Motel, 1971; Da, 1973; Thieves, 1973; Summer, 1974; Times of Wolves and Tigers, 1974; Irishmen, 1975; Time Was, 1976; A Life, 1977; Kill, 1982; Scorpions (3 stage plays), 1983; The Mask of Moriarty, 1985; Moving, 1991; Senna for Sonny, 1994; The Lily Lally Show, 1994; Chamber Music (2 plays), 1994; Magic, 1997; Love in the Title, 1998; Fillums, 1999; Colquhoun and MacBryde, 2000; *adaptations:* Great Expectations, 1995; A Tale of Two Cities, 1996; Uncle Varrick, 2004. *TV plays:* Silent Song (Italia Award, 1967); The Last Campaign, 1978; The Ring and the Rose, 1978; A Life, 1986; Hunted Down, 1989; The Celadon Cup, 1993. *TV serials:* Nicholas Nickleby, 1977; London Belongs to Me, 1977; Wuthering Heights, 1978; Strumpet City, 1979; The Little World of Don Camillo, 1980; Good Behaviour, 1983; O'Neill, 1983; The Irish RM, 1985; Troubles, 1987; Parnell and the Englishwoman, 1991. *Films:* Herself Surprised, 1977; Da, 1988; Widows' Peak, 1994; Banjaxed, 1995. *Publications:* Home Before Night (autobiog.), 1979; Out After Dark (autobiog.), 1988; Parnell and the Englishwoman (novel), 1990; Rover and other cats (memoir), 1992; The Off-Off-Shore Island (novel), 1993; The Mogs (for children), 1995; A Wild People (novel), 2000; Fillums (novel), 2004. *Recreations:* travel (esp. French canals and waterways), vintage films, lunch, dinner, friendships. *Address:* 6 Rossaun, Pilot View, Dalkey, Co. Dublin. *T:* 2809590.

LEONARD, Prof. James Vivian, PhD; FRCP, FRCPCH; Professor of Paediatric Metabolic Disease, Institute of Child Health, University of London, 1992–2004; *b* 21 Dec. 1944; *s* of Rt Rev. Mgr and Rt Hon. Graham Douglas Leonard, *qv*; *m* 1966, Dr Halcyon Sheila Deriba (*née* Disney); one *s* one *d*. *Educ:* Pembroke Coll., Cambridge (MB BChir 1970); St Thomas's Hosp. Med. Sch.; Inst. of Child Health, London (PhD 1979). FRCP 1983; FRCPCH 1997. Sen. Lectr, 1979–85, Reader, 1985–92, Inst. of Child Health; Consultant Paediatrician, Gt Ormond St Children's Hosp., 1979–2004. *Publications:* contribs on paediatric metabolic medicine. *Recreations:* gardening, travel, woodturning. *Address:* 40A Bagley Wood Road, Kennington, Oxford OX1 5LY.

LEONARD, Miles; *see* Leonard, F. M.

LEONARD, Richard Lawrence, (Dick Leonard); writer and journalist; *b* 12 Dec. 1930; *s* of late Cyril Leonard, Pinner, Middx, and Kate Leonard (*née* Whyte); *m* 1963, Irène, *d* of late Dr Ernst Heidelberger and Dr Gertrud Heidelberger, Bad Godesberg, Germany; one *s* one *d*. *Educ:* Ealing Grammar Sch.; Inst. of Education, London Univ.; Essex Univ. (MA). School teacher, 1953–55; Dep. Gen. Sec., Fabian Society, 1955–60; journalist and broadcaster, 1960–68; Sen. Research Fellow (Social Science Research Council), Essex Univ., 1968–70. Mem., Exec. Cttee, Fabian Soc., 1972–80 (Chm., 1977–78); Chm., Library Adv. Council, 1978–81. Trustee, Assoc. of London Housing Estates, 1973–78. Vis. Prof., Free Univ. of Brussels, 1988–96. European Advr, Publishers Assoc., 1987–94; Sen. Advr, Centre for European Policy Studies, 1994–99; Sen. Res. Associate, Foreign Policy Centre, London, 2003–. Contested (Lab) Harrow W, 1955; MP (Lab) Romford, 1970–Feb. 1974; PPS to Rt Hon. Anthony Crosland, 1970–74; Mem., Speaker's Conf. on Electoral Law, 1972–74. Introduced Council Housing Bill, 1971; Life Peers Bill, 1973. Asst Editor, The Economist, 1974–85; Brussels and EU correspondent, The Observer, 1989–97; Brussels correspondent, Europe magazine, 1992–2003. *Publications:* Guide to the General Election, 1964; Elections in Britain, 1968, 5th edn 2005; (ed jtly) The Backbencher and Parliament, 1972; Paying for Party Politics, 1975; BBC Guide to Parliament, 1979; (ed jtly) The Socialist Agenda, 1981; (jtly) World Atlas of Elections, 1986; Pocket Guide to the EEC, 1988; Elections in Britain Today, 1991; The Economist Guide to the European Community, 1992, 4th edn as The Economist Guide to the European Union, 1997, 9th edn 2005 (French, German, Polish, Bulgarian, Georgian, Hungarian, Romanian, Serbian, Spanish and Portuguese edns); Replacing the Lords, 1995; (jtly) Eminent Europeans, 1996; (ed) Crosland and New Labour, 1999; (ed jtly) The Pro-European Reader, 2001; A Century of Premiers: Salisbury to Blair, 2004; (ed) The Future of Socialism by Anthony Crosland, 50th anniv. edn; 19th Century Premiers: Pitt to Rosebery, 2008; contribs to Guardian, Financial Times, TLS, European Voice, The Bulletin, Prospect, and leading newspapers in USA, Canada, Japan, India, Australia and New Zealand. *Recreations:* walking, book-reviewing, family pursuits. *Address:* 32 rue des Bégonias, 1170 Brussels, Belgium. *T:* (2) 6602662. *Clubs:* Reform; Brussels Croquet.

LEORO-FRANCO, Dr Galo Alberto; Gran Cruz, National Order Al Mérito of Ecuador, 1970; Minister of Foreign Affairs, Ecuador, 1994–97; Member, Consultative Board, Ministry of Foreign Affairs, since 1997; *s* of José Miguel Leoro and Albertina Franco de Leoro; *m* 1957, Aglae Monroy de Leoro; one *s* two *d*. *Educ:* Central Univ., Quito. Licenciado in Political and Soc. Scis, 1949; Dr in Jurisprudence, Faculty of Law, 1951. Third Sec., Washington, 1955–56, Second Sec., 1956–58; First Sec., Ministry of Foreign Affairs, 1960; Counsellor, Mexico, 1961, Chargé d'Affaires, 1962; Counsellor, Alternate Rep. of Ecuador to OAS, Washington, DC, 1962–64, Minister, 1964–68; Ambassador, 1968–; Chief Legal Advisor to Ministry of Foreign Affairs, 1969–70; Undersec. Gen., Ministry of Foreign Affairs, 1970–71; Ambassador to the Dominican Republic, 1971–72; Perm. Rep. of Ecuador to OAS, 1972–79; Advisor on Internat. Orgns, Ministry of Foreign Affairs, 1979–81; Advisor on Nat. Sovereignty, Ministry of Foreign Affairs, and Rep. of the Ministry in Nat. Congress, 1981–83; Ambassador to UK, 1983–84; Ambassador and Permanent Rep. to Office of UN, Geneva, 1984–91; Chief Legal Advr, Ministry of Foreign Affairs, 1991–92; Ambassador to Holy See, 1993–94. Chairman: OAS Permanent Council, 1972–78 (Chm. of several Cttees of OAS Council and Gen. Assembly); Cttee II, Special Commn for Study of Interamerican System, Economic Co-operation problems, Washington, DC, 1973–75; INTELSAT Panel of Jurisexperts, Washington, DC, 1983–85; Rapporteur, Interamerican Conf. for Revision of TIAR; elected mem., Interamerican Juridical Cttee, Rio de Janeiro, 1981–84, Vice-Chm., 1982–83, Chm., 1985–96; Conciliator, Internat. Center for Settlement of Investment Disputes, IMF, Washington, DC, 1986–; Ecuadorian Mem., National Gp of Arbiters, Internat. Court of Arbitration, The Hague, 1987. Representative of Ecuador at over 100 internat. conferences and Chm. of the Delegation at various of them. Gran Cruz: Iron Cross, Fed. Repub. of Germany, 1970; Order of Duarte, Sánchez and Mella, Dominican Repub., 1972; Order of the Sun, Perú, 1976; 1st Class, Order of Francisco de Miranda, Venezuela, 1976; Order of Piana, Holy See; Order of San Carlos, Colombia; Order of Bernardo O'Higgins, Chile; 1st Class, Al Merito, Korea. *Publications:* contrib. Interamerican Law Year Book and Courses of Internat. Law of the OAS, Washington; various papers for Ecuadorean Year Book of Internat. Law. *Recreations:* chess, tennis. *Address:* González Suárez Avenida, N33–12 Quito, Ecuador. *Club:* Quito Tennis and Golf.

LÉOTARD, François Gérard Marie; European Union Special Envoy to Macedonia, 2001; *b* Cannes, 26 March 1942; *s* of André Léotard and Antoinette (*née* Tomasi); *m* 1992, Ysabel Duret; one *s* one *d*. *Educ:* Paris Law Univ.; Institut d'Etudes Politiques de Paris; Ecole Nationale d'Administration. Various appts in French admin, 1968–76; Mem., Nat. Assembly, 1978–86, 1988–92, 1995–2002; Minister of Culture and Communication, 1986–88; Minister of Defence, 1993–95. Mayor of Fréjus, 1977–92, 1993–97; Member: General Council, Var, 1980–88; Regl Council, Provence. Republican Party (Parti Républicain): Gen. Sec., 1982–88; Pres., 1988–90 and 1995–97; Hon. Pres., 1990–95; Pres., UDF, 1996–98. *Publications:* A Mots Découverts, 1987; Culture: les chemins de printemps, 1988; La Ville Aimée: mes chemins de Fréjus, 1989; Pendant la Crise, le Spectacle Continue, 1989; Adresse au Président des Républiques Françaises, 1991; Place de la République, 1992; Ma Liberté, 1995; Pour l'honneur, 1997; Je vous hais tous avec douceur, 2000; Paroles d'immortels, 2001; La Couleur des femmes, 2002; A mon frère qui n'est pas mort, 2003.

LEPAGE, Robert, OC 1995; OQ 1999; Director and President, RLI, since 1988; Founder, President and Artistic Director: Ex Machina Theatre Company, since 1994; In Extremis Images Inc., since 1995; *b* 12 Dec. 1957; *s* of Fernand and Germaine Lepage. *Educ:* Ecole Joseph-François Perreault, Quebec City; Conservatoire d'Art Dramatique de Québec. Joined Théâtre Repère, as actor, 1980, also Jt Artistic Dir and writer, 1986–89; Artistic Dir, Théâtre Français, Ottawa Nat. Arts Theatre, 1989–93; Artistic Dir, La Caserne, 1997–. *Stage* includes: *joint writer, director and actor:* Théâtre Repère: Circulations, 1984; La Trilogie des dragons, 1985; Vinci (one-man show), 1986; Le polygraphe, 1987; Les plaques tectoniques, 1988–91; Les aiguilles et l'opium (one-man show), 1991; La face cachée de la lune (one-man show), 2000–03; The Andersen Project (one-man show), Barbican, 2006; *director:* Carmen, Théâtre d'Bon'Humeur, 1983; Le songe d'une nuit d'été, Théâtre du Nouveau Monde, Montreal, 1988; A Midsummer Night's Dream, RNT, London, 1992; Le Cycle William Shakespeare, Quebec City, Maubeuge, Frankfurt and Paris, 1992; Macbeth and La tempête, Tokyo Globe Theatre, Tokyo, 1993; Les Sept branches de la rivière Ota (also jt writer), 1994; Elseneur (one-man show, also adapter and actor), 1995; La géométrie des miracles (world tour; also jt writer), 1998; Zulu Time, 1999; La damnation de Faust, Japan, 1999, France, 2001; 1984, Royal Opera, Covent Garden, 2005; Lipsynch, Newcastle upon Tyne, 2007; TV advertisements; *films include: writer and director:* Le confessionnal, 1995; Le polygraphe, 1996; Nô, 1998; Possible Worlds, 2000. Chevalier de l'Ordre des Arts et des Lettres (France), 1990. *Address:* c/o Lynda Beaulieu, 103 Dalhousie Street, Quebec City, QC G1K 4B9, Canada.

LE POER, Baron; Richard John Beresford; *b* 19 Aug. 1987; *s* and *heir* of Earl of Tyrone, *qv*.

LE POER TRENCH, family name of **Earl of Clancarty**.

LE PORTZ, Yves; Comdr Légion d'Honneur 1978; Grand Officier de l'Ordre National du Mérite; French financial executive; Inspector-General of Finances, 1971; *b* Hennebont, 30 Aug. 1920; *m* 1946, Bernadette Champetier de Ribes; five *c*. *Educ:* Univ. de Paris à la Sorbonne; Ecole des Hautes Etudes Commerciales; Ecole Libre des Sciences Politiques. Attached to Inspection Générale des Finances, 1943; Directeur Adjoint du Cabinet, Président du Conseil, 1948–49; Sous-Directeur, then Chef de Service, Min. of Finance and Economic Affairs, 1949–51; Directeur du Cabinet: Sec. of State for Finance and Economic Affairs, 1951–52; Minister for Posts, Telegraphs and Telephones (PTT), 1952–55; Minister for Reconstruction and Housing, 1955–57; French Delegate to UN Economic and Social Council, 1957–58; Dir-Gén., Finance, Algeria, 1958–62; Administrateur-Gén., Development Bank of Algeria, 1959–62. European Investment Bank: Vice-Pres. and Vice-Chm., Bd of Dirs, 1962–70; Pres. and Chm. Bd of Dirs, 1970–84; Hon. Pres., 1984. Chairman: Commn des Opérations de Bourse, Paris, 1984–88; Investment Funds Supervisory Cttee, Principality of Monaco, 1988–; Statutory Auditors' Ethics Cttee, 1999–. *Address:* 127 avenue de Wagram, 75017 Paris, France.

LEPPARD, Captain Keith André, CBE 1977; RN; Secretary, Institute of Brewing, 1977–90; Director Public Relations (Royal Navy), 1974–77; *b* 29 July 1924; *s* of Wilfred Ernest Leppard and Dora Gilmore Keith; *m* 1954, Betty Rachel Smith; one *s* one *d*. *Educ:* Purley Grammar Sch. MRAeS 1973; FCMI (FBIM 1973); FSAE 1985. Entered RN, FAA pilot duties, 1943; Opnl Wartime Service, Fighter Pilot, N Atlantic/Indian Oceans, 1944–45; Fighter Pilot/Flying Instr, Aircraft Carriers and Air Stns, 1946–57; CO 807 Naval Air Sqdn (Aerobatic Display Team, Farnborough), 1958–59; Air Org./Flying Trng Staff appts, 1959–63; Comdr (Air), HMS Victorious, 1963–64; Jt Services Staff Coll., 1964–65; Dir, Naval Officer Appts (Air), 1965–67; Chief Staff Officer (Air), Flag Officer Naval Air Comd, 1967–69; Chief Staff Officer (Ops/Trng), Far East Fleet, 1969–71; CO, Royal Naval Air Stn, Yeovilton, and Flag Captain to Flag Officer Naval Air Comd, 1972–74. Naval ADC to the Queen, 1976–77. *Recreations:* country life, tennis, golf. *Address:* Little Holt, Kingsley Green, Haslemere, Surrey GU27 3LW. *T:* (01428) 642797.

LEPPARD, Raymond John, CBE 1983; conductor, harpsichordist, composer; Music Director, Indianapolis Symphony Orchestra, 1987–2001; *b* 11 Aug. 1927; *s* of A. V. Leppard. *Educ:* Trinity Coll., Cambridge. Fellow of Trinity Coll., Cambridge, and Univ. Lecturer in Music, 1958–68. Hon. Keeper of the Music, Fitzwilliam Museum, 1963–82. Conductor: Covent Garden, Sadler's Wells, Glyndebourne, and abroad; Principal Conductor, BBC Northern Symphony Orchestra, 1972–80; Prin. Guest Conductor, St Louis SO, 1984–93. Hon. RAM 1972; Hon. GSM 1983; Hon. FRCM 1984. Hon. DLitt Univ. of Bath, 1972. Commendatore al Merito della Repubblica Italiana, 1974. *Publications:* realisations of Monteverdi: Il Ballo delle Ingrate, 1958; L'Incoronazione di Poppea, 1962; L'Orfeo, 1965; Il Ritorno d'Ulisse, 1972; realisations of Francesco Cavalli: Messa Concertata, 1966; L'Ormindo, 1967; La Calisto, 1969; Magnificat, 1970; L'Egisto, 1974; L'Orione, 1983; realisation of Rameau's Dardanus, 1980; Authenticity in Music, 1988; Raymond Leppard on Music, 1993; British Academy Italian Lecture, 1969, Procs Royal Musical Assoc. *Recreations:* music, theatre, books, friends. *Address:* 5040 Buttonwood Crescent, Indianapolis, IN 46228–2323, USA. *T:* (317) 259 9020, *Fax:* (317) 259 0916.

LEPPER, David; MP (Lab and Co-op) Brighton Pavilion, since 1997; *b* 15 Sept. 1945; *s* of late Henry George Lepper and Maggie Lepper (*née* Osborne); *m* 1966, Jeane Stroud; one *s* one *d*. *Educ:* St John's C of E Primary Sch., Richmond; Gainsborough Secondary Sch., Richmond; Wimbledon Co. Secondary Sch.; Univ. of Kent (BA Hons); Univ. of Sussex (PGCE); PCL (Dip. Film); Univ. of Sussex (Dip. Media). Teacher: Westlain GS, Brighton, 1968–73; Falmer Sch., Brighton, 1973–96. Mem. (Lab), Brighton BC, 1980–97 (Leader, 1986–87; Mayor, 1993–94). *Publications:* John Wayne, 1986; various articles in film and media jls. *Recreations:* cinema, music, books, watching professional cycling. *Address:* (office) John Saunders House, 179 Preston Road, Brighton BN1 6AG. *T:* (01273) 551532. *Club:* Brighton Trades and Labour.

LEPPING, Sir George (Geria Dennis), GCMG 1988; MBE 1981; Governor-General of the Solomon Islands, 1988–94; *b* 22 Nov. 1947; *e s* of Chief Dionisio Tanutanu, BEM and Regina Suluki; *m* 1972, Margaret Kwalea Teioli; two *s* four *d* (incl. twins) and one adopted *d.* *Educ:* St John's and St Peter's Primary Schs; King George VI Secondary Sch.; Agricl Coll., Vudal, PNG (Dip. Tropical Agric.); Reading Univ. (Dip. Agric.; MSc). Joined Solomon Is Public Service as Field Officer, Dept of Agric. and Rural Economy, 1968; Sen. Field Officer, then Under-Sec. (Agricl), Min. of Agric., 1979–80; Permanent Secretary: Min. of Home Affairs and Nat. Develt, 1981–84; Special Duties, as Project Dir, Rural Services Project (Develt), 1984–87; Min. of Finance, 1988. Sometime Dir, Chm. or Mem., various govt cos and authorities; Chm., Nat. Disaster Council, 1981–84. Pres., Solomon Is Amateur Athletics Union, 1970–73, 1981–82 (first Solomon Is athlete to win internat. sports medals). KStJ 1991. *Recreations:* reading, swimming, lawn tennis, snooker, snorkelling, high-speed boat driving, fishing. *Address:* PO Box 1431, Honiara, Solomon Islands.

LEPSCHY, Prof. Giulio Ciro, FBA 1987; Emeritus Professor of Italian, University of Reading, since 2000 (Professor, 1975–97; part-time Professor, 1997–2000); Visiting Research Fellow, Downing College, University of Cambridge, since 2003; *b* 14 Jan. 1935; *s* of Emilio Lepschy and Sara Castelfranchi; *m* 1962, Anna Laura Momigliano. *Educ:* Univ. of Pisa (Dott. Lett.); Scuola Normale Superiore, Pisa (Dip. Lic. and Perf.). Lib. Doc., Italy. Research, 1957–64, at Univs of Zurich, Oxford, Paris, London, Reading; Lectr 1964, Reader 1967, Univ. of Reading. Mem. Council, Philological Soc., 1984–89, 1992–96; Pres., MHRA, 2001. Corr. Mem., Accademia della Crusca, 1991. Hon. Prof., UCL, 1998. Hon. Dr, Univ. of Turin, 1998. Serena Medal, British Acad., 2000. Commendatore of the Italian Republic, 2003. *Publications:* A Survey of Structural Linguistics, 1970, new edn 1982; (jtly) The Italian Language Today, 1977, 2nd edn 1988; Saggi di linguistica italiana, 1978; Intorno a Saussure, 1979; Mutamenti di prospettiva nella linguistica, 1981; Nuovi saggi di linguistica italiana, 1989; Sulla linguistica moderna, 1989; Storia della linguistica, 1990; La linguistica del Novecento, 1992; History of Linguistics, 1994; (jtly) L'amanuense analfabeta e altri saggi, 1999; Mother Tongues and Other Reflections on the Italian Language, 2002; Parole, parole, parole e altri saggi di linguistica, 2007; contribs to learned jls. *Address:* 335 Latymer Court, Hammersmith Road, W6 7LH. *T:* and *Fax:* (020) 8748 7780.

LE QUESNE, Caroline; *see* Lucas, C.

LE QUESNE, Sir (John) Godfray, Kt 1980; QC 1962; Judge of Courts of Appeal of Jersey, 1964–97, and Guernsey, 1964–95; a Recorder, 1972–97; *b* 18 Jan. 1924; 3rd *s* of late C. T. Le Quesne, QC; *m* 1963, Susan Mary Gill; two *s* one *d.* *Educ:* Shrewsbury Sch.; Exeter Coll., Oxford (MA). Pres. of Oxford Union, 1943. Called to Bar, Inner Temple, 1947; Master of the Bench, Inner Temple, 1969, Reader, 1988, Treasurer, 1989; admitted to bar of St Helena, 1959. Dep. Chm., Lincs (Kesteven) QS, 1963–71. Chm., Monopolies and Mergers Commn, 1975–87 (a part-time Mem., 1974–75). Chm. of Council, Regent's Park Coll., Oxford, 1958–87. *Publication:* Jersey and Whitehall in the Mid-Nineteenth Century, 1992. *Recreations:* music, walking. *Address:* c/o 3 Hare Court, Temple, EC4Y 7BJ.

See also L. P. Le Quesne.

LE QUESNE, Prof. Leslie Philip, CBE 1984; DM, MCh, FRCS; Medical Administrator, Commonwealth Scholarship Commission, 1984–91; *b* 24 Aug. 1919; *s* of late C. T. Le Quesne, QC; *m* 1969, Pamela Margaret (*d* 1999), *o d* of late Dr A. Fullerton, Batley, Yorks; two *s.* *Educ:* Rugby; Exeter Coll., Oxford; Middlesex Hosp. Med. Sch. Jun. Demonstrator, Path. and Anat., 1943–45; House Surgeon, Southend Hosp. and St Mark's Hosp., 1945–47; Appointments at Middlesex Hospital: Asst, Surgical Professorial Unit, 1947–52; Asst Dir, Dept of Surgical Studies, 1952–63; Surgeon, 1960–63; Prof. of Surgery, Med. Sch., and Dir, Dept of Surgical Studies, 1963–84; Dep. Vice-Chancellor and Dean, Fac. of Medicine, Univ. of London, 1980–84. Sir Arthur Sims Commonwealth Travelling Prof., 1975. Mem. GMC, 1979–84. Arris and Gale Lectr, RCS, 1952; Baxter Lectr, Amer. Coll. Surgs, 1960. Mem., Ct of Examrs, RCS, 1971–77. Formerly Chm., Assoc. of Profs of Surgery; Pres., Surgical Res. Soc. Chm., The British Jl of Surgery. Hon. FRACS, 1975; Hon. FACS, 1982; Hon. Fellow Imperial Coll. (formerly RPMS), 1985. Moynihan Medal, 1953. *Publications:* medical articles and contribs to text books; Fluid Balance in Surgical Practice, 2nd edn, 1957. *Recreations:* fishing, reading. *Address:* Flat 1, 10 Strathray Gardens, NW3 4NY.

See also Sir J. G. Le Quesne.

LERCHE-THOMSEN, Kim Stuart, FIA; Chief Executive, Living Time, since 2004; *b* 2 Sept. 1952; *s* of Paul Lerche-Thomsen and Patricia Lerche-Thomsen (*née* Williams); *m* 1991, Emma Jane Grace Brook; one *s* one *d.* *Educ:* Sevenoaks; Brunel Univ. (BTech). FIA 1984. Dir, Pensions, Prudential, 1991–96; Man. Dir, Prudential Annuities, 1997–2001; Dir, Prudential Assurance Co. Ltd, 1999–2002; Chief Exec., Scottish Amicable, 2001–02; Chm., AssetCo (formerly Asset Investment Gp), 2003–04. FRMetS 1975. *Recreations:* ski-ing, tennis, meteorology. *Address:* (office) Davidson House, 2 Forbury Square, The Forbury, Reading, Berkshire RG1 3EU; *e-mail:* kim.lt@Living-time.co.uk. *Club:* Phyllis Court (Henley-on-Thames).

LEREGO, Michael John; QC 1995; a Recorder, since 2002; *b* 6 May 1949; *s* of late Leslie Ivor Lerego and Gwendolen Frances Lerego; *m* 1972, Susan Northover; three *d* (one *s* decd). *Educ:* Manchester Grammar Sch.; Haberdashers' Aske's Sch., Elstree; Keble Coll., Oxford (Open Schol.; Dist. Law Mods 1968; Gibbs Prize in Law 1969; BA Jurisp. 1st Cl. 1970; BCL 1st Cl. 1971; MA Oxon 1978). Called to the Bar, Inner Temple, 1972, Bencher, 2006; in practice, 1972–; Jt Hd of Chambers, Fountain Ct, 2003–07. Weekender, Queen's Coll., Oxford, 1972–78. Member: Jt Working Party of Law Soc. and Bar on Banking Law, 1987–91; Law Soc's Sub-Cttee on Banking Law, 1991–96; an Arbitrator: Lloyd's Modified Arbitration Scheme, 1988–92; Lloyd's Arbitration Scheme, 1993–. Vis. Lectr, 2006–07, Tutor, 2007–, Coll. of Law. Governor: Wroxham Sch., Potters Bar, 1995–2004. FCIArb 1997. *Publications:* (ed jtly) Commercial Court Procedure, 2000; (contrib.) The Law of Bank Payments, 3rd edn 2004; (regulatory editor) Encyclopaedia of Insurance Law, 2007–; (contrib.) Blackstone's Criminal Practice, 2008. *Recreation:* watching sport. *Address:* Fountain Court, Temple, EC4Y 9DH. *T:* (020) 7583 3335.

LERENIUS, Bo Åke, Hon. CBE 2005; Group Chief Executive, 1999–2007, non-executive Director, since 2007, Associated British Ports Holdings plc; *b* 11 Dec. 1946; *s* of Åke Lerenius and Elisabeth Lerenius; *m* 1st (marr. diss.); one *s* one *d*; 2nd, 2002, Gunilla Jöhncke. *Educ:* Malmö, Sweden; Westchester High Sch., LA; Univ. of Lund, Sweden (BA Business Admin). Div. Dir, Tarkett (part of Swedish Match Gp), 1983–85; Gp Pres. and CEO, Ernstromgruppen, 1985–92; Gp Chief Exec., Stena Line, 1992–98; Vice Chm., Stena Line and Dir, New Business Investments, Stena AB, 1998–99. Non-executive Director: Group 4 Securicor (formerly Securicor plc), 2004–; Land Securities Gp plc, 2004–; Thomas Cook Gp plc, 2007–. Chm., Swedish Chamber of Commerce for the UK, 2007–. Hon. DBA London Metropolitan, 2006. *Recreations:* golf, shooting. *Address:* 28 Stokenchurch Street, Fulham, SW6 3TR. *Clubs:* Royal Automobile; Royal Bachelors (Gothenburg); Falsterbo Golf (Sweden).

LE ROY LADURIE, Prof. Emmanuel Bernard; Commandeur de la Légion d'Honneur, 1996; Commandeur de l'Ordre des Arts et des Lettres; Professor of History of Modern Civilisation, Collège de France, 1973–99, now Honorary Professor; *b* 19 July 1929; *s* of Jacques Le Roy Ladurie and Léontine (*née* Dauger); *m* 1956, Madeleine Pupponi; one *s* one *d.* *Educ:* Univ. of Sorbonne (agrégé d'histoire); DèsL 1952. Teacher, Lycée de Montpellier, 1955–57; Res. Assistant, CNRS, 1957–60; Assistant, Faculté des Lettres de Montpellier, 1960–63; Asst Lectr, 1963, Dir of Studies, 1965–, Ecole Pratique des Hautes Etudes; Lectr, Faculté des Lettres de Paris, 1969; Prof., Sorbonne, 1970; UER Prof. of Geography and Social Sci., Univ. de Paris VII, 1971–. General Administrator, Bibliothèque Nationale, 1987–94 (Pres., Conseil scientifique, 1994–99). Mem. de l'Institut, Acad. des Scis morales et politiques, 1993–. Foreign Member: Amer. Philosophical Soc., 2000; Polish Acad. of Scis, 2000; For. Hon. Mem., American Acad. of Scis, 1984; Hon. FBA 1985. Hon. doctorate: Geneva, 1978; Michigan, 1981; Leeds, 1982; East Anglia, 1985; Leicester, York, 1986; Carnegie Mellon, Pittsburgh, 1987; Durham, 1987; Hull, 1990; Dublin, 1992; Albany, Haifa, Montréal, Oxford, 1993; Pennsylvania, 1995; HEC, Paris, 1999. *Publications:* Les Paysans du Languedoc, 1966; Histoire du climat depuis l'an mil, 1967, 2nd edn 1983; Le Territoire de l'historien, vol. 1 1973, vol. 2 1978; Montaillou: village occitan 1294–1324, 1975; (jtly) Histoire économique et sociale de la France, vol. 1 1450–1660, vol. 2 Paysannerie et Croissance, 1976; Le Carnaval de Romans 1579–1580 (Prix Pierre Lafue), 1980; L'Argent, l'Amour et la Mort en pays d'Oc, 1980; (jtly) Inventaire des campagnes, 1980; (jtly) L'Histoire urbaine de la France, vol. 3, 1981; Parmi les historiens, 1983; Pierre Prion: scribe, 1987; L'Histoire de France: l'état royal 1460–1610, 1987; (ed) Monarchies, 1987; L'Ancien Régime, 1991; Le siècle des Platter 1499–1628, vol. 1 Le mendiant et le professeur, 1995, vol. 2 Le voyage de Thomas Platter 1595–1599, 2000; (ed jtly) Mémoires de Jacques Le Roy Ladurie, 1997; Saint-Simon et le système de la cour, 1997; L'Historien, le chiffre et le texte, 1997; Histoire de la France des Régions, 2001; Histoire des paysans français de la peste noire à la Révolution, 2002; Histoire humaine et comparée du climat, vol. 1, 2004, vol. 2, 2006; Personnages et caractères, 2005; Ouverture, société, pouvoir, 2005. *Address:* Collège de France, 11 place Marcelin Berthelot, 75231 Paris cedex 05, France; (home) 88 rue d'Alleray, 75015 Paris, France.

LERWILL, Robert Earl, FCA; Chief Executive, Aegis Group plc, since 2005 (non-executive Director, 2000–05); *b* 21 Jan. 1952; *s* of Colin and Patricia Lerwill; *m* 1994, Nicola Keddie; two *s* three *d.* *Educ:* Nottingham Univ. (BA Hons Industrial Econs 1973). FCA 1977. Articled clerk to Sen. Manager, Arthur Andersen & Co., 1973–86; Gp Finance Dir, WPP Gp plc, 1986–96; Cable & Wireless plc: Exec. Dir, Finance, 1997–2002; CEO, Cable & Wireless Regl, 2000–03; Dep. Gp CEO, 2002–03. Non-executive Director: British American Tobacco plc, 2005–; Synergy Healthcare plc, 2005–. Dir/Trustee, Anthony Nolan Trust, 2002–07. *Recreations:* travel, motoring, motor cruising. *Address:* Aegis Group plc, 180 Great Portland Street, W1W 5QZ. *T:* (020) 7070 7700. *Clubs:* Old Blues Rugby (Motspur Park); Twickenham Yacht.

LESCHLY, Jan; Chairman and Chief Executive Officer, Care Capital LLC, since 2000; *b* 11 Sept. 1940; *m* 1963, Dr Lotte Engelbredt; four *s.* *Educ:* Copenhagen Coll. of Pharmacy (MSc Pharmacy); Copenhagen Sch. of Econs and Business Admin (BS Business Admin). Pharmaceutical industry, 1972–2000: Exec. Vice Pres. and Pres., Pharmaceutical Div., Novo Industries A/S, Denmark, 1972–79; Squibb Corporation: joined 1979; Vice-Pres., Commercial Develt, 1979–81; US Pres., 1981–84; Gp Vice-Pres. and Dir, 1984–86; Exec. Vice-Pres., 1986–88; Pres. and Chief Operating Officer, 1988–90; Chm., SmithKline Beecham Pharmaceuticals, 1990–94; Chief Exec., SmithKline Beecham, 1994–2000. Member, Board of Directors: Amer. Express Co.; Viacom Corp.; Ventro Corp.; Maersk Gp; Mem. Internat. Adv. Bd, DaimlerChrysler. Member: British Pharma Group; Bd of Dirs, Pharmaceutical Res. and Manufrs of America; Pharmaceutical Res. and Manufrs Foundn; Bd of Trustees, Nat. Foundn for Infectious Diseases; Dean's Adv. Council, Emory Univ. Business Sch. *Address:* Care Capital LLC, 47 Hulfish Street, Suite 310, Princeton, NJ 08542, USA.

LESCOEUR, Bruno Jean; Senior Executive Vice-President, International, Electricité de France, since 2004 (Executive Vice-President, Head of Generation, 2002–04); *b* 19 Nov. 1953; *m* 1976, Janick Dreyer; two *s* one *d.* *Educ:* Ecole Polytechnique, Paris. Electricité de France (EDF): responsible for pricing, 1978–87, for distribn of gas and electricity, Mulhouse, France, 1987–89; Rep., as Founder Mem., Electricity Pool in London, 1990; Head, Distribution Unit, EDF and GDF, South of France, 1991–93; Dep. Chief Financial Officer, 1994–98; Chm. and Chief Exec., London Electricity Gp plc, 1999–2002. Chevalier, Ordre National du Mérite (France), 2001. *Recreation:* sailing. *Address:* (office) 22–30 avenue de Wagram, 75008 Paris, France; 28 rue Washington, 75008 Paris, France.

LESIRGE, Ruth; Visiting Fellow and Head of Governance Practice, Centre for Charity Effectiveness, City University, since 2006; independent consultant, not-for-profit sectors, since 2002; Chief Executive, Mental Health Foundation, 2000–02; *b* 9 Aug. 1945; *d* of Alfred Brandler and Mirjam Brandler; *m* 1969, John Lesirge; two *s.* *Educ:* Manchester Univ. (Cert Ed 1967; Cert Children with Learning Difficulties 1972); Univ. of London Inst. of Educn (Dip. Adult and Contg Educn, 1984); Office of Public Management/ Sheffield Hallam Univ. (Post-grad. Cert. in Mgt 2000). Secondary sch. teacher of Eng. and literacy, Haringey, 1967–72; Adult Literacy Develt Worker, Islington and Haringey, 1973–83; Islington Adult Education Institute: Hd, Women's Educn, 1983–85; Hd, Soc. and Cultural Studies Dept, 1985–87; Hd of Area, Camden Adult Educn Inst., 1987–89; Principal, Adult Educn Service, London Bor. Waltham Forest, 1989–92; Chief Exec., Retail Trust charity, 1992–99. Member: Appraisal Cttee, NHS NICE, 2001–04; Private Inquiry, DoH, 2002–05. Vice-Chm., ACENVO, subseq. ACEVO, 1998–2002 (Trustee, 1995–2002); Trustee: Centre for Policy on Ageing, 1997–2002; Nat. Foundn for Entrepreneurship, 2000–. Hon. Lectr Medical Educn, Univ. of London, 1996. Churchill Fellow, 1981–82; Commonwealth Trust Bursary, 1988. *Publications:* (jtly) On Site, 1976; (jtly) Working Together: an approach to functional literacy, 1977; (jtly) Write Away, 1979; Images and Understandings: sequences for writing and discussion, 1984; (jtly) Appraising the Chief Executive, 2002. *Recreations:* theatre, gardening. *Address:* 100 Holden Road, N12 7DY. *T:* and *Fax:* (020) 8445 1864.

LESITER, Ven. Malcolm Leslie; Archdeacon of Bedford, 1993–2003, now Emeritus; *b* 31 Jan. 1937; *m*; four *d.* *Educ:* Cranleigh Sch.; Selwyn Coll., Cambridge (BA 1961; MA 1965); Cuddesdon Coll., Oxford. Ordained deacon, 1963, priest, 1964; Curate, Eastney, 1963–66; Curate, 1966–71, Team Vicar, 1971–73, St Paul, Hemel Hempstead; Vicar: All Saints, Leavesden, 1973–88; Radlett, 1988–93. RD, Watford, 1981–88. *Address:* 349 Ipswich Road, Colchester, Essex CO4 0HN.

LESLIE, family name of **Earl of Rothes**.

LESLIE, Sir Alan; *see* Leslie, Sir C. A. B.

LESLIE, (Alison) Mariot, CMG 2005; HM Diplomatic Service; Director General, Defence and Intelligence, Foreign and Commonwealth Office, since 2007; *b* Edinburgh, 25 June 1954; *d* of Stewart Forson Sanderson and Alison Mary Sanderson; *m* 1978,

Andrew David Leslie; two d. Educ: George Watson's Ladies' Coll., Edinburgh; Leeds Girls' High Sch.; St Hilda's Coll., Oxford (BA 1975). Scottish Office, 1975; joined HM Diplomatic Service, 1977: Singapore, 1978–81; Bonn, 1982–86; Paris (on secondment to Quai d'Orsay), 1990–92; Head, Envmt, Sci. and Energy Dept, FCO, 1992–93; Scottish Office Industry Dept, 1993–95; Head, Policy Planning Staff, FCO, 1996–98; Minister and Dep. Head of Mission, Rome, 1998–2001; Ambassador to Norway, 2002–06; Dir, Defence and Strategic Threats, FCO, 2006–07. Mem. Exec. Council, RUSI, 2006–. Recreations: food, travel, argument. Address: Foreign and Commonwealth Office, King Charles Street, SW1A 2AH.

LESLIE, Dr Andrew Greig William, FRS 2001; Senior Staff Scientist, MRC Laboratory of Molecular Biology, Cambridge, since 1991 (Staff Scientist, 1988–91); b 26 Oct. 1949; s of John and Margaret Leslie; m 1977, Catherine Alice Fuchs; two s one d (and one d decd). Educ: Jesus Coll., Cambridge (BA, MA); Univ. of Manchester (PhD 1974). Res. Asst, Purdue Univ., Indiana, 1974–79; Res. Asst, 1979–83, MRC Sen. Fellow, 1983–88, ICSTM. Publications: numerous contribs to scientific jls incl. Nature, Science, Cell, Molecular Cell. Recreations: walking, cycling, swimming, films, music. Address: MRC Laboratory of Molecular Biology, Hills Road, Cambridge CB2 0QH. T: (01223) 248011.

LESLIE, Dame Ann (Elizabeth Mary), DBE 2007; journalist and broadcaster; b Pakistan, 28 Jan. 1941; d of Norman Leslie and Theodora (née McDonald); m 1969, Michael Fletcher; one d. Educ: Presentation Convent, Matlock, Derbyshire; Convent of the Holy Child, Mayfield, Sussex; Lady Margaret Hall, Oxford (BA). Daily Express, 1962–67; freelance, 1967–: regular contributor to Daily Mail. Variety Club Women of the Year Award for journalism and broadcasting, 1981; British Press Awards Feature Writer of the Year, 1981, 1989; British Press Awards Commendation, 1980, 1983, 1985, 1987, 1991, 1996, 1999; Feature Writer of the Year Award, What the Papers Say, Granada Television, 1991; Lifetime Achievement Award, Media Soc., 1997; James Cameron Meml Award for internat. reporting, James Cameron Meml Trust, 1999; Gerald Barry Lifetime Achievement Award, BBC2/Granada/What the Papers Say, 2001; Edgar Wallace Award for outstanding reporting, London Press Club, 2002; Foreign Corresp. of the Year, BBC/Granada/What the Papers Say, 2004. Recreation: family life. Address: c/o Daily Mail, Northcliffe House, 2 Derry Street, Kensington, W8 5TT. T: (020) 7938 6000, Fax: (020) 7267 9914; e-mail: aemleslie@aol.com.

LESLIE, Christopher Michael; Director, New Local Government Network, since 2005; b 28 June 1972; s of Michael N. Leslie and Dania K. Leslie. Educ: Bingley Grammar Sch.; Univ. of Leeds (BA Hons Pol. and Parly Studies 1994; MA Indust. and Labour Studies 1996). Research Assistant: Rep. Bernie Sanders, US Congress, 1992; Gordon Brown, MP, 1993; Adminr, Bradford Labour Party, 1995–97; Researcher, Barry Seal, MEP, 1997. MP (Lab) Shipley, 1997–2005; contested (Lab) same seat, 2005. PPS to Minister of State, Cabinet Office, 1998–2001; Parly Sec., Cabinet Office, 2001–02; Parly Under-Sec., ODPM, 2002–03; Parly Under-Sec. of State, DCA, 2003–05. Mem. (Lab), Bradford MDC, 1994–98. Recreations: music, tennis, golf, travel. Address: New Local Government Network, 1st Floor, New City Court, 20 St Thomas Street, SE1 9RS.

LESLIE, Sir (Colin) Alan (Bettridge), Kt 1986; Commissioner, Foreign Compensation Commission, 1986–90; b 10 April 1922; s of Rupert Colin Leslie and Gladys Hannah Leslie (née Bettridge); m 1st, 1953, Anne Barbara (née Coates) (d 1982); two d; 2nd, 1983, Jean Margaret (Sally), widow of Dr Alan Cheatle. Educ: King Edward VII School, Lytham; Merton College, Oxford (MA Law). Solicitor. Commissioned, The Royal Scots Fusiliers, 1941–46. Legal practice, Stafford Clark & Co., Solicitors, 1948–60; Head of Legal Dept and Company Secretary, British Oxygen Co., later BOC International, then BOC Group, 1960–83. Law Society: Vice-Pres., 1984–85; Pres., 1985–86. Adjudicator, Immigration Appeals, 1990–94. Recreation: fishing. Address: Tye Cottage, Alfriston, E Sussex BN26 5TD. T: (01323) 870518; 36 Abingdon Road, W8 6AS. T: (020) 7937 2874. Club: Oxford and Cambridge.

LESLIE, Rt Rev. (Ernest) Kenneth, OBE 1972; b 14 May 1911; s of Rev. Ernest Thomas Leslie and Margaret Jane Leslie; m 1941, Isabel Daisy Wilson (d 1994); two s one d (and one s decd). Educ: Trinity Gram. Sch., Kew, Vict.; Trinity Coll., University of Melbourne (BA); Aust. Coll. of Theology (ThL, 2nd Cl. 1933, Th Schol. 1951, 2nd Cl. 1952). Deacon, 1934; priest, 1935; Asst Curate, Holy Trinity, Coburg, 1934–37; Priest-in-Charge, Tennant Creek, Dio. Carpentaria, 1937–38; Alice Springs with Tennant Creek, 1938–40; Rector of Christ Church, Darwin, 1940–44; Chaplain, AIF, 1942–45; Rector of Alice Springs with Tennant Creek, 1945–46; Vice-Warden, St John's Coll., Morpeth, NSW, 1947–52; Chap. Geelong Church of Eng. Gram. Sch., Timbertop Branch, 1953–58; Bishop of Bathurst, 1959–81. Hon. DLitt Charles Sturt, 1996. Recreations: walking, woodwork. Address: Hostel B4, Ilumba Gardens, Kelso, NSW 2795, Australia.

LESLIE, (Harman) John; Master, Queen's Bench Division, High Court of Justice, since 1996; b 8 April 1946; s of Percy Leslie and Sheila Mary Leslie (née Harris); m 1st, 1971, Alix Helen Cohen (marr. diss. 1980); two s; 2nd, 1986, Valerie Gibson. Educ: Dover Coll.; Clare Coll., Cambridge (BA 1968). Called to the Bar, Middle Temple, 1969, Bencher, 2001; in practice at the Bar, 1969–96. Member: Civil Procedure Rule Cttee, 1997–2002; Vice-Chancellor's Wkg Party on Civil Procedure Practice Directions, 1997–2000. Gov., Dover Coll., 1974– (Mem. Council, 1975–84). Publications: (contrib.) Halsbury's Laws of England, 4th edn, 1999, reissued 2001; (ed jtly) Civil Court Practice, 1999–; Civil Court Manual, 1999; (contrib.) Atkin's Court Forms, 2001–. Recreations: France, bridge, woodworking. Address: Royal Courts of Justice, Strand, WC2A 2LL. Club: Royal Automobile.

LESLIE, Prof. Ian Malcolm, PhD; Robert Sansom Professor of Computer Science, since 1998 and Head of Department, 1999–2004, University of Cambridge Computer Laboratory; Pro-Vice-Chancellor, University of Cambridge, since 2004; Fellow of Christ's College, Cambridge, since 1985; b 11 Feb. 1955; s of Douglas Alexander Leslie and Phyllis Margaret Leslie; m 1st, 1986, Patricia Valerie Vyoral (marr. diss. 2000); one s one d; 2nd, 2001, Celia Mary Denton (marr. diss. 2004); one d. Educ: Univ. of Toronto (BASc 1977; MASc 1979); Darwin Coll., Cambridge (PhD 1983). Asst Lectr, 1983–86, Lectr, 1986–98, Univ. of Cambridge Computer Lab. Publications: guest ed. and contrib. on selected areas in communication to IEEE Jl. Address: Christ's College, Cambridge CB2 3BU.

LESLIE, James Bolton, AC 1993 (AO 1984); MC 1944; ED 1966; Chancellor, Deakin University, 1987–96; b 27 Nov. 1922; s of Stuart Deacon Leslie and Dorothy Clare (née Murphy); m 1955, Alison Baker three s one d. Educ: Trinity Grammar Sch., Melbourne; Harvard Business Sch., Boston, USA. Served war, Australian Infantry, Pacific Theatre, 1941–46. Mobil Oil Australia Ltd: joined, 1946; Manager, Fiji, 1947–50; various postings, Australia, 1950–59; Mobil Corp., New York, 1959–61; Gen. Manager, New South Wales, 1961–66; Director, Mobil Australia, 1966–68; Chm. and Chief Exec., Mobil New Zealand, 1968–72; Chairman: Mobil Australia and Pacific, 1972–80; Qantas Airways, 1980–89; Christies Australia Ltd, 1990–95; Boral Ltd, 1991–94. Chm., Corps of

Commissionaires Aust Ltd, 1991–; Dep. Chm., Equity Trustees, 1990–97. Hon. LLD Deakin, 1997. Recreations: golf, gardening, art collecting. Address: 42 Grey Street, East Melbourne, Victoria 3002, Australia. T: (3) 94196149. Clubs: Melbourne, Melbourne Cricket, Beefsteak, Victoria Racing (Melbourne).

LESLIE, John; see Leslie, H. J.

LESLIE, Sir John (Norman Ide), 4th Bt cr 1876; b 6 Dec. 1916; s of Sir (John Randolph) Shane Leslie, 3rd Bt and Marjorie (d 1951), y d of Henry C. Ide, Vermont, USA; S father, 1971. Educ: Downside; Magdalene College, Cambridge (BA 1938). Captain, Irish Guards; served War of 1939–45 (prisoner-of-war). Kt of Honour and Devotion, SMO Malta, 1947; KCSG 1958. Publication: Never a Dull Moment (memoirs), 2006. Recreations: ornithology, ecology. Heir: nephew Shaun Rudolph Christopher Leslie [b 4 June 1947; m 1987, Charlotte Bing (marr. diss. 1989)]. Address: Castle Leslie, Glaslough, Co. Monaghan, Ireland. Clubs: Travellers; Circolo della Caccia (Rome).

LESLIE, Rt Rev. Kenneth; see Leslie, Rt Rev. E. K.

LESLIE, Mariot; see Leslie, A. M.

LESLIE, Stephen Windsor; QC 1993; b 21 April 1947; s of Leslie Leonard Leslie and Celia Leslie (née Schulsinger); m 1st, 1974, Bridget Caroline Oldham (marr. diss. 1989); two d; 2nd, 1989, Amrit Kumari Mangra (marr. diss. 2006); one s. Educ: Brighton Coll.; King's Coll. London (LLB). Called to the Bar, Lincoln's Inn, 1971, Bencher, 2001. Liveryman, Feltmakers' Co., 1998–. Publications: articles in The Times and New Law Jl. Recreations: Spanish sun, gardening, haggling for a bargain, the telephone. Address: 32 Furnival Street, EC4A 1JQ. Clubs: Carlton; Thunderers'.

LESLIE MELVILLE, family name of **Earl of Leven and Melville.**

LESOURNE, Jacques François; Officier de la Légion d'Honneur, 1993; Commandeur de l'ordre National de Mérite, 1981; Officier des Palmes Académiques, 1995; Directeur-gérant, Le Monde, 1991–94; Professor of Economics, Conservatoire National des Arts et Métiers, since 1974; b 26 Dec. 1928; s of André Lesourne and Simone Guille; m 1961, Odile Melin; one s two d (and one s decd). Educ: Ecole Polytechnique; Ecole Nationale Supérieure des Mines, Paris. Head, Econ. Dept, French Coal Mines, 1954–57; Directeur général, later Pres., SEMA, 1958–75; Dir, Interfutures Project, OECD, 1976–79. Pres., Internat. Fedn of OR Socs, 1986–88; Vice-President: Internat. Inst. for Applied Systems Analysis, 1973–79; Centre for European Policy Studies, 1987–93; Member Council: Inst. of Mgt Science, 1976–79; Eur. Econ. Assoc., 1984–89; Acad. des Technologies, 2000–; Mem., Applications Cttee, Acad. des Scis, Paris, 1999–. Harold Lander Prize, Canadian OR Soc., 1991. Publications: Technique économique et gestion industrielle, 1958 (Economic Technique and Industrial Management, 1962); Le Calcul économique, 1964; Du bon usage de l'étude économique dans l'entreprise, 1966; (jtly) Matière grise année O, 1970 (The Management Revolution, 1971); Le Calcul économique, théorie et applications, 1972 (Cost-Benefit Analysis and Economic Theory, 1975); Modèles économiques de croissance de l'entreprise, 1972; (jtly) Une Nouvelle industrie: la matière grise, 1973; Les Systèmes de destin, 1976; A Theory of the Individual for Economic Analysis, 1977; (jtly) L'Analyse des décisions d'aménagement regional, 1979; Demain la France dans le monde, 1980; Les Mille Sentiers de l'avenir, 1982 (World Perspectives—a European Assessment, 1982); (jtly) Facilitating Development in a Changing Third World, 1983; Soirs et lendemains de fête: journal d'un homme tranquille, 1981–84 (autobiog.), 1984; (jtly) La gestion des villes, analyse des décisions d'économie urbaine, 1985; (jtly) La Fin des habitudes, 1985; L'Entreprise et ses futurs, 1985; L'après-Communisme, de l'Atlantique à l'Oural, 1990 (After-communism, from the Atlantic to the Urals, 1991); L'economie de l'ordre et du désordre, 1991 (The Economics of Order and Disorder, 1992); Vérités et mensonges sur le chômage, 1995; Le modèle français, grandeur et décadence, 1998; Un homme de notre siècle, 2000; (jtly) Leçons de microéconomie evolutionniste, 2003; Démocratie, marché et gouvernance, 2004; (jtly) Evolutionary Microeconomics, 2006; (jtly) FutuRIS, la recherche et l'innovation en France, 2006. Recreation: piano. Address: 52 rue de Vaugirard, 75006 Paris, France.

LESSELS, Norman, CBE 1993; Chairman, Cairn Energy PLC, 1991–2002 (Director, 1988–2002); b 2 Sept. 1938; s of John Clark Lessels and Gertrude Margaret Ellen Lessels (née Jack); m 1st, 1960, Gillian Durward Lessels (née Clark) (d 1979); one s (and one s one d decd); 2nd, 1981, Christine Stevenson Lessels (née Hitchman). Educ: Melville Coll.; Edinburgh Acad. CA (Scotland) 1961. CA apprentice with Graham Smart & Annan, Edinburgh, 1955–60; with Thomson McLintock & Co., London, 1960–61; Partner, Wallace & Somerville, Edinburgh, merged with Whinney Murray & Co., 1969, latterly Ernst & Whinney, 1962–80; Partner, 1980–93, Sen. Partner, 1993–98, Chiene & Tait, CA. Director: Standard Life Assurance Co., 1978–2002 (Dep. Chm., 1982–88; Chm., 1988–98); Scottish Eastern Investment Trust, 1980–99; Bank of Scotland, 1988–97; Havelock Europa, 1989–98 (Chm., 1993–98); Robert Wiseman Dairies, 1994–2003; Martin Currie Portfolio Investment Trust, 1999–2001. Pres., Inst. of Chartered Accountants of Scotland, 1987–88. Recreations: golf, bridge, music. Address: 17 India Street, Edinburgh EH3 6HE. T: (0131) 225 5596. Clubs: New (Edinburgh); Hon. Company of Edinburgh Golfers, Royal & Ancient Golf.

LESSING, Charlotte; Editor of Good Housekeeping, 1973–87; freelance writer; b 14 May; m 1948, Walter B. Lessing (d 1989); three d. Educ: Henrietta Barnet Sch.; evening classes. Univ. of London Dipl. Eng. Lit. Journalism and public relations: New Statesman and Nation; Royal Society of Medicine; Lilliput (Hulton Press); Notley Public Relations; Good Housekeeping: Dep. Editor, 1964–73; Editor, 1973–87; Founder Editor, Country Living, 1985–86. PPA Editor of the Year (for Good Housekeeping), 1982; Wine Writer of the Year, Wine Guild/Taittinger, 1995. Ordre du Mérite Agricole (France), 1996. Publications: short stories, travel and feature articles; monthly wine page in The Lady, 1991–. Address: 2 Roseneath Road, SW11 6AH.

LESSING, Mrs Doris (May), CH 2000; CLit 2001; author; b Persia, 22 Oct. 1919; d of Captain Alfred Cook Tayler and Emily Maude McVeagh; lived in Southern Rhodesia, 1924–49; m 1st, 1939, Frank Charles Wisdom (marr. diss. 1943); one s one d; 2nd, 1945, Gottfried Anton Nicholas Lessing (marr. diss. 1949); one s. Associate Member: AAAL, 1974; Nat. Inst. of Arts and Letters (US), 1974. Mem., Inst. for Cultural Res., 1974. Hon. Fellow, MLA (Amer.), 1974. Hon. DLitt: Princeton, 1989; Durham, 1990; Warwick, 1994; Bard Coll., NY State, 1994; Harvard, 1995; London, 1999. Austrian State Prize for European Literature, 1981; Shakespeare Prize, Hamburg, 1982; Grinzane Cavour Award, Italy, 1989; Premio Internacional, Cataluña, 1999; David Cohen British Lit. Prize, 2001; Prince of Asturias Prize, 2001; Nobel Prize for Literature, 2007. Publications: The Grass is Singing, 1950 (filmed 1981); This Was the Old Chief's Country, 1951; Martha Quest, 1952; Five, 1953 (Somerset Maugham Award, Soc. of Authors, 1954); A Proper Marriage, 1954; Retreat to Innocence, 1956; Going Home, 1957; The Habit of Loving (short stories), 1957; A Ripple from the Storm, 1958; Fourteen Poems, 1959; In Pursuit of the English, 1960 (adapted for stage, 1990); The Golden Notebook, 1962 (Prix Médicis 1976 for French trans., Carnet d'or); A Man and Two Women (short stories), 1963; African Stories, 1964; Landlocked, 1965; The Four-Gated City, 1969; Briefing for a Descent into Hell, 1971; The Story of a Non-Marrying Man (short stories), 1972; The Summer Before the Dark, 1973; The Memoirs of a Survivor, 1975 (filmed 1981); Collected Stories: Vol. I, To Room Nineteen, 1978; Vol. II, The Temptation of Jack Orkney, 1978; Canopus in Argos: Archives: Re Planet 5, Shikasta, 1979; The Marriages Between Zones Three, Four and Five, 1980; The Sirian Experiments, 1981; The Making of the Representative for Planet 8, 1982 (libretto, 1988); The Sentimental Agents in the Volyen Empire, 1983; The Diaries of Jane Somers, 1984 (Diary of a Good Neighbour, 1983; If the Old Could..., 1984; published under pseudonym Jane Somers); The Good Terrorist, 1985 (W. H. Smith Literary Award, 1986; Palermo Prize and Premio Internazionale Mondello, 1987); The Fifth Child, 1988; Doris Lessing Reader, 1990; London Observed (short stories), 1992; Love, Again, 1996; Playing the Game, 1996; Mara and Dann: an adventure, 1999; Ben, in the World, 2000; The Sweetest Dream, 2001; The Grandmothers, 2003; The Story of General Dann and Mara's Daughter, Griot and the Snow Dog, 2005; The Cleft, 2006; Alfred and Emily, 2008; non-fiction: Going Home, 1957; Particularly Cats, 1966, rev. edn as Particularly Cats and More Cats, 1990; Prisons We Choose to Live Inside, 1986; The Wind Blows Away Our Words, 1987; African Laughter: four visits to Zimbabwe, 1992; Under My Skin: volume one of my autobiography to 1949, 1994 (James Tait Black Meml Prize, 1995; LA Times Book Prize, 1995); A Small Personal Voice, 1994; Walking in the Shade: volume two of my autobiography 1949–1962, 1997; Time Bites (essays), 2004; play: Play with a Tiger, 1962. Address: c/o Jonathan Clowes Ltd, Iron Bridge House, Bridge Approach, NW1 8BD.

LESSOF, Leila, OBE 2000; FRCP, FFPH; Chairman, Moorfields Eye Hospital NHS Trust, 1998–2001; b 4 June 1932; d of Lionel Liebster and Renée (née Segalov); m 1960, Maurice Hart Lessof, qv; one s two d. Educ: Queen's Coll., Harley St; Royal Free Hosp. Sch. of Medicine (MB BS; DMRD). FFPH (FFPHM 1986); FRCP 2000. Jun. posts, Royal Free Hosp., London Hosp. and UCH; Consultant Radiologist and Clinical Tutor, Hackney Hosp., 1964–78; Registrar in Public Health Medicine, KCH and Guy's Hosp., 1978–82; Director of Public Health: Islington HA, 1982–90; Kensington, Chelsea and Westminster HA, 1990–95; Chm., Westminster Assoc. for Mental Health, 1995–98. Recreations: opera, theatre, travel. Address: 8 John Spencer Square, N1 2LZ. T: (020) 7226 0919.

LESSOF, Prof. Maurice Hart, MD; FRCP; Professor of Medicine, University of London at United Medical and Dental Schools (Guy's Hospital), 1971–89, now Emeritus; b 4 June 1924; s of Noah and Fanny Lessof; m 1960, Leila Liebster (see L. Lessof); one s two d. Educ: City of London Sch.; King's Coll., Cambridge (MA 1945; MD 1956). Appts on junior staff of Guy's Hosp., Canadian Red Cross Memorial Hosp., Johns Hopkins Hosp., etc; Clinical Immunologist and Physician, Guy's Hosp., 1967. Chairman: SE Thames Regl Med. Audit Cttee, 1990–91; Lewisham NHS Trust, 1993–97 (Dep. Chm., Guy's and Lewisham NHS Trust, 1991–93); Royal Hospitals NHS Trust, 1998–99. Adviser on Allergy, DHSS, 1982–91. Vice-Pres. and Sen. Censor, RCP, 1987–88; Past Pres., British Soc. for Allergy. Mem. Senate, London Univ., 1981–85. Mem., Johns Hopkins Soc. of Scholars, 1991. FKC 2005. Publications: (ed) Immunological Aspects of Cardiovascular Diseases, 1981; (ed) Immunological and Clinical Aspects of Allergy, 1984 (Spanish and Portuguese edns, 1987); (ed) Clinical Reactions to Food, 1983; (ed) Allergy: an international textbook, 1987; Food Intolerance, 1992 (Spanish edn 1996); Food Allergy: issues for the food industry, 1997. Recreations: sculpting, painting. Address: 8 John Spencer Square, Canonbury, N1 2LZ. T: (020) 7226 0919. Club: Athenæum.

LESSORE, John Viviand; artist; b 16 June 1939; s of Frederick and Helen Lessore; m 1962, Paule Marie Reveille; four s. Educ: Merchant Taylors' Sch.; Slade Sch. of Fine Art. Principal exhibitions: London: Beaux Arts Gall., 1965; New Art Centre, 1971; Theo Waddington, 1981; Stoppenbach & Delestre, 1983, 1985; Nigel Greenwood, 1990; Theo Waddington and Robert Stoppenbach, 1994; Theo Waddington Fine Art, 1997; Berkeley Sq. Gall., 2002; Annely Juda Fine Art, 2004; Solomon Gall., Dublin, 1995; Miriam Shiell Fine Art, Toronto, 1997; Wolsey Art Gall., Christchurch Mansion, Ipswich, 1999; Ranger's House, Blackheath, 2000; Annandale Gall., Sydney, 2005; works in public collections include: Leicester Educn Cttee; Arts Council; Royal Acad.; Tate Gall.; Contemporary Arts Soc.; Norwich Castle; British Council; Accenture; NPG; BM. Co-founder, Prince's Drawing Sch., 2000. Trustee, Nat. Gall., 2003–. 1st Prize, Korn/Ferry Internat. Public Award, 1991; Lynn Painter-Stainers' 1st Prize and Gold Medal, 2006. Address: c/o Annely Juda Fine Art, 23 Dering Street, W1S 1AW. T: (020) 7629 7578, Fax: (020) 7491 2139; e-mail: john.lessore@lineone.net.

LESTER, family name of **Baron Lester of Herne Hill.**

LESTER OF HERNE HILL, Baron cr 1993 (Life Peer), of Herne Hill in the London Borough of Southwark; **Anthony Paul Lester;** QC 1975; QC (NI); a Recorder, 1987–93; b 3 July 1936; e s of Harry and Kate Lester; m 1971, Catherine Elizabeth Debora Wassey; one s one d. Educ: City of London Sch.; Trinity Coll., Cambridge (Exhibnr) (BA); Harvard Law Sch. (Harkness Commonwealth Fund Fellowship) (LLM). Served RA, 1955–57, 2nd Lieut. Called to Bar, Lincoln's Inn, 1963 (Mansfield scholar), Bencher, 1985; called to Bar of N Ireland, 1984; Irish Bar, 1983. Special Adviser to: Home Secretary, 1974–76; Standing Adv. Commn on Human Rights, 1975–77; UK Legal Expert, Network Cttee on Equal Pay and Sex Discrimination, EEC, 1983–93. Member: H of L Sub-Cttee, on European Law and Institutions, Inter-Govtl Conf., 1996; Mem., Parly Jt Human Rights Commn, 2001–04, 2005–. Ind. Advr to Sec. of State for Justice on aspects of constitutional reform, 2007–. Hon. Vis. Prof., UCL, 1983–; Hon. Adjunct Prof. of Law, Univ. Coll. Cork, 2007–. Lectures: Owen J. Roberts, Univ. of Pennsylvania Law Sch., 1976; F. A. Mann, London, 1983; Rubin, Columbia Law Sch., 1988; Street, Manchester, 1993; Lionel Cohen, Hebrew Univ. of Jerusalem, 1994; Stephen Lawrence, London, 2000; Thomas More, and Denning Soc., Lincoln's Inn, 2000. Mem., Bd of Overseers, Univ. of Pennsylvania Law Sch., 1978–89. Pres., Interights, 1991–; Chm., Runnymede Trust, 1991–93; Member: Council, Justice, 1977–; Amer. Law Inst., 1985–; Bd of Dirs, Salzburg Seminar, 1996–2000; Internat. Adv. Bd, Open Soc. Inst., 2000–; Co-Chm., Exec. Bd, European Roma Rights Center, Budapest, 1999–2001. Gov., British Inst. of Human Rights. Member: Adv. Bd, Inst. of European Public Law, Hull Univ. Adv. Cttee, Centre for Public Law, Univ of Cambridge, 1999–. Mem., Amer. Philos. Soc., 2003; Hon. Mem., Amer. Acad. of Arts and Scis, 2002. Mem., Bd of Govs, James Allen's Girls' Sch., 1984–94 (Chm., 1987–91); Gov., Westminster Sch., 1998–2001. Mem. Editl Bd, Public Law. Publications: Justice in the American South, 1964 (Amnesty Internat.); (co-ed.) Shawcross and Beaumont on Air Law, 3rd edn, 1964; (co-author) Race and Law, 1972; (ed) Constitutional Law and Human Rights, 1996; (co-ed) Human Rights Law and Practice, 1999, 2nd edn, 2004; contributor to: British Nationality, Immigration and Race Relations, in Halsbury's Laws of England, 4th edn, 1973, repr. 1992; The Changing Constitution (ed Jowell and Oliver), 1985, 6th edn 2007. Address: Blackstone Chambers, Blackstone House, Temple, EC4Y 9BW. T: (020) 7583 1770.

LESTER, Sir James Theodore, (Sir Jim), Kt 1996; adviser on parliamentary and government affairs; b 23 May 1932; s of Arthur Ernest and Marjorie Lester; m (marr. diss. 1989); two s; m 1989. Educ: Nottingham High School. Mem. Notts CC, 1967–74. MP (C) Beeston, Feb. 1974–1983, Broxtowe, 1983–97; contested (C) Broxtowe, 1997. An Opposition Whip, 1976–79; Parly Under-Sec. of State, Dept of Employment, 1979–81. Mem., Select Cttee on Foreign affairs, 1982–97; Vice-Chm., All Party Gp on overseas develt, 1983–97. Deleg. to Council of Europe and WEU, 1975–76. Recreations: reading, music, motor racing, travelling. Address: 9 Field House Farm, Brancaster, Norfolk PE31 8AG.

LESTER, Nicholas; Corporate Director, Services, London Councils, since 2008; b 20 March 1953; s of Frank and Eve Lester; partner, Tom Davis. Educ: Manchester Grammar Sch.; University Coll. London (BSc 1976; DipArch 1978). FCILT 1986. Architectl Asst, Sutton LBC, 1977–78; Asst Dir, 1978–80, Dir, 1980–84, Transport 2000; Greater London Council: Industry and Employment Officer, 1984–85; Public Transport Officer, 1985–86; Planning and Transport Officer, ALA, 1986–91; London Parking Dir, 1992–98; Chief Exec., Transport Cttee for London, 1998–2001; Dir, Transport, Envmt and Planning, Assoc. of London Govt, subseq. London Councils, 2001–08. Founder and Chm., London Cycling Campaign, 1978–80. Dir, Friends of the Earth Ltd, 1986–88. Chairman: London Transport Passengers' Cttee, 1983–85; Nat. Consumer Congress, 1985; Pres., British Parking Assoc., 1997–2000; Vice Pres., Europ. Parking Assoc., 2004–07. Publication: (contrib.) Travel Sickness, 1992. Recreations: food and drink, travel (especially by train and bicycle), dogs and cats (especially otterhounds), entertaining and being entertained. Address: London Councils, 59½ Southwark Street, SE1 0AL. T: (020) 7934 9905, Fax: (020) 7934 9920; e-mail: nick.lester@londoncouncils.gov.uk.

LESTER, Paul John, CBE 2007; Chief Executive, VT Group plc (formerly Vosper Thornycroft Holdings), since 2002; b 20 Sept. 1949; s of John Trevor Lester and late Joyce Ethel Lester; m 1973, Valerie Osbourn (separated); one s one d; partner, Karen Lester (née White); one d. Educ: Trent Poly. (BSc (Hons) Mech. Engrg; Dip Mgt Studies (Distinction)). Sen. Management, Dowty Group, 1968–80; Gen. Management, Schlumberger, UK, France, USA, 1980–87; Man. Dir, Defense & Air Systems, Dowty Gp, 1987–90; Chief Exec., Graseby plc, 1990–97; Gp Man. Dir, Balfour Beatty plc, 1997–2002. Dir, Vosper Thornycroft Hldgs plc, 1998–2002. Chairman: A & P Gp, 1993–99; High Integrity Solutions Ltd, 2003–08; Solent Synergy Ltd, 2006–; non-executive Director: Civica plc, 2004–08; Chloride plc, 2007–. Mem., Adv. Bd, Alchemy Partners Ltd, 1997–2008. Pres., EEF, 2000–03 (Sen. Dep. Pres., 1999–2000); Chm., Economic Policy Cttee, 1993–2000). Vis. Prof., Nottingham Trent Univ., 2003–. Member: SE England Sci., Engrg and Technol. Adv. Council, 2003–07; Govt Manufg Forum, 2004–07; Chairman: SE Regl Adv. Gp, Nat. Skills Acad. for Manufg, 2007–; SkillENG, 2007–; Chm., Solent Leadership Team, 2007–, Mem., SE Leadership Team, 2007–, BITC. President: Business Services Assoc., 2004–07; Soc. of Maritime Industries, 2005–. Gov., Barnet Coll. of Further Educn, 1993–2002; Mem. Council, Southampton Univ., 2007–. Hon. LLD Portsmouth, 2008. Recreations: tennis, weight training, running, football; life-long West Bromwich Albion supporter. Address: VT Group plc, VT House, Grange Drive, Hedge End, Southampton SO30 2DQ.

LESTER, Richard; film director; b 19 Jan. 1932; s of Elliott and Ella Young Lester; m 1956, Deirdre Vivian Smith; one s one d. Educ: Wm Penn Charter Sch.; University of Pennsylvania (BSc). Television Director: CBS (USA), 1951–54; AR (Dir TV Goon Shows), 1956. Directed The Running, Jumping and Standing Still Film (Acad. Award nomination; 1st prize San Francisco Festival, 1960). Feature Films directed: It's Trad, Dad, 1962; Mouse on the Moon, 1963; A Hard Day's Night, 1964; The Knack, 1964 (Grand Prix, Cannes Film Festival); Help, 1965 (Best Film Award and Best Dir Award, Rio de Janeiro Festival); A Funny Thing Happened on the Way to the Forum, 1966; How I won the War, 1967; Petulia, 1968; The Bed Sitting Room, 1969 (Gandhi Peace Prize, Berlin Film Festival); The Three Musketeers, 1973; Juggernaut, 1974 (Best Dir award, Teheran Film Fest.); The Four Musketeers, 1974; Royal Flash, 1975; Robin and Marian, 1976; The Ritz, 1976; Butch and Sundance: the early days, 1979; Cuba, 1979; Superman II, 1981; Superman III, 1983; Finders Keepers, 1984; The Return of the Musketeers, 1989; Get Back, 1991. Recreations: music, tennis. Address: Twickenham Film Studios, St Margaret's, Twickenham, Middx TW1 2AW.

LESTER, Sheila Mary; see Corrall, S. M.

L'ESTRANGE, Michael Gerard, AO 2007; Secretary, Department of Foreign Affairs and Trade, Australia, since 2005; b 12 Oct. 1952; m 1983, Jane Allen; five s. Educ: St Aloysius Coll., Sydney; Univ. of Sydney (BA Hons); Oxford Univ. (NSW Rhodes Schol., 1976–79; BA 1st Cl. Hons, MA). Dept of Prime Minister and Cabinet, Canberra, 1981–89; Harkness Fellow, Georgetown Univ. and Univ. of Calif, Berkeley, 1987–89; Sen. Advr, Office of Leader of Opposition, 1989–95; Exec. Dir, Menzies Res. Centre, Canberra, 1995–96; Sec. to Cabinet, and Hd, Cabinet Policy Unit, 1996–2000; High Comr for Australia in UK, 2000–05. Recreations: cricket, Rugby, golf. Address: Department of Foreign Affairs and Trade, R. G. Casey Building, John McEwen Crescent, Barton, ACT 0221, Australia.

LE SUEUR, Prof. Andrew Philip; Professor of Public Law, Queen Mary, University of London, since 2006; b 7 April 1964; s of George and Elaine Le Sueur. Educ: Hautlieu Sch., Jersey; London Sch. of Econs (LLB 1986). Called to the Bar, Middle Temple, 1987; University College London: Lectr in Laws, 1988–98; Reader in Laws, 1998–2000; Faculty of Laws; Hon. Sen. Res. Fellow, Constitution Unit, 2001–; Barber Prof. of Jurisprudence, Univ. of Birmingham, 2001–06. Specialist Adviser: H of C Constitutional Affairs Cttee, 2003–05; H of L Select Cttee on Constitutional Reform Bill, 2005; Legal Advr, H of L Constitution Cttee, 2006–. Editor, Public Law, 2002–. Publications: (with M. Sunkin) Public Law, 1997; (ed) Building the UK's New Supreme Court: national and comparative perspectives, 2004; (with Lord Woolf and J. Jowell) de Smith's Judicial Review, 6th edn 2007; articles on constitutional and administrative law. Recreation: pottering about. Address: Department of Law, Queen Mary, University of London, 339 Mile End Road, E1 4NS. T: (020) 7882 5146; e-mail: a.lesueur@qmul.ac.uk. Club: Athenæum.

LETH, Air Vice-Marshal David Richard H.; see Hawkins-Leth.

LETHBRIDGE, Prof. Robert David, PhD; Master of Fitzwilliam College, Cambridge, since 2005; Hon. Professor of Nineteenth-Century French Literature, University of Cambridge, since 2006; b 24 Feb. 1947; s of Albert Lethbridge and Muriel Alice (née de Saram); m 1970, Vera Lenore Laycock; one s one d. Educ: Mill Hill Sch.; Univ. of Kent at Canterbury (BA 1st cl. Hons 1969); McMaster Univ. (MA 1970); St John's Coll., Cambridge (MA 1973; PhD 1975). Fitzwilliam College, Cambridge: Fellow, 1973–94 (Life Fellow, 1994); Leathersellers' Fellow, 1973–78; Tutor, 1975–92, Sen. Tutor, 1982–92; Coll. Lectr (jtly with Trinity Hall), 1978–80; Asst Lectr in French, 1980–85, Lectr, 1985–94, Univ. of Cambridge; University of London: Prof. of French Lang. and Lit., 1994–2005, now Emeritus; Hd, Dept of French, 1995–97, Dean, Grad. Sch., 1997–98, Vice–Principal (Acad.), 1997–2002, Vis. Prof., 2003–05, Royal Holloway; Dir,

British Inst. in Paris, later Univ. of London Inst. in Paris, 2003–05. Visiting Professor: UCSB, 1986; Univ. of Melbourne, 2003; Hon. Prof., Queen Mary, Univ. of London, 2003–05. Chevalier des Palmes Académiques (France), 1998. *Publications:* Maupassant: Pierre et Jean, 1984; (ed with T. O'Keefe) Zola and the Craft of Fiction, 1990; (ed) Germinal, 1993; (ed with P. Collier) Artistic Relations, Literature and the Visual Arts in Nineteenth–Century France, 1994; (ed with C. Lloyd) Maupassant: conteur et romancier, 1994; (ed) L'Assommoir, 1995; (ed) Pot-Bouille, 2000; (ed) La Débâcle, 2000; (ed) Bel-Ami, 2001; (ed) Pierre et Jean, 2001; contribs to learned jls and collective works. *Recreations:* watching Rugby, contemplating the sea. *Address:* Master's Lodge, Fitzwilliam College, Cambridge CB3 0DG. *T:* (01223) 332029; *e-mail:* master@fitz.cam.ac.uk. *Club:* Oxford and Cambridge.

LETHBRIDGE, Sir Thomas (Periam Hector Noel), 7th Bt *cr* 1804; *b* 17 July 1950; *s* of Sir Hector Wroth Lethbridge, 6th Bt, and of Evelyn Diana, *d* of late Lt-Col Francis Arthur Gerard Noel, OBE; *S* father, 1978; *m* 1st, 1976, Susan Elizabeth Rocke (marr. diss. 1998); four *s* two *d*; 2nd, 2007, Mrs Ann-Marie Fenwick, *d* of Thomas Mott, Ely. *Educ:* Milton Abbey. Studied farming, Cirencester Agricultural Coll., 1969–70; Man. Dir, Art Gallery, Dorset and London, 1972–77; also fine art specialist in sporting paintings and engravings. *Recreations:* riding, shooting, swimming, bicycling. *Heir: s* John Francis Buckler Noel Lethbridge [*b* 10 March 1977; *m* 2007, Nicola Elizabeth, *e d* of Lt Col Anthony Barkas]. *Address:* c/o Drummonds, 49 Charing Cross, SW1A 2DX.

LETT, Hugh Brian Gordon; QC 2008; a Recorder of the Crown Court, since 1993; *b* Belfast, 9 Aug. 1949; *s* of Maj. Gordon Lett, DSO and Sheila Buckston Lett; *m* 1979, Angela Susan Jaques; three *s* one *d*. *Educ:* Marlborough Coll.; Council for Legal Educn. Called to the Bar, Inner Temple, 1971; in practice as barrister specialising in fraud, money laundering and serious crime. Asst Recorder, 1990–93; Hd of Chambers, South Western Chambers, Taunton, 1993–2002. Chm., Monte San Martino Trust, 1997–2005. Commendatore, Ordine al Merito della Repubblica Italiana, 2007. *Recreations:* mountain walking in Italy, re-creating POW escape routes, history of Italian War of Liberation, watching cricket and Rugby. *Address:* 2 Paper Buildings, Temple, EC4Y 7ET. *T:* (020) 7556 5500, *Fax:* (020) 7583 3423; *e-mail:* brian.lett@2pb.co.uk. *Club:* MCC.

LETTE, Kathryn Marie; author; *b* Sydney, 11 Nov. 1958; *d* of Mervyn and Val Lette; *m* 1990, Geoffrey Ronald Robertson, *qv*; one *s* one *d*. Author, playwright, satirical columnist; Writer-in-Residence, Savoy Hotel, London, 2003–04. *Publications: novels:* Puberty Blues, 1979 (jtly); Hits and Ms, 1984; Girls' Night Out, 1988; The Llama Parlour, 1991; Foetal Attraction, 1993; Mad Cows, 1996; Altar Ego, 1998; Nip 'n' Tuck, 2000; Dead Sexy, 2002; How to Kill your Husband (and other handy household hints), 2006; To Love, Honour and Betray—Till Divorce Us Do Part, 2008; *plays:* Wet Dreams, 1985; Perfect Mismatch, 1985; Grommitts, 1986; I'm So Happy for You, I Really Am, 1991. *Address:* c/o Ed Victor, 6 Bayley Street, Bedford Square, WC1B 3HB. *T:* (020) 7304 4100.

LETTS, Anthony Ashworth; President, Charles Letts Group, 1994–96 (Chairman, Charles Letts Holdings Ltd, 1977–94); *b* 3 July 1935; *s* of Leslie Charles Letts and Elizabeth Mary (*née* Gibson); *m* 1962, Rosa Maria Ciarrapico; one *s* one *d*. *Educ:* Marlborough Coll.; Cambridge Univ. (MAEcon); Yale Univ. (Industrial Admin). National Service, RE, 2 Lieut, 1954–56. Joined Charles Letts & Co. Ltd, 1960; Man. Dir, 1965 (Charles Letts family business founded by John Letts (g g g grandfather), 1796). Director: Cambridge Market Intelligence, 1994–2002; Accademia Club Ltd, 1996–2002; Gov., Westminster Kingsway (formerly Westminster) Coll., London, 1993–2002. *Recreations:* tennis, sailing, hill walking, theatre. *Address:* 95A Cambridge Street, SW1V 4PY. *T:* (020) 7828 0448. *Club:* Hurlingham.

LETTS, Melinda Jane Frances, OBE 2003; charity and health policy consultant, since 1998; accredited executive coach, since 2004; *b* 6 April 1956; *d* of Richard Letts and Jocelyn (*née* Adami); *m* 1991, Neil Scott Wishart McIntosh, *qv*; one *s* one *d*. *Educ:* Wycombe Abbey; Cheltenham Coll.; St Anne's Coll., Oxford (BA Hons, Lit Hum Cl. I). Theatre Jobs, 1978–80; Res. Asst, Brunel Univ., 1980–81; Head of Admin, CND, 1982–84, VSO, 1985–87; Prog. Funding Manager, 1987, Regl Prog. Manager, ME and S Asia, 1987–89, VSO; Staffing Manager, McKinsey & Co., 1989–91; Dep. Dir, 1991–92, Dir, later Chief Exec., 1992–98, Nat. Asthma Campaign. Chm., Long Term Medical Conditions Alliance, 1998–2004; Member: Commn for Health Improvement, 1999–2004; NHS Modernisation Bd, 2000–03; Commn for Healthcare Audit and Inspection, 2003–04; Chair, Cttee on Safety of Medicines Working Gp on Patient Information, 2003–05; Dir, Ask About Medicines, 2003–. Chair, Nat. Strategic Partnership Forum, 2005–07. Sen. Associate, Compass Partnership, 2004–. Trustee: NCVO, 1997–2002; Comic Relief, 1998–2002; General Practice Airways Gp, 2001–; Parkinson's Disease Soc., 2007–; Patron, Men's Health Forum, 2004; Member: Exec. Cttee, Tobacco Control Alliance, 1997–98; Bd, New Opportunities Fund, 1998–2001. Mem. Council, Cheltenham Coll., 1990–93; Governor, Oakley Hall Sch., Cirencester, 1993–94. Mem., ACENVO, 1992–98. MCMI (MIMgt 1992). FRSA 1996. *Recreations:* reading, swimming, gardening, crosswords. *Address:* *e-mail:* melindaletts@thecoachzone.co.uk.

See also Q. R. S. Letts.

LETTS, Quentin Richard Stephen; freelance journalist; Parliamentary Sketchwriter, since 2000, and theatre critic, since 2004, Daily Mail; *b* 6 Feb. 1963; *s* of Richard Francis Bonner Letts, schoolmaster, and Jocelyn Elizabeth Letts (*née* Adami); *m* 1996, Lois Henrietta, *d* of Patrick and Marion Rathbone; one *s* two *d*. *Educ:* Haileybury; Bellarmine Coll., Kentucky; Trinity Coll., Dublin (BA); Jesus Coll., Cambridge (Dip. Classical Archaeol.). Writer, specialist pubns, Cardiff, 1987; Daily Telegraph, 1988–95: City Diarist, 1989–90; NY Corresp., 1991; Ed., Peterborough Column, 1991–95; NY Bureau Chief, The Times, 1995–97; Parly Sketchwriter, Daily Telegraph, 1997–2000. Creator, 'Clement Crabbe', Daily Mail, 2006. Edgar Wallace Award, London Press Club, 2003; Feature Writer of Yr, What the Papers Say Awards, 2007. *Recreations:* watching cricket, singing hymns. *Address:* The Old Mill, How Caple, Herefordshire HR1 4SR. *T:* (01989) 740688. *Club:* Savile.

See also M. J. F. Letts.

LETWIN, Isabel Grace; on secondment from Treasury Solicitor's Department to Foreign and Commonwealth Office, since 2006; *b* 7 Aug. 1956; *d* of Prof. John Frank Davidson, *qv*; *m* 1984, Oliver Letwin, *qv*; one *s* one *d* (twins). *Educ:* Perse Sch. for Girls; Girton Coll., Cambridge (BA, MA). Admitted solicitor, 1981; Asst Solicitor, Private Client Dept, Macfarlanes, 1981–84; Treasury Solicitor's Department: Litigation Div., 1984–88; on secondment to HSE, 1988–91; Treasury Div., 1991–93; Central Adv. Div., 1994–99; Legal Advr to DCMS, 1999–2006. Lector (pt-time) in Family Law, Trinity Coll., Cambridge, 1981–86. *Recreations:* gardening, tennis, alpine walking. *Address:* c/o The Legal Advisers, Foreign and Commonwealth Office, King Charles Street, SW1A 2AH.

LETWIN, Rt Hon. Oliver; PC 2002; PhD; MP (C) West Dorset, since 1997; *b* 19 May 1956; *s* of Prof. William Letwin, *qv*; *m* 1984, Isabel Grace Davidson (*see* I. G. Letwin); one *s* one *d* (twins). *Educ:* Eton Coll.; Trinity Coll., Cambridge (BA, MA, PhD 1982). Vis. Fellow, Princeton Univ., 1981; Research Fellow, Darwin Coll., Cambridge, 1982–83; Special Advr, DES, 1982–83; Mem., Prime Minister's Policy Unit, 1983–86; with N. M. Rothschild & Sons Ltd, 1986–2003 (Dir, 1991–2003; non-exec. Dir, 2005–). Opposition front-bench spokesman on constitutional affairs, 1998–99, on Treasury affairs, 1999–2000; Shadow Chief Sec. to HM Treasury, 2000–01; Shadow Home Sec., 2001–03; Shadow Chancellor, 2003–05; Shadow Sec. of State for Envmt, Food and Rural Affairs, 2005; Chm., Policy Review and Chm., Conservative Res. Dept, 2005–. FRSA 1991. *Publications:* Ethics, Emotion and the Unity of the Self, 1984; Aims of Schooling, 1985; Privatising the World, 1987; Drift to Union, 1990; The Purpose of Politics, 1999; numerous articles in learned and popular jls. *Recreations:* ski-ing, tennis, walking. *Address:* House of Commons, SW1A 0AA. *T:* (020) 7219 3000. *Club:* St Stephen's.

LETWIN, Prof. William; Professor Emeritus, London School of Economics, since 1988; *b* 14 Dec. 1922; *s* of Lazar and Bessie Letwin; *m* 1944, Shirley Robin (*d* 1993); one *s*. *Educ:* Univ. of Chicago (BA 1943, PhD 1951); London Sch. of Economics (1948–50). Served US Army, 1943–46. Postdoctoral Fellow, Economics Dept, Univ. of Chicago, 1951–52; Research Associate, Law Sch., Univ. of Chicago, 1953–55; Asst. Prof. of Industrial History, MIT, 1955–60; Associate Prof. of Economic History, MIT, 1960–67; Reader in Political Science, 1966–76, Prof. of Pol Science, 1976–88, LSE. Senior Advisor: Putnam, Hayes & Bartlett, 1988–96; Spectrum Strategy Consultants, 1996–97. Chm., Bd of Studies in Economics, Univ. of London, 1971–73. *Publications:* (ed) Frank Knight, on The History and Method of Economics, 1956; Sir Josiah Child, 1959; Documentary History of American Economic Policy, 1961, 2nd edn 1972; Origins of Scientific Economics 1660–1776, 1963; Law and Economic Policy in America, 1965; (ed) Against Equality, 1983; Freeing the Phones, 1991; articles in learned jls. *Address:* 255 Kennington Road, SE11 6BY.

See also O. Letwin.

LEUCHARS, Maj.-Gen. Peter Raymond, CBE 1966; Chief Commander, St John Ambulance, 1980–89 (Commissioner-in-Chief, 1978–80 and 1985–86); *b* 29 Oct. 1921; *s* of late Raymond Leuchars and Helen Inez Leuchars (*née* Copland-Griffiths); *m* 1953, Hon. Gillian Wightman Nivison, *d* of 2nd Baron Glendyne; one *s*. *Educ:* Bradfield College. Commnd in Welsh Guards, 1941; served in NW Europe and Italy, 1944–45; Adjt, 1st Bn Welsh Guards, Palestine, 1945–48; Bde Major, 4 Guards Bde, Germany, 1952–54; GSO1 (Instr.), Staff Coll., Camberley, 1956–59; GSO1 HQ 4 Div. BAOR, 1960–63; comd 1st Bn Welsh Guards, 1963–65; Principal Staff Off. to Dir of Ops, Borneo, 1965–66; comd 11 Armd Bde BAOR, 1966–68; comd Jt Operational Computer Projects Team, 1969–71; Dep. Comdt Staff Coll., Camberley, 1972–73; GOC Wales, 1973–76. Col, The Royal Welch Fusiliers, 1974–84. Pres., Guards' Golfing Soc., 1977–2001. Chairman: St John Fellowship, 1989–95 (Vice-Pres., 1996–); Lady Grover's Fund for Officers' Families, 1991–98. FRGS 1996. BGCStJ 1989 (Bailiff of Egle, 2001). Order of Istiqlal (Jordan), 1946. *Recreations:* golf, shooting, travel, photography. *Address:* 5 Chelsea Square, SW3 6LF. *T:* (020) 7352 6187. *Clubs:* Royal and Ancient Golf; Sunningdale Golf (Captain 1975).

LEUNG Kin Pong, Andrew, SBS 2005; Founder, Andrew Leung International Consultants Ltd, since 2005; Director-General, Government Office of Hong Kong Special Administrative Region in United Kingdom, 2000–04; *b* 13 Nov. 1945; *m* 1974, Peggy Fung Lin Tong; one *s* one *d*. *Educ:* BA (ext.) London; Wolfson Coll., Cambridge (postgrad. Dip. in Develt Studies); Harvard Univ. (PMD); Solicitor's qualifying certs, England and Hong Kong. Hong Kong Civil Service: Exec. Officer, then Sen. Exec. Officer, 1967–73; Asst Sec. for Security, 1973–75; Council Office, 1976–77; Asst Financial Sec., 1979–82; on secondment to Standard Chartered Bank, 1982–83; Counsellor (Hong Kong Affairs), Brussels, 1983–87; Dep. Dir-Gen. of Industry, 1987–91; Dep. Sec. for Transport, 1991–92; Police Admin Officer, 1994–96; Dir-Gen. of Social Welfare, 1996–2000. Sen. Consultant, MEC Internat., 2005–. Distinguished Contrib., Asymmetric Threats Contingency Alliance, 2005–; Chm., China Interest Gp, Inst. of Dirs City Br., 2005–; Leader, China Gp, London Reg., RSA, 2007; Member: Royal Soc. for Asian Affairs, 2007–; Brain Trust, Evian Gp, Lausanne, 2007–; Expert, Community of Experts, Reuters Insight, 2007–. Member: Governing Council, KCL, 2004–; Adv. Bd, China Policy Inst., Nottingham Univ., 2005–. Visiting Professor: Internat. MBA Prog., Sun Yat-sen Univ., China, 2005–; Internat. MBA Prog., Lingnan Univ., China, 2006–07; NIMBAS Graduate Sch. of Mgt, Netherlands, 2006–07. Mem., Exec. Cttee, 48 Gp Club, 2004–; Network Member: Cambridge Soc., 1978–; Harvard Club UK, 2000–; China-Britain Business Council, 2005–. FRSA 2002. JP Hong Kong, 1989. SBS (Hong Kong), 2005. *Recreations:* tennis, swimming, jogging, travelling, singing, reading, Chinese calligraphy. *Address:* 1A Vincent House, Vincent Square, SW1P 2NB; *e-mail:* andrewkpleung@hotmail.com. *Club:* Hong Kong Jockey.

LEVEN, 14th Earl of, **AND MELVILLE,** 13th Earl of, *cr* 1641; **Alexander Robert Leslie Melville;** Baron Melville, 1616; Baron Balgonie, 1641; Earl of Melville, Viscount Kirkcaldie, 1690; Lord-Lieutenant of Nairn, 1969–99; *b* 13 May 1924; *e s* of 13th Earl and Lady Rosamond Sylvia Diana Mary Foljambe (*d* 1974), *d* of 1st Earl of Liverpool; *S* father, 1947; *m* 1953, Susan, *er d* of Lieut-Colonel R. Steuart-Menzies of Culdares, Arndilly House, Craigellachie, Banffshire; one *s* one *d* (and one *s* decd). *Educ:* Eton. ADC to Governor General of New Zealand, 1951–52. Formerly Capt. Coldstream Guards; retired, 1952. Vice-Pres., Highland Dist TA. Pres., British Ski Fedn, 1981–85. DL, County of Nairn, 1961; Convener, Nairn CC, 1970–74. Chm. Governors, Gordonstoun Sch., 1971–89. *Heir: g s* Hon. Alexander Ian Leslie Melville, *b* 29 Nov. 1984. *Address:* Raith, Old Spey Bridge, Grantown-on-Spey, Morayshire PH26 3NQ. *T:* (01479) 872908. *Club:* New (Edinburgh).

LEVENE, family name of **Baron Levene of Portsoken.**

LEVENE OF PORTSOKEN, Baron *cr* 1997 (Life Peer), of Portsoken, in the City of London; **Peter Keith Levene,** KBE 1989; JP; Chairman, Lloyd's, since 2002; *b* 8 Dec. 1941; *s* of late Maurice Levene and Rose Levene; *m* 1966, Wendy Ann (*née* Fraiman); two *s* one *d*. *Educ:* City of London School; Univ. of Manchester (BA Econ). Joined United Scientific Holdings, 1963; Man. Dir, 1968–85; Chm., 1982–85; Chief of Defence Procurement, MoD, 1985–91; UK Nat. Armaments Dir, 1988–91; Chm., European Nat. Armaments Dirs, 1989–90. Member: SE Asia Trade Adv. Group, 1979–83; Council, Defence Manufacturers' Assoc., 1982–85 (Vice-Chm., 1983–84; Chm., 1984–85; Pres., 2006–); Citizen's Charter Adv. Panel, 1992–93; Personal Adviser to: Sec. of State for Defence, 1984; Sec. of State for the Envmt, 1991–92; Chancellor of the Exchequer on Competition and Purchasing, 1992; Pres. of BoT, 1992–95; Prime Minister on Efficiency and Effectiveness, 1992–97. Chairman: Docklands Light Railway Ltd, 1991–94; Bankers Trust Internat. plc, 1998–99; IFSL (formerly British Invisibles), 2000–; General Dynamics UK Ltd, 2001–; Chm., Investment Banking Europe, 1999–2001, Vice-Chm., 2001–02, Deutsche Bank; Dep. Chm., Wasserstein Perella & Co. Ltd, 1991–94; Chm. and Chief Exec., Canary Wharf Ltd, 1993–96; Director: Haymarket Gp Ltd, 1997–; J. Sainsbury plc, 2001–04; non-exec. Dir, China Construction Bank, 2006–. Sen. Advr, Morgan Stanley &

Co. Ltd, 1996–98; Member: Supervisory Bd, Deutsche Börse, 2004–05; Bd, Total SA, 2005–. Chm., World Trade Centre Disaster Fund (UK), 2001–06. Member: Bd of Management, London Homes for the Elderly, 1984–93 (Chm., 1990–93); Internat. Adv. Bd, Singapore Govt Nat. Labs, 1998–99; Chairman's Council, Alcatel, 2000–03. Governor: City of London Sch. for Girls, 1984–85; City of London Sch., 1986–; Sir John Cass Primary Sch., 1985–93 (Dep. Chm., 1990–93). Mem. Court, HAC, 1984–; Mem., Court of Common Council, City of London, 1983–84 (Ward of Candlewick); Alderman, Ward of Portsoken, 1984–2005, Ward of Aldgate, 2005–; Sheriff, City of London, 1995–96; Lord Mayor of London, 1998–99; Liveryman: Carmen's Co., 1984– (Master, 1992–93); Information Technologists' Co., 1993–; Hon. Liveryman, Mgt Consultants' Co. Hon. Col Comdt, RCT, 1991–93, RLC, 1993–2006. JP City of London, 1984. Fellow, QMW, 1995. CCMI; FCIPS. Hon. FCII. Hon. DSc: City, 1998; London, 2005. KStJ 1998. Commandeur, Ordre National du Mérite (France), 1996; Kt Comdr, Order of Merit (Germany), 1998; Middle Cross, Order of Merit (Hungary), 1999. *Recreations:* skiing, watching association football, travel. *Address:* Lloyd's, 1 Lime Street, EC3M 7HA. *Clubs:* Guildhall, City Livery, Royal Automobile.

LEVENE, Ben, RA 1986 (ARA 1975); painter; *b* 23 Dec. 1938; *s* of late Mark Levene and Charlotte (*née* Leapman); *m* 1st (marr. diss. 1977); two *d*; 2nd, 1978, Susan Margaret Williams; one *s*. *Educ:* St Clement Danes Grammar Sch.; Slade School of Fine Art (DFA 1960). Boise Scholarship, 1961; lived in Spain, 1961–62; Vis. Lectr, taught painting and drawing, Camberwell Sch. of Art, 1963–89; Visiting Tutor: RA Schs, 1980–95; City & Guilds, 1990–95; Curator, RA Schs, 1995–98. Exhibited at: Thackeray Gall., 1973–81 (one man shows, 1973, 1975, 1978, 1981); Browse & Darby, London, 1986– (one man shows, 1988, 1993, 2001); one man show, Friends Room, RA, 2006; group exhibitions incl.: regular exhibitor, RA Summer Exhibn; Jasper Galls, Houston and NY; works in various private collections in England and America. *Recreation:* gardening under the supervision of my wife. *Address:* c/o Royal Academy of Arts, Piccadilly, W1V 0DS. *T:* (020) 7300 8000.

LEVENE, Jacqueline Anne; *see* Perry, J. A.

LEVENE, Prof. Malcolm Irvin, MD; FRCP; FRCPCH, FMedSci; Professor of Paediatrics and Child Health, since 1989, Chairman, Division of Paediatrics, 1992–98, University of Leeds; *b* 2 Jan. 1951; *s* of Maurice Levene and Helen Levene (*née* Kutner); *m* 1st, 1972, Miriam Bentley (marr. diss. 1990); three *d*; 2nd, 1991, Susan Anne Cave; one *s* one *d*. *Educ:* Varndean Grammar Sch., Brighton; Guy's Hosp. Med. Sch., London Univ. (MB BS 1972); MD 1981. MRCS, LRCP, 1972; MRCP 1978, FRCP 1988; FRCPCH 1996. Junior posts at Royal Sussex, Northampton General and Charing Cross Hosps, 1974–77; Registrar, Derby Children's and Charing Cross Hosps, 1977–79; Res. Lectr, RPMS, Hammersmith Hosp., 1979–82; Sen. Lectr and Reader, Dept of Paediatrics, Univ. of Leicester, 1982–88; Med. Dir, Women's and Children's Subsidiary, 1998–, Chm., Child Health Cttee, 2005–, Leeds Teaching Hosp. NHS Trust. Mem., DoH Nat. Adv. Body, Confidential Enquiry into Stillbirths and Deaths in Infancy, 1991. Chm., Scientific Adv. Cttee, Action Res., 1994–97. Ed.-in-Chief, MRCPCH Master Course, 2007. FMedSci 1999; Fellow, Acad. Perinatal Medicine, 2005. Hancock Prize, RCS, 1974; British Paediatric Association: Donald Paterson Prize, 1982; Michael Blecklow Meml Prize, 1982; Guthrie Medal, 1987; Ronnie MacKeith Prize, British Paed. Neurology Assoc., 1984; BUPA Res. Prize, 1988. *Publications:* (with H. Nutbeam) A Handbook for Examinations in Paediatrics, 1981; (jtly) Ultrasound of the Infant Brain, 1985; (jtly) Essentials of Neonatal Medicine, 1987, 3rd edn 2000; (ed jtly) Fetal and Neonatal Neurology and Neurosurgery, 1988, 3rd edn 2001; Diseases of Children, 6th edn, 1990; Paediatrics and Child Health, 1999, 2006; chapters in books and articles in learned jls on paed. topics, esp. neurology of new-born. *Recreations:* music, occasional gentle golf and gardening. *Address:* Acacia House, Acacia Park Drive, Apperley Bridge, W Yorks BD10 0PH. *T:* (0113) 250 9959.

LEVENSON, Howard; Social Security Commissioner and Child Support Commissioner, since 1997, and Pensions Appeal Commissioner, since 2005; *b* 4 Dec. 1949; *s* of Albert and Marlene Levenson; *m* 1971, Ros Botsman; one *s* one *d*. *Educ:* Tottenham Grammar Sch.; Univ. of Sheffield (BJur Hons 1970; LLM 1972); Coll. of Law, London; Birkbeck, Univ. of London (MA 2007). Admitted solicitor, 1974; Legal Officer, NCCL, 1974–77; Law Lectr, Poly., then Univ., of E London, 1977–92; Consultant, Nash and Dowell (Solicitors), 1981–91; part-time Chm., Tribunals, 1986–92; Chm., Independent Tribunal Service, 1993–97. Chm., Haldane Soc., 1980–83. *Publications:* The Price of Justice, 1981; (jtly) Social Welfare Law: Legal Aid and Advice, 1985; (jtly) Police Powers, 1985, 3rd edn 1996; contrib. vols of Atkin's Court Forms on Child Support, Judicial Review, Personal Rights, Social Security; contrib. to Modern Law Rev., Criminal Law Rev., New Law Jl, etc. *Address:* (office) Third Floor, Procession House, 55 Ludgate Hill, EC4M 7JW. *Club:* Leyton Orient Football.

LEVENTHAL, Colin David; Director, HAL Films Ltd, since 2000; *b* 2 Nov. 1946; *s* of Morris and Olga Leventhal; *m* 1995, Petrea, *d* of Thomas Hoving, *qv*; three *d*. *Educ:* Carmel Coll., Wallingford, Berks; King's Coll., Univ. of London (BA Philosophy). Solicitor of Supreme Court of England and Wales. Admitted Solicitor, 1971; BBC, 1974–81, Head of Copyright, 1978; Head of Prog. Acquisition, Channel Four TV, 1981–87; Dir of Acquisition and Sales, Channel Four TV Co., 1987–92 (Dir, 1988–92); Dir of Acquisition, Channel Four TV Corp., 1993–97; Man. Dir, Channel Four Internat. Ltd, 1993–97; Jt Chief Exec., Miramax HAL Films Ltd, 1998–2000. Mem., Film Council, 1999–2002. *Recreations:* theatre, film. *Address:* 10 Well Walk, Hampstead, NW3 1LD. *T:* (020) 7435 3038.

LEVER, Hon. Bernard Lewis; His Honour Judge Lever; a Circuit Judge, since 2001; *b* 1 Feb. 1951; *s* of Baron Lever and of Ray Rosalia, Lady Lever; *m* 1985, Anne Helen Ballingall, only *d* of Patrick Chandler Gordon Ballingall, MBE; two *d*. *Educ:* Clifton; Queen's Coll., Oxford (Neale Exhibnr; MA). Called to the Bar, Middle Temple, 1975; in practice, Northern Circuit, 1975–2001; Standing Counsel to Inland Revenue, 1997–2001. Co-founder, SDP in NW, 1981. Contested (SDP) Manchester Withington, 1983. *Recreations:* walking, music, fishing, picking up litter. *Address:* Manchester Crown Court, Minshull Street, Manchester M1 3FS. *T:* (0161) 954 7500. *Club:* Vincent's (Oxford).

LEVER, Sir Christopher; *see* Lever, Sir T. C. A. L.

LEVER, Sir Jeremy (Frederick), KCMG 2002; QC 1972; QC (NI) 1988; *b* 23 June 1933; *s* of late A. Lever; civil partnership 2006, Brian Collie. *Educ:* Bradfield Coll.; University Coll., Oxford; Nuffield Coll., Oxford. Served RA, 1951–53. 1st cl. Jurisprudence, 1956, MA Oxon; Pres., Oxford Union Soc., 1957, Trustee, 1972–77 and 1988–. Fellow, All Souls Coll., Oxford, 1957– (Sub-Warden, 1982–84; Sen. Dean, 1988–). Called to Bar, Gray's Inn, 1957, Bencher, 1985. Chairman: Oftel Adv. Body on Fair Trading in Telecommunications, 1996–2000; Appeals Panel, PRS, 1997–2002. Mem. Council, British Inst. of Internat. and Comparative Law, 1987–2004. Director (non-exec.): Dunlop Holdings Ltd, 1973–80; Wellcome plc, 1983–94. Mem., Arbitral Tribunal, US/UK Arbitration concerning Heathrow Airport User Charges, 1989–94. Vis. Prof., Wissenschaftszentrum, Berlin, für Sozialforschung, 1999. Lectures: Hamlyn, Hamlyn Trust, 1991; Lord Fletcher Meml, Law Soc., 1997; Grotius, British Inst. of Internat. and Comparative Law, 1998. Governor, Berkhamsted Schs, 1985–95. FRSA. *Publications:* The Law of Restrictive Practices, 1964; other legal works. *Recreations:* ceramics, music. *Address:* Monckton Chambers, 1 Raymond Buildings, Gray's Inn, WC1R 5NR. *T:* (020) 7405 7211, *Fax:* (020) 7405 2084; All Souls College, Oxford OX1 4AL. *T:* (01865) 279379, *Fax:* (01865) 279299; *e-mail:* chambers@monckton.com. *Clubs:* Athenæum, Garrick.

LEVER, John Darcy, MA; Headmaster, Canford School, since 1992; *b* 14 Jan. 1952; *s* of Prof. Jeffrey Darcy Lever; *m* 1981, Alisoun Margaret Yule; one *s* two *d*. *Educ:* Westminster Sch.; Trinity Coll., Cambridge (MA); Christ Church, Oxford (Cert Ed). St Edward's Sch., Oxford, 1974–76; Winchester Coll., 1976–92. *Recreations:* walking, clocks, maps. *Address:* Canford School, Wimborne, Dorset BH21 3AD. *T:* (01202) 847434.

LEVER, Kay; *see* Allen, K.

LEVER, (Keith) Mark; Chief Executive, National Autistic Society, since 2008; Director, Sackville Consulting Ltd, since 2007; *b* 20 Sept. 1960; *s* of Keith Lever and Rosemary Anne Lever (*née* Wakeley); *m* 1989, Amanda Jane Sackville Davison; four *s*. *Educ:* Wakeman Grammar Sch., Shrewsbury; Royal Holloway Coll., London (BSc Hons Physics and Mgt Sci. 1982); Cranfield Univ. Sch. of Mgt (MBA 1999). ACA 1986. Partner and Nat. Dir, Mkt Res. and Trng, Kidsons Impey, 1994; Women's Royal Voluntary Service: Dir, Trng, 1995–99; Dir, Strategic Develt, 1999–2002; Chief Exec. Officer, 2002–07. MCIM; MCIPD. *Recreations:* drinking wine with my wife, negotiating peace settlements and behaviour related pay with my four sons. *Address:* *e-mail:* marklever@aol.com. *Clubs:* Harrow Golf Society, Wanborough Amateur Golf Society.

LEVER, Sir Paul, KCMG 1998 (CMG 1991); HM Diplomatic Service, retired; Chairman, Royal United Services Institute, since 2004; *b* 31 March 1944; *s* of John Morrison Lever and Doris Grace (*née* Battey); *m* 1990, Patricia Anne, *d* of John and Anne Ramsey. *Educ:* St Paul's Sch.; The Queen's Coll., Oxford (MA; Hon. Fellow, 2006). 3rd Secretary, Foreign and Commonwealth Office, 1966–67; 3rd, later 2nd Secretary, Helsinki, 1967–71; 2nd, later 1st Secretary, UK Delegn to NATO, 1971–73; FCO, 1973–81; Asst Private Sec. to Sec. of State for Foreign and Commonwealth Affairs, 1978–81; Chef de Cabinet to Christopher Tugendhat, Vice-Pres. of EEC, 1981–85; Head of UN Dept, FCO, 1985–86; Head of Defence Dept, 1986–87; Head of Security Policy Dept, FCO, 1987–90; Ambassador and Hd, UK Delegn to Conventional Arms Control Negotiations, Vienna, 1990–92; Asst Under-Sec. of State, FCO, 1992–94; Dep. Sec., Cabinet Office, and Chm., Jt Intelligence Cttee, 1994–96; Dep. Under-Sec. of State (Dir for EU and Economic Affairs), FCO, 1996–97; Ambassador to Germany, 1997–2003. Global Develt Dir, RWE Thames Water, 2003–06. Hon. LLD Birmingham, 2001. *Recreations:* walking, art deco pottery. *Address:* Royal United Services Institute, Whitehall, SW1A 2ET.

LEVER, Sir (Tresham) Christopher (Arthur Lindsay), 3rd Bt *cr* 1911; *b* 9 Jan. 1932; *s* of Sir Tresham Joseph Philip Lever, FRSL, 2nd Bt, and Frances Yowart (*d* 1959), *d* of Lindsay Hamilton Goodwin; step *s* of Pamela Lady Lever (*d* 2003), *d* of late Lt-Col Hon. Malcolm Bowes Lyon; *S* father, 1975; *m* 1st, 1970; 2nd, 1975, Linda Weightman McDowell, *d* of late James Jepson Goulden, Tennessee, USA. *Educ:* Eton; Trinity Coll., Cambridge (BA 1954, MA 1957). FLS; FRGS. Commissioned, 17th/21st Lancers, 1950. Peat, Marwick, Mitchell & Co., 1954–55; Kitcat & Aitken, 1955–56; Dir, John Barran & Sons Ltd, 1956–64. Consultant: Zoo Check Charitable Trust, 1984–91; Born Free Foundn, 1991–2003; Chairman: African Fund for Endangered Wildlife (UK), 1987–90; UK Elephant Gp, 1991–92; Member: IUCN Species Survival Commn, 1988–; IUCN UK Cttee, 1989–; Trustee: Internat. Trust for Nature Conservation, 1980–92 (Vice-Pres. 1986–91; Pres., 1991–92); Rhino Rescue Trust, 1986–91 (Patron 1985–2003); Chm., 1990–2004, Hon. Life Pres., 2004, Tusk Trust; Chm., Ruaha Trust, 1990–95; Member Council: Soc. for Protection of Animals in N Africa, 1986–88; British Trust for Ornithology, 1988–91 (Chm., Nat. Centre Appeal, 1987–92); SOS Sahel Internat. (UK), 1995–; Director: WSPA, 1998–2003; Conservation Educn and Res. Trust, Earthwatch Inst., Europe, 2003–04; Mem., Council of Ambassadors, WWF-UK, 1999–2005 (Fellow, 2005); Patron: Lynx Educnl Trust for Animal Welfare, 1991–; Respect for Animals, 1995–; Vice-Patron, Conservation Foundn, 2005–06. Hon. Life Mem., Brontë Soc., 1988. Mem., Editl Bd, Jl of Applied Herpetology, 2005–. *Publications:* Goldsmiths and Silversmiths of England, 1975; The Naturalized Animals of the British Isles, 1977; (contrib.) Wildlife '80: the world conservation yearbook, 1980; (contrib.) Evolution of Domesticated Animals, 1984; Naturalized Mammals of the World, 1985; Naturalized Birds of the World, 1987; (contrib.) Beyond the Bars: the zoo dilemma, 1987; (contrib.) For the Love of Animals, 1989; The Mandarin Duck, 1990; They Dined on Eland: the story of the acclimatisation societies, 1992; (contrib.) The New Atlas of Breeding Birds in Britain and Ireland: 1988–1991, 1993; Naturalized Animals: the ecology of successfully introduced species, 1994; (contrib.) The Introduction and Naturalisation of Birds, 1996; Naturalized Fishes of the World, 1996; (contrib.) Stocking & Introduction of Fish, 1997; (contrib.) The EBCC Atlas of European Breeding Birds: their distribution and abundance, 1997; The Cane Toad: the history and ecology of a successful colonist, 2001; (contrib.) The Migration Atlas: movements of the birds of Britain and Ireland, 2002; Naturalized Reptiles and Amphibians of the World, 2003; (contrib.) Biological Invasions: from ecology to control, 2005; Naturalised Birds of the World, 2005; (contrib.) Silent Summer: the state of the wildlife in Britain and Ireland, 2009; The Naturalized Animals of Britain and Ireland, 2009; contribs to art, scientific and general publications. *Recreations:* watching and photographing wildlife, golf, ghillying. *Heir:* none. *Address:* Newell House, Winkfield, Berks SL4 4SE. *T:* (01344) 882604, *Fax:* (01344) 891744. *Clubs:* Boodle's; Swinley Forest Golf.

LEVERTON, Colin Allen H.; *see* Hart-Leverton.

LEVERTON, Roger Frank, FCA; Chairman, Renold plc, 1998–2006; *b* 22 April 1939; *s* of Frank Arthur Leverton and Lucia Jean Leverton (*née* Harden); *m* 1st, 1962, Patricia Jones (marr. diss.); one *s* one *d* (and one *d* decd); 2nd, 1992, Marilyn Williams. *Educ:* Haberdashers' Aske's Sch. FCA 1962. Black & Decker Manufacturing Co., 1968–84: European Dir and Gen. Manager, France, 1978–81; Gp Vice-Pres., Southern Europe, 1981–84; Chief Exec., MK Electric Gp, subseq. Pillar Electrical plc, 1984–89; Pres. and Chief Exec., Indal Ltd (RTZ Corp. plc), 1989–92; Chief Exec., Pilkington plc, 1992–97. Chairman: Infast Gp plc, 1997–2002; Betts Gp Hldgs Ltd, 1998–2005. *Recreations:* tennis, golf, theatre.

LEVESON, Lord; George James Leveson Gower; *b* 22 July 1999; *s* and *heir* of Earl Granville, *qv*.

LEVESON, Rt Hon. Sir Brian (Henry), Kt 2000; PC 2006; **Rt Hon. Lord Justice Leveson;** a Lord Justice of Appeal, since 2006; Senior Presiding Judge for England and

Wales, since 2007; *b* 22 June 1949; *er s* of late Dr Ivan Leveson and Elaine Leveson, Liverpool; *m* 1981, Lynne Rose (*née* Fishel); two *s* one *d*. *Educ:* Liverpool College, Liverpool; Merton College, Oxford (MA; Hon. Fellow, 2001). Called to the Bar, Middle Temple, 1970, Bencher, 1995; Harmsworth Scholar, 1970; practised Northern Circuit, 1971; University of Liverpool: Lectr in Law, 1971–81; Mem. Council, 1983–92; QC 1986; a Recorder, 1988–2000; a Dep. High Court Judge, 1998–2000; a Judge of the High Court, QBD, 2000–06; Presiding Judge, Northern Circuit, 2002–05; Dep. Sen. Presiding Judge for England and Wales, 2006. Mem., Parole Bd, 1992–95. Mem. Council, UCS, Hampstead, 1998–; Foundn Mem., Liverpool Coll., 2001–. Hon. LLD Liverpool, 2007. *Recreations:* walking, travel. *Address:* Royal Courts of Justice, Strand, WC2A 2LL.

LEVESON GOWER, family name of **Earl Granville**.

LEVEY, Sir Michael (Vincent), Kt 1981; LVO 1965; MA Oxon and Cantab; FRSL; FBA 1983; Director of the National Gallery, 1973–86 (Deputy Director, 1970–73); *b* 8 June 1927; *s* of O. L. H. Levey and Gladys Mary Milestone; *m* 1954, Brigid Brophy (*d* 1995), FRSL; one *d*. *Educ:* Oratory Sch.; Exeter Coll., Oxford (Hon. Fellow, 1973). Served with Army, 1945–48; commissioned, KSLI, 1946, and attached RAEC, Egypt. National Gallery: Asst Keeper, 1951–66, Dep. Keeper, 1966–68, Keeper, 1968–73. Slade Professor of Fine Art, Cambridge, 1963–64; Supernumerary Fellow, King's Coll., Cambridge, 1963–64; Slade Professor of Fine Art, Oxford, 1994–95; Hon. Fellow, Royal Acad., 1986; Foreign Mem., Ateneo Veneto, 1986. Hon. DLitt Manchester, 1989. *Publications:* Six Great Painters, 1956; National Gallery Catalogues: 18th Century Italian Schools, 1956; The German School, 1959; Painting in 18th Century Venice, 1959, 3rd edn 1994; From Giotto to Cézanne, 1962; Dürer, 1964; The Later Italian Paintings in the Collection of HM The Queen, 1964, rev. edn 1991; Canaletto Paintings in the Royal Collection, 1964; Tiepolo's Banquet of Cleopatra (Charlton Lecture, 1962), 1966; Rococo to Revolution, 1966; Bronzino (The Masters), 1967; Early Renaissance, 1967 (Hawthornden Prize, 1968); Fifty Works of English Literature We Could Do Without (co-author), 1967; Holbein's Christina of Denmark, Duchess of Milan, 1968; A History of Western Art, 1968; Painting at Court (Wrightsman Lectures), 1971; 17th and 18th Century Italian Schools (Nat. Gall. catalogue), 1971; The Life and Death of Mozart, 1971, 2nd edn 1988; The Nude: Themes and Painters in the National Gallery, 1972; (co-author) Art and Architecture in 18th Century France, 1972; The Venetian Scene (Themes and Painters Series), 1973; Botticelli (Themes and Painters Series), 1974; High Renaissance, 1975; The World of Ottoman Art, 1976; Jacob van Ruisdael (Themes and Painters Series), 1977; The Case of Walter Pater, 1978; Sir Thomas Lawrence (Nat. Portrait Gall. exhibn), 1979; The Painter Depicted (Neurath Lect.), 1981; Tempting Fate (fiction), 1982; An Affair on the Appian Way (fiction), 1984; (ed) Pater's Marius the Epicurean, 1985; Giambattista Tiepolo, 1986 (Banister Fletcher Prize, 1987); The National Gallery Collection: a selection, 1987; Men at Work (fiction), 1989; (ed) The Soul of the Eye: anthology of painters and painting, 1990; Painting and Sculpture in France 1700–1789, 1992; Florence: a portrait, 1996; The Chapel is on Fire (memoir), 2000; (ed) The Burlington Magazine: a centenary anthology, 2003; Sir Thomas Lawrence, 2005; contribs to Burlington Magazine, Apollo, etc. *Address:* 36 Little Lane, Louth, Lincs LN11 9DU.

LEVI, Andrew Peter Robert; HM Diplomatic Service; Counsellor (Economic), Moscow, since 2005; *b* 4 March 1963; *s* of Paul George Carl Levi and Paula Levi; *m* 2002, Dr Roswitha Elisabeth von Studnitz. *Educ:* Reading Blue Coat Sch. (Aldworth's Hosp.); Univ. of Manchester (BSc Hons 1985); Univ. of Freiburg im Breisgau. Entered FCO, 1987; Bonn, 1990–93; First Secretary: FCO, 1993–96; on secondment to EC (EU enlargement), 1996–98, and to OECD Secretariat, 1998; Bonn, 1998–99; on secondment to: German FO, Bonn, 1999; DCS, Stability Pact for S Eastern Europe, 1999–2001; Dep. Hd, Eastern Adriatic Dept, FCO, 2001–03; Hd, Aviation, Maritime and Energy Dept, FCO, 2003–04; Asst Dir (EU), FCO, 2004–05. *Address:* c/o Foreign and Commonwealth Office, King Charles Street, SW1A 2AH; *e-mail:* andrew.levi@fco.gov.uk.

LEVI, Malcolm Sydney; Group Chief Executive, Home Group, since 1998; *b* 3 March 1948; *s* of David and Fanny Levi; *m* 1972, Joy Poloway; two *s*. *Educ:* King Edward's Five Ways Grammar Sch., Birmingham; Mansfield Coll., Oxford (MA (Modern Hist.)). FCA 1978; MCIH 2001. Dir of Finance, Merseyside Improved Houses, 1977–82; Asst Dir of Housing, London Borough of Hammersmith and Fulham, 1982–85; Chief Executive: Paddington Churches Housing Assoc., 1985–94; Warden Housing Assoc., 1994–97; Gp Dep. Chief Exec., Home Gp, 1997–98. Mem. Bd, Newcastle Gateshead Housing Mkt Renewal Pathfinder, 2003–. Mem. Bd, Richmond Synagogue, 2002–. *Recreations:* family and friends, films, theatre, travel, walking in Northumberland. *Address:* Home Group, Ridley House, Regent Centre, Gosforth, Newcastle upon Tyne NE3 3JE. *T:* (0191) 285 0311; *e-mail:* malcolm.levi@homegroup.org.uk.

LEVI, Renato, (Sonny), RDI 1987; freelance powerboat designer; *b* 3 Sept. 1926; *s* of Mario Levi and Eleonora Ciravegna; *m* 1954, Ann Watson; two *s* one *d*. *Educ:* Collège de Cannes; St Paul's, Darjeeling. Over 50 years contributing to development of fast planing craft. *Publications:* Dhows to Deltas, 1971; Milestones in my Designs, 1992. *Recreation:* the Far East. *Address:* Sandhills, Porchfield, Isle of Wight PO30 4LH.

LEVI-MONTALCINI, Prof. Rita; research scientist; President, European Brain Research Institute; *b* 22 April 1909; *d* of Adamo Levi and Adele Montalcini. *Educ:* Turin Univ. Med. Sch. Neurological research, Turin and Brussels, 1936–41, Piemonte, 1941–43; in hiding in Florence, 1943–44; worked among war refugees, Florence, 1944–45; Univ. of Turin, 1945; with Prof. Viktor Hamburger, St Louis, USA, at Washington Univ., 1947–77 (Associate Prof., 1956, Prof., 1958–77); Dir, Inst. of Cell Biology, Italian Nat. Council of Research, Rome, 1969–79, Guest Prof., 1979–. For. Mem., Royal Soc., 1995. (Jtly) Nobel Prize for Physiology or Medicine, 1986. *Publications:* In Praise of Imperfection: my life and work (autobiog.), 1988; articles in learned jls on chemical growth factors controlling growth and development of different cell lines. *Address:* European Brain Research Institute, Via del Fosso di Fiorano 64/65, 00143, Rome, Italy.

LÉVI-STRAUSS, Claude; Grand Croix de la Légion d'Honneur, 1991; Commandeur, Ordre National du Mérite, 1971; Member of French Academy, since 1973; Professor, Collège de France, 1959–82, Hon. Professor, since 1983; *b* 28 Nov. 1908; *s* of Raymond Lévi-Strauss and Emma Lévy; *m* 1st, 1932, Dina Dreyfus; 2nd, 1946, Rose-Marie Ullmo; one *s*; 3rd, 1954, Monique Roman; one *s*. *Educ:* Lycée Janson-de-Sailly, Paris; Sorbonne. Prof., Univ. of São Paulo, Brazil, 1935–39; Vis. Prof., New School for Social Research, NY, 1941–45; Cultural Counsellor, French Embassy, Washington, 1946–47; Associate Curator, Musée de l'Homme, Paris, 1948–49. Corresp. Member: Royal Acad. of Netherlands; Norwegian Acad.; British Acad.; Nat. Acad. of Sciences, USA; Amer. Acad. and Inst. of Arts and Letters; Amer. Philos. Soc.; Royal Anthrop. Inst. of Great Britain; London Sch. of African and Oriental Studies. Hon. Dr: Brussels, 1962; Oxford, 1964; Yale, 1965; Chicago, 1967; Columbia, 1971; Stirling, 1972; Univ. Nat. du Zaïre, 1973; Uppsala, 1977; Johns Hopkins, 1978; Laval, 1979; Mexico, 1979; Visva Bharati, India, 1980; Harvard, 1986; Montreal, 1998. *Publications:* La Vie familiale et sociale des Indiens Nambikwara, 1948; Les Structures élémentaires de la parenté, 1949 (The Elementary Structures of Kinship, 1969); Race et histoire, 1952; Tristes Tropiques, 1955 (A World on the Wane, 1961; complete English edn as Tristes Tropiques, 1973); Anthropologie structurale, Vol. 1, 1958, Vol. 2, 1973 (Structural Anthropology, Vol. 1, 1964, Vol. 2, 1977); Le Totémisme aujourd'hui, 1962 (Totemism, 1963); La Pensée sauvage, 1962 (The Savage Mind, 1966); Le Cru et le cuit, 1964 (The Raw and the Cooked, 1970); Du Miel aux cendres, 1967 (From Honey to Ashes, 1973); L'Origine des manières de table, 1968 (The Origin of Table Manners, 1978); L'Homme nu, 1971 (The Naked Man, 1981); La Voie des masques, 1975 (The Way of the Masks, 1982); Le Regard éloigné, 1983 (The View from Afar, 1985); Paroles Données, 1984 (Anthropology and Myth, 1987); La Potière Jalouse, 1985 (The Jealous Potter, 1988); (with D. Eribon) De Près et de loin, 1988 (Conversations with Claude Lévi-Strauss, 1991); Histoire de Lynx, 1991 (The Story of Lynx, 1995); Regarder écouter lire, 1993 (Look, Listen, Read, 1997); Saudades do Brasil, 1994 (A Photographic Memoir, 1995); *relevant publications:* Entretiens avec Lévi-Strauss (ed G. Charbonnier), 1962; Claude Lévi-Strauss and the Making of Structural Anthropology, by Marcel Henaff, 1998; by Octavio Paz: On Lévi-Strauss, 1970; Claude Lévi-Strauss: an introduction, 1972. *Address:* 2 rue des Marronniers, 75016 Paris, France. *T:* (1) 42883471.

LEVICK, William Russell, FRS 1982; FAA; Professor, John Curtin School of Medical Research, Australian National University, 1983–96, now Emeritus Professor; *b* 5 Dec. 1931; *s* of Russell L. S. Levick and Elsie E. I. (*née* Nance); *m* 1961, Patricia Jane Lathwell; two *s* one *d*. *Educ:* Univ. of Sydney (BSc 1st Cl. Hons, MSc, MB, BS 1st Cl. Hons). Registered Medical Practitioner, State of ACT. FAA 1973. RMO, Royal Prince Alfred Hosp., Sydney, 1957–58; National Health and Med. Res. Council Fellow, Univ. of Sydney, 1959–62; C. J. Martin Travelling Fellow, Cambridge Univ. and Univ. of Calif, Berkeley, 1963–64; Associate Res. Physiologist, Univ. of Calif, Berkeley, 1965–66; Sen. Lectr in Physiol., Univ. of Sydney, 1967; Professorial Fellow of Physiology, John Curtin Sch. of Medicine, ANU, 1967–83. Fellow, Optical Soc. of America, 1977. *Publications:* articles on neurophysiology of the visual system in internat. scientific jls. *Address:* Division of Psychology, Australian National University, Canberra, ACT 0200, Australia. *T:* (2) 62950336.

LEVIEN, Robin Hugh, RDI 1995; owner, since 1999, Partner, since 2006, Studio Levien; *b* 5 May 1952; *s* of John Blomefield Levien and Louis Beryl Levien; *m* 1978, Patricia Anne Stainton. *Educ:* Bearwood Coll., Wokingham; Central Sch. of Art and Design (BA Hons 1973); Royal Coll. of Art (MA 1976). MCSD. Joined Queensberry Hunt, 1977; Partner, Queensberry Hunt, later Queensberry Hunt Levien, 1982–99. Designer of mass market products for manufrs and retailers, incl. Thomas China, Wedgwood, Ideal Standard, American Standard, Habitat, Dartington Crystal; *major products designed:* Trend (for Thomas China), 1981 (Die Gute Industrieform, Hanover, 1982; Golden Flame Award, Valencia, 1983); Studio bathroom range (for Ideal Standard), 1986; Domi bathroom taps, 1989; Symphony range of bathtubs (for American Standard), 1990 (Winner, Interior Design Product Award, Amer. Soc. of Interior Designers, 1991); Kyomi bathroom range (for Ideal Standard), 1996 (Winner, Design Week Awards, 1997); Space bathroom range (for Ideal Standard) (D&AD Silver Award; Winner, FX Internat. Interior Design Award), 1999; Home Elements range (for Villeroy & Boch), 2002. Vis. Prof., London Inst., 1997–. Mem. Council, RCA, 2001–. FRSA 1991 (Chm., Product Design, Student Design Awards, 1991–98; Paul Reilly Meml Lectr, 1998). DUniv Staffs, 2006. *Publications:* articles in Design mag. *Recreations:* Fulham farmer on 1952 Ferguson tractor, films, cooking. *Address:* Cooks Farm, North Brewham, Som BA10 0JQ. *T:* (01749) 850610.

LEVIN, David Roger; Headmaster, City of London School, since 1999; *b* 2 Oct. 1949; *s* of Jack Levin, Cape Town and Isobel Elizabeth Levin (*née* Robinson), Norfolk, England; *m* 1977, Jean Isobel, *d* of Major J. A. P. Hall. *Educ:* Kearsney Coll., Natal; Univ. of Natal (BEcon); Univ. of Sussex (MA). Gen. Manager, Cutty Sark Hotel, Scottburgh, S Africa (family business), 1972–73; Asst Master, Whitgift Sch., Croydon, 1974–75; Articled Clerk, Radcliffes & Co., Solicitors, 1976–78; Asst Master, Portsmouth Grammar Sch., 1978–80; Head of Economics, 1980–93 and Second Master, 1987–93, Cheltenham Coll.; Headmaster, Royal Grammar Sch., High Wycombe, 1993–99. Advr to Minister for London Challenge, 2002–05. FRSA. Governor: Canford Sch., 1995–; Newton Prep. Sch., 2006–; Dean Close Sch., Cheltenham, 2007–. *Recreations:* long distance swimming, theatre, hill walking, opera, military history. *Address:* City of London School, Queen Victoria Street, EC4V 3AL. *T:* (020) 7489 0291; Malden Court, Cheltenham, Glos GL52 2BL. *T:* (01242) 521692.

LEVIN, David Saul; Chief Executive, United Business Media plc, since 2005; *b* 28 Jan. 1962; *s* of late Archie Z. Levin and of Leah S. Levin, OBE; *m* 1992, Lindsay Caroline White; three *s*. *Educ:* Wadham Coll., Oxford (MA 1983); Stanford Grad. Sch. of Business (MBA 1987). Served Army, SSLC, 2nd Lieut, 1st Bn RRF, 1980. Manager, Bain & Co., 1983–89; Associate Dir, Apax Partners & Co., 1990–94; Man. Dir, Unicorn Abrasives Ltd, 1992–94; Chief Operating Officer, Euromoney Pubns plc, 1994–99; CEO, Psion plc, 1999–2002; CEO, Symbian, 2002–05. *Address:* United Business Media plc, Ludgate House, 245 Blackfriars Road, SE1 9UY.

LEVIN, Gerald Manuel; Chief Executive Officer, AOL Time Warner Inc., 2001–02; *b* 6 May 1939; *m* Barbara J. Riley. *Educ:* Haverford Coll. (BA 1960); Univ. of Pennsylvania Law Sch. (LLB 1963). Attorney, Simpson Thacher & Bartlett, NYC, 1963–67; Develt and Resources Corp., 1967–71 (Gen. Manager and Chief Operating Officer, 1969–71); Rep., Internat. Basic Economy Corp., Tehran, 1971–72; joined Time Inc., 1972: Vice-Pres., Programming, 1972–73, Pres. and CEO, 1973–76, Chm., 1976–79, Home Box Office; Gp Vice-Pres., Video, 1979–84; Exec. Vice-Pres., 1984–88; Vice-Chm. and Dir, 1988–90; merger with Warner Communications Inc. to form Time Warner, 1990: Chief Operating Officer, Vice-Chm. and Dir, 1991–92; Pres. and Co-CEO, Feb.–Dec. 1992; CEO, 1992–2001; Chm., 1993–2001; merger with AOL to form AOL Time Warner, 2001. Dir, NY Stock Exchange Inc. Member: Council on Foreign Relns; Trilateral Commn. Member, Board: NY City Partnership; Nat. Cable TV Center and Mus.; Aspen Inst.; Mus. of Jewish Heritage. Dir and Treas., NY Philharmonic. Hon. LLD: Texas Coll., 1985; Middlebury Coll., 1994; Haverford Coll.; Hon. LHD Denver, 1995. *Address:* c/o Time Warner Inc., 75 Rockefeller Plaza, New York, NY 10019–6908, USA. *T:* (212) 4848000.

LEVIN, Prof. Richard Charles, PhD; Frederick William Beinecke Professor of Economics, since 1992, President, since 1993, Yale University; *b* San Francisco, 7 April 1947; *s* of D. Derek Levin and Phylys (*née* Goldstein); *m* 1968, Jane Ellen Aries; two *s* two *d*. *Educ:* Stanford Univ. (BA 1968); Merton Coll., Oxford (LittB 1971; Hon. Fellow, 1996); Yale Univ. (PhD 1974). Yale University, 1974–: Chm., Econs Dept, 1987–92; Dean, Grad. Sch., 1992–93; Res. Associate, Nat. Bureau of Econ. Res., Cambridge, Mass, 1985–90; Program Dir, Internat. Inst. Applied System Analysis, Vienna, 1990–92. Dir, Yale–New Haven Health Services Corp. Inc., 1993–. Consultant, numerous law and business firms. Trustee: Yale–New Haven Hosp., 1993–; Tanner Lectures on Human Values, 1993–. Member: Univs Res. Assoc., 1994–; Nat. Res. Council Bd on Sci., Technol. and Econ. Policy, 1998–. Member: Amer. Econ. Assoc.; Econometric Soc. Hon.

LLD: Princeton, 1993; Harvard, 1994; Hon. DCL Oxford, 1998. *Recreations:* hiking, basket-ball. *Address:* Yale University, 105 Wall Street, New Haven, CT 06511, USA.

LEVINE, Gemma; *see* Levine, J. A.

LEVINE, James; American conductor and pianist; Principal Conductor, since 1973, Music Director, since 1976, Metropolitan Opera, New York (Artistic Director, 1986–2004); Music Director, Boston Symphony Orchestra, since 2004; *b* 23 June 1943; *s* of Lawrence Levine and Helen Levine (*née* Goldstein). *Educ:* Walnut Hills High Sch.; Juilliard Sch. of Music. Asst Conductor, Cleveland Orch., 1964–70; Music Director: Ravinia Fest., 1973–93; Cincinnati May Fest., 1974–78; UBS Verbier Fest. Youth Orch., 2000–04; Conductor: Salzburg Fest., 1975–93; Bayreuth Fest., 1982–98; Chief Conductor, Munich Philharmonic, 1999–2004. Piano début with Cincinnati SO, 1953; conducting début, Aspen Music Fest., 1961; has conducted many major orchestras throughout US and Europe, incl. Vienna Philharmonic, Berlin Philharmonic, Chicago Symphony, NY Philharmonic, Dresden Staatskapelle, Israel Philharmonic, Philharmonia, London Symphony, Boston Symphony, Philadelphia, etc. Has made numerous recordings. Smetana Medal (Czechoslovakia), 1987; nine Grammy awards; Nat. Medal of Arts, 1997; Kennedy Center Honors, 2002. *Address:* Metropolitan Opera Association Inc., Metropolitan Opera House, Lincoln Center, New York, NY 10023, USA.

LEVINE, Jennifer Ann, (Gemma); photographer; *b* 10 Jan. 1939; *d* of Ellis and Mae Mathilda Josephs; *m* 1961, Eric A. Levine (marr. diss. 1986); two *s*. *Educ:* Hasmonean Grammar Sch., London. Antique print business, 1961; interior designer, 1970–75; professional photographer, 1975–; author, 1978–. FRSA 1990. *Exhibitions:* Four Seasons, 1977; With Henry Moore, 1978, 1984; Jerusalem (photographs, poetry and watercolours), 1982, 1983; Henry Moore, 1982; Henry Moore, Wood Sculpture, 1983, 1984, 1985; Jerusalem Photographs, 1983; Tel-Aviv Faces and Places, 1984; Ethiopian Jews, 1985; Faces of the 80's, 1987; Faces of British Theatre, 1990; Gemma Levine: 20 Years of Photography, 1995; People of the 90s, 1995, 1996; Henry Moore, 1995; Memories, 1998; Retrospective to celebrate 25 years, NPG, 2001; Claridge's Within the Image, 2004; Israel Retrospective, 2005; Mayfair, Sotheby's, 2008. *Publications:* Israel: faces and places, 1978; Living with the Bible (painter in watercolour and photographer), 1978; With Henry Moore (author and photographer), 1978; We Live in Israel, 1981; Living in Jerusalem, 1982; The Young Inheritors, 1982; Henry Moore, Wood Sculpture (author and photographer), 1983; Henry Moore: an illustrated biography, by William Packer, 1985; Faces of the 80's, 1987; Faces of British Theatre, 1990; People of the 90's, 1995; Memories, 1998; My Favourite Hymn, 1999; Claridge's Within the Image, 2004; Mayfair, 2008. *Recreations:* swimming, music, gourmet eating, wine, interior design. *Address:* 32 Davies Street, W1K 4ND. *Fax:* (020) 7491 4496; *e-mail:* gemmalevine@aol.com.

LEVINE, Sir Montague (Bernard), Kt 1979; FRCGP, FRCP, FRCPI; general practitioner, 1956–87; HM Coroner, Inner South District, Greater London, 1987–97; Clinical Tutor in General Practice, St Thomas' Hospital, 1972–97; *b* 15 May 1922; *s* of late Philip Levine and of Bessie Levine; *m* 1959, Dr Rose Gold; one *s* one *d*. *Educ:* Royal Coll. of Surgeons in Ireland (LRCSI); Royal Coll. of Physicians in Ireland (MRCPI, LRCPI, LM). DMJ Clin.; FRCGP 1988; FRCPI 2000; FRCP 2002. Licentiate of Rubber Industry, 1944. Industrial physicist, rubber industry, 1939–45; House Surgeon: Royal Victoria Hosp., Bournemouth, 1955; Meath Hosp., Dublin, 1955; Metrop. Police Surg., 1960–66; Asst Dep. Coroner, Inner South London, 1974. Hon. Lectr in Coroners' Law, St Thomas' Hosp. and Guy's Hosp., 1987–97. President: British Acad. of Forensic Sciences, 1993–94; Hunterian Soc., 1997–98. Fellow, Hunterian Soc., 1990. Freeman, Borough of Southwark, 1997. Hon. DSc City, 1997. Royal College of Surgeons in Ireland: Stoney Meml Gold Medal in Anatomy, 1951; Silver Medallist, Medicine, 1953, Pathology, 1953, and Medical Jurisprudence, 1954; Macnaughton Gold Medal in Obs and Gynae., 1955; Lectr in Anat., 1956. *Publications:* Inter-parental Violence and its Effect on Children, 1975; Levine on Coroners' Courts, 1999. *Recreations:* fishing, photography, painting. *Address:* Gainsborough House, 120 Ferndene Road, Herne Hill, SE24 0AA. *T:* (020) 7274 9196. *Club:* Organon.

LEVINE, Sydney; a Recorder, North-Eastern Circuit, 1975–95; *b* 4 Sept. 1923; *s* of Rev. Isaac Levine and Mrs Miriam Levine; *m* 1959, Cécile Rona Rubinstein; three *s* one *d*. *Educ:* Bradford Grammar Sch.; Univ. of Leeds (LLB). Called to the Bar, Inner Temple, 1952; Chambers in Bradford, 1953–98. *Recreations:* music, gardening, painting, learning to use a computer. *Address:* 82A Walsingham Road, Hove, E Sussex BN3 4FF. *T:* (01273) 323590.

LEVINGE, Sir Richard (George Robin), 12th Bt *cr* 1704; farming since 1968; *b* 18 Dec. 1946; *s* of Sir Richard Vere Henry Levinge, 11th Bt, MBE, TD, and Barbara Mary (*d* 1997), *d* of late George Jardine Kidston, CMG; *S* father, 1984; *m* 1st, 1969, Hilary (marr. diss. 1978), *d* of Dr Derek Mark; one *s*; 2nd, 1978, Donna Maria d'Ardia Caracciolo; one *s* one *d*. *Educ:* Brook House, Bray, Co. Wicklow; Hawkhurst Court, West Sussex; Mahwah High School, New York; Craibstone Agricultural Coll. *Heir: s* Richard Mark Levinge, *b* 15 May 1970. *Address:* Clohamon House, Bunclody, Co. Wexford, Ireland. *T:* (54) 77253.

LEVINSON, Prof. Stephen Curtis, PhD; FBA 1988; Director, Max Planck Institute for Psycholinguistics, since 1994 (Managing Director, 1998–2001, 2007–08); Professor, Radboud University (formerly Catholic University), Nijmegen, since 1995; *b* 6 Dec. 1947; *s* of Dr Gordon A. Levinson and Dr Mary C. Levinson; *m* 1976, Dr Penelope Brown; one *s*. *Educ:* Bedales Sch.; King's Coll., Cambridge (Sen. Schol.; 1st Cl. Hons. Archaeology and Anthropology Tripos 1970); PhD Linguistics Anthropology, Calif., 1977. Asst Lectr, 1975–78, Lectr, 1978–91, Reader, 1991–94, Linguistics Dept, Cambridge; Hd, Res. Gp for Cognitive Anthropol., Max Planck Inst. for Psycholinguistics, 1991–97. Vis. Res. Fellow, ANU, 1980–82; Vis. Associate Prof., Stanford Univ., 1987–88. MAE, 2003–. *Publications:* Pragmatics, 1983; (with Dr P. Brown) Politeness, 1987; (with J. Gumperz) Rethinking Linguistic Relativity, 1996; Presumptive Meanings: the theory of generalized conversational implicature, 2000; (ed with M. Bowerman) Language Acquisition and Conceptual Development, 2001; (ed with P. Jaisson) Evolution and Culture, 2006; (ed with D. Wilkins) Grammars of Space, 2006; (ed with N. Enfield) Roots of Human Sociality, 2006; articles in books and jls. *Recreations:* Sunday painting, hiking. *Address:* Payensweg 7, 6523 MB Nijmegen, The Netherlands; Max Planck Institute for Psycholinguistics, PB 310, 6500 AH Nijmegen, The Netherlands.

LEVISON, Rev. Mary Irene; an Extra Chaplain to the Queen in Scotland, since 1993 (Chaplain, 1991–93); *b* 8 Jan. 1923; *d* of late Rev. David Colville Lusk and Mary Theodora Lusk (*née* Colville); *m* 1965, Rev. Frederick Levison (*d* 1999). *Educ:* St Leonard's Sch., St Andrews; Lady Margaret Hall, Oxford (BA); Univ. of Edinburgh (BD). Deaconess in the parish of Inveresk, Musselburgh, 1954–58; Tutor, St Colm's Coll., Edinburgh, 1958–61; Asst Chaplain, Univ. of Edinburgh, 1961–64; Asst Minister, St Andrew's and St George's Church, Edinburgh and Chaplain to the retail trade, 1978–83. Moderator of the Presbytery of Edinburgh, 1988. Vice-Pres., St Leonard's Sch., 1996–2005. Hon. DD Edinburgh, 1994. *Publication:* Wrestling with the Church, 1992. *Recreations:* music, gardening. *Address:* 2 Gillsland Road, Edinburgh EH10 5BW. *T:* (0131) 228 3118.

LEVITT, Alison Frances Josephine, (Lady Carlile of Berriew); QC 2008; a Recorder, since 2007; *b* London, 27 May 1963; *d* of Frederick David Andrew Levitt, OBE and Christian Veronica Bevington, *qv*; *m* 1st, 1993, Matthew Miller (marr. diss.); two *d*; 2nd, 2007, Baron Carlile of Berriew, *qv*. *Educ:* City of London Sch. for Girls; Univ. of St Andrews (MA Hons 1986). Called to the Bar, Inner Temple, 1988; in practice as barrister specialising in criminal law. Chm., Young Barristers Cttee, Bar Council, 1995; Sec., Criminal Bar Assoc., 2006–07. *Recreations:* crime fiction, film. *Address:* 25 Bedford Row, WC1R 4HD. *T:* (020) 7067 1500, *Fax:* (020) 7067 1507; *e-mail:* clerks@25bedfordrow.com.

LEVITT, Prof. Malcolm Harris, DPhil; FRS 2007; Professor of Physical Chemistry, University of Southampton, since 2001; *b* 10 Jan. 1957; *s* of Max and Stella Levitt; *m* 1990, Latha Kadalayil; one *d*. *Educ:* Keble Coll., Oxford (BA; DPhil 1981). Res. Scientist, MIT, 1986–92; Lectr, 1992–97, Prof. of Chemical Spectroscopy, 1997–2001, Stockholm Univ. *Publications:* Spin Dynamics: basics of nuclear magnetic resonance, 2001, 2nd edn 2007; contribs to jls. *Recreations:* electric guitar, classical guitar, politics, jazz, sketching, walking, gardening. *Address:* School of Chemistry, University of Southampton, Southampton SO17 1BJ. *T:* (023) 8059 6753, *Fax:* (023) 8059 3781; *e-mail:* mhl@soton.ac.uk.

LEVITT, Prof. Michael, PhD; FRS 2001; Professor of Structural Biology, Stanford University, California, since 1987; *b* 9 May 1947; *s* of Nathan and Gertrude Levitt; *m* 1968, Rina Harel; three *s*. *Educ:* King's Coll., London (BSc Physics 1967); Gonville and Caius Coll., Cambridge (PhD Computational Biol. 1972). Royal Soc. Exchange Fellow, Weizmann Inst., Israel, 1967–68; Staff Scientist, MRC Lab. of Molecular Biol., Cambridge, 1973–80; Prof. of Chemical Physics, Weizmann Inst., 1980–87. *Publications:* contrib. articles on computational biol. with an emphasis on structure, particularly of protein molecules. *Recreations:* cycling, ski-ing, travel. *Address:* Department of Structural Biology, Stanford School of Medicine, Stanford, CA 94305, USA. *T:* (650) 2760500, *Fax:* (650) 7238464; *e-mail:* michael.levitt@stanford.edu.

LEVITT, Tom; MP (Lab) High Peak, since 1997; *b* 10 April 1954; *s* of John and Joan Levitt; *m* 1983, Teresa Sledziewska; one *d*. *Educ:* Lancaster Univ. (BSc Hons 1975); New Coll., Oxford (PGCE 1976). Biology teacher: Wootton Bassett Sch., 1976–79; Cirencester Sch., 1980–81; Brockworth Sch., Glos., 1981–91; supply Teacher, Staffs, 1991–95; freelance res. consultant, 1993–97. Member (Lab): Cirencester Town Council, 1983–87; Stroud DC, 1990–92; Derbys CC, 1993–97. Contested (Lab): Stroud, 1987; Cotswold, EP elecn, 1989; High Peak, 1992. PPS to Minister of State, Home Office, 1999–2001, Cabinet Office, 2001, ODPM, 2001–03; PPS to Sec. of State for Internat. Develt, 2003–07. Member: Standards and Privileges Select Cttee, 1997–2003; Jt Cttee on Draft Disability Bill, 2004. Chm., Community Develt Foundn, 2004–. Trustee, RNID, 1998–2003. *Publications:* Sound Practice, 1995; Clear Access, 1997; pubns on local govt access issues for people with disabilities. *Recreations:* cricket, theatre, walking, travel. *Address:* (office) 20 Hardwick Street, Buxton, Derbys SK17 6DH. *T:* (01298) 71111.

LEVVY, (Clinton) George; management consultant, since 2004; *b* 30 Nov. 1953; *s* of late Guildford Albert Levvy and Averil Clinton Levvy (*née* Chance); *m* 1st, 1984, Irené M. Young (marr. diss. 1989); 2nd, 1991, Bethe R. Alpert; one *s* one *d*. *Educ:* Robert Gordon's Coll., Aberdeen; Univ. of Edinburgh (MB ChB). Jun. hosp. doctor, 1977–84; Med. Dir and Consultant, Excerpta Medica, Tokyo, 1984–88; Commercial Manager, Countrywide Communications Gp Ltd, 1988–91; Hd, Mktg and Communications, BRCS, 1991–94; Chief Exec., Motor Neurone Disease Assoc., 1995–2004. Member: Appraisal Cttee, NICE, 2000–06; Adv. Cttee, New and Emerging Applications of Technol., DoH, 2000–03. Trustee: Haemophilia Soc., 1999–2002; Self Help Africa, 2008–. *Publications:* contribs to jls and ed vols. *Recreations:* walking, sailing, reading, cricket. *Address:* Beam Reach Consulting Ltd, 43 Kennett Road, Oxford OX3 7BH. *T:* (01865) 766931.

LEVY, family name of **Baron Levy**.

LEVY, Baron *cr* 1997 (Life Peer), of Mill Hill in the London Borough of Barnet; **Michael Abraham Levy;** Chairman, Wireart Ltd, since 1992; *b* 11 July 1944; *s* of Samuel and Annie Levy; *m* 1967, Gilda (*née* Altbach); one *s* one *d*. *Educ:* Fleetwood Primary Sch. (Head Boy); Hackney Downs Grammar Sch. FCA 1966. Lubbock Fine (Chartered Accountants), 1961–66; Principal, M. Levy & Co., 1966–69; Partner, Wagner Prager Levy & Partners, 1969–73; Chairman: Magnet Group of Cos, 1973–88; D & J Securities Ltd, 1988–92; M & G Records, 1992–97; Chase Music (formerly M & G Music) Ltd, 1992–; Vice Chairman: Phonographic Performance Ltd, 1979–84; British Phonographic Industry Ltd, 1984–87. Chm., British Music Industry Awards Cttee, 1992–95; Patron, British Music Industry Awards, 1995–. Nat. Campaign Chm., United Jt Israel Appeal, 1982–85 (Hon. Vice Pres., 1994–2000; Hon. Pres., 2000–); Chairman: Jewish Care, 1992–97 (Pres., 1998–); Jewish Care Community Foundn, 1995–; Vice Chm., Central Council for Jewish Community Services (formerly Central Council for Jewish Social Services), 1994–99. Chairman: Chief Rabbinate Awards for Excellence, 1992–2007; Foundn for Educn, 1993–; Member: Jewish Agency World Bd of Governors, 1990–95 (World Chm., Youth Aliyah Cttee, 1991–95); Keren Hayesod World Bd of Governors, 1991–95; World Commn on Israel-Diaspora Relns, 1995–; Internat. Bd of Governors, Peres Center for Peace, 1997–; Adv. Council, Foreign Policy Centre, 1997–; NCVO Adv. Cttee, 1998–; Community Legal Service Champions Panel, 1999–; Hon. Cttee, Israel, Britain and the Commonwealth Assoc., 2000–. Personal Envoy for Prime Minister to Middle East, 1999–2007. Pres., CSV, 1998–; Trustee: Holocaust Educnl Trust, 1998–2007; Policy Network Foundn, subseq. New Policy Network Foundn, 2000–07; Mem. Exec. Cttee, Chai-Lifeline, 2001–02; Pres., Specialist Schs and Acads Trust, 2005–; Patron: Prostate Cancer Charitable Trust, 1997–; Friends of Israel Educnl Trust, 1998–; Save a Child's Heart Foundn, 2000–; Simon Marks Jewish Primary Sch. Trust, 2002–. Governor, Jews' Free Sch., subseq. JFS, 1990–95 (Hon. Pres., 1995–2001; Pres., 2001–). Hon. Patron, Cambridge Univ. Jewish Soc., 2002–. Hon. Dr Middlesex Univ., 1999. B'nai B'rith First Lodge Award, 1994; Scopus Award, Hebrew Univ. of Jerusalem, 1998; Special Recognition Award, Israel Policy Forum (USA), 2003. *Publication:* A Question of Honour (memoirs), 2008. *Recreations:* tennis, swimming. *Address:* House of Lords, SW1A 0PW.

LEVY, Rabbi Dr Abraham, OBE 2004; Spiritual Head, Spanish and Portuguese Jews' Congregation in UK, since 1983; *b* 16 July 1939; *s* of Isaac Levy and Rachel (*née* Hassan); *m* 1963, Estelle Nahum; one *s*. *Educ:* Carmel Coll.; Jews' Coll.; UCL (PhD 1978). Minister, Spanish and Portuguese Jews' Congregation, 1962–80; Communal Rabbi, 1980–. Chaplain to Lord Mayor of London, 1998–99. (With Chief Rabbi) Ecclesiastical Authy, Bd of Deputies of British Jews, 1980–. Dir, Young Jewish Leadership Inst., 1970–86; Founder and Principal, Naima Jewish Prep. Sch., 1983–; Dep. Pres., London Sch. of Jewish Studies (formerly Jews' Coll.), 1985–; Founder, Sephardi Centre, 1993. Mem., Standing Cttee, Conf. of Eur. Rabbis. Ecclesiastical Authy, London Bd of Shechitah, 2006; Vice Chm., Commn for the Licensing of Shochtim, 2006. President:

Union Anglo-Jewish Preachers, 1973–75; Jewish Child's Day; Vice President: Anglo-Jewish Assoc., 1984–; Jewish Care, 1993–; Norwood (formerly Norwood Ravenswood), 2000–; Jewish Historical Soc. of England, 2006–; British Friends of Hebrew Univ. Mem., Council of Advrs, Jewish Mus. Patron: Centre for Jewish-Christian Relations, Cambridge, 2001–; British Friends of Jerusalem Coll. of Technol.; Hospital Kosher Meals Service; Jewish Council for Racial Equality; Jewish Music Heritage Trust; Oxford Synagogue and Jewish Centre Building Appeal, 2000–; British Friends of Sarah Herzog Meml Hosp.; Jewish Med. Assoc. (UK), 2007–; Hon. Patron, Cambridge Univ. Jewish Soc. Hon. Chaplain, Jewish Lads' and Girls' Brigade. Kt Comdr (Encomienda), Order of Merit (Spain), 1993. *Publications:* The Sephardim: a problem of survival, 1972; (jtly) Ages of Man, 1985; (jtly) The Sephardim, 1992. *Recreation:* collecting antique Judaica. *Address:* 2 Ashworth Road, W9 1JY. *T:* (020) 7289 2573.

LEVY, Andrea Doreen; novelist; *b* 7 March 1956; *d* of Winston and Amy Levy; *m* William Mayblin; two step *d.* *Educ:* Middlesex Polytech. (BA Hons (Textiles) 1978). *Publications:* Every Light in the House Burnin', 1994; Never Far From Nowhere, 1996; Fruit of the Lemon, 1999; Small Island, 2004 (Orange Prize for Fiction, Whitbread Book of the Year, 2004; Commonwealth Writer's Prize, 2005). Hon. Dr Middlesex, 2006. *Recreation:* learning things. *Address:* c/o David Grossman, Literary Agency, 118B Holland Park Avenue, W11 4UA. *T:* (020) 7221 2770, *Fax:* (020) 7221 1445.

LEVY, His Honour Dennis Martyn; QC 1982; a Circuit Judge, 1991–2007; *b* 20 Feb. 1936; *s* of late Conrad Levy and Tillie (*née* Swift); *m* 1967, Rachel Jonah; one *s* one *d.* *Educ:* Clifton Coll.; Gonville and Caius Coll., Cambridge (MA). Called to the Bar, Gray's Inn, 1960, Hong Kong, 1985, Turks and Caicos Is, 1987. Granada Group Ltd, 1960–63; Time Products Ltd, 1963–67; in practice at the Bar, 1967–91; a Recorder, 1989–91. Member: Employment Appeal Tribunal, 1994–2006; Lands Tribunal, 1998. Chm., UK Assoc. of Jewish Lawyers and Jurists, 2007–. Trustee, Fair Trials Internat. (formerly Fair Trials Abroad), 2002–. *Recreations:* living in London and travelling abroad. *Address:* 25 Harley House, Marylebone Road, NW1 5HE. *T:* 07773 429372, *Fax:* (020) 7487 3231.

LEVY, Prof. John Court, (Jack), OBE 1984; FREng; FIMechE, FRAeS, FIEI; FCGI; Managing Director, Levytator Ltd, since 2001; *b* London, 16 Feb. 1926; *s* of Alfred and Lily Levy; *m* 1952, Sheila Frances Krisman; two *s* one *d.* *Educ:* Owens Sch., London; Imperial Coll., Univ. of London (BScEng, ACGI, PhD); Univ. of Illinois, USA (MS). Stressman, Boulton-Paul Aircraft, 1945–47; Asst to Chief Engr, Fullers Ltd, 1947–51. Asst Lectr, Northampton Polytechnic, London, 1951–53; Fulbright Award to Univ. of Illinois, for research into metal fatigue, 1953–54; Lectr, Sen. Lectr, Reader, Northampton Polytechnic (later City Univ.), 1954–66; also a Recognised Teacher of the Univ. of London, 1958–66; Head of Department of Mechanical Engineering, 1966–83 (now Prof. Emeritus), and Pro-Vice-Chancellor, 1975–81, City Univ.; Dir, Engrg Profession, Engrg Council, 1983–90, 1997. Consultant to Shell International Marine, 1963–85; Chairman: 1st Panel on Marine Technology, SRC, 1971–73; Chartered Engr Section, Engineers Registration Bd, CEI, 1978–82; non-exec. Dir, City Technology Ltd, 1980–91. Vice Chm., Bd of Govs, Middlesex Univ., 1997–2000; Chm., Mus. of Domestic Design and Architecture, 1999–2002. Freeman, City of London, 1991; Liveryman, Co. of Engineers, 1991. FREng (FEng 1988); FIEI 2002. Hon. DTech CNAA, 1990; DUniv: Leeds Metropolitan, 1992; Middlesex, 2005; Hon DSc City, 1994. Internat. Gold Medal for contribs to engrg educn, WFEO, 1999. *Publications:* The Engineering Dimension in Europe, 1991; papers on metal fatigue, marine technology, engrg educn, in jls of IMechE, RAeS, IEE, etc. *Recreations:* theatre, chess, exploring cities. *Address:* 18 Woodberry Way, Finchley, N12 0HG. *T:* (020) 8445 5227. *Club:* Island Sailing (Cowes, IoW).

LEVY, Paul, PhD; FRSL; author and broadcaster; Senior Contributor, Europe Leisure and Arts, Wall Street Journal, since 1993; Wine and Food Writer, You Magazine, The Mail on Sunday, since 1993; *b* 26 Feb. 1941; *er s* of late H. S. Levy and Mrs Shirley Meyers, Lexington, Ky, USA; *m* 1977, Penelope, *o c* of late Clifford and Ruby Marcus; two *d.* *Educ:* Univ. of Chicago (AB); University Coll. London; Harvard Univ. (PhD 1979); Nuffield Coll., Oxford. FRSL 1980. Teaching Fellow, Harvard, 1966–68; lapsed academic, 1971–; freelance journalist, 1974–80; Food Correspondent, 1980–82, Food and Wine Ed., 1982–92, The Observer; frequent radio and television broadcasting. Member: Soc. of Authors; PEN; Critics' Circle; Mem. Court, Oxford Brookes Univ., 2003–. Trustee: Strachey Trust, 1972–; Jane Grigson Trust, 1990–; Oxford Symposium on Food and Cooking, 2002–. Corning Award for food writing, 1980, 1981; Glenfiddich Food Writer of the Year, 1980, 1983; Glenfiddich Restaurant Critic of the Year, 1983; Specialist Writer Commendation, British Press Awards, 1985, 1987; Wine Journalist of the Year, Wine Guild of the UK, 1986. Confrèrie des Mousquetaires, 1981; Chevalier du Tastevin, 1987; Chevalier de l'ordre des Dames du Vin et de la Table, 1989; Chevalier de la Commanderie des Dindes de Lique, 1991. *Publications:* (ed) Lytton Strachey: the really interesting question, 1972; The Bloomsbury Group, in Essays on John Maynard Keynes, ed Milo Keynes, 1975; G. E. Moore and the Cambridge Apostles, 1979, 3rd edn 1989; (ed with Michael Holroyd) The Shorter Strachey, 1980, 2nd edn 1989; (with Ann Barr) The Official Foodie Handbook, 1984; Out to Lunch, 1986 (Seagrams/Internat. Assoc. of Cookery Professionals Award, USA, 1988), 2nd edn 2003; Finger-Lickin' Good: a Kentucky childhood (autobiog.), 1990; The Feast of Christmas, 1992 (also TV series); (ed) The Penguin Book of Food and Drink, 1996; (ed) Eminent Victorians: the definitive edition, 2002; (ed) The Letters of Lytton Strachey, 2005; contribs to TLS, Independent, Slate, First Post, Travel & Leisure, Observer, Guardian (Word of Mouth). *Recreations:* being cooked for, drinking better wine, trying to remember. *Address:* PO Box 35, Witney, Oxon OX29 8YT. *T:* (01993) 881312. *Club:* Groucho.

LEVY, Prof. Philip Marcus, PhD; CPsychol, FBPsS; Professor of Psychology, University of Lancaster, 1972–94, now Professor Emeritus; *b* 4 Feb. 1934; *s* of late Rupert Hyam Levy and of Sarah Beatrice Levy; *m* 1958, Gillian Mary (*née* Harker) (*d* 2003); two *d.* *Educ:* Leeds Modern School; Univ. of Leeds (BA 1955); Univ. of Birmingham (PhD 1960). Res. Fellow, Birmingham Univ., 1955–59; Psychologist, RAF, 1959–62; Sen. Res. Fellow, Lectr, Sen. Lectr, Birmingham Univ., 1962–72. Economic and Social Research Council (formerly Social Science Research Council): Mem. Council, 1983–86; Mem., Psychol. Cttee, 1976–82 (Chm., 1979–82); Chm., Educn and Human Develt Cttee, 1982–87; Chm., Human Behaviour and Develt R&D Gp, 1987–89 (Mem. Council, 1987–89). British Psychological Society: Mem. Council, 1973–80; Pres., 1978–79. Editor, Brit. Jl of Mathematical and Statistical Psychology, 1975–80. *Publications:* (jtly) Tests in Education, 1984; (jtly) Cognition in Action, 1987; numerous in psychol jls.

LEVY, Prof. Raymond, FRCPE, FRCPsych; Professor of Old Age Psychiatry, University of London at Institute of Psychiatry, 1984–96, now Emeritus Professor; Hon. Consultant, Bethlem Royal and Maudsley Hospitals, since 1984; *b* 23 June 1933; *o s* of late Gaston Levy and Esther Levy (*née* Bigio); *m* 1956, Katherine Margaret Logie (marr. diss. 1982); two *d.* *Educ:* Victoria Coll., Cairo; Edinburgh Univ. (MB, ChB 1957; PhD 1961); Univ. of London (DPM 1964). Jun. hosp. appts, Royal Infirmary, Northern Gen., Leith, Bethlem Royal and Maudsley Hosps, to 1966; Sen. Lectr and Hon. Consultant Psychiatrist, Middx Hosp. Med. Sch., 1966–71; Consultant Psychiatrist, Bethlem Royal and Maudsley Hosps, 1971–84. Mem., Med. Adv. Commn on Res. into Ageing. Pres., Internat. Psychogeriatric Assoc., 1995–98 (Mem., Bd of Dirs, 1998–2000); Vice-Pres., Eur. Assoc. Geriatric Psych.; Foundn Mem., RCPsych, 1971. Asst Editor, Internat. Jl Geriatric Psych. *Publications:* (all jtly) The Psychiatry of Late Life, 1982; Diagnostic and Therapeutic Assessment in Alzheimer's Disease, 1991; Delusions and Hallucinations in Old Age, 1992; Clinical diversity in late onset of Alzheimer's Disease, 1992; Treatment and Care in Old Age Psychiatry, 1993; Dementia, 1993; contribs to learned jls. *Recreations:* looking at pictures, drinking good wine, travelling, playing tennis. *Address:* Institute of Psychiatry, de Crespigny Park, Denmark Hill, SE5 8AF. *T:* (020) 7467 0512; 4 Hillsleigh Road, W8 7LE. *Clubs:* Campden Hill Lawn Tennis, Holland Park Lawn Tennis.

LEVY-LANG, André; Légion d'Honneur; Chairman: Compagnie Financière de Paribas, 1990–99; Banque Paribas, 1991–99; *b* 26 Nov. 1937. *Educ:* Ecole Polytechnique; Stanford Univ. (PhD Business Admin; Harkness Fellow, 1963–65). Res. physicist, French Atomic Energy Commn, 1960–62; Schlumberger Gp, 1962–74; Compagnie Bancaire: joined 1974; Mem. Bd, 1979; Chm., 1982; Chm., Adv. Bd, 1993. Director: AGF; Schlumberger; Dexia; Mem. Exec. Cttee, Pargesa Holding. Bd mem., banking and employers' assocs. *Address:* 48 boulevard Emile Augier, 75116 Paris, France.

LEW, Julian David Mathew; QC 2002; barrister and arbitrator; Partner, Herbert Smith, 1995–2005; *b* 3 Feb. 1948; *s* of Rabbi Maurice Abram Lew and Rachel Lew (*née* Segalov); *m* 1978, Margot (*née* Perk); two *d.* *Educ:* Carmel Coll.; Univ. of London (LLB Hons ext. 1969); Catholic Univ. of Louvain (PhD 1977). Barrister at Law, 1970; Solicitor, 1981; Attorney-at-Law, NY, 1981; Partner: S. J. Berwin & Co., 1986–92; Coudert Brothers, 1992–95. Dir, 1983–, Mem. Court, 2002–07, London Court of Internat. Arbitration; UK rep. to Internat. Court of Arbitration, ICC, 2006–. Vis. Prof. and Head, Sch. of Internat. Arbitration, Centre for Commercial Law Studies, QMUL (formerly QMC, then QMW), 1986–; Visiting Professor: Faculty of Law, Tel Aviv Univ., 2002; Bar Ilan Univ., Israel, 2005. *Publications:* Applicable Law on International Commercial Arbitration, 1978; (ed jtly) International Trade: law and practice, 1983, 2nd edn 1990; (ed) Contemporary Problems in International Commercial Arbitration, 1986; (ed) Immunity of Arbitrators, 1990; (ed jtly) Recognition of Foreign Judgments, 1994–; (jtly) Comparative International Commercial Arbitration, 2003; (jtly) Parallel State and Arbitral Procedures in International Arbitration, 2005; (ed jtly) Pervasive Problems in International Arbitration, 2006; (ed jtly) Arbitration Insights: twenty years of the annual lecture of the School of International Arbitration, 2007. *Address:* (chambers) 20 Essex Street, WC2R 3AL. *T:* (020) 7842 1200, *Fax:* (020) 7842 1270; *e-mail:* jlew@20essexst.com.

LEWER, Michael Edward, CBE 2002; QC 1983; a Recorder of the Crown Court, 1983–98; a Deputy High Court Judge, 1989–98; *b* 1 Dec. 1933; *s* of late Stanley Gordon Lewer and Jeanie Mary Lewer; *m* 1965, Bridget Mary Gill; two *s* two *d.* *Educ:* Tonbridge Sch.; Oriel Coll., Oxford (MA). Called to Bar, Gray's Inn, 1958, Bencher, 1992. Territorial Army: Captain, 300 LAA Regt, RA, 1955–64; APIS, Intelligence Corps, 1964–67. Chm., Home Secretary's Adv. Cttee on Local Govt Electoral Arrangements for England, 1971–73; Comr, Parly Boundary Commn for England, 1997–2008 (Asst Comr, 1965–69, 1976–88, 1992–96). Mem., Criminal Injuries Compensation Appeals Panel, 1994–2008 (Chm., 1994–2002); Mem., Criminal Injuries Compensation Bd, 1986–2000. Mem., European Parly Constituency Cttee for England, 1993–94. Member: Bar Council, 1978–81; Bar Council Professional Conduct Cttee, 1993–95 (Vice Chm., 1995). *Address:* 99 Queens Drive, N4 2BE. *T:* (020) 8800 1422.

LEWERS, Very Rev. Benjamin Hugh; Provost of Derby, 1981–97; *b* 25 March 1932; *s* of late Hugh Bunnett Lewers, DSO, OBE and Coral Helen Lewers; *m* 1957, Sara Blagden; three *s.* *Educ:* Sherborne School; Selwyn Coll., Cambridge (MA); Lincoln Theological Coll. Employee, Dunlop Rubber Co., 1953–57. Curate, St Mary, Northampton, 1962–65; Priest-in-charge, Church of the Good Shepherd, Hounslow, 1965–68; Industrial Chaplain, Heathrow Airport, 1968–75; Vicar of Newark, 1975–80, Rector 1980–81. A Church Commissioner, 1985–97. *Recreations:* cricket, music, gardening, wine and rug making, photography. *Address:* Thimble Cottage, Marshwood, Bridport, Dorset DT6 5QF. *T:* (01297) 678515.

LEWES, Bishop Suffragan of, since 1997; **Rt Rev. Wallace Parke Benn;** *b* 6 Aug. 1947; *s* of William and Lucinda Jane Benn; *m* 1978, Lindsay Develing; one *s* one *d.* *Educ:* St Andrew's Coll., Dublin; UC, Dublin (BA); Trinity Coll., Bristol (external DipTheol London Univ.). Ordained deacon, 1972, priest, 1973; Assistant Curate: St Mark's, New Ferry, Wirral, 1972–76; St Mary's, Cheadle, 1976–82; Vicar: St James the Great, Audley, Stoke-on-Trent, 1982–87; St Peter's, Harold Wood, and part-time Chaplain, Harold Wood Hosp., 1987–97. President: Fellowship of Word and Spirit, 1998–; Church of England Evangelical Council, 2000–. *Publications:* The Last Word, 1996; Jesus our Joy, 2000; The Heart of Christianity, 2004; (contrib.) Preach the Word, 2007; articles in theol jls. *Recreations:* reading, walking with my wife, Rugby, motor sports. *Address:* Bishop's Lodge, 16a Prideaux Road, Eastbourne, E Sussex BN21 2NB. *T:* (01323) 648462; *e-mail:* lewes@clara.net. *Clubs:* National; London Irish Rugby Football.

LEWES AND HASTINGS, Archdeacon of; *see* Jones, Ven. P. H.

LEWIN SMITH, Jane; Vice Lord-Lieutenant for Cambridgeshire, since 2006; *b* 18 Feb. 1950; *d* of late Brian Frederick Bartholomew and of Thelma Evelyn Bartholomew; *m* 1972, John Mann Lewin Smith; one *s* one *d.* *Educ:* Perse Sch. for Girls, Cambridge; Univ. of Bristol (BSc Soc. Sci.); Homerton Coll., Cambridge (Cert Ed). Chm., W Suffolk Co. Riding for the Disabled Assoc., 1988–96. Chm., British American Community Relns Cttee, RAF Mildenhall, 2003–. JP E Cambs 1994–2008; High Sheriff, 2002–03, DL 2003, Cambs. *Recreations:* horseracing, fishing, gardening. *Address:* Fordham Abbey, Fordham, Ely, Cambs CB7 5LL. *T:* (01638) 720477. *Club:* Royal Worlington and Newmarket Golf.

LEWINGTON, Richard George; HM Diplomatic Service, retired; Chief Technical Adviser, EU Border Management in Central Asia Programme, Dushanbe, Tajikistan, since 2007; *b* 13 April 1948; *s* of late Jack and Ann Lewington; *m* 1972, Sylviane Paulette Marie Cholet; one *s* one *d.* *Educ:* Orchard Secondary Modern Sch., Slough; Slough Grammar Sch. Joined HM Diplomatic Service, 1967; Ulaan Baatar, 1972–75; Lima, 1976–80; FCO, 1980–82; Moscow, 1982–83; First Sec. (Commercial), Tel Aviv, 1986–90; FCO, 1991–95; Dep. High Comr, Malta, 1995–99; Ambassador: to Kazakhstan and Kyrgyzstan, 1999–2002; to Ecuador, 2003–06. Hon. Sec., Tajikistan, Royal Soc. for Asian Affairs, 2003–. Trustee, Dorset Expeditionary Soc., 2004–; Mem., Soc. of Dorset Men, 2006–. *Recreations:* collecting old books and maps on Dorset, iPodding, country walks.

LEWINGTON, (Thomas) Charles, OBE 1997; Managing Director, Hanover Communications (formerly Media Strategy Ltd), since 1998; *b* 6 April 1959; *s* of Maurice Lewington and late Sheila Lewington; *m* 1995, Philippa Jane Kelly; one *d.* *Educ:* Sherborne Sch., Dorset; Univ. of Bath (BSc Econs). Reporter, Bath Evening Chronicle, 1981–86; Western Daily Press: Asst News Editor, 1986–88; Political Corresp., 1988–90; Political Corresp., Daily Express, 1990–92; Political Editor, Sunday Express, 1992–95; Dir of Communications, Cons. Party, 1995–97. Non exec. Dir, Cobra Beers Ltd, 2008–.

Recreations: reading, playing the piano. *Address:* (office) 100 Gray's Inn Road, WC1X 8AL. *T:* (020) 7400 4480; 62 Wandle Road, SW17 7DW. *T:* (020) 8672 3944. *Club:* Soho House.

LEWINTON, Sir Christopher, Kt 1993; CEng; FIMechE, FREng; Chairman, Europe, J. F. Lehman & Co., since 2000; *b* 6 Jan. 1932; *s* of Joseph and Elizabeth Lewinton; *m* 1st, Jennifer Alcock (marr. diss.); two *s*; 2nd, 1979, Louise Head; two step *s*. *Educ:* Acton Technical College. Army Service, Lieut REME. Pres., Wilkinson Sword, N America, 1960–70; Chm., Wilkinson Sword Group, 1970–85; Pres., Internat. Gp, Allegheny International, 1976–85 (Mem. Board, 1976–85); TI Gp plc: Chief Exec., 1986–97; Chm., 1989–2000; Chm., Dowty Gp PLC, 1992–2000. Non-executive Director: Reed Elsevier, 1993–99; Mannesmann AG, 1995–99; Messier-Dowty, 1994–98; Young & Rubicam, NY, 1999–2001; WPP, 2001–03; Advr, Booz Allen Hamilton, 2001–; Mem. Adv. Bd, Morgan Stanley/Metalmark Capital, 2001–; Sen. Advr, Compass Partners, 2005–. FRAeS 1993; FREng (FEng 1994). Hon. DTech Brunel, 1997. *Recreations:* golf, tennis, travel, reading. *Address:* CL Partners, 4 Grosvenor Place, 3rd Floor, SW1X 7HJ. *T:* (020) 7201 5490. *Clubs:* Boodles; Sunningdale Golf; University (New York); Everglades (Palm Beach).

LEWIS; *see* Day-Lewis.

LEWIS, family name of **Baron Lewis of Newnham** and of **Barony of Merthyr**.

LEWIS OF NEWNHAM, Baron *cr* 1989 (Life Peer), of Newnham in the County of Cambridgeshire; **Jack Lewis,** Kt 1982; FRS 1973; FRSC; (first) Warden of Robinson College, Cambridge, 1975–2001; Professor of Chemistry, University of Cambridge, 1970–95; Hon. Fellow of Sidney Sussex College (Fellow, 1970–77); *b* 13 Feb. 1928; *m* 1951, Elfreida Mabel (*née* Lamb); one *s* one *d*. *Educ:* Barrow Grammar Sch. BSc London 1949; PhD Nottingham 1952; DSc London 1961; MSc Manchester 1964; MA Cantab 1970; ScD Cantab 1977. Lecturer: Univ. of Sheffield, 1954–56; Imperial Coll., London, 1956–57; Lecturer-Reader, University Coll., London, 1957–61; Prof. of Chemistry: Univ. of Manchester, 1961–67; UCL, 1967–70. Firth Vis. Prof., Univ. of Sheffield, 1967; Vis. Prof., UCL, 1996–; Lectures: Frontiers of Science, Case/Western Reserve, 1963; Tilden, RIC, 1966; Miller, Univ. of Illinois, 1966; Shell, Stanford Univ., 1968; Venables, Univ. of N Carolina, 1968; A. D. Little, MIT, 1970; Boomer, Univ. of Alberta, 1971; AM, Princeton, 1974; Baker, Cornell, 1974; Nyholm, Chem. Soc., 1974; Chini, Italian Chem. Soc., 1980; Bailar, Illinois Univ., 1981; Dwyer, NSW Inst. of Tech., 1982; Power, Queensland Univ., 1982; Mond, Chem. Soc., 1984; Leeumaker, Wesleyan Univ., 1984; Pettit May, Texas, 1985; Nieuwland, Notre Dame, 1986; Wheeler, Dublin, 1987; Bakerian, Roy. Soc., 1989; Sir Jesse Boot Foundn, Nottingham, 1989; Garner, 1993; Gordon Stone, 1993; Shell, Edinburgh, 1994. Member: CNAA Cttee, 1964–70; Exec. Cttee, Standing Cttee on Univ. Entry, 1966–76; Schs Council, 1966–70; SERC (formerly SRC): Polytechnics Cttee, 1973–79; Chemistry Cttee (Chm., 1975–82); Science Bd, 1975–79; Council, 1979–84; SERC/SSRC Jt Cttee, 1979–84; UGC (Phys. Sci.), 1973–79; Council, Royal Soc., 1982–84 (a Vice-Pres., 1984); Vis. Cttee, Cranfield Inst. of Tech., 1982–92 (Chm., 1985–92); Royal Commn on Environmental Pollution, 1985–92 (Chm., 1986–92); Chairman: Standing Cttee on Structural Safety, 1998–2002; ESART Bd, 1998–. Mem., H of L European Communities Select Cttee, 1993–95, 1997–2001 (Chm. Sub-Cttee C, 1993–95). Pres., Royal Soc. of Chemistry, 1986–88 (Hon. Fellow, 1998); Sci. Rep. for UK on NATO Sci. Cttee, 1986–98. Trustee: Kennedy Meml Trust, 1989–99; Croucher Foundn, 1989–98. Dir, BOC Foundn, 1990–2003. Pres., Arthritis Res. Campaign, 1998–. Hon. Pres., Envmtl Industries Commn, 1996–2000. Patron, Student Community Action Develt Unit, 1985–. Hon. Mem., SCI, 1996. Chm. Govs, Leys Sch., 1997–2002. FNA 1980 (For. Fellow 1986); Foreign Member: Amer. Acad. of Arts and Science, 1983; Amer. Philos. Soc., 1994; Accademia Nazionale dei Lincei, Italy, 1995; Polish Acad. of Arts and Scis, 1996; Fellow, Indian Nat. Sci. Acad., 1985; For. Fellow, Bangladesh Acad. of Scis, 1992; For. Associate, Nat. Acad. of Sciences, USA, 1987; Hon. Fellow, Aust. Inst. of Chem., 1987. Hon. Fellow: UCL, 1990; UMIST, 1990; Central Lancs, 1993. Dr *hc* Rennes, 1980; DUniv: Open, 1982; Kingston, 1993; Hon. DSc: East Anglia, 1983; Nottingham, 1983; Keele, 1984; Leicester, 1988; Birmingham, 1988; Waterloo, Canada, 1988; Manchester, 1990; Wales (Swansea), 1990; Sheffield, 1992; Cranfield, 1993; Edinburgh, 1994; Bath, 1995; Durham, 1996; Hong Kong, 1998; NUI, 1999; Anglia, 2004. American Chem. Soc. Award in Inorganic Chemistry, 1970; Transition Metal Award, Chem. Soc., 1973; Davy Medal, Royal Soc., 1985; Mallinckrodt Award in Inorganic Chemistry, American Chem. Soc., 1986; Gold Medal, Apothecaries Soc., 1993; Paracelsus Prize and Gold Medal, New Swiss Chemical Soc., 1996; Sir Geoffrey Wilkinson Prize, Elsevier Science SA, 1997; August Wilhelm von Hofmann Denkmünze Meml Medal, German Chemical Soc., 1999; Royal Medal, Royal Soc., 2004. Chevalier, Ordre des Palmes Académiques, 1993; Commander, Cross of the Order of Merit (Poland), 1996. *Publications:* papers, mainly in Jl of Chem. Soc. *Address:* Robinson College, Grange Road, Cambridge CB3 9AN. *Club:* Oxford and Cambridge.

LEWIS, Adam Anthony Murless, CVO 2006; FRCS, FRCSE; Serjeant Surgeon to the Queen, 2001–06; Consultant Surgeon, Royal Free Hospital, 1975–2006; Surgeon: St John and Elizabeth Hospital, London, 1975–2006; King Edward VII Hospital for Officers, London, 1991–2006; *s* of late Bernard S. Lewis, CBE, DSC and Mary Lewis (*née* Murless); *m* 1964, Margaret Catherine Ann Surgey; two *s* two *d*. *Educ:* St Bartholomew's Hosp. Med. Coll. (MB, BS London 1963); FRCSE 1968; FRCS 1969. Formerly: Sen. Registrar (Surg.), Royal Free Hosp.; Post Doctoral Fellow, Stanford Univ.; Sen. Lectr (Surg.), Univ. of Benin. Surgeon to Royal Household, 1991–2001. *Publications:* papers on general and gastro-intestinal surgery.

LEWIS, Maj.-Gen. (Alfred) George, CBE 1969; *b* 23 July 1920; *s* of Louis Lewis; *m* 1946, Daye Neville, *d* of Neville Greaves Hunt; two *s* two *d*. *Educ:* St Dunstan's Coll.; King's Coll., London. Served War of 1939–45, India and Burma. Commanded 15th/19th Hussars, 1961–63; Dir, Defence Operational Requirements Staff, MoD, 1967–68; Dep. Comdt, Royal Mil. Coll. of Science, 1968–70; Dir Gen., Fighting Vehicles and Engineer Equipment, 1970–72, retired 1973. Man. Dir, 1973–80, Dep. Chm., 1980–81, Alvis Ltd; Dep. Chm., Self Changing Gears Ltd, 1976–81; Company Secretary: Leyland Vehicles, 1980–81; Bus Manufacturers (Hldgs), 1980–84; Staff Dir, BL plc, 1981–84. Mem., Governing Bd, St Dunstan's Coll. Educational Foundn, 1976–87. Hon. Col, Queen's Own Mercian Yeomanry, 1977–82. Mem., St John Council for Warwickshire, 1973–97; OStJ 1996. *Recreations:* gardening, writing, making things, croquet.

LEWIS, (Alun) Kynric; QC 1978; QC (NI) 1988; a Recorder of the Crown Court, 1979–97; *b* Harlech, 23 May 1928; 3rd *s* of late Rev. Cadwaladr O. Lewis and Ursula Lewis; *m* 1955, Bethan, *er d* of late Prof. Edgar Thomas, CBE, and Eurwen Thomas; one *s* two *d*. *Educ:* The Grammar School, Beaumaris; University Coll. of N Wales (BSc); London School of Economics (LLB). Barrister, Middle Temple, 1954, Bencher, 1988; Gray's Inn, 1961; in practice in intellectual property law chambers, 1955–98. Asst Comr, Parly Boundary Commn for Wales, 1996–99. Member: Cttees of Investigation for GB and England and Wales under Agricl Marketing Act, 1979–88; Parole Bd, 1982–85; Welsh Arts Council, 1986–92. Hon. Counsel, Welsh Books Council, 1989–2002. *Recreations:* walking, fishing, gardening. *Address:* Penrallt, Llys-faen, Caerdydd CF14 0TG; 8 New Square, Lincoln's Inn, WC2A 3QP.

LEWIS, Ann Walford, CMG 2000; HM Diplomatic Service, retired; *b* 2 May 1940; *d* of Dr Gwyn Walford Lewis and Winifred Marguerite Emma Lewis; one *s*. *Educ:* Allerton High Sch., Leeds; Leeds Univ. (BA). Teacher, translator and journalist, Finland, 1962–66; HM Diplomatic Service, 1966–2000: Research Dept, FCO, 1966–70; Second Secretary: Moscow, 1970–71; Res. Dept, FCO, 1971–72; Helsinki, 1972–74; Res. Dept, FCO, 1974–79; on secondment as Mem., Assessments Staff, Cabinet Office, 1979–82; Head of Chancery, E Berlin, 1982–85; Eastern Eur. Dept, FCO, 1985–91 (Dep. Head, 1988–91); Dep. Head, 1991–96, Head, 1996–2000, Cultural Relns Dept, FCO. Founder Dir, 1992, Dep. Chm., 1998–, English Coll. Foundn; Governor: English Coll., Prague, 1995–; St Clare's, Oxford, 2000– (Dep. Chm., 2006–). Trustee, BEARR Trust, 1999–. *Publications:* (ed) The EU and Ukraine: neighbours, friends, partners?, 2002; (ed) The EU and Belarus: between Moscow and Brussels, 2002; (ed) The EU and Moldova: on a fault-line of Europe, 2003; (ed) Old Roots, New Shoots: the story of the English College in Prague, 2004. *Recreations:* theatre, gardening, travel. *Address:* 16 Townley Road, SE22 8SR. *T:* (020) 8693 6418.

LEWIS, Anthony; *see* Lewis, J. A.

LEWIS, Anthony Meredith; Senior Partner, 1986–89, Joint Senior Partner, 1989–94, Taylor Joynson Garrett; *b* 15 Nov. 1940; *s* of Col Glyndwr Vivian Lancelot Lewis and Gillian Lewis (*née* Fraser); *m* 1970, Mrs Ewa Maria Anna Strawinska, former Social Editor of Tatler; one *s* one *d*. *Educ:* Rugby School; St Edmund Hall, Oxford (MA Law). Freshfields, 1964–70; Partner, Joynson-Hicks, 1970–86. Chief Exec., City & Thames Gp, 1994–. Panel Mem., The Prince's Trust, 1996–. *Recreations:* opera, tennis, ski-ing, golf, piano.

LEWIS, Anthony Robert, (Tony Lewis), CBE 2002; DL; writer and consultant; Marketing Consultant, Long Reach International Insurance, since 2003; *b* 6 July 1938; *s* of Wilfrid Llewellyn Lewis and Florence Marjorie Lewis (*née* Flower); *m* 1962, Joan (*née* Pritchard); two *d*. *Educ:* Neath Grammar Sch.; Christ's Coll., Cambridge (MA). Double Blue, Rugby football, 1959, cricket, 1960–62, Captain of cricket, 1962, Cambridge Univ. Glamorgan CCC: cricketer, 1955–74; Captain, 1967–72; Chm., 1988–93; Trustee, 1992–; Pres., 1999–2005; 9 Tests for England, 1972–73 (Captain of 8); Captained MCC to India, Ceylon and Pakistan, 1972–73. Presenter: sports and arts magazine programmes, HTV, 1971–82; Sport on Four, BBC Radio, 1977–86; BBC TV presenter of cricket and commentator, 1974–98; Cricket Correspondent, Sunday Telegraph, 1974–93; freelance sports contributor, Sunday Telegraph, 1993–99. Chm., World Snooker Ltd, 2003. Consultant, Univ. of Wales, Newport, 2004–07. Chm. Cttee, Assoc. of Business Sponsorship of the Arts (Wales), 1988–90; Member: Bd, Sports Council for Wales, 1967–69; Welsh Economic Council, 1994–96; Tourism Action Gp, CBI, 1994–2000; Bd, BTA, 1992–2000; Chm., Wales Tourist Bd, 1992–2000. Chm., Wales Ryder Cup bid, 2000–01. Chm., Bd, WNO, 2003–06. DL, 1994, High Sheriff, 1998–99, Mid Glam. Hon. Fellow: St David's Univ. Coll., Lampeter, 1993; Glamorgan Univ., 1995; Univ. of Wales, Swansea, 1996; Cardiff Univ., 1999; Univ. of Wales, Newport, 2008. *Publications:* A Summer of Cricket, 1976; Playing Days, 1985; Double Century, 1987; Cricket in Many Lands, 1991; MCC Masterclass, 1994; Taking Fresh Guard, 2003. *Recreations:* classical music, golf. *Clubs:* East India, MCC (Pres., 1998–2000; Trustee, 2002–03; Chm. of Cricket, 2003–07; Chm., World Cricket Cttee, 2006–); Royal Porthcawl Golf, Royal & Ancient Golf, Royal Worlington and Newmarket Golf.

LEWIS, Prof. Barry, MD, PhD; FRCP; FRCPath; Visiting Professor, Department of Medicine, Royal Prince Alfred Hospital, University of Sydney, since 2006; Consultant Physician and Professor Emeritus, University of London; *b* 16 March 1929; *s* of George Lewis and Pearl Lewis; *m* 1972, Eve Simone Rothschild; three *c*. *Educ:* Rondebosch School, Cape Town; University of Cape Town (PhD, MD). Training posts, Groote Schuur Hosp., Cape Town, 1953; lectureship and fellowships, St George's Hosp., 1959; MRC, 1963; Consultant Pathologist, St Mark's Hosp., 1967; Sen. Lectr in Chemical Pathology, hon. consultant chem. pathologist and physician, Hammersmith Hosp., 1971; Chm., Dept of Chem. Path. and Metabolic Disorders, St Thomas' Hosp., and Dir of Lipid Clinic, 1976–88. Recent research and clinical interests: causes, prevention and regression of atherosclerosis, prevention of cardiovascular disease, hyperlipidaemia. Founder Chm., Internat. Taskforce for Prevention of Coronary Heart Disease, 1987–94. Heinrich Wieland Prize, 1980. *Publications:* The Hyperlipidaemias: clinical and laboratory practice, 1976; (with Eve Lewis) The Heart Book, 1980; (with N. Miller) Lipoproteins, Atherosclerosis and Coronary Heart Disease, 1981; (jtly) Metabolic and Molecular Bases of Acquired Disease, 1990; Handbook on Prevention of Coronary Heart Disease, 1990; (with G. Assmann) Social and Economic Contexts of Coronary Disease Prevention, 1990; (jtly) Prevention of Coronary Heart Disease in the Elderly, 1991; (jtly) Prevention of Coronary Heart Disease: scientific background and clinical guidelines, 1993; (jtly) Low Blood Cholesterol: health implications, 1993; Paradise Regained: insights into coronary heart disease prevention, 1997; (jtly) Familial Hypercholesterolemia: a missed opportunity in preventive medicine; Evolution of the Lipid Clinic 1968–2008, 2008; 300 papers on heart disease, nutrition and lipoproteins in med. and sci. jls. *Recreations:* music, travel, reading. *Address:* 32/337 New South Head Road, Double Bay, NSW 2028, Australia.

LEWIS, Bernard, BA, PhD; FBA 1963; FRHistS; Cleveland E. Dodge Professor of Near Eastern Studies, Princeton University, 1974–86, now Emeritus; Director of Annenberg Research Institute, Philadelphia, 1986–90; *b* London, 31 May 1916; *s* of H. Lewis, London; *m* 1947, Ruth Hélène (marr. diss. 1974), *d* of late Overretsagfører M. Oppenhejm, Copenhagen; one *s* one *d*. *Educ:* Wilson Coll.; The Polytechnic; Universities of London and Paris (Fellow UCL 1976). Derby Student, 1936. Asst Lecturer in Islamic History, Sch. of Oriental Studies, University of London, 1938; Prof. of History of Near and Middle East, SOAS, London Univ., 1949–74 (Hon. Fellow, 1986). Served RAC and Intelligence Corps, 1940–41; attached to a dept of Foreign Office, 1941–45. Visiting Professor: UCLA, 1955–56; Columbia Univ., 1960; Indiana Univ., 1963; Collège de France, 1980; Ecole des Hautes Etudes, Paris 1983, 1988; A. D. White Prof.-at-Large, Cornell Univ., 1984–90; Hon. Incumbent, Kemal Atatürk Chair in Ottoman and Turkish Studies, Princeton Univ., 1992–93. Vis. Mem., 1969, Long-term Mem., 1974–86, Inst. for Advanced Study, Princeton, New Jersey; Lectures: Class of 1932, Princeton Univ., 1964; Gottesman, Yeshiva Univ., 1974; Exxon Foundn, Chicago, 1986; Tanner, Brasenose Coll., Oxford, 1990; Jefferson, NEH, 1990; Il Mulino, Bologna, 1991; Weizman, Rehovot, Israel, 1991; Henry M. Jackson Meml, Seattle, 1992; Merle Curti, Wisconsin, 1993. Mem., Amer. Acad. of Arts and Scis, 1983; Membre Associé, Institut d'Egypte, Cairo, 1969; Mem., Amer. Philosophical Soc., 1973; Corresp. Mem., Institut de France, Académie des Inscriptions et Belle-Lettres, 1994; Hon. Mem., Turkish Acad. of Scis, 1997. Hon. Fellow, Turkish Historical Soc., Ankara, 1972; holds 15 hon. doctorates. Certificate of Merit for services to Turkish Culture, Turkish Govt, 1973. Harvey Prizewinner, 1978; Atatürk Peace Prize, 1998; Award for Peace and Democracy, Atatürk Soc. of America, 2002; Golden Plate Award, Acad. of Achievement, Washington,

DC, 2004; Irving Kristol Award, Amer. Enterprise Inst. for Public Policy Res., 2007. *Publications:* The Origins of Ismā'īlism, 1940; Turkey Today, 1940; British contributions to Arabic Studies, 1941; Handbook of Diplomatic and Political Arabic, 1947, 1956; (ed) Land of Enchanters, 1948, 2nd edn (with S. Burstein) 2001; The Arabs in History, 1950, 6th rev. edn 1993; Notes and Documents from the Turkish Archives, 1952; The Emergence of Modern Turkey, 1961 (rev. edn, 1968); The Kingly Crown (translated from Ibn Gabirol), 1961, 2nd edn (with A. L. Gluck) 2003; co-ed. with P. M. Holt, Historians of the Middle East, 1962; Istanbul and the Civilization of the Ottoman Empire, 1963; The Middle East and the West, 1964; The Assassins, 1968; Race and Color in Islam, 1971; Islam in History, 1973, 2nd edn 2001; Islam from the Prophet Muhammad to the Capture of Constantinople, 2 vols, 1974; History, Remembered, Recovered, Invented, 1975; (ed) The World of Islam: Faith, People, Culture, 1976; Studies in Classical and Ottoman Islam, 7th-16th centuries, 1976; (with Amnon Cohen) Population and Revenue in the Towns of Palestine in the Sixteenth Century, 1978; The Muslim Discovery of Europe, 1982, 2nd edn 2001; The Jews of Islam, 1984, 2nd edn 1987; Le Retour de l'Islam, 1985; (ed, with others) As Others See Us: mutual perceptions East and West, 1985; Semites and Anti-Semites, 1986, rev. edn 1999; The Political Language of Islam, 1988; Race and Slavery in the Middle East, 1990; (ed jtly) Muslims in Europe, 1992; (ed jtly) Religionsgespräche im Mittelalter, 1992; Islam and the West, 1993; The Shaping of the Modern Middle East, 1994; Cultures in Conflict: Christians, Muslims and Jews in the Age of Discovery, 1994; The Middle East: two thousand years of history from the rise of Christianity to the present day, 1995; The Future of the Middle East, 1997; The Multiple Identities of the Middle East, 1998; A Middle East Mosaic: fragments of life, letters and history, 2000; Music of a Distant Drum, 2001; What Went Wrong?: Western Impact and Middle Eastern Response, 2002; The Crisis of Islam: holy war and unholy terror, 2003; From Babel to Dragomans: interpreting the Middle East, 2004; Political Words and Ideas in Islam, 2008; co-ed, Encyclopaedia of Islam, 1956–87; (ed, with others) The Cambridge History of Islam, vols 1a and 1b, 1970; articles in learned journals. *Address:* Near Eastern Studies Department, Jones Hall, Princeton University, Princeton, NJ 08544–1008, USA. *Club:* Athenæum; Princeton (New York).

LEWIS, Brian William; His Honour Judge Brian Lewis; a Circuit Judge, since 1997; *b* 23 July 1949; *o s* of Gilbert Pryce Lewis and Mary Williamson Lewis; *m* 1981, Maureen O'Hare; one *s*. *Educ:* Sale Co. GS for Boys; Univ. of Hull (LLB Hons). Called to the Bar, Inner Temple, 1973; Lectr, Barnet Coll., 1973–74; in practice at the Bar, Cardiff, 1974–75, Liverpool, 1976–97; Asst Recorder, 1989–93; a Recorder, 1993–97. *Recreations:* family life, sport, reading, military history. *Address:* Queen Elizabeth II Law Courts, Derby Square, Liverpool L2 1XA. *T:* (0151) 473 7373.

LEWIS, Byron; *see* Lewis, D. B.

LEWIS, Carl; *see* Lewis, F. C.

LEWIS, Very Rev. Christopher Andrew, PhD; Dean of Christ Church, Oxford, since 2003; *b* 4 Feb. 1944; *s* of Adm. Sir Andrew Lewis, KCB and late Rachel Elizabeth (*née* Leatham); *m* 1970, Rhona Jane Martindale; two *s* one *d*. *Educ:* Marlborough Coll.; Bristol Univ. (BA 1969); Corpus Christi Coll., Cambridge (PhD 1974); Westcott House, Cambridge. Served RN, 1961–66; ordained deacon, 1973, priest, 1974; Asst Curate, Barnard Castle, 1973–76; Tutor, Ripon Coll., Cuddesdon, 1976–81; Dir, Oxford Inst. for Church and Soc., 1976–79; Priest-in-charge, Aston Rowant and Crowell, 1978–81; Vice Principal, Ripon Coll., Cuddesdon, 1981–82; Vicar of Spalding, 1982–87; Canon Residentiary, Canterbury Cathedral, 1987–94; Dir of Ministerial Trng, dio. of Canterbury, 1989–94; Dean of St Albans, 1994–2003. Chm., Assoc. of English Cathedrals, 2000–. *Recreations:* guinea fowl, bicycles. *Address:* The Deanery, Christ Church, Oxford OX1 1DP. *T:* (01865) 276161, *Fax:* (01865) 276238.

LEWIS, Claire; *see* Curtis-Thomas, C.

LEWIS, Clive Buckland; QC 2006; a Recorder, since 2003; *b* 13 June 1960; *s* of John Buckland Lewis and late Vera May Lewis (*née* Prosser). *Educ:* Cwmtawe Comp. Sch.; Churchill Coll., Cambridge (BA 1981); Dalhousie Univ. (LLM 1983). Lectr, UEA, 1983–86; Fellow, Selwyn Coll., Cambridge, 1986–93; Univ. Lectr, Univ. of Cambridge, 1989–93. Called to the Bar, Middle Temple, 1987; in practice at the Bar, 1992–. First Counsel to Nat. Assembly for Wales, 2000–. Mem. Editl Bd, Public Law, 2006–. *Publications:* Judicial Remedies in Public Law, 1992, 3rd edn 2004; (ed) Civil Procedure; Remedies and the Enforcement of European Community Law, 1996. *Recreations:* travel, walking, reading, golf, bridge. *Address:* 11 King's Bench Walk, Temple, EC4Y 7EQ. *T:* (020) 7632 8500. *Clubs:* Athenæum, Royal Automobile.

LEWIS, Clive Hewitt, FRICS; President, Royal Institution of Chartered Surveyors, 1993–94; *b* 29 March 1936; *s* of Thomas Jonathan Lewis, OBE and Marguerite Eileen Lewis; *m* 1961, Jane Penelope White; two *s* one *d*. *Educ:* St Peter's Sch., York. FRICS 1963; FSVA 1979. With Goddard & Smith, 1957–62; Founder and Sen. Partner, Clive Lewis & Partners, 1963–92, when merged with Edward Erdman; Jt Chm., Colliers Erdman Lewis, 1993–95. Non-executive Director: St Modwen Properties, 1983–2002; Town Centre Securities, 1994–; Freeport Leisure, 1997–2004. Dep. Chm., Merseyside Develt Corp., 1989–98. Chm., Bank of England Property Forum, 1994–2002. Mem. Council, Internat. Year of Shelter for the Homeless, 1985–88. Mem., Gen. Council, RICS, 1987–95 (Pres., Gen. Practice Div., 1989–90); President: Eur. Council of Real Estate Professionals, 1990; UK, 1976–77, World, 1984–85, Internat. Real Estate Fedn (Mem. Exec. Cttee, 1977–92). Pres., Land Aid Charitable Trust, 1986–2003. Freeman, City of London, 1983; Liveryman, Chartered Surveyors' Co., 1983–2002. Hon. DLitt S Bank, 1993. *Recreations:* bridge, dogs, golf, cricket. *Address:* 8 The Pastures, Totteridge, N20 8AN. *T:* (020) 8445 5109. *Clubs:* MCC; S Herts Golf; Totteridge Cricket (Pres., 2005–).

LEWIS, Damian Watcyn; actor; *b* 11 Feb. 1971; *s* of Watcyn Lewis and Charlotte Lewis; *m* 2007, Helen McCrory; one *d*. *Educ:* Ashdown House Prep. Sch.; Eton Coll.; Guildhall Sch. of Music and Drama (Fellow 2006). Actor: *theatre* includes: Hamlet, Open Air Th., Regent's Park, 1994; School for Wives, Almeida, 1994; on Broadway, 1995; RSC, 1996–98; Into the Woods, Donmar, 1999; Pillars of the Community, NT, 2005; *television* includes: Warriors, 1999; Band of Brothers, 2000; Soames Forsyte in The Forsyte Saga, 2001; Life, 2007; *films* include: Dreamcatcher, 2002; An Unfinished Life, 2003; Keane, 2004; The Baker (also producer), 2008. Partner, Picture Farm Ltd, prodn co., 2004–. Ambassador for: Prince's Trust, 2002–; Christian Aid, 2005– (made report on privatization in Bolivia, 2005); Patron, Scene and Heard, 2004–. Mem., Stage Golfing Soc. *Recreations:* football, tennis, golf, gardening, bicycling, watching film, theatre, reading, travelling, day dreaming, playing piano badly. *Address:* c/o Markham & Froggatt, 4 Windmill Street, W1T 2HZ. *Clubs:* Groucho, Queen's.

LEWIS, Prof. Dan, PhD; DSc; FRS 1955; Quain Professor of Botany, London University, 1957–78, now Emeritus; Hon. Research Fellow, University College, London, since 1978; *b* 30 Dec. 1910; *s* of Ernest Albert and Edith J. Lewis; *m* 1933, Mary Phœbe Eleanor Burry (*d* 2003); one *d*. *Educ:* High Sch., Newcastle-under-Lyme, Staffs; Reading University (BSc); PhD, DSc (London). Research Scholar, Reading Univ., 1935–36; Scientific Officer, Pomology Dept, John Innes Hort. Inst., 1935–48; Head of Genetics Dept, John Innes Horticultural Institution, Bayfordbury, Hertford, Herts, 1948–57. Rockefeller Foundation Special Fellowship, California Inst. of Technology, 1955–56; Visiting Prof. of Genetics, University of Calif, Berkeley, 1961–62; Royal Society Leverhulme Visiting Professor: University of Delhi, 1965–66; Singapore, 1970; Vis. Prof., QMC, 1978–. Pres., Genetical Soc., 1968–71; Mem., UGC, 1969–74. *Publications:* Sexual Incompatibility in Plants, 1979; Editor, Science Progress; scientific papers on Genetics and Plant Physiology. *Recreation:* music. *Address:* Flat 2, 56/57 Myddelton Square, EC1R 1YA. *T:* (020) 7278 6948.

LEWIS, (David) Byron, FCA; Lord-Lieutenant of West Glamorgan, since 2008; *b* Swansea, 14 Feb. 1945; *s* of late William Edward Lewis and Eiddwen Lewis; *m* 1969, Hilary Ann Morgan; two *d*. *Educ:* Gowerton Grammar Sch., Swansea. FCA 1968. Finance Dir, various private companies; Dir, 1975–85, Asst Gp Man. Dir, 1985–91, Christie-Tyler plc; Man. Dir, subsidiaries of Hillsdown Hldgs plc, 1991–93; non-exec. Chm., various private companies, 1993–2008. Freeman, City of London, 1989. High Sheriff, W Glamorgan, 2004–05. *Recreations:* sport, music, gardening. *Address:* Bryn Newydd House, 1 Derwen Fawr Road, Sketty Green, Swansea SA2 8AN. *T:* (01792) 203012; *e-mail:* byron.lewis@btinternet.com. *Club:* Oriental.

LEWIS, Sir David Courtenay M.; *see* Mansel Lewis.

LEWIS, (David) Ralph; QC 1999; a Recorder, since 2000; *b* 29 June 1956; *s* of David Ieuan Lewis and late (Annie Mary) Eunice Lewis (*née* Evans); *m* Elizabeth Shelley; two *s* one *d*. *Educ:* Dudley Grammar Sch.; Jesus Coll., Oxford (MA). Called to the Bar, Middle Temple, 1978; an Asst Recorder, 1996–2000; Head, No 5 Chambers, 2007–. Mem., Bar Council, 1999–2002. *Recreations:* shooting, travel, ski-ing. *Address:* 5 Fountain Court, Steelhouse Lane, Birmingham B4 6DR. *T:* (0121) 606 0500. *Club:* Oxford and Cambridge.

LEWIS, David Robert; Secretary, Royal Commission on Environmental Pollution, 1992–2002; *b* 27 Nov. 1940; *o c* of William Lewis, Pembroke Dock and Kate Lewis (*née* Sperring); *m* 1965, Christine, *o d* of Leslie and Maud Tye; three *s*. *Educ:* Tiffin Sch.; New Coll., Oxford (Classical Exhibn; MA; DPhil 1970). Joined Min. of Housing and Local Govt, 1965; Sec., Central Adv. Water Cttee, 1969–73; HM Treasury, 1973–75; Asst Sec., Central Unit on Envmtl Pollution, DoE, 1975–77; Dir, Public Admin and Social Policy, CS Coll., 1978–80; Asst Sec., DoE, 1981–89; Hd, Water Services Div., DoE, 1990–92. Chm., Cymdeithas Eryri—Snowdonia Soc., 2008–; Member: Exec. Cttee, London Forum of Amenity and Civic Socs, 2003–08; Campaign (formerly Council) for National Parks, 2004– (Mem., Welsh Adv. Cttee, 2004–). Chm. Govs, Ernest Bevin Sch., later Coll., 1988–99; Chm., Sir Walter St John's Educnl Charity, 1997–2006. *Publications:* The Electrical Trades Union and the Growth of the Electrical Industry, 1970; (ed jtly) Policies into Practice, 1984. *Recreations:* exploring new places, 17th and 18th century literature. *Address:* Dolafon, Llanbedr, Gwynedd LL45 2DJ.

LEWIS, David Thomas Rowell; JP; Consultant, Norton Rose, since 2003 (Senior Partner, 1997–2003); Lord Mayor of London, 2007–08; *b* 1 Nov. 1947; *s* of Thomas Price Merfyn Lewis; *m* 1970, Theresa Susan Poole; one *s* one *d*. *Educ:* Dragon Sch., Oxford; St Edward's Sch., Oxford; Jesus Coll., Oxford (MA 1969; Hon. Fellow 1998). Admitted solicitor, 1972, Hong Kong, 1977; joined Norton Rose, 1969: articled, 1969–72; Asst Solicitor, 1972–76; Partner, 1977; Managing Partner, Hong Kong Office, 1979–82; Head: Corporate Finance, 1989–94; Professional Resources, 1994–99. Non-exec. Dir, Standard Life Assurance Co., 2003–04. Trustee: Oxford Univ. Law Foundn, 1997–2007; Oxford Inst. of Legal Practice, 2001–03; Mem., Oxford Univ. Law Develt Council, 1997– (Chm., 2003–06). Alderman, Broad Street Ward, 2001–; Sheriff, City of London, 2006–07; Liveryman: Solicitors' Co.; Fletchers' Co.; Welsh Livery Guild. JP City of London, 2002. Mem., Royal Soc. of St George, 2004–. Governor: Dragon Sch., Oxford, 1987– (Chm., 2003–08); Oxford Brookes Univ., 1995–2003; Christ's Hosp., 2001–. Mem., Law Soc. Legal Practice Course Bd, 1995–2000. President: St Edward's Sch. Soc., 1995–96; Broad Street Ward Club, 2001–. Churchwarden, St Margaret Lothbury. Hon. DCL City, 2007. KStJ 2008. *Publications:* contrib. articles in jls. *Recreations:* keeping fit, spoiling my dogs, collecting maps, travel, supporting Welsh Rugby. *Address:* Norton Rose, 3 More London Riverside, SE1 2AQ. *T:* (020) 7283 6000. *Clubs:* Achilles, Pilgrims; Hong Kong (Hong Kong).

LEWIS, David Whitfield, RDI 1995; freelance design consultant, since 1967; *b* 19 Feb. 1939; *s* of John Whitfield Lewis and Joan Lewis; *m* 1964, Marianne Mygind; one *s* one *d*. *Educ:* Central Sch. of Design, London. Employed by Danish design consultancy, working on radio and television equipment designs, incl. designs for Beolab 5000 Series Hi-Fi music systems for Bang & Olufsen, and invented slide rule motif, 1960–68; collaborated with Henning Moldenhawer on television equipment for Bang & Olufsen, and industrial processing machinery and marine products, 1968–80; work included in Design Collection, Mus. of Modern Art, NY. Hon. FRIBA, 2007. ID Prize, Danish Design Centre, 1976 (marine folding propeller), 1982 (dental tools), 1986 (television set), 1990 (push button system), 1994 (audio system); Design Prize, EC, 1988; MITI, G-Mark Grand Prix, 1991 (audio hi-fi system); Internat. Design Prize, Badenwurttemberg, 1993 (audio hi-fi system); Annual Prize, Danish Design Council, 2003. Knight of the Order of Dannebrog (Denmark), 2003. *Address:* David Lewis Designers Aps, Blegdamsvej 28,d, 2200 Copenhagen N, Denmark. *T:* 33139635; Piniehøj 2, 2960 Rungsted Kyst, Denmark.

LEWIS, Denise, OBE 2001 (MBE 1999); athlete; *b* 27 Aug. 1972; *d* of Joan Lewis; one *d* by Patrick Stevens; *m* 2006, Stephen Joseph O'Connor; one *s*. Mem., Birchfield Harriers. Heptathlon wins include: Commonwealth Games: Gold Medal, 1994, 1998; European Cup: Gold Medal, 1995, Silver Medal, 2003; Olympic Games: Bronze Medal, 1996, Gold Medal, 2000; World Championships: Silver Medal, 1997, 1999; European Championships: Gold Medal, 1998. *Publications:* Personal Best (autobiog.), 2001; The Flat Tummy Book, 2008.

LEWIS, Dr Dennis Aubrey, BSc; Director, Aslib, the Association for Information Management, 1981–89; *b* 1 Oct. 1928; *s* of Joseph and Minnie Lewis; *m* 1956, Gillian Mary Bratby; two *s*. *Educ:* Latymer Upper Sch.; Univ. of London (BSc 1st Cl. Hons Chemistry, 1953; PhD 1956). FCLIP (FIInfSc 1984). Res. Chemist, 1956–68, Intelligence Manager, 1968–81, ICI Plastics Div. Member: Adv. Council, British Library, 1976–81; Library Adv. Cttee, British Council, 1981–. Member: Welwyn Garden UDC, 1968–74; Welwyn Hatfield DC, 1974–2007 (Chm., 1976–77); Chm., Welwyn Hatfield Alliance, 2004–. Hon. LLM Herts, 2005. *Publications:* Index of Reviews in Organic Chemistry, annually 1963–; (ed jtly) Great Information Disasters, 1991; pubns on information management in Aslib Procs and other journals. *Recreations:* music, old churches, 'futurology'.

LEWIS, Derek (Compton); Chairman, Protocol Associates, since 2002; *b* 9 July 1946; *s* of late Kenneth Compton Lewis and Marjorie Lewis; *m* 1969, Louise (*née* Wharton); two *d*. *Educ:* Wrekin Coll., Telford; Queens' Coll., Cambridge (MA); London Business Sch. (MSc). Ford Motor Co., 1968–82, Dir of Finance, Ford of Europe, 1978–82; Dir of Corporate Develt and Gp Planning Man., Imperial Gp, 1982–84; Granada Group: Finance Dir, 1984–87; Man. Dir, 1988–89; Gp Chief Exec., 1990–91; Dir, Courtaulds Textiles, 1990–93; Chief Exec. and Dir Gen., HM Prison Service, 1993–95. Chairman: UK Gold Television Ltd, 1992–97; Sunsail International, 1997–99; Patientline plc, 1998–2006 (Chief Exec., 1998–2001; Pres., 2006). Chm., Drinkaware Trust, 2008–; Trustee: Patients Assoc., 1999–2002; WRVS, 2007–. Mem. Council, Univ. of Essex, 1999– (Treas., 2001–07; Pro-Chancellor, 2007–). *Publication:* Hidden Agendas, 1997. *Club:* Caledonian.

LEWIS, (Derek) Trevor; Vice-Chairman, Bradford & Bingley plc (formerly Bradford & Bingley Building Society), 1995–2003 (Director, 1990–2003); *b* 21 Oct. 1936; *s* of Lionel Lewis and Mabel (*née* Clare); *m* 1961, Pamela Jean Ratcliffe; one *s* one *d*. *Educ:* Bradford Grammar Sch.; Leeds Univ. (LLB); 2nd Cl. Hons Solicitors' Final Exam., 1960. With A. V. Hammond & Co., subseq. Hammond Suddards: articled to Sir Richard Denby, 1955–60; Asst Solicitor, 1960–63; Partner 1964–87; Jt Sen. Partner, 1987–95. Dir, W Yorks Independent Hosp., 1979–85 (Chm., 1985–88); Chairman: Little Germany Urban Village Co. Ltd, 1999–2003; Arts and Business Yorkshire Ltd, 2000–; Bradford Breakthrough Ltd, 2005–; Dep. Chm., Bradford City Centre Urban Regeneration Co. Ltd, 2003–. *Address:* Barn Elm House, Church Hill, North Rigton, N Yorks LS17 0DF. *T:* (01423) 734497.

LEWIS, Dr Dewi Meirion, FInstP; Vice President Physics, Amersham (formerly Nycomed Amersham) plc, since 1999; *b* Chester, 4 Sept. 1948; *s* of Hugh and Mair Lewis; *m* 1972, Elizabeth Mary Williams; two *s* one *d*. *Educ:* Ysgol Ardudwy Harlech, Gwynedd; UCW, Swansea (BSc 1969; PhD 1972). FInstP 1995. Res. Fellow, CERN, Geneva, 1973–74; Engr i/c, CERN ISR accelerator, 1974–79; Cyclotron Project Leader, TRC Ltd, 1979–83; Amersham International plc: Hd, Cyclotron Dept, 1983–88; Business Manager, Cyclotron and Reactor Pharmaceuticals, 1988–91; Mfg Strategy Manager, 1991–94; R&D Strategy Manager, 1994–99. Vis. Prof. of Physics, Liverpool Univ., 1997–2001. Non-exec. Dir, Reviss Services Ltd, 1992–95. Member: OECD/NEA Expert Panel on Isotopes, 1997–99; PPARC, 2000 (Chm., Audit Cttee, 2001); EPSRC Coll., 2000–; CCLRC. Chm., Tech. Cttee, ARPES, Brussels, 1993–; Scientific Advr, EC DG XII, 1994–; Mem., EMIR Network, Brussels, 2001– (Chm., Isotopes Cttee, 2001–). Mem., British Astronomical Soc., 2001. Member: Amer. Assoc. Physicists in Medicine, 2001; Eur. Assoc. Nuclear Medicine, 2001. *Publications:* contrib. articles to res. jls. *Recreations:* ski-ing, Alpine walking, golf, Rugby coaching, choral music, astronomy. *Address:* Solaise, Kiln Road, Prestwood, Bucks HP16 9DG. *T:* (01494) 543065; Amersham Health, Amersham Place, Little Chalfont, Bucks HP7 9NA. *Club:* Harewood Downs (Bucks).

LEWIS, Donald Gordon, OBE 1988; Director, National Exhibition Centre, 1982–84; *b* 12 Sept. 1926; *s* of late Albert Francis Lewis and Nellie Elizabeth Lewis; *m* 1950, Doreen Mary (*née* Gardner); one *d*. *Educ:* King Edward's Sch., Birmingham; Liverpool Univ. Dairy Industry, 1947–91; Gen. Sales Manager, Birmingham Dairies, 1961–91. Councillor (C) Birmingham CC, Selly Oak Ward, 1959, Alderman 1971–74; past Chairman, Transport and Airport Committees; West Midlands County Council: Mem., 1974–81; Chm., 1980–81; Chairman, Airport Cttee, 1974–80; Sec., Conservative Group, 1974–80; City of Birmingham District Council: Mem., 1982–95; Hon. Alderman, 1995–; Chm., Nat. Exhibn Centre Cttee, 1982–84; Chm., Birmingham Housing Cttee, 1983–84. Mem., W Midlands PTA, 1984–95; Director: Birmingham International Airport plc, 1994–96; Broader Choices for Old People, 1999–; W Midlands Special Needs Transport Ltd, 2000–; Nat. Exhibn Centre (Develts) PLC, 2005–. Gov., Heart of England NHS Foundn Trust, 2005–. Chm., Selly Oak (Birmingham) Constituency Conservative Assoc., 1975–80, Pres., 1980; Vice-Pres., Birmingham Cons. Assoc., 1987– (Chm., 1984–87). *Recreation:* eating out. *Address:* 25 Albany Gardens, Hampton Lane, Solihull B91 2PT. *T:* (0121) 705 7661.

LEWIS, His Honour Esyr ap Gwilym; QC 1971; a Circuit Judge (Official Referee), 1984–98; Senior Official Referee, 1994–98; *b* 11 Jan. 1926; *s* of late Rev. T. W. Lewis, BA, and Mary Jane May Lewis (*née* Selway); *m* 1957, Elizabeth Anne Vidler Hoffmann, 2nd *d* of O. W. Hoffmann, Bassett, Southampton; four *d*. *Educ:* Salford Grammar Sch.; Mill Hill Sch.; Trinity Hall, Cambridge (MA, LLM). Served in Intelligence Corps, 1944–47. Exhibitioner, 1944, Scholar, 1948, at Trinity Hall (Dr Cooper's Law Studentship, 1950); 1st cl. hons, Law Tripos II, 1949, 1st cl. LLB, 1950, Cambridge. Holker Sen. Schol., Gray's Inn, 1950; Called to Bar, Gray's Inn, 1951 (Bencher, 1978; Treas., 1997). Law Supervisor, Trinity Hall, 1950–55; Law Lectr, Cambridgeshire Technical Coll., 1949–50. A Recorder, 1972–84; a Dep. High Court Judge, 1978–84; Leader, Wales and Chester Circuit, 1978–81. Member: Bar Council, 1965–68; Council of Legal Education, 1967–73; Criminal Injuries Compensation Bd, 1977–84. Contested (L) Llanelli, 1964. *Publication:* contributor to Newnes Family Lawyer, 1963. *Recreations:* reading, gardening, watching Rugby football. *Address:* 2 South Square, Gray's Inn, WC1R 5HP. *T:* (020) 7405 5918. *Clubs:* Garrick; Old Millhillians.

See also M. ap G. Lewis.

LEWIS, Frederick Carlton, (Carl); athlete; *b* 1 July 1961; *s* of Bill and Evelyn Lewis. *Educ:* Univ. of Houston. Winner, 100m, 200m, and long jump, US National Athletics Championships, 1983; *Olympic Games:* Gold medals, 100m and 200m, long jump and 4×100m, 1984; Gold medals, 100m and long jump, Silver medal, 200m, 1988; Gold medals, long jump and 4×100m, 1992; Gold medal, long jump, 1996; *World Championships:* Gold medals, 100m, long jump, 4×100m, 1983; Gold medals, long jump, 4×100m, 1987; Gold medals, 100m, 4×100m, 1991. World Record: long jump (8.79m), 1983; 100m (9.86 seconds), 1991. James E. Sullivan Meml Award, Amateur Athletic Union of US, 1981; Athlete of the Century, IAAF, 1999.

LEWIS, Maj.-Gen. George; *see* Lewis, Maj.-Gen. A. G.

LEWIS, Gillian Marjorie, FMA, FIIC; heritage consultant, since 1994; *b* 10 Oct. 1945; *d* of late William Lewis and of Marjorie Lewis (*née* Pargeter). *Educ:* Tiffin Sch., Kingston upon Thames; Univ. of Newcastle upon Tyne (BA 1967); DCP, Gateshead Tech. Coll., 1969; Birkbeck Coll., London (Cert. Ecology, 1991). FIIC 1977; FMA 1988. Shipley Art Gallery, Co. Durham, 1967–69; free-lance conservator, 1969–73; Nat. Maritime Mus., 1973–94; Keeper of Conservation, 1978; Hd, Div. of Conservation and Technical Services, 1978–88; Asst Dep. Dir, 1982–86; Hd of Conservation and Registration, 1988–91; Head of Collection Projects, 1991–92; Head of External Affairs, 1992–94. Vice-Chm., UK Inst. for Conservation, 1983–84 (Mem. Cttee, 1978–80). Member: Technical Cttee, City and Guilds of London Sch. of Art, 1981–2003; Cttee, Dulwich Picture Gall., 1983–92; Wallpaintings Conservation Panel, Council for Care of Churches, 1985–88; Volunteer Steering Cttee, Office of Arts and Libraries, 1988–90; Adv. Cttee, Museums and Galleries Commn, 1988–96; Trng Standards Panel, Museums Trng Inst., 1990–93; Council, Leather Conservation Centre, 1991–92; Fabric Adv. Cttee, Southwark Cathedral, 1997–; Preservation Advr to Dean and Chapter, Peterborough Cathedral, 1994–; Adviser: Heather Trust for the Arts, 1997–2000; Royal Warrant Holders' Assoc., 1999–2003. Examiner, London Inst., Camberwell Sch. of Art, 1991–93; Assessor: Clore Small Grants Prog., 1998–2003; Attingham Trust, 2002. Trustee: Whatmore Trust, 1988–; Southwark Cathedral Millennium Trust, 1998–; Cathedral Camps, 1998–2001; Edward James Foundn, 1999–. UN50 UK Ambassador, 1995. FRSA 1987.

LEWIS, Prof. Glyn Hywel, PhD; FRCPsych; Professor of Psychiatric Epidemiology, University of Bristol, since 2001; *b* 6 Dec. 1956; *s* of Jeffrey and Marion Lewis; *m* 1982, Priscilla Hall; one *s*. *Educ:* University Coll., Oxford (MSc 1980; MA 1983); University Coll. London (MB BS 1982); Inst. of Psychiatry, London Univ. (PhD 1991). FRCPsych 1998. Registrar, Bethlem and Maudsley Hosp., 1983–86; Res. Fellow, 1986–91, Sen. Lectr, 1991–95, Inst. of Psychiatry, London Univ.; on secondment to DoH, 1991–94; Res. Fellow, LSHTM, 1993–95; Prof. of Community and Epidemiological Psychiatry, Univ. of Wales Coll. of Medicine, 1996–2001. *Address:* Division of Psychiatry, University of Bristol, Cotham House, Cotham Hill, Bristol BS6 6JL.

LEWIS, Graham D.; *see* Dixon-Lewis.

LEWIS, Prof. Gwynne, DPhil; Professor of History, 1984–97, now Emeritus, and Director, Centre for Social History, 1992–97, University of Warwick; *b* 4 Nov. 1933; *s* of Rev. Dewi Emlyn Lewis and Elizabeth May Lewis; *m* 1960, Madeline Ann Rosser; two *s* one *d*. *Educ:* Pontypridd Grammar Sch.; UCW, Aberystwyth (BA); Univ. of Manchester (MA); DPhil Oxford. Asst Lectr, 1963–65, Lectr, 1965–68, UCW, Aberystwyth; Lectr, 1968–74, Sen. Lectr, 1974–80, Reader, 1980–84, Univ. of Warwick. Hon. Vis. Fellow, Southampton Univ., 1997–2001. *Publications:* Life in Revolutionary France, 1971; The Second Vendee, 1978; The Advent of Modern Capitalism in France 1770–1840, 1993; The French Revolution: rethinking the debate, 1993; France 1715–1804: power and the people, 2004. *Recreations:* music, Rugby, walking, Paris. *Address:* 11 Castle Street, Kidwelly, Carmarthenshire SA17 5AG.

LEWIS, Henry Nathan; company director; *b* 29 Jan. 1926; *m* 1953, Jenny Cohen; one *s* two *d*. *Educ:* Hollywood Park Council Sch., Stockport; Stockport Sch.; Manchester Univ. (BA Com); LSE. Served RAF (Flt Lt), 1944–48. Joined Marks & Spencer, 1950; Dir, 1965; Jt Man. Dir responsible for textiles, 1973–76, 1983–85, for foods, 1976–83; retired 1985. Chm., Primrose Care Ltd, 1992–97; Dep. Chm., S&W Berisford, subseq. Berisford Internat., 1987–90; Director: Dixons Group, 1985–95; Hunter Saphir, 1987–91; Porter Chadburn (formerly LDH Group), 1987–2000; Delta Galil, 1988–2000; Gabicci, 1992–93; Cupid, 1993–94; Oasis, 1994–2000; Value Retail, 1994–2005; Electronics Boutique plc (formerly Rhino), 1995–2000; Uno plc, 1996–99. *Address:* Flat 15, Pavilion Court, Frognal Rise, NW3 6PZ.

LEWIS, H(erbert) J(ohn) Whitfield, CB 1968; *b* 9 April 1911; *s* of Herbert and Mary Lewis; *m* 1963, Pamela (*née* Leaford); one *s* three *d*. *Educ:* Monmouth Sch.; Welsh Sch. of Architecture. Associate with Norman & Dawbarn, Architects and Consulting Engineers; in charge of housing work, 1945–50; Principal Housing Architect, Architects Dept, London County Council, 1950–59; County Architect, Middlesex County Council, 1959–64; Chief Architect, Ministry of Housing and Local Govt, 1964–71. FRIBA; DisTP 1957. *Recreations:* music, electronics. *Address:* 8 St John's Wood Road, NW8 8RE.

LEWIS, Rt Rev. (Hurtle) John, AM 1990; SSM; Bishop of North Queensland, 1971–96; *b* 2 Jan. 1926; *s* of late Hurtle John Lewis and late Hilda Lewis. *Educ:* Prince Alfred Coll.; London Univ. (BD); ThL of ACT; Flinders Univ. (MTh 2006). Royal Australian Navy, 1943–46; Student, St Michael's House, S Aust., 1946–51; Member, SSM, 1951–; Provincial Australia, SSM, 1962–68; Prior, Kobe Priory, Japan, 1969–71. Licensed to assist, St James' Cathedral Parish, 1996–2002; permission to officiate, St John's Parish, Adelaide, 2002–. *Recreations:* rowing, horse riding. *Address:* Unit 18, 19 Barr Smith Avenue, Myrtle Bank, SA 5063, Australia.

LEWIS, Huw George; Member (Lab) Merthyr Tydfil and Rhymney, National Assembly for Wales, since 1999; *b* 17 Jan. 1964; *m* 1996, Lynne Neagle, *qv*; one *s*. *Educ:* Edinburgh Univ. (BSc Hons Chemistry). Teacher, N Berwick High Sch., and Bathgate Acad., 1987–90; House of Commons Researcher, 1990–91; Teacher, Afon Taf High Sch., 1991–94; Asst Gen. Sec., Wales Labour Party, 1994–99. Dep. Minister for Social Justice and Regeneration, 2003–07, for Regeneration, 2007, Nat. Assembly for Wales. *Address:* National Assembly for Wales, Cardiff Bay, Cardiff CF99 1NA.

LEWIS, Ian Talbot; Under Secretary (Legal), Treasury Solicitor's Office, 1982–90; *b* 7 July 1929; *s* of late Cyril Frederick Lewis, CBE and Marjorie (*née* Talbot); *m* 1st, 1962, Patricia Anne (*née* Hardy) (marr. diss. 1978); two *s*; 2nd, 1986, Susan Lydia Sargant. *Educ:* Marlborough Coll. Admitted Solicitor, 1951. National Service, 3rd The King's Own Hussars, 1952–53. Solicitor, private practice, London, 1954–57; Treasury Solicitor's Office: Legal Asst, 1957; Sen. Legal Asst, 1963; Asst Treasury Solicitor, 1977. Liveryman, Merchant Taylors' Co., 1966–. Chm., Penshurst Parish Council, 1994–96. Chm., Fordcombe Soc., 1990–94; Trustee, Fordcombe Village Hall, 1997–2007. Gov., Fordcombe C of E Primary Sch., 1991–93. Trustee, Penshurst Retreat Charity, 1993–2002. *Recreations:* sport, natural history, modern first editions, theatre. *Address:* Gables, Fordcombe, near Tunbridge Wells, Kent TN3 0RY. *T:* (01892) 740413. *Clubs:* Cavalry and Guards, MCC; Blackheath Football (Rugby Union) (Past Pres.); Blackheath Cricket (Hon. Vice Pres.); Falconhurst Cricket (Vice-Pres.); Fordcombe Cricket (Pres., 2005–07).

LEWIS, Prof. Ioan Myrddin, DPhil; FBA 1986; Professor of Anthropology, London School of Economics and Political Science, 1969–93, now Emeritus; Consultative Director, International African Institute, since 1988 (Hon. Director, 1981–88); *b* 30 Jan. 1930; *s* of John Daniel Lewis and Mary Stevenson Scott (*née* Brown); *m* 1954, Ann Elizabeth Keir; one *s* three *d*. *Educ:* Glasgow High Sch.; Glasgow Univ. (BSc 1951); Oxford Univ. (Dip. in Anthrop., 1952; BLitt 1953; DPhil 1957). Res. Asst to Lord Hailey, Chatham House, 1954–55; Colonial SSRC Fellow, 1955–57; Lectr in African Studies, University Coll. of Rhodesia and Nyasaland, 1957–60; Lectr in Social Anthrop., Glasgow Univ., 1960–63; Lectr, then Reader in Anthrop., UCL, 1963–69. Hitchcock Prof., Univ. of Calif at Berkeley, 1977; Vis. Professor: Univ. of Helsinki, Finland, 1982; Univ. of Rome, 1983; Univ. of Malaya, 1986; Univ. of Kyoto, 1986; Univ. of Naples, 1989; Univ. of Addis Ababa, 1992; CNRS, Marseille, 1993. Malinowski Meml Lectr, London, 1966; Blackwood Lectr, Oxford, 1994. Hon. Sec., Assoc. of Social Anthropologists of the Commonwealth, 1964–67; Member: Council and Standing Cttee of Council, Royal Anthropol Inst., 1965–67 and 1981–84 (Vice-Pres., 1992–96); Court of Governors and Standing Cttee, LSE, 1984–88; Internat. Cttee, Centro di Ricerca e Documentazione Febbraio '74, 1980–; Chm., African Educn Trust, 1993 (Trustee, 1992). Editor, Man (Jl of RAI), 1969–72. *Publications:* Peoples of the Horn of Africa, 1955, 3rd edn 1994; A Pastoral Democracy: pastoralism and politics among the Northern Somali of the Horn of Africa, 1961, 3rd edn 1999 (trans. Italian); (with B. W. Andrzejewski) Somali Poetry, 1964, 2nd edn 1968; The Modern History of Somaliland: from nation to state, 1965, 4th edn as A Modern History of the Somali: nation and state, 2002; Ecstatic Religion, 1971, 3rd edn 2002 (trans. Dutch, Italian, French, Portuguese and Japanese); Social Anthropology in Perspective, 1976, 4th edn 1990 (trans. Italian and Chinese); Religion in Context: cults and charisma, 1986 (trans. German and Italian), rev. edn 1996; (ed and introd) Islam in Tropical Africa, 1966, 3rd edn 1980; History and Anthropology, 1968 (trans. Spanish); Symbols and Sentiments: cross-cultural studies in symbolism, 1977; (co-ed with Fred Eggan and C. von Fürer-Haimendorf), Atlas of Mankind, 1982; Nationalism and Self-Determination in the Horn of Africa, 1983; (co-ed with Gustav Jahoda) Acquiring Culture: cross cultural studies in child development, 1988; (ed jtly) Women's Medicine: the Zar-Bori Cult in Africa and beyond, 1991; Understanding Somalia, 1993; Blood and Bone: the call of Kinship in Somali society, 1994; (co-ed with R. J. Hayward) Voice and Power: the culture of language in North-East Africa, 1996; Saints and Somalis: Islam in a clan-based society, 1998; Arguments with Ethnography: comparative approaches to history, politics and religion, 1999, 2nd edn 2004; Social and Cultural Anthropology, 2003; Understanding Somalia and Somaliland, 2008; Making and Breaking States in Africa: the Somali experience, 2008; contrib. learned jls. *Recreations:* travel, fishing. *Address:* 26 Bramshill Gardens, NW5 1JH. *T:* (020) 7272 1722.

LEWIS, Ivan; MP (Lab) Bury South, since 1997; Parliamentary Under-Secretary of State, Department for International Development, since 2008; *b* 4 March 1967; *s* of Joel and Gloria Lewis; *m* 1990, Juliette, *d* of Leslie and Joyce Fox; two *s. Educ:* William Hulme Grammar Sch.; Stand Coll.; Bury Coll. of FE. Co-ordinator, Contact Community Care Gp, 1986–89; Jewish Social Services: Community Worker, 1989–91; Community Care Manager, 1991–92; Chief Exec., 1992–97. Mem., Bury MBC, 1990–98. PPS to Sec. of State for Trade and Industry, 1999–2001; Parly Under-Sec. of State, DfES, 2001–05; Econ. Sec., HM Treasury, 2005–06; Parly Under-Sec. of State for Care Services, DoH, 2006–08. Member: H of C Deregulation Select Cttee, 1997–99; Health Select Cttee, 1999; Sec., All Party Parly Gp on Parenting, 1998–2001; Dep. Chm., Labour Friends of Israel, 1997–2001; Vice Chm., Inter-Parly Council Against Anti-Semitism, 1998–2001. Trustee, Holocaust Educnl Trust. *Recreation:* supporter of Manchester City FC. *Address:* House of Commons, SW1A 0AA; 381 Bury New Road, Prestwich, Manchester M25 1AW. *T:* (0161) 773 5500; *e-mail:* ivanlewis@burysouth.fsnet.co.uk; *web:* www.ivanlewis.org.uk.

LEWIS, James Thomas; QC 2002; a Recorder, since 2000; *b* 8 Feb. 1958; *s* of Benjamin Ivor and Kathleen Lewis; *m* 1985, Kathleen Mary Gallacher; one *s* two *d. Educ:* St John Fisher Sch., Purley; Kingston Poly. (BSc Hons); City Univ., London (DipLaw). Univ. of London OTC, 1977–80; Commnd 2nd Lieut, 1979; Royal Yeo., 1980–82; RARO, 1982–86, 1993–; HAC, 1986–93. Called to the Bar, Gray's Inn, 1987, Bencher, 2007; Attorney General's List, 2000. Mem., Criminal Cttee, Judicial Studies Bd, 2008. *Recreations:* ski-ing, clay pigeon shooting, tennis. *Address:* 3 Raymond Buildings, Gray's Inn, WC1R 5BH. *T:* (020) 7400 6400. *Clubs:* Honourable Artillery Company, Garrick.

LEWIS, Prof. Jane Elizabeth, PhD; FBA 2004; Professor of Social Policy, London School of Economics, since 2004; *b* 14 April 1950; *d* of Hedley Lewis and Dorothy Lewis (*née* Beck); *m* 1971, Mark Shrimpton. *Educ:* Reading Univ. (BA Hons 1971); Univ. of Western Ontario (PhD 1979). Department of Social Policy and Administration, London School of Economics: Lectr, 1979–87; Reader, 1987–91; Prof., 1991–96; Fellow of All Souls Coll., and Dir, Wellcome Unit for the Hist. of Medicine, Oxford, 1996–98; Prof. of Social Policy, Nottingham Univ., 1998–2000; Barnett Prof. of Social Policy and Fellow, St Cross Coll., Oxford, 2000–04. Mem., RSCan, 1995. *Publications:* The Politics of Motherhood: child and maternal welfare in England 1900–1939, 1980; (ed) Women's Welfare/Women's Rights, 1983; Women in England, 1870–1950: sexual divisions and social change, 1984; (ed) Labour and Love: women's experience of home and family 1850–1950, 1986; (ed jtly) Women and Offshore Oil in Britain, Canada and Norway, 1987; (ed) Before the Vote was Won, 1987; (jtly) Daughters Who Care: daughters looking after mothers at home, 1988; (ed jtly) The Goals of Social Policy, 1989; Women and Social Action in Victorian and Edwardian England, 1991; Women in Britain since 1945: women, family and work in the post-war years, 1992; (jtly) Whom God Hath Joined: marriage and the marital agencies 1930–1990, 1992; (ed) Women and Social Policies in Europe, 1993; The Voluntary Sector, the State and Social Work in Britain, 1995; (ed jtly) Comparing Social Welfare Systems in Europe, vol. I, 1995; (ed jtly) Protecting Women: labor legislation in Europe, the United States and Australia 1880–1920, 1995; (jtly) Implementing the New Community Care, 1996; (ed) Lone Mothers in European Welfare Regimes, 1998; (jtly) Lone Motherhood in Twentieth-Century Britain, 1998; The End of Marriage?, 2001; articles in jls. *Address:* Department of Social Policy, London School of Economics, Houghton Street, WC2A 2AE.

LEWIS, Jeffrey Allan; His Honour Judge Jeffrey Lewis; a Circuit Judge, since 2002; *b* 25 May 1949; *s* of late David Meyer Lewis and Esther (*née* Kirson); *m* 1985, Elizabeth Ann Swarbrick; one *s* one *d. Educ:* Univ. of the Witwatersrand (BA); Univ. of Leeds (LLB). Teacher, 1973–75; called to the Bar, Middle Temple, 1978; in practice, N Eastern Circuit, 1978–2002; Asst Recorder, 1993–97; Recorder, 1997–2002. Chm. (pt-time), Industrial Tribunals, Leeds Reg., 1991–95. *Recreations:* music, reading, ski-ing, gardening. *Address:* Manchester Crown Court, Minshull Street, Manchester M1 3FS. *T:* (0161) 954 7500.

LEWIS, Rt Rev. John; see Lewis, Rt Rev. H. J.

LEWIS, Sir John (Anthony), Kt 2004; OBE 1996; Principal, Dixons City Academy (formerly Technology College), Bradford, 1989–2006; *b* 9 May 1946; *s* of John D. C. Lewis and Dorothy Lewis (*née* Roberts); *m* 1969, Penny Ward; three *s. Educ:* Queens' Coll., Cambridge (BA (Hist.) 1968; MA 1971); CNAA (MSc Educnl Mgt 1982). History Teacher: Northgate GS, Ipswich, 1969–73; Appleton Hall GS, Warrington, 1973–75; Culcheth High Sch., Warrington, 1975–79; Dep. Hd, Bishop Heber High Sch., Malpas, 1979–84; Head Teacher, Birchwood High Sch., Warrington, 1984–89. *Recreations:* sport (Cambridge soccer Blue, 1968), cricket, tennis. *Address:* e-mail: ja.lewis@dsl.pipex.com.

LEWIS, Ven. John Arthur; Archdeacon of Cheltenham, 1988–98, now Archdeacon Emeritus; *b* 4 Oct. 1934; *s* of Lt-Col Harry Arthur Lewis and Evaline Helen Ross Lewis; *m* 1959, Hazel Helen Jane Morris; one *s* one *d. Educ:* Jesus College, Oxford (MA); Cuddesdon College. Assistant Curate: St Mary, Prestbury, Glos, 1960–63; Wimborne Minster, 1963–66; Rector, Eastington with Frocester, 1966–70; Vicar of Nailsworth, 1970–78; Vicar of Cirencester, 1978–88; RD of Cirencester, 1984–88. Hon. Canon, 1985–88, Canon, 1988–98, Canon Emeritus, 1998–, Gloucester Cathedral. Hon. Chaplain, Glos Constabulary, 1988–98. Chairman: Diocesan Stewardship Cttee, 1988–96; Diocesan Redundant Church Uses Cttee, 1988–98; Diocesan Bd of Educn, 1990–98. Mem. Council, Cheltenham Ladies' Coll., 1992–97. *Recreations:* travel, music, walking, gardening. *Address:* 5 Vilverie Mead, Bishops Cleeve, Cheltenham, Glos GL52 7YY. *T:* (01242) 678425.

LEWIS, John Elliott, MA; Head Master, Eton College, 1994–2002; *b* 23 Feb. 1942; *s* of John Derek Lewis and Margaret Helen (*née* Shaw); *m* 1968, Vibeke Lewis (*née* Johansson).

Educ: King's College, Auckland, NZ; Corpus Christi Coll., Cambridge (Girdlers' Company Schol.; MA Classics). Assistant Master, King's Coll., Auckland, 1964, 1966–70; Jun. Lecturer in Classics, Auckland Univ., 1965; Asst Master, 1971–80, Master in College, 1975–80, Eton College; Head Master, Geelong Grammar Sch., Australia, 1980–94.

LEWIS, Rt Rev. (John Hubert) Richard; Bishop of St Edmundsbury and Ipswich, 1997–2007; *b* 10 Dec. 1943; *s* of John Wilfred and Winifred Mary Lewis; *m* 1968, Sara Patricia Hamilton; two *s* (and one *s* decd). *Educ:* Radley; King's Coll., London (AKC). Curate of Hexham, 1967–70; Industrial Chaplain, Diocese of Newcastle, 1970–77; Communications Officer, Diocese of Durham, 1977–82; Agricultural Chaplain, Diocese of Hereford, 1982–87; Archdeacon of Ludlow, 1987–92; Bishop Suffragan of Taunton, 1992–97. Prebendary, Wells Cathedral, 1992–97. Nat. Chm., Small Farmers' Assoc., 1984–88. Mem., Gen. Synod of C of E, 1987–92. *Publication:* (ed jtly) The People, the Land and the Church, 1987. *Recreations:* bricklaying, bumble bees, kit car building.

LEWIS, Very Rev. John Thomas; Dean of Llandaff, since 2000; *b* 14 June 1947; *s* of Rev. David Islwyn Lewis and Eleanor Tranter Lewis; *m* 1976, Dr Cynthia Sheelagh McFetridge; two *s. Educ:* Dyffryn Grammar Sch., Port Talbot; Jesus Coll., Oxford (scholar; BA (Maths) 1969; Dip. Applied Stats 1970; MA 1973); St John's Coll., Cambridge (BA (Theol.) 1972; MA 1992); Westcott House, Cambridge. Ordained deacon, 1973, priest, 1974. Assistant Curate: Whitchurch, 1973–77; Lisvane, 1977–80; Chaplain, Cardiff Univ., 1980–85; Warden of Ordinands, Llandaff, 1981–85; Vicar, Brecon St David with Llanspyddid and Llanilltyd, 1985–91; Vicar, then Rector, Bassaleg, 1991–2000. Sec., Provincial Selection Panel, Church in Wales, 1987–94; Bishop of Monmouth's Chaplain for Continuing Ministerial Educn, 1998–2000. *Recreations:* hill walking, swimming, music, sport, family life. *Address:* The Deanery, The Cathedral Green, Llandaff, Cardiff CF5 2YF. *T:* (029) 2056 1545.

LEWIS, (Joseph) Anthony; writer; Chief London Correspondent, New York Times, 1965–72, editorial columnist, 1969–2001; Lecturer in Law, Harvard Law School, 1974–89; James Madison Visiting Professor, Columbia University, since 1983; *b* 27 March 1927; *s* of Kassel Lewis and Sylvia Lewis (*née* Surut), NYC; *m* 1st, 1951, Linda (marr. diss. 1982), *d* of John Rannells, NYC; one *s* two *d;* 2nd, 1984, Margaret, *d* of Bernard Charles Marshall, Osterville, Mass. *Educ:* Horace Mann Sch., NY; Harvard Coll. (BA). Sunday Dept, New York Times, 1948–52; Reporter, Washington Daily News, 1952–55; Legal Corresp., Washington Bureau, NY Times, 1955–64; Nieman Fellow, Harvard Law Sch., 1956–57. Governor, Ditchley Foundation, 1965–72. Member: Amer. Acad. of Arts and Scis, 1991; Amer. Philosophical Soc., 2005. Pulitzer Prize for Nat. Correspondence, 1955 and 1963; Heywood Broun Award, 1955; Overseas Press Club Award, 1970. Hon. DLitt: Adelphi Univ., NY, 1964; Rutgers Univ., NJ, 1973; NY Med. Coll., 1976; Williams Coll., Mass, 1978; Clark Univ., Mass, 1982; Hon. LLD: Syracuse, 1979; Colby Coll., 1983; Northeastern Univ., Mass, 1987. Presidential Citizens Medal (US), 2001. *Publications:* Gideon's Trumpet, 1964; Portrait of a Decade: The Second American Revolution, 1964; Make No Law: the Sullivan case and the First Amendment, 1991; Freedom for the Thought That We Hate: a biography of the First Amendment, 2008; articles in American law reviews. *Recreation:* dinghy sailing. *Address:* 1010 Memorial Drive, Cambridge, MA 02138, USA. *Club:* Tavern (Boston).

LEWIS, Dr Julian Murray; MP (C) New Forest East, since 1997; *b* 26 Sept. 1951; *s* of Samuel Lewis, tailor and designer, and late Hilda Lewis. *Educ:* Dynevor Grammar Sch., Swansea; Balliol Coll., Oxford (MA 1977); St Antony's Coll., Oxford (DPhil 1981). Sec., Oxford Union, 1972. Seaman, RNR, 1979–82. Res. in defence studies, 1975–77, 1978–81; Sec., Campaign for Representative Democracy, 1977–78; Res. Dir and Dir, Coalition for Peace Through Security, 1981–85; Dir, Policy Res. Associates, 1985–; Dep. Dir, Cons. Res. Dept, 1990–96. Contested (C) Swansea W, 1983. Opposition Whip, 2001–02; Shadow Defence Minister, 2002–04, 2005–; Shadow Minister for the Cabinet Office, 2004–05. Member: Select Cttee on Welsh Affairs, 1998–2001; Select Cttee on Defence, 2000–01; Exec., 1922 Cttee, 2001; Sec., Cons. Parly Defence Cttee, 1997–2001; Vice-Chairman: Cons. Parly Foreign Affairs Cttee, 2000–01; Cons. Parly European Affairs Cttee, 2000–01. Parly Chm., First Defence, 2004–. Mem., Armed Forces Parly Scheme (RAF), 1998, 2000, (RN), 2004, (RCDS), 2006. Trustee, 1998–2001, Vice-Pres., 2001–07, Pres., 2007–, British Military Powerboat Trust. Trench Gascoigne Essay Prize, RUSI, 2005 and 2007. *Publications:* Changing Direction: British military planning for post-war strategic defence 1942–47, 1988, 2nd edn 2003; Who's Left?: an index of Labour MPs and left-wing causes 1985–1992, 1992; Labour's CND Cover-up, 1992; political pamphlets. *Recreations:* history, fiction, films, music, photography. *Address:* House of Commons, SW1A 0AA. *T:* (020) 7219 3000. *Clubs:* Athenæum; Totton Conservative.

LEWIS, Keith William, AO 1994; CB 1981; Director General and Engineer in Chief, Engineering and Water Supply Department, South Australia, 1974–87; *b* 10 Nov. 1927; *s* of Ernest John and Alinda Myrtle Lewis; *m* 1958, Alison Bothwell Fleming; two *d. Educ:* Adelaide High Sch.; Univ. of Adelaide (BE Civil); Imperial Coll., Univ. of London (DIC). FTS. Engineer for Water and Sewage Treatment, Engrg and Water Supply Dept, SA, 1968–74. Chm., Pipelines Authy of SA, 1987–94; Dep. Chm., Electricity Trust of SA, 1994–95. Chairman: S Australian Water Resources Council, 1976–87; Australian Water Res. Adv. Council, 1985–90; Murray-Darling Basin Freshwater Res. Centre, 1986–91; Energy Planning Exec., 1987–93; SA Urban Land Trust, 1990–94; Member: Standing Cttee, Australian Water Resources Council, 1974–87; Electricity Trust of S Australia, 1974–84; State Planning Authority, 1974–82; Golden Grove Jt Venture Cttee, 1984–97; Bd, Amdel Ltd, 1987–94. River Murray Commissioner, representing SA, 1982–87. Hon. FIEAust 1993. Silver Jubilee Medal, 1977. *Recreations:* reading, ornithology, golf, lawn bowls. *Address:* 25 Montrose Avenue, Netherby, SA 5062, Australia. *T:* (8) 83381507, *Fax:* (8) 83382431. *Clubs:* Adelaide, Kooyonga Golf, Adelaide Oval Bowling (South Australia).

LEWIS, Kynric; see Lewis, A. K.

LEWIS, Sir Leigh (Warren), KCB 2007 (CB 2000); Permanent Secretary, Department for Work and Pensions, since 2005; *b* 17 March 1951; *s* of Harold and Ray Rene Lewis; *m* 1973, Susan Evelyn Gold; two *s. Educ:* Harrow County Grammar Sch. for Boys; Liverpool Univ. (BA Hons 1973). MIPD. Dept of Employment, 1973; Private Sec. to Parly Under Sec. of State, 1975–76; Incomes and Indust. Relations Divs, 1978–84; Principal Private Sec. to Minister without Portfolio and Sec. of State for Employment, 1984–86; Asst Sec., EC Br., 1986–87; Dir of Ops, Unemployment Benefit Service, 1987–88; Group Dir of Personnel, Cable and Wireless plc, 1988–91 (on secondment); Dir, Internat. Div., 1991–94; Dir, Finance and Resource Mgt Div., 1994–95; Dir, Finance, DfEE, 1995–96; Chief Executive: Employment Service, DfEE, then DWP, 1997–2002; Jobcentre Plus, DWP, 2002–03; Perm. Sec., Crime, Policing, Counter-Terrorism and Delivery, Home Office, 2003–05. *Recreations:* tennis, Watford Football Club. *Address:* Department for Work and Pensions, Richmond House, 79 Whitehall, SW1A 2NS.

LEWIS, Lennox Claudius, CBE 2002 (MBE 1998); professional boxer, 1989–2004; *b* 2 Sept. 1965; *s* of Violet Blake; *m* 2005, Violet Chang; one *s* one *d.* World jun. heavyweight champion, 1983; Olympic heavyweight champion (rep. Canada), 1988; European heavyweight champion, 1990; British heavyweight champion, 1991; WBC world heavyweight champion, 1993, 1997, 2002–; undisputed world heavyweight champion, 1999, 2001–02; world heavyweight champion, 2000; Founder, Lennox Lewis Coll., Hackney, London, 1994. DUniv N London, 1999. *Publications:* Lennox Lewis (autobiog.), 1993, 2nd edn 1997; (jtly) Lennox (autobiog.), 2002. *Recreations:* chess, golf, reading, listening to music.

LEWIS, Marilyn; Director, Cadw, since 2005; *b* 29 Aug. 1954; *d* of Thomas and Jacqueline Clements; *m* 1979, David Lewis. *Educ:* Univ. of Manchester (BA Hons Medieval Studies 1975); Univ. of Bangor (DAA 1976); Liverpool John Moores Univ. (MBA 1995). Asst Archivist, Suffolk CC, 1976–78; Bor. Archivist, Walsall, 1978–87; City Archivist, Chester CC, 1987–97; Shropshire County Council: Hd, Heritage, 1997–2000; Asst Dir, Cultural Services, 2000–05. *Publication:* The Book of Walsall, 1986. *Recreations:* castles, wildlife, Aston Villa Football Club, Madagascar. *Address:* Cadw, Plas Carew, 5–7 Cefn Coed, Parc Nantgarw, Cardiff CF15 7QQ; *e-mail:* marilyn.lewis@wales.gsi.gov.uk.

LEWIS, Martyn John Dudley, CBE 1997; journalist and broadcaster; Co-Founder and Chairman, Teliris Ltd, since 2001, and EU Chairman, Teliris Inc., since 2007; Chairman, NICE TV Ltd, since 2005; *b* 7 April 1945; *s* of late Thomas John Dudley Lewis and Doris (*née* Jones); *m* 1970, Elizabeth Anne Carse; two *d*. *Educ:* Dalriada High Sch., Ballymoney, NI; Trinity Coll., Dublin (BA 1967). Reporter: BBC, Belfast, 1967–68; HTV, Cardiff, 1968–70; Independent Television News: reporter, 1970–86; Head, Northern Bureau, 1971–78; presenter, News at Ten, 1981–86; Presenter: BBC One O'Clock News, 1986–87; BBC Nine O'Clock News, 1987–94; BBC TV Six O'Clock News, 1994–99; Today's the Day, BBC2, 1993–99; Crimebeat, 1996–98. Documentaries include: Battle for the Falklands; The Secret Hunters; Fight Cancer; Living with Dying; Great Ormond Street—a Fighting Chance; Health UK; A Century to Remember; series for ITV: Bethlehem—Year Zero, 1999; Dateline Jerusalem, 2000; News 40, 2000; Ultimate Questions, 2000–02. Dir, Drive for Youth, 1986–99 (Chm., 1990–99); Chm. and Founder, YouthNet UK, 1995–; Co-Founder and Chm., Global Intercasting Ltd, 1999–2007. Chm., Beacon Fellowship, 2005–07. Advr, Ogden Educnl Trust, 2000–. Member: Policy Adv. Cttee, Tidy Britain Gp, 1988–98; Volunteer Partnership (govt cttee), 1995–97; Internat. Adv. Cttee, RADA, 2007–; Director: Hospice Arts, 1989–97; CLIC UK, 1990–96; Adopt-A-Student, 1988–96; Inst. for Citizenship Studies, 1993–97; Friends of Nelson Mandela Children's Fund, 1997–2002; President: United Response, 1989–; George Thomas Centre for Hospice Care, 1996–; Vice-President: Macmillan Cancer Support (formerly Cancer Relief Macmillan Fund, then Macmillan Cancer Relief), 1988– (Dir, 1990–96); Marie Curie Cancer Care, 1990–; Help the Hospices, 1990–; British Soviet Hospice Soc., 1990–96; Demelza House Children's Hospice, 1996–; Voices for Hospices, 1996–; Barrett's Oesophagus Foundn, 2000–; Trustee: Windsor Leadership Trust, 2001–; Edutrust, 2008–; Patron: London Lighthouse, 1990–99; SW Children's Hospice, 1991–2007; Internat. Sch. for Cancer Care, 1991–99; Hope House Children's Hospice, 1992–2007; Cities in Schools, 1995–97 (Dir, 1989–95); Tomorrow Project, 1996–; For Dementia (formerly Dementia Relief Trust), 1998–; James Powell (UK) Trust, 1998–2007; Mildmay Mission Hosp., 1998–; Volunteering England (formerly Nat. Centre for Volunteering), 1998–; E Anglia Children's Hospices, 1999– (Cambridge Children's Hospice, 1989–99; Quidenham Children's Hospice, 1996–99). Freeman, City of London, 1989; Liveryman, Pattenmakers' Co., 1989–. FRSA 1990. Hon. DLitt Ulster, 1994. *Publications:* And Finally, 1983; Tears and Smiles—the Hospice Handbook, 1989; Cats in the News, 1991 (trans. Japanese, 1994); Dogs in the News, 1992 (trans. Japanese, 1996); Go For It: Martyn Lewis's essential guide to opportunities for young people (annual), 1993–97, as Book of the Site, 1998–99; Reflections on Success, 1997; Seasons of our Lives, 1999. *Recreations:* tennis, photography, piano, good food, keeping fit. *Address:* c/o Capel & Land, 29 Wardour Street, W1V 3HB. *T:* (020) 7734 2414, *Fax:* (020) 7734 8101.

LEWIS, Mary Elizabeth, (Mrs N. Woolley); Chief Executive, Institution of Highways and Transportation, since 2001; *b* 29 Dec. 1952; *d* of Kenneth Richard Lewis and Joan Lewis; *m* 1988, Nicholas Woolley. *Educ:* St Angela's Convent, Harringay; University Coll. of Wales, Aberystwyth (BA Hons English 1975). CDipAF 1991. FIHT 2006. Asst Sec., 1987–94, Dir, Finance and Personnel, 1994–98, CIB; Exec. Sec., Physiol Soc., 1999–2001. *Recreations:* embroidery, gardening, music, travel. *Address:* 92 Clinton Road, E3 4QU. *T:* (020) 8980 6308; *e-mail:* mary.lewis@iht.org.

LEWIS, Michael ap Gwilym; QC 1975; a Recorder of the Crown Court, 1976–97; *b* 9 May 1930; *s* of Rev. Thomas William Lewis and Mary Jane May Selway; *m* 1988, Sarah Turvill; two *d*, and one *d* three *s* by a previous marriage. *Educ:* Mill Hill; Jesus Coll., Oxford (Scholar). MA (Mod. History). Commnd 2nd Royal Tank Regt, 1952–53. Called to Bar, Gray's Inn, 1956, Bencher, 1986; Mem., Senate, 1979–82; South Eastern Circuit. Mem., Criminal Injuries Compensation Bd, 1993–2002. *Address:* 33 Canonbury Park North, N1 2JU. *T:* (020) 7226 6440.

See also E. ap G. Lewis.

LEWIS, Rt Rev. Michael Augustine Owen; *see* Cyprus and the Gulf, Bishop of.

LEWIS, Michael David; sports rights and programming consultant; Controller, Radio Sports Rights, BBC Sport, 1996–2007; *b* 5 June 1947; *s* of late David Lloyd Lewis and of Gwendoline Lewis; *m* 1992, Hilary Anne East; two *d*. *Educ:* Erith Grammar Sch., Kent. Dartford Reporter newspaper, 1966–70; Brighton Evening Argus, 1970–73; LBC/Independent Radio News, 1973–82; BBC Radio Sport: Duty Editor, 1982–83; Dep. Editor, 1983–84; Editor, 1984–91; Head of Sport and Outside Broadcasts, 1991–93; Dep. Controller, BBC Radio 5 Live, 1994–2000. *Recreations:* watching Arsenal, bringing up two daughters, reading newspapers. *Address:* 53 Wallingford Avenue, W10 6PZ. *T:* 07850 762259.

LEWIS, Naomi, FRSL; writer, poet, critic and broadcaster; *b* coastal Norfolk. Contributor at various times to Observer, New Statesman, New York Times, Listener, Encounter, TLS, TES, etc. *Publications:* A Visit to Mrs Wilcox, 1957; A Peculiar Music, 1971; Fantasy, 1977; The Silent Playmate, 1979; Leaves, 1980; Come With Us (poems), 1982; Once upon a Rainbow, 1981; A Footprint on the Air (poems), 1983; Messages (poems), 1985; A School Bewitched, 1985; Arabian Nights, 1987; Cry Wolf!, 1988; Proud Knight, Fair Lady, 1989; Johnny Longnose, 1989; The Mardi Gras Cat (poems), 1994; Classic Fairy Tales, 1996; Elf Hill, 1999; Rockinghorse Land, 2000; *translations* include: Hans Christian Andersen's Fairy Tales, 1981; The Snow Queen, 1988; The Frog Prince, 1990; The Emperor's New Clothes, 1997; Tales of Hans Christian Andersen, 2005; numerous introductory essays. *Recreation:* trying in practical ways to alleviate the lot of horses, camels, bears, sheep, wolves, cows, pigs and other ill-used mortals of the animal kind. *Address:* 13 Red Lion Square, WC1R 4QF. *T:* (020) 7405 8657.

LEWIS, Paul Arthur; freelance financial journalist, broadcaster and author; *b* 22 April 1948; *s* of late William Denis Lewis and of Betty Blanche Lewis; *m* 1969, Eileen Margaret Tame (marr. diss. 2002); two *s* one *d*. *Educ:* Univ. of Stirling (BA Psychology, MSc Res. Psychology 1972). Dep. Dir, Nat. Council for One Parent Families, 1976–83; Dir, Youthaid, 1983–86; Money Corresp., Saga Magazine, 1984–; Presenter, BBC: Wake Up To Money, Radio Five Live, 1998–2000; Money Box, Radio 4, 2000–. Chm., Nat. Right to Fuel Campaign, 1975–81; Gov., Pensions Policy Inst., 2002–. Sec., Wilkie Collins Soc., 1996–. Mem., Maidstone BC, 1974–84. *Publications:* Saga Rights Guide, 1988; Saga Money Guide, 1988; Your Taxes and Savings, 2002, 4th edn 2005; The Complete Money Plan, 2004; Money Magic, 2005; (ed jtly) The Public Face of Wilkie Collins, 2005; Live Long and Prosper, 2006; Understanding Taxes and Savings, 2006; Pay Less Tax, 2007; Beat the Banks, 2008; Making Your Money Work, 2008; contrib. to The Dickensian, Reader's Digest, Daily Telegraph, Radio Times, TES, Community Care. *Recreations:* annoying financial companies, making bad jokes, Wilkie Collins. *Address: e-mail:* paul@paullewis.co.uk. *T:* (020) 8747 0115.

LEWIS, Paul Keith; QC 2001; a Recorder, since 2000; *b* 26 May 1957; *s* of late John Keith Lewis and of Susan Patricia Lewis (*née* Cronin); *m* 1983, Siân Price; one *s* one *d*. *Educ:* Pontypridd Grammar Sch. for Boys; Univ. of Leicester (LLB Hons); Inns of Court Sch. of Law. Called to the Bar, Gray's Inn, 1981; in practice, Cardiff and London, 1981–; an Asst Recorder, 1998–2000. *Recreations:* sport, travel, music. *Address:* Chapel Mill, Chain Road, Abergavenny, Monmouthshire NP7 7HH. *T:* (01873) 858441; 30 Park Place, Cardiff, S Glamorgan CF10 3BS. *T:* (029) 2039 8421, *Fax:* (029) 2039 8725; *e-mail:* clerk@30parkplace.law.co.uk; 9–12 Bell Yard, WC2A 2JR. *T:* (020) 7400 1800, *Fax:* (020) 7404 1405; *e-mail:* clerks@bellyard.co.uk. *Club:* Monmouthshire Golf (Abergavenny).

LEWIS, Peter; Director, Policy Co-ordination Unit, 1994–96, and the Tax Simplification Project, 1995–96, Inland Revenue; *b* 24 June 1937; *s* of Reginald George and Edith Lewis; *m* 1962, Ursula Brigitte Kilian; one *s* one *d*. *Educ:* Ealing Grammar School; St Peter's Hall, Oxford. Royal Navy, 1955–57. Inland Revenue Inspector of Taxes, 1960–69; Inland Revenue Policy and Central Divs, 1969–85; Director: Personal Tax Div., 1986–91; Company Tax Div., 1991–95. *Address:* Glyndavas, 9 Waterloo Close, St Mawes, Cornwall TR2 5BD.

LEWIS, Peter Adrian; Director, Education, Children's Services and Leisure, since 2004, and Deputy Chief Executive, since 2008, London Borough of Enfield; *b* 9 Feb. 1954; *s* of Mrs Beryl Williams; *m* 1976, Lynn Cook. *Educ:* Madeley Coll., Keele (Cert Ed); Bristol Poly. (BEd). Teacher, Eastwood Middle Sch., Stoke on Trent, 1975–77; social worker, Staffs, Avon and Hants, 1977–88; Educn Officer, Hants CC, 1988–96; Asst Dir, Educn and Leisure Services, Southampton CC, 1996–2004. *Recreations:* opera, reading, walking, travel. *Address:* London Borough of Enfield, PO Box 56, Civic Centre, Enfield EN1 3XQ. *T:* (020) 8379 3200, *Fax:* (020) 8379 3351; *e-mail:* peter.lewis@enfield.gov.uk.

LEWIS, Peter Ronald; Director General, Bibliographic Services, British Library, 1980–89; *b* 28 Sept. 1926; *s* of Charles Lewis and Florence Mary (née Kirk); *m* 1952, June Ashley; one *s* one *d*. *Educ:* Royal Masonic Sch.; Belfast Univ. (MA). FLA; Hon. FCLIP (Hon. FLA 1989). Brighton, Plymouth, Chester public libraries, 1948–55; Head, Bibliographic Services, BoT Library, 1955–65; Lectr in Library Studies, QUB, 1965–69; Librarian: City Univ., 1969–72; Univ. of Sussex, 1972–80. Vice-Pres., 1979–85 and Hon. Treasurer, 1980–82, Library Assoc. Chm., LA Publishing Co., 1983–85. *Publications:* The Literature of the Social Sciences, 1960; The Fall and Rise of National Bibliography (Bangalore), 1982. *Recreations:* acting, editor-publisher. *Address:* Wyvern, Blackheath Road, Wenhaston, Suffolk IP19 9HD.

LEWIS, Peter Tyndale; Chairman, John Lewis Partnership, 1972–93; *b* 26 Sept. 1929; *s* of Oswald Lewis and Frances Merriman Lewis (*née* Cooper); *m* 1961, Deborah Anne, *d* of late Sir William (Alexander Roy) Collins, CBE and Priscilla Marian, *d* of late S. J. Lloyd; one *s* one *d*. *Educ:* Eton; Christ Church, Oxford (MA 1953). National service, Coldstream Guards, 1948–49; called to Bar (Middle Temple) 1956; joined John Lewis Partnership, 1959. Member: Council, Industrial Soc., 1968–79; Design Council, 1971–74; Chm., Retail Distributors' Assoc., 1972. Member: Southampton Univ. Develt Trust, 1994–2003; Council, Queen's Coll., Harley St, 1994–99. Trustee, Jt Educnl Trust, 1985–87. Governor: NIESR, 1983; Windlesham Hse Sch., 1979–95; The Bell Educnl Trust, 1987–97. *Address:* 34 Victoria Road, W8 5RG.

LEWIS, Ralph; *see* Lewis, D. R.

LEWIS, Rhodri Price; QC 2001; a Recorder, since 1998; *b* 7 June 1952; *s* of George Lewis and Nansi Lewis (*née* Price); *m* 1983, Barbara Sinden; two *d*. *Educ:* Ysgol Gymraeg Ynyswen; Cowbridge Grammar Sch.; Pembroke Coll., Oxford (MA); Sidney Sussex Coll., Cambridge (Dip. Criminol.). Called to the Bar, Middle Temple, 1975. An Asst Parly Boundary Comr, 2003–. *Publications:* Environmental Law, 2000; contrib. to Jl Planning and Envmt Law. *Recreations:* Rugby, playing the guitar, enjoying the company, coast and country of Pembrokeshire. *Address:* Landmark Chambers, 180 Fleet Street, EC4A 2HG. *Clubs:* Farmers', London Welsh Rugby Football; St David's Rugby Football.

LEWIS, Rt Rev. Richard; *see* Lewis, Rt Rev. J. H. R.

LEWIS, Very Rev. Richard; Dean of Wells, 1990–2003, now Emeritus; *b* 24 Dec. 1935; *m* 1959, Jill Diane Wilford; two *s*. *Educ:* Royal Masonic Sch.; Fitzwilliam House, Cambridge (BA 1958; MA 1961); Ripon Hall, Oxford. Asst Curate, Hinckley, Leicester, 1960–63; Priest-in-Charge, St Edmund, Riddlesdown, 1963–66; Vicar: All Saints, South Merstham, 1966–72; Holy Trinity and St Peter, Wimbledon, 1972–79; St Barnabas, Dulwich and Foundation Chaplain of Alleyn's College of God's Gift at Dulwich, 1979–90. *Publication:* (contrib.) Cathedrals Now, 1996. *Recreations:* music of all sorts, walking, gardening, reading. *Address:* Wells House, 152 Lower Howsell Road, Malvern Link, Worcester WR14 1DL. *T:* (01886) 833820; *e-mail:* Dean.Richard@wellshouse.co.uk.

LEWIS, Hon. Robin William, OBE 1988; Lord-Lieutenant of Dyfed, since 2006; *b* 7 Feb. 1941; *s* of 3rd Baron Merthyr, KBE, TD, PC, and Violet (*née* Meyrick); *m* 1967, Judith Ann Giardelli. *Educ:* Eton; Magdalen Coll., Oxford (MA; Dip. Econ. Develt). Commonwealth Develt Corp., 1964–66; Alcan Aluminium Ltd, 1967–68; Westminster Bank Ltd, 1968–72; Develt Corp. for Wales, 1972–83; Man. Dir, Novametrix Med. Systems Ltd, 1983–90; Chairman: The Magstim Co. Ltd, 1990–; J. P. Morgan US Discovery Investment Trust, 2003–. Chm., Gen. Adv. Council, IBA, 1988–90. Chairman: NT Cttee for Wales, 1994–97; Trustees, Nat. Botanic Garden of Wales, 2006–08. High Sheriff, 1987–88, DL 2002, Dyfed. CStJ 2008. *Address:* The Cottage, Cresswell Quay, Kilgetty, Pembs SA68 0TE. *Club:* Leander (Henley-on-Thames).

See also T. O. Lewis.

LEWIS, Roger Charles; Group Chief Executive, Welsh Rugby Union and Millennium Stadium, since 2006; *b* 24 Aug. 1954; *s* of late Griffith Charles Job Lewis and Dorothy Lewis (*née* Russ); *m* 1980, Dr Christine, *d* of Leslie Trollope; two *s*. *Educ:* Cynffig Comprehensive Sch., Bridgend; Univ. of Nottingham (BMus Hons 1976). Musician, 1976–80: Avon Touring Th. Co., 1977–79; Birmingham Rep. Th. Studio, 1978; Ludus

Dance in Educn Co., 1979; Scottish Ballet Workshop Co., 1979; Music Officer, Darlington Arts Centre, 1980–82; Dir, Cleveland Arts Ltd, 1982–84; Presenter, Radio Tees, 1981–84; Producer: Capital Radio, 1984–85; BBC Radio 1, 1985–87; Hd of Music, Radio 1, 1987–90; Dir, 1990–95, Man. Dir, 1995, Classical Div., EMI Records; Man. Dir, EMI Premier, 1995–97; Pres., Decca Record Co., 1997–98; Man. Dir and Prog. Controller, Classic FM, 1998–2004; Man. Dir, ITV Wales, 2004–06. Director: GWR plc, 1998–2004; The Radio Corp. Ltd, 1999–2003; Digital One, 2003–04; HTV Ltd, 2005–06; HTV Gp Ltd, 2005–06; Carltonco 120 Ltd, 2005–06; European Rugby Cup Ltd, 2007–; Celtic Rugby Ltd, 2007–; non-exec. Dep. Chm., Boosey & Hawkes, 2004–06; non-exec. Dir, Barchester Gp, 2001–06. Chairman: Classical Cttee, British Phonographic Industry Ltd, 1996–98 (Mem., 1990–96); Music and Dance Scheme Adv. Gp, DFES (formerly DFEE), 2000–04; Arts and Business Wales, 2006. Member: Bd, Liverpool European Capital of Culture, 2003–06; Bd, Wales Millennium Centre, 2004–06; Welsh Arts Review Panel, 2006. Chm., Royal Liverpool Philharmonic, 2003–06; Vice-President: London Welsh Male Voice Choir, 2004–; Welsh Music Guild, 2005–. Trustee: Masterprize (Internat. Composers' Competition), 1995–; Masterclass Charitable Trust, 2000–04; Chairman: Trustees, Ogmore Centre, 1996–2008; Classic FM Charitable Trust, 2000–04. President: Bromley Youth Music Trust, 2000–06 (Vice-Pres., 2006–); Cefn Cribwr RFC, 2007–; Member: WNO Develt Circle, 2001–06; Founder Partners Bd, Beacon Fellowship Awards, 2003–06. FRSA 2000. Hon. FRWCMD 2004; Hon. RCM 2005; Hon. Fellow, Cardiff Univ., 2007. Sony Radio Award, 1987, 1988, 1989; Grand Award Winner and Gold Medal, NY Radio Fest., 1987; One World Broadcasting Trust Award, 1989; NTL Commercial Radio Programmer of the Year, 2002. *Recreations:* Rugby, walking, ski-ing. *Address:* Welsh Rugby Union, Millennium Stadium, Westgate Street, Cardiff CF10 1NS.

LEWIS, Roger Clifford; writer; *b* 26 Feb. 1960; *e s* of late Wyndham Gardner Lewis, Bedwas, Monmouthshire; *m* 1982, Anna Margaret Jane Dickens, educational psychologist, *d* of Eric John Dickens and Iris Grace (*née* Taylor); three *s*. *Educ:* Bassaleg Comp. Sch., Newport; Univ. of St Andrews (Lawson Meml Prize, Gray Prize, Coll. Bursary, Walker Trust Award; MA 1st cl. Hons 1982); Magdalen Coll., Oxford (Charles Oldham Shakespeare Prize, Matthew Arnold Meml Prize, Chancellor's English Essay Prize; MA status 1985). University of Oxford: Jun. Res. Fellow, Wolfson Coll., 1985–89, Mem. Common Room, 1989–; Tutor, Univ. of Massachusetts Summer Sch., Trinity Coll., 1985; Lecturer and Tutor: Boston Univ. Mod. British Studies prog., St Catherine's Coll., 1986–90; Stanford Univ. and Smithsonian Instn English Lit. courses, Oxford, 1987; Lectr, Magdalen Coll., 1988. Vis. Prof., Faculty of Law, Humanities, Develt and Society, Birmingham City Univ. (formerly UCE, Birmingham), 2006–. Arts journalism: American Scholar, American Spectator, Encounter, Erotic Review, Financial Times, GQ Magazine, Independent, Listener, Mail on Sunday, New Statesman, Observer, Oldie, Opera Now, Punch, Spectator, Sunday Times, Telegraph Mag., *etc*; lead book reviewer, Express Newspapers, 2001–. Frequent interviewee on nat. and local radio and television arts and culture progs; consultant on documentaries: Larry and Viv: the Oliviers in love, C4, 2001; The Paranormal Peter Sellers, C4, 2002; Profondo Rosa: la vera storia della Pantera Rosa, Sky Italia, 2004. FRAS; FRGS; FRSA. Commnd Col by Gov. of Kentucky, 2007; Admiral, Gt Navy of State of Nebraska, 2007. *Publications:* (contrib.) The New Compleat Imbiber, 1986; (ed) Rewards and Fairies, by Rudyard Kipling (Penguin Classics), 1987; Stage People, 1989; (ed) The Memoirs and Confessions of a Justified Sinner, by James Hogg (Everyman's Liby), 1992; The Life and Death of Peter Sellers, 1994, reissued 2004 (filmed 2004 (Primetime Emmy Award 2005)); The Real Life of Laurence Olivier, 1996, reissued 2007; The Man Who Was Private Widdle: Charles Hawtrey, 2001; Anthony Burgess, 2002. *Recreations:* whistling along to gramophone records, travelling on preserved steam railways. *Address:* c/o Artellus Ltd, 30 Dorset House, Gloucester Place, NW1 5AD; *e-mail:* leslie@artellusltd.co.uk. *Clubs:* Groucho, English-Speaking Union; Players (NY).

LEWIS, Roger St John Hulton; Chairman, Berkeley Group plc, since 1999; *b* 26 June 1947; *m* 1973, Vanessa England; three *s*. *Educ:* Eton Coll. ACA 1969. KPMG 1966–72; Finance Dir, 1972–75, Man. Dir, 1975–83, Crest Homes; Gp Chief Exec., Crest Nicholson, 1983–91; Finance Dir, 1992–98, Exec. Dir, 1998–99, Berkeley Gp. *Recreations:* cricket, travel, ski-ing, food. *Address:* The Berkeley Group plc, Berkeley House, 19 Portsmouth Road, Cobham, Surrey KT11 1JG. *T:* (01932) 868555, *Fax:* (01932) 868667. *Club:* Victoria (Jersey).

LEWIS, Sean Michael, PhD; Director, British Council, Canada, 1997–2000, retired; *b* 23 Oct. 1943; *s* of Leonard Leon Lewis and Margaret Lewis (*née* Moore); *m* 1971, Jennifer M. Williams; one *s*. *Educ:* Univ. of Liverpool (BSc 1967; PhD 1971). British Council: London, 1970, 1973–75, 1978–89, 1992–97; Nigeria, 1971–73; Sri Lanka, 1975–78; Sweden, 1989–92. *Documentary films:* (co-prod.) There We Are John, 1993; (prod.) Lucky Man, 1995. *Recreations:* minimal effort downhill ski-ing, pyrotechnics, films, landscape gardening, real ale, country pubs. *Address:* 38 Ninehams Road, Caterham on the Hill, Surrey CR3 5LD. *T:* (020) 8763 1644.

LEWIS, Simon David; Group Director of Corporate Affairs, Vodafone plc, since 2004; *b* 8 May 1959; *s* of David Lewis and Sally Lewis (*née* Valentine); *m* 1985, Claire Elizabeth Anne Pendry; two *s* one *d*. *Educ:* Whitefield Comprehensive, London; Brasenose Coll., Oxford (MA); Univ. of Calif, Berkeley (Fulbright Scholar; MA). FCIPR (FIPR 1998). PR Consultant, Shandwick Consultants, 1983–86; Head: of Communications, SDP, 1986–87; of PR, S. G. Warburg Gp plc, 1987–92; Director, Corporate Affairs: NatWest Gp, 1992–96; Centrica plc, 1996–98; on secondment as Communications Sec., Buckingham Palace, 1998–2000; Man. Dir, Europe, Centrica plc, 2000–04. Mem., Fulbright Commn, 2001–. Pres., IPR, 1997. Trustee, Vodafone Gp Foundn, 2005–. Hon. Prof., Cardiff Sch. of Journalism, 2000–. FRSA. *Recreations:* family, sport, current affairs, cinema. *Address:* Vodafone plc, Vodafone House, The Connection, Newbury RG14 2FN. *Club:* Reform.

LEWIS, Stephen John B.; *see* Brimson-Lewis.

LEWIS, Susan, CBE 2008; HM Chief Inspector of Education and Training in Wales (formerly Chief Inspector of Schools in Wales), 1997–2008; *b* 7 Nov. 1947; *d* of Kenneth A. L. Lewis and Elsie (*née* Woods). *Educ:* Henry Smith Sch., Hartlepool; Univ. of Newcastle upon Tyne (BSc Hons); Univ. of Sheffield (DipEd); Sch. of Psychotherapy and Counselling, Regent's Coll., London (certified mediator, 2005, coach, 2006). Asst teacher, Bradfield Sch., WR Yorks, 1970–74; Hd of Dept and Asst Hd of Sixth Form, Shelley High Sch., Kirklees, 1974–80; Dep. Head, later Actg Head, Wisewood Sch., Sheffield, 1980–86; HM Inspector of Schools, 1986–95; Staff Inspector, Office of HM Chief Inspector, 1995–97. FRSA. *Recreations:* gardening, walking, genealogy, drawing, painting. *Address: e-mail:* hoosehoo08@tiscali.co.uk.

LEWIS, Terence; *b* 29 Dec. 1935; *s* of Andrew Lewis; *m* 1958, Audrey, *d* of William Clarke; one *s* (and one *s* decd). *Educ:* Mt Carmel Sch., Salford. Nat. service, RAMC, 1954–56. Personnel Officer. Member: Kearsley UDC, 1971–74; Bolton BC, 1976–84 (Chm., Educn Cttee, 1982–83). MP (Lab) Worsley, 1983–2005; Mem., Standards and Privileges Select Cttee, 1997–2001. *Address:* 54 Greenmount Park, Kearsley, Bolton, Lancs BL4 8NS.

LEWIS, Terence Murray, GM 1960; Commissioner of Police, Queensland, 1976–89; *b* 29 Feb. 1928; *s* of late George Murray Lewis and of Monica Ellen Lewis (*née* Hanlon); *m* 1952, Hazel Catherine Lewis (*née* Gould); three *s* two *d*. *Educ:* Univ. of Queensland (DPA 1974; BA 1978). Queensland Police Force, 1948; Criminal Investigation Br., 1950–63; Juvenile Aid Bureau, 1963–73; Inspector of Police, 1973. Member: Royal Aust. Inst. of Public Admin, 1964; Internat. Police Assoc., 1968; Internat. Assoc. of Chiefs of Police, 1977. Churchill Fellow, 1968; FAIM 1978. Hon. Correspondent for Royal Humane Soc. of Australasia, 1981. Patron, Vice-Patron, Pres., Trustee, or Mem., numerous Qld organisations. Queensland Father of the Year, 1980. Silver Jubilee Medal, 1977. *Recreation:* reading.

LEWIS, Tony; *see* Lewis, A. R.

LEWIS, Trevor; *see* Lewis, D. T.

LEWIS, Dr Trevor, CBE 1992; Director, AFRC Institute of Arable Crops Research, 1989–93; Head, 1987–93, Lawes Trust Senior Fellow, 1993–2003, Rothamsted Experimental Station; Visiting Professor in Invertebrate Zoology, University of Nottingham, 1977–98; *b* 8 July 1933; *s* of Harold and Maggie Lewis; *m* 1959, Margaret Edith Wells; one *s* one *d*. *Educ:* Univ. of Nottingham (DSc 1986); Imperial Coll. of Science and Technol., Univ. of London (PhD, DIC 1958); MA Cambridge, 1960. University Demonstr in Agricl Zoology, Sch. of Agriculture, Cambridge, 1958–61; scientific staff, Rothamsted Experimental Station, 1961–2003; seconded to ODA as Sen. Res. Fellow, Univ. of WI, Trinidad, 1970–73; Head, Entomology Dept, 1976–83; Dep. Dir, 1983–87; Hd of Crop and Envmt Protection Div., 1983–89. Special Lectr in Invertebrate Zool., Univ. of Nottingham, 1968–69 and 1973–75. AFRC Assessor to MAFF Adv. Cttee on Pesticides, 1984–89; Member: Management Bd, British Crop Protection Council, 1985–94; Bd, British Crop Protection Enterprises, 1994–; R&D Cttee, Potato Marketing Bd, 1985–89. Mem. Council, British Ecological Soc., 1982–84; Pres., Royal Entomol Soc. of London, 1985–87; Pres., Agric. and Forestry Sect., BAAS, 1997. Huxley Gold Medal, Imperial Coll. of Science and Technol., Univ. of London, 1977; British Crop Protection Council Medal, 2002. *Publications:* (with L. R. Taylor) Introduction to Experimental Ecology, 1967; Thrips—their biology, ecology and economic importance, 1973; (ed) Insect Communication, 1984; Thrips as Crop Pests, 1997; contribs to scientific jls on topics in entomology. *Recreations:* music, gardening.

LEWIS, Trevor Oswin, CBE 1983; DL; *b* 29 Nov. 1935; *s* of 3rd Baron Merthyr, KBE, TD, PC, and Violet, *y d* of Brig.-Gen. Sir Frederick Charlton Meyrick, 2nd Bt, CB, CMG; *S* father, 1977, as 4th Baron Merthyr, but disclaimed his peerage for life; also as 4th Bt (*cr* 1896) but does not use the title; *m* 1964, Susan Jane, *yr d* of A. J. Birt-Llewellin; one *s* three *d*. *Educ:* Downs Sch.; Eton; Magdalen Coll., Oxford; Magdalene Coll., Cambridge. Member: Landscape Adv. Cttee, Dept of Transport, 1968–92 (Chm., 1991–92); Countryside Commn, 1973–83 (Dep. Chm., 1980–83); Chm., Countryside Commn's Cttee for Wales, 1973–80. JP Pembs, then Dyfed, 1969–94; DL Dyfed, 1994. *Heir:* (*to disclaimed peerage*): *s* David Trevor Lewis, *b* 21 Feb. 1977. *Address:* Hean Castle, Saundersfoot SA69 9AL. *T:* (01834) 810347.

See also Hon. R. W. Lewis.

LEWIS, Dame Vera Margaret; *see* Lynn, Dame Vera.

LEWIS-BOWEN, His Honour Thomas Edward Ifor; a Circuit Judge, 1980–98; *b* 20 June 1933; *s* of late Lt-Col J. W. Lewis-Bowen and K. M. Lewis-Bowen (*née* Rice); *m* 1965, Gillian, *d* of late Reginald Brett, Puckington, Som; one *s* two *d*. *Educ:* Ampleforth; St Edmund Hall, Oxford. Called to Bar, Middle Temple, 1958. A Recorder of the Crown Court, 1974–80.

LEWIS-JONES, Janet Ann; Vice President, British Board of Film Classification, 1998–2008; Trustee (for Wales), BBC Trust, since 2006; *b* 12 May 1950; *d* of John Gwilym Jones and Elizabeth Eirliw, (Bethan), Louis Jones. *Educ:* Univ. of Liverpool (LLB 1973). VSO, PNG, 1968–69. Called to the Bar, Gray's Inn, 1974. Joined Civil Service as admin trainee, 1974; Home Office, 1974–82; Cabinet Secretariat, Cabinet Office, 1982–83; Prin. Pvte Sec. to Viscount Whitelaw, Lord Pres. of Council, Privy Council Office, 1983–85; Home Office, 1985–86; Welsh Water, 1986–90. Chm., Membership Selection Panel, Welsh Water, 2001–; Member: S4C, 1992–2003; British Waterways Bd, 1994–2004; Postal Services Commn, 2000–06; Strategic Rail Authy, 2002–05; British Transport Police Authy, 2004–05; Member, Wales Committee: UFC, 1990–92; EOC, 1994–99. Public Affairs Advr to Archbishops of Canterbury, 1991–95, 2005–06; Specialist Advr, H of L Select Cttee on the Public Service, 1996–98. Trustee: Refugee Legal Centre, 1991–92; Barnardo's, 1992–99; Community Develt Foundn, 1996–99; Baring Foundn, 1996–; Police Foundn, 1998–2004; Carnegie UK Trust, 1998–2004; Inst. of Rural Health, 2002–05. Vice Pres., Univ. of Wales, Lampeter, 1999–2001. Hon. Fellow, Aberystwyth Univ., 2008. *Recreations:* lettercutting in stone, film, walking. *Address:* 3 Camden Road, Brecon, Powys LD3 7BU. *Club:* Reform.

LEWISHAM, Archdeacon of; *see* Hardman, Ven. C. E.

LEWISOHN, His Honour Anthony Clive Leopold; a Circuit Judge, 1974–90; *b* 1 Aug. 1925; *s* of John Lewisohn and Gladys (*née* Solomon); *m* 1957, Lone Ruthwen Jurgensen; two *s*. *Educ:* Stowe; Trinity Coll., Oxford (MA). Royal Marines, 1944–45; Lieut, Oxf. and Bucks LI, 1946–47. Called to Bar, Middle Temple, 1951; S Eastern Circuit.

LEWISOHN, Neville Joseph; Director of Dockyard Manpower and Productivity (Under Secretary), Ministry of Defence, 1979–82; *b* 28 May 1922; *s* of Victor and Ruth Lewisohn; *m* 1944, Patricia Zeffertt; two *d* (and one *d* decd). *Educ:* Sutton County Sch., Surrey. Entered Admiralty as Clerical Officer, 1939; promoted through intervening grades to Principal, 1964; Dir of Resources and Progs (Ships), 1972 (Asst Sec.); Head of Civilian Management (Specialists), 2 Div., 1976. *Recreations:* music, drama.

LEWISON, Jeremy Rodney Pines; freelance curator and art consultant; Director of Collections, Tate Gallery, 1998–2002; *b* 13 Jan. 1955; *s* of late Anthony Frederick Lewison and Dinora Pines; *m* 1993, Caroline Maria Aviva Schuck; one step *s* one step *d*. *Educ:* Westminster Sch.; Magdalen Coll., Oxford (MA; Dip Hist. of Art). Curator, Kettle's Yard, Univ. of Cambridge, 1977–83; Tate Gallery: Asst Keeper, Print Collection, 1983–86; Asst Keeper, 1986–90, Dep. Keeper, 1990–97, Modern Collection. *Publications:* Anish Kapoor Drawings, 1990; Ben Nicholson, 1991; David Smith Medals for Dishonour, 1991; Brice Marden Prints 1961–91, 1992; Ben Nicholson, 1993; Shirazeh Houshiary, 1995; Karl Weschke, 1998; Interpreting Pollock, 1999; Looking at Barnett Newman, 2002; Ben Nicholson, 2002; Alice Neel, 2004; Anish Kapoor Drawings, 2005; Ra'anan Levy, 2006; Henry Moore, 2007; Ben Nicholson Prints 1928–1968: the Rentsch collection, 2007. *Recreations:* tennis, ski-ing, mountain walking, running. *Address:* 2 Fellows Road, NW3

3LP.
See also Sir K. M. J. Lewison.

LEWISON, Hon. Sir Kim (Martin Jordan), Kt 2003; **Hon. Mr Justice Lewison;** a Judge of the High Court of Justice, Chancery Division, since 2003; *b* 1 May 1952; *s* of late Anthony Frederick Lewison and Dinora Lewison (*née* Pines); *m* 1979, Helen Mary Janecek (marr. diss. 1998); one *s* one *d*; *m* 2002, Sharon Moross. *Educ:* St Paul's Sch., London; Downing Coll., Cambridge (MA 1973); Council of Legal Education. Called to the Bar, Lincoln's Inn, 1975, Bencher, 1998; QC 1991. Asst Recorder, 1994–97, Recorder, 1997–2003; a Dep. High Ct Judge, 2000–03. Mem. Council, Liberal Jewish Synagogue, 1990–96. Mem. Council, Leo Baeck Coll., 1997–2002; Gov., Anglo-American Real Property Inst., 1996–2000 (Chm., 2002). *Publications:* Development Land Tax, 1978; Drafting Business Leases, 1979, 6th edn 2000; Lease or Licence, 1985; The Interpretation of Contracts, 1989, 4th edn 2007; (Gen. Editor) Woodfall on Landlord and Tenant, 1990–. *Recreations:* visiting France, avoiding tsores. *Address:* Royal Courts of Justice, Strand, WC2A 2LL.
See also J. R. P. Lewison.

LEWITH, Dr George Thomas, FRCP; Reader in University Medicine, since 2005, and Hon. Consultant Physician, since 1995, Southampton Medical School, University of Southampton; Partner, Centre for Study of Complementary Medicine, Southampton, since 1982; *b* 12 Jan. 1950; *s* of Frank and Alice Lewith; *m* 1977, Nicola Rosemary Bazeley; two *s* one *d*. *Educ:* Queen's Coll., Taunton; Trinity Coll., Cambridge (MA); Westminster Hosp. Med. Sch. (MB BChir); DM Soton 1994. MRCGP 1980; FRCP 1999. Southampton University: Lectr in Primary Med. Care, 1979–82; Sen. Res. Fellow in Univ. Medicine, Southampton Med. Sch., 1995–2004. Vis. Prof., Univ. of Westminster, 2003–. *Publications:* contribs to numerous academic books and papers in field of complementary medicine. *Recreations:* the theatre, ski-ing, sport, sailing, gardening. *Address:* Sway Wood House, Mead End Road, Sway, Lymington, Hants SO41 6EE. *T:* (01590) 682129.

LEWSLEY, Patricia; Northern Ireland Commissioner for Children and Young People, since 2007; *b* 3 March 1957; *d* of Patrick and Mary Killen; *m* 1976, Hugh Lewsley (marr. diss. 1998); three *s* two *d*. *Educ:* St Dominic's High Sch.; Univ. of Ulster. Mem. (SDLP) Lagan Valley, NI Assembly, 1998–2007. Contested (SDLP) Lagan Valley, 2001, 2005. *Recreations:* reading, travel. *Address:* Northern Ireland Commissioner for Children and Young People, Millennium House, 17–25 Great Victoria Street, Belfast BT2 7BA.

LEWTY, (David) Ian; HM Diplomatic Service, retired; *b* 27 July 1943; *s* of late Harry Lewty and Ruby Lewty (*née* Buck); *m* 1968, Mary Law; two *d*. *Educ:* Lancing Coll.; Magdalen Coll., Oxford (MA). Third Sec., FO, 1965; MECAS, Lebanon, 1966; Third, later Second Sec., Ottawa, 1967–71; Hd, British Interests Section, Baghdad, 1971–72; First Sec., FCO, 1972–76; Hd of Chancery, Jedda, 1976–79; (on secondment) L'Ecole Nationale d'Administration, Paris, 1979–81; UK Delegn to OECD, Paris, 1981–84; FCO, 1984–87; Counsellor and Dep. Hd of Mission, Khartoum, 1987–89; Diplomatic Service Inspector, 1989–92; Hd, Migration and Visa Dept, FCO, 1992–95; Ambassador to Bahrain, 1996–99. *Address:* 38 Burlington Avenue, Richmond, Surrey TW9 4DH.

LEY, Sir Ian (Francis), 5th Bt *cr* 1905, of Epperstone, Nottingham; *b* 12 June 1934; *o s* of Sir Francis Douglas Ley, 4th Bt, MBE and Violet Geraldine Ley (*née* Johnson) (*d* 1991); *S* father, 1995; *m* 1957, Caroline Margaret (*née* Errington); one *s* one *d*. *Educ:* Eton Coll. Dep. Chm., 1972–80, Chm., 1981–82, Ley's Foundries and Engineering plc. High Sheriff, Derbyshire, 1985. *Recreation:* shooting. *Heir: s* Christopher Ian Ley [*b* 2 Dec. 1962; *m* 1999, Henrietta, *yr d* of David Nicholls]. *Club:* White's.

LEY, Prof. Steven Victor, CBE 2002; FRS 1990; BP (1702) Professor of Organic Chemistry, since 1992, and Fellow of Trinity College, since 1993, University of Cambridge. *Educ:* Loughborough Univ. of Technology (BSc 1st cl. Hons 1969; DIS 1969; PhD 1972); DSc London 1983; MA 1997, ScD 1999, Cantab. CChem, FRSC 1980; FIC 2000; CBiol, FIBiol 2003. Res. Fellow, Ohio State Univ., 1972–74; Imperial College, London: Res. Asst, 1974–75; Lectr, 1975–83; Prof. of Organic Chemistry, 1983–92; Head of Chemistry Dept, 1989–92. Royal Soc. Bakerian Lectr, 1997. Chm. Exec. Cttee, Novartis (formerly Ciba) Foundn, 1993–. Pres., Royal Soc. of Chem., 2000–02. Hon. Fellow, Cardiff Univ., 2005. Hon. DSc: Loughborough, 1994; Salamanca, 2000; Huddersfield, 2003. Royal Society of Chemistry: Hickinbottom Res. Fellow, 1981–83 (1st recipient); Corday Morgan Medal and Prize, 1980; Tilden Lectr and Medal, 1988; Award for Synthetic Chem., 1989; Pedlar Lectr and Medal, 1992; Simonsen Lectr and Medal, 1993; Award for Natural Products Chemistry, 1994; Flintoff Medal, 1996; Rhône-Poulenc Lectureship Medal and Prize, 1998; Haworth Meml Lectr, Medal and Prize, 2001; Award in Carbohydrate Chemistry, 2003; Robert Robinson Award and Medal, 2006; German Chemical Society: Adolf Windaus Medal, 1994; August Wilhelm von Hofmann Medal, 2001; Dr Paul Janssen Prize for Creativity in Organic Synthesis, European Chem. Soc., 1996; Davy Medal, Royal Soc., 2000; Pfizer Central Research: Pfizer Res. Award, 1983 (1st recipient); Pfizer Award for Innovative Science, 2001; Ernst Guenther Award, ACS, 2003; Innovation of the Year Award, CIA, 2003; iAc Award (for Innovation in Applied Catalysis), IChemE, 2004; Alexander von Humboldt Award, 2005; Yamada-Koga Prize, Japan Res. Foundn for Optically Active Compounds, 2005; Nagoya Gold Medal, Banyu Life Sci. Foundn Internat., 2006; Award for Creative Work in Synthetic Organic Chem., ACS, 2007; Paul Karrer Medal, Univ. of Zurich, 2007; Innovation Award, Soc. of Chem. Ind. (1st recipient), 2007; In hoffen Medal, Helmholtz Zentrum für Infectionsforschung, 2008. *Publications:* over 640 papers in internat. jls of chemistry. *Address:* Department of Chemistry, Lensfield Road, Cambridge CB2 1EW; *web:* http://leygroup.ch.cam.ac.uk.

LEYLAND, Sir Philip Vyvian N.; *see* Naylor-Leyland.

LEYLAND, Ronald Arthur; Chief Executive, North Yorkshire County Council, 1990–94; *b* 23 Aug. 1940; *s* of Arthur and Lucy Leyland; *m* 1962, Joan Virginia Sinclair; three *s*. *Educ:* Merchant Taylors' Sch., Crosby; Liverpool Univ. (LLB Hons 1961). Solicitor (Hons 1964). Assistant Solicitor: Bootle CBC, 1964–65; Nottingham City Council, 1965–68; Sen. Asst Solicitor, then Dir of Admin, Leeds MDC, 1968–75; County Sec., Hampshire CC, 1975–90. Dir, N Yorks TEC, 1990–94. Chm., Soc. of County Secretaries, 1986–87. *Recreation:* family history. *Address:* White House, Maunby, near Thirsk YO7 4HG. *Club:* Rotary.

LEYSER, Prof. (Henrietta Miriam) Ottoline, PhD; FRS 2007; Professor of Plant Developmental Genetics, University of York, since 2002; *b* 7 March 1965; *d* of Prof. Karl Joseph Leyser, TD, FBA and Henrietta Louise Valerie Leyser (*née* Bateman); *m* 1986, Stephen John Day; one *s* one *d*. *Educ:* Newnham Coll., Cambridge (BA Genetics 1986; PhD Genetics 1990). Post-doctoral Research Fellow: Indiana Univ., Bloomington, 1990–93; Cambridge Univ., 1993–94; Lectr, 1994–99, Reader, 1999–2002, Univ. of York. Ed., The Plant Jl, 2001–; Member, Advisory Editorial Board: Trends in Plant Sci., 1999–; Bioessays, 2001–; Current Biol., 2003–; Annual Rev. of Plant Biol., 2004–; Plant Cell Physiol., 2004–. Biotechnology and Biological Sciences Research Council: Chm., Genes and Develtl Biol. Cttee, 2004–06; Member: Strategy Bd, 2003–04; Data Policy wkg gp, 2005–06; Bioinformatics and Biol Resources Initiative Panel, 2007; Mem., MRC/BBSRC/Wellcome Trust Eur. Bioinformatics Inst. Rev. Panel, 2004; Mem., Life Sci. Interface Doctoral Trng Centres Rev. Panel, EPSRC, 2007. Treas., British Soc. for Develtl Biol., 1999–2004; Mem. Council, Internat. Soc. for Plant Molecular Biol., 2003–. K. M. Stott Res. Fellow Prize, Newnham Coll., Cambridge, 1993; President's Medal, Soc. for Exptl Biol., 2000; Rosalind Franklin Award, Royal Soc., 2007. *Publications:* (with S. Day) Mechanisms in Plant Development, 2002; chapters in: Plant Gene Isolation, 1996; Plant Cell Proliferation and its Regulation in Growth and Development, 1997; Plant Hormone Protocols, 2000; Grafting, 2005; contribs to learned jls incl. Nature, Cell, Current Biol., Development, Plant Physiol., Plant Jl. *Recreations:* singing, walking, swimming. *Address:* Department of Biology, Area 11, University of York, York YO10 5YW. *T:* (01904) 328680, *Fax:* (01904) 328682; *e-mail:* hmol1@york.ac.uk.

LEZALA, Andrew Peter, CEng, FIMechE; Managing Director, Air Rail Transit Ltd, since 2008; *b* 8 Dec. 1955; *s* of Jozef and Constance Lezala; *m* 1980, Helen Addison; one *s* two *d*. *Educ:* Derby Grammar Sch.; Univ. of Leicester (BSc Hons Eng). CEng, FIMechE 1989. British Rail: Engrg Grad. Trainee, 1977–79; bogie and suspension design engr, 1979–81; Asst Brakes Engr, 1981–84; Project Engr, 1984–86, Chief Engr, New Vehicles, 1986–87, BREL Ltd; Gp Operating and Engrg Dir, RFS Hldgs Ltd, 1987–93; Vice Pres., Business Area Metro's and Multiple Units, ABB Transportation Ltd, 1993–94; Hd of Metro's, ABB China Ltd, 1994–98; Man. Dir, Australia Ltd, 1998–99, Pres., Worldwide Metro Div., 1999–2001, Daimler Chrysler Rail Systems; Pres., Worldwide Services Div., Bombardier, 2001–04; Chief Operating Officer, Jarvis plc, 2004–05; CEO, Metronet Rail BCV Hldgs Ltd and Metronet Rail SSL Hldgs Ltd, 2005–07. Institution of Mechanical Engineers: Mem. Bd, 2000–, Chm., 2006–07, Railway Div.; Mem., Trustee Bd, 2008–. Mem. Council, Railway Ind. Assoc., 2004–07. FRSA. *Recreations:* family gatherings, motor sport, swimming, cycling, playing guitar. *Address: e-mail:* alezala@o2email.co.uk.

LI, Sir David Kwok Po, GBS; Kt 2005; OBE 1990; FCIB; FCA; Chairman, since 1997, and Chief Executive, since 1981, Bank of East Asia Ltd; *b* 13 March 1939; *s* of Li Fook Shu and Woo Tze Ha; *m* 1971, Penny Poon; two *s*. *Educ:* Univ. of Cambridge (MA). FCA 1977; FCIB 1988; FCPA. Bank of East Asia Ltd: Chief Accountant, 1969–72; Asst Chief Manager, 1973–76; Dep. Chief Manager, 1977–81; Dir, 1981–; Dep. Chm., 1995–97. Hon. Fellow: Robinson Coll., Univ. of Cambridge, 1989; Selwyn Coll., Cambridge, 1992. Hon. LLD: Cantab, 1993; Warwick, 1994; Hong Kong, 1996; Hon. DSc Imperial Coll. London, 2007. Officier de la Légion d'Honneur (France). *Recreations:* tennis, art, antiques, reading. *Address:* Bank of East Asia Ltd, 21st Floor, 10 Des Voeux Road Central, Hong Kong. *T:* 36080808. *Clubs:* Hong Kong Country, Hong Kong Golf, Hong Kong Yacht (Hong Kong); Waialae Country (Hawaii).

LI, Fook Kow, CMG 1975; JP; Chairman, Public Service Commission, Hong Kong, 1980–87, retired; *b* 15 June 1922; *s* of Tse Fong Li; *m* 1946, Edith Kwong Li (*d* 1992); four *c*. *Educ:* Massachusetts Inst. of Technology (BSc, MSc). Mem. Hong Kong Admin. Service; Teacher, 1948–54; various departmental posts and posts in the Government Secretariat, 1955–60; Asst Financial Sec., Asst Estabt Officer, Dep. Financial Sec. and Estabt Officer, 1961–69; Dep. Dir of Commerce and Industry, 1970; Dep. Sec. for Home Affairs, 1971–72; Dir of Social Welfare, 1972; Sec. for Social Services, 1973; Sec. for Home Affairs, 1977–80. JP Hong Kong, 1959. *Address:* H22 Celeste Court, 12 Fung Fai Terrace, Hong Kong. *Clubs:* Hong Kong Jockey, Hong Kong Country.
See also K. N. A. Li.

LI Ka-shing, Sir, KBE 2000 (CBE 1989); Chairman: Cheung Kong (Holdings) Ltd, since 1971; Hutchison Whampoa Ltd, since 1981; *b* Chaozhou, 1928; *m* Chong Yuet-Ming (decd); two *s*. Moved from mainland China to Hong Kong, 1940; took first job, 1942; promoted to gen. manager, 1947; founded Cheung Kong Plastics Factory, 1950; Man. Dir, Cheung Kong (Holdings) Ltd, 1971–98; acquired Hutchison Whampoa Ltd, 1979; acquired Hongkong Electric Hldgs Ltd, 1985; Cheung Kong Infrastructure Hldgs Ltd, listed 1996; business interests in China, UK, Canada, Hong Kong and many other parts of the world. HK Affairs Adviser, 1992–97; Member: Drafting Cttee for Basic Law, HKSAR, 1985–90; Preparatory Cttee for the HKSAR, 1995–97; Selection Cttee for the govt of the HKSAR, 1996. Mem., Internat. Business Adv. Council for the UK, 2006–. Established Li Ka Shing Foundn Ltd, 1980; founded Shantou Univ., 1981. Hon. Citizen: Shantou, Guangzhou, Shenzhen, Nanhai, Foshan, Zhuhai, Choazhou, Beijing. JP 1981. Hon. LLD: Hong Kong, 1986; Calgary, 1989; Chinese Univ. of Hong Kong, 1997; Cambridge, 1999; Hon. Dr Beijing, 1992; Hon. DSocSci: Hong Kong Univ. of Sci. and Technology, 1995; City Univ. of Hong Kong, 1998; Open Univ. of Hong Kong, 1999. Grand Bauhinia Medal, HKSAR, 2001; Lifetime Award for Philanthropy, Chinese Min. of Civil Affairs, 2007. Grand Officer, Order Vasco Nunez de Balboa (Panama), 1982; Commander: Order of the Crown (Belgium), 1986; Leopold Order (Belgium), 2000; Commandeur de la Légion d'honneur (France), 2005. *Recreations:* golf, boating. *Address:* Cheung Kong (Holdings) Ltd, 70/F Cheung Kong Center, 2 Queen's Road Central, Hong Kong. *Club:* Hong Kong Jockey.

LI Kwok Nang, Andrew, CBE 1993; JP; Chief Justice, and President of the Court of Final Appeal, Hong Kong, since 1997; *b* 12 Dec. 1948; *s* of Li Fook Kow, *qv*; *m* 1973, Judy M. Y. Woo; two *d*. *Educ:* St Paul's Primary Sch., Hong Kong; St Paul's Co-Educnl Coll., Hong Kong; Repton Sch.; Fitzwilliam Coll., Cambridge (MA, LLM; Hon. Fellow, 1999). Called to the Bar: Middle Temple, 1970 (Hon. Bencher, 1997); Hong Kong, 1973; QC (Hong Kong) 1988. JP Hong Kong, 1985. Hon. DLitt Hong Kong Univ. of Sci. and Technol., 1993; Hon. LLD: Baptist Univ., Hong Kong, 1994; Open Univ., Hong Kong, 1997; Univ. of Hong Kong, 2001; Griffith, 2001; NSW, 2002; Univ. of Technol., Sydney, 2005; Chinese Univ. of Hong Kong, 2006. *Recreations:* hiking, reading, tennis. *Address:* Court of Final Appeal, No 1 Battery Path, Central, Hong Kong. *T:* 21230011. *Clubs:* Athenæum; Hong Kong Jockey (Hon. Steward), Hong Kong, Hong Kong Country, Shek O Country (Hong Kong).

LI, Simon Fook Sean, GBM 1997; *b* 19 April 1922; 3rd *s* of late Koon Chun Li and Doy Hing Tam Li; *m* Marie Veronica Lillian Yang; four *s* one *d*. *Educ:* King's Coll., Hong Kong; Hong Kong Univ.; Nat. Kwangsi Univ.; University Coll., London Univ. (LLB 1950; Fellow, 1991). Barrister-at-Law, Lincoln's Inn, 1951. Crown Counsel, Attorney-General's Chambers, Hong Kong, 1953; Senior Crown Counsel, 1962; District Judge, 1966–71, Puisne Judge, 1971–80, Justice of Appeal, 1980–84, Vice-Pres., Court of Appeal, 1984–87, Hong Kong. Dir, Bank of East Asia Ltd, Hong Kong, 1987–2006. Chm., Insce Claims Complaints Bd, 1990–94; Mem., Hong Kong Special Admin. Region Basic Law Drafting Cttee, 1985–90. PR China: Hong Kong Affairs Advr, 1992–97; Dep. Dir, Preliminary Working Cttee, 1993–95, and HK Special Admin. Region Prep. Cttee, 1996–97. Hon. LLD 1986, Hon. Fellow 2002, Chinese Univ., Hong Kong. *Recreations:* hiking, swimming. *Address:* 3/F Shun Pont Comm. Bldg, 5–11 Thomson Road, Wanchai, Hong Kong. *T:* 28668680. *Clubs:* Royal Commonwealth Society; Hong Kong (Chm., 1995–96), Hong Kong Jockey (Hon. Steward) (Hong Kong).

LIANG, Prof. Wei Yao, PhD; Professor of Superconductivity, University of Cambridge, 1994–2007; President, since 2005, Fellow and Lecturer, since 1971, Gonville and Caius College, Cambridge (Life Fellow, 2007); *b* 23 Sept. 1940; *s* of late Tien Fu Liang and of Po Seng Nio Lie; *m* 1968, Lian Choo (*née* Choong); three *d*. *Educ:* Pah Chung Chinese High Sch., Jakarta; Portsmouth Coll. of Technology; Imperial Coll., London (BSc, ARCS 1st Class Hons Theoretical Physics); Univ. of Cambridge (PhD). Gonville and Caius College, Cambridge: Comyns Berkeley Unofficial Fellow, 1969–71; Dir of Studies in Natural Scis, 1975–89; University of Cambridge: Demonstrator, 1971–75; Lectr in Physics, 1975–92; Reader in high temperature superconductivity, 1992–93; Co-Dir, 1988–89, Dir, 1989–98, Interdisciplinary Res. Centre in Superconductivity. Vis. Scientist, Xerox Palo Alto Res. Centre, 1975, 1976; Visiting Professor: EPF Lausanne, 1978; Inst. of Semiconductors, Beijing, 1983; Sci. Univ. of Tokyo, 2000; Univ. of Tokyo, 2001; Xiamen Univ., 2002. *Publications:* (ed with A. S. Alexandrov and E. K. H. Salje) Polarons and Bipolarons in High Tc Superconductors and Related Materials, 1995; (ed with W. Zong) Fundamental Research in High Tc Superconductivity, 1999. *Recreations:* music, photography. *Address:* Gonville and Caius College, Cambridge CB2 1TA. *T:* (01223) 332425.

LIAO Poon-Huai, Donald, CBE 1983 (OBE 1972); company director; *b* 29 Oct. 1929; *s* of late Liao Huk-Koon and Yeo Tsai-Hoon; *m* 1963, Christine Yuen Ching-Me; two *s* one *d*. *Educ:* Univ. of Hong Kong (BArch Hons); Univ. of Durham (Dip. Landscape Design). Architect, Hong Kong Housing Authority, 1960, Housing Architect, 1966; Commissioner for Housing and Member, Town Planning Board, 1968; Director of Housing and Vice-Chm., Hong Kong Housing Authority, 1973; Sec. for Housing and Chm., Hong Kong Housing Authority, 1980; Sec. for Dist Admin, Hong Kong, 1985. Chm., HSBC China Fund, 1992–2004; Dir, TCC Hong Kong Cement Hldgs Co., subseq. TCC Internat. Hldgs Ltd, 1997–. MLC, Hong Kong, 1980; MEC, 1985. Mem., Sino-British Jt Liaison Gp, 1987–89. Fellow, Hong Kong Inst. of Architects. Hon. FIH. *Recreations:* golf, ski-ing, riding. *Address:* (residence) 55 Kadoorie Avenue, Kowloon, Hong Kong. *T:* 27155822; (office) 1515 Ocean Centre, Canton Road, Kowloon, Hong Kong. *T:* 23020820. *Clubs:* Athenæum; Hong Kong Golf, Hong Kong Jockey (Hong Kong).

LIARDET, Rear-Adm. Guy Francis, CB 1990; CBE 1985; *b* 6 Dec. 1934; *s* of Maj.-Gen. Henry Maughan Liardet, CB, CBE, DSO; *m* 1962, Jennifer Anne O'Hagan; one *s* two *d*. *Educ:* Royal Naval Coll., Dartmouth; Southampton Univ. (BA Hons 1999). Trng Comdr, BRNC, Dartmouth, 1969–70; comd HMS Aurora, 1970–72; Exec. Officer, HMS Bristol, 1974–76; Defence Policy Staff, MoD, 1978–79; RCDS, 1980; CSO (Trng), C-in-C Naval Home Comd, 1981–82; comd HMS Cleopatra and Seventh Frigate Sqn, 1983–84; Dir of Public Relations (Navy), MoD, 1984–86; Flag Officer Second Flotilla, 1986–88; Comdt, JSDC, 1988–90, retd. Dir of Public Affairs, CIA, 1990–93. Mem., RNSA, 1970–. *Publications:* contrib. Naval Review. *Recreation:* sailing. *Address:* The Downs Cottage, New Road, Meonstoke, Southampton SO32 3NN. *Club:* Royal Yacht Squadron (Cowes).

LIBBY, Donald Gerald, PhD; Under Secretary, Office of Science and Technology, Cabinet Office, and Secretary, Advisory Board for the Research Councils, 1991–94; *b* 2 July 1934; *s* of late Herbert Lionel Libby and Minnie Libby; *m* 1st, 1961, Margaret Elizabeth Dunlop McLatchie (*d* 1979); one *d*; 2nd, 1982, June Belcher. *Educ:* RMA, Sandhurst; London Univ. (BSc, PhD Physics). CEng, FIET (FIEE 1993). Department of Education and Science: Principal Scientific Officer, 1967–72; Principal, 1972–74; Asst Sec., 1974–80; Under Sec., 1980–91 (Planning and Internat. Relations Br., 1980–82, Architects, Bldg and Schs Br., 1982–86, Further and Higher Educn Br. 2, 1986–91). Adviser, Logica UK Ltd, 1995–96. *Recreations:* music, rowing, golf. *Address:* Lygon Cottage, 26 Wayneflete Tower Avenue, Esher, Surrey KT10 8QG.

LIBESKIND, Daniel, Hon. RA 2003; Architect, Studio Daniel Libeskind, New York (formerly Architectural Studio Libeskind, Berlin), since 1995; *b* Łodz, Poland, 12 May 1946; *s* of Nachman Libeskind and Dora Libeskind (*née* Blaustein); *m* 1969, Nina Lewis; two *s* one *d*. *Educ:* in Poland and Israel; Bronx High Sch. of Sci., NYC; Cooper Union Sch. of Architecture, NYC (BArch 1970); Sch. of Comparative Studies, Univ. of Essex (MA Hist. and Theory of Architecture 1971). Architectural trng in The Hague, NYC and Helsinki; Inst. for Architecture and Urban Studies, NY, 1971–72; Irving Grossman Associates, Toronto, 1972–73; Project Planners Associates, Toronto, 1973; Asst Prof. of Architecture, Univ. of Kentucky, 1973–75; Unit Master, AA, London, 1975–77; Sen. Lectr, Poly. of Central London, and Critic in Architecture, Centre of Advanced Studies in Architecture, 1975–77; Associate Prof. of Architecture, Univ. of Toronto, 1977–78; Hd, Sch. of Architecture, and Architect-in-Residence, Cranbrook Acad. of Art, Bloomfield Hills, Mich, 1978–85; Founder and Dir, *Architecture Intermundium*, Milan, 1986–89; Architect, Berlin, 1989–94, LA, 1994–95. Vis. Critic in Architecture, Houston, Lund, London, Harvard and Helsinki, 1981–84; Visiting Professor, Europe, US and Canada, 1985–, including: Bannister Fletcher Architecture Prof., Univ. of London, 1990–91; Hochschule Weissensee, Berlin, 1993–95; Sch. of Architecture and Urban Planning, UCLA, 1994–98; Hochschule fur Gestaltung, Karlsruhe; First Louis Kahn Prof., Yale Univ. Sch. of Architecture; Univ. of Pennsylvania. Ext. Examr, Bartlett Sch. of Architecture, Univ. of London, 1993. Major works include: Uozu Mt Pavilion, Japan, 1997; Polderland Gdn, Netherlands, 1997; Felix Nussbaum Haus, Osnabrück, 1998; Jewish Mus., Berlin, 1999 (German Architecture Award, 1999); Imperial War Mus. North, Manchester, 2002 (RIBA Award, 2004); London Metropolitan Univ. Graduate Centre (RIBA Award, 2004); ext. to V&A Mus.; Denver Art Mus. Mem., European Acad. of Arts and Letters, 1990. Hon. Dr: Humboldt Univ., 1997; Coll. of Arts and Humanities, Essex Univ.; Edinburgh, 2002; DePaul, Chicago, 2002; Toronto, 2004. Numerous awards, including: 1st prize, Biennale de Vinezia, 1985; Award for Architecture, AAAL, 1996; Berlin Cultural Prize, 1996; Goethe Medallion, 2000; Hiroshima Art Prize, 2001. *Publications:* Breaking Ground: adventures in life and architecture (memoir), 2004; numerous monographs. *Address:* Studio Daniel Libeskind, 2 Rector Street, New York, NY 10006, USA.

LICHFIELD, 6th Earl of, *cr* 1831; **Thomas William Robert Hugh Anson;** Viscount Anson and Baron Soberton, 1806; *b* 19 July 1978; *s* of 5th Earl of Lichfield and of Lady Leonora Grosvenor (LVO 1997), *d* of 5th Duke of Westminster, TD; *S* father, 2005. *Heir: cousin* George Rupert Anson [*b* 7 June 1960; *m* 1987, Kirsty Jane Day; two *s* one *d*].

LICHFIELD, Bishop of, since 2003; **Rt Rev. Jonathan Michael Gledhill;** *b* 15 Feb. 1949; *s* of A. Gavan Gledhill and Susan M. (*née* Roberts); *m* 1971, S. Jane Street, PhD; one *s* one *d*. *Educ:* Keele Univ. (BA Hons 1972); Bristol Univ. (MA 1975); Trinity Coll., Bristol (BCTS 1975). Ordained deacon, 1975, priest, 1976; Curate, All Saints, Marple, Gtr Manchester, 1975–78; Priest-in-charge, St George's, Folkestone, 1978–83; Vicar, St Mary Bredin, Canterbury, 1983–96; Bp Suffragan of Southampton, 1996–2003. RD, Canterbury, 1988–94; Hon. Canon, Canterbury Cathedral, 1992–96. Tutor, Canterbury Sch. of Ministry, then SE Inst. for Theol Studies, 1983–96. Member: Gen. Synod, 1995–96; Meissen Commn, 1993–97. Chm., Nat. Coll. of Evangelists, 1998–. Link Bishop, Old Catholic Churches of Union of Utrecht, 1998–. DUniv Keele, 2007. *Publication:* Leading a Local Church in the Age of the Spirit, 2003. *Recreations:* sailing, ski-ing. *Address:* Bishop's House, 22 The Close, Lichfield, Staffs WS13 7LG.

LICHFIELD, Dean of; *see* Dorber, Very Rev. A. J.

LICHFIELD, Archdeacon of; *see* Liley, Ven. C. F.

LICHFIELD, Prof. Nathaniel; Professor Emeritus, University of London, since 1978; Partner, Lichfield Planning (formerly Dalia and Nathaniel Lichfield Associates), urban and environmental planners and economists, since 1992; *b* 29 Feb. 1916; 2nd *s* of Hyman Lichman and Fanny (*née* Grecht); *m* 1st, 1942, Rachel Goulden (*d* 1968); two *d*; 2nd, 1970, Dalia Kadury; one *s* one *d*. *Educ:* Raines Foundn Sch.; University of London. BSc (EstMan), DSc (Econ), PhD (Econ); PPRTPI, FRICS. Sen. Partner, 1962–89, Chm., 1989–92, Nathaniel Lichfield & Partners Ltd, planning, develt, urban design and econ. consultants; from 1945 has worked continuously in urban and regional planning, specialising in econs of planning from 1950, with particular reference to social cost-benefit in planning, impact assessment, land policy and urban conservation; worked in local and central govt depts and private offices. Consultant commns in UK and all continents. Special Lectr, UCL, 1950; Prof. of Econs of Environmental Planning, UCL, 1966–79. Visiting Professor: Univ. of California, 1976–78; Univ. of Tel Aviv, 1959–60, 1966; Technion—Israel Inst. of Technol., 1972–74; Hebrew Univ., Jerusalem, 1980–; Univ. of Naples, 1986–; Special Prof., Univ. of Nottingham, 1989–. Chm., Econs Cttee, ICOMOS, 1988–95 (Conservation Econs Cttee report published 1993); Member: Exec. Cttee, Internat. Centre for Land Policy Studies, 1975–85; Council, Tavistock Inst. of Human Relations, 1968–93 (Vice Pres., 1993–2001); formerly Member: SSRC; CNAA; SE Econ. Planning Council; Chairman: Economics of Urban Villages Cttee, Urban Villages Forum (report published 1995); Land Assembly Cttee, DETR/Urban Villages Forum, 1998–99 (summary report 2001). Hon. Fellow, Centre for Social and Econ. Res. on Global Envmt, 1992–. Lifetime Achievement Award, RTPI, 2004. *Publications:* Economics of Planned Development, 1956; Cost Benefit Analysis in Urban Redevelopment, 1962; Cost Benefit Analysis in Town Planning: a case study of Cambridge, 1966; Israel's New Towns: a development strategy, 1971; (with Prof. A. Proudlove) Conservation and Traffic: a case study of York, 1975; (with Peter Kettle and Michael Whitbread) Evaluation in the Planning Process, 1975); (with Haim Darin-Drabkin) Land Policy in Planning, 1980; (with Leslie Lintott) Period Buildings: evaluation of development-conservation options, 1985; (with Prof. J. Schweid) Conservation of the Built Heritage, 1986; Economics in Urban Conservation, 1988; Community Impact Evaluation, 1996; papers in Urban Studies, Regional Studies, Land Economics, Town Planning Review, Restauro, Built Environment, Project Appraisal, Planning and Envmtl Law, Chartered Surveyor, Planner, Envmt and Planning, Transport and Econ. Policy. *Recreations:* finding out less and less about more and more, countering advancing age, singing. *Address:* 13 Chalcot Gardens, England's Lane, NW3 4YB. *T:* (020) 7586 0461.

LICHTER, Dr Ivan, ONZ 1997; FRCS, FRACS; Medical Director, Te Omanga Hospice, Lower Hutt, New Zealand, 1986–94; *b* 14 March 1918; *s* of Goodman Lichter and Sarah (*née* Mierowsky); *m* 1951, Heather Lloyd; three *s* one *d*. *Educ:* Univ. of Witwatersrand, Johannesburg (MB BCh). FRCS 1949; FRACS 1964. Capt., SAMC in Madagascar, Egypt, Italy and Hosp. Ship Amra, 1942–45. Postgrad. Registrar, Guy's Hosp., London, 1946; Resident Surgical Officer: Queen Mary's Hosp., London, 1947; Wembley Hosp., Middx, 1948; Registrar, and Chief Asst, Thoracic Surgical Unit, Harefield Hosp., Middx, 1948–51; Thoracic Surgeon: Johannesburg, SA, 1952–60; Otago Hosp. Bd, and Associate Prof. of Surgery, Univ. of Otago, Dunedin, 1961–84. NZ Postgrad. Travelling Fellow, 1976. Examr in Cardio-Thoracic Surgery, RACS, 1974–84. Estabd and developed palliative care services in NZ and undertook teaching and research in palliative medicine, 1974–94. Hon. FAChPM 2000. *Publications:* Palliative Care: the management of far advanced illness, 1984; Communication in Cancer Care, 1987; Ethical Dilemmas in Cancer Care, 1989; (contrib.) Oxford Textbook of Palliative Medicine, 1993, 2nd edn 1997; numerous contribs to learned jls, esp. on aspects of palliative care. *Recreations:* reading, music, walking. *Address:* 41 Kitchener Road, Milford, Auckland, New Zealand. *T:* (9) 4895340.

LICKISS, Sir Michael (Gillam), Kt 1993; DL; Chairman, VisitBritain (formerly British Tourist Authority), 2003–05; *b* 18 Feb. 1934; *s* of Frank Gillam and Elaine Rheta Lickiss; *m* 1st, 1959, Anita (marr. diss. 1979); two *s* two *d*; 2nd, 1987, Anne; one *s*. *Educ:* Bournemouth Grammar Sch.; London Sch. of Economics (BSc Econ 1955; Hon. Fellow 2006). FCA. Articled, Bournemouth, 1955–58; commissioned, Army, 1959–62; practised Bournemouth, 1962–68; Partner, Thornton Baker, Bournemouth, 1968–73, London, 1973–94: Exec. Partner, 1975; Managing Partner, 1985–89; firm's name changed to Grant Thornton, 1986; Sen. Partner, 1989–94. Chm., BTEC, subseq. Edexcel Foundn, 1994–2000 (former Mem., Council; Chm., Finance Cttee, 1985–93). DTI Inspector, jtly with Hugh Carlisle, QC, 1986–88; Lectr, UK and overseas. Chairman: Accountancy Television Ltd, 1992–94; Somerset Economic Partnership, 1994–99; West of England Develt Agency, 1994–97; South West of England RDA, 1998–2002; Director: MAI plc, 1994–96; United News and Media plc, 1996–97, and other cos. Institute of Chartered Accountants: Mem. Council, 1971–81, 1983–95; Vice-Pres., 1988–89; Dep. Pres., 1989–90; Pres., 1990–91; Past Chairman: Educn and Training, Tech. Cttee and Ethics Cttee; Professional Conduct Directorate; Chm., Somerset Rural Youth Project, 1997–99; Dir, British Trng Internat., 1998–2000. Chm., CCAB, 1990–91; Dep. Chm., Financial Reporting Council, 1990–91; Member: FEFCE, 1992–96; Copyright Tribunal, 1994–99; Senate, Engrg Council, 1996–99; Learning and Skills Nat. Council, 2000–02; Industrial Develt Adv. Bd, DTI, 2000–03. Founder President, Assoc. of Accounting Technicians, 1980–82. Chm., Genesis Project, Somerset, 2004–07. Trustee: Parnham Trust, 1992–96; RNAS Mus., 2001–03; World Heritage Coast, 2004–; Chm., Th. Royal, Plymouth, 2008–. Mem., Court of Govs, LSE, 1992–; Vice Chm., Court of Govs, Plymouth Univ., 1995–98; Mem. Council, London Univ., 1997–2003. Pres., Royal Cornwall Polytechnic Soc., 2006–. DL Somerset, 2003. Hon. DBA: Bournemouth, 1994; UWE, 2002; Hon. DEd Plymouth, 2005. *Publications:* articles in learned jls. *Recreations:* sailing, walking, gardening. *Address: e-mail:* Lickissm@aol.com. *Club:* Royal Automobile.

LICKLEY, Gavin Alexander Fraser, CA; *b* 14 Aug. 1946; *s* of Alexander Thompson Lickley and Gladys Ann Fraser (*née* Smith); *m* 1973, Anne Muir Forrester; two *d*. *Educ:* Univ. of Edinburgh (LLB Hons 1967). CA 1970. Corporate Finance Exec., GKN plc, 1971–72; with Morgan Grenfell & Co. Ltd, 1972–95: Head of Banking, 1991–95; Chm., 1996–98; Bd Mem., Global Corporates and Instns Div., Deutsche Morgan Grenfell, then Deutsche Bank AG, 1995–99. Non-exec. Dir, Paragon Gp of Cos plc, 2003. *Recreations:* golf, ski-ing. *Address:* 6 Westmoreland Road, SW13 9RY. *T:* (020) 8748 7618. *Clubs:* City of London, Roehampton; Royal Wimbledon Golf.

LICKLEY, Nigel James Dominic; QC 2006; a Recorder, since 2000; *b* 27 Aug. 1960; *s* of James Edwin and Veronica Mabel Lickley; *m* 2000, Melanie De Freitas; two *d*. *Educ:* Queen Mary's Coll., Basingstoke; University Coll. London (LLB 1982). Called to the Bar, Gray's Inn, 1983; Asst Recorder, 1998–2000. *Recreations:* fly fishing, holidays. *Address:* 3

Paper Buildings, Temple, EC4Y 7EU. *T:* (020) 7583 8055; *e-mail:* Nigel.Lickley@3paper.co.uk. *Clubs:* Athenæum; Basingstoke Rugby Football; Queens Park Cricket (Trinidad).

LICKORISH, Prof. William Bernard Raymond, ScD; Professor of Geometric Topology, University of Cambridge, 1996–2004, now Emeritus; Fellow, Pembroke College, Cambridge, 1964–2004, now Emeritus; *b* 19 Feb. 1938; *s* of William Percy Lickorish and Florence Lickorish; *m* 1962, Margaret Ann Russell; one *s* two *d. Educ:* Merchant Taylors' Sch.; Pembroke Coll., Cambridge (ScD 1991). Asst Lectr in Maths, Univ. of Sussex, 1963–64; University of Cambridge: Asst Lectr, 1964–69; Lectr, 1969–90; Reader, 1990–96; Hd, Dept of Pure Maths and Mathematical Stats, 1997–2002; Asst Dir, then Dir of Studies in Maths, Pembroke Coll., 1964–91. Visiting Professor: Univ. of Wisconsin, 1967–68; Univ. of Calif, Berkeley, 1974, Santa Barbara, 1979–80 and 1996–97; Univ. of Texas, 1989; UCLA, 1990; Univ. of Melbourne, 2002–03. Sen. Whitehead Prize, London Mathematical Soc., 1991. *Publications:* An Introduction to Knot Theory, 1997; contrib. many articles on topology. *Recreations:* gardening, to walk, to bathe. *Address:* Pembroke College, Cambridge CB2 1RF.

LIDDELL, family name of **Baron Ravensworth.**

LIDDELL, Alasdair Donald MacDuff, CBE 1997; independent consultant; Deputy Chairman, HCL plc; Senior Associate, King's Fund; *b* 15 Jan. 1949; *s* of late Donald Liddell and Barbara Liddell (*née* Dixon); *m* 1976, Jennifer Abramsky, *qv*; one *s* one *d. Educ:* Balliol College, Oxford (BA Hons Jurisp. 1970); DMS Thames Polytechnic; LHA. King's College and Royal Free Hosps, 1972–77; Administrator (Planning and Policy), Tower Hamlets HA, 1977–79; Area Gen. Administrator, Kensington and Chelsea and Westminster AHA (T), 1979–82; District Administrator, Hammersmith and Fulham HA, 1982–84; District Administrator later District Gen. Manager, Bloomsbury HA, 1984–88; Regl Gen. Manager, E Anglian RHA, 1988–94; Dir of Planning, DoH, 1994–2000. King's Fund Internat. Fellow, 1987–88. Trustee, Cambodia Trust, 1999–2004; Jt Chm. and Founder, Assoc. for Public Health, 1992–94. *Publications:* contrib. to In Dreams Begins Responsibility: a tribute to Tom Evans, 1987; Towards an Effective NHS, 1993. *Recreations:* ski-ing, playing with computers, buying French wine. *Address:* 3 Brookfield Park, NW5 1ES. *T:* (020) 7485 7465; *e-mail:* alasdair@aliddell.com.

LIDDELL, Rt Hon. Helen (Lawrie); PC 1998; High Commissioner to Australia, since 2005; *b* 6 Dec. 1950; *d* of late Hugh Reilly and Bridget Lawrie Reilly; *m* 1972, Dr Alistair Henderson Liddell; one *s* one *d. Educ:* St Patrick's High Sch., Coatbridge; Strathclyde Univ. Head, Econ. Dept, 1971–75, and Asst Sec., 1975–76, Scottish TUC; Econ. Correspondent, BBC Scotland, 1976–77; Scottish Sec., Labour Party, 1977–88; Dir, Personnel and Public Affairs, Scottish Daily Record and Sunday Mail (1986) Ltd, 1988–92; Chief Exec., Business Venture Prog., 1993–94. Contested (Lab) Fife E, Oct. 1974; MP (Lab): Monklands E, July 1994–1997; Airdrie and Shotts, 1997–2005. Opposition spokeswoman on Scotland, 1995–97; Economic Sec., HM Treasury, 1997–98; Minister of State, Scottish Office, 1998–99; Minister of Transport, 1999; Minister of State for energy and competitiveness in Europe, DTI, 1999–2001; Sec. of State for Scotland, 2001–03. *Publication:* Elite, 1990. *Recreations:* cooking, hill-walking, music, writing. *Address:* c/o Foreign and Commonwealth Office, King Charles Street, SW1A 2AH.

LIDDELL, Jennifer, (Mrs Alasdair Liddell); *see* Abramsky, Jennifer.

LIDDELL, Air Vice-Marshal Peter, CB 2002; CEng, FIET, FRAeS; Managing Director, Select Solutions Ltd, since 2003; *b* 9 Oct. 1948; *s* of late Stanley Liddell and of Mary Elizabeth Liddell (*née* Underwood); *m* 1979, Jennifer Marion, *d* of late Lt-Col Jack Prichard, DSO, MC and Eilleen Patricia Prichard; two *s* one *d. Educ:* Keswick Sch.; Manchester Univ. (BSc). FIET (FIEE 1996); FRAeS 1996. Commnd (Univ. Cadet), 1966; served No 20 Sqn, Wildenrath, 1970–73; St Mawgan, 1973–75; Swanton Morley, 1975–77; MoD, 1978–80; Marham, 1981–82; sc 1983; OC Engrg Wing, Brize Norton, 1984–85; Cranwell, 1986–88; HQ Support Comd, 1989–90; Stn Comdr, Sealand, 1991–92; rcds 1993; HQ Logistics Comd, 1994–96; HQ Strike Comd, 1997–98; AO Communications Inf. Systems and Support Services, 1999–2000; Dir Gen., Equipment Support (Air), Defence Logistics Orgn, 2000–03. *Recreations:* golf, hill walking, theatre. *Club:* Royal Air Force.

LIDDELL-GRAINGER, Ian Richard Peregrine; MP (C) Bridgwater, since 2001; *b* 23 Feb. 1959; *s* of late David Ian Liddell-Grainger of Ayton and of Anne Mary Sibylla Liddell-Grainger (*née* Smith); *m* Jill Nesbit; one *s* two *d. Educ:* Wellesley House Sch., Kent; Millfield Sch., Somerset; S of Scotland Agricl Coll., Edinburgh (NCA). Farmer, Berwicks, 1980–85; Man. Dir, property mgt and develt co., 1985–. Mem., Tynedale DC, 1989–95. Contested (C) Torridge and Devon West, 1997. Major, Queen's Div., TA (formerly with 6th (Vol.) Bn), RRF. *Address:* (office) 16 Northgate, Bridgwater, Somerset TA6 3EU; c/o House of Commons, SW1A 0AA.

LIDDIARD, Ronald; aviation, management and public administration consultant; commercial flying instructor; *b* 26 July 1932; *s* of Tom and Gladys Liddiard; *m* 1957, June Alexandra (*née* Ford); two *d. Educ:* Canton High Sch., Cardiff; Colleges of Commerce and Technology, Cardiff; Inst. of Local Govt Studies, Birmingham Univ.; Oxford Air Training Sch. Dip. Municipal Admin, Certif. Social Work; ATPL. Health Administrator, 1958–60; Social Worker, 1960–64; Sen. Welfare Administrator, 1964–70; Dir of Social Services: Bath, 1971–74; Birmingham, 1974–85; airline pilot, 1987–97. Hon. Kentucky Col, 1977. *Publications:* How to Become an Airline Pilot, 1989; chapters in: Innovations in the Care of the Elderly, 1984; Self-Care and Health in Old Age, 1986; articles in social work, aviation, management and health jls. *Recreations:* travel, reading, wines.

LIDDIMENT, David; Producer, The Old Vic Theatre Company, since 2003; Creative Director, All3Media, since 2003; a Trustee, BBC Trust, since 2006. *Educ:* Liverpool Univ. Benton and Bowles, Advertising Agency, 1974–75; Granada TV: Promotions Scriptwriter, 1975; researcher, dir, prod. and journalist; Exec. Prod., Children's Progs, 1986–88; Head of Entertainment, 1988–92; Dir of Progs, 1992–93; Head of Entertainment Gp, BBC TV, 1993–95; Dep. Man. Dir and Dir of Progs, 1995–96, Dep. Chm., 1997, LWT; Man. Dir, Granada UK Broadcasting, 1996–97; Dir of Progs, ITV Network Ltd, 1997–2002. *Address:* The Old Vic, The Cut, Waterloo, SE1 8NB.

LIDDINGTON, Sir Bruce, Kt 2000; Schools Commissioner, Department for Children, Schools and Families (formerly Department for Education and Skills), since 2006; *b* 4 Sept. 1949; *s* of Gordon Philip Liddington and Joan Liddington; *m* 1978, Carol Jane Tuttle; two *s* one *d. Educ:* Queen Mary Coll., London Univ. (BA 1971); King's Coll., Cambridge (PGCE 1972); Washington State Univ., USA (MA 1977). Teacher: Northcliffe Sch., Conisbrough, 1972–75; Westfield Sch., Wellingborough, 1975–76; Head of English, Westwood High Sch., Leek, 1977–81; Dep. Head, Ousedale Sch., Newport Pagnell, 1981–86; Headteacher, Northampton Sch. for Boys, 1986–2000. Advr, Quality Assce Unit, DfEE, 1999–2001; Professional Advr, Academies Div., DfES, 2000–06. *Recreations:* opera, reading, music, films, travel, food. *Address:* 1A Green Lane, Wolverton, Milton Keynes MK12 5HB. *T:* (01908) 310710.

LIDDLE, Caroline; *see* Thomson, C.

LIDDLE, Roger John; Chairman, Cumbria Vision, since 2007; Vice-Chairman, Policy Network, since 2007; *b* 14 June 1947; *s* of John Thwaites Liddle and Elizabeth Liddle; *m* 1983, Caroline Thomson, *qv*; one *s. Educ:* Robert Ferguson Primary Sch., Carlisle; Denton Holme Jun. Sch., Carlisle; Carlisle Grammar Sch.; Queen's Coll., Oxford (BA (Modern Hist.) 1968; MPhil (Mgt Studies) 1970). Oxford Sch. of Social and Administrative Studies, 1970–74; Ind. Relns Officer, Electricity Council, 1974–76; Special Advr to Rt Hon. William Rodgers, MP, 1976–81; Dir, Public Policy Centre, 1982–87; Man. Dir, Prima Europe Ltd, 1987–97; Special Advr on European Affairs to Prime Minister, 1997–2004; Mem., cabinet of Peter Mandelson, EC, 2004–06; Principal Advr to the Pres. of the EC, 2006–07. Mem., Oxford CC, 1971–76 (Vice-Chm., Educn Cttee, 1972–74; Dep. Leader, 1973–76). Mem., Nat. Cttee, SDP, 1981–86. *Publications:* (with Peter Mandelson) The Blair Revolution, 1996; The New Case for Europe, 2005. *Recreations:* history, politics, entertaining, holidays in Italy. *Address:* Policy Network, 11 Tufton Street, SW1P 3QB. *Club:* Reform.

LIDINGTON, David Roy, PhD; MP (C) Aylesbury, since 1992; *b* 30 June 1956; *s* of Roy N. and Rosa Lidington; *m* 1989, Helen Mary Farquhar Parry; four *s* (incl. twins). *Educ:* Haberdashers' Aske's Sch., Elstree; Sidney Sussex Coll., Cambridge (MA, PhD). British Petroleum plc, 1983–86; RTZ plc, 1986–87; Special Adviser to: Home Sec., 1987–89; Foreign Sec., 1989–90; Consultant, PPU Ltd, 1991–92. PPS to Leader of the Opposition, 1997–99; Opposition front-bench spokesman on: home affairs, 1999–2001; HM Treasury affairs, 2001–02; environment, food and rural affairs, 2002–03; NI, 2003–07; foreign affairs, 2007–. *Publications:* articles on Tudor history. *Recreations:* history, choral singing. *Address:* House of Commons, SW1A 0AA. *T:* (020) 7219 3000; 100 Walton Street, Aylesbury, Bucks HP21 7QP.

LIEBERMAN, Joseph I.; Member (Democrat) for Connecticut, US Senate, since 1989; *b* 24 Feb. 1942; *s* of Henry Lieberman and Marcia Lieberman; *m* 1983, Hadassah Freilich; one *d*; one step *s*, and one *s* one *d* from a previous marriage. *Educ:* Yale Univ. (BA 1964; JD 1967). Called to the Bar, Conn, 1967; Partner, Lieberman, Segaloff & Wolfson, New Haven, 1972–83. Mem. (Democrat), State Senate of Connecticut, 1971–81 (Majority Leader, 1975–81); Attorney-Gen., Conn, 1983–89. Democratic candidate for US Vice-President, 2000. *Publications:* The Power Broker, 1966; The Scorpion and the Tarantula, 1970; The Legacy, 1981; Child Support in America, 1986; In Praise of Public Life, 2000. *Address:* US Senate, 706 Hart Senate Office Building, Washington, DC 20510, USA.

LIEBESCHUETZ, Prof. (John Hugo) Wolfgang (Gideon), PhD; FSA; FBA 1991; Professor of Classical and Archaeological Studies, Nottingham University, 1979–92, now Professor Emeritus; *b* Hamburg, 22 June 1927; *s* of Prof. H. Liebeschuetz and Dr E. A. R. Liebeschuetz (*née* Plaut); *m* 1955, Margaret Rosa Taylor; one *s* three *d. Educ:* UCL (BA 1951; Fellow 1997); PhD London 1957. Schoolteacher, 1957–63; Leicester University: Lectr in Classics, 1963–74; Sen. Lectr, 1974–78; Reader, 1978–79. FSA 1999. Mem., Princeton Inst. for Advanced Study, 1993. Corresp. Mem., German Archaeol Inst., 1994. *Publications:* Antioch: city and imperial administration in the later Roman Empire, 1972; Continuity and Change in Roman Religion, 1979; Barbarians and Bishops: army, church and state in the age of Arcadius and Chrysostom, 1990; From Diocletian to the Arab Conquest: change in the late Roman Empire, 1990; The Decline and Fall of the Roman City, 2001; Ambrose of Milan: political letters and speeches, 2005; Decline and Change in Late Antiquity: religion, barbarians and their historiography, 2006; contribs to learned jls. *Address:* 1 Clare Valley, The Park, Nottingham NG7 1BU.

LIESNER, Hans Hubertus, CB 1980; Member, 1989–97, Deputy Chairman, 1989–95, Monopolies and Mergers Commission; *b* 30 March 1929; *e s* of Curt Liesner, lawyer, and Edith L. (*née* Neumann); *m* 1957, Jane Boland (marr. diss.); one *s* one *d*; *m* 1968, Thelma Seward. *Educ:* German grammar schs; Bristol Univ. (BA); Nuffield Coll., Oxford; MA Cantab. Asst Lectr, later Lectr, in Economics, London Sch. of Economics, 1955–59; Lectr in Economics, Univ. of Cambridge; Fellow, Dir of Studies in Economics and some time Asst Bursar, Emmanuel Coll., Cambridge, 1959–70; Under-Sec. (Economics), HM Treasury, 1970–76; Dep. Sec., and Chief Econ. Advr, DTI (formerly Industry, Trade and Prices and Consumer Protection), 1976–89. Standing Mem., Adv. Bd on Fair Trading in Telecoms, 1997–2000; Mem. Council of Mgt, NIESR, 1989–; Chm. Adv. Gp, ESRC Centre for Economic Learning and Social Evolution, 1996–. *Publications:* The Import Dependence of Britain and Western Germany, 1957; Case Studies in European Economic Union: the mechanics of integration (with J. E. Meade and S. J. Wells), 1962; Atlantic Harmonisation: making free trade work, 1968; Britain and the Common Market: the effect of entry on the pattern of manufacturing production (with S. S. Han), 1971; articles in jls, etc. *Recreations:* ski-ing, walking, gardening. *Address:* 32 The Grove, Brookmans Park, Herts AL9 7RN. *T:* (01707) 653269. *Club:* Reform.

LIEU, Prof. Judith Margaret, PhD; Lady Margaret's Professor of Divinity, University of Cambridge, since 2007; Fellow, Robinson College, Cambridge, since 2008; *b* 25 May 1951; *d* of John and Zoe Bending; *m* 1976, Samuel N. C. Lieu; one *d. Educ:* Bromley High Sch. for Girls; Univ. of Durham (BA Hons Theol. 1972, MA Theol. 1973); Univ. of Oxford (PGCE 1974); Univ. of Birmingham (PhD 1980). Hd of RE, Abbey Sch., Reading, 1974–76; Lectr in Biblical Studies, Queen's Coll., Birmingham, 1981–84; Lectr in Christian Origins and Early Judaism, 1985–95, Reader in New Testament, 1995, KCL; Sen. Lectr in Hist., 1996–98, Associate Prof., 1998, Macquarie Univ., Sydney; Prof. of New Testament Studies, KCL, 1999–2007. Editor, New Testament Studies, 2003–. *Publications:* The Second and Third Epistles of John: history and background, 1986; The Theology of the Johannine Epistles, 1991; (ed jtly) The Jews between Pagans and Greeks, 1994; Image and Reality: the Jews in the world of the Christians in the second century, 1996; The Gospel According to Luke, 1997; Neither Jew nor Greek: constructing early Christianity, 2002; Christian Identity in the Jewish and Graeco-Roman World, 2004; (ed jtly) The Oxford Handbook of Biblical Studies, 2006; (ed jtly) Biblical Traditions in Transmission, 2006; I, II, III John, 2008. *Recreations:* reading, walking, theatre, day dreaming. *Address:* Faculty of Divinity, West Road, Cambridge CB3 9BS.

LIEVEN, Prof. Dominic Christophe Bogdan, PhD; FBA 2001; Professor of Russian Government and History, London School of Economics and Political Science, University of London, since 1993 (Convenor, Department of Government, 2001–04); *b* 19 Jan. 1952; *s* of Prince Alexander Lieven and Veronica Lieven (*née* Monahan); *m* 1985, Mikiko Fujiwara; one *s* one *d. Educ:* Downside Sch.; Christ's Coll., Cambridge (BA); SSEES, London Univ. (PhD 1978). Kennedy Schol., Harvard Univ., 1973–74; FCO, 1974–75; Lectr, LSE, 1978–93. Humboldt Fellow, 1986; Visiting Professor: Univ. of Tokyo, 1992–94; Harvard Univ., 1993. Member, Editorial Board: Jl Contemporary Hist., 1994–2004; Slavonic Rev., 2000–. *Publications:* Russia and the Origins of the First World War, 1983; Russia's Rulers under the Old Regime, 1989; The Aristocracy in Europe 1815–1914, 1992; Nicholas II, 1993; Empire: the Russian Empire and its rivals, 2000;

books trans. German, Japanese and Russian. *Recreation:* collecting Russian regimental models. *Address:* Department of Government, London School of Economics, Houghton Street, WC2A 2AE. *T:* (020) 7955 7184. *Club:* Travellers.

LIEVEN, Nathalie Marie Daniella; QC 2006; barrister; *b* 20 May 1964; *d* of Alexander Lieven and Veronica Lieven; *m* 1995, Stewart Wright; one *s* two *d*. *Educ:* Godolphin and Latymer Sch.; Poly. of Central London (Dip. Law); Trinity Hall, Cambridge (BA 1986). Called to the Bar, Gray's Inn, 1989. *Recreation:* books. *Address:* Landmark Chambers, 180 Fleet Street, EC4A 2HG; *e-mail:* clerks@landmarkchambers.co.uk.

LIEW Foo Yew, PhD, DSc; FRCPath; FRSE; Gardiner Professor and Head of Department of Immunology, University of Glasgow, since 1991; *b* 22 May 1943; *s* of Liew Soon and Chai Man Ngon; *m* 1973, Dr Woon Ling Chan; one *s*. *Educ:* Monash Univ., Australia (BSc 1st cl. Hons); ANU (PhD; DSc). MRCPath 1990, FRCPath 1996. FRSE 1995. Lectr, Univ. of Malaya, 1972–77; Sen. Scientist, 1977–84, Head, Dept of Immunology, 1984–91, Wellcome Res. Lab., Beckenham. Life Mem., Nat. Biol Standards Bd, 1996. FMedSci 1999. *Publications:* Vaccination Strategies of Tropical Diseases, 1989; Immunology of intracellular parasitism, 1998; more than 250 papers in learned jls. *Recreations:* reading classical Chinese, gardening. *Address:* Department of Immunology, University of Glasgow, Glasgow G11 6NT; 37 Elwill Way, Beckenham, Kent BR3 3AB; 556 Crow Road, Glasgow G13 1NP. *T:* (0141) 211 2695.

LIFFORD, 9th Viscount *cr* 1781 (Ire.); **Edward James Wingfield Hewitt;** DL; Chairman, Rathbone Investment Management International, since 2006; *b* 27 Jan. 1949; *s* of 8th Viscount Lifford and of Alison Mary Patricia, *d* of T. W. Ashton; *S* father, 1987; *m* 1976, Alison Mary, *d* of Robert Law; one *s* two *d*. *Educ:* The Old Malthouse, Dorset; Aiglon College, Switzerland. Mem., Stock Exchange. Dir, Rathbones plc, 1996–2006. Non-exec. Dir, McKay Securities plc, 2006–. DL Hants, 2004. *Recreations:* country sports. *Heir:* *s* Hon. James Thomas Wingfield Hewitt, *b* 29 Sept. 1979. *Address:* Field House, Hursley, Hants SO21 2LE. *T:* (01962) 775203. *Clubs:* Boodle's, Pratt's.

LIFSCHUTZ, Alexander Joseph; Director, Lifschutz Davidson Sandilands (formerly Lifschutz Davidson), architects, since 1986; *b* 11 Feb. 1952; *s* of late Simon Lifschutz and of Hanna Lifschutz; *m* 1978, Monique Charlesworth; one *s* one *d*. *Educ:* St Paul's Sch.; Univ. of Bristol (BSc Jt Hons Sociology and Psychology 1974); Architectural Assoc. Foster Associates, 1981–86. *Projects* include: Broadwall Community Housing, 1994 (Royal Fine Arts Commn/Sunday Times Building of the Year, 1995; RIBA Award, 1995; Nat. Housing Design Award, DoE, 1996; Civic Trust Housing Award, 1996); mixed use develt, Oxo Tower Wharf, 1996 (Urban Regeneration Award, Royal Fine Art Commn, 1997; RIBA Award, 1997; Civic Trust Award, 1997); Oxo 8th Floor Restaurant, 1997 (RIBA Award, 1998); Royal Victoria Dock Bridge, 1999 (AJ/Bovis/Royal Acad. Award, 1997; ICE Merit Award, 1998; RIBA Award, 1999; Civic Trust Award, 2000); Hungerford Bridge, 2002 (Royal Fine Art Commn Award, 2003; Civic Trust Award, 2003); Davidson Bldg, 2003 (RIBA Award, 2004; BCO Award, 2005); *current projects* include: Telford Millennium Village; Jewish Community Centre, Doon St Leisure Centre, London's South Bank. Mem. Council, Architectural Assoc., 2002– (Vice Pres.). *Recreation:* family. *Address:* Lifschutz Davidson Sandilands Ltd, Island Studios, 22 St Peter's Square, W6 9NW.

LIGGINS, Sir Graham (Collingwood), Kt 1991; CBE 1983; FRCSE, FRACS, FRCOG; FRS 1980; FRSNZ 1976; Professor of Obstetrics and Gynaecological Endocrinology, University of Auckland, New Zealand, 1968–87, now Professor Emeritus (formerly Senior Lecturer); Consultant to National Women's Hospital, Auckland; *b* 24 June 1926; *m* 1954, Dr Cecilia Margaret Ward; two *s* two *d*. *Educ:* Univ. of NZ (MB, ChB, 1949); PhD Univ. of Auckland, 1969. MRCOG 1956; FRCSE 1958; FRACS 1960; FRCOG 1970. Is distinguished for his work on the role of foetal hormones in the control of parturition. Hon. FAGS, 1976; Hon. FACOG, 1978. Hon. MD Lund, 1983; Hon. DSc Edinburgh, 1996. Hector Medal, RSNZ, 1980. *Publications:* approx. 200 published papers. *Recreations:* forestry, sailing, fishing. *Address:* 3/38 Awatea Road, Parnell, Auckland 1, New Zealand.

LIGHT, Johanne Erica; *see* Delahunty, J. E.

LIGHT, Prof. Paul Henry, PhD; CPsychol, FBPsS; Vice Chancellor, University of Winchester (formerly Principal and Chief Executive, King Alfred's College, then University College Winchester), 2000–06; *b* 26 Aug. 1927; *s* of Ronald and Gladys Light; *m* 1970, Vivienne Mary Baker; one *s* two *d*. *Educ:* St John's Coll., Cambridge (Schol.; BA 1st cl. Natural Scis 1969; PhD Develtl Psychol. 1975); Univ. of Nottingham (MA Educnl Psychol. 1970). FBPsS 1987; CPsychol 1988. Demonstrator in Exptl Psychol., Univ. of Cambridge, 1972–74; Lectr, then Sen. Lectr, Dept of Psychol., Univ. of Southampton, 1978–87; Prof. of Educn, and Dir, Centre for Human Develt and Learning, Open Univ., 1987–92; Prof. of Psychol., Univ. of Southampton, 1992–97; Pro Vice Chancellor (Acad.), Bournemouth Univ., 1997–2000. Vis. lectureships and professorships at Univ. of NC and Univ. of Provence. FRSA 1995. *Publications:* The Development of Social Sensitivity, 1979; (with G. Butterworth) Social Cognition, 1982; (with M. Richards) Children with Social Worlds, 1986; (jtly) Learning to Think, 1991; (jtly) Becoming a Person, 1991; (jtly) Growing up in a Changing Society, 1991; (with G. Butterworth) Context and Cognition, 1993; (with K. Littleton) Learning with Computers, 1999; (jtly) Learning Sites, 1999; contrib. numerous articles to ed collections and refereed jls. *Recreations:* demolition (and, less frequently, construction), planting trees (and, less frequently, cutting them down), anything out-of-doors except sport. *Address:* Yawl Cliff, Yawl Hill Lane, Uplyme DT7 3XF. *T:* (01297) 444792; *e-mail:* paul.light@hotmail.co.uk.

LIGHTBODY, Ian (Macdonald), CMG 1974; Chairman, Public Services Commission, Hong Kong, 1978–80; *b* 19 Aug. 1921; *s* of Thomas Paul Lightbody and Dorothy Marie Louise Lightbody (*née* Cooper); *m* 1954, Noreen, *d* of late Captain T. H. Wallace, Dromore, Co. Down; three *s* one *d*. *Educ:* Queens Park Sch., Glasgow; Glasgow Univ. (MA). War service, Indian Army, India and Far East, 1942–46 (Captain); Colonial Admin. Service, Hong Kong, 1945; various admin. posts; District Comr, New Territories, 1967–68; Defence Sec., 1968–69; Coordinator, Festival of Hong Kong, 1969; Comr for Resettlement, 1971; Sec. for Housing and Chm., Hong Kong Housing Authority, 1973–77; Sec. for Admin, Hong Kong, 1977–78. MLC 1971; MEC 1977; retd from Hong Kong, 1980. Mem., Arun DC, 1983–91. *Recreation:* walking. *Address:* 29 Henty Gardens, Chichester, Sussex PO19 3DL. *Clubs:* Hong Kong, Hong Kong Jockey.

LIGHTBOWN, Ronald William, MA; FSA, FRAS; art historian and author; Keeper of the Department of Metalwork, Victoria and Albert Museum, 1985–89; *b* Darwen, Lancs, 2 June 1932; *s* of late Vincent Lightbown and Helen Anderson Lightbown (*née* Burness); *m* 1962, Mary Dorothy Webster; one *s*. *Educ:* St Catharine's Coll., Cambridge (MA). FSA, FRAS. Victoria and Albert Museum: Asst Keeper, Library, 1958–64; Asst Keeper, Dept of Metalwork, 1964–73; Dep. Keeper, 1973–76, Keeper, 1976–85, Library. Fellow, Inst. for Res. in the Humanities, Wisconsin Univ., 1974. Pres., Jewellery History Soc., 1990–93; a Vice-Pres., Soc. of Antiquaries, 1986–90 (Sec., 1979–86); Associate Trustee, Soane Mus., 1981–98. Socio dell' Ateneo Veneto, for contrib. to study of culture of Venice and the Veneto, 1987; Socio dell' Accademia Clementina, Bologna, for contribns to study of Italian art, 1988; Serena Medal for Italian Studies, British Acad., 2005. *Publications:* French Secular Goldsmiths' work of the Middle Ages, 1978; Sandro Botticelli, 1978, 2nd edn, 1989 (Prix Vasari, 1990); (with M. Corbett) The Comely Frontispiece, 1978; (ed and trans. with A. Caiger-Smith) Piccolpasso: the art of the potter, 1980, 2nd edn 2007; Donatello and Michelozzo, 1980; Andrea Mantegna, 1986; Piero della Francesca, 1992 (Prix de Mai des Libraires de France, 1992); Viaggio in un capolavoro di Piero della Francesca, 1992; (with J. Delumeau) Histoire de l'art: la Renaissance, 1995; Carlo Crivelli, 2004; (ed and introd) History of Art in 18th Century England (series of source-books on 18th century British art), 14 vols, 1970–71; V&A Museum catalogues and publications: (pt author) Italian Sculpture, 1964; Tudor Domestic Silver, 1970; Scandinavian and Baltic Silver, 1975; French Silver, 1979; (with M. Archer) India Observed, 1982; Medieval European Jewellery, 1992; contrib. to books, and many articles in learned jls, incl. Burlington Magazine, Warburg Jl and Art Bulletin. *Recreations:* reading, travel, music, conversation. *Address:* Barrowmount House, Goresbridge, Co. Kilkenny, Ireland.

LIGHTFOOT, His Honour George Michael; a Circuit Judge, 1986–2001; *b* 9 March 1936; *s* of Charles Herbert Lightfoot and Mary Lightfoot (*née* Potter); *m* 1963, Dorothy (*née* Miller); two *s* two *d*. *Educ:* St Michael's Catholic College, Leeds; Exeter College, Oxford (MA). National Service, 1955–57: York and Lancaster Regt; interpreter and interrogater, Intelligence Corps, Cyprus, 1956–57. Schoolmaster, 1962–66. Called to the Bar, Inner Temple, 1966; practised on NE circuit. Recorder, 1985–86; Dep. Circuit Judge, 2001–06. Mem., Home Farm Trust, 1980–; President: Leeds Friends of Home Farm Trust, 1987–; Mencap, Leeds, 1987–2003. Vice-Pres., Hunslet Hawks Rugby League Football Club, 1999–. *Recreations:* cricket and sport in general, gardening (labourer), learning to listen to music, reading. *Address:* *e-mail:* gmlightfoot@hotmail.com. *Clubs:* Catenian Association (City of Leeds Circle); Yorkshire CC; Northern Cricket Society.

LIGHTFOOT, Nigel Francis, FRCPath; Director, Emergency Response, Health Protection Agency, since 2003; *b* 19 March 1945; *s* of Leslie and Joyce Lightfoot; *m* 1967, Antonia Calascione; two *s* one *d*. *Educ:* Brunts Sch.; St Mary's Hospital Med. Sch., London (MB BS 1968); London Sch. of Hygiene and Tropical Medicine (MSc 1976). FRCPath 1979. MO, RN, 1966–82, served in nuclear submarines, Malta and NI, and became consultant med. microbiologist, 1979; Public Health Laboratory Service, 1982–2002: Dir, Taunton Public Health Lab.; Dir, Newcastle Public Health Lab.; Dir, PHLS North; developed chemical, biol, and radionuclear trng and exercises strategy, DoH, 2002. Hon. Consultant to RN, 1982–. Mem., Adv. Gp on Medical Countermeasures, MoD, 1995–. Visiting Professor: Cranfield Univ., 2007–; Keio Univ., Tokyo. *Publications:* Microbiological Analysis of Food and Water: guidelines for quality assurance, 1998; over 100 learned papers on microbiology and bioterrorism. *Recreations:* horses, riding to hounds, shooting, photography, cooking. *Address:* Health Protection Agency, Holborn Gate, 330 High Holborn, WC1V 7PP. *T:* (020) 7759 2700; *e-mail:* Nigel.Lightfoot@mac.com.

LIGHTING, Jane; Chief Executive Officer, Five (formerly Channel Five Broadcasting Ltd), 2003–08; *b* 22 Dec. 1956. Founder, and Man. Dir, Minotaur International, 1995–99; Man. Dir, Broadcast and Television, 1999–2002, CEO, 2002–03, Flextech. Non-exec. Dir, Trinity Mirror plc, 2008–. Chairman: British Television Distributors Assoc., 1995–96; RTS, 2006– (Trustee, 2008–). Gov., Nat. Film and Television Sch., 2001–07. *Recreations:* gardening, escaping to the country. *Club:* Groucho.

LIGHTMAN, Hon. Sir Gavin (Anthony), Kt 1994; a Judge of the High Court of Justice, Chancery Division, 1994–2008; *b* 20 Dec. 1939; *s* of Harold Lightman, QC and of Gwendoline Joan (*née* Ostrer); *m* 1965, Naomi Ann Claff; one *s* two *d*. *Educ:* University College London (LLB 1st cl. Hons 1961; Fellow, 2002); Univ. of Michigan (LLM). Called to the Bar, Lincoln's Inn, 1963, Bencher 1987, Treas., 2008–09; QC 1980. Vice Pres., Anglo Jewish Assoc., 1995– (Dep. Pres., 1986–92); Chairman: Educn Cttee, Anglo Jewish Assoc., 1986–94; Educn Cttee, Hillel House, 1992–96 (Vice-Pres., 1996–); Legal Friends, Haifa Univ., 1990–2001 (Gov., 1994); Leonard Sainer Legal Educn Foundn, 2000–. Patron: Jewish Commonwealth Council, 1994–2000 (Chm., 2000–); Hammerson Home, 1996–. *Publications:* (with G. Battersby) Cases and Statutes on Real Property, 1965; (with G. Moss) The Law Relating to the Receivers of Companies, 1986, 4th edn as The Law of Administrators and Receivers of Companies, 2007; A Report on the National Union of Miners, 1990. *Recreations:* reading, cricket, walking, travel. *Address:* Serle Court, 6 New Square, Lincoln's Inn, WC2A 3QS. *Club:* Royal Automobile.

See also S. L. Lightman.

LIGHTMAN, Ivor Harry, CB 1984; Chairman of Trustees, Autism Cymru, since 2002; *b* 23 Aug. 1928; *s* of late Abraham and Mary Lightman; *m* 1950, Stella Doris Blend; one *s*. *Educ:* Abergele Grammar Sch. Clerical Officer, Min. of Food, 1946; Officer of Customs and Excise, 1949–56; Asst Principal, then Principal, Ministry of Works, 1957–65; HM Treasury, 1965–67; Assistant Secretary: MPBW, 1967–70; CSD, 1970–73; Under Secretary: Price Commn, 1973–76; Dept of Prices and Consumer Protection, 1976–78; Dept of Industry, 1978–81; Dep. Sec., Welsh Office, 1981–88, retd. Member: Parole Bd, 1990–94; Bd of Deputies of British Jews, 2006–. Chm., First Choice Housing Assoc., 1989–94; Mem. Bd, United Welsh Housing Assoc., 1994–2003; Chm., All-Wales Adv. Panel on Services for Mentally Handicapped People, 1990–96. Chm., Cardiff Univ. of Third Age, 2000–05. *Address:* 6 Clos Coedydafarn, Lisvane, Cardiff CF14 0ER.

LIGHTMAN, Lionel; Lay Observer attached to Lord Chancellor's Department, 1986–90; *b* 26 July 1928; *s* of late Abner Lightman and late Gitli Lightman (*née* Szmul); *m* 1952, Helen, *y d* of late Rev. A. Shechter and late Mrs Shechter; two *d*. *Educ:* City of London Sch.; Wadham Coll., Oxford (MA). Nat. Service, RAEC, 1951–53 (Temp. Captain). Asst Principal, BoT, 1953; Private Sec. to Perm. Sec., 1957; Principal 1958; Trade Comr, Ottawa, 1960–64; Asst Sec. 1967; Asst Dir, Office of Fair Trading, 1973–75; Under Sec., Dept of Trade, 1975–78, DoI, 1978–81; Dir of Competition Policy, OFT, 1981–84. *Address:* 73 Greenhill, NW3 5TZ. *T:* (020) 7435 3427.

LIGHTMAN, Prof. Stafford Louis, PhD; FRCP, FMedSci; Professor of Medicine, University of Bristol, since 1993; *b* 7 Sept. 1948; *s* of Harold Lightman, QC and of Gwendoline Joan (*née* Ostrer); *m* 1977, Susan Louise Stubbs (*see* Susan Lightman) (marr. diss. 1995); three *s* one *d*. *Educ:* Repton Sch.; Gonville and Caius Coll., Cambridge (MA, MB BChir, PhD); Middlesex Hosp. Med. Sch. Vis. Sen. Scientist, MRC Neuro. Pharm. Unit, Cambridge, 1980–81; Wellcome Trust Sen. Lectr, St Mary's Hosp. Med. Sch. and Hon. Consultant Physician and Endocrinologist, St Mary's Hosp., 1981–82; Charing Cross and Westminster Medical School: Reader in Medicine, 1982–88; Prof. of Clinical Neuroendocrinology, 1988–92; Consultant Physician and Endocrinologist to Charing Cross and Westminster Hosps, 1988–92; Hon. Sen. Res. Fellow, Inst. of Neurology and Consultant Endocrinologist to Nat. Hosp. for Neurology and Neurosurgery, 1988–. Chm., Pituitary Foundn, 1995–2004. Founder FMedSci 1998. Editor-in-Chief, Jl of Neuroendocrinology, 1989–96. *Publications:* (ed with B. J. Everitt) Neuroendocrinology,

1986; (with Michael Powell) Pituitary Tumours: a handbook on management, 1996, 2nd edn 2003; (ed) Horizons in Medicine Vol. 7, 1996; (with A. Levy) Core Endocrinology, 1997; (with Graham Rook) Steroid Hormones and the T cell Cytokine Profile, 1997. *Recreations:* squash, ski-ing, hill walking, scuba diving, music, theatre, anthropology. *Address:* Henry Wellcome Laboratories, Dorothy Hodgkin Building, Whitson Street, Bristol BS1 3NY. *T:* (0117) 331 3167.

See also Hon. Sir G. A. Lightman.

LIGHTMAN, Prof. Susan Louise, PhD; FRCP, FRCPE, FRCOphth, FMedSci; Professor of Clinical Ophthalmology, Institute of Ophthalmology and Moorfields Eye Hospital, since 1993; *b* 2 Sept. 1952; *d* of John and Valerie Stubbs; *m* 1st, 1977, Prof. Stafford Louis Lightman, FRCP (marr. diss. 1995); three *s* one *d*; 2nd, 1995, Hamish Towler; one *s*. *Educ:* St Paul's Girls' Sch.; Middlesex Hosp., Univ. of London (MB BS Hons 1975); PhD London 1987. MRCP 1978, FRCP 1992; FRCOphth 1988; FRCPE 1998. Wellcome Training Fellowship: in Ophthalmology, Inst. of Ophthalmol. and Moorfields Eye Hosp., 1979–83; in Immunology, NIMR, 1983–85; MRC Travelling Fellowship and Vis. Scientist, NIH, 1985–87; MRC Sen. Clinical Fellow, 1988–90; Duke Elder Prof. of Ophthalmology, BPMF, 1990–93. FMedSci 2000. *Publications:* Immunology of Eye Diseases, 1989; Diagnosis and Management of Uveitis, 1998; HIV and the Eye, 1999; over 200 papers in peer reviewed jls. *Recreations:* walking, music, sewing, reading. *Address:* Institute of Ophthalmology, Moorfields Eye Hospital, City Road, EC1V 2PD. *T:* (020) 7566 2266.

LIGHTON, Sir Thomas (Hamilton), 9th Bt *cr* 1791 (Ire.), of Merville, Dublin; Chairman, Society of London Art Dealers, 1993–95 and 1998–2000; *b* 4 Nov. 1954; *o s* of Sir Christopher Robert Lighton, 8th Bt, MBE and his 2nd wife, Horatia Edith (*d* 1981), *d* of A. T. Powlett; *S* father, 1993; *m* 1990, Belinda, *d* of John Fergusson; twin *s* one *d* (and one *s* decd). *Educ:* Eton. *Heir: s* James Christopher Hamilton Lighton, *b* 20 Oct. 1992.

LIGRANI, Prof. Phillip Meredith, PhD; Donald Schultz Professor of Turbomachinery, Director of Rolls-Royce University Technology Centre in Heat Transfer and Aerodynamics, and Director of Thermo-Fluids Laboratory, Oxford University, since 2006; Fellow, St Catherine's College, Oxford, since 2006; *b* 2 Feb. 1952; *s* of Alfred Joseph Ligrani and Marilyn Virginia Ligrani (*née* Whittaker); one *d*. *Educ:* Univ. of Texas at Austin (BS 1974); Stanford Univ. (MS 1975; PhD 1980). Asst Prof., Turbomachinery Dept, von Karman Inst. for Fluid Dynamics, Rhode-St-Genese, Belgium, 1979–82; Vis. Sen. Res. Fellow, Dept of Aeronautics, Imperial Coll., London, 1982–84; Associate Prof., Dept of Mechanical Engrg, US Naval Postgrad. Sch., 1984–92; Prof., Dept of Mechanical Engrg, Univ. of Utah, 1992–2006. Guest Prof., Univ. of Karlsruhe, 2000. Lectr, 5th Internat. Symposium on Turbulence, Heat and Mass Transfer, Dubrovnik, 2006. Associate Editor: ASME Transactions: Jl Heat Transfer, 2003–07; ASME Transactions: Jl Fluids Engrg, 2005–08; Mem., Editl Rev. Bd, Advances in Transport Phenomena, book series, 2006–. FASME 2000. *Publications:* book chapters and contribs to learned jls incl. Internat. Jl Heat and Mass Transfer, ASME Trans: Jl Turbomachinery, ASME Trans: Jl Heat Transfer, ASME Trans: Jl Fluids Engrg, Jl Fluid Mechanics, AIAA Jl, Expts in Fluids, Physics of Fluids, AIAA Jl Heat Transfer and Thermophysics, Internat. Jl Rotating Machinery, Separation Sci. and Technol., Sensors and Acutors A: Physical, and Jl Microcolumn Separations. *Address:* Department of Engineering Science, University of Oxford, Parks Road, Oxford OX1 3PJ. *T:* (01865) 288734, *Fax:* (01865) 288756; *e-mail:* phil.ligrani@eng.ox.ac.uk.

LIIKANEN, Erkki Antero; Governor, Bank of Finland, since 2004; *b* 19 Sept. 1950; *m* 1971, Hanna-Liisa Issakainen; two *d*. *Educ:* Helsinki Univ. MP (SDP), Finland 1972–90; Minister of Finance, 1987–90; Ambassador to EU, 1990–95; Mem., EC, 1995–2004. Gen. Sec., SDP, 1981–87. *Address:* Bank of Finland, PO Box 160, 00101 Helsinki, Finland.

LIKIERMAN, Prof. Sir (John) Andrew, Kt 2001; Professor of Management Practice, London Business School, since 2001; Director, Bank of England, since 2004; *b* 30 Dec. 1943; *s* of Dolek and Olga Likierman; *m* 1987, Dr Meira, *d* of Joshua and Miriam Gruenspan; one step *s* one step *d*. *Educ:* Stowe Sch.; Univ. of Vienna; Balliol Coll., Oxford (MA). FCMA, FCCA. Divl Management Accountant, Tootal Ltd, 1965–68; Asst Lectr, 1968–69, Lectr, 1972–74, Dept of Management Studies, Leeds Univ.; Qualitex Ltd, 1969–72 (Man. Dir, Overseas Div., 1971–72); Vis. Fellow, Oxford Centre for Management Studies, 1972–74; Chm., Ex Libris Ltd, 1973–74; London Business Sch., 1974–76 and 1979–: Dir, Part-time Masters Programme, 1981–85; Dir, Inst. of Public Sector Management, 1983–88; Prof. of Accounting and Financial Control, 1987–97; Vis. Prof., 1997–2001; Dean of External Affairs, 1989–92; Dep. Principal, 1990–92; Elected Governor, 1986–89, *ex officio* Governor, 1990–93; Acting Dean, 2007. Asst Sec., Cabinet Office (Mem., Central Policy Review Staff), 1976–79, Advr, 1979–82; Advisor, H of C Select Committees: Treasury and CS, 1981–90; Employment, 1985–89; Transport, 1981, 1987–90; Social Services, 1988; Social Security, 1991; Head, Govt Accountancy Service and Chief Accountancy Advr, HM Treasury, 1993–2003; Principal Finance Officer, 1995–2000, Dir, subseq. Man. Dir, Financial Mgt, Reporting and Audit, 1995–2003, HM Treasury; Mem., various govt inquiries including: North Sea Oil Costs, 1975; Power Plant Industry, 1976; Post Office Internat. Comparisons, 1981; Accounting for Econ. Costs (Byatt Cttee), 1986; Professional Liability (Chm.), 1989. Member: Finance Cttee, Oxfam, 1974–84; Audit Commn, 1988–91; Financial Reporting Council, 1990–2003 (Observer, 1993–2003); Cttee on Financial Aspects of Corporate Governance (Cadbury Cttee), 1991–95; Council: RIPA, 1982–88; Consumers' Assoc., 1983–85; Chartered Inst. of Management Accountants, 1985–94 (Pres., 1991–92); Civil Service Coll., 1989–94; Scientific Council, Eur. Inst. of Public Admin, 1990–93; Defence Operational Analysis Centre, 1992–93; Bd, Tavistock and Portman NHS Trust, 2000–08. Non-executive Director: Barclays plc, 2004–; Market & Opinion Res. Internat. Ltd, 2004–05 (Chm., 2005); non-exec. Chm., Applied Intellectual Capital plc, 2006–. Non-exec. Dir, Economists' Bookshop, 1981–91 (non-exec. Chm., 1987–91). Mem., Steering Cttee, Governance of the UN, 2006. Hon. DBA: Southampton Business Sch., 1997; Oxford Brookes, 2006; Hon. DPhil London Metropolitan, 1999. Gold Medal, CIMA, 2002; Financial Mgt Award, 2004. *Publications:* The Reports and Accounts of Nationalised Industries, 1979; Cash Limits and External Financing Limits, 1981; (jtly) Public Sector Accounting and Financial Control, 1983, 4th edn 1992; (with P. Vass) Structure and Form of Government Expenditure Reports, 1984; Public Expenditure, 1988; (jtly) Accounting for Brands, 1989; contribs to academic and professional jls. *Recreations:* cycling, ideas, music, architecture, wine. *Address:* 5 Downshire Hill, NW3 1NR. *T:* (020) 7435 9888. *Club:* Reform.

LILEY, Ven. Christopher Frank; Archdeacon of Lichfield, and Treasurer and Canon Residentiary of Lichfield Cathedral, since 2001; *b* 1947. *Educ:* Nottingham Univ. (BEd 1970); Lincoln Theol Coll. Ordained deacon, 1974, priest, 1975; Curate, Holy Trinity, Kingswinford, 1974–79; Team Vicar, Stafford, 1979–84; Vicar, Norton, 1984–96; RD Hitchin, 1989–94; Vicar, St Chad and St Mary, and Priest i/c St Alkmund, Shrewsbury, 1996–2001. Chm., Lichfield Diocesan Bd of Ministry, 2001–. *Address:* 24 The Close, Lichfield, Staffs WS13 7LD.

LILFORD, 8th Baron *cr* 1797; **Mark Vernon Powys;** *b* 16 Nov. 1975; *s* of 7th Baron Lilford and Margaret, *d* of A. Penman; *S* father, 2005. *Heir: kinsman* Robert Charles Lilford Powys [*b* 15 Aug. 1930; *m* 1st, 1957, Charlotte Webb (marr. diss. 1972); 2nd, 1973, Janet Wightwick; (one *s* decd)].

LILFORD, Prof. Richard James, PhD; FRCP, FRCOG, FFPH; Professor of Clinical Epidemiology, University of Birmingham; *b* Cape Town, 22 April 1950; *m* 1982, Victoria Lomax; one *s* two *d*. *Educ:* St John's Coll., Johannesburg; Univ. of Witwatersrand (MB BCh 1973); PhD London 1984. MRCOG 1979, FRCOG 1996; MRCP 1981, FRCP 1998; MFPHM 1995. House officer in Medicine, Johannesburg Gen. Hosp., 1974; house officer in Surgery, Tygerberg Hosp., Cape Town, 1974–75; GP in S African Army, 1975; Groote Schuur Hospital, Cape Town: SHO in Obstetrics and Gynaecol., 1976; Registrar, 1977–78; Lecturer and Senior Registrar: Royal Free Hosp., London, 1979–80; St Bartholomew's Hosp. and Med. Coll., 1980–83; Sen. Lectr and Consultant in Obstetrics and Gynaecol., Queen Charlotte's Hosp. for Women and Inst. of Obstetrics and Gynaecol., 1983–85; University of Leeds: Prof. of Obstetrics and Gynaecol., 1985–95; Chm., Inst. of Epidemiology and Health Services Res., 1991–95; Dir of Res., United Leeds Teaching Hosps NHS Trust, 1993–95; Dir of R&D, W Midlands Regl Office, NHS Exec., DoH, 1996; Prof. of Health Services Res., Univ. of Birmingham, 1996. Hon. Prof., Univ. of Warwick. Mem., Internat. Editl Adv. Bd, Jl RSocMed, 1974–. Mem., Leeds E HA, 1989–90. Advr, NHS Nat. Clinical Trials, 1996–; Director: NHS Methodology Res. Prog.; NHS Patient Safety Res. Prog. Chm. and Mem., numerous cttees incl. DoH adv. cttees and working parties. Royal College of Obstetricians and Gynaecologists: Mem. Council, 1989–92 and 1992–95; Chm., Audit Cttee, 1992–95; Member: Scientific Adv. Cttee, 1992–95; Educn Bd, 1992–94. *Publications:* (with T. Chard) Basic Sciences for Obstetricians and Gynaecologists, 1983, 4th edn 1995; (with M. Setchell) Multiple Choice Questions in Gynaecology and Obstetrics: with answers and explanatory comments, 1985, 2nd edn 1991; Prenatal Diagnosis and Prognosis, 1990; Computing and Decision Support in Obstetrics and Gynaecology, 1990; (with T. Chard) Multiple Choice Questions in Obstetrics and Gynaecology, 1993; (with M. Levine) Fetal and Neonatal Neurology and Neurosurgery, 1994; contrib. chapters in books and numerous articles to medical and professional jls. *Address:* Department of Public Health and Epidemiology, University of Birmingham, Edgbaston, Birmingham B15 2TT.

LILL, John Richard, CBE 2005 (OBE 1978); concert pianist; Professor at Royal College of Music; *b* 17 March 1944; *s* of George and Margery Lill; *m* Jacqueline Clifton Smith. *Educ:* Leyton County High Sch.; Royal College of Music. FRCM; Hon. FTCL; FLCM; Hon. RAM 1988. Gulbenkian Fellowship, 1967. First concert at age of 9; Royal Festival Hall debut, 1963; Promenade Concert debut, 1969. Numerous broadcasts on radio and TV; has appeared as soloist with all leading British orchestras. Recitals and concertos throughout Great Britain, Europe, USA, Canada, Scandinavia, USSR, Japan and Far East, Australia, New Zealand, etc. Overseas tours as soloist with many orchestras including London Symphony Orchestra and London Philharmonic Orchestra. Complete recordings of Beethoven sonatas and concertos, Prokofiev sonatas, Brahms concertos and Rachmaninov piano music; complete Beethoven cycle, London, 1982, 1986, and Tokyo, 1988. Chappell Gold Medal; Pauer Prize; 1st Prize, Royal Over-Seas League Music Competition, 1963; Dinu Lipatti Medal in Harriet Cohen Internat. Awards; 1st Prize, Internat. Tchaikovsky Competition, Moscow, 1970. Hon. DSc Aston, 1978; Hon. DMus Exeter, 1979. *Recreations:* amateur radio, chess, walking. *Address:* c/o Askonas Holt Ltd, Lincoln House, 300 High Holborn, WC1V 7JH. *T:* (020) 7400 1700.

LILLEY, Prof. David Malcolm James, PhD; FRS 2002; FRSE; FRSC; Professor of Molecular Biology, since 1989, and Director, Cancer Research UK Nucleic Acid Structure Research Group, since 1993, University of Dundee; *b* 28 May 1948; *s* of Gerald Albert Thomas Lilley and Betty Pamela Lilley; *m* 1981, Patricia Mary Biddle; two *d*. *Educ:* Univ. of Durham (BSc 1st Cl. Hons Chemistry 1969; PhD Physical Chemistry 1973); Imperial Coll., London (MSc Biochem. 1973). FRSC 2002. Lectr, 1981–84, Reader, 1984–89, in Biochem., Univ. of Dundee. Mem., EMBO, 1984. FRSE 1988. Colworth Medal, British Biochemical Soc., 1982; Gold Medal of G. J. Mendel, Czech Acad. Scis, Prague, 1994; Prelog Gold Medal in Stereochemistry, ETH, Zürich, 1996; Award in RNA and Ribozyme Chemistry, 2001, Interdisciplinary Award, 2006, RSC. *Publications:* ed. numerous books, incl. DNA-proteins: structural interactions, 1995; Ribozymes and RNA Catalysis, 2007; (with Dr F. Eckstein) Nucleic Acids and Molecular Biology series, 1987–98; contrib. numerous scientific papers. *Recreations:* foreign languages, running, ski-ing. *Address:* MSI/WTB complex, University of Dundee, Dundee DD1 5EH. *T:* (01382) 384243; *e-mail:* d.m.j.lilley@dundee.ac.uk.

LILLEY, Prof. Geoffrey Michael, OBE 1981; CEng, FRSA, FRAeS, MIMechE, FIMA; Professor of Aeronautics and Astronautics, University of Southampton, 1964–82, now Emeritus Professor; Vice-President, INTECH (formerly Hampshire Technology Centre), since 1985; *b* Isleworth, Middx, 16 Nov. 1919; *m* 1948, Leslie Marion Wheeler (*d* 1996); one *s* two *d*. *Educ:* Isleworth Grammar Sch.; Battersea and Northampton Polytechnics; Imperial Coll. BSc(Eng) 1944, MSc(Eng) 1945, DIC 1945. RAF, 1935–36. Gen. engrg trg, Benham and Kodak, 1936–40; Drawing Office and Wind Tunnel Dept, Vickers Armstrong Ltd, Weybridge, 1940–46; Coll. of Aeronautics: Lectr, 1946–51; Sen. Lectr, 1951–55; Dep. Head of Dept of Aerodynamics, 1955, and Prof. of Experimental Fluid Mechanics, 1962–64. Visiting Professor: Stanford Univ., 1977–78; ME Technical Univ., Ankara, Turkey, 1983–90; Univ. of the Witwatersrand, 1990; Visiting Scientist: Inst. of Computer Applications in Sci. and Engrg, NASA Langley Res. Center, 1992–94, 1997–2006 (Chief Scientist, 1998–2000); Center for Turbulence Res., Stanford Univ., 1995–96. Past Member: Aeronautical Res. Council (past Mem. Council and Chm. Aerodynamics, Applied Aerodynamics, Noise Res., Fluid Motion and Performance Cttees); Noise Advisory Council (Chm., Noise from Air Traffic Working Group); Past Chm., Aerodynamics Cttee, Engrg Sci. Data Unit. Consultant to: Rolls Royce, 1959–61, 1967–84; AGARD, 1959–63 and 1988–89; OECD, 1969–71. Hon. DSc Southampton, 2004. Gold Medal for Aeronautics, RAeS, 1983; Aerodynamic Noise Medal, AIAA, 1985. *Publications:* (jt editor) Proc. Stanford Conf. on Complex Turbulent Flows; articles in reports and memoranda of: Aeronautical Research Council; Royal Aeronautical Soc., and other jls. *Recreations:* music, chess, walking. *Address:* Highbury, Pine Walk, Chilworth, Southampton SO16 7HQ. *T:* (023) 8076 9109. *Club:* Athenæum.

LILLEY, Rt Hon. Peter Bruce; PC 1990; MP (C) Hitchin and Harpenden, since 1997 (St Albans, 1983–97); *b* 23 Aug. 1943; *s* of Arnold Francis Lilley and Lilian (*née* Elliott); *m* 1979, Gail Ansell. *Educ:* Dulwich Coll.; Clare Coll., Cambridge. MA; FInstPet 1978. Economic consultant in underdeveloped countries, 1966–72; investment advisor on energy industries, 1972–84. Chm., London Oil Analysts Gp, 1979–80; Partner, 1980–86, Dir, 1986–87, W. Greenwell & Co., later Greenwell Montagu. Consultant Dir, Cons. Res. Dept, 1979–83. Chm., Bow Group, 1972–75. Contested (C) Tottenham, Oct. 1974. PPS to Ministers for Local Govt, Jan.–Oct. 1984, to Chancellor of the Exchequer, 1984–87; Economic Sec. to HM Treasury, 1987–89, Financial Sec., 1989–90; Secretary of State: for Trade and Industry, 1990–92; for Social Security, 1992–97; front bench Opposition spokesman on HM Treasury, 1997–98. Dep. Leader, Cons. Party, 1998–99.

Publications: (with S. Brittan) Delusion of Incomes Policy, 1977; (contrib.) Skidelsky: End of the Keynesian Era, 1980; various pamphlets. *Address:* House of Commons, SW1A 0AA. *T:* (020) 7219 3000. *Clubs:* Carlton, Beefsteak.

LILLEYMAN, Sir John (Stuart), Kt 2002; DSc; FRCP, FRCPE, FRCPath, FRCPCH, FMedSci; Strategic Adviser, National Research Ethics Service, since 2007; Professor of Paediatric Oncology, St Bartholomew's Hospital Medical College, subseq. Bart's and The London School of Medicine and Dentistry, Queen Mary, University of London, 1995–2004, now Emeritus; *b* 9 July 1945; *s* of Ernest Lilleyman and Frances Lilleyman (*née* Johnson); *m* 1st, 1970, Patricia Ann Traylen (marr. diss. 1996); one *s*; 2nd, 1998, Elizabeth Anne Lawrence. *Educ:* Oundle Sch.; St Bartholomew's Hosp. Med. Coll. (MB BS 1968; DSc Med. 1996). FRCP 1983; FRCPath 1984; FRCPCH 1997; FRCPE 2000. Jun. Posts at St Bartholomew's Hosp. and United Sheffield Hosps, 1968–72; Res. Fellow, Welsh Nat. Sch. of Medicine, 1972–74; Consultant Haematologist, Sheffield Children's Hosp., 1975–95; Prof. of Paediatric Haematology, Univ. of Sheffield Med. Sch., 1993–95. Med. Dir, NHS Nat. Patient Safety Agency, 2004–07. President: UK Assoc. of Clinical Pathologists, 1998–99; RCPath, 1999–2002; RSocMed, 2004–06. Vice Chairman: Acad. of Med. Royal Colls, 2000–02; Jt Consultants Cttee, 2001–02; Mem., Health Professions Council, 2002–04. FMedSci 2007. Hon. Fellow: Inst. Biomed. Sci., 1996; Faculty of Path., RCPI, 2003. Hon. MD Sheffield, 2003. *Publications:* (Chief Ed.) Pediatric Hematology, 1992, 2nd edn 2000; Childhood Leukaemia: the facts, 1994, 2nd edn 2000; contrib. articles on childhood leukaemia and blood diseases. *Recreations:* theatre, long distance walking. *Address:* Beehive Barn, Newton Lane, Sudborough, Northants NN14 3BF. *T:* (01832) 734416.

LILLFORD, Prof. Peter John, CBE 1998; PhD; Director, National Centre for Non Food Crops, since 2003; *b* 16 Nov. 1944; *s* of John Leslie Lillford and Ethel Ruth Lillford (*née* Wimlett); *m* 1969, Elisabeth Rosemary Avery; two *s*. *Educ:* King's Coll., London (BSc Hons Chemistry; PhD 1968); Cornell Univ. Res. Fellow, Cardio Vascular Res. Inst., San Francisco, 1970–71; Res. Scientist, 1971–87, Principal Scientist, 1987–99, Unilever; Chief Scientist (Foods), Unilever Research, 1999–2001; Pres., Inst. of Food Sci. and Technol., 2001–03. Special Prof. of Biophysics, Nottingham Univ., 1988–2007; Hon. Prof., Stirling Univ., 1989–2000; Visiting Professor: York Univ., 2000–; Univ. of Birmingham, 2007–. Chairman: Foresight Food and Drink Panel, OST, 1993–97; Agri-Food Cttee, BBSRC, 1997–2000; Inst. of Food Res. UK, 2007–. Fellow, Internat. Acad. of Food Sci. and Tech., 2003; McMaster Fellow, Food Sci. Australia, 2004–05; Flagship Fellow, CSIRO, 2005–08. FRSA 1996. Hon. DEng Birmingham 1999. Sen. Medal, RSC, 1991. *Publications:* Foods Structure and Behaviour, 1987; Feeding and the Texture of Food, 1991; Glassy States in Foods, 1993; (ed) Technology Foresight, Food and Drink, 1995. *Recreations:* old houses, old cars, old whisky. *Address:* The Firs, 20 Pavenham Road, Carlton, Beds MK43 7LS. *T:* (01234) 720869.

LILLIE, Stephen; HM Diplomatic Service; Head, Far Eastern Group, Foreign and Commonwealth Office, since 2006; *b* 4 Feb. 1966; *s* of Christopher Stanley Lillie and Maureen Lillie; *m* 1991, Denise Chit Lo; two *s*. *Educ:* S Wolds Comprehensive Sch., Nottingham; Queen's Coll., Oxford (MA Modern Langs 1988); Sch. of Oriental and African Studies, London and Chinese Univ. of Hong Kong (FCO Chinese lang. trng). HM Diplomatic Service: FCO, 1988–90; Hong Kong, 1990–91; Second, later First Sec., Beijing, 1992–95; First Sec., FCO, 1996–98; Dep. Hd, China Hong Kong Dept, FCO, 1998–99; Consul-Gen., Guangzhou, 1999–2003; Counsellor (Econ. and Commercial), New Delhi, 2003–06. *Recreations:* my family, reading, travel. *Address:* c/o Foreign and Commonwealth Office, King Charles Street, SW1A 2AH. *T:* (020) 7008 2647; *e-mail:* stephen.lillie@fco.gov.uk.

LILLYWHITE, Lt-Gen. Louis Patrick, MBE 1985; QHS 2002; Surgeon General, Ministry of Defence, since 2006; *b* 23 Feb. 1948; *s* of Dr William Henry Lillywhite and Annie Kate (*née* Vesey); *m* 1975, Jean Mary Daly, *d* of Bernard Daly and Margaret Mary (*née* Cooke); one *s* two *d*. *Educ:* King Edward VI Grammar Sch., Lichfield; University Coll. Cardiff and Welsh Nat. Sch. of Medicine (MB BCh 1971); London Sch. of Hygiene and Tropical Medicine (MSc Occupational Medicine 1989, top student prize). MFOM 1990. Regtl MO, 3rd Bn Parachute Regt, 1973–77; O i/c Technical Div., RAMC Trng Centre, 1977–81; RMCS and Army Staff Coll. (psc), 1982; SO, Med. Policy, Equipment and Intelligence, 1983–85; CO 23 Parachute Field Ambulance, 1985–89; Comdr Med., HQ 1 UK Armoured Div., incl. Gulf War (despatches 1991), 1990–92; Hd of Personnel, AMS, 1992–93; Mem., MoD Defence Cost Studies, 1993–95; DCS Med., HQ Land Comd, 1995–96; Med. Advr, HQ Allied Forces NW Europe, 1998–99; Dir Med. Personnel, Training and Clinical Policy, MoD, 1999–2001; Dir (CE), BF Germany Health Service, 2001–03; Dir Gen., Army Med. Services, 2003–05; Dir Gen., Med. Operational Capability, 2005–06. Comr, Royal Hosp. Chelsea, 2003–05; Gov., Royal Star and Garter Home, 2003–05. Member: BMA; SOM; Fellow, Medical Soc. of London, 1985 (Vice Pres., 2006–); FRSocMed 1999. Mem., Catenian Assoc., 1971–. Member: British Army Orienteering Club; British Army Mountaineering Assoc.; Fell Runners Assoc. *Publications:* (contrib.) Gulf Logistics: Blackadder's War, 1995; occasional contrib. to prof. jls. *Recreations:* cross country, long distance running, genealogy, hashing, computers, mountaineering. *Address:* Ministry of Defence, Level 7 Zone F, Main Building, Whitehall, SW1A 2HB. *T:* (020) 7807 8807, *Fax:* (020) 7807 8805; 4 Casways Orchard, Bratton, Westbury, Wilts BA13 4TY. *e-mail:* louis@lillywhi.demon.co.uk.

LIM FAT, Sir (Maxime) Edouard (Lim Man), Kt 1991; Professor Emeritus, University of Mauritius, since 1975; company director; *s* of V. Lim Fat and S. Lifo; *m* 1952, Y. H. Chan Wah Hak; two *s* one *d*. *Educ:* Univ. of London (BSc Chem. Eng.); Univ. of Newcastle (MSc Agric. Eng.). AEE Harwell, 1950–51; Engineer, Min. of Agriculture, Mauritius, 1951–63; Principal, Mauritius Coll. of Agriculture, 1963–68; Head, Sch. of Industrial Technology, Univ. of Mauritius, 1968–80; Director: Bank of Mauritius, 1980–92; NEDC, 1991–; two factories; Chm., Mauritius Freeport, 1992–. *Publications:* numerous articles, mainly on industrial develt and educn. *Recreations:* golf, economics, music. *Address:* 19 Rev. Lebrun Street, Rose-hill, Mauritius. *T:* (home) 4547680, *T:* (office) 4548288, *Fax:* 4545656. *Clubs:* Gymkhana, Vacoas.

LIM PIN, Professor, MD; FRCP, FRCPE, FRACP, FACP; University Professor and Professor of Medicine, National University of Singapore, since 2000; Senior Consultant, National University Hospital, since 2000; *b* 12 Jan. 1936; *s* of late Lim Lu Yeh and of Choo Siew Kooi; *m* 1964, Shirley Loo; two *s* one *d*. *Educ:* Queens' Coll., Cambridge (Queen's Schol., 1957; MA; MD 1970). FRCP 1976; FRCPE 1981; FRACP 1978; FACP 1981. MO, Min. of Health, Singapore, 1965–66; Univ. of Singapore: Lectr in Medicine, 1966–70; Sen. Lectr in Medicine, 1971–73; Associate Prof. of Medicine, 1974–77; Prof. and Head, Dept of Medicine, 1978–81; Dep. Vice-Chancellor, 1979–81; Vice-Chancellor, Nat. Univ. of Singapore, 1981–2000. Eisenhower Fellow, USA, 1982. Founder Pres., Endocrine and Metabolic Soc. of Singapore. Chairman: Nat. Wages Council, 2001–; Bio-ethics Adv. Cttee, 2001–; Nat. Longevity Insce Cttee, 2007–08; Co.-Chm., Singapore-MIT Alliance for Res. and Technol., 2007–. Chm., Mgt Bd, Tropical Marine Sci. Inst., 2001–. Member, Board of Directors: Raffles Medical Gp, 2001–; United Overseas Bank, 2001–. Mem., Bd of Govs, Chinese Heritage Centre, 1995–. Hon. Fellow: Coll. of Gen. Practitioners of Singapore, 1982; Internat. Coll. of Dentists, USA, 1999; (Dental Surgery), RCSE, 1999; Hon. FRACOG 1992; FRCPSGlas 1997; Hon. FRCSE 1997. Hon. DSc Hull, 1999. Public Administration Medal (Gold), Singapore, 1984; Meritorious Service Medal, Singapore, 1990; Friend of Labour Award, NTUC, 1995; Outstanding Service Award, NUS, 2003. DSO (Singapore), 2000; Officier, Ordre des Palmes Académiques (France), 1988. *Publications:* articles in New England Jl of Medicine, Med. Jl of Australia, BMJ, Qly Jl of Medicine, and Tissue Antigens. *Recreation:* swimming. *Address:* Department of Medicine, National University of Singapore, 5 Lower Kent Ridge Road, Singapore 119074, Republic of Singapore. *Club:* Singapore Island Country.

LIMB, Patrick Francis; QC 2006; *b* 23 June 1965; *s* of late Anthony Patrick Limb and of Yvonne Thérèse Léoncie Limb; *m* 1992, Anne Elizabeth Fentem; one *s* one *d*. *Educ:* Edinburgh Acad.; Pembroke Coll., Cambridge (Open Exhibnr; BA Hons 1986). Called to the Bar, Middle Temple, 1987; Jun. Counsel to the Crown, Provincial Panel, 2002–06. *Recreations:* running personal bests, walking through Paris, random acts of dancing. *Address:* c/o Ropewalk Chambers, 24 The Ropewalk, Nottingham NG1 5EF. *T:* (0115) 947 2581, *Fax:* (0115) 947 6532; *e-mail:* patricklimbqc@ropewalk.co.uk.

LIMBU; *see* Rambahadur Limbu.

LIMERICK, 7th Earl of, *cr* 1803 (Ire.); **Edmund Christopher Pery;** Baron Glentworth, 1790 (Ire.); Viscount Limerick, 1800 (Ire.); Viscount Pery, 1800 (Ire.); Baron Foxford, 1815; Partner, Altima Partners LLP, since 2005; *b* 10 Feb. 1963; *s* of 6th Earl of Limerick, KBE, AM and of Sylvia Rosalind Lush (*see* Sylvia, Countess of Limerick); *S* father, 2003; *m* 1st, 1990, Emily Kate (marr. diss. 2000), *o d* of Michael Thomas; two *s*; 2nd, 2002, Lydia Ann, 4th *d* of Richard Johnson. *Educ:* Eton; New Coll., Oxford (MA); Pushkin Inst., Moscow; City Univ. (Dip. Law). Called to the Bar, Middle Temple, 1987. HM Diplomatic Service, 1987–92: FCO, 1987–88; Ecole Nationale d'Administration, Paris, 1988–89; attachment to Ministère des Affaires Etrangères, Paris, 1990; Second Sec., Senegal, 1990–91, Amman, 1991–92; lawyer: with Clifford Chance, 1992–93; with Freshfields, 1993–94; solicitor with Milbank Tweed, 1994–96; Chief Rep., Morgan Grenfell (Deutsche Bank), Moscow, 1996–98; Dir, Deutsche Bank AG London, 1996–2004; Middle East Regl Manager, Man Gp, Dubai, 2004; Sen. Vice-Pres., Dubai Internat. Capital, 2005. *Recreations:* ski-ing, kitesurfing, tennis. *Heir: s* Viscount Pery, *qv*. *Address:* Chiddinglye, West Hoathly, East Grinstead, W Sussex RH19 4QT. *T:* (01342) 810987; *e-mail:* eclimerick@hotmail.com. *Clubs:* Garrick; Sussex; Dubai Kite.

LIMERICK, Sylvia Countess of; Sylvia Rosalind Pery, CBE 1991; Vice-Chairman, Foundation for the Study of Infant Deaths, since 1971; Hon. Vice-President, British Red Cross Society, since 1999; *b* 7 Dec. 1935; *e d* of Maurice Stanley Lush, CB, CBE, MC; *m* 1961, Viscount Glentworth (later 6th Earl of Limerick, KBE, AM; *d* 2003); two *s* one *d*. *Educ:* St Swithun's, Winchester; Lady Margaret Hall, Oxford (MA). Research Asst, Foreign Office, 1959–62. British Red Cross Society: Nat. HQ Staff, 1962–66; Pres., Kensington and Chelsea Div., 1966–72; a Vice-Pres., London Br., 1972–85; Vice-Chm., Council, 1984–85; Chm., 1985–95 (Chm. Emeritus, 1995–97); a Vice-Pres., Internat. Fedn of Red Cross Red Crescent Socs, 1993–97. Mem., Bd of Governors, St Bartholomew's Hosp., 1970–74; Vice-Chm., CHC, S District of Kensington, Chelsea, Westminster Area, 1974–77; Chairman: Eastman Dental Inst., 1996–99; Eastman Foundn for Oral Res. and Trng, 1996–2002; Member: Kensington, Chelsea and Westminster AHA, 1977–82; Eastman Dental Hosp. SHA, 1990–96. Non-exec. Dir, UCL Hosps NHS Trust, 1996–97. A Vice-Pres., 1978–84, Pres., 1984–2002, Health Visitors' Assoc., subseq. Community Practitioners' and Health Visitors' Assoc.; President: UK Cttee for UN Children's Fund, 1972–79 (Vice Pres., 1979–99); Nat. Assoc. for Maternal and Child Welfare, 1973–84 (Vice Pres., 1985–90). Member: Cttee of Management, Inst. of Child Health, 1976–96; Council, King Edward's Hospital Fund, 1977– (Mem., Cttee of Management, 1977–81, 1985–89); Maternity Services Adv. Cttee, DHSS, 1981–84; CS Occupational Health Service Adv. Bd, 1989–92; Vice-Chm., Jt Res. Ethics Cttee, Nat. Hosp. for Neurology and Neurosurgery/Inst. of Neurology, 1993–2004; Chm., CMO's Expert Gp to investigate Cot Death Theories, 1994–98. Trustee: Child Accident Prevention Trust, 1979–87; Voluntary Hosp. of St Bartholomew, 1993–2004; Child Health Res. Appeal Trust, 1996–2006. Reviewed National Association of Citizens Advice Bureaux, 1983. FRSocMed 1977. Hon. FRCP 1994 (Hon. MRCP 1990); Hon. FRCPCH 1996 (Hon. Mem., BPA, 1986); Hon. Fellow, Inst. of Child Health, 1996. Hon. DLitt CNAA, 1990; Hon. LLD Bristol, 1998. Hon. Freeman: Salters' Co., 1992; World Traders' Co., 2003. Humanitarian Award, European Women of Achievement, 1995. Order of Croatian Star, 2003. *Publication:* (jtly) Sudden Infant Death: patterns, puzzles and problems, 1985. *Recreations:* music, mountaineering, ski-ing. *Address:* Chiddinglye, West Hoathly, East Grinstead, W Sussex RH19 4QT. *T:* (01342) 810214.

LIMON, Sir Donald (William), KCB 1997 (CB 1993); Clerk of the House of Commons, 1994–97; *b* 29 Oct. 1932; *s* of late Arthur and Dora Limon; *m* 1987, Joyce Beatrice Clifton. *Educ:* Durham Cathedral Chorister Sch.; Durham Sch.; Lincoln Coll., Oxford (MA). A Clerk in the House of Commons, 1956–97: Sec. to House of Commons Commn, 1979–81; Clerk of Financial Cttees, 1981–84; Principal Clerk, Table Office, 1985–89; Clerk of Cttees, 1989–90; Clerk Asst, 1990–94. *Publication:* (ed jtly) Erskine May's Parliamentary Practice, 22nd edn 1997. *Recreations:* cricket, golf, singing.

LINACRE, Christina Margaret; *see* McComb, C. M.

LINACRE, Sir (John) Gordon (Seymour), Kt 1986; CBE 1979; AFC 1943; DFM 1941; Deputy Chairman, United Newspapers plc, 1981–91 (Director, 1969–91; Joint Managing Director, 1981–83; Chief Executive, 1983–88); President, Yorkshire Post Newspapers Ltd, since 1990 (Managing Director, 1965–83; Deputy Chairman, 1981–83; Chairman, 1983–90); *b* 23 Sept. 1920; *s* of John James Linacre and Beatrice Barber (*née* Seymour); *m* 1943, Irene Amy (*née* Gordon); two *d*. *Educ:* Firth Park Grammar Sch., Sheffield. Served War, RAF, 1939–46, Sqdn Ldr. Journalistic appts, Sheffield Telegraph/Star, 1937–47; Kemsley News Service, 1947–50; Dep. Editor: Newcastle Journal, 1950–56; Newcastle Evening Chronicle, 1956–57; Editor, Sheffield Star, 1958–61; Asst Gen. Man., Sheffield Newspapers Ltd, 1961–63; Exec. Dir, Thomson Regional Newspapers Ltd, London, 1963–65. Chairman: United Provincial Newspapers Ltd, 1983–88; Sheffield Newspapers Ltd, 1981–88; Lancashire Evening Post Ltd, 1982–88; Northampton Mercury Co. Ltd, 1983–88; The Reporter Ltd, 1970–88; Blackpool Gazette & Herald Ltd, 1984–88; Chameleon Television, 1992–; Dep. Chm., Express Newspapers, 1985–88; Director: United Newspapers (Publications) Ltd, 1969–88; Trident Television Ltd, 1970–84; Yorkshire Television Ltd, 1967–90. Dir, INCA/FIEJ Res. Assoc., Darmstadt, Germany, 1971–79 (Pres., 1974–77); Pres. FIEJ, 1984–88 (Mem. Bd, 1971–90). Dir, ASA, 1991–94; Member: Newspaper Soc. Council, 1966–90 (Pres., Newspaper Soc., 1978–79); Press Assoc., 1967–74 (Chm., 1970–71); Reuters Ltd, 1970–74 (Trustee, 1974–98); Evening Newspaper Advertising Bureau Ltd, 1966–78 (Chm., 1975–76); N Eastern Postal Bd, 1974–80; Adv. Bd, Yorks and Lincs, BIM, 1973–75; Health Educn Council, 1973–77; Leeds TEC, 1989–91 (Chm.). Mem., ENO,

1978–81; Chm., 1978–98, Pres., 1998–, Opera North (formerly English Nat. Opera North). Governor, Harrogate Festival of Arts and Sciences Ltd, 1973–2003 (Pres., 1992–2003). Trustee, Yorks and Lincs Trustee Savings Bank, 1972–78; Mem. Council, 1985–93, and Court, 1995–2000, Chm. Foundation, 1989–2000, Leeds Univ. CCMI (FBIM 1973). Kt, Order of White Rose (Finland), 1987; Grande Ufficiale al Merito della Repubblica Italiana, 1988 (Commendatore, 1973). *Recreations:* golf, fishing, walking. *Clubs:* Alwoodley Golf; Burnsall Angling.

LINAKER, Lawrence Edward, (Paddy); Deputy Chairman and Chief Executive, M&G Group, 1987–94; *b* 22 July 1934; *s* of late Lawrence Wignall and Rose Linaker; *m* 1963, Elizabeth Susan Elam; one *s. Educ:* Malvern College. FCA. Esso Petroleum, 1957–63; joined M&G Group, 1963; Man. Dir, 1972, Chm., 1987–94, M&G Investment Management. Chairman: Fisons, 1994–95; Marling Industries, 1996–97; Fleming Technol. Investment Trust plc, 1997–2001; Director: Fleming Mercantile Investment Trust, 1994–2005; TSB Gp, 1994–95; Lloyds TSB Gp, 1995–2001; Wolverhampton & Dudley Breweries plc, 1996–2002. Chm., Institutional Fund Managers' Assoc., 1992–94; Dir, Securities Inst., 1992–94. Trustee, Lloyds TSB Foundn for Eng. and Wales, 1995–2001; Life Trustee, Carnegie UK Trust, 1995–2005. Chm., YMCA Nat. Coll., 1992–2000; Treas., Childline, 1994–2000; Member: Council, RPMS, 1977–88; Governing Body, SPCK, 1976–95; Council, Malvern College, 1988–2003 (Treas., 1993–2002); Governing Body, Canterbury Christ Church Coll., 1993–98; Court, ICSTM, 1999–2005. *Recreations:* music, wine, gardening. *Clubs:* Athenæum, Brooks's.

LINCOLN, 19th Earl of, *cr* 1572; **Robert Edward Fiennes-Clinton;** *b* 17 June 1972; *s* of Hon. Edward Gordon Fiennes-Clinton and Julia (*née* Howson); *S* grandfather, 2001. *Heir: b* William Roy Fiennes-Clinton, *b* 1980.

LINCOLN, Bishop of, since 2001; **Rt Rev. John Charles Saxbee,** PhD; *b* 7 Jan. 1946; *s* of Charles Albert Saxbee and Florence Violet Saxbee (*née* Harris); *m* 1965, Jacqueline Margaret Carol Skym; one *d. Educ:* Cotham Grammar Sch., Bristol; Bristol Univ. (BA 1968); Durham Univ. (DipTh 1969; PhD 1976); Cranmer Hall, Durham. Ordained deacon, 1972, priest, 1973; Asst Curate, Emmanuel with St Paul, Plymouth, 1972–77; Vicar of St Philip, Weston Mill, Plymouth, 1977–81; Team Vicar, Central Exeter Team Ministry, 1981–87; Dir, SW Ministry Training Course, 1981–92; Priest-in-Charge of Holy Trinity, Wistanstow with St Michael, Cwm Head and St Margaret, Acton Scott, 1992–94; Archdeacon of Ludlow, 1992–2001; Bishop Suffragan of Ludlow, 1994–2001. Prebendary: of Exeter Cathedral, 1988–92; of Hereford Cathedral, 1992–2001. Pres., Modern Churchpeople's Union, 1997–. Religious Advr, Central TV, 1997–2006. Member: Exec., Springboard, 1998–2004; Coll. of Evangelists, 1999–. *Publication:* Liberal Evangelism: a flexible response to the decade, 1994. *Recreations:* televised sport, most kinds of music. *Address:* Bishop's House, Eastgate, Lincoln LN2 1QQ. *T:* (01522) 534701.

LINCOLN, Dean of; *see* Buckler, Very Rev. P. J. W.

LINCOLN, Archdeacon of; *no new appointment at time of going to press.*

LINCOLN, Prof. Dennis William, PhD; FRSE; Dean, Faculty of Science, University of New South Wales, 2002–03; *b* 21 July 1939; *s* of late Ernest Edward Lincoln and Gertrude Emma Holmes; one *s* one *d. Educ:* Bracondale Sch., Norwich; Essex Inst. of Agriculture; Univ. of Nottingham (BSc 1964); Corpus Christi Coll., Cambridge (MA 1966; PhD 1967); Univ. of Bristol (DSc 1974). FRSE 1992. Agricl labourer, 1955–57; Research Technician, Univ. of Nottingham, 1957–59; Res. Fellow, Corpus Christi Coll., Cambridge, 1966–67; Lectr, 1967–74, Reader, 1974–81, Prof., 1981–82, Univ. of Bristol; Dir, MRC Reproductive Biology Unit, Edinburgh, 1982–96; Hon. Prof., Edinburgh Univ., 1984–96; Dep. Vice-Chancellor (Research), Griffith Univ., Australia, 1996–2001. Short-term appts in Switzerland, The Netherlands, USA, Australia; numerous nat. and internat. duties related to promotion of reproductive health. *Publications:* papers on reproductive biology, esp. on neural mechanisms in control of lactation and fertility. *Recreations:* ornithology, international travel, wildlife photography.

LINCOLN, Paul Arthur; Director of Education, Edison Schools UK Ltd, since 2003; *b* 11 April 1946. *Educ:* Clare Coll., Cambridge (BA (Hons) History; PGCE 1969; MA 1971). Various teaching posts in secondary schools in Sussex and Essex, 1969–82; Sen. Dep. Head, William de Ferrers Sch., Essex, 1982–88; Essex County Council Education Department: Sen. Inspector, 1988–89; Principal Inspector, 1989–91; Head of Strategic Planning, 1991–92; Principal Educn Officer, Quality, 1992–93; Dep. County Educn Officer, 1994–95; Dir of Educn, 1995–97; Dir of Learning Services, Essex CC, 1997–2002; Chief Exec., Eastern Leadership Centre, Cambridge, 2003–04. *Publications:* The Learning School, 1987; Supporting Improving Primary Schools, 1999. *Recreations:* reading, walking, gardening.

LIND, Per; Swedish Ambassador to the Court of St James's, 1979–82, retired; *b* 8 Jan. 1916; *s* of Erik and Elisabeth Lind; *m* 1942, Eva Sandström; two *s* two *d. Educ:* Univ. of Uppsala. LLB 1939. Entered Swedish Foreign Service as Attaché, 1939; served in Helsinki, 1939–41; Berlin, 1942–44; Second Sec., Stockholm Foreign Ministry, 1944–47; First Sec., Swedish Embassy, Washington, 1947–51; Personal Asst to Sec.-General of UN, 1953–56; re-posted to Swedish Foreign Ministry: Chief of Div. of Internat. Organisations, 1956–59; Dep. Dir Political Affairs, 1959–64; Ambassador with special duties (*ie* disarmament questions) and actg Chm., Swedish Delegation in Geneva, 1964–66; Ambassador to Canada, 1966–69; Under-Sec. of State for Administration at Foreign Ministry, Stockholm, 1969–75; Chm. Special Political Cttee of 29th Session of Gen. Assembly of UN, 1974; Ambassador to Australia, 1975–79. *Recreation:* golf. *Address:* Gyllenstiernsgatan 7, 11526 Stockholm, Sweden.

LINDAHL, Göran; company director; *b* Umeå, Sweden, 28 April 1945; *s* of Sven Lindahl and Frida (*née* Johansson); *m* 1971, Kristina Gunnarsdotter; one *s* one *d. Educ:* Chalmers Univ. of Technology, Gothenburg (MSc Electrical Eng 1971; Hon. DSc Eng 1993). ASEA Ludvika, Sweden: High-Voltage Direct Current Div., 1971–77; Manager: High-Voltage Lab., 1977–80; Mktg and Sales, 1980–83; Pres., ASEA Transformers, 1983–85; Pres., ASEA Transmission, 1985–86, Exec. Vice-Pres. and Mem. ASEA Gp Mgt, ASEA AB, 1986–87, Västerås, Sweden; ABB Ltd, Zurich: Exec. Vice-Pres. and Mem. Gp Exec. Cttee, responsible for Power Transmission Segment, 1988–93, responsible for Power Transmission and Distribution Segment, 1993–96; Pres. and CEO, 1997–2000; Mem. Bd, ABB Ltd, 1999–2001. Chm., Alliance for Global Sustainability, 2001–02; Special Advr on Global Compact to Kofi Annan, UN Sec.-Gen., 2001–02. Member Board: Saab AB, Sweden, 1991–97; Atlas Copco AB, Sweden, 1994–97; Ericsson, Sweden, 1999–2002; DuPont, USA, 1999 (Chm., Sci and Tech. Bd Cttee, DuPont, 2000); Anglo American plc, UK, 2001; INGKA Holding BV (IKEA), Holland, 2001–; Sony Corp., Japan, 2001–05; Mem. Internat. Adv. Bd, Salomon Smith Barney Internat., USA, 1999–. Chm., World Childhood Foundn, USA, 2001 (Mem. Bd, World Childhood Foundn, Sweden, USA, Germany, 1999–2000); Vice Chairman Board: Prince of Wales Business Leaders Forum, 1998–2001; John F. Kennedy Center Corporate Fund, 1999–2001; Mem. Bd, Schwab Foundn for Social Entrepreneurship, 2001–. Chm., EU-Hong Kong Business

Co-operation Cttee, 1999–2000; Co-Chairman: ASEAN-EU Industrialists Round Table, 1998–2000; EU-Russia Industrialists Round Table, 1999–2000; US-EU-Poland Action Commn, 1999–2000; Member: EU-Japan Industrialists Round Table, 1999–2000; European Round Table of Industrialists, 2000–01. Mem. Royal Swedish Acad. of Engrg Scis, 1999; FIET (FIEE 1997). Hon. PhD Umeå, 2001. Paul Harris Fellow, Rotary Club Internat., 1997. *Recreations:* golf, astronomy. *Address:* 47 The Piper Building, Peterborough Road, SW6 3EF; *e-mail:* nstargl@aol.com.

LINDAHL, Tomas Robert, MD; FRS 1988; Principal Scientist, Cancer Research UK London Research Institute (formerly Imperial Cancer Research Fund), since 1981; *b* 28 Jan. 1938; *s* of Robert and Ethel Lindahl; *m* 1967, Alice Adams (marr. diss. 1979); one *s* one *d. Educ:* Karolinska Inst., Stockholm (MD). Research Fellow, Princeton Univ., 1964–67; Helen Hay Whitney Fellow, 1967–69, Asst Prof., 1968–69, Rockefeller Univ.; Asst Prof., 1969–75, Associate Prof., 1975–77, Karolinska Inst.; Prof. of Medical Biochemistry, Univ. of Gothenburg, 1978–81; Imperial Cancer Research Fund: Staff Scientist, 1981–83; Dir, Clare Hall Labs, 1983–2005; Asst Dir of Research, 1985–89; Associate Dir of Research, 1989–91; Dep. Dir, Res., 1991–96; Dir, Res., 1996–98; Dep. Dir, Res., 1998–2005. Croonian Lecture, Royal Soc., 1996. Member: EMBO; Royal Swedish Acad. of Scis; Norwegian Acad. of Sci. and Letters; Academia Europaea. Founder FMedSci 1998. Royal Medal, Royal Soc., 2007. *Publications:* res. papers in biochem. and molecular biol. *Recreations:* piano, wine, modern art. *Address:* Clare Hall Laboratories, South Mimms, Herts EN6 3LD.

LINDBLOM, Keith John; QC 1996; a Recorder, since 2001; *b* 20 Sept. 1956; *s* of John Eric Lindblom and June Elizabeth Lindblom (*née* Balloch); *m* 1991, Fiona Margaret Jackson; one *s* three *d. Educ:* Whitgift Sch.; St John's Coll., Oxford (MA). Called to the Bar, Gray's Inn, 1980, Bencher, 2003; called to the Bar, NI, 2002; in practice as barrister, 1981–. An Asst Parly Boundary Comr, 2000–. *Recreations:* music, reading, walking. *Address:* 2 Harcourt Buildings, Temple, EC4Y 9DB. *T:* (020) 7353 8415. *Club:* Caledonian.

LINDEN, Anya, (Lady Sainsbury of Preston Candover), CBE 2003; Ballerina, Royal Ballet, 1958–65, retired; *b* 3 Jan. 1933; English; *d* of George Charles and Ada Dorothea Eltenton; *m* 1963, John Davan Sainsbury (*see* Baron Sainsbury of Preston Candover); two *s* one *d. Educ:* Berkeley, Calif; Sadler's Wells Sch., 1947. Entered Sadler's Wells Co. at Covent Garden, 1951; promoted Soloist, 1952; Ballerina, 1958. Principal rôles in the ballets: Coppelia; Sylvia; Prince of Pagodas; Sleeping Beauty; Swan Lake; Giselle; Cinderella; Agon; Solitaire; Noctambules; Fête Etrange; Symphonic Variations; Hamlet; The Invitation; Firebird; Lady and the Fool; Antigone; Ondine; Seven Deadly Sins. Ballet coach: Royal Ballet Sch., 1989–; Rambert Sch., 1989–. Member: Nat. Council for One-Parent Families, 1978–90 (Hon. Vice-Pres., 1985–90; Mem. Appeal Cttee, 1966–87); Adv. Council, British Theatre Museum, 1975–83; Drama and Dance Adv. Cttee, British Council, 1981–83; Theatre Museum Assoc., 1984–86. Dep.-Chm. and Dir, Rambert Dance Co. (formerly Ballet Rambert), 1975–89. Trustee: Royal Opera Hse, 2003–07; Rambert Sch. of Ballet and Contemp. Dance, 2003– (Mem. Adv. Cttee, 1985–2003). Gov., Royal Ballet Sch., 1977–2004; Dep. Chm. and Mem. Council of Management, Benesh Inst. of Choreology (formerly Benesh Inst. of Movement Notation), 1986–97. Founder and Chm., Linbury Biennial Prize for Theatre Design, 1987–. Dir, Anvil Trust, 1992–98; Trustee, Galitzine—St Petersburg Library, 1993–2004. Patron: Landlife 1993–; Heatherley Sch. of Fine Art, 2007–. FRWCMD 2008. DUniv Brunel, 1995. *Recreations:* gardening, painting, photography.

LINDEN, Ian, CMG 2000; PhD; Associate Professor, School of Oriental and African Studies, University of London, since 2001; Executive Director, Catholic Institute for International Relations, 1986–2001; *b* 18 Aug. 1941; *s* of Henry Thomas William Linden and Edna Jessie Linden; *m* 1963, Jane Winder; two *s* two *d. Educ:* Southend High Sch. for Boys; St Catharine's Coll., Cambridge (MA 1966); PhD London Univ. (Middx Hosp. Med. Sch., 1966, SOAS 1975). Asst Lectr in Zoology, Nat. Univ. of Ireland, 1965–66; Res. Associate, Rockefeller Univ., NY, 1966–68; Lectr in Biology, Univ. of Malaŵi, 1968–71; Lectr, subseq. Sen. Lectr, in History, Ahmadu Bello Univ., 1973–76; Researcher, Arbeitskreis Entwicklung und Frieden, 1977–79; Prof. of African History, Univ. of Hamburg, 1979–80; Southern Africa Desk Officer and Co-ordinator of Policy Dept, Catholic Inst. for Internat. Relns, 1980–86. Hon. PhD Southampton, 1998. *Publications:* Catholics, Peasants and Chewa Resistance in Nyasaland, 1974; Church and Revolution in Rwanda, 1977; The Catholic Church and the Struggle for Zimbabwe, 1980; (jtly) Islam in Modern Nigeria, 1984; Christianisme et pouvoirs au Rwanda 1900–1990, 1999; A New Map of the World, 2004. *Recreations:* swimming, theology, walking. *Address:* 31 Royal Close, Manor Road, N16 5SE.
See also T. D. Linden.

LINDEN, Prof. Paul Frederick, PhD; FRS 2007; Blasker Professor of Environmental Science and Engineering, since 1998, and Chairman, Department of Mechanical and Aerospace Engineering, since 2004, University of California, San Diego; *b* 29 Jan. 1947; *s* of Frederick Henry Victor Linden and Muriel Constance Linden; *m* 1979, Diana Readman; two *d. Educ:* Univ. of Adelaide (BSc Hons 1967); Flinders Univ. of South Australia (MSc 1968); Emmanuel Coll., Cambridge (PhD 1972). University of Cambridge: Asst Dir of Res., 1976–91; Reader in Geophysical Fluid Dynamics, 1991–98; Dir, Fluid Dynamics Lab., 1976–98; Fellow, Downing Coll., 1977–98. Dir, Univ. of Calif, San Diego, Envmt and Sustainability Initiative, 2007–. Associate Editor, Jl Fluid Mechanics, 2005–. *Publications:* over 100 articles in refereed jls. *Recreations:* running, swimming, clarinet. *Address:* Department of Mechanical and Aerospace Engineering, University of California, San Diego, 9500 Gilman Drive, La Jolla, CA 92093–0411, USA. *T:* (858) 8222274, *Fax:* (858) 5347720; *e-mail:* pflinden@ucsd.edu. *Club:* Pacific Athletic.

LINDEN, Thomas Dominic; QC 2006; a Recorder, since 2005; *b* London, 26 Nov. 1964; *s* of Ian Linden, *qv; m* 1991, Brigit Connolly; four *d. Educ:* Beechen Cliff Comp. Sch., Bath; St Brendan's Sixth Form Coll., Bristol; Keble Coll., Oxford (BA Juris. 1st Cl. 1987; BCL 1988). Called to the Bar, Gray's Inn, 1989. *Recreations:* cycling, playing with our children. *Address:* Matrix Chambers, Griffin House, Gray's Inn, WC1R 5LN. *T:* (020) 7404 3447; *e-mail:* tomlinden@matrixlaw.co.uk.

LINDESAY-BETHUNE, family name of **Earl of Lindsay**.

LINDISFARNE, Archdeacon of; *see* Robinson, Ven. P. J. A.

LINDLEY, Bryan Charles, CBE 1982; Chairman and Chief Executive, Lord Lindley Associates, since 1990; Director, J & B Imaging, since 1998; *b* 30 Aug. 1932; *m* 1987; one *s* by former *m. Educ:* Reading Sch.; University Coll. London (Fellow 1979). BSc (Eng) 1954; PhD 1960. FIMechE 1968; FIET (FIEE 1968); FInstP 1968; FInstD 1968; FPRI 1984. National Gas Turbine Establishment, Pyestock, 1954–57; Hawker Siddeley Nuclear Power Co. Ltd, 1957–59; C. A. Parsons & Co. Ltd, Nuclear Research Centre, Newcastle upon Tyne, 1959–61; International Research and Development Co. Ltd, Newcastle upon Tyne, 1962–65; Man., R&D Div., C. A. Parsons & Co. Ltd, Newcastle upon Tyne,

1965–68; Electrical Research Assoc.: Dir, 1968–73; Chief Exec. and Man. Dir, ERA Technology Ltd, 1973–79; Dir, ERA Patents Ltd, 1968–79; Chm., ERA Autotrack Systems Ltd, 1971–79. Director: Dunlop Ltd, 1982–85; Soil-Less Cultivation Systems, 1980–85; Chm. and Dir, Thermal Conversions (UK), 1982–85; Dir of Technology, Dunlop Holdings plc, 1979–85; Director: BICC Cables Ltd, 1985–88; BICC Research and Engineering Ltd, 1985–88; Thomas Bolton & Johnson Ltd, 1986–88; Settle-Carlisle Railway Develt Co., 1992–94; Chairman: Optical Fibres, 1985–87; Linktronic Systems Ltd, 1990–92; Wetheriggs Pottery Ltd, 1992–94; SKAND Systems Ltd, 1995–97; Chief Exec., Nat. Advanced Robotics Res. Centre, 1989–90. Chm., N Lakeland Healthcare NHS Trust, 1993–97. Vis. Prof., Univ. of Liverpool, 1989–. Chairman: Materials, Chemicals and Vehicles Requirements Bd, DTI, 1982–85; RAPRA Council, 1984–85; Dir, RAPRA Technology Ltd, 1985–97; Member: Nat. Electronics Council, 1969–79; Res. and Technol. Cttee, CBI, 1974–80; Design Council, 1980–86 (Mem., Design Adv. Cttee, 1980–86); Cttee of Inquiry into Engineering Profession, 1977–80; Adv. Council for Applied Research and Develt, 1980–86; Adv. Cttee for Safety of Nuclear Installations, 1987–90; Chm., Sci. Educn and Management Div., IEE, 1974–75; Dep. Chm., Watt Cttee on Energy Ltd, 1976–80. Mem., SAE, 1984. *Publications:* articles on plasma physics, electrical and mechanical engineering, management science, impact of technological innovation, etc, in learned jls. *Recreations:* music, photography, ski-ing, walking, sailing. *Address:* Lindenthwaite, Beacon Edge, Penrith, Cumbria CA11 8BN.

LINDLEY, Prof. Dennis Victor; Professor and Head of Department of Statistics and Computer Science, University College London, 1967–77; *b* 25 July 1923; *s* of Albert Edward and Florence Louisa Lindley; *m* 1947, Joan Armitage; one *s* two *d*. *Educ:* Tiffin Boys' Sch., Kingston-on-Thames; Trinity Coll., Cambridge. MA Cantab 1948. Min. of Supply, 1943–45; Nat. Physical Lab., 1945–46 and 1947–48; Statistical Lab., Cambridge Univ., 1948–60 (Dir, 1957–60); Prof. and Head of Dept of Statistics, UCW, Aberystwyth, 1960–67, Hon. Professorial Fellow, 1978–. Hon. Prof., Univ. of Warwick, 1978–96. Vis. Professor: Chicago and Stanford Univs, 1954–55; Harvard Business Sch., 1963; Univ. of Iowa, 1974–75; Univ. of Bath, 1978–81. Fellow, Inst. Math. Statistics; Fellow, American Statistical Assoc. Wald Lectr, Inst. Math. Statistics, 1988. Guy Medal (Gold), Royal Statistical Soc., 2002. *Publications:* (with J. C. P. Miller) Cambridge Elementary Statistical Tables, 1953; Introduction to Probability and Statistics (2 vols), 1965; Making Decisions, 1971, rev. edn 1985; Bayesian Statistics, 1971; (with W. F. Scott) New Cambridge Elementary Statistical Tables, 1985, rev. edn as New Cambridge Statistical Tables, 1995; Understanding Uncertainty, 2006; contribs to Royal Statistical Soc., Biometrika, Annals of Math. Statistics. *Address:* Woodstock, Quay Lane, Minehead, Somerset TA24 5QU. *T:* (01643) 705189.

LINDLEY, Simon Geoffrey; Master of the Music, Leeds Parish Church, since 1975; Leeds City Organist, since 1976; Senior Assistant Music Officer (formerly Music and Special Projects Officer), Leeds City Council, since 1988; *b* 10 Oct. 1948; *s* of Rev. Geoffrey Lindley and Jeanne Lindley (*née* Cammaerts); *m*; three *s* one *d*. *Educ:* Magdalen Coll. Sch., Oxford; Royal Coll. of Music. FRCO(CHM), FTCL, GRSM (Lond), ARCM, LRAM. Studies with Richard Silk, David Carver, Dr Bernard Rose, Vincent Packford, Dr Philip Wilkinson and, principally, Dr John Birch. Dir of Music, St Anne & St Agnes and St Olave, London, 1968–70; Asst Master of Music, St Alban's Abbey, 1970–75; Dir of Music, St Alban's Sch., 1971–75; Sen. Lectr, Leeds Poly., 1976–88. Chorus Master: Leeds Phil. Soc., 1975–83 (Vice-Pres., 2005–); Halifax Choral Soc., 1975–87 (Vice-Pres., 1988–); Conductor: St Peter's Singers and Chamber Orch., 1977–; Univ. of Huddersfield Chamber Choir, 1997–98; Leeds Coll. of Music Choral Soc., 1999–; Chief Guest Conductor, Yorkshire Evening Post Band, 1998– (Resident Conductor, 1995–98); Music Dir, Overgate Hospice Choir, Halifax, 1997–. Special Comr, RSCM, 1975–; Centre Chm., ISM, 1976–82; Mem. Council, RCO, 1977–98, 2003– (Pres., 2000–02; Vice-Pres., 2003–); Sec., Church Music Soc., 1991–; Pres., IAO, 2003–05. Dir, English Hymnal Co. Ltd, 1996. Advr, Yorks TV Religious and Educl Progs, 1981; Artistic Advr, Leeds Summer Heritage Festivals, biennially, 1989–97. Pres., Campaign for the Traditional Cathedral Choir, 2008–. Chm., Friends of Musicians' Chapel, St Sepulchre-without-Newgate, 2004–; Trustee: Sir George Thalben-Ball Meml Trust, 1989–; Ecclesiastical Music Trust, 1998– (Chm., 2004–); Pilling Trust, 1999–. Governor: Whinmoor St Paul C of E Primary Sch., 2003– (Vice Chm., 2005–); Yorkshire Coll. of Music and Drama, 2005– (Chm., 2006–). Churchwarden, St Sepulchre-without-Newgate, 2006–. Liveryman, Co. of Musicians, 2006. Concert Organist début, Westminster Cathedral, 1969; tours of USA, France, Germany, Far East, USSR. Numerous recordings as organist and as conductor. FRSCM 2002. Hon. FGMS 1996; Hon. FGCM 2000; Hon. Fellow, Leeds Coll. of Music, 2000. DUniv Leeds Metropolitan, 2001. Spirit of Leeds Award, Leeds Civic Trust, 2006. *Compositions:* Anthems for Unison and 2 part singing, vol. 2, 1979; Ave Maria, 1980, 2003; Matthew, Mark, Luke and John, 1986; Lord, I Have Loved the Habitation of Thy House, 2002; *carols:* Come, sing and dance, 1977; How far is it to Bethlehem?, Jacob's Ladder, Now the Green Blade riseth, On Easter Morn, 1995; The Bellman's Song, Here is joy for every age, 2004. *Publications:* (ed jtly) New English Praise, 2006; contribs to Musical Times, Choir and Organ, Organists' Review, The Dalesman, The Organ. *Recreations:* churches, cathedrals, Victorian architecture, food. *Address:* 17 Fulneck, Pudsey LS28 8NT. *T:* and *Fax:* (0113) 255 6143; Learning and Leisure Department, Leeds Town Hall, The Headrow, Leeds LS1 3AD. *T:* and *Fax:* (0113) 247 8334; *e-mail:* sgl@simonlindley.org.uk. *Club:* Leeds (Leeds) (Hon. Mem., 2004).

LINDOP, Sir Norman, Kt 1973; DL; MSc; CChem, FRSC; Director, Hatfield Polytechnic, 1969–82; Chairman, Hertfordshire County Council, 1997–99 (Member (Lab), 1993–2001); *b* 9 March 1921; *s* of Thomas Cox Lindop and May Lindop, Stockport, Cheshire; *m* 1974, Jenny C. Quass; one *s*. *Educ:* Northgate Sch., Ipswich; Queen Mary Coll., Univ. of London (BSc, MSc). Various industrial posts, 1942–46; Lectr in Chemistry, Queen Mary Coll., 1946; Asst Dir of Examinations, Civil Service Commn, 1951; Sen. Lectr in Chemistry, Kingston Coll. of Technology, 1953; Head of Dept of Chemistry and Geology, Kingston Coll. of Technology, 1957; Principal: SW Essex Technical Coll. and Sch. of Art, 1963; Hatfield Coll. of Technology, 1966; Principal, British Sch. of Osteopathy, 1982–90. Chairman: Cttee of Dirs of Polytechnics, 1972–74; Council for Professions Supplementary to Medicine, 1973–81; Home Office Data Protection Cttee, 1976–78; Cttee of Enquiry into Public Sector Validation, DES, 1984–85; British Library Adv. Council, 1986–94; Herts Area Manpower Bd, 1986–88; Res. Council for Complementary Medicine, 1989–90; Member: CNAA, 1974–81; US-UK Educn (Fulbright) Commn, 1971–81; SRC, 1974–78; GMC, 1979–84. Chm. Council, Westfield Coll., London Univ., 1983–89. FCP 1980; Fellow: QMC, 1976; Hatfield Polytechnic, 1983; Hon. Fellow, Brighton Polytechnic, 1990. FRSA. DL Hertford, 1989. Hon. DEd CNAA, 1982; Hon. DSc: Ulster, 1994; Hertfordshire, 1997; Kingston, 2002. *Recreations:* mountain walking, music (especially opera). *Address:* 36 Queens Road, Hertford, Herts SG13 8AZ. *Club:* Athenæum.

LINDOP, Prof. Patricia Joyce, (Mrs G. P. R. Esdale); Professor of Radiation Biology, University of London, 1970–84, now Emeritus; Chairman, Thames Liquid Fuels (Holdings) Ltd, since 1992; *b* 21 June 1930; 2nd *c* of Elliot D. Lindop and Dorothy Jones; *m* 1957, Gerald Paton Rivett Esdale (*d* 1992); one *s* one *d*. *Educ:* Malvern Girls' Coll.; St Bartholomew's Hospital Med. Coll.; BSc (1st cl. Hons), MB, BS, PhD; DSc London 1974; MRCP 1956; FRCP 1977. Registered GP, 1954. Research and teaching in physiology and medical radiobiology at Med. Coll. of St Bartholomew's Hosp., 1955–84. UK Mem., Council of Pugwash Confs on Science and World Affairs, 1982–87 (Asst Sec. Gen., 1961–71); Mem., Royal Commn on Environmental Pollution, 1974–79; Chm. and Trustee, Soc. for Education in the Applications of Science, 1968–91; Member: Cttee 10 of ICRU, 1972–79; ESRO-NASA, 1970–74; Soc. for Radiol Protection, 1987–. Member Council: Science and Society, 1975–90; Soc. for Protection of Science and Learning, 1974–86; formerly Mem. Council, British Inst. of Radiology; Chairman: Univ. of London Bd of Studies in Radiation Biology, 1979–81; Interdisciplinary Special Cttee for the Environment, 1979–81. Governor, St Bartholomew's Hosp. Med. Coll., 1984–. Hon. Member: RCR, 1972; ARR, 1984. Ciba Award, 1957; Leverhulme Res. Award, 1984. *Publications:* in field of radiation effects. *Address:* 58 Wildwood Road, NW11 6UP. *T:* (020) 8455 5860. *Club:* Royal Society of Medicine.

LINDSAY, family name of **Earl of Crawford** and **Baron Lindsay of Birker**.

LINDSAY, 16th Earl of, *cr* 1633 (Scot.); **James Randolph Lindesay-Bethune;** DL; Lord Lindsay of The Byres, 1445; Lord Parbroath, 1633; Viscount of Garnock, Lord Kilburnie, Kingsburn and Drumry, 1703; *b* 19 Nov. 1955; *s* of 15th Earl of Lindsay and of Hon. Mary Clare Douglas-Scott-Montagu, *y d* of 2nd Baron Montagu of Beaulieu; *S* father, 1989; *m* 1982, Diana, *er d* of Major Nigel Chamberlayne-Macdonald, Cranbury Park, Winchester; two *s* three *d* (of whom one *s* one *d* are twins). *Educ:* Eton; Univ. of Edinburgh (MA Hons); Univ. of Calif, Davis. A Lord in Waiting (Govt Whip), 1995; Parly Under-Sec. of State, Scottish Office, 1995–97; elected Mem., H of L, 1999. Chairman: Assured British Meat, 1997–2001; Aquaculture Scotland, 1998–2000; Scottish Quality Salmon, 1998–2006; Genesis Quality Assurance Ltd, 2001–02; UK Accreditation Service, 2002–; Director: UA Group plc (formerly United Auctions (Scotland) Ltd), 1998–2005; Scottish Resources Gp (formerly Mining (Scotland) Ltd), 2001–; British Polythene Industries plc, 2006–; Bd Mem., Cairngorms Partnership, 1998–2003. Member: UK Round Table on Sustainable Develt, 1998–2000; Better Regulation Commn, 2006– (Vice Chm., 2007–). Trustee, Gardens for the Disabled Trust, 1984–98. Chm., Landscape Foundn, 1991–95; President: Internat. Tree Foundn, 1995–2005 (Vice-Pres., 1994–95, 2005–); RHASS, 2005–06; RSGS, 2005– (Vice-Pres., 2004–05); Mem., Adv. Council, World Resource Foundn, 1994–98. Chm., RSPB Scotland, 1998–2003 (Mem., UK Council, 1998–2003); Vice-Pres., RSPB, 2004–. Chm., Elmwood Coll., 2001–; Dir, Scottish Agricl Coll. Ltd, 2005– (Vice-Chm., 2006–07, Chm., 2007–). Vice-Pres., Royal Smithfield Club, 1999–. ARAgS 2000. DL Fife, 2007. *Publications:* (jtly) Garden Ornament, 1989; Trellis, 1991. *Heir: s* Viscount Garnock, *qv*. *Address:* Lahill, Upper Largo, Fife KY8 6JE.

See also Sir G. R. B. Wrey, Bt.

LINDSAY OF BIRKER, 3rd Baron *cr* 1945, of Low Ground, Co. Cumberland; **James Francis Lindsay;** Co-founder and Chief Technical Officer, Sun Fire Cooking, since 2004; *b* 29 Jan. 1945; *s* of 2nd Baron Lindsay of Birker and of Li Hsiao-li, *d* of Col Li Wen-chi; *S* father, 1994; *m* 1st, 1969, Mary Rose (marr. diss. 1985), *d* of W. G. Thomas, Cwmbran, Mon; no *c*; 2nd, 2000, Pamela Collett, *d* of late Lon Hutchison, Kansas City, Mo. *Educ:* Univ. of Keele (BSc 1966); Univ. of Liverpool (Post-grad. Dip. in transport design). Lectr in physics, Tunghai Univ., Taichung, Taiwan, 1967–68; exploration geophysicist, Darwin, Australia, 1969–70; Australian Foreign Service, 1972–2000; served in Chile, 1973–76; Laos, 1980–81; Bangladesh, 1982–84; Venezuela, 1987–90; Deputy High Commissioner: Pakistan, 1993–96; Kenya, 1996–2000; Dep. Perm. Rep. for Australia to UN Envmt Prog., 1996–2000. Consultant: Horn Relief (formerly Horn of Africa Relief and Develt), 2000–; Uganda Rural Develt and Trng, 2002–03. *Recreations:* hiking, tennis. *Heir: cousin* Alexander Sebastian Lindsay, *b* 27 May 1940. *Address:* 651 Oakland Avenue, Apt 2E, Oakland, CA 94611–4517, USA; *e-mail:* mukinduri@bigfoot.com.

LINDSAY, Master of; Alexander Thomas Lindsay; *b* 5 Aug. 1991; *s* and *heir* of Lord Balniel, *qv*.

LINDSAY, His Honour Crawford Callum Douglas; QC 1987; a Circuit Judge, 1998–2008; *b* 5 Feb. 1939; *s* of Douglas Marshall Lindsay, FRCOG and Eileen Mary Lindsay; *m* 1963, Rosemary Gough; one *s* one *d*. *Educ:* Whitgift Sch., Croydon; St John's Coll., Oxford. Called to the Bar, Lincoln's Inn, 1961, Bencher, 1994. A Recorder, 1982–98. Mem., Criminal Injuries Compensation Bd, 1988. *Clubs:* Garrick, MCC.

LINDSAY, Rt Rev. Hugh; Bishop (RC) of Hexham and Newcastle, 1974–92; *b* 20 June 1927; *s* of William Stanley Lindsay and Mary Ann Lindsay (*née* Warren). *Educ:* St Cuthbert's Grammar Sch., Newcastle upon Tyne; Ushaw Coll., Durham. Priest 1953; Assistant Priest: St Lawrence's, Newcastle upon Tyne, 1953; St Matthew's, Ponteland, 1954; Asst Diocesan Sec., 1953–59, Diocesan Sec., 1959–69, Hexham and Newcastle; Chaplain, St Vincent's Home, West Denton, 1959–69; Auxiliary Bishop of Hexham and Newcastle and Titular Bishop of Chester-le-Street, 1969–74. *Recreations:* walking, swimming. *Address:* Boarbank Hall, Grange-over-Sands, Cumbria LA11 7NH. *T:* (015395) 35591.

LINDSAY of Dowhill, Sir James Martin Evelyn, 3rd Bt *cr* 1962, of Dowhill, co. Kinross; 24th Representer of Baronial House of Dowhill; *b* 11 Oct. 1968; *s* of Sir Ronald Alexander Lindsay of Dowhill, 2nd Bt and of Nicoletta Lindsay; *S* father, 2004; *m* 2000, Annabel Julia, *yr d* of Dr Peter Knight; one *s* one *d*. *Educ:* Shiplake Coll.; RMA Sandhurst; UMIST (BSc). Lieut, Grenadier Guards, 1988–93. Cheshire Yeomanry, 1994– (Major). *Heir: s* Archibald Ronald Frederick Lindsay, *b* 26 Oct. 2004.

LINDSAY, Hon. Sir John (Edmund Fredric), Kt 1992; a Judge of the High Court of Justice, Chancery Division, 1992–2008; *b* 16 Oct. 1935; *s* of late George Fredric Lindsay and Constance Mary Lindsay (*née* Wright); *m* 1967, Patricia Anne Bolton; three *d*. *Educ:* Ellesmere Coll.; Sidney Sussex Coll., Cambridge (BA 1959; MA). Fleet Air Arm, 1954–56; Sub-Lt, RNVR. Called to the Bar, Middle Temple, 1961, Bencher, 1987; joined Lincoln's Inn (*ad eundem*); Junior Treasury Counsel, *bona vacantia*, 1979–81; QC 1981; a Judge of the Employment Appeals Tribunal, 1996–99; Pres., Employment Appeal Tribunal, 1999–2002; a Judge of the Administrative Court, 2002–08. Member: Senate of Inns of Court and Bar, 1979–82; Legal Panel, Insolvency Law Review Cttee (Cork Report), 1980–82; Insolvency Rules Adv. Cttee, 1985–92. *Recreation:* works of A. A. Scott, H. F. S. Morgan, L. van Beethoven and H. R. Godfrey. *Club:* Athenæum.

LINDSAY, (John) Maurice, CBE 1979; TD 1946; Consultant, The Scottish Civic Trust, 1983–2002, now Hon. Trustee (Director, 1967–83); *b* 21 July 1918; *s* of Matthew Lindsay and Eileen Frances Brock; *m* 1946, Aileen Joyce Gordon; one *s* three *d*. *Educ:* Glasgow Acad.; Scottish National Acad. of Music (now Royal Scottish Acad. of Music, Glasgow). Drama Critic, Scottish Daily Mail, Edinburgh, 1946–47; Music Critic, The Bulletin, Glasgow, 1946–60; Prog. Controller, 1961–62, Prodn Controller, 1962–64, and Features Exec. and Chief Interviewer, 1964–67, Border Television, Carlisle. Mem., Historic

Buildings Council for Scotland, 1976–87; Pres., Assoc. for Scottish Literary Studies, 1988–91; Trustee: National Heritage Meml Fund, 1980–84; New Lanark Conservation Trust, 1987–94; Hon. Vice-Pres., Scottish Envmtl Educn Council, 1984–86; Hon. Sec.-Gen., Europa Nostra, 1983–91. Hon. Gov., Glasgow Acad., 2003. Hon. FRIAS 1985. Hon. DLitt Glasgow, 1982. Atlantic Rockefeller Award, 1946. Editor: Scots Review, 1949–50; The Scottish Review, 1975–85. *Publications: poetry:* The Advancing Day, 1940; Perhaps To-morrow, 1941; Predicament, 1942; No Crown for Laughter: Poems, 1943; The Enemies of Love: Poems 1941–1945, 1946; Selected Poems, 1947; Hurlygush: Poems in Scots, 1948; At the Wood's Edge, 1950; Ode for St Andrews Night and Other Poems, 1951; The Exiled Heart: Poems 1941–1956, 1957; Snow Warning and Other Poems, 1962; One Later Day and Other Poems, 1964; This Business of Living, 1969; Comings and Goings: Poems, 1971; Selected Poems 1942–1972, 1973; The Run from Life, 1975; Walking Without an Overcoat, Poems 1972–76, 1977; Collected Poems, 1979; A Net to Catch the Winds and Other Poems, 1981; The French Mosquitoes' Woman and Other Diversions and Poems, 1985; Requiem for a Sexual Athlete and Other Poems and Diversions, 1988; Collected Poems 1940–1990, 1990; On the Face of It: Collected Poems, vol. 2, 1993; News of the World: last poems, 1995; Speaking Likenesses: a postscript, 1997; Worlds Apart, 2000; Looking Up Where Heaven Isn't, 2004; *prose:* A Pocket Guide to Scottish Culture, 1947; The Scottish Renaissance, 1949; The Lowlands of Scotland: Glasgow and the North, 1953, 3rd edn 1979; Robert Burns: The Man, His Work, The Legend, 3rd edn 1980; Dunoon: The Gem of the Clyde Coast, 1954; The Lowlands of Scotland: Edinburgh and the South, 1956, 3rd edn 1979; Clyde Waters: Variations and Diversions on a Theme of Pleasure, 1958; The Burns Encyclopedia, 1959, 4th edn 1995; Killochan Castle, 1960; By Yon Bonnie Banks: A Gallimaufry, 1961; Environment: A Basic Human Right, 1968; Portrait of Glasgow, 1972, rev. edn 1981; Robin Philipson, 1977; History of Scottish Literature, 1977, rev. edn 1992; Lowland Scottish Villages, 1980; Francis George Scott and the Scottish Renaissance, 1980; (with Anthony F. Kersting) The Buildings of Edinburgh, 1981, 2nd edn 1987; Thank You For Having Me: a personal memoir, 1983; (with Dennis Hardley) Unknown Scotland, 1984; The Castles of Scotland, 1986, rev. edn 1994; Count All Men Mortal—A History of Scottish Provident 1837–1987, 1987; Victorian and Edwardian Glasgow, 1987; Glasgow 1837, 1989; (with David Bruce) Edinburgh Past and Present, 1990; (with Joyce Lindsay) Chambers Guide to Good Scottish Gardens, 1995; Glasgow: fabric of a city, 2004; *editor:* Poetry Scotland One, Two, Three, 1943, 1945, 1946, (with Hugh MacDiarmid) Scottish Poetry Four, 1949; Sailing Tomorrow's Seas: An Anthology of New Poems, 1944; Modern Scottish Poetry: An Anthology of the Scottish Renaissance 1920–1945, 1946, 4th edn 1986; (with Fred Urquhart) No Scottish Twilight: New Scottish Stories, 1947; Selected Poems of Sir Alexander Gray, 1948; Poems, by Sir David Lyndsay, 1948; (with Hugh MacDiarmid) Poetry Scotland Four, 1949; (with Helen Cruickshank) Selected Poems of Marion Angus, 1950; John Davidson: A Selection of His Poems, 1961; (with Edwin Morgan and George Bruce) Scottish Poetry One to Six 1966–72; (with Alexander Scott and Roderick Watson) Scottish Poetry Seven to Nine, 1974, 1976, 1977; (with R. L. Mackie) A Book of Scottish Verse, 1967, 3rd edn 1983; The Discovery of Scotland: Based on Accounts of Foreign Travellers from the 13th to the 18th centuries, 1964, 2nd edn 1979; The Eye is Delighted: Some Romantic Travellers in Scotland, 1970; Scotland: An Anthology, 1974, 2nd edn 1989; As I Remember, 1979; Scottish Comic Verse 1425–1980, 1980; (with Alexander Scott) The Comic Poems of William Tennant, 1990; Thomas Hamilton, The Youth and Manhood of Cyril Thornton, 1991; (with Lesley Duncan) The Edinburgh Book of 20th Century Scottish Poetry, 2005; with Joyce Lindsay: The Scottish Dog, 1989; The Scottish Quotation Book, 1991; A Pleasure of Gardens, 1991; The Music Quotation Book, 1992; The Theatre and Opera Lovers' Quotation Book, 1993; A Mini-Guide to Scottish Gardens, 1994; The Robert Burns Quotation Book, 1994. *Recreations:* enjoying and adding to compact disc collection, cooking. *Address:* Park House, 104 Dumbarton Road, Bowling, Dunbartonshire G60 5BB. *T:* (01389) 606662.

LINDSAY, Most Rev. and Hon. Orland Ugham, OJ 1997; OD (Antigua) 1996; Archbishop of the West Indies, 1986–98; Bishop of the North-Eastern Caribbean and Aruba (formerly Antigua), 1970–98; *b* 24 March 1928; *s* of Hubert and Ida Lindsay; *m* 1959, Olga Daphne (*née* Wright); three *s*. *Educ:* Culham Coll., Oxon (Teachers' Cert.); St Peter's Coll., Jamaica; McGill Univ. BD (London) 1957. RAF, 1944–47. Teacher, Franklyn Town Govt School, Jamaica, 1949–52; Asst Master, Kingston College, 1952–53. Deacon 1956, priest 1957; Asst Curate, St Peter's Vere, Jamaica, 1956–57; Asst Master, Kingston Coll., 1958–67, Chaplain 1962–63; Priest-in-Charge, Manchioneal Cure, Jamaica, 1960; Chaplain, Jamaica Defence Force, 1963–67; Principal, Church Teachers' Coll., Mandeville, 1967–70. Sec. to Jamaica Synod, 1962–70. Hon. DD: Berkeley Divinity School at Yale, 1978; St Paul's Coll., Va, 1998; Hon. STD, Montreal Diocesan Theol Coll., 1997. *Recreations:* jazz music, photography. *Address:* Flagstaff, Crosbies, PO Box 3456, St John's, Antigua.

LINDSAY, Robert; *see* Stevenson, R. L.

LINDSAY, Shuna Taylor, (Mrs D. R. Waggott), CBE 2001; Director, Defence Management Consultancy Services, Ministry of Defence, since 2007; *b* 24 Nov. 1954; *d* of John Lindsay and late Jessie Simpson Lindsay (*née* Taylor); *m* 1979, David Reginald Waggott. *Educ:* Greenock Acad.; Univ. of Geneva (Cert. d'Etudes Françaises 1975); Univ. of Aberdeen (MA Hons French Studies 1977). Entered MoD as admin trainee, 1977; policy appts, 1977–81; Private Sec. to Air Mem. for Supply and Orgn, 1981–82; First Sec., Defence Procurement, Paris, 1989–93; Project Dir, Mil. Aircraft Projects, 1998–99; Integrated Project Team Leader for Airlift and Future Tanker Progs, 2000–01; on secondment to Rand, Calif, 2001–02; Minister, Defence Materiel, Washington, 2002–04; Dir Gen., Acquisition People, MoD, 2005–06. *Publication:* (jtly) Re-examining Military Acquisition Reform: are we there yet?, 2005. *Recreations:* music, building wooden replica model warships, collecting dolphins, walking the dog, playing golf badly. *Address:* c/o Ministry of Defence, 6.I.25, Whitehall, SW1A 2HB. *T:* (020) 7218 4086, *Fax:* (020) 7218 0223; *e-mail:* Shuna.Lindsay863@mod.uk.

LINDSAY-HOGG, Sir Michael Edward, 5th Bt *cr* 1905, of Rotherfield Hall, Rotherfield, Sussex; film and theatre director; *b* 5 May 1940; *o s* of Sir Edward William Lindsay-Hogg, 4th Bt and Geraldine Mary, *d* of E. M. Fitzgerald; *S* father, 1999, but his name does not appear on the Official Roll of the Baronetage; *m* 1st, 1967, Lucy Mary (marr. diss. 1971), *o d* of Donald Davies; 2nd, 2002, Lisa, *e d* of Benjamin Holt Ticknor III. *Films* include: Let It Be, 1970; Nasty Habits, 1977; Dr Fischer of Geneva, 1983; The Object of Beauty, 1992; Frankie Starlight, 1996; *theatre* includes: Whose Life Is It Anyway?, Mermaid, 1978, transf. NY, 1979; *television* includes: Electra, 1962; Professional Foul, 1977; (co-dir) Brideshead Revisited, 1981. *Heir:* none.

LINDSAY-SMITH, Iain-Mór; Deputy Managing Director, 1987–90, Chief Executive and Managing Director, 1991–97, and Executive Deputy Chairman, 1997–98, Lloyd's of London Press Ltd, later LLP Group Ltd; Chairman, Lloyds List, 1990–98 (Publisher, 1984–98); *b* 18 Sept. 1934; *s* of Edward Duncanson Lindsay-Smith and Margaret Wilson Anderson; *m* 1960, Carol Sara Paxman (marr. diss. 1997); one *s*. *Educ:* High Sch. of Glasgow; London Univ. (diploma course on Internat. Affairs). Scottish Daily Record, 1951–57; Commissioned 1st Bn Cameronians (Scottish Rifles), 1953–55; Daily Mirror, 1957–60; Foreign Editor, subseq. Features Editor, Daily Mail, 1960–71; Dep. Editor, Yorkshire Post, 1971–74; Editor, Glasgow Herald, 1974–77; Exec. Editor, The Observer, 1977–84. Lloyd's of London Press, subseq. LLP Ltd: Exec. Dir, 1984–87; Chm. and Chief Exec., Lloyd's, then LLP, Information Services Ltd, 1990–98; Chm., LLP Business Publishing Ltd, 1990–98; Director: LLP Incorporated, USA, 1985–97 (Chm., 1992–97); LLP Asia, 1989–98; LLP GmbH, Germany, 1989–96; Lloyd's Maritime Information Services Ltd, 1990–97 (Chm., 1993–97); Lloyd's Maritime Information Services Inc., USA, 1990–97 (Chm., 1992–97); Lutine Publications Ltd, 1984–97 (Chm., 1992–97); Internat. Art & Antique Loss Register Ltd, 1990–97; PPA, 1992–98; DYP Gp Ltd, 1995–98; IBJ Associates Ltd, 1995–98; Cotton Investments Ltd, 1995–98. Dir, Mercury Th., Colchester, 1990–95. Member: Little Horkesley Parish Council, 1987–91; PCC, 1985–92. Chm., Glasgow Newspaper Press Fund, 1974–77. Friend, RA, 2000–. Founding Fellow, Inst. of Contemp. Scotland, 2001–. FRSA 1992. *Publication:* article in Electronics and Power. *Recreations:* shooting (game and clay), playing Highland bagpipe, the outdoors. *Club:* Travellers.

LINDSELL, David Clive, FCA; Partner, Ernst & Young, since 1978; Global Director, International Financial Reporting Standards, Ernst & Young International, since 2003; *b* 9 May 1947; *s* of late Alfred and Florence Lindsell; partner, Felicity Hother; two *d*. *Educ:* Haberdashers' Aske's, Hampstead; Elstree Sch.; Christ's Coll., Cambridge (BA 1968). FCA 1972. Joined Ernst & Young, 1969; Ernst & Young International: Dir, Planning and Mktg, 1985–88; Chm., Accounting and Auditing Standards Cttee, 1989–95; Chm., Multinat. Client Gp, 1995–99; Mem. Council, Ernst & Young UK, 1991–. Institute of Chartered Accountants in England and Wales: Member: Business Law Cttee, 1989–94; Turnbull Cttee, 1999; Chm., Co. Law Sub-Cttee, 1989–94. Member: Oil Industry Accounting Cttee, 1982–85; Auditing Practices Bd for UK and Ireland, 1994–2002 (Mem., Ethics Gp, 2003–04); Bd, Eur. Financial Reporting Adv. Gp, 2004–; Standards Adv. Council, Internat. Accounting Standards Bd, 2005–; Financial Reporting Rev. Panel, 2007–. Trustee, BM, 1999– (Mem., Friends' Council, 2004–). Governor: Cranleigh Sch., 1979–85; St Albans Sch., 1995–. *Recreations:* playing and listening to jazz, museums and galleries, theatre, opera. *Address:* Ernst & Young, Becket House, 1 Lambeth Palace Road, SE1 7EU. *Club:* Oxford and Cambridge.

LINDSEY, 14th Earl of, *cr* 1626, **AND ABINGDON,** 9th Earl of, *cr* 1682; **Richard Henry Rupert Bertie;** Baron Norreys, of Rycote, 1572; *b* 28 June 1931; *o s* of Lt-Col Hon. Arthur Michael Bertie, DSO, MC (*d* 1957) and Aline Rose (*d* 1948), *er d* of George Arbuthnot-Leslie, Warthill, Co. Aberdeen, and *widow* of Hon. Charles Fox Maule Ramsay, MC; *S* cousin, 1963; *m* 1957, Norah Elizabeth Farquhar-Oliver, *yr d* of late Mark Oliver, OBE; two *s* one *d*. *Educ:* Ampleforth. Late Lieut, Royal Norfolk Regt. Insurance broker and underwriting agent at Lloyd's, 1958–92. Chm., Dawes and Henderson (Agencies) Ltd, 1988–92. Chm., Anglo-Ivory-Coast Soc., 1974–77. High Steward of Abingdon, 1963–. *Heir:* *s* Lord Norreys, *qv*. *Address:* Gilmilnscroft House, Sorn, Mauchline, Ayrshire KA5 6ND. *Clubs:* Turf, Pratt's.

LINE, Frances Mary, (Mrs James Lloyd), OBE 1996; Controller, BBC Radio 2, 1990–96; *b* 22 Feb. 1940; *d* of Charles Edward Line and Leoni Lucy Line (*née* Hendriks); *m* 1972, James Richard Beilby Lloyd. *Educ:* James Allen's Girls' Sch., Dulwich. Joined BBC as clerk/typist, 1957; Sec. in TV and Radio, 1959–67; Radio 2 producer, 1967–73; senior producer, 1973–79; Chief Assistant: Radio 2, 1979–83; Radio 4, 1983–85; Head, Radio 2 Music Dept, 1985–89. Vice-Pres., Eastbourne Soc., 1998–. Hon. Fellow, Radio Acad., 1996. *Recreations:* visual arts, travel, happy snaps. *Address:* 13 Naomi Close, Eastbourne, E Sussex BN20 7UU.

LINE, Matthew John Bardsley; Editorial Director, Craft Publishing, since 2007; *b* 22 April 1958; *s* of John Line and Jill Line (*née* Rowland); *m* 1987, Elinor Jane Fairhurst; two *d*. *Educ:* Chiswick Sch.; Exeter Univ. (BA Hons Drama). Actor, 1982; Asst Publisher, Shepheard-Walwyn Publishers, 1984–87; Production Dir, Concertina Publications, 1988; freelance journalist, 1987–92; Editor: Up Country, 1992–93; Dialogue, 1993–95; Launch Editor, Colour, 1995; Gp Editor, home interest titles, Redwood Publishing, 1996–97; Ed., Homes & Gardens, 1997–2002; Chief Exec., The Prince's Foundn, 2002–04; Ed. in Chief, relaunched She, 2004–06; Editl Consultant, Rich, 2006. Launched annual Homes & Gardens V&A Mus. Classic Design Awards, 1999–. *Publication:* Homes & Gardens Book of Design, 2000. *Recreations:* family, gardening, philosophy. *Address:* Craft Publishing, 105-106 New Bond Street, W1S 1DN.

LINE, Maurice Bernard, FCLIP; Director General (Science, Technology and Industry), British Library, 1985–88 (Deputy Director General, 1973–74, Director General, 1974–85, Lending Division); *b* 21 June 1928; *s* of Bernard Cyril and Ruth Florence Line; *m* 1954, Joyce Gilchrist; one *s* one *d*. *Educ:* Bedford Sch.; Exeter Coll., Oxford (MA). Library Trainee, Bodleian Library, 1950–51; Library Asst, Glasgow Univ., 1951–53; Sub-Librarian, Southampton Univ., 1954–65; Dep. Librarian, Univ. of Newcastle upon Tyne, 1965–68; Librarian, Univ. of Bath, 1968–71; Librarian, Nat. Central Library, 1971–73; Project Head, DES Nat. Libraries ADP Study, 1970–71. Prof. Associate, Sheffield Univ., 1977–; External Prof., Loughborough Univ., 1986–92. Member: Library Adv. Council for England, 1972–75; British Library Board, 1974–88; Pres., Library Assoc., 1990. Editor, Alexandria, 1988–2002; Gen. Editor, Librarianship and Information Work Worldwide, 1990–2000. Mem. Bd of Dirs, Engineering Information Inc., 1990–98. Fellow, Birmingham Polytech., 1992. CCMI. Hon. DLitt Heriot Watt, 1980; Hon. DSc Southampton, 1988. *Publications:* A Bibliography of Russian Literature in English Translation to 1900, 1963; Library Surveys, 1967, 2nd edn 1982; (ed jtly) Essays on Information and Libraries, 1975; (ed with Joyce Line) National Libraries, 1979; (jtly) Universal Availability of Publications, 1983; (jtly) Improving the Availability of Publications, 1984; (ed) The World of Books and Information, 1987; (ed with Joyce Line) National Libraries II, 1987; (jtly) The Impact of New Technology on Document Availability and Access, 1988; Line on Interlending, 1988; A Little Off Line, 1988; (ed) Academic Library Management, 1990; (ed with Joyce Line) National Libraries III, 1995; contribs to: Jl of Documentation; Aslib Proc.; Jl of Librarianship and Information Science, etc. *Recreations:* music, walking, other people. *Address:* 10 Blackthorn Lane, Burn Bridge, Harrogate, North Yorks HG3 1NZ. *T:* (01423) 872984.

LINEHAN, Anthony John; President, Construction Health & Safety Group, 1993–2003; *b* 27 June 1931; *s* of Daniel and Ada Linehan; *m* 1955, Oonagh Patricia FitzPatrick; two *s* two *d*. *Educ:* Bristol Univ. (BA Hons 1952). Short Service Commission, RN, 1953–57. HM Factory Inspectorate: joined 1958; HM District Inspector, 1969; Labour Adviser, Hong Kong Govt, 1973–76; Health and Safety Executive: HQ, 1976–79; Area Dir, Wales, 1979–84; HM Dep. Chief Inspector of Factories, 1984–88; Chief Inspector of Factories, 1988–92; Dir of Field Ops, 1990–92. *Recreations:* walking, reading, watching Rugby. *Address:* 2 Brookside Manor, Leigh Road, Wimborne, Dorset BH21 2BZ. *T:* (01202) 848597.

LINEHAN, Dr Peter Anthony, FBA 2002; FRHistS; Fellow, since 1966, Lecturer, since 1969, and Dean, since 1999, St John's College, Cambridge; *b* 11 July 1943; *er s* of John

James Linehan and Kathleen Margaret Linehan (*née* Farrell); *m* 1971, Christine Ann Callaghan; one *s* two *d*. *Educ:* St Benedict's Sch., Ealing; St John's Coll., Cambridge (Mullinger Schol.; BA 1st Cl. 1964, MA 1968 (Thirlwall Prizeman and Seeley Medallist), PhD 1968). FRHistS 1971. St John's College, Cambridge: Res. Fellow, 1966–69; Tutor, 1977–97; Tutor for Grad. Affairs, 1983–97; University of Cambridge: Sen. Proctor, 1976–77; affiliated lectr, Faculty of Hist., 1986–92. Woodward Lectr, Yale Univ., 1999; Birkbeck Lectr in Ecclesiastical Hist., Trinity Coll., Cambridge, 1999. Co-Ed., Jl Ecclesiastical Hist., 1979–91. Member: Accad. Senese degli Intronati, 1988; IAS, Princeton, NJ, 1988; Comissão Permanente de Aconselhamento Científico, Centro Interdisciplinar de História, Culturas e Sociedades, Univ. de Évora, Portugal, 2001; Séminaire Interdisciplinaire de Recherches sur l'Espagne Médiévale, CNRS, Univ. of Paris 13, 2000. Corresp. Mem., Real Acad. de la Historia, Madrid, 1996. Gov., Giggleswick Sch., 1983–96. Antiquary Prizeman, Univ. of Edinburgh, 1985. *Publications:* The Spanish Church and the Papacy in the Thirteenth Century, 1971 (trans. Spanish 1975); (ed with B. Tierney) Authority and Power, 1980; Spanish Church and Society 1150–1300, 1983; (ed) Proceedings of the Seventh International Congress of Medieval Canon Law 1984, 1988; Past and Present in Medieval Spain, 1992; History and the Historians of Medieval Spain, 1993; The Ladies of Zamora, 1997 (trans. French 1998, Spanish 2000, Portuguese 2008); (ed) Life, Law and Letters, 1998; (ed with J. L. Nelson) The Medieval World, 2001; The Processes of Politics and the Rule of Law, 2002; (with J. C. de Lera Maíllo) Las postrimerías de un obispo alfonsino, 2003; (with F. J. Hernández) The Mozarabic Cardinal, 2004; Spain, 1157–1300: a partible inheritance, 2008; (ed with S. Barton) Cross, Crescent and Conversion, 2008; contribs to learned jls. *Recreation:* reading obituaries, humming. *Address:* Brookside, 20 Glebe Way, Impington, Cambs CB24 9HJ. *T:* (01223) 233934; St John's College, Cambridge CB2 1TP. *T:* (01223) 338720; *e-mail:* pal35@cam.ac.uk. *Club:* Hawks (Cambridge).

LINEHAN, Stephen; QC 1993; a Recorder, since 1990; *b* 12 March 1947; *s* of Maurice Gerald Linehan and Mary Joyce (*née* Norrish); *m* 1976, Victoria Maria Rössler; one *s*. *Educ:* Mount St Mary's Coll., Spinkhill, Derbys; King's Coll., London (LLB Hons). Called to the Bar, Lincoln's Inn, 1970, Bencher, 1999. *Address:* St Philips Chambers, 55 Temple Row, Birmingham B2 5LS. *T:* (0121) 246 7000.

LINEKER, Gary Winston, OBE 1992; journalist and broadcaster; professional footballer, 1976–94; *b* 30 Nov. 1960; *s* of Barry and Margaret Lineker; *m* 1986, Michelle Cockayne (marr. diss. 2006); four *s*. Football Clubs played for: Leicester City, 1976–85; Everton, 1985–86; Barcelona, 1986–89; Tottenham Hotspur, 1989–92; Nagoya Grampus 8, 1993–94; England team, 1984–92: Captain, 1990–92; 80 appearances, 48 goals. Presenter, Match of the Day, BBC TV, 1995–. Freeman, City of Leicester, 1995. Hon. MA: Loughborough, 1992; Leicester, 1992. *Recreations:* golf, cricket, snooker. *Address:* c/o Jon Holmes Media Ltd, 5th Floor, Holborn Gate, 26 Southampton Buildings, WC2A 1PQ. *T:* (020) 7861 2550. *Clubs:* Groucho, MCC.

LINFORD, Alan C.; *see* Carr Linford.

LING, Jeffrey, CMG 1991; HM Diplomatic Service, retired; Chairman and Chief Executive, Dean & Drysdale Ltd, 1999–2007; *b* 9 Sept. 1939; *s* of Frank Cecil Ling and Mary Irene Nixon; *m* 1967, Margaret Anne Tatton; one *s*. *Educ:* Bristol Univ. BSc (Hons); FInstP; FIMgt; FBCS. FCO, 1966–69; Private Sec. to HM Ambassador, Washington, 1969–71; First Sec., Washington, 1971–73; Perm. Delegn to OECD, Paris, 1973–77; FCO, 1977–79; on secondment as Special Adviser to HM the Sultan of Brunei, 1979–82; Counsellor (Technology), Paris, 1982–86; Dir of Res., FCO, 1986–89; Asst Under-Sec. of State and Dir of Communications, subseq. of Information Systems, FCO, 1989–96; Dir Gen., Trade and Inward Investment in US, and Consul-Gen., NY, 1996–99. Dir (non-exec.), RTZ Borax and Minerals, 1991–96; Member, International Advisory Board: Buchanan Ingersoll, 2000–02; Sabatier Gp, NY, 2002–04; Chairman: Soho 4 Associates, 2000–03; Casmir Ltd, 2001–02; Special Advr to Chm. and CEO, Maxim Pharmaceuticals, 2000–05; Advisor: to CEO of Basepoint plc, 2000–03; Cedar Gp plc, 2000–01; Bd, E-Lynxx Corp., 2000–04; to Man. Dir of Dorsey and Whitney, 2002–04; to Chm. of London First, 2002–04. Chm., London New York City Alliance, 2000–01. *Recreation:* golf.

LING, Norman Arthur; HM Diplomatic Service; Ambassador to the Federal Democratic Republic of Ethiopia, Djibouti and the African Union, since 2008; *b* 12 Aug. 1952; *s* of late William Arthur Ling and of Helma Ling (*née* Blum); *m* 1979, Selma Osman. *Educ:* Sheffield Univ. (BA Hons German and Econ. Hist.). British Commercial Transport, 1975–76; Ocean Transport and Trading, 1976–78; joined Diplomatic Service, 1978; FCO, 1978–80; Second Sec., Tripoli, 1980–81; Second, later First, Sec., British Interests Section, Tehran, 1981–84; FCO, 1984–88; Dep. Consul Gen., Johannesburg, 1988–92; Dep. Head of Mission, Ankara, 1993–97; Head, Aviation, Maritime, Sci. and Energy Dept, FCO, 1997–2001; High Comr, Malaŵi, 2001–04; Change Dir, FCO, 2005–07. *Recreations:* travel, walking, organic farming. *Address:* c/o Foreign and Commonwealth Office, King Charles Street, SW1A 2AH.

LING, Prof. Roger John, PhD; FSA; Professor of Classical Art and Archaeology, University of Manchester, since 1992; *b* 13 Nov. 1942; *s* of Leslie James Ling and Kathleen Clara Ling (*née* Childs); *m* 1967, Lesley Ann Steer. *Educ:* Watford Grammar Sch.; St John's Coll., Cambridge (BA 1964; MA 1969; PhD 1970). FSA 1979. Lectr in Classics, UC of Swansea, 1967–71; University of Manchester: Lectr in History of Art, 1971–75; Sen. Lectr, 1975–83; Reader, 1983–92; Head of Dept of Hist. of Art, 1988–91. British Acad. Res. Reader, 1991–93; Balsdon Sen. Res. Fellow, British Sch. at Rome, 1994–95. *Publications:* The Greek World, 1976, 2nd edn as Classical Greece, 1988; (jtly) Wall Painting in Roman Britain, 1982; (ed) Cambridge Ancient History, vol. VII.1, 1984; Romano-British Wall Painting, 1985; Roman Painting, 1991; The Insula of the Menander at Pompeii I: the structures, 1997; Ancient Mosaics, 1998; Stuccowork and Painting in Roman Italy, 1999; (ed) Making Classical Art: process and practice, 2000; (with L. A. Ling) The Insula of the Menander at Pompeii II: the decorations, 2005; Pompeii: history, life and afterlife, 2005; numerous articles in learned jls. *Recreations:* fresh air and exercise, watching football. *Address:* School of Arts, Histories and Cultures, University of Manchester, Manchester M13 9PL. *T:* (0161) 275 3320.

LINGARD, Joan Amelia, MBE 1998; author, since 1963; *b* 1932; *d* of Henry James Lingard; *m* Martin Birkhans; three *d*. *Educ:* Bloomfield Collegiate Sch., Belfast; Moray House Coll. of Educn (Gen. Teaching Cert.). *Publications: novels:* Liam's Daughter, 1963; The Prevailing Wind, 1964; The Tide Comes In, 1966; The Headmaster, 1967; A Sort of Freedom, 1968; The Lord on Our Side, 1970; The Second Flowering of Emily Mountjoy; Greenyards; Reasonable Doubts, 1979; The Women's House, 1981; Sisters by Rite, 1984; After Colette, 1993 (Scottish Arts Council Award); Dreams of Love and Modest Glory, 1995; The Kiss, 2002; Encarnita's Journey, 2005; After You've Gone, 2007; *children's novels:* The Twelfth Day of July, 1970; Frying as Usual, 1971; Across the Barricades, 1972 (Buxtehude Bülle, 1986); Into Exile, 1973; The Clearance, 1973; A Proper Place; The Resettling; Hostages to Fortune; The Pilgrimage, 1975; The Reunion, 1977; Snake among the Sunflowers, 1977; The Gooseberry, 1978; The File on Fraulein Berg, 1980; Strangers in the House, 1981; The Winter Visitor, 1983; The Freedom Machine, 1986; The Guilty Party, 1987; Rags and Riches, 1988; Tug of War, 1989; Glad Rags, 1990; Between Two Worlds, 1991; Secrets and Surprises, 1991; Hands off Our School, 1992; Night Fires, 1993; Clever Clive and Loopy Lucy, 1993; Slo Flo and Boomerang Bill, 1994; Sulky Suzy and Jittery Jack, 1995; Lizzie's Leaving, 1996; Morag and the Lamb, 1996; Dark Shadows, 1998; A Secret Place, 1998; Tom and the Tree House, 1998 (Scottish Arts Council Award); Can You Find Sammy the Hamster?, 1998; The Egg Thieves, 1999; River Eyes, 2000; Natasha's Will, 2000; The Same Only Different, 2000; Me and My Shadow, 2001; Tortoise Trouble, 2002; Tell the Moon to Come Out, 2003; Tilly and the Wild Goats, 2005; The Sign of the Black Dagger, 2005. *Recreations:* reading, walking, travelling. *Address:* c/o David Higham Associates, 5/8 Lower John Street, Golden Square, W1R 4HA. *T:* (020) 7437 7888. *Club:* Lansdowne.

LINGARD, Robin Anthony; owner/manager, Kinnairdie Consulting, since 1997; *b* 19 July 1941; *s* of late Cecil Lingard and Lucy Lingard; *m* 1968, Margaret Lucy Virginia Elsden; two *d*. *Educ:* Felsted School; Emmanuel College, Cambridge (Exhibnr, MA). Min. of Aviation, 1963–66; Min. of Technology, 1966–70 (Private Sec. to Jt Parly Sec., 1966–68); DTI, 1971–74; DoI, 1974–83, Asst Sec., 1976; Under Sec., DTI, 1984, Cabinet Office (Enterprise Unit), 1984–85; Hd, Small Firms and Tourism Div., Dept of Employment, 1985–87; Mem. Bd, Highlands and Islands Develt Bd, 1988–91; Dir of Trng and Social Develt, 1991–93, Dir of Highlands and Is Univ. Project, 1993–97, Highlands and Islands Enterprise. Member: NEDC Sector Gp for Tourism and Leisure Industries, 1987–92; Scottish Tourist Bd, 1988–92; Management Bd, Prince's Trust and Royal Jubilee Trusts, 1989–95; Chairman: Highlands, Orkney and Western Isles Cttee, Prince's Trust, 1992–98; YouthLink Scotland, 1997–2000; BBC Scotland Appeals Adv. Cttee, 1998–2004; Fusion Scotland, 2002–05; Sustainable Develt Res. Centre, 2005–; Highland Community Care Forum, 2007–. FTS 1988. *Recreations:* reading, walking, watching birds, aviation history, dinghy sailing. *Address:* Kinnairdie House, Dingwall, Ross-shire IV15 9LL. *T:* (01349) 861044.

LINGWOOD, James; Co-Director: Artangel, since 1991; Artangel Media Ltd, since 2000; *b* 28 May 1959; *s* of Robert Lingwood and Patricia Brown; partner, Jane Hamlyn; one *s* two *d*. *Educ:* Corpus Christi Coll., Oxford (BA Hons Mod. Hist. 1979; MPhil dist. Art Hist. 1980). Curator: Inst. of Contemporary Arts, 1986–90; TSWA Sculpture Projects, 1987–90; independent curator, internat. museums, 1992–. Trustee: Paul Hamlyn Foundn, 2003–; Art Fund, 2008–. Mem. Internat. Adv. Bd, Museu Serralves, Porto. *Publications:* (jtly) Une Autre Objective, 1989; (ed) Rachel Whiteread, House, 1993; Robert Smithson: the entropic landscape, 1993; The Epic and the Everyday: contemporary photographic art, 1994; Juan Muñoz: monologues and dialogues, 1996; (ed) Vija Celmins: works 1963–1996, 1997; Juan Muñoz: Double Bind, 2001; (ed) Field Trips: Robert Smithson, Bernd and Hilla Becher, 2002; (jtly) Off Limits: 40 Artangel projects, 2002; Susan Hiller: Recall, 2004; (ed and contrib.) Francis Alÿs: Seven Walks, 2005; (ed) Gregor Schneider: Die Familie Schneider, 2006; (contrib.) Thomas Schütte: Political Work, 2007. *Address:* Artangel, 31 Eyre Street Hill, EC1R 5EW. *T:* (020) 7713 1400, *Fax:* (020) 7713 1401; *e-mail:* jl@artangel.org.uk. *Club:* MCC.

LINK, Joan Irene, LVO 1992; HM Diplomatic Service, retired; independent consultant in human resources and business coaching, since 2007; *b* 3 March 1953; *d* of William and Kathleen Mary Wilmot; *m* (marr. diss.); two *s*. *Educ:* Pear Tree Infant and Jun. Schs, Derby; Homelands Grammar Sch. for Girls, Derby; Lady Margaret Hall, Oxford (BA Mod. Langs); Open Univ. (Dip. Internat. Relns). FCIPD. Entered FCO, 1974; UK Delegn to the Cttee on Disarmament, 1980–83; Hd, Press and Inf., British Embassy, FRG, 1990–94; Hd, Resource Mgt Gp, 1996–2001, Hd, Conflict Prevention Unit, 2002–04, Hd, Conflict Issues Gp, 2004–07, FCO. Trustee: Gender Action for Peace and Security; Peace Direct. *Recreations:* talking and walking along British canals, theatre, reading, support to the cause of women in conflict countries, thinking of all the millions of other things I want to do. *Address:* c/o Foreign and Commonwealth Office, King Charles Street, SW1A 2AH.

LINKIE, William Sinclair, CBE 1989; Controller, Inland Revenue (Scotland), 1983–90; *b* 9 March 1931; *s* of late Peter Linkie and Janet Black Linkie (*née* Sinclair; she *m* 2nd, John McBryde); *m* 1955, Elizabeth Primrose Marion Reid (*d* 2003); one *s* one *d*. *Educ:* George Heriot's Sch., Edinburgh. Dept of Agriculture and Fisheries for Scotland, 1948; Inland Revenue (Scotland), 1952–90: HM Inspector of Taxes, 1961; Dist Inspector, Edinburgh 6, 1964; Principal Inspector i/c Centre I, 1975; Dist Inspector, Edinburgh 5, 1982. Pres., Inland Revenue Sports Assoc. (Scotland), 1983–90. Elder, Church of Scotland. *Recreations:* art, theatre, travel.

LINKLATER, family name of **Baroness Linklater of Butterstone**.

LINKLATER OF BUTTERSTONE, Baroness *cr* 1997 (Life Peer), of Riemore in Perth and Kinross; **Veronica Linklater;** Founder, 1991, and Executive Chairman, 1991–2004, The New School, Butterstone; *b* 15 April 1943; *d* of late Lt-Col A. M. Lyle, OBE, and Hon. Elizabeth Lyle, *y d* of 1st Viscount Thurso, KT, CMG, PC; *m* 1967, Magnus Duncan Linklater, *qv*; two *s* one *d*. *Educ:* Cranborne Chase Sch.; Univ. of Sussex; Univ. of London (DipSoc Admin). Child Care Officer, 1967–68; Co-Founder, Visitors' Centre, Pentonville Prison, 1971–77; Winchester prison project, Prison Reform Trust, 1981–82; Founder, Administrator, then Consultant, The Butler Trust, 1983–87 (Trustee, 1987–2001; Vice Pres., 2001–); Trustee, Esmée Fairbairn Foundn, 1991–; Dir, Maggie Keswick Jencks Cancer Caring Centres Trust, 1997–2004. Chm., H of L All-Party Gp on Offender Learning and Skills, 2005–06. Chm., Rethinking Crime and Punishment, 2001–; Pres., Crime Reduction Initiative, 2007–; Member: Children's Panel, Edinburgh S, 1989–97; Scottish Assoc. for the Study of Offending, 2005–. Member: Scottish Cttee, Barnardo's, 2001–04; Adv. Bd, Beacon Fellowship Charitable Trust, 2003–; Council, Winston Churchill Meml Trust, 2005–. Co-ordinator, Trustee and Vice Chm., Pushkin Prizes (Scotland), 1989–; Trustee: Lyle Charitable Trust, 2001–; Riemore Trust, 2007–; Adviser, Koestler Award Trust, 2004–. Pres., Soc. of Friends of Dunkeld Cathedral, 1989–. Patron: Airborne Initiative, 1998–2004; Nat. Schizophrenia Fellowship Scotland, 2000–; Nat. Family & Parenting Inst., 2002–; Research Autism (formerly Autism Intervention Res. Trust), 2004–; The Calyx—Scotland's Garden Trust, 2004–; Probation Bds Assoc., 2005–; Action for Prisoners' Families, 2005–; Univ. of St Andrews Medical Campaign Cttee, 2007–; PUSH, 2007–; Home Start, 2007–. Contested (Lib Dem) Perth and Kinross, May 1995. JP Inner London, 1985–88. *Recreations:* music, theatre, gardening. *Address:* 5 Drummond Place, Edinburgh EH3 6PH. *T:* (0131) 557 5705, *Fax:* (0131) 557 9757; *e-mail:* v.linklater@blueyonder.co.uk.

LINKLATER, Prof. Andrew, PhD; FBA 2005; Woodrow Wilson Professor of International Politics, Aberystwyth University (formerly University of Wales, Aberystwyth), since 2000; *b* 3 Aug. 1949; *s* of Andrew Linklater and Isabella (*née* Forsyth); *m* 1971, Jane Adam. *Educ:* Univ. of Aberdeen (MA 1971); Balliol Coll., Oxford (BPhil 1973); London Sch. of Econs (PhD 1978). Lectr, Univ. of Tasmania, 1976–81; Lectr, 1982–84, Sen. Lectr, 1985–91, Associate Prof., 1992, Monash Univ.; Prof., Keele Univ., 1993–99. *Publications:* Men and Citizens in the Theory of International Relations, 1982,

2nd edn 1990; Beyond Realism and Marxism, 1990; The Transformation of Political Community, 1998; (with H. Suganami) The English School of International Relations, 2006; Criminal Theory and World Politics: citizenship, sovereignty and humanity, 2007. *Recreations:* the Turf, Australian aboriginal art, woodland work, ECM recordings, guitar practice. *Address:* Department of International Politics, Aberystwyth University, Aberystwyth SY23 3DA. *T:* (01970) 621596; *e-mail:* adl@aber.ac.uk.

LINKLATER, Magnus Duncan, FRSE; Scotland Editor, The Times, since 2007; *b* 21 Feb. 1942; *s* of late Eric Robert Linklater, CBE, TD, and Marjorie MacIntyre; *m* 1967, Veronica Lyle (*see* Baroness Linklater of Butterstone); two *s* one *d*. *Educ:* Eton Coll.; Freiburg Univ.; Sorbonne; Trinity Hall, Cambridge (BA 2nd Cl. Hons (Mod. Lang.)). Reporter, Daily Express, Manchester, 1965–66; Diary Reporter, London Evening Standard, 1966–67; Editor: Londoner's Diary, Evening Standard, 1967–69; 'Spectrum', Sunday Times, 1969–72; Sunday Times Colour Magazine, 1972–75; Assistant Editor: News, Sunday Times, 1975–79; Features, Sunday Times, 1979–81; Exec. Editor (Features), Sunday Times, 1981–83; Man. Editor (News), The Observer, 1983–86; Editor: London Daily News, 1987; The Scotsman, 1988–94; columnist: The Times, 1994–; Scotland on Sunday, 1998–2007; broadcaster, Radio Scotland, 1994–97. Chairman: Edinburgh Book Fest., 1995–96; Scottish Arts Council, 1996–2001. Mem. judging panel, 2008 City of Culture, 2002–03. Chm., Little Sparta Trust, 2001–. FRSE 2002. Hon. DArts Napier, 1994; Hon. LLD Aberdeen, 1997; Hon. DLitt: Glasgow, 2001; Queen Margaret Univ. Lifetime Achievement Award, Scottish Daily Newspaper Soc., 2005. *Publications:* (with Stephen Fay and Lewis Chester) Hoax—The Inside Story of the Howard Hughes/Clifford Irving Affair, 1972; (with Lewis Chester and David May) Jeremy Thorpe: a secret life, 1979; Massacre: the story of Glencoe, 1982; (with the Sunday Times Insight Team) The Falklands War, 1982; (with Isabel Hilton and Neal Ascherson) The Fourth Reich—Klaus Barbie and the Neo-Fascist Connection, 1984; (with Douglas Corrance) Scotland, 1984; (contrib.) A Scottish Childhood, 1985; (with David Leigh) Not With Honour: inside story of the Westland Scandal, 1986; (with Christian Hesketh) For King and Conscience: the life of John Graham of Claverhouse, Viscount Dundee, 1989; (ed jtly) Anatomy of Scotland, 1992; (with Colin Prior) Highland Wilderness, 1993; People in a Landscape, 1997. *Recreations:* fishing, book-collecting. *Address:* 5 Drummond Place, Edinburgh EH3 6PH. *T:* (0131) 557 5705; *e-mail:* magnus.linklater@blueyonder.co.uk. *Club:* MCC.

LINLEY, Viscount; David Albert Charles Armstrong-Jones; *b* 3 Nov. 1961; *s* and *heir* of 1st Earl of Snowdon, *qv*, and *s* of HRH the Princess Margaret, CI, GCVO (*d* 2002); *m* 1993, Hon. Serena Alleyne Stanhope, *o d* of Viscount Petersham, *qv*; one *s* one *d*. *Educ:* Bedales; Parnham School for Craftsmen in Wood. Designer and Cabinet maker; Chairman: David Linley Furniture Ltd, 1985–; David Linley & Company Ltd, 1998–; Christie's UK, 2006– (Dir, Christie's International, 2005–). *Publications:* Classical Furniture, 1993, 2nd edn 1998; Extraordinary Furniture, 1996; Design and Detail in the Home, 2000. *Heir:* *s* Hon. Charles Patrick Inigo Armstrong-Jones, *b* 1 July 1999. *Address:* Linley, 60 Pimlico Road, SW1W 8LP.

See under Royal Family.

LINLITHGOW, 4th Marquess of, *cr* 1902; **Adrian John Charles Hope;** Bt (NS) 1698; Baron Hope, Viscount Aithrie, Earl of Hopetoun 1703 (Scot.); Baron Hopetoun 1809 (UK); Baron Niddry 1814 (UK); Stockbroker; *b* 1 July 1946; *s* of 3rd Marquess of Linlithgow, MC, TD, and Vivienne (*d* 1963), *d* of Capt. R. O. R. Kenyon-Slaney and of Lady Mary Gilmour; *S* father, 1987; *m* 1st, 1968, Anne (marr. diss. 1978), *e d* of A. Leveson, Hall Place, Hants; two *s*; 2nd, 1980, Peta C. Binding (marr. diss. 1997); one *s* one *d*; 3rd, 1997, Auriol Mackeson-Sandbach, former wife of Sir John Ropner, *qv*. *Educ:* Eton. Joined HM Navy, 1965. *Heir:* *s* Earl of Hopetoun, *qv*. *Address:* Philpstoun House, Linlithgow, West Lothian EH49 7NB. *T:* (01506) 834685.

LINNANE, Prof. Anthony William, AM 1995; FRS 1980; FAA; FTSE; Director, Centre for Molecular Biology and Medicine, since 1983; Professor of Biochemistry, Monash University, Australia, 1965–94, Emeritus Professor, since 1996; *b* 17 July 1930; *s* of late W. Linnane, Sydney; *m* 1956, Judith Neil (marr. diss. 1980); one *s* one *d*; *m* 1980, Daryl, *d* of A. Skurrie. *Educ:* Sydney Boys' High School; Sydney Univ. (PhD, DSc); Univ. of Wisconsin, USA. FAA 1972; FTSE 1999. Lecturer, then Senior Lectr, Sydney Univ., 1958–62; Reader, Monash Univ., Aust., 1962–65. Visiting Prof., Univ. of Wisconsin, 1976. President: Aust. Biochemical Soc., 1974–76; Fedn of Asian and Oceanic Biochemical Socs, 1975–77; 12th Internat. Congress of Biochemistry, 1982; Treasurer, Internat. Union of Biochemistry and Molecular Biol., 1988–97; Founder and Dir, 2000, Pres., 2001–, Australian Soc. for Cellular and Molecular Gerontology. Work concerned especially with the biogenesis and genetics of mitochondria, mucinous cancers and the human ageing process. Editor-in-Chief, Biochemistry and Molecular Biol. Internat., 1988–97. *Publications:* Autonomy and Biogenesis of Mitochondria and Chloroplasts, 1971; over 300 contributions to learned journals. *Address:* Centre for Molecular Biology and Medicine, Epworth Medical Centre, 2nd Floor, 185–187 Hoddle Street, Richmond, Vic 3121, Australia. *T:* (3) 94264200, *Fax:* (3) 94264201; *e-mail:* tlinnane@cmbm.com.au; 24 Myrtle Road, Canterbury, Vic 3126, Australia. *Clubs:* Athenæum; VRC; Angelsea Golf.

LINNARD, Robert Wynne; Director of Rail Strategy, Department for Transport, since 2007; *b* 18 June 1953; *s* of late John Adrian Linnard and Gwenita Linnard (*née* Johns); *m* 1974, Sally Judith Gadsden; three *s* three *d*. *Educ:* Dulwich Coll. Entered Civil Service, DoE, 1973; Principal, Dept of Transport, 1984–91; Asst Sec., 1991–99; Dir of Railways, DETR, subseq. DTLR, 1999–2002; Dir, Local Govt Finance, DTLR, then ODPM, 2002–04; Dir of Integrated and Local Transport, subseq. Regl and Local Transport Policy, DfT, 2004–07. *Recreations:* family, labradors, walking. *Address:* Department for Transport, Great Minster House, 76 Marsham Street, SW1P 4DR.

LINNELL, Andrew John, CGeog, FRGS; Head Teacher, Desborough School, since 2005; *b* 28 June 1956; *s* of Cyril Barrie Linnell and Maureen (*née* Goodyear); *m* 1989, Juliet, *d* of Prof. Oswald Hanfling and Helga Hanfling; one *s* one *d*. *Educ:* Wolstanton Grammar Sch., Staffs; Univ. of Salford (BSc); Univ. of Keele (PGCE). FRGS 1983, CGeog 2002; ACP 1988, MCollP 1988, FCollP 2005. Teacher, Howard Sch., Gillingham, Kent, 1979–86; Educn Officer, Kent CC, 1986–92; Dep. Headteacher, Sir Joseph Williamson's Mathematical Sch., Rochester, 1992–97; Head Master, Reading Sch., 1997–2005. Mem. Council, 2005–, Vice-Pres., 2006–, RGS. *Recreations:* jogging, swimming, cycling, travelling. *Address:* Desborough School, Shoppenhangers Road, Maidenhead, Berks SL6 2QB. *T:* (01628) 634505.

LINNELL, David George Thomas, CBE 1987; Chairman, 1993–96, Deputy Chairman, 1996–98, Hiscox Dedicated Insurance Fund plc, later Hiscox plc; *b* 28 May 1930; *s* of George and Marguerite Linnell; *m* 1953, Margaret Mary Paterson; one *s* one *d*. *Educ:* Leighton Park School, Reading. Managing Dir, Thomas Linnell & Sons, 1964–75; Chief Exec., Linfood Holdings, 1975–79; Chm., Spar Food Holdings, 1975–81; Chm., Eggs Authority, 1981–86; Chairman: Neighbourhood Stores, 1983–87; Birkdale Group, 1987–95; Kendell, 1994–97. Pres., Inst. of Grocery Distribution, 1980–82. Gov., St Andrew's Hosp., Northampton, 1992–2007. *Address:* The Old Rectory, Titchmarsh, Kettering, Northants NN14 3DG.

LINSTEAD, Stephen Guy; Director, Department of Trade and Industry, West Midlands Region, 1990–94; *b* 23 June 1941; *s* of late George Frederick Linstead and May Dorothy Linstead (*née* Griffiths); *m* 1st, 1971 (marr. diss.); two *s*; 2nd, 1982, Rachael Marian Feldman; two *d*. *Educ:* King Edward VII Sch., Sheffield; Corpus Christi Coll., Oxford (MA Mod. Hist.; Dip. Public and Social Admin.); Carleton Univ., Ottawa (MA Political Sci.); Huddersfield Univ. (Dip. Law). Board of Trade, 1964–76 (Private Sec. to Minister of State, 1967–69); Principal, 1969; Asst Sec., Dept of Prices and Consumer Protection, 1976–79; Dept of Trade, 1979–82; Office of Fair Trading, 1982–90; Under-Sec., DTI, 1990–94. Mem. Steering Gp, Industry '96, 1994–96. Vice-Chm., Assoc. of First Div. Civil Servants, 1982–84. Member: Exec. Cttee, Solihull Chamber of Commerce and Industry, 1996–2002 (Vice-Pres., 2000–02); Oversight Cttee, United Coll. of the Ascension, Selly Oak, 1996–2002. Reader, dio. of Birmingham, 1991–. *Publications:* Hymns of Hope for a New Millennium, 2008; contrib. Ottawa Law Review. *Recreations:* hymn writing (various hymns in Worship Live), swimming, travel, entertainment. *Address:* 20 Silhill Hall Road, Solihull, W Midlands B91 1JU. *T:* and *Fax:* (0121) 705 1376. *Club:* Royal Over-Seas League.

LINTON, Martin; MP (Lab) Battersea, since 1997; *b* 11 Aug. 1944; *s* of Sydney and Karin Linton; *m* 1975, Kathleen Stanley (*d* 1995); two *d*; *m* 2008, Sara Apps. *Educ:* Christ's Hosp.; Pembroke Coll., Oxford (MA). Journalist: Daily Mail, 1966–71; Labour Weekly, 1971–79; Daily Star, 1979–81; The Guardian, 1981–97. Mem. (Lab), Wandsworth LBC, 1971–82. PPS to Minister for the Arts, 2001–03, to Leader of Commons, 2003–05, to Lord Chancellor, 2005–. Member: Home Affairs Select Cttee, 1997–2001; Admin Cttee, 2001–05; Modernisation Cttee, 2003–05. *Publications:* The Swedish Road to Socialism, 1974; Guardian Guide to the House of Commons, 1992; Money and Votes, 1994; Was It the Sun Wot Won It?, 1995; Guardian Election Guide, 1997; Making Votes Count, 1998; Beyond 2002: long-term policies for Labour, 1999. *Recreations:* playing music, watching football. *Address:* House of Commons, SW1A 0AA. *T:* (020) 7219 4619.

LINTON, Prof. Oliver Bruce, PhD; FBA 2008; Professor of Econometrics, London School of Economics and Political Science, since 1999; *b* Gloucester, 20 Dec. 1960; *s* of Geoffrey and Margaret Linton; *m* 1990, Elisabetta Zancan; one *s* one *d*. *Educ:* London Sch. of Econs (BSc 1st cl. Hons Maths 1983; MSc Econometrics and Math. Econs 1983; Univ. of Calif, Berkeley (PhD Econs 1991). Jun. Res. Fellow, Nuffield Coll., Oxford, 1991–93; Yale University: Asst Prof., 1993–97; Associate Prof., 1997–98; Prof. of Economics, 1998–2000. Fellow, Econometric Soc., 2007; FIMS 2007. *Address:* Department of Economics, London School of Economics and Political Science, Houghton Street, WC2A 2AE. *T:* (020) 7955 7864, *Fax:* (020) 7955 6592; *e-mail:* o.linton@lse.co.uk.

LINTOTT, Robert Edward, Chief Executive, Coverdale Organisation, 1987–91; *b* 14 Jan. 1932; *s* of Charles Edward and Doris Mary Lintott; *m* 1958, Mary Alice Scott; three *s*. *Educ:* Cambridgeshire High School; Trinity College, Cambridge. BA Nat. Scis 1955, MA. Served RAF, 1950–52 (Flying Officer); joined Esso Petroleum Co. Ltd, 1955; Corporate Planning Dept, Exxon Corp., 1975–78; Exec. Asst to Chm., Exxon Corp., 1978–79; Director: Esso Petroleum Co. Ltd, 1979–84; Esso Pension Trust, 1979–87; Esso Exploration & Production UK, 1984–87; Esso UK plc, Esso Petroleum, 1984–87 (Man. Dir, 1984–86); Matthew Hall Engineering Holdings Ltd, 1987–89; CSM Parly Consultants Ltd, 1995–; MLD (Hong Kong) Ltd, 1995–; Chairman: Irish Refining Co., 1979–82; Esso Teoranta, 1982–84. Vice-Pres., UK Petroleum Industry Assoc., 1985–86; Pres., Oil Industries Club, 1986–88. Mem., Standards Bd, BSI, 1991–2000. Council Mem., 1979–, and Chm. Exec. Cttee, 1987–, Foundn for Management Educn; Member: Council for Management Educn and Develt, 1989–2000; Steering Cttee, Oxford Summer Business Sch., 1979–94 (Chm., 1987–91); Council, Manchester Business Sch., 1985–92. Councillor, Royal Bor. of Windsor and Maidenhead, 1987–91. Chm. of Govs, Queen's Coll. Taunton, 1994–2007. Chm., ESU, Taunton, 2007–. *Recreations:* cricket, vintage and modern motoring. *Address:* Huish Barton, Watchet, Somerset TA23 0LU. *T:* (01984) 640208. *Clubs:* Royal Air Force, MCC.

LIPKIN, Miles Henry J.; *see* Jackson-Lipkin.

LIPMAN, Maureen Diane, (Mrs J. M. Rosenthal), CBE 1999; actress; *b* 10 May 1946; *d* of late Maurice and Zelma Lipman; *m* 1973, Jack Morris Rosenthal, CBE (*d* 2004); one *s* one *d*. *Educ:* Newland High Sch. for Girls, Hull; London Acad. of Music and Dramatic Art. Professional début in The Knack, Watford, 1969; Stables Theatre, Manchester, 1970; National Theatre (Old Vic), 1971–73: The Front Page; Long Day's Journey into Night; The Good Natur'd Man; *West End*: Candida, 1976; Outside Edge, 1978; Meg and Mog, 1982; Messiah, 1983; Miss Skillen, in See How They Run, 1984 (Laurence Olivier Award; Variety Club of GB Award); Wonderful Town, Queen's, 1986; Re: Joyce!, Fortune, 1988, Vaudeville, 1989 and 1991, Long Wharf, Conn, USA, 1990; The Cabinet Minister, Albery, 1991; Lost in Yonkers, Strand, 1992 (Variety Club Best Stage Actress, 1993); The Sisters Rosenweig, Old Vic, 1994; Live and Kidding, Duchess, 1997; Oklahoma!, RNT, 1998, transf. Lyceum, 1999; Peggy For You, Comedy, 2000; Thoroughly Modern Millie, Shaftesbury, 2003; Aladdin, Old Vic, 2004; Glorious!, Duchess, 2005–06; other plays include: Celia, in As You Like It, RSC, 1974; Jenny, in Chapter Two, Hammersmith, 1981; Kitty McShane, in On Your Way, Riley, Stratford East, 1983; The Rivals, Manchester Royal Exchange, 1996; Sitting Pretty, Th. Royal, Bath, 2001; Martha Josie & the Chinese Elvis, touring, 2007; The Cherry Orchard, Chichester, 2008; Dir, The Sunshine Boys, Royal Lyceum, Edinburgh, 1993; *television:* plays, series and serials include: The Evacuees; Smiley's People; The Knowledge; Rolling Home; Outside Edge; Princess of France, in Love's Labour's Lost; Absurd Person Singular; Shift Work; Absent Friends; Jane Lucas, in 4 series of Agony; All at No 20 (TV Times Award, 1989); About Face, 1989 and 1990; Re: Joyce; Enid Blyton, in Sunny Stories, 1992; Eskimo Day, 1996; Cold Enough for Snow, 1997; The Fugitives, 2004; In Search of Style, 2005; Sensitive Skin, Dr Who, Casualty, 2007; He Kills Coppers, 2008; *films include:* Up the Junction, 1969; Educating Rita, 1983; Captain Jack, 1998; Solomon and Gaenor, 1999; Oklahoma! (video), 1999; Discovery of Heaven, 2001; The Pianist, 2002; Caught in the Act, 2008; *radio:* The Lipman Test (2 series), 1996, 1997; Choice Grenfell, 1998; dir, Jack Rosenthal's Last Act , 2006. BAFTA Award, for BT Commercials, 1992. Magazine columnist: Options, 1983–88; She, 1988–91 (PPA Columnist of the Year, 1991); Good Housekeeping, 1993–2003. Hon. DLitt: Hull, 1994; Sheffield, 1999; Hon. MA Salford, 1995. *Publications:* How Was it for You?, 1985; Something to Fall Back On, 1987; You Got an 'Ology?, 1989; Thank You for Having Me, 1990; When's It Coming Out?, 1992; You Can Read Me Like a Book, 1995; Lip Reading, 1999; The Gibbon's in Decline, but the Horse is Stable, 2006. *Recreation:* reading and trying to remember what I've read!

LIPNER, Prof. Julius Joseph, PhD; FBA 2008; Professor of Hinduism and the Comparative Study of Religion, University of Cambridge, since 2003; Fellow, since 1990, and Vice-President, since 2007, Clare Hall, Cambridge; *b* Patna, India, 11 Aug. 1946; *s* of Vojtech Lipner and Sylvia Teresa Lipner (*née* Coutts); *m* 1971, Anindita Neogy; one *s* one *d. Educ:* Pontifical Athenæum (Jnana Deepa Vidyapeeth), Pune, India (Licentiate in Philosophy *summa cum laude* 1969); King's Coll., London (PhD 1974); Clare Hall, Cambridge (MA 1975). Lectr in Indian Religions, Dept of Theol., Univ. of Birmingham, 1973–74; University of Cambridge: Lectr in Indian Religion and Comparative Study of Religion, 1975–99, Reader in Hinduism and Comparative Study of Religion, 1999–2003, Divinity Faculty; Fellow, St Edmund's Coll., 1976–89; Chm., Faculty Bd of Divinity, 2003–06. Visiting Professor: Univ. of Calgary, 1987, 1989, 1996; Vanderbilt Univ., Nashville, 1992; Liverpool Hope Univ., 2003–04; Hon. Prof., Kuruksetra Univ., India, 1995–97; Vis. Fellow, Vishwabharati Univ., India, 1984. Named Lectures. Member, Editorial Advisory Board: Jl Hindu-Christian Studies; Internat. Jl Hindu Studies; (Jl) Religions of S Asia. Trustee: Spalding Trusts, 1992–; Woolf Inst. (formerly Centre for Study of Jewish Christian Relations), 2001–; Teape Trust, 2008–. *Publications:* The Face of Truth: a study of meaning and metaphysics in the Vedantic theology of Ramanuja, 1986; (ed jtly) A Net Cast Wide: investigations into Indian thought in memory of David Friedman, 1986; (jtly) Hindu Ethics: purity, abortion and euthanasia, 1989; (ed jtly) The Writings of Brahmabandhab Upadhyay, vol 1, 1991, vol 2, 2002; Hindus: their religious beliefs and practices, 1994; (ed) The Fruits of our Desiring: an enquiry into the ethics of the Bhagavadgita, 1997; Brahmabandhab Upadhyay: the life and thought of a revolutionary, 1999; Bankimchandra Chatterji's Anandamath or the Sacred Brotherhood (introd., trans. and critical apparatus), 2005; (ed) Truth, Religious Dialogue and Dynamic Orthodoxy: essays in honour of Brian Hebblethwaite, 2005; contrib. articles to learned jls and edited collections. *Recreations:* following Test Cricket (especially England and India), enjoying good food, listening to Indian and Western music, reading, travel. *Address:* Divinity Faculty, University of Cambridge, West Road, Cambridge CB3 9BS. *T:* (01223) 763002.

LIPPIETT, Rear-Adm. Richard John, CB 2004; MBE 1979; Chief Executive Officer, Mary Rose Trust, since 2003; *b* 7 July 1949; *s* of late Rev. Canon Vernon Kingsbury Lippiett and Katharine F. I. S. Lippiett (*née* Langston-Jones); *m* 1976, Jennifer Rosemary Wratislaw Walker; two *s* one *d. Educ:* Brighton, Hove and Sussex Grammar Sch.; BRNC, Dartmouth. Joined RN 1967; served HM Ships Appleton, Eagle, Yarmouth, Achilles, Fife, Ambuscade and ashore at HMS Raleigh and Fleet HQ; Flag Lieut to C-in-C Fleet, 1973–74; Comd, HMS Shavington, 1975–77 and HMS Amazon, 1986–87; jsdc 1987; Naval Asst to First Sea Lord, 1988–90; Comd, HMS Norfolk and 9th Frigate Sqdn, 1991–92; rcds, 1993; COS Surface Flotilla, 1993–95; Comd, HMS Dryad and Sch. of Maritime Ops, 1995–97; Flag Officer Sea Trng, 1997–99; COS to Comdr Allied Naval Forces Southern Europe, and Sen. British Officer Southern Region, 1999–2002; Comdt, JSCSC, 2002–03. Trustee, Naval Review, 2001–. Naval Vice Pres., CCF, 2004–; Pres., Ton Class Assoc., 2007–. Patron, Nautical Trng Corps, 2007–. Younger Brother of Trinity House, 1993. *Publications:* The Type 21 Frigate, 1990; War and Peas: intimate letters from the Falklands War 1982, 2007. *Recreations:* family, classical music, gardening, sailing. *Address:* Mary Rose Trust, College Road, HM Naval Base, Portsmouth PO1 3LX.

LIPPINCOTT, Dr Kristen Clarke; Director, The Exhibitions Team, since 2007; *b* 18 Nov. 1954; *d* of Lt-Col Clifford Ellwood Lippincott and Maureen Virginia Lippincott (*née* O'Brien); *m* 1992, Gordon Stephen Barrass, *qv. Educ:* Bennington Coll., Vermont, USA (BA); Univ. of Chicago (MA, PhD). Fellowships in Italy and at Warburg Inst., 1982–90; National Maritime Museum: Curator of Astronomy, 1990 and Head of Navigational Scis, 1991–94, Old Royal Observatory; Mus. Planner and Strategist, 1994–95; Director: Display Div., 1995–96; Millennium Project, Old Royal Observatory, Greenwich, 1996–2000; Royal Observatory Greenwich, 1998–2001; Dep. Dir, Nat. Maritime Mus., 2000–06. Vis. Prof., Harvard Univ., Villa I Tatti, Florence, 2004. Council Mem., Scientific Instruments Soc., 1994–96; Trustee, Cubitt Gall., 1996–2003. Freeman, Clockmakers' Co., 2000–. FRAS 2004; FRSA 1997. *Publications:* Eyewitness Science: Astronomy, 1994; The Story of Time, 1999; numerous articles on Italian Renaissance and on history of art, of science, of scientific instruments, in learned jls. *Recreation:* travelling. *Address: e-mail:* kl@theexhibitionsteam.com.

LIPPONEN, Paavo Tapio; MP (SDP) Helsinki, Finland, 1983–87 and 1991–2006; Speaker of Parliament, 1995 and 2003–06; *b* 23 April 1941; *s* of Orvo and Hilkka Lipponen; *m* 1998, Paivi Hertzberg; two *d*, and one *d* from former marriage. *Educ:* Kuopio; Univ. of Helsinki (MScSoc 1971); Dartmouth Coll., USA. Journalist, 1963–67; SDP Res. and Internat. Affairs Sec. and Head, political section, 1967–79; Prime Minister's Sec. (Special Political Advr), 1979–92; Head, Finnish Inst. Internat. Affairs, 1989–91; Mem., Helsinki City Council, 1985–95; Prime Minister of Finland, 1995–2003. Social Democratic Party: Chm., Helsinki Dist, 1985–92; Member: Exec. Cttee, 1987–90; Party Council, 1990–93; Chm., 1993–2005. Man. Dir, Viestinta Teema Oy, 1988–95; Chm., Supervisory Bd, Outokumpo Oy, 1989–90. Member: Exec. Cttee, Internat. Commn on Employment, 1987–89; Gp of Experts on Internat. Politics of Sec.-Gen., Council of Europe, 1989–91. Hon. LLD: Dartmouth Coll., USA, 1997; Finlandia Univ., USA, 2000; Hon. Dr: Tampere Univ. of Tech., Finland, 2002; Åbo Akademi Univ., Finland, 2002; Univ. of Art and Design, Finland, 2007. Grand Cross, Order of White Rose (Finland). Holds several foreign decorations. *Publications:* Muutoksen Suunta, 1986; Kohti Eurooppaa, 2001; articles in Finnish, Swedish, English and German in domestic and foreign books, newspapers and periodicals. *Recreations:* sports activities—swimming, architecture, literature, music. *Address:* Dagmarinkatu 5B8, 00100 Helsinki, Finland. *Club:* Finnish (Helsinki).

LIPSCOMB, Rachel Elizabeth, OBE 2006; JP; a Vice President, Magistrates' Association, since 2005 (Deputy Chairman, 1999–2002, Chairman, 2002–05, of Council); *b* 24 Aug. 1948; *d* of George Edwards and Joan (*née* Button); *m* 1969, Peter W. Lipscomb, OBE; two *s* one *d. Educ:* St Felix Sch., Southwold; Middlesex Hosp., London (SRN). Magistrates' Association: Mem. Council, 1994–; Vice Chm., Family Procs Cttee, 1997–99; Chm., Sentencing Guidelines Working Party, 2002–05; Chm., Criminal Justice Cttee, 2000–02; Mem., Street Crime Action Gp, 2002–05. Member: Adv. Gp on Prison Popn, 2002–04; Audit Commn Victims and Witnesses Adv. Gp, 2002–04. Member: Lord Chancellor's Adv. Cttee, SW London, 1995–2000; Unified Admin Judicial Cttee, 2002–04; Judges Council, 2003–05. Dep. Chm., Youth and Family Panels, 1990–. Chm., Local Crime Community Sentence, 2008–; Mem. Adv. Bd, Rethinking Crime and Punishment - Implementing the Findings, Esmée Fairbairn Foundn, 2005–. Trustee, Mediation in Divorce, Richmond upon Thames, 1996–. Governor, Kingston Grammar Sch., 1996–2002. JP Kingston upon Thames, 1981. *Publications:* articles for The Magistrate and other criminal and civil justice pubns. *Recreations:* gardening, outdoor sports, family life. *Address:* c/o Magistrates' Association, 28 Fitzroy Square, W1T 6DD. *T:* (020) 7387 2353, *Fax:* (020) 7383 4020.

LIPSCOMB, Prof. William Nunn; Abbott and James Lawrence Professor of Chemistry, Harvard University, 1971–90, now Emeritus; Nobel Laureate in Chemistry, 1976; *b* 9 Dec. 1919; *s* of late William Nunn Lipscomb Sr, and of Edna Patterson Porter; *m* 1983, Jean Craig Evans; one *d*, and one *s* one *d* by previous marriage. *Educ:* Univ. of Kentucky (BS); California Inst. of Technology (PhD). Univ. of Minnesota, Minneapolis: Asst Prof. of Physical Chem., 1946–50; Associate Prof., 1950–54; Actg Chief, Physical Chem. Div., 1952–54; Prof. and Chief of Physical Chem. Div., 1954–59; Harvard Univ.: Prof. of Chemistry, 1959–71 (Chm., Dept of Chem., 1962–65). Member: Bd of Dirs, Dow Chemical Co., USA, 1982–89; Scientific Adv. Bd, Robert A. Welch Foundn, 1982–. Member: Amer. Chemical Soc. (Chm., Minneapolis Section, 1949); Amer. Acad. of Arts and Sciences, 1959–; Nat. Acad. of Sciences, USA, 1961–; Internat. Acad. of Quantum Molecular Science, 1980; Académie Européenne des Scis, des Arts et des Lettres, Paris, 1980; Foreign Mem., Netherlands Acad. of Arts and Sciences, 1976; Hon. Member: Internat. Assoc. of Bioinorganic Scientists, 1979; RSC, 1983. MA (hon.) Harvard, 1959; Hon. DSc: Kentucky, 1963; Long Island, 1977; Rutgers, 1979; Gustavos Adolphus, 1980; Marietta, 1981; Miami, 1983; Dr *hc* Munich, 1976. *Publications:* Boron Hydrides, 1963 (New York); (with G. R. Eaton) Nuclear Magnetic Resonance Studies of Boron and Related Compounds, 1969 (New York); chapters in: The Aesthetic Dimensions of Science, ed D. W. Curtin, 1982; Crystallography in North America, ed D. McLachlan and J. Glusker, 1983; contribs to scientific jls concerning structure and function of enzymes and natural products in inorganic chem. and theoretical chem. *Recreations:* tennis, chamber music. *Address:* Department of Chemistry and Chemical Biology, Harvard University, 12 Oxford Street, Cambridge, MA 02138, USA. *T:* (617) 4954098.

LIPSEY, family name of **Baron Lipsey**.

LIPSEY, Baron *cr* 1999 (Life Peer), of Tooting Bec in the London Borough of Wandsworth; **David Lawrence Lipsey;** *b* 21 April 1948; *s* of Lawrence and Penelope Lipsey; *m* 1982, Margaret Robson; one *d. Educ:* Bryanston Sch.; Magdalen Coll., Oxford (1st Cl. Hons PPE). Research Asst, General and Municipal Workers' Union, 1970–72; Special Adviser to Anthony Crosland, MP, 1972–77 (Dept of the Environment, 1974–76; FCO, 1976–77); Prime Minister's Staff, 10 Downing Street, 1977–79; Journalist, New Society, 1979–80; Sunday Times: Political Staff, 1980–82; Economics Editor, 1982–86; Editor, New Society, 1986–88; Co-founder and Dep. Editor, The Sunday Correspondent, 1988–90; Associate Ed., The Times, 1990–92; journalist, The Economist, 1992–99 (Political Ed., 1994–98); Chm., impower plc, 2001–03. Vis. Prof. in Public Policy, Univ. of Ulster, 1993–98; Vis. Fellow, Health and Social Care, LSE, 2002–04; Vis. Prof., Salford Univ., 2008–. Member: Royal Commn on Long Term Care of the Elderly, 1997–99; Ind. Commn on the Voting System, 1997–98; Licence Fee Rev. Panel (Davies Inquiry), 1999; Council, ASA, 1999–2005; Chairman: Make Votes Count, 1999–; Social Market Foundn, 2001–; Shadow Racing Trust, 2002–07; British Greyhound Racing Bd, 2004–; Financial Services Consumer Panel, 2008–. Member: Adv. Cttee, Centre for Res. into Elecns and Social Trends; Council, Constitution Unit; Adv. Bd, Centre for the Study of Gambling, Salford Univ. Secretary, Streatham Labour Party, 1970–72; Chm., Fabian Soc., 1981–82; Mem., Exec. Cttee, Charter for Jobs, 1984–86. A public interest Dir, PIA, 1994–2000; non-executive Director: Horserace Totalisator Bd, 1998–2002; LWT, 2002–03; London ITV, 2003–05. Trustee, Retired Greyhound Trust, 2003–; Pres., British Harness Racing Club, 2004–. *Publications:* Labour and Land, 1972; (ed, with Dick Leonard) The Socialist Agenda: Crosland's Legacy, 1981; Making Government Work, 1982; The Name of the Rose, 1992; The Secret Treasury: how Britain's economy is really run, 2000. *Recreations:* golf, greyhound racing, harness racing, horse racing, opera. *Address:* House of Lords, SW1A 0PW. *T:* (020) 7219 8509.

LIPSEY, Prof. Richard George, OC 1991; FRSC; Professor of Economics, Simon Fraser University, Burnaby, BC, 1989–97, now Emeritus; Fellow, Canadian Institute for Advanced Research, 1989–2002; *b* 28 Aug. 1928; *s* of R. A. Lipsey and F. T. Lipsey (*née* Ledingham); *m* 1960, Diana Louise Smart; one *s* two *d. Educ:* Univ. of British Columbia (BA 1st Cl. Hons 1950); Univ. of Toronto (MA 1953); LSE (PhD 1957). Dept of Trade and Industry, British Columbia Provincial Govt, 1950–53; LSE: Asst Lectr, 1955–58; Lectr, 1958–60; Reader, 1960–61; Prof. 1961–63; Univ. of Essex: Prof. of Economics, 1963–70; Dean of School of Social Studies, 1963–67; Sir Edward Peacock Prof. of Econs, Queen's Univ., Kingston, Ont, 1970–87. Vis. Prof., Univ. of California at Berkeley, 1963–64; Simeon Vis. Prof., Univ. of Manchester, 1973; Irving Fisher Vis. Prof., Yale Univ., 1979–80. Economic Consultant, NEDC, 1961–63; Sen. Econ. Advr, C. D. Howe Inst., Toronto, 1984–89. Member of Council: SSRC, 1966–69; Royal Economic Soc., 1968–71. President: Canadian Economics Assoc., 1980–81; Atlantic Economic Assoc., 1986–87. Editor, Review of Economic Studies, 1960–64. Fellow, Econometric Soc., 1972. FRSC 1980. Hon. LLD: McMaster, 1984; Victoria, 1985; Carleton, 1987; Queen's Univ. at Kingston, 1990; Guelph, 1993; Western Ontario, 1994; Essex, 1996; British Columbia, 1999; Simon Fraser Univ., 2007; Hon. DSc Toronto, 1992. *Publications:* An Introduction to Positive Economics, 1963, 10th edn 2003; (with P. O. Steiner) Economics, 1966, 12th edn 1999; (with G. C. Archibald) An Introduction to a Mathematical Treatment of Economics, 1967, 3rd edn 1977; The Theory of Customs Unions: a general equilibrium analysis, 1971; (with G. C. Archibald) An Introduction to Mathematical Economics, 1975; (with C. Harbury) An Introduction to the UK Economy, 1983, 5th edn 1993; (with F. Flatters) Common Ground for the Canadian Common Market, 1984; (with M. Smith): Canada's Trade Options in a Turbulent World, 1985; Global Imbalance and US Policy Response, 1987; (with R. York) A Guided Tour through the Canada-US Free Trade Agreement, 1988; (with C. Harbury) First Principles of Economics, 1988, 2nd edn 1992; (jtly) The NAFTA: what's in, what's out, what's next, 1994; (with K. Carlaw) A Structuralist Assessment of Innovation Policies, 1998; (jtly) Economic Transformations: general purpose technologies and long-term economic growth, 2005; articles in learned jls on many branches of theoretical and applied economics. *Recreations:* travel, sailing, rambling. *Address:* RR#1 Q70, Bowen Island, BC V0N 1G0, Canada; *e-mail:* rlipsey@sfu.ca.

LIPTON, Prof. Michael, CMG 2003; DLitt; FBA 2006; Research Professor, Poverty Research Unit, Sussex University, since 1994; *b* 13 Feb. 1937; *s* of Leslie and Helen Lipton; *m* 1966, Merle Babrow; one *s. Educ:* Haberdashers' Aske's Sch., London; Balliol Coll., Oxford (BA 1st Cl. Hons PPE 1960, MA 1963); Massachusetts Inst. of Technol.; DLitt Sussex 1982. Fellow, All Souls Coll., Oxford, 1961–68 and 1983–84; University of Sussex: Fellow, Inst. of Develt Studies, and Professorial Fellow, 1970–94; Founding Dir, Poverty Res. Unit, 1994–97. Dir, Consumption and Nutrition Prog., Internat. Food Policy Res. Inst., 1987–89. Employment Advr, Govt of Botswana, 1977–79; Sen. Advr, World Bank, 1981–82. Sen. Advr and topic leader, Quality of Life, ADB study of Emerging Asia, 1995–97; Lead Schol., Rural Poverty Report, IFAD, 1994–2001. Member: Wkg Party on GM crops, Bioethics Council, Nuffield Foundn, 1998–99 and 2002–03; Prog. Adv. Cttee, HarvestPlus (Biofortification) Prog. (formerly Biofortification Challenge Grant), Consultative Gp for Internat. Agricl Res., 2002–; UK and Internat. Bds, Internat. Develt Enterprises, 2004–; Bd, Centre for Chinese Agricl Policy, Chinese Acad. Scis, 2005–. Mem., Council, 2000–05, Bd, 2005–, ODI. *Publications:* Chess Problems: introduction to an art, 1963; (jtly) The Two-move Chess Problem: tradition and development, 1966; Assessing Economic Performance, 1968; Why Poor People Stay Poor: urban bias and world development, 1977, 2nd edn 1988; (with R. Longhurst) New Seeds and Poor People, 1989; (with J. Toye) Does Aid Work in India?, 1991; (ed jtly and contrib.) Including the Poor, 1993; Successes in Anti-poverty, 1998, 2nd edn 2002; contrib. learned jls. *Recreations:* chess problems (Pres., British Chess Problem Soc.,

1999–2001; Internat. Master of Chess Problem Composition, 1975–), classical music, poetry, theatre. *Address:* 15 Eaton Place, Brighton, Sussex BN2 1EH. *Club:* Lansdowne.

LIPTON, Sir Stuart (Anthony), Kt 2000; Deputy Chairman, Chelsfield LLP, since 2006; *b* 9 Nov. 1942; *s* of late Bertram Green and Jeanette Lipton; *m* 1966, Ruth Kathryn Marks; two *s* one *d.* *Educ:* Berkhamsted Sch. Director: Sterling Land Co., 1971–73; First Palace Securities Ltd, 1973–76; Man. Dir, Greycoat PLC, 1976–83; Chief Exec., Stanhope Properties PLC, 1983–95; Chief Exec., 1995–2003, Chm., 2003–06, Stanhope PLC; Chm., Stanhope Places plc, 2005–06. Advr to Hampton Site Co. for Sainsbury Bldg, Nat. Gall., 1985–91; Advr, new Glyndebourne Opera House, 1988–94; Member: Adv. Bd, Dept of Construction Management, Reading Univ., 1983–91; Property Adv. Gp, DoE, 1986–96; Mil. Bldgs Cttee, MoD, 1987–98; Barbican Centre Adv. Council, 1997–2007. Mem. Council, British Property Fedn, 1987–99. Mem., Royal Fine Art Commn, 1988–99; Chm., CABE, 1999–2004. Dir, Nat. Gall. Trust Foundn, 1998–. Trustee: Whitechapel Art Gall., 1987–94; Architecture Foundn, 1992–99 (Dep. Chm., 1992–99); Urban Land Inst., Washington, 1996–; Millennium Bridge Trust, 1998–2002; Member: English Partnerships Millennium Housing Trust Jury, 1998–99; Jury, RIBA Gold Medal Award, 1998–99. Member of Board: Royal Nat. Theatre, 1988–98; Royal Opera House, 1998–2006. Edward Bass Vis. Architectural Fellow, Yale Sch. of Architecture, 2006. Member, Governing Body: Imperial Coll., 1987–2002 (FIC 1998); LSE, 2000–06. Liveryman, Goldsmiths' Co., 1997–. Hon. Bencher, Inner Temple, 2002. Hon. RIBA 1986. Hon. LLD Bath, 2005. Bicentenary Medal, RSA, 1999. *Recreations:* architecture, crafts, art and technology, wine, opera. *Address:* (office) 53 Grosvenor Street, W1K 3HU.

LIPWORTH, Sir (Maurice) Sydney, Kt 1991; Trustee, International Accounting Standards Committee Foundation, 2000–06; Chairman, Financial Reporting Council, 1993–2001; *b* 13 May 1931; *s* of Isidore and Rae Lipworth; *m* 1957, Rosa Liwarek; two *s.* *Educ:* King Edward VII Sch., Johannesburg; Univ. of the Witwatersrand, Johannesburg (BCom, LLB). Admitted Solicitor, Johannesburg, 1955; called to the South African Bar, 1956; called to Bar, Inner Temple, 1991; in practice at the Bar, 2002–. Barrister, Johannesburg, 1956–64; non-exec. Dir, Liberty Life Assoc. of Africa Ltd, 1956–64; Director: private trading/financial gps, 1965–67; Abbey Life Assurance Gp, 1968–70; Allied Dunbar Assurance plc (formerly Hambro Life Assurance), 1971–88 (Jt Man. Dir, 1980–84; Dep. Chm., 1984–87); Chairman: Dunbar Bank, 1983–88; Allied Dunbar Unit Trusts, 1985–88 (Man. Dir, 1983–85); ZENECA Group, 1995–99 (Dir, 1994–99); Dep. Chm., Nat. Westminster Bank, 1993–2000; Director: J. Rothschild Holdings plc, 1984–87; BAT Industries plc, 1985–88; Carlton Communications plc, 1993–2004; Centrica plc, 1999–2002; Goldfish Bank Ltd, 2001–04; Cazenove Gp Ltd, 2005–. Mem., 1981–93, Chm., 1988–93, Monopolies and Mergers Commn; Member: Sen. Salaries Review Body, 1994–2002; Cttee on Financial Aspects of Corporate Governance, 1994–95. Mem. Adv. Panel, BreakThrough Breast Cancer Res. Trust, 1990–; Trustee: Allied Dunbar Charitable Trust, 1971–94; Philharmonia Orchestra, 1982– (Dep. Chm., 1986–93, Chm., 1993–, of Trustees); Royal Acad. Trust, 1988–2003; South Bank Foundn Ltd, 1996–2003; Chairman: NatWest Gp Charitable Trust, 1994–2001; Marie Curie Cancer Care 50th Anniversary Appeal, 1997–2002; Governor: Contemp. Dance Trust, 1981–87; Sadler's Wells Foundn, 1987–90. Chm., Bar Assoc. for Commerce, Finance and Industry, 1991–92. Mem., Gen. Council of the Bar, 1992–94. Hon. Bencher, Inner Temple, 1989; Hon. QC 1993. Hon. LLD Witwatersrand, 2003. *Publications:* chapters and articles on investment, life insurance, pensions and competition law. *Recreations:* tennis, music, theatre. *Address:* International Accounting Standards Board, 30 Cannon Street, EC4M 6XH. *Clubs:* Reform, Queen's.

LISBURNE, 8th Earl of, *cr* 1776; **John David Malet Vaughan;** DL; Baron Fethard, 1695; Viscount Lisburne and Lord Vaughan, 1695; barrister-at-law; *b* 1 Sept. 1918; *o s* of 7th Earl of Lisburne; *S* father, 1965; *m* 1943, Shelagh, *er d* of late T. A. Macauley, 1266 Redpath Crescent, Montreal, Canada; three *s.* *Educ:* Eton; Magdalen Coll., Oxford (BA, MA). Captain, Welsh Guards, 1939–46. Called to Bar, Inner Temple, 1947. Director: British Home Stores Ltd, 1964–87; S Wales Regional Bd, Lloyds Bank Ltd, 1978–; Divisional Dir for Wales, Nationwide Building Soc., 1982–. Chm., then Pres., Wales Council for Voluntary Action (formerly Council of Social Service for Wales), 1976–97; Hon. Life Mem., AA (Mem. Exec. Cttee, 1981–88). DL Dyfed, 1992. *Heir: s* Viscount Vaughan, *qv.* *Address:* Bringewood, Burway Lane, Ludlow SY8 1DT. *Clubs:* Beefsteak, Turf.

LISHMAN, (Arthur) Gordon, CBE 2006 (OBE 1993); Director General, Age Concern, since 2000; *b* 29 Nov. 1947; *s* of Dr Arthur Birkett Lishman and Florence May Lishman; *m* 1st, 1968, Beverley Ann Witham (marr. diss. 1972); 2nd, 1973, Stephanie Margaret Allison-Beer (marr. diss. 1984); one *s* one *d*; 3rd, 1988, Margaret Ann Brodie-Browne (*née* Long); one step *d.* *Educ:* Univ. of Manchester (BA Econ 1968). Age Concern England, 1974–: Field Officer, 1974–77; Head of Fieldwork, 1977–87; Ops Dir, 1987–2000; Dir, Age Concern Hldgs Ltd, 1995–. Member: Steering Gp for Commn on Equalities and Human Rights, 2004–06; Nat. Stakeholder Forum, DoH, 2006–; Chm., Nutrition Action Plan Delivery Bd, DoH, 2008–. Vice-Pres., Internat. Fedn on Ageing, 2004 (Dir, 2001–); Sec.-Gen., Eurolink Age, 2001–; Sec., AGE—the Eur. Older People's Platform, 2001–07 (Council Mem., 2001–08). Campaigner on age equality, 1971–; involvement in Campaign for Homosexual Law Reform/Campaign for Homosexual Equality and Stop the Seventy Tour; former Mem., Race Equality Councils in Manchester, Northants and E Lancs; Member: Liberty; Fawcett Soc.; British Humanist Assoc.; Friends of Ruskin's Brantwood. Gov., Pensions Policy Inst., 2002–. Mem., Liberal, later Liberal Democrat, Party, 1963–. Hon. Fellow, Univ. of Central Lancs, 2002. MCMI. FRSA. *Address:* Age Concern, Astral House, 1268 London Road, SW16 4ER. *T:* (020) 8765 7701. *Club:* National Liberal.

LISHMAN, Prof. William Alwyn, MD, DSc; FRCP, FRCPsych; Professor of Neuropsychiatry, Institute of Psychiatry, University of London, 1979–93, now Professor Emeritus; Consultant Psychiatrist, Bethlem Royal and Maudsley Hospitals, 1967–93; *b* 16 May 1931; *s* of George Hackworth Lishman and Madge Scott (*née* Young); *m* 1966, Marjorie Loud (*d* 2000); one *s* one *d.* *Educ:* Houghton-le-Spring Grammar Sch.; Univ. of Birmingham (BSc Hons Anatomy and Physiology, 1953; MB, ChB Hons 1956; MD 1965). DPM London, 1963; DSc London, 1985. MRCP 1958, FRCP 1972; FRCPsych 1972. House Phys. and House Surg., Queen Elizabeth Hosp., Birmingham, 1956–57; MO Wheatley Mil. Hosp., 1957–59 (Major, RAMC); Registrar, United Oxford Hosps, 1959–60; Registrar, later Sen. Registrar, Maudsley Hosp., London, 1960–66; Consultant in Psychol Medicine, Nat. Hosp. and Maida Vale Hosp., London, 1966–67; Sen. Lectr in Psychol Medicine, Hammersmith Hosp. and RPMS, 1967–69; Consultant Psychiatrist, Bethlem Royal and Maudsley Hosps, 1967–74; Reader in Neuropsychiatry, Inst. of Psychiatry, 1974–79. Vis. Fellow, Green Coll., Oxford, 1983. Advisor to Bermuda Hosps Bd, 1971; Scientific Advisor, DHSS, 1979–82; Civilian Consultant, RAF, 1987–93. Member: Neurosciences Bd, MRC, 1976–78 (Dep. Chm., 1976–77); Scientific Adv. Panel, Brain Res. Trust, 1986–93; Adv. Cttee, Mason Med. Res. Trust, 1986–93. Examiner: Univ. of Oxford (also Mem. Bd of Examrs), 1975–79; Univ. of Birmingham, 1984–87; Nat. Univ. of Malaysia, 1989. Chm., British Neuropsychiatry Assoc., 1987–93; (Hon. Life Pres., 1993); Member: Experimental Psychology Soc., 1975–95; Assoc. of British Neurologists, 1979–95; Court of Electors, and Exams Subcttee, RCPsych, 1991–96. Trustee, Psychiatry Res. Trust, 1999–2007. Gaskell Gold Medal, Royal Medico-Psychol Assoc., 1965. Member, Editorial Boards: Psychological Medicine, 1970–93; Neuropsychiatry, Neuropsychology and Behavioral Neurology, 1988–95; Cognitive Neuropsychiatry, 1996–. Guarantor of Brain, 1984–99. *Publications:* Organic Psychiatry: the psychological consequences of cerebral disorder, 1978, 3rd edn 1998; physiol and psychol papers on brain maturation, cerebral dominance, organisation of memory; clinical papers on head injury, dementia, epilepsy, neuroimaging, and alcoholic brain damage. *Recreations:* organ, piano, harpsichord, travelling.

LISLE, 9th Baron *cr* 1758 (Ire.), of Mount North, co. Cork; **John Nicholas Geoffrey Lysaght;** *b* 20 May 1960; *s* of 8th Baron Lisle and Mary Louise Lysaght (now Blackwell); *S* father, 2003. *Educ:* Lingfield. Gardener, specialising in exotic climbers; bee-keeper; charity shop volunteer. *Recreations:* collecting early 20th-century Christmas tree decorations, gardening, writing rhymes and poems. *Heir: b* Hon. David James Lysaght [*b* 10 Aug. 1963; *m* 1989, Rebecca Tamsin, *d* of Russell Charles Abbott; one *s* two *d*]. *Address:* 50 The Fairstead, Scottow, Norwich, Norfolk NR10 5AQ.

LISLE, Paul David O.; *see* Orchard-Lisle.

LISS, Prof. Peter Simon, CBE 2008; PhD; FRS 2008; Professor, School of Environmental Sciences, University of East Anglia, since 1985; *b* 27 Oct. 1942; *s* of Michael and Gertrude Liss; *m* 1967, Ruth Adler; three *s.* *Educ:* University College, Durham (BSc); Marine Science Labs, Univ. of Wales (PhD). NERC Post-doctoral Res. Fellow, Dept. of Oceanography, Southampton Univ., 1967–69; Lectr, 1969–77, Reader, 1977–85, Sch. of Envmtl Scis, UEA. Vis. Prof., Univ. of Washington, Seattle, 1977; Visiting Scientist: Ocean Chem. Lab., Canada, 1975; Grad. Sch. of Oceanography, Univ. of Rhode Island, 1989, 1990; Guest Prof., Ocean Univ., Qingdao, China, 1997–. Envmtl Chemistry Dist. Lectr, 2002, John Jeyes Lect. Award, 2003, RSC. Scientific Advisor, CEGB, London, 1979–82. Member: NERC, 1990–95; Royal Commn on Envmtl Pollution, 2005–. Treasurer, 1990–93, Chm., 1993–97, Sci. Cttee for Internat. Geosphere-Biosphere Prog.; Chairman: Scientific Steering Cttee, Surface Ocean - Lower Atmosphere Study (SOLAS), 2002–; Global Envmtl Res. Cttee, Royal Soc., 2007–09 (Vice-Chm., 1998–2007); Ind. Mem., Inter-Agency Cttee for Marine Sci. and Technol., 2000–. Pres., Challenger Soc. for Marine Sci., 2006–08 (Challenger Medal, 2000). *Publications:* Estuarine Chemistry, 1976; Environmental Chemistry, 1980; Man-Made Carbon Dioxide and Climatic Change, 1983; Quimica Ambiental, 1983; Air-Sea Exchange of Gases and Particles, 1983; Power Generation and the Environment, 1990; An Introduction to Environmental Chemistry, 1996, 2nd edn 2004; The Sea Surface and Global Change, 1997. *Recreations:* reading, music, house renovation. *Address:* 5 Chester Place, Norwich, Norfolk NR2 3DG. *T:* (01603) 623815; *e-mail:* p.liss@uea.ac.uk.

LISSACK, Richard Antony; QC 1994; a Recorder, since 1999; *b* 7 June 1956; *s* of late Victor Jack Lissack and Antoinette Rosalind Lissack; *m* 1986, Carolyn Dare Arscott; three *d* (incl. twins). *Educ:* UCS, Hampstead. Called to the Bar, Inner Temple, 1978, Bencher, 2007; an Asst Recorder, 1993–99; QC: Eastern Caribbean, 2002; New York, 2007; NI, 2007. Chairman: S & W Wilts Hunt, 1996–2002 (Pres., 2002–); Disciplinary Cttee, British Horse Trials, 2000–05. *Recreations:* breeding, competing and falling off thoroughbred horses, farming. *Address:* The Outer Temple, 222 Strand, WC2R 1BA. *T:* (020) 7353 6381. *Clubs:* Soho House; Turf; Rock Sailing.

LISTER; *see* Cunliffe-Lister, family name of Earl of Swinton.

LISTER, Andrew; *see* Lister, T. A.

LISTER, Geoffrey Richard, CBE 1994; FCA; FCIB; Joint Vice Chairman, 1996–97, Director, 1988–97, Bradford & Bingley Building Society; *b* 14 May 1937; *s* of Walter and Margaret Lister; *m* 1962, Myrtle Margaret (*née* Cooper); one *s* two *d.* *Educ:* St Bede's Grammar Sch., Bradford. Articled clerk, J. Pearson & Son, 1955–60, qual. chartered accountant, 1960; Computer and Systems Sales, Burroughs Machines Ltd, 1961–63; Audit Man., Thos Gardner & Co., 1963–65; Bradford & Bingley Building Society: Asst Accountant, 1965–67; Computer Man., 1967–70; Chief Accountant, 1970–73; Asst Gen. Man., 1973–75; Dep. Gen. Man., 1975–80; Gen. Man., 1980–84; Dep. Chief Exec., 1984–85; Chief Exec., 1985–95. Director: NHBC, 1992–97; PIA, 1994–95; Anchor Trust, 1997–99. Building Societies' Association: Mem. Council, 1984–97; Dep. Chm., 1992–93; Chm., 1993–94. CCMI. *Recreations:* walking, gardening. *Address:* Harbeck House, Harbeck Drive, Harden, Bingley, W Yorks BD16 1JG. *T:* (01535) 272350. *Clubs:* Carlton; Bradford and Bingley Sports (Bingley, W Yorks).

LISTER, Prof. (Margot) Ruth (Aline), CBE 1999; Professor of Social Policy, Loughborough University, since 1994; *b* 3 May 1949; *d* of Dr Werner Bernard Lister and Daphne (*née* Carter). *Educ:* Univ. of Essex (BA Hons Sociology); Univ. of Sussex (MA Multi-Racial Studies). Child Poverty Action Group: Legal Res. Officer, 1971–75; Asst Dir, 1975–77; Dep. Dir, 1977–79; Dir, 1979–87; Prof. of Applied Social Studies, Univ. of Bradford, 1987–93. Donald Dewar Vis. Prof. of Social Justice, Univ. of Glasgow, 2005–06. Vice-Chair, NCVO, 1991–93. Member: Opsahl Commn, 1992–93; Commn for Social Justice, 1992–94; Commn on Poverty, Participation and Power, 1999–2000; Fabian Commn on Life Chances and Child Poverty, 2004–06. Eleanor Rathbone Meml Lecture, Univ. of Leeds, 1989. Founding Academician, Acad. of Social Scis, 1999. Hon. LLD Manchester, 1987. *Publications:* Supplementary Benefit Rights, 1974; Welfare Benefits, 1981; The Exclusive Society, 1990; Women's Economic Dependency and Social Security, 1992; Citizenship: feminist perspectives, 1997, 2nd edn 2003; Poverty, 2004; (jtly) Gendering Citizenship in Western Europe, 2007; (co-ed) Why Money Matters, 2008; pamphlets, articles, and contrib. to many books on poverty, social security and women's citizenship. *Recreations:* walking, music, films, Tai Chi. *Address:* Loughborough University, Loughborough, Leics LE11 3TU; 45 Quayside Close, Nottingham NG2 3BP.

LISTER, (Robert) Patrick, CBE 1993; retired; *b* 6 Jan. 1922; *s* of Robert B. Lister; *m* 1942, Daphne Rosamund, *d* of Prof. C. J. Sisson; three *s* one *d* (and one *s* decd). *Educ:* Marlborough College; Cambridge University (MA); Harvard Business School (MBA). Captain Royal Engineers, 1942–46; Massey Harris, Toronto, 1949–51; joined Coventry Climax Ltd, 1951, Managing Director, 1971–80, Deputy Chairman, 1980–81; Dir, Climax Fork Trucks, 1981–83; Dir and Chief Exec., Engrg Employers W Midlands Assoc., 1983–84. President: Fedn Européenne de la Manutention, 1978–80; Coventry and Dist Engineering Employers' Assoc., 1979–80 and 1983; British Indust. Truck Assoc., 1980–81; Vice-Pres., Inst. of Materials Handling, later Inst. of Materials Management, 1982–93 (FILog Emeritus, 1993). Mem., 1984–97, Chm., 1986–97, Bd of Govs, and Pro-Chancellor, 1997–2005, Coventry Univ.; Gov., Coventry Technical Coll., 1984–2002. Hon. DBA Coventry, 1997. KSS 1992. *Recreations:* pastoral work, gardening, DIY. *Address:* 35 Warwick Avenue, Coventry CV5 6DJ. *T:* (024) 7667 3776.

LISTER, Ruth; *see* Lister, M. R. A.

LISTER, Prof. (Thomas) Andrew, MD; FRCP, FRCPath, FMedSci, FRCR; Professor of Medical Oncology, since 1995, and Director of Cancer Research UK (formerly Imperial Cancer Research Fund) Medical Oncology Unit, since 1995, St Bartholomew's Hospital; *b* 15 Dec. 1944; *s* of John and Eileen Lister; *m* 1969, Sarah Leigh Martin; two *s*. *Educ:* Shrewsbury; St John's Coll., Cambridge (BA Hons 1966; MB BChir 1969); St Bartholomew's Hosp. Med. Sch. FRCP 1982; FRCPath 1994; FRCR 2001. St Bartholomew's Hospital: Sen. Lectr and Hon. Consultant Physician, Dept of Med. Oncology, 1977–83; Reader in Clinical Oncology, 1983–87; Prof. of Clinical Oncology, 1987–95; Postgrad. Asst Dean, and Clinical Tutor, Med. Coll. of St Bartholomew's, 1987–93; Dir of Cancer Services and Clinical Haematol., St Bartholomew's Hosp. and Bart's and the London NHS Trust, 1994–2004. Hon. Consultant Physician, Broomfield Hosp., Chelmsford, 1979–. FMedSci 2002. *Publications:* (ed jtly) Leukemia, 6th edn 1996, 7th edn 2002; (ed jtly) The Lymphomas, 1997; contrib. Jl of Clinical Oncology, Blood, British Jl of Cancer, British Jl of Haematology, Annals of Oncology. *Recreations:* golf, bird watching. *Address:* Department of Medical Oncology, St Bartholomew's Hospital, West Smithfield, EC1A 7BE. *T:* (020) 7601 7462, *Fax:* (020) 7796 3979; *e-mail:* andrew.lister@cancer.org.uk. *Clubs:* New (Edinburgh); Honourable Company of Edinburgh Golfers.

LISTER, Tom, CBE 1978; QFSM 1977; Chief Fire Officer, West Midlands County Council, 1975–81, retired; *b* 14 May 1924; *s* of late T. Lister and Mrs E. Lister; *m* 1954, Linda, *d* of late T. J. and Mrs H. Dodds; one *d*. *Educ:* Charter House, Hull. Hull Fire Service, 1947–60; divisional officer, Lancs, 1960–62; Asst Chief Fire Officer, Warwicks, 1962–68; Chief Fire Officer, Glos, 1968–71, Bristol and Avon, 1972–75.

LISTER-KAYE, Sir John (Phillip Lister), 8th Bt *cr* 1812, of Grange, Yorks; OBE 2003; Director of the Aigas Trust, since 1979; *b* 8 May 1946; *s* of Sir John Christopher Lister Lister-Kaye, 7th Bt and Audrey Helen (*d* 1979), *d* of E. J. Carter; *S* father, 1982; direct linear descendant of Kaye Btcy *cr* 1641, of Woodsome (ext 1809); *m* 1st, 1972, Lady Sorrel Deirdre Bentinck (marr. diss. 1987), *d* of 11th Earl of Portland; one *s* two *d*; 2nd, 1989, Lucinda Anne (formerly Hon. Mrs Evan Baillie), *d* of Robin Law, Withersfield; one *d*. *Educ:* Allhallows School. Naturalist, author, lecturer. Created first field studies centre in Highlands of Scotland, 1970; Founder Director of Scottish conservation charity, the Aigas Trust, 1979; Dir, Aigas Quest Ltd, 1997–. Mem., Internat. Cttee, World Wilderness Foundn, 1983–; Chairman: Scottish Adv. Cttee, RSPB, 1986–92; Cttee for Scotland, NCC, 1989–91; NW Region, NCC for Scotland, 1991–92; NW Region, Scottish Natural Heritage, 1992–96. Pres., Scottish Wildlife Trust, 1996–2001 (Hon. Mem., 2003); Vice-Pres., Council for Protection of Rural Scotland, 1998–; Hon. Vice-Pres., RSPB, 2006–. DUniv Stirling, 1995; Hon. LLD St Andrews, 2005. *Publications:* The White Island, 1972; Seal Cull, 1979; The Seeing Eye, 1980; One for Sorrow, 1994; Ill Fares The Land, 1995; Song of the Rolling Earth, 2003; Nature's Child, 2004. *Recreations:* beach-combing, driving hydraulic diggers. *Heir:* *s* John Warwick Noel Lister-Kaye, *b* 10 Dec. 1974. *Address:* House of Aigas, Beauly, Inverness-shire IV4 7AD. *T:* (01463) 782729, *Fax:* (01463) 782097. *Club:* Caledonian.

LISTON, Gerald John, CMG 2002; Regional Director, Central and South Asia, British Council, since 2008; *b* 21 April 1949; *s* of Sidney George Liston and Ivy Mary Liston (*née* Matthews). *Educ:* Cheltenham Grammar Sch.; St Catherine's Coll., Oxford (BA Physics, MA); London Sch. of Econs (MSc Econs). Volunteer, VSO, Malaysia, 1970–71; joined British Council, 1972: Secretariat, 1972–73; Asst Regl Dir, Kumasi, Ghana, 1973–75; Asst Rep., Malaysia, 1975–80; Staff Inspr, Mgt Services, 1980–84; Director: Office Systems, 1985–88; Corporate IT, 1988–96; UK Ops, 1996–98; Resources, 1999–2003; Dir, Malaysia, 2003–08. *Recreations:* music, reading, walking, badminton, tropical plants. *Address:* c/o British Council, 10 Spring Gardens, SW1A 2BN; *e-mail:* gerry_liston@yahoo.co.uk.

LISTOWEL, 6th Earl of, *cr* 1822 (Ire.); **Francis Michael Hare;** Baron Ennismore (Ire.), 1800; Viscount Ennismore and Listowel (Ire.), 1816; Baron Hare (UK), 1869; *b* 28 June 1964; *s* of 5th Earl of Listowel, GCMG, PC and of his 3rd wife, Pamela Reid (*née* Day); *S* father, 1997. *Educ:* Westminster Sch.; Queen Mary and Westfield Coll., London Univ. (BA 1992). Elected Mem., H of L, 1999; Mem., Sub-Cttee F (Home Affairs), Select Cttee on EU, H of L, 2003–07; Treas., All-Party Parly Gp for Children; Associate, Parly Gp for Children in Care. Patron, Voice for the Child in Care. *Heir:* *b* Hon. Timothy Patrick Hare, *b* 23 Feb. 1966.

LIT, Avtar; Chairman and Chief Executive: Sunrise Radio Network, since 1989; Asia Broadcasting Corporation (Sri Lanka), since 1998; London Media Company, since 2003; *b* 7 April 1950; *s* of Gurbax Kaur Lit and Sarwan Singh Lit; *m* 1995, Anita Loomba; three *s* two *d*. *Educ:* Temple Secondary Sch., Rochester; Collingwood Naval Coll., Chatham. Man. Dir, Cable Vision, 1982–; Chairman and Chief Executive: Sunrise Radio Ltd, 1989–; Kismat Radio Network; Punjabi Radio Network; Sunrise TV; ABC Radio Network (Sri Lanka), 1998–; Dir, Sunrise Radio (Mauritius), 1994–. Hon. PhD Thames Valley, 2003. *Recreations:* new projects, travelling, para-sailing, ski-ing. *Address:* Sunrise House, Sunrise Road, Southall, Middlesex UB2 4AU. *T:* (020) 8574 6666, *Fax:* (020) 8813 9800; *e-mail:* alit@sunriseradio.com. *Club:* Reform.

LITHERLAND, Prof. Albert Edward, (Ted), FRS 1974; FRSC 1968; University Professor, 1979–93, now Emeritus, and Professor of Physics, 1966–93, University of Toronto; Director, Isotrace Laboratory, University of Toronto, since 1982; *b* 12 March 1928; *e s* of Albert Litherland and Ethel Clement; *m* 1956, (Elizabeth) Anne Allen; two *d*. *Educ:* Wallasey Grammar Sch.; Univ. of Liverpool (BSc, PhD). State Scholar to Liverpool Univ., 1946; Rutherford Memorial Scholar to Atomic Energy of Canada, Chalk River, Canada, 1953; Scientific Officer at Atomic Energy of Canada, 1955–66. Guggenheim Fellow, Toronto Univ., 1986–87. Hon. DSc Toronto, 1998. Canadian Assoc. of Physicists Gold Medal for Achievement in Physics, 1971; Rutherford Medal and Prize of Inst. of Physics (London), 1974; JARI Silver Medal, Pergamon Press, 1981; Henry Marshall Tory Medal, RSC, 1993. Izaac Walton Killam Memorial Scholarship, 1980. *Publications:* numerous, in scientific jls. *Address:* Apt #801, 120 Rosedale Valley Road, Toronto, ON M4W 1P8, Canada. *T:* (416) 9235616; *e-mail:* ted.litherland@utoronto.ca.

LITHERLAND, Robert Kenneth; *b* 23 June 1930; *s* of Robert Litherland and Mary (*née* Parry); *m* 1953, Edna Litherland; one *s* one *d*. *Educ:* North Manchester High Sch. for Boys. Formerly sales representative for printing firm. Mem., Manchester City Council, 1971 (Dep. Chm., Housing Cttee, 1979; Chm., Manchester Direct Works Cttee, 1974–78); Dep. Chm., Public Works Cttee, Assoc. of Municipal Authorities, 1977–78. MP (Lab) Manchester Central, Sept. 1979–1997. Member: Council of Europe, 1987–97; WEU, 1987–97. *Address:* 32 Darley Avenue, Didsbury, Manchester M20 8YD.

LITHERLAND, Ted; *see* Litherland, A. E.

LITHGOW, Sir William (James), 2nd Bt *cr* 1925, of Ormsary; DL; CEng; industrialist and farmer; Director, Lithgows Ltd, 1956–2006 (Chairman, 1959–84 and 1988–99); *b* 10 May 1934; *o s* of Colonel Sir James Lithgow, 1st Bt of Ormsary, GBE, CB, MC, TD, DL, JP, LLD, and Gwendolyn Amy, *d* of late John Robinson Harrison of Scalesceugh, Cumberland; *S* father, 1952; *m* 1964, Valerie Helen (*d* 1964), 2nd *d* of late Denis Scott, CBE and Mrs Laura Scott; *m* 1967, Mary Claire, (DL Argyll and Bute), *d* of Colonel F. M. Hill, CBE and Mrs Hill; two *s* one *d*. *Educ:* Winchester Coll. CEng; FRINA; CCMI (FBIM 1969; CBIM 1980). Chm., Scott Lithgow Drydocks Ltd, 1967–78; Vice-Chm., Scott Lithgow Ltd, 1968–78; Chairman: Western Ferries (Argyll) Ltd, 1972–85; Hunterston Develt Co. Ltd, 1987– (Dir, 1971–); Director: Bank of Scotland, 1962–86; Campbeltown Shipyard Ltd, 1970–96; Lithgows Pty Ltd, 1972–; Landcatch, 1981–96. Member: Council, Shipbuilding Employers Fedn, 1961–62; British Cttee, Det Norske Veritas, 1966–92; Exec. Cttee, Scottish Council Develt and Industry, 1969–85; Scottish Regional Council of CBI, 1969–76; Clyde Port Authority, 1969–71; Bd, National Ports Council, 1971–78; West Central Scotland Plan Steering Cttee, 1970–74; General Board (Royal Soc. nominee), Nat. Physical Lab., 1963–66; Greenock Dist Hosp. Bd, 1961–66; Scottish Milk Marketing Bd, 1979–83. Chm., Iona Cathedral Trustees Management Bd, 1979–83; Mem. Council, Winston Churchill Meml Trust, 1979–83. Hon. President: Mid Argyll Agricl Soc., 1976–99; Inverclyde and Dist Bn, Boys' Brigade, 1998–2000 (Vice Hon. Pres., 2000–); former Hon. Pres., W Renfrewshire Bn Boys' Brigade. Hon. Pres., Students Assoc., and Mem. Court, Univ. of Strathclyde, 1964–69. Petitioner in case of Lithgow and others *v* UK, at Eur. Court of Human Rights, 1986. Member, Queen's Body Guard for Scotland (Royal Company of Archers), 1964. Fellow: Scottish Council, 1988; Bishop Mus., Hawaii, 1969. FRSA 1990. DL Renfrewshire, 1970. Hon. LLD Strathclyde, 1979. *Publications:* lectures and papers. *Recreations:* rural life, invention, photography. *Heir:* *s* James Frank Lithgow [*b* 13 June 1970; *m* 1997, Claire, *yr d* of Nicholas du Cane Wilkinson; two *s* one *d*]. *Address:* Ormsary House, by Lochgilphead, Argyllshire PA31 8PE. *T:* (01880) 770252; Drums, Langbank, Renfrewshire PA14 6YH. *T:* (01475) 540606; RMB 125A, Karridale, WA 6288, Australia. *T:* (8) 97582261; (office) PO Box 7, Lochgilphead, Argyllshire PA31 8JH. *T:* (01880) 770711. *Clubs:* Oriental; Western (Glasgow).

LITHMAN, Nigel Mordecai Lloyd; QC 1997; a Recorder, since 2000; *b* 9 March 1952; *s* of Dr Leslie Henry Lithman, FFARCS, and Ethel Imber Lithman; *m* Debbie; three step *s*. *Educ:* Bancroft's Sch., Woodford Green; Mid Essex Coll., Chelmsford (LLB Hons). Called to the Bar, Inner Temple, 1976; in practice at the Bar, 1976–; Asst Recorder, 1996–2000. Chm., Essex Bar Mess. *Recreations:* fresh air, the arts. *Address:* Highgate, London; Stanbrook Mead, Stanbrook, Thaxted, Essex CM6 2NQ. *Club:* Lansdowne.

LITTLE, Alastair; *see* Little, R. A.

LITTLE, Allan; *see* Little, J. A. S.

LITTLE, Anthony Richard Morrell; Head Master, Eton College, since 2002; *b* 7 April 1954; *s* of Edward Little and Rosemary Margaret Little (*née* Morrell); *m* 1978, Jennifer Anne Greenwood; one *d*. *Educ:* Eton Coll.; Corpus Christi Coll., Cambridge (MA English); Homerton Coll., Cambridge (PGCE). FCollP 1990. Asst Master, Tonbridge Sch., 1977–82; Hd of English and Boarding Housemaster, Brentwood Sch., 1982–89; Headmaster: Chigwell Sch., 1989–96; Oakham Sch., 1996–2002. Governor: Northwood Coll., 1990–98; St Albans Sch., 1994–; Windsor Boys' Sch., 2002–. FRSA 1991. *Recreations:* films, theatre, music, Norfolk. *Address:* Eton College, Windsor, Berks SL4 6DL.

LITTLE, Ian; *see* Little, J. M.

LITTLE, Ian Malcolm David, CBE 1997; AFC 1943; FBA 1973; Professor of Economics of Underdeveloped Countries, University of Oxford, 1971–76; *b* 18 Dec. 1918; *s* of Brig.-Gen. M. O. Little, CB, CBE, and Iris Hermione Little (*née* Brassey); *m* 1st, 1946, Doreen Hennessey (*d* 1984); one *s* one *d*; 2nd, 1991, Lydia Segrave. *Educ:* Eton; New Coll., Oxford (MA, DPhil; Hon. Fellow, 1999). RAF Officer, 1939–46. Fellow: All Souls Coll., Oxford, 1948–50; Trinity Coll., Oxford, 1950–52; Nuffield Coll., Oxford, 1952–76, Emeritus Fellow, 1976. Dep. Dir, Economic Section, Treasury, 1953–55; Mem., MIT Centre for Internat. Studies, India, 1958–59 and 1965; Vice-Pres., OECD Develt Centre, Paris, 1965–67. Dir, Investing in Success Ltd, 1960–65; Bd Mem., British Airports Authority, 1969–74. Dir, Gen. Funds Investment Trust, 1974–76; Special Adviser, IBRD, 1976–78. Hon. DSc(SocSci) Edinburgh, 1976. *Publications:* A Critique of Welfare Economics, 1950; The Price of Fuel, 1953; (jtly) Concentration in British Industry, 1960; Aid to Africa, 1964; (jtly) International Aid, 1965; (jtly) Higgledy-Piggledy Growth Again, 1966; (jtly) Manual of Industrial Project Analysis in Developing Countries, 1969; (jtly) Industry and Trade in Some Developing Countries, 1970; (jtly) Project Analysis and Planning, 1974; Economic Development: theory, policy and international relations, 1982; (jtly) Small Manufacturing Enterprises, 1987; (jtly) Boom, Crisis and Adjustment, 1993; (jtly) India: macroeconomics and political economy 1964–1991, 1994; (jtly) India's Economic Reforms 1991–2001, 1996; (ed jtly) India's Economic Reforms and Development: essays for Manmohan Singh, 1998; Ethics, Economics and Politics, 2002; many articles in learned jls.

LITTLE, (James) Allan (Stuart); World Affairs Correspondent, BBC News, since 2005; *b* Dunragit, Wigtownshire, 11 Oct. 1959; *s* of Francis Robert Little and Elizabeth Margaret Little (*née* Clive); *m* 2006, Sheena Elizabeth McDonald. *Educ:* Univ. of Edinburgh (MA 1982). BBC: researcher, BBC Scotland, 1983; reporter: BBC Radio, 1984; Today prog., Radio Four, 1988; reporter and correspondent, BBC Foreign News, 1990–95, Iraq, 1990–91, former Yugoslavia, 1991–95; BBC Africa Corresp., Johannesburg, 1995–97 and 2000–01; Moscow Corresp., 1997–99; Presenter, Today prog., Radio Four, 1999–2003; Paris Corresp., 2003–05. Mem., Scotch Malt Whisky Soc., Edinburgh. *Publication:* (with Laura Silber) Death of Yugoslavia, 1995. *Recreations:* escaping to Scotland, books, countryside, walking. *Address:* BBC TV Centre, Wood Lane, W12 7RJ. *T:* (020) 8743 8000. *Club:* Frontline.

LITTLE, John MacCalman, (Ian), CMG 2003; CBE 1983; Chairman of Employers' Group, 2000–02, Member, 1990–2002, European Economic and Social Committee; *b* 23 Feb. 1936; *s* of John Little and Margaret Haddow Little (*née* King); *m* 1962, Irene Pirrie Frame; one *s* one *d*. *Educ:* Marr Coll., Troon. CA 1958; ACMA 1962. Financial positions: Stewarts & Lloyds Ltd, 1961–63; Pressed Steel Fisher Ltd, 1963–69; Anderson Strathclyde plc: Gp Accountant, 1969–70; Divl Financial Dir, 1971–73; Financial Dir, 1973–77; Asst Man. Dir, 1977–80; Dep. Chm. and Chief Exec., 1980–88. Dir, Scottish Exhibition Centre Ltd, 1989–96. Member: Council, CBI Scotland, 1980–89 (Chm., 1985–87); Scottish Industrial Adv. Bd, 1981–93; Accounts Commn for Scotland, 1989–97. Treas., Strathaven Rankin Parish Church, 1974–2007. *Recreations:* golf, gardening, bridge. *Address:* 8 Wateryett Loan, Strathaven, Lanarkshire ML10 6EJ. *T:* (01357) 520762; *e-mail:* jmlittle@btinternet.com. *Club:* Strathaven Golf (Chm., 2000–04).

LITTLE, (Robert) Alastair; chef and restaurant proprietor; *b* 25 June 1950; *s* of Robert Geoffrey Little and Marion Irving Little; one *s* one *d*; *m* 2000, Sharon Jacob; one *s*. *Educ:* Kirkham Grammar Sch., Lancs; Downing Coll., Cambridge (MA). Chef proprietor: Le Routier, Suffolk, 1976; Simpson's, Putney, 1979; L'Escargot, Soho, 1981; 192, London, 1983; Alastair Little, Soho, 1985; Alastair Little, Lancaster Road, 1995; proprietor, La

Cacciata, Orvieto, Italy, 1994. *Publications:* (with Richard Whittington) Keep it Simple, 1993; (with Richard Whittington) Food of the Sun, 1995; Alastair Little's Italian Kitchen, 1996; Soho Cooking, 1999. *Recreations:* reading, mycology. *Address:* 49 Frith Street, W1V 5TE. *T:* (020) 7437 6733. *Club:* Groucho.

LITTLE, Tasmin, (Mrs M. Hatch); violinist; *b* 13 May 1965; *d* of George Villiers Little and Gillian (*née* Morris); *m* 1993, Michael Hatch; one *d. Educ:* Yehudi Menuhin Sch.; Guildhall Sch. of Music (DipGSM 1986). ARCM 1984. Has performed as soloist in UK, Europe, USA, Scandinavia, S America, Hong Kong, Oman, Zimbabwe and SA. Concerto performances with leading orchestras including: Leipzig Gewandhaus; Berlin Symphony; LSO; Philharmonia; Royal Philharmonic; Hallé; Bournemouth; Royal Liverpool Philharmonic; EC Chamber Orch.; Royal Danish; Stavanger Symphony; NY Philharmonic; Cleveland; acknowledged interpreter of music of Delius. TV appearances, radio broadcasts; recordings. FGSM. Hon. DLitt Bradford, 1996; Hon. DMus Leicester, 2002. *Publication:* contrib. Delius Soc. Jl. *Recreations:* theatre, cinema, swimming, cooking, languages. *Address:* c/o Askonas Holt Ltd, Lincoln House, 200 High Holborn, WC1V 7JH. *T:* (020) 7400 1700.

LITTLE, Dr Thomas William Anthony, CBE 2001; FIBiol; Director and Chief Executive, Veterinary Laboratories Agency (formerly Central Veterinary Laboratory), Ministry of Agriculture, Fisheries and Food, 1990–2000; *b* 27 June 1940; *s* of late Thomas Lowden Little and Marjorie Annie Little; *m* 1st, 1963 (marr. diss.); one *s* one *d*; 2nd, 1985, Sally Anne Headlam; two *s. Educ:* Dame Allan's Sch., Newcastle upon Tyne; Edinburgh Univ. (BVMS); London Univ. (Dip. Bact., PhD). MRCVS 1963. General veterinary practice, March, Cambs, 1963–66; joined MAFF, 1966; Central Vet. Lab., Weybridge, 1966–82, Sen. Res. Officer 1973–82; Dep. Regl Vet. Officer, 1982–85, Vet. Head of Section, 1985–86, Tolworth; Dep. Dir, Central Vet. Lab., 1986–90. Vice-Pres., BVA, 2000–02. Chair of Govs, Fullbrook Sch., 2006–. FRSA. *Publications:* contribs to veterinary jls and text books. *Recreations:* outdoor activities. *Address:* 10 Fox Close, Pyrford, Woking, Surrey GU22 8LP.

LITTLECHILD, Prof. Stephen Charles; international consultant on privatisation, competition and regulation, since 1999; Senior Research Associate, Judge Business School (formerly Judge Institute of Management Studies), University of Cambridge, since 2004 (Principal Research Fellow, 2000–04); *b* 27 Aug. 1943; *s* of Sidney F. Littlechild and Joyce M. Littlechild (*née* Sharpe); *m* 1974, Kate Crombie (*d* 1982); two *s* one *d. Educ:* Wisbech Grammar Sch.; Univ. of Birmingham (BCom); Univ. of Texas (PhD). Temp. Asst Lectr in Ind. Econs, Univ. of Birmingham, 1964–65; Harkness Fellow, Stanford Univ., 1965–66; Northwestern Univ., 1966–68; Univ. of Texas at Austin, 1968–69; ATT Postdoctoral Fellow, UCLA and Northwestern Univ., 1969; Sen. Res. Lectr in Econs, Graduate Centre for Management Studies, Birmingham, 1970–72; Prof. of Applied Econs and Head of Econs, Econometrics, Statistics and Marketing Subject Gp, Aston Management Centre, 1972–75; Prof. of Commerce and Hd of Dept of Industrial Econs and Business Studies, Univ. of Birmingham, 1975–89; Dir Gen., Electricity Supply, 1989–98. Vis. Scholar, Dept of Econs, UCLA, 1975; Vis. Prof., New York, Stanford and Chicago Univs, and Virginia Polytechnic, 1979–80; Hon. Prof., Sch. of Business, Univ. of Birmingham, 1994–2004, now Emeritus Prof. Member: Monopolies and Mergers Commn, 1983–89; Sec. of State for Energy's Adv. Council on R&D, 1987–89; Postal Services Commn, 2006–. Hon. DSc Birmingham, 2001; Hon. DCL UEA, 2004. Zale Award, Stanford Univ., 1999; Pace Catalyst Award, UMS Gp, 2000. *Publications:* Operational Research for Managers, 1977, 2nd edn (with M. F. Shutler) as Operations Research in Management, 1991; The Fallacy of the Mixed Economy, 1978, 2nd edn 1986; Elements of Telecommunications Economics, 1979; Energy Strategies for the UK, 1982; Regulation of British Telecommunications' Profitability, 1983; Economic Regulation of Privatised Water Authorities, 1986; Privatization, Competition and Regulation in the British Electricity Industry, with Implications for Developing Countries, 2000; over 120 articles in books and jls. *Recreations:* football, genealogy. *Address:* White House, The Green, Tanworth-in-Arden B94 5AL; *e-mail:* sclittlechild@tanworth.mercianet.co.uk.

LITTLEJOHN, Bel; see Brown, C. E. M.

LITTLEJOHN, Doris, CBE 1998; JP; President, Industrial Tribunals (Scotland), 1991–2000; *b* 19 March 1935; *m* 1958, Robert White Littlejohn (decd); three *d. Educ:* Univ. of Glasgow (BL). Chm., Forth Valley Primary Care NHS Trust, until 2004. Mem., Govt Human Genetics Adv. Commn, until 1999. Non-executive Director: Law at Work (Holdings) Ltd, 2002–; Saga Radio (Glasgow) Ltd, 2004–06. Chm. Ct, Univ. of Stirling, 1999–2007. JP Stirlingshire, 1970. DUniv Stirling, 1993. *Address:* 125 Henderson Street, Bridge of Allan, Stirlingshire FK9 4RQ. *T:* (01786) 832032.

LITTLER, Sir (James) Geoffrey, KCB 1985 (CB 1981); Director, Montanaro UK Smaller Companies Investment Trust plc, 1995–2000; *b* 18 May 1930; *s* of late James Edward Littler and Evelyn Mary Littler (*née* Taylor); *m* 1958, Shirley Marsh (*see* Shirley Littler); one *s. Educ:* Manchester Grammar Sch.; Corpus Christi Coll., Cambridge (MA; Hon. Fellow, 1994). Asst Principal, Colonial Office, 1952–54; transf. to Treasury, 1954; Principal 1957; Asst Sec. 1966; Under-Sec. 1972; Dep. Sec., 1977; Second Permanent Sec. (Overseas Finance), 1983–88. Chairman: EC Monetary Cttee Deputies, 1974–77; Working Party 3, OECD, 1985–88; EC Monetary Cttee, 1987–88. Chairman: TR European Growth Trust plc, 1990–98; County NatWest Group Ltd, 1991–92; Director: NatWest Investment Bank, 1989–91; National Westminster Bank PLC, 1991–92; Chm., Israel Fund plc, 1994–99; Dir, Maritime Transport Services Ltd, 1990–93; Sen. Advr, BZW Ltd, 1993–98. *Recreation:* music. *Club:* Reform.

LITTLER, Shirley, (Lady Littler); Chairman, Gaming Board for Great Britain, 1992–98; *b* 8 June 1932; *d* of late Sir Percy William Marsh, CSI, CIE, and late Joan Mary Beecroft; *m* 1958, Sir (James) Geoffrey Littler, *qv;* one *s. Educ:* Headington Sch., Oxford; Girton Coll., Cambridge (MA; Barbara Bodichon Fellow, 2005). Assistant Principal, HM Treasury, 1953; Principal: HM Treasury, 1960; Dept of Trade and Industry, 1964; HM Treasury, 1966; Asst Secretary, National Board for Prices and Incomes, 1969; Secretary, V&G Tribunal, 1971; transf. to Home Office, 1972, Asst Under-Sec. of State, 1978–83. Joined IBA, 1983; Dep. Dir Gen., 1986–89; Dir Gen. 1990. Chm., Gaming Regulators Eur. Forum, 1996–98. Chm., Nat. Adv. Body for Health Depts' Confidential Enquiry into Stillbirths and Deaths in Infancy, 1992–99. Trustee, Police Foundn, 1992–2001. *Recreations:* history, reading.

LITTLETON, family name of **Baron Hatherton.**

LITTLEWOOD, Prof. Peter Brent, PhD; FRS 2007; Professor of Physics, since 1997, and Head, Department of Physics, since 2005, Cavendish Laboratory, University of Cambridge; Fellow, Trinity College, Cambridge, since 1997; *b* 18 May 1955; *s* of Horace Victor Littlewood and Edna May Littlewood; *m* 1978, Elizabeth Lamb; one *s* one *d. Educ:* St Olave's Sch., Orpington; Trinity Coll., Cambridge (BA 1976); Massachusetts Inst. of Technol. (Kennedy Schol.); Clare Coll., Cambridge (Denman Baynes Student; PhD

1980). Bell Laboratories, Murray Hill, New Jersey: Mem., Technical Staff, 1980–97; Hd, Theoretical Physics Res. Dept, 1992–97. Fellow, APS, 1988. *Publications:* numerous contribs to learned jls on theoretical condensed matter physics. *Recreations:* squash, music. *Address:* Cavendish Laboratory, Cambridge University, J. J. Thomson Avenue, Cambridge CB3 0HE. *T:* (01223) 337429.

LITTMAN, Mark; QC 1961; Director: Granada Group PLC, 1977–93; Burton Group plc, 1983–93; *b* 4 Sept. 1920; *s* of Jack and Lilian Littman; *m* 1965, Marguerite Lamkin, USA. *Educ:* Owen's Sch.; London Sch. of Economics (BScEcon (1st class hons) 1939); The Queen's Coll., Oxford (MA 1941). Served RN, Lieut, 1941–46. Called to Bar, Middle Temple, 1947 (Bencher, 1970, Treas., 1988); practised as Barrister-at-law, 1947–67 and 1979–; Head of Littman Chambers, 1979–2003, Chambers of Mark Littman QC, 2003–. Member: General Council of the Bar, 1968–72; Senate of Inns of Court and the Bar, 1968. Dep. Chm., BSC, 1970–79. Mem. Royal Commn on Legal Services, 1976–79. Director: Rio Tinto-Zinc Corp. PLC, 1968–91; Commercial Union Assurance Co. Ltd, 1970–81; Amerada Hess Corp. (US), 1973–86; British Enkalon Ltd, 1976–80; Envirotech Corp. (US), 1974–78. Mem., Internat. Council for Commercial Arbitration, 1978–. Mem., Ct of Governors, LSE, 1980–. *Address:* 79 Chester Square, SW1W 9DU; (chambers) 12 Gray's Inn Square, WC1R 5JP. *Clubs:* Garrick, Reform, Oxford and Cambridge, Royal Automobile; Century Association (New York).

LITTON, Andrew; conductor and pianist; Music Director, Bergen Philharmonic Orchestra, since 2005; *b* New York, 16 May 1959; *m;* one *c. Educ:* Fieldston Sch., NYC; Juilliard Sch. of Music, NYC (piano with Nadia Reisenberg; Bruno Walter Meml Conducting Scholar). Rehearsal pianist, La Scala, Milan, 1980–81; Staff Conductor, 1983–85, Associate Conductor, 1985–86, National SO, Washington; sometime Principal Conductor, Virginia Chamber Orch.; Principal Guest Conductor, 1986–88, Principal Conductor and Artistic Advr, 1988–94, Bournemouth SO, now Conductor Laureate; Music Dir, Dallas SO, 1994–2006, now Music Dir Emeritus. Début piano recital, Carnegie Hall, NY, 1979; conducting débuts include: Henry Wood Promenade Concert, 1983; RPO, 1983; Royal Opera House, Covent Garden, 1992. Winner: William Kapell Piano Comp., 1978; BBC/Rupert Foundn Internat. Conductors Comp., 1982. *Address:* Columbia Artists Management (CAMI), 1790 Broadway, New York, NY 10019–1412, USA.

LITTON, Peter Stafford; Under Secretary, Department of Education and Science, 1978–81; a General Commissioner of Income Tax, Epsom Division, 1983–96; *b* 26 Oct. 1921; *s* of late Leonard Litton and Louisa (*née* Horn); *m* 1942, Josephine Peggy Bale (*d* 2003); one *d. Educ:* Barnstaple Grammar School. Clerical Officer, Board of Education, 1938. Served in Royal Corps of Signals, 1941–46. Min. of Education, 1946; Principal Private Sec. to Secretary of State for Educn and Science, 1965–66. *Recreations:* reading, armchair astronomy. *Address:* 14 Guillards Oak, Midhurst, W Sussex GU29 9JZ. *T:* (01730) 815491.

LIU, Tsz-Ming, Benjamin, GBS 1999; a Justice of Appeal, Court of Appeal of the High Court (formerly Supreme Court), Hong Kong, 1994–99; *b* 17 May 1931; *s* of late Dr Y. T. Liu and Dorothy Mei-Kow (*née* Kwok); *m* 1954, Annemarie Marent; one *s* one *d. Educ:* Wah Yan College. Called to the Bar, Lincoln's Inn, 1957, Hong Kong, 1959; QC (Hong Kong) 1973; Judge of the District Court, Hong Kong, 1973–79; Judicial Comr, Supreme Ct, State of Brunei, 1978–89; a Judge of the High Court, Hong Kong, 1980–94. Panel Mem., Inland Revenue Bd of Review, Hong Kong, 1972; Chairman: Sub-Cttee on Bail in Criminal Proceedings, Law Reform Commn, 1985–89; Working Party on appropriate safeguards for execution of Anton Piller orders, 1992–94. Adjunct Prof., Law Faculty, Wu Nam Univ., 2003–; Vis. Prof., Law Faculty, Chung Shan Univ., 2005–; Ext. Acad. Advr, 2001–04, Adjunct Prof., 2008–, City Univ. of Hong Kong. Hon. Consultant, China Law Office, 2003–. Pres., 1992–99, Advr, 1999–, Hong Kong Local Judicial Officers' Assoc. Hong Kong Expert, China Foreign Experts Bureau, 2002; Hon. Pres., 2001–, Exec. Chm., 2005–, Hong Kong Soc. of Experts. Mem., Ethics Instnl Review Bd, Hong Kong Univ. Hosp. Authy, 2002–05; Mem. Council, UNA of China, 2002–; Hon. Advr, Hong Kong WTO Res. Inst., 2002–. Mem. Council, China Law Soc., 2004–. Director: China Overseas Friendship Assoc., 1999–2003 (Hon. Dir, 2003–); Shanghai Overseas Friendship Assoc., 2002–. *Publications:* How Are We Judged?, 2000; The Triad Societies Before and After the 1997 Change-over, 2001 (trans. Chinese, 2003); articles in press and law jls. *Address:* 1B 22 Kennedy Road, Hong Kong SAR. *T:* 28495803. *Clubs:* Hong Kong, Chinese, Hong Kong Country, Correctional Services Officers' (Hong Kong).

LIVELY, Penelope Margaret, CBE 2002 (OBE 1989); writer; *b* 17 March 1933; *d* of Roger Low and Vera Greer; *m* 1957, Jack Lively (*d* 1998); one *s* one *d. Educ:* St Anne's Coll., Oxford (BA Mod. History; Hon. Fellow, 2007). Member: Soc. of Authors, 1973–; PEN, 1985–; British Library Bd, 1993–99; Bd, British Council, 1998–2002. FRSL 1985. Hon. Fellow, Swansea Univ., 2002. Hon. DLitt: Tufts, 1992; Warwick, 1998. *Publications: children's books:* Astercote, 1970; The Whispering Knights, 1971; The Wild Hunt of Hagworthy, 1971; The Driftway, 1972; The Ghost of Thomas Kempe, 1973 (Carnegie Medal); The House in Norham Gardens, 1974; Going Back, 1975; Boy Without a Name, 1975; A Stitch in Time, 1976 (Whitbread Award); The Stained Glass Window, 1976; Fanny's Sister, 1976; The Voyage of QV66, 1978; Fanny and the Monsters, 1979; Fanny and the Battle of Potter's Piece, 1980; The Revenge of Samuel Stokes, 1981; Fanny and the Monsters (three stories), 1983; Uninvited Ghosts and other stories, 1984; Dragon Trouble, 1984; Debbie and the Little Devil, 1987; A House Inside Out, 1987; The Cat, the Crow and the Banyan Tree, 1994; Staying with Grandpa, 1997; In Search of a Homeland: the story of the Aeneid, 2001; *non-fiction:* The Presence of the Past: an introduction to landscape history, 1976; Oleander, Jacaranda: a childhood perceived, 1994; A House Unlocked (memoir), 2001; *fiction:* The Road to Lichfield, 1976; Nothing Missing but the Samovar and other stories, 1978 (Southern Arts Literature Prize); Treasures of Time, 1979 (National Book Award); Judgement Day, 1980; Next to Nature, Art, 1982; Perfect Happiness, 1983; Corruption and other stories, 1984; According to Mark, 1984; Pack of Cards, collected short stories 1978–86, 1986; Moon Tiger, 1987 (Booker Prize); Passing On, 1989; City of the Mind, 1991; Cleopatra's Sister, 1993; Heat Wave, 1996; Beyond the Blue Mountains, 1997; Spiderweb, 1998; (ed with George Szirtes) New Writing 10, 2001; The Photograph, 2003; Making It Up, 2005; Consequences, 2007; television and radio scripts. *Recreations:* gardening, landscape history, talking and listening. *Address:* c/o David Higham Associates, 5–8 Lower John Street, Golden Square, W1R 4HA. *T:* (020) 7437 7888.

LIVERMAN, Prof. Diana Margaret, PhD; Oxford Professor of Environmental Science, and Director, Environmental Change Institute, University of Oxford, since 2003; *b* 15 May 1954; *d* of John and late Peggy Liverman. *Educ:* University Coll. London (BA Geog. 1976); Univ. of Toronto (MA Geog. 1980); Univ. of Calif, LA (PhD Geog. 1984). Asst Prof. of Geog., Univ. of Wisconsin, Madison, 1984–89; Associate Prof. of Geog. and Associate Dir, Earth System Science Center, Penn State Univ., 1990–96; University of Arizona: Prof. of Geog. and Dir, Center for Latin American Studies, 1997–2003; Dean,

Coll. of Social and Behavioral Science, 2002. *Publications:* People and Pixels: linking remote sensing and social science, 1988; (jtly) World Regions in Global Context, 2002, 2nd edn 2005. *Address:* Environmental Change Institute, Oxford University Centre for the Environment, Dyson Perrins Building, South Parks Road, Oxford OX1 3QY. *T:* (01865) 275848, *Fax:* (01865) 275850.

LIVERMAN, John Gordon, CB 1973; OBE 1956; Deputy Secretary, Department of Energy, 1974–80; *b* London, 21 Oct. 1920; *s* of late George Gordon Liverman and Hadassah Liverman. *Educ:* St Paul's Sch.; Trinity Coll., Cambridge (MA). Served with RA, 1940–46. Civil servant in various government departments, 1947–80. *Address:* 12 The Stream Edge, Fisher Row, Oxford OX1 1HT. *T:* (01865) 725004.

LIVERPOOL, 5th Earl of, *cr* 1905 (2nd creation); **Edward Peter Bertram Savile Foljambe;** Baron Hawkesbury, 1893; Viscount Hawkesbury, 1905; Joint Chairman, Melbourns Brewery Ltd, since 1975 (Managing Director, 1970–87); Chairman and Managing Director, Rutland Properties Ltd, since 1987 (Director, since 1986); Chairman, Rutland Group, since 1996; *b* posthumously, 14 Nov. 1944; *s* of Captain Peter George William Savile Foljambe (killed in action, 1944) and of Elizabeth Joan (who *m* 1947, Major Andrew Antony Gibbs, MBE, TD), *d* of late Major Eric Charles Montagu Flint, DSO; *S* great uncle, 1969; *m* 1st, 1970, Lady Juliana Noel (marr. diss. 1994), *e d* of Earl of Gainsborough, *qv*; two *s*; 2nd, 1995, Marie-Ange (marr. diss. 2001), *e d* of Comte Géraud Michel de Pierredon; 3rd, 2002, Georgina, *yr d* of late Stanley and of Hilda Rubin. *Educ:* Shrewsbury School; Univ. for Foreigners, Perugia. Director: Rutland Properties Ltd, 1985–; Hart Hambleton Plc, 1986–92; J. W. Cameron & Co., 1987–90; Hilstone Developments Ltd, 1987–91; Rutland Management Ltd, 1989–. Elected Mem., H of L, 1999. *Heir: s* Viscount Hawkesbury, *qv*. *Address:* House of Lords, SW1A 0PW. *Clubs:* Turf, Pratt's, Air Squadron.

LIVERPOOL, Archbishop of, (RC), and Metropolitan of the Northern Province with Suffragan Sees, Hallam, Hexham, Lancaster, Leeds, Middlesbrough and Salford, since 1996; **Most Rev. Patrick Altham Kelly;** *b* 23 Nov. 1938; *s* of John Joseph Kelly and Mary Ann Kelly (*née* Altham). *Educ:* St Mary's Primary School, Morecambe; Preston Catholic Coll.; English College and Gregorian Univ., Rome (STL, PhL). Curate, Lancaster Cathedral, 1964–66; Lectr in Theology, 1966–79 and Rector, 1979–84, St Mary's Coll., Oscott; RC Bishop of Salford, 1984–96. *Address:* Archbishop's House, Lowood, Carnatic Road, Liverpool L18 8BY. *T:* (0151) 724 6398.

LIVERPOOL, Bishop of, since 1998; **Rt Rev. James Stuart Jones;** *b* 18 Aug. 1948; *s* of Major James Stuart Anthony Jones and Helen Jones; *m* 1980, Sarah Caroline Rosalind Marrow; three *d*. *Educ:* Duke of York's Royal Mil. Sch., Dover; Exeter Univ. (BA Hons Theol.); Wycliffe Hall, Oxford. Teacher, Sevenoaks Sch., 1970–74; Producer, Scripture Union, 1975–81; ordained deacon, 1982, priest, 1983; Curate, Christ Church, Clifton, 1982–90; Vicar, Emmanuel Church, S Croydon, 1990–94; Bishop Suffragan of Hull, 1994–98; Bishop to HM Prisons, 2007–. Took his seat in H of L, 2003. Hon. DD Hull, 1999; Hon. DLitt Lincolnshire and Humberside, 2001. *Publications:* Finding God, 1987; Why do people suffer?, 1993; The Power and the Glory, 1994; A Faith that touches the World, 1994; People of the Blessing, 1999; The Moral Leader, 2002; Jesus and the Earth, 2003. *Address:* Bishop's Lodge, Woolton Park, Woolton, Liverpool L25 6DT. *T:* (0151) 421 0831, *Fax:* (0151) 428 3055.

LIVERPOOL, Auxiliary Bishop of, (RC); *see* Williams, Rt Rev. T. A.

LIVERPOOL, Dean of; *see* Welby, Very Rev. J. P.

LIVERPOOL, Archdeacon of; *see* Panter, Ven. R. J. G.

LIVERSIDGE, Pamela Edwards, OBE 1999; DL; DSc; FREng, FIMechE; Managing Director, Quest Investments Ltd, since 1997; President, Institution of Mechanical Engineers, 1997–98; *b* 23 Dec. 1949; *d* of William H. Humphries and Dorothy Humphries; *m* 1st, 1971, Dr Dale S. Edwards (marr. diss. 1980); 2nd, 1991, Douglas B. Liversidge; two step *s* one step *d*. *Educ:* Aston Univ. (BSc Hons 1971; DSc 1998). CEng 1980; FIMechE 1988; FCGI 1997; FREng 1999. Graduate trainee and project engr, GKN plc, 1971–73; Thornton Precision Forgings: Asst Technical Manager, 1973–78; Prodn Control Manager, 1978–81; Aerofoils Product Manager, 1981–86; Sales and Mkting Dir, 1986–89; Strategic Planning Manager, E Midlands Electricity plc, 1989–93; Man. Dir, Scientific Metal Powders Ltd, 1993–97. Dir, Sheffield TEC, 1997–98; Chm., Sheffield Business Link, 1998–2001. Vis. Prof., Sheffield Univ., 1996–99. Gov., Sheffield Hallam Univ., 1994–2006. FRSA 1996. DL, 1999, High Sheriff, 2004–05, S Yorks. Liveryman, Engineers' Co., 1997– (Mem., Ct of Assts, 2000–06). A Guardian, Sheffield Assay Office, 2005–. DUniv: UCE, 1998; Sheffield Hallam, 2006; Hon. DEng: Bradford, 2000; Sheffield, 2005; Hon. DSc: Aston, 1998; Huddersfield, 2001. *Recreations:* golf, public speaking at specialist events. *Address:* Nicholas Hall, Thornhill, Bamford, Hope Valley S33 0BR. *T:* (01433) 651475, *Fax:* (01433) 659357.

LIVESEY, Bernard Joseph Edward; QC 1990; a Recorder, since 1987; a Deputy High Court Judge, since 1998; *b* 21 Feb. 1944; *s* of late Joseph Augustine Livesey and Marie Gabrielle Livesey (*née* Caulfield); *m* 1971, Penelope Jean Harper; two *d*. *Educ:* Cardinal Vaughan Sch., London; Peterhouse, Cambridge (MA, LLB). Called to the Bar, Lincoln's Inn, 1969, Bencher, 1999. Fellow, Internat. Acad. of Trial Lawyers, 1993. Mem. Adv. Bd, City Univ., 2001–. Chm. Council, Friends of Peterhouse, 2002–. *Address:* 4–5 New Square, Lincoln's Inn, WC2A 3RJ. *T:* (020) 7822 2000.

LIVESEY, David Anthony, PhD; Secretary-General, League of European Research Universities, since 2005; Fellow, since 1974, Vice-Master, since 2006, Emmanuel College, Cambridge; *b* 30 May 1944; *s* of Vincent Livesey and Marie Livesey (*née* Parr); *m* 1967, Sally Anne Vanston; one *s* two *d*. *Educ:* Derby Sch.; Imperial Coll., Univ. of London (ACGI; BSc Eng); Christ's Coll., Cambridge (PhD 1971). University of Cambridge: Res. Officer in Applied Econs, 1969–75; Lectr in Engrg, 1975–91; Sec. Gen. of Faculties, 1992–2003; Cambridge Dir, Cambridge-MIT Inst., 1999–2000; Res. Fellow, Peterhouse, 1971–74; Tutor, 1975–83, Bursar, 1983–91, Emmanuel Coll. Mem., HM Treasury Cttee on Policy Optimisation, 1976–78. Dir, Cambridge Econometrics Ltd, 1981–84 (Chm., 1982–84). Non-exec. Dir, Addenbrooke's NHS Trust, 1993–99. Trustee: Bedford Charity (Harpur Trust), 2004–; Citizens Advice, 2005– (Chm. Trustees, Cambridge and Dist CAB, 2004–). Chm., Vital Spark Forum, 2005–. Governor: St Albans RC Primary Sch., 1977–92, 2001–05 (Chm., 1984–92, 2001–05); Henley Mgt Coll., 2005–07. *Recreations:* books, swimming, trying to learn Welsh. *Address:* Emmanuel College, Cambridge CB2 3AP. *T:* (01223) 334243.

LIVESEY, Timothy Peter Nicholas; Archbishop of Canterbury's Secretary for Public Affairs, since 2006; *b* 29 June 1959; *s* of Kevin and Mary Livesey; *m* 1986, Catherine Joan Eaglestone; two *s* three *d*. *Educ:* Stonyhurst Coll.; New Coll., Oxford (BA Modern Hist. 1981). 2nd Lieut, Royal Irish Rangers, 1977–78. Asst Registrar and Dep. Sec., UMDS, Guy's and St Thomas' Hosps, 1984–87; Foreign and Commonwealth Office, 1987–2006: First Sec. (Aid), Lagos, 1989–93; Hd, Press and Public Affairs, Paris, 1996–2000; Asst Press Sec., 10 Downing St, 2000–02; on secondment as Principal Advr for Public Affairs to Cardinal Archbp of Westminster, 2002–04; Asst Dir, Information and Strategy, FCO, 2004–06. *Recreations:* family, reading, writing, rowing. *Address:* Lambeth Palace, SE1 7JU.

LIVESLEY, Prof. Brian, MD; FRCP; Professor in the Care of the Elderly, University of London at Imperial College School of Medicine (formerly Charing Cross and Westminster Medical School), 1988–2001, Professor Emeritus, 2003; Consultant Forensic Physician, since 2001; *b* 31 Aug. 1936; *s* of late Thomas Clement Livesley and Stella Livesley; *m* 1st, 1963, Beryl Hulme (*d* 1966); one *s*; 2nd, 1969, Valerie Anne Nuttall; two *d*. *Educ:* King George V Grammar Sch., Southport; Leeds Univ. Med. Sch. (MB, ChB 1960); Univ. of London (MD 1979). MRCP 1971, FRCP 1989. DHMSA 1973. Hospital appointments: Leeds Gen. Infirmary, 1961–62; Dist and Univ. Hosps, Leeds, Manchester and Liverpool, 1963–68; Harvey Res. Fellow, KCH, 1969–72; Cons. Physician in Geriatric Medicine, Lambeth, Southwark and Lewisham HA, 1973–87. Asst Dir-Gen., 1993–94, Dir-Gen., 1994–96, St John Ambulance. Clinical Examnr in Medicine, Univ. of London, 1980–94 (Sen. Examnr, 1990–94); External Examnr, Royal Free and UC Med. Sch., 1998–2001; Examiner: for Dip. in Geriatric Medicine, RCP, 1987–93; in Medicine, Soc. of Apothecaries, 1987–93; Mem., United Examng Bd for England and Scotland, 1993–96. NW Thames Regl Advr on Medicine for the Elderly, 1990–2001; Chm., N Thames Regl Trng Commn, 1993–96. Mem., Med. Commn on Accident Prevention, 1984–89 (Chm., Home and Family Safety Commn, 1988–89). NHS Exec. Assessor for NHS R&D Nat. Primary Care Awards, 2002–03. Member: British Acad. Forensic Scis, 2002–; Assoc. of Forensic Physicians, 2004–06. Lectures: Osler, 1975, Gideon de Laune, 2001, Faculty of Hist. of Medicine and Pharmacy, Soc. of Apothecaries; Hunterian, 2003; Med. Soc. of London and Osler Club (jt meeting), 2006. Freeman, City of London, 1975; Liveryman, Soc. of Apothecaries, 1980– (Yeoman, 1975; Mem. Ct of Assts, 1990–; Master, 2005–06; Immediate Past Master, 2006–07; Chm., Futures Cttee, 1999–2004; Chm., Acad. Cttee, 2000–03). JP SE London, 1983–96. KStJ 1994. *Publications:* monographs and investigations on scientific, historical, educnl and forensic problems of medicine in our ageing soc. *Recreations:* family, Christian culture study at the time of St Paul, encouraging people to think. *Address:* PO Box 295, Oxford OX2 9GD.

LIVINGSTON, Prof. Andrew Guy, PhD; FREng; Professor of Chemical Engineering, Imperial College, London, since 1999; *b* 4 Nov. 1962; *s* of Derek Heathcoat Livingston and Muriel Livingston; *m* 1996, Luisa Freitas dos Santos; one *s* one *d*. *Educ:* Univ. of Canterbury, NZ (BEng Hons Chem. 1984); PhD Cantab 1990; London Sch. of Econs (MSc Econs 1994). Company Chem. Engr, Canterbury Frozen Meat Co., NZ, 1984–86; Cambridge Commonwealth Trust Scholar, Trinity Coll., Cambridge, 1986–89; Lectr, 1990–96, Reader, 1996–99, Imperial College, London. Founder, and Man. Dir, Membrane Extraction Technology Ltd, 1996–. FREng 2006. Cremer and Warner Medal, IChemE, 1997. *Publications:* over 150 articles in learned jls and monographs. *Recreations:* fruit trees, windsurfing. *Address:* c/o Department of Chemical Engineering, Imperial College, London, SW7 2AZ. *T:* (020) 7594 5382, *Fax:* (020) 7584 5629; *e-mail:* a.livingston@imperial.ac.uk.

LIVINGSTON, Air Vice-Marshal Graham; consultant occupational health physician; *b* 2 Aug. 1928; *s* of late Neil Livingston and Margaret Anderson (*née* Graham); *m* 1970, Carol Judith Palmer; one *s* one *d* (and one *s* one *d* (and one *d* decd) of former marriage). *Educ:* Bo'ness Academy; Edinburgh Univ. (MB ChB 1951, DPH 1963); DIH (Conjoint) 1963; MFPHM (MFCM 1974); MFOM 1981. Joined RAF 1952; served N Ireland and Egypt, 1952–55; civilian GP and obst., 1956–57; rejoined RAF 1958; served Lindholme and Honington, 1958–62; post grad. study in public and indust. health, Edinburgh Univ., 1962–63; SMO, RAF Laarbruch, 1963–66; RAF Coll., Cranwell, 1966–70; served Cosford, Halton and Akrotiri, 1970–74; OC RAF Hosps, Cosford, 1974–76, Wegberg, 1976–79; Dep. Dir. Med. Personnel and Dep. Dir Med. Orgn, MoD, 1979–80; Dep. PMO, Strike Command, 1981–83; Principal Medical Officer: RAF Germany, 1983–84; RAF Support Comd, 1984–89; QHS 1985–89. Consultant in community medicine, 1984; Consultant Occupational Health Physician: NW Herts HA, 1989–94; Wycombe HA, 1991–94. Freeman, City of London, 1982. FCMI (FBIM 1986). *Recreations:* golf, gardening, dog walking. *Address:* c/o Lloyds TSB, Cox's and King's Branch, PO Box 1190, 7 Pall Mall, SW1Y 5NA. *Clubs:* Royal Air Force; Ashridge Golf.

LIVINGSTONE, Prof. David Noel, OBE 2002; PhD; FBA 1995; MRIA; Professor of Geography and Intellectual History, Queen's University of Belfast, since 1997 (Professor of Geography, 1993–97); *b* 15 March 1953; *s* of Robert Livingstone and Winifred (*née* Turkington); *m* 1977, Frances Allyson Haugh; one *s* one *d*. *Educ:* Queen's Univ. of Belfast (BA; PhD; DipEd). Queen's University, Belfast: Curator of Maps, 1984–89; Lectr, 1989–91; Reader, 1991–93; British Acad. Res. Reader, 1999–2001. Visiting Professor: Calvin Coll., Michigan, 1989–90; Univ. of Notre Dame, Indiana, 1995; Regent Coll., Vancouver, 1997, 2000, 2003; Dist. Vis. Prof., Baylor Univ., Texas, 2004–05; Vis. Noted Scholar, Univ. of BC, 1999. Lectures: Charles Lyell, BAAS, 1994–95; Hettner, Univ. of Heidelberg, 2001; Murrin, Univ. of BC, 2002; Progress in Human Geography, RGS, 2005; Appleton, Univ. of Hull, 2007; Humboldt, UCLA, 2007; Manley, Royal Holloway, Univ. of London, 2007. Mem., RAE 2001 Geog. Panel, RAE 2008 Geog. and Envmtl Studies sub-panel, HEFCE. Mem. Ct, Univ. of Ulster, 1996–2000, 2001–04. Pres., Geog. Sect., BAAS, 2005; Vice-Pres., Research, RGS, 2007–. MRIA 1998 (Mem., Nat. Cttee for Hist. and Philosophy of Sci., 1988–96, for Geography, 1996–; Mem. Council, 2001–02); FRSA 2001; MAE 2002; AcSS 2002. Adm. Back Award, RGS, 1997; Centenary Medal, RSGS, 1998; Templeton Foundn Lect. Award, 1999. *Publications:* Nathaniel Southgate Shaler and the Culture of American Science, 1987; Darwin's Forgotten Defenders, 1987; The Preadamite Theory, 1992; The Geographical Tradition, 1992; (ed jtly) The Behavioural Environment, 1989; (ed jtly) Charles Hodge, What is Darwinism, 1994; (ed jtly) Human Geography: an essential anthology, 1996; (jtly) Them and Us, 1997; (jtly) Ulster-American Religion, 1999; (ed jtly) Evangelicals and Science in Historical Perspective, 1999; (ed jtly) Geography and Enlightenment, 1999; Science, Space and Hermeneutics, 2002; Putting Science in its Place, 2003; (ed jtly) Geography and Revolution, 2005; Adam's Ancestors: race, religion and the politics of human origins, 2008; articles in learned jls. *Recreations:* music, photography. *Address:* School of Geosciences, Queen's University of Belfast, Belfast BT7 1NN. *T:* (028) 9097 5145.

LIVINGSTONE, Ian, OBE 2006; Product Acquisition Director, Eidos Interactive Ltd (formerly Creative Director, Eidos plc), since 2002 (Executive Chairman, 1995–2002); *b* 29 Dec. 1949; *s* of Neville and Anna Livingstone; *m* 1997, Frances Patricia Fletcher; two *s* one *d*. *Educ:* Stockport Coll. of Technology (HND 1970); Univ. of Surrey (BEd 1975). MCIM 1970. Co-founder and Jt Man. Dir, 1975–85, non-exec. Dir, 1985–91, Games Workshop Ltd (launched Dungeons and Dragons game in Eur.); writing books and designing board games, 1991–93; Dep. Chm., Domark Ltd, 1993–95. Non-exec. Chm., Bright Things plc, 2004–; non-exec. Dir, Skillset, 2005–. Creative Industries advr, British Council, 2003–; Chair, Computer Games Skills Forum, 2005–. Hon. DTech Abertay Dundee, 2000. Special Award, BAFTA, 2002. *Publications:* Warlock of Firetop Mountain (with Steve Jackson), 1982; Dicing with Dragons, 1982; The Forest of Doom, 1983; City of Thieves, 1983; Deathtrap Dungeon, 1984; Island of the Lizard King, 1984; Caverns of the Snow Witch, 1984; Freeway Fighter, 1985; Temple of Terror, 1985; Trial of Champions, 1986; Crypt of the Sorcerer, 1987; Casket of Souls, 1987; Armies of Death, 1988; Return to Firetop Mountain, 1992; Legend of Zagor, 1993; Darkmoon's Curse, 1995; The Demon Spider, 1995; Mudworm Swamp, 1995; Ghost Road, 1995; Eye of the Dragon, 2005. *Recreations:* golf, photography, games design, writing. *Address:* Eidos Interactive, Wimbledon Bridge House, 1 Hartfield Road, SW19 3RU; *e-mail:* ianl@eidos.co.uk. *Clubs:* Chelsea Arts, Roehampton; Wimbledon Park Golf.

LIVINGSTONE, Ian Lang, CBE 1998 (OBE 1993); DL; Chairman: Lanarkshire Health Board, 1993–2002 (Member, 1989–2002); Scottish Enterprise Lanarkshire (formerly Lanarkshire Development Agency), 1991–2000; *b* 23 Feb. 1938; *s* of John Lang Livingstone and Margaret Steele Livingstone (*née* Barbour); *m* 1967, Diane Hales; two *s*. *Educ:* Hamilton Acad.; Glasgow Univ. (BL). NP 1960. Qualified as solicitor, 1960; apprentice, Alex L. Wright & Co., Solicitors, 1957–60, legal asst, 1960–62; Ballantyne & Copland, Solicitors: Partner, 1962–70; Sen. Partner, 1970–86; Consultant, 1986–; Chm. and Dir, Bowmere Properties Ltd, 1967–; Chairman: House Sales (Motherwell) Ltd, 1978–; Islay Developments Ltd, 1989–; New Lanarkshire Ltd, 1993–; Langvale Ltd, 2001–; Kingdom FM Radio Ltd, 2008–. Chm., Scottish Local Authorities Remuneration Cttee, 2005–; Hon. Pres., Lanarkshire Chamber of Commerce, 2006–. Chm., Motherwell Coll. Bd, 1991–98. Chm., Motherwell FC, 1975–88. DL Lanarkshire, 2008. *Recreations:* football, walking, travelling, music. *Address:* Roath Park, 223 Manse Road, Motherwell, Strathclyde ML1 2PY. *T:* (01698) 253750.

LIVINGSTONE, Kenneth Robert, (Ken); Mayor of London, 2000–08 (Ind 2000–04, Lab 2004–08); *b* 17 June 1945; *s* of late Robert Moffat Livingstone and Ethel Ada Livingstone. *Educ:* Tulse Hill Comprehensive Sch.; Philippa Fawcett Coll. of Educn (Teacher's Cert.). Technician, Chester Beatty Cancer Res. Inst., 1962–70. Joined Labour Party, 1969; Reg. Exec., Greater London Lab. Party, 1974–86; Lambeth Borough Council: Councillor, 1971–78; Vice-Chm., Housing Cttee, 1971–73; Camden Borough Council: Councillor, 1978–82; Chm., Housing Cttee, 1978–80; Greater London Council: Mem. for Norwood, 1973–77, for Hackney N, 1977–81, for Paddington, 1981–86; Lab. Transport spokesman, 1980–81; Leader of Council and of Lab. Gp, 1981–86. Mem., NEC, Labour Party, 1987–89, 1997–98. Contested (Lab) Hampstead, 1979. MP (Lab) Brent East, 1987–2001. Mem., NI Select Cttee, 1997–99. Mem. Council, Zoological Soc. of London, 1994–2000 (Vice-Pres., 1996–98). FZS. *Publications:* If voting changed anything they'd abolish it, 1987; Livingstone's Labour, 1989. *Recreations:* cinema, science fiction, thinking while gardening, natural history. *Address: e-mail:* emmabeal@btopenworld.com.

LIVINGSTONE, Marilyn; Member (Lab Co-op) Kirkcaldy, Scottish Parliament, since 1999; *b* 30 Sept. 1952; *m* Peter W. Livingstone; two *d*. *Educ:* Viewforth Secondary Sch.; Fife Coll. Fife College of Further and Higher Education: Youth Trng Manager; Hd, Admin and Consumer Studies; Hd, Business Sch., until 1999. Former Member: Kirkcaldy DC; Fife Council. Chm., Scottish PLP, 1999–2003; Ministerial Parly Aid to the First Minister, 2003–07. *Address:* (office) Parliamentary Advice Centre, 3 East Fergus Place, Kirkcaldy KY1 1XT; Scottish Parliament, Edinburgh EH99 1SP.

LIVSEY, family name of **Baron Livsey of Talgarth**.

LIVSEY OF TALGARTH, Baron *cr* 2001 (Life Peer), of Talgarth in the County of Powys; **Richard Arthur Lloyd Livsey,** CBE 1994; DL; *b* 2 May 1935; *s* of Arthur Norman Livsey and Lilian Maisie (*née* James); *m* 1964, Irene Martin Earsman; two *s* one *d*. *Educ:* Talgarth County Primary Sch.; Bedales Sch.; Seale-Hayne Agricl Coll.; Reading Univ. (MSc Agric.). Develt Officer, Agric. Div., ICI, 1961–67; Farm Manager, Blairdrummond, 1967–71; farmer at Llanon; Sen. Lectr in Farm Management, Welsh Agricl Coll., Aberystwyth, 1971–85; Develt Manager, ATB Landbase Wales, 1992–95. Joined Liberal Party, 1960; contested (L): Perth and E Perth, 1970; Pembroke, 1979; Brecon and Radnor, 1983; MP (L July 1985–1988, Lib Dem 1988–92) Brecon and Radnor; MP (Lib Dem) Brecon and Radnorshire, 1997–2001. Liberal Party spokesman on agric., 1985–87; Alliance spokesman on the countryside and on agric. in Wales, and on Wales, 1987; Leader, Welsh Liberal Democrats and Party Spokesman on Wales, 1988–92 and 1997–2001; Lib Dem spokesman on agric. and rural affairs, H of L, 2002–. Mem., EU Select Cttee (D) on Agric. and the Envmt, H of L, 2002–. Pres., Wales European Movt, 2003–. Mem. Bd, Prime Cymru; Trustee, CPRW. Chm., Brecon Jazz Fest., 1993–96; Mem., Talgarth Male Voice Choir, 1993–. President: Brecon and Dist Disabled Club, 1986–; Brecknock Fedn of Young Farmers' Clubs, 2003–; Talgarth CC, 2005–; Keith Morris Fund; Vice-Pres., Cor Meibion Ystradgynlais, 2005–. Associate, BVA, 2005. DL Powys, 2004. *Recreations:* cricket, fishing. *Address:* House of Lords, SW1A 0PW.

LLANDAFF, Bishop of; *see* Wales, Archbishop of.

LLANDAFF, Assistant Bishop of; *see* Yeoman, Rt Rev. D.

LLANDAFF, Dean of; *see* Lewis, Very Rev. J. T.

LLEWELLIN, Rt Rev. (John) Richard (Allan); Head of the Archbishop of Canterbury's staff (with title of Bishop at Lambeth), 1999–2003; an Hon. Assistant Bishop, Diocese of Canterbury, since 2008; *b* 30 Sept. 1938; *s* of John Clarence Llewellin and Margaret Gwenllian Llewellin; *m* 1965, Jennifer Sally (*née* House); one *s* two *d*. *Educ:* Clifton College, Bristol; Westcott House and Fitzwilliam Coll., Cambridge (MA). Solicitor, 1960. Ordained deacon, 1964; priest, 1965; Curate at Radlett, Herts, 1964–68; Curate at Johannesburg Cathedral, 1968–71; Vicar of Waltham Cross, 1971–79; Rector of Harpenden, 1979–85; Suffragan Bishop: of St Germans, 1985–92; of Dover, 1992–99. Chm., USPG, 1994–97. *Recreations:* sailing, DIY. *Address:* 193 Ashford Road, Canterbury, Kent CT1 3XS. *T:* (01227) 789515; *e-mail:* rllewellin@clara.co.uk.

LLEWELLYN, Anthony John S.; *see* Seys Llewellyn.

LLEWELLYN, Bryan Henry; Director, Granada Travel PLC, 1989–92; *s* of Nora and Charles Llewellyn; *m* 1983, Joanna (*née* Campbell); two *s*. *Educ:* Charterhouse; Clare Coll., Cambridge (BA). Commissioned, The Queen's, 1946. Research Asst, Dept of Estate Management, Cambridge, 1954; joined Fisons Ltd, 1955; Marketing Manager, Greaves & Thomas Ltd, 1960; Regional Marketing Controller, Thomson Regional Newspapers Ltd, 1962; Marketing Dir, TRN Ltd, 1966; Managing Director: Thomson Holidays Ltd, 1969; Thomson Travel Ltd, 1972 (Chm., 1977–78); Exec. Dir, Thomson Organisation Ltd, 1972–80; Man. Dir and Chief Exec., Thomson Publications Ltd, 1977–80; Man. Dir, The Kitchenware Merchants Ltd, 1985–88. Non-exec. Dir, Orion Insurance Ltd, 1976–92.

LLEWELLYN, Sir David St Vincent, (Sir Dai), 4th Bt *cr* 1922, of Bwllfa, Aberdare, co. Glamorgan; impresario, writer and broadcaster; *b* 2 April 1946; *er s* of Sir Harry Llewellyn, 3rd Bt, CBE and Hon. Christine Saumarez, 2nd *d* of 5th Baron de Saumarez; *S* father, 1999; *m* 1980, Vanessa Mary Theresa Hubbard (marr. diss. 1987); two *d*. *Educ:* Eton; Univ. d'Aix-Marseille. Presenter, Cordially Invited, US TV show, 2002. Chevalier, l'Ordre des Côteaux de Champagne, 1992. KLJ 2000 (CLJ 1995). *Recreations:* equestrian sports, wildlife conservation. *Heir: b* Roderic Victor Llewellyn, *b* 9 Oct. 1947. *Address:* Studio Two, 2 Lansdowne Row, W1J 6HL. *T:* (020) 7413 9533.

LLEWELLYN, Prof. David Thomas; Professor of Money and Banking, and Chairman of the Banking Centre, Loughborough University, since 1976; *b* 3 March 1943; *s* of Alfred George Llewellyn and Elsie Alexandria Frith; *m* 1970, Wendy Elizabeth James; two *s*. *Educ:* William Ellis Grammar Sch., London; London Sch. of Econs and Pol Science (BSc Econ). FCIB. Economist: Unilever NV, Rotterdam, 1964; HM Treasury, London, 1965–67; Lectr in Econs, Nottingham Univ., 1967–73; Economist, IMF, Washington, 1973–76. Public Interest Dir, PIA, 1994–2001; Dir, PIA Ombudsman Bureau Ltd, 1994–2001. Visiting Professor: City Univ. Business Sch., 2001–; Cass Business Sch., London, 2003–; Swiss Finance Inst. (formerly Swiss Banking Sch.), Zurich, 2003, 2006–; IESE Business Sch., Madrid, 2006–07; Vienna Univ. of Econs and Admin, 2007–. Consultant Economist to: Harlow Butler Ueda, 1981–99; Garban Intercapital plc; ICAP plc, 2004–; Member: London Bd of Dirs, Halifax Building Soc., 1988–93; Expert Panel on Banking, Bank Indonesia, 2004–; at various times Consultant to World Bank, Building Societies Assoc., bldg socs, banks, central banks and regulatory authorities in UK and overseas. Member: Bank of England Panel of Academic Consultants; Banking Competition Task Gp, S Africa, 2003–04; Internat. Adv. Bd, Italian Bankers' Assoc., 1994–; Exec. Bd, European Financial Management Assoc., 1994–; Internat. Adv. Bd, NCR Financial Solutions (formerly NCR Financial Systems) Gp, 1997–2001; Financial Services Panel, DTI Technology Foresight Prog., 1997–2000; Consultative Gp, IMF, 2004–. Special Advr, H of C and H of L Jt Cttee on Financial Services and Markets, 1999–. Pres., Société Universitaire Européenne Recherches Financières, 2000–. TV and radio broadcasts on financial issues. Member of Editorial Board: Jl of Financial Regulation and Compliance, 2002–; Bombay Technology, 2004–; Jl of Bank Regulating, 2005–. FRSA. *Publications:* International Financial Integration, 1980; Framework of UK Monetary Policy, 1984; The Evolution of the British Financial System, 1985; Prudential Regulation and Supervision of Financial Institutions, 1986; Reflections on Money, 1989; (ed) Recent Developments in International Monetary Economics, 1991; (ed) Surveys in Monetary Economics, vols 1 and 2, 1991; Competition or Credit Controls?, 1991; (jtly) Financial Regulations: why, how and where now?, 1998; Economic Rationale of Financial Resulation, 1998; The New Economics of Banking, 1999; Competitive Strategy in the New Economics of Retail Financial Services, 2002; articles in academic and professional jls and books on monetary policy and instns, and on internat. finance. *Recreations:* DIY, culinary arts, travel, boating. *Address:* 8 Landmere Lane, Ruddington, Notts NG11 6ND. *T:* (0115) 921 6071; Economics Department, Loughborough University, Loughborough, Leics LE11 3TU. *T:* (01509) 222700; *e-mail:* D.T.Llewellyn@lboro.ac.uk; Hameau des Pins, Les Hauts du Golf, Villa 10, 8760 chemin de la Tire, 06250 Mougins, France.

LLEWELLYN, David Walter, CBE 1983; Director, Walter Llewellyn & Sons Ltd, and other companies in the Llewellyn Group, 1953–2002; *b* 13 Jan. 1930; *s* of late Eric Gilbert and Florence May Llewellyn; *m* 1st, 1955, Josephine Margaret Buxton (marr. diss. 1985); three *s*; 2nd, 1985, Tessa Caroline Sandwith. *Educ:* Radley College. FCIOB. Commissioned Royal Engineers, 1952. Industrial Adviser to Minister of Housing and Local Govt, 1967–68; Mem., Housing Corp., 1975–77; Pres., Joinery and Timber Contractors' Assoc., 1976–77; Chm., Nat. Contractors' Gp of Nat. Fedn of Building Trades Employers (now Building Employers Confedn), 1977; Chm., Building Regulations Adv. Cttee, 1977–85 (Mem. 1966–74); Dep. Chm., Nat. Building Agency, 1977–82 (Dir. 1968–82). Pres., CIOB, 1986–87. Master, Worshipful Co. of Tin Plate Workers alias Wireworkers, 1985. Governor, St Andrew's Sch., Eastbourne, 1966–78; Trustee, Queen Alexandra Cottage Homes, Eastbourne, 1973–94. Provincial Grand Master, Sussex, United Grand Lodge of Freemasons of England, 1989–97. *Recreation:* the use, restoration and preservation of historic vehicles. *Address:* Cooper's Cottage, Chiddingly, near Lewes, East Sussex BN8 6HD. *Clubs:* Reform; Devonshire (Eastbourne).

LLEWELLYN, Rear-Adm. Jack Rowbottom, CB 1974; Assistant Controller of the Navy, 1972–74; retired; *b* 14 Nov. 1919; *s* of Ernest and Harriet Llewellyn, Ashton under Lyne, Lancs; *m* 1944, Joan Isabel, *d* of Charles and Hilda Phillips, Yelverton, Devon; one *s*. *Educ:* Purley County Sch. Entered RN, 1938; RNEC, Keyham, 1939. Served War of 1939–45: HMS Bermuda, 1942; RNC, Greenwich, 1943; HMS Illustrious, 1945. Engr in Chief's Dept, Admlty, 1947; HMS Sluys, 1949; HMS Thunderer, 1951; HMS Diamond, 1953; Comdr, 1953; Asst Engr in Chief, on loan to Royal Canadian Navy, 1954; in charge Admty Fuel Experimental Station, Haslar, 1958; HMS Victorious, 1960; Asst Dir, Marine Engrg, MoD (N), 1963; Captain, 1963; in command, HMS Fisgard, 1966; Dep. Dir, Warship Design, MoD (N), 1969; Rear-Adm., 1972. *Recreations:* travel, gardening. *Address:* 3 Jubilee Terrace, Chichester, W Sussex PO19 7XT. *T:* (01243) 780180.

LLEWELLYN, John, DPhil; Senior Economic Policy Advisor, Lehman Brothers, 2006–08; *b* 13 Sept. 1944; *s* of Sir (Frederick) John Llewellyn and Joyce Llewellyn; *m* 1990, Ruth Mariette; two *s* three *d*. *Educ:* Christchurch Boys' High Sch.; Scots' Coll., Wellington; Victoria Univ. of Wellington (BA Hons 1st Cl. Econs 1966); Trinity Coll., Oxford (DPhil Econs 1970). Res. Officer, Dept of Applied Econs, 1970–74, Asst Dir of Res., Fac. of Econs, 1974–77, Univ. of Cambridge; Fellow, St John's Coll., Cambridge, 1972–77; OECD: Hd, Econ. Prospects Div., 1978–86; Dep. Dir for Social Affairs, Manpower and Educn, 1986–89; Hd, Private Office of Sec.-Gen., 1989–94; Lehman Brothers: Chief Economist Europe, 1995–96; Global Chief Economist, 1996–2006. Member: President of EC's Gp of Econ. Analysis, 2000–04; President of EC's Gp of Econ. Policy Analysis, 2005–. Member of Council: Chatham House; UK Soc. of Business Economists. Trustee, FIA Foundn for the Automobile and Society. Member, Editorial Board: OECD Economic Studies, 1983–89; Economic Modelling, 1983–93. *Publications:* (jtly) Economic Forecasting and Policy: the international dimension, 1985; (ed jtly) Economic Policies for the 1990s, 1991; (jtly) The Business of Climate Change: challenges and opportunities, 2007; (with Camille Chaix) The Business of Climate Change II: policy is accelerating, with major implications for companies and investors, 2007; articles in learned jls. *Recreations:* motorsport, writing, photography, music. *Address: e-mail:* john.llewellyn5@btinternet.com. *Clubs:* Athenæum, Royal Automobile.

LLEWELLYN, Rev. Richard Morgan, CB 1992; OBE 1979 (MBE 1976); DL; Director, Christ College, Brecon Foundation, 2001–05; *b* 22 Aug. 1937; *s* of Griffith Robert Poyntz Llewellyn and Bridget Margaret Lester Llewellyn (*née* Karslake); *m* 1964, Elizabeth Lamond (Polly) Sobey; three *s* one *d* (and one *d* decd). *Educ:* Haileybury; Imperial Service College; rcds, psc; Salisbury and Wells Theol Coll. Enlisted Royal Welch Fusiliers (Nat. Service), 1956; active service, Malaya and Cyprus, 1957–59; Instructor, Army Outward Bound Sch., 1962–63; Staff Coll., 1970; MA to CGS, 1971–72; Brigade Major, 1974–76; CO, 1st Bn RWF, 1976–79; Directing Staff, RCDS, 1979–81; Comdr, Gurkha Field Force, 1981–84; Dir, Army Staff Duties, 1985–87; GOC Wales, 1987–90; C of S, HQ UKLF, 1990–91; retired in rank of Maj.-Gen. Ordained deacon, 1993, priest, 1994; Minor Canon, Brecon Cathedral and Asst Curate, Brecon with Battle and Llanddew, 1993–95; Chaplain, Christ Coll., Brecon, 1995–2001. Regtl Col, Gurkha Transport Regt, subseq. Queen's Own Gurkha Transport Regt, 1984–94; Col, RWF,

1990–97. Chairman: Army Mountaineering Assoc., 1988–91; Gurkha Welfare Trust in Wales, 1995–; Powys Br., Army Benevolent Fund, 2001–; Armed Forces Art Soc., 2007–; Vice-Pres., Soldiers' and Airmen's Scripture Readers Assoc., 1996–. Hon. Chaplain, Univ. of Wales OTC, 2002. Welsh Vice-Patron, War Memls Trust (formerly Friends of War Memls), 1999–. DL Powys, 2006. FCMI. *Recreations:* most outdoor pursuits, gardening, painting, reading. *Address:* Llangattock Court, Llangattock, Crickhowell, Powys NP8 1PH. *Club:* Army and Navy.

LLEWELLYN, Timothy David, OBE 2007; Chairman, Burlington Magazine Ltd, since 2008 (Director, since 2006); Trustee, Burlington Magazine Foundation, since 2006; *b* 30 May 1947; *s* of late Graham David Llewellyn and Dorothy Mary Driver; *m* 1st, 1970, Irene Sigrid Mercy Henriksen (marr. diss.); one *s*; 2nd, 1978, Elizabeth Hammond. *Educ:* St Dunstan's College; Magdalene College, Cambridge. Sotheby's: Old Master Painting Dept, 1969; Director, 1974; Man. Dir, 1984–91; Chief Exec., 1991–92; Dep. Chm., Europe, 1992–94. Chm., Friends of the Courtauld Inst. of Art, 1986–2002. Mem. Council, Harvard Univ. Center for Italian Renaissance Studies, Villa I Tatti, 1996–2005 (Mem., Internat. Council, 1990–96). Co-Chm., Elgar Birthplace Appeal, 1992–99; Trustee: Elgar Foundn, 1992–99; Bd, Courtauld Inst. of Art, 1992–2001; Gilbert Collection Trust, 1998–2001; Metropole Arts Trust, 2004–, and Creative Foundn, 2008–; Samuel Courtauld Trust, 2007–; Chm., Henry Moore Sculpture Trust, 1994–99; Dir, 1994–2007, Mem. of Adv. Bd, 2007–, Henry Moore Foundn; Member: Council, Walpole Soc., 1994–99; Visual Arts Adv. Cttee, British Council, 1995–2007; Council, British Sch. at Rome, 2000–. Fellow, Ateneo Veneto, 1992. Hon. DLitt Southampton Inst., 1998. Order of Cultural Merit, Min. of Culture and Fine Arts, Poland, 1986. *Recreations:* music, fishing, travel. *Address:* 3 Cranley Mansion, 160 Gloucester Road, SW7 4QF. *T:* (020) 7373 2333, *Fax:* (020) 7244 0126; *e-mail:* timothy_llewellyn@hotmail.com. *Club:* Brooks's.

LLEWELLYN SMITH, Prof. Sir Christopher Hubert, (Sir Chris), Kt 2001; FRS 1984; Director, Culham Division, United Kingdom Atomic Energy Authority, and Head of Euratom/UKAEA Fusion Association, 2003–08; Visiting Professor, Department of Physics, University of Oxford, since 2004; *b* 19 Nov. 1942; *s* of late J. C. and of M. E. F. Llewellyn Smith; *m* 1966, Virginia Grey; one *s* one *d*. *Educ:* Wellington College; New College, Oxford (Scholar; BA 1964; DPhil 1967; Hon. Fellow, 2002; full Blue for cross-country running, 1961–63, Captain 1963; full Blue for Athletics, 1963). Royal Society Exchange Fellow, Lebedev Inst., Moscow, 1967; Fellow, CERN, Geneva, 1968; Research Associate, SLAC, Stanford, Calif, 1970; Staff Mem., CERN, 1972; Oxford University: Lectr, 1974; Reader in Theoretical Physics, 1980; Prof. of Theoretical Physics, 1987–98 (on leave of absence, 1994–98); Chm. of Physics, 1987–92; Fellow, St John's Coll., 1974–98 (Hon. Fellow, 2000); Dir-Gen., CERN, 1994–98; Provost and Pres., UCL, 1999–2002; Sen. Res. Fellow, Dept of Physics, Oxford Univ., 2002–03. Chm., Adv. Cttee on Maths Educn, 2002–04. Mem. of various policy and programme cttees for CERN (Chm., Scientific Policy Cttee, 1990–92), SLAC, Deutsches Elektronen-Synchrotron Hamburg and SERC, 1972–92; Mem., ACOST, 1989–92; Chairman: Consultative Cttee on Fusion, Euratom, 2004–; Council, Internat. Tokamak Experimental Reactor, 2007–; Pres., Council, Synchrotron Light for Experimental Sci. and Applications in the ME, 2007–. Vice-Pres., Royal Society, 2008–. MAE 1989; Fellow, APS, 1994; For. Fellow, INSA, 1998. Hon. Fellow, Cardiff Univ., 1998. Hon. FIMA 2003. Hon. DSc: Bristol, 1997; Shandong, 1997; Hon. DCien Granada, 1997. Maxwell Prize and Medal, Inst. of Physics, 1979; Medal, Japanese Assoc. of Med. Scis, 1997; Gold Medal, Slovak Acad. of Scis, 1997; Glazebrook Medal, Inst. of Physics, 1999; Distinguished Associate Award, US Dept of Energy, 1998; Distinguished Service Award, US Nat. Sci. Foundn, 1998. *Publications:* numerous articles in Nuclear Physics, Physics Letters, Phys. Rev., etc. *Recreations:* books, travel, opera. *Address:* Theoretical Physics, 1 Keble Road, Oxford OX1 3NP; *e-mail:* c.llewellyn-smith@physics.ox.ac.uk.

See also E. M. Llewellyn-Smith, Sir M. J. Llewellyn Smith.

LLEWELLYN-SMITH, Elizabeth Marion, CB 1985; Principal, St Hilda's College Oxford, 1990–2001; *b* 17 Aug. 1934; *d* of late John Clare Llewellyn Smith and of Margaret Emily Frances (*née* Crawford). *Educ:* Christ's Hospital, Hertford; Girton Coll., Cambridge (MA; Hon. Fellow, 1992). Joined Board of Trade, 1956; various appointments in Board of Trade, Cabinet Office, Dept of Trade and Industry, Dept of Prices and Consumer Protection, 1956–76; Royal Coll. of Defence Studies, 1977; Under Sec., Companies Div., Dept of Trade, later DTI, 1978–82; Dep. Dir Gen., OFT, 1982–87; Dep. Sec., DTI, 1987–90. UK Dir, EIB, 1987–90. Member: Hebdomadal Council, Oxford Univ., 1993–2000; Res. Ethics Cttee, HSE, 1993–2004; Business Appointments Panel, DTI, 1996–2002; Accountancy Investigation and Discipline Bd, Financial Reporting Council (formerly Investigation and Discipline Bd, Accountancy Foundn), 2001–; Council, Consumers' Assoc., 2002–. Trustee: Jacqueline du Pré Meml Fund, 1991–2001; Auditory Verbal UK Ltd, 2004–. Mem., Governing Body, Rugby Sch., 1991–2004. Chm., Charlotte M. Yonge Fellowship, 1995–. Hon. Fellow: St Mary's Coll., Univ. of Durham, 1999; St Hilda's Coll., Oxford, 2001. *Recreations:* travel, books, entertaining. *Address:* Brook Cottage, Taston, near Charlbury, Oxon OX7 3JL. *T:* (01608) 811874. *Club:* University Women's.

See also Sir C. H. Llewellyn Smith, Sir M. J. Llewellyn Smith.

LLEWELLYN SMITH, Sir Michael (John), KCVO 1996; CMG 1989; HM Diplomatic Service, retired; Ambassador to Greece, 1996–99; *b* 25 April 1939; *s* of late J. C. Llewellyn Smith and of M. E. F. Crawford; *m* 1967, Colette Gaulier; one *s* one *d*. *Educ:* Wellington Coll.; New Coll., Oxford; St Antony's Coll., Oxford (MA, DPhil; Hon. Fellow, 2007). FCO, 1970; Cultural Attaché, Moscow, 1973; Paris, 1976; Royal Coll. of Defence Studies, 1979; Counsellor and Consul Gen., Athens, 1980–83; Hd of Western European Dept, FCO, 1984–85; Hd of Soviet Dept, FCO, 1985–87; Minister, Paris, 1988–91; Ambassador to Poland, 1991–96. Non-exec. Dir, Coca-Cola HBC SA, 2000–. Vice-Chm., Cathedrals Fabric Commn for England, 1999–2006. *Publications:* The Great Island: a study of Crete, 1965, 2nd edn 1973; Ionian Vision: Greece in Asia Minor 1919–22, 1973, 2nd edn 1998; The British Embassy Athens, 1998; Olympics in Athens 1896: the invention of the modern Olympic Games, 2004; Athens: a cultural and literary history, 2004. *Recreations:* music, walking, wine. *Address:* 4 Frouds Close, Childrey, Wantage OX12 9NT. *Club:* Oxford and Cambridge.

See also Sir C. H. Llewellyn Smith, E. M. Llewellyn-Smith.

LLEWELYN, Sir John Michael Dillwyn-V.; *see* Venables-Llewelyn.

LLOWARCH, Martin Edge, FCA; Chairman (part-time): Transport Development Group plc, 1992–2000; Firth Rixson (formerly Johnson & Firth Brown) plc, 1993–2001; *b* 28 Dec. 1935; *s* of Wilfred and Olga Llowarch; *m* 1965, Ann Marion Buchanan; one *s* two *d*. *Educ:* Stowe Sch., Buckingham. FCA 1973. Coopers & Lybrand, 1962–68; British Steel Corporation, subseq. British Steel plc: Hd of Special Projects, 1968; Man. Dir (S Africa), 1971; Dir, Finance and Admin (Internat.), 1973; Finance Dir, Tubes Div., 1975; Finance Controller, Strip Products Gp, 1980; Man. Dir, Finance, 1983; Mem., Main Bd, 1984–91; Dep. Chief Exec., 1986; Chief Exec., 1986–91. Dep. Chm., Abbey National plc, 1994–99; non-exec. Dir, Hickson Internat., 1992–99. Mem., Accounting Standards Cttee, 1985–87. CCMI (CBIM 1985). Chairman: Govs, Stamford Endowed Schs, 1998–2004; Stamford Endowed Schs Foundn, 2005–. *Recreations:* most forms of sport, music, gardening, reading.

LLOYD OF BERWICK, Baron *cr* 1993 (Life Peer), of Ludlay in the County of East Sussex; **Anthony John Leslie Lloyd,** Kt 1978; PC 1984; DL; a Lord of Appeal in Ordinary, 1993–99; Chairman, Security Commission, 1992–99 (Vice-Chairman, 1985–92); *b* 9 May 1929; *o s* of late Edward John Boydell Lloyd and Leslie Johnston Fleming; *m* 1960, Jane Helen Violet, MBE, DL, *er d* of C. W. Shelford, Chailey Place, Lewes, Sussex. *Educ:* Eton (Schol.); Trinity Coll., Cambridge (Maj. Schol.). 1st cl. Classical Tripos Pt I; 1st cl. with distinction Law Tripos Pt II. National Service, 1st Bn Coldstream Guards, 1948. Montague Butler Prize, 1950; Sir William Browne Medal, 1951. Choate Fellow, Harvard, 1952; Fellow of Peterhouse, 1953 (Hon. Fellow, 1981); Fellow of Eton, 1974–86. Called to Bar, Inner Temple, 1955 (Bencher, 1976; Treasurer, 1999); QC 1967; Attorney-General to HRH The Prince of Wales, 1969–77; Judge of the High Court of Justice, Queen's Bench Div., 1978–84; a Lord Justice of Appeal, 1984–93. Vice-Chm., Parole Bd, 1984–85 (Mem., 1983); Mem., Criminal Law Revision Cttee, 1981. Chairman: Inquiry into Legislation against Terrorism (reported 1996); Inquiry into Gulf War Illnesses (reported 2004). Chm., Sussex Assoc. for Rehabilitation of Offenders, 1985–91; Pres., Sussex Downsmen, 1995–2004; Vice-Pres., British Maritime Law Assoc., 1983–. Mem., Top Salaries Review Body, 1971–77. Chm., H of L Select Cttee on the Speakership, 2003–05. Chm., Jt Ecclesiastical Cttee, 2003–. Trustee: Smiths Charity, 1971–94; Glyndebourne Arts Trust, 1973–94 (Chm., 1975–94); Dir, RAM, 1979– (Hon. FRAM 1985). Chm., Chichester Diocesan Bd of Finance, and Mem., Bishop's Council, 1972–76; Vice-Pres., Corp. of the Sons of the Clergy, 1997–2004. Hon. Mem., Salters' Co., 1988 (Master, 2000–01). DL E Sussex, 1983. Hon. LLD: QUB, 2005; Sussex, 2006. *Recreations:* music, carpentry; formerly running (ran for Cambridge in Mile, White City, 1950). *Address:* 68 Strand-on-the-Green, Chiswick, W4 3PF. *T:* (020) 8994 7790; Ludlay, Berwick, East Sussex BN26 6TE. *T:* (01323) 870204. *Club:* Brooks's.

LLOYD, Andrew, MBE 1995; HM Diplomatic Service; Director, Corporate Services, Foreign and Commonwealth Office, since 2008; *b* 22 Oct. 1964; *s* of Roderick Allen Lloyd and Jacqueline Lloyd (*née* Quinn); *m* 1997, Tania Mechlenborg; one *s* one *d*, and one *s* from previous marriage. *Educ:* Birkbeck Coll., London (BSc Hons Financial Econs). Joined HM Diplomatic Service, 1982; FCO, 1982–84; Washington, 1984–87; Nigeria, 1987–90; FCO, 1990–92; Second Sec. (Econ.), Korea, 1992–95; Spokesman, UK Mission to UN, NY, 1995–2000; Hd of Post, Kosovo, 2000–02; rcds 2003; Hd, Africa Dept (Southern), 2003–06, Dir (Africa), 2006–08, FCO. *Recreations:* fly-fishing, long distance running, travel, design, cooking. *Address:* c/o Foreign and Commonwealth Office, King Charles Street, SW1A 2AH.

LLOYD, Ann Judith, CBE 2008; Head of Health and Social Services, Welsh Assembly Government and Chief Executive, NHS Wales, since 2003; *b* 22 April 1948; *d* of Joseph Barnard and Beryl Greer; *m* 1998, Dr Geert Jan Koning. *Educ:* St Asaph Grammar Sch.; University Coll. of Wales, Aberystwyth (BSc (Hons)); University Coll. of Wales, Cardiff, (MSc Econ); Bristol Poly. (DMS); Univ. of Aberdeen (DipHEcon). Area Planning Dir, Dyfed HA, 1974–82; Unit Gen. Manager, Llanelli-Dinefwr, 1982–88; Dist Gen. Manager, Frenchay HA, 1988–92; Chief Executive: Frenchay Healthcare NHS Trust, 1992–99; N Bristol NHS Trust, 1999–2001; Dir, NHS Wales, 2001–03. *Publications: contributions to:* Managing Service Quality, 1992; The Health Care Management Handbook, 2nd edn 1997; NHS Handbook: 1996–1997, 1997–1998, 1998–1999; Clinical Governance: the sequel, 2000; contrib. articles in Health Service Jl, BMJ, Health Services Mgt, Croner's Health Service Manager, Health Mgt. *Recreations:* horse riding, dancing. *Address:* Maple Cottage, Church Lane, Hewelsfield, Glos GL15 6UJ; Welsh Assembly Government, Cathays Park, Cardiff CF10 3NQ. *T:* (029) 2080 1144; *e-mail:* ann.lloyd@wales.gsi.gov.uk.

LLOYD, Anthony Joseph; MP (Lab) Manchester Central, since 1997 (Stretford, 1983–97); *b* 25 Feb. 1950; *s* of late Sydney and Ciceley Beaumont Lloyd; *m* 1974, Judith Ann Tear; one *s* three *d*. *Educ:* Stretford Grammar Sch.; Nottingham Univ. (BSc Hons); Manchester Business Sch. (DipBA). Lectr, Dept of Business and Administration, Salford Univ., 1979–83. Opposition spokesman: on transport, 1988–89; on employment, 1988–92, 1993–94; on education, 1992–94; on the environment, 1994–95; on foreign and commonwealth affairs, 1995–97; Minister of State, FCO, 1997–99. Chm., PLP, 2006–. Leader, British delegn to parly assembly of Council of Europe and of WEU, 2002–07, and of OSCE, 2005–. *Address:* House of Commons, SW1A 0AA.

LLOYD, Ven. (Bertram) Trevor; Archdeacon of Barnstaple, 1989–2002; *b* 15 Feb. 1938; *s* of Bertram and Gladys Lloyd; *m* 1962, Margaret Eldey; two *s* one *d* (and one *s* decd). *Educ:* Highgate School; Hertford Coll., Oxford (schol; BA History 1960, Theology 1962; MA 1962); Clifton Theol Coll., Bristol. Curate, Christ Church, Barnet, 1964–69; Vicar, Holy Trinity, Wealdstone, 1970–84; Priest-in-charge, St Michael and All Angels, Harrow Weald, 1980–84; Vicar, Trinity St Michael, Harrow, 1984–89; Area Dean of Harrow, 1977–82; Prebendary of Exeter Cathedral, 1991–2002. Member: C of E Liturgical Commn, 1981–2002; Gen. Synod of C of E, 1990–2002 (Mem., Standing Cttee, 1996–98); Central Bd of Finance, C of E, 1990–98; Council for the Care of Churches, 1992–2001; Churches' Main Cttee, 1996–2001. Chairman: Children's Hospice South West, 1991–; Living Stones Trust, 2002–08. *Publications:* Informal Liturgy, 1972; Institutions and Inductions, 1973; The Agape, 1973; Liturgy and Death, 1974; Ministry and Death, 1974; Lay Presidency at the Eucharist?, 1977; Evangelicals, Obedience and Change, 1977; (ed) Anglican Worship Today, 1980; Ceremonial in Worship, 1981; Introducing Liturgical Change, 1984; Celebrating Lent, Holy Week and Easter, 1985; Celebrating the Agape today, 1986; The Future of Anglican Worship, 1987; A Service of the Word, 1999; Dying and Death Step by Step, 2000; (consultant ed.) Common Worship Today, 2001; Pocket Prayers for Healing and Wholeness, 2004; Introducing Times and Seasons 1, 2006; (ed) Connecting with Baptism, 2007. *Recreations:* hill walking, photography, swimming, making things from wood. *Address:* 8 Pebbleridge Road, Westward Ho!, Bideford, N Devon EX39 1HN. *T:* (01237) 424701.

LLOYD, Dr Brian Beynon, CBE 1983; Director, International Nutrition Foundation, 1990–95; Chairman of Directors, Oxford Gallery, 1967–97; Chairman, Trumedia Study Oxford Ltd, since 1985; *b* 23 Sept. 1920; *s* of David John Lloyd, MA Oxon and Olwen (*née* Beynon); *m* 1949, Reinhild Johanna Engeroff; four *s* three *d* (incl. twin *s* and twin *d*). *Educ:* Newport High Sch.; Winchester Coll. (Schol.); Balliol Coll., Oxford (Domus and Frazer Schol.; Special Certif. for BA (War) Degree in Chem., 1941; took degrees BA and MA, 1946; Theodore Williams Schol. and cl. I in Physiology, 1948); DSc Oxon 1969. Joined Oxford Nutrition Survey after registration as conscientious objector, 1941; Pres., Jun. Common Room, Balliol Coll., 1941–42; Chm., Oxford Univ. Undergraduate Rep. Council, 1942; Biochemist: SHAEF Nutrition Survey Team, Leiden, 1945; Nutrition Survey Group, Düsseldorf, 1946. Fellow of Magdalen by exam. in Physiology, 1948–52, by special election, 1952–70; Senior Tutor, 1963–64; Vice-Pres., 1967 and 1968; Emeritus

Fellow, 1970–; Chemist, Laboratory of Human Nutrition, later Univ. Lectr in Physiology, Univ. of Oxford, 1948–70; Senior Proctor, 1960–61; Dir, Oxford Polytechnic, 1970–79 (Hon. Fellow, 1991; opened Lloyd Bldg, 1984). Chairman: CNAA Health and Med. Services Bd, 1975–80; Health Educn Council, 1979–82 (Mem., 1975–82); Mem., Adv. Council on Misuse of Drugs, 1978–81. Vis. Physiologist, New York, 1963. Pres., Section I, 1964–65, Section X, 1980, British Assoc. for the Advancement of Science. Chm. of Govs, Oxford Coll. of Technology, 1963–69. Chairman: Oxford-Bonn Soc., 1973–81; Oxford Management Club, 1979–80; Pullen's Lane Assoc., 1985–95; Pres., Oxford Polytechnic Assoc., 1984–90 (Hon. Mem., 1992). *Publications:* Gas Analysis Apparatus, 1960; (jt ed) The Regulation of Human Respiration, 1962; Cerebrospinal Fluid and the Regulation of Respiration, 1965; (jt ed) Sinclair (biog.), 1990; articles in physiological and biochemical jls. *Recreations:* Klavarskribo, Correggio, round tables, the analysis of athletic records, slide rules, ready reckoners, soldering irons, home computing, collecting pictures. *Address:* High Wall, Pullen's Lane, Oxford OX3 0BX. *T:* (01865) 763353.

LLOYD, Christopher Hamilton, CVO 2002 (LVO 1996); Surveyor of The Queen's Pictures, 1988–2005; *b* 30 June 1945; *s* of Rev. Hamilton Lloyd and Suzanne Lloyd (*née* Moon); *m* 1967, Christine Joan Frances Newth; four *s*. *Educ:* Marlborough Coll.; Christ Church, Oxford (BA 1967; MA 1971; MLitt 1972). Asst Curator of Pictures, Christ Church, Oxford, 1967–68; Dept of Western Art, Ashmolean Museum, 1968–88. Fellow of Villa I Tatti, Florence (Harvard Univ.), 1972–73; Vis. Res. Curator of Early Italian Painting, Art Inst., Chicago, 1980–81. Pres., NADFAS, 2007–. Trustee: Art Fund, 2005–; Living Paintings Trust, 2005–. Gov., Gainsborough's House, 2005–. *Publications:* (ed) Studies on Camille Pissarro, 1986; The Royal Collection: a thematic exploration of the paintings in the collection of HM the Queen, 1992; (with John Berger and Michael Hofmann) Arturo di Stefano, 2001; Philip Morsberger: a passion for painting, 2007; *catalogues of permanent collections:* Catalogue of Earlier Italian Paintings in the Ashmolean Museum, 1977; (with Richard Brettell) Catalogue of Drawings by Camille Pissarro in the Ashmolean Museum, 1980; (introd. and ed) Catalogue of Old Master Drawings at Holkham Hall, by A. E. Popham, 1986; Early Italian paintings in the Art Institute of Chicago, 1993; *exhibition catalogues:* Art and its Images, 1975; Camille Pissarro, 1980; (with Richard Thomson) Impressionist Drawings from British Collections, 1986; (with Simon Thurley) Henry VIII—images of a Tudor King, 1990; The Queen's Pictures: Royal collectors through the centuries, 1991; (contrib.) Alfred Sisley, ed M. A. Stevens, 1992; Gainsborough and Reynolds: contrasts in Royal patronage, 1994; (with Vanessa Remington) Masterpieces in Little: portrait miniatures from the collection of Her Majesty Queen Elizabeth II, 1996; The Quest for Albion: monarchy and the patronage of British painting, 1998; (contrib.) Royal Treasures: a Golden Jubilee celebration, 2002; Ceremony & Celebration: Coronation Day 1953, 2003; (contrib.) George III and Queen Charlotte: patronage, collecting and Court taste, 2004; Enchanting the Eye: Dutch paintings of the Golden Age, 2004; reviews and contribs to learned jls. *Recreations:* books, theatre, cinema, music, real tennis. *Address:* Linstead Hall, Linstead Magna, Halesworth, Suffolk IP19 0QN. *T:* (01986) 785519. *Club:* Garrick.

LLOYD, Clive Hubert, AO 1985; CBE 1992; OJ 1985; OB 1986; Executive Promotion Officer, Project Fullemploy, since 1987; International Match Referee, International Cricket Council, 2002–06; *b* Georgetown, Guyana, 31 Aug. 1944; *er s* of late Arthur Christopher Lloyd and of Sylvia Thelma Lloyd; *m* 1971, Waveney Benjamin; one *s* two *d*. *Educ:* Chatham High Sch., Georgetown (schol.). Clerk, Georgetown Hosp., 1960–66. Began cricket career, Demerara CC, Georgetown, 1959; début for Guyana, 1963; first Test Match, 1966; played for Haslingden, Lancs League, 1967; Lancashire County Cricket Club: Mem., 1968–86, capped 1969; Captain, 1981–84 and 1986; Captain, W1 cricket team, 1974–78 and 1979–85; World Series Cricket in Australia, 1977–79. Made first 1st class century, 1966; passed total of 25,000 runs (incl. 69 centuries), 1981; captained WI teams which won World Cup, 1975, 1979; Manager, WI cricket tour in Australia, 1988–89; WI Team Manager, 1996–99, 2007–08. First Pres., WI Players' Assoc., 1973. West Indies Cricket Board: Mem., Bd of Dirs; Chm., Cricket Cttee. Former Dir, Red Rose Radio. Mem. (part-time), Commn for Racial Equality, 1987–90. Hon. Fellow: Manchester Polytechnic, 1986; Lancashire Polytechnic, 1986. Hon. MA: Manchester; Hull; Hon. Dr of Letters, Univ. of West Indies, Mona. Golden Arrow of Achievement (Guyana), 1975; Cacique Crown of Honours, Order of Rorima (Guyana), 1985. *Publications:* (with Tony Cozier) Living for Cricket, 1980; *relevant publications:* Clive Lloyd, by Trevor McDonald, 1985; Supercat: the authorised biography of Clive Lloyd, by Simon Lister, 2007. *Address:* c/o Harefield, Harefield Drive, Wilmslow, Cheshire SK9 1NJ.

LLOYD, Air Vice-Marshal Darrell Clive Arthur, CB 1980; Commander, Northern Maritime Air Region, 1981–83; retired; *b* 5 Nov. 1928; *s* of Cecil James Lloyd and Doris Frances Lloyd; *m* 1957, Pamela (*née* Woodside); two *s*. *Educ:* Stowe; RAF Coll., Cranwell. Commnd 1950; ADC to C-in-C, ME Air Force, 1955–57; Instr, Central Flying Sch., 1958–60; Personal Air Sec. to Sec. of State for Air, 1961–63; CO, RAF Bruggen, 1968–70; RCDS, 1972; Dir of Defence Policy, UK Strategy Div., 1973–75; Dep. Comdr, RAF Germany, 1976–78; ACAS (Ops), 1978–81. FCMI (FBIM 1972). *Recreations:* travel, golf, painting. *Address:* c/o Halifax, 63 High Street, Deal, Kent CT14 6EH. *Clubs:* Royal Air Force; Royal Cinque Ports Golf (Deal); Tandridge Golf (Oxted).

LLOYD, David Alan; Chairman, David Lloyd Associates, since 1980; Managing Director, Next Generation Clubs, since 1998; *b* 3 Jan. 1948; *s* of Dennis and Doris Lloyd; *m* 1972, Veronica Jardine; one *s* two *d*. *Educ:* Southend High Sch. Tennis player; mem., British Davis Cup team, 1973–82; ranked in Britain's top ten, 1970–81; semi-finalist, Wimbledon Championship doubles, 1973; British Wightman Cup coach, 1981; non-playing Captain, British Davis Cup team, 1995–2000. Chm., David Lloyd Leisure, 1981–96; Chm. and owner, Hull City AFC, 1997–2002. Freeman, City of London, 1985. Entrepreneur of the Year, PLC Awards, 1994. *Publications:* Improve Your Tennis Skills, 1989; Successful Tennis, 1989; Winning Tennis Fitness, 1991; How to Succeed in Business by Really Trying, 1995. *Recreations:* golf, swimming, tennis, football. *Address:* David Lloyd Associates Ltd, Cavaliers Court, Oxshott Road, Leatherhead, Surrey KT22 0BZ. *Clubs:* All England Lawn Tennis; Queenwood and Loch Lomond Cricket.

LLOYD, David Andrew, OBE 1993; HM Diplomatic Service, retired; Senior Consultant, Middle East Association, since 2001; *b* 24 Dec. 1940; *s* of John Owen Lloyd and Ellen Marjorie Howard Lloyd; *m* 1st, 1965, Janet Elizabeth Rawcliffe; one *s* one *d*; 2nd, 1979, Patricia Villa (marr. diss.); 3rd, 1987, Katharine Jane Smith; three *d*. *Educ:* Lancing Coll.; Clare Coll., Cambridge (BA Hons Arabic). Entered Foreign Office, 1964; served Kuwait, Bogotá, FCO and Madrid; First Sec., FCO, 1983–88; Head, British Trade Office, Al Khobar, Saudi Arabia, 1988–93; FCO, 1994–96; Ambassador to Slovenia, 1997–2000. Trustee and Patron, British-Slovene Soc., 2003–; Trustee, Islamic Museum, London, 2007–. Mem., Exec. Cttee, Lancing Club, 2005–. *Recreations:* indoor rowing, tennis, theatre, concerts. *Address:* New Thorntons, 150 North Road, Hertford SG14 2BZ. *T:* (01992) 583795.

LLOYD, David Bernard; Secretary, Royal College of Physicians, 1986–98; *b* 14 Jan. 1938; *s* of George Edwards and Lilian Catherine Lloyd; *m* 1968, Christine Vass; three *d*. *Educ:* Presteigne Grammar Sch.; Hereford High Sch. FCCA. Early posts in local govt, UCL, UCH Med. Sch.; Royal College of Obstetricians and Gynaecologists: Accountant, 1971–76; Secretary, 1976–82; Secretary, Nat. Inst. of Agricultural Engineering, 1982–86. Chm., Management Cttee, St Albans CAB, 1990–94 (Mem., 1985–94); Co. Sec., Harpenden Day Centre Assoc., 2000–. Member (C): Harpenden Town Council, 1992–99, 2001–03; Herts CC, 1997– (Chm., Protection Cttee, 1999–2000; Cabinet, 2001–03; Chm., Health Scrutiny Cttee, 2006–). Chm., Harpenden Trust, 1995–96. Governor: Sir John Lawes Sen. Sch., 1986–87 (also Chm.); Roundwood Jun. Sch., 1980–89 (Chm., 1985–88). Hon. FRCP 1998; Hon. FFPM 1998. *Recreations:* local charity, garden. *Address:* 16 Hartwell Gardens, Harpenden, Herts AL5 2RW. *T:* (01582) 761292, *Fax:* (01582) 467177.

LLOYD, David Mark; Head of News, Current Affairs and Business, Channel Four Television, 1997–2004; *b* 3 Feb. 1945; *s* of late Maurice Edward and Roma Doreen Lloyd; *m* 1982, Jana Tomas; one *s* one *d*, and one step *s*. *Educ:* Felsted Sch.; Brentwood Sch.; Brasenose Coll., Oxford (MA 1967). Joined BBC as Gen. Trainee, 1967: Dep. Ed., Nationwide, 1978; Editor: Money Prog., 1980; Newsnight, 1982; Sixty Minutes, 1983; Breakfast Time, 1984; Sen. Commng Editor, News and Current Affairs, Channel 4, 1988–97. Vis. Prof. of TV Journalism, City Univ., 2005–. Shell Film and TV Award, 1982; Judges Award, RTS, 2003. *Recreations:* cricket, golf, music, travel. *Address:* 9 Richmond Crescent, Islington, N1 0LZ.

LLOYD, David Rees, FRCGP; Member (Plaid Cymru) South Wales West, National Assembly for Wales, since 1999; *b* 2 Dec. 1956; *s* of Aneurin Rees Lloyd and Dorothy Grace Lloyd; *m* 1982, Dr Catherine Jones; two *s* one *d*. *Educ:* Lampeter Comprehensive Sch.; Welsh Nat. Sch. of Medicine, Cardiff (MB BCh 1980; Dip. in Therapeutics, 1995). MRCGP 1989, FRCGP 2001. Jun. hosp. med. posts, 1980–84; GP, 1984–99. National Assembly for Wales: Shadow Health Sec., 1999–2003; Shadow Finance Minister, 2003–07. *Recreation:* lay preacher. *Address:* National Assembly for Wales, Cardiff Bay, Cardiff CF99 1NA.

LLOYD, Rev. David Richard, (Rev. Denys Lloyd); Parish Priest, Our Lady and St Joseph, Sheringham and Cromer, since 2008; *b* 28 June 1939; *s* of Richard Norman Lloyd and Grace Enid Lloyd. *Educ:* Brighton College (George Long Scholar); Trinity Hall, Cambridge (Exhibitioner; BA 1961, MA 1965); Leeds Univ. (MA 1969). Asst Curate, St Martin's, Rough Hills, Wolverhampton, 1963–67; professed as Mem. of Community of Resurrection, 1969 (taking name Denys); Tutor, Coll. of Resurrection, 1970–75, Vice-Principal, 1975–84; Principal, 1984–90; Associate Lecturer, Dept of Theology and Religious Studies, Univ. of Leeds, 1972–90. Received into Roman Catholic Church at Quarr Abbey, 1990; Missionary Inst., London, 1993–94; ordained priest, 1994; Asst Priest, St Mark's, Ipswich, and RC Chaplain, Ipswich Hosp., 1994–96; Parish Priest, Our Lady's, Stowmarket, 1996–2008. Rural Dean, Bury St Edmunds, 2001–08. *Publications:* contribs to theolog. jls. *Address:* The Presbytery, 58 Cromer Road, Sheringham, Norfolk NR26 8RT.

LLOYD, Eve, (Lady Lloyd); *see* Pollard, E.

LLOYD, Frances Mary, (Mrs James Lloyd); *see* Line, F. M.

LLOYD, Sir Geoffrey (Ernest Richard), Kt 1997; PhD; FBA 1983; Professor of Ancient Philosophy and Science, University of Cambridge, 1983–2000, now Emeritus; Master of Darwin College, Cambridge, 1989–2000 (Hon. Fellow, 2000); *b* 25 Jan. 1933; *s* of William Ernest Lloyd and Olive Irene Neville Lloyd; *m* 1956, Janet Elizabeth Lloyd; three *s*. *Educ:* Charterhouse; King's Coll., Cambridge (BA 1954; MA 1958; PhD 1958). Cambridge University: Asst Lectr in Classics, 1965–67; Lectr, 1967–74; Reader in Ancient Philosophy and Science, 1974–83; Fellow, 1957–89 (Hon. Fellow, 1990), and Sen. Tutor, 1969–73, King's Coll. Bonsall Prof., Stanford Univ., 1981; Sather Prof., Berkeley, 1983–84; A. D. White Prof.-at-large, Cornell Univ., 1990–97. Chm., E Asian Hist. of Sci. Trust, 1992–2002. Fellow, Japan Soc. for the Promotion of Science, 1981. Hon. For. Mem., Amer. Acad. of Arts and Scis, 1995. Hon. LittD Athens, 2003. Sarton Medal, History of Science Soc., USA, 1987; Kenyon Medal, British Acad., 2007. *Publications:* Polarity and Analogy, 1966; Aristotle: the growth and structure of his thought, 1968; Early Greek Science: Thales to Aristotle, 1970; Greek Science after Aristotle, 1973; (ed) Hippocratic Writings, 1978; (ed) Aristotle on Mind and the Senses, 1978; Magic, Reason and Experience, 1979; Science, Folklore and Ideology, 1983; Science and Morality in Greco-Roman Antiquity, 1985; The Revolutions of Wisdom, 1987; Demystifying Mentalities, 1990; Methods and Problems in Greek Science, 1991; Adversaries and Authorities, 1996; Aristotelian Explorations, 1996; (ed) Le Savoir grec, 1996 (English edn, Greek Thought, 2000); (with N. Sivin) The Way and the Word, 2002; The Ambitions of Curiosity, 2002; In the Grip of Disease: studies in the Greek imagination, 2003; Ancient Worlds, Modern Reflections: philosophical perspectives on Greek and Chinese science and culture, 2004; The Delusions of Invulnerability: wisdom and morality in ancient Greece, China and today, 2005; Principles and Practices in Ancient Greek and Chinese Science, 2006; Cognitive Variations: reflections on the unity and diversity of the human mind, 2007; contribs to classical and philosophical jls. *Recreation:* travel. *Address:* 2 Prospect Row, Cambridge CB1 1DU; Needham Research Institute, Sylvester Road, Cambridge CB3 9AF.

LLOYD, Graham; *see* Lloyd, J. G.

LLOYD, Heather Claire, (Mrs P. N. D. Kennedy); Her Honour Judge Heather Lloyd; a Circuit Judge, since 2007; *b* Bebington, Wirral, 16 May 1957; *d* of John Howson Lloyd and late Nancy Beatrice Lloyd (*née* Barlow); *m* 1982, (Peter) Nicholas (Dodgson) Kennedy, barrister; two *s*. *Educ:* St Edmund's Coll., Liverpool; Univ. of Liverpool (LLB Hons 1978). Called to the Bar, Gray's Inn, 1979; in practice at Peel House Chambers, Liverpool, 1979–99, Chavasse Court Chambers, Liverpool, 1999–2007; Asst Recorder, 1998–2000; Recorder, 2000–07. *Recreations:* gardening, travel. *Address:* Preston Combined Court Centre, The Law Courts, Ringway, Preston PR1 2LL. *Club:* Aughton Lawn Tennis.

LLOYD, His Honour Humphrey John; QC 1979; arbitrator; a Judge of the Technology and Construction Court (formerly an Official Referee) of the High Court, 1993–2005; *b* 16 Nov. 1939; *s* of Rees Lewis Lloyd of the Inner Temple, barrister-at-law, and Dorothy Margaret Ferry (*née* Gibson); *m* 1969, Ann Findlay; one *s* one *d*. *Educ:* Westminster; Trinity Coll., Dublin (BA (Mod), LLB; MA). Called to the Bar, Inner Temple, 1963, Bencher, 1985. A Recorder, 1990–93. Chm., Architects' Registration Bd, 2002–07. Pres., Soc. of Construction Law, 1985–88. Vis. Prof., Leeds Metropolitan Univ., 2002–. Hon. Sen. Vis. Fellow, QMC, 1987; Professorial Fellow, Queen Mary, London Univ., 2005–. Hon. Fellow: Amer. Coll. of Construction Law, 1997; Canadian Coll. of Construction Lawyers, 2002. Editor-in-chief: Building Law Reports, 1977–93 (Consultant Editor, 1993–98); The Internat. Construction Law Rev., 1983–; Consultant Editor: Emden's Construction Law, 1993–; Technology and Construction Law Reports, 1999–. *Publications:* (ed) The Liability of Contractors, 1986; (contrib.) Halsbury's Laws of

England, 4th edn, 1992. *Address:* Atkin Chambers, 1 Atkin Building, Gray's Inn, WC1R 5AT. *Club:* Reform.

LLOYD, Illtyd Rhys; HM Chief Inspector of Schools (Wales), 1982–90, retired; *b* 13 Aug. 1929; *s* of John and Melvina Lloyd; *m* 1955, Julia Lewis; one *s* one *d. Educ:* Port Talbot (Glan-Afan) County Grammar Sch.; Swansea UC (Hon. Fellow, Univ. of Wales, 1987). BSc, MSc; DipStat, DipEd. Commnd Educn Br., RAF, 1951–54 (Flt Lieut). Second Maths Master, Howardian High Sch. for Boys, Cardiff, 1954–57; Hd of Maths Dept, Pembroke Grammar Sch., 1957–59; Dep. Headmaster, Howardian High Sch., 1959–63; Welsh Office: HM Inspector of Schs, 1964–70; Staff Inspector (Secondary Educn), 1971–82. Chm., Educn Resources Centre, Aberystwyth Univ., 1991–2001; Vice-Chm., S Glam FHSA, 1993–96 (Mem., 1990–96); Member: Indep. Schs Tribunal Educn Panel, 1990–2004; Exec. Cttee, Council for Educn in World Citizenship-Cymru, 1990–2003 (Treas., 1962–63; Chm., 1997–2003). Churches Together in Wales: Mem. Council, 1991–2003; Treas., 1999–2003; Mem., Finance Cttee, 1990–2003 (Vice Chm., 1995–98; Chm., 1999–2003); Baptist Union of Wales: Mem. Council, 1990–; Treas., 1992–2003; Vice-Pres., 1995–96; Pres., 1996–97; Member: Educn Cttee, Free Churches Council, 1993–2001; Finance Cttee, CTBI, 1994–2003. Member, Council: Cardiff Theol Coll., 1990–2003 (Chm., 1995–2003); Univ. of Wales, Lampeter, 1999–2004; Gov., Swansea Inst. of Higher Educn, 1990–95. Chairman: Mgt Cttee, Glyn Nest Christian Home, 1992–2003; Bryn Llifon Baptist Home, 1999–2003; Sec., Capel Gomer Church, Swansea, 1969–83; Treas., Tabernacle Welsh Baptist Church, Cardiff, 1992–. Trustee: Churches Counselling Service, 1994–2000; Churches Tourism Network Wales, 2001–05. Hon. Mem., Gorsedd of Bards, 1990. *Publications:* Geirfa Mathemateg, 1956; Secondary Education in Wales 1965–85, 1991; Gwyr y Gair, 1993; Yr Hyn a Ymddiriedwyd i'n Gofal, 1996. *Recreation:* walking. *Address:* 134 Lake Road East, Roath Park, Cardiff CF23 5NQ. *T:* (029) 2075 5296.

LLOYD, (John) Graham; consultant, 1994–96; Director of Property Services, Commission for the New Towns, 1992–94; *b* Watford, 18 Feb. 1938; *s* of late Richard and Edith Lloyd; *m* 1st, 1960, Ann (*née* Plater) (marr. diss. 1989); three *s*; 2nd, 1989, Monica (*née* Barlow). *Educ:* City of London Sch.; College of Estate Management, London Univ. (BSc Estate Management). FRICS. In private practice, London and Leamington Spa, 1959–75. Commission for the New Towns: Commercial and Industrial Manager, 1975–78, Manager, 1978–81, Hemel Hempstead; Exec. Officer/Commercial Surveyor, Corby, 1981–91; Head of Estate Management Services, 1991–92. *Recreations:* soccer, motor racing, jazz and popular music, gardening. *Address:* 4 Fairway, Kibworth Beauchamp, Leics LE8 0LB.

LLOYD, John Nicol Fortune; journalist; Contributing Editor, Financial Times, since 2006; Director of Journalism, Reuters Institute for the Study of Journalism, University of Oxford, since 2006; *b* 15 April 1946; *s* of Joan Adam Fortune and Christopher Lloyd; *m* 1983, Marcia Levy (marr. diss. 1997); one *s*; *m* 2000, Ilaria Poggiolini. *Educ:* Waid Comprehensive School; Edinburgh Univ. (MA Hons). Editor, Time Out, 1972–73; Reporter, London Programme, 1974–76; Producer, Weekend World, 1976–77; industrial reporter, labour corresp., industrial and labour editor, Financial Times, 1977–86; Editor, New Statesman, 1986–87; re-joined Financial Times, 1987; E European Editor, 1987–90; Moscow Correspondent, 1991–95; Associate Ed., New Statesman & Soc., subseq. New Statesman, 1996–2003; columnist, The Times, 1997–98; founding Editor, FT Magazine, 2003–05. Director: East-West Inst., NY, 1997–; Foreign Policy Centre, 1999–. Sen. Associate Fellow, Kennedy Sch., Harvard Univ., 1995; Sen. Associate Mem., St Antony's Coll., Oxford, 1996–99. Journalist of the Year, Granada Awards, 1984; Specialist Writer of the Year, IPC Awards, 1985; Rio Tinto David Watt Meml Prize, 1997. *Publications:* (with Ian Benson) The Politics of Industrial Change, 1982; (with Martin Adeney) The Miners' Strike: loss without limit, 1986; (with Charles Leadbeater) In Search of Work, 1987; (contrib.) Counterblasts, 1989; Rebirth of a Nation: an anatomy of Russia, 1998; Re-engaging Russia, 2000; The Protest Ethic, 2001; What the Media have done to our Politics, 2004. *Recreations:* opera, hill walking. *Address:* c/o Financial Times, One Southwark Bridge, SE1 9HL.

LLOYD, Prof. John Raymond; *see* Lloyd, M. R.

LLOYD, John Wilson, CB 1992; JP; Clerk and Head of the Office of the Presiding Officer, National Assembly for Wales, 1999–2001; *b* 24 Dec. 1940; *s* of late Dr Ellis Lloyd and Mrs Dorothy Lloyd; *m* 1967, Buddug Roberts (*d* 1996); two *s* one *d. Educ:* Swansea Grammar Sch.; Clifton Coll., Bristol; Christ's Coll., Cambridge (MA). Asst Principal, HM Treasury, 1962–67 (Private Sec. to Financial Sec., 1965–67); Principal, successively HM Treasury, CSD and Welsh Office, 1967–75 (Private Sec. to Sec. of State for Wales, 1974–75); Welsh Office: Asst Sec., 1975–82; Under Sec., 1982–88; Principal Establishment Officer, 1982–86; Hd, Housing, Health and Social Servs Policy Gp, 1986–88; Dep. Sec., 1988; Dir, Social Policy and Local Govt Affairs, 1988–98. Mem., Royal Commn on Ancient and Historical Monuments of Wales, 2002–07. JP Cardiff, 2001. *Recreations:* golf, walking, swimming. *Address:* c/o National Assembly for Wales, Cardiff Bay, Cardiff CF99 1NA. *T:* (029) 2082 5111. *Club:* Oxford and Cambridge.

LLOYD, Jonathan Bruce; composer; writer; *b* 30 Sept. 1948; *s* of Geoffrey and Nancy Lloyd; *m* 1st, 1970, Poppy Holden (marr. diss. 1975); one *s*; 2nd, 1981, Katherine Bones; two *s. Educ:* Royal Coll. of Music. Mendelssohn Scholar, 1969; Fellow, Berkshire Music Centre, Tanglewood, USA, 1973 (Koussevitzky Composition Prize); Composer-in-residence, Dartington Coll., 1978–79. *Principal works:* Cantique, 1968; Till the Wind Blows, 1969; Scattered Ruins, 1973; Everything Returns, 1977; Viola Concerto, 1979; Toward the Whitening Dawn, 1980; Waiting for Gozo, 1981; Three Dances, 1982; Mass, 1983; 5 Symphonies, 1983–89; The Shorelines of Certainty, 1984; The Adjudicator, 1985; Almeida Dances, 1986; Revelation, 1990; Wa Wa Mozart, 1991; Ballad for the Evening of a Man, 1992; Blackmail, 1993; Tolerance, 1994; Violin Concerto, 1995; And Beyond, 1996; A Dream of a Pass, 1997; Shadows of our Future Selves, 1998; The Beggar's Opera (musical adaptation), 1999; Inventing Bach, Summon the Spirit, 2000; Music to Maze, Songs, 2001; Between us a River before us the Sea, 2002. *Recreations:* tennis, walking, cycling. *Address:* c/o Boosey & Hawkes Music Publishers, 295 Regent Street, W1R 8JH. *T:* (020) 7580 2060.

LLOYD, Jonathan Salusbury; Director, since 1994, Group Managing Director, since 1995, Curtis Brown Group Ltd; *b* 1 Dec. 1946; *s* of late Reginald Lloyd and of Maureen Lloyd; *m* 1976, Marion Dickens; two *s* one *d. Educ:* Shrewsbury Sch.; Alliance Française, Paris. Joined Collins publishers as mgt trainee, 1967; export sales in Europe and Middle E, incl. Afghanistan; UK Sales Manager, 1976; Sales and Mktg Dir, 1980; Gp Rights and Contracts Dir, 1983; Managing Director: Grafton Books, 1986–91; HarperCollins, 1991–94. Vice-Pres., 1997–2000, Pres., 2000–02, Assoc. of Authors' Agents. *Recreations:* reading, sailing, theatre, opera, film, squash, running for one hour (except in the 2006 London Marathon which took longer). *Address:* c/o Curtis Brown, Haymarket House, 28–29 Haymarket, SW1Y 4SP. *T:* (020) 7393 4408, *Fax:* (020) 7393 4399; *e-mail:* jlloyd@curtisbrown.co.uk. *Clubs:* Garrick, Royal Automobile, MCC.

LLOYD, Mark; Chief Executive, Cambridgeshire County Council, since 2008; *b* 4 July 1967; *s* of David Lloyd and late Joan Lloyd (*née* Bowyer); *m* 2007, Shân Warren. *Educ:* Rhyn Park Comp. Sch., St Martins, Shropshire; Oswestry Coll.; Durham Univ. (MBA Distn 2002). Civil Service, 1985–93: actg Chief Exec., Powys TEC, 1992–93; served on Lord Justice Scott's Inquiry into defence related exports to Iraq, 1993; Dir, Educn and Trng, Central England TEC, 1994–96; Dep. Chief Exec., Bolton and Bury Chamber of Commerce, Trng and Enterprise, 1996–99; Chief Exec., Co. Durham TEC and Business Link, 1999–2000; Durham County Council: Dir, Econ. Develt and Planning, 2000–03; Man. Dir, Co. Durham Develt Company, 2000–05; Dep. Chief Exec. (Policy and Strategy), 2003–05; Chief Exec., 2005–08. *Recreations:* travel, long-distance running, photography, ski-ing, gadgets, good wine. *Address:* c/o Cambridgeshire County Council, Shire Hall, Castle Hill, Cambridge CB3 0AP. *T:* (01223) 699188; *e-mail:* mark.lloyd@cambridgeshire.gov.uk.

LLOYD, Prof. Michael Raymond; Professor, Oslo School of Architecture, 1993–96; Executive Architect/Planner, Norconsult International, Oslo, 1981–93; *b* 20 Aug. 1927; *s* of W. R. Lloyd; *m* 1957, Berit Hansen; one *s* two *d. Educ:* Wellington Sch., Somerset; AA School of Architecture. AA Dipl. 1953; ARIBA 1954; MNAL 1960. Private practice and Teacher, State School of Arts and Crafts, Oslo, 1955–60 and 1962–63; First Year Master, AA School of Architecture, 1960–62; Dean, Faculty of Arch., and Prof. of Arch., Kumasi Univ. of Science and Technology, 1963–66; Principal, AA Sch. of Architecture, 1966–71; Consultant, Land Use Consultants (Internat.) Lausanne, 1971–72; Senior Partner, Sinar Associates, Tunbridge Wells, 1973–78; Consultant Head, Hull Sch. of Architecture, 1974–77; Technical Officer, ODA, Central America, 1979–81. Prof., Bergen Sch. of Architecture, 1986–92. Leverhulme Sen. Res. Fellow, UCL, 1976–78. *Publications:* (as J. R. Lloyd) Tegning og Skissing; ed World Architecture, Vol. I Norway, Vol. III Ghana; Norwegian Laftehus; Environmental Impact of Development Activities. *Recreations:* sailing, ski-ing.

LLOYD, Sir Nicholas (Markley), Kt 1990; MA; Chairman, Brown Lloyd James, since 1997; *b* 9 June 1942; *s* of Walter and Sybil Lloyd; *m* 1st, 1968, Patricia Sholliker (marr. diss. 1978); two *s* one *d*; 2nd, 1979, Eve Pollard, *qv*; one *s. Educ:* Bedford Modern Sch.; St Edmund Hall, Oxford (MA Hons History); Harvard Univ., USA. Reporter, Daily Mail, 1964; Educn Correspondent, Sunday Times, 1966; Dep. News Editor, Sunday Times, 1968; News Editor, The Sun, 1970; Asst Editor, News of the World, 1972; Asst Editor, The Sun, 1976; Dep. Editor, Sunday Mirror, 1980; Editor: Sunday People, 1982–83; News of the World, 1984–85; Daily Express, 1986–95. Presenter, LBC, 1997–99. *Recreations:* Arsenal, golf, books, theatre. *Address:* 25 Lower Belgrave Street, SW1W 0NR.

LLOYD, Prof. Noel Glynne, PhD; Vice-Chancellor and Principal, since 2004, and Professor of Mathematics, since 1988, Aberystwyth University (formerly University of Wales, Aberystwyth); *b* 26 Dec. 1946; *s* of Joseph John Lloyd and Gwenllian Lloyd; *m* 1970, Dilys June Edwards; one *s* one *d. Educ:* Llanelli Grammar Sch.; Queens' Coll., Cambridge (BA 1968, MA 1972; PhD 1972). FTCL 1965. Res. Fellow, St John's Coll., Cambridge, 1972–74; University College of Wales, then University of Wales, Aberystwyth: Lectr, 1974–77; Sen. Lectr, 1977–81; Reader, 1981–88; Hd, Mathematics Dept, 1991–97; Dean of Sci., 1994–97; Pro Vice-Chancellor, 1997–99; Registrar and Sec., 1999–2004. Member: Bd, Mid-Wales TEC, 1999–2001; Mid-Wales Regl Cttee, Educn and Learning Wales, 2001–04; Bd, Inst. of Grassland and Envmtl Res., 2004–; Bd, UCEA, 2005–; Bd, QAA, 2005–. Sec., Capel y Morfa, Aberystwyth, 1989–2004; Chm., Ch and Soc. Bd, Presbyterian Ch of Wales. Mem. Bd, Aberystwyth Challenge Fund, 1999–. Ed., Jl of London Math. Soc., 1983–88. *Publications:* Degree Theory, 1978; numerous jl articles on Nonlinear Differential Equations. *Recreation:* music (piano, organ). *Address:* Aberystwyth University, King Street, Aberystwyth, Ceredigion SY23 2AX. *T:* (01970) 622002, *Fax:* (01970) 611446; *e-mail:* ngl@aber.ac.uk. *Club:* Oxford and Cambridge.

LLOYD, Peter Gordon, CBE 1976 (OBE 1965); retired; British Council Representative, Greece, 1976–80; *b* 20 Feb. 1920; *s* of Peter Gleave Lloyd and Ellen Swift; *m* 1952, Edith Florence (*née* Flurey) (*d* 2005); two *s* one *d. Educ:* Royal Grammar Sch., Newcastle upon Tyne; Balliol Coll., Oxford (Horsley Exhibnr, 1939; BA, MA 1948). RA (Light Anti-Aircraft), subseq. DLI, 1940–46, Captain. British Council, 1949–: Brit. Council, Belgium and Hon. Lector in English, Brussels Univ., 1949–52; Reg. Dir, Mbale, Uganda, 1952–56; Dep. Dir Personnel, 1956–60; Representative: Ethiopia, 1960–68; Poland, 1969–72; Nigeria, 1972–76. *Publications:* (introd) Huysmans, A Rebours, 1946; The Story of British Democracy, 1959; Perspectives and Identities, 1989; Destinations Over Water, 2005; critical essays on literature in periodicals. *Recreations:* literature, music, travel. *Address:* 111 Sussex Road, Petersfield, Hants GU31 4LB. *T:* (01730) 262007. *Club:* Oxford and Cambridge.

LLOYD, Rt Hon. Sir Peter (Robert Cable), Kt 1995; PC 1994; President, National Council of Independent Monitoring Boards for Prisons, 2003–07; *b* 12 Nov. 1937; *s* of late David and Stella Lloyd; *m* 1967, Hilary Creighton; one *s* one *d. Educ:* Tonbridge Sch.; Pembroke Coll., Cambridge (MA). Formerly Marketing Manager, United Biscuits plc; Chm., London English Sch. Ltd, 2007–. MP (C) Fareham, 1979–2001. Sec., Cons. Parly Employment Cttee, 1979–81; Vice-Chm., Cons. European Affairs Cttee, 1980–81; PPS to Minister of State, NI Office, 1981–82, to Sec. of State for Educn and Sci., Sir Keith Joseph, 1983–84; Asst Govt Whip, 1984–86; a Lord Comr of HM Treasury (Govt Whip), 1986–88; Parly Under-Sec. of State, Dept of Social Security, 1988–89, Home Office, 1989–92; Minister of State, Home Office, 1992–94. Member: Select Cttee on Public Affairs, 1996–97; Treasury Select Cttee, 1997–99; Chm., All Party Penal Affairs Cttee, 1997–2001; Vice-Chm., All Party Human Rights Gp, 1997–2001; Mem., H of C Commn, 1998–2000; Chm., Home Office Prisons Bds of Visitors Review Cttee, 2000–01. Vice-Chm., British Section, IPU, 1994–99; Parly Advr, Police Fedn, 1997–2001. Chairman, Bow Group, 1972–73; Editor of Crossbow, 1974–76. Jt Chm., CAABU, 1997–2001; Chm., Arab British Centre, 2001–03. Chm., New Bridge, 1994–. *Recreations:* theatre, gardening. *Address:* 32 Burgh Street, N1 8HG. *T:* (020) 7359 2871. *Club:* Players Theatre.

LLOYD, Phyllida Christian; freelance theatre director; *b* 17 June 1957; *d* of Patrick Lloyd and Margaret (*née* Douglas-Pennant). *Educ:* Birmingham Univ. (BA English and Drama 1979). Arts Council trainee dir, Wolsey Theatre, Ipswich, 1985. Cameron Mackintosh Vis. Prof. of Contemporary Th., Oxford Univ., 2006. Productions include: The Comedy of Errors, A Streetcar Named Desire, Dona Rosita the Spinster, Oliver Twist, Bristol Old Vic, 1989; The Winter's Tale, The School for Scandal, Death and the King's Horseman, Medea, Manchester Royal Exchange, 1990–91; The Virtuoso, Artists and Admirers, RSC, 1991–92; L'Etoile, La Bohème, Gloriana, Medea, Opera North, 1991–96; Six Degrees of Separation, Hysteria, Royal Court, 1992, 1993; Pericles, What the Butler Saw, The Way of the World, RNT, 1994–95; Threepenny Opera, Donmar Warehouse, 1994; Doña Rosita, Almeida, 1997; The Prime of Miss Jean Brodie, RNT, 1998; Carmen, Opera North, 1998; Macbeth, Paris Opera, 1999, Royal Opera, 2002; The Carmelites, 1999, Verdi's Requiem, 2000, ENO; Mamma Mia!, Prince Edward, 1999, and worldwide; The

Handmaid's Tale, Royal Danish Opera, 2000, ENO, 2003; Gloriana (BBC TV film), 2000 (Internat. Emmy, Royal Philharmonic Soc. award, FIPA d'or); Boston Marriage, Donmar Warehouse, transf. New Ambassadors, 2001; Albert Herring, Opera North, 2002; The Duchess of Malfi, NT, The Taming of the Shrew, Globe, 2003; The Ring Cycle, ENO, and Macbeth, Liceu Th., Barcelona, 2004; Wild East, Royal Court, 2005; Mary Stuart, Donmar Warehouse, transf. Apollo, 2005 (South Bank Award, 2005); Twilight of the Gods, ENO, 2005; The Fall of the House of Usher, Bregenz, Peter Grimes (South Bank Award, 2006), Opera North, 2006; Mamma Mia! (film), 2008. Hon. DLitt Bristol, 2006. *Address:* c/o Annette Stone, 30–31 St Peter Street, W1F 0AR. *T:* (020) 7734 0626, *Fax:* (020) 7439 2522.

LLOYD, Sir Richard (Ernest Butler), 2nd Bt *cr* 1960, of Rhu, Co. Dunbarton; Chairman: Vickers plc, 1992–97 (Director, 1978–97; Deputy Chairman, 1989–92); Argos plc, 1995–98; *b* 6 Dec. 1928; *s* of Major Sir (Ernest) Guy Richard Lloyd, 1st Bt, DSO, and Helen Kynaston (*d* 1984), *yr d* of Col E. W. Greg, CB; *S* father, 1987; *m* 1955, Jennifer Susan Margaret, *e d* of Brigadier Ereld Cardiff, CB, CBE; three *s*. *Educ:* Wellington Coll.; Hertford Coll., Oxford (MA). Nat. Service (Captain, Black Watch), 1947–49. Joined Glyn, Mills & Co., 1952; Exec. Dir, 1964–70; Chief Executive, Williams & Glyn's Bank Ltd, 1970–78; Hill Samuel & Co. Ltd: Dep. Chm., 1978–87, 1991–95; Chief Exec., 1980–87; Chm., 1987–91. Member: CBI Council, 1978–96; Industrial Develt Adv. Bd, 1972–77; Nat. Econ. Develt Council, 1973–77; Cttee to Review the Functioning of Financial Institutions, 1977–80; Overseas Projects Bd, 1981–85; Advisory Bd, Royal Coll. of Defence Studies, 1987–95; Chm., Business and Industry Adv. Cttee, OECD, Paris, 1998–99. Pres., British Heart Foundn, 1995–2004; Gov., Ditchley Foundn, 1974–2005. *Recreations:* walking, fly-fishing, gardening. *Heir: s* Richard Timothy Butler Lloyd [*b* 12 April 1956; *m* 1989, Wilhelmina, *d* of Henri Schut]. *Address:* Easton Court, Little Hereford, Ludlow SY8 4LN. *T:* (01584) 810475. *Club:* Boodle's.

LLOYD, Richard Hey; *b* 25 June 1933; *s* of Charles Yates Lloyd and Ann Lloyd (*née* Hey); *m* 1962, Teresa Morwenna Willmott; four *d*. *Educ:* Lichfield Cathedral Choir Sch.; Rugby Sch. (Music Scholar); Jesus Coll., Cambridge (Organ Scholar). MA, FRCO, ARCM. Asst Organist, Salisbury Cath., 1957–66; Organist and Master of the Choristers, Hereford Cath., 1966–74; Conductor, Three Choirs Festival, 1966–74 (Chief Conductor 1967, 1970, 1973); Organist and Master of the Choristers, Durham Cathedral, 1974–85; Dep. Headmaster, Salisbury Cathedral Choir Sch., 1985–88. Examiner, Associated Bd of Royal Schs of Music, 1967–. Mem. Council, RCO, 1974–93. *Publications:* church music. *Recreations:* cricket, theatre, travel, reading. *Address:* Duneaves, Lucton, Herefordshire HR6 9PH. *T:* (01568) 780735.

LLOYD, Robert Andrew, CBE 1991; freelance opera singer, broadcaster and writer; *b* 2 March 1940; *s* of William Edward Lloyd and May (*née* Waples); *m* 1st, 1964, Sandra Dorothy Watkins (marr. diss. 1990); one *s* three *d*; 2nd, 1992, Lynda Anne Hazell (*née* Powell). *Educ:* Southend-on-Sea High Sch.; Keble Coll., Oxford (MA Hons Mod. History; Hon. Fellow, 1990). Instructor Lieut RN (HMS Collingwood), 1963–66; Civilian Tutor, Police Staff Coll., Bramshill, 1966–68; studied at London Opera Centre, 1968–69; début in Leonore, Collegiate Theatre, 1969; Principal Bass, Sadler's Wells Opera, Coliseum, 1969–72; Principal Bass, 1972–82, Sen. Artist, 2004, Royal Opera House; Parsifal, Covent Garden, 1988; Flying Dutchman, La Scala, 1988; début at Metropolitan Opera, NY, in Barber of Seville, 1988; début at Vienna State Opera in La Forza del Destino. Guest appearances in Amsterdam, Berlin, Hamburg, Aix-en-Provence, Milan (La Scala), San Francisco, Florence, Paris, Munich, Nice, Boston, Toronto, Salzburg, Tokyo; soloist with major orchestras; over 70 recordings; associated with rôles of King Philip, Boris Godunov (first British bass to sing this rôle at Kirov Opera), Gurnemanz (opened 1991 season, La Scala), Fiesco, Banquo, King Henry; created rôle of Tyrone in Tower (opera by Hoddinott), 1999; film, Parsifal; TV productions: Six Foot Cinderella, 1988; Bluebeard's Castle (opera), 1988; Bob the Bass, 2002; 20 progs for BBC Radio 3, incl. presenter, Opera in Action, 2000–01. Vis. Prof., RCM, 1996–. President: British Youth Opera, 1989–94; Southend Choral Soc., 1996–; ISM, 2005–06; Member: Exec. Cttee, Musicians Benevolent Fund, 1988–94; Conservatoires Adv. Gp, HEFCE, 1993–97; Patron: Abertillery Orpheus Choir, 1990–; Carl Rosa Trust, 1993–. Hon. RAM 1999. FRWCMD 2005. Sir Charles Santley Award, Musicians' Co., 1997; Foreign Artist of the Year Medal, Buenos Aires, 1997; Chaliapin Commem. Medal, St Petersburg, 1998. *Publications:* contrib. miscellaneous jls. *Recreations:* sailing, straight theatre. *Address:* c/o Askonas Holt Ltd, Lincoln House, 300 High Holborn, WC1V 7JH. *Club:* Garrick.

LLOYD, Prof. Robert Glanville, DPhil; FRS 2000; Professor of Genetics, University of Nottingham, since 1990; *b* 25 June 1946; *m* Priscilla Barbara Vaughton; two *d*. *Educ:* Univ. of Bristol (BSc); Univ. of Sussex (DPhil). University of Nottingham: Lectr, 1974–85; Reader in Genetics, 1985–90; Head of Dept of Genetics, 1993–96. *Address:* Institute of Genetics, University of Nottingham, Queen's Medical Centre, Nottingham NG7 2UH; 199 Attenborough Lane, Attenborough, Nottingham NG9 6AB.

LLOYD, His Honour Stephen Harris; a Circuit Judge, 1995–2007; a Deputy Circuit Judge, since 2007; *b* 16 Sept. 1938; *s* of Thomas Richard Lloyd and Amy Irene Lloyd; *m* 1972, Joyce Eileen Baxter; two step *d*. *Educ:* Ashville Coll., Harrogate; Leeds Univ. (LLB). Dale & Newbery, solicitors: articled, 1962; admitted solicitor, 1965; Partner, 1968–85; Sen. Partner, 1985–95; Asst Recorder, 1989–93; Recorder, 1993–95. Chairman: Nat. Council for One Parent Families, 1975–83; Mediation in Divorce, 1986–90. Vice-Chm., St Peter's NHS Trust, Chertsey, 1991–95. Chm., Bd of Govs, Manor House Sch., 1987–95. Member: Morris Register, 1985–2001; Post Vintage Humber Club, 1992–2001; Alvis Owners Club, 2001–. *Recreations:* two 1936 motor cars, charity and committee work, walking, arts. *Address:* Brighton County Court, Family Centre, 1 Edward Street, Brighton BN2 2JD. *T:* (01273) 811333, *Fax:* (01273) 607638.

LLOYD, Thomas Owen Saunders, OBE 2004; DL; FSA; heritage consultant; Chairman, Historic Buildings Council for Wales, 1992–2004; *b* 26 Feb. 1955; *s* of John Audley Lloyd, MC and Mary Ivy Anna Lloyd (*née* Owen); *m* 1987, Christabel Juliet Anne Harrison-Allen (*d* 1996). *Educ:* Radley; Downing Coll., Cambridge (MA Law). FSA 1992. Solicitor, in private practice, London, 1978–87; Dir and Co. Sec., Golden Grove Book Co., Carmarthen, 1987–89; non-executive Director: Dyfed FHSA, 1990–95 (also Chm., Patients' Complaints Cttees); Wales Tourist Bd, 1995–99. Consultant (Wales), Sotheby's, 1999–. Chairman: Pembrokeshire Historical Soc., 1991–94; Buildings at Risk Trust, 1992–; Carmarthenshire Antiquarian Soc., 1999–2002; Picton Castle Trust, 2006–; Pres., Cambrian Archaeological Assoc., 2007–08. Trustee, Architectural Heritage Fund, 2006–. DL Dyfed, 2001. Hon. Fellow, Soc. of Architects in Wales, 1993. *Publications:* The Lost Houses of Wales, 1986, 2nd edn 1989; Pevsner Buildings of Wales series: (jtly) Pembrokeshire, 2004; (jtly) Carmarthenshire & Ceredigion, 2006; contribs to jls of various Welsh historical socs. *Recreation:* old books and bookplates. *Address:* Freestone Hall, Cresselly, Kilgetty, Pembrokeshire SA68 0SY. *T:* (01646) 651493.

LLOYD, Rt Hon. Sir Timothy (Andrew Wigram), Kt 1996; PC 2005; **Rt Hon. Lord Justice Lloyd;** a Lord Justice of Appeal, since 2005; *b* 30 Nov. 1946; *s* of late Thomas Wigram Lloyd and Margo Adela Lloyd (*née* Beasley); *m* 1978, Theresa Sybil Margaret Holloway. *Educ:* Winchester College; Lincoln College, Oxford (Hon. Fellow). MA. Called to the Bar, Middle Temple, 1970, Bencher, 1994; QC 1986; Mem., Middle Temple and Lincoln's Inn; a Judge of the High Ct of Justice, Chancery Div., 1996–2005. Attorney Gen., Duchy of Lancaster, 1993–96; Vice-Chancellor, County Palatine of Lancaster, 2002–05. *Publication:* (ed) Wurtzburg & Mills, Building Society Law, 15th edn 1989. *Recreations:* music, travel. *Address:* Royal Courts of Justice, Strand, WC2A 2LL.

LLOYD, Ven. Trevor; *see* Lloyd, Ven. B. T.

LLOYD, Valerie; Member (Lab) Swansea East, National Assembly for Wales, since Sept. 2001; *b* 16 Nov. 1943; *m* 1964, Robert John Lloyd; two *d*. *Educ:* Llwyn-y-Bryn High Sch. for Girls; Univ. of Wales, Swansea (BEd 1986; MEd 1992). SRN 1966; RNT 1980. Staff nurse, Swansea, 1966–69, 1971–73; nursing sister, Zambia, 1969–71; teacher: Cwmrhydyceirw Primary Sch., Swansea, 1976–77; St Christopher's Sch., Bahrain, 1977–80; Nurse Tutor, 1980–86, Sen. Nurse Tutor, 1986–92, W Glamorgan Sch. of Nursing; Sen. Lectr in Nursing, Sch. of Health Sci., Univ. of Wales, Swansea, 1992–2001. Mem. (Lab) Swansea City and County Councils, 1999–2003. *Address:* National Assembly for Wales, Cardiff CF99 1NA.

LLOYD, Wendy Jane, (Mrs M. Sellars); a District Judge (Magistrates' Courts), Greater Manchester, since 2005; *b* 31 Oct. 1960; *d* of John and Nancy Lloyd; *m* 1987, Michael Sellars; one *s* two *d*. *Educ:* Liverpool Univ. (LLB Hons). Called to the Bar, Middle Temple, 1983; in practice as barrister, Liverpool, 1984–2005; Dep. Dist Judge (Crime), 2003–05. *Recreation:* singing (mainly Gilbert and Sullivan).

LLOYD-DAVIES, Andrew; Social Security and Child Support Commissioner, since 1998; *b* 18 June 1948; *s* of late Martyn Howard Lloyd-Davies and Penelope Catherine (*née* Vevers); *m* 1989, Lucy Laetitia Anne, *d* of late Christopher William Trelawny Morshead, MC, and Hope (*née* Rodd); one *s* one *d*. *Educ:* Haileybury; St John's Coll., Oxford (BA Lit. Hum.). Called to the Bar, Lincoln's Inn, 1973; in practice at Chancery Bar, 1975–98; Dep. Social Security Comr, 1996–98. *Address:* Commissioners' Office, Third Floor, Procession House, 55 Ludgate Hill, EC4M 7JW. *Club:* MCC.

LLOYD-EDWARDS, Captain Sir Norman, KCVO 2008; RD 1971 and Bar 1980, RNR; JP; Lord-Lieutenant of South Glamorgan, 1990–2008 (Vice Lord-Lieutenant, 1986–90); *b* 13 June 1933; *s* of Evan Stanley Edwards and Mary Leah Edwards. *Educ:* Monmouth School for Boys; Quaker's Yard Grammar School; Univ. of Bristol (LLB). Joined RNVR 1952, RN 1958–60; RNR 1960–86; CO S Wales Div., RNR, 1981–84; Naval ADC to the Queen, 1984. Partner, Cartwrights, later Cartwrights, Adams & Black, Solicitors, Cardiff, 1960–93, Consultant, 1993–98. Cardiff City Councillor, 1963–87; Dep. Lord Mayor, 1973–74; Lord Mayor, 1985–86. Member: Welsh Arts Council, 1983–89; BBC Adv. Council (Wales), 1987–90. Chapter Clerk, Llandaff Cathedral, 1975–90. Chm. of Wales, 1981–96, Pres., 1996–, Duke of Edinburgh's Award; Nat. Rescue Training Council, 1983–95. Chm., Glamorgan TAVRA, 1987–90; President: Utd Services Mess, Cardiff, 1986–; S Glam Scouts, 1989–; Cardiff Assoc., National Trust, 1990–; King George's Fund for Sailors, 1990–; Christian Aid (Cardiff and Dist), 1992–; SE Wales Community Foundn, 1993–; George Thomas Hospice, 2006–; Pres., RFCA Wales, 1999–2005. Vice-Pres., RWCMD (formerly WCMD), 1995–. Founder Master, Welsh Livery Guild, 1992–95. Patron, British Red Cross (S Glam), 1991–. Hon. Colonel: 2 Bn (TA), Royal Regt of Wales, 1996–99; Royal Welsh Regt, 1999–2003; 160 (Wales) Bde, 2007–. DL S Glamorgan 1978; JP 1990. GCStJ 1996 (KStJ 1988, Prior of Wales, 1989–2005; Dep. Lord Prior, 2005–). *Recreations:* music, gardening, table talk. *Address:* Hafan Wen, Llantrisant Road, Llandaff CF5 2PU. *Clubs:* Army and Navy; Cardiff and County, United Services Mess (Cardiff).

LLOYD GEORGE, family name of **Earl Lloyd George of Dwyfor**.

LLOYD-GEORGE, family name of **Viscount Tenby**.

LLOYD GEORGE OF DWYFOR, 3rd Earl *cr* 1945; **Owen Lloyd George;** DL; Viscount Gwynedd, 1945; *b* 28 April 1924; *s* of 2nd Earl Lloyd George of Dwyfor, and Roberta Ida Freeman, 5th *d* of Sir Robert McAlpine, 1st Bt; *S* father, 1968; *m* 1st, 1949, Ruth Margaret (marr. diss. 1982; she *d* 2003), *o d* of Richard Coit; two *s* one *d*; 2nd, 1982, Cecily Josephine, *d* of late Sir Alexander Gordon Cumming, 5th Bt, MC, and of Elizabeth Countess Cawdor, *widow* of 2nd Earl of Woolton and former wife of 3rd Baron Forres. *Educ:* Oundle. Welsh Guards, 1942–47. Italian Campaign, 1944–45. Formerly Captain Welsh Guards. Carried the Sword at Investiture of HRH the Prince of Wales, Caernarvon Castle, 1969. Mem., Historic Buildings Council for Wales, 1971–94. DL Dyfed 1993. *Publication:* A Tale of Two Grandfathers, 1999. *Recreations:* shooting, gardening. *Heir: s* Viscount Gwynedd, *qv*. *Address:* Ffynone, Boncath, Pembrokeshire SA37 0HQ; 47 Burton Court, SW3 4SZ. *Clubs:* White's, Pratt's.

LLOYD-HUGHES, Sir Trevor Denby, Kt 1970; former consultant in Government/industry relations, now retired; Chairman, Lloyd-Hughes Associates Ltd, International Consultants in Public Affairs, 1970–89; *b* 31 March 1922; *er s* of late Elwyn and Lucy Lloyd-Hughes, Bradford, Yorks; *m* 1st, 1950, Ethel Marguerite Durward (marr. diss. 1971), *o d* of late J. Ritchie, Dundee and Bradford; one *s* one *d*; 2nd, 1971, Marie-Jeanne, *d* of late Marcel and Helene Moreillon, Geneva; one *d* (and one adopted *d*, a Thai girl). *Educ:* Woodhouse Grove Sch., Yorks; Jesus Coll., Oxford (MA). Commissioned RA, 1941; served with 75th (Shropshire Yeomanry) Medium Regt, RA, in Western Desert, Sicily and Italy, 1941–45. Asst Inspector of Taxes, 1948; freelance journalist, 1949; joined staff of Liverpool Daily Post, 1949; Political Corresp., Liverpool Echo, 1950, Liverpool Daily Post, 1951. Press Secretary to the Prime Minister, 1964–69; Chief Information Adviser to Govt, 1969–70. Dir, Trinity International Holdings plc (formerly Liverpool Daily Post and Echo Ltd), 1978–91. Member of Circle of Wine Writers, 1961, Chm., 1972–73. *Publications:* The Euro Trap, or Future Choices for Britain, 1999; newspaper and magazine articles on political affairs and on wine. *Recreations:* yoga, gardening, reading, walking, travel. *Address:* 52 Glen Road, Castle Bytham, Grantham, Lincs NG33 4RJ. *T:* (01780) 410001, *Fax:* (01780) 410001; *e-mail:* sirtrevorlloyd@aol.com.

LLOYD-JACOB, David Oliver, CBE 1984; Director, UK Sponsorships, Mountbatten Internship Programme, 2002–07; *b* 30 March 1938; *s* of Sir George and Lady Lloyd-Jacob; *m* 1st, 1961, Clare Bartlett; two *d*; 2nd, 1982, Carolyn Howard. *Educ:* Westminster; Christ Church, Oxford. Pres., Azcon Corp., USA, 1974–79; Man. Dir, Consolidated Gold Fields plc, 1979–81; Chm., Amcon Group Inc., USA, 1979–82; Chm. and Chief Exec. Officer, Levinson Steel Co., Pittsburgh, 1983–90; Chairman: Butte Mining plc, 1991–2000; Fibaflo Ltd, 1998–2003; Fibagroup Ltd, 2002–03; Kemp Town Enclosures Ltd, 2002–07; Fibaflo Composites Ltd, 2003–04. Chm., Britain Salutes NY, 1981–83. *Recreations:* opera, theatre, restoring old houses. *Address:* 28 Lewes Crescent, Brighton BN2 1GB. *T:* (01273) 692908. *Clubs:* Garrick; Leander (Henley-on-Thames).

LLOYD JONES, Charles Beynon; *see* Jones.

LLOYD-JONES, David Mathias; freelance conductor; *b* 19 Nov. 1934; *s* of late Sir Vincent Lloyd-Jones, and Margaret Alwena, *d* of late G. H. Mathias; *m* 1964, Anne Carolyn Whitehead; two *s* one *d*. *Educ:* Westminster Sch.; Magdalen Coll., Oxford (BA). Repetiteur, Royal Opera House, Covent Garden, 1959–60; Chorus Master, New Opera Co., 1961–64; conducted at: Bath Fest., 1966; City of London Fest., 1966; Wexford Fest., 1967–70; Scottish Opera, 1968; WNO, 1968; Royal Opera House, 1971; ENO (formerly Sadler's Wells Opera), 1969 (Asst Music Dir, 1972–78); Artistic Dir, Opera North, 1978–90; Cheltenham, Leeds and Edinburgh Fests; also conductor of BBC broadcasts, TV operas (Eugene Onegin, The Flying Dutchman, Hansel and Gretel), and operas and concerts in France, Holland, Russia, Germany, Italy, Switzerland, Bulgaria, Poland, Chile, America, Canada, Argentina, Ireland, Norway, Sweden, Japan and Australia; has appeared with most British symph. orchs. Numerous recordings with LPO, RSNO, Bournemouth SO and Sinfonietta, Royal Liverpool Philharmonic Orch. and English Northern Philharmonia (Founder Conductor). Chm., Delius Trust, 1997–. Gen. Ed., William Walton Edition, 1996–. FGSM 1992. Hon. DMus Leeds, 1986. *Publications:* (trans.) Boris Godunov (vocal score), 1968; (trans.) Eugene Onegin (vocal score), 1971; Boris Godunov (critical edn of original full score), 1975; The Gondoliers, 1986; contrib. 6th edn Grove's Dictionary of Music and Musicians, 1981; contrib. Musik in Geschichte und Gegenwart, Music and Letters, and The Listener. *Recreations:* theatre, old shrub roses, travel. *Address:* 94 Whitelands House, Cheltenham Terrace, SW3 4RA. *T:* and *Fax:* (020) 7730 8695.

LLOYD JONES, John; *see* Jones.

LLOYD-JONES, Sir (Peter) Hugh (Jefferd), Kt 1989; FBA 1966; Regius Professor of Greek in the University of Oxford and Student of Christ Church, 1960–89, now Emeritus Professor and Emeritus Student; *b* 21 Sept. 1922; *s* of Major W. Lloyd-Jones, DSO, and Norah Leila, *d* of F. H. Jefferd, Brent, Devon; *m* 1st, 1953, Frances Elisabeth Hedley (marr. diss. 1981); two *s* one *d*; 2nd, 1982, Mary Lefkowitz (Andrew W. Mellon Professor Emeritus in the Humanities, Wellesley College, Mass), *d* of Harold and Mena Rosenthal, New York. *Educ:* Lycée Français du Royaume Uni, S Kensington; Westminster Sch.; Christ Church, Oxford. Served War of 1939–45, 2nd Lieut, Intelligence Corps, India, 1942; Temp. Captain, 1944. 1st Cl. Classics (Mods), 1941; MA 1947; 1st Cl., LitHum, 1948; Chancellor's Prize for Latin Prose, 1947; Ireland and Craven Schol., 1947; Fellow of Jesus Coll., Cambridge, 1948–54; Asst Lecturer in Classics, University of Cambridge, 1950–52, Lecturer, 1952–54; Fellow and E. P. Warren Praelector in Classics, Corpus Christi Coll., Oxford, 1954–60; J. H. Gray Lecturer, University of Cambridge, 1961; Visiting Prof., Yale Univ., 1964–65, 1967–68; Sather Prof. of Classical Literature, Univ. of California at Berkeley, 1969–70; Alexander White Vis. Prof., Chicago, 1972; Vis. Prof., Harvard Univ., 1976–77. Fellow, Morse Coll., Yale Univ. Hon. Mem., Greek Humanistic Soc., 1968; Corresponding Member: Acad. of Athens, 1978 (Fellow, 2001); Nordrhein-Westfälische Akad. der Wissenschaften, 1983; Accademia di Archeologia Lettere e Belle Arti, Naples, 1984; Bayerische Akad. der Wissenschaften, 1992; Hon. Foreign Mem., Amer. Acad. of Arts and Scis, 1978; Mem., Amer. Philos. Soc., 1992. Hon. DHL Chicago, 1970; Hon. DPhil: Tel Aviv, 1984; Göttingen, 2002; Hon. PhD Thessalonica, 1999. *Publications:* Appendix to Loeb Classical Library edn of Aeschylus, 1957; Menandri Dyscolus (Oxford Classical Text), 1960; (trans.) Paul Maas, Greek Metre, 1962; (ed) The Greeks, 1962; Tacitus (in series The Great Historians), 1964; (trans.) Aeschylus: Agamemnon, The Libation-Bearers, and The Eumenides, 1970, 2nd edn 1979; The Justice of Zeus, 1971, 2nd edn 1983; (ed) Maurice Bowra, 1974; Females of the Species: Semonides of Amorgos on Women, 1975; (with Marcelle Quinton) Myths of the Zodiac, 1978; (with Marcelle Quinton) Imaginary Animals (US edn as Mythical Beasts), 1979; Blood for the Ghosts, 1982; Classical Survivals, 1982; (with P. J. Parsons) Supplementum Hellenisticum, 1983; (with N. G. Wilson) Sophoclis Fabulae, 1990; (with N. G. Wilson) Sophoclea, 1990; Academic Papers, vols 1 and 2, 1990, vol. 3, 2005; Greek in a Cold Climate, 1991; Sophocles I–II, 1994; Sophocles III, 1996; (with N. G. Wilson) Sophocles: second thoughts, 1997; Supplementum Supplementi Hellenistici, 2005; contribs to periodicals. *Recreations:* cats, remembering past cricket. *Address:* 15 West Riding, Wellesley, MA 02482, USA. *T:* (781) 2372212, *Fax:* (781) 2372246; Christ Church, Oxford OX1 1DP. *T:* (01865) 791063. *Club:* Oxford and Cambridge.

LLOYD JONES, Sir Richard (Anthony), KCB 1988 (CB 1981); Permanent Secretary, Welsh Office, 1985–93; Chairman, Arts Council of Wales, 1994–99; *b* 1 Aug. 1933; *s* of Robert and Anne Lloyd Jones; *m* 1st, 1955, Patricia Avril Mary Richmond (*d* 2002); two *d*; 2nd, 2005, Helen Margaret Yewlett (*née* Lewis). *Educ:* Long Dene Sch., Edenbridge; Nottingham High Sch.; Balliol Coll., Oxford (MA). Entered Admiralty, 1957; Asst Private Sec. to First Lord of the Admiralty, 1959–62; Private Sec. to Secretary of the Cabinet, 1969–70; Asst Sec., Min. of Defence, 1970–74; Under Sec., 1974–78, Dep. Sec. 1978–85, Welsh Office. Chairman: Civil Service Benevolent Fund, 1987–93 (Trustee, 1993–2000); Adv. Cttee on local govt staff transfers (Wales), 1993–94; Local Govt Staff Commn for Wales, 1994–97. Member: BBC Gen. Adv. Council, 1994–96; Commn for Local Democracy, 1994–95. President: Welsh Council, Ramblers' Assoc., 1993–; Groundwork Merthyr and Rhondda Cynon Taff, 1996–; Chm., Age Concern Cymru, 1999–2005 (Pres., 1996–99); Vice-Chairman: Prince of Wales' Cttee, 1993–96; Prince's Trust Bro, 1996–99; Age Concern England, 2005–. Vice Pres., Univ. of Wales, Cardiff, 1993–2004; Member: Ct, Univ. of Wales, 1995–2000; Ct, Nat. Mus. of Wales, 1996–99; Ct and Council, Cardiff Univ., 2004–. Chm., Fishguard Internat. Music Fest., 1999–2005. Hon. Fellow: UCW Aberystwyth, 1990; Trinity Coll., Carmarthen, 1996. Hon. Dr Glamorgan, 1996; Hon. LLD Wales, 2004. *Recreations:* music, railways, swimming, walking. *Address:* Radyr, Cardiff. *Clubs:* Oxford and Cambridge; Cardiff and County.

LLOYD MOSTYN, family name of **Baron Mostyn**.

LLOYD WEBBER, family name of **Baron Lloyd-Webber**.

LLOYD-WEBBER, Baron *cr* 1997 (Life Peer), of Sydmonton in the co. of Hampshire; **Andrew Lloyd Webber,** Kt 1992; composer; *b* 22 March 1948; *s* of late William Southcombe Lloyd Webber, CBE, DMus, FRCM, FRCO, and Jean Hermione Johnstone; *m* 1st, 1971, Sarah Jane Tudor (*née* Hugill) (marr. diss. 1983); one *s* one *d*; 2nd, 1984, Sarah Brightman (marr. diss. 1990); 3rd, 1991, Madeleine Astrid Gurdon; two *s* one *d*. *Educ:* Westminster Sch.; Magdalen Coll., Oxford; Royal Coll. of Music (FRCM 1988). Composer: (with lyrics by Timothy Rice): The Likes of Us, 1965; Joseph and the Amazing Technicolor Dreamcoat, 1968, rev. 1973, 1991, 2003 and 2007; Jesus Christ Superstar, 1970, rev. 1996; Evita, 1976 (stage version, 1978, rev. 2006); (with lyrics by Alan Ayckbourn) Jeeves, 1975, revived as By Jeeves, 1996; (with lyrics by Don Black) Tell Me on a Sunday, 1980, rev. 2003; Cats, 1981 (based on poems by T. S. Eliot); (with lyrics by Don Black) Song & Dance, 1982; (with lyrics by Richard Stilgoe) Starlight Express, 1984; (with lyrics by Richard Stilgoe and Charles Hart) The Phantom of the Opera, 1986; (with lyrics by Don Black and Charles Hart) Aspects of Love, 1989; (with lyrics by Christopher Hampton and Don Black) Sunset Boulevard, 1993; (with lyrics by Jim Steinman) Whistle Down the Wind, 1996; (with lyrics by Ben Elton) The Beautiful Game, 2000; (with lyrics by David Zippel) The Woman in White, 2004. Producer: *theatre*: Joseph and the Amazing Technicolor Dreamcoat, 1973, 1974, 1978, 1980, 1991; Jeeves Takes Charge, 1975; Cats, 1981; Song and Dance, 1982; Daisy Pulls It Off, 1983; The Hired Man, 1984; Starlight Express, 1984; On Your Toes, 1984; The Phantom of the Opera, 1986; Café Puccini, 1986; The Resistible Rise of Arturo Ui, 1987; Lend Me a Tenor, 1988; Aspects of Love, 1989; Shirley Valentine, 1989 (Broadway); La Bête, 1992; Sunset Boulevard, 1993; By Jeeves, 1996; Jesus Christ Superstar, 1996, 1998; Whistle Down the Wind, 1996, 1998; Bombay Dreams, 2002; The Sound of Music, 2006, and others; *film:* Phantom of the Opera, 2004. Film scores: Gumshoe, 1971; The Odessa File, 1974. Composed "Variations" (based on A minor Caprice No 24 by Paganini), 1977, symphonic version, 1986; Requiem Mass, 1985. Awards include Acad. Award (Oscar), Golden Globe, Tony, Drama Desk, Grammy, and Kennedy Center Honor. *Publications:* (with Timothy Rice) Evita, 1978; Cats: the book of the musical, 1981; (with Timothy Rice) Joseph and the Amazing Technicolor Dreamcoat, 1982; The Complete Phantom of the Opera, 1987; The Complete Aspects of Love, 1989; Sunset Boulevard: from movie to musical, 1993. *Recreations:* architecture, art. *Address:* 22 Tower Street, WC2H 9TW.
See also J. Lloyd Webber.

LLOYD WEBBER, Julian, FRCM; 'cellist; *b* 14 April 1951; *s* of late William Southcombe Lloyd Webber, CBE, DMus, FRCM, FRCO, and Jean Hermione Johnstone; *m* 1st, 1974, Celia Mary Ballantyne (marr. diss. 1989); 2nd, 1989, Princess Zohra Mahmoud Ghazi (marr. diss. 1999); one *s*; 3rd, 2001, Kheira Bourahla (marr. diss. 2007). *Educ:* University College Sch., London; Royal College of Music. ARCM 1967, FRCM 1994. Studied 'cello with: Douglas Cameron, 1965–68; Pierre Fournier, Geneva, 1972. Début, Queen Elizabeth Hall, 1972; USA début, Lincoln Center, NY, 1980. Has performed with the world's major orchestras; toured: USA, Germany, Holland, Africa, Bulgaria, S America, Spain, Belgium, France, Scandinavia, Portugal, Denmark, Australasia, Singapore, Japan, Korea, Czechoslovakia, Austria, Canada, Hong Kong and Taiwan. Has made first recordings of works by Benjamin Britten, Frank Bridge, Gavin Bryars, Michael Nyman, Delius, Rodrigo, Holst, Vaughan Williams, Haydn, Philip Glass, Sullivan, John McCabe, Malcolm Arnold; recorded: Elgar Cello Concerto (cond. Menuhin), 1985 (British Phonographic Industry Award for Best Classical Recording, 1986); Dvořák Cello Concerto with Czech Philharmonic Orchestra, 1988; also concertos by Britten, Delius, Glass, Haydn, Honegger, Lalo, Miaskovsky, Rodrigo, Saint-Saëns, Walton and Tchaikovsky Rococo Variations; Unexpected Songs. Crystal Award, World Economic Forum, Switzerland, 1998. *Publications:* Travels with My Cello, 1984; Song of the Birds, 1985; *edited:* series, The Romantic 'Cello, 1978, The Classical 'Cello, 1980, The French 'Cello, 1981; Frank Bridge 'Cello Music, 1981; Young Cellist's Repertoire, Books 1, 2, 3, 1984; Holst, Invocation, 1984; Vaughan Williams, Fantasia on Sussex Folk Tunes, 1984; Recital Repertoire for Cellists, 1987; Short, Sharp Shocks, 1990; The Great 'Cello Solos, 1992; Cello Moods, 1999; Made in England, 2004; contribs to music jls and national Press in UK, US, Canada and Australia. *Recreations:* countryside (especially British), Leyton Orient FC. *Address:* c/o IMG Artists Europe, The Light Box, 111 Power Road, Chiswick, W4 5PY. *T:* (020) 7957 5800.
See also Baron Lloyd-Webber.

LLWYD, Elfyn; MP (Plaid Cymru) Meirionnydd Nant Conwy, since 1992; *b* 26 Sept. 1951; *s* of late Huw Meirion Hughes and Hefina (*née* Roberts); surname Hughes abandoned by deed poll, 1970; *m* 1974, Eleri Llwyd; one *s* one *d*. *Educ:* Ysgol Dyffryn Conwy Llanrwst; Univ. of Wales, Aberystwyth (LLB Hons); Coll. of Law, Chester. Admitted solicitor, 1977; called to the Bar, 1997. Plaid Cymru Parly Whip, 1995–2002; Plaid Cymru Parly Leader, 1998–. Parly Ambassador to NSPCC. Pres., Gwynedd Law Soc., 1990–91. Member, Court: Univ. of Wales, Aberystwyth, 1993–; of Govs, Nat. Liby of Wales, 1994–; of Govs, Nat. Eisteddfod, 1995–; Vice-Pres., Llangollen Internat. Eisteddfod, 2000–. President: Betws-y-Coed FC; Clwb Peldroed Llanuwchllyn; Clwb Rygbi y Bala; Vice-Pres., Dolgellau Rugby Club. Pres., Estimaner Angling Soc. Fellow, Inst. of Welsh Affairs. Mem., Gorsedd of Bards. *Recreations:* pigeon breeding, Rugby, choral singing, fishing. *Address:* Ty Glyndwr, Heol Glyndwr, Dolgellau, Gwynedd LL40 1BD. *T:* (01341) 422661; Glandwr, Llanuwchllyn, Y Bala, Gwynedd LL23 7TW.

LLWYD MORGAN, Derec; *see* Morgan.

LO, Anna Manwah, MBE 2000; Member (Alliance) Belfast South, Northern Ireland Assembly, since 2007; *b* 17 June 1950; *m* (marr. diss.); two *s*. *Educ:* Univ. of Ulster (Dip. Soc. Work; MSc). Social Worker: N Down and Ards HSS Trust, 1993; Barnardo's, 1995; Chief Exec., Chinese Welfare Assoc., 1997–2007. Vice Chm. (first), NI Council for Ethnic Minorities, 1995; founding Mem., Equality Commn for NI, 1999. Chm. (first), S Belfast Partnership Bd, 1997. *Address:* Northern Ireland Assembly, Parliament Buildings, Stormont, Belfast BT4 3XX. *T:* (028) 9052 1560, *Fax:* (028) 9052 0304; *e-mail:* Anna.Lo@niassembly.gov.uk.

LOACH, Kenneth; television and film director; *b* 17 June 1936; *s* of late John Loach and of Vivien Loach (*née* Hamlin); *m* 1962, Lesley Ashton; two *s* two *d* (and one *s* decd). *Educ:* King Edward VI School, Nuneaton; St Peter's Hall, Oxford (Hon. Fellow, St Peter's Coll., 1993). BBC Trainee, Drama Dept, 1963. *Television:* Diary of a Young Man, 1964; 3 Clear Sundays, 1965; The End of Arthur's Marriage, 1965; Up The Junction, 1965; Coming Out Party, 1965; Cathy Come Home, 1966; In Two Minds, 1966; The Golden Vision, 1969; The Big Flame, 1969; After A Lifetime, 1971; The Rank and File, 1972; Days of Hope, 1975; The Price of Coal, 1977; The Gamekeeper, 1979; Auditions, 1980; A Question of Leadership, 1981; Questions of Leadership, 1983 (banned from TV); The Red and the Blue, 1983; Which Side Are You On?, 1985; The View from the Woodpile, 1988; Dispatches, 1991; Flickering Flame, 1996; Another City, 1998; The Navigators, 2001. *Films:* Poor Cow, 1968; Kes, 1970; In Black and White, 1970; Family Life, 1972; Black Jack, 1979; Looks and Smiles, 1981; Fatherland, 1987; Hidden Agenda, 1990; Riff-Raff, 1991; Raining Stones, 1993; Ladybird, Ladybird, 1994; Land and Freedom, 1995; Carla's Song, 1996; My Name is Joe, 1998; Bread and Roses, 2000; Sweet Sixteen, 2002; Ae Fond Kiss, 2004; Tickets, 2005; The Wind that Shakes the Barley, 2006 (Palme d'Or, Cannes Film Fest.); It's a Free World, 2007. BAFTA Fellow, 2006. *Address:* Sixteen Films, 2nd Floor, 187 Wardour Street, W1F 8ZB.

LOADER, Air Chief Marshal Sir Clive (Robert), KCB 2006; OBE 1996; FRAeS; Commander-in-Chief, HQ Air Command, since 2007; Air Aide-de-Camp to the Queen, since 2007; *b* 24 Sept. 1953; *s* of Ralph George Loader and Vera May Harrington; *m* 1976, Alison Anna Louise Leith. *Educ:* Judd Sch., Tonbridge; Southampton Univ. Officer/Flying Trng, 1973–76; Harrier Pilot and Weapons Instructor, 1977–87; RAF Staff Coll., 1988; Sqn Ldr, Air Offensive, MoD, 1989; Wing Comdr, Air Offensive, HQ RAF Germany, 1990–91; PSO to C-in-C Strike Command, 1991–93; Comdg Harrier Sqn and Stn, 1993–99; Air Cdre, Harrier, HQ 3 Gp (Strike Comd), 1999–2001; ACDS (Ops), MoD, 2002–04; Dep. C-in-C, RAF Strike Comd, 2004–07. FRAeS 2004. *Recreations:* golf, cricket, military history, rowing. *Address:* HQ Air Command, RAF High Wycombe, Bucks HP14 4UE. *Club:* Royal Air Force.

LOADER, Prof. Ian Spencer, PhD; Professor of Criminology, and Director, Centre for Criminology, University of Oxford, since 2005; Fellow, All Souls College, Oxford, since 2005; *b* Harrow, 2 April 1965; *s* of Tony and Pamela Loader; partner, Penelope Fraser;

three *d.* *Educ:* Park High Sch., Harrow; Lowlands Sixth Form Coll., Harrow; Univ. of Sheffield (LLB 1986); Univ. of Edinburgh (MSc 1988; PhD 1993). Lectr in Law, Liverpool Poly., 1986–87; Lectr in Criminol. and Jurisprudence, Univ. of Edinburgh, 1990–92; Keele University: Lectr, 1992–99, Sen. Lectr, 1999–2002, Reader, 2002–04, in Criminol.; Prof. of Criminol., 2004–05. Jean Monnet Fellow, European University Inst., Florence, 2004. Trustee, Police Foundn, 2007–; Mem., Commn on English Prisons Today, 2007–09. FRSA. *Publications:* (jtly) Cautionary Tales, 1994; Youth, Policing and Democracy, 1996; (jtly) Crime and Social Change in Middle England, 2000; (with Aogan Mulcahy) Policing and the Condition of England, 2003; (with Neil Walker) Civilizing Security, 2007. *Recreations:* cycling, Arsenal FC, playing with my three daughters. *Address:* Centre for Criminology, Manor Road Building, Manor Road, Oxford OX1 3UQ. *T:* (01865) 274440; *e-mail:* ian.loader@crim.ox.ac.uk.

LOADES, Prof. Ann Lomas, CBE 2001; PhD; Professor of Divinity, Durham University, 1995–2003, now Emeritus; *b* 21 Sept. 1938; *d* of Gerard Joseph Glover and Amy Lomas. *Educ:* Durham Univ. (BA Theol. 1960; PhD 1975); McMaster Univ. (MA 1965). Durham University: Lectr in Theology, 1975–81; Sen. Lectr, 1981–90; Reader, 1990–95; Chm., Bd of Studies in Theol., 1989–91. Arts and Humanities Research Board: Convenor, assessment panel for postgrad. awards in philosophy, law and religious studies, 1999–2003; Mem., Postgrad. Cttee, 1999–2003; Mem., Res. Centres Scheme Cttee, 1999–2003. Pres., Soc. for the Study of Theol., 2005 and 2006. Scholar Consultant, Christian-Muslim Forum, 2005–; Mem., Council of Archbishop's Examination in Theology, 2006–. Lay Mem., Chapter, 2001–07, Lay Canon, 2008–, Chm., Choir Assoc., 2003–, Durham Cathedral. Editor, Theology, 1991–97. *Publications:* (ed) W. A. Whitehouse, The Authority of Grace, 1981; (ed with J. C. Eaton) For God and Clarity, 1983; Kant and Job's Comforters, 1985; Searching for Lost Coins (Scott Holland Lectures), 1987; (ed) Feminist Theology: a reader, 1990; (ed with M. McLain) Hermeneutics, the Bible and Literary Criticism, 1992; (ed with L. Rue) Contemporary Classics in Philosophy of Religion, 1991; (ed) Dorothy L. Sayers, Spiritual Writings, 1993; (ed with D. W. Brown) The Sense of the Sacramental, 1995; (ed) Spiritual Classics from the late Twentieth Century, 1995; (ed with D. W. Brown) Christ: the sacramental word, 1996; Evelyn Underhill, 1997; Feminist Theology: voices from the past, 2001; (ed with J. Astley and D. W. Brown) Problems in Theology series: Creation, 2003; Evil, 2003; War and Peace, 2003; Science and Religion, 2004; God in Action, 2004. *Recreations:* going to the theatre, cooking.

LOADES, David Henry, CB 1996; FIA; Directing Actuary, Government Actuary's Department, 1983–97; *b* 16 Oct. 1937; *s* of John Henry Loades and Evelyn Clara Ralph; *m* 1962, Jennifer Glenys Stevens; one *s* two *d.* *Educ:* Beckenham and Penge County Grammar Sch. for Boys. BA. FIA 1961. Govt Actuary's Dept, 1956–97. Medal of Merit for services to the Scout Assoc., 1986. *Publications:* papers in actuarial jls. *Recreations:* painting, visiting art galleries.

LOANE, Most Rev. Marcus Lawrence, KBE 1976; *b* 14 Oct. 1911; *s* of K. O. A. Loane; *m* 1937, Patricia Evelyn Jane Simpson Knox; two *s* two *d.* *Educ:* The King's School, Parramatta, NSW; Sydney University (MA). Moore Theological College, 1932–33; Australian College of Theology (ThL, 1st Class, 1933; Fellow, 1955). Ordained Deacon, 1935, Priest, 1936; Resident Tutor and Chaplain, Moore Theological College, 1935–38; Vice-Principal, 1939–53; Principal, 1954–59. Chaplain AIF, 1942–44. Canon, St Andrew's Cathedral, 1949–58; Bishop-Coadjutor, diocese of Sydney, 1958–66; Archbishop of Sydney and Metropolitan of Province of NSW, 1966–82; Primate of Australia, 1978–82. Hon. DD Wycliffe College, Toronto, 1958. *Publications:* Oxford and the Evangelical Succession, 1950; Cambridge and the Evangelical Succession, 1952; Masters of the English Reformation, 1955, repr. 2005; Life of Archbishop Mowll, 1960; Makers of Religious Freedom, 1961; Pioneers of the Reformation in England, 1964; Makers of Our Heritage, 1966; The Hope of Glory, 1968; This Surpassing Excellence, 1969; They Were Pilgrims, 1970; Hewn from the Rock, 1976; Men to Remember, 1987. *Address:* 18 Harrington Avenue, Warrawee, NSW 2074, Australia. *T:* (2) 94892975.

LOASBY, Prof. Brian John, FBA 1994; FRSE; Professor of Management Economics, University of Stirling, 1971–84, Emeritus and Hon. Professor of Economics, since 1984; *b* 2 Aug. 1930; *s* of Frederick Thomas Loasby and Mabel Phyllis Loasby; *m* 1957, Judith Ann Robinson; two *d.* *Educ:* Kettering GS; Emmanuel Coll., Cambridge (BA 1952; MLitt 1958; MA 1998). Assistant in Pol Economy, Aberdeen Univ., 1955–58; Bournville Res. Fellow, Birmingham Univ., 1958–61; Tutor in Management Studies, Bristol Univ., 1961–67; Stirling University: Lectr in Econs, 1967–68; Sen. Lectr, 1968–71. Management Fellow, Arthur D. Little Inc., Cambridge, Mass, 1965–66; Vis. Fellow, Oxford Centre for Management Studies, 1974. Pres., Scottish Economic Soc., 1987–90; Vice-Pres., Internat. Schumpeter Soc., 2000–04. FRSE 2007. DUniv Stirling, 1998. (Jtly) Schumpeter Prize, 2000. *Publications:* The Swindon Project, 1973; Choice, Complexity and Ignorance, 1976; The Mind and Method of the Economist, 1989; Equilibrium and Evolution, 1991; (ed with N. J. Foss) Economic Organization, Capabilities and Co-ordination: essays in honour of G. B. Richardson, 1998; Knowledge, Institutions and Evolution in Economics, 1999; contrib. books, and econs and management jls. *Recreation:* gardening. *Address:* Department of Economics, University of Stirling, Stirling FK9 4LA. *T:* (01786) 467470; 8 Melfort Drive, Stirling FK7 0BD. *T:* (01786) 472124.

LOBO, António C.; *see* Costa-Lobo.

LOBO, Sir Rogerio Hyndman, (Sir Roger), Kt 1985; CBE 1978 (OBE 1972); JP; Chairman, P. J. Lobo & Co. Ltd, Hong Kong, 1946–2001; Chairman, Broadcasting Authority of Hong Kong, 1989–97; *b* 15 Sept. 1923; *s* of Dr P. J. Lobo and Branca Helena (*née* Hyndman); *m* 1947, Margaret Mary (*née* Choa); five *s* five *d.* *Educ:* Escola Central, Macao; Seminario de S Jose, Macao; Liceu Nacional Infante Dom Henrique, Macao; La Salle Coll., Hong Kong. Director: Kjeldsen & Co. (HK) (formerly Danish Fancy Food Gp), 1982–; Shun Tak Hldgs Ltd, 1994–; PCCW (formerly Pacific Century CyberWorks) Ltd, 1999–; dir of 3 other cos. Unofficial MLC, Hong Kong, 1972–85 (Sen. Mem., 1980–85); Unofficial MEC, 1978–85. Member: Urban Council, 1965–78; Housing Authority, 1967–83; Chm., Adv. Cttee on Post-Retirement Employment, 1987–98; Comr, Civil Aid Services, 1977–92 (Mem., 1955–). Hon. LLD Univ. of Hong Kong, 1982. JP Hong Kong, 1963. Silver Jubilee Medal, 1977; Civil Aid Services Long Service Medal, 1970; Civil Defence Long Service Clasp, 1982. Comdr, Order of St Gregory the Great, The Vatican, 1969. *Recreation:* golf. *Address:* Woodland Heights, E1, 2 Wongneichong Gap Road, Hong Kong. *T:* 25740779; (business) 1802, 18/F Worldwide House, 19 Des Voeux Road, Central, Hong Kong. *T:* 25269418. *Clubs:* Dynasty, Hong Kong, Rotary, Hong Kong Jockey, Hong Kong Golf, Hong Kong Country (Hong Kong).

LOCATELLI, Giorgio; Chef Proprietor, Locanda Locatelli, London, since 2002; Chef Consultant, Refettorio, Italian restaurant, Crowne Plaza City Hotel, London, since 2005; *b* 7 April 1973; *s* of Ferrucio Locatelli and Giuseppina Caletti; *m* 1995, Plaxy Exton; one *s* one *d.* Worked in local restaurants, N Italy and Switzerland; came to England and joined kitchens of Anton Edelmann at The Savoy, London, 1986; worked at Restaurant Laurent and La Tour D'Argent, Paris, 1990; returned to London as Hd Chef, Olivo, 1991; opened restaurants: Zafferano, 1995 (Michelin Star, 1999); Spighetta, 1997; Spiga, 1999; Locanda Locatelli, 2002 (Michelin Star, 2003, 2004, 2005, 2006). Television series: (with Tony Allan) Tony and Giorgio, 2000; Pure Italian, 2002. *Publications:* Tony & Giorgio (with Tony Allan), 2003; Made in Italy, 2006. *Recreations:* motorbikes, swimming. *Address:* Locanda Locatelli, 8 Seymour Street, W1H 7JZ. *T:* (020) 7486 9271, *Fax:* (020) 7486 9628; *e-mail:* info@locandalocatelli.com. *Club:* Home House.

LOCHHEAD, Richard Neilson; Member (SNP) Moray, Scottish Parliament, since April 2006; Cabinet Secretary for Rural Affairs and the Environment, since 2007; *b* 24 May 1969; *s* of Robert William Lochhead and Agnes Robertson Cloughley. *Educ:* Williamwood High Sch., Clarkston, Glasgow; Univ. of Stirling (BA Hons Political Studies, 1994). SSEB, 1987–89; Office Manager for Alex Salmond, MP, 1994–98; Develt Officer, Dundee CC, 1998–99. Contested (SNP) Gordon, 1997; MSP (SNP) NE Scotland, 1999–2006. *Recreations:* travelling, reading novels and history books, cinema, squash. *Address:* (office) 9 Wards Road, Elgin, Moray IV30 1NL.

LOCHORE, Sir Brian (James), ONZ 2007; KNZM 1999; OBE 1970; farmer; Chairman, Queen Elizabeth II Trust, since 2003; *b* 3 Sept. 1940; *s* of James Denniston Lochore and Alma Joyce Lochore (*née* Wyeth); *m* 1963, Pamela Lucy, *d* of David and Nancy Young; one *s* twin *d.* *Educ:* Opaki Primary Sch.; Wairarapa Coll. Farmer of own property, 1961–. Tennis Rep., 1957–65 and 1973–84, Rugby Rep., 1959–71, Wairarapa; Mem., NZ All Black Rugby Team, 1963–71 (Capt., 1966–70); Rugby Coach: Wairarapa Bush team, 1980–82 (Life Mem., 1988); NZ team, 1985–87 (incl. inaugural World Cup); World XV, IRB Centennial, 1986; NZ Rugby Selector, 1983–87, 2003–; Manager and Selector, World XV, 1992; Campaigns Manager, All Blacks World Cup, 1995. Mem., 1995–2002, Chm., 1998–2002, Hillary Commn. Member: Electoral Coll., Meat & Wool Bd, 1972–73; Romney Breeders' Council, 1993–97. Bd Mem., Sports Foundn, 1996–98 (Chm., High Perf. Funding Cttee, 1997–98); Mem., NZRU Selection Panel, 2004–07. Trustee: Masterton Charitable Trust, 1989–90; Halberg Trust, 1992–. Member: Mauriceville Sch. Cttee, 1973–79 (Chm., 1975–79); Masterton Secondary Schs Bd, 1980–86 (Chm., 1987–88); Comr, Kuranui Coll., 1994–95. *Recreations:* golf, tennis, thoroughbred horse breeding. *Address:* Riverlands, Paierau Road, Masterton, New Zealand. *T:* (6) 3770195.

LOCK, Prof. Andrew Raymond, PhD; CITP, FSS, FCIM; Professor of Marketing and Business Administration, since 2000, and Dean, 2000–08, now Emeritus, Leeds University Business School; *b* 23 Sept. 1947; partner, Sally Cooper; one *s* one *d.* *Educ:* Manchester Grammar Sch.; Solihull Sch.; Univ. of Leeds (BA French 1970); London Business Sch. (MSc Econ 1972; PhD 1979). Kingston Polytechnic: Lectr, then Sen. Lectr, 1972–85; Principal Lectr, 1978; Hd, Sch. of Mktg and Corp. Strategy, 1985–87; Manchester Polytechnic, subseq. Manchester Metropolitan University: Dean, Faculty of Mgt and Business, and Asst Dir, 1988–92; Dean and Pro-Vice-Chancellor, 1993–2000. Vis. Asst Prof. in Mktg, Univ. of British Columbia, 1979–80. Chm., Assoc. of Business Schs, 1998–2000. Liveryman, Co. of Marketors, 1999–. CCMI; FRSA. Hon. FIDM. *Publications:* contrib. Jl of Mktg Mgt, European Jl of Mktg, Jl of Advertising Research, Jl of OR Soc. and Mgt Learning. *Recreations:* ski-ing, classic motorcycles, watching Rugby and cricket. *Address:* 141 Hale Road, Hale, Cheshire WA15 8RT; *e-mail:* arl@lubs.leeds.ac.uk.

LOCK, David; *see* Lock, G. D.

LOCK, David Anthony; barrister; with No5 Chambers, Birmingham, London and Bristol, since 2008; Director, IM Litigation Funding Ltd (formerly Insolvency Management Ltd), since 2002; *b* 2 May 1960; *s* of late John Kirby Lock and of Jeannette Mary Lock (*née* Bridgewater); *m* 1985, Dr Bernadette Clare Gregory; one *s* two *d.* *Educ:* Jesus Coll., Cambridge (MA 1982); Central London Poly. (Dip. Law 1984). Mgt Trainee, GEC Telecommuncations, 1982–83; called to the Bar, Gray's Inn, 1985 (Wilson Schol.); started practice at the Bar, 1987; Head of Healthcare Law, Mills & Reeve, 2003–07. Mem. (Lab), Wychavon DC, 1995–97 (Chairman: Amenities and Economic Develt Cttee, 1995; Community and Leisure Cttee, 1995–97). MP (Lab) Wyre Forest, 1997–2001; contested (Lab) same seat, 2001. PPS, Lord Chancellor's Dept, 1997–98, to Lord Chancellor and Minister of State, Lord Chancellor's Dept, 1998–99; Parly Sec., Lord Chancellor's Dept, 1999–2001. Secretary: All-Party Occupational Pensions Gp, 1997–99; All Party Cycling Gp, 1998–99; Vice Chm., Textiles, Carpets and Footwear Industry Gp, 1998–99. Chm., Labour Finance & Industry Gp, 2006–. Chm., Service Authorities, Nat. Crime Squad and Nat. Criminal Intelligence Service, 2002–03. Director: Conveyancing Channel Ltd, 2002–06; Lawbook Consulting Ltd, 2002–; MDA Searchflow, 2006–. Chm., Child Advocacy Internat., 2003–07. *Recreations:* cycling, family, wine and friends, paragliding.

LOCK, David Peter, CBE 2007; Chief Planning Adviser, Department of the Environment, 1994–97; Chairman, David Lock Associates Ltd, since 1988; *b* 12 March 1948; *s* of Arthur Lovering Lock and late Kathleen Barbara (*née* Nash); *m* 1970, Jeanette Anita Jones; three *d.* *Educ:* Sir Roger Manwood's Grammar Sch., Sandwich, Kent; Nottingham Coll. of Art and Design/Trent Poly. (DipT&CP). MRTPI 1975. Area Planning Officer, Leicester CC, 1970–73; Planning Aid Officer, TCPA, 1973–78; Planning Manager, Milton Keynes Develt Corp., 1978–81; Associate Dir, Conran Roche Ltd, 1981–88. Chairman: DLA Architects Ltd, 1998–; DLA Architects Practice Ltd, 2001–; Director: City Discovery Centre Ltd, 1987–; City Discovery Centre (Trading) Ltd, 1997–; non-exec. Dir, Rapid Transport Technol. Ltd (formerly Rapid Transport Internat. plc), 1997–2004; Dir, Integrated Transport Planning Ltd, 2000–. Visiting Professor: Univ. of Central England in Birmingham, 1988–98; Univ. of Reading, 2002–. Chm., TCPA, 2001–. *Publications:* (contrib.) People and their Settlements, 1976; (contrib.) Growth and Change in the Future City Region, 1976; (contrib.) New Towns in National Development, 1980; Riding the Tiger: planning the South of England, 1989; (jtly) Alternative Development Patterns: new settlements, 1993. *Recreations:* history, geography, reading, research. *Address:* David Lock Associates Ltd, 50 North Thirteenth Street, Central Milton Keynes, Bucks MK9 3BP. *T:* (01908) 666276.

LOCK, (George) David; Managing Director, Private Patients Plan Ltd, 1975–85; *b* 24 Sept. 1929; *s* of George Wilfred Lock and Phyllis Nita (*née* Hollingworth); *m* 1965, Ann Elizabeth Biggs; four *s* one *d.* *Educ:* Haileybury and ISC; Queens' Coll., Cambridge (MA). British Tabulating Machine Co. Ltd (now ICL), 1954–59; Save & Prosper Group Ltd, 1959–69; American Express, 1969–74; Dir, Plan for Active Retirement, Frizzell Insce and Financial Services Ltd (formerly New Business Ventures, Frizzell Consumer Services Ltd), 1986–89. Director: Priplan Investments Ltd, 1979–85; Priplan Services Ltd, 1979–85; PPP Medical Centre Ltd (incorp. Cavendish Medical Centre), 1981–85. Director: Home Concern for the Elderly, 1985–87, 1989–96; The Hosp. Management Trust, 1985–92; Bd of Management, St Anthony's Hosp., Cheam, 1986–; HMT Hospitals Ltd, 1993–2005 (Vice-Pres., 2006–); Gainsborough Clinic Ltd, 2000–03; Sec., Frizzell Foundn, 1989–93. Sec., Friends of Children of Great Ormond Street, 1986. Trustee, Eynsham Trust, 1975–83; Gov., PPP Medical Trust Ltd (Dir, 1983–89). Member: Nuffield Nursing Homes Trust, 1979–; Exec. Cttee, Assoc. of Independent Hosps, 1981–87. Mem.,

RSocMed., 1979–92. Freeman, Barbers' Co., 1982–. *Recreations:* bridge, golf, music, family activities, entertaining. *Address:* Bell House, Bonfire Lane, Horsted Keynes, Sussex RH17 7AJ. *T:* (01825) 790599.

LOCK, Graham; *see* Lock, T. G.

LOCK, John Arthur, QPM 1975; Deputy Assistant Commissioner, Metropolitan Police, and National Co-ordinator, Regional Crime Squads of England and Wales, 1976–79, retired; *b* 20 Oct. 1922; *s* of Sidney George Lock and Minnie Louise Lock; *m* 1950, Patricia Joyce Lambert; two *d*. *Educ:* George Palmer Central School, Reading. Royal Air Force, 1941–46; Wireless Operator/Air Gunner; Flying Officer. Joined Metropolitan Police, 1946. *Recreation:* golf. *Club:* St Mellion Golf and Country.

LOCK, Ven. Peter Harcourt D'Arcy; Archdeacon of Rochester and Residentiary Canon of Rochester Cathedral, since 2000; *b* 2 Aug. 1944; *s* of Edward and Ruth Lock; *m* 1968, Susan Reed; one *s* one *d*. *Educ:* King's College, London (AKC 1967). Ordained deacon, 1968, priest, 1969; Curate: Meopham, 1968–72; Wigmore with Hempstead, 1972; S Gillingham, 1972–77; Rector: Hartley, 1977–83; Fawkham and Hartley, 1983–84; Vicar: Holy Trinity, Dartford, 1984–93; St Peter and St Paul, Bromley, 1993–2000; RD Bromley, 1996–2000. Mem., Gen. Synod, 1980–2000. *Recreations:* cricket, football, calligraphy, walking. *Address:* The Archdeaconry, King's Orchard, The Precinct, Rochester, Kent ME1 1TG.

LOCK, Sheila Mary; Chief Executive, Leicester City Council, since 2008; *b* 7 Dec. 1959; *d* of Thomas and Kate Donaghy. *Educ:* Our Lady's Grammar Sch., Newry; Manchester Univ. (BSc Hons; MBA). DipSW 1989; CQSW 1989. Social worker, 1987–89, Prin. Social Worker, Child Protection, 1989–91, Tameside; Prin. Officer, 1992–96, Asst Dir, 1996–98, Children's Services, Barnsley; Hd, Children's Services, Sheffield CC, 1998–2002; Hd of Student and Community Services, Calderdale MBC, 2002–06; Corporate Dir, Children & Young People's Services, 2006–08, Interim Chief Exec., 2008, Leicester CC. Dir, Nat. Space Centre, Sch. Standards and Develt Agency, 2006. *Recreations:* walking, sport, music, cooking. *Address:* Leicester City Council, New Walk Centre, Leicester LE1 6ZG.

LOCK, Stephen Penford, CBE 1991; MA, MD; FRCP; Research Associate in History, Wellcome Trust (formerly Wellcome Institute for the History of Medicine), 1992–2000; Editor, British Medical Journal, 1975–91; Volunteer assistant, Britten-Pears Library, Aldeburgh, since 2006; *b* 8 April 1929; *er s* of Wallace Henry Lock, Romford, Essex; *m* 1955, Shirley Gillian Walker, *d* of E. W. Walker, Bridlington, Yorks; one *d* (one *s* decd). *Educ:* City of London Sch.; Queens' Coll., Cambridge; St Bartholomew's Hosp., London. MA 1953; MB 1954; MD 1987; MRCP 1963; FRCP 1974; FACP 1989; FRCPE 1989. Jun. hosp. appts, 1954–63; Asst Editor, British Med. Jl, 1964–69, Sen. Asst Editor, 1969–74, Dep. Editor, 1974–75. Consulting Editor: Encyclopaedia Britannica Year Book of Medicine, 1992–99; Med. Jl of Australia, 1994–96; an Associate Ed., DNB, 1995–. Organiser and/or participant in numerous Postgrad. Courses in Med. Writing and confs in scientific editing worldwide, 1971–. Mem., Res. Ethics Cttee, KCH Medical Sch., 1992–96. Mem. Council, Harveian Soc., 1992–96 (Pres., 1994); Founder Pres., 1982–85, Mem. Council, 1985–91, European Assoc. of Sci. Editors. Vis. Prof. in Medicine, McGill Univ., 1978; Visitor, Acad. Dept of Medicine, Monash Univ., 1982; Rockefeller Scholar, Villa Serbelloni, Bellagio, 1985; Foundn Vis. Prof. in Medicine, RCSI, 1986; Vis. Prof. in Epidemiology and Biostatistics, McGill Univ., 1992; Vis. Lectr, Erasmus Summer Sch., Rotterdam, 1993–2006; Vis. Prof., Norwegian Tech. Univ., Trondheim, 2003–. Lectures: Wade, Keele Univ., 1980; Morgan, Royal Cornwall Hosp., 1984; Rock Carling, Nuffield Provincial Hosps Trust, 1985; Maurice Bloch, Glasgow Univ., 1986; Wolfson, Wolfson Coll., Oxford, 1986; Estelle Brodman, Washington Univ., St Louis, 1989; Sarah Davies, TCD, 1990; William Hey, Leeds Univ., 1990; George McGovern, Med. Library Assoc. of America, San Francisco, 1991; College, RCP, 1996; Carmichael, RCSI, 1999. Chairman: Friends of Dulwich Picture Gall., 1993–96; Aldeburgh Soc., 1998–2001 (Mem., Cttee, 1997–; Acting Sec., 2001–02; Vice-Pres., 2002–05; Pres., 2005–08); Aldeburgh Fest. Club, 2003–05 (Vice-Chm., 2001–03; Pres., 2008–). Hon. FRCPI 1987; Hon. Fellow, Amer. Med. Writers Assoc., 1994; Hon. Founder Fellow, RCPCH, 1997 (Hon. Mem., BPA, 1991). Hon. MSc Manchester, 1985. Donders Medal, Ned. Tijdsch. Geneesk, 1981; Internat. Medal, Finnish Med. Soc. Duodecim, 1981; Medal of Honour, Finnish Med. Jl, 1987; Fothergillian Medal, Med. Soc., London, 1992; Meritorious Award, Council of Biol. Eds, 1993. Officer, first cl., White Rose of Finland, 1982. *Publications:* An Introduction to Clinical Pathology, 1965; Health Centres and Group Practices, 1966; The Enemies of Man, 1968; Better Medical Writing, 1970; Family Health Guide, 1972; (ed) Personal View, 1975; Medical Risks of Life, 1976; Thorne's Better Medical Writing, 2nd edn 1977; (ed) Adverse Drug Reactions, 1977; (ed) Remembering Henry, 1977; (contrib.) Oxford Companion to Medicine, 1983; (ed) As You Were, 1984; A Difficult Balance: editorial peer review in medicine, 1985; (ed) The Future of Medical Journals, 1991; Medical Journals and Medical Progress, 1992; (ed) Fraud and Misconduct in Medical Research, 1993, 3rd edn 2001; (ed) Eighty-five Not Out: essays to honour Sir George Godber, 1993; (ed jtly) The Oxford Medical Companion, 1995; (contrib.) Oxford Illustrated History of Medicine, 1996; (ed) Ashes to Ashes, 1998; (contrib.) Our NHS, 1998; (ed) Oxford Illustrated Companion to Medicine, 2001; (contrib.) Leoš Janáček: years of a life, vol. 1, 2006, vol. 2, 2008; (contrib.) World Dictionary of Medical Biography, 2007; (contrib.) Medisinsk publisering og fagformidling, 2008; contrib. DNB and Oxford DNB. *Recreation:* reading reviews of operas I can't afford to see. *Address:* 3 Alde House, Alde House Drive, Aldeburgh, Suffolk IP15 5EE. *T:* (01728) 452411. *Club:* Royal Air Force.

LOCK, (Thomas) Graham; Chief Executive, Amalgamated Metal Corporation plc, 1983–91; *b* 19 Oct. 1931; *s* of Robert Henry Lock and Morfydd Lock (*née* Thomas); *m* 1st, 1954, Janice Olive Baker Lock (*née* Jones) (marr. diss. 1992; she *d* 1995); two *d*; 2nd, 2005, Judith Elizabeth Lucy (*née* Butterworth). *Educ:* Whitchurch Grammar School; University College of South Wales and Monmouthshire (BSc Metall); College of Advanced Technology, Aston; Harvard Business School. CEng, FIMMM. Instructor Lieut, RN, 1953–56; Lucas Industries and Lucas Electrical, 1956–61; Dir, Girling Bremsen GmbH, 1961–66; Gen. Man. and Overseas Ops Dir, Girling Ltd, 1966–73; Gen. Man. and Dir, Lucas Service Overseas Ltd, 1973–79; Man. Dir, Industrial Div., Amalgamated Metal Corp., 1979–83; non-exec. Director: Marshall's Universal plc, 1983–86; Evode Gp plc, 1985–91. CCMI. Liveryman, Co. of Gold and Silver Wyre Drawers, 1988–. Freeman, City of London, 1987. *Recreations:* sailing, music, ski-ing. *Address:* Parolas Villa, 4520 Parekklisia, near Limassol, Cyprus. *Clubs:* Army and Navy; Royal Naval Sailing Association (Portsmouth), Royal Southern Yacht (Hamble).

LOCKE, John Christopher, FRICS; Chief Executive, Property Advisers to the Civil Estate, 1997–2000; *b* 4 March 1947; *s* of late Comdr Cyril Frederick Locke, RN, CEng, FIEE and Marjorie Alice Batt Locke (*née* Collins); *m* 1st, 1969 (marr. diss. 1989); two *s*; 2nd, 1990, Maria Patricia, *d* of late Eileen Rogers (*née* Mahony). *Educ:* Pangbourne Coll.; Regent Street Poly.; Brixton Sch. of Building; Northern Poly. ARICS 1971 (Wainwright Prizewinner), FRICS 1981. Prudential Assurance Co. Ltd, 1964–88 (Dir, Estate Management, 1987–88); Divl Dir, Estate Management, Prudential Portfolio Managers Ltd, 1989–91; Director: Southbank Technopark Ltd, 1985–91 (Chm., 1989–90); City Aviation Insurance Tenancies Ltd, 1989–90; Chm., Briggait Co. Ltd, 1987–90; Surveyor, Watling Street Properties, 1989–90; Chief Exec., NHS Estate Mgt and Health Bldg Agency, 1991–97. Member: Commercial Property Cttee, RICS, 1983–89; Central Govt Support Panel, RICS, 1997–2000 (Chm., 1999–2000); Mgt Consultancy Practice Panel, RICS, 1997–2000; Govt Construction Client Panel, HM Treasury, 1997–2000 (Chm. of Strategy, Dialogue with Industry Gp, 1998–2000); Bd of Mgt, British Council for Offices, 1997–2000 (Mgt Exec., 1999–2000). Mem. Edtl Adv. Bd, Property Week, 2000. Hon. FIHEEM (Hon. FIHospE 1992). *Recreations:* opera, theatre, music, film, reading, travel, family, home. *Address:* 11 Shrewsbury Road, Beckenham, Kent BR3 4DB.

LOCKE, Patrick, CBE 1998; Secretary to Church Commissioners, 1992–98; *b* 17 March 1934; *s* of Roy Albert Locke and Nora Katherine Locke (*née* Taylor); *m* 1959, Iris Constance Cory; one *s* one *d*. *Educ:* Bristol Cathedral Sch.; Wadham Coll., Oxford (Schol.; MA). Nat. Service, 1952–54. Church Commissioners Office, 1957–98: Dep. Sec., 1985–92. Trustee, Pollen Estate, 1991– (Chm., 2002–). Gov., Pusey House, Oxford, 1999–. *Recreations:* 18th and 19th century literature, theatre. *Address:* Romans, Beggars Lane, Winchester, Hants SO23 0HE. *T:* (01962) 866386. *Club:* Athenæum.

LOCKERBIE, Catherine; Director, Edinburgh International Book Festival, since 2000; *b* 4 Sept. 1958; *d* of Prof. Samuel Ian Johnstone Lockerbie and Rowena May Lockerbie (*née* Berry); one *s*. *Educ:* Univ. of Edinburgh (MA 1st Cl. double Hons French and Philosophy). Literary Ed., 1990–2000, Chief Leader Writer, 1995–97, The Scotsman. Founding Trustee, Edinburgh UNESCO City of Literature, 2004. Hon. LLD Dundee, 2005; Hon. DLitt: Queen Margaret UC, 2006; Edinburgh, 2007; Napier Univ., 2008; DUniv Open, 2007. *Publication:* (ed) Looking for the Spark: Scottish short stories, 1994. *Recreations:* reading, reading, and learning to understand my fellow humans (through reading). *Address:* Edinburgh International Book Festival, 5a Charlotte Square, Edinburgh EH2 4DR.

LOCKETT, His Honour Reginald; a Circuit Judge, 1981–99, a Senior Circuit Judge, 1997–99; *b* 24 June 1933; *s* of George Alfred Lockett and Emma (*née* Singleton); *m* 1959, Edna (*née* Lowe); one *s* one *d*. *Educ:* Ashton-in-Makerfield Grammar Sch.; Manchester Univ.; London Univ. (LLB 1954). Solicitor, 1955. Asst Coroner for Wigan, 1963–70; Dist Registrar and County Court Registrar, Manchester, 1970–81; a Recorder of the Crown Court, 1978–81. Hon. Recorder, Borough of Preston, 1996–99; Asst Deemster, IOM, 2000–03. Pres., Manchester Law Students' Soc., 1975–77. Pres., The Boys' Bde, 1999–2003 (Vice Pres., 1978–99; Dist Pres., NW Dist, 1973–90). Reader, Anglican Church, 1970–. Editor, Butterworths Family Law Service, 1983–90; Consultant Editor, Sweet-Maxwell's High Court Litigation Manual, 1990. *Recreations:* music, photography. *Address:* 7 Blandford Rise, Lostock, Bolton BL6 4JH. *T:* (01204) 699791.

LOCKEY, John Charlton Gerard; QC 2006; barrister; *b* 8 April 1963; *s* of Bryan Lockey and Anne Lockey (*née* Conroy, now Day); *m* 1992, Louise O'Sullivan; two *d*. *Educ:* Haberdashers' Aske's Sch., Elstree; Downing Coll., Cambridge (BA 1985); Harvard Law Sch. (LLM 1986). Called to the Bar, Middle Temple, 1987; in practice, specialising in insurance and commercial law, 1988–. Chm., British Insce Law Assoc., 2004–06. *Address:* Essex Court Chambers, 24 Lincoln's Inn Fields, WC2A 3EG. *T:* (020) 7813 8000, *Fax:* (020) 7813 8080.

LOCKHART, Brian Alexander; Sheriff Principal of South Strathclyde, Dumfries and Galloway, since 2005; *b* 1 Oct. 1942; *s* of John Arthur Hay Lockhart and Norah Lockhart; *m* 1967, Christine Ross Clark; two *s* two *d*. *Educ:* Glasgow Academy; Glasgow Univ. (BL). Qualified as solicitor, 1964; Partner in Robertson Chalmers & Auld, Solicitors, Glasgow, 1966–79; Sheriff in North Strathclyde, 1979–81, in Glasgow and Strathkelvin, 1981–2005. Mem., Parole Bd for Scotland, 1997–2003. Pres., Sheriffs' Assoc., 2004–05 (Sec., 1997–2002; Vice-Pres., 2002–04). Comr, Northern Lighthouse Bd, 2005–. *Recreations:* fishing, golf, family. *Address:* 18 Hamilton Avenue, Glasgow G41 4JF. *T:* (0141) 427 1921.

LOCKHART, Brian Robert Watson; Headmaster, Robert Gordon's College, Aberdeen, 1996–2004; *b* 19 July 1944; *s* of George Watson Lockhart and Helen Lockhart (*née* Rattray); *m* 1970, Fiona Anne Sheddon, MA; one *s* two *d*. *Educ:* Leith Acad.; George Heriot's Sch.; Aberdeen Univ. (MA); Edinburgh Univ. (DipEd). History Teacher, 1968–72, Principal History Teacher, 1972–81, George Heriot's Sch.; Dep. Rector, High Sch. of Glasgow, 1981–96. Council Mem., 1988–2004, Asst Sec. and Exec. Mem., 1989–94, Headteachers' Assoc. of Scotland; Mem., Higher Still Implementation Gp, 1997–2000; Chm., UCAS Scottish Standing Cttee, 2001–02 (Mem., 1994–2003; Co-Chm., 1998–99); Mem., HMC Univs Working Party, 1999–2003; Sec., 2003, Chm., 2004, Scottish Div., HMC. University of Aberdeen: Vice-Convener, Business Cttee, 2006– (Mem., 2001–06); Mem., Audit Cttee, 2007–; Gen. Council Assessor to Court, 2008–. Mem. Bd, Voluntary Service Aberdeen, 2004–. Member: Council, St Margaret's Sch. for Girls, Aberdeen, 2004–; Bd, Hutchesons' GS, Glasgow, 2005–. Trustee, Robert Nicol Trust, 2006–. *Publications:* History of the Architecture of George Heriot's Hospital and School 1628–1978, 1978; Jinglin' Geordie's Legacy, 2003; Robert Gordon's Legacy, 2007. *Recreations:* architecture, reading biographies, sport, films, politics. *Address:* 80 Gray Street, Aberdeen AB10 6JE. *T:* (01224) 315776.

LOCKHART, His Honour Frank Roper; a Circuit Judge, 1988–2004; *b* 8 Dec. 1931; *s* of Clement and Betsy Lockhart; *m* 1958, Brenda Harriett Johnson; one *s* one *d*. *Educ:* King Edward VI Sch., Retford; Doncaster Grammar Sch.; Univ. of Leeds (LLB Hons). Asst Town Clerk, Southend-on-Sea, 1960–65; Partner, Jefferies, Solicitors, 1965–87. Chairman: Industrial Tribunal, 1983–87; Social Security Tribunal, 1970–87; a Recorder, 1985–88. *Recreations:* golf, Rack II. *Club:* Thorpe Hall Golf.

LOCKHART, Harry Eugene, (Gene), CPA; Chairman, Financial Institutions, Diamond Castle Holdings LLC, since 2005; *b* 4 Nov. 1949; *s* of Harry Eugene Lockhart, Sen., Austin, Texas, and Gladys Cummings Lockhart; *m* 1974, Terry Lockhart; one *s* three *d*. *Educ:* Univ. of Virginia (MechEng degree); Darden Graduate Bus. Sch. (MBA). CPA 1976. Sen. Cons., Arthur Anderson & Co., 1974–77; Man. Principal, Europe, Nolan Norton & Co., 1977–82; Gp Dir, Management Services, C. T. Bowring & Co., 1982–85; Vice Pres., First Manhattan Consulting Gp, 1985–87; Chief Exec., IT, 1987–88, Gp Ops, 1988–92, UK Banking, 1990–92, Midland Bank; Pres., First Manhattan Consulting Internat., 1992–94; Pres. and CEO, Mastercard International, 1994–97; Pres. and CEO, The New Power Co., 2000–03. Dir, Qsent Inc., 2003. *Recreations:* tennis, golf, running, ski-ing, photography, riding, classical music, ballet. *Address:* Diamond Castle Holdings LLC, 280 Park Avenue, 25th Floor, East Tower, New York, NY 10017, USA. *Clubs:* Blind Brook; Indian Harbor Yacht; Mill Reef.

LOCKHART, James Lawrence, FRCM, FRCO(CHM); Director of Opera, London Royal Schools' Vocal Faculty, 1992–96 (Opera Consultant, 1996–98); *b* 16 Oct. 1930; *s* of Archibald Campbell Lockhart and Mary Black Lawrence; *m* 1954, Sheila Margaret

Grogan; two s one d. *Educ:* George Watson's Boys' College; Edinburgh Univ. (BMus); Royal College of Music (ARCM, FRCM). Yorkshire Symphony Orchestra, 1954–55; Münster City Opera, 1955–56; Bavarian State Opera, 1956–57; Glyndebourne Festival Opera, 1957, 1958, 1959; Opera Workshop, Univ. of Texas, 1957–59; Royal Opera House, Covent Garden, 1959–60; BBC Scottish Orchestra, 1960–61; Scottish Opera, 1960–61; Conductor, Sadler's Wells Opera, 1961–62; Conductor and Repetiteur, Royal Opera House, Covent Garden, 1962–68; Music Dir, Welsh National Opera, 1968–73; Generalmusikdirektor: Staatstheater, Kassel, 1972–80; Koblenz Opera, 1981–88; Rheinische Philharmonie, 1981–91 (Ehrendirigent, 1991); Dir of Opera, RCM, 1986–96. Guest Conductor, Sydney Conservatorium of Music, 2005. Guest Prof. of Conducting, Tokyo Nat. Univ. of Fine Arts and Music (Tokyo Geidai), 1998–2001, now Prof. Emeritus. Hon. RAM 1993. *Recreations:* swimming, hill-walking, travel, languages. *Address:* 5 The Coach House, Mill Street, Fontmell Magna, Shaftesbury, Dorset SP7 0NU. *T:* and *Fax:* (01747) 811980.

LOCKHART, Logie B.; *see* Bruce Lockhart.

LOCKHART, Sir Simon John Edward Francis S.; *see* Sinclair-Lockhart.

LOCKHART-MUMMERY, Christopher John; QC 1986; a Recorder, 1994–2004; a Deputy High Court Judge, 1995–2004; *b* 7 Aug. 1947; *s* of Sir Hugh Lockhart-Mummery, KCVO, MD, MChir, FRCS and late Elizabeth Jean Crerar, *d* of Sir James Crerar, KCSI, CIE; *m* 1st, 1971, Elizabeth Rosamund (marr. diss. 1992), *d* of late N. P. M. Elles and of Baroness Elles, *qv*; one *s* two *d*; 2nd, 1993, Mary Lou Putley. *Educ:* Stowe; Trinity College, Cambridge (BA). Called to the Bar, Inner Temple, 1971 (Bencher, 1991). Specialist Editor, Hill and Redman's Law of Landlord and Tenant, 1974–89. *Recreations:* fishing, listening to music, opera, walking the dog. *Address:* Landmark Chambers, 180 Fleet Street, EC4A 2HG. *T:* (020) 7430 1221; 133 Abbotsbury Road, W14 8EP. *T:* (020) 7603 7200; Hookeswood House, Farnham, Blandford Forum, Dorset DT11 8DQ. *T:* (01725) 516259. *Club:* Garrick.

LOCKHEAD, Sir Moir, Kt 2008; OBE 1996; Deputy Chairman and Chief Executive, FirstGroup plc, since 1995; *b* 25 April 1945; *s* of Len and Ethel Lockhead; *m* 1966, Audrey Johnson; three *s* one *d*. Chief Engr, Strathclyde Passenger Transport Exec., 1979–85; Gen. Manager, Grampian Transport, 1985–89; led employee/mgt buyout, 1989; Exec. Chm., Grampian Transport, subseq. GRT Bus plc, FirstBus plc, then FirstGroup plc, 1989–94. *Recreations:* amateur farming and breeding Highland cattle. *Address:* FirstGroup plc, 395 King Street, Aberdeen AB24 5RP. *T:* (01224) 650102, *Fax:* (01224) 650149; *e-mail:* moir.lockhead@firstgroup.com. *Clubs:* Royal Automobile; Royal Northern University (Aberdeen).

LOCKLEY, Andrew John Harold; Head of Public Law (formerly Professional Services and Public Law), Irwin Mitchell, Solicitors, since 1996; Chairman, Special Educational Needs and Disability (formerly Special Educational Needs) Tribunal, since 1996; *b* 10 May 1951; *s* of late Ven. Harold Lockley and Ursula Margarethe Lockley, JP; *m* 1st, 1974, Ruth Mary Vigor (marr. diss.); two *s* one *d*; 2nd, 2005, Caryl Jane Berry (*née* Seymour). *Educ:* Marlborough Coll.; Oriel Coll., Oxford (BA Lit. Hum. 1973; MA 1982). Admitted a Solicitor, 1979. Res. Fellow, World Council of Churches, 1973–75; Solicitor in private practice, 1979–82; Law Society: Asst Sec., 1982–85, Sec., 1985–87, Contentious Business Dept; Dir, Legal Practice, 1987–95; Dir, Corporate and Regl Affairs, 1995–96. Legal Assessor, Fitness to Practise Panels, GMC, 2007–; Mem., Editl Adv. Bd, Educn, Public Law and the Individual, 2005–. Non-exec. Chm., Solicitors Property Centres Ltd, 1998–2000 (Dir, 1997–98). Mem., Commn on Efficiency in the Criminal Courts, 1986–93. Mem., IT and Courts Cttee, 1990–95. Gov., William Austin Sch., Luton, 1992–96. Hon. Fellow, Univ. of Sheffield, 1999. *Publications:* Christian Communes, 1976; (ed) The Pursuit of Quality: a guide for lawyers, 1993; contribs to legal periodicals. *Recreations:* growing fruit and vegetables, choral singing, swimming, walking, cooking. *Address:* Irwin Mitchell, Riverside East, Millsands, Sheffield S3 8DT. *T:* 0870 150 0100, *Fax:* (0114) 275 3306; *e-mail:* andrew.lockley@irwinmitchell.com.

LOCKLEY, Stephen Randolph, FCILT; transport consultant; *b* 19 June 1943; *s* of Randolph and Edith Lockley; *m* 1968, Angela; two *d*. *Educ:* Manchester Univ. (BScCivEng, 1st Cl. Hons). MICE; MIHT; FCILT (FCIT 1987, FILT). Lancashire County Council: North West Road Construction Unit, Highway Engrg and Planning, 1964–72; Highway/Transportation Planning, 1972–75; Lanarkshire CC, Strathclyde Regional Council: Prin. Engr (Transportation), 1975–77; Depute Dir of Policy Planning, 1977–80; Prin. Exec. Officer, 1980–86; Dir Gen., Strathclyde PTE, 1986–97. *Address:* 64 Townhead Street, Strathaven ML10 6DJ. *T:* (01357) 521774.

LOCKWOOD, Baroness *cr* 1978 (Life Peer), of Dewsbury, W Yorks; **Betty Lockwood;** DL; President, Birkbeck College, London, 1983–89; a Deputy Speaker, House of Lords, 1989–2007; *b* 22 Jan. 1924; *d* of Arthur Lockwood and Edith Alice Lockwood; *m* 1978, Lt-Col Cedric Hall (*d* 1988). *Educ:* Eastborough Girls' Sch., Dewsbury; Ruskin Coll., Oxford. Chief Woman Officer and Asst Nat. Agent of Labour Party, 1967–75; Ed., Labour Woman, 1967–71; Chm., Equal Opportunities Commn, 1975–83. Vice-Chm., Internat. Council of Social Democratic Women, 1969–75; Chm., Adv. Cttee to European Commn on Equal Opportunities for Women and Men, 1982–83. Chm., Mary Macarthur Educnl Trust, 1971–94; Pres., Mary Macarthur Holiday Trust, 1990–2002 (Chm., 1971–90). Member: Dept of Employment Adv. Cttee on Women's Employment, 1969–83; Adv. Council on Energy Conservation, 1977–80; Council, Advertising Standards Authority, 1983–93; Leeds Urban Develt Corp., 1988–95. Pres., Hillcroft Coll., 1987–95. Chancellor, Bradford Univ., 1997–2005 (Mem. Council, 1983–2005; a Pro-Chancellor, 1988–97); Leeds Univ., 1985–91; Vice Pres., UMIST, 1992–95. Chm. Bd of Trustees, Nat. Coal Mining Mus., 1995–2007. DL W Yorks, 1987. Hon. Fellow: UMIST, 1986; Birkbeck Coll., 1987. Hon. DLitt Bradford 1981; Hon. LLD Strathclyde, 1985; DUniv Leeds Metropolitan, 1999; Dr *hc* Edinburgh, 2004. *Recreations:* country pursuits, music. *Address:* 6 Sycamore Drive, Addingham, Ilkley LS29 0NY. *Club:* Soroptomist.

LOCKWOOD, Prof. David, CBE 1998; FBA 1976; Professor of Sociology, University of Essex, 1968–2001 (Pro-Vice-Chancellor, 1989–92); *b* 9 April 1929; *s* of Herbert Lockwood and Edith A. (*née* Lockwood); *m* 1954, Leonore Davidoff; three *s*. *Educ:* Honley Grammar Sch.; London Sch. of Economics. BSc(Econ) London, 1st Cl. Hons 1952; PhD London, 1957. Trainee, textile industry, 1944–47; Cpl, Intell. Corps, Austria, 1947–49. Asst Lectr and Lectr, London Sch. of Economics, 1953–60; Rockefeller Fellow, Univ. of California, Berkeley, 1958–59; Univ. Lectr, Faculty of Economics, and Fellow, St John's Coll., Cambridge, 1960–68. Visiting Professor: Dept of Sociology, Columbia Univ., 1966–67; Delhi Univ. 1975; Stockholm Univ. 1989; Vis. Fellow, ANU, 1993. Mem., SSRC (Chm., Sociol. and Soc. Admin Cttee), 1973–76; Chm., ESRC Rev. of Govt Social Classifications, 1994–98. Mem., Academia Europaea, 1990. DU Essex, 2001; Hon. LittD Cantab, 2004. *Publications:* The Blackcoated Worker, 1958, 2nd edn 1989; (jtly) The Affluent Worker in the Class Structure, 3 vols, 1968–69; Solidarity and Schism,

1992; numerous articles in jls and symposia. *Address:* 82 High Street, Wivenhoe, Essex CO7 9AB. *T:* (01206) 823530.

LOCKWOOD, Prof. Michael, PhD; FRS 2006; Chief Scientist, Space Science and Technology Department, Rutherford Appleton Laboratory, since 2001; Professor, School of Physics and Astronomy, University of Southampton, since 2000; *b* 29 April 1954; *s* of Fred T. Lockwood, CBE and Stephanie Lockwood; *m* 1976, Celia; one *s* one *d*. *Educ:* Skinners' Sch., Tunbridge Wells; Univ. of Exeter (BSc 1st Cl. Hons Physics 1975; PhD Physics 1978). FRAS 1985; CPhys, FInstP 2003. Res. Fellow, Auckland Univ., 1978–79; Higher SO, RAE, Farnborough, 1979–80; Space Sci. and Technol. Dept, Rutherford Appleton Lab., 1980–. Res. Associate, NASA/Marshall Space Flight Center, Huntsville, 1984–85. Vis. Hon. Lectr, 1987–2004, Vis. Hon. Prof., 2004–; Imperial Coll., London; Guest Lectr, Univ. Centre on Svalbard, Longyearbyen, Svalbard, 1994–. Vice Pres. (Geophysics), RAS, 1995–97; President: Div. III, Internat. Assoc. of Geomagnetism and Aeronomy, 1999–2003; Solar-Terrestrial Physics Sect., Europ. Geophysical Soc., 2000–03; Chm. Council, Internat. EISCAT Scientific Assoc., 2001–03; Mem., Astronomy Cttee, 1997–2000, Sci. Cttee, 2002–05, PPARC. Mem., American Geophysical Union, 1981. Issac Koga Gold Medal, URSI, 1990; Zel'dovich Award for Commn C (Ionospheric Phys), COSPAR, 1990; Chapman Medal, RAS, 1998; Charles Chree Medal and Prize, Inst. of Physics, 2003. *Publications:* (jtly) The Sun, Solar Analogs and the Climate, 2004; over 240 articles in jls on solar influences on the Earth. *Recreations:* playing music, watching cricket, Rugby and soccer. *Address:* Rutherford Appleton Laboratory, Chilton, Didcot, Oxon OX11 0QX. *T:* (01235) 446496, *Fax:* (01235) 445848; *e-mail:* m.lockwood@rl.ac.uk.

LOCKWOOD, Robert; General Director, Overseas Planning and Project Development, General Motors Corporation, 1982–85, retired; *b* 14 April 1920; *s* of Joseph A. Lockwood and Sylvia Lockwood; *m* 1947, Phyllis M. Laing; one *s* one *d*. *Educ:* Columbia Univ. (AB); Columbia Law Sch. (LLB). Attorney, Bar of New York, 1941; US Dist of New York and US Supreme Court, 1952. Pilot, USAAF (8th Air Force), 1944–45. Attorney: Ehrich, Royall, Wheeler & Holland, New York, 1941 and 1946–47; Sullivan & Cromwell, New York, 1947–54; Sec. and Counsel, Cluett, Peabody & Co., Inc., New York, 1955–57; Man. Dir, Cluett, Peabody & Co., Ltd, London, 1957–59; General Motors: Overseas Ops, Planning and Develt, 1960–61; Asst to Man. Dir, GM Argentina, Buenos Aires, 1962; Asst to Man. Dir, and Manager, Parts, Power and Appliances, GM Continental, Antwerp, 1964–66; Branch Man., Netherlands Br., GM Continental, Rotterdam, 1967–68; Man., Planning and Develt, GM Overseas Ops, New York, 1969–73; Vice Pres., GM Overseas Corp., and Gen. Man., Japan Br., 1974–76; Exec. Vice Pres., Isuzu Motors Ltd, Tokyo, 1976; Chm., GM European Adv. Council, 1977–82. Mem., Panel of Arbitrators, Amer. Arbitration Assoc., 1989–. *Recreations:* tennis, bridge, reading. *Clubs:* Beach and Tennis (Pebble Beach); Marines' Memorial (San Francisco).

LOCKWOOD, Rear Adm. Roger Graham, CB 2005; FCIPD; Chief Executive, Northern Lighthouse Board, since 2006; *b* 26 June 1950; *s* of Eric Garnett Lockwood and Nunda Lockwood (*née* Doak); *m* 1984, Susan Jane Cant; three *s* two *d*. *Educ:* Kimbolton Sch., Cambs; Univ. of Warwick (BA Maths). Chartered FCIPD 2001. BRNC Dartmouth, 1971; Sub Lieut, HMS Fearless, 1972; Lieut, HMS Soberton, 1973; Supply Officer (Cash), HMS Tiger, 1974–76; Captain's Sec., 2nd Submarine Sqn, 1976–78; Supply Officer, HMS Naiad, 1979–81; Flag Lieut to CDS, 1981–82; Captain's Sec., RNAS Culdrose, 1982–84; jsdc 1985; Comdr, 1985; Base Supply Officer, HMS Dolphin, 1985–87; Comdr, RN Supply Sch., 1987–89; Supply Officer, HMS Ark Royal, 1989–91; Captain, 1991; Dep. Dir, Naval Service Conditions (Pay), 1991–93; rcds 1994; Secretary to: Second Sea Lord, 1995–96; First Sea Lord, 1996–98; Cdre, 1998; Cdre, HMS Raleigh, 1998–2000; Rear Adm., 2000; COS to Second Sea Lord, and C-in-C Naval Home Comd, 2000–02; Sen. Naval Directing Staff, RCDS, and Chief Naval Supply, subseq. Chief Naval Logistics, Officer, 2002–05. Chairman: Forth Pilots Disciplinary Cttee, 2006–; Perth Sea Cadet Unit, 2006–; Associate Mem., Hon. Co. of Master Mariners, 2007–. Co. Sec., Dunblane Develt Trust, 2005–07. Area Vice Patron (Scotland), War Memorials Trust, 2007–. Gov., Kimbolton Sch., 2001–05; Comr, Queen Victoria Sch., Dunblane, 2006–. MInstD 2007. *Recreations:* family, studying the history of the SOE in France. *Address:* Northern Lighthouse Board, 84 George Street, Edinburgh EH2 3DA. *Club:* New (Edinburgh).

LOCKYER, Rear-Adm. (Alfred) Austin, LVO 1973; Chief Staff Officer (Engineering) to Commander-in-Chief Fleet, 1982–84, retired; Director General, Timber Trade Federation, 1985–92; *b* 4 March 1929; *s* of late Austin Edmund Lockyer and Jane Russell (*née* Goldman); *m* 1965, Jennifer Ann Simmons; one *s*. *Educ:* Frome County School; Taunton School; Royal Naval Engineering College. Entered RN 1947; Comdr 1965; Staff of Commander Far East Fleet, 1965–67; jssc, 1968–69; Ship Dept, 1969–71; HMY Britannia, 1971–73; Captain 1973; sowc, 1973–74; Naval Ship Production Overseer, Scotland and NI, 1974–76; Dep. Dir, Fleet Maintenance, 1976–78; Dir, Naval Officers Appointments (Engrg), 1978–80; HMS Sultan in Comd, 1980–82; ADC to the Queen, 1981; Rear-Adm. 1982. Governor: Forres Sch., Swanage, 1980–92 (Chm., 1983–92); Sherborne Sch., 1981–97. *Recreations:* gardening, golf, listening to good music. *Address:* The Old Malt House, 3 Widcombe Hill, Bath BA2 6AD. *Club:* Army and Navy.

LOCKYER, Lynda Dorothy; on secondment to Civil Contingencies Secretariat, Cabinet Office, 2002; *b* 17 Aug. 1946; *d* of Donald Lockyer and Gwendoline Lockyer (*née* Fulcher); *m* 1984, John Anthony Thompson; one *s*. *Educ:* Bromley High Sch.; Newnham Coll., Cambridge (MA Classics). Press Officer: Shell-Mex, BP Ltd, 1968–73; Sperry Univac, 1974; DHSS, later DoH, 1974–96; Home Office, 1996–; Head of Police Resources Unit, 1996–99; Dir, Corporate Resources, 1999–2000; Dir, Corporate Develt and Services, 2000–02. *Recreations:* films, theatre, opera, Europe.

LOCKYER, Roger Walter, FRHistS, FSA; Reader in History, Royal Holloway College, University of London, 1983–84, now Emeritus; *b* 26 Nov. 1927; *s* of Walter Lockyer and May Florence (*née* Cook); partner, Percy Steven. *Educ:* King's College Sch., Wimbledon; Pembroke Coll., Cambridge (Foundn Schol.; 1st cl. Hons BA 1950; Hadley Prize for Hist. 1951; MA 1955). FRHistS 1977; FSA 1981. Instructor-Lieut, RN, 1946–48; Asst d'Anglais, Lycée Louis-le-Grand, Paris, 1951–52; Hd of Hist., Haileybury and Imperial Service Coll., 1952–53; Editor, Blue Guides, Ernest Benn Ltd, 1953–54; Hd of Hist., Lancing Coll., 1954–61; Lectr, then Sen. Lectr, Royal Holloway Coll., Univ. of London, 1961–83. Vis. Prof., Univ. of Maryland, 1991. *Publications:* (jtly) A History of England, 1961; Tudor and Stuart Britain 1471–1714, 1964, 3rd edn 2004; Henry VII, 1968, 2nd edn 1997; Habsburg and Bourbon Europe 1470–1720, 1974; Buckingham: the life and political career of George Villiers, first Duke of Buckingham 1592–1628, 1981; (contrib.) For Veronica Wedgwood These: studies in Seventeenth-century history, 1986; The Early Stuarts: a political history of England 1603–1642, 1989, 2nd edn 1999; (ed jtly) Shakespeare's World: background readings in the English Renaissance, 1989; James VI & I, 1998. *Recreations:* reading, theatre, architecture, living in France. *Address:* 63 Balcombe Street, NW1 6HD. *T:* (020) 7706 1258; *e-mail:* rogerlockyer@btinternet.com.

LODDER, Peter Norman; QC 2001; a Recorder, since 2000; Chairman, Criminal Bar Association, 2008–09; *b* 3 Feb. 1958; *s* of Lt Cdr Norman George Lodder, RN and Ann Lodder; *m* 1992, Elizabeth Gummer (marr. diss. 2007); two *c*. *Educ:* King's Sch., Gloucester; Portsmouth Grammar Sch.; Univ. of Birmingham (LLB). Called to the Bar, Middle Temple, 1981 (Jules Thorn Major Schol. 1982); specialist in fraud and criminal law; Asst Recorder, 1998–2000. Mem., Gen. Council of the Bar, 1994–. *Address:* 2 Bedford Row, WC1R 4BU. *T:* (020) 7440 8888.

LODER, family name of **Baron Wakehurst**.

LODER, Sir Edmund Jeune, 4th Bt *cr* 1887, of Whittlebury, Northamptonshire, and of High Beeches, Slaugham, Sussex; *b* 26 June 1941; *er s* of Sir Giles Rolls Loder, 3rd Bt and Marie Violet Pamela Loder (*née* Symons-Jeune); *S* father, 1999; *m* 1st, 1966, Penelope Jane Forde (marr. diss. 1971); one *d*; 2nd, 1992, Susan Warren Pearl. *Address:* Eyrefield Lodge, The Curragh, Co. Kildare, Ireland.

LODGE, Anton James Corduff; QC 1989; a Recorder, since 1985; *b* 17 April 1944; *s* of Sir Thomas Lodge and Aileen (*née* Corduff). *Educ:* Ampleforth College; Gonville and Caius College, Cambridge (MA). Called to the Bar, Gray's Inn, 1966, Bencher, 1998. *Recreations:* cricket, tennis, ski-ing, music, theatre. *Address:* Park Court Chambers, 16 Park Place, Leeds LS1 2SJ. *T:* (0113) 243 3277. *Club:* Yorkshire (York).

LODGE, Prof. David John, CBE 1998; MA, PhD; FRSL; writer; Emeritus Professor of English Literature, University of Birmingham, since 2001 (Professor of Modern English Literature, 1976–87, Hon. Professor, 1987–2000); *b* 28 Jan. 1935; *s* of William Frederick Lodge and Rosalie Marie Lodge (*née* Murphy); *m* 1959, Mary Frances Jacob; two *s* one *d*. *Educ:* St Joseph's Acad., Blackheath; University College, London (Hon. Fellow, 1982). BA hons, MA (London); PhD (Birm). FRSL 1976. National Service, RAC, 1955–57. British Council, London, 1959–60. Univ. of Birmingham: Asst Lectr in English, 1960–62; Lectr, 1963–71; Sen. Lectr, 1971–73; Reader in English, 1973–76. Harkness Commonwealth Fellow, 1964–65; Visiting Associate Prof., Univ. of California, Berkeley, 1969; Henfield Writing Fellow, Univ. of E Anglia, 1977. Hon. Fellow, Goldsmiths' Coll., London, 1992. Hon. DLitt: Warwick, 1997; Birmingham, 2001. Yorkshire Post Fiction Prize, 1975; Hawthornden Prize, 1976; Whitbread Book of the Year Award, 1980; Sunday Express Book of the Year Award, 1988. Chevalier, l'Ordre des Arts et des Lettres (France), 1997. Stage plays: The Writing Game, Birmingham Rep., 1990 (adapted for television, 1996); Home Truths, Birmingham Rep., 1998. Adaptation of Dickens, Martin Chuzzlewit, for television, 1994. *Publications: novels:* The Picturegoers, 1960; Ginger, You're Barmy, 1962; The British Museum is Falling Down, 1965; Out of the Shelter, 1970, rev. edn 1985; Changing Places, 1975; How Far Can You Go?, 1980; Small World, 1984 (televised 1988); Nice Work, 1988 (adapted for television, 1989); Paradise News, 1991; Therapy, 1995; Home Truths: a novella, 1999; Thinks..., 2001; Author, Author, 2004; Deaf Sentence, 2008; *plays:* The Writing Game, 1991; Home Truths, 1998; *criticism:* Language of Fiction, 1966; The Novelist at the Crossroads, 1971; The Modes of Modern Writing, 1977; Working with Structuralism, 1981; Write On, 1986; After Bakhtin (essays), 1990; The Art of Fiction, 1992; The Practice of Writing, 1996; Consciousness and the Novel (essays), 2002; The Year of Henry James (essays), 2006; *edited:* Jane Austen's Emma: a casebook, 1968; Twentieth Century Literary Criticism, 1972; Modern Criticism and Theory, 1988, 2nd edn 1999. *Recreations:* tennis, television, cinema, theatre. *Address:* c/o Department of English, University of Birmingham, Birmingham B15 2TT. *T:* (0121) 414 3344.

LODGE, Dr Denise Valerie; Headmistress, Putney High School, GDST, since 2002; ; *m* ; one *s* one *d*. *Educ:* Bury Grammar Sch.; Royal Holloway Coll., London Univ. (BSc Botany and Zool.; PhD Zool. 1979); Chelsea Coll., London Univ. (MSc Applied Hydrobiol.); Reading Univ. (PGCE). Teacher, later Hd of Chem., Hd of Sixth Form, and Sen. Teacher, Curriculum, Sir Roger Manwood's Sch., Sandwich, 1987–96; Dep. Hd, Sheffield High Sch., GDST, 1996–99; Headmistress, Sydenham High Sch., GDST, 1999–2002. Treas., GSA, 2004–07. Mem. Ct, Imperial Coll. London, 2007–. *Recreations:* jazz, cooking, the gym, art. *Address:* Putney High School, 35 Putney Hill, SW15 6BH. *Club:* Lansdowne.

LODGE, Prof. Geoffrey Arthur, BSc, PhD; FIBiol; FRSE 1986; Professor of Animal Science, Sultan Qaboos University, Muscat, 1986–90, retired; *b* 18 Feb. 1930; *m* 1956, Thelma (*née* Calder); one *s* two *d*. *Educ:* Durham University (BSc). PhD Aberdeen. Formerly Reader in Animal Production, Univ. of Nottingham School of Agriculture, and Principal Research Scientist, Animal Research Inst., Ottawa; Strathcona-Fordyce Prof. of Agriculture, Univ. of Aberdeen, and Principal, North of Scotland Coll. of Agriculture, 1978–86. *Publications:* (ed jointly) Growth and Development of Mammals, 1968; contribs to journals and books. *Recreations:* food, malt whisky, travelling, farming. *Address:* 18 Queen Victoria Park, Inchmarlo, Banchory, Kincardineshire AB31 4AL.

LODGE, Prof. Juliet, DLitt; PhD; Professor of European Integration and Politics and Director, Jean Monnet Centre of Excellence, University of Leeds, since 1996; *b* London; *d* of Arthur and Lenore Mayer; two *s* one *d*. *Educ:* Univ. of Reading (MA; DLitt); Univ. of Hull (PhD). Fellow in Internat. Relns, LSE, 1977; Lectr in Euro Politics, Univ. of Auckland, 1978; Prof. of EU Politics, Univ. of Hull, 1978–95; Prof. of Internat. Politics, Vrije Universiteit Brussel, 1994; Prof. of EU Politics, Institut für Höhere Studien, Vienna, 1995. Vis. Prof. of EU Politics, Université Libre de Bruxelles, 1993; Vis. Lectr and Hon. Cormorant, JSDC. Freelance broadcaster and journalist on EU policies and instns. Convenor, UK Ethics Cttee on judicial co-operation in EU, 2004. Woman of Europe Award, 1992. *Publications:* The European Policy of the SPD, 1977; (jtly) European Parliament and the European Community, 1978; (ed) Terrorism: a challenge to the state, 1981; (jtly) Direct Elections to the European Parliament: community perspective, 1982; The European Community and New Zealand, 1982; Direct Elections to the European Parliament 1984, 1986; (ed) European Union: the European Community in search of a future, 1986; Threat of Terrorism, 1987; The 1989 Election of the European Parliament, 1990; (ed) The European Community and the Challenge of the Future, 1993; (ed) The 1994 Elections to the European Parliament, 1995; (ed) The 1999 Elections to the European Parliament, 2001; The European Union, 2003; The 2004 Elections to the European Parliament, 2005; (ed) Are You Who You Say You Are: the EU and biometric borders, 2007; widely publd on EU policies, biometrics, egovernance, constitution, EP and EU security in numerous prof. jls and the press. *Recreations:* art, laughing. *T:* (0113) 343 4443; *e-mail:* j.e.lodge@leeds.ac.uk. *Club:* Women of Europe.

LODGE, Oliver Raymond William Wynlayne; Regional Chairman of Industrial Tribunals, London South Region, 1980–92; *b* Painswick, Glos, 2 Sept. 1922; *e s* of Oliver William Foster Lodge and Winifred, (Wynlayne), *o d* of Sir William Nicholas Atkinson, ISO, LLD; *m* 1953, Charlotte (*d* 1990), *o d* of Col Arthur Davidson Young, CMG; one *s* two *d*. *Educ:* Bryanston Sch.; King's Coll., Cambridge. BA 1943, MA 1947. Officer-cadet, Royal Fusiliers, 1942. Called to the Bar, Inner Temple, 1945; admitted *ad eundem*, Lincoln's Inn, 1949 (Bencher, 1973; Treas., 1995); practised at Chancery Bar, 1945–74; Permanent Chairman of Industrial Tribunals, 1975–92, part-time Chm., 1992–94. Member: Bar Council, 1952–56, 1967–71; Supreme Court Rules Cttee, 1968–71. Gen. Comr of Income Tax, Lincoln's Inn, 1983–91. *Publications:* (ed) Rivington's Epitome of Snell's Equity, 3rd edn, 1948; (ed) Fraudulent and Voidable Conveyances, article in Halsbury's Laws of England, 3rd edn, 1956; contribs to legal periodicals. *Recreations:* freemasonry, walking, reading history, formerly sailing. *Address:* Southridge House, Hindon, Salisbury, Wilts SP3 6ER. *T:* (01747) 820238. *Clubs:* Garrick; Bar Yacht.

LOEHNIS, Anthony David, CMG 1988; Chairman, Alpha Bank London, since 2005 (Director, since 1994); *b* 12 March 1936; *s* of Sir Clive Loehnis, KCMG; *m* 1965, Jennifer Forsyth Anderson; three *s*. *Educ:* Eton; New Coll., Oxford (MA); Harvard Sch. of Public Administration. HM Diplomatic Service, 1960–66; J. Henry Schroder Wagg & Co. Ltd, 1967–80 (on secondment to Bank of England, 1977–79); Bank of England: Associate Dir (Overseas), 1980–81; Exec. Dir, 1981–89; Dir, S. G. Warburg Group plc, 1989–92; a Vice-Chm., S. G. Warburg & Co., 1989–92. Director: St James's Place Capital plc, 1993–2005; Mitsubishi UFJ Securities Internat., 1996–2007 (formerly Tokyo-Mitsubishi Internat., then Mitsubishi Securities Internat.); AGCO Corp. (US), 1997–2005; VTB Bank Europe plc, 2007–. A Public Works Loan Comr, 1994–2005 (Chm., 1997–2005). Exec. Dir, UK-Japan 21st Century (formerly UK-Japan 2000) Gp, 1999–2002 (Dir, 1990–2005). Member: Council: Ditchley Foundn, 1992– (Chm., F & G P Cttee, 1993–); Baring Foundn, 1994–2005; Japan Soc., 1998–2005. Chm., Villiers Park Educnl Trust, 2000–. Gov., British Assoc. for Central and Eastern Europe, 1994–2003. *Address:* 11 Cranleigh, 139 Ladbroke Road, W11 3PX. *Clubs:* Garrick, Beefsteak.

LOEWE, Raphael James, MC 1943; Goldsmid Professor of Hebrew, University College, London, 1981–86; *b* Calcutta, 16 April 1919; *s* of Herbert Loewe and Ethel Loewe (*née* Hyamson); *m* 1952, Chloe Klatzkin; two *d*. *Educ:* Dragon Sch., Oxford; Leys Sch., Cambridge; St John's Coll., Cambridge (Schol.; BA Classics 1942). Served War, Suffolk Regt, RAC. Postgrad. res. at Balliol Coll., Oxford; Lectr in Hebrew, Leeds Univ., 1949–53; Bye Fellow, Gonville and Caius Coll., Cambridge, 1953; University College London: Dir, Inst. of Jewish Studies, 1973–86; Lectr in Hebrew, 1975–78; Reader, 1978–81. Vis. Prof. in Judaica, Brown Univ., 1962–63. President: Jewish Historical Soc. of England, 1973–75; SOTS, 1980–81; British Assoc. for Jewish Studies, 1998. Actively involved in admin and pubns of Spanish and Portuguese Jews' Congregation, London (formerly Elder). *Publications:* Position of Women in Judaism, 1966; (contrib.) Encyclopaedia Judaica, 1972; (ed) The Rylands Haggadah, 1988; Solomon Ibn Gabirol, 1989; Isaac Ibn Sahula's Meshal Haqadmoni, 2004; articles on Judaism and (Anglo-) Jewish history, etc in specialist periodicals. *Recreations:* 3-way translation of poetry (English, Latin, Hebrew), walking, The Times crosswords. *Address:* 50 Gurney Drive, N2 0DE. *T:* (020) 8455 5379.

LOFTHOUSE, family name of **Baron Lofthouse of Pontefract**.

LOFTHOUSE OF PONTEFRACT, Baron *cr* 1997 (Life Peer), of Pontefract in the co. of West Yorkshire; **Geoffrey Lofthouse,** Kt 1995; JP; *b* 18 Dec. 1925; *s* of Ernest and Emma Lofthouse; *m* 1946, Sarah Lofthouse (*d* 1985); one *d*. *Educ:* Featherstone Primary and Secondary Schs; Leeds Univ. FIPD (MIPM 1984). Haulage hand in mining industry at age of 14. Personnel Manager, NCB Fryston, 1970–78. Member: Pontefract Borough Council, 1962–74 (Mayor, 1967–68); Wakefield Metropolitan District Council, 1974–79 (Chm, 1974–75; Chm., Housing Cttee). MP (Lab) Pontefract and Castleford, Oct. 1978–1997. Dep. Chm. of Ways and Means, and Dep. Speaker, H of C, 1992–97; Dep. Speaker, H of L, 1998–. Chairman: Wakefield HA, 1998–2002; Mid Yorks NHS Trust (formerly Mid Yorks Hosps NHS Trust), 2002–. Mem., NUM, 1939–64, APEX, 1970–. JP Pontefract, 1970. *Publications:* A Very Miner MP (autobiog.), 1986; Coal Sack to Woolsack (autobiog.), 1999. *Recreations:* Rugby League, cricket. *Address:* 67 Carleton Crest, Pontefract, West Yorkshire WF8 2QR.

LOFTHOUSE, Simon Timothy; QC 2006; a Recorder, since 2003; *b* 25 Aug. 1966; *s* of Adam Robert Lofthouse and Angela Anne Lofthouse (*née* Manning); *m* 1994, Sophia Ann Gawlik. *Educ:* Fernwood Comp. Sch., Nottingham; Becket Upper Sch., Nottingham; University Coll. London (LLB Hons 1987). Called to the Bar, Gray's Inn, 1988; in practice specialising in construction, energy and professional negligence law. Mem., Professional Conduct Cttee, Bar Council, 2001–04. Prosecutor, 2005–07, Vice-Chm., Complaints Cttee, 2008–, Bar Standards Bd. *Recreations:* opera, sculpture, travel. *Address:* Atkin Chambers, 1 Atkin Building, Gray's Inn, WC1R 5AT. *T:* (020) 7404 0102, *Fax:* (020) 7405 7456; *e-mail:* slofthouse@atkinchambers.com.

LOFTUS, Simon Pierse Dominic, OBE 2007; non-executive Director, Adnams plc, since 2006 (Chairman, 1996–2006); *b* 5 Aug. 1946; *s* of late Nicholas Alastair Ayton Loftus and Prudence Loftus (*née* Wootten); *m* 1980, Irène Yamato; one *d*. *Educ:* Ampleforth; Trinity Coll., Cambridge (MA). Joined Adnams, 1968, Dir, 1973. Dir, Aldeburgh Productions, 1998–; non-executive Director: 1st East, 2005–; Norwich & Peterborough Bldg Soc., 2007–. *Publications:* Anatomy of the Wine Trade, 1985; A Pike in the Basement, 1987; Puligny Montrachet, 1992; (ed) Guides to the Wines of France series, 1988–90; numerous articles in jls. *Recreations:* cooking, Anglo-Irish history, writing. *Address:* Bulcamp House, Halesworth, Suffolk IP19 9LG. *T:* (01502) 727200. *Club:* Groucho.

LOGAN, Andrew David; sculptor, since 1968; *b* 11 Oct. 1945; *s* of William Harold Logan and Irene May Logan. *Educ:* Oxford Sch. of Architecture (DipArch Oxon 1970). Founded Alternative Miss World (performance event), London, 1972; opened Andrew Logan Mus. of Sculpture, Berriew, Wales, 1991. Work in public collections: Australian Gall. of Nat. Art; NPG; Arts Council of GB; Warner Bros, UK; Costume Inst., Metropolitan Mus., NY; Curzon Tussaud, London; Cleveland Jewellery Collection, Middlesbrough; Nat. Museums and Galls on Merseyside. Member: Contemporary Glass Soc.; RSA. *Recreations:* yoga, travel, theatre. *T:* (020) 7407 6575; *e-mail:* andrewdl@andrewlogan.com.

LOGAN, Sir David (Brian Carleton), KCMG 2000 (CMG 1991); HM Diplomatic Service, retired; Director, Centre for Studies in Security and Diplomacy, and Hon. Professor, School of Social Sciences, University of Birmingham, 2002–06; *b* 11 Aug. 1943; *s* of late Captain Brian Ewen Weldon Logan, RN (Retd) and Mary Logan (*née* Fass); *m* 1967, Judith Margaret Walton Cole; one *s* one *d* (and one *s* decd). *Educ:* Charterhouse; University College, Oxford (MA). Foreign Office, 1965; served Istanbul, Ankara and FCO, 1965–70; Private Sec. to Parly Under Sec. of State for Foreign and Commonwealth Affairs, 1970–73; First Sec., 1972; UK Mission to UN, 1973–77; FCO, 1977–82; Counsellor, Hd of Chancery and Consul-Gen., Oslo, 1982–86; Hd of Personnel Ops Dept, FCO, 1986–88; Sen. Associate Mem., St Antony's Coll., Oxford, 1988–89; Minister and Dep. Head of Mission, Moscow, 1989–92; Asst Under Sec. of State (Central and Eastern Europe), 1992–94, (Defence Policy), 1994–95, FCO; Minister, Washington, 1995–97; Ambassador to Turkey, 1997–2001. Chairman: GAP Activity Projects, 2002–07; British Inst. of Archaeology, Ankara, 2007–; Member: Internat. Advisory Bd, Thames Water, 2002–07; Supervisory Bd, Efes Pilsen Internat., 2004–; Director: European Nickel plc, 2004–; Magnitogorsk Iron and Steel Co., 2007–. *Recreations:* music, reading, sailing. *Club:* Royal Ocean Racing.

LOGAN, Prof. David Edwin, PhD; Coulson Professor of Theoretical Chemistry, University of Oxford, and Fellow, University College, Oxford, since 2005; *b* 27 Aug. 1956; *s* of late James Henry Logan and Mona Elizabeth Logan; *m* 1981, Philippa Mary Walmsley; two *s* two *d*. *Educ:* Gilnahirk Primary Sch., E Belfast; Sullivan Upper Sch., Holywood; Trinity Coll., Cambridge (BA 1978; PhD Theoretical Chem. 1982). Jun. Res. Fellow, Christ's Coll., Cambridge, 1982–86; Postdoctoral Res. Associate, Univ. of Illinois, Urbana-Champaign, 1982–83; University of Oxford: Univ. Lectr in Phys. Chem., 1986–96; Prof. of Chem., 1996–2005; Official Fellow, Waters Fellow and Tutor in Phys. and Theoretical Chem., Balliol Coll., 1986–2005, Emeritus Fellow, 2005. Staff Mem., Theory Div., Institut Laue-Langevin, Grenoble, 1996. Royal Society of Chemistry: Marlow Medal and Prize, Faraday Div., 1990; Corday-Morgan Medal and Prize, 1994; Tilden Lecture and Medal, 2007. *Publications:* numerous res. articles on theoretical condensed matter chem. and phys. *Recreations:* music, poetry, weeding, liberal baiting. *Address:* Physical and Theoretical Chemistry Laboratory, South Parks Road, Oxford OX1 3QZ. *T:* (01865) 275418; *e-mail:* dlogan@physchem.ox.ac.uk.

LOGAN, Sir Donald (Arthur), KCMG 1977 (CMG 1965); HM Diplomatic Service, retired; *b* 25 Aug. 1917; *s* of late Arthur Alfred Logan and Louise Anne Bradley; *m* 1957, Irène Jocelyne Angèle, *d* of Robert Everts (Belgian Ambassador at Madrid, 1932–39) and Alexandra Comnène; one *s* two *d*. *Educ:* Solihull. Fellow, Chartered Insurance Institute, 1939. War of 1939–45: Major, RA; British Army Staff, Washington, 1942–43; Germany, 1945. Joined HM Foreign (subseq. Diplomatic) Service, Dec. 1945; Foreign Office, 1945–47; HM Embassy, Tehran, 1947–51; Foreign Office, 1951–53; Asst Political Agent, Kuwait, 1953–55; Asst Private Sec. to Sec. of State for Foreign Affairs, 1956–58; HM Embassy, Washington, 1958–60; HM Ambassador to Guinea, 1960–62; Foreign Office, 1962–64; Information Counsellor, British Embassy, Paris, 1964–70; Ambassador to Bulgaria, 1970–73; Dep. Permanent UK Rep. to NATO, 1973–75; Ambassador and Permanent Leader, UK Delegn to UN Conf. on Law of the Sea, 1976–77. Leader, UK delegn to Conf. on Marine Living Resources of Antarctica, Buenos Aires and Canberra, 1978–80. Dir, GB/E Europe Centre, 1980–87. Gov., St Clare's Coll., Oxford, 1982–2000 (Chm., 1984–93). Chairman: Jerusalem and the East Mission Trust Ltd, 1981–93; Brompton Assoc., 1986–97; Friends of Bulgaria, 1991–. Vice-Pres., Internat. Exhibitions Bureau, Paris, 1963–67. *Address:* 8 Melton Court, Onslow Crescent, SW7 3JQ. *Clubs:* Brooks's, Royal Automobile.
See also J. C. S. M. Brisby.

LOGAN, (James) Fergus (Graeme); Chief Executive, Arthritis Research Campaign, since 1998; *b* 20 June 1950; *s* of James John Forbes Moffat, (Hamish), Logan and late Lorna Jane Logan; *m* 1977, Wendy Elizabeth Plaskett, *d* of Maj.-Gen. F. J. Plaskett, *qv*; three *s* one *d*. *Educ:* Monmouth Sch. Gen. Sec., Nat. Youth Theatre, 1969–80; Head of Appeals, MENCAP, 1981–86; Head of Ops, UNICEF UK, 1986–88; Develt Dir, Bath Internat. Fest. of the Arts, 1988–90; Dir, Meml Fund for Disaster Relief, 1990; Exec. Dir, Muscular Dystrophy Gp, 1990–97. Founder and Chm., "Batteries not included" (250 charity consortium), 1992–96; Chairman: Exec. Cttee, European Neuromuscular Centre, Baarn, Netherlands, 1992–98; AMRC, 1995–99 (Mem. Exec. Council, 1992–95); Res. for Health Charities Gp, 1996–98. Trustee, Neuromuscular Centre, Winsford, Ches., 1991–97. *Recreations:* family, sport, books, beer. *Address:* Tideswell Lodge, Tideswell, near Buxton, Derbys SK17 8LH. *T:* (01298) 871919.

LOGAN, Joseph Andrew; Chairman, Hay & Kilner, Solicitors, Newcastle, Wallsend and Gosforth, 1998–2001; *b* 5 Nov. 1942; *s* of late Joseph Baird Logan and Hellen Dawson Logan (*née* Wink); *m* 1964, Heather Robertson; one *s* one *d*. *Educ:* Hilton Acad., Aberdeen. Sales Manager: Aberdeen Journals, 1958–69; Newcastle Evening Chronicle, 1969–77; Newcastle Chronicle and Journal: Exec. Asst, 1976–77; Asst Man. Dir, 1979–82; Dir, 1984–89; Man. Dir, 1985–89; Asst Man. Dir, Evening Post, Luton and Evening Echo, Watford, 1977–79; Man. Dir, Peter Reed and Co., 1982; Dep. Man. Dir, Aberdeen Journals, 1982–83 (Dir, 1984); Man. Dir, Scotsman Publications, 1989–94; Pres. and Chief Exec., Thomson Newspaper Corp., Western USA, 1994–97. Director: Weekly Courier Ltd, 1971–89; Thomson Regional Newspapers, 1984–94; Thomson Scottish Organisation Ltd, 1989–94; Northern Rock Building Soc. Scotland, 1989–94 (Dep. Chm., Northern Rock Foundn, 1989–2000). Pres., Scottish Daily Newspaper Soc., 1990–92 (Vice Pres., 1989–90); Trustee, NE Civic Trust, 1984–89; Member: British Airways Consumer Council, 1986–89; Bd, BITC, 1985–89; ScotBIC, 1989–94; Dir, Prince's Scottish Youth Business Trust, 1989–94. Mem. Council, Univ. of Newcastle upon Tyne, 1985–89. *Address:* 5 Burnside, Ponteland, Newcastle upon Tyne NE20 9AQ. *T:* (01661) 822280; *e-mail:* jalogan@onetel.com.

LOGAN, Prof. Malcolm Ian, AC 1996; PhD; Chairman, Education Gateway Holdings Ltd, since 1998; *b* 3 June 1931; *m* 1954, Antoinette, *d* of F. Lalich; one *d*. *Educ:* Univ. of Sydney (BA Hons 1951, DipEd 1952, PhD 1965). Lectr in Geography, Sydney Teachers Coll., 1956–58; Lectr in Geog., 1959–64, Sen. Lectr, 1965–67, Univ. of Sydney; Prof. of Geog. and of Urban and Regional Planning, Univ. of Wisconsin, Madison, USA, 1967–71; Monash University: Prof. of Geog., 1971–81; Pro Vice-Chancellor, 1982–85; Dep. Vice-Chancellor, 1986; Vice-Chancellor, 1987–96. Visiting Professor: Univ. of Ibadan, Nigeria, 1970–71; LSE, 1973; Nanyang Univ., Singapore, 1979. Chm., Open Learning Agency, Australia Pty Ltd, 1993–96. Australian Newspaper Australian of the Year, 1996. *Publications:* (jtly) New Viewpoints in Economic Geography, 1966; Studies in Australian Geography, 1968; New Viewpoints in Urban and Industrial Geography, 1971; Urban and Regional Australia, 1975; Urbanisation, the Australian Experience, 1980; (jtly) The Brittle Rim, 1989; contribs to Aust. Geographical Studies, Regional Studies, Land Econs, and Econ. Geography. *Address:* 1/50 Bourke Street, Melbourne, Vic 3000, Australia. *Clubs:* Athenæum, Melbourne (Melbourne).

LOGAN, Rt Rev. Vincent; *see* Dunkeld, Bishop of, (RC).

LOGAN, William Philip Dowie, MD, PhD, BSc; DPH, FRCP; epidemiological consultant to various national and international organisations, 1974–89; Director, Division of Health Statistics, WHO, 1961–74; *b* 2 Nov. 1914; *s* of late Frederick William Alexander Logan and late Elizabeth Jane Dowie; *m* 1st, Pearl (*née* Piper) (marr. diss.); four *s* two *d* (and one *s* decd); 2nd, Barbara (*née* Huneke). *Educ:* Queen's Park Sch., Glasgow; Univ. of Glasgow (BSc, DPH, MD); PhD London. RAF Med. Branch, 1940–46 (Squadron Leader). Hospital appointments in Glasgow, 1939–40 and 1946. Gen. practice in Barking, Essex, 1947–48; General Register Office, 1948–60 (Chief Medical Statistician, Adviser on Statistics to Ministry of Health, Head of WHO Centre for Classification of Diseases, and Member, WHO panel of experts on Health Statistics). *Publications:* contribs on epidemiology, vital and health statistics in official reports and medical jls. *Address:* 16 Southview Road, Bognor Regis, West Sussex PO22 7JA.

LOGIE, John Robert Cunningham, PhD; FRCS, FRCSE, FRCPSGlas; Consultant General Surgeon, Raigmore Hospital, Inverness, since 1981; Hon. Senior Lecturer in Surgery, Aberdeen University, since 1981; *b* 9 Sept. 1946; *s* of Norman John Logie and Kathleen Margaret Cameron Logie (*née* Neill); *m* 1st, 1981, Sheila Catherine Will (*d* 2001); one *s* one *d*; 2nd, 2004, Carol Joan MacDonald. *Educ:* Robert Gordon's Coll., Aberdeen; Trinity Coll., Glenalmond; Aberdeen Univ. (MB ChB 1970; PhD 1978). FRCSE 1974; FRCS 1975; FRCPSGlas 1993. Various jun. surg. hosp. posts, Aberdeen Royal Infirmary, 1970–75; Lectr in Surgery, Aberdeen Univ., 1975–81. Vice Pres., RCSE, 2006–Oct. 2009 (Mem. Council, 1991–2002; Treas., 2002–06). *Recreations:* breeding waterfowl and pheasants, railways in Britain, opera (especially Wagner). *Address:* The Darroch, Little Cantray, Culloden Moor, Inverness IV2 5EY. *T:* (01463) 792090, *Fax:* (01463) 798478; *e-mail:* john.r.c.logie@lineone.net.

LOGSDAIL, (Christopher) Nicholas (Roald); owner and Managing Director, Lisson Gallery, since 1967; *b* 21 June 1945; *s* of late John Logsdail and Else Logsdail (*née* Dahl); *m* 1st, 1968, Fiona McLean; one *s*; 2nd, 1985, Caroline Mockett; two *s* one *d*. *Educ:* Bryanston Sch.; Slade Sch., University College London. Opened Lisson Gallery, 1967; represents three generations of internationally acclaimed artists: minimal and conceptual artists, incl. Donald Judd, Sol LeWitt and Dan Graham; British sculptors, incl. Richard Deacon, Tony Cragg, Anish Kapoor, Robert Mangold, Lawrence Weiner; new generation of award-winning artists, incl. Santiago Sierra, Tim Lee, Ceal Floyer, Julian Opie, Allora and Calzadilla. Mem., Soc. of London Art Dealers. *Publications:* monographs and artists' books, 1970–. *Recreations:* collecting 20th century art and furniture, paleontology, African studies. *Address:* Lisson Gallery, 52–54 Bell Street, NW1 5DA. *T:* (020) 7724 2739.

LOGUE, Christopher, CBE 2007; writer and poet; *b* 23 Nov. 1926; *s* of John Logue and Molly Logue (*née* Chapman); *m* 1985, Rosemary Hill. *Educ:* Prior Park Coll., Bath; Portsmouth Grammar Sch. Mem., Equity. *Screen plays:* Savage Messiah (dir Ken Russell), 1972; (with Walon Green) Crusoe (based on Defoe's novel), 1989. *Broadcast:* The Arrival of the Poet in the City: a melodrama for narrator and seven musicians (music by George Nicholson), 1985; Strings (melodrama for voice and 14 musicians, with music by Jason Osborn), 1988. *Recordings:* (with Tony Kinsey and Bill Le Sage) Red Bird (poetry and jazz), 1960; Songs from The Establishment (singer Annie Ross), 1962; The Death of Patroclus (with Vanessa Redgrave, Alan Dobie and others), 1963; Audiologue (readings of own poetry set to music), 2001. *Film roles:* Swinburne, in Ken Russell's Dante's Inferno, 1966; John Ball, in John Irvin's The Peasants' Revolt, 1969; Cardinal Richelieu, in Ken Russell's The Devils, 1970; TV and stage roles. Wilfred Owen Award (first), for poetry concerning warfare, 1998. Trans. Baal, by Brecht, perf. 1985. Hon. DLitt Portsmouth, 2007. *Publications: verse:* Wand & Quadrant, 1953; Devil, Maggot & Son, 1956; Songs, 1959; Patrocleia, 1962; ABC, 1966; Pax, 1967; New Numbers, 1969; Twelve Cards, 1972; The Crocodile (illus. Binette Schroeder), 1976; Abecedary (illus. Bert Kitchen), 1977; Ode to the Dodo, 1981; War Music, 1981, Kings, 1991, The Husbands, 1995, collected into one vol. as War Music: an account of Homer's Iliad, 2001; Selected Poems, 1996; All Day Permanent Red: War Music continued, 2003; Cold Calls: War Music continued, 2005 (Whitbread Prize for Poetry, 2005); *prose:* Ratsmagic (illus. Wayne Anderson), 1976; The Magic Circus (illus. Wayne Anderson), 1979; The Bumper Book of True Stories (illus. Bert Kitchen), 1980; *plays:* The Trial of Cob & Leach, 1959; (with Harry Cookson) The Lilywhite Boys, 1959; trans. Hugo Claus, Friday, 1971; trans. Brecht and Weill, The Seven Deadly Sins, 1986; *anthologies:* The Children's Book of Comic Verse, 1979; London in Verse, 1982; Sweet & Sour, 1983; The Oxford Book of Pseuds, 1983; The Children's Book of Children's Rhymes, 1986; *autobiography:* Prince Charming: a memoir, 1999; contrib. Private Eye, The Times, The Sunday Times, etc; *as Count Palmiro Vicarion:* Lust, a pornographic novel, 1957; (ed) Count Palmiro Vicarion's Book of Limericks, 1957; (ed) Count Palmiro Vicarion's Book of Bawdy Ballads, 1957; *relevant publication:* Christopher Logue: a bibliography 1952–1997, by George Ramsden, 1998. *Address:* 41 Camberwell Grove, SE5 8JA.

LOISELLE, Hon. Gilles; PC (Can.) 1990; Advisor to the Chairman, Executive Committee, Power Corporation of Canada, since 1993; *b* 20 May 1929; *s* of Arthur Loiselle and Antoinette Lethiecq; *m* 1962, Lorraine Benoît; one *s* one *d*. *Educ:* Sacred-Heart Coll., Sudbury, Ont; BA Laval. Teacher, Tafari Makonnen Sch., Addis Ababa, 1951–53; Journalist, Le Droit, Ottawa, 1953–56; Haile Selassie First Day Sch., Addis Ababa, 1956–62; Dir, Behrane Zarie Néo Inst., Addis Ababa, 1958–62; Canadian Broadcasting Corporation: Editor, TV French Network, 1962–63; Quebec and Paris correspondent, French Radio and TV Network, 1963–67; Counsellor, Quebec House, Paris, 1967–72; Dir Gen. of Quebec Govt Communications, 1972–76; Pres., Intergovtl Deptl Cttee for Olympic Year, 1976; Dir, Interparly Relations, Quebec Nat. Assembly, 1977; Agent General for Quebec in London, with responsibility for Scandinavian countries, Iceland, and Ireland, 1977–83; Dep. Minister for federal provincial relations, 1983–84, for Cultural Affairs, Quebec, 1984–85; Agent Gen. for Quebec in Rome, 1985–88. MP (PC) Langelier, 1988–93; Minister of State for Finance, 1989–93; Pres., Treasury Bd of Canada, 1990–93; Minister of Finance, 1993. Dir, Mines Richmont Inc. Founder Mem., Assoc. France-Québec, 1969–72. Hon. Col, 55th Bde. *Recreation:* reading. *Address:* Power Corporation of Canada, 751 Victoria Square, Montreal, QC H2Y 2J3, Canada.

LOKOLOKO, Sir Tore, GCMG 1977; GCVO 1982; OBE; Chairman, Indosuez Niugini Bank, 1983–89; *b* 21 Sept. 1930; *s* of Loko Loko Tore and Kevau Sarufa; *m* 1950, Lalahaia Meakoro; four *s* six *d*. *Educ:* Sogeri High Sch., PNG. Dip. in Cooperative, India. Chm., PNG Cooperative Fedn, 1965–68; MP, 1968–77 (two terms); Minister for Health, and Dep. Chm. of National Exec. Council, 1968–72. Rep. PNG: Co-op. Conf., Australia, 1951; S Pacific Conf., Lae, 1964; attended UN Gen. Assembly, 1969, and Trusteeship Council, 1971. Governor-General of Papua New Guinea, 1977–82. KStJ 1979. *Address:* PO Box 5622, Boroko, NCD, Papua New Guinea.

LOLE, Simon Richard Anthony; freelance musician, composer and broadcaster; Director of Music and Master of the Choristers, Salisbury Cathedral, 1997–2005; *b* 23 Dec. 1957; *s* of Margaret and Dennis Lole. *Educ:* St Paul's Cathedral Choir Sch.; King's Coll., London (BMus 1978); Guildhall Sch. of Music. ARCO(CHM). Organist and Choirmaster: Barking Parish Church, 1978–80; Croydon Parish Church, 1980–85; Dir of Music, St Mary's Collegiate Church, Warwick, 1985–94; Master of the Music, Sheffield Cathedral, 1994–97; Actg Dir of Music, Jesus Coll., Cambridge, 2005. Hon. FGCM. *Publications:* many church compositions. *Recreations:* walking, reading, sport. *Address:* 141 Manor Park Road, Glossop, Derbyshire SK13 7SH. *T:* (01457) 861459; *e-mail:* simon@simonlole.com; *web:* www.simonlole.com.

LOMAS, Alfred; *b* 30 April 1928; *s* of Alfred and Florence Lomas; one *s* one *d*. *Educ:* St Paul's Elem. Sch., Stockport; various further educnl estabs. Solicitor's clerk, 1942–46; Radio Telephony Operator, RAF, 1946–49; various jobs, 1949–51; railway signalman, 1951–59; Labour Party Sec./Agent, 1959–65; Polit. Sec., London Co-op., 1965–79. MEP (Lab) London NE, 1979–99; Leader, British Lab Gp, EP, 1985–87. *Publication:* The Common Market—why we should keep out, 1970. *Recreations:* chess, arts, sport. *Address:* 28 Brookway, SE3 9BJ. *T:* (020) 8852 6689. *Club:* Hackney Labour.

LOMAS, Prof. David Arthur, ScD, PhD; FRCP, FMedSci; Professor of Respiratory Biology, University of Cambridge, since 1998; Deputy Director, Cambridge Institute for Medical Research, since 2002; Hon. Consultant Physician, Addenbrooke's and Papworth

Hospitals, since 1995; *b* 19 Feb. 1962; *s* of Peter Harry Lomas and Margaret Lomas (*née* Halsall); *m* 1987, Judith Amanda Glasbey; three *s*. *Educ:* Univ. of Nottingham (BMedSci 1983; BM BS Hons 1985); Trinity Coll., Cambridge (PhD 1993); ScD Cambridge 2004. MRCP 1988, FRCP 1997; ILTM 2000. SHO, Central Birmingham HA, 1986–88; Registrar, Gen. Hosp., Birmingham, 1988–90; MRC Trng Fellow, and Mem., Trinity Coll., Cambridge, 1990–93; MRC Clinician Scientist Fellow, Cambridge, 1993–95; Lectr in Medicine, Univ. of Cambridge, 1995–98. Croonian Lectr, RCP, 2005. FMedSci 2001. Res. Award, BUPA Foundn, 1996; Oon Internat. Prize in Preventative Medicine, Downing Coll., Cambridge, 1996; Biochem. Soc. GSK Prize, 2004. *Publications:* res. on α_1-antitrypsin deficiency and conformational diseases in med. jls. *Recreations:* family life, cricket, walking, modern literature. *Address:* Respiratory Medicine Unit, Department of Medicine, University of Cambridge, Cambridge Institute for Medical Research, Wellcome Trust/MRC Building, Hills Road, Cambridge CB2 0XY. *T:* (01223) 762818.

LOMAS, Prof. David John, FRCP, FRCR; Amersham Professor of Clinical Magnetic Resonance Imaging, University of Cambridge, since 2001; *b* 21 March 1957; *s* of Geoffrey and Sheila Lomas; *m* 1986, Rebecca Steward; two *d*. *Educ:* Emmanuel Coll., Cambridge (MA Engrg; MB BChir). MRCP 1985, FRCP 1998; FRCR 1989. Medical Registrar, Princess Margaret Hosp., Swindon, 1985–87; Radiology Registrar, 1987–93, Hon. Consultant Radiologist and Univ. Lectr, 1993–2001, Addenbrooke's Hosp., Cambridge. Vis. Scientist, Mayo Clinic, USA, 1993. *Publications:* contrib. papers to Clinical Radiol., Radiol., Science, Jl Magnetic Resonance Imaging, British Jl Radiol. *Recreations:* industrial archaeology, photography, plumbing. *Address:* University Department of Radiology, Box 219, Addenbrooke's Hospital, Hills Road, Cambridge CB2 2QQ. *T:* (01223) 336890, *Fax:* (01223) 330915.

LOMAS, Eric George; Managing Director, Gatwick Airport, 1994–97; *b* 26 June 1938; *s* of Arthur Edward Lomas and Florence Lomas; *m* 1959, Carol Letitia Davies; two *d*. *Educ:* Willesden County Grammar School; Templeton Coll., Oxford (Sen. Exec. Leadership Prog.); Cranfield Inst. (Computer Prog.). FCIT. PLA, 1954–69; served with RE, 1957–59; Associated Container Transportation, 1969–70; BAA, 1970–86, BAA plc, 1986–97; Man. Dir, Stansted Airport, 1989–94. Trustee Dir, BAA Pension Fund Co. Ltd, 2003–06. Dir, Sussex TEC, 1995–97. Mem., SE Reg., CBI, 1995–97. Chm., Lapwing Flying Club Ltd, 1979–82. Member: Petersham Book Club; Square Rigger Club. *Recreations:* reading, boating.

LOMAS, Julia Carole; Partner, Irwin Mitchell, Solicitors, since 2002 (Consultant, 2000–02); *b* 9 Dec. 1954; *d* of Charles James Lomas and Sadie Lomas; *m* (marr. diss.); one *s*. *Educ:* Lanchester Poly. (BA Business Law). Admitted solicitor, 1980. Articled clerk, London Borough of Islington, 1977–80; Dep. Borough Solicitor, London Borough of Waltham Forest, 1980–89; Borough Solicitor, London Borough of Haringey, 1989–94; Public Trustee, and Chief Exec., Public Trust Office, 1994–99. FCMI (FIMgt 1994). *Recreations:* theatre, crosswords, dining out. *Address:* Irwin Mitchell, 150 Holborn, EC1N 2NS.

LOMAS, Mark Henry; QC 2003; *b* 17 Nov. 1948; *s* of Keith and Margaret Lomas; *m* 1980, Caroline Margaret Mary Agnew; three *d*. *Educ:* Oundle Sch.; Trinity Hall, Cambridge (BA Hons, MA). Called to the Bar, Middle Temple, 1977; in practice as barrister, specialising in professional negligence, 1977–; Accredited Mediator, 2001. *Recreations:* hunting, shooting, salmon fishing. *Address:* Littleton Chambers, 3 King's Bench Walk North, Temple, EC4Y 7HR. *Club:* Boodle's.

LOMAX, (Janis) Rachel; Deputy Governor, Bank of England, 2003–08; *b* 15 July 1945; *d* of William and Dilys Salmon; *m* 1967, Michael Acworth Lomax (marr. diss. 1990); two *s*. *Educ:* Cheltenham Ladies' Coll.; Girton Coll., Cambridge (MA); LSE (MSc). HM Treasury: Econ. Assistant, 1968; Econ. Advr, 1972; Sen. Econ. Advr, 1978; Principal Pvte Sec. to Chancellor of the Exchequer, 1985–86; Under-Sec., 1986–90; Dep. Chief Econ. Advr, 1990–92; Dep. Sec. (Financial Instns and Markets), 1992–94; Dep. Sec., Cabinet Office, 1994–95; Vice Pres. and Chief of Staff, World Bank, 1995–96; Permanent Secretary: Welsh Office, 1996–99; DSS, then DWP, 1999–2002; DTLR, then Dept for Transport, 2002–03. Pres., IFS, 2007–. Mem. Bd, RNT, 2002–. Gov., De Montfort Univ., 1997–2007; Mem. Court, LSE, 2003–08. *Address:* 25 Henning Street, SW11 3DR.

LOMAX, Kevin John; Founder, Misys plc, 1979 (Chairman, 1985–2005; Chief Executive Officer, 2005–06); *b* 8 Dec. 1948; *s* of Brig. Kenneth John Lomax and Mary Lomax (*née* Foley); *m* 1975, Penelope Frances Flynn; one *s* two *d*. *Educ:* Ampleforth Coll.; Manchester Univ. (BSc Hons 1970). Advanced Project Manager, J & S Pumps Ltd, 1970–73; Asst to Divl Chm., Allied Polymer Gp, 1973–75; Managing Director: British Furnaces Ltd, 1975–77; Wellman Incandescent Ltd, 1977–80; Dir and Divl Chm., Caparo Industries (CMT) Ltd, 1980–83; Dir and Divl CEO, Electronic Components Div., STC plc, 1983–85. Non-exec. Dir, Marks & Spencer, 2000–06. Hon. DSc Birmingham, 2003. *Recreations:* golf, shooting, fishing, horse-racing, military history, music. *Address:* Hawling Manor, Hawling, Cheltenham, Glos GL54 5TA.

LOMAX, Rachel; *see* Lomax, J. R.

LOMBARD, Rt Rev. Charles F.; *see* Fitzgerald-Lombard.

LOMBE, Hon. Sir Edward Christopher E.; *see* Evans-Lombe.

LOMER, Dennis Roy, CBE 1984; Member, Central Electricity Generating Board, 1977–83; *b* 5 Oct. 1923; *s* of Bertie Cecil Lomer and Agnes Ellen Coward; *m* 1949, Audrey May Bick; one *s* one *d*. With Consulting Engineers, 1948–50; joined Electricity Supply Industry, 1950; Project Engr, Transmission Div., 1961; Asst Chief Transmission Engr, 1965; Generation Construction Div. (secondment at Dir level), 1972; Dep. Dir-Gen. (Projects), 1973; Dir-Gen., Transmission Div., 1975; Mem., Technical Review Gp for Eurotunnel, 1988–92. Dir, Davidson Gp Ltd, 1983–88. Pres., 1985–87, non-exec. Dir, 1988–94, Welding Inst; Hon. FWeldI. FIET; CIMgt. *Recreations:* golf, sailing. *Address:* Henley House, Heathfield Close, Woking, Surrey GU22 7JQ. *T:* (01483) 764656. *Club:* West Hill Golf (Surrey).

LOMER, Geoffrey John, CBE 1985; MA; FREng; FIET; Chairman, Satellite Information Services Ltd, 1993–96; Director (non-executive), Vodafone Group plc, 1992–97; *b* 5 Jan. 1932; *s* of Frederick John Lomer and Dorothy Lomer; *m* 1st, 1955, Pauline Helena May (*d* 1974); one *s* one *d*; 2nd, 1977, Antoinette Ryall (*d* 2003); one step *s* one step *d*. *Educ:* St Austell Grammar School; Queens' College, Cambridge (MA). FREng (FEng 1984). Research Engineer, EMI Research Laboratories, 1953–57; Head of Radio Frequency Div., Broadcast Equipment Dept, EMI Electronics, 1957–63; Head of Transmitter Lab., Racal Communications, 1963–68; Technical Dir, Racal Mobilcal, 1968–70; Dir in Charge, Racal Communications Equipment, 1970–76; Dep. Man. Dir, Racal Tacticom, 1976–77; Technical Dir, Racal Electronics plc, 1977–92. Vice Pres., IEE, 1991–94; Hon. FIET (Hon. FIEE 1998). *Recreations:* music, theatre. *Address:* Ventana, The Devil's Highway, Crowthorne, Berks RG45 6BJ.

See also W. M. Lomer.

LOMER, William Michael, PhD; Director, Culham Laboratory, United Kingdom Atomic Energy Authority, 1981–90, retired; *b* 2 March 1926; *s* of Frederick John Lomer and Dorothy Lomer; *m* 1952, Pamela Anne Wakelin; one *s* two *d*. *Educ:* St Austell County School; University College of the South West, Exeter (MSc London); Queens' College, Cambridge (MA, PhD). Research Scientist, UKAEA, 1952; AERE Harwell: Division Head, Theory Div., 1958–62; Division Head, Solid State Physics, 1962–68; Research Director, 1968–81; Dep. Dir, Inst. Laue Langevin, Grenoble, 1973–74. Hon. Treasurer, Inst. of Physics, 1980–82. Chm., Oxford CAB, 1994–97. Trustee, Oxford Trust, 1991–2005. FInstP. *Publications:* papers in physics and metallurgical jls. *Recreations:* gardening, walking, painting. *Address:* 7 Hids Copse Road, Cumnor Hill, Oxford OX2 9JJ. *T:* (01865) 862173.

See also G. J. Lomer.

LONDESBOROUGH, 9th Baron *cr* 1850; **Richard John Denison;** *b* 2 July 1959; *s* of John Albert Lister, 8th Baron Londesborough, TD, AMICE, and Elizabeth Ann (*d* 1994), *d* of late Edward Little Sale, ICS; *S* father, 1968; *m* 1987, Rikki Morris, *d* of J. E. Morris, Bayswater; one *s* one *d*. *Educ:* Wellington College; Exeter Univ. *Heir:* *s* Hon. James Frederick Denison, *b* 4 June 1990. *Address:* Edw Cottage, Aberedw, Builth Wells, Powys LD2 3UR.

LONDON, Bishop of, since 1995; **Rt Rev. and Rt Hon. Richard John Carew Chartres;** PC 1995; Prelate of the Order of the British Empire, since 1995; Dean of the Chapels Royal, since 1995; *b* 11 July 1947; *s* of Richard and Charlotte Chartres; *m* 1982, Caroline Mary, *d* of Sir (Charles) Alan McLintock; two *s* two *d*. *Educ:* Hertford Grammar Sch.; Trinity Coll., Cambridge (BA 1968; MA 1973); Cuddesdon Theol Coll., Oxford; Lincoln Theol Coll. Ordained: deacon, 1973; priest, 1974; Asst Curate, St Andrew's, Bedford, dio. of St Albans, 1973–75; Bishop's Domestic Chaplain, St Albans, 1975–80; Archbishop of Canterbury's Chaplain, 1980–84; Vicar, St Stephen with St John, Westminster, 1984–92; Director of Ordinands for London Area, 1985–92; Area Bishop of Stepney, 1992–95. Chairman: Churches Main Cttee, 1998–2001; C of E Heritage Forum, 1998–. Mem., Central Cttee, Conf. of European Chs. Gresham Prof. of Divinity, 1986–92. Six Preacher, Canterbury Cathedral, 1991–96. Hon. Bencher, Middle Temple, 1998. Liveryman: Merchant Taylors' Co., 1997; Drapers' Co., 2000; Hon. Freeman: Weavers' Co., 1998; Leathersellers' Co., 1999; Woolmen's Co., 2000; Vintners' Co., 2001. FSA 1999. Ehrendomprediger, Berliner Dom, 2001. BD Lambeth, 1983. Hon. DLitt London Guildhall, 1998; Hon. DD: London, 1999; City, 1999; Brunel, 1999. *Publications:* The History of Gresham College 1597–1997, 1998; Tree of Knowledge, Tree of Life, 2005. *Address:* The Old Deanery, Dean's Court, EC4V 5AA. *T:* (020) 7248 6233.

LONDON, Archdeacon of; *see* Delaney, Ven. P. A.

LONDONDERRY, 9th Marquess of, *cr* 1816; **Alexander Charles Robert Vane-Tempest-Stewart;** Baron Londonderry, 1789; Viscount Castlereagh, 1795; Earl of Londonderry, 1796; Baron Stewart, 1814; Earl Vane, Viscount Seaham, 1823; *b* 7 Sept. 1937; *s* of 8th Marquess of Londonderry and Romaine (*d* 1951), *er d* of Major Boyce Combe, Great Holt, Dockenfield, Surrey; *S* father, 1955; *m* 1st, 1958, Nicolette (marr. diss. 1971; she *d* 1993), *d* of Michael Harrison, Netherhampton, near Salisbury, Wilts; two *d*; 2nd, 1972, Doreen Patricia Wells, *qv* (marr. diss. 1989); two *s*. *Educ:* Eton. *Heir:* *s* Viscount Castlereagh, *qv*. *Address:* PO Box No 8, Shaftesbury, Dorset SP7 0LR.

LONDONDERRY, Doreen, Marchioness of; *see* Wells, D. P.

LONG, family name of **Viscount Long**.

LONG, 4th Viscount *cr* 1921, of Wraxall; **Richard Gerard Long,** CBE 1993; *b* 30 Jan. 1929; *s* of 3rd Viscount and Gwendolyn (*d* 1959), *d* of Thomas Reginald Hague Cook; *S* father, 1967; *m* 1957, Margaret Frances (marr. diss. 1984), *d* of late Ninian B. Frazer; one *s* one *d* (and one *d* decd); *m* 1984, Catherine Patricia Elizabeth Mier-Woolf (marr. diss. 1990); *m* 1990, Helen Fleming-Gibbons. *Educ:* Harrow. Wilts Regt, 1947–49. Opposition Whip, 1974–79; a Lord in Waiting (Govt Whip), 1979–97. Vice-Pres. and formerly Vice-Chm., Wilts Royal British Legion. Freeman, City of London, 1991. *Heir:* *s* Hon. James Richard Long, *b* 31 Dec. 1960. *Address:* The Island, Newquay, Cornwall TR7 1EA. *Club:* Pratt's.

LONG, Prof. Adrian Ernest, OBE 2006; PhD, DSc; FREng, FIAE; Professor of Civil Engineering, Queen's University, Belfast, 1976–2006, now Professor Emeritus; *b* 15 April 1941; *s* of Charles Long and Sylvia Long; *m* 1967, Elaine Thompson; one *s* one *d*. *Educ:* Royal Sch., Dungannon; QUB (BSc 1st cl. Hons (Civil Engrg) 1963; PhD (Structural Engrg) 1967; DSc (Civil Engrg) 1984). Bridge design engr, Foundn Engrg Co. of Canada, Toronto, 1967–68; Asst Prof., Dept of Civil Engrg, Queen's Univ., Kingston, Ont, 1968–71; Queen's University, Belfast: Lectr, 1971–76, Hd, 1977–89, Dept of Civil Engrg; Dean, Fac. of Engrg, 1988–91, 1998–2002; Dir, Sch. of Built Envmt, 1989–98. Pres., ICE, 2002–03. Hon. UK Rep., Tech. Cttee, EU Co-operation Sci. and Technol. Urban Civil Engrg, 1991–2006; Chm., Civil Engrg Sub-Panel, Res. Assessment Exercise for UK, 2008. Ed., Jl of Engrg Structures, 1986–94. FREng 1989; Founder FIAE, 1998. Hon. DSc City, 2007. (Jtly) Esso Energy Gold Medal, Royal Soc., 1994. *Publications:* over 300 tech. papers in jls and procs of confs. *Recreations:* walking, travel, gardening, occasional golf, Elder in a Presbyterian Church in Belfast. *Address:* School of Civil Engineering, Queen's University, Belfast, Belfast BT7 1NN. *T:* (028) 9097 4005, *Fax:* (028) 9066 3754; *e-mail:* a.long@qub.ac.uk.

LONG, Athelstan Charles Ethelwulf, CMG 1968; CBE 1964 (MBE 1959); Chairman, International Management Group, since 1988; Chairman, Public Service Commission, since 1987; Deputy Chairman, Public Service Pensions Board, since 1992; *b* 2 Jan. 1919; *s* of Arthur Leonard Long and Gabrielle Margaret Campbell (historical writer and novelist, Marjorie Bowen); *m* 1948, Edit Mäjken Zadie Harriet Krantz, *d* of late Erik Krantz, Stockholm; two *s*. *Educ:* Westminster Sch.; Brasenose Coll., Oxford. Served War of 1939–45: commnd into RA, 1940; seconded 7th (Bengal) Battery, 22nd Mountain Regt, IA, 1940; served Malaya; POW as Capt., 1942–45; appointed to Indian Political Service, 1946. Cadet, Burma Civil Service, 1947–48; Colonial Admin. Service (N Nigeria), 1948; Sen. District Officer, 1958; Resident, Zaria Province, 1959; Perm. Sec., Min. of Animal Health and Forestry, 1959; started new Min. of Information as Perm. Sec., 1960; Swaziland: appointed Govt Sec., 1961; Chief Sec., 1964; Leader of Govt business in Legislative Council and MEC, 1964–67; HM Dep. Comr, 1967–68; Administrator, later Governor, of the Cayman Is, 1968–71; Comr of Anguilla, March–July 1972; Admin. Sec., Inter-University Council, 1972–73. Man. Dir, Anegada Corp. Ltd, 1973–74; Pres., United Bank Internat., Cayman Is, 1976–96; Dir and Chm., Cayman Airways, 1977–81. Chairman: Planning Appeals Tribunal, 1982–84; Coastal Works Adv. Cttee, 1986–91. Chm. Governing Council, Waterford Sch., Swaziland, 1963–68. FRAS; FRGS. *Recreations:* travel, tropical farming, reading. *Address:* Box 131, Savannah, Grand Cayman, Cayman Islands, West Indies.

LONG, Christopher William, CMG 1986; HM Diplomatic Service, retired; *b* 9 April 1938; *s* of late Eric and May Long; *m* 1972, Patricia, *d* of late Dennis and May Stanbridge; two *s* one *d*. *Educ:* King Edward's Sch., Birmingham; Balliol Coll., Oxford (Deakin Scholar); Univ. of Münster, W Germany. Served RN, 1956–58. HM Diplomatic Service, 1963–98: FO, 1963–64; Jedda, 1965–67; Caracas, 1967–69; FCO, 1969–74; Budapest, 1974–77; Belgrade (CSCE), 1977; Counsellor, Damascus, 1978–80; Counsellor and Dep. Perm. Rep., UKMIS, Geneva, 1980–83; Head, Near East and N Africa Dept, FCO, 1983–85; Asst Under-Sec. of State (Dep. Chief Clerk and Chief Inspector), FCO, 1985–88; Ambassador: to Switzerland, 1988–92 and also to Liechtenstein, 1992; to Egypt, 1992–95; to Hungary, 1995–98. Dir, Foreign Service Prog., Oxford Univ., 1999–2003. Non-executive Director: Gideon Richter plc, Budapest, 1998–; KFKI Computer Systems Corp., Budapest, 2001–04. Dir, World Faiths Develt Dialogue, 2004–05. Trustee, Orders of St John Care Trust, 2003–. Gov., Prior Park Coll., Bath, 2000–. *Address:* 7 Old Pye Street, SW1P 2LD. *Club:* Athenæum.

LONG, Hubert Arthur, CBE 1970; Deputy Secretary, Exchequer and Audit Department, 1963–73; *b* 21 Jan. 1912; *s* of Arthur Albert Long; *m* 1937, Mary Louise Parker; three *s*. *Educ:* Taunton's Sch., Southampton. Entered Exchequer and Audit Department, 1930. *Address:* 2A Hawthorndene Road, Hayes, Kent BR2 7DY. *T:* (020) 8462 4373.

LONG, Ian Andrew; Director, Housing and City Support Services, Brighton and Hove City Council, since 2003; *b* 8 Nov. 1952; *s* of late Peter Long and Jean Long; *m* 2000, Sasha Cockrell; three *s* two *d*. *Educ:* Univ. of Portsmouth (BSc Social Policy 1974); Univ. of Southampton (CQSW 1977). Social Services Depts, LBCs of Haringey and Brent, 1996–83, E Sussex CC, 1983–96; Asst Dir, Adult Social Care, Brighton and Hove CC, 1996–2000; Dir, Community Care, S Downs Health NHS Trust, 2000–03. *Recreations:* various sports, reading, music, family activities. *Address:* (office) PO Box 2501, King's House, Grand Avenue, Hove, E Sussex BN3 2SS. *Fax:* (01273) 295114; *e-mail:* ian.long@brighton-hove.gov.uk.

LONG, John Richard, CBE 1987; voluntary adviser, Citizens Advice Bureau, Farnborough; *b* 9 March 1931; *s* of late Thomas Kendall Long and Jane Long; *m* 1952, Margaret (*née* Thistlethwaite); one *s* two *d*. *Educ:* Kirkham Grammar School; Dip. in EU Law, KCL, 1993. Clerical Officer, Customs and Excise, 1947; Exec. Officer, Min. of Pensions, subseq. DHSS, 1949; various posts on health functions; Asst Sec., 1978 (posts on regulation and pricing of medicines, maternity and child health, and communicable diseases); Under Sec., 1987 (NHS Personnel Div.), resigned 1988. Fundraiser at Frimley Park Hosp. *Publications:* co-author, articles on regulation of medicines. *Recreations:* golf, vegetable growing, wild life. *Address:* 77 Prospect Road, Farnborough, Hants GU14 8NT. *T:* (01252) 548525.

LONG, Martin Paul; Chairman: Churchill Properties (Southern) Ltd, since 2003; Ashworth Mairs Group, since 2005; AMG (Chartered Loss Adjusters), since 2005; M4 Underwriting Ltd, since 2006; *b* 27 Aug. 1950; *s* of Robert and Alice Long; five *s* one *d*. *Educ:* St Joseph's Coll., SE19. FCII 1981. Prudential Assce Co., 1968–69; Guardian Royal Exchange Assce Co., 1970–74; Sphere Drake Insce Co., 1975–78; Northern Star Insce Co., 1979–83; Man. Dir, Halifax Insce Co., 1983–84; Dir and Gen. Manager, Direct Line Insce, 1984–87; setting up Churchill Insce Gp, 1987–89; Founder Chm. and CEO, Churchill Insurance Gp plc, 1989–2003; Dep. Chm., Royal Bank of Scotland Insurance, 2003–04. Owner of Sweetwoods Park Golf Course. *Recreations:* sports (watching and playing), socialising, spending time with my sons. *Address:* Churchill Properties (Southern) Ltd, c/o K. A. Jeffries & Co., 18 Melbourne Grove, SE22 8RA. *T:* (01883) 650367; *e-mail:* bigm@churchill-properties.com.

LONG, Naomi Rachel; Member (Alliance) Belfast East, Northern Ireland Assembly, since 2003; *b* 13 Dec. 1971; *d* of James Dobbin Johnston and Olive Emily Johnston; *m* 1995, Michael Andrew Long. *Educ:* Mersey Street Primary Sch.; Bloomfield Collegiate Grammar Sch.; Queen's Univ., Belfast (MEng Dist. Civil Engrg 1994). Asst Engr, Parkman Consulting Engrs, 1994–96; Res. Asst, QUB, 1996–99; Graduate Civil and Envmtl Engr, Mulholland & Doherty, 1999–2003. Mem. (Alliance), Belfast CC, 2001–. Vice Chm., Cttee for Office of First and Dep. First Minister, NI Assembly, 2007–. Dep. Leader, Alliance Party of NI, 2006–. *Recreations:* Guide leader, reading, travel, choral singing. *Address:* East Belfast Alliance Constituency Office, 26 Upper Newtownards Road, Belfast BT4 3EL. *T:* (028) 9047 2004, *Fax:* (028) 9065 6408; *e-mail:* naomi.long@allianceparty.org.

LONG, Richard, RA 2001; artist; *b* 2 June 1945; *s* of Maurice Long and Frances Carpenter; *m* 1969, Denise Johnston (marr. diss. 1999); two *d*. *Educ:* West of England Coll. of Art, Bristol; St Martin's Sch. of Art, London. *Exhibitions include:* Mus. of Modern Art, NYC, 1972; Scottish Nat. Gall. of Modern Art, Edinburgh, 1974; Venice Biennale, 1976; Nat. Gall. of Victoria, Melbourne, 1977; Fogg Art Mus., Harvard Univ., 1980; Nat. Gall. of Canada, Ottawa, 1982; Century Cultural Centre, Tokyo, 1983; Guggenheim, NYC (retrospective), 1986; Tate Gall., 1990; Hayward Gall. (retrospective), 1991; ARC, Paris, 1993; Kunstsammlung Nordrhein-Westfalen, Düsseldorf, 1994; Palazzo Dell Esposizioni, Rome, 1994; Guggenheim, Bilbao, 2000; Royal Acad. (one-man), 2004; Scottish Nat. Gall. of Modern Art, 2007. Turner Prize, 1989. *Publications include:* South America, 1972; Twelve Works, 1981; Countless Stones, 1983; Stone Water Miles, 1987; (with Anne Seymour) Old World New World, 1988; Nile, 1990; Walking in Circles, 1991; Mountains and Waters, 1992; River to River, 1993; Mirage, 1997; A Walk Across England, 1997; Every Grain of Sand, 1999; Midday, 2001; Walking the Line, 2003; Walking and Sleeping, 2005; Dartmoor, 2006. *Address:* c/o Haunch of Venison, 6 Haunch of Venison Yard, W1K 5ES.

LONGAIR, Deborah Janet; *see* Howard, D. J.

LONGAIR, Prof. Malcolm Sim, CBE 2000; PhD; FRS 2004; FRSE 1981; Jacksonian Professor of Natural Philosophy, 1991–2008, Head of Department of Physics, 1998–2005, and Director of Research, since 2008, Cavendish Laboratory, University of Cambridge; Professorial Fellow, Clare Hall, Cambridge, 1991–2008, now Emeritus; *b* 18 May 1941; *s* of James Sim Longair and Lily Malcolm; *m* 1975, Prof. Deborah Janet Howard, *qv*; one *s* one *d*. *Educ:* Morgan Acad., Dundee; Queen's Coll., Dundee, Univ. of St Andrews (BSc Electronic Physics, 1963); Cavendish Lab., Univ. of Cambridge (MA, PhD 1967). Res. Fellow, Royal Commn for Exhibn of 1851, 1966–68; Royal Soc. Exchange Fellow to USSR, 1968–69; University of Cambridge: Res. Fellow, 1967–71, and Official Fellow, 1971–80, Clare Hall; Univ. Demonstrator in Phys., 1970–75; Univ. Lectr in Phys., 1975–80; Astronomer Royal for Scotland, Regius Prof. of Astronomy, Univ. of Edinburgh, and Dir, Royal Observatory, Edinburgh, 1980–90. Visiting Professor: of Radio Astronomy, Calif Inst. of Technol., 1972; of Astronomy, Inst. for Advanced Study, Princeton, 1978; Space Telescope Sci. Inst., 1997; Regents' Fellow, Carnegie Inst., Harvard Univ., 1990. Pres., RAS, 1996–98 (Editor, Monthly Notices, 1974–78). Foreign Member: Accad. Nazionale dei Lincei, 2000; Istituto Veneto di Scienze, Lettere ed Arte, 2007. Hon. LLD Dundee, 1982. Britannica Award, 1986. *Publications:* (ed) Confrontation of Cosmological Theories with Observational Data, 1974; (ed with J. Einasto) The Large-Scale Structure of the Universe, 1978; (with J. E. Gunn and M. J. Rees) Observational Cosmology, 1978; (ed with J. Warner) The Scientific Uses of the Space Telescope, 1980; High Energy Astrophysics: an informal introduction, 1980, rev. edn as High Energy Astrophysics, vol. 1: Particles, Photons and their Detection, 1992; High Energy Astrophysics, vol. 2: Stars, the Galaxy and the Interstellar Medium, 1994; (ed with H. A. Brück and G. Coyne) Astrophysical Cosmology, 1982; Theoretical Concepts in Physics, 1984, 2nd edn 2003; Alice and the Space Telescope, 1989; The Origins of Our Universe, 1991; (with A. R. Sandage and R. G. Kron) The Deep Universe, 1995; Our Evolving Universe, 1996; Galaxy Formation, 1998, 2nd edn 2008; The Cosmic Century: a history of astrophysics and cosmology, 2006; over 200 papers, mostly in Monthly Notices of RAS. *Recreations:* music, art, architecture, mountain walking. *Address:* c/o Cavendish Laboratory, J. J. Thomson Avenue, Cambridge CB3 0HE. *T:* (01223) 765953.

LONGBOTHAM, Tom; His Honour Judge Longbotham; a Circuit Judge, since 1999; *b* 9 Aug. 1942; *s* of George Ferrand Longbotham and Elizabeth Ann Longbotham; *m* 1964, Eirlys Thomas; one *s* (and one *s* decd). *Educ:* Rossall Sch.; Bristol Univ. (LLB). Admitted Solicitor, 1966; Sen. Litigation Partner, Bishop Longbotham & Bagnall, Solicitors, until 1999; Asst Recorder, 1990–95; a Recorder, 1995–99. *Recreations:* golf, gardening, hill walking, theatre. *Club:* West Wiltshire Golf.

LONGBOTTOM, Charles Brooke; company director; Chairman, Trinity Foundation for Christianity and Culture, since 2003; *b* 22 July 1930; *s* of late William Ewart Longbottom, Forest Hill, Worksop; *m* 1962, Anita, *d* of G. Trapani and Mrs Basil Mavroleon; two *d*. *Educ:* Uppingham. Contested (C) Stockton-on-Tees, 1955; MP (C) York, 1959–66; Parly Private Secretary to Mr Iain Macleod, Leader of the House, 1961–63. Barrister, Inner Temple, 1958; Chairman: Austin & Pickersgill, Shipbuilders, Sunderland, 1966–72; A&P Appledore International Ltd, 1970–79; Seascope Holdings Ltd, 1970–82; Seascope Sale & Purchase, 1970–87; Seascope Shipping Ltd, 1982–87; Seascope Insurance Holdings Ltd, 1984–86; Seascope Insurance Services Ltd, 1984–87; Illingworth Morris Pension Trustees Ltd, 1990–94; Director: Henry Ansbacher Hldgs Ltd, 1982–87; Henry Ansbacher & Co., 1982–87; Ansbacher (Guernsey) Ltd, 1982–87; British Shipbuilders, 1986–2002; Kelt Energy plc, 1988–95; MC Shipping Inc., 1989–2007 (Chm., 2004–07); Newman Martin & Buchan, 1992–2000. Member: General Advisory Council, BBC, 1965–75; Community Relations Commn, 1968–70. Trustee, 1983–2002, Chm., 1988–2001, Acorn Christian Healing Trust, then Acorn Christian Foundn. *Recreations:* golf, travel. *Address:* 66 Kingston House North, Princes Gate, SW7 1LN. *Clubs:* White's, Carlton; Berkshire.

LONGDEN, Wilson; JP; industrial relations consultant, 1987–2005; *b* 26 May 1936; *s* of late Harold and Doris Longden; *m* 1st, 1966 (marr. diss. 1982); two *s*; 2nd, 1985, Olga Longden (marr. diss. 1993). *Educ:* Chesterfield Grammar Sch.; Univ. of Hull (BA Hons, Dip Ed); Univ. of Bradford (MSc). National service, RAF, 1955–57; Teacher, Northmount High Sch., Canada, 1961–62; Lecturer: Matthew Boulton Tech. Coll., Birmingham, 1962–66; Bingley Coll. of Educn, 1966–67; Margaret McMillan Coll. of Educn, 1967–68; Hatfield Polytechnic, 1968–69; Coventry (Lanchester) Polytechnic, 1969–73; Vice-Principal, Barnfield College, Luton, 1973–87. Sec., Assoc. of Vice-Principals of Colleges, 1986–87 (Pres., 1982–84). Comr, MSC, 1983–85. JP Luton, 1980; Mem., Beds Magistrates' Courts Cttee, 1998–2000. *Publications:* The School Manager's and the School Governor's Handbook, 1977; Meetings, 1977, 2nd edn 1997; Making Secondments Work, 1990. *Recreations:* music, playing the piano, family history. *Address:* 311 Turnpike Drive, Luton LU3 3RE. *T:* (01582) 658695; *e-mail:* wilsonlongden@hotmail.com.

LONGDON, Patricia Joyce; Deputy Parliamentary and Health Service Ombudsman, 2003–08; *b* 19 Jan. 1952; *d* of Fred and Nell Morgan; *m* 1st (marr. diss. 1987); 2nd, 1995, Mick Penny; one step *s* two step *d*. *Educ:* Brighton and Hove High Sch.; UCL (BSc 1st cl. Hons 1973); Sch. of Envmtl Studies, London (MPhil 1977). DoE, 1973–80; London Rape Crisis Centre, 1980–83; Asst Dir, Local Govt Ombudsman, 1983–89; Dir, People Develt, Audit Commn, 1989–2003. *Recreations:* family and friends, reading, listening to classical music, climbing mountains, exploring the world.

LONGFIELD, Anne Elizabeth, OBE 2000; Chief Executive (formerly Director), 4Children (formerly Kids' Clubs Network), since 1994; *b* 5 July 1960; *d* of James Vincent Longfield and Jean Elizabeth Longfield; partner, Richard Reeve; one *s*. *Educ:* Prince Henry's Grammar Sch., Otley; Univ. of Newcastle upon Tyne (BA Hons History). Researcher, Save the Children Fund, 1982–83; community develt in London, 1983–87; Develt, Kids' Clubs Network, 1987–93. Performance and Innovation Unit, Cabinet Office, 2001–02. FRSA 1998. *Publications:* articles on children, families, communities and inequalities. *Recreations:* family, gardening, cycling, heritage. *Address:* c/o 4Children, City Reach, 5 Greenwich View Place, E14 9NN. *T:* (020) 7512 2112.

LONGFIELD, Dr Michael David; Vice-Chancellor, University of Teesside, 1992 (Director, Teesside Polytechnic, 1980–92), retired; *b* 28 April 1928; *s* of late Edric Douglas Longfield and Dorothy Longfield (*née* Hennessey); *m* 1st, 1952, Ann McDonnell; two *s* two *d*; 2nd, 1970, June Shirley, *d* of late Levi and Esther Beman; two *s*. *Educ:* Prince Henry's Grammar Sch., Otley; Leeds Univ. BSc, PhD; CEng, MIMechE. Lectr in Mech. Engrg, Univ. of Leeds, 1960–68; Manager, Leeds Univ. Industrial Unit of Tribology, 1968–70; Head of Dept of Mech., Marine and Production Engrg, Liverpool Polytechnic, 1970–72; Asst Dir, Teesside Poly., 1972–80. Hon. DSc Teesside, 1996. *Recreation:* the genealogy of the Longfields. *Address:* 16 Firs Road, Harrogate HG2 8RD.

LONGFORD, Earldom of; *cr* 1785; title not used by 8th Earl (*see* Pakenham, T. F. D.).

LONGHURST, Andrew Henry, FCIB; FBCS; Deputy Chairman, Royal London Assurance Society Ltd, 2000–02; *b* 23 Aug. 1939; *s* of Henry and Connie Longhurst; *m* 1962, Margaret; one *s* two *d*. *Educ:* Nottingham University (BSc Hons). FBCS 1968; FCIB (FCBSI 1990). Computer systems consultancy, 1961; Cheltenham & Gloucester Building Society: Data Processing Manager, 1967; Asst Gen. Man. (Admin), 1970; Dep. Gen. Man., 1977; Chief Exec. and Dir, 1982–95; Cheltenham & Gloucester plc: Chief Exec., 1995–96; Dir, 1995–98; Chm., 1997–98; Gp Dir Customer Finance, and Dir, Lloyds TSB Group plc, 1997–98; Chm., United Assurance Gp plc, 1998–2000. Director: Lloyds Bank plc, 1995–98; TSB Bank plc, 1995–98; Chairman, 1997–98: Lloyds UDT Ltd; Lloyds Bowmaker Ltd; United Dominions Trust Ltd; Dir, Cardnet Merchant Services Ltd, 1997–98. Non-executive Director: Hermes Focus (formerly Hermes Lens) Asset Management, 1998– (Chm., 2008–); Thames Water Plc, 1998–2000; Abbey National plc, 2005–. Mem. Council, Univ. of Glos, 2004–. CCMI (CBIM 1989); FRSA. Chm., Council of Mortgage Lenders, 1994. *Recreation:* golf. *Address:* 100 Court Road, Newton Ferrers, Plymouth PL8 1DD.

LONGHURST, Prof. James William Stuart, PhD; CEnv, FIEnvSc; Professor of Environmental Science, since 1996, and Associate Dean (Environment and External Affairs), Faculty of Environment and Technology, since 2007, University of the West of England; *b* 25 Feb. 1958; *s* of late Leonard Longhurst, DFC and bar, and of Isabella (*née*

Laing); *m* 1984, Denise Barlow; two *d. Educ:* Univ. of Plymouth (BSc Hons Envmtl Sci. 1980); Univ. of Aston (MSc Resource Utilisation and Envmtl Sci. 1981); Univ. of Birmingham (PhD 1983). Envmtl Officer, Gtr Manchester Council, 1984–86; Dir, Atmospheric Res. and Inf. Centre, Dept of Envmtl and Geographical Scis, Manchester Poly., later Manchester Metropolitan Univ., 1986–96; University of the West of England: Associate Dean and Hd, Dept of Envmtl Scis, 1996–2001; Associate Dean, Res. and Ext. Affairs, 2001–03; Associate Dean (Academic), Faculty of Applied Scis, 2003–07. Visiting posts: Swedish Envmtl Protection Agency, 1988; Academia Istropolitana, Bratislava, 1994; Univ. Poly. Catalonia, Barcelona, 1996. Series Ed., Advances in Air Pollution, 1997–; Mem., Scientific Adv. Cttee, Advances in Transport, 2000–03; Mem., Editl Adv. Bd, The Environmentalist, 1995–. Mem., 1999–2000, Chm., 2006–, QAA Benchmarking Rev. Panel for Earth Scis, Envmtl Scis and Envmtl Studies. Member: Gt Western Res. Sustainability Panel, 2005–; Bristol Envmtl Technology Partnership Bd, 2007–. Mem. Bd, Science Council, 2001–03. Mem., 1982–, Fellow, 1994, Chm. Council, 2000–06, Vice Pres., 2006–, Instn of Envmtl Scis; Mem., Nat. Soc. for Clean Air and Envmtl Protection, 1986–; Founder Mem., Inst. Air Quality Mgt, 2002–. Vice Chm., 2002–04, Chm., 2004–06, 2007–08, Cttee of Heads of Envmtl Scis. Mem., Bd of Dirs, Soc. of the Envmt, 2004–06. MIEnvSc 1982, FIEnvSc 1994; FHEA (ILTM 2001); CEnv 2004; Fellow, Wessex Inst. of GB, 2004. *Publications:* editor: Acid Deposition: sources, effects and controls, 1989; Acid Deposition: origins, impacts and abatement strategies, 1991; Air Pollution VIII, 2000; Air Quality Management, 2000; Local and Regional Aspects of Air Quality Management, 2004; (with C. A. Brebbia) Air Pollution XIV, 2006, XVI, 2008; contrib. numerous refereed scientific papers to learned jls incl. Atmospheric Envmt, Envmtl Pollution, Jl Envmtl Mgt, Urban Studies, Water, Air and Soil Pollution. *Recreations:* reading, walking in the Alps, football (sadly now only watching West Ham United). *Address:* University of the West of England, Frenchay Campus, Coldharbour Lane, Bristol BS16 1QY; 8 Kent Road, Bishopston, Bristol BS7 9DN.

LONGLEY, Mrs Ann Rosamund; Head Mistress, Roedean School, 1984–97; *b* 5 March 1942; *d* of late Jack Gilroy Dearlove and of Rhoda E. M. Dearlove (*née* Billing); *m* 1964, Stephen Roger Longley (*d* 1979); one *s* two *d. Educ:* Walthamstow Hall School, Sevenoaks; Edinburgh University (MA 1964); PGCE Bristol University, 1984. Wife and mother, 1964–; Teacher, Toorak Coll., Victoria, Australia, 1964–65; Asst Housemistress, Peninsula C of E Sch., Victoria, 1966–67; Residential Teacher, Choate School, Conn, USA, 1968–73; Teacher, Webb School, Calif, 1975–78; Headmistress, Vivian Webb School, Calif, 1981–84. FRSA 1987. DUniv Sussex, 1991. *Recreations:* film, theatre, fishing, walking.

LONGLEY, Rt Rev. Bernard; Auxiliary Bishop of Westminster, (RC), since 2003; Titular Bishop of Zarna, since 2003; *b* 5 April 1955; *s* of Frederick and Audrey Longley. *Educ:* Xaverian Coll., Manchester; RNCM; New Coll., Oxford (MA); St John's Seminary, Wonersh. Ordained priest, 1981; Asst Priest, St Joseph's, Epsom, 1982–85; English Coll., Rome, 1985–87; Theol. Tutor, St John's Seminary, Wonersh, 1987–96; Catholic Bishops' Conference: Nat. Ecumenical Officer, 1996–2003; Asst Gen. Sec. (responsible for Ecumenism and Inter Faith Affairs), 2000–03. Surrey Chm., Diocesan Commn for Christian Unity, 1991–96; Moderator, Steering Cttee, CTBI, 1999–2003. *Address:* Archbishop's House, Ambrosden Avenue, SW1P 1QJ.

LONGLEY, Clifford Edmund; JP; journalist; *b* 6 Jan. 1940; *s* of Harold Anson Longley and Gladys Vera (*née* Gibbs); *m* 1980, Elizabeth Anne Holzer; one *s* two *d. Educ:* Trinity Sch., Croydon; Univ. of Southampton (BSc Eng.). Reporter: Essex and Thurrock Gazette, 1961–64; Portsmouth Evening News, 1964–67; The Times, 1967–92 (Religious Affairs Ed., 1972–92; Asst Ed. (Leaders), 1990–92); leader writer and columnist, Daily Telegraph, 1992–95; editorial consultant and columnist, The Tablet, 1996– (Actg Ed., 1996); columnist, Daily Telegraph, 1995–2000; freelance broadcaster and author; regular contributor, BBC Radio 4: Thought for the Day, 2002–; The Moral Maze, 2005–. Chm., Portsmouth Br., NUJ, 1966–67; Father of The Times NUJ Chapel, 1972–74 and 1986–89; Chm., Docklands Br., NUJ, 1988–89. Consultant, RC Bishops' Conf. of England and Wales, 1996–. Mem. Adv. Council, Three Faiths Forum, 1995–. Select Preacher, Oxford Univ., 1988. Principal author of reports: The Common Good, for Catholic Bishops' Conf. of England and Wales, 1996; Prosperity with a Purpose, for CTBI, 2005. Mem., Steering Cttee, True Wealth of Nations Project, Inst. for Advanced Catholic Studies, Univ. of S California, 2006–. Hon. Fellow, St Mary's UC Strawberry Hill, Surrey Univ., 1999. Specialist Writer of the Year, British Press Awards, 1986; Gold Medallist, Peace Through Dialogue, Internat. CCJ, 2006. JP Bromley, 1999. *Publications:* The Times Book of Clifford Longley, 1991; The Worlock Archive, 1999; Chosen People, 2002; The Babylon Contingency, 2008; numerous articles and book chapters. *Recreations:* classical music (piano), grandchildren, reading, theology, musicology. *Address:* 24 Broughton Road, Orpington, Kent BR6 8EQ. *T:* (01689) 853189; *e-mail:* clifford.longley@ntlworld.com.

LONGLEY, Prof. Edna Mary, FBA 2006; Professor of English Literature, Queen's University Belfast, until 2002, now Emerita; *b* 24 Dec. 1940; *m* 1964, Michael George Longley, *qv*; one *s* two *d. Educ:* Trinity Coll. Dublin (BA). Lectr, Sch. of English, QUB, 1963, then Reader. *Publications:* Poetry in the Wars, 1986; Louis MacNeice: a study, 1988; The Living Stream: literature and revisionism in Ireland, 1994; Poetry and Posterity, 2000; (ed) The Bloodaxe Book of 20th Century Verse, 2000; (with Declan Kiberd) Multiculturalism: the view from the two Irelands, 2001; (contrib.) Cambridge Companion to the Literature of the First World War, 2005; *edited:* Edward Thomas: first and last poems, 1972; Selected James Simmons, 1978; Selected Paul Durcan, 1982; A Language Not to be Betrayed: selected prose of Edward Thomas, 1985; (jtly) Across a Roaring Hill: the Protestant imagination in modern Ireland, 1985; Marin Sorescu: the biggest egg in the world, 1987; Dorothy Hewett: Alice in wormland: selected poems, 1990; Culture in Ireland: division or diversity?, 1991; (jtly) Yeats Annual No 12: that accusing eye - Yeats and his Irish Readers, 1996; (jtly) Ireland (Ulster) Scotland: concepts, contexts, comparisons, 2003; Edward Thomas: the annotated collected poems, 2008. *Address:* Seamus Heaney Centre for Poetry, School of English, Queen's University Belfast, Belfast BT7 1NN.

LONGLEY, Michael George; freelance writer, since 1991; *b* 27 July 1939; *s* of Richard Cyril Longley and Constance Evelyn (*née* Longworth); *m* 1964, Edna Mary Broderick (*see* E. M. Longley); one *s* two *d. Educ:* Royal Belfast Academical Instn; Trinity Coll., Dublin (BA). Teacher, secondary schs in Dublin, Belfast and London, 1963–69; Combined Arts Dir, Arts Council of NI, 1970–91. Ireland Prof. for Poetry, 2007–. Hon. LLD: QUB, 1995; TCD, 1999; Open, 2004. Literary prizes include: Eric Gregory Award, 1966; Cholmondeley Award, 1991; Queen's Gold Medal for Poetry, 2001. *Publications:* Poems 1963–1983, 1985; Gorse Fires (Whitbread Prize), 1991; The Ghost Orchid, 1995; Selected Poems, 1998; The Weather in Japan (Hawthornden Prize, T. S. Eliot Prize), 2000; Snow Water (Librex Montale Prize), 2004; Collected Poems, 2006. *Recreations:* jazz, classical music, ornithology, botany, cooking. *Address:* c/o Lucas Alexander Whitley, 14 Vernon Street, W14 0RJ. *T:* (020) 7471 7900.

LONGMAN, Gary Leslie; Headteacher, King's Cathedral School, Peterborough, since 1994; *b* 14 April 1954; *s* of late Bernard Longman and of Betty Longman; *m* 1977, Alison Mary Shepherd; one *s* one *d. Educ:* Univ. of Nottingham (BSc Hons Botany). FCollP 1994. Assistant science teacher: Dayncourt Sch., Nottingham, 1977–79; Queen Elizabeth's Sch., Mansfield, 1979–82; Hd of Biology, 1982–85, Hd of Sci., 1985–88, Toot Hill Sch., Bingham, Notts; Dep. Head Teacher, Heysham High Sch., Morecambe, Lancs, 1988–94. *Recreations:* travel, wine-tasting, home and garden, my family. *Address:* The Ridings, Station Road, Barnack, Stamford, Lincs PE9 3DW.

LONGMAN, Michael James; His Honour Judge Longman; a Circuit Judge, since 2006; *b* 5 July 1955; *s* of Geoffrey James Longman and Beatrice Isobel Longman (*née* Dixon); *m* 1989, Gillian Sheila Nicholas; two *s* one *d. Educ:* Highgate Sch.; St John's Coll., Cambridge (BA 1977). Called to the Bar, Middle Temple, 1978; in practice, S Eastern Circuit, 1978–90, Western Circuit, 1991–2006; Recorder, 2000–06. *Recreations:* music, opera, theatre, travel. *Address:* The Law Courts, Small Street, Bristol BS1 1DA. *T:* (0117) 976 3030; *e-mail:* HHJudge.Longman@judiciary.gsi.gov.uk.

LONGMAN, Peter Martin; Consultant, The Theatres Trust, 2006–08 (Trustee, 1991–95; Director, 1995–2006); *b* 2 March 1946; *s* of Denis Martin Longman and Mary Joy Longman; *m* 1976, Sylvia June Prentice; two *d. Educ:* Huish's School, Taunton; University College, Cardiff; Univ. of Manchester. Finance Dept and Housing the Arts Officer, Arts Council, 1968–78; Dep. Dir, Crafts Council, 1978–83; Dep. Sec., 1983–84, Dir, 1984–95, Museums and Galleries Commn. Director: Caryl Jenner Productions Ltd, 1983–87; Scottish Museums Council, 1986–95; Walpole Foundn, 1997–2005; Orange Tree Theatre Ltd, 2004– (Chm., 2008–); Scarborough Th. Trust, 2005–; Charcoalblue Ltd, 2006–; Member: Council, Textile Conservation Centre Foundn, 1983– (Chm., 1998–2000; Dep. Chm., 2000–; Mem., Exec. Cttee, 1983–85, 1996–99); BTA Heritage Cttee, 1991–95; Exec., Council for Dance Educn and Trng, 1996–97; Adv. Council, Art in Churches, 1996–98; Chichester Fest. Theatre Trust, 1998–2003; Develt Cttee, ENO, 1999–2004; Covent Garden Area Trust, 2001–03; Theatre Planning and Historical Res. Cttee, Assoc. of British Theatre Technicians, 2006–. FRSA 1989. Hon. FMA 1995. *Publications:* Working Party Reports: Training Arts Administrators, Arts Council, 1971; Area Museum Councils and Services, HMSO, 1984; Museums in Scotland, HMSO, 1986; Act Now!, Theatres Trust, 2003; articles on theatre, the arts, museums. *Recreations:* discovering Britain, listening to music, studio ceramics. *Address:* 8 Eastbourne Road, Chiswick, W4 3EB. *T:* (020) 8994 5958.

LONGMORE, Rt Hon. Sir Andrew (Centlivres), Kt 1993; PC 2001; **Rt Hon. Lord Justice Longmore;** a Lord Justice of Appeal, since 2001; *b* 25 Aug. 1944; *s* of John Bell Longmore and Virginia Longmore (*née* Centlivres); *m* 1979, Margaret Murray McNair; one *s. Educ:* Winchester College; Lincoln College, Oxford (MA; Hon. Fellow, 2001). Called to the Bar, Middle Temple, 1966, Bencher, 1990. QC 1983; a Recorder, 1992–93; a Judge of the High Court, QBD, 1993–2001. Chm., Law Reform Cttee, Bar Council, 1987–90. Pat Saxton Meml Lectr, British Insce Law Assoc., 2001. *Publications:* (co-editor) MacGillivray and Parkington, Law of Insurance, 6th edn 1975, 9th edn 1997. *Recreation:* fell-walking. *Address:* Royal Courts of Justice, Strand, WC2A 2LL.

LONGRIGG, Anthony James, CMG 1992; HM Diplomatic Service, retired; Governor, Montserrat, 2001–04; *b* 21 April 1944; *m* 1967, Jane Rosa Cowlin; three *d.* Joined FCO, 1972; Second, later First, Sec., Moscow, 1975; FCO 1978; Brasilia, 1981; First Sec., FCO, 1985; Counsellor, Moscow, 1987; Counsellor, Madrid, 1991; Head, S Atlantic and Antarctic Dept, FCO, 1995–97; Minister, Moscow, 1997–2000.

LONGSDON, Col (Robert) Shaun, LVO 2006; Lieutenant, Queen's Body Guard of the Yeomen of the Guard, 2002–06; *b* 5 Dec. 1936; *s* of Wing Comdr Cyril Longsdon, Foxcote, Warwicks, and Evadne (*née* Flower); *m* 1968, Caroline Susan, *d* of late Col Michael Colvin Watson, OBE, MC, TD; three *s* one *d. Educ:* Eton. Regular Army Officer, 17th/21st Lancers, 1955–81: ADC to CIGS, 1961–62; Sen. Mil. Asst to CGS, 1975–77; CO, 17th/21st Lancers, 1977–79; GSO1 DS, NDC, 1979–81. Dir of Mktg, Knight Frank & Rutley, 1981–95; Man. Dir, Visual Insurance Protection Ltd, 1995–97. Queen's Body Guard of Yeomen of the Guard, 1985–2006: Ensign, 1987; Clerk of the Cheque and Adjutant, 1993. Col of Regt, 17th/21st Lancers, 1988–93. Gov., 1982–99, Mem. Council, 1988–99, RSC; Mem. Mgt Cttee, 1994, Chm., 1995–99, Leonard Cheshire Home, Glos; Trustee, 2000–07, Chm., Central Region, 2000–07, Leonard Cheshire. Chm., Glos Br., SSAFA Forces Help, 2004–08. *Recreation:* field sports. *Address:* Southrop Lodge, Southrop, Lechlade, Glos GL7 3NU. *T:* (01367) 850284, *Fax:* (01367) 850377; *e-mail:* longsdon_shaun@hotmail.com. *Clubs:* White's, Pratt's, Cavalry and Guards.

LONGSTONE, Lesley; Director General, Young People, Department for Children, Schools and Families, since 2007; *b* 9 Dec. 1964; *d* of John and June Broomhead; *m* 1985, Paul Longstone; two *s* one *d. Educ:* Univ. of Sheffield (BSc Hons Probability and Stats 1986). Civil Service: Manpower Services Commn, then Employment Service, later DfEE, 1985–2001; on secondment to Australian Dept of Employment, 2000–01; Department for Education and Skills: Divl Manager, Sch. Diversity, 2001–03; Actg Dir, Secondary Educn, 2003–04; Higher Educn Bill Manager and Dir, Internat. Strategy, 2004–05; Dir, Schs White Paper Implementation, subseq. Sch. Formation, 2006–07. *Recreations:* Church, family. *Address:* Department for Children, Schools and Families, Sanctuary Buildings, Great Smith Street, Westminster, SW1P 3BT. *T:* (020) 7925 5266; *e-mail:* lesley.longstone@dcsf.gsi.gov.uk.

LONGSTRETH THOMPSON, Francis Michael; *see* Thompson.

LONGUET-HIGGINS, Michael Selwyn, FRS 1963; Senior Research Physicist, University of California at San Diego, 1989–2001, now Research Physicist Emeritus; Adjunct Professor, Scripps Institution of Oceanography, La Jolla, California, since 1989; Fellow, Trinity College, Cambridge, since 1969; *b* 8 Dec. 1925; *s* of late Henry Hugh Longuet and Albinia Cecil Longuet-Higgins; *m* 1958, Joan Redmayne Tattersall; two *s* two *d. Educ:* Winchester Coll. (Schol.); Trinity Coll., Cambridge (schol.; BA); Rayleigh Prize, 1951; PhD Cantab 1951. Admiralty Research Lab., Teddington, 1945–48; Res. Student, Cambridge, 1948–51; Commonwealth Fund Fellowship, 1951–52; Res. Fellow, Trinity Coll., Cambridge, 1951–55; Nat. Inst. of Oceanography, 1954–69; Royal Soc. Res. Prof., Univ. of Cambridge, 1969–89. Visiting Professor: MIT, 1958; Institute of Geophysics, University of California, 1961–62; Univ. of Adelaide, 1964; Prof. of Oceanography, Oregon State Univ., 1967–69. Foreign Associate, US Nat. Acad. of Sci., 1979. Hon. DTech Tech. Univ. of Denmark, 1979; Hon. LLD Glasgow, 1979. Sverdrup Gold Medal, Amer. Meteorolog. Soc., 1983; Internat. Coastal Engrg Award, Amer. Soc. of Civil Engineers, 1984; Oceanography Award, Soc. for Underwater Technol., 1990. *Publications:* papers in applied mathematics, esp. physical oceanography, dynamics of sea waves and currents. *Recreations:* music, mathematical toys. *Address:* Gage Farm, Comberton, Cambridge CB23 7DH.

LONGWORTH, Ian Heaps, CBE 1994; PhD; FSA, FSAScot; Keeper of Prehistoric and Romano-British Antiquities, British Museum, 1973–95; *b* 29 Sept. 1935; *yr s* of late Joseph Longworth and Alice (*née* Heaps); *m* 1967, Clare Marian Titford; one *s* one *d*. *Educ:* King Edward VII, Lytham; Peterhouse, Cambridge. Open and Sen. Scholar, Matthew Wren Student, 1957, MA, PhD, Cantab. Temp. Asst Keeper, Nat. Museum of Antiquities of Scotland, 1962–63; Asst Keeper, Dept of British and Medieval Antiquities, Brit. Mus., 1963–69; Asst Keeper, Dept of Prehistoric and Romano-British Antiquities, Brit. Mus., 1969–73. Member: Ancient Monuments Bd for England, 1977–84; Ancient Monuments Adv. Cttee, Historic Buildings and Monuments Commn, 1991–94. Chairman: Area Archaeol. Adv. Cttee for NW England, 1978–79; Standing Conf. of London Archaeol., 2003–05. Hon. Sec., 1966–74, Vice-Pres., 1976–80, Hon. Life Mem., 2002, Prehistoric Soc.; Sec., 1974–79, Vice-Pres., 1985–89, Soc. of Antiquaries of London. Chm. Adv. Bd, Alexander Keiller Mus., Avebury, 1994–2005. *Publications:* Yorkshire (Regional Archaeologies Series), 1965; (with G. J. Wainwright) Durrington Walls—excavations 1966–68, 1971; Collared Urns of the Bronze Age in Great Britain and Ireland, 1984; Prehistoric Britain, 1985; (with I. A. Kinnes) Catalogue of the Excavated Prehistoric and Romano-British Material in the Greenwell Collection, 1985; (ed with J. Cherry) Archaeology in Britain since 1945, 1986; (with A. Ellison and V. Rigby) Excavations at Grimes Graves, Norfolk, 1972–76, Fasc. 2, 1988, (*et al.*) Fasc. 3, 1991, Fasc. 4, 1992, Fasc. 5, 1996; articles in various learned jls on topics of prehistory. *Address:* 2 Hurst View Road, South Croydon, Surrey CR2 7AG. *T:* (020) 8688 4960.

LONGWORTH, Peter, CMG 2001; HM Diplomatic Service, retired; broadcaster and critic; Director, Corporate and Government Affairs, Commonwealth Business Council, since 2002; *b* 26 May 1942; *y s* of late Frank Longworth and of Edith E. (*née* Robinson); *m* 1975, Christina Margareta, *d* of late Folke Wallin and Gun Wallin, Växjö. *Educ:* Chislehurst and Sidcup Grammar Sch.; Univ. of Sheffield (BA). Journalist, 1963–74: Labour and Ind. Corresp., Bristol Evening Post, 1964–66; Lobby Corresp., Western Daily Press., 1966–68; Diplomatic Corresp., Westminster Press., 1968–74; joined FCO, 1974; First Secretary: FCO, 1974–77; (Econ.), Bonn, 1977–81; Head of Chancery and HM Consul, Sofia, 1981–84; FCO, 1984–87; Counsellor (Econ. and Commercial), Copenhagen, 1987–91; Dep. Hd of Mission, Counsellor (Econ. and Commercial) and Consul Gen., Seoul, 1991–94; Consul-Gen., Johannesburg, and Dir of UK Trade Promotion and Investment, S Africa, 1994–98; High Comr, Zimbabwe, 1998–2001. Mem., Royal African Soc. *Club:* Reform.

LONGWORTH, Wilfred Roy, AM 1986; MSc, PhD; FRSC, FRACI; Principal Director (formerly Director), Swinburne Institute of Technology and College of Technical and Further Education, 1970–86, retired; *b* 13 Dec. 1923; *s* of Wilfred Arnold Longworth and Jessie Longworth; *m* 1951, Constance Elizabeth Dean; two *d*. *Educ:* Bolton Sch.; Manchester Univ. (BSc, MSc, PhD). FRIC 1963; FRACI 1970. Works Manager and Chief Chemist, Blackburn & Oliver, 1948–56; postgrad. res., Univ. of Keele, 1956–59; Lectr in Physical Chemistry, Huddersfield Coll. of Technol., 1959–60; Sen. Lectr in Phys. Chem., Sunderland Technical Coll., 1960–64; Head, Dept of Chem. and Biol., Manchester Polytechnic, 1964–70. Pres., World Council on Co-op. Educn, 1983–85. *Publications:* articles on cationic polymerisation in learned jls. *Recreations:* lawn bowls, gardening. *Address:* Unit 28, Fountain Court Village, 100 Station Street, Burwood, Vic 3125, Australia. *T:* (3) 98080346.

LÖNNGREN, Thomas; Executive Director, European Medicines Agency (formerly European Agency for the Evaluation of Medicinal Products), since 2001; *b* Sweden, 16 Dec. 1950; *m* 1988, Ann-Charlotte Fondelius; one *s* one *d*. *Educ:* Univ. of Uppsala (MSc Social Pharmacy 1976); Stockholm Sch. of Econs (Advanced Course in Health Econ. 1999). Pharmacist, 1976; Lectr, Pharmaceutical Faculty, Uppsala Univ., 1976–78; Sen. Pharmaceutical Officer, Dept of Drugs, Nat. Bd of Health and Welfare, Sweden, 1978–90; Sen. Pharmaceutical Consultant for Swedish health co-operation prog. in Vietnam, 1982–94; Dir of Ops, 1990–98, Dep. Dir Gen., 1998–2000, Med. Products Agency, Sweden. *Address:* EMEA, 7 Westferry Circus, Canary Wharf, E14 4HB. *T:* (020) 7418 8406, *Fax:* (020) 7418 8409; *e-mail:* thomas.lonngren@emea.europa.eu.

LONSDALE, 8th Earl of, *cr* 1807 (UK); **Hugh Clayton Lowther;** Baron and Viscount Lowther, 1797; Bt 1764; *b* 27 May 1949; *s* of 7th Earl of Lonsdale and Tuppina Cecily, *d* of late Captain G. H. Bennet; *S* father, 2006; *m* 1971, Pamela Middleton; *m* 1986, Angela M., *d* of Captain Peter J. Wyatt, RN and Mrs Christine Wyatt; *m* 1999, Elizabeth Margaret, *d* of Stanley Frazer Arnison. *Heir: half-b* Hon. William James Lowther, *b* 9 July 1957.

LONSDALE, Anne Mary, CBE 2004; President, New Hall, Cambridge, 1996–2008; Deputy Vice-Chancellor, Cambridge University, 2003–08 (Pro-Vice-Chancellor, 1998–2003); *b* 16 Feb. 1941; *d* of Dr Alexander Menzies and Mabel Menzies; *m* 1st, 1962, Geoffrey Griffin (*d* 1962); 2nd, 1964, Roger Harrison Lonsdale, *qv* (marr. diss. 1994); one *s* one *d*. *Educ:* St Anne's Coll., Oxford (BA Hons Lit. Hum. 1962; BA Hons Chinese (Oriental Studies) 1965; MA 1965; Hon. Fellow, 1996). Oxford University: Davis Sen. Schol. and Lectr in Chinese, St Anne's Coll., 1965–74; Univ. Adminr, 1974–90; Dir, External Relations, 1990–93; Sen. Associate Mem., St Antony's Coll., 1991–; Sec.-Gen., Central European Univ., Budapest, Prague, and Warsaw, 1994–96. Chairman: Conf. of Univ. Admin, UK and Ireland, 1991–93; Interdisciplinary Envmtl Studies Cttee, 1996–2001; Jt Chm., Assoc. of Univ. Admin, 1993–94; Member: Commonwealth Scholarships Commn, 1996–2002; Council of Senate, Cambridge Univ., 1997–2004; Council for Assisting Refugee Academics, 2006– (Hon. Sec., 2008–). Trustee: Open Society (formerly Inter-Univ.) Foundn, 1988–; Cambridge Commonwealth Trust, 1995–2005; Cambridge Overseas Trust, 1996–2005; Cambridge European Trust, 1998–2007; Newton Trust, 1999–2008; Moscow Sch. of Social and Econ. Scis, 1999–2008; British Assoc. for Central and Eastern Europe, 2000–08; CamFed, 2006–; European Humanities Univ., Vilnius, 2007–. Chm., Syndics, Fitzwilliam Mus., 2002–08; Syndic, CUP, 2006–08. Hon. Dr Tashkent State Univ. for Oriental Studies, 2001. Cavaliere, Order of Merit (Italy), 1988; Officier, Ordre des Palmes Académiques (France), 2002. *Recreation:* travelling. *Address:* 74 French's Road, Cambridge CB4 3LA. *T:* (01223) 501934.

See also C. J. Lonsdale.

LONSDALE, Charles John; HM Diplomatic Service; Ambassador to Armenia, since 2008; *b* Oxford, 5 July 1965; *s* of Prof. Roger Harrison Lonsdale, *qv* and Anne Mary Lonsdale, *qv*. *Educ:* Merton Coll., Oxford (BA Mod. Hist. 1987). Joined FCO, 1987; Vienna, 1988–89; FCO, 1989; Third, later Second Sec., Budapest, 1990–93; FCO, 1995; First Sec., Moscow, 1998–2003; Dep. Hd, Afghanistan Gp, 2003–05, Dep. Hd, Human Rights, Democracy and Governance Gp, 2005–08, FCO. *Recreations:* music, walking, cats. *Address:* British Embassy, 34 Baghramyan Avenue, 0019 Yerevan, Armenia. *T:* (1) 0264301, *Fax:* (1) 0264318; *e-mail:* enquiries.yerevan@fco.gov.uk.

LONSDALE, Robert Henry H.; *see* Heywood-Lonsdale.

LONSDALE, Prof. Roger Harrison, DPhil; FBA 1991; Fellow and Tutor in English, Balliol College, Oxford, 1963–2000, now Fellow Emeritus; Professor of English Literature, University of Oxford, 1992–2000; *b* 6 Aug. 1934; *s* of Arthur John Lonsdale and Phebe (*née* Harrison); *m* 1st, 1964, Anne Mary Menzies (*see* A. M. Lonsdale) (marr. diss. 1994); one *s* one *d*; 2nd, 1999, Nicoletta Momigliano. *Educ:* Hymers Coll., Hull; Lincoln Coll., Oxford (BA 1st class Hons 1957); DPhil (Oxon) 1962. National Service, RAF, commnd as Navigator, 1952–54. English Dept, Yale Univ., 1958–60; Oxford University: Bradley Jun. Res. Fellow, Balliol Coll., 1960–63; Reader in English Literature, 1990–92. *Publications:* Dr Charles Burney: a literary biography, 1965; *edited:* The Poems of Gray, Collins and Goldsmith, 1969; Vathek, by William Beckford, 1970; Dryden to Johnson, 1971; The New Oxford Book of Eighteenth-century Verse, 1984; The Poems of John Bampfylde, 1988; Eighteenth-century Women Poets: an Oxford anthology, 1989; The Lives of the English Poets, by Samuel Johnson, 2006. *Recreations:* music, book-collecting. *Address:* c/o Balliol College, Oxford OX1 3BJ.

See also C. J. Lonsdale.

LONZARICH, Prof. Gilbert George, PhD; FRS 1989; Professor of Condensed Matter Physics, since 1997, and Fellow of Trinity College, since 1977, University of Cambridge. *Educ:* Univ. of California (BA); Univ. of Minnesota (MS); PhD British Columbia; MA Cantab 1977. University of Cambridge: Demonstrator, Physics Dept, 1976; Lectr in Physics until 1990; Reader in Physics, 1990–97. *Address:* Department of Physics, Cavendish Laboratory, J. J. Thomson Avenue, Cambridge CB3 0HE. *T:* (01223) 337351; Trinity College, Cambridge CB2 1TQ; 6 Hicks Lane, Girton, Cambridge CB3 0JS. *T:* (01223) 742056.

LOOP, Bernadine P., (Mrs Floyd Loop); *see* Healy, B. P.

LOOSLEY, Brian; a District Judge (Magistrates' Courts) (formerly Metropolitan Stipendiary Magistrate), since 1989; *b* 20 Dec. 1948; *s* of late Bernard Allan Loosley and of Barbara Clara Randle; *m* 1971, Christine Mary Batt; one *s* one *d*. *Educ:* Sir William Borlase Grammar Sch., Marlow; Leeds Univ. (LLB 1971). Admitted Solicitor 1974; Prosecuting Solicitor, Thames Valley Police, 1975–78; practised privately, 1978–89. *Recreations:* history, foreign travel. *Address:* Oxford Magistrates' Court, The Court House, PO Box 37, Speedwell Street, Oxford OX1 1RZ. *T:* (01865) 448011, *Fax:* (01865) 448013.

LOPES, family name of **Baron Roborough**.

LOPES CARDOZO KINDERSLEY, Lydia Helena, (Lida); owner, Cardozo Kindersley Workshop, since 1981 (co-owner, 1981–95 and since 1998); *b* 22 July 1954; *d* of late Prof. Dr Paul Lopes Cardozo and of Ottoline Baronesse van Hemert tot Dingshof; *m* 1st, 1986, David Kindersley, MBE (*d* 1995); three *s*; 2nd, 1998, Graham F. Beck. *Educ:* Royal Acad. of Fine Arts, Den Haag, Netherlands. David Kindersley's Workshop: Lettercutter, 1976; Partner, 1981; Founder Editor, Cardozo Kindersley Editions, 1989. Associate Mem., 1999–2003, Life Mem., 2003, Clare Hall, Cambridge. Member: Assoc. Typographique Internationale, 1974–; Wynkyn de Worde Soc., 1978– (Chm., 1988; Hon. Fellow, 2001); Double Crown Club, 1996–; Cttee, Hazlitt Soc., 2005–06. Patron, Michaelhouse Project, Cambridge, 1999–. Gov., Impington Village Coll., 1997–2000. Brother, Art Workers Guild, 2000–. Fellow, 1994, Honoured Fellow, 2007, Calligraphy and Lettering Arts Soc. *Publications:* Glass & Engraver, 1983; (with David Kindersley) Letters Slate Cut, 1981, 3rd edn 2004; (with R. McKitterick) Lasting Letters, 1992; Oxford Handwriting Practice, 1993, 2nd edn 2006; The Cardozo Kindersley Workshop: a guide to commissioning work, 1996, 3rd edn 2004; (with Emma Lloyd-Jones) Letters for the Millennium, 1999, 3rd edn 2004; (with W. Graham Cannon) Kindersley at Addenbrooke's Hospital, 2000; (jtly) Optical Letter Spacing, 2001; (jtly) Apprenticeship, 2003; (with Michael Wheeler) The kindest cut of all, 2005. *Recreations:* letter writing, religion. *Address:* Cardozo Kindersley Workshop, 152 Victoria Road, Cambridge CB4 3DZ. *T:* (01223) 362170. *Club:* Athenæum.

LOPEZ CABALLERO, Alfonso; Ambassador of Colombia to the Court of St James's, 2002–06; *b* 17 Aug. 1944; *s* of Alfonso Lopez Michelsen and Cecilia Caballero de Lopez; *m* 1969, Josefina Andreu de Lopez; one *d*. *Educ:* Sch. of Foreign Service, Georgetown Univ., Washington (BSFS Internat. Affairs); INSEAD, Fontainebleau (MBA); Columbia Univ., NY (MA, MPhil Econs). Asst Manager, First Nat. City Bank of NY; Business Consultant, Arthur Young & Co.; Congressman, Colombia, 1986–90; Senator, 1990–94; Ambassador of Columbia to France, 1990–91; Minister of Agriculture, 1991–92; Ambassador to Canada, 1994–97; Minister: of the Interior, 1997–98; i/c Presidential functions (during several Presidential trips abroad). Govt negotiator with FARC guerrillas during peace process, 2000–01. *Publication:* Un nuevo modelo de desarrollo para el campo, 1988. *Address:* c/o Embassy of Colombia, 3 Hans Crescent, SW1X 0LN; *e-mail:* alopec@yahoo.com. *Clubs:* Travellers; Jockey (Bogota).

LOPPERT, Max Jeremy; writer; Associate Editor, Opera, 1986–97; *b* Johannesburg, 24 Aug. 1946; *m* 1972, Delayne Aarons. *Educ:* Univ. of Witwatersrand, Johannesburg (BA 1966); Univ. of York (BA Music 1971). Chief Music Critic, FT, 1980–96. Vis. Music Schol., Univ. of Natal, 1998–99; residency: Rockefeller Foundn Study Center, Bellagio, Italy, 2004; Centro Studi Ligure, Bogliasco, Italy, 2005. Founder, Opera Sch. and Voice Acad., Music Sch., Univ. of Natal, 1999 (opened 2002). Hon. Res. Fellow, Univ. of Kwa Zula Natal, 2007. *Publications:* contrib. to: Opera on Record (ed Alan Blyth), 3 vols, 1979, 1983, 1984; The New Grove Dictionary of Music and Musicians, 1980; The New Grove Dictionary of Opera, 1992; Who's Who in Hollywood, 1993; (ed) Words and Music, 2003. *Recreations:* cinema, cooking, pottery. *Address:* Via Molinetto 12, Refrontolo (TV), 31020, Italy.

LORAINE-SMITH, Nicholas George Edward; His Honour Judge Loraine-Smith; a Circuit Judge, since 2002; *b* 24 Jan. 1953; *s* of Maj. Bernard Lawson Loraine-Smith, MC, and Rachel Anne Loraine-Smith; *m* 1980, Annabelle Catherine Schicht; two *d*. *Educ:* Eton Coll.; Oriel Coll., Oxford (BA English). Called to the Bar, Inner Temple, 1977; Jun. Treasury Counsel, 1994–99, Sen. Treasury Counsel, 1999–2002, Central Criminal Court; Asst Recorder, 1997–2000; a Recorder, 2000–02.

LORAM, Vice-Adm. Sir David (Anning), KCB 1979; CVO 1994 (LVO 1957); Deputy Supreme Allied Commander Atlantic, 1977–80, retired; Gentleman Usher to The Queen, 1982–94, Extra Gentleman Usher, since 1994; *b* 24 July 1924; *o* surv. *s* of late Mr and Mrs John A. Loram; *m* 1st, 1958, Fiona Beloe (marr. diss. 1981); three *s*; 2nd, 1983, Diana Keigwin (marr. diss. 1990; she *d* 2008); 3rd, 1996, Sara Stead-Ellis (*née* Strickland Goodall). *Educ:* Royal Naval Coll., Dartmouth (1938–41). Awarded King's Dirk. Served War: HMS Sheffield, Foresight, Anson, Zealous, 1941–45. ADC to Governor-Gen. of New Zealand, 1946–48; specialised in Signal Communications, 1949; served in HMS Chequers, 1951; Equerry to the Queen, 1954–57; qualified helicopter pilot, 1955; commanded HMS Loch Fada, 1957; Directing Staff, JSSC, 1959–60; served in HMS Belfast, 1961; Naval Attaché, Paris, 1964–67; commanded HMS Arethusa, 1967; Dir, Naval Ops and Trade, 1970–71; commanded HMS Antrim, 1971; ADC to The Queen,

1972–73; Comdr British Forces, FO Malta, and NATO Comdr SE Mediterranean, 1973–75; Comdt, Nat. Defence Coll., 1975–77. Mem., RN Cresta Team, 1954–59. *Recreation:* fishing. *Address:* 5 Motcombe Grange, Motcombe, Shaftesbury, Dorset SP7 9HJ. *T:* (01747) 850925. *Club:* Chesapeake.

LORD, Alan, CB 1972; Deputy Chairman and Chief Executive, Lloyd's of London, 1986–92; *b* 12 April 1929; *er s* of Frederick Lord and Anne Lord (*née* Whitworth), Rochdale; *m* 1953, Joan Ogden; two *d. Educ:* Rochdale; St John's Coll., Cambridge (schol.; BA 1950 (1st Cl. Hons); MA 1987). Entered Inland Revenue, 1950; Private Sec. to Dep. Chm. and to Chm. of the Board, 1952–54; HM Treasury, 1959–62; Principal Private Sec. to First Secretary of State (then Rt Hon. R. A. Butler), 1962–63; Comr of Inland Revenue, 1969–73; Dep. Chm. Bd, 1971–73; Principal Finance Officer to DTI, subseq. to Depts of Industry, Trade, and Prices and Consumer Protection, 1973–75; Second Permanent Sec. (Domestic Econ.), HM Treasury, 1975–77. Man. Dir, 1980, Chief Exec., 1982–84, Dunlop Hldgs plc; formerly: Exec. Dir, Dunlop Hldgs; Man. Dir, Dunlop Internat. AG, 1978. Director: Allied-Lyons plc, 1979–86; Bank of England, 1983–86; Johnson Matthey Bankers, 1985–86. Chm., CBI Taxation Cttee, 1979–81. Mem. Council of Management, Henley Centre for Forecasting, 1977–82. Governor, NIESR. Pres., Johnian Soc., 1985–86. *Publications:* A Strategy for Industry (Sir Ellis Hunter Meml Lecture, Univ. of York), 1976; Earning an Industrial Living (1985 Johnian Society Lecture). *Recreations:* reading, music, gardening, rough-shooting. *Address:* Mardens, Hildenborough, Tonbridge, Kent TN11 8PA. *Club:* Reform.

LORD, Hon. Bernard, ONB 2007; Counsel, McCarthy Tétrault, since 2007; *b* 27 Sept. 1965; *s* of Ralph and Marie-Émilie Lord; *m* 1990, Diane Haché; one *s* one *d. Educ:* Mathieu-Martin High Sch., Dieppe; Univ. of Moncton, Canada (BScSoc Econs 1988; LLB 1992). Called to the Bar, New Brunswick, 1993; in private law practice, Founding Partner, LeBlanc, Desjardins, Lord, Moncton, 1995–99. MLA (Progressive C) Moncton E, NB, 1998–2007; Leader of Opposition, 1998–99; Premier of NB, 1999–2006; Pres., Exec. Council and Minister, 1999–2006: Intergovtl Affairs; resp. for NB Adv. Council on Youth; resp. for council on status of disabled persons. Leader, Progressive Cons. Party of NB, 1997–2006. Hon. LLD New Brunswick, 2001; St Thomas Univ.; Mt Allison Univ.; Hon. Dr Pol Sci. Moncton, 2002. Grand Officier, Ordre de la Pléiade, Internat. Assoc. of Francophone Parliamentarians, 2001. *Recreations:* golf, chess. *Address:* McCarthy Tétrault, Suite 2500, 1000 De La Gauchetière Street West, Montréal, QC H3B 0AZ, Canada.

LORD, Geoffrey, OBE 1989; Founder Trustee, since 1989, and Vice President, since 2000, Adapt Trust (Founder Director, 1989–96); *b* 24 Feb. 1928; *s* of Frank Lord and Edith Lord; *m* 1955, Jean; one *s* one *d. Educ:* Rochdale Grammar Sch.; Univ. of Bradford (MA Applied Social Studies). AIB. Midland Bank Ltd, 1946–58; Probation and After-Care Service, 1958–76: Dep. Chief Probation Officer, Greater Manchester, 1974–76; Sec. and Treas., Carnegie UK Trust, 1977–93. Chairman: Unemployed Voluntary Action Fund (Scotland), 1990–95; Pollock Meml Missionary Trust, 1985–2004; Pres., Centre for Envmtl Interpretation, 1984–97. Member, Scottish Arts Lottery Bd, 1994–98; Council, NYO of Scotland, 1998–. Trustee: Home-Start (formerly Home-Start Consultancy) UK, 1993–98; Faith in Older People Trust, 2007–; Sec. and Trustee, Edin. Vol. Orgns' Trusts, 1996–. FRSA 1985. Hon. Fellow, Manchester Metropolitan Univ. (formerly Manchester Poly.), 1987. *Publications:* The Arts and Disabilities, 1981; Access for Disabled People to Arts Premises: the journey sequence, 2003. *Recreations:* philately, walking, appreciation of the arts. *Address:* 9 Craigleith View, Ravelston, Edinburgh EH4 3JZ. *T:* (0131) 337 7623. *Club:* New (Edinburgh).

LORD, Sir Michael (Nicholson), Kt 2001; MP (C) Central Suffolk and North Ipswich, since 1997 (Suffolk Central, 1983–97); Second Deputy Chairman of Ways and Means and a Deputy Speaker, since 1997; *b* 17 Oct. 1938; *s* of John Lord and Jessie Lord (*née* Nicholson); *m* 1965, Jennifer Margaret (*née* Childs); one *s* one *d. Educ:* Christ's College, Cambridge. MA. FArborA. Arboricultural consultant. PPS: to Minister of State, MAFF, 1984–85; to Chief Secretary to the Treasury, 1985–87. Member: Select Cttee on Parly Comr for Admin, 1990–97; Council of Europe, 1987–91; WEU, 1987–91. *Recreations:* golf, sailing, gardening, trees. *Address:* House of Commons, SW1A 0AA.
See also T. M. Lord.

LORD, Peter Duncan Fraser, CBE 2006; Co-founder (with D. Sproxton), owner and Creative Director, Aardman Animations, since 1972; *b* 4 Nov. 1953; *s* of Peter and Margaret Lord; *m* 1976, Karen Jane Bradshaw; two *s* one *d. Educ:* Univ. of York (BA 1976). Films directed include: The Amazing Adventures of Morph, 1981–83; Conversation Pieces, 1982–83; Wat's Pig, 1996; Chicken Run, 2000. Hon. Fellow, BKSTS, 2000. Hon. Dr Design UWE, 1995; DUniv York, 2003; Hon. LLD Exeter, 2007. Chevalier, Ordre des Arts et des Lettres (France), 2001. *Publication:* Cracking Animation, 1999. *Recreations:* cricket, comic books, walking. *Address:* Aardman Animations, 1410 Aztec West Business Park, Almondsbury, Bristol BS32 4RT. *T:* (01454) 859000. *Club:* MCC.

LORD, Peter Herent, OBE 1991; FRCS; Consultant Surgeon, Wycombe General Hospital, High Wycombe, 1964–90; *b* 23 Nov. 1925; *s* of Sir Frank Lord, KBE, JP, DL and Rosalie Jeanette Herent; *m* 1952, Florence Shirley Hirst; two *s* two *d. Educ:* Manchester Grammar Sch.; St John's Coll., Cambridge (MA, MChir). St George's Hosp., Salford Royal Hosp., Christie Hosp., Manchester, St Margaret's, Epping, St George's Hosp., 1949–63 (Captain, RAMC, 1952–53). Royal College of Surgeons: H. N. Smith Research Fellow, 1964; Penrose May Teacher, 1970; Mem. Council, 1978–90; Vice-Pres., 1986–88. *Publications:* Cardiac Pacemakers, 1964; Pilonidal Sinus, 1964; Wound Healing, 1966; Haemorrhoids, 1969; Hydrocoele, 1972; Surgery in Old Age, 1980. *Recreations:* sailing, fishing. *Address:* Holly Tree House, 39 Grove Road, Beaconsfield, Bucks HP9 1PE. *T:* (01494) 674488; Bucklebury, Solva, Pembs SA62 6TB. *T:* (01437) 721263.

LORD, Richard Denyer; QC 2002; *b* 2 Jan. 1959; *s* of Arthur James Lord and Daphne Anne Lord (now Beaumont); *m* 1992, Alexandra Barnes; one *s* two *d. Educ:* Stowe Sch.; Sidney Sussex Coll., Cambridge (MA). Called to the Bar, Inner Temple, 1981. Exec. Dir, Union Foundn, 2002–; Trustee, Web of Hope, 2003–. *Publications:* Controlled Drugs: law and practice, 1984; (with Simon Salzedo) Guide to the Arbitration Act 1996, 1996. *Recreations:* cricket, reggae music, planting trees. *Address:* 7–8 Essex Street, WC2R 3LD. *T:* (020) 7379 3550, *Fax:* (020) 7379 3558; *e-mail:* lord@brickcourt.co.uk. *Club:* MCC.

LORD, Stuart; Lay Member, Fitness to Practise Panel, General Medical Council, since 2006; *b* 10 Feb. 1951; *yr s* of William Ughtred Lord and Sybil Lord (*née* Greenhalgh); *m* 1970, Dwynwen Williams; one *s* one *d. Educ:* Manchester Grammar Sch.; University Coll. of Swansea (BScEcon Hons). DHSS, later DSS, then Department for Work and Pensions, 1972–2002: Principal Private Sec. to Sec. of State, 1988–91; Asst Sec. seconded to DoE, 1991; seconded to Prudential Life and Pensions, 1993; Head of Security, Benefits Agency, 1993–94; Head of Planning and Finance Divisions, and Prin. Finance Officer, 1994–98; Head of Transport and Corporate Directorate, Govt Office for London (on secondment), 1998–2000; Dir, Modernisation Strategy, Service Strategy and Commercial Partnerships,

2000–02. Non-exec. Dir, Richmond and Twickenham PCT, 2002–06. *Publication:* (contrib.) Economics of Unemployment, 1981. *Recreations:* travel, photography, consumer electronics. *Address:* 49 Ditton Reach, Thames Ditton, Surrey KT7 0XB.

LORD, Timothy Michael; QC 2008; *b* Cambridge, 10 Feb. 1966; *s* of Sir Michael Nicholson Lord, *qv; m* 2001, Amanda Jane Green; two *s. Educ:* Bedford Modern Sch.; Christ's Coll., Cambridge (BA 1st Cl. Hons Law 1987). Admitted solicitor, 1991; Slaughter & May, 1989–92. Called to the Bar, Inner Temple, 1992; in practice at the Bar, 1993–. Sec., London Common Law and Commercial Bar Assoc., 2000–06. *Recreations:* Rugby (Cambridge blue 1986), cricket (playing Mem., MCC), sailing, ski-ing, golf. *Address:* Brick Court Chambers, 7–8 Essex Street, WC2R 3LD. *T:* (020) 7379 3550, *Fax:* (020) 7379 3558. *Club:* MCC.

LOREN, Sophia; film actress; *b* 20 Sept. 1934; *d* of Ricardo Scicolone and Romilda Villani; *m* 1957, Carlo Ponti (*d* 2007), film producer (marriage annulled in Juarez, Mexico, Sept. 1962; marriage in Paris, France, April 1966); two *s. Educ:* parochial sch. and Teachers' Institute, Naples. First leading role in, Africa sotto i Mari, 1952; acted in many Italian films, 1952–55; subsequent films include: The Pride and the Passion, Boy on a Dolphin, Legend of the Lost, 1957; The Key, Desire under the Elms, Houseboat, 1958; The Black Orchid (Venice Film Festival Award, 1958), That Kind of Woman, 1959; It Started in Naples, Heller in Pink Tights, A Breath of Scandal, 1960; The Millionairess, Two Women (Cannes Film Festival Award, 1961), Madame sans Gêne, El Cid, 1961; Boccaccio 70, 1962; Five Miles to Midnight, 1963; Yesterday, Today and Tomorrow, The Fall of the Roman Empire, Marriage, Italian Style, 1964; Operation Crossbow, Lady L, 1965; Judith, Arabesque, 1996; A Countess from Hong Kong, 1967; Sunflower, 1970; The Priest's Wife, 1971; Man of La Mancha, 1972; The Voyage, 1973; The Verdict, 1974; A Special Day, The Cassandra Crossing, 1977; Firepower, 1979; Blood Feud, 1980; Running Away, 1989; Saturday, Sunday and Monday, 1990; Prêt-à-Porter, 1994; Between Strangers, 2003. Chevalier, Legion of Honour (France), 1991. *Publications:* Eat with Me, 1972; Sophia Loren on Woman and Beauty, 1984; *relevant publication:* Sophia: living and loving, by A. E. Hotcher, 1979. *Address:* Case Postale 430, 1211 Geneva 12, Switzerland.

LORENZ, Andrew Peter Morrice; Chairman, Financial Communications Group, Financial Dynamics, since 2006; *b* 22 June 1955; *s* of Hans Viktor Lorenz and Catherine Jesse Cairns Lorenz (*née* James); *m* 1988, Helen Marianne Alway; two *s. Educ:* Stamford Sch., Lincs; Worcester Coll., Oxford (MA Mod. Hist.). The Journal, Newcastle: News Reporter, 1978–80; Educn Correspondent, 1980–81; Industrial Correspondent, 1981–82; Business Correspondent, The Scotsman, 1982–86; City Correspondent, 1986–88, Dep. City Editor, 1988–89, Sunday Telegraph; Industrial Editor, 1989–95, Business Editor, 1995, Sunday Times. Business Journalist of the Year, UK Press Awards, 1999; Business Journalist of the Year, Corp. of London, 2000. *Publications:* A Fighting Chance: British manufacturing industry in the 1980s, 1989; BZW: the first ten years, 1996; Rover Reborn: the road to BMW, 1999; (jtly) End of the Road: BMW and Rover - a brand too far, 2000, 2nd edn as End of the Road: the true story of the downfall of Rover, 2005; Kumar Bhattacharyya: the unsung guru, 2002. *Recreations:* film, music, sport. *Address:* Brook House, Monkey Island Lane, Bray, Maidenhead, Berks SL6 2ED.

LORIMER, Prof. (Andrew) Ross, CBE 2004; MD; FRCP, FRCPE, FRCPGlas, FMedSci; President, Royal College of Physicians and Surgeons of Glasgow, 2000–03; *b* 5 May 1937; *s* of James Lorimer and Katherine Lorimer (*née* Ross); *m* 1963, Fiona Marshall; three *s. Educ:* Uddingston Grammar Sch.; High Sch. of Glasgow; Univ. of Glasgow (MD Hons 1976). FRCPGlas 1972; FRCP 1978; FRCPE 1981. Res. Fellow in Medicine, Vanderbilt Univ., Nashville, 1961–63; Registrar in Medicine, Royal Infirmary, Glasgow, 1963–66; Lectr in Cardiol., Glasgow Univ., 1966–71; Consultant Cardiologist, Royal Infirmary, Glasgow, 1971–91; Hon. Prof. of Medicine, Glasgow Univ., 1991–2001. FMedSci 1998; FACP 2001; FFPH (FFPHM 2001); FRCPI 2002; Fellow, Bangladesh Coll. of Physicians and Surgeons, 2002; FRCS, FRCSE, 2003; FRACP 2004; FRCSI 2004; FCP(SoAf) 2004. DUniv Glasgow, 2001. *Publication:* Preventive Cardiology, 1988. *Recreations:* golf, cricket, hill-walking. *Address:* Woodlands Cottage, 12 Uddingston Road, Bothwell, Glasgow G71 8PH.

LORIMER, Sir Desmond; see Lorimer, Sir T. D.

LORIMER, Prof. George Huntly, FRS 1986; Professor, Department of Chemistry and Biochemistry, University of Maryland, since 1998; *b* 14 Oct. 1942; *s* of late Gordon and Ellen Lorimer; *m* 1970, Freia (*née* Schulz-Baldes); one *s* one *d. Educ:* George Watson's College, Edinburgh; Univ. of St Andrews (BSc); Univ. of Illinois (MS); Michigan State Univ. (PhD). Scientist, Max-Planck Society, Berlin, 1972–74; Research Fellow, Inst. for Advanced Studies, ANU, Canberra, 1974–77; Scientist, Society for Radiation and Environmental Research, Munich, 1977; Prin. Investigator, then Res. Leader, E. I. Du Pont de Nemours & Co., 1978–91; Dupont Fellow, Central Res. Dept, Dupont Co., Delaware, 1991–97. Adjunct Prof., Dept of Biochemistry, Univ. of Pennsylvania, 1992. Member: Amer. Soc. of Biochemistry and Molecular Biology; NAS, USA, 1997. Editor, Biochimica et Biophysica Acta, 1995; Mem Editl Bd, Jl of Biol Chem., 1998. Res. Award, Alexander von Humboldt Foundn, 1997. *Publications:* contribs to Biochemistry, Jl of Biological Chemistry, Nature, Science. *Recreations:* music, political history. *Address:* 7705 Lake Glen Drive, Glenn Dale, MD 20769–2028, USA. *T:* (home) (301) 3523679, (office) (301) 4051828, *Fax:* (home) (301) 3525539, (office) (301) 3149121; *e-mail:* GL48@ umail.umd.edu.

LORIMER, Ross; see Lorimer, A. R.

LORIMER, Sir (Thomas) Desmond, Kt 1976; Chairman, Northern Bank Ltd, 1986–97 (Director, 1983–97; Deputy Chairman, 1985); *b* 20 Oct. 1925; *s* of Thomas Berry Lorimer and Sarah Ann Lorimer; *m* 1957, Patricia Doris Samways; two *d. Educ:* Belfast Technical High Sch. Chartered Accountant, 1948; Fellow, Inst. of Chartered Accountants in Ireland, 1957. Practised as chartered accountant, 1952–74; Sen. Partner, Harmood, Banner, Smylie & Co., Belfast, Chartered Accountants, 1960–74; Chairman: Lamont Holdings PLC, 1973–96; Northern Ireland Electricity, 1991–94; Dir, Irish Distillers PLC, 1986–98. Chm., Industrial Develt Bd for NI, 1982–85; Pres., Inst. of Chartered Accountants in Ireland, 1968–69; Chairman: Ulster Soc. of Chartered Accountants, 1960; NI Housing Exec., 1971–75; Mem., Rev. Body on Local Govt in NI, 1970. *Recreations:* gardening and golf. *Address:* Windwhistle Cottage, 6A Circular Road West, Cultra, Holywood, Co. Down BT18 0AT. *T:* (028) 9042 3323. *Clubs:* Royal Belfast Golf, Royal Co. Down Golf (Co. Down).

LORNE, Marquess of; Archie Frederick Campbell; *b* 9 March 2004; *s* and *heir* of Duke of Argyll, *qv.*

LOSINSKA, Kathleen Mary, (Kate), OBE 1986; Senior Vice-President, Civil and Public Services Association, 1986–88 (President, 1979–82 and 1983–86, a Vice-President, 1982–83); *b* Croydon, Surrey, 5 Oct. 1924; *d* of late James Henry Conway, Border Regt and Dorothea Marguerite Hill; *m* 1942, Stanislaw Losinski (formerly serving Officer, Polish Air Force, subseq. 301 Bomber Sqdn, RAF, retd with rank of Sqdn Leader; awarded Polish Virtuti Militari Cross, Croix de Guerre, Cross of Lorraine, Yugoslav Cross of Valour, etc; he *d* 2002); one *s*. *Educ:* Selhurst Grammar Sch., Croydon (matriculation); university of life generally. Entered Civil Service, 1939; with Office of Population Censuses and Surveys. Delegate Mem., Council of Civil Service Unions, 1970–87 (Chm. 1980–81); Chm., CS Retirement Fellowship, 2000– (Vice-Chm., 1988–); Management Cttee, CS Benevolent Fund, 1991–. Commissioner: Trade Union TUC Nuclear Energy Review; CS Appeals Bd, 1988. Founder Mem. and Vice-Chm., Trade Union Cttee for European and Transatlantic Understanding. Chairman: White Eagle Trust, 1985; Solidarnosc Foundn. Has held all honorary positions, CPSA. Founder Mem., Resistance Internat., 1983. Governor, Ruskin Coll., 1976, 1979–86. Silver Jubilee Medal, 1977. Kt Comdr, Order of Polonia Restituta, 1987. *Recreations:* journalism, reading, music, history, travel; work for the Christian Trade Union and Moderate Trade Union Movements. *Address:* Loretto, Baggottstown West, Bruff, Co. Limerick, Ireland. *T:* (61) 382225. *Club:* Civil Service.

LOSOWSKY, Prof. Monty Seymour, FRCP; Professor of Medicine and Head of University Department of Medicine, St James's University Hospital, Leeds, 1969–96, now Emeritus Professor; *b* 1 Aug. 1931; *s* of Dora and Myer Losowsky; *m* 1971, Barbara Malkin; one *s* one *d*. *Educ:* Coopers' Company's Sch., London; Univ. of Leeds (Hons MB, ChB; MD). House appts, Leeds Gen. Infirmary, 1955–56; Registrar in Medicine, Epping, 1957–59; Asst, Externe Hôpital St Antoine, Paris, 1960; Research Fellow, Harvard Med. Unit, 1961–62; Lectr, Sen. Lectr, Reader in Medicine, 1962–69, Dean, Faculty of Medicine, 1989–94, Univ. of Leeds. Member: Leeds Eastern Health Authy, 1981–89; Specialist Adv. Cttee on General (Internal) Medicine, 1984–88; Systems Bd Grants Cttee B, MRC, 1984–88; Panel of Studies Allied to Medicine, UGC, 1982–89; British Digestive Foundn Sci. and Res. Awards Cttee, 1987–90; Yorks RHA, 1989–90; Working Gp, France Steering Gp on Undergrad. Medical and Dental Educn, DoH, 1990–94; Council, British Nutrition Foundn, 1991– (Mem. Scientific Adv. Cttee, 1987–91; Scientific Governor, 1991–); GMC, 1991–96; CVCP Rep., Acad. and Res. Staff Cttee of DoH Jt Planning and Adv. Cttee, 1990–94 (Mem., General Purposes Working Gp, 1989–94); Chm., Other Studies and Professions Allied to Medicine Panel, HEFCE, 1995–97. Lectures: Watson Smith, RCPE, 1995; Simms, RCP, 1996. Pres., British Soc. of Gastroenterol., 1993–94. Chm., Coeliac Trust, 1983–95; Governor: Coeliac Soc., 1975–2005 (Chm., Med. Adv. Council, 1995–2003); British Liver Trust, 1999–2001 (Chm., Med. Adv. Cttee, 1999–2001). Examr for Membership, RCP, 1982–96; Academic Observer and Ext. Examr, Utd Examining Bd, 1994–96. Trustee, Thackray Med. Mus., 1995– (Chm., 2000–). Gov., Leeds GS, 1988–2005. *Publications:* (jtly) Malabsorption in Clinical Practice, 1974; (ed) The Gut and Systemic Disease, 1983; (ed jtly) Advanced Medicine, 1983; (jtly) The Liver and Biliary System, 1984; (jtly) Clinical Nutrition in Gastroenterology, 1986; (jtly) Gut Defences in Clinical Practice, 1986; (jtly) Gastroenterology, 1988; Consensus in Clinical Nutrition, 1994; papers relating to haematology, hepatology and gastroenterology. *Recreations:* golf, medical history, walking, DIY, medical biography. *Club:* Royal Society of Medicine.

LOTEN, Alexander William, CB 1984; FCIBSE; Under Secretary, Department of the Environment, and Director, Mechanical and Electrical Engineering Services, Property Services Agency, 1981–85, retired; *b* 11 Dec. 1925; *s* of late Alec Oliver Loten and Alice Maud Loten; *m* 1954, Mary Diana Flint; one *s* one *d*. *Educ:* Churcher's Coll., Petersfield; Corpus Christi Coll., Cambridge Univ. (BA). CEng, FIMechE 1980; FCIBSE 1970. Served War, RNVR, 1943–46 (Air Engr Officer). Engineer: Rolls-Royce Ltd, Derby, 1950–54; Benham & Sons, London, 1954–58; Air Min. Work Directorate, 1958–64; Sen. Engr, 1964–70, Superintending Engr (Mechanical Design), 1970–75, MPBW; Dir of Works, Civil Accommodation, PSA, 1975–81. Pres., CIBS, 1976–77. Lt-Col, Engr and Railway Staff Corps RE, T&AVR, 1979–97. *Recreations:* walking, gardening, bridge. *Address:* Hockridge House, London Road, Maresfield, E Sussex TN22 2EH.

LOTEN, Graeme Neil; HM Diplomatic Service; Ambassador to Republic of Tajikistan, since 2004; *b* 10 March 1959; *s* of Richard Maurice Loten and Brenda Ivy Elizabeth Loten. *Educ:* Portsmouth Grammar Sch.; Liverpool Univ. (BA). Entered Diplomatic Service, 1981; Private Sec. to Ambassador to NATO, 1983–86; Third Sec., Khartoum, 1986–87; Second Sec., The Hague, 1988–92; Dep. Head of Mission, Almaty, 1993–97; Ambassador: to Rwanda and (non-resident) to Burundi, 1998–2001; to Mali, 2001–03; on temp. attachment to Dio. of Cyangugu, Rwanda, 2003–04. *Recreations:* travel, tennis, Portsmouth FC. *Address:* c/o Foreign and Commonwealth Office, King Charles Street, SW1A 2AH. *Clubs:* Royal Commonwealth Society, Royal Over-Seas League.

LOTERY, Prof. Andrew John, MD; FRCOphth; Professor of Ophthalmology, University of Southampton, since 2002; *b* 6 Dec. 1965; *s* of John Samuel Lotery and Caroline Lotery; *m* 1993, Helen Elizabeth Gore; two *s* one *d*. *Educ:* Queen's Univ., Belfast (MD 1997). FRCOphth 1994. Jun. hosp. appts, Belfast, 1989–91; trng in ophthalmology, Belfast, 1991–98; Molecular Ophthalmology Fellowship, 1998–2000, Asst Prof. of Ophthalmology, 2000–02, Univ. of Iowa. Current research developing novel treatments for age related macular degeneration. *Publications:* res. articles in jls incl. New England Jl of Medicine, Nature Genetics. *Recreations:* time with family, reading, running, travel. *Address:* Southampton Eye Unit, Southampton General Hospital, Tremona Road, Southampton SO16 6YD. *T:* (023) 8079 4590, *Fax:* (023) 8079 4120.

LOTHIAN, 13th Marquess of, *cr* 1701; **Michael Andrew Foster Jude Kerr, (Rt Hon. Michael Ancram);** PC 1996; DL; QC (Scot.) 1996; Lord Newbottle, 1591; Earl of Lothian, 1606; Lord Jedburgh, 1622; Earl of Ancram, Baron Kerr of Nisbet, Longnewton and Dolphinstoun, 1633; Viscount of Briene, Baron Ker of Newbattle, 1701; Baron Ker (UK), 1821; MP (C) Devizes, since 1992; *b* 7 July 1945; *s* of 12th Marquess of Lothian, KCVO and Antonella (OBE 1997), *d* of Maj.-Gen. Sir Foster Newland, KCMG, CB; *S* father, 2004; *m* 1975, Lady Jane Fitzalan-Howard, *y d* of 16th Duke of Norfolk, KG, PC, GCVO, GBE, TD, and Lavinia Duchess of Norfolk, LG, CBE; two *d*. *Educ:* Ampleforth; Christ Church, Oxford (BA); Edinburgh Univ. (LLB). Advocate, Scottish Bar, 1970. Contested (C) Edinburgh S, 1987. MP (C): Berwickshire and East Lothian, Feb.–Sept. 1974; Edinburgh S, 1979–87. Parly Under-Sec. of State, Scottish Office, 1983–87, NI Office, 1993–94; Minister of State, NI Office, 1994–97; Opposition front bench spokesman on constitutional affairs, 1997–98; Dep. Leader of the Opposition and Shadow Foreign Sec., 2001–05; Shadow Sec. of State for Internat. Affairs, 2003–05, for Defence, 2005. Member: Select Cttee on Energy, 1979–83; Intelligence and Security Cttee, 2006–. Chairman: Cons. Party in Scotland, 1980–83 (Vice-Chm., 1975–80); Cons. Party, 1998–2001. Chm., Northern Corporate Communications, 1989–91; Dir, CSM Parly Consultants, 1988–92; Mem. Bd, Scottish Homes, 1988–90. DL Roxburgh, Ettrick and Lauderdale, 1990. *Recreations:* ski-ing, photography, folksinging. *Heir:* *b* Lord Ralph William Francis Joseph Kerr [*b* 7 Nov. 1957; *m* 1st, 1980, Lady Virginia FitzRoy (marr. diss. 1987); 2nd, 1988, Marie-Claire Black; four *s* two *d*]. *Address:* House of Commons, SW1A 0AA.

LOTHIAN, Prof. Niall; Professor, Graduate Business School, Heriot-Watt University, since 1996; President, Institute of Chartered Accountants of Scotland, 1995–96; *b* 27 Feb. 1948; *s* of Revd Thomas Lothian and Jean Morgan Lothian (*née* Henderson); *m* 1971, Carol Miller; one *s* one *d*. *Educ:* Daniel Stewart's Coll.; Heriot-Watt Univ. (BA 1971). CA 1972. Lectr, Sen. Lectr, 1973–88, Prof. of Accounting, 1988–96, Director, 1991–93, Business School, Heriot-Watt Univ. Visiting Professor: IMEDE, Lausanne, 1979–80; Univ. of Witwatersrand, 1984; Mem., internat. vis. faculty, INSEAD, Fontainebleau, 1984–; Consultant: UNIDO, China, 1980; NZ Soc. of Accountants, 1992. Mem., Internat. Exec. Adv. Bd, Coll. of Finance and Accountancy, Budapest; Gov., George Watson's Coll., 1991–2004 (Chm., 1999–2004). Chm., Chiene + Tait, CA, 2005–; non-exec. Dir, Stoddard Internat. plc, 1998–2002. Chm., Adv. Audit Bd, Scottish Parly Corp. Body, 2002–. Gov., RSAMD, 2007–. Trustee, Lloyds TSB Charitable Foundn for Scotland, 1997–99. FRSA. *Publications:* How Companies Manage R&D, 1984; Measuring Corporate Performance, 1987; (jtly) Accounting, 1991; (contrib.) Ernst and Young Manager's Handbook, 2nd edn 1992; articles in professional jls. *Recreations:* graveyards, golf. *Address:* 30 Granby Road, Edinburgh EH16 5NL. *T:* (0131) 667 4429. *Clubs:* New (Edinburgh); Royal & Ancient Golf; Luffness New Golf.

LOTON, Brian Thorley, AC 1989; FTS; Chairman: Broken Hill Proprietary Co. Ltd, 1992–97; Atlas Copco Australia Pty Ltd, 1996–2001; Director, Australian Foundation Investment Co. Ltd, 1993–2001; *b* Perth, WA, 17 May 1929; *s* of Sir (Ernest) Thorley Loton and Grace (*née* Smith); *m* 1956, Joan Kemelfield; two *s* two *d*. *Educ:* Hale Sch., Perth; Trinity Coll., Melbourne Univ. (BMetEng 1953). Joined BHP as Cadet 1954; Technical Asst, 1959; Asst Chief Engr, 1961; Gen. Manager Planning and Develt, 1969, Gen. Manager Newcastle Steel Works, 1970; Exec. Gen. Manager Steel Div., 1973; Dir, 1976; Chief Gen. Manager, 1977; Man. Dir, 1982; Chief Exec. Officer, 1984, Dep. Chm., 1991. Director: Nat. Australia Bank, 1988–99 (Vice Chm., 1992–99); Amcor Ltd, 1992–99. President: Aust. Inst. of Mining and Metallurgy, 1982 (Mem. Council); Australian Mining Industry Council, 1983–84; Business Council of Aust., 1990–92; Vice-Chairman: Internat. Iron and Steel Inst., 1988, 1992–94 (Chm., 1991–92); Defence Industry Cttee, 1976–88; Member: Aust. Sci. and Technol. Council, 1977–80; Aust. Manufg Council, 1977–81; Vict. Govt Long Range Policy Planning Cttee, 1980–82; Aust. Council on Population and Ethnic Affairs, 1980–82. Internat. Counsellor, The Conf. Bd, 1984–97. Pres., Vic. Br., Scout Assoc. of Australia, 1997–2002. Mem. Faculty Engrg, Melbourne Univ., 1980–83. FIE (Aust) 1984 (Hon. Fellow); FAIM 1973; FIDA 1980. *Address:* c/o GPO Box 86A, Melbourne, Vic 3001, Australia. *Clubs:* Melbourne, Australian (Melbourne).

LOTT, (Chester) Trent, JD; US Senator from Mississippi, 1989–2007; *b* 9 Oct. 1941; *s* of Chester P. Lott and Iona Lott (*née* Watson); *m* 1964, Patricia E. Thompson; one *s* one *d*. *Educ:* Univ. of Mississippi (BPA 1963; JD 1967). Admitted to Mississippi Bar, 1967; Associate, Bryan & Gordon, 1967; Admin. Asst to Congressman William M. Colmer, 1968–72; Mem., US Congress, 1973–89; Leader, US Senate, 1996–2001 and 2002. Mem., Senate Republican Policy Cttee. *Publication:* Herding Cats: a life in politics (autobiog.), 2005. *Address:* c/o Russell Senate Office Building, Washington, DC 20510, USA.

LOTT, Dame Felicity (Ann Emwhyla), DBE 1996 (CBE 1990); FRCM; soprano; *b* 8 May 1947; *d* of John Albert Lott and Whyla (*née* Williams); *m* 1st, 1973, Robin Mavesyn Golding (marr. diss. 1982); 2nd, 1984, Gabriel Woolf; one *d*. *Educ:* Pate's Grammar Sch. for Girls, Cheltenham; Royal Holloway Coll., Univ. of London (BA Hons French; Hon. Fellow, 1995); Royal Acad. of Music (LRAM; ARAM 1976; FRAM 1986). FRCM 2006. Début: ENO, 1975; Covent Garden, 1976; Glyndebourne, 1977. Particularly associated with Mozart and Richard Strauss, whose operas she has sung in Glyndebourne, Covent Garden, Cologne, Hamburg, Brussels, Paris, Vienna, Munich, Dresden, Milan, NY, Chicago and Japan; gives recitals worldwide; many recordings. Founder Mem., The Songmakers' Almanac. Dr *hc* Sussex, 1989; Hon. DLitt Loughborough, 1996; Hon. DMus: London, 1997; RSAMD 1998; Leicester, 2000; Oxford, 2001. Bayerische Kammersängerin, 2003. Officier, Ordre des Arts et des Lettres (France), 2000 (Chevalier, 1993); Chevalier de la Légion d'Honneur (France), 2001. *Recreations:* reading, annoying the family, singing. *Address:* c/o Askonas Holt Ltd, Lincoln House, 300 High Holborn, WC1V 7JH. *T:* (020) 7400 1700.

LOTT, Trent; *see* Lott, C. T.

LOUDEN, Rt Rev. Mgr Stephen Henry, PhD; Research Associate, Centre for Theology and Education, Bangor University (formerly University of Wales, Bangor), since 1998; *b* 18 Nov. 1941; *s* of late Joseph Henry Louden and Sarah (*née* McNaughten). *Educ:* Upholland Coll. BA Open 1975; DipTh CNAA 1991; MTh Oxon 1993; PhD Wales 1998. Ordained priest, dio. Liverpool, 1968; Curate: All Saints, Anfield, 1968–73; St John's, Kirkdale, 1973–75; Our Lady's, Formby, 1975–78; Royal Army Chaplains' Department: TA Commn, 1973–78; Regular Army Commn, 1978; Dortmund Garrison, 1978–79; 8 Inf. Bde, 1979–80; Munster Garrison, 1980–82; Dhekelia Garrison, 1982–84; RC Chaplain, RMA Sandhurst, 1984–86; Berlin Inf. Bde, 1986–88; HQ NI, 1988; Hong Kong, 1988–90; Senior Chaplain RC: HQ BAOR, 1990–92; HQ NI, 1992–93; Principal RC Chaplain and VG (Army), 1993–97. Prelate of Honour, 1993. *Publications:* Chaplains in Conflict, 1996; (jtly) The Naked Parish Priest, 2003; contrib. to learned jls. *Recreations:* horology, photography, history. *Address:* 3 Ridgefield Road, Wirral, Cheshire CH61 8RS. *Club:* Army and Navy.

LOUDON, Deborah Jane, (Mrs H. Woudhuysen); Consultant, Saxton Bampfylde Hever, since 2008; Director General, Civilian Personnel, Ministry of Defence, 2005–07; *b* 4 June 1955; *d* of Joseph Buist Loudon and Joan Katherine Loudon (*née* Ede); *m* 1987, Prof. Henry Woudhuysen; two *s*. *Educ:* Malvern Girls' Coll.; Somerville Coll., Oxford (MA PPE). Home Office, 1977–2003: Private Sec. to Minister of State, 1983–84; Principal, Prison Service, 1984; Grade 5, Police Dept, 1993–99; HR Dir, 2000–03; Dir Gen., Security and Safety, MoD, 2003–05. FCIPD 2002.

LOUDON, Maj. Gen. Euan; *see* Loudon, Maj. Gen. W. E. B.

LOUDON, George Ernest; Chairman: Altius Holdings Ltd, since 1999; Altius Associates Ltd, since 2002; Pall Mall Capital Ltd, since 2001; *b* 19 Nov. 1942; *m* 1968, Angela Mary Goldsbrough; one *s* one *d*. *Educ:* Christelijk Lyceum, Zeist; Balliol Coll., Oxford (BA); Johns Hopkins Univ., Washington (MA). Lazard Frères & Cie, Paris, 1967–68; Ford Foundn, New York and Jakarta, 1968–71; McKinsey & Co., Amsterdam, 1971–76; Amro Bank, Amsterdam: Gen. Man., 1976–83; Mem., Bd of Man. Dirs, 1983–88; Dir, Midland Group, 1988–92; Chief Exec., 1988–92, Chm., 1991–92, Midland Montagu; Chm., Helix Associates Ltd, 1993–2005. Non-executive Director: M&G Gp, 1993–94; Arjo-Wiggins Appleton, 1993–2000; Harrison/Parrott Ltd, 1993–; Global Asset Management, 1994–99; Logica CMG (formerly CMG) plc, 1998–; Evolution (formerly Beeson Gregory) Gp plc, 2001–04. Mem. Bd, Multiple Sclerosis Internat. Fedn, 1999–. *Address:* PO Box 34865, W8 7WL.

LOUDON, John Duncan Ott, OBE 1988; FRCSE, FRCOG; retired; Consultant Obstetrician and Gynaecologist, Eastern General Hospital, Edinburgh, 1960–87; Senior Lecturer, University of Edinburgh, 1962–93; *b* 22 Aug. 1924; *s* of late James Alexander Law Loudon and Ursula (*née* Ott); *m* 1953, Nancy Beaton (*née* Mann); two *s*. *Educ:* John Watson's Sch., Edinburgh; Wyggeston Sch., Leicester; Univ. of Edinburgh (MB, ChB 1947). FRCSE 1954; FRCOG 1973 (MRCOG 1956). National Service, RAF, 1948–50. House appts, Edinburgh and Cambridge, 1948–52; Registrar, Sen. Registrar and Consultant Obstetrician and Gynaecologist, Simpson Maternity Pavilion and Royal Infirm., Edinburgh, 1954–66. Formerly Examiner in Obstetrics and Gynaecology: Univs of Cardiff, Manchester, Leeds, Dundee, Glasgow, Aberdeen, Newcastle upon Tyne, Cape Town, RCSI, RCSE, RCOG and RACOG. Adviser in Family Welfare to Govt of Malta, 1976–81. Vice Pres., RCOG, 1981–84 (Mem. Council, 1966–72 and 1976–81). Member: Interim Licensing Authority for IVF, 1985–91; GMC, 1986–92. *Publications:* papers to obstetric and gynaecol jls. *Recreations:* gardening, golf, travel, food and wine. *Address:* Ardbeg, 4 Kinnear Road, Edinburgh EH3 5PE. *T:* (0131) 552 1327. *Clubs:* Royal Air Force; Bruntsfield Links Golfing Society (Edinburgh).

LOUDON, Prof. Rodney, FRS 1987; Professor of Physics, Essex University, 1967, now Emeritus; *b* 25 July 1934; *s* of Albert Loudon and Doris Helen (*née* Blane); *m* 1960, Mary Anne Philips; one *s* one *d*. *Educ:* Bury Grammar Sch.; Brasenose Coll., Oxford (MA, DPhil). Postdoctoral Fellow, Univ. of California, Berkeley, 1959–60; Scientific Civil Servant, RRE Malvern, 1960–65; Member, Technical Staff: Bell Labs, Murray Hill, NJ, 1965–66, 1970; RCA Labs, Zurich, 1975; Essex University: Reader in Physics, 1966–67; Dean of Sch. of Physical Scis, 1972–74; Chm. of Physics Dept, 1976–79 and 1988–89. Visiting Professor: Yale Univ., 1975; Univ. of California, Irvine, 1980; Ecole Polytechnique, Lausanne, 1985; Univ. of Rome, 1988 and 1996; Univ. of Strathclyde, 1998–. Chm., Bd of Editors of Optica Acta, 1984–87. Fellow, Optical Soc. of America, 1994. Thomas Young Medal and Prize, Inst. of Physics, 1987; Max Born Award, Optical Soc. of Amer., 1992; Alexander von Humboldt Prize, 1998. *Publications:* The Quantum Theory of Light, 1973, 3rd edn 2000; (with W. Hayes) Scattering of Light by Crystals, 1978; (ed with V. M. Agranovich) Surface Excitations, 1984; (with D. J. Barber) An Introduction to the Properties of Condensed Matter, 1989; papers in Nature, Phys. Rev., JL Mod. Opt., Jl Phys., etc. *Recreations:* music, gardening. *Address:* 3 Gaston Street, East Bergholt, Colchester, Essex CO7 6SD. *T:* (01206) 298550.

LOUDON, Maj. Gen. (William) Euan (Buchanan), CBE 2004 (OBE 1991); Chief Executive, Edinburgh Military Tattoo, since 2007; *b* 12 March 1956; *s* of David Christie Buchanan Loudon and Doreen Mary Loudon; *m* 1981, Penelope Jane Head. *Educ:* Uddingston Grammar Sch.; Royal Military Acad., Sandhurst. Commnd Royal Highland Fusiliers, 1975; Adjt 1st Bn, 1980–83; Exchange Officer, CTC RM, 1983–85; Army Staff Coll., 1988; Bde Maj. 7th Armoured Bde, 1989–91; UN Monitoring Orgn, Zagreb, 1995; CO 1RHF, 1995–97; Mil. Sec. (A), 1997–99; Comdr 39th Inf. Bde, 1999–2001; COS and Comdr Force Troops HQ NI, 2001–03; GOC 2nd Div., and Gov., Edinburgh Castle, 2004–07. FCMI 2003. *Recreations:* field sports, fishing, golf, travel, hobby farming. *Clubs:* Caledonian; New (Edinburgh).

LOUDOUN, 14th Earl of, *cr* 1633; **Michael Edward Abney-Hastings;** Lord Campbell of Loudoun, 1601; Lord Mauchline, 1638; *b* 22 July 1942; *s* of Countess of Loudoun (13th in line) and Captain Walter Strickland Lord; assumed, by deed poll, the surname of Abney-Hastings in lieu of his patronymic, 1946; *S* mother, 2002; *co-heir* (with aunt and cousins) to Baronies of Botreaux 1368, Stanley 1456 and Hastings 1461; *m* 1969, Noelene Margaret McCormick (*d* 2002), 2nd *d* of Mr and Mrs W. J. McCormick, Barham, NSW; two *s* three *d* (of whom one *s* one *d* are twins); *m* 2008, Margaret Ann Buntin, *e d* of late H. L. Thomas; three step *s* one step *d*. *Educ:* Ampleforth. *Heir: s* Lord Mauchline, *qv*.

LOUGH, Paula Jane; *see* Radcliffe, P. J.

LOUGHBOROUGH, Lord; Jamie William St Clair-Erskine; *b* 28 May 1986; *s* and *heir* of Earl of Rosslyn, *qv*.

LOUGHBOROUGH, Archdeacon of; *see* Hackwood, Ven. P. C.

LOUGHEED, Hon. (Edgar) Peter, CC 1987; PC (Can.) 1982; QC (Can.) 1972; Counsel, Bennett Jones, barristers and solicitors, Calgary and Edmonton; *b* Calgary, 26 July 1928; *s* of late Edgar Donald Lougheed and Edna Bauld; *m* 1952, Jeanne Estelle Rogers, Edmonton; two *s* two *d*. *Educ:* public and secondary schs, Calgary; Univ. of Alberta (BA, LLB); Harvard Grad. Sch. of Business (MBA). Read law with Calgary firm of lawyers; called to Bar of Alberta, 1955, and practised law with same firm, 1955–56. Joined Mannix Co. Ltd, as Sec., 1956 (Gen. Counsel, 1958, Vice-Pres., 1959, Dir, 1960). Entered private legal practice, 1962. Chm., Quorum Funding Corp.; Director: Princeton Developments; Aon Reed Stenhouse Cos Ltd; Bechtel Canada Inc. Elected: Provincial Leader of Progressive Conservative Party of Alberta, also Member for Calgary West, 1965; Leader of the Official Opposition, 1967; Premier of Alberta, 1971–85 (re-elected 1975, 1979 and 1982). Mem., Trilateral Commn, 1999–. Mem., Canadian Adv. Bd, Carlyle Gp, 2001–. Chancellor, Queen's Univ., Ontario, 1996–2002, now Chancellor Emeritus. Hon. LLD: St Francis Xavier, 1983; Alberta, 1986; Calgary, 1986; Windsor, Lethbridge, 1988; Dalhousie, 1995; Queen's, 1996; Toronto, 1997. *Recreations:* golf, ski-ing. *Address:* (office) 4500 Bankers Hall East, 855 2nd Street SW, Calgary, AB T2P 4K7, Canada.

LOUGHRAN, Sir Gerald (Finbar), KCB 2002; Head, Northern Ireland Civil Service, 2000–02; *b* 22 Feb. 1942; *m* Gemma, (Her Honour Judge Gemma Loughran); one *s* one *d* (and one *s* decd). *Educ:* St Malachy's Coll., Belfast; QUB (BSc (Econ)). Northern Ireland Civil Service: posts in Dept of Econ. Develt and Dept of Envmt; Perm. Sec., Dept of Econ. Develt, 1991–2000. Chairman: Grafton Recruitment, 2002–; Phoenix Natural Gas, 2003–; Director: W. G. Baird Gp, 2003–; Allied Irish Bank (UK), 2005–; Kellen Investments, 2006–. Hon. Prof., QUB. Hon. DLitt Ulster, 2004.

LOUGHRAN, James; conductor; *b* 30 June 1931; *s* of James and Agnes Loughran; *m* 1st, 1961, Nancy Coggon (marr. diss. 1983; she *d* 1996); two *s*; 2nd, 1985, Ludmila (*née* Navratil). *Educ:* St Aloysius' Coll., Glasgow; Bonn, Amsterdam and Milan. FRNCM 1976; FRSAMD 1983. 1st Prize, Philharmonia Orchestra's Conducting Competition, 1961. Associate Conductor, Bournemouth SO, 1962–65; Principal Conductor: BBC Scottish SO, 1965–71; Bamberg SO, 1979–83; Prin. Conductor and Musical Advr, 1971–83, Conductor Laureate, 1983–91, Hallé Orchestra; Musical Dir, English Opera Gp, 1966 (Festivals of Drottningholm, Versailles and Aldeburgh); Chief Conductor, 1996–2003, Principal Guest Conductor, 2003–, Aarhus SO, Denmark. Guest conductor of principal orchestras of Europe, America, Australasia and Japan; conducted opera at Sadler's Wells, Royal Opera House, Scottish Opera, Netherlands Opera and Montpellier Opera; Guest Conductor, Stockholm Philharmonic, 1977–92; Guest Conductor, 1980–, Permanent Guest Conductor, 1993–, Hon. Conductor, 2006, Japan Philharmonic SO; Chief Guest Conductor, BBC Welsh SO, 1987–90. Internat. festivals and tours with Bamberg and Hallé orchestras, as well as Munich Philharmonic, BBC Symphony, Stockholm Philharmonic, London Philharmonic and Scottish Chamber orchestras; conductor, BBC Proms, 1965–89, incl. 5 last nights. Many recordings, including complete Beethoven, Brahms and Elgar symphonies. Gold Disc, EMI, 1983. Freeman, City of London, 1991; Liveryman, Musicians' Co., 1992. Hon. DMus: Sheffield, 1983; RSAMD, 2005. *Address:* 18 Hatfield Drive, Glasgow G12 0YA. *Club:* Glasgow Art (Glasgow).

LOUGHRAN, Rear-Adm. Terence William, CB 1997; Chief Executive, Sabrage Enterprises, since 1998; *b* Newcastle-upon-Tyne, 27 March 1943; parents decd; *m* (marr. diss. 1988); one *s* two *d*; *m* 1995, Philippa Mary Vernon. *Educ:* Devonport High Sch.; Britannia Royal Naval Coll. MNI 1993; FRAeS 1997. Qualified as: rotary wing pilot, 1967; flying instructor, 1971; graduated Canadian Forces Comd and Staff Coll., 1976; i/c 706 Naval Air Sqdn, 1976–77; Comdr 1979; i/c HMS Phoebe, 1980–81; Executive Officer: HMS Bristol, 1983–84; HMS Intrepid, 1984–85; Captain 1986; i/c HMS Gloucester and Comdr Armilla Patrol, Arabian Gulf Task Unit, 1986–88; Dep. Dir, Internat. Affairs in Naval Staff Duties, 1988–90; Dir, Naval Manpower Planning, 1990–92; i/c HMS Ark Royal and Comdr, Grapple Adriatic Task Gp, 1993–94; Rear-Adm., 1995; Flag Officer, Naval Aviation, 1995–98. Mem., Rona Trust, 1991– (Skipper Emeritus, 2004); Chairman of Trustees: FAA Mus., 2005–; Fly Navy Heritage Trust, 2005–. Gov., Countess Gytha Sch., 1996–2005. *Publications:* (contrib.) Royal United Services Inst. Jl. *Recreations:* sailing, motor cycling, spinning yarns. *Address:* Court Lodge, St Margarets Road, Tintinhull, Somerset BA22 8PL. *T:* and *Fax:* (01935) 824298; *e-mail:* twl@sabrage.com. *Clubs:* Royal Navy; Travellers (Newcastle); Yeovil Beefsteak and Kidney Pudding.

LOUGHREY, (Stephen Victor) Patrick; Director, Nations and Regions, BBC, since 2000; *b* 29 Dec. 1955; *s* of Eddie Loughrey and Mary Loughrey (*née* Griffin); *m* 1978, Patricia Kelly; one *s* two *d*. *Educ:* Loretto Coll., Milford; Univ. of Ulster (BA); Queen's Univ. (MA). Res. student, Trent Univ., Canada, 1977; teacher, St Colm's Draperstown, 1978–84; BBC: Producer, Educn, 1984–88; Hd, Educnl Broadcasting, 1988–91; Hd of Progs, NI, 1991–94; Controller, NI, 1994–2000. Fellow, Radio Acad., 2004–. Trustee, Teaching Awards Trust, 2008–. Jt Editor, Ulster Local Studies, 1988–91. *Publication:* People of Ireland, 1988. *Recreations:* walking, talking. *Address:* BBC White City, 201 Wood Lane, W12 7TS. *T:* (020) 8008 1220.

LOUGHTON, David Clifford; Chief Executive, The Royal Wolverhampton Hospitals NHS Trust, since 2004; *b* 28 Jan. 1954; *s* of late Clifford Loughton and of Hazel Loughton; *m* 1986, Deborah Wellington; one *s* one *d*. *Educ:* Roxet Manor Sch., Harrow; tech. colls in Harrow, Watford and Southall. MIHospE 1974; MIPlantE 1976; TEng (CEI) 1978; MHSM 1993. Asst hosp. engr, Hillingdon AHA, 1974–76; hosp. engr, Herts AHA, 1976–78; Dir and Gen. Manager, Ducost Ltd, 1978–83; Divl Manager, GEC Electrical Projects, 1984–86; Chief Exec., Walsgrave Hosps, subseq. Univ. Hosps Coventry and Warwicks, NHS Trust, 1986–2002; Develt Dir, InHealth Gp, 2002–04. Chm., Coventry and Warwicks Educn and Trng Consortium, 1996–2001; Member: NHS Confedn Nat. Council, 2007–; Adv. Bd, NHS Nat. Inst. for Health Res., 2007–. *Recreations:* home improvements, walking, sport. *Address:* The Royal Wolverhampton Hospitals NHS Trust, Hollybush House, New Cross Hospital, Wolverhampton WV10 0QP. *T:* (01902) 695951; Blacon Cottage, Norton Lindsey, Warwick CV35 8JN. *T:* (01926) 842070.

LOUGHTON, Timothy Paul; MP (C) East Worthing and Shoreham, since 1997; *b* 30 May 1962; *s* of Rev. Michael Loughton and Pamela Dorothy Loughton (*née* Brandon); *m* 1992, Elizabeth Juliet MacLauchlan; one *s* two *d*. *Educ:* Priory Sch., Lewes; Univ. of Warwick (BA 1st cl. Hons); Clare Coll., Cambridge. Joined Montagu Loebl Stanley, then Fleming Private Asset Mgt, 1984, Dir 1992–2000. Formerly: Member: Wandsworth CHC; Substance Misuse Cttee, Wandsworth HA; Battersea Sector Policing Gp; Vice-Chm., Wandsworth Alcohol Gp. Joined Conservative Party, 1977; various posts in local assocs in Lewes, Warwick Univ., Cambridge Univ. and Battersea, 1978–91; Dep. Chm., Battersea Cons. Assoc., 1994–96. Contested (C) Sheffield Brightside, 1992. Opposition spokesman: for envmt, transport and the regions, 2000–01; for health, 2001–07; for children, 2003–. Mem., Envmtl Audit Select Cttee, 1997–2001. Member: Finance Bill Standing Cttee, 1997–98; Jt House Cttee on Financial Services and Markets Bill, 1999; Treasurer: Parly Maritime Gp, 1997–; Parly Animal Welfare Gp, 2001–07; Parly Archaeology Gp, 2002–; Vice Chairman: All Party Autism Gp; All Party Cardiac Risk in the Young Gp, 2005–; Parly Gp for Children, 2005–; Chairman: All Party Gp for Wholesale Financial Mkts, 2005–; Cons. Disability Gp, 1998–2006; Jt Chm., Parly Mental Health Gp, 2005–. Captain, Commons and Lords Hockey Team, 2003–. Member: Sussex Archaeol Soc.; BM Soc. *Recreations:* archaeology, classics, wine, ski-ing, tennis, hockey. *Address:* House of Commons, SW1A 0AA.

LOUIS, Prof. (William) Roger, Hon. CBE 1999; DLitt; FBA; Kerr Professor of English History and Culture, since 1985, Distinguished Teaching Professor, since 1998, University of Texas at Austin; Supernumerary Fellow, St Antony's College, Oxford, 1986–96 (Hon. Fellow, since 1996); *b* 8 May 1936; *s* of Henry Edward and Bena May Louis; *m* 1st, 1960, Patricia Ann Leonard; one *s* one *d*; 2nd, 1983, Dagmar Cecilia Friedrich. *Educ:* Univ. of Oklahoma (Phi Beta Kappa, BA 1959); Harvard (Woodrow Wilson Fellow; MA 1960); St Antony's Coll., Oxford (Marshall Scholar; DPhil 1962); DLitt Oxon 1979. FRHistS 1984; Corresp. FBA 1993. Asst and Associate Prof., Yale, 1962–70; Humanities Research Center, University of Texas: Prof. of History and Curator, Historical Collections, 1970–85; Dir, British Studies, 1975–; Teaching Awards, 1984, 1992, 1993, 1998; National Endowment Humanities: Sen. Fellow, 1974–75; Dir, Seminars, 1985–2000. Guggenheim Fellow, 1979–80; Vis. Fellow, 1979–80, 2004, Chichele Lectr, 1990, 2002, 2003, 2006, All Souls Coll., Oxford; Vis. Fellow, Balliol Coll., Oxford, 2005; Fellow/Lecturer: Churchill Coll., Cambridge, 1985; Brookings Instn, 1989; LSE, 1992; Woodrow Wilson Internat. Center for Scholars, 1994–95, 2000; lectures: Cust, Univ. of Nottingham, 1995; British Acad. Inaugural Elie Kedourie Meml, 1996; Churchill Meml, Westminster Coll., Fulton, Mo, 1998; Antonius, Oxford Univ., 2002; Leonard Stein, Oxford, 2005; Strelitz, Tel Aviv, 2008. Dist. Vistor, Dept of Hist., Univ. of Peking, 1998; Dist. Vis. Prof., Amer. Univ. in Cairo, 2001. Founding Dir, Nat. History Center, 2001–. Chm., US Dept of State Histl Adv. Cttee, 2001–; Mem., Scholars' Council, Liby of Congress, 2006–. Pres., Amer. Historical Assoc., 2001–02. Trustee, British Empire Mus., Bristol, 2005–. Editor, British Documents on the End of Empire, 1988–; Editor-in-Chief, Oxford History of the British Empire, 1992–. Hon. DPhil Westminster Coll., 1998. *Publications:* Ruanda-Urundi, 1963; Germany's Lost Colonies, 1967; (ed with P. Gifford) Britain and Germany in Africa, 1967; (with J. Stengers) Congo Reform Movement, 1968; British Strategy in the Far East, 1971; (ed with P. Gifford) France and Britain in Africa, 1971; (ed) Nationalism Security and International Trusteeship in the Pacific, 1972; (ed) A. J. P. Taylor and his Critics, 1972; (ed) Imperialism: the Robinson and Gallagher controversy, 1976; Imperialism at Bay, 1977; (ed with W. S. Livingston) Australia, New Zealand and the Pacific Islands, 1979; (ed with P. Gifford) The Transfer of Power in Africa, 1982; The British Empire in the Middle East 1945–51, 1984 (Amer. Hist. Assoc. Prize); (ed with R. Stookey) The End of the Palestine Mandate, 1986; (ed with H. Bull) The Special Relationship, 1986; (ed with P. Gifford) Decolonization in Africa, 1988; (ed with J. A. Bill) Musaddiq, Nationalism and Oil, 1988; (ed with R. Owen) Suez 1956, 1989; (ed with R. Fernea) The Iraqi Revolution, 1991; In the Name of God Go! Leo Amery and the British Empire, 1992; (ed with R. Blake) Churchill, 1993; (ed) Adventures with Britannia: personalities, politics and culture in Britain, 1995; (ed) More Adventures with Britannia, 1998; (ed with Michael Howard) The Oxford History of the Twentieth Century, 1998; (ed with J. M. Brown) The Oxford History of the British Empire, vol. IV: the twentieth century, 1999; (ed with Roger Owen) A Revolutionary Year: the Middle East in 1958, 2002; (ed) Still More Adventures with Britannia, 2003; (ed) Yet More Adventures with Britannia, 2005; (ed) Burnt Orange Britannia, 2005; Ends of British Imperialism, 2006; (ed) Penultimate Adventures with Britannia, 2007; *festschrift:* (ed Robert King and Robin Kilson) The Statecraft of British Imperialism: essays in honor of Wm Roger Louis, 1999. *Recreation:* a German wife. *Address:* Department of History, University of Texas, Austin, TX 78712, USA. *Clubs:* Reform; Century (NY), Metropolitan (Washington).

LOUISY, Rt Hon. Sir Allan (Fitzgerald Laurent), KCMG 2005; CBE 1983; PC 1981; barrister; *b* Laborie, St Lucia, 5 Sept. 1916. Clerk, Educn Dept, St Lucia; called to the Bar, Middle Temple and St Lucia, 1949; first Supervisor of Elections, St Lucia, 1950; Crown Attorney, Magistrate, then Registrar of the Supreme Court and Court of Appeal, Jamaica; Judge of the Supreme Court, Windward and Leeward Islands, until 1973. Chm., Nat. Insurance Scheme. Mem. (St Lucia Lab) Laborie, House of Assembly, 1974–82; Leader, St Lucia Labour Party, 1974–82; Prime Minister of St Lucia, and Minister of Finance, Home Affairs, Inf. and Tourism, 1979–81; Minister without Portfolio, 1981–82; Attorney Gen., 1982. Gen. Sec., Seamen and Waterfront Workers Trade Union. Pres., St Lucia Civil Service Assoc. St Lucia Cross, 1998. *Address:* Laborie, St Lucia, West Indies.

LOUISY, Dame (Calliopa) Pearlette, Grand Cross, Order of St Lucia, 1997; GCMG 1999; Governor General, St Lucia, since 1997; *b* 8 June 1946; *d* of Rita Louisy. *Educ:* St Joseph's Convent; Univ. of West Indies (BA); Université Laval, Quebec (MA); Univ. of Bristol (PhD 1994). Principal, St Lucia A-Level Coll., 1981–86; Sir Arthur Lewis Community College: Dean, 1986–94; Vice Principal, 1994–95; Principal, 1996–97. Hon. LLD: Bristol, 1999; Sheffield, 2003. DStJ 2002. *Recreations:* horticulture, performing arts, reading. *Address:* Government House, Morne Fortune, Castries, St Lucia. *T:* 4522481.

LOUSTAU-LALANNE, Bernard Michel; barrister; international copyright consultant; *b* 20 June 1938; *s* of Michel Loustau-Lalanne, OBE, and Madeleine (*née* Boullé); *m* 1974, Debbie Elizabeth Grieve (*née* Temple-Brown) (marr. diss. 1982); one *d. Educ:* Seychelles Coll.; St Mary's Coll., Southampton; Imperial Coll., London. Called to the Bar, Middle Temple, London, 1969. Assistant Inspector, Northern Rhodesia Police, 1962–64; Crown Counsel, Seychelles, 1970–72; Sen. State Counsel and Official Notary, 1972–76; Attorney-General, Seychelles, 1976–78; High Comr for Seychelles, in London, 1978–80; concurrently Seychelles Ambassador to USA, and Seychelles Perm. Rep. to UN; Internat. Rep., PRS, 1980–90; Sec.-Gen., Eur. Fedn of Mgt Consulting Assocs, 1991–92. *Recreations:* international affairs, French literature, theatre, tennis. *Address:* 2 Albert Mansions, Luxborough Street, W1U 5BQ.

LOUTH, 16th Baron *cr* 1541; **Otway Michael James Oliver Plunkett;** *b* 19 Aug. 1929; *o s* of Otway Randal Percy Oliver Plunkett, 15th Baron, and Ethel May, *d* of Walter John Gallichan, Jersey, Channel Islands; *S* father, 1950; *m* 1951, Angela Patricia Cullinane, Jersey; three *s* two *d. Heir: s* Hon. Jonathan Oliver Plunkett, BSc, AMIEE [*b* 4 Nov. 1952; *m* 1981, Jennifer, *d* of Norman Oliver Hodgetts, Weston-super-Mare; one *s* one *d*].

LOVAT, 18th Lord (S) *cr* 1458–1464 (*de facto* 16th Lord, 18th but for the attainder); **Simon Fraser;** Baron (UK) 1837; *b* 13 Feb. 1977; *er s* of Hon. Simon Augustine Fraser, Master of Lovat (*d* 1994) and of Virginia Fraser (who *m* 1998, Frank Robert Johnson, journalist (*d* 2006)), *d* of David Grose; *S* grandfather, 1995. *Educ:* Harrow; Edinburgh Univ. *Heir: b* Jack Fraser, Master of Lovat, *b* 22 Aug. 1984.

LOVE, Andrew; MP (Lab and Co-op) Edmonton, since 1997; *b* 21 March 1949; *s* of late James Love and Olive Love (*née* Mills); *m* 1983, Ruth, *d* of late Jack and Esther Rosenthal. *Educ:* Strathclyde Univ. (BSc Hons). FCIS. Parly Officer, Co-operative Party, 1993–97. Mem. (Lab), Haringey LBC, 1980–86 (Chairman: Finance, 1984–85; Housing, 1985–86). Mem., NE Thames RHA, 1988–90. Contested (Lab and Co-op) Edmonton, 1992. PPS to Minister of State: DoH, 2001–03; for Industry and the Regions, DTI, 2003–05. Member: Public Accounts Cttee, H of C, 1997–2001; Deregulation Select Cttee, 1999–2001; Regulatory Reform Select Cttee, 2001–05; Treasury Select Cttee, 2005–. Chairman: All Party Bldg Socs and Financial Mutuals Gp (formerly All Party Building Socs Gp), 1997–2002; All Party Lebanon Gp, 2002–; All Party Small Businesses Gp, 2005– (Sec., 2000–05); Co-Chairman: All Party Homelessness and Housing Needs Gp, 2000–; All Party Sri Lanka Gp, 2004– (Sec., 1999–2004); Vice-Chm., All Party Opera Gp, 2001–. Trustee, Industrial Common Ownership Finance, 1991–. FRSA. *Publication:* (contrib.) Parliament in the 21st Century, 2004. *Recreations:* golf, opera, reading. *Address:* House of Commons, SW1A 0AA. *T:* (020) 7219 6377, *Fax:* (020) 7219 6623, *T:* (constituency office) (020) 8803 0574, *Fax:* (020) 8807 1673; *e-mail:* lovea@parliament.uk.

LOVE, Graham Carvell, FCA; Chief Executive, QinetiQ Group plc, since 2005; *b* 18 March 1954; *s* of Peter and Nancy Love; *m* (marr. diss.); one *s* one *d. Educ:* Fitzwilliam Coll., Cambridge (BA Hons Eng. 1975). Gp Financial Controller, Shandwick plc, 1988–92; Finance Dir, Defence Res. Agency, 1992–96; Chief Exec., Comax Secure Business Services, 1996–99; Chief Financial Officer, QinetiQ, 2001–05. Chm., Racing Green Cars, 1999–. *Recreations:* historic motor racing, shooting, ski-ing, sailing. *Address:* QinetiQ, Cody Technology Park, Farnborough, Hants GU14 0LX. *T:* (01252) 397588, *Fax:* (01252) 394777; *e-mail:* glove@qinetiq.com.

LOVE, Prof. Philip Noel, CBE 1983; DL; AcSS; Vice Chancellor, University of Liverpool, 1992–2002; *b* 25 Dec. 1939; *o s* of Thomas Isaac and Ethel Violet Love; *m* 1st, 1963, Isabel Leah (*d* 1993), *yr d* of Innes Taylor and Leah Wallace Mearns; three *s*; 2nd, 1995, Isobel, *widow* of David Pardey. *Educ:* Aberdeen Grammar Sch.; Aberdeen Univ. (MA 1961, LLB 1963). Admitted Solicitor in Scotland, 1963; Advocate in Aberdeen, 1963–; Partner, Campbell Connon, Solicitors, Aberdeen, 1963–74, Consultant, 1974–2004. University of Aberdeen: Prof. of Conveyancing and Professional Practice of Law, 1974–92; Dean, Faculty of Law, 1979–82, 1991–92; Vice Principal, 1986–90. Law Society of Scotland: Mem. Council, 1975–86; Examr, 1975–83 (Chm. Examrs, 1977–80); Vice-Pres., 1980–81; Pres., 1981–82. Local Chm., Rent Assessment Panel for Scotland, 1972–92; Chairman: Sec. of State for Scotland's Expert Cttee on house purchase and sale, 1982–84; Scottish Conveyancing and Executry Services Bd, 1991–96; Vice-Pres., Scottish Law Agents Soc., 1970; Member: Jt Standing Cttee on Legal Educn in Scotland, 1976–85 (Chm., 1976–80); Rules Council, Court of Session, 1968–92; Council, Internat. Bar Assoc., 1983–87 (Vice-Chm., Legal Educn Div., 1983–87); Jt Ethical Cttee, Grampian Health Bd, 1984–92 (Vice-Chm., 1985; Chm., 1986–92); Scottish Law Commn, 1986–95; Council, CVCP, then UUK, 1996–2002. Chairman: Univs and Colls Employers Assoc., 1995–2002; NW Univs Assoc., 2001–02. Chm., Aberdeen Home for Widowers' Children, 1971–92. Pres., Aberdeen Grammar Sch. Former Pupils' Club, 1987–88. Hon. Sheriff of Grampian, Highland and Islands, 1978–. Chm., Registers of Scotland Customer Adv. Gp, 1990–92. Trustee: Grampian and Islands Family Trust, 1988–92; St George's Hall Trust, 1996–; Liverpool Charity and Voluntary Services (formerly Council of Social Service), 2003–; Liverpool Philharmonic Foundn, 2005–; Mem., Merseyside Police and High Sheriff's Charitable Trust, 1998–. Chairman: Mersey Partnership, 1995–98; NW Regl Assembly, Knowledge Economy Gp, 2000–02; Mem., NW Sci. Council, 2001–02. Governor: Inst. of Occupational Medicine Ltd, 1990–; Liverpool Coll., 2003–. Dir, Rising Stars Growth Fund Ltd, 2001–05. Mem., Editl Consultative Bd for Scotland, Butterworth & Co. (Publishers) Ltd, 1990–95. DL 1997, High Sheriff, 2007–08, Merseyside. AcSS 2002. Hon. Fellow, Liverpool John Moores Univ., 2002. Hon. LLD: Abertay Dundee, 1996; Aberdeen, 1997; Liverpool, 2002. *Address:* 1 Mayfield Court, Victoria Road, Formby, Merseyside L37 7JL. *T:* (01704) 832427. *Clubs:* Artists (Liverpool); New (Edinburgh); Aberdeen Grammar School Former Pupils' Club Centre (Aberdeen); Formby Golf.

LOVE, Rear Adm. Robert Thomas, OBE 2004; Capital Ships Director, including Future Carriers (formerly Team Leader, Carrier Vehicle Future and Maritime Airborne Surveillance and Control), Defence Equipment and Support, Ministry of Defence, since 2007; Chief Naval Engineer Officer, since 2008; *b* 21 July 1955; *s* of late Bill and Ellen Love; *m* 1983, Jean Francis; two *s* one *d. Educ:* Ashton-in-Makerfield Grammar Sch.; RNEC (BSc 1978). CEng 1984; FIMarEST 1987; CMarEng 2006. HM Yacht Britannia, 1982–84; Comdr E HMS Ark Royal, 1992–94; Desk Officer, DN Plans, MoD, 1994–96; SMEO to Flag Officer Sea Trng, 1997–98; Captain 1998; Team Leader Major Warships, 2001; recovered HMS Nottingham from grounding off coast of Australia, 2003; Cdre 2003; Defence Advr to Australia, 2003–06. Mem., MENSA. FAPM 2007. *Publications:* papers at various confs. *Recreations:* cricket, golf, Rugby, fitness, food, wine, music. *Address:* Capital Ships Director, Defence Equipment and Support, Ministry of Defence, Abbey Wood, Bristol BS34 8JH. *T:* (0117) 913 4181, *Fax:* (0117) 913 5958. *Club:* MCC.

LOVEDAY, Alan (Raymond); solo violinist; *b* 29 Feb. 1928; *s* of Leslie and Margaret Loveday; *m* 1952, Ruth Stanfield; one *s* one *d. Educ:* privately; Royal College of Music (prizewinner). Made debut at age of 4; debut in England, 1946; has given many concerts, broadcasts, and made TV appearances, in this country and abroad, playing with all leading conductors and orchestras; repertoire ranges from Bach (which he likes to play on an unmodernised violin), to contemporary music. Prof., RCM, 1955–72. Formerly full-time Mem. and Soloist, Acad. of St Martin-in-the-Fields. *Recreations:* chess, bridge.

LOVEDAY, Mark Antony; Senior Partner, Cazenove & Co., 1994–2001; *b* 22 Sept. 1943; *s* of George Arthur Loveday and Sylvia Mary Loveday; *m* 1981, Mary Elizabeth Tolmie; one *s* one *d. Educ:* Winchester Coll.; Magdalen Coll., Oxford (MA). Cazenove & Co., 1966–2001; Partner, 1974–2001. Chm., Foreign & Colonial Investment Trust PLC, 2002– (Dir, 2001–). Trustee: Magdalen Coll. Develt Trust, 1982– (Chm., 2006–); Grosvenor Estate, 1999–. Liveryman, Skinners' Co., 1972. *Recreation:* golf. *Address:* 42 Royal Avenue, SW3 4QF. *T:* (020) 7730 4031, *T:* (office) (020) 7898 9109. *Clubs:* Boodle's, City University, Hurlingham, MCC; Royal St George's Golf.

LOVEGROVE, Ross Nigel, RDI 2003; FCSD; Principal, Lovegrove Design Studio, London, since 1990; *b* 16 Aug. 1958; *s* of Herbert William John Lovegrove, OBE and Mary Eileen Lovegrove; *m* 1997, Maria (*née* Miller); one *s. Educ:* Manchester Polytech. (BA 1st cl. Industrial Design 1980); Royal Coll. of Art (MDes 1983). FCSD 1990. Designer, Frog Design, W Germany, working on projects, *eg* Walkmans for Sony, computers for Apple Computers, 1980s; Consultant, Knoll Internat., Paris, 1984–87; with Atelier de Nimes, consultants to Cacharel, Louis Vuitton, Hermes and Dupont, *etc*, 1984–86; London, 1986–: projects for clients including Airbus Industries, Driade, Peugeot, Apple Computers, Issey Miyake, Olympus Cameras, Yamagiwa Corp., Tag Heuer, Hackman, Herman Miller, Japan Airlines, and Toyo Ito Architects, Japan. Has exhibited in MOMA, NY, Guggenheim Mus., NY, Axis Centre, Japan, Pompidou Centre, Paris and Design Mus., London; *work in permanent collections* including: MOMA, NY; Design Mus., London; Vitra Design Mus., Weil Am Rhein, Basel; *solo exhibitions* include: Danish Mus. of Decorative Art, Copenhagen; Stockholm; Idee, Tokyo; Yamagiwa Corp., Tokyo; Rheinauen Space, Cologne, 2001; Designosaurs, Segheria, Milan, 2004; Superliquidity, Le Bain Gall., Tokyo, 2005; Endurance, Phillips de Pury New York Chelsea Galls, 2007. Hon. Fellow, UWIC. Numerous internat. awards, including: D&AD Silver Medal, 1997; Medaille de la Ville de Paris, 1998; George Nelson Award, 1998; iF Industrie Forum Design Award, Hanover, 1999; Good Design Award, ID mag., 2000; G Mark Federal Design Prize, Japan, 2001; Janus, Paris, 2004; World Technol. Prize, San Francisco, World Technol. Network, 2005. *Publications:* Designing the 21st Century, 1998; (ed) International Design Yearbook, 2002, 2003; Supernatural: the work of Ross Lovegrove, 2004; (contrib.) Designers on Design, 2005. *Recreations:* evolution, biomimicry, paleontology, materials technology, digital architecture, form related sculpture, travel. *Address:* Lovegrove Design Studio, 21 Powis Mews, W11 1JN. *T:* (020) 7229 7104, *Fax:* (020) 7229 7032; *e-mail:* studio@rosslovegrove.com. *Club:* Groucho.

LOVEGROVE, Stephen Augustus; Chief Executive, Shareholder Executive, Department for Business, Enterprise and Regulatory Reform, since 2007; *b* Solihull, 30 Nov. 1966; *s* of John Lovegrove and Zenia Stewart Lovegrove; *m* 1997, Kate Constantia Brooke; two *d. Educ:* Warwick Sch.; Corpus Christi Coll., Oxford (BA 1989). Consultant, Hydra Associates, 1990–94; Man. Dir, Morgan Grenfell, Deutsche Bank, 1995–2004; Dir, Shareholder Exec., DTI, subseq. BERR, 2004–07. *Recreations:* bricolage, reading detective stories. *Address:* Shareholder Executive, Department for Business, Enterprise and Regulatory Reform, 1 Victoria Street, SW1H 0ET. *Clubs:* Brooks's, Tapper's Cricket.

LOVEJOY, Joseph Reginald; Football Correspondent, Sunday Times, since 1994; *b* 23 June 1951; *s* of Reginald Henry Lovejoy and Ivy May Lovejoy; *m* 1st, 1973, Cynthia Turner (marr. diss. 1990); one *s* one *d*; 2nd, 1995, Lesley Griffiths. *Educ:* Bancrofts Sch., Woodford Green; Portsmouth Tech. Coll. (NCTJ Proficiency). Reporter: Kentish Observer, 1969–73; Doncaster Evening Post, 1973; Derby Evening Telegraph, 1973–77; South Wales Echo, 1977–83; Mail on Sunday, 1983–86; Independent, 1986–94. *Publications:* Bestie: portrait of a legend, 1998; Sven Goran Eriksson, 2002; (jtly) Giggs: the autobiography, 2005. *Recreation:* darts. *Address:* Rushbrook, Forge Road, Tintern, Monmouthshire NP16 6TH. *Club:* Pontypool Rugby Football.

LOVELACE, 5th Earl of, *cr* 1838; **Peter Axel William Locke King;** Baron King and Ockham, 1725; Viscount Ockham, 1838; *b* 26 Nov. 1951; *s* of 4th Earl of Lovelace and Manon Lis (*d* 1990), *d* of Axel Sigurd Transo, Copenhagen, Denmark; *S* father, 1964; *m* 1994, Kathleen Anne Smolders, Melbourne, Aust. *Address:* Torridon House, Torridon, Ross-shire IV22 2HA.

LOVELL, Sir (Alfred Charles) Bernard, Kt 1961; OBE 1946; FRS 1955; Founder and Director of Jodrell Bank Experimental Station, Cheshire, subseq. Nuffield Radio Astronomy Laboratories, 1951–81 (renamed Jodrell Bank Observatory, 2000); Professor of Radio Astronomy, University of Manchester, 1951–80, now Emeritus Professor; *b* 31 Aug. 1913; *s* of G. Lovell, Oldland Common, Gloucestershire; *m* 1937, Mary Joyce Chesterman (*d* 1993); two *s* three *d. Educ:* Kingswood Grammar Sch., Bristol; University of Bristol. Asst Lectr in Physics, Univ. of Manchester, 1936–39; Telecommunication Res.

Establishment, 1939–45; Physical Laboratories, Univ. of Manchester and Jodrell Bank Experimental Station, Cheshire; Lectr, 1945, Sen. Lectr, 1947, Reader, 1949, in Physics. Reith Lectr, 1958; Lectures: Condon, 1962; Guthrie, 1962; Halley, 1964; Queen's, Berlin, 1970; Brockington, Kingston, Ont, 1970; Bickley, Oxford, 1977; Crookshank, RCR, 1977; Angel Meml, Newfoundland, 1977; Blackett Meml, Operational Res. Soc., 1987. Vis. Montague Burton Prof. of Internat. Relations, Univ. of Edinburgh, 1973. Member: Air Navigation Cttee, 1953–56 (Vice-Chm., 1955–56); Air Warfare Cttee, 1954–60; ARC, 1955–58; Radar & Signals Adv. Bd, 1956–59; Sci. Adv. Council, 1957–60; Guided Weapons Adv. Bd, 1958–60; SRC, 1965–70; Amer. Philosophical Soc., 1974–. Pres., RAS, 1969–71; Vice-Pres., Internat. Astronomical Union, 1970–76; Pres., British Assoc., 1975–76. Pres., Guild of Church Musicians, 1976–89; Jun. Warden, 1984–85, Sen. Warden, 1985–86, Master, 1986–87, Musicians' Co. Hon. Freeman, City of Manchester, 1977. Hon. Fellow, Society of Engineers, 1964; Hon. Foreign Member American Academy of Arts and Sciences, 1955; Hon. Life Member, New York Academy, 1960; Hon. Member: Royal Swedish Academy, 1962; RNCM, 1981; Manchester Lit. & Philos. Soc., 1988. Hon. LLD: Edinburgh, 1961; Calgary, 1966; Liverpool, 1999; Hon. DSc: Leicester, 1961; Leeds, 1966; London, 1967; Bath, 1967; Bristol, 1970; DUniv Stirling, 1974; DUniv Surrey, 1975; Hon. FIET (Hon. FIEE, 1967); Hon. FInstP, 1976. Duddell Medal, 1954; Royal Medal, 1960; Daniel and Florence Guggenheim International Astronautics Award, 1961; Ordre du Mérite pour la Recherche et l'Invention, 1962; Churchill Gold Medal, 1964; Maitland Lecturer and Silver Medallist, Institution of Structural Engineers, 1964; Second RSA American Exchange Lectr, Philadelphia, 1980; Benjamin Franklin Medal, RSA, 1980; Gold Medal, Royal Astronomical Soc., 1981; Rutherford Meml Lectr, Royal Soc., 1984. Commander's Order of Merit, Polish People's Republic, 1975. *Publications:* Science and Civilisation, 1939; World Power Resources and Social Development, 1945; Radio Astronomy, 1951; Meteor Astronomy, 1954; The Exploration of Space by Radio, 1957; The Individual and The Universe, (BBC Reith Lectures, 1958); The Exploration of Outer Space (Gregynog Lectures, 1961); Discovering the Universe, 1963; Our Present Knowledge of the Universe, 1967; (ed with T. Margerison) The Explosion of Science: The Physical Universe, 1967; The Story of Jodrell Bank, 1968; The Origins and International Economics of Space Exploration, 1973; Out of the Zenith, 1973; Man's Relation to the Universe, 1975; P. M. S. Blackett: a biographical memoir, 1976; In the Centre of Immensities, 1978; Emerging Cosmology, 1981; The Jodrell Bank Telescopes, 1985; Voice of the Universe, 1987; (with Sir Francis Graham Smith) Pathways to the Universe, 1988; Astronomer by Chance (autobiog.), 1990; Echoes of War, 1991; many publications in Physical and Astronomical journals. *Recreations:* cricket, gardening, music. *Address:* The Quinta, Swettenham, Cheshire CW12 2LD. *T:* (01477) 571254; *e-mail:* acbl@jb.man.ac.uk. *Clubs:* Athenæum, MCC; Lancashire County Cricket (Pres., 1995–96).

LOVELL-BADGE, Dr Robin Howard, FRS 2001; Head, Division of Developmental Genetics, MRC National Institute for Medical Research, since 1993; *b* 14 June 1953; *s* of Don Lovell-Badge and Eileen Betty Cator (*née* Daniels). *Educ:* Norwich Sch. (King Edward VI); University Coll. London (BSc Hons Zool. 1975; PhD Embryol. 1978). Postdoctoral research: Dept of Genetics, Univ. of Cambridge, 1978–81; EMBO Long Term Fellow, Institut Jacques Monod, Univ. Paris VII, 1981–82; Member: Scientific Staff, MRC Mammalian Develt Unit, UCL, 1982–88; MRC Scientific Staff, NIMR, 1988–. Hon. Sen. Res. Fellow, subseq. Hon. Prof., Dept of Anatomy and Develtl Biol., UCL, 1994–; Vis. Prof., Dept Biochem., Univ. of Hong Kong, 1996–. Pres., Inst. of Animal Tech., 2006–. Mem., EMBO, 1993. FMedSci 1999. Louis Jeantet Prize for Medicine, 1995; Amory Prize, Amer. Acad. Arts and Scis, 1996; Wilhelm Feldberg Prize, Feldberg Foundn, 2008. *Publications:* contribs to learned jls. *Recreations:* drawing, painting, sculpture, cooking, good food and wine. *Address:* Laboratory of Developmental Genetics, MRC National Institute for Medical Research, The Ridgeway, Mill Hill, NW7 1AA. *T:* (020) 8816 2126; *e-mail:* rlovell@nimr.mrc.ac.uk.

LOVELL-PANK, Dorian Christopher; QC 1993; a Recorder, 1989–2006; *b* 15 Feb. 1946; *s* of late Christopher Edwin Lovell-Pank, Madrid and Jean Alston de Oliva-Day (*née* McPherson), Cape Town and Buenos Aires; *m* 1983, Diana, *d* of late Michael Cady Byford and of Sonia Byford, Claret Hall, Clare, Suffolk; one *s* one *d*. *Educ:* Downside; Colegio Sarmiento, Buenos Aires; LSE; Inns of Court Sch. of Law. Called to the Bar, Inner Temple, 1971, Bencher, 1998; in practice SE Circuit; Asst Recorder, 1985–89. Mem., Panel of Chairmen, Police Discipline Appeal Tribunals, 1991–; Member: Cttee, Criminal Bar Assoc., 1989–2006 (Chm., Internat. Relations Sub-Cttee, 1993–2006); Gen. Council of Bar, 1989–92, 1998–2005 (Chm., Internat. Relations Cttee, 2001–05); Internat. Bar Assoc., 1993– (Mem. Council, 2001–05); Human Rights Inst., 1996– (Mem. Council, 2000–04); British Spanish Law Assoc., 2001–; FCO Pro Bono Lawyers Panel, 2002–. Mem., British Inst. of Internat. and Comparative Law, 2001–. Associate Mem., ABA, 1997–. Chm., Bar Conf., 1999. *Recreations:* travel, reading, things latin, swimming. *Address:* 6 King's Bench Walk, Temple, EC4Y 7DR. *T:* (020) 7583 0410, *Fax:* (020) 7353 8791; *e-mail:* clerks@6kbw.com. *Clubs:* Garrick; Aldeburgh Yacht, RNVR Yacht.

LOVELOCK, Sir Douglas (Arthur), KCB 1979 (CB 1974); First Church Estates Commissioner, 1983–93; Chairman, Central Board of Finance of the Church of England, 1983–92; *b* 7 Sept. 1923; *s* of late Walter and Irene Lovelock; *m* 1961, Valerie Margaret (*née* Lane); one *s* one *d*. *Educ:* Bec Sch., London. Entered Treasury, 1949; Min. of Supply, 1952; Private Sec. to Permanent Sec., 1953–54; Principal, 1954; Private Sec. to successive Ministers of Aviation (Rt Hon. Peter Thorneycroft and Rt Hon. Julian Amery), 1961–63; Asst Sec., 1963; Under-Sec. (Contracts), Min. of Technology, subseq. Min. of Aviation Supply, 1968–71; Asst Under-Sec. of State (Personnel), MoD, 1971–72; Dep. Sec., DTI, 1972–74, Depts of Trade, Industry, Prices and Consumer Protection, 1974–77; Chm., Bd of Customs and Excise, 1977–83. Chm., Civil Service Benevolent Fund, 1980–83. Chm., Review of Citizens' Advice Bureaux Service, 1983–84. Governor, Whitgift Foundn (Whitgift Sch., Trinity Sch., Old Palace Sch.), 1986–93 and 1998– (Chm., 1993–98). *Publication:* While I Remember, 1998. *Recreations:* walking, gardening, outdoor activities generally. *Address:* The Old House, 91 Coulsdon Road, Old Coulsdon, Surrey CR3 2LD. *T:* (01737) 555211.

LOVELOCK, Prof. James Ephraim, CH 2003; CBE 1990; FRS 1974; independent scientist, since 1964; Hon. Visiting Fellow, Green Templeton College (formerly Green College), Oxford, since 1994; *b* 26 July 1919; *s* of Tom Arthur Lovelock and Nellie Ann Elizabeth (*née* March); *m* 1st, 1942, Helen Mary Hyslop (*d* 1989); two *s* two *d*; 2nd, 1991, Sandra Jean Orchard. *Educ:* Strand Sch., London; Manchester and London Univs. BSc, PhD, DSc, ARIC. Staff Scientist, Nat. Inst. for Med. Research, 1941–61; Rockefeller Fellow, Harvard Univ., 1954–55; Yale Univ., 1958–59; Prof. of Chemistry, Baylor Univ. Coll. of Medicine, Texas, 1961–64. Vis. Prof., Univ. of Reading, 1967–90. Pres., Marine Biol Assoc., 1986–90. Mem. Sigma Xi, Yale Chapter, 1959. Hon. ScD East Anglia, 1982; Hon. DSc: Exeter, 1988; Plymouth Univ. (formerly Plymouth Poly.), 1988; Edinburgh, 1993; Kent, 1996; Univ. of E London, 1996; Colorado, 1997; Hon. DSci Stockholm, 1991. Amsterdam Prize, Roy. Netherlands Acad. of Arts and Scis, 1990; Prize, Volvo Envmt Prize Foundn, 1996; Nonino Prize, Italy, 1996; Blue Planet Prize, Asahi Glass Foundn, Tokyo, 1997; Wollaston Medal, Geol Soc., 2006. *Publications:* Gaia, 1979; (with Michael Allaby) The Great Extinction, 1983; (with Michael Allaby) The Greening of Mars, 1984; The Ages of Gaia, 1988; Gaia: the practical science of planetary medicine, 1991; Homage to Gaia: the life of an independent scientist (autobiog.), 2000; The Revenge of Gaia, 2006; numerous papers and patents. *Recreations:* walking, digital photography, reading. *Address:* Coombe Mill, St Giles on the Heath, Launceston, Cornwall PL15 9RY.

LOVELUCK, Paul Edward, CBE 1993; JP; President, National Museum Wales (formerly National Museums and Galleries of Wales), since 2002; *b* 3 Feb. 1942; *s* of Edward Henry Loveluck and Elizabeth Loveluck (*née* Treharne); *m* 1965, Lynne Gronow; one *s* one *d*. *Educ:* Maesteg Grammar Sch.; UCW, Cardiff (BA). Board of Trade, 1963–69; Welsh Office, 1969–84 (Asst Sec., 1975–84); Chief Executive: Wales Tourist Bd, 1984–95; Countryside Council for Wales, 1996–2002. Chm., Wales New Deal Task Force, 1999–2003. President: Maesteg Male Voice Choir, 1990–; Drama Assoc. of Wales, 1996–. Chair, Heritage in Action, 2003–06. JP Cardiff, 1982, Dyfed-Powys, 2006. *Recreations:* hillwalking, music. *Address:* Dôl Awel, 8 Corndon Drive, Montgomery, Powys SY15 6RG.

LOVEMAN, Stephen Charles Gardner; Under Secretary, Department of Employment, then Department for Education and Employment, 1989–96; *b* 26 Dec. 1943; *s* of Charles Edward Loveman and Edith Mary Gardner; *m* 1972, Judith Pamela Roberts; one *s* one *d*. *Educ:* Arnold Sch., Blackpool; Emmanuel College, Cambridge (BA). Dept of Employment, 1967; Private Sec. to Minister of State for Employment, 1972–74; Health and Safety Exec., 1974–77; Dept of Employment, 1977–80; Manpower Services Commn, 1980–87; Dept of Employment, 1987–88; Cabinet Office, 1988–89. *Recreations:* TV, cinema, theatre, reading, walking, swimming, voluntary work (witness support). *Address:* 24 Brincliffe Crescent, Sheffield S11 9AW.

LOVENDUSKI, Prof. Joni, PhD; FBA 2007; Anniversary Professor of Politics, Birkbeck College, University of London, since 2000; *b* 19 May 1945; *d* of Austin Lovenduski and Teresa Lovenduski (*née* Allan); *m* 1993, Prof. Alan Ware; one *s*, and one step *s*. *Educ:* Manchester Univ. (BSc Hons Econ. 1970; MA Govt 1976); Loughborough Univ. (PhD Politics 1986). Loughborough University: Lectr, then Sen. Lectr, in Politics, 1972–88; Reader in Politics, 1988–92; Prof. of Comparative Politics, 1992–94; Prof. of Politics, Southampton Univ., 1995–2000. *Publications:* (ed jtly) The Politics of the Second Electorate, 1981; (ed jtly) The New Politics of Abortion, 1986; Women and European Politics: contemporary feminism and public policy, 1986; (jtly) Politics and Society in Eastern Europe, 1987; (jtly) Contemporary Feminist Politics, 1993; (ed jtly) Gender and Party Politics, 1993; (ed jtly) Different Voices, Different Lives: gender and politics, a reader, 1994; (jtly) Political Recruitment: gender, race and class in the British Parliament, 1995; (ed jtly) Women in Politics in Britain, 1996; (ed) Feminism and Politics, 2 vols, 2000; Feminizing Politics, 2005; (ed) State Feminism and Political Representation, 2005; (jtly) Women in Parliament, 2005; contribs to British Jl Political Sci., Political Studies, Party Politics, Political Qly, Parly Affairs, Govt & Opposion, W Eur. Politics. *Recreations:* Italy, reading, gardening, bridge. *Address:* School of Politics and Sociology, Birkbeck College, Malet Street, WC1E 7HX.

LOVERANCE, Rowena Kathryn; writer and consultant; Head of Outreach and Learning Resources, then Head of e-learning, British Museum, 2001–07; *b* 4 Sept. 1952; *d* of Maurice and Wilfreda Loverance. *Educ:* Manchester High Sch. for Girls; Somerville Coll., Oxford (BA Hons Modern History; Dip. Archaeol.). Res. Fellow, Univ. of Birmingham, 1979–80; Lectr, Dept of Ancient History and Classical Archaeology, Univ. of Sheffield, 1980–83; Education Officer, 1985–98, Head of Educnl IT, 1998–2001, BM. Trustee, Culture24 (formerly 24 Hour Museum), 2006–. Pres., Churches Together in England, 1998–2001. *Publications:* Byzantium, 1988; The British Museum Christ, 2004; Christian Art, 2007. *Recreations:* Byzantine studies, archaeology.

LOVERING, John David; Chairman: Debenhams plc, since 2003; Somerfield Ltd, since 2005; *b* 11 Oct. 1949; *s* of John George and Ruby Beatrice Lovering; *m* 1971, Brenda Joan Wotherspoon; two *s* one *d*. *Educ:* Dulwich Coll.; Exeter Univ. (BA Hons); Manchester Business Sch. (MBA). Planning Manager, Spillers Internat. Div., 1975–78; Corporate Strategy Manager, Lex Service plc, 1978–83; Grand Metropolitan plc, Commercial Dir, Express Dairy Ltd, 1983–85; Head of Gp Finance and Planning, Imperial Gp plc, 1985–86; Finance Dir, Sears plc, 1986–93; Chief Operating Officer, Tarmac plc, 1993–95; Chairman: Birthdays Gp Ltd, 1996–2002; Fired Earth Ltd, 1998–2001; Homebase Ltd, 2001–02. Non-executive Chairman: Peacock Gp Ltd, 1997–2004; Odeon Cinemas Ltd, 2000–03; Laurel Pub Co., 2002–04; Fitness First, 2003–05; Vice-Chm., Barclays Capital, 2007–; Director: Aga Foodservice, 2003–06; Meyer Department Stores Pty, Australia, 2006–. Trustee and Dir, SCF, 1990–96. Member: Tonbridge Sch. Foundn, 2003–; Vice-Chancellor's Cttee, Exeter Univ., 2003–. *Recreations:* sport, walking, farming. *Club:* Alleyn (Dulwich).

LOVERING, Prof. John Francis, AO 1993; FAA; FTSE; Board Member, Southern Rural Water, since 2001; Chairman: WaterEd Australia Pty Ltd, since 2003; WaterSmart, since 2004; *b* 27 March 1930; *s* of George Francis Lovering and Dorothy Irene Mildwater; *m* 1954, Jennifer Kerry FitzGerald; two *s* one *d*. *Educ:* Canterbury High Sch., Sydney; Univ. of Sydney (MSc); Univ. of Melbourne (MSc); California Inst. of Technology (PhD). FAA 1982; FTSE (FTS 1993). Asst Curator of Minerals, Australian Museum, 1951–55; Research Fellow, Fellow and Sen. Fellow, Dept of Geophysics and Geochemistry, ANU, 1956–69; University of Melbourne: Prof. of Geology, 1969–87; Dean of Science, 1983–85; Dep. Vice-Chancellor (Research), 1985–87; Vice-Chancellor and Prof. of Geology, Flinders Univ. of SA, 1987–95. Chm., Envmt Conservation Council of Victoria, 1998–2001. Chairman of Directors: Comlabs Ltd, 1985–93; Geotrack International Pty Ltd, 1987–93; Open Learning Technology Corp., 1992–96. Pres., Murray-Darling Basin Commn, 1994–99. Hon. DSc: Flinders Univ., 1995; Melbourne Univ., 1999. Chevalier des Palmes Académiques, 1981. *Publications:* Last of Lands: Antarctica (with J. R. V. Prescott), 1979; contribs to learned jls. *Recreations:* music, wine, food. *Address:* 66a Molesworth Street, Kew, Vic 3101, Australia. *Clubs:* Melbourne, Wallaby (Melbourne).

LOVESEY, Peter Harmer; crime writer, since 1970; *b* 10 Sept. 1936; *s* of Richard Lear Lovesey and Amy Lovesey (*née* Strank); *m* 1959, Jacqueline Ruth Lewis; one *s* one *d*. *Educ:* Hampton Grammar Sch.; Reading Univ. (BA Hons 1958). Flying Officer, RAF, 1958–61; Lectr, Thurrock Technical Coll., 1961–69; Head of Gen. Educn Dept, Hammersmith & West London Coll., 1969–75. Crime Writers' Association: Chm., 1991–92; Cartier Diamond Dagger, 2000; Grand Prix de Littérature Policière (French Crime Writers' Assoc.), 1985. *Publications:* Wobble to Death, 1970 (televised 1980); The Detective Wore Silk Drawers, 1971 (televised 1980); Abracadaver, 1972 (televised 1980); Mad Hatter's Holiday, 1973 (televised 1981); Invitation to a Dynamite Party, 1974 (televised 1981); A Case of Spirits, 1975 (televised 1980); Swing, Swing Together, 1976 (televised 1980); Waxwork (Silver Dagger), 1978 (televised 1979); The False Inspector Dew (Gold Dagger), 1982; Keystone, 1983; Rough Cider, 1986; Bertie and the Tinman, 1987; On the Edge, 1989 (televised as Dead Gorgeous, 2002); Bertie and the Seven

Bodies, 1990; The Last Detective, 1991; Diamond Solitaire, 1992; Bertie and the Crime of Passion, 1993; The Summons (Silver Dagger), 1995; Bloodhounds (Silver Dagger), 1996; Upon a Dark Night, 1997; The Vault, 1999; The Reaper, 2000; Diamond Dust, 2002; The House Sitter, 2003; The Circle, 2005; The Secret Hangman, 2007; The Headhunters, 2008; *short stories:* Butchers and Other Stories of Crime, 1985; The Crime of Miss Oyster Brown and Other Stories, 1994; Do Not Exceed the Stated Dose, 1998; The Sedgemoor Strangler and Other Stories of Crime, 2001; Murder on the Short List, 2008; *non-fiction:* The Kings of Distance, 1968; (jtly) The Guide to British Track and Field Literature, 1969; The Official Centenary History of the Amateur Athletic Association, 1979; (jtly) An Athletics Compendium: an annotated guide to the UK literature of track and field, 2001; *as Peter Lear:* Goldengirl, 1977 (filmed 1979); Spider Girl, 1980; The Secret of Spandau, 1986. *Recreations:* researching athletics history, visiting teashops. *Address:* c/o Vanessa Holt Ltd, 59 Crescent Road, Leigh-on-Sea, Essex SS9 2PF. *Club:* Detection.

LOVESTONE, Prof. Simon Harold; Professor of Old Age Psychiatry, Institute of Psychiatry, King's College, London, since 2000; Director, NIHR Biomedical Research Centre for Mental Health, since 2007; *b* 16 Feb. 1961. *Educ:* Univ. of Sheffield (BSc Microbiol. 1982); Univ. of Southampton (BM 1986); PhD London 1998. MRCPsych. Sen. Lectr, 1995–99, Reader, 1999–2000, in Old Age Psychiatry, Inst. of Psychiatry, London Univ.; Hon. Consultant, Maudsley Hosp., 1995–. Dep. Dir, MRC Centre for Neurodegeneration Res., 2005–. Chm., Sci. Adv. Bd, Alzheimer's Res. Trust, 2004–. *Publications:* scientific papers on old age psychiatry and neuroscience. *Address:* Institute of Psychiatry, King's College London, De Crespigny Park, SE5 8AF.

LOVILL, Sir John (Roger), Kt 1987; CBE 1983; DL; Chairman, Sloane Square Investments, 1980–99 (Director, 1960–99); *b* 26 Sept. 1929; *s* of Walter Thomas Lovill and Elsie Lovill (*née* Page); *m* 1958, Jacqueline (*née* Parker); two *s* one *d*. *Educ:* Brighton Hove and Sussex Grammar School. S. G. Warburg, 1951–55; Dep. Gen. Manager, Securicor Ltd, 1955–60; Dir, Municipal Gen. Insce Co., 1984–95; Managing Trustee, Municipal Mutual Insce, 1988– (Chm., 1993–); Chm., Nationwide Small Business Property Trust, 1988–96; Chm., Prime Health Ltd, 1992–94. Contested (C) Ebbw Vale, 1966; Mem., East Sussex CC, 1967–89, Leader, 1973–77; Chairman: Sussex Police Authority, 1976–79; Local Authority Conditions of Service Adv. Bd, 1978–83; ACC, 1983–86; Pres., Sussex Assoc. of Local Councils, 1987–97; Vice Pres., Nat. Assoc. of Local Councils, 1991–93; Leader, Conservative Assoc. of County Councils, 1981–83. DL E Sussex 1983. *Recreations:* opera, politics, marine paintings. *Address:* Hampden House, Glynde, Lewes, Sussex BN8 6TA. *T:* (01273) 858212.

LOW, family name of **Barons Aldington** and **Low of Dalston**.

LOW OF DALSTON, Baron *cr* 2006 (Life Peer), of Dalston in the London Borough of Hackney; **Colin MacKenzie Low,** CBE 2000; Chairman, Royal National Institute of Blind People (formerly Royal National Institute for the Blind), since 2000; *b* 23 Sept. 1942; *s* of Arthur Eric Low and Catherine Cameron (*née* Anderson); *m* 1969, Jill Irene Coton; one *s* one *d*. *Educ:* Worcester Coll. for the Blind; Queen's Coll., Oxford (BA Juris, MA 1987); Churchill Coll., Cambridge (Dip. Criminol.). Lectr in Law, Univ. of Leeds, 1968–84; Dir, Disability Resource Team, 1984–94; Sen. Res. Fellow, 1994–2000, Vis. Prof., 2000–, City Univ. Member: Special Educnl Needs Tribunal, 1994–2007; Nat. Disability Council, 1996–2000; Disability Rights Task Force, 1997–99; Disability Rights Commn, 2000–02. Pres., European Blind Union, 2003–; Vice-President: Disability Alliance, 1997– (Mem. Cttee, 1974–; Chm., 1991–97); Skill, 2003– (Mem. Council, 1975–2003); Mem. Council, St Dunstan's, 2000–. *Publications:* contrib. articles to learned periodicals. *Recreations:* music, wine appreciation. *Address:* Royal National Institute of Blind People, 105 Judd Street, WC1H 9NE. *T:* (020) 7392 2205; *e-mail:* colin.low@rnib.org.uk.

LOW, Brian Buik, CBE 1994; HM Diplomatic Service, retired; High Commissioner to Papua New Guinea, 1994–97; *b* 15 Nov. 1937; *s* of Robert James Low and Helen Duncan Low; *m* 1960, Anita Joan Allum; three *d*. *Educ:* Arbroath High Sch. Served RAF, 1956–61. Joined Diplomatic Service, 1962; FO, 1962–65; Sofia, 1965–67; Sydney, 1967–69; Kuala Lumpur, 1969–73; Moscow, 1973–74; FCO, 1974–78; Singapore, 1978–81; Commercial Consul, British Trade Develt Office, NY, 1981–84; First Sec., FCO, 1984–88; Head of Chancery, Lima, 1988–91; Ambassador to Estonia, 1991–94. *Recreations:* music, reading, golf, watching sport. *Address:* Walmar Cottage, 21 Tayside Street, Carnoustie, Angus DD7 6AX. *Clubs:* Carnoustie Golf; Singapore Cricket.

LOW, Prof. Donald Anthony, AO 2005; DPhil, LittD; FRHistS, FAHA, FASSA; President of Clare Hall, 1987–94, Smuts Professor of the History of the British Commonwealth, 1983–87, and Deputy Vice-Chancellor, 1990–94, University of Cambridge; *b* 22 June 1927; *o s* of late Canon Donald Low and Winifred (*née* Edmunds); *m* 1952, Isobel Smails; one *s* two *d*. *Educ:* Haileybury and ISC; Exeter Coll., Oxford (Open Scholar in Modern History, 1944; Amelia Jackson Sen. Student, 1948; MA, DPhil; Hon. Fellow, 1992); PhD 1983, LittD 1998, Cantab. Lectr, subseq. Sen. Lectr, Makerere Coll., University Coll. of E Africa, 1951–58; Uganda corresp., The Times, 1952–58; Fellow, subseq. Sen. Fellow in History, Res. Sch. of Social Sciences, ANU, 1959–64; Founding Dean of Sch. of African and Asian Studies, and Prof. of Hist., Univ. of Sussex, 1964–72; Australian National University: Prof. of History, 1973–83; Dir, Res. Sch. of Pacific Studies, 1973–75; Vice Chancellor, 1975–82; University Fellow, 1997–2000; University of Cambridge: Fellow, Churchill Coll., 1983–87; Dir, Centre of Internat. Studies, 1985–87; Mem., Council of Senate, 1985–88. Sen. Visitor Nuffield Coll., Oxford, 1956–57; Smuts Fellow and Vis. Fellow, Clare Hall, Cambridge, 1971–72 (Hon. Fellow, 1999). Chm., Educn Adv. Cttee, Aust. Develt Assistance Bureau, 1979–82; Mem. Exec., 1976–82, Dep. Chm., 1980, Aust. Vice-Chancellors' Cttee; Member: Council, Univ. of Papua New Guinea, 1974–82; Standing Cttee, Aust. Univs Internat. Develt Program, 1975–82; Council, ACU, 1980–82; Cttee, Australian Studies Centre, London Univ., 1983–94; Governing Body: Inst. of Develt Studies, Sussex Univ., 1966–72 and 1984–91; SOAS, 1983–94; Haileybury, 1985–94; Chm., Cttee of Management, Inst. of Commonwealth Studies, London Univ., 1984–94. Hon. Fellow: Inst. of Develt Studies, UK, 1972; University House, ANU 1983. President: African Studies Assoc. of Aust. and Pacific, 1979–82; Asian Studies Assoc. of Aust., 1980–82; British Australian Studies Assoc., 1984–86; Chm., Co-ordinating Council, Area Studies Assoc., 1988–91; Vice-Pres., Australian Acad. of Humanities, 1996–98. Chm., Round Table Moot, 1992–94. Commander of the Order of Civil Merit (Spain), 1984. *Publications:* Buganda and British Overrule, 1900–1955 (with R. C. Pratt), 1960; (ed) Soundings in Modern South Asian History, 1968; (with J. C. Iltis and M. D. Wainwright) Government Archives in South Asia, 1969; Buganda in Modern History, 1971; The Mind of Buganda, 1971; Lion Rampant, 1973; (ed) Congress and the Raj 1917–1947, 1977; Oxford History of East Africa: (contrib.) Vol. I, 1963 and Vol. II, 1965; (contrib. and ed jtly) Vol. III, 1976; (ed) Constitutional Heads and Political Crises, 1988; (ed) The Indian National Congress, 1988; (ed jtly) Sovereigns and Surrogates, 1990; Eclipse of Empire, 1991; (ed) Political Inheritance of Pakistan, 1991; The Egalitarian Moment: Asia and Africa 1950–80, 1996; Britain and Indian Nationalism, 1997; (ed) Keith Hancock: legacies of an historian, 2001; articles on internat. history in jls. *Address:* 18/36 Shackleton Park, Mawson, Canberra, ACT 2607, Australia.

LOW, Dr (George) Graeme (Erick), CBE 1989; Member, 1986–91, Managing Director, Site Operations, 1990–91, United Kingdom Atomic Energy Authority; *b* Palmerston North, NZ, 29 Nov. 1928; *s* of George Eric Low and Evelyn Edith Low (*née* Gillman); *m* 1st, 1952, Marion Townsend (marr. diss. 1977); two *d*; 2nd, 1985, Joan Kathleen Swinburne. *Educ:* New Plymouth Boys' High Sch., NZ; Canterbury Coll., Univ. of NZ (BSc, MSc); Univ. of Reading (PhD, DSc). FInstP. Special Branch, RNZN, 1952–58; Research Scientist, 1958–68, Head of Materials Physics Div., 1968–70, AERE Harwell; Special Asst to Dir, UKAEA Research Gp, 1970–73; Programme Dir (Applied Nuclear), 1973–76, Research Dir (Industry), 1976–81, Dir of Environmental Research, 1981–83, AERE Harwell; Dir, AEE, Winfrith, 1983–86; Dir, AERE Harwell, 1986–87; Mem. for Estabts, UKAEA, 1987–90. Dir, UK Nirex Ltd, 1986–91. *Publications:* papers on semi-conductors, neutron beam studies of the solid state, magnetism and management. *Recreations:* reading, walking, family and friends. *Address:* 21 New Road, Reading RG1 5JD.

LOW, Gillian; Head Mistress, The Lady Eleanor Holles School, Hampton, since 2004; *b* 21 Feb. 1955; *d* of William Edward Coysh and Elizabeth Joyce Coysh (*née* Legge); one *s* two *d*. *Educ:* North London Collegiate Sch.; Somerville Coll., Oxford (Emma Clarke Beilby Schol.; BA Hons 1977, MA 1982); Trinity Coll., Cambridge (Tripos Prize; PGCE 1981). Mgt trainee, Courtaulds Ltd, 1977–79; teacher of English as foreign lang., British Coll., Reggio di Calabria, Italy, 1979–80; Asst English Teacher, then Dep. Hd of Dept, Claverham Community Coll., Battle, 1981–88; Hd of English, then Dir of Studies, Bishop Ramsey Sch., Ruislip, 1989–94; Dep. Headmistress, Godolphin and Latymer Sch., Hammersmith, 1994–98; Headmistress, Francis Holland Sch., N London, 1998–2004. Member: ASCL (formerly SHA), 1994–; GSA, 1998– (representative: Council, Internat. Confedn of Principals, 2008–; Indep. Schs Travel Assoc., 2008–); GSA/HMC Educn and Acad. Policy Cttee, 2004–. Governor: Sarum Hall Sch., Hampstead, 2003–05; Moat Sch., Fulham, 2003–06 (Chm., Educn Cttee, 2004–06); Queen's Coll., London, 2006–; Queenswood Sch., Herts, 2008–. *Recreations:* travel, reading, art. *Address:* The Lady Eleanor Holles School, Hanworth Road, Hampton, Middx TW12 3HF. *T:* (020) 8979 1601. *Clubs:* Lansdowne, University Women's.

LOW, Sir James (Richard) Morrison-, 3rd Bt *cr* 1908; DL; DFH, CEng, MIET; Director, Osborne & Hunter Ltd, Glasgow, 1956–89 (Electrical Engineer with firm, since 1952); *b* 3 Aug. 1925; *s* of Sir Walter John Morrison-Low, 2nd Bt and Dorothy Ruth de Quincey Quincey (*d* 1946); *S* father, 1955; *m* 1953, Ann Rawson Gordon (*d* 2006); one *s* three *d*. *Educ:* Ardvreck; Harrow; Merchiston. Served Royal Corps of Signals, 1943–47; demobilised with rank of Captain. Faraday House Engineering Coll., 1948–52. Chm., Scottish Cttee, Nat. Inspection Council for Electrical Installation Contracting, 1982–88; Pres., Electrical Contractors Assoc. of Scotland, 1982–84. Chm., Fife Area Scout Council, 1966–84. Hon. Pipe-Major, Royal Scottish Pipers Soc., 1981–83. Eur Ing, 1990. DL Fife, 1978. *Recreations:* shooting, piping. *Heir:* *s* Richard Walter Morrison-Low, *b* 4 Aug. 1959. *Address:* Kilmaron House, Cupar, Fife KY15 4NE. *T:* (01334) 652248. *Clubs:* New, Royal Scottish Pipers Society (Edinburgh).

LOW, Dr John Menzies, CBE 2008; Chief Executive, Charities Aid Foundation, since 2007; *b* 1 July 1953; *s* of David Low and late Helen Low (*née* Menzies); *m* 1977, Alison Jean Donald; two *d*. *Educ:* Aberdeen Acad.; Robert Gordon's Inst. of Technol. (BSc); Univ. of Aberdeen (MSc, PhD); Templeton Coll., Oxford. CEng, FIET. John Brown Engrg (UDI), 1979–84; Wm McGeogh, Birmingham, 1984–87; Booker plc (Sortex), 1988–93; Bühler AG (Sortex), 1993–99; with RNID, 1999–2007, Chief Exec., 2002–07. Mem., Assoc. of Offshore Diving Contractors Task Force on safe use of electricity underwater, 1983–84. Chm., Disability Charities Consortium, 2003–07. Trustee, ACEVO, 2003–Feb. 2009 (Chm., 2005–Feb. 2009). Deacon: Gilcomston Park Baptist Ch, 1977–84; Hertford Baptist Ch, 1991–2003 (Treas., 1994–2003). CCMI. FRSA. *Publications:* (contrib.) Instrumentation and Sensors for the Food Industry, 1993; 6 patents in optics and automated sorting; contrib. articles on speech fluency, auditory feedback, image processing, marketing and voluntary sector. *Address:* Charities Aid Foundation, St Andrew's House, 18-20 St Andrew Street, EC4A 3AY. *T:* (020) 7832 3010; *e-mail:* jlow@cafonline.org.

LOW, Prof. Martin Geoffrey, PhD; FRS 1996; Professor of Physiology and Cellular Biophysics, Columbia University, New York, since 1994; *b* 27 July 1950; *s* of Kenneth Douglas Low and Joan Elizabeth Low; *m* 1979, Eileen Ann Whalen; two *s*. *Educ:* Univ. of Newcastle upon Tyne (BSc Biochem.); Univ. of Birmingham (PhD Biochem. 1975). Postdoctoral Research Fellow: Univ. of Birmingham, 1974–77; Cornell Univ., 1977–79; Instructor, Med. Coll. of Va, 1979–81; Oklahoma Medical Research Foundation: Asst Mem., 1981–86; Associate Mem., 1986–87; Associate Prof., Columbia Univ., NY, 1987–94. *Publications:* contrib. original research and review articles in scientific jls incl. Science, Nature, Jl Biol Chem., Biochem. Jl. *Recreations:* reading, listening to music, fell walking, gardening. *Address:* Department of Physiology and Cellular Biophysics, Columbia University, 630 W 168th Street, New York, NY 10032, USA. *T:* (212) 3051707.

LOWCOCK, Andrew Charles; His Honour Judge Lowcock; a Circuit Judge, since 2001; *b* 22 Nov. 1949; *s* of Eric and Elizabeth Lowcock; *m* 1st, 1976, Patricia Anne Roberts (marr. diss. 1985); 2nd, 1985, Sarah Elaine Edwards; two *s*. *Educ:* Malvern Coll.; New Coll., Oxford (MA). Called to the Bar, Middle Temple, 1973; barrister, specialising in criminal and family law, Northern Circuit, 1974–2001; Asst Recorder, 1993–97; Recorder, 1997–2001. Gov., The Ryleys School, 1996–2007. *Recreations:* music, theatre, watching cricket and football. *Address:* The Crown Court, Minshull Street, Manchester M1 3FS. *Clubs:* MCC; Lancashire County Cricket, Nefyn Golf.

LOWCOCK, Mark Andrew; Director General, Country Programmes, Department for International Development, since 2008; *b* 25 July 1962; *s* of Brian Lowcock and Stella Connolly; *m* 1991, Dr Julia Watson; two *s* one *d*. *Educ:* Christ Church, Oxford (BA Hons 1985); Birkbeck Coll., Univ. of London (MSc Econs Dist. 1988). Grad. Fellow, Boston Univ., 1989. Overseas Development Administration, then Department for International Development 1985: Private Sec. to Minister for Overseas Develt, 1992–94; Dep., then Hd, Central Africa, Harare, 1994–97; Hd, EU Dept, 1997–99; Hd, Eastern Africa, 1999–2001; Dir, Finance and Corporate Performance, 2001–03; Dir Gen., Corporate Performance and Knowledge Sharing, 2003–06; Dir Gen., Policy and International, 2006–08. *Recreations:* Manchester United Football Club, Africa, reading, golf. *Address:* Department for International Development, 1 Palace Street, SW1E 5HE. *T:* (020) 7023 0407, *Fax:* (020) 7023 0694; *e-mail:* m-lowcock@dfid.gov.uk.

LOWDEN, Gordon Stuart; President, Institute of Chartered Accountants of Scotland, 1989–90 (Senior Vice-President, 1988–89); Chairman, Dundee Port Authority, 1979–92; *b* 22 May 1927; *s* of James Soutar Lowden and Jean Lowden; *m* 1953, Kathleen Arnot; two s one d. Educ: Dundee High Sch.; Strathallan Sch.; St John's Coll., Cambridge (MA); Univ. of St Andrews (LLB). CA. Moody Stuart & Robertson, later Peat Marwick McLintock: training, 1949–53; Partner, 1959; Office Managing Partner, 1985; retired 1988. University of Dundee: Lectr, Sen. Lectr, 1955–83; Hon. Vis. Prof., Dept of Accountancy and Business Finance, 1987. *Recreations:* golf, watching sport, bridge. *Address:* 169 Hamilton Street, Barnhill, Dundee DD5 2RE. *T:* (01382) 778360. *Club:* Royal and Ancient Golf.

LOWDEN, Prof. John Hopkins, PhD; Professor of the History of Art, Courtauld Institute of Art, London, since 2002; *b* 1 May 1953; *s* of Eric Walter and Muriel Florence Amelia Lowden; *m* 1980, Joanna Louise Cannon; *one s one d. Educ:* Leys Sch., Cambridge (Schol.); Emmanuel Coll., Cambridge (Exhibnr; MA (English) 1974); Courtauld Inst. of Art, London (MA 1977; PhD (Hist. of Art) 1980). Jun. Fellow, Dumbarton Oaks, 1979–80; Temp. Lectr, Univ. of St Andrews, 1981; Lectr, 1982–94, Reader, 1994–2002, Courtauld Inst. of Art, London. Leverhulme Sen. Res. Fellow, 1992–93; Grinfield Lectr, Univ. of Oxford, 1996–98. Otto Gründler Prize, Western Michigan Univ., 2002. *Publications:* Illuminated Prophet Books, 1988; The Octateuchs, 1992; Early Christian and Byzantine Art, 1997, 3rd edn 2003 (trans. French, Greek, Japanese, Korean); The Making of the 'Bibles Moralisées', vol. I, The Manuscripts, vol. II, The Book of Ruth, 2000; numerous contribs, primarily on manuscript illumination, to scholarly jls, standard ref. works, conf. procs, exhibn catalogues, etc. *Recreation:* family. *Address:* Courtauld Institute of Art, Somerset House, Strand, WC2R 0RN. *T:* (020) 7848 2668, *Fax:* (020) 7848 2410; *e-mail:* John.Lowden@courtauld.ac.uk.

LOWDEN, Richard Purdie; His Honour Judge Lowden; a Circuit Judge, North Eastern Circuit, since 1994; Resident Judge, Durham Crown Court, since 2001; *b* 23 April 1948; *s* of late Thomas Geoffrey Lowden, FRCS and Margaret Lowden (*née* Purdie); *m* 1973, Patricia (*d* 2002); one s two d. *Educ:* Sedbergh Sch.; Keble Coll., Oxford (MA). Called to the Bar, Inner Temple, 1971; a Recorder of the Crown Court, 1988–94; Hon. Judicial Recorder, City of Durham, 2005–. *Recreations:* fishing, fell walking, theatre. *Address:* Newcastle upon Tyne Combined Court Centre, Quayside, Newcastle upon Tyne NE1 2LA.

LOWE, Prof. (Alan) Vaughan; QC 2008; PhD; barrister; Chichele Professor of Public International Law, and Fellow of All Souls College, Oxford University, since 1999; *b* 1952; *m* Sally. *Educ:* UWIST (LLB 1973; LLM 1978; PhD 1980); MA Cantab 1991; MA Oxon 1999. Called to the Bar, Gray's Inn, 1993; in practice at the Bar, Essex Court Chambers, 1993–. Lectr, Cardiff Law Sch., 1973–79; Lectr, 1979–86, Sen. Lectr, 1986–88, Manchester Univ.; Cambridge University: Lectr, 1988–94; Reader in Internat. Law, 1994–99; Fellow of Corpus Christi Coll., 1988–99; Warden of Leckhampton, 1998–99. Visiting Professor: Duke Law Sch., USA, 1990; Tulane Law Sch., USA, 2000. Judge, European Nuclear Energy Tribunal, 2006–. Pres. or Mem., various arbitral tribunals, 2004–. *Publications:* Extraterritorial Jurisdiction, 1983; (jtly) The Law of the Sea, 1983, 3rd edn 1999; (jtly) Fifty Years of the International Court of Justice, 1996; (jtly) The Settlement of International Disputes, 1999; papers in jls. *Recreations:* ambling, rambling, music. *Address:* All Souls College, Oxford OX1 4AL. *T:* (01865) 279379.

LOWE, Prof. (Charles) Fergus, PhD; CPsychol, FBPsS; Professor of Psychology, since 1988, Deputy Vice-Chancellor, since 2004, Bangor University (formerly University College of North Wales, then University of Wales, Bangor); *b* 24 April 1946; *s* of Charles Lowe and Bridget Lowe (*née* Harte); *m* 1971, Patricia Mary Sheehy; two d. *Educ:* De La Salle Coll., Waterford; Trinity Coll., Dublin (BA Hons Phil. and Psychol.); UCNW (PhD Psychol. 1973). FBPsS 1986; CPsychol 1989. University College of North Wales, later University of Wales, Bangor: Lectr, then Sen. Lectr in Psychol., 1973–88; Hd, Sch. of Psychol., 1987–2005; Dir, Centre for Child Develt, 1990–; Dir, Bangor Food Res. Unit (Food Dude Prog.), 1989–; Pro Vice-Chancellor, 2003–04. Mem., Vice-Chancellors' Bd, Univ. of Wales, 1994–95. Res. Consultant, 1990–, Sci. Dir for Exploratory Consumer Sci., 1994–2001, Unilever. Healthy Eating Consultant for Irish Govt, 2005–. Chm., Exptl Analysis of Behaviour Gp, 1977–. Pres., Eur. Assoc. for Behaviour Analysis, 2001–02. Caroline Walker Trust Award, 1998; WHO Award for Counteracting Obesity, 2006. *Publications:* (ed jtly) Quantification of Steady-State Operant Behaviour, 1981; (ed jtly) Behaviour Analysis and Contemporary Psychology, 1985; contrib. numerous papers to scientific jls. *Recreations:* family, art, architecture, literature, classical and world music, film, wildlife, football, food. *Address:* School of Psychology, Bangor University, Bangor, Gwynedd LL57 2AS. *T:* (01248) 430410; *e-mail:* lowe@bangor.ac.uk.

LOWE, Prof. Christopher Robin, PhD; FREng; Fellow, Trinity College, Cambridge, since 1984; Director of Biotechnology, since 1984, Director, Institute of Biotechnology, since 1988, and Professor of Biotechnology, since 1999, University of Cambridge; *b* 15 Oct. 1945; *s* of late Thomas Lowe and of Hilda Lowe (*née* Moxham); *m* 1974, Patricia Margaret Reed; one s one d. *Educ:* Univ. of Birmingham (BSc 1967; PhD Biochem. 1970). FREng 2005. Postdoctoral Research Associate: Dept of Biochem., Univ. of Liverpool, 1970–73; Pure and Applied Biochem., Univ. of Lund, Sweden, 1973–74; Lectr in Biochem., 1975–82, Sen. Lectr, 1982–84, Univ. of Southampton. Visiting Professor: Univ. of Lund, 1995–; Univ. of Bath, 1996–. *Publications:* Affinity Chromatography, 1974; An Introduction to Affinity Chromatography, 1979; numerous contribs to learned jls; 60 patents. *Recreations:* antiques, travel. *Address:* Institute of Biotechnology, University of Cambridge, Tennis Court Road, Cambridge CB2 1QT. *T:* (01223) 334160; The Limes, Hempstead, Saffron Walden, Essex CB10 2PW. *T:* (01799) 599307.

LOWE, David Alexander; QC 1984; *b* Kilbirnie, Ayrshire, 1 Nov. 1942; *o s* of late David Alexander Lowe and Rea Sadie Aitchison Lowe (*née* Bridges); *m* 1972, Vivian Anne Langley; three s two d. *Educ:* Pocklington Sch., York; St John's Coll., Cambridge (schol.) MA; MacMahon Law Student). Called to Bar, Middle Temple, 1965 (Harmsworth Schol.; Bencher, 1992), *ad eundem*; Lincoln's Inn, 1975. In practice at the Chancery Bar, 1966–. *Address:* ADR Chambers (UK) Ltd, City Point, 1 Ropemaker Street, EC2Y 9HT.

LOWE, Hon. Douglas Ackley, AM 2000; Chairman, Premier's Physical Activity Council, 2004–07; Executive Officer, Tasmanian Branch, Australian Medical Association, 1992–2004; *b* 15 May 1942; *s* of Ackley Reginald Lowe and Dulcie Mary Lowe (*née* Kean); *m* 1963, Pamela June (*née* Grant); two s two d. *Educ:* St Virgil College, Hobart. Mem. Tasmanian House of Assembly, for Franklin, 1969–86: ALP, 1969–82; Ind., 1982–86. Minister for Housing, 1972; Chief Secretary, 1974; Deputy Premier, 1975–77; Chief Sec. and Minister for Planning and Reorganisation, 1975; Premier, 1977–81; Treasurer, 1980–81; Minister for: Industrial Relations, Planning and the Environment, 1976; Industrial Relations and Health, Aug. 1976; Industrial Relations and Manpower Planning, 1977–79; Economic Planning and Development, 1979–80; Energy, 1979–81; MLC (Ind.) Buckingham, Tas., 1986–92; Dep. Leader for Govt, Legislative Council, 1989–92. Australian Labor Party: State Sec. 1965–69, State Pres. 1974–75, Tasmanian Section. Tasmanian Deleg. to Aust. Constitutional Convention, 1973–85. Senator, Jaycees Internat. State Pres., Tasmanian Swimming Inc., 1990–98; Mem. Panel, Australian Swimming Disciplinary Tribunal, 1996–98. Silver Jubilee Medal, 1977; Australian Sports Medal, 2000; Centenary Medal (Tasmania), 2003; President's Award, AMA, 2004.

Publication: The Price of Power, 1984. *Address:* 1 Michele Court, Berriedale, Tas 7011, Australia.

LOWE, Air Chief Marshal Sir Douglas (Charles), GCB 1977 (KCB 1974; CB 1971); DFC 1943; AFC 1946; *b* 14 March 1922; *s* of John William Lowe; *m* 1944, Doreen Elizabeth (*née* Nichols) (*d* 2008); one s one d. *Educ:* Reading School. Joined RAF, 1940; No 75 (NZ) Sqdn, 1943; Bomber Comd Instructors' Sch., 1945; RAF Coll., Cranwell, 1947; Exam. Wing CFS, 1950; Air Min. Operational Requirements, 1955; OC No 148 Sqdn, 1959; Exchange Officer, HQ SAC, USAF, 1961; Stn Comdr Cranwell, 1963; idc 1966; DOR 2 (RAF), MoD (Air), 1967; SASO, NEAF, 1969–71; ACAS (Operational Requirements), 1971–73; AOC No 18 Group, RAF, 1973–75; Controller, Aircraft, MoD Procurement Executive, 1975–82; Chief of Defence Procurement, MoD, Sept. 1982–June 1983. Air ADC to the Queen, 1978–83. Chairman: Mercury Communications Ltd, 1984–85; Band III Hldgs, 1986–91; Director: Royal Ordnance plc, 1984–7; Rolls Royce, 1984–92. Mem. Council, St John's Sch., Leatherhead, 1984–94. CRAeS 1982; CCMI (CBIM 1984). *Recreations:* gardening, domestic odd-jobbing, photography, theatre, music. *Club:* Royal Air Force.

See also Baron Glanusk.

LOWE, Fergus; *see* Lowe, C. F.

LOWE, Sir Frank (Budge), Kt 2001; Founder, The Red Brick Road, 2006; Founder, 1981, and Chairman Emeritus, since 2003, Lowe and Partners Worldwide (formerly Lowe Howard Spink); *b* 23 Aug. 1941; *s* of Stephen and Marion Lowe; two s one d. *Educ:* Westminster School. Vis. Prof., UCL, 1990–. Founder and Chm., Capital City Acad., 2003–. Founder, Stella Artois Championships. FRSA.

LOWE, Geoffrey Colin; aviation consultant, 1980–88; *b* 7 Sept. 1920; *s* of late Colin Roderick and late Elsie Lowe; *m* 1948, Joan Stephen (*d* 1985); one d; *m* 1988, Jean Marion Bailey (*née* Wigginton) (*d* 2007). *Educ:* Reigate Grammar Sch. GPO, 1937; Exchequer and Audit Dept, 1939. Served War, RAFVR, 1941–46 (Flt-Lt). Asst Principal, Min. of Civil Aviation, 1947; Private Sec. to Permanent Sec., MCA, 1950; Principal, 1950; Colonial Office, 1954–57; Min. of Transport and Civil Aviation, 1957–61; Civil Air Attaché, SE Asia, 1961–64; Asst Sec., Overseas Policy Div., Min. of Aviation, 1964–68; Investment Grants Div., Bd of Trade, 1968–71; Counsellor (Civil Aviation), British Embassy, Washington, 1971–73; Counsellor (Civil Aviation and Shipping), Washington, 1973–74; Under Sec. (Management Services and Manpower), Depts of Industry and Trade, 1974–80. *Recreations:* theatre, crossword puzzles. *Address:* 13 Highwood, Sunset Avenue, Woodford Green, Essex IG8 0SZ. *T:* (020) 8504 7035. *Club:* Civil Service.

LOWE, Janet, CBE 2003; EdD; Member, Scottish Further and Higher Education Funding Council, since 2005; *b* South Normanton, 27 Sept. 1950; *d* of George Frederick and Sheila Lowe; *m* 1982, Dr Donald Thomas Stewart. *Educ:* Swanwick Hall Grammar Sch.; Univ. of Hull (BA Hons French and Italian 1973); Univ. of Dundee (MBA 1990); Univ. of Stirling (EdD 2005). Immigration Officer, Home Office, 1973–76; Personnel Asst, Univ. of Hull, 1976–80; Adminr, Lothian Regl Council, 1980–82; Personnel Officer, 1982–86, Asst Registrar, 1986–88, Napier Univ.; Sec. and Registrar, Duncan of Jordanstone Coll. of Art, 1988–92; Depute Principal, 1992–95, Principal, 1996–2005, Lauder Coll., Dunfermline. Member: Bd of Mgt, Scottish Further Educn Unit, 1993–2001; Scottish Consultative Council on the Curriculum, 1995–99; Scottish Cttee, Nat. Cttee of Inquiry into Higher Educn, 1996–97; Bd, Scottish Enterprise, 1998–2004; Bd, Assoc. of Scottish Colls, 2002–05; Ind. Rev. of Local Govt Finance, 2004–07. Trustee, Carnegie Trust for Univs of Scotland, 2005–. Member of Court: Heriot-Watt Univ., 1999–2005; Univ. of Dundee, 2005–. Hon. DEd Queen Margaret Univ., Edinburgh, 2007. *Recreations:* Rotary (Pres., Rotary Club of Dunfermline Carnegie, 2008–June 2009), gardening, keeping fit, reading novels, visiting Italy. *Address:* 42 Gamekeepers Road, Kinnesswood, Kinross KY13 9JR. *T:* (01592) 840277; *e-mail:* janetlowe@aol.com.

LOWE, John Evelyn, MA; FSA, FRSA; cultural consultant and author, since 1978; foreign travel specialist, journalist and photographer; *b* 23 April 1928; *s* of late Arthur Holden Lowe; *m* 1st, 1956, Susan Helen Sanderson (marr. diss. 1981); two s one d; 2nd, 1989, Yukiko Nomura; one d. *Educ:* Wellington Coll., Berks; New Coll., Oxford. Served in RAEC, 1947–49 (Sgt Instructor). Victoria and Albert Museum, Dept of Woodwork, 1953–56; Deputy Story Editor, Pinewood Studios, 1956–57; Victoria and Albert Museum: Dept of Ceramics, 1957–61; Assistant to the Director, 1961–64; Dir, City Museum and Art Gall., Birmingham, 1964–69; Dir, Weald and Downland Open Air Museum, 1969–74; Principal, West Dean College, Chichester, West Sussex, 1972–78. Vis. Prof. in British Cultural Studies, Doshisha Univ., Japan, 1979–81; Vis. Prof., Internat. Res. Centre for Japanese Studies, Kyoto, 2001–02. Literary Editor, Kansai Time Out, 1983–88. Hofer–Hecksher Bibliographical Lectr, Harvard, 1974. Pres., Midlands Fedn of Museums, 1967–69. Member: Exec. Cttee, Midland Arts Centre for Young People, 1964–69; Council of the British School at Rome, 1968–70; Crafts Adv. Cttee, 1973–78. Consultant to: Seibu Ltd, Tokyo, 1968–72; Specialtours, London, 1969–74. Trustee: Sanderson Art in Industry Fund, 1968–2005; Edward James Foundn, 1972–73; Idlewild Trust, 1972–78. Hon. Fellow, RCA, 1988. Asst Ed., Collins Crime Club, 1953–54; Founding Ed., Faber Furniture Series, 1954–56. Library of European books about Japan acquired by Nichibunken, Kyoto, 1987; eponymous collection of Japanese arts and crafts presented to Pitt Rivers Mus., 1996. *Publications:* Thomas Chippendale, 1955; Cream Coloured Earthenware, 1958; Japanese Crafts, 1983; Into Japan, 1985; Into China, 1986; Corsica: a traveller's guide, 1988; A Surrealist Life—Edward James—Poet, Patron & Eccentric, 1991; Glimpses of Kyoto Life, 1996; The Warden: a portrait of John Sparrow, 1998; Old Kyoto, 1999; major contribs to Encyclopædia Britannica and OUP Junior Encyclopedia; articles on applied arts, foreign travel, social history and Japan. *Recreations:* Japan, music, reading, book-collecting, travel. *Address:* 2 rue Jean Guiton, 47300 Villeneuve sur Lot, France. *T:* 0553417253.

LOWE, Prof. (Joseph) John, PhD; CGeol, FGS; Professor of Geography and Quaternary Science, Royal Holloway, University of London, since 1992; *b* 12 June 1946; *s* of Joseph Lowe and Margaret (*née* Rooney); *m* 1969, Jeanette P. Bell; two s. *Educ:* Univ. of St Andrews (MA 1st Cl. Hons Geog. 1970); Univ. of Edinburgh (PhD 1977). City of London Polytechnic: Lectr, 1973–77; Sen. Lectr, 1977–85; Principal Lectr and Reader, 1985–88; Prof. and Hd, Dept of Geog., 1988–89; Royal Holloway and Bedford New College, University of London: Sen. Lectr, 1989–90; Reader, 1990–92; Dean of Science, 1997–2000; Dir, Centre for Quaternary Res., Univ. of London, 1989–97 and 2006–. Pres., UK Quaternary Res. Assoc., 2005–08 (Vice-Pres., 1992–97); Vice-Pres., Internat. Union of Quaternary Assocs, 2007–. Chm., Earth Scis Cttee, NERC, 1993–96. Univ. of Helsinki Medal, 1996; Coke Medal, Geol. Soc. of London, 2003. *Publications:* Studies in the Scottish Lateglacial Environment, 1977; Studies in the Lateglacial Environment of North-West Europe, 1980; (with M. J. C. Walker) Reconstructing Quaternary Environments, 1984, 2nd edn 1997; contrib. to Nature, Jl Geol Soc., Jl Ecology, Phil. Trans Royal Soc. and others. *Recreations:* music, hill-walking, soccer (training). *Address:* Department of Geography, Royal Holloway, University of London, Egham, Surrey TW20 0EX. *T:* (01784) 443565; *e-mail:* j.lowe@rhul.ac.uk.

LOWE, Prof. Kenneth Gordon, CVO 1982; MD; FRCP, FRCPE, FRCPGlas; Physician to the Queen in Scotland, 1971–82; formerly Consultant Physician, Royal Infirmary and Ninewells Hospital, Dundee; Hon. Professor of Medicine, Dundee University, since 1969; *b* 29 May 1917; *s* of Thomas J. Lowe, MA, Arbroath, and Flora MacDonald Gordon, Arbroath; *m* 1942, Nancy Young, MB, ChB (*d* 1999), twin *d* of Stephen Young, Logie, Fife; two *s* one *d*. *Educ:* Arbroath High Sch.; St Andrews Univ. (MD Hons). Served with RAMC, 1942–46; Registrar, Hammersmith Hosp., Royal Postgrad. Med. Sch., 1947–52; Sen. Lectr in Medicine, St Andrews Univ., 1952–61. Hon. DSc St Andrews, 2003. *Publications:* (jtly) Regional Anatomy Illustrated, 1983; contribs to med. and scientific jls, mainly on renal, metabolic and cardiac disorders. *Recreations:* reading, fishing. *Address:* 36 Dundee Road, West Ferry, Dundee DD5 1HY. *T:* (01382) 778787. *Club:* Flyfishers'.

LOWE, (Nicholas) Mark; QC 1996; a Recorder, since 2000; *b* 17 June 1947; *s* of late John Lancelot Lowe, solicitor, and of Margaret Janet Lowe (*née* Hucklesby); *m* 1975, Felicity Anne Parry-Williams; two *s* one *d*. *Educ:* Colchester Royal Grammar Sch.; Leicester Univ. (LLB 1969). Called to the Bar, Gray's Inn, 1972, Bencher, 2004; in practice at the Bar, 1973–; Head of Chambers, 2006–. *Recreations:* fishing (occasional), walking, birdwatching, gardening, sheepkeeping. *Address:* 2–3 Gray's Inn Square, WC1R 5JH. *T:* (020) 7242 4986.

LOWE, Peter Alexander; Chief Information Officer and Director, Information and Workplace Services, Department for Business, Enterprise and Regulatory Reform (formerly Department of Trade and Industry), since 2006; *b* 1 March 1955; *s* of James Thomas Lowe and Dorothy Jean Bell Lowe; one *s* one *d*. *Educ:* Wallace Hall Acad.; Heriot Watt Univ. (BSc Hons Mech. Engrg). ESSO/EXXON, 1977–99: Maintenance Manager, Fawley Refinery, 1996–97; Prog. Manager, EXXON Year 2000, 1998–99; Principal Consultant, Booz Allen Hamilton, 1999–2003; Dir, IT, Home Office, 2003–06. *Recreations:* golf, running. *Address:* Department for Business, Enterprise and Regulatory Reform, Kingsgate House, 66–74 Victoria Street, SW1E 6SW. *T:* (020) 7215 3630, *Fax:* (020) 7215 3651; *e-mail:* peter.lowe@berr.gsi.gov.uk. *Club:* Bramley Golf.

LOWE, Prof. Philip David, OBE 2003; Duke of Northumberland Professor of Rural Economy, University of Newcastle upon Tyne, since 1992; Director, UK Research Councils' Rural Economy and Land Use Programme, since 2003; *b* 29 March 1950; *s* of Wilf and Lena Lowe; *m* 1972, Veronica Gibbins; one *s* one *d*. *Educ:* Exeter Coll., Oxford (MA); Manchester Univ. (MSc); Univ. of Sussex (MPhil). Res. Officer, Union of Internat. Assocs, Brussels, 1973; Lectr in Countryside Planning, 1974–89, Reader in Envmtl Planning, 1989–92, UCL; Founder and Dir, Centre for Rural Economy, Univ. of Newcastle upon Tyne, 1992–2004. Vis. Fellow, Science Centre, Berlin, 1983; Res. Fellow, Woodrow Wilson Internat. Center for Scholars, Washington, 1985. Expert Advr, H of C Select Cttee on the Envmt, 1996–99; Member: Minister of Agriculture's Adv. Gp, 1997–98; Science Adv. Council, DEFRA, 2004–; Chm., Vets' Working Gp, DEFRA, 2007–. Mem. Bd, Countryside Agency, 1999–2006; Chm., Market Towns Adv. Forum, 2001–06. *Publications:* Environmental Groups in Politics, 1983; Locality and Rurality, 1984; Countryside Conflicts, 1986; Deprivation and Welfare in Rural Areas, 1986; Rural Studies in Britain and France, 1990; Constructing the Countryside, 1993; European Integration and Environmental Policy, 1993; Moralising the Environment, 1997; British Environmental Policy and Europe, 1998; CAP Regimes and the European Countryside, 2000; The Differentiated Countryside, 2003; The Ageing Countryside, 2006. *Recreations:* cycling, cinema.

LOWE, Philip Martin; Director General for Competition, European Commission, since 2002; *b* 29 April 1947; *s* of late Leonard Ernest Lowe and Marguerite Helen Lowe (*née* Childs); *m* 1st, 1967, Gillian Baynton Forge (marr. diss. 1980); two *s*; 2nd, 1984, Nora Mai O'Connell. *Educ:* Leeds Grammar Sch.; Reading Sch.; St John's Coll., Oxford (MA in PPE); London Business Sch. (MSc Business Studies). Tube Investments, 1968–73; Commission of the European Communities, later European Commission: Directorate-Gen. for Credit and Investments, Luxembourg, 1973–82; Mem., Cabinet of President Gaston Thorn, 1982–85, of Alois Pfeiffer, 1985–86; Directorate-Gen. for Co-ordination of Structural Instruments, 1986–89; Chef de Cabinet to Rt Hon. Bruce Millan, Comr for regl policy, 1989–91; Dir, Rural Develt, 1991–93; Dir, Merger Task Force, 1993–95; Chef de Cabinet to Rt Hon. Neil Kinnock, Comr for transport, 1995–97, Vice-Pres. for admin. reform, 2000–02; Dir-Gen., Develt, 1997–2000. *Recreations:* music, running, hillwalking. *Address:* avenue Michel-Ange 18, 1000 Brussels, Belgium. *T:* (office) (2) 2965040, (home) (2) 7349665; *e-mail:* philip.lowe@ec.europa.eu.

See also Bishop Suffragan of Hulme.

LOWE, Dr Robert David; Medical Research Consultant, National Heart Foundation of Australia, 1986–89, retired; *b* 23 Feb. 1930; *s* of John Lowe and Hilda Althea Mead; *m* 1952, Betty Irene Wheeler; one *s* three *d*. *Educ:* Leighton Park Sch.; Emmanuel Coll., Cambridge; UCH Medical School. BCh, MB, MA, MD, PhD Cantab; FRCP, LMSSA. Medical Specialist, RAMC, 1955–59; Research Asst, UCH Med. Sch., 1959–61; St George's Hosp. Med. Sch.: MRC Res. Fellow, 1961–62; Wellcome Sen. Res. Fellow in Clinical Science, 1963–64; Sen. Lectr in Medicine, St Thomas' Hosp. Med. Sch., 1964–70; Hon. Consultant to St Thomas' Hosp., 1966–70; Dean, St George's Hosp. Med. Sch., 1971–82. AUCAS: Exec. Mem., 1967; Chm., 1972–78. *Publications:* (with B. F. Robinson) A Physiological Approach to Clinical Methods, 1970; papers on peripheral circulation, hypertension, adrenergic mechanisms, central action of angiotensin, control of cardiovascular system. *Recreations:* bridge, squash, hill-walking, sailing.

LOWE, Stephen; playwright; Artistic Director, Meeting Ground Theatre, since 1984; *b* 1 Dec. 1947; *s* of Harry Wright and Minnie Wright; *né* Stephen James Wright; changed name to Stephen Lowe; *m* 1st, 1975, Tina Barclay (marr. diss. 1985); one *s*; 2nd, 1999, Tanya Myers; two *d*. *Educ:* Birmingham Univ. (BA English and Theatre Studies; MA). Actor, Scarborough Theatre in the Round, 1974–78; Sen. Lectr, Writing for Performance, Dartington Coll., 1978–82; Resident Playwright, Riverside Studios, London, 1982–84. Chm., Year of Artist Adv. Gp (E Midlands), 2001–02; actg Chm., E Midlands Arts, 2001–02; Mem., Arts Council of England, then Arts Council England, and Chm., E Midlands Regl Arts Council, 2002–06. *Publications:* Touched, 1981; Ragged Trousered Philanthropists, 1983; Divine Gossip/Tibetan Inroads, 1984; Moving Pictures and Other Plays, 1985; (ed) Peace Plays, vol. 1, 1985, vol. 2, 1990; Revelations, 2004. *Recreations:* walking, snooker, history. *Address:* c/o Sara Stroud, Judy Daish Associates, 2 St Charles Place, W10 6EG. *T:* (020) 8964 8811, *Fax:* (020) 8964 8966.

LOWE, Rt Rev. Stephen Richard; *see* Hulme, Bishop Suffragan of.

LOWE, Sir Thomas (William Gordon), 4th Bt *cr* 1918, of Edgbaston, City of Birmingham; QC 2008; *b* 14 Aug. 1963; *s* of Sir Francis Reginald Gordon Lowe, 3rd Bt and of Franziska Cornelia, *d* of Siegfried Steinkopf; *S* father, 1986; *m* 1996, Mozhgan, *d* of Hassan Asilzadeh; one *s*. *Educ:* Stowe School; London School of Economics (LLB 1984); Jesus Coll., Cambridge (LLM 1986). Called to the Bar, Inner Temple, 1985. *Publications:* articles in various legal periodicals. *Heir:* *s* Theodore Christopher William Lowe, *b* 23 Aug. 2000. *Address:* Wilberforce Chambers, 8 New Square, Lincoln's Inn, WC2A 3QP.

LOWE, Vaughan; *see* Lowe, A. V.

LOWE, Veronica Ann; an Immigration Judge (formerly Immigration Appeals Adjudicator), since 2000; *b* 29 June 1951; *d* of late Arthur Ernest Bagley and Agatha (*née* Blackham); *m* 1977, Ian Stanley Lowe; one *d*. *Educ:* King Edward VI Grammar Sch. for Girls, Handsworth, Birmingham; St Hugh's Coll., Oxford (MA); Oxford Polytechnic (MIL Exams); City of Birmingham Polytechnic. Articled Clerk, Ryland, Martineau & Co., Birmingham, 1976–78; Lectr in Labour Law, Univ. of Aston in Birmingham, 1978–80; admitted solicitor, 1979; solicitor in private practice, 1979–86; Asst Area Dir, Legal Aid Area No 8, 1986–88; Area Dir (W Midlands), Legal Aid Area No 6, 1988–89; Gp Manager (Midlands), Legal Aid Bd, 1989–90; Dir, Solicitors' Complaints Bureau, 1990–95; Chief Exec., Valuation Office Agency, 1996–97; mgt consultant and author, 1998–; solicitor, Pinsent Curtis, 1999–2000; Hd of Legal Services, Oxford Brookes Univ., 2000; Sen. Legal Counsel, 2000–03, European Legal Affairs Consultant, 2003–07, Mayne Pharma (formerly Faulding Pharmaceuticals) plc. Mem. Bd, Eur. Generic Medicines Assoc., 2002–07 (Mem., Legal Affairs Cttee, 2002–07). *Publications:* contribs to publications on law for accountants and businessmen; articles on intellectual property law, generic medicines and Eur. legislation. *Recreations:* cooking, eating and drinking, reading, writing unfinished novels, listening to music, travel, talking, current affairs, being with my daughter, all historical subjects. *Address:* Phoenix Cottage, 6 Rugby Road, Dunchurch, Warwicks CV22 6PE.

LOWEN, Barry Robert; HM Diplomatic Service; Head, Engaging with the Islamic World Group, Foreign and Commonwealth Office, since 2006; *b* 9 Jan. 1964; *s* of Robert Lowen and Pamela Lowen; *m* 1989, Karin (*née* Blizard); three *s*. *Educ:* Jesus Coll., Oxford (MA PPE); Open Univ. (Dip. Mgt). Joined HM Diplomatic Service, 1986: Arab-Israeli Desk Officer, FCO, 1986; Arabic trng, 1987–89; Second Sec., Kuwait, 1989–93; Head of Section: Non-Proliferation Dept, FCO, 1993–95; ME Dept, FCO, 1995–97; First Sec., UKMIS, NY, 1997–2001; Dep. Hd, ME Dept, FCO, 2001–03; Dir, Trade and Investment, 2003–04, Dep. Hd of Mission, 2004–06, Riyadh. *Recreations:* roller-blading, tennis, family. *Address:* c/o Foreign and Commonwealth Office, King Charles Street, SW1A 2AH; *e-mail:* bklowen@yahoo.com.

LOWEN, Jonathan Andrew Michael; His Honour Judge Lowen; a Circuit Judge, since 2000; *b* 16 Aug. 1943; *s* of George Lowen, QC and Vera Fanny Lowen; *m* 1974, Eve Susan Karpf; two *s*. *Educ:* Witwatersrand Univ., Johannesburg (BA); Christ Church, Oxford (MA). Called to the Bar, Gray's Inn, 1972; a Recorder, 1995–2000.

LOWENTHAL, Prof. David, PhD; FBA 2001; Professor of Geography, University College London, 1972–85, now Professor Emeritus (Hon. Research Fellow, 1986); *b* 26 April 1923; *s* of Max Lowenthal and Eleanor Lowenthal (*née* Mack); *m* 1970, Mary Alice Lamberty; two *d*. *Educ:* Harvard (BS Hist. 1943); Univ. of Calif, Berkeley (MA Geog. 1950); Univ. of Wisconsin (PhD Hist. 1953). Served US Army (infantry, OSS, Europe), 1943–45. US State Dept, 1945–46; Asst Prof. of Hist. and Hd, Dept of Geog., Vassar Coll., 1952–56; Consultant, Inst. of Social and Econ. Studies, Dept of Hist., Univ. of WI, 1956–70; Inst. Race Relns, UK, 1961–72. Regents Prof., UC Davis, Calif, 1973; Katz Dist. Prof. of Humanities, Univ. of Washington, 1988; Visiting Professor: Univs of Calif, Berkeley, Minn, Washington, Clark and Harvard; CUNY; MIT; West Dean Coll.; St Mary's UC, Strawberry Hill; Lectures: Dist., Center of Humanities and Arts, Univ. of Georgia, 1998; A. W. Franks, BM, 1999; H. Harvey Dist., Univ. of Newfoundland, 1999; Dist., Pinchot Conservation Inst., US, 2001. Member, Editorial Boards, including: Envmt and Behaviour, 1969–76; Geog. Rev., 1973–95; London Jl, 1974–86; Progress in Geog., 1976–90; Internat. Jl Cultural Property, 1989–. Member: Council, AAAS, 1964–71; Council, Assoc. Amer. Geographers, 1968–71; US Nat. Res. Council, 1968–71; SSRC Ethnic Relns Cttee, 1972–77; Bd, Insts of Latin American Studies and Commonwealth Studies, Univ. of London, 1972–87; Landscape Res. Gp, 1984–89 (Chair). Advisor to various organisations, including: US Peace Corps on the Caribbean; UNESCO, IGU on envmtl perception; English Heritage, V&A, Sci. Mus., BM, ICOMOS, UNESCO, ICCROM on heritage. Fellowships: Fulbright, 1956–57; Guggenheim, 1965; Res. Inst. for Study of Man, Landes (US), 1992–93; Leverhulme, 1992–94. Hon. DLitt Memorial Univ., Newfoundland, 2008. Victoria Medal, RGS, 1997; Cullum Medal, Amer. Geog. Soc., 1999; RSGS Medal, 2004. *Publications:* George Perkins Marsh: versatile Vermonter, 1958 (Assoc. Amer. Geographers Award); West Indies Federation, 1961; West Indian Societies, 1972; (with M. J. Bowden) Geographies of the Mind, 1975; (with M. Binney) Our Past Before Us, 1981; The Past is a Foreign Country, 1985 (Historic Preservation (US) Book Prize); (with E. C. Penning-Rowsell) Landscape Meanings and Values, 1986; (with P. Gathercole) Politics of the Past, 1989; Heritage Crusade and the Spoils of History, 1997; George Perkins Marsh: prophet of conservation, 2000 (J. B. Jackson Book Prize, Assoc. Amer. Geographers); Passage du temps sur le paysage, 2008. *Address:* 22 Heron Place, 9 Thayer Street, W1U 3JL; 1401 LeRoy Avenue, Berkeley, CA 94708, USA.

LOWES, Peter Donald; Director, Anti-Slavery Society for Protection of Human Rights, 1987–89; *b* 13 Sept. 1926; *s* of Col J. H. Lowes and Queenie Frances Lowes (*née* Bowyer); *m* 1954, Linnea Newton (marr. diss. 1980); one *s* two *d*. *Educ:* Bradfield Coll.; Emmanuel Coll., Cambridge (MA); Univ. of British Columbia (LLB); Geneva Univ. (PhD). Served with Royal Engineers, 1946–48. Master, Wanganui Collegiate Sch., NZ, 1949, Upper Canada Coll., Toronto, 1950–51; practised law, Vancouver, 1953–55; UNRWA, Jordan, 1955–58; journalist, Canadian Broadcasting Corp., 1958; UN Narcotic Drugs, Geneva, 1959–65; External Aid, Canadian Govt, Ottawa, 1965–66; Resident Representative, United Nations Development Programme: Lesotho, 1966–68; Swaziland, 1968–71; Malaŵi, 1971–74; HQ, NY, 1974–75; Morocco, 1975–79; Co-ordinator, Internat. Drinking Water Supply and Sanitation Decade, Geneva, 1979–86. Mem. Bd, 1980–86, Consultant, 1987, Internat Reference Centre, The Hague; UNDP and World Bank Consultant, 1987–97. Adviser: CARE (UK), 1987–93; Help the Aged, 1987–93; Crisis at Christmas, 1989–99; St Ethelburga's Project, 1995–99. *Publication:* The Genesis of International Narcotics Control, 1965. *Recreations:* walking, mountaineering, history. *Address:* Apartment 34, 4 Clos Belmont, Geneva 1208, Switzerland. *T:* 7350313. *Clubs:* Alpine, Climbers'.

LOWMAN, Ven. David Walter; Archdeacon of Southend, since 2001; *b* 27 Nov. 1948; *s* of Cecil Walter Lowman and Queenie Norah Lowman. *Educ:* Crewkerne Sch., Somerset; City of London Coll. (Dip. in English Civil Law 1970); King's Coll. London (BD 1973; AKC 1973). Estate Duty Office, Inland Revenue, 1966–70. Ordained deacon, 1975, priest, 1976; Curate: Notting Hill Team Ministry, 1975–78; St Augustine, Kilburn, 1978–81; Vocations Adviser and Selection Sec., ACCM, and Chaplain, Church House, Westminster, 1981–86; Team Rector, Wickford and Runwell, Dio. Chelmsford, 1986–93; Diocesan Dir of Ordinands, and Non-residentiary Canon of Chelmsford Cathedral, 1993–2001. Mem. Wkg Pty, House of Bishops (reported on marriage in church after divorce), 1999. Chair: Vocations Adv. Panel, Ministry Div., Archbishops' Council, 2001–; N Thames Ministerial Trng Course, 2001–. Trustee, SE Essex Christian

Hospice, 2001–06. Gov., Brentwood Sch., 2001–. *Recreations:* cricket, travel (France, Italy, USA, Cyprus), opera, red wine. *Address:* The Archdeacon's Lodge, 136 Broomfield Road, Chelmsford, Essex CM1 1RN. *T:* (01245) 258257.

LOWNIE of Largo, Andrew James Hamilton; literary agent; Proprietor, Andrew Lownie Literary Agency Ltd, since 1988; writer; *b* 11 Nov. 1961; *s* of His Honour Ralph Hamilton Lownie of Largo; *m* 1998, Angela Doyle; one *s* one *d*. *Educ:* Fettes Coll.; Asheville Sch., NC (ESU Schol.); Westminster Sch.; Magdalene Coll., Cambridge (MA); Edinburgh Univ. (MSc); Coll. of Law, London. Pres., Cambridge Union Soc., 1984. Graduate trainee, Hodder & Stoughton Publishers, 1984–85; John Farquharson Literary Agents, 1985–88 (Dir, 1986–88); Director: Denniston & Lownie Ltd, 1991–93; Thistle Publishing, 1996–. Literary Agent to PEN, 2001–04. Contested (C) Monklands West, 1992. Vice-Chm., Cons. Gp for Europe, 1992–95. Sec., Biographers' Club, 1998–. Trustee, Iain MacLeod Award, 1986–. *Publications:* (ed) North American Spies, 1991; The Edinburgh Literary Guide, 1992; John Buchan: the Presbyterian Cavalier, 1995; (ed) John Buchan's Collected Poems, 1996; (ed) John Buchan: the complete short stories, vols 1–3, 1996–97; (ed) John Buchan: shorter Scottish fiction, 1997; The Literary Companion to Edinburgh, 2000; The Edinburgh Literary Companion, 2005. *Recreations:* history, music, tennis, travel. *Address:* Andrew Lownie Literary Agency Ltd, 36 Great Smith Street, SW1P 3BU. *T:* (020) 7222 7574, *Fax:* (020) 7222 7576; *e-mail:* Lownie@globalnet.co.uk.

LOWRY, John Christopher, CBE 2003; FDSRCSE, FDSRCS, FRCSE, FRCS, FFGDP(UK), FRCA; Consultant Maxillofacial and Oral Surgeon, Royal Bolton Hospital, since 1976; Dean, Faculty of Dental Surgery, Royal College of Surgeons of England, 2001–04; *b* 6 June 1942; *s* of Leslie and Betty Lowry; *m* 1968, Valerie Joyce Smethurst; one *s* one *d*. *Educ:* Altrincham Grammar Sch.; Univ. of Manchester (BDS 1963, MB ChB 1970). FDSRCS 1968; FRCSE 1984; MHSM 1994; FDSRCSE 1999; FRCS 2002; FFGDP(UK) 2005; FRCA 2007. Sen. Registrar, Manchester RHA, 1972–76; Lectr (pt-time), Univ. of Manchester, 1976–2001. Vis. Prof. of Surgery, Univ. of Central Lancs, 2004–. Hon. Consultant to the Army, 2004–. Leverhulme Travelling Fellow, 1974–75. Ed., Nat. Speciality Guidelines, 1994–97. Chairman: Central Cttee, Hosp. Dental Services, 1998–2001; Standing Dental Adv. Cttee, DoH, 2000–. Chairman: Senate of Dental Specialities, 2001–04; Jt Meeting Dental Faculties, 2001–04; Cosmetic Surgery Interspecialty Cttee, Senate of Surgery GB and Ire., 2005–08. Sec. Gen., Eur. Assoc. for Craniomaxillofacial Surgery, 1998–; Chm., British Acad. of Cosmetic Practice, 2008; President: British Assoc. of Oral and Maxillofacial Surgeons, 2001; Manchester Medical Soc., 2004–05 (Vice-Pres., 2003–04). Member: Acad. of Med. Royal Colls, 2001–04; Council, RCS, 2001–. Hon. Prof., Univ. of Bucharest, 2007. Dr *hc* Univ. of Iasi, 2006. *Publications:* (contrib.) Operative Maxillofacial Surgery, 1998; anonymous official documents for professional assocs; contrib. papers on maxillofacial reconstruction, oncology, salivary diseases and trauma, telemedicine specialisation and conscious sedation. *Recreations:* music (traditional jazz), cross-training, motor sport, walking. *Address:* The Valley House, 50 Ravens Wood, Bolton BL1 5TL. *T:* (01204) 848815, *Fax:* (01204) 845821; *e-mail:* secretary-general@eacmfs.org, johnlowry1@btinternet.com. *Club:* Royal Society of Medicine.

LOWRY, Her Honour Noreen Margaret, (Nina); a Circuit Judge, 1976–95; *b* 6 Sept. 1925; *er d* of late John Collins, MC, and Hilda Collins; *m* 1st, 1950, Edward Lucas Gardner, QC (marr. diss. 1962); one *s* one *d*; 2nd, 1963, His Honour Richard John Lowry, QC (*d* 2001); one *d*. *Educ:* Bedford High Sch.; Birmingham Univ. LLB Birmingham, 1947. Called to the Bar, Gray's Inn, 1948, Bencher, 1995. Criminal practice on S Eastern Circuit, Central Criminal Court, Inner London Sessions, etc., practising as Miss Nina Collins; Metropolitan Stipendiary Magistrate, 1967–76. Member: Criminal Law Revision Cttee, 1975–; Criminal Injuries Compensation Bd, 1995–2000. Freeman, City of London, 1985. Hon. LLD Birmingham, 1992. *Recreations:* theatre, travel.

LOWRY-CORRY, family name of **Earl of Belmore**.

LOWSON, Ven. Christopher; Director, Ministry Division, Archbishops' Council, since 2006; Priest Vicar, Westminster Abbey, since 2006; *b* 3 Feb. 1953; *s* of George Frederick Lowson, CEng, FIMarE and Isabella Annie Lowson (*née* Spence); *m* 1976, Susan Mary Osborne, RGN, RSCN, MSc; one *s* one *d*. *Educ:* Newcastle Cathedral Sch.; Consett Grammar Sch.; King's Coll. London (AKC 1975); St Augustine's Coll., Canterbury; Pacific Sch. of Religion, Berkeley, Calif (STM 1978); Heythrop Coll., Univ. of London (MTh 1996); Cardiff Law Sch. (LLM 2003). Deacon 1977, priest 1978; Asst Curate, Richmond, Surrey, 1977–82; Priest in charge, 1982–83, Vicar 1983–91, Holy Trinity, Eltham; Chaplain: Avery Hill Coll., 1982–85; Thames Poly., 1985–91; Vicar of Petersfield and Rector of Buriton, Hants, 1991–99; RD of Petersfield, 1995–99; Archdeacon of Portsmouth, 1999; Archdeacon of Portsdown, 1999–2006, Archdeacon Emeritus, 2006. Chm., Portsmouth Diocesan Bd of Ministry, 1999–2006; Bp of Portsmouth's Liaison Officer for Prisons, 1999–2003; Bp of Portsmouth's Advr to Hosp. Chaplaincy, 2003–06. Vis. Lectr, Portsmouth Univ., 1998–2004; Dir, Portsmouth Educn Business Partnership, 2000–03. Foundn Trustee, Gallipoli Meml Lecture Trust, 1985–91. *Recreations:* watching cricket, the theatre. *Address:* Ministry Division, Church House, Great Smith Street, SW1P 3NZ. *T:* (020) 7898 1390, *Fax:* (020) 7898 1000; *e-mail:* christopher.lowson@c-of-e.org.uk. *Clubs:* Athenæum, MCC.

LOWSON, Sir Ian (Patrick), 2nd Bt *cr* 1951; *b* 4 Sept. 1944; *s* of Sir Denys Colquhoun Flowerdew Lowson, 1st Bt and Hon. Patricia, OStJ, *yr d* of 1st Baron Strathcarron, PC, KC; *S* father, 1975; *m* 1979, Mrs Tanya Du Boulay, *d* of R. F. A. Judge; one *s* one *d*. *Educ:* Eton; Duke Univ., USA. OStJ. *Heir:* *s* Henry William Lowson, *b* 10 Nov. 1980. *Address:* 23 Flood Street, SW3 5ST. *Clubs:* Boodle's, Pilgrims; Brook (NY).

LOWSON, Prof. Martin Vincent, FREng; FRAeS; Chief Executive Officer, Advanced Transport Systems Ltd, since 1995; Senior Research Fellow, University of Bristol, since 2003; *b* 5 Jan. 1938; *s* of Alfred Vincent Lowson and Irene Gertrude Lowson; *m* 1961, Ann Pennicutt; one *s* one *d*. *Educ:* King's Sch., Worcester; Univ. of Southampton (BScEng, PhD). Apprentice, Vickers Armstrong (Aircraft), 1955; Res. student and Assistant, Univ. of Southampton, 1960; Head, Applied Physics, Wyle Labs, Huntsville, USA, 1964; Rolls-Royce Reader, Loughborough Univ., 1969; Westland Helicopters: Chief Scientist, 1973; Div. Dir, Corporate Develt, 1979; Bristol University: Sir George White Prof. of Aerospace Engrg, 1986–2001; Prof. of Advanced Transport, 2001–03. Chm., Flow Solutions Ltd, 1986–97. Fellow, Acoustical Soc. of America, 1971; FREng (FEng 1991); FAIAA 1996. *Publications:* numerous papers in learned jls, and patents. *Recreations:* research, squash, bluegrass music. *Address:* Alpenfels, North Road, Leigh Woods, Bristol BS8 3PJ. *T:* (0117) 973 6497.

LOWSON, Robert Campbell; on secondment from Department for Environment, Food and Rural Affairs to European Environment Agency, since 2007; *b* 7 March 1949; *s* of late George Campbell Lowson and Betty Lowson (*née* Parry); *m* 1973, Hilary Balsdon; one *s* one *d*. *Educ:* Gravesend Grammar Sch.; Brasenose Coll., Oxford (BA History 1970). Joined Ministry of Agriculture, Fisheries and Food, 1970: UK Mission, Geneva, 1977; Principal Private Sec. to Minister of Agric., Fisheries and Food, 1982; successively Head of Cereals, Milk, Animal Health, and Agric. Resource Policy Divs, 1983–94; Under Sec., 1994; Minister, UK Repn Brussels, on loan to FCO, 1995–99; Dir of Communications, MAFF, subseq. DEFRA, 1999–2001; Dir of Envmt Protection Strategy, later Envmt Strategy, 2001–07, Dir, Regulation, 2007, DEFRA. *Recreations:* all the usual things. *Address:* European Commission, BREY 9/211, 1040 Brussels, Belgium. *T:* 473186253. *Club:* Athenæum.

LOWTHER, family name of **Earl of Lonsdale** and **Viscount Ullswater**.

LOWTHER, Col Sir Charles (Douglas), 6th Bt *cr* 1824; farmer, company director; *b* 22 Jan. 1946; *s* of Lt-Col Sir William Guy Lowther, 5th Bt, OBE, and Grania Suzanne, *d* of late Major A. J. H. Douglas Campbell, OBE; *S* father, 1982; *m* 1975, Florence Rose, *y d* of Colonel Alexander James Henry Cramsie, O'Harabrook, Ballymoney, Co. Antrim; one *s* one *d*. *Educ:* Winchester College. Commissioned, Queen's Royal Irish Hussars, 1966; Regimental Duty UK and BAOR, 1974–76; Army Staff College, Camberley, 1978–79; Staff appointment, 1981; CO, QRIH, 1986–89; Officer i/c, Household Cavalry and RAC Manning and Record Office, 1989–93. Mem., HM Body Guard, Hon. Corps of Gentlemen-at-Arms, 1997–. High Sheriff, Clwyd, 1997. Racing Mem., Jockey Club, 1999. *Recreations:* fieldsports, travel. *Heir:* *s* Patrick William Lowther [*b* 15 July 1977; *m* 2006, Sarah Jane, *o d* of William Davis]. *Club:* Cavalry and Guards.

LOWTHER, James; Founding Partner, M&C Saatchi (UK), 1995 (Chairman, 2000–06); *b* 27 Jan. 1947; *s* of George Hugh Lowther and Sheila Rachel Isabelle Lowther; *m* 1987, Karen Healey Wallace; one *s* three *d*. *Educ:* Eton Coll.; Keble Coll., Oxford (MA Hons Hist.). Saatchi & Saatchi, 1977–95, Creative Dir and Dep. Chm., 1991–95. Dir, British Television Advertising Awards, 1992–; Exec. Producer, Britain's Brilliant Prodigies, 2002, 2003. Trustee, Children in Crisis, 2000–. *Publications:* (contrib.) The Copy Book, 1995; (contrib.) The 22 Irrefutable Laws of Advertising (and When to Violate Them). *Recreations:* listening to, playing and writing music, restoring beautiful but hungry historic house. *Address:* 4 Fawcett Street, SW10 9HZ. *T:* (020) 7352 2735; *e-mail:* jamesl@mcsaatchi.com; Holdenby House, Northampton NN6 8DJ. *T:* (01604) 770241; *e-mail:* jamesl@holdenby.com. *Club:* Bluebird.

LOWTHER, Sir John (Luke), KCVO 1997; CBE 1983; JP; Lord Lieutenant for Northamptonshire, 1984–98; *b* 17 Nov. 1923; *s* of Col J.G. Lowther, CBE, DSO, MC, TD and the Hon. Mrs Lowther; *m* 1952, Jennifer Jane Bevan; one *s* two *d*. *Educ:* Eton; Trinity College, Oxford. MA 1949. Served King's Royal Rifle Corps, 1942–47; worked for Singer Sewing Co., USA, 1949–51; Managing Dir, own manufacturing Co., 1951–60; farmer, 1960–. CC Northants, 1970–84 (Leader of Council, 1977–81); High Sheriff 1971, DL 1977, JP 1984, Northants. Hon. Colonel: Royal Anglian Regt (Northamptonshire), TA, 1986–89; Northants ACF, 1991–96. *Recreations:* shooting, countryman. *Address:* Nortoft Grange, Guilsborough, Northants NN6 8QB. *T:* (01604) 740289. *Club:* Boodle's.

LOWTHER, Merlyn Vivienne; a Director, Schroders plc, since 2004; *b* 3 March 1954; *d* of Norman Edward Douglas Humphrey and Joan Margaret Humphrey (*née* Hewitt); *m* 1975, David John Lowther; one *s* one *d*. *Educ:* Manchester High Sch. for Girls; Univ. of Manchester (BSc Hons Maths 1975); London Business Sch. (MSc Econs 1981); Central Sch. of Speech and Drama (MA Actor Trng and Coaching 2007). FCIB 1999. Bank of England, 1975–2004: Sen. Dealer, Gilt Edged Div., 1985–87; Head, Banking Div. and Dep. Chief Cashier, 1991–96; Personnel Dir, 1996–98; Dep. Dir and Chief Cashier, 1999–2004. Trustee: Henry Smith's Charity, 1999–; Winston Churchill Meml Trust, 2003–. FRSA 1996. Hon. LLD Manchester, 1999. *Recreations:* theatre, singing, reading, family.

LOWTHER-PINKERTON, (Anthony) James (Moxon), MVO 1986; MBE 1990; Private Secretary to Princes William and Henry of Wales, since 2005; *b* 28 Sept. 1960; *s* of Anthony Hull Lowther-Pinkerton and Sue Lowther-Pinkerton (*née* Leslie-Smith); *m* 1995, Susannah Lucy (*née* Richards); one *s* three *d*. *Educ:* Eton Coll.; RMA Sandhurst. Irish Guards, 1979–98; Equerry to HM Queen Elizabeth the Queen Mother, 1984–86; SAS Regt, 1987–94; sc 1995; Balkans desk officer, Directorate of Mil. Ops, MoD, 1996–98. Dir, Objective Team Ltd, 2001–07; Sen. Consultant, Kroll Security Gp, 2004–06. Trustee: HALO Trust, 2005–; Sentebale - The Princes' Fund for Lesotho, 2006–. Fellow, British American Project. FRGS. *Recreations:* Nelson, castles, the Suffolk coast. *Address:* Methersgate Hall, Sutton, Woodbridge, Suffolk IP12 3JL. *T:* (01394) 385928. *Clubs:* Pratt's; Frontline.

LOXDALE, Dr Hugh David, MBE 2007; CBiol; FLS; FRES; FIBiol; European Union Marie Curie Senior Research Fellow, Institute of Ecology, Friedrich Schiller University and Max Planck Institute for Chemical Ecology, Jena, Germany, since 2006; *b* 9 Sept. 1950; *s* of late John David Loxdale and Phyllis Marjorie Loxdale (*née* Duke); *m* 1993, Nicola von Mende, MSc, PhD. *Educ:* Apsley Grammar Sch., Hemel Hempstead; Univ. of Reading (ARC Bursary; BSc Hons (Zool. with Biochem. and Physiol.) 1974); Linacre Coll., Oxford (DPhil 1980). MIBiol 1974, FIBiol 2001; CBiol 1979. Entomologist, Rothamsted Experimental Station, subseq. Rothamsted Research: scientific asst, 1969–71; returned to Rothamsted, 1977; SO, 1977; HSO, 1979; SSO, 1985; Principal Res. Scientist, 1991–2005. Lectr in field; Special Lectr in insect molecular ecol., Sutton Bonington, Univ. of Nottingham, 1993–96. Mem., Co-ordination Cttee, ESF network, PARTNER (Parthenogenesis Network), 2003–05. Royal Entomological Society: Fellow, 1985; Mem. Council and Trustee, 2000–03; Vice Pres., 2003; Pres., 2004–06. Mem. Council, Systematics Assoc., 1986–89. Beds, Essex and Herts Branch, Institute of Biology: Mem. Cttee, 1998–99; Sec., 1999–2003; Chm., 2003–06. Life Gov., ICRF, 1989–2003; Hon. Fellow, CRUK, 2003–. FLS 2002. Freeman, Shrewsbury, 1993. Ed.-in-Chief, The Entomologist (Jl of Royal Entomol. Soc.), 1987–89; Mem. Editl Bd, Molecular Ecol., 2000–05; Subject Ed., Bulletin Entomol Res., 2002–05. *Publications:* (ed with J. Den Hollander) Electrophoretic Studies on Agricultural Pests, 1989; (ed with G. Lushai) Intraclonal Genetic Variation: ecological and evolutionary aspects, 2003; *natural history poetry:* The Eternal Quest: a celebration of nature in poetry, 1988, 2nd edn 2003; Blue Skies in Tuscany, 2000, 2nd edn 2003; Fascinating Felines: sixty cat poems, 2002; Bird Words: poetic images of wild birds, 2003; numerous contribs to internat. scientific jls, incl. res. and review papers, book chapters and popular articles. *Recreations:* natural history, genealogy, history, poetry, walking, debating. *Address:* 25 Pickford Hill, Harpenden, Herts AL5 5HE. *T:* (office) (Germany) (3641) 949448/571558, *Fax:* (3641) 949402/571502; *e-mail:* Hugh.Loxdale@uni-jena.de, hloxdale@ice.mpg.de.

LOY, Francis David Lindley, CBE 1997; Stipendiary Magistrate at Leeds, 1974–97; a Recorder of the Crown Court, 1983–96; *b* 7 Oct. 1927; *s* of late Archibald Loy and late Sarah Eleanor Loy; *m* 1954, Brenda Elizabeth Walker; three *d*. *Educ:* Repton Sch.; Corpus Christi Coll., Cambridge. BA Hons (Law) 1950. Royal Navy, 1946–48. Called to the Bar, Middle Temple, 1952; practised North-Eastern Circuit, 1952–72; Recorder (Northern Circuit), 1972; Stipendiary Magistrate of Leeds, 1972–74. Hon. Sec., Soc. of Provincial Stipendiary Magistrates, 1980–89, Chm., 1990–96. *Recreations:* reading, English History, walking, travel. *Address:* 4 Wedgewood Drive, Roundhay, Leeds LS8 1EF; 14 The Avenue, Sheringham, Norfolk NR26 8DG. *T:* (01263) 822697. *Club:* LSI (Leeds).

LOYD, Christopher Lewis, MC 1943; *b* 1 June 1923; 3rd and *o* surv. *s* of late Arthur Thomas Loyd, OBE, JP, Lockinge, Wantage, Berks, and Dorothy, *d* of late Paul Ferdinand Willert, Headington, Oxford; *m* 1957, Joanna, *d* of Captain Arthur Turberville Smith-Bingham, Milburn Manor, Malmesbury, Wilts; two *s* one *d*. *Educ:* Eton; King's Coll., Cambridge (MA). Served 1942–46, with Coldstream Guards, Captain. ARICS 1952, FRICS 1955. Mem., Jockey Club. Trustee, Wallace Collection, 1973–90. JP 1950, DL 1954, Oxfordshire (formerly Berks); High Sheriff of Berkshire, 1961. *Address:* Betterton Farm House, Ardington, Wantage, Oxfordshire OX12 8QP. *T:* (01235) 833265. *Club:* Boodle's.

LOYD, Sir Julian (St John), KCVO 1991 (CVO 1979); DL; FRICS; Land Agent to HM The Queen, Sandringham Estate, 1964–91; *b* 25 May 1926; *s* of General Sir Charles Loyd, GCVO, KCB, DSO, MC and Lady Moyra Loyd; *m* 1960, Mary Emma, *d* of Sir Christopher Steel, GCMG, MVO and Lady Steel; one *s* two *d* (and one *s* decd). *Educ:* Eton Coll.; Magdalene Coll., Cambridge (MA). FRICS 1955. Coldstream Guards, 1944–45. Partner in Savills, Norwich, 1955–64. Chm., King's Lynn and Wisbech NHS Trust, 1991–94. DL Norfolk, 1983. *Recreation:* fishing. *Address:* Perrystone Cottage, Burnham Market, King's Lynn PE31 8HA. *T:* (01328) 730168. *Club:* Army and Navy.

LUBA, Jan Michael Andrew; QC 2000; a Recorder, since 2000; a Judge of the Employment Appeal Tribunal (part-time), since 2002; *b* 12 Feb. 1957; *s* of Zenon and Marlene Luba; *m* 1978, Adriana; two *d*. *Educ:* London Sch. of Economics (LLB); Univ. of Leicester (LLM). Called to the Bar, Middle Temple, 1980; Legal Officer, CPAG, 1987–89; Nat. Housing Law Service, 1990–92; private practice at the Bar, England and Wales, 1992–. Patron, Croydon Housing Aid Soc., 2003–. *Publications:* (with Stephen Knafler) Repairs: Tenant's Rights, 3rd edn 1999; Housing and the Human Rights Act, 2000; (jtly) Defending Possession Proceedings, 6th edn 2006; (with Liz Davies): The Homelessness Act 2002, 2002, 2nd edn 2003; Housing Allocation and Homelessness, 2006. *Recreations:* spending time with my family, walking. *Address:* Garden Court Chambers, 57–60 Lincoln's Inn Fields, WC2A 3LS.

LUBBERS, Rudolphus Frans Marie, (Ruud); UN High Commissioner for Refugees, 2001–05; *b* Rotterdam, 7 May 1939; *s* of Paulus J. Lubbers and Wilhelmine K. Van Laack; *m* 1962, Maria E. J. Hoogeweegan; two *s* one *d*. *Educ:* Erasmus Univ., Rotterdam. Sec. to Mgt Bd, 1963–65, Co-Dir, 1965–74, Lubbers Hollandia Engrg Works; Minister of Econ. Affairs, Netherlands, 1973–77; Mem., Second Chamber of States-Gen., 1977–82; Sen. Dep. Leader, then Leader, Christian Democratic Alliance, 1977–82; Prime Minister of the Netherlands, 1982–94; Prof. on Globalisation, Faculty of Econs and Business Admin, Tilburg Univ., 1995–2000. Vis. Prof., John F. Kennedy Sch. of Govt, Harvard Univ. Internat. Pres., WWF, 1999–2000. Kt, Order of the Lion (Netherlands), 1994.

LUBBOCK, family name of **Baron Avebury**.

LUBBOCK, John David Peter, FRAM; Founder and Musical Director, Orchestra of St John's, since 1967; *b* 18 March 1945; *s* of Michael Lubbock and Diana (*née* Crawley); *m* 1st, 1977, Eleanor Sloan (marr. diss.); two *s*; 2nd, 1991, Christine Cairns; two *s*. *Educ:* St George's Choir Sch., Windsor Castle (Chorister); Radley Coll.; Royal Acad. of Music (FRAM 1999). Mem., Swingle Singers, 1971–74. Guest conductor, USA, Canada, Europe. *Recreation:* tennis. *Address:* 7 Warborough Road, Shillingford, Oxon OX10 7SA. *T:* (01865) 858210.

LUCAN, 7th Earl of, *cr* 1795 (Ire.); **Richard John Bingham;** Bt 1632; Baron Lucan, 1776; Baron Bingham (UK), 1934; *b* 18 Dec. 1934; *e s* of 6th Earl of Lucan, MC; *S* father, 1964; *m* 1963, Veronica, *d* of late Major C. M. Duncan, MC, and of Mrs J. D. Margrie; one *s* two *d*. *Educ:* Eton. Lieut (Res. of Officers) Coldstream Guards. *Heir: s* Lord Bingham, *qv*.

[The Earl has been missing since Nov. 1974 and was 'presumed deceased' in Chambers on 11 Dec. 1992. In 1999 the Lord Chancellor ruled against the application by Lord Bingham for a writ of summons to Parliament in the UK Barony of Bingham.]

LUCAS, family name of **Baron Lucas of Chilworth**.

LUCAS OF CHILWORTH, 3rd Baron *cr* 1946, of Chilworth; **Simon William Lucas;** *b* 6 Feb. 1957; *er s* of 2nd Baron Lucas of Chilworth and Ann-Marie (*née* Buck); *S* father, 2001; *m* 1993, Fiona, *yr d* of Thomas Mackintosh, Vancouver; two *s*. *Educ:* Leicester Univ. (BSc). *Heir: s* Hon. John Ronald Muir Lucas, *b* 21 May 1995.

LUCAS OF CRUDWELL, 11th Baron *cr* 1663, **AND DINGWALL,** 14th Lord *cr* 1609; **Ralph Matthew Palmer;** *b* 7 June 1951; *s* of 10th Baroness Lucas of Crudwell and 13th Lady Dingwall and of Maj. the Hon. Robert Jocelyn Palmer, MC, 3rd *s* of 3rd Earl of Selborne, PC, CH; *S* mother, 1991; *m* 1st, 1978, Clarissa Marie (marr. diss. 1995), *d* of George Vivian Lockett, TD and Alice Jeannine Lockett; one *s* one *d*; 2nd, 1995, Amanda Atha (*d* 2000); 3rd, 2001, Antonia Vera Kennedy, *d* of late Anthony Benno John Stanley Rubinstein and Anne Langford Dent; one *d*. *Educ:* Eton; Balliol Coll., Oxford (BA (Hons) Physics). BDO Binder Hamlyn, 1972–76; S. G. Warburg & Co. Ltd, 1976–88. A Lord in Waiting (Govt Whip), 1994–97; Govt spokesman on educn, 1994–95, social security and Wales, 1994–97, agric. and envmt, 1995–97; Opposition spokesman on internat. devel t, 1997–98; elected Mem., H of L, 1999. *Heir: s* Hon. Lewis Edward Palmer, *b* 7 Dec. 1987. *Address:* House of Lords, SW1A 0PW. *T:* (020) 7219 4177; *e-mail:* lucasr@parliament.uk.

LUCAS, Adrian Paul, FRCO(CHM); Organist and Master of the Choristers, Worcester Cathedral, since 1996; *b* 14 March 1962; *s* of Kenneth David Lucas and Kathleen Lucas (*née* Mash); *m* 1986, Joanna Louise Harrison; one *s* one *d*. *Educ:* St John's Coll., Cambridge (Organ Schol.; MA). FRCO(CHM) 1990. Actg Asst Organist, Salisbury Cathedral, 1980; Asst Organist, Norwich Cathedral, 1983–90; Tutor, UEA, 1985–90; Organist, Portsmouth Cathedral, 1990–96. Musical Director: Worcester Fest. Choral Soc., 1997–; Worcs SO, 2000–02; City of Birmingham Choir, 2002–. Pres., Cathedral Organists' Assoc., 2003–05. Guest Conductor, Philharmonia Orch., 2000–. Examr, Associated Bd, RSM, 1989–. Freelance recitalist, broadcaster and conductor, incl. Three Choirs Fest. Recordings incl. 4 solo organ discs and choral works with Portsmouth and Worcester Cathedral Choirs, and Choirs of Three Choirs Fest. *Publications:* various musical compositions, incl. Noël for boys' voices, harp and organ, 1998 (also recorded), Creation Canticles, 2004; contrib. to musical training books. *Recreations:* bread making, wine, gardening. *Address:* 2 Field Terrace, Worcester WR5 3BN. *T:* (01905) 352136.

LUCAS, Prof. Alan, MD; FRCP, FRCPCH, FMedSci; MRC Clinical Research Professor, and Director, MRC Childhood Nutrition Research Centre, since 1996, and concurrently Professor of Paediatric Nutrition, since 2001, Institute of Child Health, University College London; Fellow, Clare College, Cambridge, since 1982; *b* 30 June 1946; *s* of late Dr Saul H. Lucas, Maj., RAMC, and Dr Sophia Lucas; *m* 1st, 1967, Sally Wedeles (marr. diss.); 2nd, 1978, Penny Hodgson; one *s* two *d*. *Educ:* Bedales Sch., Hants; Clare Coll., Cambridge (Foundn Schol.; BA Med. & Natural Sci. Tripos 1st Cl. Hons 1968; BChir 1971, MB 1972; MA 1985); MD Cantab 1991; Oxford Univ. Med. Sch. FRCP 1991; FRCPCH 1997. Jun. posts, Radcliffe Infirmary, Oxford and Addenbrooke's Hosp., Cambridge, 1971–77; Lectr, Trinity Coll., Cambridge, 1972–76; University of Oxford: Wellcome Res. Fellow, Dept of Paediatrics, 1977–79; Lectr, St Edmund Hall, 1977–80; University of Cambridge: Clinical Lectr, 1980–82, Hon. Consultant, 1982–96, Dept of Paediatrics; Dir, Med. Studies, Peterhouse, 1980–86; Dir, Studies in Medicine and in Anatomy, Clare Coll., 1982–97; Hd, Infant and Child Nutrition, MRC Dunn Nutrition Unit, Cambridge, 1982–96; Hon. Consultant, Gt Ormond St Hosp. for Children, 1996–. Member: Panel on Child Nutrition, DHSS, 1988–96; Wkg Gp on Infant Formula, EEC, 1988; Standing Cttee on Nutrition, BPA, subseq. RCPCH, 1988–2000 (Mem., Acad. Bd, 1989–94); Physiol Medicine and Infections Bd, 1992–96, Wkg Gp on Fluoride and Osteoporosis, 1994 (Chm.) and Health Services Res. Bd, 1995–96, MRC. FMedSci 2000. Hon. Citizen, Georgia, USA (for educnl services), 1994. Guthrie Medal, RCPCH, 1982. *Publications:* over 300 scientific papers and articles, and contrib. to books, on child health, nutrition and metabolism, notably long term health effects of early nutrition. *Recreations:* art, art history, music, sports. *Address:* Institute of Child Health, 30 Guilford Street, WC1N 1EH. *T:* (020) 7905 2389.

LUCAS, Andrew, FRCO; Master of the Music, Cathedral and Abbey Church of St Alban, since 1998; *b* 19 Aug. 1958; *s* of Richard John Lucas and Vera Mary Lucas (*née* Lawrence). *Educ:* Wakeman Sch., Shrewsbury; Royal Coll. of Music (GRSM 1979; BMus (London) 1981); Sweelinck Conservatoire, Amsterdam. FRCO 1979. Dir of Music, St James', Sussex Gardens, London, 1981–85; St Paul's Cathedral: organ student, 1980–84; Asst Sub-Organist, 1985–89; Sub-Organist and Asst Dir of Music, 1990–98; Acting Organist and Master of Choristers, St Andrew's Cathedral, Sydney, Aust., 1997. Conductor, St Albans Bach Choir, 1998–; Artistic Dir, St Albans Internat. Organ Fest., 1999–2007. Pres., Asst Cathedral Organists' Assoc., 2002– (Chm., 1993–98); Mem. Council, RCO, 1997–2006. Liveryman, Co. of Musicians, 1998–. Hon. FGCM 2006. *Recreations:* theatre, travel, architecture, gardens, good food and coffee. *Address:* Cathedral and Abbey Church of St Alban, St Albans, Herts AL1 1BY. *T:* (01727) 851810; *e-mail:* andrewl01@aol.com; 31 Abbey Mill Lane, St Albans, Herts AL3 4HA.

LUCAS, Anne Katharine; *see* Stevenson, A. K.

LUCAS, Prof. Arthur Maurice, AO 2005; CBE 2002; PhD; Professor of Science Curriculum Studies, 1980–2003, and Principal, 1993–2003, King's College, London; *b* 26 Oct. 1941; *s* of Joseph Alfred Percival Lucas and May Queen Lucas (*née* Griffin); *m* 1970, Paula Jean Williams; one *s* one *d*. *Educ:* Univ. of Melbourne (BSc 1963; BEd 1968); Ohio State Univ. (PhD 1972; Fulbright Award). FIBiol 1981; FACE 1995. Appts at Yallourn and Newborough High Schs, 1964–66; Flinders Univ. of SA, 1967–70; Ohio State Univ., 1970–72; Warrnambool Inst. of Advanced Educn, 1973; Flinders University: Lectr in Sci. Educn, 1974–80; Sen. Lectr, 1976; Vice-Chm., 1976, Chm., 1977–79, Sch. of Educn; King's College, London: Asst Principal, 1987–89; Vice-Principal, 1991–93; Actg Principal, 1992; London University: Chm., Bd of Educnl Studies, 1986–88; Mem. Council, 1995–2003; Chm., Mgt Bd, Marine Biol. Stn, Millport, 1995–2002; Dep. Vice Chancellor, 1997–2002. Hon. Vis. Prof., Sch. of Educn, UEA, 2005–. Mem., Lord Chancellor's Adv. Council on Nat. Records and Archives, 2006–. Member, Council: Commonwealth Assoc. for Sci., Maths and Technol. Educn, 1981–89; Zoological Soc. of London, 1992–93 (Vice Pres., 1993); Royal Instn, 1998–2004; British Soc. for History of Sci., 1999–2002; Member: Exec. Cttee, Field Studies Council, 1986–92, 1994–2000, 2002–07; COPUS, 1993–95; Bd, Univs and Colls Employers Assoc., 1996–2003; Bd, QAA, 2002–; Parly and Scientific Cttee, 2002–03. Chm., Medicine and Soc. Panel, Wellcome Trust, 1998–2002. Mem., SE Thames RHA, 1993–94. Pres., Soc. for Hist. of Natural Hist., 2006–. *Publications:* Review of British Science Curriculum Projects (with D. G. Chisman), 1973; Environment and Environmental Education, 1979; (ed jtly) New Trends in Biology Education, 1987; (ed with P. J. Black) Children's Informal Ideas in Science, 1993; (ed jtly) Regardfully Yours: selected correspondence of Ferdinand von Mueller, vol. 1 1840–1859, 1998, vol. 2 1860–1875, 2002, vol. 3 1876–1896, 2006; numerous articles in learned jls. *Recreations:* reading, getting to know Norfolk. *Club:* Athenæum.

LUCAS, Ven. Brian Humphrey, CB 1993; Rector of Caythorpe, Fulbeck, and Carlton Scroop with Normanton, Diocese of Lincoln, 2000–03 (Priest-in-charge, 1996–2000); *b* 20 Jan. 1940; *s* of Frederick George Humphrey Lucas and Edith Mary Lucas; *m* 1966, Joy Penn; two *s* one *d*. *Educ:* St David's Coll., Lampeter (BA); St Stephen's House, Oxford. Ordained deacon 1964, priest 1965; Curate: Llandaff Cathedral, 1964–67; Parish of Neath, 1967–70; Royal Air Force: Chaplain, 1970–87; Asst Chaplain-in-Chief, 1987–91; Chaplain-in-Chief, and Archdeacon of the RAF, 1991–95, Archdeacon Emeritus, 1996; Canon and Prebendary of Lincoln Cathedral, 1991–95, now Emeritus; Priest-in-charge, St Clement Danes, 1991–95. QHC, 1989–95. Mem., Gen. Synod of C of E, 1991–95. Hon. Chaplain: Assoc. of London Clubs, 2004–; Bomber Command Assoc., 2004–; Coastal Command Assoc., 2005–; Hon. Pres., No. 3 Welsh Wing, ATC, 2007–; Chaplain to High Sheriff of Lincs, 2005–06. Vice-Pres., Clergy Orphan Corp., 1991–95; Visitor, Soldiers' and Airmen's Scripture Readers Assoc., 1991–95; Mem. Council, Bible Reading Fellowship, 1992–95. Mem. Council, RAF Benevolent Fund, 1991–95. FRSA 1993. *Recreations:* archaeology of the Near East, travel (excluding tourist areas), watching Welsh Rugby football. *Address:* Pen-y-coed, 6 Arnhem Drive, Caythorpe, Lincs NG32 3DQ. *Clubs:* Savage (Hon. Sec., 1998–2008), Royal Air Force, Civil Service.

LUCAS, Dr Caroline; Member (Green) South East Region, England, European Parliament, since 1999; *b* 9 Dec. 1960; *d* of Peter and Valerie Lucas; *m* 1991, Richard Le Quesne Savage; two *s*. Oxfam: Press Officer, 1989–91; Communications Officer for Asia, 1991–93; Policy Adviser on trade and envmt, 1993–97; on secondment to Trade Team, DFID, 1997–98; Team Leader, Trade and Investment Policy Team, 1998–99. Mem., Oxford CC, 1993–97. European Parliament: Mem., Cttee on Internat. Trade, 1999–, on Envmt, Public Health and Food Safety, 1999–; Mem., Palestine Delegn, 1999–. Green Party: Mem., 1986–; Nat. Press Officer, 1987–89; Co-Chair, 1989–90. *Publications:* (as Caroline Le Quesne): Writing for Women, 1989; Reforming World Trade: the social and environmental priorities, 1996; (as Caroline Lucas): (with Mike Wordin) Green Alternatives to Globalisation, 2004. *Recreations:* gardening, walking, piano playing. *Address:* 58 The Hop Exchange, 24 Southwark Street, SE1 1TY. *T:* (020) 7407 6281.

LUCAS, (Charles) Vivian; Chief Executive, Devon County Council, 1974–79; solicitor; *b* 31 May 1914; *s* of Frank and Mary Renshaw Lucas, Malvern, Worcs; *m* 1941, Oonah Holderness; two *s* two *d*. *Educ:* Malvern Coll.; abroad; London Univ. (LLB). Clerk, Devon County Council, 1972–74; Clerk to the Lieutenancy of Devon, 1972–79. *Recreations:* sport, bridge. *Address:* Flat 25, Hamilton Court, Salterton Road, Exmouth EX8 2BR.

LUCAS, Christopher Charles; Under Secretary, Community and International Policy Division, Department of Energy, 1977–80, retired; *b* 5 June 1920; *s* of Charles Edwin Lucas and Mabel Beatrice Read; *m* 1945, Beryl June Vincent; two *d*. *Educ:* Devonport

High Sch.; Balliol Coll., Oxford (Newman Exhibnr). Min. of Fuel, 1946; Central Econ. Planning Staff, 1948; HM Treasury, 1950–70; Cabinet Office, 1970–72; Sec., NEDC, 1973–76; Under-Sec., Dept of Energy, 1976–80. *Recreation*: riding. *Address*: Orchard Croft, Withycombe, near Minehead, Somerset TA24 6PT. *T*: (01643) 821551.

LUCAS, Christopher Tullis, CBE 1994; Development Adviser, Eastfeast; Director, Animarts; *b* 20 Dec. 1937; *s* of late Philip Gaddesden Lucas, GM and Maise Lucas; *m* 1962, Tina Colville; two *d*. *Educ*: Winchester Coll. Apprenticeship with Thomson McLintock & Co.; CA 1965; Chief Exec., ICEM Ltd, 1966–72; Sen. Radio Officer, IBA, 1972–74; first Man. Dir, Radio Forth, Edinburgh, 1974–77; Dir and Sec., RSA, and Sec., Faculty of Royal Designers for Industry, 1977–94. Mem., Aldeburgh Allotment and Garden Assoc. *Recreations*: Suffolk, creating a mini-nature reserve, theatre, carpenter, ski-ing, golf. *Address*: 60 Lebanon Park, Twickenham TW1 3DQ. *T*: (020) 8892 6584.

LUCAS, Sir Colin (Renshaw), Kt 2002; DPhil; FRHistS; Chief Executive, Rhodes Trust and Warden of Rhodes House, since 2004 (Trustee, Rhodes Trust, 1995–2004); Fellow, All Souls College, Oxford, since 2001; Vice-Chancellor, University of Oxford, 1997–2004; *b* 25 Aug. 1940; *s* of Frank Renshaw Lucas and Janine (*née* Charpentier); *m* 1st, 1964, Christiane Berchon de Fontaine Goubert (marr. diss. 1975); one *s*; 2nd, 1990, Mary Louise Hume. *Educ*: Sherborne Sch.; Lincoln Coll., Oxford (MA, DPhil; Hon. Fellow 1995). FRHistS 1974. Asst Lectr, then Lectr, Sheffield Univ., 1965–69; Vis. Asst Prof., Indiana Univ., 1969–70; Lectr, Manchester Univ., 1970–73; Fellow, Balliol Coll., Oxford, and Lectr in Modern History, Oxford University, 1973–90; Prof., 1990–94, and Dean, Div. of Social Scis, 1993–94, Chicago Univ.; Master of Balliol Coll., Oxford, 1994–2001 (Hon. Fellow, 2001). Chm. Bd, BL, 2006– (Mem., 2004–). Trustee, Andrew W. Mellon Foundn, 2001–. Mem., Hong Kong UGC, 2003–. Hon. Dr of University: Lyon, 1989; Princeton, 2002; Peking, 2002; Hon. DLitt: Sheffield, 2000; Western Australia, 2000; St Francis Xavier, 2003; Oxford Brookes, 2004; Hon. LLD: Glasgow, 2001; Warwick, 2006; Hon. DCL Oxford, 2003. Officier: Ordre des Arts et des Lettres (France), 1989; Légion d'Honneur (France), 2005 (Chevalier, 1998); Chevalier, Ordre du Mérite (France), 1994. *Publications*: The Structure of the Terror, 1973; (with G. Lewis) Beyond the Terror, 1983; (ed) The Political Culture of the French Revolution, 1988; numerous articles. *Address*: Rhodes House, South Parks Road, Oxford OX1 3RG. *T*: (01865) 270902.

LUCAS, Cristina; see Odone, C.

LUCAS, Geoffrey Haden; Secretary, Headmasters' and Headmistresses' Conference, since 2000; *b* 1 Sept. 1951; *s* of Alfred Philip Lucas and Joyce Lucas; *m* 1974, Elaine Jean Helsby; two *s* one *d*. *Educ*: Northgate Grammar Sch. for Boys, Ipswich; Univ. of Birmingham (BA Hons); Univ. of Leeds (MEd Dist.); Trinity and All Souls Coll., Leeds (PGCE). Asst teacher, then Hd of Dept, George Dixon Sch., Birmingham, 1974–80; Sen. Lectr, then Principal Lectr and Dir, PGCE Secondary Course, Trinity and All Souls Coll., Leeds, 1980–89; Professional Officer, Modern Langs/Teacher Educn, Nat. Curriculum Council, York, 1989–93; Asst Chief Exec., SCAA, 1993–97; Hd, Corporate Policy and Dir, Special Projects, QCA, 1997–2000. *Recreations*: golf, gardening, cooking, family holidays. *Club*: East India.

LUCAS, George; film director, producer and screenwriter; Chairman, Lucasfilm, since 1974; *b* 14 May 1944; *s* of George and Dorothy Lucas. *Educ*: Univ. of Southern California (Bachelor of Fine Arts, 1966). Asst to Francis Ford Coppola on The Rain People, 1967 (winner, Grand Prize, Nat. Student Film Festival for short film, THX-1138, 1967); director, co-author of screenplays: THX-1138, 1970; American Graffiti, 1973; director, author: Star Wars, 1977; director, author, executive producer: Star Wars, Episode I: the Phantom Menace, 1999; Star Wars, Episode II: Attack of the Clones, 2002; Star Wars, Episode III: The Revenge of the Sith, 2005; executive producer, author: More American Graffiti, 1979; The Empire Strikes Back, 1980; Return of the Jedi, 1983; Indiana Jones and the Temple of Doom, 1984; Willow, 1988; The Young Indiana Jones Chronicles (TV series), 1992–93; Indiana Jones and the Kingdom of the Crystal Skull, 2008; Star Wars: The Clone Wars, 2008; co-executive producer: Raiders of the Lost Ark (and co-author), 1981; Land Before Time, 1988; Indiana Jones and the Last Crusade, 1989; executive producer: Mishima, 1985; Howard the Duck, 1986; Labyrinth, 1986; Tucker, the Man and his Dream, 1988; Radioland Murders, 1994. *Publication*: Star Wars, 1976. *Address*: Lucasfilm Ltd, PO Box 2009, San Rafael, CA 94912, USA. *T*: (415) 6621800.

LUCAS, Prof. Ian Albert McKenzie, CBE 1977; Principal, 1977–88, Fellow, since 1992, Wye College, Professor, 1988, University of London, now Professor Emeritus; *b* 10 July 1926; *s* of Percy John Lucas and Janie Inglis (*née* Hamilton); *m* 1950, Helen Louise Langerman; one *s* two *d*. *Educ*: Clayesmore Sch.; Reading Univ.; McGill Univ. BSc, MSc; CBiol, FIBiol; FRAgS. Lectr, Harper Adams Agricl Coll., 1949–50; pig nutrition res., Rowett Res. Inst., Aberdeen, 1950–57 and 1958–61; Res. Fellow, Ruakura Res. Station, New Zealand, 1957–58; Prof. of Agriculture, UCNW, Bangor, 1961–77. Chm., Agricl and Vet. Cttee, British Council, 1978–87. Member: Jt Cttee on use of antibiotics in animal husbandry and vet. medicine, 1967–69; MAFF Adv. Council for Agric. and Hortic., 1969–79; Agric. and Vet. Sub-Cttee, UGC, 1972–77; CVCP, 1985–88; Cttee, Internat. Co-operation in Higher Educn, British Council, 1986–90. President: Sect. M, BAAS, 1983; Agricl Educn Assoc., 1987; Rural Educn and Develt Assoc., 1994. Member Governing Body: Grassland Res. Inst., 1970–79; Rydal Sch., 1975–77; RVC, 1978–88; E Malling Res. Station, 1978–87; Hadlow Agric. Coll., 1978–88; Inst. for Grassland and Animal Production Research, 1987–89. Hon. Life Mem., British Council, 1987. Hon. DSc McGill, 1996. *Publications*: scientific papers in Jl Agricl Science, Animal Production, Brit. Jl Nutrition and others. *Recreations*: sailing. *Address*: Valley Downs, Brady Road, Lyminge, Folkestone, Kent CT18 8DU. *T*: (01303) 863053. *Club*: Hollowshore Cruising (Oare, Kent).

LUCAS, Ian Colin; MP (Lab) Wrexham, since 2001; an Assistant Government Whip, since 2008; *b* 18 Sept. 1960; *s* of Colin and Alice Lucas; *m* 1986, Norah Anne (*née* Sudd); one *s* one *d*. *Educ*: New Coll., Oxford (BA Jurisprudence). Articled Clerk, then Solicitor, Russell-Cooke, Potter and Chapman Solicitors, Putney and Kingston, 1983–85; Solicitor: Percy, Hughes and Roberts, Chester, 1985–86; Lees, Moore and Price, Birkenhead, 1986–87; Kirwan Nicholas Jones, then Roberts Moore Nicholas Jones, Birkenhead and Wrexham, 1987–92; D. R. Crawford, Oswestry, 1992–97; Sole Principal, Crawford Lucas, Oswestry, 1997–2000; Partner, Stevens Lucas, Oswestry and Chirk, 2001. Contested (Lab) N Shropshire, 1997. Non-exec. Dir, Robert Jones and Agnes Hunt Hosp., Gobowen, Shropshire, 1997–2001. *Recreations*: history, sport, art. *Address*: (office) 41 Rhosddu Road, Wrexham LL11 2NS. *T*: (01978) 355743.

LUCAS, Irene, (Mrs John Hays), CBE 2008; Chief Executive, South Tyneside Metropolitan Borough Council, since 2002; *b* Newcastle upon Tyne, 4 Feb. 1954; *d* of Vincent and Isabelle Lucas; *m* 1997, John Hays; one *s* one *d*. *Educ*: Univ. of Sunderland (MBA). Sunderland City Council, 1977–2002: various posts incl. Asst Dir, and Dir, Community and Cultural Services; Asst Chief Exec., 1999–2002. *Recreations*: family,

football, travel. *Address*: Whitburn House, 47 Front Street, Whitburn, Sunderland SR6 7JG. *T*: (0191) 424 7010; *e-mail*: irene.lucas@southtyneside.gov.uk.

LUCAS, Hon. Ivor Thomas Mark, CMG 1980; HM Diplomatic Service, retired; Assistant Secretary-General, Arab-British Chamber of Commerce, 1985–87; *b* 25 July 1927; 2nd *s* of George William Lucas, 1st Baron Lucas of Chilworth, and Sonia Lucas; *m* 1954, Christine Mallorie Coleman; three *s*. *Educ*: St Edward's Sch., Oxford; Trinity Coll., Oxford (MA). Served in Royal Artillery, 1945–48 (Captain). BA Oxon 1951. Entered Diplomatic Service, 1951; Middle East Centre for Arab Studies, Lebanon, 1952; 3rd, later 2nd Sec., Bahrain, Sharjah and Dubai, 1952–56; FO, 1956–59; 1st Sec., Karachi, 1959–62; 1st Sec. and Head of Chancery, Tripoli, 1962–66; FO, 1966–68; Counsellor, Aden, 1968–69 (Chargé d'Affaires, Aug. 1968–Feb. 1969); Dep. High Comr, Kaduna, Nigeria, 1969–71; Counsellor, Copenhagen, 1972–75; Head of Middle East Dept, FCO, 1975–79; Ambassador to Oman, 1979–81, to Syria, 1982–84. Fellow in Internat. Politics of ME, Centre of Internat. Studies, Cambridge, 1991–94. Mem., Central Council, Royal Over-Seas League, 1988–94, 1996–2003; Chm., Anglo-Omani Soc., 1990–95 (Vice Pres., 1996–); Mem. Council, RSAA, 1988–94; Chm. Editl Bd, Asian Affairs, 1995–2002. Chm. Adv. Bd, Centre of Near and Middle Eastern Studies, SOAS, 1987–90. Trustee, Commonwealth Linking Trust, 1996–2003. *Publications*: A Road to Damascus: mainly diplomatic memoirs from the Middle East, 1997; 80 @ 80: reviews in Asian affairs 1989–2007, 2008; chapters in: Politics and the Economy in Syria, 1987; The Middle East: a handbook, 1988; various articles and reviews. *Recreations*: music, crosswords, scrabble. *Clubs*: Royal Over-Seas League, Royal Commonwealth Society.

LUCAS, John Randolph, FBA 1988; Fellow and Tutor of Merton College, Oxford, 1960–96; *b* 18 June 1929; *s* of late Rev. E. de G. Lucas, sometime Archdeacon of Durham, and Joan Mary Lucas; *m* 1961, Morar Portal, *er d* of Sir Reginald Portal, KCB, DSC; two *s* two *d*. *Educ*: St Mary's Coll., Winchester; Balliol Coll., Oxford (John Locke Schol., 1952; MA). Jun. Res. Fellow, Merton Coll., Oxford, 1953–56; Fellow and Asst Tutor, Corpus Christi Coll., Cambridge, 1956–59; Reader in Philosophy, Oxford Univ., 1990–96. Jane Eliza Procter Vis. Fellow, Princeton Univ., 1957–58; Leverhulme Res. Fellow, Leeds Univ., 1959–60. Chm., Oxford Consumers' Gp, 1961–63, 1965. Member: Archbishops' Commn on Christian Doctrine, 1967–76; Lichfield Commn on Divorce and Remarriage, 1975–78. Pres., British Soc. for the Philosophy of Sci., 1991–93. Lectures: (jtly) Gifford, Univ. of Edinburgh, 1971–73; Margaret Harris, Univ. of Dundee, 1981; Harry Jelema, Calvin Coll., Grand Rapids, 1987; Darwin, Cambridge Univ., 2000. *Publications*: Principles of Politics, 1966, 2nd edn 1985; The Concept of Probability, 1970; The Freedom of the Will, 1970; (jtly) The Nature of Mind, 1972; (jtly) The Development of Mind, 1973; A Treatise on Time and Space, 1973; Essays on Freedom and Grace, 1976; Democracy and Participation, 1976 (trans. Portuguese, 1985); On Justice, 1980; Space, Time and Causality, 1985; The Future, 1989; (jtly) Spacetime and Electromagnetism, 1990; Responsibility, 1993; (jtly) Ethical Economics, 1997; The Conceptual Roots of Mathematics, 1999; (jtly) An Engagement with Plato's Republic, 2003; Reason and Reality, 2006; various articles in learned jls. *Recreation*: walking and talking. *Address*: Lambrook House, East Lambrook, South Petherton, Som TA13 5HW. *T*: (01460) 240413; *e-mail*: john.lucas@merton.ox.ac.uk; *web*: http://users.ox.ac.uk/~jrlucas.

LUCAS, Keith Stephen; artist; *b* 28 Aug. 1924; *m* 1969, Rona Stephanie Lucas (*née* Levy); two *s* one *d* (and two step *s*). *Educ*: Royal Coll. of Art (ARCA). London Press Exchange, 1956–64; Prof. of Film and Television, Royal Coll. of Art, 1964–72 (first holder of Chair); Dir, British Film Institute, 1972–78; Television Consultant, BFI, 1979–84; Hd of Radio, Film and Television Studies, Christ Church Coll., Canterbury, 1984–89. Artistic Dir, Commonwealth Film and TV Fest. and supporting arts prog., Cyprus, 1980. Exhibitions: retrospective 1956–86, Poor Priests Hosp., Canterbury, 1986; John Nevill Gall., Canterbury, 1988; Royal Mus., Canterbury, 1990; Anna Mei Chadwick Gall., 1993, 1995; Cleary Gall., Canterbury, 1993. Chairman: Canterbury New Theatre Ltd, 1979–83; Canterbury Theatre and Festival Trust, 1983–86 (Pres., 1986); Vice-Pres., Centre Internat. de Liaison des Ecoles de Cinéma et de Télévision, 1970–72. Governor: North East London Poly., 1971–72; Canterbury Coll. of Art (formerly Canterbury Sch. of Art), 1971–74, 1981–87; Maidstone Coll. of Art, 1982–87; Kent Inst. of Art and Design, 1987–89. Hon. Fellow, Royal Coll. of Art, 1972. *Recreations*: writing, listening to music. *Address*: The Penthouse, 88 Valiant House, Vicarage Crescent, SW11 3LX. *T*: (020) 7228 5289. *Club*: Chelsea Arts.

LUCAS, Prof. Raleigh Barclay; Professor of Oral Pathology, University of London, 1954–79, now Emeritus; Consultant Pathologist, Royal Dental Hospital of London, 1950–79; *b* 3 June 1914; *s* of H. Lucas; *m* 1942, Violet Sorrell; one *d* (one *s* decd). *Educ*: George Watson's Coll.; Univ. of Edinburgh. MB, ChB (Edinburgh) 1937; DPH 1939; MD 1945; MRCP 1946; FRCPath 1963; FRCP 1974; FDS RCS 1974. Asst Bacteriologist, Edinburgh Royal Infirmary, 1939–40; Pathologist, Stoke Mandeville Hosp. and Royal Buckinghamshire Hospital, 1947–49; Reader in Pathology, University of London, 1950–54; Dean, Sch. of Dental Surgery, Royal Dental Hospital of London, 1958–73. Examiner in Pathology and Bacteriology for dental degrees, Univs of London, Glasgow, Birmingham, Sheffield, Liverpool and Wales. Served War of 1939–45, Major RAMC. FRSocMed; Fellow and Past Pres., Royal Medical Society; Mem. Pathological Soc. of Great Britain and Ireland; Mem. BMA. *Publications*: (jtly) Bacteriology for Students of Dental Surgery, 1954; Pathology of Tumours of the Oral Tissues, 1964; (jtly) Tumors of the Major Salivary Glands, 1974; (jtly) Atlas of Oral Pathology, 1985; various articles in medical and scientific journals.

LUCAS, Prof. Robert Emerson, PhD; John Dewey Distinguished Service Professor of Economics, University of Chicago, since 1980; *b* 15 Sept. 1937; *s* of Robert Emerson Lucas and Jane Templeton Lucas; *m* 1959, Rita Cohen (marr. diss.); two *s*. *Educ*: Roosevelt High Sch., Seattle; Univ. of Chicago (BA 1959; PhD 1964). Lectr, Dept of Econs, Univ. of Chicago, 1962–63; Asst Prof. of Econs, Carnegie Inst. of Technol., 1963–67; Associate Prof., 1967–70; Prof. of Econs, 1970–74, Carnegie-Mellon Univ.; University of Chicago: Ford Foundn Vis. Res. Prof., 1974–75; Prof. of Econs, 1975–80; Vice-Chm., 1975–83, Chm., 1986–88, Dept of Econs. Fellow, Amer. Acad. of Arts and Scis, 1980; Mem., NAS, USA, 1981. Nobel Prize for Economics, 1995. *Publications*: Studies in Business-cycle Theory, 1981; (with T. J. Sargent) Rational Expectations and Econometric Practice, 1981; Models of Business Cycles, 1987; (with N. L. Skokey) Recursive Methods in Economic Dynamics, 1989; Customer Service: skills and concepts for business, 1996; papers on growth theory, public finance and monetary theory. *Address*: Department of Economics, University of Chicago, 1126 East 59th Street, Chicago, IL 60637, USA.

LUCAS, Sir Thomas (Edward), 5th Bt *cr* 1887; MA; engineer, scientist, author, lecturer, complementary health practitioner, business consultant and chairman; *b* 16 Sept. 1930; *s* of late Ralph John Scott Lucas (killed in action, Libya, 1941), and Dorothy (*d* 1985), *d* of late H. T. Timson, Tatchbury Mount, Hants; *S* cousin, 1980; *m* 1st, 1958, Charmian (*d* 1970), *d* of late Col J. S. Powell; one *s*; 2nd, 1980, Ann Graham Moore. *Educ*: Wellington College; Trinity Hall, Cambridge. Consultant to European Commn DG XIII, RTZ plc,

INCRA Inc., The Hale Clinic, and to other orgns; formerly Director: SGF Properties plc; Columbia Industrial Gp; Vacuum Metallizing Processes Inc.; Oldfield Technologies plc; EMDI Ltd; Digital Health Research Ltd, and other cos. Senior Trustee: Inlight Trust; Truemark Trust. Mem., Scientific & Medical Network. *Recreations:* motor sport, art, architecture, complementary and alternative medicine. *Heir: s* Stephen Ralph James Lucas [*b* 11 Dec. 1963; *m* 1993, Charlotte Johnson; one *s* one *d*]. *Address:* c/o Drummonds Bank, 49 Charing Cross, SW1A 2DX.

LUCAS, Vivian; *see* Lucas, C. V.

LUCAS-TOOTH, Sir (Hugh) John, 2nd Bt *cr* 1920, of Bught; *b* 20 Aug. 1932; *s* of Sir Hugh Vere Huntly Duff Munro-Lucas-Tooth of Teananich, 1st Bt and Laetitia Florence, OBE (*d* 1978), *er d* of Sir John Ritchie Findlay, 1st Bt, KBE; *S* father, 1985; *m* 1955, Hon. Caroline, *e d* of 1st Baron Poole, PC, CBE, TD; three *d. Educ:* Eton College; Balliol Coll., Oxford. *Heir: cousin* James Lingen Warrand [*b* 6 Oct. 1936; *m* 1960, Juliet Rose, *yr d* of late T. A. Pearn; two *s* one *d*]. *Address:* Parsonage Farm, East Hagbourne, Didcot, Oxon OX11 9LN; 41 Lancaster Road, W11 1QJ. *Clubs:* Brooks's, Beefsteak.

LUCE, family name of **Baron Luce**.

LUCE, Baron *cr* 2000 (Life Peer), of Adur in the co. of West Sussex; **Richard Napier Luce,** KG 2008; GCVO 2000; Kt 1991; PC 1986; DL; Lord Chamberlain of HM Household, 2000–06; a Permanent Lord in Waiting to the Queen, since 2007; *b* 14 Oct. 1936; *s* of late Sir William Luce, GBE, KCMG, and Margaret, *d* of late Adm. Sir Trevylyan Napier, KCB; *m* 1961, Rose, *d* of Sir Godfrey Nicholson, 1st Bt; two *s. Educ:* Wellington Coll.; Christ's Coll., Cambridge (2nd cl. History; Hon. Fellow). Nat. Service officer, 1955–57, served in Cyprus. Overseas Civil Service, served as District Officer, Kenya, 1960–62; Brand Manager, Gallaher Ltd, 1963–65; Marketing Manager, Spirella Co. of GB; Dir, National Innovations Centre, 1968–71; Mem. European Adv. Bd, Corning Glass International, 1975–79; Director: Booker Tate, 1991–96; Meridian Broadcasting, 1991–96. Vice-Chancellor, Univ. of Buckingham, 1992–96. Contested (C) Hitchin, 1970. MP (C) Arundel and Shoreham, Apr. 1971–74, Shoreham, 1974–92. PPS to Minister for Trade and Consumer Affairs, 1972–74; an Opposition Whip, 1974–75; an Opposition spokesman on foreign and commonwealth affairs, 1977–79; Parly Under Sec. of State, 1979–81, Minister of State, 1981–82 and 1983–85, FCO; Minister of State, Privy Council Office (Minister for the Arts), 1985–90. Governor and C-in-C, Gibraltar, 1997–2000. Chairman: Commonwealth Foundn, 1992–96; Atlantic Council of the UK, 1993–96. Mem., Royal Mint Adv. Cttee, 2000–06. President: Voluntary Art Network, 1993–; Royal Over-Seas League, 2002–; King George V Fund for Actors and Actresses, 2007–. Gov., RSC, 1994–2003. Mem., Bd of Trustees, Royal Collection Trust, 2000–06; Trustee, Geographers' A–Z Map Trust, 1993–; Emeritus Trustee, RA, 2001–. DL W Sussex, 1991. *Recreations:* painting, piano. *Address:* House of Lords, SW1A 0PW. *Club:* Royal Automobile.

LUCE, Thomas Richard Harman, CB 1996; public policy consultant; Member, Regulatory Decisions Committee, Financial Services Authority, since 2001 (a Deputy Chairman, 2004–08); *b* 11 July 1939; *s* of late Air Cdre Charles Luce, DSO, and Joyce Marjorie Elizabeth Luce (*née* Johnson); *m* 1991, Virginia Manson Hunt; two step *s. Educ:* Clifton Coll.; Christ's Coll., Cambridge (BA Hons); Indiana Univ., USA. HM Inspector of Taxes, 1965–67; Asst Principal, Ministries of Aviation and Technology, 1967–69; Principal, CSD, 1969–72; Department of Health and Social Security: Principal, 1972–75; Asst Sec., 1975–84; Under Sec., 1984; seconded to HM Treasury (Head of Management Policy and Running Costs Gp), 1987–90; Dep. Dir, NHS Finance, 1990; Under Sec., Community Services Div., 1990–94, Hd of Social Care Policy, 1995–99, DoH. Chm., Home Office Review of Coroners, 2001–03. Trustee and Council Mem., CSV, 1999–2003; Trustee, Internat. Social Services (UK), 2001–04. Trustee, Hampstead and Highgate Fest., 1997–2001 (Chm. Trustees, 1997–2000). A music critic, Crosscut, Seattle, 2007–. *Publications:* articles on coroner and death certification reform; music criticism. *Recreations:* music, reading, walking, swimming. *Address:* 6 Morpeth Mansions, Morpeth Terrace, SW1P 1ER. *T:* (020) 7834 6835; 1068 East Newton, Seattle, WA 98102, USA. *e-mail:* tom.luce@btinternet.com. *Club:* Athenæum.

LUCIE-SMITH, (John) Edward (McKenzie); poet, art critic and photographer; *b* Kingston, Jamaica, 27 Feb. 1933; *s* of John Dudley Lucie-Smith and Mary (*née* Lushington); unmarried. *Educ:* King's Sch., Canterbury; Merton Coll., Oxford (MA). Settled in England, 1946. Education Officer, RAF, 1954–56; subseq. worked in advertising and as free-lance journalist and broadcaster. Curator of a number of exhibns, UK and USA, 1977–. Mem., Acad. de Poésie Européenne. FRSL. *Publications:* A Tropical Childhood and other poems, 1961 (jt winner, John Llewellyn Rhys Mem. Prize; winner, Arts Coun. Triennial Award); (ed, with Philip Hobsbaum) A Group Anthology, 1963; Confessions and Histories, 1964; (with Jack Clemo, George MacBeth) Penguin Modern Poets 6, 1964; (ed) Penguin Book of Elizabethan Verse, 1965; What is a Painting?, 1966; (ed) The Liverpool Scene, 1967; (ed) A Choice of Browning's Verse, 1967; (ed) Penguin Book of Satirical Verse, 1967; Thinking about Art, 1968; Towards Silence, 1968; Movements in Art since 1945, 1969; (ed) British Poetry Since 1945, 1970; (with Patricia White) Art in Britain 69–70, 1970; (ed) A Primer of Experimental Verse, 1971; (ed with S. W. Taylor) French Poetry: the last fifteen years, 1971; A Concise History of French Painting, 1971; Symbolist Art, 1972; Eroticism in Western Art, 1972; The First London Catalogue, 1974; The Well Wishers, 1974; The Burnt Child (autobiog.), 1975; The Invented Eye (early photography), 1975; World of the Makers, 1975; (with Celestine Dars) How the Rich Lived, 1976; Joan of Arc, 1976; (with Celestine Dars) Work and Struggle, 1977; Fantin-Latour, 1977; The Dark Pageant (novel), 1977; Art Today, 1977, revd edn 1999; A Concise History of Furniture, 1979; Super Realism, 1979; Cultural Calendar of the Twentieth Century, 1979; Art in the Seventies, 1980; The Story of Craft, 1981; The Body, 1981; A History of Industrial Design, 1983; Art Terms: an illustrated dictionary, 1984; Art in the Thirties, 1985; American Art Now, 1985; Lives of the Great Twentieth Century Artists, 1986; Sculpture since 1945, 1987; (ed) The Essential Osbert Lancaster, 1988; (with Carolyn Cohen, Judith Higgins) The New British Painting, 1988; Art in the Eighties, 1990; Art Deco Painting, 1990; Fletcher Benton, 1990; Jean Rustin, 1991; Harry Holland, 1992; Art and Civilisation, 1992; (ed) The Faber Book of Art Anecdotes, 1992; Andres Nagel, 1992; Wendy Taylor, 1992; Alexander, 1992; British Art Now, 1993; Race, Sex and Gender: issues in contemporary art, 1994; (with Elisabeth Frink) Elisabeth Frink: a portrait, 1994; American Realism, 1994; Art Today, 1995; Visual Arts in the Twentieth Century, 1996; Ars Erotica: an arousing history of erotic art, 1997; Adam, 1998; Zoo, 1998; (with Judy Chicago) Women and Art: contested territory, 1999; Judy Chicago: an American vision, 2000; Flesh and Stone (photographs), 2000; Flora, 2001; Art Tomorrow, 2002; Changing Shape (poems), 2002; Roberto Marquez, 2002; Carlo Bertocci, 2002; Stefano di Stasio, 2002; Paola Gandolfi, 2003; Ricardo Curalli, 2004; Philip Pearlstein, 2004; John Kirby, 2004; Elias Rivera, 2006; Harry Holland, 2006; contribs to Times, Sunday Times, Independent, Mail-on-Sunday, Listener, Spectator, New Statesman, Evening Standard, Encounter, London Magazine, Illustrated London News, etc. *Recreation:* the Internet. *Address:* c/o Rogers, Coleridge & White, 20 Powis Mews, W11 1JN.

LUCIER, Pierre; President, University of Quebec, 1996–2003; Fernand-Dumont Professor, Institut National de la Recherche Scientifique, Centre Urbanisation, Culture et Société, Quebec; *b* 15 Oct. 1941. *Educ:* Univ. of Montreal (BA 1963; LRelSc 1970); Jesuit Coll. Maximum (MA Philosophy 1965; MA Theology 1971); Univ. des Sciences Humaines, Strasbourg (Dr d'Etat (Phil.) 1975). Prof., Faculty of Theology, Univ. of Montreal, 1970–75; Sen. Researcher, Center for Res. in Educn, Montreal, 1975–78; Sen. Counselor, Cultural and Scientific Develt Secretariat, Exec. Council, Quebec, 1978–80; Asst Dep. Minister of Educn, Quebec, 1980–84; President: Superior Council for Educn, Quebec, 1984–89; Council of Univs, Quebec, 1989–90; Dep. Minister of Higher Educn and Sci., Quebec, 1990–93; Dep. Minister of Educn, Quebec, 1993–96. Canadian Member: Centre for Educnl Res. and Innovation, OECD, Paris, 1984–86; Cttee of Educn, OECD, Paris, 1996–97; Chm., Council of Canadian Dep. Ministers of Educn, 1993–95; Member: Sci. and Technology Council of Quebec, 1990–96; Standing Adv. Cttee for Univ. Res., Assoc. of Univs and Colls of Canada, 1998–2003; Vice-Pres., Bd of Dirs and Council of Govs, Agence Universitaire de la Francophonie, 1998–2003; Pres., Conf. of Univ. Rectors and Principals of Quebec, 2001–03 (Vice-Pres., 1997–2001). *Publications:* approx. 150 pubns, incl. a treatise on logical empiricism, and papers and articles on culture, epistemology, educn, educnl systems, instnl evaluation and higher learning. *Recreations:* reading, travelling, cinema. *Address:* INRS Urbanisation, Culture et Société, 490 rue de la Couronne, Quebec, QC G1K 9A9, Canada.

LUCK, Keith Frank; Director General, Finance, Foreign and Commonwealth Office, since 2007; *b* 18 July 1960; *s* of Jack Luck and Mauree Luck (*née* Campbell); *m* 1987, Michelle Susan Harris; one *s* one *d. Educ:* Sidney Sussex Coll., Cambridge (BA Hons 1981; MA 1985). ACMA 1986, FCMA 1993; Associate Mem., ACT, 1994. Internal audit, then financial accounting, BT, 1981–85 (CIMA Inst. Prize and Harold Wilmot Prize, 1985); BT Schol., RAPC, Worthy Down, 1983–85; Head of Financial Training, BT Mgt Coll., 1986–87; Consultant, Deloitte, Haskins & Sells, 1987–89; Business Systems Manager, 1989–90, Project Dir, 1990–91, Financial Controller, 1991–93, Midland Bank; Head of Corporate Finance, 1993–94, Asst Dir (Corporate Finance and Property) and Chief Internal Auditor, 1994–97, Tower Hamlets LBC; Dir of Finance and Support Services, Lewisham LBC, 1997–99; Dir, Support Services, Accord plc, 1999–2000; Dir of Resources, Metropolitan Police Service, 2000–06. Member: Strategic Planning Soc., 1996–99; Soc. of London Treasurers, 1997–99; London Financial Adv. Cttee, 1998–99; Steering Gp, Review of Organised Fraud, 1999; Finance and Resources Cttee, 2000–06, Reg. 8, 2000–06, ACPO; Police Allocation Formula Working Gp, 2000–06, Police Efficiency Gp, 2004–06, Home Office; Founder Mem., UK Chapter, Assoc. of Fraud Examrs, 1997–2002; Local Authy Rep., Review of Revenue Grant Distribution (England and Wales), DETR, 1999; Sec., London Team for Action against Fraud, 1998–99. Chartered Institute of Management Accountants: Mem., Adv. Panel, 2005–; Co-opted Mem. Council, 2006–; Mem., Internat. Develt Cttee, 2006–. Member: IFAC; Professional Accountants in Business, 2007–. Pres., Comets (Met. Police Sports and Social Club), 2002–06. Trustee: Civil Staff Welfare Fund, 2001–; London Gdns Scheme, 2005–. FCMI (FIMgt 1987); FRSA 2000; MInstD 2006. Business Leader of Year, CIMA, 2004. *Recreations:* family, motorcycling, motor yachting, local history, historical geography, archaeology, distance running. *Address:* Old Admiralty Buildings, SW1A 2AP; *e-mail:* keith.luck@fco.gov.uk.

LUCKETT, Dr Richard; Fellow, since 1978, and Pepys Librarian, since 1982, Magdalene College, Cambridge; *b* 1 July 1945; *s* of late Rev. Canon Gerald Archer Luckett and of Margaret Mary Luckett (*née* Chittenden). *Educ:* St John's Sch., Leatherhead; St Catharine's Coll., Cambridge (MA, PhD). Lectr, RMA, Sandhurst, 1967–69; Cambridge University: Res. Fellow, 1970–72, Fellow, 1972–78, Dean, 1974–78, St Catharine's Coll.; Univ. Asst Lectr in English, 1973–78; Lectr, 1978–2001; Precentor, Magdalene Coll., 1982–94. FSA. *Publications:* The White Generals, 1971, 2nd edn 1988; The Fabric of Dryden's Verse (Chatterton Lect.), 1981; (ed with C. Hogwood) Music in Eighteenth Century England, 1983; (contrib.) The Pepys Companion, 1983; Handel's Messiah: a celebration, 1992; (ed) The Cryes of London, 1994. *Address:* Magdalene College, Cambridge CB3 0AG. *T:* (01223) 332100. *Club:* Brooks's.

LUCRAFT, Mark; QC 2006; a Recorder, since 2003; *b* 28 Dec. 1961; *s* of Rev. Cyril William Lucraft and Ann Elizabeth Lucraft; *m* 1985, Fiona Carmel Ovington; three *s. Educ:* Wood Green Sch.; Univ. of Kent at Canterbury (BA Hons Law 1983). Called to the Bar, Inner Temple, 1984; in practice as a barrister, 1985–. *Publications:* (contrib.) Archbold: Criminal Pleading, Evidence and Practice, 1996–; (ed jtly) Encyclopedia of Road Traffic Law and Practice, 2002–. *Recreations:* cricket, classical music, gardening, good food and wine. *Address:* 18 Red Lion Court, EC4A 3EB. *T:* (020) 7520 6000, *Fax:* (020) 7520 6248; *e-mail:* mark.lucraft@18rlc.co.uk.

LUCY, Sir Edmund John William Hugh Cameron-Ramsay F.; *see* Fairfax-Lucy.

LUDDINGTON, Sir Donald (Collin Cumyn), KBE 1976; CMG 1973; CVO 1974; retired; *b* 18 Aug. 1920; *s* of late F. Norman John Luddington, Ceylon Civil Service, and late M. Myrtle Amethyst Payne; *m* 1945, Garry Brodie Johnston; one *s* one *d. Educ:* Dover Coll.; St Andrews Univ. (MA). Served War, Army, 1940–46, KOYLI and RAC, Captain. Hong Kong Govt, 1949–73; Sec. for Home Affairs, 1971–73; Governor, Solomon Islands, 1973–76. Chm., Public Services Commn, Hong Kong, 1977–78; Comr, Indep. Commn against Corruption, Hong Kong, 1978–80. *Recreation:* reading. *Clubs:* Royal Commonwealth Society; Hong Kong (Hong Kong).

LUDEMAN, Keith Lawrence; Group Chief Executive, Go-Ahead Group, since 2006; *b* 28 Jan. 1950; *s* of Joseph William Lawrence and Joan Violet Ludeman (*née* Dopson); *m* 1974, Diane June Eatock; two *d. Educ:* Newcastle Univ. (BA Hons Geog. 1971); Salford Univ. (MSc Transport Engrg and Planning 1973). Area Traffic Manager, Gtr Manchester Transport, 1974–82; Sen. Transport Officer, Hong Kong Govt, 1982–85; Sen. Consultant, MVA Consultancy, 1985–86; Managing Director: Burley & Pendle Transport & Viscount Central, 1986–88; London Gen. Transport, 1988–96; London Bus Div., Go-Ahead Gp, 1996–99; Thameslink Rail and Thames Trains, 1999–2000; Chief Exec., Rail, 2000–06, Exec. Dir, 2004–06, Go-Ahead Gp. Mem. Council, Confedn of Passenger Transport, 1997–2000; Mem., British Transport Police Authy, 2003–05. Chm., Assoc. Train Operating Cos, 2003–05. FRSA. *Recreations:* sailing, scuba diving, swimming. *Address:* Go-Ahead Group plc, Go-Ahead House, 26–28 Addiscombe Road, Croydon CR9 5GA. *T:* (020) 8929 8650, *Fax:* (020) 8929 8659; *e-mail:* keith.ludeman@go-ahead.com. *Club:* Royal Automobile.

LUDER, (Harold) Owen, CBE 1986; architect and construction industry consultant; Principal, Owen Luder Consultancy, Communication in Construction, since 1987; President, Royal Institute of British Architects, 1981–83 and 1995–97; *b* London, 7 Aug. 1928; *s* of late Edward Charles and Ellen Clara Luder; *m* 1st, 1951, Rose Dorothy (Doris) Broadstock (marr. diss. 1988); four *d* (one *s* decd); 2nd, 1989, Jacqueline Ollerton (*d* 2008).

Educ: Deptford Park Primary Sch.; Peckham Sch. for Girls; Brixton Sch. of Building; Regent St Polytechnic Sch. of Architecture. ARIBA 1954, FRIBA 1967. Private practice in architecture, 1957–87; Founder and Sen. Partner, Owen Luder Partnership, 1958–78, when it became one of the first architectural partnerships to convert to an unlimited co., Chm. and Man. Dir, 1978–87; on withdrawal from architectural practice, set up Owen Luder Consultancy (specialising in communication in construction), 1987; Director: Communication in Construction Ltd, 1990–2004; Jarvis PLC, 1995–2003. Principal architectural works in commercial and industrial architecture and environmental and urban planning in UK and abroad; consultant: to NCB for Vale of Belvoir coal mining project, 1975–87; to BR for re-use of Engrg Works, Shildon and Swindon, 1985–86; Consultant Architect, RCS, 1974–87; Architect/Planning Consultant, Marine Soc., 1990–99. Royal Institute of British Architects: Mem. Council, 1967–97; Hon. Treasurer, 1975–78; Vice-Pres., Membership Communications, 1989–90; Hon. Sec./Treasurer, Commonwealth Assoc. of Architects, 1985–87; Chm. Organising Cttee, IUA Congress 1987; Vice-Chm., 1997–2002, Chm., 2002–03, Architects Registration Bd. Pres., Norwood Soc., 1981–92. Columnist: Building magazine, 1969–78, 1983–90; Building Design magazine, 1978–81, 1994–95; Editor and Presenter, Architectural Practice Video Magazine, 1987–90; Consultant and Presenter: RIBA Technical Seminar Prog., 1985–93; Building Design Update Seminars, 1994–. Occasional radio and TV broadcaster, UK and USA. British Kart Racer, 1961–63; survivor, Lakonia cruise-liner disaster, 1963. FRSA 1984. Mem., British Acad. of Experts, 1991 (Vice Chm., 1997–99). Trustee, Children Nationwide, 1997–2001. RIBA Architecture Bronze Medal (for Eros House, Catford), 1963; various Civic Trust architectural and housing awards and commendations; Silver Jubilee Medal, for Housing Strategy for the 80s, Town Planning Assoc., 1981; Business Columnist of the Year, Publisher magazine, 1985. Arkansas Traveller, USA, 1971. *Publications:* Sports Stadia after Hillsborough, 1990; Keeping out of Trouble, 1999, 3rd edn 2005; contribs on architectural, planning and building matters to various jls. *Recreations:* writing, swimming, photography, theatre, playing golf badly, supporting Arsenal FC avidly. *Address:* (office) 702 Romney House, 47 Marsham Street, Westminster SW1P 3DS.

LUDER, Ian David; Tax Partner, Grant Thornton UK LLP, since 2002; Lord Mayor of London, 2008–Nov. 2009; *b* London, 13 April 1951; *s* of Mark Luder and Frances Luder (*née* Stillerman); *m* 1999, Lin Jane Surkitt. *Educ:* Haberdashers' Aske's Sch.; University Coll. London (BSc Econ.). FCA 1980; FTII 1983. Tax Partner, Arthur Andersen, 1989–2002. Mem., Bedford BC, 1976–99. Mem. Council, Chartered Inst. of Taxation, 1983–97 (Pres., 1994–95). City of London: Mem., Court, Common Council, 1998–; Chm., Finance Cttee, 2003–06; Alderman, Castle Baynard Ward, 2005–; Sheriff, City of London, 2007–08; Liveryman: Coopers' Co.; Tax Advisers' Co. *Recreations:* cricket, Rugby, gardening. *Clubs:* City Livery, MCC.

LUDFORD, Baroness *cr* 1997 (Life Peer), of Clerkenwell in the London Borough of Islington; **Sarah Ann Ludford;** Member (Lib Dem) London Region, European Parliament, since 1999; *b* 14 March 1951. *Educ:* Portsmouth High Sch.; London Sch. of Economics (BSc Econ; MSc Econ); Inns of Court Sch. of Law. Called to the Bar, Gray's Inn, 1979. With European Commn, 1979–85; European Advr, Lloyd's of London, 1985–87; Vice Pres., Corporate External Affairs, American Express Europe, 1987–90. Mem. (Lib Dem) Islington LBC, 1991–99. Mem., Lib Dem Federal Policy Cttee, 1990– (Vice Chm., 1992–98); Vice Chm., London Lib Dems, 1990–94. Contested: (L) Wight and Hampshire E, 1984, (Lib Dem) London Central, 1989 and 1994, EP elections; (Lib Dem) Islington N, 1992, Islington S and Finsbury, 1997. *Address:* 36b St Peter's Street, N1 8JT. *T:* (020) 7288 2526.

LUDLOW, Bishop Suffragan of, since 2002; **Rt Rev. Michael Wrenford Hooper;** Archdeacon of Ludlow, since 2002; *b* 2 May 1941; *m* 1968, Rosemary Anne Edwards; two *s* two *d*. *Educ:* Crypt Sch., Gloucester; St David's Coll., Lampeter; St Stephen's House, Oxford. Ordained deacon, 1965, priest, 1966; Asst Curate, St Mary Magdalene, Bridgnorth, Shropshire, dio. of Hereford, 1965–70; Vicar of Minsterley and Rector of Habberley, 1970–81; Rural Dean of Pontesbury, 1976–81; Rector and Rural Dean of Leominster, 1981–97; Archdeacon of Hereford, 1997–2002; Prebendary of Hereford Cathedral, 1981–2002. *Recreations:* walking, cycling, dogs, reading, music. *Address:* The Bishop's House, Corvedale Road, Craven Arms, Shropshire SY7 9BT.

LUDLOW, Archdeacon of; *see* Ludlow, Bishop Suffragan of.

LUDLOW, Caroline Mary; Her Honour Judge Ludlow; a Circuit Judge, since 1997; Designated Family Judge, Ipswich, since 2003; *b* 25 Sept. 1947; *d* of William George Hughes Woodward and Mary Josephine Woodward; *m* 1st, 1970, Brian Ludlow (marr. diss. 1976); 2nd, 1987, John Warwick Everitt; one *d*. *Educ:* Hillingdon Court; St Mary's Grammar Sch.; Queen Mary Coll., London Univ. (LLM). Called to the Bar, Inner Temple, 1970; practised on South Eastern Circuit, 1979–97; a Recorder, 1995–97. Designated Family Judge, Chelmsford County Court, 2000–04. Chm., Children's Legal Centre, 2002–. Mem., Law Sch. Adv. Cttee, 1992–, Court, 1999–, Essex Univ. (Bar Co-ordinator, Law in Action course, 1992–97). Trustee: SAFEchild, 2005–; Pact, 2006–. Guardian of the Foyer, Ipswich, 2004–. *Recreations:* reading, gardening. *Address:* East Anglian Chambers, 52 North Hill, Colchester CO1 1PY. *T:* (01206) 572756.

LUDLOW, (Ernest John) Robin, TD 1979; career consultant, since 1996; *b* 2 May 1931; *s* of late Donald Ernest Ludlow, Blandford, Dorset, and Buxted, Sussex; *m* 1st, 1970, Sonia Louise Hatfeild (marr. diss. 1993); one *s* one *d*; 2nd, 1996, Mrs Primrose June King (*née* Palmer). *Educ:* Framlingham Coll., Suffolk. RMA Sandhurst, 1949–52; commissioned RASC, 1952; Staff, RMA Sandhurst, 1954–57; retd 1957. J. Lyons & Co. Ltd, 1957–59; The Economist, 1959–72; Press Sec. to the Queen, 1972–73; Dep. Dir, Aims of Industry, 1973–77; Head of Publicity, Strutt and Parker, 1977; Man. Dir, Kiernan and Co. Ltd (Exec. Search), 1977–79; Partner, Boyden Internat. (Exec. Search), 1979–81; Managing Director: Robin Ludlow & Associates (Exec. Search), 1981–89; Management Search Internat., 1985–89; Managing Consultant, Euro Management Search, 1990–95. Governor: Clergy Orphan Corp. (St Edmund's Sch. Canterbury, St Margaret's Sch. Bushey), 1973–83; Royal Star and Garter Home for Disabled Servicemen, 1987–91; Chairman: The Yeomanry Benevolent Fund, 1981–90 (Mem. Cttee, 1975–2000); Sharpshooters Yeomanry Assoc., 1973–83 (Mem. Cttee, 1972–2000). Kent and Co. of London Yeomanry (Sharpshooters), TA, 1959–69; The Queen's Regt, TA, 1971–78 (Maj.). Vice Chm., SE, TA&VRA, 1988–91 (Mem., F and GP Cttee, 1973–91; Mem., 1973–86, Chm., 1988–91, Kent Cttee). *Recreations:* shooting, gardening, conservation, genealogy. *Address:* 19 North Row, Warminster, Wilts BA12 9AD. *T:* (01985) 217917; *e-mail:* robin.ludlow@btinternet.com.

LUDMAN, Harold, FRCS; Consultant Surgeon in Neuro-otology, National Hospital for Neurology and Neurosurgery, 1967–98; Consultant Surgeon to Ear, Nose and Throat Department, King's College Hospital, 1965–94; *b* 23 Feb. 1933; *s* of Nathan Ludman and Fanny Dinah Jerome; *m* 1957, Lorraine Israel; one *s* one *d*. *Educ:* Bradford Grammar Sch.; Sidney Sussex Coll., Cambridge (BA 1954; MB, BChir 1957; MA 1958). FRCS 1961. House Physician, UCH, 1957; House Surgeon: Royal Ear Hosp., UCH, 1957; Edgware Gen. Hosp., 1958; Royal Marsden Hosp., 1958–59; Registrar and Sen. Registrar, Ear, Nose and Throat Dept, KCH, 1960–65. President: British Assoc. Otolaryngology, 1990–93; Section of Otology, RSocMed, 1985; Chm., Soc. Audiology Technicians, 1967–75. Chm., Specialist Adv. Cttee in Otolaryngology, Jt Cttee Higher Surgical Trng, 1988–91; Mem., Intercollegiate Bd in Otolaryngology, RCS (formerly Mem. Court of Examiners); Chm., working party on deafness, MRC, 1973–77; formerly Mem., Hearing Aid Council. W. J. Harrison Prize, RSocMed, 1987; W. Jobson Horne Prize, BMA, 1990. *Publications:* (jtly) Diseases of the Ear, 1963, 6th edn 1997; (contrib.) Scott-Brown's Diseases of the Ear, Nose and Throat, 4th edn 1979, 5th edn 1987, 6th edn 1996; contribs to books on ear diseases; numerous papers to learned jls on diseases of the ear. *Recreations:* photography, computers, reading, theatre, bird watching.

LUDWIG, Christa; singer; *b* Berlin, 16 March; *d* of Anton Ludwig, singer, stage director and opera general manager and Eugenie (*née* Besalla), singer; *m* 1st, 1957, Walter Berry (marr. diss. 1970), baritone; one *s*; 2nd, 1972, Paul-Emile Deiber, actor and stage-director. *Educ:* Matura. Staedtische Buehnen, Frankfurt; Landestheater Darmstadt; Landestheater, Hannover; Vienna State Opera; guest appearances in New York, Chicago, London, Berlin, Munich, Tokyo, Milan, Rome, Lucerne, Salzburg, Epidauros, Zürich, Holland, Los Angeles, Cleveland, Saratoga, Bayreuth, Copenhagen, Gent, Montreal, Prague, Budapest and others. Kammersängerin, Austria, 1962; Grand Prix du Disque, 1966; Grammy Award, 1967; Mozart Medal, Mozartgemeinde, Vienna, 1969; First Class Art and Science, Austria, 1969; Deutscher Schallplattenpreis, 1970; Orphée d'Or, 1970; Prix des Affaires Culturelles, 1972; Vienna Philharmonic Silver Rose, 1980; Hugo Wolf Medal, 1980; Gustav Mahler Medal, 1980; Ehrenring, Staatsoper Vienna, 1980, Hon. Mem., 1981, Fidelio Medal, 1991; Golden Medal, City of Salzburg, 1988, and Vienna, 1988; Echo Prize, Germany, 1994; Musician of the Year, Musical America, 1994. Grosses Bundesverdienstkreuz (Germany), 2004. Commandeur des Arts et des Lettres (France), 1988; Chevalier, Légion d'Honneur (France), 1989; Grosses Ehrenzeichen (Austria), 1994; Commandeur, Ordre pour le Mérite (France), 1997; Officier, Légion d'Honneur (France), 2005. *Publication:* Und ich wäre so gern Primadonna gewesen (autobiog.), 1994 (French edn 1996, US edn 1999). *Recreations:* listening to music, theatre, concerts, reading. *Address:* c/o Heidrun Artmüller, Goethegasse 1, 1010 Wien, Austria.

LUDWIG, Karen Heather; *see* Vousden, K. H.

LUE, Dr Abraham Sek-Tong, CMG 1998; MBE 1984; *b* 7 Jan. 1939; *s* of Lue Phang and Chin Choy Keow; *m* 1985, Dr Adaline Mang-Yee Ko. *Educ:* King George V Sch., Hong Kong; University Coll. London (BSc); King's Coll. London (PhD 1965; FKC 1993). King's College London: Lectr and Sen. Lectr in Maths, 1962–86; Asst Principal, 1986–92, Asst Principal Emeritus, 2006. Dir, Fleming Chinese Investment Trust PLC, 1993–2004. Dir, Chelsea and Westminster NHS Healthcare Trust, 1994–96. Mem., Home Sec.'s Adv. Cttee on Race Relns, 1979–86; Chm., 1988–92, Hon. Vice Pres., 1992–, Westminster Race Equality Council. Founder and Chm., Chinese Community Centre, London, 1980–96; GB/China Centre: Mem., Exec. Cttee, 1992–2002; Hon. Treas., 1994–95; Vice Chm., 1996–2002. European Rep., K.C. Wong Educn Foundn, Hong Kong, 1987–96; Vice Chm., Lloyd George Asia Foundn, 2007–. Chm., British Liby Internat. Dunhuang Project, 1994–. *Publications:* Basic Pure Mathematics II, 1974; mathematical papers on homological algebra in learned jls. *Recreation:* reading. *Address:* 27 Magazine Gap Road, Hong Kong. *T:* 28492880, *Fax:* 28492881; 18 Randolph Road, W9 1AN. *Clubs:* Athenæum, Hurlingham; Hong Kong Jockey (Hong Kong).

LUESLEY, Prof. David Michael, MD; FRCOG; Lawson-Tait Professor of Gynaecological Oncology, University of Birmingham, since 2003; Director, Pan-Birmingham Gynaecological Cancer Centre, City Hospital, Birmingham, since 2005; *b* 14 Feb. 1952; *s* of Michael James Joseph and Elizabeth Margaret Luesley; *m* 1996, Gabrielle Patricia Downey; two *d*. *Educ:* Queen Elizabeth Grammar Sch., Wakefield; Downing Coll., Cambridge (BA 1972); Birmingham Univ. (MB ChB 1975; MD 1985). FRCOG 1993. University of Birmingham: Sen. Lectr, 1986–93, Reader, 1993–96, in Obstetrics and Gynaecol.; Prof. of Gynaecol Oncology, 1996–2003. Hon. Consultant Gynaecol Oncologist, Birmingham Women's Hosp., 2000–05. *Publications:* Intraepithelial Neoplasia of the Lower Genital Tract, 1995; Handbook of Colposcopy, 1996, 2nd edn 2002; Understanding Gynaecology: a problem solving approach, 1997; Cancer and Pre-Cancer of the Cervix, 1998; Cancer and Pre-Cancer of the Vulva, 1999; Handbook of Gynaecological Oncology, 2000. *Recreations:* food, wine, painting, photography. *Address:* 32 Chantry Road, Moseley, Birmingham B13 8DH. *T:* (0121) 249 2279, *Fax:* (0121) 449 7438; *e-mail:* d.luesley@virgin.net.

LUETCHFORD, Teresa Jane; *see* Kingham, T. J.

LUFF, Rev. Canon Alan Harold Frank; Canon Residentiary of Birmingham Cathedral, 1992–96, Canon Emeritus, 1996; *b* 6 Nov. 1928; *s* of late Frank Luff and Elsie Lilian Luff (*née* Down), Bristol; *m* 1956, Enid Meirion, *d* of late Robert Meirion Roberts and Daisy Harker Roberts; three *s* one *d*. *Educ:* Bristol Grammar School; University Coll., Oxford (BA 1951, Dip. Theol. 1952, MA 1954); Westcott House, Cambridge. ARCM 1977. Deacon, 1956; priest, 1957; Assistant Curate: St Matthew, Stretford, Manchester, 1956–59; St Peter, Swinton, Manchester (with charge of All Saints, Wardley), 1959–61; Precentor of Manchester Cathedral, 1961–68; Vicar of Dwygyfylchi (otherwise Penmaenmawr), Gwynedd, dio. Bangor, 1968–79; Precentor, 1979–92, also Sacrist, 1979–86, Westminster Abbey; licensed to officiate, dio. Llandaff, 1996–. Chm., Hymn Soc. of Great Britain and Ireland, 1987–93 (Hon. Sec., 1973–86); Vice Pres., Internat. Arbeitsgemeinschaft für Hymnologie, 1999–. Chm., Pratt Green Trust, 1988–2006. Hon. FGCM 1993 (Warden, 1984–97; Vice Pres., 1997–); ARSCM 2000. Editor, Hymn Quest, 2000–. *Publications:* Hymns and Psalms (composer and author), 1981; Welsh Hymns and their tunes, 1990; (ed) Story Song, 1993; (ed) Sing His Glory, 1997; (ed and trans.) Ann Griffiths, Hymns and Letters, 1999; (ed) Strengthen for Service: 100 years of the English Hymnal, 2005; contribs to New Christian, Musical Times, Choir and Organ, etc. *Recreations:* singing, conducting, cooking. *Address:* 12 Heol Tyn y Cae, Rhiwbina, Cardiff CF14 6DJ.

LUFF, Geoffrey Shadrack, IPFA; County Treasurer, Nottinghamshire County Council, 1984–91; *b* 12 July 1933; *s* of Shadrack Thomas Luff and Rosie Winifred Luff (*née* Lister); *m* 1st, 1956, Gloria Daphne Taylor (*d* 1992); one *s* one *d*; 2nd, 1997, Brenda Wilson. *Educ:* Mundella Grammar Sch., Nottingham; BA Hons Open, 1998. Various posts in City Treasury, Nottingham CC, 1949–67; Sen. Technical Asst and Asst Bor. Treasurer, Derby CBC, 1967–73; Asst County Treasurer, Derbyshire CC, 1973–78; Dep. County Treasurer, Nottinghamshire CC, 1978–84. *Recreations:* bowls, gardening, birdwatching, photography.

LUFF, Peter James; MP (C) Mid Worcestershire, since 1997 (Worcester, 1992–97); *b* 18 Feb. 1955; *s* of Thomas Luff and Joyce (*née* Mills); *m* 1982, Julia Jenks; one *s* one *d*. *Educ:* Windsor Grammar Sch.; Corpus Christi Coll., Cambridge (MA Econs). Research Asst to Rt Hon. Peter Walker, 1977–80; Head of Private Office to Rt Hon. Edward Heath, 1980–82; Dir, Good Relations Public Affairs, 1982–87; Special Advr to Rt Hon. Lord

Young of Graffham, 1987–89; Sen. Consultant, Lowe Bell Communications, 1989–90; Asst Man. Dir, Good Relations Ltd, 1990–92. PPS to Minister for Industry and Energy, 1993–96, to Lord Chancellor, 1996–97, to Minister of State, Home Office, 1996–97; an Opposition Whip, 2000–05; Opposition Asst Chief Whip, 2002–05; Chairman: Agriculture Select Cttee, 1997–2000; Trade and Industry Select Cttee, 2005–07; Business and Enterprise Select Cttee, 2007–; Dep. Chm., All-Party India Gp, 2006–; Chm., Cons. Parly Friends of India, 2001–05. Mem., Exec. Cttee, CPA, 2001–06. Patron, Conservative Students, 1995–98. Vice-Pres., Severn Valley Railway, 1997–. FCIPR (FIPR 1998). *Recreations:* performing arts, shooting. *Address:* House of Commons, SW1A 0AA. *T:* (01905) 763952; *e-mail:* luffpj@parliament.uk. *Club:* Worcestershire CC.

LUFFINGHAM, Prof. John Kingley, FDSRCSE; Professor of Orthodontics, University of Glasgow, 1976–93, now Emeritus; *b* 14 Aug. 1928; *s* of Alfred Hulbert Carr Luffingham and Frances Tugby; *m* 1968, Elizabeth Margaret Anderson; two *s* one *d. Educ:* Haileybury; London Hosp. Med. Coll. (BDS, PhD London); Dip. Orth RCSE. House Surgeon, London Hosp. Med. Coll., 1957–58; Registrar, KCH, 1959–61; Clinical Research Fellow, MRC, 1961–64; Sen. Registrar, Guy's Hosp., 1965–67; Sen. Lectr, Glasgow Univ., 1968–76; Consultant Orthodontist, Greater Glasgow Health Board, 1968–76. *Publications:* articles in dental jls, incl. British Jl of Orthodontics, European Jl of Orthodontics, Archives of Oral Biology. *Recreations:* ski-ing, golf.

LUFT, His Honour Arthur Christian, CBE 1988; Member, Legislative Council, Isle of Man, 1988–98; *b* 21 July 1915; *e s* of late Ernest Christian Luft and late Phoebe Luft; *m* 1950, Dorothy, *yr d* of late Francis Manley; two *s. Educ:* Bradbury Sch., Cheshire. Served Army, 1940–46. Admitted to Manx Bar, 1940; Attorney-Gen., IOM, 1972–74; Second Deemster, 1974–80; HM's First Deemster, Clerk of the Rolls, and Dep. Governor, IOM, 1980–88. Chairman: IOM Criminal Injuries Compensation Tribunal, 1974–80; Prevention of Fraud (Unit Trust) Tribunal, 1974–80; IOM Licensing Appeal Court, 1974–80; Wireless Telegraphy Appeal Bd for IOM, 1974–80; IOM Income Tax Appeal Comrs, 1980–88; IOM Gaming Control Comrs, 1988–90; Rivers Pollution Cttee, 1989–92; Data Protection Tribunal, 1990–92; IOM Arts Council, 1992–98; Member: Dept of Local Govt and Envmt, IOM, 1988–93; Dept of Agric., Fisheries and Forestry, IOM, 1993–98; Public Accounts Cttee, 1988–98; Ecclesiastical Cttee of Tynwald, 1992–98; Standing Orders Cttee of Legislative Council, 1995–98. Chm., Legislative Cttee, Diocesan Synod., 1989–98. Pres., Youth Adv. Gp, 1991–94. Pres., Manx Deaf Soc., 1975–. Pres., IOM Cricket Club, 1980–98. *Recreations:* theatre, watching cricket, gardening. *Address:* Leyton, Victoria Road, Douglas, Isle of Man IM2 6AQ. *T:* (01624) 621048.

LUKE, 3rd Baron *cr* 1929, of Pavenham, Co. Bedford; **Arthur Charles St John Lawson Johnston;** fine art dealer, since 1972; an Opposition Whip, House of Lords, since 1997; *b* 13 Jan. 1933; *e s* of 2nd Baron Luke and Barbara, *d* of Sir FitzRoy Hamilton Anstruther-Gough-Calthorpe, 1st Bt; *S* father, 1996; *m* 1st, 1959, Silvia Maria (marr. diss. 1971), *yr d* of Don Honorio Roigt; one *s* two *d*; 2nd, 1971, Sarah Louise, *d* of Richard Hearne, OBE; one *s. Educ:* Eton; Trinity Coll., Cambridge (BA Hons). Elected Mem., H of L, 1999; Opposition spokesman on defence, and on culture, media and sport, 2004–. Mem., Beds CC, 1965–70 (Chm., Staffing Cttee, 1967–70). President: Nat. Assoc. of Warehousekeepers, 1962–78; Internat. Assoc. of Book-Keepers, 1997–2001. Comdr, St John Ambulance, Beds, 1985–90 (Comr, 1972–85). Member Court: Corp. of Sons of the Clergy, 1980–2005; Drapers' Co., 1993– (Master, 2001–02). High Sheriff, Beds, 1969–70, DL Beds, 1989–2004. KStJ 1988. *Recreations:* shooting, fishing. *Heir: s* Hon. Ian James St John Lawson Johnston [*b* 3 Oct. 1963; *m* 1998, Rowena Jane, *y d* of John Aldington; two *s* one *d*]. *Address:* 46 Main Street, Middleton, Leics LE16 8YU. *T:* (01536) 772129.

LUKE, Iain Malone; *b* 8 Oct. 1951; *m* 1987, Marie. *Educ:* Dundee Coll.; Univ. of Dundee (MA 1980); Univ. of Edinburgh (DipBA 1981); Jordanhill Teacher Trng Coll. (FE Teaching Qualif.). Asst Collector of Taxes, Inland Revenue, 1969–74; Asst Sales Manager, Brown & Tawse Steel Stockholder, 1974–75; Asst Bar Manager, 1981–83; Lectr, then Sen. Lectr, Dundee Coll. of Further Educn, 1983–2001. Member (Lab): Dundee DC, 1984–96; Dundee CC, 1995–2001. MP (Lab) Dundee E, 2001–05; contested (Lab) same seat, 2005. JP Dundee, 1996–2001.

LUKES, Prof. Steven Michael, DPhil; FBA 1987; Professor of Sociology, New York University, since 1998; *b* 8 March 1941; *o s* of S. Lukes; *m* 1977, Nina Vera Mary Stanger (*d* 1999); two *s* one *d. Educ:* Royal Grammar School, Newcastle upon Tyne; Balliol Coll., Oxford (MA 1965; DPhil 1968). Student, 1962–64, Res. Fellow, 1964–66, Nuffield Coll., Oxford; Fellow of Balliol Coll., Oxford, 1966–88; Lectr in Politics, Oxford Univ., 1967–88; Prof. of Political and Social Theory, European Univ. Inst., Florence, 1987–95; Prof. of Moral Philosophy, Univ. of Siena, 1995–2000. Vis. Centennial Prof., LSE, 2001–03. *Publications:* (ed jtly) The Good Society, 1972; Emile Durkheim: his life and work, 1972; Individualism, 1973; Power: a radical view, 1974, 2nd enlarged edn 2004; Essays in Social Theory, 1976; (ed) Durkheim: Rules of Sociological Method, 1982; (ed jtly) Rationality and Relativism, 1982; (ed jtly) Durkheim and the Law, 1984; Marxism and Morality, 1985; (jtly) No Laughing Matter: a collection of political jokes, 1985; (ed) Power, 1986; Moral Conflict and Politics, 1991; The Curious Enlightenment of Professor Caritat: a comedy of ideas, 1995; Liberals and Cannibals: the implications of diversity, 2003. *Recreation:* playing jazz piano. *Address:* Department of Sociology, New York University, 269 Mercer Street, New York, NY 10003, USA; *e-mail:* steven.lukes@nyu.edu; 1 Washington Square Village, Apt 9i, New York, NY 10012, USA.

LUMET, Sidney; film director; *b* Philadelphia, 25 June 1924; *o s* of Baruch and Eugenia Lumet; *m* Rita Gam (marr. diss.); *m* 1956, Gloria Vanderbilt (marr. diss. 1963); *m* 1963, Gail Jones (marr. diss. 1978); two *d*; *m* 1980, Mary Gimbel. *Educ:* Professional Children's Sch., NY; Columbia Univ. Served US Army, SE Asia, 1942–46. Appeared as child actor: Dead End; The Eternal Road; Sunup to Sunday; Schoolhouse on the Lot; My Heart's in the Highlands; Dir, Summer Stock, 1947–49; taught acting, High Sch. of Professional Arts; Associate Dir, CBS, 1950, Dir, 1951–57. *TV shows include:* Danger; Your Are There; Alcoa: The Sacco and Vanzetti Story; Goodyear Playhouse; Best of Broadway; Omnibus. *Films directed include:* Twelve Angry Men, 1957; Stage Struck, 1958; That Kind of Woman, 1959; The Fugitive Kind, 1960; A View from the Bridge, Long Day's Journey into Night, 1962; Fail Safe, 1964; The Pawnbroker, The Hill, 1965; The Group, 1966; The Deadly Affair, 1967; Bye Bye Braverman, Last of the Mobile Hot Shots, Child's Play, The Seagull, 1969; The Anderson Tapes, 1971; The Offence, 1973; Serpico, Murder on the Orient Express, 1974; Dog Day Afternoon, 1975; Network, 1977; Equus, 1977; The Wiz, 1979; Just Tell Me What You Want, 1979; Prince of the City, 1980; Deathtrap, 1981; The Verdict, 1982; Daniel, 1983; Garbo Talks, 1984; Power, 1985; The Morning After, 1987; Family Business, 1990; Q & A, 1991; A Stranger Among Us, 1992; Guilty as Sin, 1993; Night Falls on Manhattan, 1996; Gloria, 1999; Before the Devil Knows You're Dead, 2008; *play:* Caligula, 1960. Hon. Acad. Award for Lifetime Achievement, 2005. *Address:* c/o Jeff Berg, ICM, 8942 Wilshire Boulevard, Beverly Hills, CA 90211, USA.

LUMLEY, family name of **Earl of Scarbrough**.

LUMLEY, Joanna Lamond, OBE 1995; FRGS; actress; *b* Kashmir, India, 1 May 1946; *d* of late Maj. James Rutherford Lumley, 6th Gurkha Rifles and Thyra Beatrice Rose Lumley (*née* Weir); one *s*; *m* 1st, Jeremy Lloyd (marr. diss. 1971); 2nd, 1986, Stephen William Barlow, *qv. Theatre* includes: Don't Just Lie There, Say Something, Garrick, 1972; Private Lives, tour, 1983; Hedda Gabler, Dundee, 1985; Blithe Spirit, Vaudeville, 1986; An Ideal Husband, Chichester, 1989; The Cherry Orchard, 1989; Vanilla, Brighton, transf. Lyric, 1990; The Revengers' Comedies, Strand, 1991; Who Shall I Be Tomorrow?, Greenwich, 1992; The Letter, Lyric, Hammersmith, 1995; The Cherry Orchard, Crucible, Sheffield, 2007; *television* includes: General Hospital, 1973; Coronation Street, 1973; Steptoe and Son; The New Avengers, 1976–78 (BAFTA Special Award, 2000); Sapphire and Steel, 1979; The Weather in the Streets, 1983; Mistral's Daughter; Oxbridge Blues, 1984; The Glory Boys; guest presenter, Wogan; A Perfect Hero, 1989; White Rajahs of Sarawak (documentary), 1991; Lovejoy, 1992; Absolutely Fabulous, 1992–96, 2001–03 (2 BAFTA Awards; British Comedy Award, 1993); Class Act, 1994; Girl Friday (documentary), 1994; Joanna Lumley in the Kingdom of the Thunder Dragon (documentary), 1997; Coming Home, A Rather English Marriage, 1998; Nancherrow, Dr Willoughby, MD, 1999; Mirrorball, 2000; (co-prod) The Cazalets, 2001; Up in Town, 2002; Born to be Wild, 2002; Sensitive Skin, 2005, 2007; Last Chance to Save, 2005; Jam and Jerusalem, 2006; *radio* includes: The Psychedelic Spy, 1990; The Fortunes of War, 2008; *films* include: On Her Majesty's Secret Service; The Satanic Rites of Dracula; Trail of the Pink Panther; Curse of the Pink Panther; Shirley Valentine, 1989; Innocent Lies, 1995; James and the Giant Peach, Cold Comfort Farm, 1996; Prince Valiant, 1997; Sweeney Todd, 1998; Parting Shots, Mad Cows, 1999; Maybe Baby, 2000; Ella Enchanted, The Cat's Meow, 2004; The Magic Roundabout, 2005; Corpse Bride, 2005. Hon. Patron, Trinity Coll. Dublin Philosophical Soc., 2007. Hon. DLitt: Kent, 1995; St Andrews, 2006; DUniv Oxford Brookes, 2000. *Publications:* (ed) Peacocks and Commas, 1983; Stare Back and Smile (autobiog.), 1989; Forces Sweethearts, 1993; Girl Friday, 1994; In the Kingdom of the Thunder Dragon, 1997; No Room for Secrets (autobiog.), 2004; articles in jls. *Recreations:* reading, music, travelling, granddaughters, daydreaming. *Address:* c/o Conway Van Gelder Grant Ltd, 18–21 Jermyn Street, SW1Y 6HP.

LUMLEY-SAVILE, family name of **Baron Savile**.

LUMSDAINE, Nicola Frances; *see* LeFanu, N. F.

LUMSDEN, Prof. Andrew Gino, PhD; FRS 1994; Professor of Developmental Neurobiology, King's College London School of Biomedical and Health Sciences (formerly United Medical and Dental Schools of Guy's and St Thomas' Hospitals, then Guy's, King's and St Thomas' Hospitals' Medical and Dental School, King's College London), London University, since 1989; Director, MRC Centre for Developmental Neurobiology, since 2000; *b* 22 Jan. 1947; *s* of Dr Edward Gilbert Sita-Lumsden, MD and Stella Pirie Lumsden; *m* 1st, 1970, Anne Farrington Roberg (marr. diss. 1996); two *d*; 2nd, 2002, Kathleen Marie Wets. *Educ:* Kingswood Sch., Bath; St Catharine's Coll., Cambridge (BA 1968; MA 1972; Frank Smart Scholar); Yale Univ.; PhD London 1978. Fulbright Scholar, 1968–70; Lectr in Anatomy, 1973–87, Reader in Craniofacial Biology, 1987–89, Guy's Hosp. Med. Sch. Miller Foundn Vis. Prof., Univ. of California, Berkeley, 1994; Lectr, Coll. de France, Paris, 1991; Yntema Lectr, SUNY, 1993; Howard Hughes Internat. Res. Scholar, 1993–; Jenkinson Meml Lectr, Univ. of Oxford, 1994; Seymour Kreshover Lectr, NIH, 1996; Brooks Lectr, Harvard Univ., 1996. Founder FMedSci 1998. Médaille de la Ville de Paris, 1986. *Publications:* (jtly) The Developing Brain, 2001; reports in learned jls. *Recreations:* mechanical engineering, natural history, Lotus Sevens, bridge. *Address:* MRC Centre for Developmental Neurobiology, New Hunt's House, Guy's Hospital, SE1 1UL.

LUMSDEN, Andrew Michael; Organist and Director of Music, Winchester Cathedral, since 2002; *b* 10 Nov. 1962; *s* of Sir David James Lumsden, *qv. Educ:* Winchester Coll.; Royal Scottish Acad. of Music and Drama; St John's Coll., Cambridge (MA Hons). ARCO 1979. Asst Organist, Southwark Cathedral, 1985–88; Sub-organist, Westminster Abbey, 1988–91; Organist and Master of the Choristers, Lichfield Cathedral, 1992–2002. Ext. Examr, Birmingham Conservatoire, RNCM, 1995–2005. Hon. FRCO 2004. *Recreations:* travel, flying, wine. *Address:* Cathedral Office, 1 The Close, Winchester SO23 9LS. *T:* (01962) 857200, *Fax:* (01962) 857201; *e-mail:* andrew.lumsden@winchester-cathedral.org.uk.

LUMSDEN, Sir David (James), Kt 1985; Principal, Royal Academy of Music, 1982–93; *b* Newcastle upon Tyne, 19 March 1928; *m* 1951, Sheila Daniels; two *s* two *d. Educ:* Dame Allan's Sch., Newcastle upon Tyne; Selwyn Coll., Cambridge (Hon. Fellow, 1986). Organ scholar, Selwyn Coll., Cambridge, 1948–51; BA Class I, 1950; MusB (Barclay Squire Prize) 1951; MA 1955; DPhil 1957. Asst Organist, St John's Coll., Cambridge, 1951–53; Res. Student, 1951–54; Organist and Choirmaster, St Mary's, Nottingham, 1954–56; Founder and Conductor, Nottingham Bach Soc., 1954–59; Rector Chori, Southwell Minster, 1956–59; Dir of Music, Keele, 1958–59; Prof. of Harmony, Royal Academy of Music, 1959–61; Fellow and Organist, New Coll., Oxford (Hon. Fellow, 1996), and Lectr in the Faculty of Music, Oxford Univ., 1959–76; Principal, RSAMD, Glasgow, 1976–82. Conductor: Oxford Harmonic Soc., 1961–63; Oxford Sinfonia, 1967–70; BBC Scottish Singers, 1977–80; Organist, Sheldonian Theatre, 1964–76; Choragus, Oxford Univ., 1968–72. Harpsichordist to London Virtuosi, 1972–75. Member of Board: Scottish Opera, 1977–83; ENO, 1983–88. President: Inc. Assoc. of Organists, 1966–68; ISM, 1984–85; RCO, 1986–88; Chairman: NYO, 1985–94; Early Music Soc., 1985–89. Hugh Porter Lectr, Union Theological Seminary, NY, 1967; Vis. Prof., Yale Univ., 1974–75. Hon. Editor, Church Music Soc., 1970–73. Hon. FRCO 1976; Hon. RAM 1978; FRCM 1980; FRNCM 1981; FRSAMD 1982; Hon. GSM 1984; FLCM 1985; FRSA 1985; FRSCM 1987; Hon. FTCL 1988; FKC 1991. Hon. DLitt Reading, 1990. *Publications:* An Anthology of English Lute Music, 1954; Thomas Robinson's Schoole of Musicke, 1603, 1971; Articles in: The Listener; The Score; Music and Letters: Galpin Soc. Jl; La Luth et sa Musique; La Musique de la Renaissance, etc. *Recreations:* reading, theatre, photography, travel, hill-walking, etc. *Address:* 26 Wyke Mark, Dean Lane, Winchester SO22 5DJ.

See also A. M. Lumsden.

LUMSDEN, George Innes, FRSE; CGeol, FGS; consultant in geology and scientific staff recruitment, since 1991; *b* 27 June 1926; *s* of George Lumsden and Margaret Ann Frances Lumsden (*née* Cockburn); *m* 1958, Sheila Thomson; two *s* one *d. Educ:* Banchory Academy; Aberdeen University (Lyon Prize in Geol.; BSc). Geological Survey of GB, 1949; District Geologist S Scotland, 1970, Asst Dir and Sen. Officer Scotland, 1980, Inst. of Geol Scis; British Geological Survey: CSO and Dep. Dir, 1982–85; Dir, 1985–87; Mem., CS Commn Sci. Div.'s Panel of Chairmen, 1988–91; Chm. Recruitment Bds, DRA, then DERA, 1991–2001. Member: Council of Management, Macaulay Inst. for Soil Research, 1980–87; Engineering and Sci. Adv. Cttee, Derby Coll. of Higher Educn, 1983–87; Geol. Museum Adv. Panel, 1985–87; Chm., Dirs of Western European Geol Surveys' Standing Gp on Envmtl Geology, 1984–87, Hon. Pres., 1987–, Hon. Sec., 1988–95; Sec., Forum of European Geol Surveys, 1996–2002. *Publications:* (ed) Geology and the Environment in Western Europe, 1992, 2nd edn 1994; maps, papers and books on geol topics in official Geol Survey. *Recreations:* music, theatre, sport, gardening. *Address:* 9 West Savile Gardens, Edinburgh EH9 3AB.

LUMSDEN, Iain Cobden, FFA; Group Chief Executive, Standard Life Assurance Co., 2002–04; *b* 6 June 1946; *s* of John A. Lumsden and Helen H. Lumsden (*née* Foster); *m* 1970, Rosemary Hoey; one *s* one *d. Educ:* Exeter Coll., Oxford (BA 1967; MA). FFA 1971. Standard Life Assurance Co., 1967–2004: Gp Finance Dir, 1990–2001.

LUMSDEN, James Alexander, MBE 1945; TD 1962; DL; Partner, Maclay, Murray & Spens, Solicitors, Glasgow and Edinburgh, 1947–82; *b* 24 Jan. 1915; *s* of late Sir James Robert Lumsden and Lady (Henrietta) Lumsden (*née* Macfarlane Reid); *m* 1947, Sheila, *d* of late Malcolm Cross and Evelyn Cross (*née* Newlands); three *s. Educ:* Rugby Sch.; Corpus Christi Coll., Cambridge (BA, MA 1995; LLB). Director: Bank of Scotland, 1958–85; Weir Group PLC, 1957–84; William Baird PLC, 1959–84; Murray Growth Trust PLC and other companies in Murray Johnstone Group, 1967–85 (Chm., 1971–84); Scottish Provident Instn, 1968–85 (Chm., 1977–83); Burmah Oil Co. Ltd, 1957–76 (Chm., 1971–75). Mem. Jenkins Cttee on Company Law. Mem., Queen's Body Guard for Scotland, Royal Company of Archers, 1963–. DL Dunbartonshire, 1966. *Address:* Arden-Beag, 7 Station Road, Craigendoran, Helensburgh G84 7BG. *T:* (01436) 676204. *Clubs:* New (Edinburgh); Western (Glasgow).

LUMSDEN, Prof. Keith Grant, FRSE; Director, Edinburgh Business School, since 1995; *b* 7 Jan. 1935; *s* of Robert Sclater Lumsden and Elizabeth Brow; *m* 1961, Jean Baillie Macdonald; one *s. Educ:* Univ. of Edinburgh (MA Hons Econ 1959); Stanford Univ., California (PhD 1968). FRSE 1992. Stanford University: Instructor, Dept of Econs, 1960–63; Asst Prof., Graduate Sch. of Business, 1964–67; Research Associate, Stanford Res. Inst., 1965–71; Associate Prof., Grad. Sch. of Business, 1968–75; Dir, Esmée Fairbairn Res. Centre, Heriot-Watt Univ., 1975–95. Vis. Prof., Heriot-Watt Univ., 1969–70; Affiliate Prof. of Econs, INSEAD, 1975; Acad. Dir, Sea Transport Exec. Programme, 1979; Prof. of Econs, Advanced Management Coll., Stanford Univ., 1971. Director: Economic Educn Project, 1969–74; Behavioral Res. Labs, 1970–72; Capital Preservation Fund, 1971–75; Nielsen Engineering Research, 1972–75; Hewlett-Packard Ltd, 1981–92. *Publications:* The Free Enterprise System, 1963; The Gross National Product, 1964; International Trade, 1965; (jtly) Macroeconomics, 1966, 4th edn 1981; (jtly) Macroeconomics, 1966, 4th edn 1981; (ed) New Development in the Teaching of Economics, 1967; Excess Demand and Excess Supply in World Tramp Shipping Markets, 1968; (ed) Recent Research in Economics Education, 1970; (jtly) Basic Economics: theory and cases, 1973, 2nd edn 1977; (ed) Efficiency in Universities: the La Paz papers, 1974; (jtly) Division Management Simulation, 1978; (jtly) Economics Education in the UK, 1980; (jtly) Basic Macroeconomic Models, 1981; (jtly) Running the British Economy, 1981, 6th edn 1990; (jtly) Managing the Australian Economy, 1985; (jtly) Shipping Management Model—Stratship, 1983; (jtly) Macroeconomic Database, 1984; (jtly) Strategies for Life—Stratlife, 1988; Economics, 1991; articles in professional jls. *Recreations:* tennis, deep sea game fishing. *Address:* 40 Lauder Road, Edinburgh EH9 1UE. *Clubs:* New (Edinburgh); Waverley Lawn Tennis & Squash (Edinburgh); Tantallon Golf (N Berwick).

LUNA MENDOZA, Ricardo Victor; Ambassador of Peru to the Court of St James's and concurrently Ambassador to Ireland, since 2006; *b* 19 Nov. 1940; *s* of Ricardo Luna and Victoria Mendoza; *m* 1969, Margarita Proaño; one *d. Educ:* Princeton Univ. (BA Hons Politics 1962); Columbia Univ., NY (Master Internat. Affairs 1964); Peruvian Diplomatic Acad. Diplomatic Service of Peru: served in London, Tel-Aviv, Geneva, Washington, Paris, Quito and NY, 1966–86; Ambassador, 1986; Undersec., Multi-lateral Affairs, Lima, and Co-ordinator, Contadora-Apoyo and Rio Gps, 1987–89; Ambassador: to UN, NY, 1989–92; to USA, 1992–99; Weinberg Vis. Prof. of Foreign Affairs, Princeton Univ., 2000–01; Tinker Vis. Prof. of Foreign Affairs, Columbia Univ., NY, 2002; Prof. of Internat. Affairs, Govt Inst., San Martín de Porres Univ., Lima, 2003; Advr to Peruvian Finance Minister for Internat. Affairs, 2004; Cogut Vis. Prof. of Internat. Affairs, Brown Univ., 2005; Vis. Prof. of Internat. Affairs and Co-ordinator, Latin-American Area, Fletcher Sch. of Law and Diplomacy, Tufts Univ., 2005–06. Fellow, Centre for Internat. Affairs, 1980–81, Inst. of Politics, 2006, Harvard Univ. Pan American Order, Panamerican Foundn, 1990. Commander: Order de Mayo (Argentina); Order Rio Branco (Brazil). *Publications:* Política Exterior del Perú, 1981; Carlos García Bedoya, 1993; Revaluación de la Idea del Hemisferio Occidental, 2002; contribs to jls. *Address:* Embassy of Peru, 52 Sloane Street, SW1X 9SP. *Clubs:* Athenæum, Travellers; University, Cosmos (Washington); Harvard (NY); Colonial (Princeton Univ.); Phoenix (Lima).

LUNAN, Rt Rev. David Ward; Moderator of the General Assembly of the Church of Scotland, 2008–May 2009 (designation subseq. Very Rev.); *b* London, 29 Feb. 1944; *s* of Andrew Lunan and Jean Lunan (*née* Orr); *m* 1974, Margaret Ann Fiddes Young; four *s. Educ:* Glasgow High Sch.; Univ. of Glasgow (MA 1965; BD 1968). Ordained C of S, 1970; Asst Minister, Calton New Parish, 1969–75; Minister: St Andrews Lhanbryd, Moray, 1975–87; Renfield St Stephens, Glasgow, 1987–2002; Clerk to Presbytery of Glasgow, 2002–08. Moderator: Presbytery of Moray, 1985–86; Presbytery of Glasgow, 2000–01. *Recreations:* hill walking, music, reading, travel, family. *Address:* Church of Scotland, 121 George Street, Edinburgh EH2 4YN. *T:* (0131) 225 5722; *e-mail:* moderator@cofscotland.org.uk. *Club:* Western (Glasgow).

LUNCH, John, CBE 1975; VRD 1965; FCA, FCILT; Director-General of the Port of London Authority, and Board Member, 1971–76; Chairman: Comprehensive Shipping Group, 1973–75; Transcontinental Air Ltd, 1973–75; *b* 11 Nov. 1919; *s* of late Percy Valentine Lunch and Amy (*née* Somerville); *m* 1st, 1943, Joyce Barbara Clerke (*d* 1989), *d* of late Arnold Basil O'Connell Clerke and Norah Buckley (*née* Browne); two *s*; 2nd, 1995, Fiona Charis Elizabeth Fleck, *d* of late Arthur Axel Miller, MC and Charis Harrison Martin (*née* Petty), and *widow* of Peter Hugo Fleck. *Educ:* Roborough Sch., Eastbourne. FCA 1946; FCILT (FCIT 1965). Served War, Lt RNVR, Medit. and Home Fleets, 1939–46 (N Atlantic convoys, Crete, N Africa, Malta convoys, Sicily D-Day landings; Torpedo specialist, 1944), subseq. Permanent RNVR, later RNR; Lt-Comdr RNR, retd list, 1969; Lt-Col RE (TA), Engr and Logistic Staff Corps (formerly Engr and Transport Staff Corps), 1971, Col, 1976, retd list, 1994. In business in City, 1946–48: Asst Man. Dir, Tokenhouse Securities Corp. Ltd, 1947, and dir several cos; British Transport Commn, 1948–61: road and rail transport and ancillary businesses; PLA, 1961; Dir of Finance, also Dir of Commerce, 1966; Asst Dir-Gen., responsible docks and harbour, 1969; Chairman: (and founder) PLA Port Users Consultative Cttee, 1966–71; Internat. Port Develt Cttee, Internat. Assoc. of Ports and Harbors, 1972–76; Pres., Inst. of Freight Forwarders, 1972–73. Chm., London Industrial Chartered Accountants, 1971–72; Member Council: Inst. of Chartered Accountants, 1970–77; Chartered Inst. of Transport, 1973–76; MInstRE, 2007. Mem. Cttee of Management (a Trustee), 1977–94, a Vice-Pres., 1987–94, a Life Vice-Pres., 1994, RNLI; Founder Chm., RNLI Manhood Br., 1976–78; Pres., RNLI, Hayling Island Lifeboat Station, 1978–88; Hon. Art Adviser, RNLI, 1981–99. Hon. Life Mem. Internat. Assoc. of Airport and Seaport Police, 1974. CCMI (FBIM 1971); FCIM (FInstM 1973); FILT 1999; FRSA (Council nominee) 1976; Hon. FIFP 1986. Freeman: City of London, 1970; Watermen & Lightermen's Co. of River Thames, 1970 (Court Mem., 1976–80, Hon. Court Mem., 1980–). ADC to Governor of Louisiana, with rank Adm., 1971–. Malta GC 50th Anniv. Medal, 1992. *Publications:* The Chartered Accountant in Top Management, 1965; A Plan for Britain's Ports, 1975. *Recreations:* art, opera, horse racing, sailing. *Address:* Martins, East Ashling, Chichester, West Sussex PO18 9AX. *T:* (01243) 575252. *Clubs:* Army and Navy; Itchenor Sailing (West Sussex).

LUND, John Walter Guerrier, CBE 1975; DSc, PhD; FRS 1963; FIBiol, FCIWEM; Botanist, at Windermere Laboratory of Freshwater Biological Association, 1945–78; Deputy Chief Scientific Officer; *b* 27 Nov. 1912; *s* of George E. Lund and Kate Lund (*née* Hardwick); *m* 1949, Hilda M. Canter; one *s* one *d. Educ:* Sedbergh Sch.; Univ. of Manchester; London Univ. (PhD 1939; DSc 1951). Demonstrator in Botany, Univ. of Manchester, also Queen Mary Coll. and Chelsea Polytechnic, Univ. of London, 1935–38; Temp. Lectr in Botany, Univ. of Sheffield, 1936; Staff Biologist, W Midland Forensic Science Laboratory, Birmingham, 1938–45. Hon. DSc Buckingham, 1988. *Publications:* (ed with Elizabeth Howarth) Lake Sediments and Environmental History: studies in palaeolimnology and palaeoecology in honour of Winifred Tutin, 1984; (with Hilda Canter-Lund) Freshwater Algae: their microscopic world explored, 1995; papers and articles in scientific jls, symposium vols, etc. *Recreation:* gardening. *Address:* Ellerbeck, Ellerigg Road, Ambleside, Cumbria LA22 9EU. *T:* (015394) 32369.

LUND, Mark Joseph; Chief Executive, St James's Place (formerly St James's Place Capital) plc, 2004–07; *b* 1 July 1957; *s* of Joseph and Maureen Lund; *m* 1986, Karen Will; two *s* one *d. Educ:* Liverpool Polytech. (BA Hons Social Studies); Univ. of Leeds (MA Transport Econs). Transport economist, BR, 1983–84; Management Consultant: Spicer & Oppenheim, 1984–89; Booz Allen Hamilton, 1989–91; Dir, Henderson Investors plc, 1991–2001; Chief Exec., J. P. Morgan Fundshub, 2001–03. *Recreations:* family activities, aspiring triathlete, ski-ing.

LUND, Prof. Raymond Douglas, PhD; FRS 1992; Adjunct Professor of Ophthalmology, Casey Eye Institute, Oregon Health and Science University, since 2006; *b* 10 Feb. 1940; *s* of Henry Douglas Lund and Rose Lund; *m* 1963, Jennifer Sylvia Hawes; two *s. Educ:* University College London (BSc 1st cl. Hons, PhD). LRAM. Asst Lectr, then Lectr, Anatomy Dept, UCL, 1963–66; Res. Associate, Univ. of Pennsylvania, 1966–67; Asst Prof., Anatomy Dept, Univ. of Stanford, 1967–68; Asst Prof., then Prof., Depts of Biological Structure and Neurological Surgery, Univ. of Washington, 1968–79; Prof. and Chm., Dept of Anatomy, Univ. of S Carolina, 1979–83; Prof. and Chm., Dept of Neurobiology, Anatomy and Cell Sci., Univ. of Pittsburgh, 1983–91 (Dir, Centre for Neuroscience, 1984–87); Prof. and Head of Dept of Anatomy, and Fellow of Clare College, Cambridge, 1992–95; Duke-Elder Prof. of Ophthalmology, Inst. of Ophthalmol., UCL, 1995–2000; Hatch Prof. of Ophthalmology and Res. Dir, Moran Eye Center, Univ. of Utah, 2000–06, now Prof. Emeritus. Chm. Scientific Cttee, Internat. Spinal Res. Trust, 1994–97; Trustee, Corporate Action Trust, 1997–. Founder FMedSci 1998. NIH Merit Award, 1988. *Publications:* Development and Plasticity of the Brain, 1978; contribs to learned jls. *Recreation:* music. *Address:* Casey Eye Institute, 3375 SW Terwilliger Blvd, Portland, OR 97239–4197, USA.

LUND, Rodney Cookson; Chairman: Short Brothers, 1988–90 (Director, 1988–99); National Bus Co., 1986–88 (part-time Member, 1989–92); *b* 16 June 1936; *s* of late Arthur and Doris Lund; *m* 1st, Lynda Brooks (marr. diss.); one *s*; 2nd, Hyacinth, (Miki), Wallace. *Educ:* Wallasey Grammar School; Liverpool University (BCom Hons). Served RAPC, 1957–59. Evans Medical, 1959; Carreras Rothmans, 1960–64; Partner, Urwick Orr & Partners, 1964–66 and 1969–73; Man. Dir, The Mace Voluntary Gp, 1966–69; Vice-Chm., Produce Importers Alliance, 1966–69; Executive Director: Rank Radio International, 1973–75; British Sugar Corp., 1976–82; Woolworth Holdings, 1982–86; Hazlewood Foods, 1991–2001. Mem., Nationalised Industries Chairmen's Gp, 1986–88; Chm., The Enterprise Support Gp, 1991–94. CCMI. *Recreations:* travel, opera, cooking. *Address:* 28 Chelsea Crescent, Chelsea Harbour, SW10 0XB. *T:* (020) 7352 2641.

LUNGHI, Cherie Mary; actress; *b* 4 April 1952; *d* of late Allessandro Lunghi and Gladys Corbett Lee; one *d* by Roland Joffé. *Educ:* Arts Educn Trust, London; Central Sch. of Speech and Drama. *Theatre includes:* The Three Sisters, Owners, Newcastle, 1973; She Stoops to Conquer, Nottingham Playhouse, 1974; Teeth 'n' Smiles, Royal Court, 1975; RSC, 1976–80: Much Ado About Nothing; The Winter's Tale; King Lear; Destiny; Bandits; As You Like It; Saratoga; Twelfth Night; Uncle Vanya, RNT, 1982; Holiday, Old Vic, 1987; The Homecoming, Comedy, 1991; Arcadia, RNT, 1993; Passion Play, Donmar, 1999. *Films include:* Excalibur, 1980; King David, 1984; The Mission, 1986; To Kill a Priest, 1987; Jack and Sarah, 1995; Mary Shelley's Frankenstein, 1995. *Television includes: series and serials:* The Praying Mantis, 1982; Master of the Game, 1984; The Monocled Mutineer, 1986; Ellis Island, 1987; The Manageress, 1988, 1989; The Buccaneers, 1995; Little White Lies, 1998; The Knock, 1999; Hornblower, 1999; David Copperfield, 1999; Cutting It, 2003; Casualty 1906, 2006; Casualty 1907, 2007; Secret Diary of a Call Girl, 2007; A Touch of Frost, 2008; *plays and films:* The Misanthrope, 1978; Oliver Twist, 1983; Much Ado About Nothing, 1984; Letters to an Unknown Lover, 1986; The Lady's Not for Burning, 1987; The Canterville Ghost, 1995; Le Vipère au Poing, 2004. *Address:* c/o Creative Artists Management, 55–59 Shaftesbury Avenue, W1D 6LD.

LUNN, Rt Rev. David Ramsay; Hon. Assistant Bishop, Diocese of York, since 1998; *b* 17 July 1930. *Educ:* King's College, Cambridge (BA 1953; MA 1957); Cuddesdon College, Oxford. Deacon 1955, priest 1956, Newcastle upon Tyne; Curate of Sugley, 1955–59; N Gosforth, 1959–63; Chaplain, Lincoln Theological College, 1963–66; Sub-Warden, 1966–70; Vicar of St George, Cullercoats, 1970–75, Rector, 1975–80; Rural Dean of Tynemouth, 1975–80; Bishop of Sheffield, 1980–97. *Address:* Rivendell, 28 Southfield Road, Wetwang, Driffield, E Yorks YO25 9XX. *T:* (01377) 236657.

LUNN, Peter Northcote, CMG 1957; OBE 1951; Government Service, retired 1986; *b* 15 Nov. 1914; *e s* of late Sir Arnold Lunn; *m* 1939, Hon. (Eileen) Antoinette (*d* 1976), *d* of 15th Viscount Gormanston; two *s* two *d* (and one *s* one *d* decd). *Educ:* Eton. Joined Govt Service, 1939; Malta, 1939–44; Italy, 1944–45; W Germany, 1945–46; London, 1946–48; Vienna, 1948–50; Bern, 1950–53; Berlin, 1953–56; London, 1956–57; Bonn, 1957–62; Beirut, 1962–67; London, 1967–86. Mem., Brit. International Ski team, 1931–37, Capt. 1934–37; Capt. British Olympic Ski team, 1936; competitor, Inferno downhill ski race, 1978–86, 1988–89, 1995–2005. *Publications:* High-Speed Ski-ing, 1935; Evil in High Places, 1947; A Ski-ing Primer, 1948, rev. edn 1951; The Guinness Book of Ski-ing, 1983. *Clubs:* Ski Club of Great Britain; Denham Water Ski.

LUNN-ROCKLIFFE, Victor Paul; Director, Business Group, Export Credits Guarantee Department, 2005–06; *b* 5 Dec. 1948; *s* of Col W. P. Lunn-Rockliffe, DSO, MC and J. Jéquier; *m* 1971, Felicity Ann O'Neill; two *d. Educ:* Keele Univ. (Jt Hons French History). Export Credits Guarantee Department: joined, 1973; Head, Project Underwriting Div.,

ME and N Africa, 1987; Head, Risk Management Div., 1989; Head, Claims Div., 1994; Director: Asset Mgt Gp, subseq. Portfolio and Asset Mgt Gp, 1995–2004; Credit Risk Gp, 2004–05. *Publication:* Drawing ECGD 1973–2006, 2006. *Recreations:* drawing, painting, reading, walking, ballet, cinema.

LUNNY, William Francis; Sheriff of South Strathclyde, Dumfries and Galloway, 1984–98; *b* 10 Dec. 1938; *s* of James F. Lunny and Sarah Ann Crawford or Lunny; *m* 1967, Elizabeth McDermott; two *s* one *d*. *Educ:* Our Lady's High School, Motherwell; Glasgow Univ. (MA, LLB). Solicitor, 1961–67; Depute Procurator Fiscal, 1967–74; Crown Counsel/Legal Draftsman, Antigua, 1974–76; Advocate, 1977. Barrister, Antigua, 1981. KHS 1989. *Recreations:* walking, travelling.

LUNT, Beverly Anne; Her Honour Judge Lunt; a Circuit Judge, since 2004; *b* 8 March 1954; *d* of late Thomas Gordon Lunt and of Mary Lunt. *Educ:* Oxford Polytech. (BA). Called to the Bar, Gray's Inn, 1977; in practice as a barrister, 1977–2004, Hd of Chambers, Kingsgate Chambers, Manchester, 1990–2004. *Recreations:* reading, cinema, walking, theatre, supporting animal charities (WSPA, Dogs Trust, RSPCA, IFAW). *Address:* Burnley Crown Court, Hammerton Street, Burnley BB11 1XD. *T:* (01282) 416899, *Fax:* (01282) 414911.

LUNTS, David; Executive Director, Policy and Partnerships, Greater London Authority, since 2005; *b* 31 Oct. 1957; *s* of Lawrence Henry Lunts and Kvetinka Sonja Lunts; *m*; one *s*. *Educ:* Univ. of Manchester (BA Hons Pols and Mod. Hist.). Chm., Hulme Regeneration Ltd, 1992–95; Chief Executive: Urban Villages Forum, 1995–98; Prince's Foundn, 1998–2002; Dir, Urban Policy Unit, ODPM, 2002–05. Mem., Urban Task Force, 1997–99. *Recreations:* cinema, cycling, food. *Address:* Greater London Authority, City Hall, Queen's Walk, SE1 2AA. *T:* (020) 7983 4208, *Fax:* (020) 7983 4706; *e-mail:* david.lunts@london.gov.uk.

LUPU, Radu; pianist; *b* 30 Nov. 1945; *s* of late Meyer Lupu, lawyer, and Ana Gabor, teacher of languages. *Educ:* Moscow Conservatoire. Debut at age of twelve with complete programme of own music; studied with Florica Muzicescu, Cella Delavrancea, Heinrich Neuhaus and Stanislav Neuhaus. 1st prize: Van Cliburn Competition, 1966; Enescu Internat. Competition, 1967; Leeds Internat. Pianoforte Competition, 1969; Abbiati Prize, Italian Critics' Assoc., 1989; Premio Internazionale Arturo Benedetti Michelangeli, 2006. Débuts: London, 1969; Berlin, 1971; NY and Chicago, 1972. Numerous recordings include complete Mozart violin and piano sonatas, complete Beethoven Piano Concertos, 1979. *Recreations:* history, art, sport. *Address:* c/o Terry Harrison Artists Management, The Orchard, Market Street, Charlbury, Oxon OX7 3PJ. *T:* (01608) 810330; *e-mail:* artists@harrisonturner.co.uk.

LURIE, Prof. Alison; writer; Professor of English, Cornell University, 1976–2006, now Professor Emerita; *b* 3 Sept. 1926; *d* of Harry Lurie and Bernice Stewart; *m* 1st, 1948, Jonathan Bishop (marr. diss. 1985); three *s*; 2nd, 1995, Edward Hower. *Educ:* Radcliffe Coll., Cambridge, Mass (AB). Mem., AAAL 2005. *Publications:* Love and Friendship, 1962; The Nowhere City, 1965; Imaginary Friends, 1967 (televised, 1987); Real People, 1969; The War Between the Tates, 1974; Only Children, 1979; Foreign Affairs, 1984 (Pulitzer Prize, 1985); The Truth About Lorin Jones, 1988; (ed) The Oxford Book of Modern Fairy Tales, 1993; Women and Ghosts (short stories), 1994; The Last Resort, 1998; Truth and Consequences, 2005; *non-fiction:* The Language of Clothes, 1981; Don't Tell the Grown-ups, 1990; Familiar Spirits, 2001; Boys and Girls Forever, 2003; *children's books:* Clever Gretchen, 1980; The Heavenly Zoo, 1980; Fabulous Beasts, 1981. *Address:* c/o English Department, Cornell University, Ithaca, NY 14853, USA.

LUSBY, John Martin; Adjudicator (panel member), Tribunals Service, Criminal Injuries Compensation Appeals Panel, since 1997; *b* 27 April 1943; *s* of late William Henry Lusby and of Florence Mary (*née* Wharam); *m* 1966, (Mary) Clare, *d* of late John Gargan and Ellen (*née* Myers); one *s* one *d*. *Educ:* Marist Coll., Hull; Ushaw Coll., Durham; Maryvale Inst., Birmingham (DipTh (with commendation) 1997); Open Univ. (MA Theol. (with distinction) 1998). DipHSM 1972; MHSM (AHA 1972). Entered NHS, 1961; junior appointments: De la Pole Hosp., Hull, 1961–66; County Hosp., York, 1966–67; Kettering Gen. Hosp., 1967–68; Admin. Asst, United Sheffield Hosps, 1968–70; Dep. Hosp. Sec., E Birmingham Hosp., 1970–72; Hosp. Sec., Pontefract Gen. Infirmary and Headlands Hosp., Pontefract, 1972–74; Area Gen. Administrator, Kirklees AHA, 1974–76; Asst Dist Administrator (Patient Services), 1976–79, Dist Administrator, Wandsworth and E Merton Dist, 1979–81, Merton, Sutton and Wandsworth AHA(T); Area Administrator, Doncaster AHA, 1981; Dist Administrator, 1981–84, Dist Gen. Man., 1984–90, Exec. Dir, 1990, Doncaster HA; Mem., 1990–91, Gen. Manager, 1990–95, and Exec. Dir, 1991–95, Lothian Health Bd; Chm., Indep. Review Panel, NHS Complaints Procedure, Northern and Yorks Reg., NHS Exec., 1996–97. Member: Scottish Council for Postgrad. Med. and Dental Educn, 1992–95; Health Services and Public Health Res. Cttee, Chief Scientist Orgn, SHHD, 1993–95; Scottish Implementation Gp, Jun. Doctors and Dentists Hrs of Work, 1993–95; Jt Wkg Gp on Information Services, NHS in Scotland, 1993–95. Trustee: Dementia Services Develt Centre, Univ. of Stirling, 1991–95; Scottish Dementia Appeal Trust, 1994–95. Member: Catholic Theol Assoc. of GB, 1997–2008; Catholic Biblical Assoc. of GB, 1998–; Catholic Inst. for Internat. Relations, 1999–2004; Soc. for the Study of Theology, 2000–; European Soc. for Catholic Theology, 2004–08. *Recreations:* study of theology, music, reading, travel. *Address:* Flat A, Copper Beech, 31 North Grove, N6 4SJ. *T:* (020) 8341 3426; *e-mail:* johnlusby@btinternet.com. *Club:* Middlesex CC.

LUSCOMBE, Prof. David Edward, LittD; FSA; FRHistS; FBA 1986; Professor of Medieval History, 1972–95, Research Professor of Medieval History, 2000–03, now Emeritus, University of Sheffield; *b* 22 July 1938; *s* of Edward Dominic and Nora Luscombe; *m* 1960, Megan Phillips; three *s* one *d*. *Educ:* St Michael's Sch., North Finchley; Finchley Catholic Grammar Sch.; King's Coll., Cambridge (BA, MA, PhD, LittD). Fellow, King's Coll., Cambridge, 1962–64; Fellow and Dir of Studies in History, Churchill Coll., Cambridge, 1964–72; Sheffield University: Leverhulme Personal Res. Prof. of Medieval Hist., 1995–2000; Head of Dept of History, 1973–76, 1979–84; Dep. Dean, 1983–85, Dean, 1985–87, Faculty of Arts; Pro-Vice-Chancellor, 1990–94; Chm., Humanities Res. Inst., 1992–2003; Res. Dir for Arts and Humanities, 1994–2003. Vis. Prof., Univ. of Connecticut, 1993; Leverhulme European Fellow, 1973; Vis. Fellow, All Souls Coll., Oxford, 1994; British Acad./RSC Exchange Visitor to Canada, 1991; British Acad./Japan Acad. Exchange Visitor to Japan, 1996. Raleigh Lectr, British Acad., 1988. External examiner for higher degrees in Univs. of Cambridge, Oxford, London, Liverpool, Bangor, Lancaster, ANU, Toronto, Groningen, for BA degrees at Bangor, Leicester and Leeds. Dir, Historical Assoc. Summer Vacation Sch., 1976 and 1992. Member: Governing Body, later Assoc. St Edmund's House, Cambridge, 1971–84; Cttee, Ecclesiastical History Soc., 1976–79; Council, RHistS, 1981–85; Council, British Acad., 1989–97 (Publications Sec., 1990–97; Member: Medieval Texts Cttee, 1982– (Chm., 1991–2004); Publications Cttee, 1987–97 (Chm., 1990–97); Postgrad. Studies Cttee, 1988–90; Humanities Res. Bd, 1994–96); Cttee on Acad. Res. Projects, 1990–97; Commonwealth Scholarships Commn in UK, 1994–2000; Auditor, HEQC, 1994–95. Mem. Council, Worksop Coll. and Ranby House, 1996–2008. Fellow, later Hon. Fellow, Woodard Corp. Hon. Pres., Soc. internat. pour l'étude de la philosophie médiévale, 2002– (Vice-Pres., 1987–97; Pres., 1997–2002); Mem. Cttee, Soc. for Study of Medieval Langs and Lit., 1991–96. Gen. Editor, Cambridge Studies in Medieval Life and Thought, 4th series, 1988–2004 (Adv. Editor, 1983–88); Mem., Jt Supervisory Cttee, British Acad./OUP, for Oxford DNB, 1992–99 (Associate Editor, 1993–). *Publications:* The School of Peter Abelard, 1969; Peter Abelard's Ethics, 1971 (trans. Italian, 1976); (ed jtly) Church and Government in the Middle Ages, 1976; (ed jtly) Petrus Abaelardus 1079–1142: Person, Werk und Wirkung, 1980; (jtly) David Knowles Remembered, 1991; (ed jtly) Anselm: Aosta, Bec and Canterbury, 1996; Medieval Thought, 1997 (trans. Portuguese, 2000, Greek, 2007); The Twelfth-Century Renaissance: monks, scholars and the shaping of the European mind, (in Japanese) 2000; (ed jtly) Peter Abelard, Expositio in Hexameron, 2004; (ed jtly) The New Cambridge Medieval History, vol. 4, *c* 1024–*c* 1198, parts 1 and 2, 2004; (ed jtly) Peter Abelard, Sententie, 2006; articles in learned jls. *Recreations:* grandchildren, walking, using libraries. *Address:* 28 Endcliffe Hall Avenue, Sheffield S10 3EL. *T:* (0114) 222 2555.

LUSCOMBE, Rt Rev. Lawrence Edward; Bishop of Brechin, 1975–90; Primus of the Episcopal Church in Scotland, 1985–90; *b* 10 Nov. 1924; *s* of Reginald John and Winifred Luscombe; *m* 1946, Doris Carswell Morgan, BSc, MB, ChB (*d* 1992); one *d*. *Educ:* Torquay Grammar Sch.; Kelham Theological Coll.; King's Coll., London; MA, MPhil 1991, PhD 1993, Dundee. CA 1952, ASAA 1957. FSAScot 1980. Served Indian Army, 1942–47, Major. Partner, Galbraith, Dunlop & Co., Chartered Accountants, Glasgow, 1952–63. Ordained deacon, 1963; priest, 1964; Curate, St Margaret's, Glasgow, 1963–66; Rector, St Barnabas', Paisley, 1966–71; Provost of St Paul's Cathedral, Dundee, 1971–75. Hon. Canon, Trinity Cathedral, Davenport, Iowa, 1983. A Trustee, Scottish Episcopal Ch, 1985–. Hon. Res. Fellow, Dundee Univ., 1993–. Chm. of Council, Glenalmond Coll., 1987–94. FRSA 1987. Hon. DLitt Geneva Theological Coll., 1972; Hon. LLD Dundee, 1987. OStJ 1986; ChStJ 1996. *Publications:* Matthew Luscombe, Missionary Bishop, 1992; A Seminary of Learning, 1994; The Scottish Episcopal Church in the 20th Century, 1996; Episcopacy in an Angus Glen, 2003; Steps into Freedom, 2004; Hands Across the Sea, 2006. *Address:* Woodville, Kirkton of Tealing, by Dundee DD4 0RD. *T:* (01382) 380331.

LUSH, Christopher Duncan, CMG 1983; HM Diplomatic Service, retired; Governor, British Institute of Human Rights, since 1988; Editor, Human Rights Case Digest, since 1989; *b* 4 June 1928; *s* of late Eric Duncan Thomas Lush and Iris Leonora (*née* Greenfield); *m* 1967, Marguerite Lilian (*d* 2005), *d* of Frederick Albert Bolden; one *s*. *Educ:* Sedbergh; Magdalen Coll., Oxford. Called to Bar, Gray's Inn, 1953. Asst Legal Adviser, FO, 1959–62; Legal Adviser, Berlin, 1962–65, Dep. Political Adviser, Berlin, 1965–66; FO (later FCO), 1966–69; Head of Chancery, Amman, 1969–71; Head of Aviation and Telecommunications Dept, FCO, 1971–73; Canadian Nat. Defence Coll., 1973–74; Counsellor, Paris, 1974–78; Counsellor, Vienna, 1978–82; Ambassador and UK Perm. Rep. to Council of Europe, Strasbourg, 1983–86. Médaille de Vermeil, Société d'Encouragement au Progrès, 1978. *Publications:* articles in Internat. and Compar. Law Qly, Connoisseur. *Address:* 53 Cheyne Court, Royal Hospital Road, SW3 5TS. *Clubs:* Travellers, Chelsea Arts.

LUSH, Denzil Anton; His Honour Judge Lush; Senior Judge (formerly Master) of the Court of Protection, since 1996; *b* 18 July 1951; *s* of Dennis John Lush, MBE and late Hazel June Lush (*née* Fishenden). *Educ:* Devonport High Sch., Plymouth; University Coll. London (BA, MA); Corpus Christi Coll., Cambridge (LLM); Coll. of Law, Guildford. Admitted Solicitor, England and Wales, 1978; in private practice, 1978–96; admitted Solicitor and Notary Public, Scotland, 1993. Chm., Social Security Appeals Tribunals, 1994–96. Member: Law Soc. Mental Health and Disability Sub-Cttee, 1993–96; BMA Steering Gp on advance statements about medical treatment, 1994. Trustee, Pan-European Org. of Personal Injury Lawyers Foundn, 2003–06; Patron, Solicitors for the Elderly, 2003–. Lay Reader, 1982–98. FRSocMed 2001. *Publications:* Cohabitation and Co-Ownership Precedents, 1993; Elderly Clients: a precedent manual, 1996; (with Stephen Cretney) Enduring Powers of Attorney, 4th edn 1996, 5th edn, as Cretney & Lush on Enduring Powers of Attorney, 2001; numerous contribs to legal publications. *Recreations:* supporting Plymouth Argyle FC, collecting commemorative china. *Address:* The Court of Protection, Archway Tower, 2 Junction Road, N19 5SZ. *T:* (020) 7664 7000; *e-mail:* denzil.lush@publicguardian.gsi.gov.uk. *Club:* Athenæum.

LUSH, Ian Frank; Chief Executive, Architectural Heritage Fund, since 2003; *b* 13 July 1960; *s* of Cecil and Dolly Lush; *m* 1st, 1985, Margaret Clare Hindle (marr. diss. 2002); one *d*; 2nd, 2005, Ceri-Louise Hunter; one *s*. *Educ:* King Alfred Sch., Hampstead; Univ. of York (BA Hons (Music) 1981, MA (Music) 1982); City Univ., London (Dip. Arts Admin 1986). ARCM 1982. Co-Principal Viola, Iceland SO, 1982–83; rank and file Viola, Royal Liverpool Philharmonic Orch., 1983–85; Mktg Manager, Philharmonia Orch., 1986–87; Barbican Centre: Mktg and Promotions Manager, 1987–91; Mktg Dir, 1991–93; Hd of Mktg, LSO, 1993–95; Man. Dir, London Mozart Players, 1995–2003. Dep. Chm., Heritage Link, 2006–; Director: Croydon Marketing and Development Ltd, 1996–2001; Croydon Partnership, 1997–2001; Innovative Enterprise Action, 2006–. FRSA. *Publications:* more than 120 concert progs and CD sleeve notes. *Recreations:* sport (especially fanatical devotion to Chelsea Football Club), playing tennis, theatre, cinema and concert going, urban and rural walking. *Address:* Architectural Heritage Fund, Alhambra House, 27–31 Charing Cross Road, WC2H 0AU. *T:* (020) 7925 0199, *Fax:* (020) 7930 0295; *e-mail:* ian.lush@ahfund.org.uk.

LUSH, Jane Elaine; Joint Managing Director, Splash Media, since 2005; *b* 10 Aug. 1952; *d* of Sidney and Rebecca Lush; *m* 1974, Peter Tenenbaum, landscape designer; one *s* one *d*. *Educ:* Camden Sch. for Girls. Joined BBC as trainee, 1970; BBC Television: Exec. Prod., Features Dept, 1989–90; Ed., Holiday, Commissioning Exec., Have I Got News For You, 1990; Dep. Hd, Features, 1995–2000; Controller: Daytime Television, 1998–2001; Entertainment Commissioning, 2002–05. *Recreations:* my children, family, friends, reading, holidays, Tottenham Hotspur. *Address:* *e-mail:* janelush@splashmediatv.co.uk.

LUSHINGTON, Sir John (Richard Castleman), 8th Bt *cr* 1791, of South Hill Park, Berkshire; *b* 28 Aug. 1938; *s* of Sir Henry Edmund Castleman Lushington, 7th Bt and Pamela Elizabeth Daphne, *er d* of Major Archer Richard Hunter; *S* father, 1988; *m* 1966, Bridget Gillian Margaret, *d* of late Colonel John Foster Longfield; three *s*. *Educ:* Oundle. *Heir:* *s* Richard Douglas Longfield Lushington, BA, Wing Comdr RAF [*b* 29 March 1968; *m* 1st, 2001, Christianne Jane Tipping, Flight Lieut RAF (marr. diss. 2004); 2nd, 2006, Sarah Alice Butler; one *d*]. *Address:* Kent House, Barrington, Ilminster, Somerset TA19 0JP.

LUSK, (Ormond) Felicity (Stewart); Headmistress, Oxford High School, since 1997; *b* 25 Nov. 1955; *d* of Harold Stewart Lusk, QC (NZ), and Janet Kiwi Lusk; *m* 1976 (marr. diss. 1996); two *s*. *Educ:* Marsden Coll., Wellington, NZ; Victoria Univ. (BMus); Massey Univ. (DipEd); Christchurch Teachers' Coll. (Dip Teaching); Univ. of York (Cert. Mus.

Educn). Head of Music Department: Wellington E Girls' Coll., NZ, 1980–86; Aotea Coll., NZ, 1986–89; Hasmonean High School, London: Sen. Teacher and Head of Music Dept, 1990–93; Dep. Headteacher, 1993–96. Woolf Fisher Fellowship, NZ, 1985. Councillor, London Borough of Enfield, 1990–94. Member: SHA, 1993–; GSA, 1997–. Mem. Court, Oxford Brookes Univ., 1999–; Gov., GSMD, 2000–. Mem., Adv. Council, Oxford Philomusica, 2002–. *Recreations:* reading, conversation, travel. *Address:* Oxford High School, Belbroughton Road, Oxford OX2 6XA. *T:* (01865) 559888.

LÜST, Prof. Reimar; President, Alexander von Humboldt Foundation, Bonn, 1989–99, now Hon. President; Director General, European Space Agency, 1984–90; *b* 23 March 1923; *s* of Hero Lüst and Grete (*née* Strunck); *m* 1986, Nina Grunenberg; two *s* by a previous marriage. *Educ:* Univ. of Frankfurt; Univ. of Göttingen (Dr rer. nat.). Max-Planck-Institut of Physics: Staff Scientist, 1950–60; Head of Astrophysics Dept, 1960–63; Dir, Max-Planck-Institut of Extraterrestrial Physics, 1963–72; Pres., Max-Planck-Gesellschaft zur Förderung der Wissenschaften, 1972–84. Vis. Prof., Univs of Princeton, Chicago, New York, MIT, CIT, 1955–63; Hon. Prof., Technical Univ. of Munich, 1965; Hon. Prof., Univ. of Hamburg, 1992. Chm., German Science Council, 1969–72. Chm., Bd of Govs, Internat. Univ., Bremen, 1999–2004, Hon. Chm., 2005–. Mem. and Hon. Mem. of eight academies. Dr *hc:* Sofia, 1991; Birmingham 1993. Planet No 4386 named Lüst, 1991. Adenauer-de Gaulle Prize, 1994. Grand Cross, Order of Merit (FRG), 1984; Officier, Légion d'Honneur (France), 1984; Grand Cross of Merit with Star and Shoulderblade (FRG), 1990. *Publications:* Hydrodynamik, 1955; articles in scientific jls. *Recreations:* tennis, history, ski-ing. *Address:* Max-Planck-Institute of Meteorology, Bundesstrasse 53, 20146 Hamburg, Germany. *T:* (40) 41173300.

LUSTIG, Robin Francis; Presenter, The World Tonight, BBC Radio 4, since 1989; *b* 30 Aug. 1948; *s* of Fritz Lustig and Susan (*née* Cohn); *m* 1980, Ruth Kelsey; one *s* one *d*. *Educ:* Univ. of Sussex (BA Politics). With Reuters, 1970–77: Madrid, 1971–72; Paris, 1972–73; Rome, 1973–77; The Observer, 1977–89: reporter, 1977–81; News Ed., 1981–85; ME Corresp., 1985–87; Home Affairs Ed., 1987–88; Asst Ed., 1988–89; joined BBC, 1989; progs on Radio 4 and World Service. *Address:* c/o BBC, News Centre, Wood Lane, W12 7RJ. *T:* (020) 8624 9777.

LUSZTIG, Prof. George, PhD; FRS 1983; Professor of Mathematics, Massachusetts Institute of Technology, Cambridge, USA, since 1978; *b* 20 May 1946; *s* of Akos and Erzsébet Lusztig; *m* (marr. diss.); two *d*. *Educ:* Univ. of Bucharest, Rumania; Princeton Univ. (MA, PhD). Asst, Univ. of Timisoara, Rumania, 1969; Mem., Inst. for Advanced Study Princeton, 1969–71; Univ. of Warwick: Res. Fellow, 1971–72; Lectr in Maths, 1972–74; Prof. of Maths, 1974–78. Mem., US Nat. Acad. of Scis, 1992. *Publications:* The Discrete Series of GL_n over a Finite Field, 1974; and Characters of Reductive Groups over a Finite Field, 1984; Introduction to Quantum Groups, 1993. *Address:* 106 Grant Avenue, Newton, MA 02459, USA. *T:* (617) 9648579.

LUTHER, Anne Margaret, (Mrs A. N. Brearley-Smith); Director General, Action Research, 1990–2001; *b* 19 Jan. 1946; *d* of Dermot William Richard O'Leary and Eva Margaret (*née* Christie); *m* 1st, 1969, Philip John Luther (marr. diss. 1988); two *d*; 2nd, 1992, Andrew Neville Brearley-Smith. *Educ:* Ursuline Convent, Ilford; Chelsea Coll., London (BSc 1967). King's Fund Trainee, 1967–69; PA to House Governor, Westminster Hosp., 1969–71; Dir of Res., Action Research, 1982–90. Association of Medical Research Charities: Hon. Sec., 1982–87; Mem., Exec. Council, 1991–95. Mem., Prince of Wales Adv. Gp on Disability, 1990–95. Trustee, Common Investment Funds for Charities, 1991–98. Mem., Ashridge Mgt Coll. Assoc., 1984–2001. MInstD 1994. FRSocMed. *Recreations:* music, watercolours, theatre, cookery. *Club:* Royal Society of Medicine.

LUTHER, Rt Rev. Arthur William; retired; *b* 21 March 1919; *s* of William and Monica Luther; *m* 1946, Dr Kamal Luther; one *s* two *d*. *Educ:* Nagpur University; India (MA, BT); General Theological Seminary, New York (STD 1957). Deacon, 1943; Priest, 1944; in USA and Scotland for study and parish work, 1952–54; Chaplain to Bishop of Nagpur, 1954; Head Master, Bishop Cotton School, Nagpur, 1954–57; Bishop of Nasik, 1957–70; Bishop of Bombay, 1970–73; held charge of Kolhapur Diocese concurrently with Bombay Diocese, Dec. 1970–Feb. 1972; Bishop, Church of North India, and Reg. Sec. of the Leprosy Mission, 1973–80; Promotional Sec., 1980–84. *Address:* Shripad-B, Flat 1, 60 Tulshibagwale Colony, Lane 3, Sahakar Nagar 2, Pune 411009, Maharashtra, India. *T:* 24222576.

LUTON, Jean-Marie; Officier de la Légion d'Honneur; Commandeur de l'Ordre National du Mérite; Chairman, Arianespace, 2002–07 (Chief Executive Officer, 1997–2002); Chief Executive Officer, Starsem, 2002–06; *b* Chamalières, 4 Aug. 1942; *m* 1967, Cécile Robine; three *s*. *Educ:* Ecole Polytechnique. Centre National de la Recherche Scientifique: researcher, 1964–71; Chargé de Recherches, 1971–74; Chargé de Mission, Service des Programmes des Organismes de Recherche, Min. for Industrial and Scientific Develt, 1971–73; Centre National d'Etudes Spatiales: Hd, Res. Progs Div., Progs and Indust. Policy Directorate, 1974–75; Hd, Planning and Projs Div., Progs and Indust. Policy Directorate, 1975–78; Dir, Progs and Planning, 1978–84; Dep. Dir. Gen., 1984–87; Dir for Space Progs, Space Systems Div., Aérospatiale, 1987–89; Director General: Centre National d'Etudes Spatiales, 1989–90; ESA, 1990–97. Mem., Internat. Acad. of Astronautics, 1986–. Astronautics Prize, French Assoc. for Aeronautics and Astronautics, 1985. *Recreations:* tennis, sailing. *Address:* c/o Arianespace, boulevard de l'Europe, 91006 Evry, France.

LUTZ, Marianne Christine, (Mrs C. A. Whittington-Smith); Headmistress, Sheffield High School for Girls (Girls' Public Day School Trust), 1959–83; *b* 9 Dec. 1922; *d* of Dr H. Lutz; *m* 1981, Charles Alexander Whittington-Smith, LLM, FCA (*d* 1997). *Educ:* Wimbledon High Sch., GPDST; Girton Coll., Cambridge (Schol.; MA Historical Tripos); University of London (DipEd, DipTh). Asst Mistress (History) at: Clergy Daughters' Sch., Bristol, 1946–47; South Hampstead High Sch., GPDST, 1947–59. Former Member: History Textbooks Panel for W Germany (under auspices of FO and Unesco); Professional Cttee, Univ. of Sheffield; Historical Assoc.; Secondary Heads' Assoc.; Schnauzer Club of Great Britain. *Publications:* several in connection with Unesco work and Historical Assoc. *Recreations:* crosswords, opera, art, theatre. *Address:* Evona, Hydro Close, Baslow, Bakewell, Derbyshire DE45 1SH. *T:* (01246) 582152.

LUXMOORE, Rt Rev. Christopher Charles; Bishop of Bermuda, 1984–89; Assistant Bishop of Chichester and Canon Emeritus of Chichester Cathedral, since 1991; *b* 9 April 1926; *s* of Rev. William Cyril Luxmoore and Constance Evelyn Luxmoore; *m* 1955, Judith, *d* of late Canon Verney Johnstone; four *s* one *d*. *Educ:* Sedbergh School, Yorks; Trinity Coll., Cambridge; Chichester Theol Coll. Deacon 1952, priest 1953; Asst Curate, St John the Baptist, Newcastle upon Tyne, 1952–55; Priest-in-Charge, St Bede's Ecclesiastical Dist, Newsham, 1955–57; Vicar of Newsham, 1957–58; Rector of Sangre Grande, Trinidad, 1958–66; Vicar of Headingley, Leeds, 1967–81; Proctor in Convocation and Mem. Gen. Synod, 1975–81; Hon. Canon of Ripon Cathedral, 1980–81; Precentor and Canon Residentiary of Chichester Cathedral, 1981–84; Dean of Bermuda Cathedral, 1984–89; Archdeacon of Lewes and Hastings, 1989–91. Commissary for Bishop of Trinidad and Tobago, 1968–84. Provost, Woodard Schools Southern Div., 1989–96. *Recreations:* opera, church history. *Address:* 42 Willowbed Drive, Chichester, W Sussex PO19 8JB. *T:* (01243) 784680.

LUXON, Benjamin Matthew, CBE 1986; FGSM; narrator and performer; *b* Camborne, Cornwall, 1937; US citizen, 2002; *m* 1969, Sheila Amit; two *s* one *d*; *m* 2002, Susan Crofut. *Educ:* Truro Sch.; Westminster Trng Coll.; Guildhall Sch. of Music. Teacher of Physical Education until becoming professional singer (baritone), 1963; due to severe hearing loss in 1996, eventually finished career as a professional singer. Repertoire included lieder, folk music, Victorian songs and duets, oratorio (Russian, French and English song), and operatic rôles at major opera houses at home and abroad. Major rôles included: Eugene Onegin, Don Giovanni, Wozzeck, Papageno, Julius Caesar, Posa, Gianni Schicchi, Falstaff. Numerous recordings. Appointed Bard of the Cornish Gorsedd, 1974. Third prize, Munich Internat. Festival, 1961; Gold Medal GSM, 1963. FGSM 1970; Hon. RAM, 1980; Hon. DMus: Exeter, 1980; RSAMD, 1996; Canterbury Christ Church Coll., 1997. *Recreations:* collecting English water-colours and drawings; tennis, swimming.

LUZIO, Prof. (John) Paul, PhD; FRCPath; FMedSci; Professor of Molecular Membrane Biology, since 2001, and Director, Cambridge Institute for Medical Research, since 2002, University of Cambridge; Master, St Edmund's College, Cambridge, since 2004 (Fellow, 1987–2004); *b* 15 Aug. 1947; *s* of (Fadri Gian) John Luzio and Brenda Luzio (*née* Barnwell); *m* 1st, 1977, Alison Turner (*née* Ford) (marr. diss. 1981); one *s*; 2nd, 1986, Toni Copeland (*née* Stanton) (marr. diss. 1991); 3rd, 1992, Jane Edson (*née* Geering). *Educ:* Shene Grammar Sch., London; Clare Coll., Cambridge (BA 1968; PhD 1974). MRCPath 1991, FRCPath 1998; FIBiol 2004. Lectr, Dept of Med. Biochem. (Chem. Pathol.), Welsh Nat. Sch. of Medicine, 1974–77; University of Cambridge: Sen. Res. Associate, Dept of Clin. Biochem., 1977–79; Lectr in Clinical Biochem., 1979–96; Reader in Molecular Membrane Biol., 1996–2001; Sen. Tutor, St Edmund's Coll., 1991–96. FMedSci 1999; ILTM 2002. Foundn Award, Assoc. of Clinical Biochemists, 2005. *Publications:* contribs to professional jls in biochem. and molecular cell biology. *Recreations:* gardening, fishing. *Address:* St Edmund's College, Cambridge CB3 0BN. *T:* (office) (01223) 336780; Pippin Meadow, Lowfields, Little Eversden, Cambridge CB3 7HJ; *e-mail:* jpl10@cam.ac.uk.

LUZZATTO, Prof. Lucio, MD; FRCP, FRCPath; Scientific Director, Istituto Toscano Tumori, Italy, since 2005; Professor of Haematology, University of Firenze, since 2006; *b* 28 Sept. 1936; *s* of Aldo and Anna Luzzatto; *m* 1963, Paola Caboara; one *s* one *d*. *Educ:* Genoa Univ. (MD 1959); Pavia Univ. (Spec. Haematology 1962); Lib. Doc. Italy, 1965. FRCPath 1982; FRCP 1983. Research Fellow in Haematology, Columbia Univ., 1963–64; Lectr, then Prof. of Haematology, Univ. of Ibadan, 1964–74; Dir, Internat. Inst. of Genetics and Biophysics, Naples, 1974–81; Prof. of Haematology, RPMS, 1981–94; Hon. Dir., MRC Leukaemia Res. Fund's Leukaemia Unit, 1987–93; Chm., Dept of Human Genetics, Meml Sloan-Kettering Cancer Center, NY, 1994–2000; Scientific Dir, Nat. Inst. for Cancer Res., Italy, 2000–04; Prof. of Haematology, Univ. of Genoa, 2002–06. Hon. DSc Ibadan, 1998; Hon. MD Patras, 2006. Pius XI Medal, 1976; Laurea ad hon., Univ. of Urbino, 1990; Chiron award, Italian Acad. of Medicine, 1995. *Publications:* numerous contribs to learned jls. *Address:* c/o Istituto Toscano Tumori, Via T. Alderotti 26N, 50139 Firenze, Italy. *T:* (055) 4385213; *e-mail:* lucio.luzzatto@ittumori.it.

LYALL, Andrew Gardiner, CMG 1976; Under Secretary, Department of Transport, 1981–86, retired; *b* 21 Dec. 1929; *s* of late William and Helen Lyall (*née* Gardiner); *m* 1953, Olive Leslie Gennoe White; one *s* one *d*. *Educ:* Kirkcaldy High Sch. Joined MoT, 1951; Asst Shipping Attaché, British Embassy, Washington, DC, 1961–64; Principal, Nationalised Industry Finance and Urban Transport Planning, 1965–70; Asst Sec., Railways Div., 1970–72; seconded to FCO as Counsellor, UK Representation to European Communities, 1972–75; Assistant Secretary: Land Use Planning, DoE, 1975–76; Central Unit on Environmental Pollution, 1976–77; Under Sec., PSA, 1978–81. *Recreations:* photography, travel, walking, countryside conservation. *Address:* 5 Barrowfield, Cuckfield, Haywards Heath, West Sussex RH17 5ER. *T:* (01444) 454606. *Club:* Civil Service.

LYALL, John Adrian; Managing Director, John Lyall Architects Ltd, since 1991; *b* 12 Dec. 1949; *s* of Keith Lyall and Phyllis Lyall; *m* 1991, Sallie Jean Davies; one *s* one *d*. *Educ:* Southend High Sch. for Boys; Architectural Association Sch. of Architecture, London. RIBA 1980. Partner, Alsop & Lyall, 1980–91. Major completed projects include: Leeds Corn Exchange, 1990; Cardiff Bay Visitor Centre, 1992; White Cloth Hall, Leeds, 1992; Tottenham Hale Station, 1992; N Greenwich Jubilee Line Station, 1999; Crystal Palace Park, 2000; Hammersmith Pumping Station, 2007; projects under construction: Cranfields Mill Develt, Ipswich; Dance East, Ipswich; Goldsmiths Centre, Clerkenwell; Pudding Mill Pumping Station; New World Square, Liverpool. Member: Design Panel, Cardiff Bay Develt Corp., 1989–95; Nat. Design Adv. Panel, English Partnerships, 1998–2005; Nat. Design Adv. Panel, CABE, 2007– (Enabler, 2002–). Sir Bannister Fletcher Vis. Prof., UCL, 1998. Vice Pres., RIBA, 1997, 1999; Vice Chm., RIBA Trust, 2004–; Council Mem., AA, 2005–. FRSA. *Publications:* (with W. Alsop) Architecture Projects & Drawings, 1984; (jtly) John Lyall: contexts and catalysts, 1999; contrib. Architecture Today, RIBA Jl, Architects Jl and Building Design. *Recreations:* choral singing, gardening, fruit trees. *Address:* John Lyall Architects, 13–19 Curtain Road, EC2A 3LT. *T:* (020) 7375 3324, *Fax:* (020) 7375 3325; *e-mail:* john.lyall@johnlyallarchitects.com. *Club:* Chelsea Arts.

LYALL, Katharine Elizabeth; *see* Whitehorn, K.

LYALL GRANT, Maj.-Gen. Ian Hallam, MC 1944; Director General, Supply Co-ordination, Ministry of Defence, 1970–75; retired; *b* 4 June 1915; *s* of Col H. F. Lyall Grant, DSO and Lucy Ellinor (*née* Hardy); *m* 1951, Mary Jennifer Moore (*d* 2007); one *s* two *d*. *Educ:* Cheltenham Coll.; RMA, Woolwich; Gonville and Caius Coll., Cambridge (MA). CEng, MICE 1968; FGA 1978. Regular Commission, RE, 1935; service in: India, Burma and Japan, 1938–46 (MC; twice mentioned in despatches); Cyprus and Egypt, 1951–52; CO 131 Para Engr Regt (TA), 1954–56; Instructor, JSSC, 1957–58; Imperial Defence Coll., 1961; Aden, 1962–63; Comdt, Royal School of Mil. Engineering, 1965–67; Maj.-Gen. 1966; Dep. QMG, 1967–70, retired 1970. Col Comdt, RE, 1972–77. President: Bengal Sappers Officers' Assoc., 1987–95; Burma Campaign Fellowship Gp, 1996–2002 (Chm., 1991–96). *Publications:* Burma: the turning point, 1993; (with Kazuo Tamayama) Burma 1942: the Japanese Invasion, 1999. *Recreations:* travel, flyfishing, paintings, gemmology. *Address:* 6 St Martin's Square, Chichester, W Sussex PO19 1NT. *T:* (01243) 784214. *Club:* Naval and Military.

See also Sir M. J. Lyall Grant.

LYALL GRANT, Sir Mark (Justin), KCMG 2006 (CMG 2003); HM Diplomatic Service; Political Director, Foreign and Commonwealth Office, since 2007; *b* 29 May 1956; *s* of Maj.-Gen. I. H. Lyall Grant, *qv*; *m* 1986, Sheila Jean Tresise; one *s* one *d*. *Educ:*

Eton; Trinity Coll., Cambridge (MA Law). Called to the Bar, Middle Temple, 1980; joined FCO, 1980; Second Sec., Islamabad, 1982–85; FCO, 1985–87; Private Sec. to Minister of State, FCO, 1987–89; First Sec., Paris, 1990–93; FCO 1993; seconded to European Secretariat, Cabinet Office, 1994–96; Dep. High Comr and Consul Gen., S Africa, 1996–98; Hd, EU Dept (Internal), FCO, 1998–2000; Dir, Africa, FCO, 2000–03; High Comr to Pakistan, 2003–06. *Recreations:* golf, tennis, sailing, bridge. *Address:* c/o Foreign and Commonwealth Office, SW1A 2AH. *Club:* Royal Automobile.

LYCETT GREEN, Candida; writer; *b* 22 Sept. 1942; *d* of Sir John Betjeman, CBE and Penelope, *d* of Field Marshal Lord Chetwode, GCB, OM, GCSI; *m* 1963, Rupert Lycett Green; two *s* three *d.* *Educ:* St Mary's, Wantage. TV documentary films: The Front Garden, 1979; The English Woman and the Horse, 1981; A Cottage in the Country, 1983. Mem., Historic Bldgs and Monuments Commn for England (English Heritage), 1992–2001. Mem., PRS. *Publications:* Hadrian the Hedgehog, 1969; Hadrian in the Orient, 1971; (with Christopher Booker) Goodbye London, 1972; The Front Garden, 1974; English Cottages, 1984; Brilliant Gardens, 1989; The Perfect English Country House, 1991; John Betjeman: Letters, Vol. I, 1994, Vol. II, 1995; England: travels through an unwrecked landscape, 1996; (ed) Coming Home: an anthology of prose by John Betjeman, 1997; (ed) Betjeman's Britain, an anthology of prose and verse, 1999; Country Life's 100 Favourite Houses, 1999; (with HRH Prince of Wales) The Garden at Highgrove, 2000; Over the Hills and Far Away, 2002; The Dangerous Edge of Things, 2005. *Recreation:* touring England by horse. *Address:* c/o Aitken Alexander Associates, 18–21 Cavaye Place, SW10 9PT.

See also Sir E. P. L. Green, Bt.

LYDDON, (William) Derek (Collier), CB 1984; Chief Planning Officer, Scottish Development Department, 1967–85; *b* 17 Nov. 1925; *s* of late A. J. Lyddon, CBE, and E. E. Lyddon; *m* 1949, Marian Louise Kaye Charlesworth, *d* of late Prof. J. K. Charlesworth, CBE; two *d.* *Educ:* Wrekin Coll.; University Coll., London. BA (Arch.) 1952; ARIBA 1953; DipTP 1954; AMTPI 1963; FRTPI 1973. Depute Chief Architect and Planning Officer, Cumbernauld Development Corp., 1962; Chief Architect and Planning Officer, Skelmersdale Development Corp., 1963–67. Gov., Edinburgh Coll. of Art, 1988–96; Chm., Planning Exchange, 1991–96 (Vice-Chm., 1984–88); Vice-Chairman: Edinburgh Old Town Renewal Trust, 1991–99; Edinburgh World Heritage Trust, 1999–2004. Pres., Internat. Soc. of City and Regional Planners, 1981–84. Hon. Prof., Heriot-Watt Univ., 1986; Vis. Prof., Strathclyde Univ., 1986–89. FRSGS 1996. Hon. Fellow: Univ. of Edinburgh, 1986–89; Duncan Jordanstone Coll. of Art, Dundee, 1986–. Hon. DLitt Heriot-Watt, 1981. *Recreations:* walking, reading. *Address:* 31 Blackford Road, Edinburgh EH9 2DT. *T:* (0131) 667 2266.

LYDIARD, Andrew John; QC 2003; *b* 25 Aug. 1957; *s* of George Frederick Lydiard and Beryl Lydiard (*née* Taylor); *m* 1983, Mary Adair; two *s.* *Educ:* King's Sch., Chester; University Coll., Oxford (BA); Harvard Law Sch. (LLM). Called to the Bar, Inner Temple, 1980; Tutor in Law (pt-time), Pembroke Coll., Oxford, 1982–87. *Address:* Brick Court Chambers, 7–8 Essex Street, WC2R 3LD. *T:* (020) 7379 3550, *Fax:* (020) 7379 3558; *e-mail:* andrew.lydiard@brickcourt.co.uk.

LYE, David William Frederick; Senior Civil Servant, Department of Health, since 2004; *b* 13 Jan. 1958; *s* of Frederick Hayle Lye and Barbara Criddle Lye; partner, Jacqueline Helen Warwick Karas. *Educ:* Radley Coll.; Lincoln Coll., Oxford (BA Hons Modern Hist. 1979). Joined Civil Service, 1985; Hd, NHS Trusts Unit, DoH, 1991–93; Dir, Performance Mgt, NHS W Midlands, 1993–98; Project Dir, Children and Family Court Adv. and Support Service, 1999–2001; Chief Exec., Public Guardianship Office, 2001–04. *Publications:* contrib. articles to various NHS-related jls. *Recreations:* travel, cookery, armchair sports. *Address:* Department of Health, New Kings Beam House, 22 Upper Ground, SE1 9BW. *T:* (020) 7972 4123; *e-mail:* david.lye@doh.gsi.gov.uk; 6 Clock Tower Mews, N1 7BB.

LYELL, family name of **Barons Lyell** and **Lyell of Markyate**.

LYELL, 3rd Baron *cr* 1914, of Kinnordy; **Charles Lyell;** DL; Bt 1894; *b* 27 March 1939; *s* of 2nd Baron, VC (killed in action, 1943), and Sophie, *d* of Major S. W. and Lady Betty Trafford; *S* father, 1943. *Educ:* Eton; Christ Church, Oxford. 2nd Lieut Scots Guards, 1957–59. CA Scotland. An Opposition Whip, 1974–79; a Lord in Waiting (Govt Whip), 1979–84; Parly Under-Sec. of State, NI Office, 1984–89; elected Mem., H of L, 1999. Mem., Queen's Body Guard for Scotland (Royal Company of Archers). DL Angus, 1988. *Heir:* none. *Address:* Kinnordy House, Kirriemuir, Angus DD8 5ER. *T:* (01575) 572848. *Clubs:* Turf, White's.

LYELL OF MARKYATE, Baron *cr* 2005 (Life Peer), of Markyate, in the county of Hertfordshire; **Nicholas Walter Lyell,** Kt 1987; PC 1990; QC 1980; barrister; *b* 6 Dec. 1938; *s* of late Sir Maurice Legat Lyell and Veronica Mary Lyell; *m* 1967, Susanna Mary Fletcher; two *s* two *d.* *Educ:* Stowe Sch.; Christ Church, Oxford (MA Hons Mod. Hist.). National Service, commnd Royal Artillery, 1957–59; Walter Runciman & Co., 1962–64; called to the Bar, Inner Temple, 1965, Bencher, 1986; private practice, London (Commercial and Public Law), 1965–86, 1997–; a Recorder, 1985–86 and 1997–2002. MP (C): Hemel Hempstead, 1979–83; Mid Bedfordshire, 1983–97; NE Bedfordshire, 1997–2001. Jt Sec., Constitutional Cttee, 1979; PPS to the Attorney General, 1979–86; Parly Under-Sec. of State (Social Security), DHSS, 1986–87; Solicitor General, 1987–92; Attorney General, 1992–97. Chm., Soc. of Cons. Lawyers, 1985–86, 2001–. Vice-Chm., BFSS, 1983–86. Governor, Stowe Sch., 1990– (Chm., 2001–). *Recreations:* gardening, shooting, drawing. *Address:* House of Lords, SW1A 0PW. *Clubs:* Brooks's, Pratt's, Beefsteak.

LYGO, Kevin Antony; Director of Television and Content, Channel 4, since 2007 (Director of Television, 2003–07); *b* 19 Sept. 1957; *s* of Adm. Sir Raymond Derek Lygo, *qv*; *m* 1999, Suzy Solomon; one *d*, and one step *s.* *Educ:* Cranbrook Sch.; Durham Univ. (BA Psychol.). BBC TV: comedy scriptwriter, 1981–83; gen. trainee, 1983–85; Producer, Omnibus, Wogan, 1985–96; Head of Indep. Commng Gp, 1996–97; Head of Entertainment, C4, and Controller, E4, 1998–2001; Dir of Progs, Five (formerly Channel Five TV), 2001–03. *Recreations:* Islamic art, Tibetan culture, tennis. *Address:* Channel 4 Television, 124 Horseferry Road, SW1P 2TX.

LYGO, Adm. Sir Raymond (Derek), KCB 1977; aerospace, defence and industrial consultant; *b* 15 March 1924; *s* of late Edwin T. Lygo and of Ada E. Lygo; *m* 1950, Pepper Van Osten (*d* 2004), USA; two *s* one *d.* *Educ:* Valentine's Sch., Ilford; Ilford County High Sch.; Clark's Coll., Bromley. The Times, 1940; Naval Airman, RN, 1942; Naval Pilot, 1943; CO, HMS Ark Royal, 1969–71; Vice Chief of Naval Staff, 1975–78 and Chief of Naval Staff, 1978. British Aerospace: Man. Dir, Hatfield/Lostock Div., 1978–79, Group Dep. Chm., 1980; Bd Mem., 1980–89; Chm. and Chief Exec., Dynamics Gp, 1980–82; Man. Dir, 1983–86; Chief Exec., 1986–89; Chairman: BAe Inc., 1983–88; Royal Ordnance, 1987–88; BAe Enterprises Ltd, BAe (Space Systems) Ltd, BAe Hldgs Inc., 1988–89; TNT Europe Ltd and TNT Express (UK), 1992–97; Rutland Trust PLC, 1992–99; River and Mercantile First UK Investment Trust, then Liontrust, 1997–2004; Mem., Supervisory Bd, Airbus Industrie, 1987–89. Director: James Capel Corporate Finance, 1990–92; LET, 1990–92. Dir, CBI Educn Foundn, 1985–92; Member: Council, Industrial Soc., 1985–2001; NEDC, 1989–91; Council, Foundn for Management Educn, 1992–2004. Conducted review of the management of prison service, 1991. Appeal Pres., SENSE (Nat. Deaf-Blind & Rubella Assoc.), 1983–2001; Appeal Chm., Industrial Soc., 1989–91; Dir, Southern Counties, Prince's Youth Business Trust, 1993–97; Patron, Youth Sports Trust, 1996–. Pres., FAA Officers Assoc., 1990–; Patron, Nat. FAA Assoc., 1989–. Pres., St Vincent Assoc. Freeman, City of London, 1985; Liveryman: Coachmakers' and Coach Harness Makers' Co., 1986–; Shipwrights' Co., 1988–. Life Mem., Royal Soc. of St George, 1984. FRSA; MInstD; CCMI. Hon. FRAeS; Hon. Fellow, Univ. of Westminster (formerly Poly. of Central London), 1989. *Publication:* Collision Course, 2002. *Recreations:* flying, building, gardening, joinery. *Address:* c/o Barclays Premier Banking, 1 Churchill Place, E14 5HP. *Clubs:* City Livery (Pres., 1996–97), Ambassadeurs; Royal Naval and Royal Albert Yacht (Portsmouth).

See also K. A. Lygo.

LYLE, Alexander Walter Barr, (Sandy), MBE 1987; professional golfer, since 1977; *b* 9 Feb. 1958; *s* of late Alex and Agnes Lyle; *m* (marr. diss.); two *s*; *m* 1989, Brigitte Jolande Huurman; one *s* one *d.* *Educ:* Shrewsbury local sch. Rookie of the Year, 1978; 1st in European order of merit, 1979, 1980, 1985; Open Champion, Royal St George's, 1985; won US Masters, 1988. *Publications:* Learning Golf the Lyle Way, 1986; To the Fairway Born, 2006. *Recreation:* cars.

LYLE, Sir Gavin Archibald, 3rd Bt *cr* 1929; estate manager, farmer; company director; *b* 14 Oct. 1941; *s* of late Ian Archibald de Hoghton Lyle and Hon. Lydia Yarde-Buller (who *m* 1947, as his 2nd wife, 13th Duke of Bedford; marr. diss. 1960; then Lydia Duchess of Bedford), *d* of 3rd Baron Churston; *S* grandfather, 1946; *m* 1967, Suzy Cooper (marr. diss. 1985); five *s* one *d.* *Heir:* *s* Ian Abram Lyle, *b* 25 Sept. 1968. *Address:* Glendelvine, Caputh, Perthshire PH1 4JN.

LYLE, Jonathan Henry, RCNC; Commandant, Defence College of Management and Technology, Defence Academy, since 2007; Head of Royal Corps of Naval Constructors, since 2007; *b* 25 Feb. 1959; *s* of John Henry Turner Lyle and Gillian Lucy Lyle; *m* 1981, Beverley Nichola Uren; one *s* one *d.* *Educ:* Kingswood Sch., Bath; Royal Naval Engrg Coll., Plymouth (BSc Electrical and Electronic Engrg 1979); University Coll. London (MSc Microwaves and Mod. Optics). MIET (MIEE 1984); CEng 1984. RCNC 1976; Procurement Exec., MoD, 1982–91; Cabinet Office, 1991–95; DTI, 1995–96; Defence Procurement Agency: Directorate of Mil. Aircraft Projects, 1996–2000; Integrated Project Team Leader, 2000–04; Ops Dir, Air and Weapon Systems, 2004–07; Dir Gen., Helicopters, Defence Equipment and Support, MoD, 2007. *Recreations:* orienteering, watching Bath Rugby, inland waterways. *Address:* Defence Academy of the United Kingdom, Shrivenham, Swindon, Wilts SN6 8LA. *Club:* Bristol Orienteering.

LYLE, Sandy; *see* Lyle, A. W. B.

LYLES, John, CVO 2004; CBE 1987; JP; Lord-Lieutenant of West Yorkshire, 1992–2004; *b* 8 May 1929; *yr s* of Percy George Lyles and Alice Maud Mary (*née* Robinson); *m* 1953, Yvonne (*née* Johnson); two *s* two *d.* *Educ:* Giggleswick Sch.; Leeds Univ. (BSc Textiles 1950). Chm., S. Lyles plc, 1972–95; non-exec. Dir, Hillards plc, 1983–87. Chairman: Assoc. of Yorks and Humberside Chambers of Commerce, 1975–76; Yorks and Humberside CBI, 1983–85; Industry Year 86: Yorks and Humberside Reg.; CBI Mem., Speaker's Commn on Citizenship, 1988–90; Mem., Nat. Employers' Liaison Cttee for Volunteer and Reserve Forces, 1986–92. Mem., Yorks Cttee, NT, 1988–98. Member, Court: Leeds Univ., 1988–; Bradford Univ., 1992–2004. Pres., Shrievalty Assoc., 1999– (Chm., 1993–95). President: Calderdale Community Foundn, 1994–2004; N of England Horticl Soc., 2002–04; Chairman: W Yorks Police Community Trust, 1996–2004; Northern Trng Centre Appeal, Hearing Dogs for Deaf People, 2007–. Hon. Colonel: 8th Bn, (Yorks) LI (Vols), 1993–96; King's Own Yorks Yeomanry (LI), 1996–99; Vice Pres., Yorks and Humberside TAVRA, 1992–97, 1999–2002 (Pres., 1997–99). JP Batley and Dewsbury, 1967; High Sheriff, W Yorks, 1985–86; DL W Yorks, 1987. DUniv Bradford, 1995. KStJ 1993. *Recreations:* gardening, photography, music, opera. *Address:* Thimbleby House, Hampsthwaite, Harrogate HG3 2HB. *Club:* Lansdowne.

LYMBERY, His Honour Robert Davison; QC 1967; a Circuit Judge (formerly Judge of County Courts), 1971–93; Common Serjeant in the City of London, 1990–93; *b* 14 Nov. 1920; *s* of late Robert Smith Lymbery and late Louise Lymbery; *m* 1952, (Pauline) Anne, *d* of late John Reginald and of Kathleen Tuckett; three *d.* *Educ:* Gresham's Sch.; Pembroke Coll., Cambridge. Served Army, 1940–46; commissioned 17/21 Lancers, 1941; Middle East, Italy, Greece (Royal Tank Regt), 1942–46, Major. Pembroke Coll., 1939–40, 1946–48 (MA, LLB 1st class hons). Foundation Exhibn. 1948; called to Bar, Middle Temple, 1949, Bencher, 1991; Harmsworth Law Scholar, 1949; practice on Midland Circuit, 1949–71. Recorder of Grantham, 1965–71; Chairman: Rutland QS, 1966–71 (Dep. Chm., 1962–66); Bedfordshire QS, 1969–71 (Dep. Chm., 1961–69); Commissioner of Assize, 1971. Freeman, City of London, 1983; Liveryman, Cutlers' Co., 1992–. *Recreations:* various. *Address:* c/o Central Criminal Court, EC4M 7EH. *Club:* Hawks (Cambridge).

LYMINGTON, Viscount; Oliver Henry Rufus Wallop; *b* 22 Dec. 1981; *s* and *heir* of Earl of Portsmouth, *qv*. *Educ:* Eton. *Recreations:* shooting, cars. *Clubs:* Buck's, White's.

LYNAGH, Richard Dudley; QC 1996; a Recorder, since 2000; *b* 14 Nov. 1952; *s* of Charles Lynagh and Mary Browne; *m* 1979, Regula Wegmann (*d* 2004); two *s* one *d.* *Educ:* Kettering Grammar Sch.; University Coll. London (LLB Hons). Called to the Bar, Gray's Inn, 1975, Bencher, 2004; an Asst Recorder, 1999–2000. *Address:* 2 Crown Office Row, Temple, EC4Y 7HJ.

LYNAM, Desmond Michael, OBE 2008; broadcaster; *b* 17 Sept. 1942; *s* of Edward Lynam and Gertrude Veronica Lynam (*née* Malone); *m* 1965, Susan Eleanor Skinner (marr. diss. 1974); one *s.* *Educ:* Varndean Grammar Sch., Brighton; Brighton Business Coll. ACII. Business career in insurance, until 1967; also freelance journalist; reporter for local radio, 1967–69; reporter, presenter and commentator, BBC Radio, 1969–78; presenter and commentator, BBC TV Sport, 1978–99, incl. Grandstand, Sportsnight, Match of the Day, Commonwealth and Olympic Games, and World Cup; presenter: Holiday, BBC TV, 1988–89; How Do They Do That?, BBC TV, 1994–96; The Des Lynam Show, BBC Radio, 1998–99; ITV Sport, 1999–2004; Des Meets…, BBC Radio, 2004–05; We'll Meet Again, BBC TV, 2005; The World's Greatest Sporting Legend, Sky One, 2005; Des At Wimbledon, BBC Radio, 2005; Are You Younger Than You Think?, BBC TV, 2005; Countdown, Channel 4, 2005–06. TV Sports Presenter of the Year, TRIC, 1985, 1987, 1988, 1993, 1997; Radio Times Male TV Personality, 1989; RTS Sports Presenter of the Year, 1994, 1998; Richard Dimbleby Award, BAFTA, 1994; Variety Club of GB Media Award, 1997; RTS Lifetime Achievement Award, 2003. *Publications:* Guide to

Commonwealth Games, 1986; The 1988 Olympics, 1988; The 1992 Olympics, 1992; I Should Have Been At Work! (autobiog.), 2005. *Recreations:* golf, tennis, Brighton and Hove Albion, reading, theatre. *Address:* c/o Jane Morgan Management Ltd, Thames Wharf Studios, Rainville Road, W6 9HA.

LYNCH, Christopher Charles B.; *see* Balogun-Lynch.

LYNCH, His Honour David; a Circuit Judge, 1990–2005; *b* 23 Aug. 1939; *s* of Henry and Edith Lynch; *m* 1974, Ann Knights; two *s*. *Educ:* Liverpool Collegiate Grammar School. LLB London (ext.). Served RAF, 1958–61. Sharman & Sons, Solicitors, 1955–57; Bremner Sons & Corlett, Solicitors, 1961–66; Schoolmaster, 1966–68. Called to the Bar, Middle Temple, 1968; Northern Circuit; Asst Recorder, 1983–88; a Recorder, 1988–90; Liaison Judge: St Helens Justices, 1991–2005; Liverpool John Moores Univ., 1994–2005 (Hon. Fellow, 2003). Pres., Mental Health Review Tribunals (restricted patients), 1991–2001. Northern Circuit Remembrancer, 2006–. Hon. Vice Pres., Merseyside Br., Magistrates' Assoc., 1991–2005. *Publications:* (contrib.) A Century of Liverpool Lawyers, 2002; Northern Circuit Directory 1876–2004, 2005. *Recreations:* classical guitar, golf, bookbinding, photography, history of the Northern Circuit. *Address:* c/o The Queen Elizabeth II Law Courts, Derby Square, Liverpool L2 1XA. *T:* (0151) 473 7373. *Clubs:* Athenæum (Liverpool); Caldy Golf.

LYNCH, David Keith; film director; *b* Missoula, MT, USA, 20 Jan. 1946; *m* 1st, 1967, Peggy Reavey (marr. diss. 1974); one *d*; 2nd, 1977, Mary Fisk (marr. diss. 1987); one *s*; partner, Mary Sweeney; one *s*. *Educ:* Sch. of Mus. of Fine Arts, Boston; Pennsylvania Acad. of Fine Arts. Fellow, Center for Advanced Film Studies, Amer. Film Inst., 1970. *Films:* writer and director: Eraserhead (also prod.), 1977; The Elephant Man, 1980; Dune, 1984; Blue Velvet, 1986; Wild at Heart, 1990; Twin Peaks: Fire Walk with Me (also prod.), 1992; Lost Highway, 1997; Mulholland Drive, 2002; dir, The Straight Story, 1999; Inland Empire, 2006; *television series:* writer, director and producer: Twin Peaks, 1990; On the Air, 1992.

LYNCH, Prof. James Michael, OBE 2007; PhD, DSc; CSci, CChem, FRSC; CBiol, FIBiol, FIBiotech; Distinguished Professor of Life Sciences, University of Surrey, 2004–06, now Emeritus; Chairman, Terraform plc, since 2007; Director, C-Questor plc, since 2007; *b* 24 Nov. 1945; *s* of James Michael Lynch and Constance Violet Lynch; *m* 1971, Mary Elizabeth Gibbons; two *s* two *d*. *Educ:* Wilsons Grammar Sch., London; Loughborough Univ. (BTech Chem. 1968); King's Coll. London (PhD 1971, DSc 1984, Microbiol.). CChem 1975; FRSC 1984; CBiol 1984; FIBiol 1984; FIBiotech 1993; CSci 2005. Microbiologist, Letcombe Lab., 1971–83; Hd, Microbiol. and Crop Protection, Horticultural Res. Internat., 1983–93; Prof. of Biotechnol., and Head, Sch. of Biomed. and Life Scis, Univ. of Surrey, 1993–2003. Vis. Lectr, Univ. of Oxford, 1980–84; Visiting Professor: Washington State Univ., 1981–83; KCL, 1986–93; Oregon State Univ., 1995; Univ. of Reading, 2007–. Mem., editl bds of scientific jls, 1978–. Chm., Internat. Union of Soil Sci., Soil Biol. Commn, 1990–94. Co-ordinator, OECD Prog. on Biol Resource Mgt for Sustainable Agricl Systems, 1989–2006; Sen. Advr, SEEDA, 2007–. Dir, Internat. Inst. of Biotechnol., 1998–; Bd Mem., Eur. Forestry Inst., 2006–. Vice-Chm., Blasker Award Cttee, USA, 1996–2001. FRSA 1997. Res. Award for Foreign Specialists, Japanese Govt, 1987, 1991; Prize for Microbiol. (Carlos J. Finlay Award), UNESCO, 1993. *Publications:* Soil Biotechnology: microbiological factors in crop productivity, 1983; (ed) The Rhizosphere, 1990; joint editor: Microbial Ecology: a conceptual approach, 1979; Contemporary Microbial Ecology, 1980; Microbial Adhesion to Surfaces, 1980; Microbiological Methods for Environmental Biotechnology, 1984; Micro-organisms in Action: concepts and applications in microbial ecology, 1988; Terrestrial Gene Exchange: mathematical modelling and risk assessment, 1994; Biocontrol Agents: benefits and risks, 1995; Ecotoxicology: responses, biomarkers and risk assessment, 1997; Environmental Bioremonitoring: the biotechnology ecotoxicology interface, 1998; Biological Resource Management: connecting science and policy, 2000; Innovative Soil-Plant Systems for Sustainable Agricultural Practices, 2003; Remote Sensing for Agriculture and the Environment, 2004; Forestry and Climate Change, 2007; contrib. numerous review articles and res. papers. *Recreations:* running, cycling, sailing, gardening, walking, music. *Address:* Tudor Close, 12 The Drive, Angmering on Sea, W Sussex BN16 1QH. *T:* (01903) 785534. *Clubs:* English-Speaking Union, London Athletic.

LYNCH, Jerome Cecil Alfonso; QC 2000; *b* 31 July 1955; *s* of late Clifford James Lynch and Loretta Rosa Lynch; *m* 1983, Jacqueline Theresa O'Sullivan; one *s*. *Educ:* Lancashire Poly. (BA Hons). Called to the Bar, Lincoln's Inn, 1983, Bencher, 2008; in practice at the Bar, 1983–. Co-Presenter, Nothing But the Truth, Channel 4, 1998, 1999; Presenter, Crime Team, Channel 4, 2001, 2002; Co-Presenter, The People's Court, ITV1, 2005. *Recreations:* ski-ing (well), golf (badly), drinking good wine. *Address:* Charter Chambers, 33 John Street, WC1N 2AT. *T:* (020) 7832 0300. *Club:* Royal Automobile.

LYNCH, Prof. John; Director of Institute of Latin American Studies, 1974–87 and Professor of Latin American History, 1970–87, University of London, now Professor Emeritus; *b* 11 Jan. 1927; *s* of late John P. Lynch and Teresa M. Lynch, Boldon Colliery, Co. Durham; *m* 1960, Wendy Kathleen, *d* of late Frederick and Kathleen Norman; two *s* three *d*. *Educ:* Corby Sch. Sunderland; Univ. of Edinburgh; University College, London. MA Edinburgh 1952; PhD London 1955. FRHistS 1958. Army, 1945–48. Asst Lectr and Lectr in Modern History, Univ. of Liverpool, 1954–61; Lectr in Hispanic and Latin American History, 1961–64, Reader, 1964–70, UCL. Harrison Vis. Prof., Coll. of William and Mary, Williamsburg, 1991–92. Corresp. Member: Academia Nacional de la Historia, Argentina, 1963, Academia Nacional de la Historia, Venezuela, 1980; Academia Panameña de la Historia, 1981; Academia Chilena de la Historia, 1985; Real Academia de la Historia, Spain, 1986; Sociedad Boliviana de Historia, 1987; Academia Colombiana de Historia, 2008. Dr *hc* Seville, 1990. Distinguished Service Award, Conf. on Latin American History, Amer. Histl Assoc., 1997. Comdr, Order of Isabel la Católica (Spain), 1988; Order of Andrés Bello, 1st class (Venezuela), 1995. *Publications:* Spanish Colonial Administration 1782–1810, 1958; Spain under the Habsburgs, vol. 1 1964, vol. 2 1969; (with R. A. Humphreys) The Origins of the Latin American Revolutions, 1808–1826, 1965; The Spanish American Revolutions 1808–1826, 1973; Argentine Dictator: Juan Manuel de Rosas, 1829–52, 1981; (ed) Andrés Bello: the London years, 1982; (ed) Past and Present in the Americas, 1984; Hispanoamérica 1750–1850, 1987; Bourbon Spain 1700–1808, 1989; Caudillos in Spanish America 1800–1850, 1992; Latin American Revolutions 1808–1826: old and new world origins, 1994; Massacre in the Pampas, 1872: Britain and Argentina in the age of migration, 1998; Latin America between Colony and Nation, 2001; Simón Bolívar: a life, 2006; (contrib.) Cambridge History of Latin America, vol. III 1985, vol. IV 1986; (contrib.) UNESCO Historia General de América Latina, vol. V, 2003; (contrib.) Cambridge History of Christianity, vol. VIII, 2006. *Address:* 8 Templars Crescent, N3 3QS. *T:* (020) 8346 1089.

LYNCH, Margaret; Executive Director, War on Want, 1995–98; *b* 23 Sept. 1962; *d* of William Lynch and Rosaleen Reynolds. *Educ:* Glasgow Univ. (MA Hons). Mem., Scottish Exec., Labour Party, 1986–90; former Chair, Economic and Industry Cttee, Scottish Labour Party. Founder Mem., Scotland United, 1992. *Publications:* (ed) The Forgotten Workforce, 1991; Palestinians: the forgotten victims of the Gulf War, 1991; What Price Democracy: a referendum for Scotland, 1992. *Recreations:* painting, walking, Celtic culture.

LYNCH, Prof. Michael, PhD; FRSE; Sir William Fraser Professor of Scottish History and Palaeography, University of Edinburgh, 1992–2005; *b* 15 June 1946; *s* of Francis J. and Kathleen Lynch. *Educ:* Aberdeen Grammar Sch.; Univ. of Aberdeen (MA Eng. Lit. and Hist. 1st cl. hons 1969); Inst. of Historical Res., Univ. of London (PhD 1977). Lectr in History, UCNW, Bangor, 1971–79; Lectr, 1979–88; Sen. Lectr, 1988–92, Dept of Scottish History, Univ. of Edinburgh. Chm., Ancient Monuments Bd for Scotland, 1996–2003; Publications Sec., Scottish History Soc., 1990–93; President: Historical Assoc. of Scotland, 1992–2002; Soc. of Antiquaries of Scotland, 1996–99. Trustee, Nat. Mus Scotland (formerly Nat. Mus of Scotland), 2002–. FRHistS 1982; FRSE 1995. Editor, The Innes Review, 1984–92. *Publications:* Edinburgh and the Reformation, 1981; The Early Modern Town in Scotland, 1986; The Scottish Medieval Town, 1987; Mary Stewart: Queen in three kingdoms, 1988; Scotland: a new history, 1991, 2nd edn 1992; (ed with Julian Goodare) The Reign of James VI, 2000; The Oxford Companion to Scottish History, 2002; Aberdeen before 1800: a new history, 2002. *Address:* Scottish History, School of History and Classics, University of Edinburgh, 17 Buccleuch Place, Edinburgh EH8 9LN. *T:* (0131) 650 4030.

LYNCH, Michael Francis, CBE 2008; AM 2001; Chief Executive, South Bank Centre, since 2002; *b* 6 Dec. 1950; *s* of Wilfred Brian Lynch and Joan Margaret Lynch; *m* 1st, 1967, Jane Scott (marr. diss. 1987); one *d*; 2nd, Irene Hannan; 3rd, Christine Josephine Sharp. *Educ:* Marcellin Coll., Randwick; Univ. of Sydney. Australia Council for the Arts, 1973; Gen. Manager, King O'Malley Theatre Co., Australian Theatre for Young People; Administrator, Aust. Nat. Playwrights Conf.; Gen. Manager, Nimrod Th., 1976–78; Casting Dir and Man. Partner, Forcast Pty Ltd, 1981–89; General Manager: Sydney Th. Co., 1989–94; Australia Council for the Arts, 1994–98; Chief Exec., Sydney Opera House, 1998–2002. Mem. Bd, Visit London, 2004–. Prod., film, Raw Nerve, 1988. *Address:* South Bank Centre, South Bank, SE1 8XX.

LYNCH, Michael Richard, OBE 2006; PhD; Founder and Group Chief Executive Officer, Autonomy Corporation, since 1996; *b* 16 June 1965; *s* of Michael and Dolores Lynch. *Educ:* Christ's Coll., Cambridge (BA; PhD 1991). Founder, Cambridge Neurodynamics, 1991. Non-exec. Dir, BBC, 2007–. *Recreations:* jazz saxophone, flying helicopters. *Address:* Autonomy Corporation, Cambridge Business Park, Cowley Road, Cambridge CB4 0WZ. *T:* (01223) 448000.

LYNCH, Noel; Member (Green) London Assembly, Greater London Authority, May 2003–04; *b* 20 Jan. 1947; *s* of William and Nancy Lynch; *m* 1976, Angela Enright (marr. diss. 1988); one *d*. *Educ:* Kilmallock Nat. Sch.; Charleville Christian Brothers Sch., Co. Cork; University Coll. Cork (night classes) (Dip. Social Studies). Freelance auctioneer, mainly at Hornsey Auctions, N8, and S Eastern Auctions, E Peckham, 1986–2004; shopkeeper, E Finchley, 1992–2003. Member: Metropolitan Police Authy, 2003–04; London Fire and Emergency Planning Authy, 2003–04. Chm., Standards, GLA, 2003–04. London Green Party Co-ordinator, 2001–03, 2004–. Mem., Admin. Cttee, Finchley Soc. *Publication:* Setting up Green Secondhand Shops, 1989. *Recreation:* conducting charity auctions. *Address:* c/o Green Party, 1A Waterlow Road, N19 5NJ. *T:* (020) 8340 7759; *e-mail:* noellynch@tiscali.co.uk.

LYNCH, Roderick Robertson; Chairman and Chief Executive Officer, GSS Ltd, since 2001; *b* 22 May 1949; *s* of Nanson Lynch and Catherine (*née* Robertson); *m* 1972, Christina Williams; two *s*. *Educ:* Perth Acad.; Dundee Univ. (MA 1971). Served RAC, 1966–67. British Airways, 1971–89: Gen. Manager, Southern Europe, 1983–84; Man. Dir, British Airtours, 1984–86; Head, Customer Service, 1986–89; Man. Dir, Air Europe, 1989–91; Dir, Forte Hotels, 1991–93; Man. Dir, then Chief Exec., Resources, BBC, 1993–99; CEO, Olympic Airways, 1999–2000. Bd Mem., CAA, 1993–99; Dir, NATS Ltd, 1996–99. *Recreations:* Rugby football, military history, music, aviation. *Club:* Travellers.

LYNCH-BLOSSE, Sir Richard Hely, 17th Bt *cr* 1622; RAMC, 1975–85, retired; general medical practioner, since 1985 (senior partner, since 2000); *b* 26 Aug. 1953; *s* of Sir David Edward Lynch-Blosse, 16th Bt, and of Elizabeth, *er d* of Thomas Harold Payne, Welwyn Garden City; *S* father, 1971; *m* 1st, 1976, Cara (marr. diss. 1999), *o d* of late George Sutherland, St Ives, Cambs; two *d*; 2nd, 2000, Jacqueline, *o d* of late Gordon Francis, Yardley Gobion, Northants. *Educ:* Royal Free Hosp. Sch. of Medicine. Commnd RAMC, July 1975; LRCP MRCS 1978; MB BS 1979; DRCOG 1983; MRCGP 1984. MO, European Sch., Culham, 1987–. Mem., Soc. of Ornamental Turners, 1992–. *Publication:* contrib. to Jl of RAMC. *Heir: cousin* David Ian Lynch-Blosse [*b* 14 Jan. 1950; *m* 1st, 1984, Mrs Barbara Susan McLaughlin (*d* 1985); 2nd, 1989, Nadine, *d* of John Baddeley; one *s* one *d*]. *Address:* The Surgery, Watery Lane, Clifton Hampden, Oxon OX14 3EL.

LYNCH-ROBINSON, Sir Dominick (Christopher), 4th Bt *cr* 1920, of Foxrock, co. Dublin; Global Creative Director, J. Walter Thompson, since 2004; *b* 30 July 1948; *o s* of Sir Niall Lynch-Robinson, 3rd Bt, DSC, and Rosemary Seaton; *S* father, 1996; *m* 1973, Victoria, *d* of Kenneth Weir; one *s* one *d*, and one step *d*. *Recreations:* reading, cinema. *Heir:* *s* Christopher Henry Jake Lynch-Robinson, *b* 1 Oct. 1977. *Address:* Flat 3, 34 Montagu Square, W1H 2LJ.

LYNDEN-BELL, Prof. Donald, CBE 2000; FRS 1978; Professor of Astrophysics, University of Cambridge, 1972–2001, now Emeritus; Director, Institute of Astronomy, Cambridge, 1972–77, 1982–87, and 1992–94; *b* 5 April 1935; *s* of late Lt-Col L. A. Lynden-Bell, MC and M. R. Lynden-Bell (*née* Thring); *m* 1961, Ruth Marion Truscott (*see* R. M. Lynden-Bell); one *s* one *d*. *Educ:* Marlborough; Clare Coll., Cambridge (MA, PhD). Harkness Fellow of the Commonwealth Fund, NY, at the California Inst. of Technology and Hale Observatories, 1960–62; Research Fellow and then Fellow and Dir of studies in mathematics, Clare Coll., Cambridge, 1960–65; Asst Lectr in applied mathematics, Univ. of Cambridge, 1962–65; Principal Scientific officer and later SPSO, Royal Greenwich Observatory, Herstmonceux, 1965–72. Visiting Associate, Calif Inst. of Technology and Hale Observatories, 1969–70; Visiting Professorial Fellow, QUB, 1996–; H. N. Russell Lectr, AAS, 2000. Pres., RAS, 1985–87. FHMAAAS 1985. Foreign Associate: US NAS, 1990 (J. J. Carty Award, 2000); RSSAf 1994. Hon. DSc Sussex, 1987. Eddington Medal, RAS, 1984; Brouwer Prize, AAS, 1990; Gold Medal, RAS, 1993; Bruce Medal, Astronomical Soc. of the Pacific, 1998. *Publications:* contrib. to Monthly Notices of Royal Astronomical Soc. *Recreations:* hill walking, golf, squash racquets. *Address:* Institute of Astronomy, The Observatories, Madingley Road, Cambridge CB3 0HA. *T:* (01223) 337525.

LYNDEN-BELL, Ruth Marion, PhD, ScD; FRS 2006; Professor of Condensed Matter Simulation, Queen's University, Belfast, 1995–2003, now Emeritus; *b* 7 Dec. 1937; *d* of David and Priscilla Truscott; *m* 1961, Donald Lynden-Bell, *qv*; one *s* one *d*. *Educ:*

Newnham Coll., Cambridge (BA 1959, MA 1962; PhD 1962; ScD 1989). FRSC; FInstP. Fellow, New Hall, Cambridge, 1962–65; Lectr, Univ. of Sussex, 1965–72; Fellow, New Hall, Cambridge, 1972–95, now Emerita; Coll. Lectr, St John's Coll., Cambridge, 1975–95. *Publications:* (with R. K. Harris) Nuclear Magnetic Resonance Spectroscopy, 1969; numerous articles in scientific jls. *Recreations:* gardening, walking. *Address:* University Chemical Laboratory, Lensfield Road, Cambridge CB2 1EW.

LYNDHURST, Nicholas; actor, since 1971; *b* 20 April 1961; *m* 1999, Lucy Smith; one *s. Theatre includes:* Harding's Luck, Greenwich; Trial Run, Oxford Playhouse, 1980; Black Comedy (tour); The Private Ear (tour); The Foreigner, Albery, 1987; Straight and Narrow, Wyndham's, 1992; The Dresser, Duke of York's, 2005. *Television includes:* Going Straight, 1978; Spearhead, 1978; Butterflies, 1978–83; Father's Day, 1979; To Serve Them All My Days, 1980; Fairies; Losing Her; Only Fools and Horses, 1981–91; It'll All Be Over in Half an Hour, 1983; The Two of Us, 1986–90; The Piglet Files, 1990; Goodnight Sweetheart, 1993–99; Gulliver's Travels, 1996; David Copperfield, 1999; Thin Ice, 2000; Murder in Mind, 2003; After You've Gone, 2007. *Address:* c/o Chatto & Linnit Ltd, 123A Kings Road, SW3 4PL.

LYNE, Prof. Andrew Geoffrey, PhD; FRS 1996; FRAS; Langworthy Professor of Physics, University of Manchester, since 2002; *b* 13 July 1942; *s* of Lionel Geoffrey Lyne and Kathleen Elizabeth Lyne; *m* 1st, Jennifer Anne Duckels; two *d*; 2nd, 1994, Diane Elizabeth Stanway; one step *s* one step *d. Educ:* Portsmouth GS; St John's Coll., Cambridge (MA); Manchester Univ. (PhD). Manchester University: Lectr in Radio Astronomy, 1969–79; Sen. Lectr, 1979–90; Prof. of Radio Astronomy, 1990–2002. Dir, Nuffield Radio Astronomy Labs, subseq. Jodrell Bank Observatory, 1998–2006. Vis. Scientist, CSIRO Div. of Radiophysics, Sydney, 1975–76; Leverhulme Fellow, Royal Soc., 1994. Mem., PPARC, 1997–. Herschel Medal, RAS, 1992; Sir George Thomson Gold Medal, Inst. of Measurement and Control, 1993. *Publications:* Pulsar Astronomy, 1990, 3rd edn 2006; contrib. Nature, Monthly Notes of RAS and other scientific jls. *Recreations:* tennis, golf, walking, sailing. *Address:* Tall Trees, New Road, Moreton, Congleton, Cheshire CW12 4RX.

LYNE, Colin Gwaynten; Commercial Director, Department for Constitutional Affairs, 2003–06; *b* 10 Feb. 1945; *s* of William Henry Lyne and Ada Lilian Lyne (*née* Brownsell); *m* 1978, Hilary Janet Luscombe; two *s* one *d. Educ:* Humphry Davy Grammar Sch., Penzance; Bristol Univ. (Open Schol.). Various posts in NHS, 1973–85; Co. Supplies Officer, 1985–88, Dir, Commercial Services, 1988–93, Surrey CC; Director: Commercial Services, Essex CC, 1993–99; Purchasing and Contract Mgt, LCD, 1999–2003. Non-exec. Dir, Investment and Implementation Bd, Office of Govt Commerce, HM Treasury, 2005–07. Chm., 1992–93, Pres., 1994–95, Chartered Inst. Purchasing and Supply. Chm., Eur. Council of Purchasing and Supply, 2000–02. Mem., Bd of Advrs, Southampton Univ. Sch. of Mgt, 2005–07. FCIPS 1990. FRSA 1995. *Recreations:* classical music, old books, wine, golf. *Address:* Langarth, 12 Abbey Fields, E Hanningfield, Chelmsford, Essex CM3 8XB. *T:* (01245) 403062. *Club:* Warren Golf (Danbury).

LYNE, Kevin Douglas; HM Diplomatic Service; Ambassador to Montenegro, since 2007; *b* 6 Nov. 1961; *s* of Douglas Lyne and Anne Lyne; *m* 1988, Anne Dabbadie; two *d. Educ:* Richard Hale Sch., Hertford; Portsmouth Poly. (BA Hons Latin Amer. Studies); Univ. of Essex (MA Govt and Politics). Res. Cadre, FCO, 1988–91; Second Sec., Santiago, 1991–94; Principal Res. Officer, FCO, 1994–96; First Secretary: FCO, 1996–98; UK Mission to UN, Geneva, 1998–2003; Dep. Hd of Mission, Rabat, 2003–07. *Recreation:* fishing. *Address:* c/o Foreign and Commonwealth Office, King Charles Street, SW1A 2AH.

LYNE, Richard John; HM Diplomatic Service, retired; High Commissioner to Solomon Islands, 2004–08; *b* 20 Nov. 1948; *s* of late John Arthur Lyne and Sylvia Mary Raven Lyne (*née* Knott); *m* 1977, Jennifer Anne Whitworth; one *s* one *d. Educ:* Kimbolton Sch. RAPC, 1967–70; joined HM Diplomatic Service, 1970; Archivist and Communications Officer, Belgrade, 1972–74; Accountant and Dep. Mgt Officer, Algiers, 1974–76; Third Sec., Damascus, 1977–80; Second Sec., New Delhi, 1984–87; Second, later First Sec., Stockholm, 1987–91; Dep. High Comr, Port of Spain, Trinidad, 1997–2000; Deputy Head: Conf. and Visits Gp, FCO, 2000–02; Personnel Services Dept, FCO, 2002–04. Church Warden, St Peter and St Sigfried Anglican Ch, Stockholm, 1989–91. Mem., St John Boxmoor PCC, Hemel Hempstead, 1994–96 and 2000–04. *Recreations:* family, reading, genealogy, watching sport. *Club:* Royal Over-Seas League.

LYNE, Sir Roderic (Michael John), KBE 1999; CMG 1992; HM Diplomatic Service, retired; consultant and lecturer; Special Adviser: BP Group plc, since 2005; JPMorgan Chase Bank, since 2007; *b* 31 March 1948; *s* of Air Vice-Marshal Michael Dillon Lyne, CB, AFC and Avril Joy, *d* of Lt-Col Albert Buckley, CBE, DSO; *m* 1969, Amanda Mary, *d* of Sir Howard Frank Trayton Smith, GCMG; two *s* one *d. Educ:* Legbourne County Primary Sch., Lincs; Highfield Sch., Hants; Eton Coll.; Leeds Univ. (BA Hist. 1970). FCO 1970; Army Sch. of Langs, 1971; Moscow, 1972–74; Dakar, 1974–76; Eastern European and Soviet Dept, FCO, 1976–79; Rhodesia Dept, FCO, 1979; Asst Pvte Sec. to Sec. of State for Foreign and Commonwealth Affairs, 1979–82; UK Mission to UN, NY, 1982–86; Vis. Res. Fellow, RIIA, 1986–87; Counsellor and Hd of Chancery, Moscow, 1987–90; Hd of Soviet Dept, 1990–92, Hd of Eastern Dept, 1992–93, FCO; Pvte Sec. to Prime Minister, 1993–96 (on secondment); Dir for Policy Develt, CIS ME and Africa, British Gas, 1996 (on secondment); UK Perm. Rep. to Office of UN and other internat. orgns, Geneva, 1997–2000; Ambassador to Russia, 2000–04. Hon. Prof., Moscow Sch. of Social and Economic Studies, 2001; Vis. Prof., Faculty of Business and Law, Kingston Univ., 2005–. Non-executive Director: Accor, 2006–; Aricom, 2006–; Mem., Strategic Adv. Gp, QucomHaps Hldgs Ltd, 2005–; Chm., Internat. Adv. Bd, Altimo, 2006–07; Special Rep., ITE Gp plc, 2005–. Member: Bd, Russo-British Chamber of Commerce, 2006–; Exec. Cttee, UK/Russia Round Table, 2005–07; Trilateral Commn's Task Force on Russia, 2005–07; Oxford Univ. Task Force on Energy, the Envmt and Develt, 2006–07; Chm., Adv. Cttee, Centre for E European Language Based Area Studies, 2007–. Mem. Bd, Internat. Early Music Trust, St Petersburg, 2007–. Hon. Vice-Pres., GB-Russia Soc., 2005–. Patron, AMUR, 2001–. Trustee, World Race Trust, 2004–07. Gov., Ditchley Foundn, 2005–; Mem. Bd of Govs, Kingston Univ., 2007–. Hon. Dr Rostov State Construction Univ., 2001; Hon. LLD Leeds, 2002; Hon. DBA Kingston, 2004; Hon. DLit Heriot-Watt, 2004. *Publication:* (jtly) Engaging with Russia: the next phase, 2006. *Recreations:* sport, grandchildren. *Address:* 39 Richmond Park Road, East Sheen, SW14 8JU. *Club:* Travellers.

LYNE, William Macquarie, CBE 2002 (MBE 1986); AM 2002; Director, Wigmore Hall, 1966–2003 (Assistant Manager, 1957–66), Director Emeritus, since 2006; *b* 28 Nov. 1932; *s* of Harold Baden Lyne and Marie Veronica Lyne (*née* Catalano). *Educ:* Canterbury High Sch., Sydney, Australia. Transcription Officer, Australian Broadcasting Commn, 1951–56. Mem. Bd, Henry Wood Hall, 1991–; Trustee, Geoffrey Parsons Meml Trust, 1995–; Internat. Artistic Advr, Melbourne Internat. Chamber Music Competition, 2007–; Mem. Cttee, Queen's Medal for Music, 2004–. Hon. FTCL 1997; Hon. GSM 1997; Hon. RAM 1999; Hon. RCM 1999. Evening Standard Award for Outstanding Achievement

for Classical Music, 1997; Ambassador for London Award for lifetime achievement, 1997; Cobbett Medal for Services to art of chamber music, Musicians' Co., 2001; Internat. Artists' Mgt Assoc. award, 2003. Chevalier, Ordre des Arts et des Lettres (France), 1996; Grand Cross of Honour (First Class) for Sci. and the Arts (Austria), 2001. *Publication:* (contrib.) Wigmore Hall 1901–2001: a celebration, 2001. *Recreations:* collecting gramophone records, incl. vintage; cinema, esp. films from the thirties; reading, visiting art galleries, fell walking, travel, theatre, concerts, opera. *Address:* c/o Wigmore Hall, 36 Wigmore Street, W1U 2BP; *e-mail:* Schubert@wmlyne.demon.co.uk. *Club:* Reform.

LYNK, Roy, OBE 1990; consultant in human resources, since 1996; National President, Union of Democratic Mineworkers, 1987–93; General Secretary, Nottingham Section, 1985–93; *b* 9 Nov. 1932; *s* of John Thomas Lynk and Ivy Lynk; *m* 1978, Sandra Ann; three *s* three *d. Educ:* Station Road Higher Sch. and Healdswood Sch., Sutton-in-Ashfield; Nottingham Univ. Cert. in Industrial Relations. Miner at Teversal Colliery, Nottingham, 1947; RN 1948; Miner at various collieries, Nottingham, 1950–79. National Union of Mineworkers: Branch Sec., Sutton Colliery, 1958–79; full time Area Official, Nottingham, 1979–83; Financial Sec., Nottingham Area, 1983–85, Gen. Sec., 1985; Union of Democratic Mineworkers: formed, Dec. 1985; Nat. Gen. Sec., 1985–86. Member: European Coal and Steel Community's Consultative Cttee, 1988–93; Industrial Appeal Tribunal, Nottingham, 1993–; Board, Coal Authy, 1995–98. *Recreation:* watching football. *Address:* Columbia House, 143 Huthwaite Road, Sutton-in-Ashfield, Notts NG17 2HB.

LYNN, Bishop Suffragan of, since 2004; **Rt Rev. James Henry Langstaff;** *b* 27 June 1956; *s* of Henry, (Harry), Langstaff and Jillian Langstaff (*née* Brooks, now Harper); *m* 1977, Bridget Streatfeild; one *s* one *d. Educ:* St Catherine's Coll., Oxford (BA (PPE) 1977, MA 1981); Univ. of Nottingham (BA (Theol.) 1980); St John's Coll., Nottingham (Dip. Pastoral Studies). Ordained deacon, 1981, priest, 1982; Asst Curate, St Peter, Farnborough, 1981–86; Vicar, St Matthew, Duddeston and St Clement, Nechells, 1986–96; RD, Birmingham City, 1995–96; Chaplain to Bp of Birmingham, 1996–2000; Rector, Holy Trinity, Sutton Coldfield, 2000–04; Area Dean, Sutton Coldfield, 2002–04. Tutor, Aston Trng Scheme, 1987–97. Mem., E of England Regl Assembly, 2006–. Non-exec. Dir, Good Hope Hosp. NHS Trust, 2003–04. Mem. Bd, FCH Housing and Care, 1988–2002; Chm., Flagship Housing Gp, 2006–. *Recreations:* ski-ing, walking, music, theatre, travel, current affairs. *Address:* The Old Vicarage, Castle Acre, King's Lynn, Norfolk PE32 2AA. *T:* (01760) 755553; *e-mail:* bishoplynn@norwich.anglican.org.

LYNN, Archdeacon of; *see* Gray, Ven. M. C.

LYNN, Inez Therese Philomena Alice; Librarian, The London Library, since 2002; *b* 15 March 1960; *d* of Jack Basil Lynn and Mari Therese Philomena Josephine Patricia Lynn (*née* Prendergast). *Educ:* La Sagesse Convent High Sch., Newcastle upon Tyne; Univ. of Liverpool (BA); Univ. of Toronto; Pembroke Coll., Oxford (MLitt); University Coll. London (DipLib). MCLIP (ALA 1992). SCONUL trainee, Warburg Inst., 1984–86, Inst. of Advanced Legal Studies, 1986–88, Univ. of London; London Library: Cataloguer, 1988–90; Chief Cataloguer, 1990–93; Prin. Asst Librarian, 1993–94; Dep. Librarian, 1994–2001. Trustee: Maitland Trust, 2002–06; R. M. Chambers Settlement Trust, 2002–; London Library Trust, 2002–. *Recreations:* editing Medieval Latin poetry, dressage. *Address:* The London Library, 14 St James's Square, SW1Y 4LG. *T:* (020) 7930 7705.

LYNN, Jonathan Adam; director, writer and actor; *b* 3 April 1943; *s* of Robin and Ruth Lynn; *m* 1967, Rita Merkelis; one *s. Educ:* Kingswood Sch., Bath; Pembroke Coll., Cambridge (MA). Acted in Cambridge Circus, New York, 1964; TV debut, Ed Sullivan Show, 1964; actor in repertory, Leicester, Edinburgh and Bristol Old Vic, and in London; performances include: Green Julia, 1965; Fiddler on the Roof, 1967–68; Blue Comedy, 1968; The Comedy of the Changing Years, 1969; When We Are Married, 1970; Dreyfus, 1982; actor in TV comedy programmes and plays, including: Barmitzvah Boy, 1975; The Knowledge, 1979; Outside Edge, 1982; Diana, 1984; actor in films including: Prudence and the Pill, 1967; Into the Night, 1984; Three Men and a Little Lady, 1990; Greedy (also dir.), 1994; Artistic Dir, Cambridge Theatre Co., 1977–81 (dir. 19 prodns); *director: London:* The Plotters of Cabbage Patch Corner, 1970; The Glass Menagerie, 1977; The Gingerbread Man, 1977 and 1978; The Unvarnished Truth, 1978; The Matchmaker, 1978; Songbook, 1979 (SWET Award, and Evening Standard Award, for Best Musical, 1979); Tonight at 8.30, 1981; Arms and the Man, 1981; Pass the Butler, 1982; Loot, 1984; *National Theatre:* A Little Hotel on the Side, 1984; Jacobowski and the Colonel, 1986; Three Men on a Horse, 1987 (Olivier Award for Best Comedy); *RSC:* Anna Christie, Stratford 1979, London 1980; *Broadway:* The Moony Shapiro Songbook, 1981; *films:* Mick's People (also wrote), 1982; Clue (also wrote), 1984; Nuns on the Run (also wrote), 1990; My Cousin Vinny, 1991; The Distinguished Gentleman, 1992; Greedy (also acted), 1994; Sgt Bilko, 1996; Trial and Error, 1997; The Whole Nine Yards, 2000; The Fighting Temptations, 2003; *screenplay:* The Internecine Project, 1974; *TV scriptwriter:* situation comedies, including: My Brother's Keeper, 2 series, 1974 and 1975 (also co-starred); Yes, Minister (also radio scripts), 3 series, 1980, 1981 and 1982; Yes, Prime Minister, 1986, 1987; Life After Life, 1990. Writer's Award, BAFTA, 1987; Pye TV Writers Award (for Yes, Minister and Yes, Prime Minister), 1981, 1986; Broadcasting Press Guild Award, 1980, 1986; ACE Award for Amer. Cable TV Best Comedy Writing (for Yes, Prime Minister), 1988. Hon. MA Sheffield, 1987; Hon. PsyD Amer. Behavioral Studies Inst., 2000. *Publications:* A Proper Man (novel), 1976; with Antony Jay: Yes, Minister, The Diaries of a Cabinet Minister: Vol. I, 1981; Vol. II, 1982; Vol. III, 1983; The Complete Yes Minister, 1984; Yes, Prime Minister, the Diaries of the Rt Hon. James Hacker: Vol. I, 1986; Vol. II, 1987; The Complete Yes Prime Minister, 1989; Mayday (novel), 1993. *Recreation:* changing weight. *Address:* c/o United Agents, 12–26 Lexington Street, W1F 0LE.

LYNN, Maurice Kenneth, MA; Head of French, Westminster School, 1983–88 and 1999–2008; *b* 3 March 1951. *Educ:* Thornleigh Salesian College, Bolton; Magdalen College, Oxford (Open Scholar; BA Hons 1973; MA 1977). Asst Master, Oratory Sch., 1973–79; Asst Master, Radley Coll., 1979–83; Headmaster, The Oratory Sch., 1989–91; Westminster School: Asst Master, 1992–95; Hd, Mod. Langs, 1995–99. Dir of Eur. interests for The Oratory Sch. Assoc., 1992. *Recreations:* English Catholic poetry, twentieth century French drama, soccer, ski-ing, cricket, acting and producing, cycling, travel. *Address:* 10 impasse Molière, 34300 Agde, France. *T:* 467211553.

LYNN, Michael David; Corporate Development Director, The Stationery Office Ltd, 1996–99; *b* 18 July 1942; *s* of Martin and Dorothy Lynn; *m* 1965, Hilary Smyth; one *s* one *d. Educ:* Lincoln Sch. Joined HMSO 1960; Director: Publications Distribution, 1980; Finance, 1983; Print Procurement, 1984; Dir-Gen., Corporate Services, 1987; Dep. Chief Exec., 1989; Controller and Chief Exec., 1995–96. *Recreations:* chess, crosswords.

LYNN, Prof. Richard, PhD; FBPsS; Professor of Psychology, University of Ulster, 1972–95, now Emeritus; *b* 20 Feb. 1930; *s* of Richard and Ann Lynn; *m* 1st, 1956, Susan Maher (marr. diss. 1978); one *s* two *d*; 2nd, 1990, Susan Hampson (*d* 1998); 3rd, 2004, Joyce Dora Walters, *qv. Educ:* Bristol Grammar Sch.; King's Coll., Cambridge (BA 1953;

PhD 1956; Passingham prizeman). FBPsS 1965. Lectr in Psychology, Univ. of Exeter, 1956–67; Prof. of Psychology, Dublin Economic and Social Res. Inst., 1967–72. US Mensa Award for Excellence, for work on intelligence, 1985, 1988, 1993. *Publications:* Attention, Arousal and the Orientation Reaction, 1966; The Irish Braindrain, 1969; The Universities and the Business Community, 1969; Personality and National Character, 1971; An Introduction to the Study of Personality, 1972; The Entrepreneur, 1974; (ed) Dimensions of Personality, 1981; Educational Achievement in Japan, 1987; The Secret of the Miracle Economy, 1991; Dysgenics, 1996; Eugenics: a reassessment, 2001; The Science of Human Diversity, 2001; (with T. Vanhanen) IQ and the Wealth of Nations, 2002; Race Differences in Intelligence, 2005; IQ and Global Inequality, 2006; (with T. Vanhanen) The Global Bell Curve, 2008; articles on personality, intelligence and social psychology. *Recreations:* do-it-yourself house renovation, bridge. *Address:* University of Ulster, Coleraine, Northern Ireland BT52 1SA; *e-mail:* Lynnr540@aol.com. *Club:* Oxford and Cambridge.

LYNN, Dame Vera, (Dame Vera Margaret Lewis), DBE 1975 (OBE 1969); singer; *b* 20 March 1917; *d* of Bertram Samuel Welch and Annie Welch; *m* 1941, Harry Lewis; one *d. Educ:* Brampton Rd Sch., East Ham. First public appearance as singer, 1924; joined juvenile troupe, 1928; ran own dancing school, 1932; broadcast with Joe Loss and joined Charlie Kunz, 1935; singer with Ambrose Orch., 1937–40, then went solo; voted most popular singer, Daily Express comp., 1939, and named Forces Sweetheart; own radio show, Sincerely Yours, 1941–47; starred in Applesauce, London Palladium, 1941; sang to troops in Burma, etc, 1944 (Burma Star, 1985); subseq. Big Show (radio), USA; London Laughs, Adelphi; appeared at Flamingo Hotel, Las Vegas, and many TV shows, USA and Britain, including own TV series on Rediffusion, 1955; BBC TV, 1956; BBC 2, 1970; also appearances in Holland, Denmark, Sweden, Norway, Germany, Canada, NZ and Australia; in seven Command Performances, also films and own shows on radio. 14 Gold Records; records include Auf Wiederseh'n (over 12 million copies sold), became first British artiste to top American Hit Parade. Pres., Printers' Charitable Corp., 1980. Internat. Ambassador, Variety Club Internat., 1985. Founder and Pres., Dame Vera Lynn Trust for Children with Cerebral Palsy, 2001–. Hon. Citizen: Winnipeg, 1974; Nashville, Tennessee, 1977. Freedom: City of London, 1978; City of Corner Brook, Newfoundland, 1981. FInstD. Fellow, Univ. (formerly Poly.) of E London, 1990. Hon. LLD Memorial Univ. of Newfoundland, 1977 (founded Lynn Music Scholarship, first award, 1982); Hon. MMus London, 1992. Music Publishers' Award, 1975; Show Business Personality of the Year, Grand Order of Water Rats, 1975; Ivor Novello Award, 1975; Humanitarian Award, Variety Club Internat., 1985; Lillian K. Kell Award for outstanding service by a woman during World War II, 2005. Comdr, Order of Orange-Nassau, Holland. *Publications:* Vocal Refrain (autobiog.), 1975; (jtly) We'll Meet Again, 1989; Unsung Heroines, 1990. *Recreations:* gardening, painting, sewing, swimming.

LYNNE, Elizabeth, (Liz); Member (Lib Dem) West Midlands Region, European Parliament, since 1999; *b* 22 Jan. 1948. *Educ:* Dorking Co. Grammar Sch. Started acting career, 1966; numerous theatre appearances in repertory and West End. Speech consultant, 1989–92 and 1997–99. Contested (L) Harwich, 1987. MP (Lib Dem) Rochdale, 1992–97; contested (Lib Dem) same seat, 1997. Lib Dem spokesperson: on health and community care, 1992–94; on social security and disability, 1994–97. *Address:* 55 Ely Street, Stratford upon Avon, Warwickshire CV37 6LN; c/o European Parliament, Rue Wiertz, 1047 Brussels, Belgium.

LYNNE, Gillian, CBE 1997; director, choreographer, dancer, actress; *d* of late Leslie Pyrke and Barbara (*née* Hart); *m* 1980, Peter Land, actor. *Educ:* Baston Sch., Bromley, Kent; Arts Educnl Sch. Leading soloist, Sadler's Wells Ballet, 1944–51; star dancer, London Palladium, 1951–53; role in film, Master of Ballantrae, 1952; lead in Can-Can, Coliseum, 1954–55; Becky Sharp in Vanity Fair, Windsor, 1956; guest principal dancer: Samson and Delilah, Sadler's Wells, 1957; Aida, and Tannhauser, Covent Garden, 1957; Puck in A Midsummer Night's Dream, TV, 1958; star dancer in Chelsea at Nine (featured dance segments), TV, 1958; lead in New Cranks, Lyric, Hammersmith, 1959; roles in Wanda, Rose Marie, Cinderella, Out of My Mind, and lead in revue, 1960–61; leading lady, 5 Past Eight Show, Edinburgh, 1962; conceived, dir., chor. and starred in Collages (mod. dance revue), Edinburgh Fest., 1963, transf. Savoy; *choreographed:* The Owl and the Pussycat (1st ballet), Western Theatre Ballet, 1962; Queen of the Cats, London Palladium, 1962–63; Wonderful Life (1st film), 1963–64; Every Day's a Holiday, and Three Hats for Lisa (musical films), 1964; The Roar of the Greasepaint, and Pickwick, Broadway, 1965; The Flying Dutchman, Covent Garden, 1966; Half a Sixpence (film), 1966–67 (also staged musical nos); How Now Dow Jones, Broadway, 1967; Midsummer Marriage, Covent Garden, 1968; The Trojans, Covent Garden, 1969, 1977; Breakaway (ballet), Scottish Theatre Ballet, 1969; Phil the Fluter, Palace, 1969; Ambassador, Her Majesty's, 1971; Man of La Mancha (film), 1972; The Card, Queen's, 1973; Hans Andersen, London Palladium, 1975; The Way of the World, Aldwych, 1978; My Fair Lady, national tour and Adelphi, 1979; Parsifal, Covent Garden, 1979; (also Associate Dir) Cats, New London, 1981 (Olivier Award, 1981), Broadway 1982, US nat. tour, 1983, Vienna, 1984 (Austrian Silver Order of Merit), Los Angeles, Sydney, 1985, East Berlin, 1987, Canada, Japan, Australia, Holland, Paris, 1989 (Molière Award, Best Musical), UK tour, 2003, Madrid, 2003, Moscow, 2004; Café Soir (ballet), Houston Ballet Co., 1985; Cabaret, Strand, 1986; The Phantom of the Opera, Her Majesty's, 1986, Broadway, Japan, Vienna, 1989, Stockholm, Chicago, Hamburg, Australia, Canada, 1990, Las Vegas, 2006; A Simple Man (ballet), Sadler's Wells, 1988; The Brontës (ballet), Northern Ballet Theatre, 1995; The Secret Garden, RSC, Stratford and Aldwych, 2000; Chitty Chitty Bang Bang, London Palladium, 2002, NY, 2005; Four Classical Variations, for Royal Acad. of Dance, 2005; *directed and choreographed:* The Match Girls, Globe, 1966; Bluebeard, Sadler's Wells Opera, 1966, new prodn, Sadler's Wells Opera, Coliseum, 1969; Love on the Dole (musical), Nottingham Playhouse, 1970; Liberty Ranch, Greenwich, 1972; Once Upon a Time, Duke of York's, 1972; Jasperina, Amsterdam, 1978; Cats, Vienna, 1983 (1st proscenium arch prodn; Silver Order of Merit, Austria, 1984), Paris, 1989; Valentine's Day, Chichester, 1991; Dancing in the Dark, 1991; Dance for Life Gala, 1991; Valentine's Day, Globe, 1992; What the World Needs, Old Globe, San Diego, 1997–98; Gigi, Vienna, 1999; Dick Whittington, Sadler's Wells, 1999; Some You Win (dance drama), Sadler's Wells, 2000; *directed:* Round Leicester Square (revue), Prince Charles, 1963; Tonight at Eight, Hampstead, 1970 and Fortune, 1971; Lillywhite Lies, Nottingham, 1971; A Midsummer Night's Dream (co-dir.), Stratford, 1977; Tomfoolery, Criterion, 1980; Jeeves Takes Charge, Fortune, 1980, off-Broadway, 1983, Los Angeles, 1985; To Those Born Later, New End, 1981; That's What Friends Are For!, May Fair, 1996; Avow, USA, 1996; (Additional Dir) La Ronde, RSC, Aldwych, 1982; (also appeared in) Alone Plus One, Newcastle, 1982; The Rehearsal, Yvonne Arnaud, Guildford and tour, 1983; Cabaret, Strand, 1986; I'd Like to Teach the World to Sing (Ian Adam Gala), Her Majesty's, 2008; *staged:* England Our England (revue), Princes, 1961; 200 Motels (pop-opera film), 1971; musical nos in Quilp (film), 1974; A Comedy of Errors, Stratford, 1976 (TV musical, 1977); musical As You Like It, Stratford, 1977; Songbook, Globe, 1979; Once in a Lifetime, Aldwych, 1979; new stage act for Tommy Steele, 1979; wedding sequence in Yentl (film), 1982; European Vacation II (film); Pirelli Calendar, 1988; Pickwick, Chichester and Sadler's Wells, 1993; *choreographed for television:* Peter and the Wolf (narrated and mimed all 9 parts), 1958; At the Hawk's Well (ballet), 1975; There was a Girl, 1975; The Fool on the Hill (1st Colour Special for ABC), with Australian Ballet and Sydney Symph. Orch., staged Sydney Opera House, 1975; Muppet Show series, 1976–80; (also musical staging) Alice in Wonderland, 1985; shows and specials for Val Doonican, Perry Como, Petula Clark, Nana Mouskouri, John Curry, Harry Secombe, Ray Charles, and Mike Burstein; also produced and devised Noel Coward and Cleo Laine specials; *directed for television:* Mrs F's Friends, 1981; Easy Money, 1982; Le Morte d'Arthur (also devised), 1983 (Samuel G. Engel Award, Univ. of Michigan); The Simple Man, 1987 (BAFTA award for direction and choreog.); The Look of Love, 1989; That's What Friends Are For!, 1996. Gov., Sadler's Wells Foundn, 2000–. Patron: Gordon Edwards Charitable Trust; Dancers' Career Develt Trust (formerly Independent Dancers' Resettlement Trust), 2005– (Bd Mem., 1993–); Liverpool Inst. for Performing Arts; Lang. of Dance Centre, Holland Pk; Doreen Bird Foundn; Stella Mann Coll.; British Assoc. of Choreographers; Adventures in Motion Pictures Ltd. Mr Abbott Award, Soc. of Stage Dirs and Choreographers, NY, 1999; Queen Elizabeth II Coronation Award, Royal Acad. of Dance, 2001. *Publications:* (contrib.) Cats, The Book of the Musical; articles in Dancing Times.

LYNTON, Michael Mark; Chairman and Chief Executive, Sony Pictures Entertainment, since 2004; *b* London, 1 Jan. 1960; *s* of Mark O. L. Lynton and Marion Lynton; *m* 1994, Elizabeth Jamie Alter; two *d. Educ:* Harvard Coll. (BA 1982); Harvard Business Sch. (MBA 1987). Associate, First Boston Corp., 1982–87; Pres., Disney Publg, 1987–92, Hollywood Pictures, 1992–96, Walt Disney Co.; Chm. and CEO, Penguin Gp, 1996–2000; Pres., America Online Internat., 2000–03; CEO, AOL Europe, 2001–02; Pres., Internat., AOL Time Warner, subseq. Time Warner, 2002–03. *Recreations:* tennis, ski-ing. *Address:* Sony Pictures Entertainment Inc., 10202 Washington Boulevard, Culver City, CA 90232, USA.

LYON; *see* Bowes Lyon.

LYON, Adrian Pirrie; His Honour Judge Lyon; a Circuit Judge, since 2000; *b* 18 Oct. 1952; *s* of Alexander Ward Lyon and Hilda Lyon; *m* 1976, Christina Margaret Harrison (*see* C. M. Lyon); one *s* one *d. Educ:* Leeds Grammar Sch.; Hampton Grammar Sch.; University Coll. London (LLB). Called to the Bar, Gray's Inn, 1975; Head of Chambers, 1997–2000. Mem., Bar Council, 1995–97. *Recreations:* travel, reading, theatre, computers. *Address:* c/o The Court Service, Northern Circuit, Young Street Chambers, 76 Quay Street, Manchester M3 4PR.

LYON, Christina Margaret; Her Honour Judge Lyon; a Circuit Judge, since 2007; *b* 12 Nov. 1952; *d* of Edward Arthur Harrison and Kathleen Joan Harrison; *m* 1976, Adrian Pirrie Lyon, *qv*; one *s* one *d. Educ:* Wallasey High Sch. for Girls; University Coll. London. LLB (1st Cl. Hons) 1974; admitted Solicitor, 1977. Tutor and sometime Lectr in Law, University Coll. London, 1974–75; Trainee and Asst Solicitor, Bell & Joynson, 1975–77; Liverpool University: part-time Tutor in Law, 1976–77; Lectr in Law, 1977–80; Manchester University: Lectr in Law and Law and Social Work, 1980–86; Sub-Dean, Law Faculty, 1986; Prof. of Law, Head of Dept and of Sch. of Law, Keele Univ., 1987–93; Liverpool University: Prof. of Common Law, 1993–98; Head, Dept of Law, 1993–97; Dean, Faculty of Law, 1994–97; Dir, Centre for the Study of the Child, the Family and the Law, 1995–2007; Queen Victoria Prof. of Law, 1998–2007, now Emeritus. Asst Recorder, 1998–2000; Recorder, 1999–2007. Member: ESRC Res. Grants Bd, 1988–91; Child Policy Review Gp, Nat. Children's Bureau, 1989–; Chm., Independent Representation for Children in Need, 1991–; Member: Nat. Exec. Cttee and Fundraising Cttee, Relate, 1990–94 (Pres., N Staffs Relate, 1987–93); Merseyside Panels of Guardians *ad Litem*, 1993–2002 (Vice-Chm., 1993–97); Child Protection and Family Justice Cttee, Nuffield Foundn, 1994–. Dr Barnardo's Research Fellow, 1987–92. Jt Editor, Jl of Social Welfare and Family Law (formerly Jl of Social Welfare Law), 1984–; Mem. Editl Bd, Representing Children, 1996–. FRSA 1991. *Publications:* Matrimonial Jurisdiction of Magistrates' Courts, 1981; Cohabitation without Marriage, 1983; (ed) Butterworth's Family Law Service Encyclopaedia, 1983, rev. edn 2006; Law of Residential Homes and Day Care Establishments, 1984; (ed) Child Abuse, 1990, 3rd edn 2003; The Law Relating to Children in Principles and Practice of Forensic Psychiatry, 1990; (ed with A. P. Lyon) Butterworth's Family Law Handbook, 1991; Atkins Court Forms on Infants, vols I and II, 1992; The Law Relating to Children, 1993; Legal Issues Arising from the Care and Control of Children with Learning Disabilities who also Present Severely Challenging Behaviour, vol. I, Policy Guidance, vol. II, A Guide for Parents and Carers, 1994; Child Protection and the Civil Legal Framework in The Child Protection Handbook, 1995; Children's Rights and The Children Act 1989 in Children's Rights, 1995; Working Together: an analysis of collaborative inter-agency responses to the problem of domestic violence, 1995; Law and Body Politics, 1995; (jtly) Effective Support Services for Children, 1998; (jtly) A Trajectory of Hope, 2000; Loving Smack, Lawful Assault: a contradiction in human rights and law, 2000. *Recreations:* riding, swimming, foreign travel, reading, theatre, opera.

LYON, Rt Hon. Clare; *see* Short, Rt Hon. C.

LYON, Dr (Colin) Stewart (Sinclair), FIA; FSA, FRNS; General Manager (Finance), Group Actuary and Director, Legal & General Group Plc, 1980–87; *b* 22 Nov. 1926; *s* of late Col Colin Sinclair Lyon, OBE, TD and Mrs Dorothy Winstanley Lyon (*née* Thomason); *m* 1958, Elizabeth Mary Fargus Richards; four *s* one *d. Educ:* Liverpool Coll.; Trinity Coll., Cambridge (MA; PhD 2004). FIA 1954; FSA 1972; FRNS 1955. Chief Exec., Victory Insurance Co. Ltd, 1974–76; Chief Actuary, Legal & General Assurance Soc. Ltd, 1976–85. Director: Lautro Ltd, 1987–92; Cologne Reinsurance Co. Ltd, 1987–97; City of Birmingham Touring Opera Ltd, 1987–90; Ætna Internat. (UK) Ltd, 1988–91; Pearl Gp PLC, 1991–97; UK Bd, AMP and London Life, 1991–97. Member: Occupational Pensions Bd, 1979–82; Inquiry into Provision for Retirement, 1983–85; Treasure Trove Reviewing Cttee, 1986–93. President: Inst. of Actuaries, 1982–84 (Gold Medal, 1991); British Numismatic Soc., 1966–70 (Vice-Pres., 1976–; Sanford Saltus Gold Medal, 1974). Trustee, Disablement Income Gp Charitable Trust, 1967–84; Dir, Disablement Income Gp, 1984–94 (Vice-Pres., 1995–2002); Trustee, Independent Living Fund, 1988–93. *Publications:* (with C. E. Blunt and B. H. I. H. Stewart) Coinage in Tenth-Century England, 1989; papers on Anglo-Saxon coinage, particularly in British Numismatic Jl; contrib. Jl of Inst. of Actuaries and Trans Internat. Congress of Actuaries. *Recreations:* numismatics, music, amateur radio (call sign GW3EIZ). *Address:* Ardraeth, Malltraeth, Bodorgan, Anglesey LL62 5AW. *T:* (01407) 840273. *Club:* Actuaries'.

LYON, David; *see* Lyon, J. D. R.

LYON, George; Member (Lib Dem) Argyll and Bute, Scottish Parliament, 1999–2007; *b* 16 July 1956; *s* of Alister and Mary Lyon; *m* (separated); three *d. Educ:* Rothesay Acad. Family business, farming, A. H. Lyon, 1972–94, A. K. Farms, 1994–, Isle of Bute. Mem., NFU Scotland, 1990– (Pres., 1997–99). Dep. Minister for Parly Business and for Finance and Public Services Reform, Scottish Exec., 2005–07. FRAgS 2000. *Recreations:* ski-ing, football, reading, swimming. *Club:* Farmers'.

LYON, (John) David (Richard); Chief Executive, Rexam plc (formerly Bowater Industries, then Bowater plc), 1987–96; *b* 4 June 1936; *s* of John F. A. Lyon and Elizabeth Lyon (*née* Owen); *m* 1st, 1960, Nicola M. E. Bland (marr. diss. 1986); two *s* (and one *s* decd); 2nd, 1987, Lillis Lanphier. *Educ:* Wellington College; Magdalen College, Oxford (BA Modern History 1959); Harvard Business Sch. (Advanced Management Programme, 1973). 1st Bn The Rifle Brigade, Kenya and Malaya, 1954–56 (despatches). Courtaulds, 1959–70; Rank Organisation, 1970–71; Redland, 1971–87 (Dir 1976; Man. Dir, 1982); Dir, Smiths Industries, 1991–94. Chm., Stocks Austin Sice, 1997–2002. Mem., Adv. Cttee on Business and the Envmt, 1991–93. Col Comdt, SAS Regt, 1994–2000. Non-exec. Mem., Field Army Command Gp, 2003–. Trustee, Army Museums Ogilby Trust, 1998–. FRGS (Hon. Treas., 2002–08). *Recreations:* trekking, blacksmithing. *Address:* PO Box 12, Arundel, West Sussex BN18 9ND.

LYON, John MacDonald, CB 2003; Parliamentary Commissioner for Standards, since 2008; *b* 12 April 1948; *m* Juliet Christine Southall (*see* J. C. Lyon); one *s* one *d*. *Educ:* Selwyn Coll., Cambridge (BA, MA). Home Office, 1969; Principal, 1974; Cabinet Office, 1978–80; Asst Sec., 1982; Grade 3, 1991; Director General: Police Policy, 1999; Policing and Crime Reduction Gp, 2000–03; Legal and Judicial Services Gp and Sec. of Commns, LCD, later DCA, then MoJ, 2003–07. External Mem., Nat. Trust Nominations Cttees, 2005. FRSA 2000. *Address:* House of Commons, SW1A 0AA.

LYON, Juliet Christine; Director, Prison Reform Trust, since 2000; *b* 8 April 1950; *d* of Christopher Redhead Southall and Jewel Eugenie Carr; *m* 1986, John MacDonald Lyon, *qv*; one *s* one *d*. *Educ:* Univ. of Exeter (BA Comb. Hons 1971); Univ. of London (MA Rights Dist.); Tavistock Inst. of Human Relns. Head: Adolescent Unit Sch., Exevale Hosp., 1973–76; Community Educn, Court Fields Sch., Somerset, 1976–79; Regl Manager, Richmond Fellowship Therapeutic Communities, 1980–90; Associate Dir, Trust for Study of Adolescence, 1990–99. Hon. Res. Fellow, QUB, 1994–99. Social Exclusion Unit Advr, 2001–02. Professional Advr, Childline, 1993–2003. Trustee: Children's Express, 1997–2000; Hanover Foundn, 2007–. Sec. Gen., Penal Reform Internat., 2007–. Part-time columnist and broadcaster, 2000–. *Publication:* Tell Them So They Listen: messages from young people in custody, 2000. *Recreations:* gardening, theatre, bee-keeping. *Address:* Prison Reform Trust, 15 Northburgh Street, EC1V 0JR. *T:* (020) 7251 5070, *Fax:* (020) 7251 5076; *e-mail:* juliet.lyon@prisonreformtrust.org.uk.

LYON, Mary Frances, ScD; FRS 1973; Deputy Director, Medical Research Council Radiobiology Unit, Harwell, 1982–90, retired; *b* 15 May 1925; *e d* of Clifford James Lyon and Louise Frances Lyon (*née* Kirby). *Educ:* King Edward's Sch., Birmingham; Woking Grammar Sch.; Girton Coll., Cambridge (ScD 1968; Hon. Fellow 1985). FIBiol. MRC Scientific Staff, Inst. of Animal Genetics, Edinburgh, 1950–55; MRC Radiobiology Unit, Harwell, 1955–90, Hd Genetics Div., 1962–87. Clothworkers Visiting Research Fellow, Girton Coll., Cambridge, 1970–71. Foreign Hon. Mem., Amer. Acad. Arts and Scis, 1980 (Amory Prize, 1977). Foreign Associate, US Nat. Acad. of Scis, 1979. Hon. FIBiol 2006. Royal Medal, Royal Soc., 1984; Prize for Genetics, Sanremo, Italy, 1985; Gairdner Foundn Award, 1985; Allan Award, Amer. Soc. of Human Genetics, 1986; Wolf Prize for medicine, Wolf Foundn, 1996; March of Dimes Prize in Develtl Biol., 2004; Pearl Meister Greengard Award, Rockefeller Univ., 2006; Rosenstiel Award, Brandeis Univ., 2007. *Publications:* papers on genetics in scientific jls. *Address:* MRC Mammalian Genetics Unit, Harwell, Oxon OX11 0RD. *T:* (01235) 841000.

LYON, Maj.-Gen. Robert, CB 1976; OBE 1964 (MBE 1960); Bursar, Loretto School, Musselburgh, 1979–91; *b* Ayr, 24 Oct. 1923; *s* of David Murray Lyon and Bridget Lyon (*née* Smith); *m* 1st, 1951, Constance Margaret Gordon (*d* 1982); one *s* one *d*; 2nd, 1992, Rosemary Jane, *d* of G. H. Allchin, Torquay. *Educ:* Ayr Academy. Commissioned, Aug. 1943, Argyll and Sutherland Highlanders. Served Italy, Germany, Palestine, Greece; transf. to Regular Commn in RA, 1947; Regtl Service, 3 RHA in Libya and 19 Field in BAOR, 1948–56; Instr, Mons Officer Cadet Sch., 1953–55; Staff Coll., 1957; DAQMG, 3 Div., 1958–60; jssc, 1960; BC F (Sphinx) Bty 7 PARA, RHA, 1961–62 (Bt Lt-Col); GSO1, ASD2, MoD, 1962–65 (Lt-Col); CO 4 Lt Regt, RA, 1965–67, Borneo (despatches), UK and BAOR (Lt-Col); as Brig.: CRA 1 Div., 1967–69, BAOR; IDC, 1970; Dir Operational Requirements, MoD, 1971–73; DRA (Maj.-Gen.), 1973–75; GOC SW District, 1975–78; retired 1979. Pres., Army Hockey Assoc., 1974–76; Chm., Army Golf Assoc., 1977–78. Chm., RA Council of Scotland, 1984–90. Col Comdt RA. Director: Braemar Civic Amenities Trust, 1986–90; Edinburgh Military Tattoo Ltd, 1988–98; Financial Forum, 1996–. Regl Dir Scotland, Manufacturing Forum, 1994–. HM Comr, Queen Victoria Sch., Dunblane, 1984–95. Pres., La Punta Urbanisation, Los Cristianos, 1995–98. FCMI 1982 (MBIM 1978). *Publication:* Irish Roulette, 1991. *Recreations:* golf, writing, gardening. *Address:* Woodside, Braemar, Aberdeenshire AB35 5YT. *T:* and *Fax:* (013397) 41667; *e-mail:* Lyonwoodside@ukonline.co.uk.

LYON, Hon. Sterling Rufus Webster, PC 1982; OM 2002; a Judge of the Manitoba Court of Appeal, 1986–2002; *b* 30 Jan. 1927; *s* of David Rufus Lyon and Ella May (*née* Cuthbert); *m* 1953, Barbara Jean Mayers; two *s* three *d*. *Educ:* Portage La Prairie Collegiate (Governor-General's Medal); United College (BA 1948); Univ. of Manitoba Law Sch. (LLB 1953). Crown Attorney, Manitoba, 1953–57; QC (Canada) 1960. Member, Manitoba Legislative Assembly, and Executive Council, 1958–69; Attorney-General, 1958–63 and 1966–69; Minister of: Municipal Affairs, 1960–61; Public Utilities, 1961–63; Mines and Natural Resources, 1963–66; Tourism and Recreation, Commissioner of Northern Affairs, 1966–68; Govt House Leader, 1966–69; Leader, Progressive Cons. Party of Manitoba, 1975–83; MLA: for Fort Garry, 1958–69; for Souris-Killarney, 1976–77; for Charleswood, 1977–86; Leader of the Opposition, Manitoba, 1976–77 and 1981–83; Premier of Manitoba and Minister of Dominion-Provincial Affairs, 1977–81. *Recreations:* hunting, fishing. *Club:* Albany (Toronto).

LYON, Stewart; *see* Lyon, C. S. S.

LYON, Victor Lawrence, QC 2002; a Recorder, since 2000; *b* 10 Feb. 1956; *s* of Dr J. B. Lyon. *Educ:* Marlborough Coll.; Trinity Coll., Cambridge (BA Hons 1979). Called to the Bar, Gray's Inn, 1980; Asst Recorder, 1999–2000. *Publications:* Practice and Procedure of the Commercial Court, 1st edn 1981 to 5th edn 2000. *Recreations:* tennis, swimming, golf. *Address:* Essex Court Chambers, 24 Lincoln's Inn Fields, WC2A 3EG. *T:* (020) 7813 8000, *Fax:* (020) 7813 8080; *e-mail:* vlyon@essexcourt.net. *Club:* Hurlingham.

LYON-DALBERG-ACTON, family name of **Baron Acton**.

LYONS, Maj.-Gen. Adrian William, CBE 1994; FCILT; Director General, Railway Forum, 2001–06; *b* 26 Dec. 1946; *s* of late Gp Capt. W. M. Lyons and M. P. Lyons (*née* Willis); *m* 1993, Rosemary Ann Farrer; one *d*. *Educ:* Merchant Taylors' Sch. Commnd RCT, 1966, transf. RAOC, 1972; various logistic mgt and planning appts, largely MoD based, 1977–94; psc 1980, jsdc 1986, rcds 1995; Dep. UK Mil. Rep., Brussels, 1996–98; Dir Gen. Logistic Support (Army), then Defence Logistic Support, MoD, 1998–2000. Col Comdt RLC, 2000–06; Hon. Col 168 Pioneer Regt RLC(V), 2001–07. Member: Railway Safety Adv. Bd, 2001–06 Strategy and Policy Steering Cttee, BSI, 2005–. Chairman: Hong Kong Locally Enlisted Personnel Trust, 1998–2001; Lady Grover's Fund, 2007–; Drapers' Co. and QMC City Acad. project, 2007–. Librettist for opera, Reluctant Highwayman, music by Sir Nicholas Jackson, Bt, first performed Broomhill Fest., 1995. Second Master Warden, Drapers' Co., 2008–09; Liveryman, Carmen's Co., 1998–. Chm. of Govs, Bancroft's Sch., 2003–. Pres., Rail Study Assoc., 2004–05. *Recreations:* theatre, travel, collecting (almost) anything that makes the past come alive, esp. coins (FRNS; Council Mem., British Numismatic Soc., 2005–07). *Address:* Stoke Farm, Beechingstoke, Pewsey, Wilts SN9 6HQ. *T:* (01672) 851634. *Club:* Cavalry and Guards.

LYONS, Alastair David, CBE 2001; Executive Chairman, Partners for Finance Ltd, since 2001; *b* 18 Oct. 1953; *o s* of late Alexander Lyons and of Elizabeth (*née* Eynon); *m* 1980, Judith Shauneen Rhodes; one *s* two *d*. *Educ:* Whitgift Sch.; Trinity Coll., Cambridge (Sen. Schol.; MA 2nd Cl. Hons). With Price Waterhouse & Co., 1974–79; N. M. Rothschild & Sons Ltd, 1979; H. P. Bulmer Holdings PLC, 1979–89: Gp Treas., 1979–82; Gp Financial Controller, 1983–88; Actg Gp Finance Dir, and Finance Dir, H. P. Bulmer Drinks Ltd, 1988–89; Divl Dir, Corporate Finance, Asda Gp PLC, 1989–90; Finance Dir, ASDA Stores Ltd, 1990–91; Finance Dir, 1991–94, Chief Exec., 1994–96, Nat. & Provincial Building Soc.; Man. Dir, Insurance, and Exec. Dir, Abbey National plc, 1996–97; Chief Exec., NPI, 1997–99; Dir of Corporate Projs, Nat. Westminster Gp, 1999–2000. Non-executive Chairman: Admiral Gp Ltd, 2000–; Legal Mktg Services Ltd, 2002–; In Retirement Services Ltd, 2003–; Health & Case Mgt Ltd, 2003–; Equity Release Services Ltd, 2003–; Buy-as-you-View Ltd, 2004–07; Higham Gp plc, 2005–07; Cardsave Ltd, 2007–; non-executive Director: Wishstream Ltd, 2001–02; Sesame Group Ltd, 2003–04. Non-executive Director: Benefits Agency, 1994–97; DSS, 1997–2001; DWP, 2001–02; DFT, 2002–05. Mem., Yorks Regl Cttee, NT, 1994–96. Gov., Giggleswick Sch., 1994–97. *Recreations:* cycling, running, riding, hill walking, ski-ing, collecting antiques.

LYONS, Dennis John, CB 1972; CEng, FRAeS; Director General of Research, Department of the Environment, 1971–76; *b* 26 Aug. 1916; *s* of late John Sylvester Lyons and of Adela Maud Lyons; *m* 1939, Elisabeth, *d* of Arnold and Maria Friederika Müller Haefliger, Weggis, Switzerland; five *s* two *d*. *Educ:* Grocers' Company School; Queen Mary Coll., London Univ. (Fellow, 1969). Aerodynamics Dept, Royal Aircraft Estabt, 1937; RAFVR, 1935–41; Aerodynamics Flight Aero Dept, RAE, 1941–51; Head of Experimental Projects Div., Guided Missiles Dept, RAE, 1951; Head of Ballistic Missile Group, GW Dept, 1956; Head of Weapons Dept, RAE, 1962; Dir., Road Research Laboratory, 1965–71. Member: Adv. Board for Res. Councils, 1973–76; SRC, 1973–76; Engineering Bd, SRC, 1970–76; Natural Environment Res. Council, 1973–76. Pres. OECD Road Research Unit, 1968–72. Hon. Mem., Instn Highway Engineers. *Publications:* papers in scientific jls. *Recreations:* ski-ing, pottery-making, philately. *Address:* Summerhaven, Gough Road, Fleet, Hants GU51 4LJ. *T:* (01252) 614773.

LYONS, Edward; QC 1974; LLB, BA; a Recorder of the Crown Court, 1972–98; *b* 17 May 1926; *s* of late A. Lyons and Mrs S. Taylor; *m* 1955, Barbara, *d* of Alfred Katz; one *s* one *d*. *Educ:* Roundhay High Sch.; Leeds Univ. (LLB Hons 1951; BA Hons (European Studies) 2003). Served Royal Artillery, 1944–48; Combined Services Russian Course, Cambridge Univ., 1946; Interpreter in Russian, Brit. CCG, 1946–48. Called to Bar, Lincoln's Inn, 1952, Bencher, 1983. MP (Lab 1966–81, SDP 1981–83) Bradford E, 1966–74, Bradford W, 1974–83; PPS at Treasury, 1969–70; SDP Parly spokesman: on home affairs, 1981–82; on legal affairs, 1982–83. Member: H of C Select Cttee on European Legislation, 1975–83; SDP Nat. Cttee, 1984–87; Chairman: PLP Legal and Judicial Gp, 1974–77; PLP Home Office Gp, 1974–79 (Dep. Chm., 1970–74). Contested: (Lab) Harrogate, 1964; (SDP) Bradford W, 1983; (SDP) Yorkshire West, European Parly Elecn, 1984. Mem., Exec. of Justice, 1974–89. *Recreations:* history, opera. *Address:* 59 Westminster Gardens, Marsham Street, SW1P 4JG. *T:* (020) 7834 1960; 4 Primley Park Lane, Leeds LS17 7JR. *T:* (0113) 268 5351.

LYONS, Sir John, Kt 1987; FBA 1973; Master of Trinity Hall, Cambridge, 1984–2000; *b* 23 May 1932; *s* of Michael A. Lyons and Mary B. Lyons (*née* Sullivan); *m* 1959, Danielle J. Simonet; two *d*. *Educ:* St Bede's Coll., Manchester; Christ's Coll., Cambridge. MA; PhD 1961; LittD 1988. Lecturer: in Comparative Linguistics, SOAS, 1957–61; in General Linguistics, Univ. of Cambridge, 1961–64; Prof. of General Linguistics, Edinburgh Univ., 1964–76; Prof. of Linguistics, 1976–84, Pro-Vice-Chancellor, 1981–84, Sussex Univ. DèsL (*hc*) Univ. Catholique de Louvain, 1980; Hon. DLitt: Reading, 1986; Edinburgh, 1988; Sussex, 1990; Antwerp, 1992. *Publications:* Structural Semantics, 1964; Introduction to Theoretical Linguistics, 1968; New Horizons in Linguistics, 1970; Chomsky, 1970, 3rd edn 1991; Semantics, vols 1 and 2, 1977; Language and Linguistics, 1981; Language, Meaning and Context, 1981, 2nd edn 1991; Natural Language and Universal Grammar, 1991; Linguistic Semantics, 1995; articles and reviews in learned journals.

LYONS, John, CBE 1986; General Secretary, Engineers' and Managers' Association, 1977–91, and Electrical Power Engineers' Association, 1973–91; *b* 19 May 1926; *s* of Joseph and Hetty Lyons; *m* 1954, Molly McCall; two *s* two *d*. *Educ:* St Paul's Sch.; Polytechnic, Regent Street; Cambridge Univ. (BA Econ). RN 1944–46. Asst. to Manager of Market Research Dept, Vacuum Oil Co., 1950; Research Officer: Bureau of Current Affairs, 1951; Post Office Engineering Union, 1952–57; Asst. Sec., Instn of Professional Civil Servants 1957–66, Dep. Gen. Sec. 1966–73. Member: TUC Gen. Council, 1983–91 (Chm., Energy Cttee, 1988–91); Nat. Enterprise Bd, 1975–79; Exec. Cttee PEP, 1975–78; Council, PSI, 1978–80; Adv. Council for Applied R&D, 1978–81; Engrg Council, 1982–86; PO Bd, 1980–81, British Telecommunications Bd, 1981–83; Sec., Electricity Supply Trade Union Council (formerly Employees' Nat. Cttee for Electricity Supply Industry), 1976–91; Chm., NEDO Working Party on Industrial Trucks, 1977–80. Vice-Pres., Industrial Participation Assoc., 1976–90; British rep., Econ. and Social Cttee, EU (formerly EC), 1990–98 (Vice Pres., Energy Section, 1992–98; Pres., 1994–96, Vice Pres., 1996–98, Single Market Observatory). Governor, Kingsbury High School, 1974–86; Member: Court of Governors, LSE, 1978–84; Bd of Governors, London Business Sch., 1987–88. Hitachi Lectr, Sussex Univ., 1983; addresses to: British Assoc., 1973; IEE, 1977; Internat. Monetary Conference, 1984; Newcastle Univ., 1989. FRSA 1979. Hon. Fellow, IIEXE, 1992; Hon. FIET, 2006. *Publications:* various papers and articles. *Recreations:* several.

LYONS, John; *b* 11 July 1949; one *s* one *d*. *Educ:* Woodside Secondary Sch.; Stirling Univ. (MSc 2000). Mechanical engr, 1971–88; Officer UNISON, 1988–2001. MP (Lab) Strathkelvin and Bearsden, 2001–05. Mem., Forth Valley Health Bd, 1999–2001.

LYONS, Prof. Malcolm Cameron; Sir Thomas Adams's Professor of Arabic, University of Cambridge, 1985–96; Fellow, Pembroke College, Cambridge, since 1957 (President, 1989–93); *b* Indore, India, 11 Feb. 1929; *s* of Harold William Lyons and Florence Katharine (*née* Cameron); *m* 1961, Ursula Schedler. *Educ:* Fettes Coll.; Pembroke Coll., Cambridge (Major Open Classical Schol., 1946; John Stewart of Rannoch Classical Schol.

in Latin and Greek, 1948; Browne Medallist, 1948, 1949; 1st cl. hons Pts I and II, Classical Tripos, 1948, 1949; 1st cl. hons Pts I and II, Oriental Studies, Arabic and Persian, 1953; E. G. Browne Prize, 1953; MA 1954; PhD 1957; LittD 1997). RAF, 1949–51, commissioned 1950. University of Cambridge: Asst Lectr in Arabic, 1954–59; Lectr, 1959–84; Reader in Medieval Islamic Studies, 1984–85. Seconded to FO as Principal Instructor, MECAS, Lebanon, 1961–62. Founder Editor: Arabic Technical and Scientific Texts, 1966–78; Jl of Arabic Literature, 1970–. *Publications:* Galen on Anatomical Procedures (with W. Duckworth and B. Towers), 1962; In Hippocratis de Officina Medici, 1963, and De Partibus Artis Medicativae, De Causis Contentivis, De Diaeta in Morbis Acutis (in Corpus Medicorum Graecorum), 1967; An Arabic Translation of Themistius' Commentary on Aristotle's De Anima, 1973; Aristotle's Ars Rhetorica, Arabic version, 1982; (with E. Maalouf) The Poetic Vocabulary of Michel Trad, 1968; (with J. Riley-Smith and U. Lyons) Ayyubids, Mamlukes and Crusaders, 1971; (with D. Jackson) Saladin, The Politics of the Holy War, 1982; (jtly) Meredith Dewey: diaries, letters, writings, 1992; The Arabian Epic, 1995; Identification and Identity in Classical Arabic Poetry, 1999; The Thousand and One Nights: a new translation, 2008; articles and reviews in learned jls. *Recreations:* golf, walking. *Address:* Pembroke College, Cambridge CB1 2RF. *Club:* Royal and Ancient Golf (St Andrews).

LYONS, Sir Michael (Thomas), Kt 2000; Chairman: BBC Trust, since 2007; English Cities Fund, since 2002; *b* West Ham, 15 Sept. 1949; *s* of Thomas Lyons and Lillian Lyons (*née* Stafford); *m* 1976, Gwendolene Jane Calvert; two *s* one *d*. *Educ:* Stratford Grammar Sch.; Middlesex Polytechnic (BA Soc. Scis Hons); Queen Mary Coll., London (MSc Econ; Hon. Fellow, 2003). Street market trader, 1970–72; Brand Manager, Crookes-Anestan, 1971–72; Lectr and Res. Fellow, Dept of Industrial Econs, Univ. of Nottingham, 1973–75; Sen. Res. Officer, DoE, 1975–78; W Midlands County Council: Principal Economist, 1978–82; Dep. Dir and Dir, Economic Develt, 1982–85; Chief Executive: Wolverhampton MBC, 1985–90; Notts CC, 1990–94; Birmingham CC, 1994–2001. Birmingham University: Dir, Inst. of Local Govt Studies, 2001–04; Prof. of Public Policy, 2001–06; Hon. Prof., 1999–2001 and 2006–. Sec., W Midlands Regl Chamber, 1998–2001. Councillor, Birmingham City Council, 1980–83. Director: Mouchel (formerly Parkman) plc, 2001–; Wragge & Co., 2001–; ITV (Central Indep. Television), 2002–06; SQW Ltd, 2007–. Mem., Public Services Productivity Panel, HM Treasury, 2000–07; Dep. Chm., 2003–05, Acting Chm., 2005–06, Audit Commn. Mem., Ind. Review of the Fire Service, 2002; conducted: Ind. Review of Public Sector Relocation, 2004 (report, 2004); Ind. Review of Mgt of Public Assets, 2004 (report, 2004); Ind. Review of Council Tax and the Funding of Local Govt, later Lyons Inquiry into Local Govt, 2005–07 (Final report, 2007); Chm., Cardiff CC Corporate Governance Commn, 2004. Chm., CBSO, 2001–07; Gov., RSC, 1999–2005, 2006–. FRSA. Hon. Dr: Middlesex, 1997; UCE, 2001; Wolverhampton, 2004. *Publications:* (ed with A. Johnson) The Winning Bid, 1992; (with Sir Ian Byatt) The Role of External Review in Improving Performance, 2001; contribs to professional jls. *Recreations:* music, theatre, cinema, walking. *Address:* BBC Trust, 35 Marylebone High Street, W1U 4AA; *e-mail:* m.t.lyons@btconnect.com.

LYONS, Roger Alan; Joint General Secretary, Amicus, 2002–04; Consultant, Business Services and Public Policy, since 2005; *b* 14 Sept. 1942; *s* of late Morris and Phyllis Lyons; *m* 1971, Kitty Horvath; two *s* two *d*. *Educ:* Roe Green Junior Sch., Kingsbury; Christ's Coll., Finchley; University Coll. London (BSc Hons Econ.; Fellow, 1996). Regional Officer, ASSET, then ASTMS, 1966–70; Nat. Officer 1970–87, Asst Gen. Sec. 1987–89, ASTMS; Asst Gen. Sec., 1989–92, Gen. Sec., 1992–2002, MSF; MSF merged with AEEU to form Amicus, 2002. Exec., European Metalworker Fedn, 1987–2004; Mem., Gen. Council, 1990–2004, Pres., 2003–04, TUC. Member: Central Arbitration Cttee, 2002–; Employment Appeal Tribunal, 2003–. Mem., Design Council, 1998–2004. Mem., Council, UCL, 1997–2005. Patron: Envmtl Industries Commn, 2000–; Burma Campaign, 2003–. *Recreations:* family, take-aways, cinema, football (Arsenal in particular). *Address:* 22 Park Crescent, N3 2NJ. *T:* (020) 8346 6843, *Fax:* (020) 8349 9075; *e-mail:* rogerlyons22@hotmail.com.

LYONS, Shaun, CBE 2004; **His Honour Judge Lyons;** a Circuit Judge, since 1992; a Senior Circuit Judge, since 2002; Resident Judge, Wood Green Crown Court, since 1995; *b* 20 Dec. 1942; *s* of late Jeremiah Lyons and of Winifred Ruth Lyons; *m* 1970, Nicola Rosemary, *d* of late Capt. D. F. Chilton, DSO, RN; one *s* one *d*. *Educ:* Portsmouth Grammar Sch.; Inns of Court Sch. of Law. Joined RN, 1961; Lt 1966; Lt Comdr 1974; called to the Bar, Middle Temple, 1975, Bencher, 2008; Comdr 1981; Captain 1988; Chief Naval Judge Advocate, 1989–92; retd RN, 1992. Asst Recorder and Recorder, 1988–92. Chm., Middx Adv. Cttee for Magistrates, 2004– (Dep. Chm., 1996–2004). *Clubs:* Army and Navy; Royal Yacht Squadron.

LYONS, Stuart Randolph, CBE 1993; Chairman, Airsprung Furniture Group plc, since 2005; *b* 24 Oct. 1943; 3rd *s* of late Bernard Lyons, CBE and Lucy Lyons; *m* 1969, Ellen Harriet Zion; two *s* one *d*. *Educ:* Rugby; King's Coll., Cambridge (Major Scholar). Man. Dir, John Collier Tailoring Ltd, 1969–74 (Chm., 1975–83); Dir, UDS Group plc, 1974–83 (Man. Dir, 1979–83); Chm., Colmore Trust Ltd, 1984–; Chief Exec., Royal Doulton plc, 1985–97 (Chm., 1987–93); Director: British Ceramic Res. Ltd, 1987–94; Hogg Robinson plc, 1998–2000; Aurora Computer Services Ltd, 1999–2003; Chairman: Gartmore Absolute Growth & Income Trust plc, 2004–06 (Dir, 2000–06); The Wensum Co. plc, 2003– (Dir, 2001–). Member: Leeds CC, 1970–74; Yorkshire and Humberside Econ. Planning Council, 1972–75; Clothing EDC, 1976–79; Ordnance Survey Review Cttee, 1978–79; Monopolies and Mergers Commn, 1981–85; Council, CBI, 1991–96; Nat. Manufacturing Council, 1992–95; Dir, Staffs TEC, 1990–93. Pres., BCMF, 1989–90; Chairman: British Ceramic Confedn, 1989–95; Staffs Develt Assoc., 1992–95; DTI Tableware Strategy Group, 1994–96; W Midlands Develt Agency, 1995–99; Vice-Chm., Industry 96 (W Midlands Fest. of Industry and Enterprise), 1994–96. Mem. Council, Keele Univ., 1989–97; Gov., Staffs Univ. (formerly Staffs Poly.), 1991–97. Contested (C) Halifax, Feb. and Oct. 1974. Chief Policy Advr to Shadow Sec. of State for Trade and Industry, then Health and Educn, subseq. Transport and the Envmt, 2003–05. Hon. DLitt Keele, 1994. *Publications:* The Fleeting Years: Odes of Horace, 1996; Can Consignia Deliver?, 2001; A Department for Business, 2001; Harnessing our Genius, 2003; Horace's Odes and the Mystery of Do-Re-Mi, 2007. *Address:* 50 Seymour Walk, SW10 9NF. *T:* (020) 7352 3309; *e-mail:* stuart.lyons@dsl.pipex.com. *Clubs:* Carlton, Hurlingham.

LYONS, Prof. Terence John, DPhil; FRS 2002; FRSE; Wallis Professor of Mathematics, University of Oxford, since 2000; Fellow, St Anne's College, Oxford, since 2000; *b* 4 May 1953; *s* of late Peter Lyons and of Valerie (*née* Hardie); *m* 1975, Barbara, *d* of late Joseph and Barbara Epsom; *m*; one *s* one *d*. *Educ:* St Joseph's Coll., W Norwood; Trinity Coll., Cambridge (BA Maths 1975 and 1976); Christ Church, Oxford (DPhil 1980). FRSE 1988. Jun. Res. Fellow, Jesus Coll., Oxford, 1979–81; Lectr in Maths, Imperial Coll., London, 1981–85; Colin Maclaurin Prof. of Maths, 1985–93, Hd, Dept of Maths and Stats, 1988–91, Univ. of Edinburgh; Prof. of Maths, Imperial Coll., London, 1993–2000. Hendrick Vis. Asst Prof., UCLA, 1981–82; Visiting Professor: Univ. of BC, 1990; Univs of Paris VI and XI; Univ. of Toulouse; Inst. des Hautes Etudes Scientifiques. Sen. Fellow, EPSRC, 1993–98. Vice Pres., LMS, 2000–02. Rollo Davidson Prize, 1985, Jun. Whitehead Prize, 1986, Polya Prize, 2000, LMS. *Publications:* numerous papers and articles. *Recreations:* reading, cycling, computer programming, family life. *Address:* University of Oxford Mathematical Institute, 24–29 St Giles, Oxford OX1 3LB. *T:* (01865) 273544; *e-mail:* tlyons@maths.ox.ac.uk.

LYONS, Dr Timothy John; QC 2003; *b* 27 Dec. 1957; *s* of Kenneth Sidney Lyons and Margaret Winifred Lyons (*née* Sim); *m* 1993, Patricia Anne Webb. *Educ:* Bristol Univ. (LLB Hons 1979); Queen Mary Coll., Univ. of London (LLM 1981); Queen Mary and Westfield Coll., Univ. of London (PhD 1991). FTII 1996. Called to the Bar, Inner Temple, 1980; Mem., Hon. Soc. of King's Inns and called to the Bar, Ireland, 1998; in private practice, specialising in revenue law, with partic. interest in matters relating to EC. Panel Mem., Disciplinary Tribunal, Council of Inns of Court. Asst Ed. (European Law), British Tax Review, 2004–. *Publications:* (ed) Chapman's Inheritance Tax, 7th edn, 1987, 8th edn 1990; Insolvency: law and taxation, 1989; Inheritance Tax Planning through Insurance, 1990; (jtly) Historic Buildings and Maintenance Funds, 1991; (Gen. Ed.) Capital Taxes and Estate Planning in Europe, 1991; (jtly) Capital Gains Tax Roll Over Relief for Business Assets, 1993; (ed jtly) The International Guide to the Taxation of Trusts, 1999; EC Customs Law, 2002; contrib. articles to jls incl. British Tax Rev., EC Tax Jl, European Taxation. *Recreations:* reading, music, collecting antiquarian maps. *Address:* (chambers) 15 Old Square, Lincoln's Inn, WC2A 3UE. *T:* (020) 7242 2744, *Fax:* (020) 7831 8095; *e-mail:* taxchambers@15oldsquare.co.uk. *Club:* National.

LYSAGHT, family name of **Baron Lisle**.

LYSCOM, David Edward; HM Diplomatic Service, retired; Chief Executive, Independent Schools Council, since 2008; *b* 8 Aug. 1951; *s* of late William Edward Lyscom and of Phyllis Edith May Lyscom (*née* Coyle); *m* 1973, Dr Nicole Ward; one *s* two *d*. *Educ:* Latymer Upper Sch.; Pembroke Coll., Cambridge (BA 1972). Joined HM Diplomatic Service, 1972; Vienna, 1973–76; Ottawa, 1977–79; FCO, 1979–83; First Secretary: Bonn, 1984–87; Riyadh, 1988–90; Asst Head, Aid Policy Dept, FCO, 1990–91; Counsellor, Science, Technology and Envmt, Bonn, 1991–95; Head of Envmt, Science and Energy Dept, FCO, 1995–98; Ambassador to Slovak Republic, 1998–2001; FCO, 2002–03; UK Perm. Rep. to OECD, Paris, 2004–08. *Recreations:* music, theatre, squash, tennis. *Address:* Independent Schools Council, St Vincent House, 30 Orange Street, WC2H 7HH.

LYSTER, Simon, PhD; Chief Executive (formerly Executive Director), LEAD International, since 2005 (Director of Development and Programmes, 2003–05); *b* 29 April 1952; *s* of John Neal Lyster and Marjorie Aird, (Peggy), (*née* Everard); *m* 1990, Sandra Elizabeth (*née* Charity); one *s* one *d*. *Educ:* Radley Coll.; Magdalene Coll., Cambridge (MA Hons; PhD). Admitted solicitor, 1978; Slaughter and May, 1976–78; Envmtl Defense Fund, NY, 1978–79; admitted to NY Bar, 1979; Defenders of Wildlife, Washington, 1979–81; Dir, Falklands Conservation, 1982–86; Hd, Conservation Policy, WWF UK, and Internat. Treaties Officer, WWF Internat., 1986–95; Dir-Gen., The Wildlife Trusts, 1995–2003. Non-exec. Dir, Northumbrian Water Ltd, 2006–. Mem., Darwin Adv. Cttee, 1997–2003; Trustee: Kilverstone Wildlife Charitable Trust, 2002–; World Land Trust, 2004–; Conservation Internat. - Europe, 2005–. *Publications:* International Wildlife Law, 1985; numerous articles in mags and newspapers and contribs to books. *Recreations:* natural history, tennis, cricket, walking, enthusiastic, but very bad, golf. *Address:* LEAD International, Sundial House, 114 Kensington High Street, W8 4NP. *Club:* Queen's.

LYTHGOE, Prof. Basil, FRS 1958; Professor of Organic Chemistry, Leeds University, 1953–78, now Emeritus; *b* 18 Aug. 1913; 2nd *s* of Peter Whitaker and Agnes Lythgoe; *m* 1946, Kathleen Cameron, *er d* of H. J. Hallum, St Andrews; two *s*. *Educ:* Leigh Grammar Sch.; Manchester Univ. Asst Lectr, Manchester Univ., 1938; Univ. Lectr, Cambridge Univ., 1946. Fellow of King's Coll., Cambridge, 1950. *Publications:* papers on chemistry of natural products, in Jl of Chem. Soc. *Recreation:* hill walking.

LYTTELTON, family name of **Viscount Chandos** and of **Viscount Cobham**.

LYTTLE, (James) Brian (Chambers), OBE 1996; Secretary, Probation Board for Northern Ireland, 1987–97; *b* 22 Aug. 1932; *s* of late James Chambers Lyttle and Margaret Kirkwood Billingsley; *m* 1957, Mary Alma Davidson; four *d*. *Educ:* Bangor Grammar Sch.; Trinity Coll., Dublin (BA 1st Cl. Hons Classics). Entered NI Civil Service as Asst Principal, 1954; Private Sec. to Minister of Commerce, 1960–62; Chief Exec., Enterprise Ulster, 1972–75; Dir, Employment Service, Dept of Manpower Services, 1975–77; Dir, Industrial Develt Orgn, Dept of Commerce, 1977–81; Under Secretary, Dept of Commerce, later Dept of Economic Develt, 1977–84; Under Sec., Dept of Finance and Personnel, 1984–87. Mem., Prison Arts Foundn, 1996–. *Recreations:* reading, walking, music, poetry.

LYTTON, family name of **Earl of Lytton**.

LYTTON, 5th Earl of, *cr* 1880; **John Peter Michael Scawen Lytton;** Baron Wentworth, 1529; Bt 1838; Baron Lytton, 1866; Viscount Knebworth, 1880; Sole proprietor, John Lytton & Co., Chartered Surveyors and Valuers, since 1988; *b* 7 June 1950; *s* of 4th Earl of Lytton, OBE, and Clarissa Mary, *d* of Brig.-Gen. C. E. Palmer, CB, CMG, DSO, RA; *S* father, 1985; *m* 1980, Ursula Alexandra (*née* Komoly); two *s* one *d*. *Educ:* Downside; Reading Univ. (BSc, Estate Management). FRICS 1987 (ARICS 1976); IRRV 1990; MCIArb (ACIArb 1991). President: Sussex Assoc. of Local Councils, 1997–; Nat. Assoc. of Local Councils, 1999–; Chm., Leasehold Adv. Service (formerly Leasehold Enfranchisement Adv. Service), 1994–2000. Member: Council, CLA, 1993–99 (Exec., 1994–99); Bd, Sussex Rural Community Council, 2000–; Council, S of England Agricl Soc., 2004–. Pres., Newstead Abbey Byron Soc., 1988–. Hon. FBEng 1997. *Heir: s* Viscount Knebworth, *qv*. *Address:* (office) Estate Office, Newbuildings Place, Shipley, Horsham, West Sussex RH13 8GQ. *T:* (01403) 741650.

LYTTON COBBOLD, family name of **Baron Cobbold**.

LYVEDEN, 7th Baron *cr* 1859, of Lyveden, co. Northampton; **Jack Leslie Vernon;** self-employed painter and interior decorator, since 1978; *b* 10 Nov. 1938; *e s* of 6th Baron Lyveden and of Queenie Constance Vernon (*née* Ardern); *S* father, 1999; *m* 1961, Lynette June Lilley; one *s* two *d*. *Educ:* Te Aroha District High Sch. Apprentice, painting and decorating industry, 1955–60 (NZ Trade Cert.). Life Mem., Te Aroha Fire Brigade (joined Brigade, 1959; Fire Officer, 1975; Dep. Chief Fire Officer, 1981; Chief Fire Officer, 1987–94). *Heir: s* Hon. Colin Ronald Vernon, *b* 3 Feb. 1967. *Address:* 17 Carlton Street, Te Aroha, New Zealand. *Clubs:* Te Aroha, Returned Services Association.

M

MA LIN, Hon. CBE 1983; PhD; JP; Emeritus Professor of Biochemistry, and Chairman of Board of Trustees of Shaw College, since 1986, The Chinese University of Hong Kong; *b* 8 Feb. 1925; *s* of late Prof. Ma Kiam and Sing-yu Cheng; *m* 1958, Dr Meng-Hua Chen; three *d*. *Educ:* West China Union Univ., China (BSc); Univ. of Leeds (PhD). Postdoctorate Fellow, University College Hosp. Med. Sch., London, and St James's Hosp., Leeds, 1955–56. Assistant Lectr, 1957–59, and Lectr, 1959–64, in Clinical Chemistry, Dept of Pathology, Univ. of Hong Kong; Chinese University of Hong Kong: part-time Lectr in Chemistry, 1964; Sen. Lectr, 1965–72, Reader, 1972–73, Prof., 1973–78, in Biochemistry; Dean of Faculty of Science, 1973–75; Vice-Chancellor, 1978–87. Visiting Biochemist, Hormone Research Laboratory, Univ. of California, San Francisco, 1969. FRSA 1982. Unofficial JP, 1978. Hon. DSc Sussex, 1984; Hon. DLit East Asia, 1987; Hon. LLD: Chinese Univ. of Hong Kong, 1987; Leeds, 1996; Hon. DHL SUNY, 1989; Hon. PhD Tianjin, 1998. Order of the Rising Sun, Gold Rays, with neck ribbon (Japan), 1986; Commander's Cross, Order of Merit (FRG), 1988. *Publications:* various research papers in academic jls. *Recreations:* swimming, table-tennis. *Address:* Shaw College, The Chinese University of Hong Kong, Hong Kong.

MA YING-JEOU; President of Taiwan, since 2008; *b* Hong Kong, 13 July 1950. *Educ:* National Taiwan Univ. (LLB 1972); New York Univ. (LLM 1976); Harvard Law Sch. (SJD 1981). Legal Consultant, First Nat. Bank of Boston, 1980–81; Res. Consultant, Sch. of Law, Univ. of Maryland, 1981; Associate Lawyer, Cole & Deits, NY, 1981; Government of Taiwan: Dep. Dir, First Bureau, Office of the Pres., 1981–88; Minister, Res., Develt and Evaluation Commn, 1988–91; Dep. Minister, Mainland Affairs Council, 1991–93; Minister of Justice, 1993–96; Minister without Portfolio, 1996–97; Prof. of Law, Nat. Chengchi Univ., 1998; Mayor, Taipei City, 1998–2006. Chm., Kuomintang, 2005–07. *Address:* Office of the President, No 122, Sec. 1, Chongqing S Road, Zhongzheng District, Taipei City 100, Taiwan. *T:* (2) 23113731, *Fax:* (2) 23311604; *e-mail:* public@mail.oop.gov.tw.

MA, Yo-Yo, 'cellist; *b* Paris, 7 Oct. 1955 of Chinese parentage; *m* 1978, Jill A. Horner; one *s* one *d*. *Educ:* Harvard Univ.; Juilliard Sch. of Music, NY. First public recital at age of 5 years; winner Avery Fisher Prize, 1978; has performed under many distinguished conductors with all major world orchestras including: Berlin Philharmonic; Boston Symphony; Chicago Symphony; Israel Philharmonic; LSO; NY Philharmonic; also appears in chamber music ensembles; regular participant in festivals at Tanglewood, Edinburgh, Salzburg and other major European fests. Has made numerous recordings. Dr *hc* Northeastern, USA, 1985; Harvard, 1991. Numerous Grammy Awards. *Address:* c/o ICM Artists Ltd, 40 W 57th Street, New York, NY 10019, USA. *T:* (212) 5565600.

MA, Yuzhen; Member: Board, South Centre (an organisation of developing countries), Geneva, 2002; National Committee, Chinese People's Political Consultative Conference, since 1998; *b* Sept. 1934; *s* of Ma Ziqiang and Li Jinghui; *m* 1961, Zou Jichun; one *s* one *d*. *Educ:* Beijing Inst. of Foreign Languages. Staff Mem., Inf. Dept, Min. of Foreign Affairs, People's Republic of China, 1954–63; Attaché and Third Sec., Burma, 1963–69; Dep. Div. Chief and Div. Chief, Inf. Dept, Min. of Foreign Affairs, 1969–80; First Sec. and Counsellor, Ghana, 1980–84; Dir, Inf. Dept, Min. of Foreign Affairs, 1984–88; Consul-Gen. (with rank of Ambassador), Los Angeles, 1988–91; Ambassador to the UK, 1991–95; Dep. Dir, Information Office, State Council, Beijing, 1995–97; Foreign Ministry Comr for People's Repub. of China, HKSAR, 1997–2001. Mem., Internat. Adv. Council, Asia House, 2001–. *Address:* (office) c/o Ministry of Foreign Affairs of China, International Department 2nd Division, 2 Chao Yang Men Nan Da Jie, Beijing 100701, China.

MA Zhengang; President, China Institute of International Studies, since 2004; *b* 9 Nov. 1940 (to a worker's family); *m* 1972, Chen Xiaodong; one *s*. *Educ:* Beijing Foreign Langs Univ.; post-grad. study at Ealing Tech. Coll. and LSE. Staff Mem., N American and Oceanian Affairs Dept (NAOAD), Min. of Foreign Affairs, China, 1967–70; Staff Mem., then Attaché, Yugoslavia, 1970–74; Attaché, NAOAD, 1974–81; Consul, Vancouver, 1981–85; Dep. Dir, then Dir, NAOAD, 1985–90; Counsellor, Washington, 1990–91; Dep. Dir-Gen., then Dir-Gen., NAOAD, 1991–95; Vice-Minister, Foreign Affairs Office of State Council, 1995–97; Ambassador of China to the Court of St James's, 1997–2002; Ambassador, Min. of Foreign Affairs, 2002–04. *Recreations:* table tennis, bridge, literature. *Address:* c/o China Institute of International Studies, 3 Toutiao, Taijichang, Beijing 100005, People's Republic of China.

MAAN, Bashir Ahmed, CBE 2000; JP; DL; Member, Scottish Constitutional Convention, 1988–98; Judge, City of Glasgow District Courts, 1968–97; *b* Maan, Gujranwala, Pakistan, 22 Oct. 1926; *s* of late Choudhry Sardar Khan Maan and Mrs Hayat Begum Maan; *m*; one *s* three *d*. *Educ:* D. B. High Sch., Qila Didar Singh; Panjab Univ.; Strathclyde Univ. (MSc 1994). Involved in struggle for creation of Pakistan, 1943–47; organised rehabilitation of refugees from India in Maan and surrounding areas, 1947–48; emigrated to UK and settled in Glasgow, 1953; Glasgow Founder Sec., Pakistan Social and Cultural Soc., 1955–65, Pres., 1966–69; Pres., Islamic Centre, Glasgow, 2007–; Vice-Chm., Glasgow Community Relations Council, 1970–75; Pres., Standing Conf. of Pakistani Orgns in UK, 1974–77; a Dep. Chm., Commn for Racial Equality, 1977–80; Founder Chm., Scottish Pakistani Assoc., 1984–98; Pres., Nat. Assoc. of British Pakistanis, 2000–07; Member: Overseas Pakistanis Adv. Council, Govt of Pakistan, 2001–04; President's Task Force on Human Develt of Pakistan, 2001–04; Scottish rep., Muslim Council of Britain, 1998–; Convenor, Muslim Council of Scotland, 2007–; Chairman: Strathclyde CRC, 1987–93 and 1994–96; Strathclyde Interpreting Services Adv. Cttee, 1988–96; Council of Ethnic Minority Orgns Scotland, 2002–. Member: Immigrants Prog. Adv. Cttee, BBC, 1972–80; Gen. Adv. Cttee, BBC, 1991–95; Scottish Selecting Panel, BBC, 1992–96. Hon. Res. Fellow, Univ. of Glasgow, 1988–91. Councillor, Glasgow Corp., 1970–75; City of Glasgow Dist, 1974–84 (Bailie, 1980–84); Mem., Glasgow City Council, 1995–2003 (Bailie, 1996–99); Magistrate, City of Glasgow, 1971–74; Vice-Chm. 1971–74, Chm. 1974–75, Police Cttee, Glasgow Corp.; Police Judge, City of Glasgow, 1974–75; Mem., 1995–2003, Convenor, 1999–2003, Strathclyde Jt Police Bd. Mem. Exec. Cttee, Glasgow City Labour Party, 1969–70. Contested (Lab) East Fife, Feb. 1974. Convener, Pakistan Bill Action Cttee, 1973; Member: Nat. Road Safety Cttee, 1971–75; Scottish Accident Prevention Cttee, 1971–75; Scottish Gas Consumers' Council, 1978–81; Greater Glasgow Health Bd, 1981–91; Hon. Pres., SCVO, 2001–06 (Mem., Mgt Bd, 1988–95). Chm., Organising Cttee, Glasgow Internat. Sports Festival Co. Ltd, 1987–89. Mem. Bd of Governors, Jordanhill Coll. of Educn, Glasgow, 1987–91. JP 1968, DL 1982, Glasgow. Hon Fellow, Glasgow Caledonian Univ., 2003. Hon. LLD Strathclyde, 1999; DUniv Glasgow, 2001; Hon. DLitt Glasgow Caledonian, 2002. *Publications:* The New Scots, 1992; The Thistle and the Crescent, 2008; articles, contrib. to press. *Recreations:* golf, reading. *Address:* 8 Riverview Gardens, Flat 6, Glasgow G5 8EL. *T:* (0141) 429 7689. *Club:* Douglas Park Golf.

MAATHAI, Wangari Muta, PhD; MP (National Rainbow Coalition) Tetu, Kenya, 2002–07; *b* 1 April 1940; *d* of Muta Njugi and Wanjiru Kibicho; *m* 1969, Mwangi Mathai (marr. diss.); three *c*. *Educ:* Mount St Scholastica Coll., Kansas (BS 1964); Univ. of Pittsburgh (MS 1966); Univ. of Nairobi (PhD 1971). Hd, Dept of Veterinary Anatomy, 1976, Associate Prof., 1977, Univ. of Nairobi. Dir, Kenya Red Cross, 1973–80. Mem. Bd, Nat. Council of Women of Kenya (Chm., 1981–87); Founder and Co-ordinator, Green Belt Movt, 1977–2002. Asst Minister for Envmt, Natural Resources and Wildlife, Kenya, 2003–06. Hon. FRIBA 2008. Nobel Peace Prize, 2004. *Publications:* The Canopy of Hope: my life campaigning for Africa, women and the environment, 2002; The Green Belt Movement: sharing the approach and experience, 2002; Unbowed: one woman's story, 2007. *Address:* c/o Green Belt Movement, Hughes Building, 1st Floor, Muindi Mbingu Street, Kenyatta Avenue Wing, PO Box 67545–00200, Nairobi, Kenya.

MAAZEL, Lorin, conductor; Music Director: New York Philharmonic Orchestra, 2002–June 2009; Palau de les Arts Reina Sofia, Valencia, since 2006; *b* 6 March 1930; *s* of Lincoln Maazel and Marie Varencove; *m* 3rd, 1986, Dietlinde Turban; two *s* one *d*, and one *s* three *d* by previous marriages. *Educ:* Pittsburgh University. FRCM 1981. Début as a conductor at age of 9, as violinist a few years later; by 1941 had conducted foremost US Orchestras, including Toscanini's NBC; European début as conductor, 1953; active as conductor in Europe, Latin America, Australia, Japan and USA, 1954–; performances at major festivals, including Edinburgh, Bayreuth, Salzburg and Lucerne; in USA: conducted Boston Symphony, New York Philharmonic, Philadelphia Orchestra, and at Metropolitan, 1960 and 1962; Covent Garden début, 1978. Artistic Director of Deutsche Oper Berlin, 1965–71; Chief Conductor, Radio Sinfonie Orchester, Berlin, 1965–75; Associate Principal Conductor, Philharmonia (formerly New Philharmonia) Orchestra, 1970–72, Principal Guest Conductor, 1976–80; Music Director, Cleveland Orchestra, 1972–82, Conductor Emeritus, 1982; Principal Guest Conductor, 1977–88, Music Director, 1988–90, Orchestre National de France; Director, Vienna State Opera, 1982–84; Music Director: Pittsburgh SO, 1988–96; Bayerischer Rundfunk SO, Munich, 1993–2002. Composer and conductor, 1984 (opera), Royal Opera House, 2005. Has made over 300 recordings. Hon. Dr of Music Pittsburgh Univ., 1968; Hon. Dr of Humanities Beaver Coll., 1973; Hon. Dr of Fine Arts, Carnegie-Mellon Univ., Pennsylvania; Hon. Dr of Music, RCM, 1984; Hon. DCL Univ. of South, Sewanee, 1988; Hon. Dr Indiana Univ., 1988. Sibelius Medal, Finland, 1969. Commander's Cross of Order of Merit, Federal Republic of Germany, 1977; Officier, Légion d'Honneur, France, 1981. *Address:* c/o New York Philharmonic Orchestra, Carnegie Hall, 881 Seventh Avenue, New York, NY 10019–3210, USA.

MABB, David Michael; QC 2001; *b* 12 June 1956; *s* of Kenneth George Mabb and Joyce Madeline Mabb. *Educ:* King James' Grammar Sch., Almondbury; St Nicholas Grammar Sch., Northwood; Gonville and Caius Coll., Cambridge (BA 1978; MA 1982). Called to the Bar, Lincoln's Inn, 1979. *Address:* Erskine Chambers, 33 Chancery Lane, WC2A 1EN. *T:* (020) 7242 5532.

MABB, Katherine Anne; see Green, K. A.

MABBS, Alfred Walter, CB 1982; Keeper of Public Records, 1978–82; *b* 12 April 1921; *e s* of James and Amelia Mabbs; *m* 1942, Dorothy Lowley; one *s*. *Educ:* Hackney Downs Sch. Served War, RAF, 1941–46. Asst Keeper, Public Record Office, 1950–66; Principal Asst Keeper, 1967–69; Records Admin. Officer, 1970–73; Dep. Keeper of Public Records, 1973–78. Pres., Internat. Council on Archives, 1980–82. Gen. Editor, Herts Record Soc., 1991–96. FRHistS 1954. FSA 1979. *Publications:* Guild Stewards Book of the Borough of Calne (vol. vii, Wilts Arch. and Record Soc.), 1953; The Records of the Cabinet Office to 1922, 1966; Guide to the Contents of the Public Record Office, vol. iii (main contributor), 1968; Exchequer of the Jews, vol. iv (jt contrib.), 1972; The Organisation of Intermediate Records Storage (with Guy Duboscq), 1974; articles and reviews in various jls. *Recreation:* retirement. *Address:* 32 The Street, Wallington, Baldock, Herts SG7 6SW.

MABEY, John Hedley; Controller of Financial Services, London Borough of Camden, 1996–2005; *b* 18 June 1946; *s* of Douglas Charles Mabey and Olive Ena Mabey (*née* Lipscombe); *m* 1967, Jacqueline Trudy Cassidy; two *s*. *Educ:* Chartered Inst. of Public Finance and Accountancy. Camden London Borough Council: Mgt Accountant, 1973–78; Asst Dir of Finance, 1978–92; Dep. Dir of Finance, 1992–96. *Recreations:* golf, squash.

MABEY, Richard Thomas; writer and broadcaster; *b* 20 Feb. 1941; *s* of late Thomas Gustavus Mabey and Edna Nellie (*née* Moore). *Educ:* Berkhamsted Sch.; St Catherine's

Coll., Oxford (BA Hons 1964, MA 1971). Lectr in Social Studies, Dacorum Coll. of Further Educn, 1963–65; Sen. Editor, Penguin Books, 1966–73; freelance writer, 1973–; columnist, The Times, 2004–06. Mem. Mgt Cttee, Soc. of Authors, 1998–2000. Presenter, Tomorrow's World, BBC TV, 1995. Member: Nature Conservancy Council, 1982–86; Council, Botanical Soc. of the British Isles, 1981–83; President: London Wildlife Trust, 1982–92; Richard Jefferies Soc., 1995–98; Norfolk and Norwich Naturalists' Soc., 2005–06; Vice-Pres., Open Spaces Soc., 2003–. Dir, Common Ground, 1988–. Patron: Thomas Bewick Trust, 1986–; John Clare Soc., 2006–; Mem. Adv. Council, Plantlife, 1992–. Leverhulme Trust Res. Award, 1983–84; Leverhulme Res. Fellowship, 1993–94. Hon. DSc St Andrews, 1997; DUniv Essex, 2007. Granted a civil list pension, 2008. *Publications:* (ed) Class, 1967; The Pop Process, 1969; Food for Free, 1972, 2nd edn 1989; Children in Primary School, 1972; The Unofficial Countryside, 1973; The Pollution Handbook, 1973; The Roadside Wildlife Book, 1974; Street Flowers, 1976 (TES Inf. Book Award); Plants with a Purpose, 1977; The Common Ground, 1980; The Flowering of Britain, 1980; (ed) Landscape with Figures, 1983; Oak and Company, 1983 (NY Acad. of Sci. Children's Book Award, 1984); In a Green Shade, 1983; Back to the Roots, 1983; (ed) Second Nature, 1984; The Frampton Flora, 1985; Gilbert White: a biography, 1986 (Whitbread Biography Award); Gen. Ed., The Journals of Gilbert White, 1986–89; (ed) The Gardener's Labyrinth, 1987; The Flowering of Kew, 1988; Home Country, 1990; (ed) The Flowers of May, 1990; A Nature Journal, 1991; Whistling in the Dark, 1993; Landlocked, 1994; (ed) The Oxford Book of Nature Writing, 1995; Flora Britannica (British Bk Awards Illustrated Book of the Year), 1996; Selected Writings 1974–1999, 1999; Nature Cure, 2005; (with Mark Cocker) Birds Britannica, 2005; Fencing Paradise, 2005; Beechcombings: the narratives of trees, 2007. *Recreations:* food, meandering. *Address:* c/o Sheil Land Associates, 52 Doughty Street, WC1N 2LS.

MABEY, Roger Stanley, CMG 1997; Director, Cyril Sweett Group Ltd, since 2003; *b* 11 Aug. 1944; *s* of Stanley Mabey and Edith Mabey (*née* Stride); *m* 1968, Margaret Marian Watkins; one *s* one *d*. *Educ:* Cleeve Sch., Cheltenham; Gloucestershire Coll. of Technology (HND 1964); Lancaster Coll. of Technology, Coventry; Eur. Centre of Continuing Educn, INSEAD. Joined Bovis, 1967; Project Manager, Bristol, 1967–73; Regl Dir, Harrow office, 1973–79; a Divl Dir, 1979–86; Dir, Bovis Construction Ltd, 1986–93; Asst Man. Dir, 1993–94, Man. Dir, 1994–97, Bovis Internat. Ltd; Executive Director: Bovis Construction Gp, 1998–2000; Bovis Lend Lease Ltd, 2000–03. Vice Chm., Housing Solutions Gp, 2005–. Member: DTI Adv. Gps on India, 1994, and S Africa; Market Gp, Cttee for S African Trade, 1996; BOTB, 1998. Vice Chm., Cookham Soc., 1998–2000. FCIOB 1980; FRSA 1998. *Recreations:* travel, gardening, painting, food, music, athletics, family. *Address:* Carrol Lodge, Sutton Road, Cookham, Maidenhead, Berks SL6 9RD.

MABRO, Robert Emile, CBE 1996; Fellow of St Antony's College, Oxford, 1971–2002, now Emeritus, and of St Catherine's College, Oxford, since 2007; President, Oxford Institute for Energy Studies, 2003–06, now Hon. President (Director, 1982–2003); *b* 26 Dec. 1934; *s* of Emile Mabro and Tatiana Mabro (*née* Bittar); *m* 1967, Judith Howey; two *d*. *Educ:* Coll. St Marc, Alexandria, Egypt; Univ. of Alexandria (BSc Engrg); SOAS, London Univ. (MSc Econs). Civil engr, Egypt, 1956–60; Leon Fellow, Univ. of London, 1966–67; Res. Officer, SOAS, 1967–69; Sen. Res. Officer in econs of ME, Univ. of Oxford, 1969–; Director: ME Centre, St Antony's Coll., Oxford, 1976–79; Oxford Energy Seminar, 1978–. Vice Chm. Bd, Econ. Res. Forum for Arab Countries, Iran and Turkey, 1994–97. Hon. Sec., Oxford Energy Policy Club, 1976–. Charles Hedlund Vis. Prof., Amer. Univ. in Cairo, 1997. Award, Internat. Assoc. for Energy Econs, 1990. Medal of the Pres. (Italy), 1985; Order of the Aztec Eagle (Mexico), 1997; Order of Francisco Miranda (Venezuela), 1999; Officier des Palmes Académiques (France), 2001. *Publications:* The Egyptian Economy 1952–1972, 1974; (with S. Radwan) The Industrialization of Egypt 1939–73, 1976; (ed) World Energy: issues and policies, 1980; (ed) OPEC and the World Oil Market, 1986; (jtly) The Market for North Sea Crude Oil, 1986; (with P. Horsnell) Oil Markets and Prices, 1993; (ed) Oil in the 21st Century, 2006; articles in jls. *Recreations:* cooking; collecting books, postcards, etc on Alexandria, Egypt; reading, poetry, philosophy. *Address:* (office) 57 Woodstock Road, Oxford OX2 6FA. *T:* (01865) 311377; 52 Lonsdale Road, Oxford OX2 7EP. *T:* (01865) 557623.

MABUZA, Lindiwe; High Commissioner for the Republic of South Africa to the United Kingdom, since 2001; *b* Natal, 13 Aug. 1938. *Educ:* Grailville Community Coll., Ohio (Dip. Home Econs 1959); Roma, Lesotho, Univ. of S Africa (BA 1961); Stanford Univ., Calif (MA English 1966); Univ. of Minnesota (MA American Studies 1968); Diplomatic Trng, Kuala Lumpur (Dip. 1993). Teacher, English and Zulu Lit., Manzini Central Sch., Swaziland, 1962–64; Lectr, Dept of Sociol., Univ. of Minnesota, 1968–69; Asst Prof. of Lit. and Hist., Ohio Univ., 1969–77; radio journalist with ANC's Radio Freedom (broadcasting into SA from Zambia), 1977–79; Chief Representative of ANC: to Scandinavia, based in Sweden, 1979–87 (opened ANC offices in Denmark, Norway and Finland); to US, 1989–94; Mem., first democratic Parliament, SA, 1994–95; first Ambassador for S Africa to Germany, 1995–99; High Commissioner: to Malaysia, 1999–2001 (also to Brunei and the Philippines (non-resident)). Ed., Voice of Women, Jl by ANC women, 1977–79. Chm., ANC Cultural Cttee, Lusaka, 1977–79. Hon. PhD Durban-Westville, 1997. Yari Yari Award, New York Univ., 1997. *Publications:* (ed) Malibongwe: poetry by ANC women, 1980 (trans. German and Russian); (ed) One Never Knows: short stories by ANC women in exile, 1989; From ANC to Sweden: Olof Palme poem in English and Swedish 1986 (trans. Norwegian and Finnish); Letter to Letta: selected poetry from 1970–1987, 1993; Africa to Me: poetry from 1976–1996 in English and German, 1998; Voices that Lead: poetry selection from 1976–1996, 1998; contrib. to various poetry and short story anthologies. *Address:* South African High Commission, Trafalgar Square, WC2N 5DP. *T:* (020) 7451 7299, *Fax:* (020) 7451 7284; *e-mail:* general@southafricahouse.com.

MAC; *see* McMurtry, S.

McADAM, Douglas Baxter; HM Diplomatic Service, retired; Consul General, Hamburg, 1999–2004; *b* 25 June 1944; *s* of late John Watson McAdam and Jean Cook McAdam; *m* 1965, Susan Clare Jarvis; one *s* one *d*. *Educ:* Musselburgh Burgh Sch.; Musselburgh Grammar Sch. Entered Foreign Office, 1961; served Ulan Bator, Luanda, New Delhi and FCO, 1966–78; Vice-Consul, Rio de Janeiro, 1979–82; 2nd, later 1st Sec., UK Delegn MBFR, Vienna, 1983–87; FCO, 1987–90; 1st Sec., Lagos, 1990–94; FCO, 1994–95; Ambassador to Kazakhstan and Kyrgyzstan (resident in Almaty), 1996–99. Mem., RSAA, 1997. *Recreations:* fly fishing, walking, eating well. *Address:* Colinas Verdes Lote 105, 8600–074 Bensafrim, Portugal.

McADAM, James, CBE 1995; Chairman, Signet Group plc, 1992–2006 (Chief Executive, 1992–2000); *b* 10 Dec. 1930; *s* of John Robert McAdam and Helen McAdam (*née* Cormack); *m* 1955, Maisie Una Holmes; two *d*. *Educ:* Lenzie Academy. Joined J. & P. Coats Ltd, 1945; Finance Dir, Coats Chile, 1962–66, Coats India, 1966–70, Coats Patons UK, 1972–75; Dir, 1975, Chief Exec., 1985–86, Chm., 1986–91, Coats Patons plc; Dep. Chm. and Chief Operating Officer, Coats Viyella (merged co.), 1986–91. Chm., Bisley Office Equipment Co., 1991–; Dir, Scotia Hldgs, 1991–97. Dir, London Region Post Office, 1985–87. Chairman: British Clothing Industry Assoc., 1991–2008; British Knitting and Clothing Confedn, 1991–2008; British Apparel and Textile Confedn, 1992–2008; Mem., Exec. Cttee, Scottish Council Develt and Industry, 1988–99. FRSA; CCMI. *Recreations:* theatre, travel. *Address:* 143 Whitehall Court, Westminster, SW1A 2EP. *Clubs:* Royal Automobile, Farmers.

McADAM, John David Gibson; Chairman: United Utilities, since 2008; Rentokil Initial, since 2008; *b* 30 April 1948; *s* of John McAdam and Sarah McAdam (*née* Gibson); *m* 1979, Louise Mary Mann; one *s* one *d*. *Educ:* Kelsick Grammar Sch., Ambleside; Lakes Secondary Sch., Windermere; Manchester Univ. (BSc 1st Cl. Hons Chem. Physics; Dip. Adv. Studies in Science (Physics) 1971; PhD 1973). MRC Fellowship, Manchester and Cambridge Univs; Sen. Vice Pres., Quest Internat., 1987–90; Tech. Dir, Birds Eye Walls Ltd, 1990–93; Chairman and Chief Executive Officer: Unichema Internat., 1993–97; Quest Internat., 1997; Exec. Vice-Pres., ICI plc, 1997–98; Chm. and CEO, ICI Paints, 1998–2003; Dir, 1999–2008, Chief Exec., 2003–08, ICI plc. Dir, Severn Trent plc, 2000–05; Sen. non-exec. Dir, J. Sainsbury plc, 2005–; non-exec. Dir, Rolls Royce, 2008–. Mem., Chem. Adv. Bd, Univ. of Cambridge, 2003–. *Publications:* scientific papers in scientific jls on macromolecular motion in solutions. *Recreations:* Rugby, cricket, soccer (now as a spectator), walking, listening to music. *Address:* United Utilities Group plc, 55 Grosvenor Street, W1K 3LJ.

McADAM, Prof. Keith Paul William James, FRCP, FWACP; Director, Infectious Diseases Institute, Mulago Hospital, Makerere University Medical School, Kampala, Uganda, 2004–07; Wellcome Professor of Tropical Medicine, London School of Hygiene and Tropical Medicine, London University, 1984–2004, now Emeritus (Head of Department of Clinical Sciences, 1988–94); *b* 13 Aug. 1945; *s* of Sir Ian William James McAdam, OBE, and of Mrs L. M. Hrothgaarde Bennett (*née* Gibson); *m* 1968, Penelope Ann (*née* Spencer); three *d*. *Educ:* Prince of Wales School, Nairobi; Millfield School, Som.; Clare Coll., Cambridge (MA, MB BChir); Middlesex Hosp. Med. Sch. FRSTM&H; Dip. Amer. Bd of Internal Medicine, Dip. Amer. Bd of Allergy and Clinical Immunology. Medical posts at Middlesex Hosp., Royal Northern Hosp., Brompton Hosp., Nat. Hosp. for Nervous Diseases, 1969–73; Lectr in Medicine, Inst. of Med. Research, Goroka, Papua New Guinea, 1973–75; MRC Travelling Fellow, 1975–76; Vis. Scientist, Immunology Branch, Nat. Cancer Inst., NIH, Bethesda, 1976–77; Asst Prof., Tufts Univ. Sch. of Medicine, 1977–82; Associate Prof., Divs of Allergy, Exptl Medicine and Geographic Medicine, Tufts Univ., 1982–84; Consultant Physician, Hosp. for Tropical Diseases, NW1, 1984–95; Dir, MRC Labs, The Gambia, 1995–2003 (on secondment). Adjunct Professor: Tufts New England Med. Center, Boston, 2004–07; Univ. of Minnesota Med. Sch., 2006–. *Publications:* scientific articles on immunology and tropical medicine, esp. on amyloidosis, acute phase proteins, leprosy, tuberculosis, AIDS, malaria, inflammation. *Recreations:* cricket, tennis, golf, gardening. *Address:* Oakmead, 70 Luton Lane, Redbourn, Herts AL3 7PY. *T:* (01582) 792833. *Clubs:* MCC, Jesters.

MACADIE, Jeremy James; HM Diplomatic Service; Ambassador to the Republics of Rwanda and Burundi, 2004–07; *b* 10 July 1952; *s* of Donald Jaimeson Macadie and Olga May Sheck; *m* 1975, Chantal Andrea Jacqueline Copiatti; one *d*. *Educ:* Yeovil Grammar Sch. Joined FCO, by open competition, 1972; Dakar, 1975; Addis Ababa, 1980; Sana'a, 1984; Dep. Hd of Mission, Antananarivo, 1987; Foreign Office Spokesman, 1990; Asst Private Sec. to Minister for Europe, 1995; Dep. Hd of Mission, Algiers, 1997; on secondment to African Directorate, French Ministry of Foreign Affairs, 2003. Commnd TAVR (Intelligence and Security Gp), 1983. *Recreations:* country pursuits, turning wine into water. *Address:* c/o Foreign and Commonwealth Office, SW1A 2AH.

McAFEE, Raymond Noel, CB 2002; consultant in international trade; Managing Director, UK Division, GlobalLink Trade Consulting, Washington, since 2004; *b* 15 Dec. 1943; *s* of late James Hill and Sarah McAfee (*née* O'Kane); *m* 1966, Margot McGowan; one *s* one *d*. *Educ:* Strabane Coll.; Portadown Coll. Joined HM Customs and Excise, 1963: Officer, 1963–74; Surveyor, 1974–79; Asst Collector, 1979–85; Sen. Principal, HQ London, 1985–89; Collector, NI, 1989–93; Asst Sec., HQ London, 1993–96; Dir, Central Ops, 1996–99; Comr, 1996–2003; Dir, Outfield, 1999–2001; Dir, Regl Business Services, 2001–03; Dir Gen., 2003. Mem., Standards Cttee, Tunbridge Wells BC, 2004–. FIMMM (FIM 1991). *Recreations:* golf, theatre, music. *Address: e-mail:* ray.mcafee@btinternet.com.

McAFEE, Maj.-Gen. Robert William Montgomery, CB 1999; *b* 8 Nov. 1944; *s* of Andrew Montgomery McAfee and Jane Beryl McAfee; *m* 1967, Erica-May MacLennan; one *s* one *d*. *Educ:* Inverness Royal Academy; Mons Officer Cadet Sch. Commnd, RTR, 1965; served Aden, BAOR, NI (despatches), Cyprus, Gulf, Bosnia; CO 2nd RTR, 1982–84; Instructor, Staff Coll., 1985–86; Col, Higher Command and Staff Course, 1987; Comdr 6 Armd Bde, 1988–89; ACOS (Land), HQ British Forces, ME, 1990; COS HQ 1 (BR) Corps, 1991–92; RCDS 1993; DG, Army Training, 1993–95; Comdr, Multi Nat. Div. (Central), 1996–99, retired. Dir of Admin, Norton Rose, 1999–2004. Rep. Col Comdt, RTR, 1995–99; Hon. Col Westminster Dragoons, 2003–. Comr, Duke of York's Royal Mil. Sch., 2004–. Chm., British Bobsleigh Assoc., 1998–2000; Dep. Pres., Army Rugby Union, 1994–99. *Recreations:* golf, ski-ing, watching Rugby and motor racing. *Address:* c/o Clydesdale Bank, 15 Academy Street, Inverness IV1 7JN. *Club:* Army and Navy.

MACAIRE, Robert Nigel Paul; HM Diplomatic Service; High Commissioner, Kenya, since 2008; *b* 19 Feb. 1966; *s* of James and Tatiana Macaire; *m* 1996, Alice Mackenzie; two *d*. *Educ:* Cranleigh Sch.; St Edmund Hall, Oxford (BA Modern Hist.). Gen. Staff Secretariat and Policy Studies Secretariat, MoD, 1987–90; entered FCO, 1990; Falkland Is Dept, FCO, 1990–91; Bucharest, 1992–95; Near East and N Africa Dept, then Africa Dept Southern, FCO, 1995–98; First Sec., Washington, 1998–2002; Hd, Counter Terrorism Policy Dept, FCO, 2002–04; Counsellor (Political), New Delhi, 2004–06; Dir, Consular Services, FCO, 2006–08. *Recreation:* sailing (inshore and offshore, cruising and racing). *Address:* c/o Foreign and Commonwealth Office, King Charles Street, SW1A 2AH. *Club:* Royal Ocean Racing.

McALEESE, Kevin Stanley, CBE 1998; education consultant; non-executive Director and Vice-Chairman, North Yorkshire and York Primary Care Trust, since 2006; *b* 28 Feb. 1947; *s* of late James McAleese, DFM and of Marjorie N. A. McAleese; (*née* Stromberg); *m* 1st, 1976, Dorothy Anne Nelson (*d* 1998); one *s* one *d*; 2nd, 2000, Jenny Louise Brindle (*née* Grant). *Educ:* London Nautical Sch.; Keele Univ. (BEd 1972); Univ. of Kent (MA 1985). Midshipman, subseq. Navigating Officer, Blue Funnel Line, 1964–68; Asst Teacher, West Hatch Technical High Sch., 1972–75; Head of Dept, Queen's Sch., Jt HQ Rheindahlen, 1975–78; Head of Faculty, Grange County Secondary Sch., 1978–81; Sen. Teacher, Sheppey Sch., 1981–84; Dep. Head Teacher, Geoffrey Chaucer Sch., Canterbury, 1984–87; Head Teacher: Alec Hunter High Sch., Braintree, 1987–91; Harrogate Grammar Sch., 1992–2002. Non-exec. Dir, 2002–06, Vice-Chm., 2004–06, Craven, Harrogate and Rural Dist PCT. Chm., RAF Menwith Hill British-Amer. Cttee, 2003–. FRSA 1993; FCMI (FIMgt 1995). *Publications:* Managing the Margins, 1996;

Balancing the Books, 2000; articles and series in TES and Managing Schools Today. *Recreations:* cinema, photography, music, walking, travelling. *Address:* 11 Hazel Drive, Burn Bridge, Harrogate, N Yorks HG3 1NY. *T:* (01423) 815147.

McALEESE, Mary Patricia, (Mrs Martin McAleese); President of Ireland, since 1997; *b* 27 June 1951; *d* of Patrick Leneghan and Claire (*née* McManus); *m* 1976, Martin McAleese; one *s* two *d*. *Educ:* QUB (LLB 1973); TCD (MA 1986); Dip. in Spanish, Inst. of Linguists, 1994; AIL. Called to the Bar: N Ireland, 1974; King's Inns, Dublin, 1978. Barrister, NI, 1974–75; Reid Prof. of Criminal Law, Criminology and Penology, TCD, 1975–79 and 1981–87; journalist and TV presenter, Radio Telefis Eireann, 1979–81 (part-time presenter, 1981–85); Queen's University, Belfast: Dir, Inst. of Professional Legal Studies, 1987–97; Pro Vice-Chancellor, 1994–97. Director: Northern Ireland Electricity, 1991–97; Channel 4 Television, 1992–97; Royal Gp of Hospitals HSS Trust, Belfast, 1996–97. *Publications:* (jtly) Reports on Irish Penal System, 1981; Children in Custody (ed Stewart and Tutt), 1987; (jtly) Sectarianism: a discussion document, 1993; Reconciled Being, 1997; contrib. legal and religious jls. *Recreations:* hill-walking, set dancing, reading, theology. *Address:* Aras an Uachtaráin, Phoenix Park, Dublin 8, Ireland.

McALISKEY, (Josephine) Bernadette, (Mrs Micheal McAliskey); Co-ordinator, S Tyrone Empowerment Programme; *b* 23 April 1947; *d* of late John James Devlin and Elizabeth Devlin; *m* 1973, Micheal McAliskey; three *c*. *Educ:* St Patrick's Girls' Acad., Dungannon; psychology student at Queen's Univ., Belfast, 1966–69. Youngest MP in House of Commons when elected at age of 21; MP (Ind. Unity) Mid Ulster, Apr. 1969–Feb. 1974. Founder Member and Mem. Exec., Irish Republican Socialist Party, 1975–76. Former Chm., Indep. Socialist Party, Ireland. Contested: (Ind) N Ireland, European Parlt, 1979; (People's Democracy), Dublin N Central, Dáil Eireann, Feb. and Nov. 1982. *Publication:* The Price of my Soul (autobiog.), 1969. *Recreations:* walking, folk music, doing nothing, swimming.

McALISTER, Michael Ian, FCA; Managing Director, The Tam Programme, European Bank for Reconstruction and Development, 1993–2002; *b* Leeds, Yorkshire, 23 Aug. 1930; *s* of S. McAlister, CBE, and J. A. McAlister (*née* Smith); *m* 1st, 1953, Patricia (*née* Evans) (marr. diss. 1983); four *s* three *d*; 2nd, 1984, Elizabeth Anne, *o d* of Mr and Mrs Ludwig Hehn. *Educ:* Brazil; France; St John's Coll., Oxford (MA). National Service, Lieut, Intelligence Corps (MI8), 1950–51 (Acting Capt). Articled Clerk, Price Waterhouse, London, 1954–58; Private Sec. to the Duke of Windsor, 1959–61; Investment Manager, Ionian Bank Ltd, London, 1961–67; Managing Dir, Ionian Bank Trustee Co., London, 1967–68; Slater Walker Securities (Australia): Dep. Chm., 1969–70, Chm., 1970–72; Pres., Aust. Associated Stock Exchanges, 1972–74; Director: (Middle East), Lester B. Knight and Associates, USA, 1975–79; Cluff Oil Holdings, subseq. Cluff Resources, 1979–89. Chm., Woking Cons. Assoc., 1967–68. *Recreations:* carpentry, DIY. *Address:* Kempshott, off Wilderness Road, Onslow Village, Guildford, Surrey GU2 7QP. *T:* (01483) 577258; *e-mail:* mielmcalister@aol.com.

MacALISTER, Very Rev. Randal George Leslie; Dean of St Andrews, Dunkeld and Dunblane, 1998–2006; Rector, St Kessog's, Auchterarder and St James', Muthill, 1998–2006; *b* 31 Dec. 1941; *s* of James Daniel Beaton MacAlister and Doreen MacAlister (*née* Thompson); *m* 1964, Valerie Jane Letitia Nelson; three *s*. *Educ:* Royal Sch., Armagh; Trinity Coll., Dublin (BA 1963; MA 1966; Divinity Testimonium 1964). Deacon 1964, priest 1966; Curate, St Mark's, Portadown, 1964–67; Rector: St Matthew's, Keady and Armaghbreague, 1967–74, and St John's, Derrynoose, 1973–74; St Mary's, Kirriemuir, 1974–81; St John's, Greenock, 1981–87; St John's, Forfar, 1987–95; Canon, St Ninian's Cathedral, Perth, 1993–95; Chaplain, St Mark's, Sophia Antipolis, France, 1995–98. *Recreations:* gardening, hill-walking, languages, music. *Address:* Auld Mill, Dykehead Cortachy, Kirriemuir, Angus DD8 4QN. *T:* (01575) 540216.

McALISTER, Maj.-Gen. Ronald William Lorne, CB 1977; OBE 1968 (MBE 1959); *b* 26 May 1923; 2nd *s* of late Col R. J. F. McAlister, OBE and Mrs T. M. Collins, Bath; *m* 1964, Sally Ewart Marshall; two *d*. *Educ:* Dreghorn Castle Sch., Edinburgh; Sedbergh School. Commnd 3rd QAO Gurkha Rifles, 1942; Adjt 1/3 GR Burma, 1945 (despatches); Adjt 2/10 GR Malaya, 1950–52 (despatches); Instructor, Sch. of Infantry, 1953–55; psc 1956; Bde Major 99 Gurkha Bde, Malaya, 1957–59 (MBE); jssc 1961–62; Asst Sec., Chiefs of Staff Cttee, 1962–64; 2nd in comd and CO 10th PMO Gurkha Rifles, Borneo, 1964–66 (despatches); Internal Security Duties, Hong Kong, 1967–68 (OBE); Instructor, Jt Services Staff Coll., 1968; comd Berlin Inf. Bde, 1968–71; ndc, Canada, 1971–72; Exercise Controller UK Cs-in-C Cttee, 1972–75; Dep. Commander Land Forces Hong Kong and Maj.-Gen. Brigade of Gurkhas, 1975–77; retired 1977. Col, 10th Princess Mary's Own Gurkha Rifles, 1977–85; Chm., Gurkha Brigade Assoc., 1980–90. Bursar, Wellesley House Sch., Broadstairs, 1977–88. Chm., Buckmaster Meml Home, Broadstairs, 1980–. *Publication:* (ed and contrib.) Bugle and Kukri, Vol. 2, 1986. *Recreations:* golf, gardening. *Address:* The Chalet, 41 Callis Court Road, Broadstairs, Kent CT10 3AU. *T:* (01843) 862351. *Clubs:* Army and Navy; Royal St George's Golf (Captain, 1989–90; Hon. Treas., 1991–96; Pres., 2004–08), Senior Golfers' Society.

McALISTER, William Harle Nelson; independent arts producer and consultant; Cultural Policy Adviser, Soros Foundations, 1992–97; *b* 30 Aug. 1940; *s* of Flying Officer William Nelson (*d* 1940) and Marjorie Isobel (*née* McIntyre); adopted by William Edwyn McAlister (whom she *m* 2nd); *m* 1968 (marr. diss. 1985); two *s* two *d*; one *s*. *Educ:* Sorbonne, Paris; Univ. of Copenhagen; University Coll. London (BA Hons Psychology, 1967). Dir, Almost Free Theatre, 1968–72; Dep. Dir, Inter-Action Trust, 1968–72; Founder Dir, Islington Bus Co., 1972–77; Director: Battersea Arts Centre, 1976–77; ICA, 1977–90; Creative Research Ltd, 1989–91; Beaconsfield Gall., 1999–; Ambient TV Ltd, 2000–; hiddenart.com, 2002–. Dir, Sense of Ireland Fest., 1980; Bd Dir, London International Theatre Fest., 1983; Chm. for the Arts, IT 82 Cttee, 1982. Chm., Recreational Trust, 1972–88; Co-Founder, Fair Play for Children, 1974–75; Advr, Task Force Trust, 1972–74; Trustee: Circle 33 Housing Trust, 1972–75; Moving Picture Mime Trust, 1978–80; Shape (Arts for the Disadvantaged), 1979–81. Trustee: International House, 1989–; Africa Centre, 1990–2000; World Circuit Arts, 1996–2000. Governor: Holloway Adult Educn Inst., 1974–76; Byam Shaw Sch. of Art, 2000–. Mem. Court, RCA, 1980–90. CSCE British Deleg., Krakow, Poland, 1991. *Publications:* Community Psychology, 1975; EEC and the Arts, 1978; (contrib.) Art and Society, 1999; articles on arts policy. *Recreations:* mycology, angling, tennis, travel. *Address:* 151c Grosvenor Avenue, N5 2NH. *T:* 07956 229796; *e-mail:* bill.mcalister@gmail.com.

McALLION, John; Member (Lab) Dundee East, Scottish Parliament, 1999–2003; *b* 13 Feb. 1948; *s* of Joseph and Norah McAllion; *m* 1971, Susan Jean Godlonton; two *s*. *Educ:* St Augustine's Comprehensive School, Glasgow; St Andrews Univ. (MA Hons 2nd cl. Modern and Medieval Hist. 1972); Dundee Coll. of Education. Civil Servant, Post Office, 1967–68; History Teacher, St Saviour's High Sch., Dundee, 1973–78; Social Studies Teacher, Balgowan Sch., Dundee, 1978–82; Research Asst to Bob McTaggart, 1982–86. Regional Councillor, 1984–87, Convener, 1986–87, Tayside Regional Council. MP (Lab) Dundee East, 1987–2001. Contested (Lab) Dundee E, Scottish Parlt, 2003. *Recreations:* sport, reading, music. *Address:* 3 Haldane Street, Dundee DD3 0HP. *T:* (01382) 826678.

McALLISTER, Sir Ian (Gerald), Kt 2008; CBE 1996; Chairman, Network Rail, since 2002; *b* 17 Aug. 1943; *s* of Ian Thomas McAllister and Margaret Mary McAllister (*née* McNally); *m* 1968, Susan Margaret Frances Mitchell; three *s* one *d*. *Educ:* Thornleigh College, Bolton; University College London (BScEcon). Ford Motor Co.: operations and marketing appts, 1964–79; Director: Parts Sales, 1980; Product and Marketing Parts Ops, 1981; Car Sales Ops, 1983; Marketing Plans and Programmes, 1984; Sales, Ford Germany, 1987; Gen. Marketing Manager, Lincoln Mercury Div., USA, 1989; Man. Dir, 1991–2002, and Chm. and Chief Exec., 1992–2002. Vice-President: Inst. of the Motor Industry, 1992–2002; SMMT (Pres., 1996–98). Mem. Bd and Council, BITC, 1994–2002. Non-executive Director: Scottish & Newcastle plc, 1996–; UCL Business Bd, 2007–. Mem. Adv. Bd, Victim Support, 1994. Member: Adv. Cttee on Business and the Envmt, 1996–; Welfare to Work Task Force, 1997–2001; Bd, QCA, 1997–2003 (Dep. Chm., 2000–03); Co-Chm., Cleaner Vehicles Task Force, 1997–2000; Chm., Greater Essex Prosperity Forum, 2007. Chm., Carbon Trust, 2001–. Hon. PhD: E London, 1993; Loughborough, 1999; Hon. LLD Nottingham, 1995. *Recreations:* gardening, golf, computer studies. *Address:* Network Rail, 40 Melton Street, Euston Square, NW1 2EE.

McALLISTER, John Brian; Chairman, Selbourn Care Ltd, since 2004; *b* 11 June 1941; *s* of late Thomas McAllister and of Jane (*née* McCloughan); *m* 1st, 1966, Margaret Lindsay Walker (*d* 2002); two *d*; 2nd, 2004, Lynne Patricia Oldham. *Educ:* Royal Belfast Academical Instn; Queen's Univ., Belfast (BA Hons). Joined NI Civil Service as Asst Principal, Dept of Educn, 1964; Dep. Principal, Higher Educn Div., 1968; Principal: Secondary Schs Br., 1969; Re-Organisation of Local Govt Br., 1970; Principal, Dept of Finance, 1971, Dept's Central Secretariat, 1972; Asst Sec. 1973, Sen. Asst Sec. 1976, Dep. Sec., 1978–80, Dept of Educn; Dep. Sec., later Under Sec., Dept of Finance, 1980–83; Under Sec., DoE, NI, 1983–84; Dep. Chief Exec., 1984–85, Chief Exec., 1985–88, Industrial Develt Bd for NI; Chief Exec., Crestacare (formerly Cresta Hldgs Ltd), 1990–93 (Gp Man. Dir, 1988–90); consultant, 1993–94; Chief Exec., 1994–96, Chm., 1996–99, Craegmoor Healthcare; Chief Exec., Sapphire House Ltd, 1999–2006. *Recreations:* watching sport of all kinds, reading.
See also Dame J. I. Harbison.

McALPINE, family name of **Baron McAlpine of West Green**.

McALPINE OF WEST GREEN, Baron *cr* 1984 (Life Peer), of West Green in the County of Hampshire; **Robert Alistair McAlpine;** Director, Sir Robert McAlpine & Sons Ltd, 1963–95; *b* 14 May 1942; *s* of Lord McAlpine of Moffat and Ella Mary Gardner Garnett (*d* 1987); *m* 1st, 1964, Sarah Alexandra Baron (marr. diss. 1979); two *d*; 2nd, 1980, Romilly (marr. diss.), *o d* of A. T. Hobbs, Cranleigh, Surrey; one *d*; 3rd, 2002, Athena Malpas, *d* of Capt. Malpas. *Educ:* Stowe. Joined Sir Robert McAlpine & Sons Ltd, 1958. Hon. Treasurer: Europ. Democratic Union, 1978–88; Europ. League for Econ. Co-operation, 1974–75 (Vice Pres., 1975–); Conservative and Unionist Party, 1975–90 (Dep. Chm., 1979–83). Director: George Weidenfeld Holdings Ltd, 1975–83; ICA, 1972–73. Mem., Arts Council of GB, 1981–82; Vice-President: Friends of Ashmolean Museum, 1969–; Greater London Arts Assoc., 1971–77; Vice-Chm., Contemporary Arts Soc., 1973–80. Pres., British Waterfowl Assoc., 1978–81, Patron 1981–. Member: Friends of V&A Museum, 1976–; Council, English Stage Co., 1973–75. Trustee, Royal Opera House Trust, 1974–80; Dir, Theatre Investment Fund, 1981–90 (Chm., 1985–90). Governor: Polytechnic of the South Bank, 1981–82; Stowe Sch., 1981–84; Pres., St Bartholomew's Hosp. Med. Coll., 1993–95. *Publications: as Alistair McAlpine:* The Servant, 1992; Journal of a Collector, 1994; Letters to a Young Politician, 1995; Once a Jolly Bagman (memoirs), 1997; The New Machiavelli, 1997; (jtly) Collecting and Display, 1998 Australian Memoirs, 2000; The Ruthless Leader, 2000; (jtly) The Essential Guide to Collectables, 2003. *Recreations:* the arts, horticulture, aviculture, agriculture. *Address:* House of Lords, SW1A 0PW. *Club:* Garrick.
See also Hon. Sir W. H. McAlpine, Bt.

McALPINE, Alistair; *see* Baron McAlpine of West Green.

McALPINE, Robert James, FCIOB; Director, Alfred McAlpine plc, 1957–94 (Chairman, 1983–92); *b* 6 May 1932; *s* of late Alfred James McAlpine and of Peggy (*née* Saunders); *m* 1st, Mary Jane Anton; two *s* one *d*; 2nd, Angela Bell (*née* Langford Brooke); one *d*. *Educ:* Harrow Sch. FCIOB. Director: Chester Racecourse Co., 1976– (Chm., 1994–2008); Haynes Hanson & Clark, 1978– (Chm., 1993–); Hall Engrg plc, 1985–99; Aintree Racecourse Co., 1988–2007. Chm., Export Gp for Constructional Industries, 1975–77. Mem., Jockey Club. High Sheriff, Cheshire, 1994–95. *Recreations:* racing, shooting, golf, bridge. *Address:* Tilstone Lodge, Tilstone Fearnall, Tarporley, Cheshire CW6 9HS. *Clubs:* White's, Turf, Portland, MCC.

McALPINE, Hon. Sir William (Hepburn), 6th Bt *cr* 1918, of Knott Park; FRSE; FCILT; company director; *b* 12 Jan. 1936; *s* of Lord McAlpine of Moffat (Life Peer) and Ella Mary Gardner Garnett (*d* 1987); *S* to baronetcy of father, 1990; *m* 1st, 1959, Jill Benton (*d* 2004), *o d* of Lt-Col Sir Peter Fawcett Benton Jones, 3rd Bt, OBE, ACA; one *s* one *d*; 2nd, 2004, Judy, *d* of late William Harry Sanderson and *widow* of Graham Nicholls. *Educ:* Charterhouse. Life Guards, 1954–56. Dir, Sir Robert McAlpine Ltd (formerly Sir Robert McAlpine & Sons Ltd), 1952–2007. FRSA. High Sheriff, Bucks, 1999–2000. *Recreation:* railways. *Heir:* *s* Andrew William McAlpine [*b* 22 Nov. 1960; *m* 1991, Caroline Claire, *yr d* of Frederick Hodgson; four *s*]. *Address:* Fawley Hill, Fawley Green, Henley-on-Thames, Oxon RG9 6JA. *Clubs:* Buck's, Garrick, Caledonian.
See also Baron McAlpine of West Green.

MACAN, Thomas Townley; HM Diplomatic Service, retired; Governor, British Virgin Islands, 2002–06; *b* 14 Nov. 1946; only *s* of late Dr Thomas Townley Macan and Zaida Bindloss (*née* Boddington); *m* 1976, Janet Ellen Martin, Hollidaysburg, Penn; one *s* one *d*. *Educ:* Shrewsbury Sch.; Univ. of Sussex (BA Hons Econs; Pres., Students' Union, 1967–68). MCIL (MIL 1992). Joined HM Diplomatic Service, 1969; UN Dept, FCO, 1969–71; Bonn, 1971–74; Brasilia, 1974–78; Maritime, Aviation and Envmt Dept, FCO, 1978–81; Press Sec., Bonn, 1981–86; Hd, Commonwealth Co-ordination Dept, FCO, 1986–88; Hd, Trng Dept, FCO, 1988–90; Counsellor, Lisbon, 1990–94; Ambassador to Lithuania, 1995–98; on secondment to BOC Group, 1998–99; Minister and Dep. High Comr, New Delhi, 1999–2002. *Recreations:* steam boats, sailing, church architecture, walking. *Address:* Stevney, Outgate, Ambleside, Cumbria LA22 0NH. *Clubs:* Naval; Island Cruising (Salcombe); Royal British Virgin Islands Yacht.

McANALLY, Vice-Adm. John Henry Stuart, CB 2000; LVO 1983; Naval Adviser, 2001–05, Senior Military Advisor, since 2006, to Flagship Training Ltd; National President, Royal Naval Association, since 2001; *b* 9 April 1945; *s* of late Arthur Patrick McAnally and Mrs Basil Hamilton Stuart McAnally. *Educ:* Willington Prep. Sch., Putney; Westminster Sch. FNI 1999; FRIN 1999. BRNC (RN Scholarship); HM Ships Wizard, Ashanti, Walkerton, Leverton, 1963–67; USS Moale (Exchange), 1967–68; HMS Eskimo,

1968–69; HMA Ships Melbourne and Torrens, 1971–73; CO HMS Iveston, 1973–75; Adv. Navign Course, 1975; HMS Fife, 1976–77; Staff Course, 1978; HMS Birmingham and HMY Britannia, 1979–81; MoD, 1982–83; Comd HM Ships Torquay and Alacrity, 1984–86; Staff of C-in-C Fleet, 1986–87; Captain Sixth Frigate Sqdn and CO HM Ships Ariadne and Hermione, 1987–89; Asst Dir (Warfare), Dir Naval Plans, 1989–91; RCDS 1992; HCSC 1993; Dir, Naval Logistics Staff Duties and Naval Staff Duties, MoD, 1993–95; Flag Officer Trng and Recruiting, and Chief Exec., Naval Recruiting and Trng Agency, 1996–98; Comdt, RCDS, 1998–2001. Ind. Chm., Retired Officer Selection Bds, 2001–03. Mem., Hon. Co. of Master Mariners, 2002. Younger Brother, Trinity House. MInstD. *Recreation:* golf. *Clubs:* Naval and Military, National Liberal; Royal Mid-Surrey Golf; Royal Naval and Royal Albert Yacht (Portsmouth); Hayling Golf.

See also M. B. H. McAnally.

McANALLY, Mary Basil Hamilton, (Mrs Hugh Macpherson); media consultant, since 2002; Managing Director, Meridian Broadcasting Ltd, 1996–2002; *b* 9 April 1945; *d* of late Arthur Patrick McAnally and Basil Hamilton Stuart McAnally; *m* 1979, Hugh Macpherson. *Educ:* Tiffin Girls Sch.; Wimbledon Art Sch.; London Business Sch. Internat. tennis player, 1963–67; winner, Jun. Indoor Championships of GB, 1963. Researcher, Man Alive, BBC TV, 1969; Prog. Associate, This is Your Life, Thames TV, 1969–71; Series Producer, Thames TV: Money Go Round, 1973–82; Could Do Better, What About the Workers, and The John Smith Show, 1978–80; Series Editor, For What It's Worth, Channel 4, 1982–90 (Winner, Freedom of Information Media Award, 1990); Thames TV: Editor, Daytime, 1984–87; Exec. Prod., The Time the Place, 1987–91; Head of Features, 1989–92; Meridian Broadcasting: Controller of Regl Progs and Community Affairs, 1992–94, Dir of Progs, 1994–96. Member: NCC, 1987–97; Adv. Cttee on Advertising, 1999–2002; Ind. Mem., Balancing and Settlement Code Panel, 2002–04; Ind. Dir, Exec. Bd, DTI, 2002–06; Director: Southern Screen Commn, 1997–2000; Screen South, 2002–03; Media Local Solutions Ltd, 2006–; Chm., Media and Creative Industries Task Force, 1999–2003, and Mem. Bd, 2000–07, SEEDA; Mem. Bd, SE England Cultural Consortium, 2000–03; Mem., SE Regl Assembly, 2007–. Chm., SE England Regl Sports Bd, 2003–; SE Regl Rep., 2012 Nations and Regions Cttee, 2004–; non-exec. Dir, Sport England, 2004–06. FRSA 1990; FRTS 1998. Gov., Portsmouth Univ., 1998–2000. *Publication:* (jtly) Buy Right, 1978. *Recreations:* tennis, painting, golf. *Clubs:* Arts, Forum UK; All England Lawn Tennis and Croquet (Mem., Mgt Cttee, 2002–), Cumberland Lawn Tennis, Highgate Golf, Leckford Golf.

See also J. H. S. McAnally.

MacANDREW, family name of **Baron MacAndrew**.

MacANDREW, 3rd Baron *cr* 1959, of the Firth of Clyde; **Christopher Anthony Colin MacAndrew;** farmer; *b* 16 Feb. 1945; *s* of 2nd Baron MacAndrew and Ursula Beatrice (*née* Steel) (*d* 1986); *S* father, 1989; *m* 1975, Sarah (marr. diss. 2005), *o d* of Lt-Col P. H. and Mrs Brazier; one *s* two *d*. *Educ:* Malvern. Tax Comr, 1996–. *Recreations:* golf, tennis. *Heir: s* Hon. Oliver Charles Julian MacAndrew, *b* 3 Sept. 1983. *Address:* Hall Farm, Archdeacon Newton, Darlington, Co. Durham DL2 2YB.

McANDREW, Nicolas; Chairman, Murray Johnstone Ltd, 1992–99; *b* 9 Dec. 1934; *s* of late Robert Louis McAndrew and Anita Marian McAndrew (*née* Huband); *m* 1960, Diana Leonie Wood; two *s* one *d*. *Educ:* Winchester Coll. CA 1961. Commnd Black Watch, 1953–55. With Peat, Marwick, Mitchell & Co., 1955–61; S. G. Warburg & Co. Ltd, 1962–78: Dir, 1969–78; Chm., Warburg Investment Mgt, 1975–78; Dir, Mercury Securities Ltd, 1975–78; N. M. Rothschild & Sons Ltd, 1979–88 (Man. Dir, 1980–88); Murray Johnstone Ltd, 1988–99 (Man. Dir, 1988–92). Board Member: Highlands & Islands Enterprise, 1993–97; N of Scotland Water Authy, 1995–2002. Deputy Chairman: Burn Stewart Distillers PLC, 1991–99; Liverpool Victoria Friendly Soc., 1995–2005; Chairman: Martin Currie Enhanced Income Trust (formerly Moorgate Investment Trust) PLC, 1996–2005; Guinness Flight Extra Income Trust, 1995–2002; Derby Trust PLC, 1999–2003. Chairman: Highlands and Is Rivers Assoc., 2001–05; Beauly Dist Fishery Bd, 2003–. Master, Grocers' Co., 1978–79. *Recreations:* shooting, fishing, golf, bridge. *Address:* Kilcoy Castle, Muir of Ord, Ross-shire IV6 7RX. *T:* (01463) 871393. *Club:* White's.

MACAPAGAL-ARROYO, Dr Gloria; President, Republic of the Philippines, since 2001; Senator, since 1992; *b* 5 April 1947; *d* of Diosdado Macapagal (former Pres. of the Philippines), and Dr Evangelina Macaraeg-Macapagal; *m* Jose Miguel Arroyo; two *s* one *d*. *Educ:* Georgetown Univ. (BA Econs); Assumption Coll. (BSc Commerce *magna cum laude*); Ateneo de Manila Univ. (MA Econs); Univ. of the Philippines (PhD Econs). Chair, Econs Dept, Assumption Coll.; Asst Prof., Ateneo de Manila Univ.; Sen. Lectr, Sch. of Econs, Univ. of the Philippines; Asst Sec., 1986–89, Undersec., 1989, DTI, Philippines; Sec., Dept of Social Welfare and Develt, 1998; Vice Pres., 1998–2001. Exec. Dir, Garments and Textiles Bd, 1987. Hon. Mem., Philippine Mil. Acad. Cl. of 1978. Hon. Dr: Tsinghua, China, 2001; Chulalongkorn, Thailand, 2002; Hon. LLD Waseda, Japan, 2002. *Publications:* (with V. M. Cunanan) Socio-Economic Impact of Tourism: a measurement and analysis system, 1979; (with M. San Buenaventura) The Economic and Social Impact of Tourism, 1983; The Services Sector in the Philippines, 1984; Getting Our Act Together: a President's campaign against the sexual exploitation of children, 2001; contrib. papers on tourism. *Recreations:* playing golf with the First Gentleman, watching movies with children, reading good books. *Address:* Office of the President, Malacañang Palace, San Miguel, Manila 1005, Philippines. *T:* 7356201, 5641451, *Fax:* (Exec. Sec.) 7355260; *e-mail:* corres@op.gov.ph.

MACARA, Sir Alexander (Wiseman), Kt 1998; FRCP, FRCGP, FFPH; Consultant Senior Lecturer in Epidemiology and Public Health Medicine, University of Bristol and Hon. Visiting Consultant, Bristol Royal Infirmary, 1976–97; Chairman of Council, British Medical Association, 1993–98; *b* 4 May 1932; *s* of late Rev. Alexander Macara, MA Hons and Marion Wiseman Macara (*née* Mackay); *m* 1964, Sylvia May Williams, BSc Hons, DipEd, *d* of late Edward Brodbeck and Ellen Florence Williams; one *s* one *d*. *Educ:* Irvine Royal Acad.; Glasgow Univ. (Carnegie Bursar; MB ChB 1958); LSHTM. DPH (Hecht Prize) 1960; FFPH (FFPHM 1989; FFCM 1973; MFCM 1972); FRIPH (FRIPHH 1973); FRCGP (*ad eundem gradum*) 1983; FRCP 1991; FRCPE 1997. House Physician and House Surgeon posts in Glasgow Teaching Hosps, 1958–59; General Practice experience, London and Glasgow, 1959–60; Asst MOH and Sch. MO, City and Co. of Bristol, 1960–63, then Hon. Community Physician, 1963–74; Lectr then Sen. Lectr, Univ. of Bristol, 1963–76 (Actg Head, Dept of Public Health, 1974–76). Sir Wilson Jameson Travelling Scholar, LSHTM, 1967; Vis. Prof., Univ. of Malaya, 1980; Vis. Prof. and Ext. Examnr for higher degrees, Univ. of Khartoum, 1983; Hon. Vis. Prof. in Health Studies, York Univ., 1998–2002; Ext. Examnr in Community Med. (Human Ecology), Univ. of Glasgow, 1979–82; Ext. Examnr, Inst. of Population Studies, Univ. of Exeter, 1993–97. Jt Chm., Jt Wkg Party of Med. Profession and DoH on Med. Services for Children, 1991–92, and Chm., Jt Wkg Party on Child Protection, 1993–94. General Medical Council: Mem., 1979–2002; mem. various cttees. Faculty of Community Medicine (now of Public Health Medicine): Mem. Bd, 1973–79; Treasurer, 1979–84. British Medical Association: Chm., Med. Ethics Cttee, 1982–89; Dep. Chm., 1987–89, Chm., 1989–92, Representative Body; Rep. on Standing Cttee, Doctors in the EC, 1980– (Vice-Pres., Cttee on Public Health and the Envmt, 2001–); Chm. or Mem., numerous working parties, incl. Bd of Science and Educn; Fellow, 1978. Sec.-Gen., World Fedn for Educn and Res. in Public Health, 1988–96; Dir, WHO Collaborating Centre in Envmtl Health Promotion and Ecology, 1989–97; Advr and Consultant on Educn, Trng and Health Manpower Develt, WHO, 1970–; Sec., European Collaborative Health Services Studies, 1977–89; Pres., Nat. Heart Forum, 2007– (Chm., 1998–2007). Mem. Court of Govs, LSHTM, 1993–; Gov., Redland High Sch. for Girls, Bristol, 1998–. Lectures: Long Fox Meml, Bristol Univ., 1995; Harben, RIPH & H, 1996; Gregg Meml, AMA, 1997. Founder FMedSci 1998. FRSA 1995. Hon. Member: Hungarian Soc. Social Medicine, 1989; Italian Soc. Hygiene, Preventive Medicine and Public Health (Gold Medallist), 1991; Hon. Life Fellow, Soc. Public Health, 1991; Hon. FFOM 2000. Hon. Dr Public Health and Gerasimos Alivizatos Award, Sch. of Public Health, Athens, 1992; Hon. DSc UWE, 1998. Public Health Award, 1992, John Kershaw Award, 1994, Soc. of Public Health; James Preston Meml Award, Soc. of Public Health and BMA, 1993; Médaille d'or de l'Ordre de Médecin Français, 1998; Gold Medal, BMA, 1999; Andrija Stampar Medal, Assoc. of Schs of Public Health in Eur. Reg., 2002. *Publications:* (jtly) Personal Data Protection in Health and Social Services, 1988; chapters in various books and articles and reports in med. jls on epidemiology, public health, envmtl health and ethics in medicine. *Recreations:* gardening, reading, music. *Address:* Elgon, 10 Cheyne Road, Stoke Bishop, Bristol BS9 2DH. *T:* (0117) 968 2838, *Fax:* (0117) 968 4602. *Club:* Athenæum.

McARDLE, Tony, TD 1990; Chief Executive, Lincolnshire County Council, since 2005; *b* 31 Jan. 1958; *s* of William and Olive McArdle; one *s* two *d*. *Educ:* Knockbreda Primary Sch., Belfast; Methodist Coll., Belfast; Univ. of Essex (BA Hons Govt). Free Trade Dept, Adnams plc, 1980–85; East Cambridgeshire District Council: Emergency Planning Officer, 1985–87; Asst to Chief Exec., 1987–89; Corp. Support Manager, 1989–92; Hd, Community Services, 1992–95; Asst Chief Exec., 1995–98; Chief Exec., Wellingborough BC, 1998–2005. Territorial Army, 1977–99: commnd; Royal Anglian Regt, 1979; regtl appts, 1979–95; Second i/c, Cambridge Univ. OTC, 1995–98; CO 49 Bde BSTT, 1998–99. *Address:* c/o Lincolnshire County Council, Newland, Lincoln LN1 1YQ. *T:* (01522) 514985, *Fax:* (01522) 552004; *e-mail:* tony.mcardle@lincolnshire.gov.uk.

McAREAVEY, Most Rev. John; *see* Dromore, Bishop of, (RC).

MacARTHUR, Brian; Associate Editor, The Times, 1995–2006 (Executive Editor (Features), 1991–95); Editorial Consultant, Daily Telegraph, since 2006; *b* 5 Feb. 1940; *o s* of late S. H. MacArthur and Mrs M. MacArthur; *m* 1st, 1966, Peta Deschampsneufs (*d* 1971); 2nd, 1975, Bridget Trahair (marr. diss. 1997); two *d*; 3rd, 2000, Maureen Waller. *Educ:* Brentwood Sch.; Helsby Grammar Sch.; Leeds Univ. (BA). Yorkshire Post, 1962–64; Daily Mail, 1964–66; The Guardian, 1966–67; The Times: Education Correspondent, 1967–70; Founder Editor, The Times Higher Educn Supplement, 1971–76; Home News Editor, 1976–78; Dep. Editor, Evening Standard, 1978–79; Chief Asst to the Editor, The Sunday Times, 1979–81; Exec. Editor (News), The Times, 1981–82; Jt Dep. Editor, The Sunday Times, 1982–84; Editor, Western Morning News, 1984–85; Editor-in-Chief, Today, 1986–87; Exec. Ed., The Sunday Times, 1987–91. Hon. MA Open Univ., 1976. *Publications:* Eddy Shah: Today and the Newspaper Revolution, 1988; Deadline Sunday, 1991; (ed) The Penguin Book of Twentieth Century Speeches, 1992; (ed) The Penguin Book of Historic Speeches, 1995; Requiem, 1997; (ed) The Penguin Book of Twentieth Century Protest, 1998; Gulf War Despatches, 2001; Surviving the Sword: prisoners of the Japanese 1942–1945, 2005; For King and Country: voices from the First World War, 2008. *Recreations:* vegetable gardening, cooking. *Address:* Church Farm House, The Street, Little Barningham, Norwich NR11 7AG. *T:* (01263) 577369. *Club:* Garrick.

MACARTHUR, Dame Ellen (Patricia), DBE 2005 (MBE 2001); professional offshore sailor; Director, Offshore Challenges Ltd, since 1998; *b* 8 July 1976; *d* of Kenneth John Macarthur and Avril Patricia Macarthur. *Educ:* Anthony Gell Sch., Wirksworth. RYA Yachtmaster Commercial; RYA Yachtmaster Instructor. Winner: Class II (Open 50) Route du Rhum solo trans-Atlantic race, 1998, Class I (Open 60), 2002; (Open 60) Europe 1 New Man STAR solo trans-Atlantic race, 2000; EDS Atlantic Challenge, 2001; 2nd overall, Vendée Globe non-stop solo round-the-world race, 2001; fastest solo circumnavigation of the globe (World Record, 71 days, 14 hours, 18 mins and 33 secs), 2005. Young Sailor of the Year, 1995, Yachtsman of the Year, 1999, Yachting Journalists' Assoc.; FICO World Champion, 2001; ISAF World Champion Woman Sailor, 2001. Freeman, Skye and Lochalsh, 2006. Chevalier, Légion d'Honneur (France), 2008. *Publications:* Taking on the World (autobiog.), 2002; Race Against Time, 2005. *Address:* Offshore Challenges Ltd, Cowes Waterfront - Venture Quays, Castle Street, East Cowes, Isle of Wight PO32 6EZ. *T:* 0871 063 0210, *Fax:* (020) 7681 2912; *e-mail:* ellen.macarthur@ocgroup.com.

McARTHUR, Dr John Duncan, FRCPGlas; FRCPE; Consultant Cardiologist, Nuffield Hospital, Glasgow, 1985–2007; *b* 7 Jan. 1938; *s* of Neil McPhail McArthur and Elizabeth Duncan; *m* 1963, Elizabeth Agnew Bowie (*d* 2004); two *s* one *d*. *Educ:* Univ. of Glasgow (BSc Hons 1960; MB ChB Hons 1963); DM Madras 1970. DObstRCOG 1965; MRCP 1966; MRCPG 1966; MRCPE 1967, FRCPE 1994; FRCPGlas 1980. Junior House Officer, Glasgow Royal Infirmary and Ayrshire Hosps, 1963–65; Senior House Officer and Registrar, Glasgow Royal Inf., 1965–67; Lectr, Sen. Lectr, Reader, Christian Med. Coll. Hosp., Vellore, India, as Missionary, Church of Scotland, 1968–73; Sen. Registrar, Medicine/Cardiology, Glasgow Teaching Hosps, 1973–78; Consultant Cardiologist, Western Infirmary, Glasgow, 1978–2003. Elder, Ch of Scotland. *Publications:* articles on valvular heart disease and pacemakers. *Recreations:* DIY, gardening. *Address: e-mail:* jd.mcarthur@ntlworld.com.

MacARTHUR, Judy Anne; *see* MacArthur Clark, J. A.

McARTHUR, Liam Scott; Member (Lib Dem) Orkney, Scottish Parliament, since 2007; *b* 8 Aug. 1967; *s* of William Archibald McArthur and Susan Margaret McArthur; *m* 1998, Tamsin Bailey; two *s*. *Educ:* Sanday Jun. High Sch.; Kirkwall Grammar Sch.; Univ. of Edinburgh (MA Pols 1990). Res. Asst to Jim Wallace, MP, 1990–92; Stagiaire, External Affairs, EC, 1992–93; Account Dir, APCO Worldwide, London and Brussels, 1995–2002; Special Advr to Dep. First Minister, Scottish Exec., 2002–05. Scottish Parliament: Lib Dem spokesman on enterprise, energy and tourism, 2007–; Mem., Finance Cttee, 2007–. Mem., Scottish Lib Dem Policy Cttee. *Recreations:* football, music. *Address:* Scottish Parliament, Edinburgh EH99 1SP. *T:* (0131) 348 5815; *e-mail:* liam.mcarthur.msp@scottish.parliament.uk.

McARTHUR, Dr Thomas Burns, (Tom); English teacher, since 1959; feature writer, since 1962; lecturer and writer on yoga and Indian philosophy, since 1962; author and language consultant, since 1970; Editor, English Today, 1984–2007; *b* 23 Aug. 1938; *s* of Archibald McArthur and Margaret Burns; *m* 1963, Fereshteh Mottahedin (*d* 1993); one *s* two *d*; *m* 2001, Jacqueline Lam Kam-mei. *Educ:* Glasgow Univ. (MA 1958); Edinburgh Univ. (MLitt 1970; PhD 1978). Officer-Instr, RAEC, 1959–61; Asst Master, Riland

Bedford Sch., Warwicks, 1961–63; Head of English, Cathedral and John Connon Sch., Bombay, India, 1965–67; Vis. Prof. in the English of the Media, Rajendra Prasad College of Mass Communication (Bharatiya Vidya Bhavan), Univ. of Bombay, 1965–67; Dir of Extra-Mural English Language Courses, Univ. of Edinburgh, 1972–79; Associate Prof. of English, Université du Québec à Trois-Rivières, Canada, 1979–83; Recognised Teacher (pt-time), 1986–2001, Res. Fellow, 1992–2001, Exeter Univ. Co-founder (with Reinhard Hartmann), Internat. Lexicography Course, Univ. of Exeter, 1987–2001. Consultant: Min. of Educn, Quebec, 1980–81; Société pour la promotion de l'enseignement de l'anglais (langue seconde) au Québec, 1980–83; Henson International Television (the Muppets), 1985–86; Dictionary Res. Centre, Exeter Univ., 1987–90; BBC Policy Planning Unit, 1992; also on dictionaries, encyclopedias and ELT books published by Century Hutchinson, Chambers, Collins, CUP, Longman, Macmillan, OUP and Time–Life. The Story of English (BBC radio series with D. Crystal), 1987. Member, Editorial Board: Internat. Jl of Lexicography, 1988–98; World Englishes, 1993–; Editl Advr, The Good Book Guide, 1992–; Mem., Internat. Adv. Bd, Logos, 1994–96. Hon. PhD Uppsala, 1999. *Publications:* Patterns of English series, 1972–74; English for Students of Economics, 1973; (with Beryl Atkins) Collins Dictionary of English Phrasal Verbs, 1974; (ed with A. J. Aitken) Languages of Scotland, 1979; Longman Lexicon of Contemporary English, 1981; A Foundation Course for Language Teachers, 1983; The Written Word, Books 1 and 2, 1984; Worlds of Reference, 1986; Yoga and the Bhagavad-Gita, 1986; Understanding Yoga, 1986; Unitive Thinking, 1988 (Beyond Logic and Mysticism, USA, 1990); The English Language as Used in Quebec: a survey, 1989; (ed) The Oxford Companion to the English Language, 1992, concise edn 1998; The English Languages, 1998; (ed with Alan Kernerman) Lexicography in Asia, 1998; Living Words: language, lexicography and the knowledge revolution, 1998; The English Languages, 1998; The Oxford Guide to World English, 2002. *Recreations:* reading, television, walking, cycling, travel. *Address:* 22–23 Ventress Farm Court, Cherry Hinton Road, Cambridge CB1 8HD. *T:* (01223) 245934; *e-mail:* scotsway@aol.com.

MacARTHUR CLARK, Dr Judy Anne, CBE 2004; FIBiol; Chief Inspector, Animals Scientific Procedures Inspectorate, since 2007; *b* 18 Nov. 1950; *d* of Alistair Cameron MacArthur and Elinore Muriel MacArthur (*née* Warde); *m* 1991, David Wayne Clark; two *s* two *d. Educ:* Orton Longueville Grammar Sch.; Glasgow Univ. (BVMS; DVMS 2001); DLAS 1985; DipECLAM 2001; DACLAM 2007. MRCVS 1973; FIBiol 1997. Director: G. D. Searle, 1982–86; Pfizer, UK, 1986–91; Vet. Dir, BioZone Ltd & Inc., 1992–2005; Pfizer, USA, 2005–07. Mem., BBSRC, 1996–99; Chair, Farm Animal Welfare Council, 1999–2004. Pres., RCVS, 1992–93. FRAgS 2007 (ARAgS 2002). *Publications:* numerous scientific papers. *Recreations:* gardening, exploring remote places, especially with my family. *Address:* Seacole Building, 2 Marsham Street, SW1P 4DF. *T:* (020) 7035 0751; *e-mail:* judy.macarthurclark@homeoffice.gsi.gov.uk. *Clubs:* Farmers, Royal Society of Medicine.

MacARTNEY, Sir John Ralph, 7th Bt *cr* 1799, of Lish, Co. Armagh; *b* 24 July 1945; *o s* of Sir John Barrington Macartney, 6th Bt and Amy Isobel Reinke; *S* father, 1999, but his name does not appear on the Official Roll of the Baronetage; *m* 1966, Suzanne Marie Fowler; four *d. Heir: cousin* John Alexander Macartney [*b* 1961; *m* 1986, Robyn Mary Norling (marr. diss. 2003)].

MacASKILL, Ewen; US Bureau Chief, The Guardian, since 2007; *b* 29 Oct. 1951; *s* of John Angus MacAskill and Catherine Euphemia MacAskill (*née* MacDonald); *m* 1976, Sarah Anne Hutchison; three *s. Educ:* Woodside Secondary Sch., Glasgow; Glasgow Univ. (MA Hons Modern History and Politics). Reporter, Glasgow Herald, 1973–77; VSO, working as journalist, Nat. Broadcasting Commn, Papua New Guinea, 1978–79; journalist: Reuters, 1980; Scotsman, 1981–83; China Daily, Beijing, 1984–85; Political Correspondent, 1986–90, Political Editor, 1990–96, Scotsman; Chief Pol Correspondent, 1996–99, Diplomatic Ed., 2000–07, The Guardian. Lawrence Sterne Fellow, Washington Post, 1986. Mem., St Margarets Film Club. Scotland's Young Journalist of the Year, 1974; Mem., Scoop of the Year team, What the Papers Say awards, 1999. *Recreations:* mountaineering, film, books. *Address:* 11 Norman Avenue, St Margarets, Twickenham, Middx TW1 2LY. *T:* (020) 8891 0795. *Club:* Junior Mountaineering of Scotland.

MacASKILL, Kenneth Wright; solicitor; Member (SNP) Edinburgh East and Musselburgh, Scottish Parliament, since 2007 (Lothians, 1999–2007); Cabinet Secretary for Justice, since 2007; *b* 28 April 1958; *m*; two *s. Educ:* Linlithgow Acad.; Edinburgh Univ. (LLB Hons). Consultant, Erskine, MacAskill & Co., solicitors. Mem., SNP, 1981– (Mem., Nat. Exec., 1984–2003; Treas., until 1999). Contested (SNP): Livingston, 1983, 1987; Linlithgow, 1992, 1997; Scotland Mid and Fife, EP elecns, 1989. *Address:* Scottish Parliament, Edinburgh EH99 1SP.

McASLAN, John Renwick, RIBA; ARIAS; Executive Chairman, John McAslan + Partners, since 1996; *b* Glasgow, 16 Feb. 1954; *s* of Prof. T. Crawford McAslan and Jean McAslan; *m* 1981, Dava Sagenkahn; one *s* two *d. Educ:* Dunoon Grammar Sch.; Dollar Acad.; Edinburgh Univ. (MA; DipArch). RIBA 1982; ARIAS 2005. With Cambridge Seven Associates, Boston, 1978–79; Richard Rogers and Partners, 1980–83; Troughton McAslan, 1984–95. Teaching, throughout UK and worldwide, 1990–; Prof., Welsh Sch. of Architecture, Univ. of Wales, 1998–2001; Architectural Advr to Govs, Dollar Acad., 2006–. Chm., Architect Adv. Panel, RBK&C, 2008–; Mem. Council, Tate Britain, 2008–. Numerous exhibns, 1984–. Chm., many cttees and awards gps. Internat. Associate, AIA, 2000; Mem., Japan Inst. of Architects, 1993. Founding Mem., Volubilis Foundn, Morocco, 2001. Foundation Trustee: Whitechapel Art Gall., 1989–96; John McAslan Family Charitable Trust, 1997–; RIBA/ICE McAslan Bursary, 2004–; Photographer's Gall., 2005–. Mem., Clinton Global Initiative, 2007–. FRSA 1989. Completed works include: London: RSA; Christopher Place Sch.; Trinity Coll. of Music; Swiss Cottage Liby; Peter Jones; Roundhouse; Royal Acad. of Music; other: Southampton Univ.; De La Warr Pavilion, Bexhill-on-Sea; Derngate, Northampton; Harris Acad.; Kingston Univ.; Paradise Street, Liverpool; Postgrad. Centre, Lancaster Univ.; Student Centre and Sch. of Nursing, Manchester Univ.; international: St Catherine's Coll., Kobe; Yapi Kredi HQ, Istanbul; Florida Southern Coll.; Max Mara HQ, Reggio Emilia; British Embassy, Algiers; ongoing works include: London: King's Cross Station; Marble Arch; Thomas Tallis Sch., Greenwich; RMA Woolwich; 5 Cheapside; London Olympics 2012 Energy Centres; other: Vestebene HQ, Alba; United World Coll., E Africa; Stanislavsky Centre, Moscow; Delhi Metro; RSA Acad., Tipton; Castlebrae Sch., Edinburgh; British High Commn, New Delhi. Numerous internat. architectural awards incl. Architectural Practice of the Year, Builder Gp, 1998, 1999, 2002; Civic Trust Award, 1999, 2000, 2008 (2 awards); Millennium Award, Design Council, 2000; British Construction Industry Award, 2000, 2007; Concrete Soc. Award, 2001, 2002; AIA Merit Award, 2001, 2003; RIBA Award for Architecture, 1996, 2002, 2005 (3 awards), 2007 (3 awards), 2008 (3 awards); Royal Fine Art Commn Trust Award, 2004; Roses Award, English Partnerships, 2004; EU Cultural Heritage Prize, diploma 2006, medal 2007; English Heritage Award, 2006; Camden Design Award, 2006; Architect of the Year, 2006, Masterplanning Architect of the Year, 2006, Retail Architect of the Year, 2007, Building Design. *Publications:* numerous articles and monographs. *Recreation:* spending time with family. *Address:* John

McAslan + Partners, 49 Princes Place, W11 4QA. *T:* (020) 7727 2663, *Fax:* (020) 7221 8835; *e-mail:* j.mcaslan@mcaslan.co.uk. *Clubs:* Stoke Park (Stoke Poges); Royal Bombay Yacht.

McATASNEY, Philippa Mary; QC 2006; *b* 29 Sept. 1962; *d* of Patrick Anthony McAtasney and Mary Dianne McAtasney (*née* Swateridge); *m* 2003, Richard George Leach; two *d. Educ:* Brookfield Comp. Sch.; Itchen Sixth Form Coll.; London Sch. of Econs and Pol Sci. (LLB Hons 1984). Called to the Bar, Lincoln's Inn, 1985; in practice specialising in law of sexual offences, violent crime, fraud, judicial review and police discipline work; Mem., SE and W Circuits. *Recreations:* theatre, cinema, reading, swimming, socialising with family and friends. *Address:* 9–12 Bell Yard, WC2A 2JR. *T:* (020) 7400 1800, *Fax:* (020) 7404 1405; *e-mail:* clerks@bellyard.co.uk.

McATEER, Rev. Canon Bruce James; General Secretary of the General Synod, Anglican Church of Australia, since 2004; *b* 21 Dec. 1946; *s* of Alwyn James McAteer and Olive Ellen McAteer (*née* Child); *m* 1970, Margaret Lorraine Pocock; one *s* one *d. Educ:* Australian Coll. of Theol. (DipTh); Charles Sturt Univ. (Grad. Dip. Ch Leadership and Mgt). Accountant, 1962–71; CA 1973. Ordained deacon, 1973, priest, 1975; parochial appts, dios Newcastle and Grafton, NSW, 1972–89; Gen. Manager and Bishop's Registrar, Anglican Dio. Grafton, 1989–2004; Canon in Residence, and Hon. Associate Priest, 1991–2004, Hon. Canon, 2004–, Christ Church Cathedral, Grafton. Hon. Chaplain, TS Shropshire, Grafton, 1991–2004. Mem., Australian Inst. Mgt, 1992. *Recreations:* reading, listening to music, walking. *Address:* General Synod Office, Anglican Church of Australia, Suite 2, Level 9, 51 Druitt Street, Sydney, NSW 2000, Australia; *e-mail:* generalsecretary@anglican.org.au. *Club:* NSW Masonic (Sydney).

MACAULAY OF BRAGAR, Baron *cr* 1989 (Life Peer), of Bragar in the county of Ross and Cromarty; **Donald Macaulay.** *Educ:* Univ. of Glasgow (MA, LLB). Admitted to Faculty of Advocates, 1963; QC (Scot.) 1975. Contested (Lab) Inverness, 1970. Opposition spokesman on Scottish legal affairs until 1997. Chm., SACRO, 1993–96. *Address:* House of Lords, SW1A 0PW.

McAVAN, Linda; Member (Lab) Yorkshire and the Humber Region, European Parliament, since 1999 (Yorkshire South, May 1998–99); *b* 2 Dec. 1962; *d* of Thomas McAvan and late Jean McAvan. *Educ:* St Joseph's RC Coll., Bradford; Heriot-Watt Univ. (BA Hons Interpreting and Translation 1984); Univ. Libre de Bruxelles (MA Internat. Relns 1991). Translator, Agence Europe Press Agency, Brussels, 1984–85; Co-ordinator and Adminr, Party of European Socialists, Brussels, 1985–88; Press Officer, European Youth Forum, Brussels, 1988–90; Head of Information Policy, EC Youth Exchange Bureau, Brussels, 1990–91; European Officer, Coalfield Communities Campaign, Barnsley, 1991–95; Sen. Strategy Officer on European Affairs, Barnsley BC, 1995–98. European Parliament: Lab spokesman on Envmt, Food Safety and Public Health, 2004–; Mem., Temp. Cttee on Climate Change, 2007–; Chm., Fair Trade Wkg Gp, 2004–; Dep. Leader, European Parly Lab. Party, 1999–2004; Mem., 2004–, Vice Pres. (climate change portfolio), 2006–, PES (Treas., 2004–06). Mem., Convention on the Future of Europe, 2002–03. British European Woman of the Year, 2002. *Recreations:* reading, walking, swimming. *Address:* Euro Office, 79 High Street, Wath-upon-Dearne, Rotherham, S Yorks S63 7QB. *T:* (01709) 875665.

McAVEETY, Francis; Member (Lab) Glasgow Shettleston, Scottish Parliament, since 1999; *b* 27 July 1962; *s* of Philip and Anne Marie McAveety; *m* 1985, Anita Mitchell; one *s* one *d. Educ:* Strathclyde Univ. (BA Jt Hons English and History 1983); St Andrew's Coll. of Educn, Glasgow (post grad. teaching qualification 1984). Teacher: Glasgow, 1984–94; Renfrewshire, 1994–99. Member (Lab): Glasgow DC, 1988–95; Glasgow City Council, 1995–99 (Convener, Arts and Culture, 1995–97; Leader, 1997–99). Scottish Executive: Dep. Minister for Local Govt, 1999–2000, for Health, 2002–03; Minister for Tourism, Culture and Sport, 2003–04. DL Glasgow 1998. *Recreations:* sport, reading, record collecting. *Address:* 156 Glenbuck Avenue, Glasgow G33 1LW; (constituency office) 1346 Shettleston Road, Glasgow G32 9AT.

McAVOY, Prof. Brian Ramsay, MD; FRCP, FRCGP, FRACGP, FRNZCGP, FAChAM; Specialist Medical Officer, Auckland Community Alcohol and Drug Service, since 2006; *b* 2 Jan. 1949; *s* of Thomas Ramsay McAvoy and Christine McMillan McAvoy. *Educ:* Eastwood Sen. Secondary Sch., Glasgow; Univ. of Glasgow (BSc; MB ChB); Leicester Univ. (MD). FRCGP 1988; FRCP 1992; FRNZCGP 1999; FRACGP 2000; FAChAM 2005. Vocational Trainee in Gen. Practice, Southern Gen. Hosp. Scheme, Glasgow, 1973–76; Teaching Fellow, Dept of Family Medicine, McMaster Med. Sch., Hamilton, Ont, 1976–77; Principal in General Practice: Byfield, Northants, 1977–84; Leicester, 1984–89; Guidepost, Northumberland, 1994–2000; Lectr, 1977–84, Sen. Lectr, 1984–89, in General Practice, Univ. of Leicester; Elaine Gurr Foundation Prof. of General Practice, Univ. of Auckland, NZ, 1989–94; William Leech Prof. of Primary Health Care, Univ. of Newcastle upon Tyne, 1994–2000; GP, Melbourne, 2000–06; Dir, Res. and Practice Support, RACGP, 2000–01; Dep. Dir, Nat. Cancer Control Initiative, Melbourne, 2002–06. Adjunct Prof. of Gen. Practice, Univs of Melbourne and Queensland, 2000–; Hon. Professor of General Practice: Monash Univ., 2000; Auckland Univ., 2006–. *Publications:* (ed jtly) Asian Health Care, 1990; (contrib.) Clinical Method: a general practice approach, 1988, 2nd edn 1992; (jtly) General Practice Medicine: an illustrated colour text, 2003; articles on med. educn, health care delivery, cancer, ethnic minority health, alcohol and health promotion. *Recreations:* cycling, walking, music, reading. *Address:* Auckland Community Alcohol and Drug Service, Pitman House, 50 Carrington Road, Point Chevalier, Auckland, New Zealand. *T:* (9) 8155830, *Fax:* (9) 8155851; *e-mail:* brian.mcavoy@waitematadhb.govt.nz.

McAVOY, Rt Hon. Thomas (McLaughlin), PC 2003; MP (Lab and Co-op) Rutherglen and Hamilton West, since 2005 (Glasgow, Rutherglen, 1987–2005); Treasurer of HM Household (Deputy Chief Whip), since 2008; *b* 14 Dec. 1943; *m* 1968, Eleanor Kerr; four *s.* Employee, Hoover, Cambuslang; shop steward, AEU. Mem., Strathclyde Regl Council, 1982–87; former Chm., Rutherglen Community Council. An Opposition Whip, 1990–93; Comptroller of HM Household, 1997–2008. *Address:* House of Commons, SW1A 0AA; 9 Douglas Avenue, Rutherglen, Lanarkshire G73 4RA.

McBAIN, (David) Malcolm, LVO 1972; HM Diplomatic Service, retired; Director (formerly Co-ordinator), British Diplomatic Oral History Programme, since 1995 (Leicester University, 1995–97; Churchill Archives Centre, Churchill College, Cambridge, since 1997); *b* 19 Jan. 1928; *s* of David Walker McBain and Lilian J. McBain; *m* 1951, Audrey Yvonne Evison; one *s* three *d. Educ:* Sutton County School; London School of Economics (evening student). Min. of Civil Aviation appts in Tripoli, Libya, 1949–51, New Delhi, 1953–54; Diplomatic Service: New Delhi, 1958–61; Kenya, 1963–67; Thailand, 1968–75; Brunei, 1978–81; Texas, 1981–84; Ambassador to Madagascar, 1984–87. Order of Crown of Thailand, 1972. *Recreation:* golf. *Address:* 7 Charter Court, Gigant Street, Salisbury, Wilts SP1 2LH.

MACBEATH, Prof. (Alexander) Murray, PhD (Princeton, NJ); MA (Cantab); Professor of Mathematics and Statistics, University of Pittsburgh, 1979–90; *b* 30 June 1923; *s* of late Prof. Alexander Macbeath, CBE; *m* 1951, Julie Ormrod, Lytham St Anne's; two *s*. *Educ:* Royal Belfast Academical Inst.; Queen's Univ., Belfast; Clare Coll., Cambridge. Entrance Schol., Dixon Prize in Maths, Purser Studentship, 1st class hons in Maths, BA, QUB. Bletchley Park (centre for work on breaking German Enigma codes), 1943–45. Cambridge, 1945–48; Maj. Entrance Schol., Wrangler Math. Tripos, Part II, dist. Part III, BA, Owst Prize. Commonwealth Fund Fellowship, Princeton, NJ, 1948–50; Smith's Prize, 1949; PhD Princeton, 1950. Research Fellow, Clare Coll., Cambridge, 1950–51; MA Cambridge, 1951. Lectr in Maths, Univ. Coll. of North Staffordshire, 1951–53; Prof. of Maths, Queen's Coll., Dundee, 1953–62; Mason Prof. of Pure Maths, Univ. of Birmingham, 1962–79. Visiting Professor: California Inst. of Technology, 1966–67; Univ. of Pittsburgh, 1974–75; Hon. Professor: Univ. of St Andrews, 1990–94; Univ. of Warwick, 1994–2003. *Publications:* Elementary Vector Algebra, 1964; papers in: Jl London Mathematical Soc.; Proc. London Math. Soc.; Proc. Cambridge Philosophical Soc.; Quarterly Jl of Mathematics; Annals of Mathematics; Canadian Jl of Mathematics. *Recreation:* Scottish country dancing. *Address:* 1 Church Hill Court, Lighthorne, Warwick CV35 0AR.

MacBEATH, Prof. John Ernest Carmichael, OBE 1997; Professor of Educational Leadership, since 2000, and Director of Leadership for Learning: the Cambridge Network, and Wallenberg Research Centre, University of Cambridge; Fellow of Hughes Hall, Cambridge, since 2000; *b* Bolobo, Congo, 23 May 1940; *m* Sandra; two *d*. *Educ:* Univ. of Glasgow (MA, MEd); Jordanhill Coll. (PGCE). Prof., Dept of Educnl Studies, and Dir, Quality in Educn Centre, Univ. of Strathclyde, until 2000. Mem., Govt Task Force on Standards, 1997–2001. Consultant: OECD; UNESCO; ILO; EC; Scottish Exec.; Educn Dept, HK; Govt of Switzerland; Bertelsmann Foundn; Prince's Trust; Varkey Gp, Dubai. *Publications:* (ed) Effective School Leadership: responding to change, 1998; (with K. Myers) Effective School Leaders, 1999; Schools Must Speak for Themselves: arguments for school self-evaluation, 1999; (jtly) Self-evaluation in European Schools: a story of change, 2000; (with P. Mortimore) Improving School Effectiveness, 2001; (with A. McGlynn) Self-evaluation: what's in it for schools?, 2002; (jtly) Self-evaluation in the Global Classroom, 2002; (ed with L. Moos) Democratic Learning, 2003; (jtly) Consulting Pupils about Learning. *Address:* Faculty of Education, 184 Hills Road, Cambridge CB2 8PQ; Hughes Hall, Cambridge CB1 2EW.

MACBEATH, Murray; *see* Macbeath, A. M.

McBRATNEY, George, CEng, FIMechE; Principal, College of Technology, Belfast, 1984–89; *b* 5 May 1927; *s* of George McBratney and Sarah Jane McBratney; *m* 1949, Margaret Rose Patricia, (Trissie), *d* of late John Robinson, Melbourne, Australia; one *s*. *Educ:* Coll. of Technology, Belfast (BSc(Eng) 1948); Northampton Coll. of Advanced Technol.; QUB (Dip Ed 1976). CEng, FIMechE 1971. Apprentice fitter/draughtsman, Harland and Wolff, Belfast, 1943–47; Teacher, Comber Trades Prep. Sch., 1947–54; College of Technology, Belfast: successively Asst Lectr, Lectr and Sen. Lectr, 1954–67; Asst to Principal, 1967–69; Vice-Principal, 1969–84. Council Member: IMechE, 1984–86 (Chm., NI Br., 1984–86); NI Manpower Council, 1984–; Lambeg Industrial Res. Assoc. (formerly Linen Industry Res. Assoc.), 1984–90; BTEC, 1986–89; Chm., Further Educn Adv. Cttee, Faculty of Educn, Univ. of Ulster, 1986–90. *Publications:* Mechanical Engineering Experiments, vols 1 and 2 (with W. R. Mitchell), 1962, vol. 3 (with T. G. J. Moag), 1964; (with T. G. J. Moag) Science for Mechanical Engineering Technicians, vol. 1, 1966. *Recreation:* gardening. *Address:* 16 Glencregagh Drive, Belfast BT6 0NL. *T:* (028) 9079 6123.

McBREARTY, Anthony; regeneration consultant, since 2008; Senior Research Fellow, University of East London, since 1997; *b* 26 April 1946; *s* of Patrick and Mary McBrearty; *m* 1969, Heather McGowan (marr. diss. 1994; she *d* 2003), solicitor; one *s*; two *d* by former partner. Councillor (Lab) London Borough of Haringey, 1975–86 (Chm. of Personnel Cttee, 1976–79; Chm. of Housing Cttee, 1979–82); Mem. (Lab) Enfield N, 1981–86, Chm., Housing Cttee, 1982–86, GLC. Contested (Lab) W Herts, 1987. Mem., Central Technical Unit, 1986–88; Hd of Policy, London Bor. of Newham, 1988–96; Dep. Chief Exec., Thames Gateway London Partnership, 2002–08. Mem., Mgt Cttee, Thames Reach (formerly Thames Reach Bondway) Housing Assoc., 1987–. *Recreations:* politics, history. *Address:* 56 First Avenue, Manor Park, E12 6AN. *T:* (020) 8478 8197.

McBRIDE, Alexandra Joy; *see* Stewart, A. J.

McBRIDE, Brian James; Vice-President and Managing Director, Amazon.co.uk, since 2006; *b* Glasgow, 15 Oct. 1955; *s* of Alexander and Maire McBride; *m* 1980, Linda Wilson; two *d*. *Educ:* Lourdes Secondary Sch., Glasgow; Univ. of Glasgow (MA Hons). Salesman, Xerox, 1977–81; IBM, 1981–93, latterly as Dir, Unix Marketing, IBM Europe; Man. Dir, Crosfield Electronics, 1993–95; Pres., Europe, Madge Networks, 1996–98; Vice Pres., Dell Computers, 1998–2002; Man. Dir, T-Mobile UK, 2003–05. Non-executive Director: SThree plc, 2001–08; Celtic plc, 2005–. *Recreations:* golf, tennis, watching football, music. *Club:* Camberley Heath Golf.

McBRIDE, Dianne Gwenllian; *see* Nelmes, D. G.

McBRIDE, William Griffith, AO 1977; CBE 1969; Medical Director, Foundation 41 (for the study of congenital abnormalities and mental retardation), 1972–2001; Consultant Obstetrician and Gynaecologist, St George Hospital, Sydney, 1957–93; *b* 25 May 1927; *s* of late John McBride, Sydney; *m* 1957, Patricia Mary, *d* of late Robert Louis Glover; two *s* two *d*. *Educ:* Canterbury High Sch., Sydney; Univ. of Sydney; Univ. of London. MB, BS Sydney 1950; MD Sydney 1962; FRCOG 1968 (MRCOG 1954); FRANZCOG (FRACOG 1979). Resident: St George Hosp., Sydney, 1950; Launceston Hosp., 1951; Med. Supt, Women's Hosp., Sydney, 1955–57; Cons. Gynaecologist, Bankstown Hosp., Sydney, 1957–66; Consultant Obstetrician and Gynaecologist: Women's Hosp., Sydney, 1966–83; Royal Hosp. for Women, 1983–88; Vis. Consultant, L.B.J. Tropical Medical Center, American Samoa, 1998–. Lectr in Obstetrics and Gynaecology, Univ. of Sydney, 1957–83; Examiner in Obstetrics and Gynaecology: Univ. of Sydney, 1960–83; Australian Med. Council, 2000–. Vis. Prof. of Gynaecology, Univ. of Bangkok, 1968. Mem., WHO Sub-Cttee on safety of oral contraceptives, 1971. Pres. Sect. of Obstetrics and Gynæcology, AMA, 1966–73. Fellow, Senate of Univ. of Sydney, 1976–90; FRSocMed 1988; Mem., Amer. Coll. of Toxicology, 1985. Member: Soc. of Reproductive Biology; Endocrine Soc.; Teratology Soc.; Soc. for Risk Analysis; NY Acad. of Scis, 1987; AAAS, 1992. Mem. Council, Royal Agricl Soc. of NSW, 1987–; Delegate, Council meeting of Royal Agricl Socs, Calgary, 1992; breeder and judge of Hereford cattle; judged Shropshire and W Midlands Show, 1989. Member: Bd of Dirs, Australian Opera, 1979–82; Australian Opera Council, 1982–. BP Prize of Institut de la Vie, 1971 (for discovery of the teratogenic effects of the drug Thalidomide; first person to alert the world to the dangers of this drug and possibly other drugs). *Publications:* Drugs, 1960–70; Killing the Messenger, 1994; over 100 pubns in internat. med. or scientific jls including: (on teratogenic effect of the drug Thalidomide), Lancet 1961 (London); (on mutagenic effect of Thalidomide), BMJ 1994; (on Thalidomide and DNA in rats and rabbits), Teratogenesis, Carcinogenesis, Mutagenesis, 1997; (on interaction of Thalidomide with DNA or rabbit embryos), Pharmacology & Toxicology, 1999; Bitter Pills, 2001. *Recreations:* tennis, swimming, riding, music, cattle breeding. *Address:* 1101/1 Watson Street, Neutral Bay, NSW 2089, Australia. *Clubs:* Union, Australian Jockey, Palm Beach Surf, Royal Sydney Golf, Palm Beach Golf (Sydney).

McBRIEN, Philippa Jill Olivier; *see* Harris, P. J. O.

McBURNIE, Tony; Chairman: The Strategic Index, since 1994; The Strategic Marketing Index, since 1994; *b* 4 Aug. 1929; *s* of William McBurnie and Bessie McKenzie Harvey McBurnie; *m* 1954, René Keating; one *s* one *d*. *Educ:* Lanark Grammar Sch.; Glasgow Univ. (MA). FCIM (FInstM 1984). National Service, RAF (FO), 1951–53. Divisional Manager Mullard Ltd, 1958–65; Group Marketing Dir, United Glass Ltd, 1965–69; Chairman and Managing Director: Ravenhead Co. Ltd, 1970–79; United Glass Containers Ltd, 1979–82; Man. Dir, United Glass PT&D Gp, 1982–84; Dir, United Glass Holdings PLC, 1966–84; Dir Gen., Chartered Inst. of Marketing (formerly Inst. of Marketing), 1984–89; Managing Director: Coll. of Marketing Ltd, 1985–89; Marketing Training Ltd, 1984–89; Marketing House Publishers Ltd, 1985–89. Chairman: Reed QT Search, 1989–90; Marketing Quality Assurance, 1991–95. Director: Reed Executive plc, 1987–90; Beard Dove Ltd, 1988–97; Needles Point Mgt Co. Ltd, 2003–. Pres., Assoc. of Glass Container Manufacturers, 1981–83; Chm., NJIC for Glass Industry, 1982–83; Dir, European Glass Fedn, 1979–83. *Publications:* (with David Clutterbuck) The Marketing Edge, 1987; Marketing Plus, 1989. *Recreations:* golf, swimming, theatre, the arts. *Address:* Craigwood Lodge, Prince Consort Drive, Ascot, Berks SL5 8AW. *Club:* Wentworth.

McCABE, Bernice Alda; Headmistress, North London Collegiate School, since 1997; *b* 7 Oct. 1952; *d* of Alan Collis Wood and Eileen May Wood (*née* Bolton); *m* 1st, 1971, Anthony Hugh Lowther Davis; 2nd, 1988, Thomas Patrick McCabe. *Educ:* Clifton High Sch. for Girls; Bristol Univ. (BA, PGCE); Leeds Metropolitan Univ. (MBA 1995). Asst English Teacher, Filton High Sch., Bristol, 1974–81; Head of English: Cotham Grammar Sch., Bristol, 1981–83; Collingwood Sch., Camberley, 1984–86; Dep. Headteacher, Heathland Sch., Hounslow, 1986–90; Headmistress, Chelmsford County High Sch. for Girls, 1990–97. Mem., GSA, 1997– (Mem., Univs Sub-cttee, 2001–). Gov., Orley Farm Sch., 1997–2001; Co-Dir, Prince of Wales' Educn Summer Sch., 2002–. FRSA 1995. *Recreations:* family, house in country, walking, travel, gym, running, reading. *Address:* North London Collegiate School, Canons, Edgware, Middx HA8 7RJ. *T:* (020) 8952 0912.

MACCABE, Christopher George, CB 2004; British Joint Secretary, British-Irish Intergovernmental Conference, and Political Director (formerly Associate Political Director), Northern Ireland Office, 2000–08; *b* 17 Dec. 1946; *s* of late Max Maccabe, FRSA, and of Gladys Maccabe (*née* Chalmers), MBE; *m* 1974, Jenny Livingston; one *s* two *d*. *Educ:* Royal Belfast Academical Instn; Univ. of London (LLB); Queen's Univ., Belfast (LLM). Civil Servant, 1968–: Researcher: NI Cabinet Office, 1971–72; NI Office, 1972–73; Asst Private Sec. to Chief Minister, NI Power Sharing Exec., 1973–74; Private Sec. to Minister of State, NI Office, 1974–77; NI Office, 1977–80; seconded as Special Asst to Chief Constable, RUC, 1980–84; NI Office, 1984–88; Dir of Regimes, NI Prison Service, 1988–92; Hd, Political Affairs Div., NI Office, 1992–2000. UK Special Envoy to Sri Lanka peace process, 2006–. Mem. Adv. Bd, Centre for Advancement of Women in Politics, QUB, 2001–06. Gov., Victoria Coll., Belfast, 1989– (Chm., 2002–). FRSA 2001. *Recreations:* golf, Rugby Union, reading, Anglo-Zulu War of 1879. *Clubs:* Instonians Rugby, Dunmurry Golf (Belfast).

MacCABE, Prof. Colin Myles Joseph; Professor of English and Humanities, Birkbeck, University of London, since 2006; Distinguished Professor of English and Film, University of Pittsburgh, since 2002 (Professor of English, 1985–2002); *b* 9 Feb. 1949; *s* of Myles Joseph MacCabe and Ruth Ward MacCabe; two *s* one *d*. *Educ:* Trinity College, Cambridge (BA English and Moral Scis 1971, MA 1974, PhD 1976); Ecole Normale Supérieure, 1972–73 (pensionnaire anglais). University of Cambridge: Research Fellow, Emmanuel College, 1974–76; Fellow, King's College, 1976–81; Asst Lectr, Faculty of English, 1976–81; Prof. of English Studies, 1981–85, Vis. Prof., 1985–91, Strathclyde Univ.; Head of Production, 1985–89, Head of Res., 1989–98, BFI; Prof. of English, Univ. of Exeter, 1998–2006. Chairman: John Logie Baird Centre for Research in Television and Film, 1985–91 (Dir, 1983–85); London Consortium, 1995–. Vis. Fellow, Sch. of Humanities, Griffith Univ., 1981, 1984; Mellon Vis. Prof., Univ. of Pittsburgh, 1985; Vis. Prof., Birkbeck Coll., Univ. of London, 1992–06. Mem., Editl Bd, Screen, 1973–81; Editor, Critical Qly, 1990– (Critical Editor, 1987–90). *Publications:* James Joyce and the Revolution of the Word, 1979, 2nd edn 2002; Godard: Images, Sounds, Politics, 1980; (ed) The Talking Cure: essays in psychoanalysis and language, 1981; (ed) James Joyce: new perspectives, 1982; Theoretical Essays: film, linguistics, literature, 1985; (ed jtly) The BBC and Public Sector Broadcasting, 1986; (ed) High Theory/Low Culture: analysing popular television and film, 1986; (ed) Futures for English, 1987; (ed jtly) The Linguistics of Writing, 1987; (with Isaac Julien) Diary of a Young Soul Rebel, 1991; (ed jtly) Who is Andy Warhol?, 1996; Performance, 1998; The Eloquence of the Vulgar, 1999; Godard: a portrait of the artist at 70, 2003; T. S. Eliot, 2006; The Butcher Boy, 2007. *Recreations:* eating, drinking, talking. *Address:* Department of English and Humanities, Birkbeck, University of London, 30 Russell Square, WC1B 5DP.

McCABE, Eamonn Patrick; portrait photographer; Picture Editor, The Guardian, 1988–2001; *b* 28 July 1948; *s* of James and Celia McCabe; *m* 1st, 1972, Ruth Calvert (marr. diss. 1993); one *s*; 2nd, 1997, Rebecca Smithers; one *d*. *Educ:* Challoner School, Finchley; San Francisco State Coll. FRPS 1990. Freelance photographer on local papers and with The Guardian for one year; staff photographer, The Observer, 1977–86 and 1987–88; official photographer for the Pope's visit to England, 1982; Picture Editor, Sportsweek, 1986–87. Dir, Newscast, 2001–06. Work in Nat. Portrait Gall. Hon. Prof., Thames Valley Univ., 1994. Fellow in Photography, Nat. Mus. of Photography and TV, Bradford, 1988. Hon. DLit UEA, 2007. Sports photographer of the year, RPS and Sports Council, 1978, 1979, 1981, 1984; News photographer of the year, British Press Awards, 1985; Picture Editor of the Year, Nikon Press Awards, 1992, 1993, 1995, 1997, 1998. *Publications:* Sports Photographer, 1981; Eamonn McCabe, Photographer, 1987; The Making of Great Photographs, 2006; Artists and Their Studios, 2008. *Recreations:* cycling, cinema. *Address:* c/o The Guardian, Kings Place, 90 York Way, N1 9AG. *Club:* Chelsea Arts.

McCABE, John, CBE 1985; professional musician; composer and pianist; *b* 21 April 1939; *s* of Frank and Elisabeth McCabe; *m* 1974, Monica Christine Smith. *Educ:* Liverpool Institute High Sch. for Boys; Manchester Univ. (MusBac); Royal Manchester Coll. of Music (ARMCM); Hochschule für Musik, Munich. Pianist-in-residence, University Coll., Cardiff, 1965–68; freelance musical criticism, 1966–71. Career as composer and pianist: many broadcasts and recordings as well as concert appearances in various countries. Prizewinner in Gaudeamus Competition for Interpreters of Contemporary Music, Holland, 1969. Recordings incl. 12-CD set of complete piano music by Haydn; complete piano music of Nielsen (2 records). Awarded Special Citation by Koussevitsky Internat. Recording Foundn of USA, for recording of Symph. No 2 and Notturni ed Alba, 1974; Special Award by Composers' Guild of Gt Brit. (services to Brit. music), 1975; Ivor Novello Award (TV theme tune, Sam), 1977; Distinguished Musician Award, ISM, 2003. Pres., ISM, 1983–84; Chm., Assoc. of Professional Composers, 1984–85. Hon. FRMCM; Hon. FLCM 1983; Hon. FRCM 1984; Hon. RAM 1985; Hon. FTCL 1989. Hon. DPhil Thames Valley, 2001; Hon. DMus Liverpool, 2006. *Compositions* include: seven symphonies; two operas; five ballets, incl. Edward II, and Arthur, Pts 1 and 2; concerti, incl. Horn Concerto and Cello Concerto; orchestral works incl. The Chagall Windows and Hartmann Variations, Notturni ed Alba, for soprano and orch., Fire at Durilgai for orch., Cloudcatcher Fells for brass band; chamber music, incl. The Woman by the Sea, for piano and string quartet; Les Martinets noirs, for two violins and string orchestra; keyboard works; vocal compositions. *Publications:* Rachmaninov (short biog.), 1974; Bartok's Orchestral Music (BBC Music Guide), 1974; Haydn Piano Sonatas (Ariel Music Guide), 1986; Alan Rawsthorne: portrait of a composer, 1998. *Recreations:* cricket, snooker, books, films. *Address:* c/o Novello & Co. Ltd, Music Sales, 14–15 Berners Street, W1T 3LJ.

McCABE, Ven. (John) Trevor, RD 1976; Archdeacon of Cornwall, 1996–99, now Emeritus; *b* 26 Jan. 1933; *s* of John Leslie McCabe and Mary Ena McCabe; *m* 1959, Mary Thomas; three *s* one *d*. *Educ:* Falmouth Grammar Sch.; Nottingham Univ. (BA Hons); St Catherine's Coll., Oxford; Wycliffe Hall, Oxford (DipTh). Ordained, 1959; served Plymouth and Exeter; Vicar of Capel, Surrey, 1966–71; Chaplain, Isles of Scilly, 1971–81; Residentiary Canon, Bristol Cathedral, 1981–83; Vicar, Manaccan St Anthony and St Martin in Meneage, Helston, 1983–96; RD of Kerrier, 1987–90 and 1993–96; Hon. Canon of Truro, 1993–99. Non-exec. Dir, Cornwall Partnership Trust, 1999–2005. Chm., NHS Trust for Learning Disability, 1990–99. Served RNVR/RNR, 1955–57, 1963–83. *Recreations:* shrub gardening, local Cornish history. *Address:* Sunhill, School Lane, Budock, Falmouth TR11 5DG. *T:* (01326) 378095.

McCABE, Prof. Mary Margaret Anne, PhD; Professor of Ancient Philosophy, King's College, London, since 1998; *b* 18 Dec. 1948; *d* of late Edward McCabe and Sarah Frances McCabe; *m* 1993, Martin William Denton Beddoe, *qv*; two *d*. *Educ:* Oxford High Sch. for Girls; Newnham Coll., Cambridge (BA 1970; MA 1973; PhD 1977). Fellow in Classics, New Hall, Univ. of Cambridge, 1981–90; King's College, London: Lectr in Philosophy, 1990–92; Reader in Philosophy, 1992–98; Leverhulme Trust Major Res. Fellow, 2005–08. *Publications:* (as M. M. Mackenzie) Plato on Punishment, 1981; (ed jtly, as M. M. Mackenzie) Images of Authority, 1989; Plato's Individuals, 1994; (ed jtly) Form and Argument in Late Plato, 1996; Plato and his Predecessors: the dramatisation of reason, 2000; (ed jtly) Perspectives on Perception, 2007. *Recreation:* horseracing. *Address:* Department of Philosophy, King's College London, Strand, WC2R 2LS. *T:* (020) 7848 2309; *e-mail:* mm.mccabe@kcl.ac.uk.

McCABE, Primrose Smith; *see* Scott, P. S.

McCABE, Prof. Richard Anthony, PhD; FBA 2007; Professor of English Language and Literature, University of Oxford, since 2002; Fellow, Merton College, Oxford, since 1993; *b* 2 Sept. 1954; *s* of Edward McCabe and Jenny (*née* Synnott). *Educ:* Trinity Coll., Dublin (Foundn Schol.; BA 1976 (Gold Medallist)); Pembroke Coll., Cambridge (PhD 1980). Robert Gardiner Meml Schol., Univ. of Cambridge, 1976–78. Drapers' Res. Fellow, Pembroke Coll., Cambridge, 1978–82; Lecturer: UCD, 1982–86; TCD, 1986–93; Reader in English Lang. and Lit., Univ. of Oxford, 1996–2002. Chatterton Lectr in Poetry, 1991, Res. Reader, 1999, British Acad. *Publications:* monographs: Joseph Hall: a study in satire and meditation, 1982; The Pillars of Eternity: time and providence in The Faerie Queene, 1989; Incest, Drama and Nature's Law 1550–1700, 1993; Spenser's Monstrous Regiment: Elizabethan Ireland and the poetics of difference, 2002; editor: (with H. Erskine-Hill) Presenting Poetry: Composition, Publication, Reception: essays in honour of Ian Jack, 1995; Edmund Spenser, The Shorter Poems, 1999; (with D. Womersley) Literary Milieux: essays in text and context presented to Howard Erskine-Hill, 2007. *Recreations:* book collecting, theatre going, writing, walking. *Address:* Merton College, Oxford OX1 4JD. *T:* (01865) 276289; *e-mail:* Richard.mccabe@ell.ox.ac.uk.

McCABE, Stephen James; MP (Lab) Birmingham, Hall Green, since 1997; a Lord Commissioner, HM Treasury (Government Whip), since 2007; *b* 4 Aug. 1955; *s* of James and Margaret McCabe; *m* 1991; one *s* one *d*. *Educ:* Univ. of Bradford (MA); Moray House Coll., Edinburgh (Dip. and CQSW). Social worker, Generic Team, 1977–79, Intermediate Treatment Worker, 1979–83, Wolverhampton; Manager, The Priory, Newbury, 1983–85; Lectr in Social Services, NE Worcs Coll., 1986–89; social policy researcher, BASW, and part-time child care worker, Solihull, 1989–91; Educn Advr, CCETSW, 1991–97. An Asst Govt Whip, 2006–07. *Recreations:* cooking, hill-walking, reading, football. *Address:* House of Commons, SW1A 0AA. *T:* (020) 7219 3509.

McCABE, Thomas; Member (Lab) Hamilton South, Scottish Parliament, since 1999; *b* 28 April 1954. *Educ:* St Martin's Secondary Sch., Hamilton; Bell Coll. of Technology, Hamilton (Dip. Public Sector Mgt). Light engrg, Hoover Factory, Cambuslang, 1974–93; Welfare Rights Officer, Strathclyde Regl Council and N Lanarks Council, 1993–98. Member (Lab): Hamilton DC, 1988–96 (Chm., Housing, 1990–92; Leader, 1992–96); S Lanarks Council, 1996–99 (Leader, 1996–99). Scottish Executive: Minister for Parlt and Chief Govt Whip, 1999–2001; Dep. Minister for Health and Community Care, 2003–04; Minister for Finance and Public Service Reform, 2004–07. *Recreations:* sport, golf, reading, walking, cinema. *Address:* Hamilton South Constituency Office, 23 Beckford Street, Hamilton ML3 0BT. *T:* (01698) 454018; Scottish Parliament, George IV Bridge, Edinburgh EH99 1SP.

McCABE, Ven. Trevor; *see* McCabe, Ven. J. T.

McCAFFER, Prof. Ronald, FREng; Professor of Construction Management, Loughborough University (formerly Loughborough University of Technology), since 1986; Finance Director, European Construction Institute, since 1990; *b* 8 Dec. 1943; *s* of late John Gegg McCaffer and Catherine Turner (*née* Gourlay); *m* 1966, Margaret Elizabeth, *d* of late Cyril Warner and of Mary Huntley (*née* Mason); one *s*. *Educ:* Albert Sch., Glasgow; Univ. of Strathclyde (BSc 1965; DSc 1998); PhD Loughborough 1977. FICE 1988; FCIOB 1988; MCMI (MBIM 1989); FREng (FEng 1991); Eur Ing 1990; MASCE 1999. Design Engr, Babtie, Shaw & Morton, 1965–67; Site Engineer: Nuclear Power Gp, 1967–69; Taylor Woodrow Construction Ltd, 1969–70; Loughborough University of Technology: Lectr, 1970–78; Sen. Lectr, 1978–83; Reader, 1983–86; Head of Civil Engrg, 1987–93; Dean of Engineering, 1992–97; Loughborough University: Sen. Pro-Vice-Chancellor, then Dep. Vice-Chancellor, 1997–2002; Dir, Strategic Business Partnership Innovation and Knowledge Transfer, 2002–06. Chairman: Loughborough University Utilities Ltd, 1997–02; Loughborough Univ. Enterprises Ltd, 2002–06; Loughborough Univs Innovation Center Ltd, 2002–06; Construction Industry Simulations Ltd, 2006–; Director: Loughborough Consultants Ltd, 1997–2003; Peterborough HE Co. Ltd, 1997–02; Innovative Projects Worldwide Ltd, 1998–2004; Emman Ltd, 2002–06; Imago Ltd, 2003–06. Mem., Programme Cttee, 1992–95, Educn, Trng and Competence to Practice Cttee, 1995–98, Strategy Rev. Gp, 1996, Royal Acad. of Engrg. Member: Engrg Construction Industry Trng Bd, 1994–2003; Technical Opportunities Panel, EPSRC, 2000–04; Civil Engrg Panel, 2001 RAE; Civil Engrg Sub-Panel, 2008 RAE; Associate Parly Gp for Engrg Develt, 1995–; Council Mem., E Midlands Innovation, 2005–. Visiting Professor: Univ. of Moratuwa, Sri Lanka, 1986–92; Technol Univ. of Malaysia, 1996, 2000; Sch. of Built and Natural Envmt, Glasgow Caledonian Univ., 2007–. Mem., Bd of Trustees and Advr, British Univ. in Egypt, 2005–. Moderating Examr, Engrg Council, 1988–92; past and present examr, univs in UK and overseas. Editor, Engineering, Construction and Architectural Management, 1994–. *Publications:* Modern Construction Management, 1977, 6th edn 2006; Worked Examples in Construction Management, 1978, 2nd edn 1986; Estimating and Tendering for Civil Engineering Works, 1984, 2nd edn 1991; Management of Construction Equipment, 1982, 2nd edn 1991; International Bid Preparation, 1995; International Bidding Case Study, 1995; Management of Off-highway Plant and Equipment, 2002; jl articles and conf. papers. *Recreation:* being patient with administrators. *Address:* Department of Civil Engineering, Loughborough University, Loughborough, Leics LE11 3TU. *T:* (01509) 222600, *Fax:* (01509) 223980; *e-mail:* r.mccaffer@lboro.ac.uk; *web:* www.mcaffer.com.

McCAFFERTY, Christine; MP (Lab) Calder Valley, since 1997; *b* 14 Oct. 1945; *d* of late John and Dorothy Livesley; *m* 1st, Michael McCafferty; one *s*; 2nd, David Tarlo. *Educ:* Whalley Grange Grammar Sch. for Girls, Manchester; Footscray High Sch., Melbourne. Welfare Worker (Disabled), CHS Manchester, 1963–70; Educn Welfare Officer, Manchester Educn Cttee, 1970–72; Registrar of Marriages, Bury Registration Dist, 1978–80; Project worker, Calderdale Well Women Centre, 1989–96. Member: Calderdale MBC, 1991–97; W Yorks Police Authy, 1994–97. Mem., Select Cttee on Internat. Develt, 2001–05; Chair, All-Pty Parly Gp on Population, Develt and Reproductive Health, 1999–, on Guides, 2000–, on Compassion in Dying, 2007–. Mem., Council of Europe/WEU, 1999–. Dir, Royd Regeneration Ltd, 1996–. Mem. Exec., N Reg. Assoc. for the Blind, 1993–96. Gov., Luddenden Dene Sch. *Address:* House of Commons, SW1A 0AA.

McCAFFREY, Anne Inez; writer; *b* 1 April 1926; *d* of George H. McCaffrey and Anne Dorothy McElroy-McCaffrey; *m* 1950, H. Wright Johnson (marr. diss. 1970); two *s* one *d*. *Educ:* Stuart Hall Secondary Sch.; Radcliffe Coll., Harvard Univ. (BA *cum laude* 1947). Advertising copywriter and layout artist, Liberty Music Shops, NYC, 1948–50; copywriter, then Sec. to Sales Manager, Helena Rubinstein, 1950–52. Established Equine Centre, Dragonhold Stables, Co. Wicklow, 1977. Numerous awards, including: Golden Pen Award, 1982; Science Fiction Book Club Awards, 1986, 1989, 1990, 1992, 1993, 1994, 1997; Margaret A. Edwards Award for Lifetime Literary Achievement, Amer. Liby Assoc., 1999. *Publications:* Restoree, 1967; Dragonflight, 1968; (ed) Alchemy & Academe, 1970; Mark of Merlin, 1971; Dragonquest, 1971; Ring of Fear, 1971; To Ride Pegasus, 1973; Out of This World Cookbook, 1973; The White Dragon, 1975; Kilternan Legacy, 1975; Dragonsong, 1976; Dragonsinger, 1977; Get off the Unicorn, 1977; Dragondrums, 1979; Crystal Singer, 1982; The Coelura, 1983; Moreta, Dragonlady of Pern, 1983; Stitch in Snow, 1984; Killashandra, 1985; Chronicles of Pern: First Fall, 1985; The Girl who Heard Dragons, 1986; The Year of the Lucy, 1986; Nerilka's Story, 1986; The Carradyne Touch, 1988 (US edn as The Lady); Dragonsdawn, 1988; Pern Portrait Gallery, 1988; (jtly) Guidebook to Pern, 1989, 2nd edn as The Dragonlover's Guide to Pern, 1997; Renegades of Pern, 1989; Pegasus in Flight, 1990; The Rowan, 1990; All the Weyrs of Pern, 1991; Damia, 1992; Crystal Line, 1992; Damia's Children, 1993; Lyon's Pride, 1994; The Dolphins of Pern, 1994; An Exchange of Gifts, 1995; Freedom's Landing, 1995; Black Horses for the King, 1996; A Diversity of Dragons, 1997; Dragonseye (UK title: Red Star Rising), 1997; Freedom's Choice, 1997; Masterharper of Pern, 1998; Freedom's Challenge, 1998; If Wishes Were Horses, 1998; Nimisha's Ship, 1999; The Tower & The Hive, 1999; Pegasus in Space, 2000; Skies of Pern, 2001; A Gift of Dragons, 2002; (with Todd McCaffrey) Dragon's Kin, 2003; (ed jtly) Serve it Forth: cooking with Anne McCaffrey, 2004; *variously with Margaret Ball, Jody-Lynn Nye, Elizabeth Ann Scarborough and others:* Dinosaur Planet, 1978; Dinosaur Planet Survivors, 1984; Doona series: Decision at Doona, 1969; Crisis on Doona, 1992; Treaty Planet (reissued as Treaty at Doona), 1994; Ship series: The Ship Who Sang, 1970; The Partner Ship, 1992; The Ship who Searched, 1992; The City who Fought, 1993; The Ship Who Won, 1994; The Ship Avenged, 1997; Petaybee series: Power Play, 1992; Powers that Be, 1993; Power Lines, 1994; Changelings, 2005; Acorna series: Acorna: the unicorn girl, 1997; Acorna's People, 1997; Acorna's Quest, 1998; Acorna's World, 1999; Acorna's Search, 2002; Acorna's Rebels, 2003; Acorna's Triumph, 2004; books trans. into numerous foreign langs and Braille. *Recreations:* equine events, raising Maine Coon cats, quilting. *Address:* Dragonhold-Underhill, Newcastle, Co. Wicklow, Ireland. *Club:* Sloane.

McCAFFREY, Sir Thos Daniel, (Sir Tom), Kt 1979; public affairs consultant; *b* 20 Feb. 1922; *s* of William P. and B. McCaffrey; *m* 1949, Agnes Campbell Douglas; two *s* four *d*. *Educ:* Hyndland Secondary Sch. and St Aloysius Coll., Glasgow. Served War, RAF, 1940–46. Scottish Office, 1948–61; Chief Information Officer, Home Office, 1966–71; Press Secretary, 10 Downing Street, 1971–72; Dir of Information Services, Home Office, 1972–74; Head of News Dept, FCO, 1974–76; Chief Press Sec. to Prime Minister, 1976–79; Chief of Staff to Rt Hon. James Callaghan, MP, 1979–80; Chief Asst to Rt Hon. Michael Foot, MP, 1980–83; Hd, Chief Executive's Office, BPCC, 1983–84; Dir, Public Affairs, and Special Advr to the Publisher, Mirror Gp Newspapers, 1984–85. *Address:* Balmaha, 2 The Park, Great Bookham, Surrey KT23 3JL. *T:* (01372) 454171.

McCAHILL, Patrick Gerard; QC 1996; **His Honour Judge McCahill;** a Circuit Judge, since 2001; a Specialist Chancery Circuit Judge, since 2007; *b* 6 May 1952; *s* of John McCahill and Josephine McCahill (*née* Conaghan); *m* 1979, Liselotte Gabrielle Steiner; two *d*. *Educ:* Corby GS; St Catharine's Coll., Cambridge (1st cl. Hons; MA); LLM London ext. 2003; BSc (1st cl. Hons) Open Univ. 2004. FCIArb 1992. Called to the Bar, Gray's Inn, 1975 (Bacon Schol., 1973; Atkin Schol., 1975), King's Inns, Dublin, 1990; Asst Dep. Coroner for Birmingham and Solihull, 1984–99; Asst Recorder, 1993–97; a Recorder, 1997–2001. Member: Mental Health Review Tribunal, 2000–07; Parole Bd, 2004–07. *Recreations:* humour, family history, sport. *Address:* Bristol County Court, Greyfriars, Lewins Mead, Bristol BS1 2NR.

McCAIG, Prof. Colin Darnley, PhD; FRSE; Regius Professor of Physiology, since 2002, and Head, School of Medical Sciences, since 2003, University of Aberdeen; *b* 26 June 1953. *Educ:* Univ. of Edinburgh (BSc); Univ. of Glasgow (PhD). Beit Meml Res. Fellow, Univ. of Edinburgh, 1983–86; University of Aberdeen: MRC Sen. Fellow, 1986–88; Wellcome Trust Univ. Award Lectr, 1988–93; Lectr, 1993–95; Sen. Lectr, 1995–99; Prof., 1999–2002; Hd, Dept of Biomed. Scis, 1998–2003. FRSE 2007. *Address:* School of Medical Sciences, Institute of Medical Sciences, University of Aberdeen, Foresterhill, Aberdeen AB25 2ZD.

McCAIN, John Sidney, III; US Senator from Arizona, since 1987; *b* Canal Zone, Panama, 29 Aug. 1936; *s* of John Sidney McCain and Roberta McCain (*née* Wright); *m* 1st, 1965, Carol Shepp (marr. diss. 1980); one *d*, and two step *s*; 2nd 1980, Cindy Hensley; two *s* one *d*, and one adopted *d*. *Educ:* US Naval Acad.; Nat. War Coll. Naval aviator, USN, 1958–81; POW, Vietnam, 1967–73; Capt. 1977; Dir, Navy Senate Liaison Office, Washington, 1977–81; retd USN 1981. Vice-Pres., PR, Hensley & Co., 1981–83. Mem., US House of Reps from 1st Arizona Dist, 1983–86; Senate Committees: Member: Armed Services; Sci. and Transport; Chairman: Indian Affairs, 1995–97 and 2005–07; Commerce, 1997–2001 and 2003–05. Mem., Commn on Intelligence Capabilities of US regarding weapons of mass destruction, 2004. Republican Candidate: for Presidential nomination, 2000; for Presidency of USA, 2008. Chm., Internat. Republican Inst., 1993–. Legion of Merit (USA); Silver Star (USA); Purple Heart (USA); DFC (USA); Legion of Honour (Vietnam). *Publications:* (with Mark Salter): Faith of My Fathers, 1999; Worth the Fighting For: a memoir, 2002; Why Courage Matters: the way to a braver life, 2004; Character is Destiny, 2005; Hard Call, 2007.

McCALL, Carolyn, (Mrs P. Frawley), OBE 2008; Chief Executive, Guardian Media Group plc, since 2006; *b* 13 Sept. 1961; *d* of Colleen and Arthur McCall; *m* 1986, Peter Frawley; two *s* one *d*. *Educ:* Univ. of Kent (BA Hons Hist. and Politics); Inst. of Educn, Univ. of London (PGCE); Univ. of London (MA Politics). Risk Analyst, Costain Gp plc, 1984–86; The Guardian: planner, 1986–88; advertising exec., 1988–89; advertising manager, 1989–91; Product Develt Manager, 1991–92; Display Advertising Manager, 1992; Advertising Dir, Wire UK, 1992–94; Dep. Advertising Dir, 1994–95; Advertising Dir, 1995–97; Commercial Dir, 1997–98; Guardian Newspapers Ltd: Dep. Man. Dir, 1998–2000; Chief Exec., 2000–06. Non-executive Director: New Look plc, 1999–2005; Tesco plc, 2005–08. Chair, Opportunity Now, 2005–. Member: WACL, 1995–; Mktg Gp of GB. *Address:* Guardian Media Group, 60 Farringdon Road, EC1R 3GA. *T:* (020) 7239 9711; *e-mail:* ceoffice@gmgplc.co.uk.

McCALL, Christopher Hugh; QC 1987; *b* 3 March 1944; *yr s* of late Robin Home McCall, CBE and Joan Elizabeth (*née* Kingdon); *m* 1981, Henrietta Francesca Sharpe. *Educ:* Winchester (Scholar); Magdalen Coll., Oxford (Demy; BA Maths, 1964; Eldon Law Scholar, 1966). Called to the Bar, Lincoln's Inn, 1966, Bencher, 1993. Second Jun. Counsel to the Inland Revenue in chancery matters, 1977–87; Jun. Counsel to Attorney Gen. in charity matters, 1981–87. Mem., Bar Council, 1973–76. Trustee, British Mus., 1999–2004. *Recreations:* music, travel, Egyptomania. *Address:* Maitland Chambers, 7 Stone Buildings, Lincoln's Inn, WC2A 3SZ. *T:* (020) 7406 1200; Sphinx Hill, Ferry Lane, Moulsford on Thames OX10 9JF. *T:* (01491) 652162. *Clubs:* Alpine; Leander (Henley-on-Thames).

McCALL, David Slesser, CBE 1988; DL; Chairman, Anglia Television Ltd, 1994–2001 (Director, 1970–2001; Chief Executive, 1976–94); *b* 3 Dec. 1934; *s* of Patrick McCall and Florence Kate Mary Walker; *m* 1968, Lois Patricia Elder. *Educ:* Robert Gordon's Coll., Aberdeen. Mem., Inst. of Chartered Accountants of Scotland, 1958. National Service, 1959–61. Accountant, Grampian Television Ltd, 1961–68; Company Sec., Anglia Television Ltd, 1968–76; Dir, 1970–98, Chief Exec., 1986–94, Chm., 1994–98, Anglia Television Gp. Chairman: Oxford Scientific Films Ltd, 1982–89; Greene King plc, 1995–2005; United Trustees Ltd, 1997–; 99.9 Radio Norwich Ltd, 2006–; Director: ITN, 1978–86, 1991–96; Ind. Television Publications Ltd, 1971–89; Ind. Television Assoc. Ltd, 1976–96; Sodastream Holdings Ltd, 1976–85; Norwich City Football Club, 1979–85; Channel Four Television Co., 1981–85; Radio Broadland, 1984–91; Super Channel Ltd, 1986–88; British Satellite Broadcasting, 1987–90; Regl Adv. Bd, National Westminster Bank, 1988–92; TSMS Group Ltd, 1989–96; Hodder & Stoughton Holdings Ltd, 1992–93; Cosgrove Hall Films, 1993–96; MAI plc, 1994–96; MAI Media UK Ltd, 1995–96; Meridian Broadcasting Ltd, 1994–96; Satellite Inf. Services, 1994–96; Village Roadshow Ltd, Australia, 1994–96; Bakers Dozen Inns Ltd, 1996–; Anglia FM Ltd, 1996–99; Anglo Welsh Group PLC, 1996–2000; Bernard Matthews Gp PLC, 1996–2000; Granada Pension Trust Co. Ltd, 2000–03; Bernard Matthews Hldgs Ltd, 2002–. Chm., Forum Trust Ltd (formerly Norfolk and Norwich Millennium Bid), 1996–2005; Dep. Chm., United Broadcasting and Entertainment, 1996. Mem., ITCA, subseq. Ind. Television Assoc., 1976–95 (Chm., 1986–88); Pres., Cinema and Television Benevolent Fund, 1998–2001 (Trustee, 1995–). Pres., Norfolk and Norwich Chamber of Commerce, 1988–90 (Dep. Pres., 1986–88); Chm., Norwich Playhouse Theatre, 1992–98. Treas., 1995–97, Chm. Council, 1997–2006, UEA. FRTS 1988; FRSA 1993. CCMI (CBIM 1988). DL Norfolk, 1992. Hon. DCL UEA, 2006. *Recreations:* sport, travel. *Address:* Woodland Hall, Redenhall, Harleston, Norfolk IP20 9QW. *T:* (01379) 854442.

McCALL, Duncan James; QC 2008; *b* 8 May 1965; *s* of John Berry McCall and Stella McCall. *Educ:* Magdalen Coll., Oxford (BA). Called to the Bar, Gray's Inn, 1988; in practice as barrister, 1989–. *Address:* 4 Pump Court, Temple, EC4Y 7AN. *T:* (020) 7842 5555, *Fax:* (020) 7583 2036; *e-mail:* dmccall@4pumpcourt.com.

McCALL, William; General Secretary, Institution of Professional Civil Servants, 1963–89; *b* 6 July 1929; *s* of Alexander McCall and Jean Corbet Cunningham; *m* 1955, Olga Helen Brunton; one *s* one *d*. *Educ:* Dumfries Academy; Ruskin College, Oxford. Civil Service, 1946–52; Social Insurance Dept, TUC, 1954–58; Asst Sec., Instn of Professional Civil Servants, 1958–63; Mem., Civil Service Nat. Whitley Council (Staff Side), 1963–89, Chm. 1969–71, Vice-Chm. 1983. Hon. Treasurer, Parly and Scientific Cttee, 1976–80; Part-time Mem., Eastern Electricity Board, 1977–86; Member: Cttee of Inquiry into Engrg Profession, 1977–79; PO Arbitration Tribunal, 1980–90; TUC Gen. Council, 1984–89; Pay and Employment Policy Cttee, CVCP, 1990–94; Police Complaints Authority, 1991–94. Member Council: Univ. of London, 1994–97 (Mem. Ct, 1984–94); Goldsmiths' Coll., 1989–95 (Hon. Fellow, 1996). *Address:* Foothills, Gravel Path, Berkhamsted, Herts HP4 2PF. *T:* (01442) 864974.

McCALL, Rt Rev. William David Hair; *see* Bunbury, Bishop of.

McCALL SMITH, Prof. Alexander, CBE 2007; PhD; FRSE, FMedSci; writer; Professor of Medical Law, University of Edinburgh, 1995–2005, now Emeritus; *b* 24 Aug. 1948; *s* of Sandy McCall Smith and Daphne McCall Smith (*née* Woodall); *m* 1982, Dr Elizabeth Parry; two *d*. *Educ:* Christian Brothers Coll., Bulawayo; Univ. of Edinburgh (LLB; PhD). Lectr in Law, Queen's Univ., Belfast, 1973–74; Lectr in Law, subseq. Reader in Law, Univ. of Edinburgh, 1974–95; Hd, Dept of Law, Univ. of Botswana, 1981 (on secondment). Vis. Prof. of Law, Law Sch., Southern Methodist Univ., Dallas, 1988. Vice-Chm., Human Genetics Commn, 2000–04; Mem., Internat. Bioethics Cttee, UNESCO, 1997–2004. FRSE 2001; FMedSci 2005. Hon. FRCPE 2004. Hon. DIur Parma, 2005; Hon. DLitt: Napier, 2005; Aberdeen, 2006, BC, 2006; Hon. LLD Edinburgh, 2007; Hon. DSc UEA, 2007. Saga Award, 2004; Author of the Year, British Book Awards, 2004. *Publications:* over 50 books including: (with J. K. Mason) Law and Medical Ethics, 1983, 6th edn 2002; (with K. Frimpong) The Criminal Law of Botswana, 1991; (with C. Shapiro) Forensic Aspects of Sleep, 1997; (with A. Merry) Errors, Medicine and the Law, 2001; *fiction:* Portuguese Irregular Verbs, 1997; The Finer Points of Sausage Dogs, 1998; The No 1 Ladies' Detective Agency, 1998; Tears of the Giraffe, 2000; Morality for Beautiful Girls, 2001; The Kalahari Typing School for Men, 2002; The Full Cupboard of Life, 2003; At the Villa of Reduced Circumstances, 2003; The Sunday Philosophy Club, 2004; In the Company of Cheerful Ladies, 2004; The Girl Who Married a Lion (short stories), 2004; Friends, Lovers, Chocolate, 2005; 44 Scotland Street, 2005; Espresso Tales, 2005; Blue Shoes and Happiness, 2006; Dream Angus, 2006; The Right Attitude to Rain, 2006; The Good Husband of Zebra Drive, 2007; The World According to Bertie, 2007; The Careful Use of Compliments, 2007; The Miracle at Speedy Motors, 2008; The Unbearable Lightness of Scones, 2008; The Comfort of Saturdays, 2008; books for children. *Recreation:* wind instruments. *Clubs:* New, Scottish Arts (Edinburgh).

McCALLUM, Alastair Grindlay; His Honour Judge McCallum; a Circuit Judge, since 1992; *b* 28 Feb. 1947; *s* of William and Catherine McCallum; *m* 1969, Lindsay Sheila Watkins; two *d*. *Educ:* Gilbert Rennie, Northern Rhodesia; Leeds Univ. (LLB, LLM (Com.)). Called to the Bar, Inner Temple, 1970; Asst Recorder, 1984; Recorder, 1989; Head of Chambers, 1990. *Recreations:* golf, travel, reading. *T:* (01274) 840274. *Club:* Bradford.

MacCALLUM, Prof. Charles Hugh Alexander, RIBA; FRIAS; Professor of Architecture, Glasgow University, and Head, Mackintosh School of Architecture, Glasgow School of Art, 1994–2000, now Emeritus Professor; architect in private practice, since 1973; *b* Glasgow, 24 June 1935; *s* of Alister Hugh McCallum, Pitlochry, and Jessie McLean (*née* Forsyth), Perth; *m* 1963, Andrée Simone Tonnard; two *d*. *Educ:* Hutchesons' Grammar Sch.; Glasgow Sch. of Architecture (DA); Massachusetts Inst. of Technol. (MCP 1969). RIBA 1961; FRIAS 2001. Architect, Gillespie Kidd & Coia, Glasgow, 1957–67; Sen. Architect, Dept of Architecture and Planning, Clydebank, 1969–70; Statutory Lectr, later Exec. Dir, Sch. of Architecture, University Coll., Dublin, 1969–73; Prof. of Architectural Design, Welsh Sch. of Architecture, Univ. of Wales Coll. of Cardiff, 1986–94. Architectural consultant, Scots Kirk, Paris, 2000–04. Mem. Cttee, Franco-British Union of Architects, 2000–. Médaille de la Formation, Académie d'Architecture, Paris, 2003. *Publications:* (with Françoise Hamon) Louis Visconti 1791–1853, 1991; articles on architecture and engrg, in UK, France and Russia. *Recreations:* gardening, watercolours. *Address:* 11A Charlbury Road, Oxford OX2 6UT. *Club:* Caledonian.

McCALLUM, Sir Donald (Murdo), Kt 1988; CBE 1976; FREng; FRSE; DL; General Manager, Scottish Group, 1968–85, and Director, 1970–87, Ferranti plc; Chairman, Laser Ecosse Ltd, 1990–95; *b* 6 Aug. 1922; *s* of Roderick McCallum and Lillian (*née* McPhee); *m* 1st, 1949, Barbara Black (*d* 1971); one *d*; 2nd, 1974, Mrs Margaret Illingworth (*née* Broadbent) (*d* 1997); 3rd, 2007, Mrs Jill Morgan (*née* Maxwell). *Educ:* George Watson's Boys' Coll.; Edinburgh Univ. (BSc). FIET (FIEE 1969); FREng (FEng 1982); FRAeS 1986. Admiralty Signal Establishment, 1942–46; Standard Telecommunication Laboratories, 1946; Ferranti Ltd, 1947: Chairman: Ferranti Defence Systems Ltd, 1984–87 (Hon. Pres., 1987–90); Ferranti Industrial Electronics, 1984–87 (Hon. Pres., 1987–90). Dir, Short Bros Ltd, 1981–89; Chairman: Scottish Tertiary Education Adv. Council, 1984–87; Scottish Council Develt & Industry, 1985–91 (Pres., 1991–93; Fellow, 1993). Scottish Sub-Cttee, UGC, 1987–88; Member: UFC, 1989–91 (Chm., Scottish Cttee, 1989–91); Scottish Econ. Council, 1983–92. Mem., Leeds Churches Together in Mission, 2002–07. Member: Court, Heriot-Watt Univ., 1979–85; Governing Body, Napier Polytechnic, 1988–93; Court, Napier Univ., 1993–95; Governing Body, Edinburgh Coll. of Art, 1988–93; Bd of Trustees, Nat. Liby of Scotland, 1990–96. Hon. Life Mem., Edinburgh Univ. Students' Assoc., 1984. Liveryman, Company of Engineers, 1984; Freeman, City of London. DL City of Edinburgh, 1984. CCMI (CBIM 1983). Hon. FRSGS 1993. Hon. Fellow, Paisley Coll. of Technol., 1987; Fellow, SCOTVEC, 1988. DUniv Stirling, 1985; Hon. DSc: Heriot-Watt, 1986; Napier Coll. of Commerce and Technology, Edinburgh, 1986; Hon. LLD: Strathclyde, 1987; Aberdeen, 1989. British Gold Medal, RAcS, 1985. *Recreations:* photography, reading. *Address:* Brackenhill, Newland, Ulverston LA12 7QD. *T:* (01229) 583187. *Clubs:* New (Edinburgh).

McCALLUM, Googie, (Mrs John McCallum); *see* Withers, G.

McCALLUM, Helen Mary; Director of Policy, Which? (Consumers' Association), since 2007; *b* 23 Dec. 1952; *d* of Edward James Ward and Pauline Ward; *m* 1980, Duncan Peter Finlay McCallum; two *d*. *Educ:* Queen Elizabeth's Girls' Grammar Sch., Barnet; Nottingham Univ. (BA Hons English Lit.). Sabbatical Sec., Students' Union, Univ. of Nottingham, 1973–74; Admin. Asst (PR), Univ. of Sheffield, 1974–78; PRO, Univ. of Salford, 1978–81; freelance publications work, 1981–85; Alumni Officer, Univ. of Sheffield, 1985–88; Sen. PR Manager, 1989–92, Hd of Communications, 1992–94, E Anglian RHA; Hd of Communications, NHS Exec., 1994–98; Dir of Communications, DoH, 1999–2001; Dir of Corporate Affairs, Envmt Agency, 2001–07. Mem., Assoc. of Health Care Communicators, 1989. *Recreations:* amateur dramatics, keeping moderately fit. *Address:* 79 Gilbert Road, Cambridge CB4 3NZ.

McCALLUM, Ian; *see* McCallum, R. I.

McCALLUM, Ian Stewart; Executive Sales Manager, Save & Prosper Sales Ltd, 1989–95 (Sales Manager, 1985–87, Area Manager, 1987–89); *b* 24 Sept. 1936; *s* of late John Blair McCallum and Margaret Stewart McCallum; *m* 1st, 1957, Pamela Mary (*née* Shave) (marr. diss. 1984); one *s* two *d*; 2nd, 1984, Jean (*née* Lynch); two step *d*. *Educ:* Kingston Grammar Sch. Eagle Star Insurance Co. Ltd, 1953–54; National Service, Highland Light Infantry, 1954–56; Eagle Star Insce Co. Ltd, 1956–58; F. E. Wright and Co., Insurance Brokers, 1958–63; H. Clarkson (Home) Ltd, Insurance Brokers, 1963–68; Save & Prosper Group Ltd, 1968–95. Leader, Woking Borough Council, 1972–76 and 1978–81, Dep. Leader, 1981–82; Mayor of Woking, 1976–77; Chm., Assoc. of Dist Councils, 1979–84 (Leader, 1974–79); Vice-Chairman: Standing Cttee on Local Authorities and Theatre, 1977–81; UK Steering Cttee on Local Authority Superannuation, 1974–84; Member: Local Authorities Conditions of Service Adv. Bd, 1973–84; Consultative Council on Local Govt Finance, 1975–84; Council for Business in the Community, 1981–84; Audit Commn, 1983–86; Health Promotion Res. Trust, 1983–97. Vice-Chm., Sports Council, 1980–86; Pres., European Sports Conf., 1983–85. *Recreations:* swimming, walking, reading, bowls. *Address:* 20 Perch Close, Leybourne Lakes, Larkfield, Kent ME20 6TN. *T:* (01622) 719442.

McCALLUM, John Neil, AO 1992; CBE 1971; Chairman and Executive Producer, Fauna Films, Australia, since 1967, and John McCallum Productions, since 1976; actor and producer; *b* 14 March 1918; *s* of John Neil McCallum and Lilian Elsie (*née* Dyson); *m* 1948, Georgette Lizette Withers (*see* Googie Withers); one *s* two *d*. *Educ:* Oatlands Prep. Sch., Harrogate; Knox Grammar Sch., Sydney; C of E Grammar Sch., Brisbane; RADA. Served War, 2/5 Field Regt, AIF, 1941–45. Actor, English rep. theatres, 1937–39; Stratford-on-Avon Festival Theatre, 1939; Old Vic Theatre, 1940; British films and theatre, 1946–58; films include: It Always Rains On Sunday; Valley of Eagles; Miranda; London stage plays include: Roar Like a Dove; Janus; Waiting for Gillian; J. C. Williamson Theatres Ltd, Australia: Asst Man. Dir, 1958; Jt. Man. Dir, 1959–65; Man. Dir, 1966. Appeared in: (with Ingrid Bergman) The Constant Wife, London, 1973–74; (with Googie Withers) The Circle, London, 1976–77, Australia, 1982–83; (with Googie Withers) The Kingfisher, Australia, 1978–79; The Skin Game, The Cherry Orchard, and Dandy Dick, theatrical tour, England, 1981; The School for Scandal, British Council European tour, 1984; (with Googie Withers, and dir.) Stardust, tours England, 1984,

Australia, 1984–85; The Chalk Garden, Chichester Fest., 1986; Hay Fever, Chichester Fest., 1988; The Royal Baccarat Scandal, Chichester Fest., 1988, Haymarket, 1989; (with Googie Withers) The Cocktail Hour, Australian and UK tour, 1989–90; (with Googie Withers) High Spirits, Australia, 1991; On Golden Pond, UK tour, 1992; The Chalk Garden, Sydney, 1995; An Ideal Husband, Old Vic, 1996, Australia, 1997–98; Lady Windermere's Fan, Chichester, 1997, Haymarket, 2002; A Busy Day, Bristol Old Vic and Lyric, London, 2000. Author of play, As It's Played Today, produced Melbourne, 1974. Produced television series, 1967–: Boney; Barrier Reef; Skippy; Bailey's Bird. Prod., Attack Force Z (feature film), 1980; Exec. Prod., The Highest Honor (feature film), 1982. Pres., Aust. Film Council, 1971–72. *Publication:* Life with Googie, 1979. *Recreation:* golf. *Address:* 5/19 Annam Road, Bayview, NSW 2104, Australia. *T:* (2) 99976879. *Clubs:* Melbourne (Melbourne); Australian, Elanora Country (Sydney).

McCALLUM, Martin; producer; theatre design consultant; *b* 6 April 1950; *s* of Raymond and Jessie; *m* 1st, 1971, Lesley Nunnerley (marr. diss.); one *s* one *d*; 2nd, 1986, Julie Edmett (marr. diss.); one *d*; 3rd, 1989, Mary Ann Rolfe; two *s*. *Educ:* Barfield Sch., Surrey; Frensham Heights Sch., Surrey. Entered theatre as student asst stage manager, Castle Th., Farnham, 1967; worked throughout rep. system; Prodn Manager, NT at Old Vic, 1971–75; prodns incl. Merchant of Venice, Long Day's Journey into Night, Saturday Sunday Monday; moved to S Bank, 1975; founder and Prodn Manager, The Production Office, West End, 1978–84; prodns incl. Filumena, Evita, Sweeney Todd, Cats; Man. Dir, 1981–2000, Vice-Chm., 2000–03, Cameron Mackintosh Ltd; prodns incl. Les Miserables, Phantom of the Opera, Miss Saigon, Oliver!; Director: Donmar Warehouse Th., 1992–2008 (Chm., 1996–2004); Sydney Theatre Co., 2005–. Consultant: to Glyndebourne Fest. Opera, 1980–81; to Regl Th. Scheme, Arts Council, 1980. Theatre designer and consultant: Old Fire Station Th., Oxford, 1991; Musical Hall, Stuttgart, 1994; Musical Th., Duisburg, 1996; Schaumburg Village Th., Ill, 2002; restorations: Prince Edward Th., London, 1993; Capital Th., Sydney, 1995; Th. Royal, Sydney, 1998; Auditorium Th., Chicago, 2001; Fine Arts Bldg Theatres, Chicago, 2003; Prince of Wales' Th., London, 2004; Montecasino Th., Johannesburg, 2007. Initiated Wyndham Report (on economic importance of West End theatre), 1998; initiated Theatre 2001 - Future Directions, inaugural jt theatre conference of SOLT/TMA/ITC, 2001. Mem., SOLT, 1999– (Pres. 1999–2002). Member: Drama Panel, 1999–2004, Adv. Task Gp, 2003–05, Arts Council England (formerly Arts Council of England); London's Cultural Strategy Gp, 2000–04; Th. Mus. Cttee, V&A, 2002–06. FRSA 1995. Mem., League of Amer. Theatres and Producers, 1988–. *Recreations:* the performing arts, music, art, gardens.

MacCALLUM, Very Rev. Norman Donald; Dean of Argyll and the Isles, since 2005; Provost of St John's Cathedral, Oban, and Priest-in-charge, St James', Ardbrecknish and Church of the Holy Spirit, Ardchattan, since 2000; *b* 26 April 1947; *s* of James MacCallum and Euphemia MacCallum (*née* Campbell); *m* 1972, Barbara MacColl Urquhart; one *s* one *d*. *Educ:* St John's Episcopal Sch., Ballachulish; Kinlochleven Jun. Secondary Sch.; Oban High Sch.; Edinburgh Univ. (LTh 1970); Edinburgh Theol Coll. Midlothian, E Lothian and Peebles Social Work Dept, 1970; ordained deacon, 1971, priest, 1972; Livingston Ecumenical Experiment, 1971–82; Rector, St Mary's, Grangemouth, and Priest-in-charge, St Catharine's, Bo'ness, 1982–2000; Synod Clerk, Dio. Edinburgh and Canon of St Mary's Cathedral, Edinburgh, 1996–2000. Adminr, Scottish Episcopal Clergy Appraisal Scheme, 1997–2006; Mem., Scottish Religious Adv. Cttee, BBC Scotland, 1997–2005. *Recreations:* hill-walking, photography, history. *Address:* The Rectory, Ardconnel Terrace, Oban PA34 5DJ. *T:* (01631) 562323; *e-mail:* provostoban@argyll.anglican.org.

McCALLUM, Prof. (Robert) Ian, CBE 1987; MD, DSc; FRCP, FRCPEd, FFOM; Professor of Occupational Health and Hygiene, University of Newcastle upon Tyne, 1981–85, now Emeritus; Hon. Consultant, Institute of Occupational Medicine, Edinburgh, 1985–2003; *b* 14 Sept. 1920; *s* of Charles Hunter McCallum and Janet Lyon Smith; *m* 1952, Jean Katherine Bundy Learmonth (MBE 1997), *d* of Sir James Rögnvald Learmonth, KCVO, CBE; two *s* two *d*. *Educ:* Dulwich Coll., London; Guy's Hosp., London Univ. (MD 1946; DSc 1971). FRCP 1970; FRCPEd 1985; FFOM 1979. Ho. phys., ho. surgeon, Guy's Hosp., 1943; ho. phys., Brompton Hosp., 1945. Rockefeller Travelling Fellowship in Medicine (MRC), USA, 1953–54. Reader in Industrial Health, Univ. of Newcastle upon Tyne, 1962–81. Hon. Physician, Industrial Medicine, Royal Victoria Infirmary, Newcastle upon Tyne, 1958–85; Hon. Consultant in Occ. Health to the Army, 1980–86. Mem., MRC Decompression Sickness Panel, 1962– (Chm., 1982–85). British Council: Vis. Consultant, USSR, 1977; Vis. Specialist, Istanbul, 1987; Vis. Lectr, Faculty of Medicine, Baghdad, 1987. Stanley Melville Meml Lectr, Coll. of Radiographers, 1983; Sydenham Lectr, Soc. of Apothecaries, London, 1983; Ernestine Henry Lectr, RCP, 1987. Dean, Faculty of Occ. Medicine, RCP, 1984–86; President: Sect. of Occ. Medicine, RSM, 1976–77; Soc. of Occ. Medicine, 1979–80; British Occ. Hygiene Soc., 1983–84; Mem., Adv. Cttee on Pesticides, 1975–87. Hon. Dir, North of England Industrial Health Service, 1975–84. Editor, British Jl of Industrial Medicine, 1973–79. FSAScot 1997. *Publications:* Antimony in Medical History, 1999; papers on Scottish alchemists, pneumoconiosis, decompression sickness, dysbaric bone necrosis, and antimony toxicology. *Recreation:* gardening. *Address:* 4 Chessels Court, Canongate, Edinburgh EH8 8AD. *T:* (0131) 556 7977. *Club:* Royal Society of Medicine.

McCAMLEY, Sir Graham (Edward), KBE 1986 (MBE 1981); owner, cattle properties, since 1954; *b* 24 Aug. 1932; *s* of Edward William George and Ivy McCamley; *m* 1956, Shirley Clarice Tindale; one *s* two *d*. *Educ:* Rockhampton Grammar Sch. President: Aust. Brahman Breeders, 1971–74; Central Coastal Graziers, 1974–75; Cattlemen's Union of Australia, 1976–78. Mem. Producer of Australian Meat and Livestock Co., 1982–84; Chm., Beeflands Australia Pty Ltd, 1994–97. *Recreations:* tennis, flying helicopter and fixed wing aircraft. *Clubs:* Queensland (Brisbane); Rockhampton and District Masonic.

McCANDLESS, Air Vice-Marshal Brian Campbell, CB 1999; CBE 1990; FIET; Director, Government Consultancy Services, since 2002; e-Government Director, Oracle Corporation UK, 1999–2002; *b* 14 May 1944; *s* of Norman Samuel McCandless and Rebecca Campbell; *m* 1969, Yvonne Haywood; one *s*. *Educ:* Methodist Coll., Belfast; RAF Tech. Coll., Henlow (BSc 1967); Birmingham Univ (MSc 1972); RAF Staff Coll. RAF, 1962–99: posts included: OC 26 Signals Unit, 1985–87; OC RAF Henlow, 1987–89; Dep. Chief, Architecture and Plans Div., NATO CIS Agency, Brussels, 1989–92; Dir, Comd Control and Management Inf. Systems, RAF, 1992–93; Dir, Communications and Inf. Systems, RAF, 1993–95; AO Communications and Inf. Systems, and AOC Signals Units, 1996–99. *Recreations:* bridge, music, sailing, hill walking. *Club:* Royal Air Force.

McCANNY, Prof. John Vincent, CBE 2002; PhD, DSc; FRS 2002; FREng, FIET; FIEEE; FIAE, FIEI; MRIA; Professor of Microelectronics Engineering, since 1988, Director, Institute of Electronics, Communications and Information Technology, since 2001, and Head, School of Electronics, Electrical Engineering and Computer Science, since 2005, Queen's University of Belfast; *b* 25 June 1952; *s* of Patrick Joseph McCanny and Kathleen Brigid McCanny (*née* Kerr); *m* 1979, Maureen Bernadette Mellon; one *s* one *d*. *Educ:* Univ. of Manchester (BSc Physics Hons 1973); Univ. of Ulster, Coleraine (PhD Solid State Physics 1978); Queen's Univ., Belfast (DSc Electronics Eng 1998). CPhys, MInstP 1982, FInstP 1992; CEng, MIEE 1985, FIET (FIEE 1992); MIEEE 1986, FIEEE 1999; FREng 1995; MRIA 2000; FIAE 2006; FIEI 2006. Lectr in Physics, Univ. of Ulster, Coleraine, 1977–79; Higher SO, 1979–82, SSO, 1982–84, PSO, 1984, RSRE, Malvern; Queen's University of Belfast: EPSRC IT Res. Lectr, Sch. of Electrical and Electronic Engrg, 1984–87; Reader in VLSI Signal Processing, 1987–88; Hd, Digital Signal Processing and Telecommunications Res. Div., 1988–2004. Founder, 1988, Dir, 1988–96, Audio Processing Technology Ltd; Founder, 1994, pt-time Chief Technology Officer, 1994–2004, Amphion Semiconductor Ltd (formerly Integrated Silicon Systems Ltd). Dir, Inst. of Advanced Microelectronics in Ireland, 1989–91. Mem., European Acad. of Scis, 2004. FRSA 1996. Silver Medal, Royal Acad. of Engrg, 1996; Millennium Medal, IEEE, 2000; Boyle Medal, Royal Dublin Soc./Irish Times, 2003; IT Professional of the Year, BCS (Belfast Br.), 2004; Faraday Medal, IET, 2006. *Publications:* (ed jtly) VLSI Technology and Design, 1987; (ed jtly) Systolic Array Processors, 1989; (ed jtly) VLSI Systems for DSP and Control, 1991; (ed jtly) Signal Processing Systems: design and implementation, 1997; (with Maire McLoone) System-on-Chip Architectures and Implementation for Private-Key Data Encryption, 2003; 330 scientific papers in major internat. jls and confs; 20 patents. *Recreations:* golf, soccer, Rugby, cricket, guitar, photography, films, wine. *Address:* Institute of Electronics, Communications and Information Technology, Queen's University of Belfast, Northern Ireland Science Park, Queen's Road, Queen's Island, Belfast BT3 9DT. *Club:* Clandeboye Golf.

McCARRAHER, His Honour David, VRD 1964; a Circuit Judge, 1984–95; *b* 6 Nov. 1922; *s* of Colin McCarraher and Vera Mabel McCarraher (*née* Hickley); *m* 1950, Betty Johnson (*née* Haywood) (*d* 1990); one *s* three *d*. *Educ:* King Edward VI Sch., Southampton; Magdalene Coll., Cambridge (MA Law). RN, 1941–45. Called to the Bar, Lincoln's Inn, 1948; practised Western Circuit until 1952, disbarred at own request to be articled; admitted solicitor, 1955; Sen. Partner in private practice, 1960–84; a Recorder, 1979–84. Mem. Panel, Dep. Circuit Judges, 1973–79. Pres., Hampshire Incorporated Law Soc., 1982–83. Founder Mem. and Past Pres., Southampton Junior Chamber of Commerce. Governor, King Edward VI Sch., Southampton, 1961–84 (Chm., 1983–84; Fellow, 1986). Sub-Lieut, RNVR, 1943–45, RNVSR, 1946–52; served to Captain RNR, 1969; CO Solent Div., RNR, 1969–72; ADC to the Queen, 1972–73; retired 1975. Hon. Sec., RNR Benevolent Fund, 1973–84. *Recreations:* family, golf. *Clubs:* Naval; Stoneham Golf (Southampton); Royal Naval Sailing Association (Portsmouth); Southampton Police (Hon. Mem.) (Southampton).

McCARRY, Frances Jane; *see* McMenamin, F. J.

McCARTAN, Patrick Anthony, CBE 2008; Chairman, Belfast Health and Social Care Trust, since 2006; *b* Belfast, 28 Dec. 1945; *s* of Henry McCartan and Margaret McCartan (*née* Gillespie); *m* 1972, Margaret Petrea Owens; one *s* one *d*. *Educ:* Queen's Univ. Belfast (Trade Union studies); Henley Mgt Coll.; Univ. of Ulster (MSc Dist. 1988). FCIPD 1991. NI Civil Service, 1962–72; NI Area Sec., APEX, 1972–90; Sen. Lectr and Hd of Dept, Centre for Mgt Educn, Univ. of Ulster, 1990–2002; Chairman: NW Belfast HSS Trust, 2001–06; Labour Relns Agency, 2002–08. Consultant, employment relns and mgt devel, 1990–. Chm. and Mem. Bd, Co-operation Ireland, 1991–2004; Member Board: SE Educn and Liby Bd, 1976–83; NI Econ. Council, 1978–82; IDB, 1982–89; Council for Catholic Maintained Schs, 1996–2004. Vice Chm. and Mem. Bd, St Columbanus Coll., Bangor, 1976–. *Recreations:* motorcycling (former road racer), golf, singing, playing guitar badly. *Address:* *e-mail:* pat.mccartan@belfasttrust.hscni.net. *T:* (028) 9096 0000.

McCARTHY, family name of **Baron McCarthy**.

McCARTHY, Baron *cr* 1975 (Life Peer), of Headington; **William Edward John McCarthy,** DPhil; Emeritus Fellow of Nuffield College and Associate Fellow of Templeton College, Oxford; engaged in Industrial Arbitration and Chairman of Committees of Inquiry and Investigation, since 1968; *b* 30 July 1925; *s* of E. and H. McCarthy; *m* 1957, Margaret, *d* of Percival Godfrey. *Educ:* Holloway County; Ruskin Coll.; Merton Coll.; Nuffield Coll. MA (Oxon), DPhil (Oxon). Trade Union Scholarship to Ruskin Coll., 1953; Research Fellow of Nuffield Coll., 1959; Research Dir, Royal Commn on Trade Unions and Employers' Assocs, 1965–68; Sen. Economic Adviser, Dept of Employment, 1968–71. Chm., Railway Staff Nat. Tribunal, 1973–86; Special Advisor on Industrial Relations to Sec. of State for Social Services, 1975–77; Member: Houghton Cttee on Aid to Political Parties, 1975–76; TUC Independent Review Cttee, 1976; CS Arbitration Tribunal, 1983–; Pres., British Univ. Industrial Relations Assoc., 1975–78; Special Comr, Equal Opportunities Commn, 1977–80; Dep. Chm., Teachers' Nat. Conciliation Cttee, 1979–. Chairman: TUC Newspaper Feasibility Adv. Study Gp, 1981–83; Independent Inquiry into Rover Closure Proposals, 1989–90. Adjudicator, Nursing and Midwifery Staffs Negotiating Council, 1994–; Mem., CS Arbitration Tribunal, 1996–. Mem., H of L Select Cttee on Unemployment, 1980–82; Opposition front bench spokesman on employment, 1980–97. Mem., All Party Motor Industry Gp, 1989–; Vice Chairman: All Party Friends of Music Gp, 1992–; All Party Theatre Gp, 2002–. Pres., Oxford Assoc. of Univ. Teachers, 1999–. FIPD 1995. *Publications:* The Closed Shop in Britain, 1964; The Role of Shop Stewards in British Industrial Relations, 1966; (with V. L. Munns) Employers' Associations, 1967; (with A. I. Marsh) Disputes Procedures in Britain, 1968; The Reform of Collective Bargaining at Plant and Company Level, 1971; (ed) Trade Unions, 1972, 2nd edn, 1985; (with A. I. Collier) Coming to Terms with Trade Unions, 1973; (with N. D. Ellis) Management by Agreement, 1973; (with J. F. O'Brien and V. E. Dowd) Wage Inflation and Wage Leadership, 1975; Making Whitley Work, 1977; (jtly) Change in Trade Unions, 1981; (jtly) Strikes in Post-War Britain, 1983; Freedom at Work 1985; The Future of Industrial Democracy, 1988; (with C. Jennings and R. Undy) Employee Relations Audits, 1989; (ed) Legal Intervention in Industrial Relations, 1992; New Labour at Work, 1997; Fairness at Work: past comparisons and future problems, 1999; (contrib.) Legal Regulation of the Employment Relation, 2000; articles in: Brit. Jl of Industrial Relns; Industrial Relns Jl 1995. *Recreations:* gardening, theatre, ballet, opera. *Address:* 4 William Orchard Close, Old Headington, Oxford OX3 9DR. *T:* (01865) 762016. *Club:* Reform.

McCARTHY, Anthony David; Director of People, British Airways, since 2007; *b* 14 April 1956; *s* of Robert Alan and Ena Mary McCarthy; *m* 1983, Patricia Barbara Blakey; one *s* one *d* (and one *d* decd). *Educ:* Sheffield Poly. (BA Hons (Business Studies) 1978); Salford Univ. (Postgrad. Dip. 1982). MCIPD 1980. British Aerospace, subseq. BAESYSTEMS, 1978–2003: various human resource appts; HR Dir, Royal Ordnance, 1995–97; Chm., Royal Ordnance Pensions Trustees, 1997–98; Gp HR Dir, 2001–03; Gp Dir People, Royal Mail Gp, 2003–07. *Recreations:* golf (not very well!), most sports as spectator, keen supporter of Burnley FC. *Address:* British Airways plc, Waterside, PO Box 365, Harmondsworth UB7 0GB. *Club:* Preston Golf.

McCARTHY, Arlene; Member (Lab) North West Region, European Parliament, since 1999 (Peak District, 1994–99); *b* 10 Oct. 1960; *d* of J. J. McCarthy and F. L. McCarthy; *m* 1997, Prof. David Farrell. *Educ:* South Bank Poly. (BA Hons). Researcher and Press Officer to Leader of European PLP, 1990–91; Lectr in Politics, Freie Univ., Berlin,

1991–92; Head of European Affairs, Kirklees MBC, W Yorks, 1992–94. European PLP (formerly Socialist Gp and European PLP) spokesperson on regl affairs, 1994–2004; on internat. mkt and legal affairs, 1999–2004; on internal mkt and consumer protection, 2004–; on legal affairs, 2004–. Mem., Internal Mkt and Consumer Protection Cttee, 2004– (Chm., 2006–), and Substitute Mem., Legal Affairs Cttee, 2004–, European Parlt. *Publications:* (ed jtly) Changing States: a Labour agenda for Europe, 1996; EP reports on reform of structural funds and gen. provisions of structural funds and on intellectual property and financial services; articles on European issues for local govt jls. *Recreations:* swimming, dancing, foreign languages, music. *Address:* Express Networks, 1 George Leigh Street, Manchester M4 5DL. *T:* (0161) 906 0801, *Fax:* (0161) 906 0802; *e-mail:* arlene.mccarthy@easynet.co.uk.

McCARTHY, Sir Callum, Kt 2005; PhD; Chairman, Financial Services Authority, 2003–08; a Director, Bank of England, 2003–08; *b* 29 Feb. 1944; *s* of Ralph and Nan McCarthy; *m* 1966, Penelope Ann Gee; two *s* one *d. Educ:* Manchester Grammar Sch.; City of London Sch.; Merton Coll., Oxford (BA 1965); Stirling Univ. (PhD 1971); Grad. Sch. of Business, Stanford Univ. (Sloan Fellow; MS 1982). Operations Res., ICI, 1965–72; various posts from Economic Adv. to Under Sec., DTI, 1972–85; Dir, Kleinwort Benson, 1985–89; Man. Dir, BZW, 1989–93; CEO, Barclays Bank, Japan, 1993–96, Barclays Bank, N America, 1996–98; Dir Gen., subseq. Chief Exec., Ofgem, 1999–2003 (Gas Supply, 1998–2003, Electricity Supply, 1999–2003); Chm., Gas and Electricity Mkts Authy, 2000–03. Freeman, City of London, 2008. *Publication:* (with D. S. Davies) Introduction to Technological Economics, 1967. *Recreations:* walking, cooking, reading, beekeeping.

McCARTHY, David Laurence; His Honour Judge McCarthy; a Circuit Judge, since 1995; *b* 7 April 1947; *s* of Laurence Alphonsus McCarthy and Vera May McCarthy; *m* 1981, Rosalind Marguerite Stevenson; two *s. Educ:* St Philip's Grammar Sch., Birmingham; Christ Church, Oxford (MA). Called to the Bar, Middle Temple, 1970; a Recorder, 1992; Midland and Oxford Circuit. *Recreations:* science fiction, playing the organ. *Address:* c/o Regional Manager, Midland and Oxford Circuit, The Priory Courts, Bull Street, Birmingham B4 6DW. *T:* (0121) 681 3443.

MacCARTHY, Fiona; biographer and cultural historian; *b* 23 Jan. 1940; *m* 1966, David Mellor, *qv*; one *s* one *d. Educ:* Wycombe Abbey Sch.; Lady Margaret Hall, Oxford (MA Hons Eng. Lang. and Lit.; Hon. Fellow, 2007). FRSL 1997. Design Correspondent, Guardian, 1963–69; Women's Editor, Evening Standard, 1969–70; Literary Critic: The Times, 1980–90; Observer, 1990–98; an Associate Editor, Oxford DNB, 1998–2005. Sen. Fellow, RCA, 1997 (Hon. Fellow, 1990); Hon. Fellow, Centre for 19th Century Studies, Univ. of Sheffield, 1994. Hon. DLitt Sheffield, 1996; DUniv Sheffield Hallam, 2001. Bicentenary Medal, RSA, 1986. *Publications:* All Things Bright and Beautiful: British design 1830 to today, 1972; The Simple Life: C. R. Ashbee in the Cotswolds, 1981; The Omega Workshops: decorative arts of Bloomsbury, 1984; Eric Gill, 1989; William Morris: a life for our time, 1994 (Wolfson History Prize; Yorkshire Post Art Book Award; Writer's Guild Non-Fiction Award); Stanley Spencer: an English vision, 1997; Byron: life and legend, 2002; Last Curtsey: the end of the debutantes, 2006; articles in The Guardian, TLS, New York Review of Books. *Recreations:* museums, theatre, looking at new architecture. *Address:* The Round Building, Hathersage, Sheffield S32 1BA. *T:* (01433) 650220.

McCARTHY, John Patrick, CBE 1992; journalist; *b* 27 Nov. 1956; *yr s* of late Pat and Sheila McCarthy; *m* 1999, Anna Ottewill. *Educ:* Haileybury; Hull Univ. (BA 1979). Joined UPITN (later WTN) as journalist, 1982. Kidnapped and held hostage in Beirut, 17 April 1986–8 Aug. 1991. BBC TV series (with Sandi Toksvig), Island Race, 1995; ITV series: It Ain't Necessarily So, 2001; John Meets Paul, 2003; Faultlines, 2003; ITV documentary, Out of the Shadows, 2004; BBC Radio 4 series: John McCarthy's Bible Journey, 1999; A Place Called Home, 2000. Patron, Medical Foundn for the Care of Victims of Torture. Hon. DLitt Hull, 1991. *Publications:* (with Jill Morrell) Some Other Rainbow, 1993; (with Sandi Toksvig) Island Race: improbable voyage around the coast of Britain, 1995; (with Brian Keenan) Between Extremes, 1999; A Ghost Upon your Path, 2002. *Address:* c/o LAW, 14 Vernon Street, W14 0RJ.

McCARTHY, John Sidney, MBE 1984; FCIOB; Executive Chairman, 1990–2000, non-executive Chairman, 2001–03, McCarthy & Stone; *b* 31 Dec. 1939; *s* of John James McCarthy and Helen Caroline McCarthy; *m* 1982, Gwendoline Joan Holmes; three *s* one *d.* McCarthy & Stone: Joint Founder, 1963; Chief Exec./Chm., 1963–90. Founder, 1987, and Trustee, 1996–98, McCarthy Foundn. Non-exec., Churchill Retirement Living, 2004–. *Recreations:* ski-ing, golf, shooting, polo, sailing, subaqua diving. *Clubs:* Royal Ocean Racing; Royal Guernsey Golf; Salisbury and S Wilts Golf; Rushmore Golf.

McCARTHY, Kerry; MP (Lab) Bristol East, since 2005; *b* 26 March 1965; *d* of Oliver Thomas Haughney and Sheila Ann Rix (*née* Smith); name changed to McCarthy, 1992. *Educ:* Univ. of Liverpool (BA Hons Russian, Politics and Linguistics); City of London Poly. Legal Asst, S Beds Magistrates' Court, 1986–88; Litigation Asst, Neves (Solicitors), 1988–89; trainee, Wilde Sapte, 1992–94; admitted solicitor, 1994; Lawyer, Abbey National Treasury Services plc, 1994–96; Sen. Counsel, Merrill Lynch Europe plc, 1996–99; Lawyer, Labour Party, 2001; Regl Dir, Britain in Europe, 2002–04; Hd, Public Policy, Waterfront Partnership, 2004–05. Dir, London Luton Airport Ltd, 1999–2003. PPS to Minister of State, Dept of Health, 2007, to Sec. of State for Internat. Devel t, 2007–. Mem., Treasury Select Cttee, 2005–07. Mem. (Lab) Luton BC, 1995–96 and 1999–2003. *Recreations:* travel, scuba-diving, F1 motor racing. *Address:* House of Commons, SW1A 0AA. *T:* (020) 7219 4510; *e-mail:* mccarthyk@parliament.uk; (constituency) 326a Church Road, Bristol BS5 8AJ. *T:* (0117) 939 9901, *Fax:* (0117) 939 9902. *Club:* St George Labour (Bristol).

McCARTHY, Kieran; JP; Member (Alliance) Strangford, Northern Ireland Assembly, since 1998; *b* 9 Sept. 1942; *s* of James and Elizabeth McCarthy; *m* 1967, Kathleen Doherty; two *s* two *d. Educ:* Newtownards Coll. of Technol. Formerly textile worker and sales clerk; joint partner, discount drapery, 1965–87; retailer, 1987–. Councillor, 1985–, Alderman, 1997–, Ards BC. Contested (Alliance) Strangford, 2005. JP Ards, 1990. *Recreations:* gardening, reading, cycling. *Address:* Loughedge, 3 Main Street, Kircubbin, Newtownards, Co. Down BT22 2SS. *T:* (028) 4273 8221.

McCARTHY, Prof. Mark Ian, MD; FRCP, FMedSci; Robert Turner Professor of Diabetic Medicine, University of Oxford, since 2002; Fellow of Green Templeton College (formerly Green College), Oxford, since 2002; *b* 18 July 1960; *s* of Roy Allen McCarthy and Marion Eluned McCarthy. *Educ:* Pembroke Coll., Cambridge (BA 1981; MB BChir 1985; MD 1995); St Thomas's Hosp. Med. Sch. FRCP 1999. MRC Clin. Trng Fellow, London Hosp. Med. Coll., 1991–94; MRC Travelling Fellow, Whitehead Inst., Cambridge, Mass, 1994–95; Sen. Lectr in Molecular Genetics, 1995–98, Reader, 1998–2000, Prof. of Genomic Medicine, 2000–02, Imperial Coll., Univ. of London. Hon. Consultant, Oxford Radcliffe Hosps NHS Trust, 2002–. FMedSci 2006. *Address:* Diabetes Research Laboratories, Oxford Centre for Diabetes, Endocrinology & Metabolism, Churchill Hospital, Headington, Oxford OX3 7LJ.

McCARTHY, Nicholas Melvyn, OBE 1983; HM Diplomatic Service, retired; High Commissioner to Cameroon, and also Ambassador (non-resident) to Gabon, Chad, Equatorial Guinea and the Central African Republic, 1995–98; *b* 4 April 1938; *s* of Daniel Alfred McCarthy and Florence Alice McCarthy; *m* 1961, Gillian Eileen Hill; three *s* one *d. Educ:* Queen Elizabeth's Sch., Faversham; London Univ. (BA Hons). Attaché, Saigon, 1961–64; Language Student, then Second Sec., Tokyo, 1964–69; FCO, 1969–73; First Sec., Brussels, 1973–78; FCO, 1978–80; Head of Chancery, Dakar, 1980–84; FCO, 1984–85; Consul-Gen., Osaka, 1985–90; Dep. Hd of Mission, Consul-Gen. and Counsellor, Brussels, 1990–94. *Recreations:* golf, bridge, squash, tennis, Japanese pottery. *Address:* The Old Rectory, 34 Cross Street, Moretonhampstead, Devon TQ13 8NL.

McCARTHY, (Patrick) Peter; Regional Chairman, London North, Industrial Tribunals, 1987–90; Part-time Chairman, Industrial Tribunals, 1990–92; *b* 10 July 1919; *er s* of late William McCarthy, OBE and Mary McCarthy; *m* 1945, Isabel Mary (*d* 1994), *y d* of late Dr Joseph Unsworth, St Helens; two *s* three *d. Educ:* St Francis Xavier's Coll., Liverpool; Liverpool Univ. LLB 1940, LLM 1942. Admitted Solicitor, 1942; in private practice until 1974. Part-time Chm., 1972–74, full-time Chm., 1975–90, Regl Chm., Liverpool, 1977–87, Industrial Tribunals; part-time Chm., Rent Assessment Cttee, 1972–74. JP Liverpool, 1968–74. *Address:* Brook Cottage, Sham Castle Lane, Bath BA2 6JH.

McCARTHY, Peter Herbert; independent consultant; Director, Rail Customer and Stakeholder Relations, Department for Transport, 2005–07; *b* 9 Oct. 1953; *s* of Adolf and Ursula McCarthy; *m* 2000, Angela Fleming; one *d. Educ:* Bedales Sch.; Merton Coll., Oxford (BA PPE). Joined DTI, 1979; transferred to Dept for Transport, 1983; Private Sec. to Sec. of State, 1989–92; Head: Rail Privatisation Legislation Div., 1992–96; Local Transport Policy Div., 1996–2002; Transport Finance Directorate, 2002–05. *Recreations:* reading, cycling, motoring, music, theatre. *Address:* 127 Wimbledon Park Road, SW18 5RL. *T:* (020) 8870 5710; *e-mail:* petermccarthy@talktalk.net.

McCARTHY, Richard John, FCIH; Director General, Housing and Planning (formerly Programmes, Policy and Innovation), Department for Communities and Local Government, since 2006; *b* 28 April 1958; *s* of John Anthony McCarthy and Anna Patricia (*née* Sheehan); *m* 1983, Judith Karen McCann; two *s* one *d. Educ:* Richard Challoner Sch., New Malden; Univ. of Southampton (BA Hons Geog.); Hackney Coll. FCIH 1987. Housing Officer etc, 1979–87, Ops Dir, 1987–94, Hyde Housing Assoc.; Chief Executive: S London Family Housing Assoc., 1994–99; Peabody Trust, 1999–2003; Dir Gen., Sustainable Communities, ODPM, subseq. Places, Planning and Communities, DCLG, 2003–06. Chm., Care and Repair, 1986–93. Member: Council, Nat. Housing Fedn, 1998–2003 (Chm., 2000–03); Bd, 1066 Housing Assoc., 2000–03; Housing Panel, Audit Commn, 2003. *Publications:* articles in various housing jls, incl. Housing Today and Roof. *Recreations:* theatre, music, opera, tennis, football, watching Rugby. *Address:* Department for Communities and Local Government, Eland House, Bressenden Place, SW1E 5DU. *T:* (020) 7944 3716; *e-mail:* Richard.McCarthy@communities.gsi.gov.uk.

MacCARTHY, Very Rev. Robert Brian, PhD; Dean of St Patrick's Cathedral, Dublin, since 1999 (Prebendary, 1994–99); *b* 28 March 1940; *o c* of Richard Edward MacCarthy and Dorothy MacCarthy (*née* Furney), Clonmel. *Educ:* St Columba's Coll., Rathfarnham; Trinity Coll., Dublin (BA, MA; PhD 1983); St John's Coll., Cambridge; Trinity Coll., Oxford (MA); Cuddesdon Theol Coll.; MA NUI 1965. Ordained deacon, 1979, priest, 1980; Curate, Carlow, 1979–81; Librarian, Pusey House, and Fellow, St Cross Coll., Oxford, 1981–82; Curate, 1982–83, Team Vicar, 1983–86, Bracknell; Curate, Kilkenny, 1986–88; Bp's Vicar in Kilkenny Cath., 1986–88; Domestic Chaplain to Bp of Ossory, 1986–89; Rector, Castlecomer, and RD of Carlow, 1988–95; Rector, St Nicholas' Collegiate Church, Galway and Provost of Tuam, 1995–99. *Publications:* The Estates of Trinity College, Dublin, 1992; Ancient and Modern, 1995; How Shall They Hear, 2002. *Recreation:* architectural history. *Address:* The Deanery, Upper Kevin Street, Dublin 8, Ireland. *T:* (1) 4755449. *Clubs:* Kildare Street and University (Dublin); Royal Irish Yacht (Dun Laoghaire).

McCARTHY, Suzanne Joyce; Immigration Services Commissioner, since 2005; *b* 21 Nov. 1948; *d* of Leo and Lillian Rudnick; *m* 1990, Brendan McCarthy. *Educ:* New York Univ. (BA 1970; Phi Beta Kappa); Wolfson Coll., Cambridge (Dip Social Anthropol. 1971); Lucy Cavendish Coll., Cambridge (LLM 1986). Admitted Solicitor, 1976; Solicitor in private practice, 1977–86; Lectr in Law, Univ. of Manchester, 1986–89; joined Civil Service, 1989; posts with Home Office (incl. Private Sec. to Home Sec.), Treasury, Civil Service Coll. (Dir, Policy, Govt and Europe), 1989–96; Chief Executive: HFEA, 1996–2000; Financial Services Compensation Scheme, 2000–04. Mem., Determinations Panel Pensions Regulator, 2005–. Chm., European Forum of Deposit Insurers, 2002–04 (Hon. Chm. 2008). Mem., Conduct Disciplinary Cttee, CIMA, 2006–08. Non-executive Director: Royal Brompton and Harefield NHS Trust, 1998–2006; Candoco Dance Co., 2000–04; RIBA, 2004–; Public Guardian Bd, 2007–. Mem. Panel (Dance), SOLT (Laurence Olivier) Awards, 2002. Trustee, RNIB, 2002–04. University of London: Mem. Council, 2003–08 (Dep. Chm., 2006–08); Mem., Bd of Trustees, 2008–. Freeman, City of London, 2006; Yeoman, 2006–08, Liveryman, 2008–, Co. of Ironmongers. *Recreations:* dance, travel. *Address:* Office of the Immigration Services Commissioner, 5th Floor, Counting House, 53 Tooley Street, SE1 2QN. *Club:* Athenæum.

McCARTHY, William Joseph Anthony; Director, Policy and Strategy, Department of Health, 2006–07; *b* Leeds, 14 June 1963; *s* of Shaun and Patricia McCarthy; *m* 1986, Rose Coady; four *s* one *d. Educ:* Prior Park, Bath; Queen Mary Coll., Univ. of London (BSc Econ.); London Sch. of Econs (MSc). Asst Economist, DoH, 1986–88; Analyst, Herts CC and ACC, 1988–91; rejoined Department of Health, 1991: Principal, 1991–94; Asst Sec., Primary Care, 1994–97; Head: of Public Expenditure Survey Br., 1997–99; of Finance and Performance Div. A, NHS Exec., 1999–2000; Dir of Planning and Performance, Leeds Teaching Hosps NHS Trust, 2000–02; Dir, Strategic Devel t, W Yorks Strategic HA, 2002–06. *Recreations:* playing with the children, eating out, weekends away, watching sport.

McCARTHY-FRY, Sarah; MP (Lab and Co-op) Portsmouth North, since 2005; Parliamentary Under-Secretary of State, Department for Children, Schools and Families, since 2008; *b* 4 Feb. 1955; *d* of Sidney and Constance Macaree; *m* 1st, 1973, Roger Fry (marr. diss. 1997); one *s* one d; 2nd, 1997, Anthony McCarthy. *Educ:* Portsmouth High Sch.; BPP Coll., Southampton. ACMA 2004. Financial Accountant, FPT Industries, Portsmouth, 1988–2000; GKN Aerospace Services: Financial Analyst, Farnham, 2000–03; Financial Controller, Cowes, IoW, 2003–05. Dep. Leader, Portsmouth CC, 1995–2000. *Recreations:* tap dancing, dog walking. *Address:* House of Commons, SW1A 0AA. *T:* (020) 7219 6517, *Fax:* (020) 7219 0864; *e-mail:* mccarthyfrys@parliament.uk.

McCARTIE, Rt Rev. (Patrick) Leo; Bishop of Northampton, (RC), 1990–2001, now Emeritus; *b* 5 Sept. 1925; *s* of Patrick Leo and Hannah McCartie. *Educ:* Cotton College;

Oscott College. Priest, 1949; on staff of Cotton College, 1950–55; parish work, 1955–63; Director of Religious Education, 1963–68; Administrator of St Chad's Cathedral, Birmingham, 1968–77; Aux. Bp of Birmingham, and Titular Bp of Elmham, 1977–90. Pres., Catholic Commn for Racial Justice, 1978–83; Chm., Cttee for Community Relations, Dept for Christian Responsibility and Citizenship, Bishops' Conf. on Eng. and Wales, 1983–90; Mem., Churches Main Cttee, 1996–2002. Church Representative: Churches Together in England, 1990; Council of Churches for Britain and Ireland, 1990. *Recreations:* music, walking. *Address:* Aston Hall, Aston by Stone, Staffordshire ST15 0BJ.

McCARTNEY, Gordon Arthur; consultant; Managing Director, Gordon McCartney Associates, since 1991; *b* 29 April 1937; *s* of Arthur and Hannah McCartney; *m* 1st, 1960, Ceris Ysobel Davies (marr. diss. 1987); two *d*; 2nd, 1988, Wendy Ann Vyvyan Titman. *Educ:* Grove Park Grammar Sch., Wrexham. Articled to Philip J. Walters, MBE (Town Clerk, Wrexham), 1954–59; admitted solicitor, 1959. Asst Solicitor, Birkenhead County Bor. Council, 1959–61; Asst Solicitor, 1961–63, Sen. Asst Solicitor, 1963–65, Bootle County Bor. Council; Dep. Clerk, Wrexham RDC, 1965–73; Clerk, Holywell RDC, 1973–74; Chief Exec., Delyn Bor. Council, 1974–81; Sec., Assoc. of Dist Councils, 1981–91; Associate, Succession Planning Associates, 1991–96. Dir, Nat. Transport Tokens Ltd, 1984–92. Secretary-General, British Section, IULA/CEMR, 1984–88; Chairman: CEMR Individual Members Gp, 1992–97; Local Govt Gp for Europe, 1997–2005; Co. Sec., Local Govt Internat. Bureau, 1988–91. Mem., Hansard Soc. Commn on Legislative Process, 1991–93. Director: Leisure England Ltd, 1993–; White Rock Developments Ltd, 1996–97. Organist, Elton Methodist Ch., 1991–. *Recreations:* gardening, cricket, music. *Address:* 33 Duck Street, Elton, Peterborough PE8 6RQ. *T:* (01832) 280659. *Club:* MCC.

McCARTNEY, Rt Hon. Ian; PC 1999; MP (Lab) Makerfield, since 1987; *b* 25 April 1951; *s* of late Hugh McCartney; *m* (marr. diss.); two *d* (one *s* decd); *m* 1988, Ann Parkes (*née* Kevan). *Educ:* State primary, secondary schools; Tech. Colls. Led paper boy strike, 1965; joined Labour Party, 1966; joined trade union, 1966; seaman, local govt manual worker, chef, 1966–71; unemployed, 1971–73; Labour Party Organiser, 1973–87. Councillor, Wigan Borough, 1982–87. Hon. Parly Adviser: to Greater Manchester Fire and Civil Defence Authy, 1987–92 (Mem., 1986); to Nat. Assoc. for Safety in the Home, 1989–92. Opposition spokesperson on NHS, 1992–94, on employment, 1994–96, chief spokesperson on employment, 1996–97; Minister of State: DTI, 1997–99; Cabinet Office, 1999–2001; Minister for Pensions, DWP, 2001–03; Minister without Portfolio and Chair, Labour Party, 2003–06; Minister of State, FCO and DTI, 2006–07. Mem., Parly Select Cttee on Health and Social Security, 1991–92; Jt Sec., Parly Leasehold Reform Gp. Chm., T&GWU Parly Gp, 1989–91. Sponsored by TGWU. Hon. Pres., Wigan Wheelchair Fund 1987–. *Recreations:* Wigan Rugby League fanatic (supports Wigan Warriors); head of McCartney family, a family of proud working class stock. *Address:* 2 Wyatt Grove, Ashton-in-Makerfield, Wigan WN4 8SR. *T:* (01942) 712619. *Club:* Platt Bridge Labour.

McCARTNEY, Sir (James) Paul, Kt 1997; MBE 1965; musician, composer; *b* Allerton, Liverpool, 18 June 1942; *s* of James McCartney and Mary McCartney; *m* 1st, 1969, Linda Eastman (*d* 1998); one *s* two *d*, and one step *d*; 2nd, 2002, Heather Mills (marr. diss. 2008); one *d*. *Educ:* Liverpool Inst. Mem., skiffle group, The Quarry Men, 1957–59; toured Scotland with them and Stuart Sutcliffe as the Silver Beetles, 1960; first of five extended seasons in Hamburg, Aug. 1960; made 1st important appearance as the Beatles at Litherland Town Hall, nr Liverpool, Dec. 1960; appeared as mem. of Beatles: UK, Sweden, and Royal Variety perf., London, 1963; UK, Netherlands, Sweden, France, Denmark, Hong Kong, Australia, NZ, Canada, 1964; TV appearances, USA, and later, coast-to-coast tour, 1964; UK, France, Italy, Spain, USA, Canada, 1965; West Germany, Japan, Philippines, USA, Canada, 1966; Beatles disbanded 1970; formed MPL group of cos, 1970, and own group, Wings, 1971; toured: UK, Europe, 1972–73; UK, Australia, 1975; Europe, USA, Canada, 1976; UK, 1979; Wings disbanded 1981; Europe, UK, Canada, Japan, USA, Brazil, 1989/90; USA, 2002; UK, Europe, 2003; USA, 2005. Wrote (with Carl Davis) Liverpool Oratorio, 1991; *symphony:* Standing Stone, 1997; Ecce Cor Meum (oratorio), 2006. *Songs* with John Lennon include: Love Me Do; Please Please Me; From Me To You; She Loves You; Can't Buy Me Love; I Want to Hold Your Hand; I Saw Her Standing There; Eight Days a Week; All My Loving; Help!; Ticket to Ride; I Feel Fine; I'm A Loser; A Hard Day's Night; No Reply; I'll Follow The Sun; Yesterday; For No One; Here, There and Everywhere; Eleanor Rigby; Yellow Submarine; Penny Lane; All You Need Is Love; Lady Madonna; Hey Jude; We Can Work It Out; Day Tripper; Paperback Writer; When I'm Sixty-Four; A Day in the Life; Back in the USSR; Hello, Goodbye; Get Back; Let It Be; The Long and Winding Road; subseq. *songs* include: Maybe I'm Amazed; My Love; Band on the Run; Jet; Let 'Em In; Silly Love Songs; Mull of Kintyre; Coming Up; Ebony and Ivory; Tug of War; Pipes of Peace; No More Lonely Nights; My Brave Face. *Albums* with the Beatles: Please Please Me, 1963; With The Beatles, 1963; A Hard Day's Night, 1964; Beatles for Sale, 1964; Help!, 1965; Rubber Soul, 1965; Revolver, 1966; Sgt Pepper's Lonely Hearts Club Band, 1967; Magical Mystery Tour, 1967; The Beatles (White Album), 1968; Yellow Submarine, 1969; Abbey Road, 1969; Let it Be, 1970; Anthology I, II and III, 1995–96; other albums: McCartney, 1970; Ram, 1971; Wild Life, 1971; Red Rose Speedway, 1973; Band on the Run, 1973; Venus and Mars, 1975; Wings at the Speed of Sound, 1976; Wings over America, 1976; London Town, 1978; Wings Greatest, 1978; Back to the Egg, 1979; McCartney II, 1980; Tug of War, 1982; Pipes of Peace, 1983; Give My Regards to Broad Street, 1984; Press to Play, 1986; All the Best!, 1987; CHOBA B CCCP, 1988; Flowers in the Dirt, 1989; Tripping the Live Fantastic, 1990; Unplugged: The Official Bootleg, 1991; Paul McCartney's Liverpool Oratorio, 1991; Off The Ground, 1993; Paul Is Live, 1993; Flaming Pie, 1997; Standing Stone, 1999; Run Devil Run, 1999; Wingspan, 2001; Driving Rain, 2001; Chaos and Creation in the Back Yard, 2005; Memory Almost Full, 2007. *Films* (with the Beatles): A Hard Day's Night, 1964; Help!, 1965; Magical Mystery Tour (TV), 1967; Yellow Submarine, 1968; Let It Be, 1970; (with Wings) Rockshow, 1981; (wrote, composed score, and acted in) Give My Regards To Broad Street, 1984; (wrote, composed score and produced) Rupert and the Frog Song, 1984 (BAFTA award, Best Animated Film); Get Back, 1991. *Film scores:* The Family Way, 1966; Live and Let Die, 1973 (title song only); Twice In A Lifetime, 1984 (title song only); Spies Like Us, 1985 (title song only); *TV scores:* Thingumybob (series), 1968; The Zoo Gang (series), 1974. One-man art exhibn, Walker Gall., Liverpool, 2002. Live Russian 'phone link-up, BBC Russian Service, 1989. FRCM 1995. Numerous Grammy Awards, Nat. Acad. of Recording Arts and Scis, USA, incl. Lifetime Achievement Award, 1990; Ivor Novello Awards include: for Internat. Achievement, 1980; for Internat. Hit of the Year (Ebony and Ivory), 1982; for Outstanding Contrib. to Music, 1989; PRS special award for unique achievement in popular music, 1990. Freeman, City of Liverpool, 1984. Fellow, British Acad. of Composers and Songwriters, 2000. DUniv Sussex, 1988. *Publications:* The Beatles Anthology (with George Harrison and Ringo Starr), 2000; Paintings, 2000; Blackbird Singing: poems and lyrics 1965–1999, 2001; Wingspan: Paul McCartney's band on the run, 2002; *for children:* High in the Clouds, 2005.

See also S. McCartney.

McCARTNEY, Joanne; Member (Lab) Enfield and Haringey, London Assembly, Greater London Authority, since 2004. *Educ:* Univ. of Warwick (LLB); Univ. of Leicester (LLM). Barrister, specialising in employment law; adjudicator, Housing Ombudsman. Mem. (Lab) Enfield BC, 1998–2006. *Address:* 10 Broomfield Avenue, N13 4JN; Greater London Authority, City Hall, Queen's Walk, SE1 2AA.

McCARTNEY, Robert Law; QC (NI) 1975; Member (UKU) Northern Down, Northern Ireland Assembly, 1998–2007; *b* 24 April 1936; *s* of William Martin McCartney and Elizabeth Jane (*née* McCartney); *m* 1960, Maureen Ann Bingham; one *s* three *d*. *Educ:* Grosvenor Grammar Sch., Belfast; Queen's Univ., Belfast (LLB Hons 1958). Admitted solicitor of Supreme Court of Judicature, NI, 1962; called to NI Bar, 1968. MP (UKU) N Down, June 1995–2001; contested (UKU) same seat, 2001; contested (UKU) N Down, NI Assembly, 2007. *Publications:* Liberty and Authority in Ireland, 1985; Liberty, Democracy and the Union, 2001; political reports and pamphlets. *Recreations:* reading (biography and military history), walking. *Address:* St Catherines, 2 Circular Road East, Cultra, Holywood, Co. Down, Northern Ireland BT18 0HA.

McCARTNEY, Stella; fashion designer; *b* 13 Sept. 1971; *d* of Sir (James) Paul McCartney, *qv*; *m* 2003, Alasdhair Willis; two *s* one *d*. *Educ:* Central St Martin's Coll. of Art and Design. Set up own clothing line, London, 1995; Creative Dir, Chloe, Paris, 1997–2001; estabd own fashion house, in partnership with Gucci Gp, 2001–; opened stores in NY, 2002, London, and Los Angeles, 2003. British Designer of the Year, British Fashion Awards, 2007. *Address:* (office) Peake House, 92 Golborne Road, W10 5PS.

McCAUGHRAN, John; QC 2003; *b* 24 April 1958; *s* of Desmond McCaughran and Elizabeth McCaughran (*née* Miller); *m* 1985, Catherine Françoise Marie Mondange; one *s*. *Educ:* Methodist Coll., Belfast; Trinity Hall, Cambridge (MA 1980). Called to the Bar, Gray's Inn, 1982. *Recreations:* reading, weeding, la vie française. *Address:* One Essex Court, Temple, EC4Y 9AR. *T:* (020) 7583 2000, *Fax:* (020) 7583 0118; *e-mail:* jmccaughran@oeclaw.co.uk.

McCAUGHREAN, Geraldine Margaret; author, since 1988; *b* 6 June 1951; *d* of Lesley Arthur Jones and Ethel Jones (*née* Thomas); *m* 1988, John McCaughrean; one *d*. *Educ:* Enfield County Grammar Sch. for Girls; Southgate Technical Coll.; Christ Church Coll. of Educn, Canterbury (BEd Hons 1977; Hon. Fellow, Canterbury Christ Church Univ., 2006). Sec., Thames TV, 1970–73; Sec. 1977–79, and Sub-Editor, 1983–88, Marshall Cavendish; Editorial Asst, Rothmans Internat., 1980–82; Editor, Focus, 1982. Radio play, Last Call, 1991; stage play, Dazzling Medusa, Polka Children's Theatre, 2005. *Publications:* over 140 titles, various trans. into 41 languages, including: *for children:* A Little Lower than the Angels (Whitbread Children's Book Award), 1987; A Pack of Lies (Guardian Children's Award, Carnegie Medal), 1988; Gold Dust (Whitbread Children's Book Award), 1994; Plundering Paradise (Smarties Bronze Award), 1996; Forever X (UK Reading Assoc. Award), 1997; The Stones are Hatching, 1999; Britannia, 1999; (new version) A Pilgrim's Progress, 1999 (Blue Peter Book of the Year, 2000); The Kite Rider (Smarties Bronze Award), 2001; Stop the Train (Smarties Bronze Award), 2001; Gilgamesh the Hero, 2002 (staged Bristol Old Vic, 2006); Bright Penny, 2003; The Jesse Tree, 2003; Smile! (Smarties Bronze Award), 2004; Questing Knights of the Faerie Queen, 2004; Cyrano, 2005; Peter Pan In Scarlet, 2006 (trans. 41 langs); Tamburlaine's Elephants, 2007; *for teenagers:* Not the End of the World (Whitbread Children's Book Award), 2004 (staged Bristol Old Vic, 2007); The White Darkness, 2005 (Michael L. Printz Award, 2008); *for adults:* The Maypole, 1989; Fire's Astonishment, 1990; Vainglory, 1991; Lovesong, 1996; The Ideal Wife, 1997; contribs to anthologies for children and young people. *Recreation:* theatre. *Address:* c/o David Higham Associates, 5–8 Lower John Street, Golden Square, W1R 4HA; *web:* www.geraldinemccaughrean.co.uk.

McCAUL, Colin Brownlie; QC 2003; *b* 21 Oct. 1954; *s* of Ian and Elizabeth McCaul; *m* 1988, Claire Louise Carden; two *s* three *d*. *Educ:* Dulwich Coll.; University Coll. London (LLB Hons). Called to the Bar, Gray's Inn, 1978, Bencher, 2006. *Recreations:* horses, surfing, English history. *Address:* 39 Essex Street, WC2R 3AT. *T:* (020) 7832 1111, *Fax:* (020) 7353 3978; *e-mail:* colin.mccaul@39essex.com.

McCAUSLAND, Benedict Maurice Perronet T.; *see* Thompson-McCausland.

McCAVE, Prof. (Ian) Nicholas, FGS; Woodwardian Professor of Geology, University of Cambridge, 1985–2008, now Emeritus; Fellow, St John's College, Cambridge, since 1986; *b* 3 Feb. 1941; *s* of Thomas Theasby McCave and Gwendoline Marguerite McCave (*née* Langlois); *m* 1972, Susan Caroline Adams (*née* Bambridge); three *s* one *d*. *Educ:* Elizabeth Coll., Guernsey; Hertford Coll., Oxford (MA, DSc); Brown Univ., USA (PhD). FGS 1963. NATO Research Fellow, Netherlands Inst. for Sea Research, 1967–69; Lectr 1969–76, Reader 1976–84, UEA, Norwich; Hd, Dept of Earth Scis, Univ. of Cambridge, 1988–98. Visiting Professor: Oregon State Univ., 1974; MIT, 1999; Adjunct Scientist, Woods Hole Oceanographic Instn, 1978–87. Shepard Medal for Marine Geol., US Soc. for Sedimentary Geol., 1995; Huntsman Medal for Marine Scis, Canada, 1999. *Publications:* (ed) The Benthic Boundary Layer, 1976; (ed) The Deep Sea Bed, 1990; over 150 papers in jls. *Recreations:* pottering about in the garden, rough carpentry, travel. *Address:* Marlborough House, 23 Victoria Street, Cambridge CB1 1JP.

McCLARAN, Anthony Paul; Chief Executive, Universities and Colleges Admissions Service, since 2003; *b* 5 Nov. 1957; *s* of John Edwin McClaran and Sheila Margaret McClaran (*née* Rayner); *m* 1986, Mary-Ann Helen Smith; two *s* two *d*. *Educ:* The John Lyon Sch., Harrow-on-the-Hill; Univ. of Kent (BA 1st cl. Hons (English and American Lit.) 1981). University of Warwick: Admin. Asst, 1985–89; Asst Registrar, 1989–92; Sen. Asst Registrar, 1992; University of Hull: Acad. Registrar, 1992–95; Actg Registrar and Sec., 1995; Universities and Colleges Admissions Service: Hd, Acad. Services and Develt, 1995–96; Dep. Chief Exec., 1996–2003; Actg Chief Exec., Jan.–Dec. 2003. Man. Dir, UCAS Media Ltd (formerly UCAS Enterprises), 1996–; Chm., SDS Ltd, 2003–. Mem., Bd of Dirs, Hero UK, 2001–06. Mem., Exec. Cttee, AUA, 2003–06. University of Gloucestershire: Member: Council, 1997–2005 (Mem., Standing Cttee, 2002–05); Audit Cttee, 1998–2002 (Chm., 2000–02); Governance Cttee, 1999–2005; Chair of Council and Pro-Chancellor, 2007–. Trustee and Mem., Finance and Gen. Purpose Cttee, Inspiring Futures Foundn, 2007–. FRSA; FCMI. Governor: St Edward's Sch., Cheltenham, 2003–; Nat. Star Coll., 2006–; Cheltenham Kingsmead Sch., 2007–; John Lyon Sch., 2008–. Freeman, Guild of Educators, 2007. *Publications:* articles and chapters on admissions and higher educn. *Recreations:* books, polyphony, tennis. *Address:* UCAS, Rosehill, New Barn Lane, Cheltenham, Glos GL52 3LZ. *T:* (01242) 544990, *Fax:* (01242) 544959; *e-mail:* a.mcclaran@ucas.ac.uk. *Club:* Royal Over-Seas League.

McCLARTY, David; Member (UU) Londonderry East, Northern Ireland Assembly, since 1998; *b* 23 Feb. 1951; *s* of Douglas and Helen McClarty; *m* 1973, (Alma) Norma (Yvonne) Walls; two *s*. *Educ:* Coleraine Academical Instn; Magee Coll., Londonderry. Sales Asst, NI Electricity, 1973; General Accident: Trainee Fire Underwriter, 1973; Dep. Manager, Fire Insurance Dept, 1978–84; Fire Underwriter, 1973–78; Insurance Consultant, D. McClarty & Co., 1984–98. Mem. (UU), Coleraine BC, 1989–; Mayor of Coleraine Borough, 1993–95. Freeman, City of London, 1995. *Recreations:* amateur dramatics, choral singing, sport in general. *Address:* 22 Slievebanna, Coleraine, Co. Londonderry BT51 3JG. *T:* (028) 7035 6734.

McCLAY, Sir Allen (James), Kt 2006; CBE 2000 (OBE 1994); Founder and Chairman, Almac Group, since 2001; *b* 21 March 1932. *Educ:* Cookstown High Sch.; Belfast Coll. of Technology. Sales rep., Glaxo, 1955–68; founder, Galen Ltd, 1968; retired as Pres., Galen Hldgs plc, 2001; acquired Chemical Synthesis Services from Galen, 2001, and other cos, to form Almac Gp; acquired Galen Ltd, 2004. *Address:* Almac Group, Almac House, 20 Seagoe Industrial Estate, Craigavon BT63 5QD.

McCLEAN, Prof. (John) David, CBE 1994; FBA 2003; Professor of Law, 1973–2004, now Emeritus, Public Orator, 1988–91 and 1994–2007, University of Sheffield; *b* 4 July 1939; *s* of Major Harold McClean and Mrs Mabel McClean; *m* 1966, Pamela Ann Loader; one *s* one *d*. *Educ:* Queen Elizabeth's Grammar Sch., Blackburn; Magdalen Coll., Oxford (DCL, 1984). Called to the Bar, Gray's Inn, 1963, Bencher, 2001. University of Sheffield: Asst Lectr 1961; Lectr 1963; Sen. Lectr 1968; Dean, Faculty of Law, 1978–81, 1998–2002; Pro-Vice-Chancellor, 1991–96. Vis. Lectr in Law, Monash Univ., Melbourne, 1968, Vis. Prof., 1978. Chancellor: dio. of Sheffield, 1992–; dio. of Newcastle, 1998–. Vice-Chm., C of E Bd for Social Responsibility, 1978–80. Member: Gen. Synod of C of E, 1970–2005 (Vice-Chm., House of Laity, 1979–85, Chm. 1985–95); Crown Appts Commn, 1977–87. Pres., Eur. Consortium for Church and State Res., 1995. Hon. QC 1995. *Publications:* Criminal Justice and the Treatment of Offenders (jtly), 1969; (contrib.) Halsbury's Laws of England, Vol. 8, 4th edn 1974, re-issue 1996, Vol. 2 (re-issue), 4th edn 1991; The Legal Context of Social Work, 1975, 2nd edn 1980; (jtly) Defendants in the Criminal Process, 1976; (ed jtly) Shawcross and Beaumont, Air Law, 4th edn 1977, and loose-leaf issues, 1977– (Gen. Ed., 2000–); (jtly) Recognition and Enforcement of Judgments, etc, within the Commonwealth, 1977; (ed jtly) Dicey and Morris, Conflict of Laws, 10th edn 1980, to 14th edn 2006; Recognition of Family Judgments in the Commonwealth, 1983; International Judicial Assistance, 1992; (ed) Morris, The Conflict of Laws, 4th edn 1993, to 6th edn 2005; (contrib.) Chitty, Contracts, 27th edn 1994, 28th edn 1999, 29th edn 2004; International Co-operation in Civil and Criminal Matters, 2002; Transnational Organized Crime, 2007. *Recreation:* detective fiction. *Address:* 6 Burnt Stones Close, Sheffield S10 5TS. *T:* (0114) 230 5794. *Club:* Royal Commonwealth Society.

McCLEARY, Ann Heron, (Mrs David McCleary); *see* Gloag, A. H.

McCLEARY, (William) Boyd, CVO 2004; HM Diplomatic Service; High Commissioner to Malaysia, since 2006; *b* 30 March 1949; *s* of Robert McCleary and Eleanor Thomasina McCleary (*née* Weir); *m* 2000, Jeannette Ann Collier; three *d*. *Educ:* Queen's Univ., Belfast (BA 1st Cl. Hons German Lang. and Lit. 1972). Asst, then Dep. Principal, Dept of Agric. for NI, 1972–75; First Sec. (Agric., then Chancery), Bonn, 1975–80; Western European Dept, then EC Dept (Ext.), FCO, 1981–85; First Sec., Hd of Chancery and Consul, Seoul, 1985–88; Asst Hd, Far Eastern Dept, FCO, 1988–89; Dep. Hd of Mission and Dir of Trade Promotion, Ankara, 1990–93; Counsellor (Econ. and Trade Policy), Ottawa, 1993–97; Hd, Estate Dept, FCO, 1997–2000; Consul-Gen., Düsseldorf, and Dir-Gen., Trade and Investment in Germany, 2000–05; Dir for Global Rollout of Oracle System, FCO, 2005–06. *Recreations:* spending time with my family, squash, walking, reading. *Address:* c/o British High Commission, 185 Jalan Ampang, 50450 Kuala Lumpur, Malaysia. *T:* (3) 21702200; *e-mail:* boyd.mccleary@fco.gov.uk. *Club:* Royal Over-Seas League.

McCLELLAN, John Forrest; Under Secretary, Industry Department for Scotland (formerly Scottish Economic Planning Department), 1980–85, retired; *b* 15 Aug. 1932; *s* of John McClellan and Hester (*née* Niven); *m* 1956, Eva Maria Pressel; three *s* one *d*. *Educ:* Ferryhill Primary Sch., Aberdeen; Aberdeen Grammar Sch.; Aberdeen Univ. (MA). Served Army, 2nd Lieut, Gordon Highlanders and Nigeria Regt, RWAFF, 1954–56. Entered Civil Service, 1956; Asst Principal, Scottish Educn Dept, 1956–59; Private Sec. to Perm. Under Sec. of State, Scottish Office, 1959–60; Principal, Scottish Educn Dept, 1960–68; Civil Service Fellow, Glasgow Univ., 1968–69; Asst Sec., Scottish Educn Dept, 1969–77; Asst Under Sec. of State, Scottish Office, 1977–80. Dir, 1986–2001, Trustee, 2001–, Scottish Internat. Educn Trust; Mem., Management Cttee, Hanover (Scotland) Housing Assoc., 1986–2007. Hon. Fellow, Dundee Inst. of Technology, 1988. *Publication:* Then a Soldier, 1991. *Recreations:* gardening, walking. *Address:* 7 Cumin Place, Edinburgh EH9 2JX. *T:* (0131) 667 8446. *Club:* Royal Scots (Edinburgh).

McCLELLAND, Donovan; Member (SDLP) Antrim South, 1998–2003, and Deputy Speaker, 2000–02, Northern Ireland Assembly; *b* 14 Jan. 1949; *s* of Dan and Virginia McClelland; *m* 1974, Noreen Patricia Young; two *s* one *d*. *Educ:* Queen's Univ., Belfast (BSc Econ). Lectr and researcher in Economics, QUB, 1973–75; Civil Servant, Dept of Agriculture, 1975–78; Lectr in Economics, Univ. of Ulster, 1978–98. Chm., Standards and Privileges Cttee, NI Assembly, 2000–02. *Recreation:* reading. *Address:* 18 Roseville Crescent, Randalstown, Co. Antrim BT41 2LY.

McCLELLAND, Hon. Douglas, AC 1987; Chairman, Australian Political Exchange Council, 1993–95; *s* of Alfred McClelland and Gertrude Amy Cooksley; *m* Lorna Belva McNeill; one *s* two *d*. Mem. NSW ALP Executive, 1956–62; Hon. Dir, St George Hosp., Sydney, 1957–68. Member, Australian Senate for NSW, 1962–87; Senate appointments: Minister for the Media, 1972–75; Manager, Govt Business, 1974–75; Special Minister of State, June–Nov. 1975; Opposition spokesman on Admin. Services, 1976–77; Manager, Opposition Business, 1976–77; Dep. Leader of Opposition, May–Dec. 1977; Dep. Pres. and Chm. of Cttees, 1981–82; Pres. of the Australian Senate, 1983–87; High Commissioner in UK, 1987–91; Comr-Gen., Australian Pavilion, Expo '92, Seville, Spain, 1992. Chm., Old Parliament House Redevelt Cttee, 1993–95. Chm., Bobby Limb Foundn, 1999–2002; Member: Bd of Govs, St George Foundn, 1993–2002; Bd of Govs, Mick Young Trust, 1998–2002. Patron, St George Illawarra Rugby League FC, 2002– (Chm., 1998–2000); *Recreations:* reading, making friends. *Address:* 6A Carlton Crescent, Kogarah Bay, NSW 2217, Australia. *Clubs:* City Tattersalls (Life Mem.), St George Leagues (Life Mem.), St George Rugby League Football (Life Mem.) (Sydney).

McCLELLAND, George Ewart, CB 1986; Solicitor, Department of Employment, 1982–87; *b* 27 March 1927; *s* of George Ewart McClelland and Winifred (*née* Robinson); *m* 1956, Ann Penelope, *yr d* of late Judge Arthur Henry Armstrong; one *s* two *d*. *Educ:* Stonyhurst Coll.; Merton Coll., Oxford (Classical Scholar; MA). Called to the Bar, Middle Temple, 1952. Entered Solicitor's Dept, Min. of Labour, 1953; Asst Solicitor, 1969; Principal Asst Solicitor, 1978.

McCLELLAND, Prof. (William) Grigor; former business executive and academic; *b* 2 Jan. 1922; *o c* of Arthur and Jean McClelland, Gosforth, Newcastle upon Tyne; *m* 1st, 1946, Diana Avery Close (*d* 2000); two *s* two *d*; 2nd, 2003, Caroline Mary (*née* Kent), widow of Tristram Spence. *Educ:* Leighton Park; Balliol Coll., Oxford (First Class PPE, 1948; MA). Friends' Ambulance Unit, 1941–46. Man. Dir, Laws Stores Ltd, 1949–65, 1978–85 (Chm., 1966–85); Sen. Res. Fellow in Management Studies, Balliol Coll., 1962–65; Dir, Manchester Business Sch., 1965–77, and Prof. of Business Administration,

1967–77, Univ. of Manchester; Dep. Chm., Nat. Computing Centre, 1966–68; Chm., Washington Develt Corp., 1977–88. Founding Editor, Jl of Management Studies, 1963–65. Chm., EDC for the Distributive Trades, 1980–84 (Mem., 1965–70); Member: The Consumer Council, 1963–66; Economic Planning Council, Northern Region, 1965–66; IRC, 1966–71; NEDC, 1969–71; SSRC, 1971–74; North Eastern Industrial Develt Bd, 1977–86. Hon. Vis. Prof., 1977–, and Gov., 1986–98, Durham Univ. Business Sch. Chairman: Tyne Tees Telethon Trust, 1987–93; Community Foundn for Tyne & Wear and Northumberland (formerly Tyne and Wear Foundn), 1988–93 (a Vice-Pres., 1994–); NE Adv. Panel, Nat. Lottery Charities Bd, 1995–97. Dir, Oxford Res. Gp, 2001–05. Trustee: Joseph Rowntree Charitable Trust, 1956–94 (Chm., 1965–78); Anglo-German Foundn for the Study of Industrial Soc., 1973–79; Millfield House Foundn, 1976–; Employment Inst., 1985–92; Governor: Nat. Inst. of Econ. and Social Research; Leighton Park Sch., 1952–60 and 1962–66. Mem., Soc. of Friends, 1942–. DL Tyne and Wear, 1988. MBA Manchester 1971. Hon. DCL Dunelm, 1985. CBE 1994–2003 (returned in protest at invasion of Iraq). *Publications:* Quakers Visit China (ed), 1957; Studies in Retailing, 1963; Costs and Competition in Retailing, 1966; And a New Earth, 1976; Washington: over and out, 1988; Embers of War, 1997; (ed) From Tyne to Tsar, 2007. *Recreations:* family, friends, current affairs. *Address:* 50 Reid Park Road, Jesmond, Newcastle upon Tyne NE2 2ES; *e-mail:* grigor@mcclelland.wanadoo.co.uk.

McCLEMENT, Vice Adm. Sir Tim(othy Pentreath), KCB 2006; OBE 1990; Managing Director, Flagship Superyacht Academy, since 2007; *b* 16 May 1951; *s* of late Capt. Reginald McClement, RN retd, and of Winnifred McClement (*née* Pentreath); *m* 1980, Lynne Laura Gowans; two *s*. *Educ:* Douai Sch., Berks. Joined Royal Navy, 1971: appts in various submarines, 1975–81; passed SMCC 1981; 2nd i/c HMS Conqueror during Falklands Conflict, 1982; in command: HMS Opportune, 1983–84; Staff of Captain Submarine Sea Training as a Comand Sea Rider, 1984–87; CO, SMCC, 1987–89 (Comdr); HMS Tireless, 1989–92 (surfaced at North Pole, 8 May 1990, and played cricket); HMS London, 1992–94 (Capt., Wilkinson Sword of Peace, 1993); HMS Cornwall, 1999–2001 (led Task Gp around world, May–Nov. 2000); Rear-Adm. 2001; ACNS, 2001–03; COS (Warfare) and Rear-Adm. Surface Ships, 2003–04; Vice Adm. 2004; Dep. C-in-C Fleet, 2004–06. Younger Brother, Trinity House, 2006. Freeman, City of London, 1993. MInstD. *Recreations:* swimming, tennis, dog walking. *Club:* Royal Navy of 1765 and 1785.

MACCLESFIELD, 9th Earl of, *cr* 1721; **Richard Timothy George Mansfield Parker;** Baron Parker, 1716; Viscount Parker, 1721; *b* 31 May 1943; *s* of 8th Earl of Macclesfield and Hon. Valerie Mansfield (*d* 1994), *o d* of 4th Baron Sandhurst, OBE; *S* father, 1992; *m* 1967, Tatiana Cleone, *d* of Major Craig Wheaton-Smith; three *d* (including twins); *m* 1986, Mrs Sandra Hope Mead. *Educ:* Stowe; Worcester Coll., Oxford. *Heir: b* Hon. (Jonathan) David (Geoffrey) Parker [*b* 2 Jan. 1945; *m* 1968, Lynne Valerie Butler; one *s* two *d*]. *Address:* Rectory Farmhouse, Church Lane, North Stoke, Wallingford, Oxon OX10 6BQ.

MACCLESFIELD, Archdeacon of; *see* Gillings, Ven. R. J.

McCLEVERTY, Prof. Jon Armistice; Professor of Inorganic Chemistry, 1990–2003, now Emeritus, and Senior University Research Fellow, 2003–07, University of Bristol; *b* 11 Nov. 1937; *s* of John and Nessie McCleverty; *m* 1963, Dianne Barrack; two *d*. *Educ:* Univ. of Aberdeen (BSc 1960); Imperial College, London (DIC, PhD 1963); Massachusetts Inst. of Technology. Asst Lectr, part-time, Acton Coll. of Technology, 1962–63; Asst Lectr, then Lectr, Sen. Lectr, and Reader, Univ. of Sheffield, 1964–80; Prof. of Inorganic Chem., 1980–90, and Head of Dept of Chem., 1984–90, Univ. of Birmingham. Chairman: Cttee of Heads of Univ. Chem. Depts, 1989–91; Internat. Cttee, RSC, 1994–97; Chemistry Cttee, SERC, 1990–93; Vice-Chm., Chairman of Eur. Res. Council Chemistry Cttees, 1992–93, 1995, 1997–99 (Chm., 1996–97); Member: Science Bd, SERC, 1990–93; Technical Cttee for Chemistry, Co-operation in Sci. and Technol. in Europe, EU, 1990–96; Physical Scis and Technol. Panel, NATO Sci. Affairs Div., 1999–2002 (Chm., 2001). Royal Society of Chemistry: Pres., Dalton Div., 1999–2001; Chm., Sci. and Technol. Bd, 2001–05; Chm., Awards Cttee, 2006–. Tilden Lectr, 1981, Sir Ronald Nyholm Lectr, 2001–02, RSC. RSC Medal, for work on chem. and electrochem. of transition metals, 1985. Golden Order of Merit (Poland), 1990. *Publications:* numerous articles, principally in Jl of Chem. Soc. *Recreations:* gardening, DIY, travel, traditional jazz. *Address:* School of Chemistry, University of Bristol, Cantock's Close, Bristol BS8 1TS.

McCLINTOCK, Sir Eric (Paul), Kt 1981; investment banker; *b* 13 Sept. 1918; *s* of Robert and Ada McClintock; *m* 1942, Eva Lawrence; two *s* one *d*. *Educ:* De La Salle Coll., Armidale; Sydney Univ. (DPA). Supply Dept, Dept of the Navy, Australia, 1935–47; served successively in Depts of Commerce, Agriculture, and Trade, in Washington, New York, Melbourne and Canberra, 1947–61 (1st Asst Sec. on resignation); investment banking, 1962–. Chairman: McClintock Associates Ltd; Aust. Overseas Projects Corp., 1978–84; Woolworths Ltd, 1982–87; AFT Ltd, 1984–87; Plutonic Resources Ltd, 1990–96; Malaysia Mining Corp. Australia Pty Ltd, 1993–2002; Dep. Chm., Development Finance Corp. Ltd, 1980–87; Director: Philips Industries Holdings Ltd, 1978–85; O'Connell Street Associates Pty Ltd, 1978–; Ashton Mining Ltd, 1986–93. Chm., Trade Develt Council, 1970–74. Pres., Royal Life Saving Soc. (NSW), 1987–96. Governor, Sydney Inst., 1990–95. *Recreations:* tennis, reading, travel. *Address:* Level 17, 6 O'Connell Street, Sydney, NSW 2000, Australia. *T:* (2) 92231822. *Clubs:* Australian (Sydney); Commonwealth (Canberra).

McCLINTOCK-BUNBURY, family name of **Baron Rathdonnell.**

McCLOY, Dr Elizabeth Carol, FRCP, FFOM; Chief Medical Officer and Medical Services Director, UNUM Ltd, 1997–98; *b* 25 April 1945; *d* of Edward Bradley and Ada Entwisle; *m* 1969, Rory McCloy (marr. diss. 1989); two *s*. *Educ:* Guildford Grammar Sch.; University Coll. and UCH, London (BSc Hons 1966; MB BS Hons 1969). MFOM 1988, FFOM 1993; FRCP 1995. Clinical Asst, Medicine, W Middlesex Univ. Hosp., 1972–83; Manchester Royal Infirmary: Sen. Clinical MO, Occupational Health, 1984–88; Consultant in Occupational Medicine, 1988–93; Dir of Occupational Health and Safety, Central Manchester Healthcare Trust, 1988–93; Chief Exec. and Dir, CS Occupational Health Service, later CS Occupational Health and Safety Agency, and Med. Advr to CS, 1993–96. Pres., Soc. of Occupational Medicine, 1993–94. *Publications:* (ed jtly) Practical Occupational Medicine, 1994; (contrib.) Hunters Diseases of Occupations, 7th edn 1987, 8th edn 1994; (contrib.) Oxford Textbook of Medicine, 1994; articles on hepatitis. *Recreations:* theatre, gardening, antiques.

McCLUNEY, Ian, CMG 1990; HM Diplomatic Service, retired; High Commissioner, Sierra Leone, 1993–97; *b* 27 Feb. 1937. *Educ:* Edinburgh Univ. (BSc). Served HM Forces, 1958–62. Joined FO, 1964; Addis Ababa, 1964–67; FCO, 1969–70; Baghdad, 1972–74; FCO, 1975–78; Kuwait, 1979–82; Consul-Gen., Alexandria, 1982–86; FCO, 1986–88; Ambassador to Somalia, 1989–90; Dep. High Comr, Calcutta, 1991–93. Reference Sec.,

Competition Commn, 2000–03. *Recreations:* sailing, farming in Jamaica. *Club:* Royal Over-Seas League.

McCLURE, Prof. John, OBE 2007; MD; FRCPath; Procter Professor of Pathology, University of Manchester, 1987–2003, now Emeritus; Hon. Professor, University of Ulster, since 2003; *b* 2 May 1947; *s* of Richard Burns McClure and Isabella McClure (*née* Nelson); *m* 1970, Sheena Frances Tucker; three *d*. *Educ:* Queen's Univ. Belfast (BSc Hons, MB, BCh, BAO, MD, DMJPath). Training posts in Pathology, QUB, 1972–78; Clinical Sen. Lectr and Specialist/Sen. Specialist in Pathology, Univ. of Adelaide and Inst. of Med. and Vet. Sci., Adelaide, 1978–83; University of Manchester: Sen. Lectr and Hon. Consultant in Histopathology, 1983–87; Head of Pathological Scis, 1987–95; Associate Dean, Faculty of Medicine, 1995–98. Dir, Laboratory Medicine, Central Manchester Healthcare Trust, 1996–2001. British Red Cross: Chm., Northern Regl Council, 1998–99; Mem., Nat. Bd of Trustees, 1998– (Chm., 2001–07); Pres. and Trustee, Gtr Manchester Br., 1994–99. *Publications:* papers in med. and path. jls. *Recreation:* DIY. *Address:* 39 Killymore Road, Newtownstewart, Co. Tyrone, BT78 4DT. *T:* (028) 8164 8709.

McCLURE, Joseph Robert, MBE 2000; *b* 21 Oct. 1923; *s* of Thomas Render McClure and Catherine Bridget McClure; *m* 1943, Evelyn Joice; one *d*. *Educ:* Prior Street Sch.; Oakwellgate Sch., Gateshead. Served War, Royal Marines, 1941–46. Elected Councillor (Lab): County Borough of Gateshead, 1964–73, Dep. Mayor, 1973–74; Tyne and Wear CC, 1974–82 (Chm., 1977–78). President: Tyneside Br., 1996–2001, Durham Br., 2003–, Royal Marine Assoc.; Gateshead RBL, 1971–; Vice Pres., Northumberland/Tyne and Wear County, RBL, 1997–. JP Gateshead and Blaydon, 1979–93. *Recreation:* bowls. *Address:* 170 Rectory Road, Gateshead, Tyne and Wear NE8 4RR. *T:* (0191) 477 0709.

McCLURE, Dr Judith, CBE 2003; FSAScot; Head of St George's School, Edinburgh, since 1994; *b* 22 Dec. 1945; *d* of James McClure and Vera (*née* Knight); *m* 1977, Roger John Howard Collins, DLitt, FRHistS, FSAScot. *Educ:* Newlands GS, Middlesbrough; Coll. of Law, London; Somerville Coll., Oxford (Shaw Lefevre Scholar; BA 1st Cl. Hons 1973; MA 1977; DPhil 1979). Canoness of St Augustine, Les Oiseaux, Westgate, Kent, 1964–70; Sir Maurice Powicke Meml Res. Fellow, LMH, Oxford, 1976–77; Lecturer: in Medieval Latin and Medieval History, Univ. of Liverpool, 1977–79; in History, Jesus, Somerville and Worcester Colls, Univ. of Oxford, 1979–81; School of St Helen and St Katharine, Abingdon: teacher of History and Politics, 1981–83; Head, History and Politics Dept, 1983–84; Asst Head, Kingswood Sch., Bath, 1984–87, Dir of Studies, 1986–87; Head, Royal Sch., Bath, 1987–93. Member: Governing Body, 1995–2007, Mgt Cttee, 1998–2007 (Chm., 2001–07), Scottish Council of Ind. Schs; Regl Standing Cttee for Scotland, UCAS, 1997–99; Bd of Mgt, Scottish Qualifications Authy, 1999–2000; Scottish Ministerial Strategy Cttee on Continuing Professional Develt of Teachers, 2000–03 (Chm., Leadership and Mgt Pathways Subgroup, 2001–03); Scottish Adv. Cttee on Continuing Professional Develt of Teachers, 2004–; Chm., Scottish Region, and Mem. Council, GSA, 1996–99. Member: Judicial Studies Cttee, 2006–; China Forward Planning Gp, Scottish Exec., 2006–; Convener, Scotland-China Educnl Network, 2006–. Convener, Scottish Leadership, Mgt and Admin Soc., 2004–. Mem. Adv. Cttee, Edinburgh Youth Transition and Crime Survey, 2002–. Member: Court, Bath Univ., 1989–92; Gen. Convocation, 1994–, Court, 2003–, Heriot-Watt Univ.; Adv. Bd, Open Univ. in Scotland, 2000–; Bd, Inst. of Sci. Educn in Scotland, 2003–; Bd, Confucius Inst., Univ. of Edinburgh, 2006–; Member, Board of Governors: Selwyn Sch., Gloucester, 1988–90; Clifton Hall Sch., Lothian, 1995–99; Merchiston Castle Sch., 1999–2006; The New Sch., Butterstone, 2004–05. Trustee, Hopetoun House Preservation Trust, 1997–2003. Chm., Women of Lothian Lunch, 1998–2001. FRSA 1997. *Publications:* Gregory the Great: exegesis and audience, 1979; Introduction and notes to Bede's Ecclesiastical History, 1994; articles in Jl Theol Studies, Peritia, Papers of Liverpool Latin Seminar, Prep. School and in Festschriften. *Recreations:* reading, travel, thinking about the early Middle Ages. *Address:* 12A Ravelston Park, Edinburgh EH4 3DX. *Club:* University Women's.

McCLURE, Roger Niall; Chairman, JANET (UK), since 2008; Chief Executive, Scottish Further and Higher Education Funding Council (formerly Scottish Funding Councils for Further and Higher Education), 2002–08; *b* 28 Dec. 1950; *s* of late Rev. Canon Hugh Norman McClure and Jane Paterson Brown; *m* 1974, Catherine Lynne Thomas; four *d*. *Educ:* King Edward VI Sch., Norwich; Corpus Christi Coll., Cambridge (MA); Corpus Christi Coll., Oxford (Postgrad Dip); City of London Polytechnic (Dip Public Finance & Accountancy). CPFA 1982. Auditor, Nat. Audit Office, 1978–84; Sen. Consultant, then Manager, Deloitte Haskins & Sells Mgt Consultancy, 1984–88; seconded as Financial Advr to UGC, 1985–87; Dir of Finance, PCFC, 1988–92; Dir of Finance, FEFC, 1992–96; Pro-Rector, London Inst., 1996–2002. Harkness Fellow, Center for Higher Educn Studies, Univ. of California, Berkeley, 1990–91; Special Advr, H of C Educn Sub-Cttee, 1997–98; Member, Council: KCL, 1988–97; Business and Technol. Council, 1995–98; City Literary Inst., 1998–2002. CCMI 2003. *Publication:* (contrib.) Further Education Reformed, 2000. *Recreations:* music, sport, current affairs, reading, cinema. *Address:* *e-mail:* mcclure.roger@gmail.com.

McCLURE, Ven. Timothy Elston; Archdeacon of Bristol, since 1999; *b* 20 Oct. 1946; *s* of late Kenneth Elston McClure and of Grace Helen McClure (*née* Hoar); *m* 1969, Barbara Mary Marchant; one *s* one *d*. *Educ:* Kingston Grammar Sch.; St John's Coll., Durham (BA); Ridley Hall, Cambridge. Deacon 1970, priest 1971; Curate, Kirkheaton Parish Church, Huddersfield, 1970–73; Marketing Mgr, Agrofax Labour Intensive Products Ltd, Harrow, Middx, 1973–74; Chaplain, Manchester Poly., 1974–82; Curate, St Ambrose, Chorlton-on-Medlock, 1974–79; Team Rector, Parish of Whitworth, Manchester and Presiding Chaplain, Chaplaincies to Higher Educn in Manchester, 1979–82; Gen. Sec., SCM, 1982–92; Dir, Churches' Council for Industry and Social Responsibility, Bristol, 1992–99; Hon. Canon, Bristol Cathedral, 1992–; Lord Mayor's Chaplain, Bristol, 1996–99. Chairman: Traidcraft plc, 1990–97; Christian Conference Trust, 1998–2003. *Recreations:* cooking, gardening, reading, boat restoration, sailing. *Address:* 10 Great Brockeridge, Westbury on Trym, Bristol BS9 3TY. *T:* (0117) 962 1433.

McCLUSKEY, family name of **Baron McCluskey**.

McCLUSKEY, Baron *cr* 1976 (Life Peer), of Churchhill in the District of the City of Edinburgh; **John Herbert McCluskey;** a Senator of the College of Justice in Scotland, 1984–2004; *b* 12 June 1929; *s* of Francis John McCluskey, Solicitor, and Margaret McCluskey (*née* Doonan); *m* 1956, Ruth Friedland; two *s* one *d*. *Educ:* St Bede's Grammar Sch., Manchester; Holy Cross Acad., Edinburgh; Edinburgh Univ. Harry Dalgety Bursary, 1948; Vans Dunlop Schol., 1949; Muirhead Prize, 1949; MA 1950; LLB 1952. Sword of Honour, RAF Spitalgate, 1953. Admitted Faculty of Advocates, 1955; Standing Jun. Counsel to Min. of Power (Scotland), 1963; Advocate-Depute, 1964–71; QC (Scot.) 1967; Chm., Medical Appeal Tribunals for Scotland, 1972–74; Sheriff Principal of Dumfries and Galloway, 1973–74; Solicitor General for Scotland, 1974–79. Chm., Scottish Assoc. for Mental Health, 1985–94. Independent Chairman: Scottish Football League's Compensation Tribunal, 1988–; Scottish Football Association's Appeals Tribunal, 1990–. Reith Lectr, BBC, 1986. Chm., John Smith Meml Trust, 1997–2004. Editor, Butterworth's Scottish Criminal Law and Practice series, 1988–2005. Hon. LLD Dundee, 1989. *Publications:* Law, Justice and Democracy, 1987; Criminal Appeals, 1992, 2nd edn 2000. *Recreations:* tennis, pianoforte. *Address:* c/o House of Lords, SW1A 0PW. *Club:* Royal Air Force.

McCLUSKEY, Len; Assistant General Secretary, Unite, since 2007; *b* 23 July 1950; *s* of Leonard and Margaret McCluskey. *Educ:* Cardinal Godfrey High Sch., Merseyside. Dockworker, 1968–79; Transport and General Workers' Union: District Official, Merseyside, 1979–89; Political Officer, NW Region, 1985–89; Nat. Sec., 1990–2004; Nat. Organiser, 2004–05; Asst Gen. Sec., 2005–07, when T&GWU merged with Amicus to form Unite. Mem., TUC Gen. Council and Exec., 2007–. Alumnus, Duke of Edinburgh's 8th Commonwealth Study Conf., 1998. *Recreations:* football, sport, reading, politics, chess, poetry. *Address:* Unite, 128 Theobalds Road, Holborn, WC1X 8TN.

McCLUSKIE, John Cameron, CB 1999; QC (Scot.) 1989; Consultant Parliamentary Counsel to Irish Government, since 2006; *b* 1 Feb. 1946; *m* 1970, Janis Mary Helen McArthur; one *s* one *d*. *Educ:* Hyndland Sch., Glasgow; Glasgow Univ. (LLB Hons 1967). Admitted Solicitor, Scotland, 1970; admitted Faculty of Advocates, 1974. Apprentice Solicitor, Boyds, Glasgow, 1967–69; Asst Town Clerk, Burgh of Cumbernauld, 1969–70; Legal Assistant: Macdonald, Jameson and Morris, Glasgow, 1970; SSEB, 1970–72; Asst, then Sen. Asst, Legal Sec. and Parly Draftsman, Lord Advocate's Dept, 1972–89; Legal Sec. to Lord Advocate, 1989–99; First Scottish Parly Counsel, later First Parly Counsel, Scottish Exec., 1989–2006. *Recreations:* watching mogs, walking dogs, cutting logs. *Address:* Law View, Redside Farm Steading, North Berwick, East Lothian EH39 5PE.

McCOLGAN, Elizabeth, MBE 1992; athlete and coach; Owner, Liz McColgan Health Clubs; *b* 24 May 1964; *d* of Martin and Elizabeth Lynch; *m* 1987, Peter McColgan; three *s* one *d*. *Educ:* St Saviour's High Sch., Dundee; Univ. of Alabama. Athletic achievements include: Commonwealth Games: Gold Medal, 10,000m, Edinburgh, 1986, Auckland, 1991; Bronze Medal, 3,000m, Auckland, 1991; World Cross Country Championships: Silver Medal, Warsaw, 1987; Bronze Medal, Antwerp, 1991; Silver Medal, 10,000m, Olympic Games, Seoul, 1988; Silver Medal, 3,000m, World Indoor Championships, Budapest, 1989; Gold Medal, 10,000m, World Championships, Tokyo, 1991; Gold Medal, World Half-Marathon Championships, 1992; Marathons: winner, NYC, 1991; winner, 1992, 3rd, 1996, Tokyo; 3rd, 1993, 5th, 1995, winner, 1996, 2nd, 1997 and 1998, London; retd 2001. Chair, Scottish Athletics, 2003–05. Patron, Leukaemia Res. Fund. BBC Sports Personality of the Year Award, 1991. *Recreations:* reading, movies, eating out, keeping fit. *Address:* c/o Jon Holmes Media Ltd, 5th Floor, Holborn Gate, 26 Southampton Buildings, WC2A 1PQ.

McCOLL, family name of **Baron McColl of Dulwich**.

McCOLL OF DULWICH, Baron *cr* 1989 (Life Peer), of Bermondsey in the London Borough of Southwark; **Ian McColl,** CBE 1997; MS, FRCS, FACS, FRCSE; Professor of Surgery, University of London at Guy's, King's and St Thomas' School of Medicine of King's College London (formerly United Medical Schools of Guy's and St Thomas' Hospitals), 1971–98; Director of Surgery, 1985–98, and Consultant Surgeon, 1971–98, Guy's Hospital; *b* 6 Jan. 1933; *s* of late Frederick George McColl and Winifred E. McColl, Dulwich; *m* 1960, Dr Jean Lennox, 2nd *d* of Arthur James McNair, FRCS, FRCOG; one *s* two *d*. *Educ:* Hutchesons' Grammar Sch., Glasgow; St Paul's Sch., London; Guy's Hosp., London. MB, BS 1957; FRCS 1962; FRCSE 1962; MS 1966; FACS 1975. Junior staff appts at St Bartholomew's, Putney, St Mark's, St Peter's, Great Ormond Street, Barnet, St Olave's and Guy's Hosps, 1957–67; Research Fellow, Harvard Med. Sch., and Moynihan Fellowship, Assoc. of Surgeons, 1967; Reader in Surgery, St Bartholomew's Hosp. Med. Coll., 1967 (Sub Dean, 1969–71). Visiting Professor: Univ. of South Carolina, 1974; Johns Hopkins Hosp., 1976. Consultant Surgeon: KCH, 1971–98 (FKC 2001); Edenbridge Dist Meml Hosp., 1978–91; Lewisham Hosp., 1983–90; Hon. Consultant in Surgery to the Army, 1982–98. External examiner in Surgery to Univs of Newcastle upon Tyne and Cardiff, QUB, TCD and NUI. Royal College of Surgeons: Examr in Pathology, 1970–76; Regl Advr, SE Reg., 1975–80; Mem. Council, 1986–94; Arris and Gale Lectr, 1964, 1965; Erasmus Wilson Lectr, 1972; Haig Gudenian Meml Lectr, 1988; Henry Cohen Meml Lectr, 1994; Lettsomian Lectr, Med. Soc. of London, 1993. Medical Advisor, BBC Television, 1976–92. PPS (Lord's) to the Prime Minister, 1994–97; a Dep. Speaker, H of L, 1994–2004; opposition spokesman on health, 1997–. Member: Central Health Services Council, 1972–74; Standing Medical Adv. Cttee, 1972–82; Management Cttee, King Edward VII Hospital Fund (Chm., R&D Cttee), 1975–80; Council, Metrop. Hosp. Sunday Fund, 1986–91; Council, Imperial Cancer Res. Fund, 1986–94; Exec. Council, British Limbless Ex-Service Men's Assoc., 1991–; Chairman: King's Fund Centre Cttee, 1976–86; Govt Wkg Pty on Artificial Limb and Appliance Centres in England, 1984–86; Vice Chm., SHA for Disablement Services, 1987–91. Hon. Sec., British Soc. of Gastroenterology, 1970–74. President: Soc. of Minimally Invasive Gen. Surgery, 1991–94; Limbless Assoc. (formerly Nat. Assoc. for Limbless Disabled), 1992– (Patron and Hon. Consultant, 1989–); Internat. Wheelchair Fedn, 1991–; Assoc. of Endoscopic Surgeons of GB and Ireland, 1994–98; The Hospital Saving Assoc., 1994–2001; Leprosy Mission, 1996–; REMEDI, 1996–99; Royal Med. Foundn of Epsom Coll., 2001–; Vice-Pres., John Grooms Assoc. for Disabled People, 1990–. Governor-at-Large for England, Bd of Governors, Amer. Coll. of Surgeons, 1982–88. Pres., 1985–94, Chm. Bd of Govs, 1994–2002, Mildmay Mission Hosp.; Chm., Mercy Ships UK, and Vice Chm., Mercy Ships Internat. Governor: Dulwich Coll. Prep. Sch., 1978–2002; James Allen's Girls' Sch., 1994–2004 (Chm., 1998–2004); St Paul's Sch., 2001– (Pres., Old Pauline Club, 2005–07). Trustee, Wolfson Foundn, Dulwich Estate, 1994–; Chm., Dulwich Estate Trustees, 2007– (Chm., Mgt Cttee, 2003–07). Master, Barbers' Co., 1999–2000. FKC 2002. Hon. FDSRCS 2007. Edenbridge Medal for Services to the Community, 1992; George and Thomas Hutcheson's Award, 2000; Great Scot Award, 2002; Dist. Award, Nat. Maritime Assoc., NY, 2003. *Publications:* (ed jtly) Intestinal Absorption in Man, 1975; Talking to Patients, 1982; NHS Data Book, 1984; med. articles, mainly on gastroenterology, rehabilitation and NHS management. *Recreation:* forestry. *Address:* House of Lords, SW1A 0PW. *Clubs:* Royal College of Surgeons Council, Royal Society of Medicine.

McCOLL, (Christopher) Miles; a District Judge (Magistrates' Courts) (formerly Provincial Stipendiary Magistrate), Birmingham, since 1993; *b* 18 April 1946; *s* of John Parr McColl and Lilian McColl (*née* Oddy); *m* 1971, Susan Margaret Rathbone; three *d*. *Educ:* Liverpool Coll. Admitted solicitor, 1971. Articled clerk in private practice, St Helens, 1965–69; trainee, Court Clerk, then Principal Court Clerk, Manchester City Magistrates' Court, 1969–74; Dep. Clerk to Stockport Justices, 1974–78; Clerk to Leigh Justices, 1978–93. Sec., Gtr Manchester Justices' Clerks and Courts Liaison Cttee, 1984–90; Member: Magistrates' Courts Rev. of Procedure Cttee, 1989–91; Magistrates' Courts Consultative Council, 1992–93; Children Act Procedure Adv. Gp, 1989–90; Pres. of Family Division's Cttee, 1990–92; Legal Aid Steering Cttee, 1992; Pre-trial Issues Steering Gp, 1992–93; Legal Cttee, Dist Judges (Magistrates' Cts) (formerly Jt Council of

HM Stipendiary Magistrates), 1997– (Chm., 2000–); Magistrates' Cts Rule Cttee, 2001–; Consultee, Sentencing Adv. Panel, 1998–. Secretary: S Lancs Br., Magistrates' Assoc., 1979–85; British Juvenile and Family Courts' Soc., 1980–81; Justices' Clerks' Society: Mem. Council, 1988–93; Chm., Parly Cttee, 1989; Chm., Professional Purposes Cttee, 1989–93; Pre-trial Issues Nat. Action Manager, 1991–93; Vice-Pres., Duchy of Lancaster Br., 1993. Ed., 1979–87, Jt Ed., 1987–2004, Family Law. *Publications:* Court Teasers: practical situations arising in magistrates' courts, 1978; contrib. to legal jls. *Recreations:* sport, reading, music, British countryside. *Address:* Birmingham Magistrates' Court, Victoria Law Courts, Corporation Street, Birmingham B4 6QA. *T:* (0121) 212 6600.

McCOLL, Sir Colin (Hugh Verel), KCMG 1990 (CMG 1983); HM Diplomatic Service, retired; Head of MI6, 1988–94; *b* 6 Sept. 1932; *s* of Dr Robert McColl and Julie McColl; *m* 1st, 1959, Shirley Curtis (*d* 1983); two *s* two *d*; 2nd, 1985, Sally Morgan; one *s*. *Educ:* Shrewsbury School; The Queen's College, Oxford (BA; Hon. Fellow 1996). Foreign Office, 1956; Third Secretary, Bangkok, 1958, Vientiane, 1960; Second Secretary, FO, 1962; First Secretary, Warsaw, 1966; Consul and First Secretary (Disarmament), Geneva, 1973; Counsellor, FCO, 1977. Adv. Dir, Campbell Lutyens, 1995–; Dir, Securisys Ltd, 2007–. Chairman: Peers Early Educn Trust, 1996–; Pimpernel Trust, 1997–. *Recreations:* music, walks, cycling, tennis, classics.

McCOLL, Isabella G.; Sheriff of Lothian and Borders at Edinburgh, since 2005; *b* 7 Nov. 1952. Admitted: Solicitor, 1975; Advocate, 1993; Sheriff of Tayside, Central and Fife at Dunfermline, 2000–05. *Address:* Sheriff Court House, 27 Chambers Street, Edinburgh EH1 1LB.

McCOLL, Lt Gen. Sir John Chalmers, KCB 2008; CBE 1997; DSO 2002; Deputy Supreme Allied Commander Europe, since 2007; *b* 17 April 1952. Commnd Royal Anglian Regt, 1973; sc, 1984; Staff Officer, Germany; Rifle Co. Comdr, 2nd Bn, 1987; 3rd Royal Tank Regt, 1989; Mem., Directing Staff, Staff Coll., Camberley, 1990; Comdr, 2nd Bn, 1992; COS 1st (UK) Armoured Div., 1995; Comdr, 1st Mechanized Bde, 3rd (UK) Div., 1997–99; ACOS Commitments, HQ Land Comd, 1999–2000; GOC 3rd (UK) Div., 2000–03; Comdt, JSCSC, 2003–04; Sen. British Mil. Rep., Iraq, subseq. Dep. Comdg Gen. Multinational Corps, Iraq, 2004; Comdr, Regl Forces Land Comd, 2004–07. Col Comdt, Queen's Div., 2002–. Gov., Dean Close Sch., Cheltenham, 2006–. Officer, Legion of Merit (USA), 2006. *Address:* c/o Army Personnel Centre, Kentigern House, 65 Brown Street, Glasgow G2 8EX.

McCOLL, Miles; *see* McColl, C. M.

McCOLLUM, Prof. Charles Nevin, MD; FRCS, FRCSE; Professor of Surgery, University of Manchester, since 1989; Hon. Consultant Surgeon, South Manchester University Hospitals NHS Trust; *b* 17 April 1950; *m*; two *d*. *Educ:* Tettenhall Coll.; Millfield Sch.; Medical Sch., Univ. of Birmingham (MB ChB 1972; MD 1981); Cert. Higher Surgical Trng 1981. FRCS 1976; FRCSE 1976. Registrar in Surgery, St James's Univ. Hosp., Leeds, 1976–78; Lectr in Surgery, Univ. of Birmingham, 1978–83; Sen. Lectr, 1983–88, Reader in Surgery, 1988–89, Charing Cross and Westminster Hosp. Med. Sch., London; Hon. Consultant Surgeon, Charing Cross Hosp., 1983–89. Dir, Surgicare Ltd. Examiner in Surgery: Univ. of London; Univ. of Manchester; Univ. of Glasgow. Chm., Exec. Cttee on Clinical Governance, NW Vascular Surgeons; Mem. Cttee, Venous Forum, RSocMed; Treas. and Cttee Mem., Surg. Res. Soc. of GB and Ire; Scientific Cttee, Internat. Soc. on Thrombosis and Haemostasis. Editl Bd, British Jl of Surgery. Hunterian Prof., RCS, 1985. Moynihan Prize, Assoc. of Surgeons of GB and Ire., 1979; Patey Prize, Surg. Res. Soc. of GB and Ire., 1983, 1995. *Publications:* over 40 chapters; over 240 papers on original res. *Recreations:* tennis, country sports, riding, ski-ing, sailing. *Address:* Academic Surgery Unit, Education and Research Centre, University Hospital of South Manchester, Southmoor Road, Manchester M23 9LT. *T:* (0161) 291 5853, *Fax:* (0161) 291 5854; *e-mail:* cnmcc@manchester.ac.uk. *Clubs:* Manchester Tennis and Racquet, Alderley Edge Tennis.

McCOLLUM, Rt Hon. Sir William Paschal, (Rt Hon. Sir Liam McCollum), Kt 1988; PC 1997; a Surveillance Commissioner, since 2004; *b* 13 Jan. 1933; *s* of Patrick McCollum and Mary Ellen McCollum (*née* Strain); *m* 1958, Anne Bernadette Fitzpatrick (CBE 1995); six *s* two *d*. *Educ:* Waterside School; St Columb's Coll., Derry; University College Dublin (BA 1953; LLB 1954). Called to the Bar of N Ireland, 1955; called to Irish Bar, 1963; QC 1971; High Court Judge, NI, 1987–97; a Lord Justice of Appeal, Supreme Court of Judicature, NI, 1997–2004.

McCOMB, Christina Margaret; Director, Partnerships UK plc, since 2006 (non-executive Director, 2004–06); *b* 6 May 1956; *d* of Patrick William John McComb and Margaret McComb; *m* 1980, Peter John Linacre; two *s* one *d*. *Educ:* London Sch. of Econs (BA French and Russian 1978); London Business Sch. (MBA 1989). FCO, 1978–88; Dir, 3i plc, 1989–2003; Dir, Shareholder Exec., DTI, 2003–06. Non-exec. Dir, Engage Mutual Assce, 2005–. Gov., Richmond upon Thames Coll., 1996–. *Recreations:* running, travel. *Address:* Partnerships UK plc, 10 Great George Street, SW1P 3AE. *T:* (020) 7273 8386; *e-mail:* christina.mccomb@partnershipsuk.org.uk.

McCOMB, Leonard William Joseph, RA 1991 (ARA 1987); RE, RWS, RP; painter, sculptor, printmaker, potter, draughtsman; Keeper of the Royal Academy, 1995–98; *b* 3 Aug. 1930; *s* of Archibald and Delia McComb, Glasgow; *m* 1st, 1955, Elizabeth Henstock (marr. diss. 1963); 2nd, 1966, Joan Allwork (*d* 1967); 3rd, 1973, Barbara Eleonora Gittel (marr. diss. 1999). *Educ:* Manchester Art Sch.; Slade Sch. of Fine Art, Univ. of London (Dip. Fine Art, 1960). RE 1994, Hon. RE 1995; RP 2003; Hon. RWS 1996. Teacher at art schools, Bristol, Oxford, RA schools, Slade, Goldsmiths', Sir John Cass, 1960–. *One-man exhibitions include:* Blossoms and Flowers, Coracle Press Gall., London, 1979; Drawings, Paintings and Sculpture, Serpentine Gall., London and tour, 1983; Paintings from the South, Gillian Jason Gall., London, 1989; Drawings and Paintings, Darby Gall., London, 1993; Portraits, NY Studio Sch. Gall.; The Upright Figure, Tate Modern, 2002; Leonard McComb: Drawings, Painting and Sculpture, Talbot Rice Gall., Edinburgh, 2004, Wolsey Art Gall., Ipswich, 2005; Agnew's Gall., 2006; exhibits annually, Royal Acad. of Arts; *group exhibitions include:* Arts Council, 1976, 1980, 1982, 1987; RA, 1977, 1989; Venice, 1980; Whitechapel, 1981; Tate, 1984; Hirshorn Gall., Washington, 1986; Raab Gall., Berlin, 1986; Museum of Modern Art, Brussels, 1987; Gillian Jason Gall., London, 1990, 1991; Kettles Yard Gall., 1994, 1995, 1997; Walker Art Gall., Liverpool, 1995; Aspects Gall., Portsmouth, 1997; Mus. of Modern Art, Dublin, 1997; Flowers East Gall., London, 1998; *work in public collections:* Arts Council; British Council; ICA; Cambridge Univ.; Tate; V&A; BM; Ulster Mus.; Art Galls of Birmingham, Manchester, Swindon, Worcester, Eastbourne, Bedford, Belfast; *commissions* for cos and educnl bodies include paintings, plates, tapestry, plaques. DUniv Oxford Brookes, 2004. Prizes include: Jubilee Prize, RA, 1986; Korn Ferry Award, 1990; Times Watercolour Comp. Prize, 1992, 1993; Nordstern Printmaking Prize, RA, 1992; RWS Prize, 1998; Hugh Casson Drawing Prize, 2006, Turner Watercolour Award and Medal, 2007, RA. *Recreations:* travelling and walking in the countryside.

McCOMBE, Hon. Sir Richard (George Bramwell), Kt 2001; **Hon. Mr Justice McCombe;** a Judge of the High Court of Justice, Queen's Bench Division, since 2001; Presiding Judge, Northern Circuit, 2004–07; *b* 23 Sept. 1952; *s* of Barbara Bramwell McCombe, MA, FCA; *m* 1st (marr. diss.); 2nd, 1986, Carolyn Sara Birrell; one *s* one *d*. *Educ:* Sedbergh Sch.; Downing Coll., Cambridge (MA). Called to the Bar, Lincoln's Inn, 1975, Bencher, 1996; admitted (*ad hoc*) to Bars of Singapore, 1992, Cayman Is, 1993. Second Jun. Counsel to Dir-Gen. of Fair Trading, 1982–87, First Jun. Counsel, 1987–89; QC 1989; an Asst Recorder, 1993–96, Recorder, 1996–2001; Attorney Gen., Duchy of Lancaster, 1996–2001; a Dep. High Ct Judge, 1998–2001. Mem., Senate of Inns of Court and of Bar Council, 1981–86; Chm., Young Barristers' Cttee, Bar Council, 1983–84; Co-opted Mem., Bar Council Cttees, 1986–89; Mem., Gen. Council of the Bar, 1995–97 (Chm., Internat. Relns Cttee, 1997). Head of UK Delegn to Council, Bars and Law Socs of EC, 1996–98. Inspector into affairs of Norton Group PLC, 1991–92 (report, with J. K. Heywood, 1993). Mem., Singapore Acad. of Law, 1992. Pres., Assoc. of Lancastrians in London, 2008. Gov., Sedbergh Sch., 2002–. *Recreations:* cricket, Rugby, travel, flying light aircraft. *Address:* Royal Courts of Justice, Strand, WC2A 2LL. *Clubs:* Garrick, Royal Automobile, MCC; London Scottish Football, Harlequin Football; Lancs CC.

McCOMBIE, John Alexander Fergusson, FRICS; General Manager, Glenrothes Development Corporation, 1993–96; *b* 13 Sept. 1932; *s* of Alexander William McCombie and Charlotte Mary McCombie (*née* Fergusson); *m* 1959, Seana Joy Cameron Scott; two *s* one *d*. *Educ:* Perth Acad.; Coll. of Estate Management. ARICS 1968, FRICS 1982; IRRV 1969. Nat. service, RAF, 1955–57 (MEAF). E Kilbride Develt Corp., 1959–67; Irvine Develt Corp., 1968–70; Glenrothes Develt Corp., 1970–96: Chief Estates Officer, 1970–74; Commercial Dir, 1975–93. Director: Glenrothes Enterprise Trust, 1983–94; Mid-Fife Business Trust, 1994–2003 (Chm., 1997–2003); Age Concern Glenrothes Ltd, 1996– (Chm., 1997–); Leven Valley Develt Trust, 1997–; Wolseley Register, Scottish Gp, 1999–; GIA Properties Ltd, 1999–; Chm., Ecowise Fife Ltd, 1999–2002; Dir and Sec., 1996–, Chm., 1997–, Fife Historic Bldgs Trust. Mem. Bd of Mgt, Glenrothes Coll., 1999–2003. *Recreations:* gardening, golf, philately, reading, veteran cars. *Address:* 13 Carnoustie Gardens, Glenrothes, Fife KY6 2QB. *T:* (01592) 755658. *Club:* Balbirnie Park Golf.

McCONNELL, Bridget Mary; Chief Executive, Culture & Sport Glasgow, since 2007; *b* 28 May 1958; *d* of Robert Rankin McLuckie and Patricia McLuckie (*née* Airlie); *m* 1990, Jack Wilson McConnell, *qv*; one *s* one *d*. *Educ:* St Patrick's Jun. Secondary Sch., Kilsyth; Our Lady's High Sch., Cumbernauld; St Andrew's Univ. (MA Hons 1982); Dundee Coll. of Commerce (DIA 1983); Stirling Univ. (MEd 1992). Curator, Doorstep Gall., Fife Regl Council, 1983–84; Arts Officer, Stirling DC, 1984–88; Principal Arts Officer, Arts in Fife, Fife Regl Council, 1988–96; Service Manager, Community Services/Arts, Libraries, Museums, Fife Council, 1996–98; Dir, Cultural and Leisure Services, 1998–2005, Exec. Dir (Culture and Sport), 2005–07, Glasgow CC. Chair, Scottish Assoc. of Dirs of Leisure Services, 2001–02. Member: Bd, Workshop and Artists Studio Provision Scotland Ltd, 1985–90; Combined Arts Cttee, Scottish Arts Council, 1988–94; Heritage Lottery Fund Cttee for Scotland, 2004–. Chair, Scottish Youth Dance Fest., 1993–96 (Founder Mem., 1988); Co-ordinator, Fourth Internat. Conf. in Adult Educn and the Arts, 1995. Chm., Vocal - Voice of Chief Officers of Cultural, Community and Leisure Services in Scotland, 2002–04. Mem. Bd of Govs, 2001–, Vice Chm., 2007–, RSAMD. *Publications:* (contrib.) Modernising Britain: creative futures, 1997; internat. conf. papers, ed conf. proceedings. *Recreations:* walking, playing the piano, swimming, reading. *Address:* (office) 20 Trongate, Glasgow G1 5ES. *T:* (0141) 287 5058.

McCONNELL, Prof. (Francis) Ian, PhD; FRCPath; Professor of Veterinary Science and Director of Research, Centre for Veterinary Science, Department of Veterinary Medicine (formerly of Clinical Veterinary Medicine), University of Cambridge, since 1994; Professorial Fellow of Darwin College, Cambridge, since 2003; *b* 6 Nov. 1940; *s* of Edward McConnell and Pearl McConnell (*née* Quigley); *m* 1967, Anna Farren; three *s* two *d*. *Educ:* St Aloysius' Coll., Glasgow; Univ. of Glasgow (BVMS 1965); St Catharine's Coll., Cambridge (Scholar; BA 1st Cl. Hons 1967; MA 1970; PhD 1970). MRCVS 1965; MRCPath 1981, FRCPath 1992. Fellow, Clare Hall, Cambridge, 1967–72; Wellcome Trust Res. Fellow, Inst. of Animal Physiology, Cambridge, 1970–72; Sen. Lectr in Immunology, RPMS, Hammersmith Hosp., 1972–76; MRC Sen. Scientist, MRC Lab. of Molecular Biology, Cambridge, 1976–83; Hon. Associate Lectr in Pathology, Dept of Pathology, Univ. of Cambridge, 1976–83; Prof. and Hd of Dept of Vet. Pathology, Univ. of Edinburgh, 1983–94. Chm. Review Bd, TSE Res. Prog., DEFRA, 2000–01; Member: Dirs Adv. Gp, MRC/AFRC Neuropathogenesis Unit, Edinburgh, 1984–89; AFRC Res. Grants Bd, 1984–92; Wellcome Trust Infection and Immunity Grants Bd, 1989–92; Selbourne Cttee of Enquiry into Vet. Res., 1996–98; Wellcome Trust Vet. Medicine Interest Panel, 1998–; Biosecurity Guidance Steering Gp and Expert Assessor for UK Xenotransplantation Interim Regulatory Authy, 1998–; BBSRC Immunology Rev. Gp, 1999; Govt's Spongiform Encephalopathy Adv. Cttee (SEAC), 2000–; HEFCE Panel of Experts for 2001 RAE; Marks & Spencer Adv. Gp on Zoonotic Human Infections, 2001–; TSE Epidemiology Sub-Gp, FSA, 2001–; Working Gp on TSE, Royal Soc. and Acad. of Med. Scis, 2001–02; Adv. Gp on use of Genetically Modified Animals, Royal Soc., 2001–02; Inquiry into Infectious Diseases in Livestock, Royal Soc., 2001–02; Nuffield Council for Bioethics Wkg Party on the Ethics of Res. Involving Animals, 2004–. Member: Governing Body, Inst. for Animal Health, 1988–94; Bd Govs, ICRF, 1986–92. FRSE 1987; FMedSci 1998; FRSocMed 2000. Wellcome Trust Medal for Vet. Res., 1997. *Publications:* (with M. J. Hobart) The Immune System: a course on the molecular and cellular basis of immunity, 1976, 2nd edn (with A. J. Munro and H. Waldmann) 1981; res. papers in immunology, pathology and veterinary sci. *Recreations:* ski-ing, mountain walking, family. *Address:* Centre for Veterinary Science, Department of Veterinary Medicine, University of Cambridge, Madingley Road, Cambridge CB3 0ES. *T:* (01223) 337654, *Fax:* (01223) 337671; *e-mail:* im200@cam.ac.uk. *Club:* Farmers.

McCONNELL, Rt Hon. Jack (Wilson); PC 2001; Member (Lab) Motherwell and Wishaw, Scottish Parliament, since 1999; *b* 30 June 1960; *s* of William Wilson McConnell and Elizabeth McEwan McConnell; *m* 1990, Bridget Mary McLuckie (*see* B. M. McConnell); one *s* one *d*. *Educ:* Arran High Sch., Isle of Arran; Stirling Univ. (BSc 1983; DipEd 1983). Mathematics Teacher, Alloa, 1983–92. Gen. Sec., SLP, 1992–98. Mem. (Lab) Stirling DC, 1984–93 (Treas., 1988–92; Leader, 1990–92). Contested (Lab) Perth and Kinross, 1987. Minister for Finance, 1999–2000, Minister for Educn, Europe and External Affairs, 2000–01, First Minister, 2001–07, Scottish Exec. Special Rep. of the Prime Minister on conflict resolution mechanisms, 2008–. Member: COSLA, 1988–92; Scottish Constitutional Convention, 1990–98. Pres., Gp of EU Regions with Legislative Powers, 2003–04. *Publications:* political articles in newspapers, jls and booklets. *Recreations:* music, gardening, golf, other sports. *Address:* Scottish Parliament, Edinburgh EH99 1SP.

McCONNELL, Prof. James Desmond Caldwell, FRS 1987; Professor of the Physics and Chemistry of Minerals, Department of Earth Sciences, University of Oxford, 1986–95, now Emeritus (Head of Department, 1991–95); Fellow of St Hugh's College, Oxford, 1986–95 (Hon. Fellow, 1995); *b* 3 July 1930; *s* of Samuel D. and Cathleen

McConnell; *m* 1956, Jean Elspeth Ironside; one *s* two *d*. *Educ:* Queen's Univ. of Belfast (BSc, MSc 1952); Univ. of Cambridge (MA 1955; PhD 1956); MA Oxon 1986. Univ. of Cambridge: Demonstrator, 1955; Lectr, 1960; Reader, 1972–82; Churchill College: Fellow, 1962–82; Extraordinary Fellow, 1983–88; Head of Dept of Rock Physics, Schlumberger Cambridge Research, 1983–86. Alex von Humboldt Prize, Alexander von Humboldt Stiftung, Germany, 1996. *Publications:* Principles of Mineral Behaviour (with A. Putnis), 1980, Russian edn, 1983; papers in physics jls and mineralogical jls. *Recreations:* local history, hill walking, singing. *Address:* 19 Gilmerton Court, Cambridge CB2 2HQ. *T:* (01223) 843711.

McCONNELL, John, RDI 1987; FCSD; graphic designer; freelance design practice, McConnell Design, 1963–74 and since 2005; Director, Pentagram Design, 1974–2005; *b* 14 May 1939; *s* of Donald McConnell and Enid McConnell (*née* Dimberline); *m* 1963, Moira Rose Macgregor; one *s* one *d*. *Educ:* Borough Green Secondary Modern School; Maidstone College of Art (NDD). FCSD (FSIAD 1980). Employed in advertising and design, 1959–62; Lectr, Colchester College of Art, 1962–63; co-founder, Face Photosetting, 1968. Design consultant, Boots, 1984–2002; design adviser to John Lewis Partnership, 2001–. Member: Alliance Graphique Internat., 1976; Post Office Stamp Adv. Cttee, 1984; Pres., D&AD, 1986 (President's Award, 1985); served on design competition juries, D&AD. Gold medallist at Biennale, Warsaw; Special Commendation, Prince Phillip Designer's Prize, 2002. *Publications:* (jtly) Living by Design, 1978; (jtly) Ideas on Design, 1986; (jtly) The Compendium, 1993; (ed jtly) Pentagram Book 5, 1999; Editor, Pentagram Papers. *Recreations:* house restoration, cooking. *Address:* (office) 11 Needham Road, W11 2RP. *T:* (020) 7229 3477; (home) 12 Orme Court, W2 4RL.

McCONNELL, (Sir) Robert Shean, (4th Bt *cr* 1900); *S* father, 1987, but does not use the title. *Educ:* Stowe; Queens' Coll., Cambridge (MA Urban Estate Management); Regent St Polytech. (DipTP); Univ. of BC (MSc Community and Regl Planning). FRTPI; MRICS; MCMI. Worked as a trainee surveyor in Belfast and as a town planner in UK, Canada and USA. Lectured in town planning and principles of management at univs in UK and Australia. Mem., Bruce House Appeal Cttee. Governor: South Bank Poly., 1973–75; Tulse Hill Sch., 1976–90; Stockwell Infant Jun. Sch., 1983–88; Norwood Park Primary Sch., 1996–2002; Crown Lane Primary Sch., 2003–. Councillor (Lib Dem) Lambeth BC, 1996–2006. *Publications:* Theories for Planning, 1981; (contrib.) Planning Ethics, ed Hendler, 1995; (contrib.) Housing: the essential foundations, ed Balchin and Rhoden, 1998; articles in professional jls on planning matters. *Recreation:* gardening. *Heir:* *b* James Angus McConnell [*m* Elizabeth Jillian (*née* Harris); two *s* four *d* (incl. twins)].

McCORD, Brig. Mervyn Noel Samuel, CBE 1978 (OBE 1974); MC 1951; retired; *b* 25 Dec. 1929; *s* of late Major G. McCord, MBE and Muriel (*née* King); *m* 1953, Annette Mary, *d* of C. R. W. Thomson; three *s*. *Educ:* Coleraine, NI; RMA Sandhurst. Commissioned Royal Ulster Rifles, 1949; Korea, 1950–51; School of Infantry, 1958–60; Staff Coll., Camberley, 1961–62; DAQMG, Eastern Command, Canada, 1963–65; BM, HQ 6 Infantry Brigade, 1967–69; JSSC, 1969; GSO1, HQNI, 1970–71; CO, 1st Bn The Royal Irish Rangers, 1971–74; Brig. 1975; Commander, Ulster Defence Regt, 1976–78; Dep. Comdr, Eastern Dist, 1978–81; Brig. King's Div., 1981–84. ADC to the Queen, 1981–84. Col, The Royal Irish Rangers, 1985–90 (Dep. Col, 1976–81). Chairman: SHAA, 1986–93; SHAA Retirement Homes plc, 1986–93; Dir, Sussex Housing and Care, 1994–2001. *Recreations:* cricket, athletics, country sports, gardening. *Address:* c/o Drummonds, 49 Charing Cross, SW1A 2DX. *Club:* Army and Navy.

McCORD ADAMS, Rev. Marilyn; *see* Adams.

McCORKELL, George Alexander, CB 2002; management consultant, G. A. McCorkell Ltd, since 2004; Director, Pensions Change Programme, Department for Work and Pensions, 2001–04; *b* 6 Jan. 1944; *s* of Samuel Robert McCorkell and Sarah McCorkell; *m* 1967, Nuala McCarthy; two *s*. *Educ:* Foyle Coll., Londonderry, NI; BA Math. Open, 1978; MSc Information Systems, LSE, 1982. Computer Programmer, MoD, 1967–69; Systems Analyst: Min. of Finance, 1970–74; DHSS, 1974–76; Liaison Officer, CCTA, 1976–79; Department of Health and Social Security, later Department of Social Security: Operational Systems Team Leader, 1979–83; Principal, 1983–86; Sen. Principal, 1987–88; Director: ITSA, 1988–95; Benefits Agency, 1995–99; Chief Exec., ITSA, 1999–2000; Chief Inf. Officer, 2000–01, Hd of Inf. Systems and Commercial Mgt Div., 2001, DSS. *Recreation:* golf. *Address:* 46 West Drive, Thornton-Cleveleys, Lancs FY5 2BH.

MacCORMAC, Sir Richard Cornelius, Kt 2001; CBE 1994; RA 1993; PPRIBA; Chairman, MacCormac Jamieson Prichard Ltd (formerly a Partnership, incorporated in 2002), since 1972; President, Royal Institute of British Architects, 1991–93; *b* 3 Sept. 1938; *s* of late Henry MacCormac, CBE, MD, FRCP and Marion Maud, *d* of B. C. Broomhall, FRCS; *m* 1964, Susan Karin Landen (separated 1983); one *s* (and one *s* decd). *Educ:* Westminster Sch.; Trinity Coll., Cambridge (BA 1962; Hon. Fellow, 2006); University College London (MA 1965). RIBA 1967. Served RN, 1957–59. Proj. Archt, London Bor. of Merton, 1967–69; estabd private practice, 1969. Major works include: Cable & Wireless Coll., Coventry (Royal Fine Art Commn/Sunday Times Bldg of the Year Award, 1994); Garden Quadrangle, St John's Coll., Oxford (Ind. on Sunday Bldg of the Year Award, 1994); Bowra Bldg, Wadham Coll., Oxford; Burrell's Fields, Trinity Coll., Cambridge (RIBA Regl Award, Civic Trust Award, 1997); Ruskin Liby, Lancaster Univ. (Ind. on Sunday Bldg of the Year Award, 1996; Royal Fine Art Commn/BSkyB Bldg of the Year, Univs Winner, 1998; Millennium Product status, Design Council, 1999); Southwark Stn, Jubilee Line Extension (Millennium Bldg of the Year Award, Royal Fine Art Commn Trust/BSkyB, 2000); Wellcome Wing, Science Mus. (Celebrating Construction Achievement, Regl Award for Gtr London, 2000). Taught in Dept of Arch., Cambridge Univ., 1969–75 and 1979–81, Univ. Lectr, 1976–77; Studio Tutor, LSE 1998. Visiting Professor: Univ. of Edinburgh (Dept of Architecture), 1982–85; Hull Univ., 1998–99. Dir, Spitalfields Workspace, 1981–. Chm., Good Design in Housing Awards, RIBA London Region, 1977; Mem., Royal Fine Art Commn, 1983–93; Comr, English Heritage, 1995–98. Royal Academy: Chairman: Architecture Cttee, 1997–; Exhibns Cttee, 1998–; Council, 1998–. Advisor: British Council, 1993–; Urban Task Force, 1998–. Pres., London Forum of Amenity and Civic Socs, 1997–; Trustee, Greenwich Foundn for RNC, 1998–2002. FRSA 1982. *Publications:* articles in Architectural Review and Archts Jl. *Recreations:* sailing, music, reading. *Address:* 9 Heneage Street, E1 5LJ. *T:* (020) 7377 9262.

McCORMACK, John P(atrick); General Motors Corporation, retired 1986; *b* New York, 23 Nov. 1923; *s* of John McCormack and Margaret (*née* Bannon); *m* 1952, Mari Martha Luhrs; two *s*. *Educ:* St John's Univ., Jamaica, NY (Bachelor of Business Admin); NY Univ., NYC (LLB). Joined General Motors, 1949; Gen. Clerk, Accounting Dept, NY, 1949, Sen. Clerk 1950, Sen. Accountant 1952; Asst to Treas., Djakarta Br., 1953; Asst Treas., Karachi Br., 1956; Asst Treas., Gen. Motors South African (Pty) Ltd, Port Elizabeth, 1958, Treas. 1961; Asst Finance Man., Overseas Div., NY, 1966; Treas., subseq. Man. Dir, Gen. Motors Continental, Antwerp, 1968; Finance Man., Adam Opel, 1970, Man. Dir and Chm. Bd, 1974; Gen. Dir, European Ops, Gen. Motors Overseas Corp., 1976; Vice Pres. i/c joint ventures and African ops, 1980; Vice Pres. i/c Latin American and S African Ops, 1983. *Recreations:* golf, photography. *Address:* c/o General Motors Corporation, General Motors Building, Detroit, Michigan 48202, USA; PO Box 1030, Pebble Beach, CA 93953–1030, USA.

McCORMICK, Dr Andrew Graham, FGS; Permanent Secretary, Department of Health, Social Services and Public Safety, Northern Ireland, since 2005; *b* 26 Aug. 1957; *s* of Jackson and Helen McCormick; *m* 1981, Alison Griffiths; one *s*. *Educ:* University Coll., Oxford (BA 1st Cl. Geol. 1978; MA 1989); Queen's Univ., Belfast (PhD Geochem. 1989). Joined NI Civil Service, 1980; Dept of Finance and Personnel, 1980–93; Sen. Civil Service, Dept of Educn, 1993–98; Dep. Sec., 1998–2002; Second Perm. Sec., Dept of Finance and Personnel, 2002–05. FGS 2005. *Publications:* co-author several res. papers in geochemistry. *Recreations:* hill-walking, photography, classical music. *Address:* Department of Health, Social Services and Public Safety, Castle Buildings, Stormont, Belfast BT4 3SQ. *T:* (028) 9052 0559, *Fax:* (028) 9052 0573; *e-mail:* andrew.mccormick@dhsspsni.gov.uk.

McCORMICK, Prof. Barry, PhD; Chief Economist and Director of Analysis, Department of Health, since 2004; *b* 3 Aug. 1949; *s* of Leonard McCormick and Lucy Adelaide McCormick; *m* 1975, Doreen Foti; two *s*. *Educ:* Co. High Sch., Arnold, Nottingham; Manchester Univ. (BA, MA); MIT (PhD 1976). Harkness Fellow, 1972–74, Instructor, 1974–75, MIT; Asst Lectr, Univ. of Cambridge, and Fellow, Robinson Coll., Cambridge, 1976–80; Southampton University: Lectr, 1981–87; Sen. Lectr, 1987–89; Reader, 1989–90; Prof. of Econs, 1991–2002; Dir, Econs and Ops Res., DoH, 2002–04. Sir Norman Chester Vis. Fellow, Nuffield Coll., Oxford, 1989. Academic Consultant to HM Treasury, 2001–02. Mem. Council, REconS, 2003–. *Publications:* (with G. Hughes) Housing Policy and Labour Market Performance, 2000; (jtly) Immigration Policy and the Welfare State, 2002; scientific papers on labour markets and develt policy. *Recreations:* music, supporting Rugby football, walking. *Address:* 36 Greenbank Crescent, Bassett, Southampton SO16 7FQ. *T:* (023) 8076 9486; *e-mail:* barry.mccormick@doh.gsi.gov.uk. *Club:* Oxford and Cambridge.

McCORMICK, Caroline; fundraising advisor, since 2005; Executive Director, International PEN, since 2005; *b* 14 Oct. 1971; *d* of Anthony and Marie McCormick; *m* 2001, Ian Whitaker (separated 2006). *Educ:* Astbury Primary Sch.; Heathfield High Sch.; Univ. of Sheffield (BA Hons Eng. Lit. 1993; MA Contemp. Writing 1995). Res. Officer, Rotherham TEC, 1995–96; Trust Fundraising Manager, RNID, 1996–97; Hd, Trust Fundraising, Nat. Th., 1997–99; Dir, Develt, Coin Street Community Builders, 1999–2001; Hd, Develt, Natural Hist. Mus., 2001–05. Advisor to: Green Belt Movt, 2005–06; Kids, 2005–06; Gaia Foundn, 2006–07; Old Vic Th., 2006–; Scott Prenn, 2007–. Mem. Bd, The Cholmondeleys and The Featherstonehaughs, 2003–05. *Recreations:* reading, writing, thinking, talking, swimming, theatre, film. *Address:* International PEN, Brownlow House, 50–51 High Holborn, WC1V 6ER. *T:* (020) 7405 0338, *Fax:* (020) 7405 0339; *e-mail:* executivedirector@internationalpen.org.uk.

MacCORMICK, Sir (Donald) Neil, Kt 2001; FBA 1986; Regius Professor of Public Law, University of Edinburgh, 1972–2008 (on leave of absence, 1999–2004); *b* 27 May 1941; *yr s* of J. M. MacCormick, MA, LLD (Glasgow) and Margaret I. Miller, MA, BSc (Glasgow); *m* 1st, 1965, Caroline Rona Barr (marr. diss. 1992); three *d*; 2nd, 1992, Flora Margaret Britain (*née* Milne), Edinburgh. *Educ:* High School, Glasgow; Univ. of Glasgow (MA, 1st cl. Philos. and Eng. Lit.); Balliol Coll., Oxford (BA, 1st cl. Jurisprudence; MA); LLD Edinburgh, 1982. Pres., Oxford Union Soc., 1965. Called to the Bar, Inner Temple, 1971. Lecturer, St Andrew's Univ. (Queen's Coll., Dundee), 1965–67; Fellow and Tutor in Jurisprudence, Balliol Coll., Oxford, 1967–72, and CUF Lectr in Law, Oxford Univ., 1968–72; Pro-Proctor, Oxford Univ., 1971–72; University of Edinburgh: Dean of Faculty of Law, 1973–76 and 1985–88; Provost, Faculty Gp of Law and Social Scis, 1993–97; Leverhulme Personal Res. Prof., 1997–99; Vice Principal (Internat.), 1997–99. Visiting Professor: Univ. of Sydney, 1981; Univ. of Uppsala, 1991; Anne Green Vis. Prof., Univ. of Texas, 1990; Higgins Visitor, NW Sch. of Law, Oregon, 1987. Lectures: Corry, Queen's Univ., Kingston, Ont, 1981; Dewey, NY Univ., 1982; Or Emet, Osgoode Hall, 1988; Chorley, LSE, 1992; Hart, Oxford, 1993; Stevenson, Glasgow, 1994. Contested (SNP): Edinburgh North, 1979; Edinburgh, Pentlands, 1983, 1987; Argyll and Bute, 1992, 1997; MEP (SNP) Scotland, 1999–2004. President: Assoc. for Legal and Social Philosophy, 1974–76; Soc. of Public Teachers of Law, 1983–84; Vice-President: Internat. Assoc. for Phil. of Law and Social Phil., 1991–95; RSE, 1991–94. Member: Houghton Cttee on Financial Aid to Political Parties, 1975–76; Broadcasting Council for Scotland, 1985–89; ESRC, 1995–99. Hon. QC 1999. MAE, 1995; For. Mem., Finnish Acad. of Scis, 1994. FRSE 1986. Hon. LLD: Uppsala, 1986; Saarland, 1994; Queen's Univ., Kingston, Ont, 1996; Macerata, 1998; Glasgow, 1999; Hon. DLitt Queen Margaret UC, Edinburgh, 2003. *Publications:* (ed) The Scottish Debate: Essays on Scottish Nationalism, 1970; (ed) Lawyers in their Social Setting, 1976; Legal Reasoning and Legal Theory, 1978; H. L. A. Hart, 1981; Legal Right and Social Democracy: essays in legal and political philosophy, 1982; (with O. Weinberger) Grundlagen des Institutionalistischen Rechtspositivismus, 1985; An Institutional Theory of Law, 1986 (trans. Italian, 1991); (ed jtly) Enlightenment, Right and Revolution, 1989; (ed jtly) Interpreting Statutes, 1991; Interpreting Precedents, 1997; Questioning Sovereignty, 1999; Who's Afraid of a European Constitution, 2005; Rhetoric and the Rule of Law, 2005; Institutions of Law, 2007; contribs to various symposia, jls on law, philosophy and politics. *Recreations:* hill walking, bagpiping, sailing. *Address:* 19 Pentland Terrace, Edinburgh EH10 6HA.

See also I. S. MacD. MacCormick.

McCORMICK, Prof. Francis Patrick, PhD; FRS 1996; Director, Helen Diller Family Comprehensive Cancer Center, and Cancer Research Institute, since 1997, David A. Wood Distinguished Professor of Tumor Biology and Cancer Research, since 1997, and E. Dixon Heise Distinguished Professor in Oncology, University of California, San Francisco; *b* 31 July 1950; *s* of late David and of Jane McCormick; *m* 1979, Judith Anne Demske (marr. diss. 1995). *Educ:* Univ. of Birmingham (BSc 1972); St John's Coll., Cambridge (PhD 1975). Post-doctoral Fellow: SUNY, 1975–78; ICRF, London, 1978–81; Scientist, 1981–89, Vice-Pres., Res., 1989–90, Cetus Corp.; Vice-Pres., Res., Chiron Corp., 1991–92; Founder and Vice-Pres., Res., Onyx Pharmaceuticals, 1992–96. Associate Dean, Sch. of Medicine, UCSF. Mem., Inst. of Medicine, 2005. *Publications:* (jointly): Origins of Human Cancer, 1991; The GTPase Superfamily, 1993; The ras Superfamily of GTPases, 1993. *Recreations:* motor racing, African history. *Address:* Cancer Research Institute, School of Medicine, University of California, San Francisco, CA 94115, USA. *T:* (415) 5021710.

MacCORMICK, Iain Somerled MacDonald; Database and IT Controller, Nationwide Trade Hospitality Ltd, since 2005; *b* 28 Sept. 1939; *er s* of John MacDonald MacCormick, MA, LLB, LLD and Margaret Isobel MacCormick, MA, BSc; *m* 1st, 1964, Micky Trefusis Elsom (marr. diss. 1987); two *s* three *d*; 2nd, 1988, Carole Burnett (*née* Story) (marr. diss. 1991). *Educ:* Glasgow High Sch.; Glasgow Univ. (MA). Queen's Own Lowland Yeomanry, 1957–67 (Captain). Major Account Manager, 1982, Dir Liaison Manager, 1984, BT plc; Trade Consultant, Bartering Co. Ltd, 1993–95; Agent, DataLocator Ltd, 2000. Contested (SNP) Argyll, 1970; MP (SNP) Argyll, Feb. 1974–1979; introduced, as private member's bill, Divorce (Scotland) Act, 1976. Founder Mem., SDP, 1981. Mem., Argyll and Bute District Council, 1979–80. *Recreations:* Rugby football, sailing, local history. *Address:* Flat 2, 10 Bowmont Gardens, Glasgow G12 9LW. *T:* (0141) 339 2334. *Club:* Glasgow Art (Glasgow).

See also Sir D. N. MacCormick.

McCORMICK, Prof. James Stevenson, FRCPI, FRCGP; FFPH; Professor of Community Health, Trinity College Dublin, 1973–91 (Dean of School of Physic, 1974–79); *b* 9 May 1926; *s* of Victor Ormsby McCormick and Margaretta Tate (*née* Stevenson); *m* 1954, Elizabeth Ann Dimond; three *s* one *d*. *Educ:* The Leys Sch., Cambridge; Clare Coll., Cambridge (BA, MB); St Mary's Hospital, W2. Served RAMC, 1960–62; St Mary's Hosp., 1963; general practice, 1964–73. Chairman: Eastern Health Board, 1970–72; Nat. Health Council, 1984–86. Pres., Irish Coll. of General Practitioners, 1986–87. Hon. MCFP 1982. *Publications:* The Doctor—Father Figure or Plumber, 1979; (with P. Skrabanek) Follies and Fallacies in Medicine, 1989; papers, espec. on General Practice and Ischaemic Heart Disease. *Recreation:* open air. *Address:* The Barn, Windgates, Bray, Co. Wicklow, Ireland. *T:* (1) 2874113.

McCORMICK, John, FRSE; Chairman, Scottish Qualifications Authority, since 2004; *b* 24 June 1944; *s* of Joseph and Roseann McCormick; *m* 1973, Jean Frances Gibbons; one *s* one *d*. *Educ:* St Michael's Acad., Irvine; Univ. of Glasgow (MA Modern History with Econ. History 1967; MEd 1970). Teacher, St Gregory's Secondary Sch., Glasgow, 1968–70; Education Officer, BBC School Broadcasting Council, 1970–75; Senior Education Officer, Scotland, 1975–82; Sec., and Head of Information, BBC Scotland, 1982–87; The Sec. of the BBC, 1987–92; Controller of BBC Scotland, 1992–2004. Chm., Edinburgh Internat. Film Fest., 1996–; Mem. Bd, 1997–02, Vice-Chm., 2004–05, Scottish Screen. Non-exec. Dir, Lloyds TSB Scotland, 2005–. Mem. Bd, Skillset, 2002–04. Mem., UK Electoral Commn, 2008–. Member: Glasgow Sci. Centre Charitable Trust, 1999–2005; Bd, Glasgow Sch. of Art, 2004–07; Bd, Scottish Opera, 2005– (Vice-Chm., 2008–). Dir, Irvine Bay Urban Regeneration Co., 2006–. Mem. Court, Univ. of Strathclyde, 1996–2002; Gov., RSAMD, 2003–08. FRTS 1998; FRSE 2003. Hon. DLitt Robert Gordon Univ., Aberdeen, 1997; Hon. LLD Strathclyde, 1999; DUniv: Glasgow, 1999; Paisley, 2003. *Recreation:* newspapers. *Address:* Scottish Qualifications Authority, The Optima Building, 58 Robertson Street, Glasgow G2 8DQ.

McCORMICK, John St Clair, OBE 2002; FRCSE; Medical Director, Dumfries and Galloway Royal Infirmary, 1994–2001; *b* 20 Sept. 1939; *s* of James McCormick and Claire Anne McCormick (*née* Diskett-Heath); *m* 1964, Fiona Helen McLean; two *s*. *Educ:* St Paul's Cathedral Choir Sch.; Sedbergh Sch.; Univ. of Edinburgh (MB ChB 1964). FRCSE 1967. Consultant Surgeon: Dunfermline, 1974–79; Dumfries and Galloway Royal Infirmary, 1979–99. Royal College of Surgeons of Edinburgh: Mem. Council, 1994–2003; Dir of Standards, 1997–2002; Vice Pres., 2000–03. Mem., Clinical Standards Bd, Scotland, 1999–2002. Liveryman, Co. of Wax Chandlers, 1962. *Address:* Ivy Cottage, Kirkpatrickdurham, Castle Douglas DG7 3HG.

MacCORMICK, Sir Neil; *see* MacCormick, Sir D. N.

McCOURT, Arthur David, CBE 2004; Chief Executive, The Highland Council, 1995–2007; *b* 11 July 1947; *s* of Thomas McCourt and Thomasina (*née* Taylor); *m* 1994, Jan McNaughton Smith; two *d*. *Educ:* Bell Baxter High Sch.; Edinburgh Coll. of Art; Heriot-Watt Univ. (BSc Hons Town and Country Planning, 1971). Planner, Northumberland CC, 1974–76; Team Leader, Central Regl Council, 1976–87; Sen. Policy Advr, Stirling DC, 1987–90; Asst Chief Exec., Tayside Regl Council, 1990–95. *Recreations:* keen mountaineer and walker. *Address:* Westcroft, Newtonhill, Lentran, Inverness IV3 8RN.

McCOWAN, Sir David William Cargill, 4th Bt *cr* 1934, of Dalwhat, Dumfries; *b* 28 Feb. 1934; *s* of Sir David James Cargill McCowan, 2nd Bt and of Muriel Emma Annie, *d* of W. C. Willmott; *S* brother, 1998, but his name does not appear on the Official Roll of the Baronetage; *m* 1995, Jean, *d* of A. R. McGhee; one *s* one *d*. *Heir: s* David James Cargill McCowan, *b* 2 June 1975. *Address:* Auchendennan Farm, Alexandria, Dunbartonshire G83 8RB.

McCOWEN, Alexander Duncan, (Alec), CBE 1986 (OBE 1972); actor; *b* 26 May 1925; *s* of late Duncan McCowen and Hon. Mrs McCowen. *Educ:* Skinners' Sch., Tunbridge Wells; RADA, 1941. Repertory: York, Birmingham, etc, 1943–50; Escapade, St James's, 1952; The Matchmaker, Haymarket, 1954; The Count of Clérambard, Garrick, 1955; The Caine Mutiny Court Martial, Hippodrome, 1956; Look Back in Anger, Royal Court, 1956; The Elder Statesman, Cambridge, 1958; Old Vic Seasons, 1959–61: Touchstone, Ford, Richard II, Mercutio, Oberon, Malvolio; Dauphin in St Joan; Algy in The Importance of Being Earnest; Royal Shakespeare Company, 1962–63: Antipholus of Syracuse in The Comedy of Errors; Fool, in King Lear; Father Fontana in The Representative, Aldwych, 1963; Thark, Garrick, 1965; The Cavern, Strand, 1965; After the Rain, Duchess, 1967, Golden Theatre, NY, 1967; Hadrian VII, Birmingham, 1967, Mermaid, 1968, New York, 1969; Hamlet, Birmingham, 1970; The Philanthropist, Royal Court, 1970, NY, 1971; Butley, Criterion, 1972; The Misanthrope, NT, 1973, 1975, NY 1975; Equus, NT, 1973; Pygmalion, Albery, 1974; The Family Dance, Criterion, 1976; Antony and Cleopatra, Prospect Co., 1977; solo performance of St Mark's Gospel, Riverside Studios, Mermaid and Comedy, 1978, Globe, 1981, UK tour, 1985, Half Moon, 1990; Tishoo, Wyndham's, 1979; The Browning Version, and A Harlequinade, NT, 1980; The Portage to San Cristobal of A. H., Mermaid, 1982; Kipling (solo performance), Mermaid, 1984; The Cocktail Party, Phoenix, 1986; Fathers and Sons, Waiting for Godot, NT, 1987; Shakespeare, Cole & Co. (solo performance), UK tour, 1988; The Heiress, Chichester, 1989; Exclusive, Strand, 1989; A Single Man, Greenwich, 1990; Dancing at Lughnasa, NT, 1990, transf. Phoenix, 1991; Preserving Mr Panmure, Chichester, 1991; Caesar and Cleopatra, Greenwich, 1992; Someone Who'll Watch Over Me, Hampstead, 1992, transf. Vaudeville, NY, 1992; The Tempest, Elgar's Rondo, 1993, The Cherry Orchard, 1995, RSC, Stratford; Uncle Vanya, Chichester, 1996; Tom and Clem, Aldwych, 1997; Peter Pan, RNT, 1997; Quartet, Albery, 1999. Dir, Definitely the Bahamas, Orange Tree, Richmond, 1987. Films include: Frenzy, 1971; Travels with My Aunt, 1972; Stevie, 1978; Never Say Never Again, 1983; The Age of Innocence, 1994; Gangs of New York, 2001. TV series, Mr Palfrey of Westminster, 1984. Evening Standard (later Standard) Drama Award, 1968, 1973, 1982; Stage Actor of the Year, Variety Club, 1970. *Publications:* Young Gemini (autobiog.), 1979; Double Bill (autobiog.), 1980; Personal Mark, 1984. *Recreations:* music, gardening.

McCOY, Anthony Peter, MBE 2003; National Hunt jockey; *b* 4 May 1974. Apprentice, Jim Bolgers Stables. Champion Nat. Hunt Jockey, 1995–96, 1996–97, 1997–98, 1998–99, 1999–2000, 2000–01, 2001–02, 2002–03, 2003–04, 2004–05, 2005–06, 2006–07. Winner: Cheltenham Gold Cup on Mr Mulligan, 1997; Champion Hurdle on Make A Stand, 1997, on Brave Inca, 2006; Scottish Grand National; Grand Annual Chase on Edredon Bleu, 1998; King George VI Chase on Best Mate, 2002; Irish Grand National on Butler's Cabin, 2007. Record 1700 Nat. Hunt wins, 2002; record 12 championships, 2007; first jockey to ride 2,000 Nat. Hunt winners in UK, 2004. Hon. Dr QUB, 2002. *Publications:* (with Claude Duval) The Real McCoy: my life so far, 1998; McCoy: the autobiography, 2002. *Recreations:* golf, football. *Address:* Lodge Down, Lambourn Woodlands, Hungerford, Berks RG17 7BJ.

McCOY, Hugh O'Neill, FICS; Chairman, Baltic Exchange, 1998–2000; *b* 9 Feb. 1939; *s* of Hugh O'Neill McCoy and Nora May (*née* Bradley); *m* 1964, Margaret Daphne Corfield; two *s*. *Educ:* Dudley Grammar Sch.; Sir John Cass Coll., Univ. of London (marine qualifications). Man. Dir, Horace Clarkson plc, 1993–98; Chm., H. Clarkson & Co., 1996–98. Vice Chm., Baltic Exchange, 1993–98. Non-executive Director: Gartmore Korea Fund plc, 1993–; Hadley Shipping Co., 1998–; Dir, Benor Tankers Ltd, Hamilton, Bermuda, 1998–. Pres., Inst. Chartered Shipbrokers, 1992–94. Mem., Gen. Council, Lloyd's Register of Shipping. Former Mem. Mgt, London Sea Cadets. Hon. Vice-Pres., Maritime Volunteer Service; Trustee, CAB; Chm. CAB Brentwood. Former LEA Gov., Warley Sch. Freeman, City of London; Liveryman, Co. of Shipwrights. *Recreations:* sailing, long distance walking, French wine. *Address:* 5 Heronway, Hutton, Brentwood, Essex CM13 2LX. *Clubs:* City; Royal Burnham Yacht.

McCRACKEN, Guy; *see* McCracken, P. G.

McCRACKEN, (James) Justin; Chief Executive, Health Protection Agency, since 2008; *b* 28 April 1955; *s* of Dermot and Margaret McCracken; *m* (marr. diss.); two *s* one *d*. *Educ:* Rugby Sch.; Jesus Coll., Oxford (MA Physics). Res. scientist, ICI, 1976–91; Business Manager, ICI Acrylics, 1991–97; Man. Dir, ICI Katalco, 1997–98; Regl Dir, Envmt Agency, 1998–2002; Dep. Dir Gen. (Ops), then Dep. Chief Exec. (Ops), Health and Safety Executive, 2002–08. *Recreation:* sailing. *Address:* Health Protection Agency, 7th Floor, Holborn Gate, 330 High Holborn, WC1V 7PP. *Clubs:* Royal Automobile; Coniston Sailing.

See also R. H. J. McCracken.

McCRACKEN, (Philip) Guy, LVO 2004; Chief Executive, Food Retail, Co-operative Group, since 2005; *b* 25 Nov. 1948; *m* 1972, Frances Elizabeth Addison; one *s* two *d*. *Educ:* Clee Humberston Foundn Sch., Cleethorpes; Nat. Coll. of Food Technology, Reading Univ. (BSc 1st Class Hons Food Technology). Production Manager, Mars, 1972–73; Product Development Manager, Imperial Foods, 1973–75; Marks & Spencer, 1975–2000: Man. Dir, Food Div., 1993–98; Exec. Dir, Internat. Retail and IT, 1999–2000. Chm., Duchy Originals, 1997–2004. *Recreations:* golf, ski-ing, food, travel. *Address:* Co-operative Group, New Century House, Manchester M60 4ES.

McCRACKEN, Robert Henry Joy; QC 2003; *b* 15 March 1950; *s* of Dermot McCracken, FRCP and Margaret McCracken, MB BCh. *Educ:* Rugby Sch.; Worcester Coll., Oxford (MA). Called to the Bar, Inner Temple, 1973; barrister practising in public, envmtl and planning law. Mem., Animal Procedures Cttee advising Home Sec., 1999–2003. Chm., UK Envmtl Law Assoc., 1995–97; Sec., Planning and Envmtl Bar Assoc., 1992–94. *Publications:* (jtly) Statutory Nuisance, 2000; contribs to Judicial Rev., Jl Planning and Envmtl Law. *Recreations:* painting, natural science, fell-walking. *Address:* 2 Harcourt Chambers, Francis Taylor Building, Inner Temple, EC4Y 7BY; *e-mail:* RobertMcCracken@compuserve.com. *Clubs:* Reform; Cyclists Touring, Coniston Sailing.

See also J. J. McCracken.

McCREA, Ian; Member (DemU) Mid-Ulster, Northern Ireland Assembly, since 2007; *b* 12 June 1976; *s* of Dr (Robert Thomas) William McCrea, *qv*; *m* 1998, Wanita Cardwell; two *s* one *d*. *Educ:* Magherafelt Controlled Primary Sch.; Rainey Endowed Grammar Sch.; NE Inst. for Further and Higher Educn, Magherafelt. Unipork, Cookstown, 1996–97; alarm and security installation engr, 1997–99; PA to Dr William McCrea, MP, 1997–2007. Mem. (DemU) Cookstown DC, 2001– (Vice Chm., 2005–06; Chm., 2007–). Dir, Cookstown Local Strategy Partnership, 2001–; Chm., Cookstown Dist Policing Partnership, 2006–07. *Recreation:* Chm., Coagh United FC Supporters Club. *Address:* Democratic Unionist Party Office, 10 Highfield Road, Magherafelt, Northern Ireland BT45 5JD. *T:* (028) 7963 2664, *Fax:* (028) 7930 0701; *e-mail:* office@ianmccrea.com. Cookstown Democratic Unionist Party Office, 34 Fairhill Road, Cookstown, Co. Tyrone, Northern Ireland BT80 8AG. *T:* (028) 8676 4952; *e-mail:* cookstown@ianmccrea.com.

McCREA, Rev. Dr (Robert Thomas) William; MP (DemU) Antrim South, Sept. 2000–2001 and since 2005; Member (DemU) Antrim South, Northern Ireland Assembly, since 2007 (Ulster Mid, 1998–2007); Minister, Magherafelt Free Presbyterian Church of Ulster, since 1969; *b* 6 Aug. 1948; *s* of Robert T. and Sarah J. McCrea; *m* 1971, Anne Shirley McKnight; two *s* three *d*. *Educ:* Cookstown Grammar Sch.; Theol Coll., Free Presbyterian Church of Ulster. Civil servant, 1966; Free Presbyterian Minister of the Gospel, 1967–. Dist Councillor, Magherafelt, 1973–; Mem. (DemU) Mid Ulster, NI Assembly, 1982–86. MP (DemU) Mid Ulster, 1983–97 (resigned seat Dec. 1985 in protest against Anglo-Irish Agreement; re-elected Jan. 1986); contested (DemU): Mid Ulster, 1997; Antrim S, 2001. Dir, Daybreak Recording Co., 1981–. Gospel singer and recording artist; Silver, Gold and Platinum Discs for record sales. Hon. DD Marietta Bible Coll., Ohio, 1989. *Publication:* In His Pathway—the story of the Reverend William McCrea, 1980. *Recreations:* music, horse riding. *Address:* House of Commons, SW1A 0AA. *T:* (020) 7219 8525.

See also I. McCrea.

McCREADIE, Robert Anderson; QC (Scot.) 2003; PhD; Sheriff of Tayside Central and Fife at Perth, since 2004; *b* 17 Aug. 1948; *s* of John Walker McCreadie and Jean J. M. McCreadie (*née* Ramsay). *Educ:* Univ. of Edinburgh (LLB Hons); Christ's Coll., Cambridge (PhD 1981). Lecturer in Law: Univ. of Dundee, 1974–78; Univ. of Edinburgh, 1978–92; called to Scottish Bar, 1992; Standing Junior Counsel: Dept of Transport, 1994–95; SHHD/Justice Dept, 1995–2000; Advocate Depute, 2000–02; Standing Jun. Counsel, Advocate Gen. for Scotland, 2002–03; pt-time Sheriff, 2003–04. *Recreations:* Scottish history, music, walking. *Address:* 40 Marchmont Crescent, Edinburgh EH9 1HG. *T:* (0131) 667 1383.

McCREADY, Prof. (Victor) Ralph, DSc; FRCR, FRCP; Hon. Consultant: Hammersmith Hospital, since 2004; Brighton and Sussex University Hospitals NHS Trust, since 2007; Visiting Worker, Institute of Cancer Research, since 2002; *b* 17 Oct. 1935; *s* of Ernest and Mabel McCready; *m* 1964, Susan Margaret Mellor; two *d*. *Educ:* Ballyclare High Sch., NI; Queen's Univ., Belfast (MB BCh, BAO, BSc, DSc); Guy's Hosp., London Univ. (MSc 1964). MRCP 1974, FRCP 1994; FRCR 1975. Mem., Scientific Staff, Inst. of Cancer Res., London, 1964–74, 1998–2002; Consultant, Royal Marsden Hosp., 1974–98; Hon. Consultant, Royal Marsden NHS Trust, 1998–2002. Civilian Consultant, RN, 1993–. Hon. Mem., Japanese Radiological Soc., 2002. Hon. FFR, RCSI, 1992. Barclay Prize, British Inst. of Radiology, 1973. *Publications:* med. articles, books and contribs to books on nuclear medicine, ultrasound and magnetic resonance. *Recreations:*

aviation, music. *Address:* Medical Physics Department, Royal Marsden Hospital, Sutton, Surrey SM2 5PT. *Club:* Royal Automobile.

McCREATH, Alistair William; His Honour Judge McCreath; a Circuit Judge, since 1996; Resident Judge, Worcester Crown Court, since 2006; *b* 6 June 1948; *s* of late James McCreath and Ruth Mary McCreath (*née* Kellar); *m* 1976, Julia Faith Clark; one *s* one *d*. *Educ:* St Bees Sch.; Univ. of Keele (BA Hons). Called to the Bar, Inner Temple, 1972; in practice at the Bar, 1973–96; Asst Recorder, 1986–90; Recorder, 1990–96. Hon. Recorder of Worcester, 2007–. Course Dir, Criminal Continuation (Judicial Studies Bd), 2007–. *Recreations:* golf, walking, reading, playing on computers. *Address:* Worcester Combined Court Centre, The Shire Hall, Foregate Street, Worcester WR1 1EQ. *Clubs:* Royal Troon Golf, Blackwell Golf.

McCREDIE, Ian Forbes, CMG 2004; OBE 1984; Head, Global Security, Royal Dutch Shell, since 2004; *b* 28 Dec. 1950; *s* of John and Diana McCredie; *m* 1998, Katherine Heiny; two *s*, and one *s* one *d* from previous marriage. *Educ:* Churchill Coll., Cambridge (BA 1972). Entered FCO, 1975; Third Sec., 1975; Third, later Second Sec. (Econ.), Lusaka, 1976–79; FCO, 1979–81; First Secretary: (Econ./Commercial), Tehran, 1981–83; FCO, 1983–85; Copenhagen, 1985–89; FCO, 1989–92; Counsellor: UKMIS, NY, 1992–97; FCO, 1997–99; Washington, 1999–2004. *Recreations:* squash, politics, cigars. *Club:* University.

McCREESH, Paul; Founder, Director and Conductor, Gabrieli Consort & Players; Director, Wratislavia Cantans festival, since 2006; *b* 24 May 1960; *s* of Patrick Michael McCreesh and Valerie McCreesh (*née* Connors); *m* 1983, Susan Hemington Jones; one *s* one *d*. *Educ:* Manchester Univ. (MusB 1981). Freelance conductor; founded Gabrieli Consort & Players, internat. ensemble specialising in renaissance and baroque music, 1982. Guest conductor of modern orchs incl. Budapest Fest., Gothenburg Symphony, Orch. Philharmonique de Radio France, Orch. di Santa Cecilia di Roma, Basel Chamber Orch., Zurich Tonhalle and Nederlands Philharmonic Orch. Numerous recordings and internat. recording awards. Hon. LLD Loughborough, 2005. *Recreations:* countryside, walking, children. *Address:* c/o Intermusica Artists' Management Ltd, 16 Duncan Terrace, N1 8BZ. *T:* (020) 7278 5455.

McCREEVY, Charlie; Member, European Commission, since 2004; *b* 30 Sept. 1949; *s* of Charles McCreevy and Eileen Mills. *Educ:* University Coll., Dublin (BComm). FCA 1973. Partner, Tynan, Dillon and Co., Chartered Accountants, 1974–92. Mem., Kildare CC, 1979–85. TD (FF) Kildare, 1977–2004; Minister for: Social Welfare, 1992–93; Tourism and Trade, 1993–94; frontbench spokesperson on Finance, 1995–97; Minister for Finance, Republic of Ireland, 1997–2004. *Recreations:* golf, horse-racing, Gaelic Athletic Association. *Address:* European Commission, Rue de la Loi 200, 1049 Brussels, Belgium.

McCRICKARD, Donald Cecil, FCIB; Chairman, London Town plc, 1995–2003; Group Chief Executive, TSB Group plc, 1990–92; Chief Executive, TSB Bank plc, 1989–92; *b* 25 Dec. 1936; *s* of late Peter McCrickard and Gladys Mary McCrickard; *m* 1st, 1960, Stella May, JP (marr. diss.), *d* of Walter Edward Buttle, RN retd; two *d*; 2nd, 1991, Angela Victoria Biddulph, JP, *d* of late Robert Biddulph Mitchell and of Mary Buckley Mitchell. *Educ:* Hove Grammar Sch.; LSE; Univ. of Malaya. Financial, marketing and gen. management appts to 1975; Chief Exec., American Express Co. UK, 1975, American Express Co. Asia, Pacific, Australia, 1980; Dir, American Express Internat. Inc., 1978–83; Man. Dir, UDT Holdings, later TSB Commercial Holdings, 1983; Chairman: Swan National, 1983; UDT Bank, 1983; Dir, and Dep. Group Man. Dir, 1987, Chief Exec., Banking, 1988, TSB Group; Chm., Hill Samuel Bank, 1991–92. Non-executive Chairman: TM Group Holdings Ltd, 1996–98; Verdandi Ltd (formerly SGi Gp), 1998–2006; Digitalbrain plc, 1999–2004; non-executive Director: Carlisle Gp, 1993–96; Nat. Counties Building Soc., 1995–2007 (Vice Chm., 2001–); Brit Insurance Hldgs PLC (formerly Benfield & Rea Investment Trust), 1995–2006; Allied London Properties, 1997–2000. Chm., Barnet Enterprise Trust, 1985–88. Trustee: Crimestoppers (formerly Community Action) Trust, 1991–2004; Industry in Educn, 1993–2005. *Recreations:* golf, photography, theatre, writing, restaurants, the countryside. *Club:* Royal Automobile.

McCRIRRICK, (Thomas) Bryce, CBE 1987; FREng; FIET; Director of Engineering, BBC, 1978–87; *b* 19 July 1927; *s* of late Alexander McCrirrick and Janet McCrirrick (*née* Tweedie); *m* 1953, Margaret Phyllis Yates; two *s* (and one *s* decd). *Educ:* Galashiels Academy; Heriot Watt Coll., Edinburgh; Regent Street Polytechnic, London. BBC Radio, Studio Centres in Edinburgh, Glasgow and London, 1943–46; served RAF, 1946–49; BBC Television, 1949; Engineer-in-Charge Television Studios, 1963; Head of Engineering Television Recording, and of Studio Planning and Installation Dept, 1969; Chief Engineer, Radio Broadcasting, 1970; Asst Dir of Engrg, 1971; Dep. Dir of Engrg, 1976. Technical Assessor, Investigation into Clapham Junction Rly Accident, 1989. Pres., Soc. of Electronic and Radio Technicians, 1981–85 (Vice-Pres., 1979–80); Vice-Pres., IERE, 1985–88; Pres., IEE, 1988–89 (Dep. Pres., 1986–88, Vice-Pres., 1982–86; Hon. FIEE 1995); Mem. Council, Fellowship of Engrg, 1989–92. Gov., Imperial Coll., 1985–99; Mem. Court, Heriot-Watt Univ., 1991–94; Mem. Senate, London Univ., 1992–94. FRTS 1980; FREng (FEng 1981); FBKSTS 1982; FSMPTE 1989; Hon. FIET (Hon. FIEE 1995). Hon. DSc Heriot Watt, 1987. *Recreation:* theatre. *Address:* Surrey Place, Coach House Gardens, Fleet, Hants GU51 4QX. *T:* (01252) 623422.

McCRONE, Prof. David, FBA 2005; FRSE; Professor of Sociology, since 1996, and Co-Director, Institute of Governance, since 1997, University of Edinburgh; *b* 8 Oct. 1945; *s* of Alexander McCrone and Mary McCrone; partner, Prof. Janette Webb. *Educ:* Univ. of Edinburgh (MA Hons 1969, MSc 1971). Lectr, 1975–85, Sen. Lectr, 1985–92, Reader, 1992–96, in Sociology, Univ. of Edinburgh. FRSE 2002. *Publications:* (jtly) Property and Power in a City, 1989; Understanding Scotland, 1992, 2nd edn 2001; (jtly) Scotland: the brand, 1995; The Sociology of Nationalism, 1998; (jtly) Living in Scotland: social and economic change since 1980, 2004. *Recreations:* walking, reading. *Address:* Institute of Governance, University of Edinburgh, Chisholm House, High School Yards, Edinburgh EH1 1LZ. *T:* (0131) 650 2459; *e-mail:* d.mccrone@ed.ac.uk.

McCRONE, Robert Gavin Loudon, CB 1983; FRSE 1983; General Secretary, Royal Society of Edinburgh, 2005–07 (Vice-President, 2002–05); Hon. Fellow, Europa Institute, University of Edinburgh, since 1992; *b* 2 Feb. 1933; *s* of Robert Osborne Orr McCrone and Laura Margaret McCrone; *m* 1st, 1959, Alexandra Bruce Waddell (*d* 1998); two *s* one *d*; 2nd, 2000, Olive Pettigrew Moon (*née* McNaught); two step *d*. *Educ:* St Catharine's Coll., Cambridge (Economics Tripos; MA); University Coll. of Wales, Aberystwyth (Milk Marketing Bd Research Schol. in agricl economics; MSc 1959); Univ. of Glasgow (PhD 1964). Fisons Ltd, 1959–60; Lectr in Applied Economics, Glasgow Univ., 1960–65; Economic Consultant to UNESCO, 1964; Fellow of Brasenose Coll., Oxford, 1965–72; Mem. NEDC Working Party on Agricl Policy, 1967–68; Economic Adviser to House of Commons Select Cttee on Scottish Affairs, 1969–70; Special Economic Adviser to Sec. of State for Local Govt and Regional Planning, 1970; Head of Economics and Statistics Unit, 1970–72, Under-Sec. for Regional Develt, 1972–80, Chief Econ. Advr, 1972–92, Scottish Office; Secretary: Industry Dept for Scotland, 1980–87; Scottish Office Envmt Dept (formerly Scottish Develt Dept), 1987–92. Prof. of Economics, Centre for Housing Res., Glasgow Univ., 1992–94; Vis. Prof., Dept of Business Studies, later Mgt Sch., Edinburgh Univ., 1994–2005. Member: Adv. Cttee, Constitution Unit (formerly Inquiry into Implementation of Constitutional Reform), 1995–97; Steering Gp for Review of Resource Allocation for NHS in Scotland (Arbuthnott Cttee), 1997–2000. Chm., Cttee of Inquiry into Professional Conditions of Service for Teachers' in Scotland, 1999–2000; Vice Chairman: RSE Inquiry into Foot and Mouth Disease, 2001–02; RSE Inquiry into Future of Scottish Fishing Industry, 2003–04; Chm., RSE Inquiry on the Future of Hills and Island Areas in Scotland, 2007–08. Comr, Parly Boundary Commn for Scotland, 1999–2006. Deputy Chairman: Royal Infirmary of Edinburgh NHS Trust, 1994–99; Lothian Univs Hosps NHS Trust, 1999–2001. Member Council: Royal Economic Soc., 1977–82; Scottish Economic Soc., 1982–91; ESRC, 1986–89. Member, Board: Scottish Opera, 1992–98; Queen's Hall, Edinburgh, 1999–2002; Trustee: Scottish Opera Endowment Trust, 1999–; Scottish Housing Assocs Charitable Trust, 1992–98. Hon. FRSGS 1993. Hon. LLD Glasgow 1986. *Publications:* The Economics of Subsidising Agriculture, 1962; Scotland's Economic Progress 1951–60, 1963; Regional Policy in Britain, 1969; Scotland's Future, 1969; (with Mark Stephens) Housing Policy in Britain and Europe, 1995; European Monetary Union and Regional Development, 1997; contribs to various economic jls. *Recreations:* music, walking. *Address:* 11A Lauder Road, Edinburgh EH9 2EN. *T:* (0131) 667 4766. *Club:* New (Edinburgh).

McCRORIE, Linda Esther, (Mrs Peter McCrorie); *see* Gray, L. E.

McCRUDDEN, Prof. (John) Christopher, DPhil; FBA 2008; Professor of Human Rights Law, University of Oxford, since 1999; Fellow, Lincoln College, Oxford, since 1980; *b* 29 Jan. 1952; *s* of Gerard and Theodora McCrudden; *m* 1990, Caroline Mary Pannell; one *s* one *d*. *Educ:* Queen's Univ., Belfast (LLB 1974); Yale Univ. (Harkness Fellow, 1974–76; LLM 1975); MA 1980, DPhil 1981, Oxon. Called to the Bar: Gray's Inn, 1996; NI, 2006. University of Oxford: Lectr in Law, 1976–77, Jun. Res. Fellow, 1976–80, Balliol Coll.; CUF Lectr, 1980–96; Reader in Law, 1996–99. Visiting Professor: QUB, 1994–98; Univ. of Texas Sch. of Law, 1996; Univ. of Haifa, 1996; Univ. of Mich Law Sch., 1998–; Vis. Sen. Fellow, PSI, 1987–89; Vis. Fellow and Lectr, Yale Law Sch., 1986. Member: Sec. of State for NI's Standing Adv. Commn on Human Rights, 1984–88; Expert Network on Application of Equality Directives, EC, 1986–; NI Procurement Bd, 2003–08; Specialist Advr, NI Affairs Select Cttee, H of C, 1999; Mem., Public Procurement Implementation Gp, NI Exec., 2001. Mem., Adv. Cttee, ESRC Res. Unit on Ethnic Relns, 1982–85. Jt Ed., Law in Context series, 1978–; Member, Editorial Board: Oxford Jl Legal Studies, 1983–; Internat. Jl Discrimination and the Law, 1996–; Jl Internat. Econ. Law, 1998–; European Public Law, 2003–. Hon. LLD QUB, 2006. Cert. of Merit, Amer. Soc. of Internat. Law, 2008. *Publications:* (with R. Baldwin) Regulation and Public Law, 1987; (ed) Women, Employment and European Community Law, 1988; (ed) Fair Employment Handbook, 1990, 3rd edn 1995; (jtly) Racial Justice at Work: the enforcement of the Race Relations Act 1976 in employment, 1991; Equality in Law between Men and Women in the European Community: United Kingdom, 1994; (ed with G. Chambers) Individual Rights and the Law in Britain, 1994; (ed) Equality between Women and Men in Social Security, 1994; (ed) Regulation and Deregulation, 1998; Buying Social Justice, 2007. *Recreation:* my family. *Address:* Lincoln College, Oxford OX1 3DR. *T:* (01865) 279772.

McCRUM, (John) Robert; writer; Literary Editor, The Observer, since 1996; *b* 7 July 1953; *s* of late Michael William McCrum, CBE, and of Christine Mary Kathleen (*née* fforde); *m* 1st, 1979, Olivia Timbs (marr. diss. 1984); 2nd, 1995, Sarah Lyall; two *d*. *Educ:* Sherborne Sch.; Corpus Christi Coll., Cambridge (Schol.; BA 1st Cl. Hons Hist.; MA); Univ. of Pennsylvania (Thouron Fellow; MA). House Reader, Chatto & Windus, 1977–79; Faber and Faber Ltd: Editl Dir, 1979–89; Editor-in-Chief, 1990–96. Scriptwriter and co-producer, The Story of English, BBC TV, 1980–86. Patron, Different Strokes, 2000–. By-Fellow, Churchill Coll., Cambridge, 2001–03. Tony Godwin Prize, 1979; Peabody Award, 1986; Emmy Award, 1987. *Publications:* In the Secret State, 1980; A Loss of Heart, 1982; The Fabulous Englishman, 1984; The Story of English, 1986; The World is a Banana, 1988; Mainland, 1991; The Psychological Moment, 1993; Suspicion, 1996; My Year Off, 1998; Wodehouse: a life, 2004. *Recreation:* physiotherapy. *Address:* 12 Eldon Road, W8 5PU. *Club:* Groucho.

McCUBBIN, Henry Bell; Joint Editor, Scottish Left Review, since 2000; *b* 15 July 1942; *s* of Henry McCubbin and Agnes (*née* Rankine); *m* 1967, Katie M. Campbell; three *d*. *Educ:* Allan Glen's Sch., Glasgow; BA Hons Open Univ. Film Cameraman: BBC TV, 1960–77; Grampian TV, 1977–89. MEP (Lab) Scotland NE, 1989–94; contested (Lab) Scotland NE, Eur. Parly elecns, 1994. Head, European Office, Assoc. of Gtr Manchester Authorities, 1996–99. *Recreations:* theatre, hill walking, politics. *Address:* *e-mail:* editorial@scottishleftreview.org.

McCULLAGH, Keith Graham, PhD; President and Chief Executive, Santaris Pharma A/S, since 2004; *b* 30 Nov. 1943; *s* of John Charles McCullagh and Kathleen Doreen McCullagh (*née* Walton); *m* 1967, Jean Elizabeth Milne; one *s* two *d*. *Educ:* Latymer Upper Sch.; Univ. of Bristol (BVSc); St John's Coll., Cambridge (PhD 1970). MRCVS 1965. Royal Soc. Leverhulme Schol., 1966; Medical Research Council: Mem., External Staff, Uganda, 1967; Mem., Scientific Staff, Dunn Nutrition Lab., Cambridge, 1967–69; Cleveland Clinic Foundation, USA: Res. Fellow, 1970; Mem., Res. Staff, 1971–73; Lectr in Veterinary Pathol., Univ. of Bristol, 1974–80; G. D. Searle & Co. Ltd: Dir of Biol., 1980–84; Dir of Res., 1984–86; Founder and Chief Exec., British Biotech plc, 1986–98. Vice Chm., European Assoc. of BioIndustries, 1996–98; Chairman: Phenomenon Gp plc, 1999–; Pharmacy2U Ltd, 2000–; McCullagh Associates Ltd, 2003–; Action Medical Research, 2007–; Director: MVM LLP (formerly Medical Ventures Management Ltd), 1998–2005 (Mem., Investment Cttee, 2006–); Isis Innovation Ltd, 1998–99. Chm., HM Treasury Wkg Gp on Financing of High Technol. Businesses, 1998; Mem., DTI Adv. Gp on Competitiveness and the Single Mkt, 1997–98. Chm., BioIndustry Assoc., 1993–96. Chm., British Admiral's Cup Sailing Team, 1999. *Publications:* numerous scientific articles and reviews in learned jls. *Recreations:* sailing, skiing, golf. *Address:* Cuddington Mill, Cuddington, Bucks HP18 0BP. *Clubs:* Royal Automobile; Royal Corinthian Yacht (Cowes and Burnham); Racquets Squash (Thame).

McCULLAGH, Prof. Peter, PhD; FRS 1994; John D. MacArthur Distinguished Service Professor, Department of Statistics, University of Chicago, since 2003; *b* N Ireland, 8 Jan. 1952; *s* of John A. McCullagh and Rita McCullagh (*née* Devlin); *m* 1977, Rosa Bogues; one *s* three *d*. *Educ:* Univ. of Birmingham (BSc 1974); Imperial Coll., London, (PhD 1977). Vis. Asst Prof., Univ. of Chicago, 1977–79; Lectr, Imperial Coll., London Univ., 1979–85; Prof., 1985–, Chm., 1992–98, Dept of Stats, Univ. of Chicago. FIMS, FAAAS. President's Award, Cttee of Presidents of Statistical Socs of N Amer., 1990. *Publications:* Generalized Linear Models (with J. A. Nelder), 1983, 2nd edn 1989; Tensor Methods in Statistics, 1987. *Recreation:* swimming. *Address:* Department of Statistics, University of Chicago, 5734 South University Avenue, Chicago, IL 60637, USA. *T:* (312) 7028340.

McCULLIN, Donald, CBE 1993; freelance photojournalist; *b* 9 Oct. 1935; *m* 1959 (marr. diss. 1987); two *s* one *d*; one *s* by Laraine Ashton; *m* 1995, Marilyn Bridges; *m* 2002, Catherine, *er d* of Sir Patrick Fairweather, *qv*; one *s*. *Educ:* Tollington Park Secondary Sch., Morden; Hammersmith Jun. Art Sch. Started work at 15 yrs of age after death of father; National Service (RAF), 1954–56; first pictures published by The Observer, 1958; thereafter began photographic career; worked for The Sunday Times for 18 yrs, covering wars, revolutions and travel stories. Hon. FRPS 1977. DUniv: Bradford, 1993; Open, 1994. *Publications:* Destruction Business, 1971; Is Anyone Taking Any Notice, 1971; The Palestinians, 1979; Homecoming, 1979; Hearts of Darkness, 1980; Battle Beirut, a City in Crisis, 1983; Perspectives, 1987; Skulduggery, 1987; Open Skies, 1989; (with Lewis Chester) Unreasonable Behaviour (autobiog.), 1990; Sleeping with Ghosts, 1995; India, 1999; Don McCullin, 2001; Cold Heaven: Don McCullin on AIDS in Africa, 2001; In England, 2007. *Recreations:* protecting the English countryside, travelling the world, blackberry picking.

McCULLOCH, Andrew Grant; Sheriff of Tayside, Central and Fife at Dundee, since 2004; President, Law Society of Scotland, 1996–97; *b* 10 Feb. 1952; *s* of late Frederick McCulloch and of Jean McCulloch (later McGregor); *m* 1988, Mave Curran; one *s* one *d*. *Educ:* Glasgow Acad.; Edinburgh Univ. (LLB, BSc SocSci). Joined Drummond & Co., Edinburgh, 1974; Partner, Drummond Miller, WS, 1979–2004; Solicitor-Advocate, 1994. Part-time Sheriff, 2003–04. *Recreations:* golf, opera, wine. *Address:* Westerlea, Essex Road, Edinburgh EH4 6LQ. *T:* (0131) 339 2705.

McCULLOCH, Dr Andrew William; Chief Executive, Mental Health Foundation, since 2002; *b* 21 April 1956; *s* of Ian Robert McCulloch and Marguerite Elizabeth McCulloch; partner, Louise Villeneau; one *s* one *d*. *Educ:* Eltham Coll.; Peterhouse, Cambridge (BA Natural Scis 1978); Univ. of Southampton (PhD Psychol. 1986). Principal, 1987–92, Asst Sec., 1992–96, DoH; Dir of Policy, Sainsbury Centre for Mental Health, 1996–2001. Non-exec. Dir, Haringey Healthcare NHS Trust, 1998–2001. Chair, Mental Health Media, 1999–2002. Member: Workforce Numbers Adv. Bd, DoH, 2002–04; Ministerial Adv. Gp on Vulnerable Children, 2004–05; Ministerial Adv. Gp on Mental Health, 2007–; Mental Health Advr to NESTA, 2007–; Expert Advr to Council of Europe, 2007–. *Publications:* (contrib.) Developing a National Mental Health Policy (Maudsley monograph), 2002; numerous articles on gerontology and on mental health. *Recreations:* birdwatching, reading, wine, cinema, Italy, dining, art. *Address:* Mental Health Foundation, Sea Containers House, 20 Upper Ground, SE1 9QB; *e-mail:* amcculloch@mhf.org.uk.

MacCULLOCH, Prof. Diarmaid Ninian John, DD; FBA 2001; FSA, FRHistS; Professor of the History of the Church, University of Oxford, since 1997; Fellow, St Cross College, Oxford, since 1995; *b* 31 Oct. 1951; *s* of Rev. Nigel MacCulloch and Jennie (*née* Chappell). *Educ:* Stowmarket Grammar Sch.; Churchill Coll., Cambridge (MA, PhD 1977); Univ. of Liverpool (Dip. Archive Admin 1973); DipTh Oxon 1987; DD Oxon 2001. FSA 1978; FRHistS 1981. Jun. Res. Fellow, Churchill Coll., Cambridge, 1976–78; Tutor in Hist., Librarian and Archivist, Wesley Coll., Bristol, 1978–90; Lectr, Faculty of Theol., Oxford Univ., 1995–; Sen. Tutor, St Cross Coll., Oxford, 1996–2000. Pres., C of E Record Soc., 2001–. Co-Ed., Jl Ecclesiastical Hist., 1995–. Hon. LittD UEA, 2003. *Publications:* Suffolk and the Tudors: politics and religion in an English county (Whitfield Prize, RHistS), 1986; Groundwork of Christian History, 1987, rev. edn 1994; The Later Reformation in England 1547–1603, 1990, rev. edn 2000; (ed) The Reign of Henry VIII: politics, policy and piety, 1995; Thomas Cranmer: a life (Whitbread Biography Prize, Duff Cooper Prize, James Tait Black Prize), 1996; Tudor Church Militant: Edward VI and the Protestant Reformation, 1999; Reformation: Europe's house divided 1490–1700 (Wolfson History Prize, British Academy Prize, Nat. Book Critics' Circle of US Award for non-fiction), 2003. *Recreations:* church architecture, music, drinking beer. *Address:* St Cross College, Oxford OX1 3LZ. *T:* (01865) 278458.

McCULLOCH, Prof. Ernest Armstrong, OC 1988; OOnt 2006; MD; FRSC 1974; FRS 1999; Senior Scientist Emeritus, Ontario Cancer Institute, and Princess Margaret Hospital, since 1991; University Professor, University of Toronto, 1982–91, now Emeritus; *b* 27 April 1926; *s* of Dr Albert Ernest McCulloch and Letitia Riddell McCulloch (*née* Armstrong); *m* 1953, Ona Mary Morganty; four *s* one *d*. *Educ:* Univ. of Toronto (MD Hons 1948). FRCPC 1954. Res. Fellow, Lister Inst., London, 1948–49 (Ellen Mickle Fellow); University of Toronto: Clin. Teacher, Dept of Medicine, 1954–60; Asst Prof., 1959–64, Associate Prof., 1964–66, Prof., 1966–91, Dept of Med. Biophysics; Asst Prof., 1967–68, Associate Prof., 1968–70, Prof., 1970–91, Dept of Medicine; Graduate Sec., 1969–75, Dir, 1975–79, Inst. of Med. Sci.; Asst Dean, Sch. of Graduate Studies, 1979–82; Physician, Toronto Gen. Hosp., 1960–67; Ontario Cancer Institute: Scientific Staff, 1957–91; Head, Div. of Biological Res., 1982–89; Head, Div. of Cellular and Molecular Biology, 1989–91. Vis. Prof. of Lab Medicine and Pathology, Univ. of Texas, MD Anderson Cancer Center, 1991–93; Hon. Prof., Shanxi Cancer Inst., China, 1991–. Pres., Acad. of Sci., RSC, 1987–90 (Eadie Medal, 1991). Hon. DSc Toronto, 2004. (Jtly) Annual Gairdner Award, 1969; (jtly) Albert Lasker Award, Lasker Foundn, 2005. Silver Jubilee Medal, 1977. *Publications:* more than 275 papers and reviews in med. jls. *Recreations:* sailing, gardening. *Address:* (office) 610 University Avenue, Toronto, ON M5G 2M9, Canada; (home) 480 Summerhill Avenue, Toronto, ON M4W 2E4, Canada. *Club:* Badminton and Racquet (Toronto).

McCULLOCH, Prof. Gary James, PhD; Brian Simon Professor of the History of Education, since 2003, and Assistant Director (Research, Consultancy and Knowledge Transfer), since 2007, Institute of Education, University of London; *b* 13 March 1956; *s* of Edward Joseph McCulloch and Vera Evelyn McCulloch (*née* Saunders); *m* 1984, Sarah Margaret Buyekha; one *s*. *Educ:* Caldecot Primary Sch., London; Wilson's Grammar Sch., London; Christ's Coll., Cambridge (MA, PhD History 1981). Res. Fellow, Sch. of Educn, Univ. of Leeds, 1981–83; Lectr, 1983–88, Sen. Lectr, 1988–91, in Educn, Univ. of Auckland, NZ; Prof. of Educnl Res., Lancaster Univ., 1991–94; Prof. of Educn, Univ. of Sheffield, 1994–2003; Dean of Res. and Consultancy, Inst. of Educn, Univ. of London, 2004–07. Pres., Hist. of Educn Soc. of GB, 2005–07 (Vice-Pres., 2002–04). Editor, History of Education, 1996–2003; Jt Editor, Secondary Education in a Changing World, 2003–. FRHistS 1995; FRSA 2006. *Publications:* (jtly) Technological Revolution?, 1985; The Secondary Technical School, 1989; (jtly) Schooling in New Zealand, 1990; Philosophers and Kings, 1991; (ed) The School Curriculum in New Zealand, 1992; Educational Reconstruction, 1994; (ed jtly) Teachers and the National Curriculum, 1997; Failing the Ordinary Child?, 1998; (jtly) The Politics of Professionalism, 2000; (jtly) Historical Research in Educational Settings, 2000; Documentary Research in Education, History and the Social Sciences, 2004; (ed) The Routledge Falmer Reader in the History of Education, 2005; (jtly) Succeeding with your Doctorate, 2005; Cyril Norwood and the Ideal of Secondary Education, 2007; (ed jtly) Politics and Policy-Making in Education, 2007; (ed jtly) The Death of the Comprehensive High School?, 2007; (ed jtly) Routledge International Encyclopedia of Education, 2008; (ed jtly) Social Change in the History of British Education, 2008. *Recreations:* cinema, reading, travel, walking. *Address:* Institute of Education, 20 Bedford Way, WC1H 0AL.

McCULLOCH, James Macdonald; Chief Inquiry Reporter, since 2002, and Director for Planning and Environmental Appeals, since 2007, Scottish Government (formerly Scottish Executive); *b* 3 Dec. 1948; *s* of Thomas and Jane Ann Reid McCulloch; *m* 1992, Jennifer Anne Hay; three *s*. *Educ:* Hardye's Sch., Dorchester; Lanchester Polytechnic, Coventry (BA Hons Urban & Regl Planning). MRTPI 1973. Planning Asst, Coventry Corp., 1971–73; Sen. Planner, then Prin. Planner, Scottish Develt Dept, 1973–84; Inquiry Reporter, then Prin. Reporter, subseq. Dep. Chief Reporter, Scottish Executive (formerly Scottish Office) Inquiry Reporters' Unit, 1984–2002. *Recreations:* walking, travel, eating, the people and landscapes of Spain. *Address:* Directorate for Planning and Environmental Appeals, 4 The Courtyard, Callendar Business Park, Callendar Road, Falkirk FK1 1XR. *T:* (01324) 696471, *Fax:* (01324) 696444; *e-mail:* james.mcculloch@scotland.gsi.gov.uk.

McCULLOCH, James Rae, OBE 2001; HM Diplomatic Service, retired; Ambassador to Iceland, 1996–2000; *b* 29 Nov. 1940; *s* of William McCulloch and Catherine (*née* Rae); *m* 1965, Margaret Anderson; two *s*. *Educ:* Ardrossan Acad. Joined FO, 1958; Bamako, Mali, 1962; NY, 1964; Lusaka, 1967; FCO, 1969; Algiers, 1972; Kabul, 1973; Second Sec., FCO, 1977; Luanda, 1980; Second, subseq. First Sec. (Commercial), Bangkok, 1982; First Sec., UKMIS to UN, Geneva, 1986; FCO, 1990; Dep. Hd of Mission, Hanoi, 1992–96.

MacCULLOCH, Prof. Malcolm John, MD; FRCPsych; Emeritus Professor, Wales College of Medicine, Biology, Health and Life Sciences, Cardiff University (Professor of Forensic Psychiatry, University of Wales College of Medicine, and Hon. Consultant Forensic Psychiatrist, Caswell Clinic, Bridgend & District NHS Trust, 1997–2001); *b* 10 July 1936; *s* of William MacCulloch and Constance Martha MacCulloch; *m* 1962, Mary Louise Beton (marr. diss. 1975); one *s* one *d*; *m* 1975, Carolyn Mary Reid; two *d*. *Educ:* King Edward VII Sch., Macclesfield, Cheshire; Manchester Univ. (MB, ChB, DPM, MD). Consultant Child Psychiatrist, Cheshire Child Guidance Service, 1966–67; Director Univ. Dept, Child Psychiatry and Subnormality, Birmingham Univ., 1967–70; Sen. Lectr, Adult Psychiatry, Univ. of Liverpool, 1970–75; PMO, DHSS, 1975–78; SPMO, Mental Health Div., DHSS, 1979–80; Dir. Special Hosps Res. Unit, London, 1979–86; Med. Dir, Park Lane Hosp., Liverpool, 1979–89; Res. Psychiatrist, Ashworth Hosp., Merseyside, 1990–93. Advr to Ontario Govt on Forensic Psychiatric Services, 1988–92. Vis. Prof., Clarke Inst. of Psychiatry, Toronto, 1987–88. Ed.-in-Chief, Jl of Forensic Psychiatry and Psychology, 2002–07. *Publications:* Homosexual Behaviour: therapy and assessment, 1971; Human Sexual Behaviour, 1980; numerous med. papers on aspects of psychiatry and forensic psychiatry. *Recreations:* cars, inventing, playing music. *Address:* 14 Tall Trees, Baunton Lane, Cirencester GL7 2AF. *T:* (01285) 642689.

McCULLOCH, Michael Cutler; Member, Investment Committee, Europolis Invest, since 2002; *b* 24 April 1943; *s* of late Ian James McCulloch and Elsie Margaret Chadwick; *m* 1st, 1968, Melody Lawrence (marr. diss. 1975); 2nd, 1975, Robin Lee Sussman; two *d*. *Educ:* Prince of Wales Sch., Nairobi; Clare Coll., Cambridge (BA History 1964; MA 2004); Yale Univ. (Mellon Fellow, 1964–66; MA Internat. Relations 1967). ODM, Asst Principal, 1969; Asst Private Sec. to Minister for Overseas Develt, 1972–73, Principal, 1973, ODA; First Sec. (Aid), Dhaka, FCO, 1976–78; Resident Observer, CSSB, 1978–79; Overseas Development Administration: Rayner Scrutiny and Mgt Review Team, 1979–80; E Africa Dept, 1980–83; EC Dept, 1983–84; Principal Private Sec. to Minister for Overseas Develt, 1984–85; Asst Sec., 1985; Head: Evaluation Dept, 1985–86; British Develt Div. in E Africa, 1986–89; Finance Dept, 1990–92; Know How Fund for former Soviet Union, FCO, 1992–97; UK Exec. Dir, 1997–2001, Advr to the Pres., 2003–04, EBRD. Trustee: BBC World Service Trust, 2001–; British Consultancy Charitable Trust, 2006–; Chairman of Trustees: BEARR Trust, 2003–08 (Trustee, 2001–08); Riders for Health, 2003– (Trustee, 2001–). FRSA 1995. *Recreations:* Baroque to Romantic classical music, African wildlife, photography, walking, garden design. *Address:* New Oak Barn, The Green, Bledington, Chipping Norton OX7 6XQ. *T:* (01608) 658941; *e-mail:* mcmcculloch@btinternet.com.

McCULLOCH, Rt Rev. Nigel Simeon; *see* Manchester, Bishop of.

McCULLOUGH, Sir (Iain) Charles (Robert), Kt 1981; a Surveillance Commissioner, since 1998; *b* 1931; *o s* of Thomas W. McCullough, CB, OBE and Lisette Hunter McCullough; *m* 1965, Margaret Joyce, JP, LLB, BCL, AKC, *o d* of David H. Patey, Middx Hosp.; one *s* one *d*. *Educ:* Dollar Acad.; Taunton Sch. (Exhibnr); Trinity Hall, Cambridge (Dr Cooper's Law Student, 1955; BA 1955; MA 1960). National Service, 1950–52, commnd RA; RA (TA) 1952–54. Called to the Bar, Middle Temple, 1956 (Harmsworth Law Scholar, Blackstone Pupillage Prize, J. J. Powell Prize, 1956); Bencher, 1980; Treas., 2000. Practised Midland Circuit, 1957–71, Midland and Oxford Circuit, 1972–81; a Dep. Chm., Notts QS, 1969–71; QC 1971; a Recorder of the Crown Court, 1972–81; a Judge of the High Court, QBD, 1981–98. Member: Gen. Council of the Bar, 1966–70; Criminal Law Revision Cttee, 1973–; Parole Bd, 1984–86. Trustee, Uppingham Sch., 1984–94. Pres., Trinity Hall Assoc., 1986–87. Visitor, Loughborough Univ., 2003–. *Recreations:* foreign travel, walking, watching birds. *Address:* c/o PO Box 29105, SW1V 1ZU. *Clubs:* Garrick; Pilgrims.

McCULLY, Andrew John, OBE 2001; Director, Supporting Children and Young People Group, Department for Children, Schools and Families, since 2008; *b* 14 Nov. 1963; *s* of John McCully and Lilian McCully; partner, Nicholas Howard. *Educ:* Birkenhead Sch.; Worcester Coll., Oxford (BA Hons 1986). Joined Dept of Employment as Admin Trainee, 1986; Department for Education and Employment: Sec. to New Deal Task Force, 1997–99; Manager, Learning and Skills Bill, 1999–2000; Dep. Dir, Children and Young People's Unit, 2000–02; Divl Manager, Pupil Standards Div., DFES, 2002–04; Dir, Sch. Standards Gp, DFES, subseq. DCSF, 2004–08. *Recreations:* listening to music, shopping for, cooking and eating food. *Address:* 26 Carysfort Road, N16 9AL. *T:* (020) 7254 0639; *e-mail:* andrew.mccully@dcsf.gsi.gov.uk.

McCURDY, Ven. Hugh Kyle; Archdeacon of Huntingdon and Wisbech, since 2005; *b* 9 March 1958; *s* of William Eric McCurdy and Elenor Anne McCurdy; *m* 1984, Ruth Searle; one *s* two *d*. *Educ:* Portsmouth Poly. (BA Econs 1980); Trinity Coll., Bristol (DipHE 1983); Univ. of Wales (PGCE 1984). Ordained deacon, 1985, priest, 1986; Curate: St John's, Egham, 1985–88; St John's, Woking, 1988–91; Vicar, St Andrew's, Histon, 1991–2005; Priest-in-charge, St Andrew's, Impington, 1998–2005; RD N Stowe, 1994–2005. Hon. Canon, Ely Cathedral, 2004–. *Recreations:* eating, laughing, Dr Who, sighing at my children, travel, family. *Address:* 12 Boadicea Court, Chatteris, Cambs PE16 6BN. *T:* (01354) 692142; *e-mail:* archdeacon.handw@ely.anglican.org.

McCURLEY, Anna Anderson; freelance communications consultant; Partner, Hamilton Anderson Solutions; *b* 18 Jan. 1943; *d* of George Gemmell and Mary (*née* Anderson); *m* (marr. diss.); one *d*. *Educ:* Glasgow High Sch. for Girls; Glasgow Univ. (MA); Jordanhill Coll. of Educn (Dip. in Secondary Educn); Strathclyde Univ. Secondary history teacher, 1966–72; College Methods Tutor, Jordanhill Coll. of Educn, 1972–74. Strathclyde Regional Councillor, Camphill/Pollokshaws Div., 1978–82. Sen. Exec., Dewe Rogerson, 1987–89; Head of Govt Affairs, Corporate Communications Strategy,

1990–92. Contested: (C) Renfrew W and Inverclyde, 1987; (Scottish Lib Dem) Eastwood, Scottish Parlt, 1999. MP (C) Renfrew W and Inverclyde, 1983–87. Mem., Scottish Select Cttee, 1984–87. Mem., Horserace Betting Levy Bd, 1988–97. Trustee, Nat. Galleries of Scotland, 1996–99. *Recreations:* music, cookery, cats.

McCUTCHEON, Alison; see Allden, A.

McCUTCHEON, Prof. John Joseph, CBE 1994; PhD, DSc; FFA; FRSE; Professor of Actuarial Studies, Heriot-Watt University, 1975–2001; *b* 10 Sept. 1940; *s* of James Thomson McCutcheon and Margaret (*née* Hutchison); *m* 1978, Jean Sylvia Constable. *Educ:* Glasgow Acad.; St John's Coll., Cambridge (schol.; Wright's Prize, 1960, 1962; MA 1966); Univ. of Liverpool (PhD 1969, DSc 1990). FFA 1965. Scottish Amicable Life Assce Soc., 1962–65; Consulting Actuary, Duncan C. Fraser and Co., 1965–66; Demonstrator in Pure Maths, Univ. of Liverpool, 1966–70; Associate Prof., Univ. of Manitoba, 1970–72; Heriot-Watt University: Sen. Lectr, 1972–75; Dean, Faculty of Science, 1995–98. Pres., Faculty of Actuaries in Scotland, 1992–94. FRSE 1993. *Publications:* (with W. F. Scott) An Introduction to the Mathematics of Finance, 1986; various papers on mathematics, actuarial science, mortality studies. *Recreations:* tennis, ski-ing, opera, reading, travel. *Address:* 14 Oswald Court, Edinburgh EH9 2HY. *T:* (0131) 667 7645. *Clubs:* Woodcutters Cricket, Colinton Lawn Tennis.

McCUTCHEON, Dr William Alan, FSA, MRIA; author, lecturer and consultant; Hon. Senior Research Fellow, School of Geography (formerly of Geosciences), Queen's University, Belfast, 1999–2004; *b* 2 March 1934; *s* of late William John and Margaret Elizabeth McCutcheon; *m* 1956, Margaret Craig; three *s. Educ:* Royal Belfast Academical Instn; The Queen's University of Belfast (Hugh Wisnom Scholar, 1960; BA (Hons Geog.) 1955, MA 1958, PhD 1962). FRGS (1958–94); FSA 1970; MRIA 1983. School Teacher (Geography Specialist), Royal Belfast Academical Instn, 1956–62; Director, N Ireland Survey of Industrial Archaeology, 1962–68; Keeper of Technology and Local History, Ulster Museum, Belfast, 1968–77; Dir, Ulster Museum, 1977–82; sch. teacher (geography specialist), Ditcham Park Sch., Petersfield, 1986–93. Vis. Teacher, Glenalmond Coll., 1984, 1986. Chairman: Historic Monuments Council (NI), 1980–85; Jt Cttee on Industrial Archaeology (NI), 1981–85; Member: Malcolm Cttee on Regional Museums in Northern Ireland, 1977–78; Industrial Archaeol. Cttee, Council for British Archaeol., 1981–85. *Publications:* The Canals of the North of Ireland, 1965; Railway History in Pictures, Ireland: vol. 1 1969, vol. 2 1970; (contrib.) Travel and Transport in Ireland, 1973; (contrib.) Folk & Farm, 1976; Wheel and Spindle—Aspects of Irish Industrial History, 1977; The Industrial Archaeology of Northern Ireland, 1980 (Library Assoc. high commendation as an outstanding reference book); (contrib.) Some People and Places in Irish Science and Technology, 1985; (contrib.) An Economic and Social History of Ulster 1820–1939, 1985; numerous papers. *Recreations:* reading, Schubert lieder, landscape photography, gardening. *Address:* Ardmilne, 25 Moira Drive, Bangor, Co. Down BT20 4RW. *T:* (028) 9146 5519.

McDERMID, Prof. John Alexander, PhD; FREng; FIET; Professor of Software Engineering, University of York, since 1987; *b* 5 Oct. 1952; *s* of John Alexander McDermid and Joyce Winifred McDermid (*née* Whiteley); *m* 1980, Heather Mair Denly; two *d. Educ:* Trinity Coll., Cambridge (BA 1975); Univ. of Birmingham (PhD 1981). CEng 1980, FIET (FIEE 1986). MoD student engr, then res. scientist, RSRE, Malvern, 1971–82; Computing Consultant, then Divl Manager, Systems Designers, 1982–87. Non-exec. Dir, High Integrity Solutions, 2002–08; Dir, Origin Consulting (York), 2003–. Mem., DSAC, 2004–. FBCS 1988; FRAeS 1998; FREng 2002. *Publications:* (with K. Ripken) Life Cycle Supporting in the Ada Environment, 1984; (ed) Integrated Project Support Environments, 1985; (ed) The Theory and Practice of Refinement, 1989; (ed and contrib.) Software Engineers Reference Book, 1991; (jtly) Software Engineering Environments, 1992; numerous articles in jls. *Recreations:* reading, music, walking, badminton. *Address:* Department of Computer Science, University of York, Heslington, York YO10 5DD. *T:* (01904) 432726, *Fax:* (01904) 432708; *e-mail:* john.mcdermid@cs.york.ac.uk; Yggdrasil, Scrayingham, York YO41 1JD.

McDERMID, Ven. Norman George Lloyd Roberts; Archdeacon of Richmond, 1983–93, Emeritus since 1993; *b* 5 March 1927; *s* of Lloyd Roberts McDermid and Annie McDermid; *m* 1953, Vera Wood; one *s* three *d. Educ:* St Peter's School, York; St Edmund Hall, Oxford (MA); Wells Theological Coll. Deacon 1951, priest 1952; Curate of Leeds, 1951–56, in charge of St Mary, Quarry Hill, Leeds, 1953–56; Vicar of Bramley, Leeds, 1956–64; Rector of Kirkby Overblow, 1964–80; Stewardship Adviser, Ripon Diocese, 1964–76, Bradford and Wakefield, 1973–76; Vicar of Knaresborough, 1980–83. Hon. Canon of Ripon Cathedral, 1972–93, Emeritus 1993–; RD of Harrogate, 1977–83. Member: General Synod, 1970–93; Church of England Pensions Bd, 1972–78; Redundant Churches Fund, 1977–89; Central Bd of Finance of C of E, 1985–93. Church Commissioner, 1978–83. Chairman: Ripon Diocesan House of Clergy, 1981–93; Ripon Diocesan Bd of Finance, 1988–93; Mem., Ripon Cathedral Fabric Cttee, 1990–. Mem., N Yorks County Educn Cttee, 1993–97. Chm., Bedale Probus 25 Club, 2000–03. *Recreations:* investment, historic churches, pedigree cattle, gardening. *Address:* Greystones, 10 North End, Bedale, N Yorks DL8 1AB. *T:* (01677) 422210.

MacDERMOT, Prof. John, MD, PhD; FRCP; Head of Undergraduate Medicine, Imperial College, London, 2002–06, now Professor Emeritus of Clinical Pharmacology; Undergraduate Medical Academic Links Co-ordinator, Tropical Health and Education Trust, since 2006; *b* 24 March 1947; *s* of Niall and Violet MacDermot; *m* 1976, Kay Krnakova; one *d. Educ:* Imperial Coll. of Sci. and Technol.; Charing Cross Med. Sch., Univ. of London (MD 1979); PhD Inst. of Neurology, London, 1977. FRCP 1989. Fogarty Internat. Fellow, Lab. of Biochemical Genetics, NIH, 1977–78; Wellcome Sen. Clinical Res. Fellow, RPMS, 1981–87; Professor of Pharmacology, Univ. of Birmingham, 1987–88; of Clinical Pharmacology, RPMS, later Imperial Coll., Univ. of London, 1989–99; of Medicine and Therapeutics, ICSM, 2000–02. FMedSci 1999. *Publications:* papers on processes involved in signalling from one cell to another. *Recreations:* reading, tennis, ski-ing, cooking. *Address:* Tropical Health and Education Trust, 1 Wimpole Street, W1G 0AE. *T:* (020) 7290 3888; *e-mail:* john@thet.org.

MacDERMOTT, Alasdair Tormod; HM Diplomatic Service, retired; High Commissioner, Namibia, 2002–07; *b* 17 Sept. 1945; *s* of late Norman MacDermott and Mary MacDermott; *m* 1st, 1966 (marr. diss. 1992); two *d*; 2nd, 1994, Gudrun Geiling. *Educ:* University Coll. Sch., Hampstead; lang. trng, SOAS, Univ. of London. Entered FO, later FCO, 1966; Kabul, 1971–72; FCO, 1973; Accra, 1973–77; FCO, 1977; lang. trng, Tokyo, 1978; Second Secretary: Tokyo, 1979–82; Accra, 1982–83; Political Sec., Colombo, 1983–86; First Secretary: Press Officer, Tokyo, 1986–91; FCO, 1991–95; Turkish lang. trng, 1995; (Commercial), Ankara, 1995–98; Southern African Dept, FCO, 1998–2002. Internat. Policy Advr, Europe, Leonard Cheshire Internat., 2008; Trustee, Community Action, Africa. *Recreations:* wood carving, Byzantium, Constantinople, Istanbul, Maigret, Namib desert. *Address:* 165 rue Haute, 1000 Brussels, Belgium. *Clubs:* Royal Commonwealth Society, Royal Over-Seas League; Hill (Nuwara Eliya, Sri Lanka); Ceylon Sea Anglers (Trincomalee).

McDERMOTT, Gerard Francis; QC 1999; a Recorder, since 1999; *b* 21 April 1956; *s* of late Joseph Herbert McDermott, BSc, and of Winifred Mary McDermott (*née* Limon); *m* 1992, Fiona Johnson. *Educ:* De La Salle Coll., Salford; Manchester Univ. (LLB Hons 1977). Called to the Bar, Middle Temple, 1978, Bencher, 2005; Barrister, Manchester, 1979–; Attorney-at-Law, NY, 1990. General Council of the Bar: Mem., 1983–88, 1990–96, 1998–99 and 2003–08; Chm., Internat. Relns Cttee, 1999–2000. Dir, Amer. Counsel Assoc., 1997– (Pres., 2003–04); Mem., Internat. Assoc. of Defense Counsel; Leader, European Circuit of the Bar, 2006–08. *Recreations:* travel, music. *Address:* Outer Temple Chambers, 222 Strand, WC2R 1BA. *T:* (020) 7353 6381. *Club:* Athenæum.

MacDERMOTT, Rt Hon. Sir John Clarke, Kt 1987; PC 1987; a Lord Justice of Appeal, Supreme Court of Judicature, Northern Ireland, 1987–98; *b* 1927; *s* of Baron MacDermott, PC, PC (NI), MC, and of Louise Palmer, *o d* of Rev. J. C. Johnston, DD; *m* 1953, Margaret Helen, *d* of late Hugh Dales, Belfast; four *d. Educ:* Campbell Coll., Belfast; Trinity Hall, Cambridge (BA); QUB. Called to Bar, Inner Temple and Northern Ireland, 1949; QC (NI) 1964. Judge, High Court of NI, 1973–87. *Address:* 6 Tarawood, Holywood, Co. Down BT18 0HS.

McDERMOTT, Patrick Anthony, MVO 1972; HM Diplomatic Service, retired; Deputy Bursar, Ampleforth Abbey and College, 2002–06; *b* 8 Sept. 1941; *e s* of Patrick McDermott and Eileen (*née* Lyons); *m* 1976, Christa, *d* of Emil and Anne-Marie Herminghaus, Krefeld, W Germany; two *s*, and two *s* by previous *m. Educ:* Clapham College, London. FO 1960; Mexico City, 1963; Attaché, UK Delegn to UN, NY, 1966; Vice-Consul, Belgrade, 1971; Second Sec., FCO, 1973; Second Sec., Bonn, 1973; First Sec., Paris, 1976; First Sec., FCO, 1979; Consul-Gen., and Econ. and Financial Advr to British Military Government, W Berlin, 1984; Asst Hd of Dept, FCO, 1988–89; Counsellor, Paris, 1990; Dept Head, FCO, 1995–97; Consul Gen., Moscow, and to Republic of Moldova, 1998–2001 (Chargé d'Affaires, 1998, 1999). Dir, Helmsley Walled Garden Trust, 2005–. Freeman, City of London, 1986. *Address:* Linkfoot House, 10 Acres Close, Helmsley, York YO62 5DS; *e-mail:* patrickanthonymcdermott@yahoo.co.uk.

McDEVITT, Prof. Denis Gordon, MD, DSc; Professor of Clinical Pharmacology, University of Dundee, 1984–2002, now Emeritus; Hon. Consultant Physician, Dundee teaching hospitals, 1984–2002; *b* 17 Nov. 1937; *s* of Harry and Vera McDevitt; *m* 1967, Anne McKee; two *s* one *d. Educ:* Queen's Univ., Belfast (MB ChB, BAO Hons 1962; MD 1968; DSc 1978). FRCPI 1977; FRCP 1978; FRCPE 1984. House Physician and Surg., 1962–63, SHO, 1963–64, Royal Victoria Hosp., Belfast; SHO, Registrar, Sen. Registrar, Dept of Therapeutics and Pharmacology, QUB and Belfast teaching hosps, 1964–68; Asst Prof. of Medicine and Cons. Physician, Christian Med. Coll., Ludhiana, India, 1968–71; Cons. Physician, Belfast teaching hosps, 1971–83; Queen's University, Belfast: Sen. Lectr, 1971–76, Reader, 1976–78, in Clin. Pharmacology and Therapeutics; Prof. of Clin. Pharmacology, 1978–83; Dean, Faculty of Medicine, Dentistry and Nursing, Univ. of Dundee, 1994–97. Merck Internat. Fellow in Clin. Pharmacology, Vanderbilt Univ., 1974–75. Civil Cons. in Exptl Medicine, RAF, 1987–2002. Member: British Pharmacol Soc., 1972– (SKF Medal and Lecture, 1975); Assoc. of Physicians, 1978– (Pres., 1987–88; Hon. Mem., 1988–); Medicines Commn, 1986–95 (Vice-Chm., 1992–95); GMC, 1997–2003 (Treas., 2001–03; Associate, 2003–07); Council, RCPE, 2003–08; Faculty Bd, FPM, 2003–08; Chm., Specialist Adv. Cttee on Clin. Pharmacol. and Therapeutics, 1980–83; Vice-Chm., Ethics Cttee, Centre for Human Scis, DERA, 1994–2003. FFPM 1990; FRSE 1996; FRSocMed 1996; Founder FMedSci 1998. Man. Editor, European Jl of Clin. Pharmacology, 1998–2002. *Publications:* papers on clin. pharmacology in learned jls. *Recreations:* golf, music, opera. *Address:* Mariners View, 10 Ogilvie Road, Broughty Ferry, Dundee DD5 1LU. *T:* (01382) 739483. *Club:* Royal and Ancient Golf.

MACDIARMID, Hugh Finlay, CB 2003; Solicitor to Advocate General for Scotland, 1999–2005; *b* 1 Aug. 1944; *s* of Finlay Macdiarmid and Winifred Stalker Macdiarmid; *m* 1976, Catherine Rose Smith; two *s. Educ:* Morrison's Acad., Crieff; St Andrews Univ. (MA); Edinburgh Univ. (LLB). Admitted as solicitor, 1974; Office of Solicitor to Sec. of State for Scotland, 1974–99, Divl Solicitor, 1986–99. Legal Mem., Mental Health Tribunal for Scotland, 2005–. *Recreations:* reading, contemplating. *Address:* 9 Bruntsfield Crescent, Edinburgh EH10 4EZ.

McDIARMID, Ian; actor, director; Joint Artistic Director, Almeida Theatre, 1989–2002; *b* 11 Aug. 1944; *s* of Frederick McDiarmid and Hilda (*née* Emslie). *Educ:* Morgan Acad.; St Andrews Univ.; Royal Scottish Acad. of Music and Dramatic Art (Gold Medal, 1968). *Theatre* includes: Mephisto, Round House, 1981; Insignificance, Royal Court, 1982; Tales from Hollywood, NT, 1983; The Black Prince, Aldwych, 1989; Royal Shakespeare Company: joined, 1978; Shylock in Merchant of Venice, Henry V, The Party, 1984; Red, Black and Ignorant, War Plays, The Castle, 1985; The Danton Affair, 1986; Royal Exchange, Manchester: The Wild Duck, 1983; Edward II, 1986; Don Carlos, 1987; Associate Dir, 1986–88; Jonah and Otto, 2008; Almeida: Volpone, The Rehearsal (dir), Scenes from an Execution (dir), 1990; Hippolytos, Lulu (dir), 1991; Terrible Mouth (opera), A Hard Heart (dir), 1992; School for Wives, 1993; Siren Song (opera) (dir), 1994; Tartuffe, 1996; The Cenci (opera), The Government Inspector, 1997; The Doctor's Dilemma, 1998; The Jew of Malta, 1999; The Tempest, 2000; Faith Healer, 2001, Dublin and NY, 2006 (Tony Award for best featured actor); The Embalmer, 2002; The Soldier's Tale, LSO, 1987; The King Goes Forth to France, Royal Opera House, 1987; Henry IV, Donmar, 2004; Lear, Crucible, Sheffield, 2005; John Gabriel Borkman, Donmar, 2007; Six Characters in Search of an Author, Minerva, Chichester, 2008; *films* include: The Return of the Jedi, 1983; Restoration, 1996; Star Wars, Episode I: the phantom menace, 1999; Sleepy Hollow, 2000; Star Wars, Episode II: attack of the clones, 2002, Episode III: revenge of the Sith, 2005; *television:* Karaoke, 1996; Hillsborough, 1996; Great Expectations, 1999; All the King's Men, 1999; Crime and Punishment, 2002; Charles II: The Power and the Passion, 2003; Elizabeth I, 2005; Our Hidden Lives, 2005; City of Vice, 2008. *Address:* c/o Independent Talent Group Ltd, Oxford House, 76 Oxford Street, W1D 1BS.

McDONAGH, Baroness *cr* 2004 (Life Peer), of Mitcham and of Morden in the London Borough of Merton; **Margaret Josephine McDonagh;** management consultant; *d* of Cumin McDonagh and Breda McDonagh (*née* Doogue). *Educ:* Brunel Univ. (BSc); Kingston Business Sch. (MA). Labour Party: Gen. Election Co-ordinator, 1997; Gen. Sec., 1998–2001; Gen. Manager, Express Newspapers, 2001–02. Director: TBI, 2004–; Standard Life Assurance Co., 2007–. *Address:* House of Lords, SW1A 0PW.
See also S. A. McDonagh.

MacDONAGH, Lesley Anne; Managing Partner, Lovells, Solicitors, 1995–2005; *b* 19 April 1952; *d* of Arthur George Payne and Agnes Dowie Scott; *m* 1st, 1975, John Belton (marr. diss. 1985); one *d*; 2nd, 1987, Simon Michael Peter MacDonagh; three *s. Educ:* Queen Elizabeth I Sch., Wimborne; College of Law, Guildford and London. Admitted Solicitor, 1976; Partner, Lovell White Durrant, subseq. Lovells, 1981–2006, Support Dir and Solicitor, 2005–07. Member: Council, Law Society, 1992–2001 (Mem., Planning and Envtl Cttee, 1988–95); Lands Tribunal Consultative Cttee, 1991–95; Property Adv. Gp, 1993–. Non-executive Director: Bovis Homes plc, 2003–; SEGRO (formerly Slough

Estates plc), 2007–. Trustee, Citizenship Foundn, 1991–. Vice-Chm., Envt Cttee, Knightsbridge Assoc., 1991–. Former Gov., LSE. Liveryman, Solicitors' Co., 1982– (Mem. Court, 1997–2006). Hon. Fellow, Soc. for Advanced Legal Studies, 1998. *Recreations:* family life, painting, drawing, dining. *Address:* c/o SEGRO, 234 Bath Road, Slough SL1 4EE.

McDONAGH, Siobhain Ann; MP (Lab) Mitcham and Morden, since 1997; *b* 20 Feb. 1960; *d* of Cumin McDonagh and Breda McDonagh (*née* Doogue). *Educ:* Holy Cross Convent; Essex Univ. (BA Hons 1981). Clerical Officer, DHSS, 1981–82; Wandsworth Council: Admin. Asst, 1982–83; Receptionist, Homeless Persons Unit, 1983–86; Housing Advr, Housing Aid Centre, 1986–88; Develt Co-ordinator, Battersea Churches Housing Trust, 1988–97. An Asst Govt Whip, 2007–08. Mem., South Mitcham Community Centre, 1988. *Recreations:* shopping, music, women's magazines. *Address:* 1 Crown Road, Morden SM4 5DD. *T:* (020) 8542 4835.
See also Baroness McDonagh.

MACDONALD, family name of **Barons Macdonald** and **Macdonald of Tradeston**.

MACDONALD, 8th Baron *cr* 1776; **Godfrey James Macdonald of Macdonald;** JP; DL; Chief of the Name and Arms of Macdonald; *b* 28 Nov. 1947; *s* of 7th Baron Macdonald, MBE, TD, and Anne (*d* 1988), *o d* of late Alfred Whitaker; *S* father, 1970; *m* 1969, Claire, *e d* of Captain T. N. Catlow, CBE, RN, Gabriel Cottage, Tunstall, Lancs; one *s* three *d*. JP Skye and Lochalsh, 1979; DL Ross and Cromarty, Skye and Lochalsh, 1986. *Heir: s* Hon. Godfrey Evan Hugo Thomas Macdonald of Macdonald, yr, *b* 24 Feb. 1982. *Address:* Kinloch Lodge, Isle of Skye. *Club:* New (Edinburgh).

MACDONALD OF TRADESTON, Baron *cr* 1998 (Life Peer), of Tradeston in the City of Glasgow; **Angus John Macdonald,** CBE 1997; PC 1999; Chairman, Macquarie Capital, Europe, since 2007 (Chairman, Macquarie Europe Ltd, 2004; Senior Adviser, 2005–06, Chairman, Investment Banking Group, Europe, 2006–07, Macquarie Bank Ltd); *b* 20 Aug. 1940; *s* of Colin Macdonald and Jean Macdonald; *m* 1963, Theresa, (Teen), McQuaid; two *d*. *Educ:* Allan Glen's Sch., Glasgow. Marine fitter, 1956–63; Circulation Manager, Tribune, 1964–65; journalist, The Scotsman, 1965–67; Granada Television: Editor/Exec. Producer, World in Action, 1969–75; successively Head of Current Affairs, Regl Progs, Features, 1975–82; presenter, variously, Camera, Granada 500, Party conferences, Union World; Right to Reply, Channel 4, 1982–88; Dir of Progs, 1985–90, Man. Dir, 1990–96, Chm., 1996–98, Scottish Television, subseq. Scottish Media Gp. Chm., Taylor & Francis Group, 1997–98; Director: GMTV, 1991–97; Bank of Scotland, 1998; Scottish Enterprise, 1998. Parly Under-Sec. of State (Minister for Business and Industry), Scottish Office, 1998–99; Minister of State (Minister for Transport), DETR, 1999–2001; Minister for the Cabinet Office and Chancellor of the Duchy of Lancaster, 2001–03; Mem., Select Cttee on Econ. Affairs, H of L, 2004–. Chm., All Party Parly Humanist Gp, 2005–. Mem., Steering Gp, OECD Futures Project on Global Infrastructure, 2004–07. Chm., Cairngorms Partnership Bd, 1997–98. Founder Chm., Edinburgh Television Festival, 1976; Chairman: Edinburgh Film Fest., 1994–96; ITV Broadcasting Bd, 1992–94. Vice Pres., RTS, 1994–98. Vis. Prof., Film and Media Studies, Stirling Univ., 1985–98. Governor: Nat. Film and Television Sch., 1986–97; BFI, 1997–98. Chancellor, Glasgow Caledonian Univ., 2007–; Mem. Council, Univ. of Sussex, 2006–. Patron, Dystonia Soc., 2006–. DUniv: Stirling, 1992; Glasgow, 2001; Hon. DLitt: Napier, 1997; Robert Gordon, 1998; Hon. DBA Lincoln, 2007. BAFTA Award, Best Factual Series (World In Action), 1973; Chairman of the Year, and Business Leader of the Year, Scottish Business Elite Awards, 1997; BAFTA Scotland Lifetime Achievement Award, 1997. *Publication:* Camera: Victorian eyewitness, 1979. *Recreations:* music, pictures, sports. *Address:* House of Lords, SW1A 0PW. *Club:* Royal Automobile.

McDONALD, Very Rev. Alan Douglas; Moderator of the General Assembly of the Church of Scotland, 2006–07; Minister, St Leonard's and Cameron, St Andrews, since 1998; *b* 6 March 1951; *s* of Douglas Gordon McDonald and Ray Lindsay Bishop McDonald (*née* Craig); *m* 1975, Dr Judith Margaret McDonald (*née* Allen); one *s* one *d*. *Educ:* Glasgow Acad.; Strathclyde Univ. (LLB 1972); Edinburgh Univ. (BD 1978; MTh 1996). Legal apprentice, Biggart Baillie & Gifford, 1972–74; Solicitor, Farquharson Craig, 1974–75. Community Minister, Pilton, Edinburgh, 1979–83; Minister, Holburn Central, Aberdeen, 1983–98. Convener, Church and Nation Cttee, Gen. Assembly of C of S, 2000–04. Hon. DLitt Strathclyde, 2007; Hon. DD St Andrews, 2007. *Recreations:* music, poetry, hillwalking, running, golf. *Address:* 1 Cairnhill Gardens, St Andrews, Fife KY16 8QY. *T:* (01334) 472793; *e-mail:* alan.d.mcdonald@talk21.com.

MACDONALD, Sir Alasdair (Uist), Kt 2008; CBE 2001; Headteacher, Morpeth School, Tower Hamlets, since 1992; *b* Glasgow, 15 July 1949; *s* of William Uist and Patricia Joan Macdonald; *m* 1981, Susan Catherine Roberts; two *s*. *Educ:* Morgan Primary Sch.; Morgan Acad., Dundee; Aberdeen Univ. (MA Hons Geog.); Leeds Univ. (PGCE). Teacher of English, Nkhota Kota Secondary Sch., Malawi, 1971–73; Project Manager, Christian Service Cttee, Blantyre, Malawi, 1973–74; Teacher of Geog., 1975–77, Hd of Geog., 1977–80, Dep. Hd, 1980–82, George Green's Sch., Tower Hamlets; Dep. Principal, 1983–85, Principal, 1986, Passam Nat. High Sch., Wewak, PNG; Dep. Headteacher, Quintin Kynaston Sch., Westminster, 1987–92. Consultant, Nat. Coll. of Sch. Leadership, 2006–. Unilever Fellow, London Leadership Centre, 2000. Hon. DEd E London 2008. *Recreations:* travelling with family, hiking, theatre, education, Dundee United FC, East and Central Africa. *Address:* Morpeth School, Portman Place, E2 0PX. *T:* (020) 8981 0921, *Fax:* (020) 8981 6427; *e-mail:* morpethsmt@aol.com.

MACDONALD, Alastair John Peter, CB 1989; a Civil Service Commissioner, 2001–07; Director General, Industry (formerly Deputy Secretary), Department of Trade and Industry, 1992–2000; *b* 11 Aug. 1940; *s* of late Ewen Macdonald and Hettie Macdonald; *m* 1969, Jane, *d* of late T. R. Morris; one *s* two *d*. *Educ:* Wimbledon Coll.; Trinity Coll., Oxford. Editorial staff of Spectator, 1962; Financial Times, 1963–68: Washington DC, 1965–66; Features Editor, 1966–68; joined Home Civil Service as Asst Principal, DEA, 1968; Principal, DTI, 1971; Sec., Lord Devlin's Commn into Industrial and Commercial Representation, 1971–72; Asst Sec., DoI, 1975; RCDS, 1980; Under Sec., DTI, 1981. Dep. Sec., DTI, 1985–90; Dep. Under Sec. of State, MoD (PE), 1990–92. Non-exec. Dir, Parity Gp plc, 2002–. Mem., Design Council, 2001–04. Pres., BCS, 2000–01. FBCS 1999. *Address:* 13 Burbage Road, SE24 9HJ.

McDONALD, Very Rev. Alexander; General Secretary, Board of Ministry, Church of Scotland, 1988–2002; Moderator of the General Assembly of the Church of Scotland, 1997–98; *b* 5 Nov. 1937; *s* of Alexander McDonald and Jessie Helen (*née* Low); *m* 1962, Essdale Helen (*née* McLeod); two *s* one *d*. *Educ:* Bishopriggs Higher Grade Sch.; Whitehill Senior Secondary Sch.; Stow Coll.; Scottish Coll. of Commerce; Trinity Coll., Glasgow Univ. (Dip. 1968); BA Open Univ. CMIWSc. Trainee management in timber trade, 1954–56; RAF, 1956–58; timber trade, 1958–62; Minister: St David's Church, Bathgate, 1968–74; St Mark's Church, Paisley, 1974–88. Pres., Glasgow Bn, Boys' Bde, 1998–2001. Broadcaster on TV and radio, 1969–2002. DUniv Open, 1999. *Publications:* numerous articles in jls and newspapers. *Recreations:* hill walking, swimming, reading, fishing. *Address:* 36 Alloway Grove, Paisley PA2 7DQ. *T:* (0141) 560 1937.
See also D. J. McDonald.

McDONALD, Prof. Alexander John, MA (Cantab), LLB; WS; Professor of Conveyancing, University of Dundee (formerly Queen's College), 1955–82, now Emeritus (Dean of the Faculty of Law, 1958–62, 1965); Senior Partner, Thornton, Dickie & Brand, WS, Dundee, 1978–84, Consultant to Thorntons, WS, 1984–2000; *b* 15 March 1919; *o s* of late John McDonald, and Agnes Mary Stewart McDonald; *m* 1951, Doreen Mary, *o d* of late Frank Cook, OBE; two *s* two *d*. *Educ:* Cargilfield Sch.; Fettes Coll. (open scholar); Christ's Coll., Cambridge (Classical Exhibn, BA 1942); Edinburgh Univ. (Thow Schol. and John Robertson Prize in Conveyancing; LLB with dist., 1949). Admitted as Solicitor and Writer to the Signet, 1950; Lectr in Conveyancing, Edinburgh Univ., 1952–55. *Publications:* Conveyancing Case Notes, 1981, 2nd edn 1984; Conveyancing Manual, 1982, 7th edn 2004; Registration of Title Manual, 1986. *Address:* 1 Regent Place, Broughty Ferry, Dundee DD5 1AT. *T:* (01382) 477301.

McDONALD, Alistair; Economic Development Officer, Wandsworth Borough Council, 1983–89; *b* 13 March 1925; *e s* of late John Bell McDonald and Mary McDonald; *m* 1954, Isabel Margaret Milne; two *d*. *Educ:* Fraserburgh Academy; Aberdeen Univ. (BSc 1st Cl. Hons Natural Philosophy). Served RAF and Fleet Air Arm, 1943–46. Malayan Meteorological Service, 1950–56; ICI, 1956–66; Min. of Technology, 1966–70; Dept of Trade and Industry, 1970–74; Dept of Industry, 1974–77; Director, British Shipbuilders (on secondment), 1977–79; Regional Dir, NW Region, Dept of Industry, 1979–83. *Recreation:* golf.

McDONALD, Dr Andrew John; Chief Executive, Government Skills, Cabinet Office, since 2006; *b* 27 June 1962; *s* of A. J. W. McDonald and Eileen McDonald (*née* Sharkey); *m* 1992, Louise London; one *d*. *Educ:* St John's Coll., Oxford (BA Hons (Modern Hist.) 1983); Bristol Univ. (PhD 1988). PRO, 1986–2000 (Mem., Management Bd, 1997–2000); Client Services Dir/ Actg Chief Exec., Public Guardianship Office, 2000–01; Tribunals Prog. Dir, LCD, 2001–02; Constitution Dir, DCA, 2003–05. Gwilym Gibbon Fellow, Nuffield Coll., Oxford, 1996–97; Fulbright Fellow, Inst. of Govtl Studies, Univ. of Calif, Berkeley, 2005–06. FRHistS 2000. FRSA 1999. Hon. Fellow, Sch. of Public Policy, UCL, 1998–. *Publications:* (ed with G. Terrill) Open Government, 1998; (ed) Reinventing Britain, 2007; articles on modern hist. and public policy. *Recreations:* history, sport, walking, travel. *Address:* Cabinet Office, Admiralty Arch, The Mall, SW1A 2WH. *Club:* MCC.

MACDONALD, His Honour Angus Cameron; a Circuit Judge, 1979–98; *b* 26 Aug. 1931; *o s* of late Hugh Macdonald, OBE, and Margaret Cameron Macdonald (*née* Westley); *m* 1956, Deborah Anne, *d* of late John Denny Inglis, DSO, MC, JP, and Deborah Margery Meiklem Inglis (*née* Thomson); two *d* (and one *d* decd). *Educ:* Bedford Sch.; Trinity Hall, Cambridge (BA 1954; MA 1960). Nat. service, 1950–51, commissioned, TA, 1951–57. Called to Bar, Gray's Inn, 1955; Resident Magistrate, then Crown Counsel, Nyasaland Govt, 1957–65; Sen. State Counsel, Malawi Govt, 1965–67; practised, NE Circuit, 1967–79; a Recorder of the Crown Court, 1974–79. *Recreations:* singing, fishing, shooting. *Clubs:* Northern Counties (Newcastle upon Tyne); New (Edinburgh).

MACDONALD, Angus David; Headmaster, Lomond School, since 1986; *b* Edinburgh, 9 Oct. 1950; *s* of Iain and Molly Macdonald; *m* 1976, Isabelle; two *d*. *Educ:* Jesus Coll., Cambridge (BA 1972); Edinburgh Univ. (DipEd). Teacher: Alloa Acad., 1972; Edinburgh Acad., 1973–82; Kings Sch., Paramatta, NSW, 1978; Dep. Hd, George Watson's Coll., 1982–86. *Recreations:* outdoor ed., gardening, piping. *Address:* 8 Millig Street, Helensburgh, Argyll and Bute G84 9LB. *T:* (01436) 679204; *e-mail:* a.macdonald@lomond-school.org.

MACDONALD, Prof. Averil Mary, PhD; CPhys, FInstP; Professor of Science Communication, University of Reading, since 2007; *b* Walsall, 15 Oct. 1957; *d* of Joseph Henry and Clara Eleanor Frost; *m* 1986, George Macdonald (marr. diss. 1998); two *d*; *m* 2001, Prof. Alun Vaughan. *Educ:* Univ. of York (BSc Physics 1980); Open Univ. (MA Educn Mgt 1996); Southampton Univ. (PhD Chem. 2004). CPhys 1987; FInstP 1999. Teacher of physics, Ingatestone, Essex, 1981–86; Hd of Physics, Kenilworth Sch., 1986–93; Lectr (pt-time), Univ. of Reading, 1996–2007. Educnl Consultancy business, 1996–. Trustee, NMSI, 2008–. Freeman, Horners' Co. Bragg Medal, Inst. Physics, 1999; Woman of Outstanding Achievement in Sci., UK Res. Council for Women in Sci., 2007; Plastics Industry Award for Personal Contribn to the Plastics Industry 2007. *Publications:* jointly: Reading into Science: physics, 2003; Fantastic Plastic; co-author of school textbooks in series incl. Science Web Readers, GCSE Modular Science, GCSE Gateway Science, Salters A-level Physics, Science Through Hydrogen, Essential Physics Revision. *Recreations:* talking to husband in pubs (when time permits), keeping tropical fish, 2 cats, 2 daughters and 1 husband. *Address:* JJ Thomson Physical Laboratory, University of Reading, Reading RG6 6AF. *T:* (0118) 378 8574, *Fax:* (0118) 975 0203; *e-mail:* a.m.macdonald@reading.ac.uk.

McDONALD, Beverley June; *see* Hughes, B. J.

MACDONALD, Dr Calum Alasdair; Chairman, Forestry Commission Scotland, since 2006; Vice-Chairman, Point Power & Energy Co. Ltd, since 2006; *b* 7 May 1956; *s* of Malcolm and Donella Macdonald. *Educ:* Bayble Sch.; The Nicolson Inst.; Edinburgh Univ.; Univ. of California at Los Angeles (PhD). MP (Lab) Western Isles, 1987–2005; contested (Lab) Na H-Eileanan An Iar, 2005. Parly Under-Sec. of State, Scottish Office, 1997–99. Member: TGWU; Scottish Crofting Foundn (formerly Crofters Union). *Address:* 21 New Garrabost, Isle of Lewis HS2 0PH.

MACDONALD, Charles Adam; QC 1992; **His Honour Judge Macdonald;** a Circuit Judge, since 2005; *b* 31 Aug. 1949; *s* of late Alasdair Cameron Macdonald, VRD, MB ChB, FRCP, FRCPGlas and of Jessie Catherine Macdonald, BA; *m* 1978, Dinah Jane Manns; three *d*. *Educ:* Glasgow Academy; New Coll., Oxford (MA Hons Jurisp.). Called to the Bar, Lincoln's Inn, 1972. An Asst Recorder, 1996–99; a Recorder, 1999–2005. Mem. Panel, Lloyd's Salvage Arbitrators, 2000–05. *Publication:* Butterworths Commercial Court and Arbitration Pleadings, 2005. *Recreation:* owns sport horses. *Address:* Maidstone Combined Court, Barker Road, Maidstone, Kent ME16 8EQ.

MACDONALD, Clare; *see* Moriarty, C.

MacDONALD, Colin Cameron, CB 1999; Secretary, Sound of Iona Harbours Committee, since 2004; *b* 13 July 1943; *s* of Captain Colin D. C. MacDonald and Ann MacDonald (*née* Hough); *m* 1969, Kathryn Mary Campbell. *Educ:* Allan Glen's Sch., Glasgow; Univ. of Strathclyde (BA Hons Econ. 1967). Scottish Development Department, 1967–92: Asst Sec., Housing Div., 1988–91, Management Orgn, 1991–92; Under Sec. and Principal Estab. Officer, Scottish Office, then Scottish Exec., 1992–2000; Man. Dir, Colmcille Fisheries (Iona), 2000–03. Non-exec. Dir, TSB Bank Scotland,

1994–98. *Recreations:* tennis, fishing, music. *Address:* 4 Esdaile Bank, Edinburgh EH9 2PN. *T:* (0131) 662 8457; Caol Ithe, Iona, Argyll PA76 6SP. *T:* (01681) 700344.

McDONALD, David Arthur; Chairman, Willow Housing and Care Ltd, 2004–05 and since 2006; *b* 16 Jan. 1940; *s* of late Campbell McDonald and Ethel McDonald; *m* 1st, 1963, Barbara MacCallum (marr. diss.); one *d*; 2nd, 1971, Mavis Lowe (*see* Dame Mavis McDonald); one *s*. *Educ:* Campbell College, Belfast; Trinity College, Dublin. BA (Moderatorship) Classics. Asst Master, Classics, Methodist College, Belfast, 1963–66; Press Sec. to Minister of Education, N Ireland, 1967–68; joined Min. of Housing and Local Govt, later DoE, 1970; Asst Private Sec. to Sec. of State for the Envt, 1974–76; Asst Sec., Local Govt Finance Divs, 1977–82; Dir of Information, 1982–87; Under Sec., Construction Industry, and Sport and Recreation, Directorates, 1987–90; Dir of Information, 1990–92; Under Sec., Urban Develt and Relocation Directorate, 1992–94; Under-Sec., Cities, Countryside and Private Finance Directorate, 1994. Mem., Local Govt Area Cost Adjustment Rev. Panel, 1995–96. Chairman: Network Housing Assoc., 1996–2003; Stadium Housing Assoc., 2003–06; Vice-Chm., London Strategic Housing Ltd, 1999–2002; Mem. Bd, Network Housing Gp, 2003– (Chm. Council, 2003–08). *Recreations:* golf, watching sport. *Clubs:* MCC; Wimbledon Park Golf; London Scottish Rugby.

MACDONALD, David Cameron; Chairman, National Kidney Foundation of New Zealand, 1998–2003; *b* 5 July 1936; *s* of James Fraser Macdonald, OBE, FRCS and Anne Sylvia Macdonald (*née* Hutcheson); *m* 1st, 1968, Melody Jane Coles (marr. diss. 1980); two *d*; 2nd, 1983, Mrs Sally Robertson; one *s* one *d*. *Educ:* St George's Sch., Harpenden; Newport Grammar Sch. Admitted a solicitor with Slaughter and May, 1962; joined Philip Hill Higginson Erlangers, later Hill Samuel & Co. Ltd, 1964: Dir, 1968; Dep. Chm., 1979–80; Dir, Hill Samuel Gp Ltd, 1979–80; Chief Exec., Antony Gibbs Holdings Ltd and Chm., Antony Gibbs & Sons, 1980–83; Chairman: Bath and Portland Gp, 1982–85; Pittards, 1985–97 (Dir, 1984); Sound Diffusion, 1987–89; Director: Coutts and Co., 1980–95; Sears, 1981–97; Merivale Moore, 1985–98; Cogent Elliott, 1986–97; Foster Yeoman Ltd, 1993–95. Sen. UK Advr, Credit Suisse First Boston, 1983–91. Dir Gen., Panel on Takeovers and Mergers, 1977–79. Adviser to Govt on Upper Clyde Shipbuilders crisis, 1971. Chm., Issuing Houses Assoc., 1975–77. Mem., BTA, 1971–82. Trustee, London City Ballet, 1983–87. *Recreations:* music, fishing. *Address:* Wetlands, Dawson Road, Mapua, RD1 Upper Moutere, New Zealand. *T:* (3) 5402927.

McDONALD, David John, (David Tennant); actor; *b* 18 April 1971; *s* of Very Rev. Alexander McDonald, *qv*. *Educ:* Royal Scottish Acad. Music and Drama (BA). *Theatre* includes: appearances with 7:84 Theatre Co.; Royal Shakespeare Co.: As You Like It, 1996; Romeo and Juliet, 2000; Comedy of Errors, 2000; Hamlet, 2008; Lobby Hero, Donmar and New Ambassadors, 2002; *films* include: Bright Young Things, 2003; Harry Potter and the Goblet of Fire, 2005; *television* includes: He Knew He Was Right, 2004; Blackpool, 2004; Casanova, 2005; The Doctor in Doctor Who, 2006–; Recovery, 2007. *Address:* c/o Independent Talent Group Ltd, Oxford House, 76 Oxford Street, W1D 1BS.

MACDONALD, Prof. David Whyte, DPhil, DSc; FRSE; FRGS, FIBiol; Founding Director, Wildlife Conservation Research Unit, since 1986, and Professor of Wildlife Conservation, since 2004, University of Oxford; Senior Research Fellow in Wildlife Conservation, Lady Margaret Hall, Oxford, since 1986; *b* Oxford, 30 Sept. 1951; *s* of Dr William Alexander Fraser Macdonald and Williamina Stirrat (*née* Whyte), Glasgow; *m* 1975, Jennifer Mary Wells; one *s* two *d*. *Educ:* St Lawrence Coll., Ramsgate; Wadham Coll., Oxford (Wells Schol.; BA 1972); Balliol Coll., Oxford (DPhil 1977); DSc Oxon 2004. FRGS 1978; FIBiol 1990. University of Oxford: Jun. Res. Fellow, Balliol Coll., 1976–79; Ernest Cook Res. Fellow, 1979–84, Nuffield Res. Fellow, 1984–87, Dept of Zool. A. D. White Prof.-at-Large, Cornell Univ., 1997–2003; Vis. Prof., Imperial Coll., London, 2004–. Department for Environment, Food and Rural Affairs: Mem., Adv. Cttee on Pesticides, 2002–05 (Mem., Envmtl Panel, 2003–05); Advr to UK Biodiversity Res. Adv. Gp, 2002–; Mem., 2003–04, Chm., 2004–, Darwin Adv. Cttee. Advr to Burns Inquiry into hunting with hounds, 2000; Comr, Ind. Supervisory Authy for Hunting, 2000–05. Biodiversity Advr to Esmée Fairbairn Foundn, 2002–. Founding Chm., IUCN/Species Survival Commn Canid Specialist Gp, 1985–2005. Member: Council, English Nature, 2003–05; Bd, Natural England, 2005– (Chm., Sci. Adv. Cttee, 2006–); Council, Wildfowl and Wetlands Trust, 2005–; Inter Agency Climate Change Forum, JNCC, 2007–. Trustee, Macaulay Land Use Res. Inst., 1999–2003; Mem., NERC Peer Rev. Coll., 2006–08. Vice-President: Royal Soc. of Wildlife Trusts, 1999–; RSPCA, 2001–05. Zoological Society of London: Scientific Fellow, 1993; Mem. Council, 2001–06; Vice-Pres., 2003–06. FRSE 2008; Emer. Fellow, IUCN Survival Commn, 2005. Vice Pres., Eur. Soc. of Mammalogists, 1993–2004; Mem. Council, Fauna and Flora Internat., 1995–2002. Trustee: Earthwatch Europe, 2007–; WWF UK, 2008–. Natural history films: The Night of the Fox, BBC TV, 1976; Meerkats United, BBC TV, 1987 (Wildscreen Award, 1988); One for All, All for One, 1988; The Velvet Claw (series), BBC TV, 1992. T. H. Huxley Prize, Zool Soc., 1978; Dawkins Prize for Animal Conservation and Welfare, Balliol Coll., Oxford, 2004; Merriam Prize for res. in mammalogy, Amer. Soc. of Mammalogists, 2006; Medal for outstanding services to mammalogy, Mammal Soc. of GB, 2007. *Publications:* Rabies and Wildlife: a biologist's perspective, 1980; *joint editor:* A Handbook on Biotelemetry and Radio Tracking, 1979; Social Odours in Mammals, vols 1 and 2, 1985; Carnivore Conservation, 2001; The Biology and Conservation of Wild Canids, 2004; Key Topics in Conservation Biology, 2007; *popular science:* Vulpina: story of a fox, 1977; Expedition to Borneo, 1980; Running with the Fox, 1987 (Natural Hist. Author of Year Award); The Velvet Claw: a natural history of the carnivores, 1992; Field Guide to Mammals of Britain and Europe, 1993; European Mammals: evolution and behaviour, 1995 (Natural Hist. Author of Year Award); Meerkats, 1999; Foxes, 2000; (ed) Encyclopedia of Mammals, 3rd edn 2006; contrib. learned jls incl. Nature and Science. *Recreations:* farming (sheep and sheep dogs), Burns' poetry, photography, rowing, golf, surviving. *Address:* Wildlife Conservation Research Unit, University of Oxford, Department of Zoology, Tubney House, Tubney, Oxon OX13 5QL. *T:* (01865) 393100, *Fax:* (01865) 393101; *e-mail:* david.macdonald@zoo.ox.ac.uk, wcru@zoo.ox.ac.uk. *Club:* Athenæum.

MACDONALD, Hon. Donald (Stovel); PC (Canada) 1968; CC 1994; Senior Policy Adviser, Lang Michener LLP, Toronto, since 2002; *b* 1 March 1932; *s* of Donald Angus Macdonald and Marjorie Stovel Macdonald; *m* 1st, 1961, Ruth Hutchison (*d* 1987), Ottawa; four *d*; 2nd, 1988, Adrian Merchant; three step *s* three step *d* (and one step *d* decd). *Educ:* Univ. of Toronto (BA 1951); Osgoode Hall Law Sch. 1955 (LLB *ex post facto* 1991); Harvard Law Sch. (LLM 1956); Cambridge Univ. (Dip. in Internat. Law, 1957). Called to Ont Bar, 1955; Prize in Insurance Law, Law Soc. of Upper Canada, 1955; Rowell Fellow, Canadian Inst. of Internat. Affairs, 1956; McCarthy & McCarthy, law firm, Toronto, 1957–62, Partner, 1978–88; High Comr for Canada in UK, 1988–91; Counsel, McCarthy Tétrault, 1991–2000. Special Lectr, Univ. of Toronto Law Sch., 1978–83, 1986–88. MP Rosedale, 1962–78; Parly Sec. to Ministers of Justice, Finance, Ext. Affairs, Industry, 1963–68; Minister without Portfolio, 1968; Pres., Queen's Privy Council, and Govt House Leader, 1968–70; Minister of National Defence, 1970–72; Minister of Energy, Mines and Resources, 1972–75; Minister of Finance, 1975–77. Director: McDonnell Douglas Corp., 1978–88; Du Pont Canada Inc., 1978–88; Bank of Nova Scotia, 1980–88; Alberta Energy Co. Ltd, 1981–88; MacMillan-Bloedel Ltd, 1986–88; Celanese Canada, 1991–99 (Chm., 1997–99); Sun Life Assurance Co. of Canada, 1991–2002; TransCanada Pipelines, 1991–2002; Slough Estates Canada Ltd, 1991–2001; Siemens Canada (formerly Siemens Electric) Ltd, 1991–2004 (Chm., 1991–2004); Alberta Energy Co. Ltd, 1992–2002; Hambros Canada Inc., 1994–98; BFC Construction Corp. (formerly Banister Foundn Inc.), 1994–99; Boise Cascade Corp., 1996–2004; AT&T Canada Corp., 1999; Aber Diamond Corp. (formerly Aber Resources Ltd), 1999–2003; Century Mining Corp., 2004–08. Sen. Advr, UBS Bunting Warburg, Toronto, 2000–02. Chairman: Internat. Develt Res. Centre, Canada, 1981–84; Inst. for Res. on Public Policy, Montreal, 1991–97; Design Exchange, 1993–96. Chairman: Royal Commn on Econ. Union and Develt Prospects for Canada, 1982–85; Canadian Council for Public-Private Partnerships, 1993–99; Adv. Cttee on Competition in Ont's Electricity System, 1995–96; Atlantic Council of Canada, 1998–2003. Chm. and Trustee, IPC US Income Commercial Real Estate Investment Trust, 2001–07; Trustee, Clean Power Income Trust, 2001–07. Trustee, Clan Donald Lands Trust, Armadale, Skye, 1991–2007. Chm., Canadian Friends of Cambridge, 1993–97. Freeman, City of London, 1990; Liveryman, Distillers' Co. Hon. Fellow, Trinity Hall, Cambridge, 1994. LLD (*hc*): St Lawrence, 1974; New Brunswick at Saint John, 1990; Toronto, 2000; Carleton, Ottawa, 2003; Hon. DEng Colorado Sch. of Mines, 1976. *Recreation:* silviculture. *Address:* 2709 Seventh Concession, RR4, Uxbridge, ON L9P 1R4, Canada. *T:* (905) 6492557, *Fax:* (905) 6493144; Lang Michener LLP, Suite 2500, 181 Bay Street, Toronto, ON M5J 2T7, Canada. *T:* (416) 3074241, *Fax:* (416) 3651719; *e-mail:* dmacdonald@langmichener.ca. *Clubs:* York, Toronto (Toronto).

McDONALD, Elaine Maria, OBE 1983; Director, 1993–2001, Chairman, 1997–2001, Creative Dance Artists Trust; *b* 2 May 1943; *d* of Wilfrid Samuel and Ellen McDonald. *Educ:* Convent of the Ladies of Mary Grammar Sch., Scarborough; Royal Ballet Sch., London. Walter Gore's London Ballet, 1962–64; Western Theatre Ballet, 1964–69; Principal Dancer, 1969–89, Artistic Controller, 1988–89, Scottish Ballet; has also danced with London Fest. Ballet, Portuguese Nat. Ballet, Galina Samsova and Andre Prokovsky's New London Ballet, Cuban Nat. Ballet; Associate Artistic Dir, Northern Ballet Th., 1990–92. Mem., Scottish Arts Council, 1986–90 (Mem., Dance and Mime Cttee, 1982–92). Patron, Peter Darrell Trust. Hon. LittD Strathclyde, 1990. *Relevant publication:* Elaine McDonald, ed J. S. Dixon, 1983. *Recreations:* physical therapy, theatre, travel, reading.

MACDONALD, Dr Ewan Beaton, OBE 2002; FRCP, FRCPE, FRCPGlas, FFOM, FFOMI; Hon. Senior Lecturer and Head, Healthy Working Lives Group, Public Health and Health Policy Section, University of Glasgow, since 2004 (Senior Lecturer, 1990–2004); *b* 11 Jan. 1947; *s* of Dr Duncan Macdonald, MBE and Isabel Dow Macdonald; *m* 1971, Patricia Malloy; three *s* one *d*. *Educ:* Keil Sch.; Univ. of Glasgow (MB ChB). FFOM 1988; FRCPGlas 1992; FRCP 1994; FRCPE 1996; FFOMI 1997. General medicine, Western Infirmary, Glasgow, 1971–75; National Coal Board: MO, 1975–80; PMO, Yorks, 1980–85; Hon. Consultant in Rehabilitation, Firbeck Hosp., 1980–85; IBM UK: SMO, 1986; CMO, 1987–90; Chm., IBM European Occupational Health Bd, 1988–90; Dir, SALUS (Lanarks Occupnl Health and Safety Service), 1990–. Dean, Faculty of Occupational Medicine, RCP, 1994–96; Pres., Sect. of Occupnl Medicine, Union of Eur. Med. Specialists, 2001–05 (Sec., 1997–2001). Founder and Chm., Kinloch Castle Friends Assoc., 1996–. Hon. Col, 225 Med. Support Regt (V), 2007–. *Publications:* numerous articles and chapters on occupational health. *Recreations:* mountaineering, sailing, fishing. *Address:* Public Health and Health Policy Section, 1 Lilybank Gardens, University of Glasgow, Glasgow G12 8RZ. *T:* (0141) 330 3719; *e-mail:* e.b.macdonald@clinmed.gla.ac.uk. *Club:* Loch Lomond Sailing.

MACDONALD, Very Rev. Dr Finlay Angus John; Principal Clerk, since 1996, Moderator, 2002–03, General Assembly of the Church of Scotland; a Chaplain to the Queen in Scotland, since 2001; *b* 1 July 1945; *s* of late Rev. John Macdonald, AEA, MA and Eileen Ivy Sheila (*née* O'Flynn); *m* 1968, Elizabeth Mary Stuart; two *s*. *Educ:* Dundee High Sch.; Univ. of St Andrews (MA 1967; BD 1970; PhD 1983). Pres. Students' Representative Council, St Andrews Univ., 1968–69. Licensed by Presbytery of Dundee, 1970; ordained by Presbytery of Stirling and Dunblane, 1971; Minister: Menstrie Parish Ch., 1971–77; Jordanhill Parish Ch., Glasgow, 1977–96. Convener, Business Cttee, Gen. Assembly, 1988–92. Mem., Scottish Inter-Faith Council, 2005–. Gov., Jordanhill Coll., 1988–93; Lay Mem. Court, Strathclyde Univ., 1993–96 (Fellow, 2002). Hon. DD St Andrews, 2002. *Publication:* Confidence in a Changing Church, 2004. *Recreations:* music, gardening, hill-walking. *Address:* (office) 121 George Street, Edinburgh EH2 4YN. *T:* (0131) 240 2240. *Club:* New (Edinburgh).

MacDONALD, Hon. Flora Isabel, CC 1999 (OC 1993); PC (Can.) 1979; Chairperson, HelpAge International, 1997–2001; *b* N Sydney, Nova Scotia, 3 June 1926. *Educ:* schools in North Sydney, Nova Scotia; Empire Business Coll., Sydney, NS; Canadian Nat. Defence Coll. With Nat. HQ, Progressive Cons. Party, 1957–66 (Exec. Dir, 1961–66); Nat. Sec., Progressive Cons. Assoc. of Canada, 1966–69; Administrative Officer and Tutor, Dept of Political Studies, Queen's Univ., Kingston, 1967–73; MP (Progressive C) Kingston, Ontario, 1972–88; Sec. of State for External Affairs, Canada, 1979–80; Minister of Employment and Immigration, 1984–86; Minister for Communications, 1986–88. Vis. Scholar, Centre for Canadian Studies, Univ. of Edinburgh, 1989. Special Advr, Commonwealth of Learning, 1990–91; Chairperson, Internat. Develt Res. Centre, 1992–97. Dir, C. T. Financial Services, 1989–97. Director: Care Canada, 1993–2002; Partnership Africa Canada, 1997–2004; Future Generations, Franklin, WV, 1996–. Chairman: Canadian Co-ordinating Cttee, UN Internat. Year of Older Persons, 1999; Shastri Indo-Canada Adv. Council, 1996–2004. Pres., World Federalists of Canada, 2001–04. Patron, Commonwealth Human Rights Initiative. Mem., Carnegie Commn on Preventing Deadly Conflict, Washington, 1994–98. Pres., Assoc. of Canadian Clubs, 1999–2003. Presenter, North/South (weekly TV prog.), 1990–94. Hon. degrees from Univs in Canada, US and UK. Padma Shri (India), 2004. *Publications:* papers on political subjects. *Recreations:* speedskating, mountain climbing. *Address:* #1103, 350 Queen Elizabeth Driveway, Ottawa, ON K1S 3N1, Canada.

McDONALD, F(rancis) James; Chairman, Beaumont Hospital Board of Trustees, 1992–96 (Chairman, Beaumont Hospital Foundation, 1987–92); President and Chief Operating Officer, General Motors, 1981–87; *b* Saginaw, Mich, 3 Aug. 1922; *s* of Francis and Mary McDonald; *m* 1944, Betty Ann Dettenthaler; two *s* one *d*. *Educ:* General Motors Inst.; Yale Univ. Served USN Submarine Service, 1944–46 (Lieut). Joined Saginaw Malleable Iron Plant, 1946; Transmission Div., Detroit, 1956–65; Pontiac Motor Div., 1965–68; Dir, Manufacturing Operations, Chevrolet Motor Div., 1968–69; Vice-Pres., and Mem. Admin Cttee, Gen. Motors, 1969; General Manager: Pontiac Motor Div., 1969–72; Chevrolet Motor Div., 1972–74; Exec. Vice-Pres. and a Dir, 1974; Mem. Finance Cttee, 1979; Chm., Exec. and Admin Cttees, 1981. Holds hon. degrees from univs and colls in the US, incl. Michigan State Univ. and Notre Dame Univ.

MACDONALD, Howard; *see* Macdonald, J. H.

MACDONALD, Prof. (Hugh) Ian, OC 1977; Professor, Department of Economics, and Schulich School of Business (formerly Faculty of Administrative Studies), since 1974, Director, Degree Programme in Public Administration, since 1992, York University, Toronto; President Emeritus, York University, since 1984; *b* Toronto, 27 June 1929; *s* of Hugh and Winnifred Macdonald; *m* 1960, Dorothy Marion Vernon; two *s* three *d*. *Educ:* public schs, Toronto; Univ. of Toronto; Oxford Univ. BCom (Toronto), MA (Oxon), BPhil (Oxon). Univ. of Toronto: Lectr in Economics, 1955; Dean of Men, 1956; Asst Prof., Economics, 1962. Govt of Ontario: Chief Economist, 1965; Dep. Provincial Treas., 1967; Dep. Treas. and Dep. Minister of Economics, 1968; Dep. Treas. and Dep. Minister of Economics and Intergovernmental Affairs, 1972. Pres., York Univ., 1974–84; Dir, York Internat., 1984–94. Director: the AGF Cos, 1982–; McGraw-Hill Ryerson Ltd, 1984– (Chm., 1996–). Member: Canadian Economics Assoc.; Amer. Economics Assoc.; Canadian Assoc. for Club of Rome; Inst. of Public Admin of Canada; Lambda Alpha Fraternity (Land Economics); Amer. Soc. for Public Admin. President: Empire Club of Canada, 1969–70; Ticker Club, 1971–72; Couchiching Inst. of Public Affairs, 1975–77; Canadian Rhodes Scholars Foundn, 1986–92; World Univ. Service of Canada, 1992–93; Chairman: Toronto Men's Br. of CIIA, 1959–61; Inst. for Political Involvement, 1974–76; Bd, Corp. to Promote Innovation Develt for Employment Advancement (Govt of Ontario), 1984–86; Commn on Financing of Elementary and Secondary Educn in Ontario, 1984–87; Ont. Municipal Trng and Educn Adv. Council, 1984–86; Hockey Canada, 1987–94; Annual Fund Appeal in Canada of Balliol Coll., Oxford Univ., 1992–98; The Commonwealth of Learning, 1994–2003 (Fellow, 2004). Member: Attorney General's Cttee on Securities Legislation, 1963–65; Economic Council of Canada, 1976–79; Bd, Council for Canadian Unity, 1978–99; Admin. Bd, Internat. Assoc. of Univs, 1980–90; Council and Exec. Cttee, Interamerican Orgn for Higher Educn, 1980–88 (Vice-Pres., Canada); Canadian Exec. Service Orgn, 1998–2001. Hon. Councillor, Internat. Orgn for Higher Educn, 1992. Hon. Life Mem., Canadian Olympic Assoc., 1997. KLJ 1978; Citation of Merit, Court of Canadian Citizenship, 1980. Hon. LLD Toronto, 1974; DUniv Open, 1998; Hon. DLitt: Sri Lanka Open, 1999; Dr B. R. Ambedkar Open, Hyderabad, 2001; York, 2008. Canada Centennial Medal, 1967; Silver Jubilee Medal, 1977; Commemorative Medal, 125th Anniversary of Confedn of Canada, 1992; Award of Merit, Canadian Bureau for Internat. Educn, 1994; Vanier Medal, for distinction in public service and excellence in public admin, Inst. of Public Admin of Canada, 2000; Senator Peter Boorsma Award, S Eastern Conf. for Public Admin, 2006. Golden Jubilee Medal, 2002. *Recreations:* hockey, tennis; public service in various organizations. *Address:* 7 Whitney Avenue, Toronto, ON M4W 2A7, Canada. *T:* (416) 9212908; York University, 4700 Keele Street, Toronto, ON M3J 1P3, Canada. *T:* (416) 7365632.

MACDONALD, Prof. Hugh John; Avis Blewett Professor of Music, Washington University, St Louis, since 1987 (Chair, Music Department, 1997–99); *b* 31 Jan. 1940; *s* of Stuart and Margaret Macdonald; *m* 1st, 1963, Naomi Butterworth; one *s* three *d*; 2nd, 1979, Elizabeth Babb; one *s*. *Educ:* Winchester College; Pembroke College, Cambridge (MA; PhD). FRCM 1987. Cambridge University: Asst Lectr, 1966–69; Lectr, 1969–71; Fellow, Pembroke Coll., 1963–71; Lectr, Oxford Univ., 1971–80, and Fellow, St John's Coll; Gardiner Prof. of Music, Glasgow Univ., 1980–87. Vis. Prof., Indiana Univ., 1979. Gen. Editor, New Berlioz Edition, 1966–2006. Szymanowski Medal, Poland, 1983. *Publications:* Berlioz Orchestral Music, 1969; Skryabin, 1978; Berlioz, 1981; (ed) Berlioz Selected Letters, 1995; Berlioz's Orchestration Treatise, 2002; Beethoven's Century, 2008; articles in New Grove Dict. of Music and Musicians, Musical Times, Music and Letters, Revue de Musicologie. *Recreation:* bridges. *Address:* Department of Music, Washington University, One Brookings Drive, St Louis, MO 63130–4899, USA. *T:* (314) 9355519.

MACDONALD, Iain Smith, CB 1988; MD; FRCPE, FFPH; Chief Medical Officer, Scottish Home and Health Department, 1985–88, retired; *b* 14 July 1927; *s* of Angus Macdonald, MA and Jabina Urie Smith; *m* 1958, Sheila Foster; one *s* one *d*. *Educ:* Univ. of Glasgow (MD, DPH). Lectr, Univ. of Glasgow, 1955; Deputy Medical Officer of Health: Bury, 1957; Bolton, 1959; joined Scottish Home and Health Dept, 1964, Dep. Chief Med. Officer, 1974–85. Mem., MRC, 1985–88. QHP 1984–87. *Publication:* Glencoe and Beyond: the sheep-farming years 1780–1830, 2005. *Address:* 4 Skythorn Way, Falkirk FK1 5NR. *T:* (01324) 625100.

MACDONALD, Ian; *see* Macdonald, H. I.

MACDONALD, Ian Alexander; QC 1988; *b* 12 Jan. 1939; *s* of late Ian Wilson Macdonald and Helen Nicolson, MA; *m* 1st, 1968, Judith Roberts (marr. diss.); two *s*; 2nd, 1978, Jennifer Hall (marr. diss.); one *s*; 3rd, 1991, Yasmin Sharif (marr. diss.). *Educ:* Glasgow Acad.; Cargilfield Sch., Edinburgh; Rugby Sch.; Clare Coll., Cambridge (MA, LLB). Called to the Bar, Middle Temple, 1963 (Astbury Scholar, 1962–65; Bencher, 2002); SE Circuit. Lectr in Law, Kingston Polytechnic, 1968–72; Senior Legal Writer and Research Consultant, Incomes Data Services Ltd, 1974–80 (monitoring develts in employment law). Mem., Cttee of Inquiry into disappearance of Gen. Humberto Delgado, 1965; Chm., Indep. Inquiry into Racial Violence in Manchester Schs, 1987–88. Special Advocate, Special Immigration Appeals Commn, 1999–2004. Pres., Immigration Law Practitioners' Assoc., 1984–. Mem. Editl Adv. Bd, Immigration and Nationality Law and Practice. Grand Cross, Order of Liberty (Portugal), 1995. *Publications:* Resale Price Maintenance, 1964; (with D. P. Kerrigan) The Land Commission Act 1967, 1967; Race Relations and Immigration Law, 1969; Immigration Appeals Act 1969, 1969; Race Relations: the new law, 1977; (with N. Blake) The New Nationality Law, 1982; Immigration Law and Practice, 1983, 7th edn 2008; Murder in the Playground: report of Macdonald Inquiry into Racial Violence in Manchester Schools, 1990; (contrib.) Family Guide to the Law, 1971, 1972; articles in professional jls. *Recreations:* swimming, watching football, reading. *Address:* Garden Court Chambers, 57–60 Lincoln's Inn Fields, WC2A 3LS. *T:* (020) 7993 7600. *Club:* Cumberland Lawn Tennis.

MACDONALD OF SLEAT, Sir Ian Godfrey B.; *see* Bosville Macdonald of Sleat.

MACDONALD, Prof. Ian Grant, FRS 1979; Professor of Pure Mathematics, Queen Mary College, subsequently Queen Mary and Westfield College, University of London, 1976–87, now Professor Emeritus, Queen Mary, University of London; *b* 11 Oct. 1928; *s* of Douglas Grant Macdonald and Irene Alice Macdonald; *m* 1954, Margaretha Maria Lodewijk Van Goethem; two *s* three *d*. *Educ:* Winchester Coll.; Trinity Coll., Cambridge (MA). Asst Principal and Principal, Min. of Supply, 1952–57; Asst Lectr, Univ. of Manchester, 1957–60; Lectr, Univ. of Exeter, 1960–63; Fellow, Magdalen Coll., Oxford, 1963–72; Fielden Prof. of Pure Maths, Univ. of Manchester, 1972–76. *Publications:* Introduction to Commutative Algebra (with M. F. Atiyah), 1969; Algebraic Geometry, 1969; articles in math. jls. *Address:* 56 High Street, Steventon, Abingdon, Oxon OX13 6RS.

McDONALD, Iona Sara MacIntyre; Sheriff of North Strathclyde at Kilmarnock and Paisley, since 2002; *b* 18 Nov. 1954; *d* of Thomas and Isabella MacIntyre; *m* 1978, Colin Neale McDonald (*d* 2001); one *s* one *d*. *Educ:* Glasgow Univ. (MA 1976; LLB 1978). NP 1980. Admitted solicitor, 1980; Partner, Messrs Mathie-Morton Black & Buchanan, Solicitors, Ayr, 1982–2000; Reporter to the Court, Safeguarder and Curator ad Litem, 1985–2000; Temp. Sheriff, 1995, Hon. Sheriff at Ayr, 1995–2000; All Scotland Floating Sheriff, 2000–02. *Recreations:* gardening, ski-ing, walking, travel. *Address:* Kilmarnock Sheriff Court, St Marnock Street, Kilmarnock KA1 1ED. *T:* (01563) 520211.

McDONALD, James; *see* McDonald, F. J.

MACDONALD, Most Rev. James Hector, DD; CSC; Archbishop of St John's (Newfoundland), (RC), 1991–2000, now Emeritus; *b* 28 April 1925; *s* of Alexander and Mary Macdonald. *Educ:* St Joseph's Univ., 1944–45. Ordained priest, 1953. Congregation of the Holy Cross: Mission Bank, 1954–56; Dir, Holy Cross Minor Seminary, St Joseph's, NB, 1956–62; Sec., Provincial Council, 1956–63; Dir of Vocations, 1962–63; Superior, Holy Cross House of Studies, 1964–69; Asst Provincial, 1966–72; Pastor, St Michael's, Waterloo, Ont., 1969–77; Dean, Waterloo County Priests, dio. of Hamilton, 1974–77; Aux. Bishop of Hamilton, 1978–82; Bishop of Charlottetown, 1982–91. *Address:* PO Box 1363, Bonaventure Street, St John's, NL A1C 5N5, Canada.

MACDONALD, John B(arfoot), OC 1991; DDS, MS, PhD; Chairman, Addiction Research Foundation, 1981–87 (President and Chief Executive Officer, 1976–81); Executive Director, Council of Ontario Universities, 1968–76; Professor of Higher Education, University of Toronto, 1968–76; *b* 23 Feb. 1918; *s* of Arthur A. Macdonald and Gladys L. Barfoot; *m*; two *s* one *d*; *m* 1967, Liba Kucera; two *d*. *Educ:* Univ. of Toronto, University of Illinois, Columbia Univ. DDS (with hons) Toronto, 1942; MS (Bact) Ill, 1948; PhD (Bact) Columbia, 1953. Lectr, Prev. Dentistry, University of Toronto, and private practice, 1942–44. Canadian Dental Corps, 1944–46 (Capt.) Instr, Bacteriol, University of Toronto, and private practice, 1946–47; Res. Asst, Univ. of Illinois, 1947–48; Kellogg Fellow and Canadian Dental Assoc. Res. Student, Columbia Univ., 1948–49; University of Toronto: Asst Prof. of Bacteriol., 1949–53; Assoc. Prof. of Bacteriol., 1953–56; Chm., Div. of Dental Res., 1953–56; Prof. of Bacteriol., 1956; Cons. in Dental Educn, University of BC, 1955–56; Dir, Forsyth Dental Infirmary, 1956–62 (Cons. in Bacteriol., 1962); Prof. of Microbiol., Harvard Sch., of Dental Med., 1956–62 (Dir of Postdoctoral Studies, 1960–62); President, Univ. of British Columbia, 1962–67. Consultant: Dental Med. Section of Corporate Research Div. of Colgate-Palmolive Co., 1958–62; Donwood Foundn, Toronto, 1967 (Chm. of Bd, 1972–75); Science Council of Canada, 1967–69; Addiction Research Foundn of Ontario, 1968–74 (Mem., 1974–76); Nat. Inst. of Health, 1968– (Mem., Dental Study Sect., 1961–65). Chm., Commn on Pharmaceutical Services of the Canadian Pharmaceutical Assoc., 1967; Mem. and Vice-Chm., Ontario Council of Health, 1981–84; Councillor-at-Large, Internat. Assoc. for Dental Research, 1963, Pres. 1968–69. Fellow, Mem. or Chm. of numerous assocs etc, both Canadian and international. FACD 1955; Hon. FICD 1965. Hon. AM, Harvard Univ., 1956; Hon. LLD: Univ. of Manitoba, 1962; Simon Fraser Univ., 1965; Hon DSc Univ. of British Columbia, 1967; Hon. LLD: Wilfred Laurier, 1976; Brock, 1976; W Ontario, 1977; Hon. DSc: Windsor, 1977; Toronto, 2000. *Publications:* Higher Education in British Columbia and a Plan for the Future, 1962 etc.; numerous contribs to learned jls. *Recreations:* golf, fishing. *Address:* 30 Metropolitan Crescent, Keswick, ON L4P 1L5, Canada. *Clubs:* University of BC Faculty (Vancouver); Faculty (University of Toronto).

McDONALD, Prof. John Corbett, MD; FRCP, FFCM, FFOM; Professor, Department of Occupational and Environmental Medicine, National Heart and Lung Institute (Royal Brompton Hospital), University of London, since 1986; *b* 20 April 1918; *s* of John Forbes McDonald and Sarah Mary McDonald; *m* 1942, Alison Dunstan Wells; one *s* three *d*. *Educ:* London Univ. (MD); Harvard Univ. (MS). DPH, DIH; FRCP (Canada) 1970; FRCP 1976; FFCM 1976; FFOM 1978. Served War, MO, RAMC, 1942–46. Epidemiologist, Public Health Lab. Service, 1951–64 (Dir, Epidemiol Res. Lab., 1960–64); Prof. and Head, Dept of Epidemiology and Health, McGill Univ., Montreal, 1964–76; Prof. of Occupational Health, LSHTM, London Univ., 1976–81, now Emeritus; Prof. of Epidemiol. and Hd, Sch. of Occupational Health, McGill Univ., 1981–83, Prof. Emeritus, 1988–; Chm., Dept of Clinical Epidemiology, Nat. Heart and Lung (formerly Cardiothoracic) Inst. (Royal Brompton Hosp.), Univ. of London, 1986–90. *Publications:* (ed) Recent Advances in Occupational Health, 1981; Epidemiology of Work-related Diseases, 1995, 2nd edn 2000; papers on epidemiol subjects. *Recreation:* croquet. *Address:* 26 Charlton, Chichester PO18 0HV. *Club:* Athenæum.

MacDONALD, Maj.-Gen. John Donald, CB 1993; CBE 1986 (OBE 1981); DL; Chief Executive (formerly General Secretary): The Earl Haig Fund, 1994–2003; Officers Association Scotland, 1994–2003; *b* 5 April 1938; *s* of Lt-Col John MacDonald, OBE; *m* 1964, Mary, *d* of Dr Graeme M. Warrack, CBE, DSO, TD; one *s* two *d*. *Educ:* George Watson's Coll., Edinburgh; RMA Sandhurst. Commnd, 1958; saw service with KOSB, RASC, RCT and Airborne Forces Berlin, UK, BAOR, N Africa, India (Defence Services Staff Coll.), 1958–71; ndc, 1976; Turkey NATO HQ Izmir, CO 4 Armoured Div., Transport Regt RCT, 1978–80; Instr Australian Comd and Staff Coll., 1980–82; Chief Instr and Comdt, RCT Officers' Sch., 1983; DCS 3 Armoured Div., 1983–86; Col Personnel Br. Sec., MoD, 1987–88; Comdr Transport, 1st BR Corps and Garrison Comdr Bielefeld, 1988–91; DG Transport and Movements, MoD, 1991–93. Col Comdt RLC, 1993–2003. Hon. Col, Scottish Transport Regt plc, 1997–2004. Gen. Sec., RBL, Scotland, 1994–2000. Chm., Sportsmatch, Scotland, 1993–98; Mem., Sports Council, Scotland, 1994–99. Queen's Councillor, Queen Victoria Sch., Dunblane, 1994–2004. Chm., Combined Services Rugby, 1991–93. Freeman, City of London, 1991; Hon. Mem. Ct of Assts, Carmens' Co., 1991. DL City of Edinburgh, 1996. *Recreations:* Rugby (played for Scotland, Barbarians, Combined Services and Army), ski-ing, golf, travel, music, collecting. *Address:* Ormiston Hill, Kirknewton, West Lothian EH27 8DQ. *Clubs:* Army and Navy; London Scottish, Royal & Ancient (St Andrews), Honourable Co. of Edinburgh Golfers (Muirfield), Rugby Internationalists Golfing Society.

MacDONALD, John Grant, CBE 1989 (MBE 1962); HM Diplomatic Service, retired; re-employed at Foreign and Commonwealth Office, since 1993; Representative of Secretary of State for Foreign and Commonwealth Affairs, since 1997; *b* 26 Jan. 1932; *er s* of late John Nicol MacDonald and Margaret MacDonald (*née* Vasey); *m* 1955, Jean (*d* 2003), *o c* of late J. K. K. Harrison; one *s* two *d*. *Educ:* George Heriot's School. Entered HM Foreign (later Diplomatic) Service, 1949; FO, 1949; served HM Forces, 1950–52; FO, 1952; Berne, 1954–59; Third Sec. and Vice Consul, Havana, 1960–62; FO, 1962; DSAO, 1965; Second, later First Sec. (Comm.), Lima, 1966–71; Nat. Defence Coll., Latimer, 1971–72; Parly Clerk of FCO, 1972–75; First Sec. (Comm.), Hd of Trade Promotion Sect., Washington, 1975–79; Hd of Chancery, Dhaka, 1980–81; Hd of Chancery and HM Consul, Bogotá, 1981–84; Counsellor, FCO, 1985–86; Ambassador to: Paraguay, 1986–89; Panama, 1989–92; Head UK Delegn, and Dep. Head (Political), EC Monitor Mission, 1992; temp. duty as Charter Mark Assessor, Cabinet Office, 1994, 1995; UK Mem., OSCE Observer Gp, elections in Macedonia, 1994. Vis. Lectr, Foreign

Services Inst., S Africa, 1997. *Recreations:* travel, photography, swimming. *Address:* c/o Foreign and Commonwealth Office, SW1A 2AH. *Clubs:* Naval and Military, Royal Over-Seas League.

MACDONALD, (John) Howard, CA; FCT; Director: BOC Group plc, 1991–2002; Weir Group plc, 1991–2001; *b* 5 June 1928; *s* of John and Helen Macdonald; *m* 1961, Anne Hunter; three *d. Educ:* Hermitage, Helensburgh. CA 1954. Thomson McLintock & Co. (served articles), 1949–55; Walter Mitchell & Sons, 1955–58; Aircraft Marine Products, 1958; Finance Manager, Keir & Cawder Arrow Drilling, 1958–60; Royal Dutch Shell Group, 1960–83, Group Treasurer, 1978–83; Chairman and Chief Executive: Dome Petroleum, 1983–88; NatWest Investment Bank, 1989–91; Director: National Westminster Bank, 1989–91; McDermott Internat. Inc., 1985–97; J. Ray McDermott Inc., 1985–97. Mem., Assoc. of Corporate Treasurers, 1979. *Recreations:* golf, theatre. *Address:* 18 Fairbourne, Cobham, Surrey KT11 2BP. *T:* (01932) 862281. *Club:* Caledonian.

MACDONALD, John Reginald; QC 1976; barrister-at-law; Commercial, Chancery and Administrative Lawyer; *b* 26 Sept. 1931; *s* of Ranald Macdonald and Marion Olive (*née* Kirkby); *m* 1958, Erica Stanton; one *s* one *d. Educ:* St Edward's Sch., Oxford; Queens' Coll., Cambridge. Called to Bar, Lincoln's Inn, 1955, Bencher, 1985; called to Bar of Eastern Caribbean, 1988. Represented: the people of Ocean Island, 1975; Yuri Orlov, the Soviet dissident, 1977–86; Canadian Indians, 1982; the Ilios, who were removed from Diego Garcia to make way for a US base, 1983; appeared for the people of Barbuda at the Antigua Indep. Conf. at Lancaster House in 1980; Mem., Internat. Commn of Jurists missions to investigate violence in S Africa, 1990, 1992, 1993. Drafted written constitution for the UK (We the People), proposed by Liberal Democrats, 1990, revised 1993; Mem., Jt Lib Dem Labour Cttee on Constitutional Reform, 1996–97. Contested: Wimbledon (L) 1966 and 1970; Folkestone and Hythe (L) 1983, (L/Alliance) 1987; E Kent (Lib Dem), Eur. election 1994. Chm. Council, New Kent Opera, 1996–2008. *Publication:* (ed with Clive H. Jones) The Law of Freedom of Information, 2003. *Recreation:* the theatre. *Address:* 12 New Square, Lincoln's Inn, WC2A 3SW. *T:* (020) 7419 8000. *Club:* MCC.

MacDONALD, John William; HM Diplomatic Service, retired; *b* 13 June 1938; *s* of John MacDonald and Anne Macdonald (*née* Richards); *m* 1960, Margaret Millam Burns. *Educ:* Boteler Grammar Sch.; NDC; Manchester Business Sch. Foreign Office, 1955, and 1959–94; Royal Navy, 1957–59; Dipl. Service appts include Cairo, Tokyo, Dhaka, Dar es Salaam; Consul-Gen., Shanghai, 1991–94. *Recreations:* walking, golf, listening to music. *Address:* 12 Snells Wood Court, Little Chalfont, Bucks HP7 9QT. *Club:* Little Chalfont Golf.

MACDONALD, Sir Kenneth (Carmichael), KCB 1990 (CB 1983); Chairman, Raytheon Systems Ltd (formerly Cossor Electronics, then Raytheon Cossor, Ltd), 1991–2000; *b* 25 July 1930; *s* of William Thomas and Janet Millar Macdonald; *m* 1960, Ann Elisabeth (*née* Pauer); one *s* two *d. Educ:* Hutchesons' Grammar Sch.; Glasgow Univ. MA (Hons Classics). RAF, 1952–54. Asst Principal, Air Ministry, 1954; Asst Private Sec. to Sec. of State, 1956–57; Private Sec. to Permanent Sec., 1958–61; HM Treasury, 1962–65; MoD, 1965; Asst Sec., 1968; Counsellor (Defence), UK Delegn to NATO, 1973–75; Asst Under-Sec. of State, 1975, Dep. Under-Sec. of State, 1980, Second Perm. Under-Sec. of State, 1988–90, MoD. Chairman: Raytheon (Europe) Ltd, 1991–94; Internat. Military Services Ltd, 1993–2005. Chm., Council of Voluntary Welfare Work, 1993–2005. Trustee, Chatham Historic Dockyard Trust, 1992–2000. *Recreation:* golf. *Address:* c/o Barclays Bank, 27 Regent Street, SW1Y 4UB. *Club:* Royal Air Force.

MACDONALD, Sir Kenneth (Donald John), Kt 2007; QC 1997; Director of Public Prosecutions, 2003–08; *b* 4 Jan. 1953; *s* of late Dr Kenneth Macdonald, scientist, and Maureen Macdonald (*née* Sheridan); *m* 1980, Linda Zuck, television producer; two *s* one *d. Educ:* St Edmund Hall, Oxford (BA Hons PPE 1974). Called to the Bar, Inner Temple, 1978, Bencher, 2004. A Recorder, 2001–03. Mem., Treasury Counsel Selection Cttee, Central Criminal Court, 2001–03. Criminal Bar Association: Mem. Cttee, 1997–2003; Chm., Educn Sub-Cttee, 1999–2001; Vice Chm., 2002–03; Chm., 2003; Member: Criminal Justice Adv. Panel, Justice, 1997–2003; Bar Council, 2000; Bar Public Affairs Gp, 2001–03 (Vice-Chm., 2001–02); Sentencing Guidelines Council, 2003–; Criminal Procedure Rules Cttee, 2003–. *Recreations:* 20th century history, crime fiction, film noir, Arsenal Football Club. *Address:* Matrix Chambers, Griffin Building, Gray's Inn, WC1R 5LN.

McDONALD, Most Rev. Kevin John Patrick; see Southwark, Archbishop of, (RC).

MACDONALD, Lewis; Member (Lab) Aberdeen Central, Scottish Parliament, since 1999; *b* 1 Jan. 1957; *s* of late Rev. Roderick Macdonald and of Margaret Macdonald (*née* Currie); *m* 1997, Sandra Inkster; two *d. Educ:* Inverurie Acad.; Univ. of Aberdeen (MA, PhD). Parly Researcher, office of Frank Doran, MP, 1987–92 and 1997–99; Adviser to Tom Clarke, MP, 1993–97. Mem., Exec. Cttee, SLP, 1997–99. Dep. Minister for Transport and Planning, 2001, for Enterprise, Transport and Lifelong Learning, 2001–03, for Enterprise and Lifelong Learning, 2003–04, for Envmt and Rural Develt, 2004–05, for Health and Community Care, 2005–07, Scottish Exec. Convenor, Holyrood Progress Gp, 2000–01. Contested (Lab) Moray, 1997. *Recreations:* walking, football, history. *Address:* (office) 70 Rosemount Place, Aberdeen AB25 2XJ. *T:* (01224) 646333.

MacDONALD, Madeleine Mary; see Arnot, M. M.

MacDONALD, Margo, (Mrs James Sillars); Member, Lothians, Scottish Parliament, since 1999 (SNP 1999–2003, Ind since 2003); journalist; *b* 19 April 1943; *d* of Robert and Jean Aitken; *m* 1st, 1965, Peter MacDonald (marr. diss. 1980); two *d*; 2nd, 1981, James Sillars, *qv. Educ:* Hamilton Academy; Dunfermline Coll. (Diploma of Physical Educn). Contested (SNP) Paisley, Gen. Elec., 1970; MP (SNP) Glasgow (Govan). Nov. 1973–Feb. 1974; contested (SNP): Glasgow (Govan), Gen. Elec., Feb. 1974 and Oct. 1974; Hamilton, by-election, May 1978. Vice-Chm., Scottish National Party, 1972–79 (Senior Vice-Chm., 1974–79); Mem., SNP Nat. Exec., 1980–81; Chm., SNP '79 Group, 1978–81. Director of Shelter (Scotland), 1978–81. *Recreations:* swimming, aquarobics, country music, Hibs FC. *Address:* Scottish Parliament, Edinburgh EH99 1SP.

MACDONALD, Dame Mary (Beaton), DBE 2005; Headteacher, Riverside Primary School, North Shields, since 1994; *b* 29 July 1950; *d* of Robert Beaton Skinner and Mary Ann Skinner (*née* Gregory); two *s* one *d. Educ:* Jordanhill Coll., Glasgow (DipEd (Scotland)). Primary teacher, Isle of Bute, 1970–75; career break (short-term supply work), 1975–87; Sen. Teacher, Hawthorn Primary Sch., Newcastle upon Tyne, 1987–90; Dep. Hd, Montagu Primary Sch., Newcastle upon Tyne, 1990–94. DUniv Strathclyde, 2006. *Recreations:* reading, gardening. *Address:* Riverside Primary School, Minton Lane, North Shields, Tyne & Wear NE29 6DQ. *T:* (0191) 200 5037, *Fax:* (0191) 200 5081; *e-mail:* riverside.primary@northtyneside.gov.uk.

MACDONALD, Mary Elizabeth; Registrar, Judicial Committee of the Privy Council, since 2005; *b* 2 Aug. 1958; *d* of Malcolm A. Macdonald and Anne E. Macdonald; *m* 1988,

Iain MacVay (separated); one *s. Educ:* Univ. of British Columbia (BA 1st Cl. Hons Hist. 1981); Univ. of Victoria (LLB 1986); Darwin Coll., Cambridge (LLM Internat. Law and Civil Liberties 1989). Legal researcher, Peace Tax Fund, Victoria, 1983; TEFL, Cambridge Sch., Lisbon, 1983–84; legal researcher, Hanan, Gordon & Co., Victoria, 1985; called to the Bar, British Columbia, 1987; articled law student, then lawyer, Harris, Campbell, Threlfall & O'Neill, barristers and solicitors, Burnaby, 1986–87; Crown Counsel for Province of British Columbia, 1988; Department of Justice: lawyer, Admin. Law Reform Unit, Ottawa, 1989–90; historical researcher on behalf of Justice Res. Unit (native land claims), London, 1990–91; admitted solicitor, 1991; Section Manager and Human Rights Co-ordinator, Criminal Appeal Office, Royal Courts of Justice, 1991–93, 1994–99; Sen. Crown Prosecutor, Policy Gp, Crown Prosecution Service HQ, 1993–94; Hd, Policy Initiatives Team, Women's Unit, Cabinet Office, 1999; Hd (Human Rights and Codification) Br., Criminal Justice Div., and Hd, Criminal Justice Br., Human Rights and Constitution Div., LCD, 1999–2001; Managing Lawyer, Criminal Law Team, Law Commn, 2002; Sen. Lawyer, Law Enforcement and Internat. Adv. Div., Solicitor's Office, HM Customs and Excise, 2002–04; Sen. Lawyer and Team Leader, Litigation D2a, Office of Treasury Solicitor, 2004–05. *Publication:* (jtly) Crown Law, 1991. *Recreations:* cinema, gym, literature. *Address:* Judicial Committee of the Privy Council, Downing Street, SW1A 2AJ. *T:* (020) 7276 0487, *Fax:* (020) 7276 0460; *e-mail:* mary.macdonald@jcpc.x.gsi.gov.uk.

McDONALD, Dame Mavis, DCB 2004 (CB 1998); Permanent Secretary, Office of the Deputy Prime Minister, 2002–05; Chairman, Catalyst Housing Group Ltd, since 2005; *b* 23 Oct. 1944; *d* of late Richard Henry and of Elizabeth Lowe; *m* 1971, David Arthur McDonald, *qv*; one *s. Educ:* Chadderton Grammar Sch. for Girls; London Sch. of Econs and Pol Science (BSc Econ). Min. of Housing and Local Govt, later DoE, then DETR, 1966–2000: Asst Private Sec. to Minister for Housing and Local Govt, 1969–70, to Sec. of State for the Environment, 1970–71; Private Sec. to Perm. Sec., 1973–75; Asst Sec., Central Policy Planning Unit, 1981–83; Head of Personnel Management (Envmt) Div., 1983–86; Finance, Local Authority Grants, 1986; Dep. Dir, Local Govt Finance, 1987; Under Secretary: Directorate of Admin. Resources, 1988–90; Directorate of Personnel Management, 1990–91; Directorate of Housing Resources and Management, 1990–93; Directorate of Local Govt, 1994–95; Prin. Estab. Officer, 1995; Sen. Dir, Housing, Construction, Planning and Countryside, then Dir Gen., Housing, Construction, Regeneration and Countryside Gp, 1995–2000; Perm. Sec., Cabinet Office, 2000–02. Non-exec. Dir, Tarmac Housing Div., 1988–91. Member: Cttee of Mgt, Broomleigh Housing Assoc., 1995–96; Bd, Ealing Family Housing Assoc., 2001–02. Hon. MCIH 2001. Trustee, Joseph Rowntree Foundn, 2006–. Lay Gov., Birkbeck Coll., London, 1999–.

McDONALD, Prof. Michael, PhD; CEng, FICE, FCILT; Professor of Transportation, since 1992, and Director, Transportation Research Group, since 1986, University of Southampton; *b* 10 Dec. 1944; *s* of late Douglas Frederick McDonald and Joyce Mary Kathleen McDonald (*née* Burke); *m* 1970, Millicent Elizabeth Agnew; three *s. Educ:* Univ. of Newcastle upon Tyne (BSc); Univ. of Southampton (PhD 1981). MIHT 1973; MICE 1975; CEng 1975; FCILT (FCIT 1998); FICE 2004. University of Southampton: Rees Jeffreys Lectr in Highway and Traffic Engrg, 1971–86; Sen. Lectr, 1986–88; Reader in Transportation, 1988–92; Hd, Dept of Civil and Envmtl Engrg, 1996–99. Exec. Dir, Roughton & Partners, 1985–2005; Chm., ITSUK, 2004–07. Vice-Chm., European Road Transport Res. Adv. Council, 2004–. *Address:* School of Civil Engineering and the Environment, University of Southampton, Highfield, Southampton SO17 1BJ.

MACDONALD, Morag, (Mrs Walter Simpson), CBE 1993; PhD; Secretary of the Post Office, 1985–94; *b* 8 Feb. 1947; *d* of Murdoch Macdonald Macdonald and Isobel Macdonald (*née* Black); *m* 1st, 1970, Adam Somerville; 2nd, 1983, Walter Simpson; one *d. Educ:* Bellahouston Academy, Glasgow; Univ. of Glasgow (LLB Hons 1968; PhD 2002); College of Law, London; King's Coll., London (BA 1997). Called to the Bar, Inner Temple, 1974. Joined Post Office as graduate trainee, 1968; posts in Telecommunications and Corporate HQ, 1969–79; PA to Managing Dir, Girobank, 1980; Dep. Sec., Post Office, 1983–85. Mem. Management Cttee, Industry and Parlt Trust, 1986–94. Council Mem., St George's Hosp. Med. Sch., 1994–97. Trustee, Glasgow City Heritage Trust, 2006–; Chm., Adamson Trust, 2007–. FRSA 1990. *Recreations:* walking, embroidery, very indifferent piano playing. *Address:* Ardshiel, Gwydyr Road, Crieff, Perthshire PH7 4BS. *Club:* Western (Glasgow).

McDONALD, Neil Kevin; Director, Planning for Major Infrastructure, Department for Communities and Local Government, since 2007; *b* 1 April 1957; *s* of Eric and Margaret McDonald; *m* 1982, Barbara Moyser; two *s* one *d. Educ:* Kingsbury High Sch.; Newcastle under Lyme High Sch.; St John's Coll., Cambridge (BA 1979). Entered Civil Service, 1979; Admin Trainee, Depts of Trade and Industry, 1979–82; Department of Transport, 1982–97: Principal: civil aviation, 1984–87; Driver Testing Review, 1987; LT, 1987–91; Asst Sec., Railways, 1991–93; on secondment to Office of Passenger Rail Franchising, 1994–97; Department of the Environment, Transport and the Regions: Divl Manager, Roads Policy, 1997–2000; Ed., Urban White Paper, 2000; Divl Manager, Local Authy Housing, 2000–02; Prog. Dir, Communities Plan, ODPM, 2002–03; Dir, Housing, ODPM, later DCLG, 2003–06; Dir, Home Inf. Pack Implementation, DCLG, 2006–07. *Recreations:* sailing, gardening, badminton. *Address:* Department for Communities and Local Government, Eland House, Bressenden Place, SW1E 5DU.

MACDONALD, Nigel Colin Lock; Partner, Ernst & Young, 1976–2003; *b* 15 June 1945; *s* of late Trevor William and Barbara Evelyn Macdonald; *m* 1st, 1972, Elizabeth Ruth Leaney (*d* 1981); 2nd, 1983, Jennifer Margaret Webster; one *d. Educ:* Cranleigh Sch.; Inst. of Chartered Accountants of Scotland. Thomson McLintock & Co., 1962–68; Whinney Murray & Co., 1968–70; Whinney Murray Ernst & Ernst, Netherlands, 1970–72; Whinney Murray, later Ernst & Whinney, then Ernst & Young, 1972–2003. Dir, James Lock & Co., 1976– (Chm., 1986–). Bd Mem., Coca-Cola Hellenic, 2005–. Accounting Advr, Internat. Oil Pollution Compensation Fund, 2002–. Mem. Council, 1989–93, Pres., 1993–94, Inst. of Chartered Accountants of Scotland. Member: Cadbury Cttee on corporate governance, 1991; Review Panel, Financial Reporting Council, 1991–2006; Bd, BSI, 1992–2004; Industrial Develt Adv. Bd, 1995–2001; Competition (formerly Monopolies and Mergers) Commn, 1998–2005. Trustee: Nat. Maritime Mus., 2003–; Scottish Chartered Accountants' Trust for Educn, 2006–; Scottish Accountancy Trust for Educn and Res., 2006– (Chm., 2006–). FRSA 1993. Mem., Mission Council, URC, 2005–; Elder, St Andrew's URC, Cheam, 1978–. *Recreations:* old cars, swimming, topography. *Address:* 10 Lynwood Road, Epsom, Surrey KT17 4LD. *T:* (01372) 720853. *Clubs:* Royal Automobile, City of London.

McDONALD, Dr Oonagh, CBE 1998; international regulatory and public policy consultant; *b* Stockton-on-Tees, Co. Durham; *d* of Dr H. D. McDonald, theologian. *Educ:* Roan Sch. for Girls, Greenwich; East Barnet Grammar Sch.; Univ. of London (BD Hons 1959; MTh 1962, PhD 1974, King's Coll.). Teacher, 1959–64; Lectr in Philosophy, Bristol Univ., 1965–76. Gwilym Gibbon Res. Fellow, Nuffield Coll., Oxford, 1988–89;

Sen. Res. Fellow, Univ. of Warwick, 1990. Contested (Lab): S Glos, Feb. and Oct. 1974; Thurrock, 1987. MP (Lab) Thurrock, July 1976–87. PPS to Chief Sec. to Treasury, 1977–79; Opposition front bench spokesman on defence, 1981–83, on Treasury and economic affairs, 1983–87, on Civil Service, 1983–87. Consultant, Unity Trust Bank plc, 1987–88. Non-exec. Director: Investors' Compensation Scheme, 1992–2001; Gen. Insce Standards Council, 1999–2005; Gibraltar Financial Services Commn, 1999–; SAGA Gp, 1995–98; Scottish Provident, 1999–2001; Skandia, 2001–04; British Portfolio Trust plc, 2001–; Dresdner RCM Global Investors, 2001–. Director: FSA (formerly SIB), 1993–98 (Chm., Consumer Panel, 1994–95); FSA Ombudsman Scheme, 1998–2001. Complaints Commissioner, 2001–: London Metal Exchange; IPE; Virt-x. Editor, Jl of Financial Regulation and Compliance, 1998–. *Publications:* (jtly) The Economics of Prosperity, 1980; Own Your Own: social ownership examined, 1989; Parliament at Work, 1989; The Future of Whitehall, 1992; The Future of European Retail Banking: the view from the top, 2002. *Address:* 36 Chemin de Bivouac, 06370 Mouans-Sartoux, France. *T:* (4) 92990934.

McDONALD, Patrick Anthony, CChem, FRSC; Chief Scientific Adviser, Health and Safety Executive, since 2006; *b* 22 June 1958; *s* of late Patrick Bernard and Mary Ellen McDonald; *m* 1980, Anne Holtham. *Educ:* Rutherford Comp. Sch.; Kingston Poly. (BSc Hons Applied Chem.). CChem 1983; FRSC 2005. Forensic Scientist, Lab. of Govt Chemist, 1980–87; Department of Trade and Industry: Administrator, 1987–93; Dep. Dir, 1993–2002; Dir, Key Business Technols, 2002–04; Technology Dir, 2004–06. Dir, Britech Foundn, 2004–06. FRSA. *Publications:* papers in Jl of Forensic Sci. *Recreations:* travel, early music, good food, playing cricket, drinking beer. *Address:* Health and Safety Executive, Rose Court, 2 Southwark Bridge, SE1 9HS. *T:* (020) 7717 6449, *Fax:* (020) 7717 6955; *e-mail:* patrick.mcdonald@hse.gsi.gov.uk. *Clubs:* Erith Cricket, Statics Cricket.

MACDONALD, Patrick James; Chief Executive, John Menzies plc, 2003–07; *b* 14 May 1962; *s* of Charles Patrick Macdonald and Frances Gillian Macdonald; *m* 1987, Jacqueline Ann Willis; one *s* two *d*. *Educ:* Stowe Sch.; Oriel Coll., Oxford (BA Hons Engrg Sci.); INSEAD, Fontainebleau (MBA with dist.). CEng 1990; MIMechE 1990; MIET (MIEE 1990); Eur Ing 1990. RCNC, 1984–85; Project Manager, Unilever, 1985–91; Manager, Boston Consulting Gp, 1993–97; Vice-Pres., Sourcing, GE Capital, Gen. Electric, 1997–2002. FRSA; CCMI 2004. *Recreations:* ski-ing, hill-walking, extreme gardening, family life.

MACDONALD OF CLANRANALD, Ranald Alexander; 24th Chief and Captain of Clanranald; formerly Chairman and Managing Director, Tektura Ltd; *b* 27 March 1934; *s* of late Captain Kenneth Macdonald of Inchkenneth, DSO, and late Marjory Broad Smith, Basingstoke; *S* kinsman as Chief of Clanranald, 1944; *m* 1961, Jane Campbell-Davys, *d* of late I. E. Campbell-Davys, Llandovey, Carms; two *s* one *d*. *Educ:* Christ's Hospital. Founded: Fairfix Contracts Ltd, 1963; Tektura Wallcoverings, 1970. Chm., British Contract Furnishing Assoc., 1975–76. Lieut (TA) Cameron Highlanders, 1958–68. Mem., Standing Council of Scottish Chiefs, 1957–; Pres., Highland Soc. of London, 1988–91 (Dir, 1959–80); Chief Exec., Clan Donald Lands Trust, 1978–80; Chm., Museum of the Isles, 1981–90; Founding Trustee, Lord of the Isles Galley Proj., 1989–. Vice Pres., Les Avants Bobsleigh and Toboggan Club, 1987–. *Recreation:* avoidance of boredom. *Heir:* *s* Ranald Og Angus Macdonald, younger of Clanranald, *b* 17 Sept. 1963. *Address:* 13 Eccleston Street, Belgravia, SW1W 9LX. *Clubs:* Beefsteak, Pratt's; New, Puffins (Edinburgh); British (Bangkok).

MACDONALD, Richard Auld, CBE 2002; Director General, National Farmers' Union, since 1996; *b* 31 Oct. 1954; *s* of Anthony Macdonald and Gillian Macdonald (*née* Matthews); *m* 1980, Susan Jane Reynolds; two *d*. *Educ:* Bishop's Stortford Coll.; Queen Mary Coll., London Univ. (BSc Hons Biology). National Farmers' Union: Parly Sec., 1978–85; County Sec., Devon, 1985–89; Regl Dir, SW, 1989–92; Dir, 1992–96. Chm., Associa Ltd, 2001–. FRASE 2005. *Recreations:* golf, cricket, Rugby, travel. *Address:* National Farmers' Union, Stoneleigh Park, Stoneleigh, Warwicks CV8 2TZ. *T:* (024) 7685 8600; *e-mail:* richard.macdonald@nfu.org.uk; (home) Woodpeckers, Hithercroft, South Moreton, Oxon OX11 9AL. *Clubs:* Naval and Military, Farmers; Moreton Cricket; Springs Golf.

MACDONALD, Roderick Francis; *see* Uist, Hon. Lord.

MACDONALD, Dr Rosemary Gillespie, FRCP, FRCA; Dean, Post-graduate Medical Education (Yorkshire), University of Leeds and Northern and Yorkshire NHS Executive, 1992–2001, now Emeritus; *b* 25 March 1944; *d* of John Mackenzie Paterson and Mary McCauley Paterson; *m* 1968, Hamish Neil Macdonald; one *s* one *d* (twins). *Educ:* Univ. of Glasgow (MB ChB); Univ. of Bradford (PhD 1976). FRCA 1971; FRCP 1999. Lectr in Anaesthesia, Univ. of Leeds, 1973–76; Consultant Obstetric Anaesthetist, St James's Univ. Hosp., Leeds, 1976–92. Hon. FRCPsych 2002. *Publications:* contribs to British Jl Anaesthesia, Anaesthesia, BMJ, etc. *Recreations:* cooking, walking, opera, ballet, art, human beings. *Address:* Springbank, 11 Hall Drive, Bramhope, Leeds LS16 9JF. *T:* (0113) 203 7337.

MACDONALD, Sharman; playwright, screenwriter and novelist; *b* 8 Feb. 1951; *d* of Joseph Henry Hosgood Macdonald and Janet Rowatt Williams; *m* 1976, Kevin William Knightley; one *s* one *d*. *Educ:* Hutchesons' Girls' GS, Glasgow; George Watson's Ladies' Coll., Edinburgh; Univ. of Edinburgh (MA 1972). *Theatre:* When I Was a Girl I Used to Scream and Shout, 1984; The Brave, 1988; When We Were Women, 1988; All Things Nice, 1990; Shades, 1992; The Winter Guest, 1995; Borders of Paradise, 1995; After Juliet, 1999; The Girl With Red Hair, 2005; Broken Hallelujah, 2005; *radio:* Sea Urchins, 1997 (Bronze Sony Drama Award; adapted for stage, 1998); Gladly My Cross-eyed Bear, 2000; Soft Fall the Sounds of Eden, 2004; *opera libretto:* Hey Persephone!, 1998; *films:* Wild Flowers, 1989; The Winter Guest, 1998; The Edge of Love, 2008. Most Promising Playwright Award, Evening Standard Awards, 1984. *Publications: plays:* When I Was a Girl I Used to Scream and Shout, 1984; When We Were Women, 1988; The Brave, 1988; All Things Nice, 1990; Shades, 1992; Sharman Macdonald Plays I, 1995; Sea Urchins, 1998; After Juliet, 1999; The Girl with Red Hair, 2005; *novels:* The Beast, 1986; Night Night, 1988. *Recreation:* body boarding. *Address:* c/o United Agents, 12–26 Lexington Street, W1F 0LE.

MacDONALD, Prof. Simon Gavin George, FRSE; Professor of Physics, University of Dundee, 1973–88, now Emeritus; *b* 5 Sept. 1923; *s* of Simon MacDonald and Jean H. Thomson; *m* 1948, Eva Leonie Austerlitz; one *s* one *d*. *Educ:* George Heriot's Sch., Edinburgh; Edinburgh Univ. (MA (1st Cl. Hons) Maths and Nat. Phil); PhD (St Andrews). FIP 1958, FRSE 1972. Jun. Scientific Officer, RAE, Farnborough, 1943–46; Lectr, Univ. of St Andrews, 1948–57; Senior Lecturer: University Coll. of the West Indies, 1957–62; Univ. of St Andrews, 1962–67; Visiting Prof., Ohio Univ., 1963; University of Dundee: Sen. Lectr, then Prof., 1967–88; Dean of Science, 1970–73; Vice-Principal, 1974–79. Convener, Scottish Univs Council on Entrance, 1977–83 (Dep. Convener, 1973–77); Chm., Stats Cttee, UCCA, 1989–93 (Mem. Exec. Cttee, 1977–93; Chm., Technical Cttee, 1979–83; Dep. Chm., 1983–89). Chm., Bd of Dirs, Dundee Rep. Th., 1975–89; Chm., Fedn of Scottish Theatres, 1978–80. *Publications:* Problems and Solutions in General Physics, 1967; Physics for Biology and Premedical Students, 1970, 2nd edn 1975; Physics for the Life and Health Sciences, 1975; *novels:* Death is My Mistress, 2007; The Crime Committee, 2007; Publish and Be Dead, 2007; My Frail Blood, 2007; articles in physics jls. *Recreations:* bridge, golf, fiction writing. *Address:* 7A Windmill Road, St Andrews KY16 9JJ. *T:* (01334) 478014. *Club:* Royal Commonwealth Society.

McDONALD, Simon Gerard, CMG 2004; HM Diplomatic Service; Foreign Policy Adviser to the Prime Minister and Head, Foreign and Defence Policy (formerly Overseas and Defence Secretariat), Cabinet Office, since 2007; *b* 9 March 1961; *s* of James B. McDonald and Angela (*née* McDonald); *m* 1989, Hon. Olivia Mary, *o d* of Baron Wright of Richmond, *qv*; two *s* two *d*. *Educ:* De La Salle Coll. Grammar Sch., Salford; Pembroke Coll., Cambridge (MA). Joined FCO, 1982; Jedda, 1985; Riyadh, 1985–88; Bonn, 1988–90; FCO, 1990; Private Sec. to Perm. Under-Sec. of State, FCO, 1993–95; First Sec., Washington, 1995–98; Counsellor, Dep. Hd of Mission and Consul-Gen., Riyadh, 1998–2001; Principal Private Sec. to Sec. of State for Foreign and Commonwealth Affairs, 2001–03; Ambassador to Israel, 2003–06; Dir, Iraq, FCO, 2006–07. *Recreation:* talk. *Address:* Cabinet Office, 70 Whitehall, SW1A 2AS. *T:* (020) 7276 3168; *e-mail:* the6mcdonalds@yahoo.co.uk.

McDONALD, Sir Trevor, Kt 1999; OBE 1992; DL; newscaster, 1990–2005, presenter, News at Ten, ITN, 1992–99, and ITV News at Ten, 2001–05 and since 2008; *b* Trinidad, 16 Aug. 1939; *m*; two *s* one *d*. Work on newspapers, radio and television, Trinidad, 1962–69; producer for Caribbean Service and World Service, BBC Radio, London, 1969–73; Independent Television News: reporter, 1973–78; sports corresp., 1978–80; diplomatic corresp., 1980–82; diplomatic corresp. and newscaster, 1982–87, Diplomatic Ed., 1987–89, Channel Four News; newscaster, News at 5.40, 1989–90; presenter: The ITV Evening News, 1999–2001; Tonight with Trevor McDonald, 1999–. DL Greater London, 2006. Chancellor, London South Bank (formerly S Bank) Univ., 1999–. Newscaster of the Year, TRIC, 1993, 1997, 1999; Gold Medal, RTS (for outstanding contrib. to television news), 1998. *Publications:* Clive Lloyd: a biography, 1985; Vivian Richards: a biography, 1987; Queen and Commonwealth, 1989; Fortunate Circumstances (autobiog.), 1993; (ed) Trevor McDonald's Favourite Poems, 1997; Trevor McDonald's World of Poetry (anthology), 1999. *Address:* c/o ITN, 200 Gray's Inn Road, WC1X 8XZ.

MACDONALD, Valerie Frances; *see* Gooding, V. F.

McDONALD, Very Rev. William James Gilmour; Moderator of the General Assembly of the Church of Scotland, 1989–90; Parish Minister of Mayfield, Edinburgh, 1959–92; *b* 3 June 1924; *s* of Hugh Gilmour McDonald and Grace Kennedy Hunter; *m* 1952, Margaret Patricia Watson; one *s* two *d*. *Educ:* Daniel Stewart's College, Edinburgh; Univ. of Edinburgh (MA, BD); Univ. of Göttingen. Served Royal Artillery and Indian Artillery, 1943–46. Parish Minister, Limekilns, Fife, 1953–59. Convener, Assembly Council, 1984–87. Chaplain, Edinburgh Merchant Co., 1982–2002. Warrack Lectr, Edinburgh and Aberdeen Univs, 1992, Glasgow and St Andrews Univs, 1995; Turnbull Trust Preacher, Scots Ch, Melbourne, 1993. Hon. DD Edinburgh, 1987. *Address:* 7 Blacket Place, Edinburgh EH9 1RN. *T:* (0131) 667 2100.

MACDONALD, Prof. William Weir, PhD, DSc; FIBiol; Selwyn Lloyd Professor of Medical Entomology, 1980–94, now Professor Emeritus, and Dean, 1983–88, Liverpool School of Tropical Medicine; *b* 5 Dec. 1927; *s* of William Sutherland Macdonald and Ina Weir; *m* 1950, Margaret Lawrie; two *d*. *Educ:* Univ. of Glasgow (BSc 1948). MSc 1964, PhD 1965, Univ. of Liverpool; DSc 1973, Univ. of Glasgow; FIBiol 1966. Strang-Steel Scholar, Glasgow Univ., 1948; Colonial Office Res. Scholar, 1949–50; Entomologist, E African Fisheries Res. Org., Uganda, 1950–52; Res. Fellow, Inst. for Med. Res., Kuala Lumpur, 1953–60; Lectr, Sen. Lectr, and Reader, Liverpool Sch. of Trop. Medicine, 1960–76; Prof. of Med. Entomology, London Sch. of Hygiene and Trop. Medicine, 1977–80. Consultant: WHO; various overseas govts. Chalmers Medal, Royal Soc. of Trop. Medicine and Hygiene, 1972. *Publications:* papers on med. entomology in scientific jls. *Recreations:* golf, gardening. *Address:* 10 Headland Close, West Kirby, Merseyside CH48 3JP. *T:* (0151) 625 7857.

MACDONALD-BUCHANAN, John, MC 1945; Vice Lord-Lieutenant of Northamptonshire, 1991–2000; *b* 15 March 1925; *s* of Major Sir Reginald Macdonald-Buchanan, KCVO, MBE, MC and Hon. Lady Macdonald-Buchanan, OStJ, *o c* of 1st Baron Woolavington, GCVO; *m* 1st, 1950, Lady Rose Fane (*d* 1984), *d* of 14th Earl of Westmorland; one *s* two *d*; 2nd, 1969, Mrs Jill Rosamonde Trelawnay, *d* of Maj.-Gen. Cecil Benfield Fairbanks, CB, CBE; two *d*. *Educ:* Eton; RMC, Sandhurst; RAC, Cirencester. 2nd Lt, Scots Guards, 1943; served War, 1944–45, NW Europe; Malaya, 1948–50; retired, 1952. Mem., Horserace Betting Levy Bd, 1973–76. Steward of Jockey Club, 1969–72, Sen. Steward 1979–82. High Sheriff 1963–64, DL 1978, Northants. *Address:* The Stables House, Cottesbrooke, Northampton NN6 8PH. *T:* (01604) 505732; Clunie House, Hans Place, SW1X 0EY. *T:* (020) 7581 7951. *Clubs:* White's, Turf.

MACDONALD-DAVIES, Isobel Mary; Deputy Registrar General for England and Wales, 1994–2005 (Registrar General, April–June 2000); *b* 7 Feb. 1955; *d* of Henry Alexander Macdonald and Freda Matilda Macdonald; *m* 1977, Peter Davies; one *s* two *d*. *Educ:* Bar Convent Grammar Sch., York; St Andrews Univ. (BSc 1977). CStat 1993. Asst Statistician, OPCS, 1977–84; Statistician, Dept of Educn and OPCS, 1984–94. Mem. Mgt Exec. Bd, ONS, 2001–04. *Recreations:* family, music, reading.

MACDONALD-SMITH, Maj.-Gen. Hugh, CB 1977; *b* 8 Jan. 1923; *s* of Alexander and Ada Macdonald-Smith; *m* 1947, Désirée Violet (*née* Williamson) (*d* 2004); one *s* one *d* (and one *d* decd). *Educ:* Llanelli Grammar Sch.; Llandovery Coll.; Birmingham Univ. BSc. CEng, FIET. Commissioned REME, 1944; served: India, 1945–47; Singapore, 1956–58; BAOR, 1961–63; Technical Staff Course, 1949–51; Staff Coll., Camberley, 1953; Lt-Col, 1963; Asst Dir, Electrical and Mechanical Engineering, HQ Western Comd, 1963–65; Asst Mil. Sec., MoD, 1965–66; Comd REME, 1 (BR) Corps Troops, 1966–67; Technical Gp, REME, 1967–72; Col, 1967; Brig. 1970; Dep. Dir, Electrical and Mechanical Engineering (Eng. Pol.), (Army), 1972–75; Dir, later Dir Gen., Electrical and Mech. Engrg (Army), 1975–78; retired 1978. Col Comdt, REME, 1978–83; Rep. Col Comdt, REME, 1979–80. Dir, TEMA, 1981–87 (Sec. to Council, 1979–80). Mem., Cttee of Inquiry into Engrg Profession, 1977–79. Mem. Council, IMechE, 1975–76. *Recreations:* golf, gardening, photography. *Address:* c/o Lloyds TSB, Bridport DT6 3QL.

McDONNELL, family name of **Earl of Antrim**.

McDONNELL, Dr Alasdair; MP (SDLP) Belfast South, since 2005; Member (SDLP) Belfast South, Northern Ireland Assembly, since 1998; general medical practitioner, since 1979; *b* Cushendall, Co. Antrim, 1 Sept. 1949; *s* of Charles McDonnell and Margaret (*née* McIlhatton); *m* 1998, Olivia Nugent; two *s* two *d*. *Educ:* St MacNissis Coll., Garron

Tower; University Coll., Dublin Med. Sch. (MB, BCh, BAO 1974). Jun. hosp. med. posts, 1975–79. Mem. (SDLP) Belfast CC, 1977–2001; Dep. Mayor, Belfast, 1995–96. Contested (SDLP) Belfast South, 2001. Dep. Leader, SDLP, 2004–. *Address:* House of Commons, SW1A 0AA; 22 Derryvolgie Avenue, Belfast BT9 6FN.

McDONNELL, Christopher Thomas, CB 1991; Deputy Under-Secretary of State, Ministry of Defence, 1988–91; *b* 3 Sept. 1931; *s* of Christopher Patrick McDonnell and Jane McDonnell; *m* 1955, Patricia Anne (*née* Harvey) (*d* 1967); three *s* one *d*. *Educ:* St Francis Xavier's Coll., Liverpool; Corpus Christi Coll., Oxford (MA). WO, 1954; HM Treasury, 1966–68; RCDS, 1973; Asst Under-Sec. of State, MoD, 1976–88.

McDONNELL, David Croft, CBE 2005; DL; Chief Executive Worldwide, Grant Thornton, since 2001; *b* 9 July 1943; *s* of late Leslie and Catherine McDonnell; *m* 1967, Marieke (*née* Bos); three *d*. *Educ:* Quarry Bank High School, Liverpool. FCA. Qualified Chartered Accountant, 1965; Partner, Thornton Baker, later Grant Thornton, 1972; Nat. Managing Partner, Grant Thornton, 1989–2001. Chm. Bd of Trustees, Nat. Museums Liverpool (formerly Nat. Museums and Galls on Merseyside), 1995–2005. Pres., Univ. of Liverpool, 2007–. DL Merseyside, 2003. *Recreations:* sailing, motor racing (spectating), mountain walking. *Address:* Grant Thornton, Regent's Place, 7th Floor, 338 Euston Road, NW1 3BG. *T:* (020) 7383 5100. *Club:* Athenæum.

McDONNELL, John Beresford William; QC 1984; *b* 26 Dec. 1940; *s* of Beresford Conrad McDonnell and Charlotte Mary McDonnell (*née* Caldwell); *m* 1968, Susan Virginia, *d* of late Wing Comdr H. M. Styles, DSO and of Audrey (*née* Jorgensen, who *m* 2nd, 1947, Gen. Sir Charles Richardson, GCB, CBE, DSO); two *s* one *d*. *Educ:* City of London School (Carpenter Scholar); Balliol College, Oxford (Domus Scholar; Hon. Mention, Craven Scholarship, 1958; 1st Cl. Hon. Mods 1960; 2nd LitHum 1962, 2nd Jurisp 1964; MA); Harvard Law Sch. (LLM 1965). Called to the Bar, Inner Temple, 1968; Bencher, Lincoln's Inn, 1993. Pres., Oxford Union Soc. and Amer. Debating Tour, 1962; Harkness Fellowship, 1964–66; Amer. Political Science Assoc. Congressional Fellowship, 1965–66 (attached Rep. Frank Thompson Jr, NJ and Senator George McGovern, SDak); Cons. Research Dept, 1966–69; HM Diplomatic Service, 1969–71, First Sec., Asst Private Sec. to Sec. of State for Foreign and Commonwealth Affairs, 1970–71; practising at Chancery Bar, 1972–. Cllr, Lambeth Borough Council, 1968–69. London Rowing Club Grand VIII, Henley, 1958. FRSA 1994. *Recreation:* sculling. *Address:* Mortham Tower, Rokeby, Barnard Castle DL12 9RZ. *T:* (01833) 626900; 17 Rutland Street, SW7 1EJ. *T:* (020) 7584 1498; 13 Old Square, Lincoln's Inn, WC2A 3UA. *Club:* Athenæum.

McDONNELL, John Martin; MP (Lab) Hayes and Harlington, since 1997; *b* 8 Sept. 1951; *s* of Robert and Elsie McDonnell; *m* 1st, 1971, Marilyn Jean Cooper (marr. diss. 1987); two *d*; 2nd, 1995, Cynthia Marie Pinto; one *s*. *Educ:* Great Yarmouth Grammar Sch.; Burnley Technical Coll.; Brunel Univ. (BSc); Birkbeck Coll., Univ. of London (MSc Politics and Sociology). Prodn worker, 1968–72; Research Assistant: NUM, 1976–78; TUC, 1978–82; full-time GLC Councillor, Hillingdon, Hayes and Harlington, 1982–86; Dep. Leader, GLC, 1984–85; Chm., GLC F and GP Cttee, 1982–85; Prin. Policy Advr, Camden Bor. Council, 1985–87; Secretary: Assoc. of London Authorities, 1987–95; Assoc. of London Govt, 1995–97. Editor, Labour Herald, 1985–88. Member: Gtr London Lab. Party Regl Exec. Cttee, 1982–87; for Gtr London, Lab. Party Nat. Policy Forum, 1993–; Chairman: Lab. Party Irish Soc; Labour Repn Cttee. Advr, Guildford Four Relatives Campaign, 1984–; Chair, Britain and Ireland Human Rights Centre, 1992–; Founding Mem., Friends of Ireland, 1998–. Contested (Lab): Hampstead and Highgate, 1983; Hayes and Harlington, 1992. Secretary: All Pty Britain-Kenya Gp of MPs, 1997–; All Pty Kurdish Gp, 1997–; All Pty Irish in Britain Parly Gp, 1999–; All Pty Gp on Endometriosis; Chair, All Party Punjabi Community in Britain Gp of MPs, 1999–; Secretary: Fire Brigades' Union Parly Gp; Justice Unions Parly Gp; NUJ Parly Gp; PCS Trade Union Gp; Chair: Socialist Campaign Gp of MPs, 1998–; PCS Parly Gp; Labour Repn Cttee; Left Economists Adv. Panel; Co-ordinator, RMT Parly Gp. Housefather (pt-time) of family unit, children's home, 1972–87. Chairman: Hayes and Harlington Community Develt Forum, 1997–; Barra Hall Regeneration Cttee; Friends of Lake Farm; Friends of Minet Country Park; Mem., Hayes Horticultural Show Assoc.; Hon. Vice Pres., Hayes FC; Patron, Hayes CC. *Publications:* articles and pamphlets incl. contribs to Labour Herald, Briefing, Tribune, Campaign News. *Recreations:* gardening, reading, cycling, music, theatre, cinema, Wayfarer dinghy sailing, supporting Liverpool, Hayes and Yeading Football Clubs, football refereeing; generally fermenting the overthrow of capitalism. *Address:* House of Commons, SW1A 0AA; Beverley, Cedar Avenue, Hayes, Middx UB3 2NE. *Clubs:* London Irish, Blues West 14; Hillingdon Irish Society; St Claret's, Working Men's (Hayes); Hayes and Harlington Community Centre.

McDOUGALL, Hon. Barbara Jean; PC (Can.) 1984; OC 2001; Advisor, Aird & Berlis LLP, since 2004; *b* Toronto, 12 Nov. 1937. *Educ:* Univ. of Toronto (BA Hons Econ. and Pol Sci. 1960). Chartered Financial Analyst, 1973. Worked in financial sector in Vancouver, Edmonton and Toronto; Exec. Dir, Canadian Council Financial Analysts, 1982–84; financial columnist, national magazines and on TV. MP (PC) St Paul's, Toronto, 1984–93; Minister of State: Finance, 1984–86; Privatisation, 1986–88; Minister Responsible for Status of Women, 1986–90 and for Regulatory Affairs, 1986–88; Minister, Employment and Immigration, 1988–91; Sec. of State for External Affairs, 1991–93; Chairperson, Cabinet Cttee on Foreign Affairs and Defence Policy, 1991–93; Member Cabinet Cttees: Planning and Priorities, 1991–93; Canadian Unity and Constitutional Negotiations, 1991–93. Chairperson: Morguard Real Estate Investment Trust, 1997–99; AT&T Canada Corp., 1996–99; Pres. and CEO, Canadian Inst. of Internat. Affairs, 1999–2004. Director: Corel Corp., 1998–2003; Bank of Nova Scotia, 1999–; Stelco, Inc., 1999–2006; Sun Media Corp., 1999–2001. Director: Canadian Opera Co., 1993–; Inter-Amer. Dialogue, 1994–; Internat. Crisis Gp, 1995–2006; Ind. Order of Foresters, 1998–. Mem., Internat. Adv. Bd, Council on Foreign Relns, NY, 1995–2002. Governor, York Univ., 1995–2006. Hon. LLD St Lawrence, 1992. *Address:* Aird & Berlis LLP, BCE Place, Suite 1800, PO Box 754, 181 Bay Street, Toronto, ON M5J 2T9, Canada.

McDOUGALL, Douglas Christopher Patrick, OBE 2001; Chairman: Law Debenture Corporation plc, since 2000 (Director, 1998–2000); Independent Investment Trust plc, since 2000; *b* 18 March 1944; *s* of late Patrick McDougall and Helen (*née* Anderson); *m* 1986, Carolyn Jane Griffiths, *d* of Baron Griffiths, *qv*; two *d*. *Educ:* Edinburgh Acad.; Christ Church, Oxford (MA; Hon. Student 2008). Partner, 1969–89, Sen. Partner, 1989–99, Baillie Gifford & Co., Investment Managers, Edinburgh. Chairman: Foreign and Colonial Eurotrust plc, 1999–; 3i Bioscience Investment Trust plc, 2001–06 (Dep. Chm., 2000–01); Scottish Investment Trust plc, 2003– (Dir, 1998–); Dep. Chm., Sand Aire Investments plc, 1999–2003; Director: Provincial Insce plc, 1989–94; Baillie Gifford Japan Trust plc, 1989–99; Pacific Horizon Trust plc, 1993–; Stramongate Assets plc, 2003–; Monks Investment Trust plc, 1999–; Herald Investment Trust plc, 2002–. Chairman: Institutional Fund Managers Assoc., 1994–96; Assoc. Investment Trust Cos, 1995–97; IMRO, 1997–2000 (Dir, 1988–2000). Mem., Investment Bd, Cambridge Univ., 2005–. *Address:* Linplum House, Haddington, East Lothian EH41 4PE. *T:* (01620) 810242. *Clubs:* Brooks's; New (Edinburgh); Honourable Company of Edinburgh Golfers.

MacDOUGALL, Hugh; *see* MacDougall, R. H.

MACDOUGALL, Neil; Justice of Appeal, 1989–95, and Vice-President of the Court of Appeal, 1993–95, Supreme Court of Hong Kong; *b* 13 March 1932; *s* of Norman Macdougall and Gladys Clare Kennerly; *m* 1987, Helen Lui. *Educ:* Aquinas Coll., Perth, WA; Univ. of Western Australia (LLB 1954). Admitted Barrister and Solicitor of Supreme Court, WA, 1957, and of High Court of Australia, 1958; Solicitor of Supreme Court of England, 1976, and of Supreme Court of Hong Kong, 1977. Crown Counsel, Hong Kong, 1965; Director of Public Prosecutions, Hong Kong, 1978; a Judge of the High Court, Hong Kong, 1980; Comr, Supreme Court of Brunei, 1987; a Non-Permanent Judge, Court of Final Appeal, Hong Kong, 1997–2003. Chairman: Insider Dealing Tribunal, Hong Kong, 1987–88; Air Transport Licensing Authy, Hong Kong, 1992–95. *Recreations:* classical music, study of natural history, physical training. *Club:* Hong Kong (Hong Kong).

MACDOUGALL, Patrick Lorn, FCA; Chairman: Arlington Securities plc, 1999–2005; West Merchant Bank Ltd (formerly Standard Chartered Merchant Bank, then Chartered WestLB), 1989–98 (Chief Executive, 1985–97); *b* 21 June 1939; *s* of late James Archibald Macdougall, WS, and Valerie Jean Macdougall; *m* 1st, 1967, Alison Noel Offer (marr. diss. 1982); two *s*; 2nd, 1983, Bridget Margaret Young; three *d*. *Educ:* schools in Kenya; Millfield; University Coll., Oxford (MA Jurisprudence). FCA 1976. Called to the Bar, Inner Temple, 1962. Manager, N. M. Rothschild & Sons Ltd, 1967–70; Exec. Dir, Amex Bank (formerly Rothschild Intercontinental Bank Ltd), 1970–77, Chief Exec., 1977–78; Exec. Dir, Jardine Matheson Holdings Ltd, 1978–85; Gp Exec. Dir, Standard Chartered PLC, 1988–89. Member: Internat. Adv. Bd, Creditanstalt–Bankverein, Vienna, 1982–85; Mem., Sen. Adv. Council, Seagull Energy Inc., Houston, 1996–99; Director: Global Natural Resources Inc., USA, 1994–96; Nuclear Electric plc, 1994–96; Panmure Gordon & Co. Ltd, 1996–98 (Dep. Chm., 1997–98); National Provident Instn, 1997–99. Dir and Trustee, SANE, 2001– (Chm., 2002–06). FRSA 1988. *Recreations:* opera, bridge, tough crosswords. *Address:* 110 Rivermead Court, SW6 3SB. *T:* (020) 7736 3506. *Clubs:* Athenæum, Hurlingham; Hongkong, Shek O (Hong Kong).

MacDOUGALL, Prof. (Robert) Hugh, FRCSE, FRCR, FRCPE; Bute Professor of Medicine, Head of Bute Medical School, and Dean, Faculty of Medicine, University of St Andrews, since 2002; Hon. Consultant Clinical Oncologist, Edinburgh Cancer Centre, Lothian University Hospitals, since 1986; *b* 9 Aug. 1949; *s* of Dr John David Bathgate MacDougall and Isabella Williamson MacDougall (*née* Craig); *m* 1977, Moira Jean Gray; one *s* two *d*. *Educ:* High Sch. of Dundee; Univ. of St Andrews (MB ChB 1972); Univ. of Edinburgh (DMRT 1979). FRCSE 1977; FRCR 1981; FRCPE 1996. House physician and house surgeon, Dundee Royal Infirmary, 1972–73; Registrar in Surgery, Aberdeen Royal Infirmary, and Hon. Clin. Tutor in Surgery, Univ. of Aberdeen, 1976–77; Lectr in Clin. Oncol., Univ. of Edinburgh, 1979–82; Consultant Radiotherapist and Oncologist, Tayside Health Bd, and Sen. Lectr, Univ. of Dundee, 1982–86; Sen. Lectr in Oncol., Univ. of Edinburgh, 1986–2002. *Publications:* (jtly) Helpful Essential Links to Palliative Care, 1992, 5th edn 1999; contribs to internat. jls on neutron therapy. *Recreation:* reading. *Address:* Bute Medical School, University of St Andrews, Bute Medical Buildings, St Andrews, Fife KY16 9TS. *T:* (01334) 463597/3502, *Fax:* (01334) 463482; *e-mail:* medical.dean@st-andrews.ac.uk. *Club:* New (Edinburgh).

McDOWALL, Andrew Gordon; His Honour Judge McDowall; a Circuit Judge, since 1998; *b* 2 Sept. 1948; *s* of William Crocket McDowall and Margery Haswell McDowall (*née* Wilson); *m* 1976, Cecilia Clarke; one *s* one *d*. *Educ:* Glasgow Acad.; Queen's Coll., Oxford (Open Hastings Schol.; BCL, MA). Called to the Bar, Gray's Inn, 1972; in practice at the Bar, 1972–98; a Recorder, 1993–98; South Eastern Circuit. *Recreations:* reading, music (London Orpheus Choir), squash, paronomasia. *Address:* c/o 1 King's Bench Walk, Temple, EC4Y 7DB.

McDOWALL, Maj. Gen. David, MBE 1993; General Officer Commanding Second Division, 2007–May 2009; *b* 16 Aug. 1954; *s* of David and Mary McDowall; *m* 1977, Valerie King; two *s* one *d*. *Educ:* Rephad Primary Sch.; Stranraer Acad.; RMA Sandhurst; RMCS. CO 7th Signal Regt, 1993–96; Comdr 1st Signal Bde, 2000–02; Signal Officer in Chief, 2002–04; Dir Comd and Battlespace Mgt (Army), 2004–07. FIET 2004; FBCS 2005. Chm., Army Football Assoc. *Recreations:* golf, bagpipes. *Address:* (until May 2009) Headquarters 2nd Division, Annandale Block, Craigie Hall, South Queensferry, West Lothian EH30 9TN. *Clubs:* Army and Navy, Caledonian; New (Edinburgh).

MacDOWALL, Dr David William, MA, DPhil; FSA, FRAS; Chairman, Society for South Asian Studies (formerly Society for Afghan Studies), 1982–98 (Hon. Secretary, 1972–82; Hon. Fellow, 1999); Hon. Research Fellow, Centre for Research in East Roman Studies, University of Warwick, since 1993; *b* 2 April 1930; *o s* of late William MacDowall and late Lilian May MacDowall (*née* Clarkson); *m* 1962, Mione Beryl, *yr d* of late Ernest Harold Lashmar and Dora Lashmar; two *d*. *Educ:* Liverpool Inst.; Corpus Christi Coll., Oxford; British Sch. at Rome. Hugh Oldham Scholar 1947, Pelham Student in Roman History 1951; Barclay Head Prize for Ancient Numismatics, 1953 and 1956. 2nd Lieut Royal Signals, 1952. Asst Principal, Min. of Works, 1955; Asst Keeper, Dept of Coins and Medals, British Museum, 1956; Principal, Min. of Educn, 1960; Principal, Univ. Grants Cttee, 1965; Asst Sec. 1970; Master of Univ. Coll., Durham, 1973; Hon. Lectr in Classics and in Oriental Studies, Univ. of Durham, 1975; Dir, Polytechnic of N London, 1980–85. Hon. Treasurer, Royal Numismatic Soc., 1966–73; Vice-Pres., British Archaeol Assoc., 1993–95 (Hon. Treas., 1989–93); Pres., Royal Asiatic Soc., 1994–97 (Vice-Pres., 1993–94, 1997–2000). Mem. Governing Body, SOAS, 1990–97. Trustee, UK Trust, Indian Nat. Trust for Archl and Cultural Heritage, 1994–. Corresponding Member: Istituto Italiano per il Medio ed Estremo Oriente, 1987; Amer. Numismatic Soc., 1991. Hon. Fellow, Asiatic Soc. of Mumbai, 2004. *Publications:* Coin Collections, their preservation, classification and presentation, 1978; The Western Coinages of Nero, 1979; (contrib.) Mithraic Studies, 1975; (contrib.) The Archaeology of Afghanistan, 1978; (ed jtly) Indian Numismatics: history, art and culture, 1992; (jtly) The Roman Coins, Republic and Empire up to Nerva, in the Provinciaal Museum G. M. Kam at Nijmegen, 1992; (ed jtly) Foreign Coins Found in the Indian Sub-Continent, 2003; (jtly) A Catalogue of Coins from the Excavations at Bir-kot-Ghwandai 1984–1992, 2004; articles in Numismatic Chron., Jl Numismatic Soc. India, Schweizer Münzblätter, Acta Numismatica, S Asian Archaeology, Afghan Studies, S Asian Studies, Numismatic Digest, etc. *Recreations:* travel, antiquities, photography, natural history, gardening, genealogy. *Address:* Admont, Dancers End, Tring, Herts HP23 6JY. *Club:* Athenæum.

McDOWALL, Keith Desmond, CBE 1988; Chairman, Keith McDowall Associates, 1988–2001; *b* 3 Oct. 1929; *s* of William Charteris McDowall and Edna Florence McDowall; *m* 1st, 1957, Shirley Margaret Russell Astbury (marr. diss. 1985); two *d*; 2nd, 1988, Brenda Dean (*see* Baroness Dean of Thornton-le-Fylde). *Educ:* Heath Clark Sch., Croydon, Surrey. Served RAF, National Service, 1947–49. South London Press,

1947–55; Daily Mail, 1955–67: Indust. Corresp., 1958; Indust. Editor, 1961–67; Man. Dir, Inca Construction (UK) Co. Ltd, 1967–69; Govt Information Service: successively Chief Inf. Officer, DEA, BoT, Min. of Housing and Local Govt, DoE, and Home Office, 1969–72; Dir of Inf., NI Office, 1972–74; Dir of Inf., Dept of Employment, 1974–78; Man. Dir Public Affairs, British Shipbuilders, 1978–80. Dir, Govan Shipbuilders Ltd, 1978–80. Dir of Information, 1981–86, Dep. Dir Gen., 1986–88, CBI. Chm., Kiss FM Radio, 1990–92 (Chm., steering cttee, 1989–90). Freeman, City of London, 1997; Liveryman, Shipwrights' Co., 1998–. *Publications:* articles in newspapers and various pubns. *Recreations:* sailing, cricket, mingling. *Address:* 2 Malvern Terrace, N1 1HR. *Clubs:* Reform, MCC; Medway Yacht (Rochester); Royal Cornwall Yacht (Falmouth).

MacDOWALL, Simon Charles, CD 1985; Director, Communications and Marketing, HM Revenue and Customs, since 2007; *b* 18 July 1956; *s* of Joseph and Oonagh MacDowall; *m* 1981, Gabriele Kuzaj; one *s* one *d*. *Educ:* Collège Militaire Royal, St Jean, Quebec (BA 1978). Royal Canadian Dragoons, 1978–87; Public Affairs Office, Canadian Army: Strategic Communications, 1987–91; Regl Communications, NW Canada, 1991–93; NATO: Press Officer, SHAPE, Belgium and Bosnia, 1993–94; Chief of Press and Inf., Allied Forces NW Europe, 1995–99; Communications Director: DSS, 1999–2001; DWP, 2001–06; Dir Gen., Media and Commns, MoD, 2006–07. *Publications:* Late Roman Infantryman, 1994; Late Roman Cavalryman, 1995; Germanic Warrior, 1996; Battle of Adrianople, 2001. *Recreations:* travel, running, cycling, scuba diving, good food and wine, painting historical figurines. *Clubs:* Reform, Frontline.

McDOWALL, Stuart, CBE 1984; Chairman, Fife Healthcare NHS Trust, 1994–96; economic consultant; Senior Lecturer in Economics, University of St Andrews, 1967–91; *b* 19 April 1926; *s* of Robert McDowall and Gertrude Mary Collister; *m* 1951, Margaret Burnside Woods Gyle; three *s*. *Educ:* Liverpool Institute; St Andrews University (MA hons 1950). Personnel Manager, Michael Nairn & Co., 1955–61; Lectr in Econs, St Andrews Univ., 1961–67; Master, United Coll. of St Salvator and St Leonard, 1976–80. Dep. Chm., Central Arbitration Cttee, 1976–96; Local Govt Boundary Comr for Scotland, 1983–99; Member: Monopolies and Mergers Commn, 1985–89; Restrictive Practices Court, 1993–96. Econ. Consultant to UN in Saudi Arabia, 1985–89. Sec., Scottish Economic Soc., 1970–76. *Publications:* (with P. R. Draper) Trade Adjustment and the British Jute Industry, 1978; (with H. M. Begg) Industrial Performance and Prospects in Areas Affected by Oil Developments, 1981; articles on industrial economics and regional economics. *Recreations:* golf, hill walking. *Address:* 10 Woodburn Terrace, St Andrews, Fife KY16 8BA. *T:* (01334) 473247. *Club:* Royal and Ancient Golf (St Andrews).

McDOWELL, Alexander Blair, RDI 2006; production designer, since 1980; *b* 11 April 1955; *s* of (Hamilton) Blair McDowell and Pamela McDowell (*née* Howe); *m* 1995, Kirsten Everberg; one *s* one *d*. *Educ:* Downs Sch., Colwall; Bootham Sch., York; Central Sch. of Art, London. Graphic Designer and owner, Rocking Russian Design, 1977–86; production designer: *films* designed include: The Crow, 1994; Fear and Loathing in Las Vegas, 1998; Fight Club, 1999; Minority Report, 2002; The Terminal, 2004; Charlie and the Chocolate Factory, 2005; Corpse Bride, 2005; Breaking and Entering, 2006; Bee Movie, 2007. Adv. Bd, University Art Mus., Long Beach, CA, 2005–. Vis. Artist, MIT Media Lab, 2006. Founder, Matter Art and Science, 2002–. *Recreations:* holing up, reading, eating, drinking, walking it off. *Address:* c/o Mack Agency, 4705 Laurel Canyon Boulevard, Suite 204, Valley Village, CA 91607, USA. *T:* (818) 7536300; *e-mail:* alexmcdowell1@mac.com.

See also J. B. McDowell.

MacDOWELL, Prof. Douglas Maurice, DLitt; FRSE; FBA 1993; Professor of Greek, University of Glasgow, 1971–2001, now Emeritus; *b* 8 March 1931; *s* of Maurice Alfred MacDowell and Dorothy Jean MacDowell (*née* Allan). *Educ:* Highgate Sch.; Balliol Coll., Oxford (1st Cl. Classical Mods 1952, 1st Cl. Lit. Hum. 1954; MA, DLitt). FRSE 1991. Classics Master: Allhallows Sch., 1954–56; Merchant Taylors' Sch., 1956–58; University of Manchester: Asst Lectr, Lectr and Sen. Lectr, 1958–70; Reader in Greek and Latin, 1970–71. Vis. Fellow, Merton Coll., Oxford, 1969. Sec., Council of University Classical Depts, 1974–76; Chm. Council, Classical Assoc. of Scotland, 1976–82. *Publications:* Andokides: On the Mysteries, 1962; Athenian Homicide Law, 1963; Aristophanes: Wasps, 1971; The Law in Classical Athens, 1978; Spartan Law, 1986; Demosthenes: Against Meidias, 1990; Aristophanes and Athens, 1995; (with M. Gagarin) Antiphon and Andocides, 1998; Demosthenes: On the False Embassy, 2000; Demosthenes: speeches 27–38, 2004. *Address:* 2 Grosvenor Court, 365 Byres Road, Glasgow G12 8AU. *T:* (0141) 334 7818. *Club:* Oxford and Cambridge.

McDOWELL, Sir Eric (Wallace), Kt 1990; CBE 1982; FCA; Partner, Wilson Hennessey & Crawford, later (following merger in 1973) Deloitte, Haskins & Sells, 1952–85 (Senior Partner, Belfast, 1980–85); *b* 7 June 1925; *s* of Martin Wallace McDowell and Edith Florence (*née* Hillock); *m* 1954, Helen Lilian (*née* Montgomery); one *s* two *d*. *Educ:* Royal Belfast Academical Instn. FCA 1957. Served War, 1943–46. Student Chartered Accountant, 1942, qualified 1948. Chm., Capita Mgt Consultants Ltd, 1992–98; Director: NI Transport Holding Co., 1971–74; Spence Bryson Ltd, 1986–89; TSB Northern Ireland, 1986–92; AIB Group Northern Ireland, 1992–97; Shepherd Ltd, 1992–2004. Member: Council, Inst. of Chartered Accountants in Ireland, 1968–77 (Pres., 1974–75); Industries Develt Adv. Cttee, 1971–82 (Chm., 1978–82); Adv. Cttee of NI Central Investment Fund for Charities, 1975–98 (Chm., 1980–98); NI Econ. Council, 1977–83; Industrial Develt Bd for NI, 1982–91 (Chm., 1986–91); Exec. Cttee, Relate: Marriage Guidance, NI, 1981–2002 (Chm., 1992–96); Nat. Exec. Cttee, Relate, 1992–2000; Broadcasting Council for NI, 1983–86; Financial Reporting Review Panel, 1990–94; Senate, QUB, 1993–2001. Trustee, Presbyterian Church in Ireland, 1983–. Treas., Abbeyfield Belfast Soc., 1986–99. Governor, Royal Belfast Academical Instn, 1959– (Chm. of Governors, 1977–86); President: Belfast Old Instonians Assoc., 1993–94; Confedn of Ulster Socs, 1989–98. Hon. DSc(Econ) QUB, 1989. *Recreations:* music, drama, foreign travel. *Address:* Apt 7, Newforge Manor, 11 Newforge Lane, Belfast BT9 5NT. *T:* (028) 9066 8771. *Clubs:* Royal Over-Seas League; Ulster Reform (Belfast).

McDOWELL, Prof. Gary Linn, PhD; FRHistS; Tyler Haynes Professor of Leadership Studies, Political Science and Law, University of Richmond, USA, since 2005 (Tyler Haynes Professor of Leadership Studies and Political Science, 2003–05); *b* 4 June 1949; *s* of Samuel Earl McDowell and Violet Marie McDowell (*née* Harris); *m* 1990, Brenda Jo Evans. *Educ:* Univ. of S Florida (BA 1972); Memphis State Univ. (MA 1974); Univ. of Chicago (AM 1978); Univ. of Virginia (PhD 1979). Social Studies Teacher, Dunedin Jun. High Sch., 1972–73; Asst Prof. of Political Sci., Dickinson Coll., 1979–83; Liberal Arts Fellow, Harvard Law Sch.,1981–82; Asst Prof., 1983–85, Associate Prof., 1985–86, of Political Sci., Tulane Univ.; Dir, Office of the Bicentennial of the Constitution, Nat. Endowment for the Humanities, 1984–85; Associate Dir of Public Affairs, US Dept of Justice, 1985–87; Resident Schol., Center for Judicial Studies, 1987–88; Fellow, Woodrow Wilson Internat. Center for Scholars, 1987–88; Vice Pres., Nat. Legal Center for Public Interest, 1988–89; Bradley Vis. Schol., Harvard Law Sch., 1990–92; Lectr, Harvard Univ., 1992; Dir, Inst. of US Studies, 1992–2003, and Prof. of American Studies, 1993–2003, Univ. of London. Fellow, Nat. Endowment for the Humanities, 2007–08. Mem., Fulbright Commn, 1997–2003. Member: Bd, Landmark Legal Foundn, 1992–; Bd of Visitors, Pepperdine Univ. Sch. of Public Policy, 2000–04; Soc. of Scholars, James Madison Prog. in American Ideals and Institns, Princeton Univ., 2002–. FRHistS 1996. FRSA. Dist. Educn Award, Univ. of Richmond, 2005. *Publications:* (ed jtly and contrib.) The American Founding, 1981; (ed jtly and contrib.) Taking the Constitution Seriously, 1981; Equity and the Constitution, 1982; Curbing the Courts, 1988; (jtly) Justice *vs* Law, 1993; (ed jtly and contrib.) Our Peculiar Security, 1993; (ed jtly and contrib.) Reason and Republicanism, 1997; (ed jtly) Juvenile Delinquency in the United States and the United Kingdom, 1999; (ed jtly and contrib.) America and Enlightenment Constitutionalism, 2006; numerous contribs to learned jls and other publications. *Recreations:* walking, reading, bluegrass music, martinis, mint juleps and Cuban cigars. *Address:* Jepson School of Leadership Studies, University of Richmond, Richmond, VA 23173, USA. *T:* (804) 2876085. *Club:* Reform.

McDOWELL, George Roy Colquhoun, CBE 1988; CEng, FIET; Chairman, British Standards Institution, 1985–88; *b* 1 Sept. 1922; *s* of Robert Henry McDowell and Jean McDowell; *m* 1948, Joan Annie Bryan; two *s*. *Educ:* Coleraine Academical Instn; Queen's Univ., Belfast (BSc Eng). Signals Officer, RAF, 1942–46. Works Manager, Distribn Transformer Div., subseq. Works Manager, Power Transformer Div., Ferranti Ltd, 1950–69; Dir, 1969–87, Man. Dir Designate, 1969–72, Chm. and Man. Dir, 1972–87, George H. Scholes. Director: Clipsal (UK), 1983–98 (Chm., 1985–98); Clipsal Ltd, 1997–98; Elbocks Ltd, 1997–98. Chairman: Electrical Installation Equipment Manufacturers' Assoc., 1977–80; British Electrotechnical Cttee, BSI; Electrotechnical Council, BSI, 1982–85; President: British Electrical and Allied Manufacturers' Assoc., 1981–82; Internat. Electrotechnical Commn, 1987–90; IEEIE; Institution of Electrical Engineers: Chm., Power Bd; Chm., Finance Cttee; Mem. Council. Hon. FIIE. Grand Decoration of Honour for Services to the Republic of Austria, 1978. *Recreations:* golf, Rugby, cricket. *Address:* 11 Abbey Mill, Shirleys Drive, Prestbury, Macclesfield, Cheshire SK10 4XY. *T:* (01625) 827750. *Club:* Army and Navy.

McDOWELL, Prof. John Henry, FBA 1983; FAAAS; University Professor of Philosophy, University of Pittsburgh, since 1988 (Professor of Philosophy, 1986–88); *b* 7 March 1942; *s* of Sir Henry McDowell, KBE and Norah, *d* of Walter Slade Douthwaite; *m* 1977, Andrea Lee Lehrke. *Educ:* St John's College, Johannesburg; University College of Rhodesia and Nyasaland; New College, Oxford (MA); BA London. FAAAS 1993. Fellow and Praelector in Philosophy, UC, Oxford, 1966–86, Emeritus Fellow, 1988, Hon. Fellow, 2007; Univ. Lectr (CUF), Oxford Univ., 1967–86. James C. Loeb Fellow in Classical Philosophy, Harvard Univ., 1969; Visiting Professor: Univ. of Michigan, 1975; Univ. of California, Los Angeles, 1977; Univ. of Minnesota, 1982; Jadavpur Univ., Calcutta, 1983; John Locke Lectr, Oxford Univ., 1991. Sen. Fellow, Council of Humanities, Princeton Univ., 1984. *Publications:* Plato, Theaetetus (trans. with notes), 1973; (ed with Gareth Evans) Truth and Meaning, 1976; (ed) Gareth Evans, The Varieties of Reference, 1982; (ed with Philip Pettit) Subject, Thought, and Context, 1986; Mind and World, 1994; Mind, Value, and Reality (collected articles), 1998; Meaning, Knowledge, and Reality (collected articles), 1998; articles in jls and anthologies. *Recreations:* reading, music, gardening. *Address:* c/o Department of Philosophy, University of Pittsburgh, Pittsburgh, PA 15260, USA. *T:* (412) 6245792.

McDOWELL, Jonathan Bruce, RIBA; architect; Partner, McDowell+Benedetti, since 1996; Director, McDowell+Benedetti Ltd, since 1998; *b* 18 March 1957; *s* of Hamilton Blair McDowell and Pamela (*née* Howe); *m* 2001, Rebecca Wells. *Educ:* The Downs Sch.; Bootham Sch.; Downing Coll., Cambridge (MA, DipArch); Graduate Sch. of Design, Harvard Univ. RIBA 1985. Associate, Munkenbeck & Marshall, 1986–90; Principal, Jonathan McDowell Architects, 1991–96; with Renato Benedetti, formed McDowell+Benedetti, 1996; main projects include: Smithfield Regeneration, Dublin, 1992; Oliver's Wharf Penthouse, Wapping, 1996; HQ Building, Options, London, 1997; (with YRM Architects) New Univ. of the Commonwealth, Malaysia, 1998; Assoc. of Photographers, New Gall. and HQ, London, 1998; Nursing Home for Merchant Taylors' Co., Lewisham, 2002; Suncourt Hse, 2002; Kingston Univ. Faculty of Design, 2003. Mem., CABE Enabling Panel, 2001–. FRSA 1999. *Recreation:* Balinese, Javanese and contemporary gamelan. *Address:* (office) Karen House, 1–11 Baches Street, N1 6DL.

McDOWELL, Kathryn Alexandra; Managing Director, London Symphony Orchestra, since 2005; *b* 19 Dec. 1959; *d* of late John McDowell and of Kathleen Avril McDowell; *m* 1997, Ian Charles Stewart Ritchie, *qv*. *Educ:* Belfast High Sch.; Univ. of Edinburgh (BMus 1982); Stranmillis Coll. of Education (PGCE 1983). LTCL 1980, Hon. FTCL 1996; ARCM 1981; Hon. RCM 1999. Marketing and Educn Assistant, WNO, 1984–85; Develt Manager, Scottish Chamber Orch., 1985–89; Dep. Gen. Manager, Ulster Orch., 1989–92; Music Officer, Arts Council, 1992–94; Music Dir, Arts Council of England, 1994–99; Chief Exec., Wales Millennium Centre, 1999–2001; Dir, City of London Festival, 2001–05. *Recreations:* tennis, ski-ing, travel. *Address:* London Symphony Orchestra, Barbican Centre, Silk Street, EC2Y 8DS.

McDOWELL, Prof. Linda Margaret, PhD; FBA 2008; Professor of Human Geography, University of Oxford, and Professorial Fellow, St John's College, Oxford, since 2004; *b* 1 Jan. 1949; *d* of Frederick Herbert Leigh and Olive Morgan Leigh (*née* Nicholson); *m* 1972, Christopher James McDowell; one *s* one *d*. *Educ:* Newnham Coll., Cambridge (BA Hons 1971); Bartlett Sch., University Coll. London (MPhil 1973; PhD 1986). Res. Fellow, Centre for Res. in Soc. Scis, Univ. of Kent, Canterbury, 1973–76; Res. Officer, Inst. of Community Studies, London, 1976–78; Open University: Lectr, then Sen. Lectr in Geog., 1978–92; Dep. Dean, Soc. Scis Faculty, 1989–92; University of Cambridge: Univ. Lectr in Geog., 1992–99; Fellow and Coll. Lectr, 1992–99, Vice Principal, 1997–99, Newnham Coll.; Prof. of Human Geog., LSE, 1999–2000; Prof. of Econ. Geog., UCL, 2000–04. Visiting Lecturer: Univ. of Southampton, 1976; Univ. of Kent, 1978; UCLA, 1990; UCL, 1991. AcSS 2001. Hon. Fellow, Gender Inst., LSE, 2000–. Back Award, RGS, 2001. *Publications:* (with D. Morgan) Patterns of Residence, 1979; (ed jtly) Urban Change and Conflict, 1981; (ed jtly) City, Economy and Society, 1981; (ed jtly) Geography and Gender, 1984; (ed jtly) Divided Nation: social and cultural change in Britain, 1989; (ed jtly) The Changing Social Structure, 1989; (with J. Allen) Landlords and Property, 1989; (jtly) The Transformation of Britain, 1989; (ed jtly) Defining Women: social institutions and gender divisions, 1992; Capital Culture: gender at work in the City, 1997; Undoing Place?, 1997; (ed jtly) Space, Gender, Knowledge, 1997; (ed jtly) A Feminist Glossary of Human Geography, 1999; Gender, Identity and Place, 1999; Redundant Masculinities?: employment change and white working class youth, 2003; Hard Labour: the forgotten voices of Latvian 'volunteer' workers, 2005; (ed jtly) Gender Divisions and Working Time in the New Economy, 2005; contrib. numerous book chapters and to learned jls. *Recreations:* cities, cycling, contemporary fiction, gardening. *Address:* Oxford University Centre for the Environment, South Parks Road, Oxford OX1 3QY. *T:* (01865) 275843; *e-mail:* linda.mcdowell@ouce.ox.ac.uk; St John's College, Oxford OX1 3JP. *T:* (01865) 277300.

McDOWELL, Malcolm, (Malcolm Taylor); actor; *b* 13 June 1943; *m* 1992, Kelley Kuhr; two *s*; one *s* one *d* from former marriage. *Educ:* Leeds. *Stage:* RSC Stratford, 1965–66; Entertaining Mr Sloane, Royal Court, 1975; Look Back in Anger, NY, 1980; In Celebration, NY, 1984; Holiday, Old Vic, 1987; Another Time, NY, 1993; *films:* If, 1969; Figures in a Landscape, 1970; The Raging Moon, 1971; A Clockwork Orange, 1971; O Lucky Man, 1973; Royal Flash, 1975; Aces High, 1976; Voyage of the Damned, 1977; Caligula, 1977; The Passage, 1978; Time After Time, 1979; Cat People, 1981; Blue Thunder, 1983; Get Crazy, 1983; Britannia Hospital, 1984; Gulag, 1985; Cross Creek, 1985; Sunset, 1988; Assassin of the Tsar, 1991; Milk Money, 1993; Star Trek Generations, 1994; Tank Girl, 1995; Exquisite Tenderness, 1995; Mr Magoo, 1998; Gangster No 1, 2000; Just Visiting, 2002; I Spy, 2003; The Company, 2004; Rag Tale, 2005; Never Apologise, 2008; *television:* Our Friends in the North, 1996. *Address:* c/o Markham and Froggatt, 4 Windmill Street, W1T 2HZ.

McDOWELL, Stanley; Town Clerk and Chief Executive, Belfast City Council, 1989–92; *b* 14 June 1941; *s* of William McDowell and Annie Storey; *m* 1966, Charlotte Elizabeth Stockdale; three *d*. *Educ:* Royal Belfast Academical Instn; Queen's Univ. of Belfast (BSc Econ). FCIS. Belfast City and Dist Water Comrs, 1959–70; Asst Sec. (Actg), Antrim County Council, 1971–73; Roads Service Divl Finance Officer, DoE (NI), 1973–79; Belfast City Council, 1979–92; Asst Town Clerk (Admin), 1979–89. Non-exec. Dir., Ulster Community and Hosps Trust, 1998–2002 (Chm., Audit Cttee, 1998–2002); Dep. Chm., Belfast Abbeyfield Soc. Ltd, 2002–. *Address:* 209 Bangor Road, Holywood, N Ireland BT18 0JG. *T:* (028) 9042 5132.

MACDUFF, Earl of; *see* Earl of Southesk.

MacDUFF, Hon. Sir Alistair (Geoffrey), Kt 2008; **Hon. Mr Justice MacDuff;** a Judge of the High Court of Justice, Queen's Bench Division, since 2008; *b* 26 May 1945; *s* of late Alexander MacDonald MacDuff and Iris Emma Jarvis (*née* Gardner); *m* 1st, 1969, Susan Christine Kitchener (*d* 1991); two *d*; 2nd 1993, Katherine Anne Buckley; one *s* one *d*. *Educ:* Ecclesfield Grammar Sch., Sheffield; LSE (LLB 1965); Sheffield Univ. (LLM 1967). Called to the Bar, Lincoln's Inn, 1969, Bencher, 2003. QC 1993; Asst Recorder, 1983–87; Recorder, 1987–97; Circuit Judge, 1997–2008; Sen. Circuit Judge, 2002–08; Designated Civil Judge, Birmingham Gp, 2000–08. *Recreations:* theatre, opera, wine, Rugby football. *Address:* Royal Courts of Justice, Strand, WC2A 2LL. *Club:* Painswick Rugby Football.

McDUFF, Prof. (Margaret) Dusa, PhD; FRS 1994; Distinguished Professor of Mathematics, State University of New York at Stony Brook, since 1998; *b* 18 Oct. 1945; *d* of Conrad Hal Waddington and Margaret Justin (*née* Blanco White); *m* 1st, 1968, David William McDuff (marr. diss. 1978); one *d*; 2nd, 1984, John Willard Milnor; one *s*. *Educ:* Univ. of Edinburgh (BSc Hons); Girton Coll., Cambridge (PhD 1971). Lecturer: Univ. of York, 1972–76; Univ. of Warwick, 1976–78; Asst Prof., 1978–80, Associate Prof., 1980–84, Prof. of Maths, 1984–98, SUNY at Stony Brook. Asst Prof., MIT, 1974–75; Mem., Inst. for Advanced Study, Princeton, 1976 and 1977; Vis. Prof., Univ of Calif, Berkeley, 1993. Fellow, Amer. Acad. of Arts and Scis, 1995; Mem., NAS, USA, 1999. Hon. DSc: Edinburgh, 1997; York, 2000. *Publications:* (with D. Salamon): J-Holomorphic Curves and Quantum Cohomology, 1994; Introduction to Symplectic Topology, 1995; J-Holomorphic Curves and Symplectic Topology, 2004. *Recreations:* chamber music, reading, walking. *Address:* Mathematics Department, State University of New York, Stony Brook, NY 11794–3651, USA. *T:* (631) 6328290.

MACE, Dr (Alan) Christopher (Hugh), CBE 1991; Chief of Staff, Defence Equipment and Support, Ministry of Defence, since 2007; *b* 17 Sept. 1953; *s* of late Maurice William Mace and of Josephine Mary Mace; *m* 1979, Sian Avery; one *s* one *d*. *Educ:* Weymouth Grammar Sch.; Univ. of Exeter (BSc 1975; PhD 1981). Ministry of Defence, 1979–99: rocketry and combustion res., 1979–86; novel weapon res., 1986–88; Asst Dir, Personnel, 1988–89; Project Manager procuring Army equipt, 1990–91; Director: Res. and Internat. Collaboration, 1991–94; Finance and Secretariat, Weapons and Electronic Systems Procurement, 1994–96; on secondment as Dir, Business Develt, Avery Berkel, 1996–97; Project Dir implementing resource accounting and planning systems, MoD, 1997–99; Dep. Dir Gen. (Ops), Immigration and Nationality Directorate, Home Office, 1999–2003; Chief Inspector, Immigration Service, 2000–03; Dir Gen., Logistics Resources, Defence Logistics Orgn, MoD, 2003–07. FRSA 2000. *Publications:* res. papers on combustion. *Recreations:* music, walking. *Address:* Defence Equipment and Support, MoD Abbey Wood, Maple 2C, Bristol BS34 8JH. *T:* (0117) 913 0037.

MACE, Brian Anthony; Director, Revenue Policy: Employment Initiatives, Board of Inland Revenue, 2002–04; *b* 9 Sept. 1948; *s* of late Edward Laurence Mace and Olive (*née* Bennett); *m* 1973, Anne Margaret Cornford. *Educ:* Maidstone Grammar Sch.; Gonville and Caius Coll., Cambridge (MA Mathematics). Admin trainee, Bd of Inland Revenue, 1971–73; seconded to Secretariat, Inflation Accounting Cttee, 1974–75; Inland Revenue: Principal, 1975–82; Asst Sec., 1982–90; Under Sec., 1990–2004; Dir, Savings and Investment Div., 1990–98, and Capital and Valuation Div., 1995–98; Dir, Personal Tax, 1998–2000; Dir, Study of Personal Tax, 2000–02. Mem., Tax Law Rev. Cttee, 2007–. *Recreations:* opera, chamber music and song, theatre, cricket, historic buildings. *Address:* 406 Faraday Lodge, Renaissance Walk, SE10 0QL. *T:* (020) 8305 0420.

MACE, Christopher; *see* Mace, A. C. H.

MACE, Georgina Mary, CBE 2007 (OBE 1998); DPhil; FRS 2002; Professor of Conservation Science and Director, NERC Centre for Population Biology, Imperial College London, since 2006; *m* 1985, Roderick O. Evans; one *s* two *d*. *Educ:* Univ. of Liverpool (BSc Hons 1976); Univ. of Sussex (DPhil 1979). Postdoctoral Fellow, Smithsonian Instn, Washington, DC, 1980–81; Sir James Knott Res. Fellow, Dept of Zoology, Univ. of Newcastle upon Tyne, 1981–83; Res. Fellow, Inst. of Zoology, and Hon. Fellow, Dept of Biology, UCL, 1983–89; Institute of Zoology, Zoological Society of London: Pew Scholar in Conservation and the Envmt, 1991–94; NERC Advanced Fellow, 1994–99; Dir of Sci., 2000–06. Member Council: Durrell Wildlife Conservation Trust, 1998–2004; RSPB, 2000–04; Royal Soc., 2005–06. Trustee, Nat. Hist. Mus., 2004–. *Publications:* (jtly) Creative Conservation: interactive management of wild and captive animals, 1993; (ed jtly) Conservation in a Changing World, 1999; (ed jtly) Conservation of Exploited Species, 2001; articles in learned jls. *Address:* NERC Centre for Population Biology, Imperial College at Silwood Park, Ascot, Berks SL5 7PY. *T:* (office) (020) 7594 2354.

MACE, Lt-Gen. Sir John (Airth), KBE 1990 (OBE 1974; MBE 1967); CB 1986; New Zealand Chief of Defence Force, 1987–91; *b* 29 June 1932; *m* 1962, Margaret Theodocia (*née* McCallum); one *s* one *d*. *Educ:* Ashburton High Sch., NZ; Nelson Coll., NZ; RMC Duntroon, Australia. Commissioned NZ Army, 1953; NZ SAS, 1955–57; active service in Malayan Emergency (despatches, 1958); Comd SAS Sqdn, 1960–62 and 1965; Comd Co. of 1 RNZIR 1st Bn, Borneo, 1966; Vietnam, 1967; appts include: Dir of Infantry and NZ SAS; CO, 1st Bn RNZIR, Singapore; Dir, Officer Postings; Comdr, Army Logistics Support Gp; Comdr, 1st Inf. Bde Gp; Army Staff Coll., Camberley; JSSC, Canberra; Comdr, NZ Force SE Asia, 1979–80; RCDS 1981; Dep. Chief of Defence Staff, 1982–84; Chief of General Staff, 1984–87. Hon. Col, First Bn, Royal NZ Inf. Regt, 2005–. *Recreations:* golf, walking, reading. *Club:* Wellington (Wellington).

MacEACHEN, Hon. Allan Joseph; PC (Canada) 1963; Senator (L) for Nova Scotia, 1984–96; *b* Inverness, Nova Scotia, 6 July 1921; *s* of Angus and Annie MacEachen. *Educ:* St Francis Xavier Univ. (BA 1944); Univ. of Toronto (MA 1946); Univ. of Chicago; MIT. Prof. of Economics, St Francis Xavier Univ., 1946–48; Head of Dept of Economics and Social Sciences; MP (L) Inverness-Richmond, NS, 1953–58, Inverness-Richmond, later Cape Breton-Highlands-Canso, NS, 1962–84. Special Asst and Consultant on Econ. Affairs to Hon. Lester Pearson, 1958; Minister: of Labour, 1963–65; of Nat. Health and Welfare, 1965–68; of Manpower and Immigration, 1968–70; of External Affairs, 1974–76; of Finance, 1980–82; Sec. of State for External Affairs, 1982–84; Pres., Privy Council and Govt Leader in House of Commons, Canada, 1970–74 and 1976–79; Dep. Prime Minister, 1977–79 and 1980–84; Dep. Leader of the Opposition and Opposition House Leader, 1979–80; called to Senate, 1984, Leader of Govt in Senate, 1984, Leader of Opposition in Senate, 1984–91. Co-Chm., Canada-Germany Conf., 1984–. Mem. Bd Trustees, Internat. Crisis Gp, NY, 1995–. Member, Bd of Governors: St Francis Xavier Univ.; Gaelic Coll. of Celtic Arts and Crafts, NS. Mem., Royal Celtic Soc., Edinburgh. Hon. degrees: universities: St Francis Xavier; Acadia; St Mary's; Dalhousie; Wilfrid Laurier; Loyola Coll.; Canadian Coast Guard Coll.; UC of Cape Breton. Grand Cross, Order of Merit (Germany), 1993. *Address:* RR1, Whycocomagh, NS B0E 3M0, Canada. *Clubs:* Rideau, Le Cercle Universitaire (Ottawa); Halifax (Halifax, NS); Princeton (New York).

McEACHRAN, Colin Neil; QC (Scot.) 1982; *b* 14 Jan. 1940; *s* of Eric Robins McEachran and Nora Helen Bushe; *m* 1967, Katherine Charlotte Henderson; two *d*. *Educ:* Trinity Coll., Glenalmond; Merton Coll., Oxford (BA 1961); Univ. of Glasgow (LLB 1963); Univ. of Chicago (Commonwealth Fellow; JD 1965). Admitted Solicitor, 1966; admitted to Faculty of Advocates, 1968. Advocate Depute, 1975–78. Mem., Scottish Legal Aid Bd, 1990–98; Pres., Pension Appeal Tribunals for Scotland, 1995–. Chm., Commonwealth Games Council for Scotland, 1995–99. *Recreations:* target rifle shooting (Silver Medal, Commonwealth Games, NZ, 1974), hill walking. *Address:* 13 Saxe-Coburg Place, Edinburgh EH3 5BR. *T:* (0131) 332 6820.

MACEDO, Prof. Helder Malta, PhD; Camoens Professor of Portuguese, University of London at King's College, 1982–2004, now Professor Emeritus; *b* 30 Nov. 1935; *s* of Adelino José de Macedo and Aida Malta de Macedo; *m* 1960, Suzette Armanda (*née* de Aguiar). *Educ:* Faculty of Law, Univ. of Lisbon; King's Coll., Univ. of London (BA, PhD); FKC 1991. Lectr in Portuguese and Brazilian Studies, KCL, 1971–82; Sec. of State for Culture, Portuguese Govt, 1979. Visiting Professor: Harvard Univ., 1981; Ecole des Hautes Etudes et Sciences Sociales, Paris, 1992, 1995. Pres., Internat. Assoc. of Lusitanists, 1994–99 (Hon. Pres., 2002). Fellow, Academia das Ciências de Lisboa, 1987. Editor, Portuguese Studies Jl, 1985–2002. Comendador, Ordem de Santiago da Espada (Portugal), 1993. *Publications:* Nós, Uma Leitura de Cesário Verde, 1975, 4th edn 1999; Do Significado Oculto da 'Menina a Moça', 1977, 2nd edn 1999; Poesia 1957–77, 1978; Camões e a Viagem Iniciática, 1980; The Purpose of Praise: Past and Future in The Lusiads of Luís de Camões, 1983; Cesário Verde: O Romântico e o Feroz, 1988; Partes de Africa, 1991; Viagem de Inverno, 1994; Pedro e Paula, 1998, 2nd edn 1998 (Brazilian edn, 1999); Viagens do Olhar, 1998; Vícios e Virtudes, 2000, 2nd edn 2001 (Brazilian edn, 2002); Sem Nome, 2004 (Brazilian edn, 2006); Trinta Leituras, 2007. *Address:* Department of Portuguese and Brazilian Studies, King's College London, Strand, WC2R 2LS. *T:* (020) 7873 2507.

McENERY, Judith Mary; *see* Chessells, J. M.

McENERY, Peter; actor; Associate Artist, Royal Shakespeare Co.; *b* 21 Feb. 1940; *s* of Charles and Mary McEnery; *m* 1978; one *d*. *Educ:* various state and private schs. First stage appearance, Brighton, 1956; first London appearance in Flowering Cherry, Haymarket, 1957; *stage:* rôles with RSC include, 1961–: Laertes, Tybalt, Johnny Hobnails in Afore Night Come, Bassanio, Lorenzaccio, Orlando, Sachs in The Jail Diary of Albie Sachs, Pericles, Brutus, Antipholus of Ephesus, Godber in A Dream of People; other rôles include: Rudge in Next Time I'll Sing to You, Criterion, 1963; Konstantin in The Seagull, Queen's, 1964; Harry Winter in The Collaborators, Duchess, 1973; Trigorin in The Seagull, Lyric, 1975; Edward Gover in Made in Bangkok, Aldwych, 1986; Fredrik in A Little Night Music, Chichester, transf. Piccadilly, 1989; Torvald in The Doll's House, Robert in Dangerous Corner, Chichester, 1994; Menelaus in Women of Troy, NT, 1995; Hector Hushabye in Heartbreak House, Almeida, 1997; Claudius in Hamlet, RNT, 2000; directed: Richard III, Nottingham, 1971; The Wound, Young Vic, 1972. *Films* include: Tunes of Glory, 1961; Victim, 1961; The Moonspinners, 1963; Entertaining Mr Sloane, 1970; *television:* Clayhanger, 1976; The Jail Diary of Albie Sachs, 1980; Pictures, 1983; The Collectors, 1986; The Mistress, 1986; Witchcraft, 1992. *Recreations:* steam railway preservation, ski-ing, American football. *Address:* c/o The Richard Stone Partnership, 2 Henrietta Street, WC2E 8PS.

McENROE, John Patrick; tennis player and commentator; *b* Wiesbaden, 16 Feb. 1959; *s* of John Patrick McEnroe and Katherine, (Kay), McEnroe (*née* Tresham); *m* 1st, 1986, Tatum O'Neal (marr. diss. 1994); two *s* one *d*; 2nd, 1997, Patty Smyth; two *d*, and one step *d*. *Educ:* Trinity High Sch., NYC; Stanford Univ., Calif. Amateur tennis player, 1976–78, turned professional, 1978; winner of 77 singles titles and 77 doubles titles, including: US Open (singles) 1979, 1980, 1981, 1984, (doubles) 1979, 1981, 1983, 1989; Wimbledon (singles) 1981, 1983, 1984, (doubles) 1979, 1981, 1983, 1984, 1992; Grand Prix Masters 1979, 1983, 1984. Mem., US Davis Cup team, 1978–84, 1987–89, 1991, 1992, Captain, 1999–2000. Tennis commentator, USA TV, 1992–, BBC TV, 2000–; host, TV quiz show, The Chair, 2002. Owner, John McEnroe Gall., NY. *Publication:* (with James Kaplan) Serious (autobiog.), 2002. *Address:* The John McEnroe Gallery, 41 Greene Street, New York, NY 10013, USA.

MACER, Dr Richard Charles Franklin, MA, PhD; consultant on biotechnology and genetics, 1985–95; *b* 21 Oct. 1928; *s* of Lionel William Macer and Adie Elizabeth Macer; *m* 1952, Vera Gwendoline Jeapes; three *d*. *Educ:* Worthing High Sch.; St John's Coll., Cambridge. Research, St John's Coll., Cambridge, 1949–55, Hutchinson Res. Student, 1952–53; Hd of Plant Pathology Section, Plant Breeding Inst., Cambridge, 1955–66; Dir and Dir of Res., Rothwell Plant Breeders Ltd, Lincs, 1966–72; Prof. of Crop Production, Univ. of Edinburgh, 1972–76; Dir, Scottish Plant Breeding Station, 1976–81; Gen. Manager, Plant Royalty Bureau Ltd, 1981–85. *Publications:* papers on fungal diseases of cereals. *Recreations:* hill walking, archaeology, reading.

McEVOY, His Honour David Dand; QC 1983; a Circuit Judge, 1996–2008; *b* 25 June 1938; *s* of David Dand McEvoy and Ann Elizabeth McEvoy (*née* Breslin); *m* 1974, Belinda Anne Robertson; three *d*. *Educ:* Mount St Mary's Coll.; Lincoln Coll., Oxford. BA (PPE). 2nd Lieut The Black Watch, RHR, 1958–59. Called to the Bar, Inner Temple, 1964; a

Recorder, 1979–96. *Recreations:* golf, fishing. *Clubs:* Garrick; Blackwell Golf; Seniors Golfing Society; Highland Brigade.

McEWAN, Hon. Lord; Robin Gilmour McEwan; a Senator of the College of Justice in Scotland, since 2000; *b* 12 Dec. 1943; *s* of late Ian G. McEwan and Mary McEwan, Paisley, Renfrewshire; *m* 1973, Sheena, *d* of late Stewart F. McIntyre and Lilian McIntyre, Aberdour; two *d. Educ:* Paisley Grammar Sch.; Glasgow Univ. (1st Cl. Hons LLB; PhD). Faulds Fellow in Law, Glasgow Univ., 1965–68; admitted to Faculty of Advocates, 1967; QC (Scot.) 1981. Standing Jun. Counsel to Dept of Energy, 1974–76; Advocate Depute, 1976–79; Sheriff of S Strathclyde, Dumfries and Galloway, at Lanark, 1982–88, at Ayr, 1988–2000; Temp. Judge, Court of Session and High Court of Justiciary, 1991–99. Chm., Industrial Tribunals, 1981–82; Mem., Scottish Legal Aid Bd, 1989–96. Dep. Chm., Boundary Commn for Scotland, 2007–. Mem., Scottish Civil Courts Review, 2007–. Chancellor, dio. of Glasgow and Galloway. *Publications:* Pleading in Court, 1980, 2nd edn 1995; (with Ann Paton) A Casebook on Damages in Scotland, 1983; contrib. Stair Memorial Encyclopaedia of the Laws of Scotland, 1987. *Recreation:* golf. *Address:* Court of Session, Parliament House, Parliament Square, Edinburgh EH1 1RF. *T:* (0131) 225 2595. *Clubs:* New (Edinburgh); Honourable Company of Edinburgh Golfers, Prestwick Golf.

McEWAN, Geraldine, (Mrs Hugh Cruttwell); actress; *b* 9 May 1932; *d* of Donald and Norah McKeown; *m* 1953, Hugh Cruttwell (*d* 2002); one *s* one *d. Educ:* Windsor County Girls' School. Acted with Theatre Royal, Windsor, 1949–51; Who Goes There, 1951; Sweet Madness, 1952; For Better For Worse, 1953; Summertime, 1955; Love's Labour's Lost, Stratford-on-Avon, 1956; The Member of the Wedding, Royal Court Theatre, 1957; The Entertainer, Palace, 1957–58; Stratford-on-Avon, 1958: Pericles; Twelfth Night; Much Ado About Nothing; 1961: Much Ado About Nothing; Hamlet; Everything in the Garden, Arts and Duke of York's, 1962; School for Scandal, Haymarket, and USA, 1962; The Private Ear, and The Public Eye, USA, 1963; Loot, 1965; National Theatre, 1965–71: Armstrong's Last Goodnight; Love For Love; A Flea in Her Ear; The Dance of Death; Edward II; Home and Beauty; Rites; The Way of the World; The White Devil; Amphitryon 38; Dear Love, Comedy, 1973; Chez Nous, Globe, 1974; The Little Hut, Duke of York's, 1974; Oh Coward!, Criterion, 1975; On Approval, Haymarket, 1975; Look After Lulu, Chichester, and Haymarket, 1978; A Lie of the Mind, Royal Court, 1987; Lettice and Lovage, Globe, 1988; Hamlet, Riverside Studio, 1992; The Bird Sanctuary, Abbey, Dublin, 1994; Grace Note, Old Vic, 1997; The Chairs, Royal Court Downstairs, 1997, USA 1998; Hay Fever, Savoy, 1999; National Theatre: The Browning Version and Harlequinade, 1980; The Provok'd Wife, 1980; The Rivals, 1983; Two Inches of Ivory, 1983; You Can't Take It With You, 1983; The Way of the World, 1995. Directed: As You Like It, Birmingham Rep., transf. Phoenix, 1988; Treats, Hampstead, 1989; Waiting for Sir Larry, Edinburgh, 1990; Four Door Saloon, Hampstead, 1991; Keyboard Skills, Bush, 1993. *Television includes:* The Prime of Miss Jean Brodie, 1978; The Barchester Chronicles, 1982; Mapp and Lucia, 1985, 1986; Oranges are not the only Fruit, 1990; Mulberry, 1992, 1993; The Red Dwarf, 1999; Thin Ice, 2000; Carrie's War, 2004; Agatha Christie's Marple, 2004, 2005, 2006. *Films:* The Adventures of Tom Jones, 1975; Escape from the Dark, 1978; Foreign Body, 1986; Henry V, 1989; Robin Hood, Prince of Thieves, 1991; Moses, 1996; The Love Letter, 1999; Titus, Love's Labour's Lost, 2000; The Magdalene Sisters, 2002; Pure, 2003; The Lazarus Child, 2004; Vanity Fair, 2005. *Address:* c/o Independent Talent Group Ltd, Oxford House, Oxford Street, W1D 1BS.

McEWAN, Ian Russell, CBE 2000; FRSL; author; *b* 21 June 1948; *s* of late Major (retd) David McEwan and Rose Lilian Violet Moore; *m* 1982, Penny Allen (marr. diss. 1995); two *s* two *d*; *m* 1997, Annalena McAfee. *Educ:* Woolverstone Hall Sch.; Univ. of Sussex (BA Hons Eng. Lit.); Univ. of East Anglia (MA Eng. Lit.). Began writing, 1970. Hon. Member: Amer. Acad. of Arts and Scis, 1996; Amer. Acad. of Arts and Letters, 2006. FRSL 1982; FRSA. Hon. DLitt Sussex, 1989; Hon. DLit London, 1998; Hon. LittD E Anglia, 1993. Shakespeare Prize, FVS Foundn, Hamburg, 1999. *Films:* The Ploughman's Lunch, 1983; Last Day of Summer, 1984; Soursweet, 1988; The Innocent, 1993; The Good Son, 1994. *Publications:* First Love, Last Rites, 1975 (filmed, 1997); In Between the Sheets, 1978; The Cement Garden, 1978 (filmed, 1993); The Imitation Game, 1981; The Comfort of Strangers, 1981 (filmed, 1991); Or Shall we Die? (oratorio; score by Michael Berkeley), 1982; The Ploughman's Lunch (film script), 1985; The Child in Time, 1987 (Whitbread Award; Prix Fémina, 1993); Soursweet (film script), 1989; The Innocent, 1990; Black Dogs, 1992; The Daydreamer, 1994; The Short Stories, 1995; Enduring Love, 1997 (filmed, 2004); Amsterdam (novel), 1998 (Booker Prize, 1998); Atonement, 2001 (filmed, 2006); Rose Blanche, 2004; Saturday, 2005 (James Tait Black Meml Prize, 2006); On Chesil Beach, 2007; For You (opera libretto; score by Michael Berkeley), 2008. *Recreations:* hiking, tennis. *Address:* c/o Jonathan Cape, Random Century House, 20 Vauxhall Bridge Road, SW1V 2SA.

McEWAN, Leslie James; JP; independent consultant, since 2004; Associate Consultant, Care and Health Ltd, since 2004; *b* 26 Feb. 1946; *s* of Charles and Ann McEwan; *m* 1966, Catherine Anne Currie; two *s. Educ:* St Andrews Univ. (MA); Dundee Univ. (Dip Social Admin); Univ. of Edinburgh (Dip Social Work). Midlothian, East Lothian and Peebles: Child Care Officer, Children's Dept, 1967–69; Social Worker, 1969–71; Sen. Social Worker, 1971–74; Social Work Advr, 1974–75; Divisional Director of Social Work: Midlothian-Lothian Reg., 1975–80; West Lothian, 1980–85; Lothian Region: Depute Dir of Social Work, 1985–90; Sen. Depute Dir, 1990–95; Dir, 1995–96; Dir of Social Work, City of Edinburgh Council, 1996–2003. JP Midlothian, 1973. *Recreations:* fly-fishing, golf, woodturning. *Address:* 1 Eskglades, Dalkeith, Midlothian EH22 1UZ.

McEWAN, Morag Barbara; *see* Wise, M. B.

McEWAN, Robin Gilmour; *see* McEwan, Hon. Lord.

McEWEN, Hilary Mary; *see* Mantel, H. M.

McEWEN, Prof. James, FRCP, FFPH, FFOM, FDSRCS, FMedSci; Professor of Public Health, University of Glasgow, 1989–2002, now Emeritus (Henry Mechan Professor of Public Health, 1989–2000); President, Faculty of Public Health Medicine, Royal Colleges of Physicians of the United Kingdom, 1998–2001; *b* 6 Feb. 1940; *s* of Daniel McEwen and Elizabeth Wells (*née* Dishington); *m* 1964, Elizabeth May Archibald; one *s* one *d. Educ:* Dollar Acad.; Univ. of St Andrews (MB ChB 1963). FFPH (FFPHM 1981); FFOM 1990; FRCPGlas 1991; FRCP 1999; FRCPE 1999; FDSRCS 2003. Asst MO of Health, City of Dundee, 1965–66; Lectr, Univ. of Dundee, 1966–74; Sen. Lectr, Univ. of Nottingham, 1975–81; CMO, Health Educn Council, 1981–82; Prof. of Community Medicine, King's Coll. Sch. of Medicine and Dentistry, Univ. of London, 1983–89. Hon. Consultant in Public Health Medicine, Gtr Glasgow Health Bd, 1989–2002; Hon. Civilian Advr in Public Health to the Army, 2001–06; non-exec. Dir, Glasgow Royal Infirmary and Univ. NHS Trust, 1994–99. Chm., Health Protection Adv. Gp, Scotland, 2005–. Mem., NRPB, 1996–2003. Distinguished Visitor, Univ. of Tucuman, Argentina, 1993. Hon. Chairman: UK Register for Public Health (formerly UK Voluntary Register for Public Health Specialists), 2003–; Pharmacy Health Link, 2004–07. Hon. Vice-Chm., Bd of Govs, Dollar Acad., 2003–. FCPS (Pak), 1996; Founder FMedSci 1998. Hon. FFPHMI 1997. *Publications:* (with A. Finlayson) Coronary Heart Disease and Patterns of Living, 1977; (jtly) Measuring Health Status, 1986; (ed jtly) Oxford Textbook of Public Health, 3rd edn 1997, 4th edn 2002; contrib. articles on public health, health services and quality of life. *Recreations:* Church, gardening, architectural heritage. *Address:* Auchanachie, Ruthven, Huntly AB54 4SS. *T:* (01466) 760742. *Club:* Royal Society of Medicine.

McEWEN, Sir John (Roderick Hugh), 5th Bt *cr* 1953; journalist; *b* 4 Nov. 1965; *s* of Sir Robert Lindley McEwen, 3rd Bt, of Marchmont and Bardrochat, and of Brigid Cecilia, *d* of late James Laver, CBE, and Veronica Turleigh; *S* brother, 1983; *m* 2000, Rachel, *er d* of Gerald Soane, Wallington, Surrey; two *d. Educ:* Ampleforth; University Coll. London; Glasgow Univ. (MPhil 1999). *Heir: cousin* Adam Hugo McEwen, *b* 9 Feb. 1965. *Address:* The Steadings, Polwarth, Berwickshire TD10 6YR.

MACEY, Rear-Adm. David Edward, CB 1984; *b* 15 June 1929; *s* of Frederick William Charles Macey and Florence May Macey; *m* 1st, 1958, Lorna Therese Verner (decd), *o d* of His Honour Judge Oliver William Verner; one *s* one *d*, and one step *s* two step *d*; 2nd, 1982, Fiona (marr. diss. 1994), *o d* of Vice-Adm. Sir William Beloe, KBE, CB, DSC; 3rd, 1996, Rosemary Bothway, *o d* of Percy Crotch. *Educ:* Sir Joseph Williamson's Mathematical Sch., Rochester; Royal Naval Coll., Dartmouth. Midshipman, 1948; Cruisers, Carriers, Destroyers, 1950–63; Comdr, 1963; Amer. Staff Coll., 1964; Comdr, RNC Dartmouth, 1970; Captain, 1972; Directorate Naval Plans, 1972–74; RCDS, 1975; Dir, RN Staff Coll., 1976–78; Dir, Naval Manpower, 1979–81; Rear-Adm., 1981; Dep. Asst Chief of Staff (Ops), SACEUR, 1981–84. ADC to HM the Queen, 1981. Order of the Bath: Gentleman Usher of the Scarlet Rod, 1985–90; Registrar and Sec., 1990–2001. Receiver-Gen., Canterbury Cathedral, 1984–98; Mem., Archbps' Commn on Cathedrals, 1992–94. Chm., Canterbury Choral Soc., 1992–2002. *Recreations:* walking, cricket, cooking. *Address:* Bell Tower House, Painter's Forstal, Faversham, Kent ME13 0EL. *Clubs:* Anglo-Belgian, MCC; Band of Brothers (Kent).
See also M. J. L. Kirk.

MACEY, Air Vice-Marshal Eric Harold, OBE 1975; Director General of Training (Royal Air Force), 1989–91, retired; *b* 9 April 1936; *s* of Harold Fred and Katrina Emma Mary Macey; *m* 1957, Brenda Ann Bracher; one *s* one *d. Educ:* Shaftesbury Grammar School; Southampton Tech. Coll. Asst Sci. Officer, Min. of Supply, 1953–54; RAF, 1954; commissioned, 1955; Pilot's Wings, 1956; RAF Staff Coll., 1966; RCDS 1983; AOC and Comdt, RAF Coll., Cranwell, 1985–87; ACDS (Policy and Nuclear), 1987–89. Pres., RAF Chilmark Assoc., 1994–; Vice-President: 214 Sqdn Assoc., 1990–; 101 Sqdn Assoc., 1999–; Bomber Comd Assoc., 1998–. *Recreations:* music, walking, DIY. *Address:* Ebblemead, Homington, Salisbury, Wilts SP5 4NL.

McFADDEN, Prof. Daniel L., PhD; E. Morris Cox Professor of Economics, since 1991, and Director, Econometrics Laboratory, 1991–95 and since 1996, University of California, Berkeley (Head, Department of Economics, 1995–96); *b* Raleigh, NC, 29 July 1937; *s* of Robert Sain McFadden and Alice Little McFadden; *m* 1962, Beverlee Tito Simboli; two *s* one *d. Educ:* Univ. of Minnesota (BS 1957; PhD 1962). Asst Prof. of Econs, Univ. of Pittsburgh, 1962–63; Asst Prof., 1963–66, Associate Prof., 1966–68, Prof. 1968–77, of Econs, Univ. of Calif, Berkeley; Prof. of Econs, 1977–84, James R. Killian Prof. of Econs, 1984–91, Dir, Statistics Center, 1986–88, MIT. (Jtly) Nobel Prize for Economics, 2000. *Publications:* (ed jtly) Essays on Economic Behavior Under Uncertainty, 1974; (jtly) Urban Travel Demand: a behavioural analysis, 1975; (ed jtly) Production Economics: a dual approach to theory and applications (2 vols), 1978; (ed jtly) Structural Analysis of Discrete Data with Econometric Applications, 1981; (jtly) Microeconomic Modeling and Policy Analysis: studies in residential energy demand, 1984; (ed jtly) Preferences, Uncertainty and Optimality: essays in honor of Leonid Hurwicz, 1990; (ed jtly) Handbook of Econometrics, vol. IV, 1994; contrib. learned jls. *Address:* Department of Economics, University of California, Berkeley, CA 94720–3880, USA.

McFADDEN, Jean Alexandra, CBE 1992; JP; DL; MA, LLB; Lecturer in Law, University of Strathclyde, since 1992; Vice Lord Lieutenant of City of Glasgow, 1980–92; *b* 26 Nov. 1941; *d* of John and Elma Hogg; *m* 1966, John McFadden (*d* 1991). *Educ:* Univ. of Glasgow (MA 1st Cl. Hons Classics); Univ. of Strathclyde (LLB 1st Cl. Hons). Principal Teacher of Classics, Strathclyde Schools, 1967–86; part-time Lectr in Law, Univ. of Glasgow, 1991–92. Entered Local Govt as Mem. of Glasgow Corp. for Cowcaddens Ward, 1971 then (following boundary changes) Mem., Glasgow DC for Scotstoun Ward, 1984–96; Mem., City of Glasgow Council, 1995– (Convener, 1995–96; Chair: Labour Gp, 1995–; Social Strategy Cttee, 1996–99); Chm., Manpower Cttee, 1974–77; Leader, Labour Gp, 1977–86, 1992–94; Leader, 1980–86, 1992–94, Treas., 1986–92, Glasgow DC. Convener, Scottish Local Govt Information Unit, 1984–2003; Pres., Convention of Scottish Local Auths, 1990–92; Member Board: SDA, 1989–91; Glasgow Develt Agency, 1992–2000. Convenor, Strathclyde Police Jt Bd, 2003–07. Chm., Scottish Charity Law Commn, 2000–01; Member: Health Appts Adv. Cttee, Scottish Exec. (formerly Scottish Office), 1995–2000; Ancient Monuments Bd for Scotland, 2000–03. Chm., Mayfest (Glasgow Internat. Arts Fest.), 1983–92. JP Glasgow, 1972; DL 1980. *Recreations:* cycling, theatre, walking, golf, West Highland terriers. *Address:* 16 Lansdowne Crescent, Glasgow G20 6NQ. *T:* (0141) 334 3522.

McFADDEN, Rt Hon. Patrick; PC 2008; MP (Lab) Wolverhampton South East, since 2005; Minister of State, Department for Business, Enterprise and Regulatory Reform, since 2007; *b* 26 March 1965; *s* of James and Annie McFadden. *Educ:* Holyrood Sec. Sch., Glasgow; Univ. of Edinburgh (MA Hons Pols 1988). Res. Asst to Rt Hon. Donald Dewar, MP, 1988–93; Advr to Rt Hon. John Smith, MP, 1993–94; Policy Advr to Rt Hon. Tony Blair, MP, 1994–2001; Political Sec. to the Prime Minister, 2002–05. Parly Sec. (Minister for Social Exclusion), Cabinet Office, 2006–07. *Recreations:* sport, reading. *Address:* House of Commons, SW1A 0AA. *T:* (020) 7219 4036, *Fax:* (020) 7219 5665.

McFADYEAN, Colin William; supply teacher, Gloucesterhire and South Gloucestershire, since 2003; Deputy Headteacher, Ilminster Avenue Primary School, Knowle West Bristol, 1999–2003; *b* 11 March 1943; *s* of Captain Angus John McFadyean, MC, 1st Bn London Scottish Regt (killed in action, 1944) and late Joan Mary McFadyean (*née* Irish); *m* 1970, Jeanette Carol Payne; one *s. Educ:* Plymouth Coll.; Bristol Grammar Sch.; Loughborough Coll. of Education; Keele Univ. (DLC hons, Adv. DipEd). Phys. Educn teacher, Birmingham, 1965–67; Phys. Educn Lectr, 1967–72, Sen. Lectr, 1972–74, Cheshire; Dep. Dir, Nat. Sports Centre, Lilleshall, 1974–78; Chief Coach, Jubilee Sports Centre, Hong Kong, 1979–82; Sports Master and House Master, Dulwich Coll., 1983–85; Dir Gen., NPFA, 1985–87; with Croydon Educn Authy, 1988–90; teacher, Avon, then Bristol Educn Authy, 1991–98; Dep. Headteacher, Oldbury Court Primary Sch., 1998–99. Dir Coaching, Bristol FC (Rugby Union), 1990–91; Coach, Moseley FC, 1991–93; Coach, 1992–99, Dir of Rugby, 1998–99, Cleve RFC. Internat. Rugby career includes: 11 England caps, 1966–68; 4 Tests British Lions *v* NZ, 1966; (captain) *v* Ireland, 1968; (captain) *v* Wales, 1968; scored 5 tries, 1 dropped goal (in 15 Tests); other sport: coach to Hong Kong disabled team to Olympics, Arnhem, 1980; Adviser, Hong Kong table tennis team to World Championships, Yugoslavia, 1981. Mem., Adv. Gp, RCM, 2004–07. Broadcaster with Hong Kong TV and commercial radio. *Recreations:* golf, music, theatre, gardening; supporter of Plymouth Argyle FC, 1952–. *Clubs:* British Sportsman's; England Rugby International's; Rugby Internationals Golf, Stinchcombe Hill Golf; Moseley Football (Vice-Pres.); Cleve Rugby Football (Vice-Pres.).

MacFADYEN, Alasdair Lorne; Sheriff of Grampian, Highland and Islands at Dingwall and Inverness, since 2002 and Portree, since 2005 (at Lochmaddy, 2002–05); *b* 18 Sept. 1955; *s* of Iain Archibald MacFadyen and Anna MacFadyen; *m* 1978, Lynne Ballantyne; two *d*. *Educ:* High Sch., Glasgow; Glasgow Univ. (LLB). Solicitor in private practice, 1978–2001. Temp. Sheriff, 1995–2000; pt-time Sheriff, 2000–01; all Scotland Floating Sheriff, 2001–02. Pt-time Chm., Employment Tribunals, 2000–01. *Recreation:* sailing in tall ships. *Address:* Sheriff Court, Ferry Road, Dingwall, Ross-shire IV15 9QX. *T:* (01349) 863153.

MACFADYEN, Air Marshal Ian David, CB 1991; OBE 1984; FRAeS; Lieutenant Governor, Isle of Man, 2000–05; National President, Royal British Legion, since 2006; *b* 19 Feb. 1942; *s* of Air Marshal Sir Douglas Macfadyen, KCB, CBE and of Lady Macfadyen (*née* Dafforn, now Mrs P. A. Rowan); *m* 1967, Sally Harvey; one *s* one *d*. *Educ:* Marlborough; RAF Coll., Cranwell. Joined RAF, 1960; Cranwell cadet, 1960–63 (Sword of Honour); 19 Sqdn, 1965–68; HQ, RAF Strike Command, 1969; Flying Instructor, RAF Coll., Cranwell, 1970–73; RAF Staff Coll., 1973; 111 Sqdn, 1974–75; Flt Comdr, 43 Sqdn, 1975–76; HQ 2 ATAF, RAF Germany, 1976–79; comd 29 Sqdn, 1980–84; comd 23 Sqdn, 1984; MoD, 1984–85; comd RAF Leuchars, Fife, 1985–87; RCDS, 1988; MoD, 1989–90; COS, then Comdr, HQ British Forces ME, Riyadh, 1990–91; ACDS, Op. Requirements (Air Systems), 1991–94; Dir Gen., Saudi Arabia Armed Forces Project, 1994–98; retd, 1999. Trustee, RAF Mus., 1998–2003 (Chm. Trustees, 1999–2001). Chm., Geoffrey de Havilland Flying Foundn, 2002–; Trustee, Bentley Priory Battle of Britain Trust, 2006–; Pres., Popular Flying Assoc., 2004–06. Chairman: IOM Bd, Prince's Trust, 2001–05; IOM Golden Jubilee Trust, 2002–05. Hon. Air Cdre, 606 (Chiltern) Sqdn, RAuxAF, 2007–. Liveryman, GAPAN, 1999–. QCVSA 1974. OStJ 2001. *Recreations:* aviation history, gliding, golf, photography, shooting, watercolour painting. *Address:* Collyns Mead, Hawkesbury Upton, Badminton, Glos GL9 1BB. *Clubs:* Royal Air Force; Royal & Ancient (St Andrews).

McFALL, Rt Hon. John; PC 2004; MP (Lab and Co-op) West Dunbartonshire, since 2005 (Dumbarton, 1987–2005). An Opposition Whip, 1989–91; Opposition front bench spokesman: for education and home affairs, 1992; on Scottish Affairs, 1992–97; a Lord Comr of HM Treasury (Govt Whip), 1997–98; Parly Under-Sec. of State, NI Office, 1998–99. Member, Select Committee: on Defence, 1988; on Sittings of the House, 1991; on Information, 1990–97; Chm., HM Treasury Select Cttee, 2001–; Mem. Exec. Cttee, Parly Gp for Energy Studies, 1988–97; Secretary: Retail Industry Gp, 1992–97; Hon. Sec., Parly and Scientific Cttee, 1989–92. Visiting Professor: Strathclyde Business Sch., Univ. of Strathclyde, 1991–; Glasgow Univ. Business Sch., 2004–. *Recreations:* running, golf, reading. *Address:* House of Commons, SW1A 0AA.

McFALL, Richard Graham; Chairman, 1980–86, Director, 1976–86, Fleming Enterprise Investment Trust plc (formerly Crossfriars Trust plc); *b* 31 Jan. 1920; 3rd *s* of Henry Joseph Marshall and Sarah Gertrude McFall; *m* 1945, Clara Louise Debonnaire Mitford; one *s* one *d*. *Educ:* Holmwood Prep. Sch., Lancs; Clifton Coll., Bristol. Joined Pacol Ltd, 1938; Mil. Service, HAC, 1939–40; Colonial Office, 1941–45 (Asst Sec., then Sec., W African Produce Control Bd); Motor & Air Products Ltd, 1946–48; re-joined Pacol Ltd, 1949, Dir 1951; Chm., London Cocoa Terminal Market Assoc., 1954–55; Chm., Cocoa Assoc. of London, 1958–59; Dir 1962–82, Man. Dir 1965–74, Chm., 1970–76, Vice-Chm., 1976–78, Gill & Duffus Group PLC. *Recreation:* golf. *Address:* 7 Yew Tree Walk, Effingham, Surrey KT24 5LJ. *T:* (01372) 452727. *Clubs:* Farmers'; Effingham Golf.

McFARLAND, Alan, *see* McFarland, R. A.

McFARLAND, Prof. David John, DPhil; Professor of Biological Robotics, University of the West of England, 2000–02; Fellow, Balliol College, Oxford, 1966–2000, now Emeritus; *b* 31 Dec. 1938; *s* of John Cyril and Joan Elizabeth McFarland; *m* 1962, Frances Jill Tomlin; one *s* one *d*. *Educ:* Leighton Park Sch., Reading; Liverpool Univ. (BSc 1st Cl. Hons Zoology, 1961); Oxford Univ. (DPhil Psychology, 1965). Lectr in Psychology, Durham Univ., 1964; Oxford University: Lectr in Psychology, 1966–74; Reader in Animal Behaviour, 1974–2000; Tutor in Psychology, Balliol Coll., 1966–2000. Hofmeyer Fellow, Univ. of the Witwatersrand, 1974; Visiting Professor: Dalhousie Univ., 1968; Rutgers Univ., 1971; Univ. of Penn, 1977; SUNY, Stonybrook, 1978; Univ. of Oregon, 1978; Univ. of Münster, Germany, 1989. Pres., Internat. Ethological Conf., 1981. Editor, Animal Behaviour, 1969–74. *Publications:* (with J. McFarland) An Introduction to the Study of Behaviour, 1969; Feedback Mechanisms in Animal Behaviour, 1971; (ed) Motivational Control Systems Analysis, 1974; (ed) The Oxford Companion to Animal Behaviour, 1981; (with A. Houston) Quantitative Ethology: the state space approach, 1981; (ed) Functional Ontogeny, 1982; Animal Behaviour, 1985, 3rd edn 1999; Problems of Animal Behaviour, 1989; Biologie des Verhaltens, (Germany) 1989, 2nd edn 1999; (with T. Bosser) Intelligent Behavior in Animals and Robots, (USA) 1993; Le Comportement Animal, (France) 2001; (with O. Holland) Artificial Ethology, 2001; The Oxford Dictionary of Animal Behaviour, 2006; Guilty Robots, Happy Dogs: the question of alien minds, 2008; articles in scientific learned jls. *Recreations:* keeping animals, pottery. *Address:* 55 Latchford Lane, Great Haseley, Oxon OX44 7LD; Camino Cantarilla 2, Tajaste, Tinajo, Lanzarote 35560, Spain.

McFARLAND, Sir John (Talbot), 3rd Bt *cr* 1914, of Aberfoyle, Londonderry; TD 1967; Chairman: Malvay Ltd (formerly Lanes (Business Equipment)), 1977–2001; J. T. McFarland Holdings, 1984–2001; Information and Imaging Systems Ltd, 1994–2001; *b* 3 Oct. 1927; *s* of Sir Basil Alexander Talbot McFarland, 2nd Bt, CBE, ERD, and Anne Kathleen (*d* 1952), *d* of late Andrew Henderson; *S* father, 1986; *m* 1957, Mary Scott, *d* of late Dr W. Scott Watson, Londonderry; two *s* two *d*. *Educ:* Marlborough College; Trinity Coll., Oxford. Captain RA (TA), retired 1967. Chm., R. C. Malseed & Co Ltd, 1957–90; Chairman, 1977–84: Lanes (Derry) Ltd; Lanes (Fuel) Oils Ltd; Lanes Patent Fuels Ltd; Holmes Coal Ltd; Alexander Thompson & Co. Ltd; Nicholl Ballintyne Ltd; J. W. Corbett Ltd; Wattersons Ltd. Chm., Londonderry Lough Swilly Railway Co., 1978–81; Director: Londonderry Gaslight Co., 1958–89; Donegal Holdings Ltd, 1963–85; G. Kinnaird & Son Ltd, 1981–95; Windy Hills Ltd, 1994–95; Wallcoatings Dublin Ltd, 1995–98; Taughboyne Develt Assoc., 1998–2007. Member: Londonderry County Borough Council, 1955–69; NW HMC, 1960–73; Londonderry Port and Harbour Commrs, 1965–73. Jt Chm., Londonderry and Foyle Coll., 1971–76. High Sheriff, Co. Londonderry 1958, City of County of Londonderry 1965–67; DL Londonderry 1962, resigned 1982. *Recreations:* golf, shooting. *Heir: er s* Anthony Basil Scott McFarland [*b* 29 Nov. 1959; *m* 1988, Anne Margaret, BA, ACA, *d* of T. K. Laidlaw, Gernonstown, Slane, Co. Meath. *Educ:* Marlborough Coll.; Trinity College, Dublin (BA). ACA]. *Address:* Dunmore House, Carrigans, Lifford, Co. Donegal, Ireland. *T:* (74) 40120, *Fax:* (74) 40336. *Club:* Kildare Street and University (Dublin).

McFARLAND, (Robert) Alan; Member (UU) North Down, Northern Ireland Assembly, since 1998; *b* 9 Aug. 1949; *s* of Dr Albert John Black McFarland and Mary Elizabeth Florence McFarland (*née* Campbell); *m* 1979, Celia Mary Sharp; one *s* two *d*. *Educ:* Rockport Sch., Craigavad, Co. Down; Campbell Coll., Belfast; RMA, Sandhurst. Commnd RTR, 1975; various regtl appts, 1975–81 (despatches, 1981); SO, Orgn and Deployment, HQ 4th Armd Div., 1981–83; Sqn Ldr, Challenger Tank Sqn and HQ Sqn 2nd RTR, 1983–86; SO, Public Relns, HQ SW Dist and UK Mobile Force, 1987–89; Mgt Consultant, MoD, 1989–92; retd in rank of Major, 1992. Parly Asst to Rev. Martin Smyth, MP and Rt Hon. James Molyneaux, MP, H of C, 1992–95; Dir, Somme Heritage Centre, Newtownards, 1996–98. Mem., NI Policing Bd, 2002–06. *Recreations:* military history, folk music. *Address:* c/o Parliament Buildings, Stormont, Belfast BT4 3XX.

MACFARLANE, family name of **Baron Macfarlane of Bearsden.**

MACFARLANE OF BEARSDEN, Baron *cr* 1991 (Life Peer), of Bearsden in the district of Bearsden and Milngavie; **Norman Somerville Macfarlane,** KT 1996; Kt 1983; DL; FRSE; Hon. Life President: Macfarlane Group PLC, 1999 (Chairman, 1973–98, Managing Director, 1973–90); United Distillers PLC (Chairman, 1987–96); Lord High Commissioner, General Assembly, Church of Scotland, 1992, 1993 and 1997; *b* 5 March 1926; *s* of Daniel Robertson Macfarlane and Jessie Lindsay Somerville; *m* 1953, Marguerite Mary Campbell; one *s* four *d*. *Educ:* High Sch. of Glasgow. Commnd RA, 1945; served Palestine, 1945–47. Founded N. S. Macfarlane & Co. Ltd, 1949; became Macfarlane Group (Clansman) PLC, 1973. Underwriting Mem. of Lloyd's, 1978–97; Chairman: The Fine Art Society PLC, 1976–98 (Hon. Life Pres., 1998); American Trust PLC, 1984–97; Guinness PLC, 1987–89 (Jt Dep. Chm., 1989–92); Director: Clydesdale Bank PLC, 1980–96 (Dep. Chm., 1993–96); General Accident Fire & Life Assce Corp. plc, 1984–96; Edinburgh Fund Managers plc, 1980–98. Dir, Glasgow Chamber of Commerce, 1976–79; Member: Council, CBI Scotland, 1975–81; Bd, Scottish Develt Agency, 1979–87. Chm., Glasgow Develt Agency (formerly Glasgow Action), 1985–92. Scottish Ballet: Dir, 1975–87; Vice Chm., 1983–87; Hon. Pres., 2001–; Dir, Scottish National Orch., 1977–82; Pres., Royal Glasgow Inst. of the Fine Arts, 1976–87; Mem., Royal Fine Art Commn for Scotland, 1980–82; Scottish Patron, National Art Collection Fund, 1978–; Governor, Glasgow Sch. of Art, 1976–87 (Hon. Fellow, 1993; Hon. Pres., 2001); Trustee: Nat. Heritage Meml Fund, 1984–97; Nat. Galls of Scotland, 1986–97; Dir, Culture & Sport Glasgow, 2007–. Dir, Third Eye Centre, 1978–81. Hon. Pres., Tenovus Scotland, 2006–. Hon. Pres., Charles Rennie Mackintosh Soc., 1988–. Hon. Pres., High Sch. of Glasgow, 1992– (Chm. Govs, 1979–92); Mem. Court, Univ. of Glasgow, 1979–87; Regent, RCSE, 1997–. President: Stationers' Assoc. of GB and Ireland, 1965; Co. of Stationers of Glasgow, 1968–70; Glasgow High Sch. Club, 1970–72. Patron, Scottish Licensed Trade Assoc., 1992–; Hon. Patron, Queen's Park FC. Vice Pres., PGA. Hon. Life Mem., Scottish Football League, 2006. DL Dunbartonshire, 1993. Freeman: Dumfries and Galloway, 2006; City of Glasgow, 2007. FRSE 1991; CCMI (CIMgt 1996). HRSA 1987; HRGI 1987; Hon. FRIAS 1984; Hon. FScotvec 1991; Hon. FRCPSGlas 1992. Hon. LLD: Strathclyde, 1986; Glasgow, 1988; Glasgow Caledonian, 1993; Aberdeen, 1995; DUniv Stirling, 1992; Dr (*hc*) Edinburgh, 1992. St Mungo Prize, City of Glasgow, 2005; Goodman Award, Art & Business, 2007. *Recreations:* golf, cricket, theatre, art. *Address:* Macfarlane Group PLC, Clansman House, 21 Newton Place, Glasgow G3 7PY; 50 Manse Road, Bearsden, Glasgow G61 3PN. *Clubs:* Glasgow Art (Glasgow); New (Edinburgh); Hon. Co. of Edinburgh Golfers, Glasgow Golf.

McFARLANE OF LLANDAFF, Baroness *cr* 1979 (Life Peer), of Llandaff in the County of South Glamorgan; **Jean Kennedy McFarlane;** Professor and Head of Department of Nursing, University of Manchester, 1974–88, now Professor Emeritus; *b* 1 April 1926; *d* of late James and Elvina Alice McFarlane. *Educ:* Howell's Sch., Llandaff; Bedford Coll., London (BScSoc); Birkbeck Coll., London (MA; Fellow, 1997). SRN, SCM, HV Tutor's Cert.; FRCN 1976; FCNA 1984. Staff Nurse, St Bartholomew's Hosp., 1950–51; Health Visitor, Cardiff CC, 1953–59; Royal Coll. of Nursing: Organising Tutor, Integrated Course, Educn Div., London, 1960–62; Educn Officer, Birmingham, 1962–66; Res. Project Ldr (DHSS sponsored), London, 1967–69; Dir of Educn, Inst. of Advanced Nursing Educn, London, 1969–71; Univ. of Manchester: Sen. Lectr in Nursing, Dept of Social and Preventive Medicine, 1971–73; Sen. Lectr and Head of Dept of Nursing, 1973–74. Member: Royal Commn on NHS, 1976–79; Commonwealth War Graves Commn, 1983–88. Chm., English Bd for Nursing, Midwifery and Health Visiting, 1980–83. Mem., Gen. Synod of C of E, 1990–95. Hon. FRCP 1990. Hon. MSc Manchester, 1979; Hon. DSc: Ulster, 1981; City, 2005; Hon. DEd CNAA, 1983; Hon. MD Liverpool, 1990; Hon. DLit Glamorgan, 1995; Hon. LLD Manchester, 1998. *Publications:* The Problems of Developing Criteria of Quality for Nursing Care (thesis), 1969; The Proper Study of the Nurse, 1970; (with G. Castledine) The Practice of Nursing using the Nursing Process, 1982. *Recreations:* music, walking, travelling, photography. *Address:* 5 Dovercourt Avenue, Heaton Mersey, Stockport SK4 3QB. *T:* (0161) 432 8367.

MACFARLANE, Prof. Alan Donald James, FRAI; FRHistS; FBA 1986; Professor of Anthropological Science, University of Cambridge, since 1991; *b* 20 Dec. 1941; *s* of Donald Kennedy Macfarlane and Iris Stirling Macfarlane; *m* 1st, 1966, Gillian Ions; one *d*; 2nd, 1981, Sarah Harrison. *Educ:* Sedbergh School; Worcester College, Oxford (MA, DPhil); LSE (MPhil); SOAS (PhD). University of Cambridge: Senior Research Fellow in History, King's College, 1971–74; Univ. Lectr in Social Anthropology, 1975–81; Reader in Historical Anthropology, 1981–91. Lectures: Frazer Meml, Liverpool Univ., 1974; Malinowski Meml, LSE, 1978; Radcliffe-Brown Meml, Univ. of Lancaster, 1992; Marett Meml, Univ. of Oxford, 1995; F. W. Maitland Meml, Univ. of Cambridge, 2000; Maruyama, Univ. of Calif, Berkeley, 2006; Sir Li Ka Sheng Dist., China, 2006. Rivers Meml Medal, RAI, 1984; William J. Goode Award, Amer. Sociol Assoc., 1987. Principal consultant and presenter, The Day the World Took Off (millennium series), C4, 2000. *Publications:* Witchcraft in Tudor and Stuart England, 1970; The Family Life of Ralph Josselin, 1970; Resources and Population, 1976; (ed) The Diary of Ralph Josselin, 1976; Reconstructing Historical Communities, 1977; Origins of English Individualism, 1978; The Justice and the Mare's Ale, 1981; A Guide to English Historical Records, 1983; Marriage and Love in England, 1986; The Culture of Capitalism, 1987; The Cambridge Database System User Manual, 1990; (jtly) The Nagas: hill peoples of North-east India, 1990; (ed and trans. with S. Harrison) Bernard Pignède, The Gurungs of Nepal, 1993; The Savage Wars of Peace, 1997; The Riddle of the Modern World, 2000; The Making of the Modern World, 2001; (with Gerry Martin) The Glass Bathyscaphe, 2002; (with Iris Macfarlane) Green Gold: the empire of tea, 2003; Letters to Lily: on how our world works, 2005; Japan Through the Looking Glass, 2007. *Recreations:* walking, gardening, second-hand book hunting. *Address:* 25 Lode Road, Lode, near Cambridge CB25 9ER. *T:* (01223) 811976.

MacFARLANE, Sir Alistair (George James), Kt 2002; CBE 1987; FRS 1984; FREng; FRSE; Principal and Vice-Chancellor of Heriot-Watt University, 1989–96; *b* 9 May 1931; *s* of George R. MacFarlane; *m* 1954, Nora Williams (*d* 2005); one *s*; *m* 2008, Anwen Tudor Davies. *Educ:* Hamilton Academy; Univ. of Glasgow. BSc 1953, DSc 1969, Glasgow; PhD London 1964; MSc Manchester 1973; MA 1974, ScD 1979, Cantab. FIET;

FREng (FEng 1981); FRSE 1990. Metropolitan-Vickers, Manchester, 1953–58; Lectr, Queen Mary Coll., Univ. of London, 1959–65, Reader 1965–66; Reader in Control Engrg, Univ. of Manchester Inst. of Sci. and Technology, 1966–69, Prof. 1969–74; Prof. of Engrg and Hd of Information Engrg Div., Univ. of Cambridge, 1974–88; Fellow, 1974–88, Vice-Master, 1980–88, Hon. Fellow, 1989–, Selwyn Coll., Cambridge. Chm., Cambridge Control Ltd, 1985–90; Non-Executive Director: Lothian and Edinburgh Enterprise Ltd, 1990–96; British Nuclear Fuels plc, 1995–2000. Member: Council, SERC, 1981–85; Computer Board, 1983–88; Adv. Cttee for Safety of Nuclear Installations, 1987–90; Engrg Tech. Adv. Cttee, DTI, 1991–93; BT Adv. Forum, 1997–98. Chm., Res. Councils' High Performance Computing Strategy Gp, 1995–98. Comr, Nat. Commn on Educn, 1991–93; Academic Advr, 1997–2000, CEO and Dir, 2000–01, Univ. of Highlands and Islands project; Rector, UHI Millennium Inst., 2002–04. Chairman: Scottish Univs Wkg Party on Teaching and Learning in an Expanding Higher Educn System, 1991–92 (MacFarlane Report, 1992); Scottish Council for Res. in Educn, 1992–98; Scottish Library and Information Council, 1994–98. Royal Society: Vice-Pres., 1997–99; Mem. Council, 1997–99; Chm., Educn Cttee, 2000–04. Trustee, Scottish Internat. Educn Trust, 1994–. Hon. DEng: UMIST, 1995; Glasgow, 1995; DUniv: Heriot-Watt, 1997; Paisley, 1997; Hon. DSc Abertay Dundee, 1998; Hon. DLitt Lincolnshire and Humberside, 1999. Medals: Centennial, ASME, 1980; Sir Harold Hartley, Inst. of Measurement and Control, 1982; Achievement, IEE, 1992; Faraday, IEE, 1993; Oldenburger, ASME, 2004. *Publications:* Engineering Systems Analysis, 1964; Dynamical System Models, 1970; (with I. Postlethwaite) A Complex Variable Approach to the Analysis of Linear Multivariable Feedback Systems, 1979; (ed) Frequency-Response Methods in Control Systems, 1979; (ed) Complex Variable Methods for Linear Multivariable Feedback Systems, 1980; (with S. Hung) Multivariable Feedback: a quasi-classical approach, 1982; (with G. K. H. Pang) An Expert Systems Approach to Computer-Aided Design of Multivariable Systems, 1987. *Address:* Tregarth, 2 Marine Parade, Barmouth, Gwynedd LL42 1NA; *e-mail:* alistair.macfarlane@btinternet.com.

MACFARLANE, Rev. Alwyn James Cecil; Parish Minister of Newlands (South), Church of Scotland, 1968–85; Extra Chaplain to the Queen in Scotland, since 1992 (Chaplain, 1977–92); *b* 14 June 1922; *s* of James Waddell Macfarlane and Ada Cecilia Rankin; *m* 1953, Joan Cowell Harris; one *s* one *d*. *Educ:* Cargilfield Sch.; Rugby Sch.; Oxford Univ. (MA); Edinburgh Univ. Served War: N Africa, Italy, Greece; Liaison Officer in Black Watch with 12th Bde, 1942–46. Ordained, 1951; served in parishes in Ross-shire, Edinburgh, Glasgow, Australia. *Recreations:* photography, walking. *Address:* Flat 12, Homeburn House, 177 Fenwick Road, Giffnock, Glasgow G46 6JD.

McFARLANE, Hon. Sir Andrew Ewart, Kt 2005; **Hon. Mr Justice McFarlane;** a Judge of the High Court of Justice, Family Division, since 2005; *b* 20 June 1954; *s* of Gordon McFarlane and Olive McFarlane (*née* Davies); *m* 1981, Susanna Jane Randolph; four *d*. *Educ:* Shrewsbury Sch.; Durham Univ. (BA Hons Law 1975); Univ. of Wales (LLM Canon Law 1998). Called to the Bar, Gray's Inn, 1977, Bencher, 2003; QC 1998; an Asst Recorder, 1995–99; a Recorder, 1999–2005; a Dep. High Court Judge, 2000–05; Family Div. Liaison Judge, Midland Circuit, 2006–. Chm., Family Law Bar Assoc., 2001–03. Trustee, Young Minds, 2001–08. Dep. Chancellor, Dio. of Wakefield, 2004–06; Chancellor, Dio. of Exeter, 2006–. *Publications:* (with David Hershman) Children: law and practice, 1991; (contrib.) Family Court Practice, 1993–; (with Madeleine Reardon) Child Care and Adoption Law, 2006. *Recreations:* family life, popular culture, theatre. *Address:* c/o Royal Courts of Justice, Strand, WC2A 2LL. *Club:* Garrick.

MACFARLANE, Anne Bridget; Master of the Court of Protection, 1982–95; *b* 26 Jan. 1930; *d* of late Dr David Griffith and Dr Grace Griffith; *m* 1957, James Douglas Macfarlane (*d* 1999); two *d*. *Educ:* nine schools; Bristol Univ. (LLB). Admitted Solicitor, 1954. HM Land Registry, 1966–75; Registrar, Bromley County Court, 1975–82. *Publications:* (contrib.) Atkin's Court Forms, 2nd edn 1983; Older Adults' Decision-Making and the Law, 1996. *Recreation:* collecting Victorian tiles. *Club:* Law Society (Hon. Life Mem., 1996).

MACFARLANE, Sir (David) Neil, Kt 1988; Chairman, Associated Nursing Services, 1994–2004; *b* 7 May 1936; *yr s* of late Robert and of Dulcie Macfarlane; *m* 1961, June Osmond King, Somerset; two *s* one *d*. *Educ:* St Aubyn's Prep. Sch.; Bancroft's, Woodford Green. Short Service Commission, Essex Regt, 1955–58; served TA, 265 LAA, RA, 1961–66. Joined Shell Mex and BP, 1959; contested (C): East Ham (North), 1970; Sutton and Cheam, by-election, 1972. Parly Under-Sec. of State (Dep. Minister for the Arts), DES, 1979–81; Parly Under-Sec. of State, DoE, 1981–85 (with spec. responsibility for Sport, 1981–85, for Children's Play, 1983–85). Mem., All Party Select Cttee on Science and Technology, 1974–79; MP (C) Sutton and Cheam, Feb. 1974–1992. Chairman: Rushman Lloyd PLC, 1994–97; Securicor plc, 1995–2003 (Dir, 1992–2003); Director: RMC, 1987–2001; Bradford and Bingley Bldg Soc., 1987–2000. Chairman: Sports Aid Foundn, 1986–87; Golf Fund PLC; Vice-Pres. PGA, 1985–. Trustee, England and Wales Cricket Foundn, 1997–. Mem., National Trust, 1976–. Freeman, City of London, 2000; Master, Guild of Security Professionals, 1999–2002. *Publication:* Sport and Politics: a world divided, 1986. *Recreations:* golf, cricket-watching. *Clubs:* MCC, Lord's Taverners; Essex County Cricket; Royal & Ancient Golf, Huntercombe Golf.

McFARLANE, Prof. Duncan Campbell, PhD; Professor of Service and Support Engineering, University of Cambridge, since 2006; Fellow, St John's College, Cambridge, since 1996; *b* 3 May 1963; *m* 1993, Meredith Lillian Bhathal; one *s* one *d*. *Educ:* Trinity Coll., Univ. of Melbourne (BEng Hons 1984); Queens' Coll., Cambridge (PhD 1988). BHP Co. Ltd: Cadet, 1980; Res. Officer, 1985–92; Co-ordinator, 1992–94; Lectr, 1995–2000, Sen. Lectr, 2000–03, Reader, 2003–06, in Automation Systems, Univ. of Cambridge. Dir, Distributed Automation and Inf. Lab., 2000–; Res. Dir, Auto ID Centre, 2000–03; Dir, Cambridge Auto ID Lab., 2003–07. *Publications:* (with K. Glover) Robust Controller Design Using Normalised Coprime Factor Plant Descriptions, 1990; (ed jtly) Holonic and Multi-Agent Systems for Manufacturing, 2003; (with N. Chokshi) A Distributed Coordination Approach to Reconfigurable Process Control, 2008; over 100 jl and conf. papers. *Recreations:* walking, swimming, cricket, green Penguins (collecting), bottle-top collecting. *Address:* St John's College, Cambridge CB2 1TP. *Club:* Melbourne Cricket.

McFARLANE, Sir Ian, Kt 1984; Chairman and Managing Director, Trans Pacific Petroleum NL, since 1964; *b* 25 Dec. 1923; *s* of Stuart Gordon McFarlane, CMG, MBE and Mary Grace McFarlane; *m* 1956, Ann, *d* of M. A. Shaw, Salt Lake City, USA; one *s* two *d*. *Educ:* Melbourne Grammar School; Harrow; Sydney Univ. (BSc, BE); MIT (MS). Served War of 1939–45, RANVR. Morgan Stanley & Co., 1949–59; Mem., Sydney Stock Exchange, 1959–64; Partner, Ord, Minnett, T. J. Thompson & Partners, 1959–64; Dep. Chm., Magellan Petroleum, 1964–70; Chairman and Managing Director: Southern Pacific Petroleum NL, 1968–2001; Central Pacific Minerals NL, 1968–2001; Director: Trans City Discount Ltd, 1960–64; Consolidated Rutile Ltd, 1964–68; International Pacific Corp., 1967–73; Aust. Gen. Insurance Co., 1968–74; Mercantile Mutual Insurance Co., 1969–74; Concrete Construction, 1972–74; International Pacific Aust. Investments, 1972–73; Morgan Stanley Internat., NYC, 1976–80. Mem. Council, Imperial Soc. of Knights Bachelor, 1985–. Founder, Sir Ian McFarlane Travelling Professorship in Urology, 1980. Chm., Royal Brisbane Hosp. Res. (formerly Hosp.) Foundn, 1985–93; Mem., Appeal Bd, Pain and Mgt Res. Centre, Royal North Shore Hosp., 1994–2003; Mem., 1997–2000, Vice Patron, 2001–, Nat. Trust St John's Cathedral Completion Fund, Brisbane. Co-Founder and Dep. Chm., Great Barrier Reef Res. Foundn, Brisbane, 2000–04. Life Governor, Royal Prince Alfred Hosp., Sydney, 1982; Founding Governor, St Luke's Hosp. Foundn, Sydney, 1982–. Fellow Commoner, Christ's Coll., Cambridge, 1987. Founder: Sir Ian McFarlane Scholarship for Excellence, Christ's Coll., Cambridge, 1989; Sir Ian McFarlane's Nurses' award, Royal Brisbane Hosp., 1994. Fellow, Aust. Inst. of Mining and Metallurgy, 1993. Hon. Col Kentucky, 1984–. KCGSJ 1999. *Address:* 40 Wentworth Road, Vaucluse, NSW 2030, Australia. *Clubs:* Australian (Sydney); Commonwealth (Canberra); University (NY); Royal Sydney Golf; Rose Bay Surf (Sydney).

MACFARLANE, Ian John, AC 2004; Governor, Reserve Bank of Australia, 1996–2006; *b* 22 June 1946; *s* of Gordon H. and Lilias E. M. Macfarlane; *m* 1970, Heather (*née* Payne); one *s* one *d*. *Educ:* Monash Univ. Inst. of Econs and Stats, Oxford Univ., 1971–72; OECD, Paris, 1973–78; Reserve Bank of Australia, 1979–2006: various posts, 1979–88; Head, Res. Dept, 1988–90; Asst Gov. (Economic), 1990–92; Dep. Gov., 1992–96.

McFARLANE, James Sinclair, CBE 1986; CEng, FIMMM; Director General, Engineering Employers' Federation, 1982–89; *b* 8 Nov. 1925; *s* of John Mills McFarlane and Hannah McFarlane; *m* 1951, Ruth May Harden; three *d*. *Educ:* Manchester Grammar Sch.; Emmanuel Coll., Cambridge (MA, PhD). CEng 1961; FIMMM (FIM 1961). ICI Ltd, 1949–53; Henry Wiggin & Co. Ltd, 1953–69; Chm. and Man. Dir, Smith-Clayton Forge Ltd (GKN Ltd), 1969–76; Man. Dir, Garringtons Ltd (GKN Ltd), 1976–77; Guest Keen & Nettlefolds Ltd: Gen. Man., Personnel, 1977–79; Exec. Dir, 1979–82. Mem., NEDC, 1982–89; a Civil Service Comr (pt-time), 1983–88. CCMI. *Publications:* contrib. scientific and technical jls. *Recreation:* music. *Address:* 24 Broad Street, Ludlow, Shropshire SY8 1NJ. *T:* (01584) 872495. *Club:* Caledonian.

McFARLANE, Rev. Janet Elizabeth; Director of Communications, Diocese of Norwich, since 2000; Archdeacon of Norwich, from March 2009 (designation subseq. Ven.); *b* Stoke-on-Trent, 25 Nov. 1964; *d* of David James McFarlane and Anne McFarlane; *m* 2004, Andrew Ridoutt. *Educ:* Univ. of Sheffield (BMedSci 1987); St John's Coll., Univ. of Durham (BA 1992); Cranmer Hall, Univ. of Durham (DipMin 1993). Speech Therapist, N Staffs HA, 1987–90; ordained deacon, 1993, priest, 1994; Curate, Stafford Team Ministry, 1993–96; Chaplain: Ely Cathedral, 1996–99; to Bishop of Norwich, 2000–March 2009. *Address:* (until March 2009) c/o Bishop's House, Norwich NR3 1SB; (from March 2009) 31 Bracondale, Norwich NR1 2AT.

MACFARLANE, Prof. John Thomson, DM; FRCP; Professor of Respiratory Medicine, University of Nottingham, since 2004; Consultant General and Respiratory Physician, Nottingham University Hospitals, since 1982; *b* 21 Nov. 1948; *s* of Sir George Gray Macfarlane, CB and of Barbara Grant Macfarlane; *m* 1971, Rosamund MacInnes, medical researcher and photographer; two *s*. *Educ:* Merton Coll., Oxford (BA Hons 1970); Oxford University Med. Sch. (BM BCh 1973; MA 1983; DM 1983). MRCP 1976, FRCP 1989; MRCGP 1999. Med. trng posts in Oxford, Brompton Hosp., London, and Ahmadu Bello Univ. Hosp., Zaria, Nigeria, 1974–82. Chm., British Thoracic Soc., 2006–08; Trustee and Mem. Council, RCP, 2006–08. UK Representative: on Council, Europ. Respiratory Soc., 2003–06; to Fedn of Europ. Respiratory Socs, 2006–08. *Publications:* (jtly) Legionella Infections, 1986; (jtly) Colour Atlas of Respiratory Infections, 1993; many articles, revs, guidelines and chapters in major jls and internat. textbooks, incl. Oxford Textbook of Medicine, mainly on pneumonia, legionnaires' disease and lung infections. *Recreations:* mountaineering, travel, photography, cooking, medical and military history. *Address:* Middlebeck Farm, Gray Lane, Halam, Notts NG22 8AL. *T:* (01636) 812583; *e-mail:* jtmacfarlane@googlemail.com.

MACFARLANE, Sir Neil; *see* Macfarlane, Sir D. N.

MacFARLANE, Neil; *see* MacFarlane, S. N.

MacFARLANE, Maj.-Gen. Robert Goudie, MBE 1952; FRCP, FRCPE; Deputy Secretary, Scottish Council for Postgraduate Medical Education, 1975–84; *b* 1 March 1917; *s* of late Archibald Forsyth MacFarlane and Jessie Robertson Goudie; *m* 1945, Mary Campbell Martin; three *s*. *Educ:* Hillhead High Sch., Glasgow; Glasgow Univ. MB, ChB, 1940; MD 1955; FRCPE 1964; MRCP 1970; FRCP 1979. Served War: commissioned RAMC, 1941; in Madagascar, India, Burma, 1941–45. Specialist in Medicine and Consultant Physician, 1948–; CO, British Mil. Hosp., Iserlohn, 1968–70; Prof. of Mil. Med., Royal Army Medical Coll., 1970–71; Consulting Physician, BAOR, 1971–73. Dir. of Army Medicine and Consulting Physician to the Army, 1973–74. QHP 1973. *Address:* 6 Redholm, Greenheads Road, North Berwick, East Lothian EH39 4RA.

MacFARLANE, Prof. (Stephen) Neil, DPhil; Lester B. Pearson Professor of International Relations, since 1996, and Head, Department of Politics and International Relations, since 2005, University of Oxford; Fellow, St Anne's College, Oxford, since 1996; *b* 7 March 1954; *s* of David Livingstone MacFarlane and Gertrude Cecile (*née* Straight); *m* 1981, Anne Church Bigelow; three *s* one *d*. *Educ:* Dartmouth Coll., NH (AB); Balliol Coll., Oxford (MA, MPhil, DPhil 1982). University of Virginia, USA: Asst Prof., 1984–87; Associate Prof., 1987–91; Dir, Center for Russian and E European Studies, 1990–91; Queen's University, Kingston, Ontario: Prof. of Political Studies, 1991–96; Dir, Centre for Internat. Relns, 1995–96; Dir, Centre for Internat. Studies, Oxford, 1997–2002. *Publications:* Intervention and Regional Security, 1985; The Idea of National Liberation, 1985; Western Engagement in the Caucasus and Central Asia, 1999; Politics and Humanitarian Action, 2000; Intervention in Contemporary World Politics, 2002; The United Nations and Human Security: a critical history, 2006; articles in Internat. Affairs, Internat. Jl, Survival, Post-Soviet Affairs, World Politics, Security Studies, Third World Qly. *Recreations:* cross-country ski-ing, walking, skating. *Address:* St Anne's College, Oxford OX2 6HS. *T:* (01865) 274800.

MACFARLANE, Maj.-Gen. William Thomson, CB 1981; Consultant/Administrator, Sion College, 1984–93; *b* Bath, 2 Dec. 1925; *s* of late James and Agnes Macfarlane; *m* 1955, Dr Helen D. Meredith; one *d*. Commissioned Royal Signals, 1947. Served Europe, Near East, ME, and Far East. Commanded 16th Parachute Bde Signal Squadron, 1961–63; Military Asst, Commander FARELF, 1964–66; Comd 1st Div. HQ and Signal Regt, BAOR, 1967–70; Services Mem., Cabinet Office Secretariat, 1970–72; Comd, Corps Royal Signals, 1972–73; Dir of Public Relations (Army), MoD, 1973–75; C of S, UKLF, 1976–78; Chief, Jt Services Liaison Organisation, Bonn, 1978–80. Exec. Dir, Hong Kong Resort Co. Ltd, 1981–84; Dir, Compton Manor Estates (formerly Farms) Ltd, 1990–. Col Comdt, 1980–85, Rep. Col Comdt, 1985, Royal Corps of Signals. *Club:* Naval and Military.

MacFARQUHAR, Prof. Roderick Lemonde; Professor of Government, since 1984, Leroy B. Williams Professor of History and Political Science, since 1990, Harvard University (Chairman, Department of Government, 1998–2004); *b* 2 Dec. 1930; *s* of Sir Alexander MacFarquhar, KBE, CIE, and of Berenice Whitburn; *m* 1964, Emily Jane Cohen (*d* 2001); one *s* one *d*. *Educ:* Fettes Coll.; Oxford Univ. (BA); Harvard Univ. (AM); LSE (PhD). Specialist on China, Daily Telegraph (and later Sunday Telegraph), 1955–61; Founding Editor, China Quarterly, 1959–68; Rockefeller Grantee, 1962; Reporter, BBC TV programme Panorama, 1963–64. Associate Fellow, St Antony's Coll., Oxford, 1965–68. Mem., Editorial Bd, New Statesman, 1965–69; Ford Foundation Grant, 1968; Senior Research Fellow, Columbia Univ., 1969; Senior Research Fellow, RIIA, 1971–74 (Mem. Council, 1978–83); Co-presenter, BBC Gen. Overseas Services 24 Hours prog., 1972–74, 1979–80. Governor, SOAS, 1978–83; Dir, Fairbank Center for E Asian Res., Harvard Univ., 1986–92, 2005–06. Contested: (Lab) Ealing South, 1966; (Lab) Meriden, March 1968; (SDP) Derbys S, 1983. MP (Lab) Belper, Feb. 1974–1979; PPS to Minister of State, FCO, March 1974; resignation accepted, April 1975; reappointed June 1975; PPS to Sec. of State, DHSS, 1976–78. Member: N Atlantic Assembly, 1974–79; Select Cttee for Sci. and Technology, 1976–79; Trilateral Commn, 1976–98 (Mem. Exec. Cttee, 1976–84); Exec. Cttee, Fabian Soc., 1976–80. Leverhulme Res. Fellow, 1980–83; Fellow: Woodrow Wilson Center, Smithsonian Instn, 1980–81; Amer. Acad. of Arts and Scis, 1986–. Vis. Professor: of Govt, Harvard, 1982; Lee Kuan Yew Sch. of Public Policy, Nat. Univ. of Singapore, 2005; Vis. Fellow, St Antony's Coll., Oxford, 1983; Guest Prof., Peking Univ., 1997–2000; inaugurated: Inchon Meml Lectureship, Korea Univ., 1987; Merle Goldman History Lectureship, Boston Univ., 1997; Kimsey Lectureship, Central Party Sch., Beijing, 2003. *Publications:* The Hundred Flowers, 1960; The Sino-Soviet Dispute, 1961; Chinese Ambitions and British Policy (Fabian Pamphlet), 1966; (ed) China under Mao, 1966; Sino-American Relations, 1949–71, 1972; The Forbidden City, 1972; The Origins of the Cultural Revolution: Vol. 1, Contradictions among the People 1956–1957, 1974; Vol. 2, The Great Leap Forward 1958–1960, 1983; Vol. 3, The Coming of the Cataclysm 1961–1966, 1997 (Levenson 20th Century China Prize, Assoc. for Asian Studies, 1999); (ed jtly) Cambridge History of China, Vol. 14, 1987, Vol. 15, 1991; (ed jtly) The Secret Speeches of Chairman Mao, 1989; (ed) The Politics of China 1949–1989, 1993, 2nd edn, as The Politics of China, the Eras of Mao and Deng, 1997; (ed jtly) The Paradox of China's Post-Mao Reforms, 1999; (jtly) Mao's Last Revolution, 2006; articles in Foreign Affairs, The World Today, Atlantic Monthly, Pacific Affairs, Commentary, Newsweek, NY Review of Books, etc. *Recreations:* reading, listening to music, travel. *Address:* Fairbank Center, Harvard University, Cambridge, MA 02138, USA.

McFEE, Bruce James; Director, Environmental Services Pest Control Ltd, Paisley, since 2005; *b* 18 May 1961; *s* of James and Ellen Margaret McFee; *m* 1997, Iris Lille. *Educ:* Johnstone High Sch. Formerly Customer Service Manager, Scotland's largest ind. pest control co. Member (SNP): Renfrew DC, 1988–96 (Sec., 1988–92, Leader, 1992–96, SNP Gp); Renfrewshire Council, 1995–2003 and 2007– (Leader, SNP Gp, 1995–2003). MSP (SNP) Scotland West, 2003–07. *Recreations:* travel, DIY. *Address:* 36 Troubridge Avenue, Kilbarchan, Johnstone PA10 2AU.

McFEELY, Elizabeth Sarah Ann C.; *see* Craig-McFeely.

McFERRAN, Arthur Joseph, CBE 2005; Managing Director, Northbrook Technology of NI Ltd, since 1999; *b* 30 May 1951; *s* of Dr Francis Michael Joseph McFerran and Margaret Mary Ethna McFerran; *m* 1974, Patricia McNally; two *s* one *d*. *Educ:* St Malachy's Coll., Belfast; Queen's Univ., Belfast. Salesperson, Rank Xerox, 1972–79; Man. Dir, Logicom Ltd, 1979–97; Vice-Pres., Sales and Mktg, IMRglobal Inc., 1997–99. Non-exec. Dir, Northern Bank Ltd, 2005–. Board Member: Springvale Trng Ltd, 1999–; Centre for Software Process Technol., Univ. of Ulster, 2001–; BITC NI, 2005–. Pres., NI Chamber of Commerce and Industry, 2008– (Vice-Pres., 2006–08). *Recreations:* golf, ski-ing, walking. *Address:* Northbrook Technology of NI Ltd, 9 Lanyon Place, Belfast BT1 3LZ. *T:* (028) 9034 6500, *Fax:* (028) 9034 6550; *e-mail:* amcfe@allstate.com. *Clubs:* Fortwilliam Golf (Belfast), Narin & Portnoo Golf (Co. Donegal).

McFETRICH, (Charles) Alan; Deputy Chairman, Tenon Group PLC, since 2000; Managing Partner, External Affairs, Coopers & Lybrand, 1994–96; *b* 15 Dec. 1940; *s* of late Cecil McFetrich, OBE, FCA and Kathleen M. McFetrich (*née* Proom); *m* 1990, Janet Elizabeth Henkel (*née* Munro); two *s* one *d* from previous marriage. *Educ:* Oundle Sch.; Magdalene Coll., Cambridge. FCA. Trainee Accountant, Graham Proom & Smith, 1959–61 and 1964–66; Deloitte Haskins & Sells: Accountant, 1966–68; Consultant, 1968–73; Consultancy Partner, 1973–80; seconded to Dept of Industry, 1981–82; Nat. Operations Partner, 1983–85; Nat. Managing Partner, 1985–90; Coopers & Lybrand Deloitte, later Coopers & Lybrand: Man. Partner, 1990–92; Exec. Partner, 1992–94. FRSA 1989. *Recreations:* travel, theatre.

McGAHAN, Barney; Deputy Secretary, Department for Social Development, Northern Ireland, since 2006; *b* 19 March 1954; *s* of Patrick and Rita McGahan; *m* 1976, Teresa Corrigan; three *d*. *Educ:* Queen's Univ., Belfast (BSc Maths and Computer Sci. 1976). FCCA 1986. Dir, Financial Mgt, Dept of Health and Social Services, NI, 1991–98; Dir, Ops, NI Social Security Agency, 1999–2003; Chief Exec., NI Child Support Agency, 2004–06. Chm., Armagh Coll. of Further and Higher Educn, 2002–06. *Recreations:* chess, gardening, walking. *Address:* Department for Social Development, Lighthouse Building, 1 Cromac Place, Belfast BT7 2JB. *T:* (028) 9082 9001; *e-mail:* barney.mcgahan@dsdni.gov.uk.

McGANN, Prof. Jerome John, PhD; John Stewart Bryan University Professor, University of Virginia, since 1997 (John Stewart Bryan Professor of English, 1987–97); *b* 22 July 1937; *s* of John J. McGann and Marie V. McGann (*née* Lecouffe); *m* 1960, Anne Lanni; two *s* one *d*. *Educ:* Le Moyne Coll. (BS); Syracuse Univ. (MA); Yale Univ. (PhD 1966). Asst Prof., then Prof., Univ. of Chicago, 1966–75; Professor: Johns Hopkins Univ., 1975–81; CIT, 1981–87. Fulbright Fellow, 1965–66; Guggenheim Fellow, 1970–71 and 1976–81; NEH Fellow, 1975–76 and 1987–89. Lectures: Clark, Trinity Coll., Cambridge, 1988; Carpenter, Univ. of Chicago, 1988; Alexander, Univ. of Toronto, 1986; Beckman, Univ. of Calif (Berkeley), 1992; Lansdowne, Univ. of Victoria, 1994; Patten, Indiana Univ., 1995; Byron, Univ. of Nottingham, 1998; Hulme, Univ. of London, 1998; James Murray Brown, Univ. of Aberdeen, 2007. Fellow, Amer. Acad. of Arts and Scis, 1994. Hon. DHL Chicago, 1997. Melville Kane Award, Amer. Poetry Soc., 1973; Distinguished Schol. Award, Byron Soc., 1989; Wilbur Cross Medal, Yale Univ., 1994; Richard Lyman Award, Nat. Humanities Center, 2002; James Russell Lowell Award, MLA, 2002; Lifetime Achievement Award, Mellon Foundn, 2003. *Publications:* Fiery Dust: Byron's poetic development, 1969; (ed) Pelham, or The Adventures of a Gentleman, by Edward Bulwer-Lytton, 1972; Swinburne: an experiment in criticism, 1972; Don Juan in Context, 1976; Air Heart Sermons (poems), 1976; (with J. Kauffman) Writing Home (poems), 1978; (with J. Kahn) Nerves in Patterns (poems), 1979; (ed) Byron: the complete poetical works, Vol. I 1980, Vols II and III 1981, Vols IV and V 1986, Vol. VI 1991, Vol. VII 1993; The Romantic Ideology: a critical investigation, 1983; A Critique of Modern Textual Criticism, 1983, 2nd edn 1992; The Beauty of Inflections: literary investigations in historical method and theory, 1985; (ed) Textual Studies and Literary Interpretation, 1985; (ed jtly) The Manuscripts of the Younger Romantics: Byron, Vol. I 1985, Vol. II 1986, Vols III and IV 1988; (ed) Historical Studies and Literary Criticism, 1985; (ed) The Oxford Authors Byron, 1986; Social Values and Poetic Acts, 1987; Towards a Literature of Knowledge, 1989; (ed) Victorian Connections, 1989; (ed) Postmodern Poetries, 1990; The Textual Condition, 1991; (ed) The New Oxford Book of Romantic Period Verse, 1993; Black Riders: the visible language of modernism, 1993; (ed) A Symposium on Russian Postmodernism, 1993; (ed) Byron: the Oxford poetry library, 1994; Four Last Poems (poems), 1996; Poetics of Sensibility: a revolution in literary style, 1997; (ed jtly) Letitia Elizabeth Landon: selected writings, 1997; Complete Writings and Pictures of Dante Gabriel Rossetti: a hypermedia research archive, 1999; D. G. Rossetti and The Game that Must be Lost, 2000; Radiant Textuality: literature since the World Wide Web, 2001; Byron and Romanticism, 2002; The Collected Writings of Dante Gabriel Rossetti, 2003; Algernon Charles Swinburne: major poems and selected prose, 2004; The Scholar's Art: literature and criticism in a managed world, 2006; The Point is to Change It: poetry and criticism in the continuing present, 2007. *Recreation:* squash. *Address:* PO Box 529, Ivy, VA 22945–0529, USA.

McGARRY, Ian; General Secretary, British Actors' Equity Association, 1991–2005; *b* 27 Feb. 1941; *s* of John and Jean McGarry; *m* 1964, Christine Smith (marr. diss. 1989); one *s*. *Educ:* Chichester High Sch.; Lewes County Grammar Sch. Labour Party Constituency Agent, Putney, 1964–76; Asst General Sec., Equity, 1976–91. *Recreations:* golf, football (spectator), horse racing. *Address:* The White Cottage, Barrington, Ilminster, Som TA19 0JB. *T:* (01460) 55243.

McGARVEY, Alan; independent specialist in economic and industrial development, since 1996; *b* 22 June 1942; *s* of William Johnson McGarvey and Rosina McGarvey; *m* 1st, 1967, Eileen Cook (*d* 1992); 2nd, 1997, Shirlee Ann Gleeson. *Educ:* Wallsend Grammar Sch.; Coll. of Further Educn; Newcastle Univ. (BSc); Cranfield Sch. of Management (MBA). C. A. Parsons, 1958–64 (apprentice); RTZ, 1968–71; Decca Gp, 1972–76; MK Electric, 1976–78; Director, Small Company Div., NEB, 1978–82; Chief Exec., Greater London Enterprise Bd, 1982–86; management consultant, 1986–88; Man. Dir, Greater Manchester Econ. Develt Ltd, 1987–90; regl develt specialist, 1990–93; specialist, Regl and Small and Medium Enterprises Develt, EC, 1993–96. Labour Party, 1974–; Mem., Wandsworth Borough Council, 1981–86 (Dep. Opposition Leader, 1982–83); Chm., Battersea Constituency Labour Parties, 1978–82. Exec. Mem., Wandsworth CRC, 1973–82; Board Member: Battersea Arts Centre Trust, 1982–88; Northern Chamber Orch., 1988–93; Member: Jt Governing Board, Centre for Development of Industry (EEC-ACP Lomé), 1981–90; Adv. Council, Cttee for Industrial Co-operation (EEC-ACP), 1990–96. Governor, Polytech. of South Bank, 1985–87; Chm. Govs, Medlock Sch., Manchester, 1989–91. *Recreations:* home and garden, science fiction; amateur sculptor. *Address:* Willowbank, 9 Anglesey Drive, Poynton SK12 1BT. *T:* (01625) 873869, *Fax:* (01625) 873698; *e-mail:* mcgarvey01@aol.com.

McGAUGHRIN, Anne; Legal Director, Department for Environment, Food and Rural Affairs, since 2007; *b* Glasgow, 25 Jan. 1957; *d* of John and Jean McGaughrin; *m* 1988, Michael William Cross; one *d*. *Educ:* York Univ. (BA Jt Hons English and Hist.). Admitted solicitor, 1986; Adviser: Plumstead Law Centre, 1979–84; Cullen & Co., 1984–88; PR, Canon Inc., Tokyo, 1988–91; Legal Advr, DSS, then DWP, 1992–2007. *Publication:* (ed and contrib.) Exploring Japan, 1991. *Recreations:* enjoying family, friends, the arts and the great outdoors on foot or bicycle. *Address:* Department for Environment, Area 4C, 3–8 Whitehall Place, SW1A 2HH; *e-mail:* anne.mcgaughrin@defra.gsi.gov.uk.

McGEACHY, Alistair Laird, WS; a Senior Immigration Judge, Asylum and Immigration Tribunal (formerly a Vice-President, Immigration Appeal Tribunal), since 2004; *b* 2 April 1949; *s* of William Laird McGeachy and Alice McGeachy (*née* Hill); *m* 1978, Jennifer Heather Macleod; two *s* one *d*. *Educ:* Strathallan Sch.; Univ. of Edinburgh (LLB Jt Hons Law and Hist.). Admitted solicitor: Scotland, 1974; England, 1982; WS 1975; with Fyfe Ireland, 1974–76; Refugee, then Tribunal, Counsellor, UKIAS, 1976–82; with Manches and Co., 1982–84; Partner, Macdonald Stacey, subseq. incorporated in Kidd Rapinet, 1984–97; Adjudicator of Immigration Appeals, 1997–2004. Liveryman, Gardeners' Co., 1990 (Clerk, 1985–90). *Recreations:* reading, visiting art galleries, travel. *Address:* Asylum and Immigration Tribunal, Field House, 15 Breams Buildings, EC4A 1DZ.

McGEE, Prof. James O'Donnell, FMedSci; Professor of Morbid Anatomy, University of Oxford, 1975–99, now Emeritus; Fellow of Linacre College, Oxford, since 1975; *b* 27 July 1939; *s* of Michael and Bridget McGee; *m* 1961, Anne Lee; one *s* two *d*. *Educ:* Univ. of Glasgow. MB, ChB, PhD, MD; MA (Oxon). FRCPath 1986; FRCPGlas 1989. Various appts in Univ. Dept of Pathology, Royal Infirmary, Glasgow, 1962–69; Roche Inst. of Molecular Biology, Nutley, NJ: MRC Fellow 1969–70; Vis. Scientist 1970–71; Distinguished Vis. Scientist, 1981 and 1989; Dept of Pathology, Royal Infirmary, Glasgow: Lectr 1971–74; Sen. Lectr, 1974–75. Member: Scientific Cttee, 1978–88, Grants Cttee, 1988–92, Cancer Res. Campaign; Cttee on Safety of Medicines, 1987–89 (Safety and Efficacy Sub Cttee, 1984–87); Kettle Meml Lectr, RCPath, 1980; Annual Guest Lecturer: Royal Coll. of Physicians, Ireland, 1986; Royal Acad. of Medicine (Ireland), 1985. Founder FMedSci 1998. Bellahouston Gold Medal, Glasgow Univ., 1973. *Publications:* Biopsy Pathology of Liver, 1980, 2nd edn 1988; In Situ Hybridisation: principles and practice, 1990; Oxford Textbook of Pathology, 1992: vol. 1, Principles of Pathology, vols 2a, 2b, Pathology of Systems; The Natural Immune System: The Macrophage, 1992; The Natural Killer Cell, 1992; Diagnostic Molecular Pathology, vols 1 and 2, 1992; papers in scientific jls on liver disease, breast and cervical cancers, telematics/telepathology in health care. *Recreations:* talking with my family, swimming. *Address:* Linacre College, Oxford OX1 3JA.

McGEECHAN, Ian Robert, OBE 1990; Director of Rugby, London Wasps, since 2005; *b* 30 Oct. 1946; *s* of Bob McGeechan and Hilda (*née* Shearer); *m* 1969, Judy Fish; one *s* one *d*. *Educ:* Carnegie Coll. of Physical Educn (DipPE). Teacher: Moor Grange High Sch., 1968–72; and Hd of Humanities, Fir Tree High Sch., 1972–90; Rugby player: Scottish Internat., 1972–79; Barbarians, 1973–78; British Lions, SA, 1974, NZ, 1977; coach: Headingley, 1980–83; Scotland under 21s, 1981–83; Scotland B, 1983 and 1985–88; Northampton, 1994–99; Asst Coach, Scotland, 1985–88; Nat. Coach, Scotland, 1988–93 and 1999–2003 (incl. Scotland Grand Slam, 1990, 4th place, World Cup, 1991); British Lions Coach: Australia, 1989 (won 2–1); NZ, 1993 (lost 2–1); SA, 1997 (won 2–1); Asst Coach (midweek), NZ, 2005. Chm., Sports Coach UK, 2004–. Hon. MA Nottingham, 1998; Hon. DArts Leeds Metropolitan, 2004. Parly Rugby Medal, 2004. *Publications:* Scotland's Grand Slam, 1990; So Close to Glory: Lions New Zealand, 1993; Winning Lions, South Africa, 1997. *Recreations:* photography, hill-walking with wife and two dogs. *Address:* c/o London Wasps, Twyford Avenue, Acton, W3 9QA. *T:* (020) 8993 8298, *Fax:* (020) 8993 2621; *e-mail:* ianmcgeechan@hotmail.com.

McGEEHAN, Prof. Joseph Peter, CBE 2004; PhD; FREng; Professor of Communications Engineering, Department of Electrical and Electronic Engineering, since 1985, and Director, Centre for Communications Research, since 1987, University of Bristol; Managing Director, Telecommunications Research Laboratory, Bristol, Toshiba Research Europe Ltd, since 1998; *b* 15 Feb. 1946; *s* of Joseph McGeehan and Rhoda Catherine McGeehan; *m* 1970, Jean Lightfoot; two *d*. *Educ:* Univ. of Liverpool (BEng Hons Electrical Engrg and Electronics 1967; PhD 1971; DEng 2003). FREng 1994. Sen. Scientist, Allan Clark Res. Centre, Plessey Co. Ltd, Caswell, 1970–72; Lectr, then Sen. Lectr, in Electrical Engrg, Sch. of Electrical Engrg, Univ. of Bath, 1972–85; University of Bristol: Hd, Dept of Electrical and Electronic Engrg, 1991–98; Dean of Engrg, 1998–2003. Founding Chm. and non-exec. Dir, Wireless Systems International Ltd, 1995–98; non-executive Director: Renishaw plc, 2001–; 3CR, 2003–. Non-exec. Dir, Technology Foresight Mobile Virtual Centre of Excellence, 1996–98, 2001–07. Ambassador, SW England RDA, 2003–. Governor: Bristol Grammar Sch., 2003–04; Colston Sch., Bristol, 2007–. *Publications:* more than 350 articles in internat. acad. jls and confs. *Recreations:* keeping fit, cycling, watching sport (particularly cricket, Rugby Union and F1), amateur photography, theatre, concerts.

McGEGAN, (James) Nicholas; Music Director, Philharmonia Baroque Orchestra, San Franciso, since 1985; Artistic Director, Göttingen Handel Festival, Germany, since 1991; *b* 14 Jan. 1950; *s* of late (James Edward) Peter McGegan and Christine Mary McGegan (*née* Collier). *Educ:* Corpus Christi, Cambridge (BA, MA); Magdalen Coll., Oxford. LTCL 1969. Royal College of Music: Prof., 1973–79; Dir, Early Music, 1976–80; Artist-in-Residence, Washington Univ., St Louis, Mo, 1979–85; Principal Conductor, Drottningholm Court Th., Sweden, 1993–96 (Vänners Hederstecken, 1996); Principal Guest Conductor, Scottish Opera, 1993–98. Hon. Prof., Georg-August Univ., Göttingen, 2006. Baroque series Dir, St Paul Chamber Orch., 1999–2004. Hon. RCM 1978. Has made numerous recordings, incl. opera and oratorios. Handel Prize, Halle, Germany, 1993. *Publication:* (ed) Philidor, Tom Jones, 1978. *Recreations:* history, cooking, good wine. *Address:* 722 Wildcat Canyon Road, Berkeley, CA 94708, USA. *T:* (510) 5280862; 1 Kew Terrace, Glasgow G12 0TD. *T:* (0141) 339 0786. *Clubs:* East India, Savile.

McGEOCH, Prof. Duncan James, PhD; FRSE; Director, Medical Research Council Virology Unit, Glasgow, since 1995; *b* 13 Sept. 1944; *s* of Peter and Christine McGeoch; *m* 1971, Jennifer A. Wylie; two *s*. *Educ:* Hutchesons' Grammar Sch., Glasgow; Univ. of Glasgow (BSc 1967; PhD 1971). FRSE 1987. Jane Coffin Childs Postdoctoral Fellow, Dept of Microbiology and Molecular Genetics, Harvard Med. Sch., 1971–73; Researcher, Virology Div., Dept of Pathology, Univ. of Cambridge, 1973–76; Mem. of Scientific Staff, MRC Virology Unit, Glasgow, 1976–95. Hon. Prof., Univ. of Glasgow, 1996–. Editor-in-Chief, Jl of General Virology, 1988–92. Fleming Award, Soc. for Gen. Microbiology, 1980. *Publications:* scientific papers. *Recreations:* reading, mountains and sea, ski-ing, walking, sailing.

McGEOUGH, Prof. Joseph Anthony, CEng, FIMechE, FIET; Regius Professor of Engineering, University of Edinburgh, 1983–2005, now Professor Emeritus (Head, Department of Mechanical Engineering, 1983–91; Senior Honorary Professorial Fellow, 2007–08); *b* 29 May 1940; *s* of late Patrick Joseph McGeough and Gertrude (*née* Darroch); *m* 1972, Brenda Nicholson; two *s* one *d*. *Educ:* St Michael's Coll., Irvine; Glasgow Univ. (BSc, PhD); Aberdeen Univ. (DSc). Vacation-apprentice, Malcolm & Allan Ltd, 1957–61; Research Demonstrator, Leicester Univ., 1966; Sen. Res. Fellow, Queensland Univ., 1967; Res. Metallurgist, International Research & Development Co. Ltd, Newcastle upon Tyne, 1968–69; Sen. Res. Fellow, Strathclyde Univ., 1969–72; Lectr 1972–77, Sen. Lectr 1977–80, Reader 1980–83, Dept of Engineering, Aberdeen Univ. Royal Society/SERC Industrial Fellow, 1987–89; Hon. Prof., Nanjing Univ. of Aeronautics and Astronautics, 1992–; Visiting Professor: Univ. degli Studi di Napoli Federico II, 1994; Glasgow Caledonian Univ., 1997–2003; Tokyo Univ. of Agric. and Technol., 2004; Monash Univ., 2005; Universiti Teknologi Petronas, 2007–. Institution of Mechanical Engineers: Chm., Scottish Br., 1993–95; Mem. Council, 2000–03; Mem., Trustee Bd, 2004–; Vice-Pres., 2006–. Chm., CIRP UK Bd, 2000–03 (Mem. Council, 2006–08). Editor: Procs of Internat. Confs on Computer-aided Prodn Engrg, 1986–; Processing of Advanced Materials, 1991–94; CIRP Ed., Jl of Materials Processing Technol., 1995–. FRSE 1990. *Publications:* Principles of Electrochemical Machining, 1974; Advanced Methods of Machining, 1988; (ed) Micromachining of Engineering Materials, 2001; papers mainly in Journal of Mech. Engrg Science, Proc. IMechE; contrib. Encyclopaedia Britannica, Encyclopaedia of Electrochemistry. *Recreations:* golf, hill-walking. *Address:* 39 Dreghorn Loan, Colinton, Edinburgh EH13 0DF. *T:* (0131) 441 1302.

McGHEE, George Arnott; Controller, BBC Programme Acquisition, since 2003; *b* 8 March 1956; *s* of Douglas and Myra McGhee. *Educ:* Ravensbourne Coll. of Art and Design (Dip. Media and Gen. Art Studies). Asst Film Ed., later Broadcast Exec., Scottish TV, 1979–93; Hd of Acquisitions, Channels TV Max and Max 1, Czech Republic, 1993–94; Carlton Cinema: Hd of Acquisitions, 1994–98; Dir, 1998–2003. *Recreations:* cinema, theatre, music, ski-ing, entertaining, collecting. *Address:* Room 6023, BBC TV Centre, Wood Lane, W12 7RJ; *e-mail:* george.mcghee@bbc.co.uk.

McGHEE, John Alexander; QC 2003; barrister; *b* 11 Feb. 1962; *s* of Alastair Orr McGhee and Joyce Alison McEwen McGhee (*née* Gall); *m* Marianne Richards; one *s* one *d* from a previous marriage. *Educ:* University Coll., Oxford (MA). Called to the Bar, Lincoln's Inn, 1984. *Publication:* Snell's Equity, (ed) 30th edn 1999, (gen. ed.) 31st edn 2004. *Recreation:* flute playing. *Address:* Maitland Chambers, 7 Stone Buildings, Lincoln's Inn, WC2A 3SZ.

McGHIE, Hon. Lord; James Marshall McGhie; Chairman, Scottish Land Court, since 1996; President, Lands Tribunal for Scotland, since 1996; *b* 15 Oct. 1944; *s* of James Drummond McGhie and Jessie Eadie Bennie; *m* 1968, Ann Manuel Cockburn; one *s* one *d*. *Educ:* Perth Acad.; Edinburgh Univ. (LLB Hons). Called to the Scottish Bar, 1969; QC (Scot.) 1983; Advocate-depute, 1983–86. Pt-time Chm., Medical Appeal Tribunal, 1987–92; Mem., Criminal Injuries Compensation Bd, 1992–96. *Recreations:* various. *Address:* 3 Lauder Road, Edinburgh EH9 2EW. *T:* (0131) 667 8325.

McGHIE, Duncan Clark; Chairman: Scottish Ballet, 1999–2004; Scottish Opera, 1999–2004; *b* 6 Dec. 1944; *s* of William and Helen McGhie; *m* 1969, Una Gray Carmichael; one *s* one *d*. *Educ:* George Watson's Coll., Edinburgh. BSC, 1967–78 (Financial Controller, Scottish Div., 1975–78); Gp Finance Dir, Wm Collins Plc, 1978–84; Partner, Mgt Consultancy, Coopers & Lybrand, subseq. PricewaterhouseCoopers, 1984–2000. Mem., Inland Waterways Adv. Council, 2006–. Mem., ICAS, 1967–. Elder, Ch of Scotland. *Recreations:* golf, music. *Address:* 65 Corrour Road, Newlands, Glasgow G43 2ED. *T:* (0141) 632 4502, *Fax:* (0141) 649 9030; *e-mail:* duncan.mcghie@ntlworld.com. *Clubs:* Pollok Golf, Western Gailes Golf.

McGHIE, James Marshall; *see* McGhie, Hon. Lord.

MacGIBBON, Dr Barbara Haig, (Mrs John Roberts), CB 1988; FRCPath; Chairman, Commission on Environmental Health, 1996–97; Assistant Director (Medical), National Radiological Protection Board, 1988–93; *b* 7 Feb. 1928; *d* of Ronald Ross MacGibbon and Margaret Fraser; *m* 1954, John Roberts; one *s* one *d*. *Educ:* Lady Margaret Hall, Oxford; University College Hosp. Registrar, then Res. Assistant, Dept of Haematology, Royal Postgraduate Med. Sch., 1957–64; Sen. Registrar, Sen. Lectr/Hon. Consultant, then Sen. Res. Fellow, Dept of Haematology, St Thomas' Hosp. Med. Sch., 1969–79; SMO, then PMO, Toxicology and Environmental Health, DHSS, 1979; SPMO, DHSS, 1983–88. Chm., Panel on Energy, WHO Commn on Health and Envmt, 1990–92; Consultant, MRC Inst. for Envmt and Health, 1994–97. *Publications:* (ed) Concern for Europe's Tomorrow: health and environment in the WHO European region, 1995; articles in various med. jls.

McGIBBON, Susanna Justine; Director, Legal Services B, Department for Business, Enterprise and Regulatory Reform (formerly Department of Trade and Industry), since 2006; *b* 11 Nov. 1967; *d* of Ian and Gwen McGibbon; *m* 2004, Patrick Spencer. *Educ:* Bolton Co. Grammar Sch.; Canon Slade Sch., Bolton; Univ. of Sheffield (LLB Hons 1989); Inns of Court Sch. of Law. Called to the Bar, Lincoln's Inn, 1990; in private practice at the Bar, 1990–93; FCO, 1993–98; Treasury Solicitor's Dept, 1998–2006: MoD, 1998–2000; DfES, 2000–02; Cabinet Office, 2002–06. *Recreations:* being in the mountains, at the opera or in India. *Address:* c/o Department for Business, Enterprise and Regulatory Reform, 1 Victoria Street, SW1H 0ET.

McGILL, Angus, MBE 1990; journalist; *b* 26 Nov. 1927; *s* of Kenneth and Janet McGill. *Educ:* Warehousemen, Clerks' and Drapers' Schools, Addington, Surrey. Reporter, Shields Gazette, 1944; Army service; feature writer, Evening Chronicle, Newcastle, 1948; Londoner's Diary, Evening Standard, 1957; columnist, Evening Standard, 1961–92. Chm., Knobs & Knockers, 1964–77. British Press Award, descriptive writer of the Year, 1968. *Publications:* Augusta, comic strip (drawn by Dominic Poelsma), 1968–; Yea Yea Yea (novel), 1969; (with Kenneth Thomson) Live Wires, 1982; London Pub Guide, annually 1995–97. *Address:* 83 Winchester Court, Vicarage Gate, W8 4AF. *T:* (020) 7937 2166.

MACGILL, Kerry Michael Peter; His Honour Judge Macgill; a Circuit Judge, since 2000; *b* 30 April 1950; *s* of Alan and Betty Macgill; *m* 1973, Janet Hazeldine; one *s* one *d*. *Educ:* Holborn Coll. of Law (LLB Hons London, 1971). Asst Solicitor, T. I. Clough & Co., 1975–77; Partner, Lumb & Kenningham, which later became Lumb & Macgill, criminal law practice, 1977–2000. *Recreations:* walking, golf, sailing. *Address:* Leeds Combined Court Centre, 1 Oxford Row, Leeds LS1 3BG.

McGILL, Maj.-Gen. Nigel Harry Duncan, CB 1966; Chief of Staff to Commandant-General, Royal Marines, 1967–68, retired, 1968; *b* 15 Oct. 1916; *s* of Lt-Col H. R. McGill; *m* 1944, Margaret Constance Killen; two *s* one *d*. *Educ:* Victoria Coll., Jersey. Commissioned 2nd Lt RM 1934; Maj.-Gen. 1964; Comdr, Portsmouth Group, RM, 1964–67. Representative Col Comdt RM, 1977–78. Exec., Rolls Royce Ltd, 1968–78. *Address:* Alderwood, Manor Farm Road, Fordingbridge, Hants SP6 1DY.

McGILL, Robin William, CEng; Chief Executive and Secretary, Institution of Engineering and Technology, since 2007; *b* 19 Aug. 1955; *s* of William Robertson McGill and Catherine Meikle Leitch; *m* 1977, Susan (*née* McMorran); one *s* one *d*. *Educ:* Univ. of Edinburgh (BSc 1st cl. Hons Engrg Sci. 1977). CEng, MIMechE, 1981, FIMechE; FIET. BP Chemicals, Scotland, 1977–88, Engr, then operational roles, subseq. Polythene Ops Manager; Business Manager, Boron Nitride, Carborundum Inc., Buffalo, NY, 1988–92; BP plc, 1992–2006: Strat. and Projs Manager, BP Chemicals; Distribution Sen. Bus. Advr, BP Oil Internat.; Mktg Div. Manager, Pittsburgh Pa, BP America Inc.; Mergers & Acquisitions Proj. Manager, BP Chemicals Ltd; Business Unit Leader: Plastic Fabrications Gp, BP Amoco Ltd; European Polymers, BP Chemicals Ltd; CEO, BP Solvay HDPE, 2001–04; Man. Dir, BP Grangemouth, 2004–06. Mem. Council, CBI Scotland, 1981–. *Address:* Institution of Engineering and Technology, 2 Savoy Place, WC2R 0BL. *T:* (020) 7344 5400; *e-mail:* rmgill@theiet.org.

McGILL, Stephen Phillip; Chief Executive Officer, Aon Risk Services Americas, Aon Corporation, since 2005; *b* 18 Feb. 1958; *s* of late Maj. James Osmond McGill and Joyce Courteney McGill; *m* Elizabeth Mawbey; one *s* two *d*. *Educ:* Gordon's Boys' Sch., West End, Woking. ACII 1980. Sedgwick, 1977–81; Director: Fenchurch Gp Brokers Internat., 1981–86; Willis Internat., 1986–89; Lloyd Thompson Ltd, 1989–97; Dir, 1997–2002, Gp Chief Exec., 2002–04, Jardine Lloyd Thompson Gp plc. Dir, Internat. Insce Soc. Inc., 2002–05; Pres., Insce Inst. of London, 2005–06. *Recreations:* ski-ing, swimming, tennis. *Address:* Aon Corp., 8 Devonshire Square, EC2M 4PL. *T:* (020) 7623 5500.

MacGILLIVRAY, Barron Bruce, FRCP; Consultant in Clinical Neurophysiology and Neurology, Royal Free Hospital, 1964–93 (Dean, School of Medicine, 1975–89); Consultant in Clinical Neurophysiology, National Hospital for Nervous Diseases, 1971–93; *b* 21 Aug. 1927; *s* of late John MacGillivray and of Doreene (*née* Eastwood), S Africa; *m* 1955, Ruth Valentine; two *s* one *d*. *Educ:* King Edward VII Sch., Johannesburg; Univ. of Witwatersrand (BSc Hons 1949); Univ. of Manchester; Univ. of London (MB, BS 1962). FRCP 1973. House Surg., House Phys., Manchester Royal Infirm., 1955–56; RMO, Stockport and Stepping Hill Hosp., 1957–59; Registrar, subseq. Sen. Registrar, Nat. Hosp. for Nervous Diseases, Queen Sq., London, 1959–64; Res. Fellow, UCLA, 1964–65. Pro-Vice Chancellor, Medicine, Univ. of London, 1985–87. Member: Camden and Islington AHA(T), 1975–78; NE Thames RHA, 1979–84; CVCP, 1983–87; Senate, Collegiate Council, Univ. of London; Univ. rep., Council, Sch. of Pharmacy, St George's Hosp. Med. Sch. (Treasurer, 1996–2000), and British Postgraduate Med. Fedn; Examr and Teacher, Univ. of London. Mem., Complaints Review Cttee, DHSS, 1993–94. Pres., Electrophys. Technicians Assoc., 1976–82. MRI 1975; FRSocMed; FRSA. *Publications:* papers in sci. jls on cerebral electrophysiol., epilepsy, computing and cerebral death. *Recreations:* sailing, photography. *Address:* 45 Eustace Building, 372 Queenstown Road, SW8 4NT. *T:* (020) 7498 5568; *e-mail:* bmacg@btinternet.com.

MacGILLIVRAY, Prof. Ian, MD, FRCP, FRCOG; Regius Professor of Obstetrics and Gynæcology, University of Aberdeen, 1965–84 (Dean of Medical Faculty, 1976–79), now Emeritus Professor; *b* 25 Oct. 1920; *yr s* of W. and A. MacGillivray; *m* 1950, Edith Mary Margaret Cook; one *s* twin *d*. *Educ:* Vale of Leven Academy, Alexandria; University of Glasgow (MB, ChB 1944; MD 1953); MRCOG 1949, FRCOG 1959; FRCPGlas 1973. Gardiner Research Schol., 1949–51, Lectr in Midwifery, 1951–53, Univ. of Glasgow; Senior Lecturer: in Obstetrics and Gynæcology, Univ. of Bristol, 1953–55; in Midwifery and Gynæcology, Univ. of Aberdeen, 1955–61; Prof. of Obstetrics and Gynæcology, University of London, at St Mary's Hospital Medical Sch., 1961–65. Mem., GMC, 1979–84. Founder Pres., Internat. Soc. for Study of Hypertension in Pregnancy, 1976–80; Pres., Internat. Soc. for Twin Studies, 1980–83; Mem. Council, RCOG, 1974–80. *Publications:* Outline of Human Reproduction, 1963; Combined Textbook of Obstetrics and Gynaecology, 1976; Human Multiple Reproduction, 1976; Pre-eclampsia: the hypertensive disease of pregnancy, 1983; contrib. to: British Medical Journal, Lancet, Journal of Obstetrics and Gynæcology of the British Empire; Clinical Science. *Address:* 2 White Gables, 53 Carlisle Road, Eastbourne BN21 4JR.

McGILLIVRAY, Laura Susan; Chief Executive, Norwich City Council, since 2006; *b* 29 Dec. 1953; *d* of William Watson McGillivray and Marjory Joan McGillivray (*née* Cameron); *m* 1999, Paul Robert Golding Chaplin; two *d*. *Educ:* Liverpool Univ. (BA Sociol. 1975); Birmingham Univ. (MBA Public Service Mgt 1994). Dir and Sen. Consultant, CAG Consultants, 1985–88; Dir, Manor Gdns Health and Community Centre, Islington, 1988–91; Milton Keynes Council, 1991–2000, Hd of Policy and Communications, 1996–2000; Strategic Dir, Community Services, Dacorum BC, 2000–03; Dep. Chief Exec., City of York Council, 2003–05. Member: Council, UEA, 2006–; Bd, Sainsbury Centre for the Visual Arts, 2006–. *Recreations:* lobbying for unitary status, networking, spending time with family and friends. *Address:* Norwich City Council, City Hall, Norwich NR2 1NH. *T:* (01603) 212001, *Fax:* (01603) 213001; *e-mail:* lauramcgillivray@norwich.gov.uk.

McGILLIVRAY, Robert, CEng, FICE, FCIWEM; Chairman, Fisheries (Electricity) Committee (formerly Fisheries Committee for Hydro-Electric Schemes), Scotland, 1992–2002; Chief Engineer and Under Secretary, Scottish Development Department, 1987–91; *b* 11 May 1931; *o s* of late William Gilchrist McGillivray and of Janet Love Jamieson; *m* 1955, Pauline, *e d* of late Alexander Davie; one *s*. *Educ:* Boroughmuir Sch., Edinburgh; Univ. of Edinburgh (BSc CivEng.). National Service, 1949–51. Training with J. & A. Leslie & Reid, CE, 1955–57; Asst Engr, Midlothian CC, 1957–60; CE, Dept of Agric. & Fisheries for Scotland, 1960–72; Scottish Development Department: Prin. CE, 1972–75; Engrg Inspector, 1976–80; Asst Chief Engr, 1980–85; Dep. Chief Engr, 1985–87. *Publications:* A History of the Clan MacGillivray (with George B. Macgillivray), 1973; The Clan MacGillivray, 2004. *Recreations:* music, genealogy, Highland history. *Address:* Fairview, 88/3 Barnton Park View, Edinburgh EH4 6HJ. *T:* (0131) 339 1667.

McGIMPSEY, Michael; Member (UU) Belfast South, Northern Ireland Assembly, since 1998; Minister of Health, Social Services and Public Safety, Northern Ireland, since 2007; *b* 1 July 1948; *s* of Henry and Isabel McGimpsey; *m* 1970, Maureen Elisabeth Speers; one *s* one *d*. *Educ:* Regent House Grammar Sch.; Trinity Coll., Dublin (BA 1970). Mem. (UU), Belfast CC, 1993–. Minister of Culture, Arts and Leisure, NI, 1999–2002. Contested (UU) Belfast S, 2005. *Recreations:* reading, gardening, walking. *Address:* Northern Ireland Assembly, Parliament Buildings, Stormont, Belfast BT4 3XX. *T:* (028) 9181 3948.

McGINLEY, Aideen, OBE 2000; Permanent Secretary, Department for Employment and Learning, Northern Ireland, since 2006; *b* 31 May 1954; *d* of Joseph Slevin and Terry Slevin (*née* O'Brien); *m* 1975, James McGinley; two *s* one *d*. *Educ:* Salford Univ. (BSc Hons Envmtl Sci. 1975); Univ. of Ulster (MSc Social Policy, Admin and Planning 1983). Community Services Officer: Fermanagh DC, 1976; Strabane DC, 1976–89; Fermanagh District Council: Principal Officer, Policy and Planning, 1989–92; Dir of Develt, 1992–95; Chief Exec., 1995–2000; Perm. Sec., Dept of Culture, Arts and Leisure, NI, 1999–2006. Hon. Mem. RSUA, 2004. DUniv Ulster, 1998. *Recreation:* family. *Address:* Department for Employment and Learning, Adelaide House, 39–49 Adelaide Street, Belfast BT2 8FD. *T:* (028) 9025 7833.

McGINN, Gerry; Head, Goodbody Stockbrokers, Northern Ireland, since 2007; *b* 4 May 1957. *Educ:* QUB; Columbia Graduate Business Sch., NY. Joined Nat. Westminster Bank, London; Bank of Ireland: Chief Exec., Corporate and Internat. Banking, 1990–94; Chief Exec., NI, 1994–99; Chief Exec., UK, 1999–2001; Permanent Secretary: Dept of Educn, NI, 2001–05; Dept for Regl Develt, NI, 2006–07. *Address:* Goodbody Stockbrokers, Ballsbridge Park, Dublin 4, Ireland.

McGINTY, Lawrence Stanley; Health and Science Editor, ITN, since 1989 (Science Editor, 1987–89); *b* 2 July 1948; *s* of Lawrence McGinty and Hilda (*née* Hardman); *m* 1969, Joan Allen. *Educ:* Stand Grammar Sch., Whitefield, Bury; Liverpool Univ. (BSc Zoology). Asst Editor, Chemistry in Britain, 1971–72; Technology Editor, then Health and Safety Editor, later News Editor, New Scientist, 1972–82; Science Correspondent, Channel 4 News, 1982–87. Guest Lectr, Ecole Polytechnique, Paris, 1984. Special Advisor: WHO, 2000; IAEA, 2001–03. Silver Jubilee Medal, 1977. *Recreations:* fine wine, books, walking. *Address:* ITN, 200 Gray's Inn Road, WC1X 8XZ. *T:* (020) 7430 4290.

McGIVAN, Alec John; Head, BBC Outreach, since 2007; *b* 8 Sept. 1953; *s* of Ronald McGivan and Nancy McGivan (*née* Richards); *m* 1992, Elizabeth Ann Astill; one *s* one *d*. *Educ:* Bristol Cathedral Sch.; Wadham Coll., Oxford (MA Modern Hist.). Nat. Organiser SDP, 1981–88; Events Dir, Corp. of London, 1988–90; Chief Exec., Shakespeare Globe Trust, 1990–91; Hd of Communications, Chapter One, 1991–94; Football Association: Media/Events Manager, Euro 96, 1994–96; Campaign Dir, World Cup Bid 2006, 1996–2000; Dir, Internat. Mktg, Interclubnet, 2000–02; Dir of Sport, DCMS, 2002–04; Hd, Charter Review Campaign, BBC, 2004–07. Trustee: Comic Relief, 2007–; BBC Performing Arts Fund, 2007–. *Recreations:* gardening, music, all sport, Bristol City FC, family and friends. *Address:* BBC Outreach, White City, 201 Wood Lane, W12 7TS. *T:* (020) 8752 5052; *e-mail:* alec.mcgivan@bbc.co.uk.

McGIVERN, Eugene, CB 1997; Tribunal Member, Accountancy and Actuarial Discipline Board (formerly Accountancy Investigation and Discipline Board), since 2005; Under Secretary, Board of Inland Revenue, 1986–98; *b* 15 Sept. 1938; *s* of late James and Eileen McGivern; *m* 1960, Teresa Doran; two *s* one *d*. *Educ:* St Mary's Grammar School, Belfast. Joined Inland Revenue, 1955; seconded to Welsh Office as Private Sec. to Minister of State, 1967–69; Inland Revenue, 1969–98. Mem., CSAB, 1998–2004.

McGLADE, Prof. Jacqueline Myriam, PhD; Professor, Department of Mathematics, University College London, since 2000; Executive Director, European Environment Agency, since 2003; *b* 30 May 1955; *d* of Bryan Maurice Cox and Maria Alphonsonia (*née* LeClair); *m* 1977, James McGlade (marr. diss. 1994); two *d*. *Educ:* UCNW (BSc; Hon. Fellow, Univ. of Wales, 1999); Univ. of Guelph, Canada (PhD 1981). FRICS 1989. Sen. Res. Scientist, Federal Govt of Canada, 1981–87; Adrian Fellow, Darwin Coll., Cambridge, 1987–90; Associate Prof., Cranfield Inst. of Technology, 1987–88; Schol., Internat. Fedn of Insts of Advanced Studies, Maastricht, 1988–93; Dir, and Prof. of Theoretical Ecology, Forschungszentrum Jülich, 1988–92; Prof. of Biol Scis, Univ. of Warwick, 1992–98 (Hon. Prof., 1998–2003); Dir, Centre for Coastal and Marine Scis, NERC, 1998–2000. Member: Bd, Envmt Agency, 1998–2003; Marine Foresight Panel, 1999–2002; UK-China Forum, 1999–; UK-Japan 21st Century Gp, 2002–. Trustee: Earth Centre, 1990–; Nat. Hist. Mus., 2002–. Hon. Mem., Internat. Inst. for Dynamical Systems, 1991. FRSA 1997; FLS 1998. Hon. DSc Kent, 2004. Jubileum Award, Chalmers Univ., Sweden, 1991; Minerva Prize, FZ Jülich, Germany, 1992; Masaryk Gold Medal, Univ. of Brno, 2005. *Publications:* Advanced Ecological Theory, 1999; Gulf of Guinea Large Marine Ecosystem, 2002; papers on math. biology, marine sci. informatics and governance. *Recreations:* sailing, diving, ski-ing, climbing. *Address:* 10 The Coach House, Compton Verney, Warwick CV35 9HJ.

McGLASHAN, John Reid Curtis, CBE 1974; HM Diplomatic Service, retired 1979; *b* 12 Dec. 1921; *s* of late John Adamson McGlashan and Emma Rose May McGlashan; *m* 1947, Dilys Bagnall (*née* Buxton Knight); one *s* two *d*. *Educ:* Fettes; Christ Church, Oxford (Rugger Blue, 1945). RAF (Bomber Command), 1940–45 (POW, 1941–45). Entered Foreign Service, 1953; Baghdad, 1955; Tripoli, 1963; Madrid, 1968; Counsellor, FCO, 1970–79. *Recreations:* gardening, reading. *Address:* Allendale, Selsey Bill, West Sussex PO20 9DB.

MacGLASHAN, Maureen Elizabeth, CMG 1997; HM Diplomatic Service, retired; Ambassador to the Holy See, 1995–98; *b* 7 Jan. 1938; *d* of Kenneth and Elizabeth MacGlashan. *Educ:* Luton High Sch.; Girton Coll., Cambridge (MA, LLM). Joined FO, 1961; 2nd Sec., Tel Aviv, 1964–67; FCO, 1967–72; Head of Chancery, East Berlin, 1973–75; UK Representation to EEC, 1975–77; seconded to Home Civil Service, 1977–82; Counsellor, Bucharest, 1982–86; Asst Dir, Res. Centre for Internat. Law, and bye-Fellow, Girton Coll., Cambridge Univ., 1986–90; Counsellor, Consul-Gen. and Dep. Head of Mission, Belgrade, 1990; Head, Western European Dept, FCO, 1991–92; on secondment to CSSB, 1992–95. Pres., Soc. of Indexers, 2002–05. Ed., The Indexer, 2005–. *Publications:* (trans.) Weil, Maritime Delimitation, 1989; Consolidated Index and Tables to the International Law Reports, vols 1–125, 2004. *Clubs:* Royal Over-Seas League, University Women's.

McGONIGAL, His Honour Christopher Ian; North Eastern Circuit Mercantile Judge, 1997–2003; a Deputy High Court Judge, 2003–05; *b* 10 Nov. 1937; *s* of Harold Alfred Kelly McGonigal and Cora McGonigal (*née* Bentley); *m* 1961, Sara Ann Sander; three *s* one *d*. *Educ:* Ampleforth Coll., York; Corpus Christi Coll., Oxford (MA). Coward Chance: articled clerk, 1963–65; Asst Solicitor, 1965–68; Sen. Litigation Partner, 1969–79, 1983–87; Sen. Resident Partner, Dubai, Sharjah, Bahrain and Jeddah offices, 1979–83; Clifford Chance: Jt Sen. Litigation Partner, 1987–95; Sen. Partner, Contentious Business Area, 1995–97. Asst Recorder, 1990–95; Recorder, 1995–97. *Recreations:* gardening, opera, local history. *Address:* Saltbarn, Playden, Rye, E Sussex TN31 7PH.

McGOUGAN, Donald; Director of Finance, City of Edinburgh Council, since 1995; *b* 26 Dec. 1950; *s* of Louis and Sidney McGougan; *m* 1991, Mandy Dodgson; one *s* one *d*. *Educ:* Hermitage Acad., Helensburgh. CPFA 1976. Trainee Accountant, Midlothian CC, 1971–75; Professional Asst, City of Edinburgh DC, 1975–77; Falkirk District Council: Sen. Accountant, 1977–79; Principal Asst, 1979–81; Depute Dir of Finance, 1981–87; City of Edinburgh District Council: Depute Dir of Finance, 1987–95; acting Dir of Finance, 1995–96. *Recreations:* family, golf, football. *Address:* (office) Waverley Court, 4 East Market Street, Edinburgh EH8 8BG. *T:* (0131) 469 3005.

McGOUGH, Rt Rev. David; Auxiliary Bishop of Birmingham, (RC), and Titular Bishop of Cunavia, since 2006; *b* 20 Nov. 1944; *s* of Clement and Ethel McGough. *Educ:* Cotton Coll., N Staffs; Oscott Coll., Birmingham; Ven. English Coll., Rome; Gregorian Univ., Rome (STL 1969); Pontifical Biblical Inst., Rome (LSS 1977). Ordained priest, 1970; Lectr in Biblical Studies, Oscott Coll., Birmingham, 1975–90; Parish Priest: Christ the King, Birmingham, 1986–90; Our Lady & All Saints, Stourbridge, 1990–2006; Canon of Chapter, St Chad's Cathedral, Birmingham, 2002–. Vis. Lectr, Maryvale Inst., Birmingham, 1990–2007. *Recreations:* walking, cricket. *Address:* The Rocks, 106 Draycott Road, Tean, Stoke-on-Trent ST10 4JF. *T:* (01538) 722433.

McGOUGH, Roger, CBE 2004 (OBE 1997); FRSL; poet; *b* 9 Nov. 1937; *s* of Roger Francis and Mary Agnes McGough; *m* 1st, 1970 (marr. diss. 1980); two *s*; 2nd, 1986, Hilary Clough; one *s* one *d*. *Educ:* St Mary's Coll., Crosby, Liverpool; Hull Univ. (BA, Grad. Cert. Ed.). Fellow of Poetry, Univ. of Loughborough, 1973–75. Mem. Exec. Council, Poetry Soc., 1989–. Hon. Prof., Thames Valley Univ., 1993; Hon. Fellow, John Moores Univ., 1999. FRSL 2005. Hon. MA Nene Coll., 1998; Hon. DLitt: Hull, 2004; Roehampton, 2006; Liverpool, 2006. *Television:* Kurt, Mungo, BP and Me (BAFTA Award), 1984. Lyrics for Wind in the Willows, Broadway, 1985–86; The Elements (RTS Award), 1993. *Publications:* Watchwords, 1969; After The Merrymaking, 1971; Out of Sequence, 1972; Gig, 1972; Sporting Relations, 1974; In The Glassroom, 1976; Summer with Monika, 1978; Holiday on Death Row, 1979; Unlucky For Some, 1981; Waving at Trains, 1982; Melting into the Foreground, 1986; Selected Poems 1967–1987, 1989; You at the Back, 1991; Defying Gravity, 1992; The Spotted Unicorn, 1998; The Way Things Are, 1999; Everyday Eclipses, 2002; Collected Poems, 2003; Said and Done (autobiog.), 2005; Selected Poems, 2006; *children's books:* Mr Noselighter, 1977; The Great Smile Robbery, 1982; Sky in the Pie, 1983; The Stowaways, 1986; Noah's Ark, 1986; Nailing the Shadow, 1987; An Imaginary Menagerie, 1988; Helen Highwater, 1989; Counting by Numbers, 1989; Pillow Talk, 1990; The Lighthouse That Ran Away, 1991; My Dad's a Fire-eater, 1992; Another Custard Pie, 1993; Lucky, 1993; Stinkers Ahoy!, 1995; The Magic Fountain, 1995; The Kite and Caitlin, 1996; Bad, Bad Cats, 1997; Until I Met Dudley, 1997; Good Enough to Eat, 2002; Moonthief, 2002; What on Earth?; Dotty Inventions, 2002; The Bee's Knees, 2003; All the Best, 2003; (with Brian Patten) The Monsters' Guide to Choosing a Pet, 2004; Slapstick, 2008; contributed to: Penguin Modern Poets, No 10, Mersey Sound, 1967, rev. edn 1983; Oxford Book of 20th Century Verse, 1973; The Norton Anthology of Modern Poetry, 1973; Penguin Modern Poets, No 4 (new series), 1995; edited: Strictly Private, 1981; Kingfisher Book of Comic Verse, 1986; The Kingfisher Book of Poems about Love, 1997; The Ring of Words (anthology), 1998; Wicked Poems, 2002; Sensational, 2004; You Have Been Warned, 2008. *Address:* c/o United Agents, 12–26 Lexington Street, W1F 0LE. *T:* (020) 3214 0800. *Club:* Chelsea Arts (Chm., 1984–86; Trustee, 1992–).

McGOVERN, George Stanley; United States Senator, 1963–81; US Permanent Representative to United Nations Food and Agriculture Organisation, 1998–2001; United Nations Global Ambassador on Hunger, since 2001; *b* Avon, S Dakota, 19 July 1922; *s* of Rev. Joseph C. McGovern and Francis (*née* McLean); *m* 1943, Eleanor Faye Stegeberg (*d* 2007); one *s* three *d* (and one *d* decd). *Educ:* Dakota Wesleyan Univ. (BA); Northwestern Univ. (MA, PhD). Served World War II, USAAF (DFC). Prof. of History and Govt, Dakota Wesleyan Univ., 1950–53. Exec. Sec., S Dakota Democratic Party, 1953–56; Mem., 1st Dist, S Dakota, US House of Reps, 1957–61; Dir, Food for Peace Programme, 1961–62; Senator from South Dakota, 1963–81. Democratic nominee for US President, 1972. Visiting Professor: Columbia Univ., 1977; Univ. of Pa, 1978; Northwestern Univ., 1981; Univ. of New Orleans, 1982; University Coll., Dublin, 1982; Duke Univ., 1985; Univ. of Munich, 1987. Mem., Amer. Hist. Assoc. *Publications:* The Colorado Coal Strike 1913–14, 1953; War Against Want, 1964; Agricultural Thought in the Twentieth Century, 1967; A Time of War, A Time of Peace, 1968; (with Leonard F. Guttridge) The Great Coalfield War, 1972; An American Journey, 1974; Grassroots, an Autobiography, 1978; Terry: my daughter's life-and-death struggle with alcoholism, 1996; The Third Freedom: ending hunger in our time, 2001; The Essential America, 2004.

McGOVERN, James; MP (Lab) Dundee West, since 2005; *b* 17 Nov. 1956; *s* of Thomas McGovern and Alice McGovern; *m* 1991, Norma Ward. *Educ:* Lawside RC Acad., Dundee. Apprentice glazier, 1973–77, glazier, 1977–87, Solaglas; glazier, Dundee DC, 1987–97; trade union organiser, GMB, 1997–2005. Mem., Tayside Regl Council, 1994–96. Chm., Dundee E Labour Party, 1999–2001. *Recreations:* fitness club, watching football (Celtic FC). *Address:* House of Commons, SW1A 0AA. *T:* (020) 7219 4938; *e-mail:* mcgovernj@parliament.uk.

McGOVERN, Jimmy; screenwriter; *b* Liverpool, 1949. Writer for television dramas and series: Brookside, 1983–89; Cracker, 1993, 1994, 1995, 2006; Heart and Minds, 1995; Hillsborough, 1996; The Lakes, 1997, 1999; Dockers, 1999; Sunday, 2002; Gunpowder, Treason and Plot, 2004; (also prod.) The Street, 2006, 2007; films: Priest, 1994; Go Now, 1995; Heart, 1999; Liam, 2001; musical stage show, King Cotton, Lowry, 2007. *Address:* c/o The Agency, 24 Pottery Lane, Holland Park, W11 4LZ.

McGOWAN, family name of **Baron McGowan**.

McGOWAN, 4th Baron 1937; **Harry John Charles McGowan;** *b* 23 June 1971; *o s* of 3rd Baron McGowan and Lady Gillian Angela Pepys, *d* of 7th Earl of Cottenham; *S* father, 2003; *m* 2001, Emma, *d* of Duncan Hattersley Smith; four *d. Educ:* Harrow. *Heir: uncle* Hon. Dominic James Wilson McGowan [*b* 26 Nov. 1951; *m* Brigitta Papadimitriou].

McGOWAN, Alan Patrick, PhD; Archivist, Royal Naval College, Greenwich, 1989–98; Curator Emeritus, National Maritime Museum, since 1989 (Chief Curator, 1986–88; Callender Curator, 1989–91); *b* 16 Nov. 1928; *s* of Hugh McGowan and Alice Chilton; *m* 1958, Betty Eileen, *e d* of Mr and Mrs F. L. MacDougall, Ontario; three *s. Educ:* Spring Grove Grammar Sch.; Borough Road Coll.; Univ. of Western Ontario (BA, MA); Univ. of London (PhD). Served RASC (Air Freight), 1947–49. Asst Master (History), 1953–63; Lectr, Univ. of Western Ont Summer Sch., 1964; Canada Council Fellow, 1964–66; Asst Keeper, 1967–71, Keeper, 1980, Head, 1971–86, Dept of Ships, National Maritime Museum. Associate Prof. of History, Univ. of Western Ont Summer Sch., 1977. Member: Council, Navy Records Soc., 1968–; Adv. Council on Export of Works of Art, 1972–88; Victory Adv. Technical Cttee, 1974–2005 (Chm., 1983–2005); Mary Rose Adv. Cttee, 1974–78; Ships Cttee, Maritime Trust, 1977–88; Council, Soc. for Nautical Res., 1981–; Cttee, Falkland Islands Foundn, 1981–83. Trustee, HMS Warrior (1860), 2005–. Associate RINA, 1980–88. Liveryman, Co. of Shipwrights, 1984–2003. FSA 2005. *Publications:* (ed) Jacobean Commissions of Enquiry, 1608 and 1618, vol. 113 of Navy Records Society, 1971; Royal Yachts, 1975; (with J. Fabb) The Victorian and Edwardian Navy in Photographs, 1976; (ed and prefaced) Steel's Naval Architecture, 1976; Sailor, 1977; (ed and prefaced) Steel's Rigging and Seamanship, 1978; The Century before Steam, 1980; Tiller and Whipstaff, 1981; HMS Victory 1758–1998: the career and restoration of an icon, 1999; articles in jls of history and in encyclopaedia. *Recreations:* golf, reading, music. *Address:* c/o National Maritime Museum, Greenwich, SE10 9NF.

MACGOWAN, Christopher John, OBE 2008; Chief Executive, Society of Motor Manufacturers and Traders, 1999–2007; *b* 26 April 1947; *s* of Rev. John Macgowan and Dorothy Macgowan; *m* 1st, 1968, Victoria Lindey (*d* 1989); two *d*; 2nd, 1995, Amanda Fuller (*d* 2003). *Educ:* Orwell Park; Marlborough Coll. Export Rep. (Canada), British Leyland, 1965–73; PR Manager, Massey-Ferguson, 1973–90; Sales Dir, Ransomes, 1990–94; Chief Exec., Retail Motor Ind. Fedn, 1994–99. Freeman, City of London, 1997. *Recreations:* information technology, National Hunt racing. *Club:* Royal Automobile.

McGOWAN, Prof. David Alexander, PhD; Professor of Oral Surgery, University of Glasgow, 1977–99, now Emeritus; Hon. Consultant in Oral Surgery, Greater Glasgow Health Board, 1977–99; *b* 18 June 1939; *s* of George McGowan, MBE, and Annie, (Nan), Hall McGowan (*née* Macormac); *m* 1968, Margaret Vera Macauley; one *s* two *d. Educ:* Portadown Coll.; QUB (BDS 1961; MDS 1970); London Hosp. Med. Coll., London Univ. (PhD). FDSRCS 1964; FFDRCSI 1966; FDSRCPSGlas 1978; FDSRCSE 1999. Oral Surgery trng, Royal Victoria Hosp., Belfast and Aberdeen Royal Infirmary, 1961–67; Lectr in Dental Surgery, QUB, 1968; Department of Oral and Maxillo-Facial Surgery, London Hospital Medical College: Lectr, 1968–70; Sen. Lectr, 1970–77; Sen. Tutor, 1970–73; Consultant, 1971–77; Dep. Head, 1973–77. Chm., Nat. Dental Adv. Cttee, Scotland, 1995–99. Post-grad. Advr in Dentistry for W Scotland, 1977–90; Dean: Dental Faculty, RCPSG, 1989–92; Glasgow Univ. Dental Sch., 1990–95; Senate Assessor, Court, Univ. of Glasgow, 1995–99; Mem., GDC, 1989–99 (Dep. Chm., Exec., 1995–99). Univ. Fellow, Univ. of Western Australia, 1986; Caldwell Lectr, Univ. of Glasgow, 1993. Gold Medal, Bulgarian Acad. of Medicine, 1992; University Medal: Malta, 1999; Helsinki, 2000. *Publications:* (jtly) Outline of Oral Surgery, part 1, 1985; An Atlas of Minor Oral Surgery, 1989 (trans. Italian 1991, trans. French 1993), 2nd edn 1999; (jtly) The Maxillary Sinus and its Dental Implications, 1993;(jtly) Outline of Oral Surgery, parts 1 and 2, 1998; numerous articles in jls. *Recreations:* sailing, photography, dog-walking, reading novels, listening to music. *Address:* Rhu Lodge, Rhu, Helensburgh G84 8NF. *T:* (home) (01436) 821315.

McGOWAN, Ian Duncan; Librarian, National Library of Scotland, 1990–2002; *b* 19 Sept. 1945; *s* of Alexander McGowan and Dora (*née* Sharp); *m* 1971, Elizabeth Ann Weir; two *d. Educ:* Liverpool Inst.; Exeter Coll., Oxford (BA 1st Cl. Hons Russian Lang. and Lit., 1967); Sch. of Slavonic and E European Studies, Univ. of London. National Library of Scotland: Asst Keeper, 1971–78; Keeper (Catalogues and Automation), 1978–88; Sec. of the Library, 1988–90. Chm., Nat. Preservation Adv. Cttee, 1994–96; Pres., Scottish Library Assoc., 1998 (Vice-Pres., 1996–97); Vice-Pres., Edinburgh Bibliographical Soc., 2004–. Editor, Alexandria: jl of nat. and internat. liby and inf. issues, 2003–. Chm., Britain-Russia Centre, Scotland, 1999–2002; Hon. Treas., Scotland-Russia Forum, 2003–. Chm., 2006–08, Treas., 2008–, Scottish Working People's History Trust. Founding Fellow, Inst. of Contemporary Scotland, 2000. FRSA 1999. IFLA Medal, 2002. *Recreations:* books, gardens. *Address:* 23 Blackford Road, Edinburgh EH9 2DT. *T:* (0131) 667 2432. *Club:* New (Edinburgh).

McGOWAN, John; Sheriff in Ayr, since 2000; *b* 15 Jan. 1944; *s* of Arthur McGowan and Bridget McCluskey; *m* 1966, Elise Smith; two *s. Educ:* St Joseph's Acad., Kilmarnock; Glasgow Univ. (LLB). Admitted Solicitor, 1967; Temp. Sheriff, 1986–93; Sheriff in Glasgow, 1993–2000. Chm., DHSS Appeal Tribunal, 1980–86. Mem. Council, Law Soc. of Scotland, 1982–85. *Recreations:* golf, tennis, curling, theatre. *Address:* 20 Auchendoon Crescent, Ayr KA7 4AS. *T:* (01292) 260139.

McGOWAN, Prof. Margaret Mary, (Mrs Sydney Anglo), CBE 1998; PhD; FBA 1993; Professor of French, 1974–97, Senior Pro-Vice-Chancellor, 1992–97, Research Professor, since 1997, University of Sussex; *b* 21 Dec. 1931; *d* of George McGowan and Elizabeth (*née* McGrail); *m* 1964, Prof. Sydney Anglo, *qv. Educ:* Stamford High Sch.; Univ. of Reading (BA, PhD). Lecturer: Univ. of Strasbourg, 1955–57; Univ. of Glasgow, 1957–64; University of Sussex: Lectr, 1964–68; Reader, 1968–74; Dean, Sch. of European Studies, 1977–80; Pro-Vice-Chancellor (Arts and Social Studies), 1981–86. Mem. Bd, European Strategic Mgt Unit, 1995–2003. Vice-Pres., British Acad., 1996–98. Chm., Review of Warburg Inst., Univ. of London, 2006–07. Vice-Chm. Bd, British Inst. in Paris, 1978–99; Gov., Ardingly Coll., 1994–2004. FRSA 1997. Freeman, City of Tours, 1986. Hon. DLitt Sussex, 1999. *Publications:* L'Art du Ballet de Cour, 1963; Montaigne's Deceits, 1974; Ideal Forms in the Age of Ronsard, 1985; Louis XIII's Court Ballets, 1989; Moy qui me voy: studies of the self, 1990; The Vision of Rome in Late Renaissance France, 2000. *Recreations:* music, cooking, tennis. *Address:* 59 Green Ridge, Withdean, Brighton BN1 5LU.

McGOWAN, Maura Patricia; QC 2001; a Recorder, since 1996; *b* 27 Jan. 1957; *d* of Matthew Vincent McGowan and Bridget McGowan (*née* Helebert). *Educ:* Virgo Fidelis Convent, London; St Mary's Coll., Leeds; Manchester Univ. (LLB Hons). Called to the Bar, Middle Temple, 1980, Bencher, 2005; in practice, specialising in criminal law. *Recreations:* cricket, fishing, opera, theatre, reading. *Address:* 2 Bedford Row, WC1R 4BU. *T:* (020) 7440 8888.

McGOWAN, Michael; *b* 19 May 1940; *m*; two *s* one *d. Educ:* Leicester University. Formerly: lecturer; BBC journalist; co-operative employment development officer, Kirklees Council, to 1984. MEP (Lab) Leeds, 1984–99.

McGOWAN, Neal Lowson; Rector, Larbert High School, Falkirk, since 2004; *b* 12 May 1963; *s* of late John McGowan and Elizabeth (*née* Taylor). *Educ:* Moray House Coll. of Educn, Edinburgh (Dip Tech. Ed); Univ. of Edinburgh (MEd). Teacher, Wester Hailes Educn Centre, 1985–88; Asst Principal Teacher, Lasswade High Sch., 1988–90; Principal Teacher, 1990–93, Asst Head Teacher, 1993–96, Musselburgh Grammar Sch.; Depute Rector, Selkirk High Sch., 1996–97; Head Teacher, Gracemount High Sch., Edinburgh, 1997–2002; Rector, Banchory Acad., Aberdeenshire, 2002–04. Sec. to Ministerial Discipline Task Gp, 2001. *Publications:* Standard Grade Technological Studies Revision Notes, 1990; Higher Grade Technological Studies Revision Notes, 1991; Practice Questions for Higher Grade Technological Studies, 1993. *Recreations:* golf, travel, eating out, keep fit. *Address:* Larbert High School, Carrongrange Avenue, Stenhousemuir, Larbert FK5 3BL. *T:* (01324) 554233, *Fax:* (01324) 503551; *e-mail:* neal.mcgowan@falkirk.gov.uk.

McGRADY, Edward Kevin; MP (SDLP) Down South, since 1987; *b* 3 June 1935; *y s* of late Michael McGrady and late Lilian Leatham; *m* 1959, Patricia, *d* of Wm Swail and Margaret Breen; two *s* one *d. Educ:* St Patrick's High Sch., Downpatrick. ACA 1957, FCA 1962. Former Partner, M. B. McGrady & Co., chartered accountants and insurance brokers. Councillor, Downpatrick UDC, 1961–89; Chm. of UDC, 1964–73; Vice-Chm., Down District Council, 1973, 1975–76, 1977, Chm. 1974, 1976, 1978, 1981, 1982. 1st Chm. of SDLP, 1971–73; 1st Chm. of SDLP Assembly Party; Chief Whip, SDLP, 1979–; SDLP Parly Chief Whip, 1987–; SDLP Party Assembly Chief Whip, 1998–. Member (SDLP): S Down: NI Assembly, 1973–75 (Head of Office of Exec. Planning and Co-ordination (Minister for Co-ordination, Jan.–May 1974)); NI Constitutional Convention, 1975–76; NI Assembly, 1982–86; Down S, NI Assembly, 1998–2003. Contested (SDLP) Down S, gen. elections, 1979, 1983 and 1986. Mem., NI Affairs Cttee, H of C, 1994–2005. *Recreations:* golf, badminton, choral work. *Address:* (constituency office) 32 Saul Street, Downpatrick, Co. Down BT30 6NQ. *T:* (028) 4461 2882, *Fax:* (028) 4461 9574; *e-mail:* e.mcgrady@sdlp.ie; House of Commons, SW1A 0AA. *T:* (020) 7219 4481.

McGRAIL, Prof. Seán Francis, FSA; Visiting Professor of Maritime Archaeology, University of Southampton, since 1991; Chief Archaeologist, National Maritime Museum, 1976–86; *b* 5 May 1928; *m* 1955, Ursula Anne Yates, BA; one *s* three *d. Educ:* Royal Navy (Master Mariner); Univ. of Bristol (BA); Univ. of London (PhD); Campion Hall, Oxford (MA 1987); DSc Oxon 1989. FSA 1981; MIFA 1983. Served RN, 1946–68: Seaman Officer; awarded Wings (pilot), 1952; qualified as Air Warfare Instr, 1954, as Instrument Rating Examnr, 1958; comd 849 Sqdn, FAA, 1962–63. Undergrad., Univ. of Bristol, 1968–71 (Harry Crook Scholar, 1969–71); Postgrad. Student, Inst. of Archaeology, London, 1972–73; Postgrad. Student (pt-time), UCL, 1973–78; National Maritime Museum, 1972–86, Hd of Archaeol Res. Centre, 1976–86. Leverhulme Res. Fellow, 1991–94; Visiting Professor: of Maritime Archæology, Oxford Univ., 1986–93; Danish Nat. Museum's Centre for Maritime Archaeology, Roskilde, 1994; Univ. of Haifa, 1995. Mem., Adv. Cttee on Historic Wrecks, Dept. of Nat. Heritage (formerly DoE), 1974–98. Mem., Wardour Catholic Cemetery Trust, 1976– (Treas., 1999–); Vice-Chm., Trust for Preservation of Oxford Coll. Barges, 1987–95. Prehistoric and medieval excavations, Norway, Denmark, Orkney, Ireland and Britain, 1974–93; maritime ethnographic fieldwork, Bangladesh and east coast of India, 1994–2001. Mem. Editl Bd, Mary Rose Trust, 1998–2002, 2004–. *Publications:* Building and Trials of a Replica of an Ancient Boat, 1974; Logboats of England and Wales, 1978; Rafts, Boats and Ships, 1981; Ancient Boats, 1983; Ancient Boats of North West Europe, 1987, 2nd edn 1998; Medieval Boat and Ship Timbers from Dublin, 1993; Studies in Maritime Archaeology, 1997; Boats of the World, 2001, 2nd edn 2004; Boats of South Asia, 2003; (with N. Nayling) Barland's Farm Romano-Celtic Boat, 2004; Ancient Boats and Ships, 2006; *edited:* Sources and Techniques in Boat Archaeology, 1977; Medieval Ships and Harbours, 1979; Paul Johnstone, Seacraft of Prehistory, 1980, 2nd edn 1988; Brigg 'raft' and her Prehistoric Environment, 1981; Woodworking Techniques before 1500, 1982; Aspects of Maritime Archaeology and Ethnography, 1984; (with J. Coates) Greek Trireme of 5th Century BC, 1984; (with E. Kentley) Sewn Plank Boats, 1985; Maritime Celts, Saxons and Frisians, 1990; articles in archaeological and maritime jls. *Recreations:* strategic gardening, real ale specialist. *Address:* Institute of Archaeology, 36 Beaumont Street, Oxford OX1 2PG. *T:* (01865) 278240.

McGRATH, Prof. Alister Edgar, DD; Professor of Theology, Ministry and Education, King's College London, since 2008; *b* 23 Jan. 1953; *s* of Edgar P. McGrath and Annie J. M. McGrath (*née* McBride); *m* 1980, Joanna Ruth Collicutt; one *s* one *d. Educ:* Wadham Coll., Oxford (BA 1975); Linacre Coll., Oxford; Merton Coll., Oxford (MA, DPhil 1978; BD 1983; DD 2001); St John's Coll., Cambridge. Ordained deacon, 1980, priest, 1981; Curate, St Leonard's Ch, Wollaton, Nottingham, 1980–83; Lectr, 1983–95, Principal, 1995–2004, Wycliffe Hall, Oxford; Titular Prof. of Historical Theology, 1999–2008, Dir, Centre for Evangelism and Apologetics, subseq. Oxford Centre for Christian Apologetics, 2004–06, Univ. of Oxford; Sen. Res. Fellow, Harris Manchester Coll., Oxford, 2006–08. FRSA 2005. Hon. DD Virginia Theol Seminary, 1996. *Publications:* Explaining Your Faith… Without Losing Your Friends, 1988; Justification by Faith, 1988; Justitia Dei: history of the Christian doctrine of justification, Vol. I 1989, Vol. II 1993; Doubt: handling it honestly, 1990; Luther's Theology of the Cross: Martin Luther's theological breakthrough, 1990; Cloud of Witnesses: ten great Christian thinkers, 1990; Genesis of Doctrine, 1990; Life of John Calvin: a study in the shaping of Western culture, 1990; Affirming Your Faith: exploring the Apostles' Creed, 1991; Bridge Building: creative Christian apologetics, 1992; Intellectual Origins of the European Reformation, 1992; Making Sense of the Cross, 1992; Reformation Thought: an introduction, 1992; Roots that Refresh, 1992; Suffering, 1992; (with J. McGrath) Dilemma of Self Esteem: the Cross and Christian confidence, 1992; (ed) Blackwell Encyclopedia of Modern Christian Thought, 1993; Christian Theology: an introduction, 1993; Making of Modern German Christology: from the Enlightenment to Pannenberg, 1993; Renewal of Anglicanism, 1993; Jesus: who He is and why He matters, 1994; Evangelicalism and the Future of Christianity, 1994; A Passion for Truth, 1996; (ed jtly) Doing Theology for the People of God, 1996; J. I. Packer: a biography, 1997; The Foundations of Dialogue in Science and

Religion, 1998; Historical Theology: an introduction to the history of Christian thought, 1998; T. F. Torrance: an intellectual biography, 1999; Theology for Amateurs, 2000; The Unknown God: searching for spiritual fulfilment, 2000; The Journey: a pilgrim in the lands of the spirit, 2000; (ed) Christian Literature: an anthology, 2000; In the Beginning: the story of the King James Bible, 2001; Knowing Christ, 2001; The Future of Christianity, 2001; A Scientific Theology: vol. 1, Nature, 2001, vol. 2, Reality, 2002, vol. 3, Theory, 2003; Glimpsing the Face of God, 2002; A Brief History of Heaven, 2002; The Re-enchantment of Nature, 2002; The Twilight of Atheism, 2004; Dawkins' God, 2004; Theology—The Basics, 2004; Creation, 2005; Incarnation, 2005; The Science of God: an introduction to scientific theology, 2005; The Order of Things: explorations in scientific theology, 2006; (with J. McGrath) The Dawkins' Delusion, 2007; Christianity's Dangerous Idea: the Protestant revolution, a history from the sixteenth century to the twenty-first, 2007; Resurrection, 2008; The Open Secret: a new vision for natural theology, 2008; contrib. articles to learned jls. *Recreations:* walking, Australian wines. *Address:* Department of Education and Professional Studies, King's College London, Franklin-Wilkins Building, Waterloo Road, SE1 9NH. *T:* (020) 7848 3183.

McGRATH, Sir Brian (Henry), GCVO 2001 (KCVO 1993; CVO 1988); MW; an Extra Equerry to the Duke of Edinburgh, since 1996 (Assistant Private Secretary, 1982; Private Secretary, 1982–92; Treasurer, 1984–2000); *b* 27 Oct. 1925; *s* of William Henry and Hermione Gioja McGrath; *m* 1959, Elizabeth Joan Bruce (*née* Gregson-Ellis) (*d* 1977); two *s*, and one step *d. Educ:* Eton College. Served War of 1939–45, Irish Guards, 1943–46, Lieut. Cannon Brewery Co., 1946–48; Victoria Wine Co.: joined, 1948; Dir, 1949; Chm., 1960–82; Dir, 1960, Chm., 1975–82, Grants of St James's Ltd; Dir, Allied Breweries Ltd (subseq. Allied-Lyons plc), 1970–82; Chm., Broad Street Securities, 1983–92. Younger Brother of Trinity House, 1993. MW 1956. *Recreations:* golf, gardening, shooting. *Address:* Flat 3, 9 Cheyne Gardens, SW3 5QU. *Clubs:* Boodle's, White's.

McGRATH, Prof. Elizabeth, FBA 1998; Curator, Photographic Collection, since 1991, and Professor of the History of Art, since 2000, Warburg Institute, University of London; *b* 20 March 1945; *d* of Thomas McGrath and Emilie McGrath (*née* Melvin). *Educ:* St Joseph's High Sch., Kilmarnock; Glasgow Univ. (MA 1967); PhD London 1971. Photographic Collection, Warburg Inst., London Univ., 1970–; Jt Ed., Jl of Warburg and Courtauld Insts, 1977–. Durning Lawrence Lectr, UCL, 1989; Slade Prof. of Fine Art, Oxford Univ., 1990. Mem., Flemish Acad. for Arts and Scis, 2003. Hans Reimer Prize, Hamburg Univ., 1996; Mitchell Prize for the History of Art, 1998; Eugène Baie Prize for Flemish Cultural History, Province of Antwerp. *Publications:* Rubens: Subjects from History, vol. XIII in *Corpus Rubenianum*, 1997; contrib. to Jl of Warburg and Courtauld Insts, Burlington Mag., etc. *Address:* Warburg Institute, University of London, Woburn Square, WC1H 0AB. *T:* (020) 7862 8949.

McGRATH, Ian; *see* McGrath, J. C.

McGRATH, James Aloysius; Hotspur, Racing Correspondent of the Daily Telegraph, since 1991; BBC television commentator; *b* 13 June 1952; *s* of Brian James McGrath and Kathleen May McGrath; *m* 1977, Anita Lee; two *s* two *d. Educ:* Xavier Coll., Melbourne. Cadet racing writer, The Australian, 1972–73; Racing Corresp., China Mail (Hong Kong), 1973–74; Chief Racing Writer, South China Morning Post (Hong Kong), 1975–86; writer, Racing Post, 1986–90; Racing Corresp., Sunday Telegraph, 1988–95. Racing Commentator: BBC, 1992– (Sen. Racing Commentator, 1997–); Satellite Information Services, 1993–97. Clive Graham Award for Racing Journalist of the Year, Horserace Writers' Assoc., 1992; Sports Commentator of the Year, RTS, 2001. *Recreations:* golf, ski-ing, watching cricket. *Address:* The Travers, Chobham, Woking, Surrey GU24 8SZ. *T:* (01276) 857155. *Clubs:* Carbine (founding Pres., 1997–); Hong Kong Jockey, Hong Kong Golf, Hong Kong Football (Hong Kong).

McGRATH, John Brian; Chairman, The Boots Co. plc, 2000–03 (non-executive Director, 1998–2003); *b* 20 June 1938; *m* 1964, Sandy Watson; one *s* one *d. Educ:* Brunel Univ. (BSc 1st Cl. Hons Applied Physics). UKAEA, 1962–65; NCB, 1965–67; Ford Motor Co., 1967–71; Jaguar Cars, 1971–75; Stone-Platt, 1976–82; Man. Dir, Construction and Mining Div. and Chief Exec., Compair, 1982–85; joined Grand Metropolitan PLC, 1985: Gp Dir, Watney Mann & Truman Brewers Ltd, 1985; Chm. and Man. Dir, Grand Metropolitan Brewing, 1986–88; Jt Man. Dir, Internat. Distillers & Vintners, 1988–91; IDV Ltd: Man. Dir and Chief Operating Officer, 1991–92; Chief Exec., 1992–93; Chm. and Chief Exec., 1993–96; Group Chief Executive: Grand Metropolitan PLC, 1996–97; Diageo, 1997–2000. Non-executive Director: Carlton Communications plc, 2003–04; ITV plc, 2004–07. Chm., Scotch Whisky Assoc., 1995–2000. Chm., Cicely Saunders Foundn, 2002–. Mem. Council, Brunel Univ., 2004–. *Address:* Walnut Court, Marloes Road, W8 5UB.

McGRATH, Prof. John Christie, (Ian); pharmacologist and physiologist; Regius Professor of Physiology, University of Glasgow, since 1991; *b* 8 March 1949; *s* of John Christie McGrath and Margaret Gilmore Cochrane McGrath (*née* Murray); *m* 1970, Wilma Nicol (*d* 2007); one *s* one *d. Educ:* Cross Arthurlie Primary Sch.; John Neilson Instn; Univ. of Glasgow (BSc 1st class Hons 1970; PhD 1974). Wellcome Interdisciplinary Research Fellowship, Dept of Pharmacology and Univ. Dept of Anaesthesia, Glasgow Royal Infirmary, Univ. of Glasgow, 1973–75; Institute of Biomedical and Life Sciences (formerly Institute of Physiology), University of Glasgow: Lectr, 1975; Wellcome Trust Research Leave Fellowship, 1982; Sen. Lectr, Reader, Titular Prof., 1983–91; Hd, Dept of Physiol., 1991–94; Co-Dir, Clinical Res. Initiative, 1994–99; Hd, Div. of Neurosci. and Biomed. Systems, 1997–2004. Chm. Standing Cttee, Heads of UK Physiology Depts, 2000–. Chm., Physiolog. Soc., 2006–08 (Mem., 1978; Mem. Cttee, 1988–94; Mem. Council, 2004–; Vice-Chm., 2004–06); Mem. Council, Bioscis Fedn, 2007–. Member: British Pharmacol Soc. 1975 (Sandoz Prize, 1980); Internat. Soc. for Heart Research, 1989; Amer. Soc. for Pharmacology and Experimental Therapeutics, 1991; Amer. Physiol Soc., 1994. Mem., Labour Party. Member Editorial Board: British Jl of Pharmacology, 1985–91 (Sen. Editor 2001–07); Jl of Cardiovascular Pharmacology, 1988–; Pharmacological Reviews, 1990–98; Jl of Vascular Res., 1991–; Jl of Hypertension, 2006–. 1st Pfizer Award for Biology, 1983. *Publications:* contribs to learned jls in fields of pharmacology and physiology. *Recreations:* running, cycling, politics, travel. *Address:* Institute of Biomedical and Life Sciences, University of Glasgow, Glasgow G12 8QQ. *T:* (0141) 330 4483, *Fax:* (0141) 330 2923; *e-mail:* i.mcgrath@bio.gla.ac.uk.

McGRATH, Patrick; novelist, since 1979; *b* 7 Feb. 1950; *s* of Patrick G. McGrath and Helen McGrath (*née* O'Brien); *m* 1991, Maria Penelope Katharine Aitken, *qv*; one step *s. Educ:* City of Birmingham Coll. of Commerce; Univ. of London (external BA Hons 1971). Visiting Professor: Univ. of Texas, 2006; New Sch. of Social Research, NY, 2007. *Publications:* Blood and Water and Other Tales, 1987; The Grotesque, 1988; Spider, 1990; Dr Haggard's Disease, 1993; Asylum, 1996; Martha Peake, 2000; Port Mungo, 2004; Ghost Town: tales of Manhattan then and now, 2005; Trauma, 2008. *Address:* 145 Nassau Street, 6D, New York, NY 10038, USA. *T:* (212) 7661690; *e-mail:* ppatrickmcg@aol.com. *Club:* Groucho.

McGRATH, Stephen John, CPhys; Chief Executive, Meat Hygiene Service, Food Standards Agency, since 2007; *b* 24 Jan. 1954; *s* of late John Patrick McGrath and of Helena Mary McGrath; *m* 1977, Stephanie Doreen (*née* Powell); three *s. Educ:* Southampton Univ. (BSc Hons 1976, MSc 1977). CPhys, MInstP 1978. British Gas, 1978–96: Director: Business Gas, 1993–95; Gas Supplies and Transportation, 1995–96; Ops, 1996; Operations Director: AccuRead, 1996–2001; Serviceteam, 2001–02; Chief Operating Officer, Spark Response, 2002–03; Dir, Nat. Insurance Contribns Office, Bd of Inland Revenue, subseq. HMRC, 2003–06. MInstD 1997. *Recreations:* coastal sailing, campanology, motor bike. *Address:* Meat Hygiene Service, Foss House, Kings Pool, Peasholme Green, York YO1 7PR. *T:* (01904) 455501.

McGRATH, William Joseph; Founder and Chief Executive Officer, Greenfield Services Ltd, since 1996; Managing Director, British Gas Energy Centres, since 1999; *b* 30 Sept. 1940; *s* of William George McGrath and Wallis (*née* Reinwold); *m* 1963, Mary Teresa Bridget Galvin; two *d. Educ:* St John's RC Sch., Tamworth, Staffs; Open Univ. (BA Hons). With Cunard Steamship Co. Ltd, 1956–68; G. J. Keddie & Sons Ltd, 1968–75; Director: Asda Stores Ltd, 1975–81; Comet PLC, 1981–84; Founder and Chief Exec. Officer, Builders Mate, 1984–87; Dir, Wickes PLC, 1990–93 (Dep. Chm., 1993); Chief Exec. Officer, Pentos Gp, 1994–95; Chm. and CEO, British Home Doors, 2000–04 (non-exec. Dir, 1995–2000; non-exec. Chm., 1997–2000). Non-executive Chairman: Gasflair Ltd, 1999–2003; Hiatt Ltd, 2000–; Lease 360 plc, 2006–; non-executive Director: Cashbuild, South Africa, 1995–2002; Gainsborough Building Soc., 2000–02. MInstD 1984; MCIM 1989. FRSA 1994. Wine and Spirit Educn Trust (Cert., Higher Cert. Dist. and Dip.). Compagnon de Beaujolais, 1976. KSC 1962. *Recreations:* chess, walking, gardening. *Address:* Manor House, Gringley on the Hill, Notts DN10 4RG. *T:* (01777) 817716. *Club:* East India.

MacGREGOR, family name of **Baron MacGregor of Pulham Market**.

MacGREGOR OF PULHAM MARKET, Baron *cr* 2001 (Life Peer), of Pulham Market in the County of Norfolk; **John Roddick Russell MacGregor,** OBE 1971; PC 1985; *b* 14 Feb. 1937; *s* of late Dr. N. S. R. MacGregor; *m* 1962, Jean Mary Elizabeth Dungey; one *s* two *d. Educ:* Merchiston Castle Sch., Edinburgh; St Andrews Univ. (MA, 1st cl. Hons); King's Coll., London (LLB; FKC 1988). Univ. Administrator, 1961–62; Editorial Staff, New Society, 1962–63; Special Asst to Prime Minister, Sir Alec Douglas-Home, 1963–64; Conservative Research Dept, 1964–65; Head of Private Office of Rt Hon. Edward Heath, Leader of Opposition, 1965–68. MP (C) S Norfolk, Feb. 1974–2001. An Opposition Whip, 1977–79; a Lord Comr of HM Treasury, 1979–81; Parly Under-Sec. of State, DoI, 1981–83; Minister of State, MAFF, 1983–85; Chief Sec. to HM Treasury, 1985–87; Minister of Agriculture, Fisheries and Food, 1987–89; Sec. of State for Educn and Sci., 1989–90; Lord Pres. of the Council and Leader of H of C, 1990–92; Sec. of State for Transport, 1992–94. Hill Samuel & Co. Ltd, 1968–79 (Dir, 1973–79), Dep. Chm., 1994–96; Director: Associated British Foods, 1994–2007; Slough Estates, 1995–2006; UK Food and Agric. Adv. Bd, Rabobank Gp, 1995– (Jt Chm., 2006–07); Uniq (formerly Unigate), 1996–2005; London & Manchester Gp, 1997–98; Friends Provident, 1998–2007; European Supervisory Bd, DAF Trucks NV, 2000–. Chairman: Fedn of University Cons. and Unionist Assocs, 1959; Bow Group, 1963–64; 1st Pres., Conservative and Christian Democratic Youth Community, 1963–65; Vice-President: ACC, 1995–97; LGA, 1997–99. Mem., Cttee on Standards in Public Life, 1997–2003. Member, Council: KCL, 1996–2002; IOD, 1996–; Mem., 2002–, Chm., 2007–, Cathedral Council, Norwich Cathedral (High Steward, 2007–). Dep. Chm., GBA, then Assoc. of Governing Bodies of Independent Schs, 1998–2006. Chm., St Andrew's (Ecumenical) Trust, 2005–. Hon. LLD Westminster, 1995. *Publications:* contrib. The Conservative Opportunity; also pamphlets. *Recreations:* music, reading, travelling, gardening, conjuring (Member: Magic Circle, 1989; Inner Magic Circle, 2000). *Address:* House of Lords, SW1A 0PW.

McGREGOR, Prof. Alan Michael, MD; FRCP; Professor of Medicine, since 1986, Head of Department of Diabetes, Endocrinology and Internal Medicine, and Dean of Research, since 1996, King's College London School of Medicine (formerly King's College School of Medicine and Dentistry, subseq. Guy's, King's and St Thomas' School of Medicine, King's College London); *b* 3 Aug. 1948. *Educ:* Selwyn Coll., Cambridge (BA 1971; MB, BChir 1974; MA 1982; MD 1982). MRCP 1977, FRCP 1985. MRC Trng Fellow, Royal Victoria Infirmary, Newcastle upon Tyne, 1977–80; Lectr, 1980, Wellcome Sen. Res. Fellow, 1981–86, Dept of Medicine, Univ. of Wales Coll. of Medicine. Hon. Consultant Physician, KCH NHS Trust. Mem., MRC, 1995–2000 (Chm., Physiological Medicine and Infections Bd). FKC 1997; Founder FMedSci, 1998. *Publications:* (ed) Immunology of Endocrine Diseases, 1986; contrib. learned jls. *Address:* Department of Diabetes, Endocrinology and Internal Medicine, King's College London School of Medicine, Weston Education Centre, King's Denmark Hill, Cutcombe Road, SE5 9PJ.

MacGREGOR, Alastair Rankin; QC 1994; Deputy Chairman, Criminal Cases Review Commission, since 2006 (Commissioner, since 2004); *b* 23 Dec. 1951; *s* of Alexander MacGregor and Anna MacGregor (*née* Neil); *m* 1982, Rosemary Kerslake; one *s* one *d. Educ:* Glasgow Acad.; Edinburgh Univ.; New Coll., Oxford Univ. (MA). Called to the Bar, Lincoln's Inn, 1974. *Address:* Criminal Cases Review Commission, Alpha Tower, Queensway, Birmingham B1 1TT. *T:* (0121) 633 1800.

See also R. N. MacGregor.

McGREGOR, Rev. Alistair Gerald Crichton; QC (Scot.) 1982; WS; Minister, North Leith Parish Church, Edinburgh, 1987–2002; *b* 15 Oct. 1937; *s* of late James Reid McGregor, CB, CBE, MC, and Dorothy McGregor; *m* 1965, Margaret Lees or McGregor; two *s* one *d. Educ:* Charterhouse; Pembroke Coll., Oxford (BA (Hons) Jurisprudence); Edinburgh Univ. (LLB; BD). Intelligence Corps, 1956–58. Solicitor and WS, 1965–66; Advocate, 1967–82. Clerk to Court of Session Rules Council, 1972–75; Standing Junior Counsel to: SHHD, 1977–79; Scottish Develt Dept, 1979–82. Chm., Family Care (Scotland), 1983–88; Director: Apex (Scotland), 1988–98; Kirk Care Housing Assoc., 1994–97; Palcrafts (UK) Ltd, 2003–. Governor: Dean Orphanage Trust, 1998–; Loretto Sch., 2000–06. Gen. Trustee, Ch of Scotland, 2004–. Licensed, Church of Scotland, 1986. *Recreations:* squash, tennis. *Address:* 22 Primrose Bank Road, Edinburgh EH5 3JG. *T:* (0131) 551 2802.

McGREGOR, Hon. Alistair John; QC 1997; *b* 11 March 1950; *s* of Baron McGregor of Durris; *m* 1985, Charlotte Ann East; one *s* one *d. Educ:* Haberdashers' Aske's Sch., Elstree; Queen Mary Coll., London Univ. (LLB Hons). Called to the Bar, Middle Temple, 1974. *Recreations:* music, sport. *Address:* 11 King's Bench Walk, Temple, EC4Y 7EQ. *T:* (020) 7583 0610. *Club:* Garrick.

McGREGOR, Dr Angus; Regional Medical Officer, West Midlands Regional Health Authority, 1979–88; Visiting Professor, University of Keele, 1988–94; *b* 26 Dec. 1926; *s* of Dr William Hector Scott McGregor and Dr Olwen May Richards; *m* 1951, May Burke, BA; one *d. Educ:* Solihull Sch.; St John's Coll., Cambridge. MA, MD; FRCP; FFPH;

DPH. Junior hospital posts, 1950; Army service, RAMC, 1951–52; general practice, 1953; Asst MOH, Chester, 1954–56; Deputy Medical Officer of Health: Swindon, 1957–58; Hull, 1958–65; MOH and Port MO, Southampton, 1965–74; District Community Physician, East Dorset, 1974–79. Mem. Bd, FCM, RCP, 1982–88. FRSA 1986. *Publications:* (with T. Bunbury) Disciplining and Dismissing Doctors in the NHS, 1988; contrib. papers to medical journals. *Recreation:* piano. *Address:* (home) Withyholt, 26 Lyttelton Road, Droitwich Spa, Worcestershire WR9 7AA. *T:* (01905) 776077.

McGREGOR, Ewan Gordon; actor; *b* 31 March 1971; *s* of James and Carol McGregor; *m* 1995, Eve Mavrakis; three *d*. *Theatre:* What the Butler Saw, Salisbury Playhouse, 1992; Little Malcolm, Comedy, 1998–99; Guys and Dolls, Piccadilly, 2005; Othello, Donmar Warehouse, 2007; *films:* Family Style, Being Human, 1993; Shallow Grave, 1994; Trainspotting, Swimming with the Fishes, Emma, The Pillow Book, Brassed Off, 1996; The Serpent's Kiss, Blue Juice, A Life Less Ordinary, 1997; Nightwatch, Velvet Goldmine, Little Voice, Desserts, Anno Domini, 1998; Star Wars, Episode I: The Phantom Menace, Rogue Trader, Eye of the Beholder, Tube Tales (also dir.), 1999; Nora (co-producer, 2000); Moulin Rouge, 2001; Black Hawk Down, Star Wars, Episode II: Attack of the Clones, 2002; Young Adam, Down with Love, 2003; Big Fish, 2004; Star Wars, Episode III: Revenge of the Sith, The Island, 2005; Stay, Stormbreaker, Scenes of a Sexual Nature, 2006; Miss Potter, 2007; Deception, Cassandra's Dream, 2008; *television* includes: Lipstick on Your Collar, Scarlet and Black, 1993; Doggin' Around, 1994; Karaoke, 1996; Solid Geometry, 2002; Long Way Round (series), 2004; Long Way Down (series), 2007. Hon. DLitt Ulster, 2001. *Publication:* (with Charley Boorman) Long Way Round, 2004. *Recreation:* motor bikes. *Address:* c/o Lindy King, United Agents, 12–26 Lexington Street, W1F 0LE.

McGREGOR, Prof. Gordon Peter, DPhil; Professor of Education, University of Leeds, 1991–95, now Emeritus; *b* Aldershot, Hants, 13 June 1932; 2nd *s* of William A. K. McGregor and Mary A. McGregor (*née* O'Brien); *m* 1957, Jean Olga Lewis; three *d*. *Educ:* Bishop Road Jun. Sch., Bristol; St Brendan's Coll., Bristol; Univ. of Bristol (Open Schol.; BA Hons); Univ. of East Africa (MEd); Univ. of Sussex (DPhil); Dip. Coll. of Teachers of the Blind. Educn Officer, RAF, 1953–56; Asst Master, Worcester Coll. for the Blind, 1956–59; Asst Master, King's Coll., Budo, Uganda, 1959–62; Lecturer in English Language, Makerere Univ. Coll., Uganda 1963–66; Univ. of Zambia: Sen Lecturer in Educn, 1966–68; Reader and Head of Dept of Education, 1968–70; Prof. of Educn, 1970; Principal, Bishop Otter Coll., Chichester, 1970–80; Principal, Coll., then UC, of Ripon and York St John, Leeds Univ., 1980–95. Chm., Zambia Braille Press, 1967–70. Danforth Fellow, Colorado Coll., USA, 1972; Commonwealth Educn Consultant, Sri Lanka, 1973; British Council ELT Consultant, Iraq, 1975; CUAC Consultant, univ. colls, India and Australia, 1996; Honorary Visiting Professor: Univ. of Fort Hare, 1997; Makerere Univ., 1998–; Oxford Brookes Univ., 2001–. Chairman: York Diocesan Educn Council, 1980–95; Council of Church and Associated Colls, 1990–95; Mem., UK Commn for UNESCO, 1984–86. Chm., Univs Visitation Cttee, Uganda, 2006–07. Vice-Chm. Govs, York Theatre Royal, 1992–95. Hon. Fellow, Coll. of Ripon and York St John, 2001. Hon. DLitt: Ripon Coll., Wisconsin, 1986; York Coll., Penn, 1993; Southampton, 1999; Hon. DHumLitt Union Coll., NY, 1996. *Publications:* King's College, Budo, The First Sixty Years, 1967; Educating the Handicapped, 1967; English for Education?, 1968; The Best Words (braille), 1968; Better English (braille), 1969; Teaching English as a Second Language (with J. A. Bright), 1970; English in Africa, (UNESCO), 1971; Bishop Otter College and Policy for Teacher Education 1839–1980, 1981; A Church College for the 21st Century?: 150 years of Ripon and York St John, 1991; Towards True Education, 1994; English for Life?, 2002; King's College, Budo: a centenary history, 2006; A History of York St John University: 1841–2008, 2008; numerous articles. *Recreations:* music, literature, theatre, film, travel, swimming, armchair Rugby and cricket, watching my wife bird-watching. *Address:* 4 Grangers Place, Witney, Oxon OX28 4BS. *T:* (01993) 862988.

McGREGOR, Harvey; QC 1978; DCL; Warden, New College, Oxford, 1985–96 (Fellow, 1972–85; Hon. Fellow, 1996); *b* 25 Feb. 1926; *s* of late William Guthrie Robertson McGregor and Agnes (*née* Reid). *Educ:* Inverurie Acad.; Scarborough Boys' High Sch.; Queen's Coll., Oxford (Hastings Scholar; BA 1951, BCL 1952, MA 1955, DCL 1983); Dr of Juridical Science, Harvard, 1962. Flying Officer, RAF, 1946–48. Called to the Bar, Inner Temple, 1955, Bencher, 1985; admitted to Faculty of Advocates, 1995. Bigelow Teaching Fellow, Univ. of Chicago, 1950–51; Visiting Professor: New York Univ. and Rutgers Univ., 1963–69 (various times); Univ. of Edinburgh, 1998–. Consultant to Law Commn 1966–73. Pres., Harvard Law Sch. Assoc. of UK, 1981–2001; Mem., Acad. of European Private Lawyers, 1994–; Associate Mem., Soc. of WS, 2002–. Ind. Chm., London Theatre Council and The Theatre Council (formerly Provincial Theatre Council), 1992– (Dep. Ind. Chm., 1971–92); Pres., Oxford Stage Co., 1992–; Trustee, Oxford Union Soc., 1977–2004 (Chm. Trustees, 1994–2004). Fellow, Winchester Coll., 1985–96. Trustee, Migraine Trust, 1999–. Mem. Editorial Cttee, 1967–86, Mem., Editorial Bd, 1986–, Modern Law Review. Privilegiate, St Hilda's Coll., Oxford, 2001. *Publications:* McGregor on Damages, 12th edn 1961 to 18th edn 2008; Contract Code, 1993; (contrib.) International Encyclopedia of Comparative Law, 1972; articles in legal jls. *Recreations:* music, theatre, travel. *Address:* (chambers) Hailsham Chambers, 4 Paper Buildings, Temple, EC4Y 7EX. *T:* (020) 7353 3366; (residence) Gray's Inn Chambers, Gray's Inn, WC1R 5JA. *T:* (020) 7242 4942; 29 Howard Place, Edinburgh EH3 5JY. *T:* (0131) 556 8680. *Clubs:* Garrick; New (Edinburgh).

MacGREGOR, Heather Margaret; District Judge, Principal Registry, Family Division, since 2004; *b* 14 June 1952; *d* of James Gibson and Annie Gibson (*née* Ferry); *m* 1977, Dr Arthur MacGregor; one step *s*. *Educ:* Birmingham Univ. (BA Hons Archaeol. and Ancient Hist. 1973); City Univ. (Dip. Law 1981). Archaeologist, York Archaeol Trust, 1975–79; called to the Bar, Gray's Inn, 1982; in practice as barrister, London, 1982–2004; Dep. Dist Judge, Principal Registry, Family Div., 1999–2004. *Publications:* (jtly) Medieval Tenaments in Aldwark, and Other Sites, in The Archaeology of York, vol. 10, 1988; (jtly) Excavations and Observations on the Defences and Adjacent Sites 1971–1990, in The Archaeology of York, vol. 3, 1996. *Recreations:* grand-daughter, archaeology, Scottish dancing. *Address:* Principal Registry, Family Division, First Avenue House, 42–49 High Holborn, WC1V 6NP.

MACGREGOR, Sir Ian Grant, 8th Bt *cr* 1828, of Savile Row, Middlesex; *b* 22 Feb. 1959; *s* of Sir Edwin Robert Macgregor, 7th Bt and (Margaret Alice) Jean Macgregor (*née* Peake); *S* father, 2003; *m* Cheryl, *d* of Stephen Macdonald. *Heir:* uncle Arthur Joseph Macgregor [*b* 7 Sept. 1933; *m* 1st, 1957, Carole Isabel Valens (*d* 1984); two *d*; 2nd, 1985, Brenda Margaret Hanson].

McGREGOR, Sir James David, Kt 1997; OBE 1976; ISO 1973; Member, Executive Council, Hong Kong, 1995–97; retired; *b* 30 Jan. 1924; *s* of David Nelson McGregor and Ann Horsburgh McGregor; *m* 1st, 1947, Doreen Davis (marr. diss.); one *d*; 2nd, 1963, Christine K. C. Hung; one *s* one *d*. *Educ:* Morgan Acad., Dundee; No 1 Sch. of Tech. Trng, Halton (RAF). RAF service, 1940–54 (armament specialist and aeronautical inspector). Hong Kong Government: Exec. Officer, 1954; Dep. Dir, Commerce and Industry Dept and Dep. Comr of Customs, 1972–75; Dir, Hong Kong General Chamber of Commerce, 1975–88; elected MLC, Hong Kong, 1988–95. JP Hong Kong, 1967–97. Hon. LLD Napier, 1995. *Publications:* Life and Death (short stories), 1995; numerous articles on politics, economics, Hong Kong and Asian affairs. *Recreations:* golf, snooker, writing, embroidery. *Clubs:* Hong Kong, Hong Kong Jockey; Tsawwassen Beach Grove Golf (Vancouver).

McGREGOR, James Stalker; Chairman, Honeywell Ltd, 1981–89; *b* 30 Oct. 1927; *s* of John McGregor and Jean McCabe; *m* 1953, Iris Millar Clark; one *s*. *Educ:* Dumfries Acad.; Royal Tech. Coll., Glasgow (ARTC); Glasgow Univ. BSc (Hons); CEng, MIMechE. Production Engr, Rolls Royce Ltd, 1952–56; Sales Engr, Sandvik Swedish Steels, 1956–57; Honeywell Control Systems: Assembly Manager, later Production Control Manager and Admin Manager, 1957–65; Divl Dir, Temperature Controls Gp, 1965–71; Man. Dir, 1971–86. CCMI. Hon. LLD Strathclyde, 1984. *Recreation:* golf.

MacGREGOR, Joanna Clare, FTCL, FRAM; concert pianist; *b* 16 July 1959; *d* of Alfred MacGregor and Angela (*née* Hughes); *m* 1986, Richard Williams; (one *d* decd). *Educ:* S Hampstead Sch. for Girls; New Hall, Cambridge (BA Hons); Royal Acad. of Music (FRAM 1991). FTCL 1995. Gresham Prof. of Music (jtly), 1997–2000. Has appeared as a soloist with leading orchestras, including: RPO, LSO, English Chamber Orch., BBC SO, City of London Sinfonia, NYO, London Mozart Players; has toured worldwide, incl. Netherlands, Scandinavia, Africa, Australia, NZ, USA and Far East. Classical repertoire, also jazz and new music (has commissioned and premiered over 50 new works); jtly organised Platform Fest. of New Music, ICA, 1991–93; Artistic Dir, SoundCircus, Bridgewater Hall, Manchester, 1996 and creator, SoundCircus recording label, 1998; Guest Artistic Dir, Britten Sinfonia, 2002–; has made numerous recordings. Member: Arts Council of England, 1998–2003; Adv. Bd., British Council, 2002–. Presenter: BBC Radio 3; Strings, Bow and Bellows (series), BBC TV, 1995. FRSA 2002. European Encouragement Prize for Music, 1995; South Bank Show Award for Classical Music, 2000; Royal Philharmonic Soc. Prize, 2003. *Publication:* Joanna MacGregor's Piano World (5 vols), 1999. *Address:* c/o Ingpen and Williams, 7 St George's Court, 131 Putney Bridge Road, SW15 2PA. *T:* (020) 8874 3222.

MACGREGOR, John Malcolm, CVO 1992; HM Diplomatic Service, retired; Dean, University of Kent at Brussels, since 2007; *b* 3 Oct. 1946; *s* of late Dr D. F. Macgregor and of K. A. Macgregor (*née* Adams); *m* 1982, Judith Anne Brown (*see* J. A. Macgregor); three *s* one *d*. *Educ:* Kibworth Beauchamp Grammar Sch., Leics; Balliol Coll., Oxford (BA 1967). ARCO 1965. Birmingham Univ., 1968–69; taught at Cranleigh Sch., Surrey, 1969–73; joined HM Diplomatic Service, 1973; 2nd Sec., UN Affairs, 1973–74; 1st Sec. (political), New Delhi, 1975; FCO, 1979; Pvte Sec. to Minister of State, FCO, 1981; Assistant, Soviet Dept, FCO, 1983; Dep. Head of Mission, Prague, 1986; Head of Chancery, Paris, 1990–93; Head of EU Dept (Ext.), 1993–95; Dir Gen. for Trade Promotion in Germany and Consul-Gen., Düsseldorf, 1995–98; Ambassador to Poland, 1998–2000; Dir, Wider Europe, FCO, 2000–02; Ambassador to Austria, 2003–07; UK Perm. Rep. to UN in Vienna and UK Gov. to IAEA, 2006–07. Trustee: Shannon Trust, 2007–; I Fagiolini Trust, 2007–. Gov., Chichester Univ., 2008–. *Recreations:* music, languages, bricolage, travel. *Address:* University of Kent at Brussels, Boulevard de la Plaine 5, 1050 Brussels, Belgium. *T:* (2) 6411721.

MACGREGOR, Judith Anne, LVO 1992; HM Diplomatic Service; Director for Migration, Foreign and Commonwealth Office, since 2007; *b* 17 June 1952; *d* of John Richard Brown and Beatrice Brown; *m* 1982, John Malcolm Macgregor, *qv*; three *s* one *d*. *Educ:* St Saviour's and St Olave's Grammar Sch.; Lady Margaret Hall, Oxford (BA 1st cl. Hons (Modern Hist.) 1974). Entered FCO, 1976; First Secretary: Belgrade, 1978–81; FCO, 1981–86; Prague, 1989; Paris, 1992–93; Dep. Hd, Western European Dept, FCO, 1993–95; Counsellor and Hd, Security Strategy, FCO, 2001–03; FCO Chair, CSSB, 2003–04; Ambassador to Slovakia, 2004–07. *Recreations:* walking, gardening, reading about Central Europe. *Address:* c/o Foreign and Commonwealth Office, King Charles Street, SW1A 2AH. *T:* (020) 7008 3891.

MacGREGOR OF MacGREGOR, Sir Malcolm (Gregor Charles), 7th Bt *cr* 1795, of Lanrick, co. Perth; 24th Chief of Clan Gregor; writer, photographer; *b* 23 March 1959; *er s* of Brig. Sir Gregor MacGregor of MacGregor, 6th Bt, ADC and of Fanny (*née* Butler); *S* father, 2003; *m* 1st, 1988, Cecilia Campbell (marr. diss. 2004); 2nd, 2005, Fiona, *d* of Robert Armstrong, Preston. *Educ:* Eton; Cranfield Univ. (MBA). Major, Scots Guards, retd. Mem., Queen's Body Guard for Scotland (Royal Co. of Archers). FRGS; FRPS; ABIPP. *Publications:* Wilderness Oman, 2002; Rob Roy's Country, 2003; Light over Oman, 2004; The Outer Hebrides, 2007. *Heir:* *b* Ninian Hubert Alexander MacGregor [*b* 30 June 1961; *m* 1999, Fiona Graham; one *s* one *d*]. *Address:* Bannatyne, Newtyle, Angus PH12 8TR.

MacGREGOR, Neil; *see* MacGregor, R. N.

McGREGOR, Peter, CEng, FIET; writer and consultant; Director General, Export Group for the Constructional Industries, 1984–91 (Consultant, 1991–94); *b* 20 May 1926; *s* of Peter McGregor and Margaret Thomson McGregor (*née* McAuslan); *m* 1st, 1954, Marion (*d* 2001), *d* of H. T. Downer; one *s* (one *d* decd); 2nd, 2006, Sheena Macmillan, *d* of George Lorimer McCubbin. *Educ:* Cardiff High Sch.; Univ. of Birmingham; London Sch. of Economics (BSc (Econs)). National Service, RE, 1946–48. Various appointments, Ferranti Ltd, 1950–74, incl. Works Manager, Distribution Transformer Dept, Sales Manager, Transformer Div., Gen. Manager, Power Div.; Dir, Industrie Elettriche di Legnano (Italy), 1970–74; Associate Dir, Corporate Renewal Associates Ltd, 1988–93. Dir, Oxford Univ. Business Summer Sch., 1972; first Sec. Gen., Anglo-German Foundn for Study of Industrial Soc., 1974–81; Industrial Dir (Dep. Sec.), NEDO, 1981–84. Chm., Textile Machinery EDC, 1982–86; Dir, Templeton Technol. Seminar, 1985. Member: N American Adv. Gp, BOTB, 1968–74; Europ. Trade Cttee, BOTB, 1981–83; Adv. Bd, Public Policy Centre, 1984–88; Cttee on Exchange Rate, Public Policy Centre, 1984–87. Industrial Advr to Liberal Party, 1960–73; an Industrial Advr to Social and Liberal Democrats, 1988–90; Chm., Hazel Grove Liberal Assoc., 1971–74; contested (L) Ilford South, 1964. Mem., Königswinter Conf. steering cttee, 1976–90. Hon. Treasurer, Anglo-German Assoc., 1983–91. Elder and Hon. Treas., St Columba's Ch, Oxford, 1992–97. MCIM; FCMI. *Publications:* The Retreat (novel), 1997; Lessons in Duplicity (novel), 2005; various articles and pamphlets especially on industrial relations, company structure, market economy. *Recreations:* walking, reading, listening to music, writing, conversation, gardening, drawing attention to the Emperor's lack of clothes. *Club:* Caledonian.

MacGREGOR, (Robert) Neil; Director, British Museum, since 2002; *b* 16 June 1946; *s* of Alexander MacGregor and Anna (*née* Neil). *Educ:* Glasgow Acad.; New Coll., Oxford (Hon. Fellow); Ecole Normale Supérieure, Paris; Univ. of Edinburgh; Courtauld Inst. of Art. Mem., Faculty of Advocates, Edinburgh, 1972. Lectr in History of Art and Architecture, Univ. of Reading, 1976; Editor, The Burlington Magazine, 1981–86; Dir, Nat. Gallery, 1987–2002. Trustee: Pilgrim Trust, 1990–2006; Courtauld Inst. of Art, 2002–08. Member: Supervisory Bd, Rijksmuseum, Amsterdam, 1995–2004; Internat.

Adv. Bd, Hermitage, St Petersburg, 1997–; Museums, Libraries and Archives Council, 2003–05; Arts and Humanities Res. Council (formerly Bd), 2003–Aug. 2009; Bd, RNT. Presenter of TV series: Seeing Salvation, 2000; Making Masterpieces; Painting the World. Hon. Mem., Royal Scottish Acad., 1995; Hon. FBA 2000. DUniv York, 1992; Dr *hc:* Edinburgh, 1994; Reading, Leicester, 1997; Exeter, Strathclyde, Glasgow, 1998; Hon. DLitt: Oxford, 1998; London, 1999. *Publications:* (jtly) Seeing Salvation: images of Christian art, 2000; (jtly) Britain's Paintings: the story of art through masterpieces in British collections, 2003. *Address:* British Museum, Great Russell Street, WC1B 3DG.

See also A. R. MacGregor.

MacGREGOR, Susan Katriona, (Sue), CBE 2002 (OBE 1992); Presenter for BBC Radio Four: Today, 1984–2002; A Good Read, since 2003; The Reunion, since 2003; *b* 30 Aug. 1941; *d* of late Dr James MacGregor and Margaret MacGregor. *Educ:* Herschel School, Cape, South Africa. Announcer/producer, South African Broadcasting Corp., 1962–67; BBC Radio reporter, World at One, World This Weekend, PM, 1967–72; Presenter: Woman's Hour, BBC Radio 4, 1972–87; Tuesday Call, 1973–86; Conversation Piece, 1978–94; Around Westminster, BBC TV, 1990–92. Vis. Prof. of Journalism, Nottingham Trent Univ., 1995–2003. Mem. Bd, RNT, 1998–2003. Member: RCP Cttee on Ethical Issues in Medicine, 1985–2000; Marshall Aid Commemoration Commn, 1989–98. Chair: Jury, Orange Prize for Fiction, 2002; Art Fund Museum Prize, 2008. Trustee: John Ellerman Foundn, 2002–; Young Concert Artists' Trust, 2003–; UNICEF UK, 2004–. FRSA 1983; Hon. MRCP 1995. Hon. Fellow, Harris Manchester Coll., Oxford, 2002. Hon. DLitt: Nottingham, 1996; Nottingham Trent, 2000; Staffordshire, 2001; London Metropolitan, 2002; Hon. LLD Dundee, 1997. *Publication:* Woman of Today (autobiog.), 2002. *Recreations:* theatre, cinema, ski-ing. *Address:* c/o Knight Ayton Management, 114 St Martin's Lane, WC2N 4BE. *T:* (020) 7836 5333.

McGREGOR, Wayne; choreographer; Founder and Artistic Director, Random Dance Co., since 1992 (resident company of Sadler's Wells, since 2001); Resident Choreographer, Royal Ballet, since 2006; *b* 12 March 1970; *s* of Lawrence and Ella McGregor. *Educ:* Bretton Hall Coll., Univ. of Leeds (BA 1st Cl. Hons Dance); José Limon Sch., NY. AHRB/Arts Council England Res. Fellow in Cognition and Choreography, Sch. of Exptl Psychol., Univ. of Cambridge, 2003. Choreographer in Residence, The Place Th., London, 1992–; productions for Random Dance Co. include: The Millenarium, 1997, Sulphur 16, 1998, and Aeon, 2000, commnd RFH; digit01 (commnd The Place), 2001; Nemesis (co-commnd S Hill Park, Swindon Dance, Sadler's Wells, DanceEast), 2002; Alpha, Polar Sequences (co-commnd The Place, PACT Zollverein), 2003; Ataxia (co-commnd Sadler's Wells, PACT Zollverein), 2004; AMU (co-commnd Sadler's Wells, Wellcome Trust), 2005; independent commissions include: Telenoia (Canary Wharf), 2000; (with V. Durante) Fleur de Peux, Symbiont(s) (Royal Ballet, Covent Gdn), 2000; Detritus (Rambert Dance Co.), 2001; Brainstate (Royal Ballet/ Random Dance), 2001; PreSentient (Rambert Dance Co.), 2002; 2 Human (English Nat. Ballet), Nautilus (Stuttgart Ballet), 2003; Qualia (Royal Ballet), 2004; Eden/Eden (Stuttgart Ballet), Engram (Royal Ballet), 2005; Skindex (NDT1), 2006; Chroma (Royal Ballet), 2006; *theatre:* A Little Night Music, RNT, 1996; Cleansed, Royal Court, 1998; Antony and Cleopatra, RNT, 1998; Woman in White, Palace and NY, 2004; Cloaca, 2004, Aladdin, 2005, Old Vic; You Never Can Tell, Much Ado About Nothing, Peter Hall Co., 2005; *opera* includes: Salome, ENO, 1995; Marriage of Figaro, Scottish Nat. Opera, 1995; Rinaldo, The Mikado, Grange Pk Op., 2000; Hansel and Gretel, Scottish Op., 2000; Manon, English Touring Op., 2001; Orpheus et Euridice, Scottish Nat. Op. and Scottish Opera Go Round, 2003; La Bohème, Scottish Op., 2004; The Midsummer Marriage, Chicago Lyric Op., 2005; (dir.) Dido and Aeneas, La Scala, 2006; contribs to TV progs and films. Outstanding Achievement in Dance Award, 2001, Outstanding Choreography Award, 2003, Time Out Live Awards. *Address:* Random Dance Company, Sadler's Wells Theatre, Rosebery Avenue, EC1R 4TN. *T:* (020) 7278 6015, *Fax:* (020) 7278 5469.

McGREGOR-JOHNSON, Richard John; His Honour Judge McGregor-Johnson; a Circuit Judge, since 1998; Resident Judge, Isleworth Crown Court, since 2004; *b* 11 July 1950; *s* of Maxwell and Pamela McGregor-Johnson; *m* 1974, Elizabeth Weston; one *s* one *d. Educ:* Dean Close Sch., Cheltenham; Bristol Univ. (LLB 1972). Called to the Bar, Inner Temple, 1973, Bencher, 2001; an Asst Recorder, 1990–94; a Recorder, 1994–98. *Recreations:* choral singing, sailing. *Address:* Crown Court, 36 Ridgeway Road, Isleworth, Middx TW7 5LP.

McGRIGOR, Sir James (Angus Rhoderick Neil), 6th Bt cr 1831, of Campden Hill, Middlesex; Member (C) Highlands and Islands, Scottish Parliament, since 1999; *b* 19 Oct. 1949; *er s* of Sir Charles Edward McGrigor, 5th Bt, and of Mary Bettine, *e d* of Sir Archibald Edmonstone, 6th Bt; *S* father, 2007; *m* 1st, 1987, Caroline Roboh (marr. diss. 1993); two *d*; 2nd, 1997, Emma Mary Louise Fellowes; one *s* three *d. Educ:* Cladich Sch., Argyll; Sunningdale Sch., Berks; Eton College. Shipping, 1969–71; stockbroking, 1971–74; farmer, 1975–. Mem., Queen's Body Guard for Scotland, Royal Co. of Archers, 1990. Contested (C) Argyll and Bute, 2005. *Recreations:* fishing, music, literature. Heir: *s* Alexander James Edward Lyon McGrigor, *b* 5 Aug. 1998. *Address:* Ardchonnel, by Dalmally, Argyll PA33 1BW. *Clubs:* White's, Chelsea Arts; New (Edinburgh).

McGROUTHER, Prof. (Duncan) Angus, MD; FRCS, FRCSGlas, FRCSE; Professor of Plastic and Reconstructive Surgery, University of Manchester, since 2001; Hon. Consultant Surgeon, South Manchester University Hospitals, since 2001; *b* 3 March 1946; *s* of Dr John Ingram McGrouther and Margot Christina Cooke Gray; *m;* one *s* one *d; m* 2005, Gillian Fletcher-Williams. *Educ:* Glasgow High Sch.; Univ. of Glasgow (MB ChB 1969; MD Hons 1988); Univ. of Strathclyde (MSc Bioengineering 1975). Glasgow Royal Infirmary, 1969–74; Cruden Med. Res. Fellow, Bioengrg Unit, Univ. of Strathclyde, 1972–73; Registrar and Sen. Registrar in Plastic Surgery, Canniesburn Hosp., Glasgow, 1975–78; Assistenzarzt, Klinikum Rechts der Isar, Munich, 1978; Consultant Plastic Surgeon: Shotley Bridge Gen. Hosp. and Sunderland Dist Gen. Hosp., 1979–80; Canniesburn Hosp., 1981–89; Prof. of Plastic and Reconstructive Surgery (first estabd British chair), UCL, 1989–2001. Christine Kleinert Vis. Prof., Univ. of Louisville, 1988. FMedSci 2005. Kay-Kilner Prize, British Assoc. of Plastic Surgeons, 1979; Pulvertaft Prize, British Soc. for Surgery of the Hand, 1981. *Publications:* (jtly) Principles of Hand Surgery, 1990; (ed jtly) Dupuytren's Disease, 1990; contributor to: Current Surgical Practice, vol. 6, 1992; Microvascular Surgery and Free Tissue Transfer, 1993; Gray's Anatomy, 38th edn, 1995; Bailey and Love's Short Practice of Surgery, 22nd edn, 1995; Green's Operative Surgery, 4th edn 1998, 5th edn 2004; papers on anatomy, biomechanics, plastic surgery, hand surgery, microsurgery, and wound healing. *Recreations:* mountains, sea, books. *Address:* University of Manchester, Stopford Building, Oxford Road, Manchester M13 9PT.

McGUCKIAN, John Brendan; Chairman, Ulster Television, since 1990; *b* 13 Nov. 1939; *s* of late Brian McGuckian and of Pauline (née McKenna); *m* 1970, Carmel, *d* of Daniel McGowan; two *s* two *d. Educ:* St McNissis Coll., Garrontower; Queen's Univ. of Belfast (BSc). Chairman: Cloughmills Mfg Co., 1967–; Tedcastle Hldgs, 1999–2001; Irish Continental Gp (formerly Irish Ferries) plc, 2004– (Dir, 1988–); Director: Munster & Leinster Bank, 1972–; Allied Irish Bank plc, 1976–; Harbour Group Ltd, 1978–; Aer Lingus plc, 1979–84; Unidare plc, 1987–2006; United Dairy Farmers, 2001–; Derry Development Commn, 1968–71; Dep. Chm., Laganside Corp., 1988–92; and other directorships. Chairman: Internat. Fund for Ireland, 1990–93; IDB for NI, 1991–98. Sen. Pro-Chancellor and Chm. of Senate, QUB. *Address:* Ardverna, Cloughmills, Ballymena, Co. Antrim, Northern Ireland BT44 9NL. *T:* (028) 2763 8121; Lisgoole Abbey, Culkey, Enniskillen BT92 2FP.

McGUFFIN, Prof. Peter, PhD; FRCP, FRCPsych, FMedSci; Professor of Psychiatric Genetics, since 1998, and Dean, since 2007, Institute of Psychiatry, King's College London (Director, MRC Social, Genetic and Developmental Psychiatry Research Centre, 1998–2006); *b* 4 Feb. 1949; *s* of Captain W. B. McGuffin, RD, RNR and M. M. McGuffin; *m* 1972, Prof. Anne E. Farmer; one *s* two *d. Educ:* Univ. of Leeds (MB ChB); Univ. of London (PhD). MRCP 1976, FRCP 1988; MRCPsych 1978, FRCPsych 1990. St James Univ. Hosp., Leeds, 1972–77; Registrar, Sen. Registrar, Maudsley Hosp., 1977–79; MRC Fellow, MRC Sen. Clinical Fellow, Inst. of Psychiatry, 1979–86; Hon. Consultant, Maudsley and King's Coll. Hosps, 1983–86; Prof. of Psychological Medicine, Univ. of Wales Coll. of Medicine, 1987–98. Vis. Fellow, Washington Univ., St Louis, 1981–82. Founder FMedSci 1998. Pres., Internat. Soc. of Psychiatric Genetics, 1996–2000. *Publications:* Scientific Principles of Psychopathology, 1984; A Psychiatric Catechism, 1987; Schizophrenia, the Major Issues, 1988; The New Genetics of Mental Illness, 1991; Seminars in Psychiatric Genetics, 1994; Essentials of Postgraduate Psychiatry, 1997; Behavioral Genetics, 2001, 5th edn 2008; Measuring Psychopathology, 2002; Psychiatric Genetics and Genomics, 2002; Behavioural Genetics in the Postgenomic Era, 2002; articles, research papers on psychiatry and genetics. *Recreations:* classical guitar, music, running, horse riding, farmland maintenance. *Address:* Institute of Psychiatry, de Crespigny Park, Denmark Hill, SE5 8AF; 68 Heol-y-Delyn, Lisvane, Cardiff CF4 5SR.

McGUGAN, Irene Margaret; Assistant Director, Barnardo's Scotland, since 2007; *b* 29 Aug. 1952; *d* of late James Millar Duncan and of Phyllis Margaret Duncan (née Smith, now Mrs John Nicoll); *m* 1971, James McGugan; one *s* one *d. Educ:* Robert Gordon's Inst. of Technol. (CQSW 1982; Dip. Social Work 1982); Dundee Univ. (Advanced Cert. in Child Protection Studies 1991). VSO, India, 1970–71; full-time mother and voluntary worker, 1971–80; Social Work Dept, Tayside Regl Council, 1985–96, Angus Council, 1996–99 (Manager, Community Support, 1998–99); Project Dir, Children's Services, Aberdeen CC, 2003–07. Mem. (SNP) NE Scotland, Scottish Parlt, 1999–2003. Contested (SNP) Dundee W, Scottish Parlt, 2003. Elder, Church of Scotland, 1985. *Recreations:* Gaelic, malt whisky, cycling, music, theatre. *Address:* e-mail: irene.mcgugan@snp.org.

McGUIGAN, Finbar Patrick, (Barry), MBE 1994; journalist and commentator on boxing; *b* 28 Feb. 1961; *s* of late Patrick McGuigan and of Catherine, (Kate), McGuigan; *m* 1981, Sandra Mealiff; three *s* one *d. Educ:* St Louis Convent, Clones, Co. Monaghan; Largy Sch., Clones; St Patrick's High Sch., Clones. Started boxing, 1973, Wattle Bridge ABC, then Smithborough ABC; winner: Ulster and Irish title (Juvenile), 1977; Irish Sen. title, 1978; Commonwealth Gold Medal, 1978; represented Ireland at Olympic Games, Moscow, 1980; turned professional, 1981; winner: British and European Featherweight titles, 1983; World WBA Featherweight title, 1985; made two successful defences, then lost title on third defence, 1986; retd 1989. Pres. and Founder, Professional Boxers' Assoc. (formerly Professional Boxers' Assoc., subseq. British Boxers' Assoc.), 1993–. *Publications:* (jtly) Leave the Fighting to McGuigan, 1985; (jtly) McGuigan—The Untold Story, 1991. *Recreations:* fitness, reading, etymology, relaxing with my family. *Address:* PO Box 233, Faversham, Kent ME13 9WP; *e-mail:* barrymcguigan@btinternet.com.

McGUIGAN, Rupert Iain Sutherland; HM Diplomatic Service, retired; Managing Director, Private Trust Corporation (East Africa) Ltd, 1999–2007; *b* 25 June 1941; *s* of Hugh and Sue McGuigan; *m* 1968, Rosemary Rashleigh Chaytor; two *d. Educ:* Marlborough Coll.; Magdalene Coll., Cambridge (MA Law). With BP Ltd, 1964–72; HM Diplomatic Service, 1972–97: First Secretary: New Delhi, 1974–77; Kingston, Jamaica, 1978–81; Permanent Under-Secretaries Dept, FCO, 1981–85; Bridgetown, 1985–88; Counsellor: Lagos, 1989–93; Kingston, Jamaica, 1994–96. Private Sec. to the Princess Royal, 1997–99. *Recreations:* most ball games, amateur dramatics, philately, singing in the bath. *Address:* Goodhope, Halls Lane, Waltham St Lawrence, Berks RG10 0JB. *T:* (0118) 934 0989. *Clubs:* Hawks (Cambridge); Worplesdon Golf; Muthaiga Country (Nairobi).

McGUIGAN BURNS, Simon Hugh; see Burns.

McGUINESS, Robert Clayton, PhD; Chief Executive Officer, Serco Defence, Science and Technology, since 2006; *b* 31 Dec. 1951; *s* of Robert McGuiness and Agnes McGuiness; *m* 1982, Beate Winkelmann; two *d. Educ:* Univ. of Glasgow (BSc (Hons) 1973; PhD 1976). ICI plc, 1976–2000: ICI Paints, 1976–93; Gen. Manager Marketing and Planning, ICI Autocolor, 1993–96; Vice Pres., Refinish, Glidden Co., N America, 1996–98; Chief Exec., ICI Autocolor, 1999–2000; Man. Dir, NPL Mgt Ltd, 2000–05. *Recreations:* golf, ski-ing. *Address:* Oak Lodge, Bray Road, Maidenhead, Berks SL6 1UF. *T:* (01628) 621699; Serco Defence, Science and Technology, Enterprise House, 11 Bartley Wood Business Park, Bartley Way, Hook, Hants RG27 9XB. *Club:* Maidenhead Golf.

McGUINNESS, Maj.-Gen. Brendan Peter, CB 1986; consultant in education and training, now retired; Adviser on Engineering to Schools and Colleges, University of Birmingham, 1994–96; Director of Education and Training Liaison, Engineering Employers' Federation, West Midlands, 1988–94 (Head of Educational Liaison, 1987–88); *b* 26 June 1931; *s* of Bernard and May McGuinness; *m* 1968, Ethne Patricia (née Kelly); one *s* one *d. Educ:* Mount St Mary's College. psc, rcds. Commissioned Royal Artillery, 1950; regimental duty, 1950–60; Staff, 1960–62; sc 1963; Adjutant, 1964–65; Staff, 1965–68 (despatches, Borneo, 1966); Battery Comdr, 1968–70; Staff Coll. Directing Staff, 1970–72; CO 45 Medium Regt, 1972–75; CRA 1st Armd Div., 1975–77; RCDS 1978; MoD Staff, 1979–81; Dep. Comdr, NE District, 1981–83; GOC W Dist, 1983–86. Hon. Col, Birmingham Univ. OTC, 1987–97; Hon. Regtl Col, 45 Field Regt, 1985–91. Mem. Cttee, Hereford and Worcester Br., STA, 1991–96. Project Dir, 1987–88, Gov., 1988–, The City Technol. Coll., Kingshurst; Mem. Court, Birmingham Univ., 1992–94; Governor: King's Coll. for the Arts and Technol., Guildford, 1999–; King's Internat. Coll. for Business and the Arts, Camberley, 2000–; Guest Gov., Cirencester Coll., 1998–2006. Dir, Acafess Community Trust, 1992–94 (Chm., 1992). *Recreations:* tennis, hill walking, beagling. *Address:* 107 Gloucester Street, Cirencester, Glos GL7 2DW. *T:* (01285) 657861. *Club:* Army and Navy.

McGUINNESS, Frank; playwright; Professor of Creative Writing, School of English, University College, Dublin, since 2007 (Writer in Residence, 1997–2007); *b* 29 July 1953; *s* of Patrick McGuinness and Celine O'Donnell-McGuinness. *Educ:* University College, Dublin (BA 1974; MPhil 1976). *Plays:* The Factory Girls, 1982, Observe the Sons of Ulster Marching Towards the Somme, Baglady, 1985, Abbey Th.; Innocence, Gate Th.,

1986; Carthaginians, Abbey, 1988; Peer Gynt (version), Gate, 1988; Mary and Lizzie, RSC, 1989; Three Sisters (version), Gate, 1990; Someone Who'll Watch Over Me, Vaudeville, transf. NY, 1992; The Bird Sanctuary, Abbey, 1994; A Doll's House (version), Playhouse, transf. NY, 1996; Mutabilitie, Caucasian Chalk Circle (version), 1997, RNT; Electra (version), Donmar, transf. NY, 1997; The Storm (version), Almeida, 1998; Dolly West's Kitchen, Abbey, transf. Old Vic, 1999; Miss Julie (version), Haymarket, 2000; Gates of Gold, Gate Th., Dublin, 2002; The Wild Duck, Abbey Th., 2003; Hecuba (version), Donmar, 2004; Rebecca (version), Th. Royal, Newcastle upon Tyne, 2005; Speaking Like Magpies, RSC, 2005; Phaedra, Donmar, 2006; Yerma (trans.), Arcola Th., 2006; There Came a Gypsy Riding, Almeida, 2007; Ghosts (version), Bristol Old Vic, 2007; The Lady from the Sea (version), Almeida, 2008; Oedipus, RNT, 2008; *television:* Scout, 1987; The Hen House, 1989. Hon. DLitt Ulster, 2000. Evening Standard Award, 1986; Ewart-Biggs Prize, 1987; NY Critics Circle Award, 1992; Writers' Guild Award, 1992; Ireland Fund Literary Award, 1992; Tony Award, 1997; Lifetime Achievement Award for Irish Writing, Sunday Tribune, 2007. Officier de la République française, 1996. *Publications:* The Factory Girls, 1982; Observe the Sons of Ulster Marching Towards the Somme, 1986; Innocence, 1987; Carthaginians, and Baglady, 1988; Mary and Lizzie, 1989; Someone Who'll Watch Over Me, 1992; Booterstown (poems), 1994; Plays, vol. 1, 1996; Mutabilitie, 1997; Dolly West's Kitchen, 1999; The Sea With No Ships (poems), 1999; Plays, vol. 2, 2002; Gates of Gold, 2002; The Stone Jug: poems, 2003; Dulse (poems), 2008; *versions:* Peer Gynt, 1990; Three Sisters, 1990; A Doll's House, 1996; Electra, 1997; The Storm, 1998; Miss Julie, 2000; Speaking Like Magpies, 2005; There Came a Gypsy Riding, 2007; Oedipus, 2008; The Lady from the Sea, 2008. *Recreations:* walking, horse-racing, Irish art. *Address:* Department of Anglo-Irish Literature, University College, Dublin, Belfield, Dublin 4, Ireland.

McGUINNESS, Martin; MP (SF) Ulster Mid, since 1997; Member (SF) Ulster Mid, since 1998, and Deputy First Minister, since 2007, Northern Ireland Assembly; *b* 23 May 1950. *Educ:* Christian Brothers' Tech. Coll. Mem., NI Assembly, 1982–86. Chief Negotiator, Sinn Féin. Contested (SF) Foyle, 1983, 1987, 1992. Minister of Educn, NI, 1999–2002. *Address:* Sinn Féin, 55 Falls Road, Belfast BT12 4PD.

McGUIRE, Rt Hon. Anne Catherine; PC 2008; MP (Lab) Stirling, since 1997; *b* 26 May 1949; *d* of Albert Long, CBE and Agnes Long (*née* Coney); *m* 1972, Leonard F. McGuire; one *s* one *d*. *Educ:* Our Lady and St Francis Sch., Glasgow; Univ. of Glasgow (MA Hons 1971); Notre Dame Coll. of Educn. Registrar and Sec., Court's Dept, Univ. of Glasgow, 1971–74; teacher, 1983–85; fieldworker, 1985–89, Nat. Officer, Scotland, 1989–93, CSV; Dep. Dir, Scottish Council for Voluntary Orgns, 1993–97. PPS to Sec. of State for Scotland, 1997–98; an Asst Govt Whip, 1998–2001; a Lord Comr of HM Treasury (Govt Whip), 2001–02; Parliamentary Under-Secretary of State: Scotland Office, 2002–05; DWP, 2005–08. *Recreations:* walking, Scottish traditional music, reading. *Address:* House of Commons, SW1A 0AA. *T:* (020) 7219 5014.

McGUIRE, Michael Thomas Francis; *b* 3 May 1926; *m* 1954, Marie T. Murphy; three *s* two *d*. *Educ:* Elementary Schools. Coal miner. Whole-time NUM Branch Secretary, 1957–64. Joined Lab. Party, 1951. MP (Lab): Ince, 1964–83; Makerfield, 1983–87. PPS to Minister of Sport, 1974–77. Member: Council of Europe, 1977–87; WEU, 1977–87. *Recreations:* most out-door sports, especially Rugby League football; traditional music, especially Irish traditional music. *Address:* 24 Osborne Road, Eccleston, St Helens, Lancs WA10 5JS.

McGUIRE, Prof. William Joseph, PhD; FGS; Professor of Geophysical Hazards, and Director, Benfield UCL Hazard Research Centre, University College London, since 1997; *b* 1 Dec. 1954; *s* of late John McMillan McGuire and of Audrey McGuire (*née* Wade Owens); *m* 2000, Anna Taylor; one *s*. *Educ:* St Michael's Coll., Hitchin; University Coll. London (BSc Geol 1976); CNAA (PhD 1980). FGS 1977. Lectr in Igneous Petrology and Geochem., W London Inst. of Higher Educn, 1981–90; Lectr, 1990–93, Sen. Lectr, 1993–95, Reader, 1995–97, in Volcanology and Igneous Petrology, Cheltenham and Gloucester Coll. of Higher Educn. Dir, DisasterMan Ltd, 2000–; consultant on natural hazards and climate change, HSBC Gp, 2006–. Mem. UK Govt Natural Hazard Working Gp, 2005. Chm. Volcanic Studies Gp, 1993–96, Council Mem., 1997–99, Geol Soc. of London; Mem., Sci. Media Panel, Royal Instn, 2002–. UK Nat. Corresp., Internat. Assoc. of Volcanology and Chemistry of the Earth's Interior, 1993–96; UK Rep., Europ. Volcanology Proj. Cttee, ESF, 1994; Mem., 1993–95, Sec., 1996–2000, UK Panel, IUGG. Presenter: radio: Disasters in Waiting (series), 2000, Scientists Under Pressure (series), 2001; television: The End of the World (series), 2006. FRI. Member, Editorial Board: Volcanology and Seismology, 1994–98; Acta Vulcanologica, 1995–2000; Disasters, 2002–; BBC Focus Magazine, 2005–; Philosophical Transactions A, 2007–. *Publications:* (ed jtly) Monitoring Active Volcanoes: strategies, procedures and techniques, 1995; Volcanoes of the World, 1997; Apocalypse: a natural history of global disasters, 1999; Italian Volcanoes, 2001; (jtly) Natural Hazards and Environmental Change, 2002; Raging Planet, 2002; A Guide to the End of the World: everything you never wanted to know, 2002; (with Robert Kovach) Guide to Global Hazards, 2003; (jtly) World Atlas of Natural Hazards, 2004; Surviving Armageddon: solutions for a threatened planet, 2005; Global Catastrophes: a very short introduction, 2005; Seven Years to Save the Planet, 2009; learned papers, esp. to Geol Soc. of London. *Recreations:* playing with son Fraser and cats Jetsam and Driftwood, growing vegetables, walking and mountain biking in the Peaks, worrying about the future of the planet, our race and Fraser. *Address:* Benfield UCL Hazard Research Centre, Department of Earth Sciences, University College London, Gower Street, WC1E 6BT. *T:* (020) 7679 3449, *Fax:* (020) 7679 2390; *e-mail:* w.mcguire@ucl.ac.uk.

McGURK, John Callender; journalist; *b* 12 Dec. 1952; *s* of John B. McGurk and Janet McGurk; *m* 1984, Karen Patricia Anne Ramsay (marr. diss. 2005); one *s* one *d*. *Educ:* Tynecastle Sen. Secondary Sch., Edinburgh. Trainee Journalist, Scottish County Press, 1970–73; Reporter: Evening Post, Nottingham, 1973–75; Scottish Daily News, 1975; Reporter and Broadcaster, Radio Clyde, 1975–78; Sunday Mail: Reporter, 1978–84; News Editor, 1984–88; Dep. Editor, 1988–89; Editor, Sunday Sun, Newcastle, 1989–91; Dep. Editor, Daily Record, 1991–94; broadcaster, BBC Radio Scotland, and media consultant, 1994–95; Editor: Evening News, Edinburgh, 1995–97; Scotland on Sunday, 1997–2001; Editl Dir, The Scotsman Pubns Ltd, 2001–04; Ed., The Scotsman, 2004–06; Gp Man. Ed., Daily Telegraph and Sunday Telegraph, 2006. Chm., Editors' Cttee, Scottish Daily Newspaper Soc., 2001. Mem., Press Complaints Commn, 1999–2001. *Recreations:* newspapers, dining out, travel. *Address: e-mail:* jcmcgurk@blueyonder.co.uk.

MACH, David Stefan, RA 1998; sculptor; *b* 18 March 1956; *s* of Joseph Mach and Martha (*née* Cassidy); *m* 1979, Lesley June White. *Educ:* Buckhaven High Sch.; Duncan of Jordanstone Coll. of Art (Dip. and Post Dip. in Art); Royal Coll. of Art (MA). Full-time sculptor and occasional vis. lectr, 1982–; Associate Prof., Sculpture Dept, Edinburgh Coll. of Art, 1999–; Prof. of Sculpture, Royal Acad., 2000–. Work includes Train, Darlington, largest contemp. sculpture in the UK, 1998; sculptures exhibited at galleries in England, Scotland, NY, São Paolo Biennale, Venice Biennale. Trustee, NPG, 2006–. City of Glasgow Lord Provost Prize, 1992. *Recreations:* gardening, tennis, travelling, driving, film, television. *Address:* 64 Canonbie Road, Forest Hill, SE23 3AG. *T:* (020) 8699 1668; *e-mail:* davidmach@davidmach.com. *Club:* Chelsea Arts.

McHALE, His Honour Keith Michael; a Circuit Judge, 1980–2000; *b* 26 March 1928; *s* of late Cyril Michael McHale and Gladys McHale; *m* 1966, Rosemary Margaret Arthur; one *s* one *d*. Called to the Bar, Gray's Inn, 1951. *Address:* 1 D'Arcy Place, Bromley, Kent BR2 0RY.

McHENRY, Rev. Brian Edward, CBE 2008; Curate, St Paul's, Deptford, since 2008; *b* 12 Dec. 1950; *s* of Alexander Edward McHenry and Winifred Alice McHenry (*née* Wainford); *m* 1979, Elizabeth Anne Lipsey; two *s*. *Educ:* Dulwich Coll.; New Coll., Oxford (MA); SE Inst. for Theol Educn. Called to the Bar, Middle Temple, 1976. Treasury Solicitor's Dept, 1978–92, 2000; legal advr, Monopolies and Mergers Commn, 1992–96; Solicitor: N Wales Tribunal of Inquiry into Child Abuse, 1996–97; BSE Inquiry, 1998–2000; Chief Legal Advr, Competition Commn, 2000–04; Office of Fair Trading: Solicitor, 2004–06; Gen. Counsel, 2006–08. Mem., Crown Appts Commn, 1997–2002. General Synod of Church of England: Mem., 1980–85 and 1987–2005; Vice-Chm., House of Laity, 2000–05; Chm., Standing Orders Cttee, 1991–99; Member: Standing Cttee, 1990–95; Legislative Cttee, 1981–85 and 1991–95 (Dep. Chm., 2001–05); Business Cttee, 1999–2005; Archbishops' Council, 1999–2005; Lay Vice-Pres., Southwark Diocesan Synod, 1988–96 and 1997–99; Hon. Lay Canon, Southwark Cathedral, 2004–08. A Reader, C of E, 1976–2008; ordained, 2008. *Recreations:* swimming, walking, jogging, travel, history, Arsenal FC. *Address:* 21 Maude Road, SE5 8NY. *T:* (020) 7701 9350.

McHENRY, Donald F.; Distinguished Professor in the Practice of Diplomacy, School of Foreign Service, Georgetown University, since 1998 (University Research Professor of Diplomacy and International Affairs, 1981–98); *b* 13 Oct. 1936; *s* of Limas McHenry and Dora Lee Brooks; *m* Mary Williamson (marr. diss.); one *s* two *d*. *Educ:* Lincoln Senior High Sch., East St Louis, Ill; Illinois State Univ. (BS); Southern Illinois Univ. (MSc); Georgetown Univ. Taught at Howard Univ., Washington, 1959–62; joined Dept of State, 1963; Head of Dependent Areas Section, Office of UN Polit. Affairs, 1965–68; Asst to Sec. of State, US, 1969; Special Asst to Counsellor, Dept of State, 1969–71; Lectr, Sch. of Foreign Service, Georgetown Univ.; Guest Scholar, Brookings Inst., and Internat. Affairs Fellow, Council on Foreign Relations (on leave from State Dept), 1971–73; resigned from State Dept, 1973; Project Dir, Humanitarian Policy Studies, Carnegie Endowment for Internat. Peace, Washington, 1973–76; served in transition team of President Carter, 1976–77; Ambassador and Deputy Rep. of US to UN Security Council, 1977–79, Permanent Rep., 1979; US Ambassador to UN, 1979–81. Founder and Co-Pres., IRC Gp, LLC, 1981–; Director: Internat. Paper Co., 1981–; Fleet Boston Financial Co.; Bank of Boston Corp., 1981–2004; GlaxoSmithKline (formerly SmithKline Beecham) plc, 1982–2004; Coca-Cola, 1982–; American Telephone and Telegraph, 1987–2005; Inst. for Internat. Economics, 1999–. Dir, American Ditchley Foundn; Chm., Bd of Dirs, Africare, 1989–2004; Mem. Bd of Govs, UNA of USA. Mem., American Acad. of Arts and Scis, 1992. Hon. degrees: Dennison, Duke, Eastern Illinois, Georgetown, Harvard, Illinois State, Michigan, Princeton, Southern Illinois, Tufts, and Washington Univs; Amherst, Bates, Boston and Williams Colleges. Superior Honor Award, Dept of State, 1966. Mem. Council on Foreign Relations and Editorial Bd, Foreign Policy Magazine. *Publication:* Micronesia: Trust Betrayed, 1975. *Address:* Georgetown University, 37th and O Streets, NW, Washington, DC 20057, USA.

MACHIN, Anthony; *see* Machin, E. A.

MACHIN, David; Under Treasurer, Gray's Inn, 1989–2000; *b* 25 April 1934; *s* of late Noel and Joan Machin; *m* 1963, Sarah Mary, *yr d* of late Col W. A. Chester-Master, DL; two *d*. *Educ:* Eton (Oppidan Scholar); Trinity Coll., Cambridge. National Service, 1952–54 (2nd Lieut Welsh Guards). Editor, William Heinemann Ltd, 1957–66; Literary Agent, Gregson & Wigan Ltd and London International, 1966–68; Partner, A. P. Watt & Son, 1968–70; Director: Jonathan Cape Ltd, 1970–78; Chatto, Bodley Head and Jonathan Cape Ltd, 1977–78, 1981–87; Jt Man. Dir, 1981, Man. Dir, 1982–87, The Bodley Head Ltd; Dir, Triad Paperbacks Ltd, 1983–86; Gen. Sec., The Society of Authors, 1978–81. Chm. of Trustees, Inns of Court Gainsford Trust, 1992–2000. Vice-Chm., Hammersmith Democrats, 1988–89. Chm., Lansdown Crescent Assoc., 2003–06. Hon. Bencher, Gray's Inn, 2000. *Publications:* (contrib.) Outlook, 1963; (ed) Gray's Inn 2000: a millennium record, 2002; (ed) Simon Phipps: a portrait, 2003. *Address:* 20 Lansdown Crescent, Bath BA1 5EX. *Club:* Garrick.

MACHIN, (Edward) Anthony; QC 1973; a Recorder of the Crown Court, 1976–90; *b* 28 June 1925; *s* of Edward Arthur Machin and Olive Muriel Smith; *m* 1953, Jean Margaret McKanna; two *s* one *d*. *Educ:* Christ's Coll., Finchley; New Coll., Oxford (BA 1st Cl. 1949; MA 1950; BCL 1st. Cl. 1950; Vinerian Law Scholar, 1950; Tancred Student, 1950; Cassel Scholar, 1951). Called to Bar, Lincoln's Inn, 1951, Bencher, 1980; retired from practice, 1996; Dep. High Court Judge, 1985–95; a Judge of the Courts of Appeal of Jersey and Guernsey, 1988–95. Chm., Exeter Flying Club, 1999. *Publications:* Redgrave's Factories Acts, 1962, 1966, 1972; Redgrave's Offices and Shops, 1965 and 1973; Redgrave's Health and Safety in Factories, 1976, 1982; Health and Safety at Work, 1980; Health and Safety, 1990; (contrib.) Medical Negligence, 1990 and 1994. *Recreations:* music, learning the organ, flying, web-surfing, languages. *Address:* Strand End, Strand, Topsham, Exeter EX3 0BB. *T:* (01392) 877992.

MACHIN, John Vessey; His Honour Judge Machin; a Circuit Judge, since 1997; *b* 4 May 1941; *s* of late William Vessey Machin and Dona Machin (*née* Pryce), Worksop; *m* 1967, Susan Helen, *d* of Edgar Frank Emery; one *s* one *d*. *Educ:* Dragon Sch., Oxford; Westminster Sch. Called to the Bar, Middle Temple, 1965; Midland and Oxford Circuit; Asst Recorder, 1990–94; Recorder, 1994–97. Chm., Agricl Land Tribunal (Eastern Area), 1999– (Dep. Chm., 1986–99). Judicial Mem., Lincs Probation Bd, 2006–. Governor: Worksop Coll., Notts, 1986–; Ranby House Sch., 1986–; Fellow and Midland Dir, Woodard Schs, 1988–; Foundn Gov., St Matthew's C of E Primary Sch., Normanton-on-Trent, 2005–. *Recreations:* aquatic and rural pursuits especially canambulation. *Address:* c/o Lincoln Combined Court Centre, 360 High Street, Lincoln LN5 7RL. *Clubs:* Garrick, Farmers'; Newark Rowing.

MACHIN, Kenneth Arthur; QC 1977; **His Honour Judge Machin;** a Judge, International Criminal Tribunal for Rwanda, United Nations, since 2003; *b* 13 July 1936; *o s* of Thomas Arthur Machin and Edith May Machin; *m* 1983, Amaryllis Francesca (former ballet dancer and Member of Court of Common Council, Cripplegate Ward, City of London), *o d* of Dr Donald and Lucille Bigley. *Educ:* St Albans School. Called to the Bar, 1960; South Eastern Circuit; Central Criminal Court, 1985–90 and 2001; a Recorder of the Crown Court, 1979–83; a Circuit Judge, 1983–90; a Sen. Circuit Judge, 1990–2001; a Dep. Circuit Judge, 2001–. Chief Social Security and Child Support Comr, 1990–2000. Mem., Judicial Studies Bd and Chm., Tribunals Cttee, 1992–99. Freeman,

City of London. *Recreations:* painting, Martello Towers. *Address:* c/o Central Criminal Court, Old Bailey, EC4M 7EH.

MACHIN, Prof. Stephen Jonathan, PhD; FBA 2006; Professor of Economics, University College London, since 1996; Research Director, Centre for Economic Performance, London School of Economics, since 2003; *b* 23 Dec. 1962; *s* of Raymond Edward Machin and Betty Patricia Machin; *m* 2001, Kirstine Hansen; one *s*. *Educ:* Wolverhampton Grammar Sch.; Wolverhampton Poly. (BSc 1st cl. (Econs) 1985); Univ. of Warwick (PhD 1988). Lectr, 1988–93, Reader, 1993–96, UCL. Dir, Centre for Econs of Educn, 2000–. Visiting Professor: Harvard Univ., 1993–94; MIT, 2001–02. Ed., Economic Jl, 1998–. *Publications:* papers in leading academic jls, inc. Qly Jl of Econs, Rev. of Econ. Studies, Econ. Jl, Industrial and Labor Relns Rev. and Jl of European Econ. Assoc. *Address:* Department of Economics, University College London, Gower Street, WC1E 6BT. *T:* (020) 7679 5870, *Fax:* (020) 7916 2773; *e-mail:* s.machin@ucl.ac.uk.

MACHIN, Thomas Paul Edwin; Director: MacGregor Associates, since 2000; Fraser Otis Ltd, since 2000; *b* 14 Sept. 1944; *s* of late Thomas Edwin Machin and Elizabeth Pamela Machin (*née* Collett); *m* 1970, Elizabeth-Ann Suttle. *Educ:* St Joseph's Coll., Stoke-on-Trent; London Sch. of Economics (BSc Econs). Plessey Co., 1966–69; Massey Ferguson, 1969–74; joined British Leyland, 1974; Dir, Engrg Services, 1980–82; Personnel Dir, Cowley, 1983–87; Eur. Employee Relns and Mgt Develt Dir, Lawson Mardon Gp (Europe), 1987–91; Human Resources Dir, James Neill Hldgs Ltd, 1991–92; CEO, States of Jersey Estabt Cttee, 1992–95; Chief Executive, BPIF, 1995–2000. Consultant: Negotiating Solutions, 2002–05; First Class Partnerships, 2002–. Chairman: Indust. Relns Cttee, BPIF, 1989–91; Trade Assoc. Council, CBI, 2000; Pres., Yorks Publicity Assoc., 1998. Chartered FCIPD (FIPD 1986); FRSA 1996. Freeman, City of London, 1998; Liveryman, Co. of Stationers and Newspaper Makers, 1998–2002. *Recreations:* retired Association Football referee, walking, spectator sports (especially horse racing and Association Football), politics, business, skidelling. *Address:* 271 Kenilworth Road, Balsall Common, Coventry CV7 7EL. *T:* (01676) 532546. *Club:* National Liberal.

MACHRAY, Alastair Hulbert; Editor, Liverpool Echo, since 2005; *b* 19 June 1961; *s* of Douglas Basil Machray and June Hulbert; *m* 1987, Lynne Elizabeth Ward; one *s* one *d*. *Educ:* Glasgow Acad.; Greencroft Comprehensive. Reporter, Sunderland Echo, 1979–82; sports journalist, Journal, Newcastle, 1982–85; editor, Football Pink, Newcastle, 1985–86; sports journalist, Today, 1986–88; Evening Chronicle, Newcastle: Sub Editor, 1988; Asst Chief Sub Editor, 1988–89; Dep. Chief Sub Editor, 1989–90; Design Editor, 1990–93; Asst Editor, Liverpool Echo, 1994–95; Editor: Liverpool Daily Post, 1995–2002; Daily Post in Wales, 2002–05; Ed.-in-Chief, Trinity Mirror North Wales, 2002–05. *Recreations:* golf, cricket, family, cinema, travel. *Address:* PO Box 48, Old Hall Street, Liverpool L69 3EB.

McHUGH, James, CBE 1989; FREng; Chairman, British Pipe Coaters Ltd, 1991–96; *b* 4 May 1930; *s* of late Edward McHugh and Martha (*née* Smith); *m* 1953, Sheila (*née* Cape); two *d*. *Educ:* Carlisle Grammar Sch.; various colls. FREng (FEng 1986); FIMechE, FIGEM, FInstPet. Served Army, National Service. Entered Gas Industry, 1947; technical and managerial appts in Northern and E Midlands Gas Bds; Prodn Engr 1967, Dir of Engrg 1971, W Midlands Gas Bd; British Gas Corporation, subseq. British Gas plc: Dir of Ops, 1975; Mem., 1979; Man. Dir, Prodn and Supply, 1982; Man. Dir, 1986; Gp Exec. Mem., 1986–91. Director: Lloyd's Register Quality Assurance Ltd, 1985–2002; UK Accreditation Service, 1995–2000. Member: Meteorological Cttee, MoD, 1981–85; Engrg Council, 1989–92; President: IGasE, 1986–87; Inst. of Quality Assurance, 1992–97; World Quality Council, 1997–2002. Hon. FCQI (Hon. FIQA 1997); CCMI; FRSA. Freeman, City of London, 1984; Liveryman, Engineers' Co., 1984–. *Recreations:* mountaineering, dinghy sailing. *Club:* Anglo-Belgian.

McILVEEN, Michelle Elizabeth; Member (DemU) Strangford, Northern Ireland Assembly, since 2007; *b* 21 Jan. 1971; *d* of Henry and Elizabeth McIlveen. *Educ:* Queen's Univ., Belfast (BSSc, MSSc; PGCE). Teacher of hist. and politics, 1994–97; business manager, 1997–2007. Mem. (DemU) Ards BC, 2005–. *Address:* Constituency Office, 1 Bridge Street Link, Comber, Northern Ireland BT23 5YH. *T:* (028) 9187 1441, *Fax:* (028) 9187 1494; *e-mail:* michelle.mcilveen@niassembly.gov.uk.

McINDOE, Very Rev. John Hedley; Minister of St Columba's Church, Pont Street, London, 1988–2000; Moderator of the General Assembly of The Church of Scotland, 1996–97; *b* 31 Aug. 1934; *s* of William McIndoe and May (*née* Hedley); *m* 1960, Evelyn Kennedy Johnstone (*d* 2006); three *d*. *Educ:* Greenock Acad.; Glasgow Univ. (MA Hons (Classics), 1956; BD (with distinction), 1959); Hartford Seminary, Conn, USA (STM, 1960). Ordained, 1960; Asst Minister, Paisley Abbey, 1960–63; Minister: Park Church, Dundee, 1963–72; St Nicholas Parish Church, Lanark, 1972–88. Hon. DD Glasgow, 2000. *Recreations:* theatre, films. *Address:* 5 Dunlin, Westerlands Park, Glasgow G12 0FE. *T:* (0141) 579 1366. *Club:* Caledonian.

McINERNEY, Prof. John Peter, OBE 1995; Glanely Professor of Agricultural Policy and Director of Agricultural Economics Unit, University of Exeter, 1984–2002, now Emeritus; *b* 10 Jan. 1939; *s* of Peter McInerney and Eva McInerney; *m* 1961, Audrey M. Perry; one *s* one *d*. *Educ:* Colyton Grammar Sch., Colyford, Devon; Univ. of London (BScAgric Hons); Univ. of Oxford (DipAgricEcons); Iowa State Univ. (PhD). Lectr in Agricl Econs, Wye Coll., Univ. of London, 1964–66; Lectr and Sen. Lectr in Agricl Econs, Univ. of Manchester, 1967–78; Prof. of Agricl Econs and Management, Univ. of Reading, 1978–84. Research Economist and Cons., World Bank, Washington, 1972–97. Visiting Professor: Res. Sch. of Animal Prodn and Health, Royal Vet. and Agricl Univ., Copenhagen, 1999–2005; RAC, 2001–. President: Agricl Econs Soc., 1996–97; Rural Educn and Develt Assoc., 1996–97; Member: Mgt Cttee, MAFF/DTI LINK Sustainable Livestock Prog., 1996–2002; Farm Animal Welfare Council, MAFF, 1996–2004; Bd, UK Register of Organic Food Standards, 1996–2003; Independent Scientific Gp on Cattle TB, MAFF, subseq. DEFRA, 1998–2007; Econs Panel, SW RDA, 2001–06. Trustee, Farm Animal Welfare Trust, 2008–. Governor, Silsoe Res. Inst., 1996–2003. Phi Kappa Phi 1964, Gamma Sigma Delta 1964. FRSA 1995. Hon. FRASE 1999. Massey Ferguson Nat. Agricl Award, 1998. *Publications:* The Food Industry: economics and policy (jtly), 1983; Badgers and Bovine Tuberculosis (jtly), 1986; Disease in Farm Livestock: economics and policy (jtly), 1987; Diversification in the Use of Farm Resources, 1989; Economic Analysis of Milk Quotas, 1992; Agriculture at the Crossroads, 1998; Who Cares?: a study of farmers' involvement in countryside management, 2000; What's the Damage?: costs of countryside management on farms, 2001; Animal Welfare: economics and policy, 2004; chapters in: Current Issues in Economic Policy, 1975, 2nd edn 1980; Resources Policy, 1982; Grassland Production, 1999, etc; articles in Jl of Agricl Econs, Amer. Jl of Agricl Econs, Canadian Jl of Agricl Econs, Outlook on Agric., Jl of RASE, Farm Mgt, Preventive Vet. Medicine, Agricl Progress, Nature, Jl Applied Ecol. *Recreations:* doing it myself, tentative farming, introspection. *Address:* Old Rectory Farm, Templeton, Tiverton, Devon EX16 8BN. *T:* 07764 516964; *e-mail:* J.P.McInerney@exeter.ac.uk. *Club:* Templeton Social.

MacINNES, Dame Barbara Mary; *see* Stocking, Dame B. M.

MacINNES, Hamish, OBE 1979; BEM; Founder and Leader, Glencoe Mountain Rescue Team, 1960–94; author and film consultant, major movies; Director, Glencoe Productions Ltd, since 1989; *b* 7 July 1930. Dep. Leader, British Everest Expedition, 1975. Hon. Dir, Leishman Meml Res. Centre, Glencoe, 1975–92; Mountain Rescue Cttee for Scotland (Past Sec.). Founder and Hon. Pres., Search and Rescue Dog Assoc.; Co-founder, Snow and Avalanche Foundn of Scotland, 1988; Past Pres., Alpine Climbing Group; Pres., Guide Dogs for the Blind Adventure Gp, 1986–. Patron, Equal Adventure, 2005–. Designer of climbing equipment, incl. the first all metal ice axe, terrodactyl ice tools, the MacInnes stretchers, etc. Hon. LLD: Glasgow, 1983; Dundee, 2004; Hon. DSc: Aberdeen, 1988; Heriot-Watt, 1992; DU Stirling, 1997. Great Scot Award, 2000; Mem., Scottish Sports Hall of Fame, 2003; Scottish Award for Excellence in Mountain Culture, 2009. *Publications:* Climbing, 1964; Scottish Climbs, 2 vols, 1971, 2nd edn (1 vol.) 1981; International Mountain Rescue Handbook, 1972, 5th edn 2005; Call-Out: mountain rescue, 1973, 4th edn 1986; Climb to the Lost World, 1974; Death Reel (novel), 1976; West Highland Walks, vols 1 and 2, 1979, Vol. 3, 1983, Vol. 4, 1988; Look Behind the Ranges, 1979; Scottish Winter Climbs, 1980; High Drama (stories), 1980; Beyond the Ranges, 1984; Sweep Search, 1985; The Price of Adventure, 1987; My Scotland, 1988; The Way Through the Glens, 1989; Land of Mountain and Mist, 1989; Mammoth Book of Mountain Disaster, 2003; Murder in the Glen (novel), 2008; books have been translated into Russian, Japanese and German. *Address:* Tigh A'Voulin, Glencoe, Argyll PA49 4HX.

McINNES, John Colin; DL; QC (Scot.) 1990; Sheriff Principal of South Strathclyde, Dumfries and Galloway, 2000–05; *b* 21 Nov. 1938; *s* of late Mr I. W. McInnes, WS, and of Mrs Lucy McInnes, Cupar, Fife; *m* 1966, Elisabeth Mabel Neilson; one *s* one *d*. *Educ:* Cargilfield Sch., Edinburgh; Merchiston Castle Sch., Edinburgh; Brasenose Coll., Oxford (BA); Edinburgh Univ. (LLB). 2nd Lieut 8th Royal Tank Regt, 1957–58; Lieut Fife and Forfar Yeomanry/Scottish Horse (TA), 1958–64. Advocate, 1963. In practice at Scottish Bar, 1963–73; Tutor, Faculty of Law, Edinburgh Univ., 1965–73; Sheriff of the Lothians and Peebles, 1973–74, of Tayside Central and Fife, 1974–2000. Member and Vice-President: Security Service Tribunal, 1989–2001; Intelligence Services Tribunal, 1994–2001; Mem., Investigatory Powers Tribunal, 2000–. Member: Cameron Gp on Shrieval Trng, 1995–96; Scottish Criminal Justice Forum, 1996–2000; Judicial Studies Cttee (Scotland), 1996–2000; Parole Bd for Scotland, 2005–; Chairman: Summary Justice Review Cttee, Scotland, 2001–04; Youth Court Project Gp (Scotland), 2002. Comr of Northern Lighthouses, 2000–05. Pres., Sheriffs' Assoc., 1995–97. Director: R. Mackness & Co. Ltd, 1963–70; Fios Group Ltd, 1970–72 (Chm., 1970–72). Chm., Fife Family Conciliation Service, 1988–90. Mem. Court, St Andrews Univ., 1983–91. DL Fife, 1997. Hon. LLD St Andrews, 1994. Contested (C) Aberdeen North, 1964. *Publication:* Divorce Law and Practice in Scotland, 1990. *Recreations:* shooting, fishing, ski-ing, photography.

MacINNES, Keith Gordon, CMG 1984; HM Diplomatic Service, retired; Ambassador and UK Permanent Representative to OECD, Paris, 1992–95; *b* 17 July 1935; *s* of late Kenneth MacInnes and Helen MacInnes (*née* Gordon); *m* 1st, 1966, Jennifer Anne Fennell (marr. diss. 1980); one *s* one *d*; 2nd, 1985, Hermione Pattinson. *Educ:* Rugby; Trinity Coll., Cambridge (MA); Pres., Cambridge Union Soc., 1957. HM Forces, 1953–55. FO, 1960; Third, later Second Secretary, Buenos Aires, 1961–64; FO, 1964 (First Sec., 1965); Private Sec. to Permanent Under-Sec., Commonwealth Office, 1965–68; First Sec. (Information), Madrid, 1968–70; FCO, 1970–74; Counsellor and Head of Chancery: Prague, 1974–77; Dep. Perm. Rep., UK Mission, Geneva, 1977–80; Head of Information Dept, FCO, 1980–83; Asst Under-Sec. of State and Principal Finance Officer, FCO, 1983–87; Ambassador to the Philippines, 1987–92. *Recreations:* golf, bridge.

McINTOSH, family name of **Baron McIntosh of Haringey** and **McIntosh of Hudnall**.

McINTOSH OF HARINGEY, Baron *cr* 1982 (Life Peer), of Haringey in Greater London; **Andrew Robert McIntosh;** PC 2002; President, GamCare (National Association for Gambling Care, Educational Resources and Training), since 2005; Vice-President, Royal Television Society, since 2006; Member, Gambling Commission, since 2006; *b* 30 April 1933; *s* of late Prof. A. W. McIntosh and Jenny (*née* Britton); *m* 1962, Naomi Ellen Sargant (*d* 2006); two *s*. *Educ:* Haberdashers' Aske's Hampstead Sch.; Royal Grammar Sch., High Wycombe; Jesus Coll., Oxford (MA); Ohio State Univ. (Fellow in Econs, 1956–57). Gallup Poll, 1957–61; Hoover Ltd, 1961–63; Market Res. Manager, Osram (GEC) Ltd, 1963–65; IFF Research Ltd: Man. Dir, 1965–81; Chm., 1981–88; Dep. Chm., 1988–97. Chm., SVP United Kingdom Ltd, 1983–92. Member: Hornsey Bor. Council, 1963–65; Haringey Bor. Council, 1964–68 (Chm., Develt Control); Greater London Council: Member for Tottenham, 1973–83; Chm., NE Area Bd, 1973–74, W Area Bd, 1974–76, and Central Area Bd, 1976; Opposition Leader on Planning and Communications, 1977–80; Leader of the Opposition, 1980–81. House of Lords: Opposition spokesman on educn and science, 1985–87, on industry matters, 1983–87, on the environment, 1987–92, on home affairs, 1992–97; Dep. Leader of the Opposition, 1992–97; Captain of the Yeomen of the Guard (Dep. Govt Chief Whip), 1997–2003; Minister for the Media and Heritage, DCMS, 2003–05. Chairman: Computer Sub-Cttee, H of L Offices Cttee, 1984–92; Media Sub-Cttee, 2008–; Member: Council of Europe Parly Assembly, 2005; Parly Assembly of Western EU, 2005. Vis. Res. Fellow, Policy Studies Inst., Univ. of Westminster, 2007–; Hon. Prof. of Applied Social Res., Univ. of Salford, 2008–. Mem., Metrop. Water Bd, 1967–68. Market Research Society: Ed. of Jl, 1963–67; Chm., 1972–73; Pres., 1995–98. Chairman: Assoc. of Neighbourhood Councils, 1974–80; Fabian Soc., 1985–86 (Mem., NEC, 1981–87). Principal, Working Men's Coll., NW1, 1988–97; Governor, Drayton Sch., Tottenham, 1967–83. *Publications:* Industry and Employment in the Inner City, 1979; (ed) Employment Policy in the UK and United States, 1980; Women and Work, 1981; jl articles on theory, practice and findings of survey research. *Recreations:* cooking, reading, music. *Address:* 27 Hurst Avenue, N6 5TX. *T:* (020) 8340 1496, *Fax:* (020) 8348 4641.

McINTOSH OF HUDNALL, Baroness *cr* 1999 (Life Peer), of Hampstead in the London Borough of Camden; **Genista Mary McIntosh;** arts consultant; *b* 23 Sept. 1946; *d* of late Geoffrey Tandy and Maire Tandy; *m* 1971, Neil Scott Wishart McIntosh, *qv* (marr. diss.); one *s* one *d*. *Educ:* Univ. of York (BA Philosophy and Sociology). Press Sec., York Festival of Arts, 1968–69; Royal Shakespeare Co.: Casting Dir, 1972–77; Planning Controller, 1977–84; Sen. Administrator, 1986–90; Associate Producer, 1990; Exec. Dir, RNT, 1990–96 and 1997–2002; Chief Exec., Royal Opera House, Covent Gdn, 1997; Principal, Guildhall Sch. of Music and Drama, 2002–03. Dir, Marmont Management Ltd, 1984–86. Board Member: Roundhouse Trust, 1999–; Nat. Opera Studio, 2005–; Mem. Council, RADA, 2007–. Trustee: Theatres Trust, 2002–; Southbank Sinfonia, 2003–. Hon. Fellow, Goldsmiths Coll., Univ. of London, 2003. DUniv: York, 1998; Middlesex, 2002; City, 2002. *Address:* House of Lords, SW1A 0PW.

McINTOSH, Anne Caroline Ballingall; MP (C) Vale of York, since 1997; *b* 20 Sept. 1954; *d* of Dr Alastair Ballingall McIntosh and Grethe-Lise McIntosh (*née* Thomsen); *m* 1992, John Harvey. *Educ:* Harrogate Coll., Harrogate, Yorks; Univ. of Edinburgh (LLB Hons); Univ. of Aarhus, Denmark. Admitted to Faculty of Advocates, 1982. Stagiaire,

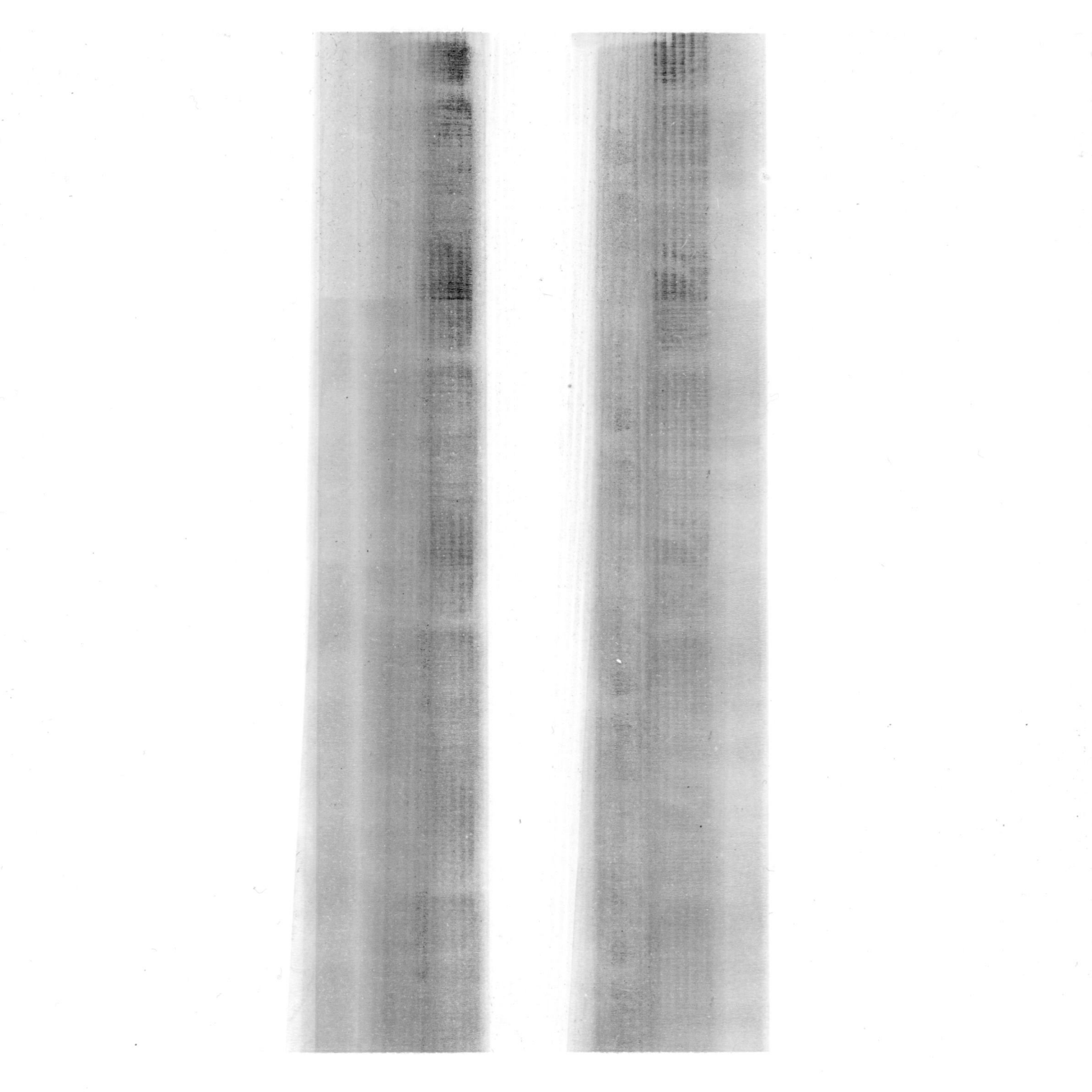

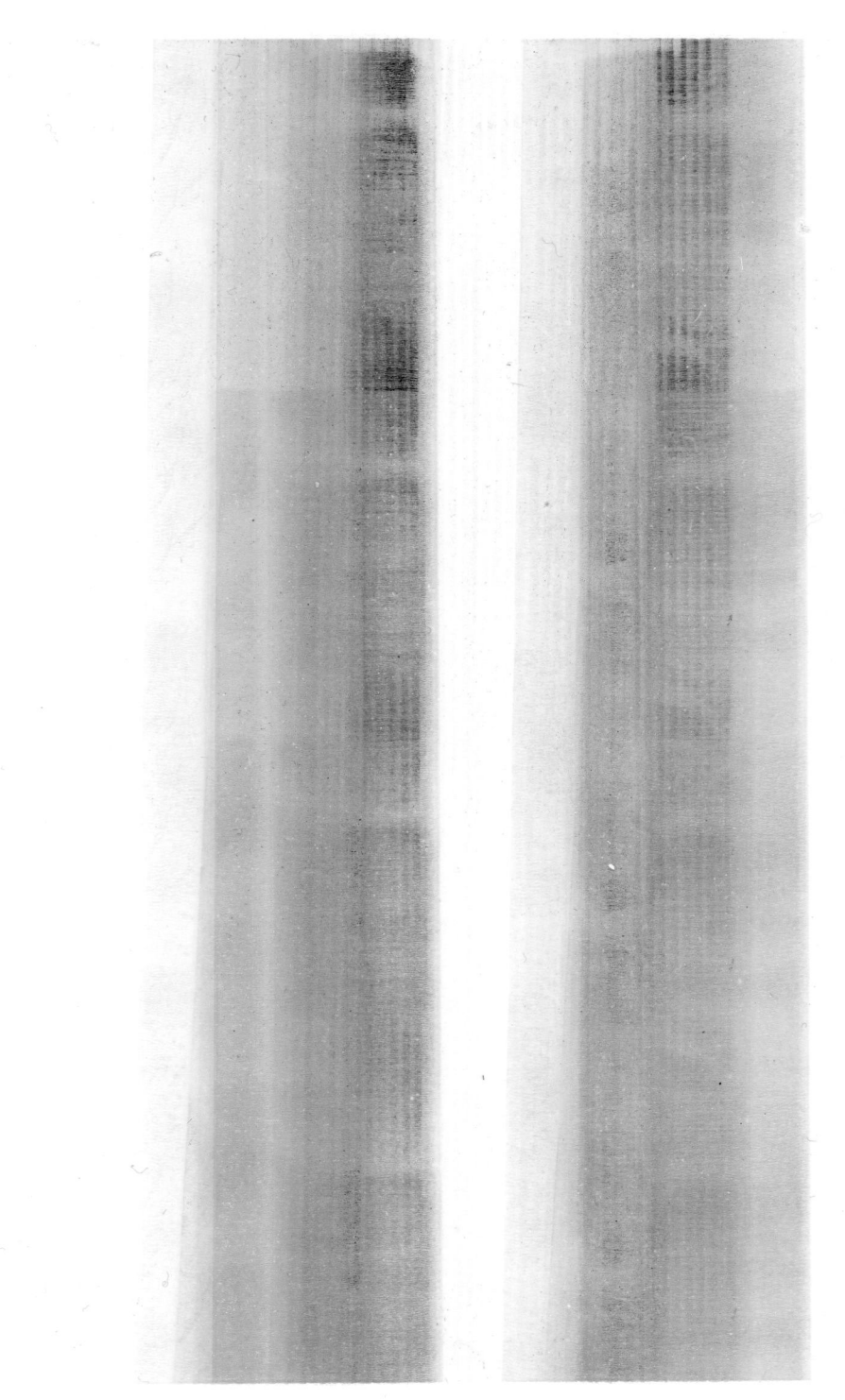

EEC, Brussels, 1978; legal advr in private EEC practice, Brussels, 1979–80; Bar apprentice with Simpson and Marwick, WS, and devilling at Scottish Bar, 1980–82; private legal practice, Brussels, specialising in EEC law, 1982–83; Secretariat Mem., responsible for transport, youth, culture, educn and tourism, and relations with Scandinavia, Austria, Switzerland and Yugoslavia, EDG, Europ. Parlt, 1983–89. European Parliament: Mem. (C), NE Essex, 1989–94, Essex N and Suffolk S, 1994–99; a Jun. Whip, EDG, 1989–92; Mem., Transport and Legal Affairs Cttees; EDG Spokesman on Rules Cttee, 1989–95, Transport and Tourism Cttee, 1992–99; Mem., Norway Parly Delegn, 1989–95, Polish Parly Delegn, 1995–97, Czech Parly Delegn, 1997–99. Shadow Minister: for Culture, Media & Sport, 2001–02; for Transport, 2002–03; for Envmt and Transport, 2003–05; for Foreign Affairs, 2005; for Work and Pensions, 2005–06; for Educn, 2006–07; for Envmt, 2007–; Opposition frontbench spokesman on envmt, food and rural affairs, 2007–. Member: Select Cttee on Envmt, Transport and the Regions, 1999–2001, on Transport, Local Govt and the Regions, 2001–02, on Transport, 2003–05, on Envmt, Food and Rural Affairs, 2007–; Exec., 1922 Cttee, 2000–01; European Scrutiny Cttee; European Standing Cttee. President: Anglia Enterprise in Europe, 1989–99; Yorkshire First, Enterprise in Yorks, 1995–99. Mem., Governing Council, Anglia Poly. Univ.; former Mem., Senate, Univ. of Essex; Gov., Writtle Coll. Hon. LLD Anglia Poly. Univ., 1997. *Recreations:* swimming, cinema, walking. *Address:* House of Commons, SW1A 0AA. *T:* (020) 7219 3000.

McINTOSH, David Angus; Senior Partner, Davies Arnold Cooper, Solicitors, 1978–2007; Consultant, Fox Solicitors, since 2007; President, Law Society, 2001–02; *b* 10 March 1944; *s* of late Robert Angus McIntosh and of Monica Joan (*née* Hillier, now Sherring); *m* 1968, Jennifer Mary Dixon; two *d*. *Educ:* Selwood Co. Sch., Frome; Coll. of Law, London. Admitted solicitor, 1969. Joined Davies Arnold Cooper, 1963. Mem., Legal Consultative Panel, Dept of Constitutional Affairs, 2003–04. Law Society of England and Wales: Mem. Council, 1996–; Chm., Exec. Cttee, 2000–; Member: Court of Appeal Users' Cttee, 1998–2000; Interim Exec. Cttee, 1999; Vice-Chm., 1997–98, Chm., 1999–2000, Civil Litigation Cttee. Chm., Cttee on Consumer Affairs, Advertising, Unfair Competition and Product Liability, Internat. Bar Assoc., 1995–99; Mem., Exec. Cttee (US), Internat. Assoc. Defense Counsel, 1995–98. Chm., Solicitors Indemnity Fund Ltd, 2006–; Chair, Legal and Professional Claims Ltd. Chm., Professional Standards Bd, Chartered Insurance Inst., 2006–. Mem. Council, Sch. of Pharmacy, Univ. of London, 2003–04. *Publications:* Personal Injury Awards in EC Countries, 1990; Civil Procedures in EC Countries, 1993; Personal Injury Awards in EU and EFTA Countries, 1994, 2003; numerous contribs on compensation, insurance and products liability to learned jls. *Recreations:* golf, trying to keep fit, choosing ties! *Address:* c/o Fox, 78 Cornhill, EC3V 3QQ. *T:* (020) 7618 2400. *Clubs:* Chigwell Golf; Real Sotogrande Golf (Spain).

MACINTOSH, Joan, CBE 1978; *b* 23 Nov. 1919; *née* Burbidge; *m* 1952, Ian Gillies Macintosh (*d* 1992); one *s* two *d* (and one *s* decd). *Educ:* Amer. and English schs; Oxford Univ. (MA Modern History). BBC, 1941–42; Amer. Div., Min. of Inf., 1942–45; HM Foreign Service, 1945–52; retd on marriage. Voluntary work in India, 1953–69; CAB Organiser, Glasgow, 1972–75. Chm. Council, Insurance Ombudsman Bureau, 1981–85; Lay Observer for Scotland (Solicitors (Scotland) Act), 1981–89; Chm., Scottish Child Law Centre, 1989–92; Mem., Royal Commn on Legal Services in Scotland, 1975–80; Mem., Scottish Constitutional Commn, 1994. Chm., Scottish Consumer Council, 1975–80; Vice-Chm., National Consumer Council, 1976–84; Vice-Pres., Nat. Fedn of Consumer Gps, 1982–97; Member: Council, Victim Support Scotland, 1992–96; Auchterarder Community Council, 1995–98. Hon. Pres., Scottish Legal Action Group, 1990. Hon. LLD: Dundee, 1982; Strathclyde, 1991; DUniv Stirling, 1988. *Recreations:* writing, local history. *Address:* Wynd End, Auchterarder, Perthshire PH3 1AD. *T:* (01764) 662499.

McINTOSH, John Charles, OBE 1996; Headmaster, The London Oratory School, 1977–2006; *b* 6 Feb. 1946; *s* of Arthur and Betty McIntosh. *Educ:* Ebury Sch.; Shoreditch Coll.; Sussex Univ. (MA). The London Oratory School: Asst Master, 1967–71; Dep. Headmaster, 1971–77. Member: Nat. Curriculum Council, 1990–93; Centre for Policy Studies Educn Gp, 1982–, and Council, 2005–; Inst. of Econ. Affairs Educn Adv. Council, 1988–91; Health Educn Council, 1985–88. Consultant Dir, Reform, 2007–. Dean, Acad. of St Cecilia, 2006–; Trustee: English Schs Orch. and Choir, 2007–; London Oratory Schola Foundn, 2007–. Mem., Catholic Union of GB, 1978–. FRSA 1981. Hon. FCP 1998. *Recreations:* playing the organ, opera, ballet, theatre. *Address:* 75 Alder Lodge, River Gardens, SW6 6NR; *e-mail:* cantemus@mac.com. *Club:* Athenæum.

MACINTOSH, Kenneth; Member (Lab) Eastwood, Scottish Parliament, since 1999; *b* 15 Jan. 1962; *s* of Dr Farquhar Macintosh, CBE; *m* 1998, Claire, *d* of Douglas and Deirdre Kinloch Anderson; two *s* three *d*. *Educ:* Royal High Sch., Edinburgh; Edinburgh Univ. (MA Hons History). Sen. Broadcast Journalist in News and Current Affairs, BBC, 1987–99. *Recreations:* sport (including football, tennis and golf), music, reading. *Address:* 238 Ayr Road, Newton Mearns, Glasgow G77 6AA. *T:* (0141) 577 0100.

McINTOSH, Lyndsay June; JP; Chairman, Central Scotland Rape Crisis and Sexual Abuse Centre, since 2003; *b* 12 June 1955; *d* of Lawrence and Mary Clark; *m* 1981, Gordon McIntosh; one *s* one *d*. *Educ:* Duncanrig Sen. Secondary Sch.; Dundee Coll. of Technology (Dip. Mgt Studies). Legal Secretary, 1973–75; Civil Servant, Inland Revenue, 1975–84; business consultant, 1996–99. Lay Inspector of Schools, 1994–99. Mem. (C) Central Scotland, Scottish Parlt, 1999–2003; Cons. spokesman on social justice, equal opportunities and women's issues, 1999–2001; Dep. Convenor, Justice 2 Cttee, 2001. Sec., Assoc. of former Mems of Scottish Parlt, 2003–. Mem., N Lanarks Justices Cttee, 2004–08. JP: N Lanarks, 1993–2008; S Strathclyde, Dumfries and Galloway, 2008. Sec., Tannochside Action Gp. *Publications:* articles on social affairs in newspapers and magazines. *Recreations:* reading, weeding, sport of kings, travel, stadium concerts, karaoke. *Address:* 35 Lynnhurst, Uddingston, Glasgow G71 6SA.

McINTOSH, Melinda Jane Frances; *see* Letts, M. J. F.

McINTOSH, Dr Neil; Edward Clarke Professor of Child Life and Health, University of Edinburgh, 1987–2007, now Emeritus; *b* 21 May 1942; *s* of William and Dorothy McIntosh; *m* 1967, Sheila Ann Clarke; two *s* one *d*. *Educ:* University College Hosp., London (MB BS; DSc Med 1995); Univ. of Southampton (BSc). Sen. Registrar in Paediatrics, UCH, 1973–78; Res. Fellow in Paediatric Endocrinology, Univ. of Calif, San Francisco, 1975–76; Sen. Lectr and Consultant Paediatrician, St George's Hosp. and Med. Sch., 1978–87; Hon. Consultant Paediatrician, Royal Hosp. for Sick Children, Edinburgh, 1987–2007; Hon. Neonatologist, Royal Infirmary, Edinburgh, 1987–2007. Consultant Advr in Neonatology to British Army, 1984–2007. Pres., European Soc. for Pediatric Res., 1993–94; Scientific Vice-Pres., RCPCH, 2002–07. Editor, Current Topics in Neonatology, 1996–2000. *Publication:* (ed with A. G. M. Campbell) Forfar and Arneil's Textbook of Paediatrics, 4th edn 1993, 7th edn (ed with P. Helms and R. Smyth) 2008. *Recreations:* music, family. *Address:* 32 Queens Crescent, Edinburgh EH9 2BA. *T:* (0131) 536 0801.

McINTOSH, Neil Scott Wishart; Chief Executive, CfBT Education Trust (formerly Centre for British Teachers), since 1990; *b* 24 July 1947; *s* of William Henderson McIntosh and Mary Catherine McIntosh; *m* 1st, 1971, Genista Mary Tandy (*see* Baroness McIntosh of Hudnall) (marr. diss. 1990); one *s* one *d*; 2nd, 1991, Melinda Jane Frances Letts, *qv*; one *s* one *d*. *Educ:* Merchiston Castle Sch., Edinburgh; Univ. of York (BA Politics); London Sch. of Econs (MSc Industrial Relations). Res. Associate, PEP, 1969–73; Res. Dir, Southwark Community Develt Proj., 1973–76; Dir, Shelter, 1976–84; Dir, VSO, 1985–90. Councillor, London Bor. of Camden, 1971–77; Chm., Housing Cttee, 1974–76. Dir, Stonham Housing Assoc., 1982–98. Vice Pres., BSA, 1985–91. Founder and Chm., Homeless Internat., 1988–91; Treasurer, Campaign for Freedom of Information, 1984– (Co-Chm., 1997–); Mem., Independent Broadcasting Telethon Trust, 1987–94. Trustee, HOST, 2004–. Gov., Langtree Sch., Oxon, 2006–. *Publication:* The Right to Manage?, 1971, 2nd edn 1976. *Recreations:* golf, sailing, theatre. *Clubs:* Reform; Goring and Streatley Golf; Plockton Sailing.

McINTOSH, Sir Neil (William David), Kt 2000; CBE 1990; JP; DL; Chairman, Judicial Appointments Board for Scotland, since 2002; *b* 30 Jan. 1940; *s* of Neil and Beatrice McIntosh; *m* 1965, Marie Elizabeth Lindsay; one *s* two *d*. *Educ:* King's Park Sen. Secondary Sch., Glasgow. ACIS 1967; FIPM 1987. J. & P. Coats, 1957–59; Outward Bound, Moray Sea Sch., 1958 (Gold Award); Honeywell Controls, 1959–62; Berks, Oxford and Reading Jt O&M Unit, 1962–64; Stewarts & Lloyds, 1964–66; Sen. O&M Officer, Lanark CC, 1966–69; Estabt/O&M Officer, Inverness CC, 1969–75; Personnel Officer, 1975–81, Dir of Manpower Services, 1981–85, Highland Regl Council; Chief Executive: Dumfries and Galloway Regl Council, 1985–92; Strathclyde Regl Council, 1992–96; Convenor, Scottish Council for Voluntary Orgns, 1996–2001. Chm., Commn on Local Govt and Scottish Parlt, 1998–99. Mem. Bd, British Telecom, Scotland, 1998–2003. Chm., Nat. Cos Contact Gp, 1996–98; Hd, COSLA Consultancy, 1996–99. Director: Training 2000 (Scotland) Ltd, 1993; Quality Scotland Foundn, 1993; Sportability Strathclyde, 1994. Scottish Advr, 2000–05, Chm., Governance Cttee, 2005–, Joseph Rowntree Foundn; Expert Advr, NI Review of Public Admin, 2002–05. Chief Counting Officer, Scottish Parlt Referendum, 1997; Mem., UK Electoral Commn, 2001–08. Trustee: Nat. Museums Scotland (formerly Nat. Museums of Scotland), 1999–; Dumfries Theatre Royal Trust, 2003–06. Mem., Comunn na Gaidhlig Wkg Gp on Status of Gaelic Lang., 2000–03. DL Dumfries, 1998; JP 1999. FRSA 1989. Hon. DHL Syracuse Univ., USA, 1993; Hon. LLD Glasgow Caledonian, 1999. *Recreations:* antique bottle collecting, bowling, local history, hill walking, dry stane dyking.

McINTOSH, Dr Robert; Director, Scotland, Forestry Commission, since 2003; *b* 6 Oct. 1951; *s* of Robert Hamilton McIntosh and Kathleen McIntosh. *Educ:* Linlithgow Acad.; Edinburgh Univ. (BSc Hons 1973; PhD 1985); MICFor 1974. Dist Officer, 1973–78, Res. Project Leader, 1979–84, Forestry Commn; Forest Dist Manager, Kielder Forest, 1984–94; Forest Enterprise: Dir, Ops, 1994–97; Chief Exec., 1997–2003. *Publications:* papers and articles in forestry jls. *Recreations:* shooting, stalking, farming. *Address:* Forestry Commission, 231 Corstorphine Road, Edinburgh EH12 7AT; East Brackley Grange, by Kinross KY13 9LU. *T:* (01577) 862057. *Club:* Farmers'.

McINTOSH, Sir Ronald (Robert Duncan), KCB 1975 (CB 1968); Chairman, APV plc, 1982–89; *b* 26 Sept. 1919; *s* of Thomas Steven McIntosh, MD, FRCPE and Christina Jane McIntosh; *m* 1951, Doreen Frances, *o d* of Commander Andrew MacGinnity, RNR and Margaret MacGinnity, Frinton-on-Sea. *Educ:* Charterhouse (Scholar); Balliol Coll., Oxford. Served in Merchant Navy, 1939–45; Second Mate, 1943–45. Assistant Principal, Board of Trade, 1947; General Manager, Dollar Exports Board, 1949–51; Commercial Counsellor, UK High Commn, New Delhi, 1957–61; Under-Secretary: BoT, 1961–64; DEA, 1964–66; Dep. Under-Sec. of State, Dept of Economic Affairs, 1966–68; Dep. Secretary, Cabinet Office, 1968–70; Dep. Under-Sec. of State, Dept of Employment, 1970–72; Dep. Sec., HM Treasury, 1972–73; Dir-Gen. Nat. Economic Development Office, and Mem. NEDC, 1973–77. Director: S. G. Warburg & Co. Ltd, 1978–90; Foseco plc, 1978–90; London & Manchester Gp plc, 1978–90. Chairman: Danish–UK Chamber of Commerce, 1990–92; British Health Care Consortium (for the former Soviet Union), 1992–97. Mem., Council, CBI, 1980–90; Co-Chm., British-Hungarian Round Table, 1980–84. Chm., Centre for Eur. Agricl Studies, Wye Coll., 1979–83. Trustee, The Tablet, 1997–2006. Companion, NEAC, 2002–. CCMI. Hon. DSc Aston, 1977. *Publications:* (contrib.) Roy Jenkins, a Retrospective, 2004; Challenge to Democracy, 2006. *Address:* The Thatched Cottage, Parsonage Farm, Throwley, Faversham, Kent ME13 0PN. *Clubs:* Royal Thames Yacht; Band of Brothers (Kent).

MacINTOSH, Sarah; HM Diplomatic Service; High Commissioner in Sierra Leone, since 2006; *b* 7 Aug. 1969. Entered FCO, 1991; Third Sec., UK Mission to UN, Vienna, 1994–95; Second Sec. (Econ./EU), Madrid, 1996–97; First Sec., FCO, 1997–2000, UK Mission to UN, NY, 2000–02; FCO, 2002–04; UN Interim Admin Mission, Kosovo, 2004–05. *Address:* c/o Foreign and Commonwealth Office, King Charles Street, SW1A 2AH.

MacINTYRE, Prof. Alasdair Chalmers; Research Professor of Philosophy, University of Notre Dame, since 2000; *b* 12 Jan. 1929; *o s* of Eneas John MacIntyre, MD (Glasgow), and Margaret Emily Chalmers, MB, ChB (Glasgow); *m* 1977, Lynn Sumida Joy; one *s* three *d* by previous marriages. *Educ:* Epsom Coll. and privately; Queen Mary Coll., Univ. of London (Fellow, 1984); Manchester Univ. BA (London); MA (Manchester); MA (Oxon). Lectr in Philosophy of Religion, Manchester Univ., 1951–57; Lectr in Philosophy, Leeds Univ., 1957–61; Research Fellow, Nuffield Coll., Oxford, 1961–62; Sen. Fellow, Council of Humanities, Princeton Univ., 1962–63; Fellow and Preceptor in Philosophy, University Coll., Oxford, 1963–66; Prof. of Sociology, Univ. of Essex, 1966–70; Prof. of History of Ideas, Brandeis Univ., 1970–72; Univ. Prof. in Philos. and Political Sci., Boston Univ., 1972–80; Luce Prof., Wellesley Coll., 1980–82; W. Alton Jones Prof. of Philosophy, Vanderbilt Univ., 1982–88; McMahon/Hank Prof. of Philosophy, Univ. of Notre Dame, Indiana, 1988–94; Arts and Scis Prof. of Phil., Duke Univ., 1995–2000. Mem., Amer. Philosophical Soc., 2006; Pres., Eastern Div., Amer. Phil Assoc., 1984. Fellow, Amer. Acad. of Arts and Scis, 1985; Corresp. FBA, 1994. Hon. Mem., Phi Beta Kappa, 1973. Hon. MRIA 2000. Hon. DHL Swarthmore, 1983; Hon. DLit: QUB, 1988; Williams Coll., Mass, 1993; DU Essex, 1990. *Publications:* Marxism and Christianity, 1954 (revised, 1968); New Essays in Philosophical Theology (ed, with A. G. N. Flew), 1955; Metaphysical Beliefs (ed), 1956; The Unconscious: a conceptual analysis, 1958; A Short History of Ethics, 1965; Secularisation and Moral Change, 1967; Marcuse: an exposition and a polemic, 1970; Sociological Theory and Philosophical Analysis (ed with D. M. Emmet), 1971; Against the Self-Images of the Age, 1971; After Virtue, 1981; Whose Justice? Which Rationality?, 1988; Three Rival Versions of Moral Enquiry, 1990; Dependent Rational Animals, 1999; Edith Stein: a philosophical prologue, 2005; The Tasks of Philosophy: selected essays vol. 1, 2006; Ethics and Politics: selected essays vol. 2, 2006. *Address:* Philosophy Department, University of Notre Dame, Notre Dame, IN 46556, USA.

McINTYRE, Prof. Alasdair Duncan, CBE 1994; FRSE 1975; Emeritus Professor of Fisheries and Oceanography, Aberdeen University, since 1986; *b* 17 Nov. 1926; *s* of Alexander Walker McIntyre and Martha Jack McIntyre; *m* 1967, Catherine; one *d. Educ:* Hermitage Sch., Helensburgh; Glasgow Univ. BSc (1st class Hons Zoology) 1948; DSc 1973. Scottish Home Department (since 1960, DAFS) Marine Laboratory, Aberdeen: Develt Commn Grant-aided Student, 1948–49; Scientific Officer, 1950; Head, Lab. Environmental Gp, 1973; Dep. Dir, 1977; Dir, 1983. Dir of Fisheries Res. Services for Scotland, Dept of Agric. and Fisheries for Scotland, 1983–86. UK Co-ordinator, Fisheries Res. and Devel t, 1986. President: Scottish Marine Biological Assoc., later Scottish Assoc. for Marine Sci., 1988–93; Estuarine and Coastal Scis Assoc., 1992–96; Sir Alister Hardy Foundn for Ocean Sci., 1992–99; Chairman: UN Gp of Experts on Scientific Aspects of Marine Pollution (GESAMP), 1981–84; Adv. Cttee on Marine Pollution, Internat. Council for the Exploration of the Sea, 1982–84; Marine Forum for Envmtl Issues, 1988–98; Atlantic Frontier Envmtl Forum, 1996–; Falkland Is Exploration and Production Envmtl Forum, 1997–; Assessor: Donaldson Inquiry into protection of UK coastline from pollution by merchant shipping, 1993–94; Donaldson Review of Salvage and Intervention Command and Control, 1997–99. Member: NCC for Scotland, 1991; Res. Bd, Scottish Natural Heritage, 1992–96. Hon. Res. Prof., Aberdeen Univ., 1983–86. Chm., Trustees of Buckland Foundn, 1994–99 (Vice Chm., 1988–94). Ed., Fisheries Research, 1988–. DUniv Stirling, 1997; Hon. DSc Napier, 2005. *Publications:* over 100 articles in scientific jls on marine ecology and pollution. *Recreations:* cooking, wine, walking. *Address:* 63 Hamilton Place, Aberdeen AB15 5BW. *T:* (01224) 645633.

McINTYRE, Sir Alister; *see* McIntyre, Sir M. A.

McINTYRE, Derrick William McEwen, TD 1980; Sheriff of Lothian and Borders at Edinburgh, since 2000; *b* 16 June 1944; *s* of Lt Col Donald and Rosemary McIntyre; *m* 1973, Janet Anna Fraser; one *d* (and one *s* one *d* decd). *Educ:* Wellington Coll.; St Andrews Univ. (LLB). Lieut, 6th Gurkha Rifles, 1966–68; Major, Black Watch (RHR), 1969–85. Solicitor in private practice, 1973–2000; Temp. Sheriff, 1982–2000. Mem., Queen's Body Guard for Scotland (Royal Co. of Archers), 1994–. *Recreations:* riding, shooting, fishing, golf. *Address:* Mainsfield, Mainsfield Avenue, Morebattle, Kelso, Roxburghshire TD5 8QW. *T:* (01573) 440254; *e-mail:* sheriff.dmcintyre@scotcourts.gov.uk.

McINTYRE, Sir Donald (Conroy), Kt 1992; CBE 1985 (OBE 1977); opera singer, freelance; *b* 22 Oct. 1934; *s* of George Douglas McIntyre and Mrs Hermyn McIntyre; *m*; three *d. Educ:* Mount Albert Grammar Sch.; Auckland Teachers' Trng Coll.; Guildhall Sch. of Music. Debut in Britain, Welsh National Opera, 1959; Sadler's Wells Opera, many roles, 1960–67; Royal Opera, Covent Garden, from 1967; also Vienna, Bayreuth, La Scala, Milan and Metropolitan, NY. *Principal roles:* Barak, in Die Frau Ohne Schatten, Strauss; Wotan and Wanderer, in The Ring, Wagner; Hollander, Wagner; Hans Sachs, in Die Meistersinger von Nurnberg, Wagner; Heyst, in Victory, Richard Rodney Bennett; Macbeth, Verdi; Scarpia, in Tosca, Puccini; Count, in Figaro, Mozart; Doctor, in Wozzeck, Berg; title role in Cardillac, Hindemith; Rocco, in Fidelio; Prospero, in Un Re in Ascolto, Berio; Balstrode, in Peter Grimes, Britten; Bayreuth: Wotan, Wanderer, Hollander; Telramund, in Lohengrin; Klingsor, Amfortas and Gurnemanz in Parsifal; Bayreuth Centenary Ring, 1976–81. *Video and films include:* Der Fliegende Holländer, 1975; Electra, 1976; Die Meistersinger, 1984; Bayreuth Centenary Ring, 1976–81; recordings include Pelléas et Mélisande, Il Trovatore, The Messiah, Oedipus Rex, The Ring, Beethoven's 9th Symphony, Damnation of Faust, Bayreuth Centenary Ring. Fidelio Award, 1989. *Recreations:* gardening, swimming, tennis, farming. *Address:* Foxhill Farm, Jackass Lane, Keston, Bromley, Kent BR2 6AN. *T:* (01689) 855368; c/o Ingpen & Williams, 7 St George's Court, 131 Putney Bridge Road, SW15 2PA.

MACINTYRE, Donald John; Assistant Editor, since 2003, and Jerusalem Correspondent, since 2004, Independent; *b* 27 Jan. 1947; *s* of Kenneth Mackenzie Campbell Macintyre and Margaret Macintyre (*née* Freeman); partner, Sarah Spankie; one *s. Educ:* Bradfield Coll.; Christ Church, Oxford (BA Lit.Hum.); UC, Cardiff (Dip. Journalism Studies). Reporter, Sunday Mercury, 1971–75; Industrial Reporter, Daily Express, 1975–77; Labour Corresp., The Times, 1977–83; Labour Editor: Sunday Times, 1983–85; The Times, 1985–86; Independent, 1986–87; Political Editor: Sunday Telegraph, 1987–89; Sunday Correspondent, 1989–90; Independent on Sunday, 1990–93; Pol Ed., 1993–96, Chief Pol Commentator, 1996–2004, Independent. *Publications:* Talking about Trade Unions, 1979; (jtly) Strike!, 1985; Mandelson and the Making of New Labour, 1999. *Recreations:* cinema, walking, bad chess. *Address:* c/o Independent, 191 Marsh Wall, E14 9RS. *Clubs:* Garrick, Soho House.

McINTYRE, Helen Jean Sutherland; *see* Fraser, H. J. S.

MacINTYRE, Prof. Iain, FMedSci; FRS 1996; Professor and Research Director, William Harvey Research Institute, Bart's and The London, Queen Mary's School of Medicine and Dentistry (formerly St Bartholomew's and the Royal London School of Medicine and Dentistry, Queen Mary and Westfield College), University of London, since 1995; *b* 30 Aug. 1924; *s* of John MacIntyre, Tobermory, Mull, and Margaret Fraser Shaw, Stratherick, Inverness-shire; *m* 1947, Mabel Wilson Jamieson, MA (*d* 2003), *y d* of George Jamieson and J. C. K. K. Bell, Largs, Ayrshire; one *d. Educ:* Jordanhill Coll. Sch., Glasgow; Univ. of Glasgow (MB, ChB 1947); PhD 1960, DSc 1970, London. MRCPath 1963 (Founder Mem.), FRCPath 1971; FRCP 1977 (MRCP 1969). Asst Clinical Pathologist, United Sheffield Hosps, and Hon. Demonstrator in Biochem., Sheffield Univ., 1948–52; Royal Postgraduate Medical School: Registrar in Chemical Pathology, 1952–54; first Sir Jack Drummond Meml Fellow, 1954–56; Asst Lectr in Chem. Path., 1956–59; Reader in Chem. Path., 1963–67; Dir, Endocrine Unit, 1967–89; Chm., Academic Bd, 1985–89; Sen. Res. Fellow, Dept of Medicine, 1989–91; Prof., Chem. Path., London Univ., 1967–89, now Emeritus; Res. Dir, William Harvey Res. Inst., St Bartholomew's Hosp. Med. Coll., 1991–94. Director: Dept of Chem. Path., Hammersmith Hosp., 1982–89; Chelsea Hosp. for Women, Queen Charlotte's Hosp. for Women, 1986–89. Vis. Scientist, Nat. Insts of Health, Bethesda, 1960–61; Commonwealth Fund Schol., Australia, 1968; Visiting Professor: San Francisco Medical Center, 1964; Melbourne Univ., 1979–80; St George's Hosp. Med. Sch., 1989–; Vis. Lectr, Insts of Molecular Biol. and Cytol., USSR Acad. of Scis, 1978. Lectures: A. J. S. McFadzean, Univ. of Hong Kong, 1981; Transatlantic, Amer. Endocrine Soc., 1987; Per Edman Meml, St Vincent's Inst. of Medical Res., Australia, 1990. Mem., Hammersmith and Queen Charlotte's SHA, 1982–89. Chm. Organizing Cttee, Hammersmith Internat. Symposium on Molecular Endocrinology, 1967–81; Member: Org Cttee, Hormone and Cell Regulation Symposia, 1976–79; Adv. Council, Workshop on Vitamin D, 1977–79. Pres., Bone and Tooth Soc., 1984–87; Member: Cttee, Soc. for Endocrinology, 1978–80; Biochem. Soc.; NIH Alumni Assoc; Assoc. of Amer. Physicians, 1998; Amer. Endocrine Soc.; Amer. Soc. for Bone and Mineral Res.; European Calcified Tissue Soc.; Assoc. of Clin. Biochemists. Vice-Pres., English Chess Assoc., 1989–. Member Editorial Board: Clinical Endocrinology, 1975–79; Molecular and Cellular Endocrinology, 1975–80; Jl of Endocrinological Investigation; Jl of Mineral and Electrolyte Metabolism; Jl of Investigative and Cell Pathol.; Jl of Metabolic Bone Disease and Related Res. Hon. Mem., Assoc. of American Physicians, 1998. Founder FMedSci 1998. Hon. MD: Turin, 1985; Sheffield, 2002. (Jtly) Gairdner Internat. Award for the discovery of the existence and origin of calcitonin, Toronto, 1967; Elsevier Award, Internat. Confs on Calcium Regulating Hormones, Inc., 1992; John B. Johnson Award, Paget Foundn, 1995; Buchanan Medal, Royal Soc., 2006. *Publications:* articles in endocrinology. *Recreations:* tennis, chess, music. *Address:* Great Broadhurst Farm, Broad Oak, Heathfield, East Sussex TN21 8UX. *T:* (01435) 883515. *Clubs:* Athenæum; Queen's, Hurlingham.

MACINTYRE, Iain Melfort Campbell, MD; FRCSE, FRCPE; FSAScot; Consultant Surgeon, Edinburgh, 1979–2004; Surgeon to the Queen in Scotland, 1997–2004; *b* 23 June 1944; *s* of John Macintyre, MA, BD, FSAScot and Mary (*née* Campbell); *m* 1969, Tessa Lorna Mary Millar; three *d. Educ:* Daniel Stewart's Coll., Edinburgh; Edinburgh Univ. (MB ChB, MD 1992). FRCSE 1974; FRCPE 1997. FSAScot 1997. Lectr in Surgery, Edinburgh Univ., 1974–78; Vis. Prof., Univ. of Natal, 1978–79; Consultant Surgeon: Leith Hosp., 1979–85; Western Gen. Hosp., 1985–2002; Royal Infirmary, Edinburgh, 2002–04. Royal College of Surgeons of Edinburgh: Mem. Council, 1991–2000; Dir of Educn and Wade Prof., 1997–2000; Hon. Sec., 2001–04; Vice Pres., 2003–06. Mem., Nat. Med. Adv. Cttee, 1992–95. *Recreations:* sailing, golf, reading. *Club:* Bruntsfield Links Golfing Society.

McINTYRE, Air Vice Marshal Ian Graeme; consultant in dental and public health for Warwickshire, and Solihull, retired; Chief Executive, Defence Dental Agency, 1997–2001; *b* 9 July 1943; *s* of Arthur McIntyre and Eileen McIntyre (*née* Patmore); *m* 1966, Joan; two *s. Educ:* Royal Masonic Sch. for Boys; Durham Univ. (BDS); BPMF, Inst. of Dental Surgery, London Univ. (MSc). MGDS RCS, DDPH RCS; FDSRCSE *ad hominem* 1998. Commnd RAF, 1961; Triservice Advr in Gen. Dental Practice, 1989; Asst Dir, Dental Service, RAF, 1991; CO, RAF Inst. of Dental Health and Trng, 1994; Dir, Clinical Services, Defence Dental Agency and Dir, RAF Dental Branch, 1995; QHDS, 1995–2001. Pres., BDA, 2003–04. *Recreations:* hill walking, gardening, watching Rugby. *Address:* Dunelm, 8 Walton Fields, Kineton, Warwicks CV35 0JP. *Club:* Royal Air Force.

McINTYRE, Ian James; writer and broadcaster; *b* Banchory, Kincardineshire, 9 Dec. 1931; *y s* of late Hector Harold McIntyre, Inverness, and late Annie Mary Michie, Ballater; *m* 1954, Leik Sommerfelt, 2nd *d* of late Benjamin Vogt, Kragerø, Norway; two *s* two *d. Educ:* Prescot Grammar Sch.; St John's Coll., Cambridge (Scholar; Med. and Mod. Langs Tripos, Pts I and II; BA 1953; MA); Coll. of Europe, Bruges. Pres., Cambridge Union, 1953. Commnd, Intelligence Corps, 1955–57. Current affairs talks producer, BBC, 1957; Editor, At Home and Abroad, 1959; Man. Trng Organiser, BBC Staff Trng Dept, 1960; Programme Services Officer, ITA, 1961; staff of Chm., Cons. Party in Scotland, 1962; Dir of Inf. and Res., Scottish Cons. Central Office, 1965; contested (C) Roxburgh, Selkirk and Peebles, 1966; long-term contract, writer and broadcaster, BBC, 1970–76; presenter and interviewer, Analysis, and other programmes on politics, for. affairs and the arts; travelled widely in Europe, N America, Africa, Asia and ME; Controller: BBC Radio 4, 1976–78; BBC Radio 3, 1978–87. Associate Ed., The Times, 1989–90. *Publications:* The Proud Doers: Israel after twenty years, 1968; (ed and contrib.) Words: reflections on the uses of language, 1975; Dogfight: the transatlantic battle over Airbus, 1992; The Expense of Glory: a life of John Reith, 1993; Dirt and Deity: a life of Robert Burns, 1995; Garrick, 1999 (Annual Book Prize, Soc. for Theatre Res., 2000); Joshua Reynolds: the life and times of the first president of the Royal Academy, 2003; Hester: the remarkable life of Dr Johnson's Dear Mistress, 2008; articles and book reviews in The Listener, The Times, The Independent, The Spectator. *Recreation:* family life. *Address:* Spylaw House, Newlands Avenue, Radlett, Herts WD7 8EL. *T:* (01923) 853532; *e-mail:* ian.mcintyre@waitrose.com. *Club:* Union (Cambridge).

McINTYRE, (John) Paul; Head, Energy Strategy and International Unit, Department of Energy and Climate Change (formerly Department of Trade and Industry, then Department for Business, Enterprise and Regulatory Reform), since 2007; *b* 4 Dec. 1951; *s* of John McIntyre and Julia McIntyre; *m* 1984, Jennifer Eastabrook; two *d. Educ:* Austin Friars, Carlisle; Churchill Coll., Cambridge (BA Econs). Joined HM Treasury, 1974: on secondment to UK Delegn to IMF/IBRD, Washington, 1977–78; Hambros Bank, City of London, 1983–85; Assistant Secretary: Social Security Policy, 1987–90; Monetary and Debt Mgt Policy, 1990–94; Dep. Dir, Internat. Finance, 1995–99; Department of Trade and Industry: Dep. Dir Gen., Enterprise and Innovation, then Regions (Business Gp), 2000–03; Hd, British Energy Team, 2003–04; Dir, Energy Strategy Unit (Energy Gp), 2004–05; Hd, Energy Policy Rev. Team, 2005–07. *Recreations:* family, cricket, reading, music. *Address:* Department of Energy and Climate Change, 1 Victoria Street, SW1P 0ET. *Clubs:* MCC; Mandarins Cricket.

McINTYRE, Sir (Meredith) Alister, Kt 1992; Chairman, Agency for Reconstruction and Development, Grenada, 2004–05; Chief Technical Advisor, Caribbean Regional Negotiating Machinery, Kingston, Jamaica, 1998–2001; *b* Grenada, 29 March 1932; *s* of Meredith McIntyre and Cynthia Eileen McIntyre; *m* Marjorie Hope; three *s* one *d. Educ:* LSE (BSc (Econ) 1st Cl. Hons 1957); Nuffield Coll., Oxford (BLitt 1963). Fulbright-Hays Fellow, Columbia Univ., 1963–64; Asst Prof., Woodrow Wilson Sch. of Public Affairs, Princeton Univ., 1962; University of the West Indies: Lectr in Economics, 1960–64; Sen. Lectr and Chm. of Social Scis, 1964–67; Dir, Inst. of Social and Econ. Res., 1964–74; Sec.-Gen., Caribbean Community Secretariat, 1974–77; Dir, Commodities Div., UNCTAD, 1977–82; Dep. Sec.-Gen., UNCTAD, 1982–87; Asst Sec.-Gen., UN, 1987–88. Vice-Chancellor, Univ. of West Indies, 1988–98. Hon. LLD: West Indies, 1980; Sheffield, 1995; Toronto, 1996. Comdr, Order of Distinction (Jamaica), 1975; Cacique's Crown of Honour (Guyana), 1978; Order of Merit (Jamaica), 1992; Order of the Caribbean Community, 1994. *Recreations:* swimming, sailing, reading. *Address:* 14 Jacks Hill Road, Kingston 6, Jamaica.

McINTYRE, Michael; *see* McIntyre, T. M.

McINTYRE, Prof. Michael Edgeworth, PhD; FRS 1990; Professor of Atmospheric Dynamics, Cambridge University, 1993–2008, now Emeritus; Co-director, Cambridge Centre for Atmospheric Science, 1992–2003; *b* 28 July 1941; *s* of Archibald Keverall McIntyre and Anne Hartwell McIntyre; *m* 1968, Ruth Hecht; one step *d* two step *s. Educ:* King's High School, Dunedin, NZ; Univ. of Otago, NZ; Trinity Coll., Cambridge. PhD Cantab 1967 (geophysical fluid dynamics); postdoctoral Fellow, Woods Hole Oceanographic Inst., 1967. Research Associate, Dept of Meteorology, MIT, 1967; Cambridge University: Asst Dir of Research, 1969; Res. Fellow, St John's Coll., 1968–71; Univ. Lectr, 1972; Reader in Atmospheric Dynamics, 1987; SERC, then EPSRC, Sen. Res. Fellow, 1992–97. Member: Atmospheric Sci. Cttee, NERC, 1989–94; Sci. Steering Gp, UK Univs Global Atmos. Modelling Prog., NERC, 1990–2002; Workshop on Tropical Cyclone Disasters, IUTAM/IUGG/ICSU, 1990–91; Scientific Steering Cttee, STRATEOLE experiment, 1992–2002; Scientific Adv. Cttee and Organizing Cttee, Prog. on Maths of Atmosphere and Ocean Dynamics, Isaac Newton Inst., 1995–96. Member: Academia Europaea, 1989; Euro. Geophys. Soc. (Julius Bartels Medal, 1999), Amer. Geophys. Union, Catgut Acoust. Soc.; FRMetS; Fellow, Amer. Met. Soc., 1991 (Carl-Gustaf Rossby Res. Medal, 1987); FAAAS 1999. *Publications:* numerous papers in professional jls, incl. papers on lucidity principles. *Recreation:* music. *Address:* Centre for Mathematical Sciences, Wilberforce Road, Cambridge CB3 0WA; *web:* www.atm.damtp.cam.ac.uk/people/mem.

McINTYRE, Prof. Neil, FRCP; Professor of Medicine, Royal Free Hospital School of Medicine, 1978–99; Hon. Consultant Physician, Royal Free Hospital, 1968–99; *b* 1 May 1934; *s* of John William McIntyre and Catherine (*née* Watkins); *m* 1966, Wendy Ann Kelsey; one *s* one *d*. *Educ:* Porth County School for Boys; King's Coll. London (BSc 1st Cl. Hons Physiol); King's Coll. Hosp. (MB BS (Hons), MD). House Officer: KCH, 1959; Hammersmith Hosp., 1960; RAF Med. Br. (Flt Lieut), 1960–63; MRC Res. Fellow, Registrar, Lectr in Medicine, Royal Free Hosp., 1963–66; MRC Travelling Fellowship, Harvard Med. Sch., 1966–68; Royal Free Hospital School of Medicine: Sen. Lectr 1968–73, Reader in Medicine 1973–78; Chm., Dept of Medicine, 1983–94; Vice Dean, 1993–96; Dir of Med. Educn, UCL Med. Sch. and Royal Free Hosp. Sch. of Med., 1993–95. Non-exec. Dir, N Middlesex Hosp. NHS Trust, 1991–96. Pres., Hist. of Medicine Soc. of Wales, 2007. MRSocMed 1968. Liveryman, Soc. of Apothecaries, 1971–. Mem., Bd of Govs, Amer. Osler Soc., 2003–06. Sam E. Roberts Medal, Univ. of Kansas Med. Sch., 1980. *Publications:* Therapeutic Agents and the Liver, 1965; The Problem Orientated Medical Record, 1979; Lipids and Lipoproteins, 1990; Clinical Hepatology, 1991; papers on liver disease, lipoprotein metabolism, med. educn. *Recreations:* reading, medical history, photographing medical statues, golf. *Address:* 7 Butterworth Gardens, Woodford Green, Essex IG8 0BJ. *Clubs:* Athenæum; Highgate Golf.

McINTYRE, Paul; see McIntyre, J. P.

MACINTYRE, Prof. Sarah Jane, (Sally), CBE 2006 (OBE 1998); PhD; FRSE; Director, MRC Social and Public Health Sciences (formerly Medical Sociology) Unit, Glasgow, since 1984; *b* 27 Feb. 1949; *d* of late Rev. Angus Macintyre and Evelyn Macintyre; *m* 1980, Dr Guy Paul Muhlemann. *Educ:* Univ. of Durham (BA 1970); Bedford Coll., London (MSc 1971); Univ. of Aberdeen (PhD 1976). FRSE 1998. Res. Fellow, Aberdeen Univ., 1971–75; non-clinical scientist, MRC Med. Sociology Unit, 1975–84. Honorary Professor: Univ. of Glasgow, 1991–; Univ. of Strathclyde, 2007–. Founder FMedSci 1998. Hon. Fellow, LSHTM, 2003. Hon. MFPHM 1993. Hon. DSc Aberdeen, 2005. *Publications:* Single and Pregnant, 1977; (jtly) Antenatal Care Assessed, 1985; contrib. jl articles on sociological and public health topics. *Recreations:* mountaineering, rock-climbing, ski-ing, running. *Address:* MRC Social and Public Health Sciences Unit, 4 Lilybank Gardens, Glasgow G12 8RZ. *T:* (0141) 357 3949; *e-mail:* sally@msoc.mrc.gla.ac.uk. *Club:* Pinnacle.

McINTYRE, (Theodore) Michael; Senior Executive, HSBC Private Banking, 1996–2001; *b* 9 Dec. 1941; *s* of James Penton McIntyre and Susan E. M. McIntyre; *m* 1969, Jill Yvonne Mander; one *s* one *d*. *Educ:* Marlborough Coll. Hongkong and Shanghai Banking Corporation Ltd: E Malaysia, Kowloon, Japan, Hong Kong and Brazil, 1959–91; Dep. CEO, 1991–92; CEO, 1992–96, UK. SBStJ 1989. *Recreations:* reading, tennis, fishing. *Address:* Flat 3, 69 Alderney Street, SW1V 4HH. *T:* (020) 7834 9719.

MACINTYRE, William Ian, CB 1992; Chairman, Council, Incorporated Froebel Educational Institute, since 2003; *b* 20 July 1943; *s* of late Robert Miller Macintyre, CBE and Florence Mary Macintyre; *m* 1967, Jennifer Mary Pitblado; one *s* two *d*. *Educ:* Merchiston Castle School, Edinburgh; St Andrews University. MA. British Petroleum Co. Ltd, 1965–72; ECGD, 1972–73; DTI, later Dept of Energy, 1973–77; seconded to ICFC, 1977–79; Asst Sec., Dept of Energy, Gas Div., 1979–83; Under-Sec. 1983, Dir-Gen., Energy Efficiency Office, 1983–87; Under Sec., Electricity Div., 1987–88, Electricity Div. B, 1988–91, Dept of Energy; Under Sec., Coal Div., Dept of Energy, then DTI, 1991–94; Head, Telecoms Div., 1994–95, Communications and Inf. Industries Directorate, 1996–2002, DTI. Dir, Templeton Estates, 2002–; Exec. Vice-Pres., Chelgate Ltd, 2004–. Dep. Chm., Froebel Inst., 2001–03 (Mem. Council, 1999–). Pro-Chancellor, Roehampton Univ. (formerly Univ. of Surrey Roehampton), 2006– (Mem. Council, 2000–06); Governor: Froebel Coll., 2001–07; Ibstock Sch., 2001– (Chm. of Govs, 2002–03).

McISAAC, Shona; MP (Lab) Cleethorpes, since 1997; *b* 3 April 1960; *d* of Angus and Isa McIsaac; *m* 1994, Peter Keith. *Educ:* St Aidan's Coll., Durham (BSc Geography). Formerly: Lifeguard, Tooting Pool; Sub-Editor: Chat; Bella; Woman; food writer, Slimmer. Mem. (Lab) Wandsworth BC, 1990–97. Mem., Select Cttee on Standards and Privileges, 1997–2001. *Recreations:* food, football, cycling, archaeology. *Address:* House of Commons, SW1A 0AA. *T:* (020) 7219 3000.

MacIVER, Matthew Macleod, CBE 2008; Chief Executive and Registrar, General Teaching Council for Scotland, since 2001; *b* Portnaguran, Isle of Lewis, 5 July 1946; *s* of Donald and Henrietta MacIver; *m* 1972, Katrina Robertson; one *s* one *d*. *Educ:* Aird Primary Sch.; Nicolson Inst., Stornoway; Edinburgh Univ. (MA 1968; DipEd 1969; MEd 1979; FEIS 2004). Teacher, Kilmarnock Acad., 1969–71; teacher, 1971–72, Principal Teacher, 1972–80, Craigmount High Sch., Edinburgh; Asst Rector, Royal High Sch., Edinburgh, 1980–83; Depute Head Teacher, Balerno High Sch., Edinburgh, 1983–86; Rector: Fortrose Acad., Ross-shire, 1986–89; Royal High Sch., Edinburgh, 1989–98; Depute Registrar (Educn), Gen. Teaching Council for Scotland, 1998–2001. Winston Churchill Travelling Fellow, 1998. Chairman: Teachers' Action Gp on Gaelic Medium Educn, 2005; Bòrd na Gàidhlig (Gaelic Lang. Bd), 2006–. Chm., Gaelic Broadcasting Cttee, 1996–2001; Member: Gaelic Television Cttee, 1991–95; for Scotland, Ofcom Content Bd, 2003–06. Chm., Highlands and Is Educnl Trust, 1994–. Hon. Prof., UHI, 2008. Hon. Life Mem., Scottish Secondary Teachers' Assoc., 2008. FEIS 2004. Hon. Dhc Aberdeen, 2008. DEd Edinburgh, 2008. *Publications:* (with A. Hogg) Industry-Coal and Iron 1700–1900, 1977; (contrib.) Scottish Education, 2nd edn 2003, 3rd edn 2008; (contrib.) Report of the Gaelic Medium Teachers' Action Group, 2005; (contrib.) Policy and Practice in Education: Gaelic Medium Education, Series 10, 2006, 2007; (with M. Nicolson) Foghlam tro Mheadhan na Gàidhlig, 2007. *Recreations:* reading, Gaelic culture, writing a monthly article for The Rudhach (community newspaper in Lewis). *Address:* 21 Durham Road, Edinburgh EH15 1NY. *T:* (0131) 669 5029.

McIVOR, Donald Kenneth; Executive-in-residence, Queen's University Business School; Director and Senior Vice-President, Exxon Corporation, Irving, Texas (formerly New York), 1985–92; *b* 12 April 1928; *s* of Kenneth MacIver McIvor and Nellie Beatrice McIvor (*née* Rutherford); *m* 1953, Avonia Isabel Forbes; four *s* one *d*. *Educ:* Univ. of Manitoba (BSc Hons in Geol.). Joined Imperial Oil, 1950; operational and res. assignments, Exploration Dept, 1950–58; gen. planning and res. management positions, 1958–68; Asst Manager and Manager, Corporate Planning, 1968–70; Exploration Manager, 1970–72; Nat. Defence Coll., 1972–73; Sen. Vice-Pres., 1973–75; Exec. Vice-Pres., 1975–77; Vice-Pres., oil and gas exploration and prodn, Exxon Corp., NY, 1977–81; Dep. Chm., Imperial Oil, 1981; Chm. and Chief Exec. Officer, Imperial Oil, 1982–85. Member: Canadian Soc. of Petroleum Geologists; American Petroleum Inst.

Publication: Curiosity's Destinations: tales and insights from the life of a geologist, 2005. *Address:* 79 Lukes Wood Road, New Canaan, CT 06840–2202, USA.

McIVOR, (Frances) Jane; District Judge (Magistrates' Courts), London, since 2001; *b* NI, 22 Oct. 1959; *d* of Rt Hon. (William) Basil McIvor, OBE, PC (NI) and (Frances) Jill McIvor, *qv*; *m* 1988, Girish Thanki; one *s* one *d*. *Educ:* sch. in Belfast; Univ. of E Anglia (LLB 1982). Called to the Bar, Inner Temple, 1983; in practice on S Eastern Circuit; Actg Metropolitan Stipendiary Magistrate, 1998–2001. Chm., Connexional Discipline Cttee, Methodist Church, 2005–. *Recreations:* entertaining, family life. *Address:* Thames Magistrates' Court, 58 Bow Road, E3 4DJ.

McIVOR, (Frances) Jill, CBE 1994; Northern Ireland Parliamentary Commissioner for Administration and for Complaints, 1991–96; *b* 10 Aug. 1930; *d* of Cecil Reginald Johnston Anderson and Frances Ellen (*née* Henderson); *m* 1953, Rt Hon. (William) Basil McIvor, OBE, PC (NI) (*d* 2004); two *s* one *d*. *Educ:* Methodist Coll.; Lurgan Coll.; Queen's Univ. of Belfast (LLB Hons). Called to Bar of Northern Ireland, 1980. Asst Librarian (Law), QUB, 1954–55; Tutor in Legal Res., Law Faculty, QUB, 1965–74; editorial staff, NI Legal Qtly, 1966–76; Librarian, Dept of Dir of Public Prosecutions, 1977–79. NI Mem., IBA, 1980–86; Dep. Chm., Radio Authy, 1990–94. Chm., Lagan Valley Regional Park Cttee, 1984–89 (Mem., 1975); Member: Ulster Countryside Cttee, 1984–89; Fair Employment Agency, 1984–89; Fair Employment Commn, 1990–91; Lay Panel, Juvenile Court, 1976–77; GDC, 1979–91; Exec., Belfast Voluntary Welfare Soc., 1981–88; Adv. Council, 1985–90, Bd, 1987–90, Co-operation North; Adv. Panel on Community Radio, 1985–86; NI Adv. Cttee, British Council, 1986–98. Chairman: Ulster–NZ Trust, 1987–; Educnl Guidance Service for Adults, 1988–90. NZ Hon. Consul for NI, 1996–2007. Mem. Bd of Visitors, QUB, 1988–. FRSA 1988–2001. DUniv Ulster, 1997. QSM 1993. *Publications:* Irish Consultant (and contrib.), Manual of Law Librarianship, 1976; (ed) Elegantia Juris: selected writings of F. H. Newark, 1973; Chart of the English Reports (new edn), 1982. *Recreations:* New Zealand, gardening. *Address:* 98 Spa Road, Ballynahinch, Co. Down BT24 8PP. *T:* (028) 9756 3534. *Club:* Royal Over-Seas League.

See also F. J. McIvor.

MACK, Prof. (Brian) John, DPhil; FSA; Professor of World Art Studies, University of East Anglia, since 2004; *b* 10 July 1949; *s* of late Brian Mack and Joan Alexandra Mack (*née* Kelly); *m* 1975, Caroline Jenkins, *d* of late Rev. Dr D. T. Jenkins; one *s* one *d*. *Educ:* Campbell Coll., Belfast; Univ. of Sussex (MA); Merton Coll., Oxford (DPhil 1975). FSA 1994. Res. Asst, 1976, Asst Keeper, 1977, Keeper, 1991–99 and 2002–04, Sen. Keeper, 1998–2002, Dept of Ethnography, BM. Vis. Prof., UCL, 1996–. Member: Council, British Inst. in Eastern Africa, 1981– (Pres., 2005–); Council, RAI, 1983–86; Council, African Studies Assoc., 1986–88; British Acad. Bd for Academy-sponsored Insts and Schs, 1996–2003; Conseil d'orientation de l'établissement publique de Musée du Quai Branly, Paris, 1999–2000; Pitt-Rivers Cttee, Univ. of Oxford, 2000–. Trustee, Horniman Mus. and Public Park, 1998–. Mem. Editl Bd, Art History, 1982–91. FRSA 2005. Nat. Art Collections Fund Award for Images of Africa, BM, 1991. *Publications:* (with J. Picton) African Textiles (Craft Adv. Council Book of the Year), 1979, 2nd edn 1989; Zulus, 1980; (with P. T. Robertshaw) Culture History in the Southern Sudan, 1982; (with M. D. McLeod) Ethnic Sculpture, 1984; Madagascar, Island of the Ancestors, 1986; Ethnic Jewellery, 1988; Malagasy Textiles, 1989; Emil Torday and the Art of the Congo 1900–1909, 1990; (with C. Spring) African Textile Design, 1991; Masks, the Art of Expression, 1994; (with K. Yoshida) Images of Other Cultures, 1997; Africa, Arts and Cultures, 2000; Museum of the Mind: art and memory in world cultures, 2003; The Art of Small Things, 2007; (with K. Yoshida) Preserving the Cultural Heritage of Africa: crisis or renaissance, 2008; articles and revs in learned jls. *Address:* School of World Art and Museology, University of East Anglia, Norwich NR4 7TJ. *T:* (01603) 592463.

MACK SMITH, Denis, CBE 1990; FBA 1976; FRSL; Extraordinary Fellow, Wolfson College, Oxford, 1987–2000 (Hon. Fellow, 2000); Emeritus Fellow, All Souls Coll., Oxford, 1987; *b* 3 March 1920; *s* of Wilfrid Mack Smith and Altiora Gauntlett; *m* 1963, Catharine Stevenson; two *d*. *Educ:* St Paul's Cathedral Choir Sch.; Haileybury Coll.; Peterhouse, Cambridge Univ. (organ and history schols). MA Cantab, MA Oxon. Asst Master, Clifton Coll., 1941–42; Cabinet Offices, 1942–46; Fellow of Peterhouse, Cambridge, 1947–62 (Hon. Fellow, 1986); Tutor of Peterhouse, 1948–58; Univ. Lectr, Cambridge, 1952–62; Sen. Res. Fellow, 1962–87, Sub-Warden, 1984–86, All Souls Coll., Oxford. Chm., Assoc. for Study of Modern Italy, 1987–. For. Hon. Mem., Amer. Acad. of Arts and Sciences, 1972. Public Orator of the Repubblica di San Marino, 1982; Hon. Citizen, Santa Margherita Ligure, 1999. Awards: Thirlwall, 1949; Serena, 1960; Elba, 1972, 1994; Villa di Chiesa, 1973; Mondello, 1975; Nove Muse, 1976; Duff Cooper Meml., 1977; Wolfson Literary, 1977; Rhegium Julii, 1983; Presidential Medal, Italy, 1984; Polifemo d'Argento, 1988; Fregene, 1990; Sileno d'Oro, 1996. Grande Ufficiale dell'Ordine al Merito della Repubblica Italiana, 1996 (Commendatore, 1978). *Publications:* Cavour and Garibaldi 1860, 1954, enlarged 2nd edn 1985; Garibaldi, 1957; (jtly) British Interests in the Mediterranean and Middle East, 1958; Italy, a Modern History, 1959; Medieval Sicily, 1968; Modern Sicily, 1968; Da Cavour a Mussolini, 1968; (ed) The Making of Italy 1796–1870, 1968, 2nd edn 1988; (ed) Garibaldi, 1969; (ed) E. Quinet, Le Rivoluzioni d'Italia, 1970; Victor Emanuel, Cavour and the Risorgimento, 1971; (ed) G. La Farina, Scritti Politici, 1972; Vittorio Emanuele II, 1972, 2nd edn 1994; Mussolini's Roman Empire, 1976; (jtly) Un Monumento al Duce, 1976; Cento Anni di Vita Italiana attraverso il Corriere della Sera, 1978; L'Italia del Ventesimo Secolo, 1978; (ed) G. Bandi, I mille: da Genova a Capua, 1981; Mussolini, 1981; (ed) F. De Sanctis, Un Viaggio Elettorale, 1983; Cavour, 1985; (jtly) A History of Sicily, 1986; Italy and its Monarchy, 1989; Mazzini, 1993; Modern Italy: a political history, 1997; La Storia Manipolata, 1998; Jt Editor, Nelson History of England, 1962–. *Address:* White Lodge, Osler Road, Headington, Oxford OX3 9BJ. *T:* (01865) 762878.

MACKAY, family name of **Earl of Inchcape, Lord Reay** and **Barons Mackay of Clashfern, Mackay of Drumadoon** and **Tanlaw.**

MACKAY OF CLASHFERN, Baron *cr* 1979 (Life Peer), of Eddrachillis in the District of Sutherland; **James Peter Hymers Mackay,** KT 1997; PC 1979; FRSE 1984; Editor-in-Chief, Halsbury's Laws of England, since 1998; Lord High Commissioner, General Assembly, Church of Scotland, 2005–06 and 2006–07; Lord Clerk Register of Scotland and Keeper of the Signet, since 2007; *b* 2 July 1927; *s* of James Mackay and Janet Hymers; *m* 1958, Elizabeth Gunn Hymers; one *s* two *d*. *Educ:* George Heriot's Sch., Edinburgh; Edinburgh Univ. (MA Hons Maths and Nat. Philosophy 1948). Lectr in Mathematics, Univ. of St Andrews, 1948–50; Major Schol., Trinity Coll., Cambridge, in Mathematics, 1947, taken up 1950; Senior Schol. 1951; BA (Cantab) 1952; LLB Edinburgh (with Distinction) 1955. Admitted to Faculty of Advocates, 1955; QC (Scot.) 1965; Standing Junior Counsel to: Queen's and Lord Treasurer's Remembrancer; Scottish Home and Health Dept; Commissioners of Inland Revenue in Scotland; Sheriff Principal, Renfrew and Argyll, 1972–74; Vice-Dean, Faculty of Advocates, 1973–76; Dean, 1976–79; Lord Advocate of Scotland, 1979–84; a Senator of Coll. of Justice in Scotland, 1984–85; a Lord of Appeal in Ordinary, 1985–87; Lord High Chancellor of GB, 1987–97. Chancellor, Heriot-Watt Univ., 1991–2005. Commissary, Univ. of Cambridge, 2003–. Part-time Mem., Scottish Law Commn, 1976–79. Hon. Master of the Bench, Inner Temple, 1979. Fellow: Internat. Acad. of Trial Lawyers, 1979; Inst. of Taxation, 1981; Amer. Coll. of Trial Lawyers, 1990. Dir, Stenhouse Holdings Ltd, 1976–77. Mem., Insurance Brokers' Registration Council, 1977–79. A Comr of Northern Lighthouses, 1975–84; Elder Brother of Trinity House, 1990. Hon. Mem., SPTL, 1986. Hon. Fellow: Trinity Coll., Cambridge, 1989; Girton Coll., Cambridge, 1990; Hon. FRCSE 1989; Hon. FRCPE 1990; Hon. FRCOG 1996; Hon. FICE 1988. Hon. LLD: Edinburgh, 1983; Dundee, 1983; Strathclyde, 1985; Aberdeen, 1987; St Andrews, 1989; Cambridge, 1989; Coll. of William and Mary, Va, 1989; Birmingham, 1990; Nat. Law Sch. of India, 1994; Bath, 1994; Glasgow, 1994; De Montfort, 1999; Hon. DCL: Newcastle, 1990; Oxford, 1998; Hon. Dr jur Robert Gordon, 2000. *Publication:* Armour on Valuation for Rating, 5th edn (Consultant Editor), 1985. *Recreations:* walking, travel. *Address:* House of Lords, SW1A 0PW. *Clubs:* Athenæum, Caledonian; New (Edinburgh).

MACKAY OF DRUMADOON, Baron *cr* 1995 (Life Peer), of Blackwaterfoot in the district of Cunninghame; **Donald Sage Mackay;** PC 1996; a Senator of the College of Justice in Scotland, since 2000; *b* 30 Jan. 1946; *s* of Rev. Donald George Mackintosh Mackay and Jean Margaret Mackay; *m* 1979, Lesley Ann Waugh; one *s* two *d*. *Educ:* George Watson's Boys' Coll., Edinburgh; Univ. of Edinburgh (LLB 1966; LLM 1968); Univ. of Virginia (LLM 1969). Law apprentice, 1969–71; Solicitor with Allan McDougall & Co., SSC, Edinburgh, 1971–76; called to the Scottish Bar, 1976; Advocate Depute, 1982–85; QC (Scot.) 1987; Solicitor-General for Scotland, 1995; Lord Advocate, 1995–97. Mem., Criminal Injuries Compensation Bd, 1989–95. Opposition spokesman on constitutional and legal affairs, H of L, 1997–2000. *Recreations:* golf, gardening, Isle of Arran. *Address:* 39 Hermitage Gardens, Edinburgh EH10 6AZ. *T:* (0131) 447 1412; Seafield, Lamlash, Isle of Arran KA27 8LG. *T:* (01770) 600646; Parliament House, Edinburgh EH1 1RQ. *T:* (0131) 225 2595, *Fax:* (0131) 225 8213. *Club:* Western (Glasgow).

MACKAY, Prof. Alan Lindsay, FRS 1988; Professor of Crystallography, Birkbeck College, University of London, 1986–91, now Emeritus; *b* 6 Sept. 1926; *s* of Robert Lindsay Mackay, OBE, MC, BSc, MD and Margaret Brown Mackay, OBE, MB ChB, JP; *m* 1951, Sheila Thorne Hague, MA; two *s* one *d*. *Educ:* Wolverhampton Grammar Sch.; Oundle Sch.; Trinity Coll., Cambridge (BA, MA); Univ. of London (BSc, PhD, DSc). Lectr, Reader, Prof., Dept of Crystallography, Birkbeck Coll., 1951–91. Visiting Professor: Univ. of Tokyo, 1969; Univ. of Tsukuba, 1980; Korean Advanced Inst. of Sci. and Tech., 1987; Hon. Professor: Central China Univ; Sichuan Inst. of Sci. Studies; China Inst. for Sci. Studies. Foreign Member: Academia Mexicana de Ciencias, 1998; Korean Acad. of Sci. and Technol., 1999. *Publications:* The Harvest of a Quiet Eye, 1977; (with A. N. Barrett) Spatial Structure and the Microcomputer, 1987; (ed) A Dictionary of Scientific Quotations, 1991; (with E. A. Lord and S. Ranganathan) New Geometries for New Materials, 2006; papers in learned jls. *Recreation:* Asian studies. *Address:* 22 Lanchester Road, N6 4TA. *T:* (020) 8883 4810.

McKAY, Allan George; Director of Information Services, British Gas, 1994–95; *b* 5 Sept. 1935; *s* of George Allan McKay and Wilhelmina McKay; *m* 1962, Margaret Currie Baxter; one *s* two *d*. *Educ:* Royal High School, Edinburgh. FCCA, ACIS, CIGEM. Accountant, Scottish Gas Board, 1961; Dir of Finance, Scottish Gas, 1975; Deputy Chairman: British Gas East Midlands, 1982; British Gas North Thames, 1987; Chairman: British Gas North Eastern, 1989; British Gas North Western, 1993. *Recreations:* golf, gardening. *Address:* Larchwood, 3 Wee Course Lane, Rosemount, Blairgowrie, Perthshire PH10 6LS.

McKAY, Allen; JP; *b* 5 Feb. 1927; *s* of Fred and Martha Anne McKay; *m* 1949, June Simpson (*d* 1997); one *s*. *Educ:* Hoyland Kirk Balk Secondary Modern School; extramural studies, Univ. of Sheffield. Clerical work, Steel Works, 1941–45; general mineworker, 1945–47; Mining Electrical Engineer, 1947–65; NCB Industrial Relations Trainee, 1965–66; Asst Manpower Officer, Barnsley Area, NCB, 1966–78. MP (Lab) Penistone, July 1978–1983; Barnsley West and Penistone, 1983–92. Opposition Whip, 1981. JP Barnsley, 1971. *Recreation:* reading. *Address:* 24 Springwood Road, Hoyland, Barnsley, South Yorks S74 0AZ. *T:* (01226) 743418.

MacKAY, Rt Hon. Andrew (James); PC 1998; MP (C) Bracknell, since 1997 (Berkshire East, 1983–97); *b* 27 Aug. 1949; *s* of Robert James MacKay and Olive Margaret MacKay; *m* 1st 1975, Diana Joy (*née* Kinchin) (marr. diss. 1996); one *s* one *d*; 2nd, 1997, Julie Kirkbride, *qv*; one *s*. *Educ:* Solihull. MP (C) Birmingham, Stechford, March 1977–1979; PPS to Sec. of State for NI, 1986–89, to Sec. of State for Defence, 1989–92; an Asst Govt Whip, 1992–93; a Lord Comr of HM Treasury (Govt Whip), 1993–95; Vice Chamberlain of HM Household, 1995–96; Treasurer of HM Household (Dep. Govt Chief Whip), 1996–97; Opposition front bench spokesman on NI, 1997–2001; Sen. Political and Parly Advr to Leader of Opposition, 2005–. Member: Environment Select Cttee, 1985–86; Standards and Privileges Cttee, 2002–05; Foreign Affairs Select Cttee, 2004–05; Sec., Cons. Parly For. Affairs Cttee, 1985–86. Dep. Chm., Cons. Party, 2004–05; Mem., Cons. Party Nat. Exec., 1979–82. *Recreations:* golf, tennis, good food. *Address:* House of Commons, SW1A 0AA. *T:* (020) 7219 4109. *Clubs:* Berkshire Golf; Aberdovey Golf; Royal & Ancient Golf (St Andrews).

MACKAY, Andrew John, OBE 2006; Head, Corporate Affairs, and Secretary to British Council, since 2008; *b* 28 July 1960; *s* of John and Margaret Mackay; *m* 1990, Margaret Allport; one *d*. *Educ:* Exeter Univ. (BA Combined Hons 1982); Reading Univ. (MA Dist. 1989); Durham Univ. (MBA 1996). British Council: Asst Dir, Teaching Centre, Cairo, 1983–87; Lang. Advr, London, 1988–89; English Lang. Officer, Peru, 1989–92; Director: Dubai, 1992–96; Barcelona, 1996–2001; USA, 2001–06; Hd of Strategy and Evaluation, Public Diplomacy Gp, FCO, 2006–08 (on secondment). FRSA 2002. *Recreations:* cinema, literature, Hispanic cultures, walking. *Address:* British Council, 10 Spring Gardens, SW1A 2BN; *e-mail:* andrewjmackay@hotmail.com.

MacKAY, Angus; Director, MacKay Hannah Ltd, since 2003; *b* 10 Sept. 1964. *Educ:* St Augustine's High Sch., Edinburgh; Edinburgh Univ. (MA Hons Politics and History, 1986). Formerly Campaign Officer, Shelter (Scotland); Parly Asst to Dr Mo Mowlam, 1990–92. Mem. (Lab) City of Edinburgh Council, 1995–99 (Convener, Finance Cttee, 1997–99). Member (Lab) Edinburgh S, Scottish Parlt, 1999–2003; Dep. Minister for Justice, 1999–2000; Minister for Finance and Local Govt, 2000–01. Contested (Lab) Edinburgh S, Scottish Parlt, 2003. *Address:* MacKay Hannah Ltd, Crichton House, 4 Crichton's Close, Edinburgh EH8 8DT.

MACKAY, Prof. Angus Iain Kenneth, PhD; FBA 1991; Professor of History, University of Edinburgh, 1985–97; *b* 1939; *m* 1962; one *s* one *d*. *Educ:* Edinburgh Univ. (MA 1962; PhD 1969). Lectr, Reading Univ., 1965–69; Lectr, then Sen. Lectr, 1969–82, Reader, 1982–85, Edinburgh Univ. *Publications:* Spain in the Middle Ages, 1977; Money, Prices and Politics in Fifteenth-century Castile, 1981; Society, Economy and Religion in late Mediaeval Castile, 1987; (with R. Bartlett) Mediaeval Frontier Societies, 1989; (with D. Ditchburn) Atlas of Medieval Europe, 1997; contribs to learned jls. *Address:* 43 Liberton Drive, Edinburgh EH16 6NL.

MACKAY, Dr Angus Victor Peck, OBE 1997; FRCPE, FRCPsych; Physician Superintendent, Argyll and Bute Hospital, since 1980; Director, Mental Health Services, Lomond and Argyll Primary Care NHS Trust, since 1999; *b* 4 March 1943; *s* of Victor P. Mackay and Christine Mackay (*née* Peck); *m* 1969, Elspeth Margaret Whitton Norris; two *s* two *d*. *Educ:* George Heriot's Sch., Edinburgh; Univ. of Edinburgh (BSc 1st Cl. Hons Pharmacol.; MB ChB 1969); Churchill Coll., Cambridge (PhD 1973). FRCPsych 1983; FRCPE 1989; TPsych 1994. Jun. Res. Fellow, 1970–73, Clin. Res. Fellow, 1973–76, Sen. Clin. Scientist, then Dep. Dir, 1976–80, MRC Neurochem. Pharmacol. Unit, Cambridge; Lector in Pharmacol., Trinity Coll., Cambridge, 1976–80. Hon. Fellow in Neurosci., Univ. of Edinburgh, 1999–; Hon. Prof. (formerly MacIntosh Lectr in Psychol Medicine), Glasgow Univ., 1982–. Mem., Mental Health Tribunal for Scotland, 2005–. Member: Cttee on Safety of Medicines and associated cttees, 1984–2002; UK Panel of Experts to Eur. Cttee on Proprietary and Medicinal Products, 1990–; Bd, Medicines and Healthcare Regulatory Agency, 2003–; Scottish Adv. Cttee on Distinction Awards, 1998–; Chm., Health Technol. Bd for Scotland, 2000–03. Member: George Heriot's First Four (Scottish Schs Rowing Champions), 1959–62; Edinburgh Univ. First Eight, 1963–66; First Eight, 1970–73, Coxless Pair, 1976–80, Churchill Coll., Cambridge. *Publications:* numerous contribs to text books and learned jls, on various aspects of neurochem. and neuropharmacol. (particularly schizophrenic illness and drug-associated movement disorder), mental health service organisation, and health technology assessment. *Recreations:* rowing, sailing (International Dragon), rhododendrons (Mem., American Rhododendron Soc.). *Address:* Lomond and Argyll Primary Care NHS Trust, Argyll and Bute Hospital, Blarbuie Road, Lochgilphead, Argyll PA312 8LD. *T:* (01546) 602323, *Fax:* (01546) 602332; *e-mail:* angus.mackay@nhs.net. *Club:* Ardrishaig Boat.

MACKAY, Charles Dorsey; Chairman: TDG plc, since 2000; Eurotunnel Group, 2001–04 (non-executive Director, 1997–2004, Deputy Chairman, 1999–2001); *b* 14 April 1940; *s* of late Brig. Kenneth Mackay, CBE, DSO and Evelyn Maud (*née* Ingram); *m* 1964, Annmarie Joder-Pfeiffer; one *s* one *d* (and one *s* decd). *Educ:* Cheltenham Coll.; Queens' Coll., Cambridge (MA); INSEAD (MBA). British Petroleum Co., 1957–69; commercial apprentice, 1957–59; univ. apprentice, Cambridge, 1959–62; marketing assistant, London, 1962–63; Regl Sales Manager, Algeria, 1963–65; Commercial Dir, Burundi/Rwanda/Congo, 1965–68; sponsored at INSEAD, France, 1968–69; McKinsey & Co. Inc., 1969–76: Consultant; Sen. Engagement Manager, 1972–76; worked in London, Paris, Amsterdam, Dar es Salaam; Pakhoed Holding NV, Rotterdam, 1976–81: Dir, 1976–77, Chm., 1977–81, Paktrans Div.; Chloride Group plc, 1981–86: Dir, 1981–86; Chm., Overseas Div., 1981–85; Chm., Power Electronics Div., 1985–86; Inchcape plc, 1986–96: Dir, 1986–96; Chief Exec., 1991–96; Dep. Chm., 1995–96; Chm., Inchcape (Hong Kong) Ltd and Dodwell and Co. Ltd, 1986–87; Chm. and Chief Exec., Inchcape Pacific Ltd, 1987–91. Chm., DSL Gp Ltd, 1996–97; Dep. Chm., Thistle Hotels Plc, 1996–2003; non-executive Director: Union Insurance Soc. of Canton Ltd, 1986–91; Hongkong and Shanghai Banking Corp. Ltd, 1986–92; Midland Bank plc, 1992–93; HSBC Holdings plc, 1992–98; British Airways plc, 1993–96; Johnson Matthey PLC, 1999–2008; Mem. Supervisory Bd, Gucci Gp NV, 1997–2001. Adv. Dir, House of Habib, 2007–. Chm. Trustees, Historic Royal Palaces, 2006–. Trustee, Develt Trust (for the mentally handicapped), 1993–. Mem. Bd, INSEAD, 2000–. *Recreations:* travel, fly-fishing, tennis, ski-ing, classical music, opera, chess. *Address:* TDG plc, 4–5 Grosvenor Place, SW1X 7HJ. *T:* (020) 7838 7775. *Clubs:* Brooks's, Piscatorial Society; Hong Kong (Hong Kong).

MacKAY, Colin, CBE 2001; FRCS, FRCSE, FRCSGlas, FRCP, FRCPI, FFPH, FRCPE; Chairman, Board of Governors, UHI Millennium Institute, since 2001; *b* 8 Nov. 1936; *s* of Kenneth MacKay and Margaret Blair Dawson MacKay; *m* 1966, Dr Helen Paul Miskimmin; one *s* two *d*. *Educ:* Univ. of Glasgow (BSc Hons; MB ChB (Commendation)). FRCS 1966; FRCSE 1966; FRCSGlas 1966; FRCP 1999; FRCPI 1999; FFPH (FFPHM 1999); FRCPE 2000. Surgical trng, Western Infirmary, Glasgow, 1961–69; MRC Travelling Fellow, Boston Univ., 1969–70; Sen. Lectr in Surgery, Univ. of Glasgow, 1970–82; Consultant Surgeon, Western Infirmary/Gartnavel Gen. Hosp., Glasgow, 1982–96. Royal College of Physicians and Surgeons of Glasgow: Mem. Council, 1972–; Hon. Treas., 1976–86; Vice Pres., Surgical, 1992–94; Visitor, 1996–97; Pres., 1997–2000. FACP 1998; FCMSA 1998; Fellow, Acad. of Medicine, Singapore 1998. *Publications:* (with I. McA. Ledingham) Textbook of Surgical Physiology, 1978, 2nd edn 1988; contribs to med. jls in field of surgical gastroenterology, in general, and peptic ulcer and gallstone disease, in particular. *Recreations:* travel, walking. *Address:* 73 Buchanan Drive, Bearsden, Glasgow G61 2EP. *T:* (0141) 942 8759. *Club:* Western (Glasgow).

MACKAY, Hon. Sir Colin (Crichton), Kt 2001; **Hon. Mr Justice Mackay;** a Judge of the High Court, Queen's Bench Division, since 2001; *b* 26 Sept. 1943; *s* of Sir James Mackerron Mackay, KBE, CB, and Katherine Millar Crichton Mackay (*née* Hamilton); *m* 1969, Rosamond Diana Elizabeth Collins; one *d* two *s*. *Educ:* Radley Coll.; Corpus Christi Coll., Oxford (Open Classical Schol; MA). Harmsworth Entrance Exhibnr, 1965, and Astbury Schol., 1967; called to the Bar, Middle Temple, 1967, Bencher, 1995; QC 1989, a Recorder, 1992–2001. Mem., Parole Bd for England and Wales, 2005–. Mem., Lambeth Horticultural Soc., 2002–. *Recreations:* opera, growing vegetables, Scotland. *Address:* Royal Courts of Justice, Strand, WC2A 2LL. *Club:* Vincent's (Oxford).

McKAY, Colin Graham; Sheriff of North Strathclyde at Kilmarnock, 2001–07; part-time Sheriff, since 2007; *b* 20 Jan. 1942; *s* of Patrick Joseph McKay and Mary Kieran; *m* 1966, Sandra Anne Coli; one *d* one *s*. *Educ:* St Aloysius' Coll., Glasgow; Clongowes Wood Coll., by Dublin; Univ. of Glasgow (MA, LLB). Admitted Solicitor, 1966; in private practice, 1966–90; Temporary Sheriff, 1985–90; Sheriff of N Strathclyde: (floater), 1990–95; at Oban and Fort William, 1995–2001.

McKAY, Daithí Gerard; Member (SF) North Antrim, Northern Ireland Assembly, since 2007; *b* 2 March 1982; *s* of Gerard and Anne McKay. *Educ:* St Patrick's Primary Sch., Rasharkin; St Louis Grammar Sch., Ballymena; N Eastern Inst. of Further and Higher Educn, Ballymena; Open Univ. (Dip Soc Scis). Customer Advr, Ulster Bank, 2001–03; Political Advr to Philip McGuigan, MLA, 2003–05. Mem. (SF) Ballymoney BC, 2005–. Mem., Gaelic Athletic Assoc. *Recreations:* Gaelic games and culture, reading, keeping fit, travelling. *Address:* 162 Bóthar na d Tullachain, Dún Lathái, Baile Meanach, Co. Antrim, Northern Ireland BT44 9AF. *T:* (028) 2765 7198; *e-mail:* daithimckay@btinternet.com.

MACKAY, David Ian; His Honour Judge Mackay; a Circuit Judge, since 1992; *b* 11 Nov. 1945; *m* 1974, Mary Elizabeth Smith; one *s* two *d*. *Educ:* Birkenhead Sch.; Brasenose Coll., Oxford (Schol.; MA 1992). Called to the Bar, Inner Temple, 1969; practised on Northern Circuit, 1970–92; Asst Recorder, 1986–89; Recorder, 1989–92. Official Referee's business, 1993–98; Provincial Judge, Technology and Construction Court, 1998–. Fellow, Soc. of Advanced Legal Studies. 2001. Gov., Birkenhead Sch., 1979–2001 (Chm., 1991–2001); Chm., Birkenhead Sch. Foundn Trust, 1998–2004. *Recreations:* history, transport, France. *Address:* Queen Elizabeth II Law Courts, Derby Square, Liverpool L2 1XA. *Club:* Athenæum (Liverpool).

MACKAY, David James, FCILT; Chief Executive, John Menzies plc, 1997–2003; Chairman, Transport Edinburgh Ltd, since 2006; *b* 20 May 1943; *s* of David Mackay and Lena Mackay (*née* Westwater); *m* 1966, Jane Brown Hunter; one *s* one *d*. *Educ:* Kirkcaldy High Sch.; post experience programmes at Edinburgh and Bradford Univs. FCILT (FCIT 1993). Various exec. posts in John Menzies plc, 1964–2003, including: Transport Manager, NI, 1965; Asst Regl Dir, Southern & London, 1973; Ops Dir, Edinburgh, 1978; Man Dir, Wholesale, 1984. Chm., Malcolm Gp, 2003–06. Chm., Adv. Gp, Glasgow's Commonwealth Games Bid, 2004–05. CCMI (CIMgt 1998). Hon. Col, Scottish Transport Regt, 2004–. Chieftain, Inverkeithing Highland Games, 2003–06. *Recreations:* golf, walking. *Address:* 4 East Harbour Road, Charlestown, Fife KY11 3EA. *Clubs:* Press (Edinburgh); Bruntsfield Golf (Edinburgh); Aberdour Golf (Fife).

MACKAY, Donald George; Hon. Research Fellow, Aberdeen University, since 1990; *b* 25 Nov. 1929; *s* of William Morton Mackay and Annie Tainsh Higgs; *m* 1st, 1965, Elizabeth Ailsa Barr (*d* 1999); two *s* one *d*; 2nd, 2005, Catherine Anne McDonald. *Educ:* Morgan Academy, Dundee; St Andrews Univ. (MA); Aberdeen Univ. (PhD). Assistant Principal, Scottish Home Dept, 1953; Principal, SHHD, 1962–66; Sec., Royal Commission on Local Govt in Scotland, 1966–69; Asst Sec., Scottish Develt Dept, 1969–79; Asst Sec., 1980–83, Under Sec., 1983–85, Dept of Agric. and Fisheries for Scotland; Under Sec., Scottish Develt Dept., 1985–88. Mem., Scottish Agricl Wages Bd, 1991–97. *Publication:* Scotland's Rural Land Use Agencies, 1995. *Recreations:* hill walking, photography, music. *Address:* 20 Ben Bhraggie Drive, Golspie, Sutherland KW10 6SX. *T:* (01408) 633975.

MacKAY, Sir Donald (Iain), Kt 1996; FRSE; FRSGS; Chairman, Scottish Mortage Trust, since 2003 (Director, since 1999); Director, Edinburgh New Income Trust (formerly Edinburgh Income and Value Trust), since 1999; *b* 27 Feb. 1937; *s* of William and Rhona MacKay; *m* 1961, Diana Marjory (*née* Raffan); two *d* (one *s* decd). *Educ:* Dollar Academy; Univ. of Aberdeen (MA). FRSE 1988. English Electric Co., 1959–62; Lectr in Political Economy, Univ. of Aberdeen, 1962–65; Lectr in Applied Economics, Univ. of Glasgow, 1965–68, Sen. Lectr, 1968–71; Prof. of Political Economy, Univ. of Aberdeen, 1971–76; Prof. of Economics, Heriot-Watt Univ., Edinburgh, 1976–82, Professorial Fellow 1982–90; Hon. Prof., 1990–. Chairman: Pieda plc, 1974–97; Scottish Enterprise, 1993–97; Grampian Hldgs, 1998–2002 (Dir, 1987–98); Malcolm Gp, 2002–03; Dir, DTZ Hldgs, 1999–2003. Mem., Scottish Econ. Council, 1985–99. Consultant to Sec. of State for Scotland, 1971–99. Gov., NIESR, 1981–. FRSGS 1996. Hon. LLD Aberdeen, 1994; DUniv Stirling, 1994. *Publications:* Geographical Mobility and the Brain Drain, 1969; Local Labour Markets and Wage Structures, 1970; Labour Markets under Different Employment Conditions, 1971; The Political Economy of North Sea Oil, 1975; (ed) Scotland 1980: the economics of self-government, 1977; articles in Econ. Jl, Oxford Econ. Papers, Manch. Sch., Scottish Jl Polit. Econ., Jl Royal Stat. Soc. *Recreations:* tennis, golf, bridge. *Address:* Newfield, 14 Gamekeeper's Road, Edinburgh EH4 6LU.

MACKAY, Douglas Ian; QC (Scot.) 1993; *b* 10 Aug. 1948; *s* of Walter Douglas Mackay and Karla Marie Anna Fröhlich; *m* 1970, Susan Anne Nicholson; two *s* one *d*. *Educ:* Inverness High Sch.; Aberdeen Univ. (LLB). Admitted advocate, 1980. *Recreations:* Scottish art, travel, mountaineering, shooting, gundogs. *Address:* St Ann's House, Lasswade, Midlothian EH18 1ND. *T:* (0131) 660 2634; Mount Pleasant Farm, Fortrose, Ross-shire IV10 8SH.

MACKAY, Eileen Alison, (Lady Russell), CB 1996; FRSE; non-executive Director, Royal Bank of Scotland Group plc, 1996–2005; *b* 7 July 1943; *d* of Alexander William Mackay and Alison Jack Ross; *m* 1983, (Alastair) Muir Russell (*see* Sir A. M. Russell). *Educ:* Dingwall Acad.; Edinburgh Univ. (MA Hons Geography). FRSE 2002. Dept of Employment, Scottish HQ, 1965–72; Scottish Office, 1972–78; HM Treasury, 1978–80; CPRS, Cabinet Office, 1980–83; Scottish Office, 1983–96: Under Sec., Housing, Envmt Dept, 1988–92; Principal Finance Officer, 1992–96. Chm., Castlemilk Partnership, 1988–92; Director: Moray Firth Maltings, 1988–99; Edinburgh Investment Trust plc, 1996–2005; Scottish TV (Regional) Ltd, 1998–99; Lothian and Edinburgh Enterprise Ltd, subseq. Scottish Enterprise Edinburgh and Lothian, 1998–2002; Scottish Financial Enterprise Ltd, 2000–06. Chm., Standing Adv. Cttee on Trunk Road Assessment, 1996–99. Mem., Commn on Local Govt and the Scottish Parlt, 1998–99. Member: Bd, Scottish Screen, 1997–99; ESRC, 1999–2003; Scottish Business and Biodiversity Gp, 1999–2002; Accountancy Review Bd, 2000–03; Bd, British Library, 2003–08; Bd of Govs, RSAMD, 2007–. Mem. Bd, Margaret Blackwood Housing Assoc., 1996–2001; Trustee: David Hume Inst., 1996–2008 (Chm. Trustees, 2002–08); Carnegie Trust for Univs of Scotland, 2000–. Mem. Court, Univ. of Edinburgh, 1997–2003. *Address:* c/o Principal's Lodging, 12 The Square, University of Glasgow, Glasgow G12 8QG. *Club:* New (Edinburgh).

MACKAY, Sir Francis Henry, Kt 2003; FCCA; Chairman: Carlton Partners, since 2006; ISS, since 2006; Founding Member, Graysons Ltd, since 2007; *b* 24 Oct. 1944; *m* 1963, Christine Leach; one *s* two *d*. FCCA 1967. Compass Group: Finance Dir, 1986–91, Chief Exec. and Dep. Chm., 1991–99; Chm., 1999–2006; Jt Dep. Chm., Granada Compass, 2000–01; Chm., Kingfisher, 2001–06. Non-exec. Dir, Centrica, 1997–2001. *Address:* Carlton Partners, Berger House, 38 Berkeley Square, W1J 5AE.

MACKAY, Air Vice-Marshal (Hector) Gavin, CB 2002; OBE 1987; AFC 1982; FRAeS; Senior Military Adviser (formerly Military Deputy) to Head of Defence Export Services, since 2002; *b* 3 Oct. 1947; *s* of John MacLean Mackay and Isobel Margaret Mackay (*née* Mackay); *m* 1971, Elizabeth Stark Bolton; one *s* one *d*. *Educ:* Dingwall Acad.; Glasgow Univ. (BSc Civil Engrg 1970); RAF Coll., Cranwell. FRAeS 1997. Qualified Flying Instructor, RAF Linton-on-Ouse, 1973–75; Harrier Pilot: No 20 Sqdn, RAF Wildenrath, 1976–77; No 3 (F) Sqdn, RAF Gutersloh, 1977–79; Flight Comdr, No 1 (F) Sqdn, RAF Wittering, 1979–82; RNSC, 1982; Central Tactics and Trials Orgn, 1983–84; OC Examng Wing, CFS, 1984–87; Concept Studies and Operational Requirements, MoD, 1987–90; Station Comdr, RAF Gutersloh, 1991–93; Dep. Dir Air Offensive, MoD, 1993; rcds 1994; ACOS Ops, HQ AIRCENT, 1995–96; Comdt, CFS, 1996–99; Hd, Jt Force 2000 Implementation Team, 1999–2000; AOC, and Comdt, RAF Coll., Cranwell, 2000–02. Hon. Air Cdre 2503 (Co. of Lincoln) Sqdn, RAuxAF Regt, 2005. Liveryman, GAPAN, 2002–. *Recreations:* flying, golf, walking. *Club:* Royal Air Force.

McKAY, Rt Hon. Sir Ian (Lloyd), KNZM 1998; PC 1992; Chartered Arbitrator; Judge of the Court of Appeal of Samoa, since 2001; Judge of the Court of Appeal of New Zealand, 1991–97; *b* 7 March 1929; *s* of Neville James McKay and Kathleen Mary (*née* McGrath); *m* 1958, Ruth Constance Younger; four *s* two *d*. *Educ:* Victoria Coll., Univ. of NZ (BA, LLB). FCIArb; FAMINZ(Arb). Barrister and Solicitor, High Court of NZ, 1952; in practice as barrister and solicitor with Swan Davies & McKay, Wellington, later Swan Davies McKay & Co., then Young Swan McKay & Co., subseq. Young Swan Morison McKay, and Kensington Swan, 1953–91; Sen. Partner, 1967–91. Chm., various govt law reform cttees, 1971–87. Dir, public and private cos, 1970–91. Fellow, Internat. Acad. Trial Lawyers, USA, 1982–. Hon. Mem., Amer. Bar Assoc., 1981. *Publications:* contrib. Defamation, to Laws of New Zealand, 1994; The Art of Piobaireachd, 1997; The Wellington Gaelic Club 75 Years, 2006; papers to nat. confs and jls of various professional bodies. *Recreations:* Highland bagpipe music, tennis. *Address:* PO Box 17028, Wellington 6147, New Zealand. *T:* (4) 4768950, *Fax:* (4) 4767950. *Club:* Wellington (Wellington, NZ).

MACKAY, Ian Stuart, FRCS; Consultant Otorhinolaryngologist, Royal Brompton Hospital and Charing Cross Hospital, London, 1977–2003; Hon. Consultant, King Edward VII Hospital for Officers, since 1995; *b* 16 June 1943; *s* of Rev. Gordon Mackay and Sylvia Mackay (*née* Spencer); *m* 1981, Madeleine Hargreaves (*née* Tull); one *d*, and one *s* one *d* from former marriage. *Educ:* Kearsney Coll., Natal, South Africa; Royal Free Hosp. Sch. of Medicine, London (MB BS 1968). FRCS 1974. Cons. Otorhinolaryngologist, Metropolitan ENT Hosp., 1977–86. Hon. Senior Lecturer: Nat. Heart and Lung Inst., 1985–; Inst. of Laryngology and Otology, Univ. of London, 1985–. Vis. Prof., Mayo Clinic, 1996. Hon. Treasurer: European Acad. of Facial Surgery, 1978–93; British Academic Conf. in Otolaryngology, 1992–; Mem. Council, Laryngology and Rhinology Section, RSocMed, 1996– (Pres., 2002–03); Founder Mem., British Allergy Foundn, 1995; Pres., British Assoc. of Otolaryngologists, 1999–2002 (Pres.-elect, 1996–99); Chm., Fedn of Surgical Specialty Assocs, 2001–03. Mem. Editl Bd, Amer. Jl of Rhinology, 1995–. *Publications:* (ed) Scott-Brown's Otolaryngology, Rhinology Vols, 5th edn 1987, 6th edn 1997; (contrib.) Facial Plastic Surgery, 1986; Otolaryngology, 1987, 2nd edn 1997; (ed) Rhinitis: mechanisms and management, 1989; chapters in books and papers, mainly on rhinoplasty and endoscopic sinus surgery. *Recreation:* sailing. *Address:* 55 Harley Street, W1G 8QR. *T:* (020) 7580 5070. *Club:* Royal Society of Medicine.

McKAY, Dr John Henderson, CBE 1987; JP; DL; Tutor and Associate Lecturer, Open University, 1993–2001; Hon. Vice President, Royal Caledonian Horticultural Society, since 1997 (Vice President, 1993–97); *b* 12 May 1929; *s* of Thomas Johnstone McKay and Patricia Madeleine Henderson; *m* 1964, Catherine Watson Taylor; one *s* one *d*. *Educ:* West Calder High School; BA Hons, PhD, Open Univ. Labourer, clerk, Pumpherston Oil Co. Ltd, 1948–50; National Service, Royal Artillery, 1950–52; Officer and Surveyor, Customs and Excise, 1952–85. Mem., 1974–77 and 1978–88, Lord Provost and Lord Lieutenant, 1984–88, City of Edinburgh DC; Chm., Edinburgh Internat. Fest. Soc., 1984–88; Jt Chm., Edinburgh Mil. Tattoo Policy Cttee, 1984–88; Councillor, Royal Caledonian Horticultural Soc., 1974–78, 1980–81, 1984–88 (Sec. and Treas., 1988–93). Convener, Business Cttee, 1992–96, Assessor on Univ. Court, 1996–99, Gen. Council of Edinburgh Univ. Chm., Scottish Wkg People's History Trust, 1992–2000; Trustee: Inst. of Occupl Medicine Res. Trust, 1992–2002; Almond Valley Collections Trust, 1994–2007; Edinburgh Quartet Trust, 1994–2002 (Chm., 1995–2000); Hon. Pres., Scottish Craftsmanship Assoc., 1987–2000; Hon. Vice-Pres., St Andrew Soc., 1989–2004; Patron, Scotland Yard Adventure Centre, 1988–2002. JP 1984, DL 1988, Edinburgh. Dr *hc* Edinburgh, 1989. *Publications:* (jtly) Pumpherston: the story of a shale oil village, 2002; (contrib.) A Sense of Place: studies in Scottish local history, 1988; (contrib.) Participating in the Knowledge Society, 2005; (contrib.) Women's Work in Industrial England, 2007; contrib. Local Population Studies. *Recreations:* gardening, listening to music. *Address:* 2 Buckstone Way, Edinburgh EH10 6PN. *T:* (0131) 445 2865. *Club:* Lothianburn Golf (Edinburgh).

MacKAY, Julie; *see* Kirkbride, J.

McKAY, Neil Stuart, CB 2001; Chief Executive, East of England Strategic Health Authority, since 2006; *b* 19 Feb. 1952; *s* of late Roy McKay and of Alison Maude McKay (*née* Dent); *m* 1978, Deirdre Mary McGinn; two *s*. *Educ:* Dame Allan's Boys' Sch., Newcastle upon Tyne. Trainee Adminr, Newcastle upon Tyne Univ. HMC, 1970–72; Asst Hosp. Sec., Dunston Hill Hosp., Gateshead HMC, 1972–74; Admin Asst, Gateshead AHA, 1974–75; Unit Adminr, Dryburn Hosp., Durham AHA, 1975–76; Commng Officer, St George's Hosp., Merton, Sutton and Wandsworth AHA, 1976–80; Dist Planning Adminr, 1980–82, Hosp. Adminr, Springfield Hosp., 1982–85, Wandsworth HA; Gen. Manager, Doncaster Royal Infirmary, 1985–88; Gen. Manager, 1988–91, Chief Exec., 1991–96, Northern Gen. Hosp. NHS Trust, Sheffield; Regl Dir, Trent Regl Office, 1996–2000, Dep. Chief Exec., 2000, NHS Exec., DoH; Chief Operating Officer, DoH, 2000–02; Chief Exec., Leeds Teaching Hosps NHS Trust, 2002–06. Hon. LLD Sheffield, 2000. *Recreations:* sport of all kinds (especially following Sunderland AFC), reading, gardening. *Address:* East of England Strategic Health Authority, Victoria House, Capital Park, Fulbourn, Cambridge CB1 5XB.

MACKAY, Neville Patrick; Chief Executive, Scottish Public Pensions Agency, since 2004; *b* 22 June 1958; *s* of Edward William Charles Mackay and Constance Evelyn Mackay; *m* 1996, Gillian Anne Prole; two *d*. *Educ:* Brentwood Sch.; Lancaster Univ. (BA Hons Geog. 1979); University Coll. London. Researcher, DoE, 1983–90; DFE, 1990–92; Department for National Heritage, later Department for Culture, Media and Sport: 1992–99; Dep. Hd, Heritage Div., 1995–97; Hd, Libraries and Inf. Div., 1997–99; Chief Exec., Resource: Council for Museums, Archives and Libraries, 2000–02; Hd, Voluntary Issues Unit, Scottish Exec., 2002–04. *Recreations:* motor sports, walking, camping, being with my family. *Address:* Scottish Public Pensions Agency, 7 Tweedside Park, Galashiels TD1 3TE.

MacKAY, Prof. Norman, CBE 1997; MD; FRCPGlas, FRCPE, FRCSE, FRCGP, FRCP; Dean of Postgraduate Medicine and Professor of Postgraduate Medical Education, University of Glasgow, 1989–2001; *b* 15 Sept. 1936; *s* of Donald MacKay and Catherine MacLeod; *m* 1961, Grace Violet McCaffer; two *s* two *d*. *Educ:* Glasgow Univ. (MB ChB, MD). FRCPGlas 1973; FRCPE 1975; FRCSE 1993; FRCGP 1993. Junior posts, Glasgow hosps, 1959–66; Lectr in Medicine, Nairobi, 1966–67; Sen. Registrar, Victoria Infirmary, Glasgow, 1967–68; Acting Sen. Lectr, Materia Medica, Univ. of Glasgow, 1968–72; Acting Consultant Physician, Falkirk, 1972–73; Consultant Physician, Victoria Infirmary, 1973–89, Hon. Consultant, 1989–94. Mem., GMC, 1999–2003. Pres., RCPSG, 1994–97 (Hon. Sec., 1973–83; Visitor, 1992–94). Vice-Chm., Copmed, 1999–2001. FCPS(Pak) 1993; FRACP; FAMS; FRCPI; FAMM; Hon. FACP 1995; Hon. FCPS Bangladesh; Hon. FRCS. *Publications:* articles in med. jls. *Recreations:* gardening, golf, soccer. *Address:* 5 Edenhall Grove, Newton Mearns, Glasgow G77 5TS. *T:* (0141) 616 2831.

MACKAY, Peter, CB 1993; Commissioner, Northern Lighthouse Board, 1999–2008 (Chairman, 2005–07); Chairman, Pacific Horizon Investment Trust plc, since 2004 (Director, since 2001); *b* Arbroath, 6 July 1940; *s* of John S. Mackay, FRCS, and Patricia M. Atkinson; *m* 1964, Sarah Holdich; one *s* two *d*. *Educ:* Glasgow High Sch.; St Andrews Univ. (MA Political Economy). Teacher, Kyogle High Sch., NSW, 1962–63; joined Scottish Office as Asst Principal, 1963; various posts, incl. Private Sec. to successive Ministers of State, 1966–68 and Secs of State, 1973–75; Nuffield Travelling Fellow, Canada, Australia and NZ, 1978–79; seconded: as Dir for Scotland, MSC, 1983–85; as Under Sec., Manpower Policy, Dept of Employment, London, 1985–86; Under Sec., Further and Higher Educn, Scottish Educn Dept, 1987–89; Principal Establishment Officer, Scottish Office, 1989–90; Sec. and Chief Exec., Scottish Office Industry Dept, 1990–95. Director: British Linen Bank, 1996–2000; Business Banking Div., Bank of

Scotland, 1999–2001. Member: Competition (formerly Monopolies and Mergers) Commn, 1996–2002; Bd, Scottish Natural Heritage, 1996–2003; Dir, Scottish Forestry Alliance, 2000–; Chm., Local Govt Boundary Commn for Scotland, 2007–. Mem. Court, Napier Univ., 1996–2004. Hon. LLD Robert Gordon's, 1996. *Recreations:* high altitudes and latitudes, dinghy sailing, sea canoeing. *Address:* Silverwood, Kincraig, by Kingussie, Inverness-shire PH21 1QE. *Clubs:* Clyde Canoe, Scottish Arctic.

MacKAY, Hon. Peter Gordon; PC (Can.) 2006; QC (Can.) 2006; MP (C) Central Nova, since 2004 ((PC) Pictou-Antigonish-Guysborough, 1997–2004); Minister of Foreign Affairs and Minister, Atlantic Canada Opportunities Agency, Canada, since 2006; *b* New Glasgow, NS, 27 Sept. 1965; *s* of Hon. Elmer M. MacKay, PC (Can.), QC (Can.) and Macha MacKay. *Educ:* Acadia Univ., NS (BA 1987); Dalhousie Univ., NS (LLB 1990). Called to the Nova Scotia Bar, 1991; in private practice specializing in criminal and family law, New Glasgow, NS, 1991–93; Crown Attorney for Central Reg., NS, 1993–97. House Leader, 1997–2003, Leader, 2003–04, PC Party of Canada; Dep. Leader, Cons. Party of Canada, 2004–06. Nat. Ambassador for Adopt-a-Liby Literacy Prog., Pictou Co., NS, 2000–. Golden Jubilee Medal, 2002. *Recreations:* silviculture, Rugby, baseball, football, ice hockey. *Address:* House of Commons, Ottawa, ON K1A 0A6, Canada. *T:* (613) 992 6022, *Fax:* (613) 992 2337; *e-mail:* MacKay.P@parl.gc.ca.

McKAY, Randal Joseph; His Honour Judge Randal McKay; QC (NI) 1989; a County Court Judge, Armagh and South Down Division, Northern Ireland, since 1994; *b* Larne, 16 April 1943; *s* of Hugh and Josephine McKay; *m* 1974, Brenda O'Neill; three *s*. *Educ:* Queen's Univ., Belfast (LLB 1969; BL 1970). In practice as barrister, 1970–94. *Recreations:* boxing, pistol shooting, crosswords, motor racing, deflating egos. *Address:* c/o Northern Ireland Court Service, Windsor House, Bedford Street, Belfast BT2 7LT; *e-mail:* rmckay.rcj@courts.ni.gov.uk.

MacKAY, Prof. Robert Sinclair, PhD; FRS 2000; FInstP, FIMA; Professor of Mathematics, University of Warwick, since 2000; *b* 4 July 1956; *s* of Donald Maccrimmon MacKay and Valerie MacKay (*née* Wood); *m* 1992, Claude Noëlle Baesens; one *s*. *Educ:* Trinity Coll., Cambridge (BA Math.; MA); Princeton (PhD Astrophys. Scis). FInstP 2000; FIMA 2003. Res. Asst, QMC, 1982–83; Vis. Researcher, Institut des Hautes Etudes Scientifiques, Bures-sur-Yvette, France, 1983–84; Lectr, 1984–90, Reader, 1990–93, Prof., 1993–95, Mathematics, Univ. of Warwick; Prof. of Nonlinear Dynamics, and Fellow of Trinity Coll., Univ. of Cambridge, 1995–2000. Nuffield Foundn Sci. Res. Fellow, 1992–93; Res. Associate, 1994–95, Vis. Prof., 1995, CNRS, Université de Bourgogne, France. (First) Stephanos Pnevmatikos Internat. Award for Res. in Nonlinear Phenomena, 1993; Jun. Whitehead Prize, London Math. Soc., 1994. *Publications:* Hamiltonian Dynamical Systems, 1987; Renormalisation in area-preserving maps, 1993; over 100 papers in learned jls. *Address:* Mathematics Institute, University of Warwick, Coventry CV4 7AL.

MACKAY, Ronald David; *see* Eassie, Rt Hon. Lord.

MACKAY, Prof. Trudy Frances Charlene, (Mrs R. R. H. Anholt), PhD; FRS 2006; William Neal Reynolds Distinguished Professor, Department of Genetics, North Carolina State University, since 1996; *b* 10 Sept. 1952; *d* of Charles Edward Mackay and Jean Somerville Mackay; *m* 1990, Robert R. H. Anholt. *Educ:* Dalhousie Univ. (BSc Hons 1974, MSc 1976); Univ. of Edinburgh (PhD 1979). Lectr, Dept of Genetics, Univ. of Edinburgh, 1980–87; Associate Prof., 1987–93, Prof., 1993–96, Dept of Genetics, N Carolina State Univ. FAAAS 2003; Fellow, Amer. Acad. of Arts and Scis, 2005. *Publications:* over 130 peer-reviewed articles in scientific jls. *Recreations:* dressage and carriage driving, listening to opera, reading mystery novels. *Address:* Department of Genetics, Campus Box 7614, North Carolina State University, Raleigh, NC 27695, USA. *T:* (919) 5155810, *Fax:* (919) 5153355; *e-mail:* trudy_mackay@ncsu.edu.

McKAY, Sir William (Robert), KCB 2001 (CB 1996); *b* 18 April 1939; *s* of late William Wallace McKay and Margaret H. A. Foster; *m* 1962, Rev. Margaret M., *d* of late E. M. Fillmore, OBE; twin *d*. *Educ:* Trinity Academy, Leith; Edinburgh Univ. (MA Hons). Clerk in the House of Commons, 1961; Clerk of Financial Cttees, H of C, 1985–87; Clerk of the Journals, H of C, 1987–91; Clerk of Public Bills, H of C, 1991–94; Clerk Asst, H of C, 1994–97; Clerk of the H of C, 1998–2002. Secretary: to the House of Commons Commn, 1981–84; to the Public Accounts Commn, 1985–87. Lay Observer, Law Soc. of Scotland, 2006–. Hon. Prof., Univ. of Aberdeen, 2003–07. *Publications:* (ed) Erskine May's Private Journal 1883–86, 1984; Secretaries to Mr Speaker, 1986; Clerks in the House of Commons 1363–1989: a biographical list, 1989; (ed) Observations, Rules and Orders of the House of Commons: an early procedural collection, 1989; (ed jtly) Erskine May's Parliamentary Practice, 22nd edn 1997, (sole editor) 23rd edn 2004; (contrib.) Stair Memorial Encyclopaedia of the Laws of Scotland, rev. edn 2002; (with M. M. McKay) A United Parish, 2002; (contrib.) Halsbury's Laws of England, 4th edn; contrib. historical jls. *Recreation:* reading Scottish history. *Address:* Knowes of Elrick Smithy, Aberchirder, Huntly, Aberdeenshire AB54 7PN.

MACKAY-DICK, Maj.-Gen. Sir Iain (Charles), KCVO 1997; MBE 1981; Clerk to the Trustees and Chief Executive, Morden College, since 1997; *b* 24 Aug. 1945; *s* of John Mackay-Dick and Margaret Edith Mackay-Dick (*née* Forty); *m* 1971, Carolynn Hilary Holmes; three *d*. *Educ:* St Edmund's Sch., Hindhead; Sherborne Sch.; RMAS; Staff Coll., Camberley (psc, hcsc). Commnd, Scots Guards, 1965; served Malaysia, Borneo, Germany, Cyprus and UK to 1986, and Falkland Is, 1982; Comdt, Jun. Div. Staff Coll., Warminster, 1986–88; Comdr, 11 Armoured Bde, 1989–91; Dep. Mil. Sec. (A), 1991–92; GOC 1st Armoured Div., Verden, 1992–93; GOC Lower Saxony Dist, Verden, 1993; Comdr British Forces Falkland Is, 1993–94; GOC London Dist and Maj. Gen. commanding Household Div., 1994–97. Mem., RUSI, 1979–2006. Hon. Col, 256 (City of London) Field Hosp., RAMC(V), 2000–07. Member: Public Schools Old Boys LTA; South Atlantic Medal Assoc. Freeman, City of London, 2000. FCMI (FIMgt 1996). Trustee, Falkland Is Meml Chapel, Pangbourne, 2005–. *Publication:* (contrib.) Central Region versus Out of Area (essays), 1990. *Recreations:* most sports (represented Army in lawn tennis and squash (Army Squash Champion, 1971)), walking, gardening, military history. *Address:* Morden College, 19 St Germans Place, Blackheath SE3 0PW. *T:* (020) 8858 3365. *Clubs:* Edinburgh Angus (Edinburgh); Jesters; Third Guards; Guards' Golfing Society, Army Golfing Society.

McKEAN, Prof. Charles Alexander, FRSE; FSAScot; Professor of Scottish Architectural History, Dundee University, since 1998 (Professor of Architecture, 1995–98); *b* 16 July 1946; *s* of John Laurie McKean and Nancy Burns Lendrum; *m* 1975, Margaret Elizabeth Yeo; two *s*. *Educ:* Fettes Coll., Edinburgh; Univ. of Bristol (BA Hons). Regional Secretary, RIBA, 1968–79; Sec. and Treas., RIAS, 1979–94; Architectural Correspondent: The Times, 1977–83; Scotland on Sunday, 1988–89; Trustee, Thirlestane Castle Trust, 1983–; Director, Workshops and Artists Studios Scotland (WASPS), 1980–85; Member: Scottish Arts Council Exhibitions Panel, 1980–83; Adv. Council for the Arts in Scotland, 1984–87; Edinburgh Common Purpose Adv. Cttee, 1990–94; Scottish Cttee, Heritage Lottery Fund, 1993–2003; Historic Envmt Adv. Council for Scotland, 2003–06; Chm., Edinburgh World Heritage Trust, 2006–; Mem. Council, and Chm. Buildings Cttee, Nat. Trust for Scotland, 1995–2003. Lectures: Bossom, RSA, 1986; RCS Prestigious, 1992. Hon. Mem., Saltire Soc. FRSE 1999; FRSA. Hon. FRIBA 1989; Hon. FRIAS 1994; Hon. FRSGS 2002. Hon. DLitt Robert Gordon, 1993. General Editor, RIAS/Landmark Trust series to Scotland, 1982–. Architectural Journalist of the Year, 1979 and 1983; Building Journalist of the Year, 1983. *Publications:* (with David Atwell) Battle of Styles, 1974; Guide to Modern Buildings in London 1965–75, 1976; Fight Blight, 1977; Architectural Guide to Cambridge and East Anglia 1920–80, 1980; Edinburgh—an illustrated architectural guide, 1982, 3rd edn 1983; (with David Walker) Dundee—an illustrated introduction through its buildings, 1984, 2nd edn 1986; Stirling and the Trossachs, 1984; The Scottish Thirties, 1987; The District of Moray—an illustrated introduction, 1987; (jtly) Central Glasgow—an illustrated architectural guide, 1989; Banff and Buchan—an illustrated architectural guide, 1990; For a Wee Country, 1990; Edinburgh: portrait of a city, 1991; Edinburgh—an illustrated architectural guide, 1992; (with David Walker) Dundee—an illustrated architectural guide, 1993; Value or Cost, 1994; Claim, 1998; The Making of the Museum of Scotland, 2001; The Scottish Château, 2001; Battle for the North, 2006. *Recreations:* gardening, topography, books and glass collecting. *Address:* 10 Hill Park Road, Edinburgh EH4 7AW. *T:* (0131) 336 2753. *Club:* Scottish Arts.

MacKEAN, His Honour Thomas Neill; a Circuit Judge, 1993–2004; *b* 4 March 1934; *s* of late Andrew Neill MacKean and Mary Dale MacKean (*née* Nichol); *m* 1962, Muriel Hodder; four *d*. *Educ:* Sherborne; Trinity Hall, Cambridge (BA). 2nd Lt, Royal Hampshire Regt, 1952–54. Partner, Hepherd Winstanley & Pugh, solicitors, Southampton, 1960–93; HM Coroner, Southampton and New Forest, 1990–93; a Recorder, 1991–93. *Recreations:* sailing, walking. *Clubs:* Royal Cruising; Royal Southern Yacht (Hamble).

McKEARNEY, Philip, CMG 1983; HM Diplomatic Service, retired; *b* 15 Nov. 1926; *s* of Philip McKearney, OBE; *m* 1950, Jean Pamela Walker; two *s*. *Educ:* City of London Sch.; Hertford Coll., Oxford. 4/7th Dragoon Guards, 1946–53; joined HM Diplomatic Service, 1953; 3rd Sec., British Embassy, Damascus, 1955–56; 1st Sec., British Legation, Bucharest, 1959–62; British Political Agent, Qatar, 1962–65; Counsellor and Consul-Gen., Baghdad, 1968–70; Counsellor, Belgrade, 1970–74; Inspector, FCO, 1975–77; Consul-General: Zagreb, 1977–80; Boston, Mass, 1980–83; Amb. to Romania, 1983–86; Dir, Foreign Service Prog., Oxford Univ., 1987–88.

McKECHIN, Ann; MP (Lab) Glasgow North, since 2005 (Glasgow, Maryhill, 2001–05); Parliamentary Under Secretary of State, Scotland Office, since 2008; *b* 22 April 1961; *d* of late William Joseph McKechin and of Anne McKechin (*née* Coyle). *Educ:* Strathclyde Univ. (LLB, DLP). Solicitor, 1983–; Partner, Pacitti Jones, Glasgow, 1990–2000. *Recreations:* films, dancing, art history. *Address:* House of Commons, SW1A 0AA. *T:* (020) 7219 8239; *web:* www.annmckechinmp.net.

MACKECHNIE, Sir Alistair (John), Kt 1993; financial consultant, since 1992; *b* 15 Nov. 1934; *s* of Frank Harper McIvor Mackechnie and Ellen Annie (*née* Brophy); *m* 1961, Countess Alexandra Kinsky, *er d* of Count Frederick-Carl Kinsky; three *d*. *Educ:* St Patrick's Coll., Wellington, NZ; Victoria Univ. of Wellington, NZ. ACA 1957. Nat. Service: commnd NZ Scottish Regt, 1955. Director: Henderson Admin, 1976–88; BSI-Thornhill Investment Mgt, 1989–2000; Hori Construction Ltd, 2000–. Twickenham Conservative Association: Chm., 1985–88; Pres., 1989–; Greater London Area Conservatives: Dep. Chm., 1988–90; Chm., 1990–93; Mem., Exec. Cttee, Nat. Union of Cons. and Unionist Assocs, 1988–96. Mem. Council, Back Care (formerly Nat. Back Pain Assoc.), 1994–. Governor: St Mary's UC, 1997–2006; St Catherine's Sch., Twickenham, 1997–2006. *Recreations:* theatre, travel, bird-watching, hill-walking. *Club:* Carlton.

McKECHNIE, George; Director of Participation and Communications, Education and Learning Wales, 2001–04; *b* 28 July 1946; *m* 1971, Janequin (*née* Morris); two *s*. *Educ:* Portobello Sen. Secondary Sch., Edinburgh. Reporter: Paisley and Renfrewshire Gazette, 1964–66; Edinburgh Evening News, 1966; Scottish Daily Mail, 1966–68; Daily Record, 1968–73; Dep. News Editor and News Editor, Sunday Mail, 1974–76; Asst Editor, 1976–81, Editor, 1981–94, Evening Times, Glasgow; Editor, The Herald, Glasgow, 1994–97; Dir of Public Affairs, Beattie Media, 1998–99; Dir of Communications, Council of Welsh TECs, 1999–2001. Director: George Outram & Co., 1986–92; Caledonian Newspaper Publishing, 1992–97. Mem., Press Complaints Commn, 1992–94. *Recreations:* reading, walking, cinema, Hearts FC. *Address:* Mumbles Hill House, Mumbles Hill, Mumbles, Swansea SA3 4HZ.

McKEE, (Charles Dean) Grant; television executive producer; Director of Programmes, Yorkshire Television, 1993–95 (non-executive Director, 2002–06); *b* 18 Aug. 1951; *s* of Comdr Eric McKee, RN, OBE and Betty (*née* Dean); *m* 1991, Jill Turton; one *d*. *Educ:* Clifton Coll.; Exeter Coll., Oxford (LLB). Journalist: Goole Times, 1974–76; Yorkshire Post, 1976–78; Yorkshire Television, 1979–95: journalist and documentary producer, 1979–88; Editor, First Tuesday, 1988–93; Controller, Documentaries and Current Affairs, 1988–93. *Publication:* (with R. Franey) Time Bomb: Irish bombers, English justice and the Guildford Four, 1988. *Recreations:* travel, cricket, countryside. *Address:* 5 Summerhouse Mews, York YO30 7ED.

McKEE, David John; writer, illustrator, painter and film maker; *b* 2 Jan. 1935; *m* Barbara Ennuss (decd); two *s* one *d*. *Educ:* Tavistock Grammar Sch.; Plympton Grammar Sch.; Plymouth Coll. of Art; Hornsey Coll. of Art. Freelance cartoonist, 1955–; films incl. Mr Benn (14 films), 1970; Founder, and Director, King Rollo Films Ltd, 1979–. *Publications:* include: Bronto's Wings, 1964; Two Can Toucan, 1964; Mr Benn series, 1967–; Elmer series, 1968–; Melric the Magician, 1970; Two Admirals, 1977; Tusk Tusk, 1978; King Rollo, 1979; Adventures of King Rollo, 1982; Not Now Bernard, 1980; I Hate My Teddy Bear, 1982; Further Adventures of King Rollo, 1983; Two Monsters, 1985; King Rollo's Letter and Other Stories, 1986; Sad Story of Veronica Who Played the Violin, 1988; Snow Woman, 1989; Zebra's Hiccups, 1991; Isabel's Noisy Tummy, 1994; Charlotte's Piggy Bank, 1996; Monster and the Teddy Bear, 1997; Prince Peter and the Teddy Bear, 1999; Mary's Secret, 1999; King Rollo's New Stockings, 2001; The Conquerors, 2004; Three Monsters, 2006; Four Red Apples, 2006. *Address:* c/o Andersen Press, 20 Vauxhall Bridge Road, SW1V 2SA.

McKEE, Grant; *see* McKee, C. D. G.

McKEE, Dr Ian Hume, MBE 2006; Member (SNP) Lothians, Scottish Parliament, since 2007; *b* 2 April 1940; *s* of late John and Marjory McKee; *m* 1992, Penelope Ann Watson (*née* Bartlett); one *s* two *d*, and one step *s* one step *d*. *Educ:* Fettes Coll., Edinburgh; Univ. of Edinburgh (MB ChB 1965); DRCOG 1970. House Officer: Ingham Infirmary, South Shields, 1965–66; Royal Infirmary, Edinburgh, 1966; MO, RAF, 1966–71; Gen. Med. Practitioner, Sighthill and Wester Hailes Health Centres, 1971–2006. Man. Dir, Hermiston Publications Ltd, 1979–95; Dir, One City Trust Ltd, 2007–. Scottish Advr, ABPI, 1985–2002. Medical Columnist: Daily Record, 1990–97; Scotsman, 2003–06.

Mem., Lord Provost of Edinburgh's Commn on Social Exclusion, 1999–2002. Mem., Merchants' Co., City of Edinburgh, 1982–; Burgess and Freeman, City of Edinburgh, 2007. *Recreations:* hill walking, boating, supporting unsuccessful football clubs, admiring finer things in life, making marmalade. *Address:* Scottish Parliament, Edinburgh EH99 1SP. *T:* (0131) 348 6815, *Fax:* (0131) 348 6818; *e-mail:* ian.mckee.msp@scottish.parliament.uk. *Clubs:* Royal Air Force; Scottish National Party (Edinburgh).

McKEE, Richard Anthony; a Senior Immigration Judge, since 2006; *b* 28 Sept. 1948; *s* of Ian and Ilse McKee. *Educ:* Campbell Coll., Belfast; Jesus Coll., Cambridge (BA Classics 1971); Sch. of Oriental and African Studies, London (MA Linguistics 1983). Lectr in Linguistics, PCL, Central Sch. of Speech and Drama, and Goldsmiths' Coll., London Univ., 1984–90. Called to the Bar, Inner Temple, 1993; in practice as barrister, 1993–2000; Immigration Adjudicator, 2000–06. *Publications:* (jtly) United Kingdom Asylum Law in its European Context, 1999; (contrib.) Butterworths Immigration Law Service, 1999; (contrib.) Immigration Law and Practice, 2001; compiler, Immigration Law Update, 2002–; numerous articles on immigration and asylum law in various jls. *Recreations:* weight training, cycling, running - in vain attempt to combat the effects of wining, dining and general conviviality. *Address:* c/o Asylum and Immigration Tribunal, Field House, Bream's Buildings, EC4A 1DZ.

McKEE, Dr Robert Andrew; Chief Executive, Chartered Institute of Library and Information Professionals (formerly Library Association), since 1999; *b* 16 Aug. 1950; *s* of Rev. Harry McKee and Nancy McKee; *m* 1976, Victoria Alexandra Lippman; one *s* one *d. Educ:* Bury Grammar Sch.; St Catherine's Coll., Oxford (BA 1971); Shakespeare Inst., Univ. of Birmingham (MA 1972; PhD 1976); Birmingham Poly. (DipLib 1977). MCLIP (ALA 1979; MIInfSc 1986). Trainee and Resources Librarian, Birmingham Liby Service, 1974–79; Tutor Librarian, Solihull Coll. of Technol., 1979–84; Principal Lectr, Dept of Liby and Inf. Studies, Birmingham Poly., 1984–88; Dir, Libraries and Arts, 1988–96, Asst Chief Exec., 1996–99, Solihull MBC. Hon. Prof., Univ. of Worcester, 2006–. Member: Council, MLA, 2003–06; PLR Adv. Cttee, 2003–; Governing Bd, IFLA, 2005–. FRSA 1991. *Publications:* The Information Age, 1985; Public Libraries into the 1990s, 1987; Planning Library Service, 1989; contribs to jl literature of liby and inf. studies. *Recreations:* walking, music, watching football (Bury FC) and cricket, enjoying the company of family and friends. *Address:* Chartered Institute of Library and Information Professionals, 7 Ridgmount Street, WC1E 7AE. *T:* (020) 7255 0691; *e-mail:* bob.mcKee@cilip.org.uk.

McKEE, Dr William James Ernest, MD; Regional Medical Officer and Advisor, Wessex Regional Health Authority, 1976–89; *b* 20 Feb. 1929; *s* of John Sloan McKee, MA, and Mrs Annie Emily McKee (*née* McKinley); *m* Josée Tucker; three *d. Educ:* Queen Elizabeth's, Wakefield; Trinity Coll., Cambridge; Queen's Coll., Oxford. MA, MD, BChir (Cantab); LRCP, MRCS, FFCM. Clinical trng and postgrad. clinical posts at Radcliffe Infirmary, Oxford, 1952–57; med. res., financed by Nuffield Provincial Hosps Trust, 1958–61; successive posts in community medicine with Metrop. Regional Hosp. Bds, 1961–69; Sen. Admin. Med. Officer, Liverpool Regional Hosp. Bd, 1970–74; Regional Med. Officer, Mersey RHA, 1974–76. Chairman: Regional Med. Officers' Gp, 1984–86; Wessex Regl Working Party to review policy for Mental Handicap Services, 1979; UK Head of Delegation, EEC Hosp. Cttee, 1988–89 (Mem., 1985–89); Member: Council for Postgrad. Med. Educn in England and Wales, 1975–85; Hunter Working Party on Med. Admin, 1972–83; DHSS Adv. Cttee on Med. Manpower Planning, 1982–85; DHSS Jt Planning Adv. Cttee on Med. Manpower, 1985–89; Bd of Faculty of Medicine, Univ. of Southampton, 1976–89. QHP 1987–90. *Publications:* papers on tonsillectomy and adenoidectomy in learned jls. *Recreations:* fly-fishing, golf. *Address:* 22a Bereweeke Avenue, Winchester SO22 6BH. *T:* (01962) 861369.

McKEE, William Stewart, CBE 2006; Chief Executive, Belfast Health and Social Care Trust, since 2007; *b* 22 Jan. 1952; *s* of James Gardiner McKee and Margaret Elisabeth McKee; *m* 1983, Ursula Byrne; one *s* one *d. Educ:* Queen's Univ., Belfast (BSc Hons); Univ. of Ulster (MBA). NHS Nat. Trng Scheme, 1976–78; various NHS mgt posts, NI, 1978–93; Chief Exec., Royal Hosps, Belfast, 1993–2006. Pres., IHM, 2000–02. *Address:* Belfast Health and Social Care Trust, Knockbracken Healthcare Park, Saintfield Road, Belfast BT8 8BH.

McKEEVER, Prof. Ian, RA 2003; artist; Professor in Painting, University of Brighton, since 2001; Professor of Drawing, Royal Academy School of Arts, London, since 2006; *b* 30 Nov. 1946; *m* 1991, Gerlinde Gabriel; one *s* one *d. Educ:* Withernsea High Sch.; Avery Hill Coll. of Educn, London (DipEd). Exhibitions include: Kunst Forum, Städtische Galerie im Lenbachhaus, Munich, 1989; Whitechapel Art Gall., 1990; Haggerty Mus. of Art, Milwaukee, 1994; Kunsthallen Brandts Klaedefabrik, Odense, 2001, 2007; Horsen Kunstmus., Horsens, 2002; Kettle's Yard, Cambridge, 2004; China Art Gall., Beijing and Nat. Gall., Shanghai, 2005; Morat Inst. für Kunst und Kunstwissenschaft, Freiburg, 2005, 2007; Ny Carlsberg Glyptotek, Copenhagen, 2006; work in collections, including: Tate Gall., London; BM; Govt Art Collection; British Council; Arts Council of GB; Scottish Nat. Gall. of Modern Art; Metropolitan Mus. of Modern Art, NY; Brooklyn Mus.; Boston Mus. of Fine Arts; Cincinnati Mus. of Modern Art; Louisiana Mus., Denmark; Mus. des 20 Jahrhunderts, Vienna. *Publication:* In Praise of Painting: three essays, 2005. *Address:* c/o Alan Cristea Gallery, 31 Cork Street, W1X 2NU.

MacKEITH, Prof. Margaret Anne, CBE 1997; PhD; FRTPI; FRGS; Consultant, MacKeith Dickinson & Partners Ltd, since 2000; Pro Vice-Chancellor, University of Central Lancashire (formerly Lancashire Polytechnic), 1995–99; *b* 26 June 1939; *d* of James and Gertrude Crane; *m* 1962, Charles Gordon MacKeith; two *s. Educ:* Shirebrook Grammar Sch., Derbyshire; Univ. of Manchester (DipTP, MA); Heriot-Watt Univ. (PhD). FRTPI 1980; FRGS 1976; MIEnvSc 1977. Planning Officer, Lancs CC, 1961–63; Consultant to MacKeith Dickinson and Partners, 1963–74; Lancashire Polytechnic: Sen., then Principal, Lectr, 1975–87; Hd, Sch. of Construction and Surveying, 1987–90; Dean, Faculty of Technol., 1987–90, Faculty of Design and Technol., 1990–95. Consultant, TradePoint Systems USA, 1999–2003. Mem., Royal Fine Art Commn, 1993–99. Member: BTEC Cttees, 1988–93; NW Cttee, OFFER, 1990–93; Landscape Adv. Cttee, Dept of Transport, 1991–93; NRA NW Cttee, 1994–97. Trustee, Nat. Museums Liverpool (formerly Nat. Museums and Galls on Merseyside), 2000–. Hon. Prof., Transylvania Univ., Romania, 1998. FRSA 1990. Dr *hc* Cluj, Romania, 1994. *Publications:* Shopping Arcades 1817–1939, 1985; History and Conservation of Shopping Arcades, 1986; articles and conf. papers on conservation, engrg educn and women in engrg and technol. *Recreations:* travel, architectural history, music, opera. *Address:* 104 Breck Road, Poulton-le-Fylde, Lancs FY6 7HT. *T:* (01253) 884774; 4 Breton House, Barbican, EC2Y 8DG.

McKELLAR, Prof. Quintin Archibald, PhD, DVM; CBiol, FIBiol, FRAgS; FRSE; Professor of Veterinary Pharmacology and Principal, Royal Veterinary College, University of London, since 2004; *b* 24 Dec. 1958; *s* of Quintin and Elizabeth McKellar; *m* 1984, Patricia Law; one *s* three *d. Educ:* Glasgow Univ. (BVMS 1981; PhD 1984; DVM 2002); Eur. Coll. Vet. Pharmacol. and Toxicol. (DipECVPT). MRCVS 1981; CBiol, FIBiol, 2001; FRAgS 2003. University of Glasgow: Lectr, 1984–96; Prof. of Veterinary Pharmacol., 1996–97; Chief Exec. and Scientific Dir, Moredun Res. Inst., 1997–2004. Chm., Regulatory Agencies Strategy Bd, 2005–; Member: Veterinary Products Cttee, 1993–2001; Council, BBSRC, 2005–. Gov., Inst. Animal Health, 2003–. FRSE 2003. *Publications:* numerous contribs to scientific literature. *Recreation:* rowing. *Address:* Royal Veterinary College, Hawkshead Lane, North Mymms, Hatfield, Herts AL9 7TA. *T:* (01707) 666829; *e-mail:* qmckellar@rvc.ac.uk. *Club:* Leander (Henley-on-Thames).

McKELLEN, Sir Ian (Murray), CH 2008; Kt 1991; CBE 1979; actor and director, since 1961; *b* 25 May 1939; *s* of late Denis Murray McKellen and Margery (*née* Sutcliffe). *Educ:* Wigan Grammar Sch.; Bolton Sch.; St Catharine's Coll., Cambridge (BA; Hon. Fellow, 1982). Cameron Mackintosh Prof. of Contemporary Theatre, Univ. of Oxford, 1991–92. Pres., Marlowe Soc., 1960–61. Elected to Council of Equity, 1971–72. Hon. DLitt Nottingham, 1989. 1st appearance (stage): Belgrade Theatre, Coventry, in a Man for all Seasons, Sept. 1961; Arts Theatre, Ipswich, 1962–63; Nottingham Playhouse, 1963–64; 1st London stage appearance, Duke of York's in A Scent of Flowers, 1964 (Clarence Derwent Award); Recruiting Officer, Chips with Everything, Cambridge Theatre Co., 1971; Founder Mem., Actors Company: Ruling the Roost, 'Tis Pity She's a Whore, Edin. Fest., 1972; Knots, Wood-Demon, Edin. Fest., 1973, and with King Lear, Brooklyn Acad. of Music, Wimbledon Theatre season, 1974; *London stage appearances:* A Lily in Little India, St Martin's; Man of Destiny/O'Flaherty VC, Mermaid Theatre; Their Very Own and Golden City, Royal Court, 1966; The Promise, Fortune, 1967 (also Broadway); White Lies/Black Comedy, Lyric; Richard II, Prospect Theatre Co., 1968 (revived with Edward II, Edin. Fest., British and European tours); Hamlet, Cambridge, 1971 (British and European tours); Ashes, Young Vic, 1975; Bent, Royal Court, Criterion, 1979 (SWET Award, 1979); Short List, Hampstead, 1983; Cowardice, Ambassadors, 1983; Henceforward, Vaudeville, 1988; Dance of Death, Lyric, 2003; Aladdin, Old Vic, 2004, 2005; The Cut, Donmar Warehouse, 2006; *with Royal National Theatre:* Much Ado About Nothing, Old Vic, 1965; Armstrong's Last Goodnight, Trelawney of the Wells, Chichester Fest., 1965; Venice Preserv'd, Wild Honey (Laurence Olivier Award, Plays and Players Award; Los Angeles and NY, 1986–87), Coriolanus (London Standard Award), South Bank, 1984–85; as Assoc. Dir, produced and acted in The Duchess of Malfi, The Real Inspector Hound with The Critic, The Cherry Orchard (Paris and Chicago), 1984–85; Bent, 1990 (also Garrick); Kent in King Lear, and title role, Richard III, 1990 (Laurence Olivier Award; Assoc. Prod. for world tour, 1990–91); Napoli Milionaria, 1991; Uncle Vanya, 1992; Richard III, US tour, 1992; An Enemy of the People, Peter Pan, 1997–98; *with Royal Shakespeare Co.:* Dr Faustus, Edin. Fest. and Aldwych, 1974; Marquis of Keith, Aldwych, 1974–75; King John, Aldwych, 1975; Too Good to be True, Aldwych and Globe, 1975; Romeo and Juliet, The Winter's Tale, Macbeth (Plays and Players Award, 1976), Stratford, 1976–77; Every Good Boy Deserves Favour, RFH, 1977, Barbican, 1982; Romeo and Juliet, Macbeth, Pillars of the Community (SWET Award, 1977), Days of the Commune, The Alchemist (SWET Award, 1978), Aldwych and RSC Warehouse, 1977–78; King Lear, The Seagull, Stratford and world tour, 2007; Prod. RSC Tour, 1978: Three Sisters, Twelfth Night, Is There Honey Still for Tea; Iago in Othello, The Other Place, Stratford and Young Vic, 1989, BBC TV (Evening Standard and London Critics' Award); *with W Yorks Playhouse, Leeds:* The Seagull, Present Laughter, 1998; The Tempest, 1999; *Directed:* Liverpool Playhouse, 1969; Watford and Leicester, 1972; A Private Matter, Vaudeville, 1973; The Clandestine Marriage, Savoy, 1975; *other performances include:* Words, Words, Words (solo recital), Edin. Fest. and Belfast Fest., 1976 (with Acting Shakespeare, Edin. and Belfast, 1977); Amadeus, Broadhurst, NY, 1980–81 (Drama Desk, NY Drama League, Outer Critics' Circle and Tony Awards); A Knight Out, NY, S Africa, UK, 1994–95; Dance of Death, NY, 2001; *Acting Shakespeare tours:* Israel, Norway, Denmark, Sweden, 1980; Spain, France, Cyprus, Israel, Poland, Romania, 1982; Los Angeles and Ritz, NYC (Drama Desk Award), 1983; San Francisco, Washington DC, Los Angeles, Olney, Cleveland, San Diego, Boston (Elliot Norton Award), 1987 Playhouse, London, 1987–88. *Films:* A Touch of Love, Alfred the Great, 1968; The Promise, 1969; Priest of Love, 1979; Scarlet Pimpernel, 1982; Plenty, Zina, 1985; Scandal, 1988; The Ballad of Little Jo, 1992; Six Degrees of Separation, Last Action Hero, 1993; The Shadow, Jack and Sarah, 1994; Restoration, 1995; Richard III (European Actor of the Year, Berlin Film Fest.), Swept from the Sea, 1996; Apt Pupil, Bent, 1997; Gods and Monsters, 1998; X-Men, 2000; The Fellowship of the Ring, 2001; The Two Towers, 2002; X-Men 2, Return of the King, 2003; Emile, 2004; Asylum, Sprung!, 2005; The Da Vinci Code, X-Men: The Last Stand, Neverwas, Flushed Away, 2006; Stardust, The Golden Compass, 2007. Has appeared on television, 1966–, incl. Walter, 1982 (RTS Performance Award for 1982); Walter and June, 1983; Mister Shaw's Missing Millions, 1993; Tales of the City, 1993; Cold Comfort Farm, 1995; Rasputin, 1996 (Golden Globe Award). *Address:* c/o Independent Talent Group Ltd, Oxford House, 76 Oxford Street, W1D 1BS. *T:* (020) 7636 6565, *Fax:* (020) 7323 0101; *web:* www.mckellen.com.

McKELVEY, Very Rev. Houston; *see* McKelvey, Very Rev. R. S. J. H.

McKELVEY, Rev. Dr Robert John; Principal, Northern College, Manchester, 1979–93; Moderator, General Assembly of the United Reformed Church, 1994–95; *b* 12 Oct. 1929; *s* of Robert John McKelvey and Eleanor McMaster McKelvey (*née* Earls); *m* 1957, Martha Esther Skelly; two *s* one *d. Educ:* Paton Congregational Coll.; Nottingham Univ. (BA 1955); Pittsburgh Theol Seminary (MTh 1956); Mansfield Coll., Oxford (DPhil 1959). Tutor, 1959–67, Principal, 1968–74, Adams United Coll., S Africa; Pres., Federal Theol Seminary of S Africa, 1970–71; Dir, Internship Trng, United Congregational Church of S Africa, 1975–78; Pres., Northern Fedn for Trng in Ministry, 1984–86. *Publications:* The New Temple: the Church in the New Testament, 1969; The Millennium and the Book of Revelation, 1999; contributor to: New Bible Dictionary, 1962; The Illustrated Bible Dictionary, 1980; New 20th Century Encyclopedia of Religious Knowledge, 2nd edn 1991; New Dictionary of Biblical Theology, 2000; Studies in the Book of Revelation, 2001; learned jls incl. NT Studies, Jl of Theol Studies. *Recreations:* gardening, walking, travel, oddjobbery. *Address:* 64 Brooklawn Drive, Withington, Manchester M20 3GZ. *T:* (0161) 434 4936.

McKELVEY, Very Rev. Dr (Robert Samuel James) Houston, TD; Dean of Belfast, since 2001; *b* 3 Sept. 1942; *s* of Robert and Annie McKelvey; *m* 1969, Eileen Roberta; one *s. Educ:* Queen's Univ., Belfast (BA 1965; MA (Ed) 1988); TCD; Garrett-Evangl Theol Seminary, Evanston, Ill. (DMin 1993; Hon. DHL 2003). Ordained deacon, 1967, priest, 1968; Curate, Dunmurry, 1967–70; Rector, Kilmakee, 1970–82; Sec., Gen. Synod Bd of Educn (NI), 1982–2001. Ed., Ch of Ire. Gazette, 1975–82. CF (TAVR), 1970–99. QVRM 2000. *Publications:* Forty Days with Jesus, 1991; The Apostles' Creed, 1992; Children at the Table, 1993; In Touch with God, 1997; God, our Children, and Us, 1999. *Recreations:* sailing, photography, travel. *Address:* Belfast Cathedral, Donegall Street, Belfast BT1 2HB. *T:* (028) 9032 8332, *Fax:* (028) 9023 8855. *Club:* Ulster (Belfast).

McKELVEY, William; *b* Dundee, 8 July 1934; *m*; two *s. Educ:* Morgan Acad.; Dundee Coll. of Technology. Joined Labour Party, 1961; formerly Sec. Organiser, Lab. Party, and full-time union official. Mem., Dundee City Council. MP (Lab) Kilmarnock, 1979–83, Kilmarnock and Loudoun, 1983–97. Chm., Select Cttee on Scottish Affairs, 1992–97.

McKELVIE, Christina; Member (SNP) Scotland Central, Scottish Parliament, since 2007; *b* Glasgow, 4 March 1968; *d* of David and Roseann Curran; two *s. Educ:* HNC Social Care. Learning Disability Services, then Learning and Develt Officer, Social Work Services, Glasgow City Council. *Recreations:* painting, hill walking, reading. *Address:* Scottish Parliament, Edinburgh EH99 1SP. *T:* (0131) 348 6681; *e-mail:* Christina.McKelvie.MSP@scottish.parliament.uk.

McKELVIE, Peter, FRCS, FRCSE; Consultant Ear, Nose and Throat Surgeon: London Hospital, 1971–98 (Hon. Consulting Surgeon, Bart's and the London (formerly Royal Hospitals) NHS Trust, since 1998); Royal National Throat, Nose and Ear Hospital, London, 1972–95 (Hon. Consulting Surgeon, since 1995); *b* 21 Dec. 1932; *s* of William Bryce McKelvie, MD, ChM, FRCSE, DLO, and Agnes E. McKelvie (*née* Winstanley), Headmistress; *m* Myra Chadwick, FRCP, Cons. Dermatologist; one *d. Educ:* Manchester Grammar Sch.; Rugby Sch.; Univ. of Manchester (MB ChB, MD, ChM). FRCS 1962, FRCSE 1989. House Surgeon: Manchester Royal Inf., 1957; Royal Nat. Throat, Nose and Ear Hosp., London, 1958; Lectr in Anatomy, KCL, 1959; Casualty Surg., St Mary's Hosp., London, 1960; Reader in Laryngology, UCL, 1968–70; Dean, Inst. of Laryngology and Otology, London, 1984–89. Examiner: London Univ.; Royal Colls of Surgeons of England, Edinburgh and Glasgow. MRSM 1966 (Pres., Laryngology Sect., 1992–93). *Publications:* numerous, on head and neck cancer. *Recreations:* mirth, watching young surgeons develop, Mediterranean Basin. *Address:* 9 Drakes Drive, Northwood, Middx HA6 2SL. *T:* (01923) 823544.

McKENDRICK, Emma Elizabeth Ann; Headmistress, Downe House, since 1997; *b* 24 June 1963; *d* of Ian and Ann Black; *m* 1987, Iain Alastair McKendrick; two *s. Educ:* Bedford High Sch.; Univ. of Liverpool (BA Hons German with Dutch); Univ. of Birmingham (PGCE). Royal School, Bath: Teacher of German, 1986–88; Head of Sixth Form and Careers, 1988–90; Housemistress for Sixth Form, 1989–90; Dep. Head, 1990–93; Headmistress, 1994–97. Mem., Exec., Ind. Schs Exam. Bd, 2006–. Governor: Hatherop Castle Prep. Sch., 1997–2002; Study Sch., Wimbledon, 1998–2006; Manor Prep. Sch., Oxford, 1998–2006; Godstowe Prep. Sch., 2000–; Cheam Prep. Sch., 2002–; King's Sch., Canterbury, 2003–; Sandroyd Prep. Sch., 2006–. *Recreations:* travel, theatre. *Address:* St Peter's House, Downe House, Cold Ash, Thatcham, Berks RG18 9JJ. *T:* (01635) 200286. *Club:* Lansdowne.

McKENDRICK, Prof. Ewan Gordon; Professor of English Private Law, since 2000 and Chair of Board, Faculty of Law, since 2004, University of Oxford; Fellow, Lady Margaret Hall, Oxford, since 2000; *b* 23 Sept. 1960; *s* of Norman and Muriel McKendrick; *m* 1983, Rosemary Grace Burton-Smith; four *d. Educ:* Univ. of Edinburgh (LLB Hons); Pembroke Coll., Oxford (BCL). Lecturer in Law: Central Lancashire Poly., 1984–85; Univ. of Essex, 1985–88; LSE, 1988–91; Fellow, St Anne's Coll., Oxford and Linnells Lectr in Law, Univ. of Oxford, 1991–95; Prof. of English Law, UCL, 1995–2000; called to the Bar, Gray's Inn, 1998; in practice as barrister, 1998–. *Publications:* Contract Law, 1990, 6th edn 2005; (with A. Burrows) Cases and Materials on the Law of Restitution, 1997; (with N. E. Palmer) Interests in Goods, 1993, 2nd edn 1997; (ed) Chitty on Contracts, 27th edn 1995, 29th edn 2004; Sale of Goods, 2000; Contract Law: text, cases and materials, 2003, 2nd edn 2005. *Recreation:* reading. *Address:* Lady Margaret Hall, Oxford OX2 6QA. *T:* (01865) 274260; 3 Verulam Buildings, Gray's Inn, WC1R 5NT. *T:* (020) 7831 8441.

McKENDRICK, Prof. Melveena Christine, PhD, LittD; FBA 1999; Professor of Spanish Golden Age Literature, Culture and Society, 1999–2008, and Pro-Vice-Chancellor for Education, 2004–08, University of Cambridge; Fellow of Girton College, Cambridge, since 1970; *b* 23 March 1941; *d* of James Powell Jones and Catherine Letitia Jones (*née* Richards); *m* 1967, Neil McKendrick, *qv*; two *d. Educ:* Neath Girls' Grammar Sch.; Dyffryn Grammar Sch., Port Talbot; King's Coll., London (BA 1st cl. Hons Spanish); Girton Coll., Cambridge (PhD 1967); LittD Cantab, 2002. Girton College, Cambridge: Jex-Blake Res. Fellow, 1967–70; Tutor, 1970–83; Sen. Tutor, 1974–81; Dir of Studies in Modern Langs, 1984–95; Lectr in Spanish, 1980–92, Reader in Spanish Lit. and Soc., 1992–99, Univ. of Cambridge; British Acad. Reader, 1992–94. Vis. Prof., Univ. of Victoria, 1997. Member: Gen. Bd, Cambridge Univ., 1993–97 (Chair, Educn Cttee, 1995–97); Humanities Res. Bd, British Acad., 1996–98; Arts and Humanities Res. Bd, 1998–99. Consultant Hispanic Ed., Everyman, 1993–99; Member, Editorial Board: Donaire, 1994–; Revista Canadiense de Estudios Hispánicos, 1995–; Bulletin of Hispanic Studies (Glasgow), 1998–. *Publications:* Ferdinand and Isabella, 1968; A Concise History of Spain, 1972; Woman and Society in the Spanish Drama of the Golden Age, 1974; Cervantes, 1980 (trans. Spanish 1986); (ed) Golden-Age Studies in Honour of A. A. Parker, 1984; Theatre in Spain 1490–1700, 1989 (trans. Spanish 1994); (jtly) El Mágico Prodigioso, 1992; The Revealing Image: stage portraits in the theatre of the Golden Age, 1996; Playing the King: Lope de Vega and the limits of conformity, 2000; Identities in Crisis: essays on honour, gender and women in the Comedia, 2002; *contributed to:* Critical Studies of Calderón's Comedias, 1973; Women in Hispanic Literature, 1983; El mundo del teatro en el siglo de oro, 1989; Teatro y prácticas escénicas en los siglos XVI y XVII, 1991; Feminist Readings on Spanish and Spanish-American Literature, 1991; Hacia Calderón, 1991; The Comedia in the Age of Calderón, 1993; Teatro y Poder, 1994; Heavenly Bodies, 1996; Texto e Imagen en Calderón, 1996; Calderón 1600–1681, 2000; Calderón: protagonista eminente del barro europeo, 2000; Spanish Theatre: studies in honour of Victor F. Dixon, 2001; Never-Ending Adventure: studies in medieval and early modern Spanish literature in honour of Peter N. Dunn, 2002; articles on Early Modern Spanish theatre in many jls. *Address:* The Manor House, 3 High Street, Burwell, Cambridge CB25 0HB.

McKENDRICK, Neil, FRHistS; historian; Master, 1996–2005, Fellow, 1958–96 and since 2005, Gonville and Caius College, Cambridge; Reader in Social and Economic History, University of Cambridge, 1995–2002; *b* 28 July 1935; *s* of late Robert Alexander McKendrick and Sarah Elizabeth Irvine; *m* 1967, Melveena Jones (*see* M. McKendrick); two *d. Educ:* Alderman Newton's Sch., Leicester; Christ's Coll., Cambridge (Entrance Schol.; BA 1st cl. Hons (with distinction) History, 1956; MA 1960; Hon. Fellow, 1996). FRHistS 1971. Cambridge University: Res. Fellow, Christ's Coll., 1958; Asst Lectr in History, 1961–64; Lectr, 1964–95; Sec. to Faculty Bd of History, 1975–77; Chm., History Faculty, 1985–87; Gonville and Caius College: Lectr in History, 1958–96; Dir of Studies in History, 1959–96; Tutor, 1961–69. Lectures: Earl, Univ. of Keele, 1963; Inaugural, Wallace Gall., Colonial Williamsburg, 1985; Chettyar Meml, Univ. of Madras, 1990. Member: Tancred's Charities, 1996–; Sir John Plumb Charitable Trust, 1999–; Properties Cttee, Nat. Trust, 1999–2005; Dr E. N. Williams' Meml Fund, Dulwich Coll., 2003–; Vice-Pres., Caius Foundn in America, 1998–; Chm., Glenfield Trust, 2002–. *Publications:* (ed) Historical Perspectives: studies in English thought and society, 1974; (jtly) The Birth of a Consumer Society: the commercialization of eighteenth century England, 1982, 2nd edn 1983; (ed jtly) Business Life and Public Policy, 1986; L'Impressa Industria Commercio Banca XIII–XVIII, 1991; The Birth of Foreign & Colonial: the world's first investment trust, 1993; Il Tempo Libero Economia e Societa Secc XIII–XVIII, 1995; (jtly) 'F & C': a history of Foreign & Colonial Investment Trust, 1999; The Hunting Diary of a Victorian and Edwardian Gentleman, Charles James Cropper: a gentleman capitalist at play, 2008; contributed to: Essays in Economic History, ed E. M. Carus Wilson, 1962; Rise of Capitalism, ed D. S. Landes, 1966; Changing Perspectives in the History of Science, ed M. Teich and R. M. Young, 1971; The Historical Development of Accounting, ed B. S. Yamey, 1978; Science and Culture in the Western Tradition, ed J. Burke, 1987; Industry and Modernization, ed Wang Jue-fei, 1989; The Social History of Western Civilization, ed R. Golden, 1992; The Other Side of Western Civilization, ed P. Stearns, 1992; The History of Enterprise, ed S. Jones and J. Inggs, 1993; The Industrial Revolution in Britain, ed J. Hoppit and E. A. Wrigley, 1994; Europäische Konsumgeschichte, ed H. Siegrist, H. Kaelble and J. Kocka, 1997; The Modern Historiography Reader: western sources, ed A. Budd, 2008; articles in learned jls, mainly on Josiah Wedgwood and the Industrial Revolution. *Recreations:* gardening, antiques, claret, photography, my wife and daughters. *Address:* Gonville and Caius College, Cambridge CB2 1TA. *T:* (01223) 332404, *Fax:* (01223) 332336; The Manor House, 3 High Street, Burwell, Cambridge CB25 0HB. *T:* (01638) 742312. *Club:* Athenæum.

McKENNA, Alison Jayne; President, Charity Tribunal, since 2008; *b* Redhill, Surrey, 12 Nov. 1963; *d* of Peter and Evelyn Lee; *m* 1998, Jack McKenna; one *d. Educ:* Poly. of the South Bank (LLB 1987); Inns of Court Sch. of Law (Bar Finals). Called to the Bar, Middle Temple, 1988; in practice as a barrister, 1988–93; Investigator, Commn for Local Admin in England, 1993–96; Legal Adviser: Criminal Appeals Office, 1996–97; Charity Commn, 1997–2002; Hd, Charities Dept, Wilsons LLP, 2002–08; admitted Solicitor-Advocate, 2003. Mem., Mental Health Act Commn, 1996–2002. *Recreation:* anything involving horses. *Address:* Charity Tribunal, PO Box 6987, Leicester LE1 6ZX. *T:* 0845 600 0877, *Fax:* (0116) 249 4253; *e-mail:* Alison.McKenna@tribunals.gsi.gov.uk.

McKENNA, Hon. Francis Joseph, (Frank); PC (Can.) 1987; Deputy Chairman, TD Bank Financial Group, since 2006; *b* 19 Jan. 1948; *s* of Durward and Olive McKenna; *m* Julie Friel; two *s* one *d. Educ:* Sussex High Sch.; St Francis Xavier Univ. (BA); Queen's Univ.; Univ. of New Brunswick (LLB). Lawyer; Mem., NB and Canadian Bar Assocs. MLA (L) Chatham, NB, 1982–97; Leader, NB Liberal Party, 1985–97; Premier of NB, 1987–97. Counsel, McInnes Cooper, 1998; Ambassador of Canada to the USA, 2005–06. Hon. DSP Moncton, 1988; Hon. LLD New Brunswick, 1988. Vanier Award, 1988. *Address:* TD Bank Financial Group, TD Tower, 66 Wellington Street West, Toronto, ON M5K 1A2, Canada.

McKENNA, Geraldine Martina Maria; Chief Executive, Maybourne Hotel Group (formerly Savoy Group), 2002–06; *b* 9 Aug. 1955; *d* of late John and Mary McKenna. *Educ:* Loreto Convent, Omagh, NI. British Airways, NI, 1976–81; Enterprise Travel (Aer Lingus), Florida, 1981–84; Belfast City Airport, 1984–87; Inter-Continental Hotel Corp., 1987–96; Gp Dir, Mktg and Sales, Savoy Gp, 1996–2002. Non-exec. Dir, GuestInvest, 2006–. FRSA 2002. Hon. DHL Schiller Internat., 2004. *Recreations:* sailing, horse-riding, travel. *Address: e-mail:* Geraldine_McKenna@hotmail.com.

McKENNA, Very Rev. Lindsay Taylor; Rector and Provost, St Paul's Cathedral, Dundee, since 2008; *b* Glasgow, 7 July 1962; *s* of Francis Christopher McKenna and Elizabeth Colquhoun McKenna (*née* Taylor). *Educ:* Univ. of Glasgow (MA Hons 1983); Univ. of Aberdeen (BD 1986); Edinburgh Theol Coll. Ordained deacon, 1987, priest, 1988; Curate, St Mary's, Broughty Ferry, 1987–90; Senior Curate, Wantage, 1990–93; Vicar, St Mary the Virgin, Illingworth, 1993–99; Pastor-Dir, CARA Trust, 1999–2002; Vicar, All Saints, Hanworth, 2002–08. *Recreations:* gardening, keeping fit, cooking, the company of friends, Modern Spanish history. *Address:* St Paul's Cathedral Rectory, 4 Richmond Terrace, Dundee DD2 1B2. *T:* (01382) 224486; *e-mail:* provost@saintpaulscathedraldundee.org.

McKENNA, Martin Nicholas; His Honour Judge McKenna; a Circuit Judge, since 2000; a Senior Circuit Judge, since 2008; *b* 19 Nov. 1955; *s* of Bernard Malcolm McKenna and Anne Rose McKenna; *m* 1st, 1979, Deborah Jane Scott (marr. diss. 1995); two *d*; 2nd, 1996, Sarah Louise Malden; two step *d. Educ:* Birmingham Univ. (LLB 1st Cl. Hons); Lincoln Coll., Oxford. Admitted Solicitor, 1980. Joined Evershed & Tomkinson, Solicitors, 1978: Associate, 1984–87; Partner, 1987–2000; Head of Litigation Dept, 1994–99. Midland Circuit. *Recreations:* Rugby, cricket, sailing, ski-ing. *Address:* Priory Courts, 33 Bull Street, Birmingham B4 6DW. *Club:* East India.

McKENNA, Prof. Patrick Gerald, (Gerry); DL; PhD; Vice-Chancellor and President, University of Ulster, 1999–2006; *b* 10 Dec. 1953; *s* of late Gerald Joseph McKenna and Mary Teresa (*née* Smyth); *m* 1976, Philomena Winifred McArdle; two *s. Educ:* Univ. of Ulster (BSc 1st Cl. Hons 1976); PhD Genetics, QUB, 1979. FIBMS 1982; FIBiol 1988; MRIA 2001; CSci 2006. Lectr, Human Biology, NUU, 1979–84; University of Ulster: Sen. Lectr, Biology, 1984–88; Dir, Biomedical Scis Res. Centre, 1985–88; Prof. and Head of Dept of Biol and Biomed. Scis, 1988–94; Dean, Faculty of Science, 1994–97; Pro-Vice-Chancellor (Res.), 1997–99. Chairman: NI Foresight, Life and Health Technologies Panel, 1995–99; Heads of Univ. Centres Biomed. Sci., 1995–97; UU-Online.com, 2000–05; Univ. of Ulster Sci. Res. Parks Ltd, 2002–04; Univs Ireland, 2003–05; Chair, UUSRP Ltd, 2002–; non-executive Director: NI Med. Physics Agency, 1995–2001; NI Sci. Park Foundn, 1999–2005; E-Univs UK Worldwide, 2000–06; E-University Hldg Co., 2001–06; UUTECH Ltd, 1997–2005 (Chair, 2002–05); Bd Mem., ILEX, 2003–05. Vice Chm., Ulster Cancer Foundn, 1999–2005. Member: Council, Inst. of Biomed. Sci., 1996–2002; Jt Med. Adv. Cttee, 2003–04; Founding Bd Mem., UK Health Educn Partnership, 2003–05. Mem., Shadow Bd for E-nursing educn, 2001–02. Member: US-Ireland R&D Taskforce, 2002–04; Bd, BITC NI, 2002–03; Sci., Engrg and Envmt Adv. Cttee, British Council, 2003–05. Freedom, Borough of Coleraine, 2001. DL Co. Londonderry, 2002. FRSA 1999. Hon. DSc NUI, 2001; Hon. LLD QUB, 2002. *Publications:* numerous scientific papers. *Recreations:* reading, the turf. *Address:* Lisban, 7 Hopefield Park, Portrush, Northern Ireland BT56 8SW. *T:* (028) 7082 1005; *e-mail:* mckennagerry@yahoo.com. *Club:* Reform.

McKENNA, Rosemary, CBE 1995; MP (Lab) Cumbernauld, Kilsyth and Kirkintilloch East, since 2005 (Cumbernauld and Kilsyth, 1997–2005); *b* 8 May 1941; *d* of Cornelius Harvey and Mary (*née* Crossan); *m* 1963, James S. McKenna; three *s* one *d. Educ:* St Augustine's, Glasgow; Notre Dame Coll. (Dip. Primary Educn). Private sec., 1958–64; teacher, various primary schs, 1974–94. Member (Lab): Cumbernauld and Kilsyth DC, 1984–96 (Leader, 1984–88 and 1992–94; Provost, 1988–92); N Lanarks Council, 1995–97. Pres., COSLA, 1994–96. PPS to Minister of State for Foreign and Commonwealth Affairs, 1998–2001. Member, Select Committee: on culture, media and sport, 2001–; on procedure, 2001–; Chm., Cttee of Selection, 2005–. Mem., Cttee of Regions of EU, 1994–98; Chm., UK and European Standing Cttees, CEMR, 1996–98. Chm., Scottish Libraries and Inf. Council, 1998–2002. *Recreations:* reading, travelling, family gatherings. *Address:* House of Commons, SW1A 0AA. *T:* (020) 7219 4003; *e-mail:* mckennar@parliament.uk.

MACKENZIE, family name of **Earl of Cromartie** and **Barons MacKenzie of Culkein** and **Mackenzie of Framwellgate**.

MACKENZIE of Gairloch; *see* Inglis of Glencorse.

MacKENZIE OF CULKEIN, Baron *cr* 1999 (Life Peer), of Assynt in Highland; **Hector Uisdean MacKenzie;** Associate General Secretary, UNISON, 1993–2000; *b* 25 Feb. 1940; *s* of George MacKenzie and Williamina Budge Sutherland; *m* 1961, Anna Morrison (marr. diss.); one *s* three *d. Educ:* Nicolson Inst., Stornoway, Isle of Lewis; Portree High Sch., Skye; Leverndale School of Nursing, Glasgow; West Cumberland School of Nursing, Whitehaven. RGN, RMN. Student Nurse, Leverndale Hosp., 1958–61; Asst Lighthouse Keeper, Clyde Lighthouses Trust, 1961–64; Student Nurse, 1964–66, Staff Nurse 1966–69, West Cumberland Hosp.; Confederation of Health Service Employees: Asst Regl Sec., 1969; Regl Sec., Yorks and E Midlands, 1970–74; Nat. Officer, 1974–83; Asst Gen. Sec., 1983–87; Gen. Sec., 1987–93. Co. Sec., UIA Insurance Ltd, 1996–2000. Pres., TUC, 1998–99. *Recreations:* reading, aviation, maritime issues, travel. *Address:* House of Lords, SW1A 0PW. *T:* (020) 7219 8515, *Fax:* (020) 7219 8712.

MACKENZIE OF FRAMWELLGATE, Baron *cr* 1998 (Life Peer), of Durham in the co. of Durham; **Brian Mackenzie,** OBE 1998; *b* 21 March 1943; *s* of Frederick George Mackenzie and Lucy Mackenzie (*née* Ward); *m* 1965, Jean Seed; two *s. Educ:* Eastbourne Sch., Darlington; London Univ. (LLB Hons 1974); FBI Nat. Acad. (graduate 1985). Durham Constabulary, 1963–98: Constable, 1963; Sgt (Trng), 1970; Det. Insp., Hd of Drug Squad, 1976; Chief Insp., Hd of Crime Computer Unit, 1979; Supt (Det.), attached to Home Office, 1980; Territorial Comdr Supt, 1983; Divl Comdr, Chief Supt, 1989–98. Nat. Pres., Police Superintendents' Assoc. of England and Wales, 1995–98 (Vice Pres., 1993–95). Vice Pres., BALPA, 2004–. Studied and lectured extensively on police methods, visiting Europe, USA and Canada. Regular broadcasts on TV and radio on law and policing issues. *Publications:* Two Lives of Brian (memoir), 2004; articles in legal and policing jls. *Recreations:* after-dinner speaking, swimming, music, travel. *Address:* House of Lords, SW1A 0PW. *Club:* Dunelm (Durham).

McKENZIE OF LUTON, Baron *cr* 2004 (Life Peer), of Luton in the County of Bedfordshire; **William David McKenzie;** Parliamentary Under-Secretary of State, Department of Work and Pensions, since 2007; *b* 24 July 1946; *s* of Donald McKenzie and Elsie May McKenzie (*née* Doust); *m* 1972, Diane Joyce (*née* Angliss). *Educ:* Bristol Univ. (BA Hons Econs and Accounting). FCA 1971. Partner, Price Waterhouse UK, 1980–86, Price Waterhouse, Hong Kong, 1993–98 (Partner-in-charge, Vietnam, 1996–98). Mem. (Lab) Luton BC, 1976–92, 1999–2005 (Leader, 1999–2003). Contested (Lab) Luton S, 1987, 1992. A Lord in Waiting (Govt Whip), 2005–07. *Recreations:* swimming, reading, music. *Address:* 6 Sunset Drive, Luton, Beds LU2 7TN. *T:* and *Fax:* (01582) 455384; *e-mail:* mckenziew@parliament.uk.

MACKENZIE, Sir Alexander Alwyne Henry Charles Brinton M.; *see* Muir Mackenzie.

McKENZIE, Alistair William, MBE 1980; HM Diplomatic Service, retired; Chief Executive, Pearl Capital (formerly Al Khazna Investments), Abu Dhabi, since 2007; *b* 19 Feb. 1945; *s* of late James McKenzie and Barbara McKenzie (*née* Anderson); *m* 1968, Margaret Emily Young; two *s. Educ:* Leith Acad., Edinburgh. Entered FCO, 1965; Budapest, 1967–69; Singapore, 1969–72; Brasilia, 1972–75; FCO, 1975–78; Vice Consul: San Salvador, 1978–80; San Jose, 1980–82; Commercial Attaché, Madrid, 1982–84; W Africa Dept, 1984–86; Dep. High Comr and Hd of Chancery, Banjul, 1986–89; Consul-Gen., Bilbao, 1990–94; First Sec., Lagos, 1994–98; Dir, British Trade Internat., 1998–2001; Counsellor and Dep. Head of Mission, Abu Dhabi, 2001–05. Chief of Protocol, Shaheen Business and Investment Gp, Amman, 2006–07. *Recreations:* golf, photography. *Club:* Royal Over-Seas League.

MACKENZIE, Archibald Robert Kerr, CBE 1967; HM Diplomatic Service, retired; *b* 22 Oct. 1915; *s* of James and Alexandrina Mackenzie; *m* 1963, Virginia Ruth Hutchison. *Educ:* Glasgow, Oxford, Chicago and Harvard Universities. Diplomatic Service, with duty at Washington, 1943–45; United Nations, 1946–49; Foreign Office, 1949–51; Bangkok, 1951–54; Cyprus, 1954; Foreign Office, 1955–57; OEEC, Paris, 1957–61; Commercial Counsellor, HM Embassy, Rangoon, 1961–65; Consul-General, Zagreb 1965–69; Ambassador, Tunisia, 1970–73; Minister (Econ. and Social Affairs), UK Mission to UN, 1973–75. Brandt Commission, 1978–80. *Publication:* Faith in Diplomacy, 2002. *Recreation:* golf. *Address:* Strathcashel Cottage, Rowardennan, near Glasgow G63 0AW. *T:* (01360) 870262.

MACKENZIE, Colin Scott; DL; part-time Sheriff, since 2004; Sheriff of Grampian, Highland and Islands at Lerwick and Kirkwall, 1992–2003; Vice Lord-Lieutenant, Western Isles, 1984–92; *b* 7 July 1938; *s* of late Major Colin Scott Mackenzie, BL and Mrs Margaret S. Mackenzie, MA; *m* 1966, Christeen Elizabeth Drysdale McLauchlan. *Educ:* Nicolson Inst., Stornoway; Fettes Coll., Edinburgh; Edinburgh Univ. (BL 1959). Admitted Solicitor and Notary Public, 1960; Procurator Fiscal, Stornoway, 1969–92. Clerk to the Lieutenancy, Stornoway, 1975–92. Dir, Harris Tweed Assoc. Ltd, 1979–95; Trustee, Western Isles Kidney Machine Trust, 1977–. Council Mem for Western Isles, Orkney, Shetland etc, Law Soc. of Scotland, 1985–92. General Assembly, Church of Scotland: Comr, Presbytery of Lewis, 1991–92; Mem., Bd of Social Responsibility, 1991–95; Convenor, Study Gp into Young People and the Media, 1991–93. Council Mem., Sheriffs' Assoc., 2002–03. DL Islands Area of Western Isles, 1975. *Publications:* The Last Warrior Band, 2002; contrib. Stair Memorial Encyclopaedia of Laws of Scotland, 1987. *Recreations:* amateur radio, boating, fishing, local history, shooting, trying to grow trees. *Address:* Park House, 8 Matheson Road, Stornoway, Western Isles HS1 2NQ. *T:* (01851) 702008. *Clubs:* New (Edinburgh); Royal Northern and University (Aberdeen).

McKENZIE, Dan Peter, CH 2003; PhD; FRS 1976; Royal Society Professor of Earth Sciences, Cambridge University, since 1996; Fellow of King's College, Cambridge, 1965–73 and since 1977; *b* 21 Feb. 1942; *s* of William Stewart McKenzie and Nancy Mary McKenzie; *m* 1971, Indira Margaret Misra; one *s. Educ:* Westminster Sch.; King's Coll., Cambridge (BA 1963, PhD 1966). Cambridge University: Sen. Asst in Res., 1969–75; Asst Dir of Res., 1975–79; Reader in Tectonics, 1979–84; Prof. of Earth Scis, 1984–96. Hon. MA Cambridge, 1966. (Jtly) Geology and Geophysics Prize, Internat. Balzan Foundn of Italy and Switzerland, 1981; (jtly) Japan Prize, Science and Technology Foundn of Japan, 1990; Royal Medal, Royal Soc., 1991; Gold Medal, RAS, 1992; Crafoord Medal, Royal Swedish Acad. of Scis, 2002. *Publications:* papers in learned jls. *Recreation:* gardening. *Address:* Bullard Laboratories, Madingley Road, Cambridge CB3 0EZ. *T:* (01223) 337177.

MACKENZIE, Rear-Adm. David John, CB 1983; FNI; Royal Navy, retired 1983; Director, Atlantic Salmon Trust, 1985–97 (Life Vice-President, 1998); *b* 3 Oct. 1929; *s* of late David Mackenzie and of Alison Walker Lawrie; *m* 1965, Ursula Sybil Balfour; two *s* one *d. Educ:* Cargilfield Sch., Barnton, Edinburgh; Royal Naval Coll., Eaton Hall, Cheshire. Cadet to Comdr, 1943–72: served in East Indies, Germany, Far East, Home and Mediterranean Fleets, and commanded: HMML 6011, HM Ships: Brinkley, Barrington, Hardy, Lincoln, Hermione; Captain 1972; Senior Officers War Course, 1972; commanded HMS Phoenix (NBCD School), 1972–74; Captain F8 in HMS Ajax, 1974–76; Director of Naval Equipment, 1976–78; Captain: HMS Blake, 1979; HMS Hermes, 1980; Rear Admiral 1981; Flag Officer and Port Admiral, Gibraltar, Comdr Gibraltar Mediterranean, 1981–83. Younger Brother of Trinity House, 1971–. Member, Queen's Body Guard for Scotland (Royal Company of Archers), 1976–. Vice Pres., Nautical Inst., 1985–93. Pres., King George's Fund for Sailors (Scotland), 1996–. *Recreations:* shooting and fishing. *Address:* Easter Meikle Fardle, Meikleour, Perthshire PH2 6EF. *Club:* New (Edinburgh).

MacKENZIE, Prof. Donald Angus, PhD; FBA 2004; FRSE; Professor of Sociology, University of Edinburgh, since 1992; *b* 3 May 1950; *s* of Angus MacKenzie and Anne MacKenzie; *m* 1998, Caroline Bamford; one *s* one *d. Educ:* Univ. of Edinburgh (BSc 1972; PhD 1978). Lectr, 1975–88, Reader, 1988–92, in Sociology, Univ. of Edinburgh. Vis. Prof. of Hist. of Sci., Harvard Univ., 1997. FRSE 2002. *Publications:* Statistics in Britain 1865–1930, 1981; Inventing Accuracy, 1990; Knowing Machines, 1995; Mechanizing Proof, 2001; An Engine, not a Camera, 2006. *Recreations:* cycling, walking, chess. *Address:* School of Social and Political Studies, University of Edinburgh, Adam Ferguson Building, George Square, Edinburgh EH8 9LL.

MacKENZIE, George Paterson; Keeper of the Records of Scotland, since 2001; *b* 22 Sept. 1950; *s* of James Sargent Porteous MacKenzie and Flora Black MacKenzie; *m* 1st, 1972, Elizabeth Hamilton (marr. diss. 1988); 2nd, 1995, Katherine Barratt (marr. diss. 2003); 3rd, 2005, Caroline Morgan. *Educ:* Univ. of Stirling (BA 1972; MLitt 1978). Asst history teacher, Larbert High Sch., 1974–75; Res. Asst, Scottish Record Office, 1975–83; Departmental Records Officer, General Register Office for Scotland, 1984–85; Hd of Records Liaison, then Preservation Services, Scottish Record Office, 1986–94; Dep. Sec. Gen., Internat. Council on Archives, Paris, 1995–96; Dir of External Relns, Nat. Archives of Scotland, 1997–2000. Adviser: on protection of archives in former Yugoslavia for UNESCO, 1995–97; on archives for World Bank, 1998–99; External Examiner in archives and records mgt, Univ. of Liverpool, 1998–2002. *Publications:* articles and conf. papers on protection of archives in armed conflict, electronic records and archives mgt. *Recreations:* reading, travel, cooking. *Address:* National Archives of Scotland, HM General Register House, Edinburgh EH1 3YY. *T:* (0131) 535 1312; *e-mail:* george.mackenzie@nas.gov.uk; Flat 2, 1 Greenhill Court, Edinburgh EH9 1BF.

MacKENZIE, Gillian Rachel, (Mrs N. I. MacKenzie); *see* Ford, G. R.

MACKENZIE, Sir Guy; *see* Mackenzie, Sir J. W. G.

MACKENZIE, Ian Clayton, CBE 1962; HM Diplomatic Service, retired; Ambassador to Korea, 1967–69; *b* 13 Jan. 1909; *m* 1948, Anne Helena Tylor (*d* 2006); one *s* one *d. Educ:* Bedford Sch.; King's Coll., Cambridge. China Consular Service, 1932–41; Consul, Brazzaville, 1942–45, Foreign Office, 1945; 1st Sec., Commercial, Shanghai, 1946–49; Santiago, Chile, 1949–53; Commercial Counsellor: Oslo, 1953–58; Caracas, 1958–63; Stockholm, 1963–66. *Address:* Koryo, Armstrong Road, Brockenhurst, Hants SO42 7TA. *T:* (01590) 623453.

MacKENZIE, James Alexander Mackintosh, CB 1988; FREng; Chief Road Engineer, Scottish Development Department, 1976–88, retired; *b* Inverness, 6 May 1928; *m* 1970, Pamela Dorothy Nixon; one *s* one *d. Educ:* Inverness Royal Acad. FICE, FIHT; FREng (FEng 1982). Miscellaneous local govt appts, 1950–63; Chief Resident Engr, Durham County Council, 1963–67; Dep. Dir, 1967–71, Dir, 1971–76, North Eastern Road Construction Unit, MoT, later DoE. *Recreations:* golf, fishing. *Address:* Pendor, 2 Dean Park, Longniddry, East Lothian EH32 0QR. *T:* (01875) 852643.

MACKENZIE, Sir James William Guy, 5th Bt *cr* 1890, of Glen Muick, Aberdeenshire; Chairman, Kerrier Direct Services, 1995–98 (Vice-Chairman, 1994–95); *b* 6 Oct. 1946; *s* of Lt-Col Eric Dighton Mackenzie, CMG, CVO, DSO (*d* 1972), 4th *s* of Sir Allan Russell Mackenzie, 2nd Bt, and Elizabeth Kathrine Mary, *d* of Captain James William Guy Innes, CBE; *S* cousin, 1993; *m* 1st, 1972, Paulene Patricia Simpson (marr. diss. 1980); two *d*; 2nd, 1996, Sally Ann (*née* Howard). *Educ:* Stowe. Vice-Pres., Crown Royale Internat., USA, 1979–81. Mem. (Ind) Kerrier DC, 1993–2003. *Recreations:* watching cricket and football, hill walking, music, unusual architecture. *Heir: b* Allan Walter Mackenzie, *b* 6 Nov. 1952. *Address:* Tresowes Hill Farm, Helston, Cornwall TR13 9SY.

MACKENZIE, Gen. Sir Jeremy (John George), GCB 1998 (KCB 1992); OBE 1982; DL; Governor, Royal Hospital, Chelsea, 1999–2006; *b* 11 Feb. 1941; *s* of late Lt-Col John William Elliot Mackenzie, DSO, QPM and of Valerie (*née* Dawes); *m* 1969, Elizabeth Lyon (*née* Wertenbaker); one *s* one *d. Educ:* Duke of York Sch., Nairobi, Kenya. psc, HCSC. Commnd Queen's Own Highlanders, 1961; Canadian Forces Staff Coll., 1974; Bde Major, 24 Airportable Bde, 1975–76; CO 1 Queen's Own Highlanders, NI and Hong Kong, 1979–82; Instructor, Staff Coll., 1982–83; Col Army Staff Duties 2, 1983–84; Comdr 12th Armoured Bde, 1984–86; Service Fellowship, King's Coll., Univ. of London, 1987; Dep. Comdt, 1987–89, Comdt, 1989, Staff Coll.; GOC 4th Armoured Div., BAOR, 1989–91; Comdr 1st (British) Corps, 1991–92; Comdr, Ace Rapid Reaction Corps, 1992–94; Dep. SACEUR, 1994–98; ADC Gen. to the Queen, 1997–98. Director: SIRVA plc, 2003–; SELEX Communications Ltd, 2004–. Mem., Adv. Bd, Blue Hackle Security, 2006–. Colonel Commandant: WRAC, 1990–92; AGC, 1992–98; Colonel: Highlanders Regt, 1994–2001; APTC, 1999–. Ensign, Queen's Body Guard for Scotland, Royal Company of Archers, 2008– (Mem., 1986–; Brig., 2001–08). Pres., Services Br., British Deer Soc., 1993–; Life Vice-Pres., Combined Services Winter Sports Assoc., 2001. DL Greater London, 2006. OStJ 2003. Comdr, US Legion of Merit, 1997 and 1999; Cross of Merit 1st Class (Czech Republic), 1998; Officers' Cross, Order of Merit (Hungary), 1998; Order of Madara Horseman, 1st Cl. (Bulgaria), 1999; Officers' Gold Medal of Merit (Slovenia), 2002. *Publication:* The British Army and the Operational Level of War, 1989. *Recreations:* shooting, fishing. *Address:* The Old Bell, 20 Long Street, Cerne Abbas, Dorset DT2 7JF. *Club:* Caledonian.

McKENZIE, John Cormack, FREng; FICE; Hon. Secretary, Overseas Affairs, Fellowship of Engineering, 1988–92; Vice-Chairman, Thomas Telford Ltd, 1982–90; Director, H. R. Wallingford plc, 1990–95; *b* 21 June 1927; *s* of William Joseph McKenzie and Elizabeth Frances Robinson; *m* 1954, Olga Caroline Cleland; three *s* one *d. Educ:* St Andrews Coll.; Trinity Coll., Dublin (MA, MAI); Queen's Univ., Belfast (MSc). FREng (FEng 1984); FIPM, FIEI, FIE(Aust). McLaughlin & Harvey, and Sir Alexander Gibb & Partners, 1946–48; Asst Lectr, QUB, 1948–50; Edmund Nuttall Ltd, 1950–82, Dir, 1967–82; Chm., Nuttall Geotechnical Services Ltd, 1967–82; Dir, British Wastewater Ltd, 1978–82. Secretary: ICE, 1982–90; Commonwealth Engineers' Council, 1983–90; Advr to Pres., World Fedn of Engrg Orgs, 2001– (Sec. Gen., 1987–97; Treas., 1997–2001); Vice-Pres., Register of Engrs for Disaster Relief. Pres., Beaconsfield Adv. Centre, 1978–2007. Hon. DSc: Tajikistan, 1993; Nottingham, 1997. *Publications:* papers: Research into some Aspects of Soil Cement, 1952; Engineers: Administrators or Technologists?, 1971; (contrib.) Civil Engineering Procedure, 3rd edn 1979; Comparison of the Market and Command Economics, 1990; Wealth Creation, 1992; Sustainable Development and the Maintenance of Economic Viability, 1994; The Contribution of Engineers to the UN International Decade for Natural Disaster Reduction, 1994; International Application of Ethics for Engineers, 1996; Beyond the Bottom Line, 1996; Quo Vadis, 1997; The Complete Engineer, 1997. *Recreations:* philately, collecting ancient pottery. *Address:* The Cottage (Annex), 20 Ledborough Lane, Beaconsfield, Bucks HP9 2PZ. *Club:* Athenæum.

McKENZIE, Prof. John Crawford; Founding Governor, University of the Arts London (formerly The London Institute), since 1996 (Rector, 1986–96); *b* 12 Nov. 1937; *s* of late Donald Walter McKenzie and Emily Beatrice McKenzie; *m* 1960, Ann McKenzie (*née* Roberts); two *s*. *Educ:* London School of Economics and Political Science (BScEcon); Bedford Coll., London (MPhil). Lecturer, Queen Elizabeth Coll., Univ. of London, 1961; Dep. Director, Office of Health Econs, 1966; Market Inf. Manager, Allied Breweries Ltd, 1968; various posts, Kimpher Ltd, 1969, finally Chief Exec., Kimpher Marketing Services, 1973; Head of Dept, London Coll. of Printing, 1975; Principal: Ilkley Coll., 1978; Bolton Inst. of Higher Educn, 1982; Rector, Liverpool Poly., 1984. Visiting Professor: Queen Elizabeth Coll., 1976–80; Univ. of Newcastle, 1981–87. Director: Antiquarian Pastimes Ltd, 1984–; New Frontiers in Educn Ltd, 1993–; Ringmaster Holdings plc, 2001–. Chm., Leeds Utd plc, 2003. Mem., Adv. Council, Univ. of Sarawak, Malaysia, 1994–; Advr, Japan Coll. of Foreign Langs, Tokyo, 1997–; Mem. Consultative Cttee, Eastern Visual Arts and Design Univ. of China, Shanghai, 2002; Sen. Vice-Pres., Shanghai Univ. of Visual Arts, 2003–. Special Advr, Shanghai Metropolitan Govt, 2002–. Chevalier de l'Ordre des Arts et des Lettres (France), 1992. *Publications:* (ed jtly) Changing Food Habits, 1964; (ed jtly) Our Changing Fare, 1966; (ed jtly) The Food Consumer, 1987; many articles in Proc. Nutrition Soc., British Jl Nutrition, Nutrition Bull., etc. *Recreation:* collecting antiquarian books and works of art. *Address:* University of the Arts London, 65 Davies Street, W1K 5DA. *T:* (020) 7514 6000. *Clubs:* Athenæum, Chelsea Arts.

McKENZIE, Rear-Adm. John Foster, CB 1977; CBE 1974 (OBE 1962); *b* Waiuku, 24 June 1923; *s* of Dr J. C. McKenzie; *m* 1st, 1945, Doreen Elizabeth (*d* 1996), *d* of Dr E. T. and Dr G. M. McElligot; one *s* one *d*; 2nd, 1996, Jocelyn Elva McIntosh. *Educ:* Timaru Boys' High Sch.; St Andrews Coll., Christchurch, NZ. Served War of 1939–45: Royal Navy; transferred to Royal New Zealand Navy, 1947; Head, Defence Liaison Staff, London, 1966–68; Imperial Defence Coll., 1969; Asst Chief of Defence Staff (Policy), Defence HQ, NZ, 1970–71; Deputy Chief of Naval Staff, 1972; Commodore, Auckland, 1973–75; Chief of Naval Staff, and Mem. Defence Council, 1975–77, retired 1977. ADC 1972–75. *Recreations:* gardening, fishing. *Address:* 1/38 Seaview Road, Remuera, Auckland 1005, New Zealand.

McKENZIE, Julia Kathleen, (Mrs Jerry Harte); actress, singer and director; *b* 17 Feb. 1941; *d* of Albion McKenzie and Kathleen Rowe; *m* 1972, Jerry Harte. *Educ:* Guildhall School of Music and Drama. Hon. FGSM, 1988. *Stage:* Maggie May, Adelphi, 1966; Mame, Drury Lane, 1969; Promises, Promises, Prince of Wales, 1970; Company, Her Majesty's, 1972; Cowardy Custard, Mermaid, 1972; Cole, Mermaid, 1974; Norman Conquests, Globe, 1975; Side by Side by Sondheim, Wyndhams, 1976, NY 1977; Ten Times Table, Globe, 1978; Outside Edge, Queens, 1979; On the 20th Century, Her Majesty's, 1980; Guys and Dolls, NT, 1982; Schweyk in 2nd World War, NT, 1982; Woman in Mind, Vaudeville, 1986; Follies, Shaftesbury, 1987; Into the Woods, Phoenix, 1990; Sweeney Todd, NT, 1993; Communicating Doors, Gielgud, 1995; Kafka's Dick, Piccadilly, 1998; The Royal Family, Th. Royal, Haymarket, 2001; The Philadelphia Story, Old Vic, 2005; directed: Stepping Out, Duke of York's, 1984; Steel Magnolias, Lyric, 1989; Just So, Watermill, Bagnor, Berks, 1989; Putting it Together, Old Fire Station, Oxford, 1992, NY, 1993; A Little Night Music, Tokyo, 1999; Honk! The Ugly Duckling, NT, 1999; Peter Pan, the Musical, RFH, 2001; Fuddy Meers, Arts Th., 2004; *films:* Ike: the war years, 1978; Shirley Valentine, 1989; The Old Curiosity Shop, 1994; Bright Young Things, 2003; Notes on a Scandal, 2006; *television films:* Those Glory Glory Days, 1980; Hotel Du Lac, 1986; Adam Bede, 1992; Jack and the Beanstalk—the Real Story, 2001; Celebration, 2006; You Can Choose Your Friends, 2007; *television series:* Maggie and Her, 1977–79; Fame is the Spur, 1982; Blott on the Landscape, 1985; Fresh Fields, 1984–86; French Fields, 1989–91; Death In Holy Orders, 2003; Cranford, 2007; Marple, 2008; *television plays:* Dear Box No, 1983; Sharing Time, 1984; Absent Friends, 1985; Julia and Company (TV special), 1986; The Shadowy Third, 1995; The Last Detective, 2002; numerous TV musicals; *radio:* Sweeney Todd, 1994; The Country Wife, A Room With a View, 1995; Mame, 1996; Follies, Gigi, 1997; Water Babies, 1998; Two Planks and a Passion, 1999; Woman in Mind, She Stoops to Conquer, 2000; On the Town, Past Forgetting, 2001; Pal Joey, On Your Toes, 2002; The Old Curiosity Shop, 2003; *directed for radio:* Rosalind, 2002; A Well Remembered Voice, Barbara's Wedding, Call Me Madam, 2003. *Recreations:* cooking, gardening. *Address:* c/o Ken McReddie, 36–40 Glasshouse Street, W1B 5DL. *T:* (020) 7439 1456, *Fax:* (020) 734 6530; *e-mail:* ken@kenmcreddie.com.

MacKENZIE, Kelvin Calder; *b* 22 Oct. 1946; *m* 1969, Jacqueline Mary Holland (marr. diss. 2006); two *s* one *d*; *m* 2008, Sarah Theresa McLean. Editor, The Sun, 1981–94; Man. Dir, British Sky Broadcasting, 1994; Dir, 1994–98, Gp Man. Dir, 1998, Mirror Group plc; Chm. and Chief Exec., Wireless Gp plc, 1998–2005; Chm., MyVideoRights.com, 2008–.

MacKENZIE, Rev. Kenneth Ian; Minister, Parish of Braemar and Crathie, since 2005; Chaplain to the Queen in Scotland, since 2007; *b* 7 April 1959; *s* of Ian Kenneth MacKenzie and Margaret Vera Matheson; *m* 1987, Jayne Louise Lovett; one *s* three *d*. *Educ:* RAC, Cirencester; Christ's Coll., Univ. of Aberdeen (BD Hons). Managing Partner, Moy Estate, Inverness, 1981–83; ordained, 1990; Asst Minister, Dyce Parish Church, Aberdeenshire, 1988–91; Associate Pastor, First Presbyterian Church, Burlingame, Calif, USA, 1991–94; Associate Minister, North Church, Perth, 1994–99; Minister, St Columba's, Budapest, 1999–2005. *Recreations:* leading charitable work teams to projects in Romania, countryside pursuits, cycling. *Address:* The Manse, Crathie, Ballater, Aberdeenshire AB35 5UL.

MacKENZIE, Kenneth John, CB 1996; Chairman, Historic Scotland Foundation, since 2001; Secretary, Scottish Executive (formerly Scottish Office) Development Department, 1998–2001; *b* 1 May 1943; *s* of John Donald MacKenzie and Elizabeth Pennant Johnston Sutherland; *m* 1975, Irene Mary Hogarth; one *s* one *d*. *Educ:* Woodchurch Road Primary School, Birkenhead; Birkenhead School; Pembroke College, Oxford (Exbnr; MA Mod. Hist.); Stanford Univ., Calif (AM Hist.). Scottish Home and Health Dept, 1965; Private Sec. to Jt Parly Under Sec. of State, Scottish Office, 1969–70; Scottish Office Regional Develt Div., 1970–73; Scottish Educn Dept, 1973–76; Civil Service Fellow, Glasgow Univ., 1974–75; Principal Private Sec. to Sec. of State for Scotland, 1977–79; Asst Sec., Scottish Economic Planning Dept, 1979–83; Scottish Office: Finance Div., 1983–85; Principal Finance Officer, 1985–88; Under Sec., Home and Health Dept, 1988–91; Under Sec., 1991–92, Sec., 1992–95, Agric. and Fisheries Dept; Cabinet Office (on secondment): Dep. Sec. (Hd of Economic and Domestic Affairs Secretariat), 1995–97; Hd, Constitution Secretariat, 1997–98. Mem., BBSRC (formerly AFRC), 1992–95. Quinquennial Reviewer for the Court Service, LCD, 2001–02. Mem., British Waterways Scotland Gp, 2002–07. Mem., Christian Aid Bd, 2005–. Hon. Prof., Dept of Politics and Internat. Relations, Univ. of Aberdeen, 2001–04. Associate Consultant, Public Admin Internat., 2002–. Elder, St Cuthbert's Parish Church. *Address:* 30 Regent Terrace, Edinburgh EH7 5BS. *Club:* Farmers'.

MACKENZIE, Lorimer David Maurice; Director, Development Strategy for Enterprises, European Commission, 1996–2002; *b* 4 Aug. 1940; *s* of William David Beveridge Mackenzie and Elizabeth Reid (*née* Peters); *m* 1959, Penelope Marsh Happer; two *s* two *d*. *Educ:* Hermitage Park Sch., Leith; Royal High Sch., Edinburgh; Edinburgh Univ. (MA Hons Mental Philosophy). Department of Agriculture and Fisheries, Scottish Office: Asst Principal, 1964–68; Principal, 1968–73; Commission of the European Communities: Head of Division: Agricl Res., 1973–77; Food Aid, 1978–82; Develt of Trade, 1982–92; Dir, Budget and Gen. Affairs, Directorate Gen. of Fisheries, 1992–96. Member: Scottish Council, Eur. Movt, 2003–; Council, Saltire Soc., 2004–. Mem., Editl Bd, Internat. Jl of Entrepreneurship and Innovation, 2001–. Chevalier de l'Ordre National du Mérite (France), 2002. *Recreations:* Scottish history and literature. *Address:* 41 Great King Street, Edinburgh EH3 6QR. *Clubs:* Royal Commonwealth Society; New (Edinburgh).

MacKENZIE, Madeleine; Scottish Parliamentary Counsel, since 2002; *b* 27 Aug. 1963; *er d* of William Gordon MacKenzie and Veronica Dorothy Rachel MacKenzie. *Educ:* Inverness High Sch.; Univ. of Aberdeen (LLB Hons; DipLP). Solicitor in private practice, 1986–90; Asst Scottish Parly Counsel, then Depute Scottish Parly Counsel, 1990–2002. *Recreations:* bridge, reading, music. *Address:* (office) Victoria Quay, Edinburgh EH6 6QQ. *T:* (0131) 244 1667; *e-mail:* madeleine.mackenzie@scotland.gsi.gov.uk. *Clubs:* Athenæum; New (Edinburgh).

MACKENZIE, Mary Margaret; *see* McCabe, M. M. A.

McKENZIE, Michael, CB 1999; QC 1991; Master of the Crown Office and Queen's Coroner and Attorney, Registrar of Criminal Appeals and of the Courts Martial Appeal Court, and Master of the Queen's Bench Division, High Court of Justice, 1988–2003; *b* Hove, Sussex, 25 May 1943; *s* of Robert John McKenzie and Kitty Elizabeth McKenzie; *m* 1964, Peggy Dorothy, *d* of Thomas Edward William Russell and Dorothy Mabel Russell; three *s*. *Educ:* Varndean Grammar Sch., Brighton. Town Clerk's Dept, Brighton, 1961–63; Asst to Clerk of the Peace, Brighton Quarter Sessions, 1963–67; Sen. Clerk of the Court, 1967–70, Dep. Clerk of the Peace, 1970–71, Middlesex Quarter Sessions; called to the Bar, Middle Temple, 1970, Bencher, 1993; Deputy to Courts Administrator, Middlesex Crown Court, 1972–73; Courts Administrator (Newcastle), NE Circuit, 1974–79; Courts Administrator, Central Criminal Court, and Coordinator for Taxation of Crown Court Costs, S Eastern Circuit, 1979–84; Dep. Circuit Administrator, SE Circuit, 1984–86; Asst Registrar, Ct of Appeal Criminal Div., 1986–88. Registrar, Civil and Commercial Court and Regulatory Tribunal, Qatar Financial Centre, 2006–. Adjunct Prof. of Law, Wake Forest Univ., NC, 2002–05. Mem., Criminal Cttee, Judicial Studies Bd, 1988–2003. Mem., Indep. Monitoring Bd, Lewes Prison, 2004–06. Life Mem., Litigation Section, State Bar, California, 2002. Freeman, City of London, 1979. FRSA 1990. Hon. Fellow, Kent Sch. of Law, Canterbury Univ., 1991. *Publication:* (ed) Rules of Court: criminal procedure, annually 1994–97; (with Lord Woolf) A Review of the Working Methods of the European Court of Human Rights, 2005. *Recreations:* Northumbrian stick dressing, fell walking. *Address:* Selwyns Wood House, Cross in Hand, East Sussex TN21 0QN.

MACKENZIE, Michael Philip; Director-General, Food and Drink Federation, 1986–2001; *b* 26 June 1937; *s* of Brig. Maurice Mackenzie, DSO, and Mrs Vivienne Mackenzie; *m* 1966, Jill (*née* Beckley); one *s* one *d*. *Educ:* Downside Sch.; Lincoln Coll., Oxford (BA); Harvard Business Sch., USA. United Biscuits plc, 1966–86: Prodn Dir, various businesses within United Biscuits, 1974–83; Man. Dir, D. S. Crawford Bakeries, 1983–86. *Recreations:* walking, gardening, opera, theatre. *Address:* Ebony Cottage, Reading Street, near Tenterden, Kent TN30 7HT. *Club:* Travellers.

MACKENZIE, Sir Peter Douglas, 13th Bt *cr* 1673 (NS), of Coul, Ross-shire; *b* 23 April 1949; *s* of Henry Douglas Mackenzie (*d* 1965) and Irene Carter Freeman; *S* kinsman, 1990, but his name does not appear on the Official Roll of the Baronetage; *m* 1st, 1982, Jennifer, *d* of Ridley Boyce (marr. diss.); two *d*; 2nd, 2000, Margo Lamond, *d* of Albert Gordon. *Heir: kinsman* Miles Roderick Turing Mackenzie [*b* 18 April 1952; *m* 1983, Hiroko Sato].

MACKENZIE, Richard Hill, CB 2002; Member, Boundary Commission for Northern Ireland, since 2002; Local Government Boundaries Commissioner for Northern Ireland, since 2006; Joint Secretary, North/South Ministerial Council, Northern Ireland, 2000–02; *b* 21 Feb. 1942; *s* of late Richard H. Mackenzie and Mary Mackenzie; *m* 1966, Jane Valerie Holmes; two *s* one *d*. *Educ:* Grosvenor High Sch., Belfast; Queen's Univ., Belfast (BSc Econs). Dep. Sec., DoE (NI), 1987–2000. Vis. Prof. in Planning, Univ. of Ulster, 2002–. Hon. MRTPI 2000. *Recreations:* choral singing, golf. *Clubs:* Ulster Reform (Belfast); Grosvenor Rugby.

MACKENZIE, Sir Roderick McQuhae, 12th Bt *cr* 1703, of Scatwell; FRCP(C); medical practitioner, pediatrician; *b* 17 April 1942; *s* of Captain Sir Roderick Edward François McQuhae Mackenzie, 11th Bt, CBE, DSC, RN and Marie Evelyn Campbell (*d* 1993), *o c* of late William Ernest Parkinson; *S* father, 1986, but his name does not appear on the Official Roll of the Baronetage; *m* 1970, Nadezhda, (Nadine), Baroness von Rorbas, *d* of Georges Frederic Schlatter, Baron von Rorbas; one *s* one *d*. *Educ:* Sedbergh; King's College London. MB, BS; MRCP; DCH. *Recreations:* classical music (violin, viola), horseback riding (3-Day eventing), windsurfing. *Heir: s* Gregory Roderick McQuhae Mackenzie, *b* 8 May 1971. *Address:* 2431 Udell Road NW, Calgary, AB T2N 4H4, Canada.

MACKENZIE, Ruth, OBE 1995; Director, Time/Room Productions, since 2002; Director General, Manchester International Festival, since 2006; *b* 24 July 1957; *d* of Kenneth Mackenzie and Myrna Blumberg. *Educ:* South Hampstead High Sch.; Sorbonne, Paris; Newnham Coll., Cambridge (MA English 1982). Editor's Asst, Time Out magazine, 1980–81; Co-founder, Dir and writer, Moving Parts Theatre Co., 1980–82; Fellow in Theatre, and Dir, Theatre in the Mill, Bradford Univ., 1982–84; Drama Officer, Arts Council of GB, 1984–86; Head of Strategic Planning, South Bank Centre, 1986–90; Exec. Dir, Nottingham Playhouse, 1990–97; Gen. Dir, Scottish Opera, 1997–99; Special Advr to Sec. of State for Culture, Media and Sport, 1999–2002. Artistic Dir, Bradford Multicultural Fest., 1983–84; Artistic Programmer, Theatr Clwyd, 1995–96; Theatre Programmer, Barbican Centre, 1995–97; Artistic Dir, Chichester Fest. Theatre, 2002–06. Member: Bd, Women in Entertainment, 1987–89; Bd, Paines Plough Theatre Co., 1990–96; Touring Panel, 1992–, Lottery Panel, 1994–97, Arts Council of GB, later Arts Council of England, subseq. Arts Council England; Dance and Drama Panel, British Council, 1992–97; Bd, London Internat. Fest. of Theatre, 1993–97; Nat. Develt Forum, ABSA, 1994–96; Bd, New Millennium Experience Co., 1997–99; Panel 2000, 1998–99; QCA Cttee on Creativity, 2001–; Chancellor's Forum, London Inst., 2001–. Gov.,

Trinity Coll. of Music, 2002–. FRSA. Hon. Fellow, Univ. of Nottingham, 1994. Hon. DLitt: Nottingham Trent, 1994; Nottingham, 1997. *Address:* Manchester International Festival, 131 Portland Street, Manchester M1 4PY.

MACKENZIE, Wallace John, OBE 1974; Director, Slough Estates plc, 1972–91 (Group Managing Director, 1975–86); *b* 2 July 1921; *s* of Wallace D. Mackenzie and Ethel F. Williamson; *m* 1951, Barbara D. Hopson; two *s* one *d.* *Educ:* Harrow Weald County Grammar Sch. Gen. Manager, Slough Estates Canada Ltd, 1952–72; Dep. Man. Dir, Slough Estates Ltd, 1972–75. Dir, Investors in Industry plc, 1982–86; Chm., Trust Parts Ltd, 1986–94 (Dir, 1985). Member: Commn for New Towns, 1978–94; London Residuary Body, 1985–95. Trustee, Lankelly Foundn, 1985–2005. *Recreations:* golf, bridge. *Address:* 1 Brampton Mews, Pound Lane, Marlow, Bucks SL7 2SY. *T:* (01628) 478310.

McKENZIE JOHNSTON, Henry Butler, CB 1981; Vice-Chairman, Commission for Local Administration in England, 1982–84 (Commissioner, 1981–84); *b* 10 July 1921; *er s* of late Colin McKenzie Johnston and late Bernardine (*née* Fawcett Butler); *m* 1949, Marian Allardyce Middleton, *e d* of late Brig. A. A. Middleton and late Winifred (*née* Salvesen); one *s* two *d.* *Educ:* Rugby. Served with Black Watch (RHR), 1940–46; Adjt 6th Bn, 1944–45; Temp. Major 1945. Staff of HM Embassy, Athens, 1946–47; entered Foreign (subseq. Diplomatic) Service, 1947; Paris, 1948–51; British High Commn, Germany, 1951–54; FO, 1954–56; 1st Sec. (Commercial), Montevideo, 1956–60; FO, 1960–63; Counsellor (Information), Mexico City, 1963–66; Dep. High Comr, Port of Spain, 1966–67; seconded to Min. of Overseas Develt, 1968–70; Consul-Gen., Munich, 1971–73; seconded to Office of Parly Comr for Admin, 1973–79, transferred permanently, 1979–81; Dep. Parly Comr for Admin, 1974–81. Mem., Broadcasting Complaints Commn, 1986–90. Mem., Social Security Appeal Tribunal, Kensington, subseq. Central London, 1985–88. Chm., British-Mexican Soc., 1977–80. *Publication:* Missions to Mexico: a tale of British diplomacy in the 1820s, 1992; Ottoman and Persian Odysseys: James Morier, creator of Hajji Baba of Ispahan, and his brothers, 1998. *Address:* 6 Pembroke Gardens, W8 6HS. *Clubs:* Athenæum, Hurlingham.

McKENZIE-PRICE, Isobel Clare; Editorial Director, housetohome.co.uk and Ideal Home magazine, since 2007; *b* 11 Jan. 1956; *d* of Edward Charles Price and Patricia Price (*née* Edgeley); *m* 1st, 1977, Andrew James Alistair McKenzie (marr. diss. 1981); 2nd, 1983, William Woods; one *s* three *d.* *Educ:* Horsham Girls High Sch.; Univ. of Leeds (BA Hons). Homes Editor, Over 21, 1979–80; Dep. Editor, Wedding and Home, 1983–85; Mem., Launch Team, Country Living, 1985–86; Dep. Editor, Essentials, 1986–90; Editor: Mother and Baby, 1990–91; Parents, 1991–92; Period Living, 1993–94; Editor in Chief, Elle Decoration, and Period Living, 1994–96; Publishing Consultant, Inspirations, 1997; Exec. Editor, Prima, and Launch Editor, Your Home, 1997–98; Ed.-in-Chief, then Editl Dir, IPC Home Interest Magazines (Ideal Home, Living etc, 25 Beautiful Homes, Homes & Gardens, Country Homes & Interiors), 1998–2004; Ed.-in-Chief, All You mag., Time Inc., NY, 2004–07. *Recreations:* family, new media, country walking. *Address:* *e-mail:* isobel_mckenzie-price@ipcmedia.com.

McKENZIE SMITH, Ian, OBE 1992; RSA 1987 (ARSA 1973); PPRSW (RSW 1981); artist (painter); President, Royal Scottish Academy, 1998–2007 (Deputy President and Treasurer, 1990–91; Secretary, 1991–98); City Arts and Recreation Officer, City of Aberdeen, 1989–96; *b* 3 Aug. 1935; *y s* of James McKenzie Smith and Mary Benzie; *m* 1963, Mary Rodger Fotheringham; two *s* one *d.* *Educ:* Robert Gordon's Coll., Aberdeen; Gray's Sch. of Art, Aberdeen; Hospitalfield Coll. of Art, Arbroath; Aberdeen Coll. of Educn. SSA 1960; AAS 1963; FSAScot 1970; ASIAD 1975; FMA 1987. Teacher of art, 1960–63; Educn Officer, Council of Industrial Design, Scottish Cttee, 1963–68; Dir, Aberdeen Art Gall. and Museums, 1968–89 (Hon. Mem., Friends of Aberdeen Art Gall., 2000). Work in permanent collections: Scottish Nat. Gall. of Modern Art; Scottish Arts Council; Arts Council of NI; Contemp. Art Soc.; Aberdeen Art Gall. and Museums; Glasgow Art Gall. and Museums; City Art Centre, Edinburgh; Perth Art Gall.; McManus Gall., Dundee; Abbot Hall Art Gall., Kendal; Hunterian Mus., Glasgow; Nuffield Foundn; Carnegie Trust; Strathclyde Educn Authority; Lothian Educn Authority; RSA; DoE; Robert Fleming Holdings; IBM; Deutsche Morgan Grenfell; Grampian Hosps Art Trust; Lord Chancellor. Mem., Cttee of Enquiry into Econ. Situation of Visual Artists, Gulbenkian Foundn, 1978. Trustee, Nat. Galls of Scotland, 1999–2007. Member: Scottish Arts Council, 1970–77 (Chm., Art Cttee, 1975–77); Scottish Museums Fedn, 1970–86; Scottish Museums Council, 1980–87 (Chm., Industrial Cttee, 1985–87); Aberdeen Univ. Museums Cttee and Music Cttee, 1970–96; ICOM Internat. Exhibns Cttee, 1986–96; Museums and Galls Commn, 1997–2000; Nat. Heritage, Scottish Gp, 1977–99; Bd of Mgt, Grampian Hosps Art Project, 1987–2000; Adv. Council on Export of Works of Art, 1991–; Curatorial Cttee, 1991–2001, Council, 1996–99, Bldgs Cttee, 1998–2001, NT for Scotland. Arts Advr, COSLA, 1976–85. Pres., RSW, 1988–98. Governor: Edinburgh Coll. of Art, 1976–88; The Robert Gordon Univ. (formerly Robert Gordon Inst. of Technology), 1989–95. External Assessor: Glasgow Sch. of Art, 1982–86; Duncan of Jordanstone Coll. of Art, 1982–86; Scottish Arts Council Gifting Scheme, 1997. Board Member: RSA Enterprises, and Friends of RSA, 1972–2007; Scottish Sculpture Workshop, 1979–2000; Aberdeen Maritime Mus. Appeal, 1981–98. Vice Pres., NADFAS, 2000–04. Trustee: Painters Workshop (Scotland), 1975–89; John Kinross Fund, 1990–2007; Alexander Naysmith Fund, 1990–2007; Spalding Fund, 1990–2007; Sir William Gillies Fund, 1990–2007; Hospitalfield Trust, 1991–2007; Marguerite McBey Trust, 2000–. FSS 1981; FRSA 1973; FRSE 2003. Hon. RA 1999; Hon. RHA 1999; Hon. RUA 1999; Hon. RWA 2000. Hon. Mem., Peacock Printmakers, 1993. Hon. LLD Aberdeen, 1991; Hon. DArt Robert Gordon, 2000. Inst. of Contemp. Prints Award, 1969; Guthrie Award, 1971, Gillies Award, 1980, RSA; ESU Thyne Scholarship, 1980; Sir William Gillies Award, RSW, 2008. *Address:* *e-mail:* i.mckenziesmith@btinternet.com. *Clubs:* Caledonian, Royal Over-Seas League, Scottish Arts (Edinburgh); Royal Northern (Aberdeen).

MACKENZIE SMITH, Peter; Managing Director, Prothero Ltd, since 2003; Director: Getenergy Ltd, since 2004; Columella Ltd, since 2004; *b* 12 Jan. 1946; *s* of late Antony and of Isobel Mackenzie Smith; *m* 1973, Sandra Gay-French; three *d.* *Educ:* Downside; Jesus Coll., Cambridge (BA Classical Tripos). Teacher: British Inst., Oporto, 1967–68; Internat. House, London, 1969; British Council, 1969–97: Asst Rep., Lagos, 1969–72; Asst Cultural Attaché, Cairo, 1972–77; Regl Dir, Southampton, 1977–80; Educnl Contracts Dept, 1980–83; Dep. Rep., Cairo, 1983–87; Director: Educnl Contracts, 1987–89; Projects Div., 1989–92; Nigeria and W Africa, 1992–94; Export Promotion, 1994–96; Africa and S Asia, 1996–97; Dir of Educn, General Electric Co., subseq. Marconi plc, 1997–2003; Export Promoter for Educn and Training, Trade Partners UK, 2001–03. Mem., Methodology Soc., 2000–. *Address:* Backfields End, Winchelsea, E Sussex TN36 4AB. *Club:* Athenæum.

McKEON, Andrew John; Managing Director (Health), Audit Commission, since 2003; *b* 22 Sept. 1955; *s* of Kenneth and Maurine McKeon; *m* 1989, Hilary Neville; one *s* one *d.* *Educ:* William Hulme's Grammar Sch., Manchester; St Catharine's Coll., Cambridge. Joined DHSS, 1976; Hd of Medicines, Pharmacy and Industry Div., 2000–02, Dir of Policy and Planning, 2002–03, DoH.

McKEOWEN, David; *see* Wills, Rt Hon. M. D.

McKEOWN, Dr John; Chief Executive Officer, United Kingdom Atomic Energy Authority, 1997–2003; Director, Hendred Strategy Ltd, 2003–06; *b* 10 March 1945; *s* of Edward McKeown and Anne McGladrigan; *m* 1967, Maureen Susan Doherty; one *s* one *d.* *Educ:* Univ. of Glasgow (BSc 1966; PhD 1971); Harvard Business Sch. CEGB Res. Fellow, 1971–73; Asst, Forward Planning, 1973–76; South of England Electricity Board: Sen. Engr, 1976–79, Principal Engr, 1979–83, Control and Instrumentation Div.; Manager: Electrical Dept, 1983–88; Nuclear Safety, 1988–90; Scottish Nuclear: Director: Safety, 1990–92; Projects, 1992–95; Safety & Envmt, 1995–96; Principal, John McKeown and Associates, 1996–97. Director: UK Nirex, 1997–2003; British Nuclear Industry Forum, 1998–2003; Oxford Economic Partnership, 1999–. *Recreations:* golf, music. *Address:* Croft Orchard, Church Street, East Hendred, Oxon OX12 8LA. *Club:* Frilford Heath Golf.

McKEOWN, Prof. Patrick Arthur, OBE 1991; MSc; FREng, FIET, FIMechE; FCQI; Professor of Precision Engineering, 1974–96, now Emeritus, Director of Cranfield Unit for Precision Engineering, 1969–96, Cranfield University (formerly Institute of Technology); Director, Pat McKeown and Associates, since 1995; *b* 16 Aug. 1930; *s* of Robert Matthew McKeown and Augusta (*née* White); *m* 1954, Mary Patricia Heath; three *s.* *Educ:* Cambridge County High Sch. for Boys; Bristol Grammar Sch.; Cranfield Inst. of Technol. (MSc). CEng, MIMechE 1969; FIET (FIProdE 1971); FCQI (FIQA 1973); FREng (FEng 1986). National Service, RE, 1949–51; Suez Campaign, 1956: Captain RE; port maintenance. Student apprentice, Bristol Aircraft Co. Ltd, Bristol, 1951–54 (HNC National State Scholarship); Cranfield Inst. of Technol., 1954–56; Société Genevoise, Newport Pagnell and Geneva, 1956–68 (Technical and Works Dir, 1965); Hd of Dept for Design of Machine Systems. Cranfield Inst. of Technol., 1975–85. Chairman: Cranfield Precision Systems Ltd, 1984–87; Cranfield Moulded Structures Ltd, 1984–91; Cranfield Precision Engrg Ltd, 1987–95 (Chief Exec., 1987–92); non-executive Director: Control Techniques plc, 1990–95; AMTRI, 1990–92; Cranfield Aerospace Ltd, 2001–03. Vice-Pres., Inst. of Qual. Assurance, 1976; Pres., CIRP (Internat. Instn for Prodn Engrg Res.), 1988–89. Member: Evaluation Panel, National Bureau of Standards, Washington, USA; Metrology and Standards Requirements Bd, DTI, 1983–86; Advanced Manufg Technol. Cttee, DTI, 1983–87; Vis. Cttee, RCA, 1984–87; ACARD working gp, 1987–88. Internat. Advr, Gintic Inst. of Manufg Technology, Singapore, 1991–97. Vis. Prof., Univ. of Calif, Berkeley, 1994. Clayton Meml Lectr, IMechE, 1986. Pres., Eur. Soc. for Precision Engrg and Nanotechnol., 1998–2000. Charter Fellow, Soc. of Manufacturing Engineers, 1985. Hon. DSc: Connecticut, 1996; Cranfield, 1996. Fulbright Award (Vis. Prof. of Mechanical Engrg, Univ. of Wisconsin-Madison), 1982; F. W. Taylor Award, Soc. of Manufacturing Engrs, 1983; Thomas Hawksley Gold Medal, IMechE, 1987; Mensforth Gold Medal, IProdE, 1988; Life Achievement Award, Amer. Soc. for Precision Engrg, 1998; Faraday Medal, IEE, 1999; Life Achievement Award, European Soc. for Precision Engrg and Nanotechnol., 2002; Internat. Prize, Japan Soc. for Precision Engrg, 2003; Georg Schlesinger Prize, Senate of State, Berlin, 2006. Freedom, City of London, 2007; Liveryman, Co. of Engrs, 2008–. *Publications:* papers in CIRP Annals; project reports and lectures for Royal Acad. of Engrg. *Recreations:* walking, travel, enjoyment of wine, good food, music, theatre. *T:* (01234) 267678; *e-mail:* patmckeown@fastmail.co.uk.

MACKERRAS, Sir (Alan) Charles (MacLaurin), AC 1997; CH 2003; Kt 1979; CBE 1974; Musical Director, Welsh National Opera, 1987–92, now Conductor Emeritus; Principal Guest Conductor: Scottish Chamber Orchestra, 1992–95, now Conductor Laureate; Philharmonia Orchestra, since 2002; President, Trinity College of Music, since 2000; *b* Schenectady, USA, 17 Nov. 1925; *s* of late Alan Patrick and Catherine Mackerras, Sydney, Australia; *m* 1947, Helena Judith (*née* Wilkins); two *d.* *Educ:* Sydney Grammar Sch.; Sydney Conservatorium of Music; student with Vaclav Talich, Prague Acad. of Music. Principal Oboist, Sydney Symphony Orchestra, 1943–46; Staff Conductor, Sadler's Wells Opera, 1948–54; Principal Conductor BBC Concert Orchestra, 1954–56; freelance conductor with most British and many continental orchestras; concert tours in USSR, S Africa, USA, 1957–66; First Conductor, Hamburg State Opera, 1966–69; Musical Dir, Sadler's Wells Opera, later ENO, 1970–77; Chief Guest Conductor, BBC SO, 1976–79; Chief Conductor, Sydney Symphony Orch., ABC, 1982–85; Principal Guest Conductor: Royal Liverpool Philharmonic Orch., 1986–88; San Francisco Opera, 1993–96 (now Conductor Emeritus); RPO, 1993–96; Czech Philharmonic Orch., 1997–2003; Mus. Dir, Orch. of St Luke's, NY, 1998–2001 (now Mus. Dir Emeritus); Conductor Laureate, Brno Philharmonic Orch., 2007; Conductor Emeritus, Orch. of the Age of Enlightenment, 2007; Guest Conductor: Vienna State Opera; Paris Opera; Munich Opera; Opera Australia; Royal Opera House Covent Garden; Metropolitan Opera; frequent radio and TV broadcasts; many commercial recordings, notably Handel, Janáček, Mozart operas and symphonies, Brahms, Dvořák, Schubert, Mahler and Beethoven symphonies; appearances at many internat. festivals and opera houses. Hon. Fellow: St Peter's Coll., Oxford, 1999; Cardiff Univ., 2003. Hon. RAM 1969; Hon. FRCM 1987; Hon. FRNCM 1999; Hon. FTCL 1999; Hon. FRWCMD 2005. Hon. DMus: Hull, 1990; Nottingham, 1991; York, Brno, Brisbane, 1994; Oxford, 1997; Prague Acad. of Music, 1999; Napier Univ., 2000; Melbourne, 2003; Sydney, 2003; Janáček Acad., Brno, 2004; London, 2005. Evening Standard Award for Opera, 1977; Janáček Medal, 1978; Gramophone Record of the Year, 1977, 1980, 1999; Gramophone Operatic Record of the Year Award, 1983, 1984, 1994, 1999; Gramophone Best Choral Record, 1986; Grammy Award for best opera recording, 1981, 2007; Chocs de l'Année Award, Le Monde de la Musique, 1998; Edison Award, 1999; Lifetime Achievement Award and Chopin Prize, Cannes, 2000; Assoc. of British Orchestras Award, 2001; Dist. Musicians Award, ISM, 2002; Gold Medal, Royal Philharmonic Soc., 2005; Queen's Medal for Music, 2005; Silver Medal, Musicians' Co., 2006; Classic FM Gramophone Lifetime Achievement Award, 2006. Medal of Merit (Czech Republic), 1996; Centenary Medal (Australia), 2003. *Publications:* ballet arrangements of Pineapple Poll (Sullivan), 1951 and of The Lady and the Fool (Verdi), 1954; reconstruction of Arthur Sullivan's lost Cello Concerto, 1986; contrib. 4 appendices to Charles Mackerras: a musicians' musician, by Nancy Phelan 1987; articles in Opera Magazine, Music and Musicians and other musical jls. *Recreations:* languages, yachting. *Address:* 10 Hamilton Terrace, NW8 9UG.

MacKERRON, Prof. Gordon Stewart; Director, Sussex Energy Group, Science and Technology Policy Research Unit, University of Sussex, since 2005; *b* 15 Jan. 1947; *s* of James and Jessie MacKerron; *m* 1997, Kara Smith; one *s* one *d.* *Educ:* St John's Coll., Cambridge (BA Econs 1968); Univ. of Sussex (MA Develt Econs). Econ. planner, ODI-Nuffield Fellow, Malaŵi, 1969–71; Fellow, SPRU, Univ. of Sussex, 1974–76; Lectr, Griffith Univ., Brisbane, 1976–78; Sen. Fellow, SPRU, Univ. of Sussex, 1978–2000; Dep. Dir, Energy Rev. Team, Perf. and Innovation Unit, Cabinet Office, 2001; Associate Dir, NERA Econ. Consulting, 2001–05. Chm., Cttee on Radioactive Waste Mgt, 2003–. *Publications:* (ed) The UK Energy Experience: a model or warning, 1996; (ed) The International Experience, 2000; contrib. jls incl. Energy Policy, Energy Jl, Revue de l'Energie. *Recreations:* singing, salsa (dance), history. *Address:* Science and Technology Policy Research Unit, Freeman Centre, University of Sussex, Brighton BN1 9QE. *T:* (01273) 876584, *Fax:* (01273) 685865; *e-mail:* g.s.mackerron@sussex.ac.uk.

McKERROW, June; charity advisor; Director, Mental Health Foundation, 1992–2000; *b* 17 June 1950; *d* of late Alexander Donald and of Lorna McKerrow; one adopted *d. Educ:* Brunel Univ. (MPhil 1977). Housing management in local govt and housing assocs, 1967–80; Dir, Stonham Housing Assoc., 1980–92. Mem. Cttee, English Rural Housing Assoc., 1997–99. Trustee and Vice-Chm., Shelter, 1985–93; Trustee: Homeless Internat., 1988–93; Cherwell Housing Trust, 1992–97; Charity Projects, 1993–97; Donnington Doorstep, 2002–; Winston's Wish, 2002–04; Change of Scene, 2008–; Dir, Soundabout, 2003–; Patron, Revolving Doors Agency, 1993–99; Chm., Housing Assocs Charitable Trust, 1998–2002; Mem. Bd, Advance Housing and Support, 2001–03. Mem., British Council, UN Internat. Year of Shelter for the Homeless, 1987. Non-exec. Dir, Oxfordshire and Buckinghamshire Mental Health Trust, 2000–07. Mem. Court, Oxford Brookes Univ., 1999–2007. *Address:* 22 Buckingham Street, Oxford OX1 4LH.

McKERROW, Neil Alexander Herdman; Bursar and Clerk to the Governors, Sedbergh School, 1997–2006; *b* 17 May 1945; *s* of late Anderson Herdman McKerrow, TD, MB ChB and of Joan Ysobel Cuthbertson (*née* Clark); *m* 1971, Penelope Mackinlay (*née* Chiene); one *s* two *d. Educ:* Sedbergh Sch.; Emmanuel Coll., Cambridge (MA). Reckitt & Colman (Overseas) Ltd, 1968–69; commnd 1st Bn Queen's Own Highlanders (Seaforth and Camerons), service in Trucial-Oman States, BAOR, 1969–73 (Capt.); Marketing Manager, Distillers Co., 1973–75; Macdonald Martin Distilleries, later Glenmorangie plc: Export Dir, 1975–81; Sales Marketing Dir, 1981–87; Man. Dir, 1987–94; Chief Exec., Forest Enterprise, Forestry Commn, 1995–96. Director: Welsh Whisky Co., 2006–; Royal Lyceum Theatre Co., 2007–. Dep. Dir, Atlantic Salmon Trust, 2006–. Member: Royal Scottish Pipers Soc., 1971–; High Constabulary, Port of Leith, 1976–; Incorp. of Malt Men, 1990–. Liveryman, Co. of Distillers, 2006–. Gov., Belhaven Hill Sch., Dunbar, 1997–2004. *Recreations:* fishing, outdoor pursuits, most sports, malt whisky, local history, traditional jazz. *Clubs:* London Scottish; New (Edinburgh); Hawks (Cambridge); Royal & Ancient Golf (St Andrews).

MACKESON, Sir Rupert (Henry), 2nd Bt *cr* 1954; *b* 16 Nov. 1941; *s* of Brig. Sir Harry Ripley Mackeson, 1st Bt, and Alethea, Lady Mackeson (*d* 1979), *d* of late Comdr R. Talbot, RN; *S* father, 1964; *m* 1968, Hon. Camilla Keith (marr. diss. 1973), *d* of Baron Keith of Castleacre. *Educ:* Harrow; Trinity Coll., Dublin (MA). Captain, Royal Horse Guards, 1967, retd 1968. *Publications:* (as Rupert Collens): (jtly) 'Snaffles' on Racing and Point-to-Pointing, 1988; (jtly) 'Snaffles' on Hunting, 1989; Look at Cecil Aldin's Dogs and Hounds, 1990; 25 Legal Luminaries from Vanity Fair, 1990; Cecil Aldin's Dog Models, 1994; (as Rupert Mackeson) Bet Like a Man, 2001. *Recreations:* art, racing. *Heir:* none. *Address:* Flat 3, 51 South Road, Weston-super-Mare, Somerset BS23 2LU.

MACKESY, Dr Piers Gerald, FRHistS; FBA 1988; Fellow of Pembroke College, Oxford, 1954–87, now Emeritus; *b* 15 Sept. 1924; *s* of Maj.-Gen. Pierse Joseph Mackesy, CB, DSO, MC and Dorothy (*née* Cook), (novelist as Leonora Starr); *m* 1st, Sarah Davies; one *s* two *d*; 2nd, Patricia Timlin (*née* Gore). *Educ:* Wellington Coll.; Christ Church, Oxford (1st cl. Hons Modern Hist., 1950; DPhil 1953; DLitt 1978). FRHistS 1965. Lieut, The Royal Scots Greys (NW Europe, 1944–47); Captain, TA, 1950–57. Robinson Schol., Oriel Coll., Oxford, 1951–53; Harkness Fellow, Harvard Univ., 1953–54; Vis. Fellow, Inst. for Advanced Study, Princeton, 1962–63; Vis. Prof., CIT, 1966; Huntington Liby, San Marino, Calif, 1967. Lectures: Lees-Knowles, Cambridge, 1972; American Bicentennial, at Williamsburg, Va, Clark Univ., Naval War Coll., US Mil. Acad., Nat. War Coll., Peabody Mus., N Eastern Univ., Capitol Historical Soc. Member, Council: Inst. for Early Amer. Hist. and Culture, 1970–73; Nat. Army Mus., 1983–92; Soc. for Army Historical Res., 1985–94 (Vice-Pres., 2003–). Chm., N of Scotland Br., Royal Scots Dragoon Guards Assoc., 1993–2007. *Publications:* The War in the Mediterranean 1803–10, 1957; The War for America 1775–83, 1964, 2nd edn 1993; Statesmen at War: the Strategy of Overthrow 1798–99, 1974; The Coward of Minden: the affair of Lord George Sackville, 1979; War without Victory: the downfall of Pitt 1799–1802, 1984; British Victory in Egypt, 1801: the end of Napoleon's conquest, 1995 (Templer Medal, Soc. for Army Histl Res., 1995); contribs to various books and jls. *Address:* Westerton Farmhouse, Dess, by Aboyne, Aberdeenshire AB34 5AY. *T:* (013398) 84415. *Club:* Army and Navy.

MACKEY, Allan Robert; Chair, Refugee Status Appeals Authority, New Zealand, since 2007; an Immigration Judge, Asylum and Immigration Tribunal (formerly a Vice President, Immigration Appeal Tribunal), since 2001; *b* 24 April 1942; *s* of Albert George Mackey and Eileen Annie Mackey; *m* 1966, Mary Anne Kirkness; two *s* one *d. Educ:* Otahuhu Coll., Auckland; Auckland Univ. (LLB 1966); Cranfield Univ. (MBA 1976). Barrister and Solicitor, NZ, 1966; Solicitor, NSW, 1968; Barrister and solicitor, Auckland, 1966–68 and 1970–74; Solicitor, Sydney, Australia, 1968–70; Mktg Manager, Todd Motors Ltd, NZ, 1975–79; Gen. Manager, Mazda Motors, NZ, 1980–86; Solicitor/ Consultant, Auckland, Hong Kong, Dubai, 1987–91; Mem., Residence, Removal and Refugee Appeal Authy of NZ, 1991–94; Chm., Refugee and Residence Appeal Authorities of NZ, 1994–2001; Legal Chair, Immigration Appeal Tribunal, UK, 1999–2001. Vis. Prof., Univ. of Tokyo, 2006. Pres., Internat. Assoc. of Refugee Law Judges, 2002–05 (Vice Pres., 2000–02). *Recreations:* yachting, walking. *Address:* c/o Asylum and Immigration Tribunal, Field House, Bream's Buildings, Chancery Lane, EC4A 1DZ. *T:* (NZ) (9) 9144172. *Club:* Wellington (Wellington, NZ).

MACKEY, Prof. James Patrick; Thomas Chalmers Professor of Theology, 1979–99, now Emeritus, and Director of Graduate School and Associate Dean, 1995–99, University of Edinburgh (Hon. Fellow, Faculty of Divinity, 1999–2002); *b* 9 Feb. 1934; *e s* of Peter Mackey and Esther Mackey (*née* Morrissey); *m* 1973, Hanorah Noelle Quinlan; one *s* one *d. Educ:* Mount St Joseph Coll., Roscrea; Nat. Univ. of Ireland (BA); Pontifical Univ. Maynooth (LPh, BD, STL, DD); Queen's Univ. Belfast (PhD); postgraduate study at Univs of Oxford, London, Strasbourg. Lectr in Philosophy, QUB, 1960–66; Lectr in Theology, St John's Coll., Waterford, 1966–69; Associate Prof. and Prof. of Systematic and Philosophical Theol., Univ. of San Francisco, 1969–79; Dean, Faculty of Divinity, Edinburgh Univ., 1984–88. Visiting Professor: Univ. of California, Berkeley, 1974; Dartmouth Coll., NH, 1989; TCD, 1999–; Curricular Consultant, UC Cork, 1999–2003. Member: Ind. Assessment Panel for NI Policing Bd, 2005; Consultative Gp on the Past (NI), 2007–08. Mem., Centre for Hermeneutical Studies, Univ. of California, Berkeley, 1974–79. Organiser, Internat. Conf. on the Cultures of Europe, Derry, 1992. *Television series:* The Hall of Mirrors, 1984; The Gods of War, 1986; Perspectives, 1986–87; radio programmes. Associate Editor: Herder Correspondence, 1966–69; Concilium (church history section), 1965–70; Horizons, 1973–79; Founding Editor, Studies in World Christianity, 1995–2002. *Publications:* The Modern Theology of Tradition, 1962; Life and Grace, 1966; Tradition and Change in the Church, 1968; Contemporary Philosophy of Religion, 1968; (ed) Morals, Law and Authority, 1969; The Church: its credibility today, 1970; The Problems of Religious Faith, 1972; Jesus: the man and the myth, 1979; The

Christian Experience of God as Trinity, 1983; (ed) Religious Imagination, 1986; Modern Theology: a sense of direction, 1987; (with Prof. J. D. G. Dunn) New Testament Theology in Dialogue, 1987; (ed) Introduction to Celtic Christianity, 1989; Power and Christian Ethics, 1993; (ed) The Cultures of Europe, 1994; The Critique of Theological Reason, 2000; (ed) Religion and Politics in Ireland, 2003; Christianity and Creation, 2006; The Scientist and the Theologian, 2007; Jesus of Nazareth, 2008; contribs to theol. and philosoph. jls. *Recreations:* yachting; rediscovery of original Celtic culture of these islands. *Address:* 15 Glenville Park, Dunmore Road, Waterford, Eire.

MACKEY, Air Vice-Marshal Jefferson; Chief Executive, Defence Dental Agency, 1996–97; *b* 24 Oct. 1936; *s* of late James Mackey and of Cicely (*née* Hitchman); *m* 1959, Sheila Mary Taylor; one *s* two *d. Educ:* Latymer Upper Sch.; Guy's Hosp. (BDS, LDS RCS). Asst Dir, Defence Dental Services, 1982–86; Officer Comdg RAF Inst. of Dental Health and Trng, 1986–87; Principal Dental Officer, RAF Support Command, 1987–90; Dir, RAF Dental Services, 1990–94; Dir, Defence Dental Services, 1992–96. QHDS 1987–97. FInstLM; FCMI; FRGS. *Address:* Takali, Oxford Road, Stone, Bucks HP17 8PB. *T:* (01296) 748823. *Clubs:* Royal Air Force; Mentmore Golf and Country.

MACKEY, Most Rev. John, CBE 1983; Bishop of Auckland, NZ, (RC), 1974–83; *b* Bray, Co. Wicklow, 11 Jan. 1918; *s* of Malachy Mackey and Kathleen (*née* Byrne). *Educ:* Auckland Univ. (MA, DipEd); Notre Dame Univ., USA (PhD). Emigrated to NZ, 1924. Ordained priest, 1941; Adminr for Auckland Diocesan Schs, 1951–71; Lectr, Holy Cross Seminary, 1972–74; formerly Professor in Theological Faculty, National Seminary of Mosgiel, Dunedin. *Publications:* The Making of a State Education System, 1967; Reflections on Church History, 1975; Looking at Ourselves, 1994. *Address:* 3 Karaka Street, Takapuna, Auckland, New Zealand.

MACKEY, William Gawen; Partner, 1952, Managing Partner UK Operations, 1981–86, Ernst & Whinney; retired 1986; *b* 22 Sept. 1924; *s* of William Gawen Mackey and Jane Mackey; *m* 1948, Margaret Reeves Vinycomb; two *s. Educ:* Dame Allan's Sch., Newcastle upon Tyne. Qualified Chartered Accountant, 1949. Served RN, 1942–45 (Sub-Lt). Joined Ernst & Whinney, 1952, Newcastle; transf. London, 1973, with responsibility for corporate restructuring and insolvency services in UK. Receiver: Airfix; British Tanners; Laker; Stone-Platt. Chm., Insolvency Sub Cttee, CCAB, 1978–82; Dir, Inst. Corporate Insolvency Courses, 1974–80. *Publications:* articles and lectures on corporate management, restructuring and insolvency. *Recreations:* opera, gardening, France. *Address:* Eynesse, Ste Foy La Grande 33220, France. *T:* 557410042, *Fax:* 557410070.

McKIBBIN, (David) Malcolm; Permanent Secretary, Department of Agriculture and Rural Development, Northern Ireland, since 2007; *b* Belfast, 20 Nov. 1956; *s* of Desmond and Iris McKibbin; *m* 1981, Susan Crook; two *d. Educ:* Univ. of Southampton (BSc Hons Civil Engrg 1978); Univ. of Ulster (DPhil 1987; MBA 1991). CCE 1982; FICE 2003; FIHT 2003. Various posts, NI Roads Service, 1978–98; Dir, Transport Policy Div., 1998–99, Regl Transport Strategy Div., 1992–2002, Dept for Regl Develt; Chief Exec., NI Roads Service, 2002–07. Mem., Bd of Govs, Royal Belfast Academical Instn, 2004–. *Recreations:* Rugby (played for many years for Instonians Rugby Club and coached Under 21 and First team squads, former Mem. Ulster Rugby Squad), playing tennis (at Belfast Boat Club and for Ulster Veterans). *Address:* Department of Agriculture and Rural Development, Dundonald House, Upper Newtownards Road, Belfast BT4 3SB. *T:* (028) 9052 4608; *e-mail:* malcolm.mckibbin@dardni.gov.uk. *Clubs:* Instonians Rugby; Belfast Boat.

McKIBBIN, Dr Ross Ian, FBA 1999; Fellow, St John's College, Oxford, 1972–2005, now Emeritus Research Fellow; *b* 25 Jan. 1942; *s* of Arnold Walter McKibbin and Nance Lilian (*née* Spence). *Educ:* Univ. of Sydney (BA, MA); St Antony's Coll., Oxford (DPhil 1970). Lectr in Hist., Univ. of Sydney, 1968–70; Jun. Res. Fellow, Christ Church, Oxford, 1970–72; CUF Lectr, Univ. of Oxford, 1972–2005; Tutor in Modern Hist., St John's Coll., Oxford, 1972–2005. *Publications:* The Evolution of the Labour Party 1910–1924, 1974, 2nd edn 1991; The Ideologies of Class, 1990; Classes and Cultures: England 1918–1951, 1998; (ed) M. Stopes, Married Love, 2004. *Recreations:* gardening, squash, tennis. *Address:* St John's College, Oxford OX1 3JP. *T:* (01865) 277344.

MACKIE, family name of **Baron Mackie of Benshie**.

MACKIE OF BENSHIE, Baron *cr* 1974 (Life Peer), of Kirriemuir; **George Yull Mackie**, CBE 1971; DSO 1944; DFC 1944; Chairman: Caithness Glass Ltd, 1966–84; Caithness Pottery Co. Ltd, 1975–84; The Benshie Cattle Co. Ltd, 1975–89; Land and Timber Services Ltd, since 1986; *b* 10 July 1919; *s* of late Maitland Mackie, OBE, Hon. LLD; *m* 1st, 1944, Lindsay Lyall Sharp (*d* 1985), *y d* of late Alexander and Isabella Sharp, OBE, Aberdeen; three *d* (one *s* decd); 2nd, 1988, Jacqueline, *widow* of Andrew Lane, and *d* of late Col Marcel Rauch. *Educ:* Aberdeen Grammar Sch.; Aberdeen Univ. Served War of 1939–45, RAF; Bomber Command, (DSO, DFC); Air Staff, 1944. Farming at Ballinshoe, Kirriemuir, 1945–89. Contested (L) South Angus, 1959; MP (L) Caithness and Sutherland, 1964–66; contested (L) Scotland NE, European Parliamentary election, 1979. Pres., Scottish Liberal Party, 1983–88 (Chm., 1965–70); Member: EEC Scrutiny Cttee (D), House of Lords; Liberal Shadow Admin; Exec., IPU; Council of Europe, 1986–97 (Mem. and Rapporteur, Cttee on Agricl and Rural Develt, 1990–97); WEU, 1986–; Liberal, then Lib Dem, Spokesman, House of Lords, 1975–2000: Devolution, Agriculture, Scotland, Industry. Chm., Cotswold Wine Co. (UK) Ltd, 1983–85. Dir, Scottish Ballet, 1986–88. Rector, Dundee Univ., 1980–83. Hon. LLD Dundee, 1982. *Publications:* Policy for Scottish Agriculture, 1963; Flying, Farming and Politics (memoir), 2004. *Address:* Benshie Cottage, Oathlaw, by Forfar, Angus DD8 3PQ. *T:* (01307) 850376. *Clubs:* Garrick, Farmers', Royal Air Force.

See also I. L. Aitken.

MACKIE, Air Cdre (Retd) Alastair Cavendish Lindsay, CBE 1966; DFC 1943 and Bar 1944; Director General, Health Education Council, 1972–82; Chairman, Ansador Ltd, 1983–2001; *b* 3 Aug. 1922; *s* of George Mackie, DSO, OBE, MD, Malvern, Worcs and May (*née* Cavendish); *m* 1944, Rachel Goodson; two *s. Educ:* Charterhouse. Royal Air Force, 1940–68; Under Treas., Middle Temple, 1968; Registrar, Architects' Registration Council, 1970; Sec., British Dental Assoc., 1971; Pres., Internat. Union for Health Educn, 1979–82. Life Pres., 3rd Parachute Bde, 6th Airborne Div. Meml Assoc., 2006. Vice-Pres., CND, 1990–. *Publication:* Some of the People All the Time, 2006. *Address:* 4 Warwick Drive, SW15 6LB. *T:* (020) 8789 4544. *Club:* Royal Air Force.

See also D. L. Mackie.

MACKIE, Prof. Andrew George; Professor of Applied Mathematics, 1968–88, Vice-Principal, 1975–80, University of Edinburgh; *b* 7 March 1927; *s* of late Andrew Mackie and Isobel Sigsworth Mackie (*née* Storey); *m* 1959, Elizabeth Maud Mackie (*née* Hebblethwaite); one *s* one *d. Educ:* Tain Royal Acad.; Univ. of Edinburgh (MA); Univ. of Cambridge (BA); Univ. of St Andrews (PhD). Lecturer, Univ. of Dundee, 1948–50; Bateman Res. Fellow and Instructor, CIT, 1953–55; Lecturer: Univ. of Strathclyde, 1955–56; Univ. of St Andrews, 1956–62; Prof. of Applied Maths, Victoria Univ. of

Wellington, NZ, 1962–65; Res. Prof., Univ. of Maryland, 1966–68. Visiting Professor: CIT, 1984; Univ. of NSW, 1985. FRSE 1962. *Publications:* Boundary Value Problems, 1965, 2nd edn 1989; numerous contribs to mathematical and scientific jls. *Recreation:* golf. *Address:* 31/7 Hermitage Drive, Edinburgh EH10 6BY. *T:* (0131) 447 2164.

MACKIE, Clive David Andrew, FCA, FSS; Secretary-General, Institute of Actuaries, 1983–92; *b* 29 April 1929; *s* of David and Lilian Mackie; *m* 1953, Averil Ratcliff; one *s* three *d. Educ:* Tiffin Sch., Kingston-on-Thames. FCA 1956; FSS 1982. Director: cos in Grundy (Teddington) Group, 1959–67; D. Sebel & Co. Ltd, 1967–70; post in admin of higher educn, 1970–73; Institute of Actuaries: Dep. Sec., 1973–77; Sec., 1977–83. Mem., Catenian Assoc., 1972–. *Recreations:* music (post 1780), cricket, carpentry, working with the Nat. Service of Talking Newspaper Assoc. of UK. *Address:* Ashes Lodge, Netherfield, E Sussex TN33 9PP. *T:* (01424) 774203. *Clubs:* Actuaries; Sussex CC.

MACKIE, David Lindsay, CBE 2004; **His Honour Judge Mackie;** QC 1998; a Deputy High Court Judge, since 1998; Senior Circuit Judge, since 2004, Judge in charge, London Mercantile Court, since 2006; *b* 15 Feb. 1946; *s* of Air Cdre Alastair Cavendish Lindsay Mackie, *qv*; *m* 1st, 1971 (marr. diss.); two *s* one *d*; 2nd, 1989. *Educ:* St Edmund Hall, Oxford (BA Modern History 1967). FCIArb 1990. Admitted Solicitor, 1971. Joined Allen & Overy, 1968, Partner, 1975–2004, Hd of Litigation, 1988–2003. A Recorder, 1992–2004. Mem., Civil and Family Cttee, Judicial Studies Bd, 1991–96; Dep. Chair, Royal Courts of Justice Advice Bureau, 1998–; Chairman: Financial Services and Markets Tribunal, 2001–; Pensions Regulator Tribunal, 2005–. Trustee, Law Works (formerly Solicitors Pro Bono Gp), 1997–. *Recreation:* climbing. *Address:* Royal Courts of Justice, Strand, WC2A 2LL.

MACKIE, Eileen Philomena Carroll; *see* Carroll, E. P.

MACKIE, Eric Dermott, OBE 1987; Executive Chairman, Swansea Dry Docks Ltd, 1995–2000; *b* 4 Dec. 1924; *s* of James Girvan and Ellen Dorothy Mackie; *m* 1950, Mary Victoria Christie; one *s* one *d. Educ:* Coll. of Technology, Belfast. CEng; MIMechE, FIMarEST, FRINA. 1st Class MoT Cert. (Steam and Diesel). Trained with James Mackie & Son (Textile Engrs), 1939–44; Design draughtsman, Harland & Wolff, Belfast, 1944–48; 2nd Engineer (sea-going) in both steam and diesel ships for Union Castle Mail Steamship Co., 1948–53; Harland & Wolff, Belfast, 1953–75: Test Engr; Manager, Shiprepair Dept; Gen. Manager i/c of Southampton branch; Gen. Manager i/c of ship prodn and ship repair, Belfast; Man. Dir, James Brown Hamer, S Africa, 1975–79; Chief Exec. and Man. Dir of Shiprepair in UK, British Shipbuilders, 1979–81; Chm. and Man. Dir, Govan Shipbuilders, later Govan Kvaerner Ltd, 1979–90. Former Mem., Governing Bd, British Marine Technology; Mem., Lloyds Gen. Cttee, 1979–, now Hon. Member. Denny Gold Medal, IMarE, 1987. *Publications:* articles for marine engrg instns on various subjects pertaining to marine engrg and gen. engrg. *Recreations:* golf, swimming, reading. *Address:* No 3 Castle Meadow, Whittingham, near Alnwick, Northumberland NE66 4SH. *T:* (01665) 574648. *Clubs:* Caledonian; Durban, Rand (Johannesburg, SA).

MACKIE, George, DFC 1944; RSW 1968; RDI 1973; freelance graphic artist and painter; Head of Design, Gray's School of Art, Aberdeen, 1958–80 (retd); *b* 17 July 1920; *s* of late David Mackie and late Kathleen Grantham; *m* 1952, Barbara Balmer, RSA, RSW, RGI; two *d*. Served Royal Air Force, 1940–46. Consultant in book design to Edinburgh University Press, 1960–87. Paintings in various private and public collections incl. HRH the Duke of Edinburgh's and Scottish Nat. Gall. of Modern Art. Major retrospective exhibitions: Books, mostly scholarly, and some Ephemera, Nat. Library of Scotland, 1991; Dartmouth Coll., NH, USA, 1991. *Publication:* Lynton Lamb: Illustrator, 1979. *Address:* 32 Broad Street, Stamford, Lincs PE9 1PJ. *T:* (01780) 753296.

MACKIE, Prof. George Owen, FRS 1991; DPhil; Professor of Biology, University of Victoria, 1968–94, Professor Emeritus since 1995; *b* 20 Oct. 1929; *s* of late Col (Frederick) Percival Mackie, CSI, OBE, IMS and Mary E. H. Mackie (*née* Owen); *m* 1956, Gillian V. Faulkner; three *s* two *d. Educ:* Oxford (BA 1954; MA 1956; DPhil 1956). FRSC 1982. Univ. of Alberta, 1957–68; Univ. of Victoria, 1968–; Chm., Biol. Dept, 1970–73. Editor, Canadian Jl of Zoology, 1980–89. Fry Medal, Canadian Soc. of Zoologists, 1989. *Publications:* (ed) Coelenterate Ecology and Behavior, 1976; numerous research articles in books and jls. *Recreations:* chamber music ('cello), earthenware pottery. *Address:* University of Victoria, Department of Biology, PO Box 3020, Victoria, BC V8W 3N5, Canada. *T:* (250) 7217146.

MACKIE, Karl Joseph, PhD; Chief Executive, Centre for Effective Dispute Resolution, since 1990; *b* 31 March 1947; *s* of John Mackie and Ethel Mackie (*née* Freeman); *m* 1st, 1968, Ann Douglas (marr. diss.); one *s* one *d*; 2nd, 2001, Eileen Philomena Carroll, *qv*; one step *d. Educ:* Buckhaven High Sch.; Univ. of Edinburgh (MA Hons), DipEd; Univ. of London (LLB ext.); Univ. of Nottingham (PhD 1987); Open Univ. (MBA 1990). CPsychol 1989; FCIArb 1992. Accredited Mediator, CEDR. Called to the Bar, Gray's Inn, 1982; Res. Associate, Univ. of Edinburgh, 1971–72; various posts, 1972–73; Lectr, then Sen. Lectr, Law and Social Psychology, Univ. of Nottingham, 1973–90; Partner, Network Associates Strategy Consultants, 1985–90. Hon. Prof. in Alternative Dispute Resolution, Univ. of Birmingham, 1994–2001; Special Prof. in Law, Univ. of Westminster, 2003–. Vice-Chm., Civil Mediation Council, 2003–. Member: Panel of Independent Mediators and Arbitrators, ACAS, 1980–; Singapore Internat. Commercial Mediators Panel, 2001–; Panel of Dist. Neutrals, Internat. Inst. for Conflict Prevention and Resolution, 2007–; Adv. Council, All Pty Parly Gp on Conflict, 2007–. Member: Educn Cttee, Bar Assoc. for Commerce, Finance and Industry, 1987–90; Law Soc. Specialisation Cttee, 1989–92. Chm., Write Away, 2003–06. FRSA 1993. Mem. editl cttee, various jls. *Publications:* (ed jtly) Learning Lawyers' Skills, 1989; Lawyers in Business and the Law Business, 1989; (ed) A Handbook of Dispute Resolution, 1991; (jtly) Commercial Dispute Resolution, 1995, 3rd edn as The ADR Practice Guide, 2007; (with E. Carroll) International Mediation: the art of business diplomacy, 2000, 2nd edn 2006; (ed jtly) The EU Mediation Atlas, 2004. *Recreations:* film, swimming, ski-ing, writing. *Address:* Centre for Effective Dispute Resolution, 70 Fleet Street, EC4Y 1EU. *T:* (020) 7536 6000.

MACKIE, Lily Edna Minerva, (Mrs John Betts), OBE 1986; Head Mistress, City of London School for Girls, 1972–86; *b* 14 April 1926; *d* of Robert Wood Mackie and Lilian Amelia Mackie (*née* Dennis); *m* 1985, John Betts (*d* 1992). *Educ:* Plaistow Grammar Sch.; University Coll., London (BA); Lycée de Jeunes Filles, Limoges; Université de Poitiers. Asst Mistress: Ilford County High Sch. for Girls, 1950–59; City of London Sch. for Girls, 1960–64; Head Mistress: Wimbledon County Sch., 1964–69; Ricards Lodge High Sch., Wimbledon, 1969–72. *Recreations:* theatre, music, gardening, travel. *Address:* Cotswold, 59–61 Upper Tooting Park, SW17 7SU.

MACKIE, Prof. Neil, CBE 1996; FRSE; international concert tenor; Professor of Singing, Royal College of Music, since 1985 (Head of Vocal Studies, 1994–2006); Professor, Fine Arts Faculty, Agder University, Kristiansand, Norway, since 2005; *b* 11 Dec. 1946; *yr s* of late William Fraser Mackie and Sheila Roberta (*née* Taylor); *m* 1973, Kathleen Mary Livingstone, soprano; two *d. Educ:* Aberdeen Grammar Sch.; Royal Scottish Acad. of Music and Drama (DipMusEd, DipRSAMD; FRSAMD 1992); Royal Coll. of Music (Foundn Scholar 1970; ARCM Hons; FRCM 1996). London recital début, Wigmore Hall, 1972; London concert début with English Chamber Orch., 1973; world premières include works by Peter Maxwell Davies, Britten, Henze and Kenneth Leighton; numerous recordings. Hon. DMus Univ. of Aberdeen, 1993. CStJ 1996. *Recreations:* reading, charity work, occasional gardening. *Address:* 70 Broadwood Avenue, Ruislip, Middx HA4 7XR. *T:* (01895) 632115; *e-mail:* neilmackie@talktalk.net. *Club:* Athenæum.

McKIE, Peter Halliday, CBE 1995; CChem, FRSC, CEng; Chairman: PHM Associates (NI) Ltd, since 1996; Health and Safety Executive for Northern Ireland, since 2005; *b* 20 March 1935; *s* of Harold and Winifred McKie; *m* 1959, Jennifer Anne Parkes; three *s* one *d. Educ:* Bangor Grammar Sch.; Queen's Univ., Belfast (BSc Chem.; Hon. DSc 1993). CChem, FRSC 1988; FCQI (FIQA 1987); CEng 1993. Shift Supervisor, Courtaulds Ltd, 1956–59; Supervisor, Du Pont Mfg, Londonderry, 1959–77; Manager, Du Pont Waynesbro Orlon Plant, USA, 1977–79; Asst Works Dir, Du Pont, Londonderry, 1979–81; Man. Dir, Du Pont Scandinavia and Du Pont Finland, 1981–84; Prodn Manager, Du Pont Europe, 1984–87; Chm., Du Pont (UK) Ltd, 1987–96; Manager, Du Pont Belle Plant, W Virginia, USA, 1995–96; Chm., QUBIS Ltd, 1998–2005. Chm., Industrial Res. & Technol. Unit, Dept. of Econ. Develt, NI, 1994–2001. Vis. Prof., Dept of Engrg, QUB, 1991–. FInstD 1987. *Recreations:* photography, sport, classic cars and motor cycles. *Address:* 3 The Rookery, Killinchy, Co. Down BT23 6SY.

McKIE, Robin Lewis; Science Editor, The Observer, since 1982; *b* Glasgow, 25 June 1950; *s* of Thomas McKie and Doreen McKie (*née* Pearson); *m* 1993, Sarah Anne Mitchell; one *s* one *d* (and one *d* decd). *Educ:* High Sch. of Glasgow; Univ. of Glasgow (BSc Hons). Trainee, Scotsman Pubns, 1974–78; Science corresp., THES, 1978–82. *Publications:* Genetic Jigsaw, 1988; (with W. Bodmer) The Book of Man, 1994; (with C. Stringer) African Exodus, 1996; Apeman, 2000; Face of Britain, 2006. *Recreations:* squash, walking, travelling on trains. *Address:* 36 Trinity Gardens, SW9 8DP. *T:* (020) 7733 7386; *e-mail:* robin.mckie@observer.co.uk. *Clubs:* Southbank Squash, Grafton Tennis.

MacKIE, Prof. Rona McLeod, (Lady Black), CBE 1999; MD, DSc; FRCP, FRCPath, FMedSci; FRSE; Professor of Dermatology, University of Glasgow, 1978–2001; *b* Dundee, 22 May 1940; *d* of late Prof. (James) Norman Davidson, CBE, FRS and Morag McLeod, PhD; *m* 1st, 1962, Euan Wallace MacKie (marr. diss. 1992); one *s* one *d*; 2nd, 1994, Sir James Whyte Black, *qv. Educ:* Channing Sch., London; Laurel Bank Sch., Glasgow; Univ. of Glasgow (MB ChB 1963; MD with commendation 1970; DSc 1994). FRCPath 1984; FRCP 1985. Junior hosp. posts, Glasgow, 1964–70; Lectr in Dermatology, Glasgow Univ., 1971–72; Consultant Dermatologist, Greater Glasgow Health Bd, 1972–78. Pres., British Assoc. of Dermatologists, 1994–95 (Sir Archibald Gray Medal, 1999); FRSE 1983 (Meeting Sec., 1994–97; Internat. Convener, 2002–); FMedSci 1998. *Publications:* textbooks and contribs to learned jls in field of skin cancer, particularly malignant melanoma. *Recreations:* family, opera, golf, gardening. *Address:* c/o University of Glasgow, Glasgow G12 8RZ; *e-mail:* R.M.Mackie@clinmed.gla.ac.uk. *Club:* Glasgow Art.

MACKILLIGIN, David Patrick Robert, CMG 1994; HM Diplomatic Service, retired; Governor, British Virgin Islands, 1995–98; *b* 29 June 1939; *s* of R. S. Mackilligin, CMG, OBE, MC and Patricia (*née* Waldegrave); *m* 1976, Gillian Margaret Zuill Walker; two *d. Educ:* St Mary's Coll., Winchester; Pembroke Coll., Oxford (2nd Cl. Hons PPE). Asst Principal, CRO, 1961–62; Third, later Second Sec., Pakistan, 1962–66; Asst Private Sec. to Sec. of State for Commonwealth Relations, 1966–68; Private Sec. to Minister Without Portfolio, 1968–69; Dep. Comr, Anguilla, 1969–71 (Actg Comr, July–Aug. 1970); First Sec., Ghana, 1971–73; First Sec., Head of Chancery and Consul, Cambodia, 1973–75 (Chargé d'Affaires at various times); FCO, 1975–80 (Asst Head of W African Dept, 1978–80); Counsellor (Commercial and Aid), Indonesia, 1980–85; NATO Defence Coll., Rome, 1985–86; Counsellor (Economic and Commercial), and Dir of Trade Promotion, Canberra, 1986–90; High Comr, Belize, 1991–95. *Recreations:* walking and swimming in remote places, ruins, second-hand bookshops, theatre, literature. *Address:* c/o Foreign and Commonwealth Office, King Charles Street, SW1A 2AH. *Clubs:* Oxford and Cambridge, Reform, Royal Commonwealth Society.

McKILLOP, Elizabeth Dorothy; Keeper, Department of Asia, since 2004, and Director of Collections, since 2007, Victoria and Albert Museum; *b* 28 May 1953; *d* of Norman R. and Mary M. McConochie; *m* 1973, Andrew C. McKillop; one *s* one *d. Educ:* Univ. of Glasgow (MA 1972); Churchill Coll., Cambridge (MA 1975); University Coll. London (MSc 2004). Ed., BBC Monitoring Service, 1979–81; Curator: Chinese Collection, BL, 1981–90; Samsung Gall. of Korean Art, V&A, 1990–93; Korean Collection, BL, 1993–2004. *Publications:* Korean Art and Design, 1992; North Korean Culture and Society, 2004. *Recreations:* food, travel. *Address:* Victoria and Albert Museum, S Kensington, SW7 2RL. *T:* (020) 7942 2000; *e-mail:* bethmckillop@hotmail.com.

McKILLOP, Prof. James Hugh, FRCP, FRCR, FMedSci; Muirhead Professor of Medicine, since 1989, and Deputy Executive Dean of Medicine, since 2007, University of Glasgow; *b* 20 June 1948; *s* of Patrick McKillop and Helen Theresa McKillop (*née* Kilpatrick); *m* 1972, Caroline Annis Oakley; two *d. Educ:* St Aloysius' Coll.; Univ. of Glasgow (BSc, MB ChB; PhD 1979). FRCPGlas 1986; FRCPE 1990; FRCP 1992; FRCR 1994. University of Glasgow: Lectr in Medicine, 1975–82; Sen. Lectr in Medicine, 1982–89; Associate Dean for Med. Educn, 2000–03; Hd, Undergraduate Med. Sch., 2003–06. Harkness Fellow, Stanford Univ., California, 1979–80. Chairman: Intercollegiate Standing Cttee on Nuclear Medicine, 1995–99; Admin of Radioactive Substances Adv. Cttee, DoH, 1996–2004; Scottish Med. and Scientific Adv. Cttee, 2001–07; NHS Educn Scotland Med. Adv. Gp, 2004–; Scottish Deans Med. Curriculum Gp, 2005–. Team Leader, GMC Quality Assurance of Basic Med. Educn, 2003–. Pres., British Nuclear Medicine Soc., 1990–92; Congress Pres., Eur. Assoc. of Nuclear Medicine, 1997; Mem., Exec. Cttee, Assoc. of Physicians of UK and Ire., 2000–03. FMedSci 1998. *Publications:* (with D. L. Citrin) Atlas of Technetium Bone Scans, 1978; (with A. G. Chalmers and P. J. Robinson) Imaging in Clinical Practice, 1988; (with I. Fogelman) Clinicians' Guide to Nuclear Medicine: benign and malignant bone disease, 1991; 250 papers mainly on nuclear medicine and cardiology. *Recreations:* opera (esp. Verdi), reading fiction, soccer. *Address:* Wolfson Medical School Building, University of Glasgow, University Avenue, Glasgow G12 8QQ. *T:* (0141) 330 8041.

McKILLOP, Murdoch Lang, CA; Partner, Kroll Talbot Hughes (formerly Talbot Hughes McKillop) LLP, since 2003; *b* 30 Oct. 1947; *s* of Graham Lang McKillop and Margaret Morris (*née* Stark); *m* 1972, Elizabeth Leith; two *d. Educ:* Kelvinside Acad., Glasgow; Univ. of Strathclyde (BA Hons 1971). CA 1975; FSPI 1996. Joined Arthur Andersen, Glasgow, as grad. trainee, 1971; Partner, 1984; Jt Administrator, Maxwell Private Gp, 1991; Joint Administrative Receiver: Leyland Daf Ltd, 1993; Ferranti Internat. plc, 1994, and others; Worldwide Head, Corporate Recovery and Turnaround, Arthur Andersen, 1996–98. Pres., Soc. of Practitioners of Insolvency, 1998–99; Jun. Vice-Pres., 2001–02, Sen. Vice-Pres., 2002–03, Pres., 2003–04, ICAS.

Recreation: sailing. *Address:* 415 Spice Quay, Butlers Wharf, 32 Shad Thames, SE1 2YL. *Club:* Royal Highland Yacht (Oban).

McKILLOP, Sir Thomas Fulton Wilson, (Sir Tom), Kt 2002; PhD; FRS 2005; FRSE; Chairman, Royal Bank of Scotland Group, since 2006 (Deputy Chairman, 2005–06); *b* 19 March 1943; *s* of Hugh McKillop and Annie (*née* Wilson); *m* 1966, Elizabeth Kettle; one *s* two *d. Educ:* Irvine Royal Acad.; Univ. of Glasgow (BSc 1st Cl. Hons; PhD Chem. 1968); Centre de Mécanique Ondulatoire Appliquée, Paris. Res. scientist, ICI Corporate Lab., 1969–75; ICI Pharmaceuticals: Hd, Natural Products Res., 1975–78; Res. Dir, France, 1978–80; Chemistry Manager, 1980–84; Gen. Manager, Res., 1984–85, Develt, 1985–89; Technical Dir, 1989–94; Zeneca Gp, then AstraZeneca: CEO, Zeneca Pharmaceuticals, 1994–99; Dir, 1996–2006; Chief Exec., 1999–2006. Non-executive Director: Amersham Internat. PLC, 1992–97; Nycomed Amersham PLC, 1997–2000; Lloyds TSB Gp PLC, 1999–2004. President: European Fedn of Pharmaceutical Industries and Assocs, 2002–04; Science Council, 2007–. Trustee, Council for Industry and Higher Educn, 2002–. Pro-Chancellor and Mem. Gen. Council, Univ. of Leicester, 1998–2007. MRI; FRSC; MACS; Mem., Soc. for Drug Res. Trustee, Darwin Trust of Edinburgh, 1995–. FMedSci 2002; FRSE 2003. Hon. Fellow: Univ. of Lancs, 2004; Manchester Interdisciplinary Biocentre, 2006; Hon. FIMechE 2006. Hon. LLD: Manchester, 1999; Dundee, 2003; Hon. DSc: Glasgow, Leicester, Huddersfield, 2000; Nottingham, 2001; St Andrews, Salford, 2004; Manchester, 2005; Lancaster, 2007; Hon. Dr: Middx, 2000; Paisley, 2006; Hon. DLitt Heriot-Watt, 2006. *Recreations:* music, sport, reading, walking, carpentry. *Address:* Royal Bank of Scotland Group, Gogarburn, Edinburgh EH12 1HQ. *Club:* Wilmslow Golf.

MACKINLAY, Andrew Stuart; MP (Lab) Thurrock, since 1992; *b* 24 April 1949; *s* of Danny Mackinlay and late Monica (*née* Beanes); *m* 1972, Ruth Segar; two *s* one *d. Educ:* Salesian Coll., Chertsey. ACIS; DMA. A clerk, Surrey CC, 1965–75; Nalgo official, 1975–92. An Opposition Whip, 1992–93; Member: Transport Select Cttee, 1992–97; Foreign Affairs Select Cttee, 1997–; Chm., All-Party Poland Gp, 1997–. *Recreations:* studying battlefields of World War I in France and Belgium, non-league football, Ireland and Poland. *Address:* House of Commons, SW1A 0AA. *T:* (020) 7219 3000. *Club:* Chadwell Working Men's.

MACKINLAY, (Jack) Lindsay; DL; Canon Treasurer, York Minster, 2000–07, now Canon Emeritus; *b* 24 Jan. 1936; *m* 1961, Catherine Elizabeth Houston; one *s* one *d.* FCA, FCMA. Rowntree plc, 1964–89 (Dir, 1973–89); Dir, 1990–2002, Chm., 1995–2002, Bradford & Bingley Bldg Soc., subseq. Bradford & Bingley plc. Dir, Argos, 1990–97; Chm., RPC Gp, 1992–2000. DL N Yorks, 2005. *Recreations:* golf, music. *Address:* The Cottage, Main Street, Stillington, York YO61 1JU.

McKINLAY, Peter, CBE 1998; Chairman, Wise Group, 1998–2001; *b* 29 Dec. 1939; *s* of late Peter McKinlay and of Mary Clegg (*née* Hamill); *m* 1963, Anne Rogerson Aitken Thomson; two *s* one *d. Educ:* Univ. of Glasgow (MA Hons). GPO HQ, Edinburgh, 1963–67; Scottish Office, 1967–91: Private Sec. to Minister of State, 1974–75; Director, Scottish Prison Service, 1988–91; Chief Executive, Scottish Homes, 1991–99. Nat. Exec., First Div. Assoc., 1977–80. Non-exec. Dir, D. S. Crawford Ltd, 1984–86; Chm., Bute Beyond 2000 (formerly Bute Partnership), 1993–98; Member: Bd, Cairngorms Partnership, 1998–99; Accounts Commn for Scotland, 2003–06. Dir, Common Purpose, 1993–97. FRSA 1998. Hon. DBA Napier, 1999. *Recreations:* family, friends, garden, TV, reading, food, drink. *Club:* Machrihanish Golf.

McKINLAY, Robert Murray, CBE 1993; FREng, FRAeS; President, Bristol Chamber of Commerce and Industry, 1994–97; *b* 12 Jan. 1934; *s* of Robert Graham McKinlay and Mary Murray; *m* 1957, Ellen Aikman Stewart; two *s. Educ:* Vale of Leven Acad.; Royal Tech. Coll., Glasgow (BSc Hons, ARTC). Flight testing and project engineering, Bristol Helicopters and Westlands, 1956–66; British Aircraft Corporation, 1966–79: Systems Develt Manager; Designer in charge; Asst Chief Engr; Asst Dir, Flight Test; Concorde Design Dir; British Aerospace, 1979–94: Dir, Airbus; Gp Dir, Man. Dir, Airbus Div.; Man. Dir, Commercial Aircraft; Chm., Airbus, 1991–94. Non-exec. Dir, B. F. Goodrich, Aerospace, Europe, 1998–2003 (Consultant, 2003–06). FREng (FEng 1992). Hon. DTech Bristol, 1991; Hon. DEng Glasgow, 2001. British Gold Medal, RAeS, 1995. *Recreations:* sailing, golf, piano, woodworking. *Address:* 43 Glenavon Park, Bristol BS9 1RW. *T:* (0117) 968 6253. *Club:* Society of Merchant Venturers (Bristol).

McKINLEY, John Key; Chairman and Chief Executive Officer, Texaco Inc., 1980–86 (President, 1971–83), retired; *b* Tuscaloosa, Ala, 24 March 1920; *s* of Virgil Parks McKinley and Mary Emma (*née* Key); *m* 1946, Helen Grace Heare; two *s. Educ:* Univ. of Alabama (BS Chem. Engrg, 1940; MS Organic Chemistry, 1941); Harvard Univ. (Graduate, Advanced Management Program, 1962). Served War, AUS, Eur. Theatre of Ops, 1941–45 (Major; Bronze Star). Texaco Inc., 1941–86: Asst Dir of Res., Beacon, NY, 1957–59; Asst to the Vice-Pres., 1959–60; Manager of Commercial Develt Processes, 1960; Gen. Man., Worldwide Petrochemicals, NYC, 1960–67, Vice-Pres., Petrochem. Dept, 1967–71 (also Vice-Pres. i/c Supply and Distribution); Sen. Vice-Pres., Worldwide Refining, Petrochems, Supply and Distbn, 1971, Pres. and Dir, 1971–83; Director: Texaco Inc., 1971–92; Merck & Co., Inc., 1982–90; Manufacturers Hanover Corp., 1980–90; Hanover Trust Co., 1980–90; Martin Marietta, 1985–90; Apollo Computer, 1987–89; Burlington Industries Inc., 1977–87; Federated Dept Stores, Inc., 1990–. Hon. Dir, Amer. Petroleum Inst. Man. Dir, Met. Opera Assoc., 1980–; National Chm., Met. Opera Centennial Fund, 1980. Dir, Americas Soc. Member: Bd of Overseers, Meml Sloan-Kettering Cancer Center, 1981–91; Brookings Council, 1986; Business Council. Fellow, Amer. Inst. of Chem. Engrs; Sesquicentennial Hon. Prof., Univ. of Alabama; Hon. LLD: Univ. of Alabama, 1972; Troy State Univ., 1974. *Address:* Tuscaloosa, AL, USA; Darien, CT 06820; Buffalo, Wyoming. *Clubs:* Brook (NYC); Wee Burn Country (Darien); Augusta National Golf (Georgia); Blind Brook (Purchase, NY); North River Yacht (Tuscaloosa).

McKINNEY, Her Honour (Sheila Mary) Deirdre; a Circuit Judge, 1981–2001; *b* 20 Oct. 1928; *d* of Patrick Peter McKinney and Mary Edith (*née* Conoley). *Educ:* Convent of the Cross, Boscombe, Bournemouth. Called to the Bar, Lincoln's Inn, 1951; a Recorder of the Crown Court, 1978–81.

MacKINNON, Charles Archibald, CB 2005; Transformation Director, Pension Service, Department for Work and Pensions, 2004–07; *b* 1 July 1950; *s* of Ian MacDougall MacKinnon and Colina (*née* Beaton); *m* 1972, Jane Halpin; one *s* two *d. Educ:* Woodside Sen. Secondary Sch.; Sheffield Hallam Univ. (MBA). Various field operational mgt roles, 1968–84; Hd of Section, Policy and Pensions, MSC, 1984–86; Project Manager, then Sen. Manager, various large projects in Employment Service, 1986–98; Benefits Agency: Dir, Field Ops (Scotland and N England), 1998–2000; Dep. Chief Exec., 2000–02; Chief Operating Officer, Pension Service, 2002–04. *Recreations:* squash, racquet ball, badminton, chess, theatre, reading, football spectator.

McKINNON, Rt Hon. Donald Charles, ONZ 2008; PC 1992; Commonwealth Secretary-General, 2000–08; *b* 27 Feb. 1939; *s* of Maj.-Gen. Walter Sneddon McKinnon, CB, CBE and Anna Bloomfield McKinnon (*née* Plimmer); *m* 1st, 1964, Patricia Maude Moore (marr. diss. 1995); three *s* one *d*; 2nd, 1995, Clare de Lore; one *s. Educ:* Lincoln Univ., New Zealand. AREINZ. Farm Manager, 1964–72; Farm Management Consultant, 1973–78; Real Estate Agent, 1974–78. MP (Nat. Party) NZ, 1978–99, for Albany, 1978–96; Dep. Leader of the Opposition, 1987–90; Dep. Prime Minister, 1990–96; Leader of the House, 1992–96; Minister: of External Relations, then Foreign Affairs, and Trade, 1990–99; of Pacific Island Affairs, 1991–98; for Disarmament and Arms Control, 1996–99; i/c War Pensions, 1998–99. *Recreations:* enthusiastic jogger and tennis player, horse riding. *Address:* c/o Commonwealth Secretariat, Marlborough House, Pall Mall, SW1Y 5HX.

McKINNON, Sir James, Kt 1992; FCMA; Director General, Office of Gas Supply, 1986–93; *b* 1929. *Educ:* Camphill School. CA 1952–2002, FCMA 1956. Company Secretary, Macfarlane Lang & Co. Ltd, Glasgow, 1955–65; Business Consultant, McLintock, Moores & Murray, Glasgow, 1965–67; Finance Director, Imperial Group plc, London, 1967–86. Chairman: Scotia Hldgs, 1992–2001; MAI plc, 1992–94; Ionica, 1993–98; Trafficmaster plc, 1994–2004; Arriva plc, 1994–99; Thorn Security Systems Ltd, 1994–96; Tyzack Precision plc, 1994–99; Discovery Trust plc, 1995–2006; Glass's Guide Ltd, 1996–98; Dep. Chm., United News & Media, 1994–2000; Director: Admiral plc, 1994–2000; F&C Private Equity Trust plc, 2005–06. Pres., Inst. of Chartered Accountants of Scotland, 1985–86. *Publications:* papers to learned jls and articles in Accountants' magazine. *Recreation:* ski-ing.

MacKINNON, Kenneth Alasdair, RD 1971; WS; NP; JP; Lord-Lieutenant of Argyll and Bute, since 2002 (Clerk of Lieutenancy, 1974–95; Vice Lord-Lieutenant, 2001–02); *b* 8 March 1936; *s* of Neil MacKinnon, WS and Janet Alison Mackenzie; *m* 1963, Anne Clare Valentine; one *s* two *d. Educ:* Edinburgh Acad.; Fettes Coll. (Pres., Old Fettesian Assoc., 1989–91); Pembroke Coll., Cambridge (BA 1959); Edinburgh Univ. (LLB 1961). Nat. Service, RN, 1954–56; Midshipman, RNVR, 1955; Lt Comdr, RNR, 1956–86. Apprentice Solicitor, Messrs Dundas & Wilson, CS, 1959–62; WS, 1962; D. M. MacKinnon, Oban: Asst Solicitor, 1962–63; Partner, 1963–96; Sen. Partner, 1989–96. Dean, Oban Faculty of Solicitors, 1995–97. Dir, Glasgow Local Bd, Commercial Union Assce, 1981–83. Hon. Sheriff, N Strathclyde at Oban, 1997. Council Member: WS Soc., 1993–96; Macmillan Cancer Relief, subseq. Macmillan Cancer Support, 2002–05 (Chm., Oban and Dist Br., 1993–). Pres., Oban Sea Cadet Unit, 2007–. Elder, C of S, 1975–2007. DL 1996, JP 2002, Argyll and Bute. Sec., 1963–76, Trustee, 2002–, Argyllshire Gathering. *Recreations:* sailing, game shooting, motoring, watching Rugby. *Address:* Ardcuam, Gallanach Road, Oban, Argyll PA34 4PE. *T:* (01631) 562325. *Club:* Royal Highland Yacht (Cdre, 1988–89, Trustee, 2003–).

McKINNON, Prof. Kenneth Richard, AO 1995; FACE; Chairman: McKinnon Walker Pty Ltd, since 1995; IMB Pty Ltd, 2000–04; Chairman, Australian Press Council, since 2000; *b* 23 Feb. 1931; *s* of Charles and Grace McKinnon; *m* 1st, 1956 (marr. diss.); one *s*; 2nd, 1981, Suzanne H., *d* of W. Milligan. *Educ:* Univ. of Adelaide; Univ. of Queensland (BA; BEd); Harvard Univ. (EdD). FACE 1972. Teacher, headmaster and administrator, 1957–65; Dir of Educn, Papua New Guinea, 1966–73; Chm., Australian Schs Commn, 1973–81; Vice-Chancellor, 1981–95, and Prof. Emeritus, Univ. of Wollongong; Vice-Chancellor: James Cook Univ. of N Qld, 1997; Northern Territory Univ., 2002–03. Chairman: Bd of Educn, Vic, 1982–85; Australian Nat. Commn for UNESCO, 1984–88; Illawara Technology Corp., 1983–; Marine Sci. and Technol. Review, 1988; Nuclear Res. Reactor Review, 1993; Reviewer, Marine Scis Orgns, 1993. Pres., AVCC, 1991–92. Member: Australia Council, 1974–77 (Dep. Chm., 1976–77); Primary Industries and Energy Res. Council, 1991–92; Prime Minister's Science Council, 1991–92. Consultant in the Arts, Aust. Govt, 1981. Dir, Coll. of Law, NSW, 1993–. Hon. DLitt: Wollongong, 1994; Deakin, 1994; NSW, 1995; DUniv James Cook, 1998. *Publications:* Realistic Educational Planning, 1973; Oceans of Wealth, 1988; Benchmarking in Universities, 2000; articles in jls and papers. *Recreations:* swimming, theatre, music, reading. *Address:* 14 Norfolk House, 1 Sutherland Crescent, Darling Point, NSW 2027, Australia. *T:* (2) 93623427, *Fax:* (2) 93632551. *Club:* Commonwealth (Canberra, Australia).

McKINNON, Malcolm; *see* McKinnon, W. M.

MACKINNON, Neil Joseph; Sheriff of Tayside Central and Fife at Falkirk, since 2005; *b* 24 Jan. 1956; *s* of late Donald Patrick Mackinnon and Catriona Traese Mackinnon (*née* Sinclair); *m* 1990, Anne Helen Gavagan; one *d. Educ:* St Aloysius' Coll., Glasgow; Univ. of Glasgow (LLB Hons 1978). Admitted solicitor, Scotland, 1980; Advocate, Scots Bar, 1984. Floating Sheriff, Edinburgh, 2000–05. Mem., Rules Council, Court of Session, 1997–99. *Recreations:* travel, hill-walking. *Address:* c/o Sheriff Court House, Main Street, Camelon, Falkirk FK1 4AR. *Club:* Broomieknowe Golf.

MACKINNON, Dame Patricia; *see* Mackinnon, Dame U. P.

MacKINNON, Prof. Roderick, MD; John D. Rockefeller Jr Professor and Head of Laboratory of Molecular Neurobiology and Biophysics, Rockefeller University, since 1996; *b* 19 Feb. 1956; *m* Alice Lee. *Educ:* Brandeis Univ. (BA 1978); Tufts Univ. (MD 1982). Harvard Univ., 1985–86; Brandeis Univ., 1986–89; Asst, later Prof., Dept of Neurobiol., Harvard Med. Sch., 1989–96; Investigator, Howard Hughes Med. Inst., 1997–. (Jtly) Nobel Prize for Chemistry, 2003. *Address:* Laboratory of Molecular Neurobiology and Biophysics, Rockefeller University, 1230 York Avenue, New York, NY 10021, USA.

MacKINNON, Rowan Dorothy; *see* Pelling, R. D.

McKINNON, Hon. Sir Stuart (Neil), Kt 1988; **Hon. Mr Justice McKinnon;** a Judge of the High Court of Justice, Queen's Bench Division, since 1988; *b* 14 Aug. 1938; *s* of His Honour Neil Nairn McKinnon, QC; *m* 1st, 1966, Rev. Helena Jacoba Sara (*née* van Hoorn) (marr. diss. 1999); two *d*; 2nd, 2001, Michelle Jean Mary Withers. *Educ:* King's Coll. Sch., Wimbledon; Council of Legal Educn; Trinity Hall, Cambridge (BA, LLB 1963; MA 1967). Called to the Bar, Lincoln's Inn, 1960, Bencher, 1987; Junior at the Common Law Bar, 1964–80; QC 1980; a Recorder, 1985–88. Chm., Lord Chancellor's Middx Adv. Cttee on JPs, 1990–97. Pres., Cambridge Univ. Law Soc., 1962–63. *Recreation:* golf. *Address:* Royal Courts of Justice, Strand, WC2A 2LL. *Club:* Royal Porthcawl Golf.

See also W. N. McKinnon.

MACKINNON, Dame (Una) Patricia, DBE 1977 (CBE 1972); *b* Brisbane, 24 July 1911; *d* of Ernest T. and Pauline Bell; *m* 1936, Alistair Scobie Mackinnon; one *s* one *d. Educ:* Glennie School and St Margaret's School, Queensland. Member Cttee of Management, Royal Children's Hospital, Melbourne, 1948–79; Vice-President, 1958; President, 1965–79; Chm., Research Bd, 1967–85. *Recreations:* gardening, reading history and biographies. *Address:* Lisson Manor, 12 Lisson Grove, Hawthorn, Vic 3122, Australia. *Club:* Alexandra (Melbourne).

McKINNON, Warwick Nairn; His Honour Judge Warwick McKinnon; a Circuit Judge, since 1998; Resident Judge, Croydon Crown Court, since 2006; *b* 11 Nov. 1947; *s* of His Honour Neil McKinnon, QC; *m* 1978, Nichola Juliet Lloyd; one *s* one *d*. *Educ:* King's Coll. Sch., Wimbeldon; Christ's Coll., Cambridge (MA). Called to the Bar, Lincoln's Inn, 1970; in practice on SE Circuit; Asst Recorder, 1991–95; Recorder, 1995–98. Chm., Essex Criminal Justice Strategy Cttee, 1999–2001; Magistrates Liaison Judge and Chm., Area Judicial Forum for SE London, 2006–. Hon. Recorder, Croydon, 2008–. *Recreations:* music, opera, travel, gardening, golf. *Address:* Croydon Combined Court Centre, The Law Courts, Altyre Road, Croydon, Surrey CR9 5AB. *T:* (020) 8410 4700.

See also Hon. Sir S. N. McKinnon.

McKINNON, (William) Malcolm; Chief Executive, SITPRO Ltd, since 2005; *b* Ilford, Essex, 14 Dec. 1953; *s* of William Malcolm McKinnon and Maureen Helena Margaret McKinnon; *m* 1978, Christine Elizabeth Platt; two *d*. *Educ:* Southend High Sch. for Boys; Inst. of Export (MIEx (Grad.) 1982). DTI, then Dept of Trade, subseq. DTI, 1973–2005; EO, Gen. Export Services, 1973–80; Third Sec., Consulate-Gen., Vancouver, 1977–78; EO, Commercial Relns with Republic of Korea, 1980–82; HEO, Internat. Trade Policy, 1983–86; Private Sec., 1987–88; Head: Trade with Soviet Union, 1988–90; EU Insce Policy, 1990–94; WTO Trade in Services, 1994–2005. Mem., Borough of Southend Swimming and Trng Club (Chm., 1992–2000 and 2003–08). Freeman, City of London, 2007. *Recreations:* travel, photography, hill and coastal walking, music, learning to ski and play golf, swimming. *Address:* SITPRO Ltd, Kingsgate House, 66–74 Victoria Street, SW1E 6SW. *T:* (020) 7215 8120, *Fax:* (020) 7215 4242; *e-mail:* malcolm.mckinnon@sitpro.org.uk.

MACKINTOSH, family name of **Viscount Mackintosh of Halifax**.

MACKINTOSH OF HALIFAX, 3rd Viscount *cr* 1957; **John Clive Mackintosh,** FCA; Bt 1935; Baron 1948; Partner, PricewaterhouseCoopers (formerly Price Waterhouse), since 1992; *b* 9 Sept. 1958; *s* of 2nd Viscount Mackintosh of Halifax, OBE, BEM; *S* father, 1980; *m* 1st, 1982, Elizabeth Lakin (marr. diss. 1993); two *s*; 2nd, 1995, Claire Jane, *y d* of Stanislaw Nowak; one *d*. *Educ:* The Leys School, Cambridge; Oriel College, Oxford (MA in PPE). FCA 1995. President, Oxford Univ. Conservative Assoc., 1979. Chartered accountant. *Recreations:* cricket, bridge, golf. *Heir: s* Hon. Thomas Harold George Mackintosh, *b* 8 Feb. 1985. *Address:* (office) 1 Embankment Place, WC2N 6RH. *Clubs:* MCC, Royal Automobile, Beefsteak; Ocean Reef (Key Largo).

MACKINTOSH, Sir Cameron (Anthony), Kt 1996; producer of musicals; Chairman, Cameron Mackintosh Ltd, since 1981; Director, Delfont/Mackintosh, since 1991; *b* 17 Oct. 1946; *s* of late Ian Mackintosh and of Diana Mackintosh. *Educ:* Prior Park Coll., Bath. Hon. Fellow, St Catherine's Coll., Oxford, 1990. Decided to be producer of musical stage shows at age 8, after seeing Slade's Salad Days; spent brief period at Central Sch. of Speech and Drama; stage hand at Theatre Royal, Drury Lane; later Asst Stage Manager; worked with Emile Littler, 1966, with Robin Alexander, 1967; produced first musical, 1969. Owner of Prince Edward, Prince of Wales, Strand, Gielgud, Wyndhams and Albery Theatres. *London productions:* Little Women, 1967; Anything Goes, 1969; Trelawney, 1972; The Card, 1973; Winnie the Pooh, 1974; Owl and Pussycat Went to See, 1975; Godspell, 1975; Side by Side by Sondheim, 1976; Oliver!, 1977, 1994, 2008; Diary of a Madam, 1977; After Shave, 1977; Gingerbread Man, 1978; Out on a Limb, 1978; My Fair Lady, 1979, 2001; Oklahoma!, 1980; Tomfoolery, 1980; Jeeves Takes Charge, 1981; Cats, 1981; Song and Dance, 1982; Blondel, 1983; Little Shop of Horrors, 1983; Abbacadabra, 1983; The Boyfriend, 1984; Les Misérables, 1985; Café Puccini, 1985; Phantom of the Opera, 1986; Follies, 1987; Miss Saigon, 1989; Just So, 1990; Five Guys Named Moe, 1991; Moby Dick, 1992; Putting It Together, 1992; Carousel, 1993; Martin Guerre, 1996; The Fix, 1997; The Witches of Eastwick, 2000; Mary Poppins, 2004. Observer Award for Outstanding Achievement in Memory of Kenneth Tynan, Olivier Awards, 1991. *Recreations:* taking holidays, cooking. *Address:* Cameron Mackintosh Ltd, 1 Bedford Square, WC1B 3RB. *T:* (020) 7637 8866. *Club:* Groucho.

MACKINTOSH, Catherine Anne, (Mrs C. D. Peel), FRCM, FRSAMD; violinist; *b* 6 May 1947; *d* of late Duncan Robert Mackintosh and Mary Isa Mackintosh; *m* 1973, Charles David Peel; one *s* one *d*. *Educ:* Cranborne Chase Sch.; Dartington Coll. of Arts; Royal Coll. of Music (ARCM; FRCM 1994). FRSAMD 1998. Prof. of Baroque and Classical Violin and Viola, Royal Coll. of Music, 1977–99. Visiting Professor of Early Music: RSAMD, 1989–; RCM; RAM; Zagreb Acad.; Vis. Prof. of Baroque Violin, Koninklijk Conservatorium, 2008–. Leader, Acad. of Ancient Music, 1973–87; Mem., Julian Bream Consort, 1978–88; Founding Mem., Purcell Quartet, 1984–; Co-Leader, Orch. of Age of Enlightenment, 1987–2007; Artistic Dir, Aestas Musica Internat. Summer Sch. of Music and Dance, Croatia, 1996–2007. *Recreations:* trombone playing, crosswords, eating. *Address:* 15 Ranelagh Road, W5 5RJ.

MACKINTOSH, Ian, FCA; Chairman, Accounting Standards Board, since 2004; *b* 18 Feb. 1946; *s* of Angus John Mackintosh and Jean Elizabeth Mackintosh (*née* Sanders); *m* 1970, Patricia Caroline (*née* McMahon) (*d* 2006); two *s*. *Educ:* Auckland Grammar Sch.; Auckland Univ. (BComm). Partner, Coopers & Lybrand, Australia, 1976–96, Consultant, 1996–2000; Chief Accountant, Australian Securities & Investment Commn, 2000–02; Manager, Financial Mgt, World Bank, 2002–04. Adjunct Prof., Univ. of Canberra, 2000–. Chm., Public Sector Cttee, Internat. Fedn of Accountants, 2000–03. FCPA. *Recreations:* golf, swimming, music, reading. *Address:* Accounting Standards Board, 5th Floor, Aldwych House, 71–91 Aldwych, WC2B 4HN. *T:* (020) 7492 2434, *Fax:* (020) 7492 2399; *e-mail:* i.mackintosh@frc-asb.org.uk.

McKINTOSH, His Honour Ian Stanley; a Circuit Judge, 1988–2007; *b* 23 April 1938; *s* of late (Herbert) Stanley and of Gertrude McKintosh; *m* 1967, (Alison) Rosemary, *e d* of Kenneth Blayney Large and Margaret Wharton Large; two *s* one *d*. *Educ:* Leeds Grammar Sch.; Exeter Coll., Oxford (MA). Admitted Solicitor of the Supreme Court, 1966. Served RAF, 1957–59. Articled to Town Clerk, Chester and to Laces & Co., Liverpool, 1962–66; Dept of Solicitor to Metropolitan Police, New Scotland Yard, 1966–69; Partner, Lemon & Co., Swindon, 1969–88; a Dep. Circuit Judge, 1976–81; a Recorder, 1981–88. Mem., Local Gen. and Area Appeals Cttees, SW Legal Aid Area, 1970–89. Mem., Stonham Housing Assoc., 1986–88 (Chm., Swindon Br.). *Recreations:* family, cricket, sailing, rowing, talking. *Clubs:* MCC, XL.

MACKINTOSH, (John) Malcolm, CMG 1975; HM Diplomatic Service, retired; *b* 25 Dec. 1921; *s* of late James Mackintosh, MD, LLD, FRCP, and Marjorie Mackintosh; *m* 1946, Elena Grafova; one *s* one *d* (and one *s* decd). *Educ:* Mill Hill; Edinburgh Academy; Glasgow Univ. MA (Hons) 1948. Served War, Middle East, Italy and Balkans, 1942–46; Allied Control Commn, Bulgaria, 1945–46. Glasgow Univ., 1946–48. Programme Organiser, BBC Overseas Service, 1948–60; Foreign Office, engaged on research, 1960–68; Asst Sec., Cabinet Office, 1968–87. Sen Fellow in Soviet Studies, IISS, 1989–91; Hon. Sen. Res. Fellow, KCL, 1987–91; Hon. Lectr in Internat. Relns, St Andrews Univ., 1991–97; Hon. Vis. Fellow, SSEES, 1994–2001. *Publications:* Strategy and Tactics of Soviet Foreign Policy, 1962, 2nd edn 1963; Juggernaut: a history of the Soviet armed forces, 1967. *Recreations:* walking, climbing. *Address:* 3 Silverbell Court, 2 Hoptree Close, N12 8LP. *T:* (020) 8445 9714. *Clubs:* Garrick, Royal Over-Seas League.

MACKINTOSH, Prof. Nicholas John, DPhil; FRS 1987; Professor of Experimental Psychology, University of Cambridge, 1981–2002; Fellow of King's College, Cambridge, 1981–2005; *b* 9 July 1935; *s* of Dr Ian and Daphne Mackintosh; *m* 1st, 1960, Janet Ann Scott (marr. diss. 1978); one *s* one *d*; 2nd, 1978, Bundy Wilson (marr. diss. 1989); two *s*; 3rd, 1992, Leonora Caroline Brosan, *d* of late Dr George Stephen Brosan, CBE, TD; one *s*. *Educ:* Winchester; Magdalen Coll., Oxford. BA 1960, MA, DPhil 1963. Univ. Lectr, Univ. of Oxford, 1964–67; Res. Fellow, Lincoln Coll., Oxford, 1966–67; Res. Prof., Dalhousie Univ., 1967–73; Prof., Univ. of Sussex, 1973–81. Visiting Professor: Univ. of Pennsylvania, 1965–66; Univ. of Hawaii, 1972–73; Bryn Mawr Coll., 1977; Univ. of NSW, 1990; Univ. de Paris-Sud, Orsay, 1993–94; Yale Univ., 2002. Editor: Qly Jl of Experimental Psychology, 1977–84; Animal Behaviour Processes sect., Jl of Experimental Psychology, 2003–. *Publications:* (ed with W. K. Honig) Fundamental Issues in Associative Learning, 1969; (with N. S. Sutherland) Mechanisms of Animal Discrimination Learning, 1971; The Psychology of Animal Learning, 1974; Conditioning and Associative Learning, 1983; Animal Learning and Cognition, 1994; Cyril Burt: fraud or framed?, 1995; IQ and Human Intelligence, 1998; papers in psychological journals. *Address:* c/o King's College, Cambridge CB2 1ST. *T:* (01223) 351386.

McKITTERICK, Dr David John, FSA, FRHistS; FBA 1995; Fellow and Librarian, Trinity College, Cambridge, since 1986; *b* 9 Jan. 1948; *s* of Rev. Canon J. H. B. McKitterick and Marjory McKitterick (*née* Quarterman); *m* 1976, Rosamond Deborah Pierce (*see* R. D. McKitterick); one *d*. *Educ:* King's Coll. Sch., Wimbledon; St John's Coll., Cambridge (Scholar; BA 1969; MA 1973; LittD 1994); University College London (DipLib 1971). Staff, Cambridge Univ. Library, 1969–70, 1971–86; Fellow, Darwin Coll., Cambridge, 1978–86; Hon. Prof. of Historical Bibliography, Cambridge Univ., 2006–. Lyell Reader in Bibliography, Univ. of Oxford, 2000; Sandars Reader in Bibliography, Univ. of Cambridge, 2001–02. Syndic, CUP, 2000–. Hon. Curator, Early Printed Books, Fitzwilliam Mus. Vice-Pres., 1990–98, Pres., 1998–2000, Bibliog. Soc.; Pres., Cambridge Bibliog. Soc., 1991–; Pubns Sec., British Acad., 2002–. Trustee, Wordsworth Trust. Gold Medal, Bibliographical Soc., 2005. *Publications:* The Library of Sir Thomas Kynvett of Ashwellthorpe 1539–1618, 1978; (ed) Stanley Morison and D. B. Updike: Selected Correspondence, 1979; (ed) Stanley Morison: selected essays on the history of letter forms in manuscript and print, 1981; (with John Dreyfus) A History of the Nonesuch Press, 1981; Four Hundred Years of University Printing and Publishing at Cambridge 1584–1984, 1984; Cambridge University Library: a history: the eighteenth and nineteenth centuries, 1986; A New Specimen Book of Curwen Pattern Papers, 1987; (ed jtly) T. F. Dibdin: *Horae Bibliographicae Cantabrigiensis*, 1988; Wallpapers by Edward Bawden, 1989; (ed) Andrew Perne: quatercentenary studies, 1991; Catalogue of the Pepys Library at Magdalene College, Cambridge, VII: facsimile of Pepys's catalogue, 1991; A History of Cambridge University Press, vol. 1: printing and the book trade in Cambridge 1534–1698, 1992, vol 2: scholarship and commerce 1698–1872, 1998, vol. 3: new worlds for learning 1873–1972, 2004; (ed) The Making of the Wren Library, 1995; Print, Manuscript and the Search for Order 1450–1830, 2003; (ed) The Trinity Apocalypse, 2005; contribs to learned jls. *Address:* Trinity College, Cambridge CB2 1TQ. *T:* (01223) 338513. *Clubs:* Roxburghe, Double Crown (President, 1994–95).

See also W. H. McKitterick.

McKITTERICK, Prof. Rosamond Deborah, FRHistS; Professor of Mediaeval History, University of Cambridge, since 1999; Fellow of Sidney Sussex College, Cambridge, since 2007; *b* Chesterfield, Derbys, 31 May 1949; *d* of Rev. Canon C. A. Pierce, OBE, MA, BD and Melissa (*née* Heaney); *m* 1976, David John McKitterick, *qv*; one *d*. *Educ:* Univ. of WA (BA 1st cl. Hons 1970); Univ. of Cambridge (MA 1977; PhD 1976; LittD 1991); Univ. of Munich (Graduate Student). FRHistS 1980; Fellow, European Medieval Acad., 1993. University of Cambridge: Asst Lectr, 1979–85; Lectr, 1985–91; Reader, 1991–97; Prof. of Early Mediaeval European Hist., 1997–99; Newnham College: Fellow, 1974–2006; Dir of Studies in Anglo-Saxon, Norse and Celtic, 1979–93; Vice-Principal, 1996–98. Hugh Balsdon Fellow, British Sch. at Rome, 2001–02; Fellow in Residence, Netherlands Inst. of Advanced Study, 2005–06; Fellow, Scaliger Inst., Univ. of Leiden, 2005–06. Guest Lectr in univs in Germany, Austria, USA, Australia, Denmark, Eire, France, Netherlands and Norway, 1978–; lecture tours: USA, 1982, 1990, 1994; Germany, 1987; UK; speaker, internat. confs on early medieval studies, Belgium, France, Netherlands, Germany, Turkey, Italy, USA, UK, Eire and Austria. Corresponding Fellow: Monumenta Germaniae Historica, Germany, 1999; Medieval Acad. of America, 2006; philosophisch-historische Klasse, Austrian Acad. Scis, 2006. FRSA 2001. Vice-Pres., RHistS, 1994–98, 2000–03. Editor: Cambridge Studies in Medieval Life and Thought; Cambridge Studies in Palaeography and Codicology, 1989–2003; Corresp. Ed., Early Medieval Europe, 1999– (Editor, 1992–99). *Publications:* The Frankish Church and the Carolingian Reforms 789–895, 1977; The Frankish Kingdoms under the Carolingians 751–987, 1983; The Carolingians and the Written Word, 1989; The Uses of Literacy in early medieval Europe, 1990; (with Lida Lopes Cardozo) Lasting Letters, 1992; Carolingian Culture: emulation and innovation, 1993; Books, Scribes and Learning in the Frankish Kingdoms, Sixth to Ninth Centuries, 1994; (ed and contrib.) The New Cambridge Medieval History II, 700–900, 1995; Frankish Kings and Culture in the Early Middle Ages, 1995; (ed jtly and contrib.) Edward Gibbon and Empire, 1996; (ed and contrib.) The Short Oxford History of Europe: the early middle ages 400–1000, 2001; (ed and contrib.) The Times Atlas of the Medieval World, 2003; History and Memory in the Carolingian World, 2004; Perceptions of the Past in the Early Middle Ages, 2006; Charlemagne: the formation of a European identity, 2008; articles in many collections of essays and conf. proc. and jls, incl. English Hist. Rev., Library, Studies in Church History, Trans of RHistS, Early Medieval Europe, Francia, Scriptorium; reviews for TLS and English and continental learned jls. *Recreations:* music, fresh air. *Address:* Sidney Sussex College, Cambridge CB2 3HU. *T:* (01223) 338800.

McKITTERICK, William Henry; Strategic Partnership Director, Plymouth Children's Services, since 2006; Children's Services and Social Care Consultant, since 2005; *b* 21 Sept. 1949; *s* of Rev. Canon J. H. B. McKitterick and M. G. McKitterick (*née* Quarterman); *m* 1972, Jennifer M. Fisher; one *s* one *d*. *Educ:* King's College Sch.; Hatfield Poly. (BA, CQSW); Bradford Univ. (MA 1982). Social Worker: Leics, 1973–75; Oldham, 1975–78; Social Services Manager: Manchester, 1978–84; Oldham, 1984–89; Wakefield, 1989–93; Head of Service, and Dep. Dir of Social Services, Wakefield, 1993–95; Dir of Social Services and Health, City and Co. of Bristol, 1995–2005. Chair, Bristol and Swindon Churches Council of Industrial and Social Responsibility, 2000–04. *Recreations:* family, walking, books. *Address:* Holly Bank, Grove Orchard, Blagdon, Bristol BS40 7DR. *T:* (01761) 463407.

See also D. J. McKitterick.

McKITTRICK, Ven. Douglas Henry; Archdeacon of Chichester, since 2002; *b* 18 Feb. 1953; *s* of Joseph Henry McKittrick and Doreen Mary (*née* Davidson). *Educ:* John Marley Sch., Newcastle upon Tyne; St Stephen's House, Oxford. Ordained deacon, 1977, priest, 1978; Curate: St Paul's, Deptford, 1977–80; St John's, Tuebrook, Liverpool, 1980–81; Team Vicar, St Stephen's, Grove Street, Liverpool, 1981–89; Vicar: St Agnes, Toxteth Park, 1989–97; St Peter's, Brighton with Chapel Royal, Chichester, 1997–2002. RD, Brighton, 1998–2002; Preb., 1998–2002, and Canon, 1998–, Chichester Cathedral. Member: Gen. Synod, 2005–; Council, Additional Curates Soc., 2005–; Nat. Healthcare Chaplaincies Council, 2006–; Ecclesiastical Law Soc. *Recreations:* long country/coastal walks, cooking, theatre, wine, Brighton and Hove Albion FC. *Address:* 2 Yorklands, Dyke Road Avenue, Hove, E Sussex BN3 6RW. *T:* (home) (01273) 505330, (office) (01273) 421021, *Fax:* (01273) 421041; *e-mail:* archchichester@diochi.org.uk.

McKITTRICK, Neil Alastair; His Honour Judge McKittrick; a Circuit Judge, since 2001; Resident Judge, Ipswich Crown Court, since 2006; *b* 1 Jan. 1948; *s* of late Ian James Arthur McKittrick and of Mary Patricia McKittrick (*née* Hobbs); *m* 1975, Jean Armstrong; one *s* one *d*. *Educ:* King's Sch., Ely; College of Law, Guildford. LLB London. Solicitor, 1972. Articled Clerk and Asst Solicitor, Cecil Godfrey & Son, Nottingham, 1967–73; Prosecuting Solicitor, Notts, 1973–77; Clerk to the Justices, 1977–89 (Darlington 1977, E Herts 1981, N Cambs 1986–89); Stipendiary Magistrate, subseq. Dist Judge (Magistrates' Courts), Middx, 1989–2001; a Recorder, 1996–2001; Magistrates' Liaison Judge, Suffolk, 2007–. Member: Council, Justices' Clerks' Soc., 1985–89 (Chm., Professional Purposes Cttee, 1987–89); Middlesex Probation Cttee, 1990–2001. Editor, Justice of the Peace, 1985–89; Licensing Editor, Justice of the Peace Reports, 1983–2003; Editor, Jl of Criminal Law, 1990–2000 (Mem., Editl Bd, 1985–2000). *Publications:* (ed jtly) Wilkinson's Road Traffic Offences, 14th edn to 18th edn, 1997; (with Pauline Callow) Blackstone's Handbook for Magistrates, 1997, 2nd edn 2000; (contrib.) Confronting Crime, 2003; papers and articles in learned jls. *Recreations:* visiting churches, racecourses. *Address:* Ipswich Crown Court, 1 Russell Road, Ipswich IP1 2AG. *T:* (01473) 228585.

MACKLEY, Ian Warren, CMG 1989; CVO 1999; HM Diplomatic Service, retired; Clerk, Select Committee on the Constitution, House of Lords, 2002–06; *b* 31 March 1942; *s* of late Harold William Mackley and of Marjorie Rosa Sprawson (*née* Warren); *m* 1st, 1968, Jill Marion (*née* Saunders) (marr. diss. 1988); three *s*; 2nd, 1989, Sarah Anne Churchley; one *s* one *d*. *Educ:* Ardingly College. FO, 1960; Saigon, 1963; Asst Private Sec. to Ministers of State, FCO, 1967; Wellington, 1969; First Sec., 1972; FCO 1973; Head of Inf. Services, New Delhi, 1976; Asst Head, UN Dept, FCO, 1979; seconded to ICI, 1982; Counsellor, Dep. Hd of UK Delegn to Conf. on Confidence- and Security-Building Measures and Disarmament in Europe, Stockholm, 1984–86; Chargé d'Affaires, Kabul, 1987–89; Dep. High Comr, Canberra, 1989–93; Head of Training, FCO, 1993–96; High Comr to Ghana and Ambassador (non-res.) to Togo, 1996–2000. Pres., Kabul Golf and Country Club, Afghanistan, 1987–89. *Recreations:* golf, armchair sport. *Address:* 21 The Beeches, Weyhill Road, Andover, Hants SP10 3EF.

MACKLIN, David Drury, CBE 1989; DL; *b* 1 Sept. 1928; *s* of Laurence Hilary Macklin and Alice Dumergue (*née* Tait); *m* 1955, Janet Smallwood; four *s*. *Educ:* Felsted Sch., Essex; St John's Coll., Cambridge. MA. Articled to Baileys Shaw & Gillett, Solicitors, 1951–54; Assistant Solicitor: Coward Chance & Co., 1954–56; Warwickshire CC, 1956–61; Devon CC, 1961–69; Dep. Clerk, Derbyshire CC, 1969–73; Chief Executive: Lincolnshire CC, 1973–79; Devon CC, 1979–88. Mem., Boundary Commn for England, 1989–99. Chm., Community Council of Devon, 1992–96; Mem., Devon and Cornwall Housing Assoc., 1989–98. Founder Mem., ViRSA Educnl Trust (Chm., 1994–98). DL Devon, 1991. *Recreations:* sailing, music, golf, theatre, walking. *Address:* The Garden Cottage, Station Road, Topsham, Exeter EX3 0DT. *T:* (01392) 873160.

MACKLIN, Prof. John Joseph, PhD; Professor of Spanish, University of Strathclyde, since 2006; *b* 9 Oct. 1947; *s* of James and Mary Macklin; *m* 1969, Pauline Ruben; one *s* two *d*. *Educ:* Queen's Univ., Belfast (BA 1st cl. French, 1st cl. Spanish; PhD 1976). University of Hull: Lectr in Hispanic Studies, 1973–85; Sen. Lectr, 1985–87; Hd of Dept, 1986–87; University of Leeds: Cowdray Prof. of Spanish, 1988–2001; Dean, Faculty of Arts, 1992–94; Dean for Res. in Humanities, 1994–99; Pro-Vice-Chancellor, 1999–2001; Principal and Vice-Chancellor, Univ. of Paisley, 2001–05. Vis. Prof., Univ. of Ulster, 2007–. Director: Scottish Enterprise, Renfrewshire, 2002–05; Council, ILT, 2003–05. Real Academia Alfonso X el Sabio, 2007. FHEA 2007. Comdr, Orden de Isabel la Católica (Spain), 1994. *Publications:* Tigre Juan and El curandero de su honra, 1980; The Modernist Fictions of Ramón Pérez de Ayala, 1988; The Scripted Self, 1995; contrib. to Bull. Hispanic Studies, MLR, Hispanic Rev., Cuadernos Hispanoamericanos, Neophilologus, Anales de la literatura española contemporánea. *Recreations:* walking, cinema, current affairs, art history. *Address:* Department of Modern Languages, University of Strathclyde, Livingstone Tower, 26 Richmond Street, Glasgow G1 1XH. *T:* (0141) 548 3406; *e-mail:* john.macklin@strath.ac.uk.

MACKLOW-SMITH, Roxanna; *see* Panufnik, R.

MACKNEY, Paul Leon John; Associate General Secretary, University and College Union, since 2007 (Joint General Secretary, 2006–07); *b* 25 March 1950; *s* of Rev. L. E. Mackney and Margaret Mackney; *m* 1st, 1969, Rosemary A. Draper (marr. diss. 1974); one *s*; 2nd, 1982, Cherry M. Sewell; one *d*. *Educ:* Exeter Univ. (BA Hons); Birmingham Poly. (RSA DipTEFL); Wolverhampton Poly. (FE CertEd); Warwick Univ. (MA Industrial Relns 1986). Trainee probation officer, 1971–73; General Studies Lectr, Poole Tech. Coll., 1974–75; Hall Green Technical College: ESOL Organiser, 1975–79; Trade Union Studies Tutor, 1980–85; Head, Birmingham Trade Union Studies Centre, S Birmingham Coll., 1986–92; W Midlands Regl Official, 1992–97, Gen. Sec., 1997–2006, NATFHE. Pres., Birmingham TUC, 1980–84 (Life Mem.); Mem., TUC Gen. Council, 2002–. *Publication:* Birmingham and the Miners' Strike, 1986. *Recreations:* music, guitar, singing. *Address:* University and College Union, 27 Britannia Street, WC1X 9JP. *T:* (020) 7837 3636. *Club:* Bread and Roses (Birmingham).

MACKRELL, Judith Rosalind; Dance Critic, The Guardian, since 1995; *b* 26 Oct. 1954; *d* of Alec Mackrell and Margaret (*née* Atkinson, later Halsey); *m* 1977, Simon Henson; two *s*. *Educ:* York Univ. (BA 1st Cl. Hons Eng. and Philosophy); Oxford Univ. Part-time Lectr in English and Dance at various estabts incl. Oxford Univ., Oxford Poly. and Roehampton Inst., 1981–86; Dance Critic, Independent, 1986–94. Freelance dance writer and arts broadcaster, 1986–. Hon. Fellow, Laban Centre for Dance, 1996. *Publications:* Out of Line, 1994; Reading Dance, 1997; (with Darcey Bussell) Life in Dance, 1998; (ed with Debra Craine) The Oxford Dictionary of Dance, 2000; Bloomsbury Ballerina: Lydia Lopokova, imperial dancer and Mrs John Maynard Keynes, 2008. *Recreations:* travel, food, music, reading, my family. *Address:* 73 Greenwood Road, E8 1NT. *T:* (020) 7249 5553.

MACKRELL, Keith Ashley Victor; Vice Chairman, Duke Corporate Education Ltd, since 2004; *b* 20 Oct. 1932; *s* of late Henry George Mackrell and Emily Winifred Mackrell (*née* Elcock); *m* 1960, June Yvonne Mendoza, *qv*; one *s* three *d*. *Educ:* Peter Symonds Sch.; London School of Economics (Harold Laski Schol.; BSc Econs 1953; Hon. Fellow, 1999). Director: Shell International, 1976–91 (Regl Co-ordinator, East and Australasia, 1979–91); BG plc, 1994–2005 (Dep. Chm., 2000–05). Non-executive Director: Standard Chartered Bank, 1991–2002; Regalian Properties, 1991–2002; Rexam (formerly Bowater) plc, 1991–98; Fairey Gp plc, 1993–99; Dresdner Emerging Markets Investment Trust, 1998–2002; Gartmore Asia Pacific (formerly Govett Asian Recovery Trust), 1998–2006; Aberdeen All Asia Trust, 2006–07. Chm., 1992–2004, Emeritus Pres., 2004, Enterprise LSE. Gov., LSE, 1991–. FInstD 1976; CCMI (CBIM 1978). Hon. LLD Nat. Univ. of Singapore, 1991. *Recreations:* tennis, theatre, reading. *Clubs:* Hurlingham, Wimbledon.

McKUEN, Rod; poet, composer, author, performer, columnist, classical composer; *b* Oakland, Calif, 29 April 1933. Has appeared in numerous films, TV, concerts, nightclubs, and with symphony orchestras. Composer: modern classical music; scores for motion pictures and TV. President: Stanyan Records; Discus Records; New Gramophone Soc.; Mr Kelly Prodns; Montcalm Prodns; Stanyan Books; Cheval Books; Biplane Books; Rod McKuen Enterprises; Vice-Pres., Tamarack Books; Dir, Animal Concern; Member, Advisory Board: Fund for Animals; Internat. Educn; Market Theatre, Johannesburg; Member, Board of Directors: National Ballet Theatre; Amer. Dance Ensemble; Amer. Guild of Authors and Composers; Exec. Pres., Amer. Guild of Variety Artists; Member: Amer. Soc. of Composers, Authors and Publishers; Writers' Guild; Amer. Fedn of TV and Radio Artists; Screen Actors' Guild; Equity; Modern Poetry Assoc.; Amer. Guild of Variety Artists; AGAC; Internat. Platform Assoc. Mem., Bd of Governors, National Acad. of Recording Arts and Sciences; Trustee: Univ. of Nebraska; Freedoms Foundn. Nat. spokesperson for Amer. Energy Awareness; Internat. spokesperson for Cttee for Prevention of Child Abuse (also Nat. Bd Mem.). Numerous awards, including: Grand Prix du Disc, Paris, 1966, 1974, 1975 and 1982; Golden Globe Award, 1969; Grammy for best spoken word album, Lonesome Cities, 1969; Entertainer of the Year, 1975; Man of the Year Award, Univ. of Detroit, 1978; awards from San Francisco, LA, Chattanooga, Topeka, Lincoln and Nebraska; Freedoms Foundn Patriot Medal, 1981; Salvation Army Man of the Year, 1982. Over 200 record albums; 41 Gold and Platinum records internationally; nominated Pulitzer Prize in classical music for The City, 1973. *Publications: poetry:* And Autumn Came, 1954; Stanyan Street and Other Sorrows, 1966; Listen to the Warm, 1967; Lonesome Cities, 1968; Twelve Years of Christmas, 1968; In Someone's Shadow, 1969; A Man Alone, 1969; With Love, 1970; Caught in the Quiet, 1970; New Ballads, 1970; Fields of Wonder, 1971; The Carols of Christmas, 1971; And to Each Season, 1972; Pastorale, 1972; Grand Tour, 1972; Come to Me in Silence, 1973; America: an Affirmation, 1974; Seasons in the Sun, 1974; Moment to Moment, 1974; Beyond the Boardwalk, 1975; The Rod McKuen Omnibus, 1975; Alone, 1975; Celebrations of the Heart, 1975; Finding my Father: one man's search for identity (prose), 1976; The Sea Around Me, 1977; Hand in Hand, 1977; Coming Close to the Earth, 1978; We Touch the Sky, 1979; Love's Been Good to Me, 1979; Looking for a Friend, 1980; An Outstretched Hand (prose), 1980; The Power Bright and Shining, 1980; Too Many Midnights, 1981; Rod McKuen's Book of Days, 1981; The Beautiful Strangers, 1981; The Works of Rod McKuen: Vol. 1, Poetry, 1950–82, 1982; Watch for the Wind…, 1982; Rod McKuen—1984 Book of Days, 1983; The Sound of Solitude, 1983; Suspension Bridge, 1984; Another Beautiful Day, 1984, vol. 2, 1985; Valentines, 1986; Intervals, 1987; A Safe Place to Land, 2001; Rusting in the Rain, 2004; *major classical works:* Symphony No One; Concerto for Guitar and Orchestra; Concerto for Four Harpsichords; Concerto for Cello and Orch.; Concerto for Bassoon and Orch.; Seascapes; Concerto for Piano and Orchestra; Adagio for Harp and Strings; Piano Variations; The Black Eagle (opera); Birch Trees (Concerto for Orch.); various other classical commns; numerous lyrics; *film and television scores:* Joanna, 1968; Travels with Charley, 1968; The Prime of Miss Jean Brodie (Academy Award Nomination), 1969; Me, Natalie, 1969; The Loner, 1969; A Boy Named Charlie Brown (Academy Award Nomination), 1970; Come to your Senses, 1971; Scandalous John, 1971; Wildflowers, 1971; The Borrowers, 1973; Lisa Bright and Dark, 1973; Hello Again, 1974; Emily, 1975; The Unknown War, 1979; Man to Himself, 1980; Portrait of Rod McKuen, 1982; The Beach, 1984. *Address:* PO Box 2783, Los Angeles, CA 90078–2790, USA.

MACKWORTH, Sir Digby (John), 10th Bt *cr* 1776, of The Gnoll, Glamorganshire; *b* 2 Nov. 1945; *s* of Sir David Arthur Geoffrey Mackworth, 9th Bt and his 1st wife, Mary Alice, (Molly), (*née* Grylles); *S* father, 1998; *m* 1971, Antoinette Francesca McKenna; one *d*. *Educ:* Wellington Coll. Lieut, Australian Army Aviation Corps, 1966; basic flying trng, 63 course, RAAF, Point Cook; helicopter pilot, 28 Commonwealth Bde, Malaysia; 161 (Indep.) Reconnaissance Flt, Australian Task Force, Viet-Nam. Pilot: Bristow Helicopters, Trinidad, Iran, 1972–77; British Airways Helicopters, Shetland, Aberdeen, China, India, 1977–89; British Airways, Heathrow, 1989–2000; easyJet, 2000–05. *Recreation:* amateur workshop practice. *Heir: kinsman* Norman Humphrey Mackworth [*b* 1917; *m* 1941, Jane Felicity Thring; two *s* one *d*]. *Address:* Blagrove Cottage, Fox Lane, Boars Hill, Oxford OX1 5DS. *T:* (01865) 735543.

MACKWORTH, Rosalind Jean, CBE 1994; Social Fund Commissioner for Great Britain, 1987–96, and for Northern Ireland, 1987–96; Senior Partner, Ashley Wilson (formerly Mackworth Rowland), Solicitors; *b* 10 Aug. 1928; *d* of Rev. Albert Walters, FRMetS and Alma Walters, sometime Comptroller to Archbishop of Canterbury; *m* 1960, Richard Charles Audley Mackworth, MA, MSc, DIC, CEng; two *d*. *Educ:* twelve small schools, following father's postings; Queen's Univ. Belfast (BA); Girton Coll., Cambridge (MA); Law Soc. professional exams. Joined Gregory Rowcliffe, Solicitors, 1956; set up own practice, 1967; amalgamated practice, Mackworth Rowland, 1982, Ashley Wilson, 2005. Mem., VAT Tribunals, 1976–. Chm., Judicial Commn, Eur. Union of Women, 1984–87 (Vice-Chm., British Section, 1986–87). *Recreations:* everything except golf. *Address:* Ashley Wilson Solicitors, 19–21 Grosvenor Gardens, SW1W 0BD. *T:* (020) 7385 4996.

McLACHLAN, Dr Andrew David, FRS 1989; Scientific Staff, Medical Research Council Laboratory of Molecular Biology, Cambridge, 1967–2000; Fellow of Trinity College, Cambridge, since 1959; *b* 25 Jan. 1935; *s* of late Donald Harvey McLachlan and Katherine (*née* Harman); *m* 1959, Jennifer Margaret Lief Kerr; three *s*. *Educ:* Winchester Coll. (Schol.); Trinity Coll., Cambridge (BA, MA, PhD, ScD). Res. Fellow, Trinity Coll., 1958; Harkness Fellow, USA, 1959–61; Lectr in Physics, Trinity Coll., 1961–87; Lectr in Chemistry, Cambridge Univ., 1965–67. Visiting Professor: CIT, 1964; Brandeis Univ., 1975; UCLA, 1989. *Publications:* (with A. Carrington) Introduction to Magnetic Resonance, 1967; papers in various jls, including Jl of Molecular Biology, Nature, and Acta Crystallographica. *Recreations:* walking, music, camping. *Address:* Trinity College, Cambridge CB2 1TQ; 12 Dane Drive, Cambridge CB3 9LP. *T:* (01223) 361318; *e-mail:* jennyandrew@fastmail.fm.

McLACHLAN, Edward Rolland; freelance cartoonist, illustrator and designer, since 1966; *b* 22 April 1940; *m* 1964, Shirley Ann Gerrard; one *s* three *d*. *Educ:* Humberstone Village Jun. Sch.; Wyggeston Boys Grammar Sch.; Leicester CAT. Cartoonist for Punch, Private Eye, Spectator, Saga mag., The Oldie, The Cartoonist, Big Issue, Building, Focus

(BBC), Roof, Property Week, IFG; illustrator for publishers, incl. Methuen, Macmillan Heinemann, Profile, John Wiley & Sons, Pearson, Penguin, OUP, Longmans and Cornelsen; television cartoon series, ITV: Simon and the Land of Chalk Drawings, 1977, and Canada, 2001; Bangers and Mash, 1989; work for many advertising agencies. *Publication:* McLachlan Book of Cartoons, 2000. *Recreations:* cycling, weight-training, gardening, pubs; long-time season ticket holder, Leicester Tigers Rugby Club. *Address:* 3 Spinney View, Coverside Road, Great Glen, Leics LE8 9EP. *T:* (0116) 259 2632, *Fax:* (0116) 259 3898; *e-mail:* mail@edmclachlan.co.uk.

McLACHLAN, Hon. Ian (Murray), AO 1989; Minister for Defence, Australia, 1996–98; Chairman, Australian Wool Innovation Ltd, since 2002; *b* 2 Oct. 1936; *s* of I. McLachlan; *m* 1964, Janet Lee; two *s* one *d. Educ:* Collegiate Sch. of St Peter, SA; Jesus Coll., Cambridge (cricket blue, 1957–58). Played cricket for SA, 1961–64. Director: SA Brewing, 1978–90 (Dep. Chm., 1983–90); Elders IXL, 1980–90. MP (L) Barker, SA, 1990–98; Shadow Minister: for Industry and Commerce, 1990–93; for Infrastructure and Nat. Develt, 1993–94; for Envmt and Heritage, 1994–95. Pres., Nat. Farmers' Fedn, 1984–88. Pres., SA Cricket Assoc., 1999–; Dir, Cricket Australia, 2004–. *Address:* 5 Fuller Court, Walkerville, Adelaide, SA 5081, Australia.

McLACHLAN, Marjory Jane; JP; Lord-Lieutenant of Stirling and Falkirk, since 2005; *b* 15 Feb. 1942; *d* of Walter and Kate Alexander; *m* 1962, Colin McLachlan; two *d. Educ:* St Leonard's Sch., St Andrews. Pres., Ladies' Br., Royal Caledonian Curling Club, 1989–90; Scottish Rep., World Curling Fedn, 1991–99. JP Falkirk, 2006. *Recreations:* family, bridge, curling, golf, travel. *Address:* Dromore, 23 Majors Loan, Falkirk FK1 5QG. *T:* (01324) 622633; *e-mail:* marjmcl@aol.com.

McLACHLIN, Rt Hon. Beverley; PC 2000; Chief Justice of Canada, since 2000; *b* Pincher Creek, Alberta, 7 Sept. 1943; *m* 1st, 1967, Roderick McLachlin (*d* 1988); one *s*; 2nd, 1992, Frank E. McArdle. *Educ:* Univ. of Alberta (MA 1968, LLB 1968). Called to the Bar: Alberta, 1969; BC, 1971; practised law: with Wood, Moir, Hyde and Ross, Edmonton, 1969–71; with Thomas, Herdy, Mitchell & Co., Fort St John, BC, 1971–72; with Bull, Housser and Tupper, Vancouver, 1972–75; Lectr, 1974–75, Associate Prof., 1975–78, Prof., 1981, Univ. of BC, 1974–81; Judge: County Court of Vancouver, 1981; Supreme Court of BC, 1981–85; Court of Appeal, BC, 1985–88; Chief Justice, Supreme Court of BC, 1988–89; Judge, Supreme Court of Canada, 1989–2000. Hon. LLD: BC, 1990; Alberta, 1991; Toronto, 1995; York, 1999; Law Soc. of Upper Canada, Ottawa, Calgary, Brock, Simon Fraser, Victoria, Alberta, 2000; Lethbridge, Bridgewater State Coll., 2001; Mt St Vincent, Prince Edward Island, 2002; Montreal, 2003; Manitoba, QUB, Dalhousie, Carleton, 2004; Maine at Fort Kent, 2005; Ateneo de Manila Univ., 2006. *Publications:* contrib. to learned jls. *Address:* Supreme Court of Canada, 301 Wellington Street, Ottawa, ON K1A 0J1, Canada.

McLAGGAN, Murray Adams; JP; Lord Lieutenant of Mid Glamorgan, 1990–2002; *b* 29 Sept. 1929; *s* of Sir John Douglas McLaggan, KCVO, FRCS, FRCSE and Elsa Violet Lady McLaggan (*née* Adams), MD, DPH; *m* 1959, Jennifer Ann Nicholl; two *s* one *d. Educ:* Winchester College; New College, Oxford (MA 1st Cl. Hons). Called to the Bar, Lincoln's Inn, 1955; Student and Tutor in Law, Christ Church, Oxford, 1957–66. Member: Parly Boundary Commn for Wales, 1980–97; Regl Adv. Bd, Wales, NRA, 1990–96 (Chm., Regl Flood Defence Cttee, 1990–97); Adv. Cttee for Wales, Environment Agency, 1996–98; former Chm., Forestry Commn Regional Adv. Cttee (Wales). Chm., Nat. Trust Cttee for Wales, 1991–93 (Dep. Chm., 1984–91). High Sheriff Mid Glamorgan, 1978–79, DL 1982; JP Glamorgan, 1968. *Recreations:* bibliophily, dendrology, amateur operatics, litter-picking. *Address:* Home Farm, Merthyr Mawr, Bridgend CF32 0LS. *T:* (01656) 653980.

McLAREN, family name of **Baron Aberconway**.

McLAREN, Clare, (Mrs Andrew McLaren); *see* Tritton, E. C.

McLAREN, David John; Chief Executive, London Oncology Clinic, since 2007; *b* 14 April 1944; *s* of late Charles Claude McLaren and Eileen Patricia (*née* Shanley); *m* 2002, Anna Maria Jacobson; one *s* three *d. Educ:* Merchant Taylors' Sch., Crosby; QMC, KCL, and Courtauld Inst., Univ. of London (BA 1965). Mather & Crowther, 1965–67; Radio Newsroom, BBC, 1967–68; Ogilvy & Mather, 1968–70; KMP Partnership, 1970–82 (Man. Dir, 1974–82); Man. Dir, Collett Dickenson Pearce, 1982–91; Hill & Knowlton: CEO, 1994–2000; Chm., 2000–04. Non-exec. Dir, Corney and Barrow Ltd, 1991–. Council Member: IPA, 1984–89; Advertising Assoc., 1984–89; Director: PRCA, 2003–06; Oxford Literary Festival, 2006–. Member: Thames & Solent Cttee, NT, 1999–; Nat. Campaign Bd, Maggies Centres, 2004–; Business Adv. Bd, Ashmolean Mus., 2005–. Trustee: Photographers' Gall., 1986–90; River & Rowing Mus., 2000– (Chm., Develt Bd, 1999–2003). FIPA 1987. FRSA 1997. *Recreations:* motoring, opera, wine, shooting, fishing, photography, books. *Clubs:* Cavalry and Guards, Groucho.

MacLAREN of MacLaren, Donald; Chief of the Clan MacLaren; HM Diplomatic Service; Ambassador to Georgia, 2004–07; *b* 22 Aug. 1954; *s* of late Donald MacLaren of MacLaren, (The MacLaren of MacLaren) and Margaret Sinclair (*née* Miller); *m* 1978, Maida-Jane Aitchison; three *s* two *d.* Joined FCO, 1978; BMG, Berlin, 1980–83; First Secretary: Moscow, 1984–87; FCO, 1987–91; Dep. Hd of Mission, Cuba, 1991–94; FCO, 1994–97; Dep. Hd of Mission, Venezuela, 1997–2000; Consul-Gen. and Dep. Hd of Mission, Ukraine, 2000–04. *Address:* c/o Foreign and Commonwealth Office, King Charles Street, SW1A 2AH.

McLAREN, Ian Alban Bryant; QC 1993; a Recorder, since 1996 (an Assistant Recorder, 1992–96); *b* 3 July 1940; *yr s* of Alban McLaren and Doris (*née* Hurst); *m* 1964, Margaret Middleton, BA; two *s* one *d. Educ:* Sandbach Sch., Blackpool Grammar Sch.; Univ. of Nottingham (LLB 1961). Called to the Bar, Gray's Inn, 1962 (Macaskie Schol.; Bencher, 2004); in practice at the Bar, 1962–; Law Tutor, Univ. of Nottingham, 1962–64; Hd of Ropewalk Chambers, 2000–06. Pres., Notts Medico-Legal Soc., 1997–98. Fellow, Soc. for Advanced Legal Studies, 2000–. Hon. LLD Nottingham Trent, 2005. *Recreations:* gardening, photography. *Address:* 24 The Ropewalk, Nottingham NG1 5EF. *T:* (0115) 947 2581.

McLAREN, Hon. Michael Duncan; QC 2002; *b* 29 Nov. 1958; *s* of 3rd Baron Aberconway and Ann Lindsay (*née* Aymer); *m* 1985, Caroline Jane, *d* of Air Chief Marshal Sir (William) John Stacey, KCB, CBE, FRAeS; two *s* one *d. Educ:* Eton Coll.; Christ's Coll., Cambridge (MA 1st Cl. Law 1980). Called to the Bar, Middle Temple, 1981; in practice at the Bar, 1981–, specialising in commercial law (aviation, shipping, etc.). *Recreations:* horticulture, music, travel. *Address:* Fountain Court Chambers, Temple, EC4Y 9DH. *T:* (020) 7583 3335, *Fax:* (020) 7353 0329; *e-mail:* mmclaren@fountaincourt.co.uk.

McLAREN, Sir Robin (John Taylor), KCMG 1991 (CMG 1982); HM Diplomatic Service, retired; Director: Invesco Asia Trust, since 1995; Fidelity Asian Values, since 1997; *b* 14 Aug. 1934; *s* of late Robert Taylor McLaren and of Marie Rose McLaren (*née* Simond); *m* 1964, Susan Ellen Hatherly; one *s* two *d. Educ:* Richmond and East Sheen County Grammar Sch. for Boys; Ardingly Coll.; St John's Coll., Cambridge (Schol.; MA). Royal Navy, 1953–55. Entered Foreign Service, 1958; language student, Hong Kong, 1959–60; Third Sec., Peking, 1960–61; FO, 1962–64; Asst Private Sec. to Lord Privy Seal (Mr Edward Heath), 1963–64; Second, later First Sec., Rome, 1964–68; seconded to Hong Kong Govt as Asst Political Adviser, 1968–69; First Sec., FCO, 1970–73; Dep. Head of Western Organisations Dept, 1974–75; Counsellor and Head of Chancery, Copenhagen, 1975–78; Head of Hong Kong and Gen. Dept, 1978–79, of Far Eastern Dept, 1979–81, FCO; Political Advr, Hong Kong, 1981–85; Ambassador to Philippines, 1985–87; Asst Under Sec. of State, FCO, 1987–90; Sen. British Rep., Sino-British Jt Liaison Gp, 1987–89; Dep. Under Sec. of State, FCO, 1990–91; Ambassador to People's Republic of China, 1991–94. Director: Batey Burn Ltd (Hong Kong), 1995–2008; Govett Asian Recovery Trust, then Gartmore Asia Pacific Trust, later Aberdeen All Asia Investment Trust, 1998–2008. Member Council: Ardingly Coll., 1996–2004 (Chm., 1999–2004); RHBNC, 1997–2004 (Chm., 1999–2004; Hon. Fellow, 2006). *Recreations:* music, reading, grandchildren. *Address:* 11 Hillside, Wimbledon, SW19 4NH. *Clubs:* Oxford and Cambridge; Hong Kong (Hong Kong).

MacLAREN, Hon. Roy; PC (Can.) 1983; High Commissioner for Canada in the United Kingdom, 1996–2000; *b* 26 Oct. 1934; *s* of Wilbur MacLaren and Anne (*née* Graham); *m* 1959, Alethea (*née* Mitchell); two *s* one *d. Educ:* schs in Vancouver, Canada; Univ. of BC (BA); Univ. of Cambridge (MA); Univ. of Harvard; Univ. of Toronto (MDiv). With Canadian Diplomatic Service, in Saigon, Hanoi, Prague, Geneva, NY (UN) and Ottawa, 1957–69; Dir, Public Affairs, Massey Ferguson Ltd, 1969–73; President: Ogilvy & Mather (Canada) Ltd, 1974–76; Canadian Business Media Ltd, 1977–93; Director: Deutsche Bank (Canada), 1984–93; London Life Assurance, 1984–93; Royal LePage Ltd, 1985–93. MP (L) Etobicoke N, 1979–96; Parly Sec., Energy, 1980–82; Minister of: State Finance, 1983; Nat. Revue, 1984; Internat. Trade, 1993–96. Non-executive Director: Standard Life, 2001–04; Brookfield, 2001–; Canadian Tire, 2001–03; Patheon, 2001–05; Algoma Central, 2001–; First Calgary Petroleums, 2008–. Commissioner: Commonwealth War Graves Commn, 1996–2000; Trilateral Commn, 2001–; Trustee, Imperial War Mus., 1996–2000; Dir, Bletchley Park Trust, 2001–04; Mem. Adv. Cttee, Scott Polar Res. Inst., 1998–2000; Gov., Ditchley Foundn, 2004–. Mem. Council, IISS, 2001–; Chairman: Canadian Inst. of Internat. Affairs, 2001–05; Canada-Europe Round Table, 2001–; Canada-India Business Council, 2001–; Atlantic Council of Canada, 2003–06. Hon. Col, 7th Toronto Regt, Royal Canadian Artillery, 1995–2005. Hon. DSL Toronto, 1996; Hon. DCL N Alabama, 2000; Hon. DLitt New Brunswick, 2001; Hon. LLD Prince Edward Island, 2003. *Publications:* Canadians in Russia 1918–1919, 1976; Canadians on the Nile 1882–1898, 1978; Canadians Behind Enemy Lines 1939–1945, 1981; Honourable Mentions, 1986; African Exploits: the diaries of William Stairs 1887–1892, 1997; Commissions High, 2006. *Recreations:* cross country walking, ski-ing. *Address:* 425 Russell Hill Road, Toronto, ON M5P 2S4, Canada. *Clubs:* White's, Pratt's; Rideau (Ottawa); Toronto; Royal Canadian Yacht.

McLAREN-THROCKMORTON, Clare; *see* Tritton, E. C.

McLATCHIE, Cameron, CBE 1996 (OBE 1988); Chairman, British Polythene Industries plc (formerly Scott & Robertson), since 1988 (Chief Executive, 1988–2003); *b* 18 Feb. 1947; *s* of Cameron McLatchie and Maggie McLatchie (*née* Maxwell Taylor); *m* 1973, Leslie Mackie; two *s* one *d. Educ:* Univ. of Glasgow (LLB). Apprentice CA, Whinney, Murray & Co., 1968–70; Admin. Asst, subseq. Prodn Manager, then Prodn Dir, Thos Boag & Co. Ltd, 1971–74; Managing Director: Anaplast Ltd, 1975–83; Scott & Robertson plc, 1983–88. Non-executive Director: Motherwell Bridge Hldgs Ltd, 1993–97; Hiscox Select plc, 1993–98 (Chm.); Royal Bank of Scotland Gp, 1998–2002. Dep. Chm., Scottish Enterprise, 1997–2000 (Mem. Bd, 1990–95). Member: Adv. Cttee on Business and the Envmt, 1991–93; Sec. of State for Scotland's Adv. Gp on Sustainable Develt, 1994–95; Bd, Scottish Envmtl Protection Agency, 1995–97. DUniv Paisley 2000. *Recreations:* golf, bridge, gardening. *Address:* c/o British Polythene Industries plc, 96 Port Glasgow Road, Greenock PA15 2RP. *T:* (01475) 501000.

McLAUCHLAN, Derek John Alexander, CBE 1998; CEng, FIET; FRAeS; FInstP; Secretary-General, Civil Air Navigation Services Organisation, Geneva, 1997–2001; *b* 5 May 1933; *s* of Frederick William McLauchlan and Nellie (*née* Summers); *m* 1960, Dr Sylvia June Smith (*see* S. J. McLauchlan); two *d. Educ:* Queen Elizabeth's Hospital, Bristol; Bristol Univ. (BSc). CEng, FIET (FIEE 1988); FRAeS 1993; FInstP 1997. BAC, 1954–66; European Space Technol. Centre, 1966–70; Marconi Space and Defence Systems, 1970–76; ICL, 1976–88; Renishaw Research, 1988–89; Dir Gen., Projects and Engrg, CAA, 1989–91; Chief Exec., NATS, 1991–97; Mem. Bd, CAA, 1991–97. Non-exec. Chm., Architecture Projects Management Ltd, 1994–96. Chm., Jt Air Navigation Services Council, 1996–97; Mem. Council, Air League, 1994–2004. Gold Medal, Czech Air Navigation Services, 2000. *Recreations:* music, theatre, walking. *Address:* 7 Holmwood Close, East Horsley, Leatherhead, Surrey KT24 6SS. *T:* (01483) 285144.

McLAUCHLAN, Prof. Keith Alan, PhD; FRS 1992; Professor of Chemistry, Oxford University, 1996–2002, now Emeritus; Fellow of Hertford College, Oxford, 1965–2002, now Emeritus; *b* 8 Jan. 1936; *s* of Frederick William McLauchlan and Nellie (*née* Summers); *m* 1958, Joan Sheila Dickenson; one *s* one *d. Educ:* Queen Elizabeth's Hosp., Bristol; Univ. of Bristol (BSc, PhD); Univ. of Oxford (MA). Post-doctoral Fellow, NRCC, Ottawa, 1959–60; Post-doctoral Fellow, then Sen. Scientific Officer, NPL, Teddington, 1960–65. Oxford University: Lectr, 1965–94; Reader in Physical Chemistry, 1994–96; Chairman: Inter-deptl Cttee for Chemistry, 1990–93; Cttee of Heads of Sci. Depts, 1991–93; Member: Gen. Bd, 1993–97; Hebdomadal Council, 1998–2000. Erskine Fellow, Univ. of Christchurch, NZ, 1997; Eminent Scientist, RIKEN, Tokyo, 2000–01. Visiting Professor: Tata Inst., Bombay, 1986; Univ. of Konstanz, Germany, 1990; Univ. of Padua, 1998; Ecole Normale Supérieure, Paris, 1998; George Willard Wheland Vis. Prof., Univ. of Chicago, 1998. Chm., Electron Spin Resonance Discussion Gp, RSC, 1989–92. Pres., Internat. Soc. for Electron Paramagnetic Resonance, 1993–96. Mem., Scientific Adv. Bd, Electro Magnetic Field Biol Res. Trust, 1995–2001. Fellow, IES, 2005. Silver Award for Chemistry, 1993, Gold Award, 2002, IES; Bruker Prize, RSC, 1997; Zavoisky Prize for Electron Spin Resonance, Tatarstan, 2001. Radio and television appearances. *Publications:* Magnetic Resonance, 1972; Molecular Physical Chemistry: a concise introduction, 2004; contrib. chaps in books; papers and review articles in Molecular Physics, Chemical Physics Letters, etc. *Recreations:* gardening, walking, ski-ing, reading. *Address:* 29 Cumnor Hill, Oxford OX2 9EY. *T:* (01865) 862570.

McLAUCHLAN, Dr Sylvia June, FFPH; Director General, The Stroke Association, 1993–97; *b* 8 June 1935; *d* of Sydney George Smith and Muriel May (*née* Treweek); *m* 1960, Derek John Alexander McLauchlan, *qv*; two *d. Educ:* High Sch. for Girls, Chichester; Univ. of Bristol (MB ChB 1959); Univ. of Manchester (MSc 1981). FFPH (FFPHM 1989). GP, Bristol, 1960–66; MO, Dept of Public Health, Portsmouth, 1970–76; Clinical MO, Macclesfield, 1976–77; Community Medicine Dept, NW RHA, 1977–86; Public Health Dept, SW Thames RHA, 1986–91; Dir of Public Health, Ealing

HA, 1991–93. Chm., Primary Care Facilitation Trust, 2000–03; Trustee, East Thames Care, 2000–04. Gov., Treloar Sch., 2001–03. *Recreations:* theatre, gardening, cooking. *Address:* 7 Holmwood Close, East Horsley, Surrey KT24 6SS.

McLAUGHLIN, Christopher John; Editor, Tribune, since 2004; *b* 11 Oct. 1955; *s* of Patrick Thomas McLaughlin and Norah Mary McLaughlin (*née* Walsh). *Educ:* St Helen's, Plaistow; St Bonaventure's, Forest Gate. Gen. reporter, Barking and Dagenham Advertiser, then Newham Recorder, 1974–78; Foreign Ed., 1978–81, Lobby Corresp., 1981–87, Labour Weekly; Parly Corresp. and Dep. Political Ed., 1987–93, European Ed., 1993–96, Scotsman; Political Corresp., Mail on Sunday, 1996–2000; Parly Columnist, Big Issue, 1999–2005; Political Ed., Sunday Mirror, 2000–04. Mem. (Lab) Newham LBC, 1978–82. *Address:* c/o Tribune, Press Gallery, House of Commons, SW1A 0AA. *T:* (020) 7433 6410, *Fax:* (020) 7433 6419; *e-mail:* tribuneweb@btinternet.com. *Club:* Soho House.

McLAUGHLIN, Eleanor Thomson; JP; DL; Lord Provost and Lord Lieutenant of Edinburgh, 1988–92; *b* 3 March 1938; *d* of Alexander Craig and Helen Thomson; *m* 1959, Hugh McLaughlin; one *s* two *d*. *Educ:* Broughton School. Mem. (Lab), Edinburgh District Council, 1974–96. Chairman: Edinburgh Festival Soc., 1988–92; Edinburgh Military Tattoo Ltd, 1988–92. JP Edinburgh, 1975; DL Edinburgh, 1993. *Recreations:* Shetland lace knitting, gardening (Alpine plants). *Address:* 28 Oxgangs Green, Edinburgh EH13 9JS. *T:* (0131) 445 4052.

McLAUGHLIN, Léonie Anne; Parliamentary Counsel, since 2003; *b* 15 Nov. 1963; *d* of Timothy Edward Nodder, *qv*; *m* 1996, Wing Comdr Andrew McLaughlin. *Educ:* Christ's Coll., Cambridge (BA English Lit. and Law 1984). Admitted solicitor, 1988; solicitor's articles with May, May & Merrimans, Gray's Inn, 1986–88; Asst, then Sen. Asst, then Dep., Parly Counsel, Parly Counsel Office, 1988–96, 2000–03; self-employed Parly draftsman, 1996–2000. *Recreations:* books, opera, fine art, travel. *Address:* Parliamentary Counsel Office, 36 Whitehall, SW1A 2AY. *T:* (020) 7210 0965, *Fax:* (020) 7210 0950; *e-mail:* lmclaughlin@cabinet-office.x.gsi.gov.uk. *Club:* Royal Air Force.

McLAUGHLIN, Dr Mark Hugh; Director of Finance and Corporate Resources, London Borough of Enfield, since 2001; *b* 20 March 1962; *s* of Raymond and Helen McLaughlin; *m* 1988, Clare Louise Hennessy; three *s*. *Educ:* Univ. of St Andrews (BSc Hons (Zool.) 1983); Univ. of Nottingham (PhD (Zool.) 1988). Res. Fellow, Inst. of Neurol., 1987; Auditor, Audit Commn, 1987–91; Principal Auditor, City of Westminster, 1991–93; Borough of Broxbourne: Asst Dir of Finance, 1993–95; Dir of Resources, 1995–98; Dir of Finance, London Borough of Hammersmith and Fulham, 1998–2001. *Recreations:* writing the great American novel, learning to roll with the punches. *Address:* Enfield Borough Council, Civic Centre, Silver Street, Enfield, Middx EN1 3XF. *T:* (020) 8379 4600; *e-mail:* mark.mclaughlin@enfield.gov.uk.

McLAUGHLIN, Prof. Martin Leonard, DPhil; Fiat Serena Professor of Italian Studies, University of Oxford, and Fellow, Magdalen College, Oxford, since 2001; *b* 4 Dec. 1950; *s* of George Vincent McLaughlin and Ann Josephine McLaughlin; *m* 1974, Catherine Ann Gallagher; one *d*. *Educ:* St Aloysius' Coll., Glasgow; Glasgow Univ. (MA); Balliol Coll., Oxford (MA; DPhil 1984). Lectr, Italian Dept, Edinburgh Univ., 1977–90; Lectr in Italian, and Student, Christ Church, Oxford, 1990–2001; Dir, Eur. Humanities Res. Centre, Univ. of Oxford, 2002–04. Reviews Ed., Italian Studies, 1989–94; Italian Ed., 1994–2001, Gen. Ed., 2001–03, Modern Lang. Rev.; Chm., Editl Bd, Legenda, 2002–. Member, Executive Committee: Soc. for Italian Studies, 1987–94 (Chm., 2004–); MHRA, 1994–. John Florio Prize for Translation, 2000. *Publications:* (ed jtly) Leopardi: a Scottis Quair, 1987; Literary Imitation in the Italian Renaissance, 1995; Italo Calvino, 1998; (trans.) Italo Calvino, Why Read the Classics?, 1999; (ed) Britain and Italy from Romanticism to Modernism, 2000; (trans.) Italo Calvino, Hermit in Paris, 2003; (trans.) Umberto Eco, On Literature, 2005; (ed jtly) Biographies and Autobiographies in Modern Italy, 2007; (ed jtly) Image, Eye and Art in Calvino: writing visibility, 2007. *Recreations:* football, travel, cinema, walking. *Address:* Magdalen College, Oxford OX1 4AU.

McLAUGHLIN, Mary, CBE 2007; Head Teacher, Notre Dame High School, Glasgow, 1990–2007; Principal, Notre Dame New Learning Community, 2003–07; *b* 18 Aug. 1948; *d* of Philip McGachey and Mary McGachey (*née* Ashe); *m* 1972, William McLaughlin; one *d*. *Educ:* Our Lady and St Joseph's Primary Sch., Glenboig; St Patrick's High Sch., Coatbridge; Univ. of Glasgow (MA); Notre Dame Coll. (DipEd). Principal Teacher, Modern Langs, St Margaret's High Sch., Airdrie, 1975–84; Asst Head, Taylor High Sch., New Stevenson, 1984–90. Member: Bd, Anniesland Coll., 1993–97; Bd, Curriculum for Excellence Prog., 2005–. Leadership in Learning Award, Becta, 2005; Glasgow Archdio. Medal for Services to Educn, 2007. *Recreations:* reading, walking, travel, theatre. *Address:* Notre Dame High School, 160 Observatory Road, Glasgow G12 9LN. *T:* (0141) 582 0190, *Fax:* (0141) 582 0191.

McLAUGHLIN, Mitchel; Member (SF) South Antrim, Northern Ireland Assembly, since 2007 (Foyle, 1998–2007); National Chairperson, Sinn Féin, since 1994; *b* 29 Oct. 1945; *m* 1975, Mary-Lou Fleming; three *s*. Mem. (SF) Derry CC, 1985–99. Sinn Féin: Mem., Nat. Exec., 1981–; peace negotiator, 1997–. Member: Civil Rights Assoc., 1968–; Nat. H-Blocks/Armagh Cttee, 1980–81. Contested (SF) Foyle, 2005. *Address:* Northern Ireland Assembly, Parliament Buildings, Belfast BT4 3XX.

MacLAURIN, family name of **Baron MacLaurin of Knebworth**.

MacLAURIN OF KNEBWORTH, Baron *cr* 1996 (Life Peer), of Knebworth in the county of Hertfordshire; **Ian Charter MacLaurin,** Kt 1989; DL; Chairman, Vodafone, 1998–99 and 2000–06; *b* Blackheath, 30 March 1937; *s* of Arthur George and Evelina Florence MacLaurin; *m* 1st, 1961, Ann Margaret (*née* Collar) (*d* 1999); one *s* two *d*; 2nd, 2002, Paula Elizabeth Brooke (*née* Morris). *Educ:* Malvern Coll., Worcs. Served in RAF, 1956–58. Joined Tesco, 1959; Dir, 1970; Man Dir, 1973–85; Dep. Chm., 1983–85; Chm., 1985–97. Non-executive Director: Enterprise Oil, 1984–90; Guinness PLC, 1986–95; National Westminster Bank plc, 1990–97; Gleneagles Hotels plc, 1992–97; Whitbread plc, 1997–2001 (Dep. Chm., 1999–2001); Vodafone (then Vodafone AirTouch, subseq. reverted to Vodafone), 1997–2006 (Dep. Chm., 1999–2000); Evolution Gp plc, 2004–; Heineken NV, 2006–. Chm., TCCB, then ECB, 1996–2002. Chm., Food Policy Gp, Retail Consortium, 1980–84; Pres., Inst. of Grocery Distribution, 1989–92. Trustee, Royal Opera House Trust, 1992. Governor and Mem. Council, Malvern Coll. (Chm. Council, 2003–); Chancellor, Univ. of Hertfordshire, 1996–2005. Mem. Cttee, MCC, 1986–96. FRSA 1986; FIMMM (FIM 1987); Hon. FCGI 1992. Liveryman, Carmen's Co., 1982–. DL Herts, 1992, Wilts, 2007. Hon. Fellow, Univ. of Wales, Cardiff, 1996. DUniv: Stirling, 1987; Bradford, 2001; Hon. LLD Hertfordshire, 1995. *Publication:* Tiger by the Tail (memoirs), 1999. *Recreation:* golf. *Address:* House of Lords, SW1A 0PW. *Clubs:* MCC, Lord's Taverners, XL, Band of Brothers; Royal & Ancient Golf (St Andrews).

MACLAY, family name of **Baron Maclay**.

MACLAY, 3rd Baron *cr* 1922, of Glasgow; **Joseph Paton Maclay;** DL; Bt 1914; Group Marketing Executive, Acomarit Group, 1993–99; *b* 11 April 1942; *s* of 2nd Baron Maclay, KBE, and of Nancy Margaret, *d* of R. C. Greig, Hall of Caldwell, Uplawmoor, Renfrewshire; *S* father, 1969; *m* 1976, Elizabeth Anne, *o d* of G. M. Buchanan, Delamere, Pokataroo, NSW; two *s* one *d*. *Educ:* Winchester; Sorbonne Univ. Managing Director: Denholm Maclay Co. Ltd, 1970–83; Denholm Maclay (Offshore) Ltd, 1975–83; Triport Ferries (Management) Ltd, 1975–83; Dep. Man. Dir, Denholm Ship Management Ltd, 1982–83; Man. Dir, Milton Timber Services Ltd, 1984–90; Dir, Denholm Ship Management (Holdings) Ltd, 1991–93. Director: Milton Shipping Co. Ltd, 1970–83; Marine Shipping Mutual Insce Co., 1982–83; Altnamara Shipping PLC, 1994–2002; Pres., Hanover Shipping Inc., 1982–83. Director: British Steamship Short Trades Assoc., 1978–83; N of England Protection and Indemnity Assoc., 1976–83. A Comr of Northern Lighthouses, 1996–2003 (Vice Chm. 2001–01, Chm., 2001–03, Bd). Chm., Scottish Br., British Sailors Soc., 1979–81; Vice-Chm., Glasgow Shipowners & Shipbrokers Benevolent Assoc., 1982–83 and 1996–97 (Pres., 1998–99); Chm., Scottish Nautical Welfare Soc., 2002–04. Chm., Scottish Maritime Mus., 1998–2005. Trustee: Cattanach Charitable Trust, 1991–; Western Isles Fisheries Trust, 2004–; Western Isles Salmon Fishing Bd, 2004–. DL Renfrewshire, 1986. *Heir: s* Hon. Joseph Paton Maclay, *b* 6 March 1977. *Address:* Duchal, Kilmacolm, Renfrewshire PA13 4RS.

McLAY, Hon. James Kenneth, (Jim), CNZM 2003; Managing Director and Principal, J. K. McLay Ltd (international business consultants), since 1987; Chairman, Macquarie Group Holdings New Zealand Ltd; *s* of late Robert McLay and Joyce McLay; *m* 1983, Marcy Farden. *Educ:* St Helier's Sch.; King's Sch.; King's Coll.; Auckland Univ. (LLB 1967); Pennsylvania State Univ. (EMP 1987). Solicitor in practice on own account, 1971; barrister 1974. MP (National Party) for Birkenhead, NZ, 1975–87; Attorney-Gen. and Minister of Justice, 1978–84; Government Spokesperson for Women, 1979–84; Dep. Prime Minister, 1984; Leader, National Party and Leader of the Opposition, 1984–86. Mem., Ministerial Wkg Party on Accident Compensation and Incapacity, 1990–91; NZ Comr, Internat. Whaling Commn, 1993–2002. Chairman: Wholesale Electricity Market Study, 1991–92; Wholesale Electricity Market Develt Gp, 1993–94. Chairman: OMNIPORT Napier Ltd, 1988–2001; Roading Adv. Gp, 1997; Project Manukau Audit Gp, 1998–; Pharmacybrands Ltd, 1999–2007; Just Water International Ltd, 2004–; Goodman (NZ) Ltd, 2005–; Metlifecare Ltd, 2006–; Director: Evergreen Forests Ltd, 1995–2002; Motor Sport New Zealand Ltd, 1996–99; Mem. Adv. Bd, Westfield NZ Ltd, 1998–2002. Founder Chm., 2004, and Patron, NZ Council for Infrastructure Develt. Hon. NZ Chm., Trans-Tasman Business Circle, 2004–08. NZ deleg., Australia/NZ Leadership Forum, 2004–08. Advr, UK Cons. Party Commn on Bank of England, 1999–2000. *Recreation:* trout fishing. *Address:* PO Box 8885, Symonds Street Post Office, Auckland 1150, New Zealand.

MacLEAN, Rt Hon. Lord; Ranald Norman Munro MacLean; PC 2001; a Senator of the College of Justice in Scotland, 1990–2005; *b* 18 Dec. 1938; *s* of late John Alexander MacLean, CBE; *m* 1963, Pamela Ross (marr. diss. 1993); two *s* one *d* (and one *s* decd). *Educ:* Inverness Royal Acad.; Fettes Coll.; Clare Coll., Cambridge Univ. (BA); Edinburgh Univ. (LLB); Yale Univ., USA (LLM). Called to the Scottish Bar, 1964; QC (Scot.) 1977; Advocate Depute, 1972–75, Home Advocate Depute, 1979–82; Standing Jun. Counsel, Health and Safety Exec. (Scotland), 1975–77; Member: Council on Tribunals, 1985–90 (Chm., Scottish Cttee, 1985–90); Scottish Legal Aid Bd, 1986–90; Scottish Judicial Appts Bd, 2002–05. Member: Stewart Cttee on Alternatives to Prosecution, 1977–82; Parole Bd for Scotland, 1998–2000, 2003; Chairman: Cttee on Serious Violent and Sexual Offenders, 1999–2000; Sentencing Commn for Scotland, 2003–05; Billy Wright Inquiry, Belfast, 2005–. Mem., Ind. Rev. Commn on Scottish Football, Scottish Football Assoc., 1995–97. Trustee, Nat. Liby of Scotland, 1967–90. Chm. of Council, Cockburn Assoc., 1988–96. Chm. Govs, Fettes Coll., 1996–2006. FSAScot 1994; FRSE 2000. Hon. LLD Aberdeen, 2003. *Publication:* (ed jtly) Gloag and Henderson, Introduction to the Law of Scotland, 7th edn 1968, 8th edn 1980. *Recreations:* hill walking, swimming. *Address:* 38 Royal Terrace, Edinburgh EH7 5AH. *Clubs:* New, Scottish Arts (Edinburgh).

MACLEAN of Dochgarroch, Very Rev. Canon Allan Murray; historian; Provost of St John's Cathedral, Oban, 1986–99; *b* 22 Oct. 1950; *o s* of late Rev. Donald Maclean of Dochgarroch and Loraine Maclean of Dochgarroch (*née* Calvert); *m* 1990, Anne (*née* Cavin), *widow* of David Lindsay; two *s* one *d*. *Educ:* Dragon School, Oxford; Trinity College, Glenalmond; Univ. of Edinburgh (MA 1st cl. Hons Scottish History); Cuddesdon Coll. and Pusey House, Oxford. Deacon 1976, Priest 1977; Chaplain of St Mary's Cathedral, Edinburgh, 1976–81; Rector of Holy Trinity, Dunoon, 1981–86; Exam. Chaplain to Bishop of Argyll and the Isles, 1983–93. Hon. Canon, St John's Cathedral, Oban, 1999–. Pres., Clan Maclean Assoc., 1994–98 (Vice-Pres., 1982–94); Chm., Clan Maclean Heritage Trust, 2001–07; Chm., Clan Chattan Assoc., 2007–. Editor: Clan Maclean, 1975–85, 2001–04; Argyll and the Isles, 1984–93; Edge, 2006–. *Publication:* Telford's Highland Churches, 1989. *Recreations:* topography, history, genealogy, architecture. *Address:* 5 North Charlotte Street, Edinburgh EH2 4HR. *T:* (0131) 225 8609; Hazelbrae House, Glen Urquhart, Inverness IV63 6TJ. *T:* (01456) 476267. *Clubs:* New, Puffin's (Edinburgh).

MACLEAN of Dunconnel, Sir Charles (Edward), 2nd Bt *cr* 1957, of Dunconnel, co. Argyll; *b* 31 Oct. 1946; *s* of Sir Fitzroy Hew Maclean of Dunconnel, 1st Bt, KT, CBE and Hon. Veronica Fraser, *d* of 16th Lord Lovat, KT, GCVO, KCMG, CB, DSO and *widow* of Lt Alan Phipps, RN; *S* father, 1996; *m* 1986, Deborah, *d* of Lawrence Young; four *d*. *Educ:* Eton; New Coll., Oxford. *Publications:* Island on the Edge of the World: story of St Kilda, 1972; The Wolf Children, 1977; The Watcher, 1983; (with C. S. Sykes) Scottish Country, 1993; Romantic Scotland, 1995; The Silence, 1996. *Heir: b* Alexander James Simon Aeneas Maclean [*b* 9 June 1949; *m* 1st, 1983, Sarah (marr. diss. 1989), *d* of Hugh Janson; 2nd, 1993, Sarah, *d* of Nicolas Thompson; two *s*]. *Address:* Strachur House, Strachur, Cairndow, Argyll PA27 8BX.

See also Maj.-Gen. J. J. J. Phipps.

MacLEAN, Colin Ross; Director (formerly Head), Children, Young People and Social Care Group, Scottish Government (formerly Scottish Executive Education Department), since 2002; *b* 22 May 1951; *s* of Maurice MacLean and Freda MacLean; *m* 1974, Ilse Youngman; two *s* one *d*. *Educ:* Univ. of Edinburgh (BSc Pure Maths 1972; DipEd (Sec. Educn) 1973; MSc Microelectronics 1980). Teacher of Maths, Edinburgh, 1973–79; Lothian Region: Asst Advr in Microelectronic Technology, 1980–82; Advr in Educnl Computing, 1982–85; Scottish Office: HM Inspector of Schs, 1985–96; Chief Statistician, 1996–99; Scottish Executive Education Department: HM Depute Sen. Chief Inspector of Schs, 1999–2000; Depute Hd, Schs Gp, 2000–02; Acting Hd of Dept, 2007; *Publication:* Computing in Schools, 1985. *Recreations:* gardening, travel, music. *Address:* Scottish Government, 2B(N), Victoria Quay, Edinburgh EH6 6QQ. *T:* (0131) 244 0859, *Fax:* (0131) 244 1475; *e-mail:* colin.maclean@scotland.gsi.gov.uk.

MACLEAN, Colin William, OBE 2000; FRCVS; Chairman, Royal Berkshire NHS Foundation Trust (formerly Royal Berkshire and Battle Hospitals NHS Trust), since 2000;

b 19 June 1938; *s* of late Kenneth Percy Maclean and Elsie Violet (*née* Middleton); *m* 1959, Jacqueline Diana Brindley; two *d*. *Educ:* William Hulme's Grammar Sch., Manchester; Liverpool Univ. Sch. of Vet. Sci. (BVSc; MVSc 1971). MRCVS 1961, FRCVS 1969. Veterinary Surgeon and Partner, veterinary practice, Thornbury, Glos, and Wickham, Hants, 1961–66; Unilever Ltd: Chief Vet. Advr, 1966–72; Manager, Pig Breeding, 1972–74; Man. Dir, Farm Mark Ltd and Masterbreeders Ltd, 1974–76; Area Gen. Manager (S), BOCM Silcock Ltd, 1980–83; Glaxo Group: Dep. Man. Dir, 1983–88; Product Develt Dir, Glaxo Animal Health Ltd, 1983–88; Technical Dir, 1988–92, Dir-Gen., 1992–99, MLC. *Publications:* contrib. to Veterinary Record, Res. Vet. Sci., Jl Comparative Pathology. *Recreations:* squash, Rugby, theatre, travel. *Address:* Crackwillow, Cock Lane, Bradfield, Reading RG7 6HW. *Club:* Farmers'.

MACLEAN, Rt Hon. David (John); PC 1995; MP (C) Penrith and the Border, since July 1983; *b* 16 May 1953. Asst Govt Whip, 1987–88; a Lord Comr of HM Treasury (Govt Whip), 1988–89; Parly Sec., MAFF, 1989–92; Minister of State: DoE, 1992–93; Home Office, 1993–97; Opposition Chief Whip, 2001–05. *Address:* House of Commons, SW1A 0AA.

McLEAN, Denis Bazeley Gordon, CMG 1989; writer; Member, New Zealand Press Council, since 1999; *b* Napier, NZ, 18 Aug. 1930; *s* of John Gordon McLean and Renée Maitland Smith; *m* 1958, Anne Davidson, Venado Tuerto, Argentina; two *s* one *d*. *Educ:* Nelson Coll., NZ; Victoria Univ. Coll., NZ (MSc); Rhodes Schol. 1954; University Coll., Oxford (MA). Jun. Lectr in Geology, Victoria UC, 1953–54; joined Dept of External Affairs of NZ Govt, London, 1957; served in: Wellington, 1958–60; Washington, 1960–63; Paris, 1963–66; Kuala Lumpur, 1966–68; Asst Sec. (Policy), MoD, Wellington, 1969–72; RCDS, 1972; Dep. High Comr, London, 1973–77; Dep. Sec. of Defence, NZ, 1977, Sec. of Defence, 1979–88; Ambassador to US, 1991–94; Warburg Prof. in Internat. Relns, Simmons Coll., Boston, Mass, 1995–98. Visiting Fellow: Strategic and Defence Studies Centre, ANU, Canberra, 1989; Guest Scholar, Woodrow Wilson Center, and Sen. Associate, Carnegie Endowment for Internat. Peace, Washington, 1990–91; Distinguished Fellow, US Inst. of Peace, 1994–95. Pres., Wellington Br., NZ Inst. of Internat. Affairs, 2002–05. *Publications:* The Long Pathway: Te Ara Roa, 1986; Peace Operations and Commonsense, 1996; The Prickly Pair: making nationalism in Australia and New Zealand, 2003; (with Maj.-Gen. W. B. Thomas) Pathways to Adventure: recollections of Major General W. B. Thomas, CB, DSO, MC and Bar, 2004; Kippenberger: dauntless spirit. *Recreations:* walking, looking at art, writing, geology. *Address:* 11 Dekka Street, Khandallah, Wellington 6004, New Zealand. *Club:* Wellington (NZ).

MACLEAN, Sir Donald (Og Grant), Kt 1985; optometrist, practising in Ayr, 1965–2001; *b* 13 Aug. 1930; *s* of Donald Og Maclean and Margaret Maclean (*née* Smith); *m* 1st, 1958, Muriel Giles (*d* 1984); one *s* one *d*; 2nd, 2002, Mrs Margaret Ross. *Educ:* Morrison's Academy, Crieff; Heriot-Watt Univ. FBOA; FCOptom. RAMC, 1952–54. Optical practice: Newcastle upon Tyne, 1954–57; Perth, 1957–65. Chm., Ayr Constituency Cons. Assoc., 1971–75; Scottish Conservative and Unionist Association: Vice-Pres., 1979–83; Pres., 1983–85; Chm., W of Scotland Area, 1977–79; Exec. Mem., Nat. Union, 1979–89; Scottish Conservative Party: Dep. Chm., 1985–89; Vice-Chm., 1989–91; Chm., Carrick, Cumnock and Doon Valley Cons. Assoc., 1998–2000. Chm., Ayrshire and Arran Local Optical Cttee, 1986–88. Chm., Ayrshire Medical Support Ltd, 1995–. Chm., Bell Hollingworth Ltd, 1996–99. Freeman: Spectacle Makers' Co., 1986 (Liveryman, 1989–); City of London, 1987. Dean of Guildry, Royal Burgh of Ayr, 1993–95. *Recreations:* coastal shipping, reading, photography, philately.

MACLEAN, Rear-Adm. Euan, CB 1986; FRINA, FIMechE; Director General Fleet Support, 1983–86; *b* 7 July 1929; *s* of John Fraser Maclean and Dorothy Mary Maclean; *m* 1954, Renée Shaw; two *d*. *Educ:* BRNC Dartmouth; RNEC Keyham/Manadon. Joined Exec. Br., RN, 1943; transf. to Engr Br., 1947; sea service in HMS Sirius, Illustrious, St Kitts, Gambia, Ocean, Indefatigable, Defender, Hermes, Eagle and Ark Royal, 1950–72; on loan to Royal Malaysian Navy, 1965–68; Prodn Dept, Portsmouth Dockyard, 1968–71; HMS Ark Royal, 1971–72; Exec. Officer, HMS Sultan, 1973; Dep. Prodn Man., Devonport Dockyard, 1974–77; Fleet Marine Engr Officer, 1977–79; student, RCDS, 1980; Prodn Man., Portsmouth Dockyard, 1981–83. ADC to the Queen, 1982. Comdr 1965, Captain 1974, Rear-Adm. 1983. *Recreations:* cycling, writing limericks (sometimes coincident).

McLEAN, Geoffrey Daniel, CBE 1988; QPM 1981; Assistant Commissioner (Territorial Operations), Metropolitan Police, 1984–90; *b* 4 March 1931; *s* of late William James McLean and Matilda Gladys (*née* Davies); *m* 1959, Patricia Edna Pope; two *s* two *d*. Following service in RA, joined Metropolitan Police, 1951; Chief Supt, 1969; Staff Officer to HMCIC, Home Office, 1970–72; Comdr, 1975; Graduate, RCDS, 1978; Dep. Asst Comr, 1979; Dep. Comdt, Police Staff Coll., 1981–83. *Recreations:* Met. Police Athletics Assoc. (Chm., 1984); Met. Police Football Club (Chm., 1984); Met. Police Race-Walking Club (Chm., 1978); riding.

McLEAN, Hector John Finlayson, CBE 1995; Secretary, Crown Appointments Commission, and Archbishops' Appointments Secretary, 1987–95; a Civil Service Commissioner, 1996–2001; *b* 10 Feb. 1934; *s* of late Dr Murdoch McLean, MB ChB and Dr Edith Muriel Finlayson McLean (*née* McGill), MB ChB, DPH, DOMS; *m* 1959, Caroline Elizabeth Lithgow; one *s* two *d*. *Educ:* Dulwich Coll.; Pembroke Coll., Cambridge (BA Hons 1958; MA 1997); Harvard Business Sch., Switzerland (SMP6 1976). Chartered FCIPD (FIPM 1965); 2nd Lieut, KOSB, 1954–55. Imperial Chemical Industries, 1958–87: Central Staff Dept, 1958; various personnel and admin. posts in Dyestuffs and Organics Divs, 1959–72; Personnel Manager, Organics Div., 1972–74; Polyurethanes Business Area Manager, 1974–75; Dir, Agricl Div., 1975–86. Non-exec. Chairman: People & Potential Ltd, 1987–97; Positive People Develt (formerly Teesside Positive People), 1987–94. Mem. Exec. Cttee, N of England Develt Council, 1978–83; Teesside Industrial Mission: Mem., Management Cttee, 1978–85; Chm., 1982–85; Dir, Cleveland Enterprise Agency, 1982–87. Mem., Northern Regl Council, CBI, 1981–85; Trustee: NE Civic Trust, 1976–88; Northern Heritage Trust, 1984–87; Family Mediation Service (N Wilts), 2000– (Chm., 2004–). Mem., Chemical and Allied Products ITB, 1979–82. Chm., Selection Panel, Wilts Police Authy, 1997–2003. Gov. Teesside Polytechnic, 1978–84; Mem. Council, Newcastle Univ., 1985–87. FRSA 1991. Pres., Alleyn Club, 1997–98 (Vice Pres., 1996–97). Hon. DSc Aston, 2004. *Recreations:* family, music (especially choral music), travel, gardening, walking. *Address:* College Farm House, Purton, near Swindon, Wilts SN5 4AE. *T:* (01793) 770525. *Club:* Royal Over-Seas League.

MACLEAN, Hector Ronald; Sheriff of Lothian and Borders, at Linlithgow, 1988–2003; *b* 6 Dec. 1931; *s* of Donald Beaton Maclean and Lucy McAlister; *m* 1967, Hilary Elizabeth Jenkins; three *d*. *Educ:* High Sch. of Glasgow; Glasgow Univ. Admitted to Faculty of Advocates, 1959. Sheriff of N Strathclyde (formerly Renfrew and Argyll), 1968–88. *Recreation:* golf. *Address:* Barrfield, Houston, Johnstone, Renfrewshire PA6 7EL. *T:* (01505) 612449.

McLEAN, Prof. Iain Sinclair, DPhil; FBA 2008; Professor of Politics, University of Oxford, and Fellow, Nuffield College, Oxford, since 1993; *b* 13 Sept. 1946; *s* of John and Louisa McLean; *m* 1984, Dr Jo Poulton; one *s* one *d*. *Educ:* Royal High Sch., Edinburgh; Christ Church, Oxford (MA, MPhil; DPhil 1972). Res. Fellow in Politics, Nuffield Coll., Oxford, 1969–71; Lectr in Politics, Univ. of Newcastle upon Tyne, 1971–78; Fellow and Praelector in Politics, University Coll., Oxford, 1978–91; Prof. of Politics, Univ. of Warwick, 1991–93. Visiting Professor: Stanford Univ., 1990; ANU, 1996, 2002; Yale Univ., 2001. Member: (Lab) Tyne and Wear MCC, 1973–79; (SDP) Oxford CC, 1982–86. Vice-Chm., Welshpool and Llanfair Light Railway, 2005–. *Publications:* Keir Hardie, 1975; Elections, 1976, 3rd edn 1983; Dealing in Votes, 1982; The Legend of Red Clydeside, 1983, 2nd edn 2000; Public Choice: an introduction, 1987; Democracy and New Technology, 1989; (ed, trans. and introd with F. Hewitt) Condorcet: foundations of social choice and political theory, 1994; (ed, trans. and introd with A. B. Urken) Classics of Social Choice, 1995; (gen. ed and contrib.) Concise Oxford Dictionary of Politics, 1996, 2nd edn 2003; (jtly) A Mathematical Approach to Proportional Representation: Duncan Black on Lewis Carroll, 1996; (ed with D. Butler) Fixing the Boundary: defining and redefining single-member electoral districts, 1996; (ed jtly) The Theory of Committees and Elections by Duncan Black and Committee Decisions with Complementary Valuation by Duncan Black and R. A. Newing, 1998; (with M. Johnes) Aberfan: government and disasters, 2000; Rational Choice and British Politics: an analysis of rhetoric and manipulation from Peel to Blair, 2001; (jtly) International Trade and Political Institutions: instituting trade in the long nineteenth century, 2001; The Fiscal Crisis of the United Kingdom, 2005; Adam Smith, 2006; numerous articles in learned jls. *Recreations:* steam railway preservation, walking, choral music. *Address:* Nuffield College, Oxford OX1 1NF.

McLEAN, His Honour Ian Graeme; a Circuit Judge, 1980–97; *b* Edinburgh, 7 Sept. 1928; *s* of Lt-Gen. Sir Kenneth McLean, KCB, KBE; *m* 1957, Eleonore Maria Gmeiner, Bregenz, Austria; two *d*. *Educ:* Aldenham Sch.; Christ's Coll., Cambridge. BA Hons Law 1950; MA 1955. Intell. Corps, 1946–48. Called to English Bar, Middle Temple, Nov. 1951; admitted Faculty of Advocates, Edinburgh, 1985; practised London and on Western Circuit, 1951–55; Crown Counsel, Northern Nigeria, 1955–59; Sen. Lectr and Head of Legal Dept of Inst. of Administration, Northern Nigeria, 1959–62; Native Courts Adviser, 1959–62; returned to English Bar, 1962; practised London and South Eastern Circuit, 1962–70; Adjudicator under Immigration Acts, 1969–70; Metropolitan Stipendiary Magistrate, 1970–80. *Publications:* Cumulative Index West African Court of Appeal Reports, 1958; (with Abubakar Sadiq) The Maliki Law of Homicide, 1959; (with Sir Lionel Brett) Criminal Law Procedure and Evidence of Lagos, Eastern and Western Nigeria, 1963; (with Cyprian Okonkwo) Cases on the Criminal Law, Procedure and Evidence of Nigeria, 1966; (with Peter Morrish) A Practical Guide to Appeals in Criminal Courts, 1970; (with Peter Morrish) The Crown Court, an index of common penalties, etc, 1972–2000, (with Peter Morrish and D. H. D. Selwood), 2001–04, (with Peter Morrish), 2005, (with Peter Morrish and S. Katkhuda), 2006, (with S. Katkhuda), 2007, 2008; (ed with Peter Morrish) Harris's Criminal Law, 22nd edn, 1972; (with Peter Morrish) The Magistrates' Court, an index of common penalties, annually 1973–92, (with Peter Morrish and John Greenhill), 1996 and 2003; (with Peter Morrish) The Trial of Breathalyser Offences, 1975, 3rd edn 1990; A Practical Guide to Criminal Appeals, 1980; A Pattern of Sentencing, 1981; (with John Mulhern) The Industrial Tribunal: a practical guide to employment law and tribunal procedure, 1982; (with Sheriff Stone) Fact-Finding for Magistrates, 1990; contrib. Archbold's Criminal Pleadings, 38th edn, and Halsbury's Laws of England, 4th edn, title Criminal Law. *Recreations:* writing, languages. *Address:* c/o First Direct, 40 Wakefield Road, Leeds LS98 1FD.

MACLEAN, Prof. Ian Walter Fitzroy, DPhil; FRHistS; FBA 1994; Titular Professor of Renaissance Studies, Oxford University, and Senior Research Fellow, All Souls College, Oxford, since 1996; *b* 9 Feb. 1945; *s* of James Walter Maclean and Elsie May Maclean (*née* Davis); *m* 1971, Pauline Jennifer Henderson; one *s* two *d*. *Educ:* Christ's Hosp.; Wadham Coll., Oxford (BA 1st Cl. Hons Mod. Lang. 1966; MA, DPhil 1971). FRHistS 1989. Sen. Scholar, Wadham Coll., Oxford, 1967–69; Lectr in French, Univ. of Leeds, 1969–72; Oxford University: CUF Lectr in French, 1972–93; Reader in French, 1994–96; Fellow, 1972–96, Supernumerary Fellow, 1996–, Queen's Coll.; Dir, European Humanities Res. Centre, 1994–99. Vis. Fellow, Humanities Res. Centre, Canberra, 1983; Vis. Scholar, Herzog August Bibliothek, Wolfenbüttel, 1986, 1995; Visiting Professor: Catholic Univ. of Nijmegen, 1993; Collège de France, 2005; Ecole Pratique des Hautes Etudes, Paris, 2007; Dist. Vis. Schol., Centre for Renaissance and Reformation Studies, Victoria Univ., Univ. of Toronto, 1994. MAE 1998. Officier, Ordre des Arts et des Lettres (France), 2005. *Publications:* Woman Triumphant: feminism in French literature, 1977; The Renaissance Notion of Woman, 1980; (ed and contrib.) Montaigne, 1982; (ed and contrib.) The Political Responsibility of Intellectuals, 1990; Meaning and Interpretation in the Renaissance: the case of law, 1992; (trans.) Potocki, The Manuscript Found in Saragossa, 1995; Montaigne philosophe, 1996; Logic, Signs and Nature in the Renaissance: the case of learned medicine, 2001; (ed and contrib.) *Res et verba* in the Renaissance, 2002; (ed) Cardano, *De Libris Propriis*, 2005; (ed and contrib.) Heterodoxy in Early Modern Science and Religion, 2006; (ed and contrib.) Transmitting Knowledge: words, images and instruments in Early Modern Europe, 2006; Le monde et les hommes selon les médecins de la Renaissance, 2006; (trans.) Descartes, A Discourse on the Method, 2006; articles and essays in learned jls, collective vols, etc. *Recreations:* music, fishing, wine. *Address:* All Souls College, Oxford OX1 4AL. *T:* (01865) 279379.

MACLEAN, Kate; Member (Lab) Dundee West, Scottish Parliament, 1999–2007; *b* 16 Feb. 1958; *d* of late Alexander Robertson and Sarah Robertson; *m* 1978 (marr. diss.); one *s* one *d*. *Educ:* Craigie High Sch., Dundee. Mem. (Lab) Dundee City Council, 1988–99 (Leader, 1992–99). Convener, Equal Opportunities Cttee, Scottish Parliament, 1999–2007. Vice-Pres., COSLA, 1996–99. *Address:* c/o Scottish Parliament, Edinburgh EH99 1SP.

McLEAN, Keith Richard, FCCA; Chairman, Harrogate Training and Development, since 2004; Partner, Birchfield Associates, since 2004; *b* 27 Oct. 1947; *s* of Bertie and Elsie McLean; *m* 1973, Patricia Ann Morrell; one *d*. *Educ:* J. Rowntree Sch., York. FCCA 1975; IPFA 1989; MHSM 1992. Hospital Management Committees: Clerical Officer, York B, 1964–67; Higher Clerical Officer, Leicester No 4, 1967–68; Internal Auditor, Nottingham No 4, 1968–70; Sen. Accountant, Huddersfield, 1970–74; Dep. Area Treas., Calderdale HA, 1974–79; Dist Finance Officer, Derbys AHA, 1979–82; North Derbyshire Health Authority: Dist Treas., 1982–85; Dist Treas. and Dep. Dist Gen. Manager, 1985–87; Dir of Finance and Corporate Strategist, Leics HA, 1987–89; Yorkshire Regional Health Authority: Regl Dir of Finance, 1990–91; Regl Gen. Manager, 1991–94; Regl Gen. Manager, Trent RHA and Regl Dir, NHS Exec., Trent, 1994–96. Director: Harrogate Mgt Centre Ltd, 1996–2004; Key Health Marketing Ltd, 1998–2004; Partner, Key Health Consulting, 1998–2005. Principal Res. Fellow, Sheffield Univ., 1996–2000. Nat. Chm., Healthcare Financial Mgt Assoc., 1992–93. FRSA 1994. *Recreation:* golf. *Address:* Harrogate Training and Development Ltd, 87 Skipton Road, Harrogate HG1 4LF. *T:* (01423) 506611.

MacLEAN, Kenneth Smedley, MD, FRCP; Consultant Physician to Guy's Hospital, 1950–79, now Emeritus; *b* 22 Nov. 1914; *s* of Hugh MacLean and Ida Smedley; *m* 1939, Joan Hardaker (*d* 2002); one *s* one *d* (and one *s* decd). *Educ:* Westminster; Clare Coll., Cambridge. MRCS, LRCP, 1939; House appts at Guy's, 1939; MB, BChir 1939. RNVR, 1939–46, Surg.-Lt and Surg.-Lt-Comdr. MRCP 1946; House Officer and Medical Registrar, Guy's Hosp., 1946–48; MD Cantab 1948; FRCP 1954; elected to Assoc. of Physicians of Great Britain and Ireland, 1956. Assistant Director, Dept of Medicine, Guy's Hospital Medical Sch., 1949, Director, 1961–63. Chm., University Hosps Assoc., 1975–78. Pres., Assurance Medical Soc., 1985–87. *Publication:* Medical Treatment, 1957. *Recreation:* golf. *Address:* Flat 1 Brackenhill, 16 Westerham Road, Limpsfield, Oxted, Surrey RH8 0ER. *T:* (01883) 716652.

MacLEAN, Kenneth Walter; QC 2002; *b* 9 Feb. 1959; *s* of Walter and Mary MacLean; *m* 1994, Jane Elizabeth; three *c*. *Educ:* Rugby Sch.; Trinity Hall, Cambridge (MA); Harvard Law Sch. (LLM). Called to the Bar, Gray's Inn, 1985. *Recreations:* ski-ing, Rugby, piping. *Address:* 1 Essex Court, Temple, EC4Y 9AR. *T:* (020) 7583 2000, *Fax:* (020) 7583 0118; *e-mail:* kmaclean@oeclaw.co.uk. *Club:* Harvard (NYC).

MACLEAN, Hon. Sir Lachlan Hector Charles, 12th Bt *cr* 1631 (NS), of Duart and Morvern; CVO 2000; DL; Major, Scots Guards, retired; 28th Chief of Clan Maclean; *b* 25 Aug. 1942; *s* of Baron Maclean, KT, GCVO, KBE, PC and of Elizabeth, *er d* of late Frank Mann; *S* to baronetcy of father, 1990; *m* 1966, Mary Helen (*d* 2007), *e d* of late W. G. Gordon; two *s* two *d* (and one *d* decd). *Educ:* Eton. DL Argyll and Bute, 1993. *Heir:* *s* Malcolm Lachlan Charles Maclean [*b* 20 Oct. 1972; *m* 1998, Anna, *e d* of Giles Sturdy; three *s*]. *Address:* Arngask House, Glenfarg, Perthshire PH2 9QA.

MACLEAN, Mavis, CBE 2002; Director, Oxford Centre for Family Law and Policy, Department of Social Policy and Social Work, University of Oxford, since 2001; *b* 31 Dec. 1943; *m* 1967, Robert Maclean; two *d*. *Educ:* St Hilda's Coll., Oxford (BA (Hist.) 1965); LSE (MSc (Econs) 1967); Univ. of N London (LLB 1990). Res. Fellow, Centre for Socio-Legal Studies, Univ. of Oxford, 1974–2001. Academic Advr to LCD, later Dept for Constitutional Affairs, 1997–; Panel Mem., Bristol Royal Infirmary Inquiry, 1998–2001. *Publications:* (with J. Eekelaar) The Parental Obligation, 1997; (ed jtly) Cross Currents, 2000; (jtly) Family Lawyers, 2000; Family Law and Family Values, 2005; contribs to Family Law, Internat. Jl Law, Policy and the Family, Law and Soc., Jl of Social Welfare and Family Law. *Recreation:* music. *Address:* Oxford Centre for Family Law and Policy, 32 Wellington Square, Oxford OX1 2ER; *e-mail:* mavis.maclean@socres.ox.ac.uk. *Club:* Athenæum.

McLEAN, Miller Roy; Group Secretary, since 1994, and General Counsel, since 2003, Royal Bank of Scotland Group; *b* Dumbarton, 4 Dec. 1949; *s* of David Peter Miller McLean and Jane Roy McLean (*née* Stenhouse); *m* 1973, Anne Gourlay; one *s* one *d*. *Educ:* Vale of Leven Acad.; Glasgow Univ. (MA); Edinburgh Univ. (LLB with Dist.). MCIBS 1972, FCIBS 1992. Royal Bank of Scotland: grad. trainee, 1970; Sec., 1983–88; Gp Sec., 1988–91; Dir, Legal and Regulatory Affairs, 1991–2000; Gp Dir, Legal and Regulatory Affairs, 2000–03. Trustee, 2000–, Chm., 2003–, Royal Bank of Scotland Gp Pension Fund; Trustee, 2006–, Chm., 2007–, Royal Bank of Scotland Insurance Pension Fund. Director: Banco Santander Portugal SA, 1991– (Vice Chm., 1993–2003); Adam & Co. Gp plc, 1998–; Newton Mgt Ltd, 1998; Ulster Bank Gp, 2001–. Mem., Financial Issues Adv. Gp, Scottish Parlt, 1998–2000; Dir, 1999–, Chm., 2001–, Whitehall and Industry Gp; Dir, Scottish Parlt and Business Exchange, 2001–08. Industry and Parliament Trust: Corporate Fellow, 1989–; Mem. Council, 1990– (Chm. Council, 1996–99); Trustee, 2000–. Chartered Institute of Bankers in Scotland: Mem. Council, 1997–; Vice-Pres., 2002–07; Pres., 2007–. Gov., Queen Margaret Univ. Coll., 2000–03. *Recreations:* golf, reading, music, forgetting family birthdays. *Address:* RBS Gogarburn, Business House G, 1st Floor, PO Box 1000, Edinburgh EH12 1HQ. *T:* (0131) 523 2223, *Fax:* (0131) 626 2997; *e-mail:* miller.mclean@rbs.com. *Club:* New (Edinburgh).

MACLEAN, Sir Murdo, Kt 2000; consultant, since 2000; *b* 21 Oct. 1943; *s* of late Murdo Maclean and of Johanna (*née* Martin). *Educ:* Glasgow. Min. of Labour Employment Exchange, Govan, Glasgow, 1963–64; BoT, 1964–67; Prime Minister's Office, 1967–72; Dept of Industry, 1972–78; Private Sec. to Govt Chief Whip, 1979–2000; Chief Exec., Tridos Solutions Ltd, 2000–02; Chm., SiScape Technology Ltd, 2001–02. Trustee, Columba 1400 Foundation, 2003–06. Freeman, City of London, 1994. FRSA 1990. *Club:* Garrick.

MACLEAN of Pennycross, Nicolas Wolfers Lorne, CMG 2002; 8th Chieftain of Maclean of Pennycross; Chief Executive, MWM, since 1999; *b* 3 Jan. 1946; *s* of late Marcel Wolfers and Audrey Wolfers (*née* Maclean of Pennycross); named Nicolas Lorne Maclean Wolfers; *S* kinsman as Maclean of Pennycross, 1993; *m* 1978, Qamar Aziz; two *s*. *Educ:* Eton; Oriel Coll., Oxford (MA PPE 1967); Univ. of Santander (Cert. Spanish). Grad. Trainee, later Manager, Eur. and Japanese Investment Section, J. Henry Schroder Wagg & Co. Ltd, 1967–71; Manager, P. N. Kemp Gee & Co., 1971–72; Samuel Montagu & Co. Ltd: Manager, London Continental Pension Unit Trust, 1972–74; Asst Dir, Project and Export Finance, 1974–82; Asst Dir, Public Finance Dept, 1982–85; Gp Advr, Midland Bank Gp, 1985–93; Sen. Advr, China, Robert Fleming PLC, 1994–97; Gp Advr, Prudential Corp. PLC and Exec. Dir, Prudential Corp. Asia Ltd, 1997–99. Initiated Wolfers Prog. with Japan (subseq. Japan Exchange and Teaching Prog.), 1976. Chm., Japan Festival Educn Trust, 2002–03 (Dep. Chm., 1992–2002). Member: RIIA, 1967–; IISS, 2002– (Sen. Fellow, 2000–07); Bd, Canada-UK Colloquia, 2007–. Fellow Emeritus, British Assoc. of Japanese Studies, 2003. *Publications:* (all jointly): Trading with China: a practical guide, 1979; Journey into Japan 1600–1868, 1981; The Eurobond and Eurocurrency Markets, 1984; Mongolia Today, 1988. *Recreations:* history, etymology, performing and visual arts, rowing, broadcasting, international affairs. *Heir:* *s* Mark Maclean, yr of Pennycross, *b* 19 July 1982. *Address:* 30 Malwood Road, SW12 8EN. *T:* (020) 8675 6725, *Fax:* (020) 8675 6886; *e-mail:* nmatmwm@hotmail.com. *Club:* Beefsteak.

MACLEAN, Prof. Norman; JP; PhD; FIBiol, FLS; Professor of Genetics, University of Southampton, 1992–2004, now Emeritus (Head of Department of Biology, 1993–97); *b* 23 Sept. 1932; *s* of late Alexander Maclean and Christine Walker; *m* 1962, Dr Jane Kay Smith; one *s* one *d*. *Educ:* George Heriot's Sch., Edinburgh; Edinburgh Sch. of Agriculture; Edinburgh Univ. (SDA, BSc 1st cl. Hons, PhD 1962). FIBiol 1990; FLS 1992. Asst Lectr in Zoology, Edinburgh Univ., 1961–64; Sir Henry Wellcome Travelling Fellow, 1964–65; Res. Associate, Rockefeller Inst., NY, 1964; Lectr in Biology, Sen. Lectr and Reader, Southampton Univ., 1965–92. Molecular Scis Ed., Jl Fish Biol., 2006–. Mem., Scientific Adv. Cttee, Aquagene Inc., Fla, 1999–. Hon. Scientific Advr, Marwell Preservation Trust (Trustee, 1995–2004). Dir, Test and Itchen Assoc. Ltd, 2006–. Edinburgh University: MacGillivray Prize in Zoology, 1956; Moira Lindsay Stuart Prize in Zoology, 1957; Gunning Victoria Jubilee Prize, 1960. JP Southampton, 1976. *Publications:* Control of Gene Expression, 1976; The Differentiation of Cells, 1977; Haemoglobin, 1978; Trout and Grayling: an angler's natural history, 1980; (jtly) DNA, Chromatin and Chromosomes, 1981; (ed jtly) Eukaryotic Genes: structure, activity and regulation, 1983; (ed) Oxford Surveys on Eurkaryotic Genes, vols 1–7, 1984–90; (jtly) Cell Commitment and Differentiation, 1987; Macmillan Dictionary of Genetic and Cell Biology, 1987; Genes and Gene Regulation, 1989, 3rd edn 1992; Animals with Novel Genes, 1994; articles in learned jls. *Recreations:* gardening, fly fishing, tennis, reading. *Address:* 10 Russell Place, Southampton SO17 1NU. *T:* (023) 8055 7649; *e-mail:* nm4@soton.ac.uk. *Club:* Abbotts Barton Angling.

McLEAN, Peter Standley, CMG 1985; OBE 1965; Head of East Asia Department, Overseas Development Administration, 1985–87; *b* 18 Jan. 1927; *s* of late William and Alice McLean; *m* 1954, Margaret Ann Minns (*d* 2002); two *s* two *d*. *Educ:* King Edward's Sch., Birmingham; Wadham Coll., Oxford (MA). Served Army, 1944–48; Lieut, 15/19th King's Royal Hussars. Colonial Service, Uganda, 1951–65, retired from HMOCS as Permanent Sec., Min. of Planning and Economic Develt; Ministry of Overseas Development: Principal, 1965; Private Sec. to Minister for Overseas Develt, 1973; Head of Eastern and Southern Africa Dept, 1975; Head of Bilateral Aid and Rural Develt Dept, 1979; Minister and UK Perm. Rep to FAO, 1980. Chm., Africa Grants Cttee, Comic Relief, 1989–92. Chm., Internat. Health Solutions Trust, 1997–. Vice-Chm., Overseas Service Pensioners Benevolent Soc., 2001–. *Recreations:* watching sport, DIY, painting. *Address:* 17 Woodfield Lane, Ashtead, Surrey KT21 2BQ. *T:* (01372) 278146.

McLEAN, Philip Alexander, CMG 1994; HM Diplomatic Service, retired; Director-General, Canning House (Hispanic and Luso-Brazilian Council), 1999–2002; *b* 24 Oct. 1938; *s* of late Wm Alexander McLean and Doris McLean (*née* Campbell); *m* 1960, Dorothy Helen Kirkby; two *s* one *d*. *Educ:* King George V Sch., Southport; Keble Coll., Oxford (MA Hons). National Service, RAF, 1956–58. Industry, 1961–68; entered HM Diplomatic Service by Open Supplementary Competition, 1968; Second, later (1969) First, Secretary, FCO; La Paz, 1970–74: Head of Chancery, 1973; FCO, 1974–76; Dep. Director of British Trade Development Office and Head of Industrial Marketing, New York, 1976–80; Counsellor and Consul-Gen., Algiers, 1981–83; Diplomatic Service Inspector, 1983–85; Hd, S America Dept, FCO, 1985–87; Consul-Gen., Boston, 1988–91; Minister and Dep. Head of Mission, Peking, 1991–94; Ambassador to Cuba, 1994–98. Robin Humphreys Vis. Res. Fellow, 1999–2000, Mem. Adv. Council, 1999–2004, Inst. of Latin American Studies, London Univ. Chm., Anglo-Bolivian Soc., 2002–06. Chm., St Luke's Housing Soc., Oxford, 2005– (Bd Mem., 2003–). Mem. Council, St Stephen's House, Oxford, 2004– (Vice Chm., 2005–). Diplomatic Advr, Carlton Tower and Lowndes Hotels, Knightsbridge, 2004–07. Hon. LLD American Internat. Coll., 1991. *Recreations:* hill walking, food and drink, friends. *Address:* Hill Cottage, Reading Road, Goring-on-Thames RG8 0LH. *Club:* Oxford and Cambridge.

MacLEAN, Ranald Norman Munro; *see* MacLean, Rt Hon. Lord.

McLEAN, Prof. Sheila Ann Manson, PhD; FRSE; FRCPE; International Bar Association Professor of Law and Ethics in Medicine, since 1990, and Director, Institute of Law and Ethics in Medicine, since 1985, Glasgow University; *b* 20 June 1951; *d* of late William Black and of Bethia Black (*née* Manson); *m* 1976, Alan McLean (marr. diss. 1987). *Educ:* Glasgow High Sch. for Girls; Glasgow Univ. (LLB 1972; MLitt 1978; PhD 1987). FRSE 1996; FRCPE 1997. Area Reporter, Children's Panel, 1972–75; Lectr, 1975–85, Sen. Lectr, 1985–90, Sch. of Law, Glasgow Univ. Chm., Scottish Criminal Cases Review Commn, 1999–2002. Chairman: Review of consent provisions of Human Fertilisation and Embryology Act, DoH, 1997–98; Ind. Review Gp on Organ Retention at Post Mortem, 2000–03; Member: UK Xenotransplantation Interim Regulatory Authy, 1997–2002; Wellcome Trust Biomedical Ethics Panel, 2002–06; Internat. Fedn of Obstetrics and Gynaecol. Ethics Cttee, 2003–; UNESCO Biomed. Ethics Cttee, 2006–; Crown Office Inspectorate Review of Organ Retention Practices, 2005–; Vice Chair, Multi-Centre Res. Ethics Cttee for Scotland, 1997–98. Member: Ethics Cttee, BMA, 2000–; Ethics and Governance Council, UK Biobank, 2004–; Adv. Cttee, ESRC Genomics Policy and Res. Forum, 2004–. Member: UKCC, 1993–98; SHEFC, 1996–98; AHRC Peer Review Coll., 2005–. Mem., Broadcasting Council for Scotland, 1991–96. FMedSci 2006. FRSA 1996. Hon. FRCGP 2003. Hon. LLD: Abertay Dundee, 2002; Edinburgh, 2002. *Publications:* (jtly) Medicine, Morals and the Law, 1983; A Patient's Right to Know: information disclosure, the doctor and the law, 1989; (jtly) The Case for Physician Assisted Suicide, 1997; Old Law, New Medicine, 1999; (jtly) Legal and Ethical Aspects of Healthcare, 2003; (jtly) Xenotransplantation: law and ethics, 2005; *edited:* Legal Issues in Medicine, 1981; (jtly) Human Rights: from rhetoric to reality, 1986; (jtly) The Legal Relevance of Gender, 1988; Legal Issues in Human Reproduction, 1989; Law Reform and Human Reproduction, 1992; Compensation for Personal Injury: an international perspective, 1993; Law Reform and Medical Injury Litigation, 1995; Law and Ethics in Intensive Care, 1996; Death, Dying and the Law, 1996; Contemporary Issues in Law, Medicine and Ethics, 1996; Medical Law and Ethics, 2002; Genetics and Gene Therapy, 2005. *Recreations:* playing guitar, singing, reading. *Address:* School of Law, The University, Glasgow G12 8QQ. *T:* (0141) 330 5577. *Club:* Lansdowne.

McLEAN, Dr Thomas Pearson, CB 1990; FRSE; CPhys, FInstP; Professor of Electrical Engineering and Science, Royal Military College of Science, Shrivenham, 1992–95; *b* Paisley, 21 Aug. 1930; *s* of Norman Stewart McLean and Margaret Pearson McLean (*née* Ferguson); *m* 1957, Grace Campbell Nokes; two *d*. *Educ:* John Neilson Instn, Paisley; Glasgow Univ. (BSc, PhD); Birmingham Univ. Royal Radar Estabt (becoming Royal Signals and Radar Estabt, 1976), 1955–80: Head of Physics Gp, 1973–77; Dep. Dir, 1977–80; Ministry of Defence: Under Sec., Dir Gen. Air Weapons and Electronic Systems, 1980–83; Dir, RARDE, 1984–86; Dep. Controller, Aircraft, 1987; Dir, Atomic Weapons Estabt, 1987–90. Member: Physics Cttee, SRC, 1968–73; Optoelectronics Cttee, Rank Prize Funds, 1972–81; Council, Inst. of Physics, 1980–84. Hon. Prof. of Physics, Birmingham Univ., 1977–80. Dep. Editor, Jl of Physics C, 1976–77. *Publications:* papers in Physical Rev., Jl of Physics, etc. *Recreations:* music, mathematics, computing.

MACLEAN, Prof. William James, MBE 2006; RSA 1991; RSW 1997; Professor of Fine Art, 1995–2001, now Emeritus Professor of Visual Art, and Research Professor, Visual Research Centre, since 2001, University of Dundee; *b* 12 Oct. 1941; *s* of Capt. John Maclean and Mary Isabella (*née* Reid); *m* 1968, Marian Leven, RSA; two *s* one *d*. *Educ:* Inverness Royal Acad.; HMS Conway MN Cadet Trng Sch., N Wales; Gray's Sch. of Art, Aberdeen (DA 1966; Post-Grad. Dip. 1967). Midshipman, Blue Funnel Line, 1957–59; school teacher, 1971–81; Lectr in Drawing and Painting, Dundee Coll. of Art, 1981–94. Solo exhibns in GB and abroad; *work in Collections of:* Arts Council of GB; British Mus.; Nat. Art Collection; Fitzwilliam Mus. and Art Gall., Cambridge; Yale Centre for British Art; Scottish Nat. Gall. of Modern Art, etc. Mem., RGI, 1996. Hon. DLitt St Andrews, 2000. *Publication:* Will Maclean: sculptures and box constructions, 1987; *relevant publication:* Symbols of Survival: the art of Will Maclean, by Prof. Duncan Macmillan, 1992. *Recreations:* reading, walking.

MacLEARY, Alistair Ronald; Hon. Professor, Heriot-Watt University, since 2004; *b* 12 Jan. 1940; *s* of Donald Herbert MacLeary and Jean Spiers (*née* Leslie); *m* 1967, Mary-Claire Cecilia (*née* Leonard); one *s* one *d*. *Educ:* Inverness Royal Acad.; Coll. of Estate Management, London; Edinburgh Coll. of Art, Heriot-Watt Univ.; Strathclyde Univ.

MSc, DipTP; FRICS, FRTPI. Gerald Eve & Co., 1963–65; Murrayfield Real Estate Co., 1965–67; Dept of Environment (on secondment), 1971–73; Wright, Partners, 1967–76; MacRobert Prof. of Land Economy, 1976–89, Dean, Faculty of Law, 1982–85, Aberdeen Univ. Univ. of Auckland Foundn Visitor and Fletcher Challenge Vis. Fellow, 1985; Memorialist, MacAuley Inst. for Soil Science, 1986–87. Mem., Cttee of Inquiry into Acquisition and Occupancy of Agricl Land, 1977–79; Chm., Watt Cttee, Energy Working Gp on Land Resources, 1977–79; Mem., Exec. Cttee, Commonwealth Assoc. of Surveying and Land Economy, 1980–85 (Chm., Bd of Surveying Educn, 1981–90); Member: Home Grown Timber Adv. Cttee, Forestry Commn, 1981–87; NERC, 1988–91 (Chm., Terrestrial and Freshwater Sci. Cttee, 1990–91); Lands Tribunal for Scotland, 1989–2005; Administrative Justice & Tribunals Council (formerly Council on Tribunals), 2005– (Chm., Scottish Cttee, 2005–Sept. 2009). Mem., Gen. Council, RICS, 1983–87 (Pres., Planning and Develt Divl Council, 1984–85). Mem., MacTaggart Chair Adv. Bd, Glasgow Univ., 1992–2000. FRSA. Hon. Fellow, Commonwealth Assoc. of Surveying and Land Economy, 1992. Founder and Editor, Land Development Studies, subseq. Jl of Property Research, 1983–90. *Publications:* (ed with N. Nanthakumeran) Property Investment Theory, 1988; National Taxation for Property Management and Valuation, 1990. *Recreations:* hill walking, field sports, golf. *Address:* St Helen's, Ceres, Fife KY15 5NQ. *T:* (01334) 828862. *Club:* Royal Northern and University (Aberdeen).

See also D. W. Bentham-MacLeary.

MacLEARY, Donald Whyte; *see* Bentham-MacLeary, D. W.

MACLEAY, Rev. John Henry James; Dean of Argyll and The Isles, 1987–99; Rector of St Andrew's, Fort William, 1978–99; retired; *b* 7 Dec. 1931; *s* of James and Isabella Macleay; *m* 1970, Jane Speirs Cuthbert; one *s* one *d*. *Educ:* St Edmund Hall, Oxford (MA); College of the Resurrection, Mirfield. Deacon 1957, priest 1958, Southwark; Curate: St John's, East Dulwich, 1957–60; St Michael's, Inverness, 1960–62, Rector 1962–70; Priest-in-charge, St Columba's, Grantown-on-Spey with St John the Baptist's, Rothiemurchus, 1970–78; Canon of St Andrew's Cathedral, Inverness, 1977–78; Canon of St John's Cathedral, Oban and Synod Clerk, Diocese of Argyll and the Isles, 1980–87. Hon. Canon, Oban Cathedral, 1999–2003. Received into RC Church, 2003. *Recreations:* fishing, reading, visiting cathedrals and churches. *Address:* 47 Riverside Park, Lochyside, Fort William PH33 7RB. *T:* (01397) 700117.

McLEAY, Hon. Leo Boyce; *b* 5 Oct. 1945; *s* of Ron and Joan McLeay; *m* 1969, Janice Delaney; three *s*. *Educ:* De La Salle Sch., Marrickville; North Sydney Technical Coll. Telephone technician, 1962–76; Asst Gen. Sec., ALP (NSW), 1976–79. MP (Lab) Grayndler, 1979–93, Watson, 1993–2004, NSW; Dep. Speaker, 1986–89, Speaker, 1989–93, House of Representatives; Chief Govt Whip, 1993–96; Chief Opposition Whip and Dep. Manager, Opposition business, 1996–2001. *Recreations:* fishing, reading. *Address:* PO Box A1420, Sydney South, NSW 1235, Australia. *Club:* Canterbury Rugby League (NSW).

McLEISH, Rt Hon. Henry (Baird); PC 2000; Member (Lab) Fife Central, Scottish Parliament, 1999–2003; *b* 15 June 1948; *s* of Harry McLeish and late Mary McLeish; *m* 1968, Margaret Thomson Drysdale (*d* 1995); one *s* one *d*; *m* 1998, Julie Fulton. *Educ:* Heriot-Watt Univ. (BA Hons planning). Research Officer, Social Work Dept, Edinburgh, 1973–74; Planning Officer, Fife County Council, 1974–75; Planning Officer, Dunfermline DC, 1975–87; part time Lectr/Tutor, Heriot-Watt Univ., 1973–87; part-time employment consultant, 1984–87. Member: Kirkcaldy DC (Chm., Planning Cttee, 1974–77); Fife Regl Council (Chm., Further Educn Cttee, 1978–82; Leader, Council, 1982–87). MP (Lab) Central Fife, 1987–2001. Minister of State, Scottish Office, 1997–99; Scottish Executive: Minister for Enterprise and Lifelong Learning, 1999–2000; First Minister, 2000–01. *Publications:* Scotland First: truth and consequences, 2004; Global Scots: voices from afar, 2005. *Recreations:* reading, malt whisky (history and development of), history, life and works of Robert Burns, Highlands and Islands of Scotland, astronomy, history of great speeches. *Address:* 49 George Street, Cellardyke, Fife KY10 3AS.

MacLELLAN, Maj.-Gen. (Andrew) Patrick (Withy), CB 1981; CVO 1989; MBE 1964; Resident Governor and Keeper of the Jewel House, HM Tower of London, 1984–89; *b* 29 Nov. 1925; *y s* of late Kenneth MacLellan and Rachel Madeline MacLellan (*née* Withy); *m* 1954, Kathleen Mary Bagnell; one *s* twin *d*. *Educ:* Uppingham. Commnd Coldstream Guards, 1944; served Palestine 1945–48, N Africa 1950–51, Egypt 1952–53, Germany 1955–56; psc 1957; DAA&QMG 4th Guards Brigade Group, 1958–59; Mil. Asst to Chief of Defence Staff, 1961–64; Instructor, Staff Coll., Camberley, 1964–66; GSO1 (Plans) Far East Comd, 1966–67; CO 1st Bn Coldstream Guards, 1968–70; Col GS Near East Land Forces, 1970–71; Comdr 8th Inf. Brigade, 1971–72; RCDS 1973; Dep. Comdr and COS, London District, 1974–77; Pres., Regular Commns Bd, 1978–80. Vice-Pres., Officers' Assoc. Mem. Cttee, Royal Humane Soc.; Mem., Adv. Council, First Aid Nursing Yeomanry (The Princess Royal's Volunteer Corps), 1979–2003 (Chm., 1997–2003). FCMI (FBIM 1970). Mem. (Walbrook Ward), Court of Common Council, City of London, 1989–2000 (Chm., Police Cttee, 1995–97). Freeman: City of London, 1984; Co. of Watermen and Lightermen; Liveryman, Fletchers' Co., 1986– (Master, 1997–98). Chevalier de la Légion d'Honneur, 1960; Order of the Sacred Treasure (Japan), 1998. *Address:* c/o Bank of Scotland, 14 Cockspur Street, SW1Y 5BL. *Clubs:* White's, Pratt's.

McLELLAN, Very Rev. Andrew Rankin Cowie; HM Chief Inspector of Prisons for Scotland, since 2002; Moderator of the General Assembly of the Church of Scotland, 2000; *b* 16 June 1944; *s* of Andrew Barclay McLellan and Catherine Hilda McLellan (*née* Cowie); *m* 1975, Irene Lamont Meek; twin *s*. *Educ:* Kilmarnock Acad.; Madras Coll., St Andrews; St Andrews Univ. (MA 1965); Glasgow Univ. (BD 1968); Union Theol Seminary, NY (STM 1969; Unitas Award, 2008). Asst Minister, St George's West, Edinburgh, 1969–71; Minister: Cartsburn Augustine, Greenock, 1971–80; Viewfield, Stirling, 1980–86; Parish Church of St Andrew and St George, Edinburgh, 1986–2002. Tutor, Glasgow Univ., 1978–82; Chaplain, HM Prison, Stirling, 1982–85. Dir, Scottish Television, 2004–. Chairman: George St Assoc. of Edinburgh, 1990–93; Scottish Religious Adv. Cttee, BBC, 1996–2001; Convener, Church and Nation Cttee, 1992–96, Parish Develt Fund, 2002–06, Gen. Assembly of the Church of Scotland. Warrack Lectr on Preaching, Divinity Faculties of Scotland, 2000. Mem., Inverclyde DC, 1977–80. Hon. DD St Andrews, 2000. *Publications:* Preaching for these People, 1997; Gentle and Passionate, 2001. *Recreations:* sport, travel, books, gardening. *Address:* 4 Liggars Place, Dunfermline, Fife KY12 7XZ. *T:* (01383) 725959.

McLELLAN, Prof. David, DPhil; Professor of Political Theory, University of Kent, 1975–99; *b* 10 Feb. 1940; *s* of Robert Douglas McLellan and Olive May Bush; *m* 1967, Annie Brassart; two *d*. *Educ:* Merchant Taylors' Sch.; St John's Coll., Oxford (MA, DPhil). University of Kent: Lectr in Politics, 1966–71; Sen. Lectr in Politics, 1972–73; Reader in Political Theory, 1973–75. Vis. Prof., State Univ. of New York, 1969; Vis. Prof. of Political Theory, Goldsmiths Coll., Univ. of London, 1999–; Guest Fellow in Politics, Indian Inst. of Advanced Studies, Simla, 1970. *Publications:* The Young Hegelians and Karl Marx, 1969 (French, German, Italian, Spanish and Japanese edns); Marx before Marxism, 1970, 2nd edn 1972; Karl Marx: The Early Texts, 1971; Marx's Grundrisse, 1971, 2nd edn 1973; The Thought of Karl Marx, 1971 (Portuguese and Italian edns); Karl Marx: His Life and Thought, 1973, 22nd edn 1976 (German, Italian, Spanish, Japanese, Swedish and Dutch edns); Marx (Fontana Modern Masters), 1975; Engels, 1977; Marxism after Marx, 1979; (ed) Marx: the first hundred years, 1983; Karl Marx: the legacy, 1983; Ideology, 1986; Marxism and Religion, 1987; Simone Weil: Utopian pessimist, 1989; Christianity and Politics, 1990; Religion and Public Life, 1992; Unto Caesar: the political relevance of Christianity, 1993; Case Law and Political Theory, 1996; (ed) Political Christianity, 1997; Karl Marx: a biography, 2006; Marxism after Marx, 2007. *Recreations:* chess, Raymond Chandler, hill walking. *Address:* c/o Rutherford College, University of Kent, Canterbury, Kent CT2 7NX.

MacLELLAN, Maj.-Gen. Patrick; *see* MacLellan, A. P. W.

MACLENNAN, family name of **Baron Maclennan of Rogart**.

MACLENNAN OF ROGART, Baron *cr* 2001 (Life Peer), of Rogart in Sutherland; **Robert Adam Ross Maclennan;** PC 1997; Barrister-at-Law; *b* 26 June 1936; *e s* of late Sir Hector MacLennan and Isabel Margaret Adam; *m* 1968, Mrs Helen Noyes, *d* of late Judge Ammi Cutter, Cambridge, Mass, and *widow* of Paul H. Noyes; one *s* one *d*, and one step *s*. *Educ:* Glasgow Academy; Balliol Coll., Oxford; Trinity Coll., Cambridge; Columbia Univ., New York City. Called to the Bar, Gray's Inn, 1962. MP Caithness and Sutherland, 1966–97 (Lab, 1966–81, SDP, 1981–88, Lib Dem, 1988–97), (Lib Dem) Caithness, Sutherland and Easter Ross, 1997–2001. Parliamentary Private Secretary: to Secretary of State for Commonwealth Affairs, 1967–69; to Minister without Portfolio, 1969–70; an Opposition Spokesman: on Scottish Affairs, 1970–71; on Defence, 1971–72; Parly Under-Sec. of State, Dept of Prices and Consumer Protection, 1974–79; opposition spokesman on foreign affairs, 1980–81; SDP spokesman on agriculture, fisheries and food, 1981–87; Leader, SDP, 1987–88; Jt Leader, SLD, 1988; Lib Dem spokesman on home affairs and the arts, 1988–94, on constitutional affairs and culture, 1994–2001; on Scotland and the Civil Service, H of L, 2005–. Member: H of C Estimates Cttee, 1967–69; Select Cttee on Scottish Affairs, 1969–70; Public Accounts Cttee, 1979–99; EU Select Cttee, H of L, 2005–. Pres., Lib Dems, 1994–98. Alternate Mem., Convention on Future of Europe, 2002–03; UK Chm., European Cultural Foundn, 2001–. Mem., Latey Cttee on Age of Majority, 1968. *Publications:* libretti: The Lie, 1992; Friend of the People, 1999. *Recreations:* theatre, music, visual arts. *Address:* House of Lords, SW1A 0PW.

MacLENNAN, Dr David Herman, OC 2001; PhD; FRS 1994; FRSC 1985; University Professor, University of Toronto, since 1993; *b* 3 July 1937; *s* of Douglas Henry MacLennan and Sigridur MacLennan (*née* Sigurdson); *m* 1965, Linda Carol Vass; two *s* (one *d* decd). *Educ:* Swan River Collegiate Inst., Canada; Univ. of Manitoba (BSA 1959); Purdue Univ. (MS 1961; PhD 1963). Postdoctoral Fellow, 1963–64, Asst Prof., 1964–68, Inst. for Enzyme Res., Univ. of Wisconsin; Banting and Best Department of Medical Research, University of Toronto: Associate Prof., 1969–74; Prof., 1974–93; Acting Chm., 1978–80; Chm., 1980–90; J. W. Billes Prof. of Med. Res., 1987–. Principal Investigator, Canadian Genetic Diseases Network, 1991–2005; Consultant, Merck, Sharp & Dohme, PA, 1992–98. Member: Med. Adv. Bd, Muscular Dystrophy Assoc., Canada, 1976–87; Scientists' Review Panel, MRC Canada, 1988–90; Univ. of Ottawa Heart Inst. Res. Review Panel, 1991–94; Chm., Molecular Biol. and Pathol. Cttee, Heart and Stroke Foundn of Canada, 1995–99; Member: Gairdner Foundn Review Panel, 1999–2001; Gairdner Foundn Med. Adv. Bd, 2001–05. Fellow, Internat. Soc. Heart Res., 2001; For. Associate, NAS, USA, 2001; Hon. Mem., Japanese Biochemical Soc., 2004. Hon. DSc Manitoba, 2001. Awards include: Ayerst Award, Canadian Biochem. Soc., 1974; Nat. Lectr Award, Biophys. Soc., 1990; Gairdner Foundn Internat. Award, 1991; Izaak Walton Killam Meml Prize for Health Scis, Canada Council, 1997; Jonas Salk Award, Ontario March of Dimes, 1998; Royal Soc. Glaxo Wellcome Prize, Medal and Lecture, 2000; Salute to the City Award, Toronto, 2002; Rick Gallop Award, Heart and Stroke Foundn of Ontario, 2002. *Publications:* ed. and contrib. to numerous learned jls, esp. on study of calcium regulation by muscle membranes. *Recreations:* collecting and restoring Canadian antique furniture, reading fiction, listening to classical music, gardening, ski-ing. *Address:* Banting and Best Department of Medical Research, University of Toronto, C. H. Best Institute, 112 College Street, Toronto, ON M5G 1L6, Canada. *T:* (416) 9785008; 292 Airdrie Road, Toronto, ON M4G 1N3, Canada. *T:* (416) 6962091.

MacLENNAN, David Ross; HM Diplomatic Service, retired; Ambassador and Consul General, Qatar, 2002–05; *b* 12 Feb. 1945; *s* of David Ross MacLennan and Agnes McConnell; *m* 1964, Margaret Lytollis; two *d*. *Educ:* West Calder High Sch. FO, 1963; ME Centre for Arab Studies, 1966–69; Third, later Second Sec., Aden, 1969–71; Second, later First Sec., FCO, 1972–75; First Sec., UK Delegn to OECD, Paris, 1975–79; First Sec., Hd of Chancery, Abu Dhabi, 1979–82; Asst Hd, N America Dept, FCO, 1982–84; EEC, Brussels, 1984–85; Counsellor, Kuwait, 1985–88; Dep. High Comr, Nicosia, 1989–90; Consul Gen., Jerusalem, 1990–93; Counsellor, Head of Africa Dept (Equatorial), FCO, and Comr, British Indian Ocean Territory, 1994–96; Ambassador to Lebanese Republic, 1996–2000. *Recreations:* conservation, gardening. *Address:* c/o Foreign and Commonwealth Office, SW1A 2AH.

MACLENNAN, Prof. Duncan, CBE 1997; FRSE; *b* 12 March 1949; *s* of James Dempster Maclennan and Mary Mackechnie (*née* Campbell); *m* (separated); one *s* one *d*. *Educ:* Allan Glen's Sch., Glasgow; Univ. of Glasgow (MA, MPhil). FRSE 1999. Lectr in Pol Econ., Aberdeen Univ., 1976–79; Glasgow University: Lectr in Applied Econs, 1979–81; Sen. Lectr, 1981–84; Titular Prof., 1984–88; Prof. of Urban Studies, 1988–90; Mactaggart Prof. of Land Economics and Finance, 1990–2004; Chief Economist: Dept of Sustainability and Envmt, Govt of Vic, Australia, 2004–05; Dept for Infrastructure and Communities, Canada. Special Advr to First Minister of Scotland, 1999–2003. Director: Centre for Housing Res. and Urban Studies, 1983–96; Cities Programme, ESRC, 1996–99. Susman Prof. of Real Estate Finance, Wharton Bus. Sch., 1988; Regent's Prof., Univ. of Calif at Berkeley, 1996; Prof. of Housing and Urban Econs, RMIT, 2004. Chm., Care and Repair (Scotland), 1987–94; Dir, Joseph Rowntree Res. Programme, 1988–94; Chairman: Joseph Rowntree Area Regeneration Steering Gp, 1996–2000; Cttee on Easing Shortages of Housing, Joseph Rowntree Foundn, 2007. Mem. Bd, Scottish Homes, 1989–99. Mem., HM Treasury Panel of Advisers, 1995–2002. Trustee, David Hume Inst., 1998–. FRSA 1993; Hon. MRTPI 2001; Hon. MCIH 2001. *Publications:* Regional Policy in Britain, 1979; Housing Economics, 1982; Paying for Britain's Housing, 1990; The Housing Authority of the Future, 1991; Fairer Subsidies, Faster Growth, 1992; Fixed Commitments, Uncertain Incomes, 1997; Changing Places, Engaging People, 2000; Cities, Competition and Economic Success, 2006; contribs to Urban Studies, Housing Studies, Economic Jl, Applied Econs. *Recreations:* walking, cooking, Rugby.

McLENNAN, Gordon; General Secretary, Communist Party of Great Britain, 1975–89; *b* Glasgow, 12 May 1924; *s* of a shipyard worker; *m*; four *c*. *Educ:* Hamilton Crescent Sch., Partick, Glasgow. Engineering apprentice, Albion Motors Ltd, Scotstoun, 1939, later engineering draughtsman. Elected Glasgow Organiser, Communist Party, 1949; Sec.,

Communist Party in Scotland, 1957; Nat. Organiser, Communist Party of GB, 1966. *Recreations:* golf and other sports; cultural interests. *Address:* c/o Unlock Democracy, 6 Cynthia Street, N1 9JF.

MacLENNAN, Graeme Andrew Yule, CA; Director, Phillips & Drew Fund Management, 1990–93; *b* 24 Aug. 1942; *s* of Finlay and Helen MacLennan; *m* 1st, 1973, Diane Marion Gibbon (*née* Fyfe) (marr. diss. 1989); two *s* two *d*; 2nd, 1989, Diana Rosemary Steven (*née* Urie). *Educ:* Kelvinside Academy, Glasgow. Asst Investment Manager, Leopold Joseph & Sons Ltd, London, 1964–68; Investment Man., Murray Johnstone & Co., Glasgow, 1969–70; Edinburgh Fund Managers: Investment Man., 1970; Dir, 1980, Jt Man. Dir, 1983–88; Investment Dir, Ivory & Sime plc, 1988–90; Hd, Investment Trust Business, LGT Asset Management, 1995–98; non-executive Director: HTR Japanese Smaller Cos Trust, 1993–96; Premium Trust, 1993–2006 (Chm., 2001–06); Noble, then Cornelian, Asset Managers, 1998–2005 (Chm., 2000–05); TriVen VCT, 1999–2003; Financial Services Compensation Scheme, 2000–06; TriVest VCT, 2000–03. *Recreations:* hill walking, fishing.

MacLENNAN, Prof. Ian Calman Muir, CBE 2005; PhD; FRCP, FRCPath; Professor of Immunology, 1979–2004, Professor Emeritus, since 2005 and Deputy Director, MRC Centre for Immune Regulation, since 2005 (Director, 1999–2004), University of Birmingham; *b* Inverness, 30 Dec. 1939; *s* of late Calman MacLennan and Mary Helen MacLennan (*née* Muir, subseq. Roxburgh) and step *s* of William Alexander Roxburgh; *m* 1965, Pamela Bennett; two *s*. *Educ:* Guy's Hosp. Med. Sch., Univ. of London (BSc Anatomy 1962; MB BS 1965; PhD 1970). FRCPath 1985; FRCP 1995. SHO, MRC Rheumatism Res. Unit, Taplow, 1966–69 (ARC Res. Fellow); Lectr, Nuffield Dept of Clin. Medicine, Oxford Univ., 1969–79; Hd, Dept of Immunology, 1979–1998, Hd, Div. of Immunity and Infection, 1998–2000, Univ. of Birmingham. Medical Research Council: Co-ordinator, trials in Multiple Myeloma, 1980–98; Chm., Wkg Party on Leukaemia in Adults, 1982–92; Dep. Chm., Cell Biol. and Disorders Bd, 1983–87 (Chm., Grants Cttee A, 1982–84); Mem. Council, and Chm., Molecular and Cellular Medicine Bd, 2000–04. Sec., British Soc. for Immunol., 1973–79. Founder FMedSci, 1998. Mem., Birmingham Med. Res. Expeditionary Soc., 1986–. Hon. Life Mem., Scandinavian Soc. Immunol., 1995. *Publications:* numerous contribs to learned jls, incl. Immunological Reviews, Nature, Annual Rev. of Immunol., Jl Exptl Medicine. *Recreations:* climbing, ski-ing, observing the natural world, listening to and supporting the City of Birmingham SO. *Address:* MRC Centre for Immune Regulation, University of Birmingham, Birmingham B15 2TT.

McLENNAN, William Patrick, CBE 1997; AM 1992; Australian Statistician, Australian Bureau of Statistics, 1995–2000; *b* 26 Jan. 1942; *s* of William Freeman McLennan and Linda Maude Shannon; *m* 1968, Christine Elizabeth Alexander (marr. diss. 2006); one *s* one *d*. *Educ:* Australian National University (BEcon Hons). Statistician, Aust. Bureau of Statistics, 1960–92; Dep. Aust. Statistician, 1986–92; Dir, CSO, and Head of Govt Statistical Service, UK, 1992–95. Vis. Fellow, Nuffield Coll., Oxford, 1992–95. Centenary Medal, Aust., 2003. *Recreation:* golf. *Address:* 325 Hindmarsh Drive, Rivett, ACT 2611, Australia.

MacLEOD, Dr Calum Alexander, CBE 1991; Chairman, Grampian Television, later stv north, 1993–2007 (Deputy Chairman, 1982–93); *b* 25 July 1935; *s* of Rev. Lachlan Macleod and Jessie Mary Morrison; *m* 1962, Elizabeth Margaret Davidson; two *s* one *d*. *Educ:* Nicolson Inst., Stornoway; Glenurquhart High Sch.; Aberdeen Univ. Partner, Paull & Williamsons Advocates, Aberdeen, 1964–80; Chairman: Aberdeen Petroleum, 1982–92; Harris Tweed Assoc. Authority, 1984–93 (Vice-Chm., 1993–95); Aberdeen Develt Capital plc, 1986–2005; Deputy Chairman: Scottish Eastern Investment Trust, 1988–99; Britannia Life, 1992–94 (Chm., 1990–92); Britannia Building Society, 1993–94 and 1999–2000 (Chm., 1994–99); Scottish Media Group, then SMG plc, 1997–2005 (acting Chm., 1998–99); Martin Currie Portfolio Investment Trust plc, 1999–2002; Director: North Bd, Bank of Scotland, 1980–2000; Bradstock Gp, 1994–98; Macdonald Hotels, 1995–2003. Member: White Fish Authy, 1973–80; N of Scotland Hydro-Electric Bd, 1976–84; Highlands and Islands Develt Bd, 1984–91; Chm., Grampian Health Bd, 1993–2000. Chairman: Chancellor's Assessor, Aberdeen Univ., 1979–90; Robert Gordon's Coll., 1981–94; SATRO North Scotland, 1986–90; Scottish Council of Indep. Schs, 1992–97; Trustee, Carnegie Trust for the Univs of Scotland, 1997–; Governor: Caledonian Res. Foundn, 1990–94; UHI Millennium Inst., 2000–. Hon LLD Aberdeen, 1986. *Recreations:* golf, fishing, motoring, Hebridean coastal walking, reading, music. *Address:* 6 Westfield Terrace, Aberdeen AB25 2RU. *T:* (01224) 641614. *Clubs:* Royal Northern and University (Aberdeen); Royal Aberdeen Golf; Nairn Golf.

McLEOD, Sir Charles Henry, 3rd Bt *cr* 1925; *b* 7 Nov. 1924; *o* surv. *s* of Sir Murdoch Campbell McLeod, 2nd Bt, and Annette Susan Mary (*d* 1964), *d* of Henry Whitehead, JP, 26 Pelham Crescent, SW7; *S* father, 1950; *m* 1957, Gillian (*d* 1978), *d* of Henry Bowlby, London; one *s* two *d*. *Educ:* Winchester. Diploma Master Brewer, 1950. Member, London Stock Exchange, 1955–. Part-time in-house proof-reader and freelancer, 1998–. Represented India, Squash Rackets Internat., 1956–58. *Heir: s* James Roderick Charles McLeod [*b* 26 Sept. 1960; *m* 1990, Helen M. Cooper, *d* of Captain George Cooper, OBE, RN; one *s* one *d*]. *Clubs:* MCC; I Zingari, Free Foresters, Jesters.

McLEOD, Prof. David, FRCS, FRCOphth; Professor of Ophthalmology, 1988–2006, now Emeritus, and Head of Department of Ophthalmology, 1988–98, University of Manchester; Hon. Consultant Ophthalmologist, Manchester Royal Eye Hospital, since 1988; *b* 16 Jan. 1946; *s* of Norman McLeod and Anne McLeod (*née* Heyworth); *m* 1967, Jeanette Allison Cross; one *s* one *d*. *Educ:* Univ. of Edinburgh (BSc 1st cl. Hons Physiology 1966; MB ChB Hons 1969). FRCS 1974; FRCOphth 1989. House Physician and Surg., Edinburgh Royal Infirmary, 1969–70; Sen. House Officer and Res. Fellow, Princess Alexandra Eye Pavilion, Edinburgh, 1970–72; Moorfields Eye Hospital: RSO, 1972–75; Fellow in Vitreoretinal Surgery and Ultrasound, 1975–78; Consultant Ophthalmic Surg., 1978–88. Civilian Consultant Ophthalmologist, RAF, 1984–2003. Vis. Prof., UMIST, 1996–2006. Vice-Pres., Royal Coll. of Ophthalmologists, 1997–2001. Mem., Club Jules Gonin, Lausanne. *Publications:* over 180 publications on retinal vascular disease, diabetic retinopathy, vitreoretinal surgery, vitreous pathology. *Recreations:* golf, ballroom dancing. *Address:* Langdale, 370 Chester Road, Woodford, Stockport, Cheshire SK7 1QG. *Club:* Bramall Park Golf.

MacLEOD, David Scott G.; *see* Gordon-MacLeod.

MacLEOD, Donald Alexander; HM Diplomatic Service, retired; study course organiser, since 1990; *b* 23 Jan. 1938; *er s* of late Col Colin S. MacLeod of Glendale, OBE, TD, and of Margaret Drysdale Robertson MacLeod; *m* 1963, Rosemary Lilian Abel (*née* Randle); two *s* two *d*. *Educ:* Edinburgh Academy; Pembroke Coll., Cambridge, 1958–61 (BA). National Service, Queen's Own Cameron Highlanders, 1956–58. HM Foreign Service, 1961; School of Oriental and African Studies, London, 1961–62; British Embassy, Rangoon, 1962–66; Private Sec. to Minister of State, Commonwealth Office, 1966–69; First Secretary, Ottawa, 1969–73; FCO, 1973–78; First Sec./Head of Chancery, Bucharest, 1978–80; Counsellor (Econ. and Commercial), Singapore, 1981–84. Dep. High Comr, Bridgetown, 1984–87; Hd of Protocol Dept, FCO, 1987–89. *Address:* Kinlochfollart, by Dunvegan, Isle of Skye IV55 8WQ.

MacLEOD, Donald Roderick; QC (Scot.) 2005; *b* 24 Sept. 1948; *s* of Ian MacCrimmon MacLeod, MB, ChB and Mairi M. E. MacLeod, MA Hons; *m* 1978, Susan Mary Fulton, LLB, solicitor; two *d*. *Educ:* High Sch. of Stirling; Univ. of Glasgow (LLB); Dip. FMS. Solicitor, 1973–77; called to Scottish Bar, 1978; in practice as counsel, 1978–. Temp. Sheriff, 1998–2000. Mem. Bd, Scottish Medico-Legal Soc.; Sec., Faculty of Advocates Criminal Bar Assoc. Contested (Lab) Kinross and W Perthshire, 1979. Founder Mem., Circle of Willis. *Publications:* The Law of Firearms and Related Legislation, 2007; contrib. occasional articles to professional jls. *Recreations:* opera, music, angling (Mem., Cobbinshaw Angling Assoc.), tying classic salmon flies, book-collecting, especially first editions of Neil M. Gunn, studying the natural history of the Highlands and Islands of Scotland and their Gaelic culture, place-names and language, hill-walking, golf, wildfowling, supporting Labour's serious and purposeful politicians, visiting historic buildings and enjoying the landscape of Scotland, savouring malt whisky. *Address: e-mail:* donald.macleod@advocates.org.uk. *T:* (0131) 260 5607.

McLEOD, Fiona Grace; Librarian, British Homeopathic Library, since 2004; *b* 3 Dec. 1957; *d* of John McLeod and Irene McLeod (*née* Robertson); *m* 1979, Dr Andrew David Rankine; one *s*. *Educ:* Glasgow Univ. (MA Hons Medieval and Modern Hist.); Strathclyde Univ. (Postgrad. DipLib). MCLIP. Librarian: Balfron High Sch., 1983–87; Glasgow North Coll. of Nursing, 1987–90; Marie Curie Centre Huntershill Liby, 1995–98. Partnership Officer, E Dunbartonshire CVS, 2004. MSP (SNP), West of Scotland, 1999–2003. Contested (SNP) Strathkelvin and Bearsden, 2003, Paisley S, 2007, Scottish Parlt. Chm., E Dunbartonshire Children's Panel Adv. Cttee, 2004–; Mem., Adv. Cttee for Scotland, Ofcom, 2004–06. *Recreations:* Scottish castles, walking.

MACLEOD, Sir Hamish; *see* Macleod, Sir N. W. H.

MACLEOD, Iain; HM Diplomatic Service; on loan as Deputy Legal Adviser, Home Office and Northern Ireland Office, since 2005; *b* 15 March 1962; *s* of Rev. Allan Macleod and Peggy Macleod (*née* Mackay); *m* 1988, Dr Alison M. Murchison; two *s* two *d*. *Educ:* Portree High Sch., Isle of Skye; Glasgow Univ. (LLB Hons 1983; Dip. Prof. Legal Practice 1985); University Coll. London (LLM 1984). Trainee solicitor, Dundas & Wilson CS, Edinburgh, 1985–87; admitted solicitor, Scotland, 1987, England & Wales, 2007; joined HM Diplomatic Service, 1987; Asst Legal Advr, FCO, 1987–91; First Sec. (Legal), UK Repn to EC, Brussels, 1991–95; Asst Legal Advr, FCO, 1995–96; Legal Counsellor: FCO, 1996–97; on loan to Law Officers' Dept, 1997–2000; FCO, 2000–01; UK Mission to UN, NY, 2001–04; FCO, 2004–05. *Publication:* (jtly) The External Relation of the European Communities, 1995. *Address:* Legal Adviser's Branch, Home Office, 2 Marsham Street, SW18 4DF. *T:* (020) 7035 1386, *Fax:* (020) 7035 6433; *e-mail:* Iain.Macleod5@homeoffice.gsi.gov.uk.

MacLEOD, Prof. Iain Alasdair, PhD; CEng, FICE, FIStructE; Professor of Structural Engineering, University of Strathclyde, 1981–2004, now Emeritus Professor; *b* 4 May 1939; *s* of Donald MacLeod and Barbara (*née* MacKenzie); *m* 1967, Barbara Jean Booth; one *s* one *d*. *Educ:* Lenzie Acad.; Univ. of Glasgow (BSc 1960, PhD 1966). CEng 1968; FIStructE 1982; FICE 1984. Asst Engr, Crouch & Hogg, Glasgow, 1960–62; Asst Lectr in Civil Engrg, Univ. of Glasgow, 1962–66; Structural Engineer: H. A. Simons Internat., Vancouver, Canada, 1966–67; Portland Cement Assoc., Skokie, USA, 1968–69; Lectr in Civil Engrg, Univ. of Glasgow, 1969–73; Prof. and Head of Dept of Civil Engrg, Paisley Coll. of Technol., 1973–81. Vice-Pres., IStructE, 1989–90; Mem., Standing Cttee on Structural Safety, IStructE and ICE, 1990–97. FRSA. Lewis Kent Award, IStructE, 1998. *Publications:* Analytical Modelling of Structural Systems, 1990; Modern Structural Analysis, 2005; over 100 published papers. *Recreations:* sailing, hill walking. *Address:* c/o Department of Civil Engineering, University of Strathclyde, Glasgow G4 0NG.

McLEOD, Brig. Ian, CMG 1999; OBE 1983; MC 1965; Division for Relations with Armed and Security Forces, International Committee of the Red Cross, since 1999; *b* 19 June 1941; *s* of David Drummond McLeod and Eleanor McLeod (*née* Williams); *m* 1966, Janet Edith Prosser Angus (*d* 2004); one *s* two *d*. *Educ:* Rhondda Co. Grammar Sch.; RMA Sandhurst; sc 1973; ndc 1991; BA Open Univ. 1990. Commnd Parachute Regt, 1961; service in 3 Para, UK, Gulf and Aden, 1961–67; Jungle Warfare Sch., Malaya, 1967–69; 2 Para, 1969–71; SC, 1971–73; HQ 44 Para Bde (V), 1974–75; 82 AB Div., US Army, 1976–77; Co. Comd, 3 Para, BAOR, 1977–79; GSO2, Defence Ops Analysis Estabt, 1979–81; CO 1 Para, 1981–84; SO1, SC, 1984–86; Col Operational Requirements, MoD, 1986–87; UK Liaison Officer, US Army, 1987–89; Comd, 42 Inf. Bde, 1989–91; Defence Advr, British High Commn, Islamabad, 1992–94; retd 1995; Mem., EC Monitor Mission to former Yugoslavia, 1995–97; Dep. Hd, Regl Office in Brcko of High Rep. for Bosnia, 1997–98; Mem., Kosovo Verification Mission, OSCE, 1998–99. Mem., Pakistan Soc., 2003–. Freeman, City of London, 1992. *Recreations:* travel, ski-ing, military history. *Address:* c/o HSBC, 33 The Borough, Farnham, Surrey GU9 7NJ.

MACLEOD, Ian Buchanan, FRCSE; Hon. Secretary, Royal College of Surgeons of Edinburgh, 1993–96; Consultant Surgeon, Royal Infirmary, Edinburgh, and Hon. Senior Lecturer, Department of Clinical Surgery, University of Edinburgh, 1969–93; Surgeon to the Queen in Scotland, 1987–93; *b* 20 May 1933; *s* of Donald Macleod, MB, ChB, and Katie Ann Buchanan; *m* 1961, Kathleen Gillean Large; one *s* one *d*. *Educ:* Wigan Grammar Sch.; Univ. of Edinburgh (BSc Hons; MB ChB Hons). FRCSE 1962. Resident appts, Royal Inf., Edinburgh, 1957–59. National Service, MO RAMC, 1959–61. Res. Fellow, Lectr and Sen. Lectr, Univ. of Edinburgh, 1962–93; Hon. and Cons. Surg., Royal Inf., Edinburgh, 1969–93. Editor, Journal of Royal College of Surgeons of Edinburgh, 1982–87. *Publications:* Principles and Practice of Surgery (with A. P. M. Forrest and D. C. Carter), 1985; (contrib.) A Companion to Medical Studies, 1968, 3rd edn 1985; (contrib.) Farquharson's Textbook of Operative Surgery, 1986; papers in surgical jls. *Recreations:* golf, photography. *Address:* 1 Southbank, Easter Park Drive, Edinburgh EH4 6SG. *T:* (0131) 336 1541. *Club:* Bruntsfield Links Golfing Society (Edinburgh).

MACLEOD, Jean Grant; *see* Scott, J. G.

McLEOD, Rev. John; Minister of Resolis and Urquhart, 1986–93; Chaplain to the Queen in Scotland, 1978–96, an Extra Chaplain, since 1996; *b* 8 April 1926; *s* of Angus McLeod and Catherine McDougall; *m* 1958, Sheila McLeod; three *s* two *d*. *Educ:* Inverness Royal Academy; Edinburgh Univ. (MA); New Coll., Edinburgh. Farming until 1952; at university, 1952–58; ordained, Inverness, 1958. Missionary in India: Jalna, 1959–68; Poona, 1969–74; involved in rural development with special emphasis on development and conservation of water resource; also responsible for pastoral work in Church of N India, St Mary's, Poona, 1970–74; Church of Scotland Minister, Livingston Ecumenical Team Ministry, 1974–86. *Recreation:* gardening. *Address:* Benview, 19 Balvaird, Muir of Ord, Ross-shire IV7 6RQ. *T:* (01463) 871286.

MacLEOD, John; Chairman, British Beet Research Organisation, since 2000; Professor of Horticulture, Royal Horticultural Society, since 2001; *b* 16 Aug. 1939; *s* of James Rae MacLeod and Mollie McKee MacLeod (*née* Shaw); *m* 1966, Janet Patricia Beavan, sculptor; one *s* (and one *s* decd). *Educ:* Nicolson Inst., Stornoway; Univ. of Glasgow (BSc Hons Agr. 1962); Michigan State Univ. (MS 1964). FRAgS 2003. NAAS, later ADAS, MAFF, 1964–90. Director: Arthur Rickwood Exptl Farm, 1982–85; ADAS Exptl Farms, MAFF, 1985–90; NIAB, Cambridge, 1990–99. Non-exec. Dir, Nat. Non Food Crops Centre, 2006–. Pres., Groupe Consultatif Internat. de Recherche sur le Colza, Paris, 1993–97; Vice-Chm., BCPC, 2000–07. Mem. Admin. Council, Internat. Inst. for Beet Res., 2003–. Chm., BASIS, 2004–. *Recreations:* long term restoration of a 16th century farmhouse and garden, sculpture, early music, walking. *Address:* British Beet Research Organisation, The Research Station, Great North Road, Thornhaugh, Peterborough PE8 6HJ; Church Farm House, Over, Cambs CB24 5NX.

McLEOD, Prof. John Bryce, DPhil; FRS 1992; Professor of Mathematics, University of Pittsburgh, 1988–2007, now Emeritus; *b* 23 Dec. 1929; *s* of John McLeod and Adeline Annie (*née* Bryce); *m* 1956, Eunice Martin Third; three *s* one *d. Educ:* Aberdeen Grammar Sch.; Univ. of Aberdeen (MA 1950); Oxford Univ. (BA 1952, MA, DPhil 1958). Rotary Foundn Fellow, Univ. of BC, 1952–53; Educn Officer, RAF, 1953–55; Harmsworth Sen. Scholar, Merton Coll., Oxford, 1955–56; Jun. Lectr in Maths, Oxford Univ., 1956–58; Lectr, Univ. of Edinburgh, 1958–60; University of Oxford: Fellow, Wadham Coll., 1960–91; Lectr in Maths, 1960–88; Jun. Proctor, 1963–64; Sen. Fellow, SERC, 1986–91. Vis. Prof., Univ. of Oxford, 2007–. *Publications:* numerous papers in mathematical jls. *Recreations:* travel, music, gardening. *Address:* 49 Northcourt Road, Abingdon, Oxon OX14 1PJ. *T:* (01235) 520239.

MacLEOD, Hon. Sir (John) Maxwell (Norman), 5th Bt *cr* 1924, of Fuinary, Morven, Co. Argyll; *b* 23 Feb. 1952; *s* of Baron MacLeod of Fuinary (Life Peer), MC and Lorna Helen Janet (*d* 1984), *er d* of late Rev. Donald Macleod; *S* to baronetcy of father, 1991. *Educ:* Gordonstoun; Bede Coll., Durham LS; Churchill Coll., Oxford. Teacher of the deaf, journalist, cartoonist for The Herald, and property developer. A Founder and Chm., Hebridean Whale and Dolphin Trust. *Heir: b* Hon. Neil David MacLeod, *b* 25 Dec. 1959. *Address:* Dowies Mill House, Dowies Mill Lane, Cramond, Edinburgh EH4 6DW; Fuinary, Morven, Argyll. *Club:* New (Edinburgh).

McLEOD, Kirsty, (Mrs Christopher Hudson); author and journalist; *b* 23 Dec. 1947; *d* of late Alexander McLeod and Elizabeth Davidson McLeod; *m* 1978, Christopher Hudson; one *s. Educ:* St Leonard's Sch., St Andrews; St Anne's Coll., Oxford (MA). Editorial staff, IPC Magazines, 1970–73; Editor, Fontana Books, 1974–76; Columnist, Daily Telegraph, 1991–93. English Heritage: Comr, 1995–2001; Chm., Historic Parks and Gardens Adv. Cttee, 1998–2001 (Mem., 1995–2001). Trustee, Kent Gardens Trust, 2002–03. *Publications:* The Wives of Downing Street, 1976; Drums and Trumpets: the House of Stuart, 1977; The Last Summer: May to September 1914, 1983; A Passion for Friendship: Sibyl Colefax and her circle, 1991; Battle Royal: Edward VIII and George VI, 1999; numerous newspaper articles. *Recreations:* gardening, visiting Italian gardens. *Address:* Domons, Higham Lane, Northiam, E Sussex TN31 6JT. *T:* (01797) 252007.

McLEOD, Prof. Malcolm Donald, CBE 2006; FRSE; Professor of African Studies, 1994–2006, Vice-Principal, 1999–2005 and Pro Vice-Principal, 2005–06, Glasgow University; Director, Hunterian Museum and Art Gallery, Glasgow, 1990–99; *b* 19 May 1941; *s* of Donald McLeod and Ellen (*née* Fairclough); *m*; two *s* one *d. Educ:* Birkenhead Sch.; Hertford and Exeter Colls, Oxford (MA, BLitt). FRSE 1995. Lectr, Dept of Sociology, Univ. of Ghana, 1967–69; Asst Curator, Museum of Archaeology and Ethnology, Cambridge, 1969–74; Lectr, Girton Coll., Cambridge, 1969–74; Fellow, Magdalene Coll., Cambridge, 1972–74; Keeper of Ethnography, British Museum, 1974–90. Member: Hist. and Current Affairs Selection Cttee, Nat. Film Archive, 1978–84; Council, Museums Assoc., 1983–86; UK Unesco Cultural Adv. Cttee, 1980–85; Chairman: Scottish Mus Council, 1996–2001; Caledonian Foundn, USA, 2003–08; Trustee, Nat. Mus Scotland (formerly Nat. Mus of Scotland), 2005–. Consultant, Manhyia Palace Mus., Kumasi, Ghana, 1994–99; Curator, RSE, 1999–2002. Hon. Lecturer: Anthropology Dept, UCL, 1976–81; Archæology Dept, Glasgow Univ., 1991–2006. Lectures: Marett, Exeter Coll., Oxford, 1982; Sydney Jones, Liverpool Univ., 1984; Arthur Batchelor, UEA, 1987; Rivers, Cambridge, 1993. Trustee: Sainsbury Unit, UEA, 1991–2000; Oriental Mus., Univ. of Durham, 1994–2000; Hunterian Collection, London, 1998–; Scottish Mus. of the Year Awards, 1999–2002; Opoku Ware Foundn Award, Ghana, 2005. *Publications:* The Asante, 1980; Treasures of African Art, 1980; (with J. Mack) Ethnic Art, 1984; (with E. Bassani) Jacob Epstein: collector, 1987; An English-Kriolu, Kriolu-English Dictionary, 1990; Collecting for the British Museum, 1994; articles and reviews in learned jls. *Address:* The Schoolhouse, Oxnam, Jedburgh TD8 6NB. *Club:* Athenæum.

McLEOD, (Margaret) Kirsty; *see* McLeod, K.

MacLEOD, Hon. Sir Maxwell; *see* MacLeod, Hon. Sir J. M. N.

MACLEOD, Sir (Nathaniel William) Hamish, KBE 1994 (CBE 1992); Financial Secretary, Hong Kong, 1991–95; *b* 6 Jan. 1940; *s* of George Henry Torquil Macleod and Ruth Natalie Wade; *m* 1970, Fionna Mary Campbell; one *s* one *d. Educ:* Univ. of St Andrews (MA Soc. Sci. Hons); Univ. of Bristol (Dip. Soc. Sci. Sociology); Birmingham Coll. of Commerce. FCIS 1995. Commercial trainee, Stewarts & Lloyds, Birmingham, 1958–62; Hong Kong Government: Admin. Officer, 1966; Dir of Trade and Chief Trade Negotiator, 1983–87; Secretary for Trade and Industry, 1987–89; Sec. for the Treasury, 1989–91. Director: Scottish Community (formerly Caledonian) Foundation, 1995–2002; Highland Distilleries, 1995–99; Scottish Oriental Smaller Cos Trust, 1995–; Chm., JP Morgan Fleming Asian Investment Trust (formerly Fleming Asian Investment Trust), 1997–2003. *Recreations:* golf, walking. *Address:* 20 York Road, Trinity, Edinburgh EH5 3EH. *T:* (0131) 552 5058. *Clubs:* Kilspindie Golf, Bruntsfield Links Golf; Hong Kong, Royal Hong Kong Yacht.

MacLEOD, Dr Norman, FGS, FLS; Keeper of Palaeontology, Natural History Museum, London, since 2001; *b* 23 Feb. 1953; *s* of Archibald Alexander MacLeod and Helen Chester MacLeod; *m* 1988, Dr Cecilia McDonald; one *d. Educ:* Univ. of Missouri, Columbia (BSc Geol. 1976); Southern Methodist Univ., Dallas (MSc Palaeontol. 1980); Univ. of Texas at Dallas (PhD Palaeontol. 1986). FGS 2002. Sci. teacher (physics, geol., astronomy, ecol.), H. Grady Spruce High Sch., Segoville, Texas, 1976–78; owner, Boreas Technical Photographers, Dallas, 1982–86; Consultant, Atlantic Richfield (ARCO) Oil and Gas, Richardson, Texas, 1984–86; Michigan Soc. Fellow and Vis. Asst Prof., Dept of Geol Scis, Univ. of Michigan, Ann Arbor, 1986–89; Researcher, Dept of Geol and Geophysical Scis, Princeton Univ., 1989–93; Natural History Museum, London, 1993–: Scientific Officer, 1993–94; SSO, 1994–96; Stratigraphy and Correlation Prog. Leader, 1995–2001; Researcher, 1996–99; Petroleum Sector Leader, 1997–2001; Associate Keeper, 2000–01; Actg Keeper, 2001. Member: Soc. Systematic Biol., 1981; Willi Hennig Soc., 1985; Centre for Evolution and Ecol., 1998; Systematics Assoc., 2001; Palaeontol Assoc., 2003 (Trustee, 2005–; Vice Pres., 2007–); Geol Soc. London, 2002. Mem., Linnean Soc., 2003. Trustee, Rotunda Mus., Scarborough, 2004–. *Publications:* The Cretaceous-Tertiary Mass Extinction: biotic and environmental changes, 1996; Morphometrics, Shape and Phylogenetics, 2002; Automated Taxon Identification in Systematics: theory, approaches and applications, 2007; contrib. numerous peer reviewed technical articles, technical reports and reviews. *Recreations:* music, theatre, wine, dining. *Address:* Department of Palaeontology, Natural History Museum, Cromwell Road, South Kensington, SW7 5BD. *T:* (020) 7942 5204, *Fax:* (020) 7942 5546.

MacLEOD, Norman Donald; QC (Scot.) 1986; MA, LLB; Advocate; Sheriff Principal of Glasgow and Strathkelvin, 1986–97; *b* 6 March 1932; *s* of late Rev. John MacLeod, Edinburgh and Catherine MacRitchie; *m* 1957, Ursula Jane, *y d* of late George H. Bromley, Inveresk; two *s* two *d. Educ:* Mill Hill Sch.; George Watson's Boys' Coll., Edinburgh; Edinburgh Univ.; Hertford Coll., Oxford. Passed Advocate, 1956. Colonial Administrative Service, Tanganyika: Dist. Officer, 1957–59; Crown Counsel, 1959–64; practised at Scots Bar, 1964–67; Sheriff of Glasgow and Strathkelvin (formerly Lanarkshire at Glasgow), 1967–86; Hon. Sheriff N Strathclyde, 1986. Vis. Prof., Law Sch., Univ. of Strathclyde, 1988–98. Comr, Northern Lighthouse Bd, 1986–97 (Chm., 1990–91). Hon. Mem., Royal Faculty of Procurators in Glasgow, 1996. *Recreations:* sailing, gardening. *Address:* Calderbank, Lochwinnoch, Renfrewshire PA12 4DJ. *T:* (01505) 843340.

MACLEOD, (Roderick) James (Andrew) R.; *see* Robertson-Macleod.

MACLEOD CLARK, Prof. Dame Jill, DBE 2000; PhD; Professor of Nursing, Head of School of Nursing and Midwifery and Deputy Dean of Faculty of Medicine, Health and Life Sciences (formerly Faculty of Medicine and Health), University of Southampton, since 1999; *b* 11 June 1944; *d* of late George William Charles Tearle Gibbs and Edith Vera Macleod Gibbs; *m* 1st, 1967, Andrew William Clark (marr. diss. 1983); two *s*; 2nd, 1989, William Arthur Bridge. *Educ:* UCH (RGN 1965); LSE (BSc Hons 1972); KCL (PhD 1982). FRCN 1997. Various clin. posts, London, Birmingham and Bedford, 1965–76; Nursing Officer, DoH, 1976–78; Res. Fellow, 1978–81, Lectr in Nursing, 1981–86, Chelsea Coll., London Univ.; King's College London: Sen. Lectr in Nursing, 1986–90; Prof. of Nursing, 1990–93; Dir, Nightingale Inst., 1993–99. FQNI 2004. Hon. DSc: Brighton, 2004; UEA, 2005. *Publications:* Research for Nursing, 1979; Communication in Nursing Care, 1981; Further Research for Nursing, 1989; numerous res. based papers in learned jls on health promotion, smoking cessation, health prof. educn and communication in health care. *Recreations:* sailing, singing. *Address:* 80 Walpole House, 126 Westminster Bridge Road, SE1 7UN. *Club:* Royal Southampton Yacht.

McLERNAN, Kieran Anthony; Sheriff of Grampian, Highland and Islands at Aberdeen, since 2000; *b* 29 April 1941; *s* of James John McLernan and Delia (*née* McEvaddy); *m* 1979, Joan Doherty Larkins; one *s* three *d. Educ:* St Aloysius' Coll., Glasgow; Glasgow Univ. (MA 1961; LLB 1965). Admitted solicitor, 1965; Tutor, Glasgow Univ., 1985–91. Temp. Sheriff, 1986–91; Sheriff of Grampian, Highland and Islands at Banff and Peterhead, 1991. KCHS 1998 (KHS 1990). *Recreations:* golf, hockey, ski-ing, etc. *Address:* Sheriff Court House, Castle Street, Aberdeen AB10 1WP; Peockstone Farm, Lochwinnoch, Strathclyde PA12 4LE. *T:* (01505) 842128.

McLETCHIE, David William; Member (C) Edinburgh Pentlands, Scottish Parliament, since 2003 (Lothians, 1999–2003); Leader, 1999–2005, Chief Whip and Business Manager, since 2007, Conservative Group, Scottish Parliament; *b* 6 Aug. 1952; *s* of James Watson McLetchie and Catherine Alexander McLetchie (*née* Gray); *m* 1st, 1977, Barbara Gemmell Baillie (*d* 1995); one *s*; 2nd, 1998, Sheila Elizabeth Foster. *Educ:* Leith Acad.; George Heriot's Sch., Edinburgh; Edinburgh Univ. (LLB Hons). Admitted solicitor, 1976; joined Tods Murray, WS, Edinburgh, 1976, Partner, 1980–2005; specialised in trusts, estates and tax. *Recreations:* golf, watching football, music, reading crime fiction and political biographies. *Address:* Scottish Parliament, Edinburgh EH99 1SP. *T:* (0131) 348 5659. *Clubs:* New (Edinburgh), Bruntsfield Links Golfing Society.

McLINTOCK, Michael George Alexander; Chief Executive, M&G Group Limited (formerly Prudential M&G Asset Management), since 1999; *b* 24 March 1961; *s* of Sir (Charles) Alan McLintock and of Sylvia Mary McLintock; *m* 1996, Nicola Fairles Ogilvy Watson; one *s* two *d. Educ:* Malvern Coll.; St John's Coll., Oxford (scholar; BA 1st cl. hons Mod. History and Econs). Morgan Grenfell & Co. Ltd, 1983; Baring Brothers & Co. Ltd, 1987; M&G Group plc, 1992, Chief Exec., 1997–99. Director: Prudential plc, 2000–; Close Brothers Gp plc, 2001–. *Recreations:* family, friends, good wine. *Address:* (office) Laurence Pountney Hill, EC4R 0HH. *T:* (020) 7626 4588. *Clubs:* Army and Navy, Boodle's, MCC.

McLINTOCK, Sir Michael (William), 4th Bt *cr* 1934, of Sanquhar, Co. Dumfries; *b* 13 Aug. 1958; *s* of Sir William Traven McLintock, 3rd Bt and Andrée, *d* of Richard Lonsdale-Hands; *S* father, 1987; *m* 1991, Jill Andrews; one *s* one *d. Heir: s* James Kieron McLintock, *b* 14 Feb. 1995.

McLOUGHLIN, Catherine Mary Anne, CBE 1998; Chair, Age Concern England; *b* 26 July 1943; *d* of Peter Patrick McLoughlin and Catherine (*née* McHugh). *Educ:* Ravenswell Convent, Bray, Co. Wicklow. Gen. nurse trng, N Middx Hosp., 1961–64; post-registration psychiatric trng, 1965–66, then specialist posts, 1966–73, Bethlem Royal and Maudsley Hosp.; Principal Nursing Officer, Bexley Hosp., 1973–77; Dep. Area Nursing Officer, Oxon, 1977–79; Chief Nursing Officer, Paddington and N Kensington HA, 1979–85; Dist Gen. Manager, Haringey HA, 1985–89; Dir of Nursing and Dep. Chief Nursing Officer, DoH, 1989–90, retd. Chair: Bromley FHSA, 1992–94; Bromley HA, 1994–99; NHS Confedn, 1997–2000; St George's Healthcare NHS Trust, 1999–2003. Chair, Nat. Network Art in Health, 2000–. Dr *hc* Middx 1995. *Recreations:* reading, art, walking, driving. *Address:* Age Concern England, Astral House, 1268 London Road, SW16 4ER. *T:* 07768 252300.

McLOUGHLIN, Elizabeth Mary, CBE 1997; consultant in public sector change management, since 2006; Command Secretary, HQ Land Command, Ministry of Defence, 2003–06; *b* 10 April 1947; *d* of Donald Norwood Menzies and late Doreen Mary Menzies (*née* Collinson); *m* 1976, John McLoughlin; three *s. Educ:* South Hampstead High Sch.; University College London (BA Hons History). Res., 1969–72; joined MoD, 1972; various posts, 1972–88; Sen. Civil Service, 1988; Comd Sec., Adjutant Gen., 1997–2002; Dir Gen., Service Personnel Policy, 2002–03. Non-exec. Dir, Great Western Ambulance NHS Trust, 2006–. Governor: King's School, Bruton; Hazlegrove Prep. Sch. *Recreations:* gardening, reading, walking the dog, music.

McLOUGHLIN, George Leeke, CB 1988; Deputy Director of Public Prosecutions for Northern Ireland, 1982–87; *b* 2 July 1921; *e s* of Charles M. McLoughlin and Rose W. McLoughlin (*née* Leeke); *m* 1953, Maureen Theresa McKaigney (*d* 1998); two *s* six *d. Educ:* St Columb's College, Londonderry; Queen's Univ. Belfast (BA). Barrister, N Ireland, practised 1945–58; joined HMOCS 1958; Resident Magistrate, 1958, Crown Counsel, 1958–63, Northern Rhodesia; Parly Draftsman, Zambia, 1965; Solicitor

General, Zambia, 1968–70, retired; Office of Law Reform, N Ireland, 1971–72; Sen. Asst Dir of Public Prosecutions, NI (Under Secretary, NI Civil Service), 1973–82. *Recreations:* photography, armchair sports following.

McLOUGHLIN, Rt Hon. Patrick (Allen); PC 2005; MP (C) West Derbyshire, since May 1986; *b* 30 Nov. 1957; *s* of Patrick and Gladys Victoria McLoughlin; *m* 1984, Lynne Newman; one *s* one *d*. *Educ:* Cardinal Griffin Roman Catholic Sch., Cannock. Mineworker, Littleton Colliery, 1979–85; Marketing Official, NCB, 1985–86. PPS to Sec. of State for Trade and Industry, 1988–89; Parly Under-Sec. of State, Dept of Transport, 1989–92, Dept of Employment, 1992–93, DTI, 1993–94; an Asst Govt Whip, 1995–96; a Lord Comr of HM Treasury (Govt Whip), 1996–97; Opposition Pairing Whip, 1997–98; Dep. Opposition Chief Whip, 1998–2005; Opposition Chief Whip, 2005–. *Address:* House of Commons, SW1A 0AA.

MACLURE, Sir John (Robert Spencer), 4th Bt *cr* 1898; Headmaster, Croftinloan School, Pitlochry, Perthshire, 1978–92 and 1997–98; *b* 25 March 1934; *s* of Sir John William Spencer Maclure, 3rd Bt, OBE, and Elspeth (*d* 1991), *er d* of late Alexander King Clark; *S* father, 1980; *m* 1964, Jane Monica, *d* of late Rt Rev. T. J. Savage, Bishop of Zululand and Swaziland; four *s*. *Educ:* Winchester College. DipEd. 2nd Lt, 2nd Bn KRRC, 1953–55, BAOR; Lt, Royal Hampshire Airborne Regt, TA. Assistant Master: Horris Hill, 1955–66 and 1974–78; St George's, Wanganui, NZ, 1967–68; Sacred Heart Coll., Auckland, NZ, 1969–70; St Edmund's, Hindhead, Surrey, 1971–74. *Heir: s* John Mark Maclure [*b* 27 Aug. 1965; *m* 1996, Emily, *d* of Peter Frean; two *s* one *d*]. *Address:* Howleigh Cottage, Blagdon Hill, Taunton, Somerset TA3 7SP. *Clubs:* MCC; Royal Green Jackets.

MACLURE, (John) Stuart, CBE 1982; Editor, Times Educational Supplement, 1969–89; *b* 8 Aug. 1926; *s* of Hugh and Bertha Maclure, Highgate, N6; *m* 1951, Constance Mary Butler; one *s* two *d*. *Educ:* Highgate Sch.; Christ's Coll., Cambridge. MA. Joined The Times, 1950; The Times Educational Supplement, 1951; Editor, Education, 1954–69. Hon. Prof. of Educn, Keele Univ., 1981–84; Dist. Vis. Fellow, PSI, 1989–90; Associate Fellow, Centre for Educn and Industry, Warwick Univ., 1991–94. President: Br. Sect., Comparative Educn Soc. in Europe, 1979; Educnl Sect., BAAS, 1983; Member: Educnl Adv. Council, IBA, 1979–84; Consultative Cttee, Assessment of Performance Unit, 1974–82. Regents' Lecturer, Univ. of California, Berkeley, 1980. Gov., Commonwealth Inst., 1991–97. Hon. Fellow, City of Sheffield Polytechnic, 1976; Hon. FCP 1985; Hon. Fellow, Westminster Coll., 1990. DUniv Open, 1991. *Publications:* Joint Editor (with T. E. Utley) Documents on Modern Political Thought, 1956; Editor, Educational Documents, 1816–1963, 1965; A Hundred Years of London Education, 1970; (with Tony Becher) The Politics of Curriculum Change, 1978; (ed with Tony Becher) Accountability in Education, 1979; Education and Youth Employment in Great Britain, 1979; Educational Development and School Building, 1945–1973, 1984; Education Re-formed, a guide to the Education Reform Act, 1988; A History of Education in London 1870–1990, 1990; Missing Links—The Challenge to Further Education, 1991; (ed with Peter Davies) Learning to Think—Thinking to Learn, 1992; The Inspectors' Calling—HMI and the Shaping of Educational Policy, 2001. *Address:* 109 College Road, Dulwich, SE21 7HN. *Club:* MCC.

McMAHON, Prof. April Mary Scott, PhD; FBA 2005; FRSE; Forbes Professor of English Language, University of Edinburgh, since 2005; *b* 30 April 1964; *d* of Irene Dugan (*née* Grant); *m* 1984, Robert McMahon; two *s* one *d*. *Educ:* Univ. of Edinburgh (MA 1986; PhD 1990). Lectr in Linguistics, and Fellow, Selwyn Coll., Cambridge, 1988–2000; Prof. of English Lang. and Linguistics, Univ. of Sheffield, 2000–04. Mem. Council, AHRC, 2005–. Pres., Linguistics Assoc. of GB, 2000–05. FRSE 2003. *Publications:* Understanding Language Change, 1994; Lexical Phonology and the History of English, 2000; Change, Chance and Optimality, 2000; (ed jtly) Time-depth in Historical Linguistics, 2 vols, 2000; An Introduction to English Phonology, 2001; (with R. McMahon) Language Classification by Numbers, 2005; (ed jtly) The Handbook of English Linguistics, 2006. *Recreations:* walking, cooking, Scottish country dancing. *Address:* Linguistics and English Language, University of Edinburgh, School of Philosophy, Psychology and Language Studies, 14 Buccleuch Place, Edinburgh EH8 9LN. *T:* (0131) 651 1999; *e-mail:* April.McMahon@ed.ac.uk.

McMAHON, Sir Brian (Patrick), 8th Bt *cr* 1817; engineer; *b* 9 June 1942; *s* of Sir (William) Patrick McMahon, 7th Bt, and Ruth Stella (*d* 1982), *yr d* of late Percy Robert Kenyon-Slaney; *S* father, 1977; *m* 1981, Kathleen Joan (marr. diss. 1991), *d* of late William Hopwood. *Educ:* Wellington. BSc, AIM. Assoc. Mem., Inst. of Welding. *Heir: brother* Shaun Desmond McMahon [*b* 29 Oct. 1945; *m* 1st, 1971, Antonia Noel Adie; 2nd, 1985, Jill Rosamund, *yr d* of Dr Jack Cherry; two *s*].

McMAHON, Sir Christopher William, (Sir Kit), Kt 1986; Director, Angela Flowers, 1992–2006; *b* Melbourne, 10 July 1927; *s* of late Dr John Joseph McMahon and late Margaret Kate (*née* Brown); *m* 1st, 1956, Marion Kelso; two *s*; 2nd, 1982, Alison Barbara Braimbridge, *d* of late Dr J. G. Cormie and late Mrs B. E. Cormie. *Educ:* Melbourne Grammar Sch.; Univ. of Melbourne (BA Hons Hist. and English, 1949); Magdalen Coll., Oxford. 1st cl. hons PPE, 1953. Tutor in English Lit., Univ. of Melbourne, 1950; Econ. Asst, HM Treasury, 1953–57; Econ. Adviser, British Embassy, Washington, 1957–60; Fellow and Tutor in Econs, Magdalen Coll., Oxford, 1960–64 (Hon. Fellow, 1986); Tutor in Econs, Treasury Centre for Admin. Studies, 1963–64; Mem., Plowden Cttee on Aircraft Industry, 1964–65; entered Bank of England as Adviser, 1964; Adviser to the Governors, 1966–70; Exec. Dir, 1970–80; Dep. Governor, 1980–85; Chief Exec. and Dep. Chm., 1986–87, Chm. and Chief Exec., 1987–91, Midland Bank. Director: Eurotunnel, 1987–91; Hongkong and Shanghai Banking Corp., 1987–91; Royal Opera House, 1989–97; Taylor Woodrow, 1991–2000 (Dep. Chm., 1997–2000); Newspaper Publishing, 1993–94; Aegis, 1993–99; FI Gp, 1994–2001; HistoryWorld, 2001–; Chairman: Coutts Consulting Gp, 1992–96; Pentos, 1993–95; Arc Dance Co., 2000–03. Mem., Gp of Thirty, 1978–84; Chairman: Working Party 3, OECD, 1980–85; Young Enterprise, 1989–92; Centre for Study of Financial Innovation, 1993–95. Mem. Court, Univ. of London, 1984–86; Gov., Birkbeck Coll., 1991–2003. Trustee: Whitechapel Art Gall., 1984–92; Royal Opera House Trust, 1984–86. Hon. Fellow, UCNW, 1988. Chevalier, Légion d'Honneur (France), 1990. *Publications:* Sterling in the Sixties, 1964; (ed) Techniques of Economic Forecasting, 1965. *Recreations:* looking at pictures, buying books, going to the movies. *Address:* The Old House, Burleigh Lane, Stroud GL5 2PQ. *Club:* Garrick.

McMAHON, Harvey Thomas, PhD; FRS 2008; Programme Leader, MRC Laboratory of Molecular Biology, Cambridge, since 1995; *b* Belfast, 31 Aug. 1965; *s* of William McMahon and Sarah Jean McMahon (*née* McCrea); *m* 1995, Kelly Lynn Hammonds; two *s*. *Educ:* Trinity College, Dublin (BA Mod. Biochem. 1987); Dundee Univ. (PhD 1990). Res. Asst, Dundee Univ., 1990–91; Postdoctoral Fellow, Howard Hughes Med. Inst., Dallas, 1991–95. *Publications:* regular contribs of papers, reviews and book chapters in scientific literature. *Recreations:* hill walking, travelling, ornithology, gardening (mostly growing weeds), community work. *Address:* MRC Laboratory of Molecular Biology, Neurobiology Division, Hills Road, Cambridge CB2 0QH. *T:* (01223) 402311, *Fax:* (01223) 402310; *e-mail:* hmm@mrc-lmb.cam.ac.uk.

McMAHON, Hugh Robertson; UK Political Editor, World Parliamentarian magazine, since 1999; Lecturer in Politics, James Watt College, since 1999; Lecturer, Office of Lifelong Learning, University of Edinburgh, since 2003; *b* 17 June 1938; *s* of Hugh McMahon and Margaret Fulton Robertson; *m* 1986, Helen Grant; one *s* one *d*. *Educ:* Glasgow University (MA Hons); Jordanhill College. Assistant Teacher: Largs High School, 1962–63; Stevenston High School, 1963–64; Irvine Royal Academy, 1964–68; Principal Teacher of History, Mainholm Academy, Ayr, 1968–71; Principal Teacher of History and Modern Studies, 1971–72, Asst Head Teacher, 1972–84, Ravenspark Academy, Irvine. MEP (Lab) Strathclyde W, 1984–99; contested (Lab) Scotland, 1999. European Parliament: Mem., Budgetary Control Cttee, 1987–92; Social Affairs, Employment and Working Envmt Cttee, 1984–99 (Vice Chm., 1992–94); Fisheries Cttee, 1994–99; Mem., Interparly Delegn with Czech Republic, 1997–99. Formerly Rep. of Scottish MEPs, Scottish Exec. Cttee, Labour Party. Mem. Bd, Centre for Russian and European Eastern Studies, 2007–. *Recreations:* golf, reading, walking, languages. *Address:* 9 Low Road, Castlehead, Paisley PA2 6AQ. *T:* (0141) 889 0885, *Fax:* (0141) 889 4790. *Clubs:* Saltcoats & Kilbirnie Labour; Irvine Bogside Golf.

McMAHON, Sir Kit; *see* McMahon, Sir C. W.

McMAHON, Rt Rev. Malcolm Patrick; *see* Nottingham, Bishop of, (RC).

McMAHON, Michael Joseph; Member (Lab) Hamilton North and Bellshill, Scottish Parliament, since 1999; *b* 18 Sept. 1961; *s* of Patrick McMahon and Bridget Clarke; *m* 1983, Margaret Mary McKeown; one *s* two *d*. *Educ:* Glasgow Caledonian Univ. (BA Hons Social Scis (Politics and Sociology) 1996). Welder, Terex Equipment Ltd, 1977–92; freelance socio-political researcher, 1996–99. *Recreations:* swimming, hill walking, supporting Celtic FC. *Address:* 7 Forres Crescent, Bellshill, Lanarkshire ML4 1HL. *T:* (01698) 306112.

McMAHON, Rt Rev. Thomas; *see* Brentwood, Bishop of, (RC).

MacMANUS, Dr Bernard Ronald; Vice-Chancellor, Bournemouth University, 1992–94; *b* 25 April 1936; *s* of Ronald MacManus and Doris Evelyn MacManus (*née* Sherriff); *m* 1959, Patricia Mary Greet; one *s* one *d*. *Educ:* St Boniface's Coll., Devon; Plymouth Poly.; Univ. of Birmingham (BScEng, PhD). Head, Dept of Mech. Production and Aeronautical Engrg, Manchester Poly., 1972–73; Dean, Faculty of Engrg, Sunderland Poly., 1973–78; Dep. Dir, Glasgow Coll. of Technology, 1978–83; Director: Dorset Inst. of Higher Educn, 1983–91; Bournemouth Poly., 1991–92. Hon. DEd Bournemouth, 2007. *Publications:* contribs to learned jls on manufacturing systems. *Recreations:* swimming, classic cars, music. *Address:* Thurlstone, Chapel Lane, Osmington, Dorset DT3 6ET.

McMANUS, Christopher; *see* McManus, I. C.

McMANUS, Declan Patrick Aloysius, (Elvis Costello); musician and composer; *b* 25 Aug. 1954; *s* of Ross McManus and Lillian McManus (*née* Costello); *m* 1974, Mary; one *s*; *m* 1986, Cait O'Riordan; *m* 2003, Diana Krall; two *s* (twins). Formed Elvis Costello and the Attractions, 1977; has collaborated with, amongst others, Brodsky Quartet, Swedish Radio Symphony Orchestra and Burt Bacharach. Dir, S Bank Centre Meltdown, 1995. Recordings include: *albums:* My Aim is True, 1977; This Year's Model, 1978; Armed Forces, 1979; Trust, 1981; Almost Blue, 1981; Imperial Bedroom, 1982; Punch the Clock, 1983; Blood and Chocolate, 1986; Spike, 1989; Mighty Like the Rose, 1991; (with Brodsky Quartet) The Juliet Letters, 1993; Brutal Youth, 1994; Extreme Honey, 1997; Painted from Memory, 1998; (with Anne Sofie von Otter) For the Stars, 2001; When I Was Cruel, 2002; North, 2003; The Delivery Man, 2004; Il Sogno, 2004; *singles:* Alison, 1977; Watching the Detectives, 1977; (I Don't Want to Go to) Chelsea, 1978; Oliver's Army, 1979; Accidents Will Happen, 1979; Good Year for the Roses, 1981; Everyday I Write the Book, 1983; Pills and Soap, 1983; The People's Limousine, 1985; Little Atoms, 1996; She, 1999.

McMANUS, Francis Joseph; solicitor; *b* 16 Aug. 1942; *s* of Patrick and Celia McManus; *m* 1971, Carmel V. Doherty, Lisnaskea, Co. Fermanagh; two *s* one *d*. *Educ:* St Michael's, Enniskillen; Queen's University, Belfast. BA 1965; Diploma in Education, 1966. Subsequently a Teacher. MP (Unity) Fermanagh and S Tyrone, 1970–Feb. 1974. Founder Mem. and Co-Chm., Irish Independence Party, 1977–. *Address:* Lissadell, 40 Drumlin Heights, Enniskillen, Co. Fermanagh, N Ireland BT74 7NR. *T:* Enniskillen (028) 6632 3401.

McMANUS, Prof. (Ian) Christopher, PhD, MD; FRCP, FRCPEd, FMedSci; Professor of Psychology and Medical Education, University College London, since 1997; *b* 1 March 1951; *s* of Robert Victor McManus and June McManus; *m* 2007, Christine Pleines; one *s* two *d*. *Educ:* Harrow Co. Grammar Sch.; Christ's Coll., Cambridge (BA 1972, MA 1977; PhD 1979); Univ. of Birmingham (MB ChB 1975); Univ. of London (MD 1985). FRCP 1998; FRCPEd 2007. University of London: Lectr in Psychol. as Applied to Medicine, Dept of Psychol., Bedford Coll., then UCL, and Dept of Psychiatry, St Mary's Hosp. Med. Sch., 1979–88; Sen. Lectr in Psychol. as Applied to Medicine, Dept of Psychol., UCL, and Dept of Psychiatry, St Mary's Hosp. Med. Sch., ICSTM, 1988–93; Prof. of Psychol., Dept of Psychol., UCL, and Dept of Psychiatry, ICSM at St Mary's, 1993–97. Examr and Educnl Advr, MRCP(UK), 1999–. C. S. Myers Lectr, BPsS, 2005. Pres., Psychol. Section, British Assoc., 2002. Fellow, Internat. Assoc. Empirical Aesthetics, 2000. Ed., Laterality, 1996–. FMedSci 2007. Ig Nobel Prize, 2002. *Publications:* Psychology in Medicine, 1992; (ed jtly) Cambridge Handbook of Psychology, Health and Medicine, 1997; Right Hand, Left Hand, 2002 (Wellcome Trust Prize, 1999; Aventis Prize, 2003). *Recreations:* all things aesthetic, all things Italian. *Address:* Department of Psychology, University College London, Gower Street, WC1E 6BT. *T:* (020) 7679 5390, *Fax:* (020) 7436 4276; *e-mail:* i.mcmanus@ucl.ac.uk.

McMANUS, Prof. James John; Professor of Criminal Justice, Glasgow Caledonian University, since 2004; *b* 23 June 1950; *s* of David McManus and Alice McManus (*née* Vallelly); *m* 1974, Catherine MacKellaig; one *s* four *d*. *Educ:* Our Lady's High Sch., Motherwell; Univ. of Edinburgh (LLB); Univ. of Dundee (PhD 1985). Lectr, UC, Cardiff, 1972–74; Lectr, 1974–76, Sen. Lectr, 1976–2004, Univ. of Dundee. Comr, Scottish Prisons Complaints Commn, 1994–99; Chm., Parole Bd for Scotland, 2000–06. Expert Advr, Cttee for Prevention of Torture, Council of Europe, 1992–. *Publications:* Lay Justice, 1992; Prisons, Prisoners and the Law, 1994. *Recreations:* golf, ski-ing. *Address:* School of Law and Social Sciences, Glasgow Caledonian University, City Campus, Cowcaddens Road, Glasgow G4 0BA.

McMANUS, John Andrew; HM Diplomatic Service; Ambassador to Guinea, since 2004; *b* 20 May 1955; *s* of Andrew McManus and Winifred (*née* Hazzard). *Educ:* Univ. of Sussex (BA Econs and Europ. Studies 1977). Joined FCO, 1977; Vice-Consul, Algiers, 1984–85; Commercial Attaché, Moscow, 1988–91; Presidency Co-ordinator, UK Perm. Repn to

EU, Brussels, 1992; First Sec., Press and Public Affairs, Berne, 1993–97; Hd of Political Section, Brussels, 2000–04. *Recreations:* athletics, food, languages. *Address:* c/o Foreign and Commonwealth Office, King Charles Street, SW1A 2AH; *e-mail:* john_mcmanus1066@hotmail.com.

McMANUS, Jonathan Richard; QC 1999; *b* 15 Sept. 1958; *s* of Frank Rostron McManus and Benita Ann McManus. *Educ:* Neale Wade Comprehensive, March; Downing Coll., Cambridge (MA). Called to the Bar, Middle Temple, 1982. *Publications:* Education and the Courts, 1998, 2nd edn 2004; contrib. Economic, Social and Cultural Rights: their implementation, in United Kingdom Law, ed Burchill, Harris and Owers, 1999. *Recreations:* music, travel, photography. *Address:* 4–5 Gray's Inn Square, Gray's Inn, WC1R 5AH. *T:* (020) 7404 5252.

McMASTER, Sir Brian (John), Kt 2003; CBE 1987; Director, Edinburgh International Festival, 1991–2006. International Artists' Dept, EMI Ltd, 1968–73; Controller of Opera Planning, ENO, 1973–76; Gen. Administrator, subseq. Man. Dir, WNO, 1976–91; Artistic Dir, Vancouver Opera, 1984–89. *Address:* 13/5 James Court, Lawnmarket, Edinburgh EH1 2PB.

McMASTER, Hughan James Michael; Chief Architect and Director of Works, Home Office, 1980–87, retired; *b* 27 July 1927; *s* of William James Michael and Emly McMaster; *m* 1950; one *s* two *d*. *Educ:* Christ's Coll., Finchley; Regent Street Polytechnic (DipArch). ARIBA 1951. Served RAF, India and Far East, 1946–48. Joined Civil Service, 1961; Navy Works, 1961–69; Whitehall Development Gp, Directorate of Home Estate Management and Directorate of Civil Accommodation, 1969–76; Defence Works (PE and Overseas), 1976–80. *Recreations:* gardening, reading, theatre, music.

McMASTER, Prof. Paul; Professor of Hepatobiliary Surgery and Transplantation, and Consultant Surgeon, Queen Elizabeth Hospital, University of Birmingham, 1980–2005; *b* 4 Jan. 1943; *s* of Dr James McMaster and Sarah Jane McMaster (*née* Lynn); *m* 1969, Helen Ruth Bryce; two *s* one *d*. *Educ:* Liverpool Coll.; Univ. of Liverpool (MB ChB 1966; ChM 1979); MA Cantab 1978. FRCS 1971. House Surgeon, subseq. House Physician, Liverpool Royal Infirmary, Univ. of Liverpool, 1966–67; SHO in Urology and Transplantation, RPMS, Hammersmith Hosp., 1967–68; Registrar in Surgery, Addenbrooke's Hosp., 1969–72; Sen. Registrar and Res. Fellow, 1972–76, Sen. Lectr in Surgery, 1976–80, Univ. Dept of Surgery, Addenbrooke's Hosp., Cambridge Univ. Visiting Professor: Univs of Rome, Genoa, Cairo, Concepción; RACS Foundn, 1998. FICS. *Publications:* numerous articles on immuno suppression, liver transplantation, develt of laparoscopic and hepatobiliary surgery, advances in major hepatic and biliary surgery. *Recreations:* gardening, sailing, reading. *Address:* c/o Liver Unit, Queen Elizabeth Hospital, Edgbaston, Birmingham B15 2TH.

McMASTER, Peter, CB 1991; Member, Lord Chancellor's Panel of Independent Inspectors, 1991–2001; *b* 22 Nov. 1931; *s* of Peter McMaster and Ada Nellie (*née* Williams); *m* 1955, Catherine Ann Rosborough; one *s* one *d*. *Educ:* Kelvinside Academy, Glasgow; RMA Sandhurst; RMCS Shrivenham. BScEng London. Called to the Bar, Middle Temple, 1969. Commissioned into Royal Engineers, 1952; served Middle and Far East; retired (major), 1970; joined Civil Service, 1970; W Midland Region, Ordnance Survey, 1970–72; Caribbean Region, Directorate of Overseas Survey, 1972–74; Headquarters, 1974–91, Dir Gen., 1985–91, Ordnance Survey. Vis. Prof., Kingston Polytechnic, subseq. Kingston Univ., 1991–93. Member Council: BCS, 1983–92; RGS, 1990–93. FIIM 1990. *Recreations:* travel, walking, chess. *Address:* Hillhead, Stratton Road, Winchester, Hampshire SO23 0JQ. *T:* (01962) 862684.
  See also Peter McMaster.

McMASTER, Peter; QC 2008; *b* Dhekelia, Cyprus, 10 Jan. 1959; *s* of Peter McMaster, *qv*; *m* 1992, Natalie Ann Adams; three *s*. *Educ:* North Bromsgrove High Sch.; Winchester Coll.; King's Coll. London (LLB 1980). Called to the Bar, Middle Temple, 1981. *Recreations:* reading, walking, shooting, cooking. *Address:* Serle Court, 6 New Square, Lincoln's Inn, WC2A 3QS. *T:* (020) 7242 6105; *e-mail:* pmcmaster@serlecourt.co.uk.

McMENAMIN, Frances Jane, (Mrs Ian McCarry); QC (Scot.) 1998; *b* 21 May 1951; *d* of Francis and Agnes McMenamin; *m* 1991, Ian McCarry. *Educ:* Our Lady of Lourdes Primary Sch., Glasgow; Notre Dame High Sch., Glasgow; Strathclyde Univ. (BA, LLB 1974). Admitted Solicitor, 1976; admitted to Faculty of Advocates, 1985. Legal Apprentice, Hughes, Dowdall & Co., Solicitors, 1974–76; Procurator Fiscal Depute, 1976–84; advocate specialising in criminal law, 1985–; Temp. Sheriff, 1991–97; Advocate Depute, 1997–2000. Mem., Adv. Gp on rape and other sexual offences, Scottish Law Commn, 2005–. Vis. Lectr, Scottish Police Coll., Tulliallan Castle, 1991–. Mem., Law Sch. Adv. Panel, 2002–, Mem. of Ct, 2005–, Univ. of Strathclyde. Dir, Faculty Services Ltd, 2003–07. *Recreations:* spending time with husband, family and friends, golf, exercise classes, reading, travelling. *Address:* (home) 59 Hamilton Drive, Glasgow G12 8DP. *T:* (0141) 339 0519; Advocates' Library, Parliament House, Parliament Square, Edinburgh EH1 1RF. *T:* (0131) 226 5071. *Club:* Hole in the Head (Edinburgh).

McMICHAEL, Sir Andrew James, Kt 2008; FRS 1992; Director, Medical Research Council Human Immunology Unit, John Radcliffe Hospital, Oxford, 1998–2000, now Hon. Director; Professor of Molecular Medicine and Director, Weatherall Institute of Molecular Medicine, Oxford University, since 2000; Fellow of Corpus Christi College, Oxford, since 2000; *b* 8 Nov. 1943; *s* of Sir John McMichael, FRS and late Sybil McMichael; *m* 1968, Kathryn Elizabeth Cross; two *s* one *d*. *Educ:* St Paul's Sch., London; Gonville and Caius Coll., Cambridge (MA; BChir 1968; MB 1969); St Mary's Hosp. Med. Sch., London. PhD 1974; MRCP 1971; FRCP 1985. House Physician, St Mary's Hosp., Royal Northern Hosp., Hammersmith Hosp. and Brompton Hosp., 1968–71; MRC Jun. Res. Fellow, National Inst. for Med. Res., 1971–74; MRC Travelling Fellow, Stanford Univ. Med. Sch., 1974–76; Oxford University: Wellcome Sen. Clin. Fellow, Nuffield Depts of Medicine and Surgery, 1977–79; University Lectr in Medicine and Hon. Consultant Physician, 1979–82; MRC Clinical Res. Prof. of Immunology, 1982–98; Prof. of Immunology, 1999–2000; Fellow, Trinity Coll., 1983–2000. Member: Adv. Bd, Beit Meml Trust, 1984–; MRC AIDS Steering Cttee, 1988–94; Res. Grants Council, Hong Kong, 1990–99; Council, Royal Soc., 1998–99. Founder FMedSci 1998. *Publications:* (ed with J. W. Fabre) Monoclonal Antibodies in Clinical Medicine, 1982; articles on genetic control of human immune response, antiviral immunity and AIDS. *Recreations:* walking and ski-ing in France.

MACMILLAN, family name of **Earl of Stockton.**

MACMILLAN OF OVENDEN, Viscount; Daniel Maurice Alan Macmillan; *b* 9 Oct. 1974; *s* and heir of Earl of Stockton, *qv*.

McMILLAN, Alan Austen, CB 1986; Solicitor to the Secretary of State for Scotland, 1984–87; *b* 19 Jan. 1926; *s* of Allan McMillan and Mabel (*née* Austin); *m* 1949, Margaret Moncur; two *s* two *d*. *Educ:* Ayr Acad.; Glasgow Univ. Served in Army, 1944–47. Qualified Solicitor in Scotland, 1949; Legal Assistant, Ayr Town Council, 1949–55;

Scottish Office: Legal Assistant, 1955–62; Sen. Legal Assistant, 1962–68; Asst Solicitor, 1968–82, seconded to Cabinet Office Constitution Unit, 1977–78; Dep. Solicitor, 1982–84. *Recreations:* reading, music, theatre.

MACMILLAN, Sir (Alexander McGregor) Graham, Kt 1983; Director, Scottish Conservative Party, 1975–84; *b* 14 Sept. 1920; *s* of James Orr Macmillan and Sarah Dunsmore (*née* Graham); *m* 1947, Christina Brash Beveridge (*d* 1998); two *s* two *d*. *Educ:* Hillhead High Sch., Glasgow. Served War, RA, 1939–46. Conservative Agent: W Lothian, 1947–50; Haltemprice, 1950–53; Bury St Edmunds, 1953–60; Dep. Central Office Agent, NW Area, 1960–61; Central Office Agent, Yorks Area, 1961–75. Chairman: M & P Financial Services Ltd, 1986–87 (Dir, 1984–87); Mid-Anglian Enterprise Agency Ltd, 1988–92 (Gov., 1987–97); Exec. Sec., YorCan Communications Ltd, 1989–94. Chairman: Bury St Edmunds Round Table, 1959–60 (Pres., 1997–2001); Bury St Edmunds Br., Multiple Sclerosis Soc., 1987–95. Mem., Transport Users' Consultative Cttee for E England, 1987–95. Hon. Sec., Suffolk Assoc. of Boys' Clubs, 1986–88. Governor, Leeds Grammar Sch., 1968–75. *Recreations:* fishing, watching cricket and rugby. *Address:* 46 Crown Street, Bury St Edmunds, Suffolk IP33 1QX. *T:* (01284) 704443.

MACMILLAN, Alexander Ross, FCIBS; Director, 1974–87, Chief General Manager, 1971–82, Clydesdale Bank PLC; *b* 25 March 1922; *s* of Donald and Johanna Macmillan; *m* 1961, Ursula Miriam Grayson; two *s* one *d*. *Educ:* Tain Royal Acad. FCIBS (FIBScot 1942). Served War, RAF, 1942–46 (despatches, King's Birthday Honours, 1945). Entered service of N of Scotland Bank Ltd, Tain, 1938; after War, returned to Tain, 1946; transf. to Supt's Dept, Aberdeen, and thereafter to Chief Accountant's Dept, Clydesdale Bank, Glasgow, 1950, on amalgamation with N of Scotland Bank; Chief London Office, 1952; Gen. Manager's Confidential Clerk, 1955; Manager, Piccadilly Circus Br., 1958; Supt of Branches, 1965; Gen. Manager's Asst, 1967; Asst Gen. Man., 1968. Director: The High Sch. of Glasgow Ltd, 1979–92; Caledonian Applied Technology Ltd, 1982–87; Highland-North Sea Ltd, 1982–2000 (Chm., 1982–); John Laing plc, 1982–86; Martin-Black PLC, 1982–85; Radio Clyde Ltd, 1982–93; Scottish Develt Finance Ltd, 1982–92; Kelvin Technology Develts Ltd, 1982–96; Compugraphics Internat. Ltd, 1982–87; Highland Deephaven Ltd, 1983–2000; TEG Products Ltd, 1986–87; New Generation Housing Soc. Ltd, 1986–95; Castle Wynd Housing Soc. Ltd, 1987–89; Wilsons Garage (Argyll) Ltd, 1987–94; Wilsons Fuels Ltd, 1987–94; EFT Gp (formerly Edinburgh Financial Trust) plc, 1987–93; Balmoral Gp Ltd, 1988–93; North of Scotland Radio Ltd, 1989–93; Radio Clyde Holdings plc, 1991–93; Gilmorhill Power Management Ltd, 1994–96; Nemoquest Ltd, 1994–96; Dumwilco Ltd, 1995–96; Chm., First Northern Corporate Finance Ltd, 1983–87. Chm., Nat. House Bldg Council (Scotland), 1982–88. Mem. Court, Univ. of Glasgow, 1981–96. Freeman, Royal Burgh of Tain, 1975. CCMI (CBIM 1980). DUniv Glasgow, 1989. *Recreation:* golf. *Address:* 4 Cochrane Court, Fairways, Milngavie, Glasgow G62 6QT.

MacMILLAN, Prof. Andrew, OBE 1992; RSA 1990; RIBA; FRIAS; Professor of Architecture, Glasgow University, and Head, Mackintosh School of Architecture, 1973–94, now Emeritus Professor; *b* 11 Dec. 1928; *s* of Andrew Harkness MacMillan of Murlaggan and Mary Jane McKelvie; *m* 1955, Angela Lillian McDowell; one *s* three *d*. *Educ:* Maryhill Public Sch.; North Kelvinside Sen. Secondary Sch., Glasgow; Glasgow Sch. of Architecture (MA 1973). FRIAS 1973. Apprenticeship, Glasgow Corp. Housing Dept, 1945–52; Architectural Asst, East Kilbride New Town Develt Corp., 1952–54; Asst Architect, 1954–63, Partner, 1966–88, Gillespie Kidd & Coia; consultant architect in private practice, 1988–. Davenport Vis. Prof., Yale Univ., 1986. Mem., Scottish Arts Council, 1978–82; Vice-Pres. for Educn, RIBA, 1981–85; Vice President: Prince and Princess of Wales Hospice, 1981–; Charles Rennie Mackintosh Soc., 1984–; Patron, Arts Educn Trust, 1988–. Royal Scottish Acad. Gold Medal, 1975; RIBA Bronze Medal, 1985; RIBA Award for Arch., 1966, 1967, 1968 and 1982; Saltire awards and Civic Trust awards at various times. *Publications:* books, papers and articles mainly dealing with urban design, urban building, architectural educn, Glasgow arch. of 20th century, and Charles Rennie Mackintosh. *Recreations:* travel, sailing, watercolours. *Address:* The Penthouse, 28 Wilson Street, Glasgow G1 1SS. *T:* (0141) 552 2481.

McMILLAN, David Loch, FRAeS; Director General, European Organisation for the Safety of Air Navigation (EUROCONTROL), since 2008; *b* 16 Sept. 1954; *s* of David and May McMillan; *m* 1977, Frances Beedham; one *s* two *d*. *Educ:* Royal High Sch., Edinburgh; Univ. of Edinburgh (MA French and Spanish). FCO, 1976; Rabat, 1978; Harare, 1980; Principal, Dept of Transport, 1984–87; First Sec. (Transport), Washington, 1987–92; Hd, Information, Dept of Transport, 1993–97; Hd, Air Traffic Div., DETR, 1997–2001; Dir, Rail Restructuring, DETR, 2001–02; Dir, Strategy and Delivery, 2002–04, Dir Gen., Civil Aviation, 2004–07, DfT. FRAeS 2008. *Recreations:* my children, reading, France. *Address:* EUROCONTROL, 96 rue de la Fusée, Brussels 1130, Belgium. *T:* (2) 7293501, *Fax:* (2) 7299100; *e-mail:* david.mcmillan@eurocontrol.int.

MACMILLAN, Deborah Millicent, (Lady Macmillan); artist; *b* Boonah, Qld, 1 July 1944; *d* of Dr Dudley Williams and Nina Deborah (*née* Darvall); *m* 1st, 1966, Denis Allard (marr. diss. 1973); 2nd, 1974, Sir Kenneth Macmillan (*d* 1992); one *d*. *Educ:* Wenona, N Sydney; Nat. Art Sch., E Sydney (Painting and Sculpture). Member: Bd, Royal Opera House, 1993–96; Exec. Cttee, Royal Acad. Dancing, 1994–; Council, Arts Council of England, 1996–98 (Chm., Dance Panel, 1996–98); Chm., Friends of Covent Gdn, 1995–96. Mem., Nat. Cttee, Houston Ballet, 1993–; Hon. Mem. Bd, American Ballet Theatre, 1993–. Gov., Nat. Youth Dance Trust, 1999–2004; Trustee, Wimbledon Sch. of Art, 2000–. Custodian, Sir Kenneth Macmillan's choreography, 1992–. *Exhibitions: solo shows:* Charlotte Lampard Gall., 1984; Turtle Key Arts Centre, 1992, 1995; Chelsea Arts Club, 1999; Gall. 27 Cork St, 2005; Water and Light Gall., 2005; *group shows:* Camden Arts Centre, 1990; Royal Acad. Summer Exhibn, 1990; Accrochage, Fischer Fine Art, 1990; Contemporary Art Soc. Mkt, 1990; Drawing Show, Thumb Gall., 1990; Art for Equality, ICA, 1991; Leicestershire Collection, 1992; Gillian Jason Contemporary Portraits Real and Imagined, 1993; Jason Rhodes Gp Show, 1995; Glyndebourne Fest. Opera, 1997–2003; Glyndebourne Ten for Ten Anniv. exhibn, 2004. *Recreations:* gardening, any displacement activity. *Address:* c/o Simpson Fox, 52 Shaftesbury Avenue, W1V 7DE. *Club:* Chelsea Arts.

MACMILLAN, Duncan; *see* Macmillan, J. D.

MACMILLAN, Very Rev. Gilleasbuig Iain, CVO 1999; FRSE; Minister of St Giles', The High Kirk of Edinburgh, since 1973; Chaplain to the Queen in Scotland, since 1979; Dean of the Order of the Thistle, since 1989; *b* 21 Dec. 1942; *s* of Rev. Kenneth M. Macmillan and Mrs Mary Macmillan; *m* 1965, Maureen Stewart Thomson; one *d*. *Educ:* Oban High School; Univ. of Edinburgh. MA, BD. Asst Minister, St Michael's Parish, Linlithgow, 1967–69; Minister of Portree Parish, Isle of Skye, 1969–73. Extra Chaplain to the Queen in Scotland, 1978–79. Hon. Chaplain: Royal Scottish Academy; Royal Coll. of Surgeons of Edinburgh; Soc. of High Constables of City of Edinburgh. FRSE 2005. Hon. FRCSE 1998. Hon. DD: Alma Coll., 1997; St Andrews, 2003; Dr *hc* Edinburgh,

1998. *Publications:* A Workable Belief, 1993; Understanding Christianity, 2004. *Address:* St Giles' Cathedral, Edinburgh EH1 1RE. *T:* (0131) 225 4363. *Club:* New (Edinburgh).

MACMILLAN, Sir Graham; *see* Macmillan, Sir A. M. G.

McMILLAN, Hamilton; *see* McMillan, N. H.

MACMILLAN, Iain Alexander, CBE 1978; LLD; Sheriff of South Strathclyde, Dumfries and Galloway at Hamilton, 1981–92; Temporary Sheriff, 1992–94; *b* 14 Nov. 1923; *s* of John and Eva Macmillan; *m* 1954, Edith Janet (*née* MacAulay); two *s* one *d*. *Educ:* Oban High Sch.; Glasgow Univ. (BL). Served war, RAF, France, Germany, India, 1944–47. Glasgow Univ., 1947–50. Subseq. law practice; Sen. Partner, J. & J. Sturrock & Co., Kilmarnock, 1952–81. Law Society of Scotland: Mem. Council, 1964–79; Pres., 1976–77. Pres., Temp. Sheriffs' Assoc., 1993–94. Chairman: Lanarkshire Br., Scottish Assoc. for Study of Delinquency, 1986–92; Victim Support, E Ayrshire, 1998–2001. Trustee, Glasgow Art Club, 2003–. Hon. LLD Aberdeen, 1975. *Recreation:* golf. *Address:* 2 Castle Drive, Kilmarnock KA3 1TN. *T:* (01563) 525864.

McMILLAN, Iain Macleod, CBE 2003; Director, CBI Scotland, since 1995 (Assistant Director, 1993–95); *b* 25 April 1951; *s* of William Catterall McMillan and Helen Macleod McMillan (*née* Paterson); *m* 1975, Giuseppina Silvana Pellegrini; three *s*. *Educ:* Bearsden Acad., Glasgow. FCIB 1991; FCIBS 1997; FAIA 2004. Bank officer and various mgt and sen. mgt posts, TSB Gp plc, 1970–93. Bd Mem., Scottish Qualifications Authy, 1997–2006 (Vice Chm., 2004–06); Chm., Scottish Business Educn Coalition, 2001–07. Non-exec. Dir, Special Health Bd, Scottish Ambulance Service, 2000–08. Chm., Adv. Bd, Business Sch. (formerly Grad. Sch. of Business), Univ. of Strathclyde, 2005–. Trustee: Industrial Mission Trust, 2000– (Chm., 2008–); Teaching Awards Trust, 2007–. Mem. or former mem., various adv. bodies and public policy cttees and working gps in Scotland. FRSA 1994; CCMI 2002; FSQA 2007. *Recreations:* walking, reading, squash. *Address:* CBI Scotland, 16 Robertson Street, Glasgow G2 8DS. *T:* (0141) 222 2184, *Fax:* (0141) 222 2187.

MacMILLAN, Jake; *see* MacMillan, John.

MacMILLAN, Dr James Loy, CBE 2004; composer and conductor; composer/conductor, BBC Philharmonic, since 2000; *b* 16 July 1959; *s* of James MacMillan and Ellen MacMillan (*née* Loy); *m* 1983, Lynne Frew; one *s* two *d*. *Educ:* Edinburgh Univ. (BMus); Durham Univ. (PhD 1987). Lectr, Univ. of Manchester, 1986–88; Composer in Residence, St Magnus Fest., Orkney, 1989; Featured Composer: Musica Nova, Glasgow, 1990; Huddersfield Contemp. Music Fest., 1991; Edinburgh Fest., 1993; Raising Sparks Fest., S Bank and Barbican, 1997; Affiliate Composer, Scottish Chamber Orch., 1990–; Artistic Dir, Philharmonia, Music of Today, 1992–2002. Vis. Prof., Univ. of Strathclyde, 1997–. FRSAMD 1996; FRNCM; FRSCM; FRSE 2007. Hon. FRIAS 1997. DUniv Paisley, 1995; Hon. DLitt: UMIST; Strathclyde, 1996; Hon. DMus: Abertay Dundee; St Andrews, 2001; Durham; Edinburgh; Glasgow; Newman Coll., Leicester; RSAMD, 2005; DUniv: Paisley; Open. Gramophone Award, 1993; Classic CD Award, 1994; Royal Philharmonic Soc. Award, 1995. *Compositions* include: Busquéda (music theatre), 1988; Visions of a November Spring (string quartet no 1), 1988; Tryst (for orch.), 1989; Tuireadh (clarinet quintet), 1991; Confession of Isobel Gowdie (for orch.), 1990; Veni, Veni Emmanuel (percussion concerto), 1992; Visitatio Sepulchri (one-act opera), 1993; Seven Last Words (chorus and strings), 1994; Britannia (overture), 1995; Ines de Castro (opera), 1996; The World's Ransoming (concerto for cor anglais), 1996; 'Cello Concerto, 1996; I—A Meditation on Iona (for chamber orch.), 1997; Ninian (clarinet concerto), 1997; 14 Little Pictures (for piano trio), 1997; Vigil (symphony), 1997; Raising Sparks (for mezzo-sop. and ensemble), 1997; Why is this night different? (string quartet no 2), 1998; Quickening (for chorus, orch., boys' choir and four soloists), 1999; Symphony no 2, 1999; Mass (chorus and organ), 2000; Parthenogenesis (for soprano, baritone, actress and small ensemble), 2000; The Birds of Rhiannon, 2001; A Deep but Dazzling Darkness (for solo violin, ensemble and tape), 2002; O Bone Jesu (a cappella chorus), 2002; Symphony no 3, 2003; Piano Concerto No. 2, 2004; A Scotch Bestiary (for organ and orch.), 2004; Tenebrae Responsaries (a cappella chorus), 2006; Sun-dogs (a cappella chorus), 2006; Stomp (with Fate and Elvira) (concert overture for orch.), 2006; From Ayrshire (for violin and orch.), 2006; The Sacrifice (opera), 2007; St John Passion (for baritone, chorus and orch.), 2008. *Recreations:* fatherhood, Glasgow Celtic FC. *Address:* c/o Boosey & Hawkes Music Publishers Ltd, Aldwych House, 71–91 Aldwych WC2B 4HN. *T:* (020) 7054 7200.

MacMILLAN, Prof. John, (Jake), PhD Glasgow; DSc Bristol; FRS 1978; CChem, ARIC; Alfred Capper Pass Professor of Organic Chemistry, 1985–90, and Head of Department of Organic Chemistry, 1983–90, University of Bristol, now Professor Emeritus and Senior Research Fellow; *b* 13 Sept. 1924; *s* of John MacMillan and Barbara Lindsay; *m* 1952, Anne Levy; one *s* two *d*. *Educ:* Lanark Grammar Sch.; Glasgow Univ. Res. Chemist, Akers Res. Labs, ICI Ltd, 1949; Associate Res. Manager, Pharmaceuticals Div., ICI Ltd, 1962; Lectr in Org. Chemistry, Bristol Univ., 1963, Reader 1968, Prof. 1978. Pres., Internat. Plant Growth Substance Assoc., 1973–76. For. Associate, Nat. Acad. of Scis, USA, 1991. *Publications:* (ed) Encyclopedia of Plant Physiology, New Series vol. 9, 1980; (ed jtly) Gibberellins, 1991; (jtly) GC-MS of Gibberellins and Related Compounds: methodology and a library of reference spectra, 1991; research papers in learned jls on natural organic products, esp. plant growth hormones. *Recreations:* gardening, theatre, music. *Address:* 7 Burrough Way, Winterbourne, S Glos BS36 1LF. *T:* (01454) 775244.

MACMILLAN, Prof. (John) Duncan, PhD; FRSE; Curator, Talbot Rice Gallery, 1979–2004, and Professor of History of Scottish Art, 1994–2001, now Emeritus, University of Edinburgh; *b* 7 March 1939; *s* of late William Miller Macmillan and Mona Constance Mary Tweedie; *m* 1971, Vivien Rosemary Hinkley; two *d*. *Educ:* Gordonstoun Sch.; St Andrews Univ. (MA Hons 1961); Courtauld Inst., London (Dip. Hist. of Art 1964); Edinburgh Univ. (PhD 1974). Lectr, 1964–81, Curator of Univ. Collections, 1987–2002, Edinburgh Univ. Art critic: The Scotsman, 1994–2000, 2002–; Business am, 2000–02. Visiting Fellow: Yale Centre for British Art, 1991; Japan Soc. for Promotion of Science, 1995. Convener, Scottish Univ. Museums Gp, 1992–99; Chm., Edinburgh Galls Assoc., 1995–98; Vice-Chm., European Union Cultural Forum; Chm., Torvean Project Steering Gp, 1997–2000; Member: Council, Edinburgh Fest. Soc., 1991–97; Cttee, Univ. Museums Gp, 1992–99; Heritage Unit Adv. Bd, Robert Gordon Univ.; comité consultatif, French Inst., Edinburgh, 1997–. Member Editorial Board: Scotlands, 1994–; British Art Jl, 1999–; Dundee Univ. Press, 2005–08. Hon. Keeper of Portraits, RCSE. Hon. RSA; FRSA; FRSE 2005 (Henry Duncan Prize, 2004). Hon. LLD Dundee, 2004. Andrew Fletcher of Saltoun Prize, Saltire Soc., 2005. *Publications:* (jtly) Miró in America, 1983; Painting in Scotland: the Golden Age 1707–1843, 1986; Scottish Art 1460–1990, 1990 (Scottish Book of the Year, Saltire Soc., 1992), 2nd edn, Scottish Art 1460–2000, 2000; Symbols of Survival: the art of Will Maclean, 1992 (Scottish Arts Council Book Award, 1993), 2nd edn 2002; The Paintings of Steven Campbell: the story so far, 1993; Scottish Art in the Twentieth Century, 1994 (Scottish Arts Council Book Award, 1995), 2nd edn as Scottish Art in the Twentieth Century: 1890–2001, 2001; (jtly) Peter Brandes: stained glass, 1994; (jtly) Eugenio Carmi, 1996; Elizabeth Blackadder, 1999; numerous exhibn catalogues, articles, etc. *Recreations:* walking, landscape photography. *Address:* 20 Nelson Street, Edinburgh EH3 6LJ. *T:* (0131) 556 7100; Wester Balnagrantach, Glen Urquhart, Inverness-shire. *T:* (01456) 450727.

MACMILLAN, John Kenneth; Regional Employment Judge (formerly Regional Chairman, Industrial, later Employment Tribunals), Nottingham, since 1997; *b* 8 July 1946; *s* of late Kenneth Lionel Macmillan, OBE and Marjorie Ethel Macmillan; *m* 1st, 1972, Mary Lister (marr. diss.); 2nd, 1977, Dawn Nelson (marr. diss.); one *d*; 3rd, 1995, Pauline Anne Swain; two step *d*. *Educ:* Carlton-le-Willows Grammar Sch., Nottingham. Admitted Solicitor, 1970; Asst Solicitor, 1970, Litigation Partner, 1971–84, Haden and Stretton, Solicitors. Pt-time Chm., 1981–87, full-time Chm., 1987–97, Industrial Tribunals, Birmingham; Mem., President's Trng Panel, 1992–2000. Ed., Employment Tribunals Members Handbook, 1999–2006; Principal Consulting Ed., Blackstone's Employment Law Practice, 2006–. Hon. Sec., RSNC, 1992–2003. Trustee, Staffs Wildlife Trust, 1982–99, 2005–. *Publication:* (contrib.) Sweet & Maxwell's Employment Court Practice, 2007. *Recreations:* nature conservation, theatre, gardening, fly fishing, philosophy. *Address:* (office) 3rd Floor, Byron House, Maid Marian Way, Nottingham NG1 6HS.

MacMILLAN, Lt-Gen. Sir John Richard Alexander, KCB 1988; CBE 1978 (OBE 1973); DL; fruit farmer; GOC Scotland and Governor of Edinburgh Castle, 1988–91; *b* 8 Feb. 1932; *m* 1964, Belinda Lumley Webb; one *s* two *d*. *Educ:* Trinity Coll., Cambridge (BA 1953; MA 1958); rcds, psc. Commnd Argyll and Sutherland Highlanders, 2nd Lieut, 1952; GSO2 (Ops Int. Trng), Trucial Oman Scouts, 1963–64; BM, HQ 24 Inf. Bde, 1967–69; Chief Recruiting and Liaison Staff, Scotland, 1970; CO, 1st Bn The Gordon Highlanders, 1971–73; GSO1 (DS), Staff Coll., 1973–75; Col GS, Mil. Ops 4, 1975–76; Brig., 1976; Bde Comd, 39 Inf. Bde, 1977–78; RCDS 1979; COS, 1 (Br.) Corps, 1980–82; Maj.-Gen., 1982; GOC Eastern Dist, 1982–84; ACGS, MoD, 1984–87; Lt-Gen., 1988. Col, The Gordon Highlanders, 1978–86; Col Comdt, Scottish Div., 1986–91; Hon. Col, Aberdeen Univ. OTC, 1987–97. Chm. Exec Cttee, Scottish Conservation Projects Trust, 1992–98; Chairman: Erskine Hosp. (formerly Princess Louise Scottish Hosp.), 1995–2000; HM Comrs for Queen Victoria Sch., Dunblane, 2000–03. DL Stirling and Falkirk, 1998–2007. *Address:* Boghall Farm, Thornhill, Stirling FK8 3QD.

MacMILLAN, Prof. Margaret Olwen, OC 2005; DPhil; Warden, St Antony's College, Oxford, since 2007; Professor of International History, University of Oxford, since 2007; *b* 23 Dec. 1943; *d* of Robert and Eluned MacMillan. *Educ:* Univ. of Toronto (BA Hons Mod. Hist. 1966); St Hilda's Coll., Oxford (BPhil Pols 1968); St Antony's Coll., Oxford (DPhil 1974; Hon. Fellow, 2003). Prof. of Hist., 1975–2002, Chair, Hist. Dept, 1987–92, Ryerson Univ.; University of Toronto: Fellow, 1999–, Provost, 2002–07, Trinity Coll.; Prof. of Hist., 2003–07; Sen. Fellow, Massey Coll., 2003. Co-Editor (pt-time), Internat. Jl, 1995–2003. FRSL 2003. Hon. DCL: King's Coll., Halifax, 2004; Royal Mil. Coll., Kingston, 2004; Hon. LLD Ryerson, 2005. *Publications:* Women of the Raj, 1988; (ed jtly) Canada and NATO: uneasy past, uncertain future, 1990; (ed jtly) The Uneasy Century: international relations 1900–1990, 1996; Peacemakers: the Paris Conference of 1919 and its attempt to end war, 2001, revised as Paris, 1919: six months that changed the world (Samuel Johnson Prize), 2002; (ed jtly and contrib.) Parties Long Estranged: Canadian-Australian relations, 2003; (jtly) Canada's House: Rideau Hall and the invention of a Canadian home, 2004; Seize the Hour: when Nixon met Mao, 2006. *Recreations:* opera, films, tennis, ski-ing, hiking. *Address:* St Antony's College, Oxford OX2 6JF. *Clubs:* Oxford and Cambridge; Toronto Lawn Tennis.

MACMILLAN, Maureen; Member (Lab) Highlands and Islands, Scottish Parliament, 1999–2007; *b* 9 Feb. 1943; *m* 1965, Michael Muirdon Macmillan, LLB; two *s* two *d*. *Educ:* Oban High Sch.; Edinburgh Univ. (MA Hons); Moray House. English Teacher, 1983–99. Co-founder, Ross-shire Women's Aid, 1980–. Mem., EIS, 1980–.

McMILLAN, Neil Macleod, CMG 1997; Director and Deputy Head, European Secretariat, Cabinet Office, since 2006; *b* 21 Oct. 1953; *s* of John Howard McMillan, CBE and Ruby Hassell McMillan (*née* Meggs); *m* 1st, 1978, Karin Lauritzen (marr. diss. 1985); 2nd, 1994, Lena Madvig Madsen; one *s*. *Educ:* Westminster City Sch.; Univ. of Regensburg; Univ. of Kiel, Germany; Exeter Univ. (BA Hons Mod. Langs 1977). Admin. Trainee, Dept of Prices and Consumer Protection, 1978–79; Dept of Industry, 1980–81; HEO (Develt), Dept of Trade, 1981–82; Private Sec. to Minister for Industry and IT, 1982–84; seconded to Govt Commn on Telecommunications Reform, Federal Min. of Research, Bonn, 1985; Principal, DTI, 1986–87; First Sec., UK Representation to EU, Brussels, 1987–91; Department of Trade and Industry: Dir, Internat. Communications Policy, 1991–98; Dir, EU Internal Trade Policy, 1998–2000; Dep. Perm. Rep., UK Mission to UN, Geneva, 2001–05; Dir, Europe, DTI, 2005–06. Chairman: European Telecommunications Regulatory Cttee, 1992–96; WTO Negotiating Gp on Basic Telecommunications Services, 1994–97; World Telecommunications Policy Forum, 1998; WTO Budget Cttee, 2002–03. *Recreations:* reading, church architecture. *Address:* c/o Cabinet Office, 70 Whitehall, SW1A 2AS. *Club:* Athenæum.

McMILLAN, (Norman) Hamilton, CMG 1997; OBE 1984; Managing Director, Zwischenzug Ltd, since 2006; *b* 28 Oct. 1946; *s* of Neil McMillan and Alma McMillan (*née* Hall); *m* 1969, Dr Carolyn Vivienne Barltrop; one *s* one *d*. *Educ:* Brentwood Sch.; Balliol Coll., Oxford. Joined HM Diplomatic Service, 1968; Third Sec., FCO, 1968–70; Third, later Second Sec., Vienna, 1970–72; Second, later First Sec., FCO, 1972–77; First Secretary: Rome, 1977–81; Dhaka, 1981–84; Cairo, 1984–86; Counsellor: (Chancery), Vienna, 1989–93; FCO, 1993–97. Dir of Ops, CIEX Ltd, subseq. Penumbra, 1997–2003; Gp Security Advr, ABN-AMRO Bank, Amsterdam, 2003–06. *Recreations:* board games, music with bite, cosmology, ceramics. *Club:* Oriental.

MACMILLAN, Dr Robert Hugh; Professor of Vehicle Design and Head of School of Automotive Studies, 1977–82, Dean of Engineering, 1980–82, Cranfield Institute of Technology; *b* Mussoorie, India, 27 June 1921; *s* of H. R. M. Macmillan and E. G. Macmillan (*née* Webb); *m* 1950, Anna Christina Roding, Amsterdam; one *s* two *d*. *Educ:* Felsted Sch.; Emmanuel Coll., Cambridge. Technical Branch, RAFVR, 1941; Flt Lt, 1945; Dept of Engrg, Cambridge Univ., 1947; Asst Prof., MIT, 1950–51; Prof. of Mech. Engrg, Swansea, 1956; Dir, Motor Industry Res. Assoc., 1964–77; Associate Prof., Warwick Univ., 1965–77. 20th Leonardo Da Vinci Lectr, 1973. Chm. Council, Automobile Div., IMechE, 1976–77; Member: Noise Adv. Council, 1970–77; Internat. Technical Commn, FIA, 1975–88; FISITA: Mem. Council, 1970–80; Chm., London Congress, 1972. Approved Lectr for NADFAS, 1985–98; official guide, Winslow Hall, 1985–97, Ascott, 1988–93; Steward, Bath Abbey, 2000–01. Member: Council, Loughborough Univ., 1966–81, 1988–91; Court, Bath Univ., 2002–. Editor, The Netherlands Philatelist, 1984–88. MIET; FIMechE; FRPSL. Hon. DTech Loughborough, 1992. Gold Medal, FISITA, 1970. *Publications:* Theory of Control, 1951; Automation, 1956; Geometric Symmetry, 1978; Dynamics of Vehicle Collisions, 1983; Netherlands Stamps 1852–1939, 1996. *Recreations:* music, philately, national heritage.

Address: 8 Portland Drive, Willen, Bucks MK15 9JU. *T:* (01908) 672417. *Clubs:* Royal Air Force, Royal Over-Seas League.

McMILLAN, Stuart; Member (SNP) Scotland West, Scottish Parliament, since 2007; *b* 6 May 1972; *s* of Henry McMillan and Janet McMillan; *m* 2003, Alexandra; one *d. Educ:* Univ. of Abertay Dundee (BA Hons Europ. Business Mgt and Langs; MBA Europ. 1997). Supply Analyst, IBM UK Ltd, 1998–2000; Parly Researcher, SNP Westminster Gp, 2000–03; Office Manager to Bruce McFee, MSP, 2003–07. *Recreations:* play bagpipes, football, music, travel, reading. *Address:* Scottish Parliament, Edinburgh EH99 1SP. *T:* (0131) 348 6807, *Fax:* (0131) 348 6809; *e-mail:* stuart.mcmillan.msp@scottish.parliament.uk.

McMILLAN-SCOTT, Edward; Member (C) Yorkshire and the Humber Region, since 1999, and Vice-President, since 2004, European Parliament (York, 1984–94; North Yorkshire, 1994–99); *b* 15 Aug. 1949; *s* of late Walter Theodore Robin McMillan-Scott, ARIBA and Elizabeth Maud Derrington Hudson; *m* 1972, Henrietta Elizabeth Rumney Hudson, solicitor; two *d. Educ:* Blackfriars School, Llanarth; Blackfriars School, Laxton; Exeter Technical College. Tour director in Europe, Scandinavia, Africa and USSR, 1968–75; PR exec., then parly consultant, 1976–84; political adviser to Falkland Islands Govt, London office 1983–84. European Parliament: Member: For. Affairs and Security Cttee, 1989–; Transport Cttee, 1989–92; Chairman: 1979 Cttee (Cons. back-bench cttee), 1994–95; Conservatives in EP, 1997–2001 (Treas., 1995); Founder, 1992, and Rapporteur, EU Initiative for Democracy and Human Rights; Chm., Election Observer Missions, Palestine 2005 and 2006, Egypt 2005. Mem. Bd, Cons. Party, 1998–2001. Trustee, BBC World Service Trust, 1999–. *Recreations:* music, reading. *Address:* European Parliament, 2 Queen Anne's Gate, SW1H 9AA.

McMINN, Prof. Robert Matthew Hay; Emeritus Professor of Anatomy, Royal College of Surgeons and University of London; *b* 20 Sept. 1923; *o s* of Robert Martin McMinn, MB, ChB, Auchinleck and Brighton, and Elsie Selene Kent; *m* 1948, Margaret Grieve Kirkwood, MB, ChB, DA; one *s* one *d. Educ:* Brighton Coll. (Schol.); Univ. of Glasgow (Scottish Univ. Champion, 440 yds hurdles, 1944). MB, ChB 1947, MD (commendation) 1958, Glasgow; PhD Sheffield 1956; FRCS 1978. Hosp. posts and RAF Med. Service, 1947–50; Demonstrator in Anatomy, Glasgow Univ., 1950–52; Lectr in Anatomy, Sheffield Univ., 1952–60; Reader 1960–66, Prof. of Anatomy 1966–70, King's Coll., London Univ.; Sir William Collins Prof. of Human and Comparative Anatomy, RCS, Conservator, Hunterian Museum, RCS, and Prof. of Anatomy, Inst. of Basic Med. Scis, London Univ., 1970–82, prematurely retd. Late Examnr to RCS, RCPSG and Univs of London, Cambridge, Edinburgh, Belfast, Singapore, Malaya and Makerere. Arris and Gale Lectr, RCS, 1960; Arnott Demonstrator, RCS, 1970. Former Treas., Anatomical Soc. of Gt Britain and Ireland (Special Presentation Award, 2000); Foundn Sec., British Assoc. of Clinical Anatomists; FRSocMed; Member: Amer. Assoc. of Anatomists; Amer. Assoc. of Clinical Anatomists; BMA; Trustee, Skin Res. Foundn. *Publications:* Tissue Repair, 1969; The Digestive System, 1974; The Human Gut, 1974; (jtly) Colour Atlas of Human Anatomy, 1977, 5th edn 2003; (jtly) Colour Atlas of Head and Neck Anatomy, 1981, 3rd edn 2004; (jtly) Colour Atlas of Foot and Ankle Anatomy, 1982, 3rd edn 2004; (jtly) Colour Atlas of Applied Anatomy, 1984; (jtly) Picture Tests in Human Anatomy, 1986; (jtly) The Human Skeleton, 1987; (ed) Last's Anatomy, 8th edn 1990, 9th edn 1994; (jtly) McMinn's Functional and Clinical Anatomy, 1995; (jtly) Concise Handbook of Human Anatomy, 1998; articles in various med. and sci. jls. *Recreations:* motoring, photography, archaeology, short-wave radio; deputy organist, Craignish Parish Church. *Address:* Achnafuaran, Ardfern, Lochgilphead, Argyll PA31 8QN. *T:* (01852) 500274.

McMULLAN, Rt Rev. Gordon; Bishop of Down and Dromore, 1986–97; *b* 1934; *m* 1957, Kathleen Davidson; two *s. Educ:* Queen's Univ., Belfast (BSc Econ 1961, PhD 1971); Ridley Hall, Cambridge; Dipl. in Religious Studies (Cantab) 1978; ThD Geneva Theol Coll., 1988; MPhil TCD, 1990; DMin Univ. of the South, USA, 1995; DPhil Ulster, 2004. Deacon 1962, priest 1963, dio. Down; Curate of Ballymacarrett, 1962–67; Central Adviser on Christian Stewardship to Church of Ireland, 1967–70; Curate of St Columba, Knock, Belfast, 1970–71; Rector of St Brendan's, East Belfast, 1971–76; Rector of St Columba, Knock, Belfast, 1976–80; Archdeacon of Down, 1979–80; Bishop of Clogher, 1980–86. Merrill Fellow/Resident Fellow, Harvard Divinity Sch., 1997–98. Hon. DCL Univ. of the South, USA, 2001. *Publications:* A Cross and Beyond, 1976; We are called …, 1977; Everyday Discipleship, 1979; Reflections on St Mark's Gospel, 1984; Growing Together in Prayer, 1990; Reflections on St Luke's Gospel, 1994; Opposing Violence/Building Bridges, 1996. *Address:* 26 Wellington Park, Bangor, Co. Down, N Ireland BT20 4PJ.

McMULLAN, His Honour Michael Brian; a Circuit Judge, 1980–95; *b* 15 Nov. 1926; *s* of late Joseph Patrick McMullan and Frances McMullan (*née* Burton); *m* 1960, Rosemary Jane Margaret, *d* of late Stanley Halse deL. de Ville; one *s* two *d. Educ:* Manor Farm Road Sch.; Tauntons Sch., Southampton; The Queen's College, Oxford (MA). Called to the Bar, Gray's Inn, 1960. National Service, Army, 1946–48. Colonial Administrative Service: Gold Coast and Ghana, Political Administration, Ashanti, Min. of Finance, Accra, Agricl Development Corp., 1949–60. In practice as Barrister, SE Circuit, 1961–80; a Recorder of the Crown Court, 1979. *Club:* Oxford and Cambridge.

McMULLEN, Prof. David Lawrence, FBA 1994; Professor of Chinese, University of Cambridge, 1989–2006, now Professor Emeritus; Fellow of St John's College, Cambridge, since 1967; *b* 10 Aug. 1939; twin *s* of late Alexander Lawrence McMullen and Muriel Felicité McMullen (*née* Sikes); *m* 1983, Sarah Jane Clarice Croft; two *d. Educ:* Monkton Combe Sch., Bath; St John's Coll., Cambridge (BA, MA, PhD). National Service, RAF, 1957–59. Taiwan Min. of Educn Schol., 1963–64; Harkness Commonwealth Fellowship, 1965–67; Asst Lectr 1967, Lectr 1972, in Chinese Studies, Cambridge Univ. Pres., British Assoc. for Chinese Studies, 1985–87. *Publications:* Concordances and Indexes to Chinese Texts, 1975; State and Scholars in T'ang China, 1988; contribs to jls of E Asian studies. *Recreation:* gardening. *Address:* Grove Cottage, 35 High Street, Grantchester, Cambridge CB3 9NF. *T:* (01223) 840206.

See also I. J. McMullen.

McMULLEN, Dr Ian James, FBA 2001; Lecturer in Japanese, University of Oxford, 1972–2006 (Pro-Proctor, 1986–87); Fellow, Pembroke College, Oxford, 1989–2006 (Vicegerent, 2003–04), Fellow Emeritus, since 2006; *b* 10 Aug. 1939; twin *s* of late Alexander Lawrence McMullen and Muriel Felicité McMullen (*née* Sikes); *m* 1970, Bonnie Shannon; one *s. Educ:* Monkton Combe Sch., Bath; St John's Coll., Cambridge (BA, MA; PhD 1969). Nat. Service, RAF, 1957–59. Schol., Min. of Educn, Japan, 1963–64; Lectr, 1965, Asst Prof., 1966–70, Associate Prof., 1970–72, Univ. of Toronto; Fellow, St Antony's Coll., Oxford, 1972–89. Pres., British Assoc. Japanese Studies, 1997–98. *Publications:* Genji Gaiden: the origins of Kumazawa Banzan's commentary on the Tale of Genji, 1991; Idealism, Protest and the Tale of Genji, 1999; contribs to jls of E Asian studies. *Recreation:* gardening. *Address:* Wilton Lodge, 44 Osberton Road, Oxford OX2 7NU. *T:* (01865) 559859.

See also D. L. McMullen.

McMULLEN, Jeremy John; QC 1994; QC (NI) 1996; **His Honour Judge McMullen;** a Circuit Judge, since 2001, a Senior Circuit Judge, since 2006; a Judge of the Employment Appeal Tribunal, since 2002; a Deputy High Court Judge, Queen's Bench Division, since 2007; *b* 14 Sept. 1948; *s* of John Ezra McMullen and late Irene McMullen; *m* 1973, Deborah Cristman; one *s* one *d. Educ:* William Hulme's Grammar Sch., Manchester; Brasenose Coll., Oxford (MA); LSE (MSc). Called to the Bar, Middle Temple, 1971, NI, 1994; Associate Attorney, New York, 1971–73; General, Municipal, Boilermakers' Union: Legal Officer, 1973–77; Regl Officer, London, 1977–84; in practice at the Bar, 1985–2001; an Asst Recorder, 1998–2000; a Recorder, 2000–01; Sports Arbitrator, 2000–. Chm. (part-time), Employment (formerly Industrial) Tribunals, 1993–2002. Chair: Industrial Law Soc., 1989–93; Employment Law Bar Assoc., 1994–95; ILO Jt Panel, 2001–02. Pres., Brasenose Soc. *Publications:* Rights at Work, 1978, 2nd edn 1983; (contrib.) Penguin Guide to Civil Liberties, 1989; Employment Tribunal Procedure, 1996, 3rd edn 2005; Employment Precedents, 1996. *Recreations:* rowing, cycling, under-gardener, family allotment. *Address:* Employment Appeal Tribunal, 58 Victoria Embankment, EC4Y 0DS. *Club:* Reform.

McMULLIN, Rt Hon. Sir Duncan (Wallace), Kt 1987; PC 1980; Judge of Court of Appeal, New Zealand, 1979–89; commercial arbitrator, since 1990; *b* 1 May 1927; *s* of Charles James McMullin and Kathleen Annie Shout; *m* 1955, Isobel Margaret, *d* of Robert Ronald Atkinson, ED; two *s* two *d. Educ:* Auckland Grammar Sch.; Univ. of Auckland (LLB). Judge of Supreme Court, 1970–79. Chm., Royal Commn on Contraception, Sterilisation and Abortion in NZ, 1975–77. Chairman: Wanganui Computer Centre Policy Cttee, 1989–93; Market Surveillance Panel, Electricity Marketing Corp., 1994–2004. Chm., NZ Conservation Authority, 1996–2000. FIArb of NZ, 1990. *Recreations:* forestry, farming, conservation, reading. *Address:* 4/456 Remuera Road, Auckland, New Zealand. *T:* (9) 5246583.

McMURRAY, Prof. Cecil Hugh, CBE 2002; FRSC, FIFST; Managing Director, Sci-Tec Consultancy, since 2003; *b* 19 Feb. 1942; *s* of late Edwin McMurray and of Margaret (*née* Smyth); *m* 1967, Ann Stuart; two *s* one *d. Educ:* Royal Belfast Academical Instn; Queen's University, Belfast (BSc 1965; BAgr 1966); PhD Bristol, 1970. FRSC 1981; FIFST 1987. Res. Fellow, Dept of Chem., Harvard Univ., 1970–72; Head of Biochem. Dept, Vet. Res. Lab., Dept of Agric. for NI, 1972–84; Prof. of Food and Agricl Chem., QUB, and concurrently DCSO, Dept of Agric. for NI, 1984–88; CSO, Dept of Agric. and Rural Develt for NI, 1988–2002. Hon. Prof., QUB, 1998–. Expert Advr, WHO, 1983, 1986; Assessor to: AFRC, 1988–94; Priorities Bd for R&D in Agric. and Food, 1988–93; Technology Bd for NI, 1988–92; NERC, 1992–93; Adv. Cttee on microbiol safety of food, 1992–2002; Dir, NI Public Sector Overseas, 1994–2002. Mem., Steering Gp on chem. aspects of food surveillance, 1992–95. Pres., Agricl Gp, BAAS, 1986–87. Mem. Cttee, Coronary Prevention Gp, 1985–89. Trustee, Agricl Inst. for NI, 1985–2002; Mem. Governing Body, Rowett Res. Inst., Aberdeen, 1986–89, 1993–2003. Mem. Editl Bd, Fertiliser Res., 1985–92. *Publications:* (ed jtly) Detection Methods for Irradiated Foods: current status, 1996; over 100 scientific publications in various jls incl. Biochemical Jl, Jl of Amer. Chemical Soc., Clin. Chem., CIBA Foundn Symposia, Jl of Chromatography, British Vet. Jl, Vet. Record, Jl Assoc. of Analytical Chem., Trace Metals in Man and Domestic Animals, Biology of Total Envmt. *Recreations:* reading, photography, walking. *Address:* 25 Sheridan Drive, Helens Bay, Bangor, Co. Down BT19 1LB. *T:* (028) 9185 3655.

McMURRAY, David Bruce, MA; Headmaster, Oundle School, 1984–99; *b* 15 Dec. 1937; *s* of late James McMurray, CBE, and Kathleen McMurray (*née* Goodwin); *m* 1962, Antonia Murray; three *d. Educ:* Loretto Sch.; Pembroke Coll., Cambridge (BA, MA). National service, Royal Scots, 1956–58, 2nd Lieut. Pembroke Coll., Cambridge, 1958–61; Asst Master, Stowe Sch., 1961–64; Fettes College: Asst Master, 1964–72; Head of English, 1967–72; Housemaster, 1972–76; Headmaster, Loretto Sch., 1976–84. Mem., Edinburgh Fest. Council, 1980–84. HM Comr, Queen Victoria Sch., Dunblane, 1977–87; Chm. of Govs, Fettes Coll., 2006–. FRSA 1989. CCF Medal, 1976, and Bar, 1984. *Recreations:* golf, sub-aqua diving, poetry. *Address:* 7 Amisfield Park, Haddington, East Lothian EH41 4QE. *T:* (01620) 825474; Apt No 1, La Punta, Los Cristianos, 38650 Arona, Tenerife, Canary Islands. *Clubs:* MCC, Free Foresters; New (Edinburgh).

McMURTRY, Sir David (Roberts), Kt 2001; CBE 1994; RDI 1989; FREng, FIMechE; Co-founder, Chairman and Chief Executive, Renishaw plc (formerly Renishaw Electrical Ltd), since 1973; *b* Dublin, 5 March 1940. CEng; FREng 2001. Formerly with Rolls Royce plc. *Address:* Renishaw plc, New Mills, Wotton-under-Edge, Glos GL12 8JR.

McMURTRY, Hon. (Roland) Roy, OOnt 2007; Counsel, Gowling Lafleur Henderson LLP; Chief Justice of Ontario, 1996–2007 (Associate Chief Justice, 1991–94, Chief Justice, 1994–96, Ontario Court of Justice (General Division)); *b* 31 May 1932; *s* of Roland Roy McMurtry and Doris Elizabeth Belcher; *m* 1957, Ria Jean Macrae; three *s* three *d. Educ:* St Andrew's Coll., Aurora, Ont; Trinity Coll., Univ. of Toronto (BA Hons); Osgoode Hall Law Sch., Toronto (LLB). Called to the Bar of Ontario, 1958; QC 1970. Partner: Benson, McMurtry, Percival & Brown, Toronto, 1958–75; Blaney, McMurtry, Stapells, 1988–91. Elected to Ontario Legislature, 1975; re-elected, 1977 and 1981; Attorney General for Ontario, 1975–85; Solicitor General for Ontario, 1978–82. High Comr in UK, 1985–88. Freeman, City of London, 1986. Hon. LLD: Ottawa, 1983; Law Soc. of Upper Canada, 1984; Leeds, 1988; York, 1991; Toronto, 1998. *Recreations:* painting, skiing, tennis. *Address:* Gowling Lafleur Henderson LLP, Suite 1600, 1 First Canadian Place, 100 King Street West, Toronto, ON M5X 1G5, Canada. *Clubs:* Albany, York (Toronto).

McMURTRY, Stanley, (Mac), MBE 2004; social and political cartoonist, Daily Mail, since 1970; *b* 4 May 1936; *s* of Stanley Harrison McMurtry and Janet Lind McMurtry; *m* 1st, 1958, Maureen Flaye (marr. diss. 1980); one *s* one *d*; 2nd, 1981, Janet Elizabeth Rattle (marr. diss. 2002); 3rd, 2003, Elizabeth Mary Vaughan. *Educ:* Sharmans Cross Secondary Sch., Birmingham; Birmingham Coll. of Art. Cartoon film animator, 1956–65; social and political cartoonist, Daily Sketch, 1968–70; freelance cartoonist, for Punch and other magazines, 1960–; TV scriptwriter with Bernard Cookson, for Tommy Cooper and Dave Allen, 1973–76. Social and Political Cartoonist of the Year, 1983, Master Cartoonist, 2000, Cartoonist Club of GB; Cartoonist of Year Award, 1982, 1984 and 1999, UK Press Gazette; Cartoonist of the Year, What the Papers Say Awards, 2003, 2007; Political Cartoonist of the Year, Cartoon Arts Trust, 2007. *Publications:* The Bunjee Venture (for children), 1977 (cartoon film, 1979); Mac's Year Books, annually, 1980–; contrib. short story to Knights of Madness, ed Peter Haining, 1998. *Recreations:* motorcycling, golf, writing. *Address:* Daily Mail, Northcliffe House, 2 Derry Street, W8 5TT. *T:* (020) 7938 6369. *Clubs:* Chelsea Arts, Saints and Sinners.

McNAB, Angela, (Mrs Carl Powell); Chief Executive, Human Fertilisation and Embryology Authority, since 2002; on secondment as Director of Public Health Delivery, Department of Health, 2007–08; *b* London, 1 April 1957; *d* of Bernard and Doris Hammond; *m* 2005, Carl Powell; two *s* two *d. Educ:* Open Univ. (BA Hons); South Bank Univ. (MSc). Nat. Hosps Coll. of Speech Scis (LCST). Speech and language therapist, subseq. managed a district-wide service, specialising in paediatrics, 1978–92; Gen.

Manager, Mid Essex Community and Mental Health Trust, 1992–99; Sen. Policy Manager, Nat. Sexual Health and HIV Strategy, DoH, 1999–2001; Chief Exec., Chingford, Wanstead and Woodford PCT, 2001–02. Mem. Bd, Council for Registration of Forensic Practitioners, 2006–. *Publications:* contrib. health and scientific jls, incl. Cell Stem Cell. *Recreations:* running, theatre, family. *Address:* 7 Tounson Court, Montaigne Close, SW1P 4AQ. *T:* 07860 114553; *e-mail:* angela.mcnab@ukonline.co.uk.

MACNAB of Macnab, James Charles; The Macnab; 23rd Chief of Clan Macnab; *b* 14 April 1926; *e s* of late Lt-Col James Alexander Macnabb, OBE, TD (*de jure* 21st of Macnab), London, SW3, and Mrs Ursula Walford (*née* Barnett), Wokingham, Berks; *S* gt uncle Archibald Corrie Macnab of Macnab, (*de facto*) 22nd Chief, 1970; *m* 1959, Hon. Diana Mary, DL, *er d* of Baron Kilmany, MC, PC, and of Monica Helen, (Lady Kilmany), OBE, JP, *o c* of late Geoffrey Lambton, 2nd *s* of 4th Earl of Durham; two *s* two *d*. *Educ:* Cothill House; Radley Coll.; Ashbury Coll., Ottawa. Served in RAF and Scots Guards, 1944–45; Lieut, Seaforth Highldrs, 1945–48. Asst Supt, then Acting Dep. Supt, Fedn of Malaya Police Force, 1948; retd, 1957. Mem., Western DC of Perthshire, 1961–64; CC, Perth and Kinross Jt County Council, 1964–75; Mem., Central Regional Council, 1978–82. Exec., subseq. Sen., Consultant, Hill Samuel Investment Services, 1982–92. Member, Royal Company of Archers, Queen's Body Guard in Scotland. Capt., Seaforth Highldrs, TA, 1960–64. JP Perthshire, 1968–75, Stirling, 1975–86. *Recreations:* shooting, travel. *Heir: s* James William Archibald Macnab, younger of Macnab [*b* 22 March 1963; *m* 1994, Dr Jane Mackintosh, *d* of late Dr David Mackintosh; one *s* one *d*]. *Address:* Leuchars Castle Farmhouse, Leuchars, St Andrews, Fife KY16 0EY. *T:* (01334) 838777. *Club:* New (Edinburgh).

McNAB, John Stanley; Chief Executive, Port of Tilbury London Ltd (formerly Port of Tilbury (Port of London Authority)), 1987–96; *b* 23 Sept. 1937; *s* of Robert Stanley McNab and Alice Mary McNab; *m* 1st, 1961, Carol Field (marr. diss. 1978); two *d*; 2nd, 1980, Jacqueline Scammell (marr. diss. 1997); 3rd, 2001, Susan Cole. *Educ:* Gravesend Grammar Sch. FCCA 1976; FCIT 1992. Nat. Service, Royal Engineers, Libya, 1956–58. Port of London Authority: joined 1954; Accountant, India and Millwall Docks, 1965, Upper Docks, 1970; Man. Dir, PLA (Thames) Stevedoring, 1973; Dir, Upper Docks, 1974; Exec. Dir (Manpower) and Group Board Mem., 1978; Dir, Tilbury, 1983. Director: Internat. Transport Ltd, 1992–96; Airflights Direct Ltd, 2000–. FRSA 1991; MCMI (MBIM 1970). Freeman: City of London, 1988; Co. of Watermen and Lightermen of River Thames, 1988. *Recreations:* golf, swimming, DIY, learning Spanish and Portuguese. *Address:* 48 Daines Way, Thorpe Bay, Essex SS1 3PQ. *T:* (01702) 587060.

McNAB JONES, Robin Francis, FRCS; Consultant Otolaryngologist, 1959–99; Surgeon: ENT Department, St Bartholomew's Hospital, 1961–87; Royal National Throat, Nose and Ear Hospital, 1962–83; *b* 22 Oct. 1922; *s* of late E. C. H. Jones, CBE, and M. E. Jones, MBE; *m* 1950, Mary Garrett; one *s* three *d*. *Educ:* Manchester Grammar Sch.; Dulwich Coll.; Med. Coll., St Bartholomew's Hosp. (MB BS 1945); FRCS 1952. Ho. Surg., St Bart's, 1946–47; MO, RAF, 1947–50; Demonstrator of Anatomy, St Bart's, 1950–52; Registrar, Royal Nat. Throat, Nose and Ear Hosp., 1952–54; Sen. Registrar, ENT Dept, St Bart's, 1954–59; Lectr, Dept of Otolaryngology, Univ. of Manchester, 1959–61; Dean, Inst. of Laryngology and Otology, Univ. of London, 1971–76; Vice-Pres., St Bart's Hosp. Med. Coll., 1984–87. Mem., Court of Examiners, 1972–78, and Mem. Council (for Otolaryngology), 1982–87, RCS; External Examiner, RCSI, 1980–83, 1988–91. Hon. Sec., Sect. of Otology, 1965–68, Pres., Sect. of Laryngology, 1981–82, RSocMed. *Publications:* various chapters in standard med. textbooks; contribs to med. jls. *Recreations:* tennis, ski-ing, golf, fishing, gardening. *Address:* 91 Barnfield Wood Road, Beckenham, Kent BR3 6ST. *T:* (020) 8650 0217.

MACNAGHTEN, Sir Malcolm Francis, 12th Bt *cr* 1836, of Bushmills House, co. Antrim; *b* 21 Sept. 1956; *s* of Sir Patrick Alexander Macnaghten, 11th Bt and of Marianne (*née* Schaefer); *S* father, 2007; *m* 1991, Yvonne Sonia-Louise Greenfield; three *d*. *Heir: b* Edward Alexander Macnaghten, *b* 24 July 1958.

McNAIR, family name of **Baron McNair**.

McNAIR, 3rd Baron *cr* 1955, of Gleniffer; **Duncan James McNair;** Director, Chelkin Ltd, since 2001; Chairman and Managing Director, Applied Learning Techniques International Ltd, since 2004; *b* 26 June 1947; *s* of 2nd Baron McNair and Vera, *d* of Theodore James Faithfull; *S* father, 1989. *Educ:* Bryanston. Former Mem., Parly Gps on Drug Misuse, Alcohol Misuse, Population Develt and Reproductive Health; Vice Chm., Parly Waterways Gp, 1995–99. Mem., Sub-Cttee E (Envmt), EC Select Cttee, H of L, 1990–92. Dir, British Anti-Trafficking Orgn Ltd, 2000–. Member: Resource Use Institute Ltd, 1994–; Adv. Bd, Effective Educn Assoc., 1996–; Council for Human Rights and Religious Freedom, 1996–; Exec. Cttee, Health Freedom Movt UK, 2002–; Exec. Cttee, Commonwealth Forum for Project Mgt, 2002–. Chm., Unitax Assoc., 1994–. Co-Vice-Patron, Nat. Police Community Trust, 2001–. *Heir: b* Hon. William Samuel Angus McNair, *b* 19 May 1958.

McNAIR, Archibald Alister Jourdan, (Archie); Co-founder, 1955, and Chairman, 1955–88, Mary Quant Group of Companies; Founder, 1971, and Chairman, 1971–88, Thomas Jourdan plc; *b* 16 Dec. 1919; *s* of late Donald McNair and Janie (*née* Jourdan); *m* 1954, Catherine Alice Jane, *d* of late John and Margaret Fleming; one *s* one *d*. *Educ:* Blundell's. Served War, 1939–45: River Thames Formation. Photographer, 1950–57. *Recreations:* sculpting, chess. *Address:* c/o McNair & Co., EBC House, Ranelagh Gardens, SW6 3PA. *Club:* Hurlingham.

See also D. B. Vernon.

MACNAIR, Charles Neville; QC (Scot.) 2002; Sheriff of Tayside, Central and Fife at Dunfermline, since 2006; *b* 18 March 1955; *s* of James T. H. Macnair, MC, and Dr Margaret E. Macnair (*née* Cameron); *m* 1987, Patricia Anne Dinning; two *d*. *Educ:* Bryanston Sch.; Aberdeen Univ. (LLB). Commnd Queen's Own Highlanders, 1977–80; served UK, NI, Hong Kong. Apprentice solicitor, Simpson & Marwick WS, Edinburgh, 1980–82; Solicitor: Brodies WS, Edinburgh, 1982–85; Peterkin's, Aberdeen, 1985–87; Advocate, 1988–; Sheriff (pt-time), 2005–06. Mem., Youth Court Feasibility Project Gp, Scottish Exec., 2002. Chm., Child and Family Law Gp, Faculty of Advocates, 2002–06. Served TA, 1980–87 and 1990–92. *Recreations:* reading, walking, sailing. *Address:* Sheriff Court House, 1/6 Carnegie Drive, Dunfermline KY12 7HJ.

McNAIR-WILSON, Sir Patrick (Michael Ernest David), Kt 1989; consultant; *b* 28 May 1929; *s* of Dr Robert McNair-Wilson; *m* 1953, Diana Evelyn Kitty Campbell Methuen-Campbell, *d* of Hon. Laurence Methuen-Campbell; one *s* four *d*. *Educ:* Eton. Exec. in French Shipping Co., 1951–53; various appointments at Conservative Central Office, 1954–58; Staff of Conservative Political Centre, 1958–61; Director, London Municipal Society, 1961–63; Executive with The British Iron and Steel Federation, 1963–64. Partner, Ferret PR and Public Affairs, 1995–2000. Dir, Photo-Me International Plc, 1996–2005. MP (C): Lewisham W, 1964–66; New Forest, Nov. 1968–1997. Opposition Front Bench Spokesman on fuel and power, 1965–66; Vice-Chm., Conservative Parly Power Cttee, 1969–70; PPS to Minister for Transport Industries, DoE, 1970–74; Opposition Front Bench Spokesman on Energy, 1974–76; Chm., Jt Lords and Commons Select Cttee on Private Bill Procedure, 1987–88; Mem., Select Cttee on Members Interests, 1985–86. Editor of The Londoner, 1961–63. *Recreations:* sailing, pottery, flying. *Address:* Godfrey's Farm, Beaulieu, Hants SO42 7YP.

McNALLY, family name of **Baron McNally**.

McNALLY, Baron *cr* 1995 (Life Peer), of Blackpool in the county of Lancashire; **Tom McNally;** PC 2005; Leader of Liberal Democrats, House of Lords, since 2004; *b* 20 Feb. 1943; *s* of John P. McNally and Elizabeth May (*née* McCarthy); *m* 1st, 1970, Eileen Powell (marr. diss. 1990); 2nd, 1990, Juliet Lamy Hutchinson; two *s* one *d*. *Educ:* College of St Joseph, Blackpool; University Coll., London (BScEcon; Fellow 1995). President of Students' Union, UCL, 1965–66; Vice-Pres., Nat. Union of Students, 1966–67; Asst Gen. Sec. of Fabian Society, 1966–67; Labour Party researcher, 1967–68; Internat. Sec. of Labour Party, 1969–74; Political Adviser to: Foreign and Commonwealth Sec., 1974–76; Prime Minister, 1976–79. Public Affairs Adviser, GEC, 1983–84; Dir-Gen., Retail Consortium, and Dir, British Retailers Association, 1985–87; Head of Public Affairs, Hill & Knowlton, 1987–93; Head of Public Affairs, 1993–96, Vice-Chm., 1996–2004, Shandwick Consultants, then Weber Shandwick Worldwide, subseq. Weber Shandwick. MP (Lab 1979–81, SDP 1981–83) Stockport S; contested (SDP) Stockport, 1983. SDP Parly spokesman on educn and sport, 1981–83. Mem., Select Cttee on Industry and Trade, 1979–83. Dep. Leader, Lib Dems, H of L, 2001–04. Pres., St Albans Lib Dems. Mem. of Court, Univ. of Hertfordshire, 2006–. FRSA; FCIPR. *Recreations:* playing and watching sport, reading political biographies. *Address:* House of Lords, SW1A 0PW.

McNALLY, Eryl Margaret; Chairman, National Energy Foundation, 2004–07; *b* 11 April 1942; *d* of late Llywelyn Williams, MP and Elsie Williams; *m* 1964, James Frederick McNally; one *s* one *d*. *Educ:* Newbridge Grammar Sch.; Bristol Univ. (BA Langs); University Coll., Swansea (PGCE). Modern langs teacher, 1964–84; advisory work, Bucks CC, 1985–93; freelance schools inspector, OFSTED, 1993–94; MEP (Lab) Beds and Milton Keynes, 1994–99, Eastern Region, England, 1999–2004. Councillor: Abbots Langley Parish Council, 1970–73; Watford RDC, 1972–74; Three Rivers DC, 1973–77; Herts CC, 1986–95. *Publications:* articles on language teaching and teacher training in professional jls. *Recreations:* learning languages, reading, world music, films. *Address:* 30 Follet Drive, Abbots Langley, Herts WD5 0LP. *T:* (01923) 662711.

McNALLY, Joseph, (Joe); Chief Executive, 1984–2001, Vice President, 1989–2001, Compaq Computer Ltd; *b* 17 July 1942; *s* of Joseph McNally and Emily McNally; *m* 1968, Anne Buglass; one *s* one *d*. *Educ:* Gateshead GS; King's Coll., Newcastle. Programmer, ICL, 1966–68; sales manager, Honeywell, 1968–79; Chief Exec. Designate, FMC/Harris, 1979–83; Founder Man. Dir, Compaq Computer UK, 1984. Non-exec. Dir, In Technology plc, 2000–. Trustee, Duke of Edinburgh's Award Scheme, 1999–. MInstD 1984. *Recreations:* shooting, fishing, gardening. *Address:* Compaq Computer Ltd, Hotham House, 1 Heron Square, Richmond, Surrey TW9 1EJ. *Clubs:* Farmers', St James's, Royal Automobile.

McNAMARA, (Joseph) Kevin; *b* 5 Sept. 1934; *s* of late Patrick and Agnes McNamara; *m* 1960, Nora (*née* Jones), Warrington; four *s* one *d*. *Educ:* various primary schools; St Mary's Coll., Crosby; Hull Univ. (LLB). Head of Dept of History, St Mary's Grammar Sch., Hull, 1958–64; Lecturer in Law, Hull Coll. of Commerce, 1964–66. MP (Lab): Kingston-upon-Hull N, Jan. 1966–1974 and 1997–2005; Kingston-upon-Hull Central, 1974–83; Hull N, 1983–97. Opposition spokesman on defence, 1982–83, on defence and disarmament, 1983–85, dep. opposition spokesman on defence, 1985–87, opposition spokesman on Northern Ireland, 1987–94, on Civil Service, 1994–95. Member: Select Cttee on For. Affairs, 1977–82 (former Chm., Overseas Develt Sub-Cttee); Parly Assembly, NATO, 1984–88; Vice-Chm., Economic Cttee, NATO, 1985–87; former Chairman: Select Cttee on Overseas Develt; PLP NI Gp; Sec., Parly Gp, TGWU. Chm., All Party Irish In Britain Gp; Vice-Chm., British-Irish Inter-Parly Body; Founder Mem., Friends of the Good Friday Agreement. Mem., UK Delegn to Council of Europe, 1976–80, 1996–2005. Commendatore, Order Al Merito della Repubblica Italiana, 1977. *Recreations:* family and outdoor activities. *Address:* 145 Newland Park, Hull HU5 2DX.

McNAMARA, Air Chief Marshal Sir Neville (Patrick), KBE 1981 (CBE 1972); AO 1976; AFC 1961; Royal Australian Air Force, retired 1984; *b* Toogoolawah, Qld, 17 April 1923; *s* of late P. F. McNamara; *m* 1950, Dorothy Joan Miller; two *d*. *Educ:* Christian Brothers Coll., Nudgee, Qld. Enlisted RAAF, 1941; commnd 1944; Fighter Pilot WWII with No 75 Sqdn, Halmaheras and Borneo; served with No 77 Sqdn in Japan on cessation of hostilities; Air Traffic Control duties, HQ NE Area, 1949; Flying Instructor, Central Flying Sch., 1951–53; operational tour with No 77 Sqdn in Korean War; Pilot Trng Officer, HQ Trng Comd, 1954–55; Staff Officer, Fighter Operations Dept Air, 1955–57; CO No 25 Sqdn W Australia, 1957–59; CO No 2 Operational Conversion Unit, 1959–61; CO and Sen. Air Staff Officer, RAAF Staff, London, 1961–63; Director of Personnel (Officers), Dept Air, 1964–66; OC RAAF Contingent, Thailand, 1966–67; Air Staff Officer, RAAF Richmond, 1967–69; Dir-Gen., Organisation Dept Air, 1969–71; Comdr RAAF Forces Vietnam, 1971–72; Aust. Air Attaché, Washington, 1972–75; Dep. Chief of Air Staff, 1975–79; Chief of Air Staff, 1979–82; Chief of Defence Force Staff, 1982–84. RAAF psc, pfc, jssc. *Publication:* The Quiet Man (autobiog.), 2005. *Recreations:* golf, fishing. *Club:* Commonwealth (Canberra).

McNAMARA, Robert Strange; Medal of Freedom with Distinction; *b* San Francisco, 9 June 1916; *s* of Robert James McNamara and Clara Nell (*née* Strange); *m* 1940, Margaret McKinstry Craig (decd); one *s* two *d*. *Educ:* University of California (AB); Harvard Univ. (MBA). Asst Professor of Business Administration, Harvard, 1940–43. Served in USAAF, England, India, China, Pacific, 1943–46 (Legion of Merit); released as Lieut-Colonel. Joined Ford Motor Co., 1946; Executive, 1946–61; Controller, 1949–53; Asst General Manager, Ford Div., 1953–55; Vice-President, and General Manager, Ford Div., 1955–57; Director, and Group Vice-President of Car Divisions, 1957–61, President, 1960–61; Secretary of Defense, United States of America, 1961–68; Pres., The World Bank, 1968–81; Director: Royal Dutch Petroleum, 1981–87; Bank of America, 1981–87; Corning, 1981–90; The Washington Post, 1981–89. Trustee: Urban Inst.; Trilateral Commn. Hon. degrees from: Harvard, Calif, Mich, Columbia, Ohio, Princeton, NY, Notre Dame, George Washington, Aberdeen, St Andrews, Fordham and Oxford Univs; Williams, Chatham and Amherst Colls. Phi Beta Kappa. Albert Pick Jr Award, Univ. of Chicago (first recipient), 1979; Albert Einstein Peace Prize, 1983; Franklin D. Roosevelt Freedom from Want Medal, 1983; Amer. Assembly Service to Democracy Award; Dag Hammarskjöld Hon. Medal; Extrepreneurial Excellence Medal, Yale Sch. of Organization and Management; Olive Branch Award for Outstanding Book on subject of World Peace, 1987; Sidney Hillman Foundn Award, 1987; Onassis Athinai Prize, 1988. *Publications:* The Essence of Security, 1968; One Hundred Countries, Two Billion People: the dimensions of development, 1975; The McNamara Years at the World Bank, 1981; Blundering into Disaster, 1987; Out of the Cold, 1990; In Retrospect: the tragedy and lessons of Vietnam, 1995; Argument Without End, 2000; Wilson's Ghost, 2001.

McNANEY, Peter Francis; Chief Executive, Belfast City Council, since 2002; *b* 8 Feb. 1959; *m* 1987, Karen McMillen; two *s* two *d*. *Educ:* Manchester Univ. (LLB Hons); Univ. of Ulster (DMS); Queen's Univ., Belfast (Cert Prof. Legal Studies; Cert Adv. Advocacy for Solicitors). Belfast City Council: Asst Solicitor, 1983–85; Sen. Solicitor, 1985–91; Asst Town Solicitor, 1991–94; Dir, Legal Services, 1994–2002. Member: Bd, Chief Execs' Forum, 2003–; NI Econ. Develt Forum, 2005–; NI Local Govt Taskforce, 2006–. Mem Editl Bd, Local Authorities Chief Execs Imprint Foundn, 2004–. *Address:* Belfast City Council, City Hall, Belfast BT1 5GS. *T:* (028) 9027 0202, *Fax:* (028) 9027 0232; *e-mail:* mcnaneyp@belfastcity.gov.uk.

McNAUGHT, His Honour John Graeme; DL; a Circuit Judge, 1987–2006; *b* 21 Feb. 1941; *s* of Charles William McNaught and Isabella Mary McNaught; *m* 1966, Barbara Mary Smith; two *s* one *d*. *Educ:* King Edward VII Sch., Sheffield; The Queen's Coll., Oxford (BA Jurisprudence, 1962). Bacon Scholar, Gray's Inn, 1962; called to the Bar, Gray's Inn, 1963; a Recorder, 1981–87; Hon. Recorder, Devizes, 1996–. Mem., Parole Bd for England and Wales, 1998–2004; Pres., Mental Health Review Tribunal, 2001–05. Chm., Wilts Criminal Justice Strategy Cttee, 2000–02. UK Council Mem., Commonwealth Magistrates' and Judges' Assoc., 1997–2000. DL Wilts, 2006. *Address:* c/o Swindon Combined Court, Islington Street, Swindon SN1 2HG.

McNAUGHTON, Andrew George, FREng; Chief Engineer, Network Rail, since 2001; Special Professor of Rail Engineering, University of Nottingham, since 2006; *b* 26 July 1956; *s* of late Arthur Alfred George, (Ian), McNaughton and Betty McNaughton; *m* 1984, Jane Evelyn Merriott; two *s*. *Educ:* Univ. of Leeds (BSc Civil Engrg 1978). CEng 1981; FICE 2001; FREng 2007. Civil Engr, SE British Rail, 1991–94; Railtrack plc: Manager, E Anglia, 1994–96; Hd, Prodn, 1997–99; Dir, Great Western, 1999–2001. Chm. Adv. Bd, Rail Research UK, 2004–. Mem., Europ. Rail Res. Council, 2004– (Chm., 2008–); Mem., Railway Heritage Cttee, 2006–; Chm., Infrastructure Commn, Internat. Railway Union, 2006–; Vice Chm., EU Transport Adv. Gp, 2006–. Liveryman, Co. of Engineers. FPWI 1975; Mem. RGS, 2004; MInstD 2004. *Recreations:* mountain walking, road cycling, studying human behaviour, growing tomatoes. *Address:* Network Rail, 40 Melton Street, NW1 2EE. *T:* (020) 7557 8313, *Fax:* (020) 7845 4412; *e-mail:* andrew.mcnaughton2@networkrail.co.uk.

McNAUGHTON, Lt-Col Ian Kenneth Arnold; Chief Inspecting Officer of Railways, Department of Transport, 1974–82; *b* 30 June 1920; *er s* of late Brig. F. L. McNaughton, CBE, DSO and Betty, *d* of late Rev. Arnold Pinchard, OBE; *m* 1946, Arthea, *d* of late Carel Begeer, Voorschoten, Holland; two *d*. *Educ:* Loretto Sch.; RMA Woolwich; RMCS Shrivenham. BScEng, CEng, FIMechE, FIRSE. 2nd Lieut RE, 1939; served War of 1939–45, NW Europe (Captain) (despatches); GHQ MELF, 1949 (Major); Cyprus, 1955; OC 8 Rly Sqdn, 1958; Port Comdt Southampton, 1959 (Lt-Col); SO I Transportation HQ BAOR, 1960; retd 1963. Inspecting Officer of Rlys, Min. of Transport, 1963. Chm., Rlys Industry Adv. Cttee, Health and Safety Commn, 1978–82. *Recreations:* gardening, foreign travel. *Address:* Chawton Glebe, Alton, Hants GU34 1SH. *T:* (01420) 83395.

MacNAUGHTON, Joan, CB 2005; Senior Vice President, Power and Environmental Policies, Alstom Power Systems, since 2007; *b* 12 Sept. 1950; *d* of Duncan McNaughton and Marion McNaughton (*née* Caldwell); *m* 1979, William Alexander Jeffrey (*see* Sir W. A. Jeffrey). *Educ:* Notre Dame Coll. Sch., Liverpool; Warwick Univ. (BSc Hons Physics). Home Office: Admin. Trainee, 1972–74; HEO (Develt), 1974–76; Asst Sec. to Royal Commn on Criminal Procedure, 1976–80; Criminal Policy Dept, 1981–85; Prin. Private Sec. to Dep. Prime Minister and Lord Pres. of the Council, 1985–87; Head, Women and Young Offenders Div., Prison Service, 1987–89; Dir, Prison Service Industries and Farms, 1989–91; Head, Criminal Policy Div., 1991–92; Prin. Private Sec. to Home Secretary, 1992–95; Chief Exec., Police IT Orgn, 1996–99; Director General: Policy, LCD, 1999–2002; Energy, DTI, 2002–06; Internat. Energy Security, DTI, 2006–07. Chm., Governing Bd, Internat. Energy Agency, 2004–05. Non-exec. Dir, Quintain Estates and Development plc, 2004–. Sen. Vis. Res. Fellow, Oxford Inst. for Energy Studies, Oxford Univ., 2006–. Mem., Bd of Govs, Argonne Nat. Lab., Univ. of Chicago, 2007–. Hon. FEI 2006. *Publication:* (contrib.) The New Economic Diplomacy. *Recreations:* reading, hill walking, watching football. *Address:* Alstom Power Systems, The Place, 175 High Holborn, WC1V 7AA. *Club:* Reform.

MACNAUGHTON, Prof. Sir Malcolm (Campbell), Kt 1986; MD; FRCPG, FRCOG, FFSRH; FRSE; Muirhead Professor of Obstetrics and Gynaecology, University of Glasgow, 1970–90, now Emeritus; *b* 4 April 1925; *s* of James Hay and Mary Robieson Macnaughton; *m* 1955, Margaret-Ann Galt; two *s* three *d*. *Educ:* Glasgow Academy; Glasgow Univ. (MD 1970). FRCOG 1966; FRCPG 1972; FFSRH (FFFP 1994); FRSE 1983. Lectr, Univ. of Aberdeen, 1957–61; Sen. Lectr, Univ. of St Andrews, 1961–66; Hon. Sen. Lectr, Univ. of Dundee, 1966–70. Pres., RCOG, 1984–87; Vice-Pres., Royal Coll. of Midwives, 1992–. Pres., British Fertility Soc., 1992–95. Hon. FACOG; Hon. FSLCOG; Hon. FRCAnaes; Hon. FRACOG. Hon. LLD Dundee, 1988. *Publications:* (ed jtly) Combined Textbook of Obstetrics and Gynaecology, 9th edn 1976; (ed and contrib.) Handbook of Medical Gynaecology, 1985; numerous papers in obstetric, gynaecological, endocrine and general medical jls. *Recreations:* fishing, walking, curling. *Address:* 9 Glenburn Road, Bearsden, Glasgow G61 4PJ. *T:* (0141) 942 1909. *Club:* Glasgow Academical (Glasgow).

McNAUGHTON, Prof. Peter Anthony, DPhil; Sheild Professor and Head of Department of Pharmacology, University of Cambridge, since 1999; Fellow of Christ's College, Cambridge, 1983–91 and since 1999; *b* 17 Aug. 1949; *s* of Anthony Henry McNaughton and Dulcie Helen McNaughton; *m* 1985, Linda Ariza; two *s* two *d*. *Educ:* Univ. of Auckland, NZ (BSc 1970); Balliol Coll., Oxford (DPhil 1974); MA Cantab 1976. University of Cambridge: Res. Fellow, Clare Coll., 1974–78; Physiological Laboratory: Elmore Med. Res. Student, 1977–78; Univ. Demonstrator, 1978–83; Univ. Lectr, 1983–91; Nuffield Sci. Res. Fellow, 1988–89; King's College London: Halliburton Prof. of Physiology, and Head of Physiology, 1991–99; Dean of Basic Med. Scis, 1993–96. Hon. Prof., Dept of Optometry and Vision Scis, Univ. of Wales, Cardiff, 1998–2002. Biotechnology and Biological Sciences Research Council: Member: Biochem. and Cell Biology Panel, 1996–2000; Neurone Initiative Panel, 2001–04; Inst. Assessment Panel, 2001; Chm., Bio-imaging Initiative Panel, 1998–2002; Member: Neurosci. Panel, Wellcome Trust, 1998–2001; Adv. Bd, MRC, 2001–; Performance Based Res. Fund Panel, NZ, 2003. Member: Physiological Soc., 1979– (Mem. Cttee, 1988–92); British Pharmacological Soc., 1999–. *Publications:* articles in fields of physiology, pharmacology and neuroscience in learned jls. *Address:* Department of Pharmacology, University of Cambridge, Tennis Court Road, Cambridge CB2 1PD.

McNEE, Sir David (Blackstock), Kt 1978; QPM 1975; Commissioner, Metropolitan Police, 1977–82; non-executive director and adviser to a number of public limited companies; *b* 23 March 1925; *s* of John McNee, Glasgow, Lanarkshire; *m* 1st, 1952, Isabella Clayton Hopkins (*d* 1997); one *d*; 2nd, 2002, Lilian Bissland Campbell (*née* Bogie). *Educ:* Woodside Senior Secondary Sch., Glasgow. Joined City of Glasgow Police, 1946. Apptd Dep. Chief Constable, Dunbartonshire Constabulary, 1968; Chief Constable: City of Glasgow Police, 1971–75; Strathclyde Police, 1975–77. Lectures: Basil Henriques, Bristol Univ., 1978; London, in Contemporary Christianity, 1979; Dallas, Glasgow, 1980; Peter le Neve Foster Meml, RSA, 1981. President: Royal Life Saving Soc., 1982–90; National Bible Soc. of Scotland, 1983–96; Glasgow City Cttee, Cancer Relief, 1987–93; Glasgow Battalion, Boys' Brigade, 1984–87; Hon. Vice-Pres., Boys' Bde, 1980–; Vice-Pres., London Fedn of Boys Clubs, 1982–. Patron, Scottish Motor Neurone Assoc., 1982–97. Hon. Col, 32 (Scottish) Signal Regt (V), TA, 1988–92. Freeman of the City of London, 1977. FCMI (FBIM 1977); FRSA 1981. KStJ 1991. *Publication:* McNee's Law, 1983. *Recreations:* fishing, golf, music. *Clubs:* Caledonian, Naval (Life Mem.).

MacNEE, Prof. William, MD; FRCPE; Professor of Respiratory and Environmental Medicine, University of Edinburgh, since 1997; Hon. Consultant Physician, NHS Lothian, since 1987; *b* Glasgow, 18 Dec. 1950; *s* of James and Elsie MacNee; *m* 1976, Edna Marina Kingsley; one *s* one *d*. *Educ:* Coatbridge High Sch.; Univ. of Glasgow (MB ChB 1975; MD Hons 1985). MRCPGlas 1978; FRCPE 1990. Hse Physician and Hse Surgeon, Glasgow and Paisley, 1975–76; SHO/Registrar in Medicine, Western Infirmary and Gartnavel Hosps, Glasgow, 1976–79; Registrar in Respiratory Medicine, City Hosp., Edinburgh, 1979–80; MRC Res. Fellow and Hon. Registrar, Dept of Respiratory Medicine, Royal Infirmary, Edinburgh, 1980–82; Lectr, Dept of Respiratory Medicine, City Hosp., Edinburgh, 1982–83; Sen. Registrar, Respiratory Medicine and Medicine, Lothian Health Bd, 1983–87; Sen. Lectr in Respiratory Medicine, 1987–93, Reader in Medicine, 1993–97, Univ. of Edinburgh; Hd, Cardiovascular/Thoracic Service, Royal Infirmary of Edinburgh, 1998–99. Clinical Director, Respiratory Medicine: Lothian Univ. Hosps NHS Trust, 1992–97; Lothian Hosps NHS Trust, 1992–2002. MRC Res. Fellow, Univ. of BC, Vancouver, 1985–86; Vis. Prof., Sch. of Life Scis, Napier Univ., Edinburgh. Mem., Scottish Thoracic Soc., 1990–93; Vice Pres., British Lung Foundn, 2007– (Hon. Sec., Scotland, 1993–2004; Chm., Scientific Cttee, 1997–2000). European Respiratory Society: Chm., Scientific Prog. Cttee, 1990–2003; Congress Chair, 2003–04; Pres., 2006–07. *Publications:* Chronic Obstructive Lung Disease, 2002, 2nd edn 2008; The Year in Respiratory Medicine, 2003; Chronic Obstructive Pulmonary Disease, 2nd edn 2003; Fast Facts Chronic Obstructive Pulmonary Disease, 2004; Clinical Management of Chronic Obstructive Pulmonary Disease, 2004; contrib. scientific papers and rev. articles on respiratory medicine topics. *Recreations:* music, walking, reading. *Address:* ELEGI Colt Research Laboratories, MRC Centre for Inflammation Research, Queen's Medical Research Institute, Level 2, Room C2.29, 47 Little France Crescent, Edinburgh EH16 6LF.

MacNEIL, Angus Brendan; MP (SNP) Na H-Eileanan An Iar, since 2005; *b* 21 July 1970; *m* 1998, Jane Douglas. *Educ:* Castlebay Secondary Sch., Isle of Barra; Nicolson Inst., Stornoway; Strathclyde Univ. (BEng 1992); Jordanhill Coll. (PGCE 1996). Civil Engr, Lilley Construction Ltd, 1992–93; reporter, BBC Radio, Inverness, 1993–95; teacher, Salen Primary Sch., Mull, 1996–98; Gaelic Develt Officer, Lochaber, 1998–99; Lectr in Educn (part-time), Inverness Coll., 1999–2000; teacher, various schs incl. Lochaber and Fort William, 2000–03; teacher and crofter, Isle of Barra, 2003–05. Contested (SNP) Inverness E, Nairn and Lochaber, 2001. *Address:* (office) 31 Bayhead, Stornoway, Isle of Lewis, Outer Hebrides HS1 2DU; House of Commons, SW1A 0AA.

McNEIL, (David) John, CBE 1988; WS; NP; Partner, Morton Fraser (formerly Morton Fraser Milligan), 1968–2002; President, Law Society of Scotland, 1986–87; *b* 24 March 1937; *s* of Donald S. McNeil and Elizabeth (*née* Campbell); *m* 1962, Georgina Avril Sargent (*d* 2005); one *s* two *d*. *Educ:* Daniel Stewart's Coll., Edinburgh; Edinburgh Univ. (MA Hons, LLB). Apprenticed to Davidson & Syme, WS, Edinburgh, 1959–62; admitted Solicitor in Scotland, 1962; WS 1964; Partner, Fraser, Stodart and Ballingall, 1964–68. Mem. Council, Law Soc. of Scotland, 1972–92. Mem., Warnock Inquiry into Aspects of Human Infertility and Embryology, 1982–84. *Recreations:* golf, snooker, music and opera, theatre. *Club:* Bruntsfield Golf (Edinburgh).

McNEIL, Duncan; Member (Lab) Greenock and Inverclyde, Scottish Parliament, since 1999; *b* 7 Sept. 1950; *m* Margaret; one *s* one *d*. Apprentice, Cartsdyke Shipyard; shipbuilder; Officer, GMB. Mem., Labour Party Scottish Exec.; Chm., Local Govt Cttee. Mem., Health Cttee, 2003–07, Scottish Parly Corporate Body, 2003–07, Scottish Parlt. *Address:* Scottish Parliament, Edinburgh EH99 1SP.

McNEIL, Ian Robert, MBE 2004; JP; FCA; Partner, Moores Rowland, Chartered Accountants, 1958–98; *b* 14 Dec. 1932; *s* of Robert and Doris Mary McNeil; *m* 1963, Ann Harries-Rees; two *d*. *Educ:* Brighton Coll. ACA 1955. Partner, Nevill Hovey Gardner (later amalgamated into Moores Rowland), 1958. Dep. Chm., Financial Reporting Council, 1991–92; Mem., Takeover Panel, 1991–92. Member: Lord Chancellor's Adv. Cttee on Legal Educn and Conduct, 1994–99; Legal Services Consultative Panel, 2000–03. Institute of Chartered Accountants in England and Wales: Vice-Pres., 1989–90; Dep. Pres., 1990–91; Pres., 1991–92. Chm., Audit Cttee, Archbishops' Council, C of E, 1999–2004. Governor, Hurstpierpoint Coll., 1999–2002. Trustee and Hon. Treas., Action Research, 1999–2000. Liveryman: Curriers' Co., 1959 (Master, 1994–95); Chartered Accountants' Co., 1989–2002. JP Hove 1967 (Chm., Hove Bench, 1988–89); Mem. Council, Magistrates' Assoc., 1983–89. *Address:* 6 The Daisycroft, Henfield, West Sussex BN5 9LH. *T:* (01273) 492606. *Club:* Athenæum.

MACNEIL OF BARRA, Prof. Ian Roderick; The Macneil of Barra; Chief of Clan Macneil and of that Ilk; Baron of Barra; Wigmore Professor of Law, Northwestern University, 1980–99, now Emeritus; *b* 20 June 1929; *s* of Robert Lister Macneil of Barra and Kathleen, *d* of Orlando Paul Metcalf, NYC, USA; *m* 1952, Nancy, *e d* of James Tilton Wilson, Ottawa, Canada; two *s* one *d* (and one *s* decd). *Educ:* Univ. of Vermont (BA 1950); Harvard Univ. (LLB 1955). Lieut, Infty, Army of US, 1951–53 (US Army Reserve, 1950–69). Clerk, US Court of Appeals, 1955–56; law practice, Concord, NH, USA, 1956–59. Cornell Univ., USA: Asst Prof. of Law, 1959–62; Associate Prof., 1962–63; Prof. of Law, 1962–72 and 1974–76; Ingersoll Prof. of Law, 1976–80; Prof. of Law, Univ. of Virginia, 1972–74. Visiting Professor of Law: Univ. of East Africa, Dar es Salaam, Tanzania, 1965–67; Harvard Univ., 1988–89; Guggenheim Fellow, 1978–79; Vis. Fellow, Wolfson Coll., Oxford, 1979. Hon. Vis. Fellow, Faculty of Law, Edinburgh Univ., 1979 and 1987. Member: Scottish Medievalists; Standing Council of Scottish Chiefs. FSAScot; Fellow, American Acad. of Arts and Scis. *Publications:* Bankruptcy Law in East Africa, 1966; (with R. B. Schlesinger, *et al*) Formation of Contracts: A Study of the Common Core of Legal Systems, 1968; Contracts: Instruments of Social Co-operation-East Africa, 1968; (with R. S. Morison) Students and Decision Making, 1970; Contracts: Exchange Transactions and Relations, 1971, 3rd edn (with P. Gudel) 2001; The New Social Contract, 1980; American Arbitration Law, 1992; (jtly) Federal Arbitration Law, 1994; The Relational Theory of Contract: selected works of Ian Macneil, ed D. Campbell, 2001. *Heir: s* Roderick Wilson Macneil, Younger of Barra [*b* 22 Oct. 1954; *m* 1988, Sau Ming, *d* of Chun Kwan, Hong Kong]. *Address:* Carlton Grange, 95/6 Grange Loan, Edinburgh EH9 2ED. *T:* (0131) 667 6068; Taigh A'Mhonaidh, Garrygall, Castlebay, Isle of Barra, Scotland HS9 5UH. *T:* (01871) 810300; (seat) Kisimul Castle, Isle of Barra.

McNEIL, John; see McNeil, D. J.

MacNEIL, Most Rev. Joseph Neil; Archbishop of Edmonton (Alberta), (RC), 1973–99, now Emeritus; b 15 April 1924; s of John Martin MacNeil and Kate MacNeil (née MacLean). Educ: St Francis Xavier Univ., Antigonish, NS (BA 1944); Holy Heart Seminary, Halifax, NS; Univs of Perugia, Chicago and St Thomas Aquinas, Rome (JCD 1958). Priest, 1948; pastor, parishes in NS, 1948–55; Chancery Office, Antigonish, 1958–59; admin. dio. Antigonish, 1959–60; Rector, Antigonish Cathedral, 1961; Dir of Extension Dept, St Francis Xavier Univ., Antigonish, 1961–69; Vice-Pres., 1962–69; Bishop of St John, NB, 1969–73. Pres., Canadian Conf. of Catholic Bishops, 1979–81 (Vice-Pres., 1977–79; Member: Commn on Ecumenism, 1985–91; Perm. Council, 1993–95; Commn on Mission, 1991–96); Chm., Alberta Bishops' Conf., 1973–99. Chancellor, Univ. of St Thomas, Fredericton, NB, 1969. Founding Mem., Inst. for Res. on Public Policy, 1968–80; Mem., Bd of Directors: The Futures Secretariat, 1981–85; Centre for Human Develt, Toronto, 1985–90. Chairman: Bd, Newman Theol Coll., Edmonton, 1973–99; Bd, St Joseph's Coll., Alberta Univ., 1973–99. Member, Bd of Management: Edmonton Gen. Hosp., 1983–92; Edmonton Caritas Health Gp, 1992–99. Address: (office) 8421–101 Avenue, Edmonton, Alberta T6A 0L1, Canada.

MacNEILL, Calum Hector Sinclair; QC (Scot.) 2007; b Elgin, 19 May 1964; s of late Malcolm Torquil MacNeill and of Morag MacNeill (née McKinnon). Educ: Robert Gordon's Coll., Aberdeen; Univ. of Aberdeen (LLB Hons 1985; DipLP 1986). Called to the Scottish Bar, 1992; Advocate Depute, 1998–2001; Standing Jun. Counsel to Scottish Exec., 2003–06. Address: Advocates' Library, Parliament House, Parliament Square, Edinburgh EH1 1RF. T: (0131) 226 5071; e-mail: calum.macneill@advocates.org.uk.

McNEILL, (Elizabeth) Jane; QC 2002; a Recorder, since 2005; b 18 March 1957; d of David McNeill and Margaret McNeill (née Lewis); m 1990, David Adams; two s. Educ: St Hilda's Coll., Oxford (BA Hons Mod. Langs); City Univ., London (Dip Law). Called to the Bar, Lincoln's Inn, 1982, Bencher, 2007. A pt-time Chm., Employment Tribunal. Recreations: bridge, Italy, ski-ing, cinema. Address: Old Square Chambers, 10–11 Bedford Row, WC1R 4BU. T: (020) 7269 0300.

McNEILL, James Walker; QC (Scot.) 1991; Judge of the Courts of Appeal of Jersey and Guernsey, since 2006; b 16 Feb. 1952; s of late James McNeill and Edith Anna Howie Wardlaw; m 1986, Katherine Lawrence McDowall; two s one d. Educ: Dunoon Grammar Sch.; Cambridge Univ. (MA); Edinburgh Univ. (LLB). Advocate 1978; Standing Junior Counsel: to Dept of Transport in Scotland, 1984–88; to Inland Revenue in Scotland, 1988–91. Session Clerk, St Andrew's and St George's Parish Ch, Edinburgh, 1999–2003; Mem. Bd, Scottish Internat. Piano Competition, 2004–. Recreations: music, hill-walking, golf, sailing, travel. Address: 28 Kingsburgh Road, Edinburgh EH12 6DZ. Clubs: New (Edinburgh); Hon. Company of Edinburgh Golfers; Isle of Colonsay Golf.

McNEILL, Jane; see McNeill, E. J.

McNEILL, Prof. John, PhD; Director Emeritus, Royal Ontario Museum, Toronto, since 1997 (Director, 1991–97; President, 1995–97); Hon. Associate, Royal Botanic Garden, Edinburgh, since 1998 (Regius Keeper, 1987–89); b 15 Sept. 1933; s of Thomas McNeill and Helen Lawrie Eagle; m 1st, 1961, Bridget Mariel Winterton (marr. diss. 1990); two s; 2nd, 1990, Marilyn Lois James. Educ: George Heriot's, Edinburgh; Univ. of Edinburgh (BSc Hons, PhD 1960). Asst Lectr and Lectr, Dept of Agricl Botany, Univ. of Reading, 1957–61; Lectr, Dept of Botany, Univ. of Liverpool, 1961–69; Plant (later Biosystematics) Research Institute, Agriculture Canada, Ottawa: Res. Scientist, 1969–77, Chief, Vascular Plant Taxonomy Sect., 1969–72; Sen. Res. Scientist, 1977–81; Prof. and Chm., Dept of Biology, Univ. of Ottawa, 1981–87; Associate Dir Curatorial, Royal Ontario Mus., Toronto, 1989–90, Acting Dir, 1990–91; Dir, George R. Gardiner Mus. of Ceramic Art, Toronto, 1991–96. Hon. Prof., Univ. of Edinburgh, 1989; Prof., Dept of Botany, Univ. of Toronto, 1990–; Adjunct Prof., Univ. of Ottawa, 1987–91. Mem. Editl Cttee, 1985–2003, Chm. Mgt Cttee, 1998–2001, Mem. Bd of Dirs, 2003–06, Emeritus Mem., 2006–, Flora North America Association; Rapporteur-général, Nomenclature section, Internat. Botanical Congresses, 1997–; Ed., Nomenclature section, Taxon (jl of Internat. Assoc. for Plant Taxonomy), 2000–. Publications include: Phenetic and phylogenetic classification (jt ed), 1964; (jtly) Grasses of Ontario, 1977; (jt ed) International Code of Botanical Nomenclature, 1983, 1988, 1994, 2000, 2006; (jtly) Preliminary Inventory of Canadian Weeds, 1988; (jt ed) Flora of North America north of Mexico, vols 1 and 2, 1993, vol. 3, 1997, vol. 22, 2000, vol. 26, 2002, vol. 23, 2003; (jt ed) International Code of Nomenclature for Cultivated Plants, 1995, 7th edn 2004; over 20 chapters or sections of sci. books and over 90 contribs to sci. res. jls. Recreation: botanical nomenclature. Address: Royal Botanic Garden, 20A Inverleith Row, Edinburgh EH3 5LR.

McNEILL, Johnston David John; Chief Executive, Rural Payments Agency, 2001–06; b 15 Aug. 1956; s of David McNeill and Mary McNeill (née Kane); m 1983, Jennifer Fowler (marr. diss. 1997); one s two d. Educ: Lurgan Coll.; Southampton Coll. of Technology (HND Mech. Engrg); Univ. of Ulster (BA); Univ. of Central Lancashire (MBA); Portsmouth Univ. (PGDipPM, MA); PGDipM. Marine engr, 1974–79; mgt posts, private sector cos, 1979–88; Dep. Gen. Manager, Lancs CC, 1988–90; Asst Dir, Southampton CC, 1990–92; Dir of Contract Services, Belfast CC, 1992–94; Chief Executive: Meat Hygiene Service, MAFF, 1994–2000; Food Standards Agency, 2000–01. FIPD. Freeman, City of London; Liveryman, Butchers' Co. Recreations: ski-ing, rowing, yacht sailing, guitar, socialising with friends and family. Club: Farmers.

McNEILL, Pauline Mary; Member (Lab) Glasgow Kelvin, Scottish Parliament, since 1999; b 12 Sept. 1962; d of John Patrick McNeill and Teresa Ward or McNeill; m 1999, William Joseph Cahill; two step s. Educ: Glasgow Coll. of Building and Printing (Dip. 1986); Strathclyde Univ. (LLB 1999). Pres., NUS, 1986–88; Regl Orgnr, GMB Scotland, 1988–99. Recreations: guitar, singing, rock music, keep fit. Address: (office) 1274 Argyle Street, Glasgow G3 8AA.

McNEILL, Peter Grant Brass; QC (Scot.) 1988; PhD; Sheriff of Lothian and Borders at Edinburgh, 1982–96, temporary Sheriff, 1996–98; writer; b Glasgow, 3 March 1929; s of late William Arnot McNeill and late Lillias Philips Scrimgeour; m 1959, Matilda Farquhar Rose, d of late Mrs Christina Rose; one s three d. Educ: Hillhead High Sch., Glasgow; Morrison's Academy, Crieff; Glasgow Univ. MA (Hons Hist.) 1951; LLB 1954; Law apprentice, Biggart Lumsden & Co., Glasgow, 1952–55; Carnegie Fellowship, 1955; Faulds Fellowship, 1956–59; Scottish Bar, 1956; PhD, 1961. Hon. Sheriff Substitute of Lanarkshire, and of Stirling, Clackmannan and Dumbarton, 1962; Standing Junior Counsel to Scottish Development Dept (Highways), 1964; Advocate Depute, 1964–65; Sheriff of Lanarks, subseq. redesignated Glasgow and Strathkelvin, at Glasgow, 1965–82. Pres., Sheriffs' Assoc., 1982–85. Chm., Review Bd, Chinook Helicopter Accident, 1988. Mem., Scottish Records Adv. Council, 1989–95. Mem. Council, Scottish Nat. Dictionary Assoc. Ltd, 1987–2002 (Chm., 1997–2001); Chairman: Scottish Legal History Gp, 1990–97; Council, Stair Soc., 1990–98 (Vice Pres., 2007); Trustee, Medievalists Colloquium for Scottish and Medieval Studies, 2007. Publications: (ed) Balfour's Practicks (Stair Society), 1962–63; (ed jtly) An Historical Atlas of Scotland c 400–c 1600, 1975; Adoption of Children in Scotland, 1982, 3rd edn 1998; (ed jtly) Atlas of Scottish History to 1707, 1996; legal and historical articles in Encyclopaedia Britannica, Juridical Review, Scots Law Times, Glasgow Herald, DNB, Oxford DNB, etc. Recreations: legal history, gardening, bookbinding. Address: 31 Queensferry Road, Edinburgh EH4 3HB. T: (0131) 332 3195.

McNEISH, Prof. Alexander Stewart, FRCP; Emeritus Professor of Clinical Science, London University, since 2001; Hon. Professor, School of Medicine, Birmingham University, since 2003; b 13 April 1938; s of Angus Stewart McNeish and Minnie Howieson (née Dickson); m 1963, Joan Ralston (née Hamilton); two s (one d decd). Educ: Glasgow Acad.; Univ. of Glasgow (MB; MPhil 2005); Univ. of Birmingham (MSc). FRCP 1977; FRCPGlas 1985; FRCPCH 1996. Sen. Lectr in Paediatrics and Child Health, Univ. of Birmingham, 1970–76; Foundn Prof. of Child Health, Univ. of Leicester, 1976–80; University of Birmingham: Leonard Parsons Prof. of Paediatrics and Child Health, 1980–95; Dir, Inst. of Child Health, 1980–93; Dean, Faculty of Medicine and Dentistry, 1987–92; Dir of R&D, W Midlands RHA, 1992–95; Dir, MRC Clinical Scis Centre, Hammersmith Hosp., 1995–97; London University: Warden, St Bart's and Royal London Sch. of Medicine and Dentistry, 1997–2001; Vice Principal, 1997–99; Dep. Principal, 1999–2001, QMW. Mem., GMC, 1984–95. Founder FMedSci 1998. Hon. Fellow, QMUL, 2007. Publications: papers on paediatric gastroenterology in Lancet, BMJ and in Archives of Disease in Childhood. Recreations: golf, music. Address: 128 Westfield Road, Edgbaston, Birmingham B15 3JQ. T: (0121) 454 6081. Clubs: Athenæum; Blackwell Golf, Rye Golf.

McNICOL, Prof. Donald; Vice-Chancellor and Principal, University of Tasmania, 1996–2002; b 18 April 1939; s of Ian Robertson McNicol and Sadie Isabelle Williams; m 1963, Kathleen Margaret Wells; one s two d. Educ: Unley High Sch.; Univ. of Adelaide (BA 1964); St John's Coll., Cambridge (PhD 1967). Fellow, Aust. Psych. Soc. Lectr in Psychology, Univ. of Adelaide, 1967–71; Research Fellow, St John's Coll., Cambridge, 1968–69; Sen. Lectr in Psych., Univ. of NSW, 1971–74; Associate Prof. in Psych., Univ. of NSW, 1975–81; Prof. of Psych., Univ. of Tasmania, 1981–86, now Emeritus Prof.; Comr for Univs and Chm., Univs Adv. Council, Commonwealth Tertiary Educn, 1986–88; Vice-Chancellor, Univ. of New England, NSW, 1988–90; Vice-Chancellor and Principal, Univ. of Sydney, 1990–96. President: AVCC, 1994–95; Assoc. of Univs of Asia Pacific, 1998–99; AHEIA, 2000–01. Publication: A Primer of Signal Detection Theory, 1972, repr. 2005. Recreations: walking, jazz, reading. Address: PO Box 1155, Sandy Bay, Tas 7006, Australia.

McNICOL, Prof. George Paul, CBE 1992; FRSE 1984; Principal and Vice-Chancellor, University of Aberdeen, 1981–91; b 24 Sept. 1929; s of Martin and Elizabeth McNicol; m 1959, Susan Ritchie; one s two d. Educ: Hillhead High Sch., Glasgow; Univ. of Glasgow (MD 1964, PhD 1965). FRCPG 1967; FRCPE 1968; FRCP 1977; FRCPath 1977. House Surg., Western Infirmary, Glasgow, 1952; House Phys., Stobhill Gen. Hosp., Glasgow, 1953; Regimental MO, RAMC, 1953–55; Glasgow Medical Sch., 1955–71: various posts in clinical acad. med., 1955–65; Hon. Cons. Phys., 1966–71; Reader in Medicine, 1970–71; Prof. of Medicine and Hon. Cons. Phys., Leeds Gen. Infirmary, 1971–81; Chm., Bd of Faculty of Medicine, Leeds Univ., 1978–81. Harkness Fellow, Commonwealth Fund, Dept of Internal Medicine, Washington Univ., 1959–61; Hon. Clinical Lectr and Hon. Cons. Phys., Makerere UC Med. Sch. Extension, Kenyatta Nat. Hosp., Nairobi (on secondment from Glasgow Univ.), 1965–66. Chm. Med. Adv. Cttee, Cttee of Vice-Chancellors and Principals, 1985–90; Member: British Council Cttee on Internat. Co-op. in Higher Educn, 1985–91; Council, ACU, 1988–91; former Mem., Adv. Council on Misuse of Drugs. Chm., Part I Examining Bd, Royal Colls of Physicians (UK). Vice-Chm., Raigmore Hosp. NHS Trust, 1993–95. Chm., Bd of Governors, Rowett Res. Inst., 1981–89; Mem., Bd of Governors, N of Scotland Coll. of Agriculture, 1981–91; Co-Pres., EU Standing Cttee for Med. Trng, 1990–93. Mem., Exec. Cttee, Scottish Council (Develt and Industry), 1989–91. Mem. Aberdeen Local Bd, Bank of Scotland, 1983–92. Hon. FACP. Hon. DSc Wabash Coll., Indiana, 1989; Hon. LLD Aberdeen, 1992. Publications: papers in sci. and med. jls on thrombosis and bleeding disorders. Address: 17 The Old Tannery, Downton, Salisbury, Wilts SP5 3FB.

MACNICOL, Malcolm Fraser, FRCS, FRCP, FRCSE(Orth); Consultant Orthopaedic Surgeon, Royal Hospital for Sick Children and Royal Infirmary, Edinburgh, since 1979; b 18 March 1943; s of Roy Simson Macnicol and Eona Kathleen Macnicol (née Fraser); m 1972, Anne Morag Docherty; two s one d. Educ: Royal High Sch., Edinburgh; Edinburgh Univ. (BSc Hons 1966, MB ChB 1969); MChOrth Liverpool 1979. FRCS 1973; FRCSE(Orth) 1979; Dip. Sports Med., RCSE, 1998; FRCP 2000. Research Fellow: Stanford Univ., 1966; Harvard Univ., 1970–71; Lectr in Orthopaedics, Edinburgh Univ., 1976–78; Sen. Orthopaedic Lectr, Univ. of W Australia, 1978–79; Sen. Orthopaedic Lectr (pt-time), Univ. of Edinburgh, 1982–. Treas., RCSE, 1987–90. Pres., British Orthopaedic Assoc., 2001–02 (Chm., Medico-legal Sub Cttee, 1998–2003; Mem., Robert Jones Orthopaedic Club); Member: British Soc. for Children's Orthopaedic Surgery, 1985–; British Assoc. for Surgery of the Knee, 1985–; British Orthopaedic Res. Soc., 1985–. Hon. Med. Advr, Scottish RU, 2004–. Mem., Malt Whisky Tasting Soc., 2000–. Publications: Princess Margaret Rose Orthopaedic Hospital 1932–1982, 1982; Aids to Orthopaedics, 1984; Basic Care of the Injured Hand, 1984; Problem Knee, 1986, 2nd edn 1993; Color Atlas and Text of Osteomy of the Hip, 1995; Children's Orthopaedics and Fractures, 1994, 2nd edn 2002; contrib. numerous peer-reviewed papers and book chapters. Recreations: tennis, walking, water-colour painting, theatre. Address: Red House, 1 South Gillsland Road, Edinburgh EH10 5DE. Clubs: Harveian Soc. (Edinburgh); Harvard Research.

McNICOLL, Air Marshal Iain Walter, CB 2006; CBE 2000; FRAeS; Deputy Commander-in-Chief Operations Air Command, since 2007; b 3 May 1953; s of Walter McNicoll and Maida Cameron McNicoll (née Readdie); m 1980, Wendelien Henriëtte Maria van den Biggelaar; one s two d. Educ: Dundee High Sch.; Univ. of Edinburgh (BSc 1975). FRAeS 2001. Commnd RAFVR, 1973, RAF, 1975; XV Sqn, 1978–81; qwi 1979; Tornado Weapons Conversion Unit 45 (Reserve) Sqn, 1982–85; 17 (Fighter) Sqn, 1985–86; 16 Sqn, 1986–89; RAF Staff Coll., 1990; PSO to Dep. C-in-C, Strike Command, 1991–92; OC 17 (Fighter) Sqn, 1992–95; MoD, 1995–98; Station Comdr, Brüggen, 1998–2000; Dir, Force Development, MoD, 2000–02; DG, Jt Doctrine and Concepts, MoD, 2002–05; AOC No 2 Gp, 2005–07. QCVSA 1989. Recreations: golf, sailing, ski-ing. Address: e-mail: mcnicoll@onetel.com. Club: Royal Air Force.

MacNISH, Alastair Jesse Head, OBE 2008; FCCA; Chairman, Accounts Commission for Scotland, 2001–07; Chairman of Board, Audit Scotland, 2001–07; b 4 Feb. 1947; m 1970, Jean Ferguson Bell; one s two d. Educ: Gourock High Sch. FCCA 1972. Chief Auditor, Renfrew CC, 1973–75; Strathclyde Regional Council: Principal Accountant, 1975–77; Asst Dir of Educn, 1977–87; Depute Dir of Social Work, 1987–95; Chief Exec., S Lanarks Council, 1995–99; Chm., Leadership Adv. Panel, Scottish Exec., 1999–2000. Clerk: Strathclyde Jt Fire Bd, 1995–99; Lanarkshire Jt Valuation Bd, 1995–99. Member:

Scotland Adv. Cttee, EOC, 1996–2000; Scottish Govt's Ministerial Panel on Fire & Rescue Services, 2007–. Chm., Bd of Dirs, Royal Caledonian Curling Club, 1999–2002. MCIPD (MIPD 1994). *Recreations:* golf, curling, bridge. *Club:* Gourock Golf (Capt. 1998–99).

McNISH, Althea Marjorie, (Althea McNish Weiss), CMT 1976; freelance textile designer, since 1957; *b* Trinidad; *d* of late J. Claude McNish, educnl reformer, and late Margaret (*née* Bourne); *m* 1969, John Weiss. *Educ:* Port-of-Spain, by her father and others; London Coll. of Printing; Central School of Art and Crafts; Royal Coll. of Art. NDD, DesRCA; FCSD (FSIA 1968, MSIA 1960). Painted throughout childhood; after design educn in London, freelance practice in textile and other design; commns from Ascher and Liberty's, 1957; new techniques for laminate murals, for SS Oriana and hosp. and coll. in Trinidad; Govt of Trinidad and Tobago travelling schol., 1962; interior design (for Govt of Trinidad and Tobago) in NY, Washington and London, 1962; Cotton Bd trav. schol. to report on export potential for British printed cotton goods in Europe, 1963; collection of dress fabric designs for ICI and Tootal Thomson for promotion of Terylene Toile, 1966; special features for Daily Mail Ideal Home Exhibn, 1966–78; (with John Weiss) etched silver dishes, 1973–; interior design for Sec.-Gen. of Commonwealth, 1975; bedlinen collection for Courtaulds, 1978; (with John Weiss) textile design develt for BRB, 1978–81; textile hangings for BRB Euston offices, 1979; banners for Design Centre, 1981; (with John Weiss) improvements to London office of High Comr for Trinidad and Tobago, 1981; advr on exhibn design for Govt of Trinidad and Tobago, Commonwealth Inst., 1982–84; fashion textile designs for Slovene textile printers, 1985–91; furnishing textile designs for Fede Cheti, Milan, 1986–91; murals and hangings for Royal Caribbean Cruise Line: MS Nordic Empress, 1990; MS Monarch of the Seas, 1991. Paintings and various work in exhibitions include: individual and gp exhibns, London, 1954–; with Caribbean Artists Movt, Th. Royal, Stratford, 1967, Digby Stuart Coll., LSE and H of C, 1968; Caribbean Artists in England, Commonwealth Inst., 1971; Island Pulse: five Caribbean-born artists, Islington Arts Factory, 1996; solo exhibn, RCA Hockney Gall., 1997; Trinidad & Tobago Through the Eye of the Artist, Commonwealth Inst., 1997; Fine Arts Soc., 198 Gall. and Six into One: Artists from the Caribbean, Morley Gall., 1998; Glebe Place, 2000; paintings, Jamaica, 1975; hangings, Kilkenny, 1981; hangings, individual exhibn, Peoples Gall., 1982; hangings, Magazine Workspace, Leicester, 1983; textile designs in exhibitions: Inprint, Manchester and London, 1964–71; Design Council/ BoT, USA and Sweden, 1969, London, 1970, London and USA, 1972; Design-In, Amsterdam, 1972–74; Design Council, 1975–80; The Way We Live Now, V&A Mus., 1978; Indigo, Lille, 1981–82; Commonwealth Fest. Art Exhibn, Brisbane, 1982; Designs for British Dress and Furnishing Fabrics, V&A Mus., 1986; Make or Break, Henry Moore Gall., 1986; Surtex, New York, 1987; Ascher, V&A Mus., 1987; Transforming the Crown: African, Asian and Caribbean Artists in Britain 1966–96, NY, 1996; work represented in permanent collection of V&A Mus. Vis. Lecturer: Central Sch. of Art and Crafts and other colls and polytechnics, 1960–; USA, 1972; Italy, W Germany and Slovenia, 1985–; Advisory Tutor in Furnishing and Surface Design, London Coll. of Furniture, 1972–90. External assessor for educnl and professional bodies, incl. CSD and NCDAD/CNAA, 1966–; Mem. jury for Leverhulme schols, 1968; Judge: Portuguese textile design comp., Lisbon, 1973; 'Living' Design Awards, 1974; Carnival selection panels, Arts Council, 1982 and 1983. Vice-Pres., SIAD, 1977–78; Design Council: Mem., selection panels for Design Awards and Design Index, 1968–80; Mem. Bd, 1974–81; Mem., Jubilee Souvenir Selection Panel, 1976; Mem., Royal Wedding Souvenir Selection Panel, 1981. Member: Fashion and Textiles Design Bd, CNAA, 1975–78; London Local Adv. Cttee, IBA, 1981–; Formation Cttee, London Inst., ILEA, 1985. Mem. Governing Body, Portsmouth Coll. of Art, 1972–81. *BBC-TV:* studio setting for Caribbean edn of Full House, 1973. Has appeared, with work, in films for COI and Gas Council. Chaconia Medal (Gold) (Trinidad and Tobago), 1976, for service to art and design; Scarlet Ibis Award (Trinidad and Tobago), 1993. *Publications:* textile designs produced in many countries, 1957–; designs and paintings illustrated in: J. Laver, The Liberty Story, 1959; Costumes, Masks and Jewellery of the Commonwealth, ed J. Debayo, 1982; Young Blood, Britain's Design Schools Today and Tomorrow, ed K. Baynes, 1983; V. D. Mendes and F. M. Hinchcliffe, Ascher, 1987; Did Britain Make It?, ed P. Sparke, 1986; M. Schoeser, Fabrics and Wallpapers, 1986; M. Schoeser and C. Rufey, English and American Textiles from 1790 to the Present, 1989; B. Philips, Fabrics and Wallpapers, 1991; S. Calloway, The House of Liberty, 1992; A. Walmsley, The Caribbean Artists Movement 1966–1972, 1992; L. Jackson, 20th Century Pattern Design: textile and wallpaper pioneers, 2002; published in Decorative Art, Designers in Britain and design jls. *Recreations:* ski-ing, travelling, music, gardening. *Address: e-mail:* althea.mcnish@virgin.net. *Club:* Soroptimist.

MACNIVEN, Duncan, TD 1985; Registrar General for Scotland, since 2003; *b* 1 Dec. 1950; *s* of late John and Jenny Macniven; *m* 1976, Valerie Margaret Clark; two *d. Educ:* Melville Coll., Edinburgh; Aberdeen Univ. (MA 1973; MLitt 1978). Joined Scottish Office, 1973; Principal, 1978–85; Asst Sec., 1986–90; Dep. Dir, Historic Scotland, 1990–95; Head of Police Div., 1995–97; Head of Police, Fire and Emergencies Gp, 1997–99; Comr and Hd of Corporate Services, Forestry Commn, 1999–2003. RE, TA, 1969–85 (Major, 1983–85). DL Robert Gordon, 2008. *Recreations:* active church membership, being outdoors, walking, ski-ing, Scottish history. *Address:* General Register Office, New Register House, 3 West Register Street, Edinburgh EH1 3YT. *T:* (0131) 314 4435.

McNULTY, Rt Hon. Anthony James; PC 2007; MP (Lab) Harrow East, since 1997; Minister of State, Department for Work and Pensions, and Minister for London, since 2008; *b* 3 Nov. 1958; *s* of James Anthony McNulty and Eileen Anne McNulty; *m* Christine Gilbert. *Educ:* Univ. of Liverpool (BA Hons); Virginia Poly. Inst. and State Univ. (MA). Business School, Polytechnic of North London: Research Asst, 1983–85; Res. Fellow and part-time Lectr, 1985–86; part-time Lectr, PCL and Kingston Poly., 1984–86; Sen. Lectr, then Principal Lectr, Business Sch., Poly. of N London, later Univ. of N London, 1986–97. Mem. (Lab), Harrow LBC, 1986–97 (Dep. Leader, 1990–96, Leader, 1996–97, Labour Gp). Mem., Regl Exec., Gtr London Labour Party, 1985–87. Mem., NI Grand Cttee. PPS to Min. of State, DfEE, 1997–99; an Asst Govt Whip, 1999–2001; a Lord Comr of HM Treasury (Govt Whip), 2001–02; Parliamentary Under-Secretary of State: ODPM, 2002–03; DfT, 2003–04; Minister of State: DfT, 2004–05; Home Office, 2005–08. *Publications:* various academic works on local govt, public sector mgt, trng and small firms. *Recreations:* eating out, theatre, films, Rugby, current affairs. *Address:* House of Commons, SW1A 0AA. *T:* (020) 7219 4108, *Fax:* (020) 7219 2417; Harrow East Labour Party, Labour Centre, 18 Byron Road, Harrow, Middx HA3 7ST. *T:* (020) 8427 2100; *e-mail:* mcnulty@parliament.uk.

McNULTY, Des(mond); Member (Lab) Clydebank and Milngavie, Scottish Parliament, since 1999; *b* Stockport, 28 July 1952; *m*; two *s. Educ:* St Bede's Coll., Manchester; York Univ.; Glasgow Univ. Subject Leader in Sociology, 1990–97, Head of Strategic Planning, 1997–99, Glasgow Caledonian Univ. Non-exec. Dir, Gtr Glasgow Health Bd, 1998–99. Member (Lab): Strathclyde Regl Council, 1990–96; Glasgow City Council, 1995–99. Dep. Minister for Communities, Scottish Exec., 2002–03, 2006–07. Scottish Parliament: shadow spokesman on transport, 2007–; Member: Transport and Envmt Cttee, 1999–2003; Corporate Body, 1999–2001; Enterprise and Lifelong Learning Cttee, 2000–01; Rural and Environment Cttee, 2007–; Convenor, Finance Cttee, 2001–02, 2003–07. Chairman: Glasgow Healthy City Partnership, 1996–99; Glasgow 1999 Fest. of Architecture and Design. Board Member: Wise Gp, 1997–; Tron Theatre Ltd, 2005–. Mem., Kemp Commn on Future of Vol. Sector in Scotland, 1995–97. Mem. Ct, Glasgow Univ., 1994–99. *Address:* Scottish Parliament, Edinburgh EH99 1SP. *T:* (0131) 348 5918; (constituency office) Clydebank Central Library, Dumbarton Road, Clydebank G81 1XH. *T:* (0141) 952 7711.

McNULTY, Sir (Robert William) Roy, Kt 1998; CBE 1992; Chairman, Civil Aviation Authority, since 2001 (Member of Board, 1999–2000); *b* 7 Nov. 1937; *s* of Jack and Nancy McNulty; *m* 1963, Ismay Ratcliffe Rome; one *s* two *d. Educ:* Portora Royal School, Enniskillen; Trinity College, Dublin (BA, BComm). Audit Manager, Peat Marwick Mitchell & Co., Glasgow, 1963–66; Accounting Methods Manager, Chrysler UK, Linwood, 1966–68; Harland & Wolff, Belfast: Management Accountant, 1968–72; Computer Services Manager, 1972–74; Management Services Manager, 1975–76; Sen. Management Consultant, Peat Marwick Mitchell & Co., Belfast, 1977–78; Short Brothers plc: Exec. Dir, Finance and Admin, 1978–85; Dep. Managing Dir, 1986–88; Man. Dir and Chief Exec., 1988–92; Pres., Shorts Gp, Bombardier Aerospace, 1992–96; Chm., 1996–99. Chairman: NATS Ltd, 1999–2001; The Odyssey Trust Co. Ltd, 1997–99; Ilex URC, 2007–; non-executive Director: Norbrook Laboratories Ltd, 1990–; Ulster Bank Ltd, 1996–2000; Acting Chm., 2006–07, Dep. Chm., 2007–, Olympic Delivery Authy. Mem., Council, SBAC, 1988–99 (Pres., 1993–94; Treas., 1995–99). Member: IDB for NI, 1992–98; Steering Gp for UK Foresight Programme, 1997–2000; Chairman: NI Growth Challenge, 1993–98; Technology Foresight Defence and Aerospace Panel, 1994–95; DTI Aviation Cttee, 1995–98. Industrial Prof., Dept of Engineering, Univ. of Warwick. Vice Pres., EEF, 1997–. CCMI; FIMI. Hon. FRAeS 1995; Hon. DSc QUB, 1999. *Recreations:* walking, golf, reading. *Address:* Civil Aviation Authority, CAA House, 45–59 Kingsway, WC2B 6TE.

McPARTLIN, Noel; Advocate, since 1976; Sheriff of Lothian and Borders at Edinburgh, since 2001; *b* 25 Dec. 1939; *s* of Michael Joseph McPartlin and Ann Dunn or McPartlin; *m* 1965, June Anderson Whitehead; three *s* three *d. Educ:* Galashiels Acad.; Edinburgh Univ. (MA, LLB). Solicitor in Glasgow, Linlithgow and Stirling, 1964–76. Sheriff of Grampian, Highland and Islands at Peterhead and Banff, 1983–85, at Elgin, 1985–2001. *Recreation:* urban and country life.

MACPHAIL, Hon. Lord; Iain Duncan Macphail, FRSE; a Senator of the College of Justice in Scotland, since 2005; *b* 24 Jan. 1938; *o s* of late Malcolm John Macphail and Mary Corbett Macphail (*née* Duncan); *m* 1970, Rosslyn Graham Lillias, *o d* of E. J. C. Hewitt, MD, TD, Edinburgh; one *s* one *d. Educ:* George Watson's Coll.; Edinburgh and Glasgow Univs. MA Hons History Edinburgh 1959, LLB Glasgow 1962. FRSE 2005. Admitted to Faculty of Advocates, 1963; in practice at Scottish Bar, 1963–73; Faulds Fellow in Law, Glasgow Univ., 1963–65; Lectr in Evidence and Procedure, Strathclyde Univ., 1968–69 and Edinburgh Univ., 1969–72; Standing Jun. Counsel to Scottish Home and Health Dept and to Dept of Health and Social Security, 1971–73; Extra Advocate-Depute, 1973; QC (Scot.) 1990; Sheriff: of Lanarks, later Glasgow and Strathkelvin, 1973–81; of Tayside, Central and Fife, 1981–82; of Lothian and Borders, 1982–89, 1995–2002; Sheriff Principal of Lothian and Borders, and Sheriff of Chancery, 2002–05. Member: Scottish Law Commn, 1990–94; Judicial Studies Cttee for Scotland, 2003–05; Chm., Sheriff Court Rules Council, 2003–05. Chm., Scottish Assoc. for Study of Delinquency, 1978–81. Arthur Goodhart Prof. in Legal Sci., Cambridge Univ., 2001–02. Comr, Northern Lighthouse Bd, 2002–05. Mem., Editl Bd, Criminal Law Review, 2001–. Hon. LLD Edinburgh, 1992. *Publications:* Law of Evidence in Scotland (Scottish Law Commn), 1979; Evidence, 1987; Sheriff Court Practice, 1988; articles and reviews in legal jls. *Address:* Court of Session, Parliament House, Parliament Square, Edinburgh EH1 1RQ. *Club:* New (Edinburgh).

McPHAIL, Angus William, MA; Warden, Radley College, since 2000; *b* 25 May 1956; *s* of Peter Bigham McPhail and Sylvia Bridget McPhail (*née* Campbell); *m* 1980, Elizabeth Hirsch; two *s* one *d. Educ:* Abingdon Sch.; University Coll., Oxford (BA Hons 1978; MA 1982). Overseas Dept, Bank of England, 1978–82; Asst Master, Glenalmond Coll., 1982–85; Head of Econs and Housemaster, Sedbergh Sch., 1985–93; Headmaster, Strathallan Sch., 1993–2000. *Recreations:* cricket, golf, music, walking. *Address:* Radley College, Abingdon, Oxon OX14 2HR. *Clubs:* East India, Lansdowne; Vincent's (Oxford); W Sussex Golf; Cryptics Cricket.

MacPHAIL, Sir Bruce (Dugald), Kt 1992; FCA; Managing Director, Peninsular and Oriental Steam Navigation Co., 1985–2003; *b* 1 May 1939; *s* of late Dugald Ronald MacPhail and Winifred Marjorie MacPhail; *m* 1st, 1963, Susan Mary Gregory (*d* 1975); three *s*; 2nd, 1983, Caroline Ruth Grimston Curtis-Bennett (*née* Hubbard). *Educ:* Haileybury Coll.; Balliol Coll., Oxford (MA); Harvard Business Sch., Mass, USA (MBA 1967). FCA 1976. Articled, Price Waterhouse, 1961–65; Hill Samuel & Co. Ltd, 1967–69; Finance Director: Sterling Guarantee Trust Ltd, 1969–74; Town & City Properties Ltd, 1974–76; Man. Dir, Sterling Guarantee Trust, 1976–85. Non-executive Director: Chelsfield Plc, 1999–2004; Chelsfield Partners, 2006–; Intelligent Engrg Ltd, 2005–; Scarborough Minerals, 2006–. Gov., Royal Ballet Sch., 1982–99; Life Gov., 1992, and Mem. Council, 1992–2004, Haileybury Coll.; Chairman: Council, Templeton Coll., Oxford, 1993–95; Council for Sch. of Management Studies, Univ. of Oxford, 1995–2001; Business Adv. Forum, Saïd Business Sch., Univ. of Oxford, 2001–08. Barclay Fellow, Green Templeton Coll. (formerly Templeton Coll.), Oxford, 1995–. Trustee, Sir Jules Thorn Charitable Trust, 1994–. *Recreations:* reading, wine, scuba diving. *Address:* Thorpe Lubenham Hall, Lubenham, Market Harborough, Leics LE16 9TR.

MACPHAIL, Iain Duncan; *see* Macphail, Hon. Lord.

McPHATE, Very Rev. Gordon Ferguson, MD, FRCPE; Dean of Chester, since 2002; *b* 1 June 1950; *s* of David and Grace McPhate; one adopted *s. Educ:* Aberdeen Univ. (MB, ChB 1974); Fitzwilliam Coll., Cambridge (BA 1977, MA 1981, MD 1988); Surrey Univ. (MSc 1986); Edinburgh Univ. (MTh 1994); Westcott House Theol Coll., Cambridge. FRCPE 1998. Ordained deacon, 1978, priest, 1979. Tutor in Physiol., Clare Coll., Cambridge, 1975–77; Lectr in Physiol., Guy's Hosp. Med. Sch., London Univ., 1978–84; Registrar in Pathol., Guildford Hosps, 1984–86; Lectr in Pathol., 1986–93, Sen. Lectr, 1993–2002, St Andrews Univ.; Fife Hospitals: Hon. Sen. Registrar in Pathol., 1988–96; Hon. Consultant Chem. Pathologist, 1996–2002; Consultant Chem. Pathologist, 2001–02. External Mem., GMC, 2000–. Hon. Curate, Sanderstead, 1978–80; Hon. Minor Canon, Southwark Cathedral, 1980–86; Hon. Chaplain, St Andrews Univ., 1986–2002. Vis. Prof. of Theol. and Medicine, Univ. of Chester (formerly UC Chester), 2003–; Hon. Reader in Medicine, Univ. of Liverpool, 2005–. FHEA 2007. *Publications:* articles in learned jls. *Recreations:* classical and choral music, 18th and 19th century Western art, cinema, reading history and biography. *Address:* The Deanery, 7 Abbey Street, Chester

CH1 2JF. *T:* (office) (01244) 500952, (home) (01244) 500971; *e-mail:* dean@chestercathedral.co.uk.

McPHEE, Robin Alasdair; a District Judge (Magistrates' Courts), since 2002; *b* 3 Sept. 1958; *s* of Kenneth Alfred McPhee and Margaret Thorpe McPhee; *m* 1982, Beverley Jayne Leggatt; one *s* one *d*. *Educ:* Goffs Sch., Cheshunt. Admitted as solicitor, 1983; Clerk: Tottenham Magistrates' Court, 1977–83; Harlow, Epping and Ongar Magistrates' Court, 1983–88; Partner, Attwater & Liell, Solicitors, Harlow, Essex, 1988–2002. *Recreations:* reading, ski-ing, hill walking. *Address:* Highbury Corner Magistrates' Court, 51 Holloway Road, N7 8JA.

MACPHERSON, family name of **Barons Macpherson of Drumochter** and **Strathcarron.**

MACPHERSON OF DRUMOCHTER, 2nd Baron *cr* 1951; **(James) Gordon Macpherson;** Chairman and Managing Director of Macpherson, Train & Co. Ltd, and Subsidiary and Associated Companies, since 1964; Chairman, A. J. Macpherson & Co. Ltd (Bankers), since 1973; founder Chairman, Castle Dairies (Caerphilly) Ltd; *b* 22 Jan. 1924; *s* of 1st Baron Macpherson of Drumochter and Lucy Lady Macpherson of Drumochter (*d* 1984); *S* father, 1965; *m* 1st, 1947, Dorothy Ruth Coulter (*d* 1974); two *d* (one *s* decd); 2nd, 1975, Catherine, *d* of Dr C. D. MacCarthy; one *s* two *d*. *Educ:* Loretto; Wells House, Malvern. Served War of 1939–45, with RAF; 1939–45 Campaign medal, Burma Star, Pacific Star, Defence Medal, Victory Medal. Founder Chm. and Patron, British Importers Confedn, 1968–72. Member: Council, London Chamber of Commerce, 1958–73 (Gen. Purposes Cttee, 1959–72); East European Trade Council, 1969–71; PLA, 1973–76; Exec. Cttee, W India Cttee, 1959–83 (Dep. Chm. and Treasurer, 1971, Chm. 1973–75); Highland Soc. of London, 1975–. Freeman of City of London, 1969; Mem., Butchers' Co., 1969–. Governor, Brentwood Sch. JP Essex, 1961–76; Dep. Chm., Brentwood Bench, 1972–76; Mem. Essex Magistrates Court Cttee, 1974–76. Hon. Game Warden for Sudan, 1974; Chief of Scottish Clans Assoc. of London, 1972–74; Member: Macpherson Clan Assoc. (Chm., 1963–64); Sen. Golfers' Soc., 1981–91. Life Managing Governor, Royal Scottish Corp., 1975–. Founder Mem., WWF, 1961. FRSA 1971; FRES 1940; FZS 1965. *Recreations:* shooting, fishing, golf, bridge. *Heir: s* Hon. James Anthony Macpherson, *b* 27 Feb. 1979. *Address:* Kyllachy, Tomatin, Inverness-shire IV13 7YA. *T:* (01808) 511212. *Clubs:* Boodle's, Shikar; Royal and Ancient (St Andrews); Thorndon Park Golf (capt. 1962–63); Hartswood Golf (Founder Pres., 1970–74).

MACPHERSON, (Agnes Lawrie Addie) Shonaig, (Mrs S. Cairns), CBE 2006; FRSE; Chairman: Scottish Council for Development and Industry, since 2004; National Trust for Scotland, since 2005; *b* 29 Sept. 1958; *d* of Harry Dempster Baird Macpherson and Margaret Douglas McClure; *m* 2002, Scott Cairns; two *s* by Roger Brown. *Educ:* Univ. of Sheffield (LLB Hons); Coll. of Law, Chester. Admitted solicitor: England and Wales (Dist.), 1984; Scotland, 1992; Solicitor: Norton Rose, 1982–85; Corporate Dept, Knapp Fisher, 1985–87; Asst Co. Sec., Storehouse plc, 1987; Hd, Legal Dept, Harrods Ltd, 1987–89; Partner, Calow Easton, 1989–91; McGrigor Donald, later McGrigors, Solicitors: Hd, IP/Technol. Team, 1991–2004; Man. Partner, Edinburgh, 1996–2001; Sen. Partner, 2001–04. Director: ITI Scotland Ltd, 2003– (Chm., 2005–); Edinburgh Internat. Conf. Centre Ltd, 2005–; Braveheart Ventures, 2005–; Braveheart Investment Gp, 2005–; Edinburgh Military Tattoo Ltd; Mem., Scottish Adv. Bd, BT plc, 2002–. Scottish Executive: non-exec. Mem., Mgt Gp, 2001–07; Culture Comr, 2004–05. Mem. Bd, SCDI, 2000–. Chm., Scottish Council Foundn, 2000–. Pres., Edinburgh Chamber of Commerce, 2002–04; Dep. Pres., British Chambers of Commerce, 2004–06. Mem. Bd, Edinburgh Internat. Film Fest., 2000–. Mem. Ct, Univ. of Edinburgh, 2001–07. Gov., Edinburgh Coll. of Art. Chm., Prince's Scottish YBT, 2007–; Trustee, Prince's Trust Scotland, 2005– (Chm., 2007). FRSE 2004; FRSA 2000. DUniv Glasgow, 2007. *Recreations:* theatre, golf, film, walking, 20th century literature. *Address:* Lochcote, Linlithgow, W Lothian EH49 6QE. *Fax:* (01506) 655231; *e-mail:* shonaigm@btconnect.com.

McPHERSON, Prof. Andrew Francis; Professor of Sociology, 1989–96, now Emeritus, and Director, Centre for Educational Sociology, 1972–96, University of Edinburgh; *b* 6 July 1942; *m* 1st, 1965, Eldwyth Mary Boyle (*d* 2000); one *s* one *d*; 2nd, 1989, Alison Jean Elphinstone Edward or Arnott (*d* 2002). *Educ:* Ripon Grammar Sch.; The Queen's Coll., Oxford (BA Hist.). DPSA; FEIS; FSCRE; FRSE. Lectr in Sociology, Univ. of Glasgow, 1965; University of Edinburgh: Res. Fellow in Education, 1968; Lectr in Sociology, 1973; Sen. Lectr, 1978; Reader, 1983. FBA 1993. *Publications:* (with G. Neave) The Scottish Sixth, 1976; (with L. Gow) Tell Them from Me, 1980; (jtly) Reconstructions of Secondary Education, 1983; (with C. Raab) Governing Education, 1988; academic articles on history and sociology of education. *Recreations:* family, music, sport. *Address:* c/o Centre for Educational Sociology, School of Education, University of Edinburgh, St John's Land, Holyrood Road, Edinburgh EH8 8AQ.

McPHERSON, Ann, CBE 2000; FRCP, FRCGP; Principal in General Practice, Oxford, 1979–2008; Fellow, Green Templeton (formerly Green) College, Oxford, since 2000; *b* 22 June 1945; *d* of late Max Egelnick and of Sadie Egelnick; *m* 1968, Prof. Klim McPherson; one *s* two *d*. *Educ:* Copthall Co. Grammar Sch.; St George's Hosp. Med. Sch., London (MB BS 1968); DCH 1972; MRCGP (with dist.) 1978, FRCGP 1993; FRCP 2001. Pt-time trng posts in paediatrics and gen. practice, London, Harvard and Oxford, 1968–76; Department of Primary Care, Oxford University: pt time Lectr, 2001–; Med. Dir, DIPEx Res. Gp of patients' experiences of health and illness, 2001–. Active in res. in women's health, teenage health and patients' experiences of illness. Co-Founder: www.dipex.org; www.youthhealthtalk.org; www.teenagehealthfreak.org. *Publications:* (with A. Anderson) Women's Problems in General Practice, 1983; (jtly) Miscarriage, 1984, 2nd edn 1990; Cervical Screening: a practical guide, 1985, 2nd edn (jtly) 1992; Fresher Pressure: how to survive as a student, 1994; (ed with D. Waller) Women's Health in General Practice, 5th edn 2003; (with N. Durham) Women's Health: by women, for women, about women, 1998; (with A. Macfarlane): Mum I Feel Funny, 1982; Diary of a Teenage Health Freak, 1987, 3rd edn 2002; I'm a Health Freak Too, 1989, 3rd edn as The Diary of the Other Health Freak, 2002; Me and My Mates, 1991; The Virgin Now Boarding, 1992; Adolescents: the Agony, the Ecstacy, the Answers: a book for parents, 1999; Healthcare of Young People: promotion in primary care, 2002; Sex: the facts, 2003; Drugs: the facts, 2003; Bullying: the facts, 2004; Relationships: the facts, 2004; The Truth: a teenager's survival guide, 2007. *Recreations:* swimming, playing tennis, reading, walking, chatting. *Address:* 25 Norham Road, Oxford OX2 6SF. *T:* (01865) 558743, *T:* (office) (01865) 240501.

MACPHERSON, Ewen Cameron Stewart; Chief Executive, 3i Group plc, 1992–97 (Director, 1989–97); *b* 19 Jan. 1942; *s* of late G. P. S. Macpherson and Elizabeth Margaret Cameron (*née* Smail); *m* 1982, Hon. Laura Anne Baring, *d* of 5th Baron Northbrook; two *s*. *Educ:* Fettes Coll., Edinburgh; Queens' Coll., Cambridge (MA; Hon. Fellow, 1996); London Business Sch. (MSc; Alumni Achievement Award, 1997). Rep., Massey-Ferguson (Export) Ltd, 1964–68; various appointments, ICFC, 1970–82; 3i Group plc and subsidiaries: Dir, City Office, 1982–90; Mem., Exec. Cttee, 1985–97; Man. Dir, Finance & Planning, 1990–92. Non-executive Director: M&G Group, 1996–99; Scottish Power, 1996–2003; Foreign & Colonial Investment Trust, 1997–2008; Booker, 1998–2000; Law Debenture Corp., 1998–2001; Glynwed Internat., 1998–2000 (Chm., 1998–2000); Pantheon Internat. Participations, 1998–2004; Sussex Place Investment Mgt, 1999–2002; Wm Grant & Sons Ltd, 2005– (Chm. Audit Cttee); Chm., Black Rock New Energy Investment Trust (formerly Merrill Lynch New Energy Technology) plc, 2000–. Indep. Trustee, Glaxo-Wellcome Pension Fund, 1997–2005 (Chm., 2000–05). Governor, NIESR, 1993–. Trustee, Develt Trust, Nat. Hist. Mus., 1998–2000. *Recreations:* gardening, sailing, classic cars. *Address:* Aston Sandford, Bucks HP17 8LP. *T:* (01844) 291335. *Clubs:* Caledonian, City of London; Royal Lymington Yacht.

McPHERSON, Graeme Paul; QC 2008; barrister; *b* Dartford, 23 Sept. 1970; *s* of Ian Bernard McPherson and Maureen Ethel McPherson (*née* Larkins); *m* 2002, Mary Seanin Gilmore; one *d*. *Educ:* Canford Sch.; Emmanuel Coll., Cambridge (BA Hons 1992). Called to the Bar, Gray's Inn, 1993; in practice as barrister specialising in indemnity and sport. Granted permit to train racehorses, 2006. *Publication:* (ed) Jackson and Powell on Professional Indemnity, 5th edn 2002, 6th edn 2007. *Recreations:* training racehorses, dreaming of winners. *Address:* 4 New Square, Lincoln's Inn, WC2A 3RJ. *T:* (020) 7822 2000, *Fax:* (020) 7822 2001; *e-mail:* g.mcpherson@4newsquare.com.

McPHERSON, James Alexander Strachan, CBE 1982; JP; FSA (Scot.); Lord-Lieutenant of Banffshire (formerly Grampian Region (Banffshire)), 1987–2002; Solicitor, since 1954; *b* 20 Nov. 1927; *s* of Peter John McPherson and Jean Geddie Strachan; *m* 1960, Helen Marjorie Perks, MA; one *s* one *d*. *Educ:* Banff Academy; Aberdeen Univ. MA, BL, LLB. National Service, 1952–54; commissioned RA. Solicitor; Partner, Alexander George & Co., Macduff, 1954–95 (Senior Partner, 1986–95; Consultant, 1995–2000). Macduff Town Council: Mem., 1958–75; Treasurer, 1965–72; (last) Provost, 1972–75; Banff County Council: Mem., 1958–75; Chm., Educn Cttee, 1967–70; Chm., Management and Finance Cttee, 1970–75; (last) Convener, County Council, 1970–75; Member: Assoc. of County Councils for Scotland, 1965–75; COSLA, 1974–86; Grampian Regional Council, 1974–90 (Chm., Public Protection Cttee, 1974–86); Police Adv. Bd for Scotland, 1974–86. Mem., Scottish Solicitors Discipline Tribunal, 1990–95; Pres., Banffshire Soc. of Solicitors, 1976–79. Former mem., numerous Scottish Cttees and Boards. Vice-Pres., Highland RFCA (formerly TAVRA), 1987–2002. Director: Banffshire Partnership, 2003–; NE Scotland Preservation Trust, 2003–; Deveron Care Services, 2003–07. Governor, Scottish Police Coll., 1974–86. Mem. Court, Aberdeen Univ., 1993–97. Elder, and Free Will Offering Treas., Macduff Parish Church. Chairman: Banff and Buchan JP Adv. Cttee, 1987–98; Aberdeenshire JP Adv. Cttee, 1998–2002; Hon. Sheriff, Grampian Highland and Islands at Banff, 1972–. JP Banff and Buchan, subseq. Aberdeenshire, 1974. *Recreations:* sailing, swimming, reading, local history. *Address:* Dun Alastair, Macduff, Banffshire AB44 1XD. *T:* (home) (01261) 832377; (office) (01261) 832201. *Clubs:* Royal Northern and University (Aberdeen); Banff Town and County.

McPHERSON, Katherine; Head of Business Development, Europe, Herbert Smith, 2005–07 (Head of Business Development, Corporate, 2004–05); Member, Archbishops' Council, since 2003; *b* 23 May 1964; *d* of Ezra Balaraj and Rebecca Balaraj (*née* Jacobs); *m* 1997, Alasdair McPherson; twin *d*. *Educ:* Nat. Univ. of Singapore (BA); Univ. of Kent, Canterbury (MBA). Ernst & Young: Project Manager, 1987–88, Mktg Manager, 1988–90, Exec. Consultant, 1990–92, Mgt Consultants, Singapore; Sen. Manager, Nat. Sales and Mktg, UK, 1992–95; Hd of Sales and Mktg, Media and Resources Office, 1996–98; Nat. Hd of Sales and Mktg, Technol., Communications and Entertainment, 1998–99; Project Dir, BBC, 1999 (on secondment); Man. Consultant, Cap Gemini Ernst & Young, 1999–2001; Business Develt Manager, 2001–02, Ops Dir, 2002, Lambeth, Lewisham and Southwark YMCA; Dir of Business Develt and Marketing, Europe, Middle East and Africa, White & Case, 2002–04. Church of England: Member: HR Panel, Archbishops' Council, 2003–; Ethical Investment Adv. Gp, 2004; Dir, Central Bd of Finance, 2003–; Mem., Gen. Synod, 2003–. Mem., PCC, St John's Ch, Blackheath, 2006–. *Recreations:* reading, cooking, music, gardening. *Address:* *e-mail:* mcpherson.katherine@gmail.com.

MACPHERSON, Mary Basil Hamilton; *see* McAnally, M. B. H.

MACPHERSON, Nicholas Ian; Permanent Secretary, HM Treasury, since 2005; *b* 14 July 1959; *s* of Ewen Macpherson and Nicolette Macpherson (*née* Van der Bijl); *m* 1983, Suky Jane Appleby; two *s*. *Educ:* Eton Coll.; Balliol Coll., Oxford; University Coll. London. Economist: CBI, 1982–83; Peat Marwick and Mitchell, 1983–85; joined HM Treasury, 1985; Principal Private Sec. to Chancellor of the Exchequer, 1993–97; Head of Work Incentives Policy, 1997–98; Dep. Dir, then Dir, (Welfare Reform), Budget and Public Finances, 1998–2001; Man. Dir, Public Services, 2001–04, Budget and Public Finances, 2004–05. Mem., Civil Service Mgt Bd, 2001–04; non-exec. Dir, HM Revenue and Customs, 2005–07. Vis. Fellow, Nuffield Coll., Oxford, 2007–. *Address:* HM Treasury, 1 Horse Guards Road, SW1A 2HQ. *T:* (020) 7270 4360.

M'PHERSON, Prof. Philip Keith, CEng, FIET; Principal, Value Measurement Practice Ltd; *b* 10 March 1927; *s* of Ven. Kenneth M'Pherson and Dulce M'Pherson; *m* 1975, Rosalie Margaret, *d* of Richard and Mary Fowler. *Educ:* Marlborough Coll.; Royal Naval Engineering Coll.; Royal Naval Coll., Greenwich; Massachusetts Inst. of Technology (SM); MA Oxon. Engineer Officer, Royal Navy, 1948–59; research in Admiralty Gunnery Estabt, 1955–59, retired as Lt-Comdr, 1959. Head, Dynamics Gp, Atomic Energy Estabt, UKAEA, 1959–65, SPSO, 1963; Fellow of St John's Coll., Oxford, 1965–67; Prof. of Systems Sci., later Systems Engrg and Management, 1967–87, and Pro-Vice-Chancellor, 1982–87, City Univ. Vis. Scholar, Internat. Inst. of Applied Systems Analysis, Austria, 1976–77; Adjunct Prof., Xian Jiaotong Univ., China, 1980–84; Visiting Professor: City Univ., 1987; RCMS, 1990. Man. Dir, MacPherson Systems Ltd, 1984–92. Member: Executive Cttee, UK Automation Council, 1964–68; SRC Control Engrg Cttee, 1970–75; Chairman: IMechE Automatic Control Gp, 1967–69; IEE Systems Engrg Gp Cttee, 1966–69; IEE Control and Automation Div., 1967–69; IEE Systems Engrg Cttee, 1984–90; Soc. for General Systems Research (UK), 1973–76. Archbishops' Commn on Rural Areas, 1988–89. Freeman, City of London, 1985; Liveryman, Engineers' Co., 1986. *Publications:* many papers in the scientific literature. *Recreations:* walking, singing, making things. *Clubs:* City Livery, Royal Over-Seas League.

MACPHERSON of Biallid, Sir (Ronald) Thomas (Stewart), (Tommy), Kt 1992; CBE (mil.) 1968; MC 1943, Bars 1944 and 1945; TD 1960; DL; Chairman: Boustead plc, since 1986; Annington Holdings PLC, since 1996; *b* 4 Oct. 1920; 5th *s* of Sir Thomas Stewart Macpherson, CIE, LLD, and Lady (Helen) Macpherson (*née* Cameron); *m* 1953, Jean Henrietta, *d* of late David Butler Wilson; two *s* one *d*. *Educ:* Cargilfield; Fettes Coll. (scholar); Trinity Coll., Oxford (1st open classical scholar; MA 1st Cl. Hons PPE). Athletics Blue and Scottish International; British Team World Student Games, Paris, 1947; represented Oxford in Rugby football and hockey, 1946–47; played Rugby for London Scottish, 1945–55; played hockey for Mid Surrey and Anglo Scots, 1956–59. Reader Middle Temple. 2nd Lieut Queen's Own Cameron Highlanders TA, 1939; Scottish

Commando, parachutist, 1940; POW, 1941–43, escaped 1943; Major 1943 (despatches). Consultant, Italo-Yugoslav Border Commn. 1946. 21 SAS TA, 1947–52; CO 1st Bn London Scottish TA, 1961–64; Col TA London Dist, 1964–67. Mem., Queen's Body Guard for Scotland (Royal Co. of Archers). Chairman: Mallinson-Denny Gp, 1981–82 (Dir, 1948–82; Man. Dir, 1967–81); Birmid Qualcast, 1982–88; Cosmopolitan Textile Co., 1983–91; Allstate Reinsurance Ltd, 1983–96; Employment Conditions Abroad Ltd, 1983–93; Webb-Bowen Internat. Ltd, 1984–94; SNTC (France), 1985–95; Owl Creek Investments plc, 1989–91; Wineworld (London) PLC, 1996–2000; Internet Network Services Ltd, 1995–99; Entuity Ltd, 2000–; Nexus Investments Ltd, 2001–; XchangePoint Ltd, 2001–05; EMAC Ltd, 2005–; Dep. Chm., Keller Group plc, 1991–99. Exec. Dir, Brooke Bond Gp plc, 1981–82; Director: Transglobe Expedition Ltd, 1976–83; Scottish Mutual Assurance Soc., 1982–91; C. H. Industrials PLC, 1983–91; NCB, 1983–86; English Architectural Glazing Ltd, 1985–99; TSB Scotland, 1986–91; Independent Insurance plc, 1987–93; Fitzwilton (UK) plc, 1990–; Soc. Générale Merchant Bank, 1991–93; Architectural Glazing (Scotland) Ltd, 1998–99; Deutsche Annington Immobilien GmbH, 2001–; UK Consultant, Sears Roebuck & Co., Chicago, 1984–98; Consultant: Bain & Co., 1987–99; Candover Investment plc, 1989–95. Member: Adv. Council, Terra Firma Capital Partners, 2001–; UK Adv. Bd, Kanbay Inc., 2006–. Founder Chm., Nat. Employment Liaison Cttee for TA and Reserves, 1986–94; Chm., ABCC, 1986–88; Pres., Eurochambres (Assoc. of European Chambers of Commerce), 1992–94, now Hon. Pres.; Vice-Pres., London Chamber of Commerce, 1985– (Chm., Council, 1980–82). Member: Council, CBI (Chm., London and SE Reg., CBI, 1975–77); Scottish Council Develt and Industry, London; Prices and Incomes Bd, 1968–69; Council, GBA, 1979–83; Council, Strathclyde Univ. Business Sch., 1982–86. Foundn Trustee, Acad. of European Law, Germany, 1994–. Chm., 1961–79, Pres., 1979–, Achilles Club; Vice-Pres., Newtonmore Camanachd Club; President: Commando Assoc., 2000–05; Friends of Scottish Rugby, 2000–; Highland Soc. of London, 2001–05; Royal Scottish Corp., 2003–. Vice Patron, POW Reserve Forces Ulysses Trust. Governor, Fettes Coll., 1984–92; Pres., London Old Fettesians, 1999–2006. Prime Warden, Co. of Dyers, 1985–86; Hon. Mem. of Court, Carpenters' Co. FRSA, FCMI. DL 1977, High Sheriff, 1983–84, Greater London. Chevalier, Légion d'Honneur, and Croix de Guerre with 2 palms and star, France; Medaglia d'Argento and Resistance Medal, Italy; Kt of St Mary of Bethlehem. *Recreations:* fishing, shooting, outdoor sport. *Address:* Craig Dhu, Newtonmore, Inverness-shire PH20 1BS. *T:* (01528) 544200, *Fax:* (01528) 544274. *Clubs:* Hurlingham, MCC; New (Edinburgh).

MACPHERSON, Shonaig; *see* Macpherson, A. L. A. S.

MACPHERSON, Prof. Stuart Gowans, OBE 2007; FRCSGlas, FRCSE, FRCS, FRCP, FRCGP; Postgraduate Dean, and Professor of Postgraduate Medicine, University of Edinburgh, since 1999; *b* 11 July 1945; *s* of John Buchanan Macpherson and Elizabeth Doris Macpherson (*née* Gowans); *m* 1970, Norma Elizabeth Carslaw; two *s* one *d. Educ:* Allan Glen's Sch., Glasgow; Univ. of Glasgow (MB ChB with Commendation 1968). FRCSGlas 1972; FRCPE 2000; FRCSE 2001; FRCS 2002; FRCGP 2005. Res. Fellow, Harvard Med. Sch., 1973–74; University of Glasgow: Sen. Lectr in Surgery, 1977–99; Associate Undergrad. Dean (Admissions), 1991–99; Associate Postgrad. Dean, 1994–99; Hon. Consultant Surgeon, Western Infirmary, Glasgow, 1977–99. *Publications:* articles on surgery, transplantation and med. educn in med. jls. *Recreations:* family, golf, travel, Isle of Arran. *Address:* 33/4 Blackford Road, Edinburgh EH9 2DT. *T:* (0131) 668 4574. *Clubs:* New (Edinburgh); Luffness New Golf; Shiskine Golf and Tennis.

MACPHERSON, Sir Thomas; *see* Macpherson, Sir R. T. S.

MACPHERSON OF CLUNY (and Blairgowrie), Sir William (Alan), Kt 1983; TD 1966; Cluny Macpherson, 27th Chief of Clan Macpherson; Judge of the High Court of Justice, Queen's Bench Division, 1983–96; *b* 1 April 1926; *s* of Brig. Alan David Macpherson, DSO, MC, RA (*d* 1969) and late Catharine Richardson Macpherson; *m* 1962, Sheila McDonald Brodie (*d* 2003); one *s* one *d* (and one *s* decd). *Educ:* Wellington Coll., Berkshire; Trinity Coll., Oxford (MA; Hon. Fellow, 1991). Called to Bar, Inner Temple, 1952; Bencher, 1978; QC 1971; a Recorder of the Crown Court, 1972–83; Presiding Judge, Northern Circuit, 1985–88; Pres., Interception of Communications Tribunal, 1990–2000; Chm., Stephen Lawrence Inquiry, 1997–99. Mem., Bar Council and Senate, 1981–83; Hon. Mem., Northern Circuit, 1987. Served, 1944–47, in Scots Guards (Capt.). Commanded (Lt-Col) 21st Special Air Service Regt (TA), 1962–65, Hon. Col, 1983–91; Mem., Queen's Body Guard for Scotland, Royal Co. of Archers, 1977–2006, Lieut 2004. Gov., Royal Scottish Corporation, 1972–96 (Vice-Pres., 1989–2005). Mem., Tay Dist Salmon Fisheries Bd, 1996–99. *Recreations:* golf, fishing, archery; Past Pres., London Scottish FC. *Heir: s* James Brodie Macpherson yr of Cluny and Blairgowrie. *Address:* Newton Castle, Blairgowrie, Perthshire PH10 6SU. *Clubs:* Caledonian, Highland Society of London (Pres., 1991–94); New (Edinburgh); Blairgowrie Golf.

MACPHIE, Maj.-Gen. Duncan Love; Executive Director, St John Ambulance, 1994–95 (Medical Director, 1993–94); *b* 15 Dec. 1930; *s* of Donald Macphie and Elizabeth Adam (*née* Gibson); *m* 1957, Isobel Mary Jenkins; one *s* two *d. Educ:* Hutchesons' Grammar Sch.; Glasgow Univ. MB ChB. Stonehouse and Hairmyres Hosps, 1957–58; commnd RAMC, 1958; RMO, 1st Bn The Royal Scots, 1958–61; GP, Glasgow, 1961–63; RMO, 3 RHA, 1963–67; CO, BMH Dharan, Nepal, 1970–72; CO, 24 Field Ambulance, 1972–75; CO, BMH Munster, 1976–78; ADMS, 4 Armd Div., 1978–80; Asst DGAMS, MoD, 1980–83; CO, Queen Elizabeth Mil. Hosp., Woolwich, 1983–85; Chief, Med. Plans Branch, SHAPE, 1985–87; Comdr Med., BAOR, 1987–90, retd. QHS 1985–90. Col Comdt, RAMC, 1990–95. Warden, St John Ophthalmic Hosp., Jerusalem, 1999. *Recreations:* gardening, Rugby, cricket, classical music, reading.

McQUAID, James, CB 1997; PhD; FREng, FIMinE; Director, Science and Technology, and Chief Scientist, Health and Safety Executive, 1996–99; *b* 5 Nov. 1939; *s* of late James and Brigid McQuaid; *m* 1968, Catherine Anne, *d* of late Dr James John Hargan and Dr Mary Helen Hargan; two *s* one *d. Educ:* Christian Brothers' Sch., Dundalk; University Coll., Dublin (BEng); Jesus Coll., Cambridge (PhD); DSc NUI 1978. MIMechE 1972; FIMinE 1986; FREng (FEng 1991). Graduate engrg apprentice, British Nylon Spinners, 1961–63; Sen. Res. Fellow 1966–68, Sen. Scientific Officer 1968–72, PSO 1972–78, Safety in Mines Res. Estabt; seconded as Safety Advr, Petrochemicals Div., ICI, 1976–77; Health and Safety Executive: Dep. Dir, Safety Engrg Lab., 1978–80, Dir, 1980–85; Res. Dir, 1985–92; Dir, Strategy and Gen. Div. and Chief Scientist, 1992–96. Mem., Envmtl Security Panel, NATO Sci. Cttee, 2005–. Chm., Electrical Equipment Certification Management Bd, 1985–92; Member: Safety in Mines Res. Adv. Bd, 1985–92; Council, Midland Inst. of Mining Engrs, 1987–98 (Vice-Pres., 1991–93, Pres., 1993–94); Council, IMinE, 1991–95; Council, Royal Acad. Engrg, 1995–98; Adv. Bd for Mech. Engrg, Univ. of Liverpool, 1987–92; Exec. Cttee, RoSPA, 1992–94; Standing Cttee on Scientific Aspects of Internat. Security, Royal Soc., 2006–; Health Protection Adv. Gp, HPA, 2006–. Mem. Court, 1985–2003, Mem. Council, 1993–2003, Vis. Prof. of Mechanical Engrg, 1996–, Univ. of Sheffield; Visiting Professor: of Sustainable Develt, Ulster Univ.,

1999–2002; of Civil Engrg, QUB, 2002–05. Pres., Sheffield Trades Hist. Soc., 1989–91. Mem., Council, S Yorks Trades Hist. Trust, 1989– (Chm., 1999–). Mem., Bd of Govs, EC Jt Res. Centre, 2001–07. FRSA 2000. Hon. DEng Sheffield, 2000. *Publications:* numerous papers in technical jls. *Recreations:* ornamental turning, model engineering, industrial archaeology. *Address:* 61 Pingle Road, Sheffield S7 2LL. *T:* (0114) 236 5349. *Club:* Athenæum.

McQUAIL, Paul Christopher; Hon. Senior Research Fellow, Constitution Unit, University College London, since 1999; consultant, various public bodies, 1994–2005; *b* 22 April 1934; *s* of Christopher McQuail and Anne (*née* Mullan); *m* 1964, Susan Adler; one *s* one *d. Educ:* St Anselm's, Birkenhead; Sidney Sussex Coll., Cambridge. Min. of Housing and Local Govt, 1957; Principal, 1962; Asst Sec., 1969; DoE, 1970; Special Asst to Permanent Sec. and Sec. of State, 1972–73; Sec., Royal Commn on the Press, 1974–77; Under Sec., DoE, 1977–88; Chief Exec., Hounslow Bor. Council, 1983–85 (on secondment); Dep. Sec., DoE, 1988–94. Member: Environment and Planning Cttee, ESRC, 1983–87; Policy Cttee, CPRE, 1995–2001; Chairman: Nat. Urban Forestry Unit, 1995–2002; Nat. Retail Planning Forum, 1995–2005; Alcohol Concern, 1996–2002. Vis. Prof., Bartlett Sch. of Architecture, 1992–2000. Trustee, Sustrans, 2002–. *Publications:* Origins of DoE, 1994; Cycling to Santiago, 1995; A View from the Bridge, 1995; (with Katy Donnelly) English Regional Government, 1996; Soviet Children's Books of the Twenties and Thirties: the Adler Collection, 2000; Unexplored Territory: elected regional assemblies in England, 2001. *Recreations:* books, hill-walking, cycling and other harmless pleasures. *Address:* 158 Peckham Rye, SE22 9QH.

McQUARRIE, Sir Albert, Kt 1987; Chairman: A. McQuarrie & Son (Great Britain) Ltd, 1946–88; Sir Albert McQuarrie & Associates Ltd, since 1988; *b* 1 Jan. 1918; *s* of Algernon Stewart McQuarrie and Alice Maud Sharman; *m* 1st, 1945, Roseleen McCaffery (*d* 1986); one *s*; 2nd, 1989, Rhoda Annie Gall. *Educ:* Highlanders Acad., Greenock; Greenock High Sch.; Royal Coll. of Science and Technology, Univ. of Strathclyde. ARCST 1939; MSE, PEng 1945. Served in HM Forces, 1939–45 (Officer in RE). Dir, Hunterston Develt Co., 1989–. Former Dean of Guild, Gourock Town Council; Chm., Fyvie/Rothienorman/ Monquhitter Community Council, 1975–79. Contested (C): Kilmarnock, 1966; Caithness and Sutherland, Oct. 1974; Banff and Buchan, 1987; Highlands and Islands, European Parly elecn, 1989. MP (C): Aberdeenshire E, 1979–83; Banff and Buchan, 1983–87. Chm., British/Gibraltar All Party Gp, 1979–87; Vice Chm., Conservative Fisheries Sub Cttee, 1979–87; Secretary: Scotch Whisky All Party Gp, 1979–87; Scottish Cons. Backbench Cttee, 1985–87; Member: Select Cttees on Scottish Affairs, 1979–83, on Agriculture, 1983–85, on Private Bill Procedure, 1987; Speaker's Panel of Chairmen, 1986–87. Mem. Council, Soc. of Engineers, 1978–87. Chm., St Georges Ltd, 2006–; Consultant, LaKOTA (EU) Internat., 2006–. Dep. Chm., Ayr Cons. Assoc., 1992–94; Hon. Pres., Banff and Buchan Cons. and Unionist Assoc., 1989–. Vice Chm., Mintlaw Community Council, 1999–2002. Pres., Gourock Horticultural Soc., 1993– (Hon. Vice-Pres., 1954–93). Vice-Pres., Gibraltar Assoc. of Europe, 1996–. Mem., Former MPs Assoc., 2005–. FRSH 1952. Freeman, City of Gibraltar, 1982. KSJ 1991; GCSJ 1999 (Grand Prior: of UK and Eire, 1999–2000; of Europe, 2000–06; Grand Councillor, 2002–06; Cross of Merit, 2000); KMLJ 2007. Granted armorial bearings, 1991. *Recreations:* golf, bridge, music, soccer, swimming, horticulture. *Address:* Kintara House, Newton Road, Mintlaw, Aberdeenshire AB42 5EF. *T:* (01771) 623955. *Clubs:* Lansdowne; Queens (San Francisco).

MacQUARRIE, (John) Kenneth; Controller, BBC Scotland, since 2004; *b* 5 June 1952; *s* of Duncan and Peggy MacQuarrie; *m* 1977, Angela Sparks; one *s* two *d. Educ:* Oban High Sch.; Univ. of Edinburgh (MA Eng. and Hist. 1973); Moray House Coll. of Educn, Edinburgh (DipEd 1974). BBC Scotland: joined as researcher, 1975; radio producer, BBC Highland, 1976–79; producer, TV, 1979–88; Head of Gaelic, 1988–92; of Gaelic and Features, 1992–97; of Broadcast, 1997–2000; of Progs, 2000–04. Board Member: Scottish Film Council, 1990–97; Gaelic Media Service, 2004–08; Vice Chm., Celtic Film and TV Assoc., 1986–93; Founder Mem., Scottish Screen Forum, 1986. *Recreations:* sailing, reading, walking. *Address:* BBC Scotland, 40 Pacific Quay, Glasgow G51 1DA. *T:* (0141) 422 6000, *Fax:* (0141) 422 7900; *e-mail:* ken.macquarrie@bbc.co.uk.

McQUATER, Ewan Alan; QC 2003; *b* 30 Oct. 1962; *s* of Angus and Doreen McQuater; *m* 1999, Caroline Hudson; two *s. Educ:* Robinson Coll., Cambridge (MA 1st cl. Hons Law 1984). Called to the Bar, Middle Temple, 1985; barrister practising in commercial law, 1986–. Asst Ed., Encyclopaedia of Banking Law, 1985–2005. *Recreations:* Rugby, blues piano. *Address:* 3 Verulam Buildings, Gray's Inn, WC1R 5NT. *T:* (020) 7831 8441, *Fax:* (020) 7831 8479; *e-mail:* emcquater@3vb.com. *Club:* Belsize Park Rugby Football.

McQUAY, Prof. Henry John, DM; FRCA, FRCPE; Nuffield Professor of Clinical Anaesthetics, University of Oxford, since 2007; Fellow, Balliol College, Oxford, since 1987; *b* 16 Sept. 1948; *s* of T. A. I. and M. D. McQuay; *m* 1st, 1971, Meryl Rhys Jones (marr. diss. 2001); two *d*; 2nd, 2002, Maureen Richfield. *Educ:* Sedbergh Sch.; Balliol Coll., Oxford (MA, BM BCl 1974; DM 1985). FRCA 1979; FRCPE 2002. Clin. Reader in Pain Relief, 1985–98, Prof. of Pain Relief, 1998–2007, Oxford Pain Relief Unit, Nuffield Dept of Anaesthetics, Univ. of Oxford. Consultant, Churchill Hosp., Oxford. Dir, R&D, Oxford Regl HA, 1992–94. Praefectus, Holywell Manor, 1997–2000. *Publications:* An Evidence-based Resource for Pain Relief, 1998; Bandolier's Little Book of Pain, 2003; Bandolier's Little Book of Making Sense of The Medical Evidence, 2006; scientific papers. *Address:* Nuffield Department of Anaesthetics, John Radcliffe Hospital, Headley Way, Oxford OX3 9DU. *T:* (01865) 231515.

McQUEEN, Alexander, CBE 2003; fashion designer; *b* Lee McQueen, 17 March 1969. *Educ:* Rokeby Comp. Sch. for Boys; Central St Martin's Coll. of Art and Design (MA 1992). Worked successively for Anderson and Sheppard, and Gieves and Hawkes (Savile Row tailors), Angels and Bermans (theatrical costumiers), Koji Tatsuno (Japanese designer), Romeo Gigli (Italian designer); est. own label, 1992; men's and ladies' collections retailed worldwide; Chief Designer, Givenchy, 1996–2001; Creative Dir, Alexander McQueen label, 2001– (Gucci acquired 51%, 2001). British Designer of the Year, British Fashion Awards, 1996, (jtly) 1997, 2000, 2001. *Address:* 1st Floor, 10 Amwell Street, EC1R 1UQ.

MACQUEEN, Angus Donald; Head of Documentaries, Channel 4 Television, since 2006; *b* 20 Oct. 1958; *s* of Angus and Elizabeth Macqueen; *m* 2004, Fiona Marie Currie; one *s. Educ:* Lincoln Coll., Oxford (BA English 1980). Lectr, Univ. of Wrocław, Poland, 1981–84; British Council Lectr, Univ. of Novosibirsk, USSR, 1984–85; Director: October Films, 2000–05; Ronachan Films, 2005–06. Documentary Director: The Hand of Stalin, 1990; The Second Russian Revolution, 1991; The Death of Yugoslavia, 1995; The People's Century, 1997; Dancing for Dollars, 1998; Loving Lenin, 1998; Gulag, 1999; Vodka, 2000; Cry for Argentina, 2001; What She Wants, 2003; The Last Peasants, 2003; Cocaine, 2005. *Recreations:* being in Kintyre, Scotland, Soviet and Eastern European politics. *Address:* c/o Channel 4 Television, 124 Horseferry Road, SW1P 2TX. *T:* (020) 7306 6436; *e-mail:* amacqueen@channel4.co.uk.

MacQUEEN, Prof. Hector Lewis, PhD; FBA 2006; FRSE; Professor of Private Law, University of Edinburgh, since 1994; *b* 13 June 1956; *s* of Prof. John MacQueen, *qv*; *m* 1979, Frances Mary Young; two *s* one *d*. *Educ:* George Heriot's Sch., Edinburgh; Univ. of Edinburgh (LLB Hons; PhD). Lectr, 1979–91, Sen. Lectr, 1991–94, Reader, 1994, Univ. of Edinburgh. Visiting Professor: Cornell Univ., 1991; Utrecht Univ., 1997; Stetson UC of Law, Florida, 2007–Feb. 2009. Mem., Adv. Panel on Public Sector Information, Cabinet Office, 2004–. Mem., Co-ordinating Cttee, Eur. Civil Code Study Gp, 1999–2008. Chairman: Scottish Records Adv. Council, 2001–08; Scottish Medievalists, 2007–. Literary Dir, Stair Soc., 1999–. *Publications:* Common Law and Feudal Society in Medieval Scotland, 1993; Atlas of Scottish History to 1707, 1996; Copyright, Competition and Industrial Design, 1989, 2nd edn 1995; Studying Scots Law, 1993, 3rd edn 2004; (with J. Thomson) Contract Law in Scotland, 2000, 2nd edn 2007; Unjustified Enrichment, 2004; (jtly) Contemporary Intellectual Property: law and policy, 2007. *Recreations:* walking, sometimes with golf clubs, more often with the wife, cricket, Scotland, conviviality. *Address:* School of Law, University of Edinburgh, Old College, South Bridge, Edinburgh EH8 9YL. *T:* (0131) 650 2060; *e-mail:* hector.macqueen@ed.ac.uk. *Club:* Heriot's Former Pupils Cricket.

MacQUEEN, Prof. John; Professor of Scottish Literature and Oral Tradition, University of Edinburgh, 1972–88, now Professor Emeritus, and Hon. Fellow, Faculty of Arts, 1993; *b* 13 Feb. 1929; *s* of William L. and Grace P. MacQueen; *m* 1953, Winifred W. McWalter; three *s*. *Educ:* Hutchesons' Boys' Grammar Sch.; Glasgow Univ.; Cambridge Univ. MA English Lang. and Lit., Greek, Glasgow; BA, MA Archaeology and Anthropology, Section B, Cambridge. RAF, 1954–56 (Flying Officer). Asst Prof. of English, Washington Univ., Missouri, 1956–59; University of Edinburgh: Lectr in Medieval English and Scottish Literature, 1959–63; Masson Prof. of Medieval and Renaissance Literature, 1963–72; Dir, Sch. of Scottish Studies, 1969–88; Endowment Fellow, 1988–92. Barclay Acheson Vis. Prof. of Internat. Relations, Macalester Coll., Minnesota, 1967; Vis. Prof. in Medieval Studies, Australian Nat. Univ., 1971; Winegard Vis. Prof., Univ. of Guelph, Ont, 1981. Chairman: British Branch, Internat. Assoc. of Sound Archives, 1978–80; Exec. Cttee, Scottish Nat. Dictionary Assoc., 1978–87; Scottish Dictionary Jt Council, 1988–92; Pres., Scottish Text Soc., 1989–92; Mem., Scottish Film Council, 1981–92 (Chm., Archive Cttee, 1980–92). FRSE 1992; FRAS 2004. Hon. DLitt NUI, 1985. Fletcher of Saltoun Award, 1990. *Publications:* St Nynia, 1961, 3rd edn 2005; (with T. Scott) The Oxford Book of Scottish Verse, 1966; Robert Henryson, 1967; Ballattis of Luve, 1970; Allegory, 1970; (ed with Winifred MacQueen) A Choice of Scottish Verse, 1470–1570, 1972; Progress and Poetry, 1982; Numerology, 1985; The Rise of the Historical Novel, 1989; (ed with Winifred MacQueen) Scotichronicon, Bks III and IV, 1989, Bks I and II, 1993, Bk V, 1995; (ed) Humanism in Renaissance Scotland, 1990; Place names of the Rhinns of Galloway and Luce Valley, 2002; Complete and Full with Numbers, 2006; (ed with Winifred MacQueen) Latin Poems of Archibald Pitcairne, 2008; Placenames of the Moors and Machars, 2008; articles and reviews in learned jls. *Recreations:* music, walking, astronomy, archaeology. *Address:* Slewdonan, Damnaglaur, Drummore, Stranraer DG9 9QN. *T:* (01776) 840637.
See also Prof. H. L. MacQueen.

McQUEEN, Steve Rodney, OBE 2002; artist; *b* 1969. *Educ:* Chelsea Sch. of Art; Goldsmiths' Coll.; Tish Sch. of Arts, NY Univ. Works incorporate film, photography and sculpture. Exhibitions in Europe and USA; solo exhibition, ICA, 1999. Works include: Bear, 1993; Five Easy Pieces, 1995; Stage, 1996; Just Above My Head, 1996; Deadpan, 1997; Drumroll, 1998; Cold Breath, 2000; Queen and Country, 2007; Hunger (film), 2008. Turner Prize, 1999. *Address:* c/o Tate Gallery, Millbank, SW1P 4RG.

McQUEEN, William Robert James, CBE 2008; Deputy Chief Executive, Crown Office and Procurator Fiscal Service, Scottish Government (formerly Executive) Justice Department, 2005–08; *b* 19 April 1951; *s* of William Robert McQueen and Mary Jane McQueen (*née* Gregson); *m* 1989, Maureen Frances Hall; two *d*. *Educ:* Queen Mary Coll., London Univ. (BSc Hons Geog.); Univ. of Calif, Los Angeles (MA); Univ. of Strathclyde (MBA). Res. Officer, Local Govt Boundary Commn for Scotland, 1974–78; Scottish Office: Sen. Res. Officer, Central Res. Unit, 1979–85; Principal: Develt Dept, 1985–88; Agric. and Fisheries Dept, 1988–91; Industry Dept, 1991; Central Services, 1991–92; Hd of Mgt and Orgn Div., 1992–95; Head, Transport Div., Scottish Exec. Develt Dept, 1995–2001; Dir, Corporate Services, Crown Office and Procurator Fiscal Service, 2001–05. *Recreations:* tennis, ski-ing, cooking. *Address:* 91 Trinity Road, Edinburgh EH5 3JX. *T:* (0131) 552 0876.

MACQUIBAN, Rev. Timothy Stuart Alexander, PhD; Minister, Wesley Methodist Church, Cambridge, and Chaplain, Wesley House, Cambridge, since 2008; *b* 11 Jan. 1952; *s* of Gordon and Beryl Macquiban; *m* 1975, Angela (*née* Spencer). *Educ:* King's Sch., Chester; Jesus Coll., Cambridge (MA); Univ. of Liverpool (DipSRAA 1974); Univ. of Bristol (MA 1986); Univ. of Birmingham (PhD 2000). Asst Archivist, Wigan MBC, 1974–77; Borough Archivist, Doncaster MBC, 1977–84; Minister, Halifax Methodist Circuit, 1987–90; Tutor in Hist., Wesley Coll., Bristol, 1990–93; Dir, Wesley and Methodist Studies Centre, Westminster Coll., Oxford, 1993–2002; Principal, Sarum Coll., Salisbury, 2002–08; Sarum Canon, 2004–08. Dep. Chm., Waldensian English Church Missions Cttee, 1999–2006. British Sec., subseq. Co-Chm., Oxford Inst. for Methodist Theol Studies, 1993–; Vice President: World Methodist Historical Soc., 1996–2006; Charles Wesley Soc., 2004–. *Publications:* Methodist Prison Chaplains, 1994; Pure Universal Love, 1995; Methodism and Education, 2000; contributions to: Historical Dictionary of Methodism, 1996; A Dictionary of British and Irish Methodism, 2000; Studies in Church History, 2002, 2004; An Encyclopedia of Protestantism, 2004; Oxford DNB, 2004. *Recreations:* choral singing, collecting Wesleyana. *Address:* 37 Maids Causeway, Cambridge CB5 8DE. *T:* (01223) 361862; *e-mail:* tmacquiban@hotmail.co.uk.

McQUIGGAN, John, MBE 1955; Executive Director, United Kingdom-South Africa Trade Association Ltd, 1978–86; retired at own request from HM Diplomatic Service, 1977; *b* 24 Nov. 1922; *s* of John and Sarah Elizabeth McQuiggan; *m* 1950, Doris Elsie Hadler; three *s* one *d*. *Educ:* St Edwards Coll., Liverpool. Served War, in RAF, 1942–47 (W Africa, Europe and Malta). Joined Dominions Office, 1940; Administration Officer, British High Commission, Canberra, Australia, 1950–54; Second Sec., Pakistan, Lahore and Dacca, 1954–57; First Sec. (Inf.), Lahore, 1957–58; Dep. Dir, UK Inf. Services, Australia (Canberra and Sydney), 1958–61; Dir, Brit. Inf. Services, Eastern Nigeria (Enugu), 1961–64; Dir, Brit. Inf. Services in Uganda, and concurrently First Sec., HM Embassy, Kigali, Rwanda, 1964–69; W African Dept, FCO, 1969–73; HM Consul, Chad, 1970–73 (first London based Consul); Dep. High Comr and Counsellor (Econ. and Commercial), Lusaka, Zambia, and sometime Actg High Comr, 1973–76. Dir-Gen., Brit. Industry Cttee on South Africa, 1986. Mem., Royal African Soc. FInstD. *Publications:* A Time to Heal (for use at Eucharist services), 2001; A Time to Heal: prayers for the sick (USA), 2003; booklets and contribs to trade and economic, technical woodworking, and religious jls. *Recreations:* tennis, carpentry, craftwork. *Address:* 7 Meadowcroft, Bickley, Kent BR1 2JD. *T:* (020) 8467 0075. *Club:* Royal Over-Seas League.

McQUILLAN, Stephen; Chief Executive, National Physical Laboratory, since 2005; *b* Glasgow, 6 Aug. 1961; *s* of Joseph McQuillan and Helen McQuillan (*née* Curran); *m* 1988, Sheena Lang; one *s*. *Educ:* Univ. of Glasgow (BSc Hons Electronics and Electrical Engrg). MIET 1998; FInstP 2006; MInstKT 2008. Engr, Conoco Inc., 1982–85; Mars, Inc.: Proj. Engr, 1985–88; Sen. Mgt Scientist, 1988–90; Internat. Distributor Manager, 1990–91; European Sales Develt Manager, 1992–94; Sales Dir, W Eur., 1994–97; Business Unit Dir, Sodeco Cash Mgt Systems, 1995–97; Global Sales Dir, Marconi Instruments, 1997–98; Man. Dir, Oxford Instruments Superconductivity Ltd, 1998–2004. Member Board: Serco Science, 2005–06; Serco Defence Ops, 2007–. Member Board: Assoc. of Ind. Res. and Technol. Orgns, 2007–; Inst. of Knowledge Transfer, 2007–. FCMI 2008. *Recreations:* running, cycling, ski-ing, cinema, theatre, biographies, travel, learning, Celtic FC. *Address:* National Physical Laboratory, Hampton Road, Teddington TW11 0LW. *T:* (020) 8943 6562, *Fax:* (020) 8614 0404; *e-mail:* steve.mcquillan@npl.co.uk.

McQUILLAN, William Rodger; HM Diplomatic Service, retired; *b* 18 March 1930; *s* of late Albert McQuillan and Isabella Glen McQuillan; *m* 1970, Sheriell May Fawcett; one *s* two *d*. *Educ:* Royal High Sch., Edinburgh; Edinburgh Univ.; Yale Univ. Served RAF, 1954–57. Asst Sec., Manchester Univ. Appointments Board, 1957–65; HM Diplomatic Service, 1965–83: First Sec., CRO, 1965; Lusaka, 1968, Head of Chancery, 1969; First Sec. (Commercial), Santiago, Chile, 1970; Counsellor and HM Consul, Guatemala City, 1974; Head of Inf. Policy Dept, FCO, 1978–81; Ambassador to Iceland, 1981–83. *Address:* Lidston House, Edderton, Ross-shire IV19 1LF.

MacQUITTY, (Joanna) Jane; freelance wine writer and broadcaster, since 1982; Wine and Drink Correspondent, The Times, since 1982; *b* 14 Oct. 1953; *d* of late William Baird MacQuitty and of Betty (*née* Bastin); *m* 1988, Philip Killingworth Hedges; one *s* two *d*. *Educ:* Benenden Sch. Wine and food writer, House & Garden, 1975–82; Editor, Which Wine Guide, and Which Wine Monthly, 1982–84; Wine Editor, Good Housekeeping, 1984–2000. Wine Lectr and Judge, 1982–. Member: Circle of Wine Writers, 1977–; Soc. of Authors, 1982–. Glenfiddich Awards: Wine Writer of the Year, 1981; Whisky Writer of the Year, 1981; Special Award (for Which Wine Guide), 1983. *Publications:* Which Wine Guide, 1983, rev. edn 1984; Jane MacQuitty's Guide to Champagne and Sparkling Wines, 1986, 3rd edn 1993; Jane MacQuitty's Guide to Australian and New Zealand Wines, 1988. *Recreations:* my family, eating, drinking, talking, sleep. *Address:* c/o The Times Week-End, 1 Pennington Street, E98 1TT.

McQUOID, Judith Mary; *see* Eve, J. M.

MacRAE, Sir (Alastair) Christopher (Donald Summerhayes), KCMG 1993 (CMG 1987); HM Diplomatic Service, retired; Assistant Professor, American Graduate School of International Relations and Diplomacy, Paris; *b* 3 May 1937; *s* of Dr Alexander Murray MacRae and Dr Grace Maria Lynton Summerhayes MacRae; *m* 1963, Mette Willert; two *d*. *Educ:* Rugby; Lincoln Coll., Oxford (BA Hons English); Harvard (Henry Fellow in Internat. Relations). RN, 1956–58. CRO, 1962; 3rd, later 2nd Sec., Dar es Salaam, 1963–65; ME Centre for Arab Studies, Lebanon, 1965–67; 2nd Sec., Beirut, 1967–68; FCO, 1968–70; 1st Sec. and Head of Chancery: Baghdad, 1970–71; Brussels, 1972–76; attached Directorate-Gen. VIII, European Commn, Brussels, on secondment from FCO, 1976–78; Ambassador to Gabon, 1978–80, and to São Tomé and Príncipe (non-resident), 1979–80; Head of W Africa Dept, FCO, 1980–83, and Ambassador (non-resident) to Chad, 1982–83; Political Counsellor and Head of Chancery, Paris, 1983–87; Minister and Head of British Interests Section, Tehran, 1987; Vis. Fellow, IISS, 1987–88; Support Services Scrutiny, FCO, 1988; Under Sec. (on secondment), Cabinet Office, 1988–91; High Comr to Nigeria, and concurrently Ambassador (non-resident) to Benin, 1991–94; High Comr to Pakistan, 1994–97; Sec. Gen., Order of St John, 1997–2000. KStJ 1997. *Address:* 4 Church Street, Wye, near Ashford, Kent TN25 5BJ.

McRAE, Frances Anne, (Mrs Hamish McRae); *see* Cairncross, F. A.

McRAE, Hamish Malcolm Donald; Associate Editor, The Independent, since 1991; *b* 20 Oct. 1943; *s* of Donald and Barbara McRae (*née* Budd); *m* 1971, Frances Anne Cairncross, *qv*; two *d*. *Educ:* Fettes College; Trinity College, Dublin (BA Hons Economics and Political Science, MA). Liverpool Post, 1966–67; The Banker, 1967–72 (Asst Editor, 1969, Dep. Editor, 1971); Editor, Euromoney, 1972–74; Financial Editor, The Guardian, 1975–89; Business and City Editor, The Independent, 1989–91. Vis. Professor: UMIST, 1999–2004; Univ. of Lancaster, 2005–. Mem. Council, REconS, 2005–. Wincott Foundn financial journalist of the year, 1979; David Watt Prize, RTZ awards, 2005; Business and Finance Journalist of the Year, British Press Awards, 2006. *Publications:* (with Frances Cairncross) Capital City: London as a financial centre, 1973, 5th edn 1991; (with Frances Cairncross) The Second Great Crash, 1975; Japan's role in the emerging global securities market, 1985; The World in 2020, 1994; (with Tadashi Nakamae) Wake-up, Japan, 1999. *Recreations:* walking, ski-ing, cooking. *Address:* The Independent, 191 Marsh Wall, E14 9RS.

MACRAE, John Esmond Campbell, CMG 1986; DPhil; HM Diplomatic Service, retired; *b* 8 Dec. 1932; *s* of Col Archibald Campbell Macrae, IMS, and Euretta Margaret Skelton; *m* 1962, Anne Catherine Sarah Strain; four *s*. *Educ:* Sheikh Bagh Sch., Kashmir; Fettes Coll., Edinburgh; Christ Church Oxford (Open Scholar); Princeton, USA. DPhil, MA. Atomic Energy and Disarmament Dept, Foreign Office, 1959–60; 2nd Sec., British Embassy, Tel Aviv, 1961–64; 1st Secretary: Djakarta, 1964; Vientiane, 1964–66; FO, NE African Dept, 1966; Central Dept, 1967–69; Southern African Dept, 1970–72; UK Mission to the UN, New York (dealing with social affairs, population and outer space), 1972–75; Counsellor, Science and Technology, Paris, 1975–80; Head of Cultural Relns Dept, FCO, 1980–85; RCDS, 1985; Ambassador: to Senegal, and (non-resident) to Mali, Cape Verde, Guinea and Guinea-Bissau, 1985–90; to Mauritania (non-resident), 1986–92 and to Morocco, 1990–92. *Recreations:* music, travel, picnics in unusual places. *Address:* Les Aires, 26110 Mirabel aux Baronnies, France.

MacRAE, Kenneth Charles; His Honour Judge MacRae; a Circuit Judge, since 1990; *b* 14 March 1944; *s* of William and Ann MacRae; *m* 1981, Hilary Vivien Williams; one *d*. *Educ:* Redruth County Grammar School; Cornwall Tech. Coll.; Fitzwilliam Coll., Cambridge (BA Hons). Called to the Bar, Lincoln's Inn, 1969; a Recorder of the Crown Court, 1985. *Recreations:* gardening, walking, music. *Address:* The Crown Court, Altyre Road, Croydon CR9 5AB.

McRAE, Lindsay; *see* Duncan, L.

MACREADIE, John Lindsay; a National Officer and Senior Policy Adviser, Public and Commercial Services Union; *b* 19 Sept. 1946; *s* of John and Mary Macreadie; *m* 1967, Roisin Ann Boden; one *s* one *d*. *Educ:* Primary and Secondary State Schools, Glasgow. Civil Servant, 1964–70; a Nat. Officer, CPSA, then PCS, 1970–; Dep. Gen. Sec., CPSA, 1987–92. Mem., TUC General Council, 1987–88. *Recreations:* politics, football, cinema. *Address:* 1 The Green, Morden, Surrey SM4 4HJ. *T:* (020) 8542 5880. *Club:* William Morris Labour (Wimbledon).

MACREADY, Sir Nevil (John Wilfrid), 3rd Bt *cr* 1923; CBE 1983; Chairman, Mental Health Foundation, 1993–97; *b* 7 Sept. 1921; *s* of Lt-Gen. Sir Gordon (Nevil) Macready, 2nd Bt, KBE, CB, CMG, DSO, MC, and Elisabeth (*d* 1969), *d* of Duc de Noailles; *S* father, 1956; *m* 1949, Mary, (Emma), (*d* 2007), *d* of late Sir Donald Fergusson, GCB; one *s* three *d*. *Educ:* Cheltenham; St John's Coll., Oxford. Served in RA (Field), 1942–47 (despatches); Staff Captain, 1945. BBC European Service, 1947–50. Vice-Pres. and Gen. Manager, Mobil Oil Française, 1972–75; Man. Dir, Mobil Oil Co. Ltd, 1975–85. Pres., Inst. of Petroleum, 1980–82. Chairman: Crafts Council, 1984–91; Horseracing Adv. Council, 1986–93; Dep. Chm., British Horseracing Bd, 1993–95. Pres., Royal Warrant Holders' Assoc., 1979–80; Trustee, V&A Museum, 1985–95. *Recreations:* racing, fishing, theatre, music. *Heir:* *s* Charles Nevil Macready [*b* 19 May 1955; *m* 1st, 1981, Lorraine McAdam (marr. diss. 1994); one *s* one *d*; 2nd, 2001, Gillian Simms]. *Address:* The White House, Odiham, Hants RG29 1LG. *T:* (01256) 702976. *Clubs:* Boodle's; Jockey (Paris).

MacROBBIE, Prof. Enid Anne Campbell, FRS 1991; FRSE; Professor of Plant Biophysics, University of Cambridge, 1987–99, now Emeritus Professor; Fellow of Girton College, since 1958; *b* 5 Dec. 1931; *d* of late George MacRobbie and Agnes Kerr MacRobbie (*née* Campbell). *Educ:* Mary Erskine Sch., Edinburgh; Univ. of Edinburgh (BSc, PhD); MA, ScD Cantab. FRSE 1998. Res. Fellow, Univ. of Copenhagen, 1957–58; Cambridge University: Res. Fellow, Botany Sch., 1958–62; Demonstrator in Botany, 1962–66; Lectr in Botany, 1966–73; Reader in Plant Biophysics, 1973–87. Mem., BBSRC, 1996–99. Foreign Associate, Nat. Acad. of Scis, USA, 1999. *Publications:* papers in sci jls. *Address:* Girton College, Cambridge CB3 0JG. *T:* (01223) 338999.

McROBERT, Rosemary Dawn Teresa, OBE 1985; Deputy Director, Consumers' Association, 1980–88; *b* Maymyo, Burma, 29 Aug. 1927; *e d* of late Lt-Col Ronald McRobert, MB, ChB, FRCOG, IMS, and Julie Rees. *Educ:* privately and at Gloucestershire College of Educn. Journalist and broadcaster on consumer subjects, 1957–63; Founder editor, Home Economics, 1954–63; Chief Information Officer, Consumer Council, 1965–70; Consumer Representation Officer, Consumers' Assoc., 1971–73; Adviser on consumer affairs in DTI and Dept of Prices and Consumer Protection, 1973–74; Dir, Retail Trading Standards Assoc., 1974–80. Member Council: Inst. of Consumer Ergonomics, 1974–81; Consumers' Assoc., 1974–79; Advertising Standards Authority, 1974–80; Member: Adv. Council on Energy Conservation, 1974–82; Design Council, 1975–84; Post Office Review Cttee, 1976; Policyholders' Protection Bd, 1976–92; Nuffield Enquiry into Pharmacy Services, 1984–86; Council for Licensed Conveyancers, 1989–94; British Hallmarking Council, 1989–97. Chm., Management Cttee, Camden Consumer Aid Centres, 1977–80. Vice-Pres., Patients Assoc., 1988–95. Director: Investors Compensation Scheme, 1988–96; CSM Parliamentary Consultants, 1988–. Liveryman, Glovers' Co., 1979. *Address:* Well House, Bolton Street, Lavenham, Suffolk CO10 9RG. *Club:* Reform.

MacRORY, Avril; Chief Executive Officer, Silverapples Media, since 2001; *b* 5 April 1956; *d* of Patrick Simon MacRory and Elizabeth (*née* Flynn); *m* 1983, Val Griffin; one *s*. *Educ:* University College, Dublin (BA Hons 1978). Producer and Director, RTE, 1979; Head of Variety, RTE, 1986; Commissioning Editor, Music, Channel 4, 1988; Head of Music Progs, 1993–98, of Millennium Event Progs, 1998–2000, BBC TV. Pres., Internat. Music Zentrum, Vienna, 1992–. *Recreations:* sailing, music, reading.

MACRORY, Prof. Richard Brabazon, CBE 2000; Professor of Environmental Law, University College, London, since 1999; Barrister-at-law; *b* 30 March 1950; *s* of Sir Patrick Macrory and Lady Marjorie Elizabeth Macrory; *m* 1979, Sarah Margaret Briant; two *s*. *Educ:* Westminster Sch.; Christ Church, Oxford (BA 1972; MA 1976). Called to the Bar, Gray's Inn, 1974; Legal Advr, Friends of the Earth Ltd, 1975–78; Imperial College, London: Lectr, 1980–89; Reader in Envmtl Law, 1989–91; Denton Hall Prof. of Envmtl Law, 1991–94; Dir, Envmtl Change Unit, Univ. of Oxford, 1994–95; Prof. of Envmtl Law, Imperial Coll., London, 1995–99. Leader, Review of Regulatory Sanctions, Cabinet Office, 2005–06. Chairman: UK Envmtl Law Assoc., 1986–88 (Patron, 2007–); Steering Cttee, European Envmtl Adv. Councils, 2001–02; Hon. Standing Counsel, CPRE, 1981–92; Member: Envmtl Adv. Bd, Shanks and McKewan plc, 1989–91; UK Nat. Adv. Cttee on Eco-labelling, 1990–91; Royal Commn on Envmtl Pollution, 1991–2003; Expert Strategy Panel, Inter-Agency Cttee for Global Envmtl Change, 1995–96; Bd, Envmt Agency, 1999–2004; Gen. Electric Ecomagination Bd, 2006–. Specialist Adviser: H of L Select Cttee on EC, 1991–92, and 1996–97; H of C Select Cttee on Envmt, 1989–92, 1993–99. Hon. Chm., Merchant Ivory Prodns Ltd, 1992–2005. Hon. Pres., Nat. Soc. for Clean Air, 2004–05. Rapporteur, UK Nat. Biotechnology Conf., 1996; UK nominated expert arbitrator, Law of the Sea Convention, 1998–2003. Hon. QC 2008. Editor, Jl of Envmtl Law, 1988–2006; Legal Corresp., Ends Report, 1982–. *Publications:* Nuisance, 1982; Water Law: principles and practice, 1985; Water Act 1989, 1989; (with D. Gilbert) Pesticide Related Law, 1989; (with S. Hollins) Bibliography of Community Environmental Law, 1995; (ed) Principles of European Environmental Law, 2004; (ed) Reflections on 30 years of EU Environmental Law, 2005; Regulation, Enforcement, and Governance of Environmental Law, 2008; articles and reviews in legal and tech. jls. *Recreations:* cinema, board-games, cycling. *Address:* Crossing Farmhouse, Tackley, Oxford OX5 3AT. *T:* (01869) 331151; Brick Court Chambers, 7–8 Essex Street, WC2R 3LD. *T:* (020) 7379 3550, *Fax:* (020) 7379 3558; Faculty of Laws, University College, Bentham House, Endsleigh Gardens, WC1H 0EG. *T:* (020) 7679 1543; *e-mail:* r.macrory@ucl.ac.uk. *Club:* Athenæum.

MACROSSAN, Hon. John Murtagh, AC 1993; Chancellor, Griffith University, 1988–2000; *b* 12 March 1930; *m* 1961, Margery Newton; one *s*. *Educ:* St Columban's Coll., Brisbane; Univ. of Queensland; Univ. of Oxford. Admitted Qld Bar, 1951; QC 1967; Judge, 1980–89, Chief Justice, 1989–98, of Supreme Court, Qld. *Address:* c/o Queensland Club, Alice Street, Brisbane, Qld 4000, Australia.

MacSHANE, Rt Hon. Denis; PC 2005; PhD; MP (Lab) Rotherham, since May 1994; *b* 21 May 1948; *e s* of late Jan Matyjaszek and of Isobel MacShane; *m* 1987, Nathalie Pham (marr. diss. 2003); one *s* three *d* (and one *d* decd). *Educ:* Merton Coll., Oxford (MA); Birkbeck Coll., London. (PhD; Hon. Fellow, 2005). BBC reporter, 1969–77; Pres., NUJ, 1978–79; Policy Dir, Internat. Metalworkers Fedn, 1980–92; Dir, European Policy Inst., 1992–94. PPS, 1997–2001, Parly Under-Sec. of State, 2001–02, Minister of State, 2002–05, FCO. Vis. Parly Fellow, St Antony's Coll., Oxford, 1998–99. Mem. Council, RIIA, 1999–; Chm., Fabian Soc., 2001–02. *Publications:* Solidarity: Poland's Independent Trade Union, 1981; François Mitterand: a political Odyssey, 1982; Black Workers, Unions and the Struggle for Democracy in South Africa, 1984; International Labour and the Origins of the Cold War, 1992; Britain's Steel Industry in the 21st Century, 1996; Edward Heath, 2006. *Recreations:* walking, family, novels, poetry. *Address:* House of Commons, SW1A 0AA.

McSHARRY, Deirdre; Editor-in-Chief, Country Living, 1986–89; *b* 4 April 1932; *d* of late Dr John McSharry and Mrs Mary McSharry. *Educ:* Dominican Convent, Wicklow; Trinity Coll., Dublin. Woman's Editor, Daily Express, 1962–66; Fashion Editor, The Sun, 1966–72; Editor, Cosmopolitan, 1973–86; Consultant, Nat. Magazine Co., and Magazine Div., The Hearst Corp., 1990–95; Ed., Countryside mag., NY, 1991–92. Curated exhibitions: American Museum in Britain, Bath: Inspirations: the textile tradition, 2001; Quilt Bonanza, 2003; Victoria Art Gallery, Bath: Blue and White Show, 2008. Mem. Council and Chm. Bath Friends, 1995–2004; Trustee, 2003–05. Patron, Holburne Mus, Bath, 2007–08. Contrib., Edwardian Revival, BBC2, 2007. Magazine Editor of the Year, PPA, 1981, 1987; Mark Boxer Award, British Soc. of Magazine Editors, 1992. *Publication:* contrib. Selvedge. *Recreation:* the arts, textiles, costume and fashion. *Address:* 8 Prior Park Buildings, Bath BA2 4NP.

MacSHARRY, Raymond; Chairman, London City Airport, 1996–2006; Director, Ryanair, 1993–2006 (Chairman, 1993–96); *b* Sligo, April 1938; *m* Elaine Neilan; three *s* three *d*. *Educ:* St Vincent's Nat. Sch., Sligo; Ballincutranta Nat. Sch., Beltra, Co. Sligo; Marist Brothers Nat. Sch., Sligo; Summerhill Coll., Sligo. TD (FF) for Sligo Leitrim, 1969–89; opposition front bench spokesman on Office of Public Works, 1973–75; Mem., Cttee of Public Accts, 1969–77; Minister of State, Dept of Finance and the Public Service, 1977–79; Minister of Agriculture, 1979–81; opposition spokesman on Agric., 1981–82; Tánaiste and Minister for Finance, 1982; Minister for Finance and the Public Service, 1987–88. Mem., Commn of EC, 1989–92. Formerly Member: New Ireland Forum; Nat. Exec., Fianna Fáil Party (later, also an Hon. Treas.). Mem. for Connaught/Ulster, Europ. Parlt, 1984–87; Mem., Council of Ministers, 1984–87. Governor, Europ. Investment Bank, 1982. Director: Jefferson Smurfit Gp, 1993–2002; Bank of Ireland, 1993–2005; Chairman: Telecom Éireann, 1999–2001; Irish Forestry Board, 1999–2002. Councillor, Sligo CC, 1967–78; Chairman: Bd of Management, Sligo Reg. Tech. Coll., 1970–78; Sligo Hosp. Exec. Cttee, 1972–78; NW Health Bd, 1974–75 (Mem., 1971–78); Member: Sligo Corp., 1967–78 (Alderman, 1974–78); Town of Sligo Vocational Educn Cttee, 1967–78; Bd of Management, Sligo-Leitrim Reg. Develt Org., 1973–78; Sligo Jun. Chamber, 1965– (PP). Freeman, Borough of Sligo, 1993. Hon. Dr NUI, 1994; Hon. DEconSc Limerick, 1994. Grand Cross, Order of Leopold II (Belgium), 1993; Alcantara, Pearse Road, Sligo, Eire.

McSHERRY, (John) Craig (Cunningham); Sheriff at Dunfermline, since 2006; *b* 21 Oct. 1949; *s* of John and Janet McSherry; *m* 1972, Elaine Beattie; two *s*. *Educ:* Ardrossan Acad.; Univ. of Glasgow (LLB Hons 1972). Lead singer, The Wilderness, 1967–68. Solicitor, 1972–92; Sen. Partner, McSherry Halliday, Solicitors, 1983–92; Advocate, 1993; Temp. Sheriff, 1997–99; Pt-time Sheriff, 2000–03; Immigration Appeals Adjudicator (pt-time), 2001–03; All Scotland Floating Sheriff, Edinburgh, 2003–05. Mem. Council, Law Soc. of Scotland, 1982–85. *Recreations:* country pursuits, ski-ing, music (classical, rock, folk), bridge, golf. *Address:* 2 Heriot Row, Edinburgh EH3 6HU. *T:* (0131) 556 8289; *e-mail:* jccmcs@hotmail.com. *Club:* New (Edinburgh).

MacSWEEN, Sir Roderick (Norman McIver), Kt 2000; MD; FRCPE, FRCPGlas, FRCPath, FMedSci; FIBiol; FRSE; Professor of Pathology, University of Glasgow, 1984–99, now Emeritus; President, Royal College of Pathologists, 1996–99; *b* 2 Feb. 1935; *s* of Murdo MacLeod MacSween and Christina (*née* McIver); *m* 1961, Dr Marjory Pentland Brown; one *s* one *d*. *Educ:* Inverness Royal Acad.; Glasgow Univ. (BSc Hons 1956; MD 1973). FRCPGlas 1972; FRCPE 1974; FRCPath 1976; FIBiol 1987; FRSE 1985. University of Glasgow: Lectr, then Sen. Lectr in Pathology, 1965–78; Titular Prof. in Pathology, 1978–84. Instructor in Pathology, Univ. of Colo, Denver, 1968–69; Otago Savings Bank Vis. Prof., Univ. of Otago, NZ, 1983. Ed., Histopathology, 1984–95. Mem., GMC, 2000–04. Chm., Unrelated Live Transplant Regulatory Authy, 2000–06. President: Royal Medico-Chirurgical Soc. of Glasgow, 1978–79; British Div., Internat. Acad. of Pathology, 1989–91; Chm., Acad. of Med. Royal Colls, 1998–2000. Hon. Librarian, RCPSG, 1985–95. Chm., Tenovus Scotland, 2006–. Founder FMedSci 1998. Hon. Fellow, Coll. of Pathologists of S Africa, 1998; Hon. FRCP 1999; Hon. FRCS 2000; Hon. FRCSE 2000. Hon. DSc Glasgow, 2007. *Publications:* (ed jtly) Pathology of the Liver, 1979, 4th edn 2002; (ed with P. P. Anthony) Recent Advances in Histopathology Nos 11–16, 1992–94; (ed with K. Whaley) Muir's Textbook of Pathology, 13th edn 1992. *Recreations:* golf, gardening, hill-walking… and more golf! *Address:* 32 Calderwood Road, Newlands, Glasgow G43 2RU. *Clubs:* Athenæum; Glasgow Golf, Dunaverty Golf (Past Capt.), Machrihanish Golf (Past Capt.).

MACTAGGART, Fiona; MP (Lab) Slough, since 1997; *b* 12 Sept. 1953; *d* of Sir Ian Auld Mactaggart, 3rd Bt and Rosemary, *d* of Sir Herbert Williams, 1st Bt, MP. *Educ:* Cheltenham Ladies' Coll.; King's Coll., London (BA Hons); Inst. of Educn, London (MA). Gen. Sec., London Students' Organisation, 1977–78; Vice-Pres., 1978–80, Nat. Sec., 1980–81, NUS; Gen. Sec., Jt Council for Welfare of Immigrants, 1982–86. Mem. (Lab) Wandsworth BC, 1986–90 (Leader of the Opposition, 1988–90). Teacher, Lyndhurst Sch., Camberwell, 1988–92; Lectr, Inst. of Educn, 1992–97. PPS to Sec. of State for Culture, Media and Sport, 1997–2001; Parly Under-Sec. of State, Home Office, 2003–06. Chm., PLP Women's Cttee, 2001–03. Chm., Liberty (NCCL), 1994–96. *Address:* House of Commons, SW1A 0AA.

MACTAGGART, Sir John (Auld), 4th Bt *cr* 1938, of King's Park, City of Glasgow; *b* 21 Jan. 1951; *s* of Sir Ian Auld Mactaggart, 3rd Bt and of Rosemary, *d* of Sir Herbert Williams, 1st Bt, MP; *S* father, 1987; *m* 1st, 1977, Patricia (marr. diss. 1990), *y d* of late Major Harry Alastair Gordon, MC; 2nd, 1991, Caroline, *y d* of Eric Williams; two *s* two *d*. *Educ:* Shrewsbury; Trinity Coll., Cambridge (MA). Chm., Western Heritable Investment Company, 1987–. *Heir:* *s* Jack Auld Mactaggart, *b* 11 Sept. 1993. *Address:* One Red Place, W1K 6PL.

See also F. Mactaggart.

MacTAGGART, Air Vice-Marshal William Keith, CBE 1976 (MBE 1956); CEng, FIMechE; FRAeS; Consultant: MPE Ltd, 1989–91 (Managing Director, 1984–89); Adwest plc, 1989–91; *b* 15 Jan. 1929; *s* of Duncan MacTaggart and Marion (*née* Keith); *m* 1st, 1949 Christina Carnegie Geddes (marr. diss. 1977); one *s* two *d*; 2nd, 1977, Barbara Smith Brown (marr. diss. 1994), *d* of Adm. Stirling P. Smith, late USN, and Mrs Smith; one step *d*; 3rd, 1995, Kathleen Mary Wilkie, *d* of William and Beatrice Booth. *Educ:* Aberdeen Grammar Sch.; Aberdeen Univ. (BScEng 1948). FIMechE 1973; FRAeS 1974. Commnd RAF, 1949; 1949–67: Engr Officer; Pilot; AWRE, Aldermaston (Montebello and Maralinga atomic trials); attended RAF Staff Coll., and Jt Services Staff Coll.; Def. Intell.; Systems Analyst, DOAE, West Byfleet, and MoD (Air); Head of Systems MDC, RAF Swanton Morley, 1968; OC RAF Newton, 1971 (Gp Captain); Dep. Comd Mech. Engr, HQ Strike Comd, 1973; Dir of Air Armament, MoD (PE), 1973 (Air Cdre); RCDS, 1977; Vice-Pres. (Air), Ordnance Bd, 1978 (Air Vice-Marshal), Pres., 1978–80. Dep. Chm., Tomash Holdings Ltd, 1980–84. FCMI (FBIM 1978). *Recreations:* music, travel. *Address:* Croft Stones, Lothmore, Helmsdale, Sutherland KW8 6HP. *T:* (01431) 821439. *Club:* Royal Air Force.

MacTHOMAS OF FINEGAND, Andrew Patrick Clayhills; 19th Chief of Clan MacThomas (Mac Thomaidh Mhor); public affairs consultant, since 2008; *b* 28 Aug. 1942; *o s* of late Captain Patrick Watt MacThomas of Finegand and Elizabeth Cadogan Fenwick MacThomas (*née* Clayhills-Henderson); *S* father, 1970; *m* 1985, Anneke Cornelia Susanna, *o d* of late Albert and of Susanna Kruyning-Van Hout; one *s* one *d*. *Educ:* St

Edward's, Oxford. FSA (Scot.) 1973. Hd, Visa (Scotland), 1975–82; Dir, Scotworld, 1982–85; Public Relations, S Africa, 1985–90; political lobbyist, 1990–97; Public Affairs Dir, Barclays PLC, 1997–2005; Develt Dir, Industry and Parliament Trust, 2005–07. Pres., Clan MacThomas Soc., 1970–; Hon. Vice-Pres., Clan Chattan Assoc., 1970–. *Publication:* History of the Clan MacThomas, 2008. *Recreations:* Clan, politics, wine and wit. *Heir:* s Thomas David Alexander MacThomas, Yr of Finegand, b 1 Jan. 1987. *Address:* c/o Barclays Bank, 22 Hide Hill, Berwick-upon-Tweed, Northumberland TD15 1AF. *Club:* Hurlingham.

MACUR, Hon. Dame Julia, DBE 2005; **Hon. Mrs Justice Macur;** a Judge of the High Court of Justice, Family Division, since 2005; Presiding Judge, Midland Circuit, since 2008; b 17 April 1957; d of Boleslaw Macur and Betsy Macur; m 1981; two s. *Educ:* Sheffield Univ. (LLB 1978). Called to the Bar, Lincoln's Inn, 1979 (Bencher, 2005); Midland and Oxford Circuit; QC 1998; a Recorder, 1999–2005. *Address:* Royal Courts of Justice, Strand, WC2A 2LL.

McVAY, Leslie Elizabeth; see Evans, L. E.

McVEIGH, Charles Senff, III; Chairman, Corporate and Investment Banking-Global Wealth Management Partnership, Citigroup (formerly Chairman, Salomon Brothers International Ltd, subseq. Salomon Smith Barney, and then Co-Chairman Schroder Salomon Smith Barney, subseq. European Investment Bank, Citigroup), since 1987; b New York, 4 July 1942; s of Charles S. McVeigh, Jr and Evelyn B. McVeigh; m 1st, 1964, Pamela Osborn (marr. diss. 1991); one s three d; 2nd, 1993, Jennifer Champneys; two s one d. *Educ:* Univ. of Virginia (BA); Long Island Univ. (MBA). Officer, Morgan Guaranty Trust Co., 1965–1971; joined Salomon Brothers, 1971: Vice-Pres. and Manager, NY Internat. Dept, 1974–75; Hd, Salomon Bros Internat., London, 1975–87; General Partner, 1977–81; Mem., European Mgt Cttee, 1981–. Non-executive Director: Savills plc, 2000–; Witan Investment Trust, 1998–2006. Mem., Fulbright Commn, 1993–2005. Member Board: LIFFE, 1983–89; London Stock Exchange, 1986–92; Clearstream (formerly CEDEL), 1994–2005; Member: City Capital Mkts Cttee, 1989–94; Legal Risk Rev. Cttee, 1990–92. *Recreations:* field sports, gardening. *Address:* Citigroup, Citigroup Centre, 33 Canada Square, Canary Wharf, E14 5LB. *Clubs:* White's, Beefsteak; The Brook, Anglers' (NYC).

McVEIGH, (Robert) Desmond; Chairman: Westwind Partners, since 2004; N. T. Energy Inc., since 2005; Advisory Board, Oriental Minerals Inc., since 2007; b 10 Jan. 1939; s of late Rev. Robert Walker McVeigh and Evelyn Mary (née McCoubrey); m 1966, Gillian Ann Nash; two s one d. *Educ:* Methodist Coll., Belfast; QUB (LLB Hons); Univ. of Michigan (LLM). Citibank, London, 1967–71; GATX, London, 1971–72; Citibank, 1972–74; First Nat. Bank, Dallas, 1974–77; Saudi Internat. Bank, London, 1977–85; Lloyds Merchant Bank, 1985–87; independent consultant, 1987–92; Chief Exec., IDB for NI, 1993–95; Man. Dir, Longdown Financial Services Ltd, 1995–2002; Exec. Chm., Asia Broadbent Inc., 2001–03; Dep. Chm., Richard Kleinwort Consultancy Group, 2002–07; non-exec. Dir, Viking Internat. Petroleum plc, 2003–05. Vis. Prof. of Finance and Industrial Relations, Warsaw Univ., 1994–. CCMI (CIMgt 1994). *Recreations:* golf, tennis, music. *Address:* Seaside Plaza, Avenue des Ligures, MC 98000, Monaco; *e-mail:* dmlfcl@gmail.com. *Club:* Automobile de Monaco.

MacVICAR, Rev. Kenneth, MBE (mil.) 1968; DFC 1944; Extra Chaplain to the Queen in Scotland, since 1991 (Chaplain in Ordinary, 1974–91); Minister of Kenmore and Lawers, Perthshire, 1950–90; b 25 Aug. 1921; s of Rev. Angus John MacVicar, Southend, Kintyre; m 1946, Isobel Guild McKay; three s one d. *Educ:* Campbeltown Grammar Sch.; Edinburgh Univ.; St Andrews Univ. (MA); St Mary's Coll., St Andrews. Mem., Edinburgh Univ. Air Squadron, 1941; joined RAF, 1941: Pilot, 28 Sqdn, RAF, 1942–45, Flt Comdr, 1944–45 (despatches, 1945). Chaplain, Scottish Horse and Fife and Forfar Yeomanry/Scottish Horse, TA, 1953–65. Convener, Church of Scotland Cttee on Chaplains to HM Forces, 1968–73. Clerk to Presbytery of Dunkeld, 1955. District Councillor, 1951–74. *Recreation:* golf. *Address:* Illeray, Kenmore, Aberfeldy, Perthshire PH15 2HE. *T:* (01887) 830514.

McVICAR, Dr Malcolm Thomas; Vice-Chancellor, University of Central Lancashire, since 1998; b 16 June 1946; s of Thomas Frederick McVicar and Rose Edith McVicar; two s; m 2002, Alison Smith; two step s. *Educ:* Univ. of Exeter (BA, MA); Univ. of London (PGCE 1975; DPA 1978; PhD 1989). Portsmouth Polytechnic: Prin. Lectr, then Hd of Dept; Dean, 1989–92; Pro-Vice-Chancellor, Univ. of Portsmouth, 1993–98. *Recreations:* ski-ing, sailing. *Address:* University of Central Lancashire, Preston, Lancs PR1 2HE. *T:* (01772) 892501; *e-mail:* mmcvicar@uclan.ac.uk.

MACVICAR, Neil; QC (Scot.) 1960; MA, LLB; Sheriff of Lothian and Borders (formerly the Lothians and Peebles), at Edinburgh, 1968–85; b 16 May 1920; s of late Neil Macvicar, WS; m 1949, Maria, d of Count Spiridon Bulgari, Corfu; one s two d. *Educ:* Loretto Sch.; Oriel Coll., Oxford; Edinburgh Univ. Served RA, 1940–45. Called to Scottish Bar, 1948. Chm., Med. Appeal Tribunals, 1961–67 and 1987–94. Chancellor, Dio. of Edinburgh, 1961–74. Chm. of Govs, Dean Orphanage and Cauvin's Trust, 1967–85. *Publications:* A Heart's Odyssey (memoirs), 1991; Grace Notes: variations on a Greek theme, 1995. *Address:* 25 Blackford Road, Edinburgh EH9 2DT. *T:* (0131) 667 2362; Kapoutsi, Gastouri, Corfu, Greece. *T:* (661) 56110. *Clubs:* New (Edinburgh); Anagnostiki Etairia (Corfu).

McVIE, Prof. (John) Gordon, MD; Director, Cancer Intelligence Ltd, since 2003; Senior Consultant, European Institute of Oncology, Milan, since 2003; Consultant to Director, International Agency for Research on Cancer, World Health Organisation, Lyon, since 2006; b 13 Jan. 1945; s of John McVie and Lindsaye Woodburn McVie (née Mair); m 1998, Claudia Joan Burke; three s by previous marriage. *Educ:* Royal High Sch., Edinburgh; Univ. of Edinburgh (BSc Hons; MB, ChB; MD 1978) MRCP 1971. Edinburgh University: MRC Fellow, 1970–71; Lectr in Therapeutics, 1971–76; CRC Sen. Lectr in Oncology, Glasgow Univ., 1976–80; Netherlands Cancer Institute, Amsterdam: Hd, Clinical Res. Unit, 1980–84; Clinical Res. Dir, 1984–89; Scientific Dir, CRC, 1989–96; Dir Gen., CRC, 1996–2002, Jt Dir Gen., Cancer Res. UK, 2002. Visiting Professor: BPMF, London Univ., 1990–96; Univ. of Glasgow, 1996–; Univ. of Wales, Cardiff, 2003–. Member: Council, Scottish Action for Smoking and Health, 1975–80; Royal College of Physicians: Collegiate Mems Cttee, 1975–80; Standing Cttee on Smoking, 1976–80; MRC Cancer Therapy Cttee UK, 1984–92; Bd of Dirs, Netherlands Cancer Inst., 1984–89; Permanent Cttee on Oncology, Min. of Health, Netherlands, 1986–89; European Organisation for Research and Treatment of Cancer: Chairman: Lung Cancer Co-operation Gp, 1981–88; Pharmacokinetics and Metabolism Gp, 1984–87 (Mem., 1981–87); Protocol Rev. Cttee, 1984–91 (Pres., 1994). Examiner: RCPE, 1976–94; RCPSG, 1978–84. Chm., UICC Fellowships Prog., 1990–98. Member: Nat. Review of Resource Allocation, Scottish Office, 1998–99; Internat. Scientific Cttee, Italian Govt, 1998; Steering Cttee, Alliance of World Cancer Res. Orgns. Mem., editl bds of numerous jls related to cancer; Editor-in-Chief, European Cancer News, 1987–97; European Ed., Jl Nat. Cancer Inst., 1994–2003; Founding Editor,

ecancermedicalscience, 2007–. FRCPE 1981; FRCPSGlas 1987; FRCP 1997; FMedSci 1999. Hon. FRCSE 2001. Hon. DSc: Abertay Dundee, 1996; Nottingham, 1997; Portsmouth, 1999; Napier Edinburgh, 2002; Ghent, 2005. *Publications:* Cancer Assessment and Monitoring, 1979; Autologous Bone Marrow Transplantation and Solid Tumours, 1984; Microspheres and Drug Therapy, 1984; Clinical and Experimental Pathology and Biology of Lung Cancer, 1985; contrib. chapters in books and jls. *Recreations:* opera, theatre, wine, grandchildren. *Club:* New (Edinburgh).

McWALTER, Tony; educational consultant (mathematics and philosophy), University of Leeds and University of Hertfordshire, since 2005; b 20 March 1945; s of late Joe McWalter and Anne Murray; m 1991, Karry Omer; one s two d. *Educ:* UC Wales, Aberystwyth (BSc 1968); McMaster Univ., Canada (MA 1969); University Coll., Oxford (BPhil 1971; MLitt 1983). School teacher, Cardinal Wiseman Sch., Greenford, 1963–64; lorry driver, E. H. Patterson Transport, 1964; Lecturer in Philosophy: Thames Poly., 1972–74; Hatfield Poly., then Univ. of Hertfordshire, 1974–97 (Dir of Computing, 1989–92). MP (Lab and Co-op) Hemel Hempstead, 1997–2005; contested same seat, 2005. Member, Select Committee: NI, 1997–2000; Sci. & Technol., 2001–05; Procedure, 2003–05. Treas., Nat. Cttee for Philosophy, 1984–97. Mem., External Adv. Bd, Faculty of Lit. Hum., Oxford Univ., 2000–; Board Member: Council for Economic and Social Aspects of Genomics, 2003–05; British Philosophical Assoc., 2004–05 (Exec. Mem., 2003–06). Hon. Vice-Pres., Herts Conservation Soc., 1997–. *Publication:* (ed jtly) Kant and His Influence, 1990. *Recreations:* tennis, bridge, croquet, theatre. *Address:* 56 St Giles Road, Codicote, Hitchin, Herts SG4 8XW.

McWEENY, Prof. Roy; Professor of Theoretical Chemistry, University of Pisa, 1982–97, Professor Emeritus, since 1998; b 19 May 1924; o s of late Maurice and Vera McWeeny; m 1947, Patricia M. Healey (marr. diss. 1979); one s one d; m 1982, Virginia Del Re. *Educ:* Univ. of Leeds; University Coll., Oxford. BSc (Physics) Leeds 1945; DPhil Oxon 1949. Lectr in Physical Chemistry, King's Coll., Univ. of Durham, 1948–57; Vis. Scientist, Physics Dept, MIT, USA, 1953–54; Lectr in Theoretical Chemistry, Univ. Coll. of N Staffs, 1957–62; Associate Dir, Quantum Chemistry Gp, Uppsala Univ., Sweden, 1960–61; Reader in Quantum Theory, 1962–64, Prof. of Theoretical Chemistry, 1964–66, Univ. of Keele; Prof. of Theoretical Chem., 1966–82, and Hd of Chemistry Dept, 1976–79, Sheffield Univ. Vis. Prof., America, Japan, Europe. Mem., Acad. Européenne des Scis, des Arts et des Lettres, 1988. Spiers Meml Medal, RSC, 2006. *Publications:* Symmetry, an Introduction to Group Theory and its Applications, 1963, repr. 2002; (with B. T. Sutcliffe) Methods of Molecular Quantum Mechanics, 1969, 2nd edn as sole author, 1989; Spins in Chemistry, 1970, repr. 2004; Quantum Mechanics: principles and formalism, 1972, repr. 2003; Quantum Mechanics: methods and basic applications, 1973; Coulson's Valence, 3rd rev. edn 1979; (contrib. and Associate Ed.) Handbook of Molecular Physics and Quantum Chemistry, 3 vols, 2002; contrib. sections in other books and encyclopædias; many research papers on quantum theory of atomic and molecular structure in Proc. Royal Soc., Proc. Phys. Soc., Phys. Rev., Revs. Mod. Phys., Jl Chem. Phys., etc. *Recreations:* drawing, sculpture, travel. *Address:* Via Consoli del Mare 3, 56126 Pisa, Italy.

McWHA, Prof. James Alexander; Vice-Chancellor and President, University of Adelaide, Australia, since 2002; b 28 May 1947; s of David McWha and Sarah Isabel McWha (née Caughey); m 1970, Jean Lindsay Farries; one s two d. *Educ:* Queen's Univ., Belfast (BSc, BAgr Hons); Glasgow Univ. (PhD Plant Physiol. 1973); PhD aeg Adelaide, 2002. Lectr in Plant Physiol., 1973–79, Hd, Dept of Plant and Microbial Scis, 1980–85, Univ. of Canterbury; Prof. of Agricl Botany, QUB and Dep. CSO, Dept of Agriculture for NI, 1985–89; Dir, DSIR Fruit and Trees (NZ), 1989–92; CEO, Horticulture and Food Res. Inst., NZ, 1992–95; Vice-Chancellor and Pres., Massey Univ., NZ, 1996–2002. Member: Council, NIAB, Cambridge, 1986–89; Bd, NZ Foundn for Res. Sci. and Technol., 1992–95; Bd, NZ Dairy Res. Inst., 1995–98; Gen. Bd, Amer. Chamber of Commerce in NZ, 2000–02. Association of Commonwealth Universities: Mem. Council, 2000–02 (NZ Rep.), 2006–07 (Aust. Rep.); Hon. Treas., 2007–July 2009; Convenor, SA Vice-Chancellors' Cttee, 2002, 2007–08; Sec. Gen., Internat. Assoc. of Univ. Presidents, 2002–05, Sec. Gen. Emeritus, 2005; Universities Australia (formerly Australian Vice-Chancellors' Cttee), 2002–; Dir, Aust. Univs Quality Agency, 2003–March 2009. Director: Industrial Res. Ltd, 1996–2001; Gp of Eight Ltd (Aust.), 2002–. Hon. DSc Massey, 2004. Centenary Medal (Aust.), 2003. *Publications:* numerous scientific and educnl articles. *Recreations:* classic cars, rallying, motor sport, Rugby Union. *Address:* University of Adelaide, Mitchell Building, North Terrace, Adelaide, SA 5005, Australia. *Clubs:* Wellington (Wellington); Union, University and Schools (Sydney); Adelaide.

McWHINNEY, Jeffrey Harold; Company Secretary, since 2003, and Managing Director, since 2004, Significan't (UK) Ltd; b 9 May 1960; s of late Harold George McWhinney and of Mabel Joan McWhinney (née Carlisle); m 1989, Brigitte François; three s one d. *Educ:* Jordanstown Schs, Belfast; Mary Hare Grammar Sch., Newbury; Kingston Univ. (Cert. Mgt 1992; Dip. Mgt 1993). Develt Officer, Breakthrough Trust, 1984–87; Head of Community Services, Disability Resources Team, 1987–91; Sen. Economic Develt Officer, Economic Develt Office, Wandsworth BC, 1991–94; Dir, Greenwich Assoc. of Disabled People, 1994–95; Chief Exec., British Deaf Assoc., 1995–2004. Dir, Sign Campaign, 1993–2003; Chief Exec., Big D Trading Co., 1996–2002; Chm., Greater London Initiatives for Disabled Entrepreneurs, 2003–05. Specialist Mem., Special Educnl Needs and Disability Tribunal, 2002–05. Trustee: UK Council on Deafness, 2001–03; RNID, 2006–. Mem., ACEVO (formerly ACENVO), 1995–2005. MInstD 1996. Deaf Acad. Award, 1996. *Publications:* Deaf Consciousness, 1992; numerous articles in various professional and specialist jls. *Recreations:* golf, reading, family activities, travel, sailing, Charlton Athletic FC. *Address:* Significan't (UK) Ltd, St Agnes House, 6 Cresswell Park, SE3 9RD.

McWHIRTER, Prof. John Graham, PhD; FRS 1999; FREng; Senior Fellow, Signal Processing Group, QinetiQ Ltd (formerly Defence Evaluation and Research Agency), since 1996; b 28 March 1949; s of late Francis David McWhirter and Elizabeth McWhirter (née Martin); m 1973, Avesia Vivianne Wolfe; one s one d. *Educ:* Newry High Sch.; Queen's Univ., Belfast (BSc 1st Cl. Hons Maths 1970; PhD 1973). CMath, FIMA 1988; FIET (FIEE 1994); FREng (FEng 1996); FInstP 1999. Royal Signals and Radar Establishment: Higher Scientific Officer, 1973–77; SSO, 1977–80; PSO, 1980–86; SPSO, 1986–96. Visiting Professor: Electrical Engrg Dept, Queen's Univ., Belfast, 1986–; Sch. of Engrg, UC, Cardiff, 1997–. Pres., IMA, 2002–03 (Vice Pres., 1998–99; Chm. and Proceedings Ed., IMA Internat. Conf. on Maths in Signal Processing, 1988, 1992, 1996 and 2000). Hon. DSc: QUB, 2000; Edinburgh, 2002. J. J. Thomson Medal, IEE, 1994. *Publications:* over 150 res. papers; inventor or jt inventor of 30 UK, European, US and Canadian patents. *Recreations:* swimming for exercise, building and flying radio-controlled model gliders. *Address:* QinetiQ Ltd, St Andrew's Road, Malvern, Worcs WR14 3PS. *T:* (01684) 895384. *Club:* Malvern Soaring Association.

McWIGGAN, Thomas Johnstone, CBE 1976; aviation electronics consultant; Secretary General, European Organisation for Civil Aviation Electronics, 1979–87; *b* 26 May 1918; *s* of late Thomas and Esther McWiggan; *m* 1947, Eileen Joyce Moughton; two *d*. *Educ:* UC Nottingham. Pharmaceutical Chemist. FIET, FRAeS, SMIEEE. Signals Officer (Radar), RAFVR, 1941–46 (despatches, 1945). Civil Air Attaché (Telecommunications) Washington, 1962–65; Dir of Telecommunications (Plans), Min. of Aviation, 1965; Dir of Telecommunications (Air Traffic Services), BoT, 1967; Dir Gen. Telecommunications, Nat. Air Traffic Services, 1969–79 (CAA, 1972–79). *Publications:* various technical papers. *Recreations:* photography, cabinet-making, gardening. *Address:* The Squirrels, Liberty Rise, Addlestone, Weybridge, Surrey KT15 1NU. *T:* (01932) 843068.

MacWILLIAM, Very Rev. Alexander Gordon; Dean of St Davids Cathedral, 1984–90; *b* 22 Aug. 1923; *s* of Andrew George and Margaret MacWilliam; *m* 1951, Catherine Teresa (*née* Bogue); one *s*. *Educ:* Univ. of Wales (BA Hons Classics, 1943); Univ. of London (BD 2nd Cl. Hons, 1946, PhD 1952, DipEd 1962). Deacon 1946, priest 1947; Curate of Penygroes, Gwynedd, 1946–49; Minor Canon, Bangor Cathedral, 1949–55; Rector of Llanfaethlu, Gwynedd, 1955–58; Head of Dept of Theology, Trinity Coll., Carmarthen, Dyfed, 1958–74; Head of School of Society Studies, Trinity Coll. (Inst. of Higher Education, Univ. of Wales), 1974–84; Canon of St Davids Cathedral and Prebendary of Trefloden, 1978. Examining Chaplain to Bishop of St Davids, 1969. Vis. Prof. of Philosophy and Theology, Central Univ. of Iowa, USA, 1983. Prov. Grand Master, S Wales Western Div., United Grand Lodge of England, 1992–. Chm., Myrddin Probus Club, Carmarthen, 2003–. *Publications:* contribs to Learning for Living (Brit. Jl of Religious Education), UCW Jl of Educn. *Recreations:* travel to archaeological sites and art centres, classical music, food and wine. *Address:* Pen Parc, Smyrna Road, Llangain, Carmarthen, Carmarthenshire SA33 5AD.

McWILLIAM, John David; *b* 16 May 1941; *s* of Alexander and Josephine McWilliam; *m* 1st, 1965, Lesley Mary Catling; two *d*; 2nd, 1994, Mary McLoughlin (marr. diss. 1997); 3rd, 1998, Helena Lovegreen. *Educ:* Leith Academy; Heriot Watt Coll.; Napier College of Science and Technology. Post Office Engineer, 1957–79. Councillor, Edinburgh CC, 1970–75 (last Treasurer of City of Edinburgh and only Labour one, 1974–75); Commissioner for Local Authority Accounts in Scotland, 1974–78. Mem., Scottish Council for Technical Educn, 1973–85. MP (Lab) Blaydon, 1979–2005. Dep. to Shadow Leader of H of C, 1983; Opposition Whip, 1984–87. Member: Select Cttee on Educn, Science and the Arts, 1980–83; Select Cttee on Procedure, 1984–87; Services Cttee (Chm., Computer sub-cttee, 1983–87); Select Cttee on Defence, 1987–99; Speaker's Panel of Chairmen, 1988–2005; Dep. Speaker, 2000–05. Mem., Gen. Adv. Council, BBC, 1984–89. JP Edinburgh, 1973. *Recreations:* reading, listening to music, angling.

McWILLIAM, Sir Michael (Douglas), KCMG 1996; Chairman, Cheltenham Festivals, since 2007 (Deputy Chairman, 2006); *b* 21 June 1933; *s* of Douglas and Margaret McWilliam; *m* 1960, Ruth Arnstein; two *s*. *Educ:* Cheltenham Coll.; Oriel Coll., Oxford (MA); Nuffield Coll., Oxford (BLitt). Kenya Treasury, 1958; Samuel Montagu & Co., 1962; joined Standard Bank, subseq. Standard Chartered Bank, 1966; Gen. Manager, 1973; Gp Man. Dir, 1983–88; Dir, SOAS, Univ. of London, 1989–96 (Hon. Fellow, 1997). Member: Bd, Commonwealth Development Corp., 1990–96; Council, ODI, 1991–94. Chm., Superannuation Fund, London Univ., 1990–97; Director: Shanghai Fund, 1992–99, Bangladesh Fund, 1993–99, Indo-Cam Gp; Simba Fund, ING Baring, 1995–2000; Indo-Cam Mosais, 1998–2001. Hon. Vice Pres., Royal African Soc., 2004– (Mem. Council, 1979–91; Chm., 1996–2004); Vice-Pres., Royal Commonwealth Soc., 2002– (Dep. Chm., 1982–91; Chm., 1996–2002); Chm., Centre for the Study of African Economies, Oxford, 1998–. Trustee, British Empire and Commonwealth Mus., Bristol, 2003– (Dep. Chm., 2003–06; Chm., 2006–08). Pres. Council, Cheltenham Coll., 1988–92 (Mem., 1977–92). *Publication:* The Development Business: a history of the Commonwealth Development Corporation, 2001. *Address:* Yew Tree Farm, Brimpsfield, Glos GL4 8LD. *Club:* Royal Commonwealth Society.

McWILLIAMS, Sir Francis, GBE 1992; FREng; conciliator and arbitrator, since 1978; Chairman, Centre for Economics and Business Research, 1992–2002; Lord Mayor of London, 1992–93; *b* 8 Feb. 1926; *s* of John J. and Mary Anne McWilliams; *m* 1950, Winifred (*née* Segger); two *s*. *Educ:* Holy Cross Acad., Edinburgh; Edinburgh Univ. (BSc Eng 1945); Inns of Court Sch. of Law. Engineer in local govt, 1945–54; Town Engineer, Petaling Jaya New Town, Malaysia, 1954–64; Consulting Civil and Struct. Engineer, Kuala Lumpur, 1964–76. Bar student, 1976–78; called to the Bar, Lincoln's Inn, 1978, Bencher, 1993. Dir, Hong Kong & Shanghai Bank (Malaysia), 1993–99. Chm., British/ Malaysian Soc., 1994–2001. Mem., Common Council, City of London, 1978–80; Alderman, Ward of Aldersgate, 1980–96; Sheriff, City of London, 1988–89. Master: Arbitrators' Co., 1985–86; Engineers' Co., 1990–91; Loriners' Co., 1995–96; Pres., Aldersgate Ward Club, 1980–96. Chm., St John's Ambulance City Br., 1992–96. Pres., Instn of Incorp. Exec. Engrs, 1994–97. Vice Chm. Trustees, Foundn for Manufg and Industry, 1994–2000. FCGI; FREng (FEng 1991). Hon. FICE. Hon. DCL City; Hon. DEng Kingston, 1994; Dr *hc* Edinburgh, 1994. KStJ 1992; KSG 1993. PJK, Selangor, Malaysia, 1963; Dato Seri Selera, Selangor, 1973. Grande Official da Ordem do Infante Dom Henrique (Portugal); Order of Merit (Senegal), 1989; Order of Independence (Cl. III) (UAE), 1989. *Publication:* Pray Silence for "Jock" Whittington (autobiog.), 2002. *Recreations:* golf, ski-ing. *Address:* Flat 7, Whittingehame House, Whittinghame, E Lothian EH41 4QA. *T:* and *Fax:* (01368) 850619. *Clubs:* Royal Over-Seas League; Hon. Company of Edinburgh Golfers, Muirfield; Royal Selangor Golf (Kuala Lumpur); Castle Park Golf (Gifford).

MADARIAGA, Prof. Isabel Margaret de, FRHistS; FBA 1990; Professor of Russian Studies, University of London at School of Slavonic and East European Studies, 1981–85, now Professor Emerita; *b* 27 Aug. 1919; *d* of late Salvador de Madariaga and Constance Archibald, MA; *m* 1943, Leonard Bertram Schapiro, CBE, FBA (marr. diss 1976; he *d* 1983). *Educ:* Ecole Internationale, Geneva; Instituto Escuela, Madrid and fifteen other schools; SSEES, Univ. of London (BA, PhD). FRHistS 1967. BBC Monitoring Service, 1940–43; Min. of Information (later COI), 1943–47; Economic Information Unit, HM Treasury, 1947–48; Editl Asst, Slavonic and East European Review, 1951–64; Asst Lectr and Lectr, LSE, intermittently, 1951–66; Lectr in Modern History, Univ. of Sussex, 1966–68; Sen. Lectr in Russian Hist., Univ. of Lancaster, 1968–71; Reader in Russian Studies, SSEES, Univ. of London, 1971–81. Corresp. Mem., Royal Spanish Acad. of History, 1991. Member, Editorial Boards: Government and Opposition, 1965–2004; Slavonic and E European Review, 1971–86; European History Qly, 1971–2004. *Publications:* Britain, Russia and the Armed Neutrality, 1963; (with G. Ionescu) Opposition, 1968; Russia in the Age of Catherine the Great, 1981 (trans. French, 1986, Italian, 1988, Russian, 2002); Catherine the Great: a short history, 1990 (trans. German, 1993, Spanish, 1994, Portuguese, 1996, Turkish, 1997, Russian, 2006); Politics and Culture in Eighteenth-Century Russia, 1998; Ivan the Terrible, 2005 (trans. Italian, 2006, Russian, 2007, Finnish, 2007, Swedish, 2008, Latvian, 2008); articles in learned jls. *Recreation:* music. *Address:* 25 Southwood Lawn Road, Highgate, N6 5SD. *T:* (020) 8341 0862. *Club:* Oxford and Cambridge.

MADDEN, (Albert) Frederick (McCulloch), DPhil, DLitt; Reader in Commonwealth Government, Oxford, 1957–84; Professorial (Charter) Fellow of Nuffield College, 1958–84, Emeritus Fellow since 1984, Pro-Proctor, 1988–89; *b* 27 Feb. 1917; *e s* of A. E. and G. McC. Madden; *m* 1941, Margaret (*d* 2004), *d* of Dr R. D. Gifford; one *s* one *d*. *Educ:* privately, by mother; Bishop Vesey's Grammar Sch.; Christ Church, Oxford (Boulter and Gladstone exhibns; BA 1938, BLitt 1939); DPhil 1950, DLitt 2005, Oxon. Dep. Sup., Rhodes House Library, 1946–48; Beit Lectr, 1947–57; Sen. Tutor to Overseas Service Courses, 1950–; Co-Dir, Foreign Service Course, 1959–72; Dir, Inst. of Commonwealth Studies, 1961–68; Vice-Chm., History Bd, 1968–73. Co-founder, Oxford Samaritans, 1961. Canadian Vis. Fellow, 1970; Vis. Prof., Cape Town, 1973; Vis. Fellow, Res. Sch., ANU, 1974. Dir, Hong Kong admin. course, 1975–86. Dir, Prospect Theatre, 1963–66. Author and actor in pageants: Marcham, 1951; Stanford, 1999; nativity and passion plays, 1995–96. FRHistS 1952. *Publications:* (with V. Harlow) British Colonial Developments, 1774–1834, 1953; (with K. Robinson) Essays in Imperial Government, 1963; chapter in Cambridge History of British Empire III, 1959; Imperial Constitutional Documents, 1765–1965, 1966; (with W. Morris-Jones) Australia and Britain, 1980; (with D. K. Fieldhouse) Oxford and the Idea of Commonwealth, 1982; Perspectives on Imperialism and Decolonisation (Festschrift), 1984; Select Documents on the Constitutional History of the British Empire: Vol. I, The Empire of the Bretaignes 1165–1688, 1985; Vol. II, The Classical Period of the First British Empire 1689–1783, 1986; Vol. III, Imperial Reconstruction 1763–1840, 1987; Vol. IV, Settler Self-government 1840–1900, 1989; Vol. V, The Dependent Empire and Ireland 1840–1900, 1991; Vol. VI, The Dominions and India since 1900, 1993; Vol. VII, The Dependent Empire 1900–48, 1994; Vol. VIII, The End of Empire 1948–97, 2000; articles and reviews in English Historical Review, etc. *Recreations:* acting (Cranmer in Quatercentenary, St Mary's, Oxford, and 186 other parts); photographing islands and highlands, hill towns, country houses, churches; Renaissance art; writing music and listening; taking services. *Address:* 1 Penstones Court, Marlborough Lane, Stanford-in-the-Vale, Oxfordshire SN7 8SW. *T:* (01367) 718068.

See also Sir D. C. A. McC. Madden.

MADDEN, Sir Charles (Jonathan), 4th Bt *cr* 1919, of Kells, co. Kilkenny; Technical Director, Wind-Ways Pty Ltd, since 2007; *b* 11 Aug. 1949; *yr s* of Lt-Col John Wilmot Madden, MC, RA, *yr s* of 1st Bt, and Beatrice Catherine (*née* Sievwright); *S* brother, 2006, but his name does not appear on the Official Roll of the Baronetage; *m* 1st, 1980, Kirsteen Victoria Ronald Noble (marr. diss. 2003); one *s* one *d*; 2nd, 2006, Dr Margaret Elaine Taylor. *Educ:* Blundell's; Portsmouth Poly.; Loughborough Univ. BSc Engrg; MTech Design; MBA Marketing. *Recreations:* playing the 'cello (Unley SO, Adelaide), sailing. *Heir: s* Samuel Charles John Madden, *b* 22 Sept. 1984. *Address:* 79 Birksgate Drive, Urrbrae, SA 5064, Australia; *e-mail:* charlie.madden@internode.au.net.

MADDEN, Rt Rev. Cuthbert, OSB; Abbot of Ampleforth, since 2005; *b* 12 Feb. 1955; *s* of James and Joan Madden. *Educ:* Middlesex Hosp. Med. Sch. (MB BS). MRCP 1982. House Surgeon, W Norwich Hosp., 1978–79; House Physician, 1979, SHO, 1979–80, Middlesex Hosp.; Rotating SHO in Medicine, Bath Utd Hosps, 1980–82; Rotating Registrar in Medicine, Royal Hallamshire Hosp., Sheffield, 1982–84; Ampleforth: entered monastic community, 1984; solemn profession, 1988; ordained priest, 1990; Housemaster, St John's, 1997–2005. Hon. FRCP 2006. *Address:* Ampleforth Abbey, York YO62 4EN. *T:* (01439) 766700/710, *Fax:* (01439) 788132.

MADDEN, Sir David (Christopher Andrew McCulloch), KCMG 2003 (CMG 1996); HM Diplomatic Service, retired; Consultant to World Society for the Protection of Animals, since 2007; *b* 25 July 1946; *s* of Dr A. F. McC. Madden, *qv* and (Alice) Margaret Madden; *m* 1970, Penelope Anthea Johnston; one *s* two *d*. *Educ:* Magdalen Coll. Sch., Oxford; Merton Coll., Oxford (Postmaster; MA); Courtauld Inst. of Art, London Univ. (MA). FCO, 1970–72; British Mil. Govt, Berlin, 1972–75; Cabinet Office, 1975–77; Moscow, 1978–81; Athens, 1981–84; FCO, 1984–87; Counsellor, 1987; Dep. Hd of Mission, Belgrade, 1987–90; Head, Southern European Dept, FCO, 1990–94; High Comr, Republic of Cyprus, 1994–99; Ambassador to Greece, 1999–2004; Pol Advr to OC EU Force, Bosnia and Hercegovina, 2004–05. Trustee, Brooke Hosp. for Animals, 2008. Hon. Dr London Metropolitan, 1999. *Recreations:* cricket, rowing, tennis, reading, writing, animal welfare. *Address:* 5 Rawlinson Road, Oxford OX2 6UE.

MADDEN, Frederick; *see* Madden, A. F. McC.

MADDEN, Dr (John) Lionel, CBE 1999; Librarian, National Library of Wales, 1994–98; *b* 8 Aug. 1938; *s* of late Cyril Madden and of Edith (*née* Mottram); *m* 1965, Georgina Mary Hardwick; one *s* one *d*. *Educ:* King Edward VII Grammar Sch., Sheffield; Lincoln Coll., Oxford (MA 1964); University Coll. London (DipLib 1963); Univ. of Leicester (PhD 1970). ALA 1964. Asst Librarian, Univ. of Hull, 1963–67; Bibliographer, Univ. of Leicester Victorian Studies Centre, 1967–72; Sen. Lectr, Coll. of Librarianship, Wales, 1973–87; Keeper of Printed Books, Nat. Liby of Wales, 1987–94. Mem., Pubns Bd, Leicester Univ. Press, 1968–72; Chm., Pubns Bd, Tennyson Soc., 1973–77. Pres., Welsh Liby Assoc., 1994–98; Chairman: Welsh Books Council, 1996–2005 (Vice-Chm., 1994–96); Liby and Inf. Services Council, Wales, 1998–2001; Capel (Welsh Chapels Heritage Soc.), 1999–. Trustee, St Deiniol's Liby, Hawarden, 1994–. Hon. Fellow, Dept of Inf. and Liby Studies, Univ. of Wales, Aberystwyth, 1989–93, Hon. Prof., 1993–; Hon. Fellow, Univ. of Wales, Lampeter, 1998–. Hon. FCLIP (Hon. FLA 1998). Hon. Mem., Gorsedd Beirdd Ynys Prydain, 1995–. *Publications:* Thomas Love Peacock, 1967; How to Find Out about the Victorian Period, 1970; Robert Southey: the critical heritage, 1972; Sir Charles Tennyson: an annotated bibliography, 1973; The Nineteenth Century Periodical Press in Britain, 1976; Primary Sources for Victorian Studies, 1977; (ed jtly) Investigating Victorian Journalism, 1990; Methodism in Wales, 2003; articles in learned jls. *Recreation:* walking. *Address:* Hafren, Cae'r Gôg, Aberystwyth SY23 1ET. *T:* (01970) 617771.

MADDEN, John Philip; film director; *b* 8 April 1949; *s* of William John Raleigh Madden and Jean Elizabeth Hunt Mills; *m* 1975, Penelope Jane Abrahams; one *s* one *d*. *Educ:* Clifton Coll., Bristol; Sidney Sussex Coll., Cambridge (MA; Hon. Fellow 2000). Artistic Dir, Oxford and Cambridge Shakespeare Co., 1970–73; Associate Prof., Yale Sch. of Drama, 1977–80. *Stage:* Wings, The Bundle, Measure for Measure, The Suicide, Terry by Terry, Grownups, Beyond Therapy, Salonika, Cinders, Between East and West, An American Comedy, Ivanov, Mrs Warren's Profession, Caritas, Proof; *films:* Ethan Frome, 1992; Golden Gate, 1994; Mrs Brown, 1997; Shakespeare in Love, 1998 (seven Academy Awards, 1998; four BAFTA Awards, 1999); Captain Corelli's Mandolin, 2001; Proof, Killshot, 2006; *television:* Poppyland, A Wreath of Roses, Sherlock Holmes, After the War, Widowmaker, Inspector Morse (four films), Prime Suspect: The Lost Child, Meat, Truth or Dare (BAFTA Scotland Award, Best Single Drama, 1997); *radio:* US National Public Radio: Wings (Prix Italia, 1978), Star Wars, The Empire Strikes Back, Return of the Jedi. Hon. DLitt Portsmouth, 2006. *Recreations:* cooking, walking, sailing. *Address:* c/o Jenne Casarotto, Casarotto Ramsey Ltd, Waverley House, 7–12 Noel Street, W1F 8GQ.

MADDEN, Max; *b* 29 Oct. 1941; *s* of late George Francis Leonard Madden and Rene Frances Madden; *m* 1972, Sheelagh Teresa Catherine Howard. *Educ:* Lascelles Secondary Modern Sch.; Pinner Grammar Sch. Journalist: East Essex Gazette; Tribune (political weekly); Sun, London; Scotsman, London; subseq. Press and Information Officer, British Gas Corp., London; Dir of Publicity, Labour Party, 1979–82. MP (Lab): Sowerby, Feb. 1974–1979; Bradford West, 1983–97.

MADDEN, Michael; Under Secretary, Ministry of Agriculture, Fisheries and Food, 1985–96, retired; *b* 12 Feb. 1936; *s* of late Harold Madden and Alice Elizabeth (*née* Grenville); *m* 1st, 1960, Marion Will (marr. diss. 1977); two *s* one *d*; 2nd, 1994, Angela Grace Abell. *Educ:* King Edward VII Sch., Sheffield. Exec. Officer, Min. of Transport and Civil Aviation, 1955; Ministry of Agriculture, Fisheries and Food: Asst Principal, 1963–67; Asst Private Sec. to Minister, 1966–67; Principal, 1967; Asst Sec. (as Head, Tropical Foods Div.), 1973; Under Sec., 1985; Head, Management Services Gp, 1985; Flood Defence, Plant Protection and Agricl Resources, 1990; Envmt Policy Gp, 1991–96. *Recreations:* walking, eating and drinking with friends, music. *Address:* 2A Brampton Road, St Albans, Herts AL1 4PW. *Club:* Farmers.

MADDEN, Prof. Paul Anthony, DPhil; FRS 2001; FRSE; Provost, Queen's College, Oxford, since 2008. *Educ:* Univ. of Sussex (BSc, DPhil). Lectr in Chemistry, then Prof. of Chemistry, 1996–2005, Univ. of Oxford; Fellow, Queen's Coll., Oxford, 1984–2004; Prof. of Chemistry and Dir, Centre for Sci. at Extreme Conditions, Univ. of Edinburgh, 2005–08. FRSE 2006. *Address:* Queen's College, Oxford OX1 4AW.

MADDEN, Paul Damian, FRGS; HM Diplomatic Service; High Commissioner to Singapore, since 2007; *b* 25 April 1959; *s* of Antony Angus Thomas Madden and Doris May Madden (*née* Brewer); *m* 1989, Sarah Pauline Thomas; two *s* one *d*. *Educ:* King's School, Ottery St Mary; Gonville and Caius Coll., Cambridge (BA Geog. 1980, MA 1983); Sch. of Oriental and African Studies, Univ. of London; Durham Univ. Business Sch. (MBA 2002). DTI, 1980–87, Private Sec. to Minister, 1984–86; Japanese Lang. Studies, SOAS and Kamakura, 1987–89; entered Diplomatic Service, 1989; First Secretary: Tokyo, 1989–92; FCO, 1992–96; Washington, 1996–2000; Dep. High Comr, Singapore, 2000–03; Hd, Public Diplomacy Dept, FCO, 2003–04; Gp Dir, UK Trade and Investment, 2004–07. Member, Court: Imperial Coll. London, 2004–07; Cranfield Univ., 2004–07. *Publication:* Raffles: lessons in business leadership, 2003. *Recreations:* travel, family. *Address:* c/o Foreign and Commonwealth Office, King Charles Street, SW1A 2AH. *Clubs:* Tanglin (Singapore); Singapore Cricket.

MADDERS, Rev. Mgr (Brian) Richard, MBE 1996; Parish Priest, Camberley and Bagshot, since 2007; *b* 12 Aug. 1949; *s* of Mervyn and Eleanor Madders. *Educ:* Mayfield Coll.; St John's Seminary, Wonersh. Employee, National Bank, 1969–71; ordained priest, 1978; Assistant Priest: Banstead, 1978–81; Brighton, 1981–84; Worthing, 1984–85; commnd RN Chaplain, 1985–2007: First Flotilla (Seagoing), 1986–87; HMS Sultan, 1987–90; Third Flotilla (Seagoing), 1990–93; Staff Chaplain, FO Surface Flotilla, 1993–95; HMS Raleigh, 1995–99; Australian Defence Force Acad., 1999; HMS Nelson, 2000–01; HMS Drake, 2001–02; Principal RC Chaplain (Naval), VG for Bishopric of the Forces (RC), and Dir, Naval Chaplaincy Service (Training and Progs), 2002–07. QHC, 2002–07. Pres., RN Motorcycle Club, 1989–2000. *Address: e-mail:* brmadders@hotmail.com. *Club:* Army and Navy.

MADDICOTT, David Sydney, (Syd); HM Diplomatic Service; British High Commissioner to Cameroon and Ambassador (non-resident) to the Central African Republic, Chad and Gabon, since 2006; *b* 27 March 1953; *s* of Patrick McCagh and Eileen Hannigan, and adopted *s* of Sydney Walter Maddicott and Catherine O'Brien; *m* 1980, Elizabeth Wynne; four *s* one *d*. *Educ:* University Coll. London (BA Hons English 1976). Various sales and mktg appts, Rank Xerox (UK) Ltd, 1976–89; Gen. Sales and Mktg Manager, Pitney Bowes (Ireland) Ltd, 1989–90; postgrad. studies, UC, Dublin, 1990–92; self-employed consultant, 1992–94; joined FCO, 1994; Hd of Section, Econ. Relns Dept/UN Dept, 1994–96; on attachment to Canadian Dept of For. Affairs and Internat. Trade, Ottawa, 1996–97; Hd, Pol, Media and Public Affairs Section, High Commn, Ottawa, 1997–2000; Dep. Hd, Latin America and Caribbean Dept, 2000–03, and Hd, Caribbean Unit, 2001–03, FCO; Sen. Duty Manager, FCO Response Centre, 2003–06. *Recreations:* singing, reading, speedway, cricket. *Address:* c/o Foreign and Commonwealth Office, King Charles Street, SW1A 2AH. *T:* (Cameroon) (2) 220545, (2) 220796, *Fax:* (2) 220148; *e-mail:* syd.maddicott@fco.gov.uk. *Clubs:* Deddington Cricket, New Edinburgh Cricket (Ottawa).

MADDICOTT, Dr John Robert Lewendon, FBA 1996; FSA; Fellow and Lecturer in Modern History, Exeter College, Oxford, 1969–2006, now Emeritus; *b* Exeter, 22 July 1943; *e s* of late Robert Maddicott, Ipplepen, Devon, and Barbara (*née* Lewendon); *m* 1965, Hilary, *d* of late Thomas and Violet Owen; two *d*. *Educ:* Cheltenham Grammar Sch.; King Edward's Sch., Bath; Worcester Coll., Oxford (BA 1st cl. 1964; DPhil 1968). FSA 1980. Jun. Lectr, Magdalen Coll., Oxford, 1966–67; Asst Lectr, Univ. of Manchester, 1967–69; Sub-Rector, Exeter Coll., Oxford, 1988–90. Vis. Prof., Univ. of S Carolina, 1983. Raleigh Lectr, British Acad., 2001; Ford's Lectr in British Hist., Oxford, 2004. Jt Editor, English Hist. Review, 1990–2000. *Publications:* Thomas of Lancaster 1307–22, 1970; The English Peasantry and the Demands of the Crown, 1294–1341, 1975; Law and Lordship: Royal Justices as Retainers in Thirteenth- and Fourteenth-Century England, 1978; Simon de Montfort, 1994; contribs to learned jls. *Recreations:* hill walking, poetry, book collecting. *Address:* Exeter College, Oxford OX1 3DP.

MADDICOTT, Syd; *see* Maddicott, D. S.

MADDISON, Prof. Angus; Professor of Economics, University of Groningen, Netherlands, 1978–96, now Emeritus; *b* 6 Dec. 1926; *s* of Thomas Maddison and Jane (*née* Walker); *m* 1st, Carol Hopkins; two *s*; 2nd, Penelope Pearce; one *d*. *Educ:* Darlington Grammar Sch.; Selwyn Coll., Cambridge (BA, MA; Hon. Fellow 1999); McGill Univ., Montreal; Johns Hopkins Univ.; Univ. Aix-en-Provence (docteur d'état). Pilot Officer, RAF, 1948–49. Lectr in Econ. Hist., Univ. of St Andrews, 1951–52; Head of Econs Div., later Dir, Develt Assistance, then Fellow, Develt Centre, OEEC and OECD, Paris, 1953–66; Dir, Res. Project on Econ. Growth, Twentieth Century Fund, NY, 1966–69; Res. Fellow and Econ. Advr, Harvard Univ. Centre for Internat. Affairs, 1969–71; Head, Central Analysis Div., OECD, Paris, 1971–78. Visiting Lecturer or Professor: Univ. of Calif, Berkeley, 1968; Nuffield Coll., Oxford, 1975; Université Paris Dauphine, 1981; ANU, 1982; St Antony's Coll., Oxford, 1988; Internat. Develt Centre, Japan, 1989; Universitá Ca' Foscari, Venice, 1990; Univ. of Turin, 1993; NY Univ., 1993; SOAS, London Univ., 1996–99; ASERI, Univ. del Sacro Cuore, Milan, 1997; Keio Univ., Fujisawa, 1998. Lectures: Kuznets Meml, Yale Univ., 1998; Wendt, Amer. Enterprise Inst., Washington, 2001; Abramovitz Meml, Stanford Univ., 2001; Colin Clark, Univ. of Qld, 2003; Ruggles, Internat. Assoc. for Res. in Income and Wealth, Cork, 2004; Arndt Meml, ANU, 2006. Consultant: EU, ECAFE, ECE, ECLAC, FAO, GATT, IADB, UNESCO, UN, UNIDO; World Bank; govts of Brazil, Ghana, Greece, Mexico and Pakistan. Corresp. FBA 1994. Foreign Hon. Member: Amer. Econ. Assoc., 1989; Amer. Acad. of Arts and Scis, 1996; Foreign Mem., Russian Acad. of Scis in Econs and Business, 1992. Hon. Dr Hitotsubashi, Japan, 2007. Medal, Univ. of Helsinki, 1986. Comdr, Order of Orange Nassau (Netherlands), 2006. *Publications:* Economic Growth in the West, 1964; Foreign Skills and Technical Assistance in Economic Development, 1965; Economic Growth in Japan and the USSR, 1969; Economic Progress and Policy in Developing Countries, 1970; Class Structure and Economic Growth: India and Pakistan since the Moghuls, 1971; Phases of Capitalist Development, 1982; Two Crises: Latin America and Asia 1929–38 and 1973–83, 1985; The World Economy in the Twentieth Century, 1989; Dynamic Forces in Capitalist Development, 1991; The Political Economy of Poverty, Equity and Growth: Brazil and Mexico, 1992; Explaining the Economic Performance of Nations: essays in time and space, 1995; Monitoring the World Economy, 1995; Chinese Economic Performance in the Long Run 1–2030, 1998, rev. 2nd edn 2007; The World Economy: a millennial perspective, 2001; The Asian Economies in the Twentieth Century, 2002; The World Economy: historical statistics, 2003; Growth and Interaction in the World Economy: the roots of modernity, 2004; Contours of the World Economy 1-2030: essays in macroeconomic history, 2007; numerous articles in econ. and financial jls. *Recreations:* collecting furniture, books and hats. *Address:* Chevincourt, 60150, France. *T:* 344760532, *Fax:* 344766514.

MADDISON, Hon. Sir David (George), Kt 2008; **Hon. Mr Justice Maddison;** a Judge of the High Court, Queen's Bench Division, since 2008; *b* 22 Jan. 1947; *s* of Claude and Clarice Maddison; *m* 1976, Indira Mary Antoinette Saverymuttu; three *s*. *Educ:* King's Sch., Chester; Grey Coll., Univ. of Durham (BA 1968). Called to the Bar, Inner Temple, 1970 (Bencher, 2005); practised on Northern Circuit, 1972–92; a Recorder, 1990–92; a Circuit Judge, 1992–2008; a Sen. Circuit Judge and Hon. Recorder of Manchester, 2003–08. Mem., Parole Bd, 1996–2002. *Publication:* (ed) Bingham's Negligence Cases, 4th edn 1996, 5th edn 2002. *Recreations:* classical music, playing the piano, singing, tennis, golf, watching football. *Address:* Royal Courts of Justice, Strand, WC2A 2LL. *Clubs:* East India; Athenæum (Liverpool); Liverpool Cricket.

MADDISON, Jane Hope; *see* Kennedy, J. H.

MADDOCK, family name of **Baroness Maddock**.

MADDOCK, Baroness *cr* 1997 (Life Peer), of Christchurch in the co. of Dorset; **Diana Margaret Maddock;** President, Liberal Democrats, 1998–99; *b* 19 May 1945; *d* of Reginald Derbyshire and Margaret Evans; *m* 1st, 1966, Robert Frank Maddock (marr. diss. 2001); two *d*; 2nd, 2001, Rt Hon. Sir Alan Beith, *qv*. *Educ:* Brockenhurst GS; Shenstone Training Coll.; Portsmouth Polytechnic. Teacher: Weston Park Girls' Sch., Southampton, 1966–69; Extra-Mural Dept, Stockholm Univ., 1969–72; Sholling Girls' Sch., Southampton, 1972–73; Anglo-Continental Sch. of English, Bournemouth, 1973–76; Greylands Sch. of English, Southampton, 1990–91. Member: (L, subseq. Lib Dem), Southampton CC, 1984–93; (Lib Dem), Northumberland CC, 2005–08; (Lib Dem) Berwick-upon-Tweed BC, 2007–April 2009. Contested (Lib Dem) Southampton Test, 1992. MP (Lib Dem) Christchurch, July 1993–1997; contested (Lib Dem) same seat, 1997. Sec., All-Party Parly Gp on Homelessness and Housing Need; Vice Chm., All-Party Parly Gp on Electoral Reform. Lib Dem spokesman on housing, H of L, 1997–2004. Member: Cttee on Standards in Public Life, 2003–; H of L Merits of Statutory Instruments Cttee, 2005–. A Vice Pres., Nat. Housing Fedn, 1997–; President: Nat. Housing Forum, 1997–; Micropower Council, 2005–; Vice Pres., Nat. Energy Action, 2000–. *Recreations:* theatre, music, reading, travel. *Address:* House of Lords, SW1A 0PW.

MADDOCKS, Anne Mary Catherine; *see* Ashworth, A. M. C.

MADDOCKS, Arthur Frederick, CMG 1974; HM Diplomatic Service, retired; Ambassador and UK Permanent Representative to OECD, Paris, 1977–82; *b* 20 May 1922; *s* of late Frederick William Maddocks and Celia Elizabeth Maddocks (*née* Beardwell); *m* 1945, Margaret Jean Crawford Holt; two *s* one *d*. *Educ:* Manchester Grammar Sch.; Corpus Christi Coll., Oxford. Army, 1942–46; Foreign (later Diplomatic) Service, 1946–82: Washington, 1946–48; FO, 1949–51; Bonn, 1951–55; Bangkok, 1955–58; UK Delegn to OEEC, 1958–60; FO, 1960–64; UK Delegn to European Communities, Brussels, 1964–68; Political Adviser, Hong Kong, 1968–72; Dep. High Comr and Minister (Commercial), Ottawa, 1972–76. Mem., OECD Appeals Tribunal, 1984–89. *Address:* Lynton House, 83 High Street, Wheatley, Oxford OX33 1XP. *Club:* Hong Kong (Hong Kong).

MADDOCKS, His Honour Bertram Catterall; a Circuit Judge, 1990–2005; *b* 7 July 1932; *s* of His Honour George Maddocks and of Mary Maddocks (*née* Day); *m* 1964, Angela Vergette Forster; two *s* one *d*. *Educ:* Malsis Hall, near Keighley; Rugby; Trinity Hall, Cambridge (schol.; MA; Law Tripos Part 2 1st Cl. 1955). Nat. Service, 2nd Lieut, RA, 1951; Duke of Lancaster's Own Yeomanry (TA), 1958–67. Called to the Bar, Middle Temple, 1956; Harmsworth Schol.; Mem., Lincoln's Inn; a Recorder, 1983–90. Pt-time Chm., VAT Tribunals, 1977–92. *Recreations:* real tennis, lawn tennis, ski-ing, bridge. *Address:* Moor Hall Farm, Prescot Road, Aughton, Lancashire L39 6RT. *T:* (01695) 421601. *Clubs:* Cavalry and Guards; Manchester Tennis and Racquet.

MADDOCKS, Fiona Hamilton; Chief Opera Critic, Music Critic and Arts Feature Writer, Evening Standard, since 2002; London Correspondent, Scherzo, Madrid, since 2004; columnist, RA Magazine, since 2006; *m* 1st, R. Cooper (marr. diss.); two *d*; 2nd, 1995, Tom Phillips, *qv*. *Educ:* Blackheath High Sch. (GPDST), London; Royal Coll. of Music; Newnham Coll., Cambridge (MA; Associate, 1985–97). Taught English Literature, Istituto Orsoline, Cortina d'Ampezzo, Italy, 1977–78; Medici Soc., London, 1978–79; News trainee, Producer and Sen. Producer, LBC, 1979–82; Founder Producer/Editor, Comment, 1982–85, Asst Commng Editor, Music, 1985–86, Channel 4; The Independent: Dep. Arts Editor, 1986–88, and writer; Music Editor and Associate Arts Editor, 1988–91; feature writer, Observer, Independent, Spectator and other pubns, 1991–; Founding Editor, 1992–97, Adv. Editor, 1997–98, BBC Music Magazine; Chief Music Critic, The Observer, 1997–2002; Editor, BBC Proms Guide, 1998–99; Exec. Editor, LSO Living Music Magazine, 1998–2003. Board Member: Opera magazine, 1998–; Unknown Public, 2006–. Member: Exec. Cttee, SPNM, 1990–91; Critics' Circle, 1995 (Mem. Council, 1997–99); Cttee, Kim Scott Walwyn Prize, 2003–; Adv. Bd, Norbert Brainin Foundn, 2006–; Adv. Gp, BBC Philharmonic, 2006–. Trustee: Masterprize, 1997–2001; Oxford Contemporary Music, 2006–. Gov., Sherborne Sch., 2001–. FRSA 2006. BP Arts Journalism Press Award, 1991. *Publication:* Hildegard of Bingen, 2001. *Address:* c/o Evening Standard, Northcliffe House, 2 Derry Street, W8 5EE.

MADDOX, Brenda Power, (Lady Maddox); writer; *b* 24 Feb. 1932; *d* of Dr Brendan W. Murphy and Edith Giamperoli Murphy; *m* 1960, Sir John Royden Maddox, *qv*; one *s* one *d*, and one step *s* one step *d*. *Educ:* High Sch., Bridgewater, Mass; Radcliffe Coll. (BA *cum laude* 1953). Press Dir, United Community Service of Boston, 1955–57; reporter and columnist, Quincy Patriot Ledger, Mass, 1957–59; UK Reporter, Reuters, 1959–60; The Economist, 1962–72 and 1975–85, latterly as Britain Ed., then Home Affairs Ed.; Media

Columnist: Daily Telegraph, 1987–94; The Times, 1994–97; biographer, writer, critic and broadcaster, 1988–. Non-exec. Dir, London Broadcasting Co., 1973–75. Member: UK Nat. Adv. Cttee for UNESCO, 1983–85; Sci. in Society Cttee, Royal Soc., 2000–04. Vice Pres., Hay Fest., 1995–; Member: British Assoc. for Sci. Writers, 1978– (Chm., 1983–84); Broadcasting Press Guild, 1983– (Chm., 1993–94); Mgt Cttee, Soc. of Authors, 1987–90; Council, RSL, 2004–. Mem., 1999–, Vice Chm., 2001–06, Shakespeare Prize Jury, Toepfer Foundn, Hamburg. FRSL 1994. Hon. Phi Beta Kappa, Harvard Univ., 1978. Hon. DHL Finch, 2004; Hon. DLitt Glamorgan, 2005. *Publications:* Beyond Babel: new directions in communications, 1972; The Half-Parent, 1975; The Marrying Kind, 1981; *biographies:* Who's Afraid of Elizabeth Taylor?, 1977; Nora: the life of Mrs James Joyce, 1988 (LA Times Biog. Prize, 1988; Silver PEN Award, 1989; Prix du Meilleur Livre Etranger, 1990) (filmed as Nora, 2000); The Married Man: a life of D. H. Lawrence, 1994 (Whitbread Biog. Award); George's Ghosts: the secret life of W. B. Yeats, 1999; Rosalind Franklin: the dark lady of DNA, 2001 (Marsh Biog. Prize, 2001; LA Times Sci. Prize, 2002); Maggie, the First Lady, 2003; Freud's Wizard: the enigma of Ernest Jones, 2006; author of reviews and articles for newspapers and mags in UK and USA. *Recreations:* giving parties, cooking, exploring mid-Wales. *Address:* 9 Pitt Street, W8 4NX. *T:* (020) 7937 9750; *e-mail:* bmaddox@pitt.demon.co.uk. *Club:* Athenæum.

See also B. M. Maddox.

MADDOX, Bronwen Maria; Chief Foreign Commentator, The Times, since 2006; *b* 7 May 1963; *d* of Sir John Royden Maddox, *qv* and Brenda Power Maddox, *qv*; one *d*. *Educ:* Westminster Sch.; St Paul's Girls' Sch.; St John's Coll., Oxford (BA PPE 1985). Analyst, Charterhouse Venture Capital, 1985–86; Dir and Hd, Media Investment Team, Kleinwort Benson Securities, 1986–91; investigative reporter, then leader writer, FT, 1991–96; The Times: US Editor and Washington Bureau Chief, 1996–99; Foreign Editor, 1999–2006. Gov., Ditchley Foundn, 2003–. *Publication:* In Defence of America, 2008. *Recreations:* walking, cooking, hiking in the US Rockies. *Address:* The Times, 1 Pennington Street, E98 1TT. *T:* (020) 7782 5234, *Fax:* (020) 7782 5140; *e-mail:* bronwen.maddox@thetimes.co.uk.

MADDOX, Sir John (Royden), Kt 1995; writer and broadcaster; Editor, Nature, 1966–73 and 1980–95; *b* 27 Nov. 1925; *s* of A. J. and M. E. Maddox, Swansea; *m* 1st, 1949, Nancy Fanning (*d* 1960); one *s* one *d*; 2nd, 1960, Brenda Power Murphy (*see* B. P. Maddox); one *s* one *d*. *Educ:* Gowerton Boys' County Sch.; Christ Church, Oxford; King's Coll., London. Asst Lecturer, then Lecturer, Theoretical Physics, Manchester Univ., 1949–55; Science Correspondent, Guardian, 1955–64; Affiliate, Rockefeller Institute, New York, 1962–63; Asst Director, Nuffield Foundation, and Co-ordinator, Nuffield Foundation Science Teaching Project, 1964–66; Man. Dir, Macmillan Journals Ltd, 1970–72; Dir, Macmillan & Co. Ltd, 1968–73; Chm., Maddox Editorial Ltd, 1972–74; Dir, Nuffield Foundn, 1975–80. Member: Royal Commn on Environmental Pollution, 1976–81; Genetic Manipulation Adv. Gp, 1976–80; British Library Adv. Council, 1976–81; Council on Internat. Develt, 1977–79; Chm. Council, Queen Elizabeth Coll., 1980–85; Mem. Council, King's Coll. London, 1985–89. Mem., Crickadarn and Gwendwr Community Council, 1981–. Hon. FRS 2000. Hon. DTech Surrey, 1982; Hon. DSc: UEA, 1992; Liverpool, 1994; Glamorgan, 1997; Hon. DLitt Nottingham Trent, 1996. *Publications:* (with Leonard Beaton) The Spread of Nuclear Weapons, 1962; Revolution in Biology, 1964; The Doomsday Syndrome, 1972; Beyond the Energy Crisis, 1975; What Remains to be Discovered, 1998. *Address:* 9 Pitt Street, W8 4NX. *T:* (020) 7937 9750; *e-mail:* john.maddox@btopenworld.com. *Club:* Athenæum.

See also B. M. Maddox.

MADDOX, Air Vice Marshal Nigel David Alan, CBE 1999; Commandant, Joint Services Command and Staff College, 2005–07; *b* 1 April 1954; *s* of Albert and Beverly Maddox; *m* 1979, Sue Elizabeth Armitage; one *d*. *Educ:* Clark's Grammar Sch.; Westcliff High Sch. for Boys; MBA Open Univ. Flight Comdr, No 12 Sqdn, 1987; RNSC, Greenwich, 1988; PSO, AOC No 18 Gp, 1989; OC Ops Wing, RAF Mount Pleasant, Falkland Is, 1990; OC No 12 Sqdn, RAF Lossiemouth, 1991; Asst Dir W, ACDS(Ops), MoD, 1993–96; Sen. RAF Officer, Germany, and Stn Comdr, RAF Brüggen, 1996–99; Air Cdre Maritime, 1999–2002; AOC No 2 Gp, 2002–05. *Recreations:* squash, golf. *Address:* 33 Kilnwood Avenue, Hockley, Essex SS5 4PR. *T:* (01702) 203294; *e-mail:* comao@aol.com. *Club:* Royal Air Force.

MADDOX, Ronald, PRI 1989 and 2004 (RI 1959); artist, illustrator and designer; *b* 5 Oct. 1930; *s* of Harold George and Winifred Maddox; *m* 1st, 1958, Camilla Farrin (*d* 1995); two *s*; 2nd, 1997, Diana Goodwin. *Educ:* Hertfordshire College of Art and Design, St Albans; London College of Printing and Graphic Art. FCSD, FSAI; Hon. RWS 1990; Hon. RBA 2002. Nat. Service, RAF, 1949–51, Air Min. Design Unit. Designer, illustrator, art director, London advertising agencies, 1951–61; private practice, 1962–; commissioned by nat. and multinat. cos and corps, govt depts, public authorities, TV; designer British postage stamps and philatelic material, 1972– (winner Prix de l'art Philatelique, 1987); exhibns, RA, RI, RBA, London and provincial galls; paintings in royal, govt and public bodies' collections. Assessor, Turner Watercolour Award/Medal (formerly Winsor & Newton Turner Watercolour Award), RA Summer Exhibn, 2002–07; Turner Watercolour Award, RI/RIWS, 2008–. Mem. Council, Artists' Gen. Benevolent Instn, 2000– (Hon. Sec., 2002–). Trustee: Royal Acad./British Institution Fund, 1996–2000; Digswell Arts Trust, 2007. Vice-Pres., RI, 1979; Governor, Fedn of British Artists, 1989–2003 (Chm., 1997); Hon. Member: Soc. of Architect Artists; Fedn of Canadian Artists; United Soc. of Artists; Campine Assoc. of Watercolours, Belgium; PS; Soc. of Graphic Artists. FRSA. Patron: Danesbury and Queen Victoria Meml Hosp., Welwyn, 1998–; Isabel Hospice, E Herts, 2000–; Trustee, Welwyn Scouts & Guides Assoc., 2005–. Freeman, City of London, 2000; Hon. Freeman, Co. of Painter-Stainers, 2000. Winsor & Newton/RI Award, 1981, 1991; Rowland Hilder landscape painting Award, RI, 1996, 2000. *Recreations:* compulsive drawing, walking, cycling, gardening. *Address:* Herons, 21 New Road, Digswell, Herts AL6 0AQ. *T:* (01438) 714884. *Club:* Arts (Hon. Mem.).

MADDOX, Stephen, OBE 2008; Chief Executive, Metropolitan Borough of Wirral, since 1997; *b* Merseyside. *Educ:* Univ. of Kent (BA 1974). Joined Wirral MBC as articled clerk, 1974; admitted as solicitor, 1977; Dep. Borough Solicitor and Sec., Wirral MBC, 1991–98. *Address:* Metropolitan Borough of Wirral, Town Hall, Brighton Street, Wallasey, Wirral CH44 8ED.

MADDRELL, Geoffrey Keggen; Chairman: Unite Group plc, since 1999; F & C UK Select Trust plc (formerly Ivory and Sime ISIS Trust, later ISIS UK Select Trust plc), since 1993; BuildStore Ltd, since 1999; Economic Lifestyle Property Investment Company, since 2007; *b* 18 July 1936; *s* of Captain Geoffrey Douglas Maddrell and Barbara Marie Kennaugh; *m* 1964, Winifred Mary Daniel Jones; two *s* one *d*. *Educ:* King William's Coll., Isle of Man (Major Cain Schol.); Corpus Christi Coll., Cambridge (MA Law and Econs); Columbia Univ., New York (MBA). Lieut, Parachute Regt, 1955–57. Shell Internat. Petroleum Co. Ltd, 1961–69; Boston Consulting Gp, Boston, USA, 1971–72; Bowater Corp., 1972–86, apptd to main bd, 1979; Pres., Bowater Europe, 1975–85; Chm., Rhenania Schiffahrtes-und-Speditions GmbH, 1973–80; joined Tootal Gp as Man. Dir, 1986, Chief Exec., 1987–91; Chief Exec., 1991–94, Chm., 1994–2003, ProShare; Chairman: Macdonald Martin Distilleries, subseq. Glenmorangie plc, 1994–2002; LDV Ltd, 1995–2004 (Dir, 2004–06); Director: Transport Develt Gp plc, 1992–97; Westbury plc, 1992–2006; Goldcrest Homes plc, 2003–; Adv. Dir, HSBC Investment Bank, 1995–98. Chm., Manchester TEC, 1988–91; Civil Service Comr, 1992–96, 2000–05. Mem., Trng and Affairs Cttee, CBI, 1989–93. Chairman: Friends of Airborne Forces, 1994–2002; UNIAID, 2001–04; Airborne Forces Charities, 2002–04; Res. Autism, 2003–; Nat. Autistic Soc. Prospects Adv. Gp, 2003–; Trustee, Help the Aged, 1983–86. Gov., UMIST, 1987–92. *Recreations:* club running, golf, travel. *Address:* 28 Sussex Street, SW1V 4RL. *T:* (020) 7834 3874.

MADDRELL, Simon Hugh Piper, PhD, ScD; FRS 1981; Fellow of Gonville and Caius College, Cambridge, 1964–2007, now Life Fellow; Hon. Professor of Integrative Physiology, Cambridge University, 2003–08, now Emeritus Hon. Professor; *b* 11 Dec. 1937; *s* of late Hugh Edmund Fisher Maddrell and Barbara Agnes Mary Maddrell; *m* 1st, 1961, Anna Myers (marr. diss. 1985, she *d* 1997); three *s* one *d*; 2nd, 1990, Katherine Mona Mapes. *Educ:* Peter Symonds' Sch., Winchester; St Catharine's Coll., Cambridge. BA, MA, PhD 1964, ScD 1978. Res. Fellow, Dalhousie Univ., Canada, 1962–64; SPSO, AFRC Unit of Invertebrate Chem. and Physiology, subseq. Unit of Insect Neurophysiology and Pharmacology, Cambridge Univ., 1968–90; College Fellow and Lectr, Gonville and Caius Coll., Cambridge, 1968–2007; Hon. Reader, Univ. of Cambridge, 1991–2003. Manager of Finances and Investments (formerly Financial Sec. and Investments Manager), Co. of Biologists Ltd, 1965–. Chm., I of M Woodland Trust, 2004–. Scientific Medal, Zool Soc. of London, 1976. *Publication:* Neurosecretion, 1979. *Recreations:* gardening, planting trees, play-reading, cinema, wine-tasting. *Address:* Gonville and Caius College, Cambridge CB2 1TA; Ballamaddrell, Ballabeg, Arbory, Isle of Man IM9 4HD. *T:* (01624) 822787.

MADEJSKI, (Robert) John, OBE 2000; DL; Chairman: Reading Football Club, since 1990; Goodhead Group plc, since 1991; Malaysian Motor Trader, since 1998; *b* 28 April 1941; *s* of Zygmunt Madejski and Joan Edith Madejski; two *d*. *Educ:* Reading Collegiate Sch. Encyclopedia salesman, Caxton Press, 1959; biscuit salesman, Huntley & Palmer, 1959–64; various jobs incl. selling Rolls Royce, Jaguar and Aston Martin cars, Calif, 1964–66; sales exec., British Motor Corp., 1966–67; Sales Dir, Stan Hope Mills, 1967–69; Classified Advertising Sales Exec., Reading Evening Post, 1969–76; founder: Auto Trader, 1976; Jt Founder, Hurst Publishing Ltd, 1977–98 (allied with Guardian/Manchester Evening News, 1982). Chairman of companies, including: Sackville Properties plc, 2001–; Royal Palm Hotel, Galapagos Is, 2002–; Reading 107 (local radio), 2002–. Chancellor, Univ. of Reading, 2007–. DL Berks 2000. Charitable funding of art galls, theatres, lecture theatres, including: Falklands Meml Chapel, Pangbourne Coll., 2000; John Madejski Fine Rooms, Royal Acad. of Arts, 2004. Hon. Fellow, Henley Mgt Coll., 2007. *Recreations:* fine dining (owner of Leatherne Bottel Restaurant, Goring-on-Thames), art (recently purchased Edgar Degas: Bronze), swimming. *Address:* Madejski Stadium, Junction 11, M4, Reading, Berks RG2 0FL. *Club:* Annabel's.

MADEL, Sir (William) David, Kt 1994; *b* 6 Aug. 1938; *s* of late William R. Madel and Eileen Madel (*née* Nicholls); *m* 1971, Susan Catherine, *d* late Lt-Comdr Hon. Peter Carew; one *s* one *d*. *Educ:* Uppingham Sch.; Keble Coll., Oxford. MA Oxon 1965. Graduate Management Trainee, 1963–64; Advertising Exec., Thomson Organisation, 1964–70. Contested (C) Erith and Crayford Nov. 1965, 1966. MP (C) S Bedfordshire, 1970–83; Bedfordshire SW, 1983–2001. PPS to Parly Under-Sec. of State for Defence, 1973–74, to Minister of State for Defence, 1974, to Rt Hon. Sir Edward Heath, KG, MBE, MP, 1991–97; an Opposition Whip, 1997–99. Chm., Cons. Backbench Educn Cttee, 1983–85; Vice-Chm., Cons. Backbench Employment Cttee, 1974–81; Member: Select Cttee on Educn, Sci. and Arts, 1979–83, on Transport, 1995–97, on Foreign Affairs, 1999–2001; H of C European Legislation Cttee, 1983–97. Mem. Ind. Monitoring Bd, HM Prison Hollesley Bay, Suffolk, 2004–. Lay Rep. for Disciplinary Hearings, Council of the Inns of Court, 2005–. Mem. Exec., CCJ, 2002–06. Mem. Court, Univ. of Luton, 1993–. *Recreations:* cricket, tennis, reading, walking, campanology (steeple-keeper's mate, St Mary's Church, Woodbridge, Suffolk). *Address:* Moor House, Middleton Moor, Saxmundham, Suffolk IP17 3PW. *Club:* Carlton.

MADELEY, Richard Holt; television presenter; *b* 13 May 1956; *s* of Christopher Holt Madeley and Mary Claire McEwan; *m* 1st, 1977, Lynda Hooley; 2nd, 1986, Judith Finnigan, *qv*; one *s* one *d*, and two step *s*. *Educ:* Coopers' Co. Grammar Sch., Bow; Shenfield Sch., Essex. Indentured jun. reporter, Brentwood Argus, 1972–74; Asst, then Dep. Ed., E London Advertiser, 1975–76; reporter, 1976–77, producer, 1977–78, BBC Radio Carlisle; reporter: Border TV, 1978–80; and presenter, Yorkshire TV, 1980–82; presenter: Granada Television, 1982–2001: programmes include: Runway, 1987–89; This Morning, 1988–2001; Eye of the Storm, 1997–2000; British Soap Awards, 1999, 2000 and 2001; Channel 4: Richard and Judy, 2001–08; British Book Awards, 2004–; ITV1: Fortune, 2007. *Publications:* Richard & Judy: the autobiography (with Judith Finnigan), 2001; Fathers and Sons, 2008. *Recreations:* cliff-walking in Cornwall, cycling, acoustic guitar, reading. *Address:* c/o James Grant Management, 94 Strand on the Green, Chiswick, W4 3NN. *T:* (020) 8742 4950. *Club:* Home House.

MADELIN, Robert; Director General for Health and Consumers (formerly for Health and Consumer Protection), European Commission, since 2004; *b* 8 May 1957; *s* of John Madelin and Kathleen Madelin (*née* Webb); *m* 1990, Marie-Christine Jalabert. *Educ:* Royal Grammar Sch., High Wycombe; Magdalen Coll., Oxford (BA (Mod. Hist. and Mod. Langs), MA); Ecole Nationale d'Admin, Paris. Principal, Multilateral Trade Policy, DTI, 1979–88; 1st Sec., UK Perm. Repn, Brussels, 1988–93; Mem., then Dep. Hd, Cabinet of Vice-Pres. of Commn, Sir Leon, later Lord, Brittan, 1993–97; Dir, Directorate Gen. of Trade, EC, 1997–2003. Hon. FRCP 2007. *Recreations:* walking, running, swimming, cooking, singing. *T:* (Belgium) (2) 2963338; *e-mail:* robert.madelin@ec.europa.eu.

MADELUNG, Prof. Wilferd Willy Ferdinand, FBA 1999; Laudian Professor of Arabic, University of Oxford, 1978–98; *b* 26 Dec. 1930; *s* of Georg Madelung and Elisabeth (*née* Messerschmitt); *m* 1963, A. Margaret (*née* Arent); one *s*. *Educ:* Eberhard Ludwig Gymnasium, Stuttgart; Univs of Georgetown, Cairo, Hamburg. PhD (Hamburg). Cultural Attaché, W German Embassy, Baghdad, 1958–60. Vis. Professor, Univ. of Texas, Austin, 1963; Privatdozent, Univ. of Hamburg, 1963–64; University of Chicago: Asst Prof., 1964; Associate Prof., 1966; Prof. of Islamic History, 1969. Guggenheim Fellowship, 1972–73; Sen. Res. Fellow, Inst. of Ismaili Studies, 1999–; Fellow, Inst. of Advanced Studies, Hebrew Univ. of Jerusalem, 2002–. Decoration of Republic of Sudan (4th cl.), 1962. *Publications:* Der Imam al-Qāsim ibn Ibrāhīm und die Glaubenslehre der Zaiditen, 1965; Religious Schools and Sects in Medieval Islam, 1985; Religious Trends in Early Islamic Iran, 1988; Religious and Ethnic Movements in Medieval Islam, 1992; The Succession to Muhammad, 1996; articles in learned jls and Encyc. of Islam. *Recreation:* travel. *Address:* 21 Belsyre Court, Oxford OX2 6HU.

MADEN, Prof. Margaret; Professor of Education, Keele University, 1995–2001; *b* 16 April 1940; *d* of Clifford and Frances Maden. *Educ:* Arnold High Sch. for Girls, Blackpool; Leeds Univ. (BA Hons); Univ. of London Inst of Educn (PGCE). Asst Teacher of Geography, Stockwell Manor Comprehensive Sch., SW9, 1962–66; Lectr, Sidney Webb Coll. of Educn, 1966–71; Dep. Head, Bicester Comprehensive Sch., Oxon, 1971–75; Headmistress, Islington Green Comprehensive Sch., 1975–82; Dir, Islington Sixth Form Centre, 1983–86; Principal Advr, Tertiary Develt, ILEA, 1986–87; Dep. County Educn Officer, 1987–88, County Educn Officer, 1989–95, Warwickshire CC. Mem., Nat. Commn on Educn, 1991–93. Member: Basic Skills Agency, 1998–2007; Prince's Trust Adv. Gp, 2001–02; Bd, Royal Opera House, 2002–; Chm., BBC Regl Adv. Council (South), 2002–05. Governor: Peers Sch., Oxford, 2006–08; Royal Ballet Sch., 2007–. Hon. Pres., BEMAS, 1995–99. Hon. FCP 1994. *Publications:* (ed jtly) Success Against the Odds, 1995; Shifting Gear: changing patterns of educational governance in Europe, 2000; (ed) Success Against the Odds—5 Years On, 2001; contributions to: Dear Lord James, 1971; Teachers for Tomorrow (ed Calthrop and Owens), 1971; Education 2000 (ed Wilby and Pluckrose), 1979; The School and the University, an International Perspective (ed Burton R. Clark), 1984; School Co-operation: new forms of Governance (ed Ransom and Tomlinson), 1994; Letters to the Prime Minister (ed Ted Wragg), 2005. *Recreations:* European painting, writing and films; politics, opera. *Address:* 12 Dale Close, Oxford OX1 1TU. *T:* (01865) 721372.

MADGE, James Richard, CB 1976; Deputy Secretary, Department of the Environment, on secondment as Chief Executive, Housing Corporation, 1973–84; *b* 18 June 1924; *s* of James Henry Madge and Elisabeth May Madge; *m* 1955, Alice June Annette (*d* 1975), *d* of late Major Horace Reid, Jamaica; two *d. Educ:* Bexhill Co. Sch.; New Coll., Oxford. Pilot in RAFVR, 1942–46. Joined Min. of Civil Aviation, 1947; Principal Private Secretary: to Paymaster-General, 1950–51; to Minister of Transport, 1960–61; Asst Secretary, Min. of Transport, 1961–66; Under-Sec., Road Safety Gp, 1966–69; Head of Policy Planning, 1969–70; Under-Sec., Housing Directorate, DoE, 1971–73. Churchwarden, St Mary Abbots, Kensington, 1987–2000.

MADGE, Nicolas John; His Honour Judge Madge; a Circuit Judge, since 2004; *b* May 1953; *s* of John Kenneth Lewis Madge and Lucy Mildred Madge; two *s. Educ:* Cannock Grammar Sch.; St Catharine's Coll., Cambridge (BA 1974). Admitted solicitor, 1978. Solicitor: Camden Community Law Centre, 1978–83; Nash and Dowell, 1984–85; Partner, Bindman and Partners, 1985–95; Dep. Dist Judge (pt-time), 1989–95; Dist Judge, W London Co. Court, 1995–2004. Mem., Civil Justice Council, 2003–06. Photographic exhibn, One World, One View, Harrow Crown Court, 2005. Contributor, 1999–, Mem., Sen. Editl Bd, 2004–, Civil Procedure (The White Book). *Publications:* Troubled by the Law?, 1978; Out of School: legal responsibility for children, 1981; (contrib.) Tribunals Practice and Procedure, 1985; (jtly) Defending Possession Proceedings, 1987, 6th edn 2006; (with D. Forbes) Debt and Housing: emergency procedures, 1993; English Roots: a family history, 1995; Housing Law Casebook, 1996, 4th edn 2008; (contrib.) Supreme Court Practice, 1999; Annotated Housing Statutes, 2003, 2nd edn 2005; one world one view (photographs), 2007; contribs to Law Soc. Gazette, New Law Jl, Solicitors' Jl, Legal Action, Justice of the Peace, Jl Housing Law, Civil Justice Qly. *Recreations:* travel and travel writing, walking, cycling, bridge, family history, photography. *Address:* Harrow Crown Court, Hailsham Drive, Harrow, Middx HA1 4TU. *T:* (020) 8424 2294.

MÁDL, Ferenc, Hon. GCMG 2002; PhD; President of Hungary, 2000–05; *b* 29 Jan. 1931; *s* of A. Mádl; *m* 1955, Dalma Némethy; one *s. Educ:* Loránd Eötvös Univ., Budapest (law degree, 1955); Univ. of Strasbourg; PhD 1974. Inst. of State and Legal Scis, Hungarian Acad. of Scis; Lectr, 1973, Dir, Inst. of Civil Law, 1978–85, Dir, Faculty of Internat. Pvte Law, 1985, Loránd Eötvös Univ., Budapest. Minister: without portfolio, 1990–93; of Culture and Educn, 1993–94. *Publications:* 20 books on law of internat. econ. relations, internat. investment law, EEC law, etc; articles on law. *Address:* c/o Office of the President, Sándor Palace, Szent György tér 1, 1014 Budapest, Hungary.

MADONNA; *see* Ciccone, M. L. V.

MAEHLER, Prof. Herwig Gustav Theodor, FBA 1986; Professor of Papyrology, University College London, 1981–2000, now Emeritus; *b* 29 April 1935; *s* of Ludwig and Lisa Maehler; *m* 1963, Margaret Anderson; two *d. Educ:* Katharineum Lübeck (Grammar Sch.); Univs of Hamburg (PhD Classics and Classical Archaeol.), Tübingen and Basel. British Council Schol., Oxford, 1961–62; Res. Assistant, Hamburg Univ., 1962–63, Hamburg Univ. Liby, 1963–64; Keeper of Greek Papyri, Egyptian Mus., W Berlin, 1964–79; Habilitation for Classics, 1975, Lectr in Classics, 1975–79, Free Univ. of W Berlin; Reader in Papyrology, UCL, 1979–81. Corresp. Mem., German Archaeol Inst., 1979; Mem., Accad. Nazionale dei Lincei, Rome, 2000. Hon. Fellow UCL, 2000. Hon. PhD: Helsinki, 2000; Budapest, 2001; Rome II (Tor Vergata), 2003. *Publications:* Die Auffassung des Dichterberufs im frühen Griechentum bis zur Zeit Pindars, 1963; Die Handschriften des S Jacobi-Kirche Hamburg, 1967; Urkunden römischer Zeit, (BGU XI), 1968; Papyri aus Hermupolis (BGU XII), 1974; Die Lieder des Bakchylides, Part 1, 2 vols, 1982, Part 2, 1997; (with G. Cavallo) Greek Bookhands of the Early Byzantine Period, 1987; Bacchylides: a selection, 2004; editions of Bacchylides and Pindar, 1970, 1987, 1989, 1992, 2003; Urkunden aus Hermupolis (BGU XIX), 2005; Schrift, Text und Bild (selected essays), 2006; articles in learned jls. *Address:* Zeltgasse 6/12, 1080 Wien, Austria.

MAFFEY, family name of **Baron Rugby**.

MAGAN, George Morgan; Deputy Governor, Bank of Ireland, since 2006 (Director, since 2003); *b* 14 Nov. 1945; *s* of Brig. William Morgan Tilson Magan, CBE and Maxine, *d* of Sir Kenneth Mitchell, KCIE; *m* 1972, Wendy Anne, *d* of Maj. Patrick Chilton, MC; two *s* one *d. Educ:* Winchester Coll. FCA. Peat Marwick Mitchell, 1964–70; Kleinwort Benson Ltd, 1971–74; Dir, Morgan Grenfell & Co. Ltd, 1974–88; Co-Founder and Chm., J. O. Hambro Magan, 1988–96; Chairman: Hawkpoint Partners, 1997–2001; Rhône Gp Ltd, 2001–; emuse (Dublin), 2001–; Lion Capital Partners, 2001–; Mallett plc, 2001–; Morgan Shipley Ltd (Dubai), 2001–; Dir, Edmiston & Co., 2001–. Treas., Conservative Pty, 2003; Trustee, Cons. Pty Foundn, 2003–. Trustee: LPO, 1992– (Chm., 1997); Royal Opera House, Covent Garden, 1995–2001; BM Develt Trust, 1999–2003. *Address:* Rhône Group 5 Princes Gate, Knightsbridge, SW7 1QJ. *T:* (020) 7761 1051. *Club:* Royal Yacht Squadron.

MAGDALINO, Prof. Paul, DPhil; FBA 2002; Professor of Byzantine History, University of St Andrews, since 1999; Professor of History, Koç University, Istanbul, since 2006; *b* 10 May 1948; *s* of Andrea and Audrey Magdalino; *m* 1973, Ruth Macrides; one *d. Educ:* Oriel Coll., Oxford (BA; DPhil Modern Hist. 1976). Jun. Fellow, Dumbarton Oaks Center for Byzantine Studies, Washington, 1974–75; Andrew J. Mellon Fellow in Early Christian Humanism, Catholic Univ. of America, 1976–77; Lectr, 1977–94, Reader, 1994–99, Univ. of St Andrews. Res. Fellow, Alexander von Humboldt Stiftung, at Inst. für Rechtsgeschichte, Frankfurt, 1980–81, and Inst. für Byzantinistik, Munich, 1983; Vis. Fellow, Humanities Res. Centre, Canberra, 1985; Vis. Prof. of Hist., Harvard Univ., 1995–96; Sen. Fellow, Dumbarton Oaks Center for Byzantine Studies, 2002–. *Publications:* (jtly) Rome and Byzantium, 1977; (ed) The Perception of the Past in Twelfth Century Europe, 1992; The Empire of Manuel I Komnenos, 1143–1180, 1993; (ed) New Constantines, 1994; Constantinople mediévale, 1996; L'Orthodoxie des Astrologues, 2006; numerous contribs to ed vols and articles to learned jls. *Recreations:* walking, swimming. *Address:* Department of Mediaeval History, University of St Andrews, 71 South Street, St Andrews KY16 9QW. *T:* (01334) 462887, *Fax:* (01334) 463334; *e-mail:* pm8@st-andrews.ac.uk.

MAGEE, Bryan; writer; Visiting Professor, King's College, London, 1994–2000 (Hon. Senior Research Fellow in History of Ideas, 1984–94); *b* 12 April 1930; *s* of Frederick Magee and Sheila (*née* Lynch); *m* 1954, Ingrid Söderlund (marr. diss.); one *d. Educ:* Christ's Hospital; Lycée Hôche, Versailles; Keble Coll., Oxford (Open Scholar; BA Modern Hist. 1952, PPE 1953; MA 1956; Hon. Fellow, 1994). Pres., Oxford Union, 1953. Henry Fellow in Philosophy, Yale, 1955–56. Music criticism for many publications, 1959–; Theatre Critic, The Listener, 1966–67; regular columnist, The Times, 1974–76. Mem., Arts Council, 1993–94 (Chm., Music Panel, 1993–94). Current Affairs Reporter on TV; Critic of the Arts on BBC Radio 3; own broadcast series include: Conversations with Philosophers, BBC Radio 3, 1970–71; Something to Say, Thames TV, 1972–73; Argument, LWT, 1973; Don't Quote Me, BBC TV 2, 1974; Men of Ideas, BBC TV 2, 1978; The Great Philosophers, BBC TV 2, 1987; What's the Big Idea?, BBC Radio 3, 1991–92. Silver Medal, RTS, 1978. Contested (Lab): Mid-Bedfordshire, Gen. Elec., 1959; By-Elec., 1960; MP (Lab 1974–82, SDP 1982–83) Leyton, Feb. 1974–1983; contested (SDP) Leyton, 1983. Elected to Critics' Circle, 1970, Pres., 1983–84. Judge: for Evening Standard annual Opera Award, 1973–84; for Laurence Olivier Annual Opera Awards, 1990–91, 1993–95; Chm. of Judges, Royal Philharmonic Soc. opera awards, 1991–2000. Lectr in Philosophy, Balliol Coll., Oxford, 1970–71; Visiting Fellow: All Souls Coll., Oxford, 1973–74; New Coll., Oxford, 1995; Merton Coll., Oxford, 1998; St Catherine's Coll., Oxford, 2000; Peterhouse, Cambridge, 2001; Clare Hall, Cambridge, 2004 (Life Mem.); Vis. Schol., 1991–93, Vis. Fellow, 1993–94, Wolfson Coll., Oxford; Vis. Schol. in Philos., Harvard, 1979, Sydney Univ., 1982, Univ. of California, Santa Barbara, 1989 (Girvetz Meml Lectr); German Marshall Fund Fellow to USA, 1989; Vis. Prof., Trinity Univ., San Antonio, Texas, 1997; Univ. of Otago, NZ, 2006. Charles Carter Lectr, Univ. of Lancaster, 1985; Bithell Meml Lectr, Univ. of London, 1989. Lecturer: Seattle Opera, 1989, 1991, 1995; Royal Opera House, 1990; San Francisco Opera, 1990; Belgian Nat. Opera, 1991; Bayreuth Festspielhaus, 1994; Los Angeles Opera, 1995 and 1997; Hawaii Opera, 2000; Glyndebourne, 2003; Royal Inst. of Philosophy, 1992, 1994, 2007. Hon. Pres., Edinburgh Univ. Philosophy Soc., 1987–88. Governor, 1979–2008, Mem. Council, 1982–2001, Ditchley Foundn; Acad. Visitor, LSE, 1994–96. Hon. Fellow, QMC, 1988; Fellow: QMW, 1989; Royal Philharmonic Soc., 1990. Hon. DLitt Leicester, 2005. *Publications:* Crucifixion and Other Poems, 1951; Go West Young Man, 1958; To Live in Danger, 1960; The New Radicalism, 1962; The Democratic Revolution, 1964; Towards 2000, 1965; One in Twenty, 1966; The Television Interviewer, 1966; Aspects of Wagner, 1968, rev. edn 1988; Modern British Philosophy, 1971; Popper, 1973; Facing Death, 1977; Men of Ideas, 1978, 2nd edn as Talking Philosophy, 2001; The Philosophy of Schopenhauer, 1983, rev. edn 1997; The Great Philosophers, 1987; Misunderstanding Schopenhauer, 1990; (with M. Milligan) On Blindness, 1995, 2nd edn, as Sight Unseen, 1998; Confessions of a Philosopher, 1997; The Story of Philosophy, 1998; Wagner and Philosophy, 2000; Clouds of Glory: a Hoxton childhood, 2003 (J. R. Ackerley Prize for Autobiog., 2004); Growing Up in a War, 2007. *Recreations:* music, theatre. *Address:* Wolfson College, Oxford OX2 6UD. *Clubs:* Garrick, Savile.

MAGEE, Sir Ian (Bernard Vaughan), Kt 2006; CB 2002; Director, St Albans Consulting Ltd; *b* 9 July 1946. *Educ:* Leeds Univ. (BA Hist.). Joined DHSS, 1969; Private Sec. to Minister for Social Security, 1976–78; seconded to Cabinet Office Enterprise Unit, 1984–86; Department of Social Security, 1986–98: Dep. to Dir of Personnel, 1986–89; Territorial Dir, Benefits Agency, 1990–93; Chief Exec., IT Services Agency, 1993–98; Chief Exec., Ct Service, LCD, 1998–2003; Second Permanent Sec. and Chief Exec., Ops, LCD, then DCA, 2003–05; Hd, Profession for Operational Delivery across Civil Service, 2004–05; Sen. Advr, Booz Allen Hamilton, 2006–. Non-exec. Dir, Live Group plc, 2008–. Mem., Adv. Bd, VAT Liaison, 2003–. *Recreations:* sport, reading. *Clubs:* MCC, Royal Automobile; Verulam Golf.

MAGINNESS, Alban Alphonsus; barrister; Member (SDLP) Belfast North, Northern Ireland Assembly, since 1998; *b* 9 July 1950; *s* of Alphonsus and Patricia Maginness; *m* 1978, Carmel McWilliams; three *s* five *d. Educ:* St Malachy's Coll., Belfast; Univ. of Ulster (BA Hons Mod. Hist. 1973); Queen's Univ., Belfast. Called to the Bar: NI, 1976; Ireland, 1984; in practice at NI Bar, specialising in civil litigation. Chm., SDLP, 1985–91. Mem. (SDLP) Belfast CC, 1985–; Lord Mayor of Belfast, 1997–98 (first SDLP Lord Mayor). Contested (SDLP) Belfast North, 1997, 2001, 2005. Member: NI Forum, 1996–98; Forum for Peace and Reconciliation, Dublin, 1994–96; NI Assembly Commn, 2007–. Mem. Bd, Belfast Harbour Comrs. *Recreations:* theatre, history, reading, walking, music. *Address:* 96 Somerton Road, Belfast BT15 4DE. *T:* (028) 9077 0558; (office) 228 Antrim Road, Belfast BT15 2AN. *T:* (028) 9022 0520; *e-mail:* a.maginness@sdlp.ie.

MAGINNIS, family name of **Baron Maginnis of Drumglass**.

MAGINNIS OF DRUMGLASS, Baron *cr* 2001 (Life Peer), of Carnteel in the County of Tyrone; **Kenneth Wiggins Maginnis;** *b* 21 Jan. 1938; *m* 1961, Joy Stewart; two *s* two *d. Educ:* Royal Sch., Dungannon; Stranmillis Coll., Belfast. Served UDR, 1970–81, commissioned 1972, Major. Party spokesman on internal security and defence. Mem., Dungannon District Council, 1981–93 and 2001–05; Mem. (UU) Fermanagh and S Tyrone, NI Assembly, 1982–86. Contested (UU) Fermanagh and S Tyrone, Aug. 1981. MP (UU) Fermanagh and S Tyrone, 1983–2001 (resigned seat Dec. 1985 in protest against Anglo-Irish Agreement; re-elected Jan. 1986). Mem., H of C Select Cttee on Defence, 1984–86, on NI, 1994–97. Vice Pres., UU Council, 1990–2005; Hon. Treas., UU Party, 2005–. Chm., Moygashel Community Develt Assoc., 1992–. Vice Pres., Autism NI, 2005–; Chm., Ind. Review Autism Services (NI), 2007–08. *Address:* House of Lords, SW1A 0PW; 1 Park Lane, Dungannon, Co. Tyrone.

MAGNUS, Sir Laurence (Henry Philip), 3rd Bt *cr* 1917, of Tangley Hill, Wonersh; Vice Chairman, Lexicon Partners Ltd, since 2001; non-executive Chairman, Xchanging ins-sure Services Ltd (formerly Ins-Sure Services Ltd), since 2001; *b* 24 Sept. 1955; *s* of Hilary Barrow Magnus, QC (*d* 1987), and of Rosemary Vera Anne Magnus (*née* Masefield); S uncle, Sir Philip Magnus-Allcroft, 2nd Bt, CBE, 1988; *m* 1983, Jocelyn Mary, *d* of R. H. F. Stanton; two *s* one *d. Educ:* Eton College; Christ Church, Oxford (MA). Corporate Finance Executive, 1977–84, Head of Corporate Finance, Singapore Branch, 1984–87, Samuel Montagu & Co. Ltd; Group Country Manager, Singapore Region, Midland Bank plc (Singapore), 1987–88; Exec. Dir, 1988–95 and Dep. Head, UK Corporate Finance Div., 1994–95, Samuel Montagu & Co. Ltd; Dir, Phoenix Securities Ltd, 1995–97 (acquired by Donaldson, Lufkin & Jenrette, 1997); Managing

Director: Donaldson, Lufkin & Jenrette Internat., 1997–2000 (acquired by Credit Suisse First Boston, 2000); Credit Suisse First Boston, 2000–01. Chm., JP Morgan Income & Capital Trust plc, 2008–; non-executive Director: Forestry Investment Mgt Ltd, 1997–; TT Electronics plc, 2001–07; J. P. Morgan (formerly J. P. Morgan Fleming) Income & Capital Investment Trust plc, 2001–08; Climate Exchange plc, 2006–; Cayenne Trust plc, 2006–. National Trust: Dep. Chm., 2005–; Mem., Finance Cttee, 1997–2005 (Chm., 2002–05); Mem., Bd of Trustees, 2005–. Chm., Eating Disorders Assoc. ('B-eat'), 2005–; Trustee, Windsor Leadership Trust, 2006–. *Recreations:* reading, fishing, walking. *Heir: s* Thomas Henry Philip Magnus, *b* 30 Sept. 1985. *Address:* c/o Lexicon Partners Ltd, No 1 Paternoster Square, EC4M 7DX. *T:* (020) 7653 6030, *Fax:* (020) 7653 6001; *e-mail:* lmagnus@lexiconpartners.com. *Clubs:* Brooks's, City of London; Millennium.

MAGNUS, Prof. Philip Douglas, FRS 1985; R. P. Doherty, Jr-Welch Regents Professor of Chemistry, University of Texas at Austin, since 1989; *b* 15 April 1943; *s* of Arthur Edwin and Lillian Edith Magnus; *m* 1963, Andrea Claire (*née* Parkinson); two *s*. *Educ:* Imperial College, Univ. of London (BSc, ARCS, PhD, DSc). Asst Lectr, 1967–70, Lectr, 1970–75, Imperial College; Associate Prof., Ohio State Univ., 1975–81; Prof. of Chemistry, 1981–87, Distinguished Prof., 1987–88, Indiana Univ. Corday Morgan Medal, RSC, 1978; Janssen Prize, Belgian Chemical Soc. and Janssen Foundn, 1992; Robert Robinson Medal, RSC, 1996. *Publications:* papers in leading chemistry jls. *Recreations:* golf, chess. *Address:* 3111D Windsor Road, Austin, TX 78703, USA. *T:* (512) 4713966.

MAGONET, Rabbi Prof. Jonathan David; Editor, European Judaism, since 2005 (Member, Editorial Board, since 1978; Co-Editor, 1992–2005); *b* 2 Aug. 1942; *s* of Alexander Philip and Esther Magonet; *m* 1974, Dorothea (*née* Foth); one *s* one *d*. *Educ:* Westminster Sch.; Middlesex Hosp. Med. Sch. (MB BS). Leo Baeck Coll.; Univ. of Heidelberg (PhD). Junior hosp. doctor, 1966–67; Leo Baeck College, subseq. Leo Baeck College—Centre for Jewish Education: Rabbinic studies, 1967–71; Head of Dept of Bible Studies, 1974–85; Principal, 1985–2005; Prof., 1996–2005, now Emeritus. Vis. Fellow, Tel Aviv Univ., 1990–91; Guest Professor: Kirchliche Hochschule, Wuppertal, Germany, 1992–93, 1995, 2004; Carl von Ossietzky Univ., Oldenburg, 1999, 2004; Univ. of Luzern, 2004; Vis. Prof., Univs of Würzburg and Augsburg, 2008. Vice-President: World Union for Progressive Judaism, 1988–2005; Movt for Reform Judaism, 2007–. Member, Editorial Board: Christian-Jewish Relations, 1987–91; Jl of Progressive Judaism, 1993–99. FRSA. Hon. DTheol Kirchliche Hochschule Wuppertal, 2005; DUniv Open, 2006; Hon. DHL Hebrew Union Coll., 2007. Verdienstkreuz (Germany), 1999. *Publications:* Form and Meaning: studies in literary techniques in the Book of Jonah, 1976; (ed jtly) Forms of Prayer, vol. I, Daily and Sabbath Prayerbook, 1977, 8th edn 2008, vol. III, Days of Awe Prayerbook, 1985, vol. II, Pilgrim Festival Prayerbook, 1995; (ed jtly) The Guide to the Here and Hereafter, 1988; A Rabbi's Bible, 1991, 2nd edn as A Rabbi Reads the Bible, 2004; Bible Lives, 1992; (jtly) How to Get Up When Life Gets You Down, 1992; (ed jtly) The Little Blue Book of Prayer, 1993; A Rabbi Reads the Psalms, 1994, 2nd edn, 2004; (jtly) Kindred Spirits, 1995; (ed) Jewish Explorations of Sexuality, 1995; The Subversive Bible, 1997; (ed) Das Jüdische Gebetbuch, 2 vols, 1997; Mit der Bibel durch das Jüdische Jahr, 1998; The Explorer's Guide to Judaism, 1998; (jtly) Sun, Sand and Soul, 1999; Abraham-Jesus-Mohammed: interreligiöser dialog aus Jüdischer perspektive, 2000; From Autumn to Summer: a Biblical journey through the Jewish year, 2000; Talking to the Other: Jewish interfaith dialogue with Christians and Muslims, 2003; Einführung ins Judentum, 2004.

MAGOS, Adam László, MD; Consultant Obstetrician and Gynaecologist, and Hon. Senior Lecturer, Royal Free Hospital, London, since 1991; Consultant Gynaecologist, King Edward VII Hospital Sister Agnes (formerly King Edward VII Hospital for Officers), London, since 1992; *b* 26 Sept. 1953; *s* of László Pál Aurel Magos and Éva Mária Magos (*née* Benjamin); *m* 1991, Anne Cyprienne Coburn; three *s*. *Educ:* Whitgift Sch., Croydon; KCL (BSc 1975); King's Coll. Hosp. Sch. of Medicine (MB BS 1978; MD 1986). MRCOG 1986, FRCOG 1998. House Officer, KCH, 1980–82; Res. Fellow in Obstetrics and Gynaecol., Dulwich Hosp., 1982–84; Registrar, KCH and Dulwich Hosp., 1984–86; Lectr, Nuffield Dept of Obstetrics and Gynaecology, John Radcliffe Hosp., Univ. of Oxford, 1986–90; Sen. Lectr and Hon. Consultant, Academic Dept of Obstetrics and Gynaecology, Royal Free Hosp., Univ. of London, 1990–91. Treas., British Soc. for Gynaecol Endoscopy, 1989–92; Member: Wkg Gp on New Technol. in Endoscopic Gynaecol Surgery, RCOG, 1993–94; MAS Trng Sub-Cttee, RCOG, 1998–2001. Hon. Member: Aust. Gynaecol Endoscopy Soc., 1994; Egyptian Soc. for Gynaecol Endoscopy, 1996. Ed., Gynaecological Endoscopy, 1990–93. Syntex Award, Internat. Soc. of Reproductive Medicine, 1988; Veress Meml Medal, Hungarian Soc. for Gynaecol Endoscopy, 1997. *Publications:* (ed jtly) Endometrial Ablation, 1993; contribs to books on premenstrual syndrome, hysteroscopic, laparoscopic and vaginal surgery, and to professional jls. *Recreations:* music, cooking, saxophone. *Address:* King Edward VII Hospital Sister Agnes, Beaumont Street, W1G 6AA. *T:* (020) 7486 4411; Royal Free Hospital, Pond Street, NW3 2QG. *T:* (020) 7431 1321.

MAGOWAN, Ven. Alistair James; Archdeacon of Dorset, since 2000; *b* 10 Feb. 1955; *s* of Samuel and Marjorie Magowan; *m* 1979, (Margaret) Louise Magowan (*née* Atkin); one *s* two *d*. *Educ:* King's Sch., Worcester; Leeds Univ. (BSc Hons Animal Physiol. and Nutrition); Trinity Coll., Bristol (DipHE); MTh Oxon 2002. Ordained deacon, 1981, priest, 1982; Curate: St John the Baptist, Owlerton, Sheffield, 1981–84; St Nicholas, Durham, 1984–89; Chaplain, St Aidan's Coll., Durham Univ., 1984–89; Vicar, St John the Baptist, Egham, 1989–2000; RD, Runnymede, 1993–98. Canon, Salisbury Cathedral, 2000–. Chairman: Guildford Diocesan Bd of Educn, 1995–2000; Salisbury Diocesan Bd of Educn, 2003–. *Recreations:* walking, fly fishing, oil painting, stamp collecting. *Address:* Little Bailie, Dullar Lane, Sturminster Marshall, Wimborne, Dorset BH21 4AD.

MAGUIRE, Adrian Edward; National Hunt jockey, retired 2002; trainer, since 2005; *b* 29 April 1971; *s* of Joseph Maguire and of late Phyllis Maguire; *m* 1995, Sabrina; one *s* one *d*. *Educ:* Kilmessan Nat. Sch.; Trim Vocational Sch. Winner: Irish Grand National, on Omerta, 1991; Hennessy Gold Cup, on Sibton Abbey, 1992; Cheltenham Gold Cup, on Cool Ground, 1992; King George VI Chase, on Barton Bank, 1993, on Florida Pearl, 2001; Queen Mother Champion Chase, on Viking Flagship, 1994; Scottish National, on Baronet, 1998, on Paris Pike, 2000; Whitbread Gold Cup, on Call It A Day, 1998; rode 1,000th winner in British racing, 2001. *Address:* Laharn Cross, Lombardstown, Mallow, Co. Cork, Ireland.

MAGUIRE, Hugh, FRAM; violinist and conductor; Director of Strings, Britten-Pears School for Advanced Music Studies, 1978–2002; Professor of Violin, Royal Academy of Music, 1957–83; *b* 2 Aug. 1926; *m* 1st, 1953, Suzanne Lewis (marr. diss. 1987), of International Ballet; two *s* three *d*; 2nd, 1988, Tricia Catchpole. *Educ:* Belvedere Coll., SJ, Dublin; Royal Academy of Music, London (David Martin); Paris (Georges Enesco). Leader: Bournemouth Symphony Orchestra, 1952–56; London Symphony Orchestra, 1956–62; BBC Symphony Orchestra, 1962–67; Cremona String Quartet, 1966–68; Allegri String Quartet, 1968–76; Melos Ensemble, 1972–85; Orch. of Royal Opera House, Covent Garden, 1983–91. Artistic Dir, Irish Youth Orch., 1970–91; String coach, European Community Youth Orch., 1980–88. Mem., Irish Arts Council, 1980–90. Hon. MMus Hull, 1975; Hon. DLitt Univ. of Ulster, 1986; Hon. DMus NUI, 1992. Harriet Cohen Internat. Award, 1963; Councils Gold Medal (Ireland), 1963; Cobbett Medal, Musicians' Co., 1982. *Address:* Chapel Cottage, Peasenhall, Suffolk IP17 2JD.

MAGUIRE, Mairead C.; *see* Corrigan-Maguire.

MAGUIRE, Maria Bernadette, (Mrs G. R. Nicholson); QC (Scot.) 2002; *b* 19 Sept. 1961; *d* of late Robert Miller Maguire, Police Inspector, and of Mary Maguire (*née* Tanham); *m* 1991, Gavin Robert Nicholson; one *s* one *d*. *Educ:* Aberdeen Univ. (LLB; DLP). Admitted to Faculty of Advocates, 1987. Standing JC to Home Office, 1999–2002. *Address:* Advocates' Library, Parliament House, Parliament Square, Edinburgh EH1 1RF. *T:* (0131) 226 5071; *e-mail:* maria.maguire@advocates.org.uk.

MAHATHIR bin MOHAMAD, Tun Dr; MHR for Kubang Pasu, 1974–2003; Prime Minister of Malaysia, 1981–2003; *b* 20 Dec. 1925; *m* Tun Dr Siti Hasmah bt Mohamad Ali; seven *c*. *Educ:* Sultan Abdul Hamid Coll.; College of Medicine, Singapore (MB BS). Medical Officer, Kedah and Perlis, 1953–57; in private practice, 1957–64. MHR for Kota Star Selatan, 1964–69; Mem., Senate, 1972–74; Minister of: Education, 1974–77; Trade and Industry, 1977–81; Home Affairs, 1986–99; Dep. Prime Minister, 1976–81. President, United Malays Nat. Orgn, 1981–2003 (Mem., Supreme Council, 1972–2003). *Publication:* The Malay Dilemma, 1969; The Way Forward (essays), 1998.

MAHER, Christina Rose, OBE 1994; Founder and Director, Plain English Campaign, since 1979; *b* 21 April 1938; *d* of late Fred Lewington and Maureen (*née* Cullen); *m* 1959, George Bernard Maher; three *s* one *d*. *Educ:* St Cecilia's Sch., Liverpool. Community worker, 1969–98. Founder: Tuebrook Bugle (first community newspaper), 1971; Liverpool News (first newspaper for people with learning difficulties), 1974. Chm., Impact Printers Foundn, 1974–98; Founder, Salford Form Market (for NCC), 1975. Hon. MA Manchester, 1995; DUniv Open, 1997. *Publications:* Plain English Story, 1980; How to Write Letters/Reports in Plain English, 1995; Decade of Drivel, 1996; Language on Trial, 1996; A to Z for Lawyers, 1996. *Recreations:* swimming, dance, theatre, keep fit. *Address:* Hillside Farm, Combs, High Peak, Derbys SK23 9UT. *T:* (01298) 815979.

MAHER, Prof. Eamonn Richard, MD; FRCP; Professor of Medical Genetics, and Head, Department of Medical and Molecular Genetics, University of Birmingham, since 1996; Consultant in Clinical Genetics, West Midlands Regional Genetics Service, Birmingham Women's Health Care NHS Trust, since 1996; *b* 20 July 1956; *s* of Richard and Edna Maher; *m* 1980, Helen Marie (*neé* Jackson); two *s* three *d*. *Educ:* Salesian High Sch., Bootle; Univ. of Manchester (BSc 1st Cl. Hons Physiol. 1977; MB ChB Hons 1980; MD 1988); Univ. of Cambridge (MA 1996). MRCP 1983, FRCP 1996. Clinical Lectr, 1988–91, Univ. Lectr, 1991–96, in Med. Genetics, Univ. of Cambridge; Consultant in Med. Genetics, Addenbrooke's Hosp., Cambridge, 1991–96. Ed., Jl of Med. Genetics, 1998–. FMedSci 2006. *Publications:* A Practical Guide to Human Cancer Genetics (with S. V. Hodgson), 1994, 3rd edn (with S. V. Hodgson, W. D. Foulkes and C. Eng) 2006; over 250 scientific articles and book chapters on clinical and molecular aspects of cancer and med. genetics. *Recreations:* Everton Football Club, taxi driver for children. *Address:* Department of Medical and Molecular Genetics, University of Birmingham School of Medicine, Institute of Biomedical Research, Edgbaston, Birmingham B15 2TT. *T:* (0121) 627 2742, *Fax:* (0121) 627 2618; *e-mail:* E.R.Maher@bham.ac.uk.

MAHER, (Elizabeth) Jane, (Mrs Peter Krook), FRCP, FRCPE, FRCR; Consultant Oncologist, Mount Vernon Cancer Centre and Hillingdon Hospital, since 1986; Hon. Professor of Cancer and Supportive Care, Complexity Management Centre, Hertfordshire University, since 2005; *b* 31 March 1953; *d* of Matthew Gerard Maher and Stella Marie Maher (*née* Griffiths); *m* 1987, Peter Arthur Larson Krook; one *d*. *Educ:* Edgbaston C of E Coll. for Girls; King's Coll., London; Westminster Med. Sch. (MB BS 1976); Westminster Hosp.; Middlesex Hosp.; Harvard Univ.; Massachusetts Gen. Hosp. MRCP 1979, FRCP 1997; FRCR 1982; FRCPE 1998. Sen. Clinical Lectr, UCL, 1990–; Med. Dir, Lynda Jackson Macmillan Centre, and Dir, Psychosocial Res., 1998–; Med. Advr, Macmillan Cancer Support (formerly Macmillan Cancer Relief), 1999–. Chairman: Nat. Cancer Inst. Consensus Meeting, palliative radiotherapy, 1992; Maher Cttee, mgt of adverse effects of radiotherapy, 1995; London Cancer Task Force, 2000–04; Lead Clinician, Cancer Services Improvement, 2000–. *Publications:* articles on breast cancer and psychosocial oncology. *Recreations:* detective fiction, medieval churches. *Address:* Lynda Jackson Macmillan Centre, Mount Vernon Hospital, Rickmansworth Road, Northwood, Middx HA6 2RN. *T:* (01923) 844681, *Fax:* (01923) 844172; *e-mail:* jane.maher@mvh-ljmc.org. *Club:* Blacks.

MAHER, His Honour Terence; a Circuit Judge, 1995–2006; *b* 20 Dec. 1941; *s* of late John Maher and of Bessie Maher; *m* 1965 (marr. diss. 1983); two *d*. *Educ:* Burnley Grammar Sch.; Univ. of Manchester (LLB Hons). Admitted Solicitor, 1966; articled to Town Clerk, Burnley; Asst Sol., City of Bradford, 1966–68; Prosecuting Sol., Birmingham Corp., 1968–70; Dep. Pros. Sol., Thames Valley Police, 1970–73; Asst Sol. and partner, Cole & Cole, Oxford, 1973–83; Metropolitan Stipendiary Magistrate, 1983–95; a Chm., Inner London Juvenile, subseq. Youth, Courts and Family Proceedings Court, 1985–95; a Recorder, 1989–95. Gen. Sec., Univ. of Manchester Students' Union, 1962–63; Chm., Chipping Norton Round Table, 1975–76; Treasurer/Vice-Chm. and Chm., Oxford and District Solicitors' Assoc., 1980–83; Mem., Law Society Standing Cttee on Criminal Law, 1980–85. Mem. Editl Bd, Jl of Criminal Law, 1982–95. *Recreations:* walking, reading, anything to do with France and the French. *Address:* c/o Luton Crown Court, 7 George Street, Luton LU1 2AA. *Club:* Frewen (Oxford).

MAHER, Terence Anthony, FCCA; Chairman: Maher Booksellers Ltd, since 1995; Race Dynamics Ltd, since 1998; *b* 5 Dec. 1935; *s* of late Herbert and Lillian Maher; *m* 1960, Barbara (*née* Grunbaum); three *s*. *Educ:* Xaverian Coll., Manchester. ACCA 1960, FCCA 1970. Carborundum Co. Ltd, 1961–69; First National Finance Corp., 1969–72; Founder, Chm. and Chief Exec., Pentos plc, 1972–93; Chairman: Dillons Bookstores, 1977–93; Athena Internat., 1980–93; Ryman, 1987–93; Tempus Publishing (formerly Chalford Publishing) Co. Ltd, 1994–98. Mem., Adv. Council on Libraries, 1997–98. Contested (L): Accrington, 1964; Runcorn, 1966. Founder Trustee, Lib Dem, 1988–2001. Trustee, Photographers' Gall., 1994–97. FRSA 1988. Led successful campaign to abolish price control on books. *Publications:* (jtly) Counterblast, 1965; (jtly) Effective Politics, 1966; Against My Better Judgement (memoir), 1994; Unfinished Business (novel), 2003; Grumpy Old Liberal: a political rant, 2005. *Recreations:* reading, ski-ing, tennis, walking, music, bridge. *Address:* 33 Montagu Square, W1H 2LJ. *T:* (020) 7723 4254; The Old House, Whichford, near Shipston-on-Stour, Warwickshire CV36 5PG. *T:* (01608) 684614. *Clubs:* Savile, Portland.

MAHLER, Dr Halfdan Theodor; Director-General, World Health Organization, 1973–88, now Emeritus; Secretary-General, International Planned Parenthood Federation, 1989–95; consultant, international health, since 1996; *b* 21 April 1923; *m*

1957, Dr Ebba Fischer-Simonsen; two s. *Educ:* Univ. of Copenhagen (MD, EOPH). Planning Officer, Internat. Tuberculosis Campaign, Ecuador, 1950–51; Sen. WHO Med. Officer, Nat. TB Programme, India, 1951–61; Chief MO, Tuberculosis Unit, WHO/HQ, Geneva, 1961–69; Dir, Project Systems Analysis, WHO/HQ, Geneva, 1969–70; Asst Dir-Gen., WHO, 1970–73. Hon. FFPHM 1975; Hon. FRSocMed 1976; Hon. FRCGP 1986; Hon. FRSTM&H, 1993; Hon. Fellow: Indian Soc. for Malaria and other Communicable Diseases, Delhi; Faculty of Community Med., RCP, 1975; Hon. Professor: Univ. Nacional Mayor de San Marcos, Lima, Peru, 1980; Fac. of Medicine, Univ. of Chile, 1982; Beijing Med. Coll., China, 1983; Shanghai Med. Univ., 1986; Bartel World Affairs Fellow, Cornell, 1988; Peking Univ., 1994; Hon. Advr, China FPA, 1994. Hon. Fellow: LSHTM, 1979; Coll. of Physicians and Surgeons, Dacca, Bangladesh, 1980; Hon. Member: Soc. médicale de Genève; Union internat. contre la Tuberculose; Société Française d'Hygiène, de Médecine Sociale et Génie Sanitaire, 1977; Med. Assoc. of Argentina, 1985; Latin American Med. Assoc., 1985; Italian Soc. of Tropical Medicine, 1986; APHA, 1988; Swedish Soc. of Medicine, 1988; Hon. Foreign Corresponding Member: Inst. of Medicine, NAS, 1989; BMA, 1990; Hon. Life Mem., Uganda Medical Assoc., 1976; Assoc. Mem., Belgian Soc. of Trop. Medicine; Mem., Inst. of Medicine, USA, 1989; List of Honour, Internat. Dental Fedn, 1984; Hon. Academician: Nat. Acad. of Medicine, Mexico, 1988; Nat. Acad. of Medicine, Buenos Aires, 1988; Acad. of Health, Peru, 2001. FRCP 1981. Hon. LLD: Nottingham, 1975; McMaster, 1989; Exeter, 1990; Toronto, 1990; Hon. MD: Karolinska Inst., 1977; Charles Univ., Prague, and Mahidol Univ., Bangkok, 1982; Aarhus, 1988; Copenhagen, 1988; Aga Khan, Pakistan, 1989; Newcastle upon Tyne, 1990; Hon. Dr de l'Univ. Toulouse (Sciences Sociales), 1977; Hon. Dr Public Health, Seoul Nat. Univ., 1979; Hon DSc: Lagos, 1979; Emory, Atlanta, 1989; SUNY, 1990; Hon. Dr Med. Warsaw Med. Acad., 1980; Hon. Dr Faculty of Medicine, Univ. of Ghent, Belgium, and Universidad Nacional Autonoma de Nicaragua, Managua, 1983; Hon. DHL CUNY, 1989; Dr *hc.* Universidad Nacional 'Federico Villarreal', Lima, Peru, 1980; Semmelweis Univ. of Medicine, Budapest, 1987. Jane Evangelisty Purkyne Medal, Prague, 1974; Comenius Univ. Gold Medal, Bratislava, 1974; Carlo Forlanini Gold Medal, 1975; Ernst Carlsens Foundn Prize, Copenhagen, 1980; Georg Barfred-Pedersen Prize, Copenhagen, 1982; Hagedorn Medal and Prize, Denmark, 1986; Freedom from Want Medal, Roosevelt Inst., 1988; Bourgeoisie d'Honneur, Geneva, 1989; UK-US Hewitt Award, RSM, 1992; Dr Ved Vias Puri Meml Award, FPA of India, 1994; UN Population Award, 1995; Andrija Stampar Award, Assoc. of Schs of Public Health in European Region, 1995. Grand Officier: l'Ordre Nat. du Bénin, 1975; l'Ordre Nat. Voltaïque, 1978; l'Ordre du Mérite, République du Sénégal, 1982; Ordre National Malgache (Madagascar), 1987; Comdr (1st cl.), White Rose Order of Finland, 1983; Commandeur, l'Ordre National du Mali, 1982; Grand Cordon, Order of the Sacred Treasure (Japan), 1988; Storkors Af Dannebrogsordenen (Denmark), 1988; Grand Cross: Order of the Falcon (Iceland), 1988; Order of Merit (Luxembourg), 1990; Ordem do Merito Medico (Brazil), 2003. *Publications:* papers etc on the epidemiology and control of tuberculosis, the political, social, economic and technological priority setting in the health sector, and the application of systems analysis to health care problems. *Recreations:* sailing, ski-ing. *Address:* 12 chemin du Pont-Céard, 1290 Versoix, Switzerland; *e-mail:* halfdan.mahler@bluewin.ch.

MAHMOOD, Khalid; MP (Lab) Birmingham Perry Barr, since 2001; *b* 13 July 1961. Formerly: engr, advr, Danish Internat. Trade Union. Mem., Birmingham CC, 1990–93. *Address:* c/o House of Commons, SW1A 0AA; (office) 1 George Street, West Bromwich, West Midlands B70 6NT.

MAHON, Alice; *b* 28 Sept. 1937; *m;* two *s. Educ:* Bradford Univ. (BA Hons). Lectr, Bradford and Ilkley Community Coll. Member: Calderdale Bor. Council, 1982–87; Calderdale DHA. MP (Lab) Halifax, 1987–2005. PPS to Sec. of State for Culture, Media and Sport, 1997. Mem., Select Cttee on Health, 1991–97. Mem., Nato Parly (formerly N Atlantic) Assembly, 1992–2005. *Address:* 125 The Hough, Northowram, Halifax, W Yorks HX3 7DE.

MAHON, His Honour Charles Joseph; a Circuit Judge, 1989–2005; *b* 16 Aug. 1939; *s* of late Frank and Amy Agnes Mahon; *m* 1974, Lavinia Gough (*née* Breaks); one *d,* and one step *s* two step *d. Educ:* Chetham's Hosp.; Gonville and Caius Coll., Cambridge (BA, LLB). Called to the Bar, Gray's Inn, 1962. Parachute Regt, TA, 1964–72. *Recreations:* music, books, walking.

MAHON, Sir (John) Denis, CH 2003; Kt 1986; CBE 1967; MA Oxon; FBA 1964; art historian; Trustee of the National Gallery, 1957–64 and 1966–73; Member, Advisory Panel, National Art-Collections Fund, since 1975; *b* 8 Nov. 1910; *s* of late John FitzGerald Mahon (4th *s* of Sir W. Mahon, 4th Bt) and Lady Alice Evelyn Browne (*d* 1970), *d* of 5th Marquess of Sligo. *Educ:* Eton; Christ Church, Oxford (Hon. Student, 1996). Has specialised in the study of 17th-Century painting in Italy and has formed a collection of pictures of the period (exhibited Nat. Gall., 1997); is a member of the Cttee of the Biennial Exhibitions at Bologna, Italy; has long campaigned for fiscal measures to encourage support from private individs for art galls and museums. Awarded Medal for Benemeriti della Cultura by Pres. of Italy for services to criticism and history of Italian art, 1957; Archiginnasio d'Oro, City of Bologna, 1968; Serena Medal for Italian Studies, British Acad., 1972. Elected Accademico d'Onore, Clementine Acad., Bologna, 1964; Sen. Fellow, RCA, 1988; Corresp. Fellow: Accad. Raffaello, Urbino, 1968; Deputazione di Storia Patria per le provincie di Romagna, 1969. Ateneo Veneto, 1987. Hon. Citizen, Cento, 1982. Hon. FRA 2002. FRSA. Hon. DLitt: Newcastle, 1969; Oxford, 1994; Rome (La Sapienza), 1998; Bologna, 2002. *Publications:* Studies in Seicento Art and Theory, 1947; Mostra dei Carracci, Catalogo critico dei Disegni, 1956 (1963); Poussiniana, 1962; Catalogues of the Mostra del Guercino (Dipinti, 1968; Disegni, 1969); (with Nicholas Turner) The Drawings of Guercino in the Collection of Her Majesty the Queen at Windsor Castle, 1989; catalogues of exhibitions for 4th centenary of Guercino's birth, 1991–92; contributed to: Actes of Colloque Poussin, 1960; Friedlaender Festschrift, 1965; Problemi Guardeschi, 1967; (consultant) Luigi Salerno, I Dipinti del Guercino, 1988; articles, including a number on Caravaggio and Poussin, in art-historical periodicals, eg, The Burlington Magazine, Apollo, The Art Bulletin, Journal of the Warburg and Courtauld Institutes, Bulletin of the Metropolitan Museum of New York, Gazette des Beaux-Arts, Art de France, Paragone, Commentari, Zeitschrift für Kunstwissenschaft; has collaborated in the compilation of catalogues raisonnés of exhibitions, eg, Artists in 17th Century Rome (London, 1955), Italian Art and Britain (Royal Academy, 1960), L'Ideale Classico del Seicento in Italia (Bologna, 1962), Omaggio al Guercino (Cento, 1967). *Address:* 33 Cadogan Square, SW1X 0HU. *T:* (020) 7235 7311, 7235 2530.

MAHON, Seán Patrick Lauritson; Chief Executive, Cattles plc, 2001–07; *b* 16 April 1946; *s* of John Patrick Mahon and Peggy Lauritson Mahon; *m* 1968, Pauline Kathleen Starling; one *s* two *d* (and one *d* decd). *Educ:* Ratcliffe Coll. FCA 1969. Partner, Coopers & Lybrand, subseq. PricewaterhouseCoopers, 1969–2000; Member: UK Bd, Coopers & Lybrand, 1992–98; UK Supervisory Bd, PricewaterhouseCoopers, 1998–2000. Accreditation Bd, ICAEW, 1982–88; Pres., Sheffield Soc. of Chartered Accountants, 1990–91. Careers Adv. Bd, Univ. of Sheffield, 1982–88. Dir, S Yorks Ambulance Trust,

1991–97; Chairman: Leeds Cares, 1998–2004; National Cares, 2004–; HRH Prince of Wales's Ambassador for Yorks Businesses, 2004–; Jerrold Hldgs, 2007–; Ind. Dir, DLA Piper, 2007–. Hon. Treas., Clubs for Young People, 1984–. Pres., Sheffield Irish Soc., 1990–91. Hon. Dr Sheffield Hallam, 2005. *Recreations:* golf, fishing, shooting. *Address:* Wyngrove, 41 Stumperlowe Crescent Road, Sheffield S10 3PR. *T:* (0114) 230 4069, *Fax:* (0114) 263 0670. *Clubs:* Walbrook; Abbeydale Golf.

MAHON, Colonel Sir William (Walter), 7th Bt *cr* 1819 (UK), of Castlegar, Co. Galway; *b* 4 Dec. 1940; *s* of Sir George Edward John Mahon, 6th Bt and Audrey Evelyn (*née* Jagger) (*d* 1957); *S* father, 1987; *m* 1968, Rosemary Jane, *yr d* of late Lt-Col M. E. Melvill, OBE, Symington, Lanarks; one *s* two *d. Educ:* Eton. Commnd Irish Guards, 1960; served UK, Germany, Malaysia, Aden, Hong Kong, Pakistan, Spain. HM Body Guard, Hon. Corps of Gentlemen at Arms: Mem., 1993–; Clerk of the Cheque and Adjutant, 2006–08; Standard Bearer, 2008–. Fundraising, Macmillan Cancer Relief, 1993–2002. Chm., Nat. Army Mus. Develt Trust, 2003. *Recreations:* shooting, collecting, military history. *Heir: s* James William Mahon, *b* 29 Oct. 1976. *Club:* Army and Navy.

MAHONEY, Dennis Leonard; Chairman, Aon Global, since 2007; *b* 20 Sept. 1950; *s* of late Frederick Mahoney; *m* 1st, Julia McLaughlin (marr. diss.); one *s* one *d;* 2nd, 1988, Jacqueline Fox; one *s* two *d. Educ:* West Hatch Technical High School; Harvard Business Sch. (PMD 1983). Chm. and CEO, Aon Group Ltd, subseq. Aon Ltd, 1997–2007. *Address:* (office) Cumberland House, 1 Victoria Street, Hamilton HM11, Bermuda.

MAHONEY, Rev. Prof. John Aloysius, (Jack), SJ; Professor of Social Theology, Georgetown University, Washington, DC, since 2008; Emeritus Professor of Moral and Social Theology, University of London, since 1999; Emeritus Professor, Gresham College, London, since 2007; *b* Coatbridge, 14 Jan. 1931; *s* of Patrick Mahoney and Margaret Cecilia Mahoney (*née* Doris). *Educ:* Our Lady's High Sch., Motherwell; St Aloysius' Coll., Glasgow; Univ. of Glasgow (MA 1951). LicPhil 1956; LicTheol 1963; DTheol *summa cum laude,* Pontifical Gregorian Univ., Rome, 1967. Entered Society of Jesus, 1951; ordained priest, 1962; Jesuit Tertianship, NY, 1963–64. Lectr in Moral and Pastoral Theology, Heythrop Coll., Oxon, 1967–70, and Heythrop Coll., London, 1970–86; Principal, Heythrop Coll., London, 1976–81 (Fellow, 2000); F. D. Maurice Prof. of Moral and Social Theology, KCL, 1986–93; Founding Dir, KCL Business Ethics Res. Centre, 1987–93; Dean, Faculty of Theol., London Univ., and Faculty of Theol. and Religious Studies, KCL, 1990–92; Dixons Prof. of Business Ethics and Social Responsibility, London Business Sch., 1993–98; Founding Dir, Lauriston Centre for Contemporary Belief and Action, Edinburgh, and Hon. Fellow, Faculty of Divinity, Edinburgh Univ., 1998–2005; Sen. Res. Associate Dir, Heythrop Inst. for Religion, Ethics and Public Life, Heythrop Coll., Univ. of London, 2005–06; Mount Street Jesuit Centre, London, 2006–08. Mercers' Sch. Meml Prof. of Commerce, Gresham Coll., London, 1987–93; Martin D'Arcy Meml Lectr, Campion Hall, Oxford, 1981–82. Vis. Scholar, Boston Coll., Mass, 2005. Mem., Internat. Theol. Commn, Rome, 1974–80; Sector Pres., Nat. Pastoral Congress, 1980; Mem., Internat. Study Gp on Bioethics, Internat. Fedn of Catholic Univs, 1984–93. Pres., Catholic Theolog. Assoc., 1984–86. Chaplain to Tablet Table, 1983–98; Domestic Chaplain to Lord Mayor of London, 1989–90. CCMI (CIMgt 1993). Hon. Fellow: Gresham Coll., City of London, 1999–2000; St Mary's UC, Strawberry Hill, 1999–. Governor, St Aloysius' Coll., Glasgow, 1999–2005 (Chm., 2000–05). Founding Editor, Business Ethics, A European Review, 1992–98. Hon. DD London, 2004. President's Medal, Georgetown Univ., Washington, DC, 2003. *Publications:* Seeking the Spirit, 1981; Bioethics and Belief, 1984; The Making of Moral Theology, 1987; The Ways of Wisdom, 1987; Teaching Business Ethics in the UK, Europe and USA, 1990; (ed) Business Ethics in a New Europe, 1992; The Challenge of Human Rights: origin, development and significance, 2006. *Address:* Wolfington Hall, Georgetown University, Washington, DC 20057–1200, USA; *e-mail:* jmlaur@aol.com.

MAHY, Brian Wilfred John, PhD, ScD; Senior Scientific Adviser, Co-ordinating (formerly National) Center for Infectious Diseases, Centers for Disease Control and Prevention, Atlanta, since 2000; Adjunct Professor, Emory University, since 1993; *b* 7 May 1937; *s* of Wilfred Mahy and Norah Dillingham; *m* 1st, 1959, Valerie Pouteaux (marr. diss. 1986); two *s* one *d;* 2nd, 1988, Penny Scott (*née* Cunningham). *Educ:* Elizabeth Coll., Guernsey; Univ. of Southampton (BSc, PhD); Univ. of Cambridge (MA, ScD 1982). Res. Biologist, Dept of Cancer Res., London Hosp. Med. Coll., Univ. of London, 1962–65; Asst Dir, Res. Virology, Dept of Pathology, Cambridge Univ., 1965–79; Fellow and Tutor, University (Wolfson) Coll., 1967–84; Librarian, Wolfson Coll., 1975–80; Huddersfield Lectr in Special Path. (Virology), 1979–84; Head, Div. of Virology, Cambridge, 1979–84; Head, Pirbright Lab., AFRC Inst. for Animal Health (formerly Animal Virus Res. Inst. and AFRC Inst. for Animal Disease Res.), 1984–89; Dir, Div. of Viral and Rickettsial Diseases, Centers for Disease Control and Prevention, Atlanta, GA, 1989–2000. Vis. Prof., Univ. of Minnesota, 1968; Eleanor Roosevelt Internat. Cancer Fellow, Dept of Microbiol., Univ. of California, San Francisco, 1973–74; Vis. Prof., Inst. für Virologie, Univ. of Würzburg, 1980–81. Convener, Virus Group, 1980–84, Mem. Council, 1983–87, Soc. for General Microbiology; Vice-Chm., 1987–90, Chm., 1990–93, Past Chm., 1994–96, Virology Div., Vice Pres., 1995–99, Pres., 1999–2002, Past Pres., 2002–05, Internat. Union of Microbiol Socs. FRSocMed 1985; Fellow: Infectious Diseases Soc. of America, 1992; Amer. Acad. of Microbiol., 1998–. Hon. DSc Southampton, 2001. Editor-in-Chief, Virus Research, 1983–; US Editor: Jl of Med. Virology, 1994–; Reviews in Med. Virology, 2000–. *Publications:* (jtly) The Biology of Large RNA Viruses, 1970; Negative Strand Viruses, 1975; Negative Strand Virus and the Host Cell, 1978; Lactic Dehydrogenase Virus, 1975; A Dictionary of Virology, 1981, 3rd edn 2001; Virus Persistence, 1982; The Microbe 1984: pt 1, Viruses, 1984; Virology: a practical approach, 1985; The Biology of Negative Strand Viruses, 1987; Genetics and Pathogenicity of Negative Strand Viruses, 1989; Concepts in Virology: from Ivanovsky to the present, 1993; Virology Methods Manual, 1996; Immunobiology and Pathogenesis of Persistent Virus Infections, 1996; (ed jtly) Topley & Wilson's Microbiology and Microbial Infections, 9th edn, Vol. 1, 1998, 10th edn, Vol. 1, 2005; numerous articles on animal virology in learned jls. *Recreations:* playing the violin in chamber and orchestral groups, gardening. *Address:* Co-ordinating Center for Infectious Diseases (C12), Centers for Disease Control and Prevention, 1600 Clifton Road, NE, Atlanta, GA 30333, USA.

MAHY, Margaret May, ONZ 1993; writer; *b* 21 March 1936; *d* of Francis George Mahy and Helen May Penlington; two *d. Educ:* Whakatane Primary and High Schs; Univ. of NZ (BA). Asst Librarian, Petone Public Library, 1959; Asst Children's Librarian, Christchurch Public Library, 1960; Librarian i/c of school requests, Sch. Library Service (Christchurch Br.), 1967; Children's Librarian, Christchurch Public Library, 1977; full time writer, 1980–. Hon. DLitt Canterbury, 1993. Carnegie Medal, 1982, 1984; Esther Glen Medal. *Publications: picture books:* The Dragon of an Ordinary Family, 1969; A Lion in the Meadow, 1969; Mrs Discombobulous, 1969; Pillycock's Shop, 1969; The Procession, 1970; The Little Witch, 1970; Sailor Jack and the Twenty Orphans, 1970; The Princess and the Clown, 1971; The Boy with Two Shadows, 1971; The Man whose Mother was a Pirate, 1972; The Railway Engine and the Hairy Brigands, 1973; Rooms for Rent/Rooms to Let, 1974; The Witch in the Cherry Tree, 1974; The Rare Spotted Birthday

Party, 1974; Stepmother, 1974; The Ultra-Violet Catastrophe, 1975; The Great Millionaire Kidnap, 1975; The Wind Between the Stars, 1976; David's Witch Doctor, 1976; Leaf Magic, 1976; The Boy who was Followed Home, 1977; Jam, 1985; The Great White Man-Eating Shark, 1989; The Tin Can Band and Other Poems, 1989; Making Friends, 1990; The Pumpkin Man and the Crafty Creeper, 1990; The Seven Chinese Brothers, 1990; The Dentist's Promise, 1991; Keeping House, 1991; The Queen's Goat, 1991; The Horrendous Hullabaloo, 1992; The Three-Legged Cat, 1993; A Busy Day for a Good Grandmother, 1993; The Christmas Tree Tangle, 1994; The Rattlebang Picnic, 1994; The Big Black Bulging Bump, 1995; Boom, Baby, Boom, Boom!, 1996; Beaten by a Balloon, 1997; Summery Saturday Morning, 1998; Simply Delicious!, 1999; Dashing Dog, 2002; Down the Back of the Chair, 2006; Bubble Trouble, 2008; *collections of stories:* three Margaret Mahy Story Books, 1972, 1973, 1975; A Lion in the Meadow, 1976; Nonstop Nonsense, 1977; The Great Piratical Rumbustification and The Librarian and the Robbers, 1978; The Chewing-Gum Rescue, 1982; The Birthday Burglar and a Very Wicked Headmistress, 1984; The Downhill Crocodile Whizz, 1986; Mahy Magic, 1986; The Three Wishes, 1986; The Door in the Air, 1988; Bubble Trouble, 1991; Tick Tock Tales, 1993; *junior novels:* Clancy's Cabin, 1974; The Bus Under the Leaves, 1975; The Pirate Uncle, 1977; Raging Robots and Unruly Uncles, 1981; The Pirates' Mixed-Up Voyage, 1983; The Blood and Thunder Adventure on Hurricane Peak, 1989; The Cousins Quartet, books 1–4, 1994; The Greatest Show off Earth, 1994; Tingleberries, Tuckertubs and Telephones: a tale of love and ice-cream, 1995; The Five Sisters, 1996; The Horribly Haunted School, 1997; Dinsmore Down in the Dump, 1999; A Villain's Night Out, 1999; *novels for older readers:* The Haunting, 1982; The Changeover, 1984; The Catalogue of the Universe, 1985; Aliens in the Family, 1986; The Tricksters, 1986; Memory, 1987; Dangerous Spaces, 1991; Underrunners, 1992; The Other Side of Silence, 1995; Operation Terror, 1997; Alchemy, 2002; *for schools:* The Crocodile's Christmas Jandals, 1982; The Bubbling Crocodile, 1983; Mrs Bubble's Baby, 1983; Shopping with a Crocodile, 1983; Going to the Beach, 1984; The Great Grumbler and the Wonder Tree, 1984; Fantail Fantail, 1984; A Crocodile in the Garden, 1985; The Crocodile's Christmas Thongs, 1985; Horrakapotchkin, 1985; *for emergent readers:* Ups and Downs, 1984; Wibble Wobble, 1984; The Dragon's Birthday, 1984; The Spider in the Shower, 1984; The Adventures of a Kite, 1985; Sophie's Singing Mother, 1985; The Earthquake, 1985; The Cake, 1985; The Catten, 1985; Out in the Big Wide World, 1985; A Vary Happy Bathday, 1985; Clever Hamburger, 1985; Muppy's Ball, 1986; Baby's Breakfast, 1986; The Tree Doctor, 1986; The Garden Party, 1986; The Man who Enjoyed Grumbling, 1986; The Trouble with Heathrow, 1986; The Pop Group, 1986; Feeling Funny, 1986; A Pet to the Vet, 1986; The New House Villain, 1986; Tai Taylor is Born, 1986; The Terrible Topsy-Turvy Tissy-Tossy Tangle, 1986; Trouble on the Bus, 1986; Mr Rumfitt, 1986; My Wonderful Aunt, 1986; The Funny, Funny Clown Face, 1986; The Haunting of Miss Cardamon, 1987; The Girl Who Washed by Moonlight, 1987; The King's Jokes, 1987; The Mad Puppet, 1987; *verse:* Seventeen Kings and Forty-Two Elephants, 1972; *non-fiction:* Look Under 'V', 1977. *Recreations:* reading, gardening. *Address:* No 1 RD, Lyttelton, New Zealand. *T:* (3) 299703.

MAI, Prof. Yiu-Wing, PhD, DSc, DEng; FRS 2008; University Chair, since 2004, Professor of Mechanical Engineering, since 2007, and Director, Centre for Advanced Materials Technology, since 1988, University of Sydney; *b* Hong Kong, 5 Jan. 1946; *s* of Lam Mai and Yuet-Yau Tsui; *m* 1980, Louisa Kit-Ling. *Educ:* Univ. of Hong Kong (BSc Engrg 1969; PhD 1972; DSc 1999); Univ. of Sydney (DEng 1999). FIEAust 1984; FTSE 1992; FHKIE 1994; FAA 2001; FHKAES 2003. Mgt and Technol. Trainer, Hong Kong Productivity Council, 1973; Postdoctoral Research Assistant: Univ. of Michigan, 1974–75; Imperial Coll., London, 1975–76; University of Sydney: Lectr, 1976–78; Sen. Lectr, 1978–82; Associate Prof., 1983–87; Prof. of Mechanical Engrg, 1987–2002; Associate Dean, R&D, 1990–93; Dir, Graduate Sch. of Engrg, 1995–98; Dir, Defence Sci. and Technol. Orgn—Airframes and Engines Div. Centre for Expertise in Damage Mechanics, 1997–2003; Pro-Dean, 1998–2004; ARC Federation Fellow, 2002–07. Prof., HKUST, 1993–95; Chair, City Univ. of Hong Kong, 2000–02; Dist. Vis. Prof., Univ. of Hong Kong, 2003–04. Pres., Australian Fracture Gp Inc., 1997. Mem. Council, Asian-Australian Assoc. for Composite Materials, 1999– (Founder Pres., 1997–98); Pres., Internat. Congress on Fracture, 2002–05 (Vice-Pres., 1997–2001). Mem., Eur. Acad. of Scis, 2008. FASME 1999. *Publications:* (with A. G. Atkins) Elastic and Plastic Fracture, 1985; (with B. Cotterell) Fracture Mechanics of Cementitious Materials, 1996; (with J. K. Kim) Engineered Interfaces in Fibre-Reinforced Composites, 1998; over 600 articles in scientific jls. *Recreations:* reading mainly Chinese literature, practising Chinese calligraphy, walking. *Address:* School of Aerospace, Mechanical and Mechatronic Engineering, Mechanical Engineering Building J07, University of Sydney, Sydney, NSW 2006, Australia. *T:* (2) 93512290, *Fax:* (2) 93513760; *e-mail:* y.mai@usyd.edu.au.

MAIANI, Prof. Luciano; President, Consiglio Nazionale delle Ricerche, Rome, since 2008; Professor of Theoretical Physics, University of Rome, since 1984; Director General, Organisation Européenne pour la Recherche Nucléaire (CERN), 1999–2003 (President of Council, 1997); *b* 16 July 1941. *Educ:* Univ. of Rome (degree in Physics 1964). Research Associate: Istituto Superiore di Sanità, 1964; Univ. of Florence, 1964; Fellow, Lyman Lab. of Physics, Univ. of Harvard, 1969; Prof., Inst. of Theoretical Physics, Univ. of Rome, 1976; Vis. Prof., Ecole Normale Supérieure, Paris, 1977; Vis. Prof., 1979–80, 1985–86, Mem. Council, 1993–97, CERN. Pres., Istituto Naz. di Fisica Nucleare, Italy, 1993–98. Fellow, APS, 1991 (J. Sakurai Prize, 1987; E. Fermi Prize, 2003). *Address:* Consiglio Nazionale delle Ricerche, Piazzale Aldo Moro 7, 00185 Rome, Italy.

MAIBAUM, Prof. Thomas Stephen Edward, PhD; CEng, FIET; Professor, Foundations of Software Engineering, and Canada Research Chair, Department of Computing and Software, McMaster University, Canada, since 2004; *b* 18 Aug. 1947; *s* of Leslie Maibaum and Olga Maibaum (*née* Klein); *m* 1971, Janet Hilless; one *s* one *d*. *Educ:* Toronto Univ. (BSc); PhD London Univ. Postdoctoral Fellow, 1973, Asst Prof., 1974–81, Univ. of Waterloo; Imperial College, University of London: Lectr, Dept of Computing, 1981–86; Reader in Computing Science, 1986–90; Hd, Dept of Computing, 1989–97; Prof., Foundns of Software Engrg, 1990–99; King's College London: Prof., Foundns of Software Engrg, 1999–2004; Hd, Dept of Computer Sci., 2001–03. Vis. Prof., Pontificia Universidade Católica de Rio do Janeiro, 1977, 1981 (Hon. Prof., 1992); Royal Soc./SERC Industrial Fellow, 1984; Marie Curie Fellowship (EU), Univ. of Lisbon, 1997–98. FRSA. Engrg Foresight Award, Royal Acad. Engrg, 1998. *Publications:* (jtly) The Specification of Computer Programs, 1987; (ed jtly) Handbook of Logic in Computer Science, vol. I, 1992, vol. II, 1992, vol. III, 1995, vol. IV, 1995, vol. V, 2000. *Recreations:* memorising the films of Mel Brooks, music, opera, travel, literature. *Address:* Department of Computing and Software, McMaster University, 1280 Main Street West, Hamilton, ON L8S 4K1, Canada; 329 Lloyminn Avenue, Ancaster, ON L9G 3Z6, Canada. *T:* (905) 5259140 ext. 26627.

MAIDEN, Sir Colin (James), Kt 1992; ME, DPhil; Chairman, Tower Insurance Ltd (formerly National Insurance Company of New Zealand Ltd), 1988–2002; Director, Fisher & Paykel Healthcare Corporation Ltd, since 2001; Vice-Chancellor, University of Auckland, New Zealand, 1971–94; *b* 5 May 1933; *s* of Henry A. Maiden; *m* 1957, Jenefor Mary Rowe; one *s* three *d*. *Educ:* Auckland Grammar Sch.; Univ. of Auckland, NZ (ME); Rhodes Scholar (NZ) 1955; Exeter Coll., Oxford (DPhil; Hon. Fellow, 1994). Post-doctorate research, Oxford Univ. (supported by AERE, Harwell), 1957–58; Head of Hypersonic Physics Section, Canadian Armament Research and Develt Estabt, Quebec City, Canada, 1958–60; Sen. Lectr in Mechanical Engrg, Univ. of Auckland, 1960–61; Head of Material Sciences Laboratory, Gen. Motors Corp., Defense Research Laboratories, Santa Barbara, Calif, USA, 1961–66; Manager of Process Engineering, Gen. Motors Corp., Technl Centre, Warren, Michigan, USA, 1966–70. Chairman: NZ Synthetic Fuels Corp. Ltd, 1980–90; Fisher & Paykel Industries Ltd, 1989–2001 (Dir, 1978); Sedgwick Gp (NZ) Ltd, 1996–98 (Dir, 1994–98); Transpower NZ Ltd, 1997–2004 (Dir, 1994–2004); DB Gp Ltd, 2003– (Dir, 1994–); Director: Mason Industries Ltd, 1971–78; Farmers Trading Co. Ltd, 1973–86; Winstone Ltd, 1978–88; Wilkins & Davies Co. Ltd, 1986–89; NZ Steel Ltd, 1988–92; Independent Newspapers Ltd, 1989–2004 (Chm., 1994–2001); ANZ Banking Gp (NZ) Ltd, 1990–93; NZ Refining Co. Ltd, 1991–2007; Progressive Enterprises Ltd, 1992–2000; Tower Ltd, 1995–2003; Foodland Associated Ltd (WA), 2000–05. Chairman: NZ Energy R&D Cttee, 1974–81; Liquid Fuels Trust Bd, 1978–86. Chm., NZ Vice-Chancellors' Cttee, 1977–78, and 1991; Hon. Treasurer, ACU, 1988–98. Member: Spirit of Adventure Trust Bd, 1972–80; NZ Metric Adv. Bd, 1973–77. NZ Agent for Joint NZ/US Sci. and Technol Agreement, 1974–81. Hon. FIPENZ 1999. Hon. LLD Auckland, 1994. Thomson Medal, Royal Soc. NZ, 1986; Medal, Univ. of Bonn, 1983; Symons Award, ACU, 1999. Silver Jubilee Medal, 1977. *Publications:* numerous scientific and technical papers. *Recreation:* tennis. *Address:* Apt 503. 10 Middleton Road, Remuera, Auckland, New Zealand. *T:* (9) 5290380. *Clubs:* Vincent's (Oxford); Northern (Auckland); Remuera Racquets, International Lawn Tennis of NZ, Auckland Golf.

MAIDEN, (James) Dennis, CEng; Director General, Federation of Master Builders, 1991–97; *b* 28 June 1932; *s* of James William Maiden and Elsie (*née* Brotherton); *m* 1953, Irene Harris; one *s* one *d*. *Educ:* Wath-upon-Dearne Grammar Sch. CEng 1966; MIMechE 1966; FFB 1987–2003. Engrg Consultant, Husband & Co., 1958–63; Chief Engr, British Shoe Corp., 1963–67; Construction Industry Training Board: Develt Manager, 1967–73; Gen. Manager, 1973–76; Dir of Trng, 1976–85; Chief Exec., 1985–90; Dir-Gen. designate, Fedn of Master Builders, 1990–91. Chief Exec., Construction Ind. Services Ltd, 1991–97; Managing Director: Nat. Register of Warranted Builders Ltd, 1991–97; Trade Debt Recovery Service Ltd, 1991–97. Pres., Kings Lynn Inst. of Mgt, 1988. Chm., Park House Hotel for Disabled People, 1983–88 and 1995–99. Trustee, Leonard Cheshire Foundn, 1987–92; Pres., Norfolk Outward Bound Assoc., 1988. Hon. Mem., C & G, 1981; CCMI (CIMgt 1986); MIPM 1971; FRSA 1987. Freeman, City of London, 1988; Liveryman, Co. of: Constructors, 1988; Plumbers, 1989. *Recreations:* golf, gardening, theatre. *Address:* Micklebring, Church Lane, Bircham, Kings Lynn, Norfolk PE31 6QW. *T:* (01485) 578336. *Club:* Hunstanton Golf.

MAIDEN, Prof. Martin David, PhD; FBA 2003; Professor of the Romance Languages, University of Oxford, since 1996; Fellow of Trinity College, Oxford, since 1996; *b* 20 May 1957; *s* of Kenneth Henry Maiden and Betty Maiden (*née* Liddiard); *m* 2005, Liliana Buruiana; one step *d*. *Educ:* King Edward VI Sch., Southampton; Trinity Hall, Cambridge (MA, MPhil, PhD). Lectr in Italian, Univ. of Bath, 1982–89; Univ. Lectr in Romance Philology, and Fellow of Downing Coll., Cambridge, 1989–96. Delegate, OUP, 2004–. Pres., Società Internazionale di Linguistica e Filologia Italiana, 1989–91; Mem. Council, Philological Soc., 1996–2000, 2003–. Associate Member: Centre for Res. on Lang. Contact, York Univ., Toronto, 2005; Associazione Italiana di Romenistica, 2006; Hon. Mem., Asociația culturală Alexandru Philippide (Iași, Romania), 2005–. Consultant Editor: Etudes romanes, 2001–; Diachronica, 2002–; Legenda Publications, 2002–; Troubadour Publications, 2002–; Studii și cercetări lingvistice, 2005–; L'Italia dialettale, 2006–; Rivista italiana di linguistica, 2006–. *Publications:* Interactive Morphonology: metaphony in Italy, 1991; (ed with J. C. Smith) Linguistic Theory and the Romance Languages, 1995; A Linguistic History of Italian, 1995; (ed with M. Parry) The Dialects of Italy, 1997; Storia linguistica dell' italiano, 1998; (with C. Robustelli) A Reference Grammar of Modern Italian, 2000, 2nd edn 2007; articles in various jls, incl. Romance Philology, Zeitschrift für romanische Philologie, Jl of Linguistics. *Recreation:* travel. *Address:* 62 Cunliffe Close, Oxford OX2 7BL. *T:* (01865) 511753.

MAIDEN, Robert Mitchell, FCIBS; Managing Director, Royal Bank of Scotland plc, and Executive Director, Royal Bank of Scotland Group plc, 1986–91; *b* 15 Sept. 1933; *s* of Harry and Georgina Maiden; *m* 1958, Margaret Mercer (*née* Nicolson). *Educ:* Montrose Acad., Tayside, Scotland. Royal Bank of Scotland: various appts, 1950–74; Supt of branches, 1974–76; Treasurer, 1976–77; Chief Accountant, 1977–81; Gen. Man. (Finance), 1981–82; Exec. Dir, 1982–86. Vice-Chm., CC-Bank AG, Germany, 1991–93; Chm., Lothian and Edinburgh Enterprise, 1994–96. Member: Accounts Commn for Scotland, 1992–99; Scottish Panel of Adjudicators, Investors in People, Scotland, 1996–2001. Gov., Napier Univ. (formerly Napier Poly.), 1988–98. Trustee, C of S Pension Scheme, 1991–96. FCMI; FRSA. *Recreations:* music, golf, reading. *Address:* Trinafour, 202 Braid Road, Edinburgh EH10 6HS. *Club:* New (Edinburgh).

MAIDLOW DAVIS, Richard Cuthbert Tolly, (Dom Leo Richard), OSB; Headmaster, Downside School, since 2003; *b* 22 April 1954; *s* of Michael Maidlow Davis and Yvette Maidlow Davis (*née* Tolley). *Educ:* Downside Sch.; Magdalene Coll., Cambridge (BA 1975); Univ. of London (BD 1982); Gregorianum, Rome (STL 1986). Professed, 1979; ordained priest, 1981; Downside School: Teacher of Classics and Religious Studies, 1982–; Novice Master, 1986–91; House Master, Smythe House, 1991–2000; Editor, Raven (Downside Sch. Mag.), 1992–; Novice Master, 2000–02. Curate, Midsomer Norton, 1982–84. *Recreations:* bicycling, woodwork. *Address:* Downside School, Stratton-on-the-Fosse, Radstock, Bath, Som BA3 4RJ. *T:* (01761) 235100.

MAIDMENT, Francis Edward, (Ted); Headmaster, Shrewsbury School, 1988–2001; *b* 23 Aug. 1942; *s* of Charles Edward and late Olive Mary Maidment. *Educ:* Pocklington Sch., York; Jesus Coll., Cambridge (Scholar). Asst Master, Lancing Coll., 1965–81 (Housemaster, 1975–81); Headmaster, Ellesmere Coll., Shropshire, 1982–88. *Recreations:* lecturing and speaking, singing, medieval history, modest tennis. *Address:* Linden Cottage, Astley, Shrewsbury SY4 4BP. *Clubs:* East India, Devonshire, Sports and Public Schools; Gilgil (Kenya).

MAIDMENT, Neil, CMG 1996; Executive Director, Glaxo Wellcome plc (formerly Glaxo Holdings plc), 1993–95 (responsible for Asia Pacific, 1993–95, and for Africa, Middle East and Turkey, 1994–95); *b* Oxford, 18 Aug. 1938; *s* of late Kenneth John Maidment, Founding Vice-Chancellor, Univ. of Auckland and Isobel Felicity Maidment (*née* Leitch); *m* 1983, Sandie Shuk-Ling Yuen. *Educ:* Magdalen Coll. Sch., Oxford; King's Sch., Auckland; King's Coll., Auckland; Univ. of Auckland (Life Mem., Students' Assoc.). Evacuated to USA with Oxford Univ. children's gp, 1940–45. South British Insurance Co. Ltd, Auckland, Singapore, Calcutta, Bombay, 1958–65; Glaxo Group: Far Eastern Surgical Rep., Singapore, Kuala Lumpur, 1965–68; Manager: Hong Kong, 1968–70;

Manila, 1971; Director and General Manager: Glaxo Hong Kong Ltd, 1971–93; Glaxo China Ltd, 1988–93; Area Dir, North Asia, 1990–93. Member: Pharmacy and Poisons Appeal Tribunal, Hong Kong, 1979–88; Sub-Cttee on Biotechnology, Hong Kong, 1988–89; UK/Hong Kong Scholarships Cttee, 1988–94. Pres., Hong Kong Assoc. of Pharmaceutical Industry, 1977–78; Chm., British Chamber of Commerce, Hong Kong, 1989–90. Non-exec. Dir, Hong Kong Inst. of Biotechnol. Ltd, 1996–2002. *Publication:* (with H. Scrimgeour and H. Williams) Arthur Scrimgeour—a life, 1990. *Recreations:* reading, travelling in China. *Address:* PO Box 23022, Wanchai, Hong Kong; Les Jumelles, 20658 Lakeshore, Baie d'Urfé, QC H9X 1R4, Canada. *Clubs:* Hong Kong, Hong Kong Jockey (Hong Kong); Saturday (Calcutta).

MAIDMENT, Ted; *see* Maidment, F. E.

MAIDSTONE, Viscount; Tobias Joshua Stormont Finch Hatton; *b* 21 June 1998; *s* and *heir* of Earl of Winchilsea and Nottingham, *qv*.

MAIDSTONE, Bishop Suffragan of, since 2001; **Rt Rev. Graham Alan Cray;** *b* 21 April 1947; *s* of late Alan Cray and Doris Mary Kathleen Cray; *m* 1973, Jacqueline Webster; two *d*. *Educ:* Leeds Univ. (BA 1968); St John's Coll., Nottingham. Ordained deacon, 1971, priest, 1972; Asst Curate, St Mark, Gillingham, 1971–75; N Area Co-ordinator, Youth Dept, CPAS, 1975–78; Asst Curate, 1978–82, Vicar, 1982–92, St Michael-le-Belfrey, York; Principal, Ridley Hall Theol Coll., 1992–2001. *Recreations:* listening to rock music, following sport, reading theology. *Address:* Bishop's House, Pett Lane, Charing, Ashford, Kent TN27 0DL.

MAIDSTONE, Archdeacon of; *see* Down, Ven. P. R.

MAIER, Prof. John Paul, DPhil; FRS 1999; Professor of Physical Chemistry, University of Basel, since 1991; *b* 15 Nov. 1947; *s* of Dr H. E. Maier and S. Maier; three *d* (one *s* decd). *Educ:* Univ. of Nottingham (BSc Hons Chemistry 1966); Balliol Coll., Oxford (DPhil Physical Chemistry 1972). University of Basel: Royal Soc. Fellow, 1973–74; Res. Associate, 1975–78; Lectr in Chemistry, 1978–81; Associate Prof. in Physical Chemistry, 1982–90. Werner Prize, Swiss Chem. Soc., 1979; Marlow Medal, RSC, 1980; Chemistry Prize, Göttingen Sci. Acad., 1986; Nat. Latsis Prize, Swiss Nat. Sci Foundn, 1987. *Recreations:* bridge, golf. *Address:* Department of Chemistry, Klingelbergstrasse 80, 4056 Basel, Switzerland. *T:* (61) 2673826, *Fax:* (61) 2673855; *e-mail:* j.p.maier@unibas.ch.

MAILER, Joanna Mary; *see* Shapland, J. M.

MAIN, Very Rev. Prof. Alan, TD 1982; PhD; Professor of Practical Theology, Aberdeen University, 1980–2001; Master, Christ's College, Aberdeen, 1992–2001; Moderator of the General Assembly of the Church of Scotland, 1998–99; *b* 31 March 1936; *s* of James E. W. Main and Mary A. R. Black; *m* 1960, Anne Louise Swanson; two *d*. *Educ:* Robert Gordon's Coll., Aberdeen; Aberdeen Univ. (MA 1957; BD 1960; PhD 1963); Union Theol Seminary, NY (STM 1961). Minister, Chapel of Garioch Parish, Aberdeenshire, 1963–70; Chaplain to Univ. of Aberdeen, 1970–80. Pres., Boys' Bde, 2005–07. Patron, Seven Incorp. Trades of Aberdeen, 2000–. Hon. DD Aberdeen, 2006. *Publications:* Worship Now, 1989; (ed) But Where Shall Wisdom Be Found?, 1995; (ed) Northern Accents, 2001; articles in jls on pastoral care and counselling, military ethics, medical ethics. *Recreations:* music (piano and organ), golf, bee-keeping. *Address:* Kirkfield, Barthol Chapel, Inverurie AB51 8TD. *Club:* Royal Northern and University (Aberdeen).

MAIN, Anne; MP (C) St Albans, since 2005; *b* 17 May 1957; *d* of late George and of Rita Wiseman; *m* 1st, 1978, Stephen Tonks (*d* 1991); one *s* two *d*; 2nd, 1995, Andrew Jonathan Main; one *s*. *Educ:* Bishop of Llandaff Secondary Sch., Cardiff; Univ. Coll. of Wales, Swansea (BA 1978); Univ. of Sheffield (PGCE 1978). Teacher of English and Drama, Feltham Comp. Sch., 1979–80; supply posts, Bristol, 1991–94. Member (C): Beaconsfield Parish Council, 1999–2002; S Bucks DC, 2001–05. *Address:* (office) 104 High Street, London Colney, St Albans, Herts AL2 1QL; House of Commons, SW1A 0AA.

MAIN, Air Vice-Marshal John Bartram, CB 1996; OBE 1979 (MBE 1977); FREng, FIET; Military Adviser, Matra Marconi Space/Astrium, 1996–2001; *b* 28 Jan. 1941; *s* of late Wing Comdr James Taylor Main, OBE and Nellie Ethel Toleman; *m* 1965, Helen Joyce Lambert; two *d*. *Educ:* Portsmouth Grammar Sch.; Birmingham Univ. (BSc Elect. Eng.); RAF Tech. Coll., Henlow. MIEE 1968, FIET (FIEE 1983). Commissioned Engr Branch, RAF, 1960; served Benson, Hiswa (Aden), Thorney Island; mentioned despatches, 1968; Dir of Sci. and Tech. Intell., MoD, 1970–74; OC No 33 Signals Unit, Cyprus, 1974–77; CO RAF Digby, 1977–79; RAF Staff Coll., 1979–80; RAF Signals Engrg Estabt, 1980–83; Head, Tech. Intell. (Air), 1983–87; RCDS 1986; Dep. Comd Aerosystems Engr, HQ Strike Comd, 1987–88; Comdt, RAF Sigs Engrg Estabt and Air Cdre Sigs, HQ RAF Support Comd, 1988–89; Dir, Command, Control, Communication and Inf. Systems (Policy and Op. Requirements), 1989–93; DG Support Services (RAF), 1993–94; AO Communications and Inf. Systems, and AOC Signals Units, HQ Logistics Comd, 1994–96. FREng 2001 (CEng 1968); FRAeS 1984. *Recreations:* gardening, cycling, sailing, reading. *Address:* Robin's Mead, 120 Manor Way, Aldwick Bay, West Sussex PO21 4HN. *Club:* Royal Air Force.

MAIN, His Honour John Roy; QC 1974; a Circuit Judge, 1976–95; *b* 21 June 1930; *yr s* of late A. C. Main, MIMechE; *m* 1955, Angela de la Condamine Davies, *er d* of late R. W. H. Davies, ICS; two *s* one *d*. *Educ:* Portsmouth Grammar Sch.; Hotchkiss Sch., USA; Brasenose Coll., Oxford (MA). Called to Bar, Inner Temple, 1954; a Recorder of Crown Court, 1972–76. Mem. Special Panel, Transport Tribunal, 1970–76; Dep. Chm., IoW QS, 1971. Pres., Transport Tribunal, 1996–97 (Chm., 1997–2000). Gov., Portsmouth Grammar Sch., 1988–2000. *Recreations:* walking, gardening, music. *Address:* 4 Queen Anne Drive, Claygate, Surrey KT10 0PP. *T:* (01372) 466380.

MAIN, Monica Maitland; Lord-Lieutenant of Sutherland, since 2005; *b* 9 Aug. 1952; *d* of Kenneth Morrison and Gwenneth Morrison (*née* Austin); *m* 1975, William George Main; one *s* one *d*. *Educ:* Dingwall Acad.; Univ. of Aberdeen (MB ChB 1975). DRCOG 1978; MRCGP 1979. General Practitioner: Kingsmills Practice, Inverness, 1982–86; Brora Med. Practice, 1992–. *Recreations:* curling, gardening, walking. *Address:* Col Bheinn, Victoria Road, Brora, Sutherland KW9 6QN. *T:* (home) (01408) 621234, (office) (01408) 621320, *Fax:* (01408) 621535.

MAIN, Peter Ramsay; QC 2003; **His Honour Judge Main;** a Circuit Judge, since 2008; *b* 17 May 1958; *s* of late Henry James Main and of Rosemary Ina Main (*née* Anderson); *m* 1988, Valerie Marie Ramsden; one *s* one *d*. *Educ:* Repton Sch.; LSE (LLB 1980); Centre for Petroleum and Mineral Law Studies, Univ. of Dundee (Dip Pet. Law 1982). Called to the Bar, Inner Temple, 1981; in practice as a barrister, Manchester, 1983–; Junior, Northern Circuit, 1986; Asst Recorder, 1999–2001; Recorder, 2001–08. *Recreations:* avid sports watcher, golf, Rhodesian ridgebacks.

MAINE, Steven; Chief Executive, Solaris Mobile, since 2008; *b* 7 Dec. 1951; s of Gerald Ivor Gordon Maine and Jean Maine; *m* 1990, Sarah Anne Kennard. *Educ:* Oriel Coll., Oxford (MA). BT, 1974–95 (Dir, India, 1994–95); Chief Exec., Kingston Communications (Hull) Ltd, 1997–2003; Dep. Chm., Spiritel plc, 2006–; non-exec. Dir, SMG plc, 2000–07. Chm., Regl CBI Yorks and Humber, 2000–. Dir, Urban Regeneration Co., Hull, 2002–. *Recreations:* golf, cycling, photography.

MAINES, James Dennis, CB 1998; CEng, FIET; Director General, Command Information Systems, Ministry of Defence, 1995–97; *b* 26 July 1937; *s* of Arthur Burtonwood Maines and Lilian Maines (*née* Carter); *m* 1st, 1960, Janet Enid Kemp (marr. diss. 1997); three *s*; 2nd, 1997, Janet Elizabeth Bussey (*née* Franks); two step *d*. *Educ:* Leigh Grammar School; City University (BSc). Joined RSRE (then RRE), Malvern, 1956 (Sandwich course in applied physics, 1956–60); Head of Guided Weapons Optics and Electronics Group, 1981; Head, Microwave and Electro-optics Group, 1983; Head, Sensors, Electronic Warfare and Guided Weapons, ARE, Portsdown, 1984–86; Dep. Dir (Mission Systems), RAE, 1986–88; Dir Gen., Guided Weapons and Electronics Systems, MoD, 1988–95. Wolfe Award for outstanding MoD research (jtly), 1973. *Publications:* (jtly) Surface Wave Filters (ed Matthews), 1977; papers in learned jls. *Recreations:* sailing, cricket, golf, music, painting, non-labour intensive gardening. *Address:* Hollybush Cottage, Folly Hill, Farnham, Surrey GU9 0DR.

MAINI, Sir Ravinder (Nath), Kt 2003; FRCP; FRS 2007; Professor of Rheumatology, Imperial College School of Medicine at Charing Cross Hospital Campus (formerly Charing Cross and Westminster Medical School), University of London, 1989–2002, now Emeritus Professor; *b* 17 Nov. 1937; *s* of Sir Amar (Nath) Maini, CBE and Saheli (*née* Mehra); *m* 1st, 1963, Marianne Gorm (marr. diss. 1986); one *s* one *d* (and one *s* decd); 2nd, 1987, Geraldine Room; two *s*. *Educ:* Sidney Sussex Coll., Cambridge (BA; MB, BChir 1962; Hon. Fellow, 2004). MRCP 1966, FRCP 1977; FRCPE 1994. Jun. med. appts, Guy's, Brompton and Charing Cross Hosps, 1962–70; Consultant Physician: St Stephen's Hosp., London, 1970–79; Rheumatology Dept, Charing Cross Hosp., 1970–81; Hon. Consultant Physician, Charing Cross Hosp., Hammersmith Hosps NHS Trust, 1981–2007; Prof. of Immunology of Rheumatic Diseases, and Hd, Dept of Immunology of Rheumatic Diseases, Charing Cross and Westminster Med. Sch., 1981–89; Dir, Kennedy Inst. of Rheumatology, 1990–2000 then Head, Kennedy Inst. of Rheumatology Div., Imperial Coll. Sch. of Medicine at Charing Cross Hosp. Campus, 2000–02 (Head, Clinical Immunology Div., 1979–2002). President: Brit. Soc. Rheumatology, 1989–90 (Heberden Orator, 1988); Brit. League Against Rheumatism, 1985–89; Chm., Res. Subcttee, 1980–85, and Mem., Scientific Co-ordinating Cttee, 1985–95, Arthritis and Rheumatism Council; Chm., Standing Cttee for Investigative Rheumatology, European League Against Rheumatism, 1992–98; Mem., Exec. Cttee, Assoc. Physicians of GB and Ire., 1988–91; Chm., Rheumatology Cttee, RCP, 1992–96 (Croonian Lectr, 1995; Lumleian Lectr, 1998); Mem., European Union of Medical Specialists, 1991– (Pres., Sect. of Rheumatology, 1994–98; Chm., Eur. Bd of Rheumatology, 1996–99). Samuel Hyde Lectr, 1998, Hon. Fellow, 2004, RSocMed. FMedSci 1999; Fellow British Soc. for Rheumatol., 2003. Member: Slovakian Rheumatol. Soc., 2003–; (Life) Indian Rheumatol. Assoc., 2003. Hon. Member: Australian Rheumatism Assoc., 1977; Norwegian Soc. for Rheumatology, 1987; Amer. Coll. of Rheumatology, 1988 (Master, 2004); Hellenic Rheumatology Soc., 1989; Hungarian Rheumatology Soc., 1990; Scandinavian Soc. for Immunology, 1996; Mexican Soc. for Rheumatology, 1996; Eur. League Against Rheumatism, 1997 (jtly, Meritorious Service Award in Rheumatology, 2005). Dr *hc* Univ. René Descartes, Paris, 1994; Hon. DSc Glasgow, 2004. Carol Nachman Prize for rheumatology (with Prof. M. Feldmann), city of Wiesbaden, 1999; Dist. Investigator Award, Amer. Coll. of Rheumatology, 1999; Crafoord Prize (with Prof. M. Feldmann), Royal Swedish Acad. of Scis, 2000; Courtin-Clarins Prize (with Prof. M. Feldmann and Prof. J.-M. Dayer), Assoc. de Recherche sur la Polyarthrite, 2000; Albert Lasker Clin. Med. Res. Award (with Prof. M. Feldmann), 2003; Outstanding Achievement in Clin. Res. Award, Inst. Clin. Res., 2004; Fothergillian Medal, Med. Soc. of London, 2004; Cameron Prize (with Prof. M. Feldmann), Edinburgh Univ., 2004; Ambuj Nath Bose Prize, RCP, 2005; Galen Medal, Soc. of Apothecaries, 2006; Japan Rheumatism Foundn Internat. RA Award (with Prof. M. Feldmann), 2007. *Publications:* Immunology of Rheumatic Diseases, 1977; (ed) Modulation of Autoimmune Disease, 1981; (contrib.) Textbook of the Rheumatic Diseases, 6th edn 1986; (ed) T cell activation in health and disease, 1989; (ed) Rheumatoid Arthritis, 1992; (contrib.) Oxford Textbook of Rheumatology, 1993; (section ed.) Rheumatology, 1993; (ed jtly) Manual of Biological Markers of Disease, Sect. A, Methods of Autoantibody Detection, 1993, Sect. B, Autoantigens, 1994, Sect. C, Clinical Significance of Autoantibodies, 1996; (contrib.) Oxford Textbook of Medicine, 2001, 4th edn 2003; articles in learned jls. *Recreations:* music appreciation, walking. *Address:* Kennedy Institute of Rheumatology, 65 Aspenlea Road, W6 8LH. *T:* (020) 8383 4444. *Club:* Reform.

MAIR, Alexander, MBE 1967; Chief Executive and Director, Grampian Television Ltd, 1970–87, retired; *b* 5 Nov. 1922; *s* of Charles Mair and Helen Dickie; *m* 1953, Margaret Isobel Gowans Rennie. *Educ:* Skene, Aberdeenshire; Webster's Business Coll., Aberdeen; Sch. of Accountancy, Glasgow. Fellow, CIMA, 1992 (Associate, 1953). Chief Accountant, Bydand Holdings Ltd, 1957–60; Company Sec., Grampian Television, 1961–70; apptd Dir, 1967; Director: ITN, 1980–87; Cablevision (Scotland) Ltd, 1983–88; TV Publication Ltd, 1970–87. Chairman: British Regional Television Assoc., 1973–75; ITCA Management Cttee, 1980–87; RGIT Ltd, 1989–98. Pres., Aberdeen Junior Chamber of Commerce, 1960–61; Mem. Council, Aberdeen Chamber of Commerce, 1973–96 (Vice-Pres., 1987–89; Pres., 1989–91). Gov., Robert Gordon's Coll., Aberdeen, 1987–2002. FRSA 1973. FRTS 1987. *Recreations:* golf, ski-ing, gardening. *Address:* Ravenswood, 66 Rubislaw Den South, Aberdeen AB15 4AY. *T:* (01224) 317619. *Club:* Royal Northern (Aberdeen).

MAIR, Alexander Stirling Fraser, (Alistair), MBE 1987; DL; Chairman, 1991–98, and Managing Director, 1977–98, Caithness Glass Ltd; *b* 20 July 1935; *s* of Alexander W. R. Mair and Agnes W. (*née* Stirling); *m* 1st, 1961, Alice Anne Garrow (*d* 1975); four s; 2nd, 1977, Mary Crawford Bolton; one *d*. *Educ:* Robert Gordon's Coll., Aberdeen; Aberdeen Univ. (BSc (Eng)); BA Hist. Open Univ. 2001. SSC, RAF, 1960–62. Rolls-Royce, Glasgow: grad. apprentice, 1957–59; various appts, until Product Centre Manager, 1963–71; Man. Dir, Caithness Glass, Wick, 1971–75; Marketing Dir, Worcester Royal Porcelain Co., 1975–77. Director: Grampian Television, 1986–2001; Crieff Hydro Ltd, 1994–2003 (Chm., 1996–2003); Murray VCT 3 PLC, 1998–2006. Vice Chm., Scottish Cons. and Unionist Party, 1992–93; Chairman: Perth Cons. and Unionist Assoc., 1999–2004; Ochil and S Perthshire Cons. and Unionist Assoc., 2005–. Mem. Council, CBI, 1985–97 (Chm., Scotland, 1989–91). Pres., British Glass Manufacturers' Confedn, 1997 and 1998; Chm., Crieff and Dist Aux. Assoc. (Richmond House), 1993–99. Hon. Pres., Perth and Kinross Assoc., Duke of Edinburgh's Award Scheme, 1993–. Mem. Court, Aberdeen Univ., 1993– (Convener, Jt Planning, Finance and Estates Cttee, 1998–2004; Chancellor's Assessor and Vice Chm., 2000–); Chm., Cttee of Chairmen of Scottish Higher Educn Instns, 2001–07. Gov., Morrison's Acad., Crieff, 1985–2006 (Chm., 1996–2006); Comr, Queen Victoria Sch., Dunblane, 1992–97. FCMI; FRSA 1986. DL Perth and Kinross, 1993. Hon. LLD Aberdeen, 2004. *Recreations:* walking, gardening, current affairs, history. *Address:* Woodend, Madderty, by Crieff, Perthshire

PH7 3PA. *T:* and *Fax:* (01764) 683210. *Club:* Royal Northern and University (Aberdeen).

MAIR, Colin David Robertson, MA; Rector, High School of Glasgow, since 2004; *b* 4 Aug. 1953; *s* of late Colin James Robertson Mair and Catherine Barbara Mair (later Welsh). *Educ:* Kelvinside Acad.; St Andrews Univ.; Glasgow Univ. (MA); Jordanhill Coll. (Cert Ed). High School of Glasgow: teacher of Latin, 1976–79; Head: of Rugby, 1977–88; of Latin, 1979–85; Bannerman Housemaster, 1982–85; Asst Rector, 1985–96; Dep. Rector, 1996–2004. Member: Council, Headmasters' Assoc. of Scotland, 1997–; UCAS Standing Gp, Scotland, 2003–. Mem., Commonweal Cttee, Trades House of Glasgow, 2005–06. *Recreations:* cricket, golf, Rugby, walking, watching Partick Thistle. *Address:* The High School of Glasgow, 637 Crow Road, Glasgow G13 1PL; *e-mail:* rector@hsog.co.uk; 17 Ladywood, Milngavie, Glasgow G62 8BE. *T:* (0141) 956 5792. *Clubs:* W of Scotland Cricket, W of Scotland Football (Glasgow); XL.

MAIR, Edward; broadcaster, BBC Radio Four, since 1998; Presenter, Newsnight, BBC2, since 2004; *b* 12 Nov. 1965; *s* of Hubert Nicolson Mair and Mary Balneaves Mair (*née* Steele). *Educ:* Whitfield Primary Sch., Dundee; Whitfield High Sch., Dundee. Broadcast Asst, Radio Tay, Dundee, 1983–87 (Host, Tay-Talk-In and Breakfast Show, 1985–87); joined BBC, 1987: sub-ed., News, Glasgow, 1987–89, Presenter, Good Morning Scotland, 1989–93, Radio Scotland; Presenter: Reporting Scotland, TV Scotland, 1989–93; Eddie Mair Live, Radio Scotland, 1993–94; Breakaway, Radio Four, 1993–94; Midday with Mair, Radio Five Live, 1994–98; (jtly) The World, World Service/WGBH Boston, 1996–98; PM, 1998–, and Broadcasting House, 1998–2003, Radio Four; host, Seven O'Clock News, BBC3, 2004–05. Diarist, The Guardian, 2001–04. Gold Award, 1994, Bronze Award, 1997, 1998 and 2000, News Journalist of Year, 2005, Gold Award for Speech Broadcaster of the Year, 2006, Sony Radio Awards; Winner, Radio Prog. of Year for Broadcasting House, BPG, 2002. *Address:* c/o Capel and Land, 29 Wardour Street, W1D 6PS. *T:* (020) 7734 2414, *Fax:* (020) 7734 8101; *e-mail:* anita@algrade.demon.co.uk. *Club:* Soho House.

MAIR, John Magnus; Director of Social Work, Edinburgh, 1969–75; Lecturer in Social Medicine, University of Edinburgh, 1959–75; *b* 29 Dec. 1912; *s* of Joseph Alexander Mair and Jane Anderson; *m* 1940, Isobelle Margaret Williamson (*d* 1969); three *s. Educ:* Anderson Inst., Lerwick; Univs of Aberdeen (MB, ChB) and Edinburgh (DPH). MFCM. Asst GP, Highlands and Islands Medical Service, 1937–40; RAMC, 1940–45; Edinburgh Public Health Dept (latterly Sen. Depute Medical Officer of Health), 1945–69. *Recreation:* golf. *Club:* Grampian (Corby).

MAIR, Prof. Robert James, PhD; FRS 2007; FREng, FICE; Professor of Geotechnical Engineering, since 1998, and Head of Civil and Environmental Engineering, since 1999, University of Cambridge; Master of Jesus College, Cambridge, since 2001; Founding Director, Geotechnical Consulting Group, London, since 1983; *b* 20 April 1950; *s* of late Prof. William Austyn Mair, CBE; *m* 1981, Margaret Mary Plowden O'Connor; one *s* one *d. Educ:* Leys Sch.; Clare Coll., Cambridge (MA 1975; PhD 1979). FICE 1990; FREng (FEng 1992). Scott Wilson Kirkpatrick and Partners, Consulting Engineers: Engr, London and Hong Kong, 1971–76; Sen. Engr, London, 1980–83; Res. Asst, Dept of Engrg, Univ. of Cambridge, 1976–79; Fellow, St John's Coll., Cambridge, 1998–2001. Special Prof., Dept of Civil Engrg, Univ. of Nottingham, 1994–97; Royal Acad. of Engrg Vis. Prof., Univ. of Cambridge, 1997–98. Member: Commn of Enquiry into Collapse of Toulon Tunnel, French Govt, 1997; Adv. Bd of Govt of Singapore on Underground Construction Projects, 2004–. Mem. Council, and various cttees, ICE, 1993–95 (Gold Medal, 2004). *Publications:* (with D. M. Wood) Pressuremeter Testing: methods and interpretation, 1987; technical papers, mainly in jls of soil mechanics and geotechnical engrg; conf. proceedings, principally on underground construction and tunnelling. *Recreations:* supporting QPR, sailing, tennis, golf, long walks. *Address:* Master's Lodge, Jesus College, Cambridge CB5 8BL. *T:* (01223) 339442, *Fax:* (01223) 339304; *e-mail:* master@jesus.cam.ac.uk, rjm50@eng.cam.ac.uk. *Clubs:* Hurlingham; Royal Solent Yacht.

MAIRS, Christopher John, FREng; FBCS; Chief Technical Officer, MetaSwitch, since 2005; *b* 14 Feb. 1957; *s* of late Gordon Mairs and Dinah Mairs (*née* Hipkin); partner, Shirley Donald. *Educ:* Nottingham High Sch.; Churchill Coll., Cambridge (BA 1st Cl. Hons Computer Sci. 1979). FREng 2006; FBCS 2006. Director, Data Connection Ltd, 1984–; Sen. Vice-Pres., Product Mgt, MetaSwitch, 2004–05. Chm., a-technic, 2001–. *Publications:* various papers and lectures on telecommunications, digital technology and inclusive design. *Recreations:* water ski-ing (including captaining British Disabled Waterski Team to victory in 3 world championships, 1989, 1997, 2001), walking, good food. *Address:* Data Connection, 100 Church Street, Enfield EN2 6BQ. *T:* (020) 8366 1177, *Fax:* (020) 8363 4478; *e-mail:* chris.mairs@metaswitch.com; 13 Macaulay Buildings, Widcombe, Bath BA2 6AT.

MAIS, Francis Thomas; Secretary, Royal Northern College of Music, 1982–90; *b* 27 June 1927; *s* of Charles Edward Mais and Emma (*née* McLoughlin); *m* 1st, Margaret Edythe Evans (*d* 1984); one *d*; 2nd, 1987, Joan Frost-Smith. *Educ:* Barnsley Grammar Sch.; Christ's Coll., Cambridge (MA). Northern Ireland Civil Service, 1951–82: Permanent Secretary: Dept of Commerce, 1979–81; Dept of Manpower Services, 1981–82. Governor, Associated Bd, Royal Schs of Music, 1985–92. Hon. RNCM 1987. *Address:* No 2 Applegarth, Fairybead Lane, Stainton, Penrith, Cumbria CA11 0DD. *T:* (01768) 210531.

MAISEY, Prof. Michael Norman, BSc, MD; FRCP; FRCR; Professor of Radiological Sciences, Guy's, King's and St Thomas' Hospitals' School of Medicine, King's College London (formerly United Medical and Dental Schools of Guy's and St Thomas's Hospitals), 1984–2002, now Emeritus; Chairman, Medical Imaging Group Ltd; *b* 10 June 1939; *s* of Harold Lionel Maisey and Kathleen Christine Maisey; *m* 1965, Irene Charlotte (*née* Askay); two *s. Educ:* Caterham Sch.; Guy's Hosp. Med. Sch. (BSc, MD). ABNM 1972; FRCP 1980; FRCR 1989. House appts, 1964–66; Registrar, Guy's Hosp., 1966–69; Fellow, Johns Hopkins Med. Instns, 1970–72; Guy's Hospital: Sen. Registrar, 1972–73; Consultant Physician, Endocrinology and Nuclear Medicine, 1973–; Med. Dir and Chm. of Mgt Bd, 1991–93; Med. Dir, Guy's and St Thomas's Hosp. NHS Trust, 1993–96. Hon. Consultant to the Army in Nuclear Medicine, 1978–. Chm., ROC and ROCME Ltd, 2004–; Dir, e-locum Services Ltd, 2003–. Pres., BIR, 2000–01. *Publications:* Nuclear Medicine, 1980; (ed jtly) Clinical Nuclear Medicine, 1983, 3rd edn 1998; (jtly) An Atlas of Normal Skeletal Scintigraphy, 1985; (jtly) An Atlas of Clinical Nuclear Medicine, 1988, 2nd edn 1994; (jtly) New Developments in Myocardial Imaging, 1993; Clinical Positron Emission Tomography, 1999; (jtly) Atlas of Clinical Positron Emission Tomography, 2006; books and papers on thyroid diseases, nuclear medicine and medical imaging. *Address:* Medical Imaging Group Ltd, Meadway House, 38A Station Road West, Oxted, Surrey RH8 9EU. *T:* (01883) 733866.

MAISNER, Air Vice-Marshal Aleksander, CB 1977; CBE 1969; AFC 1955; *b* 26 July 1921; *s* of Henryk Maisner and Helene Anne (*née* Brosin); *m* 1946, Mary (*née* Coverley) (*d* 1997); one *s* one *d. Educ:* High Sch. and Lyceum, Czestochowa, Poland; Warsaw Univ. Labour Camps, USSR, 1940–41; Polish Artillery, 1941–42; Polish Air Force, 1943–46; joined RAF, 1946; Flying Trg Comd, 1946–49; No 70 Sqdn Suez Canal Zone, 1950–52; No 50 Sqdn RAF Binbrook, 1953–55; No 230 (Vulcan) OCU, RAF Waddington, 1955–59; psa 1960; OC Flying Wing, RNZAF Ohakea, 1961–62; Dirg Staff, RAF Staff Coll., Andover, 1963–65; DD Air Plans, MoD, 1965–68; CO, RAF Seletar, Singapore, 1969–71; Asst Comdt, RAF Coll., Cranwell, 1971–73; Dir, Personnel (Policy and Plans), MoD, 1973–75; Asst Air Sec., 1975; Dir-Gen. of Personnel Management, RAF, 1976. Personnel Exec., Reed Internat. Ltd, 1977–82; Dir, Industry and Parlt Trust, 1984–87. Governor, Shiplake Coll., 1978–96. Pres., Polish Air Force Assoc., 1982–. Comdr's Cross with Star, Order of Polonia Restituta (Poland), 1990; Comdr's Cross, OM (Poland), 1992; OM with Star (Poland), 1998.

MAISONROUGE, Jacques Gaston; management consultant; *b* Cachan, Seine, 20 Sept. 1924; *s* of Paul Maisonrouge and Suzanne (*née* Cazas); *m* 1948, Françoise Andrée Féron; one *s* four *d. Educ:* Lycée Voltaire and Saint Louis, Paris. Studied engineering; gained dip. of Ecole Centrale des Arts et Manufactures. Engineer, 1948; various subseq. appts in IBM Corp., France; Chm. and Chief Exec. Officer, IBM World Trade Europe/ME/Africa Corp., 1974–81; Pres., IBM Europe, 1974–81; Sen. Vice-Pres., 1972–84, and Mem. Bd of Dirs, 1983–84, IBM Corp.; Chm., IBM World Trade Corp., 1976–84; Vice Chm., Liquid Air Corp., 1984–86; Dir-Gen. of Industry, France, 1986–87; Chm. of Bd, French Centre for Foreign Trade, 1987–89. Director: L'Air Liquide, 1964–94; IBM Europe/ME/Africa, 1987–94. Chm., Bd of Trustees, Ecole Centrale des Arts et Manufactures, 1976–87; Chancellor, Internat. Acad. of Management, 1987–93. Gov., American Hosp. of Paris, 1988–. Nat. Pres., France-US Assoc., 1994–. Grand Officier, Ordre de la Légion d'Honneur; Commander: Ordre National du Mérite; des Palmes Académiques; Order of Merit of the Italian Republic; Order of Saint Sylvester; Order of Star of North (Sweden); Grand Officer, Order of Malta. *Publication:* Inside IBM: a European's story, 1985. *Address:* 3 boulevard Flandrin, 75116 Paris, France. *Club:* Automobile of France, Cercle Interallié.

MAITLAND, family name of **Earl of Lauderdale**.

MAITLAND, Viscount, Master of Lauderdale; **Ian Maitland;** Marketing Adviser, London School of Economics and Political Science, 1995–2001; *b* 4 Nov. 1937; *s* and *heir* of Earl of Lauderdale, *qv*; *m* 1963, Ann Paule, *d* of Geoffrey Clark; one *s* one *d. Educ:* Radley Coll., Abingdon; Brasenose Coll., Oxford (MA Modern History). Various appointments since 1960; with Hedderwick Borthwick & Co., 1970–74; National Westminster Bank, 1974–95: Regl Manager, Maghreb, 1986, ME and N Africa, 1989–91; Sen. Regl Manager, Africa and ME, 1991–95. Dir, Maitland Consultancy Services Ltd, 1995–. Lecturer: NY Inst. of Finance, 1997–2000; Euromoney Instnl Investor (formerly Euromoney Publications) PLC, 1998–2006; LSE Gurukul Scholarship Course, 1999. Royal Naval Reserve (Lieutenant), 1963–73; Mem., Queen's Body Guard for Scotland, Royal Co. of Archers, 1986–. Freeman, City of London, 1998; Liveryman, Fanmakers' Co., 1998–2004. *Recreations:* photography, sailing. *Heir: s* Master of Maitland, *qv. Address:* 150 Tachbrook Street, SW1V 2NE. *Clubs:* Royal Ocean Racing; New, Puffin's (Edinburgh).

MAITLAND, Master of; Hon. John Douglas Maitland; *b* 29 May 1965; *s* and *heir* of Viscount Maitland, *qv*,; *m* 2001, Rosamund (marr. diss. 2006), *yr d* of Nigel Bennett. *Educ:* Emanuel School; Radley College; Van Mildert College, Durham (BSc). *Recreations:* cycling, camping, sailing. *Address:* 150 Tachbrook Street, SW1V 2NE.

MAITLAND, Alastair George, CBE 1966; Consul-General, Boston, 1971–75, retired; *b* 30 Jan. 1916; *s* of late Thomas Douglas Maitland, MBE, and Wilhelmina Sarah Dundas; *m* 1st, 1943, Betty Hamilton (*d* 1981); two *s* one *d*; 2nd, 1986, Hazel Margaret Porter. *Educ:* George Watson's Coll., Edinburgh; Universities of Edinburgh (MA First Class Hons), Grenoble and Paris, Ecole des Sciences Politiques. Vice-Consul: New York, 1938; Chicago, 1939; New York, 1939; Los Angeles, 1940; apptd to staff of UK High Commissioner at Ottawa, 1942; apptd to Foreign Office, 1945; Brit. Middle East Office, Cairo, 1948; Foreign Office, 1952; UK Delegation to OEEC, Paris, 1954; Consul-General: at New Orleans, 1958–62; at Jerusalem, 1962–64; at Cleveland, 1964–68; Dir-Gen., British Trade Develt Office, NY, 1968–71. Hon. LLD Lake Erie Coll., Ohio, 1971. CStJ. *Recreations:* music, golf, gardening, reading. *Address:* Box 31, Heath, MA 01346–0031, USA.

MAITLAND, Charles Alexander, (10th Bt *cr* 1918, of Clifton, Midlothian); *b* 3 June 1986; *s* of Sir Richard John Maitland, 9th Bt (*d* 1994). Has not yet established his claim to the title and his name does not appear on the Official Roll of the Baronetage.

MAITLAND, David Henry, CVO 1988; Chief Executive, 1966–81, and Chairman, 1979–81, Save & Prosper Group; *b* 9 May 1922; *s* of George and Mary Annie Maitland; *m* 1955, Judeth Mary Gold; three *d. Educ:* Eton; King's College, Cambridge. FCA. Army, 1941–46, Captain, Oxf. & Bucks Light Inf. Articled Whinney Smith & Whinney, 1946; qualified ACA 1950; Mobil Oil Co., 1952–60; Save & Prosper Group: Comptroller, 1960; Managing Dir, 1966; non-exec. Dir, 1981; retired 1987. Dir, HFC Bank, 1989–95. Chm., Unit Trust Assoc., 1973–75; Member: City Capital Markets Cttee, 1975–84; Inflation Accounting Steering Group, 1976–80; Council, Duchy of Lancaster, 1977–87; Bethlem Royal Hosp. and Maudsley Hosp. SHA, 1982–90; Royal Commn for 1851 Exhibn, 1984–97; Treloar Trust (formerly Lord Mayor Treloar Trust), 1984–2002. Vice-Chm., Crafts Council, 1989–90 (Mem., 1984–90). Mem., Cttee of Management, Inst. of Psychiatry, 1984–96 (Chm., 1987–90). *Address:* Angel House, 4 High Street, Odiham, Hants RG29 1LG.

MAITLAND, Sir Donald (James Dundas), GCMG 1977 (CMG 1967); Kt 1973; OBE 1960; Visiting Professor, Bath University, since 2000; *b* 16 Aug. 1922; *s* of Thomas Douglas Maitland and Wilhelmina Sarah Dundas; *m* 1950, Jean Marie Young, *d* of Gordon Young; one *s* one *d. Educ:* George Watson's Coll.; Edinburgh Univ. (MA). Served India, Middle East, and Burma, 1941–47 (Royal Scots; Rajputana Rifles). Joined Foreign Service, 1947; Consul, Amara, 1950; British Embassy, Baghdad, 1950–53; Private Sec. to Minister of State, Foreign Office, 1954–56; Director, Middle East Centre for Arab Studies, Lebanon, 1956–60; Foreign Office, 1960–63; Counsellor, British Embassy, Cairo, 1963–65; Head of News Dept, Foreign Office, 1965–67; Principal Private Sec. to Foreign and Commonwealth Secretary, 1967–69; Ambassador to Libya, 1969–70; Chief Press Sec., 10 Downing St, 1970–73; UK Permanent Rep. to UN, 1973–74; Dep. Under-Sec. of State, FCO, 1974–75; UK Mem., Commonwealth Group on Trade, Aid and Develt, 1975; Ambassador and UK Perm. Rep. to EEC, 1975–79; Dep. to Perm. Under-Sec. of State, FCO, Dec. 1979–June 1980; Perm. Under-Sec. of State, Dept of Energy, 1980–82. Chairman: Independent Commn for World-Wide Telecommunications Develt (Maitland Commn), 1983–85; UK Nat. Cttee for World Communications Year, 1983; HEA, 1989–94. Govt Dir, Britoil, 1983–85; Director: Slough Estates, 1983–92; Northern Engrg Industries, 1986–89. Dep. Chm., IBA, 1986–89. Chm., Charlemagne Inst. (formerly Christians for Europe), 1984–97. Mem., Commonwealth War Graves Commn, 1983–87. President: Bath Inst. for Rheumatic Diseases, 1986–95 and 1997–2003; Federal Trust for

Educn and Res., 1987–2003; Vice-Pres., Centre Européen de Prospective et de Synthèse, Paris, 1990–95; Governor, Westminster Coll., Oxford, 1990–97 (Chm., 1994–97); Pro-Chancellor, Bath Univ., 1996–2000. Private pilot, 1969–79. Hon. Fellow, Bath Spa UC, 2000. Hon. LLD Bath, 1995; Hon. DLitt UWE, 2000. *Publications:* Diverse Times, Sundry Places (autobiog.), 1996; The Boot and Other Stories, 1999; The Running Tide, 2000; Edinburgh: seat of learning, 2001; articles on internat. affairs, sovereignty, world telecommunications, public health. *Recreation:* music. *Address:* 2 Rosemary Walk, Church Street, Bradford-on-Avon BA15 1BP. *T:* (01225) 863063.

MAITLAND, Lady (Helen) Olga, (Lady Olga Hay); journalist, public affairs consultant; Chief Executive Officer, International Association of Money Transfer Networks, since 2006; *b* 23 May 1944; *er d* of Earl of Lauderdale, *qv*; *m* 1969, Robin Hay, *qv*; two *s* one *d*. *Educ:* Sch. of St Mary and St Anne, Abbots Bromley; Lycée Français de Londres. Reporter, Fleet St News Agency, Blackheath and Dist Reporter, 1965–67; journalist, Sunday Express, 1967–91, Daily Mail, 1998–2001. Consultant: Kroll Security Internat., 2004–; Sovereign Strategy, 2004–; ITT, 2008–. ILEA Candidate, Holborn and St Pancras, 1986; contested (C) Bethnal Green and Stepney, 1987. MP (C) Sutton and Cheam, 1992–97; contested (C) same seat, 1997, 2001. PPS to Minister of State, NI Office, 1996. Member, Select Committee: on Procedure, 1992–95; on Educn, 1992–96; on Social Security, 1995–96; on Health, 1996–97. Formerly Sec., Cons. back bench Defence Cttee; Sec., Cons. back bench NI Cttee, 1992–97. Founder and Chm., Families for Defence, 1983–; Pres., Defence and Security Forum, 1992–. Jt Pres., Algerian British Business Council, 2005–. *Publications:* Margaret Thatcher: the first ten years, 1989; Faith in the Family, 1997; (contrib.) Peace Studies in our Schools, 1984; (contrib.) Political Indoctrination in Schools, 1985. *Recreations:* family, the arts, travel. *Address:* 21 Cloudesley Street, N1 0HX. *T:* (020) 7837 9212.

MAITLAND-CAREW, Captain Hon. Gerald (Edward Ian); Lord-Lieutenant of Roxburgh, Ettrick and Lauderdale, since 2007; *b* 28 Dec. 1941; *s* of 6th Baron Carew, CBE and Lady Sylvia Maitland (*d* 1991), *o d* of 15th Earl of Lauderdale; assumed by Deed Poll, 1971, the surname Maitland-Carew; *m* 1972, Rosalind Averil Speke; two *s* one *d*. *Educ:* Heatherdown Prep. Sch.; Harrow Sch. Served 15th/19th King's Royal Hussars, 1960–72, Captain 1963; ADC to GOC Home Counties, 1964–67. Runs family estate, Thirlestane Castle. Chairman: Lauderdale and Galawater Br., RBL, Scotland, 1974–2004; Gurkha Welfare Trust Scotland, 1996–2004. Chm. and host, Scottish Horse Trials Championships, Thirlestane Castle, 1982–; Chairman: Lauderdale Hunt, 1980–2000; Musselburgh Racecourse, 1988–98; Mem., Jockey Club, 1987–; Vice Pres., Internat. League for the Protection of Horses, 2006– (Chm., 1999–2006). Church of Scotland: an Elder, 1977–; Mem. Architectl and Artistic Cttee, 1986–96. Trustee: Thirlestane Castle Trust, 1982–; Mellerstain House Charitable Trust, 1983–. Brig., Royal Co. of Archers, Queen's Bodyguard for Scotland, 2003–. DL Roxburgh, Ettrick and Lauderdale, 1989. *Recreations:* horses, shooting, racing. *Address:* Thirlestane Castle, Lauder, Berwickshire TD2 6RU. *T:* (01578) 722254, *Fax:* (01578) 718749; *e-mail:* maitlandcarew@thirlestanecastle.co.uk. *Clubs:* Cavalry and Guards, White's; Royal Caledonian Hunt, Jed Forest Hunt.

MAITLAND DAVIES, Keith Laurence; a District Judge (Magistrates' Courts) (formerly Metropolitan Stipendiary Magistrate), 1984–2003; *b* 3 Feb. 1938; *s* of Wyndham Matabele Davies, QC and Enid Maud Davies; *m* 1964, Angela Mary (*née* Jenkins); two *d* one *s*. *Educ:* Winchester; Christ Church, Oxford (MA). Called to the Bar, Inner Temple, 1962; private practice, 1962–84. *Address:* c/o West London Magistrates' Court, 181 Talgarth Road, W6 8DN.

MAITLAND-MAKGILL-CRICHTON, Maj.-Gen. Edward; *see* Crichton.

MAITLAND SMITH, Geoffrey; chartered accountant; *b* 27 Feb. 1933; *s* of late Philip John Maitland Smith and Kathleen (*née* Goff); *m* 1st, 1956, Winifred Patricia Lane (marr. diss. 1967); three *s* one *d*; 2nd, 1967, Gabriella Armandi (marr. diss. 1981); one *s* one *d*; 3rd, 1986, Lucinda Enid, *d* of late Lt-Col Gerald Owen Whyte. *Educ:* University Coll. Sch., London. Partner, Thornton Baker & Co., Chartered Accountants, 1960–70; Sears plc: Dir, 1971–95; Dep. Chm., 1978–84; Jt Chm., 1984; Chief Exec., 1978–88; Chm., 1985–95; Chairman: Selfridges Ltd, 1985–93; Mallett plc, 1986–89; Hammerson plc, 1993–99 (Dir, 1990–99); W. and F. C. Bonham and Sons Ltd, 1996–2000; Fiske plc, 2000–04; Dep. Chm., Midland Bank plc, 1992–96 (Dir, 1986–96); Director: Asprey plc, 1980–93; Central Independent Television plc, 1983–85; Courtaulds plc, 1983–90; Imperial Group plc, 1984–86; HSBC Holdings plc, 1992–96. Mem. Bd, Financial Reporting Council, 1990–98. Chm., 1996 British Olympic Games Appeal, 1994–97. Hon. Vice Pres., Inst. of Marketing, 1987–94. Chm. Council, University Coll. Sch., 1987–96. *Recreation:* opera. *Address:* (office) Manor Barn, Fifield, Chipping Norton, Oxon OX7 6HF. *Club:* Boodle's.

MAITLIS, Emily, (Mrs M. Gwynne); Presenter, Newsnight and News 24, BBC, since 2006; *b* 6 Sept. 1970; *d* of Prof. Peter Michael Maitlis, *qv*; *m* 2000, Mark Gwynne; two *s*. *Educ:* Queens' Coll., Cambridge (BA Hons English Lit. and Medieval Italian 1992). Documentary programme-maker, Radio 1, TVB, 1995–97; Channel 4 producer, Hong Kong handover, 1997; Business corresp., NBC, Hong Kong, 1997–98; presenter and business corresp., Sky News, 1998–2001; presenter, BBC, 2001–. *Address:* c/o Independent Talent Group Ltd, Oxford House, 76 Oxford Street, W1D 1BS. *T:* (020) 7636 6565; *e-mail:* emily.maitlis@bbc.co.uk. *Clubs:* Soho House (Mem. Cttee); Foreign Correspondents' (Hong Kong).

MAITLIS, Prof. Peter Michael, FRS 1984; Professor of Inorganic Chemistry, 1972–97, Research Professor, 1997–2002, now Emeritus, Sheffield University; *b* 15 Jan. 1933; *s* of Jacob Maitlis and Judith Maitlis; *m* 1959, Marion (*née* Basco); three *d*. *Educ:* Univ. of Birmingham (BSc 1953); Univ. of London (PhD 1956, DSc 1971). Asst Lectr, London Univ., 1956–60; Fulbright Fellow and Res. Associate, Cornell Univ., 1960–61, Harvard Univ., 1961–62; Asst Prof., 1962–64, Associate Prof., 1964–67, Prof., 1967–72, McMaster Univ., Hamilton, Ont, Canada. Chm., Chemistry Cttee, SERC, 1985–88. Fellow, Alfred P. Sloan Foundn, USA, 1968–70; Tilden Lectr, RSC, 1979–80; Sir Edward Frankland Prize Lectr, RSC, 1985; Ludwig Mond Lectr, RSC, 1996–97; Paolo Chini Lectr, Italy, 2001; Glenn T. Seaborg Meml Lectr, Univ. of Calif, Berkeley, 2004–05. Vis. Prof., Australia, Belgium, Brazil, Canada, France, Israel and Japan; Assessor for nat. res. assessments, UK, Holland, Italy, Israel and Portugal. Member: Royal Soc. of Chemistry (formerly Chem. Soc.), 1952– (Pres., Dalton Div., 1985–87); Amer. Chemical Soc., 1963–; Council, Royal Soc., 1991–93; BBC Sci. Consultative Gp, 1989–93. Foreign Mem., Accademia Nazionale dei Lincei, Italy, 1999. E. W. R. Steacie Prize (Canada), 1971; Medallist, RSC (Noble Metals and their Compounds), 1981; Kurnakov Medal, Russian Acad. of Scis, 1998. *Publications:* The Organic Chemistry of Palladium, vols 1 and 2, 1971; (jtly) Metal-catalysis in Industrial Organic Processes, 2006; many research papers in learned jls. *Recreations:* travel, music, reading, walking. *Address:* Department of Chemistry, The University, Sheffield S3 7HF. *T:* (0114) 222 9320.

See also E. Maitlis.

MAJOR; *see* Henniker-Major, family name of Baron Henniker.

MAJOR, Rt Hon. Sir John, KG 2005; CH 1999; PC 1987; Prime Minister and First Lord of the Treasury, and Leader of the Conservative Party, 1990–97; *b* 29 March 1943; *s* of late Thomas Major and Gwendolyn Minnie Coates; *m* 1970, Norma Christina Elizabeth Johnson (*see* Dame N. C. E. Major); one *s* one *d*. *Educ:* Rutlish. AIB. Banker, Standard Chartered Bank: various executive posts in UK and overseas, 1965–79. Member, Lambeth Borough Council, 1968–71 (Chm. Housing Cttee, 1970–71). Contested (C) St Pancras North (Camden), Feb. 1974 and Oct. 1974. MP (C) Huntingdonshire, 1979–83, Huntingdon, 1983–2001. PPS to Ministers of State at the Home Office, 1981–83; an Asst Govt Whip, 1983–84; a Lord Comr of HM Treasury (a Govt Whip), 1984–85; Parly Under-Sec. of State for Social Security, DHSS, 1985–86; Minister of State for Social Security, DHSS, 1986–87; Chief Sec. to HM Treasury, 1987–89; Sec. of State for Foreign and Commonwealth Affairs, 1989; Chancellor of the Exchequer, 1989–90. Jt Sec., Cons. Parly Party Environment Cttee, 1979–81. Pres., Eastern Area Young Conservatives, 1983–85. Mem., Cons. Party Adv. Council, 2003–05. Mem., European Adv. Bd, 1998–, Chm., European Bd, 2001–05, Carlyle Gp; Chm., European Adv. Council, Emerson Electric Co., 1999–; Sen. Advr, Credit Suisse (formerly Credit Suisse First Boston), 2001–; Chm., Internat. Adv. Bd, Nat. Bank of Kuwait, 2007–. Non-exec. Dir, Mayflower Corporation, 2000–03; Mem. European Bd, Siebel Systems, Inc., 2001–03. Chm., Ditchley Council, 2000–; Mem., InterAction Council, Tokyo, 1998–. President: Asthma UK (formerly Nat. Asthma Campaign), 1998–; British and Commonwealth Cricket Charitable Trust, 2002–; Vice-President: Macmillan Cancer Relief; Inst. of Sports Sponsorship, 2001–; Hon. Pres., Sight Savers Appeal, 2001–. Patron: Mercy Ships; Prostate Cancer Charity; Support for Africa, 2000; Atlantic Partnership, 2001–; FCO Assoc., 2001–; Professional Cricketers' Assoc., 2001–; Deafblind UK, 2002–; Consortium for Street Children, 2002–; 21st Century, 2002–; Goodman Fund, Chicago, 2002–; Norfolk Cricket Umpires and Scorers Assoc., 2002–; Tim Parry Johnathan Ball Foundation for Peace (formerly Tim Parry Johnathan Ball Trust), 2004–; Dickie Bird Foundn, 2004–; Vice-Patron, Atlantic Council of UK. Mem. Bd, Warden Housing Assoc., 1975–83. Member: Bd of Advrs, Baker Inst., Houston, 1998–2005; Internat. Bd of Govs, Peres Center for Peace, Israel, 1997–. Pres., Surrey CCC, 2000–02, now Hon. Life Vice-Pres. Hon. Bencher, Middle Temple, 1997. Hon. Freeman, Merchant Taylor's Co., 2002. Hon. FCIB. *Publications:* The Autobiography, 1999; More Than a Game: the story of cricket's early years, 2007. *Recreations:* music, theatre, opera, reading, travel, cricket and other sports. *Address:* PO Box 38506, SW1P 1ZW. *Clubs:* Athenæum, Buck's, Carlton, Farmers', Pratt's, MCC (Mem. Cttee, 2001–04, 2005–), Surrey CC.

MAJOR, John, LVO 1998; FRICS; consultant surveyor; General Manager, Borde Hill Estate, 2001–06; *b* 16 June 1945; *s* of John Robert Major and Vera Major; *m* 1967, (Mary) Ruth Oddy; one *s* one *d*. *Educ:* Wellingborough Sch.; RAC, Cirencester. FRICS 1980. Partner, Osmond Tricks, Bristol, 1980–85; Land Agent, Castle Howard, N Yorks, 1986–91; Land Agent to HM the Queen, Sandringham Estate, 1991–98; Chm., Clegg Kennedy Drew, Land Agents and Chartered Surveyors, 1998–99; Dir, F.P.D. Savills, 2000–01. *Recreation:* sailing, gardening. *Address:* South Green, Piddinghoe, Newhaven BN9 9AP. *Club:* Farmers.

MAJOR, Dame Malvina (Lorraine), PCNZM 2008; DBE 1991 (OBE 1985); opera singer; Professor of Voice, Canterbury University, Christchurch, New Zealand, since 2003; *b* 28 Jan. 1943; *d* of Vincent William Major and Eva Gwendolen (*née* McCaw); *m* 1965, Winston William Richard Fleming (*d* 1990); one *s* two *d*. *Educ:* Hamilton Technical Coll.; London Opera Centre. Studied with Dame Sister Mary Leo, Auckland; winner: NZ Mobil Song Quest, 1963; Melbourne Sun Aria Contest, Australia, 1964; Kathleen Ferrier Award, London, 1966. Camden Fest., London; Salzburg Fest., 1968 (internat. début as Rosina in Barber of Seville), 1969, 1991; returned to NZ, 1970; La Finta Giardiniera, Th. de la Monnaie, Brussels, 1985; Vienna, Amsterdam, New York, Antwerp, Salt Lake City, 1986; Don Giovanni, Drottningholm, Brighton Fest., 1987; Covent Garden début as Rosalinde in Die Fledermaus, 1990; with Australian Opera, and in E Berlin, 30 rôles, including: La Bohème; Madame Butterfly; Faust; Il Seraglio; Rigoletto; Don Pasquale; Lucia di Lammermoor; Magic Flute; Tosca; Merry Widow; La Traviata; Eugene Onegin; Elisabetta Regina d'Inghilterra; Marriage of Figaro; also extensive concert repertoire, TV and recordings. Established Dame Malvina Major Foundn for educn in performing arts, 1992. Entertainer and Internat. Performer of the Year, NZ, 1992; NZ Classical Disc Award, 1993 and 1994. *Recreations:* golf, sewing, family. *Address:* c/o Dame Malvina Major Foundation, PO Box 2324, Christchurch, New Zealand.

MAJOR, Dame Norma (Christina Elizabeth), DBE 1999; *b* 12 Feb. 1942; *d* of late Norman Wagstaff and Edith Johnson; *m* 1970, Rt Hon. Sir John Major, *qv*; one *s* one *d*. *Educ:* Peckham Sch. for Girls; Battersea Coll. of Domestic Science (Teachers' Cert.). Teacher, Sydenham Sch. and St Michael and All Angels Sch., Camberwell, 1963–70. Campaigned with husband, 7 Gen. Elecns, 1974–97. A Nat. Vice Pres., Mencap, 1995– (President: Mencap Challenge Fund; Mencap, Huntingdon); Mem., League of Mercy, 2004–; Patron: Crossroads Care, 1991–; Renton Foundn, 1992–; English Schs Orch., 2005–; Spinal Res. Trust; Rowan Foundn; Mercy Ships. FRSA 2004. *Publications:* Joan Sutherland, 1987; Chequers: the Prime Minister's country house and its history, 1996. *Recreations:* opera, theatre, reading. *Address:* PO Box 38506, SW1P 1ZW.

MAJOR, Pamela Ann; HM Diplomatic Service; Counsellor, Foreign and Commonwealth Office, since 2008; *b* 4 March 1959; *d* of Arthur and Mary Major; *m* 1992, (Robert) Leigh Turner, *qv*; one *s* one *d*. *Educ:* Hertford Coll., Oxford (BA Russian and French 1981); Bradford Univ. (Post-grad. Dip. Interpreting and Translating 1982); Leicester Univ. (MA Employment Relns and Labour Law 2000). Entered FCO, 1982; Second Sec., Beijing, 1986–88; FCO, 1988–92; First Sec., Moscow, 1992–95; FCO, 1995–2002 (special unpaid leave, 1998–2002); Counsellor (EU and Econ.), Berlin, 2002–06; Equality and Human Rights Commn (on secondment), 2007. *Recreations:* theatre, piano, dance, being with my children. *Address:* c/o Foreign and Commonwealth Office (PF 34909), King Charles Street, SW1A 2AH.

MAK, Prof. Tak Wah, OC 2000; OOnt 2007; FRS 1994; FRSC 1986; University Professor, University of Toronto, since 1997, Senior Scientist and Director, Advanced Medical Discovery Institute and Director, Campbell Family Institute for Breast Cancer Research, Ontario Cancer Institute, University Health Network; *b* Canton, China, 4 Oct. 1946; *s* of Kent and Linda Mak; *m* 1969, Shirley Lau; two *d*. *Educ:* Univ. of Wisconsin (BSc 1967; MSc 1969); Univ. of Alberta (PhD 1972). Research Assistant: Univ. of Wisconsin, Madison, 1967–69; Univ. of Alberta, 1969–72; University of Toronto: Postdoctoral Fellow, 1972–74; Asst Prof., 1974–78; Associate Prof., 1978–84; Prof., 1984–. Founding Dir, Amgen Inst. 1993–2002. *Publications:* (ed) Molecular and Cellular Biology of Hemopoitic Stem Cell Differentiation, 1981; (ed) Molecular and Cellular Biology of Neiplasia, 1983; (ed) Cancer: perspective for control, 1986; (ed) The T Receptor, 1987; (ed) AIDS: ten years later, 1991; contrib. Cell, Science, Nature and other learned jls. *Address:* (home) 25 Elgin Avenue, Toronto, ON M5R 1G5, Canada; (office) Princess Margaret Hospital, 620 University Avenue, Toronto, ON M5G 2C1, Canada.

MAKAROVA, Natalia; dancer and choreographer; *b* Leningrad, 21 Nov. 1940; *m* 1976, Edward Karkar; one *s*. *Educ:* Vaganova Ballet Sch.; Leningrad Choreographic Sch. Mem., Kirov Ballet, 1959–70; London début, as Giselle, Covent Garden, 1961; joined American Ballet Theatre, 1970; formed dance co., Makarova & Co., 1980; Guest Artist: Royal Ballet, Covent Garden, 1972; London Festival Ballet, 1984. Has danced many classical and contemporary rôles in UK, Europe and USA, 1970–92; appearances include: La Bayadère (which she also staged, and choreographed in part), NY Met, 1980, Manchester, 1985, Royal Opera House, Covent Gdn, 1989; On Your Toes, London and NY, 1984–86; choreographed new productions: Swan Lake, for London Fest. Ballet, London and tour, 1988; Sleeping Beauty, La Bayadère, for Royal Ballet, 2003. Honoured Artist of RSFSR, 1970. *Publications:* A Dance Autobiography, 1979; On Your Toes, 1984. *Address:* 323 Marina Boulevard, San Francisco, CA 94123–1213, USA.

MAKEHAM, Peter Derek James, CB 2003; Director General, Strategy (formerly Performance) and Reform, Home Office, since 2006; *b* 15 March 1948; *s* of Derrick James Stark Makeham and Margaret Helene Makeham; *m* 1972, Carolyne Rosemary Dawe; one *s* three *d*. *Educ:* Chichester High Sch. for Boys; Nottingham Univ. (BA); Leeds Univ. (MA Lab Econs). Economist, Dept of Employment, 1971–82; on secondment to Unilever, 1982–83; HM Treasury, 1983–84; Enterprise Unit, Cabinet Office, 1984–85; Dept of Employment, 1985–87; DTI, 1987–90; Department of Employment, then Department for Education and Employment, subseq. Department for Education and Skills, 1990–2006: Head of Strategy and Employment Policy Div., 1992–95; Director: Employment and Adult Trng, 1995–97; School Orgn and Funding, 1997–99; Teachers Gp, 1999–2000; Dir Gen., Finance and Analytical Services, 2000–06; Dir Gen., Strategy and Reform, 2006. *Recreation:* sailing. *Address:* Home Office, 2 Marsham Street, SW1P 4DF.

MAKEPEACE, John, OBE 1988; FCSD; FIMgt, FRSA; designer and furniture maker, since 1961; Founder and Director, The Parnham Trust and Parnham College (formerly School for Craftsmen in Wood), 1977–2000; *b* 6 July 1939; *m* 1st, 1964, Ann Sutton (marr. diss. 1979); 2nd, 1983, Jennie Moores (née Brinsden). *Educ:* Denstone Coll., Staffs. Study tours: Scandinavia 1957; N America, 1961; Italy, 1968; W Africa, 1972; USA, 1974; Japan, 1994; Yunnan, China, 2005. Furniture in private and corporate collections in Europe, USA, Asia and S Africa. *Public collections:* Cardiff Museum; Fitzwilliam Museum, Cambridge; Leeds Museum; Court Room, Worshipful Co. of Innholders; Board Room, Grosvenor Estate Holdings; Art Inst., Chicago; Museum für Kunsthandwerk, Frankfurt; Royal Museum of Scotland; V & A Museum; Lewis Collection, Richmond, USA; Banque Générale du Luxembourg. *Exhibitions:* Herbert Art Gall., Coventry, 1963; New Art Centre, London, 1971; Fine Art Soc., London, 1977; Interior, Kortrijk, Belgium, 1978, 1992, 1994; Royal Show, Stoneleigh, 1981–87; Crafts Council Open, 1984; National Theatre, 1980, 1986; Parnham at Smiths Gall., 1988–91; Sotheby's, 1988, 1992, 1993, 1997; New Art Forms, Chicago, 1989–92; Tokyo, 1990; ARCO, Madrid, 1993; Chicago Contemporary Art Fair, 1993–96; Art '93, London; Conservation by Design, Providence, USA, 1993; Creation, Claridge's, 1994; Banque de Luxembourg, 1995; British Embassy, Brussels, 1995; Smithsonian Instn, 1996; Rotunda, Hong Kong, 1996; Chicago Design Show, 1997; Mayor Gall., 1997; Great British Design, Cologne, 1997; Crafts Council, 1999, 2002; Maastricht Fair, 1999–2001; Sotheby's Contemporary Decorative Arts, 2000; Modern Collectibles, London, 2003; Collect, V&A Mus., 2004, 2007, 2008; Grosvenor House Art and Antiques Fair, 2005; Internat. Expo. of Sculpture, Objects and Functional Art, Chicago, 2007; Syzygy, Alpha Hse Gall., Sherborne, 2008. *Consultancies/Lectures:* Crafts Council (and Mem.), 1972–77; India Handicrafts Bd, 1975; Jammu and Kashmir Govt, 1977; Belgrade Univ., 1978; Artist in Context, V&A Mus., 1979; Chm., Wood Programme, World Crafts Conf., Kyoto, Japan, 1979; Australian Crafts Council, 1980; Oxford Farming Conf., 1990; Furniture Technols Conf., Oxford, 2000; Furniture Soc., USA, 2000; Design Fest., Barcelona, 2001; Cheongju Internat. Craft Biennale 2001, Korea. Trustee, V & A Mus., 1987–91. *Television films:* Made by Makepeace, 1975; History of English Furniture, 1978; Heritage in Danger, 1979; First Edition, 1980; Touch Wood, 1982; Tomorrow's World, 1986. Winner, Observer Kitchen Design, 1971; Hooke Park Winner, UK Conservation Award, 1987; British Construction Industry Award, 1990; Amer. Inst. of Archts Award, 1993; Award of Distinction, Furniture Soc. of USA, 2002. *Relevant publication:* John Makepeace: a spirit of adventure in craft and design, by Jeremy Myerson, 1995. *Recreations:* friends, travel, contemporary art. *Address:* Farrs, Beaminster, Dorset DT8 3NB. *T:* (01308) 862204. *Club:* Athenæum.

MAKEPEACE, Richard Edward; HM Diplomatic Service; Consul-General, Jerusalem, since 2006; *b* 24 June 1953; *s* of late Edward Dugard Makepeace and of Patricia Muriel Makepeace; *m* 1980, Rupmani Catherine Pradhan; two *s*. *Educ:* St Paul's Sch.; Keble Coll., Oxford. Joined FCO, 1976; MECAS, 1977–78; Muscat, 1979–81; Prague, 1981–85; FCO, 1985–86; Private Sec. to Parly Under-Sec. of State, FCO, 1987–88; UK Perm. Repn to EC, 1989–93; Dep. Head, Personnel Mgt Dept, FCO, 1993–95; Counsellor and Dep. Hd of Mission, Cairo, 1995–98; Ambassador to Sudan, 1999–2002; Ambassador to UAE, 2003–06. *Recreations:* travel, reading, scuba diving. *Address:* c/o Foreign and Commonwealth Office, SW1A 2AH.

MAKGILL, family name of **Viscount of Oxfuird.**

MAKGILL CRICHTON MAITLAND, Major John David; Lord-Lieutenant of Renfrewshire, 1980–94; *b* 10 Sept. 1925; *e s* of late Col Mark Edward Makgill Crichton Maitland, CVO, DSO, DL, JP, The Island House, Wilton, Salisbury, Wilts, and late Patience Irene Fleetwood Makgill Crichton Maitland (née Fuller); *m* 1st, 1954, Jean Patricia (*d* 1985), *d* of late Maj.-Gen. Sir Michael Creagh, KBE, MC, Pigeon Hill, Homington, Salisbury; one *s* one *d*; 2nd, 1987, Mary Ann Vere, *o d* of late Major Charles Herbert Harberton Eales, MC, and *widow* of Capt. James Quintin Penn Curzon. *Educ:* Eton. Served War, 1944–45, Grenadier Guards. Continued serving until 1957 (temp. Major, 1952; retd 1957), rank Captain (Hon. Major). Renfrew CC, 1961–75. DL Renfrewshire 1962, Vice-Lieutenant 1972–80. *Address:* Daluaine, Rhynie, Huntly, Aberdeenshire AB54 4WA. *T:* (01464) 861638.

MAKGOBA, Most Rev. Thabo Cecil; *see* Cape Town, Archbishop of.

MAKHLOUF, Gabriel; Director, Banking Services, HM Revenue and Customs, since 2008; *b* 3 Feb. 1960; *s* of Antoine Makhlouf and Aïda Makhlouf (née Lazian); *m* 1984, Sandy Cope; one *s*. *Educ:* Prior Park Coll., Bath; Univ. of Exeter (BA Hons Econs); Univ. of Bath (MSc Industrial Relns). Board of Inland Revenue: HM Inspector of Taxes, 1984–89; Policy Advr, 1989–92; Head of Secretariat, Change Mgt Gp, 1992–93; Head of Direct Tax Br., Fiscal Policy, HM Treasury, 1993–95; Asst Dir, Personal Tax Div., Bd of Inland Revenue, 1995–97; HM Treasury: Principal Private Sec. to Chancellor of Exchequer, 1997–98; Head, Work Incentives and Poverty Analysis, 1998; Dir, Internat., 1998–2003, Capital and Savings, 2003–05, Bd of Inland Revenue; Dir, Debt Mgt and Banking, HMRC, 2005–08. Chm., Cttee on Fiscal Affairs, OECD, 2000–04. Hon. MICM. *Address:* Debt Management and Banking, HM Revenue and Customs, 1st Floor, 100 Parliament Street, SW1A 2BQ. *T:* (020) 7147 3730.

MAKHULU, Most Rev. Walter Paul Khotso, CMG 2000; Archbishop of Central Africa, 1980–2000, now Emeritus; Bishop of Botswana, 1979–2000; *b* Johannesburg, 1935; *m* 1966, Rosemary Sansom; one *s* one *d*. *Educ:* St Peter's Theological Coll., Rosettenville; Selly Oak Colls, Birmingham. Deacon 1957, priest 1958, Johannesburg; Curate: Johannesburg, 1957–60; Botswana, 1961–63; St Carantoc's Mission, Francistown, Botswana, 1961–63; St Andrew's Coll., Selly Oak, Birmingham, 1963–64; Curate: All Saints, Poplar, 1964–66; St Silas, Pentonville, with St Clement's, Barnsbury, 1966–68; Vicar of St Philip's, Battersea, 1968–75; Secretary for E Africa, WCC, 1975–79. An Hon. Asst Bp, dio. London, 2003–. A President: WCC, 1983–91; All Africa Conf. of Churches, 1981–86. Hon. DD: Kent, 1988; Gen. Theol Seminary, NY, 1990. Officier, Ordre des Palmes Académiques (France), 1981; PH 2000.

MAKIN, Claire Margaret, FRICS; business consultant; *b* 21 March 1951; *d* of late James Ernest Makin, CBE and Mary Makin (née Morris); *m* 1978, David Anthony Bowman. *Educ:* City Univ. (MBA). FRICS 1988; ACIArb 1985. Partner, Richard Ellis, 1978–90; Consultant, Price Waterhouse, 1990–91; Partner, Bernard Thorpe, 1991–93; Dir, DTZ Debenham Thorpe, 1993–95; Chief Exec., RICS, 1995–97; Chambers Dir, 13 King's Bench Walk, 1998–2001. FRSA 1991. *Recreations:* travelling, food and wine, restoring old houses. *Address:* 128 Lexham Gardens, W8 6JE.

MAKINS, family name of **Baron Sherfield.**

MAKINSON, John Crowther, CBE 2001; Chairman and Chief Executive, Penguin Group, since 2002; *b* 10 Oct. 1954; *s* of Kenneth Crowther Makinson and Phyllis Georgina Makinson (née Miller); *m* 1985, Virginia Clare Macbeth; two *d*. *Educ:* Repton Sch.; Christ's Coll., Cambridge (BA Hons). Journalist: Reuters, 1976–79; Financial Times, 1979–86; Vice Chm., Saatchi & Saatchi (US), 1986–89; Partner, Makinson Cowell, 1989–94; Man. Dir, Financial Times, 1994–96; Finance Dir., Pearson plc, 1996–2002. Chm. Trustees, IPPR, 2008–. *Recreations:* music, cooking. *Address:* 25 Richmond Crescent, N1 0LY. *Club:* Groucho.

MAKINSON, William, CBE 1977; engineering management consultant, now retired; *b* 11 May 1915; *s* of Joshua Makinson and Martha (née Cunliffe); *m* 1952, Helen Elizabeth Parker; one *s* three *d*. *Educ:* Ashton-in-Makerfield Grammar Sch.; Manchester Univ. Asst Lecturer, Electronics, Manchester Univ., 1935–36; Education Officer, RAF Cranwell, 1936–39; RAE Farnborough, 1939–52; Hon. Squadron-Ldr, RAF, 1943–45; Superintendent, Blind Landing Experimental Unit, 1952–55; Defence Research Policy Staff, 1955–56; Managing Director, General Precision Systems Ltd, 1956–64; Group Jt Managing Director, Pullin, 1964–65; Mem., NRDC, 1967–80 (Man. Dir, 1974–80, Chief Exec., Engrg Dept, 1965–74). *Publications:* papers to Royal Aeronautical Society. *Recreation:* golf. *Address:* 2 Miller Place, West Common, Gerrards Cross, Bucks SL9 7QQ. *T:* (01753) 893219.

MAKKAWI, Dr Khalil; Chevalier, Order of Cedar, Lebanon; Chairman, Lebanese Palestinian Dialogue Committee, since 2005; Ambassador and Permanent Representative of Lebanon to the United Nations, New York, 1990–94; *b* 15 Jan. 1930; *s* of Abdel Basset Makkawi and Rosa Makkawi; *m* 1958, Zahira Sibaei; one *s* one *d*. *Educ:* Amer. Univ. of Beirut (BA Polit. Science); Cairo Univ. (MA Polit. Science); Colombia Univ., NY, USA (PhD Internat. Relations). Joined Lebanese Min. of Foreign Affairs, 1957; UN Section at Min., 1957–59; Attaché to Perm. Mission of Lebanon to UN, New York, 1959, Dep. Perm. Rep., 1961–64; First Sec., Washington, 1964–66; Chief of Internat. Relations Dept, Min. of For. Affairs, Beirut, 1967–70; Counsellor, London, 1970–71; Minister Plenipotentiary, London, 1971–73; Ambassador to: German Democratic Republic, 1973–78; Court of St James's, and Republic of Ireland, 1979–83; Dir of Political Dept, Min. of Foreign Affairs, Beirut, 1983–85; Amb. to Italy, and Permanent Rep. to UNFAO, 1985–90. Mem., Lebanese Delegn to UN Gen. Assembly Meetings, 14th–39th Session; Chairman of Lebanese Delegations to: Confs and Councils, FAO, 1985–89; Governing Councils, IFAD, 1985–89; 16th Ministerial Meeting, Islamic conf. in Fès, 1986; 8th Summit Conf. of Non-Aligned Countries, Harare, 1986; Ministerial Meeting, Mediterranean Mems, Non-Aligned Countries, Brioni, Yugoslavia, 1987; IMO Conf., Rome, 1988; Vice-Pres., Lebanese delegn to ME peace negotiations, Washington, 1993–94. A Vice-Chm., Exec. Bd, UNICEF, 1993–95, Pres., 1995–96. Grand Cross of Merit (Italian Republic). *Recreations:* sports, music. *Address:* c/o Ministry of Foreign Affairs, Beirut, Lebanon.

MAKLOUF, Raphael David; sculptor; painter; Chairman, Tower Mint, since 1975; *b* Jerusalem, 10 Dec. 1937; *m* 1968, Marillyn Christian Lewis, *d* of Gwilym Hugh Lewis, DFC; two *s* one *d*. *Educ:* studied art at Camberwell School of Art, under Karel Vogel, 1953–58. Official commissions: Tower of London, Carnegie Hall, NY, etc. Portrait effigy of the Queen on all UK and Commonwealth coinage minted 1985–97, on Britannia gold coins minted 1989–97. Bronze portraits of the Queen, 1988, at Royal Nat. Theatre, Richmond Riverside Develt and Westminster Sch. Science Building, unveiled by the Queen. 15 Stations of Cross for new Brentwood Cathedral, 1992. Sitters have included: HM Queen; HRH Prince Philip; Rt Hon. Margaret Thatcher. Designs for National Trust and English Heritage. FRSA 1985. Fellow, Univ. of the Arts London, 2003. *Address:* 3 St Helena Terrace, Richmond, Surrey TW9 1NR. *Clubs:* City Livery, Garrick, Chelsea Arts; Riverside Racquet Centre.

MAKSYMIUK, Jerzy; conductor; Chief Conductor, 1983–93, Conductor Laureate, since 1993, BBC Scottish Symphony Orchestra; *b* Grodno, Poland, 9 April 1936. *Educ:* Warsaw Conservatory. First Prize, Paderewski Piano Comp., 1964; worked at Warsaw Grand Theatre, 1970–72; founded Polish Chamber Orchestra, 1972; UK début, 1977; toured all over world incl. European festivals of Aix-en-Provence and Vienna and BBC Promenade concerts; Principal Conductor, Polish Nat. Radio Orch., 1975–77; toured extensively in E Europe and USA; has conducted orchestras in Europe, USA and Japan including: Orch. Nat. de France, Tokyo Metropolitan Symphony, Ensemble Orchestral de Paris, Israel Chamber Orch., Rotterdam Philharmonic and Hong Kong Philharmonic; in UK has conducted BBC Welsh and BBC Philharmonic Orchs, CBSO, LSO, London Philharmonic, ENO, Bournemouth Sinfonietta and Royal Liverpool Phil. Orch.; début for ENO with Don Giovanni, London Coliseum, 1990. Has made numerous recordings. Hon. DLitt Strathclyde, 1990. *Address:* c/o IMG Artists (Europe), The Light Box, 111 Power Road, Chiswick, W4 5PY.

MAKUTA, Hon. Friday Lewis; High Commissioner for Malaŵi in Zambia and Namibia, 2002–05; *b* 25 Oct. 1936; *s* of late Lewis and Anne Makuta; *m* 1962; four *s* one *d*. *Educ:* Malamulo Mission; Dedza Secondary Sch. Called to the Bar, Middle Temple, 1967. Joined Civil Service, Malaŵi, 1967; State Advocate, 1967; Chief Legal Aid Advocate, 1970; Dir of Public Prosecutions, 1972; Judge of the High Court, 1975; Attorney Gen. and Sec. for Justice, 1976; SC 1979; Dep. Sec. to the Pres. and Cabinet, 1984; Chief Justice of Malaŵi, 1985–93; Attorney Gen., 1994–95. *Address:* PO Box 320, Mulanje, Malaŵi. *T:* 465384. *Club:* Civil Service (Lilongwe, Malaŵi).

MALAHIDE, Patrick; *see* Duggan, P. G.

MALAM, Colin Albert; Football Correspondent, Sunday Telegraph, 1973–2003; *b* 16 Oct. 1938; *s* of Albert and Irene Malam; *m* 1971, Jacqueline Cope; four *s*. *Educ:* Liverpool Inst. High Sch. for Boys; Sidney Sussex Coll., Cambridge (BA Hons History). Trainee, Liverpool Daily Post and Echo, 1961–64; News Reporter, Birmingham Post, 1964–65; Press Officer: Westward TV, 1965–66; GEC (Telecommunications) Ltd, Coventry, 1966; Football Writer, later Football Correspondent, Birmingham Post, 1966–70; Football Writer, The Sun, 1970–73. *Publications:* World Cup Argentina, 1978; Gary Lineker: strikingly different, 1993; (with Terry Venables) The Best Game in the World, 1996; The Magnificent Obsession: Keegan, Sir John Hall, Newcastle and sixty million pounds, 1997; (with Malcolm Macdonald) Supermac: my autobiography, 2003; Clown Prince of Soccer?: the Len Shackleton story, 2004; The Boy Wonders: Wayne Rooney, Duncan Edwards and the changing face of football, 2006. *Recreations:* DIY, listening to music, especially jazz, reading anything, watching cricket. *Address:* (office) Sports Desk, Sunday Telegraph, 111 Buckingham Palace Road, SW1W 0DT. *T:* (020) 7931 2000.

MALAND, David; barrister; *b* 6 Oct. 1929; *s* of Rev. Gordon Albert Maland and Florence Maud Maland (*née* Bosence); *m* 1953, Edna Foulsham; two *s*. *Educ:* Kingswood Sch.; Wadham Coll., Oxford (BA Hons Mod. Hist., 1951; MA 1957; Robert Herbert Meml Prize Essay, 1959); City Univ. (Dip. Law (ext.) 1985). Nat. service commn RAF, 1951–53. Asst Master, Brighton Grammar Sch., 1953–56; Senior History Master, Stamford Sch., 1957–66; Headmaster: Cardiff High Sch., 1966–68; Denstone Coll., 1969–78; High Master, Manchester Grammar Sch., 1978–85. Schoolmaster Commoner, Merton Coll., Oxford, 1975. Chm., Assisted Places Sub-Cttee of Headmasters' Conf., 1982–83. Called to the Bar, Gray's Inn, 1986; in practice, 1987–95. Gen. Gov., British Nutrition Foundn, 1987–95. Governor: Stonyhurst Coll., 1973–80; Abingdon Sch., 1979–91; GPDST, 1984–88. *Publications:* Europe in the Seventeenth Century, 1966; Culture and Society in Seventeenth Century France, 1970; Europe in the Sixteenth Century, 1973; Europe at War, 1600–1650, 1980; (trans.) La Guerre de Trente Ans, by Pagès, 1971; articles and reviews in History. *Address:* Windrush, Underhill Lane, Westmeston, Hassocks, East Sussex BN6 8XG. *Club:* Athenæum.

MALBON, Vice-Adm. Sir Fabian (Michael), KBE 2001; Lieutenant Governor and Commander-in-Chief of Guernsey, since 2005; *b* 1 Oct. 1946; *s* of Rupert Charles Malbon and June Marion Downie; *m* 1969, Susan Thomas; three *s*. *Educ:* Brighton, Hove and Sussex Grammar Sch. Joined RN, Dartmouth, 1965; jun. postings, 1969–82; CO, HMS Torquay, 1982–84; MoD, 1984; Comdr Sea Training, 1985–87; CO, HMS Brave, 1987–88; Dir, Naval Service Conditions, MoD, 1988–90; RCDS 1991; CO, HMS Invincible, 1992–93; Naval Sec. and CE Naval Manning Agency, MoD, 1996–98; Dep. C-in-C, Fleet, 1999–2001; Dir, TOPMAST, 2001–02. President: CCF Assoc., 2003–; Royal Naval Benevolent Trust, 2007–. Mem., RNSA. *Recreation:* sailing.

MALCOLM, Hon. Lord; Colin Malcolm Campbell; a Senator of the College of Justice in Scotland, since 2007; *b* 1 Oct. 1953; *s* of Malcolm Donald Campbell and Annabella Ferguson or Campbell; *m* 1977, Fiona Anderson; one *s* one *d* (and one *d* decd). *Educ:* Grove Acad., Broughty Ferry; Univ. of Dundee (LLB). Passed Advocate, 1977; QC (Scot.) 1990. Lectr, Dept of Scots Law, Univ. of Edinburgh, 1977–79; Standing Junior Counsel: to Scottish Develt Dept (all matters other than Planning), 1984–86; to Scottish Develt Dept (Planning), 1986–90. Vice-Dean, Faculty of Advocates, 1997–2001 (Dean of Faculty, 2001–04). Part-time Mem., Mental Welfare Commn for Scotland, 1997–2001; Mem., Judicial Appts Bd for Scotland, 2002–. *Address:* Supreme Courts, Parliament House, 11 Parliament Square, Edinburgh EH1 1RQ. *T:* (0131) 225 2595.

MALCOLM, Prof. Alan David Blair, DPhil; FIBiol, FRSC, FIFST; Chief Executive, Institute of Biology, since 1998; *b* 5 Nov. 1944; *s* of late David Malcolm and Helena Malcolm (*née* Blair); *m* 1972, Susan Waller; two *d*. *Educ:* King's Coll. Sch., Wimbledon; Merton Coll., Oxford (MA, DPhil 1970). FIFST 1994; FIBiol 1997; FRSC 2004. Demonstrator, Oxford Univ., 1969–72; EMBO Fellow, Max-Planck-Institute, 1971; Lectr, Univ. of Glasgow, 1972–76; St Mary's Hospital Medical School: Lectr, 1976–79; Sen. Lectr, 1979–81; Reader, 1981–84; Prof. of Biochem., Charing Cross and Westminster Med. Sch., 1984–92; Dir Gen., Flour Milling and Baking Res. Assoc., 1992–94; Dir, BBSRC Inst. of Food Res., 1994–98. Vis. Fellow, Yale Univ., 1982; Hon. Res. Fellow, UCL, 1984–89. Vice-Chm., Technol. Foresight Food and Drink Panel, 1995–99; Member: MAFF Food Adv. Cttee, 1995–2001; EU Standing Cttee on Fruit and Vegetables, 1998–; Adv. Cttee on Novel Foods and Processes, 2002–07; UK Deleg. to Eur. Cttee of Biol Assocs, 1998–; Council, Parly Scientific Cttee, 2000– (Vice-Pres., 2003–); Expert Advisor: H of C Select Cttee on Genetically Modified Organisms, 1999; H of L Eur. Affairs Cttee on GM Labelling, 2002. Chm., Res. and Scientific Cttee, Arthritis and Rheumatism Council, 1990–92; Mem., Royal Soc. Cttee on Genetically Modified Organisms, 1998; Scientific Gov., 1995–, Vice-Chm. Council, 1996–98, Chm., 1998–2000, British Nutrition Foundn; Director: Assured Food Standards, 2002–; Sci. Council, 2003–. Chm., Biochemical Soc., 1992–95. Mem. Court, ICSTM, Univ. of London, 1998–2007. Member Editorial Board: Internat. Jl Food Science Nutrition, 1997–; Pesticide Outlook, 1998– (Chm., 2002–03); Outlook on Agriculture, 1999–; Science in Parliament, 2003–. *Publications:* Enzymes, 1971; Molecular Medicine, vol. 1, 1984, vol. 2, 1987; numerous articles, symposia, etc. *Address:* Institute of Biology, 9 Red Lion Court, EC4A 3EF. *T:* (020) 7936 5900.

MALCOLM, Prof. Hon. David Kingsley, AC 1992; QC 1980; Professor of Law, University of Notre Dame, Australia, since 2006; Lieutenant Governor of Western Australia, since 1990; Judge of the Supreme Court of Fiji, since 2004; *b* 6 May 1938; *s* of Colin Kingsley Malcolm and Jeanne (*née* Cowan); *m* 1st, 1965, Jennifer Birney (marr. diss. 1997); (one *s* decd); 2nd, 1997, Kaaren Brizland; one *d*. *Educ:* Guildford Grammar Sch.; Univ. of Western Australia (LLB 1st Cl. Hons); Wadham Coll., Oxford (Rhodes Schol.; BCL 1st Cl. Hons; Hon. Fellow, 2002). Partner, Muir Williams Nicholson, 1964–67; Counsel, Asst Gen. Counsel, Dep. Gen. Counsel, Asian Development Bank, Manila, 1967–70; Partner, Muir Williams Nicholson & Co., 1970–79; Independent Bar, 1980–88; Chief Justice, WA, 1988–2006. QC: WA, 1980; NSW, 1983. Member: Law Reform Commn of WA, 1966–67 and 1975–82 (Chm., 1976, 1979–82); Copyright Tribunal, 1978–86; Chm., Town Planning Appeal Tribunal, 1979–86. Mem., Council of Law Soc. of WA, 1966–67, 1985–88 (Vice-Pres., 1986–88); Pres., WA Bar Assoc., 1982–84; Vice Pres., Aust. Bar Assoc., 1984; Dep. Chm., 1990–95, Chm., 1995–2006, Judicial Sect., Law Assoc. for Asia and Pacific; Chm. WA Br., Internat. Commn of Jurists, 1994–2002; Chm., Conf. of Chief Justices of Asia and Pacific, Perth, 1991, Beijing, 1995, Manila, 1997, Seoul, 1999, Christchurch, 2001, Tokyo, 2003, Gold Coast, Qld, 2005. Mem. Council, Internat. Soc. for the Reform of Criminal Law, 1992–. Chairman, Advisory Board: Neuromuscular Res. Inst. of Aust., 1989–95; Crime Res. Centre, Univ. of WA, 1991–2006; Chm., Bd of Trustees, Francis Burt Legal Educn Centre and Law Mus., 1995–2006; Member: Council, Guildford Grammar Sch., 1971–98 (Dep. Chm., 1974–80; Chm., 1980–83); Senate, Univ. of WA, 1988–94; Constitutional Centenary Foundn Council, 1991–2000. Chm., Bd of Trustees, Special Airborne Services Resources Trust, 1996–. Patron, various community and sporting orgns. Hon. FRAPI 1984. Hon. Bencher, Lincoln's Inn, 1999. Paul Harris Fellow, Rotary Internat., 1997. Citizen of the Year, WA, 2000. KCSJ 2006. *Publications:* articles in various learned jls, incl. Aust. Law Jl, Aust. Bar Rev., Aust. Business Law Rev., Univ. of WA Law Rev., LAWASIA Jl. *Recreations:* Rugby Union, windsurfing. *Address:* School of Law, University of Notre Dame, Australia, PO Box 1225, Fremantle, WA 6959, Australia. *Club:* Weld (Perth, WA).

MALCOLM, Derek Elliston Michael; Film Critic: The Guardian, 1971–97; London Evening Standard, since 2003; President: International Film Critics, 1990–2001 (Chairman, UK Section, since 1982); British Federation of Film Societies, since 1993; *b* 12 May 1932; *s* of J. Douglas Malcolm and Dorothy Taylor; *m* 1st, 1962, Barbara Ibbott (marr. diss. 1966); one *d*; 2nd, 1994, Sarah Gristwood. *Educ:* Eton; Merton College, Oxford (BA Hons Hist.). Actor, amateur rider (National Hunt), 1953–56; Drama Critic, Gloucestershire Echo, 1956–62; Sub-Editor, The Guardian, 1962–69; Racing correspondent, The Guardian, 1969–71. Dir, London Internat. Film Fest., 1982–84. Gov., BFI, 1989–92. Pres., Critics' Circle of UK, 1980 (Chm., Film Section, 1978–81). Internat. Publishing Cos Critic of the Year, 1972. *Publications:* Robert Mitchum, 1984; A Century of Films, 2001; Family Secrets, 2003. *Recreations:* cricket, tennis, squash, music. *Address:* 28 Avenue Road, Highgate, N6 5DW. *T:* and *Fax:* (020) 8348 2013; The Dower House, Hull Place, Sholden, Kent CT14 0AQ. *T:* and *Fax:* (01304) 364614; *e-mail:* derekmalcolm@aol.com.

MALCOLM, Helen Katharine Lucy; QC 2006; a Recorder, since 2005; *b* 2 Jan. 1962; *d* of Dugald Malcolm and Patricia Malcolm; *m* 1987; one *s* two *d*. *Educ:* New Coll., Oxford (BA 1983). Called to the Bar, Gray's Inn, 1986. *Recreations:* food, horses, ski-ing. *Address:* 3 Raymond Buildings, Gray's Inn, WC1R 5BH. *T:* (020) 7400 6400; *e-mail:* helen.malcolm@3raymondbuildings.com.

MALCOLM, James Ian, OBE 1995; HM Diplomatic Service, retired; photographer of the Panama Canal; *b* 29 March 1946; *e s* of late William Kenneth Malcolm and Jennie Malcolm (*née* Cooper); *m* 1967, Sheila Nicholson Moore; one *s* one *d*. *Educ:* Royal High Sch., Edinburgh. Joined Foreign Office, 1966; UKDEL NATO, Brussels, 1969–72; Burma, 1972–74; FCO, 1974–77; Commercial Attaché, Kenya, 1977–80; Consul, Syria, 1980–83; Second Sec. (Commercial), Angola, 1983–85; Second, later First, Sec., FCO, 1985–87; First Secretary: (Political/Econ.), Indonesia, 1987–94; FCO, 1994–97; Dep. High Comr, Jamaica, 1997–2001; Ambassador, Panama, 2002–06. *Recreations:* reading and research in British history in Sumatra, Jamaica and Panama, golf, riding motorcycles. *Address:* 8/14 Portland Gardens, Britannia Quay, Leith, Edinburgh EH6 6NJ. *Club:* Royal Over-Seas League.

MALCOLM, Sir James (William Thomas Alexander), 12th Bt *cr* 1665 (NS), of Balbedie and Innertiel, Co. Fife; DL; *b* 15 May 1930; *s* of Lt-Col A. W. A. Malcolm, CVO (*d* 1989) and Hester Mary Malcolm (*née* Mann) (*d* 1992); *S* cousin, 1995; *m* 1955, Gillian Heather (*née* Humpherus); two *s* two *d*. *Educ:* Eton Coll.; RMA Sandhurst; Staff Coll., Camberley (psc). CO 1st Bn Welsh Guards, 1970–72; Regimental Col, Welsh Guards, 1972–76. Appeals Dir, British Heart Foundn, 1976–89. High Sheriff, 1991–92, DL 1991, Surrey. *Recreations:* golf, cricket. *Heir:* *s* Col Alexander James Elton Malcolm, OBE [*b* 30 Aug. 1956; *m* 1982, Virginia (*née* Coxon); two *s* one *d*]. *Address:* Grove House, Wrecclesham Hill, Wrecclesham, Farnham, Surrey GU10 4JN. *T:* (01252) 712167. *Clubs:* MCC; Royal St George's Golf (Sandwich); Berkshire Golf (Ascot).

MALCOLM, Noel Robert, PhD; FBA 2001; historian; Fellow of All Souls College, Oxford, since 2002; *b* 26 Dec. 1956. *Educ:* Eton; Peterhouse, Cambridge (BA 1978); Trinity Coll., Cambridge; Gonville and Caius Coll., Cambridge (MA 1981; PhD 1983). Fellow, Gonville and Caius Coll., Cambridge, 1981–88; political columnist, 1987–91, Foreign Editor, 1991–92, The Spectator; political columnist, Daily Telegraph, 1992–95. Vis. Fellow, St Antony's Coll., Oxford, 1995–96; Vis. Lectr, Harvard, 1999; Carlyle Lectr, Oxford, 2001. Chm., Bosnian Inst., 1997–. FRSL 1997. *Publications:* De Dominis 1560–1624, 1984; George Enescu: his life and music, 1990; Sense on Sovereignty, 1991; Bosnia: a short history, 1994; (ed) The Correspondence of Thomas Hobbes, 2 vols, 1994; The Origins of English Nonsense, 1997; Kosovo: a short history, 1998; (jtly) Books on Bosnia: a critical bibliography, 1999; Aspects of Hobbes, 2002. *Address:* All Souls College, Oxford OX1 4AL.

MALCOLM of Poltalloch, Robin Neill Lochnell; Chief of Clan Malcolm; Vice Lord-Lieutenant of Argyll and Bute, 1996–2001; *b* 11 Feb. 1934; *s* of Lt-Col George Ian Malcolm of Poltalloch, A&SH and Enid Gaskell; *m* 1962, Susan Freeman (*d* 2004); two *s* two *d*. *Educ:* Eton; North of Scotland Coll. of Agriculture. National Service, 1 Argyll and Sutherland Highlanders, 1952–54; TA service, 8 A&SH, 1954–64. Shipping, and British Iron & Steel Co., 1955–62; farming at Poltalloch, 1963–. Convenor, Highlands and Islands Cttee, NFU, 1972–74; Member: HIDB Consultative Council, 1973–77, 1988–91; Bd, Argyll and Isles Enterprise, 1991–98; Bd, SW Region, Scottish Natural Heritage, 1993–99. Pres., Scottish Agricl Orgn Soc. Ltd, 1983–86. Mem., Argyll and Bute DC, 1976–92. Argyll and Bute: DL, 1974–2004; JP 1976–2004. *Recreations:* shooting, swimming. *Address:* Duntrune Castle, Kilmartin, Argyll PA31 8QQ. *T:* (01546) 510283.

MALCOLM, Dr Wilfred Gordon, CBE 1994; Vice-Chancellor, University of Waikato, New Zealand, 1985–94; Chairman, Academic Audit Unit, New Zealand Universities, 2000–03; *b* 29 Nov. 1933; *s* of Norman and Doris Malcolm; *m* 1959, Edmée Ruth Prebensen; two *s* four *d*. *Educ:* Victoria Univ. of Wellington (MA, PhD); Emmanuel Coll., Cambridge (BA). Victoria University of Wellington: Lectr in Mathematics, 1960–62; Gen. Sec., Inter Varsity Fellowship of Evangelical Unions, 1963–66; Lectr/Reader in Mathematics, 1967–74; Prof. of Pure Mathematics, 1975–84. Vis. Prof., Univ. of Brunei Darussalam, 1997–99. Chm., Ministerial Adv. Cttee on Employment Relations Educn, 2001–06. DUniv Waikato 1995. *Publication:* (with Nicholas Tarling) Crisis of Identity?: the mission and management of universities in New Zealand, 2007. *Address:* 76 Hamurana Road, Omokoroa, Bay of Plenty, New Zealand.

MALCOMSON, Prof. James Martin, PhD; FBA 2000; Professor of Economics, and Fellow, All Souls College, University of Oxford, since 1999; *b* 23 June 1946; *s* of E. Watlock Malcomson and Madeline Malcomson (*née* Stuart); *m* 1979, Sally Claire Richards; (one *d* decd). *Educ:* Gonville and Caius Coll., Cambridge (BA, MA); Harvard Univ. (MA, PhD 1973). Res. Fellow in Econs, 1971–72, Lectr, 1972–83, Sen. Lectr, 1983–85, Univ. of York; Prof. of Econs, Univ. of Southampton, 1985–98. Vis. Fellow, Université Catholique de Louvain, Belgium, 1983–84. Fellow, Econometric Soc., 2005. *Publications:* (contrib.) Efficiency Wage Models of the Labor Market, 1986; (contrib.) Handbook of Labor Economics, 1999; (contrib.) Handbook of Health Economics, 2000; numerous articles in learned jls. *Recreations:* walking, music, film, theatre. *Address:* All Souls College, Oxford OX1 4AL. *T:* (01865) 279379.

MALCOMSON, Thomas Herbert; HM Diplomatic Service, retired; Executive Director, British-Peruvian Cultural Association, since 2005; *b* 9 Oct. 1937; *m* 1st, 1960, Barbara Hetherington (marr. diss. 1985); one *s* two *d*; 2nd, 1986, Blanca Ruiz de Castilla; twin *d*. *Educ:* Univ. of Glasgow. Joined FO, subseq. FCO, 1961; Bangkok, 1963; São Paulo, 1967; FCO, 1971; Colombo, 1972; Consul, Chiang Mai, 1975; FCO, 1978; Dep.

High Comr, Brunei, 1981; Acting High Comr, Solomon Is, 1984; Lima, 1985; FCO, 1989; Ambassador to Panama, 1992–96. *Address:* Av. La Floresta 331 apto. 101, Chacarilla, San Borja, Lima 41, Peru.

MALE, Anthony Hubert, (Tony), CMG 1997; FCIL; National Executive Adviser for Languages, Department for Education and Skills (formerly Department for Education and Employment), 2001–02; Director, Central Bureau for Educational Visits and Exchanges, 1986–99, and Secretary, UK Centre for European Education, 1989–99, British Council; *b* 16 March 1939; *s* of Hubert Edward Male and Louise Irene Lavinia (*née* Thomas); *m* 1960, Françoise Andrée Germaine Pinot, LèsL; one *s* one *d*. *Educ:* Yeovil Sch.; Exeter Univ. (BA, PGCE); Sorbonne. FCIL (FIL 1990). Housemaster, 1962–74, Head, Comparative Internat. Studies, 1970–74, Tiverton GS; Central Bureau for Educational Visits and Exchanges: Head, Teacher and Sch. Exchange, Europe, 1974–76; Asst Dir, 1976–78; Dep. Dir, 1978–84; Sec., 1984–86. Expert, Eur. Commn, 1977–99; Consultant, Council of Europe, 1982–99. Chm., Langs Nat. Working Gp, 2001. Pres., Fédn Internat. des Organisations de Correspondances et d'Exchanges Scolaires (FIOCES), 1986–94. Member: Adv. Panel, Langs Lead Body, 1991–98; Council, Inst. Linguists, 1997–99. Member: Bd of Dirs, Nat. Youth Jazz Orch., 1975–2004 (Hon. Vice-Pres., 2004–); Jury, Concours Internat. de Guitare, Radio France, 1993–2000. Trustee, Amer. Field Service, 1981–86; Internat. House, 1989–98; Lefèvre Trust, 1991–93; Technol. Colls Trust, 1996–99. Academic Gov., Richmond Coll., 1990–99. FRSA 1985. Hon. FCP 1993; Hon. Fellow, Westminster Coll., Oxford, 1999. Hon. Mem., British Council, 1999. Chevalier, 1977, Comdr, 1992, Ordre des Palmes Académiques (France); Chevalier, Ordre National du Mérite (France), 1984; Chevalier, Ordre de Léopold II (Belgium), 1981; Comdr, Orden del Mérito Civil (Spain), 1999. *Publications:* contrib. articles on intercultural exchange, modern langs and internat. dimension in education. *Recreations:* music, flamenco and jazz guitar, travel, photography. *Address:* *e-mail:* ahmale@aol.com. *Club:* Travellers.

MALE, David Ronald, CBE 1991; FRICS; Consultant, Gardiner & Theobald, Chartered Quantity Surveyors, since 1992 (Senior Partner, 1979–91); a Church Commissioner, 1989–93; *b* 12 Dec. 1929; *s* of Ronald Male and Gertrude Simpson; *m* 1959, Mary Louise Evans; one *s* two *d*. *Educ:* Aldenham Sch., Herts. Served RA, 2nd Lieut, 1948–49. With Gardiner & Theobald, 1950–. Mem., Gen. Council, RICS, 1976–93 (Pres., 1989–90); Pres., Quantity Surveyors Divl Council, 1977–78. Member: Bd of Dirs, Building Centre, 1970–80; Govt Construction Panel, 1973–74; EDC for Building, 1982–86; Chm., NEDC Commercial Bldg Steering Gp, 1984–88; Dir, London and Bristol Developments, 1985–91. Member: Bd of Management, Macmillan Cancer Relief (formerly Cancer Relief Macmillan Fund), 1992–2000; Court of Benefactors, RSocMed, 1986–. Mem. Bd of Govs, Wilson Centre, Cambridge, 1993–97; Governor: Aldenham Sch., 1974–93; Downe House, 2000–07; Pres., Old Aldenhamian Soc., 1986–89. Master, Chartered Surveyors' Co., 1984–85; Liveryman, Painter-Stainers' Co., 1961–93. *Recreations:* opera and ballet, golf. *Address:* Manor Farmhouse, Benham Penk, Marsh Benham, Newbury, Berks RG20 8LX. *Clubs:* Boodle's, Garrick, MCC (Mem. Cttee, 1984–96 and 1997–99; Mem., Estates Sub-Cttee, 1984–2000).

MALE, Peter Royston, (Roy), CBE 2003; Chief Executive, Blackpool, Fylde & Wyre Hospitals NHS Trust, 2002–05; *b* 16 March 1948; *s* of Royston Stanley Male and Patricia Male (*née* Kennedy); *m* 1975, Susan Bootle; one *s*. *Educ:* Nottingham High Sch.; King's Coll. Sch., Wimbledon; St John's Coll., Cambridge (BA 2nd Cl. Hons 1970; MA 1974). MHSM 1974; DipHSM 1974; MIPD 1987. Grad. trainee, NHS, Sheffield Reg., 1970–72; Doncaster Royal Infirmary, 1972–73; Fazakerley Hosp., 1973–75; Dist Personnel Officer, S Sefton, 1975–77; Area Personnel Officer, Norfolk HA, 1977–87; Director: of Personnel and Admin, Liverpool HA, 1987–90; of Personnel, Cambridge HA, 1990–92; Dep. Chief Exec., 1992–98, Chief Exec., 1998–2002, Addenbrooke's NHS Trust. Independent Member: Standards Cttee, Lancs Combined Fire and Rescue Authy, 2005–; Disciplinary Tribunals, Inst. of Legal Execs, 2005–; Chm., Probation Bd, Nat. Probation Service, Lancs, 2007–. Dir, Probation Assoc. Ltd, 2008–. *Publications:* papers and contribs to jls. *Recreations:* cricket, keyboard, gardening.

MALECELA, Cigwiyemisi John Samwel; MP (Chama cha Mapinduzi Party) Mtera, Tanzania, since 1995; *b* 20 April 1934; *m*; four *c*. *Educ:* Alliance Secondary Sch., Dodoma; St Andrews Coll., Minaki, Dar es Salaam; Univ. of Bombay (BCom); post-grad. studies, Cambridge Univ. Dist Officer, Mbeya Region, 1960–61; appts for Tanganyikan Govt, 1962–64: Consul to USA and Sec. of Mission to UN, New York, 1962–63; Regl Comr, Lake Reg., 1963–64; for Tanzania: Ambassador to UN, 1964–68, to Ethiopia, 1968; Minister: for East African Community Affairs, 1969–71; for Foreign Affairs, 1972–75; for Agriculture, 1975–80; for Minerals, 1980–82; for Communications and Transport, 1982–85; Administrator, Tanzania's Public Debt, 1985; Regional Comr, Iringa, 1987; High Comr for Tanzania in UK, and non-resident Ambassador to Ireland, 1989–90; Prime Minister and First Vice Pres., Tanzania, 1990–95; Vice Chm., Chama cha Mapinduzi, ruling party, 1992–95. Member: Internat. Ind. Commn for Worldwide Telecommunication Develt, 1983; Commonwealth Eminent Persons Group on S Africa, 1985; Gp of 34 World Eminent Persons on Disarmament and Internat. Security, Stockholm, 1988. *Address:* Box number 2324, Dodoma, Tanzania.

MALEK, Ali; QC 1996; a Recorder, since 2000; *b* 19 Jan. 1956; *s* of late Ali Akbar Malek and Irene Elizabeth (*née* Johnson); *m* 1989, Francesca Shoucair; two *d*. *Educ:* Bedford Sch.; Keble Coll., Oxford (MA, BCL). Called to the Bar, Gray's Inn, 1980, Bencher, 2003; in practice at the Bar, 1980–; Asst Recorder, 1998–2000. *Publications:* various articles on banking law. *Recreations:* running, ski-ing, golf, music. *Address:* 3 Verulam Buildings, Gray's Inn, WC1R 5NT. *T:* (020) 7831 8441. *Club:* Vincent's (Oxford).

See also H. M. Malek.

MALEK, Hodge Mehdi; QC 1999; a Recorder, since 2004; *b* 11 July 1959; *s* of late Ali Akbar Malek and Irene Elizabeth Malek (*née* Johnson); *m* 1986, Inez Dies Louise Vegelin van Claerbergen; two *s* one *d*. *Educ:* Bedford Sch.; Sorbonne, Univ. of Paris; Keble Coll., Oxford (MA 1981; BCL 1982). Called to the Bar, Gray's Inn, 1983 (Birkenhead Schol.; Atkin Schol.; Band Schol.), Bencher, 2004; in practice at the Bar, 1983–. Member: Supplementary Treasury Panel (Common Law), 1995–99; Bar Disciplinary Tribunal, 2001–. *Publications:* Gen. Ed., Phipson on Evidence, 15th edn, 2nd supp., 2002, 16th edn 2005; (contrib.) Atkins Court Forms, 2003; (with P. B. Matthews): Discovery, 1992; Disclosure, 2001, 3rd edn 2007; (contrib.) Information Rights, 2004; The Dābūyid Ispahbads and Early 'Abbāsid Governors of Tabaristān, 2004; articles on law and history. *Recreations:* swimming, ski-ing, history. *Address:* 4/5 Gray's Inn Square, Gray's Inn, WC1R 5AH. *T:* (020) 7404 5252.

See also A. Malek.

MALES, Stephen Martin; QC 1998; a Recorder, since 2000; *b* 24 Nov. 1955; *s* of Dennis Albert Males and Mary Winifred Males (*née* Bates); *m* 1982, Daphne Clytie Baker; three *s*. *Educ:* Skinners' Sch.; St John's Coll., Cambridge (MA). Called to the Bar, Middle Temple, 1978, Bencher, 2007; Asst Recorder, 1999–2000. *Recreation:* sailing. *Address:* 20 Essex Street, WC2R 3AL. *T:* (020) 7842 1200.

MALET, Sir Harry (Douglas St Lo), 9th Bt *cr* 1791, of Wilbury, Wiltshire; JP; farmer, Australia and England; *b* 26 Oct. 1936; *o s* of Col Sir Edward William St Lo Malet, 8th Bt, OBE and Baroness Benedicta von Maasburg (*d* 1979); S father, 1990; *m* 1967, Julia Gresley, *d* of Charles Harper, Perth, WA; one *s*. *Educ:* Downside; Trinity Coll., Oxford (BA Eng. Lit.). Commnd QRIH, 1958–61. JP W Somerset, 1982. *Recreation:* equestrian sports. *Heir:* *s* Charles Edward St Lo Malet [*b* 30 Aug. 1970; *m* 1997, Rachel, *d* of T. P. S. Cane; four *d*]. *Address:* Wrestwood, RMB 184, Boyup Brook, WA 6244, Australia. *Club:* Weld (Perth).

MALHADO, Noél; *see* Harwerth, N.

MALIK, Rt Rev. Ghais Abdel; President Bishop of the Central Synod of the Episcopal Church in Jerusalem and the Middle East, 1996–2000; Bishop in Egypt, 1984–2000; *b* 21 May 1930; *m* 1956, Fawzia Emsak Gouany; two *s* one *d*. *Educ:* Cairo Univ. (DipEd 1960); St George's Coll., Jerusalem. Ordained deacon 1962, priest 1963, Cairo; Curate, 1963–66, Rector, 1966–84, Jesus Light of the World Ch., Old Cairo; cons. Bishop of Egypt, with N Africa, Ethiopia, Somalia, Eritrea and Djibouti, 1984. Vice-Chm., Council of Anglican Provinces of Africa, 1992–99; Chm., Fellowship of Middle East Evangelical Churches, 1997–2001. *Recreations:* walking, reading, maintenance of harmoniums, fishing. *Address:* c/o Diocesan Office, PO Box 87, Zamalek, Cairo, Egypt.

MALIK, Khalid Taj; a District Judge, Principal Registry, Family Division, since 2006; *b* 29 Dec. 1958; *s* of Taj Ahmed Malik and Anwari Begum Malik; *m* 1986, Ruby Shabnam Khalid Malik; three *s* one *d*. *Educ:* Wyndham Primary Sch.; Kenton Comp. Sch., Newcastle upon Tyne; Univ. of Hull (BSc Hons Econs and Accountancy 1980); Newcastle upon Tyne Poly (Law Soc. finals 1991). Family clothing business, 1980–91; admitted solicitor, 1993; Goldwaters Solicitors, Newcastle upon Tyne, 1991–2006; Dep. Dist Judge, Northern Circuit, 2003–06. *Address:* Principal Registry of the Family Division, First Avenue House, 42–49 High Holborn, WC1V 6NP.

MALIK, Shahid; MP (Lab) Dewsbury, since 2005; Parliamentary Under-Secretary of State, Ministry of Justice, since 2008; *b* 24 Nov. 1967; *s* of Rafique Malik. *Educ:* London Poly.; Univ. of Durham (BA 1991). E Lancs TEC; Hd of Policy and Develt, Gtr Nottingham TEC; Chief Exec., PMC Gp; Gen. Manager, KYP Ltd; Chief Executive: Haringey Regeneration Agency, 1997–2001; Inclusive Futures. Mem., CRE, 1998–2002. Parly Under-Sec. of State, DFID, 2007–08. Mem., Lab Party NEC, 2000–05. *Address:* House of Commons, SW1A 0AA.

MALIM, Prof. Michael Henry, DPhil; FRS 2007; Professor, and Head of Department of Infectious Diseases, King's College London, since 2001; *b* 4 July 1963; *s* of Anthony and Joan Malim; *m* 1990, Dr Rebecca J. Oakey; one *s* one *d*. *Educ:* Bristol Univ. (BSc Biochem.); Oxford Univ. (DPhil Biochem. 1987). University of Pennsylvania School of Medicine: Asst Prof., Depts of Microbiol. and Medicine, 1992–98, Associate Prof. (with tenure), 1998–2001. Reported discovery of human anti-HIV gene, APOBEC3G, citation in Nature, 2002. Mem., EMBO, 2005. FMedSci 2003; Fellow, Amer. Acad. Microbiol., 2005. Elizabeth Glaser Scientist, Elizabeth Glaser Pediatric AIDS Foundn, 2001. *Publications:* articles and reviews on molecular pathogenisis of HIV/AIDS. *Recreations:* parenting, gentle sports, retired varsity golfer, cuisine, achievable DIY, cycling, hiking, bridge. *Address:* c/o Department of Infectious Diseases, King's College London, 2nd Floor, Borough Wing, Guy's Hospital, London Bridge, SE1 9RT. *T:* (020) 7188 0149, *Fax:* (020) 7188 0147; *e-mail:* michael.malim@kcl.ac.uk. *Club:* Oxford and Cambridge Golf Society.

MALIN, Dr Stuart Robert Charles; Professor of Geophysics, Bosphorus University, Istanbul, 1994–2001; *b* 28 Sept. 1936; *s* of late Cecil Henry Malin and Eleanor Mary Malin (*née* Howe); *m* 1st, 1963, Irene Saunders (*d* 1997); two *d*; 2nd, 2001, Lindsey Jean Macfarlane. *Educ:* Royal Grammar Sch., High Wycombe; King's College, London (BSc 1958); PhD 1972, DSc 1981, London. FInstP 1971; CPhys 1985; FRAS 1961 (Mem. Council, 1975–78). Royal Greenwich Observatory, Herstmonceux: Asst Exptl Officer, 1958; Scientific Officer, 1961; Sen. Scientific Officer, 1965; Institute of Geological Sciences, Herstmonceux and Edinburgh: PSO, 1970; SPSO (individual merit), 1976, and Hd of Geomagnetism Unit, 1981; Hd of Astronomy and Navigation, Nat. Maritime Museum, 1982; Maths teacher: Dulwich Coll., 1988–91, 1992–94; Haberdashers' Aske's Hatcham Coll., 1991–92. Cape Observer, Radcliffe Observatory, Pretoria, 1963–65; Vis. Scientist, Nat. Center for Atmospheric Res., Boulder, Colorado, 1969; Green Schol., Scripps Instn of Oceanography, La Jolla, 1981. Visiting Professor: Dept of Physics and Astronomy, UCL, 1983–2001; Univ. of Cairo, 1996–2002. Consultant, Rahmi M. Koç Müzesi, Istanbul, 1995–2001. Pres., Jun. Astronomical Soc., 1989–91. Associate Editor, Qly Jl, RAS, 1987–92; Editor, Geophysical Jl Internat., 1996–2004. Freeman, City of London, 2003; Liveryman, Clockmakers' Co., 2006– (Freeman, 2003). *Publications:* (with Carole Stott) The Greenwich Meridian, 1984; Spaceworks, 1985; The Greenwich Guide to the Planets, 1987; The Greenwich Guide to Stars, Galaxies and Nebulae, 1989; The Story of the Earth, 1991; (with Rahmi M. Koç) Rahmi M. Koç Müzesi Tanıtımı, 1997; The Farnol Companion, 2006; contribs to scientific jls. *Recreations:* Jeffery Farnol novels, clocks. *Address:* 30 Wemyss Road, Blackheath, SE3 0TG. *T:* (020) 8318 3712.

MALINS, Humfrey Jonathan, CBE 1997; MP (C) Woking, since 1997; lawyer and consultant; a Recorder, since 1996; *b* 31 July 1945; *s* of Rev. Peter Malins and late Lilian Joan Malins; *m* 1979, Lynda Ann; one *s* one *d*. *Educ:* St John's Sch., Leatherhead; Brasenose Coll., Oxford (MA Hons Law). College of Law, Guildford, 1967; joined Tuck and Mann, Solicitors, Dorking, 1967, qual. as solicitor, 1971; Partner, Tuck and Mann, 1973; an Asst Recorder, 1991–96; Actg Dist Judge (formerly Actg Met. Stipendiary Magistrate), 1992–. Councillor, Mole Valley DC, Surrey, 1973–83 (Chm., Housing Cttee, 1980–81). Contested (C): Toxteth Division of Liverpool, Feb. and Oct. 1974; E Lewisham, 1979. MP (C) Croydon NW, 1983–92; contested (C) same seat, 1992. PPS to Minister of State, Home Office, 1987–89, to Minister of State, DoH, 1989–92; Opposition front bench spokesman on home affairs, 2001–05. Chm. of Trustees, Immigration Adv. Service, 1993–96. *Recreations:* Rugby football, golf, gardening, soup making. *Address:* House of Commons, SW1A 0AA. *Clubs:* Vincent's (Oxford); Richmond Rugby Football; Walton Heath Golf.

See also J. H. Malins.

MALINS, Julian Henry; QC 1991; a Recorder, since 2000; *b* 1 May 1950; *s* of Rev. Peter Malins and late (Lilian) Joan Malins (*née* Dingley); *m* 1972, Joanna Pearce; three *d*. *Educ:* St John's School, Leatherhead; Brasenose College, Oxford (Boxing Blue; MA). Called to the Bar, Middle Temple, 1972, Bencher, 1996. Mem., Court of Common Council, City of London, 1981–. Governor: Mus. of London, 1998–; GSMD, 1999–. *Recreations:* fishing, walking, conversation. *Address:* 115 Temple Chambers, Temple Avenue, EC4Y 0DA. *T:* (020) 7583 5275. *Club:* Vincent's (Oxford).

See also H. J. Malins.

MALINS, Penelope, (Mrs John Malins); *see* Hobhouse, P.

MALJERS, Floris Anton, Hon. KBE 1992; Chairman, Unilever NV, and Vice Chairman, Unilever PLC, 1984–94; *b* 12 Aug. 1933; *s* of A. C. J. Maljers and L. M. Maljers-Kole; *m* 1958, J. H. Maljers-de Jongh; two *s* (one *d* decd). *Educ:* Univ. of Amsterdam. Joined Unilever, 1959; various jobs in the Netherlands until 1965; Man. Dir, Unilever-Colombia, 1965–67; Man. Dir, Unilever-Turkey, 1967–70; Chairman, Van den Bergh & Jurgens, Netherlands, 1970–74; Co-ordinator of Man. Group, edible fats and dairy, and Dir of Unilever NV and Unilever PLC, 1974–94. Member: Unilever's Special Committee, 1982–94; Supervisory Bd, KLM Royal Dutch Airlines, 1991– (Vice Chm., 1994; Chm., 2000); Supervisory Bd, Philips Electronics NV, 1993–99 (Chm., 1994); Supervisory Bd, Vendex NV, subseq. Vendex-KBB NV, 1996– (Vice Chm., 1998); Bd, Rand Europe, 1999–; Director: Guinness plc, 1994–98; Amoco Petroleum, Chicago, 1994–98; BP (formerly BP Amoco), 1998–; Diageo plc, 1998; Air France, 2004. Gov., Europ. Policy Forum, 1993–. Chm., Concertgebouw, 1987–; Mem. Bd, Nat. Mus. of Archaeology, 1993–. Chairman: Bd of Trustees, Utrecht Univ. Hosp., 1994–; Rotterdam Sch. of Mgt, Erasmus Univ., 1999–. *Address:* Vleysmanlaan 10, 2242PN Wassenaar, Netherlands.

MÄLK, Raul; Permanent Representative of Estonia to the European Union, since 2007; *b* 14 May 1952; *s* of Linda and August Mälk. *Educ:* Tartu State Univ. Res. Fellow, Inst. of Economy, Acad. of Scis, 1975–77; freelance editor, subseq. Editor in Chief, Estonian Radio, 1977–90; Dep. Head and Counsellor, Office of President of Supreme Council, 1990–92; Ministry of Foreign Affairs, Tallinn: Counsellor, 1992–93; Chief of Minister's Office, 1993–94; Dep. Permanent Under Sec. (political affairs, press and inf.), 1994–96; Ambassador to UK, 1996–2001, also to Republic of Ireland, 1996–2003; Minister of Foreign Affairs, Estonia, 1998–99; Ambassador to Portugal, 2000–03; Ministry of Foreign Affairs: Dir Gen., Policy Planning Dept, 2001; Actg Dep. Perm. Under-Sec. (EU Affairs), 2003–04, 2005–06. *Publications:* numerous articles in Estonian and Finnish newspapers; material for Estonian radio and television broadcasts, incl. comment on internat. and home news, and parly reports. *Recreations:* theatre, music, attending sports events (football, basketball, track and field). *Address:* Permanent Representation of Estonia to the EU, Rue Guimard 11/13, 1040 Brussels, Belgium.

MALKOVICH, John Gavin; actor and director; *b* Christopher, Ill, 9 Dec. 1953; *s* of late Dan Malkovich and of Joe Anne Malkovich; *m* 1982, Glenne Headley (marr. diss.); partner, Nicoletta Peyran; one *s* one *d*. *Educ:* Eastern Illinois Univ.; Illinois State Univ. Founding Mem., Steppenwolf Theatre Ensemble, Chicago 1976. *Theatre includes: actor:* True West, 1982; Death of a Salesman, 1984; Burn This, 1987 (transf. London, 1990); Slip of the Tongue, 1992 (transf. London, 1992); Libra, 1994; The Libertine, 1996; *director:* Balm in Gilead, 1980, 1984; Coyote Ugly, 1985; Arms and the Man, 1985; The Caretaker, 1986. *Films include:* The Killing Fields, Places in the Heart, 1984; Eleni, 1985; Making Mr Right, The Glass Menagerie, 1987; Empire of the Sun, Miles from Home, 1988; Dangerous Liaisons, Jane, La Putaine du Roi, 1989; The Sheltering Sky, 1990; Queen's Logic, The Object of Beauty, 1991; Of Mice and Men, 1992; Shadows and Fog, In the Line of Fire, 1993; Jennifer Eight, Alive, 1994; Beyond the Clouds, The Ogre, 1995; Mary Reilly, Mulholland Falls, 1996; Portrait of a Lady, Con Air, 1997; The Man in the Iron Mask, Rounders, 1998; Time Regained, Ladies Room, Joan of Arc, 1999; Being John Malkovich, 2000; Shadow of the Vampire, Je Rentre à la Maison, 2001; Ripley's Game, 2003; The Hitchhiker's Guide to the Galaxy, The Libertine, 2005; Eragon, 2006; Beowulf, 2007; L'Echange, 2008; *producer:* The Accidental Tourist, 1988; Somewhere Else, Ghost World, 2000; The Gun Seller, Found in the Street, 2001; *director:* The Dancer Upstairs, 2002. *Address:* c/o Finch & Partners, 6 Heddon Street, W1B 4BS.

MALLABER, (Clare) Judith; MP (Lab) Amber Valley, since 1997; *b* 10 July 1951; *d* of late Kenneth Mallaber and Margaret Joyce Mallaber. *Educ:* N London Collegiate Sch.; St Anne's Coll., Oxford (BA Hons). Res. Officer, NUPE, 1975–85; Local Govt Information Unit, 1985–96 (Dir, 1987–95). Mem., Select Cttee on Educn and Employment, 1997–2001. Mem. Adv. Council, Northern Coll., Barnsley, 1995–. *Address:* House of Commons, SW1A 0AA.

MALLABY, Sir Christopher (Leslie George), GCMG 1996 (KCMG 1988; CMG 1982); GCVO 1992; HM Diplomatic Service, retired; Chancellor of the Order of St Michael and St George, since 2005; *b* 7 July 1936; *s* of late Brig. A. W. S. Mallaby, CIE, OBE, and Margaret Catherine Mallaby (*née* Jones); *m* 1961, Pascale Françoise Thierry-Mieg; one *s* three *d*. *Educ:* Eton; King's Coll., Cambridge. British Delegn to UN Gen. Assembly, 1960; 3rd Sec., British Embassy, Moscow, 1961–63; 2nd Sec., FO, 1963–66; 1st Sec., Berlin, 1966–69; 1st Sec., FCO, 1969–71; Harvard Business Sch., 1971; Dep. Dir, British Trade Develt Office, NY, 1971–74; Counsellor and Head of Chancery, Moscow, 1975–77; Head of Arms Control and Disarmament Dept, FCO, 1977–79, Head of East European and Soviet Dept, 1979–80, Head of Planning Staff, 1980–82, FCO; Minister, Bonn, 1982–85; Dep. Sec., Cabinet Office, 1985–88; Ambassador to Germany, 1988–92; Ambassador to France, 1993–96. Man. Dir, Warburg Dillon Read, subseq. UBS Warburg, then UBS Investment Bank, 2000–06 (Adviser, 1996–2000 and 2006–); Adviser to: RMC, 1996–2000; Herbert Smith, 1997–2001; Louis Dreyfus Group, 1998–2003; Mem. Supervisory Bd, Vodafone (formerly Mannesmann) AG, 2000–; non-executive Director: Sun Life and Provincial Hldgs plc, 1996–2000; Charter Pan-European (formerly European) Investment Trust, 1996–2007. Founder, 1995 and Chm., 2001–08, Entente Cordiale Scholarships (Trustee, 1996–2001). Trustee: Tate Gall., 1996–2002; Reuters, 1998–. Chairman: Primary Immunodeficiency Assoc., 1996–2002, and 2005–06 (Pres., 2002–); Adv. Bd, GB Centre, Humboldt Univ., Berlin, 1997–2005 (Hon. Fellow, 2005); Adv. Bd, German Studies Inst., Birmingham Univ., 1998–2005; Charitable Trust of European Orgn for Res. and Treatment of Cancer (formerly Eur. Orgn for Res. and Treatment of Cancer Foundn), 2001–; Somerset House Trust, 2002–06. Hon. LLD Birmingham, 2004. Grand Cross, Order of Merit (Germany), 1992; Grand Officier, Légion d'Honneur (France), 1996; Comdr, Ordre des Palmes Académiques (France), 2004. *Recreation:* grandchildren. *Address:* 1 Shawfield Street, SW3 4BA; *e-mail:* christopher.mallaby@tiscali.co.uk. *Clubs:* Brooks's, Beefsteak, Grillions.

MALLALIEU, Baroness *cr* 1991 (Life Peer), of Studdridge in the County of Buckinghamshire; **Ann Mallalieu;** QC 1988; *b* 27 Nov. 1945; *d* of Sir (Joseph Percival) William Mallalieu and Lady Mallalieu; *m* 1979, Timothy Felix Harold Cassel (marr. diss. 2007) (*see* Sir T. F. H. Cassel, Bt); two *d*. *Educ:* Holton Park Girls' Grammar Sch., Wheatley, Oxon; Newnham Coll., Cambridge (MA, LLM; Hon. Fellow, 1992). (First woman) Pres., Cambridge Union Soc., 1967. Called to the Bar, Inner Temple, 1970, Bencher, 1992; a Recorder, 1985–93. Mem., Gen. Council of the Bar, 1973–75. Opposition spokesman on home affairs and on legal affairs, H of L, 1992–97. Chm., Ind. Council of the Ombudsman for Corporate Estate Agents, 1993–2000; Ind. Mem., British Horseracing Bd, 2004–07. Pres., Countryside Alliance, 1998–. Chm., Suzy Lamplugh Trust, 1997–2000. *Recreations:* sheep, fishing, hunting, poetry, horseracing. *Address:* House of Lords, SW1A 0PW. *T:* (020) 7219 3000.

MALLALIEU, Angela Maria; *see* Brady, A. M.

MALLET, Sir George; *see* Mallet, Sir W. G.

MALLET, John Valentine Granville, FSA; FRSA; Keeper, Department of Ceramics, Victoria and Albert Museum, 1976–89; *b* 15 Sept. 1930; *s* of late Sir Victor Mallet, GCMG, CVO, and Lady Mallet (*née* Andreae); *m* 1958, Felicity Ann Basset; one *s*. *Educ:* Winchester Coll.; Balliol Coll., Oxford (BA Modern History; Hon. Fellow, 1992). Mil. service in Army: commnd; held temp. rank of full Lieut in Intell. Corps, 1949–50. Messrs Sotheby & Co., London, 1955–62; Victoria and Albert Museum: Asst Keeper, Dept of Ceramics, 1962; Sec. to Adv. Council, 1967–73. Indep. Mem., Design Selection Cttee, Design Council, 1981–89; Member: Exec. Cttee, Nat. Art Collections Fund, 1989–2005; Art Adv. Cttee, Nat. Mus. of Wales, Cardiff, 1991–94; Wissenschaftlicher Beirat, Ceramica-Stiftung, Basel, 1990–; Arts Adv. Panel, Nat. Trust, 1996–2005; Pres., English Ceramic Circle, 1999–. Mem., Court of Assistants, Fishmongers' Co., 1970– (Prime Warden, 1983–84). *Publications:* (with F. Dreier) The Hockemeyer Collection: maiolica and glass, 1998; Xanto: pottery-painter, poet, man of the Italian Renaissance (catalogue), 2007 (Art Newspaper/AXA Prize, UK and Eire); articles on ceramics in Burlington Magazine, Apollo, Trans English Ceramic Circle, and Faenza; poems in Magma and other literary magazines. *Address:* 11 Pembroke Square, W8 6PA.

See also P. L. V. Mallet.

MALLET, Philip Louis Victor, CMG 1980; HM Diplomatic Service, retired; *b* 3 Feb. 1926; *e s* of late Sir Victor Mallet, GCMG, CVO and Christiana Jean, *d* of Herman A. Andreae; *m* 1953, Mary Moyle Grenfell Borlase; three *s*. *Educ:* Winchester; Balliol Coll., Oxford. Army Service, 1944–47. Entered HM Foreign (subseq. Diplomatic) Service, 1949; served in: FO, 1949; Baghdad, 1950–53; FO, 1953–56; Cyprus, 1956–58; Aden, 1958; Bonn, 1958–62; FO, 1962–64; Tunis, 1964–66; FCO, 1967–69; Khartoum, 1969–73; Stockholm, 1973–76; Head of Republic of Ireland Dept, FCO, 1977–78; High Comr in Guyana and non-resident Ambassador to Suriname, 1978–82. *Address:* Wittersham House, Wittersham, Kent TN30 7ED. *Club:* Brooks's.

See also J. V. G. Mallet.

MALLET, Sir (William) George, GCSL; GCMG 1997; CBE; Governor-General of St Lucia, 1996–97; *b* 24 July 1923; *m* Beryl Bernadine Leonce. *Educ:* RC Boys' Sch.; Castries Intermediate Sch. Mem., Castries City Council, 1952–64; MLC, 1958–79, MHA, 1979–96, St Lucia; Minister for Trade, Industry, Agric. and Tourism, 1964–79; Minister for Trade, Industry and Tourism, 1982–92; Dep. Prime Minister, Minister for For. Affairs, and Minister for Caribbean Community Affairs, 1992–96. *Address:* The Morne, Castries, St Lucia.

MALLETT, Conrad Richard, FRICS; Member, Lands Tribunal, 1980–92; *b* 11 May 1919; *s* of Captain Raymond Mallett, OBE, MN and Joyce Mallett (*née* Humble); *m* 1942, Elisabeth (Paulina) Williams; one *s* two *d*. *Educ:* Wellingborough Sch. Ordinary Airman to Lieut Comdr (A), RNVR, 1939–46 (despatches 1941). Partner, Montagu Evans and Son, Chartered Surveyors, London and Edinburgh, 1950–80. *Recreation:* cruising under sail. *Address:* 2 Hadley Hurst Cottages, Hadley Common, Barnet, Herts EN5 5QF. *T:* (020) 8449 5933.

MALLETT, Francis Anthony, CBE 1984; Chief Executive, South Yorkshire County Council, 1973–84; Clerk of the Lieutenancy, South Yorkshire, 1974–84; solicitor; *b* 13 March 1924; *s* of Francis Sidney and Marion Mallett; *m* 1956, Alison Shirley Melville, MA; two *s* one *d*. *Educ:* Mill Hill; London Univ. (LLB). Army, 1943–47: commissioned, Royal Hampshire Regt, 1944; served in Middle East, Italy and Germany; Staff Capt. A 160(SW) Inf. Bde, 4th Guards Bde, 1946–47. Second Dep. Clerk, Herts CC, 1966–69; Dep. Clerk, West Riding CC, 1969–74. Chairman: Assoc. of Local Authority Chief Execs, 1979–84; Crown Prosecution Service Staff Commn, 1985–87; Mem., W Yorks Residuary Body, 1985–91. *Recreations:* gardening, fishing. *Address:* Lurley Manor, Tiverton, Devon EX16 9QS. *T:* (01884) 255363. *Club:* Lansdowne.

MALLICK, Sir Netar (Prakash), Kt 1998; DL; FRCP, FRCPE; Professor of Renal Medicine, University of Manchester, 1994–2000, now Emeritus; Hon. Consultant in Renal Medicine, Manchester Royal Infirmary, 1970–2000; *b* 3 Aug. 1935; *s* of Bhawani Das Mallick and Shanti Devi Mallick; *m* 1960, Mary Wilcockson; three *d*. *Educ:* Queen Elizabeth's Grammar Sch., Blackburn; Manchester Univ. (BSc Hons 1956; MB ChB 1959; Pres., Students' Union, 1958–59). FRCP 1976; FRCPE 1992. Surgical Res. Fellow, Harvard Univ., 1960; Dept of Medicine, Welsh Nat. Sch. of Medicine, 1963–67; Manchester University: Lectr, 1967–72; Sen. Lectr, 1972–92; Hon. Prof. in Renal Medicine, 1992–94; Physician in Charge, Dept of Renal Medicine, Manchester Royal Infirmary, 1973–94. Medical Director: Central Manchester Healthcare NHS Trust, 1997–2000; Adv. Cttee on Distinction Awards, 1999–2003; Adv. Cttee on Clinical Excellence Awards, 2003–07. Vice Chm., Blackburn, Hyndburn and Ribble Valley HA, 1985–90. President: Renal Assoc., 1988–91; Manchester Med. Soc., 2005–06; Chairman: European Dialysis and Transplantation Assoc. Registry, 1991–94; Union Européenne des Médecins Specialistes, 1993–98 (Pres., Bd of Nephrology, 1993–97). Pres., Manchester Lit. and Phil. Soc., 1986–88. Patron: Nat. Kidney Fedn, 2000–; Indian Assoc., Manchester, 2003–. Hon. FRCPI 1999; Hon. FRCSE 2005. DL, 1999, High Sheriff, 2002, Greater Manchester. *Publications:* (ed) Glucose Polymers in Health and Disease, 1977; Renal Disease in General Practice, 1979; (ed) Williams, Colour Atlas of Renal Diseases, 2nd edn 1993; Atlas of Nephrology, 1994; papers on renal disease and health provision in learned jls. *Recreations:* theatre, literature, wine and food, cricket. *Address:* 43 Porchfield Square, Manchester M3 4FG. *T:* (0161) 279 1621. *Club:* Athenæum.

MALLINCKRODT, Georg Wilhelm von; *see* von Mallinckrodt.

MALLINSON, Sir James; *see* Mallinson, Sir W. J.

MALLINSON, John Russell; Speaker's Counsel, House of Commons, 1996–2000; *b* 29 June 1943; *s* of Wilfred and Joyce Helen Mallinson; *m* 1968, Susan Rebecca Jane Godfree; one *s* one *d*. *Educ:* Giggleswick Sch.; Balliol Coll., Oxford (Keasbey Schol. 1963; BA). Solicitor (Hons.), 1972. Asst Solicitor, Coward Chance, 1972–74; Sen. Legal Assistant, DTI, 1974–79; Assistant Solicitor: Law Officers' Dept, 1979–81; DTI, 1982–84; Under Sec. (Legal), DTI, 1985–89; Corporation of Lloyd's: Gen. Manager, 1989–92; Solicitor, 1992–95; Mem., Lloyd's Regulatory Bd, 1993–95. *Recreations:* reading, conversation, music, film, looking at paintings. *Address:* 4 Nunappleton Way, Hurst Green, Surrey RH8 9AW. *T:* (01883) 714775.

MALLINSON, Sir (William) James, 5th Bt *cr* 1935, of Walthamstow; DPhil; indologist; Sanskrit translator; translator, Clay Sanskrit Library; *b* 22 April 1970; *s* of Sir William John Mallinson, 4th Bt and of Rosalind Angela Mallinson (*née* Hoare, now Fishburn); *S* father, 1995; *m* 2002, Claudia Anstice Wright; one *d*. *Educ:* Eton Coll.; St Peter's Coll., Oxford (BA Sanskrit); SOAS, London Univ. (MA); Balliol Coll., Oxford (DPhil). *Publications:* (trans.) Gheranda Samhita, 2004; (trans.) Emperor of the Sorcerers, vols I and II, 2005; (trans.) Shiva Samhita, 2006; Khecarividya, 2006; (trans.) Messenger Poems, 2006; (trans.) The Ocean of the Rivers of Story, 2007. *Recreations:* juggling, yoga, paragliding. *Heir: cousin* Justin Stuart Mallinson [*b* 28 Sept. 1923; *m* 1944, Juliana Beatrice Martin; one *s* one *d*].

MALLOCH BROWN, family name of **Baron Malloch-Brown.**

MALLOCH-BROWN, Baron *cr* 2007 (Life Peer), of St Leonard's Forest in the county of West Sussex; **(George) Mark Malloch Brown,** KCMG 2007; PC 2007; Minister of State (Minister for Middle East and Africa), Foreign and Commonwealth Office, since 2008; *b* 16 Sept. 1953; *s* of George Malloch Brown and Ursula (*née* Pelly); *m* 1989, Patricia Cronan; one *s* three *d. Educ:* Magdalene Coll., Cambridge (BA 1st Cl. Hons Hist.; Hon. Fellow, 2005); Univ. of Michigan (MA Political Sci.). Political corresp., Economist, 1977–79; i/c field ops for Cambodian refugees, Thailand, 1979–81, Dep. Chief, Emergency Unit, Geneva, 1981–83, Office of UNHCR; Founder and Ed., Economist Develt Report, 1983–86; Lead Internat. Partner, Sawyer-Miller Gp, 1986–94; World Bank: Dir, Ext. Affairs, 1994–96; Vice-Pres., Ext. Affairs and for UN Affairs, 1996–99; Administrator, UNDP, 1999–2005; Chef de Cabinet to Sec.-Gen., UN, 2005–06; Dep. Sec.-Gen., UN, 2006; Vice-Chm., Soros Fund Mgt, 2007. Minister of State (Minister for Africa, Asia and UN), 2007–08. Vis. Fellow, Yale Center for the Study of Globalization, 2007. Hon. DLitt: Michigan State, 2002; Catholic Univ. of Peru, 2003; Pace, NY, 2005. *Address:* House of Lords, SW1A 0PW. *Clubs:* Groucho; Yale (New York).

MALLON, Seamus; Member (SDLP) Newry and Armagh, Northern Ireland Assembly, 1998–2003; *b* 17 Aug. 1936; *s* of Francis P. Mallon and Jane O'Flaherty; *m* 1966, Gertrude Cush; one *d. Educ:* St Joseph's Coll. of Educn. Member: NI Assembly, 1973–74 and 1982; NI Convention, 1975–76; Irish Senate, 1981–82; New Ireland Forum, 1983–84; Armagh Dist Council, 1973–86. Dep. First Minister (designate), 1998–99, Dep. First Minister, 1999–2001, NI Assembly. Dep. Leader, SDLP, 1978–2001. MP (SDLP) Newry and Armagh, Jan. 1986–2005. Member: Select Cttee on Agric., 1987–97; Anglo-Irish Inter-Parly Body, 1990–2005. Author of play, Adam's Children, prod. radio, 1968, and stage, 1969. *Recreations:* angling, gardening. *Address:* 5 Castleview, Markethill, Armagh BT60 1QP. *T:* (028) 3755 1411; (office) 2 Bridge Street, Newry, Co. Down BT35 8AE; (office) 8 Cathedral View, Armagh, Co. Armagh BT61 7QX.

MALMESBURY, 7th Earl of, *cr* 1800; **James Carleton Harris;** DL; Baron 1788; Viscount FitzHarris 1800; *b* 19 June 1946; *o s* of 6th Earl of Malmesbury, TD; *S* father, 2000; *m* 1969, Sally Ann (marr. diss. 2008), *yr d* of Sir Richard Newton Rycroft, 7th Bt; three *s* two *d. Educ:* Eton; Queen's Coll., St Andrews (MA). DL Hampshire, 1997. *Heir: s* Viscount FitzHarris, *qv. Address:* Greywell Hill, Greywell, Hook, Hants RG29 1DG. *T:* (01256) 703565.

MALMESBURY, Archdeacon of; *see* Hawker, Ven. A. F.

MALONE, Beverly; Chief Executive Officer, National League for Nursing, USA, since 2007; *b* Elizabethtown, Ky, 25 Aug. 1948; *d* of Frank Malone and Dorothy Black. *Educ:* Univ. of Cincinnati (BSN 1970; Dr in clinical psychol., 1981); Rutgers State Univ., NJ (MSN, 1972). Surgical staff nurse; own private practice, Detroit, Mich, 1973–96; clinical nurse specialist, Univ. of Cincinnati, 1973–75; Asst Administrator for nursing, Univ. of Cincinnati Hosp., 1981–86; Prof. and Dean, Sch. of Nursing, N Carolina State Univ., 1986–2000; Dep. Asst Sec. for Health, USA, 2000–01; Gen. Sec., Royal Coll. of Nursing, 2001–06. Mem., NHS Modernisation Bd, 2001–06. Pres., American Nurses Assoc., 1996–2000. *Address:* National League for Nursing, 61 Broadway, 33rd Floor, New York, NY 10006, USA.

MALONE, Dr Caroline Ann Tuke, (Mrs S. K. F. Stoddart), FSA; archaeologist; Senior Lecturer in Prehistorical Archaeology, Queen's University, Belfast, since 2007; *b* 10 Oct. 1957; *d* of Lt Col Henry Charles Malone and Margaret Hope (*née* Kayll); *m* 1983, Dr Simon Kenneth Fladgate Stoddart, *qv*; two *d. Educ:* St Mary's Sch., St Leonards on Sea; New Hall, Cambridge (MA Hons Archaeol. and Anthropol. 1984); Trinity Hall, Cambridge (PhD Archaeol. 1986). FSA 1993. Italian Govt Scholarship, Rome Univ., 1980–81; Rome Scholarship in Archaeol., Brit. Sch. in Rome, 1981–82; Curator, Alexander Keiller Mus., Avebury, 1985–87; Inspector of Ancient Monuments, English Heritage, 1987–90; Lectr, then Sen. Lectr, Univ. of Bristol, 1990–97; Cambridge University: Tutor in Archaeol., Continuing Educn, 1997–2000; Affiliated Lectr, Dept of Archaeology, 1998–2000, 2005–; Sen. Proctor, 1998–2001; Fellow, New Hall, 1997–2000; Keeper, Dept of Prehistory and Early Europe, British Mus., 2000–03; Sen. Tutor, Hughes Hall, Cambridge, 2003–07. Co Director: Gubbio Archaeol. Project, 1983–88; Gozo Project, Malta, 1987–98; Troina Project, Sicily, 1997–2001. Res. Associate Prof. of Archaeol., SUNY, Buffalo, 2004–. Mem., BASIS Cttee, British Acad., 2001–. Ed., 1998–2000, Co-Ed., 2000–02, Antiquity. Mem., Inst. of Field Archaeologists, 1986–. Fellow, McDonald Inst. for Archaeol Res., 1996–. *Publications:* (ed with S. Stoddart) Papers in Italian Archaeology, Vols 1–4, 1985; Avebury, 1989; (ed with S. Stoddart) Territory, Time and State, 1994; Neolithic Britain and Ireland, 2001; (with S. Stoddart) Mortuary Customs in Prehistoric Malta: excavations at the Brochtorff Circle at Xagtra 1987–94, 2007; contrib. numerous academic papers, articles and reviews. *Recreations:* gardening, pottery, good books, ancient monuments, antiques. *Address:* 8 Lansdowne Road, Cambridge CB3 0EU.

MALONE, (Peter) Gerald; Editor, The Sunday Times Scotland, 1989–90, Editorial Consultant, 1990; *b* 21 July 1950; *s* of P. A. and J. Malone; *m* 1981, Dr Anne S. Blyth; two *s* one *d. Educ:* St Aloysius Coll., Glasgow; Glasgow Univ. (MA, LLB). Admitted solicitor, 1972. MP (C): Aberdeen S, 1983–87; Winchester, 1992–97; contested (C) Winchester, 1997. PPS to Parly Under Secs of State, Dept of Energy, 1985, and to Sec. of State, DTI, 1985–86; an Asst Government Whip, 1986–87; Dep. Chm., Cons. Party, 1992–94; Minister of State, DoH, 1994–97. Company dir, healthcare and financial services sectors, 1997–. Dir of European Affairs, Energy and Envmtl Policy Center, Harvard Univ., 1987–90; Presenter, Talk In Sunday, Radio Clyde, 1988–90. Chm., CGA, 1991. *Recreations:* opera, motoring. *Club:* Conservative (Winchester).

MALONE, Rt Rev. Vincent; Auxiliary Bishop of Liverpool, (RC), 1989–2006; Titular Bishop of Abora, since 1989; *b* 11 Sept. 1931; *s* of Louis Malone and Elizabeth Malone (*née* McGrath). *Educ:* St Francis Xavier's Coll., Liverpool; St Joseph's Coll., Upholland; Liverpool Univ. (BSc 1959); Cambridge Univ. (CertEd 1960; DipEd 1964). FCP 1967. Chaplain to Notre Dame Training Coll., Liverpool, 1955–59; Curate, St Anne's, Liverpool, 1960–61; Asst Master, Cardinal Allen Grammar School, Liverpool, 1961–71; RC Chaplain to Liverpool Univ., 1971–79; Administrator, Liverpool Metropolitan Cathedral, 1979–89. *Address:* 17 West Oakhill Park, Liverpool L13 4BN. *T:* (0151) 228 7637, *Fax:* (0151) 228 7637; *e-mail:* vmalone@onetel.com.

MALONE-LEE, Michael Charles, CB 1995; DL; Chairman, Mid-Essex NHS Hospitals Trust, since 2008; *b* 4 March 1941; *s* of late Dr Gerard Brendan and Theresa Malone-Lee; *m* 1971, Claire Frances Cockin; two *s. Educ:* Stonyhurst College; Campion Hall, Oxford (MA). Ministry of Health, 1968; Principal Private Sec. to Sec. of State for Social Services, 1976–79; Asst Sec., 1977; Area Administrator, City and East London AHA, 1979–81; District Administrator, Bloomsbury Health Authy, 1982–84; Under Secretary, 1984, Dir, Personnel Management, 1984–87, DHSS; Prin. Fin. Officer, Home Office, 1987–90; Dep. Sec. (Dir of Corporate Affairs, NHS Management Exec.), DoH, 1990–93; Dep. Sec. (Head of Policy Gp), Lord Chancellor's Dept, 1993–95; Vice-Chancellor, Anglia Poly. Univ., 1995–2004. Non-exec. Dir, ICI (Agrochemicals), 1986–89. Dir, Essex TEC, 1996–2001; Chairman: BBC E Regl Adv. Council, 1997–99; Essex Learning and Skills Council, 2000–03. Mem., Review Body for Nursing Staff, Midwives, Health Visitors and Professions allied to Medicine, 1998–2001; non-exec. Dir, Mid-Essex PCT, 2006–08. Ecumenical Officer, Dio. Brentwood, 2005–. Chairman Governors: New Hall Sch., 1999–2002; Heythrop Coll., London Univ., 2006–. DL Essex, 2002. Hon. Fellow, Fachhochschule Für Wirtschaft, Berlin, 2004. Hon. PhD Anglia Poly. Univ., 2005. *Recreations:* natural history, marathon running. *Address:* Marshalls, Braintree CM7 2LN.

MALOUF, David George Joseph, AO 1987; writer; *b* 20 March 1934; *s* of George and Welcolme Malouf. *Educ:* Brisbane Grammar Sch.; Univ. of Queensland (BA Hons Eng Lang. and Lit.). Teacher, St Anselm's Coll., Birkenhead, 1962–68; Lectr, Dept of English, Univ. of Sydney, 1968–78. Boyer Lectr, ABC, 1998. Hon. DLitt: Macquarie, 1990; Queensland, 1991; Sydney, 1998. *Publications:* Johnno: a novel, 1975; An Imaginary Life, 1978; Child's Play, 1981; Fly Away Peter, 1981; Harland's Half Acre, 1984; Antipodes (stories), 1985; 12 Edmondstone Street, 1986; The Great World, 1990; Remembering Babylon, 1993; The Conversations at Curlow Creek, 1996; A Spirit of Play (Boyer Lectures), 1998; Untold Tales, 1999; Dream Stuff (stories), 2000; Every Move You Make (stories), 2007; The Complete Stories, 2007; *poetry:* Bicycle and Other Poems, 1970; Neighbours in a Thicket, 1974; First Things Last, 1981; Selected Poems, 1993; Revolving Days: selected poems, 2008; *libretti:* Baa Baa Black Sheep, 1993; Jane Eyre, 2000. *Address:* c/o Rogers, Coleridge & White, 20 Powis Mews, W11 1JN.

MALPAS, Prof. James Spencer, DPhil; FRCP, FRCR, FRCPCH; Master, London Charterhouse, 1996–2001; Consultant Physician, St Bartholomew's Hospital, since 1973; Professor of Medical Oncology, 1979–95, now Professor Emeritus, and Director, Imperial Cancer Research Fund Medical Oncology Unit, 1976–95, St Bartholomew's Hospital; *b* 15 Sept. 1931; *s* of Tom Spencer Malpas, BSc, MICE and Hilda Chalstrey; *m* 1957, Joyce May Cathcart; two *s. Educ:* Sutton County Grammar Sch.; St Bartholomew's Hosp., London Univ. Schol. in Sci., 1951; BSc Hons, 1952; MB BS, 1955; DPhil, 1965; FRCP 1971; FRCPCH 1978; FRCR 1983; FFPM 1989. Junior appts in medicine, St Bartholomew's Hosp. and Royal Post-Grad. Med. Sch.; Nat. Service in RAF, 1957–60; Aylwen Bursar, St Bartholomew's Hosp., 1961; Lectr in Medicine, Oxford Univ., 1962–65; St Bartholomew's Hospital: Sen. Registrar in Medicine, 1966–68; Sen. Lectr in Medicine, 1968–72; Dean, 1969–72, Gov., 1972–74, Treasurer, 1986–87, and Vice Pres., 1987–93, of Med. Coll.; Dir (Clinical), ICRF, 1986–90. Cooper Res. Schol. in Med., 1966, 1967, 1968. Examiner in Medicine: Univ. of Oxford, 1974; Univ. of London, 1985, 1986. Acad. Registrar, RCP, 1975–80; Treasurer, Postgrad. Med. Fellowship, 1984–87. Pres., Assoc. of Cancer Physicians, 1994–99. Treas., Retired Fellows Soc., RSocMed, 2008–. Trustee: St Bartholomew's and Royal London Charitable Foundn (formerly Special Trustees, St Bart's Hosp.), 1997–2007; Med. Coll. of St Bart's Hosp. Trust, 1999–; Mason-Le-Page Charitable Trust, 2001–. Lockyer Lectr, RCP, 1978; Skinner Lectr, RCR, 1986; Subodh Mitra Meml Orator, New Delhi, 1991; Louise Buchanan Lectr, Assoc. of Cancer Physicians, 1993. Editor, British Jl of Cancer, 1992–93. Fellow, Royal Instn, 2002. Freeman, City of London, 1988. Medicus Hippocraticus prize, Internat. Hippocratic Foundn of Kos, 1996. *Publications:* (ed jtly) Multiple Myeloma, 1994, 3rd edn 2003; contrib. many medical textbooks; papers in BMJ, Brit. Jl Haematology, Jl Clinical Oncology, etc. *Recreations:* travel, history, painting, sailing, amateur molecular biologist, avoiding gardening. *Address:* 253 Lauderdale Tower, Barbican, EC2Y 8BY. *T:* (020) 7920 9337. *Club:* Little Ship.

MALPAS, Sir Robert, Kt 1998; CBE 1975; FREng, FIMechE, FIChemE; Chairman, Ferghana Partners Ltd, 1998–2002; *b* 9 Aug. 1927; *s* of late Cheshyre Malpas and Louise Marie Marcelle Malpas; *m* 1st, 1956, Josephine Dickenson (*d* 2004); 2nd, 2005, Joan Holloway. *Educ:* Taunton Sch.; St George's Coll., Buenos Aires; Durham Univ. (BScMechEng (1st Cl. Hons)). Joined ICI Ltd, 1948; moved to Alcudia SA (48.5 per cent ICI), Spain, 1963; ICI Europa Ltd, Brussels, 1965; Chm., ICI Europa Ltd, 1973; ICI Main Board Dir, 1975–78; Pres., Halcon International Inc., 1978–82; a Man. Dir, BP, 1983–89; Chairman: PowerGen, 1990; Cookson Gp, 1991–98. Dir, Repsol SA, 1989–2002; non-executive Director: BOC Group, 1981–96; Eurotunnel, 1987–99 (Co-Chm., 1996–98); Enagas, Spain, 2002–06; Agcert plc, 2005–. Member: Engineering Council, 1983–88 (Vice-Chm., 1984–88); ACARD, 1983–86; Chairman: LINK Steering Gp, 1987–93; NERC, 1993–96. FREng (FEng 1978; Sen. Vice Pres., 1988–92). Hon. FRSC 1988; Hon. FIMechE 1999. FRSA. Hon. Fellow, Univ. of Westminster, 1992. Hon. DTech Loughborough, 1983; DUniv: Surrey, 1984; Sheffield Hallam, 2001; Hon. DEng Newcastle, 1991; Hon. DSc: Bath, 1991; Durham, 1997. Order of Civil Merit, Spain, 1967. *Recreations:* sport, music, theatre. *Address:* 2 Spencer Park, SW18 2SX. *Clubs:* Royal Automobile; Mill Reef (Antigua).

MALPASS, Brian William, PhD; CChem; investor and writer; Chief Executive, De La Rue Co. plc, 1987–89; *b* 12 Sept. 1937; *s* of William and Florence Malpass; *m* 1960, Hazel Anne; two *d. Educ:* Univ. of Birmingham (Open Schol.; Frankland Prize 1960; BScChem 1st Cl. Hons, PhD). MRSC. Passfield Res. Laboratories, 1963–68; De La Rue Co., 1968–89; Finance Dir, 1980–84; Man. Dir, Thomas De La Rue Currency Div., 1984–87. *Publications:* Bluff Your Way in Science, 1993; Bluff Your Way in Chess, 1993; numerous papers in scientific jls, magazine articles and book reviews. *Recreation:* grandchildren. *Address:* 13 Spinfield Mount, Marlow, Bucks SL7 2JU.

MALTBY, Antony John, MA; JP; Headmaster of Trent College, 1968–88; *b* 15 May 1928; *s* of late G. C. Maltby and Mrs Maltby (*née* Kingsnorth); *m* 1st, 1959, Jillian Winifred (*née* Burt) (*d* 2000); three *d* (and one *d* decd); 2nd, 2001, Mrs Elizabeth Mary Batin (*née* Newman); one step *s* three step *d. Educ:* Clayesmore Sch., Dorset; St John's Coll., Cambridge. BA Hons (History) 1950; MA. Schoolmaster: Dover Coll., 1951–58; Pocklington Sch., 1958–68. Mem. (Ind.), Ashford BC, 1991–2007. JP: Ilkeston, 1980; Ashford, 1992; DL Derbyshire, 1984–91. *Recreations:* community matters, travel. *Address:* Little Singleton Farm, Great Chart, Ashford, Kent TN26 1JS. *T:* (01233) 629397. *Club:* Hawks (Cambridge).

MALTBY, Colin Charles; Chairman: Princess Private Equity Holding Ltd, since 2007; Blackrock Absolute Return Strategies Ltd, since 2008; *b* 8 Feb. 1951; *s* of late George Frederick Maltby, MC and Dorothy Maltby; *m* 1983, Victoria Angela Valerie Elton; one *s* two *d. Educ:* George Heriot's Sch., Edinburgh; King Edward's Sch., Birmingham; Christ Church, Oxford (MA, MSc); Stanford Business Sch. Pres., Oxford Union, 1973; Chm., Fedn of Cons. Students, 1974–75. With N. M. Rothschild & Sons, 1975–80; Director: Kleinwort Benson Investment Mgt Ltd, 1984–95 (Chief Exec., 1988–95); Banque Kleinwort Benson SA, Geneva, 1985–88; Kleinwort Benson Gp plc, 1989–95; CCLA Investment Mgt Ltd, 1997–2003 (Chm., 1999–2003); Chm., Kleinwort Overseas Investment Trust plc, 1992–96; Chief Investment Officer, Equitas, 1996–2000; Chief Exec., BP Investment Mgt Ltd, 2000–07. Director: RM plc, 1997–99; H. Young Hldgs plc, 1997–2001. Investment Adviser: British Coal Staff Superannuation Scheme, 2001–; British Airways Pension Schemes, 2003–07. Mem., Finance Cttee, Funding Agency for

Schs, 1996–99. Fellow, Wolfson Coll., Oxford, 2002–. FRSA 1993; Fellow, Royal Instn. *Recreations:* music, ski-ing. *Address:* 1224 Chêne-Bougeries, Switzerland.

MALTHOUSE, Christopher Laurie, (Kit); Member (C) West Central, London Assembly, Greater London Authority, since 2008; Deputy Mayor of London, Policing, since 2008; *b* Liverpool, 27 Oct. 1966; *s* of John Christopher Malthouse and Susan Malthouse; *m* 2007, Juliana Farha; one *s* by a previous marriage. *Educ:* Liverpool Coll.; Newcastle Univ. (BA Jt Hons Pols and Econs). Mem., ICAEW, 1997. Touche Ross & Co., 1992–97; Finance Officer, Camode Gp, 1997–2001; Chm., County Hldgs, 2001–; Chief Exec., 2005–08, Finance Dir, 2008–, Alpha Strategic plc. Contested (C) Liverpool Wavertree, 1997. Mem., Westminster CC, 1998–2006 (Dep. Leader, 2001–05). *Publication:* (contrib.) A Blue Tomorrow, 2001. *Recreations:* baking bread and policies, writing poetry and prose, watching others dance and play. *Address:* Greater London Authority, City Hall, The Queen's Walk, SE1 2AA. *T:* (020) 7983 4099; *e-mail:* kit.malthouse@london.gov.uk.

MALTMAN, Christopher John; freelance opera singer (baritone); *b* 7 Feb. 1970; *s* of Robert John Maltman and Christine Maltman; *m* 2000, Leigh Wolf. *Educ:* Warwick Univ. (BSc Hons Biochem.); Royal Acad. of Music (LRAM, Dip. RAM, ARAM; Queen's Commendation for Excellence, 1991). Operatic roles at: Royal Opera House, Covent Gdn; ENO; WNO; Bayerische Staatsoper, Munich; Deutsche Staatsoper, Berlin; La Monnaie, Brussels; Seattle Opera; San Diego Opera; Salzburg Fest.; Glyndebourne; recitals at: Wigmore Hall; Carnegie Hall, Lincoln Centre, NY; Konzerthaus, Vienna; Concertgebouw, Amsterdam; Schwarzenberg Schubertiade; Edinburgh Fest.; Salzburg Fest.; has made numerous recordings. Lieder Prize, Cardiff Singer of the World, 1997; Young Artist of Year, Royal Philharmonic Soc., 1999; Artist of Year, Seattle Opera, 2000–01. *Recreations:* food, wine, physical fitness. *Address:* c/o Askonas Holt Ltd, Lincoln House, 300 High Holborn, WC1V 7JH. *T:* (020) 7400 1700, *Fax:* (020) 7400 1799.

MALVERN, 3rd Viscount *cr* 1955, of Rhodesia and of Bexley, Kent; **Ashley Kevin Godfrey Huggins;** *b* 26 Oct. 1949; *s* of 2nd Viscount Malvern, and of Patricia Marjorie, *d* of Frank Renwick-Bower, Durban, S Africa; *S* father, 1978. *Heir: uncle* Hon. (Martin) James Huggins, *b* 13 Jan. 1928.

MALVERN, John, FRCSE, FRCOG; Consultant Obstetrician and Gynaecologist, Queen Charlotte's and Chelsea Hospital for Women (formerly Queen Charlotte's Hospital and Chelsea Hospital), 1973–2001, now Emeritus; Hon. Consultant Gynaecologist, King Edward VII Hospital for Officers, since 1997; *b* 3 Oct. 1937; *s* of late Harry Ladyman Malvern, CBE, and Doreen Malvern (*née* Peters); *m* 1965, Katharine Mary Monica, *d* of late Hugh Guillebaud; one *s* two *d*. *Educ:* Fettes Coll., Edinburgh; Royal London Hosp. Med. Sch., Univ. of London (BSc 1st Cl. Hons 1959; MB BS 1963). FRCSE 1968; FRCOG 1984. Various jun. posts in surgery and obstetrics and gynaecology at Royal London Hosp., Plymouth Gen. Hosp., Hosp. for Women, Soho Sq., Middx Hosp., Queen Charlotte's and Chelsea Hosp. Hon. Sen. Lectr, RPMS, then ICSTM, 1973–99. Ninian M. Falkiner Lectr, Rotunda Hosp., Dublin, 1980. Chm., Acad. Gp, Inst. Obstetrics and Gynaecol., 1986–88. Royal College of Obstetricians and Gynaecologists: Officer and Hon. Treas., 1991–98; Mem. Council, 1977–83 and 1987–90; Chm., Investment Panel, 2002–06; Hon. Cellarer, 2004–; Pres., Obstetric and Gynaecol Section, RSocMed, 1989. Former Examiner for RCOG: Central Midwives Bd; Univs of London, Liverpool, Edinburgh, Manchester, Benghazi, Colombo, Khartoum and Hong Kong. Member: Central Manpower Cttee, 1981–84; PPP Healthcare Trust Ltd, 1998–2001. Member: Blair Bell Res. Soc., 1970–; Internat. Continence Soc., 1971–; Fothergill Club, 1977–; Gynaecol Vis. Soc., 1979–; Med. Soc. of London, 2004–; Hon. Mem., New England Obstetrical and Gynecol Soc., 2000. Liveryman, Soc. of Apothecaries, 1978–. FRGS 2001. Advanced Cert. in Wines and Spirits, Wine and Spirit Educn Trust level 3, 2002. *Publications:* (ed jtly) The Unstable Bladder, 1989; (ed jtly) Lecture Notes on Gynaecology, 1996; contributor to: Turnbull's Obstetrics, 1985, 2nd edn 1995; Basic Sciences in Obstetrics and Gynaecology, 1992; Gynaecology by Ten Teachers, 1995; various contribs on urogynaecology and obstetrics. *Recreations:* wine tasting, history of art, travel, croquet. *Address:* 30 Roedean Crescent, Roehampton, SW15 5JU. *T:* (020) 8876 4943. *Clubs:* Royal Society of Medicine, Hurlingham.

See also Sir H. R. Wilmot.

MALYAN, Hugh David; Member (Lab), Croydon Borough Council, 1994–2006 (Leader, 2000–05; Hon. Alderman, 2006); *b* 7 June 1959; *s* of Cyril and Brenda Malyan; *m* 1983, Ruth Margaret; one *s* one *d*. *Educ:* Strand Grammar Sch., Brixton. Trustee Savings Bank, 1975–78; fireman, London Fire Bde, 1978–92. Chm., Educn Cttee, Croydon BC, 1997–2000. Vice Chm., Assoc. of London Govt, 2002–05; Chm., Commn for London Governance, 2005–06. *Recreations:* amateur dramatics (former Mem., Downsview Players), singing, football (Crystal Palace supporter!).

MAMATSASHVILI, Teimuraz; Ambassador of Georgia to the Court of St James's, 1995–2004, and to the Republic of Ireland, 1998–2004; *b* 10 Nov. 1942; *s* of David Mamatsashvili and Maria Robakidze; *m* 1967, Irina Arkhangelskaya; two *d*. *Educ:* Georgian Polytechnical Inst. (Engineer); Acad. of Foreign Trade of USSR (Economist). Senior Engineer: Sci. Inst. of Metrology, 1965–70; USSR Trade Rep. in Australia, 1974–77; Dir, foreign trade orgn Licensintorg, Moscow, 1977–89; USSR Trade Rep., Tokyo, 1989–92; Minister of Foreign Economic Relations, Georgia, 1992–93. Rep. to IMO, 1995–; Gov., EBRD, 1996–. Orders of the Soviet Union, 1971, 1988. *Recreations:* hunting, gardening. *Club:* Les Ambassadeurs.

MAMBA, George Mbikwakhe, Hon. GCVO 1987; Minister of Foreign Affairs, Swaziland, 1988–94; *b* 5 July 1932; *s* of Ndabazebelungu Mamba and Getrude Mthwalose Mamba, and *g s* of late Chief Bokweni Mamba; *m* 1960, Sophie Sidzandza Sibande; three *s* two *d*. *Educ:* Franson Christian High Sch.; Swazi National High Sch.; Morija Teacher Trng Coll.; Cambridge Inst. of Educn; Nairobi Univ. Head Teacher, Makhonza Mission Sch., 1956–60; Teacher, Kwaluseni Central Sch., 1961–65; Head Teacher, Enkamheni Central Sch., 1966–67; Inspector of Schs, Manzini Dist, 1969–70; Welfare/Aftercare Officer, Prison Dept, 1971–72; Counsellor, Swaziland High Commn, Nairobi, 1972–77; High Comr to UK and concurrently High Comr to Malta, Ambassador to Denmark, Sweden and Norway, and Perm. Deleg. to UNESCO, 1978–88, Sen. High Comr, 1984 and Doyen of Diplomatic Corps, 1985–88. Vice-Pres., Swaziland NUT, 1966–67. Field Comr, Swaziland Boy Scouts Assoc., 1967–68, Chief Comr, 1971–72. *Publication:* Children's Play, 1966. *Recreations:* scouting, reading. *Address:* c/o Ministry of Foreign Affairs, PO Box 518, Mbabane, Swaziland.

MAMET, David Alan; writer; stage and film director; *b* 30 Nov. 1947; *s* of Bernard Morris Mamet and Lenore June Mamet (*née* Silver); *m* 1st, 1977, Lindsay Crouse (marr. diss.); 2nd, 1991, Rebecca Pidgeon. *Educ:* Goddard College, Plainfield, Vt (BA Eng. Lit. 1969); Neighbourhood Playhouse Sch., NY. Founding Mem. and first Artistic Dir, St Nicholas Theater Co., Chicago, 1974. *Plays: written and produced include:* Sexual Perversity in Chicago, 1975; American Buffalo, 1976; A Life in the Theatre, 1976; The Water Engine, 1976; The Woods, 1977; Lakeboat, 1980; Edmond, 1982; Glen Garry Glen Ross, 1984 (Pulitzer Prize for Drama, 1984; filmed, 1992); Speed the Plow, 1987; Bobby Gould in Hell, 1989; The Old Neighborhood (trilogy), 1990, UK 1998; Oleanna, 1992; The Cryptogram, 1994; *written and directed:* Boston Marriage, 1999, UK, 2001; Dr Faustus, 2004; *written:* November, 2008; Speed-the-Plow, 2008. *Films: written:* The Verdict, 1980; The Untouchables, 1986; Hoffa, 1990; Uncle Vanya on 42nd Street, 1994; The Edge, 1998; Wag the Dog, 1998; (jtly) Hannibal, 2001; *written and directed:* House of Games, 1986; (with Shel Silverstein) Things Change, 1987; Homicide, 1991; State and Main, 2001; Heist, 2001; Spartan, 2004; *directed:* The Winslow Boy, 1999. *TV series: written and directed:* The Unit, 2006. *Publications:* Writing in Restaurants, 1986; Some Freaks, 1989; The Hero Pony, 1990; On Directing Film, 1991; The Cabin, 1992; The Village, 1994; Passover, 1996; True or False—Heresy and Common Sense for the Actor, 1998; The Old Religion, 1998; Wilson: a consideration of the sources, 2000; Three Uses of the Knife, 2002; Bambi vs Godzilla: on the nature, purpose and practice of the movie business, 2007. *Address:* c/o Howard Rosenstone, Rosenstone/Wender Agency, 38 East 29th Street, 10th Floor, New York, NY 10016, USA.

MAN, Archdeacon of; *see* Smith, Ven. B.

MANASSEH, Leonard Sulla, OBE 1982; RA 1979 (ARA 1976); RWA; FRIBA; FCSD; Partner, Leonard Manasseh Partnership (formerly Leonard Manasseh & Partners), since 1950; *b* 21 May 1916; *s* of late Alan Manasseh and Esther (*née* Elias); *m* 1st, 1947 (marr diss. 1956); one *s* (and one *s* decd); 2nd, 1957, Sarah Delaforce; two *s* (one *d* decd). *Educ:* Cheltenham College; The Architectural Assoc. Sch. of Architecture (AA Dip.). ARIBA 1941, FRIBA 1964; FCSD (FSIAD 1965); RWA 1972 (Pres., 1989–94, PPRWA 1995). Asst Architect, CRE N London and Guy Morgan & Partners; teaching staff, AA and Kingston Sch. of Art, 1941–43; Fleet Air Arm, 1943–46; Asst Architect, Herts CC, 1946–48; Senior Architect, Stevenage New Town Develt Corp., 1948–50; won Festival of Britain restaurant competition, 1950; started private practice, 1950; teaching staff, AA Sch. of Architecture, 1951–59; opened office in Singapore and Malaysia with James Cubitt & Partners (Cubitt Manasseh & Partners), 1953–54. Member: Council, Architectural Assoc., 1959–66 (Pres., 1964–65); Council of Industrial Design, 1965–68; Council, RIBA 1968–70, 1976–82 (Hon. Sec., 1979–81); Council, National Trust, 1977–91; Ancient Monuments Bd, 1978–84; Bd, Chatham Historic Dockyard Trust, 1984–. Pres., Franco-British Union of Architects, 1978–79. Governor: Alleyn's Sch., Dulwich, 1987–95; Dulwich Coll., 1987–95; Dulwich Picture Gallery, 1987–94 (Chm., 1988–93). FRSA 1967; Mem., Acad. d'Architecture de France. *Work includes:* houses, housing and schools; industrial work; power stations; conservation plan for Beaulieu Estate; Nat. Motor Museum, Beaulieu; Wellington Country Park, Stratfield Saye; Pumping Station, Weymouth; British Museum refurbishment; (jtly) New Research Centre, Loughborough, British Gas. *Publications:* Office Buildings (with 3rd Baron Cunliffe), 1962, Japanese edn 1964; (jtly) Snowdon Summit Report (Countryside Commission), 1974; Eastbourne Harbour Study (Trustees, Chatsworth Settlement), 1976; New Service Yard, Hampstead Heath (Corp. of London), 1993; (jtly) planning reports and studies. *Recreations:* photography, painting, being optimistic. *Address:* 6 Bacon's Lane, Highgate, N6 6BL. *T:* (020) 8340 5528, *Fax:* (020) 8347 6313. *Clubs:* Athenæum, Arts, Royal Automobile.

MANCE, Baron *cr* 2005 (Life Peer), of Frognal, in the London Borough of Camden; **Jonathan Hugh Mance,** Kt 1993; PC 1999; a Lord of Appeal in Ordinary, since 2005; *b* 6 June 1943; *e s* of late Sir Henry Stenhouse Mance and Lady (Joan Erica Robertson) Mance; *m* 1973, Mary Howarth Arden (*see* Rt Hon. Dame M. H. Arden); one *s* two *d*. *Educ:* Charterhouse; University Coll., Oxford (MA; Hon. Fellow 2006). Called to the Bar, Middle Temple, 1965, Bencher, 1989. QC 1982; a Recorder, 1990–93; a Judge of the High Court, QBD, Commercial List, 1993–99; a Lord Justice of Appeal, 1999–2005. Worked in Germany, 1965. Chm., Banking Appeal tribunals, 1992–93. Dir, Bar Mutual Indemnity Fund Ltd, 1987–94. Chm., Consultative Council of European Judges, 2000–03. Mem., H of L Select Cttee on EU, 2007– (Chm., Sub-cttee E, Law and Instns). Chm., Hampstead Counselling Service, 2000–. Pres., British Insurance Law Assoc., 2000–02 (Dep. Pres., 1998–2000). Chm., Bar Lawn Tennis Soc., 2000–. Trustee, European Law Acad., Trier, 2003–. *Publications:* (asst editor) Chalmer's Sale of Goods, 1981; (ed jtly) Sale of Goods, Halsbury's Laws of England, 4th edn 1983; lectures and articles on insurance and other legal subjects. *Recreations:* tennis, languages, music. *Address:* House of Lords, SW1A 0PW. *Club:* Cumberland Lawn Tennis.

MANCHAM, Sir James Richard Marie, KBE 1976; international trade consultant, since 1981; Chairman, Mahé Publications Ltd, since 1984; Founding President, Republic of the Seychelles, 1976–77; Founder and Chairman, Crusade for the Restoration of Democracy in Seychelles, since 1990; Leader of revived Seychelles Democratic Party, 1992–2005; *b* 11 Aug. 1939; adopted British nationality, 1984; *e s* of late Richard Mancham and Evelyne Mancham, MBE (*née* Tirant); *m* 1963, Heather Jean Evans (marr. diss. 1974); one *s* one *d*; *m* 1985, Catherine Olsen; one *s*. *Educ:* Seychelles Coll.; Wilson Coll., London. Called to Bar, Middle Temple, 1961. Auditeur Libre à la Faculté de Droit ès Sciences Economiques, Univ. of Paris, 1962; Internat. Inst. of Labour Studies Study Course, Geneva, Spring 1968. Legal practice, Supreme Court of Seychelles. Seychelles Democratic Party (SDP), Pres. 1964; Mem. Seychelles Governing Council, 1967; Leader of Majority Party (SDP), 1967; Mem., Seychelles Legislative Assembly, 1970–76; Chief Minister, 1970–75; Prime Minister, 1975–76; Leader of Opposition, 1993–98; led SDP to Seychelles Constitutional Conf., London, 1970 and 1976. Founder, Seychelles Weekly, 1962. Lecturer, 1981, on struggle for power in Indian Ocean, to US and Eur. univs and civic gps; Lectr on geo-politics of Indian Ocean, Internat. Univ. of Japan, 1996. Promoter, Internat. Inst. of Nat. Reconciliation Between Nations, 1997. Delegate: to Conf. on Challenges of Demilitarisation of Africa in Arusha, Tanzania, 1998; to Convocation of Family Fedn for World Peace and Unification Internat., Seoul, 1999; deleg. and keynote speaker, many internat. confs on world peace. Hon. Patron, Indo-Seychelles Chamber of Commerce, 1995. Mem., Internat. Palm Soc., 1994. Hon. Trustee, Cary Ann Lindblad Intrepid Foundn, 1986–. Hon. Mem., Internat. Consultative Bd, Inst. for Strategic Studies, Brakaric Univ., Belgrade, 1998. Hon. Citizen: Dade County, Florida, 1963; New Orleans, 1965. FRSA 1968. Cert. of Merit for Distinguished Contribn to Poetry, Internat. Who's Who in Poetry, 1974; Ambassador for Peace, Internat. Fedn for World Peace, 2001; Lifetime Achievement Award, Rajiv Gandhi Foundn, 2001. Chevalier, Chaîne des Rôtisseurs, 1993. Officier de la Légion d'Honneur, 1976; Grande Médaille de la Francophonie, 1976; Grande médaille vermeille, Paris, 1976; Quaid-i-Azam Medallion (Pakistan), 1976; Gold Medal, City of Pusan, Repub. of Korea, 1976; Gold Medal for Tourism, Mexico, 1977; Gold Medal of Chamber of Commerce and Industries of France, 1977; Gold Medal des Excellences Européennes, 1977; Plaque of Appreciation, Rotary Club of Manila, Philippines, 1987; Gold Medal, Municipality of Dubai, 1995; Gold Medal, City of Bombay, 1996; Gold Key, Anchorage, Alaska, 2001. *Publications:* Reflections and Echoes from Seychelles, 1972 (poetry); L'Air des Seychelles, 1974; Island Splendour, 1980; Paradise Raped, 1983; Galloo—The undiscovered paradise, 1984; New York's Robin Island, 1985; Peace of Mind, 1989; Adages of an Exile, 1991; Oh, Mighty America, 1998; Tel est mon destin, je fais mon chemin, 2001; War on America seen from the Indian Ocean, 2002; (ed jtly) The Future of Peace in the 21st Century, 2002. *Recreations:* travel, fishing, birdfeeding, journalism, writing. *Address:* PO Box 29, Mahé,

Seychelles. *Clubs:* Royal Automobile, Annabel's, Les Ambassadeurs; Intrepids (NY); Cercle Saint Germain des Prés (Paris).

MANCHESTER, 13th Duke of, *cr* 1719; **Alexander Charles David Drogo Montagu;** Baron Montagu, Viscount Mandeville, 1620; Earl of Manchester, 1626; President, Global Atlantic, since 1983; *b* 11 Dec. 1962; *s* of 12th Duke of Manchester and Mary Eveleen (*née* McClure); *S* father, 2002; *m* 2007, Laura Ann, *d* of Marvin Smith, Michigan; one *s* one *d* by previous marriage. *Educ:* Geelong Grammar Sch., Vic; Bancroft Jun. High Sch., Calif.; Kimbolton Grammar Sch., Cambridgeshire. Director: Internal Security, 1991–; Summit Investments, 1994–; Royal Fidelity Trust, 1996–. *Heir: s* Viscount Mandeville, *qv*. *Address:* c/o British Consulate-General, 11766 Wilshire Boulevard, Los Angeles, CA 90025–6538, USA; 220 Newport Center Drive, Newport Beach, CA 92660, USA; *e-mail:* globalatlantic@aol.com.

MANCHESTER, Bishop of, since 2002; **Rt Rev. Nigel Simeon McCulloch;** Lord High Almoner to the Queen, since 1997; *b* 17 Jan. 1942; *s* of late Pilot Officer Kenneth McCulloch, RAFVR, and of Audrey Muriel McCulloch; *m* 1974, Celia Hume Townshend, *d* of Canon H. L. H. Townshend; two *d*. *Educ:* Liverpool College; Selwyn Coll., Cambridge (Kitchener Schol., BA 1964, MA 1969); Cuddesdon Coll., Oxford. Ordained, 1966; Curate of Ellesmere Port, 1966–70; Chaplain of Christ's Coll., Cambridge, 1970–73; Director of Theological Studies, Christ's Coll., Cambridge, 1970–75; permission to officiate, dio. of Liverpool, 1970–73; Diocesan Missioner for Norwich Diocese, 1973–78; Rector of St Thomas' and St Edmund's, Salisbury, 1978–86; Archdeacon of Sarum, 1979–86; Bishop Suffragan of Taunton, 1986–92; Bishop of Wakefield, 1992–2002. Prebendary of Ogbourne, Salisbury Cathedral, 1979–86, of Wanstrow, Wells Cathedral, 1986–92; Canon Emeritus of Salisbury Cathedral, 1989. Took his seat in H of L, 1997; Mem., H of L Select Cttee, on BBC Charter Review, 2005–06, on Communications, 2007–. Mem., House of Bishops, Gen. Synod of C of E, 1990–. Chairman: Finance Cttee, ACCM, 1988–92; Decade of Evangelism Steering Gp, 1989–96; C of E Communications Unit, 1993–; C of E Mission, Evangelism and Renewal Cttee, 1996–99; Gen. Synod Legislation Gp on Women Bishops, 2006–; CCJ, 2006–. Chaplain to Council of St John: Somerset, 1987–92; SW Yorks, 1992–2002; Hon. Nat. Chaplain, RBL, 2001–. Chm., Sandford St Martin Trust, 1999–. Pres., Somerset Rural Music Sch., 1986–92; Mem. Council, RSCM, 1984–2007. Chm., Somerset County Scout Assoc., 1988–92; Pres., Central Yorks Scouts, 1992–2002. Pres., St Anne's Hospice, Gtr Manchester, 2003–. Hon. DCL Huddersfield, 2003. *Publications:* A Gospel to Proclaim, 1992; Barriers to Belief, 1994. *Recreations:* music, brass bands, walking in the Lake District. *Address:* Bishopscourt, Bury New Road, Manchester M7 4LE. *Club:* Athenæum.

MANCHESTER, Dean of; *see* Govender, Very Rev. R. M.

MANCHESTER, Archdeacon of; *see* Ballard, Ven. A. E.

MANCHIPP, Amelia Anne Doris; *see* Noble, A. A. D.

MANCROFT, family name of **Baron Mancroft**.

MANCROFT, 3rd Baron *cr* 1937, of Mancroft in the City of Norwich; **Benjamin Lloyd Stormont Mancroft;** Bt 1932; *b* 16 May 1957; *s* of 2nd Baron Mancroft, KBE, TD and Diana Elizabeth (*d* 1999), *d* of late Lt-Col Horace Lloyd, DSO; *S* father, 1987; *m* 1990, Emma Louisa, *e d* of Thomas Peart; two *s* one *d*. *Educ:* Eton. MFH, Vale of White Horse Hunt, 1987–89. Chm., Inter Lotto (UK) Ltd, 1995–. Chairman: Addiction Recovery Foundn, 1989–; Drug and Alcohol Foundn, 1993–; Deputy Chairman: British Field Sports Soc., 1993–98; Phoenix House Housing Assoc., 1993–96. Dir, Countryside Alliance, 1998–. Member Executive: Nat. Union of Cons. and Unionist Assocs, 1989–95; Assoc. of Cons. Peers, 1989–95. Elected Mem., H of L, 1999. Pres., Alliance of Ind. Retailers, 1996–. Patron: Sick Dentists' Trust, 1991–; Patsy Hardy Trust, 1991–; Osteopathic Centre for Children, 1996–. *Heir: s* Hon. Arthur Louis Stormont Mancroft, *b* 3 May 1995. *Address:* House of Lords, SW1A 0PW. *Club:* Pratt's.
See also S. C. Dickinson.

MANDELA, Nelson Rolihlahla, Hon. OM 1995; President of South Africa, 1994–99; President, African National Congress, 1991–97 (Deputy President, 1990–91); *b* 1918; *s* of Chief of Tembu tribe; *m* Winnie Mandela (marr. diss. 1996); two *d*; *m* 1998, Graca, *widow* of Samora Machel. *Educ:* Univ. Coll., Fort Hare; Univ. of Witwatersrand. Legal practice, Johannesburg, 1952. On trial for treason, 1956–61 (acquitted); sentenced to five years' imprisonment, 1962; tried for further charges, 1963–64, and sentenced to life imprisonment; released, 1990. Holds hon. degrees from Oxford, Cambridge and other UK univs. Hon. QC 2000. Jawaharlal Nehru Award, India, 1979; Simon Bolivar Prize, UNESCO, 1983; Sakharov Prize, 1988; (with F. W. De Klerk) Nobel Peace Prize, 1993. *Publications:* No Easy Walk to Freedom, 1965; Long Walk to Freedom, 1994. *Address:* c/o President's Office, Private Bag X 1000, Cape Town 8000, South Africa.

MANDELSON, Baron *cr* 2008 (Life Peer), of Foy in the County of Herefordshire and Hartlepool in the County of Durham; **Peter Benjamin Mandelson;** PC 1998; Secretary of State for Business, Enterprise and Regulatory Reform, since 2008; *b* 21 Oct. 1953; *s* of late George Mandelson and Hon. Mary, *o c* of Baron Morrison of Lambeth, CH, PC. *Educ:* Hendon County Grammar Sch.; St Catherine's Coll., Oxford (Hons degree, PPE). Econ. Dept, TUC, 1977–78; Chm., British Youth Council, 1978–80; producer, LWT, 1982–85; Dir of Campaigns and Communications, Labour Party, 1985–90. MP (Lab) Hartlepool, 1992–Sept. 2004. An Opposition Whip, 1994–95; Opposition spokesman on Civil Service, 1995–97; Minister without Portfolio, Cabinet Office, 1997–98; Sec. of State for Trade and Industry, 1998, for N Ireland, 1999–2001. Mem., European Commn, 2004–08. Mem. Council, London Bor. of Lambeth, 1979–82. Industrial Consultant, SRU Gp, 1990–92. Chm., UK-Japan 21st Century Gp, 2001–. *Publications:* Youth Unemployment: causes and cures, 1977; Broadcasting and Youth, 1980; (jtly) The Blair Revolution, 1996, 2nd edn 2002. *Recreations:* swimming, country walking. *Address:* House of Lords, SW1A 0PW.

MANDELSTAM, Prof. Joel, FRS 1971; Emeritus Professor, University of Oxford, and Emeritus Fellow, Linacre College, since 1987; *b* S Africa, 13 Nov. 1919; *s* of Leo and Fanny Mandelstam; *m* 1954, Dorothy Hillier (*d* 1996); one *s* one *d*; *m* 1975, Mary Maureen Dale. *Educ:* Jeppe High Sch., Johannesburg; University of Witwatersrand. Lecturer, Medical Sch., Johannesburg, 1942–47; Queen Elizabeth Coll., London, 1947–51; Scientific Staff, Nat. Institute for Med. Research, London, 1952–66; Iveagh Prof. of Microbiology, and Fellow of Linacre College, Univ. of Oxford, 1966–87; Deptl Demonstrator, Sir William Dunn Sch. of Pathology, Univ. of Oxford, 1987–90. Fulbright Fellow, US, 1958–59; Vis. Prof., Univ. of Adelaide, 1971. Mem., ARC, 1973–83. Leeuwenhoek Lectr, Royal Soc., 1975. Editorial Board, Biochemical Journal, 1960–66. *Publications:* Biochemistry of Bacterial Growth (with K. McQuillen and I. Dawes), 1968; articles in journals and books on microbial biochemistry. *Address:* 13 Cherwell Lodge, Water Eaton Road, Oxford OX2 7QH.

MANDELSTAM, Prof. Stanley, FRS 1962; Professor Emeritus of Physics, University of California. *Educ:* University of the Witwatersrand, Johannesburg, Transvaal, South Africa (BSc); Trinity Coll., Cambridge (BA); PhD Birmingham. Formerly Professor of Math. Physics, University of Birmingham; Prof. Associé, Univ. de Paris Sud, 1979–80 and 1984–85. Fellow, Amer. Acad. of Arts and Scis., 1992. Dirac Medal and Prize, Internat. Centre for Theoretical Physics, 1991; Dannie Heinemann Prize for Mathematical Physics, APS, 1992. *Publications:* (with W. Yourgrau) Variational Principles in Dynamics and Quantum Theory, 1955 (revised edn, 1956); papers in learned journals. *Address:* Department of Physics, University of California, Berkeley, CA 94720, USA.

MANDER, Sir (Charles) Nicholas, 4th Bt *cr* 1911, of The Mount, Tettenhall, co. Stafford; *b* 23 March 1950; *er s* of Sir Charles Marcus Mander, 3rd Bt and Maria Dolores Beatrice Mander (*née* Brödermann) (*d* 2007); *S* father, 2006; *m* 1972, Karin Margareta, *d* of Arne Norin; four *s* one *d*. *Educ:* Downside; Trinity Coll., Cambridge (MA). Underwriting Mem. Lloyd's, 1972. Co-founder: Mander Portman Woodward, tutorial coll., London, 1974; Sutton Publishing, Gloucester, 1976; Dir, various land and property cos. Chm., Glos Care Partnership, 2007. Trustee: Orders of St John Care Trust; Woodchester Mansion Trust. FSA 2006. Liveryman, Fishmongers' Co. Kt of Grace and Devotion, SMO Malta. *Publications:* Varnished Leaves: a biography of the Mander family of Wolverhampton 1750–1950, 2004; Country Houses of the Cotswolds, 2008. *Recreations:* conversation, conservation, dreaming. *Heir: e s* Charles Marcus Septimus Gustav Mander, *b* 26 July 1975. *Address:* Owlpen Manor, Uley, Glos GL11 5BZ. *T:* (01453) 860261; *e-mail:* nicky@owlpen.com. *Club:* Boodle's.

MANDER, Prof. Lewis Norman, FRS 1990; Professor of Chemistry, Australian National University, since 1980; *b* 8 Sept. 1939; *s* of John Eric and Anne Frances Mander; *m* 1965, Stephanie Vautin; one *s* two *d*. *Educ:* Mount Albert Grammar Sch.; Univ. of Sydney (PhD 1965). FRACI 1980; FAA 1983. Postdoctoral Fellow, Univ. of Michigan, 1964–65; Postdoctoral Associate, Caltech, 1965–66; Lectr and Sen. Lectr in Organic Chem., Univ. of Adelaide, 1966–75; Sen. Fellow, 1975–80, Dean, 1981–86 and 1992–95, Res. Sch. of Chem., ANU. Nuffield Commonwealth Fellow, Cambridge, 1972; Fulbright Sen. Schol., Caltech, 1977, Harvard, 1986. H. G. Smith Medal, RACI, 1981; Flintoff Medal and Prize, RSocChem, 1990. *Publications:* numerous articles in learned jls, mainly on synthesis of organic molecules. *Recreations:* bushwalking, speleology. *Address:* Research School of Chemistry, Australian National University, Canberra, ACT 0200, Australia. *T:* (2) 61253761, *Fax:* (2) 61258114.

MANDER, His Honour Michael Harold; DL; a Circuit Judge, 1985–2001 (Resident Judge, Shrewsbury Crown Court, 1989–2001); *b* 27 Oct. 1936; *e s* of late Harold and Ann Mander; *m* 1960, Jancis Mary Dodd, *er d* of late Revd Charles and Edna Dodd. *Educ:* Workington Grammar School; Queen's College, Oxford (MA, 2nd cl. hons Jurisp.; Rigg Exbnr). Nat. Service, RA (2nd Lieut) to 1957. Articled clerk; solicitor, 2nd cl. hons, 1963; called to the Bar, Inner Temple, 1972. Asst Recorder, 1982–85. Dep. Chm., Agricultural Lands Tribunal, 1983–85. Freeman, City of London, 1995; Freeman, 1994, Liveryman, 2001–, Information Technologists' Co. DL Shropshire, 2000. Mem., The Magic Circle. *Recreation:* life under the Wrekin. *Address:* Garmston, Eaton Constantine, Shrewsbury SY5 6RL. *T:* (01952) 510288. *Club:* Wrekin Rotary (Hon. Mem.).

MANDER, Sir Nicholas; *see* Mander, Sir C. N.

MANDERS, Ann Beasley; *see* Beasley, A.

MANDERSON, Marcus Charles William S.; *see* Scott-Manderson.

MANDEVILLE, Viscount; Alexander Michael Charles David Francis George Edward William Kimble Drogo Montagu; *b* 13 May 1993; *s* and *heir* of Duke of Manchester, *qv*.

MANDUCA, John Alfred; High Commissioner for Malta in London, 1987–90; (concurrently) Ambassador to Norway, Sweden and Denmark, 1988–90, and to Ireland, 1990; *b* 14 Aug. 1927; *s* of Captain Philip dei Conti Manduca and Emma (*née* Pullicino); *m* 1954, Sylvia Parnis; two *s* two *d*. *Educ:* St Edward's Coll., Malta. Served 11 HAA Regt, Royal Malta Artillery (T), 1952–55 (commnd 1953). Joined Allied Malta Newspapers Ltd, 1945, Dep. Editor, 1953–62; Malta Correspondent, The Daily Telegraph and The Sunday Telegraph, 1946–62; joined Broadcasting Authority, Malta, 1962; BBC attachment, 1963; Chief Exec., Broadcasting Authority, Malta, 1963–68; Dir and Manager, Malta Television Service Ltd, 1968–71; Man. Dir, Rediffusion Gp of Cos in Malta, 1971–76; Chm., Tourist Projects Ltd, 1976–83; Dir Gen., Confedn of Private Enterprises, 1983–87; Dir, RTK Radio, 1991–93. Chairman: Malta Br., Inst. of Journalists, 1957, 1959 and 1961; Hotels and Catering Establishments Bd, 1970–71; Hon. Treas., Malta Br., Inst. of Dirs, 1975; Member: Tourist Bd, 1969–70; Broadcasting Authority, 1979–81. Trustee: Lady Strickland Trust for Malta, 1991–2005; Lady Strickland Trust for St Edward's Coll., 1997–2008. Chm. Bd of Governors, St Edward's Coll., 1995–98 (Mem., 1966–75, 1991–94). Editor, Treasures of Malta, 1994–2005. *Publications:* Tourist Guide to Malta and Gozo, 1967, 7th edn 1980; Tourist Guide to Harbour Cruises, 1974, 3rd edn 1981; Connoisseur's Guide to City of Mdina, 1975, 3rd edn 1985; Gen. Ed., Malta Who's Who, 1987; (ed) Antique Maltese Clocks, 1992; (ed) Antique Furniture in Malta, 2002; Welcome Travel Guide to City of Mdina and Rabat, 2003; Welcome Travel Guide to Malta & Gozo—Sun, Sea & History, 2003; The Bonham-Carter Diaries: what the British Governor thought of Malta and the Maltese, 2004; The Bride of Mosta: a ballad by Francis Berry, 2005; The Three Cities—Vittoriosa, Senglea and Cospicua, 2005; City of Valletta and Floriana, 2006; The Flavour of the Mintoff Era: secret negotiations made public, 2008. *Recreations:* collecting Melitensia, current affairs, gardening. *Address:* Beaulieu, Bastion Square, Citta Vecchia (Mdina) MDN 1150, Malta. *T:* 21454009, *Fax:* 21452608. *Clubs:* Royal Over-Seas League; Casino Maltese (Malta).

MANDUCA, Paul Victor Sant; Chairman: Bridgewell Group, 2006–07; UNIQ Pension Fund Trustees Ltd, since 2006; Al Futtaim Trust Co., Dubai, since 2007 (non-executive Director, since 2005); *b* 15 Nov. 1951; *s* of Victor Manduca and Elizabeth Manduca (*née* Johnson); *m* 1982, Ursula Vogt; two *s*. *Educ:* Harrow Sch.; Hertford Coll., Oxford (Hons Mod. Langs). Colegrave & Co., 1973–75; Rowe & Pitman, 1976–79; Hill Samuel Inv. Management, 1979–83; Touche Remnant, 1983–92: Dir 1986; Vice-Chm. 1987; Chm., 1989–92; Dir, Henderson (formerly TR) Smaller Cos Investment Trust (formerly Trustees Corp.), 1986–2006; Man. Dir, TR Industrial & General, 1986–88; Chm., TR High Income, 1989–94; Gp Dep. Man. Dir, Henderson Administration PLC, 1992–94; Chief Executive: Threadneedle Asset Mgt, 1994–99; Rothschild Asset Mgt, 1999–2002; CEO, Deutsche Asset Mgt (Europe), 2002–05. Exec. Chm., Gresham Trust, 1996–99 (Dir, 1994–99); non-exec. Chm., FTSE Trains, 1997–2002; Director: Eagle Star Hldgs, 1994–99; Allied Dunbar Assce, 1994–99; non-executive Director: Clydesdale Investment Trust, 1987–88; MEPC plc, 1999–2000; Wolverhampton Wanderers FC, 1999–2006; Development Securities plc, 2001– (Sen. Ind. Dir, 2006–); William Morrison Supermarkets plc, 2005– (Sen. Ind. Dir, 2006–); AON UK Ltd, 2006–; Intrinsic Ltd, 2006–; KazMunaiGaz Exploration & Production plc, 2006–. Chm., Assoc. of Investment

Trust Cos, 1991–93 (Dep. Chm., 1989–91); Mem., Takeover Panel, 1991–93. Liveryman, Bakers' Co., 1988–. *Recreations:* golf, squash, shooting. *Address:* 22 Rutland Gate, SW7 1BB. *Clubs:* White's, Lansdowne; Wentworth Golf; St George's Hill Golf.

MANDUELL, Sir John, Kt 1989; CBE 1982; FRAM, FRCM, FRNCM, FRSAMD; composer; Principal, Royal Northern College of Music, 1971–96; *b* 1928; *s* of Matthewman Donald Manduell, MC, MA, and Theodora (*née* Tharp); *m* 1955, Renna Kellaway; three *s* one *d. Educ:* Haileybury Coll.; Jesus Coll., Cambridge; Univ. of Strasbourg; Royal Acad. of Music. FRAM 1964; FRNCM 1974, CRNCM 1996; FRCM 1980; FRSAMD 1982; FRWCMD (FWCMD 1991); Hon. FTCL 1973; Hon. GSM 1986. BBC: music producer, 1956–61; Head of Music, Midlands and E Anglia, 1961–64; Chief Planner, The Music Programme, 1964–68; University of Lancaster: Dir of Music, 1968–71; Mem. Court and Council, 1972–77, 1979–83. University of Manchester: Hon. Lectr in Music, 1976–96; Mem. Court, 1990–2003. Prog. Dir, Cheltenham Festival, 1969–94; Vice-Pres., Cheltenham (formerly Cheltenham Arts) Festivals Ltd, 1995–. Arts Council: Mem. Council, 1976–78, 1980–84; Mem. Music Panel, 1971–76, Dep. Chm., 1976–78, Chm., 1980–84; Mem. Touring Cttee, 1975–80, Chm., 1976–78; Mem. Trng Cttee, 1973–77. Mem. Music Adv. Cttee, British Council, 1963–72, Chm., 1973–80; Chm. Music Panel, North West Arts, 1973–79; Man., NW Arts Bd, 1991–97. President: British Arts Fests Assoc., 1988–2004 (Vice-Chm., 1977–81, Chm., 1981–88); European Assoc. of Music Academies (now Assoc. of European Conservatoires), 1988–96 (Hon. Pres., 1996); Manchester Olympic Fest., 1990; ISM, 1991–92; Lennox Berkeley Soc., 2001–; European Music Year (1985): Dep. Chm. UK Cttee, 1982–85; Member: Eur. Organising Cttee, 1982–86; Eur. Exec. Bureau, 1982–86; Internat. Prog. Cttee, 1982–84; Mem. Exec. Cttee, Composers' Guild of GB, 1984–87 (Vice Chm., 1987–89, Chm., 1989–92); Gulbenkian Foundn Enquiry into Trng Musicians, 1978; Mem. Opera Bd, 1988–95, Mem. Bd, 1989–95, Royal Opera House; Chairman: Cttee of Heads of Music Colls, 1986–90; Nat. Curriculum Music Working Gp, 1990–91; European Opera Centre, 1995–2005; Nat. Assoc. of Youth Orchestras, 1996–2005; Governor: Chetham's Sch., 1971–2006; National Youth Orch., 1964–73, 1978–96; President: Lakeland Sinfonia, 1972–89; Jubilate Choir, 1979–91; Director: London Opera Centre, 1971–79; Associated Bd of Royal Schools of Music, 1973–96; Northern Ballet Theatre, 1973–86 (Chm., 1986–89); Manchester Palace Theatre Trust, 1978–84; London Orchestral Concert Bd, 1980–85; Young Concert Artists' Trust, 1983–93; Lake Dist Summer Music Fest., 1984– (Chm., 1996–2005); Mem. Bd, Hallé Concerts Soc. (Dep. Chm., 1997–99). Hon. Member: Roy. Soc. of Musicians, 1972; Chopin Soc. of Warsaw, 1973. Engagements and tours as composer and lectr in Canada, Europe, Hong Kong, S Africa and USA. Chairman: BBC TV Young Musicians of the Year, 1978, 1980, 1982, 1984; Munich ARD, 1979–2004; Geneva Internat. Music Comp., 1986–96; Paris Internat. Music Comp., 1992, 1994, 1996, 1998, 2003; Chm. or mem., national and internat. music competition juries. FRSA 1981; Fellow, Manchester Polytechnic, 1983. Hon. DMus: Lancaster, 1990; Manchester, 1992; RSAMD 1996. First Leslie Boosey Award, Royal Phil. Soc. and PRS, 1980. Chevalier de l'Ordre des Arts et des Lettres (France), 1990. *Publications:* (contrib.) The Symphony, ed Simpson, 1966; *compositions include:* Chansons de la Renaissance, 1956; Gradi, 1963; Diversions for Orchestra, 1970; String Quartet, 1976; Prayers from the Ark, 1981; Double Concerto, 1985; Vistas, 1997; Into the Ark, 1997; Flute Concerto, 2002; Nonet, 2005; Quartet Fulfilled, 2007; Calvary Choruses, 2007. *Recreations:* cricket, travel. *Address:* Chesham, High Bentham, Lancaster LA2 7JY. *T:* (01524) 261702. *Clubs:* Royal Over-Seas League, MCC.

MANGHAM, Maj.-Gen. William Desmond, CB 1978; Director, The Brewers' Society, 1980–90; *b* 29 Aug. 1924; *s* of late Lt-Col William Patrick Mangham and Margaret Mary Mangham (*née* Donnachie); *m* 1960, Susan, *d* of late Col Henry Brabazon Humfrey; two *s* two *d. Educ:* Ampleforth College. 2nd Lieut RA, 1943; served India, Malaya, 1945–48; BMRA 1st Div. Egypt, 1955; Staff, HQ Middle East, Cyprus, 1956–58; Instructor, Staff Coll., Camberley and Canada, 1962–65; OC 3rd Regt Royal Horse Artillery, 1966–68; Comdr RA 2nd Div., 1969–70; Royal Coll. of Defence Studies, 1971; Chief of Staff, 1st British Corps, 1972–74; GOC 2nd Div., 1974–75; VQMG, MoD, 1976–79. Colonel Commandant: RA, 1979–88; RHA, 1983–88. Advisory Governor, Ampleforth Coll., 1990–98. Mem., Gordon Foundn, 1980–2003. *Recreations:* shooting, golf. *Address:* 12 The Grange, Enborne, Newbury, Berks RG14 6RJ. *Club:* Army and Navy.

MANGO, Prof. Cyril Alexander, FBA 1976; Bywater and Sotheby Professor of Byzantine and Modern Greek, 1973–95, and Emeritus Fellow of Exeter College, Oxford University; *b* 14 April 1928; *s* of Alexander A. Mango and Adelaide Damonov; *m* 1st, 1953, Mabel Grover; one *d*; 2nd, 1964, Susan A. Gerstel; one *d*; 3rd, 1976, Maria C. Mundell. *Educ:* Univ. of St Andrews (MA); Univ. of Paris (Dr Univ Paris). From Jun. Fellow to Lectr in Byzantine Archaeology, Dumbarton Oaks Byzantine Center, Harvard Univ., 1951–63; Lectr in Fine Arts, Harvard Univ., 1957–58; Visiting Associate Prof. of Byzantine History, Univ. of California, Berkeley, 1960–61; Koraës Prof. of Modern Greek and of Byzantine History, Language and Literature, King's Coll., Univ. of London, 1963–68; Prof. of Byzantine Archaeology, Dumbarton Oaks Byzantine Center, 1968–73. FSA. *Publications:* The Homilies of Photius, 1958; The Brazen House, 1959; The Mosaics of St Sophia at Istanbul, 1962; The Art of the Byzantine Empire, Sources and Documents, 1972; Architettura bizantina, 1974; Byzantium, 1980; Byzantium and its Image, 1984; Le Développement Urbain de Constantinople, 1985; (ed) The Oxford History of Byzantium, 2002. *Address:* 12 High Street, Brill, Aylesbury, Bucks HP18 9ST.

MANGOLD, Thomas Cornelius; Reporter, BBC TV Panorama, 1976–2003; *b* 20 Aug. 1934; *s* of Fritz Mangold and Dorothea Mangold; *m* 1st, 1958, Anne (*née* Butler) (marr. diss. 1970); one *d*; 2nd, 1972, Valerie Ann Hare (*née* Dean) (marr. diss. 1991); two *d*; 3rd, 2000, Kathryn Mary Colleton Parkinson-Smith. *Educ:* Dorking Grammar Sch. Reporter, Croydon Advertiser, 1952. Served RA, 1952–54. Reporter: Croydon Advertiser, 1955–59; Sunday Pictorial, 1959–62; Daily Express, 1962–64; BBC TV News, 1964–70; BBC TV 24 Hours, later Midweek, 1970–76. *Publications:* (jtly) The File on the Tsar, 1976; (jtly) The Tunnels of Cu Chi, 1985; Cold Warrior, 1991; Plague Wars, 1999. *Recreations:* writing, playing Blues harp. *Address:* c/o A. M. Heath, 6 Warwick Court, WC1R 5DJ. *T:* (020) 7242 2811.

MANKTELOW, Rt Rev. Michael Richard John; Hon. Assistant Bishop: of Chichester, since 1994; of Gibraltar in Europe, since 1994; *b* 23 Sept. 1927; *s* of late Sir Richard Manktelow, KBE, CB, and late Helen Manktelow; *m* 1966, Rosamund Mann; three *d. Educ:* Whitgift School, Croydon; Christ's Coll., Cambridge (MA 1952); Chichester Theological Coll. Deacon 1953, priest 1954, Lincoln; Asst Curate of Boston, Lincs, 1953–57; Chaplain of Christ's Coll., Cambridge, 1957–61; Chaplain of Lincoln Theological Coll., 1961–64, Sub-Warden, 1964–66; Vicar of Knaresborough, 1966–73; Rural Dean of Harrogate, 1972–77; Vicar of St Wilfrid's, Harrogate, 1973–77; Hon. Canon of Ripon Cathedral, 1975–77; Bishop Suffragan of Basingstoke, 1977–93; Canon Residentiary, 1977–91, Vice-Dean, 1987–91, Hon. Canon, 1991–93, Canon Emeritus, 1993, Winchester Cathedral. Bursalis Prebendary, Chichester Cathedral, 1997–2002, Canon Emeritus, 2002. President: Anglican and Eastern Churches Assoc., 1980–97; Assoc.

for Promoting Retreats, 1982–87. *Publication:* Forbes Robinson: disciple of love, 1961; John Moorman: Anglican, Franciscan, Independent, 1999. *Recreations:* music, walking. *Address:* 14 Little London, Chichester, West Sussex PO19 1NZ. *T:* (01243) 531096.

MANLEY, Brian William, CBE 1994; FREng, FIET, FInstP; FCGI; Managing Partner, Manley Moon Associates, 1988–2001; President, Institute of Physics, 1996–98; *b* 30 June 1929; *s* of late Gerald William Manley and Ellen Mary Manley (*née* Scudder); *m* 1954, Doris Winifred Dane; one *s* one *d. Educ:* Shooters Hill Sch.; Woolwich Poly.; Imperial Coll. of Science and Technology (BSc, DIC). FInstP 1967; FIEE 1974, Hon. FIET (Hon. FIEE 1999); FREng (FEng 1984); FCGI 1990. Served RAF, 1947–49. Mullard Research Labs, 1954–68; Commercial Gen. Manager, Mullard Ltd, 1969–75; Managing Director: Pye Business Communications, 1975–77; TMC Ltd, 1977–82; Philips Data Systems, 1979–82; Gp Man. Dir, Philips Business Systems, 1980–83; Chm. and Man. Dir, MEL Defence Systems, 1983–86; Dir, Philips Electronic & Associated Industries Ltd, 1983–87; Chairman: AT&T Network Systems (UK) Ltd, 1986–89; Moondisks Ltd, 1994–2001. Mem. Bd, Teaching Co. Scheme, 1996–98. Pres., IEE, 1991–92; Sen. Vice Pres., Royal Acad. of Engrg, 1993–96. Centenary Fellow, Univ. of Greenwich, 1991. Sen. Pro-Chancellor and Chm. Council, Univ. of Sussex, 1995–2001. Trustee: RC dio. Arundel and Brighton, 1999–; Daphne Jackson Trust, 1999–2007. Hon. DSc: Loughborough, 1995; City, 1998; Sussex, 2002. *Publications:* many papers on electronics, communications and engrg educn. *Recreations:* walking, gardening, second-hand bookshops, searching for my Irish roots. *Address:* Hopkins Crank, Ditchling Common, Hassocks, Sussex BN6 8TP. *T:* (01444) 233734. *Club:* Athenæum.

MANLEY, David Eric; QC 2003; a Recorder, since 2000; *b* 30 April 1956; *s* of Eric and May Manley; *m* 1983, Caroline Morgan; one *s* one *d. Educ:* Leeds Univ. (BA Hons). Called to the Bar, Inner Temple, 1981; in practice, specialising in planning and environmental law. *Recreations:* gardening, reading, shooting, fishing. *Address:* King's Chambers, 36 Young Street, Manchester M3 3FT. *T:* (0161) 832 9082, *Fax:* (0161) 835 2139; *e-mail:* clerks@kingschambers.com.

MANLEY, Ivor Thomas, CB 1984; Deputy Secretary, Department of Employment, 1987–91; *b* 4 March 1931; *s* of Frederick Stone and Louisa Manley; *m* 1952, Joan Waite; one *s* one *d. Educ:* Sutton High Sch., Plymouth. Entered Civil Service, 1951; Principal: Min. of Aviation, 1964–66; Min. of Technology, 1966–68; Private Secretary: to Rt Hon. Anthony Wedgwood Benn, 1968–70; to Rt Hon. Geoffrey Rippon, 1970; Principal Private Sec. to Rt Hon. John Davies, 1970–71; Asst Sec., DTI, 1971–74; Department of Energy: Under-Sec., Principal Estabt Officer, 1974–78, Under Sec., Atomic Energy Div., 1978–81; Dep. Sec., 1981–87. UK Governor, IAEA, 1978–81; Mem., UKAEA, 1981–86. Chm., Task Force on Tourism and the Envmt, 1990–91; Board Member: Business in the Community, 1988–89; BTA, 1991–95 (Chm., Marketing Cttee, 1991–95); Volunteer Centre, UK, 1992–2000; Consortium on Opportunities for Volunteering, 1996–2000; Third Age Trust, 1999–2004 (Vice Chm., 2001–04); Chm., Univ. of Third Age, Farnborough, 2006–. *Recreations:* walking, reading, travelling, Univ. of the Third Age. *Address:* 28 Highfield Avenue, Aldershot, Hants GU11 3BZ. *T:* (01252) 322707.

MANLEY, Hon. John (Paul); PC (Can.) 1993; Senior Counsel, McCarthy Tétrault LLP, since 2004; *b* 15 Jan. 1950; *s* of John Joseph and Mildred Charlotte (Scharf) Manley; *m* 1973 Judith Mary Rae; one *s* two *d. Educ:* Carleton Univ. (BA 1971); Univ. of Ottawa (Law 1976). Law clerk for Chief Justice of Canada, 1976–77; Partner, Perley-Robertson, Panet, Hill & McDougall, lawyers, 1977–88; Chm., Ottawa-Carleton BoT, 1985–86. MP (L) Ottawa S, 1988–2004; Minister: of Industry, 1993–2000; of Western Econ. Diversification, Atlantic Canadian Opportunities Agency, 1996; of Econ. Develt for Quebec Regs, 1996–2000; of Foreign Affairs, 2000–02; of Infrastructure and Crown Corporations, and of Finance, 2002–03; Dep. Prime Minister of Canada, 2002–03; Political Minister for Ontario, 2002–03. Chairman, Cabinet Committees: on Public Security and Anti-Terrorism, 2001–03; on Econ. Union and Social Union, 2002–03. Chm., Ontario Power Gen. Review Cttee, 2004. Dir, Nortel Networks, 2004–. Newsmaker of Year, Time Mag. of Canada, 2001. *Recreation:* marathon runner. *Address:* (office) Suite 1400, The Chambers, 40 Elgin Street, Ottawa, ON K1P 5K6, Canada.

MANLEY, Simon John; HM Diplomatic Service; Director, Defence and Strategic Threats, Foreign and Commonwealth Office, since 2007; *b* 18 Sept. 1967; *s* of James and Beryl Manley; *m* 1996, Maria Isabel Fernandez Utgès; three *d. Educ:* Montpelier Primary Sch., Ealing; Latymer Upper Sch., Hammersmith; Magdalen Coll., Oxford (BA Hons Modern Hist.); Yale Univ. Grad. Sch. (MA Internat. Relns). Entered HM Diplomatic Service, 1990; UN Dept, FCO, 1990–93; on secondment to DGIV (Competition), EC, 1993; UKMIS to UN, NY, 1993–98; on secondment to EU Council of Ministers, 1998–2002; Dep. Hd, EU (Internal), FCO, 2002–03; Head: Econ. and Central Europe Team, FCO, 2003–06; Counter-Terrorism Policy Dept, FCO, 2006–07. Comdr, Order of Merit (Poland), 2004. *Recreations:* theatre, gardens, history. *Address:* c/o Foreign and Commonwealth Office, King Charles Street, SW1A 2AH.

MANLY, Timothy John; Headmaster, Hurstpierpoint College, since 2005; *b* 12 Feb. 1964; *m* 1990, Henrietta Whetstone; two *s* two *d. Educ:* Oriel Coll., Oxford (BA Hons Lit. Hum.); London Sch. of Econs (MSc); Hughes Hall, Cambridge (PGCE). Various appts in commerce, 1987–93; Sevenoaks School: Teacher, 1994–2000; Housemaster, 1996–2000; Hd of Classics Dept, 1996–99; Dep. Headmaster, Oakham Sch., 2000–04. Non-exec. Dir, Harris Fedn of S London Schs, 2007–. *Recreations:* family, cross-country and distance running, most racquet sports, bridge, books. *Address:* Hurstpierpoint College, Malthouse Lane, Hurstpierpoint, Hassocks, W Sussex BN6 9JS. *T:* (01273) 833636; *e-mail:* headmaster@hppc.co.uk.

MANN, Hon. Sir Anthony; see Mann, Hon. Sir G. A.

MANN, Prof. Anthony Howard, MD; FRCP, FRCPsych; Professor of Epidemiological Psychiatry, Institute of Psychiatry, King's College London, since 1989; *b* 11 Dec. 1940; *s* of Alfred Haward Mann and Marjory Ethel (*née* Weatherly); civil partnership 2006, Pekka Antero Vaalle. *Educ:* Rugby Sch.; Jesus Coll., Cambridge (MD 1982); St Bartholomew's Hosp. FRCPsych 1984; FRCP 1986. Res. worker, and Sen. Lectr, Inst. of Psychiatry, 1972–80; Sen. Lectr, then Prof. of Psychiatry, Royal Free Hosp., 1980–89. Associate Prof., Montpellier Univ., 2002–03. Hon. FRCGP 2001. *Publications:* numerous contribs to scientific jls on psychiatry of old age, general practice and epidemiology. *Recreations:* friends, travel. *Address:* c/o Hoare and Co., 32 Lowndes Street, SW1X 9HZ.

MANN, Prof. (Colin) Nicholas (Jocelyn), CBE 1999; PhD; FBA 1992; Dean, School of Advanced Study, 2002–07, and Pro-Vice-Chancellor, 2003–07, University of London; Senior Research Fellow, Warburg Institute, 2001–07; *b* 24 Oct. 1942; *s* of Colin Henry Mann and Marie Elise Mann (*née* Gosling); *m* 1st, 1964, Joëlle Bourcart (marr. diss. 2003); one *s* one *d*; 2nd, 2003, Helen Margaret Stevenson; two *d. Educ:* Eton; King's Coll., Cambridge (MA, PhD). Res. Fellow, Clare Coll., Cambridge, 1965–67; Lectr, Univ. of Warwick, 1967–72; Vis. Fellow, All Souls Coll., Oxford, 1972; Fellow and Tutor, Pembroke Coll., Oxford, 1973–90, Emeritus Fellow, 1991–2006, Hon. Fellow, 2006;

Dir, Warburg Inst., and Prof. of Hist. of Classical Tradition, Univ. of London, 1990–2001. Visiting Professor: Univ. of Toronto, 1996; Coll. de France, 1998. Member Council: Mus. of Modern Art, Oxford, 1984–92 (Chm., 1988–90); Contemporary Applied Arts, 1994–2005 (Chm., 1996–99); British Acad., 1995–98, 1999– (For. Sec., 1999–2006); RHBNC, 1996–98; RCA, 2001–07; Mem., British Library Adv. Council, 1997–2002. Vice-Pres., ALLEA, 2006–. Trustee, Cubitt Artists, 1996–99. Fellow, European Medieval Acad., 1993. Romance Editor, Medium Ævum, 1982–90. Hon. DLitt Warwick, 2006. *Publications:* Petrarch Manuscripts in the British Isles, 1975; Petrarch, 1984; A Concordance to Petrarch's Bucolicum Carmen, 1984; (ed jtly) Lorenzo the Magnificent: culture and politics, 1996; (ed jtly) Medieval and Renaissance Scholarship, 1996; (ed jtly) Giordano Bruno 1583–1585: the English experience, 1997; (ed jtly) The Image of the Individual: portraits in the Renaissance, 1998; (ed jtly) Photographs at the Frontier: Aby Warburg in America 1895–1896, 1998; Carnets de voyage, 2003; Pétrarque: les voyages de l'esprit, 2004; (ed jtly) Britannia Latina: Latin in the culture of Great Britain from the Middle Ages to the twentieth century, 2005; articles in learned jls. *Recreations:* yoga, poetry, sculpture. *Address:* rue du Tourneur, 46160 Cajarc, France. *T:* (5) 65349121.

MANN, David William; Deputy Chairman, Charteris plc, since 2007 (Chairman, 1996–2007); *b* 14 June 1944; *s* of William and Mary Mann; *m* 1968, Gillian Mary Edwards; two *s. Educ:* Felixstowe Grammar Sch.; Jesus Coll., Cambridge (MA). CEng; CITP; FBCS. CEIR, 1966–69; Logica: joined 1969; Dir, 1976; Man. Dir, UK Ops, 1979; Dep. Gp Man. Dir, 1982; Gp Man. Dir and Chief Exec., 1987; Dep. Chm., 1993–94. Chairman: Cambridge Display Technol., 1995–97; Flomerics Gp, 1995–2008; Velti Gp plc, 2006–; Director: Industrial Control Services Gp, 1994–2000; Druid Gp, 1996–2000; Room Solutions (formerly Room Underwriting Systems), 1996–2006; Aveva (formerly Cadcentre) Group, 1999–; Eurolink Managed Services, 1999–2000; Ansbacher Hldgs, 2000–04. Mem., Engineering Council, 1993–95. Pres., British Computer Soc., 1994–95. Master, Information Technologists' Co., 1997–98 (Chm., 2002–07, Dir, 2007–, Charitable Trust). Chm., Livery Past Masters' Assoc., 2006–08. CCMI (CIMgt 1994–2008); FInstD 1994–2006. Chm., Epping Forest Wine Soc., 2005–. *Recreations:* gardening, walking. *Address:* Theydon Copt, Forest Side, Epping, Essex CM16 4ED. *T:* (01992) 575842. *Club:* Athenæum.

MANN, Eric John; Controller, Capital Taxes Office, 1978–81; *b* 18 Dec. 1921; *s* of Percival John Mann and Marguerite Mann; *m* 1960, Gwendolen Margaret Salter (*d* 2003); one *d* (one *s* decd). *Educ:* University Coll. Sch., Hampstead; Univ. of London (LLB). Entered Inland Revenue, 1946; Dep. Controller, Capital Taxes Office, 1974. *Publications:* (ed jtly) Green's Death Duties, 5th–7th edns, 1962–71. *Address:* Lawn Gate Cottage, Moccas, Herefordshire HR2 9LF.

MANN, Dr Felix Bernard; medical practitioner; *b* 10 April 1931; *s* of Leo and Caroline Mann; *m* 1986, Ruth Csorba von Borsai. *Educ:* Shrewsbury House; Malvern Coll.; Christ's Coll., Cambridge; Westminster Hosp. MB, BChir, LMCC. Practised medicine or studied acupuncture in England, Canada, Switzerland, France, Germany, Austria and China. Founder, Medical Acupuncture Soc., 1959. *Publications:* Acupuncture; the ancient Chinese art of healing, 1962, 2nd edn 1971; The Treatment of Disease by Acupuncture, 1963; The Meridians of Acupuncture, 1964; Atlas of Acupuncture, 1966; Acupuncture: cure of many diseases, 1971; Scientific Aspects of Acupuncture, 1977; Textbook of Acupuncture, 1987; Reinventing Acupuncture, 1992, 2nd edn 2000; also edns in Italian, Spanish, Dutch, Finnish, Portuguese, German, Japanese and Swedish; contrib. various jls on acupuncture. *Recreations:* walking in the country and mountains. *Address:* 15 Devonshire Place, W1G 6HF. *T:* (020) 7935 7575. *Club:* Royal Society of Medicine.

MANN, Hon. Sir (George) Anthony, Kt 2004; **Hon. Mr Justice Mann;** a Judge of the High Court of Justice, Chancery Division, since 2004; *b* 21 May 1951; *s* of George Edgar and Ilse Beate Mann; *m* 1979, Margaret Ann Sherret; two *d. Educ:* Chesterfield Grammar Sch.; Perse Sch., Cambridge; St Peter's Coll., Oxford (BA 1973; MA 1977). Called to the Bar, Lincoln's Inn, 1974, Bencher, 2002; QC 1992; a Recorder, 2002–04. *Recreations:* French horn playing, music, computers. *Address:* Royal Courts of Justice, Strand, WC2A 2LL.

MANN, Prof. Gillian Lesley, (Jill), FBA 1990; Notre Dame Professor of English, University of Notre Dame, Indiana, 1999–2004, now Emeritus Professor; *b* 7 April 1943; *d* of late Edward William Ditchburn and Kathleen Ditchburn (*née* Bellamy); *m* 1964, Michael Mann (marr. diss. 1976); *m* 2003, Michael Lapidge. *Educ:* Bede Grammar Sch., Sunderland; St Anne's Coll., Oxford (BA 1964; Hon. Fellow, 1990); Clare Hall, Cambridge (MA; PhD 1971). Research Fellow, Clare Hall, Cambridge, 1968–71; Lectr, Univ. of Kent at Canterbury, 1971–72; University of Cambridge: Official Fellow, 1972–88; Professorial Fellow, 1988–98, Life Fellow, 1999, Girton Coll.; Asst Lectr, 1974–78; Lectr, 1978–88; Prof. of Medieval and Renaissance English, 1988–98. British Academy Research Reader, 1985–87. *Publications:* Chaucer and Medieval Estates Satire, 1973; Ysengrimus, 1987; (ed with Piero Boitani) The Cambridge Chaucer Companion, 1986, rev. edn 2003; Geoffrey Chaucer, 1991; Feminizing Chaucer, 2002; (ed) Canterbury Tales, 2005; (ed with Maura Nolan) The Text in the Community, 2006; articles on Middle English and Medieval Latin. *Recreations:* walking, travel. *Address:* Girton College, Cambridge CB3 0JG.

MANN, Jillian Rose, FRCP, FRCPCH; Consultant Paediatric Oncologist, Birmingham Children's Hospital, 1979–2002, now Emeritus; *b* 29 April 1939; *d* of William Farmcote Mann and Vera Maud Mann. *Educ:* Pate's Grammar Sch. for Girls, Cheltenham; St Thomas' Hosp. Med. Sch., London (MB BS 1962). LRCP 1962, MRCP 1966, FRCP 1980; MRCS 1962; DCH 1964; FRCPCH 1997. Postgrad. trng, St Thomas' and Great Ormond St Children's Hosps, 1963–67, and Birmingham Children's Hosp., 1967–71; Consultant Paediatrician, S Birmingham, and Consultant Associate in Haematological Diseases, Birmingham Children's Hosp., 1972–79. Hon. Prof. of Paediatric Oncology, Univ. of Birmingham, 1997–. Member: Cttee on Med. Aspects of Radiation in the Envmt, DoH, 1985–89; Standing Med. Adv. Cttee, DoH, 1986–90. Member: Leukaemia in Childhood Wkg party, MRC, 1975–2000; Med. and Scientific Adv. Panel, Leukaemia Res. Fund, 1985–88. Mem. Council, RCP, 1988–91; RCP and RCPCH: Regl Advr, 1994–99; Examr for MRCP/MRCPCH, 1994–2002. Founder Mem., 1977, Sec., 1977–81, Chm., 1983–86, UK Children's Cancer Study Gp; Chm., Educn and Trng Cttee, Soc. Internat. d'Oncologie Pédiatrique Europe and Eur. Soc. of Paediatric Haematol. and Immunol., 2000–03. Trustee, Birmingham Children's Hosp. Charities, 2003– (Chm., 2005–). Mem., Lunar Soc., Birmingham, 1994–. Eur. Women of Achievement Award, Humanitarian Section, EUW, 1996; Nye Bevan Lifetime Achievement Award, 2000. *Publications:* numerous book chapters and contribs to learned jls mostly on childhood leukaemia, cancer and blood diseases; numerous abstracts of contribs to nat. and internat. scientific meetings. *Recreations:* music, country pursuits. *Address:* Birmingham Children's Hospital Charities, Birmingham Children's Hospital, Steelhouse Lane, Birmingham B4 6NH. *T:* (0121) 333 8598.

MANN, John; MP (Lab) Bassetlaw, since 2001; *b* 10 Jan. 1960; *s* of James Mann and Brenda (*née* Cleavin); *m* 1985, Joanna White; one *s* two *d. Educ:* Manchester Univ. (BA Econ).

MIPD. Hd of Res. and Educn, AEU, 1988–90; Nat. Trng Officer, TUC, 1990–95; Liaison Officer, Nat. Trade Union and Lab Party, 1995–2000. Dir, Abraxas Communications Ltd, 1998–2001. Mem. (Lab), Lambeth BC, 1986–90. Mem., Editl Adv. Panel, People Management, 2005–. *Publications:* (with Phil Woolas) Labour and Youth: the missing generation, 1985; The Real Deal: drug policy that works, 2006. *Recreations:* football, cricket, hill walking. *Address:* House of Commons, SW1A 0AA. *Clubs:* Manton Miners'; Worksop Town.

MANN, John Frederick; educational consultant; *b* 4 June 1930; *e s* of Frederick Mann and Hilda G. (*née* Johnson); *m* 1966, Margaret (*née* Moore); one *s* one *d. Educ:* Poole and Tavistock Grammar Schs; Trinity Coll., Oxford (MA); Birmingham Univ. Asst Master, Colchester Royal Grammar Sch., 1954–61; Admin. Asst, Leeds County Bor., 1962–65; Asst Educn Officer, Essex CC, 1965–67; Dep. Educn Officer, Sheffield County Bor., 1967–78; Sec., Schools Council for the Curriculum and Exams, 1978–83; Dir of Educn, London Bor. of Harrow, 1983–88. Member: Iron and Steel Industry Trng Bd, 1975–78; Exec., Soc. of Educn Officers, 1976–78; Sch. Broadcasting Council, 1979–83; Council, British Educn Management and Admin Soc., 1979–84; Cttee, Soc. of Educn Consultants, 1990–95 (Sec., 1990–94; Vice Chm., 1994–95). Chm., Standards Cttee, Brent BC, 2002–. Governor: Welbeck Coll., 1975–84; Hall Sch., 1985–88. Chm., Brent Samaritans, 1995–99. Hon. Fellow, Sheffield Polytechnic, 1980; Hon. FCP, 1986. FRSA. JP Sheffield, 1976–79. *Publications:* Education, 1979; Highbury Fields School, 1994; To Gladly Learn, and Gladly Teach, 2004; contrib. to Victoria County History of Essex, Local Govt Studies, and Educn. *Recreations:* travel, books, theatre, gardening. *Address:* 109 Chatsworth Road, NW2 4BH. *T:* (020) 8459 5419.

MANN, Martin Edward; QC 1983; a Recorder, since 1990; a Deputy High Court Judge, Chancery Division, since 1992; *b* 12 Sept. 1943; *s* of late S. E. Mann and M. L. F. Mann; *m* 1966, Jacqueline Harriette (*née* Le Maître); two *d. Educ:* Cranleigh Sch. Called to the Bar, Gray's Inn, 1968 (Lord Justice Holker Sen. Exhibn), Lincoln's Inn, 1973 (*ad eund*); Bencher, Lincoln's Inn, 1991. Mem., Senate of the Inns of Court and the Bar, 1979–82; Chm., Bar Council Fees Collection Cttee, 1993–95. Member: Chancery Bar Assoc.; Commercial Bar Assoc.; European Circuit; Bar of Eastern Caribbean Supreme Ct. Consultant Solicitor, Palmer's Company Law Manual. *Publications:* (jtly) What Kind of Common Agricultural Policy for Europe, 1975; (contrib.) Tolley's Insolvency. *Recreations:* farming, the arts. *Address:* 24 Old Buildings, Lincoln's Inn, WC2A 3UP. *T:* (020) 7404 0946; Kingston St Mary, Somerset. *Club:* Garrick.

MANN, Rt Rev. Michael Ashley, KCVO 1989; Assistant Bishop, diocese of Gloucester, since 1989; Dean of Windsor, 1976–89; Chairman, St George's House, 1976–89; Register, Order of the Garter, 1976–89; Domestic Chaplain to the Queen, 1976–89; Prelate, Order of St John, 1980–2000; *b* 25 May 1924; *s* of late H. G. Mann and F. M. Mann, Harrow; *m* 1st, 1949, Jill Joan Jacques (*d* 1990); one *d* (one *s* decd); 2nd, 1991, Elizabeth Pepys. *Educ:* Harrow Sch.; RMC Sandhurst; Wells Theological Coll.; Graduate School of Business Admin., Harvard Univ. Served War of 1939–45: RMC, Sandhurst, 1942–43; 1st King's Dragoon Guards, 1943–46 (Middle East, Italy, Palestine). Colonial Admin. Service, Nigeria, 1946–55. Wells Theological Coll., 1955–57; Asst Curate, Wolborough, Newton Abbot, 1957–59; Vicar: Sparkwell, Plymouth, 1959–62; Christ Church, Port Harcourt, Nigeria, 1962–67; Dean, Port Harcourt Social and Industrial Mission; Home Secretary, The Missions to Seamen, 1967–69; Residentiary Canon, 1969–74, Vice-Dean, 1972–74, Norwich Cathedral; Adviser to Bp of Norwich on Industry, 1969–74; Bishop Suffragan of Dudley, 1974–76. Church Comr, 1977–85; Comr, Royal Hospital Chelsea, 1985–91. Dep. Chm., Imperial War Museum, 1990–96 (Trustee, 1980–96); Trustee: Army Museums Ogilby Trust, 1984–96; British Library, 1990–93; Military Records Soc., 1992–. Pres., Soc. of Friends of Nat. Army Mus., 1989– (Chm., 1989–97). Governor: Harrow Sch., 1976–91 (Chm., 1980–88); Atlantic Coll., 1987–91. Nat. Chaplain, Royal British Legion, 1995–2001. CCMI. GCStJ 1997 (KStJ 1990). *Publications:* A Windsor Correspondence, 1984; And They Rode On, 1984; A Particular Duty, 1986; China 1860, 1989; Some Windsor Sermons, 1989; Survival or Extinction, 1989; Regimental History of 1st Queen's Dragoon Guards, 1993; The Trucial Oman Scouts, 1994; The Veterans, 1997; Sermons for Soldiers, 1998. *Recreations:* military history, philately, ornithology. *Address:* The Cottage, Lower End Farm, Eastington, Northleach, Glos GL54 3PN. *T:* and *Fax:* (01451) 860767; *e-mail:* michaelmann@onetel.com. *Club:* Cavalry and Guards.

MANN, Murray G.; see Gell-Mann.

MANN, Nicholas; see Mann, C. N. J.

MANN, Paul; QC 2002; a Recorder, since 2001; *b* 4 Feb. 1958; *s* of George Arthur and Elsie May Mann; *m* 1988, Carol Joy Beddows. *Educ:* Trent Coll., Long Eaton, Derbyshire; Manchester Poly. (BA Hons Law). Called to the Bar, Gray's Inn, 1980; in practice as barrister, specialising in crime. Treasurer, Midland Circuit, 2002–. *Recreations:* travel, cycling, walking, amateur dramatics, wine, wheaten terriers. *Address:* 1 High Pavement, Nottingham NG1 1HF. *T:* (0115) 941 8218, *Fax:* (0115) 941 8240.

MANN, Sir Rupert (Edward), 3rd Bt *cr* 1905; *b* 11 Nov. 1946; *s* of Major Edward Charles Mann, DSO, MC (*g s* of 1st Bt) (*d* 1959), and Pamela Margaret, *o d* of late Major Frank Haultain Hornsby; *S* great uncle, 1971; *m* 1974, Mary Rose, *d* of Geoffrey Butler, Stetchworth, Newmarket; two *s. Educ:* Malvern. *Heir: s* Alexander Rupert Mann, *b* 6 April 1978. *Address:* Billingford Hall, Diss, Norfolk IP21 4HN. *Clubs:* Boodle's, MCC; Norfolk.

MANN, Prof. Stephen, DPhil; FRS 2003; Professor of Chemistry, University of Bristol, since 1998; *b* 1 April 1955; *s* of Harold and Olive Mann; *m* 1977, Jane Lucinda Musgrave; one *s* one *d. Educ:* Univ. of Manchester Inst. of Sci. and Technol. (BSc Hons Chem. 1976); Univ. of Manchester (MSc 1978); DPhil Oxford 1981. University of Bath: Lectr in Chem., 1984–88; Reader, 1988–90; Prof. of Chem., 1990–98. *Publications:* Biomineralization: principles and concepts in bioinorganic materials chemistry, 2001; numerous contribs to learned scientific jls. *Recreations:* running, electric guitar, family life. *Address:* School of Chemistry, University of Bristol, Bristol BS8 1TS. *T:* (0117) 928 9935; *e-mail:* s.mann@bris.ac.uk.

MANNERS, family name of **Baron Manners,** and **Duke of Rutland.**

MANNERS, 6th Baron *cr* 1807, of Foston, co. Lincoln; **John Hugh Robert Manners;** Partner, Macfarlanes, since 1987 (Head of Litigation, 2000–08); *b* 5 May 1956; *s* of 5th Baron Manners and Jennifer Selena, *d* of Ian Fairbairn; *S* father, 2008; *m* 2007, Juliet Elizabeth Anthea McMyn; two *d* by former marriage. *Educ:* Eton. Admitted Solicitor, 1980. *Recreations:* shooting, walking, Irish Terriers. *Heir: uncle* Richard Neville Manners [*b* 4 April 1924; *m* 1945, Juliet Mary, *d* of Lt-Col Sir Edward Hulton Preston, 5th Bt, DSO, MC; three *s* one *d*]. *Address:* North Ripley House, Avon, Christchurch, Dorset BH23 8EP; *e-mail:* willie.manners@macfarlanes.com. *Clubs:* Boodle's, Pratt's.

MANNERS, Elizabeth Maude, TD 1962; MA; Headmistress of Felixstowe College, Suffolk, 1967–79; Member, East Anglia Regional Health Authority, 1982–85; *b* 20 July 1917; *d* of William George Manners and Anne Mary Manners (*née* Sced). *Educ:* Stockton-on-Tees Sec. Sch.; St Hild's Coll., Durham Univ. (BA 1938; MA 1941). Teacher of French at: Marton Grove Sch., Middlesbrough, 1939–40; Ramsey Gram. Sch., IOM, 1940–42; Consett Sec. Sch., Durham, 1942–44; Yarm Gram. Sch., Yorks, 1944–54; Deputy Head, Mexborough Gram. Sch., Yorks, 1954–59; Head Mistress, Central Gram. Sch. for Girls, Manchester, 1959–67. Vice-President: Girl Guides Assoc., Co. Manchester, 1959–67; Suffolk Agric. Assoc., 1967–82. Member: Educn Cttee, Brit. Fedn of Univ. Women, 1966–68; Council, Bible Reading Fellowship, 1973–81; Cttee, E Br., RSA, 1974–90; Cttee, ISIS East, 1974–79. Mem. (C), Suffolk CC, 1977–85 (Member: Educn Cttee, 1977–85; Staff Joint and Personnel Cttees, 1981–85; Vice-Chm., Secondary Educn Cttee, 1981–85); Mem. (C), Felixstowe Town Council, 1991–95; Mem., Suffolk War Pensions Cttee, 1980–90. Sponsor, the Responsible Society, 1982–90. Chm. Governors, Felixstowe Deben High Sch., 1985–88. Enlisted ATS (TA), 1947; commissioned, 1949. FRSA 1972. Coronation Medal, 1953. *Publications:* The Vulnerable Generation, 1971; The Story of Felixstowe College, 1980. *Recreations:* narrow boating, choral singing, theatre, motoring, good food and wine. *Address:* 6 Graham Court, Hamilton Gardens, Felixstowe, Suffolk IP11 7ES.

MANNERS, Prof. Gerald, OBE 2005; Professor of Geography, University College London, 1980–97, now Emeritus; Chairman, Association of Charitable Foundations, 2003–07; *b* 7 Aug. 1932; *s* of George William Manners and Louisa Hannah Manners; *m* 1st, 1959, Anne (*née* Sawyer) (marr. diss. 1982); one *s* two *d*; 2nd, 1982, Joy Edith Roberta (*née* Turner); one *s*. *Educ:* Wallington County Grammar School; St Catharine's College, Cambridge (MA). Lectr in Geography, University Coll. Swansea, 1957–67; Reader in Geography, UCL, 1967–80. Vis. Schol., Resources for the Future, Inc., Washington DC, 1964–65; Vis. Associate, Jt Center for Urban Studies, Harvard and MIT, 1972–73; Vis. Fellow, ANU, 1990. Dir, Economic Associates Ltd, 1964–74. Member: Council, Inst. of British Geographers, 1967–70; LOB 1970–80; SE Economic Planning Council, 1971–79; Council, TCPA, 1980–89; Subscriber, Centre for Environmental Studies Ltd, 1981–99. Specialist Advisor to: H of C Select Cttee on Energy, 1980–92; H of L Select Cttee on Sustainable Develt, 1994–95; H of C Envmtl Audit Cttee, 1999–2001; Advr to Assoc. for Conservation of Energy, 1981–; Chairman: Regl Studies Assoc., 1981–84; RSA Panel of Inquiry into regl problem in UK, 1982–83. Trustee: City Parochial Foundn and Trust for London, 1977–2007 (Chm., Estate Cttee, 1987–2001; Chm., 1996–2004); Chelsea Physic Garden, 1980–83; Eaga Partnership Charitable Trust, 1993–. Sadler's Wells Foundn (formerly Sadler's Wells Foundn and Trust): Gov., 1978–95; Vice-Chm., 1982–86; Chm. Theatre Bd, 1986–93; Chm., 1986–95; Vice-Pres., 1995–99; Mem. Council, ENO Works, 1996–99. Mem., Investment Adv. Cttee, St Paul's Cathedral, 2000–. Mem. Court, City Univ., 1985–. *Publications:* Geography of Energy, 1964, 2nd edn 1971; South Wales in the Sixties, 1964; Changing World Market for Iron Ore 1950–1980, 1971; (ed) Spatial Policy Problems of the British Economy, 1971; Minerals and Man, 1974; Regional Development in Britain, 1974, 2nd edn 1980; Coal in Britain, 1981; Office Policy in Britain, 1986; contribs to edited volumes and learned jls. *Recreations:* music, dance, theatre, walking, undergardening. *Address:* 338 Liverpool Road, Islington, N7 8PZ. *T:* (020) 7607 7920.

MANNERS, Hon. Thomas (Jasper); Director, Lazard Brothers, 1965–89 (Deputy Chairman, 1986–89); *b* 12 Dec. 1929; *y s* of 4th Baron Manners, MC, and of Mary Edith, *d* of late Rt Rev. Lord William Cecil; *m* 1955, Sarah, *d* of Brig. Roger Peake, DSO; three *s*. *Educ:* Eton. Lazard Brothers & Co. Ltd, 1955–89; Director: Legal & General Gp, 1972–93; Scapa Gp, 1970–96; Davy Corp., 1985–91. *Recreations:* shooting, fishing. *Address:* The Old Malt House, Ashford Hill, Thatcham, Berks RG19 8BN. *T:* (0118) 981 4865. *Clubs:* Pratt's, White's.

MANNING, Prof. Aubrey William George, OBE 1998; DPhil; FRSE, FIBiol; Professor of Natural History, University of Edinburgh, 1973–97, now Emeritus; *b* 24 April 1930; *s* of William James Manning and Hilda Winifred (*née* Noble); *m* 1st, 1959, Margaret Bastock, DPhil (*d* 1982); two *s*; 2nd, 1985, Joan Herrmann, PhD; one *s*. *Educ:* Strode's School, Egham, Surrey; University Coll. London (BSc); Merton Coll., Oxford (DPhil). FRSE 1975; FIBiol 1980; FRZSScot 1997. Commnd RA, 1954–56. University of Edinburgh: Asst Lectr, 1956–59; Lectr, 1959–68; Reader, 1968–73. Mem., Bd of Trustees, Nat. Museums of Scotland, 1997–2005. Sec. Gen., Internat. Ethological Cttee, 1971–79; Member: Scottish Cttee, NCC, 1982–88; NCC Adv. Cttee on Science, 1984–88; Pop. Studies Panel, Wellcome Trust, 1995–99; President: Assoc. Study Animal Behaviour, 1983–86; Biology Sect., BAAS, 1993; Scottish Earth Sci. Educn Forum, 1999–; Royal Soc. of Wildlife Trusts, 2006–. Chm. Council, Scottish Wildlife Trust, 1990–96. Chm., Edinburgh Brook Adv. Centre, 1975–82. Patron, Optimum Population Trust, 2002–. Advr, Population and Sustainability Network, 2006–. Goodwill Ambassador, UN Internat. Year of Planet Earth, 2008. Presenter: TV series: Earth Story, 1998; Talking Landscapes, 2001; Landscape Mysteries, 2003; radio series: Unearthing Mysteries, 1999–2006; The Sounds of Life, 2004; The Rules of Life, 2005. Dr *hc* Univ. Paul Sabatier, Toulouse, 1981; DUniv Open, 2002; Hon. DSc St Andrews, 2005; Hon. MA Worcester, 2005. Dobzhansky Meml Award, Behavior Genetics Assoc., 1994; Assoc. Study Animal Behaviour Medal, 1998; Silver Medal, Zool Soc., 2003. *Publications:* An Introduction to Animal Behaviour, 1967, 5th edn (with M. Dawkins) 1998; papers on animal behaviour in learned jls. *Recreations:* woodland regeneration, hill-walking, 19th century novels. *Address:* The Old Hall, Ormiston, East Lothian EH35 5NJ. *T:* (01875) 340536.

MANNING, Sir David (Geoffrey), GCMG 2008 (KCMG 2001; CMG 1992); CVO 2007; HM Diplomatic Service; Ambassador to the United States of America, 2003–07; *b* 5 Dec. 1949; *s* of John Robert Manning and Joan Barbara Manning; *m* 1973, Catherine Marjory Parkinson. *Educ:* Ardingly Coll.; Oriel Coll., Oxford (Hon. Fellow, 2003); Johns Hopkins Sch. of Advanced Internat. Studies, Bologna (Postgrad. Diploma in Internat. Relations, 1972). FCO, 1972; Warsaw, 1974–76; New Delhi, 1977–80; FCO, 1980–84; First Sec., Paris, 1984–88; Counsellor, seconded to Cabinet Office, 1988–90; Political Counsellor and Head of Political Sect., Moscow, 1990–93; Hd of Eastern Dept, FCO, 1993–94; British Mem., Contact Gp on Bosnia, Internat. Conf. on Former Yugoslavia, April–Nov. 1994; Hd of Policy Planning Staff, FCO, 1994–95; Ambassador to Israel, 1995–98; Dep. Under-Sec. of State, FCO, 1998–2000; Perm. Rep., UK Delegn to NATO, 2000–01; Foreign Policy Advr to Prime Minister, and Hd of Defence and Overseas Secretariat, Cabinet Office, 2001–03.

MANNING, Dr Geoffrey Lewis, FRCSE; FDSRCS; Chairman, North Staffordshire Hospital NHS Trust, 1993–2000; *b* 21 Sept. 1931; *s* of late Isaac Harold Manning and Florence Hilda Manning; *m* 1978, Patricia Margaret Wilson; one *d*. *Educ:* Rossall Sch., Fleetwood, Lancs; Univ. of Birmingham (LDS, BDS 1953; MB, ChB 1961). FDSRCS 1964; FRCSE 1986. Nat. service, Capt., RADC, 1954–56. Senior Registrar: Central Middx Hosp., 1964–66; Mt Vernon Hosp., 1966–68; Parkland Meml Hosp., Dallas, 1967; Consultant Oral Surgeon, N Staffs Hosp., 1968–93. Mem., N Staffs DHA, 1986–92.

Leader, Health Task Force, Prince of Wales Business Leaders Forum, 1993–2000. Mem., British Fedn of Pottery Manufacturers. Hon. DSc Keele, 2000. *Recreations:* gardening, brick-laying, classic cars. *Address:* The Old Hall, Haughton, Stafford ST18 9HB. *T:* (01785) 780273. *Club:* Trentham Golf.

MANNING, Jane Marian, OBE 1990; freelance concert and opera singer (soprano), since 1965; *b* 20 Sept. 1938; *d* of Gerald Manville Manning and Lily Manning (*née* Thompson); *m* 1966, Anthony Edward Payne, *qv*. *Educ:* Norwich High Sch.; Royal Academy of Music (LRAM 1958); Scuola di Canto, Cureglia, Switzerland. GRSM 1960, ARCM 1962. London début (Park Lane Group), 1964; first BBC broadcast, 1965; début Henry Wood Promenade Concerts, 1972; founded own ensemble, Jane's Minstrels, 1988; regular appearances in leading concert halls and festivals in UK and Europe, with leading orchestras and conductors; many broadcasts and gramophone recordings, lectures and master classes. Specialist in contemporary music (over 300 world premières given); Warsaw Autumn Fest., 1975–78, 1987, 1992; Wexford Opera Fest., 1976; Scottish Opera, 1978; Brussels Opera, 1980. Canadian début, 1977; tours: of Australia and New Zealand, 1978, 1980, 1982, 1984, 1986, 1990, 1996, 2000, 2002; of USA, 1981, 1983, 1985, 1986, 1987, 1988, 1989, 1991, 1993, 1996, 1997. Milhaud Vis. Prof., Mills Coll. Oakland, 1983; Lucie Stern Vis. Prof., Mills Coll., Oakland, 1981 and 1986; Vis. Artist, Univ. of Manitoba, Canada, 1992; Vis. Prof., RCM, 1995–; Hon. Prof., Keele Univ., 1996–2002; AHRC (formerly AHRB) Creative Arts Res. Fellow, 2004–07, Vis. Prof., 2007–Nov. 2009, Kingston Univ. Vice Pres., SPNM, 1984–. Chm., Eye Music (formerly Nettlefold Fest.) Trust, 1990–; Member: Exec. Cttee, Musicians Benevolent Fund, 1989–; Arts Council Music Panel, 1990–95; Internat. Jury, Gaudeamus Young Interpreters Competition, Holland, 1976, 1979, 1987; Jury, Eur. Youth Competition for Composers, Eur. Cultural Foundn, 1985. Hon. ARAM 1972, Hon. FRAM 1984; FRCM 1998. DUniv York, 1988; Hon. DMus: Keele, 2004; Durham, 2007. Special award, Composers Guild of Gt Britain, 1973. *Publications:* (chapter in) How Music Works, 1981; New Vocal Repertory, vol. I, 1986, vol. II, 1998; (chapter in) A Messiaen Companion, 1996; Pierrot Lunaire: practicalities and perspectives, 2008; (chapter in) Cambridge History of Musical Performance, 2009; articles in Composer, Music and Musicians, and Tempo. *Recreations:* reading, cinema, ornithology. *Address:* 2 Wilton Square, N1 3DL. *T:* (020) 7359 1593.

MANNING, Jeremy James C.; see Carter-Manning.

MANNING, Mary Elizabeth; Executive Director, Academy of Medical Sciences, since 2000; *b* 1 Nov. 1947; *d* of late Charles Frederick Kent and Marie Lucia Kent (*née* Hall); *m* 1972, Keith Quentin Frederick Manning; two *d*. *Educ:* Stoodley Knowle Sch. for Girls, Torquay; Bedford Coll., Univ. of London (BA Hons Hist. 1968). Royal Insce Co., 1968–69; Desk Officer, 1969–72, Attaché, British High Commn, Singapore, 1972–73, MoD; English lang. teacher, La Petite Ecole Française, Sofia, 1975–78; Royal Society: Meetings Officer, 1987–95; Manager, Scientific Prog., 1995–97; Hd, Sci. Promotion, 1997–2000. Mem., Steering Gp for Public Understanding of Sci., Engrg and Technol. EPSRC, 1999–2001. Mem., BAAS, 1995–. Mem., Bd for Social Responsibility, C of E, 2001–03. *Recreations:* music, walking, family and friends, France. *Address:* Academy of Medical Sciences, 10 Carlton House Terrace, SW1Y 5AH. *T:* (020) 7969 5285.

MANNING, Maurice, DLitt; President, Irish Human Rights Commission, since 2002; Adjunct Professor of Politics, School of Politics and International Relations, University College, Dublin, since 2007; *b* 14 June 1943; *s* of Thomas and Alicia Manning; *m* 1987, Mary Hayes; one *s*. *Educ:* University Coll., Dublin (BA 1964; MA 1966; DLitt 1998). Lectr in Politics, University Coll., Dublin, 1966–2002. TD (FG), 1981–87; Senator, 1987–2002 (Leader of the Opposition, 1987–94, 1997–2002; Leader of Senate, 1994–97). Pres., European Group of National Human Rights instns, 2006–. *Publications:* The Blueshirts, 1970, 3rd edn 2006; Irish Political Parties, 1972; The Irish Electricity Industry, 1987; Betrayal (novel), 1998; James Dillon: a biography, 1999. *Recreations:* tennis, swimming, Gregorian chant, reading. *Address:* Irish Human Rights Commission, Jervis House, Jervis Street, Dublin 1, Ireland. *T:* (1) 8589601; *e-mail:* mauricemanning@ireland.com. *Clubs:* Stephen's Green Hibernian, Hypothermia (Dublin).

MANNING, Hon. Patrick Augustus Mervyn; MP (People's National Movement) San Fernando East, since 1971; Prime Minister of Trinidad and Tobago, 1991–95 and since 2001; *b* 17 Aug. 1946; *s* of late Arnold and Elaine Manning; *m* 1972, Hazel Kinsale; two *s*. *Educ:* Rose Bank Private Sch.; San Fernando Govt Sch.; Presentation Coll.; Univ. of West Indies, Jamaica (BSc Special Hons Geology 1969). Texaco Trinidad Inc.: Refinery Operator, 1965–66; Geologist, 1969–71. Parliamentary Secretary: Min. of Petroleum and Mines, 1971–73; Office of the Prime Minister, 1973–74; Min. of Planning and Develt, 1974–75; Min. of Industry and Commerce, 1975–76; Min. of Works, Transport and Communications, 1976–78; Minister: Min. of Finance (Maintenance and Public Service), 1978–81; Prime Minister's Office (Information), 1979–81; Minister of: Inf. and of Industry and Commerce, 1981; Energy and Natural Resources, 1981–86; Leader of the Opposition, 1986–90 and 1995–2001. Leader, People's National Movement, 1987–. *Recreations:* table tennis, chess, reading. *Address:* Port of Spain, Trinidad and Tobago.

MANNING, Paul Andrew, QPM 1996; Assistant Commissioner, Metropolitan Police, 1994–2000; *b* 29 May 1947; *s* of Owen Manning and Joyce Cynthia Manning (*née* Murgatroyd); *m* 1967, Margaret Anne Bucknall; two *s*. *Educ:* Forest of Needwood High Sch., Rolleston-on-Dove; Cranfield Inst. of Technology (MSc). Metropolitan Police Cadet, 1964; Constable, 1966, Chief Supt, 1985, Staffordshire Police; Asst Chief Constable, Avon and Somerset Constabulary, 1988; Dep. Chief Constable, Herts Constabulary, 1992. Chm., ACPO Traffic Cttee, 1997–2000 (Sec., 1996–97). Director: Educnl Broadcasting Services Trust, 1997–; Perseus-Global Security Technols, 2006–. Mem., Amwell Rotary Club. Mem., Guild of Freemen, City of London, 1999–. FCILT (FCIT, FILT 2000). *Recreations:* hill walking, Rotary. *Address:* 6 The Chestnuts, Hertford SG13 8AQ. *T:* (01992) 422106, *Fax:* (01992) 413080.

MANNING, Peter; Artistic Director and Conductor, Manning Camerata, since 2005; Concertmaster, Royal Opera House, Covent Garden, since 2000; Artistic Director, Musica Vitae Sweden, since 2008; *b* Manchester, 17 July 1956; *s* of Harry and Breda Manning; *m* 1st, 1980, Elizabeth (marr. diss. 1986); one *s* one *d*; 2nd, 1992, Marion; two *s*. *Educ:* Chetham's Sch., Manchester; Royal Northern Coll. of Music (GRNCM 1978; PPRNCM 1978); Indiana Univ. Prof. of Violin, RNCM, 1981–83; Leader, LPO, 1983–86; Founder and Leader, Britten String Quartet, 1986–96; Leader, RPO, 1997–99. Hon. RCM 1989. FRNCM 1992. FRSA. *Recreations:* sailing, fly fishing. *Address:* 52 Stockwell Park Road, SW9 0DA; *e-mail:* peter@manningcamerata.com. *Club:* Arts.

MANNING, Prof. Susan Lindsay, PhD; FRSE; Grierson Professor of English Literature, since 1999, and Director, Institute for Advanced Study in the Humanities, since 2005, University of Edinburgh; *b* 24 Dec. 1953; *d* of James Moncur Valentine and Honora Margaret Struan Valentine; *m* 1976, Howard John Manning; three *d*. *Educ:* Newnham Coll., Cambridge (BA 1976; PhD 1986). Res. Fellow, 1981–83, Coll. Lectr in English, 1984–99, Newnham Coll., Cambridge; Faculty of English, University of Cambridge: Univ. Asst Lectr, 1989–94; Univ. Lectr, 1994–99; Asst Chm., 1997–99. FRSE 2005;

FRSA 2006. *Publications:* The Puritan-Provincial Vision: Scottish and American literature in the nineteenth century, 1990; Fragments of Union: making connections in Scottish and American writing, 2002; Transatlantic Literary Studies, 2007; edns of works by Walter Scott, Henry Mackenzie, Nathaniel Hawthorne, Washington Irving, Hector St John de Crèvecoeur. *Address:* Institute for Advanced Studies, University of Edinburgh, Hope Park Square, Edinburgh EH8 9NW. *T:* (0131) 650 4671; *e-mail:* susan.manning@ed.ac.uk.

MANNINGHAM-BULLER, family name of **Viscount Dilhorne**.

MANNINGHAM-BULLER, Baroness *cr* 2008 (Life Peer), of Northampton in the County of Northamptonshire; **Hon. Elizabeth Lydia Manningham-Buller,** DCB 2005; Director General, Security Service, 2002–07; *b* 14 July 1948; *d* of 1st Viscount Dilhorne, PC, and Lady Mary Lilian Lindsay, 4th *d* of 27th Earl of Crawford, KT, PC. *Educ:* Benenden Sch.; Lady Margaret Hall, Oxford (MA; Hon. Fellow 2004). Entered Security Service, 1974; Dep. Dir Gen., 1997–2002. DUniv Open, 2005; Hon. DSc Cranfield, 2005. *Address:* c/o PO Box 3255, SW1P 1AE.
See also Viscount Dilhorne.

MANNION, Rosa; soprano; *b* 29 Jan. 1962; *d* of Patrick Anthony Mannion and Maria (*née* MacGregor); *m* 1985, Gerard McQuade; two *s*. *Educ:* Seafield Grammar Sch., Crosby; Royal Scottish Acad. of Music and Drama (BA). Débuts: Scottish Opera, 1984; Edinburgh Fest., 1985; ENO, 1987; Glyndebourne Fest. Opera, 1988; principal soprano: Scottish Opera, 1984–86; ENO, 1989–92; major rôles include: Gilda in Rigoletto; Violetta in La Traviata; Manon (title rôle); Magnolia in Show Boat; Pamina in Die Zauberflöte; Minka in Le Roi malgré lui; Sophie in Werther; Oscar in A Masked Ball; Atalanta in Xerxes; Constanze in Die Entführung aus dem Serail; Countess in Figaro's Wedding; Sophie in Der Rosenkavalier. Has given many concerts and recitals. Winner, Internat. Singing Competition, Scottish Opera, 1988.

MANOR, Prof. James Gilmore, DPhil; Emeka Anyaoku Professor, Institute of Commonwealth Studies, University of London, since 2007; *b* 21 April 1945; *s* of James Manor and Ann (*née* Jones); *m* 1974, Brenda Cohen; one *s*. *Educ:* Yale Univ. (BA 1967); Univ. of Sussex (DPhil 1975). Asst Lectr in History, Chinese Univ. of Hong Kong, 1967–69; Tutor, SOAS, 1973–75; Asst Prof. of History, Yale, 1975–76; Lectr in Politics, Univ. of Leicester, 1976–85; Prof. of Govt, Harvard, 1985–87; Professorial Fellow, 1987–2007, Hd of Research, 1988–91, Inst. of Develt Studies, Univ. of Sussex; Dir, and Prof. of Commonwealth Politics, Inst. of Commonwealth Studies, Univ. of London, 1994–97. V. K. R. V. Rao Prof., Inst. for Social and Economic Change, Bangalore, India, 2006–08. Sen. Res. Fellow, US Nat. Endowment for the Humanities, 1980–81; Vis Fellow, MIT, 1982. Consultant to: Dutch Govt, 1989–90; World Bank, 1994–97; Swedish Govt, 1995. Editor, Jl of Commonwealth and Comparative Politics, 1980–88. *Publications:* Political Change in an Indian State, 1977; (ed with P. Lyon) Transfer and Transformation, 1983; (ed) Sri Lanka in Change and Crisis, 1984; The Expedient Utopian, 1989; (ed) Rethinking Third World Politics, 1991; (ed with C. Colclough) States or Markets?, 1991; Power, Poverty and Poison, 1993; Nehru to the Nineties, 1994; Aid that Works, 2006. *Recreations:* reading, theatre. *Address:* Institute of Commonwealth Studies, University of London, 28 Russell Square, WC1B 5DS. *T:* (020) 7862 8844.

MANS, Keith Douglas Rowland; Chief Executive (formerly Director), Royal Aeronautical Society, since 1998; *b* 10 Feb. 1946; *s* of Maj.-Gen. Rowland Spencer Noel Mans, CBE and Veeo Mans; *m* 1972, Rosalie Mary McCann; one *s* two *d*. *Educ:* Berkhamsted School; RAF College Cranwell; Open Univ. (BA). FRAeS. Pilot, RAF, 1964–77 (Flight Lieut); Pilot, RAF Reserve, 1977–. Retail Manager, John Lewis Partnership, 1978–87. MP (C) Wyre, 1987–97; contested (C) Lancaster and Wyre, 1997. PPS to Minister of State, Dept of Health, 1990–92, to Sec. of State for Health, 1992–95. Member: H of C Environment Select Cttee, 1987–91; Select Cttee on Defence, 1995–97; Chairman: Parly Envmt Gp, 1993–97; Parly Aerospace Gp, 1994–97; Vice-Chm., Back bench Fisheries Cttee, 1987–96; Secretary: Back bench Aviation Cttee, 1987–90; Back bench Envmt Cttee, 1990–91; All Party Aviation Gp, 1991–94. Public Affairs Advr, Soc. of British Aerospace Cos, 1997–2002. Chm., Air Travel Greener By Design Cttee, 2002–. Chm., Oakhaven Hospice Charity. Member, Court: Cranfield Univ., 2002–; Southampton Univ., 2005–. Freeman, City of London, 2005. FRSA 2005. *Recreation:* flying. *Address:* Rowhurst Cottage, De La Warr Road, Milford on Sea, Lymington, Hants SO41 0PS. *Clubs:* Royal Air Force, Carlton.
See also Maj. Gen. M. F. N. Mans.

MANS, Maj. Gen. Mark Francis Noel, CBE 2005; Military Secretary, since 2008; *b* 7 March 1955; *s* of Maj.-Gen. Rowland Spencer Noel Mans, CBE and Veeo Ellen Mans; *m* 1982, Jane Goode; one *s* one *d*. *Educ:* Berkhamsted Sch. Commnd RE, 1974; CO, 21 Engr Regt, 1993–95; Comdr Engrs, 1999–2001, Asst COS Plans, 2002–04, Land Comd; Dep. Comdg Gen., Multinat. Corps, Iraq, 2005; Dep. Adjt Gen., 2005–08. Mem., Scientific Exploration Soc., 1980–. Pres., RE Rugby FC, 2000–. FCMI 1997; FCIPD 2000. Officer, Legion of Merit (USA), 2006. *Recreation:* sport, sadly increasingly as a spectator.
See also K. D. R. Mans.

MANSAGER, Felix Norman, Hon. KBE 1976 (Hon. CBE 1973); Honorary Director, Hoover Co. USA (President-Chairman, Hoover Co. and Hoover World-wide Corporation, 1966–75); Director, Hoover Ltd UK (Chairman, 1966–75); *b* 30 Jan. 1911; *s* of Hoff Mansager and Alice (*née* Qualseth); *m* Geraldine (*née* Larson); one *s* two *d*. *Educ:* South Dakota High Sch., Colton. Joined Hoover Co. as Salesman, 1929; Vice-Pres., Sales, 1959; Exec. Vice-Pres. and Dir, 1961. Dir, Belden and Blake Energy Co. Member: Council on Foreign Relations; Newcomen Soc. in N America; Trustee, Graduate Theological Union (Calif); The Pilgrims of the US; Assoc. of Ohio Commodores; Masonic Shrine (32nd degree Mason); Mem. and Governor, Ditchley Foundn; Member Board of Trustees: Ohio Foundn of Indep. Colls; Indep. Coll. Funds of America. Hon. Mem., World League of Norsemen. Marketing Award, British Inst. of Marketing, 1971. Executive Prof. of Business (Goodyear Chair), Univ. of Akron (Mem. Delta Sigma Pi; Hon. Mem., Beta Sigma Gamma). Hon. Fellow, UC Cardiff, 1973. Hon. Dr of Laws Capital Univ., 1967; Hon. LLD Strathclyde, 1970; Hon. DHL Malone Coll., Canton, Ohio, 1972; Hon. PhD Walsh Coll., Canton, 1974; Hon. Dr Humanities Wartburg Coll., Waverly, Iowa, 1976; Medal of Honor, Vassa Univ., Finland, 1973; Person of Year, Capital Univ. Chapter of Tau Pi Phi, 1981. Grand Officer, Dukes of Burgundy, 1968; Chevalier: Order of Leopold, 1969; Order of St Olav, Norway, 1971; Legion of Honour, France, 1973; Grande Officiale, Order Al Merito della Republica Italiana, 1975. *Recreation:* golf. *Address:* 3421 Lindel Court NW, Canton, OH 44718, USA. *Clubs:* Metropolitan (NYC); Congress Lake Country (Hartville, Ohio); Torske (Hon.) (Minneapolis).

MANSEL, Sir Philip, 15th Bt *cr* 1621; Chairman and Managing Director of Eden-Vale Engineering Co. Ltd, 1962–98, retired; *b* 3 March 1943; *s* of Sir John Mansel, 14th Bt and Hannah, *d* of Ben Rees; *S* father, 1947; *m* 1968, Margaret, *o d* of Arthur Docker; two *s* one *d*. *Heir:* *s* John Philip Mansel, *b* 19 April 1982. *Address:* 2 Deyncourt Close, Darras Hall, Ponteland, Northumberland NE20 9JY.

MANSEL, Prof. Robert Edward, CBE 2006; FRCS; Professor of Surgery, since 1992, and Chairman, Hospital-Based Division, since 2001, Cardiff University (formerly University of Wales College of Medicine); *b* 1 Feb. 1948; *s* of Regnier Ranulf Dabridgecourt Mansel and Mary Germaine Mansel (*née* Littlewood); *m* 1987, Elizabeth Clare, *d* of John Francis Skone and Daphne Viola (*née* Rees); two *s* four *d*. *Educ:* Llandovery Coll.; Charing Cross Hosp. Med. Sch., Univ. of London (MB BS, MS). LRCP 1971; FRCS 1975. Res. Fellow, 1976–78, Lectr and Sen. Lectr, 1979–89, Univ. of Wales Coll. of Medicine; Prof. of Surgery, Univ. of Manchester, 1989–92. Chm., Breast Speciality Gp, 1997–2002, Pres., 2004–, British Assoc. of Surgical Oncology. UICC Fellow, Univ. of Texas at San Antonio, 1982–83; Churchill Meml Fellowship, 1982; James IV Fellowship, James IV Assoc., 1989. Hunterian Prof., RCS, 1989. Hon. FRCSE 2003. *Publications:* Fibrocystic Breast Disease, 1986; (with L. E. Hughes and D. J. T. Webster) Benign Breast Disease, 1989, 3rd edn 2008; Atlas of Breast Disease, 1994; contribs to surgical jls. *Recreations:* fishing, Rugby, travel, chess. *Address:* Department of Surgery, Cardiff University, Heath Park, Cardiff CF14 4XN. *T:* (029) 2074 2749, *Fax:* (029) 2076 1623; *e-mail:* manselre@cf.ac.uk.

MANSEL-JONES, David; Chairman, Huntingdon Research Centre plc, 1978–86 (Vice-Chairman, 1974–78); *b* 8 Sept. 1926; *o s* of Rees Thomas Jones and Ceinwen Jones; *m* 1952, Mair Aeronwen Davies; one *s*. *Educ:* St Michael's Sch., Bryn; London Hospital. MB, BS 1950; MRCP 1973; FFPM 1992. Jun. Surgical Specialist, RAMC; Dep. Med. Dir, Wm R. Warner & Co. Ltd, 1957–59; Med. Dir, Richardson-Merrell Ltd, 1959–65; formerly PMO, SMO and MO, Cttee on Safety of Drugs; formerly Med. Assessor, Cttee on Safety of Medicines; Consultant to WHO, 1970–86; Senior PMO, Medicines Div., DHSS, 1971–74. Vis. Prof., Gulbenkian Science Inst., Portugal, 1981; Examiner, Dip. Pharm. Med., Royal Colls of Physicians, UK, 1980–87. *Publications:* papers related to safety of medicines. *Recreations:* music, painting. *Address:* 39 St John's Court, Princes Road, Felixstowe, Suffolk IP11 7SG. *T:* (01394) 275984.

MANSEL LEWIS, Sir David (Courtenay), KCVO 1995; JP; Lord-Lieutenant of Dyfed, 1979–2002 (Lieutenant, 1974–79; HM Lieutenant for Carmarthenshire, 1973–74); *b* 25 Oct. 1927; *s* of late Charlie Ronald Mansel Lewis and Lillian Georgina Warner, *d* of Col Sir Courtenay Warner, 1st Bt, CB; *m* 1953, Lady Mary Rosemary Marie-Gabrielle Montagu-Stuart-Wortley, OBE, JP, 4th *d* of 3rd Earl of Wharncliffe; one *s* two *d*. *Educ:* Eton; Keble Coll., Oxford (BA). Served in Welsh Guards, 1946–49; Lieut 1946, RARO. Chairman: SW Div., Royal Forestry Soc., 1963–93; S Wales Woodlands, 1969–85; Founder Chm., Carmarthen-Cardigan Cttee, 1968–, Regl Chm., S Wales, 1985–, STA. Member, Court: Nat. Mus. of Wales, 1974–91 (Mem. Council, 1987–91); UCW Aberystwyth, 1974–2002. President: Llanelli Art Soc., 1956–; Carmarthen-Cardigan Br., 1977–91, Dyfed Br., 1991–, CLA; Dyfed Wildlife Trust, 1978–2002; Gŵyl Llanelli Fest., 1979–; Dyfed Br., Magistrates' Assoc., 1979–2002; Burry Port RNLI, 1982–; Welsh Assoc. of Male Voice Choirs, 1997–; Chm., Llanelli Millennium Coastal Park Trustees, 1999–. Patron: Carmarthen RBL, 1974–; Tall Ships Council of Wales, 1991–; Commonwealth Games Council for Wales, 1996–; Wales Gurkha Villages Aid Trust, 1999–. Pres. of Trustees, Llandovery Coll., 2006– (Trustee, 1985–2001, Chm., 2001–06). President: W Wales, 1979–90, Wales, 1995–99, TAVRA; Dyfed SSAFA, 1986–2003. FRSA; Hon. Fellow, Trinity Coll., Carmarthen, 1997. High Sheriff, Carmarthenshire, 1965; JP 1969; DL 1971. KStJ (Sub Prior for Wales, 1998–2002). *Recreations:* music, sailing. *Address:* Stradey Castle, Llanelli, Dyfed SA15 4PL. *T:* (01554) 774626. *Clubs:* Cavalry and Guards, Lansdowne; Royal Yacht Squadron (Cowes); Burry Port Yacht (Founder Cdre, 1966; Pres., 1975–).

MANSELL, Ven. Clive Neville Ross; Archdeacon of Tonbridge, since 2002; *b* 20 April 1953; *s* of (Arthur James) Mervyn Mansell and June Irene Mansell (*née* Duncan); *m* 1980, Jane Margaret (*née* Sellers); one *s* two *d*. *Educ:* City of London Sch.; Leicester Univ. (LLB Hons 1974); Coll. of Law; Trinity Coll., Bristol (DipHE Theol Studies 1981). Solicitor of the Supreme Court, 1977–81. Ordained deacon, 1982, priest, 1983; Curate, Gt Malvern Priory, 1982–85; Minor Canon, Ripon Cathedral, with pastoral care of parishes of Sharow with Copt Hewick and of Marton-le-Moor, 1985–89; Rector, Kirklington with Burneston, Wath and Pickhill, 1989–2002; Area Dean, Wensley, 1998–2002. Mem., Gen. Synod of C of E, 1995–; Dep. Prolocutor, House of Clergy, Northern Convocation, 2001–02. Church Comr, 1997–. *Recreations:* cricket, music, reading, history, current affairs, photography, enjoying good meals. *Address:* 3 The Ridings, Blackhurst Lane, Tunbridge Wells, Kent TN2 4RU. *T:* (01892) 520660; *e-mail:* archdeacon.tonbridge@rochester.anglican.org.

MANSELL, Gerard Evelyn Herbert, CBE 1977; Managing Director, External Broadcasting, BBC, 1972–81; Deputy Director-General, BBC, 1977–81; retired; *b* 16 Feb. 1921; 2nd *s* of late Herbert and Anne Mansell, Paris; *m* 1956, Diana Marion Sherar; two *s*. *Educ:* Lycée Hoche, Versailles; Lycée Buffon, Paris; Ecole des Sciences Politiques, Paris; Chelsea Sch. of Art. Joined HM Forces, 1940; served in Western Desert, Sicily and NW Europe, 1942–45 (despatches). Joined BBC European Service, 1951; Head, Overseas Talks and Features Dept, 1961; Controller, BBC Radio 4 (formerly Home Service), and Music Programme, 1965–69; Dir of Programmes, BBC, Radio, 1970. Chairman: British Cttee, Journalists in Europe, 1978–95; Jt Adv. Cttee on Radio Journalism Trng, 1981–87; Sony Radio Awards Organising Cttee, 1983–87; Communications Adv. Cttee, UK Nat. Commn for UNESCO, 1983–85; Friends of UNESCO, 1986–88; Member: Communication and Cultural Studies Bd, CNAA, 1982–87; Exec. Cttee, GB–China Centre, 1986–96 (Vice-Chm., 1988–96); Franco-British Council, 1990–2002; Sandford St Martin Trust, 1991–2003. Governor, Falmouth Sch. of Art and Design, 1988–97; Chairman: New Hampstead Garden Suburb Trust, 1984–90, 1992–93; Burgh House Trust, Hampstead, 1995–98, 1999–2004. FRSA 1979. Sony Gold Award for Services to Radio, 1988. French Croix de Guerre, 1945. *Publications:* Tragedy in Algeria, 1961; Let Truth be Told, 1982. *Address:* 15 Hampstead Hill Gardens, NW3 2PH.

MANSELL, Nigel Ernest James, OBE 1991; racing driver; *b* 8 Aug. 1953; *s* of Eric and Joyce Mansell; *m* Rosanne Elizabeth Perry; two *s* one *d*. *Educ:* Wellsbourne and Hall Green Bilateral Schools; Matthew Bolton Polytechnic; Solihull Tech. Coll.; N Birmingham Polytechnic (HND). Engineering apprenticeship with Lucas; lab. technician, Lucas Aerospace, later product manager; senior sales engineer, tractor div., Girling. Began racing in karts; won 11 regional championships, 1969–76; Formula Ford and Formula Three, 1976–79; Formula Two, later Formula One, 1980; Lotus team, 1981–84; Williams-Honda team, 1985–87; Williams-Judd team, 1988; Ferrari team, 1989–90; Williams-Renault team, 1991–92 and 1994 (part time); McLaren team, 1995; first competed in a Grand Prix, Austria, 1980; won 31 Grands Prix, 1980–94 (record); Formula One World Drivers Champion, 1992; American Newman-Haas IndyCar Team, 1993; IndyCar Champion, 1993; won Grand Prix Masters, (inaugural race) Kyalomi, 2005, Qatar, 2006. President: UK Youth, 2002–; Inst. of Advanced Motorists, 2005–. Patron: Manx Cancer Help Assoc., 1983; Driving for Disabled Jersey. Grand Fellow, MIRCE

Akad. for System Operational Sci., 2000. Hon. DEng Birmingham. *Publications:* (with Derick Allsop) Driven to Win, 1988; (with Derick Allsop) Mansell and Williams, The Challenge for the Championship 1992; (with Jeremy Shaw) Nigel Mansell's IndyCar Racing, 1993; (with James Allen) Nigel Mansell, My Autobiography, 1995. *Recreations:* golf, flying.

MANSELL-JONES, Richard Mansell; Chairman, Brown, Shipley & Co., 1992–2003; *b* 4 April 1940; *s* of late Arnaud Milward Jones and Winifred Mabel (*née* Foot); *m* 1971, Penelope Marion, *y d* of Major Sir David Henry Hawley, 7th Bt. *Educ:* Queen Elizabeth's, Carmarthen; Worcester College, Oxford (MA). FCA. Articled to Price, Waterhouse & Co., 1963–68; with N. M. Rothschild & Sons, 1968–72; with Brown, Shipley & Co., 1972–88 (Dir, 1974–84; Dep. Chm., 1984–88); non-exec. Dir, 1982–88, Chm., 1988–2000, Barlow International PLC (formerly J. Bibby & Sons). Director: Brown, Shipley Holdings, 1985–92; Barlow Ltd (formerly Barlow Rand Ltd), 1988–2001; non-executive Director: Barr & Wallace Arnold Trust, 1984–93; Rand Mines Ltd, 1988–93; Barloworld Hldgs, 1990–2003; Standard Bank London, 1992–2005; Standard Internat. Holdings, 2000–05; Lifetime Gp, 2003–05; non-executive Chm., Amphion Innovations plc, 2005–. Mem. Council, CBI, 1999–2000. Mem. Bd, 2003–08, Treas., 2005–08, Royal Hosp. for Neuro-disability. Patron, Shaw Trust, 1996– (Trustee, 1990–96). MSI 1992. *Address:* c/o Private Banking, Brown, Shipley & Co. Ltd, Founders Court, Lothbury, EC2R 7HE. *T:* (020) 7606 9833. *Clubs:* Beefsteak, Boodle's, City of London.

MANSER, John; *see* Manser, P. J.

MANSER, Michael John, CBE 1993; RA 1995; architect in private practice, The Manser Practice (formerly Michael Manser Associates, then Manser Associates), since 1961; President, Royal Institute of British Architects, 1983–85; *b* 23 March 1929; *s* of late Edmund George Manser and Augusta Madge Manser; *m* 1953, Dolores Josephine Bernini; one *s* one *d*. *Educ:* Sch. of Architecture, Polytechnic of Central London (DipArch). RIBA 1954; RWA 1994. Intermittent architectural journalist and lectr; News Editor, Architectural Design, 1961–64; Architectural Correspondent, The Observer, 1961–64. TV and radio, 1963–. Councillor: RIBA, 1977–80 and 1982; RSA, 1987–93 (Founder Chm., Art for Architecture Award Scheme, 1990–93); Assessor, Art in the Workplace Awards, 1988–; Chairman: Art and Work Awards, 1996–; Nat. Home Builder Design Awards, 1998–; Stirling Prize Award, RIBA, 2000; Jury, Manser Medal, 2001–; RIBA Rep., Council, Nat. Trust, 1991–93; Member: London Transport Design Policy Cttee, 1991–95; Westminster CC Public Art Adv. Panel, 1999–; Ext. Examiner, Faculty of Architecture, Kingston Univ., 1995–98. Royal Academy: Member: Council, 1998; Architectural Cttee, 1998–; Audit Cttee, 1999–; Works Cttee, 1999–; Remuneration Cttee, 2000–. Chm., British Architectural Liby Trust, 2008. Hon. Fellow, Royal Architectural Inst. of Canada, 1985. Civic Trust Awards, 1967, 1973 and 1991; Award for Good Design in Housing, DoE, 1975; Europ. Architectural Heritage Year Award, 1975; RIBA Award and Regional Award, 1991, 1995; ICE Merit Award, 1995; Structural Steel Design Award, 1995. *Publications:* (with José Manser) Planning Your Kitchen, 1976; (contrib.) Psychiatry in the Elderly, 1991; (contrib.) Companion to Contemporary Architectural Thought, 1993. *Recreations:* going home, architecture, music, books, boats, sketching, gardening (under supervision). *Address:* 76 Whitehall Court, SW1A 2EL. *Clubs:* Brooks's, Farmers.

MANSER, (Peter) John, CBE 1992; DL; FCA; Chairman, Robert Fleming Holdings Ltd, 1997–2000 (Director, since 1972; Group Chief Executive, 1990–97); *b* 7 Dec. 1939; *s* of late Peter Robert Courtney Manser and Florence Delaplaine Manser; *m* 1969, Sarah Theresa Stuart (*née* Todd); two *d*. *Educ:* Marlborough Coll. Man. Dir, Jardine Fleming & Co. Ltd, 1975–79; Chief Exec., Save & Prosper Gp Ltd, 1983–88; Chm., Robert Fleming & Co. Ltd, 1990–97. Chairman: Delancey Estates, 1998–2001; Intermediate Capital Gp, 2001–; Shaftesbury, 2005– (Dir, 1997–); London Asia Chinese Private Equity Fund, 2006–07; Dep. Chm., Colliers CRE (formerly Fitzhardinge), 2002–; Director: Capital Shopping Centres, 1994–2000; Keppel Tatlee Bank, 2000–01; SAB Miller (formerly S African Breweries), 2001–. Dep. Chm., FIMBRA, 1984–85; Dir, SIB, 1986–93; Chm., London Investment Banking Assoc., 1994–98; Vice-Pres., BBA, 1994–98. Dir, Cancer Research Campaign, 1985–2000. Chm., Wilts Community Foundn, 1997–2002. Gov., Marlborough Coll., 2008–. Pres., Marlburian Club, 1999–2000. DL Wilts, 1999. *Recreations:* gardening, walking, shooting, saving pubs. *Address:* Chisenbury Priory, East Chisenbury, Pewsey, Wilts SN9 6AQ. *Clubs:* Boodle's, MCC.

MANSFIELD, family name of **Baron Sandhurst**.

MANSFIELD AND MANSFIELD, 8th Earl of, *cr* 1776 and 1792 (GB); **William David Mungo James Murray;** JP, DL; Baron Scone, 1605; Viscount Stormont, 1621; Baron Balvaird, 1641; (Earl of Dunbar, Viscount Drumcairn, and Baron Halldykes in the Jacobite Peerage); Hereditary Keeper of Bruce's Castle of Lochmaben; First Crown Estate Commissioner, 1985–95; *b* 7 July 1930; *o s* of 7th Earl of Mansfield and Mansfield, and of Dorothea Helena (*d* 1985), *y d* of late Rt Hon. Sir Lancelot Carnegie, GCVO, KCMG; *S* father, 1971; *m* 1955, Pamela Joan, *o d* of W. N. Foster, CBE; two *s* one *d*. *Educ:* Eton; Christ Church, Oxford. Served as Lieut with Scots Guards, Malayan campaign, 1949–50. Called to Bar, Inner Temple, 1958; Barrister, 1958–71. Mem., British Delegn to European Parlt, 1973–75; an opposition spokesman in the House of Lords, 1975–79; Minister of State: Scottish Office, 1979–83; NI Office, 1983–84. Mem., Tay Salmon Fisheries Bd, 1971–79. Director: General Accident, Fire and Life Assurance Corp. Ltd, 1972–79, 1985–98; American, then US Tracker, Trust, 1985–2002; Pinneys of Scotland, 1985–89; Ross Breeders Ltd, 1989–90. Ordinary Dir, Royal Highland and Agricl Soc., 1976–79. President: Fédn des Assocs de Chasse de l'Europe, 1977–79; Scottish Assoc. for Care and Resettlement of Offenders, 1974–79; Scottish Assoc. of Boys Clubs, 1976–79; Royal Scottish Country Dance Soc., 1977–2007; Chm., Scottish Branch, Historic Houses Assoc., 1976–79. Mem., Perth CC, 1971–75; Hon. Sheriff for Perthshire, 1974–; JP 1975, DL 1980, Perth and Kinross. Hon. Mem., RICS, 1994. *Publications:* articles on agriculture, land management and wine. *Heir:* *s* Viscount Stormont, *qv*. *Address:* Scone Palace, Perthshire PH2 6BE; 16 Thorburn House, Kinnerton Street, SW1X 8EX. *Clubs:* White's, Pratt's, Turf, Beefsteak.

MANSFIELD, Prof. Averil (Olive), (Mrs J. W. P. Bradley), CBE 1999; FRCS; FRCP; Professor of Vascular Surgery, Academic Surgical Unit, St Mary's Hospital and Imperial College School of Medicine (formerly St Mary's Hospital Medical School), 1993–2004, now Emeritus (Director, Academic Surgical Unit, 1993–99); Associate Medical Director, St Mary's Hospital, 2002–04 (Consultant Surgeon, 1982–2002); *b* 21 June 1937; *m* 1987, John William Paulton Bradley. *Educ:* Liverpool Univ. (MB 1960; ChM 1972). FRCS 1966; FRCP 2005. Consultant Surgeon: Royal Liverpool Hosp., 1972–80; Hillingdon Hosp., 1980–82; RPMS, subseq. ICSM, 1980–2002. Royal College of Surgeons: Chm., Court of Examrs, 1990–92; Mem. Council, 1990–2002; Vice-Pres., 1998–2000; President: Assoc. of Surgeons of GB and Ireland, 1992–93; Vascular Surgical Soc. of GB and Ireland, 1996–97; Sect. of Surgery, RSocMed, 1997–98. Vice-Chm., 2001–03, Chm., 2004–, Stroke Assoc. Hon. FRACS 1996; Hon. FACS 1998. Hon. MD Liverpool, 1994. *Publications:* Clinical Surgery in General, 1993; articles on vascular surgery. *Recreations:* playing the piano, walking in the Lake District, restoring old wrecks. *Address:* 31 Radnor Mews, W2 2SA.

MANSFIELD, David James; Director, Ingenious Media plc, since 2006; *b* 12 Jan. 1954; *m* 1979, Alison Patricia Pullin; two *s* one *d*. Gen. Sales Manager, Scottish TV, 1977–85; Sales and Marketing Dir, Thames TV, 1985–93; Capital Radio: Gp Commercial Dir, 1993–97; Gp Man. Dir, May–July 1997; Gp Chief Exec., Capitol Radio, then Chief Exec., GCap Media plc, 1997–2006. Non-executive Chairman: Rajar Ltd, 2007–; 1700 Gp plc, 2008–; non-executive Director: Carphone Warehouse plc, 2005–; Ingenious Ventures Ltd, 2006– (Mem., Adv. Bd, 2006).

MANSFIELD, Dr Eric Harold, FRS 1971; FREng, FRAeS, FIMA; Chief Scientific Officer (Individual Merit), Royal Aircraft Establishment, 1980–83; *b* 24 May 1923; *s* of Harold Goldsmith Mansfield and Grace Phundt; *m* 1947; two *s* one *d*; *m* 1974, Eunice Lily Kathleen Shuttleworth-Parker. *Educ:* St Lawrence Coll., Ramsgate; Trinity Hall, Cambridge (MA, ScD). Research in Structures Department, Royal Aircraft Establishment, Farnborough, Hants, 1943–83. Vis. Prof., Dept of Mechanical Engrg, Univ. of Surrey, 1984–90. Member: British Nat. Cttee for Theoretical and Applied Mechanics, 1973–79; Gen. Assembly of IUTAM, 1976–80; Council, Royal Soc., 1977–78. FREng (FEng 1976). James Alfred Ewing Gold Medal for Engrg Res., ICE, 1991; Royal Medal, Royal Soc., 1994. UK winner (with I. T. Minhinnick), World Par Bridge Olympiad, 1951. Member, Editorial Advisory Boards: Internat. Jl of Non-linear Mechanics, 1965–95; Internat Jl of Mechanical Scis, 1977–84. *Publications:* The Bending and Stretching of Plates, 1964, 2nd edn 1989; Bridge: The Ultimate Limits, 1986; contribs to: Proc. Roy. Soc., Phil. Trans., Quarterly Jl Mech. Applied Math., Aero Quarterly, Aero Research Coun. reports and memos, and to technical press. *Recreations:* duplicate bridge, palaeontology, snorkling. *Address:* Primrose Cottage, Alresford Road, Cheriton, Hants SO24 0QJ. *T:* (01962) 771280.

MANSFIELD, Guy Rhys John; QC 1994; a Recorder, since 1993; *b* 3 March 1949; *o s* of 5th Baron Sandhurst, DFC and Janet Mary (*née* Lloyd); *S* father, 2002 as 6th Baron Sandhurst, but does not use the title; *m* 1976, Philippa St Clair Verdon-Roe; one *s* one *d*. *Educ:* Harrow Sch.; Oriel Coll., Oxford (MA). Called to the Bar, Middle Temple, 1972 (Harmsworth Exhibnr, Winston Churchill Pupillage award); Bencher, 2000. Chm., Bar Council, 2005 (Member: Gen. Council of the Bar, 1998–2005; Gen. Mgt Cttee, 1998–2005; Chairman: Remuneration and Terms of Work (formerly Legal Aid and Fees) Cttee, 1998–99; Legal Services Cttee, 2000–03). Legal Assessor, GMC, 2000–06. Mem. Council, Justice, 2006–. *Publications:* (contrib.) Personal Injury Handbook, 1998, rev. edn 2001; (contrib.) Financial Provision in Family Matters, 1999–; (contrib.) An Introduction to Human Rights and the Common Law, 2000. *Recreations:* cricket, opera. *Heir:* *s* Hon. Edward James Mansfield, *b* 12 April 1982. *Address:* 1 Crown Office Row, Temple, EC4Y 7HH. *T:* (020) 7797 7500. *Clubs:* Reform, MCC; Leander (Henley-on-Thames).

MANSFIELD, Michael; QC 1989; Professor of Law, City University, since 2007; *b* 12 Oct. 1941; *s* of Frank Le Voir Mansfield and Marjorie Mansfield; *m* 1965, Melian Mansfield (*née* Bordes) (marr. diss. 1992); three *s* two *d*; 2nd, 1992, Yvette Vanson; one *s*. *Educ:* Highgate Sch.; Keele Univ. (BA Hons). Called to the Bar, Gray's Inn, 1967, Bencher, 2008. Estabd set of chambers of which head, 1984. Vis. Prof. of Law, Westminster Univ., 1997–. President: Nat. Civil Rights Movt; Haldane Soc.; Amicus. Hon. Fellow, Kent Univ., 1994. Hon. LLD: South Bank, 1995; Keele, 1995; Hertfordshire, 1995; Middx, 1999; Westminster, 2005; Ulster, 2006; Kent, 2007. *Publications:* Presumed Guilty, 1994; The Home Lawyer, 2003. *Recreations:* my children's interests. *Address:* 8 Warner Yard, Warner Street, EC4R 5EY. *T:* (020) 7405 8828.

MANSFIELD, Sir Peter, Kt 1993; FRS 1987; Professor of Physics, University of Nottingham, 1979–94, now Professor Emeritus; *b* 9 Oct. 1933; *s* of late Rose Lilian Mansfield (*née* Turner) and late Sidney George Mansfield; *m* 1962, Jean Margaret Kibble; two *d*. *Educ:* William Penn Sch., Peckham; Queen Mary Coll., London (BSc 1959, PhD 1962; Fellow, 1985). Research Associate, Dept of Physics, Univ. of Illinois, 1962–64; Lectr, Univ. of Nottingham, 1964, Sen. Lectr, 1968, Reader, 1970–79; Sen. Visitor, Max Planck Inst. für Medizinische Forschung, Heidelberg, 1972–73. Society of Magnetic Resonance in Medicine: Gold Medal, 1983; President, 1987–88. Founder FMedSci 1998. Hon. Member: Soc. of Magnetic Resonance Imaging, 1994; British Inst. of Radiology, 1993; Eur. Soc. of Magnetic Resonance in Medicine and Biol., 2002; Mem., Polish Acad. of Medicine, 2007; Hon. FRCR 1992; Hon. FInstP 1996; Hon. FRCP 2004; Hon. Fellow, Hughes Hall, Cambridge, 2004. Hon. MD Strasbourg, 1995; Hon. DSc: Kent, 1996; Nottingham, 2005; Leipzig, 2006; Warsaw, 2007; Hon. Dr Jagiellonian Univ., Krakow, 2000; DUniv Leicester, 2006. Sylvanus Thompson Lectr and Medal, 1988, Barclay Medal, 1993, British Inst. of Radiology; Gold Medal, Royal Soc. Wellcome Foundn, 1984; Duddell Medal and Prize, Inst. of Physics, 1988; Antoine Béclère Medal, Internat. Radiol Soc. and Antoine Béclère Inst., 1989; Mullard Medal and Award, Royal Soc., 1990; ISMAR Prize, 1992; Gold Medal, Eur. Assoc. of Radiol., 1995; Garmisch-Partenkirchen Prize for Magnetic Resonance Imaging, 1995; Rank Prize, 1997; (jtly) Nobel Prize for Physiology or Medicine, 2003; Nuffield Lectr and Gold Medal, RSocMed, 2006; Euromar Medal, Groupement Ampere, 2006; Galan Medal, Soc. of Apothecaries, 2006; Gold Medal, Medicas Magnus, Warsaw Univ., 2007; Mike Hogg Award, Univ. of Texas, 2007. *Publications:* NMR Imaging in Biomedicine (with P. G. Morris), 1982; (ed with E. L. Hahn) NMR Imaging, 1991; (ed) MRI in Medicine, 1995; papers in learned jls on nuclear magnetic resonance. *Recreations:* languages, reading, travel, flying (Private Pilot's Licence, Private Pilot's Licence for Helicopters). *Address:* Magnetic Resonance Centre, Department of Physics, University of Nottingham, Nottingham NG7 2RD. *T:* (0115) 951 4740, *Fax:* (0115) 951 5166.

MANSFIELD, Prof. Terence Arthur, FRS 1987; FIBiol; Professor of Plant Physiology, University of Lancaster, 1977–2001, now Emeritus; *b* 18 Jan. 1937; *s* of Sydney Walter Mansfield and Rose (*née* Sinfield); *m* 1963, Margaret Mary James; two *s*. *Educ:* Univ. of Nottingham (BSc); Univ. of Reading (PhD). FIBiol 1984. University of Lancaster: Lectr, then Reader, 1965–77; Dir, Inst. of Envmtl and Biol Scis, 1988–94; Provost of Sci. and Engrg, 1993–96. Member: AFRC, 1989–93; Eur. Envmtl Res. Orgn, 1994–. Hon. Fellow, Univ. of Lancaster, 2007. *Publications:* Physiology of Stomata, 1968; Effects of Air Pollutants on Plants, 1976; Stomatal Physiology, 1981; Plant Adaption to Environmental Stress, 1993; many contribs to books and jls in plant physiology. *Recreations:* cricket, hill walking, classical music. *Address:* 25 Wallace Lane, Forton, Preston, Lancs PR3 0BA. *T:* (01524) 791338. *Club:* Shireshead and Forton Cricket (Pres., 1993–2002).

MANSFIELD, Terence Gordon, CBE 2002; Director, 1993–2004, and a Vice President, 2000–04, Hearst Corporation USA; Consultant, Hearst Corporation UK, since 2003; *b* 3 Nov. 1938; *s* of Archer James Mansfield and Elizabeth Mansfield; *m* 1965, Helen Leonora Russell; two *d*. *Educ:* Maynard Road Jun. Sch., Essex; SW Essex Technical Sch. D. H. Brocklesby, Advertising Agents, 1954; S. H. Benson, Advertising Agents, 1956; served RAF, Christmas Island, 1957–59; Conde Nast Publications, 1960–66; Queen Magazine, 1966; National Magazine Co.: Advertisement Man., Harpers and Queen, 1969; Publisher, Harpers and Queen, 1975; Dep. Man. Dir, 1980, Pres. and CEO, 1982–2003, National

Magazine Co.; Chm., COMAG, 1984–2003; Dir, PPA, 1982–. Chm., MOBO Orgn Ltd, 2006–. Chm., Trng Bd, Periodicals Trng Council, 2000–. Member: Marketing Soc. 1975–; British Fashion Council, 1988–; Action Medical Research (formerly Action Res. for the Crippled Child, then Action Res.), 1989–; Chm., Bd of Trustees, Victim Support, 2002–05 (Mem., Adv. Bd, 1996–). Trustee: NewstrAid, 1966–; United World Coll., 1977–; St Bride's Church, 2001–. Chm., Graduate Fashion, 2006– (Vice Chm., 2005–06). Freeman, City of London, 1989; Liveryman, Stationers' & Newspaper Makers' Co., 1997–. MInstM 1969; MInstD 1976. FRSA. *Recreations:* family, running, walking dogs. *Address:* 5 Grosvenor Gardens Mews North, SW1W 0JP. *T:* (020) 7730 7740. *Clubs:* Mark's, Harry's Bar, Solus; Hanbury Manor.

MANSINGH, Lalit; Ambassador for India to the United States of America, 2001–04; *b* 29 April 1941; *s* of late Dr Mayadhar Mansingh and of Hemalata Mansingh; *m* 1976, Indira Singh; one *s* one *d.* *Educ:* Utkal Univ. (MA). Res. Fellow, Sch. of Internat. Studies, New Delhi, 1960–61; Lectr in Political Science, Utkal Univ., 1961–63; Indian Foreign Service: Probationer, 1963–64; Third, then Second Sec., Geneva, 1964–67; Under Secretary: Min. of External Affairs, 1967–69; Min. of Finance, 1969–71; Dep. Chief of Mission, Kabul, 1971–74; Dep. Sec., Min. of Finance, 1975–76; Dep. Chief of Mission, Brussels, 1976–80; Ambassador to UAE, 1980–83; Joint Secretary: Min. of External Affairs, 1983–84; Min. of Finance, 1984–85; Dir Gen., Indian Council for Cultural Relations, 1985–89; Dep. Chief of Mission, with rank of Ambassador, Washington, 1989–92; High Comr, Lagos, 1993–94; Dean, Foreign Service Inst., New Delhi, 1995–96; Sec. (West), Min. of External Affairs, 1997–98; High Comr in UK, 1998–99; Foreign Sec., Ministry for External Affairs, India, 1999–2001. *Publication:* (ed.-in-chief) Indian Foreign Policy: agenda for the 21st century, 2 vols, 1998. *Recreations:* art, culture. *Clubs:* Travellers; India International Centre, India Habitat Centre, Gymkhana (New Delhi); Bhubaneswar (Bhubaneswar); International Centre (Goa).

MANSON, Suzanne Maree; *see* Cotter, S. M.

MANSS, Thomas, FCSD; designer; Founder and Art Director, Thomas Manss & Company, since 1993; *b* Gütersloh, 11 July 1960; *s* of Karlheinz Manss and Ingrid Manss; two *s.* *Educ:* Luise Hensel Schule (primary); Evangelisch Stiftisches Gymnasium, Gütersloh; Fachhochschule Würzburg (Dipl Des). Metadesign, 1984–85; Sedley Place Design, 1985–89; Pentagram, 1989–93, Associate, 1992–93. Vis. Prof., Corporate Identity, Fachhochschule Potsdam, 1994–97. MSTD; FRSA. *Publications:* Ordnung & Eccentricity, 2002; contributed to: Design: wege zum erfolg, 1994; 26 Letters: illuminating the alphabet, 2004; Corporate Identity and Corporate Design, Neues Kompendium, 2007; Thomas Manss & Company, 2008. *Address:* Thomas Manss & Company, 3 Nile Street, N1 7LX; *web:* www.manss.com.

MANSTEAD, Prof. Antony Stephen Reid, DPhil; FBPsS; AcSS; Professor of Psychology, Cardiff University, since 2004; *b* 16 May 1950; *s* of Dr Stephen K. Manstead and Katharine E. Manstead; *m* 1997, Dr Stephanie van Goozen; one *s* one *d.* *Educ:* Univ. of Bristol (BSc Hons); Univ. of Sussex (DPhil). FBPsS 1989. Lectr in Social Psychol., Univ. of Sussex, 1974–76; Lectr, 1976–88, Sen. Lectr, 1988–90, Prof. of Psychol., 1990–92, Univ. of Manchester; Prof. of Social Psychol., Univ. of Amsterdam, 1992–2001; Prof. of Psychol. in the Social Scis, and Fellow of Wolfson Coll., Cambridge Univ., 2002–03. AcSS 2004. *Publications:* (jtly) The Accountability of Conduct: a social psychological analysis, 1983; (jtly) Introduction to Psychology: an integrated approach, 1984; (ed jtly) Handbook of Social Psychophysiology, 1989; (ed jtly) Blackwell Encyclopedia of Social Psychology, 1995; (ed jtly) Everyday Conceptions of Emotion, 1995; (ed jtly) Blackwell Reader in Social Psychology, 1997; (ed jtly) Emotions and Beliefs: how feelings influence thoughts, 2000; (ed jtly) Feelings and Emotions: the Amsterdam Symposium, 2004; (jtly) Emotion in Social Relations: cultural, group and interpersonal processes, 2005; (ed) Psychology of Emotions, 5 vols, 2008. *Recreation:* photography. *Address:* School of Psychology, Cardiff University, Tower Building, Park Place, Cardiff CF10 3AT.

MANT, Prof. David Clive Anthony, FRCP, FRCGP; Professor of General Practice and Fellow of Kellogg College, University of Oxford, since 1998. *Educ:* Churchill Coll., Cambridge (BA 1972; MA 1976); Birmingham Univ. (MB ChB 1977); London Sch. of Hygiene and Tropical Medicine (MSc (Community Medicine) 1983). MRCGP 1982, FRCGP 1999; MFPHM 1984; FRCP 1999. Trainee in gen. practice, E Oxford Health Centre, 1981–82; Registrar in Community Medicine, Oxford RHA, 1982–84; Clin. Lectr, 1984–93, and Sen. Scientist, Gen. Practice Res. Gp, 1987–93, Oxford Univ.; Prof. of Primary Care Epidemiology, Southampton University, 1993–98; Dir of R&D, S and W Reg., NHS Exec., DoH, 1996–98 (on secondment). Hon. Prof., Bristol Univ., 1996–98. FMedSci 1998.

MANTEL, Hilary Mary, (Mrs G. McEwen), CBE 2006; author; *b* 6 July 1952; *d* of Henry Thompson and Margaret Mary Thompson (*née* Foster, later Mrs Jack Mantel); *m* 1973, Gerald McEwen. *Educ:* London Sch. of Econs; Sheffield Univ. (BJur). PLR Adv. Cttee, 1997–2003. Vis. Prof., Sheffield Hallam Univ., 2006–. FRSL 1990; FEA 2007. Hon. Fellow, RHUL, 2008. Hon. LittD Sheffield, 2005. Shiva Naipaul Meml Prize, 1987; Winifred Holtby Award, RSL, 1990; Southern Arts Literature Prize, 1990; Cheltenham Fest. Prize, 1990. *Publications:* Every Day is Mother's Day, 1985; Vacant Possession, 1986; Eight Months on Ghazzah Street, 1988; Fludd, 1990; A Place of Greater Safety (Book of Year Award, Sunday Express), 1992; A Change of Climate, 1994; An Experiment in Love, 1995 (Hawthornden Prize for Literature, 1996); The Giant, O'Brien, 1998; Giving Up the Ghost: a memoir, 2003 (Book of the Year Award, MIND, 2005); Learning to Talk (short stories), 2003; Beyond Black, 2005 (Yorkshire Post Fiction Prize, 2006). *Recreation:* sleeping. *Address:* A. M. Heath & Co., 6 Warwick Court, Holborn, WC1R 5DJ.

MANTELL, Carl Nicholas; Command Secretary, Air Command, Ministry of Defence, since 2007; *b* 2 Feb. 1954; *s* of Charles Henry Purchase Mantell and Edna Joyce Mantell (*née* Bracey); *m* 1978, Janet Swinford Martin (separated); two *s* one *d.* *Educ:* Berkhamsted Sch.; Pembroke Coll., Cambridge (MA). Joined MoD, 1977; Asst Private Sec. to Minister of State for Armed Forces, 1982–83; Principal (procurement finance, procurement policy, Army equipment planning), 1983–92; Hd of Resources and Progs (Mgt Planning), 1992–94; Sec. to Support Mgt Gp, RAF Logistics Comd, 1994–97; Hd of Resources and Progs (Air), 1997–99; Dir, Capability Resources and Scrutiny, 1999–2002; Dir Gen., Central Budget, 2002–05; Command Secretary: RAF PTC, 2005–06; RAF Strike Comd/PTC, 2006–07. *Recreations:* reading, particularly history, military modelling, listening to music. *Address:* c/o Air Command, RAF High Wycombe, Bucks HP14 4UE. *T:* (01494) 497667; *e-mail:* carl.mantell635@mod.uk.

MANTELL, Rt Hon. Sir Charles (Barrie Knight), Kt 1990; PC 1997; a Surveillance Commissioner, 2006–June 2009; a Lord Justice of Appeal, 1997–2004; *b* 30 Jan. 1937; *s* of Francis Christopher Knight Mantell and Elsie Mantell; *m* 1960, Anne Shirley Mantell; two *d.* *Educ:* Manchester Grammar Sch.; Manchester Univ. (LLM). Called to the Bar, Gray's Inn, 1960, Bencher, 1990. Flying Officer, RAF, 1958–61. In practice at Bar, London and Manchester, 1961–82; a Recorder of the Crown Court, 1978–82; QC 1979; Judge of Supreme Court, Hong Kong, 1982–85; a Circuit Judge, 1985–90; Judge, High Court of Justice, QBD, 1990–97; Presiding Judge, Western Circuit, 1993–96; Judge of Courts of Appeal, Jersey and Guernsey, 2004–07; Justice of Appeal, Bermuda, 2005–07. Alternative Chm., Security Commn, 1999–; Chairman: Proscribed Orgns Appeal Commn, 2002–; Pathogens Access Appeal Commission, 2002–. *Recreations:* reading, watching cricket. *Club:* Hong Kong (Hong Kong).

MANTHORPE, John Jeremy, CB 1994; Chief Executive, 1985–96, and Chief Land Registrar, 1990–96, HM Land Registry; *b* 16 June 1936; *s* of William Broderick and Margaret Dora Manthorpe; *m* 1967, Kathleen Mary Ryan; three *s* one *d.* *Educ:* Beckenham and Penge Grammar School. HM Land Registry: Plans Branch, 1952; Principal Survey and Plans Officer, 1974; Controller (Registration), 1981–85. CCMI (CIMgt 1994); Hon. RICS (Hon. ARICS 1992). *Recreations:* walking and watching the Ashdown Forest. *Address:* Beurles, Fairwarp, Uckfield, East Sussex TN22 3BG. *T:* (01825) 712795.

MANTLE, Rt Rev. John Ambrose Cyril; *see* Brechin, Bishop of.

MANTLE, Richard John; General Director, Opera North, since 1994; *b* 21 Jan. 1947; *s* of late George William Mantle, OBE and Doris Griffiths; *m* 1970, Carol June Mountain. *Educ:* Tiffin Sch.; Ealing Coll. of Advanced Technology. Personnel Officer, Beecham Group, 1969–72; Associate Dir, J. Walter Thompson Co., 1973–79; Personnel Dir, then Dep. Man. Dir, ENO, 1980–85; Man. Dir, Scottish Opera, 1985–91; Gen. Dir, Edmonton Opera, Canada, 1991–94. Mem. Adv. Council, RSCM, 2000–. Chm., St Mary and St Anne Abbotts Bromley Foundn, 1999–. A Guardian, Shrine of Our Lady of Walsingham, 1998–. *Recreations:* music, reading, the country, English churches. *Address:* Cleveland House, Barrowby Lane, Kirkby Overblow, Harrogate, N Yorks HG3 1HQ. *T:* (01423) 815924, *Fax:* (01423) 815926; *e-mail:* richardmantle@aol.com. *Club:* Athenæum.

MANTON, 4th Baron *cr* 1922, of Compton Verney; **Miles Ronald Marcus Watson;** *b* 7 May 1958; *s* of 3rd Baron Manton and of Mary Elizabeth, twin *d* of Major T. D. Hallinan; *S* father, 2003; *m* 1984, Elizabeth, *e d* of J. R. Story; two *s* one *d.* *Educ:* Eton. Major, Life Guards. *Heir: s* Hon. Thomas Nigel Charles David Watson, *b* 19 April 1985.

MANTON, Prof. Nicholas Stephen, PhD; FRS 1996; FInstP; Professor of Mathematical Physics, since 1998, and Head of High Energy Physics Group, Department of Applied Mathematics and Theoretical Physics, since 2002, University of Cambridge; Fellow, St John's College, Cambridge, since 1997; *b* 2 Oct. 1952; *s* of Franz Eduard Sigmund Manton and Lily Manton (*née* Goldsmith); *m* 1989, Terttu Anneli Aitta; one *s.* *Educ:* Dulwich Coll.; St John's Coll., Cambridge (BA, MA, PhD 1978). FInstP 1996. Joliot-Curie Fellow, Ecole Normale Supérieure, Paris, 1978–79; Res. Fellow, MIT, 1979–81; Asst Res. Physicist, Inst. for Theoretical Physics, Univ. of Calif, Santa Barbara, 1981–84; Cambridge University: Lectr, 1987–94; Reader in Mathematical Physics, 1994–98; St John's College: Sen. Res. Student, 1985–87; Dir of Studies in Applied Maths, 1997–98; Mem., Coll. Council, 2006–. Vis. Prof., Inst. for Theoretical Physics, SUNY, Stony Brook, 1988; Scientific Associate, CERN, Geneva, 2001. Mem. Prog. Cttee, Internat. Centre for Mathematical Scis, Edinburgh, 2005–. Chm., Res. Meetings Cttee, London Mathematical Soc., 2008–. Mem., British Team, Internat. Mathematical Olympiad, 1971. Jun. Whitehead Prize, London Mathematical Soc., 1991. *Publications:* (with P. M. Sutcliffe) Topological Solitons, 2004; papers in mathematical and theoretical physics in various jls incl. Nuclear Physics, Physics Letters, Physical Rev., Communications in Mathematical Physics, Jl of Mathematical Physics, and conf. proceedings. *Recreations:* music, Finland and its culture. *Address:* Department of Applied Mathematics and Theoretical Physics, Centre for Mathematical Sciences, University of Cambridge, Wilberforce Road, Cambridge CB3 0WA. *T:* (01223) 765000; St John's College, Cambridge CB2 1TP.

MANUELLA, Sir Tulaga, GCMG 1996; MBE 1981; Governor General, Tuvalu, 1994–98; Chancellor, University of the South Pacific, 1997–2000; *b* 26 Aug. 1936; *s* of Teuhu Manuella and Malesa Moevasa; *m* 1957, Milikini Uinifaleti; two *s* three *d.* *Educ:* primary sch., Ocean Is. Gilbert and Ellice Islands Colony: sub-accountant and ledger keeper, 1953–55; clerical officer, 1955–57; Sen. Asst, then Asst Accountant, Treasury, 1957–75; Tuvalu Government: Asst Accountant, Accountant, then Actg Financial Sec., Min. of Finance, 1976–84; Financial Secretary, Financial Division: Church of Tuvalu, 1984–86; Pacific Conf. of Churches, Suva, Fiji, 1987–91; Co-ordinator of Finance and Admin, Ekalesia Kelisiano, Tuvalu, 1992–94. Patron, Pacific Islands Soc. in Britain and Ireland, 1995. *Address:* PO Box 50, Vaiaku, Funafuti, Tuvalu.

MANWARING, Randle (Gilbert), DSL; poet and author; retired company director; *b* 3 May 1912; *s* of late George Ernest and Lilian Manwaring; *m* 1st, 1941, Betty Violet (*d* 2001), *d* of H. P. Rout, Norwich; three *s* one *d*; 2nd, 2002, Mary Ratcliffe (*née* Blackburn). *Educ:* private schools; Keele Univ. (MA 1982); Mellen Univ. (DSL 2002). Joined Clerical, Medical and Gen. Life Assce Soc., 1929. War service, RAF, 1940–46, W/Cdr; comd RAF Regt in Burma, 1945. Clerical, Medical & Gen. Pensions Rep., 1950; joined C. E. Heath & Co. Ltd, 1956: Asst Dir, 1960, Dir, 1964, Man. Dir. 1969; Founder Dir (Man.), C. E. Heath Urquhart (Life and Pensions), 1966–71, and a Founder Dir, Excess Life Assce Co., 1967–75; Dir, Excess Insurance Group, 1975–78; Insurance Adviser, Midland Bank, 1971; first Man. Dir, Midland Bank Ins. Services, 1972–74, Vice-Chm., 1974–77, Dir, 1977–78. Chm., Life Soc., Corp. of Insce Brokers, 1965–66; Dep. Chm., Corp. of Insce Brokers, 1970–71; Pres., Soc. of Pensions Consultants, 1968–70. Chairman of Governors: Luckley-Oakfield Sch., 1972–83; Northease Manor Sch., 1972–84. Diocesan Reader (Chichester), 1968–, now Emeritus; Mem., C of E Evangelical Council, 1980–82; Lay Pres., Chichester Diocesan Evangelical Union, 1989–91; Mem., Diocesan Synod, 1985–98; Lay Chm., Uckfield Deanery Synod, 1993–99; Churchwarden, St Peter-upon-Cornhill, London, 1985–90. Chm., Vine Books Ltd; Dir, Crusaders Union Ltd, 1960–91 (Vice-Pres., 1983–). Vice-Pres., RAF Regt, 1990–. Chm. of Trustees, Careforce, 1980–87. Chm., Probus Club, Uckfield, 1989–90. *Publications:* The Heart of this People, 1954; A Christian Guide to Daily Work, 1963; Thornhill Guide to Insurance, 1976; The Run of the Downs, 1984; From Controversy to Co-existence, 1985; The Good Fight, 1990; A Study of Hymnwriting and Hymnsinging in the Christian Church, 1991; (for children) The Swallows, the Fox and the Cuckoo, 1998; Songs of the spirit in Poetry and Hymnology, 2004; On the Road to Mandalay, 2006; *poems:* Posies Once Mine, 1951; Satires and Salvation, 1960; Under the Magnolia Tree, 1965; Slave to No Sect, 1966; Crossroads of the Year, 1975; From the Four Winds, 1976; In a Time of Unbelief, 1977; Poem Prayers for Growing People, 1980; The Swifts of Maggiore, 1981; In a Time of Change, 1983; Collected Poems, 1986; Some Late Lark Singing, 1992; Love So Amazing, 1995; Trade Winds, 2001; Poems of the Spirit, 2004; The Making of a Minor Poet, 2007; contrib. poems and articles to learned jls in GB and Canada; contrib. hymns to several hymn books. *Recreations:* music, reading, following cricket. *Address:* Marbles Barn, Newick, Lewes, East Sussex BN8 4LG. *T:* (01825) 723845. *Clubs:* Royal Air Force, MCC; Sussex County Cricket, Sussex Martlets.

MANZE, Andrew; violinist, conductor and broadcaster; Principal Conductor, Helsingborg Symphony Orchestra, since 2006; *b* 14 Jan. 1965; *s* of Vincent and Ann

Manze. *Educ:* Bedford Sch.; Clare Coll., Cambridge (MA Classics). Violinist specialising in repertoire 1610–1830; broadcaster, BBC Radio 3, 1994–; Associate Dir, Acad. of Ancient Music, 1996–2003; Artist in Residence, Swedish Chamber Orch., 2001–; Artistic Dir, The English Concert, 2003–07. Many recordings incl. Biber Sonatas (Gramophone Award, 1996), Pandolfi Sonatas (Gramophone Award 2000) and music by Bach, Handel, Vivaldi, etc. *Recreations:* music, classics. *Address:* c/o Intermusica Artists' Management, 16 Duncan Terrace, N1 8BZ; *e-mail:* bemmerson@intermusica.co.uk.

MANZIE, Sir (Andrew) Gordon, KCB 1987 (CB 1983); Second Permanent Secretary and Chief Executive, Property Services Agency, Department of the Environment, 1984–90; *b* 3 April 1930; *s* of late John Mair and Catherine Manzie; *m* 1955, Rosalind Clay (*d* 2008); one *s* one *d*. *Educ:* Royal High Sch. of Edinburgh; London Sch. of Economics and Political Science (BScEcon; Hon. Fellow, 2003). Joined Civil Service as Clerical Officer, Scottish Home Dept, 1947. National Service, RAF, 1949. Min. of Supply: Exec. Officer (Higher Exec. Officer, 1957). Private Sec. to Perm. Sec., Min. of Aviation, 1962; Sen. Exec. Officer, 1963; Principal, 1964; Sec. to Cttee of Inquiry into Civil Air Transport (Edwards Cttee), 1967; Asst Sec., Dept of Trade and Industry, on loan to Min. of Posts and Telecommunications, 1971; Dept of Industry, 1974; Under-Sec., Dir, Office for Scotland, Depts of Trade and Industry, 1975; Under Sec., Scottish Economic Planning Dept, 1975–79; Dir, Industrial Develt Unit, 1980–81, Dep. Sec., 1980–84, Dept of Industry (Dept of Trade and Industry, 1983–84). Chairman: Anglo Japanese Construction Ltd, 1990–95; Forthspan Ltd, 1993–97; Thistle Water, 1995–97; Yorkshire Link Ltd, 1996–97; Director: Altnacraig Shipping, 1990–96; Motherwell Bridge Hldgs, 1990–97; Trafalgar House Construction Hldgs Ltd, later Kvaerner Construction, 1991–97; Trafalgar House, later Kvaerner, Corporate Develt Ltd, 1991–97; Altnamara Shipping plc, 1994–2002; Mem., Adv. Bd, LEK Partnership, 1992–2000. Gov., LSE, 1994–2005, now Emeritus (Mem., Standing Cttee and Council, 1995–2001). Trustee, Stort Trust, 1990–2001; Pres., Bishop's Stortford Caledonian Soc., 1987–93. CCMI (CBIM 1987); Hon. FCIOB 1990. *Recreations:* golf, reading, watching Rugby football. *Address:* 28 Manor Links, Bishop's Stortford, Herts CM23 5RA. *T:* (01279) 651960. *Club:* Caledonian.
See also S. G. Manzie.

MANZIE, Stella Gordon, CBE 2007 (OBE 2001); Director General, Finance and Corporate Services, Scottish Government, since 2008; *b* 13 June 1960; *d* of Sir (Andrew) Gordon Manzie, *qv* and late Rosalind (*née* Clay). *Educ:* Herts and Essex High Sch. for Girls, Bishop's Stortford; Fettes Coll., Edinburgh; Newnham Coll., Cambridge (MA English 1982); Poly. of Central London (Postgrad. DPA); Univ. of Birmingham (MSocSci 1992). Admin. Asst, ACC, 1982–84; Admin. Officer, SOLACE, 1984–86; Team Leader, Mgt Effectiveness Unit, Birmingham CC, 1987–88; Mgt Consultant, Price Waterhouse Mgt Consultants, 1988–92; Borough Dir, Redditch BC, 1992–97; Chief Executive: W Berks Council, 1997–2001; Coventry CC, 2001–08. Kieron Walsh Meml Prize, Birmingham Univ., 1997. *Recreations:* eating, drinking, socialising, travel, watching sport, reading.

MANZINI, Raimondo; Italian Ambassador to the Court of St James's, 1968–75; *b* Bologna, 25 Nov. 1913. *Educ:* Univ. of California (Berkeley); Clark Univ., Mass. (MA); Dr of Law, Bologna Univ. Entered Diplomatic Service, 1940; served San Francisco, 1940–41; Lisbon, 1941–43; Min. of Foreign Affairs in Brindisi, Salerno, Rome, 1943–44; London, 1944–47; Consul General for Congo, Nigeria and Gold Coast, 1947–50; Consul General, Baden Baden, 1951–52; Head of Information Service, CED, Paris, 1952–53; Ministry of Foreign Affairs, 1953–55; Adviser to the Minister of Foreign Trade, 1955–58; Chef de Cabinet of Minister for Foreign Affairs, 1958; Diplomatic Adviser to the Prime Minister, 1958–59; Advr to Minister of Industry, 1960–64; Perm. Rep. to OECD, Paris, 1965–68; Sec.-Gen., Min. of Foreign Affairs, 1975–78. Gran Croce, Ordine Merito Repubblica, 1968; Hon. GCVO 1969; Commandeur, Légion d'Honneur (France), 1976. *Address:* Villa Bellochio, 83 Boulevard de Garavan, Menton, France.

MANZOOR, Zahida Parveen, CBE 1998; Legal Services Ombudsman, since 2003, and Legal Services Complaints Commissioner, since 2004, for England and Wales; *b* 25 May 1958; *d* of Nazir Ahmed and Mahroof Ahmed; *m* 1984, Dr Madassar Manzoor; two *d*. *Educ:* Leeds Univ. (HVCert 1983); Bradford Univ. (MA Applied Social Studies 1989). Student nurse to Staff Nurse, W Suffolk AHA, 1977–80 (SRN 1980); Staff Nurse, then Staff Midwife, Birmingham AHA, 1980–82 (SCM 1981); Health Visitor, Durham AHA, 1983–84; Lectr, Thomas Danby Coll., 1984–86 and 1987–88; NE Regl Prog. Dir, Common Purpose Charitable Trust, 1990–92; Chm., Bradford HA, 1992–97; Regl Chm., Northern and Yorks Regl Office, NHS, DoH, 1997–2001. Co-founder and Dir, Intellisys Ltd, 1996–2003. Comr and Dep. Chm., CRE, 1993–98. Ind. Assessor, FCO, 1998–. Mem., Race Equality Adv. Panel, Home Office, 2003–. Mem., Bradford Congress, 1992–96; Dir, Bradford City Challenge, 1993–96. Trustee: W Yorks Police Community Trust, 1996–98; Uniting Britain Trust, 1996–; NSPCC, 1997–. Mem. Ct, Univ. of Bradford, 1992–98; Governor: Sheffield Hallam Univ., 1991–93; Bradford and Airedale Coll. of Health, 1992–93; Keighley Coll., 1994–95. Vice-Patron, Regl Crime Stoppers, 1998. Hon. DSc Bradford, 1999; Hon. Dr Leeds Metropolitan, 2003. *Recreations:* antiques, gardening, painting, historic buildings. *Address:* Legal Services Ombudsman's Office, 3rd Floor, Sunlight House, Quay Street, Manchester M3 3JZ.

MAOATE, Sir Tuamure Terep, KBE 2007; Deputy Prime Minister, Cook Islands, since 2005; *b* Rarotonga, Cook Is, 1 Sept. 1934; *m* 1959, Marito Mapu; five *s* one *d*. *Educ:* Fiji Sch. of Medicine (Med. Officer 1954); Auckland Univ. (Dip. Obstetrics 1973); Amsterdam Univ. (MA Public Health 1976). Gen. surgeon and Dir, Clin. Services, 1976–82. MP, Cook Is, 1983–; Minister of Health and Agric., 1983–89; Dep. Prime Minister, 1985–89; Leader of Opposition, 1998–99; Prime Minister, 1999–2002; Leader of Opposition, 2002–03; Dep. Prime Minister, 2003–04; Leader of Opposition, 2004–05. Pres., Cook Is Golden Oldies Rugby Assoc. Patron: Ngatangiia/Matavera Sports Assoc.; Ngatangiia Cook Is Christian Ch Youth. *Recreations:* Rugby, cricket, fishing, reading, tennis, table tennis, sailing. *Address:* PO Box 26, Maire Nui Drive, Rarotonga, Cook Islands. *T:* 29030, *Fax:* 29056; *e-mail:* drmaoate@dpmoffice.gov.ck.

MAPLE, Graham John; District Judge, Principal Registry of Family Division, High Court of Justice, 1991–2005; *b* 18 Dec. 1947; *s* of Sydney George and Thelma Olive Maple; *m* 1974, Heather Anderson; two *s*. *Educ:* Shirley Secondary Modern Sch.; John Ruskin Grammar Sch., Croydon; Bedford Coll., London (LLB 1973). Lord Chancellor's Dept, 1968; Sec., Principal Registry of Family Div., 1989. Member: Outer London, Court Service Cttee, 1991–96; Family Courts Forum, 1996–2005. Chm., Tenterden Counselling Service, 2007–; Mem., Ind. Monitoring Bd, HM Prison/YOI East Sutton Park, 2006–. Church Warden, St Mildred Parish Church, Tenterden, 1992–98. Consulting Editor, Rayden and Jackson on Divorce and Family Matters, 1998–2007. *Publications:* (Co-Editor) Rayden and Jackson on Divorce, 12th edn 1974, to 17th edn 1998; (Co-Editor) The Practitioner's Probate Manual, 21st edn 1979; (ed) Holloway's Probate Handbook, 8th edn 1987. *Recreations:* archaeology, Roman Britain, steam and model railways. *Address:* Westbrook, Elmfield, Tenterden, Kent TN30 6RE.

MAPLES, John Cradock; MP (C) Stratford-on-Avon, since 1997; *b* 22 April 1943; *s* of late Thomas Cradock Maples and Hazel Mary Maples; *m* 1986, Jane Corbin; one *s* one *d*. *Educ:* Marlborough Coll., Wiltshire; Downing Coll., Cambridge; Harvard Business Sch., USA. Called to the Bar, Inner Temple, 1965. Chm. and Chief Exec., Saatchi & Saatchi Govt Communications Worldwide, 1992–96; Chm., Rowland Sallingbury Casey, 1994–96. MP (C) W Lewisham, 1983–92; contested (C) W Lewisham, 1992. PPS to Financial Sec. to HM Treasury, 1987–90; Econ. Sec. to HM Treasury, 1990–92; Opposition front bench spokesman on health, 1997–98, on defence, 1998–99, on foreign affairs, 1999–2000; a Dep. Chm., Cons. Party, 1994–95 and 2006–07. *Recreations:* sailing, ski-ing. *Address:* House of Commons, SW1A 0AA.

MAPP, Derek; DL; Chairman, Sport England, 2006–07; *b* 17 May 1950; *s* of Thomas Mapp and Edna Mapp; *m* 1971, Karen Edmands; two *s* one *d*. *Educ:* Oakwood Primary Sch.; Boteler Grammar Sch. Dir, Mansfield Brewery, 1981–91; Founder and CEO, Tom Cobleigh plc, 1992–97; Chairman: Leapfrog Day Nurseries, 1998–2004; Imagesound plc, 2005–; Dir, Mapp Develts Ltd, 1996–. Non-executive Chairman: Staffline Recruitment plc, 2005–; Priority Sites Ltd, 2006–07; non-exec. Dir, 1998–, Chm., 2008–, Informa (formerly Taylor and Francis) plc (Sen. Ind. Dir, 2005–08). Chairman: E Midlands Develt Agency, 1998–2004; Mem. Bd, English Partnerships, 1998–2004. DL Derbys, 2006. Hon. DTech Loughborough, 2004; Hon. Dr Lincoln, 2004. *Recreations:* sport, reading.

MAR, Countess of (*suo jure*, 31st in line from Ruadri, 1st Earl of Mar, 1115); Premier Earldom of Scotland by descent; Lady Garioch, *c* 1320; **Margaret of Mar;** *b* 19 Sept. 1940; *er d* of 30th Earl of Mar, and Millicent Mary Salton; *S* father, 1975; recognised in surname "of Mar" by warrant of Court of Lord Lyon, 1967, when she abandoned her second forename; *m* 1st, 1959, Edwin Noel Artiss (marr. diss. 1976); one *d*; 2nd, 1976, (cousin) John Salton (marr. diss. 1981); 3rd, 1982, J. H. Jenkin, MA (Cantab), FRCO, LRAM, ARCM. Lay Mem., Immigration Appeal Tribunal, 1985–2006. Mem., EU Sub-Cttee on environment, health and consumer affairs, H of L, 1995–99, 2001–05; Dep. Speaker, H of L, 1997–2007; elected Mem., H of L, 1999. Chm., Honest Food, 2000–05. Chm., Environmental Medicine Foundn, 1997–2003. Pres., Guild of Agricl Journalists, 2007–. Patron: Dispensing Doctors' Assoc., 1985–96; Worcs Mobile Disabled Gp, 1991–2003; Gulf Veterans Assoc., 1995–; Pres., Elderly Accommodation Counsel, 1994–; patron of several ME/CFS charities. Specialist cheese maker. Governor, King's Sch., Gloucester, 1984–87. Hon. ARCVS 2006; Hon. Associate, BVA, 2007. *Heir: d* Mistress of Mar, *qv*. *Address:* St Michael's Farm, Great Witley, Worcester WR6 6JB. *T:* (01299) 896608.

MAR, Mistress of; Lady Susan Helen of Mar; interior designer; *b* 31 May 1963; *d* and *heiress* of Countess of Mar, *qv*; *m* 1989, Bruce Alexander Wyllie; two *d*. *Educ:* King Charles I School, Kidderminster; Christie College, Cheltenham. *Address:* Firethorn Farm Cottage, Plough Lane, Ewhurst Green, Cranleigh, Surrey GU6 7SG.

MAR, 14th Earl of, *cr* 1565, **and KELLIE,** 16th Earl of, *cr* 1619; **James Thorne Erskine;** DL; Baron Erskine, 1429; Viscount Fentoun, 1606; Baron Dirleton, 1603; Baron Erskine of Alloa Tower (Life Peer), 2000; Premier Viscount of Scotland; Hereditary Keeper of Stirling Castle; *b* 10 March 1949; *s* of 13th Earl of Mar and 15th Earl of Kellie, and Pansy Constance Erskine, OBE (*d* 1996); *S* father, 1993; *m* 1974, Mrs Mary Mooney, *yr d* of Dougal McD. Kirk. *Educ:* Eton; Moray Coll. of Education, 1968–71; Inverness Coll. (building course, 1987–88). Page of Honour to the Queen, 1962, 1963. Community Service Volunteer, York, 1967–68; Community Worker, Richmond-Craigmillar Parish Church, Edinburgh, 1971–73; Sen. Social Worker, Family and Community Services, Sheffield District Council, 1973–76; Social Worker: Grampian Regional Council, Elgin, 1976–77, Forres, 1977–78; Highland Regional Council, Aviemore, 1979; HM Prison, Inverness, 1979–81; Inverness W, Aug.–Dec. 1981; Community Worker, Merkinch Centre, Inverness, Jan.–July 1982; Community Service Supervisor, Inverness, 1983–87; building technician, 1989–91; project worker, SACRO Intensive Probation Project, Falkirk, 1991–93; boatbuilder, 1993. Sits in H of L as Lib Dem; Mem., H of L Select Cttee on Constitution, 2001–04, on Religious Offences, 2002–03. Contested (Lib Dem) Ochil, Scottish Parly elecn, 1999. Chm., Strathclyde Tram Inquiry, 1996; Parly Comr, Burrell Collection (lending) Inquiry, 1997. Pilot Officer, RAuxAF, 1979, attached to 2622 Highland Sqdn, RAuxAF Regt; Flying Officer, RAuxAF, 1982–86; RNXS, 1985–89. DL Clackmannan, 1991. *Recreations:* canoeing, hill walking, railways, gardening, restoration of Alloa Tower. *Heir: b* Hon. Alexander David Erskine [*b* 26 Oct. 1952; *m* 1977, Katherine Shawford, *e d* of Thomas Clark Capel; one *s* one *d*]. *Address:* Hilton Farm, Alloa, Scotland FK10 3PS. *Club:* Farmers'.

MARAN, Prof. Arnold George Dominic, MD; FRCS, FRCSE, FRCPE, FACS; Professor of Otolaryngology, University of Edinburgh, 1988–2000; *b* 16 June 1936; *s* of John and Hilda Maran; *m* 1962, Anna De Marco; one *s* one *d*. *Educ:* Daniel Stewart's Coll., Edinburgh; Univ. of Edinburgh (MB, ChB 1959; MD 1963); Univ. of Iowa. FRCSE 1962; FACS 1974; FRCPE 1989; FRCS 1991. Basic trng in surgery, Edinburgh, followed by specialty head and neck trng, Univ. of Iowa; consultant otolaryngologist, Dundee Royal Infirmary, 1967–73; Prof. of Otolaryngology, W Virginia Univ., 1974–75; consultant otolaryngologist, Royal Infirmary of Edinburgh, 1975–88. Chm., Intercollegiate Bd in Otolaryngology, 1988–91; Sec., Conf. of Royal Colls, Scotland, 1992. Royal College of Surgeons of Edinburgh: Hon. Treasurer, 1976–81; Mem. Council, 1981–86; Hon. Sec., 1988–92; a Vice-Pres., 1995–97; Pres., 1997–2000. President: Scottish Otolaryngol Soc., 1991–92; Laryngology Section, RSM, 1990. Sixteen visiting professorships; sixteen eponymous lectures. Hon. FDSRCS 1995; Hon. FCS(SoAf) 1997; Hon. FCSHK 1997; Hon. Fellow, Acad. of Medicine, Singapore, 1998; Hon. FRSocMed 2002. Hon. Member: S African Otolaryngol Soc., 1986; S African Head and Neck Soc., 1986; Irish Otolaryngol Soc., 1990 (Wilde Medal, 1990); Assoc. of Surgeons of India, 1991. Hon. DSc Hong Kong, 2004. Yearsley Medal, 1985, Semon Medal, 1990, London Univ.; Jobson Horne Prize, BMA, 1985; W. J. Harrison Prize, 1989, Howells Prize, 1991, RSM; Leon Goldman Medal, Univ. of Cape Town, 1994. Order of Gorka Dakshina Bahu (Nepal), 1998. *Publications:* Head and Neck Surgery, 1972, 4th edn 2000; Clinical Otolaryngology, 1979; Clinical Rhinology, 1990; Head and Neck Surgery for the General Surgeon, 1991; (ed) Logan Turner's Diseases of Nose, Throat and Ear, 11th edn, 1992; The Voice Doctor, 2005; Mafia: inside the dark heart, 2008; contribs to 14 textbooks; 150 articles. *Recreations:* writing, golf, playing jazz, purloining pencils. *Address:* 2 Orchard Brae, Edinburgh EH4 1NY. *T:* (0131) 332 0055; 2 Double Dykes Road, St Andrews KY16 9DX. *T:* (01334) 472939. *Clubs:* New (Edinburgh); Royal and Ancient Golf (St Andrews); Bruntsfield Golfing Society (Edinburgh).

MARBER, Patrick; writer and director; *b* 19 Sept. 1964; *s* of Brian Marber and Angela (*née* Benjamin). *Educ:* Wadham Coll., Oxford. *Plays:* Dealer's Choice, RNT and Vaudeville, 1995 (Writers' Guild and Evening Standard Awards, 1995); After Miss Julie, BBC, 1995; Closer, RNT, 1997, transf. Lyric, 1998, NY, 1999 (Evening Standard, Time Out, Critic's Circle and Olivier Best Play Awards, 1998), filmed 2005; Howard Katz, 2001, The Musicians, 2004, RNT. *Publications:* Dealer's Choice, 1995; After Miss Julie, 1995; Closer, 1997; Howard Katz, 2001.

MARCH AND KINRARA, Earl of; Charles Henry Gordon Lennox; DL; *b* 8 Jan. 1955; *s* and *heir* of Duke of Richmond, Lennox and Gordon, *qv*; *m* 1st, 1976, Sally (marr.

diss. 1989), *d* of late Maurice Clayton and of Mrs Denis Irwin; one *d*; 2nd, 1991, Hon. Janet Elizabeth, *d* of 3rd Viscount Astor and of Bronwen, *d* of His Honour Sir (John) Alan Pugh; three *s* one *d* (of whom one *s* one *d* are twins). *Educ:* Eton. DL W Sussex, 2006. *Heir: s* Lord Settrington, *qv*. *Address:* Goodwood House, Chichester, West Sussex PO18 0PY.

MARCH, Lionel John, ScD; Professor of Design and Computation, School of the Arts and Architecture, University of California, Los Angeles, 1994–2003, now Emeritus; *b* 26 Jan. 1934; *o s* of late Leonard James March and Rose (*née* Edwards); *m* 1st, 1960, Lindsey Miller (marr. diss. 1984); one *s* two *d*; 2nd, 1984, Maureen Vidler; one step *s* two step *d*. *Educ:* Hove Grammar Sch. for Boys; Magdalene Coll., Cambridge (MA, ScD). FIMA, FRSA. Nat. Service: Sub-Lt, RNVR, 1953–55. Harkness Fellow, Commonwealth Fund, Harvard Univ. and MIT, 1962–64; Asst to Sir Leslie Martin, 1964–66; Lectr in Architecture, Univ. of Cambridge, 1966–69; Dir, Centre for Land Use and Built Form Studies, Univ. of Cambridge, 1969–73; Prof., Dept of Systems Design, Univ. of Waterloo, Ontario, 1974–76; Prof. of Design, Faculty of Technology, Open Univ., 1976–81; Rector and Vice-Provost, RCA, 1981–84; Prof., Grad. Sch. of Architecture and Urban Planning, 1984–94, Hd of Architecture/Urban Design Prog. 1984–91, UCLA. Chm., Applied Res. of Cambridge Ltd, 1969–73. Mem., Governing Body, Imperial Coll. of Science and Technology, 1981–84. General Editor (with Leslie Martin), Cambridge Urban and Architectural Studies, 1970–; Founding Editor, Environment and Planning B, Planning and Design, 1974–. *Publications:* (with Philip Steadman) The Geometry of Environment, 1971; (ed with Leslie Martin) Urban Space and Structures, 1972; (ed) The Architecture of Form, 1976; (ed with Judith Sheine) R. M. Schindler: composition and construction, 1993; Architectonics of Humanism, 1998. *Address:* Spring Cottage, 20 High Street, Stretham, Ely CB6 3JQ. *T:* (01353) 649891.

MARCH, Prof. Norman Henry; Coulson Professor of Theoretical Chemistry, University of Oxford, 1977–94; Fellow of University College, Oxford, 1977–94, Emeritus since 1994; *b* 9 July 1927; *s* of William and Elsie March; *m* 1949, Margaret Joan Hoyle (*d* 1994); two *s*. *Educ:* King's Coll., London Univ. University of Sheffield: Lecturer in Physics, 1953–57; Reader in Theoretical Physics, 1957–61; Prof. of Physics, 1961–72; Prof. of Theoretical Solid State Physics, Imperial Coll., Univ. of London, 1973–77. Hon. DTech Chalmers, Gothenburg, 1980; Hon. DPhys Catania, Italy, 2003. *Publications:* The Many-Body Problem in Quantum Mechanics (with W. H. Young and S. Sampanthar), 1967; Liquid Metals, 1968; (with W. Jones) Theoretical Solid State Physics, 1973; Self-Consistent Fields in Atoms, 1974; Orbital Theories of Molecules and Solids, 1974; (with M. P. Tosi) Atomic Dynamics in Liquids, 1976; (with M. Parrinello) Collective Effects in Solids and Liquids, 1983; (with S. Lundqvist) The Theory of the Inhomogeneous Electron Gas, 1983; (with M. P. Tosi) Coulomb Liquids, 1984; (with M. P. Tosi) Polymers, Liquid Crystals and Low-Dimensional Solids, 1984; (with R. A. Street and M. P. Tosi) Amorphous Solids and the Liquid State, 1985; Chemical Bonds outside Metal Surfaces, 1986; (with P. N. Butcher and M. P. Tosi) Crystalline Semiconducting Materials and Devices, 1986; (with B. M. Deb) The Single Particle Density in Physics and Chemistry, 1987; (with S. Lundqvist and M. P. Tosi) Order and Chaos in Nonlinear Physical Systems, 1988; (with J. A. Alonso) Electrons in Metals and Alloys, 1989; Liquid Metals, 1990; Chemical Physics of Liquids, 1990; Electron Density Theory of Atoms and Molecules, 1992; (with J. F. Mucci) Chemical Physics of Free Molecules, 1993; Electron Correlation in Molecules and Condensed Phases, 1996; (with L. S. Cederbaum and K. C. Kulander) Atoms and Molecules in Intense External Fields, 1997; Electron Correlation in the Solid State, 1999; (with C. W. Lung) Mechanical Properties of Metals, 1999; (with M. P. Tosi) Introduction to Liquid State Physics, 2002; many scientific papers on quantum mechanics and statistical mechanics in Proceedings Royal Society, Phil. Magazine, Phys. Rev., Jl of Chem. Phys, etc. *Recreations:* music, chess, cricket. *Address:* 66A Lancaster Road, Carnforth, Lancs LA5 9LE.

MARCH, Valerie, (Mrs Andrew March); *see* Masterson, V.

MARCHAMLEY, 4th Baron *cr* 1908; **William Francis Whiteley;** *b* 27 July 1968; *o s* of 3rd Baron Marchamley and of Sonia Kathleen Pedrick; *S* father, 1994; *m* 2000, Amy, *yr d* of Douglas Kyle; one *s* one *d*. *Heir: s* Hon. Leon Whiteley, *b* 2004.

MARCHANT, Clare Wynne; Director of Social Services and Housing, London Borough of Bromley, 1993–2000; *b* 13 June 1941; *d* of Rev. Glyn Morgan and Elma Morgan; *m* 1980, Harold Marchant. *Educ:* Horley Endowed Sch.; Banbury Grammar Sch.; UC Wales, Aberystwyth (BA Hons Philosophy 1963); UC Wales, Cardiff (DipSocSc 1964); Birmingham Univ. (Dip. Applied Social Sci. 1965). London Borough of Lewisham: Child Care Officer, 1965–67; Team Leader, 1967–71; Social Services Dist Officer, 1971–74; Principal Social Worker, 1974–87; Asst Dir (Social Services), RBK&C, 1987–93. *Recreations:* writing, genealogy, local history, photography, enjoying myself, local environmental issues. *Address:* Shaftesbury House, 15 Royal Circus Street, Greenwich, SE10 8SN.

MARCHANT, Graham Leslie; JP; arts management consultant, since 1989; General Manager, Contemporary Dance Trust, 1994–98; *b* 2 Feb. 1945; *s* of late Leslie and Dorothy Marchant. *Educ:* King's School, Worcester; Selwyn College, Cambridge (MA). Administrator, Actors' Company, 1973–75; General Manager, English Music Theatre, 1975–78; Gen. Administrator, Opera North, 1978–82; Administrator, Tricycle Theatre, 1983–84; Chief Exec., Riverside Studios, 1984; Managing Dir, Playhouse Theatre Co., 1985–86; Dir, Arts Co-ordination, Arts Council, 1986–89; Head of Site Improvement, South Bank Centre, 1989–92. Director: Ballet Rambert Ltd, 1991–93; Lyric Theatre (Hammersmith) Trust, 1993–97; Chairman: London Dance Network, 1998–99; Nat. Dance Co-ordinating Cttee, 2000–03; Director: Shobana Jeyasingh Dance Co., 1999–2001. Trustee, Chichester Fest. Th., 2005–06. JP Thames 2003. *Recreations:* reading, gardening. *Address:* 43 Canonbury Square, N1 2AW.

MARCHANT, Ian Derek; Chief Executive, Scottish and Southern Energy plc, since 2002; *b* 9 Feb. 1961; *s* of Derek William and Rosemary Marchant; *m* 1986, Elizabeth Helen; one *s* one *d*. *Educ:* Trinity Sch., Croydon; Durham Univ. (BA Econs). ACA. Accountant: PricewaterhouseCoopers, 1983–92 (on secondment to Dept of Energy, 1989–90); Southern Electric: Corporate Finance Manager, 1992–96; Finance Dir, 1996–98; Finance Dir, Scottish and Southern Energy plc, 1998–2002. *Recreations:* golf, Rugby, including refereeing minis. *Address:* Scottish and Southern Energy plc, Inveralmond House, 200 Dunkeld Road, Perth PH1 3AQ.

MARCHANT, Ronald John, CB 2007; Chief Executive and Comptroller General, Patent Office, 2004–07; *b* 6 Nov. 1945; *s* of Arthur and Bridget Marchant; *m* 1969, Helen Ruth Walker; one *s* three *d*. *Educ:* West Ham Coll. of Technol. (BSc Hons (Chem.)). Patent Office: Examr, 1969–90; Principal Examr, 1990–92; Dir, Patents, 1992–2004. FRSA. *Recreations:* hill walking, reading.

MARCHBANK, Pearce, RDI 2004; graphic designer, since 1969; Principal Partner, design consultancy, Studio Twenty (formerly Pearce Marchbank Studio), London, since 1980; *b* 14 June 1948; *s* of late Harold George Marchbank and of Rachel Pearce Marchbank; *m* 1st, 1975, Sue Miles (marr. diss. 1981); one *s* one *d*; 2nd, 1985, Heather Page (marr. diss. 1996); two *s*; partner, Katherine Cornford. *Educ:* Bedford Sch.; Luton Coll. of Art; Central Sch. of Art and Design (BA 1st Cl. Hons). Art Director: Architectural Design mag., 1969–70; Rolling Stone mag., London, 1970; Friends mag., 1970–71; Co-ed. and designer, OZ mag., 1971 and 1974; design of complete editl set-up, style and logo, 1971–74, cover designer, 1971–80 and 1982–84, Time Out mag.; Design Dir, Music Sales music publishers, 1974–93 (incl. design of all music books for The Beatles); Dir, Omnibus Press, 1976–79; Design Consultant, Virgin Records, 1978–80; Dir and Designer, Virgin Books, 1979–81; Co-ed. and Design Dir, Event mag., 1980–81; cover designs for Marxism Today mag. up to final issue, 1990–92; Co-ed. and Designer, Les Routiers (UK), 2000–03; Designer, John Lewis Partnership own-brand packaging designs, 2003–. Clients include: nat. newspapers (designs for mag. sections of Independent, The Times, Guardian, 1988–89); art galls (Berkeley Sq. Gall., Christie's Fine Art); music publishers, Chester Music and Novello & Co. (incl. CDs and books for Phillip Glass, Sir John Tavener, Michael Nyman); restaurant designs (Zanzibar, Bank, Corney & Barrow, Opus Birmingham); wine (John Armit, Christian Moueix, Tate Modern, Le Nez Rouge). *Publications:* The Wall Sheet Journal, 1969; The Illustrated Rock Almanac, 1977; (ed) With The Beatles, 1982. *Recreations:* digital photography, medieval and Modern Movement architecture, driving in Europe. *Address:* Studio Twenty, 167 Foundling Court, Brunswick Centre, Marchmont Street, WC1N 1AN. *T:* (020) 7837 0022; *e-mail:* studiotwenty@btclick.com.

MARCHWOOD, 3rd Viscount *cr* 1945, of Penang and of Marchwood, Southampton; **David George Staveley Penny;** Bt 1933; Baron 1937; Managing Director, 1987–2004, Chairman, 1997–2004, Moët Hennessy UK Ltd (formerly Moët & Chandon (London) Ltd); *b* 22 May 1936; *s* of 2nd Viscount Marchwood, MBE and Pamela (*d* 1979), *o d* of John Staveley Colton-Fox; *S* father, 1979; *m* 1st, 1964, Tessa Jane (*d* 1997), *d* of W. F. Norris; three *s*; 2nd, 2001, Sylva, *widow* of Peter Willis Fleming. *Educ:* Winchester College. 2nd Lt, Royal Horse Guards (The Blues), 1955–57. Joined Schweppes Ltd, 1958, and held various positions in the Cadbury Schweppes group before joining Moët & Chandon. *Recreations:* Real tennis, golf, shooting, racing. *Heir: s* Hon. Peter George Worsley Penny [*b* 8 Oct. 1965; *m* 1995, Annabel, *d* of Rex Cooper; one *s* one *d*]. *Address:* Woodcock Farm, Chedington, Dorset DT8 3JA. *Club:* MCC.

MARCKUS, Melvyn; Consultant, Cardew Group (formerly Cardew & Co.), since 1998; *b* 1 Jan. 1944; *s* of late Norman Myer Marckus and Violet Frances Mary Marckus (*née* Hughes); *m* 1st, 1970, Rosemary Virden (marr. diss. 1985); one *s* one *d*; 2nd, 1987, Rachel Mary Frances, *d* of Lord King of Wartnaby. *Educ:* Worthing Grammar Sch. Journalist: Scotsman, 1962–66; Daily Mail, 1966–67; Guardian, 1967; Daily Mail, 1967–70; Daily Express, 1970–72; Sunday Telegraph, 1972–82 (Jt Dep. City Editor, 1979–82); Observer, 1982–93: City Editor, 1982–93; Editor, Observer Business, 1984–93; an Asst Editor, 1987; Exec. Dir, 1987; City Editor, The Times, 1993–96; Columnist, The Express, 1996–99. Consultant, Luther Pendragon, 1996–98. *Recreations:* fishing, films, literature. *Address:* Cardew Group, 12 Suffolk Street, SW1Y 4HG.

MARCUS, Prof. Rudolph Arthur; Arthur Amos Noyes Professor of Chemistry, California Institute of Technology, since 1978; *b* Montreal, 21 July 1923; *s* of Meyer Marcus and Esther Marcus (*née* Cohen); *m* 1949, Laura Hearne (*d* 2003); three *s*. *Educ:* McGill Univ. (BSc Chemistry 1943; PhD 1946; Hon. DSc 1988). Postdoctoral research: NRCC, Ottawa, 1946–49; Univ. of N Carolina, 1949–51; Polytechnic Institute, Brooklyn: Asst Prof., 1951–54; Associate Prof., 1954–58; Prof., 1958–64; Acting Head, Div. of Phys. Chem., 1961–62; Prof., 1964–78, Head, Div. of Phys. Chem., 1967–68, Univ. of Illinois. Vis. Prof. of Theoretical Chem., Univ. of Oxford, 1975–76; Linnett Vis. Prof. of Chem., Univ. of Cambridge, 1996; Hon. Professor: Fudan Univ., Shanghai, 1994–; Inst. of Chem., Chinese Acad. of Scis, Beijing, 1995–; Ocean Univ. of China, 2002–; Tianjin Univ., 2002–; Dist. Affiliated Prof., Tech. Univ. of Munich, 2008–. Mem., Sci. Cttees and Nat. Adv. Cttees, incl. External Adv. Bd, Nat. Sci. Foundn Center for Photoinduced Charge Transfer, 1990–; Internat. Advr in Chem., World Scientific Publishing, 1987; mem., numerous editl bds; Lectr, USA, Asia, Australia, Canada, Europe, Israel, USSR. Mem., Nat. Acad. of Sciences and other learned bodies; Foreign Member: Royal Soc., 1987; RSCan, 1993; Chinese Acad. of Scis, 1998. Hon. MRSC; Hon. Member: Internat. Soc. of Electrochemistry; Korean Chemical Soc., 1996. Hon. Fellow, UC, Oxford, 1995. Hon. DSc Oxford, 1995. Prizes incl. Wolf Prize in Chem., 1985; Nat. Medal of Science, 1989; Nobel Prize in Chem., 1992. *Publications:* contribs to sci jls, incl. articles on electrochemistry, electron transfer, unimolecular reactions, enzymes, quantum dots. *Recreations:* tennis, ski-ing, music. *Address:* Noyes Laboratory of Chemical Physics, Caltech 127–72, Pasadena, CA 91125, USA. *T:* (626) 3956566; 331 S Hill Avenue, Pasadena, CA 91106–3405, USA.

MARDELL, Mark Ian; European Political Editor, BBC, since 2005; *b* 10 Sept. 1957; *s* of Donald and Maureen Mardell; *m* 1990, Joanne Veale; two *s* one *d*. *Educ:* Priory Sch., Banstead; Epsom Coll.; Univ. of Kent at Canterbury (BA Hons Politics 1979). Journalist: Radio Tees, 1980–82; Radio Aire, 1982; Indep. Radio News, 1983–87; Industrial Ed. and Reporter, Sharp End (C4), 1987–89; Political Corresp., BBC, 1989–93; Political Ed., Newsnight, 1993–2000; Political Corresp., BBC News at Six, 2000–03; Chief Political Corresp., BBC News, 2003–05. Writer, Radio 4 short story, Judgement Day, 2004. *Publication:* How to Get On in TV (for children), 2001. *Recreations:* reading, music, swimming, cooking. *Address:* BBC Brussels, International Press Centre, Boulevard Charlemagne 1 (Boîte 50), 1041 Brussels, Belgium.

MARDER, His Honour Bernard Arthur; QC 1977; a Circuit Judge, 1983–98; President of the Lands Tribunal, 1993–98 (Member, 1989–98); *b* 25 Sept. 1928; *er s* of late Samuel and Marie Marder; *m* 1953, Sylvia Levy (MBE 1988); one *s* one *d*. *Educ:* Bury Grammar Sch.; Manchester Univ. (LLB 1951). Called to the Bar, Gray's Inn, 1952. A Recorder of the Crown Court, 1979–83. Formerly Asst Comr, Local Govt and Parly Boundary Commns; Chairman: Panel of Inquiry into W Yorks Structure Plan, 1979; Mental Health Review Tribunals, 1987–89. Pres., Land Inst., 1997–99. Mem. Bd, Orange Tree Theatre, 1986–; Trustee: Richmond Parish Lands Charity, 1987–96 (Chm., 1993–96); Richmond Museum, 1996–2003; Petersham Meadows Trust, 1999–. Hon. FSVA 1994; Hon. RICS 1999. *Recreations:* music, theatre, wine, walking.

MAREK, John, PhD; Member for Wrexham, National Assembly for Wales, 1999–2007 (Lab 1999–2003, Ind 2003–07); *b* 24 Dec. 1940; *m* 1964, Anne Pritchard (*d* 2006). *Educ:* King's Coll. London (BSc (Hons), PhD). Lecturer in Applied Mathematics, University College of Wales, Aberystwyth, 1966–83. MP (Lab) Wrexham, 1983–2001. Opposition frontbench spokesman: on health, 1985–87; on treasury and economic affairs, and on the Civil Service, 1987–92. Dep. Presiding Officer, Nat. Assembly for Wales, 2000–07. *Publications:* various research papers. *Address: e-mail:* wxm1@fsmail.net.

MARGADALE, 3rd Baron *cr* 1964, of Islay, co. Argyll; **Alastair John Morrison;** DL; *b* 4 April 1958; *er s* of 2nd Baron Margadale, TD and of Clare (*née* Barclay); *S* father, 2003; *m* 1st, 1988, Lady Sophia Louise Sydney Murphy (marr. diss. 1999), *yr d* of 11th Duke of

Devonshire, KG, PC, MC and of Dowager Duchess of Devonshire, *qv;* one *s* one *d;* 2nd, 1999, Mrs Amanda Wace, *d* of Michael Fuller. *Educ:* Harrow; RAC Cirencester. DL Wilts 2003. *Heir: s* Hon. Declan James Morrison, *b* 11 July 1993. *Address:* Estate Office, Fonthill Bishop, Salisbury, Wilts SP3 5SH.

See also Viscount Trenchard.

MARGÁIN, Hugo B., Hon. GCVO 1975; Ambassador of Mexico to the United States, 1965–70 and 1977–82; *b* 13 Feb. 1913; *s* of Cesar R. Margáin and Maria Teresa Gleason de Margáin; *m* 1941, Margarita Charles de Margáin; two *s* three *d* (and one *s* decd). *Educ:* National Univ. of Mexico (UNAM); National Sch. of Jurisprudence (LLB). Prof. of Constitutional Law, 1947, of Constitutional Writs, 1951–56, and of Fiscal Law, 1952–56, Univ. of Mexico. Govt posts include: Dir-Gen., Mercantile Transactions Tax, 1951–52, and Dir-Gen., Income Tax, 1952–59, Min. for Finance. Official Mayor, Min. for Industry and Commerce, 1959–61; Dep. Minister of Finance, Sept. 1961–Dec. 1964; Sec. of Finance, Aug. 1970–May 1973; Ambassador to the UK, 1973–77. Chm., Nat. Commn on Corporate Profit-Sharing (ie labour participation), 1963–64; Govt Rep. on Bd of Nat. Inst. for Scientific Res., 1962–63 (Chm. of Bd, 1963–64). Holds hon. degrees from univs in USA. *Publications:* Avoidance of Double Taxation Based on the Theory of the Source of Taxable Income, 1956; Preliminary Study on Tax Codification, 1957; (with H. L. Gumpel) Taxation in Mexico, 1957; Civil Rights and the Writ of Amparo in Administrative Law, 1958; The Role of Fiscal Law in Economic Development, 1960; Profit Sharing Plan, 1964; Housing Projects for Workers (Infonavit), 1971. *Recreations:* riding, swimming. *Address:* Fujiyama No 745, Col. Las Aguilas, Del. Alvaro Obregón, México 01710 DF, México.

MARGERISON, Thomas Alan; author, journalist and broadcaster on scientific subjects; Consultant, British Nuclear Forum, since 1989; *b* 13 Nov. 1923; *s* of late Ernest Alan Margerison and Isabel McKenzie; *m* 1950, Pamela Alice Tilbrook; two *s. Educ:* Huntingdon Grammar Sch.; Hymers Coll., Hull; King's Sch., Macclesfield; Sheffield University. Research Physicist, 1949; film script writer, Film Producers Guild, 1950; Scientific Editor, Butterworths sci. pubns, Ed. Research, 1951–56; Man. Editor, Heywood Pubns and National Trade Press, 1956. First Scientific Editor, The New Scientist, 1956–61; Science Corresp., Sunday Times, 1961; Dep. Editor, Sunday Times Magazine, 1962; Man. Dir, Thomson Technical Developments Ltd, 1964; Dep. Man. Dir, 1967–69, Chief Exec., 1969–71, London Weekend Television; Dir, 1966, Chm., 1971–75, Computer Technology Ltd. Formerly Dir, Nuclear Electricity Information Gp. Chm., Communications Cttee, UK Nat. Commn for UNESCO. Worked for many years with Tonight team on BBC. Responsible for applying computers to evening newspapers in Reading and Hemel Hempstead. *Publications:* articles and television scripts, indifferent scientific papers; (ed) popular science books. *Recreation:* sailing. *Club:* Savile.

MARGESSON, family name of **Viscount Margesson.**

MARGESSON, 2nd Viscount *cr* 1942, of Rugby; **Francis Vere Hampden Margesson;** *b* 17 April 1922; *o s* of 1st Viscount Margesson, PC, MC, and Frances H. Leggett (*d* 1977), New York; *S* father, 1965; *m* 1958, Helena, *d* of late Heikki Backstrom, Finland; one *s* three *d. Educ:* Eton; Trinity Coll., Oxford. Served War of 1939–45, as Sub-Lt, RNVR. A Director of Thames & Hudson Publications, Inc., New York, 1949–53. ADC to Governor of the Bahamas, 1956; Information Officer, British Consulate-General, NY, 1964–70. *Heir: s* Major the Hon. Richard Francis David Margesson, Coldstream Guards [*b* 25 Dec. 1960; *m* 1990, Wendy Maree, *d* of James Hazelton]. *Address:* 63 The Hills, Port Ewen, New York, NY 12466, USA.

MARGETSON, Sir John (William Denys), KCMG 1986 (CMG 1979); HM Diplomatic Service, retired; *b* 9 Oct. 1927; *yr s* of Very Rev. W. J. Margetson and Marion Jenoure; *m* 1963, Miranda, *d* of Sir William Menzies Coldstream, CBE and Mrs Nancy Spender; one *s* one *d. Educ:* Blundell's; St John's Coll., Cambridge (choral scholar; MA). Lieut, Life Guards, 1947–49. Colonial Service, District Officer, Tanganyika, 1951–60 (Private Sec. to Governor, Sir Edward Twining, subseq. Lord Twining, 1956–57); entered Foreign (subseq. Diplomatic) Service, 1960; The Hague, 1962–64; speech writer to Foreign Sec., Rt Hon. George Brown, MP, 1966–68; Head of Chancery, Saigon, 1968–70; Counsellor 1971, seconded to Cabinet Secretariat, 1971–74; Head of Chancery, UK Delegn to NATO, 1974–78; Ambassador to Vietnam, 1978–80; seconded to MoD as Senior Civilian Instructor, RCDS, 1981–82; Ambassador and Dep. Perm. Rep. to UN, NY, and Pres., UN Trusteeship Council, 1983–84; Ambassador to the Netherlands, 1984–87; Special Rep. of the Sec. of State for For. and Commonwealth Affairs, 1994–98. Gentleman Usher of the Blue Rod, 1992–2002. Dir, John S. Cohen Foundn, 1988–93. Chm., Foster Parents Plan (UK), 1988–90. Patron, Suffolk Internat. Trade Gp, 1988–90; Jt Pres., Suffolk and SE Cambridgeshire 1992 Club, 1988–90. Chairman: RSCM, 1988–94; Jt Cttee, London Royal Schs of Music, 1991–94; Yehudi Menuhin Sch., 1990–94; Trustee: Fitzwilliam Museum Trust, 1990–98; Ouseley Trust, 1991–97; Music in Country Churches, 1993–2000. Hon. RCM 1992; FRSCM 1994. *Recreation:* music. *Address:* 71b Cumberland Street, Woodbridge, Suffolk IP12 4AG. *Club:* Brooks's.

MARGETTS, Prof. Helen Zerlina, PhD; Professor of Society and the Internet, Oxford Internet Institute, University of Oxford, since 2004; Fellow, Mansfield College, Oxford, since 2004; *b* 15 Sept. 1961; *d* of James David Margetts and Helen Jill Scott Margetts (*née* Taylor); partner, Dr Pedro Mascuñán Pérez; one *s. Educ:* Univ. of Bristol (BSc Maths 1983); London Sch. of Econs and Pol Sci. (MSc Politics and Public Policy 1990; PhD Govt 1996). Computer programmer/systems analyst, Rank Xerox, 1984–87; Systems Analyst, Amoco Oil Co., 1987–90; Res. Officer, Dept of Govt, LSE, 1991–94; Lectr, then Sen. Lectr in Politics, Dept of Politics and Sociol., Birkbeck Coll., Univ. of London, 1994–99; University College London: Reader, 1999–2001; Prof. of Pol Sci., 2001–04; Dir, Sch. of Public Policy, 2001–04. *Publications:* (ed jtly) Turning Japanese: Britain with a permanent party of government, 1994; (jtly) Making Votes Count: replaying the 1990s General Elections under alternative electoral systems, 1997; Information Technology in Government: Britain and America, 1998; (with P. Dunleavy) Government on the Web, 1999; (with P. Dunleavy) Proportional Representation for Local Government: an analysis, 1999; (jtly) Voices of the People, 2001, 2nd edn 2005; (ed jtly) Challenges to Democracy: ideas, involvement and institutions, 2001; (with P. Dunleavy) Government on the Web II, 2002; (with P. Dunleavy) Digital Era Governance: IT corporations, the State, and e-government, 2006; (with C. Hood) The Tools of Government in the Digital Age, 2007; contrib. articles to learned jls, incl. Public Admin, Public Policy and Admin, British Jl Politics and Internat. Relns, Internat. Review of Pol Sci., Political Studies, Governance, Jl Public Admin Res. and Theory, Parly Affairs, Jl Theoretical Politics, Internat. Review of Admin. Scis. *Recreations:* art, playing with my son, horses. *Address:* Oxford Internet Institute, University of Oxford, One St Giles, Oxford OX1 3JS. *T:* (01865) 287210, *Fax:* (01865) 287211; *e-mail:* Helen.Margetts@oii.ox.ac.uk.

MARGETTS, Sir Rob(ert John), Kt 2006; CBE 1996; FREng; FIChemE; Chairman: Legal & General Group PLC, since 2000 (Vice Chairman, 1998–2000); Ensus Ltd, since 2006; Chairman, Energy Technologies Institute, since 2007; *b* 10 Nov. 1946; *s* of John William and Ellen Mary Margetts; *m* 1969, Joan Sandra Laws; three *s* one *d. Educ:* Highgate Sch.; Trinity Hall, Cambridge (BA Natural Scis and Chem. Engrg). FIChemE 1985; FREng (FEng 1988). Joined ICI, 1969: Process Design Engr, Agricl Div., Billingham, 1969; subseq. various managerial posts, including: Director: Agricl Div., 1982–85; Petrochemicals and Plastics Div., 1985; Res. and Ops, ICI Chemicals and Polymers Gp, 1987; ICI PLC: Dir, ICI Engrg, 1987–89; Gen. Manager, Personnel, 1989–90; Chm. and Chief Exec., Tioxide Gp PLC, 1991–92; Exec. Dir, 1992–97; Vice Chm., 1998–2000; Chm., ICI Pension Fund Trustee Ltd, 1994–2000. Non-exec. Dir, 1996–, Chm., Audit Cttee, 1998–2000, Legal & Gen. Gp PLC; Vice Chm., 2001–02, Chm., 2002–06, BOC Gp PLC; non-executive Director: English China Clays PLC, 1992–99; Anglo American PLC, 1999– (Chm., Remuneration Cttee, 2001–; Sen. Ind. Dir, 2003–08); Falck Renewables plc, 2007–; Chm. Europe, Huntsman Corp. (USA), 2000–; Mem., Internat. Adv. Bd, Teijin, Japan, 2004–. Chm., NERC, 2001–06. Chm., Govt Industry Forum on Non-Food Crops, 2001–04. Dir, Foundn for Sci. and Technol., 2001–. Gov., and Mem. Finance Cttee, ICSTM, 1991–2004; Member: Bd, CEFIC, 1993–95 and 1998–2000; Council, CIA, 1993–96 and 2001–; Council for Sci. and Technol., 1998–2007; Adv. Cttee on Business and the Envmt, 1999–2001; Chm., Action for Engrg, 1995–97; Trustee, Council for Ind. and Higher Educn, 1992–. Vice-Pres., Royal Acad. of Engrg, 1994–97. Mem. Ct, Univ. of Surrey, 2002–. Trustee, Brain Res. Trust, 2002–. Hon. Freeman, Salters' Co., 2004. FCGI 2001. Hon. FIC 1999; Hon. Fellow, Univ. of Cardiff, 2007. Hon. DEng Sheffield, 1997; Hon. DSc Cranfield, 2003. *Recreations:* sailing, ski-ing, tennis, watersports. *Address:* Legal & General Group PLC, One Coleman Street, EC2R 5AA.

MARGOLYES, Miriam, OBE 2002; actress; *b* 18 May 1941; *d* of late Dr Joseph Margolyes and Ruth (*née* Walters). *Educ:* Oxford High Sch.; Newnham Coll., Cambridge; Guildhall Sch. of Music and Drama (LGSM 1959). *Films* include: Rime of the Ancient Mariner, 1976; Stand Up, Virgin Soldiers, 1977; Little Shop of Horrors, 1986; The Good Father, 1987; Body Contact, 1987; Little Dorrit, 1988; Pacific Heights, 1990; I Love You to Death, 1990; The Butcher's Wife, 1991; As You Like It, 1992; Ed and His Dead Mother, 1993; The Age of Innocence, 1993; Immortal Beloved, 1994; Babe, 1995; Balto, 1995; James and the Giant Peach, 1996; Romeo and Juliet, 1996; Different for Girls, 1996; The IMAX Nutcracker, 1997; The First Snow of Winter, 1998; Left Luggage, 1998; Sunshine, 1999; Dreaming of Joseph Lees, 1999; End of Days, 1999; House!, 2000; Cats and Dogs, 2001; Harry Potter and the Chamber of Secrets, 2002; Being Julia, 2003; Ladies in Lavender, 2004; Life and Death of Peter Sellers, 2004; *theatre* includes: Dickens' Women (one-woman show), Duke of York's, 1991; She Stoops to Conquer, Queen's, 1993; The Killing of Sister George, Ambassador's, 1995; Wicked, Apollo, 2007, NY, 2008; *television* includes: Take a Letter Mr Jones, A Kick Up the Eighties, The History Man, 1981; Blackadder, 1983, 1986, 1988; Oliver Twist, 1985; Poor Little Rich Girl, 1987; The Life and Loves of a She Devil, 1990; Frannie's Turn, 1992; Cold Comfort Farm, 1995; The Phoenix and the Carpet, 1997; Supply & Demand, 1998; Vanity Fair, 1998; Dickens in America, Wallis and Edward, 2005; *radio performances* include The Queen and I, 1993. Best Supporting Actress, LA Critics Circle, 1989; Best Supporting Actress, BAFTA, 1993. *Recreations:* reading, talking, eating, Italy. *Address:* c/o United Agents, 12–26 Lexington Street, W1F 0LE.

MARGRIE, Victor Robert, CBE 1984; FCSD; studio potter; *b* 29 Dec. 1929; *s* of Robert and Emily Miriam Margrie; *m* 1st, 1955, Janet Smithers (marr. diss. 2005); three *d;* 2nd, 2005, Rosemary Ash. *Educ:* Southgate County Grammar Sch.; Hornsey Sch. of Art (NDD, ATD 1952). FSIAD 1975. Part-time teaching at various London art colls, 1952–56; own workshop, making stoneware and latterly porcelain, 1954–71; Head of Ceramics Dept, Harrow Sch. of Art, 1956–71 (founded Studio Pottery Course, 1963); Sec., Crafts Adv. Cttee, 1971–77; Dir, Crafts Council, 1977–84; Professorial appt, RCA, 1984–85; own studio, Bristol, 1985. One-man exhibns, British Craft Centre (formerly Crafts Centre of GB), 1964, 1966 and 1969; represented in V&A Mus., Ashmolean Mus. and other collections. Vice-Chm., Crafts Centre of GB, 1965; Member: Cttee for Art and Design, DATEC, 1979–84; Cttee for Art and Design, CNAA, 1981–84; Design Bursaries Bd, RSA, 1980–84; Working Party, Gulbenkian Craft Initiative, 1985–88; Fine Art Adv. Cttee, British Council, 1983–86; UK National Commn for UNESCO, 1984–85 (also Mem., Culture Adv. Cttee); Adv. Council, V&A Mus., 1979–84; Craftsmen Potters Assoc., 1960–89; Internat. Acad. of Ceramics, 1972–; Cttee, Nat. Video and Electronic Archive of the Crafts, 1993–. Ext. Examiner, Royal Coll. of Art: Dept of Ceramics and Glass, 1977; Dept of Silversmithing and Jewellery, 1978–80; Ext. Advisor, Dept of Ceramics, UWE (formerly Bristol Polytechnic), 1987–; Mem., Bd of Studies in Fine Art, Univ. of London, 1989–94; Advr, Faculty of Fine Art, Cardiff Inst. of Higher Educn, 1992–94; Vis. Prof., Univ. of Westminster (formerly Poly. of Central London), 1992–96. Governor: Herts Coll. of Art and Design, 1977–79; Camberwell Sch. of Art and Crafts, 1975–84; W Surrey Coll. of Art and Design, 1978–87; Loughborough Coll. of Art and Design, 1984–89, 1990–93. Associate Editor: Studio Pottery, 1993–2000; Ceramics in Society, 2000–05. *Publications:* contributed to: Oxford Dictionary of Decorative Arts, 1975; Europaische Keramik Seit 1950, 1979; Lucie Rie, 1981; contrib. specialist pubns and museum catalogues. *Address:* Bowlders, Doccombe, Moretonhampstead, Devon TQ13 8SS. *T:* (01647) 440264.

MARÍN-GONZALEZ, Manuel; Grand Cross of Isabel la Católica; MP for Ciudad Real, Spain, since 2000; President, Congress of Deputies, since 2004; *b* 21 Oct. 1949; *m* 1983; two *d. Educ:* Univ. of Madrid; Centre d'études européennes, Univ. of Nancy; Collège d'Europe, Bruges. MP for Ciudad Real, La Mancha, 1977–82; Sec. of State for relations with EEC, 1982–85; a Vice Pres., CEC, later EC, 1986–99. Vis. Prof., Univ. of Carlos III, Madrid, 1999. Mem., Spanish Socialist Party, 1974–, Internat. Policy Sec., 2003–04. *Address:* Congreso de los Diputados, Carrera de San Jerónimo s/n, 28071 Madrid, Spain.

MARINCOWITZ, Dr John; Headmaster, Queen Elizabeth's School, Barnet, since 1998; *b* 19 Dec. 1950; *s* of Nicholas and Diana Marincowitz; *m* 1979, Miriam Salie; one *s* one *d. Educ:* St John's Coll., Johannesburg; Witwatersrand Univ. (BA); UCW, Aberystwyth (BA Hons); SOAS, London Univ. (PhD 1985); Inst. of Educn, London Univ. (NPQH). History teacher, Trafalgar High Sch., Cape Town, 1979–82; Queen Elizabeth's School, Barnet: history teacher, 1985–86; Hd of Year, 1986–88; Hd of Sixth Form, Senior Master, 1988–98. Chm. Govs, Little Heath Sch., Herts, 1994–98. FRSA 1998. Mem., RYA, 1999. *Recreations:* sailing, non-fiction, classical music and jazz, Rugby Union (particular interest in English and S African sides). *Address:* c/o Queen Elizabeth's School, Queen's Road, Barnet, Herts EN5 4DQ. *T:* (020) 8441 4646.

MARINKER, Prof. Marshall, OBE 1991; FRCGP; Visiting Professor in General Practice, Guy's, King's and St Thomas' School of Medicine of King's College London (formerly United Medical and Dental Schools of Guy's and St Thomas' Hospitals), 1991–2006; *b* 2 March 1930; *s* of Isidor and Sarah Marinker; *m* 1st, 1955; two *s* one *d;* 2nd, 1978, Jeanette Miller. *Educ:* Haberdashers' Aske's Sch., Hampstead; Middlesex Hosp. Med. Sch., Univ. of London (MB, BS 1956). FRCGP 1972. Principal in Gen. Practice, Grays, 1959–73; Sen. Lectr, St Mary's Hosp. Med. Sch., 1971–73; Foundation Prof. of Gen. Practice and Head, Dept of Community Health, Univ. of Leicester, 1974–82; Dir, MSD Foundn, 1982–92; Dir of Medical Educn, MSD Ltd, 1992–95. Visiting Professor:

Univ. of Iowa, 1973; Univ. of Tampere, 1976; Roche Vis. Prof., NZ Coll. of GPs, 1977; Dozar Prof., Ben Gurion Univ., 1981; Sir James Wattie Meml Vis. Prof., NZ, 1982. Chm., R&D Cttee, High Security Psychiatric Services Bd, NHS, 1996–2000. Royal College of General Practitioners: Res. Registrar, 1967–70; William Pickles Lectr, 1974; Mem. Council, 1974–89; Chm., Educn Div., 1981–84; Chair, Cttee on Med. Ethics, 1987–89; George Abercrombie Prize, 1991. Chm., Council of Europe Wkg Party on the Future of Gen. Practice, 1975–77. Freeman, City of London, 1995. Hon. DM Tampere, 1982. *Publications:* (jtly) Treatment or Diagnosis?, 1970, 2nd edn 1984; (jtly) The Future General Practitioner, 1972; (ed jtly) Practice: a handbook of primary medical care, annually 1978–; (ed jtly) Teaching General Practice, 1981; (ed jtly) Towards Quality in General Practice, 1986; (ed) Medical Audit and General Practice, 1990, 2nd edn 1995; (ed) Controversies in Health Care Policy, 1995; (ed) Sense and Sensibility in Health Care, 1996; (jtly) Clinical Futures, 1998; (ed) Medicine and Humanity, 2001; (ed) Health Targets in Europe, 2002; (ed) Constructive Conversations about Health, 2006; pamphlets, lectures and papers on theory of gen. practice, med. educn, health service policy and med. ethics. *Recreations:* conversation, poetry, theatre, classical music, reading good thrillers, communing with my dog. *Address:* 8 St Peter's Church, 124 Dartmouth Park Hill, N19 5HL. *T:* (020) 7263 1586, *Fax:* (020) 7263 6759; *e-mail:* marshall@marinker.com.

MARIO, Dr Ernest; Chairman and Chief Executive Officer, Capnia, Inc., since 2007; *b* 12 June 1938; *s* of Jerry and Edith Mario; *m* 1961, Mildred Martha Daume; three *s*. *Educ:* Rutgers College of Pharmacy, New Brunswick, NJ (BSc Pharmacy); Univ. of Rhode Island (MS; PhD). Vice Pres., Manufacturing Operation, Smith Kline, 1974; E. R. Squibb & Sons: Vice Pres., Manufacturing for US Pharmaceutical Div., 1977; Vice Pres. and Gen. Man., Chemical Div., 1979; Pres., Chemical Engrg Div. and Sen. Vice Pres. of company, 1981; Pres. and Chief Exec. Officer, Squibb Medical Product, 1983; elected to Bd, 1984; joined Glaxo Inc. as Pres. and Chief Exec. Officer, 1986; apptd to Bd of Glaxo Holdings, 1988; Chief Exec., 1989–93; Dep. Chm., 1991–93; Chief Exec., 1993–2001, Co-Chm., 1993–97, Chm., 1997–2001, Alza Corp.; Chm. and CEO, Apothogen Inc., 2002; Chm., IntraBiotics Pharmaceuticals Inc., 2002–03; Chm., 2003–07 and CEO, 2003–06, Reliant Pharmaceuticals Inc. Chairman: Nat. Foundn for Infectious Diseases, Washington, 1989; American Foundn for Pharmaceutical Educn, NY, 1991. *Recreations:* golf, swimming. *Address:* Capnia, Inc., 2445 Faber Place, Suite 250, Palo Alto, CA 94303, USA.

MARJORIBANKS, John Logan, FCCA; Chairman, Local Government Boundary Commission for Scotland, 2000–07; *b* 21 Aug. 1944; *s* of William Logan Marjoribanks of that Ilk and Thelma (*née* Williamson); *m* 1976, Andrea Ruth Cox; one *s* two *d*. *Educ:* Merchiston Castle Sch.; St John's Coll., Cambridge (BA 1965, MA 1982). ACCA 1988, FCCA 1993. Scottish Agricl Industries, 1965–73; Dept of Agric., Zambia, 1973–78; Commonwealth Development Corporation: Lectr, then Sen. Lectr, Mananga Agricl Mgt Centre, Swaziland, 1979–85; Ops Exec., London, 1985–87; Country Mgr, Mozambique and Zimbabwe, 1988–93; Dir, Mananga Mgt Centre, Swaziland, 1993–95; Country Mgr, India, 1995–98; Dir, Public Affairs, 1999–2000. On-line Tutor, Imperial Coll. at Wye, 2001–04. Local Govt Political Restrictions Exemptions Adjudicator for Scotland, 2007–. Member: Cttee of Mgt, Berwickshire Housing Assoc., 2001–07; E Regl Bd, Scottish Envmtl Protection Agency, 2002–05. Vice-Chm., Berwickshire Civic Soc., 2002–. Gov., Macaulay Land Use Res. Inst., 2004–07. *Recreations:* cycling (veteran time trials), Scots heraldry, bridge. *Address:* Eden House, Gavinton, Duns, Scottish Borders TD11 3QS. *T:* (01361) 882692. *Club:* Kelso Wheelers.

MARK, Dr Alan Francis, DCNZM 2001; CBE 1989; FRSNZ 1978; Professor of Botany, University of Otago, 1975–98, now Professor Emeritus; *b* 19 June 1932; *s* of Cyril Lionel Mark and Frances Evelyn Mark (*née* Marshall); *m* 1958, Patricia Kaye Davie; two *s* two *d*. *Educ:* Univ. of New Zealand (BSc 1953; MSc 1955); Duke Univ., N Carolina (James B. Duke Fellow, 1957; Phi Beta Kappa, 1958; PhD 1958). Sen. Res. Fellow, 1960–64, Res. Advr, 1965–2000, Chm. Bd of Govs, Hellaby Indigenous Grasslands Res. Trust, 2000–; University of Otago: Lectr in Botany, 1960–65; Sen. Lectr, 1966–69; Associate Prof., 1969–75. Chm., Guardians of Lakes Manapouri, Monowai and Te Anau, 1973–99; Mem., Fiordland Marine Guardians, 2005–. Mem., Royal NZ Forest and Bird Protection Soc. *Publications:* (with Nancy M. Adams) New Zealand Alpine Plants, 1973, 3rd edn 1995; over 170 scientific papers. *Recreations:* enjoying the outdoors, nature conservation. *Address:* 205 Wakari Road, Helensburgh, Dunedin, New Zealand. *T:* (3) 4763229, (office) (3) 4797573; *e-mail:* amark@otago.ac.nz.

MARK, Sir Robert, GBE 1977; Kt 1973; QPM 1965; Commissioner, Metropolitan Police, 1972–77 (Deputy Commissioner, 1968–72); *b* Manchester, 13 March 1917; *y s* of late John Mark and Louisa Mark (*née* Hobson); *m* 1941, Kathleen Mary Leahy (*d* 1997); one *s* one *d*. *Educ:* William Hulme's Grammar Sch., Manchester. Constable to Chief Superintendent, Manchester City Police, 1937–42, 1947–56; Chief Constable of Leicester, 1957–67; Assistant Commissioner, Metropolitan Police, 1967–68. Vis. Fellow, Nuffield Coll., Oxford, 1970–78 (MA Oxon 1971). Member: Standing Advisory Council of Penal System, 1966; Adv. Cttee on Police in Northern Ireland, 1969; Assessor to Lord Mountbatten during his Inquiry into Prison Security, 1966. Royal Armoured Corps, 1942–47: Lieut, Phantom (GHQ Liaison Regt), North-West Europe, 1944–45; Major, Control Commission for Germany, 1945–47. Lecture tour of N America for World Affairs Council and FCO, Oct. 1971; Edwin Stevens Lecture to the Laity, RCM, 1972; Dimbleby Meml Lecture (BBC TV), 1973. Director: Phoenix Assurance Co. Ltd, 1977–85; Control Risks Ltd, 1982–87. Mem. Cttee, AA, 1977–87; Governor and Mem. Admin. Bd, Corps of Commissionaires, 1977–86; Hon. Freeman, City of Westminster, 1977. Hon. LLM Leicester Univ., 1967; Hon. DLitt Loughborough, 1976; Hon. LLD: Manchester, 1978; Liverpool, 1978. KStJ 1977. *Publications:* Policing a Perplexed Society, 1977; In the Office of Constable, 1978. *Address:* Esher, Surrey KT10 8LU.

MARK, Rear Adm. Robert Alan, FRIN; Principal, Booz Allen Hamilton (UK), since 2007; *b* 28 April 1955; *s* of Alexander Mark and Ruby (*née* Oliver); *m* 1978, Wendy Anne Peters; one *s* one *d*. *Educ:* Univ. of Hull (BSc Jt Hons Geol. and Phys. Geog. 1977); London Business Sch., Sloan Prog. (MSc Mgt 2001). Joined RN, 1974; HMS Wolverton, 1976; BRNC 1977; HMS Torquay, 1977–78; HMS Ajax, 1979–80; HMS Fawn (NO), 1980–82; BRNC staff, 1982–84; HMS Hecla (NO), 1984–85; RN Hydrographic Long Course, 1985; MV Bon Esprit, UK Civil Hydrographic Prog., 1985; CO, HM Survey Motor Launch Gleaner, 1986–87; Exec. Officer, HMS Fox, 1987–89; MA to Dir, US Hydrographic Dept, US Naval Oceanographic Office, 1989–91; CO, HMS Herald, 1991–93; Comdr (H), FO Surface Flotilla, 1993; SO1 (Policy), Directorate, Naval Surveying, Oceanography and Meteorol., UK, MoD, 1994–96; CO, HMS Scott, 1996–98; Asst Dir (Policy), Directorate, Naval Surveying, Oceanography and Meteorol., UK, MoD, 1998–2000; Dir of Strategy, Defence Logistics, MoD, 2001–04; BAE Systems, 2004; Sen. Directing Staff (Navy), RCDS, 2005–07. Mem. Wessex Regl Cttee, Nat. Trust, 2007–. MInstD 2004, CDir 2006. Freeman, City of London, 2004; Liveryman, Co. of Water Conservators, 2004–. *Recreations:* art, architecture, hill-walking. *Address: e-mail:* mark_bob@bah.com. *Club:* Army and Navy.

MARKESINIS, Sir Basil (Spyridonos), Kt 2005; PhD, LLD, DCL; FBA 1997; Conseiller Scientifique du Premier Président de la Cour de Cassation, France, 2002–07; non-executive Director: Alexander S. Onassis Foundation, since 2007; Alexander S. Onassis Public Benefit Foundation, since 2007; *b* 10 July 1944; *s* of Spyros B. Markesinis (former Prime Minister of Greece) and Ieta Markesinis; *m* 1970, Eugenie (*née* Trypanis); one *s* one *d*. *Educ:* Univ. of Athens (LLB, DIur); MA, PhD, LLD Cambridge; DCL Oxford. Asst Prof., Law Faculty, Univ. of Athens, 1965–68; Gulbenkian Res. Fellow, Churchill Coll., Cambridge, 1970–74; called to the Bar, Gray's Inn, 1973, Bencher, 1991; Fellow of Trinity Coll., Cambridge, and Univ. Lectr in Law, 1975–86; Denning Prof. of Comparative Law, Univ. of London, at QMC, subseq. QMW, 1986–93; Dep. Dir, Centre for Commercial Law Studies, Univ. of London, 1986–93; Prof. of Eur. Private Law, UCL, 1993–95; University of Oxford: Fellow: LMH, 1995–99; Brasenose Coll., 1999–2000; Clifford Chance Prof. of European Law, 1995–99, of Comparative Law, 1999–2000; Founder Dir, Centre, then Inst., of Eur. and Comparative Law, 1995–2000; Prof. of Common Law and Civil Law, and Chm., Inst. of Global Law, UCL, 2001–07. Prof. of Anglo-Amer. Private Law, Leiden Univ., 1986–2000, and Founder and Dir, Leiden Inst. of Anglo-American Law, 1987–2000. Advocate to Greek Supreme Court, 1976–86. Sen. Advr on European Affairs, Clifford Chance, 1999–2002. Visiting Professor: Univs of Paris I and II; Siena; Rome; Cornell; Michigan (Ann Arbor); Texas (Austin); Francqui Vis. Prof., Univ. of Gent, 1989–90, 2005–06; Jamail Regents' Prof. of Law, Univ. of Texas, Austin, 1998–. Lectures: Atkin, Reform Club, 1989; Shimizu, LSE, 1989; Lionel Cohen Meml, Hebrew Univ. of Jerusalem, 1993; Wilberforce, 1998; John Maurice Kelly Meml, 2003; Eason-Weinemann, Tulane, 2005; Peter Taylor Meml, Inner Temple, 2006; Denning, 2007. Mem., Council of Management, British Inst. of Internat. and Comparative Law, 1993–2000. Associate Fellow, Internat. Acad. of Comp. Law, 1987–98; Member: Amer. Law Inst., 1989; Acad. Internat. de Droit Comparé, 2004; Foreign Fellow: Royal Belgian Acad., 1990; Royal Netherlands Acad. of Arts and Scis, 1995; Accademia dei Lincei, Rome, 2005; Corresp. Member: Acad. of Athens, 1994; Corresp. Fellow, Inst. de France, 2004; Hon. Fellow, Greek Archaeol. Soc., 2004; Corresp. Collaborator, UNIDROIT, 1992. Hon. QC 1998. DIur (*hc*): Ghent, 1992; Paris I (Panthéon-Sorbonne), 1998; Munich, 1999; Athens, 2007. Humboldt Forschungspreise, 1996; Univ. Prize, Leiden, 1996. Officier, Ordre des Palmes Académiques (France), 1992; Comdr, Légion d'Honneur (France), 2004 (Chevalier, 1995; Officier, 2000); Kt Comdr, Order of Merit (Germany), 2003 (Comdr, 1998; Officer's Cross, 1992); Kt Grand Cross, Order of Merit (Italy), 2002 (Kt Comdr, 1999; Officer, 1995); Comdr, Order of Honour (Greece), 2000; Kt, Grand Cross, Order of Merit (France), 2006. *Publications:* The Mother's right to Guardianship according to the Greek Civil Code, 1968; The Theory and Practice of Dissolution of Parliament, 1972 (Yorke Prize); The English Law of Torts, 1976; (jtly) An Outline of the Law of Agency, 1979, 4th edn 1998; (jtly) Richterliche Rechtspolitik im Haftungsrecht, 1981; (jtly) Tortious Liability for un-intentional harm in the Common Law and the Civil Law, 2 vols, 1982; (jtly) Tort Law, 1984, 6th edn 2007; The German Law of Torts: a comparative introduction, 1986, 4th edn (jtly) as The German Law of Torts: a comparative treatise, 2002; (gen. ed. and contrib.) The Gradual Convergence: foreign ideas, foreign influences and English law on the eve of the 21st century, 1994; (ed and contrib.) Bridging the Channel, 1996; Foreign Law and Comparative Methodology: a subject and a thesis, 1997; (jtly) The German Law of Contract and Restitution, 1998; (gen. ed. and contrib.) Protecting Privacy, 1998; The Impact of the Human Rights Bill on English Law, 1998; (jtly) Tortious Liability of Statutory Bodies, 1999; Always on the Same Path: essays on foreign law and comparative methodology, 2001; (gen. ed. and contrib.) The British Contribution to the Europe of the Twenty-First Century, 2002; Comparative Law in the Courtroom and the Classroom: the story of the last thirty-five years, 2003; (jtly) Compensation for Personal Injury in English, German and Italian Law: a comparative overview, 2005; The German Law of Contract: a comparative treatise, 2006; (jtly) Foreign Law in National Courts: a new source of inspiration?, 2006; Good and Evil in Art and Law, 2007; Flawed Grandeur: the secret lives of great adventurers (in Greek), 2008; (jtly) Engaging with Foreign Law, 2009; ed. and contrib. many articles in learned jls in Belgium, Canada, England, France, Germany, Greece, Israel, Italy and USA. *Recreations:* painting, music, fund-raising, archaeological digging, chess. *Address:* Middleton Stoney House, Middleton Stoney, Bicester, Oxfordshire OX25 4TE. *T:* (01869) 343560.

MARKEY, Air Vice-Marshal Peter Desmond, OBE 1986; General Manager, NATO Maintenance and Supply Agency, Luxembourg, 1999–2004; *b* 28 March 1943; *s* of Althorpe Hazel Christopher Markey and Marjorie Joyce Markey (*née* Thomas); *m* 1966, Judith Mary Widdowson; one *s* one *d*. *Educ:* RAF Coll. Cranwell; Open Univ. (BA 1980); Cranfield Univ. (MSc 1994). RAF Supply Officer: commissioned 1964; served Singapore, France and UK to 1981; NDC, 1981–82; HQ Strike Comd, 1982–83; HQ AFCENT, Netherlands, 1983–85; MoD Carlisle, 1986–88; Station Comdr, Carlisle, 1988–89; RCDS 1990; MoD Central Staff, 1991; Dept of AMSO, 1991; HQ Logistics Comd, 1994; Dir Gen., Support Mgt, RAF, 1995–97; Dir of Resources, NATO, Luxembourg, 1997–99. Grand Cross, Order of Merit (Luxembourg), 2004. *Publications:* papers and contribs to learned jls. *Recreations:* running, mountain walking, travelling. *Address: e-mail:* Markeypd@aol.com. *Club:* Royal Air Force.

MARKHAM, Sir Alexander (Fred), Kt 2008; PhD, DSc; FRCP, FRCPath; West Riding Medical Research Trust Professor of Medicine, and Director, Molecular Medicine Unit, University of Leeds, since 1992; *b* 30 Nov. 1950; one *s* one *d*. *Educ:* Univ. of Birmingham (BSc 1971; PhD 1974; DSc 1992); Univ. of London (MB BS 1985). FRCPath 1996; FRCP 1998. ICI Pharmaceuticals, 1979–90; Nuffield Dept of Medicine, Univ. of Oxford, 1990–92; Hon. Consultant Physician, Leeds Teaching Hosps NHS Trust; Chief Executive, Cancer Research UK, 2003–07 (on secondment). Chm., NCRI, 2003–06. FMedSci 2004. *Address:* c/o School of Medicine, University of Leeds, Leeds LS2 9JT.

MARKHAM, Sir (Arthur) David, 4th Bt *cr* 1911, of Beachborough Park; *b* 6 Dec. 1950; *er s* of Sir Charles Markham, 3rd Bt and Valerie Markham (*née* Barry-Johnston); *S* father, 2006; *m* 1977, Carolyn Lorna (*née* Park) (marr. diss. 2007); two *d*. *Educ:* Milton Abbey Sch. *Recreations:* racing, travel. *Heir: b* Richard Barry Markham [*b* 18 April 1954; *m* 1985, Ann Malcolm-Smith; two *s*]. *Address:* PO Box 42263, Nairobi 00100, Kenya; *e-mail:* markham@africaonline.co.ke. *Clubs:* Muthaiga Country, Jockey (Kenya).

MARKIDES, Vanias; High Commissioner for the Republic of Cyprus in the United Kingdom, 1995–97; *b* 26 July 1937; *s* of Vias and Andromachi Markides; *m* 1962, Ioulia Michaeloudes; one *s*. *Educ:* Athens Univ. (LLB). Ministry of Foreign Affairs: Second Sec., Nicosia, 1961; Head of Consular and Cultural Affairs, Cyprus High Commn, London, 1966–68; Counsellor, 1971; Dir, First Political Div., 1975–88; Minister, Plenipotentiary, 1979; Ambassador, 1985; Permt Rep. to UN, Geneva, 1988–92; Rep. of Cyprus to UN Commn on Human Rights, 1990–92; Permt Sec., 1994–95. Dir, Office of Studies on the Cyprus Problem, 1992–95. Merito Civil Gran Cruz (Spain), 1987. *Recreations:* classical philosophy, music.

MARKL, Prof. Hubert, Dr rer. nat.; Professor of Biology, University of Konstanz, 1974–2003, now Emeritus; *b* 17 Aug. 1938; *m* Eva-Maria Markl; one *s*. *Educ:* Univ. of Munich (Dr rer. nat. 1962). Scientific Assistant: Zoological Inst., Univ. of Munich, 1962–63; Zoological Inst., Univ. of Frankfurt, 1963–67; Res. Associate, Biological Labs Harvard Univ. and Rockefeller Univ., 1965–66; Associate Prof., Zoological Inst., Univ. of Frankfurt, 1967–68; Prof. of Zoology and Dir, Zoological Inst., Technical Univ. of Darmstadt, 1968–74. Heinrich-Hertz Vis. Prof., Univ. of Karlsruhe, 1994–95. Vice Pres., Alexander von Humboldt Foundn, 1986–91; President: Deutsche Forschungsgemeinschaft, 1986–91 (Mem. Senate, 1974–77; Vice Pres., 1977–83); Ges. Deutscher Naturforscher und Ärzte, 1993–94; Berlin-Brandenburg Acad. of Scis, 1993–95; Max Planck Ges., 1996–2002. Member: Deutsche Akad. der Naturforscher Leopoldina, 1985; Berlin-Brandenburg Acad. of Scis, 1993; MAE 1988; FAAAS 1981; Corresponding Member: Bayer. Akad. der Wissenschaften, 1985; Nordrhein-Westfäl. Akad. der Wissenschaften, 1987; Akad. der Wissenschaften zu Göttingen, 1996; Foreign Member: Amer. Philos. Soc., 2000; Royal Soc., 2002; Hon. Member: Ges. Deutscher Chemiker, 1997; Max Planck Ges., 2002; Foreign Hon. Member: Amer. Acad. Arts and Scis, 1985; Indian Acad. Sci., 1991. Hon. Dr rer. nat.: Saarland, 1992; Dublin, 1997; Potsdam, 1999; Hon. DHL Jewish Theol Seminary, NY, 2000; Hon. DPhil: Tel Aviv, 2001; Hebrew Univ. of Jerusalem, 2001; Weizman Inst. Sci., 2002. Bayerische Verdienstorden, 2001. *Publications:* Biophysik, 1977 (trans. English 1983); Evolution of Social Behaviour, 1980; Natur und Geschichte, 1983; Neuroethology and Behavioral Physiology, 1983; Evolution, Genetik und menschliches Verhalten, 1986; Natur als Kulturaufgabe, 1986; Wissenschaft: zur Rede gestellt, 1989; Wissenschaft im Widerstreit, 1990; Die Fortschrittsdroge, 1992; Wissenschaft gegen Zukunftsangst, 1998; Schöner neuer Mensch?, 2002. *Address:* Universität Konstanz, Fachbereich Biologie, 78457 Konstanz, Germany. *T:* (7531) 882725; *e-mail:* hubert.markl@uni-konstanz.de.

MARKLAND, John Anthony, CBE 1999; PhD; Chairman, Scottish Natural Heritage, 1999–2006; *b* 17 May 1948; *s* of late Thomas Henry Markland and of Rita Markland (*née* Shippen); *m* 1970, Muriel Harris; four *d*. *Educ:* Bolton Sch., Lancs; Dundee Univ. (MA Geog. 1970; PhD 1975). CDipAF 1979; ACIS 1982. Demographer, Somerset CC, 1974–76; Sen. Professional Asst (Planning Res.), Tayside Regl Council, 1976–79; Fife Regional Council: PA to Chief Exec., 1979–83; Asst Chief Exec., 1983–86; Chief Exec., 1986–95; Chief Exec., Fife Council, 1995–99. Chm., Scottish Br., SOLACE, 1993–95. Chairman: Forward Scotland Ltd, 1996–2000; Scottish Leadership Foundn, 2001–; Environmental Campaigns, 2003–06. Mem., Jt Nature Conservation Cttee, 1999–2006. Vice Convener, Ct, Edinburgh Univ., 2006– (Mem., 2001–; Convener, Audit Cttee, 2004–06). Dir, Horsecross Arts Ltd, 2007–. Pres., Old Boltonians' Assoc., 2007. *Recreation:* finding the easiest way up Scotland's Munros. *Address:* 3 St Leonard's Bank, Perth PH2 8EB. *T:* (01738) 441798.

MARKOVA, Prof. Ivana, PhD; FBA 1999; FRSE; Professor of Psychology, University of Stirling, 1984–2003, now Emeritus. Formerly Lectr, Sen. Lectr, then Reader, in Psychology, and Head of Dept of Psychology, Univ. of Stirling. FRSE 1997. *Publications:* (ed) Social Context of Language, 1978; Paradigms, Thought and Language, 1982; Human Awareness: its social development, 1987; (with Klaus Foppa) Dynamics of Dialogue, 1990; (ed with Klaus Foppa) Asymmetries and Dialogue, 1991; (ed with R. M. Farr) Representations of Health, Illness and Handicap, 1994; (ed jtly) Mutualities in Dialogue, 1995; Dialogicality and Social Representations, 2003; (with Serge Moscovici) The Making of Modern Social Psychology, 2006. *Address:* Department of Psychology, University of Stirling, Stirling FK9 4LA.

MARKOWICH, Prof. Peter Alexander; Professor of Applied Mathematics, University of Cambridge, since 2007; *b* 16 Dec. 1956; *s* of Otto Markowich and Elfriede Markowich; *m*; one *d*. *Educ:* Technical Univ., Vienna (Diploma 1979; Dr Tech. 1980). Res. Asst, Internat. Inst. for Applied Systems Analysis, Austria, 1979–80; Res. Associate, Math. Res. Center, Univ. of Wisconsin-Madison, 1980–81; Asst Prof., Math. and Computer Sci. Depts, Univ. of Texas at Austin, 1981–82; Asst Prof., 1982–84, Associate Prof., 1984–89, Inst. for Applied and Numerical Math., Technical Univ., Vienna; Professor, Department of Mathematics: Technical Univ. of Berlin, 1989–90, 1991–98; Purdue Univ., 1990–91; Prof. of Math. Analysis, Johannes Kepler Univ. Linz, 1998–99; Prof. of Applied Analysis, Faculty of Math., Univ. of Vienna, 1999–2007. JSPS Fellow, Kyoto Univ., 2005. Corresp. Mem., Austrian Acad. of Scis, 2005. Wittgenstein Award, Austrian Sci. Fund, 2000. *Publications:* The Stationary Semiconductor Device Equations, 1986; (jtly) Semiconductor Equations, 1990; articles in learned jls. *Address:* Department of Applied Mathematics and Theoretical Physics, Centre for Mathematical Sciences, University of Cambridge, Wilberforce Road, Cambridge CB3 1AW; *web:* www.peter-markowich.net.

MARKOWITZ, Prof. Harry M., PhD; Professor of Finance and Economics, Baruch College, City University of New York, 1982–93; President, Harry Markowitz Company, since 1984; *b* 24 Aug. 1927; *s* of Morris Markowitz and Mildred (*née* Gruber); *m* Barbara Gay. *Educ:* Univ. of Chicago (PhB Liberal Arts 1947; MA 1950, PhD 1954 Econs). Res. Associate, Rand Corp., 1952–60 and 1961–63; Consultant, Gen. Electric Corp., 1960–61; Chm., Bd and Technical Dir, Consolidated Analysis Centres Inc., 1963–68; Prof. of Finance, UCLA, 1968–69; Pres., Arbitrage Management Co., 1969–72, Consultant, 1972–74; Vis. Prof. of Finance, Wharton Bus. Sch., 1972–74; Res. Staff Mem., T. J. Watson Res. Center, IBM, 1974–83; Adj. Prof. of Finance, Rutgers Univ., 1980–82; Consultant, Daiwa Securities, 1990–2000. Director: Amer. Finance Assoc.; TIMS. Fellow: Econometric Soc.; Amer. Acad. Arts and Sciences, 1987. Von Neumann Theory Prize, ORSA/TIMS, 1989; Nobel Prize for Economics, 1990. *Publications:* Portfolio Selection: efficient diversification of investments, 1959, 2nd edn 1991; Simscript: a simulation programming language, 1963; (jtly) Studies in Process Analysis: economy-wide production capabilities, 1963 (trans. Russian 1967); (jtly) The Simscript II Programming Language, 1969; (jtly) The EAS-E Programming Language, 1981; (jtly) Adverse Deviation, 1981; Mean-Variance Analysis in Portfolio Choice and Capital Markets, 1987; contrib. chapters to numerous books and papers in professional jls, incl. Jl of Finance, Management Science, Jl of Portfolio Management. *Recreation:* music.

MARKS, family name of **Baron Marks of Broughton**.

MARKS OF BROUGHTON, 3rd Baron *cr* 1961, of Sunningdale in the Royal Co. of Berks; **Simon Richard Marks;** *b* 3 May 1950; *s* of 2nd Baron Marks of Broughton and his 1st wife, Ann Catherine (*née* Pinto); *S* father, 1998; *m* 1982, Marion, *o d* of Peter F. Norton; one *s* three *d*. *Educ:* Eton; Balliol Coll., Oxford (BA 1971). *Heir:* *s* Hon. Michael Marks, *b* 13 May 1989.

MARKS, Bernard Montague, OBE 1984; Life President, Alfred Marks Bureau Group of Companies, 1985 (Managing Director and Chairman, 1946–84); *b* 11 Oct. 1923; *s* of Alfred and Elizabeth Marks; *m* 1956, Norma Renton (*d* 1990); one *s* (and one *s* decd). *Educ:* Highgate Public Sch.; Royal Coll. of Science. Served Somerset LI, seconded to RWAFF (Staff Capt.), 1944–46. Chm. or Vice-Chm., Fedn of Personnel Services of GB, 1965–79, 1983–84. Mem., Equal Opportunities Commn, 1984–86. *Publication:* Once Upon A Typewriter, 1974. *Recreations:* bridge, golf, theatre. *Address:* 5 Monarch Point, Lensbury Avenue, Imperial Wharf, SW6 2HW. *Clubs:* St George's Hill Golf, Coombe Hill Golf.

MARKS, Prof. David Francis, PhD; CPsychol, FBPsS; Professor of Psychology, City University, London, since 2000; *b* 12 Feb. 1945; *s* of Victor William Francis Marks and Mary Dorothy Marks; one *d* by Margaret McGoldrick; one *s* by Elsy Cecilia Clavijo. *Educ:* Southern Grammar Sch. for Boys, Portsmouth; Reading Univ. (BSc); Sheffield Univ. (PhD 1970). FBPsS 1984; CPsychol 1988; Chartered Health Psychologist, 1998. Sen. Demonstrator, Sheffield Univ., 1966–69; Lectr, 1970–74, Sen. Lectr, 1978–86, Univ. of Otago, NZ; Middlesex Polytechnic, subseq. University: Prof. of Psychology, 1986–2000; Head, Sch. of Psychology, 1986–91; Head, Health Research Centre, 1989–2000. Man. Dir, City Psychology Ltd, 2003–05; Partner, Health Psychology Consultants LLP, 2004–. Visiting Professor: Oregon, 1976; Washington, 1977; Hamamatsu Univ. Sch. of Medicine, Fukuoka Univ., Japan, 1984; Rome, 1997; Hon. Res. Fellow, UCL, 1977. Mem., DoH Scientific Cttee on Tobacco and Health, 1994–98; Convenor, Task Force on Health Psychol., Eur. Fedn of Professional Psychologists' Assocs, 1993–97. Organised internat. confs on mental imagery, 1983, 1985. Consultant to NHS, local govt and EC depts and corps. Sen. Asst Ed., Jl of Mental Imagery, 1987–96; Asst Ed., British Jl of Psychology, 1990–95; Ed., Jl Health Psychol., 1996–. Developer of first smoking cessation prog. on the internet. Gold Disk for Music Therapy, NZ Min. of Health, 1979. *Publications:* The Psychology of the Psychic, 1980, 2nd edn 2000; Theories of Image Formation, 1986; Imagery: current developments, 1990; The Quit for Life Programme, 1993; Improving the Health of the Nation, 1996; Health Psychology: theory, research and practice, 2000, 2nd edn 2005 (trans. Chinese 2004, Spanish 2008, Japanese 2009); Dealing with Dementia, 2000; The Health Psychology Reader, 2002; Research Methods for Clinical and Health Psychology, 2004; Overcoming Your Smoking Habit, 2005 (trans. French 2009); numerous book chapters and contribs to Nature, Science, Brit. Jl of Psych., Jl of Mental Imagery, and many other jls. *Recreations:* photography, film making, art, painting. *Address:* City University, Northampton Square, EC1V 0HB; *e-mail:* d.marks@city.ac.uk.

MARKS, David Joseph, MBE 2000; RIBA; Co-founder and Director, Marks Barfield Architects, since 1989; *b* 15 Dec. 1952; *s* of late Melville Mark and of Gunilla Marta (*née* Loven); *m* 1981, Julia Barbara Barfield, *qv*; one *s* two *d*. *Educ:* Architectural Assoc. RIBA 1984. Formerly architect, Richard Rogers and Partners; Founder Dir, Tetra Ltd; Co-founder and Man. Dir, London Eye Co., 1994–2006. Projects include: Millbank Millennium Pier, 2004 (RIBA Award); Spiral Café, Birmingham Bullring (Copper in Architecture Award; Civic Trust Award; Birmingham Design and Industry Awards); schools projects in Southwark. FRSA 2007. Prince Philip Special Commendation for Outstanding Achievement in Design for Business and Society, 2000; Faculty of Building Trophy, 2001; practice awards: Building Architectural Practice of the Year Award, 2001; Queen's Award for Enterprise (Innovation), 2003. *Recreations:* family, walking, ski-ing. *Address:* Marks Barfield Architects, 50 Bromells Road, Clapham Common, SW4 0BG. *T:* (020) 7501 0180, *Fax:* (020) 7498 7103; *e-mail:* dmarks@marksbarfield.com.

MARKS, Dennis Michael; broadcaster, writer and film-maker, since 1997; General Director, English National Opera, 1993–97; *b* 2 July 1948; *s* of Samuel Marks and Kitty Ostrovsky; *m*; one *s* one *d*. *Educ:* Haberdashers' Aske's Sch., Elstree; Trinity Coll., Cambridge (1st Cl. Hons English Tripos). British Broadcasting Corporation, 1969–81: TV researcher, 1969–71; Dir, TV music and arts, 1972–78; Dir/Producer, Bristol Arts Unit, 1978–81; Dir/Producer, 3rd Eye Prodns, 1981–85; BBC TV: Editor, music progs, 1985–88; Asst Head of Music and Arts Dept, 1988–91; Hd of Music Progs, 1991–93. Pres., Internat. Music Centre, Vienna, 1989–92. *Publications:* Great Railway Journeys, 1981; Repercussions, 1985. *Recreations:* cooking, travel. *Address:* 12 Camden Square, NW1 9UY.

MARKS, Frederick Charles, OBE 1983; Commissioner for Local Administration in Scotland, 1994–2000; *b* 3 Dec. 1934; *s* of James Marks and Elizabeth (*née* McInnes); *m* 1959, Agnes Miller Bruce; two *s* one *d* (and one *s* decd). *Educ:* Wishaw High Sch.; Univ. of Glasgow (MA Hons; LLB). Admitted solicitor, 1960. Legal Asst, Burgh of Motherwell and Wishaw, 1957–61; Solicitor, Burgh of Kirkcaldy, 1961–63; Depute Town Clerk, City and Royal Burgh of Dunfermline, 1963–68; Town Clerk, Burgh of Hamilton, 1968–75; Chief Exec., Motherwell Dist, 1974–83; Gen. Manager, Scottish Special Housing Assoc., 1983–89; Dep. Chm., Local Govt Boundary Commn for Scotland, 1989–94. Vice-Chairman: Queen Margaret Hosp. NHS Trust, Dunfermline, 1994–99; Fife Acute Hosps NHS Trust, 1999–2001. *Address:* 5 Queen Margaret Fauld, Dunfermline, Fife KY12 0UY.

MARKS, Prof. Isaac Meyer, MD; Professor of Experimental Psychopathology, Institute of Psychiatry, University of London, 1978–2000, now Professor Emeritus; *b* 16 Feb. 1935; *s* of Morris Norman and Anna Marks; *m* 1957, Shula Eta Winokur (*see* S. E. Marks); one *s* one *d*. *Educ:* Univ. of Cape Town (MB ChB 1956; MD 1963); Univ. of London (DPM 1963). Consultant Psychiatrist and research worker, Bethlem-Maudsley Hosp. and Inst. of Psychiatry, 1978–2000. Sen. Res. Investigator, 2000–03, Vis. Prof., 2003–, Imperial Coll. London; Vis. Prof., Vrije Univ., Amsterdam, 2005–. Salmon Medallist, NY Acad. of Medicine, 1978; IT Effectiveness Award, Health Care '98, 1998. *Publications:* Patterns of Meaning in Psychiatric Patients, 1965; Fears & Phobias, 1969; (jtly) Clinical Anxiety, 1971; (jtly) Psychotherapy, 1971; (jtly) Nursing in Behavioural Psychotherapy, 1977; Living with Fear, 1978, 2nd edn 2001; Cure and Care of Neuroses, 1981; Psychiatric Nurse Therapists in Primary Care, 1985; Behavioural Psychotherapy, 1986; (jtly) Anxiety and its Treatment, 1986; Fears, Phobias and Rituals, 1987; (ed jtly) Mental Health Care Delivery, 1990; (jtly) Problem-centred care planning, 1995; (jtly) BT Steps—Behavioural self-assessment and self care for OCD, 1996; (jtly) Hands-on-Help, 2007; 450 scientific papers. *Recreations:* hiking, gardening, theatre, cinema. *Address:* 43 Dulwich Common, SE21 7EU. *T:* (020) 8693 6611.

MARKS, John Henry, MD; FRCGP; General Practitioner, Boreham Wood, 1954–90; Chairman of Council, British Medical Association, 1984–90; *b* 30 May 1925; *s* of Lewis and Rose Marks; *m* 1954, Shirley Evelyn, *d* of Alic Nathan, OBE; one *s* two *d*. *Educ:* Tottenham County Sch.; Edinburgh Univ. MD; FRCGP; D(Obst)RCOG. Served RAMC, 1949–51. Chairman: Herts LMC, 1966–71; Herts Exec. Council, 1971–74; Member: NHS Management Study Steering Cttee, 1971–72; Standing Med. Adv. Cttee, 1984–90; Council for Postgrad. Med. Educn, 1984–90. British Medical Association: Fellow, 1976; Member: Gen. Med. Services Cttee, 1968–90 (Dep. Chm., 1974–79); Council, 1973–98; GMC, 1979–84, 1990–94; Chairman: Representative Body, 1981–84; Foundn for AIDS, 1987–99. Member, Council: ASH, 1991–99; Assurance Medical Soc., 1999–2004. *Publications:* The Conference of Local Medical Committees and its Executive: an historical view, 1979; The NHS, Beginning, Middle and End? (autobiog.), 2008; papers on the NHS and general medical practice. *Recreations:* philately, bridge, gardening. *Address:* 62 Eyre Court, 3–21 Finchley Road, NW8 9TU. *T:* (020) 7722 5955.

MARKS, Jonathan Clive; QC 1995; *b* 19 Oct. 1952; *s* of late Geoffrey Jack Marks, LDS RCS and Patricia Pauline Marks, LLB; *m* 1st, 1982, Sarah Ann Russell (marr. diss. 1991); one *s* one *d*; 2nd, 1993, (Clementine) Medina Cafopoulos; two *s* two *d*. *Educ:* Harrow;

University Coll., Oxford (BA Hons Jurisp.); Inns of Court Sch. of Law. Called to the Bar, Inner Temple, 1975; in practice, Common Law and Commercial Law, Western Circuit. Vis. Lecturer in Advocacy: Univs of Malaya and Mauritius; Sri Lanka Law Coll. Contested (SDP): Weston-Super-Mare, 1983; Falmouth and Camborne, 1987; EP elecn, Cornwall and Plymouth, 1984. Member Lib Dem Cttee for England, 1988–89; Lib Dem Federal Policy Cttee, 2004–; Chm., Lib Dem Lawyers Assoc., 2001–. Freeman, City of London, 1975; Liveryman, Patternmakers' Co., 1975– (Mem. Ct Assts, 1998–2004). *Recreations:* tennis, ski-ing, theatre, opera, food, wine, travel. *Address:* 4 Pump Court, Temple, EC4Y 7AN. *T:* (020) 7842 5555. *Club:* Royal Automobile.

MARKS, Julia Barbara; *see* Barfield, J. B.

MARKS, Laurence; writer and producer; *b* 8 Dec. 1948; *s* of late Bernard and of Lily Marks; *m* 1988, Brigitte Luise Kirchheim; one step *s. Educ:* Holloway County Sch., London; Guildhall Sch. of Music, London. Trainee journalist, Thomson Regl Newspapers, 1974; Reporter: N London Weekly Herald, 1975–77; Sunday Times, 1975–76 (freelance) and 1978–79; This Week (TV current affairs prog.), 1977–78; television scriptwriter, 1980–; (with Maurice Gran) creator and writer: Holding the Fort, 1980–82; Roots, 1981; Shine on Harvey Moon, 1982–85, 1995; Roll Over Beethoven, 1985; Relative Strangers, 1985–87; The New Statesman, 1987–91; Birds of a Feather, 1989–98; Snakes and Ladders, 1989; So You Think You've Got Troubles, 1991; Love Hurts, 1991–93; Get Back, 1992–93; Wall of Silence (film), 1993; Goodnight Sweetheart, 1993–99; Unfinished Business, 1997–98; Mosley (film), 1997; Starting Out, 2000; Dirty Work, 2000; Believe Nothing, 2002; Me, My Dad and Moorgate, 2006; Mumbai Calling, 2007. Stage plays (with Maurice Gran): Playing God, 2005; The New Statesman, 2006; radio plays (with Maurice Gran): My Blue Heaven, 2006; Dr Freud Will See You Now, Mr Hitler, 2007; My Blue Wedding, 2007. Founder (with Maurice Gran and Allan McKeown), Alomo Productions, 1988, subseq. pt of Thames TV. Pres., Pipesmokers' Council of GB, 2000. Freeman, City of London, 1994; Liveryman, Co. of Tobacco Blenders and Briar Pipe Makers, 1994. Pipesmoker of the Year, 1990. *Publications:* Moorgate: the anatomy of a disaster, 1976; Ruth Ellis: a case of diminished responsibility, 1977; A Fan for All Seasons, 1999; *with Maurice Gran:* Holding the Fort, 1981; The New Statesman Scripts, 1992; Dorien's Diary, 1993; Shine on Harvey Moon, 1995. *Recreations:* music (saxophone player), reading, English churches, tennis, medieval German, the study of Freud, Jung and Breuer, British politics, oriental philology. *Address:* c/o Linda Seifert Management, 22 Poland Street, W1F 8QQ. *T:* (020) 7292 7390, *Fax:* (020) 7292 7391; *e-mail:* inspiration@loandmo.biz. *Clubs:* Reform, Crescit.

MARKS, Lewis Adam; QC 2002; *b* 1961; *s* of Prof. Vincent Marks and Averil Marks; *m* 1986, Philippa Johnson; four *s. Educ:* City of London Freemen's Sch., Ashtead; Brasenose Coll., Oxford. Called to the Bar, Middle Temple, 1984; in practice, specialising in international divorce and big money financial relief claims. *Recreations:* family, Country and Western music, watching cricket. *Address:* Hatfield Place, Hatfield Peverel, Essex CM3 2ET; *e-mail:* lxm@hplace.fsnet.co.uk; Queen Elizabeth Building, Temple, EC4Y 9BS.

MARKS, Dr Louis Frank; film and television producer; *b* 23 March 1928; *s* of Michael Marks and Sarah Abrahams; *m* 1957, Sonia Herbstman (*d* 2006); two *d. Educ:* Christ's Coll., London; Balliol Coll., Oxford (MA, BLitt, DPhil 1957). Sen. History teacher, Beltane Sch., 1951–53; founder and editor, Books and Bookmen, 1956; freelance scriptwriter, TV series, 1958–69; joined BBC, 1970; Script Editor, Series Dept, 1970; Plays Dept, 1972; Drama Producer, 1974; producer, film and TV Drama, 1976–; over 60 productions, including: The Lost Boys (RTS Award, 1979); Play of the Month, later Festival, 1979–86, incl. Lady Windermere's Fan and Ghosts (ACE Awards, 1988, 1992); Loving, 1996; Plotlands (serial), 1997; *films* include: Silas Marner (Banff Film Fest. Award, 1986); Memento Mori (Writers' Guild Award, 1992); The Trial, 1993; *television adaptations:* Middlemarch (serial), 1994 (Writers' Guild Award, BPG TV Award for best serial, Voice of the Listener and Viewer Award for excellence in broadcasting and best TV prog., 1994); Daniel Deronda (serial), 2002 (BPG TV Award for best drama serial, 2002; Banff TV Fest. Award for best mini-series, 2003). *Publications:* (ed and trans.) Antonio Gramsci: the modern prince, 1957; articles in Archivio Storico Italiano and Italian Renaissance Studies. *Address:* Woodhall Farm, Woodhall Drive, Pinner HA5 4TG. *T:* (020) 8428 4268.

MARKS, Michael John Paul, CBE 1999; Founding Partner, NewSmith Capital Partners LLP, since 2003; *b* 28 Dec. 1941; *m* 1967, Rosemary Ann Brody; one *s* two *d. Educ:* St Paul's Sch. Joined Smith Brothers, subseq. Smith New Court, 1960; Partner, 1969–84; Dir, 1975; Man. Dir, Smith New Court International, 1984–87; Chief Exec., 1987–94, Chm., 1995, Smith New Court PLC; Dep. Chm., Jt Hd of Global Equities, and Mem. Exec. Mgt Cttee, Merrill Lynch Internat., 1995–97; Chief Operating Officer, 1997–98, Exec. Chm., 1998–2003, Merrill Lynch Europe, Middle East and Africa; Exec. Chm., Merrill Lynch Investment Mgrs and Internat. Private Client Gp, 2001–03; Exec. Vice Pres., Merrill Lynch & Co. Inc., 2001–03. Non-exec. Dir, Rothschilds Continuation, 1990–95. Director: Securities Inst., 1992–93; London Stock Exchange, 1994–2004; Trustee, Stock Exchange Benevolent Fund, 1994–97.

MARKS, Prof. Richard Charles, PhD; FSA; Professor in Medieval Stained Glass, University of York, 1992–2008, now Emeritus Professor in History of Art (Head, Department of History of Art, 2002–04); *b* 2 July 1945; *s* of Major William Henry Marks and Jeannie Eileen Marks (*née* Pigott); *m* 1970, Rita Spratley. *Educ:* Berkhamsted Sch.; Queen Mary Coll., Univ. of London (BA (Hons) History); Courtauld Inst. of Art, Univ. of London (MA, PhD, History of European Art). Research Asst for British Acad. *Corpus Vitrearum Medii Aevi* Cttee, 1970–73; Asst Keeper, Dept of Medieval and Later Antiquities, British Mus., 1973–79; Keeper of Burrell Collection and Asst Dir, Glasgow Museums and Art Galls, 1979–85; Dir, Royal Pavilion, Art Gall. and Museums in Brighton, 1985–92. Chm., Group of Directors of Museums, 1989–92; Mem. Cttee, 1985–, Pres. Internat. Bd, 1995–2004, *Corpus Vitrearum Medii Aevi*, British Academy. FSA 1977 (Mem. Council, 1990–94; Vice-Pres., 1991–94). *Publications:* (jtly) British Heraldry from its origins to *c* 1800, 1978; (jtly) The Golden Age of English Manuscript Painting, 1980; Burrell Portrait of a Collector, 1983, 2nd edn 1988; The Glazing of the Collegiate Church of the Holy Trinity, Tattershall, Lincs, 1984; (jtly) Sussex Churches and Chapels, 1989; Stained Glass in England during the Middle Ages, 1993; The Medieval Stained Glass of Northamptonshire, 1998; (jtly) Gothic: art for England 1400–1547, 2003; Image and Devotion in Late Medieval England, 2004; articles and reviews in learned jls. *Recreations:* opera, cricket, riding, parish churches, travelling in the Levant. *Address:* Hillcroft, 11 Stewkley Road, Soulbury, Bucks LU7 0DH. *Clubs:* MCC; Clydesdale Amateur Rowing (Glasgow); North British Rowing (the Borders).

MARKS, Richard Leon; QC 1999; a Recorder, since 1994; *b* 20 Nov. 1953; *s* of Harry and Denise Marks; *m* 1987, Jane Elizabeth Tordoff; one *s* one *d. Educ:* Clifton Coll.; Univ. of Manchester (LLB Hons). Called to the Bar, Gray's Inn, 1975, Bencher 2008; Leader, Northern Circuit, 2008–; an Asst Recorder, 1991–94. Pres., Restricted Patients Panel, Mental Health Review Tribunal, 2000–. *Recreations:* travel, cinema, Clarice Cliff, MUFC, cookery, collecting modern art. *Address:* Peel Court Chambers, Sunlight House, Quay Street, Manchester M3 3JZ.

MARKS, Prof. Shula Eta, OBE 1996; PhD; FBA 1995; Professor of Southern African History, School of Oriental and African Studies, University of London, 1993–2001, now Emeritus; *b* Cape Town, S Africa, 14 Oct. 1936; *d* of Chaim and Frieda Winokur; *m* 1957, Isaac Meyer Marks, *qv*; one *s* one *d. Educ:* Univ. of Cape Town (Argus Scholar, 1958–59; BA 1959); PhD London, 1967. Came to London, 1960; Lectr in the History of Southern Africa, SOAS and Inst. of Commonwealth Studies, 1963–76, Reader, 1976–83; Dir, 1983–93, Prof. of Commonwealth Hist., 1984–93, Inst. of Commonwealth Studies, London Univ.; Vice-Chancellor's Visitor to NZ, 1978. Dir, Ford Foundn Grant to Univ. of London on S African History, 1975–78; Mem., Commonwealth Scholarships Commn, 1993–. Member: Adv. Council on Public Records, 1989–94; Humanities Res. Bd, British Acad., 1997–98; AHRB, 1998–2000. Pres., African Studies Assoc. of UK, 1978; Chairman: Internat. Records Mgt Trust, 1989–2004; Council for Assisting Refugee Academics (formerly Soc. for Protection of Sci. and Learning), 1993–2004 (Mem., 1983–); Trustee, Canon Collins Educnl Trust for Southern Africa, 2004–. Editor, Jl of African History, 1971–77; Mem. Council, Jl of Southern African Studies, 1974– (Founding Mem., 1974; Chm. Bd, 1998–2002). Hon. Prof., Univ of Cape Town, 2006. Dist. Sen. Fellow, Sch. of Advanced Study, 2002, Hon. Fellow, SOAS, 2005, Univ. of London. Hon. DLitt Cape Town, 1994; Hon. DSocSc Natal, 1996. Dist. Africanist Award, African Studies Assoc. of UK, 2002. *Publications:* Reluctant Rebellion: an assessment of the 1906–8 disturbances in Natal, 1970; (ed with A. Atmore) Economy and Society in Pre-industrial South Africa, 1980; (ed with R. Rathbone) Industrialization and Social Change in South Africa, 1870–1930, 1982; (ed with P. Richardson) International Labour Migration: historical perspectives, 1983; The Ambiguities of Dependence in Southern Africa: class, nationalism and the state in twentieth-century Natal, 1986; (ed) Not either an experimental doll: the separate worlds of three South African women, 1987; (ed with Stanley Trapido) The Politics of Race, Class & Nationalism in Twentieth Century South Africa, 1987; Divided Sisterhood: race, class and gender in the South African nursing profession, 1994; chapters in Cambridge Hist. of Africa, vols 3, 4 and 6; contrib. Jl of African Hist. and Jl of Southern African Studies. *Address:* Cypress Tree House, Dulwich Common, SE21 7EU.

MARKS, Victor James; Cricket Correspondent, The Observer, since 1990; *b* 25 June 1955; *s* of late Harold George Marks and Phyllis Joan Marks; *m* 1978, Anna Stewart; two *d. Educ:* Blundell's Sch.; St John's Coll., Oxford (BA). Professional cricketer, 1975–89: played for: Oxford Univ., 1975–78 (Capt., 1976 and 1977); Somerset, 1975–89; WA, 1986–87; played in 6 Test Matches and 34 One-Day Internationals for England. Summariser, Test Match Special, BBC, 1989–. Cricket Chm., Somerset CCC, 1999–. Mem., Editl Bd, The Cricketer, 1990–2003; Associate Ed., The Wisden Cricketer, 2003–. *Publications:* Somerset Cricket Scrapbook, 1984; Marks out of XI, 1985; TCCB Guide to Better Cricket, 1987; (with R. Drake) Ultimate One-Day Cricket Match, 1988; Wisden Illustrated History of Cricket, 1989; (with R. Holmes) My Greatest Game, 1994. *Recreation:* golf. *Address:* c/o The Observer, 3–7 Herbal Hill, EC1R 5EJ.

MARKUS, Prof. Robert Austin, OBE 2000; FBA 1985; Professor of Medieval History, Nottingham University, 1974–82, now Emeritus; *b* 8 Oct. 1924; *s* of Victor Markus and Lily Markus (*née* Elek); *m* 1955, Margaret Catherine Bullen; two *s* one *d. Educ:* Univ. of Manchester (BSc 1944; MA 1948; PhD 1950). Mem., Dominican Order, 1950–54; Asst Librarian, Univ. of Birmingham, 1954–55; Liverpool University: Sub-Librarian, 1955–59; Lectr, Sen. Lectr, Reader in Medieval Hist., 1959–74. Mem., Inst. for Advanced Study, Princeton, 1986–87; Distinguished Professor of Early Christian Studies: Catholic Univ. of America, Washington, 1988–89; Univ. of Notre Dame, 1993. Pres., Assoc. Internationale d'Etudes Patristiques, 1991–95. *Publications:* Christian Faith and Greek Philosophy (with A. H. Armstrong), 1964; Saeculum: history and society in the theology of St Augustine, 1970; Christianity in the Roman world, 1974; From Augustine to Gregory the Great, 1983; The End of Ancient Christianity, 1990; Gregory the Great and his World, 1997; Christianity and the Secular, 2005; contribs to Jl of Ecclesiastical Hist., Jl of Theol Studies, Byzantion, Studies in Church Hist., etc. *Recreation:* music. *Address:* Apt 11, The Lace Mill, Wollaton Road, Beeston, Nottingham NG9 2NN. *T:* (0115) 925 5965.

MARLAND, family name of **Baron Marland**.

MARLAND, Baron *cr* 2006 (Life Peer), of Odstock, in the County of Wiltshire; **Jonathan Peter Marland;** Treasurer, Conservative Party, 2005–07; *b* 14 Aug. 1956; *s* of late Peter Greaves Marland and of Audrey Joan Marland (*née* Brierley); *m* 1983, Penelope Mary Lamb; two *s* two *d. Educ:* Shrewsbury Sch. Dir, Lloyd Thompson, then Jardine Lloyd Thompson, plc, 1982–99; Chairman: Herriot Ltd, 1989–; Grainfarmers Pension Fund, 2000–07; Janspeed Ltd, 2001–; Clareville Capital Partners LLP, 2006–; non-executive Director: Jubilee Ltd, 2002–; Essex Court Mgt Co. Ltd, 2002–; Hunter Boot Ltd; Insce Capital Partners LLP; C&UCO Properties. Treas., Boris Johnson's London Mayoral Campaign, 2007–08. Founder Chm., The Sports Nexus, 2003–; Dir, CChange, 2001–06; Chm., Harnham Water Meadows Trust, 2001–; Trustee: J. P. Marland Charitable Trust, 1995–; and Treas., Atlantic Partnership, 2001–; Guggenheim UK Charitable Trust; Invercauld Estate; Member: Adv. Cttee, Airey Neave Refugee Trust, 1992–2007; Adv. Bd, Peggy Guggenheim Mus., Venice. Contested (C) Somerton and Frome, 1997. FRSA. *Recreations:* tennis, ski-ing, shooting, wine, works of art, gardening, watching sport. *Address:* 6 Wilton Place, SW1X 8RH. *T:* (020) 7752 0177, *Fax:* (020) 7245 0778; *e-mail:* marland@odstock.net. *Clubs:* Brooks's, MCC.

MARLAND, Paul; farmer, since 1967; *b* 19 March 1940; *s* of Alexander G. Marland and Elsa May Lindsey Marland; *m* 1st, 1965, Penelope Anne Barlow (marr. diss. 1982); one *s* two *d*; 2nd, 1984, Caroline Ann Rushton. *Educ:* Gordonstoun Sch., Elgin; Trinity Coll., Dublin (BA, BComm). Hopes Metal Windows, 1964; London Press Exchange, 1965–66. MP (C) Gloucester West, 1979–97; contested (C) Forest of Dean, 1997; contested (C) South West Region, EP elecns, 1999. Jt PPS to Financial Sec. to the Treasury and Economic Sec., 1981–83, to Minister of Agriculture, Fisheries and Food, 1983–86. Chm., back bench Agric. Cttee, 1989–97. Vice-Pres., 2002–05, Pres., 2005–, Nat. Cons. Convention; Mem. Bd, Cons. Party, 2002–. *Recreations:* ski-ing, shooting, riding, fishing. *Address:* Ford Hill Farm, Temple Guiting, Cheltenham, Glos GL54 5XU.

MARLAR, Robin Geoffrey; President, Marylebone Cricket Club, 2005–06; *b* 2 Jan. 1931; *o s* of late E. A. G. Marlar and Winifred Marlar (*née* Stevens); *m* 1st, 1955, Wendy Ann Dumeresque (*d* 2000); two *s* four *d*; 2nd, 1980, Hon. Gill Taylor, 2nd *d* of Baron Taylor of Hadfield. *Educ:* King Edward Sch., Lichfield; Harrow; Magdalene Coll., Cambridge (BA). Asst Master, Eton Coll., 1953–54; Librarian, Arundel Castle, 1954–59; Captain, Sussex CCC, 1955–59; sportswriter, Daily Telegraph, 1954–60; De La Rue Co., 1960–68; Consultant and Partner, Spencer-Stuart and Associates, 1968–71; Cricket Corresp., Sunday Times, 1970–96; Founder, Marlar Group of Consultancies, 1971. Contested (C): Bolsover, 1959; Leicester NE, July 1962; contested (Referendum) Newbury, May 1993. *Publications:* The Story of Cricket, 1978; (ed) The English Cricketers Trip to USA and Canada 1859, 1979; Decision Against England, 1983. *Recreations:*

gardening, sport. *Clubs:* Garrick, MCC (Mem. Cttee, 1999–2002; Pres., 2005–06); Sussex CCC (Chm., 1997–98; Pres., 2005–07).

MARLBOROUGH, 11th Duke of, *cr* 1702; **John George Vanderbilt Henry Spencer-Churchill;** DL; Baron Spencer, 1603; Earl of Sunderland, 1643; Baron Churchill, 1685; Earl of Marlborough, 1689; Marquis of Blandford, 1702; Prince of the Holy Roman Empire; Prince of Mindelheim in Suabia; late Captain Life Guards; *b* 13 April 1926; *s* of 10th Duke of Marlborough and Hon. Alexandra Mary Hilda Cadogan, CBE (*d* 1961), *d* of late Henry Arthur, Viscount Chelsea; *S* father, 1972; *m* 1st, 1951, Susan Mary (marr. diss. 1960; she *m* 1962, Alan Cyril Heber-Percy), *d* of Michael Hornby; one *s* one *d* (and one *s* decd); 2nd, 1961, Mrs Athina Livanos (marr. diss. 1971; she *d* 1974), *d* of late Stavros G. Livanos, Paris; 3rd, 1972, Rosita Douglas; one *s* one *d* (and one *s* decd). *Educ:* Eton. Lieut Life Guards, 1946; Captain, 1953; resigned commission, 1953. Chairman: Martini & Rossi, 1979–96; London Paperweights Ltd, 1974–. Member: Council, Winston Churchill Meml Trust, 1966–; Trusthouse Charitable Trust (formerly Forte Council), 1994–. Chm., Badminton Conservation Trust, 1997–2001; Mem., Woodland Cttee, Countryside Foundn for Educn, 2001–. President: Thames and Chilterns Tourist Board, 1974–; Oxfordshire Branch, CLA, 1978–; Oxfordshire Assoc. for Young People, 1972–; Oxford Br., SSAFA, 1977–; Sports Aid Foundn (Southern), 1981–; Oxford United Football Club, 1964–; Dep. Pres., Nat. Assoc. of Boys' Clubs, 1987–. Patron, Oxfordshire Br., BRCS. CC 1961–64, Oxfordshire; JP 1962; DL 1974. *Heir: s* Marquess of Blandford, *qv*. *Address:* Blenheim Palace, Woodstock, Oxon OX20 1PX. *Clubs:* Portland, White's.

MARLER, David Steele, OBE 1984; Director, Egypt, British Council, 1997–2001; *b* 19 March 1941; *s* of Steele Edward and Dorothy Marler; *m* 1963, Belinda Mary Handisyde; two *s*. *Educ:* Brighton, Hove and Sussex Grammar Sch.; Merton Coll., Oxford (Postmaster; BA, MA). British Council, 1962–2001: seconded SOAS, 1962–63; Asst Rep., Bombay, 1963; Regional Officer, India, 1967; Dep. Rep., Ethiopia, 1970; Rep., Ibadan, Nigeria, 1974; Dir, Policy Res., 1977; Rep., Cyprus, 1980; seconded SOAS, 1984; National Univ., Singapore, 1985; Rep., China, 1987–90; Director: Asia, Pacific and Americas Div., 1990–92; Turkey, Azerbaijan and Uzbekistan, 1993–97. Chm., British Council Assoc., 2005–. *Recreations:* sailing, travel, reading, walking. *Address:* 53 The Hall, Foxes Dale, Blackheath, SE3 9BG. *T:* (020) 8318 5874. *Clubs:* Benfleet Yacht; Changi Sailing (Singapore).

MARLER, Dennis Ralph Greville, FRICS; Chairman, Falcon Property Trust, 1988–95; *b* 15 June 1927; *s* of late Greville Sidney Marler, JP, FRICS and Ivy Victoria (*née* Boyle); *m* 1952, Angela (*née* Boundy); one *s* one *d*. *Educ:* Marlborough. Served Royal Lincolnshire Regt, Palestine, 1946–48; articled pupil, Knight, Frank & Rutley, 1948–50; Partner, Marler & Marler, 1950–83; Jt Man. Dir, 1966–76, Man. Dir, 1976–85, Chm., 1985–90, Capital & Counties plc; Chairman: Knightsbridge Green Hotel Ltd, 1966–2007; Pension Fund Property Unit Trust, 1987–89. Member: NEDO Working Party for Wood Report (Public Client and Construction Industry), 1974–75; Adv. Bd, Dept of Construction Management, Univ. of Reading, 1981–88; DHSS Nat. Property Adv. Gp, 1984–91; FCO *ad hoc* Adv. Panel on Diplomatic Estate, 1985–90; RSA Art for Architecture Panel, 1990–93. A Vice-Pres., TCPA, 1983–97; Pres., British Property Fedn, 1983–84. A Vice-Pres., RNIB, 1994–99. Mem. Ct of Assistants, Merchant Taylors' Co., 1984–. CCMI; FRSA. *Recreations:* reading, golf, gardening. *Address:* Park Farm, St Minver, Cornwall PL27 6QS. *T:* (01208) 862141. *Clubs:* Royal Thames Yacht, Roehampton; St Enodoc Golf.

MARLESFORD, Baron *cr* 1991 (Life Peer), of Marlesford in the County of Suffolk; **Mark Shuldham Schreiber;** DL; political consultant, farmer and journalist; *b* 11 Sept. 1931; *s* of late John Shuldham Schreiber, AE, DL, Marlesford Hall, Suffolk and Maureen Schreiber (*née* Dent); *m* 1969, Gabriella Federica, *d* of Conte Teodoro Veglio di Castelletto d'Uzzone; two *d*. *Educ:* Eton; Trinity Coll., Cambridge. Nat. Service in Coldstream Guards (2nd Lt), 1950–51. Fisons Ltd, 1957–63; Conservative Research Dept, 1963–67; Dir, Conservative Party Public Sector Research Unit, 1967–70; Special Advr to the Govt, 1970–74; Special Adviser to Leader of the Opposition, 1974–75; Editorial Consultant, 1974–91, lobby correspondent, 1976–91, The Economist. Ind. Nat. Dir, Times Newspaper Holdings, 1991–; Director: Royal Ordnance Factories, 1972–74; British Railways (Anglia), 1988–92; Eastern Electricity plc, 1990–95. Adviser: Mitsubishi Corp. Internat. NV, 1990–2003; John Swire & Sons Ltd, 1992–. Mem., H of L Select Cttee on EU, 2003–07 (Mem., Econ. and Financial sub-cttee, 2001–05; Mem., Home Affairs sub-cttee, 2005–). Member: Govt Computer Agency Council, 1973–74; Countryside Commn, 1980–92; Rural Development Commn, 1985–93; Chm., CPRE, 1993–98. Pres., Suffolk Preservation Soc., 1997–. Mem., East Suffolk CC, 1968–70. DL Suffolk, 1991. *Recreation:* gadfly on bureaucracy. *Address:* Marlesford Hall, Woodbridge, Suffolk IP13 0AU; 5 Kersley Street, SW11 4PR. *Club:* Pratt's.

MARLING, Sir Charles (William Somerset), 5th Bt *cr* 1882; *b* 2 June 1951; *s* of Sir John Stanley Vincent Marling, 4th Bt, OBE, and Georgina Brenda (Betty) (*d* 1961), *o d* of late Henry Edward FitzRoy Somerset; *S* father, 1977; *m* 1979, Judi; three *d*.
See also D. C. Greer.

MARLOW, Antony Rivers; *b* 17 June 1940; *s* of late Major Thomas Keith Rivers Marlow, MBE, RE retd, and Beatrice Nora (*née* Hall); *m* 1962, Catherine Louise Howel (*née* Jones) (*d* 1994); three *s* two *d*. *Educ:* Wellington Coll.; RMA Sandhurst; St Catharine's Coll., Cambridge (2nd Cl. Hons (1) Mech Sciences, MA). Served Army, 1958–69; retd, Captain RE; management consultant and industrial/commercial manager, 1969–79. MP (C) Northampton North, 1979–97; contested (C) same seat, 1997. *Recreations:* farming, Rugby spectator, opera, ballet.

MARLOW, David Ellis; Chief Executive, 3i Group, 1988–92; *b* 29 March 1935; *m* 1959, Margaret Anne Smith; one *d* (one *s* decd). Chartered Accountant. Investors in Industry, subseq. 3i, 1960–92. Director: Brixton (formerly Brixton Estate) plc, 1992–2003; Trinity Mirror plc, 1992–2005. *Recreations:* playing tennis, the piano, the organ and the 'cello; ski-ing and scrambling in the Alps. *Address:* The Platt, Elsted, Midhurst, Sussex GU29 0LA. *T:* (01730) 825261. *Club:* Athenæum.

MARLOWE, Hugh; *see* Patterson, Harry.

MARMION, Prof. Barrie P., AO 1994; Visiting Professor, Department of Pathology, University of Adelaide (Adelaide Medical School), 1985–2003; *b* 19 May 1920; *s* of J. P. and M. H. Marmion, Alverstoke, Hants; *m* 1953, Diana Ray Newling, *d* of Dr P. Ray Newling, Adelaide, SA; one *d*. *Educ:* University Coll. and University Coll. Hosp., London. MD London 1947, DSc London 1963; FRCPath 1962, FRCPA 1964, FRCPE 1970, FRACP 1984; FRSE 1976. House Surg., UCH, 1942; Bacteriologist, Public Health Laboratory Service, 1943–62; Rockefeller Trav. Fellow, at Walter and Eliza Hall Inst., Melbourne, 1951–52; Foundation Prof., Microbiology, Monash Univ., Melbourne, Australia, 1962–68; Robert Irvine Prof. of Bacteriology, Univ. of Edinburgh, 1968–78; Dir, Div. of Virology, Inst. of Med. and Vet. Science, Adelaide, 1978–85, retd. Vis. Fellow, Clare Hall, Cambridge, 2004 (Life Mem., 2005). Hon. Life Member: Australian Soc. Infectious Diseases, 1985 (Pres., 1985); Australian Soc. Microbiol., 1987 (Pres., 1987); Australian Vet. Assoc., 1988; American Soc. for Rickettsiology, 2003. DUniv Adelaide, 1990. Distinguished Fellow Award (Gold Medal), RCPath Australia, 1986. *Publications:* (ed) Mackie and McCartney's Medical Microbiology, 12th edn 1975 to 14th edn 1996; numerous papers on bacteriology (Qfever and Mycoplasmas) and virology. *Recreations:* swimming, music. *Address:* 14 Birksgate Drive, Urrbrae, Adelaide, SA 5064, Australia.

MARMION, (John) Piers (Tregarthen); Chief Executive Officer, Palladian Investments, since 2006; Managing Partner, Whitehead Mann Partnership, since 2006; *b* 7 Feb. 1959; *m* 1986, Roxane; two *s* one *d*. *Educ:* Jesus Coll., Cambridge (BA 1981). Founding Dir, NB Selection, and Selector Europe, 1987–90; Chief Operating Officer and Man. Partner, Europe and Asia, Spencer Stuart, 1990–2000; Heidrick & Struggles Inc.: Pres., Internat., Europe and Asia, and Chief Operating Officer, 2000–01; Chm. and CEO, 2001–03. Non-executive Director: Blackwell Ltd, 2003–; Talent Q, 2005–; Member Advisory Board: Merryck & Co., 2003–; NSPCC, 2005–. *Recreations:* shooting, sailing, fine arts. *T:* (020) 7024 9150; *e-mail:* piers.marmion@whmllp.com.

MARMOT, Prof. Sir Michael (Gideon), Kt 2000; PhD; FRCP, FFPH, FMedSci; MRC Research Professor, Professor of Epidemiology and Public Health, University College London, since 1985 (MRC Professor, since 1995); Director, International Institute for Society and Health (formerly International Centre for Health and Society), University College London, since 1994; *b* 26 Jan. 1945; *s* of Nathan Marmot and Alice Marmot (*née* Weiner); *m* 1971, Alexandra Naomi Ferster; two *s* one *d*. *Educ:* Univ. of Sydney (BSc Hons, MB BS Hons); Univ. of California, Berkeley (PhD Epidemiology). FFPH (FFCM 1989); FRCP 1996. RMO, Royal Prince Alfred Hosp., 1969–70, Fellowship in Thoracic Medicine, 1970–71, Univ. of Sydney; Res. Fellow and Lectr, Dept of Biomedical and Envmtl Health Scis, Univ. of California, Berkeley, 1971–76 (Fellowships from Berkeley and Amer. Heart Assoc., 1972–76); Lectr and Sen. Lectr in Epidemiology, LSH&TM, 1976–85. Adjunct Prof., Dept of Soc., Human Develt and Health, Harvard Univ., 2000–; Associate, Health Policy and Mgt, Johns Hopkins Univ., 2007–08. Hon. Consultant, Public Health Medicine: Camden and Islington (formerly Bloomsbury) HA, 1980–2004; N Central London SHA, 2004–06; SHA for London, 2006–. Vis. Prof., RSocMed, 1987. Chm., DoH Scientific Ref. Gp on tackling inequalities, 2003–; Member: Royal Commn on Envmtl Pollution, 1995–2002; Ind. Inquiry into Inequalities in Health, 1997–98. Chm., Commn on Social Determinants of Health, WHO, 2005–. Vice-Pres., Academia Europaea, 2003–. Foreign Associate Mem., Inst. of Medicine, NAS, USA, 2002. Founder FMedSci 1998. Hon. FBA 2008. *Publications:* (ed jtly and contrib.) Coronary Heart Disease Epidemiology, 1992, 2nd edn 2005; (ed jtly) Social Determinants of Health, 1999, 2nd edn 2006; Status Syndrome, 2004; contribs to OPCS Medical and Population Studies; numerous papers in learned jls. *Recreations:* tennis, viola. *Address:* Department of Epidemiology and Public Health, University College London, 1–19 Torrington Place, WC1E 6BT.

MARNOCH, Rt Hon. Lord; Michael Stewart Rae Bruce; PC 2001; Senator of the College of Justice in Scotland, 1990–2005; *b* 26 July 1938; *s* of late Alexander Eric Bruce, Advocate in Aberdeen, and late Mary Gordon Bruce (*née* Walker); *m* 1963, Alison Mary Monfries Stewart; two *d*. *Educ:* Loretto Sch.; Aberdeen Univ. (MA, LLB). Admitted Faculty of Advocates, 1963; QC Scot. 1975; Standing Counsel: to Dept of Agriculture and Fisheries for Scotland, 1973; to Highlands and Islands Develt Bd, 1973; Advocate Depute, 1983–86. Mem., Criminal Injuries Compensation Bd, 1986–90. Hon. Vice Pres., Salmon and Trout Assoc., 1994– (Chm., Scotland, 1989–94). Hon. LLD Aberdeen, 1999. *Recreations:* fishing, golf. *Clubs:* New (Edinburgh); Honourable Company of Edinburgh Golfers; Bruntsfield Links Golfing Society (Edinburgh), Rosehall Golf (Turriff), Duff House Royal Golf (Banff), Nairn Golf.

MAROWITZ, Charles; Founding Artistic Director: Malibu Stage Company, since 1990; Texas Stage Company, since 1994; Director and Dramaturge, California Repertory Theatre, Long Beach, since 1996; *b* 26 Jan. 1934; Austrian mother, Russian father; *m* 1982, Jane Elizabeth Allsop. *Educ:* Seward Park High Sch.; University Coll. London. Dir, In-Stage Experimental Theatre, 1958; Asst Dir, Royal Shakespeare Co., 1963–65; Artistic Director: Traverse Theatre, 1963–64; Open Space Theatre London, 1968–81; Open Space Theatre of Los Angeles, 1982; Associate Dir, LA Theater Center, 1984–89. Drama Critic: Encore Magazine, 1956–63; Plays and Players, 1958–74; The Village Voice, 1955–; The NY Times, 1966–; West Coast critic: Theatre Week magazine, 1990–97; In-Theater magazine, 1997–; Official Drama critic, Jewish Jl, 1998–; columnist, LA View, 1994–. *West End* Director: Loot, Criterion, 1967; The Bellow Plays, Fortune, 1966; Fortune and Men's Eyes, Comedy, 1969; productions *abroad:* Woyzeck, 1965, The Shrew, 1979, Nat. Theatre, Bergen; Hedda, 1978, Enemy of the People, 1979, Nat. Theatre, Oslo; Measure for Measure, Oslo New Theatre, 1981; The Father, Trondheim, 1981; Ah Sweet Mystery of Life, Seattle, 1981; A Midsummer Night's Dream, Odense, Denmark, 1983; Tartuffe, Molde, Norway, 1985; Marat/Sade, Rutgers, 1993; Merry Wives of Windsor, Dallas Shakespeare Fest., 1993; Bashville in Love, Texas, 1995; Death of Ophelia, Copenhagen, 2006; productions in *Los Angeles:* Artaud at Rodez, 1982; Sherlock's Last Case, 1984; The Petrified Forest, 1985; The Fair Penitent, 1986; The Shrew, 1986; Importance of Being Earnest, 1987; What the Butler Saw, 1988; Wilde West, 1989; Variations on Measure for Measure, 1990; A MacBeth, 1991; Murdering Marlow, 2002; Silent Partners, 2006. Order of the Purple Sash, 1969. *Publications:* The Method as Means, 1960; The Marowitz Hamlet, 1967; A Macbeth, 1970; Confessions of a Counterfeit Critic, 1973; Open Space Plays, 1974; Measure for Measure, 1975; The Shrew, 1975; Artaud at Rodez, 1976; Variations on The Merchant of Venice; The Act of Being, 1977; The Marowitz Shakespeare, 1978; New Theatre Voices of the 50s and 60s, 1981; Sex Wars, 1982; Prospero's Staff, 1986; Potboilers (collection of plays), 1986; Recycling Shakespeare, 1991; Burnt Bridges, 1991; Directing The Action, 1992; (trans.) Cyrano de Bergerac, 1995; Alarums and Excursions, 1996; The Other Way, 1997; Boulevard Comedies, 1999; Stage Fright, 2000; Stagedust (collection of reviews), 2001; Roar of the Canon (collection of Shakespeare criticism), 2001; The Other Chekhov: biography of Michael Chekhov, 2004; Murdering Marlowe, 2004; How to Stage a Play, Make a Fortune, Win a Tony and Become a Theatrical Icon, 2006; Sounds of Music: early recording artists, 2008. *Recreation:* balling. *Address:* 3058 Sequit Drive, Malibu, CA 90265, USA.

MARQUAND, Prof. David (Ian), FBA 1998; FRHistS; Principal, Mansfield College, Oxford, 1996–2002, Hon. Fellow, 2002; *b* 20 Sept. 1934; *s* of Rt Hon. Hilary Marquand, PC; *m* 1959, Judith Mary (*née* Reed); one *s* one *d*. *Educ:* Emanuel Sch.; Magdalen Coll., Oxford (BA 1st cl. hons Mod. Hist. 1957); St Antony's Coll., Oxford (Sen. Schol.; Hon. Fellow 2003). FRHistS 1986. Teaching Asst, Univ. of Calif., 1958–59; Leader Writer, The Guardian, 1959–62; Research Fellow, St Antony's Coll., Oxford, 1962–64; Lectr in Politics, Univ. of Sussex, 1964–66. Contested: (Lab) Barry, 1964; (SDP) High Peak, 1983; MP (Lab) Ashfield, 1966–77; PPS to Minister of Overseas Develt, 1967–69; Jun. Opposition Front-Bench Spokesman on econ. affairs, 1971–72; Member: Select Cttee on Estimates, 1966–68; Select Cttee on Procedure, 1968–73; Select Cttee on Corp. Tax, 1971; British Deleg. to Council of Europe, 1970–73. Chief Advr, Secretariat-Gen.,

European Commission, 1977–78; Prof. of Contemporary History and Politics, Salford Univ., 1978–91; Prof. of Politics, 1991–96 (Hon. Prof., 1997–), and Dir, Political Economy Research Centre, 1993–96, Sheffield Univ. Vis. Scholar, Hoover Instn, Stanford, USA, 1985–86. Jt Ed., Political Qly, 1987–97. Member: Nat. Steering Cttee, SDP, 1981–88; Policy Cttee, Soc & Lib Dem, 1988–90. Trustee, Aspen Inst., Berlin, 1982–; Member: Adv. Council, Inst. of Contemporary British History, 1987–; Bd of Trustees, IPPR, 1992–2005; Adv. Council, Demos, 1993–; Social Justice Commn, 1993–94; Commn on Wealth Creation and Social Cohesion, 1994–95. Thomas Jefferson Meml Lectr, Univ. of Calif at Berkeley, 1981. FRSA. Hon. DLitt: Salford, 1996; Sheffield, 2002; Hon. Dr rer. pol. Bologna, 2002. George Orwell Meml Prize (jtly), 1980; Sir Isaiah Berlin Prize, Pol Studies Assoc., 2001. *Publications:* Ramsay MacDonald, 1977; Parliament for Europe, 1979; (with David Butler) European Elections and British Politics, 1981; (ed) John Mackintosh on Politics, 1982; The Unprincipled Society, 1988; The Progressive Dilemma, 1991, 2nd edn 1999; (ed with Anthony Seldon) The Ideas That Shaped Post-War Britain, 1996; The New Reckoning, 1997; (ed with R. Nettler) Religion and Democracy, 2000; Decline of the Public, 2004; Britain Since 1918, 2008; contrib. to: The Age of Austerity, 1964; A Radical Future, 1967; Coalitions in British Politics, 1978; Britain in Europe, 1980; The Political Economy of Tolerable Survival, 1980; The Rebirth of Britain, 1982; European Monetary Union Progress and Prospects, 1982; Social Theory and Political Practice, 1982; The Changing Constitution, 1985; Thatcherism, 1987; The Radical Challenge, 1987; The Ruling Performance, 1987; The Alternative, 1990; Debating the Constitution, 1993; Re-inventing the Left, 1994; The New Social Democracy, 1999; The Market or the Public Domain, 2001; Restating the State, 2004; articles and reviews in The Guardian, The Times, The Sunday Times, New Statesman, Encounter, Commentary, Prospect, and in academic jls. *Recreation:* walking. *Address:* 37 St Andrew's Road, Oxford OX3 9DL.

MÁRQUEZ, Gabriel García; Colombian novelist; *b* 6 March 1928; *m* Mercedes García Márquez; two *s*. *Educ:* Univ. of Bogotá; Univ. of Cartagena. Corresp., El Espectador, Rome and Paris; formed Cuban Press Agency, Bogotá; worked for Prensa Latina, Cuba, later as Dep. Head, NY office, 1961; lived in Venezuela, Cuba, USA, Spain, Mexico; returned to Colombia, 1982; divides time between Mexico and Colombia. Rómulo Gallegos Prize, 1972; Nobel Prize for Literature, 1982. *Publications:* La hojarasca, 1955 (Leaf Storm, 1973); El coronel no tiene quien la escriba, 1961 (No One Writes to the Colonel, 1971); La mala hora, 1962 (In Evil Hour, 1980); Los funerales de la Mamá Grande, 1962; Cien años de soledad, 1967 (One Hundred Years of Solitude, 1970); La increíble y triste historia de la cándida Eréndira, 1972 (Innocent Erendira and other stories, 1979); El otoño del patriarca, 1975 (The Autumn of the Patriarch, 1977); Crónica de una muerte anunciada, 1981 (Chronicle of a Death Foretold, 1982; filmed, 1987); (with P. Mendoza) El olor de la Guayaba, 1982 (Fragrance of Guava, ed T. Nairn, 1983); El amor en los tiempos del cólera, 1984 (Love in the Time of Cholera, 1988); Amores Dificiles, 1989 (Of Love and Other Demons, 1995); El General en su Laberinto, 1989 (The General in his Labyrinth, 1991); Collected Stories, 1991; Doce cuentos peregrinos, 1992 (Strange Pilgrims, 1993); Memoria de mis putas tristes, 2004 (Memories of My Melancholy Whores, 2005); *non-fiction:* Relato de un naufrago, 1970 (The Story of a Shipwrecked Sailor, 1986); La aventura de Miguel Littín, clandestina en Chile (Clandestine in Chile: adventures of Miguel Littín), 1986; Noticia de un secuestro, 1996 (News of a Kidnapping, 1997); Vivir para contarla (autobiog.), 2002 (Living to Tell the Tale, 2003). *Address:* c/o Agencia Literaria Carmen Balcelos, Diagonal 580, Barcelona, Spain.

MARQUIS, family name of **Earl of Woolton**.

MARQUIS, James Douglas, DFC 1945; Managing Director, Irvine Development Corporation, 1972–81; *b* 16 Oct. 1921; *s* of James Charles Marquis and Jessica Amy (*née* Huggett); *m* 1945, Brenda Eleanor, *d* of Robert Reyner Davey; two *s*. *Educ:* Shooters Hill Sch., Woolwich. Local Govt, 1938–41. Served War: RAF: 1941–46 (RAF 1st cl. Air Navigation Warrant, 1945), Navigation Officer, 177 Sqdn, 224 Gp, and AHQ Malaya (Sqdn Ldr 1945). Local Govt, 1946–56; Harlow Develt Corp., 1957–68; Irvine Develt Corp.: Chief Finance Officer, 1968–72; Dir of Finance and Admin., 1972. Pres., Ayrshire Chamber of Industries, 1979–80. FRMetS 1945; CPFA (IPFA 1950); FCIS 1953. *Publication:* An Ayrshire Sketchbook, 1979. *Recreations:* sketching and painting (five one-man exhibns, incl. one in Sweden; works in collections: Japan, Sweden, Norway, Denmark, Australia, USA, Canada); gardening, bonsai, suiseki. *Address:* 3 Knoll Park, Ayr KA7 4RH. *T:* (01292) 442212.

MARR, Andrew William Stevenson; Presenter: Start The Week, Radio 4, since 2002; Sunday AM, BBC TV, since 2005; *b* 31 July 1959; *s* of Donald and Valerie Marr; *m* 1987, Jacqueline Ashley, *qv*; one *s* two *d*. *Educ:* Dundee High Sch.; Craigflower, Fife; Loretto School, Musselburgh; Trinity Hall, Cambridge (BA). Trainee and gen. reporter, 1982–85, Parly Corresp., 1985–86, The Scotsman; Political Corresp., The Independent, 1986–88; Political Editor: The Scotsman, 1988; The Economist, 1989–92; political columnist and Associate Editor, 1992–96, Editor, 1996–98, Editor-in-Chief, 1998, The Independent; columnist, The Observer, and The Express, 1998–2000; Political Editor, BBC, 2000–05; columnist, Daily Telegraph, 2000–. Presenter, Andrew Marr's History of Modern Britain (series), BBC2, 2007. Columnist of the Year, What the Papers Say, 1994; Creative Media Journalist of Year, British Press Awards, 2000; Pol Journalist of Year, C4/House Mag., 2001, 2002; Specialist of the Year, RTS Awards, 2001–02; Best Individual TV Performer, Voice of the Listener and Viewer Awards, 2002; Best TV Performer, BPG, 2002; Parly Commentator of the Year, Richard Dimbleby Award, BAFTA, 2004. *Publications:* The Battle for Scotland, 1992; Ruling Britannia, 1995; The Day Britain Died, 2000; My Trade: a short history of British journalism, 2004; A History of Modern Britain, 2007. *Recreations:* reading, painting, talking. *Address:* c/o BBC, Television Centre, Wood Lane, W12 7RJ.

MARR, Douglas, CBE 2001; HM Inspector of Education, since 2004; *b* 7 Feb. 1947; *s* of Douglas N. Marr and Evelyn Marr; *m* 1990, Alison M. Gordon; one *d*. *Educ:* Aberdeen Grammar Sch.; Univ. of Aberdeen (MA Hons 1969, MEd Hons 1982). Teacher of History, Hilton Acad., Aberdeen, 1970–71; Asst Principal Teacher of Hist., Aberdeen GS, 1971–76; Principal Teacher of Hist., Hilton Acad., 1976–81; Asst Rector, Kemnay Acad., 1981–84; Depute Rector, The Gordon Schs, Huntly, 1984–87; Headteacher, Hilton Acad., 1987–88; Rector: St Machar Acad., 1988–95; Banchory Acad., 1995–2002; Schs Mgt and Curriculum Structures Co-ordinator, Aberdeenshire Council, 2002–04; Sen. Teaching Fellow, Sch. of Educn, Univ. of Aberdeen, 2004–06. Sen. Consultant, Acorn Consulting (Scotland), 2004–. Mem., Business Cttee, 2001–06, Ct, 2002–06, Univ. of Aberdeen. *Recreations:* squash, gardening, walking, occasional journalism. *Address:* Oak Lodge, Alford, Aberdeenshire AB33 8DH. *T:* (019755) 63062; *e-mail:* douglas.marr@alford.co.uk. *Club:* Leicestershire CC.

MARR, (Sir) Leslie Lynn, (2nd Bt *cr* 1919, but does not use the title); MA Cambridge; painter and draughtsman; late Flight Lieutenant RAF; *b* 14 Aug. 1922; *o s* of late Col John Lynn Marr, OBE, TD, (and *g s* of 1st Bt,) and Amelia Rachel, *d* of late Robert Thompson, Overdinsdale Hall, Darlington; *S* grandfather, 1932; *m* 1st, 1948, Dinora Delores Mendelson (marr. diss. 1956); one *d*; 2nd, 1962, Lynn Heneage (marr. diss. 2000); two *d*; 3rd, 2002, Maureen Thelma Monk (*née* Dormer). *Educ:* Shrewsbury; Pembroke Coll., Cambridge. Has exhibited at Ben Uri, Drian, Woodstock, Wildenstein, Whitechapel, Campbell and Franks Galls and Piano Nobile Fine Paintings, London; Art Sch. Gall., Shrewsbury Sch.; Mercer Art Gall., Harrogate; University Gall., Northumbria Univ.; also in Norwich, Belfast, Birmingham, Newcastle upon Tyne, Durham City Art Gall., Bristol and Paris. *Publications:* From My Point of View: personal record of some Norfolk churches, 1979; A Piano Album, 1998; A Second Album for Piano, 1998. *Heir: cousin* James Allan Marr [*b* 17 May 1939; *m* 1965, Jennifer, *yr d* of late J. W. E. Gill; two *s* one *d*]. *Address:* c/o Piano Nobile Fine Paintings, 129 Portland Road, W11 4LW.

MARR-JOHNSON, His Honour Frederick James Maugham; a Circuit Judge, 1991–2006; *b* 17 Sept. 1936; *s* of late Kenneth Marr-Johnson and Hon. Diana Marr-Johnson; *m* 1966, Susan Eyre; one *s* one *d*. *Educ:* Winchester Coll.; Trinity Hall, Cambridge (MA). Called to the Bar, Lincoln's Inn, 1962, Bencher, 1999; practised on SE Circuit, 1963–91. Judge of Mayor's and City of London Court, 1999–2006. *Recreation:* sailing. *Address:* 33 Hestercombe Avenue, SW6 5LL. *T:* (020) 7731 0412. *Clubs:* Royal Yacht Squadron (Cowes); Bar Yacht (Rear Cdre, 1999–2000).

MARRACK, Rear-Adm. Philip Reginald, CB 1979; CEng, FIMechE, FIMarEST; *b* 16 Nov. 1922; *s* of Captain Philip Marrack, RN and Annie Kathleen Marrack (*née* Proud); *m* 1954, Pauline Mary (*née* Haag); two *d*. *Educ:* Eltham Coll.; Plymouth Coll.; RNC Dartmouth; RN Engineering Coll., Manadon. War service at sea, HM Ships Orion and Argus, 1944–45; Advanced Engineering Course, RNC Greenwich, 1945–47; HM Submarines Templar and Token, 1947–50; served in Frigate Torquay, Aircraft Carriers Glory and Hermes, and MoD; Captain 1965; Commanded Admiralty Reactor Test Estab., Dounreay, 1967–70; CSO (Mat.) on Staff of Flag Officer Submarines, and Asst Dir (Nuclear), Dockyard Dept, 1970–74; Rear-Adm. 1974; Dir, Naval Ship Production, 1974–77; Dir, Dockyard Production and Support, 1977–81, retd. *Recreations:* fly fishing, gardening, viticulture, wine making.

MARRIN, John Wheeler; QC 1990; a Recorder, since 1997; *b* 24 Aug. 1951; *s* of late Dr Charles Ainsworth Marrin and of Cecilia Margaret Marrin (*née* Staveley); *m* 1984, Paquita Carmen Bulan de Zulueta; one s three *d*. *Educ:* Sherborne Sch.; Magdalene Coll., Cambridge (MA). Called to the Bar, Inner Temple, 1974, Bencher, 2002; Head of Chambers, 2005–. *Recreations:* music, ski-ing, horse-racing, travel. *Address:* Keating Chambers, 15 Essex Street, WC2R 3AA. *T:* (020) 7544 2600.

MARRINER, Sir Neville, Kt 1985; CBE 1979; conductor; Founder and Director, Academy of St Martin in the Fields, since 1956; *b* 15 April 1924; *s* of Herbert Henry Marriner and Ethel May Roberts; *m* 1955, Elizabeth Mary Sims; one *s* one *d*. *Educ:* Lincoln Sch.; Royal College of Music (ARCM). Taught music at Eton Coll., 1948; Prof., Royal Coll. of Music, 1950. Martin String Quartet, 1949; Jacobean Ensemble, 1951; London Symphony Orchestra, 1954; Music Director: Los Angeles Chamber Orchestra, 1968–77; Minnesota Orchestra, 1979–86; Stuttgart Radio Symphony Orch., 1984–89. Artistic Director: South Bank Summer Music, 1975–77; Meadow Brook Festival, Detroit Symphony Orchestra, 1979–83; Barbican Summer Festival, 1985–87. Hon. ARAM; Hon. FRCM 1983; Hon. Fellow, Hong Kong Acad. Music, 1998. Hon. MusD: RSAMD; Univ. of Hull. Kt, Order of the Star of the North (Sweden), 1984; Officer, Ordre des Arts et des Lettres (France), 1995. *Club:* Garrick.

MARRIOTT, Arthur Leslie; QC 1997; Solicitor, Dewey & LeBoeuf (formerly LeBoeuf Lamb Greene & MacRae) LLP, since 2005; a Deputy High Court Judge, since 1997; a Recorder, since 1998; *b* 30 March 1943; *s* of Arthur Leonard Marriott and Helen Gracie Marriott (*née* Patterson). *Educ:* Selhurst Grammar Sch. for Boys, Croydon; Gymnasium Christian Ernestinum, Bayreuth, Germany; Coll. of Law. FCIArb 1990; Chartered Arbitrator, 2001. Admitted Solicitor, England and Wales, 1966, Hong Kong, 1976; with Wilmer, Cutler & Pickering, 1988–97; Debevoise & Plimpton, 1997–2005. Hon. Bencher, Gray's Inn, 2001. *Publication:* (with Henry Brown) Alternative Dispute Resolution: principles and practice, 1993, 2nd edn 1999. *Recreations:* fishing, music. *Address:* Dewey & LeBoeuf LLP, 1 Minster Court, Mincing Lane, EC3R 7YL. *Clubs:* Athenæum, Royal Automobile.

MARRIOTT, Bryant Hayes; Director of Broadcasting, Seychelles Broadcasting Corporation (formerly Radio Television Seychelles), 1991–93; *b* 9 Sept. 1936; *s* of Rev. Horace Marriott and Barbara Marriott; *m* 1963, Alison Mary Eyles; one *s* two *d*. *Educ:* Tormore Sch., Upper Deal, Kent; Marlborough Coll., Wilts; New Coll., Oxford (MA). Joined BBC, 1961; Studio Manager, 1961; Producer, 1963; Staff Training Attachments Officer, 1973; Chief Asst to Controller Radio 1 and 2, 1976; Head of Recording Services, 1979; Controller, Radio Two, 1983; Controller, Special Duties, Radio BBC, 1990–91. *Recreations:* gardening, sailing, drumming. *Address:* 4 School Pasture, Burnham Deepdale, King's Lynn, Norfolk PE31 8DF. *Club:* Brancaster Staithe Sailing.

MARRIOTT, Sir Hugh Cavendish S.; *see* Smith-Marriott.

MARRIOTT, Martin Marriott; Headmaster, Canford School, 1976–92; *b* 28 Feb. 1932; *s* of late Rt Rev. Philip Selwyn Abraham, Bishop of Newfoundland, and Elizabeth Dorothy Cicely, *d* of late Sir John Marriott; *m* 1956, Judith Caroline Guerney Lubbock; one *s* two *d*. *Educ:* Lancing College; New College, Oxford. MA, DipEd. RAF Educn Branch, 1956–59. Asst Master, Heversham Grammar Sch., 1959–66; Asst Master, Housemaster, Second Master, Acting Master, Haileybury College, 1966–76. Chm., HMC, 1989. *Recreations:* grandchildren, golf, gardening. *Address:* Morris' Farm House, Baverstock, near Dinton, Salisbury, Wilts SP3 5EL. *T:* (01722) 716874; *e-mail:* marriott@waitrose.com. *Club:* East India.

MARRIOTT, Michael; furniture and product designer; Director, Michael Marriott, since 1994; *b* 7 Jan. 1963; *s* of Michael and Jean Marriott. *Educ:* London Coll. of Furniture (HND); Royal Coll. of Art (MA 1993). Pt-time tutor, RCA, 1998–. Work in exhibitions, including: RFH; Crafts Council; ICA, and countries worldwide, including Italy, Germany, Sweden, Japan and USA; work in public collections: Crafts Council; British Council; Design Mus. Jerwood Prize for Furniture, Jerwood Foundn, 1999. *Recreations:* cycling, frottage. *Address:* Unit F2, 2–4 Southgate Road, N1 3JJ; *e-mail:* mm@michaelmarriott.com. *Club:* Hat on Wall.

MARRIOTT, Richard, CVO 2006; TD 1965; Lord-Lieutenant of East Riding of Yorkshire, 1996–2005; *b* 17 Dec. 1930; *s* of late Rowland Arthur Marriott and Evelyn (*née* Caillard), Cotesbach Hall, Leics; *m* 1959, Janet (Sally) Coles; two *s*. *Educ:* Eton Coll.; Brasenose Coll., Oxford (Schol.). 2nd Lieut, Rifle Bde, 1950–51; Lt-Col comdg 21st SAS Regt (Artists) TA, 1966–69. With Brown Shipley & Co. Ltd, 1954–63; Partner, Mullens & Co. (Govt Brokers), 1964–86; Dir, Mercury Asset Mgt, 1986–96. Mem., Rural Develt Commn, Humberside, 1986–95. Vice-President: Officers' Assoc. (Chm., 1977–86); RUSI, 1993–98; Financial Adviser: Army Benevolent Fund, 1969–97 (Treas., 1997–2000); Airborne Forces Security Fund, 1972–2006; Trustee, Special Air Service

Assoc., 1994–2003. Pres., Yorks Agricl Soc., 1995–96. Member Council: Nat. Army Mus., 1991–2005; Hull Univ., 1994–2000; Vice-Pres., Brynmor Jones Liby, Hull, 1988–. Trustee: Buttle Trust, 1985–98 (Dep. Chm., 1990–96); York Minster Fund, 1987–2000; Chm., Burton Constable Foundn, 1992–. Mem., Adv. Panel, Greenwich Hosp., 1981–2002. High Sheriff, Humberside, 1991–92. DUniv Hull, 2003. *Recreations:* books, the arts, travel, field sports. *Address:* Boynton Hall, Bridlington, E Yorks YO16 4XJ. *Clubs:* Beefsteak, Special Forces, White's.

MARRIS, James Hugh Spencer; Director: Newcastle Race Course, 1994–2007; Sedgefield Racecourse, 2002–07; *b* 30 July 1937; *s* of Harry V. Marris and Agnes E. Hutchinson; *m* 1963, Susan Mary Husband; one *s* one *d. Educ:* King William's College, Isle of Man; Royal Technical College, Salford. ARTCS, CEng, FIGEM. Dir of Engineering, E Midlands Gas, 1978–82; Regional Dep. Chm., Eastern Gas, 1982–83; HQ Dir (Ops), British Gas, 1983–87; Regl Chm., British Gas, Northern, 1988–93. *Publications:* contribs to IGasE Jl. *Recreations:* golf, gardening. *Address:* 3 Apple Tree Rise, Corbridge, Northumberland NE45 5HD. *T:* (01434) 633509.

MARRIS, Robert; MP (Lab) Wolverhampton South West, since 2001; *b* 8 April 1955; *s* of Dr Charles Marris and Margaret Chetwode Marris, JP; partner, Julia Pursehouse. *Educ:* St Edward's Sch., Oxford; Univ. of British Columbia (BA Sociology and Hist. (double 1st) 1976; MA Hist. 1979). Trucker, 1977–79; trolley bus driver, 1979–82; law student, Birmingham Poly., 1982–84; articled clerk, 1985–87; solicitor, 1987–. *Recreations:* Wolves, Canadiana, bicycling. *Address:* House of Commons, SW1A 0AA. *T:* (020) 7219 8342.

MARRIS, Prof. Robin Lapthorn; Professor of Economics, 1981–86, and Head of Department of Economics, 1983–86, Birkbeck College, University of London, now Professor Emeritus; *b* 31 March 1924; *s* of Eric Denyer Marris, CB, and late Phyllis, *d* of T. H. F. Lapthorn, JP; *m* 1st, 1949, Marion Ellinger; 2nd, 1954, Jane Evelina Burney Ayres; one *s* two *d*; 3rd, 1972, Anne Fairclough Mansfield; one *d. Educ:* Bedales Sch.; King's Coll., Cambridge. BA 1946, ScD 1968, Cantab. Asst Principal, HM Treasury, 1947–50; UN, Geneva, 1950–52; Fellow of King's Coll., Cambridge, 1951–76; Lectr, 1951–72, Reader, 1972–76, in Econs, Univ. of Cambridge; Prof. 1976–81 and Chm., 1976–79, Dept of Economics, Univ. of Maryland. Visiting Professor: Univ. of California, Berkeley, 1961; Harvard, 1967; Trento Univ., Italy, 1989–91. Dir, World Economy Div., Min. of Overseas Develt, 1964–66. Consultant: Home Office, 2001–05; DfES, 2001–05; Mem., Econs Adv. Panel, Home Office, 2005–. Mem., Vis. Cttee, Open Univ., 1982–. *Publications:* Economic Arithmetic, 1958; The Economic Theory of Managerial Capitalism, 1964; The Economics of Capital Utilisation, 1964; (with Adrian Wood) The Corporate Economy, 1971; The Corporate Society, 1974; The Theory and Future of the Corporate Economy and Society, 1979; The Higher Education Crisis, 1987; Reconstructing Keynsian Economics with Imperfect Competition, 1991; Economics, Bounded Rationality and the Cognitive Revolution, 1992; How to Save the Underclass, 1996; Managerial Capitalism in Retrospect, 1998; Ending Poverty, 1999; contrib. Econ. Jl, Rev. Econ. Studies, Economica, Jl Manchester Stat. Soc., Jl Royal Stat. Soc., Amer. Econ. Rev., Qly Jl of Econs, Jl of Economic Literature, etc. *Recreations:* cooking, scuba diving, sailing. *Address:* Lingard House, Chiswick Mall, W4 2PJ; *e-mail:* robinmarris@btinternet.com.

See also S. N. Marris.

MARRIS, Stephen Nicholson; *b* 7 Jan. 1930; *s* of Eric Denyer Marris, CB, and Phyllis May Marris (*née* Lapthorn); *m* 1955, Margaret Swindells; two *s* one *d. Educ:* Bryanston School; King's College, Cambridge. MA, PhD. Nat. Inst. of Economic and Social Research, 1953–54; economist and international civil servant; with Org. for European Economic Co-operation, later Org. for Economic Co-operation and Development (OECD), 1956–83: Dir, Economics Branch, 1970; Economic Advr to Sec.-Gen., 1975; Sen. Fellow, Inst. for Internat. Econs, Washington, 1983–88. Vis. Res. Prof. of Internat. Economics, Brookings Instn, Washington DC, 1969–70; Vis. Prof., Institut d'Etudes Politiques, Paris, 1986. Hon. Dr Stockholm Univ., 1978. *Publication:* Deficits and the Dollar: the World Economy at Risk, 1985. *Address:* 8 Sentier des Pierres Blanches, 92190 Meudon, France. *T:* 146269812.

See also R. L. Marris.

MARRISON, Rev. Dr Geoffrey Edward; Senior Fellow, South East Asian Studies, University of Hull, 2000–03 (Associate, Centre for South-East Asian Studies, 1989–91; Hon. Fellow, 1992–2003); *b* 11 Jan. 1923; *s* of John and Rose Marrison; *m* 1958, Margaret Marian Millburn; one *s* three *d. Educ:* SOAS, Univ. of London (BA Malay 1948, PhD Linguistics 1967); Bishops' Coll. Cheshunt; Kirchliche Hochschule, Berlin. Indian Army, 1942–46. SOAS, 1941–42 and 1946–49; ordained Priest, Singapore, 1952; in Malaya with USPG, 1952–56; Vicar of St Timothy, Crookes, Sheffield, 1958–61; Linguistics Adviser, British and Foreign Bible Soc., 1962–67, incl. service in Assam, 1962–64; Asst Keeper, British Museum, 1967–71, Dep. Keeper 1971–74; Dir and Keeper, Dept of Oriental Manuscripts and Printed Books, British Library, 1974–83. Permission to officiate, dio. of Carlisle, 1983–; Tutor, Carlisle Diocesan Training Inst., 1984–. Res. studies on Indonesian literatures, Leiden and Indonesia, 1990–91. Hon. Canon of All Saints Pro-Cathedral, Shillong, 1963. FRAS. *Publications:* The Christian Approach to the Muslim, 1958; A Catalogue of the South-East Asian Collections of Professor M. A. Jaspan (1926–1975), 1989; A Catalogue of the South-East Asian History Collections of Dr D. K. Bassett (1931–1989), 1992; A Catalogue of the Collections of Rev. Dr Harry Parkin on Asian Religions and Batak Studies (1926–1990), 1993; A Catalogue of the Collections of Dr Roy Bruton on Sarawak, and on the Sociology of Education, 1994; Sasak and Javanese Literature of Lombok, 1999; Catalogue of Javanese and Sasak Texts, 1999; articles in Jl Malayan Branch Royal Asiatic Soc., Bible Translator. *Recreations:* ethno-linguistics of South and South East Asia, Christian and oriental art. *Address:* Emmaus, 1 Ainsworth Street, Ulverston, Cumbria LA12 7EU. *T:* (01229) 586874.

MARS-JONES, Adam; writer; Film Critic, The Times, 1999–2001; *b* 26 Oct. 1954; *s* of Hon. Sir William Mars-Jones, MBE. *Educ:* Westminster School; Trinity Hall, Cambridge (BA 1976). Film Critic, The Independent, 1986–99. *Publications:* Lantern Lecture (stories), 1981 (Somerset Maugham Award 1982); (with Edmund White) The Darker Proof (stories), 1987, 2nd edn 1988; Venus Envy (essay), 1990; Monopolies of Loss (stories), 1992; The Waters of Thirst (novel), 1993; Blind Bitter Happiness (essays), 1997; Pilcrow (novel), 2008. *Recreations:* organ-playing, baby-sitting. *Address:* 38 Oakbank Grove, Herne Hill, SE24 0AJ. *T:* (020) 7733 9757.

MARSALIS, Wynton; trumpeter; Artistic Director, Jazz at Lincoln Center, New York, since 1987; *b* New Orleans, 18 Oct. 1961; *s* of Ellis and Dolores Marsalis. *Educ:* New Orleans Center for the Creative Arts; Berkshire Music Center (Harvey Shapiro Award); Juilliard Sch., NY (Schol.). Mem., Art Blakey's Jazz Messengers, 1980–81; formed own jazz quintet, 1981; has played with major orchestras worldwide, incl. New Orleans Philharmonic, LSO, English Chamber Orch. Music Dir, Lincoln Center Jazz Orch., 1987–. *Compositions* include: In This House, On This Morning; Blood on the Fields, 1997 (Pulitzer Prize for Music, 1997); Knozz-Moe-King; Jazz (ballet score). Numerous recordings (Grammy Awards for jazz and classical performances). *Publications:* Sweet Swing Blues on the Road, 1994; Marsalis on Music, 1995; (with C. Vigeland) Jazz in the Bittersweet Blues of Life; (with S. Seyfu Hinds) To a Young Musician: letters from the road, 2004; Jazz ABZ, 2005. *Address:* Wynton Marsalis Enterprises, c/o Jazz at Lincoln Center, 33 West 60th Street, New York, NY 10023, USA; c/o Agency for the Performing Arts, 9200 West Sunset Boulevard, Suite 1200, West 12 Hollywood, CA 90069–5812, USA.

MARSCHALL JONES, Timothy Aidan; HM Diplomatic Service; HM Consul General, Lille, since 2006; *b* 5 Sept. 1962; *s* of Dr Derek Hugh Powell Jones and Thelma Anne (*née* Gray); *m* 2001, Dr Christin Marschall; one *d. Educ:* Bexhill Co. Grammar Sch.; Christ's Coll., Cambridge (BA Hons 1984). Joined HM Diplomatic Service, 1984: Vienna (CSCE), 1987–88; The Hague, 1988–92; FCO, 1992–94; EU Admin, Mostar, 1994–95; Dep. Head of Mission, Tehran, 1996–99; Ambassador to Armenia, 1999–2002; Hd of Ops, IT Strategy Unit, FCO, 2003–06. *Recreations:* swimming, cycling, idle curiosity. *Address:* c/o Foreign and Commonwealth Office, King Charles Street, SW1A 2AH.

MARSDEN, Edmund Murray; Director (formerly Minister (Cultural Affairs)), India, and Regional Director, South Asia, British Council, 2000–05; *b* 22 Sept. 1946; *s* of Christopher Marsden and Ruth Marsden (*née* Kershaw); *m* 1975, Christine Vanner (*d* 1980); *m* 1981, Megan McIntyre; one *s. Educ:* Winchester College; Trinity College, Cambridge. Partner, Compton Press, Salisbury, 1968–70; Nuffield Foundn Publications Unit, 1970–71; British Council: Ghana, 1971; Belgium, 1973; Algeria, 1975; Management Accountant, 1977; Syria, 1980; Dir, Educn Contracts, 1982; Turkey, 1987; Dir, Corporate Affairs, 1990–93; Asst Dir-Gen., 1993–99; Chm., Intermediate Technol. Develt Gp, 1995–97 and 1998–2000. *Address:* 21755 Ocean Vista Drive, Laguna Beach, CA 92651, USA; *e-mail:* emarsden01@aol.com.

MARSDEN, Gordon; MP (Lab) Blackpool South, since 1997; *b* 28 Nov. 1953; *s* of late George Henry Marsden and Joyce Marsden. *Educ:* Stockport Grammar Sch.; New Coll., Oxford (BA 1st cl. Hons History; MA); Warburg Inst., London Univ. (postgrad. res.); Harvard Univ. (Kennedy Schol. in Internat. Relations). Tutor and Associate Lectr, Arts Faculty, Open Univ., 1977–97; PR Consultant, 1980–85; Chief Public Affairs Advr, English Heritage, 1984–85; Editor, History Today, 1985–97; Consultant Ed., New Socialist, 1989–90. Chm., Fabian Soc., 2000–01. Contested (Lab) Blackpool S, 1992. PPS, Lord Chancellor's Dept, 2001–03, to Sec. of State for Culture, Media and Sport, 2003–05. Mem., Select Cttee on Educn and Employment, 1998–2001, 2005–07, on Innovation, Univs and Skills, 2007–. Vice-Pres., All Party Arts and Heritage Gp, 2000–; Chm., All Party Skills Gp, 2006–; Vice-Pres., PLP Educn and Employment Cttee, 1998–2001; Mem., Ecclesiastical Cttee, 1998–. Pres., British Resorts and Destinations (formerly British Resorts) Assoc., 1998–. Mem. Bd, Inst. of Historical Res., 1995–2001. Trustee, History Today, 2005–. Vis. Parly Fellow, St Antony's Coll., Oxford, 2003; Centenary Fellow, Historical Assoc., 2006–07. *Publications:* (ed) Victorian Values: personalities and perspectives in Nineteenth Century society, 1990, 2nd edn 1998; (contrib.) The English Question, 2000; (contrib.) The History of Censorship, 2002; contrib. History Today, Independent, Times, Tribune, THES. *Recreations:* world music, travel, medieval culture. *Address:* House of Commons, SW1A 0AA. *T:* (020) 7219 1262.

MARSDEN, Prof. Jerrold Eldon, PhD; FRS 2006; FRSC; Professor of Control and Dynamical Systems, since 1995, and Carl F. Braun Professor of Engineering, California Institute of Technology; *b* British Columbia, Canada, 1942. *Educ:* Univ. of Toronto (BSc 1965); Princeton Univ. (PhD 1968). FRSC 1991. Lectr, latterly Prof., Univ. of Calif, Berkeley, 1968–95. *Publications:* (with Michael Hoffman) Elementary Classical Analysis, 1974, 2nd edn 1993; (with Anthony Tromba) Vector Calculus, 1976, 5th edn 2003; Calculus, 2nd edn 1985; (with Alan Weinstein) Calculus Unlimited, 1981; (with Anthony Tromba and Alan Weinstein) Basic Multivariable Calculus, 1992; (with Michael Hoffman) Basic Complex Analysis, 3rd edn 1998. *Address:* Division of Engineering and Applied Science, California Institute of Technology, 1200 E California Boulevard, Pasadena, CA 91125–8100, USA.

MARSDEN, Jonathan Mark, LVO 2003; FSA; Deputy Surveyor of the Queen's Works of Art, since 1996; *b* 15 Feb. 1960; *s* of Rear-Adm. Peter Nicholas Marsden, *qv*; *m* 2002, Sarah Bernard; two *s. Educ:* Sherborne Sch.; Univ. of York (BA Hons Hist.). Asst Curator, The Treasure Houses of Britain exhibn, Nat. Gall. of Art, Washington, 1983–85; Historic Buildings Rep., Nat. Trust N Wales Reg., 1986–92, Thames and Chilterns Reg., 1992–96. Member: Exec. Cttee, Georgian Gp, 1995–2005; Council, Furniture Hist. Soc., 2002–04 (Hon. Editl Sec., 2005–); Collections Cttee, RCM, 2003–. Trustee: Household Cavalry Mus., 2003–; NACF, 2005–; Royal Yacht Britannia Trust, 2007–. FSA 2006. *Publications:* guidebooks to Penrhyn Castle, Stowe Landscape Garden, Cliveden, Chastleton, Clarence House, Buckingham Palace, Windsor Castle; contribs to exhibn catalogues and learned jls. *Recreations:* gardening, shooting, music, beach cricket. *Address:* 44 Cleaver Square, SE11 4EA.

MARSDEN, Paul William Barry; *b* 18 March 1968; *s* of Thomas Darlington Marsden and Audrey Marsden; *m* 1994, Michelle Sarah Bayley (*née* Somerville); two *s. Educ:* Open Univ. (Dip. Mgt 1995); Newcastle Coll. (Dip. Business Excellence 2000). Quality Manager: Taylor Woodrow, 1990–94; NatWest Bank, 1994–96; Mitel Telecom, 1996–97. MP (Lab, 1997–2001, Lib Dem, 2001–05) Shrewsbury and Atcham. Lib Dem spokesman on health, 2002–03, on transport, 2003–05. Mem., Select Cttee on Agric., 1997–2001, on Transport, 2003–05; Chm., All Party Gp on Mgt, 1998. Vice President: Offa's Dyke Assoc., 1997–; Heart of Wales Travellers' Assoc., 1997–. Member: Shropshire Chamber of Commerce, Trng & Enterprise, 1997–; Agric. & Rural Economy Cttee, CLA, 1997–2001. Member: DIAL Shropshire, Telford and Wrekin, 2003–; Shrewsbury and Newport Canals Trust, 2003–. Hon. Pres., W Midlands Lib Dem Youth and Students, 2003–05. MCMI (MIMgt 1996); MInstD 2002. *Publication:* (contrib.) Voices for Peace, 2001. *Recreations:* marathon running, gardening, American political history, family, rural affairs.

MARSDEN, Rear-Adm. Peter Nicholas; *b* 29 June 1932; *s* of Dr James Pickford Marsden and Evelyn (*née* Holman); *m* 1956, Jean Elizabeth Mather; two *s* one *d. Educ:* Felsted Sch., Essex. Joined RN, 1950; Commander, 1968; Captain, 1976; Commodore, Admiralty Interview Bd, 1983–84; Sen. Naval Mem., DS, RCDS, 1985–88. Exec. Dir, 21st Century Trust, 1989–92. *Recreations:* golf, beagling, gardening. *Address:* c/o National Westminster Bank, Standishgate, Wigan, Lancs WN1 1UJ. *Club:* Army and Navy.

See also J. M. Marsden.

MARSDEN, Dr Rosalind Mary, CMG 2003; HM Diplomatic Service; Ambassador to Sudan, since 2007; *b* 1950; *d* of late Major Walter Stancliffe Marsden and Winifred Howells. *Educ:* Woking County Grammar Sch. for Girls; Somerville Coll., Oxford (BA 1st Cl. Hons Mod. Hist.); St Antony's Coll., Oxford (DPhil). Joined FCO, 1974; Tokyo, 1976–80; Policy Planning Staff, 1980–82; EC Dept (Internal), 1983–84; Bonn, 1985–88; Hong Kong Dept, 1989–91; on secondment to National Westminster Bank Gp, 1991–93; Political Counsellor, Tokyo, 1993–96; Hd, UN Dept, 1996–99, Dir, Asia-Pacific,

1999–2003, FCO; Ambassador to Afghanistan, 2003–06; Consul-Gen., Basra, 2006–07. *Recreations:* mountain walking, reading, travel. *Address:* c/o Foreign and Commonwealth Office, King Charles Street, SW1A 2AH.

MARSDEN, Sir Simon (Neville Llewelyn), 4th Bt *cr* 1924, of Grimsby, co. Lincoln; fine art photographer; author; *b* 1 Dec. 1948; *s* of Sir John Denton Marsden, 2nd Bt and Hope (later Dowager Lady Marsden), *yr d* of late G. E. Llewelyn; *S* brother, 1997; *m* 1st, 1970, Catherine Thérèsa Windsor-Lewis (marr. diss. 1978); 2nd, 1984, Caroline Stanton; one *s* one *d*. *Educ:* Ampleforth Coll., Yorks; Sorbonne Univ., Paris. Photographer, 1969–; group exhibns, 1972–, include: London, NY, Paris, European and USA tour; one-man exhibns, 1975–, include: London, NY, Dublin, Paris, Brussels, Tokyo; work in collections including: Arts Council of GB, V & A Mus., Saatchi Collection, London; Bibliothèque Nationale, Paris; J. Paul Getty Mus., Malibu, Cleveland Mus. of Art, USA. Radio and TV appearances, 1986–, incl. Ghosthunter (docu-drama), Granada TV, 1992. Arts Council of GB Awards, 1975 and 1976. *Publications:* In Ruins: the once great houses of Ireland, 1980; The Haunted Realm: ghosts, witches and other strange tales, 1986; Visions of Poe, 1988; Phantoms of the Isles: further tales from the haunted realm, 1990; The Journal of a Ghosthunter: in search of the undead from Ireland to Transylvania, 1994; Beyond the Wall: the lost world of East Germany, 1999; Venice, City of Haunting Dreams, 2001; The Twilight Hour: Celtic visions from the past, 2003; This Spectred Isle: a journey through haunted England, 2005; Ghosthunter: a journey through haunted France, 2006; Memento Mori: churches and churchyards of England, 2007. *Recreations:* sport, walking, historic buildings, reading. *Heir: s* Tadgh Orlando Denton Marsden, *b* 25 Dec. 1990. *Address:* The Presbytery, Hainton, Market Rasen, Lincs LN8 6LR. *T:* (01507) 313646. *Club:* Chelsea Arts.

MARSDEN, Susan; campaigner for legal and consumer rights and for the environment; *b* 6 Dec. 1931; *d* of late John Marsden-Smedley and Agatha (*née* Bethell). *Educ:* Downe House Sch.; Girton Coll., Cambridge (MA). Called to the Bar, Middle Temple, 1957. Worked in consumer organisations in Britain and US, 1957–70; Co-founder, 1972, Exec. Dir, 1972–78, and Course Dir, 1978–81, Legal Action Gp (Editor, LAG Bulletin, 1972–78); Sec., Public Sector Liaison, RIBA, 1981–84; Asst Dir, Nat. Assoc. of CAB, 1985–86; part-time Chairman: Social Security Appeal Tribunals (Leeds), 1987–97; Disability Appeal Tribunals, 1992–97. Chair, Greater London CAB Service, 1979–85; Member: Council, National Assoc. of CAB, 1980–84; Royal Commn on Legal Services, 1976–79; Yorks Regional Rivers Adv. Cttee, Nat. Rivers Authority, 1989–96; Council, Leeds Civic Trust, 1989–92. Chair, 1988–93, Trustee, 1998–2004, EYE on the Aire. Sec., Access Cttee, WR Ramblers' Assoc., 2001–. *Publication:* Justice Out of Reach, a case for Small Claims Courts, 1969. *Recreations:* conservation along the River Aire, tree planting and preservation, gardening, walking, looking at modern buildings. *Address:* Flat 5, 28 Newlay Lane, Horsforth, Leeds LS18 4LE. *T:* (0113) 258 0936.

MARSDEN, Prof. Terry Keith, PhD; Professor of Environmental Policy and Planning, since 1995, Head, School of City and Regional Planning, since 1999, and Co-Director, Centre for Business Relationships, Accountability, Sustainability and Society (ESRC Research Centre), since 2002, Cardiff University; *b* 19 Oct. 1954; *s* of Terence Frederick and Kathleen Marsden; *m* 1982, Mary Anne Speakman; one *s* one *d*. *Educ:* Eccleshall Sec. Mod. Sch., Staffs; Univ. of Hull (BA Hons 1st Cl. Geog. and Sociol. 1976; PhD 1980). MRTPI 1998. Sen. and Principal Lectr in Planning, S Bank Poly., London, 1983–90; Co-Dir, Rural Studies Res. Centre and ESRC Countryside Change Centre, UCL, 1988–93; Reader in Human Geog., Univ. of Hull, 1993–94; Cardiff University: Dir, Res. and Graduate Sch. in the Social Scis, 2001–02; Mem. Bd, Regeneration Inst., 2000–. Visiting Professor: Dept of Rural Sociol., Univ. of Wisconsin-Madison, 1990; Econs and Sociol., Univ. of Pernambuco, Brazil, 1993, 1995; Vis. Internat. Reader in European rural develt, Swedish Sch. of Soc. Scis, Univ. of Helsinki, 2001–Dec. 2003. Special Advisor: Welsh Affairs Select Cttee, 1997–98, 2001; on rural affairs for Nat. Assembly of Wales, 2000–01. Co-Editor, Jl of Environmental Policy and Planning, 1999–. *Publications:* (ed jtly) Critical Perspectives on Rural Change, 6 vols, 1990–94; Constructing the Countryside, 1993; Reconstituting Rurality, 1995; The Condition of Sustainability, 1999; Consuming Interests: the social provision of foods, 2000; (jtly) Worlds of Food, 2006; (ed jtly) The Handbook of Rural Studies, 2006; over 100 refereed jl articles. *Recreations:* running, cycling, squash, gardening, topographical antiquarian books. *Address:* School of City and Regional Planning, Cardiff University, Glamorgan Building, King Edward VII Avenue, Cardiff CF10 3WA. *T:* (029) 2087 5736, *Fax:* (029) 2087 4845; *e-mail:* MarsdenTK@cardiff.ac.uk.

MARSDEN, William, CMG 1991; HM Diplomatic Service, retired; Chairman, Chagos Conservation Trust, since 2002; *b* 15 Sept. 1940; *s* of Christopher Marsden and Ruth (*née* Kershaw); *m* 1964, Kaia Collingham; one *s* one *d*. *Educ:* Winchester Coll.; Lawrenceville Sch., USA; Trinity Coll., Cambridge (MA); London Univ. (BSc Econs). FO, 1962–64; UK Delegn to NATO, 1964–66; Rome, 1966–69; seconded as Asst to Gen. Manager, Joseph Lucas Ltd, 1970; First Sec., FCO, 1971–76; First Sec. and Cultural Attaché, Moscow, 1976–79; Asst Head, European Community Dept, FCO, 1979–81; Counsellor, UK Representation to EEC, 1981–85; Head, E Africa Dept, FCO, and Comr, British Indian Ocean Territory, 1985–88; Ambassador to Costa Rica, and concurrently Ambassador to Nicaragua, 1989–92; Minister (Trade), Washington, 1992–94; Asst Under-Sec. of State, later Dir, (Americas), FCO, 1994–97; Ambassador to Argentina, 1997–2000. Chairman: Diplomatic Service Assoc., 1987–88; Anglo-Central American Soc., 2003–05. Internat. Advr, Coiba World Heritage Project, 2003–. Trustee, World Cancer Res. Fund, 2002–. Guest Lectr, Swan Hellenic, 2005–. *Address:* Highwood, Castlegate, Pulborough, W Sussex RH20 2NJ. *T:* (020) 7233 9538.

MARSH, family name of **Baron Marsh**.

MARSH, Baron *cr* 1981 (Life Peer), of Mannington in the County of Wiltshire; **Richard William Marsh;** PC 1966; Kt 1976; FZS; FCIT; Chairman: Mannington Management Services, since 1989; Laurentian Financial Group plc, since 1986; *b* 14 March 1928; *s* of William Marsh, Belvedere, Kent; *m* 1st, 1950, Evelyn Mary (marr. diss. 1973), *d* of Frederick Andrews, Southampton; two *s*; 2nd, 1973, Caroline Dutton (*d* 1975); 3rd, 1979, Felicity, *d* of Baron McFadzean of Kelvinside. *Educ:* Jennings Sch., Swindon; Woolwich Polytechnic; Ruskin Coll., Oxford. Health Services Officer, National Union of Public Employees, 1951–59; Mem., Clerical and Administrative Whitley Council for Health Service, 1953–59; MP (Lab) Greenwich, Oct. 1959–April 1971; promoted Offices Act 1961; Member: Select Cttee Estimates, 1961; Chm. Interdepartmental Cttee to Co-ordinate Govt Policy on Industrial Training, 1964; Parly Sec., Min. of Labour, 1964–65; Joint Parly Sec., Min. of Technology, 1965–66; Minister of Power, 1966–68; Minister of Transport, 1968–69. Chairman: British Railways Bd, 1971–76; Newspaper Publishers' Assoc., 1976–90; British Iron and Steel Consumers' Council, 1977–82; Allied Investments Ltd, 1977–81; Member: NEDC, 1971–; Freight Integration Council, 1971–; Council, CBI, 1970–. Chairman: Allied Medical Group, 1977–81; Vivat Hldgs PLC, 1982–88; TV-am, 1983–84 (Dep. Chm., 1980–83); Lopex PLC, 1986–97 (Dir, 1985–97); China & Eastern Investments Trust, Hong Kong, 1990–98 (Dir, 1987–98); Gartmore British Income & Growth Trust, 1994–; Dep. Chm., United Medical Enterprises Ltd, 1978–81; Director: Imperial Life of Canada UK, 1983–; Imperial Life Assurance Co. of Canada, 1983–; Charles Church Developments, 1987–97; Laurentian Group Corp. (Montreal), 1990–94; Advisor: Nissan Motor Co., 1981–; Fujitec, 1982–. Pres., Council ECSC, 1968. Governor: British Transport Staff Coll. (Chm.); London Business Sch. FCMI; FInstD; FInstM. *Publication:* Off the Rails (autobiog.), 1978. *Address:* House of Lords, SW1A 0PW.

MARSH, Barrie; *see* Marsh, G. B.

MARSH, Derek Richard, CVO 1999; non-executive Director: Haike Chemical Group Ltd, since 2007; China Food Co. plc, since 2007; Adviser, iFafa Tech (Manila), since 2006; *b* 17 Sept. 1946; *s* of Reginald and Minnie Marsh; *m* 1969, Frances Anne Roberts; one *s* one *d*. *Educ:* Queen's Coll., Oxford (Schol.; MA 1973). Ministry of Defence: Asst Principal, 1968–72; Asst Private Sec. to Minister of State for Defence, 1973–74; Principal, 1974–78; ndc, 1975; Admin. Sec., Sovereign Base Areas, Cyprus, 1978–81; Asst Sec., 1982–86; rcds 1987; Department of Trade and Industry: Head of Air 1 and 2, 1988–91; Director: Companies House, 1991–93; Projects Export Promotion, 1994–97; Dep. Hd of Mission and Consul-Gen., Republic of Korea, 1997–2001; Dir Gen., British Trade and Cultural Office, Taipei, 2002–05. Advr, UK Trade and Investment, 2006. Non-executive Director: Felixstowe Dock and Railway Co., 1990–91; Bovis Homes Ltd, 1992–93. *Recreations:* travel, reading, running.

MARSH, Rt Rev. Edward Frank; Bishop of Central Newfoundland, 1990–2000; Diocesan Administrator, Diocese of Central Newfoundland, 2005; *b* 25 Oct. 1935; *m* 1962, Emma Marsh; one *s* two *d*. *Educ:* Dalhousie Univ., NS (BCom 1956); Univ. of Newfoundland (BA 1960); Queen's Coll., Newfoundland (LTh 1961; BD 1969). Deacon 1959, priest 1960; Curate, Corner Brook, 1959–63; Incumbent, Harbour Breton, 1963–69; Curate, Wickford, 1969–71; Incumbent, Indian Bay, 1971–73; Curate, St John the Baptist Cathedral, St John's, 1973–77; Rector of Cartwright, dio. East Newfoundland, 1977–81; Rector, Holy Trinity, Grand Falls, 1981–90.

MARSH, Felicity Margaret Sue; *see* Goodey, F. M. S.

MARSH, Rev. (Francis) John, DPhil; Archdeacon of Blackburn, 1996–2001; *b* 3 July 1947; *s* of William Frederick and Helena Mary Marsh; *m* 1974, Gillian Popely; two *d*. *Educ:* York Univ. (BA 1969; DPhil 1976); Cert Theol Cambridge, 1975. ATCL 1965; ARCM 1966; ARCO 1971. Ordained deacon, 1975, priest, 1976; Assistant Curate: St Matthew's, Cambridge, 1975–78; Christ Church, Pitsmoor, Sheffield, 1979–81; Dir of Pastoral Trng, St Thomas', Crookes, Sheffield, 1981–85; Vicar, Christ Church, South Ossett, Wakefield, 1985–96. Rural Dean of Dewsbury, 1993–96. Mem., Gen. Synod of C of E, 1990–96, 1997–2001. Chm. Trustees, Anglican Renewal Ministries, 1989–2001. Mem., Adv. Bd, RSCM, 2000–01. *Address:* 137 Edge Lane, Dewsbury, W Yorks WF12 0HB. *T:* (01924) 451233.

MARSH, Rear-Adm. Geoffrey Gordon Ward, CB 1985; OBE 1969; jssc; Project Manager, NATO Frigate 90, Hamburg, 1988–90, retired; *m*; one *s* one *d*. *Educ:* St Albans Sch.; Queens' Coll., Cambridge. Britannia Royal Naval Coll., 1947; served on HM Ships: Indefatigable; Victorious; Carron; Norfolk; Girdle Ness; Bristol; involved in develt of Sea Dart missile; Hd of Propulsion Machinery Control, Ship Dept; Asst Dir (Surface Warfare), Naval Op. Req.; Dir, Weapons Co-ordination and Acceptance (Naval), MoD, 1978–80; i/c HMS Thunderer, 1980–82; ACNS (Op. Req.), 1982–84; Dep. Controller, Warships Equipment, MoD (Navy), 1984–87; Chief Naval Engr Officer, 1985–87. *Address:* c/o Naval Secretary, Fleet Headquarters, Whale Island, Portsmouth PO2 8BY.

MARSH, (Graham) Barrie, FCIArb; solicitor; Partner, Mace & Jones, Solicitors, Liverpool and Manchester, 1959–99 (Senior Partner, 1980–97); *b* 18 July 1935; *s* of Ernest Heaps Marsh and Laura Greenhalgh Marsh; *m* 1961, Nancy Smith; one *s* two *d*. *Educ:* Bury Grammar Sch.; Loughborough Grammar Sch.; Liverpool Univ. (LLB Hons). FCIArb 1982. Admitted as Solicitor, 1957. Nat. Chm., Young Solicitors Gp, Law Soc., 1975; President: Liverpool Law Soc., 1978–79; Solicitors' Disciplinary Tribunal, 1988–2001; Liverpool Publicity Assoc., 1980; part-time Chm., Appeals Service, 1989–2008. Chairman: Merseyside Chamber of Commerce and Industry, 1984–86; Radio City PLC, 1988–91. Non-exec. Dir, Liverpool HA, 1996–2000. Trustee, Nat. Museums and Galls on Merseyside, 1998–2006. Hon. Belgian Consul, Liverpool, and for NW, 1987–96. *Publications:* Employer and Employee: a complete and practical guide to the modern law of employment, 1977, 3rd edn 1990; contribs to legal and personnel jls on all aspects of employment law and industrial relations. *Recreations:* Liverpool Football Club, bird-watching, hill-walking. *Address:* Calmer Hey, Benty Heath Lane, Willaston, South Wirral CH64 1SA. *T:* (0151) 327 4863; *e-mail:* g.barriemarsh@tiscali.co.uk. *Club:* Army and Navy.

MARSH, Jean Lyndsey Torren; actress, writer; Artistic Director, Adelphi University Theatre, Long Island, New York, 1981–83; *b* 1 July 1934; *d* of late Henry Charles and of Emmeline Susannah Marsh; *m* 1955, Jon Devon Roland Pertwee (marr. diss. 1960; he *d* 1996). Began as child actress and dancer; *films:* Return to Oz; Willow; danced in Tales of Hoffmann, Where's Charley?, etc; Fatherland, 1995 (Cable Ace Award for Best Supporting Actress, 1996); acted in repertory companies: Huddersfield, Nottingham, etc; Broadway debut in Much Ado About Nothing, 1959; West End debut, Bird of Time, 1961; *stage:* Habeas Corpus, The Importance of Being Earnest, Too True to be Good, Twelfth Night, Blithe Spirit, Whose Life is it Anyway?, Uncle Vanya, On the Rocks, Pygmalion, Hamlet, The Chalk Garden, Blow Up does Dallas, The Old Country; Boeing, Boeing, Comedy, 2007; Portrait of a Lady, Th. Royal, Bath, 2008; *television:* series, Nine to Five; co-created and co-starred (Rose) in series Upstairs Downstairs (Emmy, 1975); co-created series, The House of Eliott; Alexei Sayle Show; The Ghost Hunter (3 series); Bremner, Bird and Fortune; Most Mysterious Murder; Sense and Sensibility; Sensitive Skin; *radio* incl. Bleak House, The Pier. Hon. DH Maryland Coll., NY, 1980. *Publications:* The Illuminated Language of Flowers, 1978; The House of Eliott, 1993; Fiennders Keepers, 1996; Iris, 1999; articles for Sunday Times, Washington Post, New York Times, Los Angeles Times, Daily Telegraph, Times. *Recreations:* walking, reading, cooking, eating, wine, music. *Address:* c/o Leslie Duff, Diamond Management, 31 Percy Street, W1T 2DD.

MARSH, Rev. John; *see* Marsh, Rev. F. J.

MARSH, John Edward; Director, Civil Service Capability Group, Cabinet Office, since 2007; *b* 18 Dec. 1963; *s* of Keith and Margaret Marsh; *m* 1990, Karen Moors; three *d*. *Educ:* Ham Dingle Primary Sch., Stourbridge; King Edward VI Coll., Stourbridge; Univ. of Bristol (BA Hons Hist. 1985); Univ. of Warwick (MA Industrial Relns 1986). FCIPD 2006. Home Office, 1986–96, Pvte Sec. to Minister of State, 1994–96; Hd of Voluntary Sector Govt Spending, Dept of Nat. Heritage, 1996–97; Sect. Leader, Public Spending Directorate, HM Treasury, 1997–99; Home Office: Hd of Personnel Mgt, HM Prison Service, 1999–2003; Dir of Human Resources, 2003–07. *Recreations:* football coaching, sports, eating out, taxi service to daughters. *Address:* Cabinet Office, Admiralty Arch, The Mall, SW1A 2WH; *e-mail:* john.marsh@cabinet-office.x.gsi.gov.uk.

MARSH, Sir John (Stanley), Kt 1999; CBE 1993; Professor of Agricultural Economics and Management, later of Agricultural and Food Economics, Reading University, 1984–97, now Emeritus; *b* 5 Oct. 1931; *s* of Stanley Albert Marsh and Elsie Gertrude Marsh (*née* Powell); *m* 1958, Kathleen Edith Casey; one *s* one *d*. *Educ:* St John's Coll., Oxford (BA PPE 1955; MA 1958); Reading Univ. (Dip. Agricl Econs 1956). CIBiol, FIBiol 1997. Res. Economist, 1956–63, Lectr, 1963–71, Reader in Agricl Econs, 1971–77, Reading Univ.; Prof. of Agricl Econs, Aberdeen Univ., and Chm. of Econs Gp, N of Scotland Coll. of Agriculture, Aberdeen, 1977–84; Reading University: Dean, Faculty of Agriculture and Food, 1986–89; Dir, Centre for Agricl Strategy, 1990–97. Chairman: Agricl Wages Bd for England and Wales, 1991–99; RURAL, 1997–; Vice-Chm., Sci. Adv. Cttee, DEFRA, 2004–07. Chm., Centre for Dairy Inf. Ltd, 2005–. Pres., British Inst. of Agricl Consultants, 1998–. FRASE 1991; FRAgS 1992. *Publications:* contribs to books; numerous articles in learned jls. *Recreations:* photography, caravanning, Methodist local preacher. *Address:* 15 Adams Way, Earley, Reading, Berks RG6 5UT. *T:* (0118) 986 8434. *Clubs:* Farmers'; Caravan (East Grinstead).

MARSH, Kevin John; Editor, BBC College of Journalism, since 2006; *b* 14 Nov. 1954; *s* of John Marsh and Elizabeth Jill Marsh; *m* 1979, Melissa Sue Fletcher; one *s* one *d*. *Educ:* Doncaster Grammar Sch.; Christ Church, Oxford (MA). Joined BBC, 1978; Radio 4: Editor: PM, 1989–92; World at One, 1992–96; World at One and PM, 1996–98; launched Broadcasting House, 1998; Editor, Today, 2002–06. Attended Salzburg Seminar, 1984; panelist and moderator, World Econ. Forum, Davos, 2004, 2005, 2006, Warsaw, 2005; Vis. Fellow, Bournemouth Univ., 2005–. Alumnus, Prince of Wales Business and the Envmt Prog., 2005–. Mem., RIIA. FRSA. Sony Radio Awards, 1991, 1992, 2003, 2004, 2005; Amnesty Internat. Media Award, 2001. *Publications:* contrib. various articles. *Recreations:* Rugby, opera. *Address:* BBC College of Journalism, White City, W12 7TQ; *e-mail:* kevin.marsh.01@bbc.co.uk; *web:* http://storycurve.blogspot.com. *Club:* Wasps Rugby Football.

MARSH, Prof. Leonard George, OBE 1992; MEd; DPhil; Principal, Bishop Grosseteste College, 1974–96; *b* 23 Oct. 1930; third *c* of late Ernest Arthur Marsh and Anne Eliza (*née* Bean); *m* 1953, Ann Margaret Gilbert; one *s* one *d*. *Educ:* Ashford (Kent) Grammar Sch.; Borough Road Coll., London Inst. of Educn (London Univ. Teachers' Certif. and Academic Dip.); Leicester Univ. (MEd); DPhil York, 1988. Lectr in Educn and Mathematics, St Paul's Coll., Cheltenham, 1959–61; Lectr, 1961–63, Sen. Lectr, 1963–65, Principal Lectr and Head of Postgraduate Primary Educn Dept, 1965–74, Goldsmiths' Coll., London. Hon. Prof., Hull Univ., 1987–96. Visiting Lectr, Bank Street Coll., New York, and Virginia Commonwealth Univ.; former Consultant, OECD, Portugal; Educnl Consultant, Teacher Trng Proj., Botswana, 1981; Dir, Sindh Pakistan Primary Educn Develt Prog., 1992–96; Specialist tour to India for British Council; Mem., SCAA, 1993–97. Dir (non-exec.), A & C Black plc, 1994–2000. Member: Gen. Adv. Council, IBA, 1977–82; N Lincolnshire AHA, 1984–90; Chm., Nat. Assoc. for Primary Educn, 1981–83. Gov., Canterbury Christ Church Coll., 1997–2001. FRSA. Hon. FCP (FCP 1989). Hon. DLitt Hull, 1996. *Publications:* Let's Explore Mathematics, Books 1–4, 1964–67; Children Explore Mathematics, 1967, 3rd edn 1969; Exploring Shapes and Numbers, 1968, 2nd edn 1970; Exploring the Metric System, 1969, 2nd edn 1969; Exploring the Metric World, 1970; Approach to Mathematics, 1970; Alongside the Child in the Primary School, 1970; Let's Discover Mathematics, Books 1–5, 1971–72; Being A Teacher, 1973; Helping your Child with Maths—a parents' guide, 1980; The Guinness Mathematics Book, 1980; The Guinness Book for Young Scientists, 1982. *Recreations:* photography, theatre, walking, films. *Address:* Broomfields, 16 The Meadow, Chislehurst, Kent BR7 6AA. *T:* (020) 8467 6311. *Club:* Athenæum.

MARSH, Dame Mary (Elizabeth), DBE 2007; Founding Director, Clore Social Leadership Programme, Clore Duffield Foundation, since 2008; *b* 17 Aug. 1946; *d* of George Donald Falconer and Lesley Mary (*née* Wilson); *m* 1968, Juan Enrique Marsh (*d* 1999); four *s*. *Educ:* Birkenhead High Sch., GPDST; Univ. of Nottingham (BSc; Hon. Pres., Students Union, 2005–); London Business Sch. (MBA). Teacher, Icknield High Sch., 1968; St Christopher School, Letchworth: teacher, 1969–72; Dep. Hd, 1980–90; Head: Queens' Sch., Watford, 1990–95; Holland Park Sch., 1995–2000; Dir and Chief Exec., NSPCC, 2000–08. Mem., Learning and Skills Council, 2005–. *Recreations:* swimming, reading, music, good company, walking in mountains and by the sea. *Address:* c/o Clore Duffield Foundation, Studio 3, Chelsea Manor Studios, Flood Street, SW3 5SR. *Club:* Reform.

MARSH, Norman Stayner, CBE 1977; QC 1967; Law Commissioner, 1965–78; Member, Royal Commission on Civil Liability and Compensation for Personal Injury, 1973–78; *b* 26 July 1913; 2nd *s* of Horace Henry and Lucy Ann Marsh, Bath, Som; *m* 1939, Christiane Christinnecke (*d* 2000), 2nd *d* of Professor Johannes and Käthe Christinnecke, Magdeburg, Germany; two *s* two *d*. *Educ:* Monkton Combe Sch.; Pembroke Coll., Oxford (2nd Class Hons, Final Honour Sch. of Jurisprudence, 1935; 1st Cl. Hons BCL; Hon. Fellow, 1978). Vinerian Scholar of Oxford Univ., Harmsworth Scholar of Middle Temple, called to Bar, 1937; practice in London and on Western Circuit, 1937–39; Lieut-Col Intelligence Corps and Control Commission for Germany, 1939–46. Stowell Civil Law Fellow, University Coll., Oxford, 1946–60; University Lecturer in Law, 1947–60; Estates Bursar, University Coll., 1948–56; Secretary-General, International Commission of Jurists, The Hague, Netherlands, 1956–58. Member: Bureau of Conference of Non-Governmental Organisations with Consultative Status with the United Nations, 1957–58; Internat. Cttee of Legal Science (Unesco), 1960–63. Dir of British Institute of International and Comparative Law, 1960–65. Mem., Younger Cttee on Privacy, 1970–72. Hon. Vis. Prof. in Law, KCL, 1972–77. Vice-Chm., Age Concern, England, 1979–86. General editor, International and Comparative Law Quarterly, 1961–65, Mem., Editorial Board, 1965–93. *Publications:* The Rule of Law as a supra-national concept, in Oxford Essays in Jurisprudence, 1960; The Rule of Law in a Free Society, 1960; Interpretation in a National and International Context, 1974; (editor and part-author) Public Access to Government-held Information, 1987; articles on common law and comparative law in English, American, French and German law jls. *Address:* 10 Trinity Close, The Pavement, Clapham, SW4 0JD. *T:* (020) 7622 2865.
See also B. K. Cherry.

MARSH, Paul Henry; Consultant, Downs Solicitors LLP, Dorking, since 2007; President, Law Society of England and Wales, 2008–July 2009 (Vice President, 2007–08); *b* 6 Sept. 1947; *s* of Cyril Samuel Marsh and Ellen Victoria Marsh; *m* 1972, Sheila Slater; one *s* two *d*. *Educ:* Raynes Park Grammar Sch.; BA Business Law. Partner, Bells Solicitors, Kingston upon Thames, 1976–2007. Law Society: Mem. Council, 1987–; Chm., Solicitors Indemnity Fund, 2003–06. Hon. LLD Kingston, 2008. *Recreations:* gardening, vintage cars, the family. *Address:* The Law Society, 113 Chancery Lane, WC2A 1PL. *T:* (020) 7320 5602; *e-mail:* paul.marsh@lawsociety.org.uk; *Clubs:* Bentley Drivers, Vintage Sports Car.

MARSH, Prof. Paul Rodney; Professor of Finance, London Business School, 1985–2006, now Emeritus (Professor of Management and Finance, 1985–98, Esmée Fairbairn Professor of Finance, 1998–2002); *b* 19 Aug. 1947; *s* of Harold Marsh and Constance (*née* Miller); *m* 1971, Stephanie (*née* Simonow). *Educ:* Poole Grammar Sch.; London School of Economics (BScEcon, 1st Cl. Hons); London Business Sch. (PhD). Systems Analyst, Esso Petroleum, 1968–69; Scicon, 1970–71; London Business School, 1974–: Bank of England Res. Fellow, 1974–85; Dir, Sloan Fellowship Prog., 1980–83; non-exec. Dir, Centre for Management Develt, 1984–90; Mem. Gov. Body, 1986–90; Faculty Dean, 1987–90; Dep. Principal, 1989–90; Associate Dean, Finance Progs, 1993–2006. Member: CBI Task Force on City-Industry Relationships, 1986–88; Exec. Cttee, British Acad. of Management, 1986–88. Non-executive Director: M&G Investment Management Ltd, 1989–97; M&G Gp, 1998–99; Majedie Investments, 1999–2006; Aberforth Smaller Cos Trust, 2004–; Dir, Hoare Govett Indices Ltd, 1991–. Gov. Examg Bd, Securities Inst., 1994–2002. *Publications:* Cases in Corporate Finance, 1988; Managing Strategic Investment Decisions, 1988; Accounting for Brands, 1989; Short-termism on Trial, 1990; The Millennium Book: a century of investment returns, 2000; Triumph of the Optimists, 2002; The HGSC Smaller Companies Index, annually 1987–; (with E. Dimson) Global Investment Returns Yearbook, annually 2000–; numerous articles in Jl of Financial Econs, Jl of Finance, Jl of Business, Harvard Business Review, Jl of Inst. of Actuaries, Res. in Marketing, Mergers and Acquisitions, Financial Analysts Jl, Jl of Apples Corporate Finance, Long Range Planning, etc. *Recreations:* gardening, investment. *Address:* London Business School, Regent's Park, NW1 4SA. *T:* (020) 7000 7000; *e-mail:* pmarsh@london.edu.

MARSH, Richard St John Jeremy, PhD; Director, Improving Accountability, Clarity and Transparency (ImpACT) Coalition, since 2007; *b* 23 April 1960; *s* of late Gordon Victor Marsh ; *m* 1984, Elizabeth Mary Mullins (marr. diss. 2006); one *s* one *d*. *Educ:* Trinity Sch. of John Whitgift; Keble Coll., Oxford (BA 1982; MA 1986); Coll. of the Resurrection, Mirfield; Durham Univ. (PhD 1991). Deacon 1985, priest 1986; Curate, Grange St Andrew, Runcorn, 1985–87; Chaplain and Solway Fellow, UC, Durham, 1987–92; Asst Sec. for Ecum. Affairs to Abp of Canterbury, 1992–95, Sec., 1995–2001; Canon Residentiary and Dir, Internat. Study Centre, subseq. Canon Librarian and Dir of Educn, Canterbury Cathedral, 2001–05. Licensed to officiate, Dio. London, 1993–2001; Canon, Dio. Gibraltar in Europe, 1995–2001; Non-Res. Canon, Canterbury Cathedral, 1998–2001. Vis. Sen. Lectr, Canterbury Christchurch UC, 2003–. Chm., St Augustine's Foundn, 2003. *Publications:* Black Angels, 1998; (contrib.) Ink and Spirit, 2000; (with Katherine Marshall) Millennium Challenges for Development and Faith Institutions, 2003; (ed) Prayers from the East, 2004. *Recreations:* music, cooking. *Address:* Institute of Fundraising, Park Place, 12 Lawn Lane, SW8 1UD. *T:* (020) 7840 1038; *e-mail:* richardm@institute-of-fundraising.org.uk. 6 Barrack Square, Winchelsea, E Sussex TN36 4EG.

MARSH, Roger; Director-General, Strategic Finance and Operations, Cabinet Office, 2007–09, on secondment from PricewaterhouseCoopers; *b* 19 Sept. 1953; *s* of Peter and Connie Marsh; *m* 1981, Susan Smith (marr. diss. 2002); three *d*; partner, Sally Thomson; one *d*. *Educ:* Stockton C of E Grammar Sch.; Univ. of Leeds (BSc Hons Metallurgy 1976). FCA 1990. Price Waterhouse, subseq. PricewaterhouseCoopers: joined, 1976; Partner, 1988; latterly Sen. Business Recovery Partner, Leeds. *Recreations:* collecting fine wines, fast cars. *Address:* PricewaterhouseCoopers, Benson House, 33 Wellington Street, Leeds LS1 4JP; *e-mail:* roger.marsh@uk.pwc.com, roger.marsh@cabinet-office.x.gsi.gov.uk. *Club:* Reform.

MARSH, Susanna; *see* Nicklin, S.

MARSHALL, family name of **Marshall of Knightsbridge**.

MARSHALL OF KNIGHTSBRIDGE, Baron *cr* 1998 (Life Peer), of Knightsbridge in the City of Westminster; **Colin Marsh Marshall**, Kt 1987; Chairman: Pirelli UK Ltd, since 2003; Nomura International, since 2004; *b* 16 Nov. 1933; *s* of Marsh Edward Leslie and Florence Mary Marshall; *m* 1958, Janet Winifred (*née* Cracknell); one *d*. *Educ:* University College Sch., Hampstead. Progressively, cadet purser to Dep. Purser, OSNC, 1951–58; Hertz Corp., 1958–64: management trainee, Chicago and Toronto, 1958–59; Gen. Man., Mexico, Mexico City, 1959–60; Asst to Pres., New York, 1960; Gen. Manager: UK London, 1961–62; UK Netherlands and Belgium, London, 1962–64; Avis Inc., 1964–79: Reg. Man./Vice-Pres., Europe, London, 1964–66; Vice-Pres. and Gen. Man., Europe and ME, London, 1966–69; Vice-Pres. and Gen. Man., International, London, 1969–71; Exec. Vice-Pres. and Chief Operating Officer, New York, 1971–75; Pres. and Chief Operating Officer, New York, 1975–76; Pres. and Chief Exec. Officer, New York, 1976–79; Co-Chm., 1979–81; Exec. Vice-Pres., Norton Simon Inc., New York, 1979–81; Dir and Dep. Chief Exec., Sears Holdings plc, 1981–83; British Airways, 1983–2004: Chief Exec., 1983–95; Dep. Chm., 1989–93; Chm., 1993–2004. Chairman: Inchcape plc, 1996–2000; Siebe, subseq. BTR Siebe, then Invensys, plc, 1998–2003; Dep. Chm., British Telecommunications plc, 1996–2001. Board Member: HSBC Holdings, 1992–2004; US Air, 1993–96; Qantas, 1993–96 and 2000–01; NY Stock Exchange, 1994–2000; Royal Automobile Club Ltd, 1998–99. Chm., Visit Britain, 2005–06. Dep. Chm., Financial Reporting Council, 1996–99. Chm. Trustees, Conference Bd, NY, 2000–04. Member: Council, Inst. of Dirs, 1982–2006; Chartered Inst. of Marketing, 1989–96 (Pres., 1989–94); Marketing Council, 1995–2004 (Chm., 1995–96); Vice Pres., Advertising Assoc., 1988–; Pres., 1996–98, Dep. Pres., 1998–99, CBI. Vice Chm., World Travel & Tourism Council, 1990–99; Pres., Commonwealth Youth Exchange Council, 1998–. Chm., London Development Partnership, 1998–2000. Chm., RIIA (Chatham House), 1999–2003. President: Knightsbridge Assoc., 2003–; Westminster City Academy, 2007–. Mem., Hong Kong Assoc., 1996–2000. Trustee, RAF Museum, 1991–2000. Chm. of Govs, Birkbeck Coll., London Univ., 2003–. Hon. DHL Suffolk, Boston, USA, 1984; Hon. LLD: Bath, 1989; American Univ. in London, Richmond Coll., 1993; Lancaster, 1997; Hon. DSc: Buckingham, 1990; Cranfield, 1997; Hon. DCL Durham, 1997; Hon. LittD Westminster, 1999; Hon. Dr Business London Guildhall, 2000. *Recreation:* tennis. *Address:* Pirelli UK Ltd, 15 Grosvenor Street, W1K 4QZ. *T:* (020) 7355 0701, *Fax:* (020) 7355 0727; *e-mail:* anne.hensman@pirelli.com. *Clubs:* Royal Automobile, All England Lawn Tennis and Croquet, Queen's (Chm., 2007–).

MARSHALL, Alan Ralph; Managing Director, ARM Educational Consultants Ltd, 1991–94; *b* 27 July 1931; *s* of Ralph Marshall and Mabel Mills; *m* 1958, Caterina Gattico; one *s* one *d*. *Educ:* Shoreditch College (Teacher's Cert. 1953); London Univ. (Dip Ed 1959; MPhil 1965); Eastern Washington State Univ. (MEd 1964); Stanford Univ. (MA 1969). Teacher, schools in UK and USA, 1954–62; Lectr, Shoreditch Coll., 1962–68; Vis. Prof., Eastern Washington State Univ., 1964–65; Field Dir, Project Technology, Schools Council, 1970–72; Editor, Nat. Centre for School Technology, 1972–73; Course Team Chm., Open Univ., 1973–76; HM Inspector, DES, 1976–91, HM Chief Inspector of Schools, 1985–91. Hon. DEd CNAA, 1990. *Publications:* (ed) School Technology in Action, 1974; (with G. T. Page and J. B. Thomas) International Dictionary of Education, 1977; Giving Substance to a Vision, 1990; articles in jls. *Recreations:* painting, reading.

MARSHALL, Arthur Stirling-Maxwell, CBE 1986 (OBE 1979); HM Diplomatic Service, retired; *b* 29 Jan. 1929; *s* of Victor Stirling-Maxwell Marshall and Jeannie Theodora Hunter; *m* 1st, 1955, Eleni Kapralou, Athens (*d* 1969); one *s* two *d*; 2nd, 1985, Cheryl Mary Hookens, Madras; one *d*. *Educ:* Daniel Stewart's Coll., Edinburgh. Served Royal Navy, 1947–59. Foreign Office, 1959; Middle East Centre for Arab Studies, Lebanon, 1959–61; Political Officer, British Political Agency, Bahrain and Registrar of HBM Court for Bahrain, 1961–64; Attaché, Athens, 1964–67; Information Officer, Rabat, Morocco, 1967–69; Commercial Secretary: Nicosia, Cyprus, 1970–75; Kuwait, 1975–79; Deputy High Commissioner, Madras, 1980–83; Counsellor, Kuwait, 1983–85; Ambassador to People's Democratic Republic of Yemen, 1986–89. *Recreations:* music, nature. *Address:* 2 The Larches, Rickmansworth Road, Northwood, Middx HA6 2QY.

MARSHALL, Prof. Barry James, AC 2007; FRS 1999; FRACP; Clinical Professor, University of Western Australia, since 2000; *b* 30 Sept. 1951; *s* of Robert and Marjorie Marshall; *m* 1972, Adrienne Joyce Feldman; one *s* three *d*. *Educ:* Univ. of Western Australia (MB BS). FRACP 1983. Clinical asst (res.), Gastroenterology Dept, Royal Perth Hosp., 1985–86; University of Virginia: Res. Fellow in Medicine, Div. of Gastroenterology, 1986–87; Asst Prof. of Medicine, 1988–92, Associate Prof., 1992, Prof., 1993; Clinical Prof., 1993–96; Prof. of Res. in Internal Medicine, 1996–2000; Clinical Prof. of Medicine, 1997–2000, NH&MRC Burnet Fellow and Clinical Prof. of Medicine, 1998–2000, Univ. of WA. Hon. Res. Fellow in Gastroenterology, Sir Charles Gairdner Hosp., 1997. (Jtly) Warren Alpert Prize, Harvard Med. Sch., 1995; Albert Lasker Award, NYC, 1995; (jtly) Paul Ehrlich Prize, Frankfurt, 1997; Kilby Prize, Dallas, 1997; Dr A. H. Heineken Prize for Medicine, Amsterdam, 1998; Florey Medal, Aust. Inst. for Pol Sci., Canberra, 1998; Buchanan Medal, Royal Soc., 1998; Benjamin Franklin Medal for Life Sci., Philadelphia, 1999; Prince Mahidol Award, 2001; (jtly) Nobel Prize in Physiology or Medicine, 2005. *Publications:* Campylobacter pylori, 1988; Helicobacter pylori in peptic ulceration and gastritis, 1991; Helicobacter Pylori, 1990 (Proc. 2nd Internat. Symposium), 1991; Gastroenterology Clinics of North America, 2000; contribs to jls incl. The Lancet, Amer. Jl Gastroenterol., Jl Infectious Diseases, Jl Nuclear Medicine, Jl Clinical Pathol., Digestive Diseases and Scis, Gastroenterol., Scandinavian Jl Gastroenterol., Jl Clinical Microbiol., Alimentary Pharmacol. and Therapeutics. *Recreations:* computers, photography, electronics. *Address:* Helicobacter Pylori Research Laboratory, Department of Microbiology, University of Western Australia, QE2 Medical Centre, Nedlands, WA 6009, Australia. *T:* (8) 93464815.

MARSHALL, Hon. (Cedric) Russell, CNZM 2001; President, New Zealand Institute of International Affairs, since 2007; High Commissioner for New Zealand in the United Kingdom, also accredited to Nigeria, and as Ambassador of New Zealand to Ireland, 2002–05; *b* 15 Feb. 1936; *s* of Cedric Thomas Marshall and Gladys Margaret Marshall; *m* 1961, Barbara May Watson; two *s* one *d*. *Educ:* Nelson Coll.; Christchurch Teachers Coll.; Auckland Univ. (DipTeaching, 1966); BA Victoria Univ., 1992. Primary teacher, Nelson, 1955–56; Trinity Methodist Theol Coll., 1958–60; Methodist Minister: Christchurch, Spreydon, 1960–66; Masterton, 1967–71; teacher, Wanganui High Sch., 1972. MP (Lab) Wanganui, 1972–90; Opposition education spokesman, 1976–84; Sen. Opposition Whip, 1978–79; Minister of Education, 1984–87, for the Environment, 1984–86, of Conservation, 1986–87, of Disarmament and Arms Control, 1987–89, of Foreign Affairs, 1987–90, for Pacific Island Affairs, 1988–90. Chairman: Commonwealth Observer Mission to Seychelles election, 1993; Commonwealth Observer Mission to South Africa, 1994; Mem., Commonwealth Observer Mission to Lesotho elections, 1993. Chairman: NZ Commn for UNESCO, 1990–99; Polytechnics Internat. New Zealand, 1994–2001; Education New Zealand, 1998–2002; Tertiary Educn Adv. Commn, 2000–02; Tertiary Educn Commn, NZ, 2005–07; Member: UNESCO Exec. Bd, 1995–99 (Chm., Finance and Admin Commn, 1997–99); Public Adv. Cttee for Disarmament and Arms Control, 1997–2000; Growth and Innovation Adv. Bd, 2005–07; Mem. Council, 1994–2001, Pro-Chancellor, 1999, Chancellor, 2000–01, Victoria Univ. of Wellington. Chairman: Cambodia Trust (Aotearoa-NZ), 1994–2001; Cambodia Trust (UK), 2002–05 (Trustee, 2000–05); Trustee, Africa Information Centre, 1978–95 (Chm., 1991–95). *Recreations:* reading, listening to music, genealogy. *Address:* 5 Whitianga View, Paremata, Porirua, New Zealand. *T:* (4) 2336608.

MARSHALL, Charles Michael John; Senior NHS Specialist, District Audit, 2001; *b* 25 Sept. 1954; *s* of George William Marshall and Lucy Cameron Marshall (*née* MacInnes); *m* 1985, Margaret Hutchinson (marr. diss. 1990). *Educ:* Royal Grammar Sch., Newcastle upon Tyne; King's Coll. London. Civil Servant, Lord Chancellor's Dept, MoD and Privy Council Office, 1976–86 (Private Sec. to Lord Privy Seal and Leader of H of C, 1983–85); General Manager: Dulwich Hosp., 1986–88; King's Coll. and Dulwich Hosps, 1988–89; Dist Gen. Manager, Newcastle HA, 1989–92; Chief Exec., UCL Hosps NHS Trust, 1992–98; Dir, Charles Marshall Consulting Ltd, 1998. Vis. Prof. in Health Service Mgt, UCL, 1995; Vis. Fellow, King's Fund Coll., 1994–96. Member: Council, Nat. Assoc. for Educn of Sick Children, 1995–97; Trusts Council, NAHAT, 1996–97; Council, St Oswald's Hospice, 1998; Hon. Sec., Middx Hosp. Special Trustees, 1994–98. Mem. Ct of Govs, LSHTM, 1999.

MARSHALL, Prof. Christopher John, DPhil; FRS 1995; Director, Cancer Research UK (formerly Cancer Research Campaign) Centre for Cell and Molecular Biology, Institute of Cancer Research, since 1994; *b* 19 Jan. 1949; *s* of Lillian and James Marshall; *m* 1st, 1973, Vivien Roma Morrall (marr. diss. 1997); two *s* one *d*; 2nd, 2005, Lesley Ford. *Educ:* King Henry VIII Sch., Coventry; Churchill Coll., Cambridge (MA); Lincoln Coll., Oxford (DPhil). Postdoctoral Fellow: ICRF, 1973–78; Sidney Farber Cancer Inst., Boston, USA, 1978–80; Research Scientist, Inst. of Cancer Research, 1980–. Gibb Life Fellow, CRC (later Cancer Res. UK), 1992. Choh Hao Li Meml Lectr, Univ. of Calif, Berkeley, 2002. Mem., EMBO, 1993; Founder FMedSci 1998. Novartis Prize and Medal, Biochemical Soc., 1999. *Publications:* contribs to learned jls. *Recreation:* cycling. *Address:* Chester Beatty Laboratories, Institute of Cancer Research, 237 Fulham Road, SW3 6JB. *T:* (020) 7352 9772. *Club:* Norwood Paragon Cycling.

MARSHALL, Daniel; *see* Marshall, T. D.

MARSHALL, David; former transport worker; *b* 7 May 1941; *m*; two *s* one *d*. *Educ:* Larbert, Denny and Falkirk High Schs; Woodside Sen. Secondary Sch., Glasgow. Joined Labour Party, 1962; former Lab. Party Organiser for Glasgow; Mem., TGWU, 1960–. MP (Lab): Glasgow, Shettleston, 1979–2005; Glasgow East, 2005–June 2008. Chairman, Select Committee: Transport, 1987–92 (Mem., 1985–92); Scottish Affairs, 1997–2001 (Mem., 1981–83, 1994–97); Mem., Chairmen's Panel, 2005–08. Former Chairman: All Party ANZAC Gp; British Canadian Gp; S Pacific Gp; Aviation Gp; Gardening and Horticulture Gp. Hon. Sec. and Hon. Treas., Scottish Gp of Labour MPs, 1981–2001. Private Member's Bill, The Solvent Abuse (Scotland) Act, May 1983. Chairman: British Gp, IPU, 1997–2000; Exec. Cttee, UK Br., CPA, 2003–08. Mem., UK Delegn to Council of Europe and WEU, 2001–08. Member: Glasgow Corp., 1972–75; Strathclyde Reg. Council, 1974–79 (Chm., Manpower Cttee); formerly: Chm., Manpower Cttee, Convention of Scottish Local Authorities; Mem., Local Authorities Conditions of Service Adv. Bd. *Recreations:* gardening, music.

MARSHALL, David Arthur Ambler, CBE 2003; CEng; FRAeS; Director General, Society of British Aerospace Companies, 1997–2003; *b* 4 April 1943; *s* of Henry R. Marshall and Joan E. Marshall; *m* 1968, Karen Elizabeth Marker; two *d*. *Educ:* Brighton Coll.; Churchill Coll., Cambridge (MA). FRAeS 1994; CEng 2005. Joined Rolls Royce Ltd as Apprentice, 1961; Develt Engr, 1970–73; Co. Rep., Airbus, 1973–75; Manager, Eur. Sales, 1975–78; Commercial Manager, 1978–83; Head of Business Planning, 1983–87; Gen. Manager, Mktg, 1987–89; Dir, Business Planning, 1989–90; Commercial Dir, 1990–93; Dir, Business Develt, 1993–96. Pres. RAeS, 2007–08. FRSA 1998. Freeman, City of London, 1999; Liveryman, Fan Makers' Co. *Recreations:* garden railways, music. *Address:* Pémirol, 31290 Vieillevigne, France.

MARSHALL, Sir Denis (Alfred), Kt 1982; solicitor; with Barlow Lyde & Gilbert, 1937–83; *b* 1 June 1916; *s* of Frederick Herbert Marshall and Winifred Mary Marshall; *m* 1st, 1949, Joan Edith Straker (*d* 1974); one *s*; 2nd, 1975, Jane Lygo (*d* 2002). *Educ:* Dulwich Coll. Served War: HAC, 1939; XX Lancs Fusiliers (Temp. Major), 1940–46. Articled to Barlow Lyde & Gilbert, Solicitors, 1932–37; admitted Solicitor, 1937. Mem. Council, Law Soc., 1966–86, Vice-Pres., 1980–81, Pres., 1981–82. Member: Insurance Brokers Registration Council, 1979–91; Criminal Injuries Compensation Bd, 1982–90; Council, FIMBRA, 1986–90. *Recreation:* gardening. *Address:* 15 Coombe Road, Dartmouth, Devon TQ6 9PQ.

MARSHALL, Hon. Denis William Anson, QSO 2000; Secretary-General, Commonwealth Parliamentary Association, 2002–06; *b* 23 Sept. 1943; *s* of Lionel Henry Swainson Marshall and Mabel Alice Okeover Marshall; *m* 1965, Annette Kilmister (separated); one *s* two *d*. *Educ:* Christ's Coll., Christchurch, NZ. MP (Nat. Party) Rangitikei, NZ, 1984–99; Minister: of Conservation, 1990–96; of Sci., 1990–93; of Lands, 1993–96; of Survey and Land Inf., 1993–96; Associate Minister: of Agric., 1990–96; of Employment, 1990–96. Chairman: NZ Rural Communities Trust, 2000–01; NZ Nat. Parks and Conservation Foundn, 2000–02. *Recreations:* hiking, boating, gardening, reading.

MARSHALL, Dr Edmund Ian; Lecturer in Management Science, University of Bradford, 1984–2000; *b* 31 May 1940; *s* of Harry and Koorali Marshall; *m* 1969, Margaret Pamela, *d* of John and Maud Antill, New Southgate, N11; one *d*. *Educ:* Magdalen Coll., Oxford (Mackinnon Schol.; Double 1st cl. hons Maths, and Junior Mathematical Prize, 1961); PhD Liverpool, 1965. Various univ. appts in Pure Maths, 1962–66; mathematician in industry, 1967–71. Mem., Wallasey County Borough Council, 1963–65. Contested (L) Louth Div. of Lincs, 1964 and 1966; joined Labour Party, 1967. MP (Lab) Goole, May 1971–1983; PPS to Sec. of State for NI, 1974–76, to Home Sec., 1976–79; Chm., Trade and Industry sub-cttee of House of Commons Expenditure Cttee, 1976–79; Mem., Chairmen's Panel in House of Commons, 1981–82; Opposition Whip, 1982–83; joined SDP, 1985. Contested (SDP/Alliance) Bridlington, 1987. Chair, Wakefield and Dist Lib Dems, 2005. Non-exec. Dir, Wakefield FHSA, 1990–96; Dir, Wakefield Healthcare Commn, 1994–96. Member: British Methodist Conf., 1969–72, 1980 and 1985–97 (Vice-Pres., 1992); World Methodist Conf., 1971; British Council of Churches, 1972–78; Sec., Associate (formerly All-Party) Parly Gp related to Council of Church Colls, 1994–2001; Bishop of Wakefield's Advr for Ecumenical Affairs, 1998–2007. Methodist Local Preacher, 1959–; Reader in C of E, 1994–. Mem., Gen. Synod of C of E, 2000–. Governor: Woodhouse Grove Sch., Bradford, 1986–94; Wakefield Grammar School Foundn, 1989–97. *Publications:* (jtly) Europe: What Next? (Fabian pamphlet), 1969; Parliament and the Public, 1982; Business and Society, 1993; (jtly) The Times Book of Best Sermons, 1995; various papers in mathematical and other jls. *Recreations:* word games, music. *Address:* 37 Roundwood Lane, Harpenden, Herts AL5 3BP. *Clubs:* Royal Over-Seas League; Middlesex CC.

MARSHALL, Dr Frank Graham, FIET; technology consultant, since 1998; Group Research and Development Director, Colt Group Ltd, 1990–98; *b* 28 March 1942; *s* of Frank and Vera Marshall; *m* 1965, Patricia Anne (*née* Bestwick); two *s* one *d*. *Educ:* Birmingham Univ. (BSc Physics); Nottingham Univ. (PhD Physics). FIET (FIEE 1984). Joined Royal Signals and Radar Estabt (MoD) (Physics and Electronic Device Res.), 1966; Sen. Principal Scientific Officer, 1975–80; seconded to HM Diplomatic Service as Science and Technology Counsellor, Tokyo, 1980–82. Man. Dir, Plessey Electronic Systems Res., later Plessey Res. Roke Manor, 1983–87; Technical Dir, Plessey Naval Systems, 1987–90. (Jtly) IEEE Best Paper award, 1973; (jtly) Wolfe Award, 1973. *Publications:* numerous papers on electronic signal processing devices in various jls. *Recreations:* country life, electronics.

MARSHALL, Very Rev. Geoffrey Osborne; Dean of Brecon, since 2008; *b* Rossett, Denbighshire, 5 Jan. 1948; *s* of Dr Harry Marshall and Joan Marshall (*née* Harris); *m* 1972, Hazel Caunce; one *s* two *d*. *Educ:* Repton Sch.; St John's Coll., Univ. of Durham (BA); Coll. of the Resurrection, Mirfield. Ordained deacon, 1973, priest, 1974; Vicar: Christ Church, Belper, 1978–86; Spondon, Derby, 1986–93; Rural Dean, Derby N, 1990–95; Sub-Dean, Derby Cathedral, 1993–2002; Rector, Wrexham, 2002–08; Area Dean, Wrexham, 2002–08. Trustee, Shelter Cymru, 2002–. Chaplain, Derby High Sch., 1987–2001. *Recreations:* leading pilgrimages to the Middle East, archaeology, walking. *Address:* The Deanery, The Cathedral Close, Brecon, Powys LD3 9DP. *T:* (01874) 623857, *Fax:* (01874) 623716; *e-mail:* admin@breconcathedral.org.uk.

MARSHALL, Prof. Gordon, CBE 2003; DPhil; FBA 2000; AcSS; Vice-Chancellor, University of Reading since 2003; *b* 20 June 1952; *s* of Robert Marshall and Ina Marshall (*née* McPhie); *m* 1975, Heather Alexander (marr. diss. 1999); one *s*; partner, Marion Headicar. *Educ:* Falkirk High Sch.; Univ. of Stirling (BA 1st Cl. Hons Sociol. 1974); Nuffield Coll., Oxford (DPhil 1978). Postdoctoral Res. Fellow, Nuffield Coll., Oxford, 1977–78; Lectr and Sen. Lectr, Dept of Sociol., Univ. of Essex, 1978–90; Prof. of Sociol., Univ. of Bath, 1990–93; Official Fellow in Sociol., Nuffield Coll., Oxford, 1993–99; Chief Exec. and Dep. Chm., ESRC, 2000–02. Chm., Higher Educn Statistics Agency, 2007–. British Acad./Leverhulme Trust Sen. Res. Fellow, 1992–93. AcSS 2000. *Publications:* Presbyteries and Profits, 1980; In Search of the Spirit of Capitalism, 1982; (jtly) Social Class in Modern Britain, 1987; In Praise of Sociology, 1990; (jtly) Oxford Dictionary of Sociology, 1994, 3rd edn 2005; (jtly) Against the Odds?, 1997; (jtly) Repositioning Class, 1997; contrib. numerous articles to jls and symposia. *Recreations:* in my dreams. *Address:* The University of Reading, Whiteknights, PO Box 217, Reading RG6 6AH. *T:* (0118) 378 6226, *Fax:* (0118) 987 4062; *e-mail:* g.marshall@reading.ac.uk.

MARSHALL, Hazel Eleanor; QC 1988; **Her Honour Judge Marshall;** a Senior Circuit Judge, since 2006; a Deputy High Court Judge, since 1994; *b* 14 Jan. 1947; *d* of Geoffrey Briddon and late Nancy Briddon; *m* 1st, 1969, Robert Hector Williamson (marr. diss. 1980); 2nd, 1983, Harvey Christopher John Marshall; one step *s*. *Educ:* Wimbledon High Sch.; St Hilda's Coll., Oxford (MA Jurisprudence). FCIArb 1992. Atkin Scholar, Gray's Inn. Called to the Bar, Gray's Inn, 1972, Bencher, 1996; Asst Recorder, 1993–96;

a Recorder, 1996–2006. Acting Deemster, I of M, 1999–2006. Chm., Chancery Bar Assoc., 1994–97. Mem., DfT (formerly DoE, subseq. DETR, then DTLR) Property Adv. Gp, 1994–2003. Hon. Mem., ESU. *Publication:* (with Harvey Marshall) Law and Valuation of Leisure Property, 1994. *Recreations:* gardening, opera, occasional off-shore sailing. *Address:* Central London Civil Justice Centre, 26 Park Crescent, W1B 1HT. *Club:* Royal Over-Seas League (Hon. Mem.).

MARSHALL, Howard; *see* Marshall, I. H.

MARSHALL, Rev. Canon Hugh Phillips; Vicar of Wendover, 1996–2001; *b* 13 July 1934; *s* of Dr Leslie Phillips Marshall and Dr (Catherine) Mary Marshall; *m* 1962, Diana Elizabeth Gosling; one *s* three *d. Educ:* Marlborough Coll.; Sidney Sussex Coll., Cambridge (BA, MA); Bishop's Hostel, Lincoln. RN, 1952–54. Ordained deacon 1959, priest 1960, Dio. London; Curate, St Stephen with St John, Westminster, 1959–65; Vicar of St Paul, Tupsley, Hereford, 1965–74; Vicar and Team Rector of Wimbledon, 1974–87; Rural Dean of Merton, 1979–85; Vicar of Mitcham, Surrey, 1987–90; Chief Sec., ABM, 1990–96. Hon. Canon: Southwark Cathedral, 1989, Hon. Canon Emeritus, 1990; St John's Cathedral, Bulawayo, 1996. Commissary to Bishop of Matabeleland, 1989–. Mem., SE Reg. Awards Cttee, Nat. Lottery Charities Bd, 1998–2002. Chm., Betty Rhodes Fund, 1996–2007 (Mem., 1989–2007). Foundn Gov., Deddington Vol. Aided Sch., 2002–. Hon. Sec., Oxford Diocesan Bd of Patronage, 2001–. *Recreations:* DIY, cooking, gardening, writing, travel. *Address:* 7 The Daedings, Deddington, Banbury, Oxon OX15 0RT. *T:* (01869) 337761.

MARSHALL, Prof. (Ian) Howard, PhD; Professor of New Testament Exegesis, University of Aberdeen, 1979–99, now Professor Emeritus and Hon. Research Professor; *b* 12 Jan. 1934; *s* of Ernest Ewart Marshall and Ethel Marshall (*née* Curran); *m* 1961, Joyce Elizabeth Proudfoot; one *s* three *d. Educ:* Univ. of Aberdeen (MA 1955; BD 1959; PhD 1963); Fitzwilliam Coll., Cambridge (BA 1959); Univ. of Göttingen. Asst Tutor, Didsbury Coll., Bristol, 1960–62; pastoral work, Darlington, 1962–64; University of Aberdeen: Lectr, 1964–70; Sen. Lectr, 1970–77; Reader, 1977–79. Hon. DD Asbury, Kentucky, 1996. *Publications:* Eschatology and the Parables, 1963, 2nd edn 1978; Pocket Guide to Christian Beliefs, 1963, 3rd edn 1978, repr. 1989; The Work of Christ, 1969, 2nd edn 1994; Kept by the Power of God, 1969, 3rd edn 1995; Luke: historian and theologian, 1970, 3rd edn 1989; The Origins of New Testament Christology, 1976; (ed) New Testament Interpretation, 1977, 2nd edn 1979; I Believe in the Historical Jesus, 1977; The Gospel of Luke, 1978; The Epistles of John, 1978; Acts, 1980; Last Supper and Lord's Supper, 1980; Biblical Inspiration, 1982, 2nd edn 1995; 1 and 2 Thessalonians, 1983; (ed) Christian Experience in Theology and Life, 1988; Jesus the Saviour: studies in New Testament theology, 1990; 1 Peter, 1991; The Acts of the Apostles, 1992; The Epistle to the Philippians, 1992; (with K. P. Donfried) The Theology of the Shorter Pauline Letters, 1993; (ed with D. Peterson) Witness to the Gospel: the theology of the Book of Acts, 1998; (with P. H. Towner) A Critical and Exegetical Commentary on the Pastoral Epistles, 1999; (contrib.) Exploring the New Testament: Vol. 2: The Letters and Revelation, 2002; (ed) Moulton and Geden: Concordance to the Greek New Testament, 6th edn 2002; New Testament Theology: many witnesses, one Gospel, 2004; (jtly) Beyond the Bible: moving from scripture to theology, 2004; Aspects of the Atonement, 2007. *Recreations:* hill walking, gardening, music, reading. *Address:* School of Divinity, History and Philosophy, King's College, Aberdeen AB24 3UB. *T:* (01224) 272388, *Fax:* (01224) 273750; *e-mail:* i.h.marshall@abdn.ac.uk.

MARSHALL, James; Assistant Auditor General, National Audit Office, 1993–2002; *b* 16 March 1944; *s* of James Marshall and late Winifred Marshall (*née* Hopkins); *m* 1980, Patricia Anne Smallbone; one *s. Educ:* Sacred Heart Coll., Droitwich; King Charles I Grammar Sch., Kidderminster; Jesus Coll., Cambridge (MA). Joined Inland Revenue, 1966: Asst Principal, 1966–69; Private Sec. to Chm. of Bd, 1969–70; Principal, 1970–74; First Sec., Budget and Fiscal, UK Repn to EC, Brussels, 1974–77; First Asst, UK Mem. of Court, European Court of Auditors, 1977–80; Asst Sec., Inland Revenue, 1980–88; Consultant, CJA Mgt Recruitment, 1988–89; Dir, Nat. Audit Office, 1989–93. *Recreations:* reading, walking, cooking, entertaining, music. *Address:* 56 Melody Road, SW18 2QF. *T:* (020) 8870 3308. *Club:* Oxford and Cambridge.

MARSHALL, Jeremy; *see* Marshall, John J. S.

MARSHALL, Prof. John, CBE 1990; FRCP, FRCPE; Professor of Clinical Neurology in the University of London, 1971–87, now Emeritus; *b* 16 April 1922; *s* of James Herbert and Bertha Marshall; *m* 1946, Margaret Eileen Hughes; two *s* three *d. Educ:* Univ. of Manchester (MB ChB 1946, MD 1951, DSc 1981). FRCPE 1957, FRCP 1966; DPM 1952. Sen. Registrar, Manchester Royal Infirmary, 1947–49; Lt-Col RAMC, 1949–51; MRC research worker, 1951–53; Sen. Lectr in Neurology, Univ. of Edinburgh, 1954–56; Reader in Clinical Neurology, Univ. of London, 1956–71. Chm., Disability Living (formerly Attendance) Allowance Bd, 1982–93. Knight of the Order of St Sylvester (Holy See), 1962, KCSG 1986 (KSG 1964). Auenbrugger Medal, Univ. of Graz, 1983. *Publications:* The Management of Cerebrovascular Disease, 1965, 3rd edn 1976; The Infertile Period, Principles and Practice, 1963, 2nd rev. edn 1969; Love One Another, 1995. *Recreations:* gardening, walking. *Address:* Flat 15, 85 Worple Road, SW19 4JH. *T:* (020) 8247 3513.

MARSHALL, Prof. John, PhD; FRCPath; Frost Professor of Ophthalmology and Chairman, Department of Ophthalmology, King's College London School of Medicine (formerly United Medical and Dental Schools of Guy's and St Thomas' Hospitals, then Guy's, King's and St Thomas' School of Medicine, King's College London), since 1991; Director, Laser Institute of America, since 2004; *b* 21 Dec. 1943; *s* of Henry Thomas George Marshall and Ellen Emily Martha Marshall; *m* 1972, Judith Anne Meadows. *Educ:* Inst. of Ophthalmology, Univ. of London (BSc; PhD 1968). FRCPath 2007. Institute of Ophthalmology: Lectr in Anatomy, 1968–73; Sen. Lectr in Visual Sci., 1973–80; Reader in Exptl Pathology, 1981–83; Sembal Prof. of Exptl Ophthalmology, 1983–91; Hon. Consultant in Ophthalmology, St Thomas' Hosp., 1992–. Hon. Dist. Prof., Sch. of Optometry and Visual Sci., Univ. of Cardiff, 2008–. Ed., numerous scientific jls, 1985–. Advr on lasers to WHO, 1974–80, to Internat. Red Cross, 1989–95. Director: DIOMED, 1991–97; Ellex R&D, 2007–; Ellex Medical Ltd, 2007–. Trustee: Brit. Retinitis Pigmentosa Soc., 1978–; Devereux House, 1999–; Co. of Spectacle Makers' Charity, 2004–; Frost Charitable Trust, 2007–. Ambassador, Fight for Sight, 2008. Gov., Moorfields Eye Hosp., 1988–90. Mem., Ct of Assts, Spectacle Makers' Co., 2001–. Numerous patents on applications of lasers to eye surgery, 1968–. Fellow, Academia Ophthalmologica Europeae, 2004. FRSA 1989. Hon. Fellow: Coll. of Optometrists, 1997; Univ. of Cardiff, 2005; Hon. FRCOphth, 2005. Nettleship Medal, 1980, Ashton Medal, 1993, RCOphth; Mackenzie Medal, Tennant Inst. of Ophthalmol., Glasgow, 1985; Raynor Medal, Intraocular Implant Soc., UK, 1988; Ridley Medal, Internat. Soc. for Cataract and Refractive Surg., 1990; Wilkening Award, Laser Inst. of Amer., 1999 (Fellow, 2003); Ida Mann Medal, Oxford, 2000; Lord Crook Gold Medal, Spectacle Makers' Co., 2001; Doyne Medal, Oxford Congress of Ophthalmol., 2001; Barraquer Medal, Internat. Soc. of Refractive Surg., 2001; Euretina Award, European Soc. of

Retinal Specialists, 2003; Innovator Award, Amer. Soc. Cataract & Refractive Surgeons, 2004; Lim Medal, Singapore Nat. Eye Centre, 2004; Sen. Achievement Award, Amer. Acad. of Ophthalmol., 2005. *Publications:* Hazards of Light, 1986; Laser Technology in Ophthalmology, 1988; Vision and Visual Systems, 1991; Annual of Ophthalmic Laser Surgery, 1992; numerous papers in scientific jls, concerning effect of lasers, light and aging on ocular tissues. *Recreations:* work!, reading. *Address:* Wildacre, 27 Cedar Road, Farnborough, Hants GU14 7AU. *T:* (01252) 543473. *Clubs:* Athenæum, Royal Automobile.

MARSHALL, John Alexander, CB 1982; General Secretary, Distressed Gentlefolk's Aid Association, 1982–89; *b* 2 Sept. 1922; *s* of James Alexander Marshall and Mena Dorothy Marshall; *m* 1947, Pauline Mary (*née* Taylor); six *s. Educ:* LCC elem. sch.; Hackney Downs School. Paymaster General's Office, 1939; FO, 1943; HM Treasury, 1947: Principal, 1953; Asst Sec., 1963; Under-Sec., 1972; Cabinet Office, 1974–77; Northern Ireland Office, 1977–82, Dep. Sec., 1979–82. *Recreations:* literature, music. *Address:* 48 Long Lane, Ickenham, Middx UB10 8TA. *T:* (01895) 672020.

MARSHALL, John Gibb, (John Sessions); actor, writer; *b* 11 Jan. 1953; *s* of John Marshall and Esmé Richardson. *Educ:* Univ. of Wales (MA). Plays and one-man shows, 1982–85; *television:* Spitting Image, 1986; Porterhouse Blue, 1987; A Day in Summer, 1988; Whose Line is it Anyway?, 1988; Single Voices, 1990; Ackroyd's Dickens, 1990; Jute City, 1991; Life with Eliza, 1992; A Tour of the Western Isles, 1993; Citizen Locke, 1994; The Treasure Seekers, 1996; Tom Jones, 1997; My Night with Reg, 1997; Stella Street (4 series), 1997, 1998, 2000, 2001; In the Red, 1998; The Man, 1999; Gormenghast, 2000; Randall & Hopkirk Deceased, 2000; Murder Rooms, 2001; Well-Schooled in Murder, 2002; Judge John Deed, 2002 and 2005; Midsomer Murders, 2002; The Lost Prince, 2002; Dalziel and Pascoe, 2002; The Key, 2003; George Eliot: a life, 2003; QI, 2003, 2004, 2006; Hawking, 2004; The Legend of the Tamworth Two, 2004; Absolute Power, 2005; The English Harem, 2005; The Moving Finger, 2006; Low Winter Sun, 2006; Jackanory, 2006; The Ronni Ancona Show, 2006; Oliver Twist, 2007; one-man shows: New Year Show, 1988; On the Spot, 1989; Tall Tales, 1991; Likely Stories, 1994; *theatre:* The Life of Napoleon, Albery, 1987; The Common Pursuit, Phoenix, 1988; The American Napoleon, Phoenix, 1989; Die Fledermaus, Royal Opera House, 1990; Travelling Tales, Haymarket, 1991; Tartuffe, Playhouse, 1991; The Soldier's Tale, Barbican, 1993, 2003; My Night with Reg, Royal Court, 1994; Paint, said Fred!, Royal Acad., 1996; *films:* The Bounty, 1984; Whoops Apocalypse, 1986; Castaway, 1987; Henry V, 1989; Sweet Revenge, 1990; The Pope Must Die, 1991; Princess Caraboo, 1994; In the Bleak Midwinter, 1995; The Scarlet Tunic, 1998; Cousin Bette, 1998; A Midsummer Night's Dream, 1999; One of the Hollywood Ten, 2000; High Heels and Low Life, 2001; Gangs of New York, 2002; A Flight of Fancy, 2002; Stella Street: the movie, 2003; Five Children and It, 2003; The Merchant of Venice, 2004; Rag Tale, 2005; The Good Shepherd, 2006; Intervention, 2007; Inconceivable, 2008; *radio:* Whose Line is it Anyway?, 1988; Beachcomber, 1989; Mightier than the Sword, 1992; Figaro gets Divorced, 1993; Poonsh, 1993; The Good Doctor, 1994; Private Passions, 1997–2002; The Reith Affair, 1998; Saturday Night Fry, 1998; The Destiny of Nathalie X, 1998; Season's Greetings, 1999; The Man who came to Dinner, 2000; Reconstructing Louis, 2000; Dante's Inferno, 2001; The Haunting, 2002; The Titanic Enquiry, 2002; In the Company of Men, 2003; St Graham and St Evelyn—Pray for Us, 2003; The Possessed, 2006; Eternal Sunshine, 2008. *Recreation:* dinner parties. *Address:* c/o Markham & Froggatt, 4 Windmill Street, W1P 1HF. *T:* (020) 7636 4412. *Club:* Groucho.

MARSHALL, (John) Jeremy (Seymour); DL; Chairman, Trans Siberian Gold plc, 2001–06; *b* 18 April 1938; *s* of late Edward Pope Marshall and Nita Helen Marshall (*née* Seymour); *m* 1962, Juliette Butterley; one *s* two *d. Educ:* Sherborne Sch.; New Coll., Oxford (MA Chem.). Nat. Service, Royal Signals, 1956–58. Wiggins Teape, 1962–64; Riker Labs, 1964–67; CIBA Agrochemicals, 1967–71; Hanson Trust: Managing Director: Dufaylite Developments, 1971–76; SLD Olding, 1976–79; Chief Executive: Lindustries, 1979–86; Imperial Foods, 1986–87; BAA plc, 1987–89; De La Rue Co. plc, 1989–98. Director: John Mowlem & Co., 1991–97; Camelot Gp, 1993–98; BTR plc, 1995–98; Hillsdown Holdings, 1998–2000. Dir, Fleet Exec. Bd, RN, 2002–05. Hon. Treas., Design Museum, 2000–06 (Trustee, 1996–2006). Chm., Varrier-Jones Foundn, 2006–. Chm., St John Council, Cambs, 2007–. Mem. Council, Sch. of Mgt Studies, Oxford Univ., 1995–2002. High Sheriff 2006–07, DL 2007, Cambs. CCMI (CBIM 1991); FCILT 1989. *Recreations:* squash, lawn tennis, shooting, music. *Address:* Willow House, Bourn, Cambridge CB23 2SQ. *T:* (01954) 719435. *Club:* Royal Automobile.

MARSHALL, John Leslie; Chairman, Beta Global Emerging Markets Investment Trust plc, 2000–01 (Director, 1990–2001); *b* 19 Aug. 1940; *s* of late Prof. William Marshall and Margaret Marshall; *m* 1978, Susan Elizabeth (marr. diss. 2000), *d* of David Mount, Petham, Kent; two *s. Educ:* Glasgow Academy; St Andrews Univ. (MA). ACIS. Asst Lecturer in Economics, Glasgow Univ., 1962–66; Lectr in Economics, Aberdeen Univ., 1966–70; Mem., Internat. Stock Exchange; Carr Sebag & Co., 1979–82; Partner, 1983–86, Dir, 1986–90, Analyst, 1990–93, Carr Kitcat & Aitken; Analyst: London Wall Equities, subseq. Mees Pierson Securities (UK) Ltd, 1993–97; New Japan Securities, 1998–99. Sen. Financial Journalist, Shares mag., 1999–. Member (C): Aberdeen Town Council, 1968–70; Ealing Borough Council, 1971–86 (Chm., Finance Bd, 1978–82; Chm., Local Services Cttee, 1982–84); Barnet LBC, 1998– (Chm., Cons. Gp, 1998–2000, 2004–05); Chm., Council Policy Conference, 2002–03; Dep. Mayor, 2004; Cabinet Mem. for Investment in Educn (formerly Educn and Lifelong Learning), 2004–08; Mayor, 2008–). Contested (C): Dundee East, 1964 and 1966; Lewisham East, Feb. 1974. MEP (C) London N, 1979–89; Asst Whip, EDG, Eur. Parlt, 1986–89. MP (C) Hendon South, 1987–97; contested (C) Finchley and Golders Green, 1997, 2001. PPS to Minister for the Disabled, Dept of Social Security, 1989–90, to Sec. of State for Social Security, 1990–92, to Leader of H of C, 1992–95. Mem., Select Cttee on health, 1995–97; Vice Chm., All Pty Mental Health Gp, 1996–97. Chm., British Israel Parly Gp, 1991–97; Vice Pres., Anglo-Israel Assoc., 2001– (Chm., 1994–2000). Consultant, Bus and Coach Council, 1991–97. Chm., Friends of the Northern Line, 1994–97. Chm., Dermatrust Appeal, 1998–2005. *Publications:* articles on economics in several professional jls; pamphlets on economic questions for Aims. *Recreations:* watching cricket, football and Rugby; gardening, bridge, theatre. *Address:* 66 Sandringham Gardens, N12 0PJ. *Clubs:* St Stephen's, MCC; Middlesex County Cricket.

MARSHALL, John Roger; Chairman: Building Software Ltd, since 1997; Supply Chain Partnering, since 1996; *b* 20 April 1944; *s* of John Henry Marshall and Betty Alaine Rosetta Marshall; *m* (marr. diss.); one *s* two *d. Educ:* Rendcomb College; Bristol Univ. (BSc Hons Civil Eng.). MICE, CEng, FIHT. Balfour Beatty Consultants, W. C. French and R. McGregor & Sons, 1966–70; Mears Construction, 1970–78; Henry Boot, 1978–83; Man. Dir, Mowlem Management, 1983–87; Dir, 1987–95, Man. Dir, 1989–94, Chief Exec., 1994–95, John Mowlem and Co. PLC. Non-executive Director: St Aldwyns Enterprises (subseq. Resources) Ltd, 1996–2002; BRE Ltd, 1998–2001. *Recreation:* arts (visual, dramatic and operatic). *Address:* Carpenter's House, Westonbirt, Tetbury, Glos GL8 8QG.

MARSHALL, Dr John Walton, CBE 2004; DL; former Chairman, Cardea Group; Regional Appointments Commissioner, Northern and Yorkshire Region, NHS Executive, 2001–03; *b* 3 Feb. 1931; *s* of Harry and Gladys Marshall; *m* 1958, Glenison Mills; three *s*. *Educ:* University of Manchester (BSc 1952, PhD 1955). Scientific Officer, UKAEA, 1955–58; Tech. Officer, ICI, 1958–65; Vice-Pres., 1965–68, Pres., 1968–74, Katalco Corp.; Business Area Manager, ICI, 1974–78; Director: ICI Agricl Div., 1978–89; Durham Univ. Business Sch., 1989–94; Chm. (pt-time), Magneco-Metrel UK Ltd, 1994–2001. Part-time Chairman: S Durham HA, 1994–96; Co. Durham HA, 1996–2001. Chm. (pt-time), Darlington CAB. Hon. Chairman of Governors: Macmillan CTC, 1998–2004; Durham Sch., 2001–. DL Co. Durham, 2002. *Recreations:* mountaineering, music, theatre. *Address:* Lea Close, Roman Way, Middleton-St-George, Co. Durham DL2 1DG. *T:* (01325) 332215, *Fax:* (01325) 332632. *Clubs:* Farmers; Rucksack (Manchester).

MARSHALL, Katharine Jane, (Mrs H. J. Stevenson); Her Honour Judge Katharine Marshall; a Circuit Judge, since 2008; *b* 11 Aug. 1958; *d* of Ian David Gordon Lee and Ivy Margaret Lee (*née* Cox); *m* 1st, 1981, David Forrest Marshall (marr. diss. 1985); one *s*; 2nd, 1996, Huw John Stevenson; one *s* one *d*. *Educ:* Sidney Sussex Coll., Cambridge (Taylor Schol.; MA Natural Scis/Law 1980); Council for Legal Educn; Greenwich Univ. (DMS Dist. 1998). Called to the Bar, Inner Temple, 1983; Dep. Justices Clerk, E Berks, 1997–2001; Actg Stipendiary Magistrate, then Dep. Dist Judge, 1999–2002; District Judge (Magistrates' Courts), 2002–06; Recorder, 2007–08. Mem., Family Procedure Rule Cttee, 2004–08. *Publication:* Wilkinson's Road Traffic Referencer, 2007, rev. edn 2008. *Recreations:* living a life I love with those I love, 70's rock music, walking in faraway isolated locations; fascinated by life of Napoleon (particularly exile on St Helena). *Address:* Portsmouth Combined Court Centre, Courts of Justice, Winston Churchill Avenue, Portsmouth PO1 2EB. *Club:* Oxford and Cambridge.

MARSHALL, Kathleen Anne; Commissioner for Children and Young People in Scotland, 2004–April 2009; *b* 4 June 1953; *d* of Matthew Gallagher and Christina McEvoy; *m* 1974, Robert Hunter Marshall; two *s* one *d*. *Educ:* Univ. of Glasgow (LLB 1973); Open Univ. (BA Hons 1979); Maryvale Inst., Birmingham (BA Hons (Divinity) 2003). Legal Apprentice, then Solicitor, Glasgow Corp., subseq. Glasgow DC, 1973–77; full-time mother, 1977–89; Co-Dir, then Dir, Scottish Child Law Centre, 1989–94; child law consultant, 1994–2004. Visiting Professor: Queen's Coll., Glasgow, subseq. Glasgow Caledonian Univ., 1992–95; Glasgow Centre for the Child and Society, Univ. of Glasgow, 1997–. Mem., Law Soc. of Scotland, 1975–. *Publications:* Children's Rights in the Balance: the participation-protection debate, 1997; (with Paul Parvis) Honouring Children: the human rights of the child in Christian perspective, 2004; numerous articles in jls. *Recreation:* dreaming about not being a workaholic. *Address:* Scotland's Commissioner for Children and Young People, 85 Holyrood Road, Edinburgh EH8 8AU. *T:* (0131) 558 3733, *Fax:* (0131) 556 3378; *e-mail:* kathleen.marshall@sccyp.org.uk.

MARSHALL, His Honour Laurence Arthur; a Circuit Judge, 1991–2003; *b* 1 June 1931; *s* of Reginald Herbert Marshall and Nora Marshall; *m* 1st, 1959, Marian Charlotte Mowlem Burt (marr. diss. 1979); two *s* two *d*; 2nd, 1980, Gloria Elizabeth Kindersley (*d* 2007). *Educ:* Ardingly Coll.; King's Coll., London (LLB). Called to the Bar, Gray's Inn, 1956. *Recreation:* building. *Address:* The Old Post Office, Stourton, Shipston on Stour, Warwicks CV36 5HG. *T:* (01608) 686363. *Club:* Royal London Yacht.

MARSHALL, Margaret Anne, OBE 1999; concert and opera singer; soprano; *b* 4 Jan. 1949; *d* of Robert and Margaret Marshall; *m* 1970, Dr Graeme Griffiths King Davidson; two *d*. *Educ:* High School, Stirling; Royal Scottish Academy of Music and Drama (DRSAMD). Recital début, Wigmore Hall, 1975; performs regularly with all major British orchs, also with ENO and Scottish Opera; opera début as Euridice, in Orfeo, Florence; major rôles include: Countess Almaviva in The Marriage of Figaro; Fiordiligi in Così fan Tutte; Elvira and Donna Anna in Don Giovanni; Violetta in La Traviata; Marschallin in Der Rosenkavalier; Constanze in The Seraglio; many concert and opera performances in Europe and N America; numerous recordings. First Prize, Munich International Competition, 1974. Gulliver Award, 1992. *Recreations:* squash, golf. *Address:* Woodside, Main Street, Gargunnock, Stirling FK8 3BP. *Club:* Gleneagles Country.

MARSHALL, Mark Anthony, CMG 1991; HM Diplomatic Service, retired; Ambassador to the Republic of Yemen (formerly Yemen Arab Republic) and the Republic of Djibouti, 1987–93; *b* 8 Oct. 1937; *s* of late Thomas Humphrey Marshall, CMG and of Nadine, *d* of late Mark Hambourg; *m* 1970, Penelope Lesley Seymour; two *d*. *Educ:* Westminster Sch.; Trinity Coll., Cambridge (BA). MECAS, 1958; Third Sec., Amman, 1960; FO, 1962; Commercial Officer, Dubai, 1964; FO, 1965; Aden, 1967; First Sec., 1968; Asst Dir of Treasury Centre for Admin. Studies, 1968; UK Delegn to Brussels Conf., 1970; First Sec./Head of Chancery, Rabat, 1972; First Sec., FCO, 1976; Counsellor: Tripoli, 1979–80; Damascus, 1980–83; Head of Finance Dept, FCO, 1984–87. *Recreations:* swimming, fell walking, bridge.

MARSHALL, Prof. Martin Neil, CBE 2005; MD; FRCGP; Medical Director, The Health Foundation, since 2007; *b* 2 Sept. 1961; *s* of Dr Geoffrey Marshall and Mary Marshall; *m* 1988, Susan Miles. *Educ:* University Coll. London (BSc Immunol. 1984); Charing Cross and Westminster Hosp. Med. Sch., Univ. of London (MB BS 1987; MD 1997); Univ. of Exeter (MSc Health Care 1994). DRCOG 1990; DCH 1991; MRCGP 1991, FRCGP 1998. Exeter Vocational Trng Scheme for Gen. Practice, 1988–91; Partner in Gen. Practice, Mt Pleasant Health Centre, Exeter, 1991–99; Lectr in Gen. Practice, Univ. of Exeter, 1994–97; Harkness Fellow in Health Care Policy, Rand Corp., Calif, 1998–99; Hd, Community Health Scis Div., Univ. of Exeter, 1999; University of Manchester: Hon. Res. Fellow, 1998–99, Sen. Clin. Res. Fellow, 2000–01, Nat. Primary Care R&D Centre; Prof. of Gen. Practice, 2001–06; Hd, Div. of Primary Care, 2005–06; Principal in Gen. Practice (pt-time), Robert Darbishire Practice, Manchester, 2000–06; Dep. Chief Med. Officer for England, DoH, 2006–07. Mem. Council, RCGP, 2005–06. Pres., Eur. Soc. for Quality Improvement in Family Practice, 2005–06. Hon. FRCP 2005. *Publications:* numerous contribs relating to quality and safety in health care. *Recreation:* being outside. *Address:* The Health Foundation, 90 Long Acre, WC2E 9RA. *T:* (020) 7257 8000.

MARSHALL, Prof. Mary Tara, OBE 1997; Director, Dementia Services Development Centre, University of Stirling, 1989–2005; *b* 13 June 1945; *d* of Percy Edwin Alan and Phyllis April Trix Johnson-Marshall. *Educ:* Edinburgh Univ. (MA); London School of Economics (DSA); Liverpool Univ. (Dip. in Applied Social Studies). Child Care Officer, Lambeth, 1967–69; Social Worker, Liverpool Personal Service Soc. Project, 1970–74; Organiser, res. project, Age Concern, Liverpool, 1974–75; Lectr in Applied Social Studies, Liverpool Univ. 1975–83; Dir, Age Concern, Scotland, 1983–89. Mem., Royal Commn on Long Term Care for the Elderly, 1998–99. Member: Liverpool Housing Trust, 1976–; Edinvar Housing Assoc., 1988–; Gov., PPP Foundation (formerly Healthcare Med. Trust Ltd), 1998–2003. Member: Centre for Policy on Ageing, 1986– (Gov., 1994–2000); BASW, 1970–; British Soc. of Gerontology, 1977–; 21st Century Social Work Rev. Gp, 2004–05; Ind. Funding Review of Free Personal and Nursing Care. Sessional Inspector, Social Work Inspection Agency. FRSE 2003. AcSS 1999. FRSA 2003. Hon. DEd Queen Margaret Coll., 1998; Hon. DSocSc Edinburgh, 2004; DUniv Stirling, 2006. *Publications:* Social Work with Old People, 1983, 4th edn (with J. Phillips and M. Ray), 2006; "I Can't Place This Place At All": working with people with dementia and their carers, 1996, 2nd edn (with M.-A. Tibbs) as Social Work and People with Dementia, 2006; (ed) Food, Glorious Food: perspectives on food and dementia, 2003; (ed) Perspectives on Rehabilitation and Dementia, 2005; (ed with K. Allan) Dementia: walking not wandering, 2006; book reviews, papers, reports and articles. *Recreations:* birdwatching, photography. *Address:* 24 Buckingham Terrace, Edinburgh EH4 3AE. *T:* (0131) 343 1732.

MARSHALL, Rt Rev. Michael Eric, MA; Bishop in Residence, since 1997, Rector, since 2002, Holy Trinity, Sloane Street; an Assistant Bishop: Diocese of London, since 1984; Diocese of Chichester, since 1992; *b* Lincoln, 14 April 1936. *Educ:* Lincoln Sch.; Christ's Coll., Cambridge (Tancred Scholar, Upper II: Hist. Pt 1 and Theol Pt 1a, MA); Cuddesdon Theological Coll. Deacon, 1960; Curate, St Peter's, Spring Hill, Birmingham, 1960–62; Tutor, Ely Theological Coll. and Minor Canon of Ely Cath., 1962–64; Chaplain in London Univ., 1964–69; Vicar of All Saints', Margaret Street, W1, 1969–75; Bishop Suffragan of Woolwich, 1975–84; Founding Episcopal Dir, Anglican Inst., St Louis, Missouri, 1984–92; Dir of Evangelism, Chichester Theol Coll., 1991–97; Preb. of Wightring in Chichester Cathedral and Wightring Theol Lectr, 1990–99. Archbishops' Advr on Evangelism, 1992–97; Leader, Springboard, 1992–97. Founder and Director: Inst. of Christian Studies, 1970; Internat. Inst. for Anglican Studies, 1982; Dir, Trinity Inst. for Christianity and Culture, 2003–; Trustee, Trinity Foundn, 2003–. Exam. Chap. to Bp of London, 1974. Member: Gen. Synod, 1970, also Diocesan and Deanery Synods; Liturgical Commn; Anglican/Methodist Liaison Commn until 1974; SPCK Governing Body; USPG Governing Body. Has frequently broadcast on BBC and commercial radio; also lectured, preached and broadcast in Canada and USA. *Publications:* A Pattern of Faith, 1966 (co-author); Glory under Your Feet, 1978; Pilgrimage and Promise, 1981; Renewal in Worship, 1982; The Anglican Church, Today and Tomorrow, 1984; Christian Orthodoxy Revisited, 1985; The Gospel Conspiracy in the Episcopal Church, 1986; The Restless Heart, 1987; The Gospel Connection, 1991; The Freedom of Holiness, 1992; Free to Worship, 1996; Flame in the Mind: a journey of spiritual passion, 2002; Founder and co-editor, Christian Quarterly. *Recreations:* music, cooking. *Address:* 53 Oakley Gardens, Chelsea SW3 5QQ.

MARSHALL, Michael John, CBE 1999; DL; Chairman, Marshall of Cambridge (Holdings) Ltd, since 1990; *b* 27 Jan. 1932; *s* of Sir Arthur Gregory George Marshall, OBE and Rosemary Wynford Marshall; *m* 1st, 1960, Bridget Wykham Pollock (marr. diss. 1977); two *s* two *d*; 2nd, 1979, Sibyl Mary Walkinshaw (*née* Hutton); two step *s*. *Educ:* Eton Coll.; Jesus Coll., Cambridge (MA Hist.; rowing Blue, 1954, rep. GB in Eur. championships, 1955). IEng; FRAeS; FIMI. Nat. Service, Flying Officer, RAF, 1950–52. Joined Marshall of Cambridge (Eng) Ltd, 1955: Dep. Chm. and Man. Dir, Marshall (Cambridge) Ltd, 1964–90. Dir, Eastern Electricity Bd, 1971–77; Chm., BL Cars Distributor Council, 1977, 1983 (Mem., 1975–84); Vice-President: Inst. Motor Ind., 1980–; EEF, 1993–2003; Chm., Cambs Manpower Cttee, 1980–83. Vice-Chm., Cambs Youth Involvement Cttee, Silver Jubilee Fund, 1977–78; Chm., Cambridge Olympic Appeal, 1984; Mem., Ely Cathedral Restoration Appeal Cttee, 1987–; Pres., Cambridge Soc. for Blind, 1989–92; Chm., Prince's Trusts' Cambs Appeal Cttee, 1991–92; Pres., Cambridge '99 Rowing Club, 1996–2003. Chairman: Civilian Cttee, 104 (City of Cambridge) Sqdn, ATC, 1975–; Beds and Cambs Wing, ATC, 1987–93 (Hon. Pres., 2008–); Member: Air Cadet Council, 1994–2006; Council, Air League, 1995– (Chm., 1998–2003; Pres., 2004–); Air Squadron, 1998–. Hon. Air Cdre, No 2623 (East Anglian) Sqdn, RAuxAF, 2003–. Hon. Vice Patron, Royal Internat. Air Tattoo, 2003–. CCMI (CIMgt 1997); FRSA. Freeman, City of London, 1988; Liveryman, GAPAN, 1989–. Cambridgeshire: High Sheriff, 1988–89; DL 1989; Vice Lord-Lieutenant, 1992–2006. DUniv Anglia Poly., 2001. *Recreations:* flying, reading. *Address:* (office) c/o Marshall of Cambridge (Holdings) Ltd, The Airport, Newmarket Road, Cambridge CB5 8RX. *T:* (01223) 373245, *Fax:* (01223) 324224; *e-mail:* mjm@marcamb.co.uk. *Clubs:* Royal Air Force, Air Squadron; Hawks, Cambridge County (Cambridge); Leander (Henley-on-Thames); Eton Vikings.

MARSHALL, Prof. Sir (Oshley) Roy, Kt 1974; CBE 1968; High Commissioner for Barbados in the United Kingdom, 1989–91; Vice-Chancellor, Hull University, 1979–85, Emeritus Professor since 1985; *b* 21 Oct. 1920; *s* of Fitz Roy and Corene Carmelita Marshall; *m* 1st, 1945, Eirwen Lloyd (*d* 1998); one *s* three *d*; 2nd, 2000, Hon. Marie Elizabeth Bourne Hollands, CHB. *Educ:* Harrison Coll., Barbados, WI; Pembroke Coll., Cambridge; University Coll., London (Fellow, 1985). Barbados Scholar, 1938; BA 1945, MA 1948 Cantab; PhD London 1948. Barrister-at-Law, Inner Temple, 1947. University Coll., London: Asst Lecturer, 1946–48; Lecturer, 1948–56; Sub-Dean, Faculty of Law, 1949–56; Prof. of Law and Head of Dept of Law, Univ. of Sheffield, 1956–69, Vis. Prof. in Faculty of Law, 1969–80; on secondment to University of Ife, Ibadan, Nigeria, as Prof. of Law and Dean of the Faculty of Law, 1963–65; Vice-Chancellor, Univ. of West Indies, 1969–74; Sec.-Gen., Cttee of Vice-Chancellors and Principals, 1974–79. Chairman: Commonwealth Educn Liaison Cttee, 1974–81; Cttee on Commonwealth Legal Co-operation, 1975; Commonwealth Standing Cttee on Student Mobility, 1982–94; Council for Educn in the Commonwealth, 1985–91; Review Cttee on Cave Hill Campus, Univ. of WI, 1986; Constitutional Commn on the Turks and Caicos Islands, 1986; Barbados National Commission on Law and Order, 2002–; Member: Police Complaints Bd, 1977–81; Council, RPMS, 1976–83; Council, ACU, 1979–85; Management Cttee, Universities Superannuation Scheme Ltd, 1980–85; UGC for Univ. of S Pacific, 1987; Chm., Bd of Governors, Hymers Coll., Hull, 1985–89; Vice-Chm., Governing Body of Commonwealth Inst., 1980–81; Mem., Bd of Governors, Commonwealth of Learning, 1988–91; Trustee, Commonwealth Foundn, 1981. Hon. LLD: Sheffield, 1972; West Indies, 1976; Hull, 1986; Hon. DLitt CNAA, 1992. *Publications:* The Assignment of Choses in Action, 1950; A Casebook on Trusts (with J. A. Nathan), 1967; Theobald on Wills, 12th edn, 1963. *Recreations:* racing and cricket. *Address:* Evanston, Nelson Road, Navy Gardens, Christ Church BB 14031, Barbados, West Indies. *T:* 426 2474. *Club:* Royal Commonwealth Society.

MARSHALL, Peter David, CMG 2002; OBE 1990; Consultant, Forensic Seismology and Arms Control Research Programmes, Atomic Weapons Establishment, Blacknest, since 2002; *b* 13 June 1937; *s* of Jonathan Marshall and Grace Florence Marshall (*née* Mayes); *m* 1957, Pamela Margaret Rose Champion; one *d*. *Educ:* Dagenham Co. High Sch.; Durham Univ. (MSc Geophysics). Min. of Supply, AERE Harwell, 1953; AWE Foulness, UKAEA, 1955; with Forensic Seismology Gp, AWE Blacknest, UKAEA, 1963–72; MoD, 1972–92 (PSO, 1980; SPSO, 1992); Vis. Scientist, Lawrence Livermore Nat. Lab., Calif., 1975–76; Tech. Advr to UK Delegn, Tri-lateral Test Ban Negotiations, 1977–81; Dep. Hd, 1982–2001, Hd, 2001–02, Forensic Seismology Gp, AWE Blacknest; Dist. Scientist, AWE, 2000. UK Delegate, UN Conf. of Disarmament (CD) Gp of Scientific Experts, Geneva, 1976–93; Technical Advisor: on verification techniques to UK CD Delegn, 1971–96; UK CD Delegn to negotiate a Comprehensive Nuclear Test Ban Treaty, and Chm., Gp of Scientific Experts, during negotiations, 1994–96. Consultant,

CTBTO, Vienna, 1997–. Hon. Treas., 2006–07, Chm., 2007–, Oxford Transplant Foundn. *Publications:* contrib. numerous peer-reviewed papers on technical issues related to solving problems of detecting, locating and identifying nuclear test explosions. *Recreations:* reading, cryptic crosswords, philately, gardening. *Address:* 2 Appletree Close, Newbury, Berks RG14 6HR; *e-mail:* petermpam@aol.com.

MARSHALL, Sir Peter (Harold Reginald), KCMG 1983 (CMG 1974); CVO 2003; Chairman, Joint Commonwealth Societies Council, 1993–2003; *b* 30 July 1924; 3rd *s* of late R. H. Marshall; *m* 1st, 1957, Patricia Rendell Stoddart (*d* 1981); one *s* one *d*; 2nd, 1989, Judith, *widow* of E. W. F. Tomlin. *Educ:* Tonbridge; Corpus Christi Coll., Cambridge (Hon. Fellow 1989). RAFVR, 1943–46. HM Foreign (later Diplomatic) Service, 1949–83: FO, 1949–52; 2nd Sec. and Private Sec. to Ambassador, Washington, 1952–56; FO, 1956–60; on staff of Civil Service Selection Board, 1960; 1st Sec. and Head of Chancery, Baghdad, 1961, and Bangkok, 1962–64; Asst Dir of Treasury Centre for Administrative Studies, 1965–66; Counsellor, UK Mission, Geneva, 1966–69, Counsellor and Head of Chancery, Paris, 1969–71; Head of Financial Policy and Aid Dept, FCO, 1971–73; Asst Under-Sec. of State, FCO, 1973–75; UK Rep. on Econ. and Social Council of UN, 1975–79; Ambassador and UK Perm. Rep. to Office of UN and Other Internat. Organisations at Geneva, 1979–83; Commonwealth Dep. Sec. Gen. (Econ.), 1983–88. Chm., Commonwealth Trust and Royal Commonwealth Soc., 1988–92; Pres., Queen Elizabeth House, Oxford, 1990–94; Vice Pres., Council for Educn in World Citizenship, 1985–98; Member: ICRC Consultative Gp of Internat. Experts, 1984–86; Exec. Cttee, Pilgrims, 1986–2001 and 2004–; Council, VSO, 1989–95; ODI, 1989–99; Governor, E-SU of the Commonwealth, 1984–90; Trustee: King George VI and Queen Elizabeth Foundn of St Catharine's, 1987–2001; Magna Carta Trust, 1993–2004. Mem., Panel of Judges, WorldAware Business Awards, 1988–2002. Chm., Nikaean Club, 1992–2002. Vis. Lectr, Diplomatic Acad. of London, 1989–2001. Hon. Fellow, Univ. of Westminster, 1992. Hon. Vice-Pres., Aircrew Assoc., 2005. *Publications:* The Dynamics of Diplomacy, 1990; (contrib.) The United Kingdom—The United Nations (ed Jensen and Fisher), 1990; (ed) Diplomacy Beyond 2000, 1996; Positive Diplomacy, 1997; (ed) Are Diplomats Really Necessary?, 1998; (ed) The Information Explosion: a challenge for diplomacy, 1998; (ed) Diplomacy and Divinity, 2006; numerous articles on Commonwealth questions. *Recreations:* good music, bad golf, Euro-gazing. *Address:* 26 Queensdale Road, W11 4QB. *Clubs:* Travellers, Royal Commonwealth Society.

MARSHALL, Prof. Peter James, CBE 2002; DPhil; FBA 1992; Rhodes Professor of Imperial History, King's College, London, 1980–93, now Emeritus; *b* 28 Oct. 1933; *s* of Edward Hannaford Marshall and Madeleine (*née* Shuttleworth). *Educ:* Wellington College; Wadham Coll., Oxford (BA 1957; MA, DPhil 1962; Hon. Fellow, 1997). Military service, King's African Rifles, Kenya, 1953–54. Assistant Lecturer, Lecturer, Reader, Professor, History Dept, King's Coll., London, 1959–80 (FKC 1991). Mem., History Wkg Gp, National Curriculum, 1989–90. Pres., RHistS, 1996–2000 (Vice-Pres., 1987–91; Hon. Vice-Pres., 2000–). Hon. For. Mem., Amer. Historical Assoc., 2003–. Editor, Journal of Imperial and Commonwealth History, 1975–81; Associate Editor, Writings and Speeches of Edmund Burke, 1976–. Hon. DLitt: Bristol, 2008; London, 2008. *Publications:* Impeachment of Warren Hastings, 1965; Problems of Empire: Britain and India 1757–1813, 1968; (ed, with J. A. Woods) Correspondence of Edmund Burke, vol. VII, 1968; The British Discovery of Hinduism, 1972; East India Fortunes, 1976; (ed) Writings and Speeches of Edmund Burke, vol. V, 1981, vol. VI, 1991, vol. VII, 2000; (with Glyndwr Williams) The Great Map of Mankind, 1982; Bengal: the British bridgehead (New Cambridge History of India, Vol. II, 2), 1988; Trade and Conquest: studies on the rise of British dominance in India, 1993; (ed) Cambridge Illustrated History of the British Empire, 1996; (ed) Oxford History of the British Empire, Vol. II, The Eighteenth Century, 1998; A Free Though Conquering People: eighteenth-century Britain and its empire, 2003; (ed) The Eighteenth Century in Indian History: evolution or revolution?, 2003; The Making and Unmaking of Empires: Britain, India and America, *c* 1750–1783, 2005; articles in Economic History Rev., History, Modern Asian Studies, etc. *Address:* 7 Malting Lane, Braughing, Ware, Herts SG11 2QZ. *T:* (01920) 822232.

MARSHALL, Peter James, CMG 1996; HM Diplomatic Service, retired; Consul General, Atlanta, USA, 1997–2001; *b* 25 June 1944; *s* of George Aubrey Marshall and Joan Marshall; *m* 1966, Roberta Barlow; one *s* three *d*. *Educ:* Ripon Grammar Sch. Min. of Aviation, 1963–64; CRO, 1964–65; seconded to Commonwealth Secretariat, 1965–67; served Malta, 1967–70; Vice Consul (Commercial), Johannesburg, March–Dec. 1970; 2nd Sec. (Commercial/Information), Kaduna, 1970–74; Vice Consul (Commercial), San Francisco, 1974–79; First Sec., FCO, 1979–83; Dep. High Comr, Malta, 1983–88; First Sec., FCO, 1988–90; Dep. Head, News Dept, FCO, 1990–94; Counsellor, Consul Gen. and Dep. Head of Mission, later Chargé d'Affaires, Algiers, 1994–95; Ambassador to Algeria, 1995–96. *Recreations:* grandchildren, gardening, travel, flying. *Address:* 2 Hemlock Close, Kingswood, Surrey KT20 6QW.

MARSHALL, Very Rev. Peter Jerome; Dean of Worcester, 1997–2006, now Emeritus; *b* 10 May 1940; *s* of Guy and Dorothy Marshall; *m* 1965, Nancy Jane Elliott; one *s* two *d*. *Educ:* St John's, Leatherhead; Upper Canada Coll., Toronto; McGill Univ.; Westcott House, Cambridge. Ordained deacon, 1963, priest, 1964; Curate, St Mary, E Ham, 1963–66; Curate, St Mary, Woodford, and Curate i/c, St Philip and St James, S Woodford, 1966–71; Vicar, St Peter, Walthamstow, 1971–81; Dep. Dir of Training, dio. of Chelmsford, 1981–84; Canon Residentiary, Chelmsford Cathedral, 1981–85; Dio. Dir of Training, Ripon, and Canon Residentiary, Ripon Cathedral, 1985–97. Chm. Pastoral Cttee, dio. of Worcester, 1997–2006. Chm., Barking and Havering AHA, 1976–82. *Recreations:* swimming, walking, sailing, films. *Address:* 433 Gordon Avenue, Peterborough, ON K9J 6G6, Canada. *T:* (705) 8763371; *e-mail:* petermarshall10@cogeco.ca.

MARSHALL, Philip Scott; QC 2003; *b* 6 June 1965; *s* of Arthur and Elizabeth Marshall; *m* 1993, Barbara James; two *s* one *d*. *Educ:* Merchiston Castle Sch., Edinburgh; Queens' Coll., Cambridge (MA Hons); Harvard Law Sch. (LLM). Called to the Bar, Lincoln's Inn, 1987; Fellow, Queens' Coll., Cambridge, 1991–94; in practice as barrister, specialising in commercial, company and insolvency law, 1991–. *Publications:* Practice and Procedure of the Companies Court, 1997; (contrib.) Civil Appeals, 2002; contribs to various legal jls. *Recreations:* horse racing, golf. *Address:* (chambers) Serle Court, 6 New Square, Lincoln's Inn, WC2A 3QS. *T:* (020) 7242 6105, *Fax:* (020) 7405 4004.

MARSHALL, Robert Leckie, OBE 1945; Principal, Co-operative College, and Chief Education Officer, Co-operative Union Ltd, 1946–77; *b* 27 Aug. 1913; *s* of Robert Marshall and Mary Marshall; *m* 1944, Beryl Broad; one *s*. *Educ:* Univ. of St Andrews (MA Mediaeval and Modern History; MA 1st Cl. Hons English Lit.); Commonwealth Fellow, Yale Univ. (MA Polit. Theory and Govt). Scottish Office, 1937–39. Served War, 1939–46: RASC and AEC; finally Comdt, Army Sch. of Educn. Pres., Co-op. Congress, 1976. Missions on Co-op. develt to Tanganyika, Nigeria, India, Kenya, S Yemen and Thailand. Member: Gen. Adv. Council, and Complaints Rev. Bd, IBA, 1973–77; Monopolies and Mergers Commn, 1976–82; Distributive Studies Bd, Business Educn Council, 1976–79; Treas., Council for Educnl Advance, 1974–77; Chm., Quest House, Loughborough, 1980–86; Vice-Chm., Charnwood Community Council, 1980–90. Mem. Court, Loughborough Univ. of Technol., 1981–91. Hon. MA Open Univ., 1977; Hon. DLitt Loughborough Univ. of Technol., 1977. Jt Editor, Jl of Soc. for Co-operative Studies, 1967–95. *Publications:* Lippen on Angus—a celebration of North Angus Co-operative Society, 1983; contribs to educnl and co-op jls. *Recreations:* walking, reading, sharing in community life. *Address:* c/o 28 Denmark Road, Ealing, W13 8RG.

MARSHALL, Prof. Robin, PhD; FRS 1995; Professor of Experimental Physics, 1992–2005, Research Professor of Physics and Life Sciences, since 2005, University of Manchester; *b* 5 Jan. 1940; *s* of Robert Marshall and Grace Eileen Marshall (*née* Ryder); *m* 1963 (marr. diss. 2003); two *s* one *d*. *Educ:* Ermysted's Grammar Sch., Skipton; Univ. of Manchester (BSc 1962; PhD 1965). DSIR Research Fellow, 1965–67; Vis. Scientist, Deutsches Elektronen Synchrotron, Hamburg, 1967–68; Res. Scientist, MIT, 1968–70; Scientist, Daresbury Lab., 1970–78; PSO, 1978–86, Sen. Principal (IM), 1986–92, Rutherford Appleton Lab. Dir and Co. Sec., Frontiers Science and Television Ltd, 1999–. Mem., Bd of Govs, Museum of Sci. and Industry, Manchester, 2003–. Max Born Medal and Prize, German Physical Soc., 1997. *Publications:* High Energy Electron-Positron Physics, 1988; Electron-Positron Annihilation Physics, 1990; numerous scientific papers. *Recreation:* nurturing ducks on Manchester's inner city canals. *Address:* Department of Physics and Astronomy, University of Manchester, Manchester M13 9PL. *T:* (0161) 275 4170.

MARSHALL, Sir Roy; *see* Marshall, Sir O. R.

MARSHALL, Roy Thomas, PhD; Chief Information Officer and Director, Knowledge, Information Technology and Working Environment, Department for Communities and Local Government, since 2006; *b* Wolverhampton, 6 Oct. 1955; *s* of Thomas and Brenda Marshall; *m* 1979, Alison Mary Marian Shirley; two *s* one *d*. *Educ:* Univ. of Exeter (BSc 1st cl. Hons Maths and Theoretical Phys 1977; PhD Maths 1980). Geophysicist, BP Exploration, 1980–84; Head, Mapping and Modelling: BP Alaska, 1984–87; BPX London, 1987–92; Head, Systems Integration, Data Services, BPX London, 1992–94; Business Inf. Manager, BP Abu Dhabi, 1994–99; Head, Inf. Systems Gp, National Grid, 1999–2001; Dir, Deanfield Consultancy Ltd, 2003–04; Chief Inf. Officer and Head, ICT, ODPM, subseq. DCLG, 2004–06. Sen. Responsible Officer, Govt Connect, 2006–08. Founder Mem., Govt CIO Council, 2004–. *Recreations:* gardening, DIY. *Address:* Department for Communities and Local Government, Eland House, Bressenden Place, SW1E 5DU. *T:* (020) 7944 8796; *e-mail:* roy.marshall@communities.gsi.gov.uk.

MARSHALL, Hon. Russell; *see* Marshall, Hon. C. R.

MARSHALL, Stephen; Deputy Minister of Education, Ontario, since 2008; *b* Adelaide, 3 March 1954; *s* of late Frank and Barbara Marshall; *m* 1981, Karyn Thompson; two *s* one *d*. *Educ:* Deakin Univ., Geelong (MEducAdmin, MBA); South Australia Coll. of Educn (Dip. Teaching (Primary), Grad. Dip. Curr. Develt, Grad. Dip. Professional Develt, Cert. Human Achievement Skills). Teacher, Elizabeth Vale Primary Sch., 1977–85; Project Officer, Primary Educn Review, 1986–87, Primary Educn, 1988–89, SA Dept of Educn; Principal (Class 1), Murray Bridge S Primary Sch., 1989–92; Dist Supt of Educn, Murrylands, SA Dept of Educn, 1992–94; Asst Gen. Manager, Central Highlands/Wimmera Reg., 1994–96; Gen. Manager Schs, Loddon/Campaspe/Mallee Reg., 1998–99; Gen. Manager, Sch. and Regl Ops, SA Dept of Educn, 1999–2001; Regl Dir, Western Metropolitan Reg., Victoria Dept of Educn, Employment and Trng, 2001–02; CEO, Dept of Educn and Children's Services, S Australia, 2002–06; Welsh Assembly Government: Member: Mgt Bd, 2006; Ministerial Adv. Gp for Educn, Lifelong Learning and Skills, 2006; Dir, Educn, Lifelong Learning and Skills, subseq. Children, Educn, Lifelong Learning and Skills, 2006–08. Mem., Govt Adv. Cttee, Internat. Baccalaureate Orgn, 2006–. *Address:* Ministry of Education, 2nd Floor, 880 Bay Street, Toronto, ON M7A 1N3, Canada.

MARSHALL, Steven, FCMA; Chairman: Balfour Beatty plc, since 2008 (non-executive Director, 2005–08); Delta plc, since 2005 (Senior Independent Director, 2004–05); *b* 11 Feb. 1957; *s* of late Victor Marshall and of Kathleen Marshall. *Educ:* Isleworth Grammar Sch. Mgt accountant, BOC Gp, 1977–81; Marketing Analyst, then Systems Accountant, Black & Decker, 1981–84; Treasury Controller, then Sector Financial Controller, Burton Gp, 1984–87; Dep. Gp Finance Dir, and Co. Sec., Parkdale Hldgs plc, 1987–89; Gp Investor Relns Dir, then Eur. Finance Dir, IDV, Grand Metropolitan plc, 1990–95; Gp Finance and Commercial Dir, 1995–98, Gp Chief Exec., 1998–99, Thorn plc; Gp Finance Dir, 1999–2000, Gp Chief Exec., 2000–02, Railtrack Gp plc; Exec. Chm., Queens Moat Houses plc, 2003–04. Chm., Torex Retail plc, 2007. Non-exec. Dir, Southern Water Services, 2005–. Special Advr to CIMA, 2002–05. Trustee, Chimpanzee Rehabilitation Trust, 2002–. FCMA 1987. *Recreations:* wildlife conservation and welfare, natural history, travel. *Address:* Balfour Beatty plc, 130 Wilton Road, SW1V 1LQ.

MARSHALL, (Thomas) Daniel; Member (Lab), Newcastle City Council, 1986–2004; Lord Mayor of Newcastle, 1998–99; *b* 6 Nov. 1929; *s* of James William and Leonora Mary Marshall; *m* 1st, 1953, Eileen James (*d* 1995); one *s*; 2nd, 2000, Catherine Fix, San Diego. *Educ:* St George's RC Elementary Sch., Bell's Close, Newcastle upon Tyne; Ruskin Coll.; Open Univ. Post Office, then Nat. Assistance Board, 1960; DHSS, 1966. Councillor, Newburn UDC, 1967; Mem., Tyne and Wear CC, 1974–86 (Chm., 1978–79). Chairman: Newburn Riverside Recreation Assoc. Ltd, 1980–; Tyne and Wear Enterprise Trust, 1981–2006; Nat. Resource for Innovative Trng, Res. and Employment Ltd, 1985–; Throckley Community Hall Ltd, 1991–; Tyne and Wear PTA, 1995–2004 (Mem., 1986–2004); Grange Day Centre Ltd, 1994–; Director: Bowes Railway Co., 1982–2005; Newburn Sports Services Ltd, 1984–; Managed Business Services, 2003–. Trustee: Grange Welfare Assoc., 1970–; Building Preservation Trust Ltd, 1978–2007 (Vice Chm.). DL Tyne and Wear, 1999. Hon. Alderman, Newcastle CC, 2005. *Recreation:* reading. *Address:* 7 Hallow Drive, Throckley, Newcastle upon Tyne NE15 9AQ. *T:* (0191) 267 0956. *Clubs:* Grange Welfare; Newburn Memorial (Newcastle).

MARSHALL, Valerie Margaret; Managing Director, Stratagem CFS Ltd, since 2003; *b* 30 March 1945; *d* of Ernest Knagg and Marion Knagg; *m* 1972, Alan Roger Marshall (marr. diss. 1996); two *s* one *d*. *Educ:* Brighton and Hove High Sch.; Girton Coll., Cambridge (MA); London Graduate Sch. of Business Studies (MSc). LRAM. FSI. Financial Controller, ICFC, 1969–80; Scottish Development Agency: Investment Exec., 1980–84; Investment Man., 1984–88; Head of Business Enterprise, 1988–90; Director: Renfrew Development Co. Ltd, 1988–90; Scottish Food Fund, 1988–90; Grieg, Middleton & Co., 1990–2001; Sitka Capital Partners, 2001–02; Photopharmica Ltd, 2002–03; Fusion Lifestyle (formerly Southwark Community Leisure) Ltd, 2003–. Non-executive Director: Veryan Medical Ltd, 2004–07; Nano Biodesign Ltd, 2006–. Member: Scottish Cttee, Design Council, 1975–77; Monopolies and Mergers Commn, 1976–81. Chm., Scottish Music Inf. Centre, 1986–90. University of Kent: Mem. Council, 2003– (Treas., 2004–05; Chm., 2005–); Pro-Vice-Chancellor, 2005–. Governor: Glasgow Sch.

of Art, 1989–90; Tonbridge GS for Girls, 1993–97. *Recreations:* music, ballet, walking, entertaining. *Address:* 6 Egdean Walk, Sevenoaks, Kent TN13 3UQ.

MARSHALL, Wayne; organ recitalist and solo pianist, conductor and composer; *b* 13 Jan. 1961; *s* of Wigley Marshall and Costella (*née* Daniel). *Educ:* Chetham's Sch., Manchester; Royal Coll. of Music; Vienna Hochschule. Organ Schol., Manchester Cathedral and St George's Chapel, Windsor. Dir, W11 Opera Gp, 1991; Associate Music Dir and Conductor, Carmen Jones, Old Vic, 1991; Guest Chorus Dir, Royal Opera Hse, 1992; Organist-in-Residence, Bridgewater Hall, Manchester, 1996–. Organ, solo piano, and duo recitals throughout UK, and overseas incl. US, European and Far East concert series; festivals performed at incl. Bregenz Opera, Austria, 2003, 2004, Braunschweig Classix, Germany; conductor and soloist with leading orchestras in UK and overseas, incl. CBSO, RPO, Philharmonia, London Philharmonic, BBCSO, Berlin Philharmonic, LA Philharmonic, Rotterdam Philharmonic, Suisse Romande, Orch. Nat. de Lyon, Toronto Symphony and Vienna Symphony. Has made numerous recordings incl. organ music, and works by Hindemith and Gershwin. Artist of Year Award, BBC Music Mag., 1998; ECHO Award, 1998. *Address:* c/o Askonas Holt Ltd, Lincoln House, 300 High Holborn, WC1V 7JH. *T:* (020) 7400 1700, *Fax:* (020) 7400 1799; *e-mail:* info@askonasholt.co.uk.

MARSHALL-ANDREWS, Robert Graham; QC 1987; MP (Lab) Medway, since 1997; a Recorder of the Crown Court, since 1982; *b* 10 April 1944; *s* of late Robin and Eileen Nora Marshall; *m* 1968, Gillian Diana Elliott; one *s* one *d*. *Educ:* Mill Hill Sch.; Univ. of Bristol (LLB; winner, Observer Mace Nat. Debating Competition, 1965). Called to the Bar, Gray's Inn, 1967, Bencher, 1996; Oxford and Midland Circuit. Contested (Lab) Medway, 1992. Founder Mem., Old Testament Prophets, 1996. Dep. Chm., Theatre Council, 1997–. Trustee: George Adamson Trust, 1988–; Geffrye Museum, 1990–. Chm. of Govs, Grey Court Sch., 1988–94. *Publications:* The Palace of Wisdom (novel), 1989; A Man without Guilt (novel), 2002; contrib. political articles to nat. periodicals. *Recreations:* theatre, reading, Rugby (watching), travelling about. *Address:* House of Commons, SW1A 0AA; Carmelite Chambers, 9 Carmelite Street, EC4Y 0DR. *T:* (020) 7936 6300. *Clubs:* Garrick; Druidston (Broadhaven, Pembrokeshire).

MARSHALL EVANS, David; *see* Evans.

MARSHAM, family name of **Earl of Romney**.

MARSHAM, Viscount; David Charles Marsham; *b* 18 April 1977; *s* and *heir* of Earl of Romney, *qv*. Captain, Scots Guards.

MARSLEN-WILSON, Lorraine Komisarjevsky; *see* Tyler, L. K.

MARSLEN-WILSON, Prof. William David, PhD; FBA 1996; Director, MRC Cognition and Brain Sciences Unit (formerly MRC Applied Psychology Unit), Cambridge, since 1997; Fellow, Wolfson College, Cambridge, since 2000; *b* Salisbury, Wilts, 5 June 1945; *s* of David William Marslen-Wilson and Pera (*née* Funk); *m* 1982, Lorraine Komisarjevsky Tyler, *qv*; one *s* one *d*; one *d*. *Educ:* St John's Coll., Oxford (BA 1st cl. Philosophy and Psychology 1967); PhD MIT 1973. Asst Prof., Cttee on Cognition and Communication, Dept of Behavioral Scis, Chicago Univ., 1973–78; Scientific Associate, Max Planck Inst. for Psycholinguistics, Nijmegen, 1977–82; Lectr, Dept of Exptl Psychol., Cambridge Univ., 1982–84; Co-Dir, Max Planck Inst. for Psycholinguistics, 1985–87; Sen. Scientist, MRC Applied Psychol. Unit, Cambridge, 1987–90; Prof. of Psychology, 1990–97, College Fellow, 2000–, Birkbeck Coll., London Univ. Hon. Prof. of Language and Cognition, Cambridge Univ., 2002–. MAE 1996. *Publications:* (ed) Lexical Representation and Process, 1989; over 150 contribs to learned jls incl. Science, Nature, Psychological Rev., Jl of Exptl Psychol., Cognition, Lang. and Cognitive Processes. *Recreations:* photography, cooking, gardening. *Address:* MRC Cognition and Brain Sciences Unit, 15 Chaucer Road, Cambridge CB2 7EF. *T:* (01223) 355294, *Fax:* (01223) 500250.

MARSON, Anthony; Finance Director, C. B. Marketing and Investments Ltd, 1997, retired; *b* 12 Jan. 1938; *m* 1963, Margaret Salmond; three *s*. *Educ:* Bristol Univ. (BA). Finance Dir, Pharmaceutical Div., Beecham Gp, 1968–90; Gp Finance Dir, PSA Services, DoE, 1990–93. *Address:* Bullbeggars House, Church Hill, Woking, Surrey GU21 4QE.

MARSON, Geoffrey Charles; QC 1997; **His Honour Judge Marson;** a Circuit Judge, since 2005; *b* 30 March 1952; *s* of Charles Marson and Muriel Annie Marson; *m* 1992, Denise Lynn Gresty; two *s*. *Educ:* Malton Grammar Sch.; King's Coll. London (LLB Hons). Called to the Bar, Gray's Inn, 1975; Asst Recorder, 1991–95; a Recorder, 1995–2005; Head of Chambers, 1997–2005. Pt-time Pres., Mental Health Review Tribunals (Restricted Panel), 2000–. *Recreations:* family, wine, cooking, travel. *Address:* Leeds Combined Court Centre, 1 Oxford Row, Leeds LS1 3BG.

MARSTON, Nicholas Richard; His Honour Judge Marston; a Circuit Judge, since 2005; a Deputy High Court Judge, since 2007; Designated Family Judge, Hampshire and Isle of Wight, since 2008; *b* 24 March 1952; *s* of late Lt Comdr Max Marston, MBE, DSC, RN retd and of Iris May Marston; *m* 1985, Suzanne Amanda Lyons; one *s* one *d*. *Educ:* UWIST (LLB Hons). Called to the Bar, Middle Temple, 1975; Asst Recorder, 1998–99; a Recorder, 1999–2005. *Recreations:* keen historian and traveller, food, wine and friends, cricket, a largely misplaced devotion to the Welsh Rugby team. *Address:* Portsmouth County Court, Winston Churchill Avenue, Portsmouth PO1 2EB.

MARTIENSSEN, Prof. Robert Anthony, PhD; FRS 2006; Professor of Plant Genetics, Cold Spring Harbor Laboratory, since 1995; *b* 21 Dec. 1960. *Educ:* Emmanuel Coll., Cambridge (BA 1982; PhD 1986). Univ. of Calif, Berkeley, 1986–88; Cold Spring Harbor Lab., 1989–. Co-founder and Dir, Orion Genomics. *Publications:* articles in learned jls. *Address:* Cold Spring Harbor Laboratory, 1 Bungtown Road, Cold Spring Harbor, NY 11724, USA.

MARTIN, Prof. Alan Douglas, PhD; FRS 2004; Professor of Theoretical Physics, University of Durham, 1978–2003, now Emeritus; *b* 4 Dec. 1937; *s* of Frederick Charles Martin and Emily May Martin (*née* Berkley); *m* 1st, 1964, Penelope Johnson (marr. diss. 1999); one *s* two *d*; 2nd, 2000, Robin Louise Thodey. *Educ:* Eltham Coll.; UCL (BSc 1958; PhD 1962). CPhys 1989, FInstP 1989. Res. Associate, Univ. of Illinois, 1962; University of Durham: Lectr, 1964–71; Sen. Lectr, 1971–74; Reader, 1974–78; Hd, Dept of Physics, 1989–93; Derman Christopherson Res. Fellow, 1995–96. Res. Associate, CERN, Geneva, 1971–73. Erskine Fellow, Univ. of Canterbury, NZ, 2003; Leverhulme Emeritus Fellow, 2004–06. Max Born Medal and Prize, Inst. of Physics and German Physical Soc., 2007. *Publications:* (with T. D. Spearman) Elementary Particle Theory, 1969; (with F. Halzen) Quarks and Leptons, 1984; (with P. D. B. Collins) Hadron Interactions, 1984; (jtly) Particle Physics and Cosmology, 1989; more than 300 res. papers in scientific jls. *Recreations:* gardening, ski-ing, tennis, listening to music. *Address:* 8 Quarry Heads Lane, Durham City, DH1 3DY. *T:* (office) (0191) 334 3672, *Fax:* (0191) 334 3658; *e-mail:* A.D.Martin@durham.ac.uk.

MARTIN, (Arthur) Bryan, CB 1987; Member of Health and Safety Executive, 1985–88, and Director, Resources and Planning Division, 1977–88; Head of UK Delegation, and Alternate Chairman, Channel Tunnel Safety Authority, 1989–92; *b* 16 July 1928; *s* of Frederick Arthur Martin and Edith Maud Martin; *m* 1953, Dyllis Naomi Eirne Johnstone-Hogg; two *s*. *Educ:* Bristol Grammar Sch.; Royal Mil. Coll. of Science (BSc). Joined Army, REME, 1948; commnd, 1948; Lt-Col, 1967–69; served in UK, Germany, Malaya (despatches, 1959), Cyprus and Aden; joined Civil Service (Dept of Employment), 1969, as direct entrant principal; Asst Sec., Factory Inspectorate, 1973; Under Sec., HSE, 1977. Director: Docklands Light Railway, 1993–98; Angel Train Contracts, 1996–99.

MARTIN, Barry Robert; Headmaster, Hampton School, since 1997; *b* 18 July 1950; *s* of late Robert Martin and Peggy Martin; *m* 1983, Fiona MacLeod; one *s* one *d*. *Educ:* Kingston Grammar Sch.; St Catharine's Coll., Cambridge (MA; Hockey Blue 1973); Inst. of Education, London Univ. (PGCE); Loughborough Univ. (MBA). Asst Master, Kingston GS, 1973–75; Bank of England Overseas Dept, 1975–77; Hd of Econs and Business Studies and Housemaster, Caterham Sch., 1978–83; Hd of Econs, Repton Sch., 1983–85; Housemaster and Dir of Studies, Mill Hill Sch., 1985–92; Principal, Liverpool Coll., 1992–97. Chief Examr, Cambridge A Level Business Studies, 1988–2002. Mem., HMC, 1992– (Hon. Treas., 2007–); Dir, ISC, 2007–. Gov., King's House Sch., 2004–. FRSA 1994; FCMI (FIMgt 1997). *Publications:* jointly: The Complete A–Z Business Studies Handbook, 1994, 4th edn 2003; The Complete A–Z Economics and Business Studies Handbook, 1996, 3rd edn 2003; Business Studies, 1999, 2nd edn 2003; articles in Business Rev. *Recreation:* Cornwall. *Address:* Hampton School, Hanworth Road, Hampton, Middx TW12 3HD. *T:* (020) 8979 5526. *Clubs:* East India; Hawks (Cambridge).

MARTIN, Prof. Benjamin Raymond; Professor of Science and Technology Policy Studies, since 1996, and Director, Science and Technology Policy Research, Science Policy Research Unit, 1997–2004, University of Sussex; *b* 9 Aug. 1952; *s* of Adrian Sidney Martin, MBE and Joan Dorothy (*née* Mingo); *m* 1973, Valerie Ann Bennett; two *s* one *d*. *Educ:* Blundell's Sch.; Churchill Coll., Cambridge (Kitchener Schol.; BA, MA); Univ. of Manchester (MSc). VSO sci. teacher, Nigeria, 1973–75; Science Policy Research Unit, University of Sussex: Fellow, 1978–86; Lectr, 1983–90; Sen. Fellow, 1986–96; Sen. Lectr, 1990–96. Vis. Lectr, Imperial Coll., London, 1983–84; Vis. Fellow, Max-Planck-Inst. für Gesellschaftsforschung, 1987. Member: Steering Gp, UK Technol. Foresight Prog., 1993–2000; Technol Opportunities Panel, EPSRC, 2001–04. Mem. Senate, 1997–2004, and Council, 1997–2002, Univ. of Sussex. Derek de Solla Price Medal for Sci. Studies, Scientometrics jl, 1997. *Publications:* (with J. Irvine) Foresight in Science, 1984; (with J. Irvine) Research Foresight, 1989; (jtly) Investing in the Future, 1990; (jtly) Equipping Science for the 21st Century, 1997; (jtly) Science in Tomorrow's Europe, 1997; (with P. Nightingale) The Political Economy of Science, Technology and Innovation, 2000; (jtly) Creative Knowledge and Environments, 2004; numerous papers in learned jls. *Recreations:* indoor rowing (10th place, World Indoor Rowing Championships, Boston, 1998), ski-ing, reading, DIY, gardening, family - balancing demands of two professional careers and three children! *Address:* Linden Lea, 4 Foxglove Gardens, Purley, Surrey CR8 3LQ. *T:* (020) 8660 0329; *e-mail:* B.Martin@sussex.ac.uk.

MARTIN, Sir Bruce; *see* Martin, Sir R. B.

MARTIN, Bryan; *see* Martin, A. B.

MARTIN, Campbell; freelance journalist, since 2007; Member Scotland West, Scottish Parliament, 2003–07 (SNP, 2003–04, Ind, 2004–07); *b* 10 March 1960; *s* of Campbell Martin and Jeanie, (Bunty), Martin; *m* 1993, Carol Marshall; one *s* one *d*. *Educ:* Ardrossan Acad.; James Watt Coll., Greenock (HNC Social Scis). Craft apprenticeship, ICI, Ardeer, Ayrshire, 1976–80; various posts, 1980–93; mature student, 1993–94; Buyer, Prestwick, 1995–97, Purchasing Liaison, Manchester, 1997–99, British Aerospace; Parly Asst and Whip's Administrator, SNP Parly Gp, Scottish Parlt, 1999–2003. *Recreation:* reading. *Address:* 3 Stanley Drive, Ardrossan, Ayrshire KA22 8NX.

MARTIN, Charles Edmund, MA; Headmaster, Bristol Grammar School, 1986–99; *b* 19 Sept. 1939; *s* of late Flight Lieut Charles Stuart Martin and of Sheila Martin; *m* 1966, Emily Mary Bozman; one *s* (one *d* decd). *Educ:* Lancing College; Selwyn College, Cambridge (Hons English; MA); Bristol University (PGCE). VSO, Sarawak, 1958–59; Asst Master, Leighton Park School, Reading, 1964–68; Day Housemaster and Sixth Form Master, Sevenoaks School, 1968–71; Head of English Dept and Dep. Headmaster, Pocklington School, 1971–80; Headmaster, King Edward VI Camp Hill Boys' School, Birmingham, 1980–86. Sec., 1992–93, Chm., 1993–94, HMC SW Div.; Divl Rep., HMC Cttee, 1992–94; Member: ISC Assisted Places Cttee, 1997–99; HMC Bridges and Partnership Cttee, 1998–99. Chief Examnr, A-level English, UCLES, 1978–83. VSO selector, 1999–. Gov., John Cabot Academy (formerly John Cabot City Technol. Coll.), 2000–07 (Vice Chm., 2007–). Mem., Sarawak Assoc., 2008–. *Recreations:* travel, hill walking, theatre, ornithology. *Address:* 47 Hampton Park, Redland, Bristol BS6 6LQ.

MARTIN, Christine Jane; Resident Senior Immigration Judge, Asylum and Immigration Tribunal, Stoke on Trent and Nottingham, since 2006; *b* 20 Jan. 1957; *d* of John Stewart Wreford and Peggy Patricia Wreford (*née* Clark); *m* 1986, Lawford Patrick William Martin; one *s* one *d*. *Educ:* Univ. of Keele (BA Hons 1979); Chester Coll. of Law (Law Soc. Finals 1980). Admitted Solicitor, 1982, then partner in private practice, 1982–2002; Immigration Adjudicator, then Immigration Judge, Manchester, 2003–06. Pres. (pt-time), Mental Health Rev. Tribunal, 1996–2006. *Recreations:* Guide Association (Brownie Guider), archery instructor, reading, cooking, theatre. *Address:* Stoke Asylum and Immigration Tribunal, Bennett House, Town Road, HAnley, Stoke-on-Trent ST1 2QB. *T:* (01782) 200163. *Club:* British Pottery Manufacturers Federation.

MARTIN, Christopher; *see* Martin, K.

MARTIN, Christopher George; management consultant; Director of Personnel, British Broadcasting Corporation, 1981–89, retired; *b* 29 May 1938; *s* of George and Lizbette Martin; *m* 1st, 1960, Moira Hughes (marr. diss. 1975); one *s* one *d*; 2nd, 1981, Elizabeth Buchanan Keith; one *s* decd. *Educ:* Beckenham Sch., Kent. Royal Marines, 1956–62. Group Personnel Manager: Viyella Internat., 1964–70; Great Universal Stores, 1970–74; Personnel Dir, Reed Paper & Board, 1974–76; UK Personnel Dir, Air Products Ltd, 1976–78; Gp Personnel Controller, Rank Organisation Ltd, 1978–81. CCMI (CBIM 1984); FIPM 1984. *Publication:* contrib. Jl of Textile Inst. *Recreations:* music, sailing. *Address:* Roquevail, 11400 Peyrens, France. *T:* (4) 68230369.

MARTIN, Christopher Jon; Director, Public Services and Environment, HM Treasury, since 2007; *b* West Bromwich, 15 May 1973; *s* of Peter and Gwenda Martin; *m* 2005, Christina Scott. *Educ:* Univ. of Bristol (BSc Hons Pols, BSc Physics 1996). Private Sec. to Financial Sec. to HM Treasury, 1999–2002; Sen. Manager, London Bor. of Hackney, 2002; HM Treasury: Asst Sec., Gen. Expenditure Policy, 2003–04; Hd, Productivity Team, 2004–06; Press Sec. to the Chancellor of the Exchequer and Head of

Communications, 2006–07. *Recreations:* running, baking bread, reading history, visiting Italy. *Address:* HM Treasury, 1 Horse Guards Road, SW1A 2HQ. *T:* (020) 7270 4459; *e-mail:* chris.martin@hm-treasury.gov.uk. *Club:* Arsenal Football.

MARTIN, Christopher Sanford; Headmaster, Millfield School, 1990–98; *b* 23 Aug. 1938; *s* of late Geoffrey Richard Rex Martin and Hazel Matthews; *m* 1968, Mary Julia Parry-Evans (marr. diss. 2006); one *s* one *d. Educ:* St Andrews Univ. (MA Mod. Langs; PGCE). Commissioned 2/10 Gurkha Rifles, 1957. Taught at Westminster Sch., 1963–78, at Philips, Exeter Acad., USA, 1966; Head Master, Bristol Cathedral Sch., 1979–90. Member: Privy Council Educnl Panel, 1986–96; Engrg Council Educn Cttee, 1988–96; Adv. Gp on teaching as a profession, Teacher Trng Agency, 1995–98. Chairman: SW Div., HMC, 1987; Choir Schools' Assoc., 1987–89; HMC/SHA Working Party on teacher shortage, 1987–90; Students Partnership Worldwide, 1998–2005; Nat. Rep., HMC Cttee, 1987–89. Founded Textbooks for Africa scheme (ODA), 1988. Chairman: Mental Health Foundn, 2000–04; Hanover Foundn, 2001–; Bottletop, 2008–. Pres., Nat. Assoc. for Gifted Children, 2003–. Gov., Coram Family, 1999–2007. *Publication:* Millfield: a school for all seasons, 2007. *Recreations:* travel, cycling. *Address:* Place House, Kington Langley, Wilts SN15 5NH.

MARTIN, Claire; jazz singer; Presenter, Jazz Line Up, BBC Radio 3, since 2000; *b* 6 Sept. 1967; *d* of David and Carole Godwin; adopted surname Martin as stage name; one *d. Educ:* Carshalton Coll. Jazz educator. Has performed with Hallé Orch., Liverpool SO, BBC Big Band, London Jazz Orch., Pete Long Big Band, Laurence Cottle Big Band, HR Big Band (Frankfurt), John Wilson Orch., Rias Big Band (Berlin). *Album recordings:* The Waiting Game, 1992; Devil May Care, 1993; Old Boyfriends, 1994; Offbeat, 1995; Make this City Ours, 1997; Take My Heart, 1999; Perfect Alibi, 2000; Every Now and Then, 2001; Too Darn Hot, 2002; Secret Love, 2004; When Lights are Low, 2005; He Never Mentioned Love, 2007. Best Vocalist, British Jazz Awards, 1996, 1998, 2000, 2002, BBC Jazz Awards, 2003. *Recreations:* yoga, tennis, jazz clubs. *Address:* 33 Derek Avenue, Hove, Sussex BN3 4PE; *e-mail:* clairemartinjazz@btopenworld.com.

MARTIN, Dr Claude; Chancellor, International University in Geneva, since 2006; *b* 20 July 1945; *s* of Julien and Anna Martin-Zellweger; *m* 1985, Judith Füglister; two *s* two *d. Educ:* Univ. of Zurich (MSc; PhD Wildlife Ecol.). Field project executant, WWF/IUCN, India, 1971–73; Dir, Bia Nat. Park, Ghana, 1975–78; World Wildlife Fund, subseq. World Wide Fund for Nature: Dir, Switzerland, 1980–90; Dep. Dir Gen. (Prog.), Internat., 1990–93; Dir Gen., WWF Internat., 1993–2005. Comdr, Golden Ark (Netherlands), 2003; Officier, Ordre National (Madagascar), 2003. *Publication:* Die Regenwälder Westafrikas, 1989, trans. as The Rainforests of West Africa, 1991. *Recreations:* mountain climbing, restoration of ancient buildings. *Address:* International University in Geneva, ICC 20, route de Pré-Bois, 1215 Geneva 15, Switzerland.

MARTIN, Sir Clive (Haydn), Kt 2001; OBE 1981; TD; DL; Chairman, MPG Ltd (formerly Staples Printers Ltd), since 1978; Lord Mayor of London, 1999–2000; *b* 20 March 1935; *s* of Thomas Stanley Martin and Dorothy Gladys Martin; *m* 1959, Linda Constance Basil Penn; one *s* three *d. Educ:* St Albans Sch.; Haileybury and Imperial Service Coll.; London Sch. of Printing and Graphic Arts. FCIS 1966; FCMA 1971. Nat. Service, Germany, commnd RE (Survey), 1956–58. Man. Dir, Staples Printers Ltd, 1972–85. ADC to The Queen, 1982–86. City of London: Alderman, Aldgate Ward, 1985–2005; Sheriff, 1996–97. Master: Stationers' and Newspaper Makers' Co., 1997–98; Chartered Secs' and Administrators' Co., 2004–05. Hon. Artillery Company: CO, 1978–80; Regtl Col, 1981–83; Master Gunner, Tower of London, 1981–83. Vice-Pres., RFCA for Greater London, 2003–. Hon. Colonel: 135 Ind. Geographic Sqn, RE, 1999–2004; London Regt, 2001–06. Trustee, Morden Coll., 1999–. Hon. DCL City, 1999; Hon. Dr London Inst., 2001. Comdr 1st Degree, Order of Dannebrog (Denmark). *Recreations:* sailing, cycling, walking. *Address:* Weatherbury, 16 Heath Road, Potters Bar, Herts EN6 1LN. *Clubs:* Oriental, Royal Ocean Racing.

MARTIN, Rev. Prof. David Alfred, PhD; FBA 2007; International Fellow (formerly Senior Professorial Fellow), Institute for the Study of Economic Culture, Boston University, since 1990; Professor of Sociology, London School of Economics and Political Science, London University, 1971–89, now Emeritus; *b* 30 June 1929; *s* of late Frederick Martin and late Rhoda Miriam Martin; *m* 1st, 1953, Daphne Sylvia Treherne (*d* 1975); one *s*; 2nd, 1962, Bernice Thompson; two *s* one *d. Educ:* Richmond and East Sheen Grammar Sch.; Westminster Coll. (DipEd 1952); BSc (ext.) 1st Cl. Hons, London Univ., 1959; PhD 1964; Westcott House, Cambridge. School teaching, 1952–59; postgrad. scholar, LSE, 1959–61; Asst Lectr, Sheffield Univ., 1961–62; Lectr, LSE, 1962–67, Reader, 1967–71. JSPS Scholar, Japan, 1978–79; Scurlock Prof. of Human Values, Southern Methodist Univ., Dallas, Texas, 1986–90; Hon. Prof., Lancaster Univ., 1993–2006; Adjunct Prof., Liverpool Hope Univ., 2006–. Lectures: Cadbury, Birmingham Univ., 1973; Ferguson, Manchester Univ., 1977; Gore, Westminster Abbey, 1977; Firth, Nottingham Univ., 1980; Forwood, Liverpool Univ., 1982; Prideaux, Exeter Univ., 1984; F. D. Maurice, KCL, 1991; Sarum, Oxford Univ., 1994–95; Gunning, Edinburgh Univ., 1997; Select Preacher, Cambridge Univ., 1979. Pres., Internat. Conf. of Sociology of Religion, 1975–83. Ordained deacon, 1983, priest 1984; Hon. Asst Priest, Guildford Cathedral, 1983–. Hon. DTheol Helsinki, 2000. *Publications:* Pacifism, 1965; A Sociology of English Religion, 1967; The Religious and the Secular, 1969; Tracts against the Times, 1973; A General Theory of Secularisation, 1978; Dilemmas of Contemporary Religion, 1978; (ed) Crisis for Cranmer and King James, 1979; The Breaking of the Image, 1980; (ed jtly) Theology and Sociology, 1980; (ed jtly) No Alternative, 1981; (ed jtly) Unholy Warfare, 1983; Divinity in a Grain of Bread, 1989; Tongues of Fire, 1990; The Forbidden Revolutions, 1996; Reflections on Sociology and Theology, 1997; Does Christianity Cause War?, 1997; Pentecostalism—The World Their Parish, 2001; Christian Language and its Mutations, 2002; Christian Language in the Secular City, 2002; On Secularization: towards a revised general theory, 2005; contrib. Encounter, TLS, THES, Daedalus, TES. *Recreation:* piano accompaniment. *Address:* Cripplegate Cottage, 174 St John's Road, Woking, Surrey GU21 7PQ. *T:* (01483) 762134.

MARTIN, David John Pattison; barrister; Partner, A., D., P. & E. Farmers, since 1968; *b* 5 Feb. 1945; *s* of late John Besley Martin, CBE and Muriel Martin; *m* 1977, Basia Dowmunt; one *s* three *d* (and one *d* decd). *Educ:* Norwood Sch., Exeter; Kelly College; Fitzwilliam College, Cambridge (BA Hons 1967). Governor, Dummer Academy, USA, 1963–64; called to the Bar, Inner Temple, 1969; practised until 1976; returned to the Bar, 1998; formerly Dir, family caravan and holiday business. Teignbridge District Councillor (C), 1979–83. Contested Yeovil, 1983. MP (C) Portsmouth South, 1987–97; contested (C) same seat, 1997; PPS to Minister of State, Defence Procurement, 1990, to Sec. of State, Foreign and Commonwealth Affairs, 1990–94. Contested (C): South West Region, EP elecns, 1999; Rugby and Kenilworth, 2001; Bristol W, 2005. *Recreations:* music, golf. *Address:* Queen Square Chambers, 56 Queen Square, Bristol BS1 4PR. *Club:* Hawks (Cambridge).

MARTIN, (David) Paul; Chief Executive, London Borough of Sutton, since 2005; *b* 10 Aug. 1961; *s* of late Leslie John and of Dora Marguerite Martin; *m* 1984, Lynne Margaret Allwright; two *d. Educ:* Ilford Co. High Sch. for Boys; UCW, Aberystwyth (BA Hons); Anglia Business Sch. (MSc). Asst Librarian, Notts CC, 1982–85; Community Services Librarian, Bolton MBC, 1985–87; Area Organiser of Cultural Services, Manchester CC, 1987–91; Hd, Policy and Review, 1991–93, Asst Chief Exec., 1993–97, Cambs CC; Dir, Community Services, 1997–99, Chief Exec., 1999–2002, Peterborough CC; Regl Dir, Govt Office for the SE, 2002–05. *Recreations:* music, theatre, English and American literature, travel, keeping fit. *Address:* London Borough of Sutton Civic Offices, St Nicholas Way, Sutton SM1 1EA.

MARTIN, David Weir; Member (Lab) Scotland, European Parliament, since 1999 (Lothians, 1984–99); *b* 26 Aug. 1954; *s* of William Martin and Marion Weir. *Educ:* Liberton High School; Heriot-Watt University (BA Hons Econs); Leicester Univ. (MA 1997). Stockbroker's clerk, 1970–74; animal rights campaigner, 1975–78. Lothian Regional Councillor, 1982–84. European Parliament: Leader, British Lab. Gp, 1987–88; a Vice Pres., 1989–2004. Vice-Pres., Internat. Inst. for Democracy; Vice-President: Nat. Playbus Assoc., 1985–; Advocates for Animals (formerly Scottish Soc. for Prevention of Vivisection), 1993–. Dir, St Andrew Animal Fund, 1986–. *Publications:* Europe: an ever closer union, 1991; Fabian pamphlets on the Common Market and on EC enlargement; Wheatley pamphlet on European Union. *Recreations:* soccer, reading. *Address:* (office) PO Box 27030, Edinburgh EH10 7YP. *T:* (0131) 654 1606.

MARTIN, Prof. Derek H.; Professor of Physics, Queen Mary and Westfield College (formerly Queen Mary College), University of London, 1967–94, Emeritus Professor since 1995 (Hon. Fellow, 1996); *b* 18 May 1929; *s* of Alec Gooch Martin and Winifred Martin; *m* 1951, Joyce Sheila Leaper; one *s* one *d. Educ:* Hitchin Boys' Grammar Sch.; Eastbourne Grammar Sch.; Univ. of Nottingham (BSc; PhD). Queen Mary College, London: Lectr, 1954–58, 1962–63; Reader in Experimental Physics, 1963–67; Dean, Faculty of Science, 1968–70; Head of Dept of Physics, 1970–75. DSIR Res. Fellow, 1959–62; Visiting Professor: Univ. of Calif, Berkeley, 1965–66; Univ. of Essex, 1995–97. Member: Astronomy, Space and Radio Bd, SRC, 1975–78; Bd, Athlone Press, 1973–79; Royal Greenwich Observatory Cttee, 1977–80; Senate, Univ. of London, 1981–86; Court, Univ. of Essex, 1986–98. Fellow, Inst. of Physics (Hon. Sec., 1984–94); Mem., Internat. Astronomical Union. NPL Metrology Award, 1983. Editor, Advances in Physics, 1974–84. *Publications:* Magnetism in Solids, 1967; Spectroscopic Techniques, 1967; numerous articles and papers in Proc. Royal Soc., Jl of Physics, etc. *Address:* 14 Avon Mill Place, Pershore, Worcs WR10 1AZ. *T:* (01386) 555301. *Club:* Athenæum.

MARTIN, Most Rev. Diarmuid; *see* Dublin, Archbishop of, and Primate of Ireland, (RC).

MARTIN, Dominic David William, CVO 2007; HM Diplomatic Service; UK Permanent Representative to Organisation for Economic Co-operation and Development, Paris (with rank of Ambassador), since 2008; *b* 25 Nov. 1964; *s* of Christopher Martin and Felicity Martin (*née* Weston); *m* 1996, Emily Walter; three *d. Educ:* Westminster Sch.; Oriel Coll., Oxford (BA Hons). Joined HM Diplomatic Service, 1987; FCO, 1987–89; Third, later Second Sec., New Delhi, 1989–92; FCO, 1992–96; First Secretary: Buenos Aires, 1996–99; FCO, 1999–2001; Political Counsellor, and Hd, Political Dept, New Delhi, 2001–04; Counsellor (Political, Press and Public Affairs), Washington, 2004–07. *Address:* c/o Foreign and Commonwealth Office, King Charles Street, SW1A 2AH. *Club:* Barnes Cricket.

MARTIN, Evelyn Fairfax, OBE 1994; Company Secretary, National Council of Women of GB, 1992–2000 (National President, 1986–88); Co-Chair, Women's National Commission, 1991–93; *b* 12 Aug. 1926; *d* of late Kenneth Gordon Robinson and Beatrice Robinson (*née* Munro); *m* 1949, Dennis William Martin; three *d* (and one *d* decd). *Educ:* Belvedere Girls' Sch., Liverpool; Huyton Coll. for Girls, Liverpool; Mrs Hoster's Secretarial Coll. Foster parent, 1960–71. Chairman: Battered Wives Hostel, Calderdale, 1980–82; Calderdale Well Woman Centre, 1982–86; Calderdale CHC, 1982–84; Women's Health and Screening Delegn, 1985–91. FRSA 1991. *Recreations:* gardening, foreign travel, animals. *Address:* 32 Clifton Road, Halifax HX3 0BT. *T:* (01422) 360438; *e-mail:* evelynfairfax@tiscali.co.uk. *Club:* University Women's.

MARTIN, Francis James, (Frank); HM Diplomatic Service; High Commissioner to Botswana, since 2005; *b* 3 May 1949; *s* of Brian and Elizabeth Martin; *m* 1970, Aileen Margaret Shovlin; two *s* two *d. Educ:* St Ninian's High Sch., Kirkintilloch; Bourne Sch., Kuala Lumpur; St John's, Singapore. Joined FCO, 1968; Third Sec., Reykjavík, 1971–73; Vice Consul (Commercial), Stuttgart, 1973–76; FCO, 1976–78; Vice-Consul (Political/Inf.), Cape Town, 1979–83; Second, later First, Sec. (Instns), UK Representation to EC, Brussels 1983–88; FCO, 1988; Dep. High Comr, Freetown, 1988–91; FCO, 1991; on secondment to DTI, 1992–95; lang. student, 1995; Dep. Hd of Mission, Luanda, 1995–98; First Sec., and Hd, Commercial Dept, Copenhagen, 1998–2001; FCO, 2001–02; High Comr to Lesotho, 2002–05. *Recreations:* fishing, hashing, walking. *Address:* c/o Foreign and Commonwealth Office, King Charles Street, SW1A 2AH.

MARTIN, (Francis) Troy K.; *see* Kennedy Martin.

MARTIN, Frank; Change Manager, Tax Policy Project, HM Treasury, 2003–06; *b* 1 April 1946; *s* of Frank and Sylvia Martin; *m* 1975, Jean Richardson; one *s* one *d. Educ:* Alsop High Sch. for Boys, Liverpool; Sidney Sussex Coll., Cambridge (BA Hist.); LSE (MSc Internat. Relns). COI, 1969–73; DTI, 1973–76; HM Treasury, 1976–2006: Dep. Dir, Central Unit on Purchasing, 1987–89; on secondment as Principal Establishment and Finance Officer, CSO, 1989–93, and TTA, 1999–2001; Second Treasury Officer of Accounts, 1994–98; Dir, Corporate Services, Commonwealth Secretariat, 2001–03 (on secondment). *Recreations:* walking, reading, gardening, listening to music.

MARTIN, Geoffrey; *see* Martin, T. G.

MARTIN, Prof. Geoffrey Almeric Thorndike, PhD, LittD; FSA; Edwards Professor of Egyptology and Head of Department of Egyptology, University College London, 1988–93, now Emeritus; *b* 28 May 1934; *s* of late Albert Thorndike Martin and Lily Martin (*née* Jackson). *Educ:* Palmer's Sch., Grays Thurrock; University Coll. London (Sir William Meyer Prize, 1961; BA 1963); Corpus Christi Coll., Cambridge; Christ's Coll., Cambridge (MA 1966; PhD 1969; LittD 1994). Chartered Librarian (ALA, 1958–60); FSA 1975. Cataloguer, Brit. Nat. Bibliography, 1957–60; Lady Wallis Budge Res. Fellow in Egyptology, Christ's Coll., Cambridge, 1966–70; University College London: Lectr in Egyptology, 1970–78; Reader in Egyptian Archaeology, 1978–87; Prof. (*ad hominem*) of Egyptology, 1987–88. Wilbour Fellow, Brooklyn Museum, 1969; Rundle Fellow, Aust. Centre for Egyptology, Macquarie Univ., 1985, 1995, 2000; Jane and Morgan Whitney Art Hist. Fellow, Met. Mus. of Art, NY, 1999–2001. Vis. Prof., Collège de France, 1986. Glanville Lectr, Cambridge, 1990. Assisted at excavations of Egypt Exploration Society at: Buhen, Sudan, 1963; Saqqara, Egypt, 1964–68, 1970–71 (Site Dir, 1971–74; Field Dir, 1975–98); Field Director: Epigraphic Mission, Amarna, Egypt, 1969, 1980; Leiden Excavations, Saqqara, 1999–2000 (Hon. Dir, 2001–); Jt Field Dir, 1998–2001, Field Dir,

2002, Amarna Royal Tombs Project, Valley of the Kings, Thebes; Field Dir, Cambridge Expedn to Valley of the Kings, 2005–. Mem. Cttee, Egypt Exploration Soc., 1969–97; Rep. for GB, Council of Internat. Assoc. Egyptologists, 1976–82; Mem. Cttee, Bd of Management, Gerald Averay Wainwright Near Eastern Archaeol Fund, Oxford Univ., 1985–89; Christ's College, Cambridge: Hon. Keeper of Muniment Room, 1997–2004; Hon. Keeper of the Plate, 2000–; Hon. Keeper of the Archives, 2004–; Fellow Commoner, 1998–. Patron, Thurrock Local History Soc., 1996–. Corresp. Mem., German Archaeol Inst., 1982. Ed., Egypt in Miniature series (Oxford Expedition to Egypt), 2006–. *Publications:* Egyptian Administrative and Private-Name Seals, 1971; The Royal Tomb at El-Amarna, vol. 1, 1974, vol. 2, 1989; The Tomb of Hetepka, 1979; The Sacred Animal Necropolis at North Saqqara, 1981; (with V. Raisman) Canopic Equipment in the Petrie Collection, 1984; Scarabs, Cylinders and other Ancient Egyptian Seals, 1985; The Tomb Chapels of Paser and Raia, 1985; Corpus of Reliefs of the New Kingdom, vol. 1, 1987; (with A. El-Khouly) Excavations in the Royal Necropolis at El-Amarna, 1987; The Memphite Tomb of Horemheb, 1989; The Hidden Tombs of Memphis, 1991 (German edn 1994); Bibliography of the Amarna Period and its aftermath, 1991; The Tomb of Tia and Tia, 1997; The Tombs of Three Memphite Officials, 2001; Stelae from Egypt and Nubia in the Fitzwilliam Museum, Cambridge, 2005; contribs to learned and other jls and to Festschriften. *Recreations:* travel, English history, bibliography. *Address:* c/o Christ's College, Cambridge CB2 3BU.

MARTIN, Sir George (Henry), Kt 1996; CBE 1988; Chairman: AIR Group of companies, 1965–2006; Heart of London Radio, 1994–2005; Director, Chrysalis Group, 1978–2006; *b* 3 Jan. 1926; *s* of Henry and Bertha Beatrice Martin; *m* 1st, 1948, Sheena Rose Chisholm; one *s* one *d*; 2nd, 1966, Judy Lockhart Smith; one *s* one *d*. *Educ:* St Ignatius Coll., Stamford Hill, London; Bromley County Sch., Kent; Guildhall Sch. of Music and Drama (Hon. FGSM 1998). Sub-Lieut, FAA, RNVR, 1944–47. BBC, July 1950; EMI Records Ltd, Nov. 1950–1965; formed AIR Gp of cos (originally Associated Independent Recordings Ltd), 1965; built AIR Studios, 1969; built AIR Studios, Montserrat, 1979; completed new AIR Studios, Lyndhurst Hall, Hampstead, 1992; company merged with Chrysalis Gp, 1974; produced innumerable records, including all those featuring The Beatles; scored the music for fifteen films; nominated for Oscar for A Hard Day's Night, 1964; Grammy Awards, USA, 1964, 1967 (two), 1973, 1993, 1996; Ivor Novello Awards, 1963, 1979. Hon. RAM 1999; Hon. FGSM 2000. Hon. DMus: Berklee Coll. of Music, Boston, Mass, 1989; Leeds, 2007; Hon. MA Salford, 1992. Music Industry Trusts' Award, 1998; Lifetime Achievement Award, Ghent, 2002. *Publications:* All You Need Is Ears, 1979; Making Music, 1983; Summer of Love, 1994; Playback: an illustrated memoir, 2002. *Recreations:* boats, sculpture, tennis, snooker. *Address:* 55 Lancaster Gate, W2 3NA. *Clubs:* Oriental; Alderney Sailing.

MARTIN, Prof. (George) Steven, PhD; FRS 1998; Richard and Rhoda Goldman Distinguished Professor, Department of Molecular and Cell Biology, since 2002, and Research Virologist, Cancer Research Laboratory, since 1983, University of California at Berkeley (Professor of Molecular and Cell Biology, since 1989); *b* 19 Sept. 1943; *s* of Kurt and Hanna Martin; *m* 1969, Gail Zuckman; one *s*. *Educ:* Queens' Coll., Cambridge (MA 1966; PhD 1968). Postdoctoral Fellow, Virus Lab., Univ. of Calif, Berkeley, 1968–71; staff mem., ICRF, London, 1971–75; University of California, Berkeley: Asst Prof., 1975–79, Associate Prof., 1979–83, Prof. of Zoology, 1983–89, Dept of Zool.; Asst Res. Virologist, 1975–79, Associate Res. Virologist, 1979–83, Cancer Res. Lab. Jane Coffin Childs Meml Fund Fellow, 1968–70; Amer. Cancer Soc. Dernham Fellow, 1970–71; John Simon Guggenheim Meml Foundn Fellow, 1991–92. Scholar Award in Cancer Res., Amer. Cancer Soc., 1991–92. *Publications:* contribs to Nature, Science, Cell and other scientific jls. *Recreations:* hiking, bicycling, reading. *Address:* University of California at Berkeley, Department of Molecular and Cell Biology, 16 Barker Hall #3204, Berkeley, CA 94720-3204, USA. *T:* (510) 6421508.

MARTIN, Gerard James; QC 2000; a Recorder, since 2000; *b* 27 May 1955; *m* 1980, Deirdre Martin; three *s*. *Educ:* St Joseph's Coll., Blackpool; Trinity Hall, Cambridge (BA Law). Called to the Bar, Middle Temple, 1978; Asst Recorder, 1997–2000. *Recreations:* most sports, good food and wine. *Address:* Exchange Chambers, Pearl Assurance House, Derby Square, Liverpool L2 9XX.

MARTIN, Iain; Deputy Editor, Sunday Telegraph, since 2006; Group Executive Editor, Telegraph Media Group, since 2007; *b* 2 Oct. 1971; *m* Fiona; one *s*. *Educ:* Castlehead High Sch., Paisley; Univ. of Glasgow (MA 1993). Reporter, Sunday Times Scotland, 1993–97; Political Ed., then Asst Ed., Scotland on Sunday, 1997–2000; Asst Ed. and political commentator, The Scotsman, 2000–01; Dep. Ed., Scotland on Sunday, 2001; Ed., The Scotsman, 2001–04; Ed., Scotland on Sunday, 2004–06. *Address:* c/o Telegraph Media Group, 111 Buckingham Palace Road, SW1W 0DT; *e-mail:* iain.martin@telegraph.co.uk.

MARTIN, Ian; Special Representative of the United Nations Secretary-General, Nepal, since 2007; *b* 10 Aug. 1946; *s* of Collin and Betty Martin. *Educ:* Brentwood Sch.; Emmanuel Coll., Cambridge; Harvard Univ. Ford Foundn Representative's Staff, India, 1969–70, Pakistan, 1970–71, Bangladesh, 1972; Community Relations Officer, Redbridge Community Relations Council, 1973–75; Gen. Sec., Jt Council for the Welfare of Immigrants, 1977–82 (Dep. Gen. Sec., 1976–77; Exec. Cttee Mem., 1982–86); Gen. Sec., The Fabian Soc., 1982–85; Sec. Gen., Amnesty Internat., 1986–92 (Hd, Asia Res. Dept, 1985–86). Dir for Human Rights, UN/OAS Internat. Civilian Mission in Haiti, 1993, 1994–95; Chief, UN Human Rights Field Op., Rwanda, 1995–96; Special Advr, UN High Comr for Human Rights, 1998; Dep. High Rep. for Human Rights, Bosnia and Herzegovina, 1998–99; Special Rep. of UN Sec.-Gen., East Timor Popular Consultation, 1999; Dep. Special Rep. of UN Sec.-Gen., UN Mission in Ethiopia and Eritrea, 2000–01; Vice-Pres., Internat. Center for Transitional Justice, NY, 2002–05; Rep. of UN High Comr for Human Rights, Nepal, 2005–06. Sen. Associate, Carnegie Endowment for Internat. Peace, 1993, 1994; Visiting Fellow: Human Rights Centre, Univ. of Essex, 1996–97; Internat. Peace Acad., NY, 2000. Member: Exec. Cttee, NCCL, 1983–85; Redbridge and Waltham Forest AHA, 1977–82; Redbridge HA, 1982–83. Councillor, London Borough of Redbridge, 1978–82. *Publications:* Immigration Law and Practice (with Larry Grant), 1982; Self-Determination in East Timor, 2001; *contributed to:* Labour and Equality, Fabian Essays, 1980; Civil Liberties, Cobden Trust Essays, 1984; Hard Choices (ed J. Moore), 1998; Honoring Human Rights (ed A. Henkin), 2000; The United Nations and Regional Security (ed M. Pugh and W. P. S. Sidhu), 2003; Humanitarian Intervention and International Relations (ed J. M. Welsh), 2004; The UN Security Council (ed D. Malone), 2004. *Address:* 346 Ben Jonson House, Barbican, EC2Y 8NQ.

MARTIN, Ian Alexander; Chairman, SSL International PLC, 2001–05; Executive Chairman, Heath Lambert Holdings Ltd, 2003–05; *b* 28 Feb. 1935; *s* of Alexander Martin and Eva (*née* Gillman); *m* 1963, Phyllis Mitchell-Bey; one *s* two *d*. *Educ:* Univ. of St Andrews (MA). Mem., Inst. of Chartered Accountants, Scotland. Dir, Mine Safety Appliances Co. Ltd, 1969–72; Div. Dir, ITT Europe, 1977–79; Grand Metropolitan: Dir, 1985–94; Gp Man. Dir, 1991–93; Dep. Chm., 1993–94; Chairman: Intercontinental Hotels, 1986–88; Burger King Corp., 1989–93; Pillsbury Co., 1989–93; Internat. Distillers and Vintners, 1992–93; Chm. and Chief Exec., Glenisla Gp Ltd, 1994–97; Chm., 1995–2001, Chief Exec., 2001, Unigate, then Uniq; Chairman: Baxi Gp (formerly Newmond), 1997–2002; Heath Lambert Fenchurch Hldgs (formerly Erycinus), 1997–2005; William Hill, 1999–; 365 Corporation PLC, 1999–2002; Director: St Paul Companies Inc., 1989–96; Grocery Manufacturers of America, 1989–93; Granada Group, 1992–98; House of Fraser, 1994–2000; Nat. Commn on Children, USA, 1990–93. Chm., Europe Cttee, CBI, 1993–94; Mem. Adv. Cttee, Ian Jones & Partners, 1998–. Trustee, Duke of Edinburgh's Award Scheme, 1991–98; Dir, Friends of the Youth Award Inc., 1991–98. Freeman, City of London, 1982. CCMI (CBIM 1986). *Recreations:* angling, golf, music.

MARTIN, James, FCCA; Chairman, A J Bell Ltd, since 2007; Christie Hospital NHS Foundation Trust, since 2007; *b* 9 Dec. 1942; *s* of Warwick Hammond Martin and Elsie Eileen Martin; *m* 1964, Jean Iveson (*d* 2006); two *s*. FCCA 1972. Chief Exec., 1982–2002, Dep. Chm., 2002–05, N Brown Group plc. Non-executive Director: Redrow plc, 1997–2007; Styles & Wood Gp, 2006–; Chm., Alexon plc, 2005–08. Mem., NW Business Leadership Team, 2000–05; NW Inst. of Direct Marketing, 2002–05. *Recreations:* sport, fishing, shooting, golf. *Address:* The Coach House, Great Budworth, Cheshire CW9 6HB. *T:* (01606) 891436, *Fax:* (01606) 892496; *e-mail:* jimmartin@martinhouse.fsnet.co.uk.

MARTIN, James Brown; Police Complaints Commissioner for Scotland, since 2007; *b* 6 Dec. 1953; *s* of James and Annie Martin; *m* 1975, Anne McNaughton; one *s* one *d*. *Educ:* Larbert Village and High Schs; Heriot-Watt Univ. (BAEcon); Moray House College of Educn. Teacher, Falkirk High Sch., 1975–79; Field Officer 1979–83, Asst Sec. 1983–88, Gen. Sec., 1988–95, EIS. Member: Gen. Council, Scottish TUC, 1987; Exec., ETUCE, 1988; Exec., Education International, 1993. Mem., Forth Valley Enterprise Bd, 1989. *Recreations:* Hibernian FC, watching football. *Address:* 1 Orchard Grove, Polmont, Stirlingshire FK2 0XE.

MARTIN, Janet, (Mrs K. P. Martin); Relief Warden (Assisted Independence), Test Valley Housing, 1988–91; *b* Dorchester, Dorset, 8 Sept. 1927; *d* of James Wilkinson and Florence Steer; *m* 1951, Peter Martin, sometime of Southampton HA and Senior Consultant AT&T (ISTEL) Ltd (*d* 2004); one *s* one *d*. *Educ:* Dorchester Co. Sch. for Girls, Dorset; Weymouth Tech. Coll.; occupational training courses. PA to Group Sec., Herrison HMC, 1949; admin./clerical work, NHS and other, 1956; social research fieldwork, mainly NHS (Wessex mental health care evaluation team), and Social Services (Hants CC and Nat. Inst. for Social Work), 1967–76; residential social worker (children with special needs), Southampton, 1976–78; Social Services Officer, Test Valley, 1978–86; Senior Residential Care Officer (Elderly), Test Valley Social Services, 1986–87. Interviewer, MRC 'National' Survey, 1970–85; Psychosexual Counsellor, Aldermoor Clinic, 1981–84. Mem., Press Council, 1973–78. *Recreations:* buildings, books. *Address:* The Old Stables, Linden Avenue, Dorchester, Dorset DT1 1EJ. *T:* (01305) 269839.

MARTIN, Dame Joan Margaret; *see* Higgins, Dame J. M.

MARTIN, John; *see* Martin, L. J.

MARTIN, John Alfred Holmes; His Honour Judge Martin; QC (NI) 1989; a County Court Judge, Northern Ireland, since 1990; Chief Social Security Commissioner, and Chief Child Support Commissioner, Northern Ireland, since 1997; Chief Pensions Appeal Commissioner, Northern Ireland, since 2005; *b* 31 May 1946; *s* of Very Rev. Dr Alfred Martin and Doris Muriel Martin; *m* 1983, Barbara Elizabeth Margaret Kyle; one *s* one *d*. *Educ:* Finaghy Primary Sch.; Royal Belfast Academical Instn; Queen's Univ., Belfast (LLB 1969; Dip. Law 1970). Called to the Bar, NI Inn of Court, 1970, Gray's Inn, 1974, King's Inns, 1975; a Dep. Co. Court Judge, 1983–88; Crown Court Judge, 1990–97; Recorder of Londonderry, 1993–94; Additional Judge for Co. Court Belfast, 1994–97. Pt-time Chm., 1981–88, Chm., 1988–89, Vice Pres., 1990, Industrial Tribunals, NI; Vice Pres., Fair Employment Tribunal, NI, 1990; Chm. and Pres., Pensions Appeal Tribunals, NI, 2001–; Dep. Social Security Comr, GB, 2005–. Member: NI Bar Council, 1983; Council of HM County Court Judges, 1990– (Hon. Sec., 1995–97); Council of HM Social Security and Child Support Comrs of the UK, 2004–. Pres., Irish Legal Hist. Soc., 2004–06. Gov., Presbyterian Orphan Soc., 1991–. Vice Pres., Irish Amateur Rowing Assoc., 1978–79; Mem. Jury and Umpire, rowing events, Olympic Games, 1980 and Commonwealth Games, 1986. *Recreations:* rowing, hill-walking, gardening, reading. *Address:* Office of the Social Security Commissioners, Headline Building, 10–14 Victoria Street, Belfast BT1 3GG. *T:* (028) 9072 8731, *Fax:* (028) 9031 3510. *Clubs:* Ulster Reform; Leander.

MARTIN, Vice-Adm. Sir John (Edward Ludgate), KCB 1972 (CB 1968); DSC 1943; FNI; retired; Lieutenant-Governor and Commander-in-Chief of Guernsey, 1974–80; *b* 10 May 1918; *s* of late Surgeon Rear-Admiral W. L. Martin, OBE, FRCS and Elsie Mary Martin (*née* Catford); *m* 1942, Rosemary Ann Deck; two *s* two *d*. *Educ:* RNC, Dartmouth. Sub Lt and Lt, HMS Pelican, 1938–41; 1st Lt, HMS Antelope, 1942; navigation course, 1942; Navigation Officer, 13th Minesweeping Flotilla, Mediterranean, 1943–44, including invasions N Africa, Sicily, Pantelleria, Salerno; RNAS Yeovilton, 1944; Navigation Officer: HMS Manxman and HMS Bermuda, 1944–46; HMS Nelson, 1947; HMS Victorious, 1948; Staff Coll., 1949; Navigation Officer, HMS Devonshire, 1950–51; Dirg Staff, Staff Coll., 1952–54; Jt Services Planning Staff, Far East, 1954–55; Exec. Off., HMS Superb, 1956–57; Jt Services Staff Coll., 1958; Dep. Dir Manpower Planning and Complementing Div., Admty, 1959–61; Sen. Naval Off., W Indies, 1961–62; Comdr Brit. Forces Caribbean Area, 1962–63; Capt. Britannia Royal Naval Coll., Dartmouth, 1963–66; Flag Officer, Middle East, 1966–67; Comdr, British Forces Gulf, 1967–68 (despatches); Dir-Gen., Naval Personal Services and Training, 1968–70; Dep. Supreme Allied Comdr, Atlantic, 1970–72. Comdr 1951; Captain 1957; Rear-Adm. 1966; Vice-Adm. 1970. Pres., Nautical Inst., 1975–78. *Recreations:* fishing, shooting, beagling (Jt Master Britannia Beagles, 1963–66), sailing. *Clubs:* Army and Navy; Royal Naval Sailing Association; Royal Yacht Squadron.

MARTIN, Prof. John Francis, MD; FRCP; British Heart Foundation Professor of Cardiovascular Medicine, since 1996, and Leader, Institute of Cardiovascular Science, since 2007, University College London; Hon. Consultant Physician, University College Hospitals NHS Trust, since 1996; *b* 8 July 1943; *s* of Francis Martin and Marie-Antoinette Martin (née Bessler); *m* 1979, Íde Leddy (marr. diss. 1987); *m* 1991, Elisabeth Gaillochet (marr. diss. 1995). *Educ:* English Coll., Valladolid, Spain; Univ. of Sheffield (MB ChB 1973; MD 1981). FRCP 1989. Lectr in Medicine, Sheffield Univ., 1975–79; Sen. Lectr, Univ. of Melbourne, 1979–81; Hon. Consultant Physician, St Vincent's Hosp., Melbourne, 1979–81; Sen. Lectr, Sheffield Univ., 1981–86; Hon. Consultant Physician, Hallamshire Hosp., 1981–86; Hd, Cardiovascular Res., Wellcome Foundn Res. Labs, 1986–96; Sen. Lectr, 1986–90, BHF Prof. of Cardiovascular Sci., 1990–96, KCL; Hon. Consultant Physician, KCH, 1986–96. Queen Victoria Eugenia Chair, Complutense Univ., Madrid, 2004–05. CSO and Dir, Ark Therapeutics (formerly Eurogene), 2000– (Founder, 1997). Mem., Animal Procedures Cttee, Home Office, 1998–2006. Pres., Eur.

Soc. for Clinical Investigation, 1992–95; Vice Pres., Eur. Soc. Cardiology, 2000–02 (FESC 1995; Mem. Bd, 1998–2006; Chm., European Union Relations Cttee (formerly European Affairs Cttee), 2001–06; Gold Medal, 2008). Captain, RAMC(V), 1977–83, Major, 1983–86; now RARO. FMedSci 2000. *Publications:* Platelet Heterogeneity, Biology and Pathology, 1990; The Origin of Loneliness: poems and short stories, 2004; contrib. articles to learned jls on cardiovascular biol. and medicine, particularly arteriosclerosis, thrombosis and acute coronary syndromes and gene therapy. *Recreations:* poetry, Mediaeval philosophy. *Address:* British Heart Foundation Laboratories, Department of Medicine, University College London, 5 University Street, WC1E 6JJ. *T:* (020) 7209 6532; 21 West Square, SE11 4SN. *T:* (020) 7735 2212. *Club:* Athenæum.

MARTIN, John Howard Sherwell, FRICS; Senior Partner, Knight Frank, 1996–2004; *b* 7 Aug. 1945; *s* of John Robert Henry Martin and Lilian Vera Sherwell; *m* 1971, Linda Susan Johnson; one *s* two *d*. *Educ:* Emanuel Sch. FRICS 1971. Trainee Surveyor, GLC, 1965–71; joined Knight Frank & Rutley, 1971: Partner, 1978–96. Non-exec. Dir, Baltic Exchange, 1993–98. Trustee, St Clement Danes Holborn Estate Charity, 1987–2000. *Recreations:* travel, antiques, gardening. *Address:* Rowlands Court, Newchapel Road, Lingfield, Surrey RH7 6BJ. *Club:* Oriental.

MARTIN, John Neville, FREng, FICE, FIStructE; Chairman, Ove Arup Partnership, 1992–95; *b* 9 April 1932; *s* of Reginald Martin and Dorothy Sylvia Martin (*née* Bray); *m* 1964, Julia Mary Galpin; three *s* one *d*. *Educ:* Royal Grammar Sch., Guildford. FICE 1957; FIStructE 1957; FREng (FEng 1988). Articled pupil with Engr and Surveyor, Woking UDC, 1949–52; Nat. Service, RE, 1952–54; Asst Engr, Sir William Halcrow & Partners, Consulting Engrs, 1954–57; with Ove Arup Partnership, Consulting Engrs, 1957–95. Chm., Ove Arup Foundn, 1996–2000. Chm., Haslemere Dist Scout Council, 1995–2002. *Publications:* various papers for engrg jls (IStructE). *Recreations:* Scouting, mountain-walking, music, country dancing.

MARTIN, John Paul; Director for Employment, Labour and Social Affairs, Organisation for Economic Co-operation and Development, since 2002; *b* 6 April 1948; *s* of Denis Martin and Veronica Martin; *m* 1972, Jacqueline Davida Gunn; two *s* one *d*. *Educ:* University Coll., Dublin (MA Econ); MPhil Oxford. Res. Asst, Econ. and Social Res. Inst., Dublin, 1970–72; Lectr in Econs, Merton Coll., Oxford, 1974–77; Res. Fellow, Nuffield Coll., Oxford, 1975–77; Lectr in Econs, Univ. of Buckingham, 1975–77; Organisation for Economic Co-operation and Development, Paris: Administrator, 1977–80; Principal Administrator, 1980–83; Hd of Div. and Editor of OECD Employment Outlook, 1983–87; Hd of Div., Econs Dept, 1987–93, and Editor, OECD Economic Outlook, 1992–93; Dep. Dir for Employment, Labour and Social Affairs, 1993–2000; Dir for Educn, Employment, Labour and Social Affairs, 2000–02. Pt-time Prof., Institut d'Etudes Politiques de Paris, 1993–; Res. Fellow, Inst. for the Study of Labour, Univ. of Bonn, 2005–. Mem., French Prime Minister's Conseil de l'orientation pour l'emploi, 2005–; Mem., Expert Gp on Future Skills Needs, Irish Govt, 2007–. Mem., Adv. Bd, World Demographic Assoc., 2006–. *Publications:* Trade and Payments Adjustment Under Flexible Exchange Rates, 1977; Youth Unemployment, 1980; The Nature of Youth Unemployment, 1984; many articles in jls such as Economic Jl, Economica, Oxford Economic Papers, Rev. of Econs and Stats, Jl of Internat. Economics, OECD Observer, and OECD Economic Studies. *Recreations:* tennis, reading, wine-tasting. *Address:* Organisation for Economic Co-operation and Development, 2 rue André Pascal, 75775 Paris Cedex 16, France. *T:* (1) 45249358, *Fax:* (1) 45249198; *e-mail:* john.martin@oecd.org.

MARTIN, John Sharp Buchanan, FIHT; transport consultant, since 2004; appeals adjudicator for Department of Transport, since 2006; Head of Transport (formerly Transport and Planning) Group, Scottish Executive (formerly Scottish Office) Development Department, 1998–2004; *b* 7 July 1946; *s* of David Buchanan Martin and Agnes Miller Martin (*née* Craig); *m* 1971, Catriona Susan Stewart Meldrum; one *s* one *d*. *Educ:* Bell-Baxter High Sch., Cupar, Fife; Univ. of St Andrews (BSc). FIHT 2003. Asst Principal, Scottish Educn Dept, 1968–71; Private Sec. to Parly Under-Sec. of State for Scotland, 1971–73; Scottish Office: Principal, 1973–80, seconded to Rayner Scrutinies, 1979–80; Asst Sec., 1980–92; Under-Sec., Sch. Educn and Sport, Educn, subseq. Educn and Industry Dept, 1992–98. Mem., SE Scotland Transport Partnership, 2006–. Mem. Adv. Bd, Transport Res. Inst., Napier Univ., 2005–. *Recreations:* tennis, golf, cricket, philately. *Clubs:* Colinton Lawn Tennis, Merchants of Edinburgh Golf, Woodcutters Cricket (Edinburgh).

MARTIN, John Sinclair, CBE 1977; farmer; Chairman, Anglian Flood Defence Committee, Environment Agency (formerly National Rivers Authority), 1989–97; *b* 18 Sept. 1931; *s* of Joseph and Claire Martin, Littleport, Ely; *m* 1960, Katharine Elisabeth Barclay, MB, BS; three *s* one *d*. *Educ:* The Leys Sch., Cambridge; St John's Coll., Cambridge (MA, Dip. in Agriculture). Chairman: Littleport and Downham IDB, 1971–88; JCO Arable Crops and Forage Bd, 1973–76; Eastern Regional Panel, MAFF, 1981–86 (Mem., 1972–78); Great Ouse Local Land Drainage Cttee, AWA, 1983–88; Anglian Drainage Cttee, 1988–89; Member: Eastern Counties Farmers' Management Cttee, 1960–70; ARC, 1968–78; Great Ouse River Authority, 1970–74; Lawes Agricl Trust Cttee, 1982–84; MAFF Priorities Bd, 1984–88; Anglian Water Authority, 1988–89; Vice-Pres., Assoc. of Drainage Authorities, 1986–. Chairman: Ely Br., NFU, 1963; Cambs NFU, 1979. High Sheriff, Cambs, 1985–86. *Address:* Denny Abbey, Waterbeach, Cambridge CB25 9PQ. *T:* (01223) 860282. *Club:* Farmers'.

MARTIN, John Vandeleur; QC 1991; a Judge of the Courts of Appeal of Jersey and Guernsey, since 2007; *b* 17 Jan. 1948; *s* of Col Graham Vandeleur Martin, MC and Margaret Helen (*née* Sherwood); *m* 1974, Stephanie Johnstone Smith; two *s* one *d*. *Educ:* Malvern Coll.; Pembroke Coll., Cambridge (MA). Called to the Bar, Lincoln's Inn, 1972, Bencher, 1999. Dep. High Court Judge, Chancery Div., 1993. Liveryman, Drapers' Co., 1973. *Recreations:* almost any opera, swimming in warm water. *Address:* Wilberforce Chambers, 8 New Square, Lincoln's Inn, WC2A 3QP. *T:* (020) 7306 0102.

MARTIN, John William Prior; HM Diplomatic Service, retired; Counsellor, Foreign and Commonwealth Office, 1985–89; *b* 23 July 1934; *er s* of late Stanley Gordon Martin and Frances Heather (*née* Moore); *m* 1960, Jean Fleming; three *s* one *d*. *Educ:* CIM Sch., Chefoo and Kuling; Bristol Grammar Sch.; St John's Coll., Oxford (MA). National Service, 1953–55 (2nd Lieut Royal Signals). Joined FO, 1959; Beirut, 1960; Saigon, 1963; Language Student, Hong Kong, 1965–67; Dar es Salaam, 1968; FCO, 1971; Singapore, 1974; FCO, 1978; Kuala Lumpur, 1982. *Recreations:* conservation, travel, ornithology.

MARTIN, Jonathan Arthur, OBE 1995; sports broadcasting consultant; Controller, Television Sport, BBC Broadcast, 1996–98; *b* 18 June 1942; *s* of Arthur Martin and Mabel Gladys Martin (*née* Bishop); *m* 1967, Joy Elizabeth Fulker; two *s*. *Educ:* Gravesend Grammar School; St Edmund Hall, Oxford (BA 1964, English; MA 1992). Joined BBC as general trainee, 1964; producer, Sportsnight, 1969; producer, Match of the Day, 1970; editor, Sportsnight and Match of the Day, 1974; exec. producer, BBC TV Wimbledon tennis coverage, 1979–81; producer, Ski Sunday and Grand Prix, 1978–80; managing

editor, Sport, 1980; Head of Sport, 1981–87, Head of Sport and Events, 1987–96, BBC TV. Vice-Pres., EBU Sports Gp, 1984–98. *Recreations:* ski-ing, golf, watching sport, especially Watford FC. *Address:* Arkle, Valentine Way, Chalfont St Giles, Bucks HP8 4JB. *Club:* Harewood Downs Golf.

MARTIN, Kevin Joseph; President, Law Society, 2005–06 (Vice-President, 2004–05); *b* 15 June 1947; *s* of James Arthur Martin and Ivy Lilian Martin; *m* 1971, Maureen McCormack; two *s*. *Educ:* Sacred Heart Sch., Coventry; Cotton Coll., N Staffs; Coll. of Law, Guildford. Admitted solicitor, 1970. Articled clerk, Tafft & James, Coventry, 1964–70; Solicitor/Partner, Mackintosh & Co., Birmingham, 1970–79; Partner, K. J. Martin & Co., Balsall Common, Solihull, 1979–2001; Consultant, Lodders, Stratford-upon-Avon, 2001–. Council Mem. for Coventry and Warwickshire, Law Soc., 1996–. *Recreations:* golf, ski-ing, classical music, cricket, Rugby. *Address:* 10 Elm Court, Arden Street, Stratford-upon-Avon, Warks CV37 6PA; *e-mail:* kevinj_martin@btinternet.com. *Clubs:* Royal Automobile; Coventry Drapers (Coventry); Ladbrook Park Golf; Coventry and N Warwickshire Cricket.

MARTIN, Kit; Projects Consultant, The Prince's Regeneration Trust; *b* 6 May 1947; *s* of Sir (John) Leslie Martin, RA, and Sadie Speight, architect; *m* 1st, 1970, Julia Margaret Mitchell (marr. diss. 1978); 2nd, 1980, Sally Martha, *d* of late Sqdn Ldr Edwin Brookes; one *d*. *Educ:* Eton; Jesus Coll., Cambridge (BA 1969; DipArch 1972; MA 1973). Started Martin & Weighton, architectural practice, 1969–76; partner involved in numerous projects to restore and save listed bldgs in UK, France and Italy; Dir, Kit Martin (Historic Houses Rescue) Ltd, 1974–; initiated rescue and conversion of listed bldgs of outstanding architectural interest, including: Dingley Hall, Northants, 1976–79; Gunton Park, Norfolk, 1980–84; Cullen House, Banffshire, 1982–85; Tyninghame House, E Lothian, 1988–92; Burley on the Hill, Rutland, 1993–97; Formakin, Renfrewshire, 1994–99; Maristow, Devon, 1995–99 (several schemes have won local, nat. or European awards); Dir, Historic Bldgs Rescue Ltd, 1993–2002; initiated rescue and conversion of several listed bldgs, including Royal Naval Hosp., Norfolk to housing, and a chapel. Dir, The Prince of Wales's Phoenix Trust (UK Historic Building Preservation Trust), 1997–2001. Mem., Historic Bldgs Council for Scotland, 1987–99. Trustee, Save Europe Heritage, 1994–. Hon. FRIBA 2000. *Publications:* The Country House: to be or not to be, 1982; Save Jamaica's Heritage (UNESCO Award), 1990. *Recreations:* ski-ing, squash, private flying with wife, landscape gardening, including restoration of Gunton Park according to historic principles. *Address:* (office) Park Farm, Gunton Park, Hanworth, Norfolk NR11 7HL.

MARTIN, Sir Laurence (Woodward), Kt 1994; DL; Senior Adviser, Center for Strategic and International Studies, Washington, since 2000 (Arleigh Burke Professor of Strategy, 1998–2000); *b* 30 July 1928; *s* of Leonard and Florence Mary Martin; *m* 1951, Betty Parnall (*d* 2005); one *s* one *d*. *Educ:* St Austell Grammar Sch.; Christ's Coll., Cambridge (MA); Yale Univ. (MA, PhD). Flying Officer, RAF, 1948–50; Instr, Yale Univ., 1955–56; Asst Prof., MIT, 1956–61; Rockefeller Fellow for Advanced Study, 1958–59; Associate Prof., Sch. of Advanced Internat. Studies, The Johns Hopkins Univ., 1961–64; Wilson Prof. of Internat. Politics, Univ. of Wales, 1964–68; Prof. of War Studies, King's Coll., Univ. of London, 1968–77, Fellow 1983–; Vice-Chancellor, Univ. of Newcastle upon Tyne, 1978–90, Emeritus Prof., 1991; Dir, RIIA, 1991–96. Research Associate, Washington Center of Foreign Policy Research, 1964–76, 1979–. Lees-Knowles Lectr, Cambridge, 1981; BBC Reith Lectr, 1981. Member: SSRC, 1969–76 (Chm. Res. Grants Bd); Internat. Res. Council, Center for Internat. and Strategic Studies (formerly Georgetown Center of Strategic Studies), 1969–77, 1979– (Co-Chm., 1998–); Council, IISS, 1975–83. Consultant, Sandia Labs. DL Tyne and Wear, 1986. Hon. DCL Newcastle, 1991. *Publications:* The Anglo-American Tradition in Foreign Affairs (with Arnold Wolfers), 1956; Peace without Victory, 1958; Neutralism and Non-Alignment, 1962; The Sea in Modern Strategy, 1967; (jtly) America in World Affairs, 1970; Arms and Strategy, 1973; (jtly) Retreat from Empire?, 1973; (jtly) Strategic Thought in the Nuclear Age, 1979; The Two-Edged Sword, 1982; Before the Day After, 1985; The Changing Face of Nuclear Warfare, 1987; (jtly) British Foreign Policy, 1997. *Address:* 35 Witley Court, Coram Street, WC1N 1HD.

MARTIN, (Leonard) John, CBE 1995; Consulting Actuary, Watson Wyatt (formerly R. Watson & Sons), since 1954; *b* 20 April 1929; *s* of Leonard A. Martin and Anne Elisabeth Martin (*née* Scudamore); *m* 1st, 1956, Elisabeth Veronica Hall Jones (*d* 2006); one *s* one *d*; 2nd, 2007, Jill Corradi. *Educ:* Ardingly Coll.; Open Univ. (BSc Hons 2005). FIA, FSS, FPMI. Joined R. Watson & Sons, 1952, Partner 1954, Sen. Partner 1984–94. Dir, NPI Insurance Co., 1993–99. Pres., Inst. of Actuaries, 1992–94; Chm., Consultative Group of Actuaries in Europe, 1988–91; Rapporteur, Cttee of Actuaries, UN, 1988–2006. FRSA. Liveryman, GAPAN. *Recreations:* flying, sailing, singing. *Address:* Pitt House, Ducie Avenue, Bembridge, Isle of Wight PO35 5NF. *Club:* Naval.

MARTIN, Leslie Vaughan; Directing Actuary (Superannuation and Research), Government Actuary's Department, 1974–79; *b* 20 March 1919; *s* of late Hubert Charles Martin and late Rose Martin (*née* Skelton); *m* 1949, Winifred Dorothy Hopkins; one *s* one *d*. *Educ:* Price's Sch., Fareham. FIA 1947. Served with RAMC and REME, 1940–46. Deptl Clerical Officer, Customs and Excise, 1936–38; joined Govt Actuary's Dept, 1938; Asst Actuary, 1949; Actuary, 1954; Principal Actuary, 1962. Mem. Council, Inst. of Actuaries, 1971–76; Vice-Chm., CS Medical Aid Assoc., 1976–79. Churchwarden, St Barnabas, Dulwich, 1965–70, 1977–79, Vice-Chm. of PCC, 1970–79; Treasurer: Morchard Bishop Parochial Church Council, 1980–83; Cadbury Deanery Synod, 1981–88; Chulmleigh Deanery Synod, 1989–97; Lapford PCC, 1991–93. *Recreations:* crosswords, mathematical puzzles. *Address:* Pickwick House, Down St Mary, Crediton, Devon EX17 6EQ. *T:* (01363) 84581.

MARTIN, Lewis Vine; Executive Director, 1995–2002, Chief Executive, Priory of England and Islands, 1999–2002, St John Ambulance; *b* 14 Nov. 1939; *s* of Lewis and Else Martin; *m* 1964, Patricia Mary Thorne; two *d*. *Educ:* Clarks Coll., Cardiff. Exec. posts in marketing, investment, admin, major projects and gen. management, UK and Europe, Mobil Oil Co. Ltd, 1955–95. *Recreations:* keep fit, swimming, gardening, Rugby (spectator now).

MARTIN, Louise Livingstone, CBE 2003; nutritionist; Chairman, Commonwealth Games Council for Scotland, 1999–2008; Hon. Secretary, Commonwealth Games Federation, since 1999; *b* 2 Sept. 1946; *d* of James Stewart Campbell and Minnie Campbell; *m* 1973, Ian Alexander Martin; one *s* one *d*. *Educ:* Dunfermline High Sch.; Edinburgh Coll. of Domestic Science (Dip. Dom. Sci. Food and Nutrition). Lectr in Nutrition, Edinburgh Coll. of Domestic Science, subseq. Queen Margaret Coll., 1969–72; Head of Department: Glenrothes High Sch., 1972–73; Millburn Acad., Inverness, 1973–75. Tutor, Nat. Coaching Foundn, 1990–; Vis. Lectr in Sports Nutrition, Heriot-Watt Univ. and Univ. of Edinburgh, 1994–2001. Board Member: SportScotland, 1997–2005; UK Sport, 2002–; Active Stirling, 2006–. Hon. Pres., Scottish Gymnastics, 1999 (Pres., 1993–99). Hon. DArts Abertay, 2007. *Recreations:* hill-walking, swimming, reading, travel, classical music. *Address:* Commonwealth Games Federation, 138 Piccadilly, W1J 7NK; *e-mail:* email@louise-martin.com.

MARTIN, Michael C.; *see* Craig-Martin.

MARTIN, Rt Hon. Michael John; PC 2000; MP Glasgow North East; Speaker of the House of Commons, since 2000; *b* 3 July 1945; *s* of Michael and Mary Martin; *m* 1966, Mary McLay; one *s* one *d.* *Educ:* St Patrick's Boys' Sch., Glasgow. Sheet metal worker; AUEW Shop Steward, Rolls Royce, Hillington, 1970–74; Trade Union Organiser, 1976–79; Mem., and sponsored by, AEEU. MP Glasgow, Springburn, 1979–2005, Glasgow NE, 2005– (Lab 1979–2000, when elected Speaker). PPS to Rt Hon. Denis Healey, MP, 1981–83; Member: Select Cttee for Trade and Industry, 1983–86; Speaker's Panel of Chairmen, 1987–2000; First Dep. Chm. of Ways and Means, and a Dep. Speaker, H of C, 1997–2000. Chm., Scottish Grand Cttee, 1987–97. Councillor: for Fairfield Ward, Glasgow Corp., 1973–74; for Balornock Ward, Glasgow DC, 1974–79. Mem., Coll. of Piping, 1989–. DUniv Glasgow. *Recreations:* hill walking, local history, piping. *Address:* Speaker's House, Westminster, SW1A 0AA.
See also P. Martin.

MARTIN, Paul; Member (Lab) Glasgow Springburn, Scottish Parliament, since 1999; *b* 17 March 1967; *s* of Rt Hon. Michael John Martin, *qv*; *m* 1997, Fiona Allen. *Educ:* All Saints Secondary Sch.; Barmulloch Coll., Glasgow. Mem. (Lab) City of Glasgow Council, 1995–99. *Address:* Scottish Parliament, Edinburgh EH99 1SP.

MARTIN, Paul, PhD; Fellow, 1985–86 and 2001–04, Senior Member, since 2004, Wolfson College, Cambridge; writer, since 2001; *b* 11 May 1958; *s* of Joseph and Pamela Martin; *m*; two *s* one *d.* *Educ:* Christ's Coll., Cambridge (MA, PhD). Harkness Fellow and Postdoctoral Schol., Stanford Univ., 1982–83; Asst Lectr, Cambridge Univ., 1984–86; MoD, 1986–2000; Dir of Communication, Cabinet Office, 2000–01. *Publications:* (with Patrick Bateson) Measuring Behaviour, 1986, 3rd edn 2007; The Sickening Mind, 1997; (with Patrick Bateson) Design for a Life, 1999; Counting Sheep, 2002; (with Kristina Murrin) What Worries Parents, 2004; Making Happy People, 2005; Sex, Drugs and Chocolate, 2008.

MARTIN, Paul; *see* Martin, D. P.

MARTIN, Rt Hon. Paul (Edgar Philippe); PC (Canada) 1993; MP (L) for Lasalle-Emard, Quebec, since 1988; Prime Minister of Canada, 2003–06; *b* Windsor, Ont, 28 Aug. 1938; *s* of Paul Joseph James Martin and Eleanor Alice Martin; *m* 1965, Sheila Ann Cowan; three *s.* *Educ:* Univ. of Ottawa; Univ. of Toronto (BA Philos. and Hist. 1962); Univ. of Toronto Law Sch. (LLB 1965). Merchant seaman on salvage ops in Arctic; worked in Legal Dept, ECSC, Luxembourg; with Osler, Hoskin & Harcourt, Toronto; called to the Bar, Ontario, 1966; with Power Corp. of Canada; Chm. and Chief Exec. Officer, Canada Steamship Lines; Corporate Dir for several major cos. Critic for: Treasury Bd and Urban Develt, until 1991; Envmt and Associate Finance Critic, 1991–93; Minister responsible for Federal Office of Regl Develt, 1993–97; Finance Minister, Canada, 1993–2002. First Chm., G-20, 1999–2002. Liberal Party of Canada: Co-Chm., Nat. Platform Cttee, 1993; Leader, 2003–06. *Address:* House of Commons, Parliament Buildings, Ottawa, ON K1A 0A6, Canada.

MARTIN, Paul James, (Paul Merton); comedian, actor, writer; *b* 9 July 1957; *s* of Albert and Mary Martin; *m* 1991, Caroline Quentin, *qv* (marr. diss. 1999); *m* 2000, Sarah Parkinson (*d* 2003). *Educ:* Wimbledon Coll. Civil Servant, Dept of Employment. *Stage:* stand-up comic: London Comedy Store, 1981–; London cabaret circuit, 1982–88; toured England, Scotland and Ireland, 1993; London Palladium, 1994; Live Bed Show, Garrick, 1994; presenter, Paul Merton's Silent Clowns, UK tour, 2007; *television* includes: series: Comedy Wavelength, 1987; Whose Line is it Anyway?, 1989–93; Have I Got News For You, 1990–; Paul Merton—the series, 1991, 1993; Paul Merton's Life of Comedy, 1995; Paul Merton's Palladium Story (2 programmes), 1995; Paul Merton in Galton & Simpson, 1996, 1997; The Paul Merton Show, 1996; Room 101, 1999–2007; Paul Merton in China, 2007; Thank God You're Here, 2008; *films:* An Evening with Gary Lineker, 1994; The Suicidal Dog, 2000 (writer and dir); *radio* series include: Just a Minute, 1988–; I'm Sorry I Haven't a Clue, 1993–; The Masterson Inheritance, 1993–96; Two Priests and a Nun go into a Pub, 2000; Late, 2001. BAFTA Award, Best Entertainer, 2003. *Publications:* (with Julian Clary) My Life with Fanny the Wonderdog, 1988; Paul Merton's History of the 20th Century, 1993; Have I Got News For You, 1994; My Struggle, 1995; Silent Comedy, 2007. *Recreations:* tropical fish, walking, film comedy. *Address:* c/o International Artistes Ltd, 4th Floor, Holborn Hall, 193–197 High Holborn, WC1V 7BD. *T:* (020) 7025 0600, *Fax:* (020) 7404 9865.

MARTIN, Peter; *see* Martin, R. P.

MARTIN, Peter Anthony; Financial Adviser to Association of Police Authorities, since 2005; *b* 8 Dec. 1946; *s* of Frank and Renie Martin; *m* 1970, Jennifer Margaret (*née* Shaw); one *s* four *d.* *Educ:* Nottingham High Sch.; St John's Coll., Oxford (BA Hons); Univ. of Kent at Canterbury (MA Management). CIPFA 1973. Accountant, Derbyshire CC, 1969–76; Asst County Treasurer, W Sussex CC, 1976–81; Kent County Council: Dep. County Treas., 1981–86; County Treas., later Finance Dir, 1986–97; Dir, Peter Martin Consultancy Ltd, 1997–2001. Treasurer: Kent Police Authy, 1995–2000; Metropolitan Police Authy, 2000–05. Pres., Police Authy Treasurers Soc., 2004–05. Local Authy Assocs' Revenue Support Grant Principal Negotiator, 1991–94. Pres., Soc. of Co. Treasurers, 1996–97. *Recreations:* cricket, reading, family. *Address:* Woodside, Hadlow Park, Hadlow, Tonbridge, Kent TN11 0HZ.

MARTIN, Peter William, CBE 2006; Managing Director, Journeyman Resolutions, since 2007; *b* 15 May 1947; *s* of Ronald William Martin and Rosemary Joan Damaris Martin; *m* 1981, Rhonda Mary Craker; two *s* one *d.* *Educ:* King's College Sch., Wimbledon; Goldsmiths' Coll., London. Winston Churchill Travelling Fellow, 1986. Regl Dir, Phoenix House, 1978–90; Chief Exec., Addaction, 1990–2005. Non-exec. Dir, Kent and Medway NHS and Social Care Trust, 2007–. Member: Parole Bd of England and Wales, 1994–2000; Adv. Council for the Misuse of Drugs, 2000–. *Recreations:* singing badly, field pursuits, tractor driving, being a good neighbour, reading and poetry recitations. *Address:* Forge Cottage, Cudham TN14 7QB; *e-mail:* peter.martin@iconism.net. *Club:* Royal Automobile.

MARTIN, Prof. Raymond Leslie, AO 1987; MSc, PhD, ScD, DSc; FRACI, FRSC, FTSE, FAA, FAIM; Professor of Chemistry, Monash University, Melbourne, 1987–92, now Emeritus (Vice-Chancellor, 1977–87); Chairman, Australian Science and Technology Council, 1988–92; *b* 3 Feb. 1926; *s* of Sir Leslie Harold Martin, CBE, FRS, FAA and late Gladys Maude Elaine, *d* of H. J. Bull; *m* 1954, Rena Lillian Laman; three *s* one *d.* *Educ:* Scotch Coll., Melbourne; Univ. of Melb. (BSc, MSc); Sidney Sussex Coll., Cambridge (PhD, ScD). FRACI 1956; FRSC (FRIC 1974); FTSE (FTS 1989); FAA 1971; FAIM 2003. Resident Tutor in Chemistry, Queen's Coll., Melb., 1947–49 (Fellow, 1979–2004, Sen. Fellow, 2005–); Sidney Sussex Coll., Cambridge: 1851 Exhibn Overseas Scholar, 1949–51; Sen. Scholar, 1952–54; Res. Fellow, 1951–54; Sen. Lectr, Univ. of NSW, 1954–59; Section Leader, 1959–60, and Associate Res. Manager, 1960–62, ICIANZ; Prof. of Inorganic Chem., 1962–72, and Dean of Faculty of Science, 1971, Univ. of Melb.; Australian National University, Canberra: Prof. of Inorganic Chem., Inst. of Advanced Studies, 1972–77, Prof. Emeritus 1977; Dean, Res. Sch. of Chem., 1976–77; DSc. Vis. Scientist: Technische Hochschule, Stuttgart, 1953–54; Bell Telephone Labs, NJ, 1967; Vis. Prof., Columbia Univ., NY, 1972. Royal Aust. Chemical Institute: Smith Medal, 1968; Olle Prize, 1974; Inorganic Medal, 1978; Leighton Medal, 1989; Fed. Pres., 1968–69. Chm., Internat. Commn on Atomic Weights and Isotopic Abundances, IUPAC, 1983–87; Mem., Prime Minister's Science Council, 1989–92. Director: Circadian Technologies Ltd, 1986–2002; Heide Park and Art Gall., 1988–92; Winston Churchill Meml Trust, 1983–2006 (Nat. Chm., 1995–2000; Nat. Pres., 2001–06); Chairman: Syngene Ltd, 1996–; Optiscan Pty Ltd, 1997–2002; Trustee, Selby Scientific Foundn, 1990–. Council Mem., Victorian Coll. of the Arts, 1984–98 (Dep. Pres., 1991; Pres., 1992–95). Hon. LLD Monash, 1992; Hon. DSc Melbourne, 1996. Queen's Silver Jubilee Medal, 1977; Centenary Medal, Australia, 2003. *Publications:* papers and revs on physical and inorganic chem. mainly in jls of London, Amer. and Aust. Chem. Socs. *Recreations:* ski-ing, golf, lawn tennis (Cambridge Univ. team *v* Oxford, Full Blue; Cambs County Colours). *Address:* PO Box 98, Mount Eliza, Vic 3930, Australia. *Clubs:* Melbourne (Melbourne); Hawks (Cambridge); Frankston Golf (Victoria); Royal South Yarra Lawn Tennis.

MARTIN, Richard Graham; Vice-Chairman, Allied-Lyons, 1988–92 (Director, 1981–92; Chief Executive, 1989–91); *b* 4 Oct. 1932; *s* of Horace Frederick Martin, MC and Phyllis Jeanette Martin; *m* 1958, Elizabeth Savage; two *s* one *d.* *Educ:* Sherborne School; St Thomas's Hosp. Med. Sch., 1953–54. 2nd Lt, RA, 1951–52. Joined Friary Holroyd & Healy's Brewery, 1955, Dir, 1959; Dir, Friary Meux, 1963–66; Managing Dir, Ind Coope (East Anglia), 1966–69; Director: Joshua Tetley & Son, 1969–72; Allied Breweries, 1972–92; Chief Exec., Joshua Tetley & Son, 1972–78; Vice-Chm., Joshua Tetley & Son and Tetley Walker, 1978–79; Chm., Ind Coope, 1979–85; Man. Dir, 1985–86, Chm. and Chief Exec., 1986–88, Allied Breweries; Chairman: J. Lyons & Co. Ltd, 1989–91; Hiram Walker, 1991 (Dir, 1989–91); Allied-Lyons, later Allied-Domecq, Pensions and Trustee Services, 1992–95; non-exec. Dir, Gibbs Mew plc, 1995–98. Chm., Brewers' Soc., 1991–92 (Vice-Chm., 1989–91). Pres., Shire Horse Soc., 1981–82. *Recreations:* travel, music, food.

MARTIN, Sir (Robert) Bruce, Kt 1992; QC 1977; Chairman, The Bob Martin Co., since 1980; *b* 2 Nov. 1938; *s* of late Robert Martin and Fay Martin; *m* 1967, Elizabeth Georgina (*née* Kiddie) (marr. diss. 1995); one *s* one *d.* *Educ:* Shrewsbury Sch.; Liverpool Univ. (LLB Hons 1959). Called to the Bar, Middle Temple, 1960; a Recorder of the Crown Court, 1978–86. Vice-Chm., Mersey RHA, 1986–88 (Mem., 1983–88); Chairman: N Western RHA, 1988–94; NHS Litigation Authy, 1996–99. *Recreations:* music, golf, ski-ing. *Address:* 4 Montpelier Terrace, SW7 1JP. *Clubs:* Reform; Royal Birkdale Golf; Inanda (Johannesburg).

MARTIN, Robert George H.; *see* Holland-Martin.

MARTIN, Robert Logan, (Roy); QC (Scot.) 1988; QC 2008; *b* 31 July 1950; *s* of Robert Martin and Dr Janet Johnstone Logan or Martin; *m* 1984, Fiona Frances Neil; one *s* two *d.* *Educ:* Paisley Grammar Sch.; Univ. of Glasgow (LLB). Solicitor, 1973–76; admitted to Faculty of Advocates, 1976 (Vice Dean, 2001–04; Dean, 2004–07); Mem., Sheriff Court Rules Council, 1981–84; Standing Junior Counsel to Dept of Employment in Scotland, 1983–84; Advocate-Depute, 1984–87; Temporary Sheriff, 1988–90. Admitted to Bar of NSW, 1987; called to the Bar, Lincoln's Inn, 1990. Chairman: Industrial Tribunals, 1991–96; Police Appeals Tribunal, 1997–. Mem., Judicial Appointments Bd for Scotland, 2007–. Chm., Scottish Planning, Local Govt and Envmtl Bar Gp, 1991–96; Co-Chairman: Forum for Barristers and Advocates, 2002–; Internat. Council of Advocates and Barristers, 2004–. Hon. Prof., Sch. of Law, Univ. of Glasgow, 2006–. Affiliate, RIAS, 1995. Trustee, Nat. Liby of Scotland, 2004–07. Hon. Sec., Wagering Club, 1982–91. Gov., Loretto Sch., 2002– (Chm., 2007–). *Recreations:* shooting, ski-ing, modern architecture, vintage motor cars. *Address:* Kilduff House, Athelstaneford, North Berwick, East Lothian EH39 5BD. *Club:* New (Edinburgh).

MARTIN, Robin Geoffrey; Director, Hewetson plc, 1980–98 (Chairman, 1980–88); *b* 9 March 1921; *s* of Cecil Martin and Isabel Katherine Martin (*née* Hickman); *m* 1946, Margery Chester Yates; two *s* one *d.* *Educ:* Cheltenham Coll.; Jesus Coll., Cambridge (MA). FIQ. Tarmac Ltd: Dir 1955; Gp Man. Dir 1963; Dep. Chm. 1967; Chm. and Chief Exec., 1971–79; Dir, Serck Ltd, 1971, Dep. Chm., 1974, Chm., 1976–81; Director: Burmah Oil Co,. 1975–85; Ductile Steels Ltd, 1977–82. Mem., Midlands Adv. Bd, Legal and General Assurance Soc. Ltd, 1977–84. Chm., Ironbridge Gorge Develt Trust, 1976–78. Life Governor, Birmingham Univ., 1970–85. *Recreations:* gardening, bridge.

MARTIN, Robin Rupert, CB 2004; Director, Tax Law Rewrite Project, HM Revenue and Customs (formerly Board of Inland Revenue), 2003–06; *b* 28 Feb. 1946; *s* of late Rupert Claude Martin and Ellen Martin (*née* Wood); *m* 1972, Jane Elizabeth Mackenzie Smith; three *s.* *Educ:* Harrow Sch.; Worcester Coll., Oxford (MA Hons). VSO: Thailand, 1964–65; India, 1969–70; joined Home Civil Service, 1970: Private Sec. to Chm., Bd of Inland Revenue, 1973–74; Office of Chancellor of Duchy of Lancaster, Cabinet Office, 1976–79; Asst Sec., 1981; Under Sec., 1993; Principal Finance Officer, 1993–2000, Dir, Cross-Cutting Policy, 2000–03, Bd of Inland Revenue. Dir, CS Healthcare, 2003–. Member: Methodology Soc., 2007–; Southwold Sailors' Reading Room Assoc. *Recreations:* infrequent leisurely hill-walking, cricket, second-hand books. *Club:* MCC.

MARTIN, Roger John Adam; formerly HM Diplomatic Service; Vice-President, Somerset Wildlife Trust, since 2001; *b* 21 Jan. 1941; *s* of late Geoffrey (Richard Rex) Martin and of Hazel (*née* Matthews); *m* 1972, Ann Cornwell (*née* Sharp); one *s.* *Educ:* Westminster School; Brasenose College, Oxford (BA). VSO, Northern Rhodesia, 1959–60; Commonwealth Office, 1964–66; Second Sec., Djakarta, 1967, Saigon, 1968–70; First Sec., FCO, 1971–74, Geneva, 1975–79; seconded to Dept of Trade, as Head of Middle East/North Africa Br., 1981–83; Dep. High Comr, Harare, 1983–86; resigned. Vis. Fellow, Univ. of Bath. Mem., Nat. Exec., VSO, 1988–96; Dir, Som Trust for Nature Conservation, subseq. Som Wildlife Trust, 1988–2001. Member: Regional Committees: Envmt Agency, 1990–; MAFF, 1993–97; Planning Conf., 1996–2000; Heritage Lottery Fund, 2001–06. Founder Mem., SW Regl Assembly, 1998. Mem., Exmoor Nat. Park Authy, 1998–; Chm., SW Reg., 2001–06, Trustee, 2003–07, CPRE; Pres., Mendip Soc., 2001–. Hon. DSc UWE, 2001. *Publication:* Southern Africa: the price of apartheid, 1988. *Recreations:* environmental issues, walking, archaeology. *Address:* Coxley House, Coxley, near Wells, Somerset BA5 1QS. *T:* (01749) 672180.

MARTIN, Prof. Ronald Leonard, PhD; FBA 2005; AcSS; Professor of Economic Geography, University of Cambridge, since 2000; Fellow, St Catharine's College, Cambridge, since 2000; *b* 17 April 1948; *s* of Bertie Leonard Martin and Joan Gladys Martin (*née* Claypole); *m* 1974, Lynda Mary Hunt. *Educ:* Gilberd Sch., Colchester; Trinity

Coll., Cambridge (BA 1st Cl. Hons Geog.; MA; PhD Geog. 1978). University of Cambridge: Asst Lectr in Geog., 1974–79; Lectr in Geog., 1979–98; British Acad. Thank-offering to Britain Fellow, 1997–98; Reader in Econ. Geog., 1998–2000; Leverhulme Major Res. Fellowship, 2007–. Fellow, Cambridge-MIT Inst., 2002. AcSS 2001. *Publications:* Towards the Dynamic Analysis of Spatial Systems, 1978; Regional Wage Inflation and Unemployment, 1981; Recollections of a Revolution: geography as spatial science, 1984; The Geography of Deindustrialisation, 1986; Regional Development in the 1990s, 1992; Human Geography: society, space and the social sciences, 1994; Money, Power and Space, 1994; Union Retreat and the Regions, 1996; Money and the Space Economy, 1999; The Reader in Economic Geography, 1999; Geographies of Labour Market Inequality, 2003; Putting Workforce in Place, 2005; Clusters and Regional Development, 2006; The Competitive Advantage of Regions, 2006; (ed) Critical Concepts in Economic Geography, 5 vols, 2007; Handbook of Evolutionary Economic Geography, 2008; Economic Geography, 2008; contrib. numerous articles to various jls, incl. Trans IBG, Envmt and Planning, Jl Econ. Geog., Regl Studies, Econ. Geog., Cambridge Jl Econs. *Recreations:* Italian opera, wine, astronomy, garden design, rabbits, reading everything and anything. *Address:* The Vines, Redgate Road, Girton, Cambridge CB3 0PP. *T:* (01223) 277244; St Catharine's College, Cambridge CB2 1RL. *T:* (01223) 338316; *e-mail:* rlm1@cam.ac.uk.

MARTIN, Ronald Noel, CB 1998; FRCVS; Chief Veterinary Officer, Department of Agriculture for Northern Ireland, 1990–98; *b* 15 Dec. 1938; *s* of Robert John and Margretta Martin; *m* 1962, Alexandrina Margaret McLeod; two *s. Educ:* Royal (Dick) Sch. of Veterinary Studies, Univ. of Edinburgh (BVMS). FRCVS 1995 (MRCVS 1961). Private veterinary practice, 1960–64; Ministry of Agriculture, later Department of Agriculture, for Northern Ireland: Vet. Officer, 1964–69; Divl Vet. Officer, 1969–73; Sen. Principal Vet. Officer, 1973–78; Dep. Chief Vet. Officer, 1978–90. Chm., NI Food Chain Certification Cttee, 2001–. *Recreations:* gardening, walking, cycling. *Address:* 8 Whiteside, Mountain Road, Newtownards, Co. Down BT23 4UP. *T:* (028) 9181 3962.

MARTIN, Roy; *see* Martin, Robert L.

MARTIN, (Roy) Peter, MBE 1970; author and critic; *b* 5 Jan. 1931; *s* of Walter Martin and Annie Mabel Martin; *m* 1st, 1951, Marjorie Peacock (marr. diss. 1960); 2nd, Joan Drumwright (marr. diss. 1977); two *s;* 3rd, 1978, Catherine Sydee. *Educ:* Highbury Grammar Sch.; Univ. of London (BA 1953, MA 1956); Univ. of Tübingen. Nat. Service (RAF Educn Branch), 1949–51. Worked as local govt officer, schoolteacher and tutor in adult educn; then as British Council officer, 1960–83; service in Indonesia, Hungary (Cultural Attaché) and Japan (Cultural Counsellor). *Publications:* (with Joan Martin) Japanese Cooking, 1970; The Chrysanthemum Throne, 1997; (as James Melville): The Wages of Zen, 1979; The Chrysanthemum Chain, 1980; A Sort of Samurai, 1981; The Ninth Netsuke, 1982; Sayonara, Sweet Amaryllis, 1983; Death of a Daimyo, 1984; The Death Ceremony, 1985; Go Gently Gaijin, 1986; The Imperial Way, 1986; Kimono For A Corpse, 1987; The Reluctant Ronin, 1988; A Haiku for Hanae, 1989; A Tarnished Phoenix, 1990; The Bogus Buddha, 1990; The Body Wore Brocade, 1992; Diplomatic Baggage, 1994; The Reluctant Spy, 1995; (as Hampton Charles): Miss Seeton At The Helm, 1990; Miss Seeton, By Appointment, 1990; Advantage Miss Seeton, 1990. *Recreations:* music, books. *Address:* c/o Curtis Brown, 28/29 Haymarket, SW1Y 4SP. *Clubs:* Travellers, Detection.

MARTIN, Stanley William Frederick, CVO 1992 (LVO 1981); JP; HM Diplomatic Service, retired; Extra Gentleman Usher to the Queen, since 1993; Protocol Consultant, Foreign and Commonwealth Office, since 1993; Chairman, Royal Over-Seas League, since 2005; *b* 9 Dec. 1934; *s* of Stanley and Winifred Martin; *m* 1960, Hanni Aud Hansen, Copenhagen; one *s* one *d. Educ:* Bromley Grammar Sch.; University Coll., Oxford (MA Jurisprudence; Pres., OU Law Soc., 1957); Inner Temple (student Scholar). Nat. Service, 2nd Lieut RASC, 1953–55. Entered CRO, 1958; Asst Private Sec. to Sec. of State, 1959–62; First Secretary: Canberra, 1962–64; Kuala Lumpur, 1964–67; FCO (Planning Staff and Personnel Dept), 1967–70; seconded to CSD (CSSB), 1970–71; HM Asst Marshal of the Diplomatic Corps, 1972–81; First Asst Marshal, 1981–92; Associate Head of Protocol Dept, FCO, 1986–92. Vis. Prof., Diplomatic Acad., Poly. of Central London, subseq. Univ. of Westminster, 1987– (Hon. Fellow, 1998). Diplomatic Consultant: Hyde Park Hotel, then Mandarin Oriental Hyde Park, 1993–99; Grosvenor House, 1999–2002. Member: Cttee, London Diplomatic Assoc., 1972–; Council, Oxford Univ. Soc., 1993–2002; Adv. Council, Spanish Inst. of Protocol Studies, 1997–; Cttee, European-Atlantic Gp, 2003–. Trustee: Attlee Foundn, 1993–99; Toynbee Hall, 1996–99; Jt Commonwealth Socs Trust, 2005–; Patron, Apex Trust, 2002– (Vice-Patron, 1995–2002). Adviser: Consular Corps of London, 1993–; London Mayors' Assoc., 2004– (Hon. Mem., 2006). Mem., Commonwealth Observer Gp, Guyana elecns, 1997. Gov., Goodenough Coll. for Overseas Graduates, 2005–. Freelance lectr, 1993–. FRSA 1985. JP Inner London, 1993–2000. Freeman of the City of London, 1988. Companion, Order of Distinguished Service (Brunei), 1992. *Publications:* (jtly) Royal Service: history of the Royal Victorian Order, Medal and Chain, vol. I 1996, vol. II 2001; The Order of Merit: one hundred years of matchless honour, 2006; (contrib.) Diplomatic Handbook, 2nd edn 1977 to 8th edn 2004; contribs to Jl of Orders and Medals Res. Soc., Jl of Royal Over-Seas League, Diplomat mag. *Recreations:* collecting books, manuscripts and obituaries, historical research and writing, walking, siestas, watching old films in the afternoon. *Address:* 14 Great Spilmans, Dulwich, SE22 8SZ. *T:* (020) 8693 8181. *Clubs:* Royal Over-Seas League, Oxford and Cambridge, Danish.

MARTIN, Stephen Harcourt; Chief Executive, Higher Education Funding Council for Wales, 2000–03; *b* 4 Sept. 1952; *s* of Robert Harcourt Martin and Joan Winifred Martin (*née* Carpenter); *m* 1988, Amanda Suna Hodges (marr. diss. 2002); one *s* one *d. Educ:* Watford GS for Boys; Haywards Heath GS; Hull Univ. (Pol Studies). Nursing Assistant, De La Pole Psych. Hosp., Willerby, 1973–74; Welsh Office: Exec. Officer, Town and Country Planning Div., 1974–77; Admin Trainee, Health and Industry Depts, 1977–79; Pvte Sec. to successive Perm. Secs, 1979–81; Principal: Health Dept, 1981–85; Housing Div., 1985–87; Asst Sec., Health and Social Services Divs, 1987–92; Under Sec., later Dir, Educn Dept, 1992–97; Prin. Establishments Officer, 1997–99; Sec. and Dir of Policy, Welsh Fourth Channel Authy, 1999–2000; Chief Executive: Further Educn Funding Council for Wales, 2000–01; Nat. Council for Educn and Trng for Wales, 2000–03. *Recreations:* music, literature.

MARTIN, Prof. Hon. Stephen Paul; Pro Vice-Chancellor (International), Victoria University, Melbourne, since 2005; *b* 24 June 1948; *s* of Harold and Vera Martin; *m;* one *s* three *d. Educ:* ANU (BA); Univ. of Alberta (MA); Sydney Univ. (MTCP); Univ. of NSW (Dip. Ed); PhD Wollongong. High School teacher, 1970–74; Univ. Lectr, 1975–77; Town Planner, NSW Dept of Planning and Environment, 1977–84. MP (Lab) Cunningham, NSW, 1984–2002; Chm., Banking, Finance and Public Administration Cttee, 1987–91; Parly Sec. to Minister for Foreign Affairs and Trade, 1991–93; Speaker, House of Reps, Aust., 1993–96; Shadow Minister: for Sport and Tourism, and for Veterans' Affairs, 1996–97; for Small Business, Customs, Sport and Tourism, 1997–98; for Defence, 1998–2001; for Trade and Tourism, 2001–02. Professorial Fellow, Grad. Sch. of Business and Professional Develt, Univ. of Wollongong, 2002–03; CEO, Univ. of Wollongong in Dubai, 2004–05. *Recreations:* swimming, Rugby League, movies. *Address:* Victoria University, PO Box 14428, Melbourne, Vic 8001, Australia.

MARTIN, Steven; *see* Martin, G. S.

MARTIN, (Thomas) Geoffrey, OBE 2002; Adviser, responsible for Strategic Relationships, Office of the Commonwealth Secretary-General, since 2005; *b* 26 July 1940; *s* of Thomas Martin and Saidee Adelaide (*née* Day); *m* 1968, Gay (Madeleine Annesley) Brownrigg; one *s* three *d. Educ:* Queen's Univ., Belfast (BSc Hons). President, National Union of Students of England, Wales and Northern Ireland, 1966–68; City of London: Banking, Shipping, 1968–73; Director, Shelter, 1973–74; Diplomatic Staff, Commonwealth Secretariat, 1974–79; Head of EC Office, NI, 1979–85; Head of EC Press and Inf. Services, SE Asia, 1985–87; Hd of External Relations, EC Office, London, 1987–93; Hd of Repn of EC in UK, 1994–2002; Office of Commonwealth Sec.-Gen., 2002–. Vis. Prof., Leeds Univ., 2003–. Hon. DSc Plymouth, 2000. *Address:* Commonwealth Secretariat, Marlborough House, Pall Mall, SW1Y 5HX. *Club:* Travellers.

MARTIN, Prof. Thomas John, AO 1996; MD, DSc; FRACP, FRCPA; FRS 2000; FAA; Director, St Vincent's Institute of Medical Research, University of Melbourne, 1988–2002; *b* 24 Jan. 1937; *s* of Thomas Michael and Ellen Agnes Martin; *m* 1964, Christine Mayo Conroy (*d* 1995); two *s* four *d. Educ:* Xavier Coll.; Univ. of Melbourne (MB BS 1960; MD 1969; DSc 1979). FRACP 1969; FRCPA 1985; FAA 1996. Registrar and Res. Fellow, RPMS, London, 1965–66; Sen. Res. Fellow, 1967–68, Sen. Lectr, 1968–73, Dept of Medicine, Univ. of Melbourne; Prof. of Chemical Pathology, Univ. of Sheffield, 1974–77; Prof. of Medicine, Univ. of Melbourne, 1977–98, now Emeritus (Chm., Dept of Medicine, 1985–98). Vis. Prof., RPMS, 1973. Hon. MD Sheffield, 1992. *Publications:* more than 400 scientific papers, reviews and book chapters on endocrinology, bone cell biology, cancer and clinical medicine. *Recreations:* music, golf, fly-fishing, travel. *Address:* 1/6 Findon Crescent, Kew, Vic 3101, Australia. *T:* (3) 98528424. *Club:* Melbourne.

MARTIN, Timothy Randall; Founder, 1979, and Chairman, since 1983, J. D. Wetherspoon plc; *b* 28 April 1955; *s* of Ray and Olive Martin; *m* Felicity Owen; one *s* three *d. Educ:* Nottingham Univ. (LLB). Called to the Bar, 1980. *Address:* J. D. Wetherspoon plc, Wetherspoon House, Central Park, Reeds Crescent, Watford, Herts WD24 4QL. *T:* (01923) 477777. *Club:* Exeter Squash.

MARTIN, Tom; JP; President, since 2006, and non-executive Director, since 1996, ARCO Ltd; Vice Lord-Lieutenant, East Riding of Yorkshire, since 2006; *b* 22 March 1936; *s* of Thomas Martin and Marjorie Martin; *m* 1960, Anne, *er d* of Thomas W. Boyd, CBE, DSO and Barbara Boyd; one *s* three *d. Educ:* Bramcote Sch., Scarborough; Winchester Coll.; Emmanuel Coll., Cambridge (BA Hons Law 1959). National Service, RNVR (Sub Lt), 1954–56. ARCO Ltd: Dir, 1965–96; Jt Man. Dir, 1969–96; Chm., 1981–2006. Gen. Comr of Income Tax, 1998–2006. Mem. Council, CBI, 1992–99. Mem. (C), Humberside CC, 1977–84. Mem., Magistrates' Adv. Council, 1985–93. Dir, Humber Forum, 2000–; Founder Chm., E Riding Community Safety Partnership, 1996–; Trustee, Humberside Police Tribune Trust, 2001–. Patron, NSPCC, 2004–. Gov., Humberside Univ., 1993–96. JP Hull, 1972; High Sheriff, 1996–97, DL, 1998, ER of Yorks. *Recreations:* a veritable tribe of grandchildren, shooting, travel, antiquarian horology, and in an earlier life rowing, sailing and walking. *Address:* Newbegin House, 14–16 Newbegin, Beverley, E Yorks HU17 8EG. *T:* (01482) 869552, *Fax:* (01482) 887945; *e-mail:* tom.martin@arco.co.uk. *Clubs:* Naval; Leander; Hawks (Cambridge); Royal Yorks Yacht.

MARTIN-JENKINS, Christopher Dennis Alexander; Chief Cricket Correspondent, The Times, 1999–2008; BBC cricket commentator, since 1972; *b* 20 Jan. 1945; *s* of late Dennis Frederick Martin-Jenkins, TD and Dr Rosemary Clare Martin-Jenkins (*née* Walker); *m* 1971, Judith Oswald Hayman; two *s* one *d. Educ:* Marlborough; Fitzwilliam Coll., Cambridge (BA (Modern Hist.); MA). Dep. Editor, The Cricketer, 1967–70; sports broadcaster, 1970–73, Cricket Correspondent, 1973–80, 1984–91, BBC; Editor, 1981–88, Editl Dir, 1988–91, The Cricketer International; Cricket Correspondent, Daily Telegraph, 1991–99. President: Rugby Fives Assoc., 1993–95; W Sussex Assoc. of Umpires and Scorers, 1995–; Cricket Soc., 1998–2008. Trustee, Brian Johnston Meml Trust, 1995– (Chm., 1998–2000). *Publications:* Testing Time, 1974; Assault on the Ashes, 1975; MCC in India, 1977; The Jubilee Tests and the Packer Revolution, 1977; In Defence of the Ashes, 1979; Cricket Contest, 1980; The Complete Who's Who of Test Cricketers, 1980; The Wisden Book of County Cricket, 1981; Bedside Cricket, 1981; Twenty Years On: Cricket's years of change, 1984; Cricket: a way of life, 1984; (ed) Cricketer Book of Cricket Eccentrics, 1985; (ed) Seasons Past, 1986; (ed jtly) Quick Singles, 1986; Grand Slam, 1987; Cricket Characters, 1987; Sketches of a Season, 1989; Ball by Ball, 1990; (jtly) Summers Will Never Be the Same, 1994; The Spirit of Cricket (anthology), 1994; World Cricketers, 1996; An Australian Summer, 1999; Men For All Seasons, 2001. *Recreations:* cricket, golf, music, theatre, walking. *Clubs:* East India, MCC; I Zingari, Free Foresters, Arabs, Marlborough Blues, Cranleigh Cricket, Albury Cricket, Rudgwick Cricket, Horsham Cricket; West Sussex Golf, Royal St George's Golf.

MARTINEAU, David Nicholas Nettlefold; His Honour Judge Martineau; a Circuit Judge, since 1994; *b* 27 March 1941; *s* of Frederick Alan Martineau and Vera Ruth Martineau (*née* Naylor); *m* 1968, Elizabeth Mary Allom; one *s* (one *d* decd). *Educ:* Eton; Trinity Coll., Cambridge (MA, LLM). Called to the Bar, Inner Temple, 1964; Asst Recorder, 1982–86; Recorder 1986–94. Mem., Exec. Cttee, Cystic Fibrosis Trust, 1990–2004. *Recreations:* ski-ing, water ski-ing, wind-surfing, music, wine and food. *Address:* Blackfriars Crown Court, Pocock Street, SE1 0BJ. *T:* (020) 7922 5800. *Clubs:* MCC; Hawks (Cambridge).

MARTINEAU, Malcolm John; pianist, accompanist; Professor, Royal Academy of Music, since 1987; *b* 3 Feb. 1960; *s* of George Martineau and Hester Dickson. *Educ:* George Watson's Coll., Edinburgh; St Catharine's Coll., Cambridge (BA 1981); Royal Coll. of Music. Début, Wigmore Hall, 1984; has accompanied many leading singers, incl. Thomas Allen, Dame Janet Baker, Barbara Bonney, Della Jones, Dame Felicity Lott, Ann Murray, Bryn Terfel, Anne Sofie von Otter, Frederica von Stade, and instrumentalists, incl. Emma Johnson; has accompanied master classes, Britten-Pears Sch. Presented song recital series: Debussy and Poulenc, St John's, Smith Square; Britten, Wigmore Hall; Jt Artistic Dir, Liederreise, St John's, Smith Sq., 1998. Recordings incl. complete folk song settings of Beethoven and Britten, instrumental and vocal music incl. Arnold, Brahms, Fauré, Schubert, Schumann, Strauss and song recitals, with various artists. Hon. RAM 1998; Hon. Dr RSAMD, 2004. Accompanist's Prize, Walther Grüner Internat. Lieder Competition, 1983. *Recreations:* theatre-going, cooking. *Address:* c/o Askonas Holt, Lincoln House, 300 High Holborn, WC1V 7JH. *T:* (020) 7400 1700.

MARTINEAU-WALKER, Roger Antony; *see* Walker.

MARTINEZ, Arthur C.; Chairman and Chief Executive Officer, Sears, Roebuck and Co., 1995–2000, now Emeritus; *b* 25 Sept. 1939; *s* of Arthur F. Martinez and Agnes M. Martinez (*née* Caulfield); *m* 1966, Elizabeth Rusch; one *s* one *d*. *Educ:* Polytechnic Univ. (BSME); Harvard Univ. (MBA 1965). Exxon Chemical Co., 1960; Dir of Planning, Internat. Paper Co., 1967–69; Asst to Pres., Talley Industries, 1969–70; Dir of Finance, 1970–73, Vice-Pres., 1973–80, RCA Corp.; Sen. Vice-Pres. and Chief Financial Officer, 1980–84, Exec. Vice-Pres., 1984–87, Vice-Chm., 1990–92, Saks Fifth Avenue; Gp Chief Exec., Retail Div., and Sen. Vice Pres., Batus Inc., 1987–90; Chm. and Chief Exec. Officer, Sears Merchandise Gp, 1992–95. Director: PepsiCo Inc., 1999–; Internat. Flavors & Fragrances Inc., 2000–; Chm., Federal Reserve Bank of Chicago, 1999–2001; Mem., Supervisory Bd, ABN AMRO, 2002– (Vice-Chm.). Chm., Nat. Minority Supplier Develt Council, 1994–97. Chm., Bd of Trustees, Polytechnic Univ., 1994–99; Trustee: Northwestern Univ.; Art Inst. of Chicago; Chicago Symphony Orch.; Northwestern Univ. Hosp. *Publication:* (jtly) The Hard Road to the Softer Side, 2001.

MARTINI, His Eminence Cardinal Carlo Maria, SJ; Archbishop of Milan, 1980–2002, now Emeritus; *b* 15 Feb. 1927; *s* of Leonardo and Olga Maggia. *Educ:* Pontifical Gregorian Univ. (DTheol); Pontifical Biblical Inst. (Doctorate in holy scripture). Ordained priest, 1952; Rector, Pontifical Biblical Inst., 1969–78; Rector, Gregorian Univ., 1978–79. Cardinal 1983. Pres., Consilium Conferentiarum Episcopalium Europae, 1987–93.

MARTLEW, Eric Anthony; MP (Lab) Carlisle, since 1987; *b* 3 Jan. 1949; *m* 1970, Elsie Barbara Duggan. *Educ:* Harraby Secondary School, Carlisle; Carlisle Tech. Coll. Nestlé Co. Ltd, 1966–87: joined as lab. technician; later Personnel Manager, Dalston Factory, Carlisle. Member: Carlisle County Borough Council, 1972–74; Cumbria CC, 1973–88 (Chm., 1983–85). Mem., Cumbria Health Authy, later E Cumbria HA, 1977–87 (Chm., 1977–79). Opposition spokesman on defence, 1992–95; an Opposition Whip, 1995–97; PPS to Chancellor of Duchy of Lancaster, 1997–98, to Leader of H of L, 1998–2001. Chm., All Party Animal Welfare Gp; Joint Chair: W Coast Main Line All Party Gp; All Party Rail Gp; Mem., Chairman's Panel. Patron: Animal Sanctuary, Moorhouse, Carlisle, 2004–; Animal Refuge, 2005; Cerebral Palsy Cumbria, 2005–; Motor Neurone Disease Assoc., 2006–. *Recreations:* photography, fell walking, horse racing. *Address:* 3 Chatsworth Square, Carlisle, Cumbria CA1 1HB. *T:* (01228) 511395.

MARTONMERE, 2nd Baron *cr* 1964; **John Stephen Robinson;** *b* 10 July 1963; *s* of Hon. Richard Anthony Gasque Robinson (*d* 1979) and of Wendy Patricia (who *m* subseq. Ronald De Mara), *d* of late James Cecil Blagden; *S* grandfather, 1989; *m* 2001, Marion Elizabeth Wills, *d* of Ian Wills, Toronto; one *s*. *Educ:* Lakefield College School; Senaca College. *Heir:* *s* Hon. James Ian Robinson, *b* 26 Feb. 2003. *Address:* 67 Donwoods Drive, Toronto, ON M4N 2G6, Canada.

MARTYN, (Charles) Roger (Nicholas); Master of the Supreme Court, 1973–95; part-time Adjudicator, Immigration Appellate Authority, 1991–95; *b* 10 Dec. 1925; *s* of Rev. Charles Martyn; *m* 1960, Helen, *d* of Frank and Florence Everson; two *s* one *d*. *Educ:* Charterhouse, 1939–44; Merton Coll., Oxford, 1947–49. MA (Hons) Mod. Hist. Joined Regular Army, 1944; commissioned 60th Rifles (KRRC), 1945; CMF, 1946–47; special release, 1947. Articles, 1950–52, and admitted as solicitor, 1952. Sherwood & Co., Parly Agents (Partner), 1952–59; Lee, Bolton & Lee, Westminster (Partner), 1961–73; Notary Public, 1969. Mem. and Dep. Chm., No 14 Legal Aid Area Cttee, 1967–73; Hon. Legal Adviser to The Samaritans (Inc), 1955–73. Chairman: Family Welfare Assoc., 1973–78 (Chief Trustee of 129 public charities and 6 almshouses); NHS Complaints Panel for Gtr London, 1999–2004; Member: Gtr London Citizens' Advice Bureaux Management Cttee, 1974–79; Council, St Gabriel's Coll. (Further Education), Camberwell, 1973–77 (Vice-Chm.); Council, Goldsmiths' Coll., Univ. of London, 1988–94 (Mem., Delegacy, 1977–88). Freeman, City of London, 1995. *Recreations:* walking, sailing (Vice-Cdre, Thames Barge Sailing Club, 1962–65), observing people, do-it-yourself, nigrology. *Address:* 29 St Albans Road, NW5 1RG. *T:* (020) 7267 1076.

MARTYN-HEMPHILL, family name of **Baron Hemphill**.

MARTYR, Peter McCallum; Partner, since 1985, and Chief Executive, since 2002, Norton Rose; *b* 31 March 1954; *s* of John Walton Martyr and Jean Wallace Robertson; *m* 1978, Carol Frances Busby; one *s* one *d*. *Educ:* University Coll., Cardiff (LLB Jt Hons). Admitted solicitor, 1979; Mem., Exec. Cttee, Norton Rose, 1997–. *Recreations:* Rugby (watching), ski-ing, music, classic cars. *Address:* Norton Rose, Kempson House, Camomile Street, EC3A 7AN. *T:* (020) 7283 6000, *Fax:* (020) 7283 6500; *e-mail:* peter.martyr@nortonrose.com.

MARWICK, George Robert, CVO 2007; JP; farmer and company director; Lord-Lieutenant of Orkney, 1997–2007 (Vice Lord-Lieutenant, 1995–97); *b* 27 Feb. 1932; *s* of late Robert William Marwick, BSc Hons, MICE, Civil Engr, and Agnes Kemp Marwick (*née* Robson); *m* 1st, 1958, Hanne Jensen (marr. diss. 1989); three *d*; 2nd, 1990, Norma Gerrard (*née* Helm). *Educ:* Port Regis, Dorset; Bryanston Sch., Dorset; Edinburgh Sch. of Agriculture (SDA 1953). Chm. and Man. Dir, Swannay Farms Ltd, 1972–; Chairman: Campbeltown Creamery Ltd, 1974–90; Campbeltown Creamery (Hldgs) Ltd, 1974–90; Director: North Eastern Farmers Ltd, 1968–98; Orkney Islands Shipping Co., 1972–87. Chm., N of Scotland Water Bd, 1970–73; Member: Scottish Agricl Cons. Panel (formerly Winter Keep Panel), 1964–98; Countryside Commn for Scotland, 1978–86; Council, NT for Scotland, 1979–84. Ind. Mem., Orkney CC, then Orkney Is Council, 1968–78 (Vice-Convenor, 1970–74; Convenor, 1974–78). JP, 1970, DL, 1976, Orkney. Hon. Sheriff of Grampian, Highlands and Is, 2000. *Recreations:* shooting, motor sport. *Address:* Swannay House, by Evie, Orkney KW17 2NP. *T:* (01856) 721263, *Fax:* (01856) 721227. *Club:* New (Edinburgh).

MARWICK, Patricia, (Tricia); Member (SNP) Fife Central, Scottish Parliament, since 2007 (Mid Scotland and Fife, 1999–2007); *b* 5 Nov. 1953; *m* 1975, Frank Marwick; one *s* one *d*. *Educ:* Fife. Former public affairs officer, Shelter. Mem., SNP, 1985– (Mem. NEC, 1997–2000). Contested (SNP) Fife Central, 1992, 1997. *Address:* Scottish Parliament, Edinburgh EH99 1SP.

MARWOOD, Anthony; violinist; *b* 6 July 1965; *s* of Michael Travers Marwood and Anne (*née* Chevallier). *Educ:* King Edward VI Grammar Sch., Chelmsford; Royal Acad. of Music; Guildhall Sch. of Music and Drama. Mem., Florestan Trio, 1995–; Artistic Dir, Irish Chamber Orch., 2006–; internat. engagements as solo violinist; collaborator with dancers and actors. Vis. Prof., GSMD, 1997–. Has made recordings as soloist and chamber musician. Instrumentalist Award, Royal Philharmonic Soc., 2006. *Recreations:* theatre, finding myself in Cape Town. *Address:* c/o Owen White Management, Top Floor, 59 Lansdowne Place, Hove, E Sussex BN3 1FL.

MARYCHURCH, Sir Peter (Harvey), KCMG 1985; Chairman, Associated Board of the Royal Schools of Music, 1994–2000; Director, Government Communications Headquarters, 1983–89; *b* 13 June 1927; *s* of Eric William Alfred and Dorothy Margaret Marychurch; *m* 1965, June Daphne Ottaway (*née* Pareezer). *Educ:* Lower School of John Lyon, Harrow. Served RAF, 1945–48. Joined GCHQ, 1948; Asst Sec. 1975; Under Sec. 1979; Dep. Sec. 1983. Chairman: Cheltenham Arts Festivals, 1994–2000; Cheltenham Internat. Fest. of Music, 1993–97; Cheltenham and Cotswold Relate, 1990–97; Pres., Cheltenham Arts Council, 1998–2007. FRSAMD 1998. Hon. RNCM 2000. Medal for Distinguished Public Service, US Dept of Defense, 1989. *Recreations:* theatre, music (especially opera), gardening. *Address:* HSBC, 2 The Promenade, Cheltenham, Glos GL50 1LS. *Club:* Naval and Military.

MARYON DAVIS, Dr Alan Roger, FRCP; FFPH; FFSEM; President, Faculty of Public Health, Royal Colleges of Physicians of the UK, since 2007; Hon. Professor of Public Health, King's College London, since 2007; *b* 21 Jan. 1943; *s* of Cyril Edward Maryon Davis and Hilda May Maryon Davis; *m* 1981, Glynis Anne Davies; two *d*. *Educ:* St Paul's Sch.; St John's Coll., Cambridge (MA 1968; MB BChir 1970); St Thomas's Hosp. Med. Sch. (LRCP, MRCS 1969); London Sch. of Hygiene and Tropical Medicine. MSc (Social Med.) London 1978. MRCP 1972; FFPH (FFCM 1986; MFCM 1978); FRIPH (FRIPHH 1989); FRCP 2005; FFSEM 2007. Early med. career in gen. medicine and rheumatology, later in community medicine; MO, 1977–84, CMO, 1984–87, Health Educn Council; Sen. Med. Adviser, Health Educn Authority, 1987–88; Hon. Consultant, Paddington and N Kensington HA, 1985–88; Hon. Sen. Lectr in Community Medicine, St Mary's Hosp. Med. Sch., 1985–88; Hon. Sen. Lectr in Public Health, UMDS, then KCL, 1988–2007; Consultant in Public Health Med., W Lambeth, then SE London, subseq. Lambeth, Southwark and Lewisham, HA, 1988–2002; Dir of Public Health, Southwark PCT, 2002–07. Vice Chm., Nat. Heart Forum, 2005–; Chair, RIPH, 2006– (Vice Chm., 2002–06). Writer and broadcaster on health matters, 1975–; BBC radio series include Action Makes the Heart Grow Stronger (Med. Journalist's Assoc. Radio Award), 1983; BBC television series include: Body Matters, 1985–89; Health UK, 1990–91. Editor-in-Chief, Health Education Jl, 1984–88; Med. Advice Columnist, Woman magazine, 1988–2005. *Publications:* Family Health and Fitness, 1981; Body Facts, 1984; (with J. Thomas) Diet 2000, 1984; (with J. Rogers) How to Save a Life, 1987; PSSST—a Really Useful Guide to Alcohol, 1989; Cholesterol Check, 1991; The Good Health Guide, 1994; Ruby's Health Quest, 1995; The Body-clock Diet, 1996; Feeling Good, 2007. *Recreations:* eating well, drinking well, singing (not so well) in the humorous group Instant Sunshine. *Address:* Friary Court, The Friary, Salisbury SP1 2HU. *T:* (01722) 341786.

MASCHLER, Fay, MBE 2004; restaurant critic, Evening Standard, since 1972; *b* 15 July 1945; *d* of Mary and Arthur Frederick Coventry; *m* 1970, Thomas Michael Maschler, *qv* (marr. diss. 1987); one *s* two *d*; *m* 1992, Reginald Bernard John Gadney. *Educ:* Convent of the Sacred Heart, Greenwich, Conn. Copywriter, J. Walter Thompson, 1964; journalist, Radio Times, 1969. *Publications:* Cooking is a Game You Can Eat, 1975; A Child's Book of Manners, 1979; Miserable Aunt Bertha, 1980; Fay Maschler's Guide to Eating Out in London, 1986; Eating In, 1987; Howard & Maschler on Food, 1987; Teach Your Child to Cook, 1988; Evening Standard Restaurant Guides, annually, 1993–. *Address:* 12 Fitzroy Square, W1T 6BU. *Clubs:* Groucho, Car Clamp.

MASCHLER, Thomas Michael; Publisher, Jonathan Cape Children's Books, since 1991; Director, Jonathan Cape Ltd, since 1960 (Chairman, 1970–91); Founder, Booker Prize for Fiction, 1969; *b* 16 Aug. 1933; *s* of Kurt Leo Maschler and of Rita Masseron (*née* Lechner); *m* 1970, Fay Coventry (*see* Fay Maschler) (marr. diss. 1987); one *s* two *d*; *m* 1988, Regina Kulinicz. *Educ:* Leighton Park School. Production Asst, Andre Deutsch, 1955; Editor, MacGibbon & Kee, 1956–58; Fiction Editor, Penguin Books, 1958–60; Jonathan Cape: Editorial Dir, 1960; Man. Dir, 1966. Associate Producer, The French Lieutenant's Woman (film), 1981. *Publications:* (ed) Declarations, 1957; (ed) New English Dramatists Series, 1959–63; Publisher (memoirs), 2005. *Address:* 18 Lennox Gardens, SW1X 0DG.

MASCIE-TAYLOR, Prof. (Bryan) Hugo, FRCP, FRCPI; Medical Director, Leeds Teaching Hospitals NHS Trust, since 1998; *b* 21 Aug. 1947; *s* of (Henry) Hugo and (Madeline) Eira Mascie-Taylor; *m* 1st, 1972, Heather Chapman (marr. diss. 1994); one *s*; 2nd, 1994, Louise Thomas; two *s*. *Educ:* Sir Thomas Rich's Sch., Gloucester; Univ. of Leeds; Univ. of California, San Francisco; Ashridge Mgt Coll.; Henley Coll. of Mgt (ADipC 1997). FRCPI 1992; FRCP 1994; MIHM (MHSM 1996). Consultant Physician: St James Univ. Hosp., Leeds, 1986–91; (and Clinical Dir), Seacroft Hosp., Leeds, 1991–94; Dir, Strategic Develt, Leeds Community and Mental Health Trust, 1992–94; Med. Dir, 1994–96, Dir, Commng, 1996–98, Leeds HA. University of Leeds: Hon. Sen. Clin. Lectr, 1986–; Vis. Prof., Sch. of Medicine, 2004–; Vis. Fellow, Univ. of York, 1996–. External Examiner: (Masters/Gerontol.), Univ. of Hull, 1996–99; (Masters/Clin. Mgt), Univ. of Durham, 2003–. Chm., Overseas Partnership and Trng Initiative (OPTIN), 2004–. Member, Board: British Assoc. of Med. Managers; NHS Employers Policy Bd. *Publications:* articles in clinical and mgt jls. *Recreations:* English furniture, ski-ing. *Address:* Trust Headquarters, Leeds Teaching Hospitals NHS Trust, Leeds LS9 7TF. *T:* (0113) 206 5192, *Fax:* (0113) 206 5424; *e-mail:* hugo@mascie-taylor.org.

MASCORD, Dr David John; Headmaster, Bristol Grammar School, since 1999; *b* 18 Oct. 1950; *s* of George and Evelyn Mascord; *m* 1974, Veronica Mary Chalton Peers; two *s*. *Educ:* York Univ. (BA 1st Cl. Hons Chemistry 1972); St John's Coll., Cambridge (PhD 1976; PGCE with Dist.). Head of Chemistry, Wellington Coll., 1981–86; Sen. Teacher, Aylesbury GS, 1986–89; Asst Hd, 1989–98, Dep. Hd, 1998–99, Bristol GS. *Publications:* contrib. articles in Faraday Discussions of Chem. Soc., Molecular Physics, Jl Chem. Industry. *Recreations:* walking, swimming, personal computing, cooking, reading, particularly Charles Dickens, sketching, painting. *Address:* Bristol Grammar School, University Road, Bristol BS8 1SR. *T:* (0117) 973 6006, *Fax:* (0117) 946 7485.

MASEFIELD, Sir Charles (Beech Gordon), Kt 1997; CEng, FRAeS, FIMechE; President, BAE SYSTEMS, 2003–07 (Group Marketing Director, 1999–2002, Vice-Chairman, 2002–03); *b* 7 Jan. 1940; *s* of Sir Peter (Gordon) Masefield and Patricia Doreen (*née* Rooney); *m* 1970, Fiona Anne Kessler; two *s*. *Educ:* Eastbourne Coll.; Jesus Coll., Cambridge (MA). CEng 1984; FRAeS 1980; FIMechE 1984. Sales Exec. and Test Pilot, Beagle Aircraft, 1964–70; Hawker Siddeley Aviation: Test Pilot, 1970–76; Dep. Chief Test Pilot, Manchester, 1976–78; British Aerospace, Manchester: Chief Test Pilot, 1978–80; Project Dir, 1980–81; Prodn Dir, 1981–84; Gen. Manager, 1984–86; Man. Dir, BAe Hatfield, Manchester, Prestwick, 1986–92; Pres., BAe Commercial Aircraft, 1992–93; Sen. Vice-Pres. and Commercial Dir, Airbus Industrie, Toulouse, 1993–94; Hd, Defence Export Services Orgn, 1994–98; Vice-Chm., GEC, 1998–99. Chairman: Microsulis Ltd, 2003–07; Helvetia Wealth Mgt, Switzerland, 2004–; non-executive Director: Banque Piguet, Switzerland, 2002–04; Qator Foundn, 2003–. Pres., RAeS, 1994–95. FRSA 1999. Hon. FIMechE 2005. *Recreation:* golf. *Address:* Old Hall, Markyate, Herts AL3 8AR. *T:* (01582) 763901.

MASEFIELD, (John) Thorold, CMG 1986; HM Diplomatic Service, retired; Governor and Commander-in-Chief of Bermuda, 1997–2001; *b* 1 Oct. 1939; *e s* of late Dr Geoffrey Bussell Masefield, DSc and of Mildred Joy Thorold Masefield (*née* Rogers); *m* 1962,

Jennifer Mary, MBE, *d* of late Rev. Dr H. C. Trowell, OBE and late K. M. Trowell, MBE; two *s* one *d* (and one *d* decd). *Educ:* Dragon Sch., Oxford; Repton Sch.; St John's Coll., Cambridge (Scholar) (MA). Joined CRO, 1962; Private Sec. to Permanent Under Sec., 1963–64; Second Secretary: Kuala Lumpur, 1964–65; Warsaw, 1966–67; FCO, 1967–69; First Sec., UK Delegn to Disarmament Conf., 1970–74; Dep. Head, Policy Planning Staff, FCO, 1974–77; Far Eastern Dept, FCO, 1977–79; Counsellor, Head of Chancery and Consul Gen., Islamabad, 1979–82; Head of Personnel Services Dept, FCO, 1982–85; Head, Far Eastern Dept, FCO, 1985–87; Fellow, Center for Internat. Affairs, Harvard Univ., 1987–88; seconded to CSSB, 1988–89; High Comr, Tanzania, 1989–92; Asst Under-Sec. of State, FCO, 1992–94; High Comr, Nigeria, also concurrently Ambassador (non-resident) to the Republics of Benin and of Chad, 1994–97. Dep. Chm., Bermuda Soc., 2006–07. Mem., Brockenhurst Parish Council, 2005– (Vice-Chm., 2006–07; Chm., 2007–). KStJ 1997. *Publication:* article in International Affairs. *Recreations:* fruit and vegetables. *Club:* Brockenhurst Probus.

MASERI, Attilio, MD; FRCP; FACC; President, Heart Care Foundation ONLUS; *b* 12 Nov. 1935; *s* of Adriano and Antonietta Albini, Italian nobles; *m* 1960, Countess Francesca Maseri Florio di Santo Stefano (*d* 2000); one *s*. *Educ:* Classic Lycée Cividale, Italy; Padua Univ. Med. Sch. Special bds in Cardiology, 1963, in Nuclear Medicine, 1965, Italy. Research fellow: Univ. of Pisa, 1960–65; Columbia Univ., NY, 1965–66; Johns Hopkins Univ., Baltimore, 1966–67; University of Pisa: Asst Prof., 1967–70; Prof. of Internal Medicine, 1970; Prof. of Cardiovascular Pathophysiology, 1972–79; Prof. of Medicine (Locum), 1977–79; Sir John McMichael Prof. of Cardiovascular Medicine, RPMS, Univ. of London, 1979–91; Prof. of Cardiology, and Dir, Inst. of Cardiology, Catholic Univ. of Rome, 1991–2001; Prof. of Cardiology and Dir, Cardiovascular and Thoracic Dept, Vita-Salute San Raffaele Univ., Milan, 2001–08. King Faisal Prize for Medicine, 1992; Dist. Scientist Award, Amer. Coll. of Cardiology, 1997; Grand Prix Scientifique, Inst de France, 2004. Chevalier d'honneur et devotion, SMO Malta. *Publications:* Myocardial Blood Flow in Man, 1972; Primary and Secondary Angina, 1977; Perspectives on Coronary Care, 1979; Ischemic Heart Disease: a rational basis for clinical practise and clinical research, 1995; articles in major internat. cardiological and med. jls. *Recreations:* ski-ing, snowboarding, windsurfing, tennis, sailing. *Address:* Heart Care Foundation ONLUS, Via La Marmora 36, 50121 Florence, Italy. *Club:* Queen's.

MASHAM, Lord; Mark William Philip Cunliffe-Lister; *b* 15 Sept. 1970; *s* and *heir* of Earl of Swinton, *qv*; *m* 2000, Felicity Shadbolt.

MASHAM OF ILTON, Baroness *cr* 1970 (Life Peer); **Susan Lilian Primrose Cunliffe-Lister, (Susan, Countess of Swinton);** DL; *b* 14 April 1935; *d* of Sir Ronald Sinclair, 8th Bt and Reba Blair (who *m* 2nd, 1957, Lt-Col H. R. Hildreth, MBE; she *d* 1985), *d* of Anthony Inglis, MD; *m* 1959, Lord Masham (later 2nd Earl of Swinton) (*d* 2006); one *s* one *d* (both adopted). *Educ:* Heathfield School, Ascot; London Polytechnic. Has made career in voluntary social work. Mem., Peterlee and Newton Aycliffe New Town Corp., 1973–85. Mem., Select Cttee on Sci. and Technol., 1997–. All-Party Parliamentary Committees: Vice-Chairman: Drug Misuse, 1984–; AIDS, 1988–; Member: Disablement, 1970–; Penal Affairs, 1975–; Member, All-Party Parliamentary Groups on: Children, 1982–; Breast Cancer, 1993–; Skin, 1994–; Epilepsy, 1994–; Primary Care and Public Health, 1998–; British Council Associate Parly Gp, 1999–; Associate Parly Health Gp (formerly Forum), 2001–. President: N Yorks Red Cross, 1963–88 (Patron, 1989–); Yorks Assoc. for the Disabled, 1963–98; Spinal Injuries Assoc., 1982–; Chartered Soc. of Physiotherapy, 1975–82; Papworth and Enham Village Settlements, 1973–85; Registration Council of Scientists in Health Care, 1991–; Countrywide Workshops Charitable Trust, 1993–97; Vice-President: British Sports Assoc. for the Disabled; Disabled Drivers Assoc.; Assoc. of Occupnl Therapists; Action for Dysphasic Adults; Hosp. Saving Assoc.; Chairman: Bd of Dirs, Phoenix House (Drug Rehabilitation), 1986–92 (Patron, 1992–); Home Office Working Gp on Young People and Alcohol, 1987; Member: Yorks RHA, 1982–90; N Yorks FHSA, 1990–95; Bd of Visitors, Wetherby Young Offenders Instn (formerly Wetherby Youth Custody Centre), 1963–94; Winston Churchill Meml Trust, 1980–2007; Council, London Lighthouse, 1991–98; Trustee, Spinal Res. Trust; Patron many orgns in area of health and disability, including: Disablement Income Gp; Yorks Faculty of GPs; Mem. and Governor, Ditchley Foundn, 1980–; former Mem., Volunteer Centre. Freedom, Borough of Harrogate, 1989. DL North Yorks, 1991. Hon. FRCGP 1981; Hon. FCSP 1996; Hon. Fellow, Bradford and Ilkley Community Coll., 1988. Hon. MA Open, 1981; DUniv York, 1985; Hon. LLD: Leeds, 1988; Teesside, 1993; Hon. DSc Ulster, 1990; Hon. DLitt Keele, 1993; Hon. DCL UEA, 2001. *Publication:* The World Walks By, 1986. *Recreations:* breeding highland ponies, swimming, table tennis, fishing, flower decoration, gardening. *Address:* Dykes Hill House, Masham, near Ripon, N Yorks HG4 4NS. *T:* (01765) 689241; 46 Westminster Gardens, Marsham Street, SW1P 4JG. *T:* (020) 7834 0700.

MASHELKAR, Raghunath Anant, PhD; FRS 1998; Council of Scientific & Industrial Research Bhatnagar Fellow, India, since 2007; *b* 1 Jan. 1943; *s* of late Anant Tukaram Mashelkar and Anjani Anant Mashelkar; *m* 1970, Vaishali R. Mashelkar; one *s* two *d*. *Educ:* Univ. of Bombay (BChemEngrg 1966; PhD 1969). Sen. Scientist, 1976–86, Dir, 1989–95, Nat. Chemical Lab., Pune; Dir Gen., Council of Scientific and Industrial Res., and Sec., Dept of Scientific and Industrial Res., India, 1995–2006. Pres., Indian Sci. Congress, 1999–2000. Fellow: Indian Acad. of Scis, 1983 (Vice Pres., 1995–97); Indian Nat. Sci. Acad., 1984 (Viswakarma Medal, 1988); Maharashtra Acad. of Scis, 1985 (Pres., 1991–94); Third World Acad. of Scis, 1994. Hon. DSc: Salford, 1993; Kanpur, 1995; Delhi, 1998; Guwahati Anna (Chennai), Pretoria, 2000; London, 2001; Wisconsin, 2002; Allahabad, 2002; Varanasi, 2002; Baroda, 2003; Kalyani, 2004; Narendra Deva, Faizabad, 2004; Govind Ballabh Pant, Pantnagar, 2004; Maharishi Dayanand, Rohtak, 2005; Guru Nanak Dev, Amritsar, 2005; Mohanlal Sukhadia, Udaipur, 2006; Lucknow, 2006; Hon. DLit Santiniketan, 2006. Herdillia Award, Indian Inst. of Chem. Engrs, 1982; K. G. Naik Gold Medal, 1985; Republic Day Award, NRDC, 1995; Atur Sangtani Award, Atur Foundn, 1998; Lifetime Achievement Award, Indian Analytical Instruments Assoc., 1998; Shanti Sharup Bhatnagar Medal, INSA, 2001; Nat. Award, Lal Bahadur Shastri Inst. of Mgt for Excellence in Public Admin and Mgt Studies, 2002; Medal of Engrg Excellence, WFEO, 2003; New Millennium Innovation Award, Associated Chambers of Commerce and Industry of India, 2003; Lifetime Achievement Award, 2004, Asutosh Mookherjee Meml Award, 2005, Indian Sci. Congress Assoc.; Stars of Asia Award, Business Week, USA, 2005; TWAS Medal, Acad. of Scis for Developing World (TWAS), 2005; Suryadatta Nat. Award, Suryadatta Gp of Insts, 2006. Padmashri, 1991; Padmabhushan, 2000. *Publications:* (ed jtly) Advances in Transport Processes, vol. 1, 1980, vol. 2, 1982, vol. 3, 1983, vol. 4, 1986, vol. 8, 1992, vol. 9, 1993; (ed jtly and contrib.) Frontiers in Chemical Reaction Engineering, vols 1 and 2, 1984; (ed jtly) Transport Phenomena in Polymeric Systems, vol. 1, 1987, vol. 2, 1989; (ed jtly) Advances in Transport Phenomena in Fluidizing Systems, 1987; (ed jtly) Recent Trends in Chemical Reaction Engineering, vols 1 and 2, 1987; (ed jtly) Reactions and Reaction Engineering, 1987; (ed jtly and contrib.) Heat Transfer Equipment Design, 1988; (ed jtly) Readings in Solid State Chemistry, 1994; (ed jtly and contrib.) Dynamics of Complex Fluids, 1998; (ed jtly and contrib.) Structure and Dynamics in the Mesoscopic Domain, 1999; (jtly) Intellectual

Property and Competitive Strategies in the 21st Century, 2004; numerous articles in jls and contribs to books. *Address:* National Chemical Laboratory, Pune 411008, India. *T:* 25902197, 25902605, *Fax:* 25902607.

MASIRE, Quett Ketumile Joni, Hon. GCMG 1991; Naledi Ya Botswana; President of Botswana, 1980–98; Congo Facilitator, Southern African Development Community, since 1999; *b* 23 July 1925; *m* 1957, Gladys Olebile; three *s* three *d*. *Educ:* Kanye; Tiger Kloof. Founded Seepapitso Secondary School, 1950; reporter, later Dir, African Echo, 1958; Mem., Bangwaketse Tribal Council, Legislative Council (former Mem., Exec. Council); founder Mem., Botswana Democratic Party (Editor, Therisanyo, 1962–67); Member, Legislative Assembly (later National Assembly): Kanye S, 1966–69; Ngwaketse-Kgalagadi, 1974–79; Dep. Prime Minister, 1965–66; Vice-Pres. and Minister of Finance and Development Planning, 1966–80. African Pres. in Residence, Boston Univ., 2006–07. *Publication:* Very Brave or Very Foolish: memoirs of an African diplomat. *Address:* PO Box 70, Gaborone, Botswana. *T:* 353391.

MASKELL, Prof. Duncan John, PhD; Marks and Spencer Professor of Farm Animal Health, Food Science and Food Safety, since 1996, and Head, Department of Veterinary Medicine, since 2004, University of Cambridge; Fellow, Wolfson College, Cambridge, since 1998; *b* 30 May 1961; *s* of Leslie George Maskell and Mary Sheila Horsburgh Maskell; *m* 1992, Dr Sarah Elizabeth Peters; one *s* one *d*. *Educ:* Gonville and Caius Coll., Cambridge (MA, PhD). Res. Scientist, Wellcome Biotech, 1985–88; Res. Fellow, Inst. of Molecular Medicine, John Radcliffe Hosp., Univ. of Oxford, 1988–92; Lectr, Dept of Biochemistry, Imperial Coll., London Univ., 1992–96. Food Standards Agency: Member: Res. Review Gp, 2000–01; Adv. Cttee on Res., 2002–07; Gen. Adv. Cttee on Sci., 2008–. Member: Agri-Food Cttee, 1997–2003 (Chm., 2000–03), Strategy Bd, 2000–03, BBSRC; Council, RCVS, 2004–. Co-founder, Arrow Therapeutics Ltd, 1998; non-exec. Dir, Moredun Res. Inst., 2006–. *Publications:* papers in learned jls on molecular microbiol. and bacterial infectious diseases. *Recreations:* watching cricket, Manchester United, cooking, fine wine, music. *Address:* Department of Veterinary Medicine, University of Cambridge, Madingley Road, Cambridge CB3 0ES. *T:* (01223) 339868.

MASKEY, Alexander; Member (SF) Belfast South, Northern Ireland Assembly, since 2003 (Belfast West, 1998–2003); Lord Mayor of Belfast, 2002–03; *b* 8 Jan. 1952; *s* of Alexander and Teresa Maskey; *m* 1976, Elizabeth McKee; two *s*. *Educ:* Christian Brothers' Primary Sch.; Donegall Street, Belfast; St Malaghy's Coll., Belfast. Mem. (SF), Belfast CC, 1983–. Member: Nat. Cttee, Ard Chomairle, 1994–; NI Forum, 1996–98; NI Policing Bd, 2007–. Contested (SF) Belfast S, 2001, 2005. *Recreations:* photography, reading. *Address:* 178 Ormeau Road, Belfast BT7 2ED.

MASKIN, Prof. Eric Stark, PhD; Albert O. Hirschman Professor of Social Science, Institute for Advanced Study, Princeton, since 2000; *b* New York, 12 Dec. 1950; *s* of Meyer and Bernice Rabkin Maskin; *m* 1983, Dr Gayle Sawtelle; one *s* one *d*. *Educ:* Harvard Univ. (AB Maths 1972; AM Applied Maths 1974; PhD 1976). Res. Fellow, Jesus Coll., Cambridge, 1976–77; Prof., MIT, 1981–84; Prof., 1985–2000, Louis Berkman Prof. of Econs, 1997–2000, Harvard Univ. Guggenheim Fellow, 1980–81; Sloan Res. Fellow, 1983–85. Lectures: Churchill, Cambridge Univ., 1994; Arrow, Stanford Univ., 1998; Schwartz, Northwestern Univ., 2002; Toulouse, Univ. of Toulouse, 2004; Zeuthen, Univ. of Copenhagen, 2004; Marshall, Cambridge Univ., 2007; Klein, Univ. of Penn, 2007. Fellow: Econometric Soc., 1981 (Pres., 2003); Amer. Acad. of Arts and Scis, 1994. Corresp. FBA 2003. Hon. Fellow, St John's Coll., Cambridge, 2004. Mem., NAS, 2008. Hon. MA Cantab, 1977; Hon. DHL Bard Coll., 2008; Dhc Corvinus Univ. of Budapest, 2008. Galbraith Teaching Prize, Harvard Univ., 1990, 1992; Nobel Prize in Econs, 2007; Erik Kempe Award, Kempe Foundn, 2007. *Publications:* contrib. learned jls incl. Rev. of Econ. Studies, Qly Jl of Econs, Econometrica, Jl of Political Economy. *Recreation:* music. *Address:* Institute for Advanced Study, Einstein Drive, Princeton, NJ 08540, USA. *T:* (609) 7348309, *Fax:* (609) 9514457; *e-mail:* maskin@ias.edu.

MASLIN, David Michael E.; see Eckersley-Maslin.

MASLIN, Prof. Mark Andrew, PhD; Professor of Physical Geography, since 2006, Director, Environment Institute, since 2006, and Head, Department of Geography, since 2007, University College London; *b* London, 14 March 1968; *s* of Christopher Alan and Catherine Anne Maslin; *m* 1998, Johanna Lucy Andrews; two *d*. *Educ:* Univ. of Bristol (BSc 1st Cl. Hons); Darwin Coll., Cambridge (PhD 1993). Res. Scientist, Kiel Univ., 1993–95; Lectr in Geog., 1995–2002, Reader in Geog., 2002–06, UCL. Exec. Dir, UCL Carbon Auditors Ltd, 2007–. Trustee and co-Dir, TippingPoint: Art and Climate Change, 2006–. *Publications:* Restless Planet (series): Floods (with Emma Durham), 1999, Storms, 1999, Earthquakes, 1999; Global Warming, 2002, 2nd edn 2007; The Coming Storm, 2002; Global Warming: a very short introduction, 2004, 2nd edn 2008; over 90 articles in jls incl. Science, Nature, Paleoceanography and Geology. *Recreation:* travel. *Address:* UCL Environment Institute, Pearson Building, Gower Street, University College London, WC1E 6BT. *T:* (020) 7679 2000; *e-mail:* mmaslin@geog.ucl.ac.uk.

MASOJADA, Bronislaw Edmund, (Bronek); Chief Executive Officer, Hiscox Ltd, since 2006; *b* 31 Dec. 1961; *s* of Milek Edmund Masojada and Shirley Mary Masojada (*née* Johnston); *m* 1986, Jane Elizabeth Ann Lamont; three *s* two *d*. *Educ:* Univ. of Natal, SA (BSc Civil Engrg 1982; MPhil Mgt Studies 1987); Trinity Coll., Oxford (Rhodes Schol. 1985). Nat. Service, Engrg Corps, S African Army, 1983–84. McKinsey & Co., Sydney, London and Tokyo: Jun. Associate, then Associate, 1989–91; Engagement Manager, 1992–93; Managing Director: Hiscox Gp, 1993–95; Hiscox plc, 1996–2006. Dir, Xchanging Insure Services, 2003–06. Dep. Chm. Council, Lloyd's, 2001–07; Lloyd's Underwriting Agents Association: Mem. Cttee, 1993–98; Chm., 2000–01; Mem., Cttee, Lloyd's Mkt Assoc., 2000–01. Dep. Pres., 2003–04, Pres., 2004–05, Insce Inst. of London. Trustee, Lloyd's Tercentenary Fund, 2007–. *Recreations:* kite surfing, ski-ing. *Address:* Hiscox Ltd, 45 Reid Street, Hamilton HM12, Bermuda. *T:* 2788300, *Fax:* 2788301; *e-mail:* bronek.masojada@hiscox.com. *Club:* Stormriders Kiteboarding.

MASON, family name of **Baron Mason of Barnsley.**

MASON OF BARNSLEY, Baron *cr* 1987 (Life Peer), of Barnsley in South Yorkshire; **Roy Mason;** PC 1968; DL; *b* 18 April 1924; *s* of Joseph and Mary Mason; *m* 1945, Marjorie, *d* of Ernest Sowden; two *d*. *Educ:* Carlton Junior Sch.; Royston Senior Sch.; London Sch. of Economics (TUC Scholarship). Went underground at 14 years of age, 1938–53; NUM branch official, 1947–53; mem. Yorks Miners' Council, 1949. MP (Lab): Barnsley, March 1953–1983; Barnsley Central, 1983–87. Labour party spokesman on Defence and Post Office affairs, 1960–64; Minister of State (Shipping), Bd of Trade, 1964–67; Minister of Defence (Equipment), 1967–April 1968; Postmaster-Gen., April–June 1968; Minister of Power, 1968–69; President, Bd of Trade, 1969–70; Labour party spokesman on Civil Aviation, Shipping, Tourism, Films and Trade matters, 1970–74; Secretary of State for: Defence, 1974–76; Northern Ireland, 1976–79; opposition spokesman on agriculture, fisheries and food, 1979–81. Mem., Council of Europe and WEU, 1973. Chm., Yorkshire Gp of Labour MPs, 1972–74; Chm., Miners

Gp of MPs, 1974, Vice-Chm., 1980. Chairman: Prince's Trust, S Yorks, 1985–; Barnsley Business and Innovation Centre, 1990–. DL South Yorks, 1992. DUniv Sheffield Hallam, 1993; Hon. DCL Northumbria, 2005. *Recreations:* work, provided one stays on top of it, fly-fishing, cravatology (tie-designing). *Address:* 12 Victoria Avenue, Barnsley, S Yorks S70 2BH. *Club:* Lords and Commons Fly-Fishing (founder, and Pres., 1983–).

MASON, Alastair Michael Stuart, FRCP; Chairman, SSL Ltd, 1996–2003; Partner, Partners in Care, 1996–2003; *b* 4 March 1944; *s* of late Adair Stuart and of Rosemary Mason; *m* 1967 (marr. diss. 2006); two *s* two *d. Educ:* Downside Sch.; London Hosp., London Univ. MB BS. MRCP, FRCP 1993; MRCS; FFPH (FFPHM 1991). Hosp. junior appts, 1967–73; Sen. Medical Officer, Dept of Health, 1974–84; Sen. Manager, Arthur Andersen & Co., 1984–88; RMO, S Western RHA, 1988–94. *Publications:* (ed) Walk don't run, 1985; Information for Action, 1988. *Recreations:* walking, reading, theatre. *Address:* 5 The Cobblers Close, Gotherington, Glos GL52 9HF.

MASON, Hon. Sir Anthony (Frank), AC 1988; KBE 1972 (CBE 1969); Chancellor, University of New South Wales, 1994–99; Chief Justice, High Court of Australia, 1987–95; *b* Sydney, 21 April 1925; *s* of F. M. Mason; *m* 1950, Patricia Mary, *d* of Dr E. N. McQueen; two *s. Educ:* Sydney Grammar Sch.; Univ. of Sydney (BA, LLB). RAAF Flying Officer, 1944–45. Admitted to NSW Bar, 1951; QC 1964. Commonwealth Solicitor-General, 1964–69; Judge, Court of Appeal, Supreme Court of NSW, 1969–72; Justice, High Court of Australia, 1972–87; Judge, Supreme Court of Fiji, 1995–2000; Non-permanent Judge, HK Court of Final Appeal, 1997–; Pres., Solomon Islands Court of Appeal, 1997–99. Mem., Permanent Court of Arbitration, 1987–99. Mem., Panel of Arbitrators and Advrs, INTELSAT, 1965–69; Presiding Arbitrator, Internat. Centre for Settlement of Investment Disputes (dispute under N Amer. Free Trade Agreement), 1999–2001. Nat. Fellow, Res. Sch. of Social Scis, ANU, 1995–99 (Dist. Vis. Fellow, 2000–); Arthur Goodhart Prof. in Legal Sci., and Vis. Fellow, Gonville and Caius Coll., Cambridge, 1996–97. Vice-Chm., UN Commn on Internat. Trade Law, 1968. Chairman: Nat. Liby of Australia, 1995–98; Adv. Bd, Nat. Inst. for Law, Ethics and Public Affairs, Griffith Univ., 1995–99; Member: Council of Management, British Inst. of Internat. and Comparative Law, 1987–98; Council, ANU, 1969–72; Pro-Chancellor, ANU, 1972–75. Mem., Amer. Law Inst., 1995. FASSA 1989. Hon. Bencher, Lincoln's Inn, 1987. Hon. LLD: ANU, 1980; Sydney, 1988; Melbourne, 1992; Monash, 1995; Griffith, 1995; Deakin, 1995; NSW, 2000; Hong Kong 2005; Hon. DCL Oxford, 1993. *Recreations:* gardening, tennis, swimming. *Address:* 1 Castlereagh Street, Sydney, NSW 2000, Australia.

MASON, Sir (Basil) John, Kt 1979; CB 1973; FRS 1965; DSc (London); Director-General of the Meteorological Office, 1965–83; Chancellor, University of Manchester Institute of Science and Technology, 1994–96 (President, 1986–94); *b* 18 Aug. 1923; *s* of late John Robert and Olive Mason, Docking, Norfolk; *m* 1948, Doreen Sheila Jones; two *s. Educ:* Fakenham Grammar Sch.; University Coll., Nottingham. Commissioned, Radar Branch RAF, 1944–46. BSc 1st Cl. Hons Physics (London), 1947, MSc 1948; DSc (London) 1956. Shirley Res. Fellow, Univ. of Nottingham, 1947; Asst Lectr in Meteorology, 1948, Lectr, 1949, Imperial Coll.; Warren Res. Fellow, Royal Society, 1957; Vis. Prof. of Meteorology, Univ. of Calif, 1959–60; Prof. of Cloud Physics, Imperial Coll. of Science and Technology (Univ. of London), 1961–65. Dir, Royal Soc. prog. on Acidification of Surface Waters, 1983–90; Sen. Advr, Centre for Envmtl Technol. (formerly Global Envt Res. Centre), Imperial Coll., 1990–2000; Chairman: WMO/ICSU Scientific Cttee, World Climate Res. Prog., 1984–88; Co-ordinating Cttee, Marine Science and Technol., 1988–91. Hon. Gen. Sec. British Assoc., 1965–70; President: Physics Section, British Assoc., 1965; Inst. of Physics, 1976–78; BAAS, 1982–83; Nat. Soc. for Clean Air, 1989–91; Assoc. for Science Educn, 1992; Pres., 1968–70, Hon. Mem., 1985, Royal Meteorol. Soc.; Sen. Vice-Pres., 1976–86, and Treasurer, 1976–86, Royal Soc.; Pres., Soc. of Envmtl Engrs, 1999–2003. UK Perm. Rep., World Meteorological Orgn, 1965–83 (Mem. Exec. Cttee, 1966–75 and 1977–83). Member: ABRC, 1983–87; Astronomy, Space Radio Bd, SERC, 1981–85. Chm. Council, 1970–75, Pro-Chancellor, 1979–85, Surrey Univ. Lectures: James Forrest, ICE, 1967 and 1993; Kelvin, IEE, 1968; Dalton, RIC, 1968; Bakerian, Royal Soc., 1971; Hugh MacMillan, IES, 1975; Symons, Royal Meteorol. Soc., 1976; Halley, Oxford, 1977; Jesse Boot, Nottingham, 1987; Rutherford, Royal Soc., Larmor, Cambridge and Belfast, Linacre, Oxford, H. L. Welch, Toronto, and Cockcroft, Manchester, 1990; Loretto, Edinburgh, 1993; Sir Henry Tizard, Westminster Sch., 1999. Mem., Academia Europaea, 1989; Hon. Mem., Amer. Meteorol Soc., 1988; Foreign Mem., Norwegian Acad. of Sci. and Letters, 1993. Hon. Fellow: Imperial Coll. of Science and Technology, 1974; UMIST, 1979; Hon. FInstP, 2009. Hon. DSc: Nottingham, 1966; Durham, 1970; Strathclyde, 1975; City, 1980; Sussex, 1983; Plymouth Polytechnic, 1990; Heriot-Watt Univ., 1991; UMIST, 1994; Reading, 1998; Hon. ScD East Anglia, 1988. Hugh Robert Mill Medal, Royal Meteorol. Soc., 1959; Charles Chree Medal and Prize, Inst. Physics and Phys. Soc., 1965; Rumford Medal, Royal Soc., 1972; Glazebrook Medal, Inst. Physics, 1974; Symons Meml Gold Medal, Royal Meteorol. Soc., 1975; Royal Medal, Royal Soc., 1991. *Publications:* The Physics of Clouds, 1957, 2nd edn 1971; Clouds, Rain and Rain-Making, 1962, 2nd edn 1975; The Surface Waters Acidification Programme, 1990; Acid Rain, 1992; more than 250 papers in physics and meteorological journals. *Recreations:* foreign travel, music, gardening. *Address:* 64 Christchurch Road, East Sheen, SW14 7AW.

MASON, Benedict; composer, sound artist and film maker. *Educ:* King's Coll., Cambridge (schol.; MA); Royal Coll. of Art (MA). Guido d'Arezzo, 1988; John Clementi Collard Fellowship, 1989; Fulbright Fellow, 1990; Deutsche Akademischer Austauschdienst Künstlerprogramm, Berlin, 1994. *Compositions* include: Hinterstoisser Traverse, 1986; 1st String Quartet, 1987; Lighthouses of England and Wales, 1987 (Britten Prize, 1988); Oil and Petrol Marks on a Wet Road are sometimes held to be Spots where a Rainbow Stood, 1987; Horn Trio, 1987; Six Piano Etudes, 1988; Chaplin Operas, 1989; Sapere Aude for Eighteenth Century Period Instrument Orchestra, 1989; Dreams that do what they're told, 1990; Concerto for the Viola Section accompanied by the Rest of the Orchestra, 1990; Nodding Trilliums and Curve-lined Angles, 1990; Self Referential Songs and Realistic Virelais, 1990; Rilke Songs, 1991; Animals and the Origins of the Dance, 1992; Quantized Quantz, 1992; !, 1992; Colour and Information, 1993; 2nd String Quartet, 1993; Playing Away: an opera about Germany, Opera, Pop Music and Football, 1994. *Sound/theatre installations:* Ohne Missbrauch der Aufmerksamkeit, 1993; Second Music for a European Concert Hall: Ensemble Modern/Freiburg Barockorchester/Benoît Régent/Mozartsaal, 1994; third music for a european concert hall (espro: eic: i love my life), 1994; Clarinet Concerto, 1995; ASKO/PARADISO: the Fifth Music. Résumé with C. P. E. Bach, 1995; Schumann-Auftrag: Live Hörspiel ohne Worte, 1996; SEVENTH. (for David Alberman and Rolf Hind) PIANO.WITH.VIOLIN.TO.TOUR.ALL. HALLS.MUSIC, 1996; Carré, Nederlands Kamerkoor, Schoenberg Ensemble, Eighth Music for a European Concert Hall (First Music for a Theatre), 1996; Steep Ascent within and away from a Non European Concert Hall: Six Horns, Three Trombones and a Decorated Shed, 1996; Trumpet Concerto, 1997; The Four Slopes of Twice among Gliders of her Gravity (two Steinway model D pianos, two Ampico player pianos and one human being), 1997; Szene für Jean Nouvel (drei Frauenstimmen, drei Spiegelstimmen, Orch., Sampler und Film), 1998. Solo exhibn, gastronomic amorous gymnastic etc music, Berlin, 1997. *Films:* Horn, 1980; Doppler Between, 1983; Resonating Toner, 1985; all stages, 1987; Leading Articles, 1990; Reassurance, 1991; Disclaimer, 1995. Ernst von Siemens Prize, 1992; Paul Fromm Award, 1995; Britten Award, 1996. *Publication:* outside sight unseen and opened, 2nd edn, 2002. *Recreation:* litigation.

MASON, Colin Rees, OBE 2003; TD 1982; Managing Director, Chiltern Broadcast Management (trading name of Aurora World Ltd), since 1997; Vice Lord-Lieutenant for Bedfordshire, since 2005; *b* 19 Aug. 1943; *s* of Clifford Harold Mason and Ann Mason (*née* Jones); *m* 1968, Grace Angela St Helier Tweney; one *s* one *d. Educ:* Gwent Coll., Newport; UCW, Aberystwyth (BA Hons); Magdalene Coll., Cambridge (MPhil); Harvard Grad. Sch. of Business (OPM). Producer, BBC, 1969–74; Prog. Dir, Swansea Sound, 1974–80; Asst Man. Dir, Standard Broadcasting, 1980–82; Man. Dir, Chiltern Radio plc, 1981–95; Dep. Chm., Choice FM, 1995–2004. Dir, Alderney Broadcasting Corp. Ltd, 2003–. Royal Welsh Regt (formerly Royal Regt of Wales), TA: Lt Col 1984, Col 2000; CO, Pool of Public Information Officers, 1990–93; served Saudi Arabia, Kuwait, 1991, Kosovo, 1999–2000, Sierra Leone, Macedonia, 2001, Afghanistan, 2002, Iraq, 2003; Co. Comdt, 2000–04; Hon. Col, 15 (UK) Psychol Ops Gp, 2004–. High Sheriff, 2002–03, DL 2002, Beds. *Recreations:* travel, ski-ing. *Address:* c/o Coutts Bank, 440 Strand, WC2R 0QS; *e-mail:* masonradio@aol.com. *Clubs:* Army and Navy, Reform.

MASON, David Arthur; Director of Social Services, Warwickshire County Council, 1991–97; *b* 13 May 1946; *s* of Arthur J. Mason and Vera M. Mason. *Educ:* Birmingham Polytechnic (Cert. Social Work, 1970); Univ. of Aston in Birmingham (MSc Public Sector Management, 1981). Social worker, 1966–70; Sen. Social worker, Hounslow, 1970–72; Unit Organiser, Birmingham Family Service Unit, 1972–75; Area Man., Birmingham, 1975–81; Divl Dir of Social Services, Warwickshire, 1981–84; Director of Social Services: Knowsley, 1985–87; Liverpool CC, 1987–91.

MASON, Sir David (Kean), Kt 1992; CBE 1987; BDS, MD; FRCSGlas, FDSRCPS Glas, FDSRCSE, FRCPath; FRSE; Professor of Oral Medicine and Head of the Department of Oral Medicine and Pathology, University of Glasgow Dental School, 1967–92, now Professor Emeritus; Dean of Dental Education, University of Glasgow, 1980–90; *b* 5 Nov. 1928; *s* of George Hunter Mason and Margaret Kean; *m* 1967, Judith Anne Armstrong; two *s* one *d. Educ:* Paisley Grammar Sch.; Glasgow Acad.; St Andrews Univ. (LDS 1951, BDS 1952); Glasgow Univ. (MB, ChB 1962, MD (Commendation) 1967). FDSRCSE 1957; FDSRCPS Glas 1967 (Hon. FDSRCPS Glas 1990); FRCSGlas 1973; FRCPath 1976 (MRCPath 1967); FRSE 1999. Served RAF, Dental Br., 1952–54. Registrar in Oral Surgery, Dundee, 1954–56; gen. dental practice, 1956–62; Vis. Dental Surgeon, Glasgow Dental Hosp., 1956–62, Sen. Registrar 1962–64; Sen. Lectr in Dental Surgery and Pathology, Univ. of Glasgow, 1964–67; Hon. Consultant Dental Surgeon, Glasgow, 1964–67. Chm., National Dental Consultative Cttee, 1976–80 and 1983–87; Member: Medicines Commn, 1976–80; Dental Cttee, MRC, 1973–80; Physiol Systems Bd, MRC, 1976–80; Jt MRC/Health Depts/SERC Dental Cttee, 1984–87; GDC, 1976–94 (Mem., Disciplinary Cttee, 1980–85; Health Cttee, 1985–89; Pres., 1989–94); Dental Cttee, UGC, 1977–87 (Chm., 1983–87); Supervised Trng Gp, UGC, 1984–86; Dental Rev. Wkg Party, UGC, 1986–87; Jt Cttee for Higher Trng in Dentistry, 1977–84; Dental Strategy Rev. Gp, 1980–81; Scientific Prog. Cttee, FDI, 1980–87; Consultant to Commn on Dental Res., FDI, 1973–80. President: W of Scotland Br., BDA, 1983–84; British Soc. for Dental Res., 1984–86; British Soc. for Oral Medicine, 1984–86; GDC, 1989–94; Convener, Dental Council, RCPGlas, 1977–80. Lectures: Charles Tomes, RCS, 1975; Holme, UCH, London, 1977; Caldwell Meml, Univ. of Glasgow, 1983; Evelyn Sprawson, London Hosp. Med. Coll., 1984. Hon. Member: BDA, 1993; Amer. Dental Assoc., 1994. Hon. FFDRCSI 1988; Hon. FRCSE 1995; Hon. FDSRCS 2002. Hon. DDS Wales, 1991; Hon. LLD Dundee, 1993; Hon. DSc Western Ontario, 1997; DUniv Glasgow, 1998. John Tomes Prize, RCS, 1979; Colyer Medal, RCS, 1992. *Publications:* (jtly) Salivary Glands in Health and Disease, 1975; (jtly) Introduction to Oral Medicine, 1978; (jtly) Self Assessment: Manual I, Oral Surgery, 1978; Manual II, Oral Medicine, 1978; (ed jtly) Oral Manifestations of Systemic Disease, 1980, 2nd edn 1990; (jtly) World Workshop on Oral Medicine, 3 vols, 1988, 1993, 1999. *Recreations:* golf, tennis, gardening, enjoying the pleasures of the countryside. *Address:* Cherry Tree Cottage, Houston Road, Kilmacolm, Renfrewshire PA13 4NY. *Clubs:* Royal & Ancient Golf, Elie Golf House, Kilmacolm Golf; Western (Glasgow).

MASON, Frances Jane G.; *see* Gumley-Mason.

MASON, His Honour (George Frederick) Peter; QC 1963; FCIArb 1986; a Circuit Judge, 1970–87; *b* 11 Dec. 1921; *s* of George Samuel and Florence May Mason, Keighley, Yorks; *m* 1st, 1950 (marr. diss. 1977); two *s* two *d* (and one *d* decd); 2nd, 1981, Sara, *er d* of Sir Robert Ricketts, 7th Bt. *Educ:* Lancaster Royal Grammar Sch.; St Catharine's Coll., Cambridge. Open Exhibnr St Catharine's Coll., 1940. Served with 78th Medium Regt RA (Duke of Lancaster's Own Yeo.) in Middle East and Italy, 1941–45, latterly as Staff Capt. RA, HQ 13 Corps. History Tripos Pt 1, 1st cl. hons with distinction, 1946; called to Bar, Lincoln's Inn, 1947; MA 1948; Cholmeley Schol., 1949. Asst Recorder of Huddersfield, 1961; Dep. Chairman: Agricultural Land Tribunal, W Yorks and Lancs, 1962; West Riding of Yorks Quarter Sessions, 1965–67; Recorder of York, 1965–67; Dep. Chm., Inner London QS, 1970; Dep. Chm., NE London QS, 1970–71; Senior Judge: Snaresbrook Crown Ct, 1974–81; CCC, 1982; Inner London Crown Court, 1983–87. Member: Council, Assoc. of Futures Brokers and Dealers, 1987–91; London Court of Internat. Arbitration, 1990–2000; Bd, Securities and Futures Authy, 1991–93; Amer. Arbitration Assoc., 1992–2002; Bd, Internat. Petroleum Exchange, 1993–98; Special Cttee, London Metal Exchange, 1995–2006. Freeman, City of London, 1977. Liveryman, Wax Chandlers' Co., 1980–. *Publication:* Next Please: a judge's daybook, 2001. *Recreations:* reflection, survival. *Address:* Lane Cottage, Amberley, Glos GL5 5AB. *T:* (01453) 872412, *Fax:* (01453) 878557; *e-mail:* peter@masonamberley.co.uk. *Clubs:* Athenæum; Hawks (Cambridge).

MASON, Sir Gordon (Charles), Kt 1993; OBE 1982; JP; *b* 8 Nov. 1921; *s* of Joseph Henry Mason and May Louisa Mason; *m* 1944, Tui Audrey King; two *s* one *d. Educ:* Kaipara Flats. In local government, New Zealand, 1960–92: Dep. Chm., 1965–72, Co. Chm., 1972–89; Mayor, Rodney DC, 1989–92. Chm., Local Govt Trng Bd, 1981–89; Pres., NZ Counties Assoc., 1984–87. Past Master: Rodney Masonic Lodge; Rotary; Lions. JP NZ, 1968. *Recreations:* travel, gardening. *Address:* 40 Alnwick Street, Warkworth, New Zealand. *T:* (9) 4258878. *Clubs:* Bowling (NZ); RSA (Warkworth, NZ).

MASON, (James) Stephen, CB 1988; Counsel to the Speaker, House of Commons, 1994–2000; *b* 6 Feb. 1935; *s* of Albert Wesley Mason and Mabel (*née* Topham); *m* 1961, Tania Jane Moeran (*see* T. J. Mason); one *s* two *d. Educ:* Windsor County Grammar Sch.; Univ. of Oxford (MA, BCL). Called to the Bar, Middle Temple, 1958; in practice, 1961–67; Office of Parly Counsel, 1967–94: Parly Counsel, 1980–94. *Recreations:* reading, playing the piano, compulsory gardening. *Address:* Amberley House, Church Street, Amberley, West Sussex BN18 9NF.

MASON, Jane; *see* Mason, T. J.

MASON, Sir John; *see* Mason, Sir B. J.

MASON, John Fingland; MP (SNP) Glasgow East, since July 2008; *b* 1957. CA 1980. Mem. (SNP), Glasgow CC, 1998–2008 (Leader of the Opposition, 1999–2008). *Address:* House of Commons, SW1A 0AA.

MASON, John Kenneth; Director for Climate Change and Water Industry, and for Environmental Quality, Scottish Government (formerly Scottish Executive), since 2007; *b* 26 June 1956; *s* of Kenneth George Mason and Helen Mary Mason (*née* Green); *m* 1990, Alison Margaret Cruickshanks; one *s* two *d*. *Educ:* Hertford Coll., Oxford (BA Hons Geog. 1978); University Coll. London (MPhil Town Planning 1981). MCIPD 1997. Senior Town Planner: Kent CC, 1980–85; DoE, 1985–87; Principal: DoE, 1988–90; Scottish Office, 1990–94; Dep. Chief Exec., Registers of Scotland, 1994–96; Asst Sec., Enterprise and Industry, Scottish Office, 1996–2000; Prin. Private Sec. to First Minister, Scottish Exec., 2001–02; Under Sec. and Hd, Tourism, Culture and Sport Gp, Scottish Exec. Educn Dept, 2002–05; Under Sec. and Hd, Envmt Gp, Scottish Exec. Envmt and Rural Affairs Dept, subseq., Dir, Scottish Exec. Envmt Gp, 2006–07. Non-executive Director: Scottish Swimming, 2006–; Edinburgh Internat. Film Festival, 2007. *Recreations:* photography, enjoying the best of Scotland. *Address:* Scottish Government, Victoria Quay, Edinburgh EH6 6QQ; *e-mail:* john.mason@scotland.gsi.gov.uk.

MASON, Prof. John Kenyon French, CBE 1973; MD; FRSE; Regius Professor of Forensic Medicine, University of Edinburgh, 1973–85, now Emeritus; *b* 19 Dec. 1919; *s* of late Air Cdre J. M. Mason, CBE, DSC, DFC and late Alma French; *m* 1943, Elizabeth Latham (decd); two *s*. *Educ:* Downside Sch.; Cambridge Univ.; St Bartholomew's Hosp. MD, FRCPath, FRCPE 2002, DMJ, DTM&H; LLD Edinburgh 1987. FRSE 1995. Joined RAF, 1943; Dir of RAF Dept of Aviation and Forensic Pathology, 1956; retd as Group Captain, Consultant in Pathology, 1973. Pres., British Assoc. in Forensic Medicine, 1981–83. Hon. LLD Edinburgh, 2005. L. G. Groves Prize for Aircraft Safety, 1957; R. F. Linton Meml Prize, 1958; James Martin Award for Flight Safety, 1972; Douglas Weightman Safety Award, 1973; Swiney Prize for Jurisprudence, 1978; Lederer Award for Aircraft Safety, 1985. *Publications:* Aviation Accident Pathology, 1962; (ed) Aerospace Pathology, 1973; Forensic Medicine for Lawyers, 1978, 4th edn 2001; (ed) The Pathology of Violent Injury, 1978, 3rd edn as The Pathology of Trauma, 2000; Law and Medical Ethics, 1983, 7th edn 2005; Butterworth's Medico-Legal Encyclopaedia, 1987; Human Life and Medical Practice, 1989; Medico-legal Aspects of Reproduction, 1990, 2nd edn 1998; The Courts and the Doctor, 1990; (ed) Forensic Medicine: an illustrated text, 1993; Legal and Ethical Aspects of Healthcare, 2003; The Troubled Pregnancy, 2007; papers in medical and legal jls. *Address:* 66 Craiglea Drive, Edinburgh EH10 5PF. *Club:* Royal Air Force.

MASON, Sir John (Peter), Kt 1994; CBE 1989; DL; solicitor; Chairman, National Union of Conservative and Unionist Associations, 1992–93 (Vice Chairman, 1989–92); *b* 25 Dec. 1940; *m* Margaret Jehu; one *s* two *d*. *Educ:* Scunthorpe GS. Admitted solicitor, 1964; Sen. Partner, Mason Baggott & Garton, solicitors, Scunthorpe, 1976–. Chairman: Scunthorpe HA, 1981–93; Scunthorpe and Goole Hosps NHS Trust, 1993–2001; N Lincs PCT, 2001–06. Conservative Party: Chm., E Midlands Area, 1985–89; Dep. Chm., Bd of Finance, 1994–; Mem., Nat. Union Exec. Cttee, 1977–98 (Chm., European Cttee, 1989–92). Chm., Humberside ProHelp Gp, 2006–. Board Member: N Lincs Local Strategic Partnership, 2007–; Lincs Wildlife Trust, 2007–. President: Scunthorpe and Dist Choral Soc., 1978–; Scunthorpe and Dist Scouts Assoc., 1989–. DL Lincs, 2006. *Address:* Mason, Baggott & Garton, 13/19 Wells Street, Scunthorpe, N Lincs DN15 6HN.

MASON, Prof. (John) Stanley, PhD; CEng; Principal and Vice-Chancellor, Glasgow Caledonian University, 1993–97 (Principal, Glasgow College of Technology, then Glasgow Polytechnic, 1988–93); *b* 30 Jan. 1934; *s* of George and Grace Mason; *m* Florence; two *s*. *Educ:* Wigan Grammar Sch.; Nottingham Univ. (BSc 1st cl. Hons Mining Engrg 1958); Liverpool Poly. (PhD 1972). With NCB, 1950–54 and 1958–59; Maths Master, Leeds Grammar Sch., 1959–62; Lt, RN, 1963–66 (ME and RNEC, Manadon); Prin. Lectr in Mechanical Engrg, Liverpool Poly., 1966–68; Sen. Res. Fellow, Nottingham Univ., 1968–69; Hd, Fluid Mechanics and Thermodynamics Div., Liverpool Poly., 1969–73; Hd, Sch. of Mechanical Engrg and Dean, Faculties of Engrg and Technol., Thames Poly., 1973–87; Depute Dir, Glasgow Coll., 1987–88. Mem., SERC, 1990–94. Silver Plate, USA Powder and Bulk Solids Conf., 1985. *Publications:* (jtly) Bulk Solids Handling Technology, 1987; numerous papers. *Recreations:* travel, sport.

MASON, Rt Rev. Kenneth Bruce, AM 1984; retired; Chairman, Australian Board of Missions, General Synod of the Anglican Church of Australia, 1983–93; *b* 4 Sept. 1928; *s* of Eric Leslie Mason and Gertrude Irene (*née* Pearce); unmarried. *Educ:* Bathurst High Sch.; Sydney Teachers' Coll.; St John's Theological Coll., Morpeth (ThL 1953); Univ. of Queensland (BA DipDiv 1964). Primary Teacher, 1948–51; deacon, 1953; priest, 1954; Member, Brotherhood of the Good Shepherd, 1954; Parish of: Gilgandra, NSW, 1954–58; Darwin, NT, 1959–61; Alice Springs, NT, 1962; student, Univ. of Qld, 1963–64; resigned from Brotherhood, 1965; Trinity Coll., Melbourne Univ.: Asst Chaplain, 1965; Dean, 1966–67; Bishop of the Northern Territory, 1968–83. Member, Oratory of the Good Shepherd, 1962, Superior, 1981–87. *Recreations:* attending opera, listening to music, walking, railways. *Address:* PO Box 544, Glebe, NSW 2037, Australia. *T:* (2) 95664427; *e-mail:* kmason@ogs.net.

MASON, Rev. Canon Kenneth Staveley; Canon Theologian, Scottish Episcopal Church, 1995–96; Canon of St Mary's Cathedral, Edinburgh, 1989–96, now Canon Emeritus; *b* 1 Nov. 1931; *s* of Rev. William Peter Mason and Anna Hester (*née* Pildrem); *m* 1958, Barbara Thomson; one *s* one *d*. *Educ:* Imperial College of Science, London (BSc, ARCS); BD (ext.) London; Wells Theological Coll. Assistant Curate: St Martin, Kingston upon Hull, 1958; Pocklington, 1961; Vicar of Thornton with Allerthorpe and Melbourne, 1963; Sub-Warden and Librarian, KCL, at St Augustine's Coll., Canterbury, 1969; Dir, Canterbury Sch. of Ministry, 1977, Principal, 1981. Examining Chaplain to Archbp of Canterbury, 1979–91; Six Preacher in Canterbury Cath., 1979–84; Hon. Canon of Canterbury, 1984–89; Principal, Edinburgh Theol Coll., later Dir, Theol Inst., Scottish Episcopal Church, 1989–95. *Publications:* George Herbert, Priest and Poet, 1980; Anglicanism, a Canterbury essay, 1987; Priesthood and Society, 1992; Catholic Tradition and the Ordination of Women, 1993; A Great Joy, 2001. *Recreation:* bird-watching. *Address:* 2 Williamson Close, Ripon HG4 1AZ. *T:* (01765) 607041.

MASON, Prof. Malcolm David, MD; FRCP, FRCR; Cancer Research Wales Professor of Clinical Oncology, Cardiff University (formerly University of Wales College of Medicine), since 1997; *b* 31 May 1956; *s* of Seymour and Marion Mason; *m* 1983, Lee-Anne Isaacs; two *d*. *Educ:* Westminster Sch.; Med. Coll. of St Bartholomew's Hosp. (MB BS 1979; MD 1991). FRCR 1987; FRCP 1997. Lectr in Radiotherapy and Oncol., Inst. of Cancer Res. and Royal Marsden Hosp., 1989–91; Consultant Clinical Oncologist, 1992–96, Hon. Consultant, 1996–, Velindre Hosp., Cardiff. Dir, Wales Cancer Bank, 2004–. Member (pt-time): NRPB, 2000–05; Cttee on Med. Aspects of Radiation in the Envmt, 2003–. *Publications:* (with L. Moffatt) Prostate Cancer: the facts, 2003; numerous contribs to learned jls. *Recreation:* playing the piano music of the great classical masters from Bach to Rachmaninov. *Address:* Velindre Hospital, Whitchurch, Cardiff CF14 2TL. *T:* (029) 2031 6964, *Fax:* (029) 2052 9625; *e-mail:* masonmd@cardiff.ac.uk.

MASON, Dame Monica, DBE 2008 (OBE 2002); Director, Royal Ballet, since 2002 (Principal Répétiteur, 1984–91, Assistant Director, 1991–2002); *b* 6 Sept. 1941; *d* of Richard Mason and Mrs E. Fabian; *m* 1968, Austin Bennett. *Educ:* Johannesburg, SA; Royal Ballet Sch., London. Joined Royal Ballet in Corps de Ballet, 1958; Sen. Principal until 1989; created role of Chosen Maiden in Rite of Spring, 1962; also created roles in: Diversions, Elite Syncopations, Electra, Manon, Romeo and Juliet, Rituals, Adieu, Isadora, The Four Seasons, The Ropes of Time. Assistant to the Principal Choreographer, Royal Ballet, 1980–84. DUniv Surrey, 1996. *Address:* Royal Opera House, Covent Garden, WC2E 9DD.

MASON, Dr Pamela Georgina Walsh, FRCPsych; Vice-Chairman, Taunton and Somerset NHS Trust, 1991–97; Senior Principal Medical Officer (Under Secretary), Department of Health and Social Security, 1979–86, retired; re-employed as Senior Medical Officer, Department of Health, 1986–90; *d* of late Captain George Mason and Marie Louise Walsh; god-daughter and ward of late Captain William Gregory, Hon. Co. of Master Mariners; *m* 1st, 1949, David Paltenghi (*d* 1961); two *s*; 2nd, 1965, Jan Darnley-Smith (*d* 1996). *Educ:* Christ's Hosp. Sch.; Univ. of London, Royal Free Hosp. Sch. of Medicine (MRCS, LRCP, 1949; MB, BS 1950). DPM 1957; MRCPsych 1971. Various appointments at: Royal Free Hosp., 1951–53; Maudsley Hosp. and Bethlem Royal Hosp., 1954–58; Guy's Hosp., 1958–60; Home Office, 1961–71; DHSS, later DoH, 1971–90. Vis. Psychiatrist, Holloway Prison, 1962–67; Adviser: C of E Children's Soc., 1962–; Royal Philanthropic Soc., 1962–; WRAF Health Educn Scheme, 1962–67. Consultant to: Law Commn, 1991–93; Carnegie Inquiry into the Third Age, 1991–92; Nat. Audit Office, 1992–94. Chairman: WHO Working Gp on Youth Advisory Services, 1976; WHO Meeting of Nat. Mental Health Advrs, 1979. Member: Council of Europe Select Cttee of Experts on Alcoholism, 1976–77; Cttee of Experts on Legal Problems in the Medical Field, 1979–80; UK Delegn to UN Commn on Narcotic Drugs, 1980–86; Organising Cttee, World Summit of Ministers of Health on Progs for AIDS Prevention, 1988; Review of Prison Med. Services, 1990. Chm. Appeals Cttee, Somerset Red Cross, 1999–2001. FRSocMed. QHP 1984–87. *Publications:* contribs to various professional jls and Govt pubns. *Recreations:* antiquities, humanities, ballet, films, tennis, seafaring and expeditions. *Address:* Apartment 8, The Elms, Weston Park West, Bath BA1 4AR.

MASON, Paul; Chief Executive Officer, Somerfield Group, since 2006; *b* 14 Feb. 1960; *s* of John and Joan Mason; *m* 1984, Juliet Greenway; three *s*. *Educ:* Univ. of Manchester (BA 1st Cl. Hons). Various posts, Mars GB Ltd, 1982–90; Buying and Logistics Dir, B&Q plc, 1990–94; Dir, Mgt Bd, Asda plc, 1994–99; Chief Operating Officer, 1999–2000, Pres. and CEO, 2000–01, Asda Walmart UK; President: Matalan plc, 2002–04; Levi Strauss & Co. Europe, 2004–06. *Address:* Somerfield plc, Somerfield House, Whitchurch Lane, Bristol BS14 0TJ.

MASON, Prof. Paul James, CB 2003; PhD; FRS 1995; Professor of Meteorology and Director, NCAS Universities Weather and Environment Research Network, University of Reading, 2003–06, now Professor Emeritus; *b* 16 March 1946; *s* of Charles Ernest Edward Mason and Phyllis Mary Mason (*née* Swan); *m* 1968, Elizabeth Mary Slaney; one *s* one *d*. *Educ:* Univ. of Nottingham (BSc Physics 1967); Univ. of Reading (PhD Geophysics 1972). Meteorological Office: SO, 1967–71; SSO, 1971–74; PSO, 1974–79; Head, Meteorological Res. Unit, Cardington, 1979–85; Asst Dir, Boundary Layer Br., 1985–89; Dep. Dir, Physical Res., 1989–91; Chief Scientist, 1991–2002. Vis. Prof., Univ. of Surrey, 1995–. Chm., Global Climate Observing System Steering Cttee, 2001–. Member: Editing Cttee, Qly Jl Meteorology, 1983–88; Editl Bd, Boundary Layer Meteorology, 1988–2000. Royal Meteorological Society: Mem. Council, 1989–90; Vice Pres., 1990–92 and 1994–95; Pres., 1992–94. L. G. Groves Prize for Meteorology, MoD, 1980; Buchan Prize, RMetS, 1986. *Publications:* scientific papers in meteorology and fluid dynamics jls. *Recreations:* walking, exploring the countryside. *Address:* Department of Meteorology, University of Reading, PO Box 243, Reading RG6 6BB. *T:* (0118) 931 8954.

MASON, Peter; *see* Mason, G. F. P.

MASON, Peter Geoffrey, MBE 1946; High Master, Manchester Grammar School, 1962–78; *b* 22 Feb. 1914; *o s* of Harry Mason, Handsworth, Birmingham; *m* 1st, 1939, Mary Evelyn Davison (marr. diss.); three *d*; 2nd, 1978, Elizabeth June Bissell (*d* 1983); 3rd, 1985, Marjorie Payne. *Educ:* King Edward's Sch., Birmingham; Christ's Coll., Cambridge (Scholar). Goldsmith Exhibitioner, 1935; Porson Scholar, 1936; 1st Class, Classical Tripos, Pts 1 and 2, 1935, 1936. Sixth Form Classical Master, Cheltenham Coll., 1936–40, Rugby Sch., 1946–49; Headmaster, Aldenham Sch., 1949–61. War Service, 1940–46: commissioned into Intelligence Corps, 1940; various staff appointments including HQ 21 Army Group; later attached to a dept of the Foreign Office. Member: Advisory Cttee on Education in the Colonies, 1956; ITA Educnl Adv. Council, 1964–69; Council, University of Salford, 1969–87; Council, British Volunteer Programme (Chm., 1966–74); Chairman: Council of Educn for World Citizenship, 1966–83; Reg. Conf. on IVS, 1972–82; (first), Eur. Council of Nat. Assocs of Indep. Schs, 1988–94, Hon. Life Pres., 1994; Hon. Dir of Research, ISCis (formerly ISIS), 1981–. *Publications:* Private Education in the EEC, 1983; Private Education in the USA and Canada, 1985; Private Education in Australia and New Zealand, 1987; Independent Education in Southern Africa, 1990; Independent Education in Western Europe, 1992, 2nd edn 1997; articles and reviews in classical and educational journals. *Recreations:* travel, fly-fishing, walking. *Address:* Leeward, Longborough, Moreton-in-Marsh, Glos GL56 0QR. *T:* and *Fax:* (01451) 830147; *e-mail:* xbf15@dial.pipex.com. *Club:* East India.

MASON, Sir Peter (James), KBE 2002; non-executive Chairman, Thames Water, since 2006; Chief Executive Officer, AMEC plc, 1996–2006; *b* 9 Sept. 1946; *s* of Harvey John Mason and Jenny Mason (*née* Wilson); *m* 1st, 1969, Elizabeth Ann McLaren (marr. diss. 1992); two *s*; 2nd, 1997, Beverly Ann Hunter. *Educ:* Marr Coll., Troon; Univ. of Glasgow (BSc Hons Engrg 1968). Norwest Holst Group Ltd, 1980–92: Man. Dir, Civil Engrg Div., 1980–85; CEO, 1985–92; BICC plc, 1992–96: Dir, 1992–96; CEO, 1992–96, Chm., 1994–96, Balfour Beatty Ltd. Sen. Ind. Dir, BAE Systems plc, 2003–; non-exec. Dir, Acergy, 2006–. Board Mem., UK Trade and Investment (formerly British Trade Internat.), 2000–04; Mem., Olympic Delivery Authy, 2006–. *Recreations:* opera, sailing, gardening. *Address:* c/o Thames Water, Clearwater Court, Vastern Road, Reading RG1 8DB.

MASON, Rt Rev. Peter Ralph; Director of Development, Wycliffe College, Toronto, since 2003; *b* 30 April 1943; *s* of late Ralph Victor Mason and of Dorothy Ida Mullin; *m* 1965, Carmen Ruth Ruddock; one *s* two *d*. *Educ:* McGill Univ., Montreal (BA 1964; BD 1967; MA 1971); Princeton Univ. (DMin 1983). Ordained deacon, 1967, priest, 1968;

Asst Curate, St Matthew's, Montreal, 1967–69; Incumbent, parish of Hemmingford, 1969–71; Rector: St Clement's, Montreal, 1971–74; St Peter's, Montreal, 1975–80; St Paul's, Halifax, NS, 1980–85; Principal, Wycliffe Theol Coll., Univ. of Toronto, 1985–92; Bishop of Ontario, 1992–2002. Hon. DD Montreal Diocesan Theol Coll., 1987; Hon. DD: Trinity Coll., Toronto, 1992; Wycliffe Coll., Toronto, 1994. *Recreations:* golf, sailing, ski-ing, opera. *Address:* Wycliffe College, 5 Hoskin Avenue, Toronto, ON M5S 1H7, Canada; 35 Prinyer's Drive, RR4, Picton, ON KOK 2TO, Canada.

MASON, Philippa; *see* Gregory, P.

MASON, Air Vice-Marshal Richard Anthony, (Tony), CB 1988; CBE 1981; DL; Leverhulme Emeritus Fellow, University of Birmingham, 2002–05; *b* 22 Oct. 1932; *s* of William and Maud Mason; *m* 1956, Margaret Stewart; one *d*. *Educ:* Bradford Grammar Sch.; St Andrews Univ. (MA); London Univ. (MA); DSc Birmingham 1997. Commissioned RAF, 1956; Director of Defence Studies, 1977; Director of Personnel (Ground), 1982; Deputy Air Secretary, 1984; Air Sec., 1985–89; Dir, Centre for Studies in Security and Diplomacy, 1988–2001, Hon. Prof., 1996–, Univ. of Birmingham. Leverhulme Airpower Res. Dir, Foundn for Internat. Security, 1989–94. Advr to H of C Defence Cttee, 2001–06. Hon. Freeman, Bor. of Cheltenham, 2001. DL Glos, 2002. Hon. FRAeS 2006. *Publications:* Air Power in the Next Generation (ed), 1978; Readings in Air Power, 1979; (with M. J. Armitage) Air Power in the Nuclear Age, 1981; The RAF Today and Tomorrow, 1982; British Air Power in the 1980s, 1984; The Soviet Air Forces, 1986; War in the Third Dimension, 1986; Air Power and Technology, 1986; To Inherit the Skies, 1990; Air Power: a centennial appraisal, 1994; Air and Space Power: revised roles and technology, 1998; articles in internat. jls on defence policy and strategy. *Recreations:* Rugby, writing, gardening. *Address:* c/o Lloyds TSB, Montpelier Walk, Cheltenham GL50 1SH. *Club:* Royal Air Force.

MASON, Prof. Sir Ronald, KCB 1980; FRS 1975; Professor of Chemistry, University of Sussex, 1971–86 (Pro-Vice-Chancellor, 1977); Chairman: British Ceramic Research Ltd, 1990–96; University College Hospitals NHS Trust, 1992–2001; *b* 22 July 1930; *o s* of David John Mason and Olwen Mason (*née* James); *m* 1952, E. Pauline Pattinson; three *d*; *m* 1979, Elizabeth Rosemary Grey-Edwards. *Educ:* Univ. of Wales (Fellow, University College Cardiff, 1981); London Univ. (Fellow, UCL, 1996). CChem, FRSC; FIMMM (FIM 1993). Research Assoc., British Empire Cancer Campaign, 1953–61; Lectr, Imperial Coll., 1961–63; Prof. of Inorganic Chemistry, Univ. of Sheffield, 1963–71; Chief Scientific Advr, MoD, 1977–83. Vis. Prof., Univs in Australia, Canada, France, Israel, NZ and US, inc. A. D. Little Prof., MIT, 1970; Univ. of California, Berkeley, 1975; Ohio State Univ., 1976; North Western Univ., 1977; Prof. associé, Univ. de Strasbourg, 1976; Erskine Vis. Prof., Christchurch, NZ, 1977; Prof., Texas, 1982; Vis. Prof. of Internat. Relns, UCW, 1985–95. Schmidt Meml Lectr, Israel, 1977. SRC: Mem., 1971–75; Chm. Chemistry Cttee, 1969–72; Chm. Science Bd, 1972–75; Consultant and Council Mem., RUSI, 1984–88; UK Mem., UN Commn of Disarmament Studies, 1984–92; Chairman: Council for Arms Control, 1986–90; Engrg Technol. Cttee, DTI, 1991–93. Pres., BHRA, 1986–94 (Chm., BHR Gp, 1990–95); Member: ABRC, 1977–83; BBC Adv. Group, 1975–79. Chairman: Hunting Engineering Ltd, 1987 (Dep. Chm., 1985–87); Science Applications Internat. Corp. (UK) Ltd, 1993–96; Xtreamis plc, 1998–2000; Advanced Messaging Ltd, 2004–06. Pres., Inst. of Materials, 1995–96. Foundation Chm., Stoke Mandeville Burns and Reconstructive Surgery Res. Trust, 1990–94; Chm., UCL Hosps Charities, 2004–07. Hon. FIMechE 1997. Hon. DSc: Wales, 1986; Keele, 1992. Corday-Morgan Medallist, 1965, and Tilden Lectr, 1970, Chemical Society; Medal and Prize for Structural Chem., Chem. Soc., 1973. *Publications:* (ed) Advances in Radiation Biology, 1964 (3rd edn 1969); (ed) Advances in Structure Analysis by Diffraction Methods, 1968 (6th edn 1978); (ed) Physical Processes in Radiation Biology, 1964; many papers in Jl Chem. Soc., Proc. Royal Soc., etc, and on defence issues.

MASON, Samantha Mary Constance; *see* Beckett, S. M. C.

MASON, Stanley; *see* Mason, J. S.

MASON, Stephen; *see* Mason, J. S.

MASON, (Tania) Jane; Regional Chairman of Employment Tribunals, London Central Region, 2000–01; *b* 25 Sept. 1936; *d* of late Edward Warner Moeran, sometime MP, and of Pymonie (*née* Fincham); *m* 1961, James Stephen Mason, *qv*; one *s* two *d*. *Educ:* Frensham Heights Sch. Called to the Bar, Inner Temple, 1961. Law Reporter, Judicial Cttee of Privy Council, 1976–83; Asst Legal Advr, British Council, 1983–86; full-time Chm. of Industrial Tribunals, 1986–92; Regional Chairman: Industrial Tribunals, London S Reg., 1992–97; Industrial, later Employment, Tribunals, London N Reg., 1997–2000. *Recreations:* country life, English novels. *Address:* Amberley House, Church Street, Amberley, West Sussex BN18 9NF. *Club:* Reform.

MASON, Timothy Ian Godson; arts and heritage consultant; Director, Museums & Galleries Commission, 1995–2000; *b* 11 March 1945; *s* of late Ian Godson Mason and Muriel (*née* Vaile); *m* 1975, Marilyn Ailsa Williams; one *d* one *s*. *Educ:* St Alban's Sch., Washington, DC; Bradfield Coll., Berkshire; Christ Church, Oxford (MA). Assistant Manager, Oxford Playhouse, 1966–67; Assistant to Peter Daubeny, World Theatre Season, London, 1967–69; Administrator: Ballet Rambert, 1970–75; Royal Exchange Theatre, Manchester, 1975–77; Director: Western Australian Arts Council, 1977–80; Scottish Arts Council, 1980–90; Consultant on implementation of changes in structure of arts funding, Arts Council of GB, 1990–91; Chief Exec., London Arts Bd, 1991–95. Member: Gen. Adv. Council, BBC, 1990–96; Gen. Council, Commonwealth Assoc. of Museums, 2003–. Trustee, Civic Trust, 2004–06. Gov., KCH, 2006–. *Publications:* Shifting Sands, 2003; Design Reviewed: urban housing, 2004; Designed with Care, 2006. *Recreations:* family, travelling, the arts. *Address:* 30 Chatsworth Way, SE27 9HN. *T:* (020) 8761 1414.

MASON, Air Vice-Marshal Tony; *see* Mason, Air Vice-Marshal R. A.

MASON, William Ernest, CB 1983; Deputy Secretary (Fisheries and Food), Ministry of Agriculture, Fisheries and Food, 1982–89, retired; *b* 12 Jan. 1929; *s* of Ernest George and Agnes Margaret Mason; *m* 1959, Jean (*née* Bossley); one *s* one *d*. *Educ:* Brockley Grammar Sch.; London Sch. of Economics (BScEcon). RAF, 1947–49; Min. of Food, 1949–54; MAFF, 1954; Principal 1963; Asst Sec. 1970; Under Sec., 1975; Fisheries Sec., 1980. Dir, Food and Agric. Div., NATO Central Supplies Agency (West), 1983–93. Dir, Allied-Lyons, then Allied Domecq, PLC, 1989–98; consultant on food and drink industry, 1989–98. Member: Econ. Devlt Cttee for Distrib. Trades, 1975–80; Econ. Devlt Cttee for Food and Drink Manufg Inds, 1976–80; Adv. Bd, Inst. of Food Res., 1993–98. Chm. of Govs, Prendergast Sch. for Girls, 1974–86. FRSA 1989; FIGD 1989; Hon. FIFST 1989. Hon. Keeper of the Quaiche, 1989–. *Recreations:* music, reading, modern British painting. *Address:* 3 Cranleigh House, 16 Overbury Avenue, Beckenham, Kent BR3 6PY. *T:* (020) 8650 8241. *Club:* Reform.

MASRI, Taher Nashat, Order of the Renaissance (Jewelled), Jordan, 1991; Order of Al-Kawkab, Jordan, 1974; Hon. GBE 1988; Member of Senate, Jordan, since 1998; *b* 5 March 1942; *s* of Nashat Masri and Hadiyah Solh; *m* 1968, Samar Bitar; one *s* one *d*. *Educ:* North Texas State Univ. (BBA 1965). Central Bank of Jordan, 1965–73; MP Nablus District, Jordan, 1973–74, 1984–88, 1989–97; Minister of State for Occupied Territories Affairs, 1973–74; Ambassador to: Spain, 1975–78; France, 1978–83; Belgium (non-resident), 1978–80; Britain, 1983–84; Perm. Delegate to UNESCO, 1978–83; Foreign Minister, 1984–89 and 1991; Dep. Prime Minister and Minister of State for Economic Affairs, April–Aug. 1989; Chm., Foreign Relations Cttee, 1989–91; Prime Minister of Jordan and Minister of Defence, June–Nov. 1991; Speaker of Lower House of Parlt, 1993–94. Rapporteur, Royal Commn for Drafting of Nat. Charter, 1989–90. Chm., Bd of Trustees, Jordan Univ. of Sci. and Technol., 1999–. Grand Cross, Order of Civil Merit, Spain, 1977; Order of Isabel the Catholic, Spain, 1978; Commander, Legion of Honour, France, 1981. *Address:* PO Box 5550, Amman 11183, Jordan. *T:* (6) 5920600, (office) 4642227, *Fax:* (6) 4642226.

MASSE, Hon. Marcel, OQ 1995; PC (Can.) 1984; Président, Commission franco-québécoise sur les lieux de mémoire communs, since 1997; *b* 1936; *s* of Rosaire Masse and Angeline Masse; *m* 1960, Cécile, *d* of René and Clementine Martin; one *s* one *d*. *Educ:* Ecole Normale Jacques-Cartier, Montréal; Univ. de Montréal; Inst. of Pol Sci., Paris; Sorbonne, Paris; City of London Coll.; Inst. Européen d'Admin. des Affaires, Fontainebleau. History teacher, Joliette, Québec, 1962–66; Mem., Québec Nat. Assembly, 1966–73 (Minister, 1966–70); Dir, Lavalin Inc., Montréal, 1974–84; MP (Progressive C) Frontenac, Québec, 1984–93; Minister of Communications, Canada, 1984–86, 1989–91; Minister of Energy, Mines and Resources, 1986–89; Minister of National Defence, 1991–93; Quebec Deleg. Gen. in Paris, 1996–97. Pres., Commn des biens culturels du Québec, 1997–2000. Officer, Legion of Honour (France), 1999. *Recreations:* reading, music, fishing, ski-ing. *Address:* CP 1030, Saint-Donat, QC J0T 2C0, Canada. *Club:* Garnison (Quebec).

MASSENET, Natalie; Founder and Chairman, Net-a-porter.com, since 2000; *b* Los Angeles, 13 May 1965; *d* of Bob Rooney and Barbara Rooney; *m* Arnaud Massenet; two *d*. *Educ:* Univ. of Calif, Los Angeles (BA Eng. Lit.). In film business, 1988–90; Moda mag., Italy, 1990–93; W Coast Fashion Ed., WWD and W, 1993–96; Sen. Fashion Ed., Tatler, 1996–99. Entrepreneur of the Year, Harper's Bazaar and Chanel, 2006, CNBC Eur. Business Leaders Awards, 2008. *Address:* Net-a-porter.com, The Dome, Whiteleys Centre, 151 Queensway, W2 4YN. *T:* (020) 7255 4500, *Fax:* (020) 7255 4599. *Clubs:* Soho House, Babington House.

MASSER, Prof. David, PhD; FRS 2005; Professor of Mathematics, University of Basel, since 1992; *b* 8 Nov. 1948; *s* of William and Rose Masser; *m* 1988, Hedda Freudenschuss. *Educ:* Trinity Coll., Cambridge (BA Hons 1970, MA 1974; PhD 1974). University of Nottingham: Lectr, 1973–75 and 1976–79; Reader, 1979–83; Res. Fellow, Trinity Coll., Cambridge, 1975–76; Prof., Univ. of Michigan, Ann Arbor, 1983–92. *Publications:* Elliptic Functions and Transcendence, Lecture Notes in Mathematics, Vol. 437, 1975; about 75 papers in math. jls. *Address:* Nadelberg 17, 4051 Basel, Switzerland.

MASSER, Prof. (Francis) Ian, PhD; Professor of Urban Planning, International Institute for Aerospace Survey and Earth Sciences, Netherlands, 1998–2003; *b* 14 Sept. 1937; *s* of late Francis Masser and Isabel Masser (*née* Haddaway); *m* 1st, 1962, Alexandra Arnold (*d* 1988); two *d*; 2nd, 1996, Susan Parkin. *Educ:* Malton Grammar Sch.; Univ. of Liverpool (BA, MCD, PhD 1975; LittD 1993). MRTPI 1964. Leverhulme Res. Fellow, UC of Rhodesia and Nyasaland, 1960–61; Associate Planner, Shankland Cox Associates, 1962–64; Lectr, then Sen. Lectr, Univ. of Liverpool, 1964–75; Prof. and Hd of Inst. of Urban and Regional Planning, Univ. of Utrecht, 1975–79; University of Sheffield: Prof. of Town and Regl Planning, 1979–98; Hd, Dept of Town and Regional Planning, 1979–86; Dean, Faculty of Architectural Studies, 1981–84 and 1992–95; Chm., Sheffield Centre for Envmtl Res., 1979–92. Visiting Professor: Hitotsubashi Univ., Tokyo, 1986; Poly. of Turin, 1993–94; Univ. of Utrecht, 1998–; UCL, 2003–; Univ. of Melbourne, 2004–. Ed., Papers of Regl Sci. Assoc., 1975–80. Nat. Co-ordinator, ESRC Regl Res. Lab. Initiative, 1986–91; Co-Dir, ESF GISDATA scientific prog., 1991–97. Councillor: Regl Sci. Assoc., 1975–78 (Vice-Pres., 1980–81); Assoc. for Geographic Information, 1991–94, 1999–2003; Chm., Res. Assessment Evaluation Cttee on Geographical and Envmtl Sci., Assoc. of Univs in Netherlands, 1995–96; President: European Umbrella Orgn for Geographic Information, 1999–2003; Global Spatial Data Infrastructure Assoc., 2002–04. FRSA 1983. *Publications:* Analytical Models for Urban and Regional Planning, 1972; Inter-regional Migration in Tropical Africa, 1975; (ed) Spatial Representation and Spatial Interaction, 1978; (ed) Evaluating Urban Planning Efforts, 1983; (ed) Learning from Other Countries, 1985; (ed) Handling Geographic Information, 1991; Geography of Europe's Futures, 1992; (ed) Diffusion and Use of Geographic Information Technologies, 1993; (ed) Planning for Cities and Regions in Japan, 1994; Geographical Information Systems and Organisations, 1995; (ed) GIS Diffusion, 1996; Governments and Geographic Information, 1998; GIS Worlds: creating spatial data infrastructures, 2005; Building European SDIs, 2007. *Recreations:* walking, travel. *Address:* Town End House, Taddington, Buxton, Derbys SK17 9UF. *T:* (01298) 85232.

MASSEREENE, 14th Viscount *cr* 1660, **AND FERRARD,** 7th Viscount *cr* 1797; **John David Clotworthy Whyte-Melville Foster Skeffington;** Baron Loughneugh (Ire.), 1660; Baron Oriel (Ire.), 1790; Baron Oriel (UK), 1821; stockbroker with M.D. Barnard & Co.; *b* 3 June 1940; *s* of 13th Viscount and Annabelle Kathleen, *er d* of H. D. Lewis; *S* father, 1992; *m* 1970, Ann Denise, *er d* of late Norman Rowlandson; two *s* one *d*. *Educ:* St Peter's Court, Millfield; Institute Monte Rosa. Grenadier Guards, 1958–61. Stock Exchange, 1961–64; motor trade, 1964–70; Stock Exchange, 1970–; various dirships; landowner. *Recreations:* vintage cars, stalking, shooting. *Heir: s* Hon. Charles John Clotworthy Whyte-Melville Foster Skeffington, *b* 7 Feb. 1973. *Clubs:* Turf, Pratt's.

MASSEVITCH, Prof. Alla Genrikhovna; Chief Scientist of the Astronomical Institute of the Russian Academy of Sciences, since 1988 (Vice-President, 1952–88); Professor of Astrophysics, Moscow University, since 1946; *b* Tbilisi, Georgia, USSR, 9 Oct. 1918; *d* of Genrick Massevitch and Natalie Zhgenti; *m* 1942, Joseph Friedlander; one *d*. *Educ:* Moscow Univ. Lectured at the Royal Festival Hall, London, and at the Free Trade Hall, Manchester, etc., on The Conquest of Space, 1960; in charge of network of stations for tracking Sputniks, in Russia, 1957–93. Pres. Working Group 1 (Tracking and Telemetring) of COSPAR (Internat. Cttee for Space Research) 1961–66. Pres., Commission 35 (Internal Structure of Stars) of the Internat. Astronom. Union, 1967–70; Dep. Sec. Gen., UNISPACE 82 (UN Conf. on Exploration and Peaceful Uses of Outer Space), Vienna, 1981–83. Chm., Space Science Studies Cttee, Internat. Acad. of Astronautics, 1983–86; Associate Editor, Astrophysics and Space Science, 1987–94; Mem. Editorial Bd, Astrophysics (Russian), 1985–; Editor of series: Vital Problems of Astrophysics, 1987–99; Vital Problems of Space Research, 1987–99. Foreign Member: Royal Astronomical Soc., 1963; Indian Nat. Acad. of Sciences, 1979; Austrian Acad. Scis, 1985; Internat. Acad. Astronautics, 1964. Vice-President: Inst. for Russian-American

Relations (formerly Soviet-American Relations), 1967–; USSR Peace Cttee, 1977–92 (Mem. Bd, 1965–92); Mem. Bd, Internat. Peace Cttee, 1965–92. Hon. Mem., Russian Acad. of Cosmonautics, 1996. Internat. Award for Astronautics (Prix Galabert), 1963. Medals of 2nd World War; Govtl decorations, USSR, Sign of Honour, 1963, Red Banner, 1975; Govt Order with Star (Poland), 1985; USSR State Prize, 1975. Hon. Scientist Emeritus, 1978. *Publications:* Use of Satellite Tracking Data for Geodesy (monograph), 1980; Physics and Evolution of Stars (monograph), 1988; 159 scientific papers on the internal structure of the stars, stellar evolution, and optical tracking of artificial satellites, in Russian and foreign astronomical and geophysical journals. *Address:* 48 Pyatnitskaya Street, Moscow 119017, Russia. *T:* (095) 2313980, *Fax:* (095) 2302081; Pushkarev per 6, Apt 4, Moscow 103045, Russia; *e-mail:* vmyakutin@inasan.rssi.ru. *Club:* Club for Scientists (Moscow).

MASSEY, family name of **Baroness Massey of Darwen**.

MASSEY OF DARWEN, Baroness *cr* 1999 (Life Peer), of Darwen in the county of Lancashire; **Doreen Elizabeth Massey;** Chairman, National Treatment Agency, since 2002; *b* 5 Sept. 1938; *d* of Mary Ann Hall (*née* Sharrock) and Jack Hall; *m* 1966, Dr Leslie Massey; two *s* one *d. Educ:* Darwen Grammar Sch., Lancs; Birmingham Univ. (BA Hons French 1961); DipEd 1962; Inst. of Educn, London Univ. (MA 1985). Graduate service overseas, Gabon, 1962–63; teacher: S Hackney Sch., 1964–67; Springside Sch., Philadelphia, 1967–69; Pre-School Play Group Association, 1973–77; teacher, Walsingham Sch., London, 1977–83 (co-ordinator Health Educn, Head of Year, senior teacher); advisory teacher for personal, social and health educn, ILEA, 1983–85; Manager, Young People's Programme, Health Educn Council, 1985–87; Dir of Educn, 1987–89, Dir, 1989–94, FPA. Co-Chm., All-Party Parly Gp for Children, 2001–. Member: Brook Adv. Centres; Nat. Trust; Dir, Adv. Council on Alcohol and Drug Educn; Trustee, Trust for Study of Adolescence; Mem., The Lady Taverners, 2004–; school governor. FRSA 1992. *Publications:* Sex Education: Why, What and How?, 1988; Sex Education Factpack, 1988; (jtly) Sex Education Training Manual, 1991; (ed) Sex Education Resource Book, 1994; (ed) The Lover's Guide Encyclopedia, 1996; articles on sex educn, family planning, health educn. *Recreations:* reading, cinema, theatre, opera, art and design, yoga, pilates, sports, vegetarian cookery, travel. *Address:* House of Lords, SW1A 0PW.

MASSEY, Vice Adm. Alan Michael, CBE 2003; Second Sea Lord and Commander-in-Chief Naval Home Command, since 2008; Flag Aide-de-Camp to the Queen, since 2008; *b* 9 March 1953; *s* of Harry Massey and Astrid Ellen Irene Massey (*née* Lange); *m* 1987, Julie Samantha Smith; two *s* two *d. Educ:* Northgate Grammar Sch., Ipswich; Univ. of Liverpool (BA Hons 1975); Keswick Hall Coll. of Educn (PGCE 1976). HMS: Bulwark, 1979; Norfolk, 1980; Leander, 1981; Brazen, 1984; Ark Royal, 1987; RN staff course, 1989; MoD, London, 1990; NATO, Brussels, 1991; CO, HMS Newcastle, 1993; MoD, London, 1995; CO, HMS Campbeltown, 1996; rcds, 1998; MoD, London, 1998; NATO SACLANT, 1999; Commanding Officer: HMS Illustrious, 2001; HMS Ark Royal, 2002; PJHQ Northwood, 2003–05; ACNS, MoD, 2005–08. Vice-Pres., RN Soccer. Cdre, RNSA. *Recreations:* sailing, guitar, languages, family. *Address:* Fleet Headquarters, Whale Island, Portsmouth PO2 8BY. *T:* (023) 9262 5273, *Fax:* (023) 9262 5933; *e-mail:* alan.massey972@mod.uk. *Clubs:* Royal Navy of 1765 and 1785; Fleet Air Arm Officers' Assoc.

MASSEY, Anna (Raymond), CBE 2005; actress; *b* 11 Aug. 1937; *d* of late Raymond Massey and Adrianne Allen; *m* 1st, 1958, Jeremy Huggins (marr. diss. 1963; he *d* 1995); one *s*; 2nd, 1988, Uri Andres. *Educ:* London; New York; Switzerland; Paris; Rome. *Plays:* The Reluctant Debutante, 1955; Dear Delinquent, 1957; The Elder Statesman, 1958; Double Yolk, 1959; The Last Joke, 1960; The Miracle Worker, 1961; The School for Scandal, 1962; The Doctor's Dilemma, 1963; The Right Honourable Gentleman, 1964; The Glass Menagerie, 1965; The Prime of Miss Jean Brodie, 1966; The Flip Side, 1967; First Day of a New Season, 1967; This Space is Mine, 1969; Hamlet, 1970; Spoiled, 1971; Slag, 1971; Jingo, 1975; Play, 1976; The Seagull, 1981; Broadway Bound, 1991; A Hard Heart, 1992; Grace, 1992; Moonlight, 1993; *at National Theatre:* Heartbreak House, 1975; Close of Play, 1979; Summer; The Importance of Being Earnest; A Kind of Alaska, and Family Voices, in Harold Pinter trio Other Places, 1982; King Lear, 1986; Mary Stuart, 1996. *Films:* Gideon's Day, 1957; Peeping Tom, 1960; Bunny Lake is Missing, 1965; The Looking Glass War, 1969; David Copperfield, 1969; De Sade, 1971; Frenzy, 1972; A Doll's House, 1973; Sweet William, 1979; The Corn is Green, 1979; Five Days One Summer, 1982; Another Country, 1984; The Chain, 1985; Le Couleur du Vent, 1988; The Tall Guy, 1989; Haunted, 1995; The Grotesque, 1995; The Slab Boys, 1997; Déjà Vu, 1997; Captain Jack, 1999; Mad Cows, 1999; Room to Rent, 2001; Dark Blue World, 2002; The Importance of Being Earnest, 2002; The Machinist, 2004; The Oxford Murders, 2008; *films for television:* Journey into the Shadows, Sakharov, 1984; Sacred Hearts, 1985; Hotel du Lac, 1986; The Christmas Tree, 1987; Sunchild, 1988; A Tale of Two Cities, 1989; Man From the Pru, 1990; The Sleeper, 2000; numerous appearances in TV plays, including Shalom, Joan Collins, 1990; A Respectable Trade (series), 1998; He Knew He Was Right (series), 2004; The Web of Belonging, 2004; The Robinsons (series), 2005; A Good Murder, 2006; Pinochet in Suburbia, 2006; Oliver Twist, 2007; Affinity, 2008. *Publication:* Telling Some Tales (autobiog.), 2006. *Address:* c/o Markham and Froggatt Ltd, 4 Windmill Street, W1T 2HZ.

MASSEY, Prof. Doreen Barbara, FBA 2002; AcSS; Professor of Geography, Open University, since 1982; *b* Manchester, 3 Jan. 1944; *d* of Jack Massey and Nancy Massey (*née* Turton). *Educ:* St Hugh's Coll., Oxford (BA 1st Cl. Hons Geog. 1966; Hon. Fellow, 2000); Univ. of Pennsylvania (MA Regl Sci. 1972). Centre for Envmtl Studies, 1968–80; SSRC Fellow in Industrial Locn Res., 1980–82. Vis. Researcher, Inst. Nacional de Investigaciones Economicas y Sociales, Managua, 1985–86. Hettner Lectr, Univ. of Heidelberg, 1998. Mem., Editl Bd, Catalyst Trust, 1998–; Co-founder and Ed., Soundings: a jl of politics and culture, 1995–. Member: Bd, Gtr London Enterprise Bd, 1982–87; Adv. Cttee, Centre for Local Econ. Strategies, 1986–88. Mem. Bd, Nat. Inst. for Regl and Spatial Analysis, Ireland, 2001–. Hon. Vice Pres., Geographical Assoc., 1989–93. Trustee, Lipman-Miliband Trust, 1986–. AcSS 1999; FRSA 2000. Hon. DSc Edinburgh, 2006; Hon. DLitt NUI, 2006. Victoria Medal, RGS, 1994; Prix Vautrin Lud, Fest. Internat. de Géographie, 1998; Anders Retzius Gold Medal, Swedish Soc. for Anthropology and Geography, 2003; Centenary Medal, RSGS, 2003. *Publications:* (ed jtly) Alternative Approaches to Analysis, 1975; (with A. Catalano) Capital and Land: landownership by capital in Great Britain, 1978; (with R. Meegan) The Geography of Industrial Reorganisation, 1979; (with R. Meegan) The Anatomy of Job Loss, 1982; Spatial Divisions of Labour: social structures and the geography of production, 1984, 2nd edn 1995; (ed jtly) Geography Matters!, 1984; (ed jtly) Politics and Method: contrasting studies in industrial geography, 1985; Nicaragua: some urban and regional issues in a society in transition, 1987; (ed jtly) The Economy in Question, 1988; (ed jtly) Uneven Re-Development, 1988; (jtly) High-Tech Fantasies, 1992; Space, Place and Gender, 1994; (ed jtly) Geographical Worlds, 1995; (ed jtly) A Place in the World?: places, cultures and globalisation, 1995; (ed jtly) Re-thinking the Region, 1998; (ed jtly) Human Geography Today, 1999; (ed jtly) City Worlds, 1999; (ed jtly) Unsettling Cities, 1999;

Power-geometries and the Politics of Space-time, 1999; (jtly) Cities for the Many not the Few, 2000; (jtly) Decentering the nation: a radical approach to regional inequality, 2003; For Space, 2005; (ed jtly) A World in the Making, 2006; World City, 2007; Samanaikainen Tila, 2008; contrib. articles to learned jls on urban and regl issues, globalisation and the conceptualisation of space and place. *Recreations:* travelling, walking, bird-watching, photography, reading, talking with friends. *Address:* Faculty of Social Sciences, Open University, Walton Hall, Milton Keynes MK7 6AA. *T:* (01908) 654475, *Fax:* (01908) 654488.

MASSEY, Col Hamon Patrick Dunham; Clerk, Ironmongers' Company, since 2005; *b* 18 Aug. 1950; *s* of Lt Col Patrick Massey, MC and Bessie Lee Massey; *m* 1988, Cate Campbell; one *s* three *d. Educ:* Harrow; RMA Sandhurst; Army Staff Coll., Camberley. Commnd Blues and Royals, 1970; Adjutant, 1977–79; Army Staff Coll., 1982; CO, Household Cavalry Mounted Regt, 1992–94; Defence Attaché, Buenos Aires, 1997–2000; Comdr, Household Cavalry and Silver Stick in Waiting, 2000–05. *Recreations:* fishing, gardening, dry stone walls. *Address:* Ironmongers' Hall, Shaftesbury Place, Barbican, EC2Y 8AA. *T:* (020) 7776 2304, *Fax:* (020) 7600 3579; *e-mail:* clerk@ironhall.co.uk. *Club:* Turf.

See also W. G. S. Massey.

MASSEY, (Robert) Graham; Managing Director, The Science Archive Ltd, 1996–2001; *b* 28 Sept. 1943; *s* of Robert Albert Massey and Violet Edith Massey (*née* Smith); *m* 1965, Allison Ruth Duerden; one *s* one *d. Educ:* Manchester Grammar Sch.; Balliol Coll., Oxford (BA 1st Cl. Hons History). Joined BBC 1965 as general trainee; Producer, Science and Features Dept, 1970; Producer, 1972, Editor, 1981–85, Horizon; Series Producer, Making of Mankind (with Richard Leakey), 1979–81; Head, Special Features Unit, BBC Drama, 1985–89; Head, Science and Features Dept, BBC, 1989–91; Dir, Co-productions, 1991–92, Dir, Internat., 1992–94, BBC Enterprises. *Recreations:* theatre, cinema, cooking. *Address:* 2 Gregory Place, W8 4NG.

MASSEY, Roy Cyril, MBE 1997; Organist and Master of the Choristers, Hereford Cathedral, 1974–2001; *b* 9 May 1934; *s* of late Cyril Charles Massey and Beatrice May Massey; *m* 1975, Ruth Carol Craddock Grove. *Educ:* Univ. of Birmingham (BMus); privately with David Willcocks. FRCO (CHM); ADCM; ARCM; FRSCM (for distinguished services to church music) 1972. Organist: St Alban's, Conybere Street, Birmingham, 1953–60; St Augustine's, Edgbaston, 1960–65; Croydon Parish Church, 1965–68; Warden, RSCM, 1965–68; Conductor, Croydon Bach Soc., 1966–68; Special Comr of RSCM, 1964–74; Organist to City of Birmingham Choir, 1954–74; Organist and Master of Choristers, Birmingham Cath., 1968–74; Dir of Music, King Edward's Sch., Birmingham, 1968–74. Conductor, Hereford Choral Soc., 1974–2001; Conductor-in-Chief, alternate years Associate Conductor, Three Choirs Festival, 1975–2001; Adviser on organs to dioceses of Birmingham and Hereford, 1974–. Mem. Council and Examiner, RCO, 1970–94 and 1997–2006; Mem., Adv. Council, 1976–78, Council, 1984–98, RSCM; Mem. Council, Friends of Cathedral Music, 1999–2002. President: Birmingham Organists' Assoc., 1970–75; Cathedral Organists' Assoc., 1982–84; IAO, 1991–93; RCO, 2003–05. Fellow, St Michael's Coll., Tenbury, 1976–85. Hon. FGCM 2001. DMus Lambeth, 1990. *Recreations:* motoring, old buildings, walking the dog. *Address:* 2 King John's Court, Tewkesbury, Glos GL20 6EG. *T:* (01684) 290019; *e-mail:* drroymassey@ukonline.co.uk.

MASSEY, William Greville Sale; QC 1996; barrister; *b* 31 Aug. 1953; *s* of late Lt Col Patrick Massey, MC and Bessie Lee Massey (*née* Byrne); *m* 1978, Cecilia D'Oyly Awdry; three *s. Educ:* Harrow; Hertford Coll., Oxford (Entrance Schol.; MA). Called to the Bar, Middle Temple, 1977 (Harmsworth Exhibnr), Bencher, 2004. Member: Revenue Bar Assoc., 1978–; Chancery Bar Assoc., 1980–; London Commercial and Common Law Bar Assoc., 1980–. Governor: Summer Fields Sch., 1996–; Harrow Sch., 2000–; John Lyon Sch., 2002–. *Recreations:* chess, cricket, opera, gardening, ski-ing. *Address:* Pump Court Tax Chambers, 16 Bedford Row, WC1R 4EF. *T:* (020) 7414 8080, *Fax:* (020) 7414 8099.

See also H. P. D. Massey.

MASSIE, Allan Johnstone, FRSL; author and journalist; *b* 19 Oct. 1938; *s* of late Alexander Johnstone Massie and Evelyn Jane Wilson Massie (*née* Forbes); *m* 1973, Alison Agnes Graham Langlands; two *s* one *d. Educ:* Drumtochty Castle Sch.; Trinity College, Glenalmond; Trinity College, Cambridge (BA). Schoolmaster, Drumtochty Castle Sch., 1960–71; TEFL, Rome, 1972–75; fiction reviewer, The Scotsman, 1976–; Creative Writing Fellow: Edinburgh Univ., 1982–84; Glasgow and Strathclyde Univs, 1985–86; columnist: Glasgow Herald, 1985–88; Sunday Times Scotland, 1987–91; Daily Telegraph, 1991–; The Scotsman, 1992–; Daily Mail, 1994–; Sunday Times Scotland, 1996–. Mem., Scottish Arts Council, 1989–91. Trustee, Nat. Museums of Scotland, 1995–98. Hon. Pres., Classical Assoc. of Scotland, 2003–05. FRSL 1982; Hon. FRIAS 1997. *Publications: fiction:* Change and Decay In All Around I See, 1978; The Last Peacock, 1980; The Death of Men, 1981; One Night in Winter, 1984; Augustus, 1986; A Question of Loyalties, 1989; The Hanging Tree, 1990; Tiberius, 1991; The Sins of the Fathers, 1991; Caesar, 1993; These Enchanted Woods, 1993; The Ragged Lion, 1994; King David: a novel, 1995; Shadows of Empire, 1997; Antony, 1997; Nero's Heirs, 1999; The Evening of the World, 2001; Arthur The King, 2003; Caligula, 2003; Charlemagne and Roland, 2007; *non-fiction:* Muriel Spark, 1979; Ill-Met by Gaslight, 1980; The Caesars, 1983; A Portrait of Scottish Rugby, 1984; Colette, 1986; 101 Great Scots, 1987; Byron's Travels, 1988; Glasgow, 1989; The Novel Today, 1990; Edinburgh, 1994; The Thistle and the Rose, 2005; *plays:* Quintet in October; The Minstrel and the Shirra; First-Class Passengers. *Recreations:* reading, lunching, watching cricket, Rugby, horse-racing, smoking, walking the dogs. *Address:* Thirladean House, Selkirk TD7 5LU. *T:* (01750) 20393. *Clubs:* Academy; Selkirk RFC.

MASSIE, Sir Herbert William, (Sir Bert), Kt 2007; CBE 2000 (OBE 1984); Chairman, Bert Massie Ltd, since 2007; Commissioner for the Compact, since 2008; *b* 31 March 1949; *s* of Herbert Douglas and Lucy Joan Massie; *m* 2007, Maureen Lilian Shaw. *Educ:* Portland Trng Coll. for Disabled, Mansfield; Hereward Coll., Coventry; Liverpool Poly. (BA Hons 1977); Manchester Poly. (CQSW). Wm Rainford Ltd, 1967–68; W Cheshire Newspapers Ltd, 1968–70; Liverpool Assoc. for Disabled, 1970–72; Disabled Living Foundn, 1977; RADAR, 1978–99 (Dir, 1990–99). Member: Management Cttee, Disabled Drivers Assoc., 1968–71; Exec. Cttee, Assoc. of Disabled Professionals, 1979 (Trustee, 1979–94 Vice Chm., 1986–94); Careers Service Adv., Council for England, 1979–83; Voluntary Council for Handicapped Children (later Council for Disabled Children), 1980–93 (Vice-Chm., 1985–93); Exec. Cttee, OUTSET, 1983–91; MSC Wkg Party to Review Quota Scheme for Employment of Disabled People, 1984–85; Access Cttee for England, 1984–93; Disabled Persons Tspt Adv. Cttee, 1986–2002; BR Adv. Gp on Disabled People, 1986–94; Tripscope, 1986–2006 (Vice-Chm., 1989–2006); Nat. Adv. Council on Employment of People with Disabilities, 1991–98; Independent Commn on Social Justice, 1993–94; DSS Panel of Experts on Incapacity Benefit, 1993–94; Cabinet Office Adv. Panel on Equal Opportunities in Sen. CS, 1994–2001; Nat. Disability

Council, 1996–2000 (Dep. Chm., 1997–2000); Bd, Eur. Disability Forum, 1996–2000; Adv. Cttee, New Deal Task Force, 1997–2000; Disability Rights Task Force, 1997–99; Chm., Disability Rights Commn, 2000–07; Mem., Commn for Equality and Human Rights, 2006–Oct. 2009. 1990 BEAMA Foundation for Disabled People: Sec., 1986–90; Trustee, 1990–2000. Vice Pres., Foundn for Assistive Technol., 2000–; UK Nat. Sec., 1993–2000, Dep. Vice-Pres., Europe, 1996–2000, Rehabilitation Internat. Patron: Disabled Living Services (Manchester), 1990–; Heswall Disabled Children's Holiday Fund, 2003–; Merseyside Neurological Trust, 2004–; Trustee: Independent Living Fund, 1990–93; Habinteg Housing Assoc., 1991–; Mobility Choice, 1998–; Inst. for Employment Studies, 2000–07; United Trusts, 2006–08; RAISE, Liverpool, 2008–. Governor: Pensions Policy Inst., 2002–07; Motability, 2002–; Liverpool John Moores Univ., 2008–. Non-exec. Dir, Appleshaw Ltd, 2007–. FRSA 1988. Freeman, City of London, 2008; Mem., Wheelwrights' Co., 2008–. Hon. Fellow, Liverpool John Moores Univ., 2002. Hon. LLD Bristol, 2005; DUniv Staffs, 2007. Snowdon Award, 1995; Master Wheelwrights Award, Co. of Wheelwrights, 2002; Duncan Medal, Duncan Soc., Liverpool, 2003; Gold Award for Further Educn Alumni, Assoc. of Colls, 2003. *Publications:* (with M. Greaves) Work and Disability, 1977, 1979; Aspects of the Employment of Disabled People in the Federal Republic of Germany, 1982; (with M. Kettle) Employer's Guide to Disabilities, 1982, 2nd edn 1986; (jtly) Day Centres for Young Disabled People, 1984; Travelling with British Rail, 1985; (with J. Weyers) Wheelchairs and their Use, 1986; (with J. Male) Choosing a Wheelchair, 1990; (with J. Isaacs) Seat Belts and Disabled People, 1990; Social Justice and Disabled People, 1994; Getting Disabled People to Work, 2000; reports and numerous articles. *Recreations:* photography, reading. *Address:* (home) 2 North Sudley Road, Liverpool L17 0BG. *T:* (0151) 727 3252; *e-mail:* bert@massie.com. Commission for the Compact, 77 Paradise Circus, Queensway, Birmingham B1 2DT. *T:* (0121) 237 5903; *e-mail:* bert.massie@thecompact.org.uk.

MASSINGHAM, John Dudley, CMG 1986; HM Diplomatic Service, retired; Consul General and Director of Trade Promotion, Johannesburg, 1987–90; *b* 1 Feb. 1930; *yr s* of Percy Massingham and Amy (*née* Sanders); *m* 1952, Jean Elizabeth Beech (*d* 1995); two *s* two *d*. *Educ:* Dulwich Coll.; Magdalene Coll., Cambridge (MA); Magdalen Coll., Oxford. HM Overseas Civil Service, N Nigeria, 1954–59; BBC, 1959–64; HM Diplomatic Service, 1964–90: First Secretary, CRO, 1964–66; Dep. High Comr and Head of Chancery, Freetown, 1966–70; FCO, 1970–71; seconded to Pearce Commn, Jan.–May 1972; First Sec. (Information), later Aid (Kuala Lumpur), 1972–75; First Sec. and Head of Chancery, Kinshasa, 1976–77; Chief Sec., Falkland Islands Govt, 1977–79; Consul-General, Durban, June–Dec. 1979; Counsellor (Economic and Commercial), Nairobi, 1980–81; Governor and C-in-C, St Helena, 1981–84; High Comr to Guyana and non-resident Ambassador to Suriname, 1985–87. *Recreations:* bird watching, nature conservation work. *Address:* 24 Cherry Orchard, Pershore, Worcs WR10 1EL.

MASSY, family name of **Baron Massy**.

MASSY, 10th Baron *cr* 1776 (Ire.); **David Hamon Somerset Massy;** *b* 4 March 1947; *s* of 9th Baron Massy and of Margaret Elizabeth (*née* Flower); *S* father, 1995. *Educ:* St George's Coll., Weybridge. Late Merchant Navy. *Heir:* *b* Hon. John Hugh Somerset Massy [*b* 2 Jan. 1950; *m* 1978, Andrea West; one *s*].

MASTER, Simon Harcourt; Group Managing Director, 1989–90, Group Deputy Chairman, 1989–2004, Chairman, General Books Division, 1992–2004, and non-executive Director, 2004–08, Random House (formerly Random Century) Group; *b* 10 April 1944; *s* of Humphrey Ronald Master and Rachel Blanche Forshaw (*née* Plumbly); *m* 1969, Georgina Mary Cook Batsford, *d* of Sir Brian Batsford; two *s*. *Educ:* Ardingly Coll.; Univ. de La Rochelle. Hatchards Booksellers, 1963; Pan Books Ltd, 1964, Sen. Editor, 1967; Sen. Editor, B. T. Batsford Ltd, 1969; Pan Books Ltd: Editorial Dir, 1971; Publishing Dir, 1973; Man. Dir, 1980–87; Chief Exec., Random House UK Ltd, 1987–89; Vice Pres., Internat. Random House Inc., 1987–90; Chm. and Chief Exec., Arrow, 1990–92; Vice Pres., Random House (Delaware) Ltd, 1997–99. Non-exec. Dir, HMSO, 1990–95; non-exec. Chm., London Book Fair, 2006–08; Mem., British Book Awards Acad. Bd, 2006–08. Publishers Association: Mem. Council, 1989–95, Mem. Bd, 1997–98; Vice Pres., 1995–96 and 2000–01; Pres., 1996–97 and 2001–02. *Recreations:* gardening, golf, old cars. *Address:* c/o Random House Group, 20 Vauxhall Bridge Road, SW1V 2SA. *Clubs:* Groucho; Sherborne Golf.

MASTERMAN, Crispin Grant, FCIArb; **His Honour Judge Masterman;** a Circuit Judge, since 1995; *b* 1 June 1944; *s* of late Osmond Janson Masterman and Anne Masterman (*née* Bouwens); *m* 1976, Clare Fletcher; one *s* two *d*. *Educ:* St Edward's Sch., Oxford; Univ. of Southampton (BA). FCIArb 1991. Called to the Bar, Middle Temple, 1971; a Recorder, 1988–95; Designated Family Judge, Cardiff and Pontypridd, 2006–. Mem., Council, Cardiff Univ., 1995–2004 (Vice-Chair, 1998–2004). *Recreations:* family and friends, walking, golf. *Address:* 28 South Rise, Llanishen, Cardiff CF14 0RH. *T:* (029) 2075 4072.

MASTERS, Brian Geoffrey John; author; *b* 25 May 1939; *s* of Geoffrey Howard Masters and Mabel Sophia Charlotte (*née* Ingledew). *Educ:* Wilson's Grammar Sch., London; University Coll., Cardiff (BA 1st cl. Hons 1961); Université de Montpellier. FRSA 1989. *Publications:* Molière, 1969; Sartre, 1969; Saint-Exupéry, 1970; Rabelais, 1971; Camus: a study, 1973; Wynyard Hall and the Londonderry Family, 1974; Dreams about HM The Queen, 1974; The Dukes, 1975; Now Barabbas Was A Rotter: the extraordinary life of Marie Corelli, 1978; The Mistresses of Charles II, 1980; Georgiana, Duchess of Devonshire, 1981; Great Hostesses, 1982; Killing for Company: the case of Dennis Nilsen, 1985 (Gold Dagger Award, CWA); The Swinging Sixties, 1985; The Passion of John Aspinall, 1988; Maharana: the Udaipur Dynasty, 1990; Gary, 1990; The Life of E. F. Benson, 1991; The Shrine of Jeffrey Dahmer, 1993; (ed and trans.) Voltaire's Treatise on Tolerance, 1994; Masters on Murder, 1994; The Evil That Men Do, 1996; She Must Have Known: the trial of Rosemary West, 1996; Thunder in the Air: great actors in great roles, 2000; Getting Personal: a biographer's memoir, 2002. *Recreations:* etymology, stroking cats. *Address:* 47 Caithness Road, W14 0JD. *T:* (020) 7603 6838; 6 Place E. Granier, 34160 Castries, France. *T:* (4) 67875834. *Clubs:* Garrick, Beefsteak, Pratt's, Aspinall's.

MASTERS, Dr Christopher, CBE 2002; Chairman, Sagentia AG, since 2007; *b* 2 May 1947; *s* of Wilfred and Mary Ann Masters; *m* 1971, Gillian Mary (*née* Hodson); two *d*. *Educ:* Richmond Sch.; King's Coll. London (BSc, AKC); Leeds Univ. (PhD). Research Chemist, Shell Research, Amsterdam, 1971–77; Corporate Planner, Shell Chemicals UK, 1977–79; Business Develt Manager, Christian Salvesen, 1979–81; Dir of Planning, Merchants Refrigerating Co., NY, 1981–82; Managing Director: Christian Salvesen Seafoods, 1983–86; Christian Salvesen Industrial Services, 1984–89; Chief Exec., Christian Salvesen PLC, 1989–97; Exec. Chm., Aggreko plc, 1997–2002; Chairman: Voxar Ltd, 2002–04; Babtie Gp Ltd, 2002–04; SMG plc, 2004–07. Director: British Assets Trust plc, 1990–; Scottish Widows' Fund or Life Assurance Soc., 1992–2000; Wood Gp, 2002–; Alliance Trust, 2002–; Crown Agents, 2005–. Chm., Young Enterprise Scotland, 1993–96; Mem., SHEFC, 1995–2005 (Chm., 1998–2005). Chm., Festival City Theatres Trust, 2002–; Director: Scottish Opera, 1994–99 (Vice Chm., 1996–99); Scottish Chamber Orch., 1995–. Master, Merchant Co., City of Edinburgh, 2007–. FRSE 1996. Hon. DBA Strathclyde, 2006; Hon. DLaws St Andrews, 2006; Hon. Dhc Edinburgh 2007; Hon. DEd Abertay Dundee, 2007. *Publications:* Homogeneous Transition—Metal Catalysis, 1981, Russian edn 1983; numerous research papers and patents. *Recreations:* music, wine.

MASTERS, Guy; *see* Masters, T. G.

MASTERS, Robert James; Headmaster, Judd School, since 2004; *b* 14 July 1964; *s* of Thomas Masters and Judith Lindsey Masters (*née* Boothman); *m* 1988, Rachel Clare Pugh; two *s* one *d*. *Educ:* Univ. of Reading (BSc 1st Cl. Hons Maths); Univ. of Bristol (PGCE Maths with Games). Teacher of maths, Gravesend GS for Boys, 1986–97 (Head: of Middle Sch., 1990–93; of Maths, 1993–97); Dep. Headmaster, Torquay Boys' GS, 1997–2004. Additional Mem., HMC, 2007–. *Recreations:* hockey, cryptic crosswords. *Address:* The Judd School, Brook Street, Tonbridge, Kent TN9 2PN. *T:* (01732) 770880, *Fax:* (01732) 771661; *e-mail:* headmaster@judd.kent.sch.uk.

MASTERS, Sheila Valerie; *see* Baroness Noakes.

MASTERS, Prof. (Thomas) Guy, PhD; FRS 2005; Professor of Geophysics, Institute of Geophysics and Planetary Physics, University of California, San Diego, since 1985; *b* 5 Oct. 1954; *s* of Thomas James Masters and Joyce Masters; *m* 1982, Virginia Fleming; one *s* one *d*. *Educ:* Victoria Univ. of Manchester (BSc 1st Cl. 1975); King's Coll., Cambridge (PhD 1979). University of California, San Diego: Green Schol., 1979–80, res. geophysicist, 1981–85, IGPP; Dir, Earth Scis, 1999–2002 and 2005–06. Fellow, Amer. Geophysical Union, 1995. *Publications:* numerous contribs to leading jls. *Recreations:* horse-riding, ski-ing, gardening. *Address:* Institute of Geophysics and Planetary Physics, Scripps Institution of Oceanography, University of California, San Diego, 9500 Gilman Drive, La Jolla, CA 92093–0225, USA. *T:* (858) 5344122, *Fax:* (858) 5345332; *e-mail:* gmasters@ucsd.edu.

MASTERSON, Valerie, (Mrs Andrew March), CBE 1988; opera and concert singer; *d* of Edward Masterson and Rita McGrath; *m* 1965, Andrew March; one *s* one *d*. *Educ:* Holt Hill Convent; studied in London and Milan on scholarship, and with Edwardo Asquez. Début, Landestheater Salzburg; appearances with: D'Oyly Carte Opera, Glyndebourne Festival Opera, ENO, Royal Opera, Covent Garden, etc; appears in principal opera houses in Paris, Aix-en-Provence, Toulouse, Munich, Geneva, Barcelona, Milan, San Francisco, Chile, etc; leading roles in: La Traviata, Le Nozze di Figaro, Manon, Faust, Alcina, Die Entführung aus dem Serail, Così fan tutte, La Bohème, Semele (SWET award, 1983), Die Zauberflöte, Julius Caesar, Rigoletto, Romeo and Juliet, Carmen, Count Ory, Mireille, Louise, Idomeneo, Les Dialogues des Carmélites, The Merry Widow, Xerxes, Orlando, Lucia di Lammermoor. Recordings include: La Traviata; Elisabetta, Regina d'Inghilterra; Der Ring des Nibelungen; The Merry Widow; Julius Caesar; Scipione; several Gilbert and Sullivan operas. Broadcasts regularly on radio and TV. Pres., British Youth Opera, 1995–2001 (Vice-Pres., 2001–). Patron, Mousehole Male Voice Choir, 2002. Hon. Pres., Rossini Soc., Paris. FRCM 1992; Hon. RAM 1993. Hon. DLitt South Bank, 1999.

MASTERTON, Gordon Grier Thomson, FREng; FRSE; Vice President (formerly Managing Director) Environment, Jacobs UK Ltd (formerly Babtie Group Ltd, later Jacobs Babtie), since 2003; *b* 9 June 1954; *s* of late Alexander Bain Masterton and Mary Masterton; *m* 1976, Lynda Christine Jeffries; one *s* one *d*. *Educ:* Dunfermline High Sch.; Univ. of Edinburgh (BSc, BA); Imperial Coll., London (MSc; DIC 1981). CEng, FREng 2006; FICE; FIStructE; FIES; MCIWEM. Joined Babtie Shaw & Morton, 1976; Dir, 1993, Man. Dir of Facilities, 2002–03, Babtie Group Ltd. Chm., Construction Industry Council, Scotland, 2002–04; Mem., Royal Commn on Ancient and Historical Monuments of Scotland, 2003–. Vice-Pres., 2001–05, Pres., 2005–06, ICE. Vis. Prof., Univ. of Paisley, 1998–2003. Pres., Glasgow Grand Opera Soc., 1991–94. FRSE 2007. Mem., Engineers' Co., 2007–. Hon. DTech Glasgow Caledonian, 2007. *Publications:* (ed) Bridges and Retaining Walls—broadening the European horizons, 1994; author of 3 technical design guides on concrete foundations and retaining walls, 1995, 1997, 1999; over 30 technical papers. *Recreations:* music, engineering, history. *Address:* Jacobs UK Ltd, 95 Bothwell Street, Glasgow G2 7HX. *T:* (0141) 243 8317, *Fax:* (0141) 243 8753; *e-mail:* gordon.masterton@jacobs.com. *Club:* Western (Glasgow).

MASTERTON-SMITH, Cdre Anthony Philip, RN; CEng; Chairman, Penwood Management Ltd, since 2005; Chief Executive, Royal College of Physicians, 1998–2005; *b* 2 Aug. 1944; *s* of late Edward Masterton-Smith and Pauline Masterton-Smith (*née* Pilgrim); *m* 1975, Jennifer Sue Sprigings; one *s* one *d*. *Educ:* UCS, Hampstead; BRNC Dartmouth; RNEC Manadon. CEng, MIET (MIEE 1973). Royal Navy, 1962–98: HM Ships Fiskerton, Victorious, Llandaff, Bacchante, Scylla, Southampton; Staff of FO Sea Training, 1978–80; CO, HMS Royal Arthur, 1982–84; jsdc, 1986; Dep. Dir, Naval Recruiting, 1988–91; Defence and Naval Attaché, Tokyo, 1992–95; Cdre, BRNC Dartmouth, 1995–98. Director: RCP Regent's Park Ltd, 2001–05; Vale Health Ltd, 2006–. FRSA 2002. Hon. FRCP 2006. *Recreations:* opera, gardening, walking, sport. *Address:* Penwood, Whiteleaf, Bucks HP27 0LU. *Clubs:* Monks Risborough Cricket, Whiteleaf Golf.

MASUI, Prof. Yoshio, OC 2003; PhD; FRSC 2003; FRS 1998; Professor, University of Toronto, 1978–97, now Emeritus; *b* Kyoto, 6 Oct. 1931; adopted Canadian nationality, 1983; *s* of Fusa-jiro Masui and Toyoko Masui; *m* 1959, Yuriko Suda; one *s* one *d*. *Educ:* Kyoto Univ. (BSc 1953; MSc 1955; PhD 1961). Lectr, 1958–65, Asst Prof., 1965–68, Prof. Emeritus, 1999, Konan Univ., Japan; Staff Biologist, 1966–68, Lectr, 1969, Yale Univ.; Associate Prof. of Zoology, Univ. of Toronto, 1969–78. Hon. DSc Toronto, 1999. Albert Lasker Basic Medical Res. Award (jtly), for pioneering studies of regulation of cell divisions, 1998. *Address:* Department of Zoology, University of Toronto, 25 Harbord Street, Toronto, ON M5S 3G5, Canada. *T:* (416) 9783493.

MASUR, Kurt; German conductor; Principal Conductor, London Philharmonic Orchestra, 2000–07; Music Director, Orchestre National de France, 2002–08; *b* 18 July 1927; *m* 3rd, Tomoko Sakurai, soprano; one *s*; four *c* by previous marriages. *Educ:* Nat. Music Sch., Breslau; Leipzig Conservatory. Orch. Coach, Nat. Theatre of Halle, Saxony, 1948–51; Conductor: Erfurt City Theatre, 1951–53; Leipzig City Theatre, 1953–55; Dresden Philharmonic Orch., 1955–58; Music Director: Mecklenburg State Theatre, Schwerin, 1958–60; Komische Oper, E Berlin, 1960–64; Chief Conductor, Dresden Philharmonic Orch., 1967–72; Artistic Dir, Gewandhaus Orch. of Leipzig, 1970–96 (Hon. Mem., 1981; Conductor Laureate, 1996); Music Dir, NY Philharmonic Orch., 1992–2002, now Emeritus (Guest Conductor, 1982–92); Guest Conductor: Cleveland Orch., 1974; Philadelphia Orch.; Boston SO; Berlin Philharmonic Orch.; Leningrad Philharmonic Orch.; l'Orchestre de Paris; RPO. Prof., Leipzig Acad. of Music, 1975–.

MATACA, Most Rev. Petero; *see* Suva, Archbishop of, (RC).

MATANE, Sir Paulias (Nguna), GCL 2005; GCMG 2005 (CMG 1980); Kt 1986; OBE 1975; writer; Governor-General, Papua New Guinea, since 2004; *b* 21 Sept. 1931; *s* of Ilias Maila Matane and Elsa Toto; *m* 1957, Kaludia Peril Matane; two *s* two *d. Educ:* Teacher's College (Dip. Teaching and Education). Asst Teacher, Tauran Sch., PNG, 1957, Headmaster, 1958–61; School Inspector, 1962–66; Dist Sch. Inspector and Dist Educn Officer, 1967–68; Supt, Teacher Educn, 1969; Foundn Mem., Public Service Bd, 1969–70; Sec., Dept of Business Develt, 1971–74; Ambassador to USA, Mexico and UN, and High Comr to Canada, 1975–80; Sec., Foreign Affairs, PNG, 1980–85. Chairman: Treid Pacific (PNG) Pty Ltd, 1986–90; Newton Pacific (PNG) Pty Ltd, 1995–. Chairman: Review Cttee on Philosophy of Educn, 1986; Cocoa Industry Investigating Cttee, 1987; Foundn for Peoples of South Pacific, PNG, 1989–94; PNG Censorship Bd, 1990–97; Children, Women and Families in PNG: a situation analysis, 1996. Producer of regular progs for TV, 1990–2004, and radio, 1998. Hon. DTech Univ. of Technol., Lae, 1985; Hon. PhD Univ. of PNG, 1986; Hon. DLitt Univ. of PNG, 2008. UN 40th Anniv. Medal, 1985. KStJ 2005. *Publications:* Kum Tumun of Minj, 1966; A New Guinean Travels through Africa, 1971; My Childhood in New Guinea, 1972; What Good is Business?, 1972; Bai Bisnis I Helpim Yumi Olsem Wanem?, 1973; Exploring South Asia, vol. 1, Two New Guineans Travel through SE Asia, 1974, 2001, vol. 2, 2001; Aimbe the Challenger, 1974; Aimbe the School Dropout, 1974; Aimbe the Magician, 1976; Aimbe the Pastor, 1979; Two Papua New Guineans Discover the Bible Lands, 1987; To Serve with Love, 1989; Chit Chat, vol. 1, 1991, vol. 2, Let's Do It PNG, 1994, vol. 3, 2000; East to West—the longest train trip in the world, 1991; Trekking Through the New Worlds, 1995; Voyage to Antarctica, 1996; Laughter Made in PNG, 1996; Amazing Discoveries in 40 Years of Marriage, 1997; The Other Side of Port Moresby—in pictures, 1998; A Trip of a Lifetime, 1998; The Word Power, 1998; Waliling United Church: then and now, 1998; Coach Adventures Down Under, 1999; Management Problems in Papua New Guinea: some solutions, 2000; Further Management Problems in Papua New Guinea: their solutions, 2000; Management for Excellence, 2001; Exploring the Holy Lands, 2001; Humour in Papua New Guinea, 2002; Ripples in the South Pacific Ocean, 2002; India: a splendour in cultural diversity, 2004; Papua New Guinea: land of natural beauty and cultural diversity, 2005; The Time Traveller, 2005; Fifty Golden Years: saga of true love in marital and national life, 2006; Travelling Through Australia by Coach, 2007; Cultural Diversity of India, 2007; Education for Integral Human Development, 2008; Aimbe Braves Through Challenges, 2008; Public Addresses to be Privately Addressed, 2008. *Recreations:* reading, gardening, squash, fishing, writing. *Address:* PO Box 79, Port Moresby, NCD, Papua New Guinea. *Clubs:* Tamukavar, Tauran Ex Student and Citizens' (Papua New Guinea).

MATE, Rt Rev. Martin; Bishop of Eastern Newfoundland and Labrador, 1980–92; *b* 12 Nov. 1929; *s* of John Mate and Hilda Mate (*née* Toope); *m* 1962, Florence Hooper, Registered Nurse; two *s* three *d. Educ:* Meml Univ. of Newfoundland; Queen's Coll., St John's, Newfoundland (LTh); Bishop's Univ., Lennoxville, PQ. BA (1st Cl. Hons), MA. Deacon 1952, priest 1953; Curate, Cathedral of St John the Baptist, St John's, Newfoundland, 1952–53; Deacon-in-charge and Rector, Parish of Pushthrough, 1953–58; Incumbent, Mission of St Anthony, 1958–64; Rural Dean, St Barbe, 1958–64; Rector of Cookshire, Quebec, 1964–67; Rector of Catalina, Newfoundland, 1967–72; RD of Bonavista Bay, 1970–72; Rector of Pouch Cove/Torbay, 1972–76; Treasurer, Diocesan Synod of E Newfoundland and Labrador, 1976–80. *Publication:* Pentateuchal Criticism, 1967. *Recreations:* carpentry, hunting, fishing, camping. *Address:* 57 Penney Crescent, St John's, NL A1A 5J5, Canada.

MATEAR, Comr Elizabeth Anne; Territorial Leader and President, Women's Ministries, Salvation Army, United Kingdom with the Republic of Ireland, since 2006; Moderator, Free Church Council, since 2007; *b* 16 Aug. 1952; *d* of Jack and Elizabeth Kowbus; *m* 1978, John Matear; one *s. Educ:* Ladybank Primary Sch.; Bell Baxter High Sch.; Jordanhill Coll. (DipSW); Internat. Coll. for Officers, Salvation Army. Social worker: in addiction services, 1973–75, in alcohol assessment, 1977–78; Salvation Army Officer, 1977–; Commanding Officer: Godalming, 1978–80; Reading E, 1980–83; Hove, 1983–85; Chester-le-Street, 1985–87; Divl Youth Work, 1987–1990; Church Growth Consultant, 1990–94; CO, Bradford, 1994–95; Dir of Personnel, Yorks Div., 1996–97; Personnel Co-ordinator, UK Territorial HQ, 1997–99; Divl Leader, E Midlands Div., 1999–2001; Caribbean Territorial Leader and Territorial Pres., Women's Ministries, 2001–06; Co-Pres., Churches Together in England. *Recreations:* walking, reading, crossword puzzles, people. *Address:* Salvation Army Territorial Headquarters, 101 Newington Causeway, SE1 6BN. *T:* (020) 7367 4603; *e-mail:* elizabeth.matear@ salvationarmy.org.uk.

MATES, James Michael; Senior News Correspondent, ITN, since 2002; *b* 11 Aug. 1961; *s* of Rt Hon. Michael John Mates, *qv; m* 1991, Fiona Margaret Bennett; two *s* one *d. Educ:* Marlborough Coll.; Farnham Coll.; Leeds Univ. (BA Hons). Joined Independent Television News, 1983: Tokyo corresp., 1989–91; North of England corresp., 1991–92; Moscow corresp., 1992–94; Diplomatic Ed., 1994–97; Washington corresp., 1997–2002. *Recreations:* bridge, tennis, mountain biking. *Address:* c/o Independent TV News, 200 Gray's Inn Road, WC1X 8XZ.

MATES, Lt-Col Rt Hon. Michael (John); PC 2004; MP (C) East Hampshire, since 1983 (Petersfield, Oct. 1974–1983); *b* 9 June 1934; *s* of Claude John Mates; *m* 1st, 1959, Mary Rosamund Paton (marr. diss. 1980); two *s* two *d*; 2nd, 1982, Rosellen (marr. diss. 1995); one *d*; 3rd, 1998, Christine, *d* of Count and Countess Moltke, Copenhagen. *Educ:* Salisbury Cathedral Sch.; Blundell's Sch.; King's Coll., Cambridge (choral schol.). Joined Army, 1954; 2nd Lieut, RUR, 1955; Queen's Dragoon Guards, RAC, 1961; Major, 1967; Lt-Col, 1973; resigned commn 1974. Minister of State, NI Office, 1992–93. Vice-Chm., Cons. NI Cttee, 1979–81 (Sec., 1974–79); Chairman: Select Cttee on Defence, 1987–92 (Mem., 1979–92); Select Cttee on NI, 2001–05; Cons. Home Affairs Cttee, 1987–88 (Vice-Chm., 1979–87); All-Party Anglo-Irish Gp, 1979–92; Sec., 1922 Cttee, 1987–88, 1997–; Mem., Intell. and Security Cttee, 1994–; Mem., Butler Review of Intelligence on Weapons of Mass Destruction, 2004; introduced: Farriers Registration Act, 1975; Rent Amendment Act, 1985. Farriers' Co.: Liveryman, 1975–; Asst, 1981; Master, 1986–87. *Address:* House of Commons, SW1A 0AA.
See also J. M. Mates.

MATEV, Dr Lachezar Nikolov; Ambassador of Bulgaria to the Court of St James's, since 2005; *b* 5 Aug. 1951; *s* of Nikola Matev and Roza Mateva; *m* 1977, Bisserka Petrova; one *s* one *d. Educ:* Technical Univ., Sofia (MSc Automation and Telemechanics); Sofia Univ. (MSc Applied Maths); Diplomatic Acad., Moscow (MA High Hons Internat. Politics; PhD Internat. Relns 1991). Joined Bulgarian Diplomatic Service, 1982; First Sec., Prague, 1982–89; Diplomatic Acad., Moscow, 1989–91; Internat. Econ. Orgns Directorate, 1991–92; Co-founder and Man. Dir, Internat. Business Develt mag., and Man. Dir, Vecco Ltd, 1992–93; Hd, UN Agencies Sect., Foreign Econ. Policy Dept, 1993–95; Counsellor, Madrid, 1995–98; Mem., Accession Negotiations Team, Eur. Integration Directorate, Foreign Affairs Ministry, 1998–2002; Minister, London, 2002–05. Perm. Rep. of Bulgaria to IMO, 2007–. Kt Comdr, Royal Order of Francis I. *Recreations:* art, music (classical,

opera), theatre, sport, gardening, business and finance. *Address:* Bulgarian Embassy, 186–188 Queen's Gate, SW7 5HL. *T:* (020) 7591 0781, *Fax:* (020) 7584 4948; *e-mail:* ambass.office@bulgarianembassy.org.uk.

MATHER, Lt-Col Anthony Charles McClure, CVO 1998; OBE 1990 (MBE 1965); Secretary, Central Chancery of the Orders of Knighthood and Assistant Comptroller, Lord Chamberlain's Office, 1991–99; *b* 21 April 1942; *s* of late Eric James Mather and Stella Mather (*née* McClure); *m* 1966, Gaye, *d* of late Dr Eric Lindsay Dickson and Mrs Louise Tillett; one *s* two *d. Educ:* Eton College. Commissioned, Grenadier Guards, 1962; served UK, British Guyana, Germany and Hong Kong; retired 1991. An Extra Equerry to the Queen, 1992–. Freeman, City of London, 1998. *Recreations:* gardening, fishing, music. *Address:* The Horseshoes, Chirton, near Devizes, Wilts SN10 3QR. *T:* (01380) 840261. *Club:* Army and Navy.

MATHER, Christopher Paul; a Senior Immigration Judge, Asylum and Immigration Tribunal, since 2005; a Legal Member, Special Immigration Appeals Commission, since 2006; a Recorder of the Crown Court, since 1996 (Assistant Recorder, 1991–96); *b* 20 June 1947; *s* of Bertrand and Jean Barker Mather; *m* 1970, Pauline Mary Man; twin *s* and *d. Educ:* Ellesmere Coll., Shropshire. Admitted solicitor, 1973; Partner and Consultant, Penningtons, 1994–2000. Mem., Hants and IoW Valuation Tribunal, 1988–94; Dep. Dist Judge, 1989–91; Immigration Adjudicator, 2000–03; a Vice Pres., Immigration Appeal Tribunal, 2003–05. *Recreation:* managing and improving a 10 acre estate. *Address:* Asylum and Immigration Tribunal, Field House, 15 Breams Buildings, EC4A 1DZ. *T:* (020) 7073 4032; *e-mail:* chris.mather@judiciary.gsi.gov.uk. *Club:* Bristol Owners.

MATHER, Clive; see Mather, H. C.

MATHER, Graham Christopher Spencer; solicitor; President: European Policy Forum, since 1992; European Media Forum, since 1997; European Financial Forum, since 1999; *b* 23 Oct. 1954; *er s* of Thomas and Doreen Mather; *m* 1st, 1981, Fiona Marion McMillan (marr. diss. 1995), *e d* of Sir Ronald McMillan Bell, QC, MP and of Lady Bell; two *s*; 2nd, 1997, Geneviève, *widow* of James Seton Fairhurst. *Educ:* Hutton Grammar School; New College, Oxford (Burnet Law Scholar); MA Jurisp. Institute of Directors: Asst to Dir Gen., 1980; Head of Policy Unit, 1983; Institute of Economic Affairs: Dep. Dir, 1987; Gen. Dir, 1987–92. MEP (C) Hampshire N and Oxford, 1994–99. Mem., HM Treasury Working Party on Freeports, 1982. Member: Monopolies and Mergers Commission, 1989–94; Competition Appeal Tribunal (formerly Appeal Tribunal, Competition Commn), 2000–; Ofcom Consumer Panel, 2004–. Vis. Fellow, Nuffield Coll., Oxford, 1992–2000. Mem., Westminster City Council, 1982–86; contested (C) Blackburn, 1983. Radio and television broadcaster. Consultant: Tudor Investment Corp., 1992–; Elliott Associates, 2007–; Advr, BIFU, 1997–99; non-executive Director: Greenham Common Community Trust, 2000–; Zamyn Cultural Foundn, 2005–. Vice-Pres., Assoc. of Dist Councils, 1994–97. Trustee, Social Market Foundn, 2008–. Past Asst Grand Registrar, United Grand Lodge of England, 1997. *Publications:* lectures, papers and contribs to jls; contribs to The Times. *Address:* European Policy Forum, 125 Pall Mall, SW1Y 5EA. *T:* (020) 7839 7565, *Fax:* (020) 7839 7339; *e-mail:* graham.mather@ epfltd.org. *Club:* Oxford and Cambridge.

MATHER, (Harold) Clive; Lead Director, Iogen Corporation, Ottawa, since 2007; Chairman: The Matthew 25:35 Trust, since 2007; Tearfund, since 2008; Shell Pensions Trust Ltd, since 2008; *b* 19 Sept. 1947; *m* 1976, Ann (*née* Mason); one *s* two *d. Educ:* Warwick Sch.; Lincoln Coll., Oxford (BA 1969). With Shell, 1969–2007: early career in UK, Brunei and Gabon; Retail Regl Manager, Shell UK, 1984–86; Dir of Personnel and Public Affairs, Shell South Africa, 1986–91; Dir of Human Resources and Admin, Shell UK Ltd, and Dir, Shell Res. Ltd, 1991–95; Chief Inf. Officer, Shell Internat., 1995–97; Dir, Internat., Shell, 1997–99; Chief Exec., Shell Services Internat., 1999–2002; Chm., Shell UK Ltd, and Hd of Global Learning, Shell, 2002–04; Pres. and CEO, Shell Canada, 2004–07. Chm., Lensbury Ltd, 1999–2004; Dir, Place Dome Inc., 2005–. Chm., Petroleum Employers' Council, 1994–96. Commr, EOC, 1991–94; Member: Adv. Bd, Relationships Foundn, 1996–2004; Supervisory Bd, Office of Govt and Commerce 2002–04; President's Cttee, CBI, 2002–04; British N American Cttee, 2005–; Chairman: Corporate Social Responsibility Acad., 2003–05; IMD Business Council, 2003–. Chm., Lambeth Educn Action Zone Forum, 1998–2003; Dep. Chm., Windsor Leadership Trust, 1994–2005. Trustee, Royal Anniversary Trust, 2003–. MCIPD 2004; CCMI 2004. FRSA 1992. *Recreations:* sport, good food and wine. *Address:* PO Box 1077, Guildford, Surrey GU1 9HQ.

MATHER, James Stuart, CA; Member (SNP) Argyll and Bute, Scottish Parliament, since 2007 (Highlands and Islands, 2003–07); Minister for Enterprise, Energy and Tourism, since 2007; *b* 6 March 1947; *s* of James Stuart Mather and Sarah Morag Mather (*née* MacKenzie); *m* 1980, Maureen Anne (*née* Drysdale); one *s* one *d. Educ:* Paisley Grammar Sch.; Greenock High Sch.; Glasgow Univ. Director: Computers for Business (Scotland) Ltd, 1986–96; Business for Scotland, 1997–; Scotland in Europe, 2001–. Opposition spokesman on enterprise and the econ., Scottish Parlt, 2003–07. Nat. Treas., SNP, 2000–. Mem., ICAS, 1971. *Recreations:* cycling, golf, hill-walking, reading. *Address:* Scottish Parliament, Edinburgh EH99 1SP. *T:* (0131) 348 5701; *e-mail:* jim.mather.msp@ scottish.parliament.uk; Kaims, Roshven, by Lochailort, Inverness-shire PH38 4NB. *T:* (01687) 470244. *Club:* Traigh Golf (Arisaig).

MATHER, John Douglas, FCILT; Chief Executive, National Freight Consortium plc, 1984–93; *b* 27 Jan. 1936; *s* of John Dollandson and Emma May Mather; *m* 1958, Hilda Patricia (*née* Kirkwood); one *s* (one *d* decd). *Educ:* Manchester Univ. (BACom, MAEcon). MIPM. Personnel Management: Philips Electrical, 1959–66; Convoys Ltd, 1966–67; Personnel Management, Transport Management, National Freight Company, 1967–93. Chairman: Cranfield Ventures, 2000–06; CIT Hldgs, 2000– (Dir, 1994–); non-executive Director: Charles Sidney plc (formerly Bletchley Motor Gp), 1993–98; Computer Management Gp, 1993–98; Miller Gp, 1993–2003; St Mary's (Paddington) NHS Trust, 1995–97. Chairman: Bedfordshire TEC, 1991–93; Camden Business Partnership, 1991–; London Regeneration Consortium plc, 1993–95. Member: Adv. Bd, Cranfield Sch. of Management, 1992–97; Council, Cranfield Univ., 1993–2006. Trustee, Help The Aged, 1993– (Chm., 1995–2004). Mem., Co. of Carmen. CCMI. *Recreations:* golf, gardening, travel. *Address:* Roundhale, Love Lane, Kings Langley, Hertfordshire WD4 9HW. *T:* (01923) 263063. *Club:* Woburn Golf and Country.

MATHER, Richard Martin; Principal, Rick Mather Architects, since 1973; *b* 30 May 1937; *s* of late Richard John Mather and Opal Mather (*née* Martin). *Educ:* Sch. of Architecture and Allied Arts, Univ. of Oregon (BArch); Dept of Urban Design, Architectural Assoc. Teacher, UCL, Univ. of Westminster, and Harvard Grad. Sch. of Design, 1967–88; RIBA External Examiner to univs and colls in England and Scotland, 1986– (Mem. Council, RIBA, 1998–2000). Consultant Architect: Architectural Assoc., 1978–92 (Mem. Council, 1992–96); UEA, 1988–92; Univ. of Southampton, 1996–2006. Trustee: V & A Mus., 2000–; British Architectural Library Trust, 2004–. Thomas Jefferson Prof., Univ. of Virginia, 2003. Projects include: Times Newspaper HQ, London (RIBA

Award, 1992); further UEA buildings (RIBA Award, 1994; Civic Trust Award, 1995); All Glass Structure, London (RIBA Nat. Award, 1994); ARCO Building, Keble Coll., Oxford (RIBA Award, 1996; Civic Trust Award, 1997); The Priory, Hampstead (RIBA Nat. Award, 1998; AIA Award, 1997; Civic Trust Award, 1998); ISMA Centre, Univ. of Reading (RIBA Award, Civic Trust Award, 1999); Neptune Court, Nat. Maritime Mus. (Civic Trust Award, 2000); Wallace Collection, 2000; Dulwich Picture Gall. (RIBA Conservation Award, 2001; AIA Business Week/Arch. Record Award, 2001; Civic Trust Award, 2002); London South Bank Centre Masterplan, 2000–; Lindley Library, RHS, 2001; Virginia Mus. of Fine Arts, 2001; Sloane Robinson Bldg, Keble Coll., Oxford, 2002; Central Milton Keynes Residential Quarter, 2002–; Ashmolean Mus., Oxford Masterplan, 2002; Greenwich World Heritage Site Masterplan, 2002; Lincoln Sch. of Architecture, 2004; Lyric Th., Hammersmith, 2004; new Girls' Boarding House, Stowe Sch., 2007; Art & Design Acad., John Moores Univ., Liverpool, 2008; Culture Centre, Eastbourne, 2008. *Recreations:* gardens, food, ski-ing. *Address:* Rick Mather Architects, 123 Camden High Street, NW1 7JR. *T:* (020) 7284 1727.

MATHERS, Peter James, LVO 1995; HM Diplomatic Service, retired; High Commissioner to Jamaica, 2002–05; *b* 2 April 1946; *s* of Dr James Mathers and Margaret Mathers (*née* Kendrick); *m* 1983, Elisabeth Hoeller; one *s* one *d*. *Educ:* Bradfield Coll., Berks. Army SSC, 1968–71. Joined HM Diplomatic Service, 1971: SOAS (Persian), 1972–73; Tehran, 1973–75; Bonn, 1976–78; FCO, 1978–81; Copenhagen, 1981–85; Tehran, 1986–87; FCO, 1987–88; on secondment to UN Office, Vienna, 1988–91; FCO, 1991–95; Dep. High Comr, Barbados and Eastern Caribbean, 1995–98; Counsellor, Commercial and Economic, Stockholm, 1998–2002. *Address:* Doles Ash, Knott Park, Oxshott, Surrey KT22 0HS.

MATHERS, Sir Robert (William), Kt 1981; *b* 2 Aug. 1928; *s* of William Mathers and Olive Ida (*née* Wohlsen); *m* 1957, Betty Estelle Greasley; three *d*. *Educ:* Church of England Grammar Sch., E Brisbane. FAIM; FRMIA 1982. Chm. and Man. Dir, Mathers Enterprises Ltd, 1973–88; Chm., Kinney Shoes (Australia) Ltd, 1988–90; Dep. Chm., Bligh Coal Ltd, 1981–88; Director: Finlayson Timber & Hardware Pty Ltd, 1986–98; Nat. Mutual Life Assoc. of Australasia, 1988–96; Kidston Gold Mines, 1988–96; Buderim Ginger, 1989–95; Coles Myer, 1992–96; Leutenegger, 1992–95; Touraust Funds Management, 1994–96; Australian Tourism Co., 1994–96. Mem., Aust. Adv. Bd, Kmart Corp., USA, 1991–94. Life Mem., Retailers Assoc. of Qld, 1990 (Mem. Council, 1952–90); Pres., Footwear Retailers Assoc., 1960–63. Member: Council, Australian Bicentennial Authority, 1980–89; Finance Adv. Cttee for XII Commonwealth Games, 1979; Australiana Fund, 1980–94; Brisbane Adv. Bd, Salvation Army, 1990–96; Adv. Bd, Bond Univ. Sch. of Business, 1991–96; Councillor: Griffith Univ., 1978–88; Enterprise Australia, 1983–92; Deputy Chairman: Nat. Finance Cttee, Australian Stockman's Hall of Fame and Outback Heritage Centre, 1984–89; Organising Cttee, Brisbane Bid for 1992 Olympics, 1985–88. Liberal Party: Treas., Qld Br., 1976–90; Member: State Exec., Qld, 1976–90; Federal Council, 1977–90; Life Member: Qld Div., 1984; Young Liberal Movt, Qld Div., 1984. Trustee: WWF, Australia, 1981–87; Queensland Art Gall., 1983–87 (Founding Cttee Mem., Qld Art Gall. Foundn, 1979). Hon. FAMI 1984; FRSA 1989. DUniv Griffith, 1992. Cavaliere, Order of Merit (Italy), 1983. *Recreations:* golf, tennis, swimming. *Address:* Unit 2 Waterford, 88 Macquarie Street, St Lucia, Qld 4067, Australia. *T:* (7) 38703339. *Clubs:* Rotary, Royal Queensland Yacht Squadron, Tattersalls, Brisbane Polo, Queensland Rugby Union, Indooroopilly Golf (Brisbane).

MATHESON, Alexander, OBE 1990; JP; FRPharmS; Lord-Lieutenant of the Western Isles, 2001–07 (Vice Lord-Lieutenant, 1994–2001); Chairman: Highlands and Islands Airports Ltd, 2001–07; Harris Tweed Authority, 2001–07; *b* 16 Nov. 1941; *s* of Alex Matheson, MB ChB and Catherine Agnes Matheson (*née* Smith), MA; *m* 1965, Irene Mary Davidson, BSc Hons, MSc; two *s* two *d*. *Educ:* Nicolson Inst., Stornoway; Robert Gordon Inst. of Technol., Aberdeen. MRPharmS 1965, FRPharmS 1993. Pharmacist. Man. Dir, 1966–82 and Chm., 1967–, Roderick Smith Ltd. Member: Stornoway Town Council, 1967–75 (Provost, 1971–75); Ross and Cromarty CC, 1967–75. Member: Stornoway Trust Estate, 1967– (Chm., 1971–81); Stornoway Port Authy (formerly Pier and Harbour Commn), 1968– (Chm., 1971–72 and 1991–2001); Western Isles Island Council, 1974–94 (Convener, 1982–90); Western Isles Health Bd, 1974–2001 (Chm., 1993–2001). Pres., Islands Commn of Peripheral Maritime Regions of Europe, 1988–93. JP Western Is, 1971; Hon. Sheriff, Stornoway, 1972. *Recreations:* genealogy, research and lecturing on local history. *Address:* 33 Newton Street, Stornoway, Isle of Lewis HS1 2RW. *T:* (01851) 702082, *Fax:* (01851) 700415.

MATHESON of Matheson, yr, Lt Col Alexander Fergus; Secretary, Central Chancery of the Orders of Knighthood, since 2005; *b* 26 Aug. 1954; *o s* and *heir* of Major Sir Fergus John Matheson of Matheson, Bt, *qv*; *m* 1983, Katharine Davina Mary, *d* of Sir (William Richard) Michael Oswald, *qv*; two *s* one *d*. *Educ:* Eton Coll.; Durham Univ.; RMA Sandhurst; Army Staff Coll. Coldstream Guards, 1973–2001; Temp. Equerry to the Queen, 1982–84; COS, British Forces, Belize, 1992–94; Adjt, RMA Sandhurst, 1995–96; Bde Major, Household Div., 1996–98. CO Oxford Univ. OTC, 1998–2000. Exec. Dir, BSES Expeditions, 2001–05. Extra Equerry to the Queen, 2006–. *Recreations:* birds, bicycle, bagpipes. *Address:* Central Chancery of the Orders of Knighthood, St James's Palace, SW1A 1BH. *T:* (020) 7930 4832. *Club:* Pratt's.

MATHESON, Duncan, MA, LLM; QC 1989; **His Honour Judge Matheson;** a Circuit Judge, since 2000. *Educ:* Rugby Sch.; Trinity Coll., Cambridge. Bencher, Inner Temple, 1994. Jun. Counsel in Legal Aid Matters, Law Soc., 1981–89; a Recorder, 1985–2000. Chairman, Legal Aid Area Committee: London S, 1989–92; London, 1992–95. *Address:* Kingston upon Thames Crown Court, 6–8 Penrhyn Road, Kingston upon Thames, Surrey KT1 2BB.

MATHESON of Matheson, Major Sir Fergus (John), 7th Bt *cr* 1882, of Lochalsh, Co. Ross; Chief of Clan Matheson; *b* 22 Feb. 1927; *yr s* of Gen. Sir Torquhil George Matheson, 5th Bt, KCB, CMG and Lady Elizabeth Matheson, ARRC (*d* 1986), *o d* of 8th Earl of Albemarle; *S* brother, 1993; *m* 1952, Hon. Jean Elizabeth Mary Willoughby, *yr d* of 11th Baron Middleton, KG, MC; one *s* two *d*. *Educ:* Eton. Major, Coldstream Guards, 1944–64. One of HM Body Guard of the Hon. Corps of Gentlemen-at-Arms, 1979–97 (Standard Bearer, 1993–97). Pres., St John Ambulance, Norfolk, 1993–96. *Heir:* (to baronetcy and chiefship): *s* Lt-Col Alexander Fergus Matheson of Matheson, yr, *qv*. *Address:* The Old Rectory, Hedenham, Norfolk NR35 2LD.

MATHESON, Michael; Member (SNP) Falkirk West, Scottish Parliament, since 2007 (Central Scotland, 1999–2007); *b* 8 Sept. 1970; *s* of Edward and Elizabeth Matheson. *Educ:* Queen Margaret Coll., Edinburgh (BSc Occupational Therapy); Open Univ. (BA; Dip. Applied Social Scis). Health Profession Council State Registered Occupational Therapist. Community Occupational Therapist: Social Work Dept, Highland Regl Council, 1991–93; Central Regl Council, 1993–97; Social Work Services, Stirling Council, 1997–99. SNP dep. spokesperson on health and social policy, 1997–98; Dep. Opposition spokesman for justice and land reform, Scottish Parlt, 1999–2004; Opposition spokesman for culture and sport, 2004–07. Scottish Parliament: Mem., Health and Sport Cttee, 2007–; Cross Party Gp on Cuba, 2002–; Co-Convenor, Cross Party Gp on Malawi, 2006–; Mem., Cross Party Gp on Sport, 2001–. Member: Ochils Mountain Rescue Team; BSES. *Recreations:* mountaineering, travel, supporting Partick Thistle FC. *Address:* Scottish Parliament, Edinburgh EH99 1SP. *T:* (0131) 348 5671, *Fax:* (0131) 348 6474; (constituency office) 15a East Bridge Street, Falkirk FK1 1YD. *T:* (01324) 629271, *Fax:* (01324) 635576.

MATHESON, Stephen Charles Taylor, CB 1993; Deputy Secretary, 1989–2000, and Deputy Chairman, Inland Revenue, 1993–2000; *b* 27 June 1939; *s* of Robert Matheson and Olive Lovick; *m* 1960, Marna Rutherford Burnett; two *s*. *Educ:* Aberdeen Grammar Sch.; Aberdeen Univ. (MA hons English Lang. and Lit., 1961). HM Inspector of Taxes, 1961–70; Principal, Bd of Inland Revenue, 1970–75; Private Sec. to Paymaster General, 1975–76, to Chancellor of the Exchequer, 1976–77; Board of Inland Revenue, 1977–2000; Project Manager, Computerisation of Pay As You Earn Project; Under Sec., 1984; Dir of IT, 1984; Comr, 1989; Dir Gen. (Management), 1989–94, (Policy and Technical), 1994–2000. CITP; FBCS (Pres., 1991–92); FIPPM (FBIPM 1996). Hon. DBA De Montfort Univ., 1994. *Publications:* Maurice Walsh, Storyteller, 1985; (contrib.) The Listowel Literary Phenomenon, 1994. *Recreations:* Scottish and Irish literature, book collecting, cooking, music.

MATHEW, Brian Frederick, MBE 2005; Editor, Curtis's Botanical Magazine, 1993–2002; *b* 30 Aug. 1936; *s* of Frederick Mathew and Ethel Mathew (*née* Baines); *m* 1966, Helen Margaret Briggs; one *s*. *Educ:* Oxted County Grammar Sch.; RHS Sch. of Horticulture (RHS Dip. in Horticulture (Hons) 1962). Botanist, Royal Botanic Gardens, Kew, 1967–92, Hon. Res. Fellow, 1999. Mem., RHS Horticultural Bd, 2002–04. VMH 1992. *Publications:* Dwarf Bulbs, 1973; The Genus Daphne, 1976; The Larger Bulbs, 1978; A Field Guide to Bulbs of Europe, 1981; The Iris, 1981, 2nd edn 1989; The Crocus, 1982; A Field Guide to the Bulbous Plants of Turkey, 1984; Hellebores, 1989; The Genus Lewisia, 1989; Allium Section Allium, 1996; Growing Bulbs, 1997; Bulbs: the four seasons, 1998. *Recreations:* gardening, photography.

MATHEW, John Charles; QC 1977; *b* 3 May 1927; *s* of late Sir Theobald Mathew, KBE, MC, and Lady Mathew; *m* 1952, Jennifer Jane Mathew (*née* Lagden); two *d*. *Educ:* Beaumont Coll. Served, Royal Navy, 1945–47. Called to Bar, Lincoln's Inn, 1949; apptd Junior Prosecuting Counsel to the Crown, 1959; First Sen. Prosecuting Counsel to the Crown, 1974–77. Elected a Bencher of Lincoln's Inn, 1970. *Recreations:* golf, shooting, cinema. *Address:* 45 Abingdon Court, 17 Abingdon Villas, W8 6BT. *T:* (020) 7937 7535. *Club:* Garrick.

MATHEW, Robert Knox, (Robin); QC 1992; *b* 22 Jan. 1945; *s* of late Robert Mathew, TD, MP and Joan Leslie (*née* Bruce); *m* 1968, Anne Rosella Elliott; one *d*. *Educ:* Eton Coll.; Trinity Coll., Dublin (BA 1967). City and financial journalist, 1968–76. Called to the Bar, Lincoln's Inn, 1974. Asst Parly Boundary Comr, 1992–98. *Recreations:* country pursuits, racing, ski-ing. *Address:* 12 New Square, Lincoln's Inn, WC2A 3SW; Church Farm, Little Barrington, Burford, Oxon OX18 5TE. *T:* (01451) 844311, *Fax:* (01451) 844768. *Club:* Boodle's.

MATHEWS, Rear Adm. Andrew David Hugh, CB 2008; Director General Submarines, Defence Equipment and Support, 2005–May 2009; Chief of Materiel (Fleet) and Chief of Fleet Support to Navy Board (in rank of Vice Adm.), from May 2009; *b* Stanford le Hope, Essex, 27 June 1958; *s* of Hugh Leslie Mathews, OBE and Pamela Lorna Mathews (*née* Edwards); *m* 1987, Beverley Yvette Taylor; one *s* one *d*. *Educ:* Newcastle Royal Grammar Sch.; RNEC, Manadon (BSc Hons); RNC, Greenwich (MSc). BRNC, Dartmouth, 1976; nuclear engrg appts at sea and ashore; RN Staff Course, RNC Greenwich, 1989; MEO, HMS Trenchant, 1990–92; MEO, subseq. Captain Sea Trng, 1992–95; Second Sea Lord's Dept, 1995–97; Asst Dir, Nuclear Propulsion Safety, 1997–99; RCDS 2000; Mil. Asst to Chief of Defence Procurement, 2000–02; Naval Base Comdr, Devonport, 2002–05. Pres., Navy Rowing, 2006. *Recreations:* dinghy sailing, cycling, gardening, Cornwall. *Club:* Army and Navy.

MATHEWS, Jeremy Fell, CMG 1989; Attorney General of Hong Kong, 1988–97; *b* 14 Dec. 1941; *s* of George James and Ivy Priscilla Mathews; *m* 1st, 1968, Sophie Lee (marr. diss. 1992); two *d*; 2nd, 1992, Halima Guterres. *Educ:* Palmer's Grammar Sch., England. Qualified as solicitor, London, 1963; private practice, London, 1963–65; Dep. Dist Registrar in the High Court of Australia, Sydney, 1966–67; Hong Kong Government: Crown Counsel, 1968; Dep. Law Draftsman, 1978; Dep. Crown Solicitor, 1981; Crown Solicitor, 1982. Dep. Dist Chm., Appeals Service, 1998–2003. Chm. Council, Overseas Service Pensioners' Assoc., 2004–. *Recreations:* reading, gardening, music. *Club:* Hong Kong.

MATHEWS, Marina Sarah Dewe, (Mrs John Dewe Mathews); *see* Warner, M. S.

MATHEWS, Michael Robert; Partner, Clifford Chance, 1971–2000; President, Law Society of England and Wales, 1998–99; *b* 3 Nov. 1941; *s* of George Walter Mathews and Betty Mathews (*née* Willcox); *m* 1966, Ann Gieve; two *s* one *d*. *Educ:* Uppingham Sch.; King's Coll., Cambridge (MA). Admitted solicitor, 1966; joined Coward Chance (later Clifford Chance), 1963. Vice Pres. and Chm., City of London Law Soc., 1992–95; Law Society of England and Wales: Mem. Council, 1995–2004; Dep. Vice Pres. and Treas., 1996–97; Vice Pres., 1997–98. Master: City of London Solicitors' Co., 1999–2000; Carpenters' Co., 2007–08. Hon. LLD City, 1999. *Recreations:* walking, watching good cricket. *Address:* 12 Clare Lawn Avenue, East Sheen, SW14 8BG.

MATHEWS, Peter Michael, CMG 2002; Chairman and Managing Director, Black Country Metals Ltd, since 1986; *b* 26 Oct. 1946; *s* of Cyril and Audrey Mathews; *m* 1980, Gillian Anne (*née* Hatfield); one *s* one *d*. *Educ:* Ellesmere Coll., Shropshire; Mt Radford Sch., Exeter. UK Trade & Investment (formerly Trade Partners UK): Mem., Bd, 2001–04; Mem., Internat. Trade Develt Adv. Panel, 2001–; Chm., Engrg Sector Adv. Gp, 2006–07; Chm., Advanced Engrg Adv. Bd, 2007–. Pres., Midlands World Trade Forum, 2001–. Mem., Business Forum for Multilinguism, EC. Member: Adv. Bd, Bureau of Internat. Recycling, Brussels, 1995–2006; Bd, British Metals Recycling Assoc., 2002–; Bd, Internat. Reinforcing Bar Assoc., Istanbul; Chm., Convention Cttee Bureau of Internat. Recycling. Nat. Pres., British Metal Fedn, 1997–99. Pres., Dudley Chamber of Commerce, 2002–05; Member: Bd, Black Country Chamber of Commerce, 2002– (Pres., 2007–); Council, Birmingham Chamber of Commerce, 2002–. MIex 1996; Mem., Inst. of Cast Metal Engrs, 2002; FInstD 1997. FRSA 1990. Hon. Life Mem., Ulster Metals Assoc., 1990. *Recreations:* theatre, golf, snooker, travel. *Address:* c/o Black Country Metals Ltd, Stambermill House, 1 Bagley Street, Lye, Stourbridge, W Midlands DY9 7AY. *T:* (01384) 893893, *Fax:* (01384) 891504; *e-mail:* peter@bcmetals.com.

MATHEWSON, Sir George (Ross), Kt 1999; CBE 1985; BSc, PhD, MBA; FRSE; CEng, MIEE; Chairman: Royal Bank of Scotland Group, 2001–06 (Director, 1987–2006; Deputy Chairman, 2000–01); Royal Bank of Scotland, 2001–06 (Director, 1987–2006); National Westminster Bank, 2001–06; Cheviot Asset Management Ltd, since 2006; Wood

Mackenzie Ltd, since 2007; *b* 14 May 1940; *s* of George Mathewson and Charlotte Gordon (*née* Ross); *m* 1966, Sheila Alexandra Graham (*née* Bennett); two *s*. *Educ*: Perth Academy; St Andrews Univ. (BSc, PhD); Canisius Coll., Buffalo, NY (MBA). Assistant Lecturer, St Andrews Univ., 1964–67; various posts in Research & Development, Avionics Engineering, Bell Aerospace, Buffalo, NY, 1967–72; joined Industrial & Commercial Finance Corp., Edinburgh, 1972; Area Manager, Aberdeen, 1974, and Asst General Manager and Director, 1979; Chief Exec. and Mem., Scottish Develt Agency, 1981–87; Royal Bank of Scotland Group: Dir of Strategic Planning and Develt, 1987–90; Dep. Gp Chief Exec., 1990–92; Gp Chief Exec., 1992–2000. Director: Scottish Investment Trust Ltd, 1981–; IIF Inc., 2001–; Santander Central Hispano, 2001–04. Chm., Council of Econ. Advrs to the Scottish Govt, 2007–; Mem., Financial Reporting Council, 2004–. Pres., BBA, 2002–04. Chm., Bd of Trustees, Royal Botanic Garden, Edinburgh, 2007–. FCIBS 1994; CCMI (CBIM 1985); FRSE 1988. Hon. LLD: Dundee, 1983; St Andrews, 2000; DUniv Glasgow, 2001; Dr *hc* Edinburgh, 2002. *Publications*: various articles on engineering/finance. *Recreations*: Rugby, tennis, business. *Address*: Royal Bank of Scotland Group, PO Box 1000, Gogarburn, Edinburgh EH12 1HQ. *Club*: New (Edinburgh).

MATHEWSON, Hew Byrne, FDSRCSE; Principal Dental Surgeon, Edinburgh, since 1977; President, General Dental Council, since 2003; *b* 18 Nov. 1949; *s* of Alexander M. Mathewson and Dorothy W. Mathewson; *m* 1971, Lorna A. M. McConnachie; one *s* one *d*. *Educ*: High Sch. of Glasgow; Glasgow Univ. (BDS 1974); Univ. of Wales, Cardiff (LLM 1990). DGDP 1992; FDSRCSE 1995; FDSRCS 2007. Associate Dental Surgeon, Wishaw and Canterbury, 1974–77. Asst Dir, Dental Studies, Univ. of Edinburgh, 1987–99; Regl Gen. Practice Vocational Trng Advr, SE Scotland, 1988–96. Chm., Scottish Gen. Dental Services Cttee, 1991–97; Vice-Chm., UK Gen. Dental Services Cttee, 2000–03; Chm. Bd, Mental Health Tribunal for Scotland Admin. Member: GDC, 1996– (Jt Chair, Professional Conduct Cttee, 2001–03); Council for Regulation of Health Care Professionals, 2003– (Vice-Chm., 2005–06); Council for Registration of Forensic Practitioners, 2006–; Pres., Conf. of Orders and Assimilated Bodies of Dental Practitioners in Europe, 2006–08. Mem., Appeals Cttee, ICAEW, 2006–. Mem. Editl Bd, British Dental Jl, 1992–2003. *Recreations*: walking, carpentry, theatre and cinema, travel. *Address*: General Dental Council, 37 Wimpole Street, W1G 8DQ.

MATHEWSON, Iain Arthur Gray, CMG 2004; HM Diplomatic Service, retired; non-executive Director, Candole Partners, since 2007; Adviser: Detica plc, since 2007; Citigroup, since 2007; *b* 16 March 1952; *s* of late John Gray Mathewson and of Jane Mathewson (now Murray); *m* 1983, Jennifer Bloch; one *s* one *d*. *Educ*: Downside Sch.; Corpus Christi Coll., Cambridge. HM Customs and Excise, 1974–77; DHSS, 1977–80; FCO, 1980; First Secretary: UK Mission to UN, NY, 1981–84; Warsaw, 1985–88; FCO, 1989–93; Counsellor: Prague, 1993–96; FCO, 1996–2006. Mem., British Wireless Dinner Club. *Recreations*: golf, music. *Address*: e-mail: iain@mathewson.co.uk. *Clubs*: Travellers; Berkshire Golf.

MATHIAS, Prof. Christopher Joseph, DPhil, DSc; FRCP, FMedSci; Professor of Neurovascular Medicine, University of London, since 1991, at Imperial College London (St Mary's Hospital) (formerly Imperial College School of Medicine (St Mary's Hospital), Imperial College of Science, Technology and Medicine), and Institute of Neurology, University College London; Consultant Physician, since 1982: St Mary's Hospital; National Hospital for Neurology and Neurosurgery; *b* 16 March 1949; *s* of late Lt Elias Mathias, IN and Hilda Mathias (*née* Pereira); *m* 1977, Rosalind (Lindy) Margaret, *d* of late Ambrose Jolleys, Cons. Paediatric Surgeon and of Betty Jolleys; two *s* one *d*. *Educ*: St Aloysius Sch., Visakhapatnam; St Joseph's E. H. Sch., Bangalore; St John's Med. Coll., Bangalore Univ. (MB BS 1972); Worcester Coll., Oxford; Wolfson Coll., Oxford (DPhil 1976); Univ. of London (DSc 1995). LRCSE, LRCPSGlas 1974; MRCP 1978, FRCP 1987. Rhodes Schol., 1972–75; Res. Officer and Hon. Registrar, Dept of Neurology, Churchill Hosp., Oxford, 1972–76; Clinical Asst and Res. Fellow, Nat. Spinal Injuries Centre, Stoke Mandeville Hosp., 1973–76; Sen. Hse Officer, Dept of Medicine, RPMS/Hammersmith Hosp., 1976–77; Registrar in Medicine, St Mary's Hosp., Portsmouth and Dept of Renal Medicine, Univ. of Southampton, 1977–79; Wellcome Trust Sen. Res. Fellow in Clinical Sci. at St Mary's Hosp. Med. Sch., 1979–84; Wellcome Trust Sen. Lectr in Med. Sci., St Mary's Hosp. Med. Sch. and Inst. of Neurol., 1984–92. Consultant Physician, Western Eye Hosp., 1982–98. Prof. Ruitinga Foundn Award and Vis. Prof., Acad. Med. Centre, Univ. of Amsterdam, 1988; Nimmo Vis. Prof., Univ. of Adelaide, 1996; Visiting Professor: Univ. of Hawaii, 1999; Univ. of Hong Kong, 2008. Dr J. Thomas Meml Oration, St John's Med. Coll., Bangalore Univ., 1988; Lectures: Lord Florey Meml, and Dorothy Mortlock, Royal Adelaide Hosp., Univ. of Adelaide, 1991; BP Regl, RCP, 1992; Thailand Neurological Soc., 1995; Sir Hugh Cairns Meml, Adelaide, 1996; Allan Birch Meml, London, 1997; Abbie Meml, Univ. of Adelaide, 1999; Coll., RCP, 2001; Sir Robert Menzies Meml Foundn, Sydney, 2001; Wahler Meml, London Jewish Med. Soc., 2002; Inaugural, Portuguese Autonomic Soc., Lisbon, 2002; Prof. Dr R. L. Müller Meml, Univ. of Erlangen, 2002; Prof. Athasit Vejajiva, Bangkok, 2003; Sir Roger Bannister, 2004, Chelsea Therapeutics, 2007, Jt Eur. Fedn of Autonomic Socs and Amer. Autonomic Soc.; Sir Gordon Holmes, London, 2004; Prof. Krishnamoorthy, Srinivas, Chennai, 2005; Keynote, 58th Congress of Japanese Neurovegetative Soc., Chiba, 2005; Valsalva, Bologna, 2006; 20th Shri K. Gopalakrishna, Chennai, 2006; Roche, Internal Medicine Assoc. of Aust. and NZ, 2007; Northern Communities Health Foundn, Adelaide, 2007; Swiss Autonomic Soc., Berne, 2008; G. M. Mascarenhas Oration, St John's Medical Coll. N Atlantic Chapter, Florida, 2008. Chairman: Clinical Autonomic Res. Soc., 1987–90 (first Sec., 1982–86); Res. Cttee, World Fedn of Neurol., 1993–97 (Mem., 1989–93); Chm., Scientific Panel, 1994–99, Mem., Task Force, 2004–06, Lead, Task Force on Orthostatic Intolerance, 2008–, European Fedn of Neurol Socs; Pres., Eur. Fedn of Autonomic Socs, 1998–2004; Member: Scientific Cttee, Internat. Spinal Res. Trust, 1996–2008; Bd of Dirs, Amer. Autonomic Soc., 1996–2004; Sec. of State's Hon. Med. Adv. Panel on Driving and Disorders of the Nervous System, 2004–; Task Force, Amer. Spinal Injury Assoc., 2004–07; Mem. and Chm., MSA-Autonomic Gp, Consensus Conference on MSA, Amer. Acad. of Neurology, Boston, 2007. Consultant, ESA, 1997–2000; Mem., Jt ESA/NASA Neuroscience Rev. Panel, 1997. Non-exec. Dir, W London Mental Health Trust, 2008–. Mem., NW Thames Regl Adv. Cttee for Distinction Awards, 1999–2001; Chm., Dr P. M. Shankland (Pushpa Chopra) Charitable Trust Prize Fund, 1998–. Mem., Bd of Govs, Nat. Soc. for Epilepsy, 2004–08. Patron: Autonomic Disorders Assoc. Sarah Matheson Trust, 1997–; STARS (Syncope Trust), 2001–. FMedSci 2001. Founder Editor-in-Chief, Clinical Autonomic Res., 1991–; Member, Editorial Board: Hypertension, 1990–93; Jl of Pharmaceutical Medicine, 1991–95; Functional Neurol., 1990–2003; High Blood Pressure and Cardiovascular Prevention, 1992–; Jl of Hypertension, 1994–97; Parkinsonism and Related Disorders, 1995–2005, 2008–; Internat. Jl of Evidence-Based Healthcare, 2007–. Dr *hc* Lisbon, 2007. *Publications*: (ed jtly) Mild Hypertension: current controversies and new approaches, 1984; (ed jtly) Concepts in Hypertension: a festschrift for Prof. Sir Stanley Peart, 1989; (ed with Sir Roger Bannister) Autonomic Failure: a textbook of clinical disorders of the autonomic nervous system, 3rd edn 1992, 4th edn 1999; chaps in neurol. and cardiovascular textbooks; papers on nervous system and hormonal control of circulation in neurological, cardiovascular and other medical disorders. *Recreations*: gardening, badminton, watching cricket and football, observing human (and canine) behaviour. *Address*: Meadowcroft, West End Lane, Stoke Poges, Bucks SL2 4NE; e-mail: c.mathias@imperial.ac.uk. *Clubs*: Athenæum, Royal Society of Medicine; Vincent's (Oxford).

MATHIAS, Surg. Rear-Adm. (D) Frank Russell Bentley; retired 1985; Director, Naval Dental Services, 1983–85, and Deputy Director of Defence Dental Services (Organisation), Ministry of Defence, 1985; *b* 27 Dec. 1927; *s* of Thomas Bentley Mathias and Phebe Ann Mathias; *m* 1954, Margaret Joyce (*née* Daniels); one *s* one *d*. *Educ*: Narberth Grammar Sch.; Guy's Hosp., London. LDSRCS Eng. 1952. House Surgeon, Sussex County Hosp., Brighton, 1952–53; joined RN, 1953; principal appointments: Staff Dental Surgeon, Flag Officer Malta, 1972; Flotilla Dental Surgeon, Flag Officer Submarines, 1972–74; Comd Dental Surgeon, Flag Officer Naval Air Comd, 1974–76; Dep. Dir, Naval Dental Services, 1976–80; Comd Dental Surgeon to C-in-C Naval Home Comd, 1980–83. QHDS 1982–85. OStJ 1981.

MATHIAS, (Jonathan) Glyn; Member, Electoral Commission, 2001–08; *b* 19 Feb. 1945; *s* of late Roland Glyn Mathias and Mary Annie (*née* Hawes); *m* 2000, Ann Bowen (*née* Hughes); one *s* two *d*. *Educ*: Llandovery Coll., Carmarthenshire; Jesus Coll., Oxford (MA); Univ. of Southampton (MSc). Reporter, South Wales Echo, 1967–70; News Asst, BBC Southampton, 1970–73; ITN: Political Reporter, London, 1973–81; Political Editor, 1981–86; Asst Editor, 1986–91; Controller, Public Affairs, 1991–93; Chief Political Correspondent, 1993–94; BBC Wales: Political Editor, 1994–99; Manager, Public Affairs, 1999–2000. Sen. Lectr, British Politics, UWIC, 2001–03 (Hon. Fellow, 2004). *Publications*: (ed) ITN Election Factbook, 1987; (contrib.) Televising Democracies, 1992. *Recreation*: family life. *Address*: Harddfan, Avenue Court, Brecon, Powys LD3 9BE. *T*: (01874) 623368; e-mail: glynmathias@btinternet.com. *Club*: Reform.

MATHIAS, Pauline Mary; Headmistress, More House School, 1974–89; *b* 4 Oct. 1928; *d* of Francis and Hilda Donovan; *m* 1954, Prof. Anthony Peter Mathias; two *s*. *Educ*: La Retraite High School; Bedford College, London (BA Hons; DipEd). Head of English Dept, London Oratory Sch., 1954–64; Sen. Lectr in English and Admissions Tutor, Coloma Coll. of Education, 1964–74. Mem., ITC, 1991–96. Pres., GSA, 1982–83; Vice-Pres., Women's Careers Foundn, 1985–89; Chairman: ISIS, 1984–86; GBGSA, 1994–98 (Dep. Chm., 1992–94). Governor: Westminster Cathedral Choir Sch., 1978–2003; ESU, 1986–92; St Felix Sch., Southwold, 1986–95 (Chm., 1990–95); London Oratory Sch., 1987– (Dep. Chm., 1994–2000); St Mary's Sch., Ascot, 1995–2002 (Trustee, 2006–); Godolphin and Latymer Sch., 1995–98. *Address*: 18 Lee Road, Aldeburgh, Suffolk IP15 5HG.

MATHIAS, Dr Peter, CBE 1984; MA, DLitt; FBA 1977; Master of Downing College, Cambridge, 1987–95 (Hon. Fellow, 1995); *b* 10 Jan. 1928; *o c* of John Samuel and late Marian Helen Mathias; *m* 1958, Elizabeth Ann, *d* of Robert Blackmore, JP, Bath; two *s* one *d*. *Educ*: Colston's Sch., Bristol; Jesus Coll., Cambridge (Schol.; Hon. Fellow, 1987). 1st cl. (dist) Hist. Tripos, 1950, 1951; DLitt: Oxon, 1985; Cantab, 1987. Research Fellow, Jesus Coll., Cambridge, 1952–55; Asst Lectr and Lectr, Faculty of History, Cambridge, 1955–68; Dir of Studies in History and Fellow, Queens' Coll., Cambridge, 1955–68 (Hon. Fellow, 1987); Tutor, 1957–68; Senior Proctor, Cambridge Univ., 1965–66; Chichele Prof. of Economic History, Oxford Univ., and Fellow of All Souls Coll., Oxford, 1969–87; Emeritus Fellow, 1987–. Mem., Council of the Senate, Cambridge Univ., 1991–94. Visiting Professor: Univ. of Toronto, 1961; School of Economics, Delhi, 1967; Univ. of California, Berkeley, 1967; Univ. of Pa, 1972; Virginia Gildersleeve, Barnard Coll., Columbia Univ., 1972; Johns Hopkins Univ., 1979; ANU, Canberra, 1981; Geneva, 1986; Leuven, 1990; San Marino, 1990; Waseda, 1996; Osaka Gakuin, 1998; Free Univ., Bolzano, 1999; Kansai, 2006. Asst Editor, Econ. Hist. Rev., 1955–57; Gen. Editor, Debates in Economic History, 1967–86. Chairman: Business Archives Council, 1968–72 (Vice-Pres., 1980–84 and 1995–; Pres., 1984–95); Econ. and Social History Cttee, SSRC, 1975–77 (Mem., 1970–77); Acad. Adv. Council, University Coll., Buckingham, 1979–84 (Mem., 1984–98); Wellcome Trust Adv. Panel for History of Medicine, 1981–88; Friends of Kettle's Yard, 1989–95; Fitzwilliam Mus. Enterprises Ltd, 1990–99; Syndic of Fitzwilliam Mus., 1987–98; Bd of Continuing Educn, 1991–95; Nat. Adv. Council, British Library, 1994–2000 (Mem., Adv. Cttee (Humanities and Social Scis), 1990–94); Central European Univ. Press, 2000–; Member: ABRC, 1983–89; Round Table, Council of Industry and Higher Educn, 1989–94; Beirat Wissenschaftskolleg, Berlin, 1992–98; Bd of Patrons, Eur. Banking Hist. Assoc., 1995–. Treasurer, Econ. Hist. Soc., 1968–88 (Pres., 1989–92; Vice Pres., 1992–); Hon. Treasurer, British Acad., 1980–89; International Economic History Association: Sec., 1959–62; Pres., 1974–78; Hon. Pres., 1978–; Vice Pres., Internat. Inst. of Economic History Francesco Datini, Prato, 1987–99 (Mem. Exec. Cttee, 1972–99; Comitato d'Honore, 1999–); Jerusalem Cttee, 1978–93; Mem., Academia Europaea, 1989; Trustee and Mem. Council, GB Sasakawa Foundn, 1994– (Chm., 1997–2005; Pres., 2006–); Foreign Member: Royal Danish Acad., 1982; Royal Belgian Acad., 1988. Curator, Bodleian Library, 1972–87. FRHistS 1972 (Vice-Pres., 1976–80; Hon. Vice-Pres., 2001). Hon. DLitt: Buckingham, 1985; Birmingham, 1988; Hull, 1992; Warwick, 1995; De Montfort, 1995; East Anglia, 1999; Hon. DSc Russian Acad. of Scis, 2002; Hon. Dr Kansai, 2006. Order of the Rising Sun with Gold Rays (Japan), 2003. *Publications*: The Brewing Industry in England 1700–1830, 1959, repr. 1993; English Trade Tokens, 1962; Retailing Revolution, 1967; The First Industrial Nation, 1969, rev. edn 1983; (ed) Science and Society 1600–1900, 1972; The Transformation of England, 1979; L'Economia Britannica dal 1815 al 1914, 1994; Cinque Lezioni di Teoria e Storia, 2003; General Editor, Cambridge Economic History of Europe, 1968–93. *Recreation*: travel. *Address*: 33 Church Street, Chesterton, Cambridge CB4 1DT. *T*: (01223) 329824.

MATHIAS, Sean Gerard; writer and director; *b* 14 March 1956; *s* of John Frederick Mathias and Anne Josephine Patricia Mathias (*née* Harding). *Educ*: Bishop Vaughan Comprehensive Sch., Swansea. *Writer: plays*: Cowardice, Ambassadors, 1983; A Prayer for Wings, and Infidelities, Edinburgh Fest., 1985; Poor Nanny, King's Head, Islington, 1989; Swansea Boys, RNT Studio, 1991; *screenplay*: The Lost Language of Cranes, 1991. *Director: film*: Bent, 1996 (Prix de la Jeunesse, Cannes, 1997); *plays*: Exceptions, New End, 1989; Bent, RNT, transf. Garrick, 1990; Uncle Vanya, RNT, 1992; Ghosts, Sherman Th., Cardiff, 1993; Les Parents Terribles, RNT, 1994; Design for Living, Donmar, transf. Gielgud, 1994; Indiscretions, NY, 1995; A Little Night Music, RNT, 1995; Marlene, Oldham, transf. Lyric, 1996, NY, 1999; Antony and Cleopatra, RNT, 1998; Suddenly Last Summer, Comedy, 1999; Servicemen, NY, 2001; Dance of Death, NY, 2001, Lyric, 2003, Sydney, 2004; The Elephant Man, NY, 2002; Company, Washington, 2002; Antigone, Cape Town, 2004; Aladdin, Old Vic, 2005; Shoreditch Madonna, Soho Th., 2005; The Cherry Orchard, LA, 2006; Triptych, Johannesburg, 2007, Southwark Playhouse, 2008; Ring Round the Moon, Playhouse, 2008. Dir of the Year, Evening Standard Awards, and Critics' Circle Awards, 1994. *Publications: plays*: A Prayer for Wings,

1985; Infidelities, 1985; *novella*: Manhattan Mourning, 1989. *Address*: c/o Judy Daish Associates, 2 St Charles Place, W10 6EG. *T*: (020) 8964 8811.

MATHIES, Monika W.; *see* Wulf-Mathies.

MATHIESON, Rt Hon. Dame Janet Hilary; *see* Smith, Rt Hon. Dame J. H.

MATLHABAPHIRI, Gaotlhaetse Utlwang Sankoloba; MP (Democratic Party), Botswana, since 2004; Assistant Minister, Ministry of Health, Botswana, since 2008; *b* 6 Nov. 1949; *s* of late Sankoloba and Khumo Matlhabaphiri; four *d*. *Educ*: Diamond Corporation Training Sch.; London; Friederick Ebert Foundn, Gaborone (Labour Economics). Clerk, Standard Chartered Bank, 1971–72; teacher, also part-time Dep. Head Master, Capital Continuation Classes, Gaborone, 1971–72; diamond sorter valuator, 1973–79. MP, Botswana, 1979–84 and 1989–94; Gen. Sec., Botswana Democratic Party Youth Wing, 1978–85, 1992–96 and 1996–98; Asst Minister of Agriculture, 1979–85; Mem., Central Cttee, Botswana Democratic Party, 1982–85, 1991–95 and 1995–99 (Chm., Labour Cttee, 1991); Ambassador of Botswana to Nordic countries, 1985–86; High Comr for Botswana in UK, 1986–88 (concurrently Ambassador (non-resident) to Romania and Yugoslavia); High Comr of Botswana to Namibia and Ghana, and Ambassador to Angola, 2000–04; Asst Minister of Labour and Home Affairs, 2007–08. Asst Gen. Sec., Bank Employees Union, 1972; Gen. Sec., Botswana Diamond Sorters Valuators Union, 1976–79; Chairman: Botswana Fedn of Trade Unions, 1979; Parly Public Accounts Cttee, 1993–94; Law Reform Cttee, 1993–94; Citizen Cttee of Botswana, 1998–2000. Mem. Bd, Botswana Develt Corp., 1998–2000. Member: CPA; Botswana Br., IPU Cttee, 1993; UEESA. Conductor/Dir, Botswana Democratic Party Internat. Choir. Governor, IFAD, 1980–84. *Recreations*: footballer, athlete; choral music. *Clubs*: Royal Over-Seas League, Royal Commonwealth Society; Gaborone Township Rollers.

MATLOCK, Prof. Jack Foust; American career diplomat; George F. Kennan Professor, Institute for Advanced Study, Princeton, 1996–2001; *b* 1 Oct. 1929; *s* of late Jack F. Matlock and of Nellie Matlock (*née* McSwain); *m* 1949, Rebecca Burrum; four *s* one *d*. *Educ*: Duke Univ. (BA 1950); Columbia Univ. (MA 1952). Editor and translator on Current Digest of the Soviet Press, 1952–53; Russian language and literature Instructor, Dartmouth Coll., 1953–56; joined US Foreign Service, 1956; served in Moscow, Austria, Ghana, Zanzibar, Tanzania; Vis. Prof. of Political Science, Vanderbilt Univ., 1978–79; Dep. Dir, Foreign Service Inst., 1979–80; Chargé d'Affaires, Moscow, 1981; Ambassador to Czechoslovakia, 1981; Special Asst to President for Nat. Security Affairs and Sen. Dir, European and Soviet Affairs on Nat. Security Council Staff, 1983–86; Ambassador to Soviet Union, 1987–91. Kathryn and Shelby Cullom Davis Prof., Columbia Univ., 1993–96. Vis. Prof. Princeton Univ., 2001–04; Sol Linowitz Prof. of Internat. Relns, Hamilton Coll., 2006. Masaryk Award, 1983; Superior Honor Award, Dept of State, 1981; Presidential Meritorious Service Award, 1984, 1987. *Publications*: Handbook to Russian edn of Stalin's Works, 1972; Autopsy on an Empire: the American Ambassador's account of the collapse of the Soviet Union, 1995; Reagan and Gorbachev: how the Cold War ended, 2004; articles on US–Soviet relations. *Address*: 940 Princeton-Kingston Road, Princeton, NJ 08540, USA; 32 Wagoner Hill Road, Fayetteville, TN 37334, USA. *Club*: Century Association (NY).

MATOKA, Dr Peter Wilfred, GCCF 2006; Senior Lecturer, Department of Social Development Studies, University of Zambia, since 1995; *b* 8 April 1930; *m* 1957, Grace Joyce; two *s* one *d*. *Educ*: Mwinilunga Sch.; Munali Secondary Sch.; University Coll. of Fort Hare (BA Rhodes); American Univ., Washington (Dipl. Internat. Relations); Univ. of Zambia (MA); Univ. of Warwick (PhD 1994). MP Mwinilunga, Parlt of Zambia, 1964–78; Minister: of Information and Postal Services, 1964–65; of Health, 1965–66; of Works, 1967; of Power, Transport and Works, 1968; of Luapula Province, 1969; High Comr for Zambia in UK and Ambassador to the Holy See, 1970–71; Minister of Health, 1971–72; Minister of Local Govt and Housing, 1972–77; Minister of Economic and Technical Co-operation and Pres., Africa, Caribbean and Pacific Gp of States, 1977; retd from active politics, 1992; Sen. Regl Advr, Econ. Commn for Africa, UN, Addis Ababa, 1979–83; High Comr in Zimbabwe, 1984–89. Mem. Central Cttee, United National Independence Party, 1971–78 and 1984–91 (Chairman: Social and Cultural Cttee, 1989–90; Sci. and Technol. Cttee, 1990–91). Life Mem., CPA, 1974. Pres., AA of Zambia, 1969–70. Kt of St Gregory the Great, 1964; Mem., Knightly Assoc. of St George the Martyr, 1986–. *Publication*: Child Labour in Zambia, 1999. *Recreations*: reading, walking, watching television. *Address*: PO Box 50101, Lusaka, Zambia; (home) 26D Ibex Hill Township, Lusaka, Zambia.

MATOLENGWE, Rt Rev. Patrick Monwabisi; a Bishop Suffragan of Cape Town, 1976–88, retired; Director, Reconciliation and Healing Programme, South African Council of Churches, 1997; *b* 12 May 1937; *s* of David and Emma Matolengwe; *m* 1967, Crecencia Nompumelelo (*née* Nxele); three *s* two *d*. *Educ*: Healdtown Institution, Fort Beaufort (matric.); Lovedale Teacher Training Coll., Alice; Bishop Gray Coll., Cape Town; Federal Theol Sem., Alice (Cert. Theol.). MTh and DD, Nashotah House Seminary, 1992; DMin, United Theol Seminary, 1996. Teaching, 1959–60; Court Interpreter, 1960–61; theological studies, 1962–65; Curacy at Herschel, Dio. Grahamstown, 1965–68; Rector of Nyanga, Dio. Cape Town, 1968–76; Rector of St Luke's Church, Whitewater, 1988–89, Dean and Assisting Bishop, All Saints' Cathedral, 1990–97, Dio. of Milwaukee. *Recreations*: scouting, singing, music, reading, tennis. *Address*: South African Council of Churches, PO Box 62098, Marshalltown 2107, South Africa.

MATRENZA, Richard Anthony; High Commissioner for Malta in London, 1997–99; *b* 17 Oct. 1936; *s* of Domenic and Esther Sultana; *m* 1957, Doris Mercieca; one *s* one *d*. *Educ*: St Michael's Teacher Training Coll., Malta; Univ. of Oxford (Dip. Politics and Econs 1965). Teacher, 1954–60; Trade Union Negotiator, 1960–69; Management Consultant and Industrial Relations Specialist, 1970–96. MInstD. *Publications*: Libraries in Malta, 1956; L-Istorja ta' Louis Pasteur, 1959; professional papers. *Recreations*: industrial archaeology, collecting comics (late 1940s and early 1950s). *Address*: 41 Triq Kristofru, Valletta, Malta VLTO3. *T*: 240584.

MATSUURA, Koïchiro; Director-General of UNESCO, since 1999; *b* 29 Sept. 1937; *s* of Seichi and Kiyoko Matsuura; *m* 1967, Takako Kirikae; two *s*. *Educ*: Univ. of Tokyo; Havenford Coll., USA (MBA). Counsellor, Embassy of Japan, USA, 1977–80; Consul Gen., Hong Kong, 1985–88; Dir-Gen., Econ. Co-operation Bureau, 1988–90, N American Affairs Bureau, 1990–92, Min. of Foreign Affairs; Dep. Minister for Foreign Affairs (Sherpa for Japan at G-7 Summit), 1992–94; Ambassador of Japan to: Djibouti, 1994–99; France, 1994–99; Andorra, 1996–99. Chm., World Heritage Cttee, UNESCO, 1998–99. Bintang Jasa Utama (Indonesia), 1993; Grand Officer, Nat. Order of Merit (France), 1994; Comdr, Nat. Order of 27 June (Djibouti), 1997. *Publications*: In the Forefront of Economic Co-operation Diplomacy, 1990; History of Japan–United States Relations, 1992; Focusing on the Future: Japan's global role in a changing world, 1993; The G-7 Summit: its history and perspectives, 1994; Development and Perspectives of the Relations between Japan and France, 1995; Japanese Diplomacy at the Dawn of the 21st Century, 1998. *Recreations*: Go, tennis, golf, mountain climbing. *Address*: UNESCO, 7 Place de Fontenoy, 75352 Paris, France. *T*: (1) 45681310.

MATT; *see* Pritchett, Matthew.

MATTAJ, Iain William, PhD; FRS 1999; FRSE; Director General, European Molecular Biology Laboratory, since 2005; *b* 5 Oct. 1952; *s* of George Eugeniusz Mattaj and Jane Margaret Mattaj; *m* 1974, Ailsa McCrindle. *Educ*: Edinburgh Univ. (BSc); Leeds Univ. (PhD 1980). Postdoctoral research: Freidrich Miescher Inst., Basel, 1979–82; Biocentre, Basel Univ., 1982–85; Gp Leader, 1985–90, Programme Co-ordinator, 1990–99, Scientific Dir, 1999–2005, EMBL, Heidelberg. Exec. Ed., EMBO Jl, 1990–. Mem., EMBO, 1989. Pres., Ribonucleic Acid Soc., 1998–2000. FRSE 2000. *Publications*: numerous contribs to scientific jls. *Recreations*: squash, music, literature. *Address*: European Molecular Biology Laboratory, Meyerhofstrasse 1, 69117 Heidelberg, Germany. *T*: (6221) 387393.

MATTHEW, Chessor Lillie, FRIBA, FRIAS; Principal, Duncan of Jordanstone College of Art, Dundee, 1964–78, retired; *b* 22 Jan. 1913; *s* of William Matthew and Helen Chessor Matthew (*née* Milne); *m* 1939, Margarita Ellis; one *s*. *Educ*: Gray's School of Art; Robert Gordon's Coll., Aberdeen. Diploma in Architecture; MRTPI 1948; FRIBA 1958; FRIAS 1958. Lectr, Welsh Sch. of Architecture, Cardiff, 1936–40. Served RAF, 1940–46, Flt-Lt. Sen. Lectr, Welsh Sch. of Architecture, Cardiff, 1946–57; Head of Sch. of Architecture, Duncan of Jordanstone Coll. of Art, Dundee, 1958–64. Mem., Royal Fine Art Commn for Scotland, 1966–78. JP 1974. *Recreations*: hill walking, foreign travel. *Address*: Craigmhor, 36 Albany Road, West Ferry, Dundee DD5 1NW. *T*: (01382) 778364.

MATTHEWMAN, His Honour Keith; QC 1979; a Circuit Judge, 1983–2001; *b* 8 Jan. 1936; *e s* of late Lieut Frank Matthewman and Elizabeth Matthewman; *m* 1962, Jane (*née* Maxwell); one *s*. *Educ*: Long Eaton Grammar Sch.; University College London (LLB). Called to the Bar, Middle Temple, 1960. School teacher, Barking, Essex, 1958–59, and Heanor, Derbys, 1960–61; Commercial Assistant, Internat. Div., Rolls-Royce Ltd, 1961–62; practice at the Bar, 1962–83, Midland Circuit, later Midland and Oxford Circuit; a Recorder of the Crown Court, 1979–83. Newspaper columnist, Beeston Express (Notts), 2004–06. Mem. Cttee, Council of HM's Circuit Judges, 1984–89. Member: Notts Probation Cttee, 1986–2001; Parole Bd, 1996–2002 (Judge Appraiser, 2002–04). A Pres., Mental Health Review Tribunals, 1993–99. Ext. Examr, Bar vocational course, Nottingham Trent Univ., 2000–03. Inaugural Pres., Friends of the Galleries of Justice (Nottingham), 1998–2007. Patron, Criminal Justice Assoc., 2003–. Patron, Nottingham Cartoon Fest., 2002–. Mem. (Lab), Heanor UDC, 1960–63. TV appearances include Crimestalker, Central TV, 1993. *Recreations*: gardening, reading. *Address*: c/o Crown Court, Nottingham NG1 7EJ. *Club*: Beeston Fields Golf (Bramcote).

MATTHEWS, Hon. Lord; Hugh Matthews; a Senator of the College of Justice in Scotland, since 2007; *b* 4 Dec. 1953; *s* of Hugh Matthews and Maureen Matthews (*née* Rea); *m* 2000, Lindsay M. A. Wilson. *Educ*: St Columba's Primary Sch., Kilmarnock; St Joseph's Acad., Kilmarnock; Glasgow Univ. (LLB Hons). Admitted to Faculty of Advocates, 1979; QC (Scot.) 1992; Standing Jun. Counsel, Dept of Employment, Office in Scotland, 1984–88; Advocate-depute, 1988–93; temp. Sheriff, 1993–97; Sheriff of Glasgow and Strathkelvin, 1997–2007; temp. Judge, 2004–07. *Recreations*: ancient history, golf, football, animal husbandry, astronomy, theatre. *Clubs*: The Club (Kilmarnock); Pollok Golf (Glasgow).

MATTHEWS, Rt Rev. Anthony Francis Berners H.; *see* Hall-Matthews.

MATTHEWS, Colin, DPhil; FRNCM, FRCM; composer; Prince Consort Professor of Composition, Royal College of Music, since 2001; *b* 13 Feb. 1946; *s* of Herbert and Elsie Matthews; *m* 1977, Belinda Lloyd; one *s* two *d*. *Educ*: Univ. of Nottingham (BA Classics, MPhil Composition); Univ. of Sussex (DPhil). Studied composition with Arnold Whittall and Nicholas Maw, 1967–70; collaborated with Deryck Cooke on performing version of Mahler's Tenth Symphony, 1964–74; asst to Benjamin Britten, 1971–76; worked with Imogen Holst, 1972–84; taught at Univ. of Sussex, 1971–72, 1976–77. Associate Composer: LSO, 1990–99; Hallé Orch., 2001–. Distinguished Vis. Fellow, Univ. of Manchester, 2001–; Special Prof. of Music, Univ. of Nottingham, 2007–. Dir, Holst Estate and Holst Foundn, 1973–; Trustee, Britten-Pears Foundn, 1983– (Music Dir, 2008–); Dir, Britten Estate, 1983– (Chm., 2000–); Mem. Council and Exec. Cttee, SPNM, 1981–93, 1994–99; Exec. Mem. Council, Aldeburgh Foundn, 1984–93; Dir, PRS, 1992–95; Mem. Council, RPS, 2005–. Founder, NMC Recordings Ltd, 1988. Gov., RNCM, 2000–08. Patron, Musicians against Nuclear Arms, 1985–. FRNCM 2003; FRCM 2007. Hon. DMus Nottingham, 1998. Scottish National Orch. Ian Whyte Award, 1975; Park Lane Group Composer Award, 1983; Royal Philharmonic Soc. Award, 1996. *Principal works*: Fourth Sonata, 1974; Night Music, 1976; Sonata no 5 'Landscape', 1977–81; String Quartet no 1, 1979; Oboe Quartet, 1981; The Great Journey, 1981–88; Divertimento for Double String Quartet, 1982; Toccata Meccanica, 1984; Night's Mask, 1984; Cello Concerto, 1984; Suns Dance, 1985; Five Duos, 1985; Three Enigmas, 1985; String Quartet no 2, 1985; Pursuit (ballet), 1986; Monody, 1986–87; Eleven Studies in Velocity, 1987; Two Part Invention, 1987; Cortège, 1988; Hidden Variables, 1989; Quatrain, 1989; Second Oboe Quartet, 1990; Five Concertinos, 1990; Chiaroscuro, 1990; Machines and Dreams, 1990; Broken Symmetry, 1990–91; Renewal, 1990–96; Contraflow, 1992; Memorial, 1992; String Quartet no 3, 1994; ...through the glass, 1994; 23 Frames, 1995; Cello Concerto no 2, 1996; Renewal, 1996; My Life So Far (film score), 1998; Two Tributes, 1999; Aftertones, 2000; Pluto, 2000; Continuum, 2000; Horn Concerto, 2001; Debussy Preludes, 2001–07; Reflected Images, 2003; A Voice to Wake, 2005; Berceuse for Dresden, 2005; Turning Point, 2006; Alphabicycle Order, 2007; The Island, 2008. *Publications*: contribs to Musical Times, Tempo, TLS, etc. *Recreations*: wine, very amateur astrophysics. *Address*: c/o Faber Music Ltd, 3 Queen Square, WC1N 3AU. *T*: (020) 7278 6881, *Fax*: (020) 7278 3817; *e-mail*: promotion@fabermusic.co.uk. *Club*: Leyton Orient Supporters'.
See also D. J. Matthews.

MATTHEWS, Brother Daniel (Fairbairn), SSF; Minister General, Society of Saint Francis, since 1997; *b* 7 Sept. 1936; *s* of Maxwell and Mary Matthews. *Educ*: S Shields Marine Coll. (1st Cl. Marine Engrg); Bishop Patteson Theological Coll., Kohimarama, Solomon Is (DipTh). Chief Engr (Marine), 1957–63; joined Society of St Francis, 1964: Guardian, Solomon Is, 1975–81; Minister Provincial, Australia and NZ, 1981–97. *Recreations*: walking, reading. *Address*: Society of Saint Francis, The Friary, Hilfield, Dorchester, Dorset DT2 7BE.

MATTHEWS, David; *see* Matthews, William D.

MATTHEWS, David John; composer; *b* 9 March 1943; *s* of Herbert and Elsie Matthews; *m* 1st, 1995, Jean Hasse (marr. diss. 2002); 2nd, 2005, Jenifer Wakelyn. *Educ*: Bancroft's

Sch., Woodford; Univ. of Nottingham (BA Classics). Studied composition with Anthony Milner, 1967–69; Asst to Benjamin Britten, 1966–70. Musical Dir, Deal Fest., 1989–2003; Composer in Association, Britten Sinfonia, 1997–2001. Collaborated with Deryck Cooke on performing version of Mahler's Tenth Symphony, 1964–74. Hon. DMus Nottingham, 1997. *Compositions include:* 3 songs for soprano and orchestra, 1968; String Quartet No 1, 1970; Symphony No 1, 1975; String Quartet No 2, 1976; Symphony No 2, 1977; String Quartet No 3, 1977; September Music, for small orch., 1979; Ehmals und Jetzt, 6 songs for soprano and piano, 1979; The Company of Lovers, 5 choral songs, 1980; String Quartet No 4, 1981; Serenade, for chamber orch., 1982; Violin Concerto No 1, 1982; The Golden Kingdom, 9 songs for high voice and piano, 1983; Piano Trio No 1, 1983; Clarinet Quartet, 1984; Symphony No 3, 1985; In the Dark Time, for orch., 1985; Variations for strings, 1986; The Flaying of Marsyas, for oboe and string quartet, 1987; Chaconne, for orch., 1987; Cantiga, for soprano and chamber orch., 1988; The Ship of Death, for chorus, 1989; Piano Sonata, 1989; String Trio, 1989; Romanza, for 'cello and small orch., 1990; The Music of Dawn, for orch., 1990; Symphony No 4, 1990; Capriccio, for 2 horns and strings, 1991; String Quartet No 6, 1991; Oboe Concerto, 1992; The Sleeping Lord, for sop. and ensemble, 1992; A Vision and a Journey, for orch., 1993; Piano Trio No 2, 1993; A Congress of Passions, for voice, oboe and piano, 1994; Vespers, for soli, chorus and orch., 1994; Skies now are Skies, for tenor and string quartet, 1994; A Song and Dance Sketchbook, for piano quartet, 1995; Sinfonia, for orch., 1995; Moments of Vision, for chorus, 1995; Two Pieces for Strings: Little Chaconne, 1996, Fall Dances, 1999; Hurrahing in Harvest, for chorus, 1997; Variations, for piano, 1997; Burnham Wick, for small orch., 1997; Violin Concerto No 2, 1998; String Quartet No 8, 1998; Symphony No 5, 1999; String Quartet No 9, 2000; Aubade, for chamber orch., 2001; String Quartet No 10, 2001; After Sunrise, for chamber orch., 2001; Cello Concerto, 2002; Fifteen Fugues for solo violin, 2002; String Trio No 2, 2003; L'Invitation au voyage, for voice and piano quartet, 2003; Aequam memento, for chorus, 2004; Piano Quintet, 2004; Journeying Songs, for 'cello, 2004; Piano Trio No 3, 2005; Movement of Autumn, for sop. and chamber orch., 2005; Fanfares and Flowers, for symphonic wind band, 2006; Terrible Beauty, for voice and ensemble, 2007; Symphony No 6, 2007; Adonis, for violin and piano, 2007; One Foot in Eden, for tenor and piano quintet, 2008. *Publications:* Michael Tippett, 1980; Landscape into Sound, 1992; Britten, 2003; contribs to Musical Times, Tempo, TLS. *Recreations:* walking, sketching. *Address:* c/o Faber Music Ltd, 3 Queen Square, WC1N 3AU.

See also C. Matthews.

MATTHEWS, Prof. David Richard, DPhil; FRCP; Professor of Diabetes Medicine, University of Oxford, since 2002; Medical Tutor and Fellow, Harris Manchester College, Oxford, since 1998; *b* 22 Sept. 1947; *s* of William John Matthews and Ena Matthews (*née* Brading); *m* 1970, Clare Tegla; one *s* two *d*. *Educ:* Chigwell Sch.; Corpus Christi Coll., Oxford (Sen. Schol. 1970; MA, DPhil 1973; BM BCh 1975). FRCP 1994. Oxford University: Nuffield Jun. Res. Fellow, Balliol Coll., 1981–84; Joan and Richard Doll Sen. Res. Fellow, Green Coll., 1984–88; Hon. Consultant Physician, Diabetes Res. Labs, 1988–92; Consultant Physician, Oxford Radcliffe Hosps NHS Trust, 1992–; Chm., Oxford Centre for Diabetes, Endocrinology and Metabolism, 2000–; Co-dir, UK Diabetes Res. Network, 2007–. Mem., Assoc. of Physicians. FRSocMed. Methodist lay preacher, 1977–. *Publications:* over 200 peer-reviewed papers in field of diabetes. *Recreation:* science and religion, gardening. *Address:* Oxford Centre for Diabetes, Endocrinology and Metabolism, Churchill Hosp., Oxford OX3 7LJ; *e-mail:* david.matthews@ocdem.ox.ac.uk.

MATTHEWS, Douglas, FRSL; FCLIP; Librarian, The London Library, 1980–93; *b* 23 Aug. 1927; *s* of Benjamin Matthews and Mary (*née* Pearson); *m* 1968, Sarah Maria Williams (marr. diss. 1991); two *d*. *Educ:* Acklam Hall Sch., Middlesbrough; Durham Univ. (BA). FRSL 1999. Assistant: India Office Library, 1952–62; Kungl. Biblioteket, Stockholm, 1956–57; Librarian, Home Office, 1962–64; Dep. Librarian, London Library, 1965–80. Trustee, Royal Literary Fund, 1993–. Mem. Court, Univ. of Sussex, 1983–94. *Address:* 1 Priory Terrace, Mountfield Road, Lewes, Sussex BN7 2UT. *T:* (01273) 475635. *Club:* Garrick.

MATTHEWS, Duncan Henry Rowland; QC 2002; *b* 1 Sept. 1961; *m* 1991, Hon. Emma Elizabeth, *d* of Lord Griffiths, *qv*; one *s* one *d*. *Educ:* Westminster Sch. (Queen's Schol.); Magdalen Coll., Oxford (MA Modern Hist.); City Univ. (Dip. Law); Inns of Court Sch. of Law. Called to the Bar, Gray's Inn, 1986, Bencher, 2006. Chm., Bar Council Educn and Trng Cttee. *Recreations:* Real tennis, tennis, bridge, theatre, reading, history. *Address:* (chambers) 20 Essex Street, WC2R 3AL. *T:* (020) 7842 1200, *Fax:* (020) 7842 1270; *e-mail:* clerks@20essexst.com. *Clubs:* Garrick, Hurlingham.

MATTHEWS, Geoffrey Vernon Townsend, OBE 1986; Director of Research and Conservation, 1955–88, and Deputy Director, 1973–88, Wildfowl Trust, Slimbridge; *b* 16 June 1923; *s* of Geoffrey Tom Matthews and Muriel Ivy Townsend; *m* 1st, 1946, Josephine (marr. diss. 1961), *d* of Col Alured Charles Lowther O'Shea Bilderbeck; one *s* one *d*; 2nd, 1964, Janet Kear (marr. diss. 1978; she *d* 2004); 3rd, 1980, Mary Elizabeth, *d* of William Evans; one *s* one *d*. *Educ:* Bedford Sch.; Christ's Coll., Cambridge (MA, PhD). RAF Operational Res., Bomber and SE Asia Comds (Sci. Officer/Flt Lieut), 1943–46. Post-doctoral res., Cambridge Univ., 1950–55; Special Lectr, Bristol Univ., 1965–88; Hon. Lectr 1966–69, Professorial Fellow 1970–90, UC, Cardiff. Dir, Internat. Waterfowl Res. Bureau, 1969–88, Counsellor of Honour, 1989–. Served on numerous non-govtl and govtl cttees; travelled widely. Pres., Assoc. for the Study of Animal Behaviour, 1971–74; Vice-Pres., British Ornithologists' Union, 1972–75, Union Medal, 1980. FIBiol, 1974; Corresp. Fellow, Amer. Ornithologists Union, 1969–. RSPB Medal, 1990. Officer, Dutch Order of Golden Ark, 1987. *Publications:* Bird Navigation, 1955, 2nd edn 1968; The Ramsar Convention on Wetlands, 1993 (trans. German and Japanese); chapters contributed to 45 multi-authored books; more than 100 papers in sci. and conservation jls. *Recreations:* fossil hunting, collecting zoological stamps, reading, household maintenance. *Address:* 32 Tetbury Street, Minchinhampton, Glos GL6 9JH. *T:* (01453) 884769. *Club:* Victory.

MATTHEWS, Hugh; *see* Matthews, Hon. Lord.

MATTHEWS, Jeffery Edward, MBE 2004; FCSD; freelance graphic designer and consultant, since 1952; *b* 3 April 1928; *s* of Henry Edward Matthews and Sybil Frances (*née* Cooke); *m* 1953, (Sylvia Lilian) Christine (*née* Hoar) (*d* 1994); one *s* one *d*. *Educ:* Alleyn's; Brixton Sch. of Building (Interior Design; NDD). AIBD 1951; FCSD (FSIAD 1978). Graphic designer with J. Edward Sander, 1949–52; part-time tutor, 1952–55. Lettering and calligraphy assessor for SIAD, 1970–. Designs for Post Office: decimal to pay labels, 1971; fount of numerals for definitive stamps, 1981; stamps: United Nations, 1965; British bridges, 1968; definitives for Scotland, Wales, NI and IOM, 1971; Royal Silver Wedding, 1972; 25th Anniversary of the Coronation, 1978; London, 1980; 80th birthday of the Queen Mother, 1980; Christmas, 1980; Wedding of Prince Charles and Lady Diana Spencer, 1981; Quincentenary of College of Arms, 1984; 60th birthday of the Queen, 1986; Wedding of Prince Andrew and Sarah Ferguson, 1986; Order of the Thistle Tercentenary of Revival, 1987; 150th Anniversary of the Penny Black, 1990; self-adhesive definitives, 1993; The Queen's Beasts, 1998; Jeffery Matthews miniature sheet, 2000; End of War miniature sheet, 2005; Machin definitives 40th Anniversary miniature sheet, 2007; also first-day covers, postmarks, presentation packs, souvenir books and posters; one of three stamp designers featured in PO film, Picture to Post, 1969. Other design work includes: title banner lettering and coat of arms, Sunday Times, 1968; cover design and lettering for official prog., Royal Wedding, 1981; The Royal Mint, commemorative medal, Order of the Thistle, 1987; Millennium commemorative crown piece, 1999; End of War commemorative medal, 2005; stained glass window for Forest Hill Methodist Ch. and accompanying film (Light Through Geometry), 2007; official heraldry and symbols, HMSO; hand-drawn lettering, COI; calligraphy, packaging, promotion and bookbinding designs, logotypes, brand images and hand-drawn lettering, for various firms including Unicover Corp., USA, Harrison & Sons Ltd, Metal Box Co., John Dickinson, Reader's Digest Assoc. Ltd, Encyc. Britannica Internat. Ltd, ICI and H. R. Higgins (Coffee-man) Ltd. Work exhibited in A History of Bookplates in Britain, V&A Mus., 1979; contrib. Oral History of the Post Office collection, British Liby, 2001. Citizen and Goldsmith of London (Freedom by Patrimony), 1949. FRSA 1987. Rowland Hill Award for Outstanding Contribution, 2004, Phillips Gold Medal for Stamp Design, 2005, Royal Mail. *Publications:* (contrib.) Designers in Britain, 1964, 1971; (contrib.) 45 Wood-engravers, 1982; (contrib.) Royal Mail Year Book, 1984, 1986, 1987, 1998; (contrib.) Queen Elizabeth II: a Jubilee portrait in stamps, 2002. *Recreations:* furniture restoration, playing the guitar, gardening, DIY.

MATTHEWS, John, CBE 1990; FRAgS; Director, Institute of Engineering Research, Agricultural and Food Research Council (formerly National Institute of Agricultural Engineering), 1984–90; *b* 4 July 1930; *s* of John Frederick Matthews and Catherine Edith Matthews (*née* Terry); *m* 1982 (marr. diss. 1993); two *d*; *m* 2000, June Robinson. *Educ:* Royal Latin School, Buckingham. BSc (Physics) London. CPhys, FInstP; CEng; FIAgrE 1970 (Hon. FIAgrE 1994). Scientist, GEC Res. Labs, 1951–59; National Institute of Agricultural Engineering: joined 1959; Head of Tractor Performance Dept, 1967–73; Head of Tractor and Cultivation Div., 1973–83; Asst Dir, 1983–84; Dir, 1984–90. Vis. Prof., Cranfield Inst. of Technology, 1987. Vice Chm., Ceredigion and Mid-Wales NHS Trust, 2000–03 (Dir, 1992–03). Mem., Bd of Management, AFRC, 1986–90. Formerly Chm., Technical Cttees, Internat. Standards Orgn and OECD; Pres., Inst. of Agricl Engineers, 1986–88. Pro-Chancellor, Univ. of Luton, 1993–98 (Chm. of Govs, Luton Coll. of Higher Educn, 1989–93). Fellow: Ergonomics Soc.; Academie Georgofili, Italy, 1991. Mem., RAFA; Chm., Teifiside Probus Club, 2002–06. Research Medal, RASE, 1983. Max Eyth Medallion (Germany), 1990; Chevalier de Merite Agricole (France), 1992. *Publications:* (contrib.) Fream's Elements of Agriculture, 1984; (ed) Progress in Agricultural Physics and Engineering, 1991; contribs to other books and jls on agricultural engineering and ergonomics. *Recreations:* gardening, travel. *Address:* Carron, Aberporth, Cardigan, Ceredigion SA43 2DA.

MATTHEWS, Prof. John Burr Lumley, (Jack), FRSE; Director, 1988–96 and Secretary, 1988–99, Scottish Association for Marine Science (formerly Scottish Marine Biological Association) (Hon. Fellow, 1999); *b* 23 April 1935; *s* of Dr John Lumley Matthews and Susan Agnes Matthews; *m* 1962, Jane Rosemary Goldsmith; one *s* two *d*. *Educ:* Warwick Sch.; St John's Coll., Oxford (MA, DPhil). FRSE 1988. Res. Scientist, Oceanographic Lab., Edinburgh, 1961–67; University of Bergen: Lectr, Sen. Lectr, Marine Biology, 1967–78; Prof., Marine Biology, 1978–84; Dep. Dir, Scottish Marine Biol Assoc., 1984–88; Dir, Dunstaffnage Marine Lab., NERC, 1988–94. Vis. Prof., Oceanography, Univ. of British Columbia, 1977–78; Hon. Prof., Biology, Univ. of Stirling, 1984–. Member: Cttee for Scotland, Nature Conservancy Council, 1989–91; SW Regl Bd, Scottish Natural Heritage, 1992–97 (Dep. Chm., 1994–97). Sec., Internat. Assoc. of Biol Oceanography, 1994–2002. Mem., Bd and Acad. Council, Univ. of the Highlands and Islands Ltd, 1993–96. Trustee: Internat. Sch., Bergen, 1980–84; Oban Hospice, 1999–2005; Hebridean Whale & Dolphin Trust, 2000– (Chm., 2001–); Nadair Trust, 2003–07. Founding Fellow, Inst. for Contemp. Scotland, 2000; FRSA 1989. *Publications:* (ed jtly) Freshwater on the Sea, 1976; Aquatic Life Cycle Strategies, 1999; (ed jtly and contrib.) Achievements of the Continuous Plankton Recorder Survey and a Vision for its Future, 2003; contribs to marine sci. jls. *Recreations:* hill-walking, cross-country ski-ing, pethau cymreig. *Address:* The Well, 18 Manse Road, Milnathort, Kinross KY13 9YQ. *T:* (01577) 861066.

MATTHEWS, Dr John Duncan, CVO 1989; FRCPE; retired; Consultant Physician, Royal Infirmary, Edinburgh, 1955–86; Hon. Senior Lecturer, University of Edinburgh, 1976–86; *b* 19 Sept. 1921; *s* of Joseph Keith Matthews and Ethel Chambers; *m* 1945, Constance Margaret Moffat; two *s*. *Educ:* Shrewsbury; Univ. of Cambridge (BA); Univ. of Edinburgh (MB, ChB). FRCPE 1958. Surgeon, High Constables and Guard of Honour, Holyroodhouse, 1961–87, Moderator, 1987–89. Hon. Consultant in Medicine to the Army in Scotland, 1974–86; Examr in Medicine, Edinburgh and Cambridge Univs and Royal Colleges of Physicians. Vice-Pres., RCPE, 1982–85; Mem./Chm., various local and national NHS and coll. cttees. Sec., Edinburgh Medical Angling Club, 1963–86. *Publications:* occasional articles in med. jls on diabetes and heart disease. *Recreations:* cricket (Free Foresters, Grange, and Scotland), fishing, golf, gardening. *Address:* 3 Succoth Gardens, Edinburgh EH12 6BR.

MATTHEWS, Prof. John Frederick, DPhil; FRHistS; FSA; FBA 1990; Professor of Roman History, Departments of Classics and History, since 1996, John M. Schiff Professor of Classics and History, since 2001, Yale University (Chair of Classics, 1998–2005); *b* 15 Feb. 1940; *s* of Jack and Mary Matthews; *m* 1st, 1965, Elaine Jackson (marr. diss. 1995); two *d*; 2nd, 1995, Veronika Grimm. *Educ:* Wyggeston Boys' Sch., Leicester; Queen's Coll., Oxford (MA 1965; DPhil 1970). FRHistS 1986; FSA 1993. Oxford University: Dyson Jun. Res. Fellow in Greek Culture, Balliol Coll., 1965–69; Conington Prize, 1971; Univ. Lectr in Middle and Late Roman Empire, 1969–90; Reader, 1990–92; Prof. of Middle and Later Roman History, 1992–96; Official Fellow, Corpus Christi Coll., 1969–76; Fellow, and Praelector in Ancient History, Queen's College, Oxford, 1976–96. Inst. for Advanced Study, Princeton, 1980–81; British Acad. Reader in Humanities, 1988–90; Fellow, Nat. Humanities Center, N Carolina, 1995–96. Vis. Prof., Sch. of Archaeology and Ancient History, Univ. of Leicester, 2006–. Chm. of Govs, Cheney Sch., Oxford, 1986–91. Hon. DLitt Leicester, 2003. *Publications:* Western Aristocracies and Imperial Court AD 364–425, 1975; (with T. J. Cornell) Atlas of the Roman World, 1982; Political Life and Culture in late Roman Society, 1985; The Roman Empire of Ammianus, 1989; (with Peter Heather) The Goths in the Fourth Century, 1991; Laying Down the Law: a study of the Theodosian Code, 2000; The Journey of Theophanes: travel, business and daily life in the Roman East, 2006 (James Henry Breasted Prize, American Historical Assoc., 2007). *Recreations:* playing the piano, listening to music, suburban gardening. *Address:* 160 McKinley Avenue, New Haven, CT 06515, USA. *T:* (203) 3898137.

MATTHEWS, John Waylett; Chairman, Regus Group plc, since 2002; *b* 22 Sept. 1944; *s* of late Percy Victor Matthews and Phyllis Edith Matthews (*née* Waylett); *m* 1972, Lesley

Marjorie Halliday; two *s* one *d*. *Educ:* Forest Sch. FCA 1967. Dixon Wilson & Co., 1961–69; N. M. Rothschild & Sons, 1969–71; County Natwest, 1971–88 (Sen. Dir, 1984–88); Dep. Chm./CEO, Beazer plc, 1988–91; CEO, Indosuez Capital, 1991–94; Chm., Crest Nicholson plc, 1996–2007. Non-executive Director: Rotork plc, 1998–; SDL plc, 2001–; Diploma plc, 2003–; Minerva plc, 2007–. Gov., Forest Sch., 1998– (Chm., 2001–). *Recreations:* golf, shooting, ski-ing. *Address:* Regus Group plc, 3000 Hillswood Drive, Chertsey, Surrey KT16 0RS. *T:* (01932) 895135, *Fax:* (01932) 895263; *e-mail:* john.matthews@regus.com. *Clubs:* City of London, Royal Automobile, MCC.

MATTHEWS, Margaret; *see* Gilmore, M.

MATTHEWS, Michael Gough; pianist, teacher, adjudicator and consultant; Director, 1985–93, Vice President, since 1994, Royal College of Music, 1985–93; *b* 12 July 1931; *s* of late Cecil Gough Matthews and Amelia Eleanor Mary Matthews. *Educ:* Chigwell School; Royal College of Music (Open Scholarship, 1947; Hopkinson Gold Medal, 1953; ARCM, FRCM 1972); ARCO; Diploma del Corso di Perfezionamento St Cecilia, Rome. Diploma of Honour and Prize, Chopin Internat. Piano Competition, 1955; Italian Govt Scholarship, 1956; Chopin Fellowship, Warsaw, 1959. Pianist; recitals, broadcasts, concerts, UK, Europe and Far East. Supervisor Junior Studies, RSAMD, 1964–71; Royal College of Music: Dir, Junior Dept, and Prof. of Piano, 1972–75; Registrar, 1975; Vice-Dir, 1978–84. Teacher and adjudicator of internat. competitions; Chm. Adjudicators, Royal Over-Seas League Competition, 2005–07. Hon. Dir, Royal Music Foundn, Inc., USA, 1985–. Member: NYO GB; Royal Philharmonic Soc., 1985–; Music Study Gp, EEC, 1989–; Comité d'Honneur, Presence de l'Art, Paris, 1990–; Council, Purcell Tercentenary Trust, 1992. Vice-President: RCO, 1985–; Nat. Youth Choir, 1986–; Herbert Howells Soc., 1987–; Hon. Vice-Pres., Royal Choral Soc., 1992–. Chm., Parkhouse Award, 1997–99. Consultant to HM the Sultan of Oman, 1993–2000, to Jaguar Cars, 1993–. Hon. FLCM 1976; Hon. RAM 1979; FRSAMD 1986; FRNCM 1991; Hon. GSM 1987. Recordings of piano music by Fauré, 1995 and 1997, and Brahms, 1999. *Publications:* various musical entertainments; arranger of educational music. *Recreation:* gardening. *Address:* 608 The Bridge, 334 Queenstown Road, Battersea, SW8 4NR. *T:* (020) 7720 3235. *Club:* Athenæum.

MATTHEWS, Paul Bernard, LLD; Consultant Solicitor, Withers LLP, since 1996; HM Coroner, City of London, since 2002; Deputy Master of the High Court of Justice, Chancery Division, since 2008; *b* 21 Aug. 1955; *s* of Leonard William Matthews, KSG and late Noreen Elizabeth Matthews; *m* 1986, Katie Bradford. *Educ:* St Peter's Sch., Bournemouth; UCL (Charlotte Ashby Prize, Andrews Prize, 1976; LLB 1977); St Edmund Hall, Oxford (BCL 1979); Univ. of London (LLD 1995); Inns of Court Sch. of Law (Exam. Prize, Council of Legal Educn, 1981). Called to the Bar, Gray's Inn, 1981; admitted Solicitor: England and Wales, 1987; Ireland, 1997; Solicitor-Advocate (Higher Courts: Civil), 2001. In private practice as barrister, 1982–84; Hopkins & Wood, London: Legal Asst, 1984–87; Partner, 1987–92; Consultant Solicitor, 1992–96; Deputy Coroner: City of London, 1994–2002; Royal Household, 2002–06; (*ad hoc*) N London, 2004–07. Tutor (pt-time), 1978–79, Lectr in Law, 1979–83, UCL; Tutor (pt-time), St Edmund Hall, Oxford, 1979–80. Visiting Lecturer: City Univ., 1981–84; UCL, 1985–86; Inst. de Droit des Affaires, Univ. d'Aix-Marseille, 1991–99; Vis. Sen. Lectr, 1991–94, Vis. Prof., 1995–, KCL. Mem., Common Core of Eur. Private Law Project, Univ. of Trento, 2001–. Dep. Chm., Trust Law Cttee, 2005– (Mem., Wkg Parties on Trustees' Exoneration and Trustees' Indemnity, 1997–99); Member: Guernsey Trust Law Review Cttee, 2000–; Wkg Party on Coroners and Inquests, Law Soc., 2003–; EC Gp of Experts on property consequences of marriage and on wills and succession in EU, 2005–08; Specialist Advr, H of C Constitutional Affairs Cttee, 2006–; Coroner Mem., Review Bodies, 2006–. Member: Soc. of Legal Scholars, 1979–; British Inst. of Internat. and Comparative Law, 1989–; Coroners' Soc. of England and Wales, 1994–; Soc. of Trust and Estate Practitioners, 1996–; Internat. Acad. of Estate and Trust Lawyers, 2004–. Member: Selden Soc., 2002–; Stair Soc., 2003–. FRSocMed 2005. FRSA 1994. Liveryman, City of London Solicitors' Co., 1992–. Trustee, David Isaacs Fund, 2002–. Jt Ed., Trust Law Internat., 2005– (Asst Ed., 1995–2004); Mem. Editl Bd, Jersey Law Review, 1997–. *Publications:* Jervis on Coroners, 10th edn 1986 to 12th edn 2002 (10th and 11th edns with J. C. Foreman); (with T. Sowden) The Jersey Law of Trusts, 1988, 3rd edn 1994; (with S. C. Nicolle) The Jersey Law of Property, 1991; (with H. M. Malek) Discovery, 1992, 2nd edn as Disclosure, 2000, 3rd edn 2007; (with D. Millichap) A Guide to the Leasehold Reform, Housing and Urban Development Act 1993, 1993; (with H. Barraclough) A Practitioner's Guide to the Trusts of Land and Appointment of Trustees Act 1996, 1996; (ed with K. Bradford) Butterworths Business Landlord and Tenant Handbook, 1996, 4th edn 2007; Trusts: migration and change of proper law, 1997; Trust and Estate Disputes, 1999; (ed with D. Hayton and C. Mitchell) Underhill & Hayton's Law of Trusts and Trustees, 17th edn 2006; contrib. Halsbury's Laws of England, 4th edn reissue; articles, notes and reviews in learned jls. *Recreations:* reading, music, local history, cinema, languages. *Address:* City of London Coroner's Court, Walbrook Wharf, 78–83 Upper Thames Street, EC4R 3TD; *e-mail:* coroner@cityoflondon.gov.uk; School of Law, King's College, Strand, WC2R 2LS; *e-mail:* paul.matthews@kcl.ac.uk. *Club:* Athenæum.

MATTHEWS, Prof. Peter Bryan Conrad, FRS 1973; MD, DSc; Professor of Sensorimotor Physiology, 1987–96, now Emeritus and Student of Christ Church, 1958–96, now Emeritus, University of Oxford; *b* 23 Dec. 1928; *s* of Prof. Sir Bryan Matthews, CBE, FRS; *m* 1956, Margaret Rosemary Blears; one *s* one *d*. *Educ:* Marlborough Coll.; King's Coll., Cambridge; Oxford Univ. Clinical School. Oxford University: Univ. Lectr in Physiology, 1961–77; Reader, 1978–86; Tutor, Christ Church, 1958–86. Sir Lionel Whitby Medal, Cambridge Univ., 1959; Robert Bing Prize, Swiss Acad. of Med. Science, 1971. *Publications:* Mammalian Muscle Receptors and their Central Actions, 1972; papers on neurophysiology in various scientific jls. *Address:* University Laboratory of Physiology, Parks Road, Oxford OX1 3PT. *T:* (01865) 272500.

MATTHEWS, Prof. Peter Hugoe, LittD; FBA 1985; Professor of Linguistics, University of Cambridge, 1980–2001, now Emeritus (Head of Department of Linguistics, 1980–96); Fellow, since 1980, Praelector, 1987–2001, St John's College, Cambridge; *b* 10 March 1934; *s* of John Hugo and Cecily Eileen Emsley Matthews; *m* 1984, Lucienne Marie Jeanne Schleich; one step *s* one step *d*. *Educ:* Montpellier Sch., Paignton; Clifton Coll.; St John's Coll., Cambridge (MA 1960; LittD 1988). Lectr in Linguistics, UCNW, 1961–65 (on leave Indiana Univ., Bloomington, 1963–64); University of Reading: Lectr in Linguistic Science, 1965–69; Reader, 1969–75; Prof., 1975–80 (on leave as Fellow, King's Coll., Cambridge, 1970–71, and as Fellow, Netherlands Inst. of Advanced Study, Wassenaar, 1977–78). Pres., Philological Soc., 1992–96 (Vice-Pres., 1996–). Hon. Mem., Linguistic Soc. of America, 1994–. An Editor, Jl of Linguistics, 1970–79. *Publications:* Inflectional Morphology, 1972; Morphology, 1974, 2nd edn 1991; Generative Grammar and Linguistic Competence, 1979; Syntax, 1981; Grammatical Theory in the United States from Bloomfield to Chomsky, 1993; The Concise Oxford Dictionary of Linguistics, 1997, 2nd edn 2007; A Short History of Structural Linguistics, 2001; Linguistics: a very short introduction, 2003; Syntactic Relations, 2007; articles and book chapters. *Recreations:* cycling, gardening. *Address:* 10 Fendon Close, Cambridge CB1 7RU. *T:* (01223) 247553; 22 Rue Nina et Julien Lefevre, 1952 Luxembourg. *T:* 224146.

MATTHEWS, Philip Rodway B.; *see* Bushill-Matthews.

MATTHEWS, Prof. Robert Charles Oliver, (Robin), CBE 1975; FBA 1968; Master, Clare College, Cambridge, 1975–93, now Emeritus; Professor of Political Economy, Cambridge University, 1980–91, now Emeritus; *b* 16 June 1927; *s* of Oliver Harwood Matthews, WS, and Ida Finlay; *m* 1948, Joyce Hilda Lloyds (*d* 2006); one *d*. *Educ:* Edinburgh Academy; Corpus Christi Coll., Oxford (Hon. Fellow, 1976). Student, Nuffield Coll., Oxford, 1947–48; Lectr, Merton Coll., Oxford, 1948–49; University Asst Lectr in Economics, Cambridge, 1949–51, and Univ. Lectr, 1951–65; Fellow of St John's Coll., Cambridge, 1950–65; Drummond Prof. of Political Economy, Oxford, and Fellow of All Souls Coll., 1965–75. Vis. Prof., Univ. of California, Berkeley, 1961–62. Chm., SSRC, 1972–75. A Managing Trustee, Nuffield Foundn, 1975–96; Trustee, Urwick Orr and Partners Ltd, 1978–86. Pres., Royal Econ. Soc., 1984–86; Mem., OECD Expert Group on Non-inflationary Growth, 1975–77. Chm., Bank of England Panel of Academic Consultants, 1977–93. FIDE Internat. Master of chess composition, 1965. For. Hon. Mem., Amer. Acad. of Arts and Scis, 1985; Hon. Mem., Amer. Econ. Assoc., 1993. Hon. DLitt: Warwick, 1980; Abertay Dundee, 1996. *Publications:* A Study in Trade Cycle History, 1954; The Trade Cycle, 1958; (with M. Lipton and J. M. Rice) Chess Problems: introduction to an art, 1963; (with F. H. Hahn) Théorie de la Croissance Economique, 1972; (ed) Economic Growth: trends and factors, 1981; (with C. H. Feinstein and J. C. Odling-Smee) British Economic Growth 1856–1973, 1982; (ed with G. B. Stafford) The Grants Economy and Collective Consumption, 1982; (ed) Slower Growth in the Western World, 1982; (ed with J. R. Sargent) Contemporary Problems of Economic Policy: essays from the CLARE Group, 1983; (ed) Economy and Democracy, 1985; Mostly Three-Movers: collected chess problems, 1995; articles in learned journals. *Address:* Clare College, Cambridge CB2 1TL. *Club:* Reform.

MATTHEWS, Suzan Patricia, (Mrs A. R. Matthews); QC 1993; **Her Honour Judge Suzan Matthews;** a Circuit Judge, since 2003; a Deputy High Court Judge, since 2000; *b* 5 Dec. 1947; *y c* of late Sidney Herbert Clark and Susan Hadnett Clark (*née* Mathews); *m* 1970, Anthony Robert Matthews; one *s*. *Educ:* Univ. of Bradford (BSc Hons Business Admin 1972). Called to the Bar, Middle Temple, 1974. Asst Recorder, 1991–95; a Recorder, 1995–2003. Asst Boundary Comr, 1992–2003. Councillor, SE Region, Gas Consumers' Council, 1987–96. Member: Criminal Injuries Compensation Appeals Panel, 1996–2003; Adv. Bd on Family Law, 1997–2002; Criminal Injuries Compensation Bd, 1999–2000; Mental Health Rev. Tribunal (Restricted Patients) Panel, 1999–2003; Dep. Chm., Criminal Injuries Compensation Appeals Panel, 2000–03. Chm., Inquiry into Richard Neale for Sec. of State for Health, 2002–04. Pres., The Valley Trust, 2000–. FRSA. *Recreations:* historical research, music, gardening. *Address:* The Crown Court at Kingston, 6–8 Penrhyn Road, Kingston-upon-Thames KT1 2BB. *T:* (020) 8240 2500.

MATTHEWS, Sir Terence (Hedley), Kt 2001; OBE 1994; FREng, FIET; Chairman, Mitel Networks, since 2001; Chief Executive Officer, March Networks Corporation; *b* 6 June 1943. *Educ:* Univ. of Wales, Swansea (BSc). Co-founder, Mitel Corp., 1972–85; Founder, Chm. and CEO, Newbridge Networks Corp., 1986–2000. Founder and Investor, Celtic House Internat., 1994–; Chairman: Covendia Corp.; DragonWave; Tundra Semiconductor Corp.; Celtic Manor Resort, Wales. FREng (FEng 1998). *Address:* Mitel Networks, 350 Legget Drive, PO Box 13089, Kanata, ON K2K 2W7, Canada.

MATTHEWS, Timothy John; Chief Executive, Remploy Ltd, since 2008; *b* 24 June 1951; *s* of Kenneth James Matthews and Vera Joan Matthews (*née* Fittall); *m* 1984, Sally Vivien Davies; two *s*. *Educ:* Peterhouse, Cambridge (BA Hons History). Admin. Trainee, DHSS, 1974; Private Sec. to Perm. Sec., DHSS, 1978–79; Dist Gen. Administrator, Bloomsbury HA, 1984; Gen. Manager, Middlesex Hosp., 1985; Dist Gen. Manager, Maidstone HA, 1988; Chief Executive: St Thomas' Hosp., 1991; Guy's and St Thomas' Hosp. Trust, 1993–2000; Chief Exec., Highways Agency, 2000–03; Man. Dir, Parsons Brinckerhoff Ltd, 2003–08. Dir, J. Laing plc, 2004–07. Director: S Bank Careers, 1996–2000; Focus Central London TEC, 1997–2001; S Bank Employers' Gp, 1998–2000. Trustee, Kent Community Housing Trust, 1991–94. *Recreations:* allotment gardening, opera. *Club:* Surrey CC.

MATTHEWS, Trevor John; Chief Executive Officer, Friends Provident, since 2008; *b* Sydney, 25 March 1952; *s* of Jack and Vinda Latham Matthews; *m* 1999, Michele; two *s*; one *s* from previous marriage. *Educ:* Macquarie Univ., Sydney (MA 1978). FIA 1975. Legal & General Assce Hldgs Australia, 1972–89, Man. Dir, 1989–96; Gen. Manager, Personal Financial Services, National Australia Bank, 1996–98; Exec. Gen. Manager, Canadian Ops, Manulife, 1998–2001; Pres. and CEO, Manulife Japan, 2001–04; Chief Exec., UK Financial Services, Standard Life, 2004–08. *Recreations:* travel, reading, family. *Address:* Friends Provident, 100 Wood Street, EC2V 7AN. *T:* 0870 608 3678; *e-mail:* trevor.matthews@friendsprovident.co.uk. *Clubs:* Union, University and Schools of Sydney; Royal Sydney Yacht Squadron.

MATTHEWS, Rt Rev. Victoria; *see* Christchurch, Bishop of.

MATTHEWS, Rev. Canon William Andrew; Vicar of Bradford-on-Avon, since 1981; Chaplain to the Queen, since 2001; *b* 8 Jan. 1944; *s* of Charles and Olive Matthews; *m* 1969, Jean Elizabeth McNicholas; one *s*. *Educ:* Malmesbury Grammar Sch.; Univ. of Reading (BA 1965; MA 1994); St Stephen's House, Oxford. Ordained deacon, 1967, priest, 1968; Curate: St Alban's, Westbury Park, Bristol, 1967–70; Marlborough, 1970–73; Priest i/c, 1973–75, Vicar, 1975–81, Winsley. RD, Bradford-on-Avon, 1984–94; Canon and Preb., Salisbury Cath., 1988–. *Address:* Holy Trinity Vicarage, 18A Woolley Street, Bradford-on-Avon, Wilts BA15 1AF. *T:* (01225) 864444; *e-mail:* w.a.matthews@btinternet.com.

MATTHEWS, His Honour (William) David; a Circuit Judge, 1992–2008; *b* 19 Nov. 1940; *s* of Edwin Kenneth William Matthews and Bessie Matthews; *m* 1965, Pauline Georgina May Lewis; two *s*. *Educ:* Wycliffe Coll. Admitted Solicitor, 1964; Partner, T. A. Matthews & Co., 1965–92; a Recorder, 1990–92. Mem., Mental Health Review Tribunal, 2001–08. Chm., W Mercia Criminal Justice Strategy Cttee, 2000–03. Pres., Herefordshire, Breconshire and Radnorshire Incorp. Law Soc., 1988–89. Mem. Council, Three Counties Agricl Soc., 1978–2001. Gov., Wycliffe Coll., 1985–90. *Recreations:* cricket, boats, National Hunt racing.

MATTHIAS, David Huw; QC 2006; FCIArb; *b* Cardiff, 13 Feb. 1954; *s* of David and Joan Matthias; *m* 1981, Sarah Widdows; three *s* one *d*. Lieut, RTR, 1973–76. Called to the Bar, Inner Temple, 1980; in practice as barrister, specialising in commercial litigation and arbitration, judicial review. FCIArb 1999. *Recreations:* supporting Welsh Rugby, sailing, running and walking with my dogs, cooking and eating out, theatre-going. *Address:* 2–3 Gray's Inn Square, WC1R 5JH. *T:* (020) 7242 4986, *Fax:* (020) 7405 1166; *e-mail:* dmatthias@2-3gis.co.uk.

MATTHÖFER, Hans; Member of the Bundestag (Social Democrat), 1961–87; *b* Bochum, 25 Sept. 1925; *m* Traute Matthöfer (*née* Mecklenburg). *Educ:* primary sch.; studied economics and social sciences in Frankfurt/Main and Madison, Wis, USA, 1948–53 (grad. Economics). Employed as manual and clerical worker, 1940–42; Reich Labour Service, 1942; conscripted into German Army, 1943 (Armoured Inf.), final rank NCO. Joined SPD (Social Democratic Party of Germany), 1950; employed in Economics Dept, Bd of Management, IG Metall (Metalworkers' Union) and specialized in problems arising in connection with automation and mechanization, 1953 (Head of Educn Dept, 1961). Member, OEEC Mission in Washington and Paris, 1957–61; Vice-Pres., Gp of Parliamentarians on Latin American Affairs (Editor of periodical Esprés Español until end of 1972); Mem., Patronage Cttee of German Section of Amnesty Internat.; Pres., Bd of Trustees, German Foundn for Developing Countries, 1971–73; Parly State Sec. in Federal Min. for Economic Co-operation, 1972; Federal Minister for Research and Technology, 1974, of Finance, 1978–82, for Posts and Telecommunications, 1982. Mem. of Presidency and Treasurer, SPD, 1985–87. Chm., Exec. Bd, Beteiligungsges. der Gewerkschaften (formerly für Gemeinwirtschaft) AG, trade union holding, 1987–97. Counsellor to Govt of Bulgaria, 1997–2000. Publisher, Vorwärts, 1985–88. *Publications:* Der Unterschied zwischen den Tariflöhnen und den Effektivverdiensten in der Metallindustrie der Bundesrepublik, 1956; Technological Change in the Metal Industries (in two parts), 1961–62; Der Beitrag politischer Bildung zur Emanzipation der Arbeitnehmer—Materialien zur Frage des Bildungsurlaubs, 1970; Streiks und streikähnliche Formen des Kampfes der Arbeitnehmer im Kapitalismus, 1971; Für eine menschliche Zukunft—Sozialdemokratische Forschungs—und Technologiepolitik, 1976; Humanisierung der Arbeit und Produktivität in der Industriegesellschaft, 1977, 1978, 1980; Agenda 2000: Vorschläge zur Wirtschafts- und Gesellschaftspolitik, 1993; numerous articles on questions of trade union, development, research and finance policies. *Relevant publication*: Hans Matthöfer: Gewerkschafter, Politiker, Unternehmer, by W. Abelshauser, 2007. *Address:* Augustinum, Appartment 306, Georg Rückert Strasse 2, 65812 Bad Soden am Taunus, Germany.

MATTILA, Karita Marjatta; opera singer, soprano; *b* 5 Sept. 1960; *d* of Erkki and Arja Mattila; *m* 1992, Tapio Kuneinen. *Educ:* Sibelius Acad., Helsinki; private studies in London. Début: Finnish Nat. Opera, 1983; Royal Opera House, Covent Garden, 1986; Metropolitan Opera, NY, 1990; has performed in opera houses worldwide; has performed with conductors incl. Abbado, Haitink, Mehta and Solti; has worked with theatre directors incl. Luc Bondy and Lev Dodin; concert and recital performances. Has made numerous recordings. Outstanding Perf. Award, Evening Standard, 1997; François Reichenbech Prize, Académie du Disque Lyrique, 1997. *Address:* c/o Universal Music Classical Management & Productions, Bond House, 347–353 Chiswick High Road, W4 4HS. *T:* (020) 8742 5408.

MATTINGLEY, Brig. Colin Grierson, CBE 1985 (OBE 1980); Clerk to the Grocers' Company, 1988–98; *b* 12 Oct. 1938; *s* of Lt-Col Wallace Grierson Mattingley, KOSB and Jeanette McLaren Mattingley (*née* Service); *m* 1964, Margaretta Eli Kühle; two *d*. *Educ:* Wellington Coll.; RMA Sandhurst. rcds, ndc, psc. Commnd KOSB, 1958; sc 1971; comd 1st Bn KOSB, 1979–81; Jun. Directing Staff, RCDS, 1981–82; Comdr, 8 Inf. Bde, 1982–84; Dir, Army Service Conditions, 1985–87; retd 1988. Col, KOSB, 1990–95. *Recreations:* sketching, walking, landscape gardening. *Address:* Stockers House, Broad Street, Somerton, Som TA11 7NH. *Clubs:* Army and Navy, St James's.

MATTINGLY, Prof. David John, PhD; FSA; FBA 2003; Professor of Roman Archaeology, University of Leicester, since 1998; *b* 18 May 1958; *s* of Harold B. Mattingly and Erica R. Mattingly (*née* Stuart); *m* 1981, Jennifer Warrell-Bowring; one *s* two *d*. *Educ:* Univ. of Manchester (BA 1st Cl. Hons History 1980; PhD 1984). British Acad. Postdoctoral Fellow, Inst. of Archaeol., Univ. of Oxford, 1986–89; Asst Prof., Dept of Classical Studies, Univ. of Michigan, 1989–91; Lectr, 1991–95, Reader, 1995–98, Sch. of Archaeol. and Ancient Hist., Univ. of Leicester. British Acad. Res. Reader, 1999–2001. Chm., Soc. for Libyan Studies, 1996–2001. FSA 1993. *Publications:* (ed jtly) Town and Country in Roman Tripolitania, 1985; (ed jtly) Libya: research in archaeology, environment, history and society, 1989; (with B. Jones) An Atlas of Roman Britain, 1990, rev. edn 1993; (ed jtly) Leptiminus (Lamta): a Roman port city in Tunisia, Report No 1, 1992; Tripolitania, 1995; (ed jtly) Farming the Desert: the UNESCO Libyan Valleys Archaeological Survey, Vols 1 and 2, 1996 (J. Wiseman Book Award); (ed) Dialogues in Roman Imperialism: power, discourse and discrepant experience in the Roman Empire, 1997; (ed jtly) Life, Death and Entertainment in Ancient Rome, 1999; (ed jtly) Geographical Information Systems and Landscape Archaeology, 1999; (ed jtly) Economies Beyond Agriculture in the Classical World, 2001; (jtly) Leptiminus (Lamta): the east baths, cemeteries, kilns, Venus mosaic, site museum and other studies, Report No 2, 2001; (jtly) The Archaeology of Fazzan, Vol. 1, Synthesis, 2003, Vol. 2, Gazetteer, Pottery and Other Finds, 2007; (ed jtly) The Libyan Desert: natural resources and cultural heritage, 2006; An Imperial Possession: Britain in the Roman Empire, 2006; (ed jtly) Cambridge Dictionary of Classical Civilization, 2006; (ed jtly) Archaeology and Desertification: the Wadi Faynan landscape survey, southern Jordan, 2007. *Recreations:* family, book group. *Address:* School of Archaeology and Ancient History, University of Leicester, Leicester LE1 7RH. *T:* (0116) 252 2610, *Fax:* (0116) 252 5005; *e-mail:* djm7@le.ac.uk.

MATTINGLY, Dr Stephen, TD 1964; FRCP; Consultant Physician, Middlesex Hospital, 1958–81, now Emeritus; Consultant Physician, 1956–82 and Medical Director, 1972–82, Garston Manor Rehabilitation Centre; Hon. Consultant in Rheumatology and Rehabilitation to the Army, 1976–81; *b* 1 March 1922; *s* of Harold Mattingly, CBE and Marion Grahame Meikleham; *m* 1945, Brenda Mary Pike; one *s*. *Educ:* Leighton Park Sch.; UCH (MB, BS); Dip. in Physical Med., 1953. FRCP 1970. House-surg., UCH, 1947; Regtl MO, 2/10 Gurkha Rifles, RAMC Far East, 1947–49; House-surg. and Registrar, UCH, 1950–55; Sen. Registrar, Middx Hosp., 1955–56. Reg. Med. Consultant for London, S-Eastern, Eastern and Southern Regions, Dept of Employment, 1960–74. Mem., Attendance Allowance Bd, 1978–83. Lt-Col RAMC TA, 1952–67. *Publications:* (contrib.) Progress in Clinical Rheumatology, 1965; (contrib.) Textbook of Rheumatic Diseases, ed Copeman, 1969; (contrib.) Fractures and Joint Injuries, ed Watson Jones, 5th edn 1976, 6th edn 1982; (ed) Rehabilitation Today, 1977, 2nd edn 1981; Aspects of Brington: a Northamptonshire Country Parish, 1997, 2nd edn 1998. *Recreation:* gardening. *Address:* Highfield House, Steeple Lane, Little Brington, Northants NN7 4HN. *T:* (01604) 770271.

MATTINSON, Deborah Susan; Joint Chairman, Chime Research and Engagement Division, since 2000; *b* 17 Sept. 1956; *d* of R. R. and J. M. Mattinson; *m* 1989, David Arnold Pelly; two *s* one *d*. *Educ:* Bristol Univ. (LLB). Account Manager, McCann Erickson, 1978–83; Account Dir, Ayer Barker, 1983–85; Co-founder, Gould Mattinson, 1985–90; Founder, GMA Monitor, 1990–92; Jt CEO, Opinion Leader Res., 1992–2007. Comr, EOC, 2002–07. Trustee: Green Alliance, 2004–; Dance Umbrella, 2008–. *Recreations:* family, reading, walking, theatre. *T:* (work) (020) 7861 2540.

MATUSSEK, Thomas; Permanent Representative of Germany to the United Nations, since 2006; *b* 18 Sept. 1947; *m* 1975, Ursula Schütten; one *s* two *d*. *Educ:* Sorbonne, Paris; Univ. of Bonn. Judge's Asst and Asst Lectr, Univ. of Bonn, 1973–75; entered German Foreign Service, 1975; Foreign Office, Bonn, 1975–77; London, 1977–80; Federal Chancellery, European Affairs, Bonn, 1980–83; New Delhi, 1983–86; Lisbon, 1986–88; Foreign Office, Bonn, 1988–92; Chief of Staff and Hd of Foreign Minister's Private Office, Bonn, 1992–94; Dep. Chief of Mission, Washington, 1994–99; Dir Gen., Political Affairs, Foreign Office, 1999–2002; Ambassador to UK, 2002–06. *Recreations:* mountaineering, ski-ing. *Address:* Permanent Mission of Germany to the UN, 871 UN Plaza, New York, NY 10017, USA. *Clubs:* Athenæum, Royal Automobile, Naval and Military, Travellers.

MATUSZEWSKI, Zbigniew, Silver Cross of Merit, 1976; Knight's Cross of the Order of Merit, 1996; Ambassador of the Republic of Poland to the Court of St James's, 2004–06; *b* 10 Feb. 1946; *s* of Stefan Matuszewski and Maria Matuszewska (*née* Zielińska); *m* 1976, Ewa; two *s*. *Educ:* Warsaw Univ. (LLM 1968). Warsaw Univ., 1968–80, Man. Dir, 1978–80; Polish Ministry of Foreign Affairs, 1980–: Political Counsellor, London, 1986–91; Dir, Foreign Minister's Cabinet, 1991–93; Minister Plenipotentiary, Dep. Perm. Rep. of Poland to the UN, NY, 1993–2000; Dep. Dir, Internat. Office, Chancellery of the President, 2000–01; Dir Gen., Foreign Service, 2001–04. *Clubs:* Athenæum, Army and Navy, Travellers.

MATUTES JUAN, Abel; President, Fiesta Hotel Group S.L.; Minister for Foreign Affairs, Spain, 1996–2000; *b* 31 Oct. 1941; *s* of Antonio Matutes and Carmen Juan; *m* Nieves Prats Prats; one *s* three *d*. *Educ:* University of Barcelona (Law and Economic Sciences). Prof., Barcelona Univ., 1963; Vice-Pres., Employers Organization for Tourism, Ibiza-Formentera, 1964–79; Mayor of Ibiza, 1970–71; Senator, Ibiza and Formentera in Alianza Popular (opposition party), 1977–82; Vice-Pres., Partido Popular (formerly Alianza Popular), 1979– (Pres., Economy Cttee); Mem., EEC, 1986–94; MEP for Spain, 1994–96; Pres., Commn for External Relations and Security, EP, 1994–96. Pres., Nat. Electoral Cttee; Spokesman for Economy and Finance, Grupo Popular in Congress (Parlt). Member: Bd, Banco Santander; Adv. Bd, TUI. *Recreation:* tennis. *Address:* POB 416, Ibiza. *Clubs:* Golf Rocalliza (Ibiza); de Campo Tennis (Ibiza).

MAUCERI, John Francis; Chancellor, North Carolina School of the Arts, since 2006; Founding Director, Hollywood Bowl Orchestra, since 2006 (Director, 1991–2006; Conductor, 1991–96; Principal Conductor, 1997–2006); *b* 12 Sept. 1945; *s* of Gene B. Mauceri and Mary Elizabeth (*née* Marino); *m* 1968, Betty Ann Weiss; one *s*. *Educ:* Yale Univ. (BA, MPhil). Music Dir, Yale Symphony Orch., 1968–74; Associate Prof., Yale Univ., 1974–84; Music Director: Washington Opera, 1979–82; Orchestras, Kennedy Center, 1979–91; Amer. Symphony Orch., NYC, 1985–87; Scottish Opera, 1987–93; Teatro Regio, Torino, 1994–98; Pittsburgh Opera, 2001–06; Leonard Bernstein Fest., LSO, 1986; Conductor, Amer. Nat. Tour, Boston Pops Orch., 1987; co-Producer, musical play, On Your Toes, 1983; Musical Supervisor, Song and Dance, Broadway, 1985. Vis. Prof., Yale Univ., 2001. Dir, Charles Ives Soc., 1986–91 (Mem., 1986–); Mem., Adv. Bd, Amer. Inst. for Verdi Studies, 1986–; Consultant: for Music Theater, Kennedy Center for Performing Arts, Washington, 1982–91; Leonard Bernstein Orgn, 2006–; Trustee, Nat. Inst. for Music Theater, 1986–91. Member Advisory Board: Kurt Weill Edn, 1996–; Leonard Bernstein Center for Learning, 2006–; Film Music Soc., 2006–. Fellow, Amer. Acad. Berlin, 1999. Television appearances; numerous recordings (Grammy award for Candide recording, 1987; Edison Klassiek Award, 1991; Deutsche Schallplatten Prize, 1991, 1994; Cannes Classical Award for Kurt Weill's Der Protagonist, 2003); soundtrack to film Evita, 1996. Antoinette Perry Award, League of NY Theatres and Producers, 1983; Drama Desk Award, 1983; Outer Critics Circle Award, 1983; Arts award, Yale Univ., 1985; Olivier award for Best Musical for Candide, adaptation for Scottish Opera/Old Vic prodn, 1988; Wavenden All Music Award for Conductor of the Year, 1989; Emmy Award, 1994, 1998; Soc. for Preservation of Film Music Award, 1995; Diapason d'Or, 1997; Treasures of LA Award, 2007. *Publications:* (contrib.) Sennets and Tuckets: a Bernstein celebration (ed Ledbetter), 1988; (contrib.) Atti di Convegno Internazionale: Verdi 2001, 2003; various articles for Scottish Opera programmes, newspapers, magazines and jls. *Address:* c/o Columbia Artists Management, 1790 Broadway, New York, NY 10019–1412, USA.

MAUCHLINE, Lord; Simon Michael Abney-Hastings; *b* 29 Oct. 1974; *s* and *heir* of Earl of Loudoun, *qv*. *Address:* Wangaratta, Vic 3677, Australia.

MAUD, Hon. Sir Humphrey (John Hamilton), KCMG 1993 (CMG 1982); FRCM; HM Diplomatic Service, retired; Chairman, Commonwealth Disaster Management Agency Ltd, since 1999; *b* 17 April 1934; *s* of Baron Redcliffe-Maud, GCB, CBE and Jean, *yr d* of late J. B. Hamilton, Melrose; *m* 1963, Maria Eugenia Gazitua; three *s*. *Educ:* Eton (Oppidan Scholar); King's Coll., Cambridge (Scholar; Classics and History); MA. Mem., NYO, 1949–52. Instructor in Classics, Univ. of Minnesota, 1958–59; entered Foreign Service, 1959; FO, 1960–61; Madrid, 1961–63; Havana, 1963–65; FO, 1966–67; Cabinet Office, 1968–69; Paris, 1970–74; Nuffield Coll., Oxford (Econs), 1974–75; Head of Financial Relations Dept, FCO, 1975–79; Minister, Madrid, 1979–82; Ambassador, Luxembourg, 1982–85; Asst Under Sec. of State, FCO, 1985–88; High Comr, Cyprus, 1988–90; Ambassador to Argentina, 1990–93. Dep. Sec. Gen. (Econ. and Social Affairs) of the Commonwealth, 1993–99. Chairman: Emerging Markets Partnership—Financial Advisors, 1999–2002; Pall Mall Initiatives, 2001–. Member, Council: British Diabetic Assoc., 1986–90; RCM, 1987–2002. Dir, Orchestra of St John's, 1997–2002. Trustee, Parkhouse Award, 1994–; Mem., Queen's Medal for Music Cttee, 2004–. FRCM 2002. *Recreations:* golf, music ('cellist), bird-watching. *Address:* 31 Queen Anne's Grove, W4 1HW. *Clubs:* Oxford and Cambridge, Garrick; Royal Mid-Surrey Golf.

MAUDE, family name of **Viscount Hawarden**.

MAUDE, Rt Hon. Francis (Anthony Aylmer); PC 1992; MP (C) Horsham, since 1997; *b* 4 July 1953; *s* of Baron Maude of Stratford-upon-Avon, TD, PC; *m* 1984, Christina Jane, *yr d* of late Peter Hadfield, Shrewsbury; two *s* three *d*. *Educ:* Abingdon Sch.; Corpus Christi Coll., Cambridge (MA (Hons) History; Avory Studentship; Halse Prize). Called to Bar, Inner Temple, 1977 (scholar; Forster Boulton Prize). Councillor, Westminster CC, 1978–84. MP (C) Warwicks N, 1983–92; contested (C) Warwicks N, 1992. PPS to Minister of State for Employment, 1984–85; an Asst Government Whip, 1985–87; Parly Under Sec. of State, DTI, 1987–89; Minister of State, FCO, 1989–90; Financial Sec. to HM Treasury, 1990–92; Shadow Chancellor, 1998–2000; Shadow Foreign Sec., 2000–01; Chm., Conservative Party, 2005–07; Shadow Minister for the Cabinet Office and Shadow Chancellor of the Duchy of Lancaster, 2007–. Chm., Govt's Deregulation Task Force, 1994–97. Director: Salomon Brothers, 1992–93; Asda Gp, 1992–99; Man. Dir, 1993–97, Adv. Dir, 1997–98, Morgan Stanley & Co.; Dep. Chm., Benfield Gp, 2003–; Chairman: Incepta Gp, 2004–06; Mission Marketing Gp, 2006–. *Recreations:* ski-ing, cricket, reading, music. *Address:* House of Commons, SW1A 0AA.

MAUDSLAY, Richard Henry, CBE 2006; CEng, FREng; FIEE; Chairman, Defence Science and Technology Laboratory, Ministry of Defence, since 2005; Deputy Chairman, Hardy & Greys Ltd, since 1999; *b* 19 Nov. 1946; *s* of Cecil Winton Maudslay and Charity Magdalen (*née* Johnston); *m* 1968, Rosalind Elizabeth Seville; two *d*. *Educ:* Christ's Hosp., Horsham; Edinburgh Univ. (BSc Electrical Engrg). CEng 1977; FIEE 1985; FREng 1994. Grad. trainee, Scottish Electrical Trng Scheme, 1968–69; Systems Analyst, Parsons Peebles, 1969–71; Systems Manager: Reyrolle Belmos, 1971–72; and Corporate Planner, Parsons Peebles, 1972–74; Prodn Manager, Parsons Peebles Power Transformers, 1974–78; Gen. Manager, Transformadores Parsons Peebles de Mexico, 1978–85; Managing Director: NEI Parsons, 1985–92; Rolls-Royce Industrial Power Gp, 1992–97 (Mem. Bd, Rolls-Royce Plc, 1994–97). Non-executive Director: dominick hunter Gp plc, 2000–05; N G Bailey Gp Ltd, 2001–. Mem. Bd, One NorthEast (RDA), 1999–2004 (Dep. Chm., 2002–04). Chm., N E Sci. and Industry Council, 2004–. Mem., Business Chamber, Enterprise Policy Gp, EC, 2007–. Pres., BEAMA, 1996–98. *Recreations:* music (Chm., Brinkburn Music Fest.), restoring 100-year old houses. *Address:* c/o Hardy & Greys Ltd, Willowburn, Alnwick, Northumberland NE66 2PF. *T:* (01665) 602771, *Fax:* (01665) 602225.

MAUGHAN, Air Vice-Marshal Charles Gilbert, CB 1976; CBE 1970; AFC; Independent Panel Inspector, Department of the Environment, 1983–94; *b* 3 March 1923. *Educ:* Sir George Monoux Grammar Sch.; Harrow County Sch. Served War, Fleet Air Arm (flying Swordfishes and Seafires), 1942–46. Joined RAF, 1949, serving with Meteor, Vampire and Venom sqdns in Britain and Germany; comd No 65 (Hunter) Sqdn, Duxford, Cambridgeshire (won Daily Mail Arch-to-Arc race, 1959). Subseq. comd: No 9 (Vulcan) Sqdn; flying bases of Honington (Suffolk) and Waddington (Lincs); held a staff post at former Bomber Comd, Air Staff (Ops), Strike Command, 1968–70; Air Attaché, Bonn, 1970–73; AOA Strike Command, 1974–75; SASO RAF Strike Command, 1975–77. Gen. Sec., Royal British Legion, 1978–83. *Address:* Whitestones, Tresham, Wotton-under-Edge, Glos GL12 7RW.

MAUGHAN, Sir Deryck C., Kt 2002; Managing Director, Kohlberg Kravis Roberts & Company, since 2005; Chairman, KKR Asia, since 2005; *b* 20 Dec. 1947; *s* of Renwick Maughan and Muriel Maughan; *m* 1981, Va; one *d*. *Educ:* King's Coll., London (BA Hons 1969); Stanford Univ. (MS 1978). HM Treasury, 1969–79; Chief Executive Officer: Salomon Bros, 1992–97; Salomon Smith Barney, 1997–98; Vice Chm., Citigroup Inc., 1998–2004. Vice-Chm., NY Stock Exchange, 1996–2000. Harkness Fellow, 1977–78. *Address:* 9 West 57 Street, New York, NY 10019, USA. *Club:* Metropolitan (New York).

MAULEVERER, (Peter) Bruce; QC 1985; FCIArb 1997; a Recorder, 1985–2004; a Deputy High Court Judge, 1992–2004; *b* 22 Nov. 1946; *s* of late Major Algernon Arthur Mauleverer and Hazel Mary Mauleverer; *m* 1971, Sara (*née* Hudson-Evans); two *s* two *d*. *Educ:* Sherborne School; University College, Univ. of Durham (BA 1968). Called to the Bar, Inner Temple, 1969, Bencher 1993; Hd of Chambers, 4 Pump Ct, 1992–2000. Vice-Chm., Internat. Law Assoc., 1993– (Hon. Sec.-Gen., 1986–93). Vice-Pres., Internat. Social Sci. Council, UNESCO, 1998–2000. Trustee: UNICEF UK, 2002–08; Tavistock Centre for Couple Relationships, 2005–; Jubilee Sailing Trust, 2006–. *Recreations:* sailing, ski-ing, travel. *Address:* Eliot Vale House, 8 Eliot Vale, Blackheath, SE3 0UW. *T:* (020) 8852 2070. *Clubs:* Garrick, Royal Ocean Racing.

MAUNDER, Prof. Leonard, OBE 1977; BSc; PhD; ScD; FREng; FIMechE; Professor of Mechanical Engineering, 1967–92, now Emeritus (Professor of Applied Mechanics, 1961), Dean of the Faculty of Applied Science, 1973–78, University of Newcastle upon Tyne; *b* 10 May 1927; *s* of Thomas G. and Elizabeth A. Maunder; *m* 1958, Moira Anne Hudson (*d* 2005); one *s* one *d*. *Educ:* Bishop Gore Grammar Sch., Swansea; University Coll. of Swansea (BSc; Hon. Fellow, 1989); Edinburgh Univ. (PhD); Massachusetts Institute of Technology (ScD). Instructor, 1950–53, and Asst Prof., 1953–54, in Dept of Mech. Engrg, MIT; Aeronautical Research Lab., Wright Air Development Center, US Air Force, 1954–56; Lecturer in Post-Graduate Sch. of Applied Dynamics, Edinburgh Univ., 1956–61. Christmas Lectr, Royal Instn, 1983. Member: NRDC, 1976–81; SRC Engrg Bd, 1976–80; Adv. Council on R&D for Fuel and Power, Dept of Energy, 1981–92; British Technology Gp, 1981–92; ACOST, 1987–93; Dep. Chm., Newcastle Hospitals Management Cttee, 1971–73. President: Internat. Fedn Theory of Machines and Mechanisms, 1976–79; Engrg, BAAS, 1980; Vice-Pres., IMechE, 1975–80; Chm., Engrg Educn (formerly Continuum) Exec. Bd, Royal Acad. of Engrg, 1997–2003. Hon. Foreign Mem., Polish Soc. Theoretical and Applied Mechanics, 1984. Hon. Fellow, UC, Swansea, 1989. *Publications:* (with R. N. Arnold) Gyrodynamics and Its Engineering Applications, 1961; Machines in Motion, 1986; numerous papers in the field of applied mechanics. *Address:* 46 Moorside South, Newcastle upon Tyne NE4 9BB.

MAUNG, U Hla; Ambassador of the Union of Myanmar to the Court of St James's, 1992–96, concurrently accredited to Denmark, Norway and Sweden; *b* 8 Nov. 1932; *s* of U Pya and Daw Amar; *m* 1955, Daw Khin Myint; four *s* two *d*. *Educ:* Univ. of Yangon (BA Econs); Vanderbilt Univ., USA (MA Econs; Dip. in Econ. Develt). Ministry of Planning and Finance, Yangon: Asst Dir, 1966–72; Dir-Gen., 1972–78; Asian Development Bank, Manila: Alternate Exec. Dir, 1978–80; Exec. Dir, 1981–83; Dir-Gen., Min. of Planning and Finance, Yangon, 1983–84; Ambassador to: Philippines, 1984–87; Yugoslavia, 1987–92. Kyein Wut Pi Pya Ye/Taya U Pade So Mo Ye Tazeik, 1989; Pyi Thu Wun Htan Taziek, 1989; Naingngandaw Ayechan Thayarye Tazeik, 1989; Pyi Thu Wun Htan Kaung Taziek, 1992. *Publications:* articles on econs to Myanmar monthly jls. *Recreations:* reading, swimming. *Address:* c/o Ministry of Foreign Affairs, Prome Court, Prome Road, Yangon, Myanmar.

MAUNSELL, (Caroline) Harriet, OBE 1994; non-executive Director, Serious Fraud Office, since 2004; *b* 22 Aug. 1943; *d* of Dr Geoffrey Sharman Dawes and Margaret Joan (*née* Monk); *m* 1986, Michael Brooke Maunsell, *qv*. *Educ:* Somerville Coll., Oxford (MA 1965). Called to the Bar, Middle Temple, 1973; Solicitor, 1978. Courtaulds Ltd, 1965–77; Lovell White & King, subseq. Lovells, 1977–97, Partner, 1980–97. Member: Occupational Pensions Bd, 1987–97 (Dep. Chm., 1992–97; Chm., 1993); Council, Occupational Pensions Adv. Service, 1990–93; OPRA, 1997–2005 (Chm., 2001–05). Co-founder and first Chm., Assoc. of Pension Lawyers, 1984–85 (Mem. cttees, 1984–97). Dir, Ambache Chamber Orchestra, 1996–2002; Council Mem., Cheltenham Ladies' Coll., 1998–2001; Member: Somerville Develt Bd, 2004– (Chm., 2005–); With-Profits Cttee, Norwich Union, 2007–. *Publication:* (with Jane Samsworth) Guide to the Pensions Act 1995, 1995. *Recreations:* reading, gardening, opera, travel, playing the piano, singing in a choral society. *Address:* 41 Colebrooke Row, N1 8AF.

MAUNSELL, Michael Brooke; Administrator, City Solicitors Educational Trust, 2000–08; *b* 29 Jan. 1942; *s* of Captain Terence Augustus Ker Maunsell, RN and Elizabeth (*née* Brooke); *m* 1st, 1965, Susan Pamela Smith (*see* S. P. Maunsell) (marr. diss. 1986); 2nd, 1986, (Caroline) Harriet Dawes (*see* C. H. Maunsell). *Educ:* Monkton Combe Sch.; Gonville and Caius Coll., Cambridge (MA, LLB). Admitted Solicitor, 1967; with Lovell White & King (Solicitors), 1967–88: Partner, 1971–88; Admin Partner, 1978–83; Partner, 1988–97, Managing Partner, 1993–97, Lovell White Durrant; Sen. Fellow, British Inst. of Internat. and Comparative Law, 1998–2000. Dir, J. M. Jones & Sons (Holdings) Ltd, 1981–91. Chm., Educn and Trng Cttee, City of London Law Soc., 1978–91; Mem., London (No 13) Local, then Area, Legal Aid Cttee, 1971–89. Mem., Determinations Panel, Pensions Regulator, 2005–. Trustee: Highgate Cemetery Charity, 1988–95; Kings Corner Project (Islington), 1997–. Governor: Grey Coat Hosp., Westminster, 1997–2005; Bishopsgate Foundn, 2002– (Dep. Chm., 2007–08; Chm., 2008–). Liveryman, City of London Solicitors' Co., 1973–. *Recreations:* opera, theatre, travel, good living. *Address:* 41 Colebrooke Row, N1 8AF. *T:* (020) 7226 7128.

MAUNSELL, Susan Pamela; Policy Co-ordinator, 2002–05, Inquiry Secretary, 2007, Competition Commission; *b* 30 Jan. 1942; *d* of George Cruickshank Smith and Alice Monica Smith (*née* Davies); *m* 1965, Michael Brooke Maunsell, *qv* (marr. diss. 1986). *Educ:* Nottingham High Sch. for Girls (GPDST); Girton Coll., Cambridge (schol.; BA classics; MA). Ministry of Health: Asst Principal, 1964; Private Sec. to Perm. Sec., 1967, to Parly Sec., 1968; Department of Health and Social Security: Principal, 1969; Asst Sec., 1976; Regl Controller, London S Social Security Reg., 1981–85; various HQ policy posts, 1985–89; Under Sec., Policy Div. A, DSS, 1989–92; Dir, Office of Parly Comr for Admin, 1993–2001. Mem., CSAB, 1993–99. Chair, Age Concern Bromley, 1997–2001. FRSA 1995. *Recreations:* travel, books, theatre, riding, food, wine. *Address:* 27 Longton Avenue, SE26 6RE. *T:* (020) 8778 5605; *e-mail:* SusanMaunsell@aol.com.

MAURICE, Rt Rev. Peter David; *see* Taunton, Bishop Suffragan of.

MAURICE, Dr Rita Joy; Director of Statistics, Home Office, 1977–89; *b* 10 May 1929; *d* of A. N. Maurice and F. A. Maurice (*née* Dean). *Educ:* East Grinstead County Sch.; University Coll., London. BSc (Econ) 1951; PhD 1958. Asst Lectr, subseq. Lectr in Economic Statistics, University Coll., London, 1951–58; Statistician, Min. of Health, 1959–62; Statistician, subseq. Chief Statistician, Central Statistical Office, 1962–72; Head of Economics and Statistics Div. 6, Depts of Industry, Trade and Prices and Consumer Protection, 1972–77. Member: Council, Royal Statistical Soc., 1978–82; Parole Bd, 1991–94; Retail Prices Index Adv. Cttee, 1992–94. *Publications:* (ed) National Accounts Statistics: sources and methods, 1968; articles in statistical jls. *Address:* 10 Fairfax Place, Swiss Cottage, NW6 4EH.

MAUROY, Pierre; Senator, Nord, since 1992; *b* 5 July 1928; *s* of Henri Mauroy and Adrienne Mauroy (*née* Bronne); *m* 1951, Gilberte Deboudt; one *s*. *Educ:* Lycée de Cambrai; Ecole normale nationale d'apprentissage de Cachan. Joined Young Socialists at age of 16 (Nat. Sec., 1950–58); teacher of technical educn, Colombes, 1952; Sec.-Gen., Syndicat des collèges d'enseignement technique de la Fédération de l'Education nationale, 1955–59; Sec., Fedn of Socialist Parties of Nord, 1961; Mem., Political Bureau, 1963, Dep. Gen. Sec., 1966, Socialist Party; Mem. Exec. Cttee, Fédération de la gauche démocratique et socialiste, 1965–68; First Sec., Fedn of Socialist Parties of Nord and Nat. Co-ordination Sec., Socialist Party, 1971–79; First Sec., Socialist Party, 1988–92. Member, from Le Cateau, and Vice-Pres., Conseil Gen. du Nord, 1967–73; Town Councillor and Deputy Mayor of Lille, 1971, Mayor, 1973–2001, Vice-Pres., Town Corp., 1971–81; Deputy, Nord, 1973–81, 1986–92; Prime Minister of France, 1981–84. Pres., Regional Council, Nord-Pas-de-Calais, 1974–81; Socialist Rep. and Vice-Pres., Political Commn, EEC, 1979–81. Political Dir, Action Socialiste Hebdo, 1979–81; President: Communauté Urbaine de Lille, 1989–; Fédération nationale Léo Lagrange; Fédération Nationale des Elus Socialistes et Républicains, 1987–90; Socialist International, 1992–99; Fondation Jean Jaurès, 1992–. *Publications:* Héritiers de l'avenir, 1977; C'est ici le chemin, 1982; A gauche, 1985; Parole de Lillois, 1994; Léo Lagrange, 1996; Mémoires, 2003. *Address:* Sénat, 75291 Paris Cedex 06, France; 17–19 rue Voltaire, 59800 Lille, France.

MAVOR, Prof. John, FREng; FRSE; Vice-President (Physical Science and Engineering), Royal Society of Edinburgh, 2004–07; Principal and Vice-Chancellor, Napier University, 1994–2002; *b* 18 July 1942; *s* of Gordon Hattersley Mavor and Wilhelmina Baillie McAllister; *m* 1968, Susan Christina Colton; two *d*. *Educ:* City Univ., London; London Univ. (BSc, PhD, DSc(Eng)); Edinburgh Univ. (MPhil). FInstP; FIEEE; FIET. AEI Res. Labs, London, 1964–65; Texas Instruments Ltd, Bedford, 1968–70; Emihus Microcomponents, Glenrothes, 1970–71; University of Edinburgh: Lectr, 1971; Reader, 1979; Lothian Chair of Microelectronics, 1980; Head of Dept of Electrical Engrg, 1984–89; Prof. of Electrical Engrg, 1986–94; Dean, 1989–94, and Provost, 1992–94, Faculty of Sci. and Engrg. Hon. DSc: Greenwich, 1998; City, 1998. *Publications:* MOST Integrated Circuit Engineering, 1973; Introduction to MOS LSI Design, 1983; over 150 technical papers in professional electronics jls. *Recreations:* gardening, walking, steam railways. *Address:* 8 Heriot Row, Edinburgh EH3 6HU.

MAVOR, Michael Barclay, CVO 1983; MA; Headmaster, Loretto School, 2001–08; *b* 29 Jan. 1947; *s* of late William Ferrier Mavor and Sheena Watson Mavor (*née* Barclay); *m* 1970, Jane Elizabeth Sucksmith; one *s* one *d*. *Educ:* Loretto School; St John's Coll., Cambridge (Exhibn and Trevelyan Schol.; Pres., Johnian Soc., 2000). MA (English); CertEd. Woodrow Wilson Teaching Fellow, Northwestern Univ., Evanston, Ill, 1969–72; Asst Master, Tonbridge Sch., 1972–78; Course Tutor (Drama), Open Univ., 1977–78; Headmaster, Gordonstoun Sch., 1979–90; Head Master, Rugby Sch., 1990–2001. Chm., HMC, 1997. Mem., Queen's Body Guard for Scotland, Royal Co. of Archers, 1997–. *Recreations:* theatre, writing, archery, golf, fishing. *Clubs:* Hawks (Cambridge); New (Edinburgh).

MAW, (John) Nicholas; composer; *b* 5 Nov. 1935; *s* of Clarence Frederick Maw and Hilda Ellen (*née* Chambers); *m* 1960, Karen Graham; one *s* one *d*. *Educ:* Wennington Sch., Wetherby, Yorks; Royal Academy of Music. Studied in Paris with Nadia Boulanger and Max Deutsch, 1958–59. Fellow Commoner in Creative Arts, Trinity Coll., Cambridge, 1966–70; Visiting Professor of Composition: Yale Music Sch., 1984–85, 1989; Boston Univ., 1986; Prof. of Music, Milton Avery Grad. Sch. of Arts, Bard Coll., NY, 1990–99; Prof. of Composition, Peabody Conservatory of Music, Baltimore, 1999–2008. Midsummer Prize, Corp. of London, 1980; Konssevitsky Foundn Award, 1990; Sudler Internat. Wind Band Prize, John Philip Sousa Soc., 1992; Stoeger Prize for Chamber Music, Chamber Music Soc., Lincoln Center, 1993. *Compositions include: operas:* One-Man Show, 1964; The Rising of The Moon, 1970; Sophie's Choice, 2002; *for orchestra:* Sinfonia, 1966; Sonata for Strings and Two Horns, 1967; Serenade, for small orchestra, 1973, 1977; Life Studies, for 15 solo strings, 1973; Odyssey, 1974–86; Summer Dances, 1981; Spring Music, 1983; The World in the Evening, 1988; Shahnama, 1992; Dance Scenes, 1995; Variations in Old Style, 1995, subseq. retitled Voices of Memory; Concert Suite from Sophie's Choice, 2004; *for instrumental soloist and orchestra:* Sonata Notturna, for cello and string orchestra, 1985; Little Concert, for oboe and chamber orchestra, 1987; Violin Concerto, 1993; Cor Anglais Concerto, 2004; *for voice and orchestra:* Nocturne, 1958; Scenes and Arias, 1962; *for wind band:* American Games, 1991; *chamber music:* String Quartet, no 1, 1965, no 2, 1983, no 3, 1994, no 4, 2005; Chamber Music for wind and piano quintet, 1962; Flute Quartet, 1981; Ghost Dances, for chamber ensemble, 1988; Piano Trio, 1991; String Sextet, 2006; *instrumental music:* Sonatina for flute and piano, 1957; Essay for organ, 1961; Personae for piano, nos I-III, 1973, IV–VI, 1985; Music of

Memory, for solo guitar, 1989; Sonata for solo violin, 1997; Narration for solo cello, 2001; *vocal music:* The Voice of Love, for mezzo soprano and piano, 1966; Six Interiors, for high voice and guitar, 1966; La Vita Nuova, for soprano and chamber ensemble, 1979; Five American Folksongs, for high voice and piano, 1988; Roman Canticle, for mezzo soprano, flute, viola and harp, 1989; *choral music:* Five Epigrams, for chorus, 1960; Round, for chorus and piano, 1963; Five Irish Songs, for mixed chorus, 1973; Reverdie, five songs for male voices, 1975; Te Deum, for treble and tenor soli, chorus, congregation and organ, 1975; Nonsense Rhymes; songs and rounds for children, 1975–76; The Ruin, for double choir and solo horn, 1980; Three Hymns, for mixed choir and organ, 1989; One Foot in Eden Still, I Stand (motet for choir and soloists), 1990; Hymnus, for chorus and orch., 1996. *Address:* c/o Faber Music Ltd, 3 Queen Square, WC1N 3AU.

MAWBY, Colin (John Beverley); conductor and composer; Conductor, National Irish Chamber Choir, 1996–2001; *b* 9 May 1936; *e s* of Bernard Mawby and Enid Mawby (*née* Vaux); *m* 1987, Beverley Courtney; two *s*. *Educ:* St Swithun's Primary Sch., Portsmouth; Westminster Cathedral Choir Sch.; Royal Coll. of Music. Organist and Choirmaster of Our Lady's Church, Warwick St, W1, 1953; Choirmaster of Plymouth Cath., 1955; Organist and Choirmaster of St Anne's, Vauxhall, 1957; Asst Master of Music, Westminster Cath., 1959; Master of Music, 1961–75; Dir of Music, Sacred Heart, Wimbledon, 1978–81; Choral Dir, Radio Telefis Eireann, 1981–95. Conductor: Westminster Chamber Choir, 1971–78; Westminster Cathedral String Orchestra, 1971–78; New Westminster Chorus, 1972–80; Horniman Singers, 1979–80. Prof. of Harmony, Trinity Coll. of Music, 1975–81. Director (Catholic) Publisher, L. J. Cary & Co., 1963; Vice-Pres., Brit. Fedn of *Pueri Cantores*, 1966; Member: Council, Latin Liturgical Assoc., 1969; Adv. Panel, Royal Sch. of Church Music, 1974; Music Sub-Cttee, Westminster Arts Council, 1974. Hon. FGCM 1988. Broadcaster and recording artist; freelance journalism. KSG 2006. *Publications:* Church music including twenty-six Masses, anthems, motets, two children's operas and Holy Week music. *Recreations:* gardening, wine drinking. *Address:* 30a Disraeli Road, Forest Gate, E7 9JP. *T:* (020) 8555 6010; *e-mail:* colinmawby@btinternet.com.

MAWBY, Peter John; Headmaster, Lancaster Royal Grammar School, 1983–2001; *b* 17 Aug. 1941; *s* of Norman James Mawby and May Mawby (*née* Huse); *m* 1968, Gillian Fay Moore; one *s* one *d*. *Educ:* Sedbergh Sch.; Queens' Coll., Cambridge (MA 1966). Assistant Teacher: Shrewsbury Sch., 1964–65; St John's Sch., Leatherhead, 1965–68; Head of Biology, Edinburgh Acad., 1968–79; Head of Science, Cheltenham Coll., 1979–83. Member: Council, Brathay Exploration Gp, 1989–95; Court, Lancaster Univ., 1989–2001; Headteacher Mentoring Exec. Cttee, Grant-Maintained Schs' Centre, 1992–99. Consultant, Rydal Hall, Dio. of Carlisle, 2003–05. Chm., Lancs br., Cambridge Soc., 2006–; Pres., Old Lancastrian Club, 2006–07. *Publications:* (with M. B. V. Roberts) Biology 11–13, 1983; Biology Questions, 1985; Longman Science 11–14: Biology, 1991, 3rd edn 1996. *Recreations:* sport, music, ornithology. *Address:* Lowhill, Haverbreaks Road, Lancaster LA1 5BJ.

MAWDSLEY, Harry Paul, OBE 2003; JP; DL; Chairman, Magistrates' Association, 1999–2002; *b* 21 July 1939; *s* of Harry and Jessie Mawdsley; *m* 1970, Anne Horton Rigby; two *s*. *Educ:* Univ. of Massachusetts (MSc 1969); Univ. of Manchester (MEd 1974). Teacher, Birmingham schs, 1961–66; Lectr, Alsager Trng Coll., Cheshire, 1966–85; Principal Lectr and Hd, Dept of Sport Sci., Crewe and Alsager Coll. of Higher Educn, 1985–88; Hd, Admissions and Mktg, Manchester Metropolitan Univ., 1988–99. Vice-Pres., British Univs Sports Assoc., 2000–. JP South Cheshire, 1975; DL Cheshire 2003. *Recreations:* jogging, gardening, foreign travel. *Club:* Army and Navy.

MAWER, Sir Philip (John Courtney), Kt 2002; Prime Minister's Independent Adviser on Ministerial Interests, since 2008; *b* 30 July 1947; *s* of Eric Douglas and Thora Constance Mawer; *m* 1972, Mary Ann Moxon; one *s* two *d*. *Educ:* Hull Grammar Sch.; Edinburgh Univ. (MA Hons Politics 1971); DPA (London Univ. External) 1973. Senior Pres., Student Representative Council, 1969–70. Home Office, 1971; Private Sec. to Minister of State, 1974–76; Nuffield and Leverhulme Travelling Fellowship, 1978–79; Sec., Lord Scarman's Inquiry into Brixton disturbances, 1981; Asst Sec., Head of Industrial Relations, Prison Dept, 1984–87; Principal Private Sec. to Home Sec. (Rt Hon. Douglas Hurd), 1987–89; Under-Secretary, Cabinet Office, 1989–90; Secretary-General: Gen. Synod of C of E, 1990–2002; Archbishops' Council, 1999–2002; Parly Comr for Standards, 2002–07. Non-exec. Dir, Ecclesiastical Insce Gp, 1996–2002, 2008–. Trustee: All Churches Trust, 1992–; Foundn for Church Leadership, 2003–; Mem. Governing Body, SPCK, 1994–2002. Patron: Church Housing Trust, 1996–; Isabel Hospice, 2004–. Hon. Lay Canon, St Alban's Cathedral, 2003. FRSA 1991–2007. Hon. DLitt Hull, 2006; Hon. LLD Hertfordshire, 2007. *Recreations:* family and friends. *Address:* c/o Propriety and Ethics Team, Cabinet Office, 70 Whitehall, SW1A 2AS.

MAWER, Ronald K.; *see* Knox-Mawer.

MAWHINNEY, family name of **Baron Mawhinney**.

MAWHINNEY, Baron *cr* 2005 (Life Peer), of Peterborough, in the county of Cambridgeshire; **Brian Stanley Mawhinney,** Kt 1997; PC 1994; *b* 26 July 1940; *s* of Frederick Stanley Arnot Mawhinney and Coralie Jean Mawhinney; *m* 1965, Betty Louise Oja; two *s* one *d*. *Educ:* Royal Belfast Academical Instn; Queen's Univ., Belfast (BSc); Univ. of Michigan, USA (MSc); Univ. of London (PhD). Asst Prof. of Radiation Research, Univ. of Iowa, USA, 1968–70; Lectr, subsequently Sen. Lectr, Royal Free Hospital School of Medicine, 1970–84. Mem., MRC, 1980–83. Mem., Gen. Synod of C of E, 1985–90. MP (C): Peterborough, 1979–97; Cambs NW, 1997–2005. PPS to Ministers in HM Treasury, Employment and NI, 1982–86; Under Sec. of State for NI, 1986–90; Minister of State: NI Office, 1990–92; DoH, 1992–94; Sec. of State for Transport, 1994–95; Minister without Portfolio, 1995–97; Opposition front bench spokesman on home affairs, 1997–98. Pres., Cons. Trade Unionists, 1987–90 (Vice-Pres., 1984–87); Chm. of Cons. Party, 1995–97. Mem., AUT. Contested (C) Stockton on Tees, Oct. 1974. Non-exec. dir of cos in England; Chm., Football League, 2003–08. Freedom, City of Peterborough, 2008. *Publications:* (jtly) Conflict and Christianity in Northern Ireland, 1976; In the Firing Line, 1999. *Recreations:* sport, reading. *Address:* House of Lords, SW1A 0PW.

MAWHOOD, Caroline Gillian, (Mrs J. P. Nettel); Assistant Auditor General, National Audit Office, since 1996; *b* 17 July 1953; *d* of John Lennox Mawhood and Joan Constance Dick; *m* 1980, Julian Philip Nettel, *qv*; two *s*. *Educ:* Queen Anne's Sch., Caversham; Bristol Univ. (BScSoc Geography). CIPFA. Joined Exchequer and Audit Dept, 1976, Dep. Dir, 1989–92; Office of the Auditor General, Canada, 1992–93; Dir of Corporate Policy, Nat. Audit Office, 1993–95. *Publication:* (contrib.) State Audit in the European Union, 1996. *Recreations:* golf, tennis, swimming, bridge. *Address:* National Audit Office, 157–197 Buckingham Palace Road, SW1W 9SP. *T:* (020) 7798 7533. *Clubs:* Anglo-Belgian; Roehampton, Wimbledon Park Golf.

MAWREY, Richard Brooks; QC 1986; a Recorder of the Crown Court, since 1986; a Deputy High Court Judge, since 1995; *b* 20 Aug. 1942; *s* of Philip Stephen Mawrey and Alice Brooks Mawrey; *m* 1965, Gillian Margaret Butt, *d* of Francis Butt and Alice Margaret Butt; one *d*. *Educ:* Rossall School; Magdalen College, Oxford (BA, 1st class Hons Law, 1963; Eldon Law Scholar, 1964; MA 1967). Albion Richardson Scholar, Gray's Inn, 1964; called to the Bar, Gray's Inn, 1964, Bencher, 2004; Lectr in Law, Magdalen College, Oxford, 1964–65, Trinity College, Oxford, 1965–69. An Election Comr, 1995–. Co-Founder and Trustee, Historic Gardens Foundn, 1995–; Chm., Oxfordshire Gardens Trust, 2002–06. *Publications:* Computers and the Law, 1988; specialist editor: Consumer Credit Legislation, 1983; Butterworths County Court Precedents, 1985; Bullen & Leake & Jacob's Precedents of Pleadings, 13th edn 1990, 16th edn 2007; Butterworths Civil Court Pleadings, 1999–; Goode: Consumer Credit Law and Practice, 2006–; Blackstone's Guide to the Consumer Credit Act 2006, 2006. *Recreations:* history, opera, cooking. *Address:* 2 Harcourt Buildings, Temple, EC4Y 9DB. *T:* (020) 7583 9020.

MAWSON, family name of **Baron Mawson**.

MAWSON, Baron *cr* 2007 (Life Peer), of Bromley-by-Bow, in the London Borough of Tower Hamlets; **Andrew Mawson,** OBE 2000; *b* 8 Nov. 1954; *s* of Jack and Mary Mawson; *m* 1975, Susan Barnes; two *s* one *d*. *Educ:* Manchester Univ. (BA 1979; MPhil 1987). Church Minister, United Reformed Church, 1984–. Founder, 1984, Chief Exec., now Pres., Bromley-by-Bow Centre; Co-Founder, 1998, Exec. Dir, now Pres., Community Action Network. Founder Chm., 1996, now Pres., Stanton Guildhouse, Glos. Founder, Water City Gp, E London. Dir, Leaside Regeneration Ltd. *Publications:* (jtly) Church and the City, 1975; (jtly) People before Structures, 1999; The Social Entrepreneur, 2008. *Recreations:* sailing, music, walking, reading. *Address:* House of Lords, SW1A 0PW. *T:* (020) 7219 3000; *e-mail:* mawsona@parliament.uk.

MAWSON, David, OBE 1990; JP; DL; FSA; Partner, Feilden and Mawson, Architects, Norwich, 1957–90, Consultant, since 1990; *b* 30 May 1924; *s* of John William Mawson and Evelyn Mary Mawson (*née* Bond); *m* 1951, Margaret Kathlyn Norton; one *s* one *d*. *Educ:* Merchant Taylors' Sch., Sandy Lodge; Wellington Coll., NZ; Auckland Univ., NZ; Kingston-upon-Thames Coll. of Art. Royal Navy, 1945–47. Architect, 1952–. Architect: Norwich Cathedral, 1977–90; St Giles Cathedral, Edinburgh, 1977–81. Chairman: Norfolk Soc. (CPRE), 1971–76 (Vice Pres., 1976–96, 2001–; Pres., 1996–2000); 54 Gp, 1982–; Norfolk ProHelp (formerly Norfolk Professional Firms Gp), BITC, 1994–2004; Friends of Norwich Museums, 1985–2000 (Vice-Pres., 2002–); Founder and Chm., British Assoc. of Friends of Museums, 1973–89 (Vice-Pres., 1989–); Founder Pres., World Fedn of Friends of Museums, 1975–81, Past Pres., 1981–; Pres., Costume and Textile Assoc. for Norfolk Museums, 1989–. Mem., Cttee of Nat. Heritage, 1973–89; Trustee: Norfolk Historic Bldgs Trust, 1975–90 (Dir, 1990–); Theatre Royal, Norwich, 1991–99; Dep. Pres., Norfolk Gardens Trust, 2005– (Founder, and Chm., 1988–91; Vice-Pres., 1991–2005); Council Mem., Assoc. of Gardens Trusts, 1994–98. Mem., Norfolk Assoc. of Architects, 1952–94 (Pres., 1979–81); Hon. Treas., Heritage Co-ordination Gp, 1981–87. Trustee, Wymondham Bridewell Preservation Trust, 1994–. First Gov., Wymondham Coll., 1991–99. Pres., Norwich Venta Probus Club, 2001–02. Chm., Townclosians (Alumni of Town Close House Sch., Norwich), 2003–07. JP Norwich, 1972; DL Norfolk, 1986. FSA 1983. Hon. MA UEA, 1995. *Publication:* paper on British Museum Friends Socs in Proc. of First Internat. Congress of Friends of Museums, Barcelona, 1972; contrib. Jl of Royal Soc. of Arts. *Recreations:* gardening, sailing. *Club:* Norfolk (Norwich) (Pres., 1986–87).

MAXEY, Peter Malcolm, CMG 1982; HM Diplomatic Service, retired 1986; *b* 26 Dec. 1930; *m* 1st, 1955, Joyce Diane Marshall; two *s* two *d*; 2nd, Christine Irene Spooner. *Educ:* Bedford Sch.; Corpus Christi Coll., Cambridge. Served HM Forces, 1949–50. Entered Foreign Office, 1953; Third Sec., Moscow, 1955; Second Sec., 1956; First Sec., Helsinki, 1962; Moscow, 1965; First Sec. and Head of Chancery, Colombo, 1968; seconded to Lazard Bros, 1971; Inspector, 1972; Deputy Head UK Delegation to CSCE, Geneva, 1973; Head of UN Dept, FCO, 1974; NATO Defence Coll., Rome, 1977; Dublin, 1977; on secondment as Under Sec., Cabinet Office, 1978–81; Ambassador, GDR, 1981–84; Ambassador and Dep. Perm. Rep. to UN, NY, 1984–86. Editorial Dir, Global Analysis Systems, 1986–88.

MAXTON, family name of **Baron Maxton**.

MAXTON, Baron *cr* 2004 (Life Peer), of Blackwaterfoot in Ayrshire and Arran; **John Alston Maxton;** *b* Oxford, 5 May 1936; *s* of late John Maxton, agr. economist, and Jenny Maxton; *m* 1970, Christine Maxton; three *s*. *Educ:* Lord Williams' Grammar Sch., Thame; Oxford Univ. Lectr in Social Studies, Hamilton Coll. Chm., Assoc. of Lectrs in Colls of Educn, Scotland; Member: Educnl Inst. of Scotland; Socialist Educnl Assoc.; MSF. Joined Lab. Party, 1970. MP (Lab) Glasgow, Cathcart, 1979–2001. Opposition spokesman on health, local govt, and housing in Scotland, 1985–87, on Scotland, 1987–92; Scottish and Treasury Whip, 1984–85. Member: Scottish Select Cttee, 1981–83; Public Accounts Cttee, 1983–84; Culture, Media and Sport (formerly Nat. Heritage) Select Cttee, 1992–2001; Speaker's Panel of Chairmen, 1994–97. *Recreations:* family, listening to jazz, running.

MAXWELL, family name of **Barons de Ros** and **Farnham**.

MAXWELL, David Campbell F.; *see* Finlay-Maxwell.

MAXWELL, Ian Robert Charles; Publisher, 1995–98, Editorial Consultant, since 1998, Maximov Publications; *b* 15 June 1956; *s* of late (Ian) Robert Maxwell, MC; *m* 1st, 1991, Laura Plumb (marr. diss. 1998); 2nd, 1999, Tara Dudley Smith; one *s*. *Educ:* Marlborough; Balliol Coll., Oxford (MA). Pergamon Press, 1978–83; Prince's Charitable Trust, 1983–84; British Printing & Communication Corporation, later Maxwell Communication Corporation, 1985–91 (Jt Man. Dir, 1988–91); Chm., Agence Centrale de Presse, 1986–89; Chairman and Publisher: Mirror Gp Newspapers, 1991 (Dir, 1987–91); The European Newspaper, 1991 (Dir, 1990–91). Mem., Nat. Theatre Develt Council, 1986–91; Pres., Club d'Investissement Media, 1988–91. Vice Chm., Derby County Football Club, 1987–91 (Chm., 1984–87). *Recreations:* music, ski-ing, water ski-ing, football.

See also K. F. H. Maxwell.

MAXWELL, Prof. James Rankin, PhD, DSc; FRS 1997; Senior Research Fellow, University of Bristol, since 1999 (Professor of Organic Geochemistry, 1990–99, now Emeritus); *b* 20 April 1941; *s* of John J. and Helen M. T. Maxwell; *m* 1964, Joy Millar Hunter; one *d* (one *s* decd). *Educ:* Univ. of Glasgow (BSc; PhD 1967); DSc Bristol 1982. Research Asst, Univ. of Glasgow, 1967; Postdoctoral Res. Chemist, Univ. of Calif, Berkeley, 1967–68; University of Bristol: Postdoctoral Fellow, 1968–69; Res. Associate, 1969–72; Lectr, 1972–78; Reader, 1978–90; Hd, Envmtl and Analytical Chem. Section, 1991–99. Geochemistry Fellow, Geochem. Soc., USA and European Assoc. Geochem., 1996. J. Clarence Karcher Medal, Univ. of Oklahoma, 1979; Treibs Medal, Geochem.

Soc., USA, 1989. *Publications:* numerous papers in learned jls. *Recreations:* walking, gardening, cooking. *Address:* School of Chemistry, University of Bristol, Cantock's Close, Bristol BS8 1TS. *T:* (0117) 928 7669.

MAXWELL, John Frederick Michael; His Honour Judge Maxwell; a Circuit Judge, since 2005; *b* 20 May 1943; *s* of Frederic Michael and Mabel Doreen Maxwell; *m* 1986, Jayne Elizabeth Hunter; one *s* one *d*, and two step *s*. *Educ:* Dover Coll.; New Coll., Oxford (MA Juris.). Called to the Bar, Inner Temple, 1965; a Dep. Stipendiary Magistrate, 1978–90; Asst Recorder, 1990–95; a Recorder, 1995–2005. Standing Counsel to: HM Customs and Excise, 1995–2005; Revenue and Customs Prosecutions Office, 2005. Chm., Birmingham Karma Ling, 1991–; Trustee, Rokpa Trust, 1996–. Mem., RYA. *Recreations:* music, yachting. *Address:* Stafford Crown and County Courts, Victoria Square, Stafford ST16 2QQ. *T:* (01785) 610730. *Clubs:* Portishead Cruising; Old Gaffers Assoc.

MAXWELL, John Hunter, CA; Chairman, DX Services plc, 2004–06; *b* 25 Sept. 1944; *s* of late John Hunter Maxwell, OBE and of Susan Elizabeth Una Smith; *m* 1967, Janet Margaret Frew; three *s*. *Educ:* Melville Coll., Edinburgh; Dumfries Acad.; Edinburgh Univ. CA 1967. T. Hunter Thompson & Co., CA, Edinburgh, 1962–67; Regl Dir, Far East, Rank Xerox Ltd, 1967–83; Gp Financial Controller, Grand Metropolitan plc, 1983–86; Chief Executive: Provincial Gp, 1986–92; BPB Industries plc, 1992–93; non-exec. Dir, Alliance & Leicester, 1993–94; Corporate Develt Dir, Prudential Corp. plc, 1994–96; Dir Gen., AA, 1996–2000; Chm., Wellington Underwriting plc, 2000–03. Non-executive Director: RAC, 2000–; Provident Financial, 2000–; The Big Food Gp plc, 2001–05; Parity Gp plc, 2002–05; Royal & Sun Alliance plc, 2003–; Homeserve plc, 2004–; MSA, 2007–. Chm., IAM, 2002–07 (Mem. Council, 1997–2007). CCMI (CIMgt 1992); FIMI 1997; FRSA 1997. Trustee, RAF Benevolent Fund, 2004–07. Gov., Royal Ballet Sch., 2000–06. Hon. Treas., Cruising Assoc., 1973–74. Freeman, City of London, 1998; Liveryman, Coachmakers' and Coach Harness Makers' Co., 1998–. *Recreations:* sailing, classic cars, travel, arts. *Address:* 8 Caroline Terrace, SW1W 8JS. *Clubs:* Royal Automobile (Mem. Cttee, 2004–), Royal Thames Yacht.

MAXWELL, Kevin Francis Herbert; Chairman, Corunna Estates Ltd, since 2007; *b* 20 Feb. 1959; *s* of late (Ian) Robert Maxwell, MC; *m* 1984, Pandora Deborah Karen Warnford-Davis; two *s* five *d*. *Educ:* Marlborough Coll.; Balliol Coll., Oxford (MA Hons). Chairman: Maxwell Communication Corporation, 1991 (Dir, 1986–91); Macmillan Inc., 1991 (Dir, 1988–91); Dir, Guinness Mahon Hldgs, 1989–92; Chm., Telemonde Inc., 1999–2002. Chm., Oxford United FC, 1987–92. Trustee, New Sch. for Social Research, NYC, 1989–92. *Recreations:* water colour painting, football.
See also I. R. C. Maxwell.

MAXWELL, Sir Michael (Eustace George), 9th Bt *cr* 1681 (NS), of Monreith, Wigtownshire; MRICS; *b* 28 Aug. 1943; *s* of Major Eustace Maxwell (*d* 1971) and late Dorothy Vivien, *d* of Captain George Bellville; *S* uncle, 1987. *Educ:* Eton; College of Estate Management. *Recreations:* microlights, curling, tennis, ski-ing. *Address:* 56 Queensmill Road, SW6 6JS. *Clubs:* Stranraer Rugby; Port William Tennis.

MAXWELL, Sir Nigel Mellor H.; *see* Heron-Maxwell.

MAXWELL, Prof. Patrick Henry, DPhil; FRCP; Professor of Medicine and Head of Division of Medicine, University College London, since 2008; Hon. Consultant Nephrologist, Royal Free Hospital, since 2008; Hon. Consultant Physician, University College London Hospitals, since 2008; Registrar, Academy of Medical Sciences, since 2006; *b* 12 March 1962; *s* of Robert James Maxwell, *qv*; *m* 1989, Margaret Jane Hughes; two *s* one *d*. *Educ:* Eton (King's Schol.); Corpus Christi Coll., Oxford (BA Physiol Scis 1983; DPhil 1994); St Thomas's Hosp. Med. Sch., London (MB BS Distn 1986). MRCP 1989, FRCP 1995. House Officer, St Thomas' Hosp. and Worthing Hosp., 1986–87; Sen. House Officer, Hammersmith Hosp. Renal Unit, St Thomas' Hosp., Nat. Heart Hosp. and Nat. Hosp. for Neurology and Neurosurgery, 1987–89; Registrar, Lewisham Hosp. and Guy's Hosp., 1989–91; University of Oxford: MRC Trng Fellow, Inst. of Molecular Medicine, 1991–94; Clinical Lectr, 1994–96; Univ. Lectr, and Hon. Consultant Nephrologist, 1996–2000; Reader in Nephrology, 2000–02; Prof. of Nephrology, Imperial Coll., London, 2002–08; Hon. Consultant Physician, Imperial Coll. Healthcare NHS Trust (formerly Hammersmith Hosps), 2002–08. Member: Renal Assoc.; Assoc. of Physicians of GB and Ire. FMedSci 2005. *Publications:* Medical Masterclass: nephrology, 2001; articles in learned jls on erythropoietin, HIF-1 and oxygen sensing. *Recreations:* sailing, losing to my children at chess. *Address:* Rayne Institute, University College London, 5 University Street, WC1E 6JJ. *T:* (020) 7679 6351, *Fax:* (020) 7679 6211; *e-mail:* p.maxwell@ucl.ac.uk.

MAXWELL, Richard; QC 1988; a Recorder, since 1992; a Deputy High Court Judge, since 1998; *b* 21 Dec. 1943; *s* of Thomas and Kathleen Marjorie Maxwell; *m* 1966, Judith Ann Maxwell; two *s* two *d*. *Educ:* Nottingham High Sch.; Hertford College, Oxford (MA). Lectr in Law, 1966–68; called to the Bar, Inner Temple, 1968. An Asst Recorder, 1989–92. *Recreations:* fly fishing, ski-ing, mountain-biking, golf, wine, single malt whisky. *Clubs:* Nottingham and Notts United Services; Nottingham Squash Rackets; Darley Dale Flyfishers' (Chm.); Beeston Fields Golf; Peak Forest Angling.

MAXWELL, Robert James, CVO 1998; CBE 1993; FRCPE; Chairman, The Gloucestershire Partnership NHS Trust, 2002–08; *b* 26 June 1934; *s* of Dr George B. Maxwell, MC and Cathleen Maxwell; *m* 1960, Jane FitzGibbon; three *s* two *d*. *Educ:* Leighton Park Sch.; New Coll., Oxford (BA 1st Cl. Hons, MA; Newdigate Prize for Poetry); Univ. of Pennsylvania (MA); LSE (PhD); Univ. of Tromsø (Dip. in Health Econs). FCMA; FRCPE 1997; 2nd Lieut, Cameronians (Scottish Rifles), 1952–54. Union Corp., 1958–66; McKinsey & Co., 1966–75; Administrator to Special Trustees, St Thomas' Hosp., 1975–80; Sec. and Chief Exec., The King's Fund, 1980–97. Pres., European Healthcare Management Assoc., 1985–87; Pres., Open Section, RSocMed, 1986–88; Chm. Council, Foundn for Integrated Medicine, 1998–2001. Chm., Court, LSHTM, 1985–95; Mem. Council, London Univ., 2004–08; Governor: NISW, 1981–98; UMDS, 1989–98; Director: Guy's and Lewisham Trust, 1990–93; Lewisham NHS Trust, 1993–98; Severn NHS Trust, 1998–2002; Mem., Bd of Management, Med. Defence Union, 1990–98 (Hon. Fellow, 1998). Chm., Leighton Park Sch., 1981–2001. FRSA 1995. Hon. FRCGP 1994; Hon. MRCP 1987; Hon. Mem., Assoc. of Anaesthetists, 1990. Trustee: Joseph Rowntree Foundn, 1994–; Thrive (formerly Horticultural Therapy), 1998–; Pharmacy Practice Res. Trust, 1999–2005. JP Inner London Youth and Family Courts (Chm.), 1971–98; JP S Glos, 1999–2004. DUniv Brunel, 1993; Hon. DLitt West of England, 1993. *Publications:* Health Care: the growing dilemma, 1974; Health and Wealth, 1981; Reshaping the National Health Service, 1988; Spotlight on the Cities, 1989; An Unplayable Hand?: BSE, CJD and British Government, 1997. *Recreations:* poetry, walking, stained glass, not quite catching up with correspondence. *Address:* Pitt Court Manor, North Nibley, Dursley, Glos GL11 6EL. *Clubs:* Brooks's, Royal Society of Medicine.
See also P. H. Maxwell.

MAXWELL, Simon Jeffrey, CBE 2007; Director, Overseas Development Institute, since 1997; *b* 1 May 1948; *s* of Frederick Norman Maxwell and Ruth Maxwell (*née* Salinsky); *m* 1973, Catherine Elizabeth Pelly; three *s*. *Educ:* Lycée d'Anvers; Solihull Sch.; St Edmund Hall, Oxford (BA PPE 1970); Univ. of Sussex (MA Develt Econs 1973). United Nations Development Programme: Jun. Professional Officer, Nairobi, 1970–72; Asst Res. Rep., New Delhi, 1973–77; Agricl Economist, ODA, Santa Cruz, Bolivia, 1978–81; Fellow, Inst. of Develt Studies, Univ. of Sussex, 1981–97. Member: Oxfam Field Cttee for Latin America, 1981–84; Ind. Gp on British Aid, 1982–; UN Adv. Gp on Nutrition, 1990–96; Program Adv. Panel, Foundn for Develt Co-operation, 1997–. External Examiner, Wye Coll., Univ. of London, 1995–98; Gov., Inst. of Develt Studies, 1996–97. Mem. Council, Develt Studies Assoc. of UK and Ireland, 1998–2005 (Pres., 2001–05). Trustee, Action for Conservation through Tourism, 1998–2004; Patron, One World Broadcasting Trust, 1998–; Mem., Adv. Cttee, Charter 99, 1999–2002. Fellow, World Econ. Forum, 2003–; Hon. Fellow, Foreign Policy Assoc., NY, 2003–. *Publications:* numerous pubns on poverty, food security, aid and agricl develt. *Address:* Overseas Development Institute, 111 Westminster Bridge Road, SE1 7JD. *T:* (020) 7922 0300; 20 West Drive, Brighton, E Sussex BN2 0GD.

MAXWELL, (William) Stewart; Member (SNP) West of Scotland, Scottish Parliament, since 2003; Minister for Communities and Sport, since 2007; *b* 24 Dec. 1963; *s* of William Maxwell and Margaret Maxwell; *m* 1995, Mary Stevenson; one *d*. *Educ:* Glasgow Coll. of Technol. (BA Hons Soc. Sci.). Wilmax Ltd (family business), 1986–88, 1991–93; Admin. Officer, Scottish Training Foundn, 1988–91; Strathclyde Fire Brigade: Industrial Trng Manager, 1993–94; Sen. Admin. Officer, 1994–2001; Mgt Inf. System Project Manager, 2001–03. Scottish Parliament: Shadow Dep. Minister for Health, 2004–06; Shadow Minister for Sport, Culture and Media, 2006–07; Dep. Convener, Justice 1 Cttee, 2003–04; Member: Subordinate Legislation Cttee, 2003–07; Justice 2 Cttee, 2004–06; Enterprise and Culture Cttee, 2006–07. Vice Convener, Publicity, 2003–04, Mem., NEC, 2003–04, SNP. *Recreations:* cinema, theatre, Rugby (debenture holder at Murrayfield), swimming, reading, eating out. *Address:* Scottish Parliament, Edinburgh EH99 1SP. *T:* (0131) 348 5000; *e-mail:* Stewart.Maxwell.msp@scottish.parliament.uk.

MAXWELL DAVIES, Sir Peter, Kt 1987; CBE 1981; composer and conductor; Master of the Queen's Music, since 2004; *b* 8 Sept. 1934; *s* of Thomas and Hilda Davies. *Educ:* Leigh Grammar Sch.; Manchester Univ. (MusB (Hons) 1956); Royal Manchester Coll. of Music. FRNCM 1978. Studied with Goffredo Petrassi in Rome (schol. 1957); Harkness Fellow, Grad. Music Sch., Princetown Univ., NJ, 1962–64. Dir of Music, Cirencester Grammar Sch., 1959–62; lecture tours in Europe, Australia, NZ, USA, Canada and Brazil; Visiting Composer, Adelaide Univ., 1966; Prof. of Composition, RNCM, 1975–80; Vis. Fromm Prof. of Composition, Harvard Univ., 1985. Founder and Co-Dir, with Harrison Birtwistle, of Pierrot Players, 1967–71; Founder and Artistic Director: The Fires of London, 1971–87; St Magnus Fest., Orkney Is, 1977–86 (Pres., 1986–); Artistic Dir, Dartington Hall Summer Sch. of Music, 1979–84; Associate Composer/Conductor: Scottish Chamber Orch., 1985–94 (Composer Laureate, 1994–); RPO, 1992–2000; Conductor/Composer, BBC Philharmonic Orch., 1992–2001. Retrospective Festival, South Bank Centre, 1990. President: Schs Music Assoc., 1983–; N of England Educn Conf., 1985; Composers' Guild of GB, 1986–; Making Music (formerly NFMS), 1989–; Cheltenham Arts Fests, 1994–96; SPNM, 1995–. Series for Schools Broadcasts, BBC Television. FRCM 1994; FRSAMD 1994; Fellow, British Acad. of Composers and Songwriters, 2005. Member: Accademica Filarmonia Romana, 1979; Royal Swedish Acad. of Music, 1993; Bavarian Acad. of Fine Arts, 1998. Hon. Member: RAM, 1979; Guildhall Sch. of Music and Drama, 1981; Royal Philharmonic Soc., 1987; RSA, 2001. Hon. FRIAS 1994. Hon. Fellow, Univ. of Highlands and Islands, 2004. Hon. DMus: Edinburgh, 1979; Manchester, 1981; Bristol, 1984; Open Univ., 1986; Glasgow, 1993; Durham, 1994; Hull, 2001; Oxford, 2005; Kingston, 2005; Hon. LLD Aberdeen, 1981; Hon. DLitt: Warwick, 1986; Salford, 1999; DUniv Heriot-Watt, 2002. Cobbett Medal, for services to chamber music, 1989; (first) Award, Assoc. of British Orchs, 1991; Gulliver Award, 1991; Charles Groves Award, NFMS, 1995; Dist. Musicians Award, ISM, 2001. Officier de l'Ordre des Arts et des Lettres (France), 1988. *Major compositions include: orchestral:* First Fantasia on an In Nomine of John Taverner, 1962, Second Fantasia, 1964; St Thomas Wake, 1968; Worldes Blis, 1969; Stone Litany, 1973; Symphony No 1, 1976; Black Pentecost, 1979; Symphony No 2, 1980; Sinfonia Concertante, 1982; Into the Labyrinth, 1983; Symphony No 3, 1985; An Orkney Wedding, with Sunrise, 1985; Violin Concerto, 1985; Concerto for trumpet and orch., 1988; Symphony No 4, 1989; Ojai Festival Overture, 1991; The Turn of the Tide, 1992; A Spell for Green Corn: The MacDonald Dances, 1993; Symphony No 5, 1994; Cross Lane Fair, 1994; The Beltane Fire, 1995; Symphony No 6, 1996; Concerto for piccolo, 1996; Concerto for piano, 1997; Mavis in Las Vegas, 1997; Sails in St Magnus, retitled Orkney Saga, I and II, 1997, III, 1999, V, 2000; Strathclyde Concertos: No 1, 1986; No 2, 1988; No 3, for horn, trumpet and orch., 1989; No 4, for clarinet and orch., 1990; No 5 for violin, viola and string orch., 1991; No 6, for flute and orch., 1991; No 7, for double bass and orch., 1992; No 8, for bassoon and orch., 1993; No 9, for woodwind and strings, 1994; No 10, for orch., 1996; A Reel of Seven Fishermen, 1998; Rome Amor, 1998; Horn Concerto, 1999; Symphony No 7, and No 8 (Antarctic), 2000; *instrumental and ensemble:* Sonata for trumpet and piano, 1955; Alma redemptoris mater, 1957; Revelation and Fall, 1966; Antechrist, 1967; Missa super L'Homme Armé, 1968; From Stone to Thorn, 1971; Ave Maris Stella, 1975; A Mirror of Whitening Light, 1977; Image, Reflection, Shadow, 1982; Trumpet Quintet, 1999; Crossing King's Reach, 2001; De Assumtione Beatae Mariae Virginis, 2001; Mass, 2001; Naxos Quartet No 1, 2002, No 2 and No 3, 2003, No 4 and No 5, 2004, No 6, No 7 and No 8, 2005; Piano Trio, 2002; *opera:* Taverner, 1970; The Martyrdom of Saint Magnus, 1976; The Two Fiddlers, 1978; The Lighthouse, 1979; Cinderella, 1979; Piano Sonata, 1981; Brass Quintet, 1981; Resurrection, 1987; The Doctor of Myddfai, 1995; *music theatre:* Eight Songs for a Mad King, 1969; Vesalii Icones, 1969; Miss Donnithorne's Maggot, 1974; Le Jongleur de Notre Dame, 1978; The No 11 Bus, 1984; The Great Bank Robbery, 1989; Mr Emmet Takes a Walk, 1999; *ballet:* Salome, 1978; Caroline Mathilde, 1990; *choral:* Five Motets, 1959; O Magnum Mysterium, 1960; Solstice of Light, 1979; The Three Kings, 1995; Job, 1997; The Jacobite Rising, 1997; Sea Elegy, 1998; Canticum Canticorum, 2001; Mass, 2002. *Address:* c/o Intermusica, 16 Duncan Terrace, N1 8BZ.

MAXWELL-HYSLOP, Kathleen Rachel, FSA; FBA 1991; archaeologist, retired; *b* 27 March 1914; *d* of Sir Charles Clay, CB, FBA and Hon. Lady Clay; *m* 1938, Aymer Robert Maxwell-Hyslop (*d* 1993); one *s* two *d*. *Educ:* Downe House Sch.; Sorbonne; London Univ. (Acad. Postgrad. Dip. in Archaeology of Western Asia). FSA 1950. Institute of Archaeology, University of London: Asst Lectr, 1947–52; Lectr in W Asiatic Archaeology, 1952–66. Archaeol research and travel in Turkey, Cyprus, Iraq, Jordan, Israel, 1950–89; lectured in Philadelphia, MIT, Teheran, Amman; excavations in British Isles, Turkey, Cyprus, Iraq and Iran, 1936–90. *Publications:* Western Asiatic Jewellery *c.* 3000–612 BC, 1971; articles in Iraq, Levant, Jl of Archaeol Science, Anatolian Studies and jls in USA and Turkey. *Recreations:* gardening, painting, piano. *Address:* Water Lane House, Little Tew, Chipping Norton, Oxon OX7 4JG. *T:* (01608) 683226.

MAXWELL-HYSLOP, Sir Robert John, (Sir Robin), Kt 1992; *b* 6 June 1931; 2nd *s* of late Capt. A. H. Maxwell-Hyslop, GC, RN, and late Mrs Maxwell-Hyslop; *m* 1968, Joanna Margaret, *er d* of Thomas McCosh; two *d*. *Educ:* Stowe; Christ Church, Oxford (MA). Hons Degree in PPE Oxon, 1954. Joined Rolls-Royce Ltd Aero Engine Div., as graduate apprentice, Sept. 1954; served 2 years as such, then joined Export Sales Dept; PA to Sir David Huddie, Dir and GM (Sales and Service), 1958; left Rolls-Royce, 1960. Contested (C) Derby (North), 1959; MP (C) Tiverton Div. of Devon, Nov. 1960–1992. Member: Trade and Industry Select Cttee, 1971–92; Standing Orders Cttee, 1977–92; Procedure Select Cttee, 1978–92. Former Chm., Anglo-Brazilian Parly Gp. Politician of the Year Award (first recipient), Nat. Fedn of Self-employed and Small Businesses, 1989. Hon. Associate, BVA, 1977. *Publication:* (ed) Secretary to the Speaker: Ralph Verney's correspondence, 1999. *Recreation:* naval and South American history. *Address:* 2 Lime Tree Mead, Tiverton, Devon EX16 4PX.

MAXWELL MACDONALD, Dame Anne Stirling, Btss (11th in line) *cr* 1682 (NS), of Pollok, Renfrewshire; *b* 8 Sept. 1906; *o d* of Sir John Maxwell Stirling-Maxwell, 10th Bt, KT and Ann Christian, *d* of Rt Hon. Sir Herbert Maxwell, 7th Bt; *S* father who *d* 1956, after which Btcy was dormant until succession recognised by Lyon Court in 2005 under the terms of the 1707 special remainder; *m* 1930, John Moreton-Macdonald (later Maxwell Macdonald) (*d* 1995); two *s*. *Heir: er s* John Ronald Maxwell Macdonald [*b* 22 May 1936; *m* 1964, Eleanor Ruth (*née* Laird); two *s* one *d*].

MAXWELL SCOTT, Sir Dominic James, 14th Bt *cr* 1642, of Haggerston, Northumberland; *b* 22 July 1968; *s* of Sir Michael Fergus Maxwell Scott, 13th Bt and of Deirdre Moira, *d* of late Alexander McKechnie; *S* father, 1989; *m* 2004, Emma Jane, *d* of late Keith Perry; one *d*. *Educ:* Eton; Sussex Univ. *Heir: b* Matthew Joseph Maxwell Scott, *b* 27 Aug. 1976.

MAXWELL-TIMMINS, Nicholas James; *see* Timmins.

MAY, family name of **Barons May** and **May of Oxford**.

MAY, 4th Baron *cr* 1935, of Weybridge, co. Surrey; **Jasper Bertram St John May;** Bt 1931; *b* 24 Oct. 1965; *o s* of 3rd Baron May and of Jillian Mary (*née* Shipton); *S* father, 2006. *Educ:* Harrow.

MAY OF OXFORD, Baron *cr* 2001 (Life Peer), of Oxford in the County of Oxfordshire; **Robert McCredie May,** OM 2002; AC 1998; Kt 1996; FRS 1979; Royal Society Research Professor, Department of Zoology, Oxford University, and Imperial College, London, since 1988; Fellow of Merton College, Oxford, 1988–2001, now Emeritus; President, Royal Society, 2000–05; *b* 8 Jan. 1936; *s* of Henry W. May and Kathleen M. May; *m* 1962, Judith (*née* Feiner); one *d*. *Educ:* Sydney Boys' High Sch.; Sydney Univ. BSc 1956, PhD (Theoretical Physics) 1959. Gordon Mackay Lectr in Applied Maths, Harvard Univ., 1959–61; Sydney Univ.: Sen. Lectr in Theoretical Physics, 1962–64; Reader, 1964–69; Personal Chair, 1969–73; Princeton University: Prof. of Biology, 1973–88; Class of 1877 Prof. of Zoology, 1975–88; Chm., Univ. Res. Bd, 1977–88; Chief Scientific Advr to the Govt and Hd of the OST, 1995–2000. Vis. Prof., Imperial Coll., 1975–88; visiting appointments at: Harvard, 1966; California Inst. of Technology, 1967; UKAEA Culham Lab., 1971; Magdalen Coll., Oxford, 1971; Inst. for Advanced Study, Princeton, 1972; King's Coll., Cambridge, 1976. Pres., British Ecol Soc., 1992–93; Chm., Natural History Mus., 1994–98 (Trustee, 1991–93); Trustee: WWF (UK), 1990–94; Royal Botanic Gardens, Kew, 1991–96; Nuffield Foundn, 1993–. Member: Smithsonian Council, USA, 1988–91; Jt Nature Conservation Council, 1989–95; Bd of Trustees, British Council, 2001–06. Founder FMedSci 1998. Hon. FInstP 2002; Hon. FREng 2005; Hon. FIBiol 2006. Overseas Mem., Australian Acad. of Sci., 1991; For. Associate, US Nat. Acad. of Scis, 1992. Linnean Medal, 1991; Crafoord Prize, Royal Swedish Acad. of Scis, 1996; Swiss-Italian Balzan Prize, 1998; Japanese Blue Planet Prize, 2001; Copley Medal, Royal Soc., 2007. *Publications:* Stability and Complexity in Model Ecosystems, 1973, 2nd edn 1974; Theoretical Ecology: Principles and Applications, 1976, 3rd edn 2007; Population Biology of Infectious Diseases, 1982; Exploitation of Marine Communities, 1984; Perspectives in Ecological Theory, 1989; Infectious Diseases of Humans: dynamics and control, 1991; Extinction Rates, 1994; Evolution of Biological Diversity, 1999; Virus Dynamics, 2000; articles in mathematical, biol and physics jls. *Recreations:* tennis, running, bridge. *Address:* Department of Zoology, Tinbergen Building, South Parks Road, Oxford OX1 3PS.

MAY, Prof. Anthony Dormer, OBE 2004; FREng; Professor of Transport Engineering, University of Leeds, since 1977; *b* 29 Feb. 1944; *s* of Albert James Gooding May and Beatrice Mary May; *m* 1968, Jennifer Margaret Caroline Hesketh. *Educ:* Bedford Sch.; Pembroke Coll., Cambridge (BA 1st cl. Hons (Mech. Scis) 1966, MA 1969); Yale Univ. 1967. CEng 1972; FICE 1993. Gp Planner Roads, GLC, 1967–77. Dir, MVA Ltd, 1985–2001. FREng 1995. *Publications:* over 60 papers in academic jls. *Recreations:* choral singing, canals, gardening, travel. *Address:* Cleaves House, Thirlby, YO7 2DQ. *T:* (01845) 597606.

MAY, Rt Hon. Sir Anthony (Tristram Kenneth), Kt 1991; PC 1998; **Rt Hon. Lord Justice May;** a Lord Justice of Appeal, since 1997; President, Queen's Bench Division, High Court of Justice, since 2008 (Vice-President, 2002–08); *b* 9 Sept. 1940; *s* of late Kenneth Sibley May and Joan Marguérite (*née* Oldaker); *m* 1968, Stella Gay Pattisson; one *s* two *d*. *Educ:* Bradfield Coll.; Worcester Coll., Oxford (Trevelyan Scholar 1960, Hon. Scholar 1962; MA; Hon. Fellow, 1999). Called to the Bar, Inner Temple, 1967 (Scholar, 1965; Bencher, 1985; Reader, 2007; Treas., 2008); QC 1979; a Recorder, 1985–91; a Judge of the High Court of Justice, QBD, 1991–97; Dep. Hd of Civil Justice, 2000–03. Jun. Counsel to DoE for Land Commn Act Matters, 1972–75; Chm., Commn of Inquiry, Savings and Investment Bank Ltd, IoM, 1990. A Judge, Employment Appeal Tribunal, 1993–97; Judge in Charge, Non-Jury List, 1995–97. Chm., Security Vetting Appeals Panel, 1997–2000. Vice-Chm., Official Referees Bar Assoc., 1987–91. Mem., Civil Procedure Rule Cttee, 1997–2003. President: Technol. and Construction Bar Assoc., 2002–; Soc. of Construction Law, 2004–. Vice-Pres., Guildford Choral Soc., 1991– (Chm., 1980–91). Mem. Council, Wycombe Abbey Sch., 1997–. *Publication:* (ed) Keating on Building Contracts, 5th edn 1991, 6th edn 1995. *Recreations:* gardening, music, books, bonfires. *Address:* Royal Courts of Justice, Strand, WC2A 2LL. *Club:* Garrick.

MAY, Brian Harold, CBE 2005; guitarist, songwriter and producer; *b* Hampton, Middx, 19 July 1947; *s* of Harold and Ruth May; *m* 1st, 1976, Christine Mullen (marr. diss. 1988); one *s* two *d*; 2nd, 2000, Anita Dobson. *Educ:* Hampton Grammar Sch.; Imperial Coll. London (BSc 1974; PhD Astrophysics 2008). Founding Mem., Queen, 1970–; albums: Queen, 1973; Queen II, 1974; Sheer Heart Attack, 1974; A Night at the Opera, 1975; A Day at the Races, 1976; News of the World, 1977; Jazz, 1978; Live Killers, 1979; The Game, 1980; Flash Gordon Original Soundtrack, 1980; Hot Space, 1982; The Works, 1984; A Kind of Magic, 1986; The Miracle, 1989; Innuendo, 1991; Made in Heaven, 1995; solo albums: Back to the Light, 1993; Another World, 1998. Writer of music, Macbeth, for Red and Gold Th. Co., 1987; Prod. and Music Dir, We Will Rock You, Dominion Th., 2002 and worldwide. Trustee, Mercury Phoenix Trust, 1992–. Chancellor, Liverpool John Moores Univ., 2008–. *Publication:* (jtly) Bang! The Complete History of the Universe, 2006. *Address:* Duck Productions Ltd, PO Box 141, Windlesham, Surrey GU20 6YW.

MAY, Charles Alan Maynard, FREng, FIET; lately Senior Director, Development and Technology, British Telecom; retired 1984; *b* 14 April 1924; *s* of late Cyril P. May and Katharine M. May; *m* 1947, Daphne, *o d* of late Bertram Carpenter; one *s* two *d*. *Educ:* The Grammar Sch., Ulverston, Cumbria; Christ's Coll., Cambridge (Mech. Sciences tripos 1944, MA). FIET (FIEE 1967); FREng (FEng 1982). Served REME and Indian Army, 1944–47. Entered Post Office Engrg Dept, 1948; Head of Electronic Switching Gp, 1956; Staff Engr, Computer Engrg Br., 1966; Dep. Dir (Engrg), 1970; Dir of Research, Post Office, later British Telecom, 1975–83. Dir, SIRA Ltd, 1982–89. Chm., IEE Electronics Divl Bd, 1977–78; Member: Council, IEE, 1970–72 and 1976–80; BBC Engrg Adv. Cttee, 1978–84; Adv. Cttee on Calibration and Measurement, 1978–83; Adv. Cttee, Dept of Electronic and Electrical Engrg, Sheffield Univ., 1979–82; Communications Systems Adv. Panel, Council of Educnl Technology, 1980–83; Ind. Adv. Bd, Sch. of Eng. and Applied Scis, Sussex Univ., 1981–84; Council, ERA Technology, 1983–88. Graham Young Lectr, Glasgow Univ., 1979. Vis. Examr, Imperial Coll., Univ. of London, 1980–82; External Examnr, NE London Polytechnic, 1982–86. Governor, Suffolk Coll. of Higher and Further Educn, 1980–83. *Publications:* contribs on telecommunications to learned jls. *Recreations:* gardening, snooker, bridge. *Address:* Corner Cottage, High Park Avenue, East Horsley, Leatherhead, Surrey KT24 5DD. *T:* (01483) 282521.

MAY, Christine; business development and public affairs consultant; Chair: Scottish Library and Information Council; Unifi (Scotland); *b* Dublin, 23 March 1948; *m* William May; one *s* one *d*. *Educ:* Coll. of Catering and Domestic Sci., Dublin. Dip. Inst. Mgt. Catering manager, Dublin and London, 1965–81; Lectr, Fife Coll., 1987–94. Formerly Member, Board: Scottish Homes; Scottish Enterprise. Member (Lab): Kirkcaldy DC, 1988–96 (Leader, 1993–96); Fife Council, 1995–2003 (Leader, 1998–2003). MSP (Lab Co-op) Fife Central, 2003–07. *Address: e-mail:* christinemay@blueyonder.co.uk.

MAY, David; *see* May, M. D.

MAY, Douglas James; QC (Scot) 1989; FRPS; a Social Security Commissioner and a Child Support Commissioner, since 1993; *b* 7 May 1946; *s* of Thomas May and Violet Mary Brough Boyd or May. *Educ:* George Heriot's Sch., Edinburgh; Edinburgh Univ. Advocate 1971. Temporary Sheriff, 1990–99. Contested (C): Edinburgh E, Feb. 1974; Glasgow Cathcart, 1983. Pres., Edinburgh Photographic Soc., 1996–99. FRPS 2002. *Recreations:* golf, photography, travel, concert going. *Address:* Office of the Social Security Commissioners, George House, 126 George Street, Edinburgh EH2 4HH. *T:* (0131) 271 4310. *Clubs:* Merchants of Edinburgh Golf (Captain, 1997–99), Bruntsfield Links Golfing Society, Luffness New Golf.

MAY, Gordon Leslie, OBE 1982; retired solicitor; *b* 19 Nov. 1921; *s* of A. Carveth May and Isobella May; *m* 1945, Nina Cheek (*d* 2002); one *s* two *d*. *Educ:* Worcester College for the Blind; Manchester Univ. War service, 1939–45. Admitted Solicitor, 1947; South Eastern Gas Board: Solicitor, 1956; Secretary, 1961; Executive Board Member, 1968; British Gas Corporation: Dep. Chairman, SW Region, 1974; Corp. Sec., 1977–84; Mem. Executive, 1982–84. Consultant, Keene Marsland, solicitors, 1984–87. Mem. Exec. Council, RNIB, 1975–89. Chm. Bd of Governors, Worcester Coll. for the Blind, 1980–87. Liveryman, Solicitors' Co., 1963. *Recreation:* sailing. *Clubs:* Medway Yacht (Upnor); Alderney Sailing.

MAY, Graham; retired from Civil Service, 1981; *b* 15 Dec. 1923; *s* of Augustus May; *m* 1952, Marguerite Lucy Griffin; four *s*. *Educ:* Gravesend County Sch. for Boys; Balliol Coll., Oxford (BA). War Service, Royal Artillery, 1942–46. Asst Principal, Min. of Works, 1948, Principal 1952; seconded to Treasury, 1961–63; Asst Sec., MPBW, 1963; Under Sec., DoE, 1972–81.

MAY, James Nicholas Welby; Director-General, UK Offshore Operators Association, 1997–2003; *b* 21 Feb. 1949; *s* of Richard Percy May and Caroline Rosemary Welby May (*née* Jack); *m* 1979, Diana Mary Tamplin; two *s*. *Educ:* Sherborne Sch., Dorset; Southampton Univ. (BSc 1970); College of Law. Called to the Bar, Lincoln's Inn, 1974. Programme Officer, UNEP, 1976–77; Project Officer, IUCN, 1977–78; Legal Officer, Friends of the Earth, 1978–79; Legal Adviser, NFU, 1980–89; Dir-Gen., British Retail Consortium, 1989–97. Sec., Footwear Distributors' Fedn, 1989–97. Member: Countryside Commn Common Land Forum, 1984–86; Nat. Retail Trng Council, 1989–97; Distributive Occupational Standards Council, 1993–97; Council, 1996–2003, Trade Assoc. Council, 1998–2003, CBI; Meteorological Cttee, 1997–99; HSE Open Govt Complaints Panel, 2003–05. Non-exec. Dir, Meteorological Office, 2000–07; non-exec. Chm., Common Data Access Ltd, 2000–03; non-executive Member: Land Command Bd, 2004–07 (Chm., Audit Cttee, 2004–07); Defence Audit Cttee, 2005–07. Trustee, Sherborne Sch. Foundn, 1999–2004. *Recreations:* travel, tennis, ski-ing. *Address: e-mail:* james.diana@blueyonder.co.uk. *Club:* Roehampton.

MAY, Air Vice-Marshal John Anthony Gerard, CB 1995; CBE 1993; FRAeS; Air Officer Training and Air Officer Commanding Training Group, Headquarters Personnel and Training Command, and Chief Executive, Training Group Defence Agency, 1994–97; *b* 12 Nov. 1941; *s* of late Anthony Frederick May and Beatrice Mary (*née* Niblett); *m* 1964, Margaret Anne Chester; two *s*. *Educ:* City of London Sch. FRAeS 1997. Joined RAF 1961; flying trng, then Qualified Flying Instr, Linton-on-Ouse; Lightning aircraft, 1966; served with Nos 56, 5 and 19 Sqns; Staff Coll., Camberley, 1977; Chief Flying Instr, RAF Cranwell, 1979; Stn Comdr, Binbrook, 1985; Dep. Dir of Air Defence, MoD, 1987; Air Cdre Policy and Plans, RAF Support Comd, 1989; AOC No 38 Gp, and SASO, HQ Strike Comd, 1993–94. Dir, RAF Alpine Teams, 2004–. Vice-Chm. (Air), E Anglia RFCA, 2003–. QCVSA 1971. *Recreations:* alpine ski-ing, classic cars, RAFVR(T) air experience flying for cadets. *Address:* 157 Sapley Road, Hartford, Huntingdon, Cambs PE29 1YT. *Club:* Royal Air Force.

MAY, Jonathan Charles; Executive Director, Policy and Strategy, Office of Fair Trading, since 2006; *b* 12 Aug. 1949; *s* of Edward Kelly May and Sheila Joy May; *m* 1984, Florence Pauline Cowmeadow; one *s*. *Educ:* Reading Univ. (BA Hons Econ); LSE (MSc Econ). Res. Officer, LSE, 1973–75; Sen. Res. Officer, planning issues, DoE, 1975–84; overseas aid and Home Office expenditure work, 1984–94; Hd of competition, regulation and energy team, HM Treasury, 1994–99; Dir, UK Competition Policy, DTI, 1999–2001; Dir, Markets and Policy Initiatives, OFT, 2001–06. *Recreations:* family, friends, reading, relaxation, music. *Address:* Office of Fair Trading, 2–6 Salisbury Square, EC4Y 8JX. *T:* (020) 7211 8712, *Fax:* (020) 7211 8391; *e-mail:* jonathan.may@oft.gsi.gov.uk.

MAY, Prof. (Michael) David, DSc; FRS 1991; Professor and Head of Department of Computer Science, Bristol University; *b* Holmfirth, 24 Feb. 1951; *s* of Douglas May. *Educ:*

Queen Elizabeth's GS, Wakefield; King's Coll., Cambridge (BA 1972; MA 1976); DSc Southampton. Lectr, Dept of Computer Sci., Warwick Univ.; Technology Manager (Computer Architecture), Inmos Ltd, Bristol. Vis. Prof. of Engrg Design, Oxford Univ., 1991. *Publication:* (ed jtly) Networks, Routers and Transputers: function, performance and application, 1993. *Address:* Department of Computer Science, University of Bristol, Merchant Venturers' Building, Woodland Road, Bristol BS8 1UB. *T:* (0117) 954 5134; 9 Eaton Crescent, Clifton, Bristol BS8 2EJ. *T:* (0117) 974 2586.

MAY, Stuart; *see* May, W. H. S.

MAY, Rt Hon. Theresa Mary; PC 2003; MP (C) Maidenhead, since 1997; *b* 1 Oct. 1956; *d* of Rev. Hubert Brasier and Zaidee Brasier (*née* Barnes); *m* 1980, Philip John May. *Educ:* St Hugh's Coll., Oxford (MA). Bank of England, 1977–83; Inter-Bank Res. Orgn, 1983–85; Assoc. for Payment Clearing Services, 1985–97 (Hd of European Affairs Unit, 1989–96). Mem. (C), Merton LBC, 1986–94. Contested (C): Durham NW, 1992; Barking, June 1994. Opposition frontbench spokesman on educn and employment, 1998–99; Shadow Secretary of State: for Educn and Employment, 1999–2001; for Transport, Local Govt and the Regions, 2001–02; for Transport, 2002; for Envmt and Transport, 2003–04; for the Family, 2004–05, also for Culture, Media and Sport, 2005; Chm., Cons. Party, 2002–03; Shadow Leader, H of C, 2005–; Shadow Minister for Women, 2007–. *Recreations:* walking, cooking. *Address:* House of Commons, SW1A 0AA. *Club:* Maidenhead Conservative.

MAY, Valentine Gilbert Delabere, CBE 1969; *b* 1 July 1927; *s* of Claude Jocelyn Delabere May and Olive Gilbert; *m* 1st, 1955, Penelope Sutton; one *d*; 2nd, 1980, Petra Schroeder; one *d*. *Educ:* Cranleigh Sch.; Peterhouse Coll., Cambridge. Trained at Old Vic Theatre Sch. Director: Ipswich Theatre, 1953–57; Nottingham Playhouse, 1957–61; Bristol Old Vic Company, 1961–75; plays directed at Bristol which transf. to London incl.: War and Peace, 1962; A Severed Head, 1963; Love's Labour's Lost, 1964 (also British Council European tour); Portrait of a Queen, 1965; The Killing of Sister George, 1965; The Italian Girl, 1968; Mrs Mouse, Are You Within, 1968; Conduct Unbecoming, 1969; It's a Two-Foot-Six Inches Above the Ground World, 1970; Poor Horace, 1970; Trelawny, 1972; The Card, 1973. Directed at Old Vic: Richard II, 1959; Mourning Becomes Electra, 1961; Tribute to the Lady, 1974–75. Dir, Yvonne Arnaud Theatre, Guildford, 1975–92; plays directed which transferred to London: Baggage, 1976; Banana Ridge, 1976; The Dark Horse, 1978; House Guest, 1981. Directed: Little Me, Prince of Wales, 1984; Royal Baccarat Scandal, Chichester Fest., 1988, London, 1989; Henry IV (by Pirandello), London, 1990; The Accused, Haymarket Theatre Royal, 2000. Dir, Ludlow Festival, 1993–96: The Taming of the Shrew, Richard III, King Lear. Overseas prodns include: Romeo and Juliet, and Hamlet (NY and USA tour); The Taming of the Shrew (Hong Kong Fest. and Latin America tour); Broadway prodns: A Severed Head; Portrait of a Queen; The Killing of Sister George; Conduct Unbecoming; Murder Among Friends; Pygmalion. Hon. MA Bristol, 1975. *Recreations:* reading, architecture, music, astronomy. *Address:* Manor House Farm, Peasmarsh, Guildford, Surrey GU3 1LY. *T:* (01483) 563547.

MAY, (William Herbert) Stuart; Senior Partner, Theodore Goddard, Solicitors, 1989–97; *b* 5 April 1937; *s* of Arthur Douglas May and Jean Reid; *m* 1966, Sarah Margaret (*née* Maples); four *s*. *Educ:* Taunton School; Wadham College, Oxford (MA). Qualified Solicitor, 1965, with Theodore Goddard, Partner 1970. *Recreations:* gardening, walking, reading, golf.

MAYALL, Prof. James Bardsley Lawson, FBA 2001; Sir Patrick Sheehy Professor of International Relations, University of Cambridge, 1998–2004; Fellow, 1998–2004, now Emeritus, and Director of Studies in Social and Political Sciences, since 2004, Sidney Sussex College, Cambridge (Vice-Master, 2003–04); *b* 14 April 1937; *s* of Robert Cecil Mayall and Rhoda Anne (*née* Stote); *m* 1st, 1964, Margaret Berry (marr. diss. 1990); one *d*; 2nd, 1991, Avril Doris Whalley. *Educ:* Shrewsbury Sch.; Sidney Sussex Coll., Cambridge (BA Hist. Tripos 1960; MA 1998). Sir John Dill Fellow, Princeton Univ., NJ, 1960–61; BoT, 1961–64; British High Commn, New Delhi, 1964–65; London School of Economics: Dept of Internat. Relns, 1966–98; Prof. of Internat. Relns, 1991–98, Prof. Emeritus, 1998–; Chm., Steering Cttee, Centre for Internat. Studies, 1991–98. Mem. Council, RIIA, 1992–98 (Associate Editor, Survey and Documents of Internat. Affairs, 1967–71). Chm., Adv. Bd, Inst. of Commonwealth Studies, Univ. of London, 2006–; Academic Advr, RCDS, 2008–. *Publications:* Africa and the Cold War, 1971; (Associate Ed.) Survey of International Affairs 1963, 1977; (ed jtly) A New International Commodity Regime, 1979; (ed jtly) The End of the Post-War Era: documents on Great Power relns 1968–75, 1980; (ed) The Community of States: a study in international political theory, 1982; Nationalism and International Society, 1990; (ed jtly) The Fallacies of Hope: the post Colonial record of the Commonwealth Third World, 1991; (ed) The New Interventionism 1991–94: United Nations experience in Cambodia, Former Yugoslavia and Somalia, 1996; World Politics: progress and its limits, 2000 (ed jtly) International Human Rights in the 21st Century: protecting the rights of groups, 2003. *Recreations:* cooking, gardening, watching cricket, walking the dog. *Address:* Sidney Sussex College, Sidney Street, Cambridge CB2 3HU. *T:* (01223) 767228. *Club:* MCC.

MAYBLIN, Andrea Doreen; *see* Levy, A. D.

MAYER, Anthony; *see* Mayer, R. A. J.

MAYER, (Anthony) David, FRCS; Consultant Hepatobiliary and Liver Transplant Surgeon, Queen Elizabeth Hospital, Birmingham, and Honorary Consultant Liver Transplant Surgeon, Birmingham Children's Hospital, since 1990; *b* 11 Jan. 1950; *s* of John Mayer and Sheila Mayer (*née* Lesser); *m* 1977, Helen Rastall; three *d*. *Educ:* Tonbridge Sch.; Univ. of Sussex (BSc 1971); Guy's Hosp., Univ. of London (MB BS 1976; MS 1986). FRCS 1980. House Officer, 1976–77, SHO, 1977, Guy's Hosp.; SHO, Brighton Gen. Hosp. and Royal Sussex Co. Hosp., 1978–80; Registrar, Scarborough Hosp., 1980–81; Res. Fellow, Leeds Gen. Infirmary, 1982–84; Registrar, Walsgrave Hosp., Coventry, 1985–86; Sen. Registrar, Queen Elizabeth Hosp., Birmingham, 1986–88; Vis. Fellow, UCSD, 1988–89. Hon. Sen. Lectr, Univ. of Birmingham, 1990–. Chm., Liver Adv. Gp to UK Transplant, 2003–; Pres., Transplantation Section, RSM, 2003–09. *Publications:* various articles on transplantation and surgery in med. jls, inc. Lancet, BMJ, New England Jl of Medicine and British Jl of Surgery. *Recreations:* cycling, music, literature, theatre. *Address:* Liver Unit, 3rd Floor, Nuffield House, Queen Elizabeth Hospital, Birmingham B15 2TH. *Club:* Royal Society of Medicine.

MAYER, Prof. Colin Peter; Peter Moores Dean, since 2006, Professor of Management Studies, since 1994, Saïd Business School (formerly School of Management Studies), University of Oxford; Fellow of St Edmund Hall, Oxford, since 2006; *b* 12 May 1953; *s* of late Harold Charles Mayer and Anne Louise Mayer; *m* 1979, Annette Patricia Haynes; two *d*. *Educ:* St Paul's Sch.; Oriel College, Oxford (Hon. Fellow, 2006); Wolfson College, Oxford (MA, MPhil, DPhil); Harvard Univ. HM Treasury, 1976–78; Harkness Fellow, Harvard, 1979–80; Fellow in Economics, St Anne's College, Oxford, 1980–86 (Hon. Fellow, 1993); Price Waterhouse Prof. of Corporate Finance, City Univ. Business Sch., 1987–92; Prof. of Econs and Finance, Univ. of Warwick, 1992–94; Fellow, Wadham Coll., Oxford, 1994–2006. Chairman: ESF Network in Financial Markets, 1989–94; Oxford Economic Research Associates, subseq. OXERA Hldgs, Ltd, 1987–; Dir, Oxford Financial Res. Centre, 1998–2006. Delegate, OUP, 1996–2006 (Chm., Audit Cttee, 2002–06). Mem. Exec. Cttee, REconS, 2002–06. Inaugural Fellow, European Corporate Governance Inst., 2002–. Gov., St Paul's Sch., London, 2002–. Associate Editor: Jl of Internat. Financial Management; Jl of European Financial Management; Review of Finance; Fiscal Studies; Oxford Review of Economic Policy. *Publications:* (with J. Kay and J. Edwards) Economic Analysis of Accounting Profitability, 1986; (with J. Franks) Risk, Regulation and Investor Protection, 1989; (with A. Giovannini) European Financial Integration, 1991; (with X. Vives) Capital Markets and Financial Intermediation, 1993; (with T. Jenkinson) Hostile Takeovers, 1994; (with J. Franks and L. C. da Silva) Asset Management and Investor Protection, 2002; (with X. Freixas and P. Hartmann) Handbook of European Financial Markets and Institutions, 2008; articles in economic and finance jls. *Recreations:* piano, jogging, reading philosophy and science. *Address:* Saïd Business School, University of Oxford, Park End Street, Oxford OX1 1HP. *T:* (01865) 288811.

MAYER, David; *see* Mayer, A. D.

MAYER, John; *see* Mayer, R. J.

MAYER, (Ralph) Anthony (Jeffrey), CBE 2000; Chair, Office for Tenants and Social Landlords, since 2008; *b* 24 Feb. 1946; *s* of George Mayer and Margaret (*née* Jones); *m* 1971, Ann Gowen; one *s* one *d*. *Educ:* City of Bath Boys' Sch.; Lycée Michelet, Paris; St Edmund Hall, Oxford (BA Hons PPE). Ministry of Housing and Local Government, subseq. Department of the Environment, 1967–85: Asst Principal, 1967–72; seconded as Pvte Sec. to Parly Sec., CSD, 1971–72; Principal, 1972–81; seconded as Mem., CPRS, 1974–76, and as Prin. Pvte Sec. to Sec. of State for Transport, 1980–82; Asst Sec., 1981–85; Asst Dir, N. M. Rothschild and Sons, 1985–87; Man. Dir (Finance and Admin), Rothschild Asset Management, 1987–91; Chief Exec., Housing Corp., 1991–2000; Actg Chief Exec., Transport for London, 2000; Chief Exec., GLA, 2000–08. *Recreations:* hill walking, bridge, cycling, yachting. *Address:* 37 Copthall Gardens, Twickenham, Middlesex, TW1 4HH.

MAYER, Prof. Roland George, PhD; Professor of Classics, King's College London, since 1996; *b* Annapolis, Md, 24 July 1947; *s* of Roland George Mayer, Jr and Mary Clare Devine. *Educ:* Univ. of Calif at Berkeley (BA 1967); Peterhouse, Cambridge (BA 1972; PhD 1977). Res. Fellow, Bedford Coll., Univ. of London, 1976–79; Lectr, 1979–88, Sen. Lectr, 1988–89, Birkbeck Coll., Univ. of London; Sen. Lectr, KCL, 1989–96. Editor, Classical Review, 1994–2001. *Publications:* Seneca: Phaedra, 2002; *edited:* Lucan, Civil War 8, 1982; Horace, Epistles 1, 1994; Tacitus, Dialogus, 2001; (with M. Coffey) Seneca, Phaedra, 1990. *Recreations:* opera, South German Baroque churches. *Address:* Department of Classics, King's College London, Strand, WC2R 2LS. *T:* (020) 7848 2058; *e-mail:* roland.mayer@kcl.ac.uk.

MAYER, Prof. (Roland) John, FRCPath; Professor of Molecular Cell Biology, since 1986 and Head of Molecular Cell Biology, School of Biomedical Sciences, since 1997, University of Nottingham; *b* 30 April 1943; *s* of George and Ethel Mayer; *m* 1967, Elaine Ing; two *s*. *Educ:* Univ. of Birmingham (BSc 1st Cl., 1965; PhD 1968); DSc Nottingham 1980. Lectr, Sen. Lectr and Reader, Univ. of Nottingham, 1970–86. *Publications:* (with J. H. Walker) Immunochemical Methods in the Biological Sciences: enzymes and proteins, 1980; (with J. H. Walker) Immunochemical Methods in Cell and Molecular Biology, 1987; (with F. J. Doherty) Intracellular Protein Degradation, 1992; contribs to learned jls. *Recreation:* golf. *Address:* School of Biomedical Sciences, University of Nottingham Medical School, Queen's Medical Centre, Nottingham NG7 2UH. *T:* (0115) 970 9369.

MAYER, Thomas, CBE 1985; FREng; Chairman: Pelicam Ltd, since 2004; Eldonray Ltd, 1990–2004; *b* 17 Dec. 1928; *s* of Hans and Jeanette Mayer; *m* 1st, 1956 (marr. diss. 1975); one *s* one *d*; 2nd, 1975, Jean Patricia Burrows. *Educ:* King's Sch., Harrow; Regent Street Polytechnic (BScEng). FIET (FIEE 1964); FRTS 1968; FREng (FEng 1987); CRAeS 1990. Broadcasting Div., Marconi Co. Ltd, 1948–68; Man. Dir, Marconi Elliott Micro-Electronics Ltd, 1968–69; Man. Dir, Marconi Communication Systems Ltd, 1969–81; Man. Dir, 1981–86, Chm., 1981–90, THORN EMI Electronics Ltd; Chief Exec., THORN EMI Technology Gp, 1986–88; Exec. Dir, THORN EMI plc, 1987–90. Chairman: THORN EMI Varian Ltd, 1981–89; Holmes Protection Gp, 1990–91; ITT Defence Ltd, 1993–97; Director: Thorn Ericsson, 1981–88; Systron Donner Corp., 1983–90; Inmos Corp., 1985–88; Babcock Thorn Ltd, 1985–90; THORN EMI Australia, 1987–88; non-executive Director: Devonport Management Ltd, 1990–97; Eurodis Electron (formerly Electron House) plc, 1991–2002. Chm., UK Nat. Widescreen Television Forum, DTI, 1991–97. Member: Council, IEE, 1971–74; Council, Electronic Engrg Assoc., 1974–75, 1981–87 (Pres., 1982–83); Nat. Electronics Council, 1983–98; SBAC, 1984–90 (Pres., 1987–88). Liveryman, Worshipful Co. of Engineers, 1984–. *Recreations:* golf, swimming, theatre. *Address:* 1590 A.D., Burton Lane, Monks Risborough, Bucks HP27 9JF. *T:* (01844) 344194. *Club:* Ellesborough Golf.

MAYER, Vera; Her Honour Judge Mayer; a Circuit Judge, since 2002; *b* 11 June 1948; *d* of Milan and Suzanna Mayer; two *d*. *Educ:* Bar-Ilan Univ., Israel (BA Psychol.); Inst. of Educn, Univ. of London (MSc Child Develt). Called to the Bar, Gray's Inn, 1978; Asst Recorder, 1998–2000; Recorder, 2000–02. Mem., Professional Conduct Cttee, Bar Council, 2000–02. *Recreations:* child-rearing, and in remaining time, action-packed travel, music, theatre. *Address:* Barnet County Court, St Mary's Court, Regent's Park Road, N3 1BQ; *e-mail:* HHJudge.Mayer2@judiciary.gsi.gov.uk.

MAYES, Maj.-Gen. Frederick Brian, CB 1995; FRCS; Director General, Army Medical Services, 1993–96; *b* 24 Aug. 1934; *s* of late Harry Frederick and Constance Enid Mayes; *m* 1962, Mary Anna Georgina Roche; one *s* two *d* (and one *s* decd). *Educ:* Wyggeston Grammar Sch., Leicester; St Mary's Hosp. Med. Sch. (MB BS London 1958). Commissioned Lieut RAMC, 1960; served Aden, E Africa, BAOR, UK; Consultant in Surgery, 1972; CO, BMH Hannover, 1984–87; CO, Cambridge Mil. Hosp., Aldershot, 1987–88; Consultant Surgeon, HQ BAOR, 1988–90; Comdr Med., HQ BAOR, 1990–93. QHS, 1991–96. Pres., St John's Ambulance, Germany, 1990. CStJ 1993. *Recreations:* off-shore sailing, bridge, mountaineering. *Address:* Mornington, 9 Searle Road, Farnham, Surrey GU9 8LJ. *T:* (01252) 715453.

MAYES, Ian; QC 1993; *b* 11 Sept. 1951; marr. diss.; two *s*. *Educ:* Highgate Sch. (Foundation Schol.); Trinity Coll., Cambridge. Called to the Bar, Middle Temple, 1974 (Harmsworth Schol.; Bencher, 2001). Dept of Trade Inspection, London Capital Group Ltd, 1975–77; Standing Counsel to Inland Revenue, 1983–93. Chm., Disciplinary Tribunal, Lloyd's of London. Mem., Justice Cttee on Fraud Trials. Chm., Art First. *Recreation:* photography. *Address:* 3 (North) King's Bench Walk, Temple, EC4Y 7HR. *T:* (020) 7797 8600. *Club:* Garrick.

MAYES, Rt Rev. Michael Hugh Gunton; Bishop of Limerick and Killaloe, 2000–08; *b* 31 Aug. 1941; *s* of Thomas David Dougan Mayes and Hilary Gunton; *m* 1966, Elizabeth Annie Eleanor Irwin; one *s* two *d*. *Educ:* The Royal Sch., Armagh; Trinity Coll., Dublin (BA); Univ. of London (BD). Ordained, 1964; Assistant Curate: St Mark's, Portadown, 1964–67; St Columba's, Portadown, 1967–68; Missionary, Japan, 1968–74; Incumbent: St Michael's, Cork, 1975–86; Moviddy, Cork, 1986–88; Rathcooney, Cork, 1988–93; Archdeacon of Cork, Cloyne and Ross, 1986–93; Bishop of Kilmore, Elphin and Ardagh, 1993–2000. *Recreations:* reading, music, photography, walking. *Address:* 4 Langford Place, Langford Row, Cork, Ireland. *T:* (21) 1967688; *e-mail:* bpkilm@iol.ie.

MAYFIELD, Rt Rev. Christopher John; Bishop of Manchester, 1993–2002; Hon. Assistant Bishop, Diocese of Worcester, since 2002; *b* 18 Dec. 1935; *s* of Dr Roger Bolton Mayfield and Muriel Eileen Mayfield; *m* 1962, Caroline Ann Roberts; two *s* one *d*. *Educ:* Sedbergh School; Gonville and Caius Coll., Cambridge (MA 1961); Linacre House, Oxford (Dip. Theology); MSc Cranfield Univ. 1984. Deacon 1963, priest 1964, Birmingham; Curate of St Martin-in-the-Bull Ring, Birmingham, 1963–67; Lecturer at St Martin's, Birmingham, 1967–71; Chaplain at Children's Hospital, Birmingham, 1967–71; Vicar of Luton, 1971–80 (with East Hyde, 1971–76); RD of Luton, 1974–79; Archdeacon of Bedford, 1979–85; Bishop Suffragan of Wolverhampton, 1985–93. Mem., H of L, 1998–2002. *Recreations:* family, gardening, walking. *Address:* 54 Primrose Crescent, St Peter's, Worcester WR5 3HT.

MAYHEW, family name of **Baron Mayhew of Twysden**.

MAYHEW OF TWYSDEN, Baron *cr* 1997 (Life Peer), of Kilndown in the co. of Kent; **Patrick Barnabas Burke Mayhew,** Kt 1983; PC 1986; QC 1972; DL; *b* 11 Sept. 1929; *o* surv. *s* of late A. G. H. Mayhew, MC; *m* 1963, Rev. Jean Elizabeth Gurney, OBE 1997, MA (Cantab), BD (Lond), FKC, *d* of John Gurney; four *s*. *Educ:* Tonbridge; Balliol Coll., Oxford (MA). President, Oxford Union Society, 1952. Commnd 4th/7th Royal Dragoon Guards, national service and AER, captain. Called to Bar, Middle Temple, 1955, Bencher 1980. Non-exec. Dir, Western Provident Assoc., 1997– (Vice-Chm., 2000–). Contested (C) Camberwell and Dulwich, 1970. MP (C): Royal Tunbridge Wells, Feb. 1974–1983; Tunbridge Wells, 1983–97. Parly Under Sec. of State, Dept of Employment, 1979–81; Minister of State, Home Office, 1981–83; Solicitor General, 1983–87; Attorney General, 1987–92; Sec. of State for NI, 1992–97. Member of Executive: 1922 Cttee, 1976–79; Assoc. of Cons. Peers, 1998–2006. Chm., Prime Minister's Adv. Cttee on Business Appts, 2000–08. DL Kent, 2001. *Address:* House of Lords, SW1A 0PW. *Clubs:* Garrick, Pratt's, Beefsteak; Tunbridge Wells Constitutional.

MAYHEW, David Lionel; Chairman: Cazenove Group, since 2001; JPMorgan Cazenove Holdings, since 2005; Cazenove Capital Holdings Ltd, since 2005; *b* 20 May 1940; *s* of Lionel Geoffrey Mayhew and Biddy Vowe Mayhew; *m* 1966, Virginia Ann Wonnacott; two *s* one *d*. *Educ:* Eton Coll. With Panmure Gordon, 1961–69; Cazenove & Co., subseq. JPMorgan Cazenove Ltd, 1969–, Partner, 1971–2001. Chm., Rio Tinto plc, 2000–. *Recreations:* farming, country pursuits. *Address:* (office) 20 Moorgate, EC2R 6DA. *T:* (020) 7588 2828. *Clubs:* Boodle's, City of London; Swinley Golf; New Zealand Golf.

MAYHEW, Dame Judith; *see* Mayhew Jonas, Dame J.

MAYHEW, Kenneth; Reader in Economics, University of Oxford, since 1996; Fellow and Tutor in Economics, Pembroke College, Oxford, since 1976 (Vicegerent, 2000–03); Director, ESRC Research Centre on Skills, Knowledge and Organisational Performance, since 1998; *b* 1 Sept. 1947; *s* of late Albert Chadwick Mayhew and Alice Mayhew (*née* Leigh). *Educ:* Manchester Grammar Sch.; Worcester Coll., Oxford (MA); London School of Economics (MScEcon). Economic Asst, HM Treasury, 1970–72; Res. Officer, Queen Elizabeth House, Oxford, 1972; Asst Res. Officer, then Res. Officer, Inst. of Economics and Statistics, Oxford, 1972–81; Economic Dir, NEDO, 1989–91. Vis. Associate Prof., Cornell Univ., 1981. Advr, CBI, 1983. Editor, Oxford Bull. of Econs and Stats, 1976–88; Associate Editor: Oxford Review of Economic Policy, 1984–; Oxford Economic Papers, 1997–. *Publications:* Trade Unions and the Labour Market, 1983; (ed with D. Robinson) Pay Policies for the Future, 1983; (ed with A. Bowen) Improving Incentives for the Low Paid, 1990; (ed with A. Bowen) Reducing Regional Inequalities, 1991; (ed jtly) Providing Health Care, 1991; (ed jtly) Britain's Training Deficit, 1994; (ed jtly) The Economics of Skills Obsolescence, 2002; (ed jtly) Low Wage Work in the UK, 2008; reports and numerous articles on labour econs and industrial relns in learned jls. *Recreations:* travel, literature. *Address:* Pembroke College, Oxford OX1 1DW. *T:* (01865) 276434. *Club:* Reform.

MAYHEW, Prof. Leslie Dennis, PhD; Professor of Statistics, Cass Business School (formerly City University Business School), since 2002; Managing Director, Mayhew Associates Ltd, since 2001; *b* 7 Nov. 1947; *s* of Charles and Violet Mayhew; *m* 1984, Karin Sigmund; two *s* one *d*. *Educ:* Birkbeck Coll., London (BSc Hons (1st class); PhD 1979). Dir of OR, later Business Develt Manager, Benefits Agency, and sen. post in Finance/Planning, DHSS, then DSS, 1979–93; Dir of Central Services and Prin. Estabts and Finance Officer, CSO, 1993–96; Gp Dir for Admin. Services and Registration, ONS, 1996–98; Prof. of Geography, Birkbeck Coll., London Univ., 1998–2001. Res. Schol., Internat. Inst. for Applied Systems Analysis, Vienna, 1980–82 and 1999–; Vis. Prof., Birkbeck Coll., London Univ., 1995–98. Hon. FFPH 2002; Hon. FIA 2004. *Publications:* Urban Hospital Location, 1986; (jtly) The Economic Impacts of Population Ageing in Japan, 2004; contrib. learned jls and periodicals in health, transport, geography and operational res. (current research: ageing, pensions, disability, neighbourhood statistics, population statistics). *Recreations:* tennis, music, travelling. *Address:* Faculty of Actuarial Science and Insurance, Cass Business School, 106 Bunhill Row, EC1Y 8TZ; *e-mail:* lesmayhew@googlemail.com.

MAYHEW JONAS, Dame Judith, DBE 2002; Chair, Private Investment Commission, London Development Agency, since 2000; Chairman, Independent Schools Council, since 2008; *b* 18 Oct. 1948; *m* 1st, 1976 (marr. diss. 1986); 2nd, 2003, Christopher William Jonas, *qv*. *Educ:* Univ. of Otago, NZ (LLM 1973). Barrister and Solicitor, NZ, 1973; admitted Solicitor, England and Wales, 1993. Lectr in Law, Univ. of Otago, 1970–73; Lecturer in Law and Sub Dean: Univ. of Southampton, 1973–76; King's Coll., London, 1976–89; Dir, Anglo Franch law degree, Sorbonne, Paris, 1976–89; Dir of Training and Employment Law, Titmuss Sainer Dechert, 1989–94; Dir of Educn and Trng, Wilde Sapte, 1994–99; Provost, King's Coll., Cambridge, 2003–06. Non-exec. Dir, Merrill Lynch & Co. Inc., USA, 2006– (Advr, 2003–06); Special Advisor: to Chm., Clifford Chance, 2000–03; City and Business Advr to Mayor of London, 2000–04. Corporation of London: Mem., Court of Common Council, 1986–2004; Chm., Educn Cttee, 1989–95; Chm., 1997–2003, Dep. Chm., 2003–04, Policy and Resources Cttee. Director: Gresham Coll., 1990–; ESU, 1993–99; Geffrye Mus., 1995–99; Internat. Financial Services London (formerly British Invisibles), 1996–2004; City Disputes Panel, 1996–99; London First Centre, 1996–2002; London First, 1997–2003; 4Ps, 1997–2004; London Development Partnership, 1998–2000; London Develt Agency, 2000–04; Tower Hamlets Educn Business Partnership, 2001–03. Trustee, Natural History Mus., 1998–2006; Mem. Council, BM Develt Trust, 2001–02. Chm., Royal Opera House, 2003–08. Governor: London Guildhall Univ., 1992–99, 2000–03; Birkbeck Coll., London Univ., 1993–2004 (Chm., 1999–2003; Fellow, 2003); Imperial Coll., London Univ., 2001–04. Fellow, London Business Sch., 2003; FCGI 2004. Hon. FICPD 2004. Hon. DLaws: Otago, 1998; City, 1999; London Metropolitan, 2003. *Recreations:* opera, theatre, old English roses, tennis. *Address:* 25 Victoria Square, SW1W 0RB. *Club:* Guildhall.

MAYHEW-SANDERS, Sir John (Reynolds), Kt 1982; MA; FCA; Chief Executive, 1975–83, and Chairman, 1978–83, John Brown PLC (Director, 1972–83); *b* 25 Oct. 1931; *e s* of Jack Mayhew-Sanders, FCA; *m* 1958, Sylvia Mary (*d* 1995), *d* of George S. Colling; three *s* one *d*. *Educ:* Epsom Coll.; RNC, Dartmouth; Jesus Coll., Cambridge (MA Engrg). FCA 1958. RN, 1949–55. Mayhew-Sanders & Co., Chartered Accountants, 1955–58; P-E Consulting Gp Ltd, 1958–72 (Dir, 1968–72). Director: Dowty Gp, 1982–85; Rover Gp (formerly BL plc), 1980–89; Chm., Heidrick and Struggles UK, 1985–87; Chief Exec., Samuelson Gp, 1987. Member: Management Bd, Engineering Employers' Fedn, 1977–81; BOTB, 1980–83; BBC Consultative Gp on Industrial and Business Affairs, 1981–83; Chm., Overseas Projects Bd, 1980–83; Pres., British-Soviet Chamber of Commerce, 1982–88; Vice-Pres., Inst. of Export, 1982. Governor, Sadler's Wells Foundn, 1983–89. CCMI (CBIM 1980); FRSA 1983. *Recreations:* fishing, shooting, astronomy, music. *Address:* Great Deptford House, High Bickington, Umberleigh, N Devon EX37 9BP.

MAYLAND, Rev. Canon Ralph, VRD 1962 and bar 1972; non-stipendiary Priest-in-Charge, Brancepeth, 1994–96; *b* 31 March 1927; *s* of James Henry and Lucy Mayland; *m* 1959, Rev. Jean Mary Goldstraw; one *d* and one adopted *d*. *Educ:* Cockburn High Sch., Leeds; Leeds City Training Coll.; Westminster Coll., London Univ.; Ripon Hall, Oxford. Schoolteacher, 1945–46; RN, 1946–51; perm. commn, RNR, 1952, Chaplain, 1961–82; 3rd yr student, 1951–52; schoolteacher, 1952–57; theol student, 1957–59. Curate of Lambeth, 1959–62; Priest-in-charge, St Paul's, Manton, Worksop, 1962–67; Vicar, St Margaret's, Brightside, 1968–72; Chaplain, Sheffield Industrial Mission, 1968–75; Vicar, St Mary's, Ecclesfield, 1972–82; Chaplain to Master Cutler, 1979–80; Canon and Treasurer, York Minster, 1982–94, Canon Emeritus, 1994–. Hon. Chaplain, HMS York, 1989–; Chaplain, 8th Destroyer Assoc., 2000–. Life Mem., Royal Naval Assoc. *Recreation:* collecting Victorian children's literature. *Address:* Minster Cottage, 51 Sands Lane, Barmston, Driffield, East Yorkshire YO25 8PQ. *T:* (01262) 468709. *Club:* Nikaean.

MAYNARD, Prof. Alan Keith; Professor of Health Economics, since 1997, Director, York Health Policy Group, since 1998, University of York; *b* 15 Dec. 1944; *s* of Edward Maynard and Hilda (*née* McCausland); *m* 1968, Elizabeth Shanahan; two *s* two *d*. *Educ:* Univ. of Newcastle upon Tyne (BA Hons 1st cl. 1967); Univ. of York (BPhil 1968). Asst Lectr and Lectr, Univ. of Exeter, 1968–71; University of York: Lectr in Econs, 1971–77; Sen. Lectr, then Reader in Econs and Dir, Grad. Programme in Health Econs, 1977–83; Prof. of Econs and Founding Dir, Centre for Health Econs, 1983–95; Sec., Nuffield Provincial Hosps Trust, 1995–96. Vis. Prof., LSE, 1995–2004; Hon. Prof., Univ. of Aberdeen, 2000–06; Adjunct Prof., Technol. Univ. of Sydney, 2003–. Founding Ed., Health Economics, 1992–. Mem., York HA, 1982–91; non-exec. Mem., York Hosp. NHS Trust, 1991–97; Chm., York NHS Trust, 1997–. Member: ESRC, 1986–88; Health Services Res. Cttee, MRC, 1986–92; Police Foundn Inquiry into 1971 Misuse of Drugs Act, 1997–2000; Chm., Evaluation Panel, Fourth Health and Med. Res. Programme, EC, 1990–91; Specialist Advr, H of C Select Cttee on Health, 2006–. FMedSci 2000. Hon. MFPHM. Hon. DSc Aberdeen, 2004; Hon. LLD Northumbria, 2006. *Publications:* Health Care in the European Community, 1976; (ed jtly) The Public Private Mix for Health, 1982, 2005; (with A. B. Atkinson and C. Trinder) Parents and Children, 1983; (ed jtly) Preventing Alcohol and Tobacco Problems, 1989; (ed jtly) Controlling Legal Addictions, 1990; (ed jtly) Competition in Health Care, 1991; (ed jtly) Purchasing and Providing Cost Effective Health Care, 1993; (ed with Iain Chalmers) Non Random Reflections on Health Services Research, 1997; (ed jtly) Being Reasonable about the Economics of Health, 1997; contrib. numerous articles to various jls. *Recreations:* walking, reading, watching cricket, football. *Address:* York Health Policy Group, Department of Health Sciences, University of York, Heslington, York YO10 5DD. *Clubs:* Royal Society of Medicine, Royal Commonwealth Society.

MAYNARD, Edwin Francis George; Overseas Business Consultant; Member, Export Council Advisory Panel; HM Diplomatic Service, retired; Deputy High Commissioner, Calcutta, 1976–80; *b* 23 Feb. 1921; *s* of late Edwin Maynard, MD, FRCS, DPH, and late Nancy Frances Tully; *m* 1945, Patricia Baker; one *s* one *d*; *m* 1963, Anna McGettrick; two *s*. *Educ:* Westminster. Served with Indian Army (4/8th (PWO) Punjab Regt and General Staff) (Major, GSO II), Middle East and Burma, 1939–46. BBC French Service, 1947; Foreign Office, 1949; Consul and Oriental Sec., Jedda, 1950; Second, later First, Sec., Benghazi, 1952; FO 1954; Bogota, 1956; Khartoum, 1959; FO, 1960; Baghdad, 1962; Founder Dir, Diplomatic Service Language Centre, 1966; Counsellor, Aden, 1967; Counsellor, New Delhi, 1968–72; Minister (Commercial), 1972–76, Chargé d'Affaires, 1974–75, Buenos Aires. *Recreations:* shooting, fishing, languages, gardening. *Address:* Littlebourne Court, Littlebourne, Canterbury, Kent CT3 1TU. *Club:* Brooks's.

MAYNARD, Prof. Geoffrey Walter; Economic Adviser, Investcorp International Ltd, 1986–2003; Director of Economics, Europe and Middle East, Chase Manhattan Bank, 1977–86 (Economic consultant, 1974); Director, Chase Manhattan Ltd, 1977–86; *b* 27 Oct. 1921; *s* of Walter F. Maynard and Maisie Maynard (*née* Bristow); *m* 1949, Marie Lilian Wright; two *d*. *Educ:* London School of Economics. BSc(Econ); PhD. Served War, 1941–46, RAF. Lectr and Sen. Lectr, UC of S Wales, Cardiff, 1951–62; Economic Consultant, HM Treasury 1962–64; Economic Advr, Harvard Univ. Develt Adv. Gp in Argentina, 1964–65; University of Reading: Reader, 1966–68; Prof. of Economics, 1968–76; Vis. Prof. of Economics, 1976–. Editor, Bankers' Magazine, 1968–72; Under-Sec. (Econs), HM Treasury, 1972–74 (on leave of absence); Dep. Chief Economic Advr, HM Treasury, 1976–77; occasional consultant, IBRD, Overseas Develt Administration of FCO. Mem., Econ. Affairs Cttee, ESRC, 1982–85. Mem. Governing Body, Inst. of Develt Studies, Sussex, 1984–91; Mem. Council, Inst. of Fiscal Studies, 1988–2000. *Publications:* Economic Development and the Price Level, 1962; (jtly) International Monetary Reform and Latin America, 1966; (jtly) A World of Inflation, 1976; The Economy under Mrs Thatcher, 1988; chapters in: Development Policy: theory and practice, ed G. Papanek, 1968; Commonwealth Policy in a Global Context, ed Streeten and Corbet, 1971; Economic Analysis and the Multinational Enterprise, ed J. Dunning, 1974; Special Drawing Rights and Development Aid (paper), 1972; articles in Economic Jl, Oxford Economic Papers, Jl of Development Studies, World Development, etc. *Address:* 219 Queens Quay, 58 Upper Thames Street, EC4V 3EH. *Club:* Reform.

MAYNARD, Roger Paul; Director of Investment and Alliances (formerly Investment and Joint Ventures), British Airways, since 1996; Director, Iberia, since 2000; Chairman, British Airways Pension Investment Management Ltd, since 2005; *b* 10 Feb. 1943; *s* of Leonard John Maynard and May Gertrude Blake; *m* 1966, Ruth Elizabeth Wakeling (marr. diss. 2004); three *s* (including twin *s*). *Educ:* Purley Grammar Sch., Surrey; Queens' Coll., Cambridge (MA Hons Economics). Asst Principal, Bd of Trade, 1965; Second Secretary, UK Mission to UN and Internat. Organisations, Geneva, 1968; Principal: Dept of Industry, Shipbuilding Division, 1972; Dept of Trade, Airports Policy, 1975; Asst Sec., Dept of Industry, Air Division, 1978; Counsellor, Aviation and Shipping, British Embassy, Washington, 1982; British Airways: Vice Pres., Commercial Affairs, N America, 1987–89; Exec. Vice Pres., N America, 1989; Dir, Investor Relations and Marketplace Performance, 1989–91; Dir, Corporate Strategy, 1991–96. Director: US Air, 1993–96; Qantas, 1993–2004. *Recreations:* cricket, golf, music. *Address:* 43 Rosebank, Holyport Road, Fulham, SW6 6LQ. *T:* (office) (020) 8738 6013.

MAYNE, Ann, (Mrs Roger Mayne); *see* Jellicoe, P. A.

MAYNE, Prof. David Quinn, FRS 1985; FREng; Professor of Electrical and Computer Engineering, University of California, Davis, 1989–96, now Professor Emeritus; Senior Research Fellow, Department of Electrical and Electronic Engineering, Imperial College London, since 1996; *b* 23 April 1930; *s* of Leslie Harper Mayne and Jane Quin; *m* 1954, Josephine Mary Hess; three *d*. *Educ:* Univ. of the Witwatersrand, Johannesburg (BSc (Eng), MSc); DIC, PhD, DSc London. FIET, FIEEE; FREng (FEng 1987). Lectr, Univ. of Witwatersrand, 1950–54, 1956–59; R&D Engineer, British Thomson Houston Co., Rugby, 1955–56; Imperial College: Lectr, 1959–67, Reader, 1967–71; Prof. of Control Theory, 1971–89, now Prof. Emeritus; Sen. Sci. Res. Fellow, 1979–80; Hd of Dept of Electrical Engrg, 1984–88. Research Consultant, 1974–, at Univs of California (Berkeley, and Santa Barbara), Lund, Newcastle NSW, and Wisconsin. Res. Fellow, Harvard Univ., 1970; Vis. Prof., Academia Sinica, Beijing, Shanghai and Guangzhou, 1981; Hon. Prof., Beihang Univ., Beijing, 2006. Corresp. Mem., Nacional Acad. de Ingenieria, Mexico, 1983. FIC 2000; Fellow, IFAC, 2006. Hon. DEng Lund Univ., 1995. *Publications:* Differential Dynamic Programming, vol. 24 in Modern Analytic and Computational Methods in Science and Mathematics (with D. H. Jacobson, ed R. Bellman), 1970; Geometric Methods in System Theory, proc. NATO Advanced Study Inst., (ed. with R. W. Brockett), 1973; contribs to learned jls. *Recreations:* walking, cross-country ski-ing. *Address:* 123 Elgin Crescent, W11 2JH.

MAYNE, Eric; Under Secretary, General Functions Group, Department of Economic Development, Northern Ireland, 1986–87, retired; *b* 2 Sept. 1928; *s* of Robert P. Mayne and Margaret Mayne; *m* 1954, Sarah Boyd (*née* Gray); three *s* two *d*. *Educ:* Bangor Grammar Sch. Univ. of Reading (BSc); Michigan State Univ. (MS). Horticultural Advisor, Min. of Agriculture, NI, 1949–56; Kellogg Foundation Fellow, 1956–57; Horticultural Advisor, HQ Min. of Agriculture, NI, 1957–64; Principal Officer, 1964–67; Gen. Manager, NI Agric. Trust, 1967–74; Sen. Asst Secretary, Dept of Agriculture, NI, 1974–79; Dep. Sec., Dept of Manpower Services, NI, 1979–82; Under Sec., Dept of Econ. Develt, NI, 1982–87. *Recreations:* gardening, winemaking.

MAYNE, John Fraser, CB 1986; Principal Establishment and Finance Officer, Department of Health and Social Security, then Department of Health, 1986–90; *b* 14 Sept. 1932; *s* of late John Leonard Mayne and Martha Laura (*née* Griffiths); *m* 1958, Gillian Mary (*née* Key); one *s* one *d*. *Educ:* Dulwich Coll.; Worcester Coll., Oxford. National Service, Royal Tank Regt, 1951–53. Air Min., 1956–64; HM Treasury, 1964–67; MoD, 1967–70; Asst Private Sec. to Sec. of State for Defence, 1968–70; Cabinet Office and Central Policy Rev. Staff, 1970–73; MoD, 1973–78; Private Sec. to Sec. of State for Def., 1975–76; Asst Under-Sec. of State (Air Staff), 1976–78; Principal Establishments and Finance Officer, NI Office, 1979–81; Dir Gen. of Management Audit, MoD, 1981–83; Dep. Sec., Cabinet Office (MPO), 1984–86. Non-exec. Mem., Hampstead HA, 1991–93. Associate, PA Consulting Group, 1990–95; Dir, Carnegie Young People Initiative, 1996–98. Member: Council, RUSI, 1986–89; Public Policy Unit, 1992–97. Trustee, Nat. AIDS Trust, 1992–2007. Chm., Friends of Scottish Opera, 2004–; Mem. Bd, Scottish Opera, 2005–. Freeman, City of London, 1983. *Recreations:* listening to music, restoring furniture, cooking. *Address:* Hazlefield House, Auchencairn, Castle Douglas DG7 1RF; 4/1 Carlton Terrace, Edinburgh EH7 5DD. *Club:* New (Edinburgh).

MAYNE, Richard (John); writer; broadcaster; *b* 2 April 1926; *s* of John William Mayne and Kate Hilda (*née* Angus); *m* 1st, Margot Ellingworth Lyon; 2nd, Jocelyn Mudie Ferguson; two *d*. *Educ:* St Paul's Sch., London; Trinity Coll., Cambridge (1st Cl. Hons Pts I and II, Hist. Tripos; MA and PhD). War service, Royal Signals, 1944–47. Styring, Sen., and Res. Scholar, and Earl of Derby Student, Trinity Coll., Cambridge, 1947–53; Leverhulme European Scholar, Rome, and Rome Corresp., New Statesman, 1953–54; Asst Tutor, Cambridge Inst. of Educn, 1954–56; Official: ECSC, Luxembourg, 1956–58; EEC, Brussels, 1958–63; Dir of Documentation Centre, Action Cttee for United States of Europe, and Personal Asst to Jean Monnet, Paris, 1963–66; Paris Corresp., Encounter, 1966–71, Co-Editor, 1985–90, Contributing Editor, 1990–91. Vis. Prof., Univ. of Chicago, 1971; Dir of Federal Trust for Educn and Res., 1971–73; Head of UK Offices, 1973–79, Special Advr, 1979–80, EEC. Hon. Professorial Fellow, UCW, Aberystwyth, 1986–89. Film critic: Sunday Telegraph, 1987–89; The European, 1990–98. Officier, Ordre des Arts et des Lettres (France), 2002. *Publications:* The Community of Europe, 1962; The Institutions of the European Community, 1968; The Recovery of Europe, 1970 (rev. edn 1973); The Europeans, 1972; (ed) Europe Tomorrow, 1972; (ed) The New Atlantic Challenge, 1975; (trans.) The Memoirs of Jean Monnet, 1978 (Scott-Moncrieff Prize, 1979); Postwar: the dawn of today's Europe, 1983; (ed) Western Europe: a handbook, 1986; Federal Union: the pioneers, 1990; (trans.) Europe: a history of its peoples, 1990; (trans.) A History of Civilisations, 1993; (trans.) Illustrated History of Europe, 1993; The Language of Sailing, 2000; In Victory Magnanamity, in Peace Goodwill: a history of Wilton Park, 2003; (ed) Cross Channel Currents, 2004; Nuances, 2006. *Recreations:* travel, sailing, singing. *Address:* Albany Cottage, 24 Park Village East, Regent's Park, NW1 7PZ. *T:* (020) 7387 6654. *Clubs:* Groucho; Les Misérables (Paris).

MAYNE, William; writer; *b* 16 March 1928; *s* of William and Dorothy Mayne. *Educ:* Cathedral Choir Sch., Canterbury, 1937–42 (then irregularly). Has pursued a career as novelist and has had published a large number of stories for children and young people—about 120 altogether, beginning in 1953 and going on into the foreseeable future. Lectr in Creative Writing, Deakin Univ., Geelong, Vic, Aust., academic years, 1976 and 1977; Fellow in Creative Writing, Rolle Coll., Exmouth, 1979–80. Library Assoc.'s Carnegie Medal for best children's book of the year (1956), 1957; Guardian Award for Children's Fiction, 1993; (jtly) Kurt Maschler Award, 1997. *Address:* c/o David Higham Associates, 5–8 Lower John Street, Golden Square, W1F 9HA.

MAYO, 11th Earl of, *cr* 1785; **Charles Diarmuidh John Bourke;** Baron Naas, 1776; Viscount Mayo, 1781; *b* 11 June 1953; *e s* of 10th Earl of Mayo and his 1st wife, Margaret Jane Robinson Harrison; S father, 2006; *m* 1st, 1975, Marie Antoinette Cronnelly (marr. diss. 1979); one *d*; 2nd, 1985, Marie Veronica Mannion; two *s*. *Educ:* St Aubyn's, Rottingdean; Portora Royal Sch., Enniskillen; QUB; Bolton Street Coll. of Technology, Dublin. *Heir: s* Lord Naas, *qv*. *Address:* Derryinver, Beach Road, Clifden, Co. Galway, Eire.

MAYO, Col (Edward) John, OBE 1976; Director General, Help the Aged, 1983–96; *b* 24 May 1931; *s* of late Rev. Thomas Edward Mayo, JP, and Constance Muriel Mayo; *m* 1st, 1961, Jacqueline Margaret Anne Armstrong, MBE 1985, Lieut WRAC (*d* 1993), *d* of late Brig. C. D. Armstrong, CBE, DSO, MC; one *s*; 2nd, 1998, Pamela Joyce Shimwell. *Educ:* King's Coll., Taunton. Commissioned into Royal Regt of Artillery, 1951; served Malta and N Africa 36 HAA Regt, 1951–55; ADC to Governor of Malta, 1953–54; 2nd Regt RHA, BAOR, 1955–58; ADC to C-in-C BAOR/Comdr Northern Army Gp, 1958–60; 20 Field Regt, RA UK, 1960–61; Adjt 20 Field Regt, RA Malaya, 1961–63; Adjt 254 (City of London) Regt RA(TA), 1963–64; Instr RMA, Sandhurst, 1964–66; GS03 Mil. Operations, MoD, 1966–68; Second in Comd 20 Heavy Regt, RA BAOR, 1968–70; GS02 Instr Staff Coll., 1970–72; commanded 17 Trng Regt and Depot RA, 1972–74, and The Depot Regt RA, 1974–75; GS01 Public Relations MoD, 1976–79; Col GS; Public Information BAOR, 1979–83; retired 1983. Dir, Executive Communication Consultants (IOM) Ltd, 1999–. Chm. Comrs, Jurby, IOM, 2002–04. Mem. Bd, HelpAge Sri Lanka, 1985–; Trustee: HelpAge Kenya, 1984–; HelpAge India, 1985–99; Global Cancer, 1998–2004; Combat Stress, 1993–2005. Patron: The Homeless Fund, 1996–2001; Gesture, 2002–03; Employers Retirement Assoc., 2003–. MCIPR (MIPR 1981). FRSA 1987. *Publications:* miscellaneous articles on military matters. *Recreations:* fishing, gardening, sailing, travelling, collecting and restoring antiques. *Address:* Ballamoar Castle, Sandygate, Isle of Man IM7 3AJ. *T:* (01624) 897504, *Fax:* (01624) 898144; *e-mail:* mayo@manx.net. *Clubs:* Army and Navy, Special Forces, Woodroffe's, MCC.

MAYO, Col John; *see* Mayo, Col E. J.

MAYO, Simon Andrew Hicks; Presenter, BBC Radio 5 Live Afternoon Show, since 2001; *b* 21 Sept. 1958; *s* of Derek Leslie Mayo and Gillian Mary Mayo; *m* 1986, Hilary Mary Bird; two *s* one *d*. *Educ:* Solihull Sch.; Worthing Grammar Sch.; Warwick Univ. (BA Hons). Presenter: Breakfast Show, 1988–93, Morning Show, 1993–2001, Radio 1; Album Chart Show, Radio 2, 2001–; television: Scruples, 1988; Best of Magic, 1989; Confessions, 1994, 1995, 1996, 1997; The Big End, 1999; Winning Lines, 1998–2000; Dig!, 2005. Hon. Vice-Pres., Melchester Rovers, 1989. Hon. DLitt Warwick, 2005. *Publications:* (with S. Jenkins) Breakfast in the Holy Land, 1988; Confessions, 1991; Further Confessions, 1992; (with M. Wroe) Snogging, 1992; (with M. Wroe) The Big Match, 1993; Very Worst of Confessions, 1993; Classic Confessions, 1994. *Recreations:* etymology, astronomy, the school run, walking in bad weather, thinking up quizzes. *Address:* c/o PBJ Management, 7 Soho Street, W1D 3DQ.

MAYO, Simon Herbert; Vice President, Court of Appeal of the High Court, Hong Kong, 2000–03; *b* 15 Nov. 1937; *s* of late Herbert and Marjorie Mayo; *m* 1966, Catherine Yin Ying Young; one *s* one *d*. *Educ:* Harrow Sch. Admitted a solicitor, England and Wales, 1961, Hong Kong, 1963; called as barrister and solicitor, W Australia, 1967. Asst Legal Advr, GEC, 1961; Asst Solicitor, Deacons, Solicitors, Hong Kong, 1963; in private practice, WA, 1967; Asst Registrar, 1968, Registrar, 1976, Supreme Court of Hong Kong; a Judge of the High Court, Hong Kong, 1980–95; Justice of Appeal, Court of Appeal of Supreme, then High, Court, Hong Kong, 1995–2000. *Recreations:* golf, music, literature, walking. *Clubs:* Hong Kong, Sheko Country (Hong Kong).

MAYO, Simon Peter; QC 2008; *b* London, 23 Sept. 1961; *s* of Peter and Anita Mayo; *m* 1996, Jayne Sugg; one *d*, and two step *s*. *Educ:* Beal Grammar Sch.; Univ. of N London (BA Hons Law). Called to the Bar, Inner Temple, 1985; in practice as barrister specialising in criminal law, 1985–. *Recreations:* Rugby, motorsport, running, dancing in public and anything else to embarrass my daughter. *Address:* 187 Fleet Street, EC4A 2AT. *T:* (020) 7430 7430.

MAYOR, His Honour Hugh Robert; QC 1986; a Circuit Judge, 1992–2007; *b* 12 Oct. 1941; *s* of George and Grace Mayor; *m* 1970, Carolyn Ann Stubbs; one *s* one *d*. *Educ:* Kirkham Grammar Sch.; St John's Coll., Oxford (MA). Lectr, Univ. of Leicester, 1964 (MA). Called to the Bar, Gray's Inn, 1968; a Recorder, 1982–92.

MAYOR ZARAGOZA, Federico; Director-General of UNESCO, 1987–99; *b* Barcelona, 27 Jan. 1934; *s* of Federico Mayor and Juana Zaragoza; *m* 1956, Maria Angeles Menéndez; two *s* one *d*. *Educ:* Madrid Complutense Univ. Granada University: Prof. of Biochemistry, 1963–73; Rector, 1968–72; Prof. of Biochemistry, Univ. Autónoma, Madrid, 1973. Dir, 1974–78, Scientific Chm., 1983–87, Molecular Biology Centre, Higher Council for Scientific Research. Under-Sec., Min. for Educn and Science, 1974–75; Pres., Commn for Study of Special Set of Rules for the four Catalan Provinces, 1976; Mem., Cortes (Parliament) for Granada, 1977–78; Dep. Dir-Gen., UNESCO, 1978–81; Minister for Educn and Science, Spain, 1981–82; Special Advr to Dir-Gen., UNESCO, 1982; Dir, Inst. of Sciences of Man, Madrid, 1983–87. Mem., European Parlt, 1987. Pres., Foundn for Culture of Peace, Madrid, 1999–. *Address:* Mar Caribe, 15 Interland, Majadahonda, 28220 Madrid, Spain.

MAYOU, Prof. Richard Anthony, FRCP, FRCPsych; Professor of Psychiatry, University of Oxford, 1997–2004 and Fellow, Nuffield College, Oxford, 1976–2005, now Emeritus; *b* 23 Nov. 1940; *s* of Cecil Richard Mayou and Kathleen (*née* Batt); *m* 1981, Ann Foster (*née* Bowler); one step *s* one step *d*. *Educ:* King Edward's Sch., Birmingham; St John's Coll., Oxford (open scholar; BM, MSc, MA); Inst. of Psychiatry, London Univ. (MPhil). FRCPsych 1979; FRCP 1985. House Officer, Queen Elizabeth Hosp., Birmingham, 1966–67; House Physician, Hammersmith and Brompton Hosps, London, 1967–68; Registrar, then Sen. Registrar, Maudsley & Bethlem Royal Hosps, London, 1968–72; Lectr and Clinical Reader in Psychiatry, Oxford, 1973–97. Chm., Friends of Oxford Univ. Botanic Garden, 2004–. *Publications:* Shorter Oxford Textbook of Psychiatry, 1983, 4th edn 2001; Psychiatry Core Text, 1994, 3rd edn 2004; contribs to learned jls on psychological aspects of medical symptoms and disorders. *Recreations:* countryside, gardening, architecture, the arts. *Address:* Hill House, Shabbington, Aylesbury, Bucks HP18 9HQ. *T:* (01844) 201885; *e-mail:* richard.mayou@nuffield.ox.ac.uk. *Club:* Athenæum.

MAYR-HARTING, Prof. Henry Maria Robert Egmont, DPhil; FBA 1992; Regius Professor of Ecclesiastical History, University of Oxford, 1997–2003, now Emeritus; Co-Censor of Degrees, Christ Church, Oxford, since 2004 (Lay Canon, 1997–2003); *b* 6 April 1936; *s* of Herbert Mayr-Harting and Anna Mayr-Harting (*née* Münzer), Prague; *m* 1968, Caroline Henry; one *s* one *d*. *Educ:* Douai School; Merton Coll., Oxford (BA Mod. Hist. 1957; MA; DPhil 1961). Asst Lectr and Lectr in Medieval History, Univ. of Liverpool, 1960–68; Fellow, and Tutor in Medieval History, 1968–97, Emeritus Fellow, 1997, St Peter's Coll., Oxford; Reader in Medieval History, Oxford Univ., 1993–97. Vis. Fellow, Peterhouse, Cambridge, 1983; Slade Prof. of Fine Art, Oxford Univ., 1987–88; Brown Foundn Fellow, Univ. of the South, Tennessee, 1992. Corresp. Mem., Austrian Acad. of Scis, 2001. Hon. DLitt: Lawrence Univ., Wisconsin, 1998; Univ. of the South, Tennessee, 1999. *Publications:* The Acta of the Bishops of Chichester 1075–1207, 1965; The Coming of Christianity to Anglo-Saxon England, 1972, 3rd edn 1991; What to do in the Penwith Peninsula, Cornwall, in less than perfect weather, 1987, 2nd edn 1988; Ottonian Book

Illumination: an historical study, 2 vols, 1991 (trans. German 1991), 2nd edn 1999; Two Conversions to Christianity: the Bulgarians and the Anglo-Saxons, 1994; (ed with Richard Harries) Christianity: two thousand years, 2001; Church and Cosmos in Early Ottonian Germany: the view from Cologne, 2007; articles in learned jls. *Recreations:* music, especially playing keyboard instruments; watching cricket. *Address:* St Peter's College, Oxford OX1 2DL; 29 Portland Road, Oxford OX2 7EZ. *Club:* Athenæum.

MAYS, Colin Garth, CMG 1988; HM Diplomatic Service, retired; Bursar, Yehudi Menuhin School, 1991–97; *b* 16 June 1931; *s* of William Albert Mays and Sophia May Mays (*née* Pattinson); *m* 1956, Margaret Patricia, *d* of Philemon Robert Lloyd and Gladys Irene (*née* Myers); one *s*. *Educ:* Acklam Hall Sch.; St John's Coll., Oxford (Heath Harrison Scholar, MA). Served in Army, 1949–51; entered HM Foreign (subseq. Diplomatic) Service, 1955; FO, 1955–56; Sofia, 1956–58; Baghdad, 1958–60; FO, 1960; UK Delegn to Conf. of 18 Nation Cttee on Disarmament, Geneva, 1960; Bonn, 1960–65; FO, 1965–69; Prague, 1969–72; FCO, 1972–77; Head of Information Administration Dept, 1974–77; Counsellor (Commercial), Bucharest, 1977–80; seconded to PA Management Consultants, 1980–81; Diplomatic Service Overseas Inspector, 1981–83; High Commissioner: Seychelles, 1983–86; Bahamas, 1986–91. Liveryman, Painter-Stainers' Co., 1981. *Recreations:* sailing, travel. *Club:* Travellers.

MAYSTADT, Dr Philippe; President, and Chairman, Board of Directors, European Investment Bank, since 2000; *b* 14 March 1948; *s* of Auguste Maystadt and Marie-Thérèse Deblon; *m* 1970, Suzanne Franquin; two *s* one *d*. *Educ:* Catholic Univ. of Louvain, Belgium (PhD Law 1970); Claremont Grad. Sch., LA (MA Public Admin). Asst Prof., Catholic Univ. of Louvain, 1970–77; MHR, Charleroi, Belgium, 1977–91, 1995–98; Mem., Senate, 1998–99; Sec. of State for Walloon Reg., 1979–80; Minister: for CS and Scientific Policy, 1980–81; of Budget, Scientific Policy and Planning, 1981–85; of Econ. Affairs, 1985–86; Dep. Prime Minister and Minister of Econ. Affairs, 1986–88; Minister of Finance, 1988–95; Minister of Finance and Foreign Trade, June–Sept. 1995; Dep. Prime Minister and Minister of Finance and Foreign Trade, 1995–98. Pres., Parti Social Chrétien, 1998–99. Chairman: G-10 Ministers of Finance, 1990–91; Council of Ministers of Economy and Finance of EC, 1993; Interim Cttee, IMF, 1993–98; Council of Governors, EBRD, 1997–98. Part-time Prof., Faculty of Law, Catholic Univ. of Louvain, 1989–. *Publications:* (with A. Jacquemin) Les aspects juridiques de l'intervention de l'Etat dans la vie économique, 1975 (Prix spécial de l'Association des juristes d'entreprises); Ecouter et puis Décider, 1988; (with F. Dermine-Minet) Comprendre l'économie: le marché et l'Etat à l'heure de la mondialisation, 1998, 4th edn 2007. *Address:* European Investment Bank, 100 Boulevard Konrad Adenauer, 2950 Luxembourg. *T:* 437994464.

MAZANKOWSKI, Rt Hon. Donald (Frank); PC (Can.) 1979; OC 2000; AOE 2003; Deputy Prime Minister of Canada, 1986–93; Minister of Finance, 1991–93; *b* 27 July 1935; *s* of late Frank Mazankowski and Dora (*née* Lonowski); *m* 1958, Lorraine Poleschuk; three *s*. *Educ:* High Sch., Viking, Alberta. MP (Progressive Conservative), Vegreville, 1968–93; Minister for Transport and Minister responsible for Canadian Wheat Bd, 1979–80; Minister of Transport, 1984–86; Pres. of Queen's Privy Council for Canada, 1986–91; Minister of Agriculture, 1988–91; Minister responsible for Privatization, 1988; Govt House Leader and Pres. of Privy Council, 1986–91. Director: Shaw Communications Inc., 1993–; Investors Group, 1994–; Great West Life Co., 1994–; Power Corp. of Canada, 1996–; Weyerhaeuser Co., 1997–; ATCO Gp, 1999–; Canadian Oilsands Trust, 2002–; Dir and Trustee, Yellow Pages Gp, 2003–. Chairman: Canadian Genetics Diseases Network, 1998–2004; Premier's Adv. Council on Health, Alberta, 2000–02. Hon. DEng Technical Univ. of Nova Scotia, 1987; Hon. LLD Alberta, 1993. *Address:* 80 Nottingham Inlet, Sherwood Park, AB T8A 6N2, Canada; *e-mail:* donmaz@shaw.ca.

MAZRUI, Prof. Ali A., DPhil; Albert Schweitzer Professor in the Humanities, since 1989, and Director, Institute of Global Cultural Studies, State University of New York, Binghamton; *b* Kenya, 24 Feb. 1933; *s* of Al'Amin Ali Mazrui, Judge of Islamic Law, and Safia Suleiman Mazrui; marr. diss.; three *s*; two *s* by Pauline Uti. *Educ:* Univ. of Manchester (BA with distinction 1960); Columbia Univ. (MA 1961); Oxford Univ. (DPhil 1966). Makerere University, Kampala, Uganda: Lectr, 1963–65; Prof. and Head of Dept of Political Science, 1965–73; Dean, Faculty of Social Sciences, 1967–69; Res. Prof., Univ. of Jos, Nigeria, 1981–86; Prof. of Pol Science and of Afroamerican and African Studies, Univ. of Michigan, 1974–91; Andrew D. White Prof.-at-Large, Cornell Univ., 1986–92, Emeritus and Sen. Scholar, 1992–; Ibn Khaldun Prof.-at-Large, Sch. of Islamic and Social Scis, Leesburg, 1997–. Vis. Prof., Univs of London, Manchester, Sussex, Leeds, Harvard, Calif (LA), Northwestern, Stanford, Colgate, Ohio State, Bridgewater State Coll., Mass, Denver, Pennsylvania State, McGill, Canada, Nairobi, Cairo, Baghdad, Singapore and Australian National, 1965–; Walter Rodney Vis. Prof., Univ. of Guyana, 1997–98. Expert Adviser: World Bank, 1988–91; UN Commn on Transnational Corps, 1987–92. Member: Adv. Cttee, Trans-Africa Run for Wildlife Foundn, Inc., 1987–; Adv. Bd of Dirs, Detroit Chapter, AFRICARE, 1987–; Pan-African Adv. Council to UNICEF, 1988–. Pres., African Studies Assoc. of USA, 1978–79; Vice-President: Internat. Congress of African Studies, 1978–; Internat. African Inst., 1987–; World Congress of Black Intellectuals, 1988–. BBC Reith Lectr, 1979; Presenter, The Africans (BBC TV series), 1986. *Publications:* Towards a Pax Africana, 1967; The Anglo-African Commonwealth, 1967; On Heroes and Uhuru-Worship, 1967; Violence and Thought, 1969; (with R. I. Rotberg) Protest and Power in Black Africa, 1970; The Trial of Christopher Okigbo (novel), 1971; Cultural Engineering and Nation-Building in East Africa, 1972; (with Hasu Patel) Africa in World Affairs: the next thirty years, 1973; World Culture and the Black Experience, 1974; Soldiers and Kinsmen in Uganda, 1975; The Political Sociology of the English Language: an African perspective, 1975; A World Federation of Cultures: an African perspective, 1976; Africa's International Relations, 1977; The Warrior Tradition in Modern Africa, 1978; Political Values and the Educated Class in Africa, 1978; The African Condition (The Reith Lectures), 1980; (with Michael Tidy) Nationalism and New States of Africa, 1984; The Africans: a triple heritage, 1986; Cultural Forces in World Politics, 1990; Africa since 1935 (Vol. VIII, UNESCO General History of Africa), 1993; (with A. M. Mazrui) The Power of Babel: language and governance in Africa's experience, 1998; (ed jtly) The African Diaspora, 1999; (with A. M. Mazrui) Political Culture of Language, 1999; Africanity Redefined, collected essays, vol. 1, 2002; Africa and Other Civilizations, collected essays, vol. 2, 2002; The Titan of Tanzania: Julius K. Nyerere's legacy, 2002; (with A. M. Mazrui) Black Reparations in the Era of Globalization, 2002; The African Predicament and the American Experience, 2004; A Tale of Two Africas, 2006. *Address:* Institute of Global Cultural Studies, Binghamton University, PO Box 6000 LNG–100, Binghamton, NY 13902, USA. *T:* (607) 7774494; 313 Murray Hill Road, Vestal, NY 13850, USA.

MBEKEANI, Nyemba W.; Chief Executive, Mkulumadzi Farm Bakeries Ltd, since 1981; Chairman, Spearhead Holdings Ltd, since 1987; *b* 15 June 1929; Malawi parentage; *m* 1950, Lois Moses (*née* Chikankheni); two *s* three *d*. *Educ:* Henry Henderson Institute, Blantyre; London Sch. of Economics (Economic and Social Administration, 1963). Local Government Officer, 1945–58; political detention in Malawi and Southern Rhodesia, 1959–60; Business Executive, 1960–61; Local Govt Officer, 1963–64; Foreign Service, 1964; High Commissioner for Malawi in London, 1964–67; Ambassador to USA and Permanent Rep. at the UN, 1967–72; Ambassador to Ethiopia, 1972–73; Gen. Manager, Malaŵi Housing Corp., 1973–81. Farmer, company director, tea broker, baker, confectioner. Chm., Petroleum Control Commn, 1987–93; Comr, Malaŵi Electoral Commn, 1998–99. Board Member: Lingadzi Farming Co., 1987–; Sable Farming Co., 1987–. Trustee, Small Farmers Fertilizer Revolving Fund, 1988–. Counsellor, Malaŵi Univ. Council, 1984–93; Chm., Malaŵi Polytechnic Bd of Govs, 1988–93. *Recreation:* flower gardening. *Address:* PO Box 2095, Blantyre, Malaŵi. *T:* 08831060; *Telex:* 44847 Lumadzi MI.

MBEKI, Thabo Mvuyelwa, Hon. GCMG 2000; President of South Africa, 1999–2008 (Deputy President, 1994–99); President, African National Congress, 1997–2007 (Deputy President, 1994–97); *b* 18 June 1942; *s* of late Govan and of Epainette Mbeki; *m* 1974, Zanele Dlamini. *Educ:* St John's High Sch., Umtata; Lovedale Inst.; Sussex Univ. (MA Econs; Hon. LLD 1995). Youth organiser, ANC, Johannesburg, 1961–62; left S Africa, 1962; worked in ANC Offices, London, 1967–70; mil. training, USSR, 1970; African National Congress: Asst Sec., Revolutionary Council, 1971–72; Mem., NEC, 1975–2007; Acting Rep., Swaziland, 1975–76; Rep. Nigeria, 1976–78; Political Sec., President's Office, 1978; Dir, Information and Publicity, 1984–89; Hd, Dept of Internat. Affairs, 1989–94 (Hd, delegn talks with S African Govt which led to unbanning of ANC and release of political prisoners, 1989; Mem., delegn concerning talks with S African Govt, 1990); Chm., 1993.

M'BOW, Amadou-Mahtar; Director-General of Unesco, 1974–87; *b* 20 March 1921; *s* of Fara-N'Diaye M'Bow and N'Goné Casset, Senegal; *m* 1951, Raymonde Sylvain; one *s* two *d*. *Educ:* Univ. of Paris. Teacher, Rosso Coll., Mauritania, 1951–53; Dir, Service of Fundamental and Community Educn, Senegal, 1953–57; Min. of Education and Culture, 1957–58; Teacher at Lycée Faidherbe, St-Louis, Senegal, 1958–64; Prof., Ecole Normale Supérieure, Dakar, 1964–66; Minister of Educn, 1966–68; Mem. Nat. Assembly, Senegal, 1968–70; Minister of Culture, Youth and Sports 1968–70; Asst Dir-Gen. for Educn, UNESCO, 1970–74. Member: Acad. des Sciences d'Outre-Mer, 1977; Acad. of Kingdom of Morocco, 1981; Hon. Mem., Royal Acad. Fine Arts, San Temo, Spain, 1977; For. Mem., Acad. of Athens, 1983. Hon. Professor: Ecole normale supérieure, Dakar, 1979; Indep. Univ. of Santo Domingo, 1978; Nat. Indep. Univ. of Mexico, 1979. Hon. Dr: Buenos Aires, 1974; Granada (Lit. and Phil.), Sherbrooke (Educn), West Indies (Laws), 1975; Open, Kliment Okhridski, Sofia, Nairobi (Lit.), 1976; Malaya (Lit.), Philippines (Laws); Venice (Geog.), Uppsala (Soc. Scis), Moscow (Soc. Scis), Paris I, 1977; Andes (Philos.), Peru (Educn Scis), Haiti, Tribhunvan Univ., Nepal (Lit.), State Univ., Mongolia, Khartoum (Law), Sri Lanka, 1978; Charles Univ., Prague (Phil.), Tashkent, Québec, 1979; Nat. Univ. of Zaïre, Madras, Belgrade, Ivory Coast, Sierra Leone, 1980; Univ. Gama Filho, Brazil, 1981; Nat. Univ. of Lesotho, 1981; Univ. of Benin, 1981; Technical Univ. of Middle East, Ankara, 1981; Univ. of Ankara, 1981, Univ. of Gand, Belgium, 1982; Nat. Univ. of Seoul, 1982; State Univ. of Kiev, 1982; Laval Univ., Quebec, 1982; Quaid-i-Azam Univ., Islamabad, 1983; Jawaharlal Nehru Univ., New Delhi, 1983; Aix-Marseilles Univ., 1983; Beijing Univ., China, 1983; Kim Il Sung Univ., PDR of Korea (Pedagogy), 1983; Lucknow Univ., India (Lit.), 1983; Chulalongkorn Univ., Thailand (Pedagogy), 1983; Sokoto Univ., Nigeria (Lit.), 1984; Malta Univ., 1986; Polytechnic Univ. of Catalonia, Cauca Univ. Popayan (Colombia), Univ. of Mayor, Real y Pontificia de San Francisco Xavier de Chuquisara, Sucre (Bolivia), 1987; Grand Tribute, Univ. Candido Mendes, Brazil, 1981. Order of Merit, Senegal; Grand Cross: Order of the Liberator, Order of Andres Bello and Order of Francisco de Miranda, Venezuela; Order of Merit and Juan Montalvo National Order of Merit (Educn), Ecuador; Order of Miguel Antonio Caro y Rufino José Cuervo, Colombia; Order of Stara Planina, Bulgaria; Order of the Sun, Peru; Order of Merit of Duarte, Sanchez and Mella, Dominican Republic; National Order of the Lion, Senegal; Order of Alphonso X the Sabio, Spain; Order of the Southern Cross and Order of Merit of Guararapes, Brazil; Order of Distinguished Diplomatic Service Merit, Republic of Korea; Order of Sikatuna, Philippines; Order of Merit, Indonesia; Order of Merit, Syrian Arab Republic; Order of Merit, Jordan; Order of the Arab Republic of Egypt; Order of Felix Varela, Cuba; Grand Cross: Order of Nat. Flag (PDR of Korea); Order of Meritorious Action (Libya); Nat. Order of Andean Condor (Bolivia); Grand Order of Education (Bolivia); Grand Officer: National Order of Ivory Coast; National Order of Guinea; Order of Merit, Cameroon; National Order of Merit, Mauritania; Order of Independence, Tunisia; Commander: Order of Academic Palms; National Order of Upper Volta; Order of the Gabonese Merit; Order of Arts and Letters, France; Grand Medal, Order of the Inconfidência, State of Minas Gerais, Brazil; Medal: Order of Merit of Caetés, Olinda, Brazil; Order of Manual José Hurtado, Panama; Superior Decoration for Education, Jordan. Man and his World Peace Prize, Canada, 1978; Gold Medal of Olympic Order, 1981; Gold Medal of ALECSO (Arab Educnl, Cultural and Scientific Orgn), 1981; Internat. Dimitrov Prize, 1982; Gold Medal: Champion of Africa, 1986, of Andalucia, 1987. *Publications:* Le temps des peuples, ed R. Laffont, 1982; Where the Future Begins, 1982; Hope for the Future, 1984; Unesco: universality and international intellectual co-operation, 1985; numerous monographs, articles in educnl jls, textbooks, etc. *Address:* Fondation Paix et Développement, BP 3473, Bd Djily Mbaye & Macadou Ndiaye, Imm Fahd 14ème étage, Dakar, Senegal.

MEACHER, family name of **Baroness Meacher**.

MEACHER, Baroness *cr* 2006 (Life Peer), of Spitalfields in the London Borough of Tower Hamlets; **Molly Christine Meacher;** Chairman, East London NHS Foundation Trust (formerly East London and The City Mental Health NHS Trust), since 2004; *b* 15 May 1940; *d* of William F. and Lucy M. Reid; *m* 1991, Peter Richard Grenville Layard (*see* Baron Layard); two *s* two *d* by a former *m*. *Educ:* Berkhamsted Sch. for Girls; York Univ. (BScEcon); Univ. of London (DipSoc; CQSW). Campaign Dir and Res. Officer, CPAG, 1970–72; Projects Officer, Mental Health Foundn, 1973–78; Approved Social Worker, 1980–82; Mgr, Nat. Assoc. of CABx, 1982–84; Parly Officer, BASW, 1984–87; CEO, Campaign for Work, 1987–92; Advr to Russian Govt, 1991–94; Mem., later Dep. then Acting Chm., Police Complaints Authy, 1994–2002; Chm., Security Industry Authy, 2002–04. Mental Health Act Comr, 1987–92; non-exec. Dir, Tower Hamlets Healthcare NHS Trust, 1994–98. *Publications:* Scrounging on the Welfare, 1970; (jtly) To Him Who Hath, 1971; New Methods of Mental Health Care, 1979; (contrib.) The Mentally Disordered Offender, 1991. *Recreations:* music, golf, tennis, grandchildren. *Address:* East London NHS Foundation Trust, Eastone, 22 Commercial Street, E1 6LP. *T:* (020) 7655 4061.

MEACHER, Rt Hon. Michael (Hugh); PC 1997; MP (Lab) Oldham West and Royton, since 1997 (Oldham West, 1970–97); *b* 4 Nov. 1939; *s* of late George Hubert and Doris May Meacher; *m* 1st, 1962, Molly Christine (*née* Reid) (marr. diss. 1987) (*see* Baroness Meacher); two *s* two *d*; 2nd, 1988, Mrs Lucianne Sawyer. *Educ:* Berkhamsted Sch., Herts; New College, Oxford (Greats, Class 1 1962); LSE (DSA 1963). Sec. to Danilo Dolci Trust, 1964; Research Fellow in Social Gerontology, Univ. of Essex, 1965–66; Lecturer in Social Administration: Univ. of York, 1967–69; London Sch. of Economics, 1970.

Parly Under-Secretary of State: DoI, 1974–75; DHSS, 1975–76; Dept of Trade, 1976–79; Mem., Shadow Cabinet, 1983–97; chief opposition spokesman on health and social security, 1983–87, on employment, 1987–89, on social security, 1989–92, on development and co-operation, 1992–93, on Citizen's Charter, 1993–94, on transport, 1994–95, on employment, 1995–96, on envmtl protection, 1996–97; Minister of State (Minister for the Envmt), DETR, 1997–2001, DEFRA, 2001–03. Mem., Treasury Select Cttee, 1980–83 (a Chm. of its sub-cttee). Chm., Labour Co-ordinating Cttee, 1978–83; Member: Campaign for Press Freedom; Labour Party NEC, 1983–88. Vis. Prof., Univ. of Surrey, Dept of Sociology, 1980–87. *Publications:* Taken for a Ride: Special Residential Homes for the Elderly Mentally Infirm, a study of separatism in social policy, 1972; Fabian pamphlets incl. The Care of the Old, 1969; Wealth: Labour's Achilles Heel, in Labour and Equality, ed P. Townsend and N. Bosanquet, 1972; Socialism with a Human Face, 1981; Diffusing Power: the key to Socialist revival, 1992; numerous articles. *Recreations:* music, sport, reading. *Address:* House of Commons, SW1A 0AA; 34 Kingscliffe Gardens, SW19 6NR.

MEAD, Deryk, CBE 2003; Chief Executive, NCH (formerly NCH Action for Children), 1996–2004; *b* 3 July 1945; *s* of Joe and Ruth Mead; *m* 1967, Susan Margaret Kay; two *s*. *Educ:* Univ. of Manchester (BSc, MSc); Univ. of Leeds (DipPSW); CQSW. Approved Sch. Officer, Burnley, 1969–74; Principal Officer, Social Services, Lancs, 1974–79; Deputy Director of Social Services: Rochdale, 1979–87; Cumbria, 1987–91; Dir of Social Services, Gloucestershire, 1991–96. Member: Meat Hygiene Bd, 2005–; Bd, Passenger Focus, 2005–; Bd, W Midlands Strategic HA, 2007–; Public Mem., Network Rail, 2007–. *Publications:* contrib. to numerous publications. *Recreations:* fell running, rock and ice climbing, sea kayaking. *Address:* The Barn House, Old Church Road, Colwall, Malvern, Worcs WR13 6EZ.

MEAD, Dr Keith Owen, CB 2000; CEng, FIET; CMath, FIMA; Director of Technology and Engineering, Government Communications Headquarters, 1994–2000; *b* 14 Oct. 1945; *s* of Kenneth Stanley Mead and Constance Louise Mead; *m* 1971, Fiona McDonald McCall; one *s* one *d*. *Educ:* Southend High Sch. for Boys; Sussex Univ. (BSc); Liverpool Univ. (PhD 1971). CEng 1996, FIET (FIEE 1996); CMath 1996, FIMA 1996; ATCL (MusEd) 2001. Joined GCHQ, 1970; PSO, 1975; Asst Sec., 1987; RCDS 1990; Under Sec., 1994. Mem. Council, IMA, 1999–2002. *Publications:* maths res. papers in learned jls. *Recreations:* playing the piano, teaching and arranging music, walking. *Address: e-mail:* me@keithmead.name.

MEAD, Dr Timothy John; Registrary, University of Cambridge, 1997–2007, now Emeritus; Fellow, Wolfson College, Cambridge, since 1997; Secretary, Cambridge Commonwealth and Overseas Trusts, since 2008; *b* 31 May 1947; *s* of Ernest Arthur Mead and Catherine Beryl Louisa Mead (*née* Midlane); *m* 1971, Anne Frances Glasson; one *s* one *d*. *Educ:* Queen Mary Coll., Univ. of London (BSc Hons 1969); Churchill Coll., Cambridge (PhD 1972). Admin. Asst, Univ. of Sheffield, 1972–75; University of Southampton: Asst Registrar, 1976–79; Asst Sec., 1979–82; Sen. Asst Registrar, 1982–86; Dep. Registrar and Academic Sec., Univ. of Nottingham, 1986–91; Registrar, 1991–97, and Sec., 1996–97, Univ. of Kent at Canterbury. Dir, Univs and Colls Staff Develt Agency, 1996–2004. Governor: Hills Rd Sixth Form Coll., Cambridge, 2001–08 (Chm., 2003–08); Addenbrooke's Hosp. NHS Foundn Trust, 2004–07. *Publications:* articles in Jl of Chemical Soc. *Recreations:* music, natural history. *Address:* Wolfson College, Cambridge CB3 9BB. *Club:* Oxford and Cambridge.

MEAD, Prof. William Richard, FBA 1994; Professor and Head of Department of Geography, University College, London, 1966–81, now Emeritus Professor; *b* 29 July 1915; *s* of William Mead and Catharine Sarah Stevens; unmarried. *Educ:* Aylesbury Gram. Sch. (Foundation Governor, 1981–); London Sch. of Economics (Hon. Fellow 1979). PhD 1946, DSc(Econ) 1968, London. Served RAF, 1940–46. Asst Lectr and Lectr, University of Liverpool, 1947–49; Rockefeller Fellowship, held in Finland, 1949–50; Lectr, 1950, Reader, 1953, University Coll., London. Chm. Council, Sch. of Slavonic and E European Studies, 1978–80. Chm., Anglo-Finnish Soc., 1966–95; President: Inst. of British Geographers, 1971 (Hon. Mem., 1989); Geog. Assoc., 1981–82 (Hon. Mem., 1991); Bucks Archaeol. Soc., 2001–; Hon. Sec., Royal Geographical Society, 1967–77 (Vice Pres., 1977–81, Hon. Vice-Pres., 1981–). Pres., Crabtree Foundn, 1997–98. Brown Meml Lectr, Univ. of Minnesota, 1983. Hon. Member: Finnish Geog. Soc.; Fenno-Ugrian Soc.; Porthan Soc.; Sydsvenska geografiska sällskapet; Det norske Videnskaps. Akademi, 1976; Det Norske Geografiske Selskab; Foreign Mem., Finnish Acad. of Science and Letters. Gill Memorial Award, 1951, Founder's Medal, 1980, RGS; Wahlberg Gold Medal, Swedish Geographical Soc., 1983; Fennia Medal, Finnish Geographical Soc., 1988; Res. Medal, RSGS, 1988. Dr *hc*: University of Uppsala, 1966; Turku, 2003; DPhil *hc* Univ. of Helsinki, 1969; PhD *hc* Lund, 1987. Chevalier, Swedish Order of Vasa, 1962; Comdr, Orders of: Lion of Finland, 1963 (Chevalier, 1953); White Rose of Finland, 1976; Polar Star of Sweden, 1977. *Publications:* Farming in Finland, 1953; Economic Geography of Scandinavian States and Finland, 1958; (with Helmer Smeds) Winter in Finland, 1967; Finland (Modern Nations of the World Series), 1968; (with Wendy Hall) Scandinavia, 1972; The Scandinavian Northlands, 1973; (with Stig Jaatinen) The Åland Islands, 1974; An Historical Geography of Scandinavia, 1981; An Experience of Finland, 1993; Aylesbury: a personal memoir from the 1920s, 1996; Aylesbury Grammar School 1598–1998, 1997; A Celebration of Norway, 2002; Pehr Kalm: a Finnish visitor to the Chilterns 1748, 2003; Adopting Finland, 2006; other books on Norway, Sweden, Canada and USA. *Recreations:* riding, music. *Address:* 6 Lower Icknield Way, Aston Clinton, near Aylesbury, Bucks HP22 5JS.

MEADE, family name of **Earl of Clanwilliam.**

MEADE, Eric Cubitt, FCA; Senior Partner, Deloitte Haskins & Sells, Chartered Accountants, 1982–85; *b* 12 April 1923; *s* of William Charles Abbott Meade and Vera Alicia Maria Meade; *m* 1960, Margaret Arnott McCallum; two *s* one *d*. *Educ:* Ratcliffe College. FCA 1947. Served War, Hampshire Regt, 1942–46; N Africa, Italy, prisoner of war, 1944–45; Captain. Chartered Accountant, 1947. Mem. Council, Inst. of Chartered Accountants in England and Wales, 1969–79 (Chm., Parly and Law Cttee, 1974–76; Chm., Investigation Cttee, 1976–77); Chm., Consultative Cttee., Accountancy Bodies Ethics Cttee, 1977–83; Mem. Council, FIMBRA, 1986–87; Lay Mem., Solicitors Complaints Bureau, 1986–89; Mem., Audit Commn, 1986–89. *Recreations:* tennis, bowls. *Address:* 56 Hurlingham Court, Ranelagh Gardens, Fulham, SW6 3UP. *T:* (020) 7736 5382. *Club:* Hurlingham.

MEADE, Richard David; QC 2008; *b* London, 14 Nov. 1966; *s* of Prof. Thomas Wilson Meade, *qv*; *m* 2003, Sara Louise Payne; one *s* two *d*. *Educ:* William Ellis Sch., London; University Coll., Oxford (BA Juris.). Called to the Bar, Lincoln's Inn, 1991; in practice as barrister specialising in intellectual property, 1991–. *Publication:* (ed jtly) Kerly's Law of Trade Marks and Trade Names, 13th edn 2001, 14th edn 2005. *Recreations:* poker, family. *Address:* 8 New Square, Lincoln's Inn, WC2A 3QP. *Club:* Barracuda, Victoria Sporting.

MEADE, Richard John Hannay, OBE 1974; Bureau Member, and Chairman of Northern European Group of Nations, International Equestrian Federation, 1990–98; *b* 4 Dec. 1938; *s* of John Graham O'Mahony Meade and late Phyllis Brenda Meade; *m* 1977, Angela Dorothy Farquhar; two *s* one *d* (and one *s* decd). *Educ:* Lancing College; Magdalene College, Cambridge (Engineering Degree). Competed for GB in 3-day equestrian events, 1963–82; won 3 Olympic gold medals: team gold, 1968; team and individual gold, Munich, 1972; World Championships individual medals include: silver, Burghley, 1996; silver, Punchestown, 1970; World Championships team medals include: gold, Punchestown, 1970; gold, Luhmühlen, 1982; European Championships team medals include: gold, Punchestown, 1967; gold, Burghley, 1971; gold, Horsens, 1981; won Burghley 1964 and Badminton 1970 and 1982. Mem., 3-day Event Cttee, Internat. Equestrian Fedn, 1977–80; Pres., British Equestrian Fedn, 1989–92; Chairman: British Horse Foundn, 1991–; Internat. Eventing Officials Club, 2003–. *Publication:* Fit for Riding, 1984. *Address:* Church Farm, West Littleton, Chippenham, Wilts SN14 8JB. *T:* (01225) 891226.

MEADE, Prof. Thomas Wilson, DM; FRCP, FMedSci; FRS 1996; Emeritus Professor of Epidemiology, Department of Epidemiology and Population Health, London School of Hygiene and Tropical Medicine, since 2001; *b* 21 Jan. 1936; *s* of James Edward Meade, CB, FBA, and Elizabeth Margaret (*née* Wilson); *m* 1962, Helen Elizabeth Perks; one *s* two *d*. *Educ:* Westminster Sch.; Christ Church, Oxford; St Bartholomew's Hosp. Sen. Lectr, Dept of Public Health, LSHTM, 1968–70 (on secondment to Schieffelin Leprosy Research Sanatorium, S India, 1969–70); Dir, MRC Epidemiol. and Med. Care Unit, Northwick Park Hosp., then Wolfson Inst. of Preventive Medicine, 1970–2001, and Prof. of Epidemiol., St Bart's Hosp. Med. Coll., then St Bart's and The Royal London Hosp. Sch. of Medicine and Dentistry, 1992–2001, QMW. Member: MRC Physiological Systems and Disorders Bd, 1974–78; MRC Health Services Res. Panel and Cttee, 1981–90; Wellcome Trust Physiology and Pharmacology Panel, 1990–95; Council, Royal Soc., 1998–99. Founder FMedSci 1998. Internat. Balzan Prize, Fondazione Internazionale Premio E. Balzan, 1997; MRC Millennium Medal, 2002. *Publications:* papers on thrombosis and arterial disease. *Recreation:* allotment. *Address:* 28 Cholmeley Crescent, N6 5HA. *T:* (020) 8340 6260. *Club:* Leander (Henley-on-Thames).

See also R. D. Meade.

MEADES, Jonathan Turner; journalist, writer and television performer; *b* 21 Jan. 1947; *s* of late John William Meades and Margery Agnes Meades (*née* Hogg); *m* 1st, 1980, Sally Dorothy Renée (marr. diss. 1986), *d* of Raymond Brown; twin *d*; 2nd, 1988, Frances Anne (marr. diss. 1997), *d* of Sir William Bentley, KCMG; two *d*; 3rd, 2003, Colette Claudine Elizabeth, *d* of Michael Forder. *Educ:* King's Coll., Taunton; RADA; Bordeaux Univ. Editor, Event, 1981–82; Features Editor, Tatler, 1982–85; Restaurant Critic, The Times, 1986–2001. Columnist, The Times, 2001–05; contributor to magazines and newspapers, 1971–, including: Books and Bookmen, Time Out, Observer, Architects Jl, Sunday Times, Harpers and Queen, Vogue, Literary Review, Tatler, A La Carte, Independent, Sunday Correspondent, Mail on Sunday, Evening Standard. *Television: series:* The Victorian House, 1987; Abroad in Britain, 1991; Further Abroad, 1994; Even Further Abroad, 1997; Meades Eats, 2003; Abroad Again in Britain, 2006; Jonathan Meades: Abroad Again, 2007; Magnetic North, 2008; *films:* Jerry Building, 1994; Heart Bypass, 1998; Travels with Pevsner: Worcestershire, 1998; Victoria Died in 1901 and is Still Alive Today, 2001; tvSSFBM EHKL, 2001; Joebuilding, 2006; *film script:* L'Atlantide, 1991. *Publications:* This is Their Life, 1979; An Illustrated Atlas of the World's Great Buildings, 1980; Filthy English (short stories), 1984; Peter Knows what Dick Likes, 1989; Pompey (novel), 1993; The Fowler Family Business (novel), 2002; Incest and Morris Dancing, 2002. *Recreations:* buildings, mushrooms, woods. *Address:* c/o Capel and Land Ltd, 29 Wardour Street, W1D 6PS. *T:* (020) 7734 2414; *e-mail:* jtm.juvarra@orange.fr. *Clubs:* Groucho, Academy.

MEADOW, Sir (Samuel) Roy, Kt 1997; FRCP, FRCPE, FRCPCH; Professor and Head of Department of Paediatrics and Child Health, University of Leeds, 1980–98, now Emeritus Professor; *b* 9 June 1933; *m* 1st, 1962, Gillian Margaret Maclennan; one *s* one *d*; 2nd, 1978, Marianne Jane Harvey. *Educ:* Wigan Grammar Sch.; Bromsgrove Sch.; Worcester Coll., Oxford (BA Hons Physiol. 1957; MA, BM BCh 1960). DRCOG 1962; DCH 1963; MRCP 1964, FRCP 1974; FRCPE 1996; FRCPCH 1997. Partner GP, Banbury, 1962–64; junior appts at Guy's Hosp., Evelina Children's Hosp., Hosp. for Sick Children, London and Royal Alexandra Hosp., Brighton, 1964–67; MRC Sen. Res. Fellow, Birmingham Univ., 1967–68; Sen. Lectr and Consultant Paediatrician, Leeds Univ., 1970–80. Consultant Advr to CMO, DoH, 1997–2000. Blackwell Vis. Prof., NZ Paediatric Assoc., 1989; Kildorrory Lectr, Irish Paed. Assoc., 1987; Charles West Lectr, RCP, 1993. Chm., Assoc. for Child Psychology and Psychiatry, 1983–84; President: BPA, 1994–96 (Chm., Acad. Bd, 1990–94); RCPCH, 1996–97. Enuresis Resource and Inf. Centre, 1996–2004. Editor, Archives of Diseases in Childhood, 1979–87. Dawson Williams Prize, BMA, 1994; James Spence Medal, RCPCH, 1999. *Publications:* Lecture Notes on Paediatrics, 1973, 7th edn 2001; Bladder Control and Enuresis, 1973; The Child and His Symptoms, 1978; ABC of Child Abuse, 1989, 4th edn 2007; Paediatric Kidney Disease, 1992; reports and papers on teratogenicity of anticonvulsant drugs, Munchausen Syndrome by proxy child abuse, childhood urinary tract disorders and child abuse. *Recreation:* gardening.

MEADOWCROFT, Michael James; politician, writer and public affairs consultant; *b* 6 March 1942; marr. diss.; one *s* one *d*; *m* 2nd, 1987, Elizabeth Bee. *Educ:* King George V Sch., Southport; Bradford Univ. (MPhil 1978). Chm., Merseyside Regl Young Liberal Orgn, 1961; Liberal Party Local Govt Officer, 1962–67; Sec., Yorks Liberal Fedn, 1967–70; Asst Sec., Joseph Rowntree Social Service Trust, 1970–78; Gen. Sec., Bradford Metropolitan Council for Voluntary Service, 1978–83. Senior Vis. Fellow, PSI, 1989. Dir, Electoral Reform Consultancy Services, 1992–94. Columnist, Yorkshire Post, 2004–. Member: Leeds City Council, 1968–83; W Yorks MCC, 1973–76, 1981–83. Dir, Leeds Grand Theatre and Opera House, 1971–83. Chm., Liberal Party Assembly Cttee, 1977–81; Pres. Elect, 1987–88, Pres., 1993–2002, Liberal Party. Contested (L) Leeds W, Feb. and Oct. 1974, 1987, 1992. MP (L) Leeds W, 1983–87. Chm., Electoral Reform Soc., 1989–93. Has undertaken 48 missions to 35 new and emerging democracies; Co-ordinator: UN Electoral Assistance Secretariat, Malawi, 1994; OSCE Internat. Observer Mission, Russian Presidential elecn, 1996, Bulgaria, 1996, Bosnia Refugee Vote, 1996; EU Observation Unit, Suriname Nat. Assembly elecns, 2000; EU Chief Observer, Zambian Presidential elecns, 2001; Advr on Jerusalem, EU Electoral Unit, Palestinian Assembly elecns, 1995–96; Consultant, Cttee for Free and Fair Elections, Cambodia, 1997; European Co-Dir, EC Support to Democratic Electoral Process in Cambodia, 1998; Post-Electoral Advr, Indonesian Assembly elecns, 1999; Consultant to: EC's TACIS project in Uzbekistan, 2002; Indep. Electoral Commn, Dem. Rep. of Congo, 2004–05; Electoral Commn, Benin, 2006; Nat. Democratic Inst. project, Bangladesh, 2008. Hon. Alderman, City of Leeds, 2002. Chevalier, Commanderie de Faugères, 1998. *Publications:* Liberal Party Local Government Handbook (with Pratap Chitnis), 1963; Success in Local Government, 1971; Liberals and a Popular Front, 1974; Local Government Finance, 1975; A Manifesto for Local Government, 1975; The Bluffer's Guide to Politics, 1976; Liberal

Values for a New Decade, 1980; Social Democracy—Barrier or Bridge?, 1981; Liberalism and the Left, 1982; Liberalism and the Right, 1983; Liberalism Today and Tomorrow, 1989; The Politics of Electoral Reform, 1991; Diversity in Danger, 1992; The Case for the Liberal Party, 1992; (with E. Bee) Faugères: a guide to the Appellation, 1996, 3rd edn 2005 (French edn 2006); Focus on Freedom, 1997, 3rd edn 2001. *Recreations:* music (including jazz), French philately. *Address:* Waterloo Lodge, 72 Waterloo Lane, Bramley, Leeds LS13 2JF. *T:* (0113) 257 6232, *Fax:* (0113) 257 9009; *e-mail:* meadowcroft@bramley.demon.co.uk. *Clubs:* National Liberal (Hon. Librarian); Leeds (Chm., 2000–04), Armley Liberal, Bramley Liberal, Burley Liberal, Upper and Lower Wortley Liberal (Leeds).

MEADOWS, Prof. (Arthur) Jack, FInstP; FCLIP; Professor of Library and Information Studies, Loughborough University, 1986–2001, now Emeritus; *b* 24 Jan. 1934; *s* of Arthur Harold Meadows and Alice Elson; *m* 1958, Isobel Jane Tanner Bryant; one *s* two *d*. *Educ:* New Coll., Oxford (MA Physics; DPhil Astronomy); University Coll. London (MSc History and Philosophy of Science). Fulbright Schol., Vis. Fellow, Mt Wilson and Palomar Observatories, Asst Prof., Univ. of Illinois, 1959–61; Lectr, Univ. of St Andrews, 1961–63; Asst Keeper, British Mus., 1963–65; University of Leicester: Hd of Dept and Prof., Astronomy and History of Science Depts, 1965–86; Hd of Primary Communications Res. Centre, 1975–86; Hd of Office for Humanities Communication, 1982–86; Loughborough University: Hd, Library and Inf. Stats Unit, 1986–97; Hd, Computers in Teaching Initiative Centre for Liby and Inf. Studies, 1989–97; Pro-Vice-Chancellor, 1995–96. Hon. Life Vice-Pres., LA, 1995. Hon. FCLIP 2002. Hon. DSc City, 1995. *Publications:* Stellar Evolution, 1967; The High Firmament: a survey of astronomy in English literature, 1969; Early Solar Physics, 1970; Science and Controversy, 1972; Communication in Science, 1974; Greenwich Observatory: recent history (1836–1975), 1975; The Scientific Journal, 1979; (jtly) Dictionary of New Information Technology, 1982; (jtly) The Lamp of Learning: Taylor & Francis and the development of science publishing, 1984; (jtly) Maxwell's Equations and their Applications, 1985; Space Garbage, 1985; (jtly) Dictionary of Computing and Information Technology, 1987; The Origins of Information Science, 1987; (jtly) The History of Scientific Discovery, 1987; (jtly) Principles and Practice of Journal Publishing, 1987, rev. edn as Journal Publishing, 1997; Infotechnology, 1989; Innovation in Information, 1994; (jtly) Front Page Physics, 1994; (jtly) Project ELVYN, 1995; Communicating Research, 1998; Understanding Information, 2001; The Victorian Scientist, 2004; The Future of the Universe, 2007; about 250 articles. *Recreation:* sleeping in church services. *Address:* 47 Swan Street, Seagrave, Leics LE12 7NL. *T:* (01509) 812557.

MEADOWS, Graham David; Director General, Regional Policy, Commission of European Communities, 2004–06 (Director, 1989–2003; Acting Director General, 2003–04); *b* 17 Dec. 1941; *s* of late Albert Edward Meadows and Jessica Maude Titmus; two *d*. *Educ:* Edinburgh Univ. MA Hons Political Economy. Journalist, 1958–69, specialising latterly in agric. affairs; European corresp., Farmers' Weekly (based in Brussels), 1973–75; EC 1975–; Mem., agric. policy unit; adviser on agricl, fisheries and envmt policy, Office of Pres. of EEC (Gaston E. Thorn), 1981–84; Chef de Cabinet of Stanley Clinton Davis, Mem. of EEC responsible for transport, envmt and nuclear safety, 1985–89. *Recreations:* mountain walking, reading in the history of economic thought.

MEADOWS, Jack; *see* Meadows, A. J.

MEADOWS, Pamela Catherine, (Mrs P. A. Ormerod); Visiting Fellow, National Institute of Economic and Social Research, since 1998; Chairman, Synergy Research and Consulting, since 2004; *b* 9 Jan. 1949; *d* of late Sidney James Meadows, OBE and of Hilda Catherine (*née* Farley); *m* 1975, Paul Andrew Ormerod; one *s*. *Educ:* Kenya High Sch., Nairobi; Penrhos Coll., Colwyn Bay; Univ. of Durham (BA Econs 1970); Birkbeck Coll., Univ. of London (MSc Econs 1978). Research Officer, NIESR, 1970–74; Sen. Econ. Asst, then Econ. Advr, Home Office, 1974–78; Department of Employment: Econ. Advr, 1978–88; Grade 5, 1988–92; Chief Economic Advr, and Hd of Econs, Res. and Evaluation Div., 1992–93; Dir, PSI, 1993–98. Vis. Prof., Arbetslivsinstitutet, Stockholm, 1998–2000. Mem., Better Regulation Task Force, 1997–2000. Trustee, Employment Policy Inst., 1995–2000; Mem. Exec. Cttee, Public Mgt and Policy Assoc., 1998–2001. Gov., Birkbeck Coll., 1997–2001. *Address:* c/o National Institute of Economic and Social Research, 2 Dean Trench Street, Smith Square, SW1P 3HE.

MEADWAY, (Richard) John, PhD; Under Secretary, Department of Trade and Industry, 1989–96; *b* 30 Dec. 1944; *s* of late Norman Pardey Meadway and of Constance Meadway (now Kellaway); *m* 1968, Rev. Dr Jeanette Valerie (*née* Partis); two *d*. *Educ:* Collyer's Sch., Horsham; Peterhouse, Cambridge (MA NatScis); Edinburgh Univ. (PhD); Oxford Univ. (MA). Asst Principal, Min. of Technology, 1970; Private Secretary: to Minister for Trade and Consumer Affairs, 1973; to Sec. of State for Prices and Consumer Protection, 1974; to the Prime Minister, 1976–78; Asst Sec., Dept of Trade, later DTI, 1979–89; Hd of Overseas Trade Div. 2, 1989–94, Hd of Export Control and Non-Proliferation Div., 1994–96, DTI. UK Gov., IAEA, 1994–96. Dir of Fitness to Practise, GMC, 1997–98. Chm., Newham Mind, 1998–2003. Trustee, Refugee Legal Centre, 1999–2006. FRSA 1995. *Publications:* papers on the amino-acid sequences of proteins. *Recreations:* reading, travel. *Address:* 4 Glebe Avenue, Woodford Green, Essex IG8 9HB. *T:* (020) 8504 1958. *Club:* Reform.

MEAGER, Michael Anthony; Director of Estates, Department of Health, 1989–91; *b* 15 Feb. 1931; *s* of Arthur Pattison Meager and Dora Edith Meager (*née* Greeves); *m* 1954, Val Cranmer Benson, *d* of H. C. Benson; two *s* one *d*. *Educ:* Royal Naval Coll., Dartmouth; Clacton County High Sch.; Architectural Assoc. Sch. of Architecture. ARIBA 1955; AADip 1956. National Service, RE, 1955–57: commnd 1956, served Cyprus, 1956–57. HMOCS, Kenya, 1958–63; architect in private practice, 1964–66; Department of Health (formerly MoH and DHSS), 1966–91: Chief Arch., 1986–88; Dir of Health Building, 1988–89. *Club:* Royal Over-Seas League.

MEAGHER, Prof. Thomas Robert, PhD; Professor of Plant Biology, since 1999, and Director, Centre for Evolution, Genes and Genomics, since 2004, University of St Andrews; *b* Oakland, Calif, 23 Nov. 1952; *s* of William Richard Meagher and Martha Meagher (*née* Bischoff); *m* 1977, Dr Laura Reinertsen. *Educ:* Univ. of S Florida (BA Hons Botany 1973); Duke Univ., N Carolina (PhD 1978). Duke University: teaching asst, Botany Dept, 1973–74; NIH Grad. traineeship, Univ. Prog. in Genetics, 1974–78; Res. Associate, 1978–82, Res. Scientist, 1983, Botany Dept; Temp. Instructor, Zool. Dept, 1984; Res. Scientist, Botany Dept, 1984–87; Asst Prof., 1987–90, Associate Prof., 1990–98, Prof., 1998–99, Rutgers Univ. Fulbright Schol., Dept of Pure Maths and Math. Stats, Univ. of Cambridge, 1982–83. Vis. Scientist, Univ. of Edinburgh, Royal Botanic Gdn, 1995–96; Hon. Prof., Scottish Crop Res. Inst., 2003–. Member: Sci. Adv. Council, DEFRA, 2004–; NERC, 2007–. *Publications:* contributor: Plant Reproductive Ecology: patterns and strategies, 1988; Sexual Dimorphism in Plants, 1999; (with C. Vassiliadis) Genes in the Environment, 2003; contrib. learned jls incl. Amer. Naturalist, Amer. Jl of Botany, Annals of Botany, Biological Conservation, Biological Jl Linnean Soc., Conservation Letters, Crop Sci., Ecology, Ecol. Applications, Evolution, Evolutionary Ecology Res., Genetics, Genetic Res., Heredity, Jl of Evolutionary Biology, New Phytology, Phil Transactions of Royal Soc., Theoretical Applied Genetics. *Recreation:* French horn (Mem., Scottish Vienna Horn Soc.). *Address:* School of Biology, University of St Andrews, St Andrews, Fife KY16 9TH. *T:* (01334) 463364, *Fax:* (01334) 463366; *e-mail:* trm3@st-and.ac.uk.

MEAKINS, Prof. Jonathan Larmonth, OC 2000; MD; DSc; Nuffield Professor of Surgery, University of Oxford, 2002–08; Fellow, Balliol College, Oxford, since 2002; *b* 8 Jan. 1941; *s* of Jonathan Fayette Meakins and Mildred Dawson Meakins (*née* Larmonth); *m* 1972, Dr Jacqueline McClaran. *Educ:* McGill Univ. (BSc 1966); Univ. of Western Ontario (MD 1966); Univ. of Cincinnati (DSc 1972). Royal Victoria Hospital, Montreal: Consultant Surgeon, 1974–2002; Surgeon in Chief, 1988–98; McGill University: Asst Prof. of Surgery and Microbiol., 1974–79; Associate Prof., 1979–81; Prof. of Surgery and Microbiol., 1981–2002; Prof. of Surgery, 1988–93 and 1998–2002; Surgeon in Chief, McGill Univ. Health Centre, 1998–2002. Regent, 1993–2002, Vice Chair, 2000–02, Amer. Coll. of Surgeons. KM 1993. *Publications:* Surgical Infection in Critical Care Medicine, 1985; (with J. C. McClaran) Surgical Care of the Elderly, 1988; (jtly) ACS Surgery: principles and practice, 1988, 5th edn 2003; (jtly) Host Defence Dysfunction in Trauma, Shock and Sepsis: mechanisms and therapeutic approaches, 1993; Surgical Infections: diagnosis and treatment, 1994. *Recreations:* tennis, golf, gardening, cooking, art history. *Address:* The Linton, 1509 Sherbrooke Street West, Montreal, QC H3G 1M1, Canada. *Clubs:* University (Montreal); Royal Montreal Golf, Montreal Indoor Tennis; Frilford Heath Golf (Oxford).

MEALE, (Joseph) Alan; MP (Lab) Mansfield, since 1987; *b* 31 July 1949; *s* of late Albert Henry and Elizabeth Meale; *m* 1983, Diana Gilhespy; one *s* one *d*. *Educ:* St Joseph's RC School; Ruskin College, Oxford; Sheffield Hallam Univ. (MA 1997). Seaman, British Merchant Navy, 1964–68; engineering worker, 1968–75; Nat. Employment Develt Officer, NACRO, 1977–80; Asst to Gen. Sec., ASLEF, 1980–83; Parly and Political Advisor to Michael Meacher, MP, 1983–87. An Opposition Whip, 1992–94; PPS to Dep. Leader of Lab. Party, 1994–97, to Dep. Prime Minister, 1997–98; Parly Under-Sec. of State, DETR, 1998–99. Mem., Select Cttee on Home Affairs, 1989–92; Treas., Parly All Party Football Gp, 1989; Chm., British Cyprus Cttee, 1992–; Treas., British Section, CPA Cyprus Gp. Member: Parly Court of Referees; MSF Parly Cttee, 1997–. Mem., Commonwealth War Graves Commn, 2002–. *Recreations:* reading, writing. *Address:* 85 West Gate, Mansfield, Notts NG18 1RT. *T:* (01623) 660531; House of Commons, SW1A 0AA. *Clubs:* Woodhouse Working Men's, Bellamy Road Working Men's, Mansfield Town Association Football (Mansfield).

MEANTI, Dr Luigi; Chairman, ENI SpA, Rome, 1993–96; *b* Milan, 14 Aug. 1928; *m*; two *s*. *Educ:* Poly. of Milan (Dr Ing). Asst Prof., Poly. of Milan, 1954–57; SNAM SpA, Milan: mem. staff, R&D dept, 1958–65; with gas planning dept, 1966–69; Dep. Gen. Manager, 1970–72; Gen. Manager, 1973–80; Vice-Pres. and Man. Dir, 1981–91; Hon. Pres., 1991–. Pres., Internat. Gas Union, Zürich, 1991–94; Vice Pres., EUROGAS, 1991–93. Hon. Member: IGasE, 1992; Assoc. Technique de l'Industrie du Gaz, Paris, 1993.

MEAR, Stephen; choreographer; *b* 19 Feb. 1964; *s* of Albert and Fay Mear; partner, Mark Smith. *Educ:* London Studio Centre. Dancer, later dance captain, in West End musicals, incl. 42nd Street, Cats, Follies, Some Like It Hot, Anything Goes, 1984–90; choreographer: Of Thee I Sing, Bridewell, 1999; A Little Night Music, Bouncers; Woman in Love; Grapevine (world première); Shakers; Love Off the Shelf; Snoopy; Grease; Ruthie Henshall in Concert; She Loves Me (Canada); Gary Wilmot's Showstoppers Tour; Whitelight Tradeshow; Singin' in the Rain, W Yorks Playhouse, NT and tour, 2000; Stepping Out, Half a Sixpence, W Yorks Playhouse, 2000; (with Bob Avian) The Witches of Eastwick, Th. Royal, Drury Lane, 2001; Don Giovanni, Royal Opera House, 2002; Honk, Japan; The Three Musketeers, Germany, 2003; Anything Goes, NT and Th. Royal, Drury Lane, 2003–04; Tonight's the Night, Victoria Palace, 2004; Acorn Antiques, Th. Royal, Haymarket, 2005; Putting It Together, Just So and How to Succeed..., Chichester Fest. Th., 2005; On the Town, ENO, 2005; (with Matthew Bourne) Mary Poppins, Prince Edward, 2005 (Olivier Award for Best Choreography); Sinatra at the Palladium, 2006. *Recreations:* theatre, film, music. *Address:* *e-mail:* mearstephen@hotmail.com.

MEARA, Rev. Canon David Gwynne; Rector, St Bride's Church, Fleet Street, since 2000; *b* 30 June 1947; *s* of Gwynne and Winifred Meara; *m* 1973, Rosemary Anne, *d* of John and Audrey Alexander; two *s* two *d*. *Educ:* Merchant Taylors' Sch., Northwood; Oriel Coll., Oxford (BA Lit. Hum. 1970; BA Theol. 1972; MA 1973); Cuddesdon Theol Coll., Oxford. Lambeth Dip. 1975. Ordained deacon, 1973, priest, 1974; Curate, Christchurch, Reading, 1973–77; Chaplain, Univ. of Reading, 1977–82; Vicar, Basildon, Aldworth and Ashampstead, 1982–94; RD, Bradfield, 1990–94; Rector, 1994–2000, Area Dean, 1996–2000, Buckingham. Sec., 1980–2000, Chm., 1990–2000, Oxford Diocesan Adv. Gp on Mission; Mem., Oxford DAC, 1998–2000. Hon. Canon, Christ Church Cathedral, Oxford, 1997–; Chaplain: Co. of Stationers and Newspaper Makers, 2000–; Co. of Marketors, 2000–; Co. of Turners, 2001–; Publicity Club of London, 2001–; London Press Club, 2001–. Chaplain, Co. of Spectacle Makers, 2006–07. Pres., Monumental Brass Soc., 2002–. FSA 1994; FRSA 2001. *Publications:* The Foundation of St Augustine at Reading, 1982; Victorian Memorial Brasses, 1983; A. W. N. Pugin and the Revival of Memorial Brasses, 1991; Modern Memorial Brasses, 2008; *contributions to:* Blue Guide to English Parish Churches, (Berkshire), 1985; Catalogue of Pugin Exhibition, V & A Mus., 1994; Catalogue of Pugin Exhibition, NY, 1995; Monumental Brasses as Art and History, 1996. *Recreations:* church-crawling, opera, theatre, art galleries, amateur dramatics, malt whisky. *Address:* St Bride's Rectory, Fleet Street, EC4Y 8AU. *T:* (020) 7427 0133. *Club:* Athenæum.

MEARS, Dr Adrian Leonard, CBE 2005; CPhys, FInstP; Chairman, Scienogy Ltd, since 2005; *b* 27 May 1944; *s* of Leonard Mears and Marjorie (*née* Isaac); *m* 1969, Barbara Bayne; two *s*. *Educ:* Highgate Sch.; Christ Church, Oxford (DPhil, MA). Res. Associate, Univ. of Md, USA, 1969–71; joined RRE (later Royal Signals and Radar Establishment), 1971: worked on display technology, optoelectronics and lasers, 1971–81; Hd, Signal Processing, 1981–86; Dir of Science (Comd, Control, Communications and Inf. Systems), MoD, 1987–89; Dep. Dir and Commercial Dir, RSRE, 1990–91; Tech. and Quality Dir, DRA, 1991–95; Tech. Dir, 1995–2001, Chief Knowledge Officer, 1998–2000, DERA; Tech. Dir and Chief Tech. Officer, QinetiQ, 2001–04. *Recreations:* walking, theatre, music. *Address:* Scienogy Ltd, 21 Collum End Rise, Leckhampton, Glos GL53 0PA. *T:* (01242) 521050.

MEARS, Rt Rev. John Cledan; Bishop of Bangor, 1983–92; *b* 8 Sept. 1922; *s* of Joseph and Anna Lloyd Mears; *m* 1949, Enid Margaret; one *s* one *d*. *Educ:* Univ. of Wales, Aberystwyth (BA Philosophy 1943); Wycliffe Hall, Oxford; St Deiniol's Library, Hawarden. MA Wales 1948 (research, Blaise Pascal). Deacon 1947, priest 1948, St Asaph; Curate: Mostyn, 1947–49; Rhosllannerchrugog, 1949–55; Vicar of Cwm, 1955–58; Lecturer, St Michael's Coll., Llandaff and Univ. of Wales, Cardiff, 1959–73; Chaplain,

1959–67; Sub-warden, 1967–73; Vicar of St Mark's, Gabalfa, Cardiff, 1973–82. Examining Chaplain, 1960–73; Hon. Canon of Llandaff Cathedral, 1981–82; Sec. of Governing Body, Church in Wales, 1977–82. *Publications:* reviews in Theology, articles in Efrydiau Athronyddol, Diwynyddiaeth, and Barn. *Recreations:* hiking, mountaineering. *Address:* 25 Avon Ridge, Thornhill, Cardiff CF14 9AU. *T:* (029) 2061 5505.

MEARS, Martin John Patrick; solicitor in private practice; President of the Law Society, 1995–96; *b* 12 Feb. 1940; *s* of J. F. Mears and E. Mears; seven *c. Educ:* St Illtyd's College, Cardiff; Wadham Coll., Oxford (MA, BCL). Solicitor, 1966. Editor, legal satirical jl, Caterpillar. *Publications:* numerous articles in national, regional and legal press. *Recreations:* Law Society, journalism, travel, reading. *Address:* Mears Hobbs & Durrant, 6 Queen Street, Great Yarmouth, Norfolk NR30 2QP; Old Rectory, Haddiscoe, Norwich NR14 6PG. *Clubs:* Oxford and Cambridge; Norfolk (Norwich).

MEATH, 15th Earl of, *cr* 1627; **John Anthony Brabazon;** Baron Ardee (Ire.) 1616; Baron Chaworth (UK) 1831; *b* 11 May 1941; *er s* of 14th Earl of Meath, and of Elizabeth Mary (*née* Bowlby); *S* father, 1998; *m* 1973, Xenia Goudime; one *s* two *d. Educ:* Harrow. Page of Honour to the Queen, 1956–58. Served Grenadier Guards, 1960–63. *Heir: s* Lord Ardee, *qv. Address:* Killruddery, Bray, Co. Wicklow, Ireland.

MEATH, Bishop of, (RC), since 1990; **Most Rev. Michael Smith;** *b* 6 June 1940; *s* of John Smith and Bridget Fagan. *Educ:* Gilson Endowed Sch., Oldcastle; St Finian's Coll., Mullingar; Lateran Univ., Rome (DCL 1966). Ordained priest, 1963; Curate, Clonmellon, 1967–68; Chaplain: St Loman's Hosp., 1968–74; Sacred Heart Hosp., 1975–84; Auxiliary Bp of Meath, 1984–88; Coadjutor Bp of Meath, 1988–90. Diocesan Sec., dio. of Meath, 1968–84; Sec., Irish Bishops' Conf., 1984– (Asst Sec., 1970–84). *Recreations:* golf, walking. *Address:* Bishop's House, Dublin Road, Mullingar, Co. Westmeath, Ireland. *T:* (44) 48841, 42038, *Fax:* (44) 43020; *e-mail:* bishop@dioceseofmeath.ie.

MEATH AND KILDARE, Bishop of, since 1996; **Most Rev. Richard Lionel Clarke,** PhD; *b* 25 June 1949; *s* of Dudley Hall Clarke and Norah Constance (*née* Quine); *m* 1975, Linda Margaret Thompson; one *s* one *d. Educ:* Trinity Coll., Dublin (MA 1979; PhD 1990); King's Coll., London (BD 1975). Ordained deacon, 1975, priest, 1976; Assistant Curate: Holywood, Down, 1975–77; St Bartholomew with Christ Church, Leeson Park, Dublin, 1977–79; Dean of Residence, Trinity Coll., Dublin, 1979–84; Rector, Bandon Union of Parishes, dio. of Cork, 1984–93; Dean of Cork and Incumbent of St Fin Barre's Union of Parishes, Cork, 1993–96. *Publications:* And Is It True?, 2000; A Whisper of God, 2006. *Recreation:* music. *Address:* Bishop's House, Moyglare, Maynooth, Co. Kildare, Ireland. *T:* (1) 6289354.

MEDAWAR, His Honour Nicholas Antoine Macbeth; QC 1984; a Circuit Judge, 1987–2005; *b* 25 April 1933; *e s* of Antoine Medawar and Innes (*née* Macbeth); *m* 1st, 1962, Joyce Catherine (*née* Crosland-Boyle) (marr. diss. 1977); one *s* (one *d* decd); 2nd, 1977, (Caroline) Mary, *d* of Harry Samuel Collins, of Nottingham and Buckley. *Educ:* Keswick Grammar School; Trinity College, Dublin (BA Mod., LLB); Hague Acad. of Internat. Law (dip.). Called to the Bar, Gray's Inn, 1957. Nat. Service, RASC, 1957–59, 2nd Lieut. In practice at the common law bar, 1959–87; Recorder of the Crown Court, 1985–87; Dep. High Court Judge, 1987–2005. A Legal Assessor, Gen. Optical Council, 1984–87. Mem. Ethnic Minorities Adv. Cttee, Judicial Studies Bd, 1993–96. Non-exec. Dir, Cine Tele Sound Ltd, 1959–72. *Recreations:* divers. *Address:* 2/11 Wedderburn Road, Hampstead, NW3 5QS.

MEDD, David Leslie, OBE 1964; Consultant Architect, Department for Education (formerly Department of Education and Science), since 1978; *b* 5 Nov. 1917; *s* of Robert Tate Medd and Dorothy (*née* Rogers); *m* 1949, Mary Beaumont Crowley, OBE, architect (*d* 2005). *Educ:* Oundle; Architectural Assoc. (AA Dip. Hons). ARIBA 1941. Architects' Dept, Herts CC, 1946–49. Develt Gp, Architects and Building Br., Min. of Educn, later DES, 1949–78; private architectural work, 1978–. Commonwealth Fund Fellowship, 1958–59. Hon. DSc: Edinburgh, 1974; Hull, 1993. SADG Medal (France), 1941; Distinguished Service Certificate, BSI, 1992. *Publications:* School Furniture, 1981; contrib. to numerous learned jls, incl. HMSO building bulletins. *Recreations:* art, music, furniture making, gardening. *Address:* 5 Pennyfathers Lane, Harmer Green, Welwyn, Herts AL6 0EN. *T:* (01438) 714654. *Club:* Royal Over-Seas League.

MEDHURST, Brian; Managing Director (International Division), Prudential Corporation plc, 1985–94; *b* 18 March 1935; *s* of late Eric Gilbert Medhurst and Bertha May (*née* Kinggett); *m* 1960, Patricia Anne Beer; two *s* one *d. Educ:* Godalming Grammar Sch.; Trinity Coll., Cambridge (MA). FIA 1962 (Mem. Council, 1982–87). Joined Prudential Assurance Co. Ltd, 1958; Deputy Investment Manager, 1972; Investment Manager, 1975; Jt Chief Investment Manager, 1981; Gen. Manager, 1982. *Recreations:* chess, golf, piano duets, tree felling. *Address:* Woodcroft, Yelverton, Devon PL20 6HY. *T:* (01822) 853337. *Clubs:* North Hants Golf, Yelverton Golf.

MEDINA, Earl of; Henry David Louis Mountbatten; *b* 19 Oct. 1991; *s* and *heir* of Marquess of Milford Haven, *qv*.

MEDLEY, George Julius, OBE 1989; Director, WWF-UK (World Wide Fund for Nature) (formerly World Wildlife Fund (UK)), 1978–93; *b* 2 Aug. 1930; *s* of late Brig. Edgar Julius Medley, DSO, OBE, MC and Norah Medley (*née* Templer); *m* 1952, Vera Frances Brand; one *s* one *d. Educ:* Winchester College; Wye College, Univ. of London. BSc (Hort.). Fruit farmer, 1952–56; Manager, Chemical Dept, Harrisons & Crosfield, Colombo, 1957–63; Dir, Fisons (Ceylon), 1960–63; Tech. Develt Manager, Tata Fison, Bangalore, 1963–64; Gen. Manager Pesticides Div., Tata Fison Industries, Bombay, 1964–68; Sales Manager, Western Hemisphere, Agrochemicals, Fisons Internat. Div., 1968–69; Overseas Manager, Fisons Agrochemical Div., 1970–71; Dep. Managing Dir, Glaxo Labs, India, 1972–73, Managing Dir, 1973–77. Chm., Alexis Productions Ltd, 1994–98; Director: Edward Jewson Services to Charities Ltd, 1993–2001; Tisbury Halls, 2006–. Member: Radioactive Waste Management Adv. Cttee, 1991–98; UK Ecolabelling Bd, 1995–99. Vice-Pres., Organisation of Pharmaceutical Producers of India, 1974–77; Founder Mem. and Vice-Chm., Inst. of Charity Fundraising Managers, 1983 (Chm., 1984–85); Treasurer: Wilts Country Markets Ltd (formerly Wilts WI Market Soc.), 1993–99, 2004–07; Wilts Wildlife Trust, 1994–99 (Pres., 1999–2003); Trustee: Farming and Wildlife Adv. Gp, 1984–93; Internat. Inst. for Envmt and Develt, 1989–93; Falkland Islands Foundn, 1985–92. Mem., Tisbury Parish Council, 2001–07 (Vice-Chm., 2002–07). FCMI; FICFM 1988. Officer, Order of Golden Ark (Netherlands), 1993. *Publications:* contrib. to Strategic Planning Soc. Jl. *Recreations:* gardening, DIY. *Address:* Hoddinotts House, Tisbury, Wilts SP3 6QQ. *T:* (01747) 870677.

MEDLICOTT, Michael Geoffrey; Chief Executive (formerly Managing Director), Servus (formerly Opus) Holdings plc, 1997–2001; *b* 2 June 1943; *s* of Geoffrey Henry Medlicott and Beryl Ann Medlicott (*née* Burchell); *m* 1st, 1973, Diana Grace Fallaw (marr. diss. 1998); one *s* three *d*; 2nd, 1999, Susan Caroline Whittall. *Educ:* Downside School; Lincoln College, Oxford (Scholar; MA). Management Trainee, P&O-Orient Lines, 1965–66; Shipping Asst, Mackinnon, Mackenzie & Co., Bombay, 1966–68, Tokyo, 1968–69; Asst to Management, P&O-Orient Lines, 1969–71; P&O Cruises: Develt Analyst, 1971–73; Asst Fleet Manager, 1973–75; Gen. Manager, Fleet, 1975–80; Gen. Manager, Europe, 1980–83; Dir, Europe, 1983–86; Man. Dir, Swan Hellenic, 1983–86; Man. Dir, P&O Air Holidays, 1980–86; Dir, P&O Travel, 1980–84; Chief Exec., BTA, 1986–93; Vice Pres., Europe, 1993–96, Europe and Asia, 1996–97, Delta Airlines Inc. Chairman: Delta Aeroflot Travel Enterprises (Moscow), 1996–97; Servus Facilities Mgt Ltd, 1998–2001; Servus b2b Ltd, 2000–01; Transaction Dir, Nomura Internat. Principal Finance Gp, 1997–2000; Director: Deltair UK Investments, 1995–96; Lesteris Ltd, 1995–96; Gatwick Handling Internat. Ltd, 1995–96; Grand Facilities Mgt Holdings Ltd, 1998–2000; Member, Board: Manchester Airport plc, 2002–04; Manchester Airports Gp plc, 2004–; John Laing plc, 2004–06; Laing Rail Ltd, 2006–08; M&O Trains Ltd, 2006–08; OCS Gp Ltd, 2006– (Chm., Audit Cttee, 2008–); Chairman: Investors Cttee, ING REIM Ltd Infrastructure Fund, 2007–; Caring Homes Gp, 2008–. Chm., European Travel Commn, 1992–93 (Chm., Planning Cttee, 1990–92). Member: Council of Management: Passenger Shipping Assoc., 1983–86; Heritage of London Trust, 1987–; London Tourist Bd, 1992–93; Council, Tidy Britain Gp, 1988–; Bd, British-Amer. Chamber of Commerce, 1996–97; Bd, Nat. Savings & Investments, HM Treasury, 2003– (Chm., Audit Cttee, 2005–07; Appts and Remuneration Cttee, 2007–). Member: Adv. Panel, Languages Lead Body, Dept of Employment, 1990–93; Adv. Council, Univ. of Surrey Tourism Dept, 1991–; Hon. Bd, Univ. Center of Hellenic and European Studies, Piraeus, 1994–. Trustee, British Travel & Educnl Trust, 1986–93. LEA Gov., Ecchinswell and Sydmonton C of E Primary Sch., 1999–2003. Mem., Royal Philatelic Soc. FRSA 1986. CRAeS 1994. Queen Mother's Birthday Award for Envmtl Improvement, 1993, 1995. *Publications:* (contrib.) Facility Management: risks and opportunities, 2000; contribs to British West Indies Study Circle Bulletin, 1970–. *Recreations:* philately, opera, travelling in perfect company. *Club:* Oxford and Cambridge.

MEDLYCOTT, Sir Mervyn (Tregonwell), 9th Bt *cr* 1808, of Ven House, Somerset; *b* 20 Feb. 1947; *s* of Thomas Anthony Hutchings Medlycott (*d* 1970) (2nd *s* of 7th Bt) and Cecilia Mary Medlycott, *d* of late Major Cecil Harold Eden; *S* uncle, 1986. Genealogist; FSG 1990; Pres., Somerset and Dorset Family History Soc., 1986– (Founder and Hon. Sec., 1975–77; Chm., 1977–84; Vice-Pres., 1984–86). *Heir:* none. *Address:* The Manor House, Sandford Orcas, Sherborne, Dorset DT9 4SB. *T:* (01963) 220206.

MEDVEDEV, Dmitry Anatolyevich, PhD; President of Russia, since 2008; *b* Leningrad, 14 Sept. 1965; *m* Svetlana Vladimirovna; one *s. Educ:* Leningrad State Univ. (PhD Law 1990). Lectr, St Petersburg State Univ., 1990–99; Advr to Chm., Leningrad CC, 1990–95; Expert Consultant to Cttee for Ext. Affairs, St Petersburg City Hall, 1990–95; Dep. Govt COS, 1999; Dep. COS, 1999–2000, First Dep. COS, 2000–03, COS, 2003–05, Presidential Exec. Office; First Dep. Prime Minister, 2005–08. Chm., 2000–01 and 2002–, Dep. Chm., 2001–02, OAO Gazprom. *Address:* Office of the President, The Kremlin, Kremlevskaya Naberezhnaya, Moscow 103073, Russia.

MEDWAY, Lord; John Jason Gathorne-Hardy; *b* 26 Oct. 1968; *s* and *heir* of 5th Earl of Cranbrook, *qv*.

MEEK, Elizabeth Jane, CBE 2000; Regional Director, Government Office for the North West, since 2008; *b* 5 Sept. 1950; *d* of Patrick and Gladys Cox; *m* 1975, Innes Meek; three *d. Educ:* John Port Sch., Etwall, Derbyshire; Univ. of Exeter (BA Hons English). Joined Civil Service (fast stream entry), 1972; Department of the Environment, then of Environment, Transport and the Regions, subseq. for Transport, Local Government and the Regions: Asst Private Sec. to Sec. of State, DoE, 1978–79; First Sec., British High Commn, Lagos, 1979–81 (on secondment); Govt link with Manchester Olympic Bid, 1991–93; Hd, London Policy Unit, 1993–94; Hd, Strategy and Co-ordination Unit, 1994–97, Dir, GLA Div. (setting up Mayor and Assembly of London), 1997–2000, Govt Office for London; Interim Dir Communications and Public Affairs, Transport for London, 2000–01 (on secondment); Regl Dir, Govt Office for London, 2001–07. *Publication:* Survive Lagos, 1982. *Recreations:* mountain walking, ski-ing. *Address:* Government Office for the North West, City Tower, Piccadilly Plaza, Manchester M1 4BE. *T:* (0161) 952 4002, *Fax:* (0161) 952 4004; *e-mail:* liz.meek@gonw.gsi.gov.uk.

MEEK, Marshall, CBE 1989; RDI 1986; FREng, FRINA; Chairman, Argonautics Maritime Technologies Ltd, 1995–2002; Director, North of England (formerly European) Microelectronics Institute, 1996–2002; President, Royal Institution of Naval Architects, 1990–93 (Vice President, 1979–90); *b* 22 April 1925; *s* of Marshall Meek and Grace R. Smith; *m* 1957, Elfrida M. Cox; three *d. Educ:* Bell Baxter School, Cupar; Glasgow University (BSc Naval Arch. 1946). FIES 1963; FREng (FEng 1990). Caledon Shipbuilding Co., 1942–49; Asst Naval Architect, BSRA, 1949–53; Naval Architect, Ocean Fleets, 1953–79 (Dir, 1964–79); Head of Ship Technology, British Shipbuilders, 1979–84; Managing Dir, National Maritime Inst., 1984–85; Dep. Chm., British Maritime Technology, 1985–86. Visiting Professor in Naval Architecture: Strathclyde Univ., 1972–83; UCL, 1983–86. Mem., Lloyds Register of Shipping Technical Cttee, 1979–2001. Chm., Marine Technology Bd, 1984–88; Member: Defence Scientific Adv. Council, 1989–94; Marine and Coastguard Agency (formerly Surveyor General's, then Marine Safety Agency) Res. Cttee, Dept of Transport, 1992–98; Cadland (Royal Yacht replacement) Cttee, 1996–2000. Pres., NECInst., 1984–86. Chm., NE Coast Engrg Trust, 1994–96. Master, RDI, 1997–99. Mem., Northumberland Br., Gideons International in UK, 1986– (Chm., 2000–03); Trustee, Northumberland and Newcastle upon Tyne Police Court Mission Fund, 1990–. JP City of Liverpool, 1977–79. FRSA 1968 (Mem. Council, 1995–99; Vice Pres., 1997–99; Mem., Design Adv. Gp, 1997–99; Chm., Student Engrg Design Award Panel, 1997–2000; Chm., NE Reg., 1992–97). Hon. DSc Strathclyde, 2005. *Publications:* There Go the Ships (memoirs), 2003, 2nd edn 2007; numerous papers to RINA and other marine jls. *Recreations:* gardening, reading, church activities. *Address:* Coppers, Hillside Road, Rothbury, Morpeth, Northumberland NE65 7PT. *T:* (01669) 621403. *Club:* Caledonian.

MEEK, Stephen Donald Andrew; Principal, Geelong Grammar School, Australia, since 2004; *b* 27 Nov. 1952; *s* of George Edward Meek and Joan Meek; *m* 1987, Christine Sanders; two *s. Educ:* St John's Sch., Leatherhead; St Andrews Univ. (MA 1st Cl. Hons Mediaeval and Modern Hist.); Worcester Coll., Oxford (PGCE). History teacher, Dulwich Coll., 1978–85; Sherborne School, 1985–95: Hd of Hist., 1985–90; Housemaster, School House, 1990–95; Headmaster, Hurstpierpoint Coll., 1995–2004. *Recreations:* house in France, golf, bridge. *Address:* Geelong Grammar School, 50 Biddlecombe Avenue, Corio, Vic 3214, Australia. *T:* (3) 52739247; *e-mail:* principal@ggs.vic.edu.au.

MEEK, Stephen Graham; Director of Strategy, Department for Children, Schools and Families (formerly Department for Education and Skills), since 2006; *b* 4 Aug. 1965; *s* of Gerald Arthur Meek and Judith Ann Meek; *m* 1994, Juliet Louise Greer; one *s* (and one *s* decd). *Educ:* Rugby Sch.; Univ. of Edinburgh (MA Hons Pols and Hist. 1988); Univ. of Essex (MA Philos. 1989). HM Treasury, 1992–2005: Private Sec. to Economic Sec.,

1994–95; Policy Advr, Social Security Team, 1997–2000; Hd, Home Financial Services Team, 2001–03; Hd, Educn, Trng and Culture Team, 2003–05; Prog. Dir for Children and Young People, LGA, 2005–06. *Address:* Department for Children, Schools and Families, Sanctuary Buildings, Great Smith Street, SW1P 3BT. *T:* 0870 001 2345; *e-mail:* stephen.meek@dcsf.gsi.gov.uk.

MEEKE, (Robert) Martin (James); QC 2000; a Recorder, 1996; *b* 25 Dec. 1950; *s* of James Alexander Meeke and Mildred Alverta Meeke; *m* 1973, Beverley Ann Evans; one *s* one *d. Educ:* Allhallows Sch., Devon; Bristol Univ. (LLB Hons). Called to the Bar, Gray's Inn, 1973. *Address:* Colleton Chambers, Colleton Crescent, Exeter EX2 4DG. *T:* (01392) 274898.

MEERES, Norman Victor, CB 1963; Under-Secretary, Ministry of Defence, 1971–73, retired; *b* 1 Feb. 1913; *m* 1938, Elizabeth Powys Fowler; two *s* one *d. Educ:* Sloane Sch., Chelsea; Magdalene Coll., Cambridge. Asst Principal, Air Ministry, 1935; Principal, 1940, Asst Sec., 1944, Ministry of Aircraft Prod.; Asst Sec., Min. of Supply, 1946; Under Secretary: Min. of Supply, 1956; Min. of Aviation, 1959–67; seconded to Dipl. Service in Australia, with title Minister (Defence Research and Civil Aviation), 1965–68; Under-Sec., Min. of Technology, 1969–70. ARCM (piano teaching), 1974. *Recreations:* music, lawn tennis. *Address:* 89 Grove Way, Esher, Surrey KT10 8HF. *T:* (020) 8398 1639.

MEESE, Edwin, III; lawyer; Distinguished Fellow, Heritage Foundation, Washington, since 1988; Distinguished Visiting Fellow, Hoover Institution, Stanford University, California, since 1988; *b* Oakland, Calif, 1931; *s* of Edwin Meese Jr and Leone Meese; *m* 1958, Ursula Herrick; one *s* one *d* (and one *s* decd). *Educ:* Oakland High Sch.; Yale Univ. (BA 1953); Univ. of Calif at Berkeley (JD 1958). Dep. Dist Attorney, Alameda County, 1959–67; Sec. of Legal Affairs to Gov. of Calif, Ronald Reagan, 1967–69; Exec. Assistant and C of S to Gov. of Calif, 1969–75; Vice-Pres., Rohr Industries, 1975–76; Attorney at Law, 1976–80; Dir, Center for Criminal Justice Policy and Management, Univ. of San Diego, 1977–81; Prof. of Law, Univ. of San Diego Law Sch., 1978–81; Counsellor to Pres. of USA, 1981–85; Attorney Gen. of USA, 1985–88. Hon. LLD: Delaware Law Sch.; Widener Univ.; Univ. of San Diego; Valparaiso Univ.; California Lutheran Coll.; Universidad Francisco Marroquin, Guatemala. *Publications:* With Reagan: the inside story, 1992; Judicial Tyranny: the new kings of America, 2005; contribs to professional jls. *Address:* The Heritage Foundation, 214 Massachusetts Avenue, NE, Washington, DC 20002, USA.

MEESON, Nigel Keith; QC 2002; a Recorder, since 2004; Head of Litigation, Conyers Dill & Pearman, Cayman Islands, since 2007; acting Judge of Grand Court, Cayman Islands; *b* 10 Feb. 1959; *s* of Arthur Edward Meeson and Beryl Grace Meeson; *m* 1st, 1982, Beverley Christine Frank (marr. diss. 2006); two *d*; 2nd, 2007, Gaylene Brereton; one *d. Educ:* St Alban's Sch., Herts; Magdalen Coll., Oxford (BA Hons Juris., MA). Called to the Bar, Middle Temple, 1982; Attorney, State Bar of Calif, 1990; Accredited Mediator, CEDR, 1993; FCIArb 2006; in practice as Barrister, 1983–2007; admitted to the Bar of Cayman Is, 2007. Vis. Lectr, UCL, 1994–2005. *Publications:* The Practice and Procedure of the Admiralty Court, 1986; Ship and Aircraft Mortgages, 1989; Admiralty Jurisdiction and Practice, 1993, 3rd edn 2003; (contrib.) Ship Sale and Purchase, 2nd edn 1993, 3rd edn 1998. *Recreations:* sailing, ski-ing, golf. *Address:* Conyers Dill & Pearman, Cricket Square, Hutchins Drive, PO Box 2681, Grand Cayman KY1–1111, Cayman Islands. *T:* 9453901, *Fax:* 9453902; *e-mail:* nigel.meeson@conyersdillandpearman.com. *Clubs:* Bar Yacht; Aldeburgh Yacht.

MEGAHEY, Leslie; writer and director, film, television and theatre; *b* 22 Dec. 1944; *s* of Rev. Thomas and Beatrice Megahey. *Educ:* King Edward VI Grammar Sch., Lichfield; Pembroke Coll., Oxford. BBC general trainee, 1965; radio drama, script editor, producer, 1967; director, producer, TV arts series, 1968–; Exec. Producer, Arena, 1978–79; Editor, Omnibus, 1979–81, Co-Editor, 1985–87; Head of Music and Arts, BBC TV, 1988–91; other *television:* The Orson Welles Story, 1982; Artists and Models, 1986; The RKO Story, 1987; Leonardo, 2003; numerous drama-documentaries; *films:* Schalcken the Painter, 1979; Cariani and the Courtesans, 1987; Duke Bluebeard's Castle (filmed opera), 1988; The Hour of the Pig, 1993; Earth (co-writer, narration script), 2007; *theatre:* (dir and co-author) Jack—a night on the town, Criterion, 1994, NY, 1996. Mem., Arts Council Adv. Panel, Film and TV, 1985–89. Awards: BAFTA, 1980; Prague, 1975; Asolo, 1985; NY, 1987; Banff, 1987; Royal Philharmonic, 1989; Prix Italia, 1989; Argentine Film Critics', 1999; Lifetime Achievement, Montréal FIFA Fest., 2001. *Address:* c/o The Agency, 24 Pottery Lane, W11 4LZ.

MEGAHY, Thomas; *b* 16 July 1929; *s* of Samuel and Mary Megahy; *m* 1954, Jean (*née* Renshaw); three *s. Educ:* Wishaw High Sch.; Ruskin Coll., Oxford, 1953–55; College of Educn (Technical), Huddersfield, 1955–56 and 1968–69; London Univ. (external student), 1959–63. BScEcon London; DipEcon and PolSci Oxon; DipFE Leeds. Left school at 14 to work on railway; National Service, RN, 1947–49; railway signalman, 1950–53. Lecturer: Rotherham Coll. of Technology, 1956–59; Huddersfield Technical Coll., 1960–65; Park Lane Coll., Leeds, 1965–79. MEP (Lab) SW Yorks, 1979–99. European Parliament: Vice Pres., 1987–89; Dep. Leader, British Labour Group of MEPs, 1985–87; Member: Social Affairs Cttee, 1984–99; Transport and Tourism Cttee, 1989–99; Hungarian Jt Cttee, 1992–99; Substitute Mem., Social Affairs Cttee, 1984. Active member of Labour Party, 1950–; Chm., Scottish Labour League of Youth; Executive Mem., Dewsbury CLP, 1962–. Councillor, Mirfield UDC, 1963–74; Leader, Kirklees Metropolitan Borough Council, 1973–76; Opposition Leader, 1976–78. Member, Yorks and Humberside REPC, 1974–77; Vice-President: AMA, 1979–97; Yorks and Humberside Develt Assoc., 1981–. *Address:* 6 Lady Heton Grove, Mirfield, West Yorks WF14 9DY. *T:* (01924) 492680.

MEGGESON, Michael; Solicitor and Notary Public; Senior Partner, Warner, Goodman & Streat, 1986–94; a Recorder of the Crown Court, 1981–92; *b* 6 Aug. 1930; *s* of Richard Ronald Hornsey Meggeson and Marjorie Meggeson; *m* 1975, Alison Margaret (*née* Wood). *Educ:* Sherborne; Gonville and Caius Coll., Cambridge (BA 1953; MA 1963). Nat. Service, RA, 1949–50; 5th Bn Royal Hampshire Regt, TA, 1950–63. Admitted a Solicitor, 1957; Asst Solicitor, 1957–59, Partner, 1959–94, Warner & Sons, subseq. Warner Goodman & Co., and Warner, Goodman & Streat; Dep. Circuit Judge, 1978–81. Mem. Cttee, Solicitors Staff Pension Fund, 1980–2004 (Chm., Cttee of Management, 1988–92); Pres., Hampshire Incorp. Law Soc., 1981–82. *Recreations:* sailing, golf, gardening, music. *Address:* Church Farm, Langrish, near Petersfield, Hants GU32 1RQ. *T:* (01730) 264470. *Clubs:* Royal Southern Yacht (Hamble); Hayling Island Golf, Liphook Golf.

MEGHIR, Prof. Konstantinos Ektor Dimitrios, (Costas), PhD; FBA 2005; Professor of Economics, University College London, since 1992; *b* 13 Feb. 1959; *s* of John and Marie-Jose Meghir; *m* 1987, Sofia Skalistiri; one *s* one *d. Educ:* Univ. of Manchester (BA Econ, MA Econ; PhD 1985). Res. Schol., Internat. Inst. for Applied Systems Analysis, Vienna, 1982–83; Temp. Lectr, Univ. of Manchester, 1983–84; University College London: Res. Officer, 1984–85; Lectr, 1985–91; Reader, 1991–92; Hd, Dept of Econs, 2005–08. Dep. Res. Dir, 1991–2005, Co-Dir, 2005–, ESRC Centre, Inst. of Fiscal Studies. Mem. Council, REconS, 2007–. Jt Man. Ed., Econ. Jl, 1996–2001; Co-ed., Econometrica, 2001–06. *Publications:* contribs to learned jls. *Recreations:* sailing, ski-ing, photography. *Address:* Department of Economics, University College London, Gower Street, WC1E 6BT. *T:* (020) 7679 5877, *Fax:* (020) 7323 4780; *e-mail:* c.meghir@ucl.ac.uk.

MEHAFFEY, Rt Rev. James; Bishop of Derry and Raphoe, 1980–2002; *b* 29 March 1931; *s* of John and Sarah Mehaffey; *m* 1956, Thelma P. L. Jackson; two *s* one *d. Educ:* Trinity College, Dublin (MA, BD); Queen's University, Belfast (PhD). Curate Assistant: St Patrick's, Belfast, 1954–56; St John's, Deptford, London, 1956–58; Minor Canon, Down Cathedral, 1958–60; Bishop's Curate, St Christopher's, Belfast, 1960–62; Incumbent: Kilkeel, Diocese of Dromore, 1962–66; Cregagh, Diocese of Down, 1966–80. Hon. DLitt Ulster, 1999. *Address:* 10 Clearwater, Londonderry BT47 6BE. *T:* (028) 7134 2624; *e-mail:* james.mehaffey@btinternet.com.

MEHMET, Alper, MVO 1990; HM Diplomatic Service, retired; Ambassador to Iceland, 2004–08; *b* Cyprus, 28 Aug. 1948; *s* of Bekir Mehmet and Leman Mehmet; *m* 1968, Elaine Susan Tarrant; two *d. Educ:* Parmiter's Grammar Sch.; Bristol Poly. Entered Home Office, 1970; Immigration Service, 1970–79; Lagos, 1979–83; transf. to HM Diplomatic Service; Asst Pvte Sec. to Parly Under-Sec. of State, FCO, 1983–85; Second Sec., Bucharest, 1986–89; Dep. Hd of Mission, Reykjavík, 1989–93; FCO, 1993–98; First Sec., Bonn, 1999, Berlin, 1999–2003. *Address: e-mail:* alpm2001@yahoo.co.uk.

MEHTA, Bharat, OBE 2000; Chief Executive (formerly Clerk to the Trustees), City Parochial Foundation, since 1998; *b* 5 March 1956; *s* of Maganlal Jinabhai Mehta and Rattanben Mehta; *m* 1990, Sally Anne Chambers; two *d. Educ:* Plymouth Poly. (BA Hons Psychology 1979); UCL (MSc Ergonomics 1981). Researcher, MRC, 1979–80; Community Develt Worker, Pensioners Link, 1981–84; Policy Officer, NCVO, 1984–86; Principal Officer, Waltham Forest LBC, 1987–89; Dir of Develt, 1989–93, CEO, 1993–98, Nat. Schizophrenia Fellowship. Chm., Active Community Unit Adv. Gp, Home Office, 2003–04. Mem., HM Treasury and Cabinet Office spending review of future role of third sector in econ. and social regeneration, 2006–07. Non-exec. Dir, N Middlesex Univ. Hosp. NHS Trust, 2005– (Vice Chm., 2008–). Patron, Revolving Doors Agency, 1998–. Mem. Bd, Joseph Rowntree Foundn, 2003–. Chm., Governing Body, Bowes Primary Sch., 2000–05. Judge, Charity Awards, 2005–. Fellow, British American Proj., 1996. FRSA 2003. *Publication:* contrib. British Jl of Psychology. *Recreations:* field hockey, swimming, history. *Address:* City Parochial Foundation, 6 Middle Street, EC1A 7PH. *Clubs:* Southgate Adelaide Hockey (Vice Pres., 2002–), Griffins Hockey.

MEHTA, Prof. Goverdhan, Padma Shri 2000; PhD; FRS 2005; FNA; CSIR Bhatnagar Fellow, Department of Organic Chemistry, Indian Institute of Science, since 2005 (Professor of Chemistry and Director, 1998–2005). *Educ:* Univ. of Pune (PhD). Res. Associate, Michigan State and Ohio State Univs, 1967–69; Lectr, then Asst Prof., Indian Inst. of Technol., 1969–77; Prof. of Chemistry, 1977–98, Founder Dean, 1977–86, Vice-Chancellor, 1994–98, Univ. of Hyderabad. President: INSA, 1999–2001; ICSU, 2005–. *Address:* Department of Organic Chemistry, Indian Institute of Science, Bangalore 560012, India.

MEHTA, Ved (Parkash); writer; *b* Lahore, 21 March 1934; 2nd *s* of late Dr Amolak Ram Mehta (former Dep. Director General of Health Services, Govt of India), and Shanti Devi Mehta (*née* Mehra); naturalized citizen of USA, 1975; *m* 1983, Linn Fenimore Cooper Cary, *d* of late William L. Cary and of Katherine Cary; two *d. Educ:* Arkansas Sch. for the Blind; Pomona Coll. (BA 1956); Balliol Coll., Oxford (Hazen Fellow, 1956–59; BA Hons Mod. Hist. Oxon, 1959; MA 1962; Hon. Fellow, 1999); Harvard Univ. (MA 1961). Phi Beta Kappa, 1955. Harvard Prize Fellow, 1959–60; Residential Fellow, Eliot House, Harvard Univ., 1959–61; Guggenheim Fellow, 1971–72, 1977–78; Ford Foundn Travel and Study Grantee, 1971–76, Public Policy Grantee, 1979–82; MacArthur Prize Fellow, 1982–87. Staff writer, The New Yorker, 1961–94. Yale University: Rosenkranz Chair in Writing, 1990–93; Lectr in History, 1990, 1991, 1992; Lectr in English, 1991–93; Residential Fellow, 1990–93, Berkeley Coll. Vis. Schol., Case Western Reserve Univ., 1974; Beatty Lectr, McGill Univ., 1979; Vis. Prof. of Literature, Bard Coll., 1985, 1986; Noble Foundn Vis. Prof. of Art and Cultural History, Sarah Lawrence Coll., 1988; Vis. Fellow (Literature), Balliol Coll., 1988–89; Vis. Prof. of English, NY Univ., 1989–90; Arnold Bernhard Vis. Prof. of English and History, Williams Coll., 1994; Randolph Distinguished Vis. Prof. of English and History, Vassar Coll., 1994–96; Sen. Fellow, Freedom Forum, Media Studies Center, 1996–97; Fellow, Center for Advanced Study in Behavioral Scis, 1997–98. Arkansas Traveler Lect., Univ. of Arkansas, 2006. Mem. Council on Foreign Relations, 1979–. Member: Usage Panel, Amer. Heritage Dictionary, 1982; Johnsonians, 2006. Fellow, NY Inst. for Humanities, 1988–92. Hon. DLit: Pomona, 1972; Bard, 1982; Williams, 1986; Bowdoin, 1995; DUniv Stirling, 1988. Assoc. of Indians in America Award, 1978; Silver Medal, Signet Soc., Harvard, 1983; Distinguished Service Award, Asian/Pacific Americans Liby Assoc., 1986; NYC Mayor's Liberty Medal, 1986; Centenary Barrows Award, Pomona Coll., 1987; Literary Lion Medal, 1990, Literary Lion Centennial Award, 1996, NY Public Liby; NY State Asian-American Heritage Month Award, 1991. *Publications:* Face to Face, 1957 (Secondary Educn Annual Book Award, 1958; serial reading on BBC Light prog., 1958, dramatization on Home prog., 1959; reissued 1967, 1978); Walking the Indian Streets, 1960 (rev. edn 1971); Fly and the Fly-Bottle, 1963, 2nd edn 1983 introd. Jasper Griffin; The New Theologian, 1966; Delinquent Chacha (fiction), 1967; Portrait of India, 1970, 2nd edn 1993; John Is Easy to Please, 1971; Mahatma Gandhi and His Apostles, 1977, reissued 1993; The New India, 1978; Photographs of Chachaji, 1980; A Family Affair: India under three Prime Ministers, 1982; Three Stories of the Raj (fiction), 1986; Rajiv Gandhi and Rama's Kingdom, 1995; A Ved Mehta Reader: the craft of the essay, 1998; Continents of Exile (autobiography): Daddyji, 1972; Mamaji, 1979; Vedi, 1982; The Ledge Between the Streams, 1984; Sound-Shadows of the New World, 1986; The Stolen Light, 1989; Up at Oxford, 1993; Remembering Mr Shawn's New Yorker: the invisible art of editing, 1998; All For Love, 2001; Dark Harbor: building house and home on an enchanted island, 2003; The Red Letters, 2004; numerous translations; articles and stories in Amer., British and Indian newspapers and magazines, 1957–. Writer and commentator of TV documentary film Chachaji: My Poor Relation, PBS, 1978, BBC, 1980 (DuPont Columbia Award for Excellence in Broadcast Journalism, 1977–78). *Recreation:* listening to Indian and Western music. *Address:* 139 East 79th Street, New York, NY 10075, USA. *T:* (212) 7377487, *Fax:* (212) 4727220. *Clubs:* Century Association (NY) (Trustee, 1973–75; Mem. Wine Cttee, 2000–04); Tarratine (Dark Harbor, Maine).

MEHTA, Zubin; Music Director for life, Israel Philharmonic Orchestra (Musical Adviser, 1962–78); Artistic Director, Maggio Musicale Fiorentino, since 1986; General Music Director, Bavarian State Opera, 1998–2006; *b* 29 April 1936; *s* of Mehli Mehta; *m* 1st, 1958, Carmen Lasky (marr. diss. 1964); one *s* one *d*; 2nd, 1969, Nancy Kovack. *Educ:* St Xavier's Coll., Bombay; Musikakademie, Vienna. First Concert, Vienna, 1958; first prize internat. comp., Liverpool, 1958; US debut, Philadelphia Orch., 1960; debut with Israel and Vienna Philharmonic Orchs, 1961; apptd Music Director, Montreal Symphony Orch., 1961; European tour with this orch., 1962; guest conducting, major European Orchs, 1962; Music Director: Los Angeles Philharmonic Orch., 1962–78; New York Philharmonic, 1978–91. Opera debut, Montreal, Tosca, 1964; debut Metropolitan Opera, Aida, 1965; operas at Metropolitan incl.: Tosca, Turandot, Otello, Carmen, Mourning becomes Elektra (world première), Trovatore, etc. Tours regularly with Israel Philharmonic Orchs and occasionally with Vienna Phil. Orch.; regular guest conducting with Vienna Phil., Berlin Phil., Orch. de Paris. Hon. Doctorates: Colgate Univ.; Brooklyn Coll.; Westminster Coll.; Occidental Coll.; Sir George Williams Univ., Canada; Weizmann Inst. of Science, Israel; Tel-Aviv Univ. Holds numerous awards; Israel Wolf Foundn Prize, 1996; Padma Bhushan (India), 1967; Commendatore of Italy; Médaille d'Or Verneil, City of Paris, 1984. *Address:* 27 Oakmont Drive, Los Angeles, CA 90049–1901, USA. *T:* (310) 4443111.

MEIER, Maj.-Gen. Anthony Leslie, CB 1995; OBE 1981; Director-General, Management and Support of Intelligence, Ministry of Defence, 1991–94; *b* 3 Sept. 1937; *s* of late Eric Leslie Francis Meier and Vera Madge Meier (*née* Terry); *m* 1973, Susanne Jennifer Manley; two *s* one *d*. *Educ:* Latymer Upper Sch.; RMA Sandhurst. Commissioned RASC, 1957, later RCT; regtl appts, Germany and on secondment to Brigade of Gurkhas, Far East, 1958–68; Staff Coll., 1969; MoD, 31 Sqn GTR, NDC, HQ BAOR, CO 8 Regt RCT, to 1981; Col GS Coord (COS), Staff Coll., 1981–84; NATO Defence Coll., Rome, 1984–85; HQ AFCENT, 1985–87; Dir of Intell. (Warsaw Pact), MoD, 1988–90. Dir, Macmillan Appeal for Brighton and Hove Hospice, 1994–96; non-exec. Dir, Eastbourne Hosps NHS Trust, 1994–2002. Adjudicator, Criminal Injuries Compensation Appeals Panel, 1997–2007. Chm., Bd of Govs, St Bede's Prep. Sch., Eastbourne, 1994–99; Dep. Chm., 1999–2008, Chm., 2008–, Bd of Govs, St Bede's Sch., Sussex; Special Comr, Duke of York's Royal Mil. Sch., 1998– (Chm., 2003–08). *Publications:* Notes on the Soviet Ground Forces, 1972; articles in Internat. Defense Review. *Recreation:* sport. *Address:* c/o National Westminster Bank, 5 Meads Street, Eastbourne, E Sussex BN20 7QT.

MEIER, His Honour David Benjamin; a Circuit Judge, 1993–2003; Designated Care Judge for Buckinghamshire; *b* 8 Oct. 1938; *s* of Arnold Meier, PhD and Irma Meier; *m* 1964, Kathleen Lesly Wilton; one *d*. *Educ:* Bury Grammar Sch.; King's College London (LLB). Admitted Law Society, 1964; Solicitor. Metropolitan Stipendiary Magistrate, 1985–93; a Recorder, 1991–93. Pres., Mental Health Tribunals, 1988–2000; Chairman: Juvenile Court, 1988–93; Family Panel, 1991–93. Pres., N Middx Law Soc., 1984–85. *Recreations:* riding, cricket, golf. *Address:* c/o Milton Keynes County Court, 351 Silbury Boulevard, Witan Gate East, Milton Keynes MK9 2DT.

MEIER, Richard Alan; principal architect, Richard Meier & Partners (formerly Richard Meier & Associates, New York), since 1963; *b* Newark, NJ, 12 Oct. 1934; *s* of Jerome Meier and Carolyn Meier (*née* Kaltenbacher); *m* 1978, Katherine Gormley (marr. diss. 1987); one *s* one *d*. *Educ:* Cornell Univ. (BAArch 1957). FAIA. Architect with: Frank Grad & Sons, NJ, 1957; Davis Brody & Wisniewski, NY, 1958–59; Skidmore, Owings & Merrill, 1959–60; Marcel Breuer & Associates, 1960–63. Adjunct Prof. of Architecture, Cooper Union, 1963–73; Visiting Professor: Yale Univ., 1975, 1977, 2008; Harvard Univ., 1977; UCLA, 1987, 1988. *Major works* include: Smith House, Darien, Conn, 1967, and houses in Harbor Springs, E Hampton, Malibu, Dallas, New York, Florida, Pittsburgh and Naples; Bronx Developmental Center, NY, 1977; Atheneum, New Harmony; High Mus. of Art, Atlanta, 1983; Mus. für Angewandte Kunst (formerly Kunsthandwerk), Frankfurt, 1984; City Hall and Central Liby, The Hague; Canal Plus HQ, Paris, 1992; Mus. of Contemp. Art, Barcelona, 1995; Getty Center, LA, 1997; 173/176 Perry St, NY, 2002; 66 Restaurant, NY, 2003; Center for Possibility Thinking, California, 2003; Jubilee Church, Rome, 2003; Burda Collection Mus., Baden-Baden, 2004; San Jose City Hall, 2005; 165 Charles St, NY, 2006; Ara Pacis Mus., Rome, 2006; Arp Museum, Rolandseck, Germany, 2006. *Exhibitions* include: XV Triennale, Milan, 1973; Mus. of Modern Art, NY, 1975, 1981; Princeton Univ., 1976; Cooper-Hewitt Mus., NY, 1976–77; Athens, 1982–83; Tokyo, 1988; Naples, 1991; Rome, 1993; Nagoya, 1996; Paris, 1999. 5 Architectural Record awards, 1964–77; 68 AIA Awards, 1968–2006; Pritzker Prize for Architecture, 1984; RIBA Gold Medal, 1988; 5 Progressive Architecture awards, 1979–95; AIA Gold Medal, 1997; Praemium Imperiale, Japan, 1997. Comdr, Ordre des Arts et Lettres (France), 1992 (Officier, 1984). *Publications:* On Architecture, 1982; Richard Meier, Architect, vol. 1 1984, vol. 2 1991, vol. 3 1999; vol. 4 2004; Richard Meier Museums, 2006; Richard Meier Houses and Apartments, 2008; contribs to professional jls. *Address:* 475 10th Avenue, Floor 6, New York, NY 10018–1120, USA.

MEIN, Very Rev. James Adlington; Dean of the Episcopal Church, Diocese of Edinburgh, 2001–04, now Dean Emeritus; Rector of Christ Church, Morningside, 1990–2004; *b* 29 Dec. 1938; *s* of James Helliwell Mein and Kathleen Elsie Mein (*née* Dawson); *m* 1966, Helen Shaw (*née* Forrester-Paton); one *s* one *d*. *Educ:* Nottingham Univ. (BA Hons Theol. 1960); Westcott House, Cambridge. Ordained deacon, 1963, priest, 1964; Curate, St Columba, Edinburgh, 1963–67; Chaplain to Bp of Edinburgh, 1965–67; Sec., Christian Service Cttee, Malaŵi, 1967–72; Rector, St Mary, Grangemouth, 1972–82, with Bo'ness, 1976–82; Team Priest, Livingston, 1982–90; Canon, St Mary's Cathedral, Edinburgh, 1990–2001. *Recreations:* walking, golf, reading, television. *Address:* Cardhu, Bridgend, Linlithgow EH49 6NH. *T:* (01506) 834317; *e-mail:* jim@meins.plus.com.

MEINERTZHAGEN, Peter Richard; Chairman, Hoare Govett, 1991–2004 and 2005–07; *b* 16 April 1946; *s* of late Daniel Meinertzhagen and Marguerite Meinertzhagen (*née* Leonard); *m* 1967, Nikki Phillips; five *d*. *Educ:* Eton College; Sorbonne. Hoare & Co.: joined 1965; Partner, 1973; Dir, Institutional Sales, 1973–90. Dir, London Stock Exchange, 1998–2008. *Recreations:* golf, tennis, horse-racing, music. *Address:* 20 Tite Street, SW3 4HZ. *T:* (020) 7352 6806. *Club:* White's.

MEIRION-JONES, Prof. Gwyn Idris, FSA 1981; author and consultant on historic buildings; Professor Emeritus, London Metropolitan University; *b* 24 Dec. 1933; *e s* of late Maelgwyn Meirion-Jones and Enid Roberts, Manchester; *m* 1961, Monica (*d* 2003), *e d* of late George and Marion Havard, Winchester. *Educ:* North Manchester Grammar School; King's College London (BSc, MPhil, PhD). National Service, RAF, 1954–56. Schoolmaster, 1959–68; Lectr in Geography, Kingston Coll. of Technology, 1968; Sir John Cass College, later City of London Polytechnic: Sen. Lectr i/c Geography, 1969; Principal Lectr i/c, 1970; Head of Geography, 1970–89; Personal Chair, 1983–89, then Prof. Emeritus; Hon. Research Fellow, 1989–98. Leverhulme Research Fellow, 1985–87; Vis. Prof. of Archaeol., Univ. of Reading, 1995–2007. Dir, Soc. of Antiquaries, 2001–02. British Assoc. for the Advancement of Science: Sec., 1973–78, Recorder, 1978–83, Pres., 1992–93, Section H (Anthropology and Archaeology); Mem. Council, 1977–80; Mem. Gen. Cttee, 1977–83; Ancient Monuments Society: Mem. Council, 1974–79 and 1983–94; Hon. Sec., 1976–79; Vice-Pres., 1979–; Editor, 1985–94. Member: Comité Scientifique des Musées du Finistère, 1984–; Royal Commn on Historical Monuments of England, 1985–97; Adv. Cttee on Bldgs and Domestic Life, Welsh Folk Mus., 1991–95. Hon. Pres., Domestic Buildings Res. Gp (Surrey), 1991– (Pres., 1986–91). Editor, Medieval Village Res. Gp, 1978–86. Liveryman, Welsh Livery Guild, 2007–. Hon. Corresp. Mem., Soc. Jersiaise, 1980–90 and 1990–; Corresponding Member: Cie des Architectes en Chef des Monuments Historiques, 1989–; Soc. d'Histoire et d'Archéol. de Bretagne, 1997–. Exhibitions: vernacular architecture of Brittany, on tour 1982–89; Architecture vernaculaire en Bretagne (15e–20e siècles), Rennes and tour, 1984–89. *Publications:* La Maison traditionnelle (bibliog.), 1978; The Vernacular Architecture of Brittany, 1982; (with Michael Jones) Aimer les Châteaux de Bretagne, 1991 (trans. English and German); (with Michael Jones) Les Châteaux de Bretagne, 1992; (jtly) Manorial Domestic Buildings in England and Northern France, 1993; Historic Buildings and Dating by Dendrochronology, 1997; (jtly) La Ville de Cluny et ses Maisons XIe–XVe siècles, 1997; (jtly) The Seigneurial Residence in Western Europe AD *c* 800–1600, 2002; papers in sci., archaeol and ethnol jls. *Recreations:* food, wine, music, walking, fly-fishing. *Address:* 11 Avondale Road, Fleet, Hants GU51 3BH. *T:* (01252) 614300; *e-mail:* gwynmj@orange.fr. *Clubs:* Athenæum; Royal Scots (Edinburgh).

MEISEL, Prof. John, CC 1999 (OC 1989); PhD; FRSC; President, Royal Society of Canada, 1992–95; Sir Edward Peacock Professor of Political Science, Queen's University, Canada, 1983–94, now Emeritus; Co-Editor (formerly Editor), International Political Science Review, 1979–95; *b* 23 Oct. 1923; *s* of Fryda S. Meisel and Anne Meisel (*née* Heller); *m* 1949, Murie A. Kelly (decd). *Educ:* Pickering Coll.; Univ. of Toronto (BA, MA); LSE (PhD). FRSC 1974. Political scientist; Queen's University, Canada: Instructor to Prof., 1949–79; Hardy Prof. of Political Science, 1963–79. Vis. Prof., Yale, 1976–77; Commonwealth Dist. Vis. Prof., UK, 1978. Chm., Canadian Radio-TV and Telecommunications Commn, 1980–83. President: Canadian Pol. Sci. Assoc., 1973–74; Social Sci. Fedn of Canada, 1975–76. Hon. LLD: Brock; Calgary; Carleton; Queen's; Guelph; Toronto; Regina; DU Ottawa; Hon. DLitt Waterloo; Hon. DSS Laval. Canada Medals: Confedn Centennial, 1967; 125th Anniv. Confedn, 1992; Silver Jubilee Medal, 1977. *Publications:* The Canadian General Election of 1957, 1962; Papers on the 1962 Election, 1964; Working Papers on Canadian Politics, 1972; (with Vincent Lemieux) Ethnic Relations in Canadian Voluntary Associations, 1972; Cleavages, Parties and Values in Canada, 1974; (with Jean Laponce) Debating the Constitution, 1994; numerous articles in acad. jls. *Recreations:* visual and performing arts, swimming, cross-country ski-ing, hiking, bird watching, flower admiring, indoor gardening, printed word. *Address:* Colimaison, Tichborne, ON K0H 2V0, Canada. *T:* (613) 2792380; (winter) 70a Johnson Street, Kingston, ON K7L 1X7. *T:* (613) 5463102; Queen's University, Kingston, ON K7L 3N6, Canada. *T:* (613) 5336227, *Fax:* (613) 5336848; *e-mail:* meiselj@queensu.ca. *Club:* University (Toronto).

MEIXNER, Helen Ann Elizabeth, (Mrs Helen Thornton), CMG 2001; Regional Director, South-East Europe and Director, Romania, 1997–2001, British Council; *b* 26 May 1941; *d* of Henry Gerard and Valerie Meixner; *m* Jack Edward Clive Thornton, CB, OBE (*d* 1996). *Educ:* Sydney C of E Grammar Sch. for Girls, Darlinghurst; Univ. of Queensland (BA 1961); Sch. of Slavonic and East European Studies, UCL (MA 2004). Teacher, Abbotsleigh Girls' Sch., Wahroonga, 1962; Educn Asst, ABC, 1963–64; joined British Council, 1966; Recruitment Unit, Zagreb Office, Exchanges, Courses, Staff Recruitment, Dir-Gen's and Personnel Depts; Head, Design, Production and Publishing Dept, 1984–86; Dep. Dir, Personnel and Head, Personnel Dept, 1986–91; Dir of Libraries, Books and Information Div., 1991–94; Dep. Dir, Professional Services and Head, Consultancy Gp, 1994–96; Dir, Central Europe, 1996–97. Member: Council, Ranfurly Liby Service, 1991–94; Exec. Cttee, VSO, 1995–97; Council, Book Aid Internat., 2001–. Dir, Cornerhouse, Manchester, 1993–95. Trustee, AngloRomanian Educnl Trust, 2002–. Gov., Langford Primary Sch., Hammersmith, 2002– (Chm., 2008–). JP Inner London, 1988–98. *Recreations:* music, reading, walking, travel. *Address:* 131 Dalling Road, W6 0ET. *T:* (020) 8748 7692.

MELANESIA, Archbishop of, since 1994; **Most Rev. Ellison Leslie Pogo,** KBE 2000; Bishop of Central Melanesia, since 1994; *b* 9 Dec. 1947; *s* of Stephen Zaku and Sarah Duri; *m* 1978, Roslyn (*née* Kairopo); one *s* two *d*. *Educ:* Bishop Patteson Theol Coll., Kohimarama, Solomon Is; St John's Theol Coll., Auckland, NZ (LTh). Asst Priest, Anderson's Bay, Dunedin, 1979–81; Bishop of Ysabel, Solomon Is, 1981–94. Mem., Exec. Cttee, Pacific Conf. of Churches, 1984–; Comr for Pacific Region, Unit IV (Sharing and Service), WCC, 1989–; Ex Officio Mem., Pacific Ecumenical Regl Gp, 1989–. Chm., Bd of Govs, Pacific Theol Coll., Suva, Fiji, 1994–. *Recreations:* reading, gardening. *Address:* Archbishop's House, PO Box 19, Honiara, Solomon Islands. *T:* (office) 21892, 21137, (home) 22339.

MELANESIA, CENTRAL, Bishop of; *see* Melanesia, Archbishop of.

MELBOURNE, Archbishop of, since 2006; **Most Rev. Philip Leslie Freier,** PhD; *b* 9 Feb. 1955; *m* 1976, Joy Launder; two *s*. *Educ:* Qld Inst. of Technol. (BAppSc 1975); Univ. of Qld (DipEd 1976); St John's Coll., Morpeth (Associate Dip. in Theol 1984); Melbourne Coll. of Divinity (BD 1984); Univ. of Newcastle (MEdSt 1984); James Cook Univ., Townsville (PhD 2000). Teacher, Qld Educn Dept, 1976–81. Ordained deacon, 1983, priest, 1984; Deacon in Charge, Ch of the Ascension, Kowanyama, 1983–84, Priest in Charge, 1984–88; Rector: St Oswald, Banyo, 1988–93; Christ Ch, Bundaberg, 1993–99; Bishop of Northern Territory, 1999–2006. Area Dean: Brisbane N, 1992–93; the Burnett, 1995–98; Examining Chaplain to Archbp of Brisbane, 1993–99. Member: Diocesan Council, Dio. Carpentaria, 1986–88; Gen. Synod, 1987–98 (Mem., Missionary and Ecumenical Commn, 1995–98); Provincial Synod, 1987–98 (Mem., Standing Cttee, 1988–); Diocesan Council, Dio. Brisbane, 1991–94. *Publications:* Thaw Pathn a Palal Nguwl, 1978; (with E. J. Freier) Kupmari, A Picture Book, 1978; Science Program for Aboriginal Community Schools, 1980; (jtly) Mathematical Program for Schools in Aboriginal and Torres Strait Islander Communities, 1983; articles in jls. *Address:* The Anglican Centre, 209 Flinders Lane, Melbourne, Vic 3000, Australia.

MELBOURNE, Archbishop of, (RC), since 2001; **Most Rev. Denis James Hart;** *b* Melbourne, 13 May 1941; *s* of Kevin James Hart and Annie Eileen (*née* Larkan). *Educ:* Xavier Coll., Kew; Corpus Christi Coll., Werribee; Corpus Christi Coll., Glen Waverley. Ordained priest, 1967; Chaplain, Repatriation Hosp., Heidelberg, 1967–68; Asst Priest, N Balwyn, 1968; Asst Priest and Master of Ceremonies, St Patrick's Cathedral, Melbourne, 1969–74; Prefect of Ceremonies, Archdio. Melbourne, 1970–96; Advocate and Notary, Regional Matrimonial Tribunal, 1975–85; Exec. Sec., Nat. Liturgical Commn, Aust. Catholic Bps' Conf., 1975–90; Parish Priest, St Joseph's, W Brunswick, 1987–96; Vicar Gen. and Moderator of the Curia, 1996–2001; Aux. Bp, Archdio. Melbourne, 1997–2001; Titular Bp of Vagada, 1997–2001. Mem., Cttee for Liturgy, 2000–, Cttee for Finance, 2002–, Aust. Catholic Bps' Conf. *Recreations:* walking, music, reading. *Address:* St Patrick's Cathedral, Melbourne, Vic 3002, Australia. *T:* (3) 99265612.

MELBOURNE, Assistant Bishops of; *see* Hale, Rt Rev. S. J.; Huggins, Rt Rev. P. J.; White, Rt Rev. P. R.

MELCHETT, 4th Baron *cr* 1928; **Peter Robert Henry Mond;** Bt 1910; Policy Director, Soil Association, since 2001; *b* 24 Feb. 1948; *s* of 3rd Baron Melchett and of Sonia Elizabeth Sinclair, *qv*; *S* father, 1973. *Educ:* Eton; Pembroke Coll., Cambridge (BA); Keele Univ. (MA). Res. Worker, LSE and Addiction Res. Unit, 1973–74. A Lord in Waiting (Govt Whip), 1974–75; Parly Under-Sec. of State, DoI, 1975–76; Minister of State, NI Office, 1976–79. Chm., working party on pop festivals, 1975–76; Chm., Community Industry, 1979–85; Chm., 1986–89, Exec. Dir, 1989–2000, Greenpeace UK. Special Lectr, Sch. of Biological Scis, Nottingham Univ., 1984–2002. Chairman: Wildlife Link, 1979–87; Greenpeace Japan, 1994–2001; Mem. Bd, Greenpeace Internat., 1989, 2001; Member: Govt Organic Action Plan Gp, 2002–; BBC Rural Affairs Cttee, 2004–; Govt Sch. Meals Review Panel, 2005. Vice-Pres., Ramblers' Assoc., 1984– (Pres., 1981–84). *Address:* Courtyard Farm, Ringstead, Hunstanton, Norfolk PE36 5LQ.

MELDING, David Robert Michael; Member (C) South Wales Central, National Assembly for Wales, since 1999; *b* 28 Aug. 1962; *s* of David Graham Melding and Edwina Margaret Melding (*née* King). *Educ:* Dwr-y-felin Comprehensive Sch., Neath; UC Cardiff (BScEcon); Coll. of William and Mary, Virginia (MA). Cons. Res. Dept, 1986–89; Dep. Dir, Welsh Centre for Internat. Affairs, 1989–96; Manager, Carers Nat. Assoc. in Wales, 1996–99. *Recreations:* swimming, golf, reading, campaigning to restore Pluto as a planet. *Address:* National Assembly for Wales, Cardiff Bay, Cardiff CF99 1NA. *T:* (029) 2089 8328.

MELDRUM, Sir Graham, Kt 2002; CBE 1994; QFSM 1989; FIFireE; Chairman, West Midlands Ambulance Service NHS Trust, since 2007; *b* 23 Oct. 1945; *s* of George Meldrum and Agnes (*née* Gordon); *m* 1964, Catherine Meier; one *s* one *d*. *Educ:* Inverurie Acad., Aberdeenshire. FIFireE 1995. Fireman to Station Officer, London Fire Bde, 1963–73; Instructor, in the rank of Asst Divl Officer, Fire Service Coll., 1973–74; Divl Officer III, Hants Fire Service, 1974–76; Tyne and Wear: Divl Officer II, 1976–79; Divl Officer I, 1979–80; Sen. Divl Officer, 1980–83; West Midlands: Asst Chief Officer, 1983–84; Dep. Chief Fire Officer, 1984–90; Chief Fire Officer, 1990–97; HM Chief Inspector of Fire Services, 1998–2007. Pres., Chief and Asst Chief Fire Officers' Assoc., 1994–95; Chairman: Fire Services Nat. Benevolent Fund, 1994; CACFOA (Research) Ltd, 1988–; CACFOA (Services) Ltd, 1988–. DUniv 1997. OStJ 1998. *Publications:* papers on fire engrg in jls. *Recreations:* computers, motor-cycling, railways, industrial archaeology, community work. *Address:* 1 Palmers Leys, Kineton, Warwicks CV35 0JG.

MELDRUM, Hamish Robin Peter, FRCGP, FRCPE; Chairman of Council, British Medical Association, since 2007; *b* Edinburgh, 14 April 1948; *s* of James S. Meldrum and May I. Meldrum (*née* MacGregor); *m* 1974, Mhairi M. K.; two *s* one *d*. *Educ:* Stirling High Sch.; Edinburgh Univ. (BSc Med. Sci. 1969; MB ChB 1972). DRCOC 1977; FRCGP 2001; FRCPE. Hse physician, Edinburgh Royal Infirmary, 1972–73; Med. SHO, then Registrar, Torbay Hosp., Devon, 1973–76; GP trainee, Harrogate, 1976–78; Principal in Gen. Practice, Bridlington, E Yorks, 1978–. Mem., GPs Cttee, BMA, 1991– (Chm., 2004–07). *Publications:* contrib. med. jls incl. BMJ. *Recreations:* sport (watching most, playing tennis and running), hill walking, music (varied), wine appreciation, good company and discussion. *Address:* Holly Farm, 9 St John's Close, Bridlington, E Yorks YO16 4SQ. *T:* (home) (01262) 400019, (office) (020) 7883 6000, 07889 036275; *e-mail:* hmeldrum@bma.org.uk.

MELDRUM, James; Keeper, Registers of Scotland, since 2003; *b* 9 Aug. 1952; *s* of late George and Marion Meldrum. *Educ:* Lenzie Academy; Glasgow Univ. (MA Hons). Joined Scottish Office 1973; Principal, 1979–86; Dep. Dir, Scottish Courts Admin, 1986–91; Head, Investment Assistance Div., Scottish Office Industry Dept, 1991–94; Registrar General for Scotland, 1994–99; Dir, Admin. Services, Scottish Exec., 1999–2002; Dir of Business Mgt and Area Business Manager, Glasgow Crown Office and Procurator Fiscal Service, 2002–03. FRSA 2008. *Recreations:* reading, music. *Address:* Registers of Scotland, Meadowbank House, 153 London Road, Edinburgh EH8 7AU. *T:* (0131) 659 6111, *Fax:* (0131) 459 1221. *Club:* Royal Commonwealth Society.

MELDRUM, Keith Cameron, CB 1995; veterinary consultant, since 1997; Chief Veterinary Officer, Ministry of Agriculture, Fisheries and Food, 1988–97; *b* 19 April 1937; *s* of Dr Walter James Meldrum and Mrs Eileen Lydia Meldrum; *m* 1st, 1962, Rosemary Ann (*née* Crawford) (marr. diss. 1980); two *s* one *d*; 2nd, 1982, Vivien Mary (*née* Fisher). *Educ:* Uppingham; Edinburgh Univ. Qualified as veterinary surgeon, 1961; general practice, Scunthorpe, 1961–63; joined MAFF, Oxford, 1963; Divl Vet. Officer, Tolworth, 1972, Leamington Spa, 1975; Dep. Regional Vet. Officer, Nottingham, 1978; Regional Vet. Officer, Tolworth, 1980; Asst Chief Vet. Officer, Tolworth, 1983; Dir of Vet. Field Service, 1986. UK Deleg., Office Internat. des Epizooties, 1988–97. Mem. Council, RCVS, 1988–97. Gov., Inst. of Animal Health, 1988–97. Trustee, Animal Health Trust, 2002–07. Hon. FRSH 2000. Bledisloe Vet. Award, RASE, 1995. *Recreations:* outdoor activities. *Address:* The Orchard, Swaynes Lane, Merrow, Guildford, Surrey GU1 2XX. *Club:* Farmers'.

MELGUND, Viscount; Gilbert Francis Elliot-Murray-Kynynmound; *b* 15 Aug. 1984; *s* and *heir* of Earl of Minto, *qv*. *Educ:* Marlborough Coll.

MELHUISH, Prof. Edward Charles, PhD; Professor of Psychology, Birkbeck, University of London, since 2001; *b* 3 April 1950; *s* of Robert Hector Melhuish and Elsie Beatrice Melhuish; one *s* four *d*. *Educ:* Univ. of Bristol (BSc); Univ. of London (PhD 1980). Researcher, Univ. of London, 1981–86; Lectr, UCNW, Bangor, 1987–94; Prof., Cardiff Univ., 1994–2000. Exec. Dir, Nat. Evaluation of Sure Start, 2001–. *Publications:* Day Care for Young Children: international perspectives, 1991; Early Childhood Care and Education, 2006; The National Evaluation of Sure Start: does area-based early intervention work?, 2007. *Recreations:* reading, music, film, Rugby, travel.

MELHUISH, Sir (Michael) Ramsay, KBE 1993; CMG 1982; HM Diplomatic Service, retired; *b* 17 March 1932; *s* of late Henry Whitfield Melhuish and Jeanette Ramsay Pender Melhuish; *m* 1961, Stella Phillips; two *s* two *d*. *Educ:* Royal Masonic Sch., Bushey; St John's Coll., Oxford (BA). FO, 1955; MECAS, 1956; Third Sec., Bahrain, 1957; FO, 1959; Second Sec., Singapore, 1961; First Sec. (Commercial) and Consul, Prague, 1963; First Sec. and Head of Chancery, Bahrain, 1966; DSAO (later FCO), 1968; First Sec., Washington, 1970; Counsellor, Amman, 1973; Head of N America Dept, FCO, 1976; Counsellor (Commercial), Warsaw, 1979–82; Ambassador, Kuwait, 1982–85; High Comr, Zimbabwe, 1985–89; Ambassador, Thailand, 1989–92. Head, EC Monitor Mission, Zagreb, July–Dec. 1992. *Recreations:* tennis, golf. *Address:* Longwood Lodge, Leatherhead Road, Oxshott, Surrey, KT22 0ET. *Club:* Oxford and Cambridge.

MELIA, Dr Terence Patrick, CBE 1993; Chairman, Learning and Skills Development Agency, 2000–03; *b* 17 Dec. 1934; *s* of John and Kathleen Melia (*née* Traynor); *m* 1976, Madeline (*née* Carney); one *d*. *Educ:* Sir John Deane's Grammar Sch., Northwich; Leeds Univ. (PhD). CChem, FRSC. Technical Officer, ICI, 1961–64; Lectr, then Sen. Lectr, Salford Univ., 1964–70; Principal, North Lindsey Coll. of Technology, 1970–74; HM Inspector of Schools, 1974–92: Regional Staff Inspector, 1982–84; Chief Inspector, Further and Higher Educn, 1985–86; Chief Inspector, Higher Educn, 1985–91; Sen. Chief Inspector, HM Inspectorate of Schs, 1991–92; Chief Inspector, FEFC, 1993–96. Vis. Prof., Leeds Metropolitan Univ., 1993–. Chairman: Further Educn Staff Develt Forum, 1996–99; Further Educn Develt Agency, 1997–2000; Further Educn NTO, 1999–2001; Educn Policy Cttee, RSA Exams, 1996–99. Gov., Hills Road Sixth Form Coll., Cambridge, 2001–04. Hon. DSc Salford, 1998; Hon. DEd: Bradford, 2005; Plymouth, 2006. *Publications:* Masers and Lasers, 1967; papers on thermodynamics of polymerisation, thermal properties of polymers, effects of ionizing radiation, chemical thermodynamics, nucleation kinetics, thermal properties of transition metal compounds and gas kinetics. *Recreations:* golf, gardening.

MELINSKY, Rev. Canon (Michael Arthur) Hugh; Principal, Northern Ordination Course, 1978–88; *b* 25 Jan. 1924; *s* of late M. M. Melinsky and Mrs D. M. Melinsky; *m* 1949, Renate (*née* Ruhemann); three *d*. *Educ:* Whitgift Sch., Croydon; Christ's Coll., Cambridge (BA 1947, MA 1949); London Univ. Inst. of Education (TDip 1949); Ripon Hall, Oxford. Inter-Services Special Intelligence Sch., 1943–44; Japanese Intelligence in FE, 1944–46. Asst Master: Normanton Grammar Sch., 1949–52; Lancaster Royal Grammar Sch., 1952–57. Ordained deacon, 1957, priest, 1959; Curate: Wimborne Minster, 1957–59; Wareham, 1959–61; Vicar of St Stephen's, Norwich, 1961–68; Chaplain of Norfolk and Norwich Hosp., 1961–68; Hon. Canon and Canon Missioner of Norwich, 1968–73; Chief Sec., ACCM, 1973–77. Chairman: C of E Commn on Euthanasia, 1972–75; Inst. of Religion and Medicine, 1973–77; Mem., Social Policy Cttee, C of E Bd for Social Responsibility, 1982–92; Mem. Cttee for Theological Educn, ACCM, 1985–88. Hon. Res. Fellow, Dept of Theol Studies, Manchester Univ., 1984. *Publications:* The Modern Reader's Guide to Matthew, 1963; the Modern Reader's Guide to Luke, 1963; Healing Miracles, 1967; (ed) Religion and Medicine, 1970; (ed) Religion and Medicine 2, 1973; Patterns of Ministry, 1974; (ed) On Dying Well, 1975, 2nd edn 2000; Foreword to Marriage, 1984; (contrib.) The Weight of Glory, 1991; The Shape of the Ministry, 1992; (contrib.) Tentmaking: perspectives on self-supporting ministry, 1998; A Code-breaker's Tale, 1998. *Address:* 15 Parson's Mead, Norwich, Norfolk NR4 6PG. *T:* (01603) 455042.

MELLAART, James, FBA 1980; Lecturer in Anatolian Archaeology, Institute of Archaeology, University of London, 1964–91; *b* 14 Nov. 1925; *s* of J. H. J. Mellaart and A. D. Van Der Beek; *m* 1954, Arlette Meryem Cenani; one *s*. *Educ:* University College, London. BA Hons (Ancient Hist. and Egyptology) 1951. Archaeol field surveys in Anatolia as Scholar and Fellow of British Inst. of Archaeol. at Ankara, 1951–56; excavations at Hacilar, 1957–60; Asst Dir, British Inst. of Archaeol. at Ankara, 1959–61; excavations at Çatal Hüyük, Turkey, 1961–63 and 1965; Foreign Specialist, Lectr at Istanbul Univ., 1961–63. Corresp. Mem., German Archaeol Inst., 1961. *Publications:* Earliest Civilisations of the Near East, 1965; The Chalcolithic and Early Bronze Ages in the Near East and Anatolia, 1966; Çatal Hüyük, a Neolithic Town in Anatolia, 1967; Excavations at Hacilar, 1970; The Neolithic of the Near East, 1975; The Archaeology of Ancient Turkey, 1978; Çatal Hüyük and Anatolian Kilims, 1989; (with Ann Murray) Beycesultan, vol. III 2, 1995; chapters in Cambridge Ancient History; numerous articles in Anatolian Studies, etc. *Recreations:* geology, Turkish ceramics, clan history, Gaelic and classical music, Seljuk art. *Address:* 13 Lichen Court, 79 Queen's Drive, N4 2BH. *T:* (020) 8802 6984.

MELLARS, Prof. Paul Anthony, ScD; FBA 1990; Fellow, Corpus Christi College, Cambridge, since 1981 (President, 1992–2000); Professor of Prehistory and Human Evolution, Cambridge University, 1997–2007, now Emeritus; *b* 29 Oct. 1939; *s* of Herbert and Elaine Mellars; *m* 1969, Anny Chanut. *Educ:* Woodhouse Grammar Sch., Sheffield; Fitzwilliam Coll., Cambridge (Exhibnr; BA 1st Cl. Hons Archaeol. and Anthropol. 1962; MA 1965; PhD 1967; ScD 1988). FSA 1977. Sir James Knott Res. Fellow, Univ. of Newcastle upon Tyne, 1968–70; University of Sheffield: Lectr in Prehistory and Archaeol., 1970–75; Sen. Lectr, 1975–80; Reader, 1980–81; University of Cambridge: Lect, 1981–91; Reader in Archaeology, 1991–97. British Academy: Res. Reader, 1989–91; Reckitt Archaeol. Lectr, 1991; Vis. Prof., SUNY (Binghamton), 1974; Vis. Fellow, ANU, 1981; Danish Res. Council Vis. Lectr, Copenhagen and Aarhus Univs, 1985. President: Hunter Archaeol. Soc., 1975–80; Prehistoric Soc., 1998– (Vice Pres., 1992–95); Chm., Archaeol. Sci. Cttee, Council for British Archaeol., 1980–87; Mem. Council, British Acad., 1994–97 (Chm., Archaeol. Sect., 1995–). MAE 1999. Hon. Mem., Italian Inst. of Prehistoric & Proto-historic Sciences, 1997. *Publications:* (ed) The Early Postglacial Settlement of Northern Europe, 1976; Excavations of Oronsay, 1987; (ed) Research Priorities of Archaeological Science, 1987; (ed) The Human Revolution, 1989; (ed) The Emergence of Modern Humans, 1990; The Middle Palaeolithic: adaptation, behaviour & variability, 1991; (ed) The Origin of Modern Humans and the Impact of Science-based Dating, 1992; The Neanderthal Legacy, 1996; (ed) Modelling the Early Human Mind, 1996; Star Carr in Context, 1998; articles in archaeol. jls. *Recreations:* music, foreign travel. *Address:* Long Gable, Elsworth, Cambs CB3 8HX. *T:* (01954) 267275; Department of Archaeology, University of Cambridge, Downing Street, Cambridge CB2 3DZ. *T:* (01223) 333520.

MELLENEY, Clare Patricia; *see* Montgomery, C. P.

MELLING, Dr Jack; consultant and contractor, US Government Accountability Office, Washington, since 1998; *b* 8 Feb. 1940; *s* of John Melling and Mary (*née* Marsden); *m* 1967, Susan Ewart. *Educ:* Rivington and Blackrod Grammar Sch.; Manchester Univ. (BSc, MSc); Bath Univ. (PhD). FRPharmS 1977; FIBiol 1979; FRCPath 1996. Res. Asst, Bath Univ., 1965–68; Lectr, Heriot-Watt Univ., 1968–69; SSO, then PSO, MoD, 1969–79; Dir, Vaccine Res. and Prodn Lab., PHLS, 1979–87; Dep. Dir, 1987–93, Dir, 1993–96, Centre for Applied Microbiology and Res., Porton Down; Dir, Biologicals Develt Center, Salk Inst. for Biol Studies, USA, 1996–2001; Dir (part-time), Karl Landsteiner Inst., Vienna, 2001–03; Sen. Project Manager (part-time), Battelle Meml Inst., Columbus, Ohio, 2001–05; Sen. Sci. Fellow, Center for Arms Control and Non-Proliferation, Washington, 2004–. Visiting Professor: Rutgers Univ., 1979–84; Aston Univ., 1981–96; Westminster Univ., 1995–2005; Gastprofesseur, Inst. for Social and Preventive Medicine, Univ. of Zürich, 1999–2006. Society of Chemical Industry: Mem. Council, 1983–86, 1998–2001; Sec., 1975–81, Chm., 1981–83, Biotechnology Gp; Chm. Pubns Cttee, 1999–2004; Hon. Treas., 2004–. Member: British Nat. Cttee for Microbiol., 1978–84; MRC Cttee on Develt of Vaccines and Immunol Products, 1979–96; Cttee on Safety of Medicines Biologicals Subcttee, 1982–99; Ind. Register Defence Scientific Adv. Council, 1994–98; Res. Adv. Cttee on Gulf War Veterans' Illnesses, US Dept of Veterans' Affairs, 2002–. Sec., British Co-ordinating Cttee for Biotechnol., 1981–85; Sen. Scientific Advr, Internat. AIDS Vaccine Initiative, 1999–2006. Editor, Jl of Chem. Technol. and Biotechnol., 1985–; Mem. Editl Bd, Vaccine, 1983–. Lampitt Medal, SCI, 1993. *Publications:* Continuous Culture Applications and New Fields, 1977; Adhesion of Micro-organisms to Surfaces, 1979; The Microbial Cell Surface and Adhesion, 1981; Biosafety in Industrial Technology, 1994; papers in scientific jls. *Recreations:* ski-ing, shooting, walking. *Address:* US Government Accountability Office, 441 G Street NW, Washington,

DC20548, USA; *e-mail:* mellingj@gao.gov. *Clubs:* Athenæum, Royal Society of Medicine; Parkstone Yacht (Poole).

MELLITT, Prof. Brian, FREng; Chairman, Building Research Establishment, since 1998; *b* 29 May 1940; *s* of John and Nellie Mellitt; *m* 1961, Lyn Waring; one *s* one *d.* *Educ:* Loughborough Univ.; Imperial College, London Univ. (BTechEng, DIC). FIET, FIMechE, FIRSE; FREng (FEng 1990). Student apprentice, 1956, Junior Engineer, 1962, R&D Engineer, 1964, English Electric Co.; Lectr and Sen. Lectr, Huddersfield Polytechnic, 1966–67; Research Dept, British Rlys Bd, 1968–70; University of Birmingham: Lectr, 1971; Sen. Lectr, 1979; Prof., 1982; Head of Dept of Electronic and Electrical Engrg, 1986; Dean, Faculty of Engrng, 1987–88; Hon. Prof. of Electronic Engrg, 1989; Dir Engrg, London Underground Ltd, 1989–95; Dir, Metro Power, 1990–95; Dir of Engrg and Prodn, Railtrack PLC, 1995–99; Engrg Advr, Railtrack (UK), 1999–2000. Consultant Engineer, railway related organisations, 1972–88. Chairman: BMCONSULT Ltd, 1999–; Metro-Consulting Ltd, 2000–02; SIRA Ltd, 2001–06; Director: Railway College Ltd, then Catalis Rail Trng, 1998–2000; Jarvis plc, 2002–; Rail Advr, NM Rothschild, 1999–. President: Welding Inst., 2000–01; IEE, 2001–02 (Vice Pres., 1996–99; Dep. Pres., 1999–2001). Editor, IEE Procs (B), 1978–. Hon. Fellow, Assoc. of Project Managers, 1998. Hon. DTech Loughborough, 1991; Hon. DSc Huddersfield, 1998; Hon. DEng Birmingham, 1999. Leonardo da Vinci Award, Italian Assoc. for Industrial Design, 1989. *Publications:* contribs on electric railway topics to learned jls. *Recreation:* bridge. *Address:* The Priory, 36 Church Street, Stilton, Cambs PE7 3RF. *T:* (01733) 240573. *Club:* Athenæum.

MELLON, Sir James, KCMG 1988 (CMG 1979); HM Diplomatic Service, retired; Chairman: Charlemagne Capital (UK) Ltd (formerly Regent Europe Asset Management), since 2000; Lancashire Digital Ltd, since 2004; *b* 25 Jan. 1929; *m* 1st, 1956, Frances Murray (*d* 1976); one *s* three *d*; 2nd, 1979, Mrs Philippa Shuttleworth (*née* Hartley). *Educ:* Glasgow Univ. (MA). Dept of Agriculture for Scotland, 1953–60; Agricultural Attaché, Copenhagen and The Hague, 1960–63; FO, 1963–64; Head of Chancery, Dakar, 1964–66; UK Delegn to European Communities, 1967–72; Counsellor, 1970; Hd of Sci. and Technol. Dept, FCO, 1973–75; Commercial Counsellor, East Berlin, 1975–76; Head of Trade Relations and Export Dept, FCO, 1976–78; High Comr in Ghana and Ambassador to Togo, 1978–83; Ambassador to Denmark, 1983–86; Dir-Gen. for Trade and Investment, USA, and Consul-Gen., New York, 1986–88. Chairman: Scottish Homes, 1989–96; Thamesmead Town, 1993–96; Regent Pacific Corp. Finance, 1999–2001. *Publications:* A Danish Gospel, 1986; Og Gamle Danmark, 1992; (ed and trans.) Per Federspiel, 2005. *Address:* Charlemagne Capital (UK) Ltd, 39 St James's Street, SW1A 1JD. *Club:* New (Edinburgh).

MELLOR, Christopher John; Chairman, Northern Ireland Water Ltd, since 2006; Deputy Chairman, Monitor, Independent Regulator of NHS Foundation Trusts, since 2004; *b* 3 March 1949; *s* of late John Whitaker Mellor and Mary Mellor (*née* Thompson); *m*; five *d.* Chartered Accountant, 1972. Various posts in local govt finance, 1967–79; with Anglian Water Authy, subseq. Anglian Water PLC, then awg plc, 1979–2003: Sen. Accountant, 1979–85; Principal Accountant, 1985–87; Hd, Privatisation Unit, 1987–88; Hd, Finance and Planning, 1988–90; Principal Accountant, then Head, Financial Planning, 1988–90; Gp Finance Dir, 1990–98; Gp Man. Dir, 1998–2000; Chief Exec., 2000–03. Non-exec. Dir, Addenbrooke's Hosp. NHS Trust, 1994–98. Non-exec. Dir, Grontmij UK Ltd, 2004–. *Recreations:* music, painting, golf. *Address:* c/o Monitor, 4 Matthew Parker Street, SW1H 9NL.

MELLOR, David, CBE 2001 (OBE 1981); DesRCA; RDI 1962; FCSD; designer, manufacturer and retailer; Chairman, Crafts Council, 1982–84; *b* 5 Oct. 1930; *s* of Colin Mellor; *m* 1966, Fiona MacCarthy, *qv*; one *s* one *d.* *Educ:* Sheffield College of Art; Royal College of Art (DesRCA and Silver Medal, 1953, Hon. Fellow 1966); British School at Rome. Set up silver-smithing workshop, Sheffield, 1954; designer and maker of silver for Worshipful Co. of Goldsmiths, Cutlers' Co., Southwell Minster, Essex Univ., Darwin Coll., Cambridge, among others, and range of silver tableware for use in British embassies; designer of fountain in bronze for Botanic Gdns, Cambridge, 1970; concurrently opened industrial design office. Consultancies, 1954–, include: Walker & Hall, Abacus Municipal, Glacier Metal, ITT, Post Office, British Rail, James Neill Tools; Magis Furniture; Cons. to DoE on design of traffic signals, 1965–70. Trustee: V&A Museum, 1984–88; Peak Park Trust, 1992–96. Work in collections: Goldsmiths' Co., V&A, Millennium Galls, Sheffield, Mus. of Modern Art, NY; retrospective exhibn, Design Mus., 1998; permanent exhibn, David Mellor Design Mus., Hathersage, 2006. Liveryman, Goldsmiths' Co., 1980; Freeman, Cutlers' Co. of Hallamshire, 1981. FCSD (FSIAD 1964; CSD Medal 1988). Hon. Fellow, Sheffield City Polytechnic, 1979; Hon. DLitt Sheffield Univ., 1986; Hon. DDes De Montfort, 1997; Hon. Dr RCA, 1999; Hon. DTech Loughborough, 2006. Awards: Design Centre: 1957, 1959, 1962, 1965, 1966; Design Council: 1974, 1977; RSA Presidential Award for Design Management, 1981; V&A Lifetime Achievement Award, 2006. *Address:* The Round Building, Hathersage, Sheffield S32 1BA. *T:* (01433) 650220.

MELLOR, Prof. David Hugh; Pro-Vice-Chancellor, University of Cambridge, 2000–01; Professor of Philosophy, University of Cambridge, 1986–99; Fellow, Darwin College, Cambridge, 1971–2005 (Vice-Master, 1983–87); *b* 10 July 1938; *s* of Sydney David Mellor and Ethel Naomi Mellor (*née* Hughes). *Educ:* Manchester Grammar School; Pembroke College, Cambridge (BA Nat. Scis and Chem. Eng, 1960; MA; PhD 1968; ScD 1990; MEng 1992); Univ. of Minnesota (Harkness Fellowship; MSc Chem. Eng, 1962). Technical Officer, ICI Central Instruments Lab., 1962–63; Cambridge University: Research Student in Philosophy, Pembroke Coll., 1963–68; Fellow, Pembroke Coll., 1965–70; Univ. Asst Lectr in Philosophy, 1965–70; Univ. Lectr in Philosophy, 1970–83; Univ. Reader in Metaphysics, 1983–85. Vis. Fellow in Philosophy, ANU, 1975; Radcliffe Trust Fellow in Philosophy, 1978–80. Hon. Prof. of Philosophy, Univ. of Keele, 1989–92. President: British Soc. for the Philos. of Science, 1985–87; Aristotelian Soc., 1992–93. Chm., Analysis Trust, 2000–. Editor: British Journal for the Philosophy of Science, 1968–70; Cambridge Studies in Philosophy, 1978–82. FBA 1983–2008. Hon. FAHA, 2003. Hon. PhD Lund, 1997. *Publications:* The Matter of Chance, 1971; Real Time, 1981; Matters of Metaphysics, 1991; The Facts of Causation, 1995; Real Time II, 1998; Probability: a philosophical introduction, 2005; articles in Mind, Analysis, Philosophy of Science, Philosophy, Philosophical Review, Ratio, Isis, British Jl for Philosophy of Science, Jl of Philosophy. *Recreation:* theatre. *Address:* 25 Orchard Street, Cambridge CB1 1JS. *T:* (01223) 740017.

MELLOR, Rt Hon. David John; PC 1990; QC 1987; broadcaster, journalist and international business adviser; *b* 12 March 1949; *s* of late Mr and Mrs Douglas H. Mellor; *m* 1974, Judith Mary Hall (marr. diss. 1995); two *s.* *Educ:* Swanage Grammar Sch.; Christ's Coll., Cambridge (BA Hons 1970). FZS 1981. Called to the Bar, Inner Temple, 1972; in practice thereafter. Chm., Cambridge Univ. Conservative Assoc., 1970; contested West Bromwich E, Oct. 1974; MP (C) Putney, 1979–97; contested (C) same seat, 1997. PPS to Leader of Commons and Chancellor of the Duchy of Lancaster, 1981; Parly Under-Sec. of State, Dept of Energy, 1981–83, Home Office, 1983–86; Minister of State: Home Office, 1986–87; Foreign and Commonwealth Office, 1987–88; Dept of Health, 1988–89; Home Office, 1989–90; Privy Council Office (Minister for the Arts), 1990; Chief Sec. to the Treasury, 1990–92; Sec. of State for Nat. Heritage, 1992. Sec., Cons. Parly Legal Cttee, 1979–81; Vice-Chm., Greater London Cons. Members Cttee, 1980–81. Chairman: Sports Aid Foundn, 1993–97; Football Task Force, 1997–99. Special Trustee, Westminster Hosp., 1980–87; Trustee, Fund for the Replacement of Animals in Medical Experiments, 2004– (Co-Patron, 2005–). Mem. Council, NYO, 1981–; Mem. Bd, ENO, 1993–95; Pres., Bournemouth SO, 2000–. Presenter: 6.06, 1993–99, Mellor, 1999–2001, BBC Radio 5; Vintage Years (series), BBC Radio 3, 1993–2000; The Midnight Hour, BBC2, 1997–99; Across the Threshold (series), Classic FM, 1998–. Music Critic, Mail on Sunday, 2000–; columnist: The Guardian, 1992–94; The People, 1998–2003; sports columnist, Evening Standard, 1997–. BBC Radio Personality of the Year, Variety Club of GB, 1995. Hon. Associate, BVA, 1986. *Recreations:* classical music, reading, football.

MELLOR, Derrick, CBE 1984; HM Diplomatic Service, retired; re-employed at Foreign and Commonwealth Office, since 1984; Occasional Lecturer, School of Oriental and African Studies, since 1987; *b* 11 Jan. 1926; *s* of William Mellor and Alice (*née* Hurst); *m* 1954, Kathleen (*née* Hodgson); two *s* one *d.* Served Army, 1945–49. Board of Trade, 1950–57; Trade Commission Service, 1958–64: served Kuala Lumpur and Sydney; HM Diplomatic Service, 1964–: served Copenhagen, Caracas, Asuncion (Ambassador, 1979–84) and London; Trng Consultant, FCO, 1987–. Project Dir for S Amer., GAP Activity Projects (GAP) Ltd, 1993–. *Recreations:* tennis, golf, ski-ing. *Address:* Summerford Farmhouse, Withyham, E Sussex TN7 4DA. *T:* (01892) 770707. *Club:* Army and Navy.

MELLOR, Fiona; *see* MacCarthy, F.

MELLOR, Hugh Wright; Secretary and Director, National Corporation for Care of Old People (now Centre for Policy on Ageing), 1973–80; *b* 11 Aug. 1920; *s* of late William Algernon and Katherine Mildred Mellor; *m* 1944, (Winifred) Joyce Yates. *Educ:* Leys Sch., Cambridge; London Univ. (BScEcon). Friends Relief Service, 1940–45; Sec., St Albans Council of Social Service, 1945–48; Community Develt Officer, Hemel Hempstead Develt Corp., 1948–50; Asst Sec., Nat. Corp. for Care of Old People, 1951–73. Pres., Hanover Housing Assoc., 1994–99 (Chm., 1980–85). *Publications:* The Role of Voluntary Organisations in Social Welfare, 1985; (with Joyce Mellor) Quakers in High Wycombe 1650–2000: a brief history, 2003. *Recreations:* walking, reading, music. *Address:* Lark Rise, Risborough Road, Great Kimble, Aylesbury, Bucks HP17 0XS. *Club:* Royal Commonwealth Society.

MELLOR, Ian, MA; Headmaster, Stockport Grammar School, 1996–2005; *b* 30 June 1946; *s* of William Crompton Mellor and Annie Mellor; *m* 1969, Margery Ainsworth; three *s.* *Educ:* Manchester Grammar Sch.; Sidney Sussex Coll., Cambridge (MA, DipEd). Asst Modern Langs teacher, King's Sch., Chester, 1968–73; Head of Modern Languages: Kirkham Grammar Sch., Lancs, 1974–76; Bristol Grammar Sch., 1976–84; Dep. Head, Sale Boys' Grammar Sch., 1984–90; Head, Sir Roger Manwood's Sch., Sandwich, 1991–96. *Recreations:* Association football, cricket, reading, music of the 1960s, philatelic flaws and watermark varieties, bridge. *Address:* Bryn Issa, 10 Boot Street, Whittington, Shropshire SY11 4DG.

MELLOR, Dame Julie (Thérèse), DBE 2006; Partner, PricewaterhouseCoopers, since 2005; *b* 29 Jan. 1957; *d* of Gp Capt. Edward Vernon Mellor and late Patricia Ann Mellor; *m* 1990, Nick Reed; one *s* one *d.* *Educ:* Winchester Co. High Sch. for Girls; Brasenose Coll., Oxford (BA Hons Exptl Psychol.; Hon. Fellow, 2003). Eleanor Emerson Fellow in Labour Educn, Cornell Univ., NY and teacher, Inst. for Educn Res. on Women and Work, 1979–81; Employee Relns Advr, Shell UK, 1981–83; Econ. Develt Officer, London Borough of Islington, 1983–84; Sen. Employment Policy Advr and Dep. Hd, Contract Compliance, Equal Opportunities Unit, ILEA, 1984–89; Equal Opportunities Manager, TSB Gp, 1989–91; Dir of Equal Opportunities and Corporate Human Resources Dir, British Gas, 1992–96; owner and principal consultant, Julie Mellor Consultants, 1996–99; Chair, EOC, 1999–2005. Mem., CRE, 1995–2002. Member: Minister's Nat. Adv. Council on Employment of Disabled People, 1993–95; Bd, Employers' Forum on Disability, 2001–; Bd, NCC, 2001–07; Bd, DIUS, 2008–. Chair, Fatherhood Inst. (formerly Fathers Direct), 2005–. FCGI 2003. Hon. DPhil Anglia, 2003. *Recreations:* theatre, travel, food, family. *Address:* PricewaterhouseCoopers, 80 Strand, WC2R 0AF.

MELLOR, Very Rev. (Kenneth) Paul; Dean of Guernsey, Rector of St Peter Port and Priest-in-Charge of Sark, since 2003; *b* 11 Aug. 1949; *s* of William Lewis and Frances Emma, (Peggy), Mellor; *m* 1972, Lindsey Helen Vinall; three *s.* *Educ:* Ashfield Sch., Kirkby-in-Ashfield; Southampton Univ. (BA Theol. 1971); Leeds Univ. (MA Theol. 1972); Cuddesdon Coll. Ordained deacon, 1973, priest, 1974; Curate: St Mary the Virgin, Cottingham, 1973–76; All Saints, Ascot, 1976–80; Vicar: St Mary Magdalen, Tilehurst, 1980–85; St Lalluwy, Menheniot, 1985–94; Canon Treasurer and Canon Residentiary, Truro Cathedral, 1994–2003 (Hon. Canon, 1990–94). RD, W Wivelshire, 1990–94; Chm., Truro Diocesan Bd for Mission and Unity, 1990–95. Member: Gen. Synod, 1994–; Cathedral Fabric Commn for England, 1995–2000. Hon. Canon, Winchester Cathedral, 2003–. *Recreations:* walking, reading (esp. modern fiction), theatre, travel. *Address:* The Deanery, St Peter Port, Guernsey, CI GY1 1BZ. *T:* (01481) 720036; *e-mail:* paul@townchurch.org.gg.

MELLOR, His Honour Kenneth Wilson; QC 1975; a Circuit Judge, 1984–97; *b* 4 March 1927; *s* of Samuel Herbert Mellor; *m* 1957, Sheila Gale; one *s* three *d.* *Educ:* King's College Cambridge (BA 1949; LLB 1950; MA 1951). RNVR, 1944–47 (Sub Lieut). Called to the Bar, Lincoln's Inn, 1950. Dep. Chm., Hereford QS, 1969–71; a Recorder, 1972–84. Chm., Agricultural Land Tribunal (West Midlands).

MELLOR, Very Rev. Paul; *see* Mellor, Very Rev. K. P.

MELLOR, Ronald William, CBE 1984; FREng, FIMechE; Secretary, Institution of Mechanical Engineers, 1987–93; *b* 8 Dec. 1930; *s* of William and Helen Edna Mellor; *m* 1956, Jean Sephton; one *s* one *d.* *Educ:* Highgate School; King's College London (BSc Eng). FIMechE 1980; FREng (FEng 1983). Commnd RA, 1950. Ford Motor Co.: Manager Cortina Product Planning, 1964; Manager Truck Product Planning, 1965; Chief Research Engineer, 1969; Chief Engine Engineer, 1970; Chief Body Engineer, Ford Werke AG, W Germany, 1974; Vice Pres. Car Engineering, Ford of Europe Inc., 1975–87; Dir, Ford Motor Co. Ltd, 1983–87. Mem., Bd of Govs, Anglia Polytechnic Univ., 1993–2002 (Hon. Fellow, 2004). Liveryman, Co. of Carmen, 1990–. Thomas Hawksley Lectr, IMechE, 1983. *Recreation:* yachting.

MELLOWS, Prof. Anthony Roger, OBE 2003; TD 1969; PhD, LLD; Solicitor of the Supreme Court, 1960–2001; Professor of the Law of Property in the University of London, 1974–90, now Emeritus; Lord Prior, Order of St John, since 2008 (Vice Lord Prior, 2005–08); *b* 30 July 1936; *s* of L. B. and M. P. Mellows; *m* 1973, Elizabeth, DStJ, *d* of Ven. B. G. B. Fox, MC, TD, and of Hon. Margaret Joan Fox, *d* of 1st Viscount Davidson, PC, GCVO, CH, CB. *Educ:* King's Coll., London (AKC 1957; LLB 1957; LLM 1959; PhD 1962; BD 1968; LLD 1973; Fellow 1980). Commissioned Intelligence Corps (TA), 1959, Captain 1964; served Intell. Corps (TA) and (T&AVR) and on the Staff, 1959–71; RARO, 1971–91. Admitted a solicitor, 1960; private practice, 1960–2001; Sen. Partner, 1962–96, Consultant, 1996–2001, Alexanders; Consultant, Hunters, 2001–04. Asst Lectr in Law, King's Coll., London, 1962, Lectr, 1964, Reader, 1971; Dir of Conveyancing Studies, 1969; Dean, Fac. of Laws, Univ. of London, 1981–84, and of Fac. of Laws, KCL, 1981–85; Hd of Dept of Laws, KCL, 1984–87; Mem. Council, KCL, 1972–80. Mem., Archbishops' Millennium Adv. Gp, 1995–2000; Chm., Archbishops' Rev. of Bishops' Needs and Resources, 1999–2002. Chm., St John and Red Cross Defence Med. Welfare Service, 2001–05. Trustee: Kincardine Foundn, 1972–84; Nineveh Trust, 1985–90; London Law Trust, 1968– (Chm. Trustees); Lambeth Fund, 1995–; Marit and Hans Rausing Charitable Foundn, 1996–2006; Order of St John and British Red Cross Soc. Jt Cttee, 1987– (Vice Chm. Trustees, 2001–); The Choral Foundn of the Chapel Royal, HM Tower of London, 2005–; The Constable's Fund, 2005–. FRSA 1959. Freeman of the City of London, 1963. GCStJ 1991 (KStJ 1988; CStJ 1985; OStJ 1981; Mem. Council, 1981–88; Registrar, 1988–91; Chancellor, 1991–99; Dep. Lord Prior, 1999–2005); Comdr, Ordine Pro Merito Melitensi, SMO Malta, 1999. *Publications:* Local Searches and Enquiries, 1964, 2nd edn 1967; Conveyancing Searches, 1964, 2nd edn 1975; Land Charges, 1966; The Preservation and Felling of Trees, 1964; The Trustee's Handbook, 1965, 3rd edn 1975; Taxation for Executors and Trustees, 1967, 6th edn 1984; (jtly) The Modern Law of Trusts, 1966, 5th edn 1983; The Law of Succession, 1970, 4th edn 1983; Taxation of Land Transactions, 1973, 3rd edn 1982. *Address:* 22 Devereux Court, Temple Bar, WC2R 3JJ. *Club:* Athenæum.

MELLOWS, Heather Jean, (Mrs A. Johnson), FRCOG; Consultant Obstetrician and Gynaecologist, Doncaster and Bassetlaw Hospitals NHS Foundation Trust, since 1988; *b* 13 March 1951; *d* of late A. Paul Mellows, DFC, MA, LLB and of Jean Mellows (*née* Wells); *m* 1982, Anthony Johnson; two step *s*. *Educ:* Royal Free Hosp. Sch. of Medicine (MB BS 1974). FRCOG 1993; FFFP 2007. Regl Assessor in Obstetrics, Confidential Enquiry into Maternal Deaths, 1993–; Mem. Panel, Sec. of State's Inquiry into Quality and Practice within the NHS, arising from the actions of Rodney Ledward, 1999–2000 (reported, 2000). Co-Chm., Maternity Module, Children's Nat. Service Framework, 2002–04; Advr, Obstetrics and Gynaecol., DoH, 2006–08. Royal College of Obstetricians and Gynaecologists: Mem. Council, 1986–92, 1994–96 and 1999–2001; Chm., Hosp. Recognition Cttee, 1994–96; Jun. Vice Pres., 2001–04. *Address:* Brookhouse Hall, Laughton, Sheffield S25 1YA. *T:* (01909) 562399.

MELLY, Rear Adm. Richard Graham, (Dick); Clerk, Goldsmiths' Company, since 2005; *b* 31 Dec. 1953; *s* of Peter Emerson Melly and Shirley Julia Melly (*née* Higham); *m* 1987, Lynne Griffiths; two *d*. *Educ:* Winchester House Sch.; Stowe Sch.; Univ. of Manchester (BSc (Mech. Engrg) 1974); RNEC (MSc (Marine Engrg) 1980). CEng 1987. Her Majesty's Ships: Devonshire, 1976–78; Hermes, 1980–82; Nottingham, 1988–90; staffing duties, MoD, 1993–95; Superintendent Ships, Portsmouth, 1995–98; rcds 2000; Dir, Naval Manning, 2001–03; COS to Second Sea Lord and C-in-C, Naval Home Comd, 2003–05. Trustee, Falkland Is Meml Chapel Trust. Member: British Hallmarking Council, 2005–; Council, Goldsmiths Coll., 2005–. Trustee, Goldsmiths Centre, 2007–. *Recreations:* ski-ing, computing, DIY. *Address:* The Goldsmiths' Company, Goldsmiths' Hall, Foster Lane, EC2V 6BN. *T:* (020) 7606 7010.

MELMOTH, Sir Graham (John), Kt 2002; Chief Executive, Co-operative Group (CWS) Ltd (formerly Co-operative Wholesale Society), 1996–2002; *b* 18 March 1938; *s* of Harry James Melmoth and Marjorie Doris Melmoth (*née* Isitt); *m* 1967, Jennifer Mary Banning; two *s*. *Educ:* City of London Sch. FCIS 1972. National Service, 1957–59 (Lieut), RA. Asst Sec., Chartered Inst. of Patent Agents, 1961–65; Sec., BOC-AIRCO, 1965–69; Dep. Sec., Fisons, 1969–72; Sec., Letraset, 1972–75; CWS, then Co-operative Group (CWS) Ltd, 1975–: Director: Co-operative Bank plc, 1992–2003; Co-operative Press Ltd, 1994–98; Co-operative Insurance Soc. Ltd, 1996–2003. Chm., Ringway Developments plc, 1995–2002 (Dir, 1988–2002); Dir, Unity Trust Bank plc, 1992–98. Chairman: Manchester TEC Ltd, 1999–2001 (Dir, 1997–2001); Manchester Enterprises Ltd, 2001–03 (Dir, 1997–2000, Chm., 1999–2000, Manchester TEC Ltd). Chm., NCVO, 2004–. Mem. Council, NACRO, 1998–2004. Trustee: New Lanark Conservation Trust, 1987–2004; Nat. Mus. of Labour History, 1995–2001; Charities Aid Foundn, 2004–. Pres., Internat. Co-operative Alliance, Geneva, 1995–97. FIGD 1996; FRSA 1996; CCMI (CIMgt 1997). *Recreations:* opera, theatre, Co-operative history. *Address:* Greengarth, Dockray, Cumbria CA11 0LS. *Club:* Reform.

MELTON, Christopher; QC 2001; a Recorder, since 2005; *b* 15 Nov. 1958; *s* of Derek Edward and Margaret Melton; *m* 1990, Karen Jacqueline Holder; two *s* two *d*. *Educ:* Manchester Grammar Sch. Called to the Bar, Gray's Inn, 1982; in practice, specialising in medical law. *Recreations:* tennis, ski-ing, Francophile. *Address:* (chambers) 12 Byrom Street, Manchester M3 4PP; *e-mail:* chris.melton@virgin.net. *Club:* Bowdon Lawn Tennis.

MELVILL JONES, Prof. Geoffrey, FRS 1979; FRSC 1979; FCASI; FRAeS; Emeritus Professor, McGill University, since 1992; Adjunct Professor, since 1992, Research Professor, since 2001, University of Calgary; *b* 14 Jan. 1923; *s* of Sir Bennett Melvill Jones, CBE, AFC, FRS and Dorothy Laxton Jotham; *m* 1953, Jenny Marigold Burnaby; two *s* two *d*. *Educ:* King's Choir Sch.; Dauntsey's Sch.; Cambridge Univ. (BA, MA, MB, BCh). Appointments in UK, 1950–61: House Surgeon, Middlesex Hosp., 1950; Sen. Ho. Surg., Otolaryngology, Addenbrooke's Hosp., Cambridge, 1950–51; MO, RAF, 1951; Scientific MO, RAF Inst. of Aviation Medicine, Farnborough, Hants, 1951–55; Scientific Officer (external staff), Medical Research Council of Gt Britain, 1955–61; McGill University: Dir, Aviation, later Aerospace Med. Res. Unit, 1961–88; Associate Prof., 1961–68; Full Prof., 1968–91; Hosmer Res. Prof. of Physiol., 1978–91. Fellow, Aerospace Medical Assoc., 1969; FCASI 1965; FRAeS 1981. First recipient, Dohlman Medal for research in the field of orientation and postural control, 1986; Robert Bárány Jubilee Gold Medal for most significant research on vestibular function during past 5 years; Ashton Graybiel Lectureship Award, US Navy, 1989; Stewart Meml Lectureship Award, RAeS, 1989; Buchanan-Barbour Award, RAeS, 1990; McLaughlan Medal, RSCan, 1991. *Publications:* Mammalian Vestibular Physiology, 1979 (NY); Adaptive Mechanisms in Gaze Control, 1985; research papers in physiological jls. *Recreations:* outdoor activities, music. *Address:* Department of Clinical Neurosciences, Faculty of Medicine, University of Calgary, 3330 Hospital Drive NW, Calgary, AB T2N 4N1, Canada. *T:* (403) 220 8764/4307, *Fax:* (403) 283 8731.

MELVILLE; *see* Leslie Melville, family name of Earl of Leven and Melville.

MELVILLE, 9th Viscount *cr* 1802; **Robert David Ross Dundas;** Baron Duneira 1802; *b* 28 May 1937; *s* of Hon. Robert Maldred St John Melville Dundas (2nd *s* of 7th Viscount) (killed in action, 1940), and of Margaret Connell (who *m* 2nd, 1946, Gerald Bristowe Sanderson), *d* of late Percy Cruden Ross; *S* uncle, 1971; *m* 1982, Fiona Margaret Stilgoe, *d* of late Roger and of Mrs Stilgoe, Stogumber, Som; two *s*. *Educ:* Wellington College. District Councillor, Lasswade, Midlothian; Mem., Midlothian CC, 1964–67. Pres., Lasswade Civic Soc. Lieutenant, Ayrshire Yeomanry; Captain (Reserve), Scots Guards. *Recreations:* fishing, shooting, golf, chess. *Heir: s* Hon. Robert Henry Kirkpatrick Dundas, *b* 23 April 1984. *Address:* Frith Wood, Far Oakridge, Stroud, Glos GL6 7PG. *Clubs:* Cavalry and Guards; House of Lords Motor; Midlothian County; Bonnyrigg and Lasswade District Ex-Servicemen's.

MELVILLE, Anthony Edwin; Headmaster, The Perse School, Cambridge, 1969–87; *b* 28 April 1929; *yr s* of Sir Leslie Galfreid Melville, KBE; *m* 1964, Pauline Marianne Surtees Simpson, *d* of Major A. F. Simpson, Indian Army; two *d*. *Educ:* Sydney Church of England Grammar Sch.; Univ. of Sydney (BA); King's Coll., Cambridge (MA). Sydney Univ. Medal in English, 1950; Pt II History Tripos, 1st cl. with dist., 1952; Lightfoot Schol. in Eccles. History, 1954. Asst Master, Haileybury Coll., 1953. *Recreations:* reading, gardening, music. *Address:* 4 Field Way, Cambridge CB1 8RW. *Club:* East India.

MELVILLE, Sir David, Kt 2007; CBE 2001; PhD; CPhys, FInstP; Vice-Chancellor, University of Kent, 2001–07; *b* 4 April 1944; *s* of late Frederick George Melville and Mary Melville; *m*; one *s* two *d*. *Educ:* Clitheroe Royal Grammar Sch.; Sheffield Univ. (BSc 1st Cl. Hons 1965; PhD 1969); Columbia Univ. CPhys, FInstP 1978. Southampton University: Lectr in Physics, 1968–78; Sen. Lectr, 1978–84; Lancashire Polytechnic: Prof. of Physics and Head, Sch. of Physics and Astronomy, 1985–86; Asst Dir, 1986–89; Vice-Rector, 1989–91; Dir, Middlesex Polytechnic, 1991–92; Vice-Chancellor, Middlesex Univ., 1992–96; Chief Exec., FEFC, 1996–2001. ICI Res. Fellow, 1968; Visiting Professor: Univ. of Parma, Italy, 1974–80; Oporto Univ., Portugal, 1983; Univ. of Warwick, 1997–2003; Visiting Scientist: ICI Corporate Lab., Runcorn, 1975; Consiglio Nazionale delle Ricerche, Italy, 1976–80. Mem. Bd, British Non-Ferrous Metals Ltd, 1987–92. Vice-Chm., CVCP, 1995–96. Member: Council, BNF Metals Technol. Centre, 1986–92; SERC Materials Commn, 1988–92; SERC Condensed Matter Sub-Cttee, 1986–88; SERC Physics Cttee, 1988–92; SERC Metals and Magnetic Materials Cttee, 1988–92; Council for Industry and Higher Educn, 1994–96, 2001–07; Council, Inst. of Employment Studies, 1998–2001; Jt DfEE/DCMS Educn and Libraries Task Gp, 1999–2000; Bd, Higher Educn Stats Agency, 2002–07 (Chm., 2003–07); Bd, The Place, 2002–08; Kent Ambassadors, 2002–; Bd, Higher Educn Prospects, 2002–07; DfES 14–19 Curriculum and Qualifications Adv. Cttee, 2003–04; DfES Foundn Degree Task Force, 2003–04; Kent Strategic Partnership, 2003–07; SE England Regl Assembly, 2003–06; SE England Sci., Engrg and Technol. Adv. Council, 2003–06; Bd, Lifelong Learning UK, 2004– (Chm., 2006–); QCA Quals and Skills Adv. Gp, 2004–; DfES Rev. of Further Educn Colls, 2005–06; Bd, Medway Renaissance Partnership, 2005–07; Bd, Edexcel, 2005–; Bd, Inst. of Financial Services, 2005–; DIUS Higher Educn Project Bd; DIUS Sci., Technol., Engrg and Math. High Level Strategy Gp, 2007–. Chairman: SERC Magnetism and Magnetic Materials Initiative, 1989–91; UK and Republic of Ireland Chapter, Magnetics Soc., IEEE, 1988–93; Internat. Congress on Magnetism, Edinburgh, 1991; Health and Safety Cttee, Univs and Colleges Employers Assoc., 2003–07; Univs Race Equality Consultation Project, 2003–05; Univ. Vocational Awards Council, 2003–08; Higher Educn in SE, 2003–06; Kent and Medway LSC, 2006–08; Cttee of Inquiry into Changing Learner Experience, 2008–; Vice-Chm., Kent Public Service Bd, 2004–07. Hon. Pres., Co. of Middx Trust, 1992–; Trustee, Learning from Experience Trust, 2001–; Vice-Chm., Trustees, Marlowe and Folkestone Academies, 2005–. DUniv: Middlesex, 1997; Derby, 2000; Hon. DSc: Sheffield, 1997; Southampton, 2001; Hon. DLitt, Kent 2008. *Publications:* articles on magnetism, magnetic materials and biophysics in scientific and engrg jls. *Recreations:* sailing, walking, ski-ing, plumbing. *Address:* 55A Chilbolton Avenue, Winchester, Hants SO22 5HJ.

MELVILLE, David; *see* Melville, R. D.

MELVILLE, James; *see* Martin, R. P.

MELVILLE, (Richard) David; QC 2002; barrister; *b* 22 April 1953; *s* of Col Robert Melville and late Joan Emerton Melville (*née* Hawkins); *m* 1981, Catharine Mary Wingate; one *s* one *d*. *Educ:* Wellington Coll.; Pembroke Coll., Cambridge (BA 1974, MA 1978). Called to the Bar, Inner Temple, 1975, Bencher, 2007. *Recreations:* sailing, ski-ing, painting, piano. *Address:* 39 Essex Street, WC2R 3AT. *T:* (020) 7832 1111, *Fax:* (020) 7353 3978. *Clubs:* Bar Yacht; Royal Corinthian Yacht; Itchenor Sailing; West Wittering Sailing; West Wittering Windsurfing.

MELVILLE-ROSS, Timothy David, CBE 2005; Chairman: Higher Education Funding Council for England, since 2008; DTZ Holdings plc, since 2000; *b* 3 Oct. 1944; *s* of late Antony Stuart Melville-Ross and of Anne Barclay Fane; *m* 1967, Camilla Mary Harlackenden; two *s* one *d*. *Educ:* Uppingham School; Portsmouth College of Technology (Dip Business Studies). British Petroleum, 1963–73; Rowe, Swann & Co., stockbrokers, 1973–74; joined Nationwide Building Soc., 1974: Dir and Chief Gen. Man., 1985–87; Dir and Chief Exec., 1987–94; Dir Gen., Inst. of Dirs, 1994–99; Chm., Investors in People UK, 1999–2006. Dep. Chm., Monument Oil and Gas plc, 1997–99 (Dir, 1992–99); Chairman: NewsCast Ltd, 2000–04; Bank Insinger de Beaufort NV, 2000–05; Manganese Bronze plc, 2003– (Dir, 2000–); Royal London Mutual Insce Ltd, 2005– (Dir, 1999–; Dep. Chm., 2002–05); Bovis Homes Gp plc, 2005–08 (Dir, 1998–2008). Member Council: Industrial Soc., 1986–95; Inst. of Business Ethics, 1994–; Essex Univ., 1995–2007. Pro-Chancellor and Chm. of Council, Univ. of Essex, 2000–07. Trustee, Uppingham Sch., 1988–2000. FRSA; CCMI (Pres., 2006–07); FCIS; FCIB. *Recreations:* music, reading, bridge, tennis, the countryside.

MELVYN HOWE, Prof. George; *see* Howe.

MENARY, Andrew Gwyn; QC 2003; a Recorder, since 2002; *b* 29 March 1959; *m* 1982, Joy Michelle; one *s* one *d*. *Educ:* BA Hons Law. Called to the Bar, Inner Temple, 1982; in practice as barrister, Liverpool, 1982–. *Recreations:* playing the tuba, beginner's level golf. *Address:* (chambers) 7 Harrington Street, Liverpool L2 9YH. *T:* (0151) 236 5818, *Fax:* (0151) 236 2800; *e-mail:* andrew.menary@7hs.co.uk.

MENCHÚ, Rigoberta; human rights activist; Goodwill Ambassador, UNESCO, since 1996; *b* 1959; *d* of late Vicente Menchú, Mayan resistance leader and founder, Cttee of Peasant Unity (CUC), Guatemala, and Juana Menchú; *m* 1995, Angel Canil. Works for indigenous peoples' rights; founded Rigoberta Menchú Tum Foundn, Guatemala City; Member: CUC; United Representation of Guatemalan Opposition; Five Hundred Years of Resistance Campaign; UN Working Group on Indigenous Populations; UN Internat. Indian Treaty Council. Pres., Indigenous Initiative for Peace, UN, 1999. Nobel Peace Prize, 1992. *Publications:* (with Elisabeth Burgos-Debray) I, Rigoberta Menchú, 1983 (trans. English 1984; in 12 other langs); (with Gianni Minà y Dante Liano) Rigoberta: grandson of the Mayas, 1998 (trans. Italian and English).

MENDEL, Paul David, MBE 2000; Director, Council of Christians and Jews, 1992–98; broadcaster and speaker; *b* 14 Oct. 1930; *s* of late Eric Lazarus Mendel and Esther (*née* Graber); *m*; one *s* one *d*; *m* 1989, Rosalind Alder. *Educ:* St Christopher's Sch., Letchworth.

Nat. Service, 1949–51, Capt. RMP. Former Member: Middx CC; Barnet BC. Dep. Dir, Defence and Gp Relns, Bd of Deputies of British Jews, 1982–84; Council of Christians and Jews: Asst Dir, 1985–87; Dep. Dir, 1987–92. Mem., Interfaith Network Exec., 1987–. JP Juvenile and W Central PSD, 1955–83 (sometime Chm.). *Recreations:* travel, reading, people. *Address:* 100 Lyncroft Mansions, Lyncroft Gardens, NW6 1JY. *T:* (020) 7794 6989.

MENDELSOHN, Robert Victor, JD; Group Chief Executive and Director, Royal & Sun Alliance Insurance Group plc, 1997–2002; *b* NYC, 18 July 1946; *s* of Harold Victor Mendelsohn and Mary Ellen (*née* Muldoon); *m* 1968, Patricia Fielding; one *s* one *d*. *Educ:* Georgetown Univ. (AB 1968); Harvard Univ. (JD 1971). Called to the Bar, NY, 1971; Attorney, Willkie Farr & Gallagher, NYC, 1971–74; Pres. and Dir, W. R. Berkley Corp., Greenwich, Conn, 1974–93; Chief Exec., 1994–97, Chm., 1997, Royal & Sun Alliance USA, Inc., Charlotte, NC. Director: Amer. Insce Assoc., 1994– (Chm., 1999–2000); Internat. Insce Soc., 1999–; Chm. Council, Insce Co. Execs, 1998–2000. Mem., UK-China Forum, 1999. Mem., Bd of Regents, Georgetown Univ., Washington, 1999–. Trustee, Jose Limon Dance Foundn, 1979–95, now Emeritus. *Recreations:* golf, walking, ski-ing, sailing.

MENDELSON, Prof. Maurice Harvey; QC 1992; DPhil; barrister; Professor of International Law, University of London at University College London, 1987–2001, now Emeritus; *b* 27 Aug. 1943; *s* of William Maizel Mendelson and Anne (*née* Aaronson); *m* 1968, Katharine Julia Olga Kertesz; two *d*. *Educ:* St Marylebone Grammar Sch.; New Coll., Oxford (BA 1st Cl. Hons Jurisprudence 1964; MA; DPhil 1971). Called to the Bar, Lincoln's Inn, 1965 (Bencher, 2000); Internat. Law Fund Schol., 1966; Leverhulme European Res. Schol., 1966–67; Lectr in Laws, KCL, 1968–74; Kennedy Law Schol., Lincoln's Inn, 1970–73; Official Fellow and Tutor in Law, St John's Coll., Oxford, and Univ. Lectr in Law, Oxford, 1975–86. Fulbright Vis. Schol., Harvard Law Sch., 1977; Visiting Professor: Univ. of N Carolina, 1982; Univ. of Pennsylvania, 1986; Univ. of Paris II, 1993; Univ. of NSW, 1999; Univ. of Paris X, 2002–03. Mem., Bd of Editors, British Yearbook of Internat. Law, 1995–. Mem., Amer. Law Inst., 2000. FRGS 1995. Officier, Ordre de la Valeur (Cameroon), 2003. *Publications:* articles in internat. law jls, etc; reports to Internat. Law Assoc. *Recreations:* the arts, painting, swimming, tennis (Real and lawn), riding. *Address:* Blackstone Chambers, Blackstone House, Temple, EC4Y 9BW. *T:* (020) 7583 1770. *Club:* Athenæum.

MENDES, Samuel Alexander, CBE 2000; Co-Founder, and Director, Neal Street Productions, since 2003; *b* 1 Aug. 1965; *s* of Valerie Hélène Mendes (*née* Barnett) and James Peter Mendes; *m* 2003, Kate Elizabeth Winslet, *qv*; one *s*. *Educ:* Magdalen Coll. Sch., Oxford; Peterhouse, Cambridge (BA English, 1st Cl. Hons). Asst Dir, Chichester Festival, 1987–88, Artistic Director, Minerva Studio Theatre, 1989: productions included: Summerfolk, 1989; Love's Labour's Lost, 1989; Artistic Dir, Donmar Warehouse Th., 1992–2002; productions at *Donmar Warehouse* include: Assassins, 1992; Translations, 1993; Cabaret, 1993, NY (Tony Award for Best Revival of Musical), 1998; Glengarry Glen Ross, 1994; The Glass Menagerie (Olivier Award), 1995; Company (Olivier Award), 1995; Habeas Corpus, 1996; The Fix, 1997; The Front Page, 1997; The Blue Room, 1998, NY, 1999; To the Green Fields and Beyond, 2000; Twelfth Night, 2002, NY, 2003; Uncle Vanya, 2002, NY, 2003; productions as freelance director: *Royal Shakespeare Co.:* Troilus and Cressida, 1990; The Alchemist, 1991; Richard III, 1992; The Tempest, 1993; *Royal National Theatre:* The Sea, 1991; The Rise and Fall of Little Voice, 1992; The Birthday Party, 1994; Othello, 1997; The Cherry Orchard, Aldwych, 1989; London Assurance, Haymarket, 1989; Kean, Old Vic, 1990; The Plough and the Stars, Young Vic, 1991; Oliver!, Palladium, 1994; Gypsy, NY, 2003; The Vertical Hour, NY, 2006. *Films:* American Beauty (Academy Award for Best Dir and Best Picture), 1999; Road to Perdition, 2002; Jarhead, 2006. Numerous other awards. *Address:* c/o Neal Street Productions Ltd, 26–28 Neal Street, WC2H 9QQ.

MENDOZA, June Yvonne, AO 1989; OBE 2004; RP; ROI; artist; *d* of John Morton and Dot (*née* Mendoza), musicians; *m* 1960, Keith Ashley Victor Mackrell, *qv*; one *s* three *d*. *Educ:* Lauriston Girls' Sch., Melbourne; St Martin's Sch. of Art. Member: RP 1970; ROI 1968. Portraits for govt, regts, industry and commerce, academia, medicine, theatre, sport (*eg* Chris Evert for Wimbledon Mus.), and in public and private collections internationally. These include: Queen Elizabeth II; Queen Elizabeth the Queen Mother; Prince and Princess of Wales; Margaret Thatcher; John Major; Prime Minister of Australia, Sir John Gorton; Prime Minister of Fiji, Ratu Sir Kamisese Mara; Prime Minister of Singapore, Goh Chok Tong; former Prime Minister of Singapore, Lee Kuan Yew; Pres. of Iceland, Vigdis Finnbogadottir; Pres. of Philippines, Corazón Aquino; Donald Coggan, Robert Runcie, and George Carey, severally, while Archbishop of Canterbury; large group paintings include: The House of Commons in Session, 1986; House of Representatives, for new Parliament building in Canberra; private series of musicians include: Sir Yehudi Menuhin; Sir Georg Solti; Dame Joan Sutherland; Sir Colin Davis; Sir Charles Mackerras; Sir Michael Tippett. Lectures internationally; appearances on art programmes, TV and radio. Hon. Mem., Soc. of Women Artists, 1986. Hon. DLitt: Bath, 1986; Loughborough, 1994; DUniv Open, 2003. *Address:* 34 Inner Park Road, SW19 6DD.

MENDUS, Prof. Susan Lesley, FBA 2004; Professor of Political Philosophy, University of York, since 1996; *b* 25 Aug. 1951; *d* of John and Beryl Coker; *m* 1977, Andrew Mendus. *Educ:* UC of Wales, Aberystwyth (BA); Lady Margaret Hall, Oxford (BPhil). University of York: Lectr in Philos., 1975–90; Sen. Lectr in Political Philos., 1990–95; Dir, Morrell Studies in Toleration Prog., 1995–2000. *Publications:* Toleration and the Limits of Liberalism, 1989; Impartiality in Moral and Political Philosophy, 2002. *Recreations:* theatre, swimming, birdwatching. *Address:* Politics Department, University of York, York YO10 5DD. *T:* (01904) 433195; *e-mail:* slm6@york.ac.uk.

MENEM, Carlos Saúl; President of Argentina, 1989–99; *b* 2 July 1935; *s* of Saúl Menem and Mohibe Akil; *m* 1966, Zulema Fátima Yoma (marr. diss.); one *d* (one *s* decd); *m* 2001, Cecilia Bolloco (marr. diss. 2008); one *s*. *Educ:* Córdoba Univ. Legal Advr, Confederación General del Trabajo, La Rioja, 1955–70; lawyer, La Rioja, 1958; Gov., La Rioja, 1973–76, 1983–89; imprisoned, 1976–81. Pres., Partido Justicialista, La Rioja, 1963–. Vice Pres., Confedn of Latin American Popular Parties, 1990–. Founder, Juventud Peronista (Peronist youth gp), 1955. *Publications:* Argentina, Now or Never; Argentina Year 2000; (jtly) The Productive Revolution.

MENEVIA, Bishop of, (RC), since 2001; **Rt Rev. (John) Mark Jabalé,** OSB; *b* 16 Oct. 1933; *s* of John and Arlette Jabalé. *Educ:* Belmont Abbey Sch.; Fribourg Univ. (LèsL); St Mary's Coll., London (DipEd). Belmont Abbey School: Games Master and House Master, 1963–69; Headmaster, 1969–83; built Monastery of the Incarnation, in Tambogrande, Perú; Prior, 1986–93, Abbot, 1993–2000, Belmont Abbey; Bp Coadjutor of Menevia, 2000–01. Steward, Henley Royal Regatta. *Recreations:* computers, rowing. *Address:* Bryn Rhos, 79 Walter Road, Swansea SA1 4PS. *T:* (01792) 650534. *Club:* Leander (Henley-on-Thames).

MENHENNET, Dr David, CB 1991; Librarian of the House of Commons, 1976–91; Visiting Research Fellow, Goldsmiths College, London University, 1990–2002; *b* 4 Dec. 1928; *s* of William and Everill Menhennet, Redruth, Cornwall; *m* 1954, Audrey, *o d* of William and Alice Holmes, Accrington, Lancs; two *s*. *Educ:* Truro Sch., Cornwall; Oriel Coll., Oxford (BA 1st Cl. Hons 1952); Queen's Coll., Oxford. Open Scholarship in Mod. Langs, Oriel Coll., Oxford, 1946; Heath Harrison Trav. Scholarship, 1951; Bishop Fraser Res. Scholar, Oriel Coll., 1952–53; Laming Fellow, Queen's Coll., Oxford, 1953–54; Zaharoff Trav. Scholarship, 1953–54. MA 1956, DPhil 1960, Oxon. Library Clerk, House of Commons Library, 1954; Asst Librarian i/c Res. Div., 1964–67; Dep. Librarian, 1967–76. Member: Study of Parliament Gp, 1964–90; Bd of Mgt, H of C, 1979–91. Chm. Adv. Cttee, Bibliographic Services, British Library, 1986–92 (Mem., 1975–86); Mem. Exec. Cttee, Friends of Nat. Libraries, 1991–96. FRSA 1966 (Life Fellow 2001). Freeman, City of London, 1990; Liveryman, Stationers' Co., 1990. Gen. Editor, House of Commons Library Documents series, 1972–90. *Publications:* (with J. Palmer) Parliament in Perspective, 1967; The Journal of the House of Commons: a bibliographical and historical guide, 1971; (ed with D. C. L. Holland) Erskine May's Private Journal, 1857–1882, 1972; (contrib.) The House of Commons in the Twentieth Century, ed S. A. Walkland, 1979; (contrib.) The House of Commons: Services and Facilities 1972–1982, ed M. Rush, 1983; The House of Commons Library: a history, 1991, 2nd edn 2002; Essays and Articles on Bernardin de Saint-Pierre 1737–1814, 1998; articles in Lib. Assoc. Record, Parliamentarian, Parly Affairs, Polit. Qly, New Scientist, Contemp. Rev., Jl of Librarianship, Jl of Documentation, Book Collector. *Recreations:* National Trust activities, visiting Cornwall, French literature. *Address:* Meadow Leigh, 3 Westfield Close, Bishop's Stortford, Herts CM23 2RD. *T:* (01279) 755815. *Club:* Athenæum.

MENIN, Rt Rev. Malcolm James; Bishop Suffragan of Knaresborough, 1986–97; Hon. Assistant Bishop, diocese of Norwich, since 2000; *b* 26 Sept. 1932; *s* of Rev. James Nicholas Menin and Doreen Menin; *m* 1958, Jennifer Mary Cullen; one *s* three *d*. *Educ:* Dragon School; St Edward's School; University Coll., Oxford (MA); Cuddesdon Coll. Curate: Holy Spirit, Southsea, 1957–59; St Peter and St Paul, Fareham, 1959–62; Vicar of St James, Norwich, later St Mary Magdalene with St James, Norwich, 1962–86; RD Norwich East, 1981–86; Hon. Canon, Norwich Cathedral, 1982–86. *Recreations:* walking, photography, carpentry. *Address:* 32c Bracondale, Norwich NR1 2AN. *T:* (01603) 627987.

MENKES, Suzy Peta, (Mrs S. P. Menkes-Spanier), OBE 2005; Fashion Editor, International Herald Tribune, since 1988; *b* 24 Dec. 1943; *d* of Edouard Gerald Lionel Menkès and Betty Curtis Lightfoot; *m* 1969, David Graham Spanier (*d* 2000); three *s* (one *d* decd). *Educ:* Univ. of Cambridge (MA). Editor, Varsity newspaper, Cambridge, 1966; Jun. Reporter, The Times, 1966–69; Fashion Editor, Evening Standard, 1969–77; Women's Editor, Daily Express, 1977–80; Fashion Editor: The Times, 1980–87; The Independent, 1987–88. Freeman: City of Milan, 1986; City of London, 1987. Chevalier, Légion d'Honneur (France), 2005. British Press Awards Commendations, 1983 and 1984; Eugenia Sheppard Award for Fashion Journalism, Council of Fashion Designers of America, 1995. *Publications:* The Knitwear Revolution, 1983; The Royal Jewels, 1985, 3rd edn 1988; The Windsor Style, 1987; Queen and Country, 1992. *Recreations:* family life, reading, opera, Royal history. *Address:* c/o International Herald Tribune, 6 bis rue des Graviers, 92521 Neuilly Cedex, France. *T:* (1) 41439428.

MENNELL, Stuart Leslie; Clerk, Hawkwell Parish Council, since 2002; *b* 17 Oct. 1948; *s* of Albert Edward Mennell and Iris Mennell (*née* Jackson); *m* 1970, Margaret Hirst (*d* 2000); three *d*. *Educ:* Barlby High Sch., E Yorks. Ministry of Social Security, 1968–72; HM Customs & Excise: Preventive Duties, 1972–75; VAT, 1975–78; Regl Personnel Officer, 1978–82; Statistical Office, 1982–84; HQ Personnel Manager, 1984–86; Estate Manager, 1986–88; National Maritime Museum: Estabt Officer, 1988–89; Personnel & Corporate Planning Manager, 1989–93; Dir, Collections and Mus. Services Div., 1993–2001; Dir, Strategic Develts, 2001. MIPD 1989; MCMI (MIMgt 1992). *Recreations:* classic motor cycles, walking. *Address:* 10 Hever Close, Hockley, Essex SS5 4XB. *T:* (01702) 205464.

MENON, Prof. David Krishna, MD; PhD; FRCP, FRCA, FMedSci; Professor of Anaesthesia, University of Cambridge, since 2000; Fellow, Queens' College, Cambridge, since 2002; *b* 21 Aug. 1956; *s* of Parakat Govindan Kutty Menon and Violet Rebecca Menon; *m* 1988, Wendy Humphreys; one *s*. *Educ:* Univ. of Madras (MB BS, MD 1992); RPMS, Univ. of London (PhD 1995). FRCA 1988; FRCP 1999. Residency in Internal Medicine, Jawaharlal Inst., Pondicherry, India, 1978–83; Registrar: in Medicine, Professorial Med. Unit, Leeds Gen. Infirmary, 1984–86; in Anaesthetics, Royal Free Hosp., London, 1987–88; MRC Res. Fellow, Robert Steiner Magnetic Resonance Unit, Hammersmith Hosp., 1989–91; Clinical Lectr, 1992–93, Lectr in Anaesthesia, 1993–2000, Univ. of Cambridge; Lead Consultant and Dir, Neurocritical Care, Addenbrooke's Hosp., 1997–2001. Mem. Council, Intensive Care Soc., 2002–. Founder FMedSci 1998. *Publications:* Textbook of Neuroanaesthesia and Critical Care, 1998; contrib. to several textbooks, incl. Oxford Textbook of Critical Care, 1999, and Oxford Textbook of Medicine, 2001; contribs to various jls on topics of critical care and neuroscis. *Recreations:* basketball, science fiction, cooking, Lego. *Address:* University Department of Anaesthesia, Box 93, Addenbrooke's Hospital, Hills Road, Cambridge CB2 2QQ. *T:* (01223) 217889. *Club:* Royal Society of Medicine.

MENON, Prof. Mambillikalathil Govind Kumar, MSc, PhD; FRS 1970; Advisor to the Indian Space Research Organization, Department of Space, Government of India, since 2004 (Dr Vikram Sarabhai Distinguished Professor, 1999–2004); President, International Council of Scientific Unions, 1988–93; *b* 28 Aug. 1928; *s* of Kizhekepat Sankara Menon and Mambillikalathil Narayaniamma; *m* 1955, Indumati Patel; one *s* one *d*. *Educ:* Jaswant Coll., Jodhpur; Royal Inst. of Science, Bombay (MSc); Univ. of Bristol (PhD). Tata Inst. of Fundamental Research: Reader, 1955–58; Associate Prof., 1958–60; Prof. of Physics and Dean of Physics Faculty, 1960–64; Senior Prof. and Dep. Dir (Physics), 1964–66, Dir, 1966–75. Chm., Electronics Commn, and Sec., Dept of Electronics, Govt of India, 1971–78; Scientific Advr to Minister of Defence, Dir-Gen. of Defence Res. and Develt Orgn, and Sec. in the Ministry of Defence for Defence Res., 1974–78; Dir-Gen., Council of Scientific and Industrial Res., 1978–81; Sec. to Govt of India, Dept of Science and Technology, 1978–82, Dept of the Envmt, 1980–81; Chm., Commn for Addtnl Sources of Energy, 1981–82; Mem., Planning Commn, 1982–89; Chm., Science Adv. Cttee to the Cabinet, 1982–85; Scientific Advr to the Prime Minister, 1986–89; Minister of State for Sci. and Technology, India, 1989–90; MP (Janata Dal) Rajasthan, Rajya Sabha, 1990–96. M. N. Saha Dist. Fellow, Nat. Acad. of Scis, India, 1994–99. Pres., India Internat. Centre, 1983–88, 2007–; Member: UN Sec.-Gen.'s Adv. Cttee on Application of Sci. and Technol. to Develt, 1972–79 (Chm. for 2 yrs); Bd of Dirs, Internat. Fedn of Insts for Advanced Study, Stockholm, 1992–99. President: Indian Sci. Congress Assoc., 1981–82; Indian Statistical Inst., 1990–. Chairman: Indian Inst. of Technology, Bombay, 1997–2003; Indian Inst. of Technology, Delhi, 2003–06. Fellow: Indian Acad. of Sciences (Pres., 1974–76); Indian Nat. Science Acad. (Pres., 1981–82); Founding Fellow, Third World Acad. of Sciences; Hon. Fellow: Nat. Acad. of Sciences,

India (Pres., 1987–88); Indian Inst. of Sciences, Bangalore; Hon. FInstP 1998; For. Hon. Member: Amer. Acad. of Arts and Scis; Russian Acad. of Scis; Mem., Pontifical Acad. of Scis, Vatican; Hon. Pres., Asia Electronics Union; Hon. Mem., Instn of Electrical & Electronics Engrs Inc., USA. Member: Governing Council, UN Univ., 1986–92; Bd, Inst. for Advanced Studies, UN Univ., Tokyo, 1996–2004 (Chm., 1996–2001). Hon. DSc: Jodhpur Univ., 1970; Delhi Univ., 1973; Sardar Patel Univ., 1973; Allahabad Univ., 1977; Roorkee Univ., 1979; Banaras Hindu Univ., 1981; Jadavpur Univ., 1981; Sri Venkateswara Univ., 1982; Indian Inst. of Tech. Madras, 1982; Andhra Univ., 1984; Utkal Univ., 1984; Aligarh Muslim Univ., 1986; Bristol Univ., 1990; N Bengal Univ., 1989; Indian Inst. of Technology, Kharagpur, 1990; Guru Nanak Dev. Univ., 1996; Hon. Dr Engrg Stevens Inst. of Tech., USA, 1984; Hon. LLD IASE, Rajasthan, 2005. Royal Commn for Exhibn of 1851 Senior Award, 1953–55; Shanti Swarup Bhatnagar Award for Physical Sciences, Council of Scientific and Industrial Research, 1960; Khaitan Medal, RAS, 1973; Pandit Jawaharlal Nehru Award for Sciences, Madhya Pradesh Govt, 1983; G. P. Chatterjee Award, 1984; Om Prakash Bhasin Award for Science and Technol., 1985; C. V. Raman Medal, INSA, 1985; J. C. Bose Triennial Gold Medal, Bose Inst., 1983; (first) Ashutosh Mukherjee Gold Medal, Indian Science Congress Assoc., 1988; Gujar Mal Modi Foundn Award, New Delhi, 1994; Abdus Salam Award, Third World Acad. of Scis, 1997. National Awards: Padma Shri, 1961; Padma Bhushan, 1968; Padma Vibhushan, 1985. *Publications:* 150, on cosmic rays and elementary particle physics. *Recreations:* photography, bird-watching. *Address:* C-178 Sarvodaya Enclave, New Delhi 110017, India; *e-mail:* mgkmenon@nic.in. *Clubs:* National Liberal; India International Centre (New Delhi).

MENSAH, Barbara; Her Honour Judge Mensah; a Circuit Judge, since 2005; a Senior Immigration Judge, Asylum and Immigration Tribunal (formerly a Vice-President, Immigration Appeal Tribunal), since 2003; *b* 6 March 1959; *d* of Benjamin Amponsah Mensah and Victoria (*née* Apomasu). *Educ:* Wadhurst Coll., Kent; Millfield Sch.; UC of Swansea (BSc Philos.); City Univ. (Dip Law); Council of Legal Educn (Bar Finals); Queen Mary and Westfield Coll., London (LLM). Called to the Bar, Lincoln's Inn, 1984, Bencher, 2005. Lawyer, International Tobacco (Ghana) Ltd, 1987–89; pt-time Sen. Lectr, Inns of Court Sch. of Law, 1990–2000; Immigration Adjudicator, 1995; Dep. District Judge (Magistrates' Courts), 1998; a Recorder, 2003–05. Member: Adv. Bd on Restricted Patients, 1999–2002; Legal Services Consultative Panel, 2000–02. Mem., Disciplinary Panel, Bar Council, 2001. ACIArb, 1994–2000. *Publications:* The Prison Guide (with Andrew Goodman), 1999; European Human Rights Case Locator 1960–2000, 2000; European Human Rights Case Summaries, 2001; contrib. to Inns of Court Sch. of Law Bar Manuals. *Recreations:* swimming, reading, music. *Address:* Luton Crown Court, 7 George Street, Luton, Beds LU1 2AA.

MENSAH, Evelyn Justina A.; *see* Asante-Mensah.

MENTETH, Sir James (Wallace) Stuart-, 6th Bt *cr* 1838; *b* 13 Nov. 1922; *e s* of 5th Bt and Winifred Melville (*d* 1968), *d* of Daniel Francis and *widow* of Capt. Rupert G. Raw, DSO; *S* father, 1952; *m* 1949, Dorothy Patricia, *d* of late Frank Greaves Warburton; two *s*. *Educ:* Fettes; St Andrews Univ.; Trinity Coll., Oxford (MA). Served War of 1939–45, with Scots Guards, 1942–44; on active service in North Africa and Italy (Anzio) (severely wounded). *Recreations:* gardening, ornithology. *Heir: s* Charles Greaves Stuart-Menteth [*b* 25 Nov. 1950; *m* 1976, Nicola St Lawrence; four *d*].

MENTZ, Donald, AM 1994; Chief Executive Officer, Mentz International Trading, since 2004; *b* 20 Oct. 1933; *s* of Stanley Mentz and Marie Agnes (*née* Bryant); *m* 1959, Mary Josephine (*née* Goldsworthy); one *s* two *d*. *Educ:* Hampton High School, Victoria; Dookie Agricultural College, Victoria (DDA); Melbourne Univ. (BAgSci); Australian Nat. Univ. (BEcon). Dept of External Territories, Australia, 1969–73; Aust. Develt Assistance Bureau, Dept of Foreign Affairs, 1973–77; Dept of Business and Consumer Affairs, 1977–78; Dir of Operations, Asian Develt Bank, Philippines, 1979–81; Dep. Sec., Dept of Business and Consumer Affairs, Aust., 1981–82; Dep. Sec., Dept of Territories and Local Govt, 1983–84; Dir Gen., Commonwealth Agricl Bureaux, later CAB Internat., 1985–92; Man. Dir, Mentz Internat. Trading, 1993–99; Exec. Dir, Crawford Fund for Internat. Agricl Res., Aust., 1999–2001; Man. Dir, Mentak Granite and Marble Pty Ltd, 2000–03. *Recreations:* ski-ing, gardening. *Address:* 10 Bonwick Place, Garran, ACT 2605, Australia. *Clubs:* Athenæum; Commonwealth (Canberra).

MENZIES, Hon. Lord; Duncan Adam Young Menzies; a Senator of the College of Justice in Scotland, since 2001; *b* 28 Aug. 1953; *s* of late Douglas William Livingstone Menzies and Margaret Adam (*née* Young); *m* 1979, Hilary Elizabeth McLauchlan Weston; two *s*. *Educ:* Cargilfield; Glenalmond (schol.); Wadham Coll., Oxford (schol.; MA); Edinburgh Univ. (LLB). Admitted Advocate, 1978; Standing Junior Counsel to Admiralty, 1984–91; QC (Scot.) 1991; Temp. Sheriff, 1996–97; Home Advocate Depute, 1998–2000. Chm., Scottish Planning, Local Govt and Envmtl Bar Gp, 1997–2001. Contested (C): Midlothian, 1983; Edinburgh Leith, 1987. Mem., von Poser Soc. of Scotland, 1996–. Founder, Scottish Wine Soc., 1976. *Recreations:* shooting, golf, wine. *Address:* Court of Session, Parliament House, Parliament Square, Edinburgh EH1 1RQ. *Clubs:* Saintsbury; New (Edinburgh); Honourable Company of Edinburgh Golfers.

MENZIES, Duncan Adam Young; *see* Menzies, Hon. Lord.

MENZIES, Lt-Gen. Robert Clark, CB 2002; OBE 1989; FRCPE, FRCPath, FFPH; Chief Commander, St John Ambulance, 2005–06 (Chief Medical Officer, 2002–05); *b* 1 June 1944; *s* of late Flt Lieut Robert Clark Menzies and Jane, (Jean), Reid Menzies; *m* 1st, 1967, Joanna, (Joan), Letitia Lindsay Dunning (marr. diss. 2006); one *s* one *d*; 2nd, 2006, Dr Hausa Thakker. *Educ:* Kilmarnock Acad.; Glasgow Univ. (MB ChB 1967); DMJ (Pathology) 1976. MRCPath 1980, FRCPath 1992; FFPH (FFPHM 1999); FRCPE 2000. OC, Med. Reception Stn, Warminster, 1969; Trainee Pathologist, Leishman Lab., Cambridge Mil. Hosp., 1971–72; Pathologist, BMH, Rinteln, 1973–75; Registrar in Pathology, Queen Alexandra Mil. Hosp., 1975–76; British Army Exchange Pathologist, Armed Forces Inst. of Pathology, Washington, 1976–78 (Chief, Missile Trauma Pathology Br. and Hon. Professional Lectr, George Washington Univ.); Sen. Registrar in Pathology, Leishman Lab., Cambridge Mil. Hosp., 1978–81; Lectr in Forensic Medicine, Charing Cross Hosp. Med. Sch., 1981–83; Consultant Pathologist, Leishman Lab., 1983–85; Prof. of Mil. Pathology, Royal Army Med. Coll. and RCPath, 1985–89; CO, BMH Rinteln, 1989–92; Dir of Army Pathology, 1992–94; CO, 217 (London) Gen. Hosp. RAMC(V), 1994–95; Commander Medical: HQ London Dist, 1995–96; HQ Land Comd, 1996–99; Dir Gen., AMS, 1999–2000; Surgeon Gen. to the Armed Forces, 2000–02. QHS 1996–2003. Pres., Stapleford & Berwick St James Br., RBL, 2003–06. Freeman, City of London, 1995. CStJ 2006 (Trustee and Dir, Priory of England and the Islands, Order of St John, 2004–06). *Publications:* articles on pathology, particularly forensic pathology, in jls. *Recreations:* walking, travelling, photography, reading, music. *Club:* Army and Navy.

MENZIES-WILSON, William Napier, CBE 1985; Chairman, Ocean Transport & Trading plc, Liverpool, 1980–86 (Director, 1973–88); *b* 4 Dec. 1926; *s* of James Robert Menzies-Wilson and Jacobine Napier Williamson-Napier; *m* 1953, Mary Elizabeth Darnell Juckes; two *s* one *d*. *Educ:* Winchester; New Coll., Oxford (MA); North Western Univ., Chicago. Joined Stewarts & Lloyds Ltd, 1950; Managing Director, Stewarts & Lloyds of South Africa Ltd, 1954–61, Chairman, 1961; Director, Stewarts & Lloyds Ltd, 1964; Dir, Supplies & Transport, British Steel Corporation, 1967–73; Chairman: Wm Cory & Son Ltd, 1973–77; Viking Resources Trust, 1986–89; Director: Overseas Containers Holdings, 1979–86; Dunlop Holdings, 1982–84; NFC, 1986–95. Pres., Gen. Council of British Shipping, 1984–85; Mem. Exec. Bd, Lloyd's Register of Shipping, 1984–87. Trustee, Help the Aged, 1984– (Chm., Bd of Trustees, 1988–95). *Recreations:* shooting, golf, gardening. *Address:* Chaftonhop, Wacton Lane, Bredenbury, Bromyard, Herefords HR7 4TF. *T:* (01885) 483267. *Club:* Hon. Co. of Edinburgh Golfers.

MEON, Archdeacon of The; *see* Hancock, Ven. P.

MER, Francis Paul; Minister of Economy, Finance and Industry, France, 2002–04; *b* 25 May 1939; *s* of René Mer and Yvonne Casalta; *m* 1964, Catherine Bonfils; three *d*. *Educ:* Ecole Nationale Supérieure des Mines, Paris; Ecole Polytechnique. Mining engr, Ministry of Industry, 1966; tech. advr, Abidjan, 1967–68; joined St-Gobain Pont-à-Mousson Gp, 1970: St-Gobain Industries: Dir of Planning, 1971–73; Dir-Gen. Planning, 1973; Manager, 1974–78; St-Gobain Pont-à-Mousson: Dir of Planning, 1973; Asst Dir-Gen., 1978–82; Pres. Dir-Gen., Pont-à-Mousson SA, 1982–86; Pres. Dir-Gen., Usinor-Sacilor, 1986–2002; Chm., Usinor Gp, 2001–02; Co-Chm., Arcelor, 2002–. Director: Credit Lyonnais, 1997–2002; Electricité de France, 1997–; Air France, 1997–2002; Rhodia, 2004–; Adecco, 2004–. Chairman: Eurofer, 1990–97; IISI, 1997–98. President: French Steel Fedn, 1988–2002; Nat. Tech. Res. Assoc., 1991–2002; formerly President: Entreprise pour l'environnement; Cercle de l'industrie. Officier: Légion d'Honneur (France); Ordre Nat. du Mérite (France).

MERCER, Prof. Alan; Professor of Operational Research, University of Lancaster, 1968–98, now Emeritus; *b* 22 Aug. 1931; *s* of Harold Mercer and Alice Ellen (*née* Catterall); *m* 1954, Lillian Iris (*née* Pigott); two *s*. *Educ:* Penistone Grammar Sch.; Cambridge Univ. (MA; DipMathStat); London Univ. (PhD). NCB, 1954–56; UKAEA, 1956–62; Armour & Co. Ltd, 1962–64; Univ. of Lancaster, 1964–: Chm., Sch. of Management and Organisational Scis, 1982–85. Mem., Central Lancashire Develt Corp., 1971–85; Mem., 1985–89, Chm., 1986–89, Warrington and Runcorn Develt Corp. Chm., Employers' Side of Whitley Council for New Towns Staff, 1979–89 (Mem., 1971–89); Mem., Management and Industrial Relns Cttee, SSRC, 1972–76, 1980–82; Chm., Industry and Employment Cttee, ESRC, 1984–87 (Vice Chm., 1982–84); Mem., NW Econ. Planning Council, 1973–79. Jt Editor, European Journal of Operational Research, 1977–98. *Publications:* Operational Distribution Research (jtly), 1978; Innovative Marketing Research, 1991; numerous papers in learned jls. *Recreations:* travel, sport. *Address:* South Cottage, Calton, Airton, Skipton, North Yorks BD23 4AD. *T:* (01729) 830542.

MERCER, (Christine) Ruth; Headmistress, Godolphin and Latymer School, since 2009; *b* Preston, 19 June 1962; *d* of George Mercer and Joan Evelyn Mercer (*née* Stopforth); *m* 1988, Colin B. Horsley; one *s* one *d*. *Educ:* Bedford Coll., London (BA Hons Hist. 1983); St Catherine's Coll., Oxford (PGCE 1984); Dept of Contg Educn, Univ. of Oxford (Adv. Dip. Local Hist. 2006). Hd of Hist. and Politics, Notting Hill and Ealing High Sch., 1992–98; Dep. Headmistress, Godolphin and Latymer Sch., 1998–2002; Headmistress, Northwood Coll., 2002–08. *Recreations:* travel, fell walking, genealogy, reading, history, swimming. *Address:* The Godolphin and Latymer School, Iffley Road, Hammersmith, W6 0PG. *T:* (020) 8741 1936.

MERCER, His Honour Geoffrey Dallas; a Circuit Judge, South Eastern Circuit, 1991–2005; *b* 17 Dec. 1935; *s* of Leon Dallas Mercer, FRCS and Veronica Kathleen Mary Lillian Mercer (*née* Pitt-Lancaster). *Educ:* Clifton Coll., Bristol; St John's Coll., Cambridge (MA, LLM). Called to the Bar, Gray's Inn, 1960; practised at the Bar, 1961–91; Hd of Chambers, 1985–91; an Asst Recorder, 1986; a Recorder, 1990. Former English Youth International and Cheshire County golfer. *Recreations:* golf, music. *Clubs:* Royal Automobile; Burhill Golf; Worplesdon Golf.

MERCER, Giles; *see* Mercer, R. G. G.

MERCER, Hugh Charles; QC 2008; barrister; *b* Barnard Castle, Co. Durham; *s* of Keith and Gabrielle Mercer; *m* 1995, Isabelle Corbeel; two *s* (one *d* decd). *Educ:* Downing Coll., Cambridge (BA 1984); Université Libre de Bruxelles (Licence spéciale en droit européen). Called to the Bar, Middle Temple, 1985; in practice as barrister specialising in EU and internat. law; Chambers of Mark Littman, QC, 1987–95; Essex Court Chambers, 1995–; Circuit Junior, Eur. Circuit, Bar of England and Wales, 2001–. Hd, UK Delegn to Council of Bars and Law Socs of Europe, 2007–. *Publications:* Commercial Debt in Europe: recovery and remedies, 1991; European Civil Practice, 2004. *Recreations:* squash, mountain walking, gardening. *Address:* Essex Court Chambers, 24 Lincoln's Inn Fields, WC2A 3EG. *T:* (020) 7813 8000, *Fax:* (020) 7813 8080. *Clubs:* Royal Automobile; Achille Ratti Climbing.

MERCER, Prof. Ian Dews, CBE 1996; Secretary General, Association of National Park Authorities, 1996–2001; Hon. Professor of Rural Conservation Practice, University of Wales, since 1991; *b* 25 Jan. 1933; *s* of Eric Baden Royds Mercer and Nellie Irene Mercer; *m* 1st, 1957, Valerie Jean Hodgson; four *s*; 2nd, 1976, Pamela Margaret Gillies (*née* Clarkson). *Educ:* King Edward VI Sch., Stourbridge; Univ. of Birmingham (BA Hons). Sub-Lieut RNR, 1954–56. Field Centre appts, Preston Montford, 1956–57, Juniper Hall, 1957–59; Warden, Slapton Ley, 1959–68; Lectr, St Luke's Coll., Exeter, 1968–70; Warden, Malham Tarn Field Centre, 1970–71; County Conservation Officer, Devon CC; 1971–73; National Park Officer, Dartmoor, 1973–90; Chief Exec., Countryside Council for Wales, 1990–95. Chairman: Envmtl Trng Orgn, 1996–98; Devon Foot and Mouth Disease Inquiry, 2001–02; SW Forest Partnership, 2002–08; Dartmoor Commoners Council, 2004–; Devon Rural Network, 2005–08; Member: Inland Waterways, Amenity Adv. Council, 1995–2001; Devon and Cornwall Cttee, Nat. Trust, 1996–2005. President: Field Studies Council, 1986–; Devon Wildlife Trust, 1986–; Vice-Pres., Council for Nat. Parks, 2001–. Governor: Univ. of Plymouth, 1996–2005; Stover Sch., 1996–2004 (Chm., 2003–04). FRAgS 1999; Hon. FLI 1997. Hon. LLD Exeter, 1994; Hon. DSc Plymouth, 1995. *Publications:* Nature Guide to the West Country, 1981; chapters in books on conservation, education and national park matters. *Recreations:* painting, golf, gardening in France, teaching adults birds and landscape. *Address:* Ponsford House, Moretonhampstead, Devon TQ13 8NL. *T:* (01647) 440612. *Clubs:* Farmers'; Symonds.

MERCER, Patrick John, OBE 1997 (MBE 1992); MP (C) Newark and Retford, since 2001; *b* 26 June 1956; *s* of late Rt Rev. Eric Arthur John Mercer and of Rosemary Wilma (*née* Denby); *m* 1990, Catriona Jane Beaton; one *s*. *Educ:* King's Sch., Chester; Exeter Coll., Oxford (MA Mod. Hist. 1980). Commnd 1st Bn Worcs and Sherwood Foresters, 1975: served NI, 1975–77; Captain: BAOR and W Belfast, 1980–83 (despatches); Instructor, Brecon, 1984–86; Major: Chief Instructor, Ugandan Sch. of Inf., 1986; Jun. Inf. Bn, Shorncliffe, 1986–88; sc, Camberley, 1988; Co. Comdr, Omagh, NI, 1989–90

(GOC's Commendation); SO2 G3 (Ops), HQ NI, 1991–92; Chief Instructor, Platoon Comdr's Course, 1993; Lieut Col, SO1 Instructor, Staff Coll., Camberley, 1994–95; CO, Tidworth, Bosnia, Canada, 1995–97; Col, Hd of Strategy, Army Trng and Recruitment Agency, 1997–99; Defence Corresp., Today prog., BBC Radio 4, 1999. Mem., KCL team tasked with writing defence policy for E Timor, 2000. Opposition front bench spokesman on home, constitutional and legal affairs, 2003–07, on homeland security, 2004–07. Hon. Col, Notts ACF, 2007. *Publications:* Inkermann: the soldiers' battle, 1997; Give Them a Volley and Charge, 1997; contrib. jls and newspapers. *Recreations:* watercolour painting, history, bird watching, country sports. *Address:* House of Commons, SW1A 0AA; Newark and Retford Conservative Association, London Road, Newark, Notts NG24 1TN. *T:* (01636) 703269. *Clubs:* Army and Navy; Newark Working Men's.

MERCER, Dr (Robert) Giles (Graham); Headmaster, Prior Park College, 1996–Aug. 2009; *b* 30 May 1949; *s* of late Leonard and Florence Elizabeth Mercer; *m* 1974, Caroline Mary Brougham; one *s*. *Educ:* Austin Friars School, Carlisle; Churchill College, Cambridge (Scholar; 1st cl. Hist. Tripos, Pts I and II; MA); St John's College, Oxford (Sen. Schol., DPhil). Head of History, Charterhouse, 1974–76; Asst Principal, MoD, 1976–78; Dir of Studies and Head of History, Sherborne School, 1979–85; Headmaster, Stonyhurst Coll., 1985–96. Life Mem., Catholic Union, 1985. Chm., 2000–04, Vice-Pres., 2006–, Catholic Ind. Schs Conf. Governor: All Hallows Prep. Sch., Shepton Mallett, 1999–; St Mary's Sch., Shaftesbury, 2005–07. FRSA 2005. KSG 2004. *Publication:* The Teaching of Gasparino Barzizza, 1979. *Recreations:* art, music, travel, swimming. *Address:* c/o Prior Park College, Bath, Avon BA2 5AH. *T:* (01225) 835353; *e-mail:* rggmercer@aol.com. *Club:* East India.

MERCER, Rt Rev. Robert William Stanley, CR; Diocesan Bishop, Anglican Catholic Church of Canada, 1989–2005 (Assistant Bishop, 1988–89); *b* 10 Jan. 1935; *s* of Harold Windrum Mercer and Kathleen Frampton. *Educ:* Grey School, Port Elizabeth, S Africa; St Paul's Theological Coll., Grahamstown, SA (LTh). Deacon 1959, priest 1960, Matabeleland; Asst Curate, Hillside, Bulawayo, 1959–63; Novice, CR, 1963; professed, 1965; at Mirfield, 1963–66; at St Teilo's Priory, Cardiff, 1966–68; Prior and Rector of Stellenbosch, S Africa, 1968–70; deported from SA, 1970; Chaplain, St Augustine's School, Penhalonga, Rhodesia, 1971–72; Rector of Borrowdale, Salisbury, Rhodesia, 1972–77; Bishop of Matabeleland, 1977–87. Sub-Prelate, Order of St John of Jerusalem, 1981. *Address:* 3 The Limes, St Botolph's Road, Worthing, W Sussex BN11 4HY.

MERCER, Roger James, OBE 2005; FSA, FSAScot; FRSE; Secretary, Royal Commission on the Ancient and Historical Monuments of Scotland, 1990–2004; *b* 12 Sept. 1944; *o s* of Alan Mercer and Patricia (*née* Hicks); *m* 1970, Susan Jane Fowlie; one *s* one *d*. *Educ:* Harrow County Grammar Sch.; Edinburgh Univ. (MA). Inspector of Ancient Monuments, DoE, 1969–74; Lectr and Reader, Dept of Archaeology, Univ. of Edinburgh, 1974–89. Mem., Ancient Monuments Bd for Scotland, 1988–2004; Pres., Soc. of Antiquaries of Scotland, 2005–08 (Vice Pres., 1988–91); Vice President: Council for British Archaeology, 1990–94; Prehistoric Soc., 1989–92. British Acad. Readership, 1989; Hon. Professor of Archaeology: Univ. of Durham, 1996–; Univ. of Edinburgh, 1999–. FSAScot 1971; FSA 1976; FRSE 1995. Hon. MIFA 2004. *Publications:* Beaker Studies in Europe (ed), 1979; Hambledon Hill—a Neolithic Landscape, 1980; Grimes Graves—Excavations 1971–72, 1981; Carn Brea—a Neolithic Defensive Complex, 1981; (ed) Farming Practice in British Prehistory, 1981; Causewayed Enclosures, 1990; articles and reviews in learned jls. *Recreations:* music, books, good food. *Address:* Home House, 4 Old Church Lane, Duddingston, Edinburgh EH15 3PX. *T:* (0131) 661 2931.

MERCER, Ruth; *see* Mercer, C. R.

MERCHANT, Eileen; JP; Headmistress, Putney High School (GDST), 1991–2002; *b* 20 Feb. 1944; *d* of Jeremiah and Ellen McGill; *m* 1966, John Richard Merchant, *qv*; two *s*. *Educ:* Sheffield Univ. (BSc 1st Cl. Chem.). Dir of Studies, Bedford High Sch., 1974–86; Dep. Hd, Latymer Sch., Edmonton, 1986–91. JP Wimbledon, 1999–2003, Sussex, 2005. *Recreations:* birdwatching, reading, walking.

MERCHANT, John Richard; consultant; Director of Resources, Voluntary Service Overseas, 1995–2003; *b* 4 June 1945; *s* of William Henry Merchant and Eileen Merchant; *m* 1966, Eileen McGill (*see* E. Merchant); two *s*. *Educ:* Gravesend Grammar Sch.; Sheffield Univ. (BSc); Cranfield Inst. of Technol. (MSc). Lyons Bakery Ltd, 1966–69; Lectr, Cranfield Inst. of Technol., 1969–75; Statistician, MoD, 1975–79; Chief Statistician, CS Coll., 1979–82; Asst Sec., Cabinet Office (MPO), 1982–84; Principal Finance and Estabt Officer, DPP, 1984–86, Crown Prosecution Service, 1986–88; Under Sec., 1985; Sec. and Dir, Council Policy and Admin, SERC, 1988–94; Grade 3, Office of Public Service and Science, 1994. *Recreations:* gliding, Nigerian postal history, birdwatching.

MERCHANT, Piers Rolf Garfield; *b* 2 Jan. 1951; *s* of Garfield Frederick Merchant and Audrey Mary Rolfe-Martin; *m* 1977, Helen Joan Burrluck; one *s* one *d*. *Educ:* Nottingham High Sch.; Univ. of Durham (BA (Hons) Law and Politics, MA Political Philosophy). Reporter, Municipal Correspondent, Chief Reporter, Dep. News Editor, 1973–80, News Editor, 1980–82, The Journal; Editor, Conservative Newsline, 1982–84. Dir of Corporate Publicity, NEI plc, 1987–90; Dir of Public Affairs, The Advertising Assoc., 1990–92; Man. Dir, Cavendish Gp plc, 1998–2000 (non-exec. Dir, 2000–01); Exec. Dir, Made in London, 2000–04; Dir of Campaigns, LCCI, 2001–04; Actg Chief Exec., UKIP, 2004. Contested (C) Newcastle upon Tyne Central, 1979. MP (C): Newcastle upon Tyne Central, 1983–87; Beckenham, 1992–Oct. 1997. PPS to Sec. of State for Social Security, 1992–97. Co-Chm., Freeflow of Information Cttee, Internat. Parly Gp, 1986–91; Vice-Chm., All-Party Parly Cttee on AIDS, 1987. Contested (UK Ind), North-East, EP, 2004. Pol Advr to Roger Knapman, Ldr of UKIP, 2002–06. Non-executive Director: Eur. Public Health Foundn, 1993–2004; Tyne and Wear Waste Saver Ltd, 1996–98; London Asset Mgt Ltd, 2000–04; 91 St George's Drive Co. Ltd, 2006–. Member: London Business Bd, 2001–02; London Sports Bd, 2001–03; Team London, 2002–04; London Fund Manager's Adv. Bd, 2002–04; Econs Res. Adv. Bd, GLA, 2003–04. Mem., Sen. Common Room, UC, Durham. *Publications:* newspaper articles and features. *Recreations:* swimming, walking, genealogy, electronics, computers. *Address:* *e-mail:* pmerchant@yahoo.co.uk.

MERCIECA, Most Rev. Joseph, STD, JUD; Archbishop of Malta, (RC), 1976–2006; *b* Victoria, Gozo, 11 Nov. 1928. *Educ:* Gozo Seminary; Univ. of London (BA); Gregorian Univ., Rome (STD); Lateran Univ., Rome (JUD). Priest, 1952; Rector of Gozo Seminary in late 1960s; Permanent Judge at Sacred Roman Rota and Commissioner to Congregation for the Sacraments and Congregation for the Doctrine of the Faith, 1969; Auxiliary Bishop of Malta, and Vicar-General, 1974–76. Consultor, Supreme Tribunal of Apostolic Segnatura suis, 1992–. *Address:* c/o Archbishop's Curia, PO Box 29, Valletta, Malta.

MEREDITH, Most Rev. Bevan; Archbishop of Papua New Guinea, Primate of the Province of Papua New Guinea, 1990–95; Bishop of New Guinea Islands, 1977–95; licensed to officiate, diocese of Brisbane; Hon. Assistant, St Faith's Parish, Strathpine, since 1995; *b* Alstonville, NSW, 14 Aug. 1927; 3rd *c* of Stanley Meredith and Edith Meredith (*née* Witchard). *Educ:* Univ. of Queensland; St Francis Theol Coll., Brisbane. Teacher, Slade Sch., Warwick, Qld and Housemaster, Highfields House, 1948–53; Staff, Martyrs' Meml Sch., PNG, 1954–58; deacon 1961, priest 1962, St Thomas, Toowong; Priest-in-charge, Managalas, PNG, 1963–67; Asst Bp of New Guinea, 1967–77. *Recreations:* music, photography, philately. *Address:* 23 Coronet Drive, Bray Park, Qld 4500, Australia. *T:* and *Fax:* (7) 38896993.

MEREDITH, David Michael; District Judge (Magistrates' Courts) (formerly Stipendiary Magistrate), Leicestershire, since 1995; *b* 2 May 1945; *s* of George and Phyllis Maude Meredith; *m* 1977, Lynn Graham; one *s*. *Educ:* King Edward VII Sch., Sheffield; St Edmund Hall, Oxford (BA, DipEd). Asst Teacher, Chorlton High Sch., 1969–70, and King Edward VII Sch., Sheffield, 1970–74; admitted solicitor, 1977; Articled Clerk and Asst Solicitor, 1975–81, Partner, 1981–95, Graysons, Sheffield. *Recreations:* football, bad golf, theatre, travel. *Address:* Leicester Magistrates' Court, Pocklington's Walk, Leicester LE1 9BE. *T:* (0116) 255 3666. *Club:* Vincent's (Oxford).

MEREDITH, Richard Alban Creed, MA; Head Master, Monkton Combe School, 1978–90; *b* 1 Feb. 1935; *s* of late Canon R. Creed Meredith; *m* 1968, Hazel Eveline Mercia Parry; one *s* one *d*. *Educ:* Stowe Sch.; Jesus Coll., Cambridge. Asst Master (Modern Langs), 1957–70, Housemaster, 1962–70, King's Sch., Canterbury; Headmaster, Giggleswick Sch., 1970–78. CMS Area Sec., dios of Derby, Leicester and Southwell, 1990–98. *Recreations:* walking, foreign travel, music, gardening. *Address:* Beacon Knoll, 334 Beacon Road, Loughborough LE11 2RD. *T:* (01509) 212008.

MEREDITH DAVIES, (James) Brian; *see* Davies.

MERES, Lisa Moreen; *see* Opie, L. M.

MERIFIELD, Sir Anthony (James), KCVO 2000; CB 1994; The Ceremonial Officer, Cabinet Office, 1994–2000; *b* 5 March 1934; *s* of late Francis Bertram Merifield and Richardina (*née* Parker); *m* 1980, Pamela Pratt. *Educ:* Chesterfield Sch.; Shrewsbury Sch.; Wadham Coll., Oxford (MA). National Service, 1952–54, Royal Tank Regt. HM Overseas Civil Service, Kenya, 1958–65; Department of Health and Social Security: Principal, 1965–71; Asst Sec., 1971–77; Under Secretary, 1978–82; Under Sec., NI Office, 1982–85; Dir of Regl Liaison, NHS Management Bd, DHSS, subseq. NHS Management Exec., DoH, 1986–91; Head of Sen. and Public Appts Gp, Cabinet Office, 1991–94. Chm., KCH Charity (formerly Charitable Trust), 2004–. *Address:* c/o Lloyds TSB, High Street, Oxford OX1 4AA. *T:* (home) (020) 8670 1546. *Clubs:* Athenæum, Royal Commonwealth Society; Achilles; Dulwich and Sydenham Hill Golf.

MERKEL, Dr Angela Dorothea; Member, Bundestag, since 1990; Chancellor, Federal Republic of Germany, since 2005; Chairman, Christian Democratic Union, since 2000; *b* Hamburg, 17 July 1954; *d* of Horst Kasner and Herlinde Kasner; *m* 1998, Prof. Dr Joachim Sauer. *Educ:* Univ. of Leipzig; Zentralinstitut für physikalische Chemie, East Berlin (Dr rer. nat. Physics 1986). Res. Associate in Quantum Chemistry, Zentralinstitut für Physikalische Chemie, East Berlin, 1978–90; joined Demokratischer Aufbruch, 1989, Press Spokesperson, 1990, Dep. Spokesperson for Govt of Lothar de Maizière, March–Oct. 1990; joined CDU, 1990; Dep. Federal Chm., 1991–98; Chm., CDU, Fed. State of Mecklenburg-Vorpommern, 1993–2000; Gen. Sec., CDU, 1998–2000; Chm., CDU/CSU Parly Gp, Bundestag, 2002–05. Federal Minister: for Women and Young People, 1991–94; for Environment, Nature Conservation and Nuclear Safety, 1994–98. *Publications:* Der Preis des Überlebens: Gedanken und Gespräche über zukünftige Aufgaben der Umweltpolitik, 1997; Europa und die deutsche Einheit: Zehn Jahre Wiedervereinigung: Bilanz und Ausblick, 2000; (with Hugo Müller-Vogg) Mein Weg: ein gespräch mit Hugo Müller-Vogg, 2005. *Recreations:* reading, hiking, gardening. *Address:* c/o Bundeskanzleramt, Willy Brandt Strasse 1, 10557 Berlin, Germany. *T:* (30) 40000, *Fax:* (30) 40002357; *e-mail:* internetpost@bundeskanzlerin.de.

MERLO, David, CEng, FIET; Director of Research, British Telecommunications plc, 1983–89; *b* 16 June 1931; *s* of Carlo G. Merlo and Catherine E. Merlo (*née* Stringer); *m* 1952, Patricia Victoria Jackson; two *s*. *Educ:* Kilburn Grammar Sch., London; London Univ. (BScEng 1st Cl. Hons 1954); W. B. Esson schol. of IEE, 1953, and IEE Electronics Premium, 1966. CEng 1967, FIEE 1973. Post Office Research Br., 1948; Executive Engineer, 1955; Sen. Scientific Officer, 1959; Principal Sci. Officer, 1967; Head of Division, 1974; Dep. Director of Research, 1977. Visiting Lecturer: Northampton Polytechnic, 1955–61; Regent Street Polytechnic, 1960–69; Governor, Suffolk College of Higher and Further Education, 1984–89. Served on numerous technical committees in telecommunications field. FRSA 1988. Patent award, 1970. *Publications:* miscellaneous contribs to learned jls. *Recreations:* reading, photography, wine. *Address:* Heather Lodge, Levington, Ipswich IP10 0NA. *T:* (01473) 659508.

MERRICKS, Walter Hugh, CBE 2007; Chief Ombudsman, Financial Ombudsman Service, since 1999; *b* 4 June 1945; 2nd *s* of late Dick and Phoebe Merricks, Icklesham, Sussex; *m* 1982, Olivia Montuschi; one *s* one *d*, and one step *s*. *Educ:* Bradfield College, Berks; Trinity College, Oxford. MA Hons (Jurisp). Articled Clerk with Batt, Holden, 1968–70; admitted Solicitor, 1970; Hubbard Travelling Scholar, Montreal, 1971; Dir, Camden Community Law Centre, 1972–76; Lectr in Law, Brunel Univ., 1976–81; legal affairs writer, New Law Journal, 1982–85; Law Society: Sec., Professional and Public Relations, 1985–87; Asst Sec.-Gen. (Communications), 1987–95; Dir, Professional and Legal Policy, 1995–96; Insurance Ombudsman, 1996–99. Member: Royal Commn on Criminal Procedure, 1978–81; Fraud Trials (Roskill) Cttee, 1984–86; Victim Support Wkg Party on Financial Compensation, 1992–93. Pres., British Insce Law Assoc., 2006–; Chairman: British and Irish Ombudsman Assoc., 2001–04; Nat. Gamete Donation Trust, 2000–01; Internat. Network of Financial Ombudsman Schemes, 2007–; Mem., HFEA, 2002– (Chm., 2007–08); Membership Sec., Donor Conception Network. Mem. Council, Justice, 2004–; Hon. FCII 2004. Hon. LLD London Guildhall, 2001. Achievement Award, British Insce Awards, 2004. *Address:* c/o Financial Ombudsman Service, South Quay Plaza, 183 Marsh Wall, E14 9SR. *T:* (020) 7964 1000; *e-mail:* enquiries@financial-ombudsman.org.uk.

MERRILL, Dame Fiona Claire; *see* Reynolds, Dame F. C.

MERRIMAN, Air Vice-Marshal (Henry) Alan, CB 1985; CBE 1973; AFC 1957, and Bar 1961; DL; defence and aerospace consultant; *b* 17 May 1929; *s* of Henry Victor Merriman and Winifred Ellen Merriman; *m* 1965, Mary Brenda Stephenson; three *d*. *Educ:* Hertford Grammar Sch.; RAF Coll., Cranwell. Graduate, Empire Test Pilots Sch. FRAeS 1977. Commnd, 1951; Qual. Flying Instr, 263 F Sqdn, Empire Test Pilots Sch., Fighter Test Sqdn, A&AEE, Central Fighter Estabt, and RAF Staff Coll., 1952–63; Personal Air Sec. to Minister of Defence for RAF, 1964–66; Jt Services Staff Coll., 1966; OC Fighter Test Sqdn, A&AEE, 1966–69; HQ 38 Gp, 1969–70; Stn Comdr, RAF Wittering, 1970–72; RCDS, 1973; CO Empire Test Pilots Sch., 1974–75; Comdt, A&AEE, 1975–77; Dir, Operational Requirements (1), 1977–81; Mil. Dep. to Head of Defence Sales, 1981–84. Pres., NW Essex Aircrew Assoc., 1990–; Vice-Pres., N Herts Aircrew

Assoc., 1992–; Herts County Rep., RAF Benevolent Fund, 1995. Queen's Commendation for Valuable Services in the Air, 1956. DL Herts, 1995. *Recreations:* classic cars and aircraft, gardening. *Club:* Royal Air Force.

MERRIMAN, Nicholas John, PhD; Director, Manchester Museum, University of Manchester, since 2006; *b* 6 June 1960; *s* of Michael and Pamela Merriman; *m* (marr. diss.); two *s*. *Educ:* King Edward's Sch., Birmingham; St John's Coll., Cambridge (BA Archaeol. 1982; PhD 1989); Univ. of Leicester (Cert. Mus. Studies). AMA; FSA. Museum of London: Asst Keeper, Prehistory, 1986–91; Hd, Dept of Early London Hist. and Collections, 1991–97; University College London: Sen. Lectr, then Reader, in Mus. Studies, Inst. of Archaeol., 1997–2006; Curator, 1998–2006, Dir, 2006, Mus and Collections. Pres., Council for British Archaeol., 2005–08. FRSA. *Publications:* Beyond the Glass Case: the past, the heritage and the public in Britain, 1991; The Peopling of London, 1993; Making Early Histories in Museums, 1999; Public Archaeology, 2004. *Recreations:* running, family. *Address:* Manchester Museum, Oxford Road, Manchester M13 9PL. *T:* (0161) 275 2649, *Fax:* (0161) 275 2676; *e-mail:* nick.merriman@manchester.ac.uk.

MERRITT, Prof. John Edward; Emeritus Professor, The Open University, since 1987; *b* 13 June 1926; *s* of Leonard Merritt and Janet (*née* Hartford); *m* 1948, Denise Edmondson; two *s*. *Educ:* Univ. of Durham (BA); Univ. of London (DipEdPsychol). AFBPsS; FRSA. Sandhurst, 1945–46; Trng Officer, Border Regt, 1946–48. Educnl Psychologist, Lancs LEA, 1957–59; Sen. Educnl Psychologist, Hull LEA, 1959–63; Lectr, Inst. of Educn, Univ. of Durham, 1964–71; Prof. of Teacher Educn, Open Univ., 1971–85, retd. Hon. Res. Fellow, Charlotte Mason Coll., Ambleside, 1986–88. Pres., UK Reading Assoc., 1969–70; Chm., 5th World Congress on Reading, Vienna, 1974; Mem., Nat. Cttee of Inquiry into Reading and Use of English (Bullock Cttee), 1973–75. Hon. FCP 1994. *Publications:* Reading and the Curriculum (ed), 1971; A Framework for Curriculum Design, 1972; (ed jtly) Reading Today and Tomorrow, 1972; (ed jtly) The Reading Curriculum, 1972; Perspectives on Reading, 1973; What Shall We Teach, 1974; numerous papers in educnl jls. *Recreations:* fell walking, orienteering, climbing, ski-ing, theatre. *Address:* Highfield, 5 Cross Street, Keswick, Cumbria CA12 4DE. *T:* (01768) 774875.

MERRITT, Lindsay; *see* Nicholson, L.

MERRITT, Prof. Neil; Vice-Chancellor, University of Portsmouth, 1992–94 (President, Portsmouth Polytechnic, 1991–92); *b* 3 March 1939; *s* of the late Leslie Alfred Merritt and Gladys Irene (*née* Green); *m* 1961, Jean Fisher (former Headmistress, Heathfield Sch., GPDST, Pinner); one *s* one *d*. *Educ:* Ilford County High Sch.; Univ. of Hull (LLB). Asst Lectr, City of London Coll., 1962–63; Lectr, Slough Coll., 1963–65; Staff Tutor, Further Educn Staff Coll., 1965–68; Head, Faculty of Management and Arts, Norfolk Coll. of Arts and Technology, 1968–73; Vice-Principal, Mid-Essex Technical Coll., 1973–74; Pro-Dir, Chelmer Inst. of Higher Educn, 1975–76; Vis. Prof. of Law, Indiana Univ., 1974 and 1976; Dir, Ealing Tech. Coll., later Ealing Coll. of Higher Educn, then Polytechnic of W London, 1977–91 (Prof. *ad hominem*, 1989). Secretary, then Chairman: Assoc. of Law Teachers, 1965–71; Standing Conf. of Principals, 1977–91; Member: Adv. Cttee on Legal Educn, 1972–76; CNAA Legal Studies Bd, 1978–84; Nat. Adv. Body for Public Sector Higher Educn Bd, 1982–88. Chm., Hillingdon Hosp. Trust, 1991–94. FRSA. *Publications:* (with E. G. H. Clayton) Business Law, 1966; articles in professional jls on law, and higher educn policy. *Recreations:* music, travelling, France.

MERRIVALE, 4th Baron *cr* 1925, of Walkhampton, Co. Devon; **Derek John Philip Duke;** *b* 16 March 1948; *s* of 3rd Baron Merrivale and of Colette, *d* of John Douglas Wise, Bordeaux, France; *S* father, 2007; *m* 1976, Guillemette; one *s*. *Heir: s* Hon. Thomas Duke, *b* 25 March 1980.

MERRON, Gillian Joanna; MP (Lab) Lincoln, since 1997; Parliamentary Under-Secretary of State, Foreign and Commonwealth Office, since 2008; *b* 12 April 1959. *Educ:* Wanstead High Sch.; Univ. of Lancaster (BSc Hons (Mgt Scis) 1981). Business Develt Advr, 1982–85; Local Govt Officer, 1985–87; E Midlands full-time Official, NUPE and UNISON, 1987–95; Sen. Officer, UNISON, Lincolnshire, 1995–97. Mem., Lab. Pty, 1982–. PPS to Minister of State for the Armed Forces, 1998–99, to Minister of State for Defence Procurement, 1999–2001, MoD, to Sec. of State for NI, 2001–02; an Asst Govt Whip, 2002–04; a Lord Comr of HM Treasury (Govt Whip), 2004–06; Parly Under-Sec. of State, DfT, 2006–07; a Parly Sec., Cabinet Office, and Minister for the E Midlands, 2007–08; Parly Under-Sec. of State, DFID, 2008. Mem., Select Cttee on Trade and Industry, 1997–98. Vice-Chm., PLP Back bench Cttee on Foreign and Commonwealth Affairs, 1997–98; Chm., E Midlands Gp of Lab. MPs, 1999–2002; Associate, British-Irish Inter-Parly Body, 2001–02. Mem. Bd, Westminster Foundn for Democracy, 1998–2001. Grad., Armed Forces Parly Scheme (RAF), 1997–98; Fellow, Industry and Parlt Trust, 2002–. Dir, E Midlands Sport, 2000–03. *Recreations:* gym, running, films, Lincoln City FC. *Address:* House of Commons, SW1A 0AA.

MERRY, David Byron, CMG 2000; HM Diplomatic Service, retired; High Commissioner, Gaborone, 2001–05; *b* 16 Sept. 1945; *s* of late Colin Merry and Audrey Merry (*née* Handley); *m* 1967, Patricia Ann Ellis; one *s* two *d*. *Educ:* King Edward VII Sch., Sheffield; Ecclesfield Grammar Sch. Min. of Aviation, 1961–65; entered HM Diplomatic Service, 1965; Bangkok, 1969–73; Budapest, 1974–77; FCO, 1977–81; First Sec. (Econ.) and Civil Air Attaché, Bonn, 1981–85; Head of Chancery, E Berlin, 1985–88; FCO, 1989–93; Counsellor and Dep. Head of Mission, Manila, 1993–97; Dep. High Comr, Karachi, 1997–2000; FCO, 2000–01. *Recreations:* swimming, walking. *Address:* 22 Orchard Close, Hawley, Camberley, Surrey GU17 9EX.

MERRYLEES, Prof. Andrew, RSA 1991; RIBA; FRIAS, FCSD; consultant in private architectural practice, Hypostyle Architects; *b* 13 Oct. 1933; *s* of Andrew Merrylees and Mary McGowan Craig; *m* 1959, Maie Crawford; two *s* one *d*. *Educ:* Glasgow Sch. of Architecture (BArch 1956; DipTP 1957). RIBA 1958; FRIAS 1977; FCSD 1978. Joined Sir Basil Spence, Glover & Ferguson, 1952: student, 1952–57; architect, 1957–68; Associate, 1968; Partner, 1972–85; Principal, Andrew Merrylees Associates, then Andrew Merrylees Grierson & Robertson, subseq. Merrylees & Robertson, 1985–2000, merged with Hypostyle, 2001. Consultant Architect: SCONUL, 1964–79; UC Dublin, 1973–91. Hon. Prof. of Architecture, Univ. of Dundee, 1998–. Member: Adv. Council for Arts in Scotland, 1989–97; Council, RIAS, 1991–94. Mem., Edinburgh Fest. Soc., 1979–. *Major projects* include: university buildings at Edinburgh (Civic Trust Award, for Univ. Liby, 1969), Heriot-Watt, Dublin, Liverpool, Newcastle and Aston in Birmingham; Scottish HQ for AA; Sorting Office for PO, Edinburgh (Art in Architecture Award, Saltire Soc., 1983); Nat. Liby of Scotland (SCONUL Award, 1996); British Golf Mus., St Andrews; Motherwell Heritage Centre. FRSA 1993. Winner, numerous design competitions, including: UC Dublin Liby; Liverpool Univ. Arts Liby; Conf. Centre, Heriot-Watt Univ.; John Logie Baird Visions Centre, Glasgow; Dundee Sci. Centre. Numerous awards, including: Bronze Medal, RIBA, 1968; Gold Medal, Royal Scottish Acad., 1984. *Recreations:* architecture, painting, cooking. *Club:* Scottish Arts (Edinburgh).

MERSEY, 5th Viscount *cr* 1916, of Toxteth; **Edward John Hallam Bigham;** Lord Nairne 1681; Baron Mersey 1910; *b* 23 May 1966; *s* of 4th Viscount Mersey and of Joanna (*née* Murray); *S* father, 2006; *m* 1st, 1994, Claire Haigh (marr. diss. 1996); 2nd, 2001, Clare, *d* of Robert Schaw Miller; two *d*. *Educ:* Eton; Balliol Coll., Oxford; Trinity Coll. of Music, London. *Heir: uncle* Hon. David Edward Hugh Bigham [*b* 14 April 1938; *m* 1965, Anthea Rosemary Seymour; three *s* one *d*].

MERTHYR, Barony of (*cr* 1911); title disclaimed by 4th Baron; *see under* Lewis, Trevor Oswin.

MERTON, Viscount; Simon John Horatio Nelson; *b* 21 Sept. 1971; *s* and *heir* of 9th Earl Nelson, *qv*.

MERTON, John Ralph, MBE (mil.) 1942; draughtsman, portrait painter, inventor (of military, domestic and fun inventions), engineer; *b* 7 May 1913; *s* of late Sir Thomas Merton, KBE, FRS; *m* 1939, Viola Penelope von Bernd; two *d* (and one *d* decd). *Educ:* Eton; Balliol Coll., Oxford. Served War of 1939–45 in Far East (MBE); Asst to Mountbatten's Scientific Advr in Kandy, Ceylon; Air Photo reconnaissance research, Lieut-Col 1944. Works include: Mrs Daphne Wall, 1948; The Artist's daughter, Sarah, 1949; Altar piece, 1952; The Countess of Dalkeith, at Drumlanrig, 1958; A myth of Delos, 1959; Clarissa, 1960; Mrs Julian Sheffield, 1970; Sir Charles Evans, 1973; Iona Colquhoun Duchess of Argyll, 1982; Triple Portrait of Sir David Piper, 1984 (in Nat. Portrait Gall.); James Meade, 1987; Triple Portrait of HRH The Princess of Wales (for Cardiff City Hall), 1987; HM The Queen (at Buckingham Palace), 1989; Paul H. Nitze (in Johns Hopkins Univ.), 1991; Triple Portrait of Duke of Grafton (for Nat. Portrait Gall.), 1992; Peregrine Churchill, 1993; John Lewis (Chm. of the Trustees, Wallace Collection), 1995, his daughter Lily Lewis, 2003; Lord and Lady Romsey with a mirror reflecting Broadlands, 1997; double portrait drawing of two children, 1999 (exhibited RA, 2000); two paintings, from own photos, of coral trees under S China Sea off Tioman Is, N Malaysia: vertical tree (a mile off shore), 2000; horizontal tree (in shallower water), 2001; retrospective exhibn, Fine Art Soc., London, 2003; Lyndsay Wicksham, age 6, USA; Roy Bohana; large paintings from own 35mm transparencies, incl. S of France, Scotland, John Dory fish underwater in Kimmeridge Bay (Dorset), Paleokrastritsa (Corfu), Pound House pond; small paintings from underwater slides in Tioman Island, Malaysia. Legion of Merit (USA), 1945. *Publication:* A Journey Through an Artist's Life, 1994, part 2, 2003. *Recreations:* music, making things. *Address:* Pound House, Oare, near Marlborough, Wilts SN8 4JA. *T:* (01672) 563539.

See also Hon. Sir R. A. Morritt.

MERTON, Paul; *see* Martin, P. J.

MERTON, Prof. Robert C., PhD; John and Natty McArthur University Professor, Graduate School of Business, Harvard University, since 1998; *b* 31 July 1944; *s* of late Robert K. Merton and Suzanne C. Merton; *m* 1966, June Rose (separated 1996); two *s* one *d*. *Educ:* Columbia Univ. (BS Engrg Math. 1966); California Inst. of Technology (MS Applied Math. 1967); MIT (PhD Econs 1970). Massachusetts Institute of Technology: Asst Prof., 1970–73, Associate Prof., 1973–74, Prof., 1974–80, of Finance; J. C. Penney Prof. of Management, 1980–88; George Fisher Baker Prof. of Business Admin, Graduate Sch. of Business, Harvard Univ., 1988–98. Mem., NAS, 1993; Fellow: Amer. Acad. of Arts and Scis; Econometric Soc.; Internat. Assoc. of Financial Engrs; Inst. for Quantitative Res. in Finance; Financial Mgt Assoc.; Amer. Finance Assoc. Hon. Prof., Hautes Etudes Commerciales, France, 1995; Hon. LLD Chicago, 1991; Hon. DEconSc Lausanne, 1996; Dr *hc* Paris Dauphine, 1997; Hon. Dr Mgt Sci., Nat. Sun Yat-sen Univ., Taiwan, 1998; Hon. DSc Athens Univ. of Econs and Business, 2003. Leo Melamed Prize, Univ. of Chicago, 1983; Financial Engr of the Year Award, Internat. Assoc. of Financial Engrs, 1993; Internat. Prize, Accademia Nazionale dei Lincei, 1993; Nobel Prize for Economics, 1997; Michael I. Pupin Medal for Service to the Nation, Columbia Univ., 1998; Distinguished Alumni Award, CIT, 1999; Nicholas Molodovsky Award, Assoc. for Investment Mgt and Res., 2003. *Publications:* Continuous-Time Finance, 1990, rev. edn 1992; (jtly) Casebook in Financial Engineering: applied studies of financial innovation, 1995; (jtly) The Global Financial System: a functional perspective, 1995; (jtly) Finance, 2000; contribs to scientific jls. *Address:* Morgan Hall 397, Harvard Business School, Soldiers Field, Boston, MA 02163, USA. *T:* (617) 495 6678, *Fax:* (617) 495 8863.

MERVYN DAVIES, David Herbert; *see* Davies.

MERZ, (Joachim) Friedrich; Member (CDU/CSU) Bundestag, since 1994; *b* 11 Nov. 1955; *m* 1981, Charlotte Gass; one *s* two *d*. *Educ:* Univ. of Bonn. Mil. service, 1975–76. Practical trng in judicial and other legal work, Saarbrücken and Johannesburg, SA, 1982–85; magistrate, Saarbrücken, 1985–86; lawyer, 1986–: German Chemical Industry Assoc., Bonn, Frankfurt, 1986–89; Partner, Mayer, Brown LLP, Berlin, Frankfurt, Cologne, 2005–. MEP (CDU/CSU) S Westfalia, 1989–94. Mem., Finance Cttee and Cttee for Eur. Affairs, Bundestag, 1994–. CDU/CSU Parliamentary Group: co-ordinator, on Finance Cttee, 1996–98; Dep. Chm., 1998–2000, 2002–04; Chm., 2000–02; Member: Bd, CDU Nordrhein-Westfalen, 1997–; Fed. Bd, 1998–2000, Presidium, 2002–04, CDU party. *Address:* Bundeshaus, Platz der Republik, 11011 Berlin, Germany.

MESHER, John; Social Security Commissioner and Child Support Commissioner, since 1993; *b* 25 June 1947; *s* of late Percy Charles Mesher and Dorothy Mesher; *m* 1973, Hilary Anne Wilkens; one *s* and *d* (and one *d* decd). *Educ:* Bancroft's Sch.; University Coll., Oxford (BA Jurisp, BCL); Yale Law Sch. (LLM). Called to the Bar, Gray's Inn, 1970; Lectr in Laws, QMC, 1969–76; University of Sheffield: Lectr in Law, Sen. Lectr and Reader, 1976–93; Simmons & Simmons Res. Fellow in Pensions Law, 1988–93; Prof. Associate, 1993–. Part-time Chm. of Social Security, Medical, and Disability Appeals Tribunals, 1981–93, Pensions Appeal Tribunals, 1995–2004; Dep. Social Security Comr, 1991–93. Editor, Occupational Pensions Law Reports, 1992–97; Section Editor, Encyclopedia of Employment Law, 1991–97. *Publications:* Compensation for Unemployment, 1976; CPAG's Supplementary Benefit Legislation Annotated, 1983, 10th edn, as Income-Related Benefits: the Legislation, 1993; (contrib.) Rayden and Jackson on Divorce and Family Matters, 17th edn 1997; contribs to learned jls. *Address:* The Commissioners' Office, 3rd Floor, Procession House, 55 Ludgate Hill, EC4M 7JW. *T:* (020) 7029 9850.

MESHOULAM, Melanie; *see* Clore, M.

MESIĆ, Stjepan, Hon. GCMG 2001; President, Republic of Croatia, since 2000; *b* 24 Dec. 1934; *s* of Josip and Mandica Mesić; *m* 1961, Milka; two *d*. *Educ:* Univ. of Zagreb (LLB). Mayor, Orahovica, Croatia, 1967–71; MP Socialist Republic of Croatia, 1965–71; involved in Croatian Spring movt and served one-year jail sentence; Sec., 1990, Hd, Exec. Cttee, 1992, Croatian Democratic Union; Prime Minister, Socialist Republic of Croatia, May–Aug. 1990; last Pres., Yugoslavia, May–Dec. 1991; Speaker, Parlt of Republic of Croatia, 1992–94; Founder, Croatian Indep. Democrats Party (HND), 1994; Mem., Croatian Nat. Party (HNS), 1997–2000 (Exec. Vice-Pres. and Pres., Zagreb Br.). Charles

Univ. Medal, 2001. Homeland War Meml Medal (Croatia), 1993; State Order of Star of Romania, 2000; Grand Star, Decoration of Honour for Merit (Austria), 2001; Golden Order, Gjergj Kastrioti Skënderbeu (Albania), 2001; Grand Cross, Order of Saviour (Greece), 2001; Order of White Double Cross, 1st class (Slovakia), 2001; Knight Grand Cross, Order of Merit with Grand Cordon (Italy), 2001; Grand Cross with Collar, Order of the Republic (Hungary), 2002; Dostyk Order, 1st degree (Kazakhstan), 2002; Order of the Crown (Malaysia), 2002. *Publication:* The Break-up of Yugoslavia: political memoirs, 1992, 2nd edn 1994. *Recreations:* Nanbudo, swimming. *Address:* Office of the President of the Republic of Croatia, Pantovčak 241, 10 000 Zagreb, Croatia. *T:* (1) 4565191, *Fax:* (1) 4565299.

MESSEL, Prof. Harry, AC 2006; CBE 1979; BA, BSc, BMilSci; PhD (NUI) 1951; Professor and Head of the School of Physics, and Director of Science Foundation for Physics, University of Sydney, Australia, 1952–87, now Emeritus Professor; Chancellor, Bond University, 1992–97 (Executive Chancellor, 1993–96); *b* 3 March 1922. *Educ:* Rivers Public High Sch., Rivers, Manitoba. Entered RMC of Canada, 1940, grad. with Governor-General's Silver Medal, 1942. Served War of 1939–45: Canadian Armed Forces, Lieut, Canada and overseas, 1942–45. Queen's Univ., Kingston, Ont., 1945–48 (BA 1st Cl. Hons in Mathematics, 1948; BSc Hons in Engineering Physics, 1948); St Andrews Univ., Scotland, 1948–49; Institute for Advanced Studies, Dublin, Eire, 1949–51; Sen. Lectr in Mathematical Physics, University of Adelaide, Australia, 1951–52. CPhys, FInstP; FAAAS 1983. Mem., Aust. Atomic Energy Commn, 1974–81; Sen. Vice-Chm., Species Survival Commn, IUCN, 1978–2001 (Chm., Crocodile Specialist Gp, 1989–2004). Life Mem., Royal Instn of GB, 1991. FRSA 1972. Hon. DSc: Sydney; Royal Mil. Coll. of Canada, 2006; Hon. DHL Schiller Internat., 1994. Tall Poppy Award, NSW Australian Inst. of Political Sci., 2004; Sir Peter Scott Medal for Conservation Merit, IUCN/Species Survival Commn, 2004. *Publications:* Chap. 4, Progress in Cosmic Ray Physics, vol. 2, (North Holland Publishing Company), 1953; co-author and editor of: A Modern Introduction to Physics (Horwitz-Grahame, Vols I, II, III, 1959, 1960, 1962); Selected Lectures in Modern Physics, 1958; Space and the Atom, 1961; A Journey through Space and the Atom, 1962; The Universe of Time and Space, 1963; Light and Life in the Universe, 1964; Science for High School Students, 1964; Time, 1965; Senior Science for High School Students, 1966; (jt) Electron-Photon Shower Distribution Function, 1970; (jt) Multistrand Senior Science for High School Students, 1975; Australian Animals and their Environment, 1977; Time and Man, 1978; Tidal Rivers in Northern Australia and their Crocodile Populations (20 monographs), 1979–87; The Study of Populations, 1985; editor of: From Nucleus to Universe, 1960; Atoms to Andromeda, 1966; Apollo and the Universe, 1967; Man in Inner and Outer Space, 1968; Nuclear Energy Today and Tomorrow, 1969; Pioneering in Outer Space, 1970; Molecules to Man, 1971; Brain Mechanisms and the Control of Behaviour, 1972; Focus on the Stars, 1973; Solar Energy, 1974; Our Earth, 1975; Energy for Survival, 1979; The Biological Manipulation of Life, 1981; Science Update, 1983; The Study of Population, 1985; Highlights in Science, 1987; numerous papers published in: Proc. Physical Soc., London; Philosophical Magazine, London; Physical Review of America. *Recreations:* conservation, water ski-ing, hunting, fishing and photography. *Address:* 74 Montevideo Drive, Clear Island Waters, Qld 4226, Australia. *T:* (7) 55755873, *Fax:* (7) 55755874.

MESSER, Cholmeley Joseph; Chairman, Hamilton Insurance, 1995–2000; Director, HFC Bank plc, 1993–99; *b* 20 March 1929; *s* of late Col Arthur Albert Messer, DSO. CBE, FRIBA, and Lilian Hope Messer (*née* Dowling); *m* 1956, Ann Mary Power; two *d. Educ:* Wellington Coll. Solicitor. Served KRRC, 2nd Lieut, 1948–49. Articled Lawrance Messer & Co., Solicitors, London 1949–54; Partner, 1957–66; Save & Prosper Group: Exec. Dir, 1967–72; Dep. Man. Dir, 1973–80; Man. Dir, 1980–84; Chm., 1981–89. Chm., Code of Advertising Practice Cttee, Advertising Standards Authority, 1977–78; Vice-Chm., Internat. Bar Assoc. Cttee on Investment Cos Funds and Trusts, 1978–81; Chm., Unit Trust Assoc., 1981–83; Mem., 1989–92, Chm., 1992–98, London Pension Funds Authy. Chm., British Bobsleigh Assoc., 1989–92. *Recreations:* armchair sport, gardening, golf, collecting military postcards. *Address:* The Manor House, Normandy, Guildford, Surrey GU3 2AP. *T:* (01483) 810910. *Clubs:* City of London, MCC.

MESSERVY-WHITING, Maj.-Gen. Graham Gerald, CBE 2003 (MBE 1980); Deputy Director, Centre for Studies in Security and Diplomacy, University of Birmingham, since 2003; Member, Pensions Appeal Tribunal, since 2005; *b* 20 Oct. 1946; *s* of late Gerald and Kathleen Messervy-Whiting; *m* 1969, Shirley Hitchinson; one *s. Educ:* Lycée Français de Londres; Army Staff Coll.; RAF Staff Coll. Commnd Intelligence Corps, 1967; Regtl duty, 1 KOSB, Germany, Libya, Cyprus, Hong Kong, 1968–82; jsdc 1984; Secretariat Chiefs of Staff, 1984–86; CO, Intelligence and Security Gp, Germany, 1986–88; Briefing Officer, SACEUR, 1988–91; rcds 1992; Mil. Advr to Lord Owen, 1992–93; Res. Fellow, KCL, 1993; Dir, Defence Commitments Staff, 1994–95; COS, WEU, 1995–98; Asst Dir, Ops, GCHQ, 1998–2000; C of S, EU Mil. Staff, 2000–03. FRUSI 1996. Associate Fellow, Chatham House, 2003–07. *Publications:* contrib. London Defence Studies (King's Coll.) and jl of RUSI. *Recreations:* working gundogs, bridge, travel. *Address:* University of Birmingham, Edgbaston, Birmingham B15 2TT; *e-mail:* g.messervywhiting@bham.ac.uk. *Club:* Army and Navy.

MESSITER, Malcolm Cassan; oboist; Founder and Managing Director: Messiter Software, since 1985; Trans-Send International Ltd, since 1992; *b* 1 April 1949; *s* of late Ian and of Enid Messiter; *m* 1972, Christine (marr. diss. 1990); one *d. Educ:* Bryanston Sch.; Paris Conservatoire; Royal Coll. of Music (ARCM Hons 1971). First Oboe: BBC Concert Orchestra, 1971–77; London Mozart Players, 1977–83; London Festival Orchestra, 1985–; many solo concerts. Several recordings. Founder, Virtual Orchestra Co. Ltd, 1999. *Publications:* personal computer software and manuals. *Recreations:* wine, music, opera, model helicopters. *Address:* 47 Sutton Crescent, Barnet, Herts EN5 2SW.

MESTEL, Prof. Leon, PhD; FRS 1977; Professor of Astronomy, University of Sussex, 1973–92, now Emeritus; *b* 5 Aug. 1927; *s* of late Rabbi Solomon Mestel and Rachel (*née* Brodetsky); *m* 1951, Sylvia Louise Cole; two *s* two *d. Educ:* West Ham Secondary Sch., London; Trinity Coll., Cambridge (BA 1948, PhD 1952). ICI Res. Fellow, Dept of Maths, Univ. of Leeds, 1951–54; Commonwealth Fund Fellow, Princeton Univ. Observatory, 1954–55; University of Cambridge: Univ. Asst Lectr in Maths, 1955–58; Univ. Lectr in Maths, 1958–66; Fellow of St John's Coll., 1957–66; Vis. Mem., Inst. for Advanced Study, Princeton, 1961–62; J. F. Kennedy Fellow, Weizmann Inst. of Science, Israel, 1966–67; Prof. of Applied Maths, Manchester Univ., 1967–73. Eddington Medal, 1993, Gold Medal, 2002, RAS. *Publications:* Magnetohydrodynamics (with N. O. Weiss), 1974 (Geneva Observatory); Stellar Magnetism, 1999; papers, revs and conf. reports on different branches of theoretical astrophysics. *Recreations:* reading, music. *Address:* 13 Prince Edward's Road, Lewes, E Sussex BN7 1BJ. *T:* (01273) 472731.

MESTON, family name of **Baron Meston**.

MESTON, 3rd Baron *cr* 1919, of Agra and Dunottar; **James Meston;** QC 1996; **His Honour Judge Meston;** a Circuit Judge, since 1999; *b* 10 Feb. 1950; *s* of 2nd Baron Meston and Diana Mary Came, *d* of Capt. O. S. Doll; *S* father, 1984; *m* 1974, Jean Rebecca Anne, *d* of John Carder; one *s* two *d. Educ:* Wellington College; St Catharine's Coll., Cambridge (MA); Leicester Univ. (LLM). Barrister, Middle Temple, 1973; Jun. Counsel to Queen's Proctor, 1992–96; a Recorder, 1997–99. Legal Assessor, 1991–99, Sen. Legal Assessor, 1999, UKCC. Appeal Steward, BBB of C, 1993–2001. Pres., British Soc. of Commerce, 1984–92. *Heir: s* Hon. Thomas James Dougall Meston, *b* 21 Oct. 1977. *Address:* Queen Elizabeth Building, Temple, EC4Y 9BS. *Club:* Hawks (Cambridge).

METCALF, Christopher Sherwood John; His Honour Judge Metcalf; a Circuit Judge, since 2001; *b* 18 May 1945; *s* of Bernard Metcalf and Margaret Metcalf; *m* 1977, Pamela Falconer; two *s* two *d. Educ:* The Leys Sch., Cambridge; W Georgia Coll., USA (Rotary Internat. Schol. 1963). Called to the Bar, Middle Temple, 1972; in practice on Midland and Oxford Circuit, 1972–2001; Asst Recorder, 1991–95; Recorder, 1995–2001. *Recreations:* foreign travel, church architecture, private enterprise, games, choral music. *Address:* Leicester Combined Court Centre, 90 Wellington Street, Leicester LE1 6HG.

METCALF, Prof. David Harry, CBE 2008; PhD; Professor of Industrial Relations, London School of Economics, since 1985; Ombudsman, European Bank for Reconstruction and Development, since 1997; *b* 15 May 1942; *s* of Geoffrey and Dorothy Metcalf; *m* 1968, Helen Pitt (Dame Helen Metcalf, DBE, *d* 2003); one *s. Educ:* Manchester Univ. (BA Econ 1964; MA 1966); London Univ. (PhD 1971). Apprentice welder, English Electric, 1959–61; Lectr in Econs, LSE, 1967–75; Special Advr to Minister for Social Security, 1976–79; Prof. of Econs, Kent Univ., 1978–85. Comr, Low Pay Commn, 1997–2007; Dir, Starting Price Regulatory Commn, 2005–. Chm., Home Office Migration Adv. Cttee, 2007–. Editor, British Jl Industrial Relns, 1990–95. Jockey Club Steward, Sandown, Plumpton and Folkestone. *Publications:* Low Pay, Occupational Mobility and Minimum Wage Policy in Britain, 1983; New Perspectives on Industrial Disputes, 1993; Trade Unions: resurgence or demise?, 2005; articles in Econ. Jl, Industrial and Labor Relns Rev., etc. *Recreations:* horse-racing (owner and investor), watching Tottenham Hotspur FC. *Address:* 18 St Georges Avenue, N7 0HD. *T:* (020) 7607 5902; *e-mail:* d.metcalf@lse.ac.uk. *Club:* MCC.

METCALF, Prof. David Michael, DPhil, DLitt; Professor of Numismatics, University of Oxford, 1996–98; Keeper of Heberden Coin Room, Ashmolean Museum, Oxford, 1982–98; Fellow of Wolfson College, Oxford, 1982–98, now Emeritus; *b* 8 May 1933; *s* of Rev. Thomas Metcalf and Gladys Metcalf; *m* 1958, Dorothy Evelyn (*née* Uren); two *s* one *d. Educ:* St John's College, Cambridge. MA, DPhil, DLitt; FSA. Asst Keeper, Ashmolean Museum, 1963. President: Royal Numismatic Soc., 1994–99 (Sec., and Editor, Numismatic Chronicle, 1974–84); UK Numismatic Trust, 1994–99. *Publications:* Coinage in South-eastern Europe 820–1396, 1979; Coinage of the Crusades and the Latin East, 1983, 2nd edn 1995; (ed with D. H. Hill) Sceattas in England and on the Continent, 1984; Coinage in Ninth-century Northumbria, 1987; Thrymsas and Sceattas in the Ashmolean Museum, Oxford: vol. 1, 1993, vol. 2, 1993, vol. 3, 1994; Corpus of Lusignan Coinage, vol. 2, 1996, vol. 1, 1998, vol. 3, 2000; Suevic Coinage, 1997; An Atlas of Anglo-Saxon Coin Finds, 1998; Byzantine Lead Seals from Cyprus, 2004; (with W. Op den Velde) The Monetary Economy of the Netherlands *c* 690–*c* 715, 2007; articles on numismatics in various jls. *Address:* 20 The Shawl, Leyburn, N Yorks DL8 5DG.

METCALF, Prof. Donald, AC 1993 (AO 1976); FRS 1983, FRACP, FRCPA, FAA; Assistant Director and Head of Cancer Research Unit, Walter and Eliza Hall Institute of Medical Research, Melbourne, 1965–96; Research Professor of Cancer Biology, University of Melbourne, 1986–96, now Professor Emeritus; *b* 26 Feb. 1929; *s* of Donald Davidson Metcalf and Enid Victoria Metcalf (*née* Thomas); *m* 1954, Josephine Emily Lentaigne; four *d. Educ:* Sydney University. MD, BSc (med). Resident MO, Royal Prince Alfred Hosp., Sydney, 1953–54; Surgeon-Lieut, RANR, 1953–58; Carden Fellow in Cancer Res., Walter and Eliza Hall Inst. of Med. Res., 1954–65. Vis. Fellow, Harvard Med. Sch., 1956–58; Visiting Scientist: Roswell Park Meml Inst., Buffalo, 1966–67; Swiss Inst. for Experimental Cancer Res., Lausanne, 1974–75; Radiobiological Res. Inst., Rijswijk, 1980–81; Royal Soc. Guest Res. Fellow, Cambridge Univ., 1981. *Publications:* The Thymus, 1966; (with M. A. S. Moore) Haemopoietic Cells, 1971; Hemopoietic Colonies, 1977; Hemopoietic Colony Stimulating Factors, 1984; The Molecular Control of Blood Cells, 1988; (with N. A. Nicola) The Hemopoietic Colony Stimulating Factors, 1995; numerous scientific papers on cancer and leukaemia. *Recreations:* music, tennis. *Address:* 268 Union Road, Balwyn, Victoria 3103, Australia. *T:* (3) 98361343.

METCALF, Malcolm, MC 1944; DL; Chairman, Surrey County Council, 1978–81; *b* 1 Dec. 1917; *s* of Charles Almond Metcalf and Martha Fatherly Atkins Metcalf; *m* 1945, Charis Thomas (*d* 2003); two *s. Educ:* Merchant Taylors' Sch., Crosby. ACIS. Army service, 1939–46. Contested (C) Barrow-in-Furness, 1959; Mem., Surrey CC, 1965–89 (Leader, 1973–77; Vice-Chm., 1977–78); Member: Metrop. Water Board, 1965–74 (Vice-Chm. 1971–72); Thames Conservancy, 1970–74; Thames Water Authority, 1973–78, 1981–87. Mem., Assoc. of County Councils, 1975–88. DL Surrey, 1979. *Address:* 1 The Lodge, Watts Road, Thames Ditton KT7 0DE. *T:* (020) 8398 3057. *Clubs:* MCC, Burhill Golf (Walton-on-Thames).

METCALF, Ven. Robert Laurence; Priest-in-charge, St Michael, Garston, 2004–06; Archdeacon of Liverpool, 1994–2002, now Emeritus; *b* 18 Nov. 1935; *s* of late Victor Noel Metcalf and Phyllis Maud Metcalf (*née* Dunwell); *m* 1964, Rachel Margaret Herring; two *s* three *d. Educ:* St John's Coll., Durham Univ. (BA 1960; rowing colours, 1960); Cranmer Hall, Durham (DipTheol 1962); Cardiff Univ. (LLM 2002). Nat. Service, REME, 1955–57. Ordained deacon, 1962, priest, 1963; Curate: Christ Church, Bootle, 1962–65; i/c St John's, Widnes, 1965–67; Vicar, St Catharine, Wigan, 1967–75; Dir, Wigan Br., Samaritans, 1970–75; Rector, Holy Trinity, Wavertree, 1974–94; Chaplain: Liverpool Royal Sch. for the Blind, 1975–94; Blue Coat Sch., Liverpool, 1975–94; Diocesan Dir of Ordinands, Liverpool, 1982–94; Hon. Canon, Liverpool Cathedral, 1988. Chm., Pre-theol Educn Panel, Ministry Div., Archbps' Council, 1999–2006. Mem., Toxteth Rotary Club (Pres., 1995–96). Chm., Liverpool Welsh Choral, 2005–08. Occasional broadcaster, BBC Radio Merseyside. *Publications:* contrib.: Prayers for Today's Church, 1972; For All the Family, 1984; Prayers for Today's World, 1993; Reconciliation. *Recreations:* walking, rowing, reading novels (political intrigue!), holidaying. *Address:* 32 Storrsdale Road, Liverpool L18 7JZ. *T:* (0151) 724 3956, *Fax:* (0151) 729 0587; *e-mail:* bob.metcalf@uwclub.net.

METCALFE, Adrian Peter, OBE 2001; international sport and media consultant; *b* 2 March 1942; *s* of Hylton and Cora Metcalfe; *m* Catherine, Baroness von Delvig; one *s* one *d* by former marriage. *Educ:* Roundhay Sch., Leeds; Magdalen Coll., Oxford. Reporter, Sunday Express, 1964; Dep. Editor, World of Sport, ABC TV, 1965; Producer, Sports Arena, LWT, 1968; Presenter, CBS Sports Spectacular, 1972–76; Man. Dir, AMO Productions, 1976; Sen. Commissioning Editor, Sport and Features, Channel 4 TV, 1981; Commentator, ITV, 1966–87; Director of Programmes: Eurosport, 1989–91; Tyne Tees Television Ltd, 1991–92; Dir, Venue Production, Atlantic Olympic Games, 1994–96; Chm., API Television, 1996–98; Exec. Publr, worldsport.com, 1998–2000; Chm.,

AMDM Agency, 2003–; Dir, World Professional Billiards and Snooker Assoc., 2004–. GB Record, 400m, 45·7, ranked No 1 in the world at 400m, 1961; Gold Medal, 400m and 4×400m, World Student Games, 1963; Silver Medal, 4×400m, Tokyo Olympics, 1964; 7 British Records, 4 European Records, 1961–64. Pres., OUAC, 1962–63. Mem., UK Sport, 1998– (Chm., Major Events Steering Gp, 1999–2003); Life Vice-Pres. and Trustee, Sports Aid Foundn, 1990–. *Recreations:* still running, Russian culture. *Address:* 5 King Lane, Leeds LS17 5NT. *T:* (0113) 268 3841.

METCALFE, Prof. David Henry Harold, OBE 1989; Professor of General Practice, University of Manchester School of Medicine, 1978–92, now Professor Emeritus; *b* 3 Jan. 1930; *s* of Henry R. Metcalfe and Mary Metcalfe (*née* Evans); *m* 1957, Anne (*née* Page); three *s. Educ:* Leys School, Cambridge; Cambridge Univ. (clinical course at Liverpool) (MA, MB, BChir); MSc Manchester. FRCGP; FFPH. United Liverpool Hosps, 1956–58; Principal in gen. practice, Hessle, E Yorks, 1960–70; Asst Prof. in Family Medicine, Univ. of Rochester, NY, 1970–72; Sen. Lectr (GP), Dept of Community Health, Nottingham Univ. Med. Sch., 1972–78. Dir, DHSS Urban Primary Care Res. Unit, 1978–92. Vice-Chm., RCGP, 1983–84. *Publications:* papers on medical information handling, doctor-patient communication, patterns of general practice, and medical educn. *Recreations:* photography, sailing, hill walking. *Address:* Westgate Barn, Milburn, Penrith, Cumbria CA10 1TW. *T:* (01768) 361947.

METCALFE, Prof. James Charles, PhD; Professor of Mammalian Cell Biochemistry, University of Cambridge, 1996–2007, now Emeritus; Fellow, Darwin College, Cambridge, 1975–2000; *b* 20 July 1939; *s* of Cyril Tom Metcalfe and Olive Kate (*née* Ayling); *m* 1st, 1969, Susan Milner (marr. diss.); one *s* one *d*; 2nd, 1983, Aviva Miriam Tolkovsky. *Educ:* St Paul's Sch.; Sidney Sussex Coll., Cambridge (MA; PhD 1965). Research Fellow, Dept of Pharmacology, Cambridge Univ. and Dept of Pharmacology, Harvard Med. Sch., 1965–67; Mem. Scientific Staff, MRC Molecular Pharmacology Unit, Dept of Pharmacology, Cambridge, 1967–72; Res. Fellow, Dept of Chemistry, Stanford Univ., 1968; Perm. MRC appt, 1970; Div. of Molecular Pharmacology, NIMR, 1972–73; Univ. Lectr, Dept of Pharmacology, Cambridge, 1974; Sir William Dunn Reader, Dept of Biochem., Cambridge, 1974–96. Chm., Scientific Cttee, CRC, 1995–2000. Mem., EMBO, 1981. Fogarty Internat. Schol., NIH, 1979. Colworth Medal, Biochem. Soc., 1973. *Publications:* papers in scientific jls. *Recreations:* walking in France, reading, ski-ing. *Address:* Department of Biochemistry, University of Cambridge, Tennis Court Road, Downing Site, Cambridge CB2 1QW. *T:* (01223) 333633.

METCALFE, Prof. (John) Stanley, CBE 1993; AcSS; Stanley Jevons Professor of Political Economy and Cobden Lecturer, School of Economic Studies, since 1980, Director, Policy Research in Engineering, Science and Technology, since 1984, and Co-Executive Director, ESRC Centre for Research on Innovation and Competition (Executive Director, 1997), University of Manchester; *b* 20 March 1946; *m* 1967, Joan Shrouder; one *s* one *d. Educ:* Liverpool Collegiate High Sch.; Univ. of Manchester (BA 1967; MSc 1968). Lectr in Econs, Univ. of Manchester, 1967–74; Lectr, then Sen. Lectr in Econs, Univ. of Liverpool, 1974–80; University of Manchester: Hd, Dept of Econs, 1986–89; Dean of Faculty, 1992–95; Mem. Court, 1992– (Mem., Finance Cttee, 1977–); Interim Dean, Faculty of Med. and Human Scis, 2004. Member: ACARD, 1983–87; ACOST, 1987–92; MMC, 1991–97. AcSS 2003. FRSA. *Publications:* (contrib.) The UK Economy, 1975; (jtly) Post Innovation Performance, 1986; (jtly) New Electronic Information: the UK database industry in its international context, 1987; (ed jtly) Barriers to Growth in Small Firms, 1989; The Enterprise Challenge: overcoming barriers to growth in small firms, 1990; (ed jtly) Evolutionary Theories of Economic and Technological Change, 1991; (ed jtly) Wealth from Diversity, 1996; Evolutionary Economics and Creative Destruction, 1998. *Address:* ESRC Centre for Research on Innovation and Competition, University of Manchester, Harold Hankins Building, Booth Street West, Manchester M13 9QH.

METCALFE, Julian Edward; Founder, 1986, Creative Director, since 2003, Pret a Manger; *b* 14 Dec. 1959; *s* of David Metcalfe and Alexa (*née* Boycun); *m* 1993, Melanie Willson; two *s. Educ:* Harrow; Central London Poly. (BSc). *Recreation:* eating. *Address:* (office) 1 Hudson's Place, SW1V 1PZ. *T:* (020) 7827 8888. *Club:* White's.

METCALFE, Julian Ross; HM Diplomatic Service; Deputy Permanent Representative, UK Mission to the United Nations and other international organisations, Geneva, since 2005; *b* 24 Feb. 1956; *s* of late Patrick Ross Metcalfe and Marjory Gillian Metcalfe (*née* Gaze); *m* 1983, Rachel Mai Jones; one *d. Educ:* Horris Hill Sch.; Cheltenham Coll.; Univ. of Bristol (BSc Pols and Econs 1978); Univ. of Sussex (MA Econs 1981). Project Trust Volunteer, mentally handicapped children, S Africa, 1975; ODI Fellow serving as Health Planning Officer, Govt of Malaŵi, 1978–81; consultant, Commodities Res. Unit, 1982–83; FCO Econ. Advr, 1983–87; First Sec., Cairo, 1987–91; Southern Africa Dept, 1991–93, Eastern Adriatic Dept, 1993–95, FCO; Hd, UK Delegn, EC Monitoring Mission to Former Yugoslavia, 1995; Dep. Hd of Mission, Zagreb, 1995–97; Jt Hd, Eastern Adriatic Dept (dealing with Balkans), FCO, 1997–2000; Hd, Estate Strategy Unit, FCO, 2000–04. *Recreations:* camping, helping in garden. *Address:* BFPO 5279, HA4 6EP; *e-mail:* Julian.metcalfe@fco.gov.uk. *Club:* Royal Commonwealth Society.

METCALFE, Stanley; *see* Metcalfe, J. S.

METCALFE, Stanley Gordon; Chairman: Queens Moat Houses plc, 1993–2001; Ranks Hovis McDougall PLC, 1989–93, retired (Managing Director, 1981–89, Chief Executive, 1984–89, and Deputy Chairman, 1987–89); *b* 20 June 1932; *s* of Stanley Hudson Metcalfe and Jane Metcalfe; *m* 1968, Sarah Harter; two *d. Educ:* Leeds Grammar Sch.; Pembroke Coll., Oxford (MA). Commnd Duke of Wellington's Regt, 1952. Trainee, Ranks, Hovis McDougall, 1956–59; Director, Stokes & Dalton, Leeds, 1963–66; Managing Director, McDougalls, 1966–69; Director, Cerebos Ltd, 1969–70; Managing Director: RHM Overseas Ltd, 1970–73; RHM Cereals Ltd, 1973–79; Director, Ranks Hovis McDougall Ltd, 1979. Member: Exec. Cttee, FDF, 1987–93 (Pres., 1990–92); Priorities Bd for R&D in Agriculture and Food, 1987–92; CBI President's Cttee, 1990–93; Council, Business in the Community, 1990–93. Chm., Adv. Bd, Inst. of Food Research, 1988–90. President, Nat. Assoc. of British and Irish Millers, 1978. *Recreations:* cricket, golf, theatre. *Address:* The Oast House, Lower Froyle, Alton, Hants GU34 4LX. *T:* (01420) 22310. *Clubs:* Boodle's, MCC; IZ, Arabs.

METGE, Dame (Alice) Joan, DBE 1987; research anthropologist and writer; *b* 21 Feb. 1930; *d* of Cedric Leslie Metge and Alice Mary (*née* Rigg). *Educ:* Auckland Univ. (MA); London School of Economics (PhD). Jun. Lectr, Geography Dept, Auckland Univ., 1952; research and doctoral study, 1953–61; Lectr, Univ. Extension, Auckland Univ., 1961–64; University of Wellington: Sen. Lectr, Anthropology Dept, 1965–67, Associate Prof., 1968–88. Fifth Captain James Cook Res. Fellow, 1981–83. Hon. DLitt Auckland, 2001. Hutchinson Medal, LSE, 1958; Elsdon Best Meml Medal, Polynesian Soc., 1987; Te Rangi Hiroa Medal, Royal Soc. of NZ, 1997; Asia-Pacific Mediation Peace Prize, 2006. *Publications:* A New Maori Migration, 1964; The Maoris of New Zealand, 1967, rev. edn 1976; (with Patricia Kinloch) Talking Past Each Other, 1978; In and Out of Touch, 1986; Te Kohao o Te Ngira, 1990; New Growth From Old, 1995; Korero Tahi-Talking Together, 2001. *Recreations:* theatre, music, reading, gardening. *Address:* 3 Mariri Road, Onehunga, Auckland 1061, New Zealand. *T:* (9) 6345757.

METHAM, Patricia; HM Inspector of Schools, since 2006; *b* Cairo, 1 March 1945; *d* of John (Jack) Andrews and Jane Starrett Andrews; *m* 1st, 1966, Nicholas Hern (marr. diss.); two *d*; 2nd, 1986, Dr Tim Metham. *Educ:* Upper Chine Sch., Isle of Wight; Bristol Univ. (BA English and Drama). English and Drama Teacher: Dartford Girls' Grammar Sch., 1966–67; Sir Leo Schultz High Sch., Hull, 1967; Newland High Sch., Hull, 1967–72; Wimbledon High Sch., 1975–82 (School-Teacher Fellow, Merton Coll., Oxford, 1981); Head of English and Sixth Form, Francis Holland Sch., London, 1982–87; Head: Farlington Sch., Horsham, 1987–92; Ashford, Sch., 1992–97; Roedean Sch., 1997–2002; Principal, Internat. Regent's Sch., Thailand, 2003–05. Vice Chm., Ind. Schs Exams Bd, 1999. JP, Horsham, then Ashford, 1991–97. *Publications:* editor of seven critical play texts. *Recreations:* theatre, choral singing, travel to centres of archaeological and cultural interest (in Europe, particularly), good food and good wine.

METHUEN, family name of **Baron Methuen**.

METHUEN, 7th Baron *cr* 1838; **Robert Alexander Holt Methuen;** electrical engineer, retired from Roll-Royce plc, 1994; *b* 22 July 1931; *y s* of 5th Baron Methuen and Grace (*d* 1972), *d* of Sir Richard Durning Holt, 1st Bt; *S* brother, 1994; *m* 1st, 1958, Mary Catharine Jane (marr. diss. 1993), *o d* of late Ven. C. G. Hooper; two *d*; 2nd, 1994, Margrit Andrea, *o d* of Friedrich Hadwiger. *Educ:* Shrewsbury; Trinity Coll., Cambridge. Elected Mem., H of L, 1999. Member: EC sub-cttee B, 1995–99; Admin and Works sub-cttee, 1997–2000; Sci. and Technol. Cttee, 2000–03; Library and Computers sub-cttee, 2000–03; Merits of Statutory Instruments Cttee, 2003–. *Heir: cousin* James Paul Archibald Methuen-Campbell, *b* 25 Oct. 1952.

METHUEN, Very Rev. John Alan Robert; Dean of Ripon, 1995–2005; *b* 14 Aug. 1947; *s* of late Rev. Alan Robert Methuen and Ruth Josephine Tyrrell Methuen; *m* 1970, Bridget Mary (*née* Andrews); two *d. Educ:* Upton Prep. Sch., Windsor; Eton Coll. Choir Sch.; St John's Sch., Leatherhead; Brasenose Coll., Oxford (Colquitt Exhibnr 1966; BA 1969; MA 1972); Cuddesdon Coll., Oxford. Asst Curate, Fenny Stratford and Water Eaton Team Ministry, Milton Keynes, 1971–74; Asst Chaplain, Eton Coll., 1974–77; Priest-in-Charge, St James, Dorney and Warden of Dorney Parish-Eton Coll. Conf. Centre, 1974–77; Vicar, St Mark, Reading, 1977–83; Rector, The Ascension, Hulme, Manchester, 1983–95. Church Comr, 1998–2004. Master, Ripon Hosps of St John the Baptist and St Mary Magdalen, 1995–2005. Member: Egypt Exploration Soc., 1991–; N Yorks Ancient Egyptian Soc., 1996–; Thames Valley Ancient Egypt Soc., 2005–; Actors Church Union, 2006–. Writer and Dir, The Christian Life (series of 8 educnl videos), 1990–93; lecturer: Interchurch Travel, 1975–95; Swan Hellenic Cruises, 1996–; Voyages of Discovery, 2007–; Ancient World Tours, 2007–; Saga Holidays 2008–; Petrie Museum, 2008–. Gerald Avery Near Eastern Archaeol. Prize, Oxford Univ., 1965. *Publications:* various lectures, reviews and papers. *Recreations:* drama and theatre, concerts and music-making; film-making, directing, writing and broadcasting; history and archaeology; pilgrimage and travel (especially as leader and lecturer). *Address:* Dean's Lodge, 108 Honeypot Lane, NW9 9QX. *Clubs:* Leeds City (Leeds); Ripon City (Ripon).

METHUEN, Richard St Barbe; QC 1997; a Recorder, since 2002; *b* 22 Aug. 1950; *s* of late John Methuen and of Rosemary Methuen; *m* 1974, Mary Catherine Griffiths, LLB, MA, *d* of David Howard Griffiths, OBE; one *s* two *d. Educ:* Marlborough College. Called to the Bar, Lincoln's Inn, 1972. Head of Chambers, 2000–05. Mediator in personal injury and clinical negligence work. *Address:* 12 King's Bench Walk, Temple, EC4Y 7EL; *e-mail:* methuen@12kbw.co.uk.

METTERS, Dr Jeremy Stanley, CB 1994; FRCOG; Deputy Chief Medical Officer, Department of Health, 1989–99; *b* 6 June 1939; *s* of late Thomas Lee Metters and Henrietta Currey; *m* 1962, Margaret Howell; two *s* one *d. Educ:* Eton; Magdalene College, Cambridge; St Thomas' Hosp. (MB BChir 1963, MA 1965). MRCOG 1970, FRCOG 1982. House officer posts, St Thomas' Hosp. and Reading, 1963–66; Lectr in Obst. and Gyn., St Thomas' Hosp., 1968–70; Registrar in Radiotherapy, 1970–72; DHSS 1972; SPMO (Under Sec.), 1984; Dep. Chief Scientist, DHSS, later Dept of Health, 1986–89. Member: Council of Europe Cttee on Bioethics (formerly Ethical and Legal Problems relating to Human Genetics), 1983–89; ESRC, 1986–88. *Publications:* papers in med. and sci. jls. *Recreations:* DIY, steam preservation.

METTYEAR, Michael King; His Honour Judge Mettyear; a Circuit Judge, since 1992; *b* 22 Sept. 1946; *s* of Charles Frank Henry King and Vera May (*née* Moore); *m* 1984, Gail Stafford; one *s* one *d. Educ:* LLB London (external). Called to the Bar, Middle Temple, 1973; a Recorder, 1990–92; Hon. Recorder, Kingston upon Hull and ER of Yorks, 2003–. Member: Sentencing Adv. Panel, 1999–2004; Sentencing Guidelines Council, 2004. *Recreations:* tennis, travel, ski-ing. *Address:* Hull Combined Court Centre, Lowgate, Hull HU1 2EZ. *T:* (01482) 586161.

METZ, David Henry, PhD; Visiting Professor, Centre for Transport Studies, University College London, since 2005; *b* 11 March 1941; *s* of Lewis and Esther Metz; *m* 1st, 1966, Marilyn Ann Yeatman (marr. diss. 1980); one *s*; 2nd, 1994, Monica Mary Threlfall. *Educ:* City of London Sch.; University Coll. London (BSc Chem, MSc Biochem); King's Coll. London (PhD Biophysics). Virology Division, National Institute for Medical Research, 1967–76: Fellow, Helen Hay Whitney Foundn, 1967–69; Mem., MRC Scientific Staff, 1969–76; Res. Fellow, Dept of Microbiol., Harvard Med. Sch., and Children's Hosp. Med. Center, Boston, 1972–73; Dept of Energy, 1976–86; Dep. Dir-Gen., Office of Gas Supply, 1986–89; Dept of Energy, 1989–92; Chief Scientist, Dept of Transport, 1992–97; Dir, AgeNet, Wolfson Inst. of Preventive Medicine, 1997–2000. Vis. Prof., Centre for Ageing and Public Health, LSHTM, 2000–06. Non-executive Director: Camden and Islington Community Health Services NHS Trust, 2001–02; Camden PCT, 2002–. Member: Mgt Bd, TRRL, 1993–96; Res. and Technol. Cttee, BR, 1994–96; Res. Adv. Council, NATS, 1997–99; Financial Services Consumer Panel, 2005–. Mem. Mgt Bd, Oxford Dementia Centre, 1999–2001. *Publications:* Older, Richer, Fitter (with M. Underwood), 2005; The Limits to Travel, 2008; papers in sci. jls. *Recreations:* cooking, riding. *Address:* 14 Montpelier Grove, NW5 2XD.

MEWIES, Sandra Elaine, (Sandy); Member (Lab) Delyn, National Assembly for Wales, since 2003; *b* 16 Feb. 1950; *d* of Tom Oldland and Margaret Owens; *m* 1976, Paul Mewies; one *s. Educ:* Grove Park Girls' Grammar Sch.; Open Univ. (BA Hons). Journalist, 1967–87; marketing/PR, 1988–90; Community Care Co-ordinator, Clwyd, 1991–93; Lay Inspector of Schs, 1993–2002. Mem., Wrexham CBC, 1988–2004 (Mayor, 2000–01). Dir, Wales European Centre, 1997–2003; Bd Mem., N Wales Probation, 2000–03. Hon. Fellow, NE Wales Inst., 2002–. *Recreation:* reading. *Address:* National Assembly for Wales, Cardiff Bay, Cardiff CF99 1NA. *T:* (029) 2089 8280, *Fax:* (029) 2089 8281; *e-mail:* sandy.mewies@wales.gov.uk; (constituency office) 64 Chester Street, Flint CH6 5DH. *T:* (01352) 763398.

MEXBOROUGH, 8th Earl of, *cr* 1766; **John Christopher George Savile;** Baron Pollington, 1753; Viscount Pollington, 1766; *b* 16 May 1931; *s* of 7th Earl of Mexborough, and Josephine Bertha Emily (*d* 1992), *d* of late Captain Andrew Mansel Talbot Fletcher; *S* father, 1980; *m* 1st, 1958, Lady Elizabeth Hariot (marr. diss. 1972; she *d* 1987), *d* of 6th Earl of Verulam; one *s* (one *d* decd); 2nd, 1972, Mrs Catherine Joyce Vivian, *d* of late J. K. Hope, CBE, DL; one *s* one *d*. MIMI. *Heir: s* Viscount Pollington, *qv*. *Address:* Arden Hall, Hawnby, York YO6 5LS. *T:* (01439) 798348; 14 Lennox Gardens Mews, SW1X 0DP. *T:* (020) 7589 3669. *Clubs:* White's; All England Lawn Tennis and Croquet; Air Squadron; Mill Reef (Antigua).

MEYER, Sir (Anthony) Ashley (Frank), 4th Bt *cr* 1910, of Shortgrove, Newport, Essex; *b* 23 Aug. 1944; *s* of Sir Anthony Meyer, 3rd Bt and of Barbadee Violet Meyer (*née* Knight); *S* father, 2004; *m* 1966, Susan Mathilda (marr. diss. 1980), *d* of Charles Freestone; one *d*. *Educ:* Goldsmiths' Coll., London Univ. *Heir:* none.

MEYER, Sir Christopher (John Rome), KCMG 1998 (CMG 1988); HM Diplomatic Service, retired; Chairman, Press Complaints Commission, since 2003; *b* 22 Feb. 1944; *s* of Flight Lieut R. H. R. Meyer (killed in action 1944) and late Mrs E. P. L. Meyer (subseq. Mrs S. Landells); *m* 1976, Françoise Elizabeth Hedges (marr. diss.), *d* of Air Cdre Sir Archibald Winskill, KCVO, CBE, DFC, AE; two *s*, and one step *s*; *m* 1997, Catherine Laylle; two step *s*. *Educ:* Lancing College; Lycée Henri IV, Paris; Peterhouse, Cambridge (MA History; Hon. Fellow, 2002); Johns Hopkins Sch. of Advanced Internat. Studies, Bologna. Third Sec., FO, 1966–67; Army Sch. of Education, 1967–68; Third, later Second, Sec., Moscow, 1968–70; Second Sec., Madrid, 1970–73; First Sec., FCO, 1973–78; First Sec., UK Perm. Rep. to European Communities, 1978–82; Counsellor and Hd of Chancery, Moscow, 1982–84; Head of News Dept, FCO, 1984–88; Fellow, Center for Internat. Affairs, Harvard, 1988–89; Minister (Commercial), 1989–92, Minister and Dep. Hd of Mission, 1992–93, Washington; Press Sec. to Prime Minister (on secondment to Cabinet Office), 1994–96; Ambassador: to Germany, 1997; to USA, 1997–2003. Non-executive Director: GKN, 2003–; Arbuthnot Banking Gp, 2007–. Gov., ESU, 2006–. Mem., Exec. Cttee, Pilgrims Soc., 2005–. *Publication:* DC Confidential, 2005. *Address:* c/o Press Complaints Commission, Halton House, 20/23 Holborn, EC1N 2JD. *Clubs:* Garrick; Metropolitan (Washington).

MEYER, Rev. Canon Conrad John Eustace; *b* 2 July 1922; *s* of William Eustace and Marcia Meyer; *m* 1960, Mary Wiltshire; no *c*. *Educ:* Clifton Coll.; Pembroke Coll., Cambridge; Westcott House. BA 1946, MA 1948. Served War of 1939–45: Royal Navy (commissioned from lower deck), 1942–46. Lieut (S) RNVR, post war, until apptd Chaplain, RNVR, 1950–54. Deacon, 1948; Priest, 1949; Asst Curate: St Francis, Ashton Gate, Bristol, 1948–51; Kenwyn, Truro, 1951; Falmouth Parish Church, 1954; Vicar of Devoran, Truro, 1956–65; Diocesan Youth Chaplain, 1956; Asst Dir of Religious Educn, 1958; Diocesan Sec. for Educn, 1960–69; Archdeacon of Bodmin, 1969–79; Hon. Canon of Truro, 1966–79; Examining Chaplain to Bishop of Truro, 1973–79; Bishop Suffragan of Dorchester, 1979–87 (Area Bishop, 1985–87); Hon. Asst Bishop, dio. of Truro, 1990–94. Received into RC Ch, 1994; ordained priest, 1995; Hon. Canon, Plymouth RC Cathedral, 2001. Hon. Diocesan Sec., Nat. Soc., 1960–69. Society for Promoting Christian Knowledge: Mem. Governing Body, 1972–90; Chairman: Projects Cttee, 1973–87; Appeals Cttee, 1987–90; Vice Chm., 1988–90; Vice-Pres., 1990–. Chairman: Federation of Catholic Priests, 1976–79; Church Union Exec. Cttee, 1979–84; The Churches' Group on Funerals at Cemeteries and Crematoria, 1980–89. Fellow, Woodard Corp. of Schools, 1967–92; Provost, Western Div., Woodard Corp., 1970–92 (Hon. Fellow, 1993–94). Hon. FICDDS. *Recreations:* swimming, walking, military history, civil defence, archaeology. *Address:* Hawk's Cliff, 38 Praze Road, Newquay, Cornwall TR7 3AF. *Club:* Royal Commonwealth Society.

MEYER, Julie; Founder and Chief Executive Officer, Ariadne Capital, 2000–07; *b* 28 Aug. 1966. *Educ:* Valparaiso Univ. (BA Dist. 1988); INSEAD (MBA 1997). Consultant: AC3, Paris, 1989–91; Meyer Gp, Paris, 1992–93; Account Manager, Cunningham Communication, 1994–97; Associate, Roland Berger & Partner, Paris, 1997; independent consultant, London and Paris, 1997–98; Jt Founder, 1998 and Chief Marketing Officer, 1998–2000, First Tuesday; Asst Dir, NewMedia Investors, 1998–99. *Recreations:* Pastis and Amaretto, any kind of sport, taking weekend trips and sleeping late, genealogy, carrying on family traditions, finding John Galt. *Address:* Ariadne Capital, 28 Queen Street, EC4R 1BB.

MEYER, Michael Siegfried; Chairman, Remote Controlled Lighting Ltd, since 2001; Chairman and Chief Executive Officer, Direct Message plc, since 2002; *b* 2 May 1950; *s* of late Ernest Meyer and of Gretta Gillis; *m* 1st, 1984, Jill Benedict (marr. diss. 1990); one *d*; 2nd, 1994, Livia Hannah, *o d* of Maj.-Gen. Monty Green. *Educ:* South African College School, Cape Town. FCIS. Company Secretary, Heenan Beddow International, 1973–75; Director, 1976–79, Chief Exec., 1980–82, Chm. and Chief Exec., 1983–2000, EMESS plc; Man. Dir, Brilliant Hldgs GmbH, Germany, 1987–2000; Pres., Alsy Lighting Inc., 1988–2000; Chairman: Supervisory Bd, Eclatec SA, France, 1989–2000; Domes of Silence Hldgs, 2005–; Director: Meyer Leclerc & Co., 1982–; Royal Sovereign Group, 1986–90; Henderson Smaller Cos Investment Trust, 1990–2002; Walker Greenbank, 1991–97; Design Trust, 1994–2001; Construct London, 2005–07; Aluminum Shapes Ltd, 2005–; Windmill Extrusions Ltd, 2005–; Partner, EMESS Capital 202 LLP, 2007–. *Recreations:* cricket, Rugby, theatre. *Address:* 10 The Factory, 1 Nile Street, N1 7LX. *T:* (020) 3043 0125. *Clubs:* Naval and Military, MCC, Lansdowne; Western Province Cricket (Cape Town); Wanderers (Johannesburg).

MEYER, Roelof Petrus, (Roelf Meyer); Chairman, Civil Society Initiative, since 2000; Executive Deputy Chairman, Tilca Infrastructure Corporation, since 2002; *b* 16 July 1947; *m* 2002, Michéle Krüger (*née* de la Rey); two *s* two *d* by former marriage. *Educ:* Ficksburg High Sch.; Univ. of OFS (BComm, LLB). Practised as attorney, Pretoria and Johannesburg, until 1980; MP (Nat. Party) S Africa, 1979–97 (for Johannesburg West, 1979–94); MP (UDM), 1999–2000; Deputy Minister, S Africa, 1986–91; Minister of: Defence, 1991–92; Constitutional Develt, 1992–96; Provincial Affairs, 1994–96. Co-Founder, 1997, Dep. Pres., 1998–2000, United Democratic Movt. *Recreations:* reading, jogging, cycling. *Address:* PO Box 2271, Brooklyn Square, Pretoria, 0075, South Africa. *T:* (12) 4204437, *Fax:* (12) 4203886; *e-mail:* rmeyer@lantic.net.

MEYER, Dr Rolf Arthur; Chairman of the Board, and Chief Executive Officer, Ciba Specialty Chemicals Inc., 1997–2000; *b* Switzerland, 31 Oct. 1943; *m* 1969, Elisabeth Lehmann; one *s*. *Educ:* Univ. of St Gallen, Switzerland (MBA 1967; PhD Political Sci. 1973). Various mkting and financial posts in Swiss textile ind., 1967–73; joined Ciba, 1973: financial analyst, HQ, Basle, 1973–76; Controller, Gp Co., SA, 1976–79; Manager, strategic planning and control and mkting and prodn depts, Basle, 1979–85; Corporate Vice-Pres., Ciba-Geigy Corp., USA, 1985–92 (Dir, US Corp., 1991–92); Chief Financial Officer and Mem., Exec. Cttee, 1992–97. Director: Swiss Stock Exchange, 1992–99; UBS, 1992–; Diethelm Keller Siber Hegner (formerly Siber Hegner), 1996–; COS, 2001–04. Chm., Alumni Adv. Cttee on Educn, Univ. of St Gallen, 2003–.

MEYER, Stephen Richard; Chief Inspector, Marine Accident Investigation Branch, Department for Transport (formerly Department for Transport, Local Government and the Regions), since 2002; *b* 28 Aug. 1950; *s* of Ernest Frederick Meyer and Rita Agnes Meyer (*née* Humphrey); *m* 1977, Erica Michelle Diana, *d* of Captain N. Hall, Jersey; two *d*. *Educ:* Merchant Taylors' Sch., Crosby; BRNC, Dartmouth. Joined RN, 1968; served HMS Tenby, Charybdis, Beachampton, Apollo, and USS Raleigh, 1969–74; loaned Sultan of Oman's Navy, i/c Sultan's Naval Vessel Al Mansur, 1975; comd HMS Bildeston, 1975–77; Flag Lieut to Adm. Sir Henry Leach, 1977–79; qualified principal warfare officer, 1980; served HM ships Coventry and Broadsword, 1980–83; commanded: HMS Galatea, 1985–86; HMS Liverpool, 1986–88; HMS Fearless, 1990–91; Head of Maritime Intelligence, 1992–93; Dir of Navy Plans, 1994–97; comd, HMS Illustrious, 1997–98; Head of Jt Force 2000 Study Team, 1998; Military Advr to High Representative, Sarajevo, 1999–2000; Comdr UK Task Gp, UK Maritime Forces, and Comdr Anti Submarine Warfare Striking Force, 2000–01; Chief of Staff, Permt Jt HQ, 2001–02; retd in rank of Rear-Adm. Trustee, CHIRP Charitable Trust, 2003–. FNI. *Recreations:* family, home, friends. *Address:* Marine Accident Investigation Branch, Carlton House, Carlton Place, Southampton SO15 2DZ.

MEYJES, Sir Richard (Anthony), Kt 1972; DL; President, Association of Optometrists, 1995–2000; *b* 30 June 1918; *s* of late Anthony Charles Dorian Meyjes and Norah Isobel Meyjes; *m* 1939, Margaret Doreen Morris; three *s*. *Educ:* University College School, Hampstead. War Service, RASC, Sept. 1939–Jan. 1946 (temp. Captain). Qualified as Solicitor, June 1946; Legal Dept, Anglo-Saxon Petroleum Co., 1946–56; Manager, Thailand and Vietnam Division, Shell International Petroleum Co., 1956–58; Marketing Manager, Shell Co. of Philippines, Ltd, Manila, 1958–61; President, 1961–64; Head of Regional Marketing Div., Shell International Petroleum Co., London, 1964–66; Marketing Coordinator, 1966–70; seconded to HM Govt (Mr Heath's Admin) as Head of Business Team, 1970–72; Dir and Group Personnel Co-ordinator, Shell International Petroleum Co. Ltd, 1972–76. Director: Foseco Minsep, later Foseco plc, 1976–89 (Dep. Chm., 1986–89); Coates Bros plc, 1976–83 (Chm., 1978–83); Portals Hldgs, 1976–88. Vice-Pres., Assoc. of Optometrists, 1988–95. Chm. Council, Univ. of Surrey, 1980–85. DL, 1983, High Sheriff, 1984, Surrey. Master, Worshipful Co. of Spectacle Makers, 1985–87. CCMI; FInstD; Hon. FCOptom; FRSA. DUniv Surrey, 1988. Officer of Philippine Legion of Honour, 1964. *Recreations:* gardening, walking. *Address:* 31 Mayfield, Rowledge, Farnham, Surrey GU10 4DZ. *T:* (01252) 794726. *Clubs:* Royal Over-Seas League, Institute of Directors.

MEYLER, John William F.; *see* Forbes-Meyler.

MEYNELL, Benedict William; Hon. Director-General, Commission of the European Communities, since 1981; *b* 17 Feb. 1930; *s* of late Sir Francis Meynell, RDI, and of Lady (Vera) Meynell, MA; *m* 1st, 1950, Hildamarie (*née* Hendricks) (marr. diss. 1965); two *d*; 2nd, 1967, Diana (*née* Himbury) (marr. diss. 1971). *Educ:* Beltane Sch.; Geneva Univ. (Licencié-ès-sciences politiques); Magdalen Coll., Oxford (Doncaster schol.; MA). Asst Principal, Bd of Inland Revenue, 1954–56; Asst Principal, BoT, 1957–59, Principal, 1959–68; Principal British Trade Commissioner, Kenya, 1962–64; Board of Trade: Principal Private Sec. to Pres., 1967–68; Asst Sec., 1968–70; Commercial Counsellor, Brit. Embassy, Washington, DC, 1970–73; a Dir, EEC, responsible for relations with Far East, and for commercial safeguards and textiles negotiations, 1973–77, for relations with N America, Japan and Australasia, 1977–81. *Publications:* (paper) International Regulation of Aircraft Noise, 1971; contribs: Japan and Western Europe, ed Tsoukalis and White, 1982; A Survey of External Relations, in Yearbook of European Law 1982; Servir l'Etat, 1987 (Cahiers de l'Homme series). *Address:* New Cottage, Greatham Lane, Pulborough, West Sussex RH20 2ES. *T:* (01798) 872688. *Club:* Savile.

MEYRIC HUGHES, Henry Andrew Carne; independent curator and consultant; President, International Foundation Manifesta (formerly European Visual Arts Manifestation), since 1995 (Board Member, since 1993; Chairman, 1995–2006); International President, Association of Art Critics, Paris, since 2002; *b* 1 April 1942; *s* of late Reginald Richard Meyric Hughes and of Jean Mary Carne Meyric Hughes (*née* Pratt); *m* 1968, Alison Hamilton Faulds; one *s* one *d*. *Educ:* Shrewsbury Sch.; Univs of Rennes and Munich; University Coll., Oxford (BA Hons); Univ. of Sussex (MA). British Council, 1968–92: Berlin, Lima, Paris, Milan, London; Dir, Fine Arts Dept, later Visual Arts Dept, 1986–92; Dir of Exhibns, South Bank Centre (Hayward Gall., Nat. Touring Exhibns, Arts Council Collection), 1992–96. British Comr, Venice Biennale and São Paulo Bienal, 1986–92; Official Comr, XXIII Council of Europe exhibn, London, Barcelona and Berlin, 1995–96; Cypriot Pavilion, Venice Biennale, 2003; Co-curator: The Romantic Spirit in German Art, 1790–1990, Edinburgh, London, Munich, 1994; Blast to Freeze: British Art in the Twentieth Century, Wolfsburg and Toulouse, 2002–03; Associate Curator, The Age of Modernism, Berlin, 1997. Dir, Riverside Trust, 1986–95; Mem. Court, RCA, 1986–92; Mem., Faculty of Fine Arts, British Sch. at Rome, 1988–94. Board Member: Internat. Assoc. of Curators of Contemp. Art, 1992–97; Inst. of Internat. Visual Arts, 1995–; Konsthallen, Göteborg, 1995–2000; Pres., British Sect., AICA, 1988–91. Mem., Gp of Consultants, Council of Europe exhibns, 2006–. Pres. of Jury, Diploma examinations, École Nationale Supérieure des Beaux-Arts, Paris, 2004. Member, Scientific Committee: Museum Moderner Kunst Stiftung Ludwig Wien, 2001–02; Galleria d'Arte Moderna, Bologna, 2001–05; Archive de la Critique d'Art, 2002–; Dox Centre for Contemporary Art, Prague, 2004–. Trustee, Arnolfini Gall., Bristol, 2006–. Member, Jury: Turner Prize, 1988; Biennale de Cetinje, 2002; Caribbean Biennial, 2003; Gwangju Biennale, 2004 (Chm.); Premio Furla, Bologna, 2005; Dakar Biennial, 2006. Silver Medal, Czech Soc. for Internat. Cultural Relations, 1986. Officier, l'Ordre Nat. des Arts et des Lettres (France), 1997; Bundesverdienstkreuz (Germany), 2002. *Publications:* articles on visual arts and cultural relations, UK and overseas, 1966–. *Recreations:* music, Europe. *Address:* 13 Ashchurch Grove, W12 9BT. *T:* and *Fax:* (020) 8749 4098; *e-mail:* henry@meyrichughes.homechoice.co.uk.

MEYRICK, Very Rev. (Cyril) Jonathan; Dean of Exeter, since 2005; *b* 23 April 1952; *s* of Christopher and Isolde Meyrick; *m* 1984, Rebecca Keatley; one *s* two *d*. *Educ:* Lancing Coll.; St John's Coll., Oxford (BA Hons 1973, MA 1977); Salisbury and Wells Theol Coll. Ordained deacon, 1976, priest, 1977; Curate, Bicester, 1976–78; Domestic Chaplain to Bishop of Oxford, 1978–81; Tutor in Old Testament Studies, Codrington Coll., Barbados, 1981–84; Team Vicar, Taplow, Burnham Team Ministry, 1984–90; Team Rector, Tisbury, 1990–98; RD, Chalke Valley, 1997–98; Canon Residentiary, Rochester Cathedral, 1998–2005; Acting Dean, Rochester, 2003–05. *Publications:* Old Testament Syllabus for Developing Ministries Programme, Diocese of Rochester, 2001; (contrib.) Cultural Diversity Guide, 2001, rev. edn 2003; Rochester Cathedral Official Guidebook, 2004; A Carol of Hope, 2008. *Recreations:* acting, singing, punting, croquet, tennis. *Address:* The Deanery, 10 Cathedral Close, Exeter EX1 1EZ. *T:* (office) (01392) 273509, *Fax:* (01392) 285986; *e-mail:* dean@exeter-cathedral.org.uk. *Club:* Garrick.

MEYRICK, Sir George (Christopher Cadafael Tapps Gervis), 7th Bt *cr* 1791, of Hinton Admiral; *b* 10 March 1941; *s* of Sir George David Eliott Tapps Gervis Meyrick,

6th Bt, MC and Ann, *d* of late Clive Miller; *S* father, 1988; *m* 1968, Jean Louise, *d* of late Lord William Montagu Douglas Scott and of Lady William Montagu Douglas Scott; two *s* one *d*. *Educ:* Eton; Trinity College, Cambridge (MA). FRICS. *Heir: s* George William Owen Tapps Gervis Meyrick [*b* 3 April 1970; *m* 2006, Candida Clark]. *Address:* Hinton Admiral, Christchurch, Dorset BH23 7DU; Bodorgan, Isle of Anglesey LL62 5LW. *Club:* White's.

MEYRICK, Very Rev. Jonathan; *see* Meyrick, Very Rev. C. J.

MEYRICK, (Sir) Timothy (Thomas Charlton), (5th Bt *cr* 1880, of Bush, Pembrokeshire, but does not use the title); *b* 5 Nov. 1963; *s* of Sir David John Charlton Meyrick, 4th Bt and of Penelope Anne (*née* Marsden-Smedley); *S* father, 2004. *Educ:* Eton; Bristol Univ. *Heir: b* Simon Edward Meyrick [*b* 20 Sept. 1965; *m* 1989, Jennifer Amanda Irvine; one *s* one *d*].

MIAKWE, Hon. Sir Akepa, KBE 1989 (OBE 1982); Chairman, Eastern Highlands Development Corporation, Papua New Guinea, since 1982; *b* 1934; *s* of Umakue Miakwe and Obio Opae; *m* Kora Maho; seven *s* five *d*. *Educ:* Grade 3, Kabiufa Primary Sch. Local Govt Councillor, 1960–77 (Pres., 1962–64, Sen. Vice-Pres., 1965–72); MP Goroka, 1972–76, Unggai/Bena, 1977–82; Minister for Correctional Services and Liquor Licensing under Nat. Party. Mem. Bd Dirs, Eastern Highlands Capital Authority, 1989–; Dir, New Guinea Highlands Coffee Exports Pty Ltd, 1992–. Mem. Council, Univ. of Papua New Guinea, 1991–94. *Address:* Eastern Highlands Development Corporation Pty Ltd, PO Box 971, Goroka, Eastern Highlands Province, Papua New Guinea. *T:* 7322057, *Fax:* 7321961.

MICHAEL, Rt Hon. Alun (Edward); PC 1998; JP; MP (Lab and Co-op) Cardiff South and Penarth, since 1987; *b* 22 Aug. 1943; *m* 1966, Mary Crawley; two *s* three *d*. *Educ:* Colwyn Bay GS; Keele Univ. (BA Hons English and Phil.). Journalist, South Wales Echo, 1966–71; Youth and Community Worker, Cardiff, 1972–84; Area Community Education Officer, Grangetown and Butetown, 1984–87. Mem., Cardiff City Council, 1973–89 (sometime Chm., Finance, Planning, Performance Review, and Econ. Develt, and Chief Whip, Labour Gp). Dir, Cardiff and Vale Enterprise. Mem. (Lab and Co-op) Wales Mid and West, and First Sec. for Wales, Nat. Assembly for Wales, 1999–2000. An Opposition Whip, 1987–88; Opposition frontbench spokesman: on Welsh Affairs, 1988–92; on Home Affairs and the voluntary sector, 1992–97; Minister of State, Home Office, 1997–98; Sec. of State for Wales, 1998–99; Minister of State (Minister for Rural Affairs and Local Envmtl Quality, DEFRA, 2001–05; Minister of State, DTI, 2005–06. Chairman: Co-operative Parly Gp, 1988–92; Parly Friends of Co-operative Ideal, 1988–92; Member: Nat. Exec., Co-op. Party, 1988–92; Parly Cttee, Co-op. Union, 1988–94. Chairman: All-Party Gp on Alcohol Misuse, 1991–93, 1998–; All-Party, Penal Affairs Gp; Parly Friends of WNO, 1991–97; Jt Chm., All-Party Gp on Somalia, 1989–97; Vice-Chm., All-Party Penal Affairs Gp, 1991–97; Jt Sec., All-Party Gp for Further and Tertiary Educn, 1990–97; Sec., All-Party Panel for Personal Social Services, 1990–93. Formerly: Mem. Bd, Crime Concern; Vice-Pres., YHA; Mem. Exec., Nat. Youth Bureau. Formerly Vice-Pres., Bldg Socs Assoc. Dep. Chm., Cardiff Bay Opera House Trust, 1994–96; Mem. Bd, Cardiff and Vale Enterprise, 1982–93; plays leading role locally in community develt projects. FRSA 2003. JP Cardiff, 1972 (Chm., Cardiff Juvenile Bench, 1986–87; formerly Mem., S Glam Probation Cttee). *Recreations:* long-distance running, mountain walking, opera, listening to classical music, member of the Parliamentary Choir, reading. *Address:* House of Commons, SW1A 0AA. *T:* (020) 7219 3441. *Clubs:* Penarth Labour; Grange Stars; Earlswood.

MICHAEL, Sir Duncan, Kt 2001; PhD; FREng; Chairman, Ove Arup Partnership, 1995–2000 (Director, 1977–2002; Trustee, 1977–2006; Chairman of Trustees, 1995–2004); Trustee, Ove Arup Foundation, since 1995; *b* 26 May 1937; *s* of Donald Michael and Lydia Cameron MacKenzie; *m* 1960, Joan Clay; two *s* one *d*. *Educ:* Beauly Public School; Inverness Royal Academy. BSc Edinburgh; PhD Leeds. FICE 1975; FIStructE 1975; FREng (FEng 1984); FHKIE 1981; FRSE 2005. Lectr, Leeds Univ., 1961; Engr, Ove Arup Partnership, 1962. Member: Council, IStructE, 1977–80, 1983–89; Jt Bd of Moderators of Engrg Instns, 1985–92; SE Asia Trade Adv. Group, BOTB, 1982–85; Civil Engineering Cttee, SERC, 1980–83; Council, Royal Acad. Engrg, 1994–2005 (Chm., Awards Cttee, 1995–99; Vice Pres., 1999–2005; new HQ project bd, 2004–); Vice-Chm., Council of Tall Buildings & Urban Habitat, 1980–96; Member: Educn and Trng Affairs Cttee, CBI, 1997–2003; State of the Nation Assessment Panel, ICE, 2000–03; Adv. Bd, Master of Research, Univ. of Dundee, 2000–07 (Chm., 2000–04); Chm., Engrg Adv. Bd, Aberdeen Univ., 1998–; Mentor: Professors of Design for Sustainable Engrg, Univ. of Cambridge, 2000–05; Imperial Coll., London, 2001–08; Member: Industrial Adv. Cttee, Churchill Coll., Cambridge, 2000–05; Academic Adv. Bd, Univ. of Highlands and Islands proj., 1999–2001; Bd, Housing Corp., 2000– (Chairman: Investment Cttee, 2002–; Gold Awards Judging Panel, 2005–); Mgt Bd, Scottish Res. Partnership in Engrg, 2007–; land assets advr to Chm., UCL Health Trust, 2005–08. Fellowship of Engrg Vis. Prof., Aberdeen Univ., 1989–94; Vis. Prof., Leeds Univ., 1990–94. Trustee, Lydia Michael Trust, 2000–. Fellow, Inst. of Scottish Shipbldrs and Engrs, 2000; Mem., Smeatonian Soc. of Civil Engrs, 2001. Hon. DEng: Abertay Dundee, 1997; UMIST, 1999; Hon. DSc: Aberdeen, 2001; Robert Gordon, 2003; Strathclyde, 2005; Edinburgh, 2007. Gold Medal, IStructE, 2000. *Publications:* Skyscrapers, 1987; lectures and engineering papers in technical jls. *Recreations:* garden, Scottish archaeology, opera. *Address:* 3 High Cedar Drive, SW20 0NU. *Clubs:* Caledonian, London Scottish Wimbledon.

MICHAEL, George; singer, songwriter and producer; *b* Georgios Kyriacos Panayiotou, 25 June 1963; *s* of Jack Kyriacus Panayiotou and late Lesley Panayiotou. *Educ:* Bushey Meads Sch. Formed band, The Executive, 1981; co-singer, Wham!, 1981–86; solo singer, 1986–; nat. and internat. tours. *Albums include:* with Wham!: Fantastic, 1983; Make it Big, 1984; Music from the Edge of Heaven. 1985; The Final, 1986; solo: Faith, 1987; Listen Without Prejudice, 1989; Older, 1996; Songs from the Last Century, 1999; Patience, 2004. *Publication:* (with Tony Parsons) Bare: George Michael, his own story, 1990. *Address:* c/o Connie Filippello Publicity, 49 Portland Road, W11 4LJ; c/o Sony Music Entertainment, 10 Great Marlborough Street, W1F 7LP.

MICHAEL, Prof. Ian David Lewis; King Alfonso XIII Professor of Spanish Studies, University of Oxford, 1982–2003, now Emeritus; Fellow, Exeter College, Oxford, 1982–2003, now Emeritus; *b* 26 May 1936; *o s* of late Cyril George Michael and Glenys Morwen (*née* Lewis). *Educ:* Neath Grammar Sch.; King's Coll., London (BA First Class Hons Spanish 1957; FKC 2002); PhD Manchester 1967. University of Manchester: Asst Lectr in Spanish, 1957–60; Lectr in Spanish, 1960–69; Sen. Lectr in Spanish, 1969–70; University of Southampton: Prof. of Spanish and Hd of Spanish Dept, 1971–82; Dep. Dean, Faculty of Arts, 1975–77, 1980–82; Sen. Curator and Chm., Univ. Library Cttee, 1980–82; Oxford University: Curator, Taylor Instn, 1994–2000; Chm., Faculty Bd of Mod. Langs, 1999–2000. Leverhulme Faculty Fellow in European Studies (at Madrid), 1977–78; first British-Spanish Foundn Vis. Prof., Complutensian Univ., Madrid, 1993–94. Member: Gp of Three for Spain (Humanities research review), Eur. Science Foundn, 1987; Welsh Acad. (Eng. Lang. Section), 1995–. Pres., Assoc. of Hispanists of GB and Ire., 1990–92; Pres., Oxford Medieval Soc., 2002–03. Comdr, Order of Isabel la Católica (Spain), 1986. *Publications:* The Treatment of Classical Material in the Libro de Alexandre, 1970; Spanish Literature and Learning to 1474, in, Spain: a Companion to Spanish studies, 1973, 3rd edn 1977; The Poem of the Cid, 1975, new edn 1984; Poema de Mio Cid, 1976, 2nd edn 1979; Gwyn Thomas, 1977; chapter on Poem of My Cid in New Pelican Guide to English Literature. I ii, 1983; (ed) Sound on Vision: studies on Spanish cinema, 1999; (ed) Context, Meaning and Reception of Celestina, 2000; Gonzalo de Berceo, Miracles of Our Lady, 2006; articles in various learned jls and Festschriften; *as David Serafín:* Saturday of Glory, 1979 (John Creasey Meml Award, CWA, 1980); Madrid Underground, 1982; Christmas Rising, 1982; The Body in Cadiz Bay, 1985; Port of Light, 1987; The Angel of Torremolinos, 1988. *Recreations:* writing pseudonymous fiction; opera. *Address:* Calle Goya, 57 (buzón 10), 28001 Madrid, Spain. *T:* (91) 5769218; *e-mail:* idlm@ya.com. *Club:* Organon.

MICHAEL, Ian (Lockie), CBE 1972; Deputy Director, Institute of Education, University of London, 1973–78; *b* 30 Nov. 1915; 4th *c* of late Reginald Warburton Michael and Margaret Campbell Kerr; *m* 1942, Mary Harborne Bayley (*d* 2007), *e c* of late Rev. William Henry Bayley; one *s* one *d*. *Educ:* St Bees Sch.; private study. BA (London) 1938; PhD (Bristol) 1963. Schoolmaster: St Faith's Sch., Cambridge, 1935–40; Junior Sch., Leighton Park, 1941–45, Headmaster, 1946–49; Lectr in Educn, Bristol Univ., 1950–63; Prof. of Educn, Khartoum Univ., 1963–64; Vice-Chancellor, Univ. of Malaŵi, 1964–73. Leverhulme Emeritus Fellowship, 1978–79, 1979–80; Vis. Prof. of Educn, Univ. of Cape Town, 1981. Hon. DLitt Malaŵi, 1974. *Publications:* English Grammatical Categories and the Tradition to 1800, 1970; The Teaching of English from the Sixteenth Century to 1870, 1987; Early Textbooks of English, 1993; Literature in School 1700–1830, 1999. *Address:* 6 Jessop Crescent, Westbury Fields, Westbury-on-Trym, Bristol BS10 6TQ. *T:* (0117) 950 5621.

See also Sir J. Michael.

MICHAEL, Sir Jonathan, Kt 2005; FRCP; Deputy Managing Director, Healthcare, BT Health, since 2007; *b* 21 May 1945; *s* of Ian Lockie Michael, *qv*; *m* 1st, 1975, Jacqueline Deluz (marr. diss. 1992); one *s* three *d*; 2nd, 2005, Karen E. Young. *Educ:* Bristol Grammar Sch.; St Thomas's Hosp. Med. Sch., London Univ. (MB BS 1970). MRCS 1970; MRCP 1973, FRCP 1985. Consultant Physician and Nephrologist, Queen Elizabeth Hosp., Birmingham, 1980–2000; Med. Dir, 1994–97, Chief Exec., 1997–2000, University Hosp. Birmingham NHS Trust; Chief Exec., Guy's and St Thomas' Hosp. NHS Trust, then NHS Foundn Trust, 2000–07. Chairman: Assoc. UK Univ. Hosps, 2004–07; Bd of NHS Foundn Trust Network, 2006–07. Gov., Edgbaston High Sch. for Girls, Birmingham, 1988–2000 (Chm. Govs, 1997–2000; Vice-Pres., 2000–05). FKC 2005. *Publications:* contrib. articles on nephrology and medical science. *Address:* BT Global Services, 7th Floor, Fleet Place House, 2 Fleet Place, Holborn Viaduct, EC4M 7RT. *T:* (020) 7105 9271.

MICHAEL, Peter Anthony, CBE 1998; Acting Director, Central Policy, HM Revenue and Customs, since 2008; *b* 2 July 1954; *s* of Taxis Michael and Helen Marie Teresa Michael; *m* 1989, Joanne Elizabeth Angel; two *d*. *Educ:* Pierrepont Sch.; City of London Univ. (Dip. English Law 1976). HM Treasury: Policy Advr, Industrial Policy Div., 1978–79; Private Secretary: to Minister of State (Lords), 1981; to Minister of State (Commons), 1982; Board of Inland Revenue, later HM Revenue and Customs: Policy Adviser: Capital Taxes Div., 1985–89; Internat. Div., 1989–90; Asst Dir, EC Unit, Internat. Div., 1990–98; Director: EU Div., 1998–2000; EU Coordination and Strategy, Internat., 2000–01; Tax Law Rewrite Project, 2001–03; Revenue Policy: Strategy and Co-ordination, 2003–05; Dep. Dir (formerly Dir, Policy Improvement and Professionalism), Central Policy, 2005–08. *Recreations:* music, fishing, IT. *Address:* HM Revenue and Customs, 100 Parliament Street, SW1A 2BQ.

MICHAEL, Sir Peter (Colin), Kt 1989; CBE 1983; Chairman: Classic FM, 1993–2008 (Director, 1991–2008); Pilot Investment Trust, 1993–97; *b* 17 June 1938; *s* of Albert and Enid Michael; *m* 1962, Margaret Baldwin; two *s*. *Educ:* Whitgift Sch., Croydon; Queen Mary Coll., Univ. of London (BSc Elec. Engrg; Fellow, 1983). Chairman: Micro Consultants Group, 1969–85; Quantel Ltd, 1974–89; Databasix Ltd, 1986–88; UEI plc, 1986–89 (Dep. Chm., 1981–85); Cray Electronics, 1989–93. Dir, Rutherford Asset Management, 1995–97; non-executive Director: GWR Gp plc, 1996–2005; Neverfail Holdings Ltd, 2001–; GCap Media plc, 2005–08. Chairman: Peter Michael Winery, Calif, 1982–; Donnington Valley Hotel, 1991–; The Vineyard at Stockcross, 1997–; Pelican Cancer Centre, 1999–; Virtual Music Stores Ltd, 2000–08. Member: Adv. Council for Applied R&D, 1982–85; NCB, 1983–86; ACARD Sub-Gp on Annual Review of Govt Funded R&D, 1985–86; Technol. Requirements Bd, DTI, 1986–88; Adv. Cttee, Royal Mint, 1999–2007; Modern Collection Cttee, 2006–, Wine Sub-cttee, 2006–, Goldsmiths' Co. Paper on City financing of electronics companies to PITCOM, 1988. Chairman: Royal Soc. of British Sculptors Appeal, 1992; Chelsea Harbour '93 Internat. Sculpture Exhibn Appeal; The Sculpture Company, 1995–99. Chm., Greenham Common Community Trust, 1996–. Humphrey Davies Lecture, QMC, 1984. Freeman, City of London, 1984; Liveryman, Goldsmiths' Co., 1988 (Freeman, 1984). CCMI (CBIM 1982). FRSA 1984. Hon. FBKSTS 1981. Hon. LLD Reading, 2004. The Guardian Young Businessman of the Year, 1982. *Recreations:* tennis, opera, classical music, wine, sculpture, writing rhyme. *Address:* (office) Buckingham House, West Street, Newbury, Berks RG14 1BE. *T:* (01635) 552502.

MICHAELS, Prof. Leslie, MD; FRCPath, FRCP(C); Professor of Pathology, Institute of Laryngology and Otology, London University, 1973–90 (Dean, 1976–81); Emeritus Professor, Department of Histopathology, Royal Free and University College Medical School, University of London (formerly University College and Middlesex School of Medicine, then University College London Medical School), since 1990; *b* 24 July 1925; *s* of Henry and Minnie Michaels; *m* Edith (*née* Waldstein); two *d*. *Educ:* Parmiter's Sch., London; King's Coll., London; Westminster Med. Sch., London (MB, BS; MD). FRCPath 1963, FRCP(C) 1962. Asst Lectr in Pathology, Univ. of Manchester, 1955–57; Lectr in Path., St Mary's Hosp. Med. Sch., London, 1957–59; Asst Prof. of Path., Albert Einstein Coll. of Medicine, New York, 1959–61; Hosp. Pathologist, Northern Ont, Canada, 1961–70; Sen. Lectr, Inst. of Laryngol. and Otol., 1970–73. *Publications:* Pathology of the Larynx, 1984; Ear, Nose and Throat Histopathology, 1987, 2nd edn 2001; scientific articles in jls of medicine, pathology and otolaryngology. *Recreations:* reading, music, walking. *Address:* Romany Ridge, Hillbrow Road, Bromley, Kent BR1 4JL.

MICHAELS-MOORE, Anthony; *see* Moore.

MICHEL, Prof. (Christopher) Charles, DPhil; Professor of Physiology, Imperial College School of Medicine (formerly St Mary's Hospital Medical School), 1984–2000, now Emeritus; Senior Research Investigator, Imperial College London, since 2000; *b* 23 March 1938; *s* of late Maurice and May Michel; *m* 1965, Rosalind McCrink; one *s* one *d*. *Educ:* Leeds Grammar Sch.; Queen's Coll., Oxford (BA 1959, 1st cl. Physiol.; MA,

DPhil 1962; BM BCh 1965). MRCP 1986, FRCP 1996. US Public Health Postdoctoral Res. Fellow, 1962; Oxford University: Deptl Demonstrator in Physiol., 1964–67; Univ. Lectr in Physiol., 1967–84; Fellow and Praelector in Physiol., Queen's Coll., 1966–84. Lectures: Oliver-Sharpey, RCP, 1985; Annual Prize Review, Physiol. Soc., 1987; Starling Centenary, World Congress for Microcirculation, 1996; Haliburton, KCL, 2000; Zweifach Meml, UCSD, 2001. Sec., Physiol Soc., 1980–83; Chm., RN Personnel Res. Cttee, 1991–96, Army Personnel Res. Cttee, 1993–94, MRC. Hon. Member: Amer. Physiol. Soc., 1993; Brit. Microcirculation Soc., 2001; Physiol Soc., 2001. Malpighi Prize, Eur. Soc. for Micro-circulation, 1984. *Publications:* (ed with E. M. Renkin) American Handbook of Physiology: the microcirculation, 1984; articles in learned jls. *Recreations:* walking, ornithology, reading. *Address:* Sundial House, High Street, Alderney, Channel Islands GY9 3UG.

MICHEL, Prof. Dr Hartmut; Director, Max Planck Institut of Biophysics, Frankfurt am Main, since 1987; *b* Ludwigsburg, W Germany, 18 July 1948; *s* of Karl Michel and Frieda Michel; *m* (marr. diss.); one *s* one *d*. *Educ:* Universities of: Tübingen (Dip. in biochem.); Würzburg (PhD); Munich (habilitation for biochemistry, 1986). Res. associate with D. Oesterhelt, Univ. of Würzburg, 1977–79; group leader in D. Oesterhelt's dept, Max-Planck-Inst. of Biochemistry, Martinsried, until 1987. For. Mem., Royal Soc., 2005. Various prizes, including: Biophysics Prize of Amer. Phys. Soc., 1986; Otto Klung Prize for Chemistry, 1986; (jtly) Otto Bayer Prize, 1988; (jtly) Nobel Prize for Chemistry, 1988. *Publication:* (ed) Crystallization of Membrane Proteins, 1990. *Recreations:* nature, wild life, physical exercise, readings on history and travel. *Address:* Max Planck Institut für Biophysik, Max von Laue Strasse 3, 60438 Frankfurt am Main, Germany. *T:* (69) 63031001, *Fax:* (69) 63031002.

MICHEL, Louis; Member, European Commission, since 2004; *b* 2 Sept. 1947; *m*; two *c*. German lang. teacher, 1968; Lectr, Inst. Supérieur de Commerce, St Louis; Prof. of Dutch, English and German Lit., Ecole Normale Provinciale, Jodoigne, 1968–78. MHR (PRL), Belgium, 1978–99; Mem., parly commns on Finance, Budget, Instnl Reforms, and Commn on supervising electoral expenditures; elected to Senate, 1999, 2003, 2004; Dep. Prime Minister and Minister of Foreign Affairs, Belgium, 1999–2004. Mem., Benelux Interparly Consultative Council. Dep. Pres., Liberal Internat. Mem. Bd, ELDR. Liberal Reform Party (PRL): Sec.-Gen., 1980–82; Pres., 1982–90 and 1995–99; Pres., Parly Gp in Council of Walloon Reg., 1991–92; Parly Gp in House of Reps, 1992–95. Alderman, 1977–, Mayor, 1983–, Jodoigne. Comdr, Order of Leopold (Belgium), 1995; Grand-Croix: Order of Infante Dom Henrique (Portugal), 1999; Ordre of Orange-Nassau (Netherlands), 2000; Order of Isabel la Católica (Spain), 2000; Ordre Royal de l'Etoile Polaire (Sweden), 2001; Grand Officier, Légion d'Honneur, 2003. *Publications:* (with D. Ducarme) Le défi vert, 1980; (with P. Monfils) L'enfant, 1984; Libres et forts-projet éducatif pour réussir le futur, 1986; Wallons et optimistes, 1997; De echte Walen, 1997; Rendre Confiance, 1998; Objectif 100 La Wallonnie j'y crois!, 1998; Lettre aux citoyens de mon pays, 1999. *Address:* European Commission, 200 Rue de la Loi, 1049 Brussels, Belgium. *T:* (2) 5018211.

MICHELL, John; *see* Michell, M. J.

MICHELL, Keith; actor, since 1948; *b* Adelaide; *s* of Joseph Michell and Alice Maud (*née* Aslat); *m* 1957, Jeannette Sterke; one *s* one *d*. *Educ:* Port Pirie High Sch.; Adelaide Teachers' Coll.; Sch. of Arts and Crafts; Adelaide Univ.; Old Vic Theatre Sch. Formerly taught art. *Stage:* First appearance, Playbox, Adelaide, 1947; Young Vic Theatre Co., 1950–51; first London appearance, And So To Bed, 1951; Shakespeare Meml. Theatre Co., 1952–56, inc. Australian tour, 1952–53 (Henry IV Part 1, As You Like It, Midsummer Night's Dream, Troilus and Cressida, Romeo and Juliet, Taming of the Shrew, All's Well That Ends Well, Macbeth, Merry Wives of Windsor); Don Juan, Royal Court, 1956; Old Vic Co., 1956 (Antony and Cleopatra, Much Ado about Nothing, Two Gentlemen of Verona, Titus Andronicus); Irma La Douce, Lyric, 1958, Washington, DC, 1960 and Broadway, 1960–61; The Chances, Chichester Festival, 1962; The Rehearsal, NY, 1963; The First Four Hundred Years, Australia and NZ, 1964; Robert and Elizabeth, Lyric, 1964; The King's Mare, 1966; Man of La Mancha, 1968–69, NY, 1970; Abelard and Heloise, 1970, Los Angeles and NY, 1971; Hamlet, Globe, 1972; Dear Love, Comedy, 1973; The Crucifer of Blood, Haymarket, 1979; On the Twentieth Century (musical), Her Majesty's, 1980; Pete McGynty and the Dreamtime (own adap. of Peer Gynt), Melbourne Theatre Co., 1981; Captain Beaky Christmas Show, Lyric, Shaftesbury Ave., 1981–82; The Tempest, Brisbane, 1982; opened Keith Michell Theatre, Port Pirie, with one-man show, 1982; Amadeus (UK tour), 1983; La Cage Aux Folles, San Francisco and NY, 1984, Sydney and Melbourne, 1985; Portraits, Malvern Fest. and Savoy, 1987; Aspects of Love, Edmonton and Toronto, 1991–92, Chicago, 1992; Scrooge, Melbourne, 1993; Caesar and Cleopatra, Edmonton, 1994; Brazilian Blue, Brisbane, 1995; various one-man shows, Family Matters, and All the World's a Stage, UK tour, S Australia Adelaide Fest. and Keith Michell Th., Port Pirie, 2000–04; Bernadino Ramazzini - The Artisan's Archangel, RSocMed London, 2005; *Chichester Festival Theatre:* Artistic Director, 1974–77; Tonight We Improvise, Oedipus Tyrannus, 1974; Cyrano de Bergerac, Othello, 1975; (dir and designed) Twelfth Night, 1976; Monsieur Perrichon's Travel, 1976; The Apple Cart, 1977; (dir and designed) In Order of Appearance, 1977; Murder in the Cathedral (Chichester Cathedral), 1977; Henry VIII, 1991; toured Australia with Chichester Co., 1978 (Othello, The Apple Cart); acted in: On the Rocks, 1982; Jane Eyre, 1986; The Royal Baccarat Scandal, 1988, transf. Theatre Royal Haymarket, 1989; Henry VIII, 1991; Monsieur Amilcar (Minerva), 1995. *Films include:* Dangerous Exile; The Hell Fire Club; Seven Seas to Calais; The Executioner; House of Cards; Prudence and the Pill; Henry VIII and his Six Wives; Moments, The Deceivers. *Television includes:* Henry VIII in the Six Wives of Henry VIII (series), 1972; Keith Michell at Chichester, 1974; My Brother Tom, 1986; Captain James Cook, 1987; Murder She Wrote (series), 1990. Many recordings. First exhibn of paintings, 1959; subseq. one-man exhibns at John Whibley Gall., London, Wright Hepburn and Webster Gall., NY, Century Gall., Henley-on-Thames, Wylma Wayne Gall., London, Vincent Gall., Adelaide. Many awards. *Publications:* (ed and illus.) Twelve Shakespeare Sonnets (series of lithographs produced 1974), 1981; illus. and recorded Captain Beaky series, 1975; (compiled and illus.) Practically Macrobiotic, 1987, 3rd edn 2000. *Recreations:* gardening, photography, swimming, cooking.

MICHELL, Michael John; Director: Prestbury Enterprises Ltd; Eni UK Ltd; *b* 12 Dec. 1942; *s* of late John Martin Michell and of Pamela Mary Michell; *m* 1st, 1965, Pamela Marianne Tombs (marr. diss. 1978); two *s* (one *d* decd); 2nd, 1978, Alison Mary Macfarlane (marr. diss. 2005); two *s*; 3rd, 2005, Janice Margaret Bintcliffe. *Educ:* Marlborough College; Corpus Christi College, Cambridge (BA 1964). Min. of Aviation, 1964; Private Sec. to Sir Ronald Melville, 1968–69; Concorde Div., 1969–73; Sec. to Sandilands Cttee on inflation accounting, 1973–75; Private Sec. to Sec. of State for Industry, 1975–77; HM Treasury, 1977–80; Industrial Policy Div., Dept of Industry, 1980–82; RCDS 1983; Department of Trade and Industry: Head, Air Div., 1984–88; Chief Exec., Radio Div., subseq. Radiocommunications Agency, 1988–93; Head, Oil and Gas Div., 1993–98. *Address:* 10 Ebury Bridge Road, SW1W 8PZ.

MICHELL, Prof. Robert Hall, FRS 1986; Royal Society Research Professor at the University of Birmingham, 1987–2006, now Emeritus; *b* 16 April 1941; *s* of Rowland Charles Michell and Elsie Lorna Michell; two *s* one *d*. *Educ:* Crewkerne School, Somerset; Univ. of Birmingham (BSc Med. Biochem. and Pharmacol. 1962; PhD Med. Biochem. 1965; DSc 1978). Research Fellow, Birmingham, 1965–66, 1968–70, Harvard Med. Sch., 1966–68; Birmingham University: Lectr in Biochemistry, 1970–81; Sen. Lectr, 1981–84; Reader, 1984–86; Prof. of Biochemistry, 1986–87. Mem., Physiol. Systems and Disorders Bd, 1985–90, Chm., Grants Cttee B, 1988–90, MRC; Member: Fellowships Cttee, BHF, 1992–97; Fellowships Selection Panel, Lister Inst. of Preventive Medicine, 1999–2005; Fellowship Review Panel, Human Frontiers Sci. Prog., 1999–2001. Mem., Biochem. Panel, 1996 RAE, Biol Scis Panel, 2001 and 2008 RAEs, HEFCE. Member: Adv. Bd, Beit Meml Trust, 1993–2006; Council, Royal Soc., 1996–97; Adv. Bd, EMF Res. Trust, 2000–. Pres., Med. Scis Sect., BAAS, 1993–94. Mem., EMBO, 1991. Morton Lectr, Biochem. Soc., 2002. Member, Editorial Boards: Jl Neurochem., 1974–80; Cell Calcium, 1979–89; Biochem. Jl, 1983–88; Current Opinion in Cell Biology, 1988–; Procs Royal Soc. B, 1989–97; Jl of Molecular Endocrinology, 1992–99; Molecular Membrane Biology, 1993–. FMedSci 2002. CIBA Medal, Biochemical Soc., 1988. *Publications:* (with J. B. Finean and R. Coleman) Membranes and their Cellular Functions, 1974, 3rd edn 1984; (ed with J. B. Finean) Membrane Structure, vol. 1 of New Comprehensive Biochemistry, 1981; (ed with J. W. Putney, Jr) Inositol Lipids in Cellular Signalling, 1987; (ed with M. J. Berridge) Inositol Lipids and Transmembrane Signalling, 1988; (ed jtly) Inositol Lipids and Cellular Signalling, 1989; contribs to Nature, Biochem. Jl and sci. jls. *Recreations:* birdwatching, wilderness, pottery. *Address:* 59 Weoley Park Road, Birmingham B29 6QZ. *T:* (0121) 472 1356.

MICHELL, Roger Harry; director; *b* 5 June 1956; *s* of H. D. Michell, DFC, and Jillian Green; *m* 1992, Kate Buffery (marr. diss. 2002); one *s* one *d*. *Educ:* Clifton Coll., Bristol; Queens' Coll., Cambridge (BA Hons). With Royal Court Th., 1978–80, Royal Shakespeare Th., 1985–91. Judith E. Wilson Sen. Fellow, Cambridge Univ., 1990. *Plays* include: Private Dick, Edinburgh and Whitehall, 1980; The Catch, Royal Court, 1981; White Glove, Lyric, Hammersmith, 1982; Marya, Old Vic., 1990; My Night with Reg, Royal Court and Criterion, 1995; Some Sunny Day, Hampstead, 1996; Old Times, 2004, Betrayal, 2007, Donmar Warehouse; The Female of the Species, Vaudeville, 2008; Royal Shakespeare Company: Merchant of Venice, 1986; Dead Monkey, 1986; Hamlet, 1987; Temptation, 1987; Conversation, 1987; Constant Couple, 1988; Restoration, 1988; Some Americans Abroad, 1989; Redevelopment, 1989; Two Shakespearian Actors, 1990; Royal National Theatre: The Coup, 1991; Under Milk Wood, 1995; The Homecoming, 1997; Blue/Orange, 2000; Honour, 2003; Landscape with Weapon, 2007; *television* includes: Buddha of Suburbia, 1994; Ready When You Are, Mr Patel, 1995; My Night with Reg, 1997; Michael Redgrave, My Father, 1998; *films:* Persuasion, 1995; Titanic Town, 1999; Notting Hill, 1999; Changing Lanes, 2002; The Mother, 2003; Enduring Love, 2004; Venus, 2007. *Recreations:* children, cooking, wines of Southern Rhône. *Address:* c/o Independent Talent Group Ltd, Oxford House, 79 Oxford Street, W1D 1BS.

MICHELMORE, Clifford Arthur, CBE 1969; television broadcaster and producer; *b* 11 Dec. 1919; *s* of late Albert, (Herbert), Michelmore and Ellen Alford; *m* 1950, Jean Metcalfe (Broadcaster) (*d* 2000); one *s* one *d*. *Educ:* Cowes Senior Sch., Isle of Wight. Entered RAF, 1935; commnd 1940; left RAF 1947. Head, Outside Broadcasts and Variety, BFN, 1948; Dep. Station Dir, BFN, also returned to freelance as Commentator and Producer, 1949. Entered Television, 1950. Managing Director: Michelmore Enterprises Ltd, 1969–2000; Communication Consultants Ltd, 1969–84; RM/EMI Visual Programmes, 1971–81; Dir, CP Video, 1988–96. Has taken part in numerous radio and television programmes in Britain, Europe and the USA. Introduced: "Tonight" series, 1957–65; 24 Hours series, 1965–68; General Election Results programmes, 1964, 1966, 1970; So You Think…, 1966–72; Our World, 1967; With Michelmore (interviews); Talkback; Apollo Space Programmes, 1960–70; Holiday, 1969–86; Chance to Meet, 1970–73; Wheelbase, 1972; Getaway, 1975; Globetrotter, 1975; Opinions Unlimited, 1977–79; Presenter: Day by Day (Southern TV), 1980; Sudden Change (HTV), 1982; Cliff Michelmore Show (BBC Radio), 1982–83; Home on Sunday (BBC TV), 1983–90; Waterlines (BBC Radio Four), 1984–94; Lifeline (BBC TV), 1986–96; Coastline (BBC Radio Four), 1991–94; Cliff's Country, 1992 (BBC Radio Four); Scrapbook, 1996; A Year to Remember, 1996–2000 (BBC Radio Two). Made films: Shaping of a Writer, 1977; Hong Kong: the challenge, 1978. FRSA 1975. Television Society Silver Medal, 1957; Guild of TV Producers Award, Personality of the Year, 1958; TV Review Critics Award, 1959; Variety Club Award, 1961. *Publications:* (ed) The Businessman's Book of Golf, 1981; Cliff Michelmore's Holidays By Rail, 1986; (with Jean Metcalfe) Two-Way Story (autobiog.), 1986; Some of These Days, 1987; contribs to Highlife, Financial Weekly; various articles on television, broadcasting and travel. *Recreations:* golf, doing nothing. *Address:* Northend Barn, South Harting, Petersfield, Hants GU31 5NR. *T:* (01730) 825665. *Club:* Royal Air Force.

MICHELS, Sir David (Michael Charles), Kt 2006; Senior European Strategist, Strategic Hotels & Resorts, since 2007; *b* 8 Dec. 1946; *s* of Klaus Peter and Thelma Sadie Michels; *m* 1973, Michele Ann Arnold; one *s* one *d*. *Educ:* Hendon Coll. FIH. Grand Metropolitan, 1966–81; Ladbrokes: Sales and Marketing Dir, Hotels, 1981–83; Man. Dir, Leisure Div., 1983–85; Man. Dir, Ladbroke Hotels, 1985–87; Hilton International: Sen. Vice-Pres., Sales and Marketing, 1987–89; Dep. Chm., Hilton UK and Exec. Vice-Pres., Hilton Worldwide, 1989–91; Chief Exec., Stakis plc, 1991–99; Chief Executive: Hilton Internat. Hotels, 1999–2000; Hilton Gp plc, 2000–06. Dep. Chm., Marks and Spencer Gp plc, 2008–; non-exec. Dir, British Land Co. plc, 2003–; Sen. Ind. Dir, EasyJet plc. Trustee, Anne Frank Trust. Hon. DLitt Glasgow Caledonian, 1993. *Recreations:* tennis, poker, reading.

MICHIE, Prof. David Alan Redpath, OBE 1997; RSA 1972 (ARSA 1964); RGI 1984; Head, School of Drawing and Painting, Edinburgh College of Art, 1982–90; Professor Emeritus, Heriot-Watt University, 1991; *b* 30 Nov. 1928; *s* of late James Michie and late Anne Redpath, OBE, ARA, RSA; *m* 1951, Eileen Anderson Michie; two *d*. *Educ:* Edinburgh Coll. of Art (DA). National Service, 1947–49; Edinburgh Coll. of Art, 1949–53 (studied painting); travelling scholarship, Italy, 1953–54; Lectr in Painting, Gray's Sch. of Art, Aberdeen, 1958–62; Lectr in Painting, Edinburgh Coll. of Art, 1962–82, Vice-Principal, 1974–77. Visiting Professor of Painting: Acad. of Fine Art, Belgrade, 1979; Univ. of Calif, Santa Barbara, 1992. Member: Gen. Teaching Council for Scotland, 1976–80; Edinburgh Festival Soc., 1976–; Museums and Galls Commn, 1991–96. Mem. Court, Heriot-Watt Univ., 1979–82. Pres., Soc. of Scottish Artists, 1961–63. One Man Exhibitions: Mercury Gallery, London, 1967, 1969, 1971, 1974, 1980, 1983, 1992, 1996, 1999; Mercury Gall., Edinburgh, 1986; Lothian Region Chambers, 1977; Scottish Gall., Edinburgh, 1980, 1994, 1998, 2003, 2008; Kasteel de Hooge Vuursche, Baarn, Netherlands, 1991. RWA 1991–2000. FRSA 1990; FFCS 2000. *Recreation:* music. *Address:* 17 Gilmour Road, Edinburgh EH16 5NS. *T:* (0131) 667 2684.

MICHIE, Prof. Jonathan, DPhil; Director, Department for Continuing Education, University of Oxford, and President, Kellogg College, Oxford, since 2008; *b* 25 March

1957; *s* of late Prof. Donald Michie and (Dame) Anne Laura McLaren, DBE, FRS; *m* 1988, Carolyn Grace Downs, *qv*; two *s*. *Educ:* Balliol Coll., Oxford (BA 1st Cl. Hons PPE); Queen Mary Coll., London (MSc Econ (Dist.)); DPhil Econ Oxon 1985. Lectr, Univ. of Oxford, 1983; Res. Officer, Econ. Dept, TUC, 1983–88; Expert to EC, Brussels, 1988–90; Fellow in Econs, St Catharine's Coll., Cambridge, 1990–92; Lectr in Accounting and Finance, Judge Business Sch., Univ. of Cambridge, 1992–97; Dir, Contracts and Competition Prog., ESRC, 1992–97; Sainsbury Prof. of Mgt, Birkbeck Coll., Univ. of London, 1997–2004; Prof. of Mgt and Dir, Business Sch., Univ. of Birmingham, 2004–08. Non-exec. Dir, Sandwell and W Birmingham Hosps NHS Trust, 2006–08 (Chm., Audit Cttee, 2006–08). Mem. Council, ACAS, 2007– (Chm., Audit Cttee, 2007–). Member: Council, Univ. of Birmingham, 2005–08 (Mem., Investments Cttee, 2005–08); Nat. Exec. Cttee, Assoc. of Business Schs, 2005– (Treas., 2005–). *Publications:* Wages in the Business Cycle, 1987; The Political Economy of Competitiveness, 2000; A Reader's Guide to Social Science, 2001; Systems of Production, 2002; The Handbook of Globalisation, 2003. *Recreations:* supporting Manchester United, campaigning for supporter control of football clubs. *Address:* The Garden House, Apley Hall, Bridgnorth WV15 5NE. *T:* (01952) 730897, *Fax:* (01952) 730896; *e-mail:* jonathanmichie@yahoo.co.uk.

MICHIE, William; *b* 24 Nov. 1935; *m* 1st, 1957 (marr. diss. 1982); two *s*; 2nd, 1987, Judith Ann (*née* Frost); one step *s* one step *d*. *Educ:* Abbeydale Secondary Sch., Sheffield; Sheffield Polytechnic. Nat. Service, RAF, 1957–59. Formerly: apprentice electrician; maintenance electrician; Lab. Technician, Computer Applications; unemployed, 1981–83. Joined Labour Party, 1965; Co-op. Party, 1966. Mem., Amicus (formerly AUEW, then AEU, then AEEU), 1952– (former Br. Trustee; former Standing Orders Cttee Deleg., Lab. Party Yorks Regl Conf.). Member: Sheffield City Council, 1970–84 (Chairman: Planning, 1974–81; Employment, 1981–83; Gp Sec./Chief Whip, 1974–83); South Yorks CC, 1974–86 (Area Planning Chm., 1974–81). MP (Lab) Sheffield, Heeley, 1983–2001. Member: Privileges Select Cttee, 1994–96; Members' Interests Select Cttee, 1993–96; Jt Cttee on Parly Privilege, 1997–2001. Chm., AEEU Parly Gp, 1997–2001 (Mem., 1983–2001). *Recreations:* darts, gardening, Sheffield Wednesday.

MICKELSON, Philip Alfred; golfer; *b* San Diego, 16 June 1970; *s* of Philip Mickelson and Mary Mickelson; *m* Amy McBride; one *s* two *d*. *Educ:* Arizona State Univ. Winner, Northern Telecom Open (as amateur), 1991; professional golfer, 1992–; wins include: Buick Invitational, 1993, 2000, 2001; Mercedes Championship, 1994, 1998; Northern Telecom Open, 1995; NEC World Series Golf, 1996; AT&T Pebble Beach Nat. Pro-Am, 1998, 2005; BellSouth Classic, 2000, 2005; PGA Tour Championship, 2000; US Masters Tournament, 2004 and 2006; PGA Championship, 2005; Member: US Ryder Cup Team, 1995, 1997, 1999 (winners), 2002, 2004; President's Cup Team, 1994 (winners), 1996 (winners), 1998, 2000 (winners), 2003. *Address:* c/o Gaylord Sports Management, Suite 230, 14646 North Kierland Boulevard, Scottsdale, AZ 85254, USA; c/o PGA Tour, 112 PGA Tour Boulevard, Ponte Vedra Beach, FL 32082, USA.

MICKLETHWAIT, (Richard) John; Editor, The Economist, since 2006; *b* 11 Aug. 1962; *s* of Richard Miles Micklethwait and Jane Evelyn Micklethwait (*née* Codrington); *m* 1992, Fevronia Read; three *s*. *Educ:* Ampleforth Coll., York; Magdalen Coll., Oxford (BA Modern Hist.). The Economist: Finance corresp., 1987–90; W Coast Bureau Chief, 1990–93; Business ed., 1993–97; NY Bureau Chief, 1997–2000; US ed., 2000–06. *Publications:* with Adrian Wooldridge: The Witch Doctors, 1996; A Future Perfect, 2000; The Company, 2003; The Right Nation, 2004. *Recreations:* sport, dog walking. *Address:* The Economist, 25 St James's Street, SW1A 1HG. *T:* (020) 7830 7032, *Fax:* (020) 7839 2968; *e-mail:* rjm@economist.com. *Club:* Royal Automobile.

MICKLEWHITE, Sir Michael; *see* Caine, Sir Michael.

MIDDLE, Anne Hilary; *see* Shinwell, A. H.

MIDDLEBURGH, Rabbi Dr Charles Hadley; Rabbi: Dublin Jewish Progressive Congregation, since 2002; Cardiff Reform Synagogue, since 2005; Senior Lecturer in Rabbinics, Leo Baeck College, since 2003; Lecturer, Irish School of Ecumenics, Trinity College, Dublin, since 2002; *b* 2 Oct. 1956; *s* of late Hyman Middleburgh and of Elizabeth Middleburgh; *m* 1984, Gilly Blyth. *Educ:* Brighton Coll.; University Coll. London (BA Hons, PhD 1982); Leo Baeck Coll. Lay reader, Brighton and Hove Progressive Synagogue, 1975–77; Minister, Kingston Liberal Synagogue, 1977–83; ordained 1986; Rabbi, Harrow and Wembley Progressive Synagogue, 1983–97; Exec. Dir, ULPS, 1997–2002; Rabbi, Progressive Judaism in Denmark, 2002–05. Leo Baeck College: Lectr in Bible, Aramaic, Rabbinic Practice, 1985–2002; Interim Dir of Rabbinic Studies, 2005–06. Occasional broadcaster, BBC Radio 4 and World Service, 1997–, RTE, Radio Eireann. FZS 1997; FRSA 1998. *Publications:* (Associate Ed.) Union of Liberal and Progressive Synagogues Daily, Sabbath and Festival Prayer Book, 1995; (ed jtly) Union of Liberal and Progressive Synagogues High Holy Days Prayerbook, 2003. *Recreations:* animal photography, running, cycling, needlepoint, horse-riding, playing with tigers. *Address:* *e-mail:* charles@middleburgh.co.uk; *web:* www.middleburgh.co.uk.

MIDDLEHURST, Tom; Member (Lab) Alyn and Deeside, National Assembly for Wales, 1999–2003; *b* 25 June 1936; *s* of late James Middlehurst and Agnes Middlehurst; *m* 1986, Patricia Mary; one *s* one *d* from a previous marriage. *Educ:* Ormskirk Grammar Sch.; Wigan Tech. Coll.; Liverpool Poly. Engrg apprentice, 1952–57; Underground Engr, NCB, 1957–63; engr, 1963–71; Local Govt Officer, Flintshire, later Clwyd, CC, 1971–93. Mem. (Lab), Alyn and Deeside DC, 1986–95; Mem. (Lab), Clwyd CC, 1993–95 (Chm., Housing Cttee; Chm., Personnel Cttee); Leader (Lab), Flintshire CC, 1995–99. Chm., Welsh Local Govt Assoc., 1997–99. National Assembly for Wales: Sec. for Post-16 Educn and Training, 1999–2000; Member: N Wales Cttee, 1999–2003; European Affairs Cttee, 2000–03; Local Govt and Housing Cttee, 2000–03; Envmt, Planning and Transport Cttee, 2000–03. Mem., Labour Party, 1961–; Mem. Bd of Dirs, Wales European Centre. Chm. Govs, Clwyd Theatr Cymru, 1995–99.

MIDDLEMAS, Prof. Robert Keith; Professor of History, University of Sussex, 1986–98, now Emeritus; *b* 26 May 1935; *s* of late Robert James Middlemas, Solicitor and of Eleanor Mary (*née* Crane), Howick, Northumberland; *m* 1958, Susan Mary, *d* of Laurence Edward Paul Tremlett and Marjorie Isobel Derrington Bell; one *s* three *d*. *Educ:* Stowe Sch.; Pembroke Coll., Cambridge (Exhibnr, scholar, BA 1st cl. History 1958); DPhil 1972, DLitt 1982, Sussex. 2nd Lieut, Northumberland Fusiliers, 1954–55 (served in Kenya); Clerk, House of Commons, 1958–66; Lectr in History, Univ. of Sussex, 1966–76, Reader, 1976–86. Visiting Professor: Stanford Univ. and Hoover Instn, Stanford, 1984; Univ. of Beijing, 1989. Member: UK Nat. Cttee, Unesco, 1980–86; Council, Inst. of Contemporary British History; Council and Res. Cttee, Foundn for Manufg and Industry, 1993–96; Conseil de Surveillance, ESL and Network, Paris, 1997–2006; Chm., ESL and Network (UK) Ltd, 2002–06. FRSA. Co-Founder and Editor, Catalyst: a jl of public debate, 1985–87. *Publications:* The Master Builders, 1963; The Clydesiders, 1965; (with John Barnes) Baldwin, 1969; Diplomacy of Illusion, 1972; (ed) Thomas Jones: Whitehall Diary, vols I and II, 1969–70, vol. III, 1972; Politics in Industrial Society, 1979; Cabora Bassa, 1975; Power and the Party, 1980; Industry, Unions and Government, 1984; Power, Competition and the State, vol. I, Britain in Search of Balance 1940–61, 1986, vol. 2, Threats to the Post-War Settlement: Britain 1961–74, 1990; vol. 3, The End of the Post-War Era: Britain since 1974, 1991; Orchestrating Europe: informal politics of the European Community since 1973, 1995; articles and reviews in learned jls. *Recreations:* sports, sailing, fishing, landscape gardening; Member, UK Nat. Rifle Team, Canadian tour, 1958. *Address:* West Burton House, West Burton, Pulborough, West Sussex RH20 1HD. *T:* (01798) 831516. *Club:* Flyfishers'.

MIDDLESBROUGH, Bishop of, (RC), since 2008; **Rt Rev. Terence Patrick Drainey;** *b* Manchester, 1 Aug. 1949; *s* of Joseph Patrick Drainey and Mary Elizabeth Drainey (*née* Roebuck). *Educ:* Augustinian Theol Studium, Pontifical Univ. of Comillas, Valladolid (STB). Ordained priest, 1975; St Wulstan, Great Harwood, 1975–80; St Thomas of Canterbury, Higher Broughton, Salford, 1980–85; Immaculate Conception and St Philip Neri, Radcliffe, 1985–86; Priest (*fidei donum*), Archdiocese of Kisumu, Western Kenya, 1986–91; Parish Priest: Holy Cross, Patricroft, 1991–94; St Bernadette's, Whitefield, 1994–97; Spiritual Dir, 1997–2003, Dir of the Propaedeutic Prog., 1998–2003, Royal English Coll. of St Albans, Valladolid; Pres., St Cuthbert's Coll., Ushaw, 2003–07. Mem., Bishops' Conference Dept of Catholic Educn and Formation, 2008–. Appointed Papal Chaplain by His Holiness Pope Benedict XVI, 2006. *Recreations:* music, especially choral, walking, gardening. *Address:* (residence) Bishop's House, 16 Cambridge Road, Middlesbrough TS5 5NN. *T:* (01642) 818253; (office) Curial Office, 50a The Avenue, Linthorpe, Middlesbrough TS5 6QT. *T:* (01642) 850505.

MIDDLESEX, Archdeacon of; *see* Welch, Ven. S. J.

MIDDLETON, 12th Baron *cr* 1711; **Digby Michael Godfrey John Willoughby,** MC 1945; DL; Bt 1677; *b* 1 May 1921; *er s* of 11th Baron Middleton, KG, MC, TD, and Angela Florence Alfreda (*d* 1978), *er d* of Charles Hall, Eddlethorpe Hall, Malton, Yorks; *S* father, 1970; *m* 1947, Janet, *o d* of General Sir James Marshall-Cornwall, KCB, CBE, DSO, MC; three *s*. *Educ:* Eton; Trinity Coll., Cambridge. BA 1950; MA 1958. Served War of 1939–45: Coldstream Guards, 1940–46; NW Europe, 1944–45 (despatches, MC, Croix de Guerre); Hon. Col, 2nd Bn Yorkshire Volunteers, TAVR, 1976–88. Mem., H of L Select Cttee on Europ. Communities, 1985–97; Chm., H of L Sub-Cttee D, Agriculture and Food, 1989–92, 1994–97. Pres., CLA, 1981–83; Member: Yorks and Humberside Econ. Planning Council, 1968–79; Nature Conservancy Council, 1986–89. DL 1963, JP 1958, CC 1964–74, ER of Yorks; CC N Yorks, 1974–77. *Heir: s* Hon. Michael Charles James Willoughby [*b* 14 July 1948; *m* 1974, Hon. Lucy Sidney, *y d* of 1st Viscount De L'Isle, VC, KG, GCMG, GCVO, PC; two *s* three *d*]. *Address:* Birdsall House, Malton, N Yorks YO17 9NR. *Club:* Boodle's.

MIDDLETON, Bishop Suffragan of, since 2008; **Rt Rev. Mark Davies;** *b* 12 May 1962; *s* of late Cyril and of Gwen Davies; *m* 1991, Joanne Winrow; one *s*. *Educ:* UC of Ripon and York St John (BA Hons Leeds 1985); Coll. of Resurrection, Mirfield (Cert. Pastoral Theol. 1986). Ordained deacon, 1989, priest, 1990; Asst Curate, Barnsley St Mary, 1989–92; Priest-in-charge, Barnsley St Paul, 1992–95; Rector of Hemsworth, 1995–2006; Asst Diocesan Dir of Ordinands, Wakefield, 1998–2006; RD, Pontefract, 2000–06; Archdeacon of Rochdale, 2006–08. Proctor in Convocation, 2000–06; Hon. Canon, Wakefield Cathedral, 2002–06. *Recreations:* music, food, walking. *Address:* The Hollies, Manchester Road, Rochdale OL11 3QY. *T:* (01706) 358550; *e-mail:* bishopmark@manchester.anglican.org.

MIDDLETON, Bernard Chester, MBE 1986; self-employed book restorer and designer bookbinder, since 1953; *b* 29 Oct. 1924; *s* of late Regent Marcus Geoffrey Middleton and Doris Hilda Middleton (*née* Webster); *m* 1951, Dora Mary Davies (*d* 1997). *Educ:* Central Sch. of Arts and Crafts, London; apprenticed to British Museum Bindery (1940); City and Guilds of London Inst. (Silver Medal (1st prize) 1943). Served: Home Guard, 1941–43; RN, 1943–46. Craftsman-Demonstrator, RCA, 1949–51; Manager, Zaehnsdorf Ltd, 1951–53. Chief Examr in General Bookbinding, CGLI, 1957–63. Has conducted workshops for restoration of leather bindings in Belgium, Brazil, Switzerland, The Netherlands, USA and Venezuela; gold-tooled bindings are in many major libraries incl. BL, Royal Liby, The Hague, V&A Mus. and Wormsley Liby. Member: Art Workers Guild, 1961; Assoc. Internationale de Bibliophilie, 2002; Fellow, Designer Bookbinders, 1955 (Pres., 1973–75). FRSA 1951; FSA 1967. Hon. Fellow, Soc. of Bookbinders, 2002; Hon. Member: Guild of Book Workers, USA, 2003; Inst. of Conservation, 2006. *Publications:* A History of English Craft Bookbinding Technique, 1963, 4th edn 1996; The Restoration of Leather Bindings, 1972, 4th edn 2004; You *Can* Judge a Book by Its Cover, 1994; Recollections: my life in bookbinding, 1995; Recollections: a life in bookbinding, 2000; contribs to craft jls and introductions to books and exhibn catalogues. *Recreations:* reading, enjoying the past from a safe distance. *Address:* 3 Gauden Road, Clapham, SW4 6LR. *T:* (020) 7622 5388, *Fax:* (020) 7498 2716.

MIDDLETON, David Fraser; Head, Scotland Office, since 2007; *b* 23 June 1956; *s* of late Fraser Middleton and Margaret Middleton; *m* 1992, Diane Lamberton; one *d*. *Educ:* Univ. of Glasgow (MA Hons (Modern Hist. and Political Econ.)). Joined Scottish Office, as administrative trainee, 1978: Private Sec. to successive Ministers of State, 1982–84; on secondment to Cabinet Office, 1984; Br. Hd, Finance Gp (Housing and Educn), 1984–89; Head, Whitfield Urban Partnership, Dundee, 1989–91; Hd of Div., Scottish Develt Dept, 1991–96; Hd Policy, Finance and Strategy Div., Roads Directorate, 1996–97; Hd, Personnel, 1997; Dir of Implementation, Scottish Exec., Jan.–June 1998; Head: Local Govt Gp, 1999–2001; Local Govt and External Relns, 2001–02; Rural Gp, Scottish Exec. Envmt and Rural Affairs Dept, 2002–06; Dir of Special Projects, UHI (on attachment), 2006–07; Deputy Chief Exec. and Dir of Corporate Services, Crown Office and Procurator Fiscal Service, Scottish Exec., then Scottish Govt, 2007. *Recreations:* golf, gardening. *Address:* Scotland Office, 1 Melville Crescent, Edinburgh EH3 7HW. *Club:* Royal Musselburgh Golf.

MIDDLETON, (David) Miles, CBE 1992; Chairman, Tees Valley Learning and Skills Council, 2000; Partner, Middleton Associates, since 1993; *b* 15 June 1938; *s* of late Harry Middleton and of Dorothy Hannah Middleton (*née* Nisbet); *m* 1st, 1962, Mary Gale (marr. diss. 1979); one *s* one *d*; 2nd, 1980, Elizabeth, (Bobbie), Lancaster; two step *s* two step *d*. *Educ:* Sedbergh Sch. ACA 1962, FCA 1972. Articled Clerk, Strachan & Co., 1956–61; Audit Sen., Coopers Brothers & Co., 1962–64; Coopers & Lybrand: Manager, Zürich, 1964–68; Newcastle upon Tyne office, 1968–71, 1986–90; Middlesbrough office, 1971–86; Partner, 1974; Sen. Partner, NE Practice, 1990–93. Chairman: Northern Enterprise Ltd, 1988–; Rural Develt Commn, 1997–99; Hadrian's Wall Tourism Partnership, 2000–. Member Board: NE Regl Develt Agency, 1999–2001; Countryside Agency, 1999–2000; Tynedale Housing, 2000–. Pres., British Chamber of Commerce, 1990–92. *Address:* Ingleboro, St Helen's Lane, Corbridge, Northumberland NE45 5JD. *T:* (01434) 633545; (office) 19 Dacre Street, SW1H 0DH. *T:* (020) 7340 2900. *Clubs:* Royal Over-Seas League; Northern Counties (Newcastle upon Tyne); Hexham Golf; Bassenthwaite Sailing.

MIDDLETON, Donald King, CBE 1981; HM Diplomatic Service, retired; Chairman, Leominster Abbeyfield Society, 1993–97; *b* 24 Feb. 1922; *s* of late Harold Ernest Middleton and Ellen Middleton; *m* 1st, 1945, Marion Elizabeth Ryder (*d* 1988); one *d*; 2nd, 1996, Mary Elaine Aston. *Educ:* King Edward's Sch., Birmingham; Saltley College. Min. of Health, 1958–61; joined Commonwealth Relations Office, 1961; First Sec., British High Commn, Lagos, 1961–65; Head of Chancery, British Embassy, Saigon, 1970–72; British Dep. High Commissioner, Ibadan, 1973–75; HM Chargé d'Affaires, Phnom Penh, 1975; seconded to NI Office, Belfast, 1975–77; High Comr, Papua New Guinea, 1977–82. *Address:* 17 Apple Meadow, Weobley, Herefordshire HR4 8RZ.

MIDDLETON, Edward Bernard; Partner, PKF (UK) LLP, Chartered Accountants; *b* 5 July 1948; *s* of Bernard and Bettie Middleton; *m* 1971, Rosemary Spence Brown; three *s*. *Educ:* Aldenham Sch., Elstree; Chartered Accountant, 1970. Joined London office of Pannell Kerr Forster, 1971; Nairobi office, 1973; Audit Manager, London office, 1975; Partner, 1979; seconded to DTI as Dir, Industrial Develt Unit, 1984–86. Dir, PKF Hotel Consultancy Services, 1996–. Mem. sub-cttee, Consultative Cttee of Accountancy Bodies, 1980–84. Hon. Treas., Hospitality Action (formerly Hotel and Catering Benevolent Assoc.), 1992–; Mem. Council, British Assoc. of Hospitality Accountants, 1997–2007. Liveryman, Co. of Spectacle Makers, 2004. *Recreations:* sailing, photography. *Address:* Barrans, Bury Green, Little Hadham, Ware, Herts SG11 2ES. *T:* (01279) 658684. *Club:* Reform.

MIDDLETON, Dame Elaine (Madoline), DCMG 1998; MBE 1976; Executive Director, National Committee for Families and Children, Belize, 1994–98; *d* of Elstan Kerr and Leolyn Kerr Gillett; *m* 1961, Winston Middleton; one *s* two *d*. *Educ:* Belize Teachers' Trng Coll. (Teacher's Cert 1957); UC, Swansea (Dip. Social Welfare and Admin 1961; Dip. Applied Social Studies 1966); Univ. of the Union Inst., Ohio (BA in Social Work 1990). Primary Sch. Teacher, Salvation Army Sch. and Methodist Schs, Belize City, Dangriga and Gales Point, Manatee, 1947–57; Social Development Department, Belize: Probation Officer, 1957–62; Dep. Head, 1963–68; Head of Dept, 1969–81; Dir-Gen., Belize Red Cross Soc., 1981–83; lived and worked in USA, 1983–94. Member: Consortium for Belizean Develt, 1985–; Women's Commn of Belize, 1997–. Sec., Bd of Mgt, Wesley Coll., 2000–; Pres., YWCA of Belize, 2001–. *Recreations:* reading, community work. *Address:* 16 4th Street, King's Park, Belize City, Belize. *T:* (2) 234760.

MIDDLETON, Sir John (Maxwell), Kt 2002; OBE 1978; Planter of Kulili Estates, Karkar Island; *b* 19 July 1930; *s* of William Maxwell Middleton and Alice Victoria (*née* Tregent); *m* 1961, Anna Maria Kadava; two *s*. *Educ:* Sydney C of E Grammar Sch. Chm., Dylup Plantation Ltd, 1977–86; Dir, Dylup Investment Corp., 1986–91; Foundn Dir, Ramu Sugar Ltd, 1981–. Mem., PNG House of Assembly and Parliament, 1968–77. Chairman: PNG Fiscal Commn, 1978–83; PNG Kokonas Indastri Koporasen (Copra Ind. Corp.), 2003–04. Mem. and Dep. Chm., PNG Cocoa Bd, 1978–92. *Recreations:* game fishing, sea activities. *Address:* Kulili Estates, PO Box 486, Madang 511, Papua New Guinea. *T:* 8537461, *Fax:* 8537473; *e-mail:* wmm@global.net.pg. *Clubs:* Papua, Madang, Madang Country (PNG).

MIDDLETON, Rear-Adm. (John) Patrick (Windsor), CB 1992; Secretary, Royal Commission for the Exhibition of 1851, 1995–2002; *b* 15 March 1938; *s* of late Comdr John Henry Dudley Middleton, RN and Norna Mary Tessimond (*née* Hitchings); *m* 1962, Jane Rodwell Gibbs; one *s* one *d*. *Educ:* Cheltenham College; BRNC Dartmouth; RNEC Manadon. CEng, MIMechE, MIMarEST. Entered Royal Navy 1954; CSO(E) to Flag Officer Submarines, 1981; CSO(E) Falkland Islands, 1983; Captain Naval Drafting, 1984; Dir, In Service Submarines, 1987; CSO (Engrg), later (Support), to C-in-C Fleet, 1989–92, retd. Trustee, CARE for People with Learning Disabilities, 1993–2007 (Chm. Trustees, 1998–2007). Liveryman: Armourers and Brasiers' Co., 1971– (Mem. Ct of Assts, 1995–; Master, 2001–02). Gov., Chilmark and Fonthill Bishop Primary Sch., 2003–07. *Recreations:* sailing, walking, gardening, writing. *Address:* Manora, Chilmark, Wilts SP3 5AH. *T:* (01722) 716231; *e-mail:* mimanora@aol.com. *Club:* Royal Naval Sailing Association (Portsmouth).

MIDDLETON, Lawrence John, CMG 1985; PhD; HM Diplomatic Service; Ambassador to the Republic of Korea, 1986–90, retired; *b* 27 March 1930; *s* of John James Middleton and Mary (*née* Horgan); *m* 1963, Sheila Elizabeth Hoey; two *s* one *d*. *Educ:* Finchley Catholic Grammar Sch.; Regent Street Poly. (BSc (ext.) 1949); King's Coll., London (BSc Special Hons 1951, PhD 1954). Scientific Officer, ARC, 1954–60 and 1962–63; Asst Specialist, Univ. of Calif, Berkeley, 1959–60; on secondment as Cons. to FAO and to UN Cttee on Effects of Atomic Radiation, 1960–62 and to CENTO Inst. of Nuclear Science, 1963–65; Principal, Min. of Agriculture, 1966–68; First Sec., FO, 1968; Washington, 1969–71; Kuala Lumpur, 1971–74; Counsellor (Commercial), Belgrade, 1974–78; Dir of Research, FCO, 1978–80; Cabinet Office, 1980–82; Counsellor, UK Delegn to Conf. on Disarmament, Geneva, 1982–84; Sen. DS, RCDS, 1984–86. Mem. Council, 1994–2001, Vice-Pres., 1998–2001, Royal Asiatic Soc. (FRAS 1992); Chm., Anglo-Korean Soc., 1995–2002. Chm., N Oxford Defence Assoc., 1995–2000. *Publications:* articles on plant physiology and nuclear science in biology, 1954–63. *Address:* 12 Polstead Road, Oxford OX2 6TN. *Club:* Frilford Heath Golf.

MIDDLETON, Rear Adm. Linley Eric, CB 1986; DSO; FRAeS; *m* 1965, Pamela Mannerings (*née* Lewis); three *s*. *Educ:* Dale Coll., Kingwilliamstown. Qualified as FAA pilot, 1952; served HMS Indefatigable, HMS Centaur, HMS Bulwark, HMS Eagle, HMS Mounts Bay, HMS Victorious and HMS Ark Royal, 1952–63; BRNC Dartmouth, 1964–65; CO, 809 Naval Air Squadron in HMS Hermes, 1966–67; Naval Staff, MoD, 1968–69; CO, HMS Whitby, 1970–71; Staff of Flag Officer, Naval Air Comd, 1971–73; Capt. 2nd Frigate Sqn and CO, HMS Undaunted, 1973–74, and CO, HMS Apollo, 1974–75; Chief Staff Officer to Flag Officer Carriers & Amphibious Ships, 1975–77; Dir, Naval Air Warfare, 1978–79; CO, HMS Hermes, 1980–82; Asst Chief of Naval Staff (Ops), 1983–84; Flag Officer, Naval Air Comd, 1984–87, retired. Man. Dir, British Internat. Helicopters, 1987–92. Liveryman: Coach Makers' and Coach Harness Makers' Co., 1983; GAPAN, 1993.

MIDDLETON, Michael Humfrey, CBE 1975; Director, Civic Trust, 1969–86; *b* 1 Dec. 1917; *s* of Humfrey Middleton and Lilian Irene (*née* Tillard); *m* 1954, Julie Margaret Harrison (*d* 2003); one *s* two *d*. *Educ:* King's Sch., Canterbury. Art Critic, The Spectator, 1946–56; Art Editor and Asst Editor, Picture Post, 1949–53; Exec. Editor, Lilliput, 1953–54; Editor, House and Garden, 1955–57; Sec. and Dep. Dir, Civic Trust, 1957–69; Mem. Council, Soc. of Industrial Artists and Designers, 1953–55, 1968–70; UK Sec.-Gen., European Architectural Heritage Year, 1972–75. Member: Adv. Cttee on Trunk Road Assessment, 1977–80; UK Commn for UNESCO, 1976–80. Hon. Fellow: RIBA, 1974; Landscape Inst., 1986. Film scripts include A Future for the Past, 1972. Council of Europe Pro Merito Medal, 1976. *Publications:* Soldiers of Lead, 1948; Group Practice in Design, 1967; Man Made the Town, 1987; Cities in Transition, 1991; contributor to many conferences and jls, at home and abroad, on art, design and environmental matters. *Recreation:* looking. *Address:* c/o 47 Tunley Road, SW17 7QH. *T:* (020) 8673 7221.

MIDDLETON, Rev. Canon Michael John; Canon of Westminster, 1997–2004, now Canon Emeritus; Treasurer, 1997–2004, and Almoner, 2000–04, Westminster Abbey; *b* 21 July 1940; *s* of Bernard and Gladys Middleton; *m* 1965, Anne Elisabeth Parker; two *s* one *d*. *Educ:* Weymouth Grammar Sch.; St Cuthbert's Soc., Durham (BSc); Fitzwilliam Coll., Cambridge (MA); Westcott House, Cambridge. Ordained: deacon, 1966; priest, 1967; Curate, St George's Jesmond, Newcastle, 1966–69; Chaplain: St George's Grammar Sch., Cape Town, 1969–72; King's School, Tynemouth, 1972–77; Vicar, St George's, Jesmond, Newcastle, 1977–85; Rector of Hexham, 1985–92; Archdeacon of Swindon, 1992–97. Hon. Canon of Newcastle, 1990. Proctor in Convocation, 1980–92. *Recreations:* walking, Westerns. *Address:* 37 High Fellside, Kendal, Cumbria LA9 4JG. *T:* (01539) 729320.

MIDDLETON, Miles; *see* Middleton, D. M.

MIDDLETON, Rear-Adm. Patrick; *see* Middleton, Rear-Adm. J. P. W.

MIDDLETON, Sir Peter (Edward), GCB 1989 (KCB 1984); Director, 1991–2004 and Chairman, 1999–2004, Barclays Bank (Deputy Chairman, 1991–98; Chairman, BZW Banking Division, 1991–98); Chairman: Camelot Group plc, since 2004; MMC UK, since 2007; *b* 2 April 1934; *m* 1st, 1964, Valerie Ann Lindup (*d* 1987); one *d* (one *s* decd); 2nd, 1990, Constance Owen. *Educ:* Sheffield City Grammar Sch.; Sheffield Univ. (BA; Hon. DLitt 1984); Bristol Univ. Served RAPC, 1958–60. HM Treasury: Senior Information Officer, 1962; Principal, 1964; Asst Director, Centre for Administrative Studies, 1967–69; Private Sec. to Chancellor of the Exchequer, 1969–72; Treasury Press Secretary, 1972–75; Head of Monetary Policy Div., 1975; Under Secretary, 1976; Dep. Sec., 1980–83; Permanent Sec., 1983–91. Director: Bass PLC, 1992–2001; General Accident Fire & Life Assurance Corp. plc, later CGU plc, 1992–98; United Utilities PLC (formerly NW Water Gp), 1994–2007 (Vice-Chm., 1998–99; Chm., 1999–2000; Dep. Chm., 2000–07); MTS OJSC, 2005–07; UK Chm., Marsh & McLennan Gp, 2007– (Mem., Internat. Adv. Bd, 2005–); Chairman: Marsh Ltd, 2005–; Reyniers & Co., 2005–. Mem., Adv. Bd, Financial Dynamics, 2004–; Sen. Advr, Fenchurch Adv. Partners, 2005–. Chairman: Sheffield Urban Regeneration Co. Ltd (Sheffield 1), 2000–05; Creative Sheffield, 2006–. Chm., CEDR, 2004–. Dir, Internat. Monetary Conf., 2001–03; Mem. Adv. Council, Monetary Authy of Singapore, 2001–05. Member: Adv. Bd, Nat. Econ. Res. Associates 1991; Exec. Cttee, Centre for Econ. Policy Res. Pres., British Bankers' Assoc., 2004–06. Vis. Fellow, Nuffield Coll., Oxford, 1981–89. Dir, Inst. of Contemporary British History, 2001–03 (Chm., 1992–2001). Mem. Council, 1991–, Chancellor, 1999–, Univ. of Sheffield (Pro-Chancellor, 1997–99); Mem. Council, Manchester Business Sch., 1985–92; Governor: London Business Sch., 1984–90; Ditchley Foundn, 1985–; NIESR, 1991–2007. Dir, English Chamber Orch. and Music Soc., 1992–2003. Cdre, Civil Service Sailing Assoc., 1984–92. *Recreations:* hill walking, music, outdoor sports. *Address:* Camelot Group plc, Tolpits Lane, Watford, Herts WD18 9RN. *Club:* Reform.

MIDDLETON, Peter James; Chairman, GTL Resources plc, 2002–07 (Director, 2000–07); *b* 10 Feb. 1940; *s* of Roy and Freda Middleton; *m* 1st, 1968, Yvonne Summerson (marr. diss. 1996); two *s* one *d*; 2nd, 1996, Anita Mehra; two *s* one *d* (of whom one *s* one *d* are twins). *Educ:* Univ. of Paris; Univ. of Hull (BA Hons). HM Diplomatic Service, 1969–85: Second Sec., Jakarta, 1969–71; First Sec., Dar-es-Salaam, 1973–74; Paris, 1978–82; Midland Bank, 1985–87, Head of Banking Ops, 1986–87; Gp Chief Exec., Thomas Cook Gp, 1987–92; Chief Executive: Lloyd's of London, 1992–95; Salomon Brothers Internat., later Salomon Smith Barney, 1995–98; Chm., Football League, 1998–2000; Chief Exec., World Snooker Assoc., 1999–2000; Transaction Dir, Nomura Internat. plc, 2000–02. Chairman: London Luton Airport, 1999–2000; Rockingham Motor Speedway, 2000–02; Tees Valley Urban Regeneration Co., 2002. *Recreations:* soccer, horse-racing, music.

MIDDLETON, Prof. Richard, DPhil; FBA 2004; Professor of Music, University of Newcastle upon Tyne, 1998–2005, now Emeritus; *b* 4 Feb. 1945; *s* of Harold and Joan Middleton; *m* 1969, Jane Pescod Harding; three *d*. *Educ:* Clare Coll., Cambridge (BA 1966); Univ. of York (DPhil 1970). Staff Tutor in Music, Dept of Extramural Studies, Univ. of Birmingham, 1970–72; Open University: Lectr, 1972–79; Sen. Lectr, 1979–95; Reader in Music and Cultural Studies, 1995–97. Hon. DHL Chicago, 2006. *Publications:* Pop Music and the Blues, 1972; Studying Popular Music, 1990; (ed) Reading Pop, 2000; (ed jtly) The Cultural Study of Music: a critical introduction, 2003; Voicing the Popular, 2006. *Recreation:* farming. *Address:* Beechburn Grange, High Grange, Crook, Co. Durham DL15 8AX; *e-mail:* richard.middleton@ncl.ac.uk.

MIDDLETON, Stanley; novelist; *b* Bulwell, Nottingham, 1 Aug. 1919; *y s* of Thomas and Elizabeth Ann Middleton; *m* 1951, Margaret Shirley, *y d* of Herbert and Winifred Vera Welch; two *d*. *Educ:* High Pavement Sch.; University Coll., Nottingham (later Univ. of Nottingham). Served Army (RA and AEC), 1940–46. Head of English Dept, High Pavement Coll., Nottingham, 1958–81. Judith E. Wilson Vis. Fellow, Emmanuel Coll., Cambridge, 1982–83. FRSL 1998. Hon. MA Nottingham, 1975; MUniv Open, 1995; Hon. DLitt: De Montfort, 1998; Nottingham Trent, 2000. *Publications:* novels: A Short Answer, 1958; Harris's Requiem, 1960; A Serious Woman, 1961; The Just Exchange, 1962; Two's Company, 1963; Him They Compelled, 1964; Terms of Reference, 1966; The Golden Evening, 1968; Wages of Virtue, 1969; Apple of the Eye, 1970; Brazen Prison, 1971; Cold Gradations, 1972; A Man Made of Smoke, 1973; Holiday (jtly, Booker Prize), 1974; Distractions, 1975; Still Waters, 1976; Ends and Means, 1977; Two Brothers, 1978; In A Strange Land, 1979; The Other Side, 1980; Blind Understanding, 1982; Entry into Jerusalem, 1983; The Daysman, 1984; Valley of Decision, 1985; An After Dinner's Sleep, 1986; After a Fashion, 1987; Recovery, 1988; Vacant Places, 1989; Changes and Chances, 1990; Beginning to End, 1991; A Place to Stand, 1992; Married Past Redemption, 1993; Catalysts, 1994; Toward the Sea, 1995; Live and Learn, 1996; Brief Hours, 1997; Against the Dark, 1998; Necessary Ends, 1999; Small Change, 2000; Love in the Provinces, 2002; Brief Garlands, 2004; Sterner Stuff, 2005; Mother's Boy, 2006; Her Three Wise Men, 2008. *Recreations:* music, listening, argument, water-colour painting. *Address:* 42 Caledon Road, Sherwood, Nottingham NG5 2NG. *T:* (0115) 962 3085. *Club:* PEN.

MIDDLETON, Timothy John; Director in the Legal Service, Council of the European Union, since 2003; *b* 15 Sept. 1953; *s* of William Smith Middleton and Brenda Mary Middleton; *m* 1983, Janet Kathleen Elliott; one *s* two *d*. *Educ:* King Edward VII Grammar Sch., Coalville, Leics; Balliol Coll., Oxford (MA Jurisprudence); Coll. of Law. Called to the Bar, Gray's Inn, 1977; Legal Asst, 1979–83, Sen. Legal Asst, 1983–85, MAFF; on secondment to Directorate Gen. VI (Agriculture), CEC, 1985–87; Lawyer: MAFF, 1987–89; Legal Secretariat to Law Officers, 1989–92; Legal Dir, Intervention Bd, 1992–94; Hd of a Legal Div., MAFF, 1994–97; Dep. Legal Advr, Home Office, 1997–2001; Solicitor to Equitable Life Inquiry, 2001–03. Gov., Broadwater Sch., Godalming, 1999–2003. Churchwarden, St John the Evangelist, Farncombe, 2000–03. *Recreations:* modern literature, theatre, cooking. *Address:* Council of the European Union, Rue de la Loi 175, 1048 Brussels, Belgium.

MIDLETON, 12th Viscount *cr* 1717 (Ire.); **Alan Henry Brodrick;** Baron Brodrick of Midleton, Co. Cork 1715; Baron Brodrick of Peper Harow 1796; Museum Manager, British Horological Institute, since 2001 (Chairman, 1999–2000); *b* 4 Aug. 1949; *s* of Alan Rupert Brodrick (*d* 1972) (*g g s* of 7th Viscount) and of Alice Elizabeth, *d* of G. R. Roberts; *S* uncle, 1989; *m* 1st, 1978, Julia Helen (marr. diss. 2002), *d* of Michael Pitt; two *s* one *d*; 2nd, 2002, Maureen Susan, *d* of Joseph Sime. *Educ:* St Edmund's School, Canterbury. Keeper of Horology, John Gershom Parkington Collection of Time Measurement Instruments, Bury St Edmunds, 1986–2002. British Horological Institute: FBHI; Mem. Council, 1993; Chm. Museum and Liby Cttee, 1994; Chm., Mus. Trust, 1995. *Recreation:* bicycling. *Heir: s* Hon. Ashley Rupert Brodrick, *b* 25 Nov. 1980.

MIDORI; *see* Goto, Mi Dori.

MIDWINTER, Eric Clare, OBE 1992; MA, DPhil; writer; *b* 11 Feb. 1932; *m*; two *s* one *d*. *Educ:* St Catharine's Coll., Cambridge (BA Hons History); Univs of Liverpool (MA Educn) and York (DPhil). Educational posts, incl. Dir of Liverpool Educn Priority Area Project, 1955–75; Head, Public Affairs Unit, Nat. Consumer Council, 1975–80; Dir, Centre for Policy on Ageing, 1980–91, Chm., 2002–. Chairman: Council, Adv. Centre for Educn, 1976–84; London Transport Users Consultative Cttee, 1977–84; London Regl Passengers' Cttee, 1984–96; Community Educn Develt Centre, 1995–2001. Mem., POW Adv. Cttee on Disability, 1990–95. Vis. Prof. of Educn, Univ. of Exeter, 1993–2002. Pres., Assoc. of Cricket Statisticians and Historians, 1997–2004. Chm., Cricket Soc. Book of the Year Award, 2002–. DUniv Open, 1989. *Publications:* Victorian Social Reform, 1968; Law and Order in Victorian Lancashire, 1968; Social Administration in Lancashire, 1969; Nineteenth Century Education, 1970; Old Liverpool, 1971; Projections: an education priority project at work, 1972; Social Environment and the Urban School, 1972; Priority Education, 1972; Patterns of Community Education, 1973; (ed) Teaching in the Urban Community School, 1973; (ed) Pre-School Priorities, 1974; Education and the Community, 1975; Education for Sale, 1977; Make 'Em Laugh: famous comedians and their world, 1978; Schools and Society, 1980; W. G. Grace: his life and times, 1981; Age is Opportunity: education and older people, 1982; (ed) Mutual Aid Universities, 1984; The Wage of Retirement: the case for a new pensions policy, 1985; Fair Game: myth and reality in sport, 1986; Caring for Cash: the issue of private domiciliary care, 1986; Redefining Old Age, 1987; The Lost Seasons: wartime cricket 1939–1945, 1987; (ed) Retired Leisure, 1987; Polls Apart? Older Voters and the 1987 General Election, 1987; New Design for Old, Function, Style and Older People, 1988; Red Roses Crest the Caps: a history of Lancashire cricket, 1989; Creating Chances: arts by older people, 1990; Old Order: crime and older people, 1990; Out of Focus: old age, the press and broadcasting, 1991; Brylcreem summer: the 1947 cricket season, 1991; An Illustrated History of County Cricket, 1992; Lifelines, 1994; The Development of Social Welfare in Britain, 1994; First Knock: cricket's opening pairs, 1994; European Year '93, 1995; 150 Years: a celebration: Surrey CCC, 1995; Thriving People: the growth and prospects of the U3A in the UK, 1995; Darling Old Oval: history of Surrey County Cricket Club, 1995; State Educator: the life and enduring influence of W. E. Forster, 1996; Pensioned Off: retirement and income examined, 1997; Yesterdays: the way we were, 1998; The Billy Bunter Syndrome: or why Britain failed to create a relevant secondary school system, 1998; (ed) MCC Yearbook, 1998, 1999, MCC Annual, 2000–06; From Meadowland to Multinational: a review of cricket's social history, 2000; Yesterdays: our finest hours, 2001; Quill on Willow: cricket in literature, 2001; Best-remembered: a hundred stars of yesteryear, 2002; As One Stage Door Closes: the story of John Wade, jobbing conjuror, 2002; Novel Approaches: a guide to the popular classic novel, 2003; 500 Beacons: the USA story, 2004; Red Shirts and Roses: the story of the two Old Traffords, 2005; The People's Jesters: Twentieth Century British comedians, 2006; Lord Salisbury, 2006; Parish to Planet: how football came to rule the world, 2007; George Duckworth, Warrington's Ambassador at Large, 2007; An Outline of Political Thought and Practice, 2008. *Recreations:* sport, comedy. *Clubs:* Savage, MCC; Lancashire CCC.

MIDWINTER, Prof. John Edwin, OBE 1984; PhD; FRS 1985; FREng; Pender Professor of Electronic Engineering, University College London, 1991–2004, now Professor Emeritus; *b* 8 March 1938; *s* of Henry C. and Vera J. Midwinter; *m* 1961, Maureen Anne Holt; two *s* two *d*. *Educ:* St Bartholomew's Grammar Sch., Newbury, Berks; King's Coll., Univ. of London (BSc Physics, 1961; AKC 1961). PhD Physics, London (ext.), 1968. MInstP 1973; FIET (FIEE 1980); FIEEE 1983; FREng (FEng 1984). Joined RRE, Malvern, as Scientific Officer, 1961 (research on lasers and non-linear optics); Sen. Scientific Officer, 1964–68; Perkin Elmer Corp., Norwalk, Conn, USA, 1968–70; Res. Center, Materials Research Center, Allied Chemical Corp., Morristown, NJ, USA, 1970–71; Head of Optical Fibre Develt, PO Res. Centre, Martlesham, 1971–77; Head, Optical Communications Technol., British Telecom Res. Labs, 1977–84; University College London: BT Prof. of Optoelectronics, 1984–91; Head, Dept of Electronic Engrg, later of Electronic and Electrical Engrg, 1988–98; Vice Provost, 1994–99. Pres., IEE, 2000–01 (Vice Pres., 1994; Dep. Pres., 1998–2000; Chm., Electronics Div., 1991–92). Lectures: Bruce Preller, RSE, 1983; Clifford Patterson, Royal Soc., 1983; Cantor, RSA, 1984. Hon. DSc: Nottingham, 2000; Loughborough, 2001; QUB, 2004. Electronics Div. Premium, 1976, J. J. Thompson Medal, 1987, Faraday Medal, 1997, IEE; Eric Sumner Award and Medal, IEEE, 2002. *Publications:* Applied Non-Linear Optics, 1972; Optical Fibers for Transmission, 1979 (Best Book in Technol. Award, Amer. Publishers' Assoc., 1980); over 200 papers on lasers, non-linear optics and optical communications. *Recreations:* country and mountain walking, ski-ing. *Address: e-mail:* john.midwinter@btopenworld.com.

MIDWINTER, Stanley Walter, CB 1982; Chief Planning Inspector (Director of Planning Inspectorate), Departments of the Environment and Transport, 1978–84; *b* 8 Dec. 1922; *s* of late Lewis Midwinter and Beatrice (*née* Webb); *m* 1954, Audrey Mary Pepper (*d* 1988); one *d*. *Educ:* Regent Street Polytechnic Sch.; Sch. of Architecture (DipArch, ARIBA 1948); Sch. of Planning and Res. for Regional Develt (AMTPI 1952, FRTPI 1965); Dip. in Sociol., Univ. of London, 1976. Served War, RE, 1942–46: N Africa, Italy, Greece. Planning Officer, LCC, 1949–54; Bor. Architect and Planning Officer, Larne, NI, 1955–60; joined Housing and Planning Inspectorate, 1960; Dep. Chief Inspector, 1976. Assessor at Belvoir Coalfield Inquiry, 1979. Town Planning Institute: Exam. Prize, 1952; Thomas Adams Prize, 1955; President's Prize, 1958. *Publications:* articles in TPI Jl.

MIERS, Sir (Henry) David (Alastair Capel), KBE 1985; CMG 1979; HM Diplomatic Service, retired; Chairman, Society of Pension Consultants, 1998–2006; *b* 10 Jan. 1937; *s* of late Col R. D. M. C. Miers, DSO, QO Cameron Highlanders, and Honor (*née* Bucknill); *m* 1966, Imelda Maria Emilia, *d* of Jean-Baptiste Wouters, Huizingen, Belgium; two *s* one *d*. *Educ:* Winchester; University Coll., Oxford. Tokyo, 1963; Vientiane, 1966; Private Sec. to Minister of State, FO, 1968; Paris, 1972; Counsellor, Tehran, 1977–79; Hd, Middle Eastern Dept, FCO, 1980–83; Ambassador to Lebanon, 1983–85; Asst Under-Sec. of State, FCO, 1986–89; Ambassador: to Greece, 1989–93; to Netherlands, 1993–96. Chairman: British-Lebanese Assoc., 1998–; Anglo-Hellenic League, 1999–2007.

MIESENBÖCK, Prof. Gero, MD; Waynflete Professor of Physiology, University of Oxford, since 2007; *b* 15 July 1965; *s* of Dr Gottfried and Hannelore Miesenböck; *m* 1997, Barrie Dolnick; one *d*. *Educ:* Bundesgymnasium Wels, Austria; Univ. of Innsbruck (MD 1993); Umeå Univ., Sweden. Postdoctoral Fellow, 1992–98, Asst Mem. and Hd, Lab. of Neural Systems, 1999–2004, Meml Sloan-Kettering Cancer Center, NY; Asst Prof. of Cell Biol., Genetics and Neurosci., Weill Med. Coll. of Cornell Univ., NY, 1999–2004; Associate Prof. of Cell Biol. and Cellular and Molecular Physiol., Yale Univ. Sch. of Medicine, 2004–07. Alfred P. Sloan Fellow, 2000; Searle Schol., 2000; Beckman Young Investigator, 2000. Hon. MA Yale, 2007. *Publications:* contribs to Annual Rev. of Neuroscience, Cell, Nature, Neuron, Science. *Recreations:* literature, travel, history of science. *Address:* Department of Physiology, Anatomy and Genetics, University of Oxford, Sherrington Building, Parks Road, Oxford OX1 3PT.

MIFLIN, Dr Benjamin John, PhD; Chairman, Crop Evaluation Ltd, since 2000; Director, 1994–99, Lawes Trust Fellow, 1999–2006, Institute of Arable Crops Research and IACR-Rothamsted; *b* 7 Jan. 1939; *s* of late Stanley Miflin and Kathleen (*née* Davies); *m* 1964, Hilary Newman; three *d*. *Educ:* Univ. of Nottingham (BSc); Univ. of Illinois (MS); QMC and Imperial Coll., London (PhD 1965). FRAgS 1988; FIBiol 1997. Lectr in Plant Scis (Plant Biochem.), Sch. of Agric., Univ. of Newcastle upon Tyne, 1965–73; Hd, Biochem. Dept, 1973–85, and Div. of Molecular Scis, 1983–85, Rothamsted Exptl Stn, Harpenden; Hd, Internat. R & D, Ciba-Geigy Seeds, Basle, 1986–93. Vis. Prof., Univ. of Nottingham, 1981–85 and 1994–2000. Mem., Adv. Cttee on Novel Foods and Processes, 1995–98. Corresp. Mem., Amer. Soc. of Plant Physiologists, 1986. *Publications:* (ed) The Biochemistry of Plants, Vol. 5, 1980, (ed with P. J. Lea) Vol. 16, 1990; (ed) Oxford Surveys of Plant Cell and Molecular Biology, Vols 1–7, 1984–91; numerous papers in field of plant biochem. and related subjects. *Recreations:* ski-ing, gardening, photography. *Address:* The Studio, 4 Dean Court Road, Rottingdean, Brighton BN2 7DH.

MIFSUD BONNICI, Dr Carmelo, BA, LLD; Prime Minister of Malta, 1984–87; *b* 17 July 1933; *s* of Dr Lorenzo Mifsud Bonnici, and Catherine (*née* Buttigieg). *Educ:* Govt sch. and Lyceum, Malta; Univ. of Malta (BA, LLD); University Coll. London. Lectr in Industrial and Fiscal Law, Univ. of Malta, 1969–86. Legal Consultant, General Workers' Union, 1969–83; Dep. Leader, Labour Party, responsible for Party affairs, 1980–82; Designate Leader of the Labour Movement, 1982; co-opted to Parlt, 1983, Minister of Labour and Social Services, 1983; Sen. Dep. Prime Minister, 1983–84; Leader, Labour Party, 1984–92; MP First District, 1987–96. *Recreation:* reading. *Address:* Hamrun, Malta.

MIFSUD BONNICI, Dr Ugo; President of Malta, 1994–99; *b* 8 Nov. 1932; *m* 1959, Gemma Bianco; two *s* one *d*. *Educ:* Lyceum, Malta; Univ. of Malta (BA 1952; LLD 1955). Elected MP, 2nd Electoral Div., 1966–94; Shadow Minister of Educn, 1971; President: General Council, 1976; Admin. Council, 1976; Minister of: Educn, 1987; Educn and the Interior, 1987–92; Educn and Human Resources, 1992. Companion of Honour, Nat. Order of Merit (Malta). *Publications:* Biex il-Futur Jerga' Jibda, 1976; Il-Linja t-Tajba, 1980; Biex il-Futur Rega' Beda, 1992; Il-Manwal tal-President, 1997; Kif Sirna Repubblika, 1999. *Recreations:* reading, writing, listening to music. *Address:* 18 Triq Erin Serracino Inglott, Bormla, Malta. *Club:* Casino Maltese.

MILAN, Archbishop of, (RC), since 2002; **His Eminence Cardinal Dionigi Tettamanzi;** *b* 14 March 1934. Ordained priest, 1957; Bishop of Ancona-Osimo, 1989–91; Gen. Sec., Italian Episcopal Conf., 1991–95; Archbishop of Genoa, 1995–2002; apptd Cardinal, 1998; Cardinal-Priest, SS Ambrose and Charles, 1998. *Address:* Piazza Fontana 2, 20122 Milano, Italy.

MILAŠINOVIĆ, Tanja, PhD; Ambassador of Bosnia and Herzegovina to the Court of St James's, 2005–08; *b* 28 June 1962; *d* of Rade and Radosava Milašinović. *Educ:* Univ. of Zagreb (MSc 1988); Univ. of Ljubljana (PhD 1992). Asst, Fac. of Mining, Geol. and Petroleum, Univ. of Zagreb, 1986–87; res. work, 1987–91, Asst, 1989–91, Inst. of Experimental Physics, Ludwig Maximilians Univ., Munich; Asst Prof., Faculties of Agric. and of Forestry, Univ. of Belgrade, 1992–98; Asst Minister, Min. of Foreign Econ. Affairs, Rep. of Srpska Govt, 1998–2001; Minister Counsellor and Chargé d'Affaires, Mission of Bosnia and Herzegovina to EU, Min. of Foreign Affairs, 2001–05. *Publication:* articles in learned jls. *Recreation:* tennis. *Address:* c/o Embassy of Bosnia and Herzegovina, 5–7 Lexham Gardens, W8 5JJ. *Club:* Athenæum.

MILAZI, Ibrahim Laston Bwanausi; High Commissioner of Malaŵi in the United Kingdom, 2004–05; *b* 20 Oct. 1959; *s* of late Lowless Bwanausi Milazi and Salma Pilo; *m* 1983, Amina Mahmoud Kamwaza; four *s* two *d*. *Educ:* Univ. of Malaŵi (Dip. Business Studies 1983; BA Human Resource Mgt 1998). Exec. Sec. and Admin Sec., Muslim Assoc. of Malaŵi, 1983–91; Educn Rep., Pretoria N Muslim Educn Inst., 1991–93; Wamy Muslim Youth Dir for Southern Africa, 1993–99; Ambassador to Libya, Morocco and Tunisia, 2000–04. Member: Bd, Malaŵi Bureau of Standards, 1995–98; Council, Univ. of Malaŵi, 1999–. *Address:* c/o Malaŵi High Commission, 33 Grosvenor Street, W1K 4QT; *e-mail:* imilazi@hotmail.com.

MILBANK, Prof. (Alasdair) John, PhD, DD; Research Professor of Religion, Politics and Ethics, University of Nottingham, since 2004; *b* 23 Oct. 1952; *s* of John Douglas Milbank and Jean Hyslop Milbank; *m* 1978, Alison Grant Legg; one *s* one *d*. *Educ:* Queen's Coll., Oxford (MA); PhD Birmingham 1986; DD Cantab 1998. Christendom Trust Teaching Fellow, Lancaster Univ., 1983–91; University of Cambridge: Lectr in Theol., 1991–96; Reader in Philosophical Theol., 1996–98; Fellow, Peterhouse, 1993–98; Frances Myers Ball Prof. of Philosophical Theol., Univ. of Virginia, 1999–2004. *Publications:* Theology and Social Theory, 1990, 2nd edn 2006; The Religious Dimension in Vico's Thought, Part I 1991, Part II 1992; The Word Made Strange: theology, language, culture, 1996; The Mercurial Wood (poems), 1997; (ed jtly) Radical Orthodoxy: a new theology, 1998; (with C. Pickstock) Truth in Aquinas, 2001; Being Reconciled: ontology and pardon, 2002; The Suspended Middle, 2005; (with S. Zizek) The Absolute Truth, 2008; The Legend of Death (poems), 2008; Proposing Theology, 2009. *Recreations:* walking, poetry, photography, cinema, reading fiction, early music, archaeology. *Address:* Burgage Hill Cottage, Burgage, Southwell, Notts NG25 0EP. *T:* (01636) 819224, *Fax:* (office) (0115) 951 5887; *e-mail:* john.milbank@nottingham.ac.uk.

MILBANK, Sir Anthony (Frederick), 5th Bt *cr* 1882; DL; farmer and landowner since 1977; *b* 16 Aug. 1939; *s* of Sir Mark Vane Milbank, 4th Bt, KCVO, MC, and Hon. Verena Aileen, Lady Milbank (*d* 1995), *yr d* of 11th Baron Farnham, DSO; *S* father, 1984; *m* 1970, Belinda Beatrice, *yr d* of Brig. Adrian Gore, DSO; two *s* one *d*. *Educ:* Eton College. Brown, Shipley & Co. Ltd, 1961–66; M&G Securities Ltd, 1966–77. Chairman: Moorland Assoc., 1987–2001; Northern Uplands Moorland Regeneration Project, 1999–2001; Member: NCC Cttee for England, 1989–91; CLA Exec. Cttee, 1989–94; Council, RSPB, 1993–98, 2007–. Pres., Yorks Wildlife Trust, 2000–03. High Sheriff of Durham, 1991–92; DL N Yorks, 1998. *Recreations:* various. *Heir: s* Edward Mark Somerset Milbank, *b* 9 April 1973. *Address:* Barningham Park, Richmond, N Yorks DL11 7DW.

MILBANK, John; *see* Milbank, A. J.

MILBERG, Dr Joachim; Chairman, Supervisory Board, BMW AG, since 2004 (Member, 2002–04); *b* Verl, Westfalia, 10 April 1943. *Educ:* Bielefeld State Engrg Coll.; Berlin Tech. Univ. (Dr ing 1971). Apprentice machine fitter, 1959–62; Res. Asst, Inst. Machine Tool and Prodn Technol., Berlin Tech. Univ., 1970–72; Exec. Manager, 1972–78, Hd, Automatic Turning Machines Div., 1978–81, Werkzeugmaschinenfabrik Gilderneister AG; Prof. of Machine Tools and Mgt Sci., Munich Tech. Univ., 1981–93; BMW AG: Member Board of Management: Prodn, 1993–98; Engrg and Prodn, 1998–99; Chm., Bd of Mgt, 1999–2002. *Address:* BMW Haus, Petuelring 130, 80788 Munich, Germany.

MILBORNE-SWINNERTON-PILKINGTON, Sir Thomas Henry; *see* Pilkington.

MILBOURN, Dr Graham Maurice; Director, National Institute of Agricultural Botany, 1981–90, retired; *b* 4 Sept. 1930; *s* of late Frank McLaren Milbourn, BSc and Winifred May Milbourn; *m* 1956, Louise Lawson, BSc Hons; three *s*. *Educ:* Reading Univ. (BSc, MSc, PhD). Served RN, 1948–50. Asst Lectr, Reading Univ., 1953–56; SO, ARC Radiobiological Lab., 1956–61; Sen. Lectr, Crop Production, Wye Coll., London Univ., 1961–77; Prof. of Crop Production, Sch. of Agric., Edinburgh Univ., 1977–81. Vis. Prof., Silsoe Coll., Cranfield Univ. (formerly Inst. of Technology), 1991–2003. Pres., Assoc. Applied Biologists, 1991. *Publications:* papers on physiology of cereals and vegetables, uptake of radio-nucleides by crops. *Recreation:* sailing.

MILBURN, Rt Hon. Alan; PC 1998; MP (Lab) Darlington, since 1992; *b* 27 Jan. 1958; *m* 2007, Dr Ruth Briel; two *s*. *Educ:* Stokesley Comprehensive Sch.; Lancaster Univ. (BA). Co-ordinator, Trade Union Studies Information Unit, Newcastle, 1984–90; Sen. Business Development Officer, N Tyneside MBC, 1990–92. Opposition front bench spokesman on health, 1995–96, on Treasury and econ. affairs, 1996–97; Minister of State, DoH, 1997–98; Chief Sec. to HM Treasury, 1998–99; Sec. of State for Health, 1999–2003; Chancellor, Duchy of Lancaster, 2004–05. Mem., Public Accounts Cttee, 1994–95; Chair, PLP Treasury Cttee, 1992–95. *Address:* House of Commons, SW1A 0AA.

MILBURN, Sir Anthony (Rupert), 5th Bt *cr* 1905; landowner; *b* 17 April 1947; *s* of Major Rupert Leonard Eversley Milburn (*yr s* of 3rd Bt) (*d* 1974) and of Anne Mary, *d* of late Major Austin Scott Murray, MC; *S* uncle, 1985; *m* 1977, Olivia Shirley, *y d* of Captain Thomas Noel Catlow, CBE, DL, RN; two *s* one *d*. *Educ:* Hawtreys, Savernake Forest; Eton College; Cirencester Agricultural Coll. MRICS. *Recreations:* sporting and rural pursuits. *Heir: s* Patrick Thomas Milburn, *b* 4 Dec. 1980. *Address:* Newton Fell House, Newton, Stocksfield, Northumberland NE43 7XB. *T:* (01661) 842867. *Club:* New (Edinburgh).

MILBURN, Donald B.; *see* Booker-Milburn.

MILDMAY, Sir Walter John Hugh St J.; *see* St John-Mildmay.

MILDON, His Honour Arthur Leonard; QC 1971; a Circuit Judge, 1986–96; *b* 3 June 1923; *er s* of late Rev. Dr W. H. Mildon, Barnstaple; *m* 1950, Iva, *er d* of late G. H. C. Wallis, Plymouth; one *s* one *d*. *Educ:* Kingswood Sch., Bath; Wadham Coll., Oxford (MA). Pres., Oxford Univ. Liberal Club, 1948. Army Service, 1942–46: Lieut, 138th (City of London) Field Regt, RA; Captain, 1st Army Group, RA. Called to Bar, Middle Temple, 1950, Bencher, 1979, Lent Reader, 1999; Member of Western Circuit; Dep. Chm., Isle of Wight QS, 1967–71; a Recorder, 1972–85. Mem., Bar Council, 1973–74. Pres., Medico-Legal Soc., 1994–96. *Recreation:* sailing. *Address:* c/o 4 New Square, Lincoln's Inn, WC2A 3RJ. *T:* (020) 7822 2000. *Club:* Royal Solent Yacht.

See also D. W. Mildon.

MILDON, David Wallis; QC 2000; *b* 19 Sept. 1955; *s* of His Honour Arthur Leonard Mildon, *qv*; *m* 1983, Lesley Mary Richardson; one *s* one *d*. *Educ:* Emmanuel Coll., Cambridge (LLB; MA). Called to the Bar, Middle Temple, 1980; in practice at the Bar, 1980–. *Recreations:* music, sailing. *Address:* Essex Court Chambers, 24 Lincoln's Inn Fields, WC2A 3ED. *T:* (020) 7813 8000.

MILDON, Russell; Director, Common Market Organisations, European Commission, since 2005; *b* 22 Aug. 1949; *s* of R. F. Mildon and J. Mildon (*née* Kröpfl); *m* 1973, Micheline Williams; two *s* one *d*. *Educ:* Royal Holloway Coll., London Univ. (Open Schol.; BSc Hons); Brunel Univ. (MTech). With Commission of the European Communities, 1974–: Statistics, studies and reports (Agricl), 1974–81; Gen. Affairs Gp, 1981–83; Private Sec. to Dep. Dir Gen., Agricl Markets, 1983–86; Advr to Vice-Pres., 1986–89; Head: Unit for Analysis of Situation of Agricl Holdings, 1989; Unit for Oilseeds and Protein Crops, 1989–93; Director: Internat. affairs relating to agric., 1993–96; orgn of markets in specialised crops, 1996–2001; Audit of Agricl Expenditure, Personnel and Admin, 2001–02; orgn of markets in crops, 2002–05. *Recreations:* chess, travel. *Address:* European Commission, 1049 Brussels, Belgium. *T:* (2) 2953224.

MILEDI, Prof. Ricardo, MD; FRS 1970; Distinguished Professor, University of California, Irvine, since 1984; *b* Mexico City, 15 Sept. 1927; *m* 1955, Ana Carmen (Mela) Garces; one *s*. *Educ:* Univ. Nacional Autónoma, Mexico City. BSc 1945; MD 1955. Research at Nat. Inst. of Cardiology, Mexico, 1952–54; Rockefeller Travelling Fellowship at ANU, 1956–58; research at Dept of Biophysics, UCL, 1958–84. Fellow, Amer. Acad. of Arts and Scis, 1986; Mem., Nat. Acad. of Scis, 1989; Hon. Member: Hungarian Acad. of Scis, 1988; Mexican Acad. of Medicine, 1995; Corresp. Mem., Mexican Acad. of Scis, 1991; Titular Mem., Eur. Acad. of Arts, Scis and Humanities, 1992. Dr *hc* Universidad del País Vasco, Spain, 1992; Univ. Nacional Autonoma de Mexico, 2007. Luigi Galvani Award, 1987; Internat. Prize for Science, King Faisal Foundn, 1988; Royal Medal, Royal Soc., 1998. *Address:* Laboratory of Cellular and Molecular Neurobiology, Department of Neurobiology and Behavior, 1215 and 1140 McGaugh Hall, University of California, Irvine, CA 92697–4550, USA. *T:* (949) 8244730, *Fax:* (949) 8246090; *e-mail:* rmiledi@uci.edu; 9 Gibbs Court, Irvine, CA 92612, USA. *T:* (714) 8562677.

MILEHAM, Peter; DL; President, British Chambers of Commerce, 2006–08 (Director, 2002–08); *b* 31 March 1943; *s* of William John Mileham and Mary Margaret, (Mayda), Mileham (*née* Kerrigan); *m* 1973, Shelagh Frances Preston; two *d*. *Educ:* Scarborough Tech. Coll. (HND Bldg 1965); Hull and York Tech. Colls. MIOB. Dir, Liquid Plastics Ltd, Preston, 1973–. Chm., Preston and NW, Yorkshire Bank, 2005–. Mem., Parly All Party Corporate Governance Gp, 2007–. Dir, NW Lancs Chamber of Commerce, 1992–. Vice Pres., Eurochambres Brussels, 2006–. Dir, UK India Business Council, 2008–. DL Lancs, 2004. *Publications:* various papers and articles in leading construction industry press. *Recreations:* gardening, arts, classical music. *Address:* Bucklebury, Lightfoot Lane, Fulwood, Preston PR2 3LR. *T:* (01772) 862220, *Fax:* (01772) 255034; *e-mail:* pm@liquidplastics.co.uk.

MILES, Anthony John; Executive Publisher, Globe Communications Corporation, Florida, USA, 1985–90; *b* 18 July 1930; *s* of Paul and Mollie Miles; *m* 1975, Anne Hardman. *Educ:* High Wycombe Royal Grammar Sch. On staff of (successively): Middlesex Advertiser; Nottingham Guardian; Brighton Evening Argus. Daily Mirror: Feature writer, 1954–66; Asst Editor, 1967–68; Associate Editor, 1968–71; Editor, 1971–74; Mirror Group Newspapers: Editorial Dir, 1975–84; Dep. Chm., 1977–79 and 1984; Chm., 1980–83. Dir, Reuters Ltd, 1978–84. Member: Press Council, 1975–78; British Exec. Cttee, IPI, 1976–84; Council, CPU, 1983–84; Life Vice-Pres., Newspaper Press Fund (Appeal Chm., 1982–83). *Address:* 6 Dukes Point, Dukes Head Yard, Highgate Village, N6 5JQ; Millennium Cottage, Dunster, Som TA24 6SY. *Clubs:* Reform, Savile.

MILES, Lieut-Comdr Brian, CBE 1994; RD 1970; FNI; RNR (retired); Director, Royal National Lifeboat Institution, 1988–98; *b* 23 Feb. 1937; *s* of Terence Clifford Miles and Muriel Irene Terry; *m* 1964, Elizabeth Anne Scott; one *s* two *d*. *Educ:* Reed's School, Cobham; HMS Conway; Merchant Navy Cadet School. Master Mariner (Foreign Going) Cert. P&O Orient Lines: Cadet, 1954–57; Deck Officer, 1958–64; RNLI: Divl Inspector, 1964–73; Asst to Director, 1974–79; Ops Staff Officer, 1979–81; Dep. Dir, 1982–87. Chairman: Friends of Dolphin Trust, 1989–; Poole Arts Trust, 1996–2003; Member Council: Royal Nat. Mission to Deep Sea Fishermen, 1999– (Dep. Chm., 2001–05, Chm., 2005–); Dorset Br., BRCS, 2000–03. FNI 1989; CCMI (CIMgt 1994). Freeman, City of London, 1993; Mem., Master Mariners' Co., 1994–. Younger Brother, Trinity House, 1994. Comdr, Order of Lion (Finland), 1997. *Address:* 8 Longfield Drive, West Parley, Ferndown, Dorset BH22 8TY. *T:* (01202) 571739.

MILES, Prof. Charles William Noel, CBE 1980; Head of Department of Land Management and Development, 1968–81, Dean of Faculty of Urban and Regional Studies, 1972–75, and Professor Emeritus, 1981, University of Reading; Chairman, Agricultural Wages Board for England and Wales, 1972–81; *b* 3 Nov. 1915; 2nd *s* of late Lt-Col Sir Charles W. Miles, 5th Bt; *m* 1940, Jacqueline, (Dickie), Cross (*d* 1998); one *d* (one *s* decd). *Educ:* Stowe Sch.; Jesus Coll., Cambridge (MA). FRICS. Army Service, 1939–46; Univ. Demonstrator and Univ. Lectr, Dept of Estate Management, Cambridge, 1946–54; Chief Agent to Meyrick Estates in Hants and Anglesey, 1954–68; Agent to Bisterne Estate, 1957–68. Pres., Chartered Land Agents Soc., 1965–66; Mem., Cambs AEC, 1953–54; Mem., SE Region Adv. Cttee of Land Commn, 1967–70. Mem., Yates Cttee on Recreation Management Trng, 1977–82. Leverhulme Trust Emeritus Fellowship, 1982–84. *Publications:* Estate Finance and Business Management, 1953, 4th edn 1981; Estate Accounts, 1960; Recreational Land Management, 1977, 2nd edn 1992; (co-ed) Walmesley's Rural Estate Management, 6th edn, 1978; Running an Open house, 1986; Going Public, 1991; (jtly) Aspects of Rural Estate Management, 1995. *Recreations:* walking, gardening, theatre. *Address:* AEHA Ltd, Suite 42, Clare Park, Farnham, Surrey GU10 5DT. *Club:* Farmers'.

See also Sir W. N. M. Miles, Bt.

MILES, Prof. Christopher John; film director and producer; *b* 19 April 1939; *s* of late John Miles, MC and Clarice Baskerville (*née* Remnant); *m* 1967, Susan Helen Howard Armstrong; one *d*. *Educ:* Winchester Coll.; Institut des Hautes Etudes Cinématographiques, Paris. Dir, Milesian Film Productions, 1962–; *films* include: Six Sided Triangle, 1963; The Virgin and the Gypsy, 1970 (Best Film Award, US and UK Critics, 1970); Time for Loving, 1972; The Maids, 1974; That Lucky Touch, 1976; Alternative Three, 1977; Priest of Love: life of D. H. Lawrence, 1981; Lord Elgin and some stones of no value, 1985; Cyclone Warning Class 4, 1994; The Clandestine Marriage, 1999; *theatre:* Skin of our Teeth, Chicago, 1973; *television:* Zinotchka, 1973; Neck, 1978; Love in the Ancient World, 1996; Fire from Olympia, 2004. Prof. of Film and Television, RCA, 1989–93. Lecture tours: India, for British Council, 1985; USA, 1986. FRCA 1989. Patron, Marlowe Soc., 1995–. *Publications:* Alternative Three, 1977 (trans. 5 langs); (with John Julius Norwich) Love in the Ancient World, 1996; (contrib.) H of C Report on Film, 1982; contrib. Image et Son, D. H. Lawrence Soc. Jl. *Recreations:* film-making, long walks and sketching in Arcadia. *Address:* Calstone House, Calstone, Calne, Wilts SN11 8PY. *Club:* Garrick.

MILES, David, FSA, FSAScot; Chief Archaeological Advisor, English Heritage, since 2005 (Chief Archaeologist, 1999–2005); *b* 6 Dec. 1947; *s* of Tom and Norah Miles; *m* 1969, Gwyn Morgan (*see* Gwyn Miles); one *s* one *d*. *Educ:* St Gregory's Grammar Sch., Huddersfield; King Edward VI Grammar Sch., Nuneaton; Birmingham Univ. (BA Hons). Dir of Excavations, M5 Excavation Cttee, 1970–71; Res. Asst, Bristol Univ., 1971–72; Director of Excavations: Abingdon Excavation Cttee, 1972–73; Upper Thames Excavation Cttee, 1973–74; Dep. Dir, 1974–87, Dir, 1987–99, Oxford Archaeological Unit. FSA 1984; FSAScot 2000. MIFA 1988. *Publications:* (with D. Benson) The Upper Thames Valley, 1974; An Introduction to Archaeology, 1977; (ed) The Romano-British Countryside, 1982; (ed with B. Cunliffe) Aspects of the Iron Age in Central Southern Britain, 1984; (ed with K. Branigan) The Economies of Romano-British Villas, 1987; (jtly) Two Oxfordshire Anglo-Saxon Cemeteries: Berinsfield and Didcot, 1995; (jtly) The Anglo-Saxon Cemetery at Butler's Field, Lechlade, Gloucestershire, 1998; (jtly) Uffington White Horse and its Landscape, 2003; The Tribes of Britain, 2005; (jtly) Iron Age and Roman Settlement in the Thames Valley, 2007; contrib. to learned jls, newspapers and magazines. *Recreations:* reading, gardening, arts. *Address:* 118 Millbank Court, 24 John Islip Street, SW1P 4LQ. *T:* (020) 7828 5781; Pailler de la Devezette, 30460 Lasalle, France; *e-mail:* david.miles@english-heritage.org.uk.

MILES, Prof. David Kenneth, PhD; Managing Director in Economic Research and Chief UK Economist, Morgan Stanley, since 2004; *b* 6 Oct. 1959; *s* of Kenneth Douglas Miles and Rebecca Owen; *m* 1997, Faye Dimdore; one *s* two *d*. *Educ:* Bishop Gore Sch., Swansea; University Coll., Oxford (BA PPE 1981); Nuffield Coll., Oxford (MPhil Econs 1983); Birkbeck Coll., London (PhD Econs 1993). Economist, Bank of England, 1983–89; Lectr, then Reader, Birkbeck Coll., London, 1989–93; Econ. Advr, Bank of England, 1993–94; Chief UK Economist, Merrill Lynch, 1994–96; Prof. of Financial Econs, 1996–2004, Vis. Prof., 2004–, Imperial Coll., London. Ed., Fiscal Studies, 1997–2004. Non-exec. Dir, FSA, 2004–; Specialist Advr, Treasury Select Cttee, 1999–. Fellow, Centre for Econ. Policy Res., 1992–; Mem. Council, NIESR, 2004–; Gov., Pensions Inst., 2002–. *Publications:* Housing, Financial Markets and the Wider Economy, 1994; (with A. Scott) Macroeconomics: understanding the wealth of nations, 2001, 2nd edn 2004; (ed jtly) The Economics of Public Spending, 2003; The Miles Review of the UK Mortgage Market, 2004; articles in econs jls and chapters in books. *Recreations:* cinema, squash, Rugby, wine, children. *Address:* Morgan Stanley, 20 Bank Street, Canary Wharf, E14 4AD. *T:* (020) 7425 1820; *e-mail:* david.miles@morganstanley.com.

MILES, (Frank) Stephen, CMG 1964; HM Diplomatic Service, retired; *b* 7 Jan. 1920; *s* of Harry and Mary Miles; *m* 1953, Margaret Joy (*née* Theaker); three *d*. *Educ:* Hermitage Sch., Helensburgh; John Watson's Sch., Edinburgh; Daniel Stewart's Coll., Edinburgh; St Andrews Univ. (MA); Harvard Univ. (Commonwealth Fellowship; MPA). Served with Fleet Air Arm, 1942–46 (Lt (A) RNVR). Scottish Home Dept, 1948; FCO (previously CRO), 1948–80; served in: New Zealand, 1949–52; E and W Pakistan, 1954–57; Ghana,

1959–62; Uganda, 1962–63; British Dep. High Commissioner, Tanzania, 1963–65 (Acting High Commissioner, 1963–64); Acting High Commissioner in Ghana, March–April 1966; Consul-Gen., St Louis, 1967–70; Dep. High Comr, Calcutta, 1970–74; High Comr, Zambia, 1974–78; High Comr, Bangladesh, 1978–79. A Dir of Studies, Overseas Services Unit, RIPA, 1980–83. Councillor: Tandridge DC, Surrey, 1982–90; Limpsfield Parish Council, 1983–95 (Chm., 1987–89). *Recreations:* cricket, tennis, golf. *Address:* 25 Sycamore Court, Hoskins Road, Oxted, Surrey RH8 9JQ. *T:* (01883) 713132. *Clubs:* Royal Commonwealth Society, MCC; Tandridge Golf.

MILES, Gwyn; Director, Somerset House Trust, since 2006; *b* 17 Nov. 1947; *d* of Sir Morien Morgan, CB, FRS and of Lady Morgan (*née* Axford); *m* 1969, David Miles, *qv*; one *s* one *d*. *Educ:* Bristol Univ. (BSc Physiol.); Bath Univ. (DipEd); Museums Assoc. (Cert. in Conservation). Research Assistant: McGill Univ., Montreal, 1969; Bristol Univ., 1969–70; Science Teacher, St Mary Redcliffe and Temple Sch., Bristol, 1971; Department of Antiquities, Ashmolean Museum, Oxford: Conservator, 1972–82; Head of Conservation, 1982–85; Victoria and Albert Museum: Dep. Keeper of Conservation, 1985–89; Surveyor of Collections, 1989–95; Dir of Major Projects, 1995–2002; Dir, Projects and Estate, 2002–05. Trustee: The Making, 2004–. *Publications:* Traditional Knitting in the British Isles, 1979; articles on conservation, collections management and gardening. *Recreations:* arts, architecture, gardening. *Address:* 118 Millbank Court, 24 John Islip Street, SW1P 4LQ. *T:* (020) 7828 5781; Le Pailler de la Devezette, 30460 Lasalle, France.

MILES, Prof. Hamish Alexander Drummond, OBE 1987; Barber Professor of Fine Arts and Director of the Barber Institute, University of Birmingham, 1970–90, Professor at Large and Emeritus Director, 1990–91, Emeritus Professor, since 1992; *b* 19 Nov. 1925; *s* of J. E. (Hamish) Miles and Sheila Barbara Robertson; *m* 1957, Jean Marie, *d* of T. R. Smits, New York; two *s* two *d*. *Educ:* Douai Sch.; Univ. of Edinburgh (MA); Balliol Coll., Oxford. Served War: Army, 1944–47. Asst Curator, Glasgow Art Gallery, 1953–54; Asst Lectr, then Lectr in the History of Art, Univ. of Glasgow, 1954–66; Vis. Lectr, Smith Coll., Mass, 1960–61; Prof. of the History of Art, Univ. of Leicester, 1966–70. Trustee, National Galleries of Scotland, 1967–87; Mem., Museums and Galleries Commn, 1983–87. *Publications:* (jtly) The Paintings of James McNeill Whistler, 2 vols, 1980; sundry articles and catalogues. *Recreation:* woodland management. *Address:* 31 Drummond Place, Edinburgh EH3 6PW; Burnside, Kirkmichael, Blairgowrie, Perthshire PH10 7NA.

MILES, (Henry) Michael (Pearson), OBE 1989; Chairman: Schroders, since 2003; Johnson Matthey PLC, 1998–2006 (Director, 1990–2006); *b* 19 April 1936; *s* of late Brig. H. G. P. Miles and Margaret Miles; *m* 1967, Carol Jane Berg; two *s* one *d*. *Educ:* Wellington Coll. National Service, Duke of Wellington's Regt, 1955–57. Joined John Swire & Sons, 1958; Dir, John Swire & Sons (HK) Ltd, 1970–99 (Chm., 1984–88); Managing Director: John Swire & Sons (Japan) Ltd, 1973–76; Cathay Pacific Airways Ltd, 1978–84 (Chm., 1984–88); Chm., Swire Pacific, 1984–88; Exec. Dir, 1988–99, Advr to Board, 1999–, John Swire & Sons Ltd. Director: Baring PLC, 1989–95 (Jt Dep. Chm., 1994–95); Portals Holdings, 1990–95; BP, 1994–2006; ING Baring Hldgs Co., 1995–2002; BICC, 1996–2002. Chm., Hong Kong Tourist Assoc., 1984–88. Vice Pres., China Britain Business Gp, 1995–2000. Gov., Wellington Coll., 1988–2005. *Recreations:* golf, tennis. *Address:* Schroders plc, 31 Gresham Street, EC2V 7QA. *Clubs:* White's; Queen's; Royal and Ancient Golf; Berkshire Golf; Sunningdale Golf.

MILES, Jenefer Mary; *see* Blackwell, J. M.

MILES, Prof. John Richard; Professor of Fashion and Textiles, 2002–07, Visiting Professor, since 2007, Bath Spa University (formerly Bath Spa University College); *b* 22 June 1944; *s* of Thomas William Miles and Hilda Mary Miles (*née* Davis); *m* 1963, Judith Bud (marr. diss.). *Educ:* Croydon Coll. of Art; Royal Coll. of Art (MDes). Set up design studio, Miles Calver and Pound (now Calver and Pound), 1973–78 (Director); Founder Dir, Peppermint Prints, 1978–82; founded John Miles Partnership, 1996. Head, Textiles and Fashion, Brighton Polytechnic, 1979–85; Design Dir, Courtaulds, 1985–87; Gen. Manager, Next, 1987–89; Prof. of Fashion and Textiles, RCA, 1989–97; Dir of Product Mkting, DMC, France, 1997–2000; Prof. of Design, Southampton Univ., 2001–02. Consultant, Studio Claire and Lyn; Dir, Miles Whiston and Wright, 1989–96. Chm., Textile and Fashion Panel, CNAA, 1983–96; Mem., Industrial Lead Body, 1991–95. Governor, Winchester Sch. of Art, 1989–94. Hon. Dr of Design, Southampton, 1998. *Recreations:* gardening, films, cooking, reading. *Address:* The Old School House, 54 Main Street, South Rauceby, Sleaford, Lincs NG34 8QQ.

MILES, John Seeley, FCSD, FSTD; typographer and graphic designer; *b* 11 Feb. 1931; *s* of Thomas William Miles and Winifred (*née* Seeley); *m* 1955, Louise Wilson; one *s* two *d*. *Educ:* Beckenham and Penge Grammar Sch.; Beckenham School of Art. FCSD (FSIAD 1973); FSTD 1974. UN travelling schol. to Netherlands to practise typography and punch cutting under Jan van Krimpen and S. L. Hartz, 1954–55; Assistant to Hans Schmoller at Penguin Books, 1955–58; joined Colin Banks to form design partnership, Banks and Miles, 1958, Partner, 1958–96; Dir, Parsimony Press, 1999–2003. Consultant to: Zoological Soc., Regent's Park and Whipsnade, 1958–82; Expanded Metal Co., 1960–83; Consumers' Assoc., 1964–93; British Council, 1968–83; The Post Office, 1972–83; E Midlands Arts Assoc., 1974–79; Curwen Press, 1970–72; Basilisk Press, 1976–79; Enschedé en Zn, Netherlands, 1980–94; British Telecom, 1980–89; British Airports Auth., 1983–87; typographic advisor, HMSO, 1985–96; design advisor: Agricl Inf. Workshop, Udaipur, India, 1973; Monotype Corp., 1985–92; hon. design advisor: UEA, 1990–97; UNHCR, Geneva, 1994–99; Internat. Assoc. Univs, Paris, 2000–03; Aston-Mansfield Charities, 2001–03; Memorial Arts Charity, 2005–. Designed banknote series Netherlands Antilles, 1987. Member: PO Design Adv. Cttee, 1972–76; Icograda Internat. Archive Cttee, 1993–2003. American Heritage Lectr, New York, 1960; held seminar, Graphic Inst., Stockholm, 1977 and 1986. Chairman: Wynkyn de Worde Soc., 1973–74; Arbitration Cttee, Assoc. Typographique Internationale, 1984–2002; Mem., Soc. Roy. des Bibliophiles et Iconophiles de Belgique, 1991–94. Governor, Central School of Arts and Crafts, 1978–85; External examiner: London Coll. of Printing, 1984–88; Technische Hoogschool Delft, 1986–87; Reading Univ., 1990–93; De Montfort Univ., 1994–99; Plymouth Univ., 2004–07. Mem. CGLI, 1986. Exhibitions: London, 1971, 1978; Amsterdam and Brussels, 1977; Hamburg, 1991. FRSA 1988. (With Colin Banks) Green Product Award, 1989; BBC Envmtl Award, 1990. *Publications:* Design for Desktop Publishing, 1987; articles and reviews in professional jls. *Recreations:* gardening, painting, reading aloud. *Address:* Pit Cottage, Tunstall Common, Woodbridge, Suffolk IP12 2JR. *T:* (01728) 688889. *Club:* Double Crown.

MILES, Michael; *see* Miles, H. M. P.

MILES, Oliver; *see* Miles, R. O.

MILES, Sir Peter (Tremayne), KCVO 1986; an Extra Equerry to HM the Queen, since 1988; *b* 26 June 1924; *er s* of late Lt-Col E. W. T. Miles, MC; *m* 1956, Philippa Helen Tremlett; two *s* one *d*. *Educ:* Eton Coll.; RMC, Sandhurst. First The Royal Dragoons, 1944–49; J. F. Thomasson & Co., 1949–59; Gerrard & National Discount Co. Ltd, 1959–80 (Managing Director, 1964–80). Director: P. Murray-Jones Ltd, 1966–75; Astley & Pearce Holdings Ltd, 1975–80 (Chm., 1978–80). Keeper of the Privy Purse and Treas. to the Queen, 1981–87; Receiver-Gen., Duchy of Lancaster, 1981–87; Mem., Prince of Wales' Council, 1981–87. *Clubs:* Cavalry and Guards, Pratt's, White's.

MILES, Raymond Reginald; Chief Executive, CP Ships Ltd, 1988–2005; *b* 2 Aug. 1944; *s* of Reginald Gonville Miles and Ellen Mary Miles (*née* Gower); *m* 1966, Susan Georgina Barrow, *d* of George Barrow; two *d*. *Educ:* Lanchester Poly. (BA Econs); London Business Sch. (MBA 1972). Ocean Group plc, Liverpool: Corporate Planner, 1972–75; Divl Finance Dir, 1975–78; Wilh. Wilhelmsen, Norway, USA and London: Exec. Vice Pres., Barber Blue Sea, 1978–86; Man. Dir, Global Equipt Mgt, 1986–88. Sen. Ind. Dir, Provident Financial plc, 2003–06; Chm., Southern Cross Healthcare Gp plc, 2006–; Lead Ind. Dir, Stelmar Shipping Ltd, USA, 2004–05; Adv. Dir, Stena AB, Sweden, 2006–; Dep. Chm., Internat. Personal Finance plc, 2006–. Chm., World Shipping Council, 2001–05. Dir, W of England Protection and Indemnity Club, 1994–2004; Chm., Box Club, 2003–05. Trustee: Nat. Maritime Mus., Greenwich, 1998–2006; Nat. Maritime Mus., Cornwall, 2001–; Garden Opera, 2003– (Chm., 2008–); Country Holidays for Inner City Kids, 2006–; Chm., Devon Community Foundn, 2006–. *Recreations:* Chelsea FC, opera, theatre, shooting. *Address:* *e-mail:* ray.miles@woodtown.org. *Club:* Reform.

MILES, (Richard) Oliver, CMG 1984; HM Diplomatic Service, retired; Chairman, MEC International Ltd, since 2000 (Director, since 1997); Senior Consultant, mi2g, since 1997; *b* 6 March 1936; *s* of George Miles and Olive (*née* Clapham); *m* 1968, Julia, *d* of late Prof. J. S. Weiner; three *s* one *d*. *Educ:* Ampleforth Coll.; Merton Coll., Oxford (Oriental Studies). Entered Diplomatic Service, 1960; served in Abu Dhabi, Amman, Aden, Mukalla, Nicosia, Jedda; Counsellor, Athens, 1977–80; Head of Near East and N Africa Dept, FCO, 1980–83; Ambassador to: Libya, 1984; Luxembourg, 1985–88; Under-Sec. on loan to NI Office, Belfast, 1988–90; Asst Under Sec. of State (Economic), FCO, 1990–91; Dir Gen. of Jt Directorate, Overseas Trade Services, FCO/DTI, 1991–93; Ambassador to Greece, 1993–96. Non-exec. Dir, Vickers Defence Systems, 1990–93. Dep. Chm., Libyan British Business Council, 2004–. Chm., Host (Hosting for Overseas Students), 1998–2004; Pres., Soc. for Libyan Studies, 1998–2005. Dist. Vis. Prof., Amer. Univ., Cairo, 2005. *Recreations:* bird-watching, reading poetry, playing the flute. *Club:* Travellers.

MILES, Robert John; QC 2002; *b* 29 Nov. 1962; *s* of David and Marion Miles; *m* 1999, Lisabel Mary Macdonald. *Educ:* Christ Church, Oxford (MA, BCL). Called to the Bar, Lincoln's Inn, 1987, Bencher, 2007; in practice, specialising in company and commercial law. *Address:* 4 Stone Buildings, Lincoln's Inn, WC2A 3XT. *T:* (020) 7242 5524. *Club:* Garrick.

MILES, Roger Steele, PhD, DSc; Head, Department of Public Services, The Natural History Museum (formerly British Museum (Natural History)), 1975–94; *b* 31 Aug. 1937; *s* of John Edward Miles and Dorothy Mildred (*née* Steele); *m* 1960, Ann Blake; one *s* one *d*. *Educ:* Malet Lambert High Sch., Hull; King's Coll., Univ. of Durham (BSc, PhD, DSc). Sen. Res. Award, DSIR, 1962–64; Sen. Res. Fellow, Royal Scottish Museum, 1964–66, Sen. Scientific Officer, 1966–68; Sen. Sci. Officer, BM (Nat. Hist.), 1968–71, Principal Sci. Officer, 1971–74. Hon. Fellow, Columbia Pacific Univ., 1983. *Publications:* Palaeozoic Fishes, 2nd edn, 1971 (1st edn, J. A. Moy-Thomas, 1939); (ed, with P. H. Greenwood and C. Patterson) Interrelationships of Fishes, 1973; (ed, with S. M. Andrews and A. D. Walker) Problems in Vertebrate Evolution, 1977; (with others) The Design of Educational Exhibits, 1982, 2nd edn 1988; (ed with L. Zavala) Towards the Museum of the Future, 1994 (trans. Spanish and revised, 1995); papers and monographs on anatomy and palaeontology of fishes, articles on museums, in jls. *Recreations:* music, twentieth century art and architecture. *Address:* 3 Eagle Lane, Snaresbrook, E11 1PF. *T:* (020) 8989 5684.

MILES, Roy; dealer in British fine paintings and writer; *b* 9 Feb. 1935; *s* of Edward Marsh and Elsa McKinley (who later *m* George Miles); *m* 1970, Christine Rhodes (*d* 1997). *Educ:* Bembridge Sch., Isle of Wight; Sorbonne, Paris. Gold Medal for painting, Liverpool Watercolour Soc., 1945. Set world record prices for British paintings, such as Stubbs and Canaletto, 1970; subseq. instrumental in creation of Victorian art market. Dir and prop., Roy Miles Gall., 1975–98; first dealer to put on exhibitions of Russian art, early 1980s. Encourages young artists; works with various charities. *Publications:* Priceless: a life in art (autobiog.), 2003; articles in magazines, newspapers and jls. *Recreation:* classical music. *Address:* 10 Ennismore Gardens, SW7 1NP. *T:* (020) 7581 7969.

MILES, Stephen; *see* Miles, F. S.

MILES, Wendy Ann; *see* Henry, W. A.

MILES, William; Chief Executive, West Yorkshire County Council, and Clerk to the Lieutenancy, West Yorkshire, 1984–86; *b* 26 Sept. 1933; *s* of William and Gladys Miles; *m* 1961, Jillian Anne Wilson; three *s*. *Educ:* Wyggeston School, Leicester; Trinity Hall, Cambridge (MA, LLM). Solicitor. Asst Solicitor, Leicester, Doncaster and Exeter County Boroughs, 1960–66; Asst Town Clerk, Leicester Co. Borough, 1966–69; Dep. Town Clerk, Blackpool Co. Borough, 1969–73; City Legal Adviser, Newcastle upon Tyne, 1973–74; Chief Exec., Gateshead Borough Council, 1974–84. Mem., Local Govt Residuary Body (England), 1995–99. Mem., Cheltenham Rotary Club. *Recreations:* bridge, hill walking, sport. *Address:* 3 St Stephen's Manor, Cheltenham, GL51 3GF. *T:* (01242) 575840.

MILES, Sir William (Napier Maurice), 6th Bt *cr* 1859; retired architect; *b* 19 Oct. 1913; *s* of Sir Charles William Miles, 5th Bt, OBE; *S* father, 1966; *m* 1946, Pamela, *d* of late Capt. Michael Dillon; one *s* two *d*. *Educ:* Stowe; University of Cambridge (BA). Architectural Assoc. Diploma, 1939; RIBA 1940. Mem., Dignity in Dying (formerly Voluntary Euthanasia Soc.). *Recreation:* surviving. *Heir:* *s* Philip John Miles, *b* 10 Aug. 1953. *Address:* Old Rectory House, Walton-in-Gordano, near Clevedon, North Somerset BS21 7AW. *T:* (01275) 873365.
See also Prof. C. W. N. Miles.

MILFORD, 4th Baron *cr* 1939, of Llanstephan, co. Radnor; **Guy Wogan Philipps;** QC 2002; Bt 1919; *b* 25 July 1961; *e s* of 3rd Baron Milford and Hon. Mary Makins (now Viscountess Norwich), *e d* of 1st Baron Sherfield, GCB, GCMG, FRS; *S* father, 1999; *m* 1996, Alice Sherwood; two *s*. *Educ:* Eton Coll. (KS); Magdalen Coll., Oxford (Roberts-Gawen Scholar; 1st cl. Classical Hon. Mods; 1st cl. Lit. Hum.; MA). Called to the Bar, Inner Temple, 1986; in practice, 1987–. *Heir:* *s* Hon. Archie Sherwood Philipps, *b* 12 March 1997. *Address:* 68 Westbourne Park Road, W2 5PJ. *T:* (020) 7229 1844; Llanstephan House, Llanstephan, Brecon, Powys LD3 0YR. *T:* (01982) 560693; *e-mail:* lordmilford@hotmail.com.

MILFORD, John Tillman; QC 1989; **His Honour Judge Milford;** a Circuit Judge, since 2002; Liaison Judge to Northumberland and North Tyneside Justices, since 2003; *b*

4 Feb. 1946; *s* of late Dr Roy Douglas Milford, Strathtay, Perthshire, and Jessie Milford (*née* Rhind), JP; *m* 1975, Mary Alice, *d* of late Dr E. A. Spriggs of Wylam, Northumberland; three *d*. *Educ:* The Cathedral School, Salisbury; Hurstpierpoint; Exeter Univ. (LLB). Called to the Bar, Inner Temple, 1969, Bencher, 1998; in practice on NE Circuit, 1970–2002. Head, Trinity Chambers, Newcastle upon Tyne, 1985–99; a Recorder, 1985–2002; a Dep. High Court Judge, 1994–2002. Chm., Northumbria Area Judicial Forum, 2005–. County Chairman: British Field Sports Soc. for South Northumberland, 1996–98; Countryside Alliance for South Northumberland, 1998–99; Regl Chm., Countryside Alliance for NE England, 1999–2002. Chairman: River Tyne Fishing Festival, 1997; Bywell Country Fair, 1999, 2000; Vice-Chm., Newcastle and Dist Beagles, 1999–2005. Trustee, Get Hooked on Fishing, 2003– (Chm., 2005–). *Recreations:* fishing, shooting, gardening, stalking, collecting. *Address:* 12 Trinity Chare, Newcastle upon Tyne NE1 3DF. *T:* (0191) 232 1927; The Law Courts, Quayside, Newcastle upon Tyne NE1 3LA. *Clubs:* Northern Counties (Newcastle upon Tyne) (Chm., 2003–07); Durham County (Durham).

MILFORD HAVEN, 4th Marquess of, *cr* 1917; **George Ivar Louis Mountbatten;** Earl of Medina, 1917; Viscount Alderney, 1917; *b* 6 June 1961; *s* of 3rd Marquess of Milford Haven, OBE, DSC, and of Janet Mercedes, *d* of late Major Francis Bryce, OBE; *S* father, 1970; *m* 1989, Sarah Georgina (marr. diss. 1996), *d* of George A. Walker, *qv*; one *s* one *d*; *m* 1997, Clare Wentworth-Stanley. *Heir:* *s* Earl of Medina, *qv*.

MILIBAND, Rt Hon. David (Wright); PC 2005; MP (Lab) South Shields, since 2001; Secretary of State for Foreign and Commonwealth Affairs, since 2007; *b* 15 July 1965; *s* of late Ralph Miliband and of Marion Miliband (*née* Kozak); *m* 1998, Louise Shackelton; two adopted *s*. *Educ:* Corpus Christi Coll., Oxford (BA 1st Cl. Hons PPE); Massachusetts Inst. of Technol. (Kennedy Schol.; MSC Political Sci.). Res. Fellow, Inst. of Public Policy Res., 1989–94; Head of Policy, Office of Leader of the Opposition, 1994–97; Dir of Policy, 1997, Head, 1998–2001, Prime Minister's Policy Unit; Minister of State: DfES, 2002–04; Cabinet Office, 2004–05; Minister of State (Minister for Communities and Local Govt), ODPM, 2005–06; Sec. of State for Envmt, Food and Rural Affairs, 2006–07. Sec., Commn on Social Justice, 1992–94. *Publications:* (ed) Re-inventing the Left, 1994; (ed jtly) Paying for Inequality: the economic cost of social injustice, 1994. *Recreation:* supporting Arsenal and S Shields FC. *Address:* House of Commons, SW1A 0AA. *Clubs:* Whiteleas Social, Cleadon Social.

See also Rt Hon. E. Miliband.

MILIBAND, Rt Hon. Edward; PC 2007; MP (Lab) Doncaster North, since 2005; Secretary of State for Energy and Climate Change, since 2008; *b* 24 Dec. 1969; *s* of late Ralph Miliband and of Marion Miliband (*née* Kozak). *Educ:* Corpus Christi Coll., Oxford (BA); London Sch. of Economics (MSc (Econ)). TV journalist; speechwriter and researcher for Harriet Harman, MP, 1993, for Rt Hon. Gordon Brown, MP, 1994–97; Special Advr to Chancellor of the Exchequer, 1997–2002; Lectr in Govt, Harvard Univ., 2002–04; Chm., Council of Econ. Advrs, HM Treasury, 2004–05. Parly Sec., Cabinet Office, 2006–07; Chancellor of the Duchy of Lancaster and Minister for the Cabinet Office, 2007–08. *Address:* House of Commons, SW1A 0AA.

See also Rt Hon. D. W. Miliband.

MILINGO, Most Rev. Emanuel; Former Archbishop of Lusaka (Archbishop, (RC), 1969–83); *b* 13 June 1930; *s* of Yakobe Milingo Chilumbu and Tomaide Lumbiwe Miti; *m* 2001, Maria Sung. *Educ:* Kachebere Seminary, Malawi; Pastoral Inst., Rome; University Coll., Dublin. Curate: Minga Parish, Chipata Dio., 1958–60; St Mary's Parish, 1960–61; Chipata Cathedral, 1963–64; Parish Priest, Chipata Cathedral, 1964–65; Sec. for Communications at Catholic Secretariat, Lusaka, 1966–69. Founder, The Daughters of the Redeemer, Congregation for young ladies, 1971. Dep. Hd, Pontifical Council for Migrants and Itinerants, 1983–99. *Publications:* Amake-Joni, 1972; To Die to Give Life, 1975; Summer Lectures for the Daughters of the Redeemer, 1976; The Way to Daughterhood; My God is a Living God, 1981; Lord Jesus, My Lord and Saviour, 1982; Demarcations, 1982; The Flower Garden of Jesus the Redeemer; My Prayers Are Not Heard; Precautions in the Ministry of Deliverance. *Recreation:* music. *Address:* c/o Archdiocese of Lusaka, PO Box 32754, 41 Wamulwa Road, Lusaka, Zambia.

MILL, Douglas Russell; Secretary and Chief Executive (formerly Secretary), Law Society of Scotland, 1997–2008; *b* 3 Jan. 1957; *s* of Alan M. L. Mill and Anna B. Mill (*née* Russell); *m* 1982, Christine Rankin; two *s* one *d*. *Educ:* Paisley Grammar Sch.; Glasgow Univ. (LLB, BA, MBA). Apprentice, Wright & Crawford, 1978–80; Partner: Cameron Pinkerton Haggarty, 1980–85; MacFarlane Young & Co., 1985–96. Dep. Dir, Univ. of Strathclyde Centre for Professional Legal Studies, 1993–96. DUniv Paisley, 2000. *Publication:* Successful Practice Management, 1992. *Recreations:* Rugby, golf. *Club:* Duntar Golf.

MILL, Ian Alexander; QC 1999; *b* 9 April 1958; *s* of Ronald MacLauchlan Mill and Thelma Anita Mill; *m* 1987, Mary Emma Clayden; three *s*. *Educ:* Epsom Coll.; Trinity Hall, Cambridge (MA Classics and Law). Called to the Bar, Middle Temple, 1981; in practice at the Bar, 1982–. *Recreations:* cricket, golf, opera, theatre, good food and wine. *Address:* Blackstone House, Temple, EC4Y 9BW. *T:* (020) 7583 1770. *Club:* MCC.

MILLAIS, Sir Geoffroy Richard Everett, 6th Bt *cr* 1885, of Palace Gate, Kensington and Saint Ouen, Jersey; *b* 27 Dec. 1941; *s* of Sir Ralph Regnault Millais, 5th Bt and his 1st wife, Felicity Caroline Mary Ward (*née* Warner) (*d* 1994), *d* of Brig.-Gen. W. W. Warner, CMG; *S* father, 1992. *Heir:* *cousin* John Frederic Millais [*b* 17 Sept. 1949; *m* 1991, Susan Clayton; two *d*].

MILLAN, Rt Hon. Bruce; PC 1975; Member, Commission of the European Communities, 1989–95; *b* 5 Oct. 1927; *s* of David Millan; *m* 1953, Gwendoline May Fairey; one *s* one *d*. *Educ:* Harris Academy, Dundee. Chartered Accountant, 1950–59. Contested: West Renfrewshire, 1951, Craigton Div. of Glasgow, 1955. MP (Lab): Glasgow, Craigton, 1959–83; Glasgow, Govan, 1983–88; Parly Under-Sec. of State: for Defence, (RAF), 1964–66, for Scotland, 1966–70; Minister of State, Scottish Office, 1974–76; Sec. of State for Scotland, 1976–79; opposition spokesman on Scotland, 1979–83. *Address:* 1 Torridon Avenue, Glasgow G41 5LA. *T:* (0141) 427 6483.

MILLAR, family name of **Baron Inchyra**.

MILLAR, Anthony Bruce; Chairman, Canadian Zinc (formerly San Andreas Resources) Corporation, 1994–2000; *b* 5 Oct. 1941; *s* of late James Desmond Millar and of Josephine Georgina Millar (*née* Brice); *m* 1964, Judith Anne (*née* Jester); two *d*. *Educ:* Haileybury and Imperial Service College. FCA 1974 (ACA 1964). Asst to Group Management Accountant and Group Treasurer, Viyella Internat. Fedn, 1964–67; United Transport Overseas Ltd, Nairobi, and London (Dep. Group Financial Controller), 1967–72; Finance Dir, Fairfield Property Co. Ltd, 1972–75; Consultant, 1975–77; Managing Dir, Provincial Laundries Ltd, 1977–81; Dep. Chm., Hawley Group, 1981–82; Chm., 1982–92, Hon. Pres., 1992–2000, The Albert Fisher Gp. Freeman, City of London, 1993–; Liveryman, Fruiterers' Co., 1993– (Hon. Assistant and Mem. Ct, 2001–03). *Recreations:* swimming, scuba diving, walking, bridge, travel. *Address:* Frensham Vale House, Lower Bourne, near Farnham, Surrey GU10 3JB. *Club:* Mark's.

MILLAR, Betty Phyllis Joy; Regional Nursing Officer, South Western Regional Health Authority, 1973–84, retired; *b* 19 March 1929; *o d* of late Sidney Hildersly Millar and May Phyllis Halliday. *Educ:* Ursuline High Sch. for Girls; Dumbarton Academy; Glasgow Royal Infirm.; Glasgow Royal Maternity Hosp.; Royal Coll. of Nursing, London. RGN 1950; SCM 1953; NA (Hosp.) Cert. 1961. Theatre Sister, Glasgow Royal Infirm., 1953–54; Ward and Theatre Sister, Henry Brock Meml Hosp., 1954–55; Nursing Sister, Iraq Petroleum Co., 1955–57; Clinical Instructor, Exper. Scheme of Nurse Trng, Glasgow, 1957–60; Admin. Student, Royal Coll. of Nursing, 1960–61; 2nd Asst Matron, Glasgow Royal Infirm., 1961–62; Asst Nursing Officer, Wessex Regional Hosp. Bd, 1962–67; Matron, Glasgow Royal Infirm., 1967–69; Chief Regional Nursing Officer, SW Regional Hosp. Bd, 1969–73. WHO Fellowship to study nursing services in Scandinavia, 1967. Mem. Jt Bd of Clinical Nursing Studies, 1970–82. *Address:* Pinedrift, 45 Stoneyfields, Easton-in-Gordano, Bristol BS20 0LL. *T:* (01275) 372709.

MILLAR, Douglas George, CB 2007; Clerk Assistant, since 2003, and Director General, Chamber and Committee Services, since 2008, House of Commons; *b* 15 Feb. 1946; *s* of late George Millar and Doris Mary Millar (*née* Morris); *m* 1st, 1967, Susan Mary Farrow (marr. diss. 1986); one *s* one *d*; 2nd, 1987, (Jane) Victoria Howard Smith; one *s* one *d*. *Educ:* City of Norwich Sch.; Bristol Univ. (BA Hons History 1967); Reading Univ. (MA Politics 1968). A Clerk, H of C, 1968–; Clerk of Defence Cttee, 1979–83; Clerk i/c Private Members' Bills and Divs, 1983–87; Clerk of Home Affairs Cttee, 1987–89; Principal Clerk and Clerk of Financial Cttees and Treasury and Civil Service Cttee, 1989–91; Sec. to Public Accounts Commn, 1989–91; Second Clerk, Select Cttees, 1991–94; Clerk of Select Cttees, 1994–97; Departmental Finance Officer, 1994–2003; Prin. Clerk, Table Office, 1998–2001; Clerk of Legislation, 2001–02. Jt Sec., Assoc. of Secs Gen. of Parlts, 1971–77. *Publications:* articles and reviews in parly and political jls. *Recreations:* watching Norwich City, family, golf. *Address:* House of Commons, SW1A 0AA. *T:* (020) 7219 3311. *Club:* Roehampton.

MILLAR, Prof. Fergus Graham Burtholme, DPhil; DLitt; FSA; FBA 1976; Camden Professor of Ancient History, University of Oxford, and Fellow of Brasenose College, Oxford, 1984–2002, Emeritus Fellow, 2002; *b* 5 July 1935; *s* of late J. S. L. Millar and of Jean Burtholme (*née* Taylor); *m* 1959, Susanna Friedmann; two *s* one *d*. *Educ:* Edinburgh Acad.; Loretto Sch.; Trinity Coll., Oxford (1st Cl. Lit. Hum.; Hon. Fellow, 1992); DPhil 1962, DLitt 1988, Oxon. Fellow: All Souls Coll., Oxford, 1958–64; Queen's Coll., Oxford, 1964–76 (Hon. Fellow, 1999); Prof. of Ancient History, UCL, 1976–84. Leverhulme Emeritus Fellow, Oriental Inst., Oxford, 2002–04; Sather Prof. of Classical Lit., Univ. of Calif, Berkeley, 2003. President: Soc. for the Promotion of Roman Studies, 1989–92 (Vice-Pres., 1977–89, 1992–2001; Hon. Vice-Pres., 2001); Classical Assoc., 1992–93; Pubns Sec., British Acad., 1997–2002. FSA 1978. Corresponding Member: German Archaeol. Inst., 1978; Bavarian Acad., 1987; Finnish Acad., 1989; Russian Acad., 1999; Amer. Acad. of Arts and Scis, 2003. Ed., Jl of Roman Studies, 1975–79. Hon. DPhil Helsinki, 1994; Hon. DLitt St Andrews, 2004. Conington Prize, Univ. of Oxford, 1963; Cultori di Roma Prize, Comune di Roma, 2005; Kenyon Medal for Classical Studies, British Acad., 2005. *Publications:* A Study of Cassius Dio, 1964; The Roman Empire and its Neighbours, 1967; (ed with G. Vermes) E. Schürer, history of the Jewish people in the age of Jesus Christ (175 BC–AD 135), Vol. I, 1973, Vol. II, 1979, Vol. III, parts 1 and 2 (ed with G. Vermes and M. D. Goodman), 1986–87; The Emperor in the Roman World (31 BC–AD 337), 1977, 2nd edn 1992; (ed with E. Segal) Caesar Augustus: seven aspects, 1984; The Roman Near East, 1993; The Crowd in Rome in the Late Republic, 1998; Rome, the Greek World and the East, vol. I, 2002, vol. 2, 2004, vol. 3, 2006; The Roman Republic in Political Thought, 2002; A Greek Roman Empire: power and belief under Theodosius II (408–450), 2006. *Address:* Oriental Institute, Pusey Lane, Oxford OX1 2LE; 80 Harpes Road, Oxford OX2 7QL. *T:* (01865) 515782.

MILLAR, Fiona; Columnist, Education Guardian, since 2003; Chairman of Trustees, Family and Parenting Institute, since 2004; *b* London, 2 Jan. 1958; *d* of Robert Millar and Audrey Millar; partner, Alastair John Campbell, *qv*; two *s* one *d*. *Educ:* Camden Sch. for Girls; University Coll. London (BSc Econs and Econ. Hist.). Graduate trng scheme, Mirror Gp, 1980–82; Daily Express, 1982–88; freelance journalist, 1988–94; Office of the Leader of the Opposition, 1995–97; Special Advr to the Prime Minister, 1997–2003. Television programmes: writer and presenter, The Best for My Child, 2004; presenter: Involving Parents, 2005; The Parents' Guide, 2006; Admissions Code, 2007. Chm., Comprehensive Future, 2008–. Chairman of Governors: Gospel Oak Prim. Sch., 2000–; William Ellis Sch., 2008–. *Publications:* (with Glenys Kinnock) By Faith and Daring, 1993; (with Melissa Benn) A Comprehensive Future, 2006. *Recreations:* swimming, reading, my children and their friends, walking the dog. *Address:* 13 Estelle Road, NW3 2JX; *e-mail:* fiona.millar1@btinternet.com.

See also G. J. Millar.

MILLAR, Gavin James; QC 2000; a Recorder, since 2003; *b* 10 July 1959; *s* of Robert and Audrey Millar; partner, Carmel Mary Elizabeth Fitzsimons; one *s* three *d*. *Educ:* St Peter's Coll., Oxford (BA Jurisprudence). Called to the Bar, Lincoln's Inn, 1981; Founder Mem., Doughty St Chambers, 1990. Mem., Public Affairs Cttee, Bar Council, 1995–97; Vice-Chm., Soc. of Labour Lawyers, 1999–2001. Mem. (Lab) Westminster CC, 1985–94. *Publication:* (jtly) Media Law and Human Rights, 2001. *Recreations:* family, football, painting. *Address:* Doughty Street Chambers, 10–11 Doughty Street, WC1N 2PL. *T:* (020) 7404 1313. *Club:* Manchester United Football.

MILLAR, Graeme Stewart, CBE 2006; FRPharmS; Director, Graeme Millar Ltd, since 1982; Chairman, Fletcher Jones Ltd, since 2000; *b* 20 Feb. 1955; *s* of Stewart and Louise Millar; *m* 1978, Fay Cooper Kennedy; three *s*. *Educ:* Heriot-Watt Univ. (BSc Hons Pharmacy). FRPharmS 1999. Director: Dunfermline Bldg Soc., 2001– (Vice Chm., 2007); Essentia Gp Ltd, 2003–08; Lomax Mobility Ltd, 2005–07. Dir, NCC, and Chm., Scottish Consumer Council, 2000–06; Chairman: Scottish Construction Forum, 2004–; Scottish Food Adv. Cttee, 2006–; Dir, Food Standards Agency, 2005–. Non-exec. Dir, Scottish Rugby Union, 2006. Chm., Sick Kids Friends Foundn, 2000–. Hon. Prof. of Pharmacy, Robert Gordon's Univ., Aberdeen, 2006–. *Recreations:* Rugby (spectator), golf, family and friends, good food and wine. *Address:* 2 Campbell Avenue, Edinburgh EH12 6DS. *T:* and *Fax:* (0131) 337 0608; *e-mail:* millargraeme@yahoo.co.uk. *Clubs:* Home House; New (Edinburgh); Royal Burgess Golfing Society (Edinburgh); Golf House (Elie, Fife).

MILLAR, Rt Rev. Preb. John Alexander Kirkpatrick, (Sandy); Bishop, Church of Uganda, since 2005; an Assistant Bishop (Bishop in Mission), Diocese of London, since 2006; Priest-in-charge, St Mark's, Tollington Park, since 2003; *b* 13 Nov. 1939; *s* of Maj.-Gen. Robert Kirkpatrick Millar of Orton, CB, DSO and Frances (*née* Beyts); *m* 1971, Annette Fisher; one *s* three *d*. *Educ:* Eton; Trinity Coll., Cambridge (BA 1962; MA 1966); Univ. of Durham (DipTh). Deacon 1976; priest 1977; Curate, 1976–85, Vicar,

1985–2005, Holy Trinity Brompton, with St Paul, Onslow Square; Area Dean, Chelsea, 1989–94; Prebendary, St Paul's Cathedral, 1997–. *Address:* 1 Moray Road, N4 3LD. *T:* (020) 7561 5462.

MILLAR, John Stanley, CBE 1979; County Planning Officer, Greater Manchester Council, 1973–83; *b* 1925; *s* of late Nicholas William Stanley Millar and late Elsie Baxter Millar (*née* Flinn); *m* 1st, 1961, Patricia Mary (*née* Land) (*d* 1992); one *d*; 2nd, 1993, Christine (*née* Riley). *Educ:* Liverpool Coll.; Univ. of Liverpool. BArch, DipCD, PPRTPI, RIBA. Planning Asst, then Sen. Asst Architect, City of Liverpool, 1948–51; Sectional Planning Officer, then Dep. Asst County Planning Officer, Lancs CC, 1951–61; Chief Asst Planning Officer, then Asst City Planning Officer, City of Manchester, 1961–64; City Planning Officer, Manchester, 1964–73. *Publications:* papers in professional and technical jls. *Recreations:* walking, listening to music, travel, the sea. *Address:* 55 Stanneylands Drive, Wilmslow, Cheshire SK9 4EU. *T:* (01625) 523616.

MILLAR, Air Vice-Marshal Peter, CB 1998; Director, Carbon Trading, C-Questor PLC, since 2005; Chairman, C-Green Fuels Ltd, since 2006; *b* 20 June 1942; *s* of Air Cdre John Christopher Millar, RAF and Patricia Millar (*née* Allen); *m* 1966, Annette McMillan; one *s* two *d*. *Educ:* Malvern Coll.; RAF Coll., Cranwell. Served RAF: No 20 Sqn, Singapore, 1964–66; No 4 FTS, RAF Valley, 1967–69; Central Flying Sch., RAF Kemble, 1969–71; 560 Trng Sqn, Randolph AFB, Texas, 1971–74; RAF Staff Coll., 1974; Flight Commander: No 20 Sqn, Wildenrath, 1975–77; No 4 Sqn, Gutersloh, 1977–78; MoD, 1978–79; Sqn Comdr, No 233 OCU, RAF Wittering, 1979–82; USAF Air Warfare Coll., Maxwell AFB, Alabama, 1982–83; Brit. Defence Staff, Washington, 1983–84; Stn Comdr, RAF Wittering, 1985–86; RCDS 1987; on staff, UK Mil. Rep., NATO HQ, 1988–90; Dir NATO, MoD, 1990–93; HQ AAFCE, Ramstein AFB, Germany, 1993–95; Administr, Sovereign Base Areas and Comdr, British Forces Cyprus, 1995–98; retd 1998. Dir of Security, Medical World Inc., and Dir, Internat. Admin, Medical Mall Ltd, 1998–99. Mem. Adv. Bd, World Challenge Expeditions Ltd, 2000–04; Dir, Ops, Intellectual Property Rights Protection Ltd, 2003–06. Chairman: Biotrans Consortium, 2004–; Terrafuels Ltd, 2006–. Gov., Queen Alexandra's Hosp. Home, 2005–. FRAeS 1997; MInstD 1997. *Recreations:* ski-ing, golf, off-shore sailing. *Club:* Royal Air Force.

MILLAR, Peter Carmichael, OBE 1978; Deputy Keeper of HM Signet, 1983–91; *b* 19 Feb. 1927; *s* of late Rev. Peter Carmichael Millar, OBE, DD and of Ailsa Ross Brown Campbell or Millar; *m* 1953, Kirsteen Lindsay Carnegie, *d* of late Col David Carnegie, CB, OBE, TD, DL, Dep. Gen. Manager, Clydesdale Bank; two *s* two *d*. *Educ:* Aberdeen Grammar Sch.; Glasgow Univ.; St Andrews Univ.; Edinburgh Univ. MA, LLB; WS. Served RN, 1944–47. Partner in law firms, Messrs W. & T. P. Manuel, WS, 1954–62; Aitken, Kinnear & Co., WS, 1963–87; Aitken Nairn, WS, 1987–92. Clerk to Soc. of Writers to HM Signet, 1964–83. Chairman: Church of Scotland Gen. Trustees, 1973–85; Mental Welfare Commn for Scotland, 1983–91; (part-time) Medical Appeal Tribunals, 1991–99; Pension Appeal Tribunals, 1992–99. Convener, Scottish Child and Family Alliance, later Children in Scotland, 1992–95. *Recreations:* golf, hill-walking, music. *Address:* 25 Cramond Road North, Edinburgh EH4 6LY. *T:* (0131) 336 2069. *Clubs:* New (Edinburgh); Hon. Co. of Edinburgh Golfers, Bruntsfield Links Golfing Society.

MILLAR, Robert Brandon, CA; Chief Executive, New City Vision, since 2004; *b* 30 March 1950; *m* 1975, Sandra Falconer; one *s* one *d*. *Educ:* George Heriot's Sch.; Edinburgh Univ. (MA Hons Econs). Gen. Mgt, BT, 1972–74; CA apprenticeship, Touche Ross & Co., 1974–78; Accountant, Bredero UK, 1978–79; Financial Controller, Castle Rock HA, 1979–83; Manager Registration, Housing Corp., 1983–89; Dir of Strategy, Scottish Homes, 1989–97; Finance Dir, Miller Homes, 1997–99; Chief Exec., Scottish Homes, subseq. Communities Scotland, 2000–03. *Recreation:* various sports. *Address:* New City Vision, 13 Newton Place, Glasgow G3 7PR. *Clubs:* Merchants of Edinburgh Golf, Granton on Spey Golf, Thistle Tennis.

MILLAR, Samira; *see* Ahmed, S.

MILLAR, Rt Rev. Preb. Sandy; *see* Millar, Rt Rev. Preb. J. A. K.

MILLARD, Anthony Paul; founder and Chairman, Anthony Millard Consulting, since 2001; Headmaster, Giggleswick School, 1993–2001; *b* 21 Sept. 1948; *s* of Leonard William Millard and Marjorie Ethel Millard (*née* Manley); *m* 1971, Lesley Margaret Baker; one *s* three *d*. *Educ:* Solihull Sch.; LSE (BSc Econ); Balliol Coll., Oxford (PGCE). Teaching in Zambia, 1971–74; Stagiaire (specialist trainee) with EC, 1974–75; Wells Cathedral School: Asst Master, 1975–77; Housemaster, 1977–86; Dep. Headmaster, 1982–86; Headmaster, Wycliffe Coll., Glos, 1987–93. Non-exec. Dir, Servicespan Ltd, 2001–04; Man. Dir, Schools Div., Nord Anglia plc, 2002–03. Chairman: ISIS (Central), 1990–92; Services Cttee, HMC, 1995–2000; Boarding Schs Assoc., 2000 (Mem. Exec. Cttee, 1995–2001); Vice Chm., Bloxham Project Cttee, 1991–96; Mem. Council, ISCO, 1995–98. Contested (C) Wirral South, 2001. Chm. Govs, British Internat. Sch., NY, 2006–. FRSA 1986. *Recreations:* tennis, travel, mountains. *Address:* Brookside Cottage, Ewen, Cirencester, Glos GL7 6BU. *T:* (01285) 770365; *e-mail:* anthonymillard@yahoo.co.uk. *Clubs:* East India, Devonshire, Sports and Public Schools.

MILLARD, Sir Guy (Elwin), KCMG 1972 (CMG 1957); CVO 1961; HM Diplomatic Service, retired; *b* 22 Jan. 1917; *s* of Col Baldwin Salter Millard, and Phyllis Mary Tetley; *m* 1st, 1946, Anne, *d* of Gordon Mackenzie; one *s* one *d*; 2nd, 1964, Mary Judy, *d* of late James Dugdale and Pamela Dugdale (*née* Coventry); two *s*. *Educ:* Charterhouse; Pembroke Coll., Cambridge. Served RN, World War II. HM Diplomatic Service, 1939–76: Ambassador to Hungary, 1967–69; Minister, Washington, 1970–71; Ambassador to Sweden, 1971–74; Ambassador to Italy, 1974–76. Chm., British-Italian Soc., 1977–83. Grand Officer, Order of Merit, Italy, 1981. *Address:* Fyfield Manor, Southrop, Glos GL7 3NZ. *T:* (01367) 850234.

MILLEDGE, Peter Neil; Legal Adviser and Deputy Counsel to the Chairman of Committees, House of Lords, since 2005; *b* 4 March 1955; *s* of late Frederick Milledge and Mary Kirkwood Milledge (*née* Cree); *m* 1979, Jennifer Miriam Greenall; two *s*. *Educ:* Newport (Essex) Grammar Sch.; King's Coll. London (LLB 1976). Called to the Bar, Middle Temple, 1977; joined Govt Legal Service, 1979; Legal Asst, 1979–82, Sen. Legal Asst, 1982–85, Asst Solicitor, 1985, DHSS; seconded to Law Officers' Dept, 1987–89; Asst Dir, Legal Services, DSS, subseq. DWP, 1989–2005. Gov., Newport Free GS, Saffron Walden, 2008–. *Publications:* (contrib.) Tribunals: practice and procedure, 1986; contribs to legal jls. *Recreations:* walking, gardening, local history, bellringing. *Address:* House of Lords, SW1A 0PW. *T:* (020) 7219 3211. *Club:* Civil Service.

MILLEN, Brig. Anthony Tristram Patrick; Defence Advisor to British High Commissioner, Ottawa, Canada, 1980–83, retired; *b* 15 Dec. 1928; *s* of Charles Reginald Millen and Annie Mary Martin; *m* 1954, Mary Alice Featherston Johnston (*d* 2008); three *s* two *d* (and two *s* decd). *Educ:* Mount St Mary's Coll. 5th Royal Inniskilling Dragoon Guards, 1948; served in Germany, Korea, Cyprus, N Ireland, Hong Kong, USA. *Publications:* articles in US military jls. *Recreation:* sailing. *Address:* Victoria Stables, East End, Ampleforth, N Yorks YO62 4DA. *T:* (01439) 788982.

MILLER, family name of **Baronesses Miller of Chilthorne Domer** and **Miller of Hendon**.

MILLER OF CHILTHORNE DOMER, Baroness *cr* 1998 (Life Peer), of Chilthorne Domer in the co. of Somerset; **Susan Elizabeth Miller;** *b* 1 Jan. 1954; *d* of Frederick Oliver Meddows Taylor and Norah Langham; *m* 1st, 1980, John Miller (marr. diss. 1998); one *d* (and one *d* decd); 2nd, 1999, Humphrey Temperley. *Educ:* Sidcot Sch.; Oxford Polytech. David & Charles, Publishers, 1975–77; Weidenfeld & Nicholson, 1977; Penguin Books, 1977–79; bookshop owner, Sherborne and Yeovil, 1979–89. Lib Dem spokesman on envmt, food and rural affairs, H of L, 1999–2007, on home affairs, 2007; Vice-Chm., All Party Parly Gps on Latin America, Mexico and Bolivia; Chm., All Party Parly Gp on Street Children. Member (Lib Dem): S Somerset DC, 1991–98 (Leader, 1996–98); Somerset CC, 1997–2005. Parish Councillor, Chilthorne Domer, 1987–. *Recreations:* walking, sailing, reading, friends. *Address:* House of Lords, SW1A 0PW.

MILLER OF HENDON, Baroness *cr* 1993 (Life Peer), of Gore in the London Borough of Barnet; **Doreen Miller,** MBE 1989; JP; *b* 13 June 1933; *d* of Bernard Henry Feldman and Hetty Feldman; *m* 1955, Henry Miller; three *s*. *Educ:* Brondesbury and Kilburn High Sch.; LSE. Chairman and Managing Director, 1971–88: Universal Beauty Club Ltd (UK); Cosmetic Club International GmbH (Germany); Universal Beauty Club (Pty) Ltd (Australia). Nat. Chm. and Exec. Dir, The 300 Group, 1985–88; Chm., Women Into Public Life Campaign, 1987–; Human Rights Advr, Soroptimist International, 1987–90. A Baroness in Waiting (Govt Whip), 1994–97; an Opposition Whip, 1997–99; Opposition spokesman on trade and industry, 1999–2007. Crown Agent, 1990–94. Chairman: Barnet FHSA, 1990–94; Nat. Assoc. of Hosp. and Community Friends (formerly Nat. Assoc. of Leagues of Hosp. Friends), 1997–2003. Mem., Monopolies and Mergers Commn, 1992–93. Trustee, Menerva Educnl Trust, 1992–. Jt Treas., 1990–93, Chm., 1993–96, Pres., 1996–98, Greater London Area, Nat. Union of Conservative & Unionist Party. FRSA. JP Brent, 1971. *Publication:* Let's Make Up, 1975. *Recreations:* politics, reading, football, sitting by sunlit swimming pools given the opportunity. *Address:* House of Lords, SW1A 0PW.

MILLER, Sir Albert (Joel), KCMG 2002; LVO 1994; MBE 1963; QPM 1970; CPM 1965; President, 1976–2003, Co-Chairman, 1998–2003, and Chief Executive Officer, since 2006, Grand Bahama Port Authority Ltd; *b* 23 Feb. 1926; *s* of late Joseph Edward Miller and Nellie Miller; *m* 1949, Laurie; two *s* one *d*. *Educ:* private tutorage, St Augustine's Coll., Nassau. Joined Royal Bahamas Police Force, 1943: Detective Corporal, 1950; Detective Sergeant, 1953; Detective Inspector, 1955; Asst Supt, 1957; Dep. Supt, 1961; Supt, 1962; Asst Comr, 1964; Dep. Comr, 1968–71, resigned. Vice-Pres., 1971–74, Pres., 1974–, Bahamas Amusements Ltd. Hon. ADC to Governor of the Bahamas. *Recreations:* fishing, boating, swimming, reading. *Address:* PO Box F-44270, Freeport, Bahamas. *T:* (242) 3527770, *Fax:* (242) 3523702; *e-mail:* ajmiller.modalena@coralwave.com. *Clubs:* Les Ambassadeurs; Rotary of Freeport (Bahamas).

MILLER, Amelia, (Mrs Michael Miller); *see* Freedman, A.

MILLER, Prof. Andrew, CBE 1999; PhD; FRSE; Principal and Vice-Chancellor, Stirling University, 1994–2001, Professor Emeritus, since 2001; Secretary and Treasurer, Carnegie Trust for the Universities of Scotland, since 2004; *b* 15 Feb. 1936; *s* of William Hamilton Miller and Susan Anderson (*née* Auld); *m* 1962, Rosemary Singleton Hannah Fyvie; one *s* one *d*. *Educ:* Beath High Sch.; Edinburgh Univ. (BSc Hons 1958; PhD 1962); Wolfson Coll., Oxford (MA 1967; Hon. Fellow, 1995). Postdoctoral Fellow, CSIRO, Melbourne, 1962–65; Tutor in Chemistry, Ormond Coll., Melbourne Univ., 1963–65; Staff Scientist, MRC Lab. of Molecular Biol., Cambridge, 1965–66; Lectr in Molecular Biophysics, Oxford Univ., 1966–83; Fellow, Wolfson Coll., Oxford, 1967–83; on secondment as Hd, EMBL, Grenoble, 1975–80; Edinburgh University: Prof. of Biochem., 1984–94; on secondment as Dir of Res., European Synchrotron Radiation Facility, Grenoble, 1986–91; Vice-Dean of Medicine, 1991–93; Vice-Provost of Medicine and Veterinary Medicine, 1992–93; Vice-Principal, 1993–94. Gen. Sec., RSE, 2001–05, 2007; Interim Chief Exec., Cancer Research UK, 2001–02. Chm., Internat. Centre for Math. Scis, Edinburgh, 2001–05. Leverhulme Emeritus Fellowship, 2001–03. Member: Action Gp on Standards in Scottish Schs, DFEE, 1997–99; Scottish Exec. Sci. Strategy Gp, 1999–; Bd, Food Standards Agency, 2003–05; Dep. Chm., Scottish Food Adv. Cttee, 2003–05. Dir, Scottish Knowledge plc, 1997–2002. Advr, Wellcome Trust, on UK-Wellcome-French-Synchrotron, 1999–2000. Mem. Council, Open Univ., 2001–05. FRSE 1986 (Mem. Council, 1997–2005). DUniv: Stirling, 2002; Open, 2007. *Publications:* (ed jtly) Minerals in Biology, 1984; numerous papers on collagen and muscle in scientific jls incl. Nature, Jl Molecular Biol. *Recreations:* music, walking, reading, wondering. *Address:* 5 Blackford Hill Grove, Edinburgh EH9 3HA.

MILLER, Andrew Peter; MP (Lab) Ellesmere Port and Neston, since 1992; *b* 23 March 1949; *s* of late Ernest William Thomas Miller and of Daphne May Miller; *m* Frances Ewan; two *s* one *d*. *Educ:* Hayling Island Secondary Sch.; LSE (Mature Student; Dip. Indust. Relations 1976). Lab. Technician, Dept of Geology, Portsmouth Poly., specialising in X-RF and X-RD analysis, 1967–76; Divl Officer, ASTMS, subseq. MSF, 1977–92. PPS, DTI, 2001–05. Mem., Science and Technol. Select Cttee, 1992–97; Chairman: Regulatory Reform Select Cttee, 2005–; PITCOM, 2005–; Vice Chm., PLP Cttee on Science and Technol., 1993–97; Treas., 1997–2000, Vice Pres., 2000–03, Parlt and Sci. Cttee. Ldr, PLP Leadership Campaign Team, 1997–98. Dir, Eur. Informatics Market, 1996–98. Pres., Computing for Labour, 1993–. *Publication:* (jtly) North West Economic Strategy, 1987. *Recreations:* walking, photography. *Address:* Hollytree Cottage, Commonside, Alvanley, Cheshire WA6 9HB. *T:* (01928) 722642; *e-mail:* millera@parliament.uk.

MILLER, Arjay; Dean, and Professor of Management, Graduate School of Business, Stanford University, 1969–79, now Dean Emeritus; Vice-Chairman, Ford Motor Company, 1968–69 (President, 1963–68); *b* 4 March 1916; *s* of Rawley John Miller and Mary Gertrude Schade; *m* 1940, Frances Marion Fearing; one *s* one *d*. *Educ:* University of California at Los Angeles (BS with highest hons, 1937). Graduate Student and Teaching Asst, University of California at Berkeley, 1938–40; Research Technician, Calif. State Planning Bd, 1941; Economist, Federal Reserve Bank of San Francisco, 1941–43. Captain, US Air Force, 1943–46. Asst Treas., Ford Motor Co., 1947–53; Controller, 1953–57; Vice-Pres. and Controller, 1957–61; Vice-Pres. of Finance, 1961–62; Vice-Pres., Staff Group, 1962–63. Mem. Bd of Dirs, Public Policy Inst., Calif; Trustee: Brookings Instn, Washington; Internat. Exec. Service Corps; Urban Inst. Mem. Bd of Dirs, SRI International. Councillor, The Conference Board. Fellow, Amer. Acad. of Arts and Scis, 1990. Hon. LLD: Univ. of California (LA), 1964; Whitman Coll., 1965; Univ. of Nebraska, 1965; Ripon Coll., 1980; Washington Univ., St Louis, 1982. *Address:* 225 Mountain Home Road, Woodside, CA 94062, USA. *Clubs:* Bohemian, Pacific Union (San Francisco).

MILLER, Hon. (Arthur) Daniel; consultant; Premier, British Columbia, 1999–2000; *b* 24 Dec. 1944; *s* of Arthur William Miller and Evelyn Estelle Miller (*née* Lewis); *m* 1987, Beverly Gayle Ballard (*née* Bartram); three *s* two *d.* *Educ:* N Vancouver Secondary Sch. Millwright. Former Mem. Council, Prince Rupert City. Government of British Columbia: MLA (NDP) North Coast, 1986–2001; Minister of: Forests, 1991–93; Skills, Training and Labour, 1993–96; Municipal Affairs, 1996–97; Dep. Premier, 1996–99; Minister: of Employment and Investment, 1997–98; of Energy and Mines, and resp. for Northern Develt, 1998–2001. *Address:* 1234 Richardson Street, Victoria, BC V8V 3E1, Canada.

MILLER, Barry; Director General Service Personnel Policy, Ministry of Defence, 1999–2002; *b* 11 May 1942; *s* of Lt-Col Howard Alan Miller and Margaret Yvonne Richardson; *m* 1968, Katrina Elizabeth Chandler; one *s* one *d.* *Educ:* Lancaster Royal Grammar Sch. Ministry of Defence: Exec. Officer, RAE Farnborough, 1961; Asst Principal, MoD, London, 1965; Principal: Defence Policy Staff, 1969; Naval Personnel Div., 1969; Equipment Secretariat (Army), 1972; Defence Secretariat, 1973; CSD, 1975; Asst Secretary: Civilian Management, 1977; Defence Secretariat, 1980; RCDS 1984; Asst Sec., Management Services (Organisation), 1985; Director General: Defence Quality Assurance, 1986; Test and Evaluation, 1992; Asst Under Sec. (Finance), PE, 1994; Dir Gen., Finance, 1995; Command Sec. to Second Sea Lord and C-in-C Naval Home Command, and Asst Under-Sec. of State (Naval Personnel), 1996–99. Director: Royal Naval Film Corp., 1969–72; BSI, 1986–89; 3rd Gunwharf Gate Mgt Co. Ltd, 1997–99; RNM Functions Ltd, 2003–. Hon. Dep. Sec., First Div. Assoc., 1969–73. Chairman: Finance Cttee, Greenwich Hosp., 1996–99; DHE Audit Cttee, 2002–04; Mem., Defence Estates Audit Cttee, 2004. Deputy Chairman: Trustees, Royal Naval Mus., Portsmouth, 2003–; Governors, Royal Hosp. Sch., Holbrooke, 1996–99. Chm., Friends of Torbay (Musical Weekend), 2007–; Mem. Council, King George V Fund for Sailors, 2002– (Chm., Distribution Cttee, 2005–); Trustee: Tunbridge Wells Internat. Young Concert Artists Competition, 2003–; Midday Music, 2004–; Hon. Treas., Green Room Music, 1997–. *Club:* Civil Service (Chm., 1990–95).

MILLER, Bill; *b* 22 July 1954; *s* of George and Janet Miller; one *s* one *d.* *Educ:* Paisley Coll.; Kingston Poly. (BSc Land Econs). DipTP; MRICS. Surveyor, Glasgow DC, 1978–94. Councillor (Lab) Strathclyde, 1986–94. MEP (Lab) Glasgow, 1994–99, Scotland, 1999–2004. *Recreations:* record collecting, Kilmarnock Football Club, golf. *Address:* c/o John Smith House, 145–165 West Regent Street, Glasgow G2 4RZ. *Club:* Castlemilk Labour (Glasgow).

MILLER, Bruce; *see* Miller, J. D. B.

MILLER, Carolyn; Chief Executive, Merlin, since 2005; *b* 20 Nov. 1951; *d* of Norman and Irene Miller. *Educ:* Southampton Univ. (BSc); City Univ., London (DipTP). Local govt, 1973–84; Sen. Advr to Ministry of Planning, Nicaragua, 1984–87; Save the Children: Prog. Dir, Mozambique/Angola, 1987–89; Hd, Southern Africa Regl Office, 1989–91; Dir, Asia, Latin America and Caribbean, ME, 1991–96; Dir of Progs, 1996–2001; Dir, Eastern Europe and the Western Hemisphere, subseq. Europe, ME and Americas, DFID, 2001–04. *Recreations:* walking, arts. *Address:* (office) 12th Floor, 207 Old Street, EC1V 9NR. *T:* and *Fax:* (020) 7014 1610; *e-mail:* carolyn.miller@merlin.org.uk.

MILLER, Cheryl; *see* Miller, D. C.

MILLER, Colin Brown; Sheriff for South Strathclyde, Dumfries and Galloway, since 1991; *b* 4 Oct. 1946; *s* of late James Miller and Isabella Brown or Miller; *m* 1972, Joan Elizabeth Blyth; three *s.* *Educ:* Paisley Grammar Sch.; Glasgow Univ. (LLB 1967). Solicitor in private practice, 1969–91. Mem. Council, Law Soc. of Scotland, and Convener of various cttees, 1983–91. Dean, Faculty of Procurators in Paisley, 1991. *Recreations:* walking, family, railways, ships, motor vehicles, photography. *Address:* Sheriffs' Chambers, Wellington Square, Ayr KA7 1EE. *T:* (01292) 268474.

MILLER, Hon. Daniel; *see* Miller, Hon. A. D.

MILLER, David; journalist and author; columnist, Daily Telegraph, since 1997; Chief Sports Correspondent, The Times, 1983–97; *b* 1 March 1935; *er s* of Wilfred Miller and Everilda Miller (*née* Milne-Redhead); *m* 1957, Marita Marjorie Malyon; one *s* one *d.* *Educ:* Charterhouse; Peterhouse, Cambridge (Nat. Sci. Tripos; CUAFC *v* Oxford, 1954–55). Sub-editor, The Times, 1956–59; Sports Correspondent: Daily Telegraph, 1960–73; Sunday Telegraph, 1961–73; Chief Sports Corresp., Daily Express, 1973–82. Has covered 19 Summer and Winter Olympic Games and 13 Football World Cups, attended 56 FA Cup Finals, over 400 England football internationals and 47 Wimbledon Championships. Member: Press Commn of IAAF, 1988–2004; FIFA Press Commn, 1993–97. Chm., Sports Writers' Assoc. of GB, 1981–84; Mem., Internat. Soc. of Olympic Historians, 1993–. Sports Writer of Year Award, What the Papers Say, 1986; Doug Gardner Services to Journalism Award, Sports Writers' Assoc., 2001; FIFA Centenary Jules Rimet Award, 2004. *Publications:* Father of Football: biography of Sir Matt Busby, 1970; World Cup, 1970; World Cup, 1974; The Argentina Story, 1978; Cup Magic, 1981; (with Sebastian Coe) Running Free, 1981; The World to Play For, 1982; Coming Back, 1984; England's Last Glory, 1986; Sports Writers' Eye (anthology), 1989; Stanley Matthews, 1990; Born to Run, 1992; (jtly) History of IAAF, 1992; Olympic Revolution: biography of Juan Antonio Samaranch, 1992 (trans. 8 langs); Our Sporting Times, 1996; (co-author) Opus: a history of Arsenal FC, 2007; Official IOC books: Seoul '88; Albertville '92; Lillehammer '94; Atlanta '96; Nagano '98; Athens to Athens: official history, 1894–2004, of the International Olympic Committee and the Olympic Games, 2003, revised edn as Athens to Beijing, 2008. *Recreations:* sailing, reading. *Address:* Box 14, NR25 7SL. *Fax:* (01263) 588293. *Clubs:* Royal Thames Yacht; Hawks (Cambridge); Achilles; Corinthian Casuals Football; Middlesex Wanderers; Pegasus Football (Oxford).

MILLER, Prof. David Andrew Barclay, FRS 1995; W. M. Keck Foundation Professor of Electrical Engineering, since 1997 (Professor of Electrical Engineering, since 1996), Director, Solid State and Photonics Laboratory, since 1997, and Co-Director, Stanford Photonics Research Centre, Stanford University; *b* 19 Feb. 1954; *s* of Matthew Barclay Miller and Martha Sanders Miller (*née* Dalling); *m* 1976, Patricia Elizabeth Gillies; one *s* one *d.* *Educ:* St Andrews Univ. (BSc Hons 1976); Heriot-Watt Univ. (PhD Phys 1979). FIEEE 1995. Res. Associate, 1979, Lectr, 1980–81, Heriot-Watt Univ.; Technical Staff, 1981–87, Head of Advanced Photonic Res. Dept, 1987–96, AT&T Bell subseq. Bell, Laboratories, Holmdel, NJ; Dir, E. L. Ginzton Lab., 1997–2006, Stanford Univ. Pres., IEEE Lasers and Electro-Optics Soc., 1995. Fellow: Amer. Phys. Soc.; Optical Soc. of America (Adolph Lomb Medal, 1986; R. W. Wood Prize, 1988); Corresp. FRSE 2002. Internat. Prize in Optics, Internat. Commn for Optics, 1991; Third Millennium Medal, IEEE, 2000. Hon. Dr Natural and Applied Scis, Free Univ. Brussels, 1997; Hon. DEng Heriot-Watt, 2003. *Publications:* numerous papers in learned jls. *Recreation:* clarinet and saxophone playing. *Address:* Ginzton Laboratory, 450 Via Palou, Stanford University, Stanford, CA 94305–4088, USA. *T:* (650) 7230111, *Fax:* (650) 7259355; 815 San Francisco Court, Stanford, CA 94305, USA.

MILLER, David Ivimey, OBE 1991; HM Diplomatic Service, retired; Senior Consultant, MEC International Ltd, since 2003; *b* 26 March 1937; *y s* of late Reginald James Miller and Helen Joyce (*née* Leech), Cambridge; *m* 1966, Caroline Ethel Jackson; two *d.* *Educ:* Aldenham Sch.; Sch. of Slavonic and East European Studies, London Univ.; Magdalen Coll., Oxford. Served FO, subseq. FCO, and Moscow, 1964–72; Berlin, 1972–74; CSCE, Geneva, 1974, Belgrade, 1977; First Sec. and Head of Chancery, Belgrade, 1978–81; seconded to Cabinet Office, 1982–85, to NATO Secretariat, Brussels, 1985–90; Asst Dir of Research, FCO, 1990–95; Ambassador to Armenia, 1995–97. Political Advr, OSCE, Tirana, 2000. Associate Fellow, RUSI, 1997. *Address:* Sharon, Chalkhouse Green Road, Kidmore End, Reading RG4 9AS. *Club:* Oxford and Cambridge.

MILLER, Prof. David Leslie, DPhil; FBA 2002; Professor of Political Theory, University of Oxford, since 2002; Fellow in Social and Political Theory, Nuffield College, Oxford, since 1979; *b* 8 March 1946; *s* of Leslie Miller and Alice (*née* Renfrew); *m* 1982, Susan Deborah Hersh; two *s* one *d.* *Educ:* Canford Sch.; Selwyn Coll., Cambridge (BA, MA); Balliol Coll., Oxford (BPhil, DPhil 1974). Lecturer in Politics: Univ. of Lancaster, 1969–76; UEA, 1976–79; Jun. Proctor, Univ. of Oxford, 1988–89. *Publications:* Social Justice, 1976; Philosophy and Ideology in Hume's Political Thought, 1981; (with L. Siedentop) The Nature of Political Theory, 1983; Anarchism, 1984; (jtly) The Blackwell Encyclopaedia of Political Thought, 1986; Market, State and Community: theoretical foundations of market socialism, 1989; Liberty, 1991; (with M. Walzer) Pluralism, Justice and Equality, 1995; On Nationality, 1995; Principles of Social Justice, 1999; Citizenship and National Identity, 2000; (with S. Hashmi) Boundaries and Justice: diverse ethical perspectives, 2001; Political Philosophy: a very short introduction, 2003. *Recreations:* tennis, hiking, theatre, music. *Address:* Nuffield College, Oxford OX1 1NF. *T:* (01865) 278569, *Fax:* (01865) 278621; *e-mail:* david.miller@nuffield.ox.ac.uk.

MILLER, Prof. David Louis, MD; FRCP, FFPH; Professor of Public Health Medicine, St Mary's Hospital Medical School, University of London, 1983–95, now Emeritus Professor; *b* 16 Sept. 1930; *s* of John Henry Charles Miller and Muriel (*née* Rogers); *m* 1955, Wendy Joy Clark; three *s* one *d.* *Educ:* The Leys, Cambridge; Peddie Sch., Hightstown, NJ, USA; Clare Coll., Cambridge (BA 1952, MA 1955; MB, BChir 1955; MD 1965); St Thomas's Hosp. Med. Sch. (Scholar). DPH 1964; FRCP 1978 (MRCP 1973); FFPH (FFCM 1972). House Officer, St Thomas' Hosp., 1956–57; MO, RAF, 1957–60; Research Asst, RPMS, 1960–62; Epidemiologist, PHLS, 1962–71; US Public Health Service Internat. Res. Fellow, Johns Hopkins Sch. of Hygiene and Public Health, Md, 1965–66; Prof. of Community Medicine, Middlesex Hosp. Med. Sch., 1972–82. Hon. Sen. Res. Fellow, UMDS of Guy's and St Thomas' Hosp., then GKT, 1995–2002. Aneurin Bevan Meml Fellowship, Govt of India, 1981. Pres., Sect. Epidemiology, RSocMed, 1986–88; Acad. Registrar, FPHM, RCP, 1989–94. Life Mem., Soc. of Scholars, Johns Hopkins Univ., 1983. President: Central YMCA, 1986–2002 (Chm., 1977–99); Metropolitan Union of YMCAs, 2001–. *Publications:* (jtly) Lecture Notes on Epidemiology and Public Health Medicine, 1975, 5th edn 2004; Epidemiology of Diseases, 1982; pubns on epidemiology, esp. respiratory infections, vaccines, HIV and health services. *Recreations:* walking, music, youth and community. *Club:* Royal Society of Medicine.

See also R. C. W. Miller.

MILLER, His Honour David Quentin; a Circuit Judge, 1987–2000; *b* 22 Oct. 1936; *s* of Alfred Bowen Badger and Mair Angharad Evans. *Educ:* Ellesmere Coll., Shropshire; London Sch. of Econs and Pol. Science, London Univ. (LLB Hons 1956). Called to the Bar, Middle Temple, 1958; admitted Barrister and Solicitor of the Supreme Court of NZ, 1959. In practice, SE Circuit, 1960–82; Metropolitan Stipendiary Magistrate, 1982–87; a Recorder, 1986–87. *Recreations:* history, walking, gardening, art, music, Trollope Society. *Address:* Highfields, Bullinghope, Hereford HR2 8EB. *T:* (01432) 273995.

MILLER, Sir Donald (John), Kt 1990; FRSE; FREng, FIMechE, FIET; Chairman, ScottishPower (formerly South of Scotland Electricity Board), 1982–92; *b* 9 Feb. 1927; *s* of John Miller and Maud (*née* White); *m* 1973, Fay Glendinning Herriot; one *s* two *d.* *Educ:* Banchory Academy; Univ. of Aberdeen (BSc(Eng)). FEng 1981. Metropolitan Vickers, 1947–53; British Electricity Authority, 1953–55; Preece, Cardew and Rider (Consulting Engrs), 1955–66; Chief Engr, North of Scotland Hydro-Electric Bd, 1966–74; Dir of Engrg, then Dep. Chm., SSEB, 1974–82. Chairman: Premium Trust, 1993–98; Nat. Cycle Network Steering Cttee, 1995–2001. Chm., Power Div., IEE, 1979. Hon. Mem., British Nuclear Energy Soc., 1989. DUniv Strathclyde, 1992; Hon. DSc Aberdeen, 1997. *Publications:* papers to IEE. *Recreations:* reading, gardening, sailing.

MILLER, (Dorothy) Cheryl, CBE 2002; Chief Executive (formerly Head of Paid Service), East Sussex County Council, since 1994; *b* 31 Aug. 1954; *d* of Sidney Radcliffe and Dorothy (*née* Ainsworth); *m* 1976, Graham Edwin Miller; one *s* one *d.* *Educ:* Preston Park Sch., Lancs; Preston Sixth Form Coll.; Manchester Univ. (BA Hons). Admin. Trainee, CSD, 1975–77; HEO(D) and Asst Private Sec. to Lord Privy Seal and Leader of House of Lords, 1977–78; Personnel Policy Br., CSD, 1979–80; Mem., PM's Advr on Efficiency (Lord Rayner) Scrutiny Team, 1980; Cabinet Office: Head, CS Policy on Retirement and Redundancy Conduct and Discipline Br., 1980–84; Head, Constitutional Br., Machinery of Govt Div., 1984–85; Asst Dir, then Dep. Dir, CSSB, 1986–90; Head, Staff Develt, DTI, 1991; County Personnel Officer, 1991–93 and Head, Exec. Office, 1992–93, E Sussex CC. Member: Royal Commn on Envmtl Pollution, 2000–03; Stakeholder Gp, Foresight Flood and Coastal Defence Project, OST, 2003–04; Geographic Inf. Panel, ODPM, 2005–. Non-executive Director: Sussex Enterprise, 1994–2002; Wired Sussex, 1999–2002. Mem., SEEDA Adv. Council, 1998–. Chm., ACCE, 2000–01; Pres., SOLACE, 2004–05 (Vice-Pres., 2002–04). Chairman: E Sussex Youth Offending Bd, 2000–; E Sussex Drug and Alcohol Action Team, 2000–; Board Member: E Sussex Economic Partnership, 1996–2005; E Sussex Strategic Partnership, 2001–06. *Recreations:* theatre, music, literature, women's equality issues, family activities, cooking, entertaining. *Address:* East Sussex County Council, County Hall, St Anne's Crescent, Lewes, East Sussex BN7 1SW. *T:* (01273) 481560.

MILLER, Ven. Geoffrey Vincent; Archdeacon of Northumberland, since 2005; *b* 26 Jan. 1956; *s* of late Harold and Vera Miller; *m* 1993, Elaine; one *s.* *Educ:* Sharston High Sch., Manchester; Durham Univ. (BEd 1978); St John's Coll., Nottingham (DPS 1983); Newcastle Univ. (MA with distinction 1994). Ordained deacon, 1983, priest, 1984; Curate, Jarrow, 1983–86; Team Vicar, St Aidan and St Luke, Billingham, 1986–92; Diocesan Urban Develt Officer, Dio. Durham, 1991–99; Community Chaplain, Stockton-on-Tees, 1992–94; Priest-in-charge, 1994–96, Vicar, 1996–99, St Cuthbert, Darlington; Diocesan Urban Officer and Residentiary Canon, St Nicholas Cathedral, Newcastle upon Tyne, 1999–2005. Chm., British Cttee, French Protestant Industrial Mission, 2000–. *Recreation:* looking on the brighter side. *Address:* 80 Moorside North, Fenham, Newcastle upon Tyne NE4 9DU. *T:* (0191) 273 8245, *Fax:* (0191) 226 0286; *e-mail:* g.miller@newcastle.anglican.org.

MILLER, Sir Hal; *see* Miller, Sir Hilary D.

MILLER, Rt Rev. Harold Creeth; *see* Down and Dromore, Bishop of.

MILLER, Sir Harry, 12th Bt *cr* 1705, of Chichester, Sussex; hill country farmer, New Zealand, 1942–89; *b* 15 Jan. 1927; *yr s* of Sir Ernest Henry John Miller, 10th Bt and Netta Mehalah Miller (*née* Bennett) (*d* 1980); *S* brother, 1995; *m* 1954, Gwynedd Margaret Sheriff; one *s* two *d*. RNZAF 1945 (volunteer pilot). *Recreations:* mountain climbing, golf, forestry management. *Heir:* *s* Anthony Thomas Miller [*b* 4 May 1955; *m* 1990, Barbara Battersby (*née* Kensington); two *s*, and two step *s* one step *d*]. *Address:* 53 Koha Road, Taupo, New Zealand. *T:* (7) 3780905.

MILLER, Sir Hilary Duppa, (Sir Hal), Kt 1988; DL; Chairman, Cosmopolitan Holdings Ltd, since 1991; *b* 6 March 1929; *s* of late Lt-Comdr John Bryan Peter Duppa-Miller, GC; *m* 1st, 1956, Fiona Margaret McDermid; two *s* two *d*; 2nd, 1976, Jacqueline Roe, *d* of T. C. W. Roe and of Lady Londesborough; one *s* one *d*. *Educ:* Eton; Merton Coll., Oxford; London Univ. MA (Oxon) 1956; BSc (Estate Management) (London), 1962. With Colonial Service, Hong Kong, 1955–68. Company Director. Chief Exec., SMMT, 1991–93. Contested: (C), Barrow-in-Furness, 1970; Bromsgrove by-elec. May 1971; MP (C) Bromsgrove and Redditch, Feb. 1974–1983, Bromsgrove, 1983–92. PPS to Sec. of State for Defence, 1979–81, to Chancellor of the Duchy of Lancaster, 1981, resigned; Vice-Chm., Conservative Party Orgn, and PPS to the Chm., 1984–87; Mem., UK delegn to Council of Europe, 1974–76. Jt Chm., All Party Motor Industry Gp, 1978. Chm., Nat. Clubs Assoc., 2001–. Mem. Council, RFU, 2003–. Fellow, Econ. Develt Inst. of World Bank, Washington. DL Worcs, 2000. *Recreations:* sailing, fell walking, cricket, Rugby. *Address:* Moorcroft Farm, Sinton Green, Worcester, Worcs WR2 6NW. *Clubs:* Oxford and Cambridge; Vincent's (Oxford); Aston Fields Royal British Legion (Bromsgrove); Eton Ramblers, Free Foresters, Blackheath Football (Pres., 1999–2003).

MILLER, Ian Harper Lawson; Sheriff of Glasgow and Strathkelvin at Glasgow, since 2001; *b* 16 Jan. 1954; *s* of late Henry Young Miller and Jean Watson Harper Miller (*née* Lyall); *m* 1987, Sheila Matthews Howie; one *s* three *d*. *Educ:* Robert Gordon's Coll., Aberdeen; Univ. of Aberdeen (MA Hons Hist. 1976; LLB 1978). Solicitor, 1980–91; Partner, Burnett & Reid, Solicitors, Aberdeen, 1986–91; called to the Scottish Bar, 1992; Temp. Sheriff, 1998; Sheriff of Grampian Highland and Islands at Aberdeen, 1998–2001. Pt-time Tutor, Dept of Scots Law, Univ. of Aberdeen, 1981–91. Mem., Sheriff Court Rules Council, 1987–91. *Recreations:* reading, music, family life, golf. *Address:* Sheriff's Chambers, Glasgow Sheriff Court, 1 Carlton Place, Glasgow G5 9DA. *T:* (0141) 429 8888; 25 Wester Coates Avenue, Edinburgh EH12 5LS. *T:* (0131) 346 1853. *Clubs:* Royal Northern and University (Aberdeen); Royal Aberdeen Golf.

MILLER, Dr Jacques Francis Albert Pierre, AC 2003 (AO 1981); FRS 1970; FAA 1970; Head of Experimental Pathology Unit, Walter and Eliza Hall Institute of Medical Research, 1966–96; Professor of Experimental Immunology, University of Melbourne, 1990–97, now Emeritus; *b* 2 April 1931; French parents; *m* 1956, Margaret Denise Houen. *Educ:* St Aloysius' Coll., Sydney. BSc (Med.) 1953, MB, BS 1955, Sydney; PhD 1960, DSc 1965, London. Sen. Scientist, Chester Beatty Res. Inst., London, 1960–66; Reader, Exper. Pathology, Univ. of London, 1965–66. Croonian Lectr, Royal Soc., 1992. For. Mem., Académie Royale de Médicine de Belgique, 1969; For. Associate, US Nat. Acad. Scis, 1982. Hon. MD Sydney, 1986. Langer-Teplitz Cancer Research Award (USA), 1965; Gairdner Foundn Award (Canada), 1966; Encyclopaedia Britannica (Australia) Award, 1966; Scientific Medal of Zoological Soc. of London, 1966; Burnet Medal, Austr. Acad. of Scis, 1971; Paul Ehrlich Award, Germany, 1974; Rabbi Shai Shacknai Meml Prize, Hadassah Med. Sch., Jerusalem, 1978; Saint-Vincent Internat. Prize for Med. Res., Italy, 1983; first Sandoz Immunology Prize, 1990; first Medawar Prize, Transplantation Soc., 1990; J. Allyn Taylor Internat. Prize for Medicine, John Robarts Res. Inst., 1995; Florey-Faulding Medal and Prize, Australian Inst. of Pol Sci., 2000; Copley Medal, Royal Soc., 2001; PM's Prize for Science, Australia, 2003. *Publications:* over 400 papers in scientific jls and several chapters in books, mainly dealing with thymus and immunity. *Recreations:* music, photography, art, literature. *Address:* Walter and Eliza Hall Institute of Medical Research, 1G Royal Parade, Parkville, Victoria 3050, Australia. *T:* (3) 93452555.

MILLER, James, CBE 1986; Chairman, Miller Group Ltd (formerly James Miller & Partners), 1970–99; *b* 1 Sept. 1934; *s* of Sir James Miller, GBE, and Lady Ella Jane Miller; *m* 1st, 1959, Kathleen Dewar; one *s* two *d*; 2nd, 1969, Iris Lloyd-Webb; one *d*. *Educ:* Edinburgh Acad.; Harrow Sch.; Balliol Coll., Oxford (MA Engrg Sci.). Joined James Miller & Partners, 1958; Board Mem., 1960; Man. Dir, 1970–91. Director: Life Assoc. of Scotland, 1981–93; British Linen Bank, 1983–99 (Chm., 1997–99); Britoil, 1988–90; Bank of Scotland, 1993–2000; Mem., Scottish Adv. Bd, British Petroleum, 1990–2001. Pres., FCEC, 1990–93 (Chm., 1985–86). Dir, Royal Scottish Nat. Orchestra, 1996–2002 (Chm., 1997–2002). Chm., Court, Heriot-Watt Univ., 1990–96. Hon. Consul for Austria, 1994–2003; Dean, Consular Corps in Edinburgh, Leith, 1999–2001. *Recreation:* shooting. *Address:* Alderwood, 49 Craigcrook Road, Edinburgh EH4 3PH. *T:* (0131) 332 2222, *Fax:* (0131) 332 1777. *Club:* City Livery.

MILLER, James Francis Xavier; Headmaster, Royal Grammar School, Newcastle upon Tyne, 1994–2008; *b* 3 March 1950; *yr s* of Lt-Col John Francis Miller and Barbara Mary Miller (*née* Cooke); *m* 1976, Ruth Ellen Rowland (*née* Macbeth); two *s*. *Educ:* Douai Sch.; Merton Coll., Oxford (BA Classical Mods and PPE; MA). Winchester College: Asst Master, 1972–89; Hd of Econs, 1978–82; Housemaster, 1982–89; Headmaster, Framlingham Coll., 1989–94. Chm., Amazing Grades Ltd (formerly study-links.com), 2000–. Councillor, Winchester CC, 1976–83 (Chm., Health and Works Cttee, 1979–82). FRSA 1994. *Recreations:* golf, cricket, opera, crosswords. *Address:* Orchard Cottage, Eardisland, Leominster, Herefordshire HR6 9BJ. *Clubs:* East India; Free Foresters.

MILLER, Prof. J(ohn) D(onald) Bruce; Executive Director, Academy of the Social Sciences in Australia, 1989–91; Professor of International Relations, Research School of Pacific Studies, Australian National University, 1962–87, now Emeritus; *b* 30 Aug. 1922; *s* of Donald and Marion Miller, Sydney, Australia; *m* 1st, 1943, Enid Huthnance; one *s*; 2nd, 1957, Margaret Martin; one *s*; 3rd, 1990, Judith Bennet. *Educ:* Sydney High Sch.; University of Sydney. BEc, 1944; MEc 1951; MA Cantab 1978. Announcer and Talks Officer, Australian Broadcasting Commission, Sydney and Canberra, 1939–46; Staff Tutor, Department of Tutorial Classes, University of Sydney, 1946–52; Asst Lecturer in Political Science and International Relations, London Sch. of Economics, 1953–55; Lecturer in Politics, University Coll., Leicester, 1955–57; Prof. of Politics, University of Leicester, 1957–62; Dean of Social Sciences, 1960–62; Public Orator, 1961–62. Res. Associate, Chatham House, 1965, 1969, 1973. Visiting Professor: Indian Sch. of International Studies, 1959; Columbia Univ., New York, 1962, 1966, 1981; Yale, 1977; Princeton, 1984, 1986; Overseas Vis. Fellow, St John's Coll., and Smuts Vis. Fellow, Cambridge Univ., 1977–78; Macrossan Lectr, University of Queensland, 1966. Member: Aust. Population and Immigration Council, 1975–81; Aust. Res. Grants Cttee, 1975–81. Joint Editor, Journal of Commonwealth Political Studies, 1961–62; Editor, Australian Outlook, 1963–69; Chm., Editorial Adv. Bd for Austr. documents on foreign relations, 1971–77; Austr. Nat. Commn for UNESCO, 1982–84, 1990–93. Canberra correspondent, The Economist, 1962–87. FASSA 1967 (Treas., 1979–83). *Publications:* Australian Government and Politics, 1954, 4th edn with B. Jinks 1970; Richard Jebb and the Problem of Empire, 1956; Politicians (inaugural), 1958; The Commonwealth in the World, 1958; The Nature of Politics, 1962; The Shape of Diplomacy (inaugural), 1963; Australia and Foreign Policy (Boyer Lectures), 1963; (ed with T. H. Rigby) The Disintegrating Monolith, 1965; Britain and the Old Dominions, 1966; Australia, 1966; The Politics of the Third World, 1966; (ed) India, Japan, Australia: Partners in Asia?, 1968; Survey of Commonwealth Affairs: problems of expansion and attrition 1953–1969, 1974; (ed) Australia's Economic Relations, 1975; The EEC and Australia, 1976; The World of States, 1981; Ideology and Foreign Policy, 1982; Norman Angell and the Futility of War, 1986; (ed) Australians and British, 1987; (ed with L. J. Evans) Policy and Practice, 1987; (ed with R. J. Vincent) Order and Violence, 1990. *Recreation:* staying alive. *Address:* 1 Mountbatten Park, Yarralumla, ACT 2600, Australia. *T:* (2) 62825599.

MILLER, Very Rev. John Dunlop; Minister, Castlemilk East Parish Church, Glasgow, 1971–2007; Moderator of the General Assembly of the Church of Scotland, 2001–02; *b* 11 Nov. 1941; *s* of Rev. Ian Robert Newton Miller and Dr Jessie Sinclair Miller (*née* Dunlop); *m* 1968, Mary Glen Robertson; one *s* two *d*. *Educ:* Kilmarnock Acad.; Merchant Taylor's Sch.; Corpus Christi Coll., Oxford (BA 1964); New Coll., Edinburgh (BD 1967); Union Theol Seminary, NY (STM 1970). Ordained 1971. Hon. DD Glasgow, 2001. *Publications:* Ministry and Mission in Working Class Areas, 1976; Buildings and Mission in Working Class Areas, 1986; Reflections on the Beatitudes, 2002; Silent Heroes, 2004. *Recreation:* cycling. *Address:* 98 Kirkcaldy Road, Glasgow G41 4LD.

MILLER, John Harmsworth, CBE 2006; architect in private practice; *b* 18 Aug. 1930; *s* of Charles Miller and Brenda Borrett; *m* 1st, 1957, Patricia Rhodes (marr. diss. 1975); two *d*; 2nd, 1985, Su Rogers. *Educ:* Charterhouse; Architectural Assoc. Sch. of Architecture (AA Dip. Hons 1957). ARIBA 1959. Private practice, Colquhoun and Miller, 1961–90, John Miller and Partners, 1990–; works include: Forest Gate High Sch., West Ham (Newham), 1965; Chemistry Labs, Royal Holloway Coll., London Univ., 1970; Melrose Activity Centre, Milton Keynes Develt Corp. (Commendation, Steel Awards, 1975); Pillwood House, Feock, Cornwall (RIBA Regional Award, 1975); housing, Caversham Road/Gaisford Street, Camden, 1978; single person flats, Hornsey Lane, Haringey, 1980; Oldbrook, Milton Keynes (Silver Award, Architectural Design, 1987; Highly Commended, Housing Design and Civic Trust Awards); Whitechapel Art Gall. extension, 1985 (RIBA Regl Award, 1988; Civic Trust Award, 1988); Gulbenkian Gall. for RCA, 1989; Stevens Bldg for RCA, and Nomura Gall. and bookshop for Tate Gall., 1991; Queen's building, UEA (RIBA Nat. Award) and new 20th century galls for Nat. Portrait Gall., 1993; Elizabeth Fry building, UEA, 1995 (RIBA Regl Award); Ramphal building, Warwick Univ., 1996; Serpentine Gall., 1998; Shackleton Meml Library, Scott Polar Res. Inst., Cambridge Univ., 1999 (RIBA Regl Award); Tate Gall. Centenary Develt, Tate Britain, 2001 (RIBA Nat. Award); Library, Newnham Coll., Cambridge, and Courtyard Develt, Fitzwilliam Mus., Cambridge, 2004 (RIBA Nat. Award, 2005); Playfair Project, Nat. Galls of Scotland, 2004; Brindley Arts Centre, 2005 (RIBA Nat. Award; Civic Trust Award). Exhibition Designs: Dada and Surrealism Reviewed, 1978; Ten Modern Houses, 1980; Picasso's Picassos, 1981; Adolf Loos, 1985; Matisse Picasso, 2002; Anthony Caro, 2006. Tutor: RCA and AA, 1961–73; Cambridge Sch. of Arch., 1969–70; Prof. of Environmental Design, RCA, 1975–85, Fellow 1976, Hon. Fellow, 1985. FRSA 1985. Vis. Prof., Sch. of Arch., UC Dublin, 1985. Visiting Critic: Cornell Univ. Sch. of Arch., Ithaca, 1966, 1968 and 1971; Princeton Univ. Sch. of Arch., NJ, 1970; Dublin Univ. Sch. of Arch., 1972–73; Univ. of Toronto, 1985. European Prize for Architecture, 1988. *Publications:* contribs to architect. jls. *Address:* Apt 10, The Beauchamp Building, Brookes Market, EC1N 7SX. *T:* (020) 7242 2404.

MILLER, Jonathan; Foreign Affairs Correspondent, Channel 4 News, since 2003; *b* 21 Oct. 1962; *s* of John Miller and Sheila Rankin; *m* 1994, Cornelia Dobb; one *d*. *Educ:* Monkton Combe Sch., Bath; Durham Univ. (BA Hons Geog.). Journalist, South mag., 1986–89; freelance journalist and guidebook writer, SE Asia, 1989–92; journalist, BBC World Service, 1992–94; Indochina Corresp., 1994–95, Bangkok Corresp., 1995–97, BBC; ind. documentary-maker and reporter, 1997–2003. Specialist Journalist of the Year, 2006, Internat. News Award, 2006, RTS; TV News Award, Amnesty Internat., 2006. *Recreations:* travelling, cooking, mountain walking. *Address:* Channel 4 News, ITN, 200 Gray's Inn Road, WC1X 8XZ. *T:* (020) 7430 4606; *e-mail:* jonathan.miller@itn.co.uk.

MILLER, Sir Jonathan (Wolfe), Kt 2002; CBE 1983; stage director, writer and broadcaster; *b* 21 July 1934; *s* of late Emanuel Miller, DPM, FRCP; *m* 1956, Helen Rachel Collet; two *s* one *d*. *Educ:* St Paul's Sch.; St John's Coll., Cambridge (MB, BCh 1959; Hon. Fellow 1982). FRCP 1997; FRCPE 1998. Research Fellow: in Hist. of Med., UCL, 1970–73; in Neuropsychol., Univ. of Sussex. Associate Director, Nat. Theatre, 1973–75; Artistic Dir, Old Vic, 1988–90. Mem., Arts Council, 1975–76. Vis. Prof. in Drama, Westfield Coll., London, 1977; Fellow, UCL, 1981–. Co-author and appeared in Beyond the Fringe, 1961–64; stage directing in London and NY, 1965–67; *television:* Editor, BBC Monitor, 1965; directed films for BBC TV (incl. Alice in Wonderland), 1966; Exec. Producer, BBC Shakespeare series, 1979–81; writer and presenter, TV series, including: The Body in Question, 1978; Madness, 1991; Opera Works, 1997; Jonathan Miller's Brief History of Disbelief, 2004; *radio:* Self-Made Things (series), Radio 4, 2005; *stage:* School for Scandal, 1968, The Seagull, 1969, The Malcontent, 1973, Nottingham Playhouse; King Lear, The Merchant of Venice, Old Vic, 1970; The Tempest, Mermaid, 1970; Hamlet, Arts Theatre, Cambridge, 1970; Danton's Death, 1971, School for Scandal, 1972, Measure for Measure, 1974, Marriage of Figaro, 1974, The Freeway, 1974, Nat. Theatre; The Taming of the Shrew, 1972, The Seagull, 1973, Chichester; Family Romances, 1974, The Importance of Being Earnest, 1975, All's Well That Ends Well, 1975, Greenwich; Three Sisters, Cambridge, 1976; She Would If She Could, Greenwich, 1979; Long Day's Journey Into Night, Haymarket, 1986; The Taming of the Shrew, RSC, Stratford, 1987, Barbican, 1988; (jtly adapted and directed) The Emperor, Royal Court, 1987 (televised, 1988); Andromache, One Way Pendulum, Bussy D'Ambois, The Tempest, Candide, Old Vic, 1988; King Lear, The Liar, Old Vic, 1989; The Way of the World, Gate Theatre, Dublin, 1992; A Midsummer Night's Dream, Almeida, 1996; As You Like It, Gate Theatre, Dublin, 2000; The Cherry Orchard, Crucible, Sheffield, 2007; Hamlet, Tobacco Factory, Bristol. 2008; *film:* Take a Girl Like You, 1970; *operas:* Arden Must Die, Sadler's Wells Theatre, 1974; The Cunning Little Vixen, Glyndebourne, 1975 and 1977; English National Opera: The Marriage of Figaro, 1978; The Turn of the Screw, 1979, 1991; Arabella, 1980; Otello, 1981; Rigoletto, 1982, 1985, 1995; Don Giovanni, 1985; The Magic Flute, 1986; Tosca, 1986; The Mikado, 1986, 1988, 1993, 2004, 2006; The Barber of Seville, 1987, 2006; Der Rosenkavalier, 1994; Carmen, 1995; La Traviata, 1996; Kent Opera: Così Fan Tutte, 1975; Rigoletto, 1975; Orfeo, 1976; Eugene Onegin, 1977; La Traviata, 1979; Falstaff, 1980, 1981; Fidelio, 1982, 1983, 1988; La Scala: La Fanciulla del West, 1991; Manon Lescaut, 1992; Maggio Musicale, Florence: Don Giovanni, 1990; Così fan Tutte, Tosca, 1991; Marriage of Figaro, 1992; Idomeneo, 1996; Metropolitan Opera, New York: Katya Kabanova, 1991; Pelléas et Mélisande, 1995; Marriage of Figaro, Vienna State Opera, 1991; Roberto Devereux, Monte Carlo, 1992; Die Gezeichnete, Zürich, 1992; Maria Stuarda, Monte Carlo, 1993; The Secret Marriage, Opera North, 1993; Falstaff, Zürich, 1993; L'Incoronazione di Poppea, Glimmerglass Opera, 1994; Così fan tutti, Royal Opera House, and Rome, 1995; The Beggar's Opera, Wilton's Music Hall, 1999; Don Pasquale, Royal Opera House, 2004; La Clemenza di Tito, Zürich, 2005; St Matthew Passion, Brooklyn Acad. of Music, 2006; *exhibitions:* Mirror Image: Jonathan Miller on reflection, Nat. Gall., 1998; Metal, wood and paper constructions, Boundary Gall., 2003. Hon. Fellow, RA, 1991; Hon. DLitt: Leicester, 1981; Cambridge, 1996. Silver Medal, Royal TV Soc., 1981; Albert Medal, RSA, 1990. *Publications:* McLuhan, 1971; (ed) Freud: the man, his world, his influence, 1972; The Body in Question, 1978; Subsequent Performances, 1986; (ed) The Don Giovanni Book: myths of seduction and betrayal, 1990; On Reflection, 1998. *Recreation:* deep sleep. *Address: e-mail:* jwmiller@btinternet.com.

MILLER, Judith Henderson; author and publishing consultant; *b* 16 Sept. 1951; *d* of Andrew and Bertha Cairns; *m* 1978, Martin John Miller, *qv* (marr. diss. 1992); two *d. Educ:* Galashiels Acad.; Edinburgh Univ. (MA Hons English, 1973). Copywriter, WHT Advertising, Auckland, NZ, 1973–74; Editor, Lyle Publications, Galashiels, 1974–75; Occupational Guidance Officer, Dept of Employment, 1975–79; Man. Dir and Editor, Miller Publications, 1979–98; with Martin Miller opened Chilston Park Hotel, 1985; Man. Dir, MJM Publishing Projects, 1985–92; Co-Founder, Miller's Magazine, 1991. Television appearances include The House Detectives, The Art and Antiques Hour, The Antiques Trail, The Martha Stewart Show, Antiques Roadshow. *Publications:* Miller's Antiques and Collectables: the facts at your fingertips, 1993; Miller's Classic Motorcycles Price Guide, annually, 1993–98; Miller's Art Nouveau and Art Deco Buyer's Guide, 1995; Miller's Pine and Country Furniture Buyer's Guide, 1995; Period Kitchens, 1995; Period Fireplaces, 1995; How to Make Money out of Antiques, 1995; Period Soft Furnishings, 1996; Country Finishes and Effects, 1997; Miller's Clocks and Barometers Buyer's Guide, 1997; Wooden Houses, 1997; Care and Repair of Antiques and Collectables, 1997; The Style Sourcebook, 1998; Classic Style, 1998; Miller's Antiques Encyclopaedia, 1998; Period Details Sourcebook, 1999; A Closer Look at Antiques, 2000; Colour, 2000; Dorling Kindersley Antiques Price Guide, annually, 2003–; Collectables Price Guide, annually, 2003–; (with John Wainwright) Dorling Kindersley Collectors Guide to Costume Jewellery, 2003; Art Nouveau, 2004; Twentieth Century Glass, 2004; Arts and Crafts, 2005; Art Deco, 2005; Dorling Kindersley Furniture, 2005; Twentieth Century Roadshow, 2005; Buy, Keep or Sell, 2005; Tribal Art, 2006; Handbags, 2006; Perfume Bottles, 2006; Sixties Style, 2006; Metal Toys, 2006; Decorative Arts, 2006; Antiques Detective, 2007; with Martin Miller: Miller's Antiques Price Guide, annually 1979–98; The Antiques Directory—Furniture, 1985; Period Details, 1987; Miller's Pocket Antiques Fact File, 1988; Period Style, 1989; Understanding Antiques, 1989; Miller's Collectables Price Guide, annually 1989–98; Country Style, 1990; Miller's Collectors Cars Price Guide, annually 1991–98; Miller's Art Deco Checklist, 1991; Furniture Checklist, 1991; Period Finishes and Effects, 1992; Victorian Style, 1993. *Recreations:* antiques!, bridge. *Club:* Groucho.

MILLER, Julian Alexander, CB 2003; Director General, Resources and Plans, Ministry of Defence, since 2006; *b* 14 July 1955; *s* of Allan Douglas Stewart Miller and Mavis Jean Miller; *m* 1986, Roslin Mair; one *s* one *d. Educ:* Farnham Grammar Sch.; Sussex Univ. (BSc); Leeds Univ. (PhD 1980). Joined MoD, 1980: on loan to CSD, 1988; Private Sec. to Armed Forces Minister, 1990–92; on loan to FCO as First Sec., then Counsellor, UK Delegn to NATO, 1992–96; Hd, Resources and Programmes, Army, then Prog. Develt, 1996–99; Private Sec. to Defence Sec., 1999–2001; on loan to Cabinet Office as Chief, Assessments Staff, 2001–03; Dir Gen., Service Personnel Policy, MoD, 2003–06. *Recreations:* reading, photography. *Address:* c/o Ministry of Defence Main Building, Whitehall, SW1A 2HB.

MILLER, Prof. Karl Fergus Connor; Lord Northcliffe Professor of Modern English Literature, University College London, 1974–92; Editor, 1979–89, and Co-Editor, 1989–92, London Review of Books; *b* 2 Aug. 1931; *s* of William and Marion Miller; *m* 1956, Jane Elisabeth Collet; two *s* one *d. Educ:* Royal High School, Edinburgh; Downing Coll., Cambridge. Asst Prin., HM Treasury, 1956–57; BBC TV Producer, 1957–58; Literary Editor, Spectator, 1958–61; Literary Editor, New Statesman, 1961–67; Editor, Listener, 1967–73. FRSL 1992. *Publications:* (ed) Poetry from Cambridge, 1952–54, 1955; (ed, with introd.) Writing in England Today: The Last Fifteen Years, 1968; (ed) Memoirs of a Modern Scotland, 1970; (ed) A Listener Anthology, August 1967–June 1970, 1970; (ed) A Second Listener Anthology, 1973; (ed) Henry Cockburn, Memorials of his Time, 1974; Cockburn's Millennium, 1975; (ed, with introd.) Robert Burns, 1981; Doubles: studies in literary history, 1985; Authors, 1989; Rebecca's Vest (autobiog.), 1993; Boswell and Hyde, 1995; Dark Horses: an experience of literary journalism (autobiog.), 1998; Electric Shepherd: a likeness of James Hogg, 2003. *Recreation:* watching football. *Address:* 26 Limerston Street, SW10 0HH.

MILLER, Keith William; Director, Keith Miller Consultants Ltd, since 2007; *b* 25 Sept. 1952; *s* of late William George Ernest Miller and of Doris Julia Miller (*née* Stapleton); *m* 1973, Vivien Jean Holding; one *s* one *d. Educ:* Luton Grammar Sch.; Luton Sixth Form Coll.; Univ. of Salford (BSc Civil Engrg 1973). CEng 1979; MICE 1980, FICE 2004; MIHT 1980, FIHT 2004. Norwest Holst, 1973–74; Luton BC, 1974–79; Department of Transport: Project Engr, 1979–86; Principal Private Sec. to Minister of State for Transport, 1986–88; Principal Engr, 1988–93; Projects Dir, 1993–96; Highways Agency: IT Dir, 1996–2000; Divl Dir, 10-Year Strategy, 2000, Lands and Ops Mgt, 2000–03, Dir of Major Projects, 2003–07. Mem. Council, ICE, 2006–. *Publications:* minor contribs in technical press and jls. *Recreations:* meeting friends, painting muddy watercolours, playing games with my grandsons. *Address:* 1 Hartham Close, Grafham, Huntingdon, Cambs PE28 0ED.

MILLER, Dr Kenneth Allan Glen, CBE 1988; FREng, FIMechE; Director General, Engineering Council, 1982–88; *b* 27 July 1926; *s* of Dr Allan Frederick Miller and Margaret Hutchison (*née* Glen); *m* 1st, 1954, Dorothy Elaine Brown (marr. diss. 1999); three *s*; 2nd, 1999, Betty Nanette Hatton (*née* Bridgwater). *Educ:* Upper Canada Coll., Toronto; Trinity Hall, Cambridge (BA 1946; MA 1950; Hon. Fellow, 1992); PhD Wales, 1949. FIMechE 1965; FREng (FEng 1981). Res. Asst to Prof. of Physics, Aberystwyth, 1946; joined ICI, Billingham, 1949; various posts on production and design, 1949–59; seconded to BTC, 1959–60; Asst Tech. Manager, 1960, Engrg Manager, 1963, Engrg Dir, 1965, HOC Div., ICI; Engrg Advr, ICI, 1971; Managing Director: APV Co., 1974; APV Holdings, 1977–82. Chm., Pollution Control and Measurement (Europe), subseq. PCME, Ltd, 1993–2002. Deputy Chairman: ECCTIS 2000 Ltd, 1990–96; standing Conf. on Schs' Sci. and Technology, 1990–96. Member: Cttee for Industrial Technol., 1972–76; UGC, 1981–83; Chm., Steering Cttee for Manufrg Adv. Service, 1977–82. Member Council: Fellowship of Engrg, 1982–85; CRAC, 1987–96. FInstD 1974; CCMI (CIMgt 1985). *Publication:* The Outspoken Dr Miller (memoirs), 2006. *Recreations:* theatre, photography. *Address:* 66 Trematon Place, Broom Road, Teddington, Middx TW11 9RH. *T:* (020) 8943 3561. *Club:* Leander.

MILLER, Kenneth William, FCA; Chairman, Colt Group, since 2000; *b* 4 Feb. 1939; *s* of Albert William Miller and Winifred (*née* Ashworth); *m* 1st, 1964, Carol Susan Hislop (marr. diss. 1987); one *s* one *d*; 2nd, 1988, Jean Helen McPhail McInnes. *Educ:* Surbiton County Grammar Sch. FCA 1961. Company Sec., Hunting Associated Industries, 1965–73; Asst Finance Dir, Hunting Gp, 1969–73; Commercial Dir, E. A. Gibson & Co. Ltd, 1973–78; Hunting Petroleum Services plc: Dir, 1978–87; Man. Dir, 1987–89; Chief Exec., Hunting plc, 1989–2000. *Recreations:* reading, sport, music. *Address:* Colt Group, New Lane, Havant, Hants PO9 2LY. *T:* (023) 9245 1111. *Club:* Royal Automobile.

MILLER, Leszek; Deputy (Dem. Left Alliance) for Łódź, 1991–2005; Prime Minister of Poland, 2001–04; *b* Zyrardów, 3 July 1946; *m* 1969, Aleksandra Borowiec; one *s. Educ:* Higher Sch. of Social Scis, Warsaw (MPolSci.). Electrician, Enterprise of Linen industry, Zyrardów, 1963–70; became social and trade union activist, 1970; Polish United Workers' Party (PUWP): Youth Div., 1977–84, staff mem., 1988–99, Central Cttee; First Sec., Voivodeship's Cttee, 1985–88; Mem., Politburo Central Cttee, 1989–90. Minister: of Labour and Social Policy, 1993–96; and Hd, Council of Ministers' Office, 1996; of Internal Affairs and Admin, 1997. Socialdemocracy party, now Democratic Left Alliance: Gen. Sec., 1990–93; Vice-Chm., 1993–97; Chm., 1997–2001. Goodwill Ambassador, Polish Cttee, UNICEF, 2000–. Golden Cross of Merit, 1979; Kt's Cross, Polonia Restituta (Poland), 1984. *Recreations:* angling, literature.

MILLER, Prof. Marcus Hay, PhD; Professor of Economics, University of Warwick, since 1974; *b* 9 Sept. 1941; *s* of J. Irvine Miller and Rose H. (*née* Moir); *m* 1967, Margaret Ellen Hummel (marr. diss.; she *d* 2001); two *d. Educ:* Price's Sch., Fareham, Hants; University Coll., Oxford (BA 1st Cl. PPE); Yale Univ. (Henry Fellowship, MA, PhD Econ). Lecturer, London School of Economics, 1967–76; Prof. of Economics, Univ. of Manchester, 1976–78. Economist, 1972–73, Houblon-Norman Fellow, 1981–82, Bank of England; Vis. Associate Prof. of Internat. Finance, Univ. of Chicago, 1976; Vis. Prof. of Public and Internat. Affairs, Princeton Univ., 1983; Res. Fellow, Centre for Economic Policy Res., 1983– (Co-Dir, Internat Macroeconomics Prog., 1986–91); Vis. Fellow, Inst. for Internat. Econs, Washington, 1986–. Member, Academic Panel, HM Treasury, 1976– (Chm., 1979–80); Adviser, House of Commons Select Cttee on the Treasury and Civil Service, 1980–81. Mem. Management Cttee, NIESR, 1980–91. *Publications:* joint editor: Monetary Policy and Economic Activity in West Germany, 1977; Essays on Fiscal and Monetary Policy, 1981; Targets and Indicators: a blueprint for the international co-ordination of economic policy, 1993; Exchange Rate Targets and Currency Bands 1992; The Asian Financial Crisis, 1999; articles in professional jls, mainly on domestic and internat. macroecons. *Recreations:* sailboarding, contemporary dance. *Address:* Department of Economics, University of Warwick, Coventry CV4 7AL; *e-mail:* m.h.miller@warwick.ac.uk. *Club:* Reform.

MILLER, Maria Frances Lewis; MP (C) Basingstoke, since 2005; *b* 26 March 1964; *d* of John and June Lewis; *m* 1990, Iain Miller; two *s* one *d. Educ:* London Sch. of Econs (BSc Hons Econs 1985). Advertising Exec., Grey Advertising, 1985–90; Advertising and Mktg Manager, Texaco, 1990–95; Director: Grey Advertising, 1995–2000; Rowland Co., then PR21, 2000–02. Pres., Wolverhampton NE Cons. Assoc., 2001–; Chm., Wimbledon Cons. Assoc., 2002–03. *Recreation:* three children under the age of 12. *Address:* House of Commons, SW1A 0AA. *T:* (020) 7219 3000; *e-mail:* millerm@parliament.uk.

MILLER, Martin John; Chairman, City Diaries, since 1997; Co-Founder and Managing Director, Milroy Estates Ltd, since 1983; *b* 24 Nov. 1946; *s* of Marcus and Phyllis Miller; *m* 1st, 1966, Elaine (marr. diss. 1975); three *d*; 2nd, 1978, Judith Henderson Cairns (*see* J. H. Miller) (marr. diss. 1992); two *d*; 3rd, 2001, Ioana Beju. *Educ:* West Tarring Secondary Modern Sch., Worthing. Freelance photographer, 1965–68; Co-Founder, Lyle Publications, 1968–74; semi-retirement, 1974–79; Co-Founder, MJM Publications, 1979; Co-Founder, and Publisher, Miller's Magazine, 1991–95; Co-Founder, Martin Miller's Gin, 1999; with Judith Miller opened Chilston Park Hotel, 1985; opened: Miller's Residence, Notting Hill, 1997; Miller's Academy of Arts and Science, 2006; Glencot House Hotel, Somerset, 2007. *Publications:* Miller's Collectables Price Guide (with Judith Miller, annually, 1989–98); Antiques Source Book (annually, 2000–06); Antiques: furniture, 2002; Antiques Collectables, 2002; 20th Century Antiques, 2003; The Complete Guide to Antiques, 2003; Disjointed Noughts: collected poems, 2006; with Judith Miller: Miller's Antiques Price Guide, annually, 1979–98; The Antiques Directory—Furniture, 1985; Period Details, 1987; Miller's Antique Pocket Fact File, 1988; Period Style, 1989; Understanding Antiques, 1989; Country Style, 1990; Miller's Collectors Cars Price Guide, annually 1991–98; Miller's Art Deco Checklist, 1991; Furniture Checklist, 1991; Period Finishes and Effects, 1992; Victorian Style, 1993. *Recreations:* shooting, indulging in fine wines and gourmet food. *Club:* Groucho.

MILLER, Dame Mary Elizabeth H.; *see* Hedley-Miller.

MILLER, Michael A.; *see* Ashley-Miller.

MILLER, Rev. Canon Paul; Vicar of Shortlands, Bromley, since 2001; Chaplain to the Queen, since 2005; *b* 24 Feb. 1949; *s* of late Sidney George Miller and Florence Lilian Miller; *m* 1976, Lynette Jane Warren; three *s. Educ:* Cannock Sch., Chelsfield; Bromley Grammar Sch. for Boys; Oak Hill Theol Coll. Ordained deacon 1974, priest 1975; Assistant Curate: Upton, dio. Exeter, 1974–77; Farnborough, dio. Guildford, 1977–78; Vicar: St Luke, Torquay, 1978–86; Green Street Green and Pratts Bottom, 1986–2001; Rural Dean of Orpington, 1996–2001. Hon. Canon, Rochester, 2000–; Anglican Ecumenical Borough Dean, Bromley, 2006–. SBStJ 1984. *Recreations:* cricket, golf, football, travel, philately. *Address:* The Vicarage, 37 Kingswood Road, Shortlands, Bromley BR2 0HG. *T:* (020) 8460 4989, *Fax:* (020) 8289 7577; *e-mail:* canonpmiller@aol.com.

MILLER, Sir Peter (North), Kt 1988; Chairman, Lloyd's, 1984–87; Chairman, The Miller Insurance Group Ltd (formerly Thos R. Miller & Son (Holdings)), 1971–83 and 1988–96; *b* 28 Sept. 1930; *s* of Cyril Thomas Gibson Risch Miller, CBE and Dorothy Alice North Miller, JP; *m* 1991, Jane Herbertson; one *s* and two *s* one *d* by previous marriage. *Educ:* Rugby (1st XV and Capt. of running); Lincoln Coll., Oxford (MA Hons; full blue, cross country; Hon. Fellow, 1992); City Univ. (DSc). National Service, Intelligence Corps, 1949–50. Joined Lloyd's, 1953; qualified as barrister, 1954; Partner, Thos R. Miller & Son (Insurance), 1959, Sen. Partner, 1971–96. Dep. Chm., Lloyd's Insurance Brokers' Assoc., 1974–75, Chm. 1976–77; Mem., Cttee of Lloyd's, 1977–80 and 1982–89 (Mem. Council of Lloyd's, 1983–89); in charge of team responsible for passage of Lloyd's Bill (Fisher), 1980–82. Member: Baltic Exchange, 1966–; Insurance Brokers' Registration Council, 1977–81; Vice-Pres., British Insce Brokers' Assoc., 1978–96; Chm., British Cttee of Bureau Veritas, 1980–2002. Chm. of Trustees, Lloyd's Tercentenary Foundn, 1989–2007. One of HM's Lieutenants for the City of London, 1987–. Mem., Chief Pleas, Sark, 1969–. Mem., Rector's Council, Lincoln Coll., Oxford, 1992–. Commendatore, Ordine al Merito della Repubblica Italiana, 1989. Hon. DSc City, 1987. *Recreations:* all sport (except cricket), including tennis, running, sailing; wine, music, old churches, gardening. *Address:* c/o Miller Insurance Group, Dawson House, 5 Jewry Street, EC3N 2PJ. *Clubs:* City of London, Travellers; Vincent's (Oxford); Thames Hare and Hounds.

MILLER, Prof. Richard Albert, OBE 1976; FRAeS; FCMI; Chairman, DGB Sterling (formerly Dinol (GB)) Ltd, since 1998; *b* 12 July 1936; *s* of Albert and Emily Kate Miller; *m* 1959, Beryl Marjorie Thompson; one *s* one *d*. *Educ:* Northampton Grammar Sch.; Coll. of Art, Nottingham; Open Univ. (DipEd, BA Hons); Poly. of E London (MA, MSc). Royal Air Force, 1956–82, Pilot; Flying Duties, 1957–70; RAF Advanced Staff Course, 1970; MoD, 1971–72; OC 36 Sqn, RAF Lyneham, 1973–75; Station Comdr, RAF Benson and Dep. Captain of Queen's Flight, 1976–78; ADC to the Queen, 1976–78; RAF Diamond Jubilee Fellow, Univ. of S Calif and Fitzwilliam Coll., Cambridge, 1979; Dir, Dept of Air Warfare, RAF Coll., 1980; Dir, Air Staff Briefing, MoD, 1981–82; Dir, PR (RAF), MoD, 1982–84; retired (Air Cdre). Executive Air Weapons, BAe Inc., USA, 1985–86; Dir, Defence Procurement Management Gp, 1986–88, Dean, Continuing Educn, 1987–89, Dir, Sch. of Defence Management, 1988–95, RMCS; Dir of Strategic Mgt, Sch. of Defence Mgt, RMCS, Cranfield Univ., 1995–97. Visiting Professor: Cranfield Univ., 1997–2006; Bath Univ., 1999–. Freedom, City of London, 1982. QCVSA 1965, 1970. *Recreations:* reading, significant DIY, computing. *Address:* 4 Walnut Tree Grove, Brampton, Huntingdon, Cambs PE28 4UG. *T:* (01480) 451485. *Club:* Royal Air Force.

MILLER, Richard Charles William; Executive Director, ActionAid UK, since 2004; *b* 5 March 1962; *s* of Prof. David Louis Miller, *qv*; *m* 1992, Sally Gardner; three *s*. *Educ:* Leys Sch., Cambridge; Univ. of Bristol (BSc Hons Soc. Admin and Pols 1984). Catholic Agency for Overseas Development: Africa Progs Officer, 1986–92; Dep. Dir, 1992–98; S Africa Regl Rep., 1998–2003. Mem., Adv. Bd, Traidcraft Exchange, 1986–89. Trustee: IVS, 1984–87; Disasters Emergency Cttee, 2004–. *Recreations:* family, travel, African music, watching my sons play sport. *Address:* ActionAid, Hamlyn House, Macdonald Road, N19 5PG. *T:* (020) 7561 7561, *Fax:* (020) 7272 0899; *e-mail:* richard.miller@actionaid.org.

MILLER, Richard Hugh; QC 1995; *b* 1 Feb. 1953; *s* of Sir Stephen James Hamilton Miller, KCVO, FRCS and Lady (Heather) Miller. *Educ:* Charterhouse; Univ. of Sussex (BSc Chem. Physics). Called to the Bar, Middle Temple, 1976, Bencher, 2007; specialising in patent matters. Chm., Intellectual Property Bar Assoc., 2005– (Vice-Chm., 2004–05); Member: Bar Council, 2006– (Mem., European Cttee, 2005–, Professional Practice Cttee, 2008–); Council, UK Gp, Internat. Assoc. for Protection of Intellectual Property, 2006–. *Publication:* (ed jtly) Terrell on the Law of Patents, 14th edn 1994 to 16th edn 2006. *Recreations:* travel, films. *Address:* 3 New Square, Lincoln's Inn, WC2A 3RS. *T:* (020) 7405 1111.

MILLER, Richard Morgan; Chief Executive, Willis Corroon Group plc, 1990–94; *b* Nashville, Tenn, 1931; *m* 1953, Betty Ruth Randolph; one *s* two *d*. *Educ:* Montgomery Bell Acad., Nashville; Vanderbilt Univ., Nashville (BA 1953); Wharton Sch., Univ. of Pennsylvania. Served Korean War, 1953–55, Lt US Marine Corps; retired from US Marine Corps Reserve, 1960, Capt. Salesman, Dominion Insce Agency, 1955–58; established Richard M. Miller & Co., 1958, Pres., 1958–70; merger with Synercon Corp., 1970: Founder, Dir, Pres. and Chief Exec. Officer, 1970–76 (also Pres. and Chief Exec. Officer subsid. cos); Synercon Corp. merged into Corroon & Black Corp., 1976: Exec. Vice-Pres., Chief Operating Officer and Dir, 1976–78; Pres., Chief Operating Officer and Dir, 1978–88; Chief Exec. Officer, Pres. and Dir, 1988–89; Chm. Bd, Chief Exec. Officer and Dir, 1990–93; Corroon & Black Corp. merged into Willis Faber plc, 1990. Member, National Associations of: Casualty and Surety Agents; Insurance Brokers; Surety Bond Producers; Mem., Nat. Fedn of Independent Business; Director: Consumer Benefit Life Insce Co.; Meridian Insce Co. (Bermuda); Third Nat. Bank; Third Nat. Corp. Trustee and Member Executive Committee: Insce Inst. of America; Amer. Inst. for Property and Liability Underwriters. *Recreation:* golf. *Clubs:* City Midday, New York Athletic (New York); Belle Meade Country, Cumberland, Nashville City, Tennessee (Nashville, Tennessee); John's Island (Florida); Mid Ocean (Bermuda).

MILLER, Robert Alexander Gavin D.; *see* Douglas Miller.

MILLER, Robin Anthony; a Recorder of the Crown Court, 1978–2003; *b* 15 Sept. 1937; *s* of William Alexander Miller, CBE, BEM, and Winifred Miller; *m* 1962, Irene Joanna Kennedy; two *s* one *d*. *Educ:* Devonport High Sch., Plymouth; Wadham Coll., Oxford (MA). Called to the Bar, Middle Temple, 1960. *Address:* St Michael's Lodge, 192 Devonport Road, Stoke, Plymouth, Devon PL1 5RD. *T:* (01752) 564943.

MILLER, Sir Robin (Robert William), Kt 2003; Chairman: Boosey & Hawkes Music Publishers Ltd; Edge Performance VCT, since 2005. Joined East Midlands Allied Press as jun. reporter, Motor Cycle News, 1965; various sen. editl roles; Man. Dir, Mag. Div., 1974; Mem. Bd, 1976–2003; Chief Exec., 1985–98 and 2001–03, non-exec. Chm., 1998–2001, Emap plc. Non-exec. Chm., HMV Gp, 2004–05; non-executive Director: Moss Bros plc, 1998–2001; Channel 4 TV; former non-exec. Dir, Horserace Totalisator Bd. Chm., E Regl Sports Bd, Sport England, 2003–05; Mem. Panel, UK Sports Inst., 2000–. *Address:* (office) Aldwych House, 71–91 Aldwych, WC2B 4HN.

MILLER, Sir Ronald (Andrew Baird), Kt 1993; CBE 1985; CA; *b* 13 May 1937; *m* 1965, Elizabeth Ann Gordon; one *s* one *d*. *Educ:* Daniel Stewart's Coll.; Univ. of Edinburgh (BSc). With Dawson Internat., 1968–95: Dir, 1976; Chm. and Chief Exec., 1982–91; Exec. Chm., 1991–95. Director: Securities Trust of Scotland, 1983–2001; Christian Salvesen, 1987–97; Aggreko, 1997–2002; Mem. Bd, Scottish Amicable, 1997–2003 (Dir, Scottish Amicable Life Assce Soc., 1987–97, Dep. Chm., 1994–97). Chairman: British Knitting and Clothing Export Council (later British Fashion Exports), 1993–97 (Mem., 1987–98; Vice Pres., 1997–); Scottish Textile Assoc., 1992–95 (Mem., 1992–98); Cttee of Chairmen of Scottish Higher Educn Instns, 1999–2001; Member: N Amer. Adv. Gp, DTI, 1986–96; ScotBIC, 1990–95; Quality Scotland, 1991–95; Scottish Council, CBI, 1992–95; British Apparel and Textile Confedn, 1993–95; SHEFC, 1992–95; Quality Assurance Agency for Higher Educn, 1997–2003 (Chm., Scottish Cttee, 1998–2003); Walpole Cttee, 1992–95; SCOTrust, 1994–99. Mem. Court, Napier Univ., 1992–2001 (Chm. Court, 1998–2001). Liveryman, Woolmen's Co., 1992–. FRSA; CCMI. DSc *hc* Heriot-Watt, 1992; DUniv Napier, 2001. *Club:* Caledonian.

MILLER, Ronald Kinsman, CB 1989; Solicitor of Inland Revenue, 1986–90, retired; part-time Chairman, VAT and Duties Tribunals, 1991–2002; *b* 12 Nov. 1929; *s* of William Miller and Elsie May Kinsman; *m* 1952, Doris Alice Dew; one *s* one *d*. *Educ:* Colchester Royal Grammar Sch. Served RN, 1948–50. Called to the Bar, Gray's Inn, 1953. Joined Inland Revenue, 1950; Asst Solicitor, 1971; Law Officers' Dept, 1977–79; Principal Asst Solicitor, 1981–86. *Recreations:* gardening, reading, music. *Address:* 4 Liskeard Close, Chislehurst, Kent BR7 6RT. *T:* (020) 8467 8041. *Club:* Athenæum.

MILLER, Dr Roy Frank; Vice-Principal, 1985–98, Hon. Research Fellow in Physics, since 1998, Royal Holloway and Bedford New College, University of London; *b* 20 Sept. 1935; *s* of Thomas R. Miller and Margaret Ann Tattum; *m* 1961, Ruth Naomi Kenchington; one *s*. *Educ:* Wembley County Grammar Sch.; University Coll. SW England, Exeter; Royal Holloway Coll. BSc, PhD; CPhys, FInstP. Teacher, Halbutt Secondary Modern Sch., 1957; Royal Holloway College: Demonstrator, 1957, Asst Lectr, 1960, Lectr, 1963, Sen. Lectr, 1973, Physics Dept; Vice-Principal, 1978–81; Acting Principal, 1981–82; Principal, 1982–85; Hon. Fellow, 2000. Research Associate and Teaching Fellow, Case Western Reserve Univ., Ohio, USA, 1967–68. Mem. Senate, Univ. of London, 1981–85; Chm., Bd, Inst. of Classical Studies, Univ. of London, 1983–2001; Trustee and Governor, Strode's Foundn, Strode's Coll., Egham, 1982–. MRI. *Publications:* articles in Jl Phys C, Phil. Mag., Vacuum. *Recreations:* mountaineering, squash, music. *Club:* Athenæum.

MILLER, Sidney James, MA; Citizens' Advice Bureau Adviser, Bedford, since 1995; *b* 25 Jan. 1943; *s* of Sidney Tomsett Miller and Mary Ada Miller (*née* Marshall); *m* 1971, Judith Branney (*née* Passingham); three *s* one *d*. *Educ:* Clifton Coll., Bristol; Jesus Coll., Cambridge (MA); Harvard Univ. VIth Form Classical Master and House Tutor, Clifton Coll., Bristol, 1965–68; Asst Master and Classical Tutor, Eton Coll., 1968–73, Head of Classical Dept, 1971–73; Dep. Headmaster (Organisation), Bridgewater Hall, Stantonbury Campus, Milton Keynes, 1974–77; Headmaster, Kingston Grammar Sch., Kingston upon Thames, 1977–86; Head Master, Bedford Sch., 1986–88; Professional Officer, Sch. Exams and Assessment Council, 1988–89; HEO, DES, later DFE, 1989–95. Mem., Gen. Synod of C of E, 1994–95. Dir, Bedford Concern for the Homeless and Rootless, 1996– (Chm., 2005–). Founder Mem., Bedford Millennium Probus Club, 1999– (Chm., 2007–08). *Publications:* (ed jtly) Greek Unprepared Translation, 1968; (ed jtly) Inscriptions of the Roman Empire AD14–117, 1971; article in Didaskalos, 1972. *Recreations:* watching sports, learning languages, walking. *Address:* 43 Waterloo Road, Bedford MK40 3PG. *Clubs:* MCC; Achilles; Bedford Rugby.

MILLER of Glenlee, Sir Stephen (William Macdonald), 8th Bt *cr* 1788, of Glenlee, Kirkcudbrightshire; FRCGP; General Practitioner, since 1986; *b* 20 June 1953; *s* of Sir Macdonald Miller of Glenlee, 7th Bt and Marion Jane Audrey Pettit, (Audrey, Lady Miller of Glenlee); *S* father, 1991; *m* 1st, 1978, Mary (*d* 1989), *d* of G. B. Owens; one *s* one *d*; 2nd, 1990, Caroline Clark (*née* Chasemore); one step *s* one step *d*. *Educ:* Rugby Sch.; St Bartholomew's Hosp. MB; FRCS 1981; MRCGP 1986, FRCGP 1995. Surgical Registrar, Sheffield, 1979–81; Orthopaedic Registrar, Newcastle, 1982–84. *Publications:* various papers in med. jls. *Recreations:* gardening, fishing. *Heir:* *s* James Stephen Macdonald Miller, *b* 25 July 1981. *Address:* The Lawn, Shebbear, Beaworthy, Devon EX21 5RU.

MILLER, Terence George, TD 1960; MA Cantab; Director, Polytechnic of North London, 1971–80; *b* 16 Jan. 1918; *o s* of late George Frederick Miller, Cambridge, and late Marion Johnston, Port William, Wigtownshire; *m* 1944, Inga Catriona, 3rd *d* of Austin Priestman, MD, Folkestone, Kent; one *s* three *d*. *Educ:* Perse (foundn schol.); Jesus Coll., Cambridge (schol.; Nat. Sci. Tripos, pt 1 cl. 1, pt 2 cl. 1). Wiltshire Prizeman, 1939. Served War of 1939–45: RA, Glider Pilot Regt; RE (TA), 1947–67 (Lt-Col 1964). Harkness Scholar, 1948; Research Fellow, Jesus Coll., 1949–54. University Demonstrator, 1948; Lectr in Geology, Univ. of Keele, 1953; Sen. Lectr, 1963, Prof. of Geography, Univ. of Reading, 1965–67; Principal, University Coll. of Rhodesia, 1967–69; Vis. Prof., Reading Univ., 1969–71. *Publications:* Geology, 1950; Geology and Scenery in Britain, 1953; scientific papers in various jls. *Recreations:* studying command problems in war, beachcombing, listening. *Address:* Plough House, Docking Road, Sedgeford, Norfolk PE36 5LR.

MILLER, Prof. William Lockley, PhD; FBA 1994; FRSE; Edward Caird Professor of Politics, Glasgow University, since 1985; *b* 12 Aug. 1943; *s* of William Lockley Miller and Florence Ratcliffe; *m* 1967, Fiona Thomson; two *s* one *d*. *Educ:* Edinburgh Univ. (MA 1st Cl. Maths and Nat. Phil. 1965); Newcastle Univ. (PhD Computing 1970). Lectr in Politics, Sen Lectr and Prof., Strathclyde Univ., 1968–85. Vis. Prof. in Politics, Virginia Tech., Blacksburg, 1983–84. FRSE 1999. *Publications:* Electoral Dynamics, 1977; The End of British Politics?, 1981; The Survey Method, 1983; (with Martin Harrop) Elections and Voters, 1987; Irrelevant Elections?, 1988; (jtly) How Voters Change, 1990; Media and Voters, 1991; (jtly) Alternatives to Freedom, 1995; (jtly) Political Culture in Contemporary Britain, 1996; (jtly) Values and Political Change in Postcommunist Europe, 1998; (jtly) Models of Local Governance, 2000; (jtly) A Culture of Corruption?, 2001 (Ukrainian edn, 2004); (ed) Anglo-Scottish Relations from 1900 to Devolution and Beyond, 2005; (jtly) Multicultural Nationalism: Islamophobia, Anglophobia and devolution, 2006; (jtly) The Open Economy and its Enemies: public attitudes in east Asia and eastern Europe, 2006. *Recreation:* hill walking. *Address:* Department of Politics, Adam Smith Building, The University, Glasgow G12 8RT. *T:* (0141) 339 8855.

MILLER SMITH, Charles; Chairman: Asia House, since 2007; Artsource Solutions UK Ltd, since 2008; *b* 7 Nov. 1939; *s* of William Smith and Margaret Pettigrew Brownlie Wardrope; adopted grandfather's surname, Miller Smith, 1963; *m* 1st, 1964, Dorothy Agnes Wilson Adams (*d* 1999); one *s* two *d*; 2nd, 2004, Debjani Jash. *Educ:* Glasgow Acad.; St Andrews Univ. (MA). ACCA. Unilever: Financial Dir, Vinyl Products, 1970–73; Head of Planning, 1974; Finance Dir, Walls Meat Co., 1976; Vice-Chm., Hindustan Lever, 1979–81; Speciality Chemicals Group, 1981; Chief Executive: PPF Internat., 1983; Quest Internat., 1986; Financial Dir, Unilever Board, 1989; Exec., Unilever Foods, 1993–94; Imperial Chemical Industries: Dir, 1994–2001; Chief Exec., 1995–99; Chm., 1999–2001; Dep. Chm., 1999–2000, Chm., 2000–07, Chm., Adv. Bd, 2007–, Scottish Power plc. Non-executive Director: Midland Bank, 1994–96; HSBC Hldgs plc, 1996–2001; Firstsource Solutions Ltd, 2001–; Advr, Goldman Sachs, 2002–05; Senior Adviser: Warburg Pincus, 2005–; Deutsche Bank (RREEF Infrastructure), 2007–. Mem. Mgt Bd, MoD, 2002–07. Hon. LLD St Andrews, 1995. *Recreations:* reading, walking. *Address:* Scottish Power plc, 1st Floor, 85 Buckingham Gate, SW1E 6PD. *T:* (020) 7651 2000. *Club:* National.

MILLETT, family name of **Baron Millett**.

MILLETT, Baron *cr* 1998 (Life Peer), of St Marylebone in the City of Westminster; **Peter Julian Millett,** Kt 1986; PC 1994; a Lord of Appeal in Ordinary, 1998–2004; a non-permanent Judge, Court of Final Appeal, Hong Kong, since 2000; *b* 23 June 1932; *s* of late Denis Millett and Adele Millett; *m* 1959, Ann Mireille, *d* of late David Harris; two *s* (and one *s* decd). *Educ:* Harrow; Trinity Hall, Cambridge (Schol.; MA; Hon. Fellow, 1994). Nat. Service, RAF, 1955–57 (Flying Officer). Called to Bar, Middle Temple, 1955, *ad eundem* Lincoln's Inn, 1959 (Bencher, 1980, Treas., 2004), Singapore, 1976, Hong Kong, 1979; at Chancery Bar, 1958–86; QC 1973; a Judge of the High Court of Justice, Chancery Div. 1986–94; a Lord Justice of Appeal, 1994–98. Examnr and Lectr in Practical Conveyancing, Council of Legal Educn, 1962–76. Junior Counsel to Dept of Trade and Industry in Chancery matters, 1967–73. Mem., General Council of the Bar, 1971–75. Outside Mem., Law Commn on working party on co-ownership of matrimonial home, 1972–73; Mem., Dept of Trade Insolvency Law Review Cttee, 1977–82. Pres., West London Synagogue of British Jews, 1991–95. Editor-in-Chief, Encyc. of Forms and Precedents, 1988–. Hon. LLD London, 2000. *Publications:* contrib. to Halsbury's Laws of England; articles in legal jls. *Recreations:* philately, bridge, The Times crossword. *Address:* House of Lords, SW1A 0PW; 18 Portman Close, W1H 6BR. *T:* (020) 7935 1152; St

Andrews, Kewhurst Avenue, Cooden, Bexhill-on-Sea, East Sussex TN39 3BH.
See also R. L. Millett.

MILLETT, Anthea Christine, CBE 2000; Commissioner, Civil Service Commission, since 2007; *b* 2 Nov. 1941; *d* of Rupert Millett and Lucy Millett. *Educ:* Erdington Grammar School for Girls, Birmingham; Bedford Coll., Univ. of London (BA Hons). Teacher: Channing School, Highgate, 1963–65; Bournville Grammar Tech. Sch., Birmingham, 1965–67; Solihull High Sch., 1967–71 (Head of Dept); Dep. Head, Tile Hill Comprehensive Sch., Coventry, 1972–77; HM Inspectorate of Schools, subseq. OFSTED, 1978–95: Chief Inspector, 1987–92; Dir of Inspection, 1993–95; Chief Exec., TTA, 1995–99. Chairman: Wilts HA, 2000–02; Avon, Glos and Wilts Strategic HA, 2002–06. Mem., Cttee of Enquiry, Mgt and Govt of Schools, 1975–77. Trustee, Francis Holland Schs, 1995–2006. FRGS; FRSA. *Recreations:* travel, walking, gardening, DIY.

MILLETT, Prof. Martin John, DPhil; FSA; FBA 2006; Laurence Professor of Classical Archaeology, University of Cambridge, since 2001; Fellow, Fitzwilliam College, Cambridge, since 2001; *b* 30 Sept. 1955; *s* of John Millett and Sybil Vera Millett (*née* Paine); *m* 2005, Joanna Story; one *d*. *Educ:* Inst. of Archaeology, Univ. of London (BA 1977); Merton Coll., Oxford (DPhil 1983). FSA 1984. Asst Keeper of Archaeol., Hants Co. Mus. Service, 1980–81; University of Durham: Lectr, 1981–91; Sen. Lectr, 1991–95; Prof. of Archaeol., 1995–98; Prof. of Classical Archaeol., Univ. of Southampton, 1999–2001. Dir, Soc. of Antiquaries, 2001–07 (Treas., 2007–). Asst Ed., 1986–89, Ed., 1989–94, Archaeological Jl. *Publications:* The Romanization of Britain, 1990; Roman Britain, 1995; ed monographs and papers on Roman archaeology; contrib. numerous articles to learned jls. *Recreations:* food, wine, the outdoors. *Address:* Faculty of Classics, University of Cambridge, Sidgwick Avenue, Cambridge CB3 9DA. *T:* (01223) 335161, *Fax:* (01223) 335409; *e-mail:* mjm62@cam.ac.uk.

MILLETT, Peter Joseph; HM Diplomatic Service; High Commissioner to Cyprus, since 2005; *b* 23 Jan. 1955; *m* 1981, June Harnett; three *d*. Entered FCO, 1974; Vice Consul, Caracas, 1978–80; Second Sec., Doha, 1981–85; FCO, 1986–89; First Sec., UK Repn to EU, Brussels, 1989–93; Hd, Personnel Policy Unit, FCO, 1993–96; Dep. Hd of Mission, Athens, 1997–2001; Hd, Security Strategy Unit, FCO, 2002–05. *Address:* c/o Foreign and Commonwealth Office, King Charles Street, SW1A 2AH.

MILLETT, Hon. Richard (Lester); QC 2003; *b* 29 Sept. 1961; *s* of Baron Millett, *qv*; *m* 1988, Patricia Mary Natalie Spencer; one *s* two *d*. *Educ:* Harrow Sch.; Trinity Hall, Cambridge (BA Hons Classical Tripos Pt 1, Law Tripos Pt 2; lightweight rowing blue, 1983). Called to the Bar, Lincoln's Inn, 1985 (Megarry Prize for Landlord and Tenant Law); Standing Jun. Counsel to the Crown (Treasury A Panel), 2001–03. *Publications:* (with G. Andrews) The Law of Guarantees, 1992, 4th edn 2004; contrib. Law Qly Rev. *Recreations:* Alpinism, gastronomy, fishing. *Address:* 53 Gloucester Avenue, NW1 7BA. *T:* (020) 7267 9804; Essex Court Chambers, 24 Lincoln's Inn Fields, WC2A 3EG. *Clubs:* Royal Automobile, Cumberland Lawn Tennis; Leander (Henley-on-Thames).

MILLGATE, Prof. Michael Henry, PhD; FRSC; FRSL; University Professor of English, Emeritus, Toronto University, since 1994; *b* 19 July 1929; *s* of Stanley Millgate and Marjorie Louisa (*née* Norris); *m* 1960, Jane, *d* of Maurice and Marie Barr. *Educ:* St Catharine's Coll., Cambridge (MA); Michigan Univ.; Leeds Univ. (PhD). Tutor-Organizer, WEA, E Lindsey, 1953–56; Lectr in English Lit., Leeds Univ., 1958–64; Prof. of English and Chm. of the Dept, York Univ., Ont, 1964–67; Prof. of English, Toronto Univ., 1967–94 (University Prof., 1987–94). Killam Sen. Res. Schol., 1974–75, Killam Res. Fellow, 1986–88; John Simon Guggenheim Meml Fellow, 1977–78. FRSC 1982; FRSL 1984. Pierre Chauveau Medal, RSC, 1999. *Publications:* William Faulkner, 1961; (ed) Tennyson: Selected Poems, 1963; American Social Fiction, 1964; (ed jtly) Transatlantic Dialogue, 1966; The Achievement of William Faulkner, 1966; (ed jtly) Lion in the Garden, 1968; Thomas Hardy: his career as a novelist, 1971; (ed jtly) The Collected Letters of Thomas Hardy, vols I-VII, 1978–88; Thomas Hardy: a biography, 1982, rev. and expanded edn as Thomas Hardy: a biography revisited, 2004; (ed) The Life and Work of Thomas Hardy, 1985; (ed) William Faulkner Manuscripts 20, 21, 22 and 23, 1987; (ed) New Essays on Light in August, 1987; (ed) Thomas Hardy: selected letters, 1990; Testamentary Acts: Browning, Tennyson, James, Hardy, 1992; (ed jtly) Thomas Hardy's 'Studies, Specimens &c' Notebook, 1994; (ed) Letters of Emma and Florence Hardy, 1996; Faulkner's Place, 1997; (ed) Thomas Hardy's Public Voice, 2001; (ed jtly) Thomas Hardy's Poetical Matter Notebook, 2008. *Address:* 1 Balmoral Avenue, Apt 809, Toronto, ON M4V 3B9, Canada. *T:* (416) 920 3717.

MILLIGAN, Eric; JP; Member (Lab), City of Edinburgh Council, since 1995; Convener, Lothian and Borders Police Board, 2003–07; *b* 27 Jan. 1951; *m* Janis. *Educ:* Tynecastle High Sch.; Napier Coll. Former printer. Member (Lab): Edinburgh DC, 1974–78; Lothian Regl Council, 1978–96 (Chm., Finance Cttee, 1980–82, 1986–90; Convener, 1990–96); Convener, Edinburgh City Council, 1995–96; Lord Provost and Lord-Lieutenant of Edinburgh, 1996–2003. Mem., COSLA, 1980–82, 1986–96 (Pres., 1988–90). Dir, Edinburgh Fest. Soc., 1996–2003; Chm., Edinburgh Military Tattoo Ltd, 1996–2003. JP Edinburgh, 1996. Hon. FRCSE 2000. Hon. DBA Napier, 1999; DUniv Heriot-Watt, 2004. Chevalier, Ordre Nat. du Mérite (France), 1996. *Recreations:* watching football and Rugby as played by Heart of Midlothian FC and Boroughmuir RFC, listening to music. *Address:* c/o City of Edinburgh Council, City Chambers, High Street, Edinburgh EH1 1YJ. *T:* (0131) 200 2000. *Clubs:* Caledonian; Royal Over-Seas League, Royal Scots, Edinburgh Press (Edinburgh); Boroughmuir Rugby Football.

MILLIGAN, Iain Anstruther; QC 1991; *b* 21 April 1950; *s* of late Wyndham Macbeth Moir Milligan, MBE, TD; *m* 1979, Zara Ann Louise Spearman; one *s* two *d*. *Educ:* Eton; Magdalene College, Cambridge (MA); College of Law. Called to the Bar, Inner Temple, 1973, Bencher, 2002. Head of Chambers, 1999–. *Recreations:* farming, forestry, walking. *Address:* 20 Essex Street, WC2R 3AL. *T:* (020) 7842 1200; Dunesslin, Dunscore, Dumfries DG2 0UR. *T:* (01387) 820345.

MILLIGAN, Scott Gregor; Director, Legal Services Group, Department for Business, Enterprise and Regulatory Reform (formerly Department of Trade and Industry), since 2001; *b* 28 Oct. 1951; *s* of late Gregor Stormont Milligan and Marylla Milligan (*née* Jolles); *m* 1984, Elizabeth Mary Cliff; one *s* two *d*. *Educ:* Christ's Hosp. Sch.; Mansfield Coll., Oxford (BA Modern Hist. 1973). Called to the Bar, Middle Temple, 1975; joined Govt Legal Service, 1977; Legal Asst, 1977–81, Sen. Legal Asst, 1981–85, Dept of Employment; Asst Solicitor, advising Dept of Employment, Treasury Solicitor's Dept and Dept of Energy, 1985–92; Asst Solicitor, DTI, 1992–2001. Chm., Whitehall Prosecutors' Gp, 2001–04. *Recreations:* cycling, singing, squash, Spring Grove Fringe theatre, family activities. *Address:* Department for Business, Enterprise and Regulatory Reform, 10 Victoria Street, SW1H 0NN. *T:* (020) 7215 3144, *Fax:* (020) 7215 3122; *e-mail:* s.milligan@berr.gsi.gov.uk.

MILLIGAN, His Honour Timothy James; a Circuit Judge, 1991–2008; *b* 16 March 1940; *s* of Dr Peter James Wyatt Milligan and Rosemary Elizabeth Ann (*née* Dutton); *m* 1976, Sally Marcella (*née* Priest) (marr. diss. 1999); two step *s*. *Educ:* Frilsham House Prep. School; Winchester Coll.; Grenoble Univ. (1st and 2nd Foreigner's Degrees). Articled Clerk, Taylor Garrett, 1960–65; admitted Solicitor, 1967; Asst Solicitor, Leeds Smith, Beds, 1967–69; Asst Solicitor, then Partner, Triggs Turner, Guildford, 1969–73; Solicitor, then Partner, Warner & Richardson, Winchester, 1973–91; HM Coroner, Central Hants, 1982–91; a Recorder of the Crown Court, 1988–91. Hon. Mem., Coroners Soc. of GB, 1991; Mem. of various Old Wykehamist clubs and assocs. Chm. Disciplinary Cttee of Rackets Cttee, Tennis and Rackets Assoc., 1998–. *Recreations:* rackets, cricket, football, reading, music, theatre, cinema. *Clubs:* MCC; Hampshire CC (Mem. Cttee, 1993–); Jesters; Tennis and Rackets Association (Mem., Rackets Cttee, 1988–98).

MILLIKEN, Hon. Peter (Andrew Stewart); MP (L) Kingston and the Islands, since 1988; Speaker, House of Commons, Canada, since 2001; *b* Kingston, Ont., 12 Nov. 1946; *s* of John Andrew Milliken and Catherine Margaret (*née* McCuaig). *Educ:* Queen's Univ. (BA Hons 1968); Wadham Coll., Oxford (BA 1970, MA 1978); Dalhousie Univ. (LLB 1971). Called to the Bar, Ont., and Solicitor, Supreme Court of Ont., 1973; in practice with Cunningham Swan, Carty, Little & Bonham, 1973–88. Parly Sec. to Govt House Leader, 1993–96; Dep. Chm., Cttees of Whole House, 1996–97; Dep. Speaker and Chm., Cttees of Whole House, 1997–2001. Mem., Coroners' Council, Ont., 1985–88. *Address:* Speaker's Office, House of Commons, Ottawa, ON K1A 0A6, Canada; *e-mail:* milliken@petermilliken.org.

MILLIKEN-SMITH, Mark Gordon; QC 2006; a Recorder of the Crown Court, since 2004; *b* 4 July 1963; *s* of John Michael Milliken-Smith and Gillian Frances Milliken-Smith (*née* Woods, now Bird); *m* 1991, Sybella Anne Wilson; one *s* one *d*. *Educ:* Wellington Coll.; Univ. of Bristol (LLB Hons 1985). Called to the Bar, Gray's Inn, 1986; in practice, specialising in criminal law. *Recreations:* family, variously watching, playing and coaching cricket, Rugby and football. *Address:* 2 Bedford Row, WC1R 4BU. *T:* (020) 7440 8888, *Fax:* (020) 7242 1738; *e-mail:* mmilliken-smith@2bedfordrow.co.uk. *Clubs:* MCC; Hankley Common Golf.

MILLING, Michael Crowley C.; *see* Crowley-Milling.

MILLINGTON, Anthony Nigel Raymond; Director General, Tokyo Office, European Automobile Manufacturers Association, since 1995; *b* 29 Jan. 1945; *m* 1969, Susan Carolyn (*née* Steilberg); two *s*. *Educ:* Ipswich School; Univ. of Grenoble; Trinity College, Cambridge (BA); Univ. of Chicago. HM Diplomatic Service, 1968–94: FCO, 1968; Tokyo, 1969–76; FCO, 1976–80; Paris, 1980–84; Japanese National Defence College, 1984–85; Head of Chancery, Tokyo, 1985–88; Head of Far Eastern Dept, FCO, 1989–90; Rolls-Royce PLC, 1990; Pres., Rolls-Royce (Far East) Ltd, 1990–94 (on leave of absence); FCO, 1994. Mem., Japanese Prime Minister's Regulatory Reform Commn, 1998–2002. Advr to Bd of Dirs, Japan Automobile Importers' Assoc., 2001–. Chm. Bd of Trustees, British Sch. in Tokyo, 2004–. *Recreations:* golf, tennis, walking in the countryside. *Address:* c/o European Automobile Manufacturers Association, PO Box 564, Ark Mori Building, 1–12–32 Akasaka, Minato-ku, Tokyo 107–6030, Japan. *T:* (3) 35054963, *Fax:* (3) 35054871; *e-mail:* anrm@miinet.or.jp. *Clubs:* Royal Automobile; Tokyo Lawn Tennis (Director).

MILLINGTON, Christopher John; QC 2001; a Recorder, since 1995; *b* 31 Oct. 1951; *s* of Dennis Millington and Christine Millington; *m* 1976, Jane Elisabeth Bucknell; one *s* one *d*. *Educ:* Birmingham Univ. (LLB, LLM). Called to the Bar, Gray's Inn, 1976; in chambers, Birmingham, 1976–. *Recreations:* tennis, golf, travel, music, especially rock guitar. *Address:* St Philip's Chambers, 55 Temple Row, Birmingham B2 5LS. *T:* (0121) 246 7000. *Clubs:* Edgbaston Priory Tennis, Blackwell Golf.

MILLINGTON, Wing Comdr Ernest Rogers, DFC 1945; advisor on training, Youth Training Scheme, 1980–90; Teacher in charge of Teachers' Centre, London Borough of Newham, 1967–80, retired; Founder, and Editor, Project, 1967–80; *b* 15 Feb. 1916; *s* of Edmund Rogers Millington and Emily Craggs; *m* 1st, 1937 (marr. diss. 1974); four *d*; 2nd, 1975, Ivy Mary Robinson. *Educ:* Chigwell Sch., Essex; College of S Mark and S John, Chelsea; Birkbeck Coll., London Univ. Clerk; Accountant; Company Sec.; served War of 1939–45, soldier, gunner officer, pilot RAF, instructor and heavy bomber, CO of a Lancaster Sqdn. MP (Commonwealth) for Chelmsford, 1945–50. Re-joined Royal Air Force, 1954–57. Head of Social Educn, Shoreditch Comprehensive Sch., London, 1965–67. *Publications:* (edited): A Study of Film, 1972; The Royal Group of Docks, 1977; A Geography of London, 1979; National Parks, 1980; Was That Really Me? (autobiog.), 2005. *Recreation:* healthy living - ambition to survive to 100! *Address:* Villa Martine, Couze St Front, 24150 Lalinde, France. *T:* 553249431.

MILLINGTON, Tamara; *see* Ingram, T.

MILLION, Clive Ernest; a District Judge, Principal Registry of the Family Division of the High Court, since 1993; a Recorder, since 1999; *b* 7 Sept. 1946; *s* of Arthur Ernest Million and Phyllis May Million; *m* 1975, Pauline Margaret Lock; three *s*. *Educ:* St Dunstan's Coll.; Birmingham Coll. of Art and Design (BA Hons Industrial Design (Engrg) 1969). Called to the Bar, Middle Temple, 1975; an Asst Recorder, 1995–99. *Recreation:* anything legal, but non-legal. *Address:* (office) First Avenue House, 42–49 High Holborn, WC1V 6NP. *T:* (020) 7947 6934.

MILLON, Charles; Ambassador of France to UN Food and Agriculture Organization, since 2003; *b* Belley, Ain, 12 Nov. 1945; *s* of Gabriel Millon and Suzanne Millon (*née* Gunet); *m* Chantal Delsol; six *c*. *Educ:* Lamartine Instn, Belley; Saint-Marie Sch., Lyon. Asst Lectr, 1969; legal and fiscal consultant, 1969–. Deputy (UDF-PR) for Belley-Gex, elected 1978, 1981, 1986, 1988, 1993, 1995, 1997; Mem., Regl Council for Rhône-Alpes, elected 1981, 1986 (Pres., 1988–98); Mem., Gen. Council of the Ain (Canton of Belley), 1985–88; French National Assembly: Vice-Pres., 1986–88; Mem., Foreign Cttee, 1988; Pres., Parly Gp of UDF, 1989–95; Minister of Defence, 1995–97. Pres., Departmental Fedn, PR and UDF, 1983–85; Mem., Pol Bd, PR, 1984–95. Founder, 1998, Pres., 1998–99, Leader, 1999–, Droite Libérale Chrétienne. Mayor of Belley, 1977–2001; Municipal Councillor and Urban Community Councillor, Lyon, 2001–. *Publications:* L'extravagante histoire des nationalisations, 1984; L'alternance-Vérité, 1986; La tentation du conservatisme, 1995; La Paix Civile, 1998; Lettre d'un ami impertinent à Jacques Chirac, 2002. *Address:* (office) 52 Corso del Rinascimento, 00186 Rome, Italy; 46 Boulevard St Michel, 75006 Paris, France.

MILLS, family name of **Viscount Mills**.

MILLS, 3rd Viscount *cr* 1962; **Christopher Philip Roger Mills;** Bt 1953; Baron 1957; Area Manager, Thames Region, Environment Agency, since 1996; *b* 20 May 1956; *s* of 2nd Viscount Mills and Joan Dorothy (*d* 1998), *d* of James Shirreff; *S* father, 1988; *m* 1980, Lesley Alison, *er d* of Alan Bailey. *Educ:* Oundle School; Univ. of London (BSc Hons Biol Scis; MSc Applied Fish Biology); Plymouth Poly. Biologist at Salmon Research Trust of Ireland, 1980–89; National Rivers Authority: Technical Asst, 1989–91; Area Fisheries, Recreation and Ecology Man., NW Region, 1991–95; Area Man., Thames Reg.,

1995–96. Member Council: Inst. of Fisheries Mgt, 1993–; RSPB, 1995–2000. *Publications:* papers in Aquaculture, Aquaculture and Fisheries Management, Fish Biology. *Recreations:* flyfishing, fine wines.

MILLS, Prof. Anne Jane, CBE 2007; PhD; Professor of Health Economics and Policy, since 1995, and Head, Department of Public Health and Policy, since 2006, London School of Hygiene and Tropical Medicine; *b* 26 Jan. 1951; *d* of Maurice and Anthea Mills; *m* 1979, Patrick Corran; two *s. Educ:* Aston Clinton Primary Sch.; Aylesbury High Sch.; Oxford High Sch.; St Hilda's Coll., Oxford (MA Hist. and Econs 1973); Leeds Univ. (Dip. Health Services Studies 1976); PhD Health Econs London Univ. 1990. Fellow, ODI, 1973–75; Res. Officer, Nuffield Inst. for Health Services Studies, 1976–79; Lectr, 1979–86, Sen. Lectr, 1986–92, Reader, 1992–95, in Health Econs, LSHTM. Co-Chm., Wkg Gp 5, Commn on Macroecons and Health, 2000–02. Foreign Associate, Inst. of Medicine, 2006–. FHEA 2007. *Publications:* (with K. Lee) Policy Making and Planning in the Health Sector, 1982; (ed with K. Lee) The Economics of Health in Developing Countries, 1983; (ed jtly) Health System Decentralization Concepts, Issues and Country Experience, 1990; (ed with K. Lee) Health Economics Research in Developing Countries, 1993; (ed jtly) Private Health Providers in Developing Countries: serving the public interest?, 1997; (ed) Reforming Health Sectors, 2000; (jtly) The Challenge of Health Sector Reform: what must governments do?, 2001; (ed jtly) International Public Health, 2001, 2nd edn 2005; (ed jtly) Priorities in Health, 2006; (ed jtly) Disease Control Priorities in Developing Countries, 2nd edn 2006; (ed jtly) Health, Economic Development and Household Poverty: from understanding to action, 2007. *Recreations:* music, walking, cooking. *Address:* London School of Hygiene and Tropical Medicine, Keppel Street, WC1E 7HT. *T:* (020) 7927 2354, *Fax:* (020) 7436 3611; *e-mail:* anne.mills@lshtm.ac.uk.

MILLS, Dame Barbara (Jean Lyon), DBE 1997; QC 1986; QC (NI) 1991; The Adjudicator, since 1999; *b* 10 Aug. 1940; *d* of John and Kitty Warnock; *m* 1962, John Angus Donald Mills; four *c. Educ:* St Helen's Sch., Northwood; Lady Margaret Hall, Oxford (Gibbs Scholar, 1961; MA; Hon. Fellow, 1991). Called to the Bar, Middle Temple, 1963, Bencher, 1990. Jun. Treasury Counsel, Central Criminal Court, 1981–86; a Recorder, 1982–92; Dir, Serious Fraud Office, 1990–92; DPP, 1992–98. Member: Criminal Injuries Compensation Bd, 1988–90; Parole Bd, 1990; Legal Assessor to GMC and GDC, 1988–90; DVO Complaints Assessor, 2001–04. Member: Gen. Adv. Council, BBC, 1991–92; Reporting Panel, Competition Commn, 2001–. Chairman: Forum UK, 1999–2001; Women's Liby Council, 2000–07. Non-exec. Dir, Royal Free Hampstead NHS Trust, 2000–07. Governor, London Metropolitan (formerly London Guildhall) Univ., 1999–2007. Trustee, Victim Support, 1999–2004. Hon. Fellow, Soc. for Advanced Legal Studies, 1997. Hon. LLD: Hull, 1993; Nottingham Trent, 1993; London Guildhall, 1994. *Recreation:* my family. *Address:* (office) 8th Floor, Euston Tower, Euston Road, NW1 3US. *T:* (020) 7667 1382, *Fax:* (020) 7930 2298; *e-mail:* adjudicators@gtnet.gov.uk.

MILLS, Prof. Bernard Yarnton, AC 1976; DSc Eng; FRS 1963; FAA 1959; Professor of Physics (Astrophysics), University of Sydney, 1965–85, Emeritus Professor, 1986; *b* 8 Aug. 1920; *s* of Ellice Yarnton Mills and Sylphide Mills. *Educ:* King's Sch., New South Wales; University of Sydney. BSc 1940, DSc Eng 1959 (Sydney). Joined the then Council for Scientific and Industrial Research and worked on Develt of mil. radar systems; after working for many years on radioastronomy he joined Sydney Univ. to form a radioastronomy group in Sch. of Physics, 1960; Reader in Physics, 1960–65; responsible for Mills Cross radio-telescope, near Hoskinstown, NSW. Lyle Medal of Australian Academy of Science, 1957. *Publications:* (jtly) A Textbook of Radar, 1946; many contribs to sci. jls in Australia, England and America, mainly on subjects of radioastronomy and astrophysics. *Address:* 52 Victoria Street, Roseville, NSW 2069, Australia.

MILLS, David John; Chief Executive, Post Office Ltd, 2002–05; Chairman, My Home Move Ltd, since 2007; *b* 9 Feb. 1944; *s* of John Henry Mills and Violet Germaine Mills; *m* 1967, Lesley Jacqueline Wand; one *s* two *d. Educ:* London Business Sch. (Dist. Sloan Fellow). Joined Midland Bank, later HSBC, 1962; Gen. Manager, HSBC, 1989–2002; Dir, Royal Mail Gp Hldgs, 2002–05. Director: Camelot Gp plc, 2003–06; Cardpoint plc, 2007–. Dir, PIA, 1995–2000. Chm., Employers' Forum on Disability Ltd, 2004–07; Mem., Nat. Disability Council, 1993–95. Trustee, RADAR, 2004–; Vice Pres., Vitalise, 2005–. *Recreations:* family, wine, fishing, motorsport. *Address: e-mail:* david@davidjmills.com. *Club:* Royal Automobile.

MILLS, Prof. Eric William, AM 1986; CChem, FRSC; FRACI; Director, South Australian Institute of Technology, 1978–85, retired; *b* 22 April 1920; *s* of William and Lucy Margaret Mills; *m* 1st, 1945, Inge Julia Königsberger (*d* 1986); three *d*; 2nd, 1993, Natalya Bakaeva; one *d. Educ:* Liverpool Institute; Univ. of Liverpool (BSc, PhD). Chemist, British Insulated Cables, 1941–45; Research Chemist, British Oxygen Co., 1948–49; Sen. Lectr, Birmingham College of Advanced Technology, 1949–52; Head of Dept, Rutherford Coll. of Technology, 1952–57; Principal: Carlisle Technical Coll., 1958–60; Chesterfield Coll. of Technology, 1960–63; Asst Dir, SA Inst. of Technology, 1964–77. *Address:* 3 Pam Street, Beaumont, SA 5066, Australia. *T:* (8) 83796674.

MILLS, Geoffrey Thomas; Headmaster, Latymer School, 1983–98; *b* 13 Nov. 1935; *s* of Thomas Henry Mills and Margaret Jane (*née* Lewington); *m* 1970, Dorothy Anne Williams; one *s* three *d. Educ:* Enfield Grammar Sch.; Clare Coll., Cambridge (MA). Nat. Service, Corporal Clerk, RASC, 1954–56. Foreign lang. asst, Lyons, France, 1960–61; teacher of French and Spanish, Guthlaxton Grammar Sch., Leicester, 1961–62; Hd of Spanish, Sweyne Grammar Tech. Sch., Rayleigh, Essex, 1962–65; Head of Modern Languages: Coborn Sch. for Girls, Bow, 1965–69; Woodhouse Grammar Sch., Finchley, 1969–73; Dir of Studies, Longdean Sch., Hemel Hempstead, 1973–78; Headmaster, Manhood High Sch. and Community Centre, Selsey, W Sussex, 1978–83. Ind. Chm., Standards Cttee, London Borough of Enfield, 1999–. *Recreations:* golf (Blue, 1958), bridge, crosswords, reading. *Address:* 59 Wades Hill, Winchmore Hill, N21 1BD. *T:* (020) 8360 7335. *Club:* Mid Herts Golf (Wheathampstead).

MILLS, Sir (George) Ian, Kt 2001; FCA, FIMC, CMC, FIHM; Commissioner, London Region, NHS Executive, Department of Health, 2001–03; Member, NHS Appointments Commission, 2001–03; *b* 19 Nov. 1935; *s* of George Haxton Mills and Evelyn Mary (*née* Owen); *m* 1968, Margaret Elizabeth Dunstan; one *s* one *d* (and one *s* decd). *Educ:* Taunton's Grammar Sch., Southampton. FCA 1960; FIMC 1964; LHSM 1985; FIHM 1990; CMC 2000. Articled to Beal, Young & Booth, Southampton, 1954–60; Price Waterhouse, London, 1960–65; seconded to World Bank team assisting Govt of Pakistan Treasury, 1962; Chief Accountant, Univ. of Ibadan, Nigeria, 1965–68; rejoined Price Waterhouse, 1968; London Office, 1968–70; Newcastle upon Tyne Office, as Manager i/c Northern and Scottish Management Consultancy Ops, 1970–73; Partner, 1973; London Office, 1973–85: i/c Africa Management Consultancy Services, 1975–83; Nat. Dir, Central Govt Services, 1983–85; Nation Health Service Management Board, 1985–89: Dir of Financial Management, 1985–88; Dir of Resource Management, 1988–89; rejoined Price Waterhouse, 1989; Sen. Partner, Business Development Europe, 1989–91. Chairman: Lewisham and N Southwark HA, 1991–93; SE London HA, 1993–96; SE London Commissioning Agency, 1991–93; Lambeth, Southwark and Lewisham Health Commn, then HA, 1993–96; N Thames, then London, Reg., NHS Exec., DOH, 1996–2001. Mem., NHS Policy Bd, then Sec. of State for Health's Regl Chairmen's Adv. Cttee, 1996–2001. Mem., Ind. Remuneration Panel, London Borough of Lewisham, 2001– (Chm., 2001–). Member: Blackheath Preservation Trust Ltd, 1991–2004; Bd of Govs, UMDS of Guy's and St Thomas' Hosps, 1991–96; IHSM Consultants, 1992–96; Bd of Govs, St Christopher's Hospice, 1993–2003 (Chm., 2000–03); Delegacy, KCH Med. Sch., 1993–96; Bd of Trustees, Blackheath Historic Bldgs Trust, 2003– (Chm., 2003–). Trustee, SE London Community Foundn, 1995–2000. FRSA. Member: Editl Adv. Bd, Health Services Jl, 1992–96; Editl Bd, British Jl of Health Care Mgt, 1996–2003. *Publications:* St Margaret, Lee: a new guide, 1996; Rebirth of a Building, 2000; Craftsmen of St Margaret, 2006; articles in financial, educnl and med. jls. *Recreations:* classical music, photography, travel, heritage. *Address:* 60 Belmont Hill, SE13 5DN. *T:* (020) 8852 2457. *Clubs:* Royal Commonwealth Society; Royal Society of Arts.

MILLS, Maj.-Gen. Giles Hallam, CB 1977; CVO 1984; OBE 1964; retired; *b* 1 April 1922; 2nd *s* of late Col Sir John Digby Mills, TD, Bisterne Manor, Ringwood, Hampshire, and Lady Mills; *m* 1947, Emily Snowden Hallam (*d* 2005), 2nd *d* of late Captain W. H. Tuck, Perrywood, Maryland, USA, and Mrs Tuck; two *s* one *d. Educ:* Eton Coll. Served War: 2nd Lieut, KRRC, 1941; 1st Bn, KRRC, N Africa, Italy (Adjt, despatches), 1943–47. Staff Coll., 1951; Armed Forces Staff Coll. (US), 1959; Mil. Asst to CIGS, 1961–63; CO, 2 Green Jackets, KRRC, 1963–65; Admin. Staff Coll., Henley, 1965; Regtl Col, Royal Green Jackets, 1966–67; Comd, 8 Infty Bde, 1968–69; IDC 1970; Comd, British Army Staff and Mil. Attaché, Washington, 1971–73; Divl Brig., The Light Div., 1973–74; Dir of Manning (Army), 1974–77, retd. Major and Resident Governor, HM Tower of London, and Keeper of the Jewel House, 1979–84. *Publications:* Annals of The King's Royal Rifle Corps, vol. VI (with Roger Nixon), 1971, vol. VII, 1979.

MILLS, Gloria Helenly, CBE 2005 (MBE 1999); National Secretary, UNISON, since 2006; *b* 1958; *d* of James and Olga Mills. *Educ:* Open Univ. (Prof. Cert. Mgt 2003; Prof. Dip. Mgt 2004; MBA 2007). MCIPD 2004. NUPE: Regl Area Officer, 1985; Sen. Nat. Officer, Equal Rights, 1987; UNISON: Dir of Equal Opportunities, then of Equalities, 1993–2006; Nat. Organiser (Equalities), 1999–2006; Mem., Sen. Mgt Gp, 2004–. Trades Union Congress: Member: Women's Cttee, 1989–; General Council, 1994–; Exec. Cttee, 2000–; Pres., 2005–06; Chairman: Race Relns Cttee, 1995, 2000–; Women's Conf., 1999; Mem., Gen. Council, ITUC, 2006–. Member: Race Relns Forum, 1998–2003, Race Equality Adv. Panel, 2003–, Home Office; Race, Employment and Educn Forum, DFEE, 1998–2001; Employment Appeal Tribunal, 2000–; Commn for Racial Equality, 2002–07. Public Services International: Exec. Bd, 2002–; Chm., Eur. TUC Women's Cttee, 2003; Vice-Chm., World Women's Cttee, 2004. Mother of Chapel: NATSOPA, 1980–85; SOGAT, 1982–85. FRSA 1998. MCMI 2008. Hon. LLD Staffordshire, 2006. *Publications:* various articles on race equality and gender inc. article on combating institutional racism in Industrial Law Jl. *Recreations:* reading, cricket, football, Arsenal. *Address:* UNISON, 1 Mabledon Place, WC1H 9AJ. *T:* (020) 7551 1409; *e-mail:* glormlls@aol.com, g.mills@unison.co.uk.

MILLS, Harold Hernshaw, CB 1995; Chairman, Caledonian MacBrayne Ltd, 1999–2006; *b* 2 March 1938; *s* of late Harold and Margaret Mills; *m* 1973, Marion Elizabeth Beattie, MA. *Educ:* Greenock High Sch.; Univ. of Glasgow (BSc, PhD). Cancer Research Scientist, Roswell Park Memorial Inst., Buffalo, NY, 1962–64; Lectr, Glasgow Univ., 1964–69; Principal, Scottish Home and Health Dept, 1970–76; Asst Secretary: Scottish Office, 1976–81; Privy Council Office, 1981–83; Scottish Development Dept, 1983–84; Under Sec., Scottish Develt Dept, 1984–88; Prin. Finance Officer, Scottish Office, 1988–92; Sec., Scottish Office Envmt Dept, 1992–95; Sec. and Hd of Dept, Scottish Office Develt Dept, 1995–98. Mem. Bd, Home in Scotland, 1998–2004 (Chm., 2000–04). Director: Northlink Orkney and Shetland Ferries Ltd, 2000–; Edinburgh City Centre Partnership, 2002–06; Northlink Ferries Ltd, 2006–. Chairman: LandTrust, 1998–; Edinburgh World Heritage Trust, 1999–2006; Trustee: Scottish Maritime Mus., 1998–; Edinburgh Old Town and South Side Trust, 1999–2006; Dir, City of Adelaide Charitable Trust, 2005–. Gov., Queen Margaret UC, Edinburgh, 1998–2004. *Publications:* scientific papers in jls of learned socs on the crystal structure of chemical compounds. *Address:* 21 Hatton Place, Edinburgh EH9 1UB. *T:* (0131) 667 7910.

MILLS, Sir Ian; *see* Mills, Sir G. I.

MILLS, Prof. Ian Mark, FRS 1996; Professor of Chemical Spectroscopy, University of Reading, 1966–95, now Emeritus; *b* 9 June 1930; *s* of John Mills, MD and Margheurita Alice Gertrude Mills (*née* Gooding); *m* 1957, Margaret Mary Maynard; one *s* one *d. Educ:* Leighton Park Sch.; Univ. of Reading (BSc); St John's Coll., Oxford (DPhil). Res. Fellow, Univ. of Minnesota, 1954–56; Res. Fellow in Theoretical Chem., Corpus Christi Coll., Cambridge, 1956–57; University of Reading: Lectr in Chemistry, 1957–64; Reader, 1964–66; Leverhulme Emeritus Res. Fellow, 1996–98. Mem. and Chm. of various cttees, IUPAC, 1985–2000; Royal Society of Chemistry: Vice-Pres., Faraday Div., 1984–86; Mem., British Nat. Cttee for IUPAC, 1992–2000 (Chm., 1998–2000); Mem. Council, Royal Instn, 2000–03 and 2006–. Pres., Consultative Cttee on Units, Bureau Internat. des Poids et Mésures, 1995–; Chm., Cttee on Symbols and Units, BSI, 1996–2003. Lomb Medal 1960, Fellow 1974, Lippincott Medal 1982, Optical Soc. of America; Spectroscopy Award, RSC, 1990. Editor, Molecular Physics, 1972–77 and 1995–2004. *Publications:* (ed jtly) Quantities, Units and Symbols in Physical Chemistry, 1988, 3rd edn 2006; papers in learned jls. *Recreations:* walking, sailing. *Address:* 57 Christchurch Road, Reading RG2 7BD. *T:* (0118) 987 2335; *e-mail:* i.m.mills@reading.ac.uk; Department of Chemistry, University of Reading, RG6 6AD. *T:* (0118) 378 8456.

MILLS, John Frederick, CBE 2008; Director, Rural Policy, Department for Environment, Food and Rural Affairs, 2003–07; *b* 6 Sept. 1950; *s* of Henry Alfred Mills and Jean Margaret Aitchison; *m* 1st, 1974, Jean Marie Correia (*d* 1999); one *s* three *d*; 2nd, 2003, Imogen Stephanie Nicholls. *Educ:* Highgate Sch.; The Queen's Coll., Oxford (MA, BLitt (Mod. Hist.)); Merton Coll., Oxford (Domus Sen. Schol.). Department of Trade and Industry, 1974–92: Private Sec. to Minister of State for Industry, 1976–78; seconded to Govt of Hong Kong, 1981–85; Hd of Internat. Telecommunications Policy, 1986–89; Mem., Prime Minister's Policy Unit, 1989–92; Under Sec. and Dir of Consumer Affairs, OFT, 1992–95; Chief Executive: Cornwall CC, 1995–99; Policy and Resources Dept, States of Jersey, 1999–2003. Non-exec. Dir, Royal Cornwall Hosps NHS Trust, 2007– (Vice-Chm.). Mem., OFT Adv. Panel, 2001–03. Gov., Highgate Sch., 1993– (Treasurer and Chm., 1999–). *Address:* Le Picachon, Les Varines, St Saviour, Jersey JE2 7SB. *T:* (01534) 732374.

MILLS, Jonathan Edward Harland; Director, Edinburgh International Festival, since 2007; *b* 21 March 1963; *s* of Dr Frank Mills, AO and Elayne Mary Mills. *Educ:* Univ. of Sydney (BMus Composition); RMIT Univ. (MArch Acoustic Design); studied composition with Peter Sculthorpe, Sydney, and piano and composition with Lidia Arcuri-Baldecchi and Bruno Bettinelli, Italy. Artistic Dir, Blue Mountains Fest., 1988–90;

Composer-in-Residence and Res. Fellow in Envmtl Acoustics, RMIT Univ., 1992–97; Artistic Advr, Brisbane Biennial Internat. Music Fest., 1995–97; Artistic Dir, Melbourne Fest. (incl. Dir, Melbourne's Millennium Eve celebrations, 31 Dec. 1999 and Federation Fest., 2001), 2000–01; Composer-in-Residence, Bundanon Trust, 2002; Dir, Alfred Deakin Innovation Lects, 2003–05; Artistic Advr, Recital Centre and Elisabeth Murdoch Hall, Melbourne, 2005–. Adjunct Professor: Envmtl Acoustics, RMIT Univ., 1998–2003; La Trobe Univ., 2004–07; Vice Chancellor's Fellow, Univ. of Melbourne, 2006. Member: Australian Internat. Cultural Council, 1998–2003; Australian Heritage Commn, 2002–04; New Media Arts Bd, 2003–05, Maj. Performing Arts Bd, 2005, Australia Council; Australian Heritage Council, 2004–06; Board Member: Synergy Percussion, 2001–06; Melbourne Recital Hall, 2004–05; Art Exhibns Australia, 2005; Chairman: Commonwealth Govt Review into Australian Youth Orch. and Australian Nat. Acad. of Music, 2004–05; Review of Opera for Victoria Govt, 2005. Member Jury: Pratt Prize for Music Th., 2002–; Ian Potter Foundn Music Commns, 2003–05. Patron, Leigh Warren & Dancers, 2001–. Works and performances include: Ethereal Eye (electro-acoustic dance opera), 1996; The Ghost Wife (chamber opera, libretto by Dorothy Porter), 1999; Sandakan Threnody (for solo tenor, chorus and orch.), 2001, theatrical version, 2004; The Eternity Man (chamber opera, libretto by Dorothy Porter), 2003; various other works for radio, film, theatre and concert perf. FRSA. Centenary Medal, Australia, 2002; Prix Italia, 2005. *Address:* c/o Edinburgh International Festival, The Hub, Castlehill, Edinburgh EH1 2NE.

MILLS, Sir Keith (Edward), Kt 2006; DL; Chairman: Loyalty Management Group, since 1992; Loyalty Management UK Ltd, since 2001; Deputy Chairman, London Organising Committee, 2012 Olympic Games, since 2006; Team Principal, TEAMORIGIN, British Americas Cup Series, 2007; *b* 15 May 1950; *s* of Edward James Mills and Margaret Catherine Mills; *m* 1974, Maureen Elizabeth Simmons; one *s* one *d*. *Educ:* St Martin's, Brentwood. Mktg Exec., Economist newspaper, 1969–74; Mktg Manager, Financial Times, 1974–77; Account Dir, Newton & Godin Advertising, 1977–80; Man. Dir, Nadler & Larimer Advertising, 1980–84; Chm. and CEO, Mills Smith & Partners, 1984–89; CEO, Air Miles UK Ltd, 1988–92. Internat. Pres. and CEO, London 2012 Ltd, 2003–06. Director: Breakthrough Breast Cancer Charity, 2006–; AT Racing Ltd, 2006–. DL Kent, 2008. Hon. PhD Loughborough, 2006. *Recreations:* sailing, ski-ing, music, travelling. *Address:* 1 Curzon Square, W1J 5UB. *T:* (office) (020) 7152 4700, *Fax:* (020) 7152 4300; *e-mail:* k.mills@loyalty.co.uk. *Club:* Royal Ocean Racing.

MILLS, Lawrence William Robert; Managing Owner, Oscar Mills & Associates, since 1994; Director, Kids' Gallery Co. Ltd, Hong Kong, since 2005; *b* London, 7 May 1934; *m* 1992, Amira Hamdy (*née* Elsayed); one *d* and two *d* by previous marriage. *Educ:* Reigate Grammar Sch., Surrey; Open Univ. (MBA 1997; LLB Hons 2004). National Service: RN, 1953; Intell. Corps, 1954. Formerly, Jun. Exec., K. F. Mayer Ltd, London. Hong Kong Govt (Mem. of HMOCS): Exec. Officer, Cl. II, 1958; Asst Trade Officer, 1960; Trade Officer, 1964; Sen. Trade Officer, 1968; Principal Trade Officer, 1969; Asst Dir of Commerce and Industry, 1971; Chief Trade Negotiator, 1974–75, 1977–79, 1981–83; Counsellor (Hong Kong Affairs), UK Mission, Geneva, 1976–77; Director of Trade, Hong Kong, 1977–79, 1981–83; Comr of Industry, 1979–81; Regional Sec., Hong Kong and Kowloon, 1983; Official MLC, Hong Kong, 1983; retired from Hong Kong Govt Service, 1983. Chief Exec., Laws Fashion Knitters Ltd, Hong Kong and Sri Lanka, 1983–85; Dir Gen., Fedn of Hong Kong Industries, 1985–89; Chief Exec., Dubai Commerce and Tourism Promotion Board, 1989–93; Sen. Enterprise Advr, UN Develt Prog., China, 1994–97; Gen. Manager, Mohamed Hareb Al Otaiba, Dubai, 1997–98; Instnl/Mkting Advr, USAID/DAI Market Access Prog. for West Bank and Gaza Strip, on secondment as Chief Operating Officer, Palestine Trade Center, 1999–2000; Advr, EU Assistance Project, Jordan Tourism Bd, Amman, 2001–02. *Recreation:* music (classical jazz). *Address:* 21/F Coda Plaza, 51 Garden Road, Central, Hong Kong. *Clubs:* Naval and Military; Hong Kong, Hong Kong Country (Hong Kong).

MILLS, Leif Anthony, CBE 1995; General Secretary, Banking, Insurance and Finance Union (formerly National Union of Bank Employees), 1972–96; Chairman, Covent Garden Market Authority, 1998–2005; *b* 25 March 1936; *s* of English father and Norwegian mother; *m* 1958, Gillian Margaret Smith (*d* 2003); two *s* two *d*. *Educ:* Balliol Coll., Oxford. MA Hons PPE. Commnd in Royal Military Police, 1957–59. Trade Union Official, Nat. Union of Bank Employees, 1960–96: Research Officer, 1960; Asst Gen. Sec., 1962; Dep. Gen. Sec., 1968. Mem. various arbitration tribunals; Member: TUC Non-Manual Workers Adv. Cttee, 1967–72; TUC Gen. Council, 1983–96 (Pres., 1994–95); Office of Manpower Economics Adv. Cttee on Equal Pay, 1971; Cttee to Review the Functioning of Financial Instns, 1977–80; CS Pay Res. Unit Bd, 1978–81; Armed Forces Pay Review Body, 1980–87; Monopolies and Mergers Commn, 1982–91; Financial Reporting Council, 1990–96; Ind. Review Cttee on Higher Educn Pay & Conditions, 1998–99; Chairman: TUC Financial Services Cttee, 1983–96; TUC Educn and Training Cttee, 1989–94. Member: BBC Consultative Gp on Social Effects of Television, 1978–80; Council, NCVQ, 1992–96; Bd, Investors in People, 1992–96; PIA Ombudsman Council, 1994–2000 (Dep. Chm., 1997–2000); Bd, Employment Tribunal Service, 1996–2001; Council, Consumers' Assoc., 1996–2002. Contested (Lab) Salisbury, 1964, 1965 (by-elecn). Mem. Governing Body, London Business Sch., 1988–92. Trustee, Civic Trust, 1988–96. FRGS 1992. *Publications:* biography (unpublished), Cook: A History of the Life and Explorations of Dr Frederick Albert Cook, SPRI ms 883, Cambridge, 1970; (published) Frank Wild, Antarctic explorer, 1999; Men of Ice: two polar biographies, 2008. *Recreations:* rowing, chess. *Address:* 31 Station Road, West Byfleet, Surrey KT14 6DR. *T:* (01932) 342829. *Clubs:* Oxford and Cambridge; Oxford University Boat, Weybridge Rowing.

MILLS, Mark Fortescue P.; *see* Platts-Mills.

MILLS, Rt Rev. Murray John; Bishop of Waiapu, 1991–2002; *b* 29 May 1936; *s* of Robert Claude Mills and Mabel Winifred Mills; *m* 1961, Judith Anne Cotton; two *s* three *d*. *Educ:* Auckland Univ. (BA, MA); St John's Theol Coll. (LTh (First Cl. Hons)). Ordained: Deacon, 1960; Priest, 1961 (dio. of Auckland); Assistant Curate: Papakura, 1960–63; Whangarei, 1963–65; Vicar: Bay of Islands, 1965–70; Matamata, 1970–75; Archdeacon of Waikato, 1976–81; Vicar-Gen., dio. of Waikato, 1978–84; Vicar: Tokoroa, 1981–84; St John's Cathedral, Napier (dio. of Waiapu) and Dean of Waiapu, 1984–91. Examining Chaplain to Bishop of Waikato, 1974–84; Advr in Christian Educn, 1976–81. Liaison Bp, Oceania Mission to Seafarers, 1988–2002; Pres., Conf. of Churches in Aotearoa, NZ, 2000–03. Mem., Assoc. of Christian Spiritual Dirs, 2003–. *Publication:* History of Christ Church, Papakura, 1961. *Recreations:* tramping, gardening, drama, politics, music, reading. *Address:* 12 Clyde Road, Napier, New Zealand. *T:* (6) 8350884; *e-mail:* muju@Xtra.co.nz.

MILLS, Neil McLay; Chairman, Sedgwick Group plc, 1979–84; *b* 29 July 1923; *yr s* of late L. H. Mills; *m* 1950, Rosamund Mary Kimpton, *d* of Col and Hon. Mrs A. C. W. Kimpton; two *s* two *d*. *Educ:* Epsom Coll.; University Coll. London. Served War, 1940–46: commnd RN; Lieut RNVR; Coastal Forces (mentioned in despatches, 1944). Joined Bland Welch & Co. Ltd, 1948; Exec. Dir, 1955; Chm., 1965–74; Chm., Bland Payne Holdings Ltd, 1974–79. Underwriting Mem. of Lloyd's, 1955–91. Director: Montagu Trust Ltd, 1966–74; Midland Bank Ltd, 1974–79; Wadlow Grosvenor International Ltd, 1984–88; Threadneedle Publishing Co., 1987–93. Vice-President: Insurance Inst. of London, 1971–84; British Insurance Brokers Assoc., 1978–84 (Mem., Internat. Insurance Brokers Cttee); Mem. Cttee, Lloyd's Insurance Brokers Assoc., 1974–77. Member: Church Army Board, 1957–64 (Vice-Chm., 1959–64); Council, Oak Hill Theol Coll., 1958–62. Trustee and Governor, Lord Mayor Treloar Trust, 1975–81. Freeman, City of London, 1984; Liveryman, Insurers' Co., 1984–86. *Recreations:* reading and reflecting. *Address:* The Old Post House, 23 Broad Street, Alresford, Hants SO24 9AR. *T:* (01962) 732464. *Club:* Pilgrims.

MILLS, Oliver Arthur Seymour; Managing Director, Adult Social Services, Kent County Council, since 2006; *b* 11 Oct. 1951; *s* of Seymour Herbert Hatten Mills and Mary Patricia Mills; *m* 1990, Janice Reay; two *s*, and one step *d*. *Educ:* Tonbridge Sch.; Univ. of Warwick (BA Hons Hist. 1973); Wadham Coll., Oxford (MSc Applied Soc. Studies 1979; CQSW 1979). Social worker, London Bor. of Camden, 1980–84; Team Leader, London Bor. of Lewisham, 1984–87; Kent County Council, 1987–: Social Services Directorate: Asst Dir, 1992–98; Dir, Ops, 1998–2005; Strategic Dir, Social Services, 2005–06. *Recreations:* playing tennis, music, allotment. *Address:* Kent Adult Social Services, Brenchley House, 123/135 Week Street, Maidstone ME14 1RF. *T:* (01622) 694888, *Fax:* (01622) 694910; *e-mail:* Oliver.Mills@kent.gov.uk.

MILLS, Sir Peter (Frederick Leighton), 3rd Bt *cr* 1921; *b* 9 July 1924; *s* of Major Sir Frederick Leighton Victor Mills, 2nd Bt, MC, RA, MICE, and Doris (*née* Armitage); *S* father, 1955; *m* 1954, Pauline Mary, *d* of L. R. Allen, Calverton, Notts; one *s* (one adopted *d* decd). *Educ:* Eastbourne Coll.; Cedara Coll. of Agriculture, University of Natal (BSc Agric.). Served HM Forces, 1943–47. CS, Fedn Rhodesia and Nyasaland, 1953; with Rhodesia Min. of Agric., 1964, Zimbabwe Min. of Agric., 1980–90. *Heir: s* Michael Victor Leighton Mills [*b* 30 Aug. 1957; *m* 1981, Susan, *d* of J. Doig, Harare, Zimbabwe]. *Address:* PO Box A474, Avondale, Harare, Zimbabwe.

MILLS, Rev. Peter Watson, QHC 2001; Chaplain-in-Chief and Director General Chaplaincy Services, Royal Air Force, since 2006; *b* 9 Feb. 1955; *s* of late Peter Watson Mills and of Janet (*née* Lonsdale); *m* 1979, Sheila Anderson; two *d*. *Educ:* Christ's Coll., Univ. of Aberdeen (BD 1983, CPS 1983). Police Constable, Grampian Police, 1974–78. Licensed 1983, ordained, 1984; Asst Minister, Montrose, 1983–84; RAF Chaplain, 1984–; Principal Chaplain, C of S and Free Churches, 2001–06. *Recreations:* computing, reading, music, electric guitar. *Address:* Chaplaincy Services (RAF), Building 4, RAF High Wycombe HP14 4UE. *T:* (01494) 493801. *Club:* Royal Air Force.

MILLS, Peter William; QC (Can.) 1985; company director and business consultant, since 1999; *b* 22 July 1942; *s* of Joseph Roger Mills and Jane Eveyln (*née* Roscoe); *m* 1967, Eveline Jane (*née* Black); two *s*. *Educ:* Dalhousie Univ. Law Sch. (LLB); Dalhousie Univ. (BComm). ICD.D 2005. Barrister and solicitor, Ont, Canada; with McInnes, Cooper and Robertson, Halifax, 1967; Solicitor, Canadian Pacific Ltd, Montreal and Toronto, 1967–71; Dir, Cammell Laird Shipbuilders Ltd, 1971–76; Mem., Org Cttee for British Shipbuilders, 1976–77; Manager, Currie, Coopers & Lybrand Ltd, Toronto, 1977–79; The Woodbridge Co. Ltd: Gen. Counsel, 1980–98; Vice-Pres., 1980–87; Dir, 1982–98; Sen. Vice-Pres., 1988–98. Director: Corporate Develt, FP Publications Ltd, 1979–80; Augusta Newsprint Co., 1981–; Hudson's Bay Co., 1985–2006; Markborough Properties Inc., 1986–97; Cambridge Shopping Centres Ltd, 1997–2001; Cadillac Fairview Corp. Ltd, 2001–; Torstar Corp., 2004–06. Dir, St John's Rehabilitation Hosp. Foundn, 2002–03; Chm., Hudson's Bay Co. History Foundn, 2005–06. Dir, Canadian Inst. of Chartered Accts, 2004–. *Recreations:* golf, sailing, travel, reading. *Address:* 390 Glencairn Avenue, Toronto, ON M5N 1V1, Canada. *Fax:* (416) 4820754; *e-mail:* pwmills@sympatico.ca. *Clubs:* York Downs Golf and Country (Toronto); Royal Liverpool Golf (Hoylake).

MILLS, Richard Michael; Chairman and Chief Executive, Delfont Mackintosh Theatres Ltd, 1991–96; *b* 26 June 1931; *s* of Richard Henry Mills and Catherine Keeley; *m* 1st, 1960, Lynda Taylor (marr. diss. 1967); one *d*; 2nd, 1983, Sheila White; two *s*. Commenced working in the theatre as an Assistant Stage Manager in 1948, and worked in every capacity, including acting and stage management. Joined Bernard Delfont Ltd, 1962; Dir, 1967; Dep. Chm., 1970–79; Chm., 1979–91; Chief Exec., 1970–91; Managing Director: Prince of Wales Theatre, 1970–96; Prince Edward Theatre, 1978–96. Director: EMI Film & Theatre Corp., 1970–81; Trust House Forte Leisure, 1980–83; First Leisure Corp., 1983–93. Member: Nat. Theatre Bd, 1976–91; Finance and Gen. Purposes Cttee, NT, 1976–91; Drama Panel, Arts Council of GB, 1976–77; English Tourist Bd, 1982–85. Pres., Stage Golfing Soc., 2004–05. Shows worked on in the West End, 1948–62, include: I Remember Mama, Tuppence Coloured, Medea, Adventure Story, Anne Veronica, The Devil's General, I Capture the Castle, No Escape, Misery Me, Three Times a Day, The Sun of York, To my Love, Be my Guest, Hunter's Moon, The Iceman Cometh, Brouhaha, Detour after Dark, The Ginger Man, Sound of Murder, Will You Walk a Little Faster, Pool's Paradise, Belle, Come Blow your Horn. Whilst Gen. Manager and Dir with Bernard Delfont Ltd: Never Too Late, Pickwick, 1962; Caligula, Maggie May, Little Me, Our Man Crichton, 1963; The Roar of the Greasepaint (NY), Pickwick (NY), Twang, Barefoot in the Park, 1964; The Owl and the Pussycat, The Matchgirls, Funny Girl, Joey Joey, The Odd Couple, 1965; Queenie, Sweet Charity, The Four Musketeers, 1966; Golden Boy, Look Back in Anger (revival), 1967; Mame, Cat Among the Pigeons, 1968; Carol Channing, Danny La Rue at the Palace, 1969; Kean, Lulu, 1970; Applause, The Unknown Soldier and his Wife, 1971. With Lord Delfont presented in the West End: The Good Old Bad Old Days, Mardi Gras, Brief Lives, Queen Daniella, Cinderella, Henry IV, Harvey, Sammy Cahn's Songbook, Streetcar Named Desire, Good Companions, It's All Right if I Do It, Charley's Aunt, An Evening with Tommy Steele, Gomes, The Wolf, Danny La Rue Show, Beyond the Rainbow, Dad's Army, Plumber's Progress, Paul Daniels Magic Show, Underneath the Arches, Little Me, The Best Little Whorehouse in Texas, and over 100 pantomimes and summer season shows. *Recreations:* golf, poker. *Clubs:* Royal Automobile; Richmond Golf.

MILLS, Robert Ferris; Under Secretary, Department of Finance and Personnel, Northern Ireland, 1990–96, retired; *b* 21 Sept. 1939; *s* of Robert and Rachel Mills; *m* 1st, 1968, Irene Sandra Miskelly (marr. diss. 1978); one *s* one *d*; 2nd, 1984, Frances Elizabeth Gillies; two step *d*. *Educ:* Sullivan Upper School, Holywood, Co. Down; Queen's Univ., Belfast (BA Hons). Inland Revenue, 1961–64; Min. of Commerce, NI, 1964–68; Dept of Housing and Local Govt, 1968–71; Dept of the Environment, NI, 1971–75; Asst Sec., 1975–83, Under Sec., 1983–90, Dept of Health and Social Services, NI. *Recreations:* golf, tennis, travel, the arts.

MILLS, Stratton; *see* Mills, W. S.

MILLS, Rt Hon. Tessa Jane Helen Douglas, (Mrs David Mills); *see* Jowell, Rt Hon. T. J. H. D.

MILLS, (William) Stratton; Senior Partner, 1974–2000, Consultant, 2000–05, Mills, Selig, Solicitors, Belfast (Partner, 1959–2000); company director; Chairman, Hampden Group PLC (formerly Hampden Homecare plc), 1992–99; *b* 1 July 1932; *o s* of late Dr J. V. S. Mills, CBE, Resident Magistrate for City of Belfast, and Margaret Florence (*née* Byford); *m* 1959, Merriel E. R. Whitla, *o d* of late Mr and Mrs R. J. Whitla, Belfast; three *s. Educ:* Campbell Coll., Belfast; Queen's Univ., Belfast (LLB). Vice-Chm., Federation of University Conservative and Unionist Assocs, 1952–53 and 1954–55; admitted a Solicitor, 1958. MP (UU) Belfast N, Oct. 1959–Dec. 1972; MP (Alliance) Belfast N, Apr. 1973–Feb. 1974; PPS to Parly Sec., Ministry of Transport, 1961–64; Member: Estimates Cttee, 1964–70; Exec. Cttee, 1922 Cttee, 1967–70, 1973; Hon. Sec. Conservative Broadcasting Cttee, 1963–70, Chm., 1970–73; Mem., Mr Speaker's Conference on Electoral Law, 1967. Mem., One Nation Gp, 1972–73. Member: Adv. Bd, Public Records Office, NI, 1996–; Bd, Historic Bldgs Council for NI, 2004–. Chm., Ulster Orchestra Soc. Ltd, 1980–90; Mem. Bd, Castleward Opera., 1988–98; Dir, Opera Rara, 1998–. Mem. Council, Winston Churchill Meml Trust, 1990–95. Arnold Goodman Award, for encouragement of business sponsorship of the arts, 1990. *Address:* 17 Malone Park, Belfast BT9 6NJ. *T:* (028) 9066 5210. *Clubs:* Carlton, MCC; Reform (Belfast).

MILLS-EVANS, Carole Denise; Corporate Director of Resources, Nottingham City Council, since 2007; *b* Coventry, 7 Dec. 1963; *d* of Peter and Pauline Mills; *m* (marr. diss.); one *s. Educ:* Wolverhampton Poly. CPFA 1992. Coventry HA, 1983–86; Coventry CC, 1986–88; Walsall Metropolitan Borough Council: various posts, 1988–2002; Actg Chief Financial Officer, 2002–03; Exec. Dir, Corporate Services, 2003–07. Chartered Institute of Public Finance and Accountancy: Mem. Council, 2007–08; Vice Pres., 2005–07, Pres., 2007–April 2009, Midlands. Chm., Finance Adv. Gp, W Midlands, LGA, 2004–07. Accredited peer, IDeA, 2005–. Gov., Bishop Vesey Grammar Sch., 2003–07 (Chm., Finance and Estates Cttee, 2005–07). *Recreations:* professional networks, coaching and mentoring, yoga, cycling, active CIPFA member. *Address:* Irnham Road, Four Oaks, Sutton Coldfield B74 2TG. *T:* (office) (0115) 915 8504; *e-mail:* carole@evans211.freeserve.co.uk.

MILLSON, Tony; JP; HM Diplomatic Service, retired; Counsellor, Foreign and Commonwealth Office, 2001–03; *b* 25 Nov. 1951; *s* of Donald Millson and Joan (*née* Whittle). *Educ:* Grimsby Wintringham Grammar Sch. Entered HM Diplomatic Service, 1970; MECAS, 1973; Third Sec. (Commercial), Tripoli, 1974–76; Third, later Second Sec. (Develt), Amman, 1976–80; FCO, 1980–83; Second Sec., BMG Berlin, 1983–86; First Sec., FCO, 1986–88; Hd of Chancery, Kuwait, 1988–90; FCO, 1991–93; Ambassador to Macedonia, 1993–97; Counsellor, FCO, 1997–98; High Comr, The Gambia, 1998–2000; Dep. High Comr, Abuja, 2000–01. JP London, 2004. *Recreations:* reading, listening to music. *Address:* 33 Ormond House, Medway Street, SW1P 2TB. *T:* (020) 7222 3641.

MILMAN, Andrée, (Mrs David Milman); see Grenfell, A.

MILMAN, Sir David (Patrick), 10th Bt *cr* 1800, of Levaton-in-Woodland, Devonshire; educational consultant, since 1999; *b* 24 Aug. 1945; *er s* of Lt-Col Sir Derek Milman, 9th Bt and Christine Margaret Milman (*née* Whitehouse); *S* father, 1999; *m* 1969, Christina Hunt; one *s* one *d. Educ:* London Univ. (Teacher's Cert. 1st cl. 1968; BEd (Hons) 1969; MA 1976). Headteacher, 1981–89; Headteacher Trng Co-ordinator, ILEA, 1988–89; Asst Dir, Sch. Mgt South, 1989–91; Area Advr, 1991–93; Sen. Area Advr, 1993–98, NW Kent; District Adv. Officer, Dartford, 1998–99. *Publications:* Teachers' Guidelines to Take Part Readers Series, 1973; Take a Look Series, 1974; What do you think?, 1976; Senior Manager's Personal Profile, 1991. *Recreations:* ornithology, reading. *Heir: s* Thomas Hart Milman, *b* 7 Oct. 1976. *Address:* 71 Camden Road, Sevenoaks, Kent TN13 3LU. *T:* (01732) 459089.

MILMINE, Rt Rev. Douglas, CBE 1983; an Assistant Bishop, diocese of Chichester, since 1992; *b* 3 May 1921; *s* of Alexander Douglas Milmine and Rose Gertrude Milmine (*née* Moore); *m* 1945, Margaret Rosalind, *d* of Edward and Gladys Whitley, Kilmorie, Meadfoot, Torquay; three *s* one *d. Educ:* Sutton Valence School; St Peter's Hall, Oxford (MA 1946); Clifton Theological Coll. RAFVR, 1941–45; POW, 1943–45. Deacon 1947, priest 1948; Curate: SS Philip and James, Ilfracombe, 1947–50; St Paul's, Slough, 1950–53; missionary with South American Missionary Society: Maquehue, Chile, 1954; Temuco, 1955–60; Santiago, 1961–68; Archdeacon of N Chile, Bolivia and Peru, 1964–68; Hon. Canon of Chile, 1969–72; Midland Area Sec. of SAMS, 1969–72; Bishop in Paraguay, 1973–85; retired 1986. *Publications:* Stiff Upper Smile (autobiog.), 1993; La Comunión Anglicana en América Latina, 1993. *Recreation:* study of current affairs. *Address:* 1c Clive Court, 24 Grand Parade, Eastbourne, East Sussex BN21 3DD. *T:* (01323) 734159.

MILMO, John Boyle Martin; QC 1984; **His Honour Judge Milmo;** a Circuit Judge, since 2004; *b* 19 Jan. 1943; *s* of late Dermod Hubert Francis Milmo, MB BCh and Eileen Clare Milmo (*née* White). *Educ:* Downside Sch.; Trinity Coll., Dublin (MA, LLB). Called to the Bar, Lincoln's Inn, 1966, Bencher, 1992; a Recorder, 1982–2004; a Dep. High Ct Judge, 1993–2004. Mem., Parole Bd, 2005–. Mem., Bar Council, 1992–2002 (Chm., Legal Aid and Fees Cttee, 1996–97). Trustee, Historic Singers Trust, 2004–. *Recreations:* opera, discography. *Address:* c/o Nottingham Crown Court, 60 Canal Street, Nottingham NG1 7EL. *Club:* United Services (Nottingham).

MILMO, Patrick Helenus; QC 1985; *b* 11 May 1938; *s* of Sir Helenus Milmo; *m* 1968, Marina, *d* of late Alexis Schiray and of Xenia Schiray, rue Jules Simon, Paris; one *s* one *d. Educ:* Downside; Trinity Coll., Cambridge (BA 1961; MA 1997). Harmsworth Scholar; called to the Bar, Middle Temple, 1962 (Bencher, 1994; Reader, 2005). Part-time employment judge, 1998–. Asst Comr, Parly Boundary Commn, 2000–. Dep. Chm., Disciplinary Cttee, RPSGB, 2008–. *Publication:* (ed jtly) Gatley on Libel and Slander, 9th edn 1998, 10th edn 2004. *Recreations:* wine, horse-racing, cinema. *Address:* 5 Raymond Buildings, Gray's Inn, WC1R 5BP; 7 Baalbec Road, N5 1QN.

MILNE, family name of **Baron Milne.**

MILNE, 3rd Baron *cr* 1933, of Salonika and of Rubislaw, co. Aberdeen; **George Alexander Milne;** self-employed chair caner (Ablecaner); *b* 1 April 1941; *s* of 2nd Baron Milne, TD and of Cicely Abigail Milne (*née* Leslie); *S* father, 2005. *Educ:* Winchester. Liveryman, Grocers' Co. *Recreations:* sailing, bicycling, golf. *Heir: b* Hon. Iain Charles Luis Milne [*b* 16 Sept. 1949; *m* 1987, Berta Guerrero; two *s*]. *T:* (020) 8977 9761; *e-mail:* george.milne2@btinternet.com. *Club:* Pilgrims.

MILNE, Alasdair David Gordon; Director-General, BBC, 1982–87; *b* 8 Oct. 1930; *s* of late Charles Gordon Shaw Milne and Edith Reid Clark; *m* 1954, Sheila Kirsten Graucob (*d* 1992); two *s* one *d. Educ:* Winchester Coll.; New Coll., Oxford (Hon. Fellow, 1985). Commnd into 1st Bn Gordon Highlanders, 1949. Hon. Mods Oxon 1952; BA Oxon Mod. Langs, 1954. Joined BBC, 1954; Dep. Editor, 1957–61, Editor, 1961–62, of Tonight Programme; Head of Tonight Productions, 1963–65; Partner, Jay, Baverstock, Milne & Co., 1965–67; rejoined BBC, Oct. 1967; Controller, BBC Scotland, 1968–72; Dir of Programmes, 1973–77, Man. Dir, 1977–82, BBC TV; Dep. Dir-Gen., BBC, 1980–82. Chm., Darrell Waters Ltd, 1988–90. Chm., Gaelic Broadcasting Task Force, 1999–2000. Vis. Prof., Univ. of Miami, 1989. Vice-Pres., RTS, 1986–87. Chm., John MacFadyen Meml Trust, 1980–93. DUniv Stirling, 1983. Cyril Bennett Award, RTS, 1987. *Publication:* DG: the memoirs of a British broadcaster, 1988. *Recreations:* piping, salmon fishing, golf. *Address:* 30 Holland Park Avenue, W11 3QU. *Club:* Travellers.

MILNE, David Calder; QC 1987; FCA; a Recorder, 1994–2006 (Assistant Recorder, 1989–94); *b* 22 Sept. 1945; *s* of late Ernest and of Helena Milne; *m* 1978, Rosemary Bond (marr. diss. 1999); one *d*; partner, Jackie Power; one *s. Educ:* Harrow Sch.; Oxford Univ. (MA). ACA 1969; FCA 1974. Articled to Whinney Murray & Co., chartered accountants, 1966–69; called to the Bar, Lincoln's Inn, 1970, Bencher, 1996. Trustee, Wildfowl and Wetlands Trust, 2002–. *Recreations:* natural history, music, golf, Rugby. *Address:* (chambers) 16 Bedford Row, WC1R 4EF. *T:* (020) 7414 8080. *Clubs:* Garrick, Hurlingham, Gnomes; Walton Heath Golf.

MILNE, Ian Innes, CMG 1965; OBE 1946; a Senior Clerk, House of Commons, 1969–76; *b* 16 June 1912; *e s* of Kenneth John Milne, CBE, and Maud Innes; *m* 1939, Marie Mange (*d* 1989); one *d. Educ:* Westminster Sch.; Christ Church, Oxford. Advertising, 1935–40; RE, 1940–46 (Lt-Col). FO, 1946–68; 2nd Sec., Teheran, 1948–51; 1st Sec., Berne, 1955–56; 1st Sec., Tokyo, 1960–63; retired 1968. US Legion of Merit (Off.), 1946. *Recreations:* gardening, music.

MILNE, Maj. Gen. John, CB 2000; Registrar, St Paul's Cathedral, since 2001; *b* 13 Oct. 1946; *s* of Donald William Milne and Evelyn (*née* Ayrer); *m* 1970, Cherrill Rosemary Tookey; two *s* one *d. Educ:* Lowestoft Grammar Sch.; Royal Coll. of Defence Studies. Commnd, Royal Artillery, 1966: helicopter pilot, 1970–74; Mil. Asst, CoS Northern Army Gp, 1980–82; Comdr, 2 Field Regt, 1986–88; Dep. Comdr, 7 Armd Bde, Saudi Arabia, 1990; Comdr, 1 Artillery Bde, 1992–93; Dir, Army Recruiting, 1994–97; Dep. Comdr for Logistics, Stabilisation Force, Bosnia Herzogovina, 1997; Dir for Support, Allied Land Forces, Central Europe, 1998–99; COS Kosovo Force, Pristina, 1999–2000. Col Comdt, RA, 2001–07. Chm. of Trustees, Royal Sch. Hampstead, 2004–. Freeman, City of London, 2001; Liveryman, Masons' Co., 2002–. FCMI (FInstM 1993). Bronze Star (US), 1991. *Recreations:* tennis, golf, bridge. *Address:* Lloyds TSB, 174 Fleet Road, Fleet, Hants GU13 8DD. *Club:* Army and Navy.

MILNE, Sir John (Drummond), Kt 1986; Chairman, Alfred McAlpine plc, 1992–96; *b* 13 Aug. 1924; *s* of Frederick John and Minnie Elizabeth Milne; *m* 1948, Joan Akroyd; two *s* two *d. Educ:* Stowe Sch.; Trinity Coll., Cambridge. Served Coldstream Guards, 1943–47. APCM (now Blue Circle Industries): management trainee, 1948; Asst to Director i/c Overseas Investments, 1953; President, Ocean Cement, Vancouver, 1957; Director, APCM, 1964, Man. Dir and Chief Exec., 1975; Blue Circle Industries: Chm. and Managing Director, 1983; Chm., 1983–90 (non-exec., 1987–90). DRG plc (formerly The Dickinson Robinson Group): Dir, 1973–89; Chm., 1987–89; Director: Royal Insurance, 1982–95; Witan Investment Co., 1988–96; Avon Rubber, 1989–95; Solvay & Cie SA, 1990–96. *Recreations:* golf, shooting. *Address:* Chilton House, Chilton Candover, Hants SO24 9TX. *Clubs:* Boodle's, MCC; Berkshire Golf, Swinley Forest Golf.

MILNE, Judith Frances; see English, J. F.

MILNE, Nanette Lilian Margaret, OBE 1994; Member (C) Scotland North East, Scottish Parliament, since 2003; *b* 27 April 1942; *d* of Harold G. Gordon and Hannah L. C. Gordon (*née* Stephen); *m* 1965, Alan Ducat Milne; one *s* one *d. Educ:* Aberdeen High Sch. for Girls; Univ. of Aberdeen (MB ChB 1965). FFARCS 1969. Medical Officer, Grampian Health Board, later Aberdeen Royal Hospitals NHS Trust: anaesthetics, 1966–73; oncology research, 1980–92. Mem. (C), City of Aberdeen DC, 1988–96, Aberdeen CC, 1995–99. Vice-Chm., Scottish Cons. and Unionist Party, 1989–93. JP Aberdeen, 1993. *Publications:* contrib. to BMJ on cardiovascular effects of laparoscopy and on colorectal cancer. *Recreations:* gardening, sports. *Address:* Scottish Parliament, Holyrood, Edinburgh EH99 1SP. *T:* (0131) 348 5652; *e-mail:* nanette.milne.msp@scottish.parliament.uk.

MILNE, Nikola Caroline; see Stewart, N. C.

MILNE, Peter Alexander, PhD; Eur Ing; CEng, FIMechE, FIMarEST; Senior Consultant, AMRIE, 1996–2000 (Director, 1994–96); *b* 23 April 1935; *s* of late Alexander Ogston Milne and of Lilian Winifred Milne (*née* Murray); *m* 1961, Beatrice Taylor Reid; two *d. Educ:* Tynemouth Sch.; Harwell Reactor Sch.; BSc Marine Engrg Univ. of Durham 1957; PhD Applied Sci. Univ. of Newcastle 1960. Practical experience with apprenticeship at Wallsend Slipway & Engineering and at sea with Union Castle Mail Steamship; Trainee Manager, Swan Hunter Gp, 1961; Technical Dir, Swan Hunter Shipbuilders, 1970–74, Man. Dir, 1974–77; British Shipbuilders HQ at formation of Corp., 1977; Man. Dir, Shipbuilding Ops, 1978–80, Mem. Bd, 1981–90 (Bd Mem. for Engrg, 1981–83, for Merchant Ship and Enginebuilding, 1985–90), Man. Dir, Merchant and Composite Div., 1984, British Shipbuilders; Man. Dir, BMT Cortec, 1990–94. Director: Vosper Thornycroft, 1978–80; Tyneside Maritime and Engrg, 1996–98. Bd Mem., SMRTB, 1971–75; Chm., BSI Ind. Cttee, 1972–76; Dir, Lloyds Register of Shipping, 1984–91; Chm., Northern Engrg Centre, 1990–94. Vis. Lectr in Marine Engrg, Newcastle Univ., 1970–75. Pres., NECInst, 1986–88. Freeman, City of London, 1984; Liveryman, Shipwrights' Co., 1984–98. *Publications:* papers related to science and industry. *Recreations:* watching Rugby, cricket, hill-walking, enjoying grandchildren. *Address:* 14 Woodland Close, Earsdon Village, Whitley Bay, Tyne and Wear NE25 9LL. *T:* (0191) 252 2708.

MILNE, Ronald Robert, FRSE; FCLIP; Director of Scholarship and Collections, British Library, since 2007; *b* 14 Feb. 1957; *s* of Robert Hally Milne and Joyce (*née* McRobbie). *Educ:* Perth Acad.; Berwickshire High Sch.; Univ. of Edinburgh (MA 1979); University Coll. London (MA 1983); MA Oxon 2003. FCLIP (FLA 2002). SCONUL trainee, Cambridge Univ. Liby, 1981–82; Sen. Liby Asst, Univ. of London Liby Resources Co-ordinating Cttee, 1983–85; Asst Librarian, Glasgow Univ. Liby, 1985–90; Sub-Librarian, Trinity Coll., Cambridge, 1990–94; Asst Dir of Liby Services, KCL, 1994–98; Dir, Res. Support Libraries Prog., 1998–2002; Dep. to Dir, Univ. Liby Services and to Bodley's Librarian, 2002–04; Acting Dir and Bodley's Librarian, 2004–07, Oxford Univ.; Fellow, Wolfson Coll., Oxford, 2003–07. Mem., Legal Deposit Adv. Panel, DCMS, 2007–. Dir, Consortium of Res. Libraries, 2005–07. Chairman: Nat. Preservation Office Bd, 2005–07; Digital Preservation Coalition, 2006–; Internat. English Short Time Catalogue Cttee, 2007–. Mem., UK Literary Heritage Wkg Gp, 2007–. FRSA 2000; FRSE 2006. *Publications:* contribs to professional jls and books. *Recreations:* hill-walking, listening to music, photography. *Address:* British Library, 96 Euston Road, NW1 2DB. *T:* (020) 7412 7530, *Fax:* (020) 7412 7093; *e-mail:* ronald.milne@bl.uk. *Club:* Reform.

MILNE, Prof. William Ireland, PhD; FREng, FIET, FIMMM; Professor of Electrical Engineering, since 1996, Head of Electrical Division, since 1999, and Director, Centre for Advanced Photonics and Electronics, since 2005, University of Cambridge; Fellow, Churchill College, Cambridge, since 1977; *b* 15 Feb. 1948; *s* of William Ireland Milne and Jenelia Foy Kelso Milne (*née* Reid); *m* 1st, 1971, Jennifer Stovell (marr. diss. 1991); one *s* one *d*; 2nd, 1992, Catharina Jacqueline Ann Baker; one step *s* one step *d*. *Educ:* Forfar Acad.; St Andrews Univ. (BSc Hons 1970); Imperial Coll., London DIC, PhD 1973). FIET (FIEE 1989); FIMMM (FIM 1999). Sen. Scientist, then Principal Scientist, Plessey Res. Centre, Caswell, 1973–76; Engineering Department, University of Cambridge: Asst Lectr, 1976–80; Lectr, 1980–90; Reader, 1990–96. Visiting Professor: Tokyo Inst. of Technol., 1985; Nanyang Technol Univ., Singapore, 1993; Gifu Univ., Japan, 2001; South East Univ., Nanying, 2007–; Dist. Vis. Prof., Nat. Univ. of Singapore, 2008; Hon. Prof., Coll. of Sci. and Technol. of Huazhang Normal Univ., 2007–. FREng 2006. Hon. DEng Univ. of Waterloo, Toronto, 2003. *Recreations:* golf, tennis, travel. *Address:* Electrical Division Building, Engineering Department, Cambridge University, 9 J. J. Thomson Avenue, Cambridge CB3 0FA.

MILNE-WATSON, Sir Andrew (Michael), 4th Bt *cr* 1937, of Ashley, Longbredy, co. Dorset; Proprietor, A. D. R. Associates Ltd, since 1993; *b* 10 Nov. 1944; *o s* of Sir Michael Milne-Watson, 3rd Bt, CBE and Mary Lisette Gunion Milne-Watson (*née* Bagnall); *S* father, 1999; *m* 1st, 1970, Beverley Jane Gabrielle Cotton (marr. diss. 1981); one *s* one *d*; 2nd, 1983, Gisella Stafford (*née* Tisdall); one *s*. *Educ:* Eton. Sales and Mgt Trainee, Sidney Flavel & Co. Ltd, 1965–68; Mgt Trainee, E Midlands Gas Bd, 1968–69; Ogilvy & Mather (UK): Trainee, 1969; Account Mgr, 1970; Account Dir, 1973–79; Managing and Client Service Director: Mathers Advertising Ltd, 1979–82; Phoenix Advertising Ltd, 1982–84; Dep. Chm., Lewis Broadbent Advertising Ltd, 1984–87; founded: Minerva Publications Ltd, 1987–89; MW Communications Ltd, 1989–90; Dir of Advertising and Mktg, Inc. Publications, 1990–93. Liveryman, Grocers' Co. *Recreations:* cooking, gardening, building renovation. *Heir: s* David Alastair Milne-Watson [*b* 24 Aug. 1971; *m* 2000, Sandra M. Geraldi, Campinas, Brazil]. *Address:* 22 Musgrave Crescent, SW6 4QE. *T:* (020) 7731 4488. *Club:* Garrick.

MILNER, family name of **Baron Milner of Leeds**.

MILNER OF LEEDS, 3rd Baron *cr* 1951; **Richard James Milner;** *b* 16 May 1959; *s* of 2nd Baron Milner of Leeds, AE and Sheila Margaret (*née* Hartley); *S* father, 2003; *m* 1988, Margaret, *y d* of G. F. Voisin; two *d*. *Educ:* Charterhouse; Surrey Univ. (BSc). Freeman, City of London, 1988; Liveryman, Clothworkers' Co., 1988. Mem., Vins Sans Frontières, Jersey. *Heir:* none. *Address:* Roche d'Or, Trinity, Jersey, CI JE3 5JA.

MILNER, Prof. Arthur David, PhD; FRSE; Professor of Cognitive Neuroscience, University of Durham, since 2000; *b* 16 July 1943; *s* of Arthur Milner and Sarah Ellen Milner (*née* Gaunt); *m* 1965, Christine Armitage; two *s*. *Educ:* Bradford Grammar Sch.; Lincoln Coll., Oxford (Open Schol.; BA 1965; MA 1970); Inst. of Psychiatry, London (DipPsych 1966; PhD 1971). Res. Asst, Inst. of Psychiatry, London, 1966–70; University of St Andrews: Lectr, 1970–82, Sen. Lectr, 1982–85, in Psychology; Reader in Neuropsychology, 1985–90; Prof. of Neuropsychology, 1990–2000; Chm., Dept of Psychology, 1983–88; Dean, Faculty of Science, 1992–94; Head, Sch. of Psychology, 1994–97. *Publications:* The Neuropsychology of Consciousness, 1992; The Visual Brain in Action, 1995, 2nd edn 2006; Comparative Neuropsychology, 1998; Cognitive and Neural Bases of Spatial Neglect, 2002; Sight Unseen, 2004 (BPsS Book Award, 2005); The Roots of Visual Awareness, 2004; sci. articles in learned jls and books, mainly on brain mechanisms underlying visual perception, visual guidance of movement, and bilateral co-ordination. *Recreations:* walking, cinema, jazz. *Address:* Department of Psychology, University of Durham, Science Laboratories, South Road, Durham DH1 3LE. *T:* (0191) 334 0433.

MILNER, Prof. Arthur John Robin Gorell, FRS 1988; FRSE; Professor of Computer Science, 1995–2001, now Professor Emeritus, and Fellow of King's College, since 1995, Cambridge University; *b* 13 Jan. 1934; *s* of John Theodore Milner and Muriel Emily (*née* Barnes-Gorell); *m* 1963, Lucy Petronella Moor; two *s* one *d*. *Educ:* Eton Coll.; King's Coll., Cambridge (BA Maths, 1957). FRSE 1993. Maths teacher, Marylebone Grammar Sch., 1959–60; Ferranti Ltd, London, 1960–63; Lectr in Maths and Computing, City Univ., London, 1963–68; Research Fellow: University Coll., Swansea, 1968–70; Artificial Intelligence Lab., Stanford Univ., Calif, 1970–72; Edinburgh University: Lectr, 1973–75; Sen. Lectr, 1975–78; Reader, 1978–84; Prof. of Computation Theory, 1984–94. Founder Mem., Academia Europaea, 1988; For. Mem., French Acad. of Scis, 2007. Hon. DSc(Eng) Chalmers Univ., Gothenburg, Sweden, 1988. A. M. Turing Award, ACM, 1991; Royal Medal, RSE, 2004. *Publications:* Calculus for Communication and Concurrency, 1989; The Definition of Standard ML, 1990, 2nd edn 1997; Commentary on Standard ML, 1990; Communicating and Mobile Systems: the π calculus, 1999; contribs to Computer Science on mechanised logic of computation and on calculus of communicating systems. *Recreations:* music, carpentry, walking. *Address:* 24 Lyndewode Road, Cambridge CB1 2HN.

MILNER, Prof. Brenda (Atkinson), CC 2004 (OC 1984); OQ 1985; FRS 1979; FRSC 1976; Professor of Psychology, Department of Neurology and Neurosurgery, McGill University, since 1970; Dorothy J. Killam Professor, Montreal Neurological Institute, since 1993 (Head of Neuropsychology Research Unit, 1970–91); *b* 15 July 1918; *d* of Samuel Langford and Clarice Frances Leslie (*née* Doig). *Educ:* Univ. of Cambridge (BA, MA, ScD); McGill Univ. (PhD). Experimental Officer, Min. of Supply, 1941–44; Professeur Agrégé, Inst. de Psychologie, Univ. de Montréal, 1944–52; Res. Associate, Psychology Dept, McGill Univ., 1952–53; Lectr, 1953–60, Asst Prof., 1960–64, Associate Prof., 1964–70, Dept of Neurology and Neurosurgery, McGill Univ. Hon. LLD: Queen's Univ., Kingston, Ont, 1980; Cambridge, 2000; Hon. DSc: Manitoba, 1982; Lethbridge, 1986; Mount Holyoke, 1986; Toronto, 1987; McGill, 1991; Wesleyan, 1991; Acadia, 1991; St Andrews, 1992; Hartford, 1997; McMaster, 1999; Memorial, 2002; Columbia, 2002; Ryerson, 2008; Hon. DScSoc Laval, 1987; Hon. Dr Montreal, 1988; Hon. DHumL Mount St Vincent, 1988; DU Ottawa, 2004. Izaak Walton Killam Prize, Canada Council, 1983; Hermann von Helmholtz Prize, Inst. for Cognitive Neuroscience, USA, 1984; Ralph W. Gerard Prize, Soc. for Neuroscience, 1987; Wilder Penfield Prize, PQ, 1993; Metropolitan Life Foundn award, 1996; John. P. McGovern Award, AAAS, 2001; D. O. Hebb Award, Canadian Soc. for Brain, Behaviour and Cognitive Sci., 2001; Neurosci. Award, NAS, 2004; Gairder Foundn Award in Health Res., 2005. Grand Dame of Merit, Order of Malta, 1985. *Publications:* mainly articles in neurological and psychological jls. *Address:* Montreal Neurological Institute, 3801 University Street, Montreal, QC H3A 2B4, Canada. *T:* (514) 3988503, *Fax:* (514) 3988540.

MILNER, Rt Rev. Ronald James; Bishop Suffragan of Burnley, 1988–93; Hon. Assistant Bishop, diocese of Southwell and Nottingham (formerly diocese of Southwell), since 1994; *b* 16 May 1927; *s* of Maurice and Muriel Milner; *m* 1950, Audrey Cynthia Howard; two *s* two *d* (and one *d* decd). *Educ:* Hull Grammar School; Pembroke Coll., Cambridge (MA); Wycliffe Hall, Oxford. Ordained deacon, 1953, priest, 1954; Succentor, Sheffield Cathedral, 1953–58; Vicar: Westwood, Coventry, 1958–64; St James, Fletchamstead, Coventry, 1964–70; Rector of St Mary's, Southampton, 1970–73; Rector of the Southampton Team Ministry, 1973–83; Archdeacon of Lincoln, 1983–88. *Recreations:* ornithology, walking, music. *Address:* 7 Crafts Way, Southwell, Notts NG25 0BL.

MILNER, Dr Simon Trevor; Director, Media and Convergence Policy, BT plc, since 2008; *b* 23 April 1967; *s* of Trevor Winston Milner and Christine Mary Milner; *m* 1991, Sarah Wells; two *s* one *d*. *Educ:* Bradford Grammar Sch.; Wadham Coll., Oxford (BA Hons Hist. and Econs); London Sch. of Econs (MSc Industrial Relns, PhD Industrial Relns 1993). London School of Economics: Res. Officer, Centre for Econ. Performance, 1990–94; Lectr, Dept of Industrial Relns, 1994–95; Sec., Commn on Public Policy and British Business, IPPR, 1995–97; Sen. Advr, Policy and Planning, 1997–99, Secretary, 2000–05, BBC; Hd, Ext. Relns, Equality of Access Office, BT plc, 2005–08. *Publication:* New Perspectives on Industrial Disputes, 1993. *Recreations:* children, football. *Address:* BT plc, 81 Newgate Street, EC1A 7AJ.

MILNER, Sir Timothy William Lycett, (Sir Tim), 10th Bt *cr* 1717, of Nun Appleton Hall, Yorkshire; *b* 11 Oct. 1936; *er s* of Sir (George Edward) Mordaunt Milner, 9th Bt and Barbara Audrey (*d* 1951), *d* of Henry Noel Belsham; *S* father, 1995. *Heir: b* Charles Mordaunt Milner [*b* 18 May 1944; *m* 1965, Lady Charlene French, *e d* of 3rd Earl of Ypres; three *s*]. *Address:* c/o Natte Valleij, Box 4, Klapmuts 7625, South Africa.

MILNER-GULLAND, Prof. Robert Rainsford, (Robin), FBA 2002; FSA; Professor of Russian and East European Studies, 1993–2001, Research Professor in Russian, since 2001, School of Humanities (formerly School of European Studies), University of Sussex; *b* 24 Feb. 1936; *s* of late Laurence Harry Milner-Gulland and Ruth (Nancy) Milner-Gulland (*née* Bavin); *m* 1966, Alison Margaret Taylor; one *s* two *d*. *Educ:* Westminster Sch. (Schol.); New Coll., Oxford (Schol., then Sen. Schol.; BA Modern Langs, MA); Moscow Univ. University of Sussex: Asst Lectr, then Lectr, Sch. of Eur. Studies, 1962–74; Reader in Russian and E Eur. Studies, 1974–93. Member: Cttee, British Univs Assoc. of Slavists, 1970–78; Sussex Historic Churches Trust, 2002–. FSA 1988. Coronation Medal, 1953. *Publications:* Soviet Russian Verse: an anthology, 1964; (with M. Dewhirst) Russian Writing Today, 1974; (with J. Bowlt) An Introduction to Russian Art and Architecture, 1980; Cultural Atlas of Russia, 1989, 2nd edn 1998; (ed and trans.) The Life of Zabolotsky, 1994; The Russians, 1997, 2nd edn 1999; (ed and trans.) Icon and Devotion, by O. Tarasov, 2002; contrib. articles to learned jls on many aspects of Russian studies and on Romanesque art of Sussex. *Recreations:* walking, archaeology. *Address:* Arts Building, University of Sussex, Falmer, Brighton, Sussex BN1 9QN. *T:* (01273) 877340; *e-mail:* r.r.milner-gulland@sussex.ac.uk.

MILNES, Rodney; *see* Blumer, Rodney Milnes.

MILNES COATES, Prof. Sir Anthony (Robert), 4th Bt *cr* 1911; BSc, MB BS, MD; FRCPath, FRCP; Professor of Medical Microbiology, St George's Hospital Medical School, since 1989; *b* 8 Dec. 1948; *s* of Sir Robert Edward James Clive Milnes Coates, 3rd Bt, DSO, and Lady Patricia Ethel, *d* of 4th Earl of Listowel; *S* father, 1982; *m* 1978, Harriet Ann Burton; one *s* two *d*. *Educ:* Eton; BSc London 1970; St Thomas's Hospital, London Univ. (MB BS 1973; MD 1984). MRCS 1973; MRCP 1978, FRCP 1998; FRCPath 1999. MRC Trng Res. Fellow, Dept of Bacteriology, RPMS, 1979–82; Sen. Registrar in Bacteriology, RPMS, 1982–84; Sen. Lectr (Hon. Consultant), Dept of Medical Microbiology, London Hosp. Medical Coll., 1984–90. Councillor, 1980–, Mayor, 2002–03, Royal Borough of Kensington and Chelsea. *Heir: s* Thomas Anthony Milnes Coates, *b* 19 Nov. 1986. *Address:* Hereford Cottage, 135 Gloucester Road, SW7 4TH. *Club:* Brooks's.

MILNOR, (Margaret) Dusa; *see* McDuff, M. D.

MILROY, Prof. (Ann) Lesley, PhD; Fellow, Centre for Linguistics and Philology, University of Oxford, since 2005; Hans Kurath Collegiate Professor of Linguistics, University of Michigan, 2000–05, now Professor Emerita; *b* 5 March 1944; *d* of Thomas Keddie Cross and Janet Elizabeth Cross; *m* 1965, Prof. James R. D. Milroy; three *s*. *Educ:* Univ. of Manchester (BA 1st Cl. Hons English 1965; MA 1967); Univ. of Belfast (PhD 1979). Various lecturing posts, Ulster Poly., 1972–82; Sen. Simon Research Fellow, Univ. of Manchester, 1982–83; University of Newcastle upon Tyne: Lectr in Linguistics, 1983–85; Sen. Lectr, 1985–88; Prof. of Sociolinguistics, 1988–98 (on leave of absence, 1994–98); Prof. of Linguistics, Univ. of Michigan, 1994–2000. Vis. Fellow, Univ. of Canterbury, Christchurch, NZ, 1992. *Publications:* Language and Social Networks, 1980, 2nd edn 1987; Observing and Analysing Natural Language, 1987; (with J. Milroy) Authority in Language: investigating language prescription and standardisation, 1987, 3rd edn 1998; (with R. Lesser) Linguistics and Aphasia: psycholinguistic and pragmatic aspects of intervention, 1993; (ed with J. Milroy) Real English: the grammar of English dialects in the British Isles, 1993; (ed with P. Muysken) One Speaker, Two Languages: cross-disciplinary perspectives on codeswitching, 1995; (with M. Gordon) Sociolinguistics: method and interpretation, 2003; contrib. articles to learned jls. *Recreations:* swimming, walking, reading. *Address:* Stable Cottage, Hempton Road, Deddington, Oxon OX15 0TL.

MILROY, Very Rev. Dominic Liston, OSB; MA; Headmaster, Ampleforth College, 1980–92; *b* 18 April 1932; *s* of Adam Liston Milroy and Clarita Burns. *Educ:* Ampleforth Coll.; St Benet's Hall, Oxford (1st Cl. Mod. Langs, MA). Entered Ampleforth Abbey, 1950; teaching staff, Ampleforth Coll., 1957–74; Head of Mod. Langs, 1963–74; Housemaster, 1964–74; Prior of Internat. Benedictine Coll. of S Anselmo, Rome, 1974–79. Chm., HMC, 1992. *Address:* Ampleforth Abbey, York YO62 4EN. *T:* (01439) 766714.

MILROY, Lesley; *see* Milroy, A. L.

MILROY, Lisa Katharine, RA 2005; painter; *b* Vancouver, 16 Jan. 1959; *d* of Reginald Charles Milroy and Leona Vera Milroy (*née* Demchuk); partner, Lewis Biggs, *qv*. *Educ:* St Martin's Sch. of Art; Goldsmiths' Coll., Univ. of London (BA 1st Cl. Hons Fine Arts 1982). *Solo exhibitions* include: Nicola Jacobs Gall., London, 1984, 1986, 1988; Cartier Art Foundn, Paris, 1984; John Berggruen Gall., San Francisco, 1989, 1992; Galerie Luis Campaña, Frankfurt, 1991, Cologne, 1993, 1997, 2003; Waddington Galls, London, 1993, 1998; Galerie Jennifer Flay, Paris, 1993, 1996, 1999; Gall. Shoko Nagai, Tokyo, Kyoto City Univ. of Arts, 1994; British Sch. at Rome, 1995; Alan Cristea Gall., London, 1998, 2000, 2003, 2005; Sadler's Wells Th., London, 2000; Tate Gall., Liverpool, 2001; Galerie Xippas, Paris, 2005; New Art Centre Sculpture Park and Gall., Roche Court, Wilts, Galerie Lelong, Zürich, 2006; *group exhibitions* include: Sydney Biennale, 1986, 1998; John Moores Liverpool Exhibns, Walker Art Gall., Liverpool, 1985, 1987, 1989, 2002, 2004; Carnegie Internat., 1991; Tate Gall., 1992, 1995; Calouste Gulbenkian Foundn, Lisbon, 1992, 1997; Vienna and Hamburg, 1993; Scottish Nat. Gall. of Modern Art, Edinburgh, 1995; Tate Gall., Liverpool, 1996, 1998; Whitechapel Art Gall., 2000; Jerwood Space, London, 2002; Galerie Lelong, Zürich, 2004; Tate Modern, 2004; *work* *in public collections* including: Arts Council of GB; British Council; Calouste Gulbenkian Foundn, Lisbon; Contemporary Art Soc.; Metropolitan Mus. of Art, NY; Tate Gall., London; Tokyo Metropolitan Art Collection. 1st prize, John Moores, 1987; D&AD Silver Award for Royal Mail Millennium Stamp, 2000. *Recreation:* hiking. *Address:* c/o Royal Academy of Arts, Burlington House, Piccadilly, W1J 0BD.

MILSOM, Stroud Francis Charles; QC 1985; FBA 1967; Professor of Law, Cambridge University, 1976–90; Fellow of St John's College, Cambridge, since 1976; *b* 2 May 1923; *yr s* of late Harry Lincoln Milsom and Isobel Vida Collins; *m* 1955, Irène (*d* 1998), *d* of late Witold Szereszewski, Wola Krysztoporska, Poland. *Educ:* Charterhouse; Trinity Coll., Cambridge. Admiralty, 1944–45. Called to the Bar, Lincoln's Inn, 1947, Hon. Bencher, 1970; Commonwealth Fund Fellow, Univ. of Pennsylvania, 1947–48; Yorke Prize, Univ. of Cambridge, 1948; Prize Fellow, Fellow and Lectr, Trinity Coll., Cambridge, 1948–55; Fellow, Tutor and Dean, New Coll., Oxford, 1956–64; Prof. of Legal History, London Univ., 1964–76. Selden Society: Literary Dir, 1964–80; Pres., 1985–88. Mem., Royal Commn on Historical Manuscripts, 1975–98. Vis. Lectr, New York Univ. Law Sch., several times, 1958–70; Visiting Professor: Yale Law Sch., several times, 1968–; Harvard Law Sch. and Dept of History, 1973; Charles Inglis Thomson Prof., Colorado Univ. Law Sch., 1977. Maitland Meml Lectr, Cambridge, 1972; Addison Harris Meml Lectr, Indiana Univ. Law Sch., 1974; Vis. Prof. and Wilfred Fullagar Lectr, Monash Univ., 1981; Ford's Lectr, Oxford, 1986; Carpentier Lectr, Columbia Univ., 1995. Foreign Mem., Amer. Phil Soc., 1984. Hon. LLD: Glasgow, 1981; Chicago, 1985; Cambridge, 2003. Ames Prize, Harvard, 1972; Swiney Prize, RSA/RCP, 1974. *Publications:* Novae Narrationes (introd., trans. and notes), 1963; introd. reissue Pollock and Maitland, History of English Law, 1968; Historical Foundations of the Common Law, 1969, 2nd edn 1981; The Legal Framework of English Feudalism, 1976; Studies in the History of the Common Law (collected papers), 1985; A Natural History of the Common Law, 2003. *Address:* St John's College, Cambridge CB2 1TP; 113 Grantchester Meadows, Cambridge CB3 9JN. *T:* (01223) 354100. *Club:* Athenæum.

MILTON, Anne Frances; MP (C) Guildford, since 2005; *b* 3 Nov. 1955; *d* of late Patrick Turner and Nesta Turner; *m* Dr Graham Henderson; three *s* one *d*. *Educ:* Haywards Heath Grammar Sch.; St Bartholomew's Hospital Sch. of Nursing (RGN 1977). Staff Nurse, 1977–78, Research Nurse, 1978–81, St Bartholomew's Hosp.; District Nursing Sister: City and Hackney HA, 1981–83; St Thomas' Hosp., London, 1983–85; Med. Advr on Housing for E London and City HA, 1985–2000; self-employed med. advr to social housing providers, 2000–05. Member: CPRE; Countryside Alliance. *Publication:* contrib. Lancet. *Recreations:* gardening, reading, music. *Address:* House of Commons, SW1A 0AA. *T:* (020) 7219 8392; *e-mail:* miltona@parliament.uk.

MILTON, Maj.-Gen. Anthony Arthur, CB 2002; OBE 1995; Commandant General Royal Marines, and Commander United Kingdom Amphibious Forces, 2002–04; *b* 19 Aug. 1949; *s* of W. W. Milton; *m* 1972, Nova Mary Biscombe; three *d*. *Educ:* King Edward VI Sch., Chelmsford; St John's Coll., Cambridge (MPhil Internat. Relns). Commnd Royal Marines, 1967; Subaltern, 42, 45 and 40 Commando, serving in Far East, Norway, Caribbean, Cyprus and NI, 1970–76; exchange tour with USMC, 1976–78; CTC, Lympstone, 1978–81; Army Staff Coll., 1982; MoD, 1983–84; Equerry to the Duke of Edinburgh, 1983–84; Co. Comdr, 42 Commando, 1985–86; COS, 3 Commando Bde, 1987–89; MoD, 1991–92; CO, 40 Commando, Norway and NI, 1992–94; rcds 1995; Comdr, 3 Commando Bde, 1995–97; Dir, N Atlantic and Western Europe, 1997–98; ADC to the Queen, 1997–99; Dir Gen., Jt Doctrine and Concepts, MoD, 1999–2002. Vis. Fellow, Cambridge Univ., 2007. FRGS 1992. *Publications:* academic articles. *Recreations:* sailing, music, mountains. *Club:* Army and Navy.

MILTON, Derek Francis, CMG 1990; HM Diplomatic Service, retired; student of Polish affairs; *b* 11 Nov. 1935; *s* of Francis Henry Milton and Florence Elizabeth Maud Kirby; *m* 1st, 1960, Helge Kahle; two *s*; 2nd, 1977, Catherine Walmsley. *Educ:* Preston Manor County Grammar Sch., Wembley; Manchester Univ. (BA Hons Politics and Modern History, 1959). RAF, 1954–56. Colonial Office, 1959–63; Asst Private Sec. to Commonwealth and Colonial Sec., 1962–64; Commonwealth Prime Ministers' Meeting Secretariat, 1964; First Secretary: CRO (later FO), 1964–67; UK Mission to UN, New York, 1967–71; Rome, 1972–75; FCO, 1975–77; Counsellor: Civil Service Res. Fellow, Glasgow Univ., 1977–78; Caracas, 1978–79; Dept of Trade, 1980–82; Overseas Inspectorate, 1982–84; Minister-Counsellor, Mexico City, 1984–87; RCDS, 1988; High Comr, Kingston, Jamaica, and non-resident Ambassador to Haiti, 1989–95. Americas Res. Gp, Res. Analysts, FCO, 1995–99 (on contract). *Recreations:* QPR Football Club, travel, swimming. *Address:* 31 Park Road, Beckenham BR3 1QG.

MILTON, Peter James Denis, MD; FRCOG; Consultant Obstetrician and Gynaecologist, Addenbrooke's Hospital, Cambridge, and Associate Lecturer, University of Cambridge, 1976–2002, now Consultant Emeritus; Internal Professional Advisor, NHS Ombudsman, since 2002; *b* 17 Jan. 1938; *s* of James Hugh Milton, CEng, FInstMarE, and Dorothy Winifred Milton (*née* Nelson); *m* 1968, Rosemary Jane Phillips; two *s* one *d*. *Educ:* Merchant Taylors' Sch., Crosby, Liverpool; King's Coll., London; St George's Hosp. Med. Sch., Univ. of London (MB BS; MD 1978); MA Cantab 1978. MRCS, LRCP 1963; DA 1969; MRCOG 1970, FRCOG 1983. Jun. med. and surgical posts, St George's, Winchester, Canterbury and St Thomas' Hosps, 1963–70; Ships Surgeon, Blue Star Line, 1968; Registrar, Obstetrics and Gynaecology, St Thomas' Hosp. and Groote Schuur Hosp., Cape Town, 1970–72; Lectr and Sen. Registrar, St Thomas' Hosp., 1972–76; Res. Associate, Imperial Cancer Res. Lab., Lincoln's Inn, 1972–76. Editor and reviewer, obstetric and gynaecological specialist books and jls. Royal College of Obstetricians and Gynaecologists: Fellows' Rep., Council, 1993–98; Chm., Continuing Med. Educn Cttee, 1995–98; Mem., various cttees; Sen. Vice Pres., 1998–2001. Pres., Sect. Obstetrics and Gynaecol., RSocMed, 2004–05 (Hon. Sec., 1992–93; Vice-Pres., 1993–96). Examiner: RCOG; Univs of Cambridge, London, Edinburgh, Liverpool, Manchester, Glasgow, W Indies, Colombo and Khartoum. *Publications:* papers and chapters on pre-natal diagnosis, pre-malignant disease, menopause and other obstetric and gynaecol topics in British and overseas specialist jls. *Recreations:* sailing, ski-ing, second-hand bookshops, walking dogs and more distant travel. *Address:* King's Head House, Duxford, Cambridge CB22 4RP. *T:* (01223) 832238. *Clubs:* Athenæum, Royal Society of Medicine; Royal Fowey Yacht; Aldeburgh Yacht; Gynaecological Travellers of UK and Ireland.

MILTON, Sir Simon (Henry), Kt 2006; Deputy Mayor of London, Policy and Planning, since 2008; *b* 2 Oct. 1961; *s* of Clive Milton and Ruth Milton (*née* Klein). *Educ:* Gonville and Caius Coll., Cambridge (BA Hons Hist 1983); Cornell Univ. (Master Professional Studies). Man. Dir, 1995–99, Chm., 1999–2001, Apco UK Ltd. Mem. (C), Westminster CC, 1988–2008 (Leader, 2000–08). Dep. Chm., Central London Partnership, 2002–. Dep. Chm., 2005–07, Chm., 2007–08, Sen. Advr, Planning, 2008, LGA; Bd Mem., Leadership Centre for Local Govt, 2005–. *Recreation:* city management. *Address:* Greater London Authority, City Hall, Queen's Walk, SE1 2AA.

MILTON-THOMPSON, Surg. Vice-Adm. Sir Godfrey (James), KBE 1988; FRCP; Warden, St Katharine's House, Wantage, 1993–98; Medical Director General (Naval), 1985–90; Surgeon General, Ministry of Defence, 1988–90; *b* 25 April 1930; *s* of Rev. James Milton-Thompson and May LeMare (*née* Hoare); *m* 1952, Noreen Helena Frances, *d* of Lt-Col Sir Desmond Fitzmaurice, CIE; three *d*. *Educ:* Eastbourne Coll.; Queens' Coll., Cambridge (MA); St Thomas' Hosp. (MB BChir); FRCP 1974 (MRCP 1961); DCH 1963. Joined Royal Navy, 1955; after general service and hosp. appts at home and abroad, Cons. Phys., RN Hosp., Plymouth, 1967–70 and 1972–75; Hon. Research Fellow, St Mark's Hosp., London, 1969–71; Prof. of Naval Medicine, 1975–80; RCDS 1981; Dep. Medical Director General (Naval), 1982–84; Surg. Rear-Adm. (Operational Med. Services), 1984–85; Dep. Surg. Gen. (Research and Trng), MoD, 1985–87. QHP, 1982–90. Chm., Cornwall Community Healthcare Trust, 1991–93. Member: Medical Research Soc., 1971–; British Soc. of Gastroenterology, 1972–; Vice Pres., British Digestive Foundn, 1993–. Hon. Col, 211 (Wessex) Field Hosp., RAMC(V), 1990–95. Chm., Liskeard DFAS, 2001–. Gov., St Mary's Sch., Wantage, 1995–2006 (Chm., 1996–2006). Errol-Eldridge Prize, 1974; Gilbert Blane Medal, 1976. KStJ 1989 (Mem., Chapter Gen., 1988–95; Hospitaller, 1991–95; Chm., St John Council, Cornwall, 2000–; Mem., English Priory Chapter, 2000–). *Publications:* on clinical pharmacology of the gastro-intestinal tract and therapy of peptic ulcer, etc, in med. jls. *Recreations:* fishing, paintings and painting, literature. *Address:* Pool Hall, Menheniot, Liskeard, Cornwall PL14 3QT. *Club:* Naval and Military.

MILVERTON, 2nd Baron *cr* 1947, of Lagos and of Clifton; **Rev. Fraser Arthur Richard Richards;** Rector of Christian Malford with Sutton Benger and Tytherton Kellaways, 1967–93; *b* 21 July 1930; *s* of 1st Baron Milverton, GCMG, and Noelle Benda, *d* of Charles Basil Whitehead; *S* father, 1978; *m* 1957, Mary Dorothy, BD, *d* of late Leslie Fly, ARCM, Corsham, Wilts; two *d*. *Educ:* De Carteret Prep. Sch., Jamaica; Ridley Coll., Ontario; Clifton Coll.; Egerton Agric. Coll., Kenya; Bishop's Coll., Cheshunt. Royal Signals, 1949–50; Kenya Police, 1952–53. Deacon 1957, priest 1958, dio. Rochester; Curate: Beckenham, 1957–59; St John Baptist, Sevenoaks, 1959–60; Great Bookham, 1960–63; Vicar of Okewood with Forest Green, 1963–67. Chaplain, Wilts ACF, 1968–81. Trustee and Dir, Voice (UK) Ltd. Gov., Clifton Coll. *Recreations:* family, reading, current affairs and history; enjoys music and walking; interested in tennis, swimming, cricket and Rugby Union. *Heir: b* Hon. Michael Hugh Richards [*b* 1 Aug. 1936; *m* 1960, Edna Leonie (*d* 2001), *y d* of Col Leo Steveni, OBE, MC; one *s*].

MILWARD, Prof. Alan Steele, FBA 1987; Official Historian, Cabinet Office, 1993–2007; Professor Emeritus of Economic History, London School of Economics, since 1997; *b* 19 Jan. 1935; *s* of Joseph Thomas Milward and Dorothy Milward (*née* Steele); *m* 1st, 1963, Claudine Jeanne Amélie Lemaître (marr. diss. 1994); 2nd, 1998, Frances M. B. Lynch; two *d*; one *d*. *Educ:* University College London (BA 1956); LSE (PhD 1960); MA Manchester 1981. Asst Lectr in Indian Archaeology, Univ. of London, 1959; Lectr in Economic History, Univ. of Edinburgh, 1960; Sen. Lectr in Social Studies, Univ. of East Anglia, 1965; Associate Prof. of Economics, Stanford Univ., 1969; Prof. of European Studies, UMIST, 1971; Prof. of Contemp. Hist., Eur. Univ. Inst., 1983–86 and 1996–2002; Prof. of Econ. History, LSE, 1986–96. Visiting Professor: Stanford Univ., 1966; Ecole Pratique des Hautes Etudes, 1977, 1990; Univ. of Illinois, 1978; Univ.-Gesamthochschule, Siegen, 1980; Oslo Univ., 1990; Aarhus Univ., 1992; Trondheim Univ., 1993–2000; Sen. Vis. Fellow, St John's Coll., Oxford, 2002–03. Hon. Fellow, Royal Norwegian Acad. of Scis and Letters, 1994. *Publications:* The German Economy at War, 1965; The New Order and the French Economy, 1970; The Social and Economic Effects of the Two World Wars on Britain, 1971, 2nd edn 1984; The Fascist Economy in Norway, 1972; (with S. B. Saul) The Economic Development of Continental Europe 1780–1870, 1973; (with S. B. Saul) The Development of the Economies of Continental Europe 1870–1914, 1977; War, Economy and Society, 1977; The Reconstruction of Western Europe 1945–1951, 1984, 2nd edn 1987; (with B. Martin) Landwirtschaft und Ernährung im Zweiten Weltkrieg, 1984; The European Rescue of the Nation-State, 1992; The Frontier of National Sovereignty, 1993; (with G. Brennan) Britain's Place in the World: a historical enquiry into import controls 1945–60, 1996; The Rise and Fall of a National Strategy 1945–1963, 2002. *Recreation:* theatre. *Address:* 5 Richmond Crescent, N1 0LZ.

MILWARD, Timothy Michael, FRCS; Consultant Plastic Surgeon to Leicester Royal Infirmary, Pilgrim Hospital, Boston, and Lincoln County Hospital, 1976–2002, now Emeritus; *b* 24 March 1937; *s* of Francis John and Rosemary Gwendoline Milward; *m* 1970, Susan Isabel; four *d* (incl. twins). *Educ:* Rugby Sch.; Clare Coll., Cambridge (MB, BCh, MA); St Thomas' Hosp. President: British Assoc. of Aesthetic Plastic Surgeons, 1987–88; BAPS, 1996; Mem., Senate of Surgery of GB and Ireland, 1995–98. Fellow, Acad. of Experts. *Publications:* contrib. British Jl of Plastic Surgery. *Recreations:* squash, tennis, walking with friends. *Address:* Spire Leicester Hospital, Gartree Road, Leicester LE2 2FF. *T:* (0116) 265 3678, *Fax:* (0116) 265 3679.

MIMPRISS, Peter Hugh Trevor, CVO 2001; Charities Adviser to HRH the Prince of Wales, 2004–06; *b* 22 Aug. 1943; *s* of Hugh Trevor Baber Mimpriss and Gwyneth Mary Mimpriss (*née* Bartley); *m* 1st, 1971, Hilary Ann Reed (marr. diss. 1992); two *d*; 2nd, 1992, Elisabeth Lesley Molle. *Educ:* Sherborne Sch. Admitted solicitor, 1967. Joined Allen & Overy, 1968; Partner, 1972–2002; univ. solicitor, Univ. of London, 1995–2002; Dir, Edmond J. Safra Philanthropic Foundn, 2002–04. Chairman: Charity Law Assoc., 1992–97; Chariguard Gp of Common Investment Funds, 1994–2000. Director: Leeds Castle Foundn, 1980–2006; Chatham Historic Dockyard Trust, 1986–2000; Weston Park Foundn, 1986–2001; Lawcare (formerly Solcare), 1997–2002; PYBT, 1997–99; Prince's Regeneration Trust, 2002–08; Member, Council: Prince's Trust, 1998–2007; King George Jubilee Trust, 2000–06; Queen's Silver Jubilee Trust, 2000–; Trustee: Inst. of Philanthropy, 2000–07; World Trade Centre Disaster Fund, 2001–06; Prince's Foundn for Children and the Arts, 2004–; Prince's Sch. of Traditional Arts, 2005–; Autism Speaks (formerly Nat. Alliance of Autism Res.), 2005– (Dep. Chm., 2005–); Sir Edward Heath Charitable Foundn, 2005–; Jewish Mus., 2006–. Hon. DCL Durham, 2003. *Recreations:* walking, maritime history, vintage cars, collecting books. *Clubs:* Athenæum, Garrick.

MIMS, Prof. Cedric Arthur, MD, FRCPath; Professor of Microbiology, Guy's Hospital Medical School, London, 1972–90; *b* 9 Dec. 1924; *s* of A. H. and Irene Mims; *m* 1952, Valerie Vickery; two *s* two *d*. *Educ:* Mill Hill Sch.; University Coll. London (BSc (Zool)); Middlesex Hosp. Med. Sch. (MB, BS, MD). Medical Research Officer, East African Virus Research Inst., Entebbe, Uganda, 1953–56; Research Fellow and Professorial Fellow, John Curtin Sch. of Med. Research, Australian Nat. Univ., Canberra, 1957–72; Rockefeller Foundn Fellow, Children's Hosp. Med. Centre, Boston, USA, 1963–64; Visiting Fellow, Wistar Inst., Philadelphia, USA, 1969–70. *Publications:* (jtly) The Biology of Animal Viruses, 1974; Mims' Pathogenesis of Infectious Disease, 1976, 5th edn 2000; (with D. O. White) Viral Pathogenesis and Immunology, 1984; (jtly) Medical Microbiology, 1993, 4th edn 2008; When We Die, 1998; The War Within Us, 2000; Love and Old Age, 2003; Fouling the Nest, 2006; The Story of Food, 2008; numerous papers on the pathogenesis of virus infections. *Address:* 1/10 Murray Crescent, Griffith, ACT 2603, Australia.

MINA, Jacqueline Kathleen; goldsmith and jewellery designer; *b* 5 Feb. 1942; *d* of John Frederick Bartlett and Kay Crome and step *d* of Emanuel Hurwitz; *m* 1966, Michael Christou Minas; one *d*. *Educ:* Hornsey Coll. of Art and Crafts; Royal Coll. of Art (DesRCA 1965). Has worked from own studio/workshop, 1965–. Part-time teaching posts include: Harrow Sch. of Art, 1965–70; Farnham Sch. of Art and Design, 1965–75; RCA, 1972–94; Leicester Coll. of Art, 1975–84. External examiner: Edinburgh Coll. of Art, 1989–91; Glasgow Sch. of Art, 1992–96; Bucks UC, 1997–2000. Mem., Jury, Jerwood Prize for Applied Arts (Jewellery), 2007. Mem., Assoc. for Contemporary Jewellery, 1997. FRSA 1999. Freeman, 1985, Lady Liveryman, 1995, Co. of Goldsmiths. Trustee, Bishopsland Educnl Trust, 2001–. Work in exhibitions in UK, Europe and USA, including: Oxford Gall., 1980; Byzantium, NY, 1985; V&A Mus., 1985; Goldsmiths' Hall, London, 1997; Crafts Council Shop at V&A, 2000; World Craft Forum, Kanazawa, Japan, 2003; Collect, V&A Mus., annually, 2004–08; Orgold, Flow Gall., 2004, Scottish Gall., Ruthin Crafts Centre, Wales, 2005; L'or, Bijoux d'Europe, France, 2005; The Goldmark, Thomas Goode, London, 2006; Diamonds, Contemporary Applied Arts, London, 2008; work in public collections in UK and USA, including: Cooper Hewitt Mus., NY; Goldsmiths' Hall; Nat. Mus. of Scotland, Edinburgh; V&A Mus.; Crafts Council, London; Cleveland Contemp. Jewellery Collection, Middlesbrough Inst. of Modern Art. Jerwood Prize for Applied Arts (Jewellery), Jerwood Foundn, 2000. *Publications:* (contrib.) V&A 150th Anniversary Album, 2007; contrib. articles to jls incl. Crafts mag., Jewellery Studies, Findings. *Recreations:* music (appreciation), contemporary dance (appreciation), gardening, cooking, swimming, grannying. *Address:* c/o The Scottish Gallery, 16 Dundas Street, Edinburgh EH3 6HZ. *T:* (0131) 558 1200, *Fax:* (0131) 558 3900.

MINDHAM, Prof. Richard Hugh Shiels, MD; FRCP, FRCPsych; Nuffield Professor of Psychiatry, 1977–2000, now Emeritus, and Dean, Faculty of Medicine, Dentistry and Health, 1996–97, University of Leeds; *b* 25 March 1935; *s* of Thomas Raper Mindham and Winifred Gertrude Mindham; *m* 1971, Barbara Harris Reid; one *s* one *d*. *Educ:* Guy's Hosp. Medical Sch.; Inst. of Psychiatry, Univ. of London; Univ. of Leeds (MA Hist. and Theory of Architecture 2004). MD 1974; FRCPsych 1977; FRCPE 1978; FRCP 2000. Nottingham University Medical School: Sen. Lectr in Psychiatry, 1972–76; Reader, 1976–77; Dean of Postgrad. Studies, Univ. of Leeds, 1994–96. Vis. Prof., Johns Hopkins Univ., 1982. Chief Examr, RCPsych, 1995–98. *Publications:* papers on psychiatry, psychopharmacology and Parkinson's disease. *Recreations:* music, architecture, walking. *Address: e-mail:* r.h.s.mindham@btinternet.com. *Clubs:* Royal Society of Medicine; Leeds.

MINFORD, Prof. (Anthony) Patrick (Leslie), CBE 1996; Professor of Economics, Cardiff Business School, Cardiff University, since 1997; *b* 17 May 1943; *s* of Leslie Mackay Minford and Patricia Mary (*née* Sale); *m* 1970, Rosemary Irene Allcorn; two *s* one *d*. *Educ:* Horris Hill; Winchester Coll. (scholar); Balliol Coll., Oxford (schol.; BA); London Sch. of Economics (grad. studies; MScEcon, PhD). Economic Asst, Min. of Overseas Development, London, 1966; Economist, Min. of Finance, Malawi, 1967–69; Economic Adviser: Director's Staff, Courtaulds Ltd, 1970–71; HM Treasury, 1971–73, and HM Treasury Delegn in Washington, 1973–74; Visiting Hallsworth Fellow, Manchester Univ., 1974–75; Editor, NIESR Review, 1975–76; Edward Gonner Prof. of Applied Econs, Liverpool Univ., 1976–97. Vis. Prof., Cardiff Business Sch., 1993–97. Dir, Merseyside Develt Corp., 1988–89. Mem., Monopolies and Mergers Commn, 1990–96. Mem., HM Treasury's Panel of Economic Forecasters, 1993–96. Mem. Bd, WNO, 1993–98. *Publications:* Substitution Effects, Speculation and Exchange Rate Stability, 1978; (jtly) Unemployment—Cause and Cure, 1983, 2nd edn 1985; (jtly) Rational Expectations and the New Macroeconomics, 1983; (jtly) The Housing Morass, 1987; The Supply Side Revolution in Britain, 1991; (jtly) The Cost of Europe, 1992; Rational Expectations Macroeconomics, 1992; Markets Not Stakes, 1998; (jtly) Britain and Europe: choices for change, 1999; (jtly) Advanced Macroeconomics: a primer, 2002; (jtly) Money Matters: essays in honour of Alan Walters, 2004; (jtly) Should Britain Leave the EU?: an economic analysis of a troubled relationship, 2005; An Agenda for Tax Reform, 2006; articles in learned jls on monetary and internat. economics. *Address:* Cardiff Business School, Cardiff University, Cardiff CF1 3EU.

MINGAY, (Frederick) Ray, CMG 1992; Chief Executive, Trade Development Services, since 1997; consultant to various companies and other organisations; *b* 7 July 1938; *s* of Cecil Stanley and Madge Elizabeth Mingay; *m* 1963, Joan Heather Roberts (*d* 2001); three *s* one *d*. *Educ:* Tottenham Grammar Sch.; St Catharine's Coll., Cambridge (Open Exhibnr; MA); London Univ. (Postgrad. Pub. Admin.); Min. of Educn Cert. of Teaching Competence. Nat. Service, 1959–61: 2nd Lieut RAEC; attached RIF, Kenya. Administration, St Thomas' Hosp., 1961; schoolmaster, 1961–62; Min. of Transport, 1962–64; BoT, 1964; Chrysler (UK) Ltd, 1968–70; Consul (Commercial), Milan, 1970–73; Asst Sec., Dept of Trade, 1973–78; Counsellor (Commercial), Washington, 1978–83; Under Secretary: Mechanical and Electrical Engrg Div., DTI, 1983–86; Investment and Develt Div., DTI, 1986–88; Consul-Gen., Chicago, 1988–92; Head of Overseas Trade Div. DTI, 1992–93; Dir-Gen., Export Promotion, DTI, 1993–97 (concurrently Asst Under Sec. of State, FCO (Jt Export Promotion Directorate), 1993–96). Appts Assessor, Dept for Business, Enterprise and Regulatory Reform (formerly DTI), 2002–; Ind. Mediator, 2006–. Dir, Cove Holidays Ltd, 1977–80; non-executive Director: Aalco, 1983–87; Amari World Steel, 1987–88. Mem., BOTB, 1993–97. Mem., Mid-West Marshall Scholar Selection Cttee, 1988–92. Churchill Fellow, Westminster Coll., Fulton, Mo, 1991. FCMI; MIEx; FRSA. Hon. Citizen, Minneapolis, 1990. *Club:* Reform.

MINGOS, Prof. (David) Michael (Patrick), DPhil; FRS 1992; CChem, FRSC; Principal, St Edmund Hall, Oxford, 1999–Sept. 2009; Professor of Chemistry, University of Oxford, since 2000; *b* 6 Aug. 1944; *s* of Vasso Mingos and Rose Enid Billie Hayes (*née* Griffiths); *m* 1967, Stacey Mary Hosken; one *s* one *d*. *Educ:* Univ. of Manchester (BSc); Univ. of Sussex (DPhil). CChem 1983; FRSC 1983. Fulbright Fellow, Northwestern Univ., 1968–70; ICI Fellow, Sussex Univ., 1970–71; Lectr, QMC, 1971–76; University of Oxford: Lectr, 1976–90; Reader, 1990–92; Fellow, Keble Coll., 1976–92 and by special election, 1993 (Hon. Fellow, 1999); Univ. Assessor, 1991–92; Sir Edward Frankland BP Prof. of Inorganic Chemistry, Imperial Coll., Univ. of London, 1992–99; Dean, Royal Coll. of Sci., 1996–99. Dist. Prof., Xi'an Petroleum Inst., China, 1994–; Wilhelm Manchot Res. Prof. and prize, Munich, 1995; Vis. Prof., Imperial Coll., London, 1999–2002; Univ. of Auckland Foundn Visitor, 2000. Lee Meml Lecture, Univ. of Chicago, 1997. Vice Pres., Dalton Div., RSC, 1993–96. Gov., Harrow Sch., 1994–2004. Hon. DSc: UMIST, 2000; Sussex, 2001. Corday Morgan Medal, 1980, Tilden Medal, 1988, Chemistry of Noble Metals Award, 1983, RSC; M. J. Collins Prize, for innovation in microwave chemistry, CEM Corp., 1996; Alexander von Humboldt Stiftung Forschungspreis, 1999. Regl Editor, Jl of Organometallic Chem., 1996–2006; Member, Editorial Board: Transition Metal Chem., 1975–2006; Structure and Bonding, 1983– (Man. Ed., 2002–); New Jl of Chem., 1986–96; Jl of Organometallic Chem., 1991–; Chemical Soc. Rev., 1992–97; Advances in Inorganic Chem., 1992–2000; Inorganic Chemistry, 1997–99. *Publications:* Introduction to Cluster Chemistry, 1990; Essentials of Inorganic Chemistry 1, 1995; Essential Trends in Inorganic Chemistry, 1997; (ed) Structural and Electronic Paradigms in Cluster Chemistry, 1997; Essentials of Inorganic Chemistry 2, 1998; (ed) Liquid Crystals, Vols 1 and 2, 1999; (ed) Supramolecular Assembly via Hydrogen Bonds, Vols 1 and 2, 2004; (Ed.-in-Chief) Comprehensive Organo-metallic Chemistry III, Vols 1–13, 2007; contribs to jls of learned socs. *Recreations:* cricket, tennis, walking. *Address:* St Edmund Hall, Oxford OX1 4AR. *T:* (01865) 279003; *e-mail:* michael.mingos@seh.ox.ac.uk.

MINKOWSKI, Prof. Christopher Zand, PhD; Boden Professor of Sanskrit, University of Oxford, since 2005; Fellow of Balliol College, Oxford, since 2005; *b* May 1953; *s* of Jan M. Minkowski and Anne Minkowski. *Educ:* Gilman Sch., Baltimore; Harvard Coll. (AB English 1975); Univ. of Delhi (Dip. Hindi 1976); Harvard Univ. (AM 1980; PhD Sanskrit and Indian Studies 1986). Vis. Asst Prof. of Asian Langs and Lits, Univ. of Iowa, 1984–85; Instructor in Sanskrit, Brown Univ., 1985–87; Jun. Res. Fellow in Indology, Wolfson Coll., Oxford, 1988–89; Asst Prof., then Associate Prof., subseq. Prof., of Asian Studies and Classics, Cornell Univ., 1989–2006. *Publications:* Priesthood in Ancient India, 1991; numerous articles in learned jls on Vedic ritual, religion and literature, Sanskrit epics, hist. of astronomy and cosmology, and intellectual hist. of early Mod. S Asia. *Recreations:* walking, gardening, further adventures in the improbable. *Address:* Balliol College, Oxford OX1 3BJ.

MINOGUE, Prof. Kenneth Robert; Professor of Political Science, London School of Economics and Political Science, University of London, 1984–95, now Emeritus; *b* 11 Sept. 1930; *s* of Denis Francis Minogue and Eunice Pearl Minogue (*née* Porter); *m* 1954, Valerie Pearson Hallett (marr. diss. 2001); one *s* one *d*. *Educ:* Sydney Boys' High Sch.; Sydney Univ. (BA); London School of Economics (BScEcon; Hon. Fellow, 2002). Asst Lectr, Univ. of Exeter, 1955–56; London School of Economics: Asst Lectr, 1956; Sen. Lectr, 1964; Reader, 1971. Centenary Medal for services to political science (Australia), 2003. *Publications:* The Liberal Mind, 1961; Nationalism, 1967; The Concept of a University, 1974; Alien Powers: the pure theory of ideology, 1985; Politics: a very short introduction, 1995; (ed and contrib.) Conservative Realism, 1996; The Silencing of Society, 1997; Waitangi Morality Reality, 1998; numerous contribs to learned jls. *Recreations:* opera, walking. *Address:* 43 Perrymead Street, SW6 3SN. *T:* (020) 7731 0421. *Club:* Garrick.

MINOGUE, Maj.-Gen. Patrick John O'Brien; retired; *b* 28 July 1922; *s* of Col M. J. Minogue, DSO, MC, late East Surrey Regt, and Mrs M. V. E. Minogue; *m* 1st, 1950, June Elizabeth (*née* Morris) (*d* 2000); one *s* two *d*; 2nd, 2005, Carol Olga Lee; three step *d*. *Educ:* Brighton Coll.; RMCS. FBCS, FIWSP, FIMH; jssc, psc, ato. Indian Army, 1942–46; East Surrey Regt, 1947; RAOC, 1951; served UK, BAOR, USA, Cyprus; Col, 1969; Brig., 1971; Insp. RAOC, 1971–73; Comdt, Central Ord. Depot, Bicester, 1973–75; Maj.-Gen. 1975; Comdr, Base Orgn, RAOC, 1975–78. Hon. Col, RAOC (TAVR), 1975–78; Col Comdt, RAOC, 1980–87. Group Systems Controller, Lansing Bagnall Ltd, 1978–81; Chm., LT Electronics, 1979–81. Mem., Spanish Golf Fedn, 1982–. CCMI (FBIM 1976, CBIM 1980). *Recreations:* cricket, sailing (Cdre Wayfarer Class, UK, 1975; RYA Coach), golf, shooting, gun-dogs, athletics, lawn bowling. *Address:* 26 Pegasus Court, South Street, Yeovil BA20 1ND. *Clubs:* MCC; Army Sailing Association; Royal Logistic Corps Yacht; Milocarian Athletic; Staff College (Camberley); Yeovil Golf; Cabrera Lawn Bowling (Pres., 1987–92).

MINSON, Prof. Anthony Charles, PhD; Professor of Virology, since 1991, and Pro-Vice-Chancellor, since 2003, University of Cambridge; Fellow of Wolfson College, Cambridge, since 1982; *b* 8 Feb. 1944; *s* of Charles Minson and Esney Minson (*née* Lewis); *m* 1976, Jennifer Mary Phillips; one *s* one *d*. *Educ:* Ilford High Sch.; Birmingham Univ. (BSc); Australian Nat. Univ. (PhD 1969). Lectr, Univ. of Birmingham, 1974–76; Res. Fellow, 1976–82, Lectr, 1982–91, Univ. of Cambridge. Mem. Council, Soc. of Gen. Microbiol., 1990–93, 2003–. Mem., Governing Body, Inst. of Animal Health, 1997–2003. FMedSci 2002. *Publications:* scientific papers on biology and pathogenesis of animal and plant viruses. *Recreation:* sailing. *Address:* University of Cambridge, The Old Schools, Trinity Lane, Cambridge CB2 1TN. *T:* (01223) 765695, *Fax:* (01223) 765693; *e-mail:* acm@mole.bio.cam.ac.uk.

MINTER, Graham Leslie, LVO 1983; HM Diplomatic Service, retired; Senior Consultant, Responsible Business Solutions (formerly Corporate Policy and Practice), International Business Leaders' Forum, since 2005; *b* 4 Jan. 1950; *s* of Norman Leslie Minter and Beryl Winifred Minter; *m* 1975, Peter Anne Scott; one *s* one *d*. *Educ:* Orange Hill County Grammar Sch. HM Diplomatic Service, 1968–2005: FCO, 1968–71; Anguilla, 1971–72; Latin American Floater, 1973–75; Asunción, 1975–78; FCO, 1978–79; First Secretary: (Econ.), Mexico City, 1979–84; FCO, 1984–90; Canberra, 1990–94; FCO, 1994–98; Ambassador to Bolivia, 1998–2001; Dep. Hd, Economic Policy Dept, FCO, 2002–04; Gp Hd, Global Business Gp, FCO, 2004–05. *Recreations:* travel, music, walking, reading, genealogy, birdwatching, table tennis, tennis, football. *Address:* Ringlestone, Goudhurst Road, Marden, Kent TN12 9JY.

MINTO, 7th Earl of, *cr* 1813; **Gilbert Timothy George Lariston Elliot-Murray-Kynynmound;** Bt 1700; Baron Minto, 1797; Viscount Melgund, 1813; *b* 1 Dec. 1953; *s* of 6th Earl of Minto, OBE and Lady Caroline, *d* of 9th Earl of Jersey; *S* father, 2005; *m* 1983, Diana, *yr d* of Brian Trafford; two *s* one *d* (and one *s* decd). *Educ:* Eton; North East London Polytechnic (BSc Hons 1983). MRICS. Lieut, Scots Guards, 1972–76. Mem., Royal Co. of Archers, Queen's Body Guard for Scotland, 1983–. *Heir:* *s* Viscount Melgund, *qv*. *Clubs:* White's, Shikar.

MINTO, Dr Alfred, FRCPsych; Consultant Psychiatrist (Rehabilitation), Southern Derbyshire Health Authority, 1988–90, retired 1991; *b* 23 Sept. 1928; *s* of Alfred Minto and Marjorie Mavor Goudie Leask; *m* 1949, Frances Oliver Bradbrook; two *s* two *d*. *Educ:* Aberdeen Central Sch.; Aberdeen Univ. (MB ChB 1951); MA History, Univ. of Nottingham, 1996. DPM RCS&P London 1961; MRCPsych 1972, FRCPsych 1974. House Physician, Huddersfield Royal Inf., 1952; Sen. House Officer/Jun. Hosp. Med. Officer, Fairmile Hosp., Wallingford, 1952–56; Sen. Registrar, St Luke's Hosp., Middlesbrough, 1956–59; Sen. Hosp. Med. Officer, 1959–63, Conslt Psychiatrist, 1963, Mapperley Hosp., Nottingham; Conslt Psychiatrist i/c, Alcoholism and Drug Addiction Service, Sheffield RHB, 1963–68; Conslt Psychiatrist, St Ann's and Mapperley Hosps, 1968–81; Med. Dir, Rampton Hosp., 1981–85; Associate Prof. of Psychiatry, Univ. of Calgary, and Clinical Dir of Forensic Psychiatry, Calgary Gen. Hosp., Alberta, 1986–87. Clinical Teacher, Nottingham Univ. Med. Sch., 1971–85; Special Lectr in Forensic Psych., Nottingham Univ., 1982–85. Conslt Psychiatrist, CS Comrs, 1964–85. *Publications:* Key Issues in Mental Health, 1982; papers on alcoholism, community care, toxoplasmosis. *Recreations:* books, people. *Address:* 76 Walsingham Road, Nottingham, NG5 4NR.

MINTOFF, Hon. Dominic, (Dom), BSc, BE&A, MA, A&CE; Prime Minister of Malta, 1971–84; Leader of Malta Labour Party, 1949–84; *b* Cospicua, 6 Aug. 1916; *s* of Lawrence Mintoff and late Concetta (*née* Farrugia); *m* 1947, Moyra de Vere Bentick (decd); two *d*. *Educ:* Govt Elem. Sch., Seminary and Lyceum, Malta; Univ. of Malta (BSc 1937; BE&A, A&CE 1939); Hertford Coll., Oxford (Govt Travelling Scholar; Rhodes Scholar; MA Engrg Science). Practised as civil engineer in Britain, 1941–43, and as architect in Malta, 1943–. Gen. Sec. Malta Labour Party, 1936–37; Mem., Council of Govt and Exec. Council, 1945; MP (Lab) Malta, 1947–98 (did not seek re-election following disagreement with current Lab Party policies); Dep. Prime Minister and Minister for Works and Reconstruction, 1947–49 (resigned); Prime Minister and Minister of Finance, 1955–58; resigned office in 1958 to lead the Maltese Liberation Movement; Leader of Opposition, 1962–71; Minister of Foreign Affairs, 1971–81; Minister of the Interior, 1976–81 and 1983–84. Mem., Labour delegns to UK, 1945, 1947, 1948 and 1949. Negotiated removal of British Military base, 1971 and other foreign mil. bases by 1979. Co-chairman: Malta Peace Movement, 2003–; Malta Arise Front, 2003–. Dr *hc* Univ. of Pol. Studies, Ponterios, Greece, 1976. Order of the Republic, Libya, 1971; Grand Cordon: Order of the Republic, Tunisia, 1973; Order of Ouissam Alaouite, 1978. *Publications:* scientific, literary and artistic works. *Recreations:* horse-riding, swimming, water ski-ing, bocċi. *Address:* The Olives, Tarxien, Malta.

MINTON, Kenneth Joseph, CBE 1995; Executive Chairman, 4 Imprint plc, since 2004; Director: Solvay SA, 1996–2006; Pay Point plc, since 2004; *b* 17 Jan. 1937; *s* of late Henry Minton and Lilian Minton (*née* Moore); *m* 1961, Mary Wilson; one *s*. *Educ:* Leeds Univ. (BSc 1st cl. Hons Mining Engrg). Management positions with: Unilever, UK and France, 1960–68; Laporte plc, 1968–95 (Chief Exec. and Man. Dir, 1979–95); Chm., SGB Gp plc, 1997–2000 (non-exec. Dir, SGB, 1997–2000); Executive Chairman: Arjo Wiggins Appleton plc, 1997–2001; Inveresk plc, 2001–02; non-executive Director: Caradon plc, 1991–99; Jeyes Gp plc, 1989–98 (Chm., 1993–96); John Mowlem & Co. PLC, 1994–98 (Chm., 1995–98); Sentrachem Ltd, 1996–97; Tomkins plc, 2000–06. Mem. Bd, CEFIC, 1991–95. Trustee, Industry and Parlt Trust, 1998– (Founder Mem., 1977; Chm., Mgt Council, 1993–96). Pres., SCI, 1996–98. SCI Centenary Medal, 1994. *Recreations:* gardens, fine art, walking, South Africa, charities. *Address:* 7 Midway, St Albans, Herts AL3 4BD.

MINTON, Yvonne Fay, CBE 1980; mezzo-soprano; *er d* of R. T. Minton, Sydney; *m* 1965, William Barclay; one *s* one *d*. *Educ:* Sydney Conservatorium of Music. Elsa Stralia Scholar, Sydney, 1957–60; won Canberra Operatic Aria Competition, 1960; won Kathleen Ferrier Prize at s'Hertogenbosch Vocal Competition, 1961. Joined Royal Opera House as a Principal Mezzo-Soprano, 1965. Major roles include: Octavian in Der Rosenkavalier; Dorabella in Cosi Fan Tutte; Marina in Boris Godunov; Helen in King Priam; Cherubino in Marriage of Figaro; Orfeo in Gluck's Orfeo; Sextus in La clemenza di Tito; Dido in The Trojans at Carthage; Kundry in Parsifal; Charlotte in Werther; Countess Geschwitz in Lulu. Recordings include Octavian in Der Rosenkavalier, Mozart Requiem, Elgar's The Kingdom, etc. Guest Artist with Cologne Opera Company, Oct. 1969–. Hon. RAM 1975. *Recreations:* reading, gardening. *Address:* c/o Ingpen and Williams, 7 St George's Court, 131 Putney Bridge Road, SW15 2PA. *T:* (020) 8874 3222.

MINZLY, Angela Christine Mary; *see* Heylin, A. C. M.

MIQUEL, Raymond Clive, CBE 1981; Chairman and Managing Director, Lees Foods plc (formerly Lees Group Ltd), since 1992; Chairman, Scottish Sports Council, 1987–91; Member, Sports Council, 1988–91; *b* 28 May 1931; *m* 1958; one *s* two *d*. *Educ:* Allan Glen's Sch., Glasgow; Glasgow Technical Coll. Joined Arthur Bell & Sons Ltd as Works Study Engineer, 1956; Production Controller, 1958; Production Director, 1962; Dep. Man. Dir, 1965; Man. Dir, 1968–85; Dep. Chm., 1972; Chm., 1973–85. Chairman: Towmaster Transport Co. Ltd, 1974–86; Canning Town Glass Ltd, 1974–86; Wellington Importers Ltd, USA, 1984–86; Gleneagles Hotels PLC, 1984–86; Chm. and Chief Exec., Belhaven plc, 1986–88. Dir, Golf Fund Plc, 1989–94. Vis. Prof. in Business Develt, Glasgow Univ., 1985–. Member: British Internat. Sports Cttee, 1987–91; CCPR, 1984–. Governor, Sports Aid Foundn, 1979–2000. CCMI (CBIM 1981). *Publication:* Business as Usual: the Miquel way (autobiog.), 2000. *Address:* Whitedene, Caledonian Crescent, Gleneagles, Perthshire, Scotland PH3 1NG. *T:* (01764) 662642.

MIRMAN, Sophie, (Mrs R. P. Ross); Joint Managing Director, Trotters Childrenswear and Accessories, since 1990; *b* 28 Oct. 1956; *d* of late Simone and Serge Mirman; *m* 1984, Richard Philip Ross; one *s* two *d*. *Educ:* French Lycée, London. Marks & Spencer, 1974–81; Gen. Manager, 1981–82, Man. Dir, 1982–83, Tie Rack; Co-Founder, Sock Shop International, 1983; Chm. and Joint Man. Dir, Sock Shop International plc, 1983–90. *Recreations:* family, sport. *Address:* Unit 7, Talina Centre, Bagleys Lane, SW6 2BW. *T:* (020) 7371 5973.

MIRO, Victoria; Founder, and Director, Victoria Miro Gallery, since 1985; *b* 1 July 1945; *d* of Montagu and Jane Cooper; *m* 1970, Warren Miro; one *s* one *d*. *Educ:* Slade Sch. of Fine Art. Represents artists, including Chris Ofili, Peter Doig, Isaac Julien, Doug Aitken, Thomas Demand, Grayson Perry, Ian Hamilton Finlay. *Recreations:* food, fashion. *Address:* Victoria Miro Gallery, 16 Wharf Road, N1 7RW. *T:* (020) 7336 8109, *Fax:* (020) 7251 5596; *e-mail:* victoria@victoria-miro.com.

MIRRÉ, Federico; Ambassador of the Argentine Republic to the Court of St James's, 2003–08; Permanent Representative to International Maritime Organisation, 2003; *b* 7 Aug. 1938; *s* of Emilio Juan Mirré and Marie Teresa (*née* Gavaldá-Lavin); *m* 1966; two *d*; *m* 2002, Cecilia Duhau. *Educ:* Manuel Belgrano Sch. of Marist Brothers; Univ. of Buenos Aires (LLB); Inst. of Foreign Service, Buenos Aires. Asst Prof. of Public Internat. Law, Univ. of Buenos Aires, 1977–79; Counsellor, Delegn to Papal Mediation, Vatican, 1979–81; Southern Patagonia Diplomatic Liaison Officer with Internat. Red Cross, 1982; Mem., Delegn to British-Argentine Negotiations on Malvinas, Berne, 1984; Minister, Paris, 1985–88; Ambassador to Ivory Coast, Burkina Fasso and Niger, 1988–91; Agent for Argentina on Laguna del Desierto boundary case with Chile, 1991–94; Ambassador to Norway and Iceland, 1994–99; Legal Advr, Min. of Foreign Affairs, 1999; Dir, Internat. Security, Min. of Labour, 2000–02; Hd, Dept of Western Europe, Min. of Foreign Affairs, 2002–03. Dir, Fundación Andina, 1991–94. Pres., Professional Assoc. of Foreign Service, 1992–94. Ed., Perspectiva Internacional, 1991–94. *Recreations:* yachting, golf. *Clubs:* Canning, Caledonian, White's.

MIRREN, Dame Helen, DBE 2003; actress; *b* 26 July 1945; *m* 1997, Taylor Hackford. *Theatre includes: RSC:* Troilus and Cressida, Much Ado About Nothing, 1968; Richard III, Hamlet, The Two Gentlemen of Verona, 1970; Miss Julie, 1971; Macbeth, 1974; Henry VI parts I, II and III, 1977; Antony and Cleopatra, The Roaring Girl, 1983; *other:* Teeth 'n' Smiles, Royal Court, 1974; The Bed Before Yesterday, Lyric, 1976; Measure for Measure, Riverside, 1979; The Duchess of Malfi, Manchester Royal Exchange, 1980; Faith Healer, Royal Court, 1981; Extremities, Duchess, 1984; Two Way Mirror, Young Vic, 1988; Sex Please, We're Italian, Young Vic, 1991; A Month in the Country, Albery, and Roundabout, Broadway, 1994; Antony and Cleopatra, RNT, 1998; Collected Stories, Haymarket, 1999; Orpheus Descending, Donmar, 2000; Dance of Death, NY, 2001; Mourning Becomes Electra, NT, 2003. *Films include:* Age of Consent, 1969; Savage Messiah, 1971; O Lucky Man, 1973; Caligula, 1977; The Long Good Friday, 1980; Excalibur, 1981; Cal, 1984; 2010, 1985; White Nights, Heavenly Pursuits, 1986; The Mosquito Coast, 1987; Pascali's Island, When the Whales Came, 1988; Bethune: The Making of a Hero, 1989; The Cook, The Thief, his Wife and her Lover, 1989; The Comfort of Strangers, 1989; Where Angels Fear to Tread, 1990; The Madness of King George, 1994; Some Mother's Son, 1996; Teaching Mrs Tingle, 1998; Greenfingers, The Pledge, 2001; Last Orders, Gosford Park, 2002; Calendar Girls, 2003; The Clearing, 2004; The Queen, 2006 (Best Actress, Oscar award, 2007). *TV includes:* Prime Suspect (7 series), 1991–96, 2003, 2006 (Emmy Award, 2007); Painted Lady, 1997; Ayn Rand, 1998; Losing Chase; The Roman Spring of Mrs Stone; Elizabeth I; (dir) Happy Birthday (USA). *Publication:* In the Frame: my life in words and pictures, 2007. *Address:* c/o Ken McReddie Ltd, 36–40 Glasshouse Street, W1B 5DL.

MIRRLEES, Sir James (Alexander), Kt 1997; FBA 1984; Professor of Political Economy, University of Cambridge, 1995–2003; Fellow of Trinity College, Cambridge, since 1995; *b* 5 July 1936; *s* of late George B. M. Mirrlees; *m* 1961, Gillian Marjorie Hughes (*d* 1993); two *d*; *m* 2001, Patricia Wilson. *Educ:* Douglas-Ewart High Sch., Newton Stewart; Edinburgh Univ.; Trinity Coll., Cambridge. MA Edinburgh Maths, 1957; BA Cantab Maths, 1959; PhD Cantab Econs, 1963. Adviser, MIT Center for Internat. Studies, New Delhi, 1962–63; Cambridge Univ. Asst Lectr in Econs and Fellow of Trinity Coll., 1963, University Lectr, 1965; Adviser to Govt of Swaziland, 1963; Res. Assoc., Pakistan Inst. of Develt Econs, Karachi, 1966–67; Edgeworth Prof. of Econs, and Fellow, Nuffield Coll., Oxford Univ., 1968–95. Visiting Professor: MIT, 1968, 1970, 1976, 1987; Univ. of California, Berkeley, 1986; Yale Univ., 1989; Dist. Prof.-at-large, Chinese Univ. of Hong Kong, 2002–; Laureate Prof., Univ. of Melbourne, 2005–. Mem., Treasury Cttee on Policy Optimisation, 1976–78. Econometric Society: Fellow, 1970; Vice-Pres., 1980, Pres., 1982; Chm., Assoc. of Univ. Teachers of Econs, 1983–87; President: Royal Economic Soc., 1989–92; European Economic Assoc., 2000. For. Hon. Mem., Amer. Acad. of Arts and Scis, 1981; Hon. Mem., Amer. Economic Assoc., 1982; Foreign Associate, US Nat. Acad. of Scis, 1999. Hon. FRSE, 1998. Hon. DLitt: Warwick, 1982; Portsmouth, 1997; Oxford, 1998; Hon. DSocSc Brunel, 1997; Hon. DSc Edinburgh, 1997. Nobel Prize for Economics, 1996. *Publications:* (joint author) Manual of Industrial Project Analysis in Developing Countries, 1969; (ed jtly) Models of Economic Growth, 1973; (jt author) Project Appraisal and Planning, 1974; articles in economic jls. *Recreations:* reading detective stories and other forms of mathematics, playing the piano, travelling, listening. *Address:* c/o Trinity College, Cambridge CB2 1TQ.

MIRRLEES, Robin Ian Evelyn Stuart de la Lanne-; Richmond Herald of Arms, 1962–67; *b* Paris, 13 Jan. 1925; grandson of Ambassador La Lanne; godson of 11th Duke of Argyll; one *s*. *Educ:* Merton Coll., Oxford (MA). Several language diplomas. Served India, 1942–46; Captain RA, 1944; Gen. Staff, New Delhi, 1946; Embassy Attaché, Tokyo, 1947; Rouge Dragon Pursuivant of Arms, 1952–62 (and as such attended Coronation). Co-editor, Annuaire de France, 1966–. ADC to HM the King of Yugoslavia, 1963–70. Has raised substantial funds for humanitarian organisations (incl. own private donations); undertook restoration of Inchdrewer Castle, Scotland, and others; Laird of Island of Bernera, pop. *c* 250. Freeman of City of London, 1960. Patrician of San Marino, 1964. Succeeded to the title of Comte de Lalanne (France), 1962 and titular Prince of Coronata. Various foreign orders of knighthood. *Recreations:* piloting, travelling, painting, mystic philosophy. *Address:* Bernera Lodge, Great Bernera Island, by Stornoway, Outer Hebrides, Scotland. *Clubs:* Lansdowne; Travellers (Paris).

MIRSKY, Prof. Rhona Mary, PhD; Professor of Developmental Neurobiology, 1990–2004, now Emeritus, and Research Associate, since 2004, University College London; *b* 29 May 1939; *d* of Thomas Gibson Pearson and Lynda Pearson (*née* Williams); *m* 1963, Jonathan Mirsky (marr. diss. 1985); *m* 2006, Kristján R. Jessen. *Educ:* New Hall, Cambridge (BA 1961; PhD 1964). Biochemistry Department, Dartmouth Medical School, USA: Instr, 1966–69; Asst Prof., 1969–73; Res. Associate (Asst Prof.), 1973–75; University College London: Vis. Scientist, 1974, Associate Res. Fellow, 1975–81, MRC Neuroimmunology Project, Dept of Zoology; Lectr, 1981–85, Reader, 1985–90, Dept of Anatomy and Develtl Biology. Mem. Council, MRC, 1998–2001. FMedSci 2001. *Publications:* numerous papers in scientific jls. *Address:* Department of Anatomy and Developmental Biology, University College London, Gower Street, WC1E 6BT. *T:* (020) 7679 3380.

MIRZOEFF, Edward, CVO 1993; CBE 1997; television director, executive producer and consultant; *b* 11 April 1936; *s* of late Eliachar Mirzoeff and of Penina (*née* Asherov); *m* 1961, Judith Topper; three *s*. *Educ:* Hasmonean Grammar Sch.; Queen's Coll., Oxford (Open Scholarship in Mod. History; MA). Market Researcher, Social Surveys (Gallup Poll) Ltd, 1958–59; Public Relns Exec., Duncan McLeish & Associates, 1960–61; Asst Editor, Shoppers' Guide, 1961–63; with BBC Television, 1963–2000: director and producer of film documentaries incl. (with Sir John Betjeman) Metro-land, 1973, A Passion for Churches, 1974, and The Queen's Realm, 1977; Police - Harrow Road, 1975; The Regiment, 1977; The Front Garden, 1979; The Ritz (BAFTA Award for Best Documentary), 1981; The Englishwoman and The Horse, 1981; Elizabeth R (British Video Award), 1992; Torvill and Dean: facing the music, 1994; Treasures in Trust, 1995; John Betjeman - the last laugh, 2001; Series Editor: Bird's-Eye View, 1969–71; Year of the French, 1982–83; In At The Deep End, 1983–84; Just Another Day, 1983–85; Real Lives, 1985; Editor, 40 Minutes, 1985–89 (BAFTA Awards for Best Factual Series, 1985, 1989; Samuelson Award, Birmingham Fest., 1988); Executive Producer: Fire in the Blood, Pandora's Box, 1992; The Ark, 1993; True Brits, 1994; Situation Vacant, 1995; The House, 1996 (Royal Philharmonic Soc. Music Award for Radio, TV and Video, 1996; BPG Award for Best Documentary Series, 1996; Internat. Emmy, 1996); Full Circle with Michael Palin, 1997; The 50 Years War: Israel and the Arabs, 1998; Children's Hospital, 1998–2000; Michael Palin's Hemingway Adventure, 1999; Queen Elizabeth the Queen Mother, 2002; The Lord's Tale, 2002; A Very English Village, 2005; The Lie of the Land, 2007. Trustee: BAFTA, 1999–2006 (Vice-Chm., TV, 1991–95; Chm., 1995–97); David Lean BAFTA Foundn, 2006–. Chm., Grierson (formerly Grierson Meml) Trust, 2002–06 (Trustee, 1999–; Vice-Chm., 2000–02). Mem., Salisbury Cathedral Council, 2002–. Dir, Dirs' and Producers' Rights Soc., 1999–2007. Vice-Pres., Betjeman Soc., 2006–. BFI TV Award, 1988; Alan Clarke Award for Outstanding Creative Contribn to Television, BAFTA, 1995. *Recreations:* lunching with friends, mowing lawns. *Address:* 9 Westmoreland Road, SW13 9RZ. *T:* (020) 8748 9247. *Club:* Garrick.

MISCAMPBELL, Gillian Margaret Mary, OBE 1982; DL; Chairman, Stoke Mandeville Hospital NHS Trust, 1995–2001; *b* 31 Dec. 1935; *d* of late Brig. Francis William Gibb and Agnes Winifred Gibb; *m* 1958, Alexander Malcolm Miscampbell; three *s*. *Educ:* St Leonard's Sch. Member: Area Manpower Bd, 1985–88; Milton Keynes Develt Corp. Bd, 1990–92. Chm., Aylesbury Vale HA, 1981–93; Mem., Bucks HA, 1993–95. Mem. (C), Bucks CC, 1977–93 (Chm., 1989–93; Chm., Educn Cttee, 1985–89). Chm.,

Aylesbury Cons. Assoc., 1975–78; Vice Chm., Nat. Women's Adv. Cttee, Cons. Party, 1979–80. University of Buckingham: Mem. Council, 1985–2005 (Vice Chm., 1994–2005); Chm., F and GP Cttee, 1993–98. Chm., Cancer Care and Haematol. Fund, Stoke Mandeville Hosp., 2004–. Dir, Buckinghamshire Foundn, 1999–2006; Chm., Aylesbury Grammar Sch. Foundn, 2005–. DL Bucks, 1993. DUniv Buckingham, 1998. *Address:* Rosemount, 15 Upper Street, Quainton, Aylesbury, Bucks HP22 4AY. *T:* (01296) 655318.

MISCHLER, Norman Martin; Chairman: Hoechst UK Ltd, 1975–84; Hoechst Ireland Ltd, 1976–84; Berger Jenson & Nicholson Ltd, 1979–84; *b* 9 Oct. 1920; *s* of late Martin Mischler and Martha Sarah (*née* Lambert); *m* 1949, Helen Dora Sinclair (*d* 2007); one *s* one *d*. *Educ:* St Paul's Sch., London; St Catharine's Coll., Cambridge (MA). Cricket Blue, 1946. Indian Army, 1940; served in Burma Campaign; released, rank of Major, 1946. Joined Burt, Boulton & Haywood, 1947, Vice-Chm. 1963; Dep. Man. Dir, Hoechst UK Ltd, 1966; Chairman: Harlow Chemical Co. Ltd, 1972–74; Kalle Infotec Ltd, 1972–74; Director: Berger, Jenson & Nicholson Ltd, 1975–84; Ringsdorff Carbon Co. Ltd, 1968–84; Vice-Chm., German Chamber of Industry and Commerce in London, 1974–84; Mem. Council, Chemical Industries Assoc. Ltd, 1975–84. Freeman, City of London. Officer's Cross, German Order of Merit, 1985. *Recreations:* cricket, opera, and theatre. *Address:* Scott House, Earsham Street, Bungay, Suffolk NR35 1AF. *Club:* Hawks (Cambridge).

MISKIN, Charles James Monckton; QC 1998; a Recorder, since 1998; *b* 29 Nov. 1952; *s* of late Nigel Monckton Miskin and Hilda Meryl Miskin (*née* Knight); *m* 1st, 1982, Karen Elizabeth Booth (marr. diss. 1995); one *s* three *d*; 2nd, 2005, Angharad Jocalyn Start; one *s* two *d*. *Educ:* Charterhouse Sch. (Sutton Prizewinner); Worcester Coll., Oxford (Open Exhibnr; BA Hons Juris. 1974; MA 1978). Called to the Bar, Gray's Inn, 1975, Bencher, 2005; in practice as barrister, 1977–, Hd of Chambers, 2003–06; Mem., S Eastern Circuit; Asst Recorder, 1992–98; Standing Counsel to Inland Revenue, 1993–98. Mem., Criminal Bar Assoc., 1977–. Chm., Bar Theatrical Soc., 1986–. Liveryman: Wax Chandlers' Co., 1975–; Armourers' and Braziers' Co., 1986–. *Recreations:* travel, opera, history, the children, laughter. *Address:* 23 Essex Street, WC2R 3AS. *T:* (020) 7413 0353. *Clubs:* Travellers, Hurlingham.

MISRA, Arnu Kumar; Chief Executive Officer, Cannons Group, since 2005 (Chief Operating Officer, 2003–05); *b* 8 Jan. 1962; *s* of Kulbushan Misra and Pushpa Misra; *m* 1990, Neelam Bhardwaj; one *s*. *Educ:* Univ. of Bradford (BSc 1st Cl. Hons 1983); Bradford Mgt Centre (MBA 1987); INSEAD (AMP 2005). MMM Logistics Consultancy, 1987–89; various exec. and sen. exec. roles, ASDA Gp plc, 1990–2003. *Recreations:* fair-weather cricket, hill walking, spinning. *Address:* Cannons Group Ltd, Cannons House, 40–44 Coombe Road, New Malden, Surrey KT3 4QF. *T:* (020) 8336 8365, *Fax:* (020) 8336 8300; *e-mail:* arnu.misra@cannons.co.uk.

MISTRY, Dhruva, Hon. CBE 2001; RA 1991; FRBS; sculptor, painter and printmaker; *b* 1 Jan. 1957; *s* of Pramodray and Kantaben Mistry. *Educ:* Maharaja Sayajirao Univ. of Baroda (MA 1981); RCA (British Council schol.; MA 1983). Artist-in-residence, Kettle's Yard, and Fellow of Churchill Coll., Cambridge, 1984–85; Sculptor-in-residence, V&A Mus., 1988; Prof., Hd of Sculpture and Dean, Faculty of Fine Arts, MS Univ. of Baroda, 1998–2002. First solo exhibn, Art Heritage, New Delhi, transf. to Jehangir Art Gall., Bombay, 1982. Rep. Britain at 3rd Rodin Grand Prize Exhibn, Japan, 1990. Works in public collections including: Lalit Kala Akademi, New Delhi; Tate Gall., Arts Council, British Council and V&A Mus., London; Nat. Mus. of Wales, Cardiff; Fukuoka Asian Art Mus., Japan; open air collections include sculptures at Goodwood, Yorks Sculpture Park and Hakone Open Air Mus., Japan; works of art for: Victoria Square, Birmingham, commnd by Birmingham CC, 1992; Tamano City Project, Uno, Japan, 2002; LNG Petronet, Dahej, 2003; Delhi Univ., 2005. FRBS 1993. *Recreations:* photography, reading, walking.

MITCALFE, (Joan) Kirsteen; Vice Lord-Lieutenant of Moray, since 2005; *b* 23 July 1936; *d* of Douglas and Jenny Mackessack; *m* 1959, Hugh Mitcalfe; four *d*. *Educ:* Oxenfoord Castle Sch., Midlothian; Open Univ. (BA Hons). Secretary: Moray and Nairn Br., Pony Club, 1971–96; Forres Br., Riding for the Disabled, 1972–90; Burgie Internat. Horse Trials, 1988–2003. Gov., Gordonstoun Sch., 1981–94. Voluntary work with hospice movt, WRVS and as church sec. *Recreations:* ski-ing, fishing, travelling, music. *Address:* Milton Brodie, Forres, Moray IV36 2UA. *T:* (01343) 850281; *e-mail:* k.mitcalfe@btinternet.com.

MITCHARD, (Gerald Steven) Paul; QC 2008; Head of European Arbitration and Litigation, Skadden, Arps, Slate, Meagher & Flom (UK) LLP, since 2001; *b* Paulton, 2 Jan. 1952; *s* of Gerald Mitchard and Janet Mitchard; *m* 1987, Dorothy Grant; two *s*. *Educ:* Lincoln Coll., Oxford (MA Juris. 1974). Slaughter and May, 1977–84; Simmons & Simmons: Partner, 1984–99; Head of Litigation, 1993–99; Partner, Wilmer, Cutler & Pickering, 1999–2001. *Recreations:* hiking, reading. *Address:* Skadden, Arps, Slate, Meagher & Flom (UK) LLP, 40 Bank Street, Canary Wharf, E14 5DS. *T:* (020) 7519 7050, *Fax:* (020) 7519 7070; *e-mail:* paul.mitchard@skadden.com. *Club:* Vincent's (Oxford).

MITCHELL, family name of **Baron Mitchell**.

MITCHELL, Baron *cr* 2000 (Life Peer), of Hampstead in the London Borough of Camden; **Parry Andrew Mitchell;** *b* 6 May 1943; *s* of Leon and Rose Mitchell; *m* 1st, 1972, Doreen Hargreaves (marr. diss.); one *d*; 2nd, 1988, Hannah Ruth Lowy; two *s* (twins). *Educ:* Christ's Coll., Finchley; Univ. of London (BSc ext.); Columbia Univ., NY (MBA). Chm., United Leasing plc, 1976–87. Mem., H of L Select Cttee on Sci. and Technol., 2003–07, on EU, Sub-Cttee B, Internal Market, 2007–. Chairman: Syscap plc, 1992–2006; Weizmann UK, 2005–. Chm., eLearning Foundn, 2006–. *Recreations:* fiddling with computers, scuba diving, jazz, opera. *Address:* House of Lords, SW1A 0PW. *T:* (020) 7433 3238; *e-mail:* parrym@mac.com.

MITCHELL, Adrian; writer; *b* 24 Oct. 1932; *s* of James Mitchell and Kathleen Fabian. *Educ:* Greenways Sch.; Dauntsey's Sch.; Christ Church, Oxford. Worked as reporter on Oxford Mail, Evening Standard, 1955–63; subseq. free-lance journalist for Daily Mail, Sun, Sunday Times, New Statesman; Granada Fellow, Univ. of Lancaster, 1968–69; Fellow, Center for Humanities, Wesleyan Univ., 1972; Resident Writer, Sherman Theatre, Cardiff, 1974–75; Vis. writer, Billericay Comp. Sch., 1978–80; Judith E. Wilson Fellow, Cambridge Univ., 1980–81; Resident writer, Unicorn Theatre for Children, 1982–83; Fellow in Drama, Nanyang Univ., Singapore, 1995; Dylan Thomas Fellow, UK Festival of Literature, 1995. Poetry Editor, New Statesman and Society, 1994–96. FRSL 1987. Hon. DArts N London, 1997. Apptd shadow poet laureate by Red Pepper mag., 2003. *Plays:* Marat/Sade (stage adaptation), RSC, 1964; Tyger, NT Co. at New Theatre, 1971; Man Friday, 7:84 Theatre Co., 1973 (TV 1972, Screenplay 1975); Mind Your Head, Liverpool Everyman, 1973; Daft as a Brush (TV), 1975; A Seventh Man, Hampstead, 1976; White Suit Blues, Nottingham, Edinburgh and Old Vic, 1977; Houdini, Amsterdam, 1977; Glad Day (TV), 1978; Uppendown Mooney, Welfare State Theatre Co., 1978; The White Deer, Unicorn Theatre, 1978; Hoagy, Bix and Wolfgang Beethoven Bunkhaus, King's Head Theatre, 1979; In the Unlikely Event of an Emergency, Bath, 1979; Peer Gynt (adaptation), Oxford Playhouse, 1980; You Must Believe All This (TV), 1981; The Tragedy of King Real, Welfare State Theatre Co., 1982; Mowgli's Jungle, Contact Theatre, Manchester, 1982; A Child's Christmas in Wales (with Jeremy Brooks), Great Lakes Fest., 1983; The Wild Animal Song Contest, Unicorn Theatre, 1983; Life's a Dream (adaptation with John Barton), RSC Stratford, 1983, Barbican, 1984; C'Mon Everybody, Tricycle Theatre, 1984; The Great Theatre of the World (adaptation), Mediaeval Players, 1984; Satie Day/Night, Lyric Studio, Hammersmith, 1986; Mirandolina (adaptation), Bristol Old Vic, 1987; The Last Wild Wood in Sector 88, Rugby Music Centre, 1987; Anna on Anna, Th. Workshop, Edinburgh, 1988; Woman Overboard, The Patchwork Girl of Oz, Palace Th., Watford, 1988; The Snow Queen, NY, 1990; Vasilisa The Fair (adaptation), NY, 1991; Pieces of Peace (TV), 1991; Unicorn Island, Dartington, 1992; The Blue, Walk the Plank, Fitzcarraldo Theatre Ship, Glasson Dock, Lancs and other UK ports, 1992; A New World and The Tears of the Indians (adaptation), Nuffield Theatre, Southampton, 1992; Meet the Baron, Dartington, 1993; Sir Fool's Quest, Dartington and nat. tour, 1994; Tyger Two, Boston, USA, 1995; Tom Kitten and his Friends, Unicorn Th., 1995; The Siege, Nat. Playwright Commissioning Gp, 1996–97; The Little Violin (adaptation), Tricycle Th., 1998; The Lion, the Witch and the Wardrobe (adaptation), RSC, 1998; Start Again, Morecambe, 1998; Jemima Puddleduck and her Friends, Unicorn Th., 1998; The Heroes (trilogy), Kageboushi Th., Japan, 1999; The Mammoth Sails Tonight, Dream Factory, Warwick, 1999; All Shook Up, Tricycle Th., 2001; Alice in Wonderland (adaptation), RSC, 2001; Peter Rabbit and his Friends, Unicorn Th., 2002; Aladdin, Doublejoint, Belfast, 2005; King of Shadows, NY, 2005; Nobody Rides the Unicorn, Puppetcraft, Devon, 2005; Perseus and the Gorgon's Head, Puppetcraft, Devon, 2006; The Fear Brigade, Global Village, Kent, 2006; Maudie and the Green Children, Playhouse, 2008; To the River (radio), 2008; National Theatre: The Mayor of Zalamea (adaptation), 1981; Animal Farm (lyrics), 1984; The Government Inspector, 1985; The Pied Piper, 1986; Love Songs of World War Three, 1987; Fuente Ovejuna (adaptation), 1989; Triple Threat, 1989. *Publications: novels:* If You See Me Comin', 1962; The Bodyguard, 1970; Wartime, 1973; *poetry:* Poems, 1964; Out Loud, 1968; Ride the Nightmare, 1971; The Apeman Cometh, 1975; For Beauty Douglas, (Collected Poems 1953–1979), 1982; On the Beach at Cambridge, 1984; Nothingmas Day, 1984; Love Songs of World War Three, 1988; All My Own Stuff, 1991; Adrian Mitchell's Greatest Hits—The Top Forty, 1991; Blue Coffee, 1996; Heart on the Left, 1997; All Shook Up, 2000; (ed) Blackbird Singing: lyrics and poems of Paul McCartney, 2001; The Shadow Knows, 2004; *for children:* The Baron Rides Out, 1985; The Baron on the Island of Cheese, 1986; The Baron All At Sea, 1987; Leonardo the Lion from Nowhere, 1987; Our Mammoth, 1987; Our Mammoth Goes to School, 1987; Our Mammoth in the Snow, 1988; The Pied Piper, 1988; Strawberry Drums, 1989; The Thirteen Secrets of Poetry, 1993; (ed) The Orchard Book of Poems, 1993; Maudie and the Green Children, 1996; Gynormous!, 1996; Balloon Lagoon, 1997; Robin Hood and Marian, 1998; Twice My Size, 1998; My Cat Mrs Christmas, 1998; Nobody Rides the Unicorn, 1999; (ed) Dancing in the Street, 1999; Zoo of Dreams, 2001; (ed) A Poem A Day, 2001; Daft as a Doughnut, 2004; also plays. *Address:* c/o United Agents, 12–26 Lexington Street, W1F 0LE. *Club:* Chelsea Arts.

MITCHELL, Alec Burton, MA; CEng, MIMechE, FRINA; Director, Admiralty Marine Technology Establishment, 1977–84, retired; Scientific Adviser to Director General Ships, Ministry of Defence, 1981–84; *b* 27 Aug. 1924; *er s* of Ronald Johnson Mitchell and Millicent Annie Mitchell; *m* 1952, Barbara, *d* of Arthur Edward and Katie Florence Jane Archer; three *s*. *Educ:* Purley County Sch.; St John's Coll., Cambridge (MA). Mechanical Sciences Tripos, Cambridge, 1944. Aeronautical Engineer with Rolls Royce Ltd, Hucknall, 1944–46; Grad. apprentice and gas turbine design engr with English Electric Co. Ltd, Rugby, 1946–48. Joined RN Scientific Service, 1948; Dep. Head of Hydrodynamic Research Div., Admty Research Lab., 1961; promoted Dep. CSO, 1966; Dep. Dir, Admty Research Laboratory, 1973, Dir, 1974–77. *Publications:* numerous scientific papers on hydrodynamics and under-water propulsion systems. *Recreations:* golf, horology, wood-work. *Address:* 32 Ormond Crescent, Hampton, Middx TW12 2TH.

MITCHELL, Alexander Graham, CBE 1973; DFM 1945; Governor, Turks and Caicos Islands, 1973–75 (Administrator, 1971–73); *b* 2 Nov. 1923; *s* of Alexander Mitchell and Evelyn Mitchell (*née* Green); *m* 1954, Pamela Ann Borman; three *d*. *Educ:* Dulwich College; Downing Coll., Cambridge. Served RAF, 1942–45. Sudan Government Civil Service, 1951–55; HM Overseas Civil Service, 1955; Western Pacific High Commission: various posts in British Solomon Islands Protectorate and British Residency, New Hebrides, 1955–71; Sec., Financial Affairs, British Residency, 1968–71; retired June 1977. Clerk to Governors, Dame Allan's Schools, Newcastle, 1977–88. *Recreations:* ancient and military history. *Address:* 2 Corchester Towers, Corbridge, Northumberland NE45 5NP. *Club:* Royal Over-Seas League.

MITCHELL, Andrew John Bower; MP (C) Sutton Coldfield, since 2001; Director, Lazard Brothers & Co. Ltd, since 1997; *b* 23 March 1956; *s* of Sir David Bower Mitchell, *qv* and late Pamela Elaine (*née* Haward); *m* 1985, Sharon Denise (*née* Bennett); two *d*. *Educ:* Rugby; Jesus Coll., Cambridge (MA History). 1st RTR (Short Service (Limited) Commission), 1975; served with UNFICYP. Pres., Cambridge Union, 1978; Chm., Cambridge Univ. Conservatives, 1977; rep. GB in E-SU American debating tour, 1978. Internat. and Corp. business, Lazard Brothers & Co., 1979–87, Consultant, 1987–92. Senior Strategy Adviser: Boots Co., 1997–2001; Accenture (formerly Andersen Consulting), 1997–. Director: Miller Insce Gp, 1997–2001; Commer Gp, 1998–2002; Financial Dynamics Holdings, 1998–2002. Advr to Bd, Hakluyt, 1998–2001. Contested (C) Sunderland South, 1983. MP (C) Gedling, 1987–97; contested (C) same seat, 1997. A Vice-Chm., Cons. Party, with special responsibility for candidates, 1992–93; an Asst Govt Whip, 1992–94; a Lord Comr of HM Treasury (Govt Whip), 1994–95; Parly Under Sec. of State, DSS, 1995–97; Opposition front bench spokesman: economic affairs, 2003–04; police and home affairs, 2004–05; Shadow Sec. of State for internat. develt, 2005–. Sec., One Nation Gp of Conservative MPs, 1989–92, 2005–. Chm., Coningsby Club, 1983; President: Islington North Conservatives, 1996–2006 (Chm., 1983–85); Gedling Cons. Assoc., 2004–. Vice-Chm., Alexandra Rose Charity, 1998–. Member Council: SOS Sahel, 1991–; GAP, 2000–05. *Recreations:* ski-ing, music, travel. *Address:* 30 Gibson Square, N1 0RD. *T:* (020) 7226 5519; 8 Tudor Road, Sutton Coldfield B73 6BA. *T:* (0121) 355 5519. *Clubs:* Pratt's; Cambridge Union Society (Cambridge); Carlton and District Constitutional (Gedling); Sutton Coldfield Conservative.

MITCHELL, Andrew Jonathan; HM Diplomatic Service; Ambassador to Sweden, since 2007; *b* 7 March 1967; *s* of Michael John Mitchell and Patricia Anne Mitchell; *m* 1996, Helen Sarah Anne Magee; two *s* one *d*. *Educ:* St Mary's Coll., Crosby, Liverpool; Queen's Coll., Oxford (BA 1st Cl. Hons Mod. Langs 1990; Laming Scholar, Queen's Coll. Bursary, Markham Prize for French). Joined FCO, 1991; Second Sec., Bonn, 1993; First Sec., FCO, 1996; Dep. Hd of Mission, Kathmandu, 1999; Counsellor, FCO, 2002–07. *Recreations:* enjoy cricket as player, spectator and general bore, passionate supporter of Liverpool Football Club, love the sea and the mountains, good books, great ideas and fine wine. *Address:* British Embassy, Skarpögatan 6–8, Box 27819, 11593 Stockholm, Sweden. *T:* (8) 6713100; *e-mail:* andrew.mitchell@fco.gov.uk; c/o Foreign and Commonwealth Office, SW1A 2AH. *Clubs:* MCC, Soho House; Vincent's (Oxford).

MITCHELL, Andrew Robert; QC 1998; a Recorder, since 1999; *b* 6 Aug. 1954; *s* of late Malcolm Mitchell and of Edna Audrey Mitchell; *m* 1st, 1982, Patricia Ann Fairburn (marr. diss. 1991); 2nd, 1992, Carolyn Ann Blore; one *s* one *d*. *Educ:* Haberdashers' Aske's Sch. Called to the Bar, Gray's Inn, 1976, Bencher, 2005; in practice at the Bar, 1976–; Asst Recorder, 1995–99. Head of Chambers, 1990–. Mem., Gen. Council of Bar, 2003– (Treas., 2008–). Mem. (C) Haringey LBC, 1984–94 (Leader of the Opposition, 1989–91). Contested (C) Islington S and Finsbury, 1987. Gov., Highgate Primary Sch., 1984–99 (Chm. of Govs, 1997–98). *Publications:* Confiscation and Proceeds of Crime, 1993, 3rd edn 2002; Concise Guide to Criminal Procedure Investigations Act 1996, 1997; (contrib.) Administrative Court: practice *v* procedure, 2006. *Recreations:* playing tennis, watching football and cricket. *Address:* Furnival Chambers, 32 Furnival Street, EC4A 1JQ. *T:* (020) 7405 3232; *e-mail:* arm@furnivallaw.co.uk. *Clubs:* Royal Automobile, MCC.

MITCHELL, Angus; *see* Mitchell, J. A. M.

MITCHELL, Anthony Paul; His Honour Judge Tony Mitchell; a Circuit Judge, since 2000; *b* 9 Aug. 1941; *s* of Arthur Leslie Mitchell and Ivy Muriel Mitchell (*née* Simpson); *m* 1st, 1972, Shirley Ann Donovan (marr. diss. 1985); one *s* one *d*, and one step *s* one step *d*; 2nd, 1989, Julia Fryer (*d* 2000); one step *s* one step *d*; 3rd, 2003, Bethan Henderson; one step *s* one step *d*. *Educ:* Whitgift Sch., Croydon; Coll. of Law, London. Articled, Routh Stacey & Co.; qualified, 1965; admitted Solicitor, 1966; Partner, Toller Hales Collcutt, 1969–2000; Dep. Dist Judge, 1982–2000; Asst Recorder, 1991–95; Recorder, 1995–2000. *Recreations:* music, theatre, cinema, ballet, Rugby, cricket, motor racing, keeping fit, personal development and things spiritual with a small s. *Address:* c/o The Court Service, Midland Circuit, The Priory Courts, 33 Bull Street, Birmingham B4 6DW. *Club:* Lansdowne.

MITCHELL, Austin Vernon, DPhil; MP (Lab) Great Grimsby, since 1983 (Grimsby, April 1977–1983); *b* 19 Sept. 1934; *s* of Richard Vernon Mitchell and Ethel Mary Mitchell; *m* 1st, Patricia Dorothea Jackson (marr. diss.); two *d*; 2nd, Linda Mary McDougall; one *s* one *d*. *Educ:* Woodbottom Council Sch.; Bingley Grammar Sch.; Manchester Univ. (BA, MA); Nuffield Coll., Oxford (DPhil). Lectr in History, Univ. of Otago, Dunedin, NZ, 1959–63; Sen. Lectr in Politics, Univ. of Canterbury, Christchurch, NZ, 1963–67; Official Fellow, Nuffield Coll., Oxford, 1967–69; Journalist, Yorkshire Television, 1969–71; Presenter, BBC Current Affairs Gp, 1972–73; Journalist, Yorkshire TV, 1973–77; Co-presenter, Target, Sky TV, 1989–98. PPS to Minister of State for Prices and Consumer Protection, 1977–79; Opposition front bench spokesman on trade and industry, 1987–89. Member, Select Committee: on Treasury and Civil Service, 1983–87; on agric., 1997–2001; on envmt, food and rural affairs, 2001–05; Public Accounts, 2006–. Mem., Public Accounts Commn, 1997–. Chair, Yorks and Humber Seafood Gp, Yorks Forward, 2007–. Mem., OT Prophets. Associate Ed., House Magazine. ONZM 2001. *Publications:* New Zealand Politics In Action, 1962; Government By Party, 1966; The Whigs in Opposition 1815–1830, 1969; Politics and People in New Zealand, 1970; Yorkshire Jokes, 1971; The Half-Gallon Quarter-Acre Pavlova Paradise, 1974; Can Labour Win Again, 1979; Westminster Man, 1982; The Case for Labour, 1983; Four Years in the Death of the Labour Party, 1983; Yorkshire Jokes, 1988; Teach Thissen Tyke, 1988; Britain: beyond the blue horizon, 1989; Competitive Socialism, 1989; Accounting for Change, 1993; Election '45, 1995; Corporate Governance Matters, 1996; The Common Fisheries Policy: end or mend?, 1996; (with David Wienir) Last Time: Labour's lessons from the sixties, 1997; (with Anne Tate) Fishermen: the rise and fall of deep water trawling, 1997; Parliament in Pictures, 1999; Farewell My Lords, 1999; Austin Mitchell's Yorksher, 2002; Pavlova Paradise Revisited, 2002; Austin Mitchell's Yorkshire Sayings, 2004; Taming the Corporations, 2005; The Pensions Scandal, 2007. *Recreation:* worriting (*sic*). *Address:* 13 Bargate, Grimsby, South Humberside DN34 4SS. *T:* (01472) 342145; House of Commons, SW1A 0AA. *T:* (020) 7219 4559; *e-mail:* Mitchellav@parliament.uk.

MITCHELL, Prof. Basil George, DD; FBA 1983; Nolloth Professor of the Philosophy of the Christian Religion, Oxford University, 1968–84; Fellow of Oriel College, 1968–84, now Emeritus; *b* 9 April 1917; *s* of George William Mitchell and Mary Mitchell (*née* Loxston); *m* 1950, Margaret Eleanor Collin; one *s* three *d*. *Educ:* King Edward VI Sch., Southampton; Queen's Coll., Oxford (Southampton Exhibitioner. 1st cl. Lit Hum 1939). Served Royal Navy, 1940–46; Lt RNVR 1942, Instructor Lt RN 1945. Lectr, Christ Church, Oxford, 1946–47; Fellow and Tutor in Philosophy, Keble Coll., Oxford, 1947–67, Emeritus Fellow, 1981; Sen. Proctor, 1956–57; Hebdomadal Council, 1959–65. Visiting Professor: Princeton Univ., 1963; Colgate Univ., 1976. Lectures: Stanton, in Philosophy of Religion, Cambridge Univ., 1959–62; Edward Cadbury, University of Birmingham, 1966–67; Gifford, Glasgow Univ., 1974–76; Nathaniel Taylor, Yale, 1986; Martin, Univ. of Hong Kong, 1987; Norton, Southern Baptist Theol Seminary, Louisville, 1989; Sarum, Oxford Univ., 1992. Member: C of E Working Parties on Ethical Questions, 1964–78; Doctrine Commn, 1978–84. Hon. DD Glasgow, 1977; Hon. DLitHum Union Coll., Schenectady, 1979. *Publications:* (ed) Faith and Logic, 1957; Law, Morality and Religion in a Secular Society, 1967; Neutrality and Commitment, 1968; (ed) The Philosophy of Religion, 1971; The Justification of Religious Belief, 1973; Morality: Religious and Secular, 1980; How to Play Theological Ping Pong, 1990; Faith and Criticism, 1994; (with J. R. Lucas) Engaging with Plato's Republic, 2003; articles in philosophical and theological periodicals. *Recreations:* gardening, flower arrangement. *Address:* Bartholomew House, 9 Market Street, Woodstock, Oxford OX20 1SU. *T:* (01993) 811265.

MITCHELL, Bryan James, CB 2006; Director, Business and Information Management Directorate, Welsh Assembly Government, 2003–05; *b* 1 March 1945; *s* of Herbert Mitchell and Hilda (*née* Grant); *m*; four *d*. *Educ:* Robert Clack Technical Sch., Dagenham; Open Univ. (BA). MoT, 1967–74; CSD, 1974–76; DoE, 1976–78; Welsh Office, 1978–99; Dep. Clerk to Nat. Assembly for Wales, 1999–2000; Welsh Assembly Government, 2000–05.

MITCHELL, Charles Julian Humphrey; *see* Mitchell, Julian.

MITCHELL, Charlotte Isabel; *b* 3 May 1953; *d* of (John) Angus (Macbeth) Mitchell, *qv* and Ann Katharine (*née* Williamson), MA, MPhil, author; *m* 1st, 1972 (marr. diss. 2000); one *s* one *d*; 2nd, 2002, Paul Southall. *Educ:* St George's Sch. for Girls, Edinburgh; Birmingham Coll. of Art (DipAD 1974); Dip Wine and Spirits 1991. Exhibn organiser, Scottish Craft Centre, 1974–76; Director: Real Foods Ltd, 1976–97; Go Organic Ltd, 1998–2003; organic food consultant, Waitrose plc, 1998–2002; Disability Equality Trainer, Capability Scotland, 2004–05. Trustee, 1987–2005, Dir, 1990–92, Chm., 1990–97, Hon. Vice-Pres., 2006–, Soil Assoc. Trustee, Knockando Wool Mill, Speyside, 2004–. Hon. Mem., BBC Scotland Adv. Council for Rural and Agricl Affairs, 1994–98. *Publication:* The Organic Wine Guide, 1987. *Recreations:* food, wine, music, books, gardening.
See also J. J. Mitchell.

MITCHELL, Christopher Richard; His Honour Judge Christopher Mitchell; a Circuit Judge, since 2003; Resident Judge, Basildon Combined Court Centre, since 2008; *b* 16 Sept. 1942; *e s* of late Anthony Geoffrey Fulton Mitchell and of Cynthia Grace Mitchell (*née* Charlton); *m* 1980, Elisabeth Jeanne Antonine Pineau, *e d* of late Jean Pineau; one *d*. *Educ:* St Dunstan's Coll.; King's Coll. London (LLB 1964). Treasury Solicitor's Dept, 1965–69; called to the Bar, Gray's Inn, 1968; in practice at the Bar, London and S Eastern Circuit (crime), 1969–2003; Asst Recorder, 1987–91, Recorder, 1991–2003; Immigration Appeal Adjudicator, 1998–2003. Asst Comr, Parly Boundary Commn, 1993–94. *Recreations:* hill-walking, books, European railways, cycling, building sheds. *Address:* c/o Basildon Crown Court, The Gore, Basildon, Essex SS14 2EU. *T:* (01268) 458000.

MITCHELL, Sir David (Bower), Kt 1988; DL; *b* June 1928; *er s* of James Mitchell, Naval Architect; *m* 1954, Pamela Elaine Haward (separated; she *d* 2005); two *s* one *d*. *Educ:* Aldenham. Farming, 1945–50; businessman, wine merchant, 1951–79. Chm., El Vino Co. Ltd, 1992–2001. MP (C) Basingstoke, 1964–83, Hampshire North West, 1983–97. An Opposition Whip, 1965–67; PPS to Sec. of State for Social Services, 1970–74; Parly Under Sec. of State, DoI, 1979–81, NI Office, 1981–83, Dept of Transport, 1983–85; Minister of State for Transport, 1986–88. Chm., Cons. Parly Smaller Business Cttee, 1974–79. Founder, Small Business Bureau, 1976. DL Hants, 1994. *Recreations:* gardening, walking, wine-tasting, travel. *Club:* Carlton.
See also A. J. B. Mitchell.

MITCHELL, David Charles; His Honour Judge David Mitchell; a Circuit Judge, South Eastern Circuit, since 2001; Designated Civil Judge, London, since 2007; *b* 4 May 1950; *s* of Charles and Eileen Mitchell; *m* 1973, Susan Cawthera; one *s* one *d*. *Educ:* state schs; St Catherine's Coll., Oxford (MA Juris.). Called to the Bar, Inner Temple, 1972; barrister-at-law, Bradford Chambers, 1972–99, Pump Court, Temple, 1999–2001; specialised in civil and family law, crime and personal injury; Asst Recorder, 1989–93; a Recorder, 1993–2001; Chm., Mental Health Rev. Tribunal (Restricted Panel), 2003–05; Designated Civil Judge, Kent, 2003–07. *Recreations:* hill-walking, ski-ing, the theatre, listening to classical music, anything connected with France. *Address:* Central London Civil Justice Centre, 26 Park Crescent, W1B 1HT.

MITCHELL, David McKenzie, MD; FRCP; Consultant Physician, St Mary's Hospital, Paddington, since 1987, and Medical Director, Imperial College Healthcare NHS Trust (formerly St Mary's NHS Trust), since 1998; *b* 27 July 1948; *s* of John Bernard Mitchell and Elizabeth Mitchell; *m* 1977, Elizabeth Gaminara (marr. diss. 2005); one *s* one *d*. *Educ:* Mostyn House Sch.; Oundle Sch.; Gonville and Caius Coll., Cambridge (MB BChir 1974; MD 1983); Middlesex Hosp.; London Univ. (BA (Philos.) 1983, ext.); Keele Univ. (MBA 1998). FRCP 1991. Trng posts in gen. and respiratory medicine, Hammersmith Hosp., Brompton Hosp., UCH, London Chest Hosp., 1973–87; Res. Fellow in Immunology, ICRF, 1980–82. Liveryman, Musicians' Co., 2005. *Publications:* Respiratory Medicine Revision, 1986; AIDS and the Lung, 1990; Recent Advances in Respiratory Medicine, 1991; papers on various aspects of respiratory medicine. *Recreations:* playing jazz saxophone, classical music, opera, philosophy, travel. *Address:* Imperial College Healthcare NHS Trust, Praed Street, W2 1NY. *T:* (020) 7886 1082, *Fax:* (020) 7886 7833; *e-mail:* david.mitchell@imperial.nhs.uk. *Club:* Athenæum.

MITCHELL, David William, CBE 1983; Chairman, 2001–04, Hon. President, since 2005, Scottish Conservative and Unionist Party; *b* 4 Jan. 1933; *m* 1965, Lynda Katherine Marion Guy; one *d*. *Educ:* Merchiston Castle School, Edinburgh. Nat. Service, 1950–52 (commnd RSF; seconded to 4th Nigerian Regt, RWAFF). Western RHB, 1968–75; Director: Mallinson, Denny (Scotland), 1975–89; Hunter Timber (Scotland), 1989–92; Jt Man. Dir, M & N Norman (Timber) Ltd, 1992–96. Chm., Cumbernauld New Town Develt Corp., 1987–97. Member: Exec. Cttee, Scottish Council Develt and Industry, 1979–95; Scottish Council, CBI, 1980–85; Scottish Exec. Cttee, Inst. of Directors, 1984–91. President: Timber Trade Benevolent Soc., 1974; Scottish Timber Trade Assoc., 1984. Pres., Scottish Cons. and Unionist Assoc., 1980–82; Treasurer, Scottish Cons. Party, 1990–93, 1998–2001. Gov., Craighalbert Centre for Children with Motor Neurone Disease, 1992–95. *Recreations:* golf, shooting, fishing. *Address:* The Old Mill House, Symington, Ayrshire KA1 5QL. *T:* (01563) 830851. *Clubs:* Western (Glasgow); Royal and Ancient Golf, Prestwick Golf; Queen's Park Football.

MITCHELL, Sir Derek (Jack), KCB 1974 (CB 1967); CVO 1966; Second Permanent Secretary (Overseas Finance), HM Treasury, 1973–77; *b* 5 March 1922; *s* of late Sidney Mitchell, Schoolmaster, and Gladys Mitchell; *m* 1944, Miriam (*d* 1993), *d* of late F. E. Jackson; one *s* two *d*. *Educ:* St Paul's Sch.; Christ Church, Oxford. Served War of 1939–45: Royal Armoured Corps and HQ London District, 1942–45. Asst Principal HM Treasury, 1947; Private Sec. to Economic Sec., 1948–49; Private Sec. to Permanent Sec. and Official Head of Civil Service (Sir Edward Bridges), 1954–56; Principal Private Secretary to: Chancellor of Exchequer (Mr Reginald Maudling), 1962–63; The Prime Minister (Mr Harold Wilson, previously Sir Alec Douglas-Home), 1964–66; Under-Sec., 1964; Dep. Under-Sec. of State, DEA, 1966–67; Dep. Sec., MAFF, 1967–69; Economic Minister and Head of UK Treasury and Supply Delegn, Washington, (also UK Exec. Dir for IMF and IBRD), 1969–72. Director: Guinness Mahon & Co., 1977–78; Bowater Corp., 1979–84; Bowater Industries, 1984–89; Bowater Inc., 1984–93; Standard Chartered, 1979–89; Indep. Dir, The Observer Ltd, 1981–93; Sen. Advr, Shearson Lehman Brothers Internat., 1979–88; Chm., Jocelyn Burton Silversmith & Goldsmith Ltd, 1991–98. Mem., PLA, 1979–82. Dir, Peter Hall Production Co. Ltd, 1989–90; Mem. Bd, NT, then RNT, 1977–95; Chm., Royal Nat. Theatre Foundn, 1989–2002 (Treas., 1982–89); Bd Mem., French Theatre Season, London 1997, 1996–99. Mem. Council, University Coll. London, 1978–82; Governing Trustee, Nuffield Trust (formerly Nuffield Provincial Hospitals Trust), 1978–98; Trustee, Royal Nat. Theatre Endowment Fund, 1990–2000. *Recreations:* opera, theatre, music, motoring on minor roads. *Club:* Garrick.

MITCHELL, Donald Charles Peter, CBE 2000; PhD; FRCM; musicologist; Life President and Director, Britten Estate Ltd, since 2000 (Chairman, 1986–2000); Trustee, Britten-Pears Foundation, 1986–2000, now Trustee Emeritus; *b* 6 Feb. 1925; *s* of Frederick George Mitchell and Kathleen Mary Mitchell (*née* Charles); *m* 1956, Kathleen Livingston (*née* Burbidge); one step *s* and two foster *s*. *Educ:* Brightlands Prep Sch.; Dulwich Coll.; Univ. of Durham (1949–50); Univ. of Southampton (PhD 1977). Advisory Reader (new fiction), Gainsborough Pictures (1928) Ltd, 1942–43; Non-Combatant Corps, 1943–45; Asst Master, Oakfield Sch., London, 1946–48; Founding Editor, Music Survey, 1947, Jt Editor, 1949–52; Music Critic: Musical Times, 1953–57; Musical Opinion, 1953–57; Head of Music Dept, Faber & Faber, 1958; Editor, Tempo, 1958–62; Music Staff, Daily Telegraph, 1959–64; Music Advr, Boosey & Hawkes, 1963–64; Music Critic, Listener, 1964; Man. Dir, Faber Music, 1965–71 (Vice-Chm., 1976–77; Chm., 1977–86, Pres., 1988–95); founding Prof. of Music, Univ. of Sussex, 1971–76; Executor, Benjamin Britten's estate, 1976. Guest Artistic Dir, Aldeburgh Fest.,

1991. Visiting Professor of Music: Univ. of Sussex, 1977; Univ. of York, 1991; KCL, 1995–99; Hon. Res. Fellow, RCM, 2000–; Hon. Prof., Shanghai Conservatory of Music, 2006. Britten-Pears School for Advanced Musical Studies: Chm., Educn Cttee, 1976; Dir of Study Courses, 1977; Dir of Academic Studies, 1977–90; Hon. Dir, 1995. Director: Performing Right Soc., 1973 (Jt Dep. Chm., 1987–89, Chm., 1989–92, Hon. Mem. Council, 1992); Music Copyright (Overseas) Services Ltd, 1977–92; English Music Theatre, 1973; Nexus Opera, 1986–91; Chm. Exec. Cttee, Mahler Fest., Concertgebouw, Amsterdam, 1995. Member: BBC Central Music Adv. Council, 1967; Council, Aldeburgh Foundn, 1977–94; Adv. Bd, Musical Quarterly, NY, 1985; Adv. Bd, Kurt Weill Edition, NY, 1992; Editl Bd, Muziek & Wetenschap, 1997–2002. Vice-Pres., CISAC, 1992–94. Gov., 1988, Council of Honour, 2000–, RAM (Hon. RAM 1992); Gov., NYO, 1989–90. FRCM 2004. Hon. DMus Srinakharinwirot, Bangkok, 2001. Gustav Mahler Medal of Honor, Bruckner Soc., USA, 1961; Medal of Honour, Internat. Gustav Mahler Soc.; Gustav Mahler Medal of Honour, Vienna, 1987; Royal Philharmonic Soc. Award, 1992; Univ. of Toronto Distinguished Visitor Award, 1999; Charles Flint Kellog Award, NY, 2002. *Publications:* (jtly) Benjamin Britten: a commentary on his works, 1952, 2nd edn 1972; (jtly) The Mozart Companion, 1956, 2nd edn 1965; Gustav Mahler: the early years, 1958, 4th edn 2003; The Language of Modern Music, 1963, 4th edn 1993; Alma Mahler: Gustav Mahler Memories and Letters, 1968, (jtly) 4th edn 1990; (jtly) The Faber Book of Nursery Songs, 1968; (jtly) The Faber Book of Children's Songs, 1970; Gustav Mahler: the Wunderhorn years, 1975, 3rd edn 2005; (jtly) Benjamin Britten: pictures from a life 1913–1976, 1978; Britten and Auden in the Thirties: the year 1936, (T. S. Eliot Meml Lectures), 1981, 2nd edn 2000; Gustav Mahler: songs and symphonies of life and death, 1985, 2nd edn 2002; Benjamin Britten: Death in Venice, 1987; (jtly) Letters from a Life: selected letters and diaries of Benjamin Britten, vols 1 and 2, 1991, vol. 3, 2004, vol. 4, 2008; Cradles of the New: writings on music 1951–1991, ed Mervyn Cooke, 1995; Gustav Mahler: the world listens, 1995; (jtly) Mahler's Seventh Symphony, facsimile edn 1995; (ed) New Sounds, New Century: Mahler's Fifth Symphony and the Royal Concertgebouw Orchestra, 1997; (jtly) The Mahler Companion, 1999; Discovering Mahler: writings on Mahler 1955–2005, 2007; articles in jls. *Recreations:* travelling, reading, cooking, collecting pottery and paintings, studying the classical music of Thailand. *Address:* 83 Ridgmount Gardens, Torrington Place, WC1E 7AY. *T:* (020) 7580 1241, *Fax:* (020) 7436 7964; La Tour Quiterne, Rue de l'église, 16420 Brigueuil, Charente, France. *T:* (5) 45 290 779. *Club:* Garrick.

MITCHELL, Douglas Svärd; Controller of Personnel and Administrative Services, Greater London Council, 1972–78; *b* 21 Aug. 1918; *er s* of late James Livingstone Mitchell and Hilma Josefine (*née* Svärd); *m* 1943, Winifred Thornton Paterson (*d* 2002), *d* of late William and Ellen Paterson; one *s* two *d*. *Educ:* Morgan Academy, Dundee. Royal Ordnance Factories, 1937–51; Principal, Min. of Supply, 1951–55; Dir of Personnel and Admin., in Industrial, Production and Engineering Groups, UKAEA, 1955–63; Authority Personnel Officer for UKAEA, 1963–64; Dir of Establishments, GLC, 1964–72. *Address:* The Manor House, Horncastle, Lincolnshire LN9 5HF. *T:* (01507) 523553.

MITCHELL, Fergus Irvine; His Honour Judge Fergus Mitchell; a Circuit Judge, since 1996; *b* 30 March 1947; *s* of Sir George Irvine Mitchell, CB, QC (Scot.) and Elizabeth Mitchell (*née* Leigh Pemberton), JP; *m* 1972, Sally Maureen, *yr d* of Sir Derrick Capper, QPM and Muriel Capper; one *s* one *d*. *Educ:* Tiffin Boys' Sch., Kingston-upon-Thames. Called to the Bar, Gray's Inn, 1971; Asst Recorder, 1989; Recorder, 1993. Member: Gen. Council of the Bar, 1992–95; Professional Conduct Cttee, 1993–95; Bar Race Relations Cttee, 1994–95. *Recreations:* farm in Aveyron, France, opera. *Address:* Kingston-upon-Thames Crown Court, 6–8 Penrhyn Road, Kingston-upon-Thames, Surrey KT1 2BB.

MITCHELL, Rear-Adm. Geoffrey Charles, CB 1973; retired 1975; Director, The Old Granary Art and Craft Centre, Bishop's Waltham, Hants, 1975–86; *b* 21 July 1921; *s* of William C. Mitchell; *m* 1st, 1955, Jocelyn Rainger (*d* 1987), Auckland, NZ; one *s* two *d*; 2nd, 1990, Dr Hilary Gardiner. *Educ:* Marlborough College. Joined RN 1940; Captain 1961; Director Officer Recruiting, 1961–63; Captain (F), 2nd Frigate Sqdn, 1963–65; Director Naval Ops and Trade, 1965–67; Comdr, NATO Standing Naval Force Atlantic, 1968–69; Director Strategic Policy, to Supreme Allied Comdr Atlantic, 1969–71; Rear Adm. 1971; Dep. Asst Chief of Staff (Ops), SHAPE, 1971–74; Chm., RNR and Naval Cadet Forces Review Bd, 1974–75. *Recreations:* golf, painting, music, languages, sailing. *Address:* 10 Nelson Close, Stockbridge, Hants SO20 6ES. *T:* (01264) 810365.

MITCHELL, George Edward, CBE 2006; Chief Executive, Corporate, HBOS, 2001–05, and Governor, 2003–05, Bank of Scotland; *b* 7 April 1950; *m* 1971, Agnes Rutherford; three *d*. *Educ:* Forrester High Sch., Edinburgh. Joined Bank of Scotland, 1966: held a wide range of posts, incl. periods in Hong Kong, NY and London; Chief Exec., Bank of Scotland Retail Bank, 1999–2000. *Recreations:* football, tennis.

MITCHELL, Hon. George John, Hon. GBE 1999; lawyer; *b* 20 Aug. 1933; *s* of George and Mary Mitchell; *m* 1959, Sally L. Heath (marr. diss.); one *d*; *m* 1994, Heather MacLachlan; one *s* one *d*. *Educ:* Bowdoin Coll. (BA 1954); Georgetown Univ. (LLB 1960). Served US Army, 1954–56 (1st Lieut). Admitted to Bar of Maine and of Washington, 1960, to DC Bar, 1960; Trial Attorney, Anti-Trust Div., Dept of Justice, Washington, 1960–62; Exec. Asst to Senator Edmund Muskie, 1962–65; Partner, Jensen, Baird, Gardner, Donovan & Henry, Portland, 1965–77; US Attorney, Maine, 1977–79; US Dist Judge, N Maine, 1979–80; US Senator (Democrat) from Maine, 1980–95; Majority Leader, US Senate, 1988–95. Chm., Irish Peace Talks, 1995–98. Chancellor, QUB, 1999–. Hd, Internat. Adv. Council, Thames Water, 1999–. Hon. LLD QUB, 1997. Presidential Medal of Freedom (USA), 1999. *Publications:* (jtly) Men of Zeal: a candid inside story of the Iran-Contra Hearings, 1988; World on Fire, 1990; Not For America Alone: the triumph of democracy and the fall of communism, 1997; Making Peace, 1999. *Address:* DLA Piper, 1251 Avenue of the Americas, New York, NY 10020–1104, USA. *T:* (212) 8356002.

MITCHELL, Gordon Scotland; Director, Starburst Consulting Ltd, since 2006; *b* 30 Dec. 1956. *Educ:* Univ. of Edinburgh (MA Hons); Univ. of Newcastle upon Tyne (BPhil); Bristol Business Sch., UWE (MBA 1997). Posts in nat. voluntary sector, 1982–92; Hd, Policy and Corporate Relns, Newport CBC, 1992–97; Chief Executive: Bracknell Forest BC, 1998–2003; Nottingham CC, 2003–06. Gov., Nottingham Trent Univ., 2005–. *Recreations:* good food and wine, lying in the sun. *Address:* 36 William Bancroft Building, Roden Street, Nottingham NG3 1GU.

MITCHELL, Gregory Charles Mathew; QC 1997; PhD; a Recorder, since 2000; *b* 27 July 1954; *s* of John Matthew Mitchell, *qv*; three *s* one *d*. *Educ:* King's Coll., London (BA Hons; PhD); City Univ. (Dip. Law). Called to the Bar, Gray's Inn, 1979, Bencher, 2005. *Recreations:* ski-ing, scuba diving, tennis. *Address:* 3 Verulam Buildings, Gray's Inn, WC1R 5NT. *T:* (020) 7831 8441.

MITCHELL, Harry; QC 1987; Company Secretary, The Wellcome Foundation Ltd, 1976–92, and Wellcome plc, 1985–92; *b* 27 Oct. 1930; *s* of Harry and Lily Mitchell; *m* 1960, Mrs Megan Knill (*née* Watkins); one step *s* one step *d*. *Educ:* Bolton School; Corpus Christi College, Cambridge (BA). FCIS. Called to the Bar, Gray's Inn, 1968. Asst District Comr, Colonial Service, Sierra Leone, 1954–59; Company Sec., Asbestos Cement, Bombay, 1960–64; Asst Company Sec., British Aluminium Co., 1964–66; Legal Manager/Exec. Dir Legal, Hawker Siddeley Aviation, 1966–76. Chm., Bar Assoc. for Commerce, Finance and Industry, 1984–85 (Vice-Pres., 1986–); Mem. Senate of Inns of Court and Bar and Bar Council, 1978–81, 1983–86; Part-time Immigration Adjudicator, 1992–2002. Director: Berkeley Square Pension Trustee Co. Ltd, 2004–; Berkeley Square Common Investment Fund Ltd, 2005–. Mem., Adv. Council, Migrationwatch UK, 2003–. Mem., CBI London Regional Council, 1990–92. Board Member: Sarsen Housing Assoc., Devizes, 1994–2006 (Chm., 1995–2001); Silbury Gp Ltd, 2003–05; Ridgeway Community Housing Assoc., 2003–04. Trustee, Migraine Trust, 1995–2005. *Publications:* Remote Corners: a Sierra Leone memoir, 2002; articles in New Law Jl, Business Law Review and Jl of Immigration, Asylum and Nationality Law. *Recreations:* playing piano, opera, reading, travel. *Address:* The Mount, Brook Street, Great Bedwyn, Marlborough, Wilts SN8 3LZ. *T:* (01672) 870898; *e-mail:* harrymitchellqc@hotmail.com.

MITCHELL, Helen Josephine, (Mrs Michael Mitchell); *see* Watts, H. J.

MITCHELL, Iain Grant; QC (Scot.) 1992; Chairman: Scottish Lawyers' European Group, since 2002; Scottish Society for Computers and Law, since 2007 (Vice-Chairman, 2001–07); *b* 15 Nov. 1951; *s* of late John Grant Mitchell and Isobel (*née* Gilhespie). *Educ:* Perth Acad.; Edinburgh Univ. (LLB Hons 1973). Called to the Scottish Bar, 1976; Temp. Sheriff, 1992–97. Chm., IT Gp, Faculty of Advocates, 1999–. Exec. Ed., Scottish Parlt Law Rev., 1999–2003; Jt Ed., E-Law Rev., 2001–04. Cons. local govt cand. on various occasions, 1973–82; contested (C): Falkirk W, 1983; Kirkcaldy, 1987; Cumbernauld and Kilsyth, 1992; Dunfermline East, 1997; Dundee E, Scottish Parlt, 1999; Scotland, EP elecns, 1999; Edinburgh North & Leith, 2001; Falkirk W, Scottish Parlt, 2003. Hon. Secretary: Scottish Cons. & Unionist Assoc., 1993–98; Scottish Cons. & Unionist Party, 1998–2001; Chm., Edinburgh Central Cons. Assoc., 2003–05. Chm., N Queensferry Community Council, 2007– (Vice-Chm., 2004–07). Member, Executive Committee: Scottish Council, European Movement, 1992–; Perth Civic Trust, 1999–2002. Dir, Scottish Baroque Ensemble Ltd, 1985–2003 (Chm., 1999–2003); Chairman: Trust for an Internat. Opera Theatre of Scotland, 1984–; N Queensferry Arts Trust, 2005–; N Queensferry Railway Station Preservation Trust, 2006–; Perthshire Public Arts Trust, 2007– (Trustee, 2000–07); Mem., Forth Bridge Meml Cttee, 2005–. Reader, Ch of Scotland, 2005–. FSA (Scot) 1974; FRSA 1988. *Recreations:* music and the arts, photography, cinema, walking, travel, finding enough hours in the day. *Address:* Advocates' Library, Parliament House, High Street, Edinburgh EH1 1RF. *T:* (0131) 226 5071.

MITCHELL, James; Social Security Commissioner, 1980–95; a Child Support Commissioner, 1993–95; *b* 11 June 1926; *s* of James Hill Mitchell and Marjorie Kate Mitchell (*née* Williams); *m* 1957, Diane Iris Mackintosh; two *d*. *Educ:* Merchiston Castle Sch., Edinburgh; Brasenose Coll., Oxford, 1944–45 and 1948–51 (Open Exhibnr, BCL, MA). Served RAFVR, 1945–48. Assistant Master, Edge Grove Preparatory Sch., Herts, 1952–55; called to the Bar, Middle Temple, 1954; private practice as barrister/solicitor, Gold Coast/Ghana, 1956–58; practice as barrister, London, 1958–80. Most Hon. Order of Crown of Brunei, 3rd Cl. 1959, 2nd Cl. 1972. *Recreations:* sailing, walking, railways, the Jacobites.

MITCHELL, Rt Hon. Sir James (Fitz Allen), KCMG 1995; PC 1985; Prime Minister of St Vincent and the Grenadines, 1984–2000; *b* 15 May 1931; *s* of Reginald and Lois Mitchell; *m* (marr. diss.); four *d*. *Educ:* Imperial College of Tropical Agriculture (DICTA); University of British Columbia (BSA). MIBiol 1965; CBiol. Agronomist, 1958–65; owner, Hotel Frangipani, Bequia, 1966–, and other cos. MP for Grenadines, 1966–2001; Minister of Trade, Agriculture and Tourism, 1967–72; Premier, 1972–74; Minister of Foreign Affairs, 1984–92; Minister of Finance, 1984–98. Founder and Pres., New Democratic Party, 1975–; Chm., Caribbean Democrat Union, 1991–; Vice-Chm., Internat. Democrat Union, 1992–; Chm., Caribbean Community, 2000. Chm., Commonwealth Observer Gp, Lesotho Gen. Election, 2002. Alumni Award of Distinction, 1988, Centenary Award, 2008, Univ. of BC. Chevalier d'honneur, Chaîne des Rôtisseurs, 1995. Order of the Liberator (Venezuela), 1972; Order of Propitious Clouds (Taiwan), 1995; Gran Cruz, Order of Infante Dom Henrique (Portugal), 1997; Grand Cross, Order of Knights of Malta, 1998. *Publications:* World Fungicide Usage, 1967; Caribbean Crusade, 1989; Guiding Change in the Islands, 1996; A Season of Light, 2001; Beyond the Islands (autobiog.), 2006. *Recreations:* gardening, sailing. *Address:* Bequia, St Vincent, West Indies. *T:* 4573602. *Clubs:* St Vincent Nat. Trust; Bequia Sailing.

MITCHELL, (Janet) Margaret; JP; Member (C) Scotland Central, Scottish Parliament, since 2003; *b* 15 Nov. 1952; *d* of late John Aitken Fleming and of Margaret McRae Fleming (*née* Anderson); *m* 1978, Henry Thomson Mitchell. *Educ:* Coatbridge High Sch.; Hamilton Teacher Training Coll. (DipEd); Open Univ. (BA); Strathclyde Univ. (LLB; DipLLP); Jordanhill Coll. (Dip Media Studies). Primary school teacher, Airdrie and Bothwell, 1974–93. Mem. and Cons Gp Leader, Hamilton DC, 1988–96. Non-exec. Dir, Stonehouse and Hairmyres NHS Trust, 1993–97; Special Advr to David McLetchie, MSP and James Douglas Hamilton, MSP, 1999–2002. Scottish Cons. justice spokesman, 2003–07; Scottish Parliament: Convener: Equal Opportunities Cttee, 2007–; Dyslexia Cttee; Vice-Convener, Tibet Cttee. Mem., Scottish Cons. Party Exec., 2002–03. Hon. Member: Psoriasis Scotland Arthritis Link Volunteers, 2004–; Bd of Advrs, ThinkScotland.org, 2007–. JP South Lanarks, 1990. *Recreations:* music, cycling, photography. *Address:* Huntly Lodge, Fairfield Place, Bothwell G71 8RP; Scottish Parliament, Edinburgh EH99 1SP; *e-mail:* Margaret.Mitchell.msp@scottish.parliament.uk.

MITCHELL, Jeremy George Swale Hamilton; consumer policy adviser; *b* 25 May 1929; *s* of late George Oswald Mitchell and late Agnes Josephine Mitchell; *m* 1st, 1956, Margaret Mary Ayres (marr. diss. 1988); three *s* one *d*; 2nd, 1989, Janet Rosemary Powney. *Educ:* Ampleforth; Brasenose and Nuffield Colls, Oxford (MA). 2nd Lt, RA, 1948–49. Dep. Research Dir, then Dir of Information, Consumers' Assoc. (Which?), 1958–65; Asst Sec., Nat. Econ. Develt Office, 1965–66; Scientific Sec., then Sec., SSRC, 1966–74; Under Sec., and Dir of Consumer Affairs, Office of Fair Trading, 1974–77; Under Sec. and Dir, Nat. Consumer Council, 1977–86. Member: Economic Develt Cttee for the Distributive Trades, 1981–86; Independent Cttee for Supervision of Telephone Information Services, 1989–97; Direct Mail Services Standards Bd, 1990–95; Bd, PIA, 1994–2000; Scottish Consumer Council, 1995–2000; Telecoms Ombudsman Service Council, 2002–06; Scottish Solicitors' Discipline Tribunal, 2004–; Consumer Panel, OFCOM, 2006–; Vice-Chm., Nat. Council on Gambling, 1981–; Chm., Scottish Adv. Cttee on Telecommunications, 1998–2003; Comr for Scotland, Broadcasting Standards Commn, 1999–2000. *Publications:* (ed) SSRC Reviews of Research, series, 1968–73; (ed jtly) Social Science Research and Industry, 1971; Betting, 1972; (ed) Marketing and the Consumer Movement, 1978; (ed jtly) The Information Society, 1985; (ed) Money and the Consumer, 1988; Electronic Banking and the Consumer, 1988; The Consumer and

Financial Services, 1990; Banker's Racket or Consumer Benefit?, 1991; (ed jtly) Television and the Viewer Interest, 1994. *Recreations:* Swinburne, racing. *Address:* 19 Eglinton Crescent, Edinburgh EH12 5BY.

MITCHELL, Prof. Joan Eileen, (Mrs James Cattermole); Professor of Political Economy, University of Nottingham, 1978–85; *b* 15 March 1920; *d* of late Albert Henry Mitchell, Paper Merchant, and Eva Mitchell; *m* 1956, James Cattermole (*d* 2007); one *s* one *d*. *Educ:* Southend-on-Sea High Sch.; St Hilda's Coll., Oxford. Economist, Min. of Fuel and Power, 1942; Tutor, St Anne's Coll., Oxford, 1945; Economist, BoT, 1947; Research Officer, Labour Party, 1950; Lectr in Econs, Nottingham Univ., 1952, Reader in Econs, 1962. Mem., NBPI, 1965–68; personal economic adviser to Sec. of State for Prices and Consumer Protection, 1974–76. Member: Cttee to Review the Functioning of Financial Institutions, 1977–80 (Chm. Res. Panel); Standing Commn on Pay Comparability, 1979–81. *Publications:* Britain in Crisis 1951, 1963; Groundwork to Economic Planning, 1966; The National Board for Prices and Incomes, 1972; Price Determination and Prices Policy, 1978. *Recreations:* gardening, cooking. *Address:* c/o 34 Streatham Common South, SW16 3BX.

MITCHELL, John; *see* Mitchell, R. J.

MITCHELL, (John) Angus (Macbeth), CB 1979; CVO 1961; MC 1946; Secretary, Scottish Education Department, 1976–84; *b* 25 Aug. 1924; *s* of late John Fowler Mitchell, CIE and Sheila Macbeth, MBE; *m* 1948, Ann Katharine Williamson, MA, MPhil, author; two *s* two *d*. *Educ:* Marlborough Coll.; Brasenose Coll., Oxford (Junior Hulme Scholar); BA Modern Hist., 1948. Served Royal Armoured Corps, 1943–46: Lieut, Inns of Court Regt, NW Europe, 1944–45; Captain East African Military Records, 1946. Entered Scottish Education Dept, 1949; Private Sec. to Sec. of State for Scotland, 1958–59; Asst Sec., Scottish Educn Dept, 1959–65; Dept of Agriculture and Fisheries for Scotland, 1965–68; Scottish Development Dept, 1968; Asst Under-Secretary of State, Scottish Office, 1968–69; Under Sec., Social Work Services Gp, Scottish Educn Dept, 1969–75; Under Sec., SHHD, 1975–76. Chairman: Scottish Marriage Guidance Council, 1965–69; Working Party on Social Work Services in NHS, 1976; Working Party on Relationships between Health Bds and Local Authorities, 1976; Consultative Cttee on the Curriculum, 1976–80; Stirling Univ. Court, 1984–92; Scottish Action on Dementia, 1985–94; Vice-Convener, Scottish Council for Voluntary Orgs, 1986–91; Member: Commn for Local Authority Accounts in Scotland, 1985–89; Historic Buildings Council for Scotland, 1988–94; Co-ordinator, Recording Scottish Graveyards Project, 1992–99; Sec., Greyfriars Kirkyard Trust, 1992–. Mem., Dementia Services Develt Trust, 1988–2000. Hon. Vice-Pres., Scottish Genealogy Soc., 2007–. Hon. Fellow, Edinburgh Univ. Dept of Politics, 1984–88. Hon. LLD Dundee, 1983; DUniv Stirling, 1992. Kt, Order of Oranje-Nassau (Netherlands), 1946. *Publications:* Procedures for the Reorganisation of Schools in England (report), 1987; Monumental Inscriptions in SW Midlothian, 2005. *Recreations:* old Penguins, genealogy, gravestones. *Address:* 31/5 Kinnear Road, Edinburgh EH3 5BS. *T:* (0131) 552 3454. *Club:* New (Edinburgh).
See also C. I. Mitchell, J. J. Mitchell.

MITCHELL, Dr John Francis Brake, OBE 2001; FRS 2004; FRMetS; FIMA; Director, Climate Science, Meteorological Office, since 2007; *b* 7 Oct. 1948; *s* of Norman Brake Mitchell and Edith Alexandra Mitchell (*née* Reside); *m* 1973, Catriona Rogers; one *s* two *d*. *Educ:* Down High Sch., Downpatrick; Queen's Univ., Belfast (BSc Applied Maths 1970; PhD Theoretical Physics 1973). FRMetS 1973. Joined Meteorological Office, 1973: HSO, 1973–75; SSO, 1975–78; PSO, 1978–88; Grade 6, 1988–2002; Chief Scientist, 2002–07. Vis. Prof., Sch. of Maths, Meteorol. and Physics, Univ. of Reading, 2004–; Hon. Prof. of Envmtl Scis, UEA, 2003; Hon. Vis. Prof., Sch. of Engrg, Univ. of Exeter, 2007–. Symons Meml Lectr, RMetS, 2003. Mem., NERC, 2007–. Mem., Editl Bd, Climate Dynamics, 1994–. MAE 1998; FIMA 2003. L. G. Groves Trust Fund Prize for Meteorol., 1984; (jtly) Mumm Gerbier Award, 1997 and 1998; Hans Oeschger Medal, European Geophysical Soc., 2004. *Publications:* contrib. scientific papers on climate and climate change. *Recreations:* sport, outdoor pursuits, photography. *Address:* Meteorological Office, Fitzroy Road, Exeter EX1 3PB. *T:* (01392) 884604, *Fax:* 0845 300 1300; *e-mail:* john.f.mitchell@metoffice.gov.uk.

MITCHELL, John Gall; QC (Scot.) 1970; a Deputy Social Security Commissioner and a Deputy Child Support Commissioner, 1999–2001 (a Social Security (formerly National Insurance) Commissioner, 1979–99; a Child Support Commissioner, 1993–99); *b* 5 May 1931; *s* of late Rev. William G. Mitchell, MA; *m* 1st, 1959, Anne Bertram Jardine (*d* 1986); three *s* one *d*; 2nd, 1988, Margaret, *d* of late J. W. Galbraith. *Educ:* Royal High Sch., Edinburgh; Edinburgh Univ. (MA, LLB). Commn, HM Forces, 1954–56 (Nat. Service). Advocate 1957. Standing Junior Counsel, Customs and Excise, Scotland, 1964–70; Chairman: Industrial Tribunals, Scotland, 1966–80; Legal Aid Supreme Court Cttee, Scotland, 1974–79; Pensions Appeals Tribunal, Scotland, 1974–80. Hon. Sheriff: of Lanarkshire, 1970–74; of S Strathclyde, 1975–79. *Address:* Rosemount, Park Road, Dalkeith, Midlothian EH22 3DH.

MITCHELL, John Logan; QC (Scot.) 1987; *b* 23 June 1947; *s* of Robert Mitchell and Dorothy Mitchell; *m* 1973, Christine Brownlee Thomson; one *s* one *d*. *Educ:* Royal High School, Edinburgh (Past Pres., Former Pupils' Club); Edinburgh Univ. (LLB Hons). Called to the Bar, 1974; Standing Junior Counsel: to Dept of Agriculture and Fisheries for Scotland, 1979; Forestry Commission for Scotland, 1979; Advocate Depute, 1981–85. *Recreation:* golf. *Address:* 17 Braid Farm Road, Edinburgh. *T:* (0131) 447 8099. *Clubs:* Mortonhall Golf, Craigielaw Golf, Luffness New Golf.

MITCHELL, John Matthew, CBE 1976; PhD; Assistant Director-General, 1981–84, Senior Research Fellow, 1984–85, British Council; retired; *b* 22 March 1925; *s* of Clifford George Arthur Mitchell and Grace Maud Jamson; *m* 1952, Eva Maria von Rupprecht; three *s* one *d*. *Educ:* Ilford County High Sch.; Worcester Coll., Oxford; Queens' Coll., Cambridge (MA). PhD Vienna. Served War, RN, 1944–46. British Council: Lectr, Austria, 1949–52 and Egypt, 1952–56; Scotland, 1957–60; Dep. Rep., Japan, 1960–63; Reg. Dir, Zagreb, 1963–66; Reg. Rep., Dacca, 1966–69; Dep. Controller, Home Div., 1969–72; Rep., Federal Republic of Germany, 1973–77; Controller, Educn, Medicine and Sci. Div., 1977–81. Vis. Fellow, Wolfson Coll., Cambridge, 1972–73; former Lectr, univs of Vienna, Cairo and Tokyo. Fellow, Chartered Inst. of Linguists (Chm. Council, 1996–99; Pres., 2004–07; Vice-Pres., 2007–). *Publications:* International Cultural Relations, 1986; verse, short stories and trans. from German and French. *Recreations:* golf, theatre, cinema, opera. *Address:* The Cottage, Pains Hill Corner, Pains Hill, Limpsfield, Surrey RH8 0RB. *T:* (01883) 723354. *Club:* Tandridge Golf.
See also G. C. M. Mitchell.

MITCHELL, Jonathan James; QC (Scot.) 1992; *b* 4 Aug. 1951; *s* of (John) Angus (Macbeth) Mitchell, *qv* and Ann Katharine (*née* Williamson); *m* 1987, Melinda McGarry; one *s* one *d*. *Educ:* Marlborough Coll.; New Coll., Oxford (BA); Edinburgh Univ. (LLB). Advocate, 1979; Temp. Sheriff, 1988–95. Dep. Social Security Comr, 1994–2002. Mem., Scotch Malt Whisky Soc. *Publication:* Eviction and Rent Arrears, 1994. *Address:* 30 Warriston Crescent, Edinburgh EH3 5LB. *T:* (0131) 557 0854, *Fax:* (0131) 557 3210; *e-mail:* jonathanmitchell@mac.com.
See also C. I. Mitchell.

MITCHELL, Julian; writer; *b* 1 May 1935; *s* of late William Moncur Mitchell and of Christine Mary (*née* Browne). *Educ:* Winchester; Wadham Coll. Oxford. Nat. Service in Submarines, 1953–55; Temp. Acting Sub-Lieut, RNVR. Member: Literature Panel, Arts Council, 1966–69; Welsh Arts Council, 1988–92 (Chm. Drama Cttee, 1989–92). Curator, Joshua Gosselin exhibn, Chepstow, 2003. Wolfson Lecture, Oxford, 2003. John Llewellyn Rhys Prize, 1965; Somerset Maugham Award, 1966. Television plays include: Shadow in the Sun; A Question of Degree; Rust; Abide With Me (Internat. Critics Prize, Monte Carlo, 1977); Survival of the Fittest; Consenting Adults (Scottish BAFTA 2007); adaptations of: Persuasion; The Alien Corn; Staying On; The Good Soldier; The Mysterious Stranger; The Weather in the Streets; Inspector Morse; series, Jennie, Lady Randolph Churchill, 1974; television documentary: All the Waters of Wye, 1990. Films: Arabesque, 1965; Vincent and Theo, 1990; Wilde, 1997. Theatre: Adelina Patti, 1987. *Publications: novels:* Imaginary Toys, 1961; A Disturbing Influence, 1962; As Far As You Can Go, 1963; The White Father, 1964; A Circle of Friends, 1966; The Undiscovered Country, 1968; *biography:* (with Peregrine Churchill) Jennie: Lady Randolph Churchill, 1974; *autobiography:* A Disgraceful Anomaly (C. M. Bowra), 2003; *translation:* Henry IV (Pirandello), 1979 (John Florio Prize, 1980); *plays:* Half-Life, 1977; The Enemy Within, 1980; Another Country, 1981 (SWET play of the year, 1982; filmed, 1984); Francis, 1983; After Aida (or Verdi's Messiah), 1986; Falling Over England, 1994; August, 1994 (adapted from Chekhov's Uncle Vanya; filmed, 1996); (adapted from Ivy Compton-Burnett): A Heritage and Its History, 1965; A Family and a Fortune, 1975; (contrib.) History and Fiction, ed by R. L. O. Tomlin, 2005; contribs to: Welsh History Review, The Monmouthshire Antiquary. *Recreations:* local history, fishing. *Address:* 47 Draycott Place, SW3 3DB.

MITCHELL, Katrina Jane, (Katie); freelance director; Associate Director, Royal National Theatre, since 2003; *b* 23 Sept. 1964; *d* of Michael and Sally Mitchell. *Educ:* Magdalen Coll., Oxford (MA Eng. Lit. and Lang.). Asst Dir, 1989–90, Associate Dir, 1996–98, RSC; Associate Dir, Royal Court Th., 2001–04. Productions directed: Gate Theatre, Notting Hill: Vassa Zheleznova, 1991; Women of Troy, 1991; The House of Bernarda Alba, 1992; Royal Shakespeare Company: The Dybbuk, 1992; Ghosts, 1993; Henry VI, 1995; Easter, 1995; The Phoenician Women, 1996; Beckett Shorts, 1997; Uncle Vanya, 1998; Royal Court: Live Like Pigs, 1993; The Country, 2000; Mountain Language, Ashes to Ashes, 2001; Nightsongs, Face to the Wall, 2002; Forty Winks, 2004; The City, 2008; Abbey Theatre, Dublin: The Last Ones, 1993; Iphigenia at Aulis, 2001; National Theatre: Rutherford and Son, 1994; Machine Wreckers, 1995; The Oresteia, 1999; Ivanov, 2002; Three Sisters, 2003; Iphigenia at Aulis, 2004; A Dream Play, 2005; The Seagull, Waves, 2006; Women of Troy, 2007; The Idiot, 2008; Welsh National Opera: Don Giovanni, 1996; Jenufa, 1998; Katya Kabanova, 2001; Jephtha, 2003, restaged, ENO, 2005; The Sacrifice, 2007; End Game, Donmar Warehouse, 1996; The Maids, Young Vic, 1999; Easter, 2001, Krapp's Last Tape, 2004, The Maids, 2008, Royal Dramatic Th., Stockholm; television: Widowing of Mrs Holroyd, 1995; Turn of the Screw, 2004. *Address:* c/o Leah Schmidt, The Agency, 24 Pottery Lane, W11 4LZ.

MITCHELL, Keith Kirkman, OBE 1979; Lecturer in Physical Education, University of Leeds, 1955–90; *b* 25 May 1927; *s* of John Stanley Mitchell and Annie Mitchell; *m* 1950, Hannah Forrest; two *s*. *Educ:* Loughborough Coll. (Hons Dip. in Physical Educn). Phys. Educn Master, Wisbech Grammar Sch., 1950–52; Dir of Phys. Recreation, Manchester YMCA, 1952–55. Chm. Exec. Cttee, CCPR, 1981–87; Mem., Sports Council, 1976–87. Dir, 1953–84, Pres., 1985, now Pres. Emeritus and Patron, England Basketball (formerly English Basketball Assoc.). *Recreations:* basketball, photography, gardening, golf. *Address:* 6 Kirkbourne Grove, Baildon, Shipley BD17 6HW. *T:* (01274) 584907.

MITCHELL, Margaret; *see* Mitchell, J. M.

MITCHELL, Michael James Ross, PhD; Director General, Rail and National Networks (formerly Rail), Department for Transport, since 2005; *b* 22 Feb. 1948; *s* of James and Margaret Mitchell; *m* 1971, Jillian Mary Tomory; two *s*. *Educ:* Univ. of Aberdeen (MA Hons 1970; PhD 1993); Univ. of Edinburgh (MBA 1987). CMILT (MCIT 1977). With BR, 1970–86 (Area Manager, Coventry, 1978–80); Eastern Scottish Omnibuses Ltd, 1986–94 (Ops Dir, 1990–94); Man. Dir, Grampian Regl Transport, later FirstBus plc, 1994–97; FirstGroup plc: Divl Dir, 1997; Man. Dir, First Great Western, 1998; Dir, Rail, 1999; Chief Operating Officer, 2001–04; Business Develt Dir, 2004–05. *Publications:* Aberdeen Suburban Tramways, 1980, revd edn 1981; Aberdeen District Tramways, 1983; Fae Dee to Don and Back Again: 100 years of Aberdeen transport, 1998. *Recreations:* vintage bus restoration, photography, travel. *Address:* Department for Transport, Great Minster House, 76 Marsham Street, SW1P 4DR. *T:* (020) 7944 4155; *e-mail:* mike.mitchell@dft.gsi.gov.uk.

MITCHELL, Nicolas John; His Honour Judge Nicolas Mitchell; a Circuit Judge, since 1996; *b* 12 May 1940; *s* of Leslie George Tudor Mitchell and Emma Mitchell; *m* 1962, Marion Davies; two *s*. *Educ:* Bancroft's Sch. Admitted solicitor, 1962; in private practice, 1962–96; a Recorder, 1992–96. Sheffield Prize, Law Soc., 1962. *Recreations:* walking, gardening, outdoor pursuits, reading, opera. *Address:* c/o Midland and Oxford Circuit Office, The Priory Courts, 33 Bull Street, Birmingham B4 6DW.

MITCHELL, Very Rev. Patrick Reynolds, KCVO 1998; Dean of Windsor, 1989–98; Register, Order of the Garter, 1989–98; Domestic Chaplain to the Queen, 1989–98; *b* 17 March 1930; *s* of late Lt-Col Percy Reynolds Mitchell, DSO; *m* 1st, 1959, Mary Evelyn (*née* Phillips) (*d* 1986); three *s* one *d*; 2nd, 1988, Pamela, *d* of late A. G. Le Marchant and *widow* of Henry Douglas-Pennant; one step *s* one step *d* (and two step *s* decd). *Educ:* Eton Coll.; Merton Coll., Oxford (MA Theol); Wells Theol Coll. Officer in Welsh Guards (National Service), 1948–49. Deacon, 1954; priest, 1955; Curate at St Mark's, Mansfield, 1954–57; Priest-Vicar of Wells Cathedral and Chaplain of Wells Theological Coll., 1957–60; Vicar of St James', Milton, Portsmouth, 1961–67; Vicar of Frome Selwood, Somerset, 1967–73; Dean of Wells, 1973–89; Director of Ordination Candidates for Bath and Wells, 1971–74. Res. Fellow, Merton Coll., Oxford, 1984. Chm., Cathedral Libraries and Archives Assoc., 1997–2001. Member: Adv. Bd for Redundant Churches, 1978–92; Cathedrals Adv. Commn for England, 1981–91. Governor, Wellington Coll., 1994–98. Hon. Freeman, City of Wells, 1986. FSA 1981. *Address:* Wolford Lodge, Dunkeswell, Honiton, Devon EX14 4SQ. *T:* (01404) 841244. *Club:* Oxford and Cambridge.

MITCHELL, (Richard) John; His Honour Judge John Mitchell; a Circuit Judge, since 2005; *b* 28 Oct. 1948; *s* of Kenneth Frank Mitchell and Edith Mitchell; *m* 1977, Marlene Le Saint; two *s*. *Educ:* Brentwood Sch.; Peterhouse, Cambridge (MA 1972). Called to the Bar, Middle Temple, 1972; a District Judge, 1999–2005. *Publication:* Children Act Private Law Proceedings: a handbook, 2003, 2nd edn 2006. *Recreations:* walking, theatre. *Address:* Clerkenwell and Shoreditch County Court, The Gee Street Courthouse, 29–41 Gee Street, EC1V 3RE.

MITCHELL, Prof. Stephen, DPhil; FBA 2002; Leverhulme Professor of Hellenistic Culture, University of Exeter, since 2002; *b* 26 May 1948; *s* of David and Barbara Mitchell; *m* 1974, Matina Weinstein; three *s*. *Educ:* St John's Coll., Oxford (BA 1970; MA, DPhil 1975). Lectr, 1976, Sen. Lectr, 1984, Reader, 1989, Prof., 1993–2001, UC of Swansea, subseq. Univ. of Wales, Swansea. Vis. Fellow, Inst. of Advanced Study, Princeton, 1983–84; British Acad. Res. Reader, 1990–92. Hon. DTheol Humboldt Univ., Berlin, 2006. *Publications:* Anatolia: land, men and gods in Asia Minor, 1993; Cremna in Pisidia: an ancient city in peace and in war, 1995; Pisidian Antioch: the site and its monuments, 1998; A History of the Later Roman Empire 284–641, 2007. *Recreations:* walking, travel, wine. *Address:* Department of Classics and Ancient History, University of Exeter, Exeter EX4 4QH; *e-mail:* S.Mitchell@ex.ac.uk.

MITCHELL, Hon. Sir Stephen (George), Kt 1993; a Judge of the High Court of Justice, Queen's Bench Division, 1993–2003; President, National Security Appeals Panel, Information Tribunal, 2004–07; *b* 19 Sept. 1941; *s* of Sydney Mitchell and Joan Mitchell (*née* Dick); *m* 1978, Alison Clare (*née* Roseveare) (*d* 1998); two *d*. *Educ:* Bedford Sch.; Hertford Coll., Oxford (MA). Called to the Bar, Middle Temple, 1964, Bencher, 1993; Second Prosecuting Counsel to the Crown, Inner London Crown Court, 1975; Central Criminal Court: a Junior Prosecuting Counsel to the Crown, 1977; a Senior Prosecuting Counsel to the Crown, 1981–86; QC 1986; a Recorder, 1985–89; a Circuit Judge, 1989–93. Dep. Chm., Security Vetting Appeals Panel, 2001–04. Mem., Judicial Studies Bd, 1991–93. *Publications:* (ed) Phipson on Evidence, 11th edn, 1970; (ed) Archbold's Criminal Pleading Evidence and Practice, 1971–88; The Marks on Chelsea-Derby and Early crossed-batons Useful Wares 1770–*c*1790, 2007. *Address:* Royal Courts of Justice, Strand, WC2A 2LL.

MITCHELL, Stephen Graham; Head of News Programmes, BBC, since 2007; *b* 14 July 1949; *s* of Derek Mitchell and Phyllis Mitchell (*née* Rigden); *m* 1977, Barbara Gilder; one *s* one *d*. *Educ:* Loughborough Grammar Sch.; Manchester Univ. (BA Hons). Reporter, Thompson Newspapers, Newcastle Jl, S Wales Echo, The Times, 1971–74; BBC: producer, reporter, Radio Newsroom, and Duty Editor, Today prog., 1974–84; Dep. Foreign News Ed., 1985; Ed., Parly Output, 1986–88; Ed., then Man. Ed., Radio Newsroom, 1988–93; Ed., Radio News Progs, 1993–97; Dep. Hd, News Progs (Bimedia), 1997–99; Hd, Radio News, 2000–07. *Recreations:* my family, reading. *Address:* 30 Amenbury Lane, Harpenden, Herts AL5 2DF.

MITCHELL, Terence Croft; Keeper of Western Asiatic Antiquities, British Museum, 1985–89; *b* 17 June 1929; *s* of late Arthur Croft Mitchell and Evelyn Violet Mitchell (*née* Ware). *Educ:* Holderness School, New Hampshire, USA; Bradfield Coll., Berks; St Catharine's Coll., Cambridge (MA 1956). REME Craftsman, 1947–49. Asst Master, St Catherine's Sch., Almondsbury, 1954–56; Resident Study, Tyndale House, Cambridge, 1956–58; European Rep., Aust. Inst. of Archaeology, 1958–59; Dept of Western Asiatic Antiquities, British Museum, 1959, Dep. Keeper, 1974, Acting Keeper, 1983–85. Chm., Faith and Thought (formerly Victoria Inst.), 1986–; Vice Chm., British Inst. at Amman for Archaeology and History, 1990–93. Lay Chm., Chelsea Deanery Synod, 1981–84. Editor, Palestine Exploration Fund Monograph Series, 1990–2000. *Publications:* Sumerian Art at Ur and Al-'Ubaid, 1969; (ed) Sir Leonard Woolley, Ur Excavations VIII, The Kassite Period and the Period of the Assyrian Kings, 1965; VII, The Old Babylonian Period, 1976; (ed) Music and Civilization, 1980; chapters on Israel and Judah in Cambridge Ancient History, vol. 3, part 1, 1982, part 2, 1991; The Bible in the British Museum: interpreting the evidence, 1988, rev. edn 1996, rev. and enlarged edn 2004; (with Ann Searight) Catalogue of the Western Asiatic Seals in the British Museum, 2007; Stamp Seals III: impressions of Stamp Seals on Cuneiform Tablets, Clay Bullae and Jar Handles, 2007; articles and reviews. *Recreations:* music, reading, landscape gardening. *Address:* 32 Mallord Street, Chelsea, SW3 6DU. *T:* (020) 7352 3962. *Club:* Athenæum.

MITCHELL, Valerie Joy, OBE 2001; Director-General, English-Speaking Union of the Commonwealth, since 1994; *b* 2 March 1941; *d* of Henry Frederick Twidale and Dorothy Mary (*née* Pierce), MBE; *m* 1st, 1962, Henri Pierre Eschauzier (marr. diss. 1970); two *s*; 2nd, 1972, Graham Rangeley Mitchell; one *d*. *Educ:* Beaufront Sch., Camberley; McGill Univ., Montreal (BA Hons). PA to Asst Dean of Arts and Sci., McGill Univ., Montreal, 1962–64; PR Consultant to Mayer-Lismann Opera Workshop, 1970–80; English-Speaking Union: Asst, Educn Dept, 1980–83; Dir of Branches and Cultural Affairs, 1983–94; Dep. Dir-Gen., 1989–94; Sec.-Gen., Internat. Council of ESU Worldwide, 1994–. Member: Internat. Cttee, Shakespeare Globe Centre, 2000–05; Exec. Cttee, European Atlantic Gp, 2001–; Pilgrims Soc., 2003–; Trustee: Shakespeare Globe Trust, 2006–; Longborough Fest. Opera, 2006–; RAD, 2007–; Prince Galitzine-St Petersburg Trust, 2007–; Harvard House Meml Trust, 2008–. FRSA 1987. *Recreations:* music, theatre, tennis, walking. *Address:* English-Speaking Union, Dartmouth House, 37 Charles Street, W1J 5ED. *T:* (020) 7529 1550.

MITCHELL, Warren; *b* 14 Jan. 1926; *s* of Montague and Annie Misell, later Mitchell; *m* 1952, Constance Wake; one *s* two *d*. *Educ:* Southgate Co. Sch.; University Coll., Oxford; RADA. Demobbed RAF, 1946. First professional appearance, Finsbury Park Open Air Theatre, 1950; Theophile in Can-Can, Coliseum, 1954; Crookfinger Jake in The Threepenny Opera, Royal Court and Aldwych, 1956; Mr Godboy in Dutch Uncle, Aldwych, 1969; Satan in Council of Love, Criterion, 1970; Herbert in Jump, Queen's, 1971; Ion Will in The Great Caper, Royal Court, 1974; The Thoughts of Chairman Alf, Stratford E, 1976; Willie Loman in Death of a Salesman, Nat. Theatre, 1979; Ducking Out, Duke of York's, 1983; Harpagon in The Miser, Birmingham Rep., 1986; Max in The Homecoming, 1991; West Yorkshire Playhouse: King Lear, 1996; Visiting Mr Green, 2000; Art, Wyndhams, 2000; The Price, Tricycle, 2002, Apollo, 2003 (Best Supporting Actor, Olivier Awards, 2004); *films include:* Diamonds Before Breakfast; Assassination Bureau; Best House in London; Till Death Us Do Part; Moon Zero Two; Whatever Happened to Charlie Farthing; Jabberwocky; Stand Up Virgin Soldiers; Meetings with Remarkable Men; Norman Loves Rose; The Chain; *television:* Alf Garnett in Till Death Us Do Part, BBC, 1966–78, and In Sickness and in Health, BBC, 1985, 1986; The Thoughts of Chairman Alf (series), 1998; Shylock in Merchant of Venice, BBC, 1981; Till Death (series), ITV, 1981; The Caretaker, BBC, 1981; So You Think You've Got Troubles (series), BBC, 1994; Wall of Silence, BBC, 1995; Death of a Salesman, BBC, 1996; Gormenghast, BBC, 2000. TV Actor of the Year Award, Guild of Film and TV Producers, 1966; Actor of Year Award: Evening Standard, 1979; Soc. of West End Theatres, 1979; Plays and Players, 1979. *Recreations:* sailing, tennis, playing clarinet. *Address:* c/o Ken McReddie, 36–40 Glasshouse Street, W1B 5DL.

MITCHELL, Rev. Mgr William Joseph; Parish Priest, St Michael's Tetbury, since 2001; *b* 4 Jan. 1936; *s* of late William Ernest and Catherine Mitchell. *Educ:* St Brendan's Coll., Bristol; Corpus Christi Coll., Oxford (MA); Séminaire S Sulpice, Paris; Gregorian Univ., Rome (LCL). Ordained Priest, Pro-Cathedral, Bristol, 1961; Curate, Pro-Cathedral, Bristol, 1963–64; Secretary to Bishop of Clifton, 1964–75; Parish Priest, St Bernadette, Bristol, 1975–78; Rector, Pontifical Beda Coll., Rome, 1978–87; VG, 1987–2001, Judicial Vicar, 2002–07, dio. Clifton; Parish Priest: St John's, Bath, 1988–90; St Antony's, Bristol, 1990–96; St Mary's, Bristol, 1996–97; Adminr, subseq. Dean, Clifton Cathedral, Bristol, 1997–2001. Canon, Clifton Cathedral Chapter, 1987–. Prelate of Honour, 1978. KHS 2003. *Address:* St Michael's Presbytery, 31 Silver Street, Tetbury, Glos GL8 8DH. *T:* (01666) 502367; *e-mail:* billmitchell@tetbury31.freeserve.co.uk.

MITCHELL COTTS, Sir Richard Crichton; *see* Cotts.

MITCHELL-INNES, Alistair Campbell; Chairman, Next Pension Trustees Ltd, 1991–2005; *b* 1 March 1934; *s* of Peter Mitchell-Innes; *m* 1957, Penelope Ann Hill; one *s* two *d*. *Educ:* Charterhouse; Stanford Business Sch. (Executive Program). Dir, Brooke Bond Gp plc, 1979–84; Chief Exec., Nabisco Gp Ltd, 1985–88; Chief Exec., Isosceles plc, 1991–93; Dep. Chm., H. P. Bulmer (Holdings) plc, 1990–2001; Chairman: Sidney C. Banks plc, 1994–2000; Anglo & Overseas Trust PLC, 1996–2004. Non-exec. Dir, 1989–2004, Dep. Chm., 2002–04, Next plc. *Recreations:* golf, cricket, military history. *Address:* 9 Market Street, Rye, E Sussex TN31 7LA. *Clubs:* Caledonian, MCC; Berkshire Golf.

MITCHELL-THOMSON, family name of **Baron Selsdon**.

MITCHINER, Dr John Edward; HM Diplomatic Service, retired; High Commissioner to Sierra Leone, and Ambassador (non-resident) to Liberia, 2003–06; *b* 12 Sept. 1951; *s* of late Geoffrey Morford Mitchiner and Ursula Angela Mitchiner (*née* Adolph); *m* 1983, Elizabeth Mary Ford, MA, MNIMH. *Educ:* John Fisher Sch., Purley; Beaumont Coll., Old Windsor; Bristol Univ. (BA 1972); Sch. of Oriental and African Studies, London Univ. (MA 1973; PhD 1977). ACU Res. Fellow, Visva Bharati Univ., Santiniketan, 1977–78; Bipradas Palchaudhuri Fellow, Calcutta Univ., 1978–79; joined FCO, 1980; Third, later Second Sec. (Information), Istanbul 1982–85; FCO, 1985–87; Second Sec. (Develt), New Delhi, 1987–91; Second, later First Sec. (Political), Berne, 1991–95; Head, Japan Section, FCO, 1995–96; Ambassador to Armenia, 1997–99; Dep. High Comr, Kolkata, India, 2000–03. MRAS. *Publications:* Studies in the Indus Valley Inscriptions, 1978; Traditions of the Seven Rsis, 1982, 2nd edn 2000; The Yuga Purana, 1986, 2nd edn 2002; Guru: the search for enlightenment, 1992; contribs to learned jls. *Recreations:* sheep farming and breeding llamas, bridge, tennis, family history, karabash. *Address:* Bower Farm, Whitland SA34 0QX. *Club:* Royal Commonwealth Society.

MITCHISON, Avrion; *see* Mitchison, N. A.

MITCHISON, Prof. Denis Anthony, CMG 1984; Professor of Bacteriology, Royal Postgraduate Medical School, 1971–84, Professor Emeritus, London University, since 1984; at St George's, University of London (formerly St George's Hospital Medical School), since 1993; Director, Medical Research Council's Unit for Laboratory Studies of Tuberculosis, 1956–84; *b* 6 Sept. 1919; *e s* of Baron Mitchison, CBE, QC, and late Naomi Margaret Mitchison, CBE, writer; *m* 1st, 1940, Ruth Sylvia (*d* 1992), *d* of Hubert Gill; two *s* two *d*; 2nd, 1993, Honora, *d* of Christopher Carlin. *Educ:* Abbotsholme Sch.; Trinity Coll., Cambridge; University Coll. Hosp., London (MB, ChB). House Physician: Addenbrooke's Hosp.; Royal Berkshire Hosp.; Asst to Pathologist, Brompton Hosp.; Prof. of Bacteriology (Infectious Diseases), RPMS, 1968–71. Member, Scientific Advisory Committee: TB Alliance, 1998–; Medicine in Need, 2006–. FRCP; FRCPath. *Publications:* numerous papers on bacteriology and chemotherapy of tuberculosis. *Address:* 14 Marlborough Road, Richmond, Surrey TW10 6JR. *T:* (020) 8940 4751.

See also J. M. Mitchison, N. A. Mitchison.

MITCHISON, Prof. John Murdoch, ScD; FRS 1978; FRSE 1966; Professor of Zoology, University of Edinburgh, 1963–88, now Professor Emeritus and Hon. Fellow; *b* 11 June 1922; *s* of Baron Mitchison, CBE, QC, and late Naomi Margaret Mitchison, CBE, writer; *m* 1947, Rosalind Mary Wrong (*d* 2002); one *s* three *d*. *Educ:* Winchester Coll.; Trinity Coll., Cambridge. Army Operational Research, 1941–46; Sen. and Research Scholar, Trinity Coll., Cambridge, 1946–50; Fellow, Trinity Coll., Cambridge, 1950–54; Edinburgh University: Lectr in Zoology, 1953–59; Reader in Zoology, 1959–62; Dean, Faculty of Science, 1984–85; Mem. of Court, 1971–74, 1985–88. J. W. Jenkinson Memorial Lectr, Oxford, 1971–72. Member: Council, Scottish Marine Biol. Assoc., 1961–67; Exec. Cttee, Internat. Soc. for Cell Biology, 1964–72; Biol Cttee, SRC, 1972–75; Royal Commn on Environmental Pollution, 1974–79; Science Bd, SRC, 1976–79; Working Gp on Biol Manpower, DES, 1968–71; Adv. Cttee on Safety of Nuclear Installations, Health and Safety Exec., 1981–84. Pres., British Soc. for Cell Biology, 1974–77. Mem., Academia Europaea, 1989. FInstBiol 1963. *Publications:* The Biology of the Cell Cycle, 1971; papers in scientific jls. *Address:* Great Yew, Ormiston, East Lothian EH35 5NJ. *T:* (01875) 340530.

See also D. A. Mitchison, N. A. Mitchison.

MITCHISON, Prof. (Nicholas) Avrion, FRS 1967; Senior Fellow, Department of Immunology, University College London, since 1996; *b* 5 May 1928; 3rd *s* of Baron Mitchison, CBE, QC, and late Naomi Margaret Mitchison, CBE, writer; *m* 1957, Lorna Margaret, *d* of Maj.-Gen. J. S. S. Martin, CSI; two *s* three *d*. *Educ:* Leighton Park Sch.; New Coll., Oxford (MA 1949). Fellow of Magdalen College, 1950–52; Commonwealth Fund Fellow, 1952–54; Lecturer, Edinburgh Univ., 1954–61; Reader, Edinburgh Univ., 1961–62; Head of Div. of Experimental Biology, Nat. Inst. for Med. Research, 1962–71; Jodrell Prof. of Zoology and Comparative Anatomy, UCL, 1970–89 (Hon. Fellow, 1993); Scientific Dir, Deutsches Rheuma-Forschungszentrum Berlin, 1990–96. Hon. MD Edinburgh, 1977. *Publications:* articles in scientific journals. *Address:* 14 Belitha Villas, N1 1PD; Department of Immunology, University College London, Windeyer Building, 46 Cleveland Street, W1P 6DB. *T:* (020) 7380 9349, *Fax:* (020) 7380 9357; *e-mail:* n.mitchison@ucl.ac.uk.

See also D. A. Mitchison, J. M. Mitchison.

MITFORD, family name of **Baron Redesdale**.

MITFORD-SLADE, Patrick Buxton, OBE 2000; Partner, Cazenove & Co., 1972–96; *b* 7 Sept. 1936; *s* of late Col Cecil Townley Mitford-Slade and Phyllis, *d* of E. G. Buxton; *m* 1964, Anne Catharine Stanton, *d* of late Major Arthur Holbrow Stanton, MBE; one *s* two *d*. *Educ:* Eton Coll.; RMA Sandhurst. Commissioned 60th Rifles, 1955, Captain; served Libya, NI, Berlin and British Guyana; Adjt, 1st Bn The Royal Green Jackets, 1962–65; Instructor, RMA Sandhurst, 1965–67. Stockbroker, Cazenove & Co., 1968–96; Man. Dir, Cazenove Money Brokers, 1986–96. Director: Clive Securities Group Ltd, 1996–99; John Govett Holdings Ltd, 1996–97; Clive Discount Co. Ltd, 1996–98; Investec Bank (UK) Ltd, 1996–98; AIB Asset Management Hldgs Ltd, 1997–98; SG Hambros Bank (formerly SG Hambros Bank & Trust Co.) Ltd, 2001–08. Asst Sec., Panel on Takeovers and Mergers, 1970–72; Mem., Stock Exchange, 1972–86, Internat. Stock Exchange, 1986–92 (Mem. Council, 1976–91; Dep. Chm., 1982–85); Chairman: City Telecommunications Cttee, 1983–92; Securities Industry Steering Cttee on Taurus, 1988–90; Money Brokers Assoc., 1990–96; Dep. Chm., Stock Borrowing and Lending Cttee, 1996–98. Chm., St Luke's Hosp. for the Clergy, 2001– (Hon. Treas., 1994–2001). Vice Pres., Officers' Assoc., 1985– (Chm., 1985–2000); Mem., Benevolent and Strategy

Cttee, RBL, 1998–2005; Hon. Recorder, Royal (formerly British) Commonwealth Ex-Services League, 2005– (Hon. Treas., 1993–2005). Chairman: Royal Green Jackets Administrative Trustees, 2005–08 (Trustee, 1996–); The Rifles Regtl Trustees, 2007–; Gov., Reed's Sch., 2001–08 (Chm., 2002–08). *Recreations:* shooting, fishing. *Address:* The White House, Wivelrod, Alton, Hants GU34 4AR.

MITHANI, Abbas; His Honour Judge Mithani; a Circuit Judge, since 2006; *b* 27 Feb. 1958; *s* of late Hussein Mithani and of Lailabanu Mithani; *m* 1982, Sajeda Nurmohomed; two *s* one *d. Educ:* Univ. of Newcastle upon Tyne (LLB Hons); Univ. of Keele (LLM). Admitted solicitor (with Hons), 1981; Licensed Insolvency Practitioner, 1987; Civil Higher Court Advocate, 1994; Dep. Bankruptcy Registrar, 1994. Dep. Dist Judge, 1993–99; Dist Judge, 1999–2006; a Recorder, 2000–06. Hon. Prof. of Law, Univ. of Birmingham, 2000–. Mem. Court, Univ. of Newcastle upon Tyne, 2005–. Asian Jewel Award for Legal Excellence for Central Britain, Inst. of Asian Professionals, 2003. *Publications:* Islamic Wills, 1994; Mithani and Wheeler, 1995, 2nd edn as Mithani: Directors' Disqualification, 1998; *contributor:* Encyclopaedia of Forms and Precedents, 5th edn; Atkin's Court Forms, 2nd edn; Civil Court Service, 2000–; Kelly's Draftsman, 18th edn 2002; numerous contribs to Law Soc.'s Gazette, Insolvency Law and Practice and other jls on commercial litigation, insolvency and directors' duties. *Recreations:* keen interest in history and literature, watching all kinds of sports.

MITHEN, Prof. Steven John, PhD; FBA 2004; FSA, FSAScot; Professor of Early Prehistory, since 2000, and Head, School of Human and Environmental Sciences, since 2003, University of Reading; *b* 16 Oct. 1960; *s* of William Mithen and Patricia Mithen; *m* 1985, Susan Orton; one *s* two *d. Educ:* Slade Sch. of Fine Art; Univ. of Sheffield (BA 1st cl. Hons (Prehist. and Archaeol.) 1983); Univ. of York (MSc (Biol Computation) 1984); Univ. of Cambridge (PhD (Archaeol.) 1987). University of Cambridge: Res. Fellow in Archaeol., Trinity Hall, 1987–90; Lectr in Archaeol. (temp.), 1989–91; Res. Associate in Archaeol., McDonald Inst., 1991–92; University of Reading: Lectr, 1992–96, Sen. Lectr, 1996–98, in Archaeol.; Reader in Early Prehistory, 1998–2000. FSAScot 1993; FSA 1998. *Publications:* Thoughtful Foragers: a study of prehistoric decision making, 1990; The Prehistory of the Mind: a search for the origins of art, science and religion, 1996; (ed) Creativity in Human Evolution and Prehistory, 1998; (ed) Hunter-Gatherer Landscape Archaeology: the Southern Hebrides Mesolithic Project 1988–1998, 2 vols, 2001; After the Ice: a global human history 20,000–5,000 BC, 2003; The Singing Neanderthals, 2005; The Early Prehistory of Wadi Faynan, 2007; articles in jls incl. Antiquity, Jl of Archaeol Sci., Jl of Human Evolution, Current Anthropol. and Levant. *Recreations:* family, lepidoptery. *Address:* School of Human and Environmental Sciences, University of Reading, PO Box 227, Reading RG6 6AB. *T:* (0118) 378 6102, *Fax:* (0118) 931 0279; *e-mail:* s.j.mithen@reading.ac.uk.

MITSAKIS, Prof. Kariofilis; Professor of Modern Greek Literature, University of Athens, 1978–99, now Emeritus; *b* 12 May 1932; *s* of Christos and Crystalli Mitsakis; *m* 1966, Anthoula Chalkia; two *s. Educ:* Univs of Thessaloniki (BA, PhD), Oxford (MA, DPhil) and Munich. Scientific Collaborator, National Research Foundn of Greece, 1959–62; Associate Prof. of Byzantine and Modern Greek Literature, Univ. of Maryland, 1966–68; Chm. of Dept of Comparative Literature, Univ. of Maryland, 1967–68; Sotheby and Bywater Prof. of Byzantine and Modern Greek Language and Literature, Univ. of Oxford, 1968–72; Prof. of Modern Greek Lit., Univ. of Thessaloniki, 1972–75; Dir, Inst. for Balkan Studies, Thessaloniki, 1972–80. Hon. DLitt and Ph Johannesburg, 2001. Gottfried Herder Prize, Vienna Univ., 2000. *Publications:* Problems Concerning the Text, the Sources and the Dating of the Achilleid, 1962 (in Greek); The Greek Sonnet, 1962 (in Greek); The Language of Romanos the Melodist, 1967 (in English); The Byzantine Alexanderromance from the Cod. Vindob. theol. gr. 244, 1967 (in German); Byzantine Hymnography, 1971 (in Greek); Petrarchism in Greece, 1973 (in Greek); Introduction to Modern Greek Literature, 1973 (in Greek); Homer in Modern Greek Literature, 1976 (in Greek); George Viziynos, 1977 (in Greek); Modern Greek Prose: the Generation of the '30s, 1978 (in Greek); Modern Greek Music and Poetry, 1979 (in Greek and English); March Through the Time, 1982; The Living Water, 1983; Points of Reference, 1987 (in Greek); The Cycles with their trails that rise and fall, 1991 (in Greek); The Boston Essays, 1993 (in Greek); The Oxford Essays, 1995 (in Greek); The Alexanderromance, 2001 (in Greek); Modern Greek Miscellany, 2001 (in Greek); In Imagination and in Word: studies on the poet C. P. Cavafy, 2001 (in Greek); Pan the Great: studies on the poet A. Sikelianos, 2001 (in Greek); contribs to Balkan Studies, Byzantinisch-Neugriechische Jahrbücher, Byzantinische Zeitschrift, Comparative Literature Studies, Diptycha, Etudes Byzantines–Byzantine Studies, Glotta, Hellenika, Jahrbuch der Oesterreichischen Byzantinischen Gesellschaft, Nea Hestia, etc. *Recreations:* music, travelling. *Address:* 25 Troados Street, Aghia Paraskevi, 153 42 Athens, Greece.

MITTAL, Lakshmi Niwas; President and Chief Executive Officer, ArcelorMittal, since 2006 (Chairman and Chief Executive Officer, Mittal Steel Company Ltd, 2004–06); *b* 15 June 1950; *s* of Mohan Lal and Guta Mittal; *m* 1971, Usha; one *s* one *d. Educ:* St Xavier's Coll., Calcutta (BCom). Founded The LNM Group, Indonesia, 1976 (Chm.); subseq. expanded operations into Trinidad and Tobago, Mexico, Canada, Germany, Kazakhstan, USA, France, Algeria, Romania, S Africa and Czech Repub.; former Chm. and CEO, Ispat Internat. NV and LNM Holdings NV; Chm. and CEO of many group mem. cos. Has championed development of integrated mini-mills and use of direct reduced iron (DRI) as scrap substitute for steelmaking. Founder, LNM Foundn for charitable progs in India. Steelmaker of the Year, New Steel Magazine, 1996; Willy Korf Steel Vision Award, American Metal Market/World Steel Dynamics, 1998. *Recreations:* yoga, swimming. *Address:* ArcelorMittal, 7th Floor, Berkeley Square House, Berkeley Square, W1J 6DA.

MITTING, Hon. Sir John Edward, Kt 2001; **Hon. Mr Justice Mitting;** a Judge of the High Court of Justice, Queen's Bench Division, since 2001; *b* 8 Oct. 1947; *s* of late Alison Kennard Mitting and Eleanor Mary Mitting; *m* 1977, Judith Clare (*née* Hampson); three *s. Educ:* Downside Sch.; Trinity Hall, Cambridge (BA, LLB). Called to the Bar, Gray's Inn, 1970, Bencher, 1996; QC 1987; a Recorder, 1988–2001; Chm., Special Immigration Appeal Commn, 2007–. *Recreations:* wine, food, bridge. *Address:* Royal Courts of Justice, Strand, WC2A 2LL. *Club:* Garrick.

MITTLER, Prof. Peter Joseph, CBE 1981; MA, PhD, MEd; CPsychol; FBPsS; Professor of Special Education, 1973–95, Professor Emeritus, since 1995, and Dean, Faculty of Education and Director, School of Education, 1991–94, University of Manchester; *b* 2 April 1930; *s* of Dr Gustav Mittler and Gertrude Mittler; *m* 1st, 1955, Helle Katscher (marr. diss. 1997); three *s;* 2nd, 1997, Penelope Anastasia Platt. *Educ:* Merchant Taylors' Sch., Crosby; Pembroke Coll., Cambridge (MA); PhD London; MEd Manchester. Clinical Psychologist, Warneford and Park Hosps, Oxford, 1954–58; Principal Psychologist, Reading Area Psychiatric Services, 1958–63; Lectr in Psychology, Birkbeck Coll., Univ. of London, 1963–68; Manchester University: Dir, Hester Adrian Res. Centre, 1968–82; Dir, Centre for Educnl Guidance and Special Needs, Dept of Educn, 1977–91; Dep. Dir, Sch. of Educn, 1989–91. Vis. Prof., Manchester Metropolitan Univ., 1996–97; Distinguished Vis. Prof., Univ. of Hong Kong, 1997–98; Fellow, Centre

for Policy Studies, Dartington, 1995–. Chm., Nat Develt Gp for Mentally Handicapped, 1975–80; Mem., Schs Exams and Assessment Council, 1988–90. Pres., Internat. League of Socs for Persons with Mental Handicap, 1982–86 (Vice-Pres., 1978–82); Mem., Prince of Wales Adv. Gp on Disability, 1984–90; Chm. Trustees and Council, British Inst. of Learning Disabilities, 1995–97; Advr on disability to UN, UNESCO, WHO, ILO, UNICEF. FIASSID 2000. *Publications:* ed, Psychological Assessment of Mental and Physical Handicaps, 1970; The Study of Twins, 1971; ed, Assessment for Learning in the Mentally Handicapped, 1973; ed, Research to Practice in Mental Retardation (3 vols), 1977; People not Patients, 1979; (jtly) Teaching Language and Communication to the Mentally Handicapped, (Schools Council), 1979; (ed jtly) Advances in Mental Handicap Research, 1980; (ed) Frontiers of Knowledge in Mental Retardation (2 vols), 1981; (ed jtly) Approaches to Partnership: professionals and parents of mentally handicapped people, 1983; (ed jtly) Aspects of Competence in Mentally Handicapped People, 1983; (ed jtly) Staff Training in Mental Handicap, 1987; (jtly) Inset and Special Educational Needs: running short, school-focused inservice courses, 1988; (ed jtly) Special Needs Education (World Yearbook of Education), 1993; Teacher Education for Special Educational Needs, 1993; (jtly) Innovations in Family Support for People with Learning Difficulties, 1994; (ed jtly) Teacher Education for Special Needs in Europe, 1995; (ed) Changing Policy and Practice for People with Learning Disabilities, 1995; (jtly) Disability and the Family, 1995; Working Towards Inclusive Education: social contexts, 2000; papers in psychol and educnl jls. *Recreations:* music, travel. *Address:* 8 Drayton Manor, Parrs Wood Road, Manchester M20 5GJ. *T:* and *Fax:* (0161) 434 5625.

MIURIN, Fields W.; *see* Wicker-Miurin.

MIYAKE, Kazunaru, (Issey); fashion designer; *b* 22 April 1938. *Educ:* Tama Art Univ., Tokyo; Chambre Syndicale de la Couture, Paris. Assistant Designer: Guy Laroche, Paris, 1966–68; Hubert de Givenchy, Paris, 1968–69; Designer, Geoffrey Beene, NY, 1969–70; established Miyake Design Studio, Tokyo, 1970; first Paris fashion show, 1973; Founder: Pleats Please, 1993; A-POC, 1999. *Exhibitions:* Bodyworks - Fashion Without Taboos, Tokyo, San Francisco, LA, London, 1985; Musée des Arts Décoratifs, Paris, 1988; Issey Miyake Making Things, Paris, 1998, NY, 1999, Tokyo, 2000. Numerous awards. Hon. Dr: RCA, 1993; Lyon, 1999. Chevalier, Légion d'honneur (France), 1993; Bunka Korosha (Japan), 1998. *Publications:* East Meets West, 1978; Issey Miyake Bodyworks, 1983. *Address:* Issey Miyake Design Studio, 1–23 Oyama-cho, Shibuya-ku, Tokyo 151, Japan.

MKAPA, Benjamin William; President, United Republic of Tanzania, 1995–2005; *b* 12 Nov. 1938; *s* of William Matwani and Stephania Nambanga; *m* 1966, Anna Joseph Maro; two *s. Educ:* Lupaso Primary Sch.; Ndanda Secondary Sch.; Kigonsera Seminary; St Francis Coll., Pugu (Cambridge Sch. Cert.); Makerere UC (BA Hons 1962); Sch. of Internat. Affairs, Columbia Univ. Admin. Officer, subseq. Dist Officer, then Foreign Service Officer, Dodoma, 1962; Managing Editor: The Nationalist and Uhuru, 1966–72; The Daily News, and The Sunday News, 1972–74; Press Sec. to President, 1974–76; Founding Dir, Tanzania News Agency, 1976; High Comr to Nigeria, 1976–77; nominated MP, 1977–82, 1984–85; elected MP for Nanyumbu, 1985, re-elected 1990; Minister for Foreign Affairs, 1977–82, 1984–90; Minister for Information and Culture, 1980–82; High Comr to Canada, 1982–83; Ambassador to USA, 1983–84; Minister for Information and Broadcasting, 1990–92; Minister for Science, Tech. and Higher Educn, 1992–95. Chm., 1996–2006, Mem., 1977–, Chama cha Mapinduzi (Revolutionary Party). *Address:* Office of the Former President, PO Box 7652, Dar es Salaam, Tanzania.

MKONA, Callisto Matekenya, Hon. GCVO 1985; Senior Principal Secretary for Home Affairs, Malaŵi, 1994, retired; *b* 4 June 1930; *s* of late Benedicto Mkona and of Martha Matekenya Mkona; *m* 1971, Helen Victoria (*née* Sazuze); two *s* two *d. Educ:* Zomba, Malaŵi; Urbanian Univ., Rome (DCL, Dip. Soc. Scis). Secondary School teacher, 1962–64; Mission Educn Liaison Officer, 1964–67; Educn Attaché (First Sec.), Washington and London, 1967–71; Ambassador to Ethiopia, 1971–72; Minister, Washington, 1972–73; High Comr in Zambia, 1973–75; Ambassador in Bonn, 1975–78; Dep. Principal Sec., Min. of External Affairs, 1978–79; Principal Sec., Office of the President and Cabinet, 1979–81; High Comr in London, also concurrently accredited to Denmark, France, Norway, Portugal, Sweden and Switzerland, 1981–87; Chm., Malaŵi Public Service Commn, 1987–88; High Comr in Nairobi, concurrently accredited to Egypt, Israel and Uganda, 1988–93; Permanent Representative to: UN Centre for Human Settlements (HABITAT), 1988–93; UNEP, 1988–93. Republic of Malaŵi 6th July 1966 Medal, 1966; Malaŵi Silver Jubilee of Independence Award, 1989. *Recreations:* reading, walking, tennis, golf. *Address:* Chigumula, PO Box 5643, Limbe, Malaŵi.

MLINARIC, David; interior decorator and designer, 1964–2004; founded David Mlinaric Ltd, 1964, became Mlinaric, Henry and Zervudachi Ltd, 1989; *b* 12 March 1939; *s* of Franjo and Mabel Mlinaric; *m* 1969, Martha Laycock; one *s* two *d. Educ:* Downside Sch.; Bartlett Sch. of Architecture; University Coll. London. Private and commercial interior designing and decorating, often in historic bldgs. Work includes: rooms in Nat. Gall. and NPG, London, 1986; Spencer House, London, 1990; Wellcome Building, London, 1992; Royal Opera House, Covent Garden; British Galls, V&A Mus. Fellow, BIDA; FRSA. Hon. Fellow, RCA, 1987. *Recreations:* gardening, sightseeing. *Address:* 38 Bourne Street, SW1W 8JA. *T:* (020) 7730 9072.

MO, Timothy Peter; writer; *b* 30 Dec. 1950; *s* of Peter Mo Wan Lung and Barbara Helena Falkingham. *Educ:* Convent of the Precious Blood, Hong Kong; Mill Hill School; St John's Coll., Oxford (BA; Gibbs Prize 1971). *Publications:* The Monkey King, 1978 (Geoffrey Faber Meml Prize, 1979); Sour Sweet, 1982 (Hawthornden Prize, 1983; filmed, 1989); An Insular Possession, 1986; The Redundancy of Courage, 1991 (E. M. Forster Award, Amer. Acad. and Inst. of Arts and Letters, 1992); Brownout on Breadfruit Boulevard, 1995; Renegade or Halo[2] (James Tait Black Meml Prize), 1999. *Recreations:* scuba diving, weight training, gourmandising. *Address:* BCM Paddleless, WC1N 3XX; *e-mail:* timothymo@eudoramail.com.

MOATE, Sir Roger (Denis), Kt 1993; *b* 12 May 1938; *m* 1st; one *s* one *d;* 2nd, Auriol (*née* Cran) (MBE 2003); one *d. Educ:* Latymer Upper Sch., Hammersmith. Insurance Broker; with J. H. Minet, in S Africa and Kenya, 1957–60; Director: Walker Moate & Co., 1961–66; Alexander Howden Insce Brokers Ltd, 1967–70. Contested (C) Faversham, 1966. MP (C) Faversham, 1970–97; contested (C) Sittingbourne and Sheppey, 1997. Mem., Select Cttee on Agric., 1995–97. Hon. Sec., British-Amer. Parly Gp, 1974–81; Chm., British-Norwegian Parly Gp, 1987–97. Chm., Brentford and Chiswick Young Conservatives; Vice-Chm., Greater London Area Young Conservatives, 1964. Comdr, Royal Norwegian Order of Merit, 1994. *Recreations:* ski-ing, tennis, gardening. *Address:* New Calico, Newnham, Sittingbourne, Kent ME9 0LN.

MOBERLY, Dr Patricia Jane; JP; Chairman, Guy's and St Thomas's Hospital NHS Foundation Trust (formerly NHS Trust), since 1999. *Educ:* Univ. of Liverpool (BA Hons Eng. Lang. and Lit.); King's Coll., London (PhD 1985). Teacher: Chikola Sch., Zambia; Roan Sch., Greenwich; Mary Datchelor Sch., Camberwell; Sen. Teacher and Hd, Sixth

Form, Pimlico Sch., 1974–98. Mem., Lambeth BC 1971–78. Member: Lambeth Southwark and Lewisham AHA 1976–81; Lambeth DHA, 1981–90. Mem., GMC, 2002–. Governor: Maudsley and Bethlem Hosp., 1976–78; UMDS, 1988–90. Mem., Nat. Cttee, Anti-Apartheid Movement. JP Inner London, 1976.

MOBERLY, Sir Patrick (Hamilton), KCMG 1986 (CMG 1978); HM Diplomatic Service, retired; Ambassador to South Africa, 1984–87; *b* 2 Sept. 1928; *yr s* of G. H. Moberly; *m* 1955, Mary Penfold; two *s* one *d. Educ:* Winchester; Trinity Coll., Oxford (MA). HM Diplomatic Service, 1951–88; diplomatic posts in: Baghdad, 1953; Prague, 1957; Foreign Office, 1959; Dakar, 1962; Min. of Defence, 1965; Commonwealth Office, 1967; Canada, 1969; Israel, 1970; FCO, 1974; Asst Under-Sec. of State, 1976–81; Ambassador to Israel, 1981–84. *Recreations:* opera, congenial travel. *Address:* 38 Lingfield Road, SW19 4PZ.

MOCHAN, Charles Francis; HM Diplomatic Service, retired; High Commissioner to Fiji, and also (non-resident) to Kiribati, Tuvalu and Nauru, 2002–06; *b* 6 Aug. 1948; *s* of Charles Mochan and Margaret Mochan (*née* Love); *m* 1970, Ilse Sybilla Carleon Cruttwell; one *s* one *d. Educ:* St Patrick's High Sch., Dumbarton. MoD (Navy), 1966; joined FCO 1967; Port Elizabeth, S Africa, 1970–72; Kingston, Jamaica, 1972–74; FCO, 1974–77; Seoul, 1977–80; Second, later First Sec., Helsinki, 1981–84; FCO, 1984–87; Dep. High Comr, Mauritius, 1988–91; FCO, 1991–95; Consul-Gen., Casablanca, 1995–98; Ambassador to Republic of Madagascar, 1999–2002, and concurrently to Federal Islamic Republic of Comoros, 2001–02. *Recreations:* soccer, ornithology, music, walking, golf.

MODARRESSI, Anne, (Mrs T. M. Modarressi); *see* Tyler, A.

MOELWYN-HUGHES, Edmwnd Goronwy; Vice Judge Advocate General, 1994–2004; a Recorder, 1990–2003; *b* 29 Aug. 1937; twin *s* of late Dr E. A. Moelwyn-Hughes and of Mair Elen Moelwyn-Hughes (*née* Evans); *m* 1964, Carolyn, *o d* of late John Sanders and Beryl (*née* Hobday); one *s* two *d. Educ:* The Leys Sch., Cambridge; Trinity Hall, Cambridge (MA). Nat. Service, 1956–58, 2nd Lieut Royal Welch Fusiliers. Called to the Bar, Inner Temple, 1968; practised Wales and Chester Circuit, 1968–73. Dep. Judge Advocate, 1973–78; Asst JAG, 1978–94; Standing Civilian Court Magistrate, 1982–96; an Asst Recorder, 1984–90; DJAG, British Forces in Germany, 1989–91. Governor: The Leys Sch., 1996–2001; St Faith's Sch., Cambridge, 1996–2001. *Recreations:* reading, music, walking, theatre. *Clubs:* Army and Navy, Royal Commonwealth Society.

MOFFAT, Captain (Alexander) Iain (Black), RD 1980 (and Bar 1988); CEng; FGS; RNR retired; Vice Lord-Lieutenant for Northumberland, since 2002; Professorial Fellow in Dam Engineering, University of Newcastle upon Tyne, since 2004 (Visiting Fellow, 2000–04); *b* 29 March 1938; *s* of late Alexander Moffat and Margaret D. H. Moffat (*née* Black); *m* 1963, Madeline Wright; one *s* one *d. Educ:* Edinburgh Acad.; Univ. of Edinburgh (BSc). CEng, MICE 1970; FGS 1987. Civil Engr posts, 1962–66; University of Newcastle upon Tyne: Lectr, 1966–74; Sen. Lectr, 1974–2000; Dep. Head, Dept of Civil Engrg, 1991–98. Vis. Sen. Lectr, Univ. of Durham, 1998–2001. Chm., 1994–2003, Pro-Chm., 2003–, Northumbrian Univ. Mil. Educn Cttee; Mem., ICE Panel for Historic Engrg Works, 2005–. Vice-Chm. (RN and RM), RFCA for N of England, 1996–2003. Trustee: Ocean Youth Trust (NE), 2007–; HMS Trincomalee Trust, 2008–. CO, Tyne Div., RNR, HMS Calliope, 1982–86. DL Northumberland, 1990. *Publications:* (jtly) Hydraulic Structures, 1990, 4th edn 2007; numerous contribs/papers to professional jls and conf. proc. in UK and overseas on issues in dam engrg, geotechnics, etc. *Recreations:* walking, history (technology, naval, military, social (19th and 20th Century)), travel, reading. *Address:* 43 Bishops Hill, Acomb, Hexham, Northumberland NE46 4NH. *T:* (01434) 605243; *e-mail:* aibmoffat@aol.com, a.i.b.moffat@ncl.ac.uk.

MOFFAT, Alistair Murray; author and broadcaster; *b* 16 June 1950; *s* of John and Ellen Moffat; *m* 1976, Lindsay Anne Reid Thomas; one *s* two *d. Educ:* Kelso High Sch.; St Andrews Univ. (MA Hons); Edinburgh Univ. (CertEd); London Univ. (MPhil). Administrator, Edinburgh Festival Fringe, 1976–81; Scottish Television, subseq. Scottish Media Group: Arts Corresp., 1981–86; Controller of Features, 1987–90; Dir of Progs, 1990–93; Chief Exec., then Man. Dir, Scottish Television Enterprises, 1993–99. Chm., Scottish TV Regl Bd, 1999–2003. *Publications:* The Edinburgh Fringe, 1978; Kelsae: a history from earliest times, 1985; Remembering Charles Rennie Mackintosh, 1989; Arthur and the Lost Kingdoms, 1999; The Sea Kingdoms, 2001; The Borders, 2002; Homing, 2003; Heartland, 2004; Before Scotland, 2005; Tyneside, 2005; East Lothian, 2006; The Reivers, 2007; Fife: a history, 2007. *Recreation:* apprentice groom. *Address:* The Henhouse, Selkirk TD7 5EY.

MOFFAT, Anne; MP (Lab) East Lothian, since 2001; *b* 30 March 1958; *d* of Francis Hunter Moffat and late Wilma Hoxton Moffat; *m* 1984, David Adair Harold Picking (marr. diss. 2003); one *s. Educ:* Woodmill High Comprehensive Sch. Nurse: Fife Health Bd, 1975–80; NI Eastern Health and Social Service, 1980–83 (staff nurse, 1982–83); staff nurse, then nursing sister, E Kent Community Health Care NHS Trust, 1984–2001. Mem., NEC, COHSE, 1990; Mem., NEC, 1993–2001, Nat. Pres., 1999–2000, UNISON. Mem. (Lab), Ashford BC, 1994–98. *Address:* (office) 65 High Street, Tranent, East Lothian EH33 1LN; c/o House of Commons, SW1A 0AA.

MOFFAT, Sir Brian (Scott), Kt 1996; OBE 1982; Deputy Chairman, HSBC Holdings plc, 2001–08 (Director, 1998–2008); *b* 6 Jan. 1939; *s* of Festus and Agnes Moffat; *m* 1964, Jacqueline Mary Cunliffe; one *s* one *d* (and one *s* decd). *Educ:* Hulme Grammar School. FCA. Peat Marwick Mitchell & Co., 1961–68; British Steel Corp., then British Steel plc, subseq. Corus Gp, 1968–2003: Man. Dir, Finance, 1986–91; Chief Exec., 1991–99; Chm., 1993–2003. Non-executive Director: Enterprise Oil, 1995–2002; Bank of England, 2000–06; Macsteel Global Hldgs (formerly Nosmas Investment Hldgs) BV, 2003–. Hon. DSc: Warwick, 1998; Sheffield, 2001. *Recreations:* farming, fishing, shooting. *Club:* Flyfishers'.

MOFFAT, David Andrew, FRCS; Consultant Neurotologist and Skull Base Surgeon, Addenbrooke's Hospital, Cambridge, since 1981; Lecturer, University of Cambridge, since 1981; *b* 27 June 1947; *s* of Graham and Myra Moffat; *m* 1970, Jane Elizabeth; two *s* one *d. Educ:* St Nicholas Sch., Northwood; London Hospital Med. Coll. (BSc Hons 1968; MB BS 1971); MA Cantab 1984. MRCS 1971, FRCS 1977; LRCP 1971. Consultant Surgeon, Westminster Hosp., 1979–80. Chm., Intercollegiate Specialty Bd and Panel of Examiners, 1998–2001; Mem., Specialist Adv. Cttee in Otolaryngology, 2001–06. Master, British Academic Conf. in Otolaryngology, 2006–. *Publications:* (ed jtly) Recent Advances in Otolaryngology, 7, 1995, 8, 2007; 150 papers in learned jls on neurology and skull base surgery including acoustic neuroma, meningioma, glomus jugulare tumours, squamous cell carcinomas of temporal bone, méniere disease, electrophysiology. *Recreations:* fast cars, golf, ski-ing, ballet. *Address:* Department of Otoneurological and Skull Base Surgery, Box 48, Addenbrooke's Hospital, Cambridge University Hospitals NHS Foundation Trust, Hills Road, Cambridge CB2 2QQ. *T:* (01223) 586638, *Fax:* (01223) 217559; *e-mail:* dam26@cam.ac.uk. *Club:* Gog Magog.

MOFFAT, Rev. Canon George; Rector, Priory Church of St Mary and St Cuthbert, Bolton Abbey, since 2007; Hon. Chaplain to the Queen, since 2000; *b* 31 July 1946; *s* of George and Mary Moffat; *m* 1975, Peta Ollen; two *d. Educ:* Edinburgh Theol Coll.; New Coll., Edinburgh (BD 1977); Open Univ. (BA Hons 1987); Bradford Univ. (MA 2004). Ordained deacon, 1972, priest, 1973; Curate: Christ Church, Falkirk, 1973–76; St Peter, Lutton Place, Edinburgh, 1976–81; Anglican Chaplain, Edinburgh Univ., 1977–81; Curate, St Leonard and All Saints, Heston, 1981–84; Vicar, St Mary the Virgin, S Emsall, 1984–93; Team Rector, Manningham, 1993–2007. Hon. Canon, Bradford Cathedral, 2002–. Non-exec. Dir, Bradford City Teaching PCT, 2003–06. *Recreations:* country walking, supporting creative modern dance. *Address:* The Rectory, Bolton Abbey, Skipton, N Yorks BD23 6AL. *T:* (01756) 710326.

MOFFAT, Captain Iain; *see* Moffat, Captain A. I. B.

MOFFAT, Lt-Gen. Sir (William) Cameron, KBE 1985 (OBE 1975); FRCS; *b* 8 Sept. 1929; *s* of William Weir Moffat and Margaret Garrett; *m* 1953, Audrey Watson; one *s. Educ:* King's Park Sch., Glasgow; Univ. of Glasgow, Western Infirmary (MB ChB). DTM&H. House Surgeon, Western Inf., Glasgow, 1952; Ship's Surg., Anchor Line, 1953; MO Seaforth Highlanders, 1954; SMO Edinburgh, 1956–57; Hammersmith Hosp., 1962; Birmingham Accident Hosp., 1964; Surg., RAAF Hosp. Malaya, 1965–67; Cons. Surg., BMH Rinteln, 1968–70; Prof. Military Surgery, RAM Coll. and RCS, 1970–75; CO BMH Rinteln, 1978–80; Comd MED HQ 1 (Br) Corps, 1980–83; PMO, UKLF, 1983–84; Surg. Gen./Dir Gen. Army Med. Servs, MoD, 1985–87, retired. QHS 1984–88. Chief Med. Advr, BRCS, 1988–94. Hon. DSc Glasgow, 1991. CStJ 1985. *Publications:* contribs to surgical text books and jls on missile wounds and their management. *Recreations:* golf, travel, bird-watching. *Address:* Kippax, Pound Green, Freshwater, Isle of Wight PO40 9HH.

MOFFATT, Prof. (Henry) Keith, ScD; FRS 1986; FRSE; Professor of Mathematical Physics, University of Cambridge, 1980–2002, now Professor Emeritus (Head of Department of Applied Mathematics and Theoretical Physics, 1983–91); Fellow, Trinity College, Cambridge, 1961–76, and since 1980; *b* 12 April 1935; *s* of late Frederick Henry Moffatt and Emmeline Marchant Fleming; *m* 1960, Katharine, (Linty), Stiven, *d* of late Rev. D. S. Stiven, MC, DD; one *s* two *d* (and one *s* decd). *Educ:* George Watson's Coll., Edinburgh; Edinburgh Univ. (BSc); Cambridge Univ. (BA, PhD, ScD). Lectr in Maths, Cambridge Univ., and Dir of Studies in Maths, Trinity Coll., 1961–76 (Tutor, 1971–75, Sen. Tutor, 1975); Prof. of Applied Maths, Bristol Univ., 1977–80; Dir, Isaac Newton Inst. for Mathematical Scis, Cambridge Univ., 1996–2001. Visiting appts, Stanford Univ. and Johns Hopkins Univ., 1965, Univ. of Paris VI, 1975–76, Institut de Mécanique, Grenoble, 1986, Univ. of California, San Diego, 1987, Santa Barbara, 1991, Ecole Polytechnique Palaiseau, 1992–99, Kyoto Univ., 1993; Blaise Pascal Internat. Chair, Ecole Normale Supérieure, Paris, 2001–03. Pres., IUTAM, 2000–04. Co-editor, Journal of Fluid Mechanics, 1966–83. Foreign Mem., Royal Netherlands Acad. of Arts and Scis, 1991; Associé Etranger, Acad. des Sciences, Paris, 1998; Socio Straniero, Acad. Nazionale dei Lincei, Rome, 2001. MAE 1994. FRSE 1988; Fellow, Amer. Phys. Soc., 2003. Hon. FIMA 2007. D*hc* Inst. Nat Polytechnique de Grenoble, 1987; Hon. DSc: SUNY, 1990; Edinburgh, 2001; Eindhoven Tech. Univ., 2006; Glasgow, 2007. Panetti-Ferrari Prize and Gold Medal, 2001; Euromech Fluid Mechanics Prize, 2003; Sen. Whitehead Prize, LMS, 2005; Hughes Medal, Royal Soc., 2005. Officier des Palmes Académiques, 1998. *Publications:* Magnetic Field Generation in Electrically Conducting Fluids, 1978; (jt ed) Topological Fluid Mechanics, 1990; Topological Aspects of the Dynamics of Fluids and Plasmas, 1992; Tubes, Sheets and Singularities in Fluid Dynamics, 2003; papers in fluid mechanics and dynamo theory in Jl Fluid Mech. and other jls. *Recreation:* bread baking. *Address:* Trinity College, Cambridge CB2 1TQ.

MOFFATT, John, MA, DPhil; Provost, The Queen's College, Oxford, 1987–93, Hon. Fellow, 1993; *b* 12 Oct. 1922; *s* of Jacob and Ethel Moffatt; *m* 1949, Una Lamorna Morris (*d* 1992); one *d. Educ:* Keighley Boys' Grammar Sch.; Magdalen Coll., Oxford (MA, DPhil). Radar research with British Thomson-Houston Co. Ltd, Rugby, 1942–46; Oxford University: Sen. Res. Officer, Clarendon Lab., 1950; Lectr, Dept of Nuclear Physics, 1965; The Queen's College: Fellow and Praelector in Physics, 1950; Sen. Tutor, 1972–76. *Publications:* articles on physics in various scientific jls. *Address:* 2 Cumnor Rise Road, Cumnor Hill, Oxford OX2 9HD.

MOFFATT, Keith; *see* Moffatt, H. K.

MOFFATT, Laura Jean; MP (Lab) Crawley, since 1997; *b* 9 April 1954; *d* of Stanley and Barbara Field; *m* 1975, Colin Moffatt; three *s. Educ:* Hazelwick Comprehensive Sch., Crawley; Crawley Coll. of Technology. SRN, 1975–97. Mem. (Lab), Crawley BC, 1984–97 (Mayor, 1989–90). Contested (Lab) Crawley, 1992. Parliamentary Private Secretary: to Lord Chancellor, 2001–04; to Sec. of State, DWP, 2005–06; to Minister of State, DfES, 2006; to Sec. of State, DfES, 2006–07; to Sec. of State, DoH, 2007–. *Recreations:* pets, walking, holidays with family. *Address:* 6 The Broadway, Crawley, Sussex RH10 1DS. *T:* (01293) 526005.

MOFFETT, David Leslie; Chief Executive, Welsh Rugby Union, 2002–05; *b* 17 May 1947; *s* of Henry Albert Moffett and Barbara Moffett, later Pinkney; *m* 1970, Lauren Jacqueline Dartnell; one *s* one *d. Educ:* Nairobi Primary Sch.; Prince of Wales Sch., Nairobi; Brisbane Boys' Coll. Man. Dir, Pacific Waste Management, Sydney, 1981–86; Exec. Dir, NSW Rugby, 1992–95; Chief Executive Officer: SANZAR, 1995–96; NZ RFU, 1996–99; Nat. Rugby League, Australia, 1999–2001; Sport England, 2002. *Recreations:* walking, reading, cycling, photography.

MOFFETT, Peter; actor (stage name Peter Davison); *b* 13 April 1951; *s* of Claude and late Sheila Moffett; *m* 2003, Elizabeth Heery; two *s*, and one *d* from previous marriage. *Educ:* Winston Churchill Comprehensive Sch., Woking; Central Sch. of Speech and Drama (Acting Dip.). *Television* series: All Creatures Great and Small, 1978; Dr Who, 1981–84; A Very Peculiar Practice, 1986–87; Campion, 1989; Ain't Misbehavin', 1993; At Home with the Braithwaites, 2000; Last Detective, 2003; Too Good to be True, 2003; Distant Shores, 2005; The Complete Guide to Parenting, 2006; Fear, Stress and Anger, 2007 (Best Comedy Actor, Monte Carlo TV Fest., 2007); *stage:* King Arthur in Spamalot, Palace Th., 2007. Top Man of Year Award, Multi-coloured Swap Shop, 1982. *Recreation:* sailing down the Thames.

MOFFITT, Prof. Terrie Edith, PhD; FBA 2004; FMedSci; Knut Schmidt Nielsen Professor of Psychology and Neuroscience, Duke University, since 2008; *b* 9 March 1955; *d* of Terry W. Moffitt and Glenda Macon Moffitt; *m* 1990, Prof. Avshalom Caspi, *qv. Educ:* Univ. of NC, Chapel Hill (BA 1977); USC (PhD 1984). Postdoctoral Fellow, UCLA, 1984; Res. Asst Prof., USC and Vis. Scholar, Univ. of Otago, NZ, 1985–86; Prof., Dept of Psychol., Univ. of Wisconsin, Madison, 1987–2007; Associate Dir, Dunedin Multidisciplinary Health and Develt Study, Dunedin Sch. of Medicine, Univ. of Otago, 1991–; Prof. of Social Behaviour and Develt, Inst. of Psychiatry, KCL, 1997–2007; Prof., Dept of Psychol. and Neurosci., Duke Univ., 2007–08. MAE 2005; FMedSci 1999;

Fellow: Amer. Soc. of Criminology, 2003; Amer. Psychopathol Assoc., 2005. Stockholm Prize in Criminology, 2007. *Publications:* Sex Differences in Antisocial Behaviours, 2001; over 200 articles in jls incl. Science, Lancet, JAMA, Archives of General Psychiatry, etc. *Recreations:* trekking and camping in the world's 'orange' countries on a scale from 'blue' (Scandinavia) to 'red' (Angola and Iraq). *Address:* Department of Psychology and Neuroscience, Duke University, Grey House, 2020 Main Street, Durham, NC 27708, USA; *e-mail:* terrie.moffitt@duke.edu.

MOGER, Christopher Richard Derwent; QC 1992; a Recorder, since 1993 (an Assistant Recorder, 1990–93); a Deputy High Court Judge, since 1999; *b* 28 July 1949; *s* of late Richard Vernon Derwent Moger and Cecile Eva Rosales Moger (*née* Power); *m* 1st, 1974, Victoria Trollope (marr. diss. 1991); three *s*; 2nd, 1991, Prudence Da Cunha. *Educ:* Sherborne School; Bristol Univ. (LLB Hons). FCIArb 1997. Called to the Bar, Inner Temple, 1972, Bencher, 2001. Member: Western Circuit; London Common Law Bar Assoc.; Commercial Bar Assoc.; Official Referee's Bar Assoc.; Barristers' Overseas Advocacy Cttee. *Recreations:* fishing, walking. *Address:* 4 Pump Court, Temple, EC4Y 7AN. *T:* (020) 7842 5555. *Club:* Garrick.

MOGFORD, Jeremy Lewis; Managing Director: Mogford Ltd, since 1998; Mogford Hotels Ltd, since 1998; *b* 9 Oct. 1947; *s* of Peter Charles Mogford and Pamela Margaret Mogford (*née* Bennett); *m* 1971, Hilary Jane Raymond; one *s* one *d*. *Educ:* Canford Sch.; Royal Grammar Sch., High Wycombe; Univ. of Surrey (BSc Hotel and Catering Admin). MIH (MHCIMA 1971). Founder, owner and Man. Dir, 1973–97, Consultant, 1997–, Browns Restaurants Ltd; Director: Peachey Productions, 1998–2000; Ruso Ltd, 2001–. Mem. Exec. Cttee, Restaurant Assoc. of GB, 1998–2003. Dir and Sponsor, Discerning Eye Art Exhibn, 1995–97; Sponsor, Oxford Lit. Fest., 1995. DUniv Oxford Brookes, 2001. Independent Gp Restaurateur of the Year, Caterer and Hotelkeeper mag., 1997. *Recreations:* topiary, fly fishing, 20th century British art. *Address:* c/o Drummonds, 49 Charing Cross, SW1A 2DX. *Clubs:* Garrick, Groucho, Soho House.

MOGG; *see* Rees-Mogg, family name of Baron Rees-Mogg.

MOGG, family name of **Baron Mogg**.

MOGG, Baron *cr* 2008 (Life Peer), of Queen's Park in the County of East Sussex; **John Frederick Mogg,** KCMG 2003; non-executive Chairman, and Member, Gas and Electricity Markets Authority, since 2003; *b* 5 Oct. 1943; *s* of Thomas W. Mogg and Cora M. Mogg; *m* 1967, Anne Smith; one *d* one *s*. *Educ:* Bishop Vesey's Grammar Sch., Sutton Coldfield; Birmingham Univ. (BA Hons). Rediffusion Ltd, 1965–74; Principal: Office of Fair Trading, 1974–76; Dept of Trade (Insurance Div.), 1976–79; First Sec., UK Perm. Representation, Brussels, 1979–82; Department of Trade and Industry: Asst Sec., Minerals and Metals Div., 1982–85; PPS to Sec. of State for Trade and Industry, 1985–86; Under Secretary: European Policy Div., 1986–87; Industrial Materials Market Div., 1987–89; Dep. Hd, European Secretariat, Cabinet Office, 1989–90; Dep. Dir Gen., DGIII, EC, 1990–93; Dir Gen., DGXV, subseq. DG Internal Mkt, EC, 1993–2003. Vis. Prof., Univ. of Parma, Italy, 2006–. Chm., Govs, Univ. of Brighton, 2006–. Trustee, Brighton Philharmonic Orch., 2006–. *Address:* Office of Gas and Electricity Markets, 9 Millbank, SW1P 3GE.

MOGGACH, Deborah; novelist, journalist and script-writer; *b* 28 June 1948; *d* of late Richard Alexander Hough, writer and of Helen Charlotte (*née* Woodyatt); *m* 1971, Anthony Austin Moggach (marr. diss. 1988); one *s* one *d*. *Educ:* Camden Sch. for Girls; Bristol Univ. (BA Hons English); Inst. of Educn, Univ. of London (BEd English). Mem., Exec. Cttee, English PEN, 1992–95; Chm., Soc. of Authors, 1999–2001 (Mem., Broadcasting Cttee, 1995–97, Mgt Cttee, 1998–2000). Television includes: Crown Court, 1983; To Have and to Hold, 1986; Stolen, 1990; Goggle Eyes (adaptation; Writers' Guild Award for Best Adapted Serial), 1993; Seesaw, 1998; Close Relations, 1998; Love in a Cold Climate (adaptation), 2001; Final Demand, 2003; stage play, Double Take, Liverpool Playhouse, 1990, Chichester Fest. Theatre, 1993; film script, Pride and Prejudice (adaptation), 2005. Young Journalist of the Year, Westminster Arts Council, 1975. FRSL 1998. Hon. DLitt Bristol, 2005. *Publications:* You Must Be Sisters, 1978; Close to Home, 1979; A Quiet Drink, 1980; Hot Water Man, 1982; Porky, 1983; To Have and To Hold, 1986; Smile and other stories, 1987; Driving in the Dark, 1988; Stolen, 1990; The Stand-In, 1991; The Ex-Wives, 1993; Changing Babies, 1995; Seesaw, 1996; Close Relations, 1997; Tulip Fever, 1999; Final Demand, 2001; These Foolish Things, 2004; In The Dark, 2007. *Recreation:* walking around London looking into people's windows. *Address:* c/o Curtis Brown, 28–29 Haymarket, SW1Y 4SP. *T:* (020) 7396 6600.

MOGGRIDGE, Harry Traherne, (Hal), OBE 1986; PPLI; FIHort; Consultant, Colvin and Moggridge, Landscape Consultants (established 1922), since 1997 (Partner, 1969–97; Senior Partner, 1981–97); *b* London, 2 Feb. 1936; *s* of late Lt-Col Harry Weston Moggridge, CMG, and Helen Mary Ferrier Taylor; *m* 1963, Hon. Catherine Greville Herbert, *yr d* of 2nd Baron Hemingford; two *s* one *d*. *Educ:* Tonbridge Sch.; Architectural Assoc. (Dip.); evening lectures in landscape design under Prof. P. Youngman. Notts CC, 1960; Asst to Geoffrey Jellicoe, 1961–63; Site architect for Sir Wm Halcrow & Ptrs, Tema Harbour, Ghana, 1964–65; Landscape asst, GLC, 1966–67; own practice; entered into partnership with late Brenda Colvin, CBE, PPILA, 1969, continuing in partnership with Christopher Carter, ALI, and staff of fifteen. Prof. of Landscape Architecture, Univ. of Sheffield, 1984–86. Member: Royal Fine Art Commn, 1988–99; Nat. Trust Architectural Panel, 1991–. Mem. Council, Landscape Inst., 1970–83 (Hon. Sec., Vice Pres., Pres. 1979–81) and 1987–93 (Deleg. to Internat. Fedn of Landscape Architects, 1980–90 and 2002–06; Chm., Internat. Cttee, 1986–92); Chm., Landscape Foundn, 1995–99. Corresponding Mem., ICOMOS-IFLA Internat. Cttee on Historic Gdns and Cultural Landscapes, 2000–; Mem., ICOMOS-UK Cultural Landscapes and Historic Gdns Cttee, 2003–. Chm., Penllergare Trust, 2000–. Landscape works include: Brenig Reservoir, Clwyd; White Horse Hill, a new car park and restoration of grass downland; Gale Common Hill, Yorkshire, woods and fields over 100 million cubic metres of waste ash and shale built over 60 years; quarries; countryside studies; reclamation; public and private gardens; Aldermaston Ct, near Reading, grounds for a new co. headquarters; restoration of historic parks (eg Blenheim, Knole, Castle Hill, Dinefwr, Aberglasney garden), creation of new parks and consultancy for Inner Royal Parks of London; master plans for RHS Wisley Gdns and for Welsh Nat. Botanic Gdns. FRSA. VMH 2000; President's Medal, Landscape Inst., 2002; Europa Nostra Medal, 2003. *Publications:* numerous articles and chapters of books describing works or technical subjects. *Recreations:* looking at pictures, gardens, buildings, towns, landscapes and people in these places; walking, theatre, grandchildren. *Address:* Filkins, Lechlade, Glos GL7 3JQ. *T:* (01367) 860225. *Club:* Farmers.

See also Lady Goodhart.

MOGREN, Dr Håkan Lars; Deputy Chairman, AstraZeneca PLC, since 1999; *b* 17 Sept. 1944; *s* of late Ivan and Märta Mogren; *m* 1975, Anne Marie (*née* Hermansson); two *s*. *Educ:* Royal Inst. of Technol., Stockholm (DSc Biotechnol. 1969). President and Chief Executive Officer: AB Marabou (Sweden), 1977–88; Astra AB (Sweden), 1988–99. Chairman: Reckitt Benckiser plc, 2001–03; Affibody AB, 2002–; Vice Chm., Gambro AB, 1996–; Director: Investor AB, 1990–; Norsk Hydro ASA, 2001–; Groupe Danone SA, 2003–; Mem. Supervisory Bd, Rémy-Cointreau SA, 2003–. Chairman: Res. Inst. of Industrial Econs, Sweden, 1993–2003; Sweden-Japan Foundn, Sweden, 1998–2003 (Dir, 1991–); Sweden-America Foundn, Sweden, 2000–; British-Swedish Chamber of Commerce, Sweden, 2001–03; Dir, Marianne and Marcus Wallenberg Foundn, 1999–. Member: Swedish Gastronomic Acad., 1985–; Royal Swedish Acad. of Engrg Scis, 1988–. Hon. DSc Leicester, 1998. King's Medal with Ribbon, Order of Seraphims (Sweden), 1998; Chevalier, Légion d'Honneur (France), 1995. *Address:* AstraZeneca PLC, 15 Stanhope Gate, W1K 1LN. *T:* (020) 7304 5121.

MOHYEDDIN, Zia; actor; Chairman, National Academy of Performing Arts, Pakistan, since 2004; *b* 20 June 1931. *Educ:* Punjab University (BA Hons). Freelance directing for Aust. broadcasting, 1951–52; RADA, 1953–54; Pakistan stage appearances, 1956–59; UK stage, 1959–71; Dir Gen., Pakistan Nat. Performing Ensemble, to 1977; producer and dir, Central TV, 1980–94; *stage:* appearances include: A Passage to India, 1960; The Alchemist, 1964; The Merchant of Venice, 1966; Volpone, 1967; The Guide, 1968; On The Rocks, 1969; Measure for Measure, 1981; Film, Film, Film, 1986; *films:* Lawrence of Arabia, 1961; Sammy Going South, 1963; The Sailor from Gibraltar; Khartoum, 1965; Ashanti, 1982; Assam Garden, 1985; Immaculate Conception, 1992; The Odyssey; Doomsday Gun, 1993; L'Enfant des Rues, 1994; *television series:* The Hidden Truth, 1964; Gangsters, 1979; Jewel in the Crown, 1983; King of the Ghetto, 1986; Mountbatten, 1988; Shalom Salaam, 1989; creator, Family Pride, Channel Four, 1990. *Recreations:* reading, bridge, watching cricket. *Address:* c/o Plunket Greene/James Sharkey Associates, PO Box 8365, W14 0GL. *T:* (020) 7603 2227, *Fax:* (020) 7603 2221. *Club:* Savile.

MOI, Daniel arap; President of Kenya, 1978–2002; Minister of Defence, 1979–2002; *b* Rift Valley Province, 2 Sept. 1924. *Educ:* African Inland Mission Sch., Kabartonjo; Govt African Sch., Kapsabet. Teacher, 1946–56. MLC, 1957; Mem. for Baringo, House of Representatives, 1963–78; Minister for Educn, 1961; Minister for Local Govt, 1962–64; Minister for Home Affairs, 1964–67; Vice-Pres. of Kenya, 1967–78. Chm., Kenya African Democratic Union (KADU), 1960; Pres., Kenya African Nat. Union (KANU) for Rift Valley Province, 1966; Pres. of KANU, 1978–. Chm., Rift Valley Provincial Council. Former Member: Rift Valley Educn Bd; Kalenjin Language Cttee; Commonwealth Higher Educn Cttee; Kenya Meat Commn; Bd of Governors, African Girls' High Sch., Kikuyu. EGH, EBS. *Address:* c/o State House, PO Box 40530, Nairobi, Kenya.

MOIR, Arthur Hastings; Clerk to the Northern Ireland Assembly, 2001–07; *b* 18 Oct. 1948; *s* of Arthur and Kathleen Moir; *m* 1987, Catherine Quinn; three *d*. *Educ:* Belfast Royal Acad.; Queen's Univ., Belfast (LLB Hons 1971). Admitted solicitor, 1974; Partner: Alex Stewart & Son Solicitors, 1978–84; McConnell and Moir Solicitors, 1984–88; Legal Advr, Land Registry of NI, 1988–93; Registrar of Titles and Land Purchase Trustee, 1993–2001; Chief Exec., Land Registers of NI, 1995–2001. *Publication:* The Land Registration Manual, 1994, 2nd edn 2005. *Recreations:* playing bridge, humouring people. *Address:* Lincoln Building, Great Victoria Street, Belfast BT2 7SL.

MOIR, Sir Christopher Ernest, 4th Bt *cr* 1916, of Whitehanger, Fernhurst, co. Sussex; *b* 22 May 1955; *e s* of Sir Ernest Ian Royds Moir, 3rd Bt and of Margaret Hanham, *d* of George Eric Carter; *S* father, 1998; *m* 1983, Mrs Vanessa Kirtikar, *yr d* of V. A. Crosby; twin *s*, and one step *d*. *Educ:* King's College Sch., Wimbledon. FCA 1976. *Heir: er s* Oliver Royds Moir, *b* 9 Oct. 1984. *Address:* Three Gates, 174 Coombe Lane West, Kingston upon Thames, Surrey KT2 7DE.

MOIR, Dorothy Carnegie, CBE 2003; MD; FRCP, FFPH, FICS; Director of Public Health and Chief Administrative Medical Officer, Lanarkshire Health Board, since 1994; *b* 27 March 1942; *d* of Charles Carnegie Coull and Jessie Coull (*née* Ritchie); *m* 1970, Alexander David Moir; three *s*. *Educ:* Albyn Sch. for Girls, Aberdeen; Aberdeen Univ. (MB ChB 1965; MD 1970); Open Univ. (MBA 2000). FFPH (FFPHM 1988); FRCP 1996; FICS 2001. Resident Med. House Officer, Aberdeen Royal Infirmary, 1965–66; Resident Surg. House Officer, Royal Aberdeen Childrens' Hosp., 1966; Res. Fellow in Therapeutics, 1966–69, Lectr in Community Medicine, 1970–79, Univ. of Aberdeen; Community Medicine Specialist, Grampian Health Bd, 1979–88; Unit MO, Acute Services, Aberdeen Royal Infirmary, 1984–88; Dir of Public Health and Chief Admin. MO, Forth Valley Health Bd, 1988–94. *Publications:* (jtly) The Prescription and Administration of Drugs in Hospital: a programmed learning text, 1970, 3rd edn 1988; many articles in med. and pharmaceut. jls. *Address:* 14 Beckford Street, Hamilton ML3 0TA. *T:* (01698) 281313.

MOIR, James William Charles, CBE 2003; LVO 2002; Controller, BBC Radio 2, 1995–2003; *b* 5 Nov. 1941; *s* of William Charles Moir and Mary Margaret Moir (*née* Daly); *m* 1966, Julia (*née* Smalley); two *s* one *d*. *Educ:* Gunnersbury Catholic Grammar School; Univ. of Nottingham (BA). Joined BBC TV Light Entertainment Group, 1963; Producer, Light Entertainment, 1970, Exec. Producer, 1979; Head of Variety, 1982–87; Head of Gp, 1987–93; Dep. Dir, Corporate Affairs, BBC, 1993–95. Chm., EBU Working Pty on Light Entertainment, 1992–94. Mem., Internat. Media Centre, Univ. of Salford, 2001–. Trustee, Symphony Hall, Birmingham, 1996–. Hon. Mem. Council, NSPCC, 1990–. Hon. Pres., Students' Union, Univ. of Nottingham, 2002–05. FRTS 1990; Fellow, Radio Acad., 1998 (Outstanding Contrib. to Music Radio, 2001). Hon. DLitt Nottingham, 2004. Gold Badge of Merit, British Acad. Composers & Songwriters, 1993; Outstanding Contrib. to Broadcasting, BPG, 2002. KSG 2004. *Address:* The Lawn, Elm Park Road, Pinner, Middx HA5 3LE. *Clubs:* Reform, Garrick.

MOIR, Judith Patricia; Her Honour Judge Moir; a Circuit Judge, since 1999; *b* 2 Dec. 1954; *d* of Norman and Stephanie Edwardson; *m* 1977, Charles Geoffrey Moir; two *s* one *d*. *Educ:* Central Newcastle High Sch.; Somerville Coll., Oxford (BA Jurisp.). Called to the Bar, Gray's Inn, 1978; in practice at the Bar, NE Circuit, 1978–99. *Recreation:* family. *Address:* Newcastle Combined Court Centre, Quayside, Newcastle upon Tyne NE1 3LA.

MOISEIWITSCH, Prof. Benjamin Lawrence, (Benno); Professor of Applied Mathematics, Queen's University of Belfast, 1968–93, now Emeritus; *b* London, 6 Dec. 1927; *s* of Jacob Moiseiwitsch and Chana Kotlerman; *m* 1953, Sheelagh Mary Penrose McKeon; two *s* two *d*. *Educ:* Royal Liberty Sch., Romford; University Coll., London (BSc, 1949, PhD 1952). Sir George Jessel Studentship in Maths, UCL, 1949; Queen's University, Belfast: Lectr and Reader in Applied Maths, 1952–68; Dean, Faculty of Science, 1972–75; Hd, Dept of Applied Maths and Theoretical Physics, 1977–89. MRIA 1969. *Publications:* Variational Principles, 1966, repr. 2004; Integral Equations, 1977, repr. 2005; articles on theoretical atomic physics in scientific jls. *Address:* 21 Knocktern Gardens, Belfast, Northern Ireland BT4 3LZ. *T:* (028) 9065 8332.

MOLE, Christopher David; MP (Lab) Ipswich, since Nov. 2001; an Assistant Government Whip, since 2008; *b* 16 March 1958; *m* 1996, Shona Gibb; two *s*. *Educ:* Dulwich Coll.; Univ. of Kent (BSc 1979). Technologist, Plessey Res., 1979–81; Res.

Manager, BT Labs, Martlesham, 1981–98. Mem. (Lab) Suffolk CC, 1985–2001 (Leader of Council, 1993–2001); Mem., Gen. Assembly, LGA. Dep. Chm., E of England Develt Agency, 1998–2001. PPS to Minister for Local Govt, 2005–06, 2007–08. Mem., Select Cttee, ODPM, 2003–05, on Sci. and Technol., 2007. *Address:* (office) 33 Silent Street, Ipswich IP1 1TF; House of Commons, SW1A 0AA.

MOLE, David Richard Penton; QC 1990; **His Honour Judge Mole;** a Circuit Judge, since 2002; *b* 1 April 1943; *s* of late Rev. Arthur Penton Mole and Margaret Isobel Mole; *m* 1969, Anu-Reet (*née* Nigol); three *s* one *d*. *Educ:* St John's School, Leatherhead; Trinity College, Dublin (MA); LSE (LLM). City of London College, 1967–74 (Sen. Lectr, 1971); called to the Bar, Inner Temple, 1970; Standing Junior Counsel to Inland Revenue in rating valuation matters, 1984; a Recorder, 1995–2002; Jt Hd of Chambers, 2000–02; authorised to act as High Ct Judge in Admin Ct, 2004. Legal Mem., Lands Tribunal, 2006–; Mem., Parole Bd, 2003–09. Part-time cartoonist, 1979–83. *Publications:* contribs to Jl of Planning Law. *Recreations:* walking, drawing, painting. *Address:* Harrow Crown Court, Hailsham Drive, Harrow HA1 4TU. *T:* (020) 8424 2294.

MOLE, Stuart Gordon, OBE 1984; Director-General, Royal Commonwealth Society, 2000–09; *b* 15 Jan. 1949; *s* of late Rev. Arthur Penton Mole and Margaret Isobel Mole; *m* 1st, 1971 (marr. diss. 1977); 2nd, 1982, Katherine Madeleine Anthea Little (marr. diss. 1996); two *s*; partner, Helen Catherine Vines; one *d*. *Educ:* St Paul's Cathedral Choir Sch.; St John's Sch., Leatherhead (music schol.); Univ. of Nottingham (BA 1970); Hertford Coll., Oxford (PGCE 1971); Birkbeck Coll., Univ. of London (MSc 1974). Lectr, Chelmsford Coll., 1971–75; Parly Press Officer, Liberal Party, 1975–77; Dir, OUTSET youth and disability charity, 1977–80; Hd, Office of Leader of Liberal Party, 1980–83; political lobbyist and speechwriter, 1983–84; Commonwealth Secretariat: Special Asst to Sec.-Gen., 1984–90; Dir, Sec.-Gen's Office, 1990–2000. Mem. (Lib Dem), Chelmsford BC, 1972–87 (Chm., P & R Cttee, 1983–87). Contested: (L) Chemsford, Feb. and Oct. 1974, 1979, 1983, 1987; (Lib Dem) N Essex and S Suffolk, European Parlt, 1994. Hd, Leader's Gen. Election Campaign Tour, 1993. Dir and Mem. Editl Bd, The Round Table, 1994–. *Recreations:* choral music, singing. *Address:* c/o Royal Commonwealth Society, 25 Northumberland Avenue, WC2N 5AP. *T:* (020) 7766 9200. *Clubs:* Royal Commonwealth Society, Royal Over-Seas League; Bristol Commonwealth Society.

See also D. R. P. Mole.

MOLESWORTH, family name of **Viscount Molesworth**.

MOLESWORTH, 12th Viscount *cr* 1716 (Ire.); **Robert Bysse Kelham Molesworth;** Baron Philipstown 1716; businessman; *b* 4 June 1959; *s* of 11th Viscount Molesworth and Anne Florence (*née* Cohen; *d* 1983); *S* father, 1997. *Educ:* Cheltenham; Sussex Univ. (BA Philosophy). *Recreations:* ballroom dancing, travel, carpentry. *Heir: b* Hon. William John Charles Molesworth, *b* 20 Oct. 1960.

MOLESWORTH, Allen Henry Neville; management consultant; *b* 20 Aug. 1931; *s* of late Roger Bevil Molesworth (Colonel RA), and of Iris Alice Molesworth (*née* Kennion); *m* 1970, Gail Cheng Kwai Chan. *Educ:* Wellington Coll., Berks; Trinity Coll., Cambridge (MA). FCA, FIMC. 2nd Lt, 4th Queen's Own Hussars, Malaya, 1950. Project Accounts, John Laing & Sons (Canada) Ltd, 1954–58; Singleton Fabian & Co., Chartered Accountants, 1959–63; Consultant: Standard Telephones & Cables Ltd, 1963–67; Coopers & Lybrand Associates Ltd, 1967–76: India, 1970; Kuwait, 1971; France, 1972; New Hebrides, 1972; Laos, 1974; Tonga, 1975; Financial and Admin. Controller, Crown Agents, 1976–84; Chief Accountant, British Telecom Property, 1984–90. *Recreations:* shooting, ski-ing, music, restoring antiques. *Address:* c/o Lloyds TSB, 8–10 Waterloo Place, SW1Y 4BE. *Clubs:* 1900, Coningsby.

MOLESWORTH-ST AUBYN, Sir William, 16th Bt *cr* 1689, of Pencarrow, Cornwall; *b* 23 Nov. 1958; *s* of Sir Arscott Molesworth-St Aubyn, 15th Bt, MBE and of Iona Audrey Armatrude, *d* of Adm. Sir Francis Loftus Tottenham, KCB, CBE; *S* father, 1998; *m* 1988, Carolyn, *er d* of William Tozier; two *s* one *d*. *Educ:* Harrow. Late Captain, The Royal Green Jackets. *Heir: s* Archie Hender Molesworth-St Aubyn, *b* 27 March 1997.

MOLINA, Prof. Mario Jose, PhD; Professor, Department of Chemistry and Biochemistry, University of California, San Diego, since 2004; President, Mario Molina Center, Mexico City, since 2004; *b* 19 March 1943; *s* of Roberto Molina-Pasquel and Leonor Henriquez de Molina; *m* 1st, 1973, Luisa Yu Tan (marr. diss.); one *s*; 2nd, 2006, Guadalupe Alvarez. *Educ:* Univ. Nacional Autónoma de México (Ingeniero Quimico 1965); Univ. of Calif, Berkeley (PhD 1972). Asst Prof., Univ. Nacional Autónoma de México, 1967–68; Res. Associate, Univ. of Calif, Berkeley, 1972–73; Res. Associate, 1973–74, Asst Prof., 1975–79, Associate Prof., 1979–82, Univ. of Calif, Irvine; Sen. Res. Scientist, Jet Propulsion Lab., Calif, 1983–89; Prof., Dept of Earth, Atmospheric and Planetary Scis and Dept of Chemistry, MIT, 1989–2004. Mem., US Nat. Acad. of Scis, 1993. Tyler Ecology and Energy Prize, USA, 1983; (jtly) Nobel Prize for Chemistry, 1995. *Publications:* articles in jls and chapters in books. *Recreations:* music, tennis. *Address:* Department of Chemistry and Biochemistry, University of California, San Diego, 9500 Gilman Drive MC 0356, La Jolla, CA 92093, USA.

MOLITOR, Edouard, Hon. KCMG 1976; Grand Officier, Ordre du Mérite (Luxembourg), 1990; Grand Officier, Ordre de la Couronne de Chêne, 1996; Officier, Ordre Civil et Militaire d'Adolphe de Nassau, 1977; Ambassador of Luxembourg: to Italy, 1993–96; to Malta, 1995–96; Permanent Representative to UN Food and Agriculture Organisation, 1993–96; *b* Luxembourg City, 14 Feb. 1931; *s* of Joseph Molitor and Lucie Michels; *m* 1960, Constance Scholtes; three *s*. *Educ:* Univs of Grenoble, Nancy and Paris. Dr en droit. Barrister, Luxembourg, 1955–60; joined Diplomatic Service, 1960 (Political Affairs); First Sec. and Rep. to UNESCO, Paris, 1964–69; Counsellor and Consul-Gen., Brussels, 1969–73; Dir of Protocol and Juridical Affairs, Min. of Foreign Affairs, 1973–78; Mem., Commn de Contrôle, EC, 1973–77; Ambassador to the Holy See, 1976–79; Ambassador to Austria, 1978–89; Perm. Rep. to UNIDO, IAEA, 1978–89; Head of Luxembourg Delegn, MBFR Conf., 1978–89 and at CSCE Conf., Vienna, 1986–89; Ambassador to UK, Ireland and Iceland, and Perm. Rep. to Council of WEU, 1989–92. Mem., Rotary Club, Luxembourg. Foreign Decorations from: Norway, 1964; Italy, W Germany, Belgium, 1973; Greece, 1975; Denmark, Tunisia, Senegal, Netherlands, France, 1978; Vatican, Austria, 1989; Iceland, 1990; Italy 1996. *Recreations:* swimming, hiking, ski-ing, shooting, music, literature. *Address:* 47 allée Léopold Goebel, 1635 Luxembourg.

MOLKOV, Prof. Vladimir Valentine, PhD, DSc; Professor of Fire Safety Science, University of Ulster, since 1999; *b* 21 Nov. 1953; *s* of Valentine Ivan Molkov and Praskovya Ivanovna Molkova; *m* 1974, Galina Victorovna Molkova; one *d*. *Educ:* Moscow Univ. of Physics and Technol. (MSc Gen. and Applied Physics 1977; PhD Chem. Physics 1984); DSc Fire Safety, All-Russian Res. Inst for Fire Protection, 1997. Researcher, then Sen. Researcher, 1978–92, Hd of Dept, 1992–99, VNIIPO (All-Russian Res. Inst. for Fire Protection). Vis. Prof., Toho Univ., Japan, 1997; JSPS Fellow, Univ. of Tokyo, Japan, 1997. Co-Founder, Internat. Seminar on Fire and Explosion Hazards, 1995. Dep. Editor-in-Chief, Fire and Explosion Safety Jl, 1992; Mem. Editl Bd, Fire Safety Jl, 1999. *Publications:* over 100 articles. *Recreations:* friends, swimming, music. *Address:* 22 Rosemount Park, Newtownabbey, Co. Antrim, Northern Ireland BT37 0NL. *T:* (028) 9036 8731, *Fax:* (028) 9036 8726; *e-mail:* v.molkov@ulster.ac.uk.

MØLLER, Dr Per Stig; MP (C) Gentofte, 1983–87, Frederiksberg, since 1987, Denmark; Minister for Foreign Affairs, Denmark, since 2001; *b* 27 Aug. 1942; *s* of Poul and Lis Møller. *Educ:* Univ. of Copenhagen (MA Comparative Lit. 1967, PhD 1973). Cultural Ed., Radio Denmark, 1973–74; Lectr, Sorbonne, Paris, 1974–76; Dep. Hd, Culture and Society Dept, 1974 and 1976–79, Chief of Progs for Dir of Progs, 1979–84, Radio Denmark; Vice-Chm., 1985–86, Chm., 1986–87, Radio Council. Commentator, Berlingske Tidende, 1984–2001. Minister for the Envmt, 1990–93; Mem., Foreign Policy Cttee, 1994–2001; Chm., Security Policy Cttee, 1994–96; foreign policy spokesman, 1998–2001. Mem., Council of Europe, 1987–90, 1994–97 and 1998–2001. Danish Conservative Party: Mem., Exec. Cttee, 1985–89 and 1993–98; Chm., 1997–98; Political Leader, Parly Party, 1997–98. Chm., Popular Educn Assoc., 1983–89. Georg Brandes Award, Soc. of Danish Lit. Critics, 1996; Einar Hansen Res. Fund Award, 1997; Cultural Award, Popular Educn Assoc., 1998; Raoul Wallenberg Medal, 1998; Kaj Munk Award, 2001; Rosenkjær Award, 2001; Robert Schuman Medal, 2003. Comdr, 1st Cl., Order of Dannebrog (Denmark), 2002; Chevalier, Ordre National du Lion (Senegal), 1975; Grosskreuz des Verdienstordens (Germany), 2002; Comdr, Ordre National (Benin), 2003; Grand Cross, Order of Crown of Oak (Luxembourg), 2003; Gold Nersornaat (Greenland), 2005; Order of Stara Planina, 1st Cl. (Bulgaria), 2006; Comdr Grand Cross, Order of Polar Star (Sweden), 2007; Grand Cross, Order of South Cross (Brazil), 2007; Grand Cross of Comdr, Order for Merits to Lithuania, 2007. *Publications:* La Critique dramatique et littéraire de Malte-Brun, 1971; Malte-Bruns litterære Kritik og dens Plads i Transformationsprocessen, 1973; Erotismen, 1973; København-Paris t/r, 1973; På Sporet af det forsvundne Menneske, 1976; Livet i Gøgereden, 1978; Fra Tid til Anden, 1979; Tro, Håb og Fællesskab, 1980; Midt i Redeligheden, 1981; Orwells Håb og Frygt, 1983; Nat uden Daggry, 1985; (jtly) Mulighedernes Samfund, 1985; Stemmer fra Øst, 1987; Historien om Estland, Letland og Litauen, 1990; Kurs mod Katastrofer?, 1993; Miljøproblemer, 1995; Den naturlige Orden - Tolv år der flyttede Verden, 1996; Spor. Udvalgte Skrifter om det åbne Samfund og dets Værdier, 1997; Magt og Afmagt, 1999; Munk, 2000; Mere Munk, 2003. *Address:* Royal Danish Ministry of Foreign Affairs, 2 Asiatisk Plads, 1448 Copenhagen, Denmark. *T:* 33920000, *Fax:* 32540933; *e-mail:* um@um.dk.

MOLLISON, Prof. Patrick Loudon, CBE 1979; MD; FRCP, FRCPath, FRCOG; FRS 1968; Professor of Hæmatology, St Mary's Hospital Medical School, London University, 1962–79, now Emeritus Professor; *b* 17 March 1914; *s* of William Mayhew Mollison, Cons. Surgeon (ENT), Guy's Hospital; *m* 1st, 1940, Dr Margaret D. Peirce (marr. diss., 1964); three *s*; 2nd, 1973, Dr Jennifer Jones. *Educ:* Rugby Sch.; Clare Coll., Cambridge; St Thomas' Hosp., London. MD Cantab 1944; FRCP 1959; FRCPath 1963; FRCOG *ad eund*, 1980. House Phys., Medical Unit, St Thomas' Hosp., 1939; Medical Officer, S London Blood Supply Depot, 1939–43; RAMC, 1943–46; Dir, MRC Blood Transfusion Res. Unit, Hammersmith Hosp., 1946–60; part-time Dir, MRC Experimental Hæmatology Unit, 1960–79; Hon. Lectr, then Sen. Lectr, Dept of Medicine, Post-grad. Medical Sch., 1948; Consultant Hæmatologist: Hammersmith Hosp., 1947–60; St Mary's Hosp., 1960–79. Hon. FRSocMed 1979; Landsteiner Meml Award, USA, 1960; P. Levine Award, USA, 1973; Oehlecker Medal, Germany, 1974. *Publications:* Blood Transfusion in Clinical Medicine, 1951, 10th edn (jtly) 1997; papers on red cell survival and blood group antibodies. *Recreations:* music, gardening. *Address:* 60 King Henry's Road, NW3 3RR. *T:* (020) 7722 1947.

MOLLO, Joseph Molelekoa Kaibe; Corporate Affairs Manager, Gencor, Johannesburg; *b* 7 May 1944; *s* of Kaibe and Cyrian Mollo; *m* 1972, Makaibe; two *s* two *d*. *Educ:* Univ. of Botswana, Lesotho and Swaziland (BA Admin); Univ. of Saskatchewan (MCEd); Carleton Univ. (working on a Master's degree in Political Science since 1978). Asst Sec., Min. of Finance, 1971; Comr of Co-operatives, 1973; Dep. Perm. Sec., Finance, 1975; High Comr, Canada, 1976; Perm. Sec., Finance, 1980; High Comr in London, 1982–83; Ambassador to Denmark (also accredited to Sweden, Norway, Finland, Iceland, GDR and Poland), 1983–86; Man. Dir, Trading Corp. of Lesotho, 1986–88; Ambassador of Lesotho to Republic of South Africa, 1992–94. Unpublished thesis: Profit versus Co-operation: the struggle of the Western Co-operative College. *Recreations:* jogging, dancing, music, soccer.

MOLLON, Prof. John Dixon, DSc; FRS 1999; Professor of Visual Neuroscience, University of Cambridge, since 1998; Fellow of Gonville and Caius College, Cambridge, since 1996; *b* 12 Sept. 1944; *s* of Arthur Greenwood Mollon and Joyce Dorothy Mollon. *Educ:* Scarborough High Sch.; Hertford Coll., Oxford (BA 1966; DPhil 1970). Sen. Schol., Wadham Coll., Oxford, 1967–69; Post-doctoral Fellow, Bell Telephone Labs, NJ, 1970; Lectr in Psychology, Corpus Christi Coll., Oxford, 1971–72; University of Cambridge: Univ. Demonstrator, 1972–76; Lectr, 1976–93, Reader, 1993–98, in Exptl Psychology. Hon. Sec., Experimental Psychology Soc., 1974–78. Fellow, Optical Soc. of America, 1984. *Publications:* (with H. B. Barlow) The Senses, 1982; (with L. T. Sharpe) Colour Vision: physiology and psychophysics, 1983; (with J. Pokorny and K. Knoblauch) Normal and Defective Colour Vision, 2003. *Recreations:* book collecting, historical research. *Address:* Gonville and Caius College, Cambridge CB2 1TA.

MOLLOY, Michael John; writer; *b* 22 Dec. 1940; *s* of John George and Margaret Ellen Molloy; *m* 1964, Sandra June Foley; three *d*. *Educ:* Ealing School of Art. Sunday Pictorial, 1956; Daily Sketch, 1960; Daily Mirror, 1962–85: Editor, Mirror Magazine, 1969; Asst Editor, 1970; Dep. Editor, 1975; Editor, Dec. 1975–1985; Editor, Sunday Mirror, 1986–88; Mirror Group Newspapers: Director, 1976–90; Editor in Chief, 1985–90. Exhibitions of paintings: Galerie Aalders, S France, 2001; Walton Gall., London, 2003. *Publications:* The Black Dwarf, 1985; The Kid from Riga, 1987; The Harlot of Jericho, 1989; The Century, 1990; The Gallery, 1991; Sweet Sixteen, 1992; Cat's Paw, 1993; Home Before Dark, 1994; Dogsbody, 1995; The Witch Trade, 2001; The Time Witches, 2002; Wild West Witches, 2003; The House on Falling Star Hill, 2004; Peter Raven Under Fire, 2005. *Recreations:* reading, writing, painting. *Address:* 62 Culmington Road, W13 9NH. *Club:* Savile.

MOLONEY, Patrick Martin Joseph; QC 1998; **His Honour Judge Moloney;** a Circuit Judge, since 2007; *b* 2 July 1953; *s* of late Dr Eamon Moloney and Jean Moloney (*née* Handley); *m* 2003, Sarah Harrison; one step *s* two step *d*. *Educ:* Prior Park Coll., Bath; St Catherine's Coll., Oxford (Open Schol.; BA Hons Jurisp. 1973; BCL 1974). Vis. Asst Prof., Univ. of British Columbia, 1974–75; called to the Bar, Middle Temple, 1976 (Harmsworth Schol.; Bencher, 2006); in practice at the Bar, specialising in libel law, 1978–2007; a Recorder, 2000–07. Mem. Bar, NI, 1999. FRGS 2003. *Publication:* (contrib.) Halsbury's Laws of England, 1997. *Recreation:* independent travel. *Address:* Peterborough Combined Court Centre, Crown Buildings, Rivergate, Peterborough, Cambs PE1 1EJ.

MOLONY, (Thomas) Desmond; (3rd Bt *cr* 1925 of the City of Dublin); *S* father, 1976, but does not use the title, and his name is not on the Official Roll of the Baronetage.

MOLYNEAUX OF KILLEAD, Baron *cr* 1997 (Life Peer), of Killead in the co. of Antrim; **James Henry Molyneaux,** KBE 1996; PC 1983; Leader, Ulster Unionist Party, 1979–95; *b* 27 Aug. 1920; *s* of late William Molyneaux, Seacash, Killead, Co. Antrim; unmarried. *Educ:* Aldergrove Sch., Co. Antrim. RAF, 1941–46. Vice-Chm., Eastern Special Care Hosp. Man. Cttee, 1966–73; Chm. Antrim Br., NI Assoc. for Mental Health, 1967–70; Hon. Sec., S Antrim Unionist Assoc., 1964–70; Vice-Pres., Ulster Unionist Council, 1974–79. MP (UU): Antrim S, 1970–83; Lagan Valley, 1983–97. Leader, UU Party, House of Commons, 1974–95. Mem. (UU) S Antrim, NI Assembly, 1982–86. Dep. Grand Master of Orange Order and Hon. PGM of Canada. JP Antrim, 1957–87; CC Antrim, 1964–73. *Recreations:* gardening, music. *Address:* Aldergrove, Crumlin, Co. Antrim, N Ireland BT29 4AR.

MOLYNEUX, Anne; Her Honour Judge Molyneux; a Circuit Judge, since 2007; *b* Southport, 12 Jan. 1959; *d* of Robert Molyneux and Audrey Molyneux (*née* Young); *m* 2006, George Jonathan Morris; one *s* one *d* by a previous marriage. *Educ:* Univ. of Sheffield (LLB Hons 1979); Chester Coll. of Law. Admitted solicitor, 1983; Recorder, 2000–07. Mem., Parole Bd, 2003–07. Mem., Law Soc. *Recreations:* walking, reading (Mem., Ealing and Fulham Book Club), family. *Address:* The Crown Court, Woodall House, Lordship Lane, Wood Green, N22 5LF; *e-mail:* HHJudge.Molyneux@hmcourts-service.gsi.gov.uk.

MOLYNEUX, Prof. David Hurst, DSc; Professor of Tropical Health Sciences, University of Liverpool, since 1991 (Director, Liverpool School of Tropical Medicine, 1991–2000); *b* 9 April 1943; *s* of Reginald Frank Molyneux and Monica Foden Molyneux; *m* 1969, Anita Elisabeth Bateson; one *s* one *d*. *Educ:* Denstone Coll.; Emmanuel Coll., Cambridge (BA 1965; PhD 1969; MA 1969; DSc 1992). FIBiol 1984. Lectr, Dept of Parasitology, Liverpool Sch. of Tropical Medicine, 1968–77; seconded as Research Officer to Nigerian Inst. for Trypanosomiasis, Kaduna, 1970–72, as Project Manager to UNDP/WHO, Bobo Dioulasso, Burkino Faso, 1975–77; Prof. of Biology, Univ. of Salford, 1977–91. Dir, DFID/Glaxo SmithKline Lymphatic Filariasis Support Centre, 2000–. Member: WHO Cttees incl. Onchocerciasis, Guinea worm, Parasitic Diseases; Internat. Commn on Disease Eradication, 2001–. Mem., Bd of Trustees, 1999–2008, Chm. Bd, 2005–08, Pres., 2005–07, JRS Biodiversity Foundn (formerly Biosis, subseq. JRS Foundn), Philadelphia. Trustee, Nat. Museums and Galls on Merseyside, 1995–2000. President: British Soc. of Parasitology, 1992; RSTM&H, 2007–09. Mem., Governing Body, Inst. of Animal Health, 2001–. Hon. FRCP 2006. Chalmers Medal, RSTM&H, 1987; Wright Medal, British Soc. of Parasitology, 1989; McKay Medal, Amer. Soc. of Tropical Medicine, 2007. *Publications:* The Biology of Trypanosoma and Leishmania: parasites of man and domestic animals (with R. W. Ashford), 1983; (ed) Control of Human Parasitic Diseases, 2006; numerous contribs to professional jls. *Recreations:* golf, music, travel, primitive art. *Address:* Liverpool School of Tropical Medicine, Pembroke Place, Liverpool L3 5QA. *T:* (0151) 708 9393; Kingsley Cottage, Town Well, Kingsley, Cheshire WA6 8EZ. *T:* (01928) 788397. *Club:* Delamere Forest Golf (Captain, 2007–08).

MOLYNEUX, Helena; Consultant, Telos Partners Ltd, since 2004; *b* 17 Aug. 1948; *d* of Joseph and Mary Molyneux. *Educ:* Manchester Univ. (BSc); Cranfield Inst. of Technol. (MBA). FIPD. United Biscuits, 1969–73; Univ. of Sierra Leone, 1973–76; Bank of America: Personnel Manager, Bank of Amer. Internat., 1979–80; Divl Personnel Manager, NT & SA, San Francisco, 1980–82; Head, Employee Relns and Personnel Planning, Eur., ME and Africa Div., 1982–87; Bankers Trust Co.: Head, Employee Relns and Staffing, Eur., 1987–89; Dir, Corporate Personnel, Eur., 1989–93; Dir of Personnel, British Council, 1993–2000; Consultant, HelenaMolyneux Consulting, 2000–04. Vice-Chm., 1997–2001, Chm., 2001–, Progressio (formerly Catholic Inst. for Internat. Relations). FRSA. *Recreations:* Dorset, ski-ing, travel.

MOLYNEUX, James Robert M.; *see* More-Molyneux.

MOLYNEUX, Peter Douglas, OBE 2005; designer, producer and programmer of computer games; Co-founder, and Managing Director, Lionhead Studios, since 1997; *b* 5 May 1959; *s* of George and Myrna Molyneux; *m* 2007, Emma Margaret Douglas; one *s*. *Educ:* Bearwood Coll., Wokingham; Farnborough Tech. Coll.; Southampton Univ. (BSc Computer Scis). Co-founder, Bullfrog Prodns, Guildford, 1987; designer and programmer: Populous, 1989; Powermonger, 1990; Populous 2, 1991; designer and producer: Syndicate, 1993; (and programmer) Theme Park, 1994; Magic Carpet, 1994; (and programmer) Dungeon Keeper, 1997; designer and programmer, Black & White, 2001. Hon. DTech: Abertay Dundee, 2003; Bournemouth, 2005; Southampton, 2007; DUniv Surrey, 2007. Chevalier, Order of Arts and Letters (France), 2007. *Recreation:* playing poker and board games. *Address:* Lionhead Studios, 1 Occam Court, Occam Road, Surrey Research Park, Guildford GU2 7YQ. *T:* (01483) 401000, *Fax:* (01483) 401001; *e-mail:* pmolyneux@lionhead.com.

MONAGHAN, Charles Edward, CA; Chairman, Aegon UK, 1999–2005; President, Institute of Chartered Accountants of Scotland, 1999–2000; *b* 20 June 1940; *s* of Charles Monaghan and Elspeth Margaret Monaghan; *m* 1971, Dorothy Evelyn Hince; one *s*. *Educ:* Loretto Sch.; Edinburgh Univ. (BSc). CA 1965. Unilever, 1965–98: Ops Mem., E Asia Pacific, 1991–95; Head, Exec. Cttee Secretariat, 1996–98; Dir, Scottish Equitable, 1995. *Recreations:* squash, ski-ing, golf. *Address:* 10 Wool Road, Wimbledon, SW20 0HW. *T:* (020) 8946 8825. *Clubs:* Caledonian, Wimbledon; Royal Wimbledon Golf.

MONAGHAN, Karon; QC 2008; *b* London, 21 June 1963. *Educ:* Ealing Coll. of Higher Educn (LLB). Called to the Bar, Inner Temple, 1989; in practice as barrister specialising in equity law. *Publication:* Equity Law, 2007. *Address:* Matrix Chambers, Griffin Building, Gray's Inn, WC1R 5LN.

MONBIOT, George Joshua; freelance author and journalist, since 1987; columnist, The Guardian, since 1995; *b* 27 Jan. 1963; *s* of Raymond Geoffrey Monbiot, *qv*. *Educ:* Brasenose Coll., Oxford (BA, MA Zool.). BBC radio producer, 1985–87. Vis. Fellow, Green Coll., Oxford, 1993–95; Visiting Professor: Univ. of E London, 1997–99; Univ. of Bristol, 1999; Hon. Professor: Univ. of Keele, 1999–2000; Oxford Brookes Univ., 2003–. Hon. Fellow, Univ. of Cardiff, 2007. DU Essex, 2007. Sony Award for Radio Production, 1987; Lloyds Nat. Screenwriters Award, 1987; Sir Peter Kent Award, 1991; UN Global 500 Award, 1995; OneWorld Trust Media Award, 1996. *Publications:* Poisoned Arrows, 1989, 2nd edn 2003; Amazon Watershed, 1991; No Man's Land, 1994, 2nd edn 2003; Captive State, 2000, 2nd edn 2001; The Age of Consent, 2003, 2nd edn 2004; Heat, 2006; Bring on the Apocalypse: six arguments for global justice, 2008. *Recreations:* natural history, kayaking, ultimate frisbee, apple growing, gardening, cooking, conversation. *Address:* Y Goeden Eirin, Newtown Road, Machynlleth SY20 8EY. *T:* (01654) 702758; *e-mail:* g.monbiot@zetnet.co.uk.

MONBIOT, Raymond Geoffrey, CBE 1994 (MBE 1981); Deputy Chairman, Conservative Party, 2003–06; Chairman, Rotherfield Management Ltd, since 1988; *b* 1 Sept. 1937; *s* of Maurice and Ruth Monbiot; *m* 1961, Rosalie Vivien Gresham (*née* Cooke), OBE; one *s* one *d* (and one *d* decd). *Educ:* Westminster Sch.; London Business Sch. From pastry chef to Man. Dir of three subsids, J. Lyons & Co. Ltd, 1956–78; Man. Dir, Associated Biscuits, 1978–82; Chm., Campbell's Soups UK, 1982–88. Chairman: Nat. Cons. Convention, 2003–06; Finance Cttee, Cons. Party, 2004–06. Chm., Northants and Berks, Duke of Edinburgh Award Industrial Projects, 1976–86. Fellow, Mktg Soc. Freeman, City of London; Liveryman, Butchers' Co. David Ogilvy Award for Mktg, Campbell's Soups UK, 1985. *Publications:* How to Manage Your Boss, 1981; The Burnhams Book of Characters, 2002; The Characters of North Norfolk, 2003. *Recreations:* gardening, cooking, writing. *Address:* Eastgate House, Burnham Market, Norfolk PE31 8HH. *T:* (01328) 730928, *Fax:* (01328) 730368; *e-mail:* rmonbiot@rotherfieldmgmnt.demon.co.uk. *Clubs:* Farmers; Leander.
See also G. J. Monbiot.

MONCADA, Dr Salvador Enrique, FRCP, FMedSci; FRS 1988; Director, Wolfson Institute for Biomedical Research (formerly Institute for Strategic Medical Research (Cruciform Project)), University College London, since 1996; *b* 3 Dec. 1944; *s* of Dr Salvador Eduardo Moncada and Jenny Seidner; *m* 1st, 1966; one *d*; 2nd, 1998, HRH Princess Esmeralda of Belgium; one *s* one *d*. *Educ:* Univ. of El Salvador (DMS 1970); London Univ. (DPhil 1973; DSc 1983). FRCP 1994. GP, Social Service of El Salvador, 1969; Associate Prof. of Pharmacol. and Physiol., Univ. of Honduras, 1974–75; Wellcome Research Laboratories, 1971–73 and 1975–95: Sen. Scientist, 1975–77; Hd of Dept of Prostaglandin Res., 1977–85; Dir, Therapeutic Res. Div., 1984–86; Dir of Res., Wellcome Foundn, 1986–95. Croonian Lect., Royal Soc., 2005. Mem., British Pharmacol Soc., 1974. Founder FMedSci 1998. Associate Fellow, Third World Acad. of Sciences, 1988; For. Associate, Nat. Acad. of Scis, USA, 1994. Dr *hc:* Univ. of Complutense de Madrid, 1986; Univ. of Honduras, 1987; Univ. of Cantabria, 1988; Hon. DSc: Sussex, 1994; Mt Sinai Sch. of Medicine, NY, 1995; Nottingham, 1995; Univ. Pierre & Marie Curie, Paris, 1997. Peter Debeye Prize (jtly), Limburg Univ., 1980; Prince of Asturias Prize for Science and Technology, 1990; Royal Medal, Royal Soc., 1994; Amsterdam Prize for Medicine, 1997. *Publications:* (Scientific Ed.) British Medical Bulletin, 39 pt 3: Prostacyclin, Thromboxane and Leukotrienes, 1983; Nitric oxide from L-arginine: a bioregulatory system, 1990; (ed jtly) The Biology of Nitric Oxide, pts 3 and 4, 1994, pt 5, 1996, pt 6, 1998, pt 7, 2000; (ed jtly) Nitric Oxide and the Vascular Endothelium, 2006. *Recreations:* music, literature, theatre. *Address:* Wolfson Institute for Biomedical Research, University College London, Gower Street, WC1E 6BT.

MONCASTER, John Anthony; Master of the Supreme Court, Chancery Division, since 1992; *b* Louth, Lincs, 15 Oct. 1939; *o c* of Jack Moncaster and Muriel (*née* Butterick); *m* 1966, Gillian Ann, *o d* of Rev. Royston York; two *s* two *d*. Called to the Bar, Gray's Inn, 1961; practised at Chancery Bar. *Recreation:* books. *Address:* Dukes, Layer Marney, Essex CO5 9UZ. *T:* (01206) 330184.

MONCEL, Lt-Gen. Robert William, OC 1968; DSO 1944; OBE 1944; CD 1944; retired 1966; *b* 9 April 1917; *s* of René Moncel and Edith Brady; *m* 1939, Nancy Allison, *d* of Ralph P. Bell; one *d*. *Educ:* Selwyn House Sch.; Bishop's Coll. Sch. Royal Canadian Regt, 1939; Staff Coll., 1940; Bde Major 1st Armd Bde, 1941; comd 18th Manitoba Dragoons, 1942; GSO1, HQ 2 Cdn Corps, 1943; comd 4th Armd Bde, 1944; Dir Canadian Armd Corps, 1946; Nat. War Coll., 1949; Canadian Jt Staff, London, 1949–54; Comdr 3 Inf. Bde, 1957; QMG, 1960; GOC Eastern Comd, 1963; Comptroller Gen., 1964; Vice-Chief of the Defence Staff, Canada, 1965–66. Col, 8th Canadian Hussars. Chm., Fishermen's Memorial Hosp., 1980–84; Dir, Nova Scotia Rehabilitation Center, 1986. Mem. Bd of Regents, Mount Allison Univ., 1983. Croix de Guerre, France, 1944; Légion d'Honneur, France, 1944. Hon. LLD Mount Allison Univ., 1968. *Recreations:* fishing, sailing, golf. *Club:* Royal Nova Scotia Yacht.

MONCK, family name of **Viscount Monck**.

MONCK, 7th Viscount *cr* 1801; **Charles Stanley Monck;** *S* father, 1982 but does not use the title. **Heir:** *b* Hon. George Stanley Monck.

MONCK, Elizabeth Mary, (Lady Monck), PhD; Senior Research Officer, Thomas Coram Research Unit, Institute of Education, since 1997; *b* 7 Aug. 1934; *d* of Geoffrey Dugdale Kirwan and Molly Kirwan (*née* Morrow); *m* 1960, Sir Nicholas Jeremy Monck, *qv*; three *s*. *Educ:* Godolphin Sch., Salisbury; Newnham Coll., Cambridge (MA); UCL (PhD 1996). MRC Social Psychiatry Res. Unit, Inst. Psychiatry, 1957–62; EIU, 1969–73; Research Officer: Centre for Envmtl Studies, 1974–80; Acad. Dept Child Psychiatry, Inst. Child Health, 1980–95; Associate, Newnham Coll., Cambridge, 1997–. Mem., ILEA, 1986–90. Trustee, National Gall., 1993–99. Mem., 1990–93, Chm., 1993–97, Regl Customer Service Cttee (Thames), OFWAT; Ind. Mem., Cttee on Chemicals and Materials in Public Water Supply, Drinking Water Inspectorate, 1998–2001; Reporting Mem., Competition Commn, 1999–2004. Trustee, Family Rights Group. *Publications:* books include: (with R. Dobbs) The Great Ormond Street Adolescent Life Events Dictionary of Contextual Threat Ratings, 1985; (ed and contrib.) Emotional and Behavioural Problems in Adolescents: a multi-disciplinary approach to identification and management, 1988; (with A. Kelly) Managing Effective Schools, 1992; evaluation studies in child abuse and adoption. *Recreations:* walking, gardening, listening to music. *Address:* 31 Lady Margaret Road, NW5 2NG.

MONCK, Sir Nicholas (Jeremy), KCB 1994 (CB 1988); Permanent Secretary, Employment Department Group, 1993–95; *b* 9 March 1935; *s* of Bosworth Monck and Stella Mary (*née* Cock); *m* 1960, Elizabeth Mary Kirwan (*see* E. M. Monck); three *s*. *Educ:* Eton; King's Coll., Cambridge; Univ. of Pennsylvania; LSE. Asst Principal, Min. of Power, 1959–62; NEDO, 1962–65; NBPI, 1965–66; Senior Economist, Min. of Agriculture, Tanzania, 1966–69; HM Treasury, 1969–92: Asst Sec., 1971; Principal Private Sec. to Chancellor of the Exchequer, 1976–77; Under Sec., 1977–84; Dep. Sec. (Industry), 1984–90; Second Perm. Sec. (Public Expenditure), 1990–92. Dir, Standard Life, 1997–2005. Member: BSC, 1978–80; IMRO, 1995–2000; Council of Mgt, NIESR, 2002–. Chm., British Dyslexia Assoc., 1995–2000. Member: Finance Cttee, Nat. Trust, 1990–2005; UCL Hosps NHS Foundn Trust, 2005–. Trustee, Glyndebourne Arts Trust, 1996–2004. Chm., Oxford Policy Inst., 2004–. *Address:* 31 Lady Margaret Road, NW5 2NG. *T:* (020) 7485 8474.

MONCKTON, family name of **Viscount Galway** and **Viscount Monckton of Brenchley**.

MONCKTON OF BRENCHLEY, 3rd Viscount *cr* 1957; **Christopher Walter Monckton;** Director, Christopher Monckton Ltd, consultants, 1987–2006; *b* 14 Feb. 1952; *s* of 2nd Viscount Monckton of Brenchley, CB, OBE, MC and Marianna Laetitia (*née* Bower); *S* father, 2006; *m* 1990, Juliet Mary Anne, *y d* of Jørgen Malherbe Jensen. *Educ:* Harrow; Churchill Coll., Cambridge (BA 1973, MA 1977); University Coll.,

Cardiff; Dip. Journalism Studies (Wales), 1974. Standing Cttee, Cambridge Union Soc., 1973; Treas., Cambridge Univ. Conservative Assoc., 1973. Reporter, Yorkshire Post, 1974–75, Leader-Writer, 1975–77; Press Officer, Conservative Central Office, 1977–78; Editor-designate, The Universe, 1978, Editor, 1979–81; Managing Editor, Telegraph Sunday Magazine, 1981–82; Leader-Writer, The Standard, 1982; Special Advr to Prime Minister's Policy Unit, 1982–86; Asst Editor, Today, 1986–87; Consulting Editor, 1987–92, Chief Leader-Writer, 1990–92, Evening Standard. Freeman, City of London, and Liveryman, Worshipful Co. of Broderers, 1973–. Member: Internat. MENSA Ltd, 1975–; St John Amb. Brigade (Wetherby Div.), 1976–77; Hon. Soc. of the Middle Temple, 1979–; RC Mass Media Commn, 1979–; Sec. to Econ., Forward Strategy, Health, and Employment Study Gps, Centre For Policy Studies, 1980–82. Vis. Lectr in Business Studies, Columbia Univ., NY, 1980. Editor, Not the Church Times, 1982. Kt SMO, Malta, 1973; OStJ 1973. DL Greater London, 1988–96. *Publications:* The Laker Story (with Ivan Fallon), 1982; Anglican Orders: null and void?, 1986; The Aids Report, 1987; Sudoku X, 2005; Sudoku X-mas, 2005; Sudoku Xpert, 2005; Junior Sudoku X, 2005; Sudoku Xtreme, 2005. *Recreation:* romance. *Heir: b* Hon. Timothy David Robert Monckton [*b* 15 Aug. 1955; *m* 1984, Jennifer Carmody; three *s*]. *Address:* Carie, Rannoch, Perthshire PH17 2QJ. *T:* (01882) 632341, *Fax:* (01882) 632776; *e-mail:* monckton@mail.com. *Clubs:* Brooks's, Beefsteak, Pratt's.

See also Hon. R. M. Monckton.

MONCKTON, Hon. Rosa(mond) Mary, (Hon. Mrs Dominic Lawson); Chairman, Asprey & Garrard UK Ltd, 2002–05 (Chief Executive, 2000–02); *b* 26 Oct. 1953; *d* of 2nd Viscount Monckton of Brenchley, CB, OBE, MC; *m* 1991, Hon. Dominic Ralph Campden Lawson, *qv*; two *d*. *Educ:* Ursuline Convent, Tildonk, Belgium. Asst Man. Dir, Cartier, London, 1979; Sales and Exhibn Manager, Tabbah Jewellers, Monte Carlo, 1980; Promotions Manager, Asprey, 1982–85; Man. Dir, 1986–97, Pres., 1997–2000, Tiffany, London. Chm., KIDS, 1999–2004 (Pres., 2004–); Mem., Diana, Princess of Wales Meml Cttee, 1997– (Chm., Fountain Design Cttee, 2001–). Liveryman, Goldsmiths' Co., 2000–. *Address:* Cox's Mill, Dallington, Heathfield, E Sussex TN21 9JG.

MONCKTON-ARUNDELL, family name of **Viscount Galway**.

MONCREIFF, family name of **Baron Moncreiff**.

MONCREIFF, 6th Baron *cr* 1873, of Tulliebole, co. Kinross; Bt (NS) 1626, (UK) 1871; **Rhoderick Harry Wellwood Moncreiff;** *b* 22 March 1954; *o s* of 5th Baron Moncreiff and Enid Marion Watson (*née* Locke); *S* father, 2002; *m* 1982, Alison Elizabeth Anne, *d* of J. D. A. Ross; two *s*. *Heir: s* Hon. Harry James Wellwood Moncreiff, *b* 12 Aug. 1986.

MONCREIFFE of that Ilk, Hon. Peregrine David Euan Malcolm; *b* 16 Feb. 1951; *s* of Sir Iain Moncreiffe of that Ilk, 11th Bt, CVO, DL, QC (Scot.) and Countess of Erroll, 23rd in line; *m* 1988, Miranda Fox-Pitt; two *s* four *d*. *Educ:* Eton; Christ Church, Oxford (MA Modern Hist.). Lieut, Atholl Highlanders, 1978. Investment banker: with White Weld & Co. Ltd/Credit Suisse First Boston Ltd, 1972–82; Lehman Brothers Kuhn Loeb/Shearson Lehman, 1982–86; E. F. Hutton & Co., 1986–88; Chief Exec., Buchanan Partners Ltd, 1990–99. Mem., Royal Commn on Ancient and Historical Monuments of Scotland, 1989–94. Chm., Scottish Ballet, 1988–90. Trustee, Save the Rhino, 1991–2000. Mem., Royal Co. of Archers (Queen's Body Guard for Scotland), 1979–. Freeman, City of London; Liveryman, Co. of Fishmongers, 1987–. *Address:* Easter Moncreiffe, Bridge of Earn, Perth PH2 8QA. *T:* (01738) 812338. *Clubs:* White's, Turf, Pratt's; New (Edinburgh); Leander (Henley); Brook (New York).

MONCRIEFF, Rear Adm. Ian; National Hydrographer, United Kingdom Hydrographic Office, since 2006; *b* 5 Jan. 1955; *s* of Donald and Ellen Moncrieff; *m* 1986, Marion McLennan; two *s*. *Educ:* Kirkham High Sch.; Preston VI Form Coll.; Univ. of Keele (BA Hons Geog. and Geol. 1977); BRNC Dartmouth. Served in HM Ships Sheffield, Arrow, Yarnton and Nottingham, 1978–85; qualified as Principal Warfare Officer and specialist in communications, 1985; Principal Warfare Officer, HMS Glasgow, 1986; i/c new entry radio operator trng, HMS Mercury, 1986–88; Royal Cypher Officer and Flag Lieut, HMY Britannia, 1988–90; Desk Officer, Directorate of Naval Plans and Progs, MoD, 1990–92; CO, HMS Nottingham, 1992–94; DACOS Policy and Progs to C-in-C Fleet, 1994–97; Comdr, HMS Invincible, 1997–98; Captain 1998; CSO Plans and Policy to CGRM, 1998–2001; CO, HMS Endurance, 2001–03; Cdre 2003; Dir, Navy Communications and Inf. Systems, 2003–04; HCSC 2005; Comdr British Forces South Atlantic, 2005–06; Rear Adm., 2006. Mem. Council, RNLI, 2007–. Mem., Hon. Co. of Master Mariners, 2000–. Younger Brother, Trinity House, 2007–. MInstD 1996; MRIN 2008. *Recreations:* golf, sailing, tennis, wildlife photography. *Address:* United Kingdom Hydrographic Office, Admiralty Way, Taunton, Somerset TA1 2DN. *T:* (01823) 723432, *Fax:* (01823) 325522; *e-mail:* ian.moncrieff@ukho.gov.uk.

MOND, family name of **Baron Melchett**.

MONDALE, Walter Frederick; American Ambassador to Japan, 1993–96; *b* Ceylon, Minnesota, 5 Jan. 1928; *s* of Rev. Theodore Sigvaard Mondale and Claribel Hope (*née* Cowan); *m* 1955, Joan Adams; two *s* one *d*. *Educ:* public schs, Minnesota; Macalester Coll., Univ. of Minnesota (BA *cum laude*); Univ. of Minnesota Law Sch. (LLB). Served with Army, 1951–53. Admitted to Minn. Bar, 1956; private law practice, Minneapolis, 1956–60; Attorney-Gen., Minnesota, 1960–65; Senator from Minnesota, 1965–76; Vice-Pres., USA, 1977–81; Counsel with Winston & Strawn, 1981–87; Partner with Dorsey & Whitney, 1987–93. Democratic Candidate for Vice-Pres., USA, 1976, 1980; Democratic Candidate for Pres., USA, 1984. Chm., Nat. Democratic Inst. for Internat. Affairs, 1987–93. Mem., Democratic Farm Labor Party. *Publication:* The Accountability of Power. *Address:* c/o Dorsey & Whitney LLP, # 1500, 50 South 6th Street, Minneapolis, MN 55402–1498, USA.

MONDS, Prof. Fabian Charles, CBE 1997; PhD; Professor of Information Systems, 1987–2000, now Emeritus, and Pro-Vice-Chancellor (Planning), 1993–2000, University of Ulster; Chairman, Northern Ireland Centre for Trauma and Transformation, since 2002; *b* 1 Nov. 1940; *s* of Edward James Monds and Mary Brigid (*née* McPoland); *m* 1967, Eileen Joan Graham; two *d*. *Educ:* Queen's Univ., Belfast (BSc; PhD). CEng, MIET, MBCS. Vis. Asst Prof., Purdue Univ., USA, 1965, 1966; Lectr, 1967–77, Sen. Lectr, 1977–78, Reader, 1978–86, QUB; Dean, Faculty of Informatics, 1989–93, Provost, Magee Coll., Londonderry, 1995–2000, Univ. of Ulster. Gov. for NI, BBC, 1999–2006; Chairman: NI Inf. Age Initiative, 1999–2002; Univ. of Ulster Sci. Res. Parks Ltd, 1999–2002; NI Industrial Res. and Technol. Unit, 2000–01; Omagh 2010 Task Force, 2001–02; Invest Northern Ireland, 2002–05; Co-Chm., US-Ireland R&D Partnership, 2005–. Trustee, UK Teaching Awards Trust, 1999–2006. CCMI. *Publications:* Minicomputer Systems, 1979; (with R. McLaughlin) An Introduction to Mini and Micro Computers, 1981, 2nd edn 1984; The Business of Electronic Product Development, 1984; two patents; contrib. learned jls. *Recreation:* general aviation. *Address:* NICTT, 2 Retreat Close, Omagh, BT79 0HW.

MONE, Rt Rev. John Aloysius; Bishop of Paisley, (RC), 1988–2004, now Emeritus; *b* 22 June 1929; *s* of Arthur Mone and Elizabeth Mone (*née* Dunn). *Educ:* Holyrood Secondary School, Glasgow; Séminaire Saint Sulpice, Paris; Institut Catholique, Paris (Faculty of Social Studies). Ordained Priest, Glasgow, 1952; Assistant Priest: St Ninian's, Knightswood, Glasgow, also hosp. and sch. chaplain, 1952–74; Our Lady and St George's, Glasgow, 1975–79; Parish Priest, St Joseph's, Tollcross, Glasgow, 1979–84; Auxiliary Bishop of Glasgow, 1984–88. Episcopal Vicar, Marriage, 1981–83; Dir, Ministry to Priests Prog., 1982–84. Scottish National Chaplain, Girl Guides, 1971–; Dir, Scottish Catholic Internat. Aid Fund, 1974– (Chm., 1974–75, Pres./Treas., 1984–2004); Chm., Scottish Catholic Marriage Advisory Council, 1982–84; President: Scottish Justice and Peace Commn, 1987–2004; Pastoral and Social Care Commn, 1996–2004. Advr to Nat. Child Protection Team, 2004–. Pres., Paisley Family Soc., 2007. *Recreations:* watching soccer (attending if possible), playing golf (when time!), playing the piano. *Address:* 30 Esplanade, Greenock, Renfrewshire PA16 7RU.

MONEO VALLÉS, Prof. José Rafael, (Prof. Rafael Moneo); architect; Josep Lluis Sert Professor of Architecture, Graduate School of Design, Harvard University, since 1991; *b* Tudela, Spain, 9 May 1937; *s* of Rafael Moneo and Teresa Vallés; *m* 1963, Belén Feduchi; three *d*. *Educ:* Tech. Sch. of Madrid (degree in arch., 1961). Fellow, Spanish Acad., Rome, 1963–65; Asst Prof., Technical Sch. of Architecture, Madrid, 1966–70; Prof. of Architectural Theory, Technical School of Architecture, Barcelona, 1970–80; Prof. of Composition, Tech. Sch. of Madrid, 1980–85; Chm., Dept of Architecture, Harvard Univ., 1985–90. Projects include: Diestre Factory, Zaragoza, 1967; Pamplona Bull Ring, 1967; Urumea Residential Building, San Sebastián, 1971; (with Ramón Bescós) Bankinter Bank, Madrid, 1976; Logroño Town Hall, 1976; Nat. Mus. of Roman Art, Mérida, 1986; Previsión Española Insurance Co., Seville, 1987; Bank of Spain, Jaén, 1988; San Pablo Airport, Seville, 1992; Architectural Assoc. of Tarragona, 1992; Atocha Railway Stn, Madrid, 1992; Thyssen-Bornemisza Mus., Madrid, 1992; Pilar and Joan Miró Foundn, Palma de Mallorca, 1992; Davis Art Mus., Wellesley Coll., Mass, 1993; (with Manuel de Solá-Morales) Diagonal Buildings, Barcelona, 1993; Don Benito Cultural Centre, Badajoz, 1997; Museums of Modern Art and Architecture, Stockholm, 1998; Town Hall extension, Murcia, 1998; Barcelona Concert Hall, 1999; Kursaal Auditorium and Congress Centre, San Sebastián, 1999; Potsdamer Platz Hotel and office building, Berlin; Audrey Jones Beck Building, Mus. of Fine Arts, Houston, 2000; Cathedral of Our Lady of the Angels, Los Angeles, 2002; (with Belén Moneo) new studios, Cranbrook Acad. of Art, 2002; Arenberg Campus Liby, Catholic Univ. Leuven, 2002; Chivite Winery, Arinzano, Navarra, 2002; Gregorio Marañón Mother's and Children's Hosp., Madrid, 2003; Gen. and Royal Archive of Navarra, Pamplona, 2003; CDAN/Beulas Foundn, Huesca, 2004; (with José Antonio Martínez Lapeña and Elías Torres) apts, Sabadell, 2005; (with Alberto Nicolau) apts, La Haya, 2006; extension, Bank of Spain, Madrid, 2006; extension, Prado Mus., Madrid, 2007; Lab. for Integrated Sci. and Engrg, Harvard Univ., 2007; Mus. of Roman Th., Cartagena, 2008; Aragonia commercial center, apts, hotel and offices, 2008; Panticosa Resort Hotels, 2008; Novartis Lab., Basel, 2008. Gold Medal for Achievement in Fine Arts (Spain), 1992; Gold Medal: French Acad. of Architecture, 1996; Internat. Union of Architects, 1996; Pritzker Prize, 1996; Royal Gold Medal, RIBA, 2003. *Publications include:* (jtly) Grand Hyatt Berlin, 2000; (jtly) Theoretical Anxiety and Design Strategies in the Work of Eight Contemporary Architects, 2004; articles in learned jls. *Address:* Cinca 5, Madrid 28002, Spain; Department of Architecture, Harvard Graduate School of Design, 48 Quincy Street, Cambridge, MA 02138, USA.

MONEY, Ernle (David Drummond), CBE 1996; Barrister-at-Law; *b* 17 Feb. 1931; *s* of late Lt-Col E. F. D. Money, DSO, late 4th Gurkha Rifles, and Sidney, *o d* of D. E. Anderson, Forfar; *m* 1st, 1960, Susan Barbara (marr. diss. 1985), *d* of Lt-Col D. S. Lister, MC, The Buffs; two *s* two *d*; 2nd, Bella Maharaj (*d* 1993), barrister-at-law. *Educ:* Marlborough Coll.; Oriel Coll., Oxford (open scholar). Served in Suffolk Regt, 1949–51, and 4th Bn, Suffolk Regt (TA), 1951–56; MA Hons degree (2nd cl.) in mod. hist., 1954. Tutor and lecturer, Swinton Conservative Coll., 1956. Called to Bar, Lincoln's Inn (Cholmeley Scholar), 1958. Mem., Bar Council, 1962–66. MP (C) Ipswich, 1970–Sept. 1974; Opposition Front Bench Spokesman on the Arts, 1974; Sec., Parly Cons. Arts and Amenities Cttee, 1970–73, Vice-Chm., 1974; Vice-Pres., Ipswich Cons. Assoc., 1979–81. Regular columnist, East Anglian Daily Times, for some years. Governor, Woolverstone Hall Sch., 1967–70; co-opted Mem., GLC Arts Cttee, 1972–73; Member: GLC Arts Bd, 1974–76; Cttee, Gainsborough's Birthplace, Sudbury; Acquisitions sub-cttee, 2001–, Exec. cttee, 2002–, Patrons of British Art, Tate Gall. Fine Arts Correspondent, Contemporary Review, 1968–88. Pres., Ipswich Town Football Club Supporters, 1974–80; Vice-Pres., E Suffolk and Ipswich Branch, RSPCA, 1974–77. Mem., Primrose League. *Publications:* (with Peter Johnson) The Nasmyth Family of Painters, 1970; Margaret Thatcher, First Lady of the House, 1975; regular contrib. various periodicals and newspapers on antiques and the arts. *Recreations:* music, pictures and antiques, watching Association football. *Address:* 33a Bishops Road, Highgate Village, N6 4HP. *T:* (020) 8348 5391. *Clubs:* Carlton, Beefsteak, Dinosaurs; Norfolk (Norwich).

MONEY, Hon. George Gilbert, CHB 1986; FCIB; Director, Barclays Bank International Ltd, 1955–81 (Vice-Chairman, 1965–73); *b* 17 Nov. 1914; 2nd *s* of late Maj.-Gen. Sir A. W. Money, KCB, KBE, CSI and late Lady Money (*née* Drummond). *Educ:* Charterhouse Sch. Clerk, L. Behrens & Soehne, Bankers, Hamburg, 1931–32; Clerk, Barclays Bank Ltd, 1932–35, Dir 1972–73; joined Barclays Bank DCO (now Barclays Bank PLC), London, 1935; served in Egypt, Palestine, Cyprus, Ethiopia, Cyrenaica, E Africa, 1936–52; Local Dir, W Indies, 1952; Director: Barclays Bank of California, 1965–75; Bermuda Provident Bank Ltd, 1969–89; Barclays Bank of the Netherlands, Antilles NV, 1970–86; Republic Finance Corp. Ltd, 1972–88; Republic Bank Ltd, 1972–88; Barclays Bank of Jamaica Ltd, 1972–77; Barclays Australia Ltd, 1972–75; New Zealand United Corp., 1972–75; Chairman: Bahamas Internat. Trust Co. Ltd, 1970–72; Cayman Internat. Trust Co. Ltd, 1970–72; Mem., Caribbean Bd, Barclays Bank PLC, 1952–88. *Publication:* Nine Lives of a Bush Banker, 1990. *Recreations:* water ski-ing, fishing, bridge. *Address:* Saltram, St Joseph, Barbados.

MONEY-COUTTS, family name of **Baron Latymer**.

MONEY-COUTTS, Sir David (Burdett), KCVO 1991; Chairman, Coutts & Co., 1976–93; *b* 19 July 1931; *s* of late Hon. Alexander B. Money-Coutts (2nd *s* of 6th Baron Latymer, TD), and Mary E., *er d* of Sir Reginald Hobhouse, 5th Bt; *m* 1958, Penelope Utten Todd; one *s* two *d*. *Educ:* Eton (Hon. Fellow, 1996); New Coll., Oxford (MA). National Service, 1st Royal Dragoons, 1950–51; Royal Glos Hussars, TA, 1951–67. Joined Coutts & Co., 1954; Dir, 1958–96; Man. Dir, 1970–86. Director: National Discount Co., 1964–69; Gerrard Gp (formerly Gerrard & National), 1969–99 (Dep. Chm. 1969–89); United States & General Trust Corp., 1964–73; Charities Investment Managers (Charifund), 1964–2000 (Chm., 1984–2000); Dun & Bradstreet, 1973–87; National Westminster Bank, 1976–90 (Regl Dir, 1969–92, Chm., SE Reg., 1986–88; Chm., S Adv. Bd, 1988–92; Mem., UK Adv. Bd, 1990–92); Phoenix Assurance, 1978–85 (Dep. Chm., 1984–85); Sun Alliance & London Insurance, 1984–90; M & G Gp, 1987–97

(Chm., 1990–97). Member: Kensington and Chelsea and Westminster AHA, 1974–82 (Vice-Chm., 1978–82); Bloomsbury HA, 1982–90 (Vice-Chm., 1982–88); Health Educn Council, 1973–77. Middlesex Hospital: Governor, 1962–74 (Dep. Chm. Governors, 1973–74); Chm., Finance Cttee, 1965–74; Mem., Med. Sch. Council, 1963–88 (Chm., 1974–88; Special Trustee, 1974–2000 (Chm., 1974–97)). Chm., Inst. of Sports Medicine, 1997–2006. Mem., Council, UCL, 1987–97. Trustee: Multiple Sclerosis Soc., 1967–99; Scout Foundn, 1992–2001 (Chm., 1994–2001). Hon. Treas., Nat. Assoc. of Almshouses, 1960–92; Hon. Sec., Old Etonian Trust, 1969–76, Chm. Council, 1976–2001; Trustee, Mansfield Coll., Oxford, 1988–95. *Recreations:* odd jobs, living in the country. *Address:* Magpie House, Peppard Common, Henley-on-Thames, Oxon RG9 5JG. *T:* (01491) 628005. *Club:* Leander (Henley-on-Thames).

MONHEMIUS, Prof. (Andrew) John, PhD; CEng; Roy Wright Professor of Mineral and Environmental Engineering, 1996–2004, now Professor Emeritus, and Dean, Royal School of Mines, 2000–04, Imperial College of Science, Technology and Medicine, London University; *b* 3 Oct. 1942; *s* of Frank Andre Monhemius and Edna Rowland Monhemius; *m* 1966, Johanna Werson; one *s* one *d. Educ:* Univ. of Birmingham (BSc); Univ. of British Columbia (MASc); Imperial Coll., Univ. of London (PhD; DIC). CEng. Royal School of Mines, Imperial College: Lectr, 1966–86; Reader, 1986–96. Vis. Prof. of Extractive Metallurgy, Federal Univ. of Rio de Janeiro, 1973–75. FIMMM (FIMM 1984). Mem., Chaps Club. *Publication:* (ed with J. E. Dutrizac) Iron Control in Hydrometallurgy, 1986. *Address:* Royal School of Mines, Imperial College of Science, Technology and Medicine, SW7 2BP. *T:* (020) 7594 7329, *Fax:* (020) 7594 7444; *e-mail:* j.monhemius@ ic.ac.uk. *Club:* Twickenham Yacht.

MONIER-WILLIAMS, His Honour Evelyn Faithfull; a Circuit Judge, 1972–92; continued sitting in Crown and County Courts until 1995; *b* 29 April 1920; *o s* of late R. T. Monier-Williams, OBE, Barrister-at-Law, and Mrs G. M. Monier-Williams; *m* 1948, Maria-Angela Oswald (*d* 1983); one *s* one *d. Educ:* Charterhouse; University Coll., Oxford (MA). Admitted to Inner Temple, 1940; served Royal Artillery, 1940–46 in UK, Egypt, Libya, Tunisia, Sicily (8th Army), France, Low Countries and Germany; called to Bar, Inner Temple, 1948; South Eastern Circuit; Master of the Bench, Inner Temple, 1967, Reader, 1987, Treas., 1988; Mem. Senate of Four Inns of Court, 1969–73; Mem. Council, Selden Soc., 1970– (Vice Pres., 1990–96); Mem., Council of Legal Educn, 1971–87, Vice Chm., 1974–87; Mem., Lord Chancellor's Adv. Cttee on Legal Educn, 1979–87; Mem., Council of the Inns of Court, 1987–88. Livery, Glaziers' Company, 1974. *Recreation:* collecting old books. *Address:* Inner Temple, EC4Y 7HL.

MONK, Alec; *see* Monk, D. A. G.

MONK, Rear-Adm. Anthony John, CBE 1973; Appeals Organizer, The Royal Marsden Hospital Cancer Fund, 1984–87; *b* 14 Nov. 1923; *s* of Frank Leonard and Barbara Monk; *m* 1951, Elizabeth Ann Samson; four *s* (one *d* decd). *Educ:* Whitgift Sch.; RNC Dartmouth; RNEC Keyham. MSc, BScEng, CEng, FIMarEST, FRAeS, FIMechE. Engr Cadet, 1941; served War of 1939–45, Pacific Fleet; flying trng, Long Air Engrg Course, Cranfield, 1946; RN Air Stn Ford; RNEC Manadon, 1950; Prodn Controller and Man., RN Aircraft Yard, Belfast, 1953–56; Mem. Dockyard Work Measurement Team, subseq. Engr Officer HMS Apollo, Techn. Asst to Dir-Gen. Aircraft, Sqdn Engr Officer to Flag Officer Aircraft Carriers, 1963–65; Asst Dir of Marine Engrg, 1965–68; Dir of Aircraft Engrg, 1968; Comd Engrg Officer to Flag Officer Naval Air Comd; Naval Liaison Officer for NI and Supt RN Aircraft Yard, Belfast, 1970; Port Admiral, Rosyth, 1974–76; Rear-Adm. Engineering to Flag Officer Naval Air Comd, 1976–78. Comdr 1956; Captain 1964; Rear-Adm. 1974. Dir Gen., Brick Develt Assoc., 1979–84. Liveryman, Co. of Engrs, 1998–. MRI. FRSA. *Recreation:* swimming (ASA teacher). *Address:* Morning Glory, Kingsdown, Deal, Kent CT14 8AT.

MONK, Arthur James; Director, Components, Valves and Devices, Ministry of Defence, 1981–84, retired; *b* 15 Jan. 1924; *s* of late Rev. Arthur S. Monk, AKC, and late Lydia E. Monk; *m* 1953, Murial V. Peacock; one *s* two *d. Educ:* Latymer Upper School, Hammersmith; London Univ. BSc Hons Physics 1953; FIET 1964. Served RAF, 1943–48. Services Electronic Research Labs, 1949–63; Asst Director (Co-ord. Valve Development), MoD, 1963–68; Student, Imperial Defence Coll., 1969; idc 1970; Admiralty Underwater Weapons Establishment, 1970–73; Dep. Director, Underwater Weapons Projects (S/M), MoD, 1973–76; Counsellor, Def. Equipment Staff, Washington, 1977–81. *Publications:* papers on electronics in jls of learned societies. *Recreations:* photography, family history and genealogy. *Address:* 65 Wyke Road, Weymouth, Dorset DT4 9QN. *T:* (01305) 782338.

MONK, (David) Alec (George); Chairman, Charles Wells Ltd, 1998–2003 (Director, 1989–2003); *b* 13 Dec. 1942; *s* of Philip Aylmer and Elizabeth Jane Monk; *m* 1965, Jean Ann Searle; two *s* two *d. Educ:* Jesus College, Oxford (MA (PPE); Hon. Fellow, 1999). Research Staff, Corporate Finance and Taxation, Sheffield Univ., 1966 and London Business Sch., 1967; Senior Financial Asst, Treasurer's Dept, Esso Petroleum Co., 1968; various positions with The Rio Tinto-Zinc Corp., 1968–77, Dir, 1974–77; Vice-Pres. and Dir, AEA Investors Inc., 1977–81; Chm. and Chief Exec., The Gateway Corp. (formerly Dee Corp.) PLC, 1981–89; CEO, Tri-Delta Corp. Ltd, 1990–93. Dir, Scottish Eastern Investment Trust, 1985–98. Mem., NEDC, 1986–90. Pres., Inst. of Grocery Distribution, 1987–89. Vis. Indust. Fellow, Manchester Business Sch., 1984. Hon. Fellow, St Hugh's Coll., Oxford, 1985; Foundn Fellow, New Hall, Cambridge, 2001. Hon. LLD Sheffield, 1988. *Publication:* (with A. J. Merrett) Inflation, Taxation and Executive Remuneration, 1967. *Recreations:* sports, reading.

MONK, Dame Susan Catherine Hampshire-; *see* Leather, Dame S. C.

MONK BRETTON, 3rd Baron *cr* 1884; **John Charles Dodson;** DL; *b* 17 July 1924; *o s* of 2nd Baron and Ruth (*d* 1967), 2nd *d* of late Hon. Charles Brand; *S* father, 1933; *m* 1958, Zoë Diana Scott; two *s. Educ:* Westminster Sch.; New Coll., Oxford (MA). DL E Sussex, 1983. *Heir: s* Hon. Christopher Mark Dodson [*b* 2 Aug. 1958; *m* 1988, Karen, *o d* of B. J. McKelvain, Fairfield, Conn; two *s* one *d*]. *Address:* Chemin de la Becque 24, 1814 La Tour de Peilz, Switzerland. *T:* (21) 9442912.

MONKS, John Stephen; General Secretary, European Trades Union Confederation, since 2003; *b* 5 Aug. 1945; *s* of Charles Edward Monks and Bessie Evelyn Monks; *m* 1970, Francine Jacqueline Schenk; two *s* one *d. Educ:* Ducie Technical High Sch., Manchester; Nottingham Univ. (BA Econ). Joined TUC, 1969; Hd of Orgn and Industrial Relns Dept, 1977–87; Dep. Gen. Sec., 1987–93; Gen. Sec., 1993–2003. Member: Council, ACAS, 1979–95; ESRC, 1988–91. Vice-Chm., Learning and Skills Council, 2001–04. Chm. Trustees, People's History Museum (formerly Nat. Museum of Labour History), 2004– (Trustee, 1988–). Vis. Prof., Sch. of Mgt, Univ. of Manchester (formerly at UMIST), 1996–. Mem., Court, Henley Mgt Coll. *Recreations:* squash, hiking, music. *Address:* European Trade Union Confederation, 5 Boulevard Roi Albert II, 1210 Brussels, Belgium.

MONKSWELL, 5th Baron *cr* 1885; **Gerard Collier;** *b* 28 Jan. 1947; *s* of William Adrian Larry Collier and Helen (*née* Dunbar); *S* to disclaimed barony of father, 1984; *m* 1974, Ann Valerie Collins; two *s* one *d. Educ:* Portsmouth Polytechnic (BSc Mech. Eng, 1971); Slough Polytechnic (Cert. in Works Management 1972). Massey Ferguson Manfg Co. Ltd: Product Quality Engineer, 1972; Service Administration Manager, 1984–89. Mem. (Lab), Manchester City Council, 1989–94. Mem., H of L, 1985–99. *Recreations:* politics, swimming, movies. *Heir: s* Hon. James Adrian Collier, *b* 29 March 1977. *Address:* 183 Egerton Road South, Manchester M21 0XD.

MONMOUTH, Bishop of, since 2003; **Rt Rev. Dominic Edward William Murray Walker,** OGS; *b* 28 June 1948; *s* of Horace John and Mary Louise Walker. *Educ:* Plymouth Coll.; King's Coll. London (AKC); Heythrop Coll., London (MA); Univ. of Wales (LLM). Ordained priest, 1972; Asst Curate, St Faith, Wandsworth, 1972–73; Domestic Chaplain to the Bishop of Southwark, 1973–76; Rector, Newington, 1976–85; Rural Dean, Southwark and Newington, 1980–85; Vicar, Team Rector, and Rural Dean of Brighton, 1985–97; Canon and Prebendary, Chichester Cathedral, 1985–97; Area Bishop of Reading, 1997–2003. Mem., CGA, 1967–83; Mem., OGS, 1983– (Superior, 1990–96). Vice-Pres., RSPCA, 2001. Governor: Univ. of Wales Newport, 2003–; St Michael's Coll., Llandaff. Hon. DLitt Brighton, 1998. *Publication:* The Ministry of Deliverance, 1997. *Address:* Bishopstow, Stow Hill, Newport NP20 4EA. *T:* (01633) 263510, *Fax:* (01633) 259946; *e-mail:* bishop.monmouth@churchinwales.org.uk.

MONMOUTH, Dean of; *see* Fenwick, Very Rev. R. D.

MONRO, (Andrew) Hugh; Principal, Bristol Cathedral Choir School (formerly Headmaster, Bristol Cathedral School), since 2007; *b* 2 March 1950; *s* of late Andrew Killey Monro, FRCS and Diana Louise (*née* Rhys); *m* 1974, Elizabeth Clare Rust; one *s* one *d. Educ:* Rugby School; Pembroke College, Cambridge (MA; PGCE). Graduate trainee, Metal Box, 1973; Haileybury College, 1974–79; Noble & Greenough School, Boston, Mass, 1977–78; Loretto School, 1979–86; Headmaster: Worksop College, 1986–90; Clifton College, 1990–2000; Master, Wellington College, 2000–05. *Recreations:* golf, American literature. *Club:* Hawks (Cambridge).

MONRO, Hugh; *see* Monro, A. H.

MONRO, Maj.-Gen. Hon. Seymour Hector Russell Hale, CBE 1996; Director, Atlantic Salmon Trust, since 2004; *b* 7 May 1950; *s* of Rt Hon. Lord Monro of Langholm, AE, PC, DL and (Elizabeth) Anne (*née* Welch); *m* 1977, Angela Sandeman; three *s. Educ:* Cargilfield Sch.; Glenalmond Coll.; RMA, Sandhurst. MA to Comdr 1st Br. Corps, 1982–84; Co. Comdr, 1st Bn Queen's Own Highlanders, 1984–86; Instr, All Arms Tactics, Warminster, 1986–87; Directing Staff, Army Staff Coll., 1987–89; CO, 1st Bn, Queen's Own Highlanders, 1989–91; Col, Gen. Staff, MoD, 1991–94; Comdr, 39 Inf. Bde, 1994–95; Pres., Regular Commns Bd, 1996–97; Dep. Chief, Jt Ops, HQ SFOR, 1997; Dir, Infantry, 1998–2001. ADC to the Queen, 1998–2001. Adjutant, Queen's Bodyguard for Scotland, 2001–; Dep. Comdr, NATO Rapid Deployable Corps (Italy), 2001–03. Chairman: Highlands and Islands Bd, Prince's Trust, 2004–07; Highland Heritage Appeal, 2007–. Mem. Council, Glenalmond Coll., 1993–2003. *Recreations:* shooting, fishing, stalking, golf, photography, conservation, travel. *Address:* Atlantic Salmon Trust, King James VI Business Centre, Friarton Road, Perth PH2 8DG. *Club:* New (Edinburgh).

MONRO, Stuart Kinnaird, OBE 2007; PhD; Scientific Director, Our Dynamic Earth, Edinburgh, since 2004; *b* 3 March 1947; *s* of William Kinnaird Monro and Williamena Milne Monro; *m* 1971, Shiela Dowie Wallace; three *s* one *d. Educ:* Aberdeen Acad.; Univ. of Aberdeen (BSc 1970); Univ. of Edinburgh (PhD 1982; Hon. Fellow 2005). FGS 1990; CGeol 1991; FHEA 2007 (ILTM 2001). Principal Geologist, British Geol Survey, 1970–2004; Tutor in Earth Scis (pt-time), Open Univ., 1982–. Vis. Prof., Sch. of Geoscis, Univ. of Edinburgh, 2008–. Member: Scottish Sci. Adv. Cttee, 2003– (Ind. Co-Chm., 2007–); Young People's Cttee, RSE, 2005–; non-exec. Dir, Edinburgh Internat. Sci. Fest., 2004–; Trustee, Nat. Mus Scotland (formerly Nat. Mus of Scotland), 2005–. Member: Council, Open Univ., 1994–2002; Court, Univ. of Edinburgh, 2007–. President: Westmorland Geol Soc., 1994–2005; Edinburgh Geol Soc., 2006–07. Hon. Geol Advr, John Muir Trust, 2005–. FRSSA 1998 (Pres., 2002–05). *Publications:* Geology of the Irvine District, 1999; various scientific papers and reports. *Recreations:* theatre, travel, the great outdoors—especially the rocks! *Address:* 34 Swanston Grove, Edinburgh EH10 7BW. *T:* (0131) 445 4619; *e-mail:* stuart.monro@dynamicearth.co.uk. *Club:* Rotary (Edinburgh).

MONRO DAVIES, His Honour William Llewellyn; QC 1974; a Circuit Judge, 1976–99; *b* 12 Feb. 1927; *s* of Thomas Llewellyn Davies and Emily Constance Davies; *m* 1956, Jean, *d* of late E. G. Innes; one *s* one *d. Educ:* Christ Coll., Brecon; Trinity Coll., Oxford (MA, LitHum). Served in RNVR, 1945–48 (Sub-Lt). Called to the Bar, Inner Temple, 1954. Mem., Gen. Council of the Bar, 1971–75. A Recorder of the Crown Court, 1972–76. *Recreations:* the theatre and cinema; watching Rugby football.
See also N. A. Stewart.

MONSON, family name of **Baron Monson**.

MONSON, 11th Baron *cr* 1728; **John Monson;** Bt *cr* 1611; *b* 3 May 1932; *e s* of 10th Baron and of Bettie Northrup (who *m* 1962, Capt. James Arnold Phillips), *d* of late E. Alexander Powell; *S* father, 1958; *m* 1955, Emma, *o d* of late Anthony Devas, ARA, RP; three *s. Educ:* Eton; Trinity Coll., Cambridge (BA). Elected Mem., H of L, 1999. Pres., Soc. for Individual Freedom. *Heir: s* Hon. Nicholas John Monson [*b* 19 Oct. 1955; *m* 1st, 1981, Hilary (marr. diss. 1996), *o d* of Kenneth Martin, Nairobi and Diani Beach; one *s* one *d*; 2nd, 2002, La Ilustrisima Maria Victoria Nicklin Perez]. *Address:* The Manor House, South Carlton, Lincoln LN1 2RN. *T:* (01522) 730263.

MONSON, (John) Guy (Elmhirst); Managing Partner and Chief Information Officer, Sarasin & Partners LLP, since 2008; *b* London, 11 Sept. 1962; *s* of Hon. Jeremy David Alfonso John Monson and Patricia Mary, *yr d* of late Maj. George Barker, MFH; *m* 1995, Lady Olivia Rose Mildred FitzRoy, *y d* of Duke of Grafton, *qv. Educ:* Eton Coll.; Lady Margaret Hall, Oxford (BA PPE 1984). Joined Sarasin Investment Management Ltd, 1984; Dir, 1989–; Chief Investment Officer, 1993–2007; CEO, 2007; Chief Investment Officer, Bank Sarasin Gp, 1997–2007; Partner, Bank Sarasin & Co., 2001–02. *Recreations:* flying, steam engines. *Address:* Sarasin & Partners LLP, Juxon House, 100 St Paul's Churchyard, EC4M 8BU. *T:* (020) 7038 7000, *Fax:* (020) 7038 6858. *Clubs:* White's, Pratt's.

MONSON, Prof. John Rowat Telford, MD; FRCS, FRCSI, FACS; Professor of Surgery and Head of Department, Academic Surgical Unit, University of Hull, since 1993; *b* 14 Jan. 1956; *s* of Desmond Monson and Ann Monson; *m* 1980, Aideen White, MB; two *s* one *d. Educ:* Sandford Park Secondary Sch., Dublin; Trinity Coll. Dublin (MB BCh, BAO 1979; MD 1987). FRCSI 1983; FRCS 1987; FACS 1992; FRCSE (*ad hominem*) 2004. Pre-registration house officer, Royal City of Dublin Hosp., 1979; pre-Fellowship surgical trng, Dublin, 1980–83; post Fellowship surgical trng, Leeds, 1983–84; Res.

Fellow, Univ. of Leeds, 1984–86; Sen. Registrar, Surgical Trng, Dublin, 1986–89; Fellow in Surgical Oncology, Mayo Clinic, USA, 1989–90; Asst Dir and Sen. Lectr in Surgery, St Mary's Hosp. Med. Sch., London, 1990–93. Surgical Res. Soc. Internat. Travelling Fellow, 1986; Edward Halloran Bennett Travelling Fellow in Surgery, 1989; James IV Assoc. Internat. Fellow, 1996. Visiting Professor: UCLA; Univ. of Texas; Monash Univ.; Sir Edwin Tooth Vis. Prof., Univ. of Queensland, 2003. Mem. Council, British Jl of Surgery, 1997–2004. Vice-Pres., British Assoc. of Surgical Oncology, 1997; Hon. Sec., Surgical Res. Soc. of GB and Ireland, 1998–; Mem., James IV Assoc. of Surgeons, 1999–. (Dir, 2000–); Member: Special Adv. Cttee for Gen. Surgery in UK, 2000–06; Health Innovation Council, 2007–; Advr, NHS Modernisation Agency, 2002–; Bd Mem., BUPA Foundn, 2006–; Nat. Co-ordinator, Laparoscopic Colorectal Trng Prog. Examiner, Intercollegiate Bd in Gen. Surgery, 2000–; Ext. Examiner, Univ. of Malaysia, 2001. 14th Millin Lectr, RCSI, 1990; Robert Smith Lectr, RCSI, 2006. Hon. FRCSGlas, 1998; Hon. Fellow, Soc. of Univ. Surgeons, USA, 2002. *Publications:* (ed with A. Darzi) Laparascopic Inguinal Hernia Repair, 1994; (ed jtly) Atlas of Surgical Oncology, 1994; (with A. Darzi) Laparascopic Colorectal Surgery, 1995; (ed jtly) Surgical Emergencies, 1999; numerous contribs on subjects of colorectal surgery, tumour immunology and laparascopic surgery in jls incl. Lancet, Brit. Jl Surgery and Brit. Jl Cancer. *Recreations:* wine, classic cars, historic motor racing, armchair sport, bad golf. *Address:* Academic Surgical Unit, Castle Hill Hospital, Hull, E Yorks HU16 5JQ. *T:* (01482) 623225, *Fax:* (01482) 623274.

MONTAGNIER, Prof. Luc; Professor, Pasteur Institute, Paris, 1985–2000 (Head of Viral Oncology Unit, 1972–2000); Director of Research, Centre national de la recherche scientifique, since 1974; *b* 18 Aug. 1932; *s* of Antoine Montagnier and Marianne (*née* Rousselet); *m* 1961, Dorothea Ackermann; one *s* two *d. Educ:* Collège de Châtellerault; Univ. de Poitiers; Univ. de Paris. Asst, 1955–60, Attaché, 1960, Head, 1963, Head of Research, 1967, Faculty of Science, Paris; Head of Lab., Inst. of Radium, 1965–71. Dist. Prof. and Dir, B. and G. Salick Center for Molecular and Cellular Biol., Queens Coll., CUNY, 1997–2001. Co-discoverer of AIDS virus, 1983. Commandeur: Légion d'honneur; Ordre national du Mérite. *Publications:* Vaincre le Sida, 1986; Des virus et des hommes, 1994; Virus, 2000; Les Combatsole le vie, 2008; scientific papers on research into AIDS, molecular biology, virology, etc. *Address:* 1 rue Miollis, 75732 Paris Cedex 15, France.

MONTAGU; *see* Douglas-Scott-Montagu.

MONTAGU, family name of **Duke of Manchester**, **Earl of Sandwich**, and **Baron Swaythling**.

MONTAGU OF BEAULIEU, 3rd Baron *cr* 1885; **Edward John Barrington Douglas-Scott-Montagu;** Chairman, Historic Buildings and Monuments Commission, 1983–92; *b* 20 Oct. 1926; *o s* of 2nd Baron Montagu of Beaulieu and Pearl (who *m* 2nd, 1936, Captain Hon. Edward Pleydell-Bouverie, RN, MVO, *s* of 6th Earl of Radnor; she *d* 1996), *d* of late Major E. B. Crake, Rifle Brigade, and Mrs Barrington Crake; *S* father, 1929; *m* 1st, 1959, Elizabeth Belinda (marr. diss. 1974), *o d* of late Capt. the Hon. John de Bathe Crossley, and late Hon. Mrs Crossley; one *s* one *d*; 2nd, 1974, Fiona Herbert; one *s. Educ:* St Peter's Court, Broadstairs; Ridley Coll., St Catharines, Ont; Eton Coll.; New Coll., Oxford. Late Lt Grenadier Guards; released Army, 1948. Elected Mem., H of L, 1999. Founded Montagu Motor Museum, 1952 and World's first Motor Cycle Museum, 1956; created Nat. Motor Museum Trust, 1970, to administer new Nat. Motor Museum at Beaulieu, opened 1972. Mem., Develt Commn, 1980–84. President: Assoc. of British Transport and Engrg Museums, 1964–; Historic Houses Assoc., 1973–78; Southern Tourist Bd, 1977–2004; Union of European Historic Houses, 1978–81; Fédération Internationale des Voitures Anciennes, 1980–83; Museums Assoc., 1982–84; Fedn of British Historic Vehicle Clubs, 1989–; Tourism Soc., 1991–2000 (now Pres. Emeritus); UK Vineyards Assoc., 1996–; Millennium Pres., Inst. of Journalists, 2000; Hon. Fellow, Inst. of Motor Industry, 1996; Chancellor, Wine Guild of UK, 1983–; Patron, Assoc. of Independent Museums, 1978–. Freeman, City of London, 2003. FRSA 1981; FCIPR (FIPR 1998). Hon. FMA, 1988. Commodore: Nelson Boat Owners' Club; Beaulieu River Sailing Club; Vice Cdre, H of L Yacht Club. Founder and Editor, Veteran and Vintage Magazine, 1956–79. Hon. DTech Nottingham Trent, 1998. *Publications:* The Motoring Montagus, 1959; Lost Causes of Motoring, 1960; Jaguar, A Biography, 1961, rev. edn, 1986; The Gordon Bennett Races, 1963; Rolls of Rolls-Royce, 1966; The Gilt and the Gingerbread, 1967; Lost Causes of Motoring: Europe, vol. i, 1969, vol. ii, 1971; More Equal than Others, 1970; History of the Steam Car, 1971; The Horseless Carriage, 1975; Early Days on the Road, 1976; Behind the Wheel, 1977; Royalty on the Road, 1980; Home James, 1982; The British Motorist, 1987; English Heritage, 1987; The Daimler Century, 1995; Wheels Within Wheels (autobiog.), 2000. *Heir: s* Hon. Ralph Douglas-Scott-Montagu [*b* 13 March 1961; *m* 2005, Ailsa, *e d* of Kenneth Camm, Brecht, Belgium]. *Address:* Palace House, Beaulieu, Hants SO42 7ZN. *T:* (01590) 614701, *Fax:* (01590) 612623; Flat 11, 24 Bryanston Square, W1H 2DS. *T:* (020) 7262 2603, *Fax:* (020) 7724 3262. *Clubs:* Historical Commercial Vehicle (Pres.), Disabled Drivers Motor (Pres.), and mem. of many historic vehicle clubs.

See also Earl of Lindsay.

MONTAGU, Jennifer Iris Rachel, LVO 2006; PhD; FBA 1986; Curator of the Photograph Collection, Warburg Institute, 1971–91, now Hon. Fellow; *b* 20 March 1931; *d* of late Hon. Ewen Edward Samuel Montagu, CBE, QC. *Educ:* Brearley Sch., New York; Benenden Sch., Kent; Lady Margaret Hall, Oxford (BA; Hon. Fellow 1985); Warburg Inst., London (PhD). Assistant Regional Director, Arts Council of Gt Britain, North West Region, 1953–54; Lecturer in the History of Art, Reading Univ., 1958–64; Asst Curator of the Photograph Collection, Warburg Inst., 1964–71. Slade Prof., and Fellow of Jesus Coll., Cambridge, 1980–81; Andrew W. Mellon Lectr, Nat. Gall. of Art, Washington, 1991; Invited Prof., Collège de France, 1994. Member: Academic Awards Cttee, British Fedn of University Women, 1963–89; Executive Cttee, National Art-Collections Fund, 1973–2005; Consultative Cttee, Burlington Magazine, 1975–; Cttee, The Jewish Museum, 1983–; Reviewing Cttee on Export of Works of Art, 1987–96. Trustee: Wallace Collection, 1989–2001; BM, 1994–2001. Hon. Academician, Accademia Clementina, Bologna, 1988. Serena Medal for Italian Studies, British Acad., 1992; Accademica Cultora, Accademia di San Luca, Rome, 2000; Premio Cultore di Roma, 2001; Premio Daria Borghese, 2001; Socio Onorario dell'Università e Nobil Collegio degli Orefici Gioiellieri Argentieri dell'Alma, Città di Roma, 2003. Officier, Ordre des Arts et des Lettres (France), 1991; Chevalier de la Légion d'honneur (France), 1999; Ufficiale dell'Ordine al Merito (Italy), 2003. *Publications:* Bronzes, 1963; (with Jacques Thuillier) Catalogue of exhibn Charles Le Brun, 1963; Alessandro Algardi, 1985 (special Mitchell Prize); Roman Baroque Sculpture: the industry of art, 1989; The Expression of the Passions, 1994; Gold, Silver and Bronze: metal sculpture of the Roman Baroque, 1996; (ed and contrib.) Algardi: l'altra faccia del Barocco, 1999; (ed and contrib.) Ori e argenti: Capolavori del '700 da Arrighi a Valadier, 2007; articles in learned periodicals. *Address:* 10 Roland Way, SW7 3RE. *T:* (020) 7373 6691; Warburg Institute, Woburn Square, WC1H 0AB.

MONTAGU, Sir Nicholas (Lionel John), KCB 2001 (CB 1993); Chairman, Board of Inland Revenue, 1997–2004; *b* 12 March 1944; *s* of late John Eric Montagu and Barbara Joyce Montagu, OBE; *m* 1974, Jennian Ford Geddes, *o d* of late Ford Irvine Geddes, MBE; two *d. Educ:* Rugby Sch.; New Coll., Oxford (MA). Asst Lectr 1966–69, Lectr 1969–74, in Philosophy, Univ. of Reading; Department of Social Security (formerly Department of Health and Social Security): Principal, 1974–81 (seconded to Cabinet Office, 1978–80); Asst Sec., 1981–86; Under Sec., 1986–90; Deputy Secretary, 1990 (seconded to Dept of Transport, 1992–97): Public Transport, 1992–94; Infrastructure, 1994–95; Railways, 1995–97; Hd, Econ. and Domestic Secretariat, Cabinet Office, 1997. Adviser: PricewaterhouseCoopers, 2004–; IDDAS, 2005–; non-exec. Director: Xafinity, 2005–; PIC Hldgs, 2006–; Chm., With-Profits Cttee, Norwich Union, 2007–. DUniv: Middlesex, 2001; Bradford, 2003. *Publication:* Brought to Account (report of Rayner Scrutiny on National Insurance Contributions), 1981; The Pale Yellow Amoeba (report of peer review of DCMS), 2000; articles in newspapers and magazines. *Recreations:* cooking, walking.

MONTAGU DOUGLAS SCOTT, family name of **Duke of Buccleuch**.

MONTAGU-DOUGLAS-SCOTT, Douglas Andrew; *see* Scott.

MONTAGU-POLLOCK, Sir Giles Hampden; *see* Pollock.

MONTAGU STUART WORTLEY, family name of **Earl of Wharncliffe**.

MONTAGUE, family name of **Baron Amwell**.

MONTAGUE, Sir Adrian (Alastair), Kt 2006; CBE 2001; Chairman: British Energy Group plc, since 2002; Michael Page International, since 2002; Infrastructure Investors Ltd, since 2005; Friends Provident plc, since 2005; *b* 28 Feb. 1948; *s* of late Charles Edward Montague and Olive Montague (*née* Jones); *m* 1st, 1970, Pamela Evans (marr. diss. 1982; she *d* 2000); one *s* two *d*; 2nd, 1986, Penelope Webb; one *s. Educ:* Trinity Hall, Cambridge (MA). Admitted Solicitor, 1973; with Linklaters & Paines, Solicitors, 1971–94 (Partner, 1979); Dir, Kleinwort Benson, subseq. Dresdner Kleinwort Benson, 1994–97; Chief Exec., Private Finance Initiative Task Force, HM Treasury, 1997–2000; Deputy Chairman: Partnerships UK, 2000–01; Network Rail, 2001–04; Chm., Cross London Rail Links Ltd, 2004–05. Non-executive Director: CellMark AB, 2000–; London First, 2007–; Skanska AB, 2007–. Mem., Strategic Rail Authy, 2000–01. *Address:* British Energy, 1 Sheldon Square, Paddington Central, Paddington, W2 6TT.

MONTAGUE, Robert Joel, CBE 1990; Founder, Chairman and Chief Executive, Axis Intermodal plc, since 1999; *b* 22 June 1948; *s* of late Robert and of Freda Montague; *m* 1972 (marr. diss.); two *s* one *d*; *m* 1990, Silke Kruse; two *s* one *d. Educ:* Bedstone Sch., Shropshire; Caius Sch., Brighton. Esso Petroleum Co. Ltd, 1964–69; Cables Montague Ltd, 1969–80; Founder, Chm. and Chief Exec., Tiphook plc, 1978–94. *Recreations:* children, fishing, opera, ballet.

MONTAGUE, Air Cdre Ruth Mary Bryceson; Director, Women's Royal Air Force, 1989–94; *b* 1 June 1939; *d* of late Griffith John Griffiths and Nancy Bryceson Griffiths (*née* Wrigley); *m* 1966, Roland Arthur Montague. *Educ:* Cavendish Grammar Sch. for Girls, Buxton; Bedford Coll., Univ. of London (BSc). Commissioned RAF, 1962; UK and Far East, 1962–66; UK, 1966–80; HQ Strike Command, 1980–83; RAF Staff Coll., 1983–86; Dep. Dir, WRAF, 1986–89. ADC to the Queen, 1989–94. Mem., Council and F and GP Cttee, RAF Benevolent Fund, 1994–2003; Chm., Adv. Bd, Princess Marina House Care Home, 2003–07. Mem. Council, Royal Holloway, London Univ., 1994–2003 (Hon. Fellow, 2006). FRSA 1993. *Recreations:* cookery, tapestry, gardening, swimming, world travel. *Address:* c/o National Westminster Bank, PO Box 873, 7 High Street, Marlow, Bucks SL7 1BZ. *Club:* Royal Air Force.

MONTAGUE, Sarah Anne Louise, (Mrs C. Brooke); Presenter, Today Programme, BBC Radio 4, since 2002; *b* 8 Feb. 1966; *d* of Col John and Mary Montague; *m* 2002, Christoph Brooke; three *d. Educ:* Blanchelande Coll., Guernsey; Univ. of Bristol (BSc Hons Biol.). County Natwest, 1987–89; Charles Tyrwhitt Shirts, 1990–91; Channel TV, 1991–94; Reuters, 1994–95; Sky News, 1995–97; BBC, 1997–: BBC News 24, 1997–2001; Hardtalk, 1999–; BBC Newsnight, 2000; BBC Breakfast, 2001–02. *Recreations:* musicals, diving, ski-ing, jigsaws, gardens. *Address: e-mail:* Sarah.Montague@bbc.co.uk.

MONTAGUE BROWNE, Sir Anthony (Arthur Duncan), KCMG 2000; CBE 1965 (OBE 1955); DFC 1945; HM Diplomatic Service, retired; a Managing Director, Gerrard and National PLC, 1970–83 (Director, 1967–70); *b* 8 May 1923; *s* of late Lt-Col A. D. Montague Browne, DSO, OBE, Bivia House, Goodrich, Ross-on-Wye, and Violet Evelyn (*née* Downes); *m* 1st, 1950, Noel Evelyn Arnold-Wallinger (marr. diss. 1970); one *d*; 2nd, 1970, Shelagh Macklin (*née* Mulligan). *Educ:* Stowe; Magdalen Coll., Oxford (William Doncaster Schol.); abroad. Pilot RAF, 1941–45. Entered Foreign (now Diplomatic) Service, 1946; Foreign Office, 1946–49; Second Sec., British Embassy, Paris, 1949–52; seconded as Private Sec. to Prime Minister, 1952–55; seconded as Private Sec. to Rt Hon. Sir Winston Churchill, 1955–65; Counsellor, Diplomatic Service, 1964; seconded to HM Household, 1965–67. Dir, Columbia (British) Productions, 1967–77. Trustee, Winston Churchill Memorial Trust; Vice-Pres., Univs Fedn for Animal Welfare, 1987–93 (Mem., Council, 1985–91). Freeman, City of London, 1987. Hon. DL Westminster Coll., Fulton, Missouri, 1988. *Publication:* Long Sunset: memoirs of Winston Churchill's last Private Secretary, 1995. *Address:* Podkin Wood, High Halden, Ashford, Kent TN26 3HS. *T:* (01580) 291902. *Clubs:* Boodle's, Pratt's.

MONTEAGLE OF BRANDON, 6th Baron *cr* 1839; **Gerald Spring Rice;** late Captain, Irish Guards; one of HM Body Guard, Hon. Corps of Gentlemen-at-Arms, 1978–96; *b* 5 July 1926; *s* of 5th Baron and Emilie de Kosenko (*d* 1981), *d* of Mrs Edward Brooks, Philadelphia, USA; *S* father, 1946; *m* 1949, Anne, *d* of late Col G. J. Brownlow, Ballywhite, Portaferry, Co. Down; one *s* three *d* (of whom two are twins). *Educ:* Harrow. Member: London Stock Exchange, 1958–76; Lloyd's, 1978–98. *Heir: s* Hon. Charles James Spring Rice [*b* 24 Feb. 1953; *m* 1987, Mary Teresa Glover; four *d*]. *Address:* Glenamara, Stradbally, Co. Waterford, Ireland. *Clubs:* Cavalry and Guards, Pratt's; Kildare Street and University (Dublin).

MONTEFIORE; *see* Sebag-Montefiore.

MONTEITH, Brian; Member, Scotland Mid and Fife, Scottish Parliament, 1999–2007 (C 1999–2005, Ind. 2005–07); *b* 8 Jan. 1958; *s* of Donald MacDonald Monteith and Doreen Campbell Monteith (*née* Purves); *m* 1984, Shirley Joyce Marshall; twin *s. Educ:* Portobello High Sch.; Heriot Watt Univ. Chm., Fedn of Conservative Students, 1982–83; Public Relations Consultant: Michael Forsyth Associates, London, 1983–84 and 1985–86; Dunseath Stephen Associates, Edinburgh, 1984–85; Man. Dir, Leith Communications Ltd, 1986–91; PR Dir, Forth Mktg Ltd, 1991–94; Scottish Dir, Communication Gp, 1994–96; sole proprietor and Consultant, Dunedin PR, 1996–99. Scottish Parliament:

Convener, Audit Cttee, 2003–07; Cons. spokesman on educn, culture and sport, 1999–2003, on finance and local govt, 2003–05. Mem., Tuesday Club. *Recreation:* football. *Club:* Duddingston Golf (Edinburgh).

MONTEITH, Prof. John Lennox, FRS 1971; FRSE 1972; Emeritus Professor of Environmental Physics, University of Nottingham, 1989; *b* 3 Sept. 1929; *s* of Rev. John and Margaret Monteith; *m* 1955, Elsa Marion Wotherspoon; four *s* one *d*. *Educ:* George Heriot's Sch.; Univ. of Edinburgh (BSc 1951; Hon. DSc 1989); Imperial Coll., London. DIC, PhD; FInstP, FIBiol. Mem. Physics Dept Staff, Rothamsted Experimental Station, 1954–67; Prof. of Environmental Physics, 1967–86, Dean of Faculty of Agricl Sci., 1985–86, Nottingham Univ.; Dir, Resource Management Programme, Internat. Crops Res. Inst. for the Semi-Arid Tropics, 1987–91 (Vis. Scientist, 1984); Sen. Vis. Fellow, NERC, 1992–94. Adjunct Prof., Depts of Agricl Engrg and Agronomy, Univ. of Florida, 1991–; Vis. Prof., Reading Univ., 1992–95; Hon. Prof., Edinburgh Univ., 1992–. Governor: Grassland Res. Inst., 1976–83; Silsoe Res. Inst., 1993–97. Vice Pres., British Ecological Soc., 1977–79; Pres., Royal Meteorol Soc., 1978–80; Fellowship Sec., RSE, 1997–99. Member: NERC, 1980–84; British Nat. Cttee for the World Climate Programme, 1980–86; Lawes Agricl Trust Cttee, 1983–86. Nat. Res. Council Senior Res. Associate, Goddard Space Flight Center, Md, USA, 1985; Clive Behrens Lectr, Leeds Univ., 1986; York Distinguished Lectr, Univ. of Florida, 1991. Buchan Prize, 1962, Symon's Meml Medal, 1995, RMetS; Solco Tromp Award, Internat. Soc. of Biometeorology, 1983; Rank Fund Nutrition Prize, 1989. *Publications:* Instruments for Micrometeorology (ed), 1972; Principles of Environmental Physics, 1973, 3rd edn (with M. H. Unsworth), 2007; (ed with L. E. Mount) Heat Loss from Animals and Man, 1974; (ed) Vegetation and the Atmosphere, 1975; (ed with C. Webb) Soil Water and Nitrogen, 1981; (ed with R. K. Scott and M. H. Unsworth) Resource Capture by Crops, 1994; papers on Micrometeorology and Crop Science in: Quarterly Jl of RMetSoc.; Jl Applied Ecology, etc. *Recreations:* music, photography. *Address:* 34 St Alban's Road, Edinburgh EH9 2LU.

MONTGOMERIE, family name of **Earl of Eglinton**.

MONTGOMERIE, Lord; Hugh Archibald William Montgomerie; Business Sales Consultant, Dell Computers, since 2004; *b* 24 July 1966; *s* and *heir* of 18th Earl of Eglinton and Winton, *qv*; *m* 1991, Sara Alexandra (marr. diss. 1998), *e d* of Niel Redpath; *m* 2001, Carol Anne Robinson, *yr d* of R. Donald Robinson Jr, Brentwood, Tenn; one *s* two *d*. *Educ:* Univ. of Edinburgh (MBA 2000). RN officer, 1988–92. Ops Manager, Gander & White Shipping Ltd, 1996–97. Intelligence Officer, 51 Highland Bde, 1997–98. Project Manager, ReServ Construction Co. Inc., 2000–04. Bd Mem., Soc. of Scottish Armigers. *Heir: s* Hon. Rhuridh Seton Archibald Montgomerie, *b* 4 March 2007. *Address: e-mail:* balhomie@bellsouth.net.

MONTGOMERIE, Colin Stuart, OBE 2005 (MBE 1998); professional golfer, since 1987; *b* Glasgow, 23 June 1963; *s* of James Montgomerie; *m* 1st, 1990, Eimear Wilson (marr. diss. 2004); one *s* two *d*; 2nd, 2008, Gaynor Knowles. *Educ:* Strathallen Sch., Perth; Leeds Grammar Sch.; Houston Baptist Univ., Texas. Wins include: Scottish Amateur Stroke-Play Championship, 1985; Scottish Amateur Championship, 1987; Portuguese Open, 1989; Scandinavian Masters, 1991, 1999, 2001; Dutch Open, 1993; Volvo Masters, 1993, (jtly) 2002; Spanish Open, 1994; English Open, 1994; German Open, 1994, 1995; Lancôme Trophy, 1995; Alfred Dunhill Cup, 1995; Million Dollar Challenge, 1996; European Masters, 1996; Dubai Desert Classic, 1996; Irish Open, 1996, 1997, 2001; King Hassan II Trophy, 1997; European Grand Prix, 1997; World Cup (Individual), 1997; World Championship of Golf, 1997; PGA Championship, 1998, 1999, 2000; German Masters, 1998; British Masters, 1998; Benson & Hedges Internat. Open, 1999; Loch Lomond Invitational, 1999; BMW Internat. Open, 1999; Cisco World Matchplay, 1999; French Open, 2000; Skins Game, USA, 2000; Australian Masters, 2001; TCL Classic, 2002; Macau Open, 2003; Caltex Masters, Singapore, 2004; Dunhill Links Championship, 2005; Hong Kong Open, 2006; European Open, 2007; World Cup (Team), 2007; 1st in European Order of Merit, annually, 1993–99, 2005. Member: Alfred Dunhill Cup team, 1988, 1991–2000; World Cup Team, 1988, 1991–93, 1997–99, 2006–07; Ryder Cup team, 1991, 1993, 1995, 1997, 1999, 2002, 2004, 2006; UBS Cup Team, 2003, 2004; Seve Trophy team, 2000, 2002, 2003, 2005, 2007. *Publications:* (with Lewine Mair) The Real Monty (autobiog.), 2002; The Thinking Man's Guide to Golf, 2003. *Address:* c/o IMG, McCormack House, Burlington Lane, W4 2TH.

MONTGOMERY, family name of **Viscount Montgomery of Alamein**.

MONTGOMERY OF ALAMEIN, 2nd Viscount *cr* 1946, of Hindhead; **David Bernard Montgomery,** CMG 2000; CBE 1975; Chairman, Baring Puma Fund, 1991–2002; *b* 18 Aug. 1928; *s* of 1st Viscount Montgomery of Alamein, KG, GCB, DSO, and Elizabeth (*d* 1937), *d* of late Robert Thompson Hobart, ICS; *S* father, 1976; *m* 1st, 1953, Mary Connell (marr. diss. 1967); one *s* one *d*; 2nd, 1970, Tessa, *d* of late Gen. Sir Frederick Browning, GCVO, KBE, CB, DSO, and Lady Browning, DBE (Dame Daphne du Maurier). *Educ:* Winchester; Trinity Coll., Cambridge (MA). Shell International, 1951–62; Dir, Yardley International, 1963–74; Man. Dir, Terimar Services (Overseas Trade Consultancy), 1974–99; Dir, Korn/Ferry International, 1977–93; Chm., Antofagasta (Chile) and Bolivia Railway Co., 1980–82; Dir, NEI, 1981–87. Mem., Exec. Cttee, British Gp, IPU, 1987–99; Deleg., OSCE Parly Assembly, 1991–2000. Elected crossbench Mem., H of L, 2005. Editorial Adviser, Vision Interamericana, 1974–94. Chm., Economic Affairs Cttee, Canning House, 1973–75; Pres., British Industrial Exhibition, Sao Paulo, 1974. Councillor, Royal Borough of Kensington and Chelsea, 1974–78. Hon. Consul, Republic of El Salvador, 1973–77. President: Anglo-Argentine Soc., 1977–87; Anglo-Belgian Soc., 1994–2006; Chairman: Hispanic and Luso Brazilian Council, 1978–80 (Pres., 1987–94); Brazilian Chamber of Commerce in GB, 1980–82; European Atlantic Gp, 1992–94 (Pres., 1994–97). Pres., Cambridge Univ. Engrs Assoc., 2001–06. Patron: D-Day and Normandy Fellowship, 1980–95; 8th Army Veterans Assoc., 1985–2002. President: Redgrave Theatre, Farnham, 1977–89; Restaurateurs Assoc. of GB, 1982–90 (Patron, 1991–99); Acad. of Food and Wine Service, 1995–98; Centre for International Briefing, Farnham Castle, 1985–2003. Pres., Amesbury Sch., 1992– (Gov., 1976–92). Gran Oficial: Orden Bernardo O'Higgins (Chile), 1989; Orden Libertador San Martin (Argentina), 1992; Orden Nacional Cruzeiro do Sul (Brazil), 1993; Orden de Isabel la Católica (Spain), 1993; Commander's Cross, Order of Merit (Germany), 1993; Order of Aztec Eagle (Mexico), 1994; Order of Leopold II (Belgium), 1997; Orden de San Carlos (Colombia), 1998; Orden del Libertador (Venezuela), 1999. *Publication:* (with Alistair Horne) The Lonely Leader: Monty 1944–45, 1994. *Heir: s* Hon. Henry David Montgomery [*b* 2 April 1954; *m* 1980, Caroline, *e d* of Richard Odey, Hotham Hall, York; three *d*]. *Address:* 2/97 Onslow Square, SW7 3LU. *T:* (020) 7589 8747. *Clubs:* Garrick, Canning.

MONTGOMERY, Alan Everard, CMG 1993; PhD; HM Diplomatic Service, retired; Member, Immigration Services Tribunal, since 2001; *b* 11 March 1938; *s* of Philip Napier Montgomery and Honor Violet Coleman (*née* Price); *m* 1st, 1960, Janet Barton (*d* 1994); one *s* one *d*; 2nd, 1999, Florence Belle Liebst. *Educ:* Royal Grammar Sch., Guildford; County of Stafford Training Coll. (Cert. of Educn); Birkbeck Coll., London (BA Hons, PhD). Served Middx Regt, 1957–59. Teacher, Staffs and ILEA, 1961–65; Lectr, Univ. of Birmingham, 1969–72; entered FCO, 1972; 1st Secretary: FCO, 1972–75; Dhaka, 1975–77; Ottawa, 1977–80; FCO, 1980–83; Counsellor GATT/UNCTAD, UKMIS Geneva, 1983–87; Counsellor, Consul-Gen. and Hd of Chancery, Jakarta, 1987–89; Head of Migration and Visa Dept, FCO, 1989–92; Ambassador to the Philippines, 1992–95; High Comr to Tanzania, 1995–98. Trade Policy Advr, Commonwealth Business Council, 1998–99. Mem., Fitness to Practice Cttee (formerly Professional Conduct Cttee), GMC, 2000–08; Lay Member: Immigration Services Tribunal, 2001–08; Complaints Commn, 2001–04, Professional Standards Cttee, 2004–05, Rules Cttee, 2006, Gen. Council of the Bar; Professional Conduct Panel, RICS, 2003–07; Professional Conduct Panel, British Assoc. for Counselling and Psychotherapy, 2003–08. Mem. Bd, FARM Africa, 1998–2001. Gp Leader, RCDS Africa tour, 2001–03. *Publications:* (contrib.) Lloyd George: 12 essays, ed A. J. P. Taylor, 1971; (contrib.) Commonwealth Banking Almanac, 1999; contrib. Cambridge Hist. Jl. *Recreations:* historic buildings, jazz, theatre, opera, gardening.

MONTGOMERY, Sir (Basil Henry) David, 9th Bt *cr* 1801, of Stanhope; CVO 2007; JP; Lord-Lieutenant of Perth and Kinross, 1996–2006; Chairman, Forestry Commission, 1979–89; *b* 20 March 1931; *s* of late Lt-Col H. K. Purvis-Montgomery, OBE, and of Mrs C. L. W. Purvis-Russell-Montgomery (*née* Maconochie Welwood); *S* uncle, 1964; *m* 1956, Delia, *o d* of Adm. Sir (John) Peter (Lorne) Reid, GCB, CVO; one *s* four *d* (and one *s* decd). *Educ:* Eton. National Service, Black Watch, 1949–51. Member: Nature Conservancy Council, 1973–79; Tayside Regional Authority, 1974–79. Comr, Mental Welfare Commn for Scotland, 1990–91. Trustee, Municipal Mutual Insurance Ltd, 1980–96. Hon. LLD Dundee, 1977. DL Kinross-shire, 1960, Vice-Lieutenant 1966–74; JP 1966; DL Perth and Kinross, 1975. *Heir: s* James David Keith Montgomery [*b* 13 June 1957; *m* 1983, Elizabeth, *e d* of late E. Lyndon Evans, Pentyrch, Mid-Glamorgan; one *s* one *d*. Served The Black Watch, RHR, 1976–86]. *Address:* Home Farm, Kinross KY13 8EU. *T:* (01577) 863416.

MONTGOMERY, Rear Adm. Charles Percival Ross, CBE 2006; Naval Secretary and Chief of Staff (Personnel) to Commander-in-Chief Fleet, since 2007; *b* 12 April 1955; *s* of Phillip Stuart Montgomery and Eileen Beryl Montgomery; *m* 1982, Adrienne Julie; three *s* one *d*. *Educ:* Univ. of Sheffield (BEng Hons 1976). CO HMS Beaver, 1991–93; Directorate of Defence Policy, 1993–95; Private Sec. to Sec. of State, 1995–97; Trng Dir, Naval Recruiting and Trng Agency, 1997–2000; Hd, NRTA Estate Rev. Team, 2000; Asst Dir of Naval Staff (Strategy), 2000–02; rcds, 2003; Dir Naval Personnel Strategy, 2003–06; Cdre Maritime Warfare Sch. and CO HMS Collingwood, 2006–07. Younger Brother, Trinity House, 2007–. *Recreations:* cricket, golf, Rugby, hockey, gardening, outdoor pursuits. *Address:* Mail Point 3.1, Leach Building, Whale Island, Portsmouth PO2 8BY. *Clubs:* Royal Navy of 1765 and 1785; St Cross Cricket (Winchester).

MONTGOMERY, Clare Patricia; QC 1996; a Recorder, since 2000; a Deputy High Court Judge, since 2003; a Judge of the Courts of Appeal of Jersey and Guernsey, since 2007; *b* 29 April 1958; *d* of Stephen Ross Montgomery and Ann Margaret Barlow; *m* 1991, Victor Melleney; two *d*. *Educ:* Millfield Sch.; UCL (LLB). Called to the Bar, Gray's Inn, 1980, Bencher, 2002. An Asst Recorder, 1999–2000. Mem., Supplementary Panel (Common Law), 1992–96. *Publication:* (ed) Archbold Criminal Pleading Evidence and Practice, annually, 1993–. *Address:* Matrix Chambers, Gray's Inn, WC1R 5LN. *T:* (020) 7404 3447.

MONTGOMERY, Sir David; *see* Montgomery, Sir B. H. D.

MONTGOMERY, David, CMG 1984; OBE 1972; Foreign and Commonwealth Office, 1987–91; *b* 29 July 1927; *s* of late David Montgomery and of Mary (*née* Walker Cunningham); *m* 1955, Margaret Newman; one *s* one *d*. Royal Navy, 1945–48. Foreign Office, 1949–52; Bucharest, 1952–53; FO, 1953–55; Bonn, 1955–58; Düsseldorf, 1958–61; Rangoon, 1961–63; Ottawa, 1963–64; Regina, Saskatchewan, 1964–65; FCO, 1966–68; Bangkok, 1968–72; Zagreb, 1973–76; FCO, 1976–79; Dep. High Comr to Barbados, 1980–84, also (non-resident) to Antigua and Barbuda, Dominica, Grenada, St Kitts and Nevis, St Lucia, St Vincent and the Grenadines, 1980–84; FCO, 1984–85. *Recreations:* golf, music (light and opera). *Address:* 8 Ross Court, Putney Hill, SW15 3NY.

MONTGOMERY, David John; Chairman, Mecom Group Plc (formerly Mecom UK Management Ltd), since 2000; *b* 6 Nov. 1948; *s* of William John and Margaret Jean Montgomery; *m* 1st, 1971, Susan Frances Buchanan Russell (marr. diss. 1987); 2nd, 1989, Heidi Kingstone (marr. diss. 1997); 3rd, 1997, Sophie Countess of Woolton, *d* of Baron Birdwood, *qv*; one *s*. *Educ:* Queen's University, Belfast (BA Politics/History). Sub-Editor, Daily Mirror, London/Manchester, 1973–78; Assistant Chief Sub-Editor, Daily Mirror, 1978–80; Chief Sub-Editor, The Sun, 1980; Asst Editor, Sunday People, 1982; Asst Editor, 1984, Editor, 1985–87, News of the World; Editor, Today, 1987–91 (Newspaper of the Year, 1988); Man. Dir, News UK, 1987–91; Chief Exec., 1991, Dir, 1991–, London Live Television; Chief Exec., Mirror Gp Newspapers, 1992–99. Director: Satellite Television PLC, 1986–91; News Group Newspapers, 1986–91; Caledonian Publishing Co. (Glasgow Herald & Times), 1991–92; Donohue Inc., 1992–95; Newspaper Publishing (The Independent, Independent on Sunday), 1994–98; Scottish Media Gp (formerly Scottish Television), 1995–99; Press Assoc., 1996–99; Chairman: Tri-mex Gp, 1999–2002; Yava, 2000–03; Africa Lakes plc, 2000–07; West 175 Media plc, 2002–06; Moyle Hldgs Ltd, 2003–08; NI Energy Hldgs, 2005–08; Berliner Verlag (Germany), 2005–; Media Gp Limburg (Netherlands), 2006–. Pres., Integrated Educn Fund Develt Bd (NI), 2000–. Member: QUB Foundn Bd, 2002–05; Campaign for Peace and Democratic Reconstruction for NI, 2002–; Chm., Team NI, 2003–08. *Address:* 15 Collingham Gardens, SW5 0HS.

MONTGOMERY, Sir Fergus; *see* Montgomery, Sir W. F.

MONTGOMERY, Hugh Bryan Greville; non-executive Director, Andry Montgomery group of companies (organisers, managers and consultants in exhibitions), since 1994 (Managing Director, 1952–88; Chairman, 1988–94); *b* 26 March 1929; *s* of Hugh Roger Greville Montgomery, MC, and Molly Audrey Montgomery, OBE (*née* Neele). *Educ:* Repton; Lincoln Coll., Oxford (MA PPE; Fleming Fellow, 1996). Founder member, Oxford Univ. Wine and Food Soc. Consultant and adviser on trade fairs and developing countries for UN; Consultant, Internat. Garden Festival, Liverpool, 1984. Chairman: Brit. Assoc. of Exhibn Organisers, 1970; Internat. Cttee, Amer. Nat. Assoc. of Exposition Managers, 1980–82 and 1990–93; British Exhibn Promotion Council, 1982–83; World Trade Centers Assoc., NY, 2000– (Founder, World Trade Center, Novosibirsk, Russia, 1993); Pres., Union des Foires Internat., 1994–97 (Vice Pres., 1987–94). Member: Adv. Bd, Hotel Inst. for Management, Montreux, 1986–2002; London Regl Cttee, CBI, 1987–90; BOTB, 1991–94. Mem. Council, Design and Industries Assoc., 1983–85. Chm. of Trustees of ECHO (Supply of Equipment to Charity Hosps Overseas), 1978–89; Chairman: Interbuild Fund, 1972–2006; The Building Museum, 1988–2000; British Architectural Library Trust, 1989–2000; Vice-Pres., Bldg Conservation Trust, 1992–94 (Vice-Chm., 1979–92); Trustee: The Cubitt Trust, 1982–99; Music for the World,

1990–92; Hon. Treas., Contemporary Art Soc., 1980–82; Councillor, Acad. of St Martin-in-the-Fields Concert Soc., 1988–2000. Member Executive Committee: CGLI, 1974–2003; Nat. Fund for Research into Crippling Diseases, 1970–92. Common Councilman, Dowgate Ward, City of London, 1999–2004. Mem. Court, Co. of World Traders, 1992–2003 (Master, 1995); Liveryman, 1952, Master, 1980–81, Co. of Tylers and Bricklayers (Trustee, Charitable and Pension Trusts, 1981–2000). Hon. FRIBA 2001; Hon. FCGI 2002. Hon. DHL Endicott Coll., Mass, 2003. Silver Jubilee Medal, 1977; Pro Cultura Hungaria Medal, 1991; Brooch, City of Utrecht, 1992; Gold Medal, Belgrade Fair, 1995; Leadership Award, Internat. Council for Caring Communities, UN, 2000. *Publications:* Industrial Fairs and Developing Countries (UNIDO), 1975; Going into Trade Fairs (UNCTAD/GATT), 1982; Exhibition Planning and Design, 1989 (Russian edn 1991, Chinese edn 2001); The Montgomery Painting Collection at Museum of Fine Art in Budapest, 1999; contrib. to Internat. Trade Forum (ITC, Geneva). *Recreation:* commissioning contemporary sculpture. *Address:* 9 Manchester Square, W1U 3PL. *T:* (020) 7886 3123; Snells Farm, Amersham Common, Bucks HP7 9QN. *Clubs:* Oxford and Cambridge, City Livery, Guildhall.

MONTGOMERY, John; Sheriff of South Strathclyde, Dumfries and Galloway, since 2003, at Ayr since 2005; *b* 17 Sept. 1951; *s* of Robert and Jessie Montgomery; *m* 1978, Susan Wilson Templeton; one *s* three *d. Educ:* Stevenston High Sch.; Ardrossan Acad.; Glasgow Univ. (LLB Hons). NP. Solicitor, 1976–2003. Temp. Sheriff, 1995–99; Sheriff (pt-time), 2000–03. *Recreations:* family, walking, gardening, travel. *Address:* Sheriff Court, Wellington Square, Ayr KA7 1DR.

MONTGOMERY, John Duncan; Member, Monopolies and Mergers Commission, 1989–95; *b* 12 Nov. 1928; *s* of Lionel Eric Montgomery and Katherine Mary Montgomery (*née* Ambler); *m* 1956, Pauline Mary Sutherland; two *d. Educ:* King's College Sch., Wimbledon; LSE (LLB, LLM). Admitted Solicitor 1951; Treasury Solicitor's Dept, 1960–68; Legal Adviser, Beecham Products, 1974–75; Head, Legal Div., Shell UK, 1975–88 and Company Sec., Shell UK, 1979–88. Former Chm., Youth Orgns, Merton. Freeman, City of London, 1987; Mem., Loriners' Co., 1988. JP SW London, 1985–98. *Recreations:* dinghy sailing, photography. *Address:* 6 White Lodge Close, Sutton, Surrey SM2 5TQ. *Clubs:* MCC; Surrey CC.

MONTGOMERY, John Matthew; Clerk of the Salters' Company, 1975–90; *b* 22 May 1930; *s* of Prof. George Allison Montgomery, QC, and Isobel A. (*née* Morison); *m* 1956, Gertrude Gillian Richards; two *s* one *d. Educ:* Rugby Sch.; Trinity Hall, Cambridge (MA). Various commercial appointments with Mobil Oil Corporation and First National City Bank, 1953–74. Member Council: Surrey Trust for Nature Conservation Ltd, 1965–89 (Chm., 1973–83; Vice-Pres., 1983–); Royal Soc. for Nature Conservation, 1980–89; Botanical Soc. of British Isles, 1991–95; Founder Mem., London Wildlife Trust, 1981–. Member, Executive Committee: Nat. Assoc. of Almshouses, 1980–91; Age Concern Gtr London, 1985–96 (Chm., 1988–91; Vice-Pres., 1996–2001). *Recreations:* various natural history interests. *Address:* 4 Rosehill, Claygate, Esher, Surrey KT10 0HL. *T:* (01372) 464780.

MONTGOMERY, Prof. Jonathan Robert; Professor of Health Care Law, University of Southampton, since 2001; Chairman: Advisory Committee on Clinical Excellence Awards, since 2005; Hampshire Primary Care Trust, since 2006; *b* 29 July 1962; *s* of Robert William Montgomery and Margaret Elizabeth Montgomery (*née* Exell); *m* 1986, Elsa Mary Wells Harnett; two *d. Educ:* King's College Sch., Wimbledon; Gonville and Caius Coll., Cambridge (BA 1983; LLM 1984). Lectr, 1984–98, Reader, 1998–2001, Univ. of Southampton. Non-exec. Dir, 1992–98, Chm., 1998–2001, Southampton Community Health Services NHS Trust; Chairman: W Hants NHS Trust, subseq. Hants Partnership NHS Trust, 2001–04; Hants and IoW Strategic HA, 2004–06. Member: Med. Ethics Cttee, BMA, 2003–; Ethics Adv. Gp to Care Records Develt Bd, NHS Prog. for IT, 2004–. Chm., Winchester Diocesan Council for Social Responsibility, 1997–98; Lay Examining Chaplain for Bishop of Portsmouth, 2003–. Patron, CISters (Childhood Incest Survivors). General Editor: (with R. Sax) Butterworths Family Law Service, 1996–; Butterworths Family and Child Law Bulletin, 1997–2006. Hon. FRCPCH 2005. *Publications:* Health Care Law, 1997, 2nd edn 2003; (with P. Alderson) Health Care Choices: making decisions with children, 1996; numerous book chapters and contribs to learned jls. *Recreations:* family and friends, active member of the Church of England, church youth work. *Address:* School of Law, University of Southampton, Highfield, Southampton SO17 1BJ; *e-mail:* J.R.Montgomery@soton.ac.uk.

MONTGOMERY, Joseph, CB 2006; Director General, Places and Communities, Department for Communities and Local Government, since 2006; *b* 1 Feb. 1961. *Educ:* Becket Sch., Nottingham; Aston Univ. (BSc 1983). Asst Sec., Cadbury Trust, 1986–89; Leader, Deptford Task Force, DTI, 1989–92; Chief Exec., Deptford City Challenge, 1992–94; Dir, Leisure, Economy and Envmt, 1994–99, Exec. Dir for Regeneration, 1999–2001, Lewisham BC; Dir Gen., Neighbourhood Renewal Unit, DTLR, then at ODPM, subseq. Tackling Disadvantage Gp, ODPM, then at DCLG, 2001–06. *Address:* Department for Communities and Local Government, Eland House, Bressenden Place, SW1E 5DU.

MONTGOMERY, Sir (William) Fergus, Kt 1985; *b* 25 Nov. 1927; *s* of late William Montgomery and Winifred Montgomery; *m* Joyce, *d* of George Riddle. *Educ:* Jarrow Grammar Sch.; Bede Coll., Durham. Served in Royal Navy, 1946–48; Schoolmaster, 1950–59. Nat. Vice-Chm. Young Conservative Organisation, 1954–57, National Chm., 1957–58; contested (C) Consett Division, 1955; MP (C): Newcastle upon Tyne East, 1959–64; Brierley Hill, April 1967–Feb. 1974; contested Dudley W, Feb. 1974; MP (C) Altrincham and Sale, Oct. 1974–1997. PPS to Sec. of State for Educn and Science, 1973–74, to Leader of the Opposition, 1975–76. Chm., H of C Cttee of Selection, 1992–97; Mem. Exec. Cttee, British American Parly Gp, 1991–97. Mem. Executive, CPA, 1983–97. Councillor, Hebburn UDC, 1950–58. Has lectured extensively in the USA. *Recreations:* bridge, reading, going to theatre. *Address:* 181 Ashley Gardens, Emery Hill Street, SW1P 1PD. *T:* (020) 7834 7905; 6 Groby Place, Altrincham, Cheshire WA14 4AL. *T:* (0161) 928 1983.

MONTGOMERY CAMPBELL, Philip Henry; *see* Campbell.

MONTGOMERY CUNINGHAME, Sir John Christopher Foggo, 12th Bt *cr* 1672, of Corsehill, Ayrshire and Kirktonholm, Lanarkshire; Director, Primentia Inc., and other companies; *b* 24 July 1935; 2nd *s* of Col Sir Thomas Montgomery-Cuninghame, 10th Bt, DSO (*d* 1945), and of Nancy Macaulay (his 2nd wife), *d* of late W. Stewart Foggo, Aberdeen (she *m* 2nd, 1946, Johan Frederik Christian Killander); *b* of Sir Andrew Montgomery-Cuninghame, 11th Bt; *S* brother, 1959; *m* 1964, Laura Violet, *d* of Sir Godfrey Nicholson, 1st Bt; three *d. Educ:* Fettes; Worcester Coll., Oxford (MA). 2nd Lieut, Rifle Brigade (NS), 1955–56; Lieut, London Rifle Brigade, TA, 1956–59. *Recreation:* fishing. *Heir:* none. *Address:* The Old Rectory, Brightwalton, Newbury, Berks RG20 7BL.

MONTI, Dr Mario; Chairman, Brussels European and Global Economic Laboratory, since 2005; *b* 19 March 1943; *m*; two *c. Educ:* Bocconi Univ. (Dr); Yale Univ. Bocconi University, Italy: Asst, 1965–69; Prof. of Monetary Theory and Policy, 1971–85; Prof. of Economics and Dir, Economics Inst., 1985–94; Founder, Paolo Baffi Centre for Monetary and Financial Economics, 1985; Rector, 1989–94, Pres., 1994, Innocenzo Gasparini Inst. of Economic Res. Mem., European Commn, 1995–2004. *Address:* (office) 33 Rue de la Charité, Box 4, 1210 Brussels, Belgium.

MONTLAKE, Henry Joseph; solicitor; Senior Partner, H. Montlake & Co., 1954–2000; a Recorder of the Crown Court, 1983–98; *b* 22 Aug. 1930; *s* of Alfred and Hetty Montlake; *m* 1952, Ruth Rochelle Allen; four *s. Educ:* Ludlow Grammar Sch., Ludlow; London Univ. (LLB 1951). Law Soc.'s final exam., 1951; admitted Solicitor, 1952. National Service, commnd RASC, 1953. Dep. Registrar of County Courts, 1970–78; Dep. Circuit Judge and Asst Recorder, 1978–83. Pres., West Essex Law Soc., 1977–78. Mem. Ethics Cttee, BUPA Roding Hosp. IVF Unit, 1991–2000. Chm., Ilford Round Table, 1962–63; Pres., Assoc. of Jewish Golf Clubs and Socs, 1984–94 (Sec., 1977–84). Gov., Redbridge Coll. of Further Educn, 1991–92. *Recreations:* golf, The Times crossword, people, travel. *Address:* Chelston, 5 St Mary's Avenue, Wanstead, E11 2NR. *T:* (020) 8989 7228, *Fax:* (020) 8989 5173; *e-mail:* henry@chelston.org. *Clubs:* Dyrham Park Golf; Abridge Golf (Chm. 1964, Captain 1965).

MONTREAL, Archbishop of, (RC), since 1990; **His Eminence Cardinal Jean-Claude Turcotte;** *b* 26 June 1936. Ordained priest, 1959; consecrated bishop, 1982; Cardinal, 1994. *Address:* Office of the Archbishop, 2000 Sherbrooke Street West, Montreal, QC H3H 1G4, Canada.

MONTREAL, Bishop of, since 2004; **Rt Rev. Barry Bryan Clarke;** *b* Montreal, 10 Oct. 1952; *m* 1997, Leslie James; one *d* from previous marriage. *Educ:* McGill Univ. (BTh 1977); Montreal Theol Coll. (Dip. Min. 1978). Ordained 1978; Asst Curate, St Matthias, Westmount, 1978–80; Rector: Trinity Church, St Bruno, 1980–84; St Michael and All Angels, 1984–93; St Paul's, Lachine, 1993–2004. Regional Dean: Ste Anne, 1988–92; Pointe Claire, 1997–2003; Archdeacon, St Lawrence, 2003–04. *Address:* (office) 1444 Union Avenue, Montreal, QC H3A 2B8, Canada. *T:* (514) 8436577, *Fax:* (514) 8433221; *e-mail:* bishops.office@montreal.anglican.ca.

MONTROSE, 8th Duke of, *cr* 1707; **James Graham;** Lord Graham 1445; Earl of Montrose 1505; Bt (NS) 1625; Marquis of Montrose 1644; Duke of Montrose, Marquis of Graham and Buchanan, Earl of Kincardine, Viscount Dundaff, Lord Aberuthven, Mugdock, and Fintrie 1707; Earl and Baron Graham (Eng.) 1722; *b* 6 April 1935; *e s* of 7th Duke of Montrose, and Isobel Veronica (*d* 1990), *yr d* of Lt-Col T. B. Sellar, CMG, DSO; *S* father, 1992; *m* 1970, Catherine Elizabeth MacDonell, *d* of late Captain N. A. T. Young, and of Mrs Young, Ottawa; two *s* one *d. Educ:* Loretto. Elected Mem., H of L, 1999; Opposition Whip, H of L, 2001–; Opposition spokesman on Scottish affairs, 2001–. Captain, Royal Company of Archers (Queen's Body Guard for Scotland), 2005– (Mem., 1965–). Area Pres., Scottish NFU, 1986 (Mem. Council, 1981–86 and 1987–90); Pres., RHAS, 1997–98. OStJ 1978. *Heir: s* Marquis of Graham, *qv. Address:* Auchmar, Drymen, Glasgow G63 0AG. *T:* (01360) 660307.

MONTY, Simon Trevor; QC 2003; *b* 9 Dec. 1959; *s* of Cyril Monty and Gina (*née* Dixon); *m* 1985, Susan Andrea Goldwater; two *s* one *d. Educ:* Alleyn's Sch., Dulwich; Manchester Univ. (LLB Hons 1981). Called to the Bar, Middle Temple, 1982, Bencher, 2004; in practice as barrister, 1983–, specialising in professional negligence litigation. *Publication:* (contrib.) Jackson & Powell's Professional Liability Precedents, 2000. *Recreations:* ski-ing, music, walking. *Address:* Four New Square, Lincoln's Inn, WC2A 3RJ. *T:* (020) 7822 2000, *Fax:* (020) 7822 2001; *e-mail:* s.monty@4newsquare.com.

MOODY, David Barker; Lord-Lieutenant of South Yorkshire, since 2004; Chairman: J. Shipman Properties Ltd, since 1998; South Yorkshire Investment Fund, since 2001; *b* 7 April 1940; *s* of Norman William Barker Moody and Dorothy Moody (*née* Beetham); *m* 1966, Carolyn Susan Lindop Green; one *s* three *d. Educ:* Worksop Coll.; Pembroke Coll., Oxford (MA Mod. Hist.); London Business Sch. (Sloan Fellow 1971). Asst Master, Sussex House Prep. Sch., 1959–60; graduate apprentice, United Steel Cos Ltd, 1963–64; Samuel Fox & Company Limited: Mgt Develt Officer, 1964–70; Manager Billet Finishing, 1970–72; Sales Manager, 1972–75; Commercial Dir, Spartan Redheugh Ltd, 1975–81; Chm. and Man. Dir, Spartan Sheffield Ltd, 1981–99. President: Sheffield Chamber of Commerce and Industry, 1998–99; S Yorks Community Fund, 2004–; Army Benevolent Fund S Yorks, 2004–; Wentworth Castle and Stainborough Park Heritage Trust, 2004–; S and W Yorks, Order of St John, 2004–; Friends of Sheffield Cathedral, 2006– (Vice-Pres., 2004–06); Vice-Pres., S and W Yorks, RBL, 2004–. Governor: Worksop Coll., 1975– (Chm. of Govs, 1992–2001); Ranby House Sch., 1975– (Chm. of Govs, 1992–2001); Fellow and Dir, Woodard Schs Ltd, 1981–2005. High Sheriff, S Yorks, 2003–04. *Recreations:* Burgundy, grandchildren, landscape, Romanesque, Schubert. *Address:* Ivas Wood, Round Green Lane, Stainborough, Barnsley, Yorks S75 3EL. *T:* (01226) 205325, *Fax:* (01226) 785420; *e-mail:* davidmoody@stainborough.freeserve.co.uk. *Club:* Royal Over-Seas League.

MOODY, Ian Charles Hugh, OBE 1996; DL; Commissioner-in-Chief, St John Ambulance, 1991–95; *b* 25 April 1928; *s* of William Thomas Charles Moody and Roberta (*née* Baxter); *m* 1952, Angela de Lisle Carey (*d* 2007); one *s* two *d. Educ:* Cheltenham Coll.; RMA, Sandhurst. Served RWF, 1947–50. Industrial relations and personnel appointments with: Compania Shell de Venezuela, 1951–54; Shell Trinidad Ltd, 1954–59; Shell BP Nigeria Ltd, 1959–60; PT Shell Indonesia, 1960–64; Pakistan Shell Oil Ltd, 1964–68; Personnel Manager, Shell Nigeria Ltd, 1968–72; Employee Relations, Shell Internat. Petroleum Co. Ltd, 1974–76; Personnel Manager, Shell Internat. Trading Co., 1976–83; retd 1983. St John Ambulance, Devon: Comr, 1983–88; Comdr, 1988–91; Chm., 1995–98. Chm., E Devon Cons. Assoc., 1997–2000. FCIPD. DL Devon, 1991. KStJ 1991. *Recreations:* cricket, sailing, gardening. *Address:* The Queen Anne House, The Strand, Lympstone, Devon EX8 5JW. *T:* (01395) 263189. *Club:* MCC.

MOODY-STUART, Sir Mark, KCMG 2000; PhD; FGS; FRGS; Director, Shell Transport and Trading Company plc, 1991–2005 (Chairman, 1997–2001); Chairman, Anglo American plc, since 2002; *b* 15 Sept. 1940; *s* of Sir Alexander Moody-Stuart, OBE, MC and Judith (*née* Henzell); *m* 1964, Judith McLeavy; three *s* one *d. Educ:* Shrewsbury Sch.; St John's Coll., Cambridge (MA, PhD; Hon. Fellow, 2001). Joined Shell, 1966; worked for various Shell companies in: Holland, 1966; Spain, 1967; Oman, 1968; Brunei, 1968–72; Australia, 1972–76; UK, 1977–78; Brunei, 1978–79; Nigeria, 1979–82; Turkey, 1982–86; Malaysia, 1986–89; Holland, 1990–94; Gp Man. Dir, 1991–2001, Chm., Cttee of Man. Dirs, 1998–2001, Royal Dutch/Shell Group. Director: HSBC Hldgs plc, 2001–; Accenture, 2001–; Saudi Aramco, 2007–. Co-Chm., G-8 Task Force on Renewable Energy, 2000–01. Member: UN Sec.-Gen's Adv. Council on Global Compact, 2001–04; Bd, Global Reporting Initiative, 2001–07; UN Global Compact Bd, 2006– (Vice Chm., 2007–); Chm., Global Compact Foundn, 2006–. Vice-Pres., 1997–2001, Pres., 2001–, Liverpool Sch. of Tropical Medicine. Gov., Nuffield Hosps, 2001–08. Mem., Soc. of

Petroleum Engrs, 1990–; FGS 1966 (Pres., 2002–04); FInstPet 1997 (Cadman Medal, 2001); FRGS 1999. Hon. FIChemE 1997. Hon. DBA Robert Gordon, 2000; Hon. LLD Aberdeen, 2004; Hon. DSc London, 2007. *Publications:* papers in Geol Mag., Jl of Sedimentary Petrology, Bull. Amer. Assoc. Petrology and Geol., Norsk Polarinstitut, Proceedings of Geologists' Assoc., Corporate Environmental Strategy. *Recreations:* sailing, travel, reading. *Address:* 9 Gun House, 122 Wapping High Street, E1W 2NL. *Clubs:* Travellers, Cruising Association.

MOOLLAN, Sir (Abdool) Hamid (Adam), Kt 1986; QC (Mauritius) 1976; Chairman, Law Reform Commission, Mauritius, 1996–2003; *b* 10 April 1933; *s* of Adam Sulliman Moollan and Khatija Moollan; *m* 1966, Sara Sidiot; three *s. Educ:* Soonee Surtee Musalman Society Aided School; Royal College School; King's College London (LLB); Faculté de Droit, Univ. de Paris. Called to the Bar, Middle Temple, 1956; joined Mauritian Bar, 1960. Chm., Bar Council, Mauritius, 1970, 1993. Mem., Presidential Commn for reform of judicial and legal system, Mauritius, 1997. *Recreations:* tennis, horse racing, hunting, fishing. *Address:* (home) Railway Road, Phoenix, Mauritius. *T:* 6864983; (chambers) 43 Sir William Newton Street, Port-Louis, Mauritius. *T:* 2083881. *Clubs:* Royal Over-Seas League; Mauritius Gymkhana, Mauritius Turf.

MOOLLAN, Sir Cassam (Ismael), Kt 1982; Chief Justice, Supreme Court of Mauritius, 1982–88, retired; Acting Governor-General, several occasions in 1984, 1985, 1986, 1987, 1988; Commander-in-Chief of Mauritius, 1984; *b* 26 Feb. 1927; *s* of Ismael Mahomed Moollan and Fatimah Nazroo; *m* 1954, Rassoulbibie Adam Moollan; one *s* two *d. Educ:* Royal Coll., Port Louis and Curepipe; London Sch. of Econs and Pol. Science (LLB 1950). Called to the Bar, Lincoln's Inn, 1951. Private practice, 1951–55; Dist Magistrate, 1955–58; Crown Counsel, 1958–64; Sen. Crown Counsel, 1964–66; Solicitor Gen., 1966–70; QC (Mauritius) 1969; Puisne Judge, Supreme Court, 1970; Sen. Puisne Judge, 1978. Editor, Mauritius Law Reports, 1982–84. Chevalier, Légion d'Honneur (France), 1986. *Recreations:* bridge, Indian classical and semi-classical music. *Address:* Chambers, 43 Sir William Newton Street, Port Louis, Mauritius. *T:* 2120794, 2083881, *Fax:* 2088351; 22 Hitchcock Avenue, Quatre Bornes, Mauritius. *T:* 4546949.

MOON, Angus; *see* Moon, P. C. A.

MOON, Brenda Elizabeth, FRSE; FCLIP; University Librarian, University of Edinburgh, 1980–96; *b* 11 April 1931; *d* of Clement Alfred Moon and Mabel (*née* Berks). *Educ:* King Edward's Grammar Sch. for Girls, Camp Hill, Birmingham; St Hilda's Coll., Oxford (MA); MPhil Leeds; PhD Hull 2002. FCLIP (FLA 1958); FRSE 1992. Asst Librarian, Univ. of Sheffield, 1955–62; Sub-Librarian, 1962–67, Dep. Librarian, 1967–79, Univ. of Hull. Curator, Royal Soc. of Edinburgh, 2002–05. *Publications:* Mycenaean Civilisation: publications since 1935, 1957; Mycenaean Civilisation: publications 1956–1960, 1961; Periodicals for South-East Asian Studies: a union catalogue of holdings in British and selected European libraries, 1979; More Usefully Employed: Amelia B. Edwards (biography), 2006; articles in prof. and other jls. *Recreations:* travel and the history of travel. *Address:* 4 Cobden Road, Edinburgh EH9 2BJ. *T:* (0131) 667 0071.
See also M. M. Moon.

MOON, Madeleine; MP (Lab) Bridgend, since 2005; *b* 27 March 1950; *d* of Albert Edward and Hilda Ironside; *m* Stephen John Moon; one *s. Educ:* Madeley Coll. (Cert Ed 1971); Keele Univ. (BEd 1972); University Coll., Cardiff (CQSW, DipSW 1980). Social Services Directorate: Mid Glamorgan CC, 1980–96; City and Co. of Swansea, 1996–2002; Care Standards Inspectorate for Wales, 2002–05. Member (Lab): Porthcawl Town Council, 1990–2000 (Mayor, 1992–93, 1995–96); Ogwr BC, 1991–96; Bridgend CBC, 1995–2005. *Recreations:* travel, theatre, films, reading, walking our dog, shopping, looking for things I have put in a safe place! *Address:* House of Commons, SW1A 0AA; *e-mail:* moonm@parliament.uk.

MOON, Mary Marjorie; Head Mistress, Manchester High School for Girls, 1983–94; *b* 28 Sept. 1932; *d* of Clement Alfred Moon and Mabel Moon (*née* Berks). *Educ:* King Edward's Grammar Sch. for Girls, Camp Hill, Birmingham; Univ. of Manchester (BA Hons, MEd); Univ. of London Inst. of Education (PGCE). Asst English Teacher, 1955–59, Head of English Dept, 1959–63, Orme Girls' Sch., Newcastle-under-Lyme; Head of English, Bolton Sch. (Girls' Div.), 1963–71; Head Mistress, Pate's Grammar Sch. for Girls, Cheltenham, 1971–83. Mem. Court, Univ. of Manchester, 1985–2000. *Recreations:* photography, sketching, travel. *Address:* 18 South Parade, Bramhall, Stockport, Cheshire SK7 3BH.
See also B. E. Moon.

MOON, Michael, RA 1994; artist; *b* 9 Nov. 1937; *s* of Donald and Marjorie Moon; *m* 1977, Anjum Khan; two *s. Educ:* Chelsea Sch. of Art; RCA. One-man shows include: Tate Gall., 1976; Waddington Galls, London, 1969, 1970, 1972, 1978, 1984, 1986, 1992; Macquarie Galls, Sydney, 1982; Christine Abrahams Gall., Melbourne, 1983; Pace Prints, NY, 1987; Kass/Meridien Gall., Chicago, 1988; Linda Goodman Gall., Johannesburg, 1994; Alan Cristea Gall., 1996; Serge Sirocco Gall., San Francisco, 1997; work in public collections include: Tate Gall.; Australian Nat. Gall., Canberra; Mus. of WA, Perth; Art Gall. of NSW, Sydney; Power Inst., Sydney; Walker Art Gall., Liverpool; Birmingham City Art Gall.; V&A Mus. *Address:* 61 Kirkwood Road, SE15 3XU. *T:* (020) 7639 6651.

MOON, Sir Peter Wilfred Giles Graham-, 5th Bt *cr* 1855; *b* 24 Oct. 1942; *s* of Sir (Arthur) Wilfred Graham-Moon, 4th Bt, and 2nd wife, Doris Patricia, *yr d* of Thomas Baron Jobson, Dublin; *S* father, 1954; *m* 1st, 1967, Sarah Gillian Chater (marr. diss.) (formerly *m* Major Antony Chater; marr. diss. 1966), *e d* of late Lt-Col Michael Lyndon Smith, MC, MB, BS, and Mrs Michael Smith; two *s*; 2nd, 1993, Mrs Terry de Vries, Cape Town, S Africa. *Recreations:* shooting, golf. *Heir: s* Rupert Francis Wilfred Graham-Moon, *b* 29 April 1968. *Club:* Royal Cork Yacht.

MOON, (Philip Charles) Angus, QC 2006; barrister; *b* 17 Sept. 1962; *s* of Charles Moon and Liggy Quyke; *m* 1996, Florence; one *s* three *d. Educ:* King's Coll., Taunton; Christ's Coll., Cambridge (BA 1984). Called to the Bar, Middle Temple, 1986; in practice as a barrister, 1986–, specialising in medical and employment law. Editor, Life Sciences Law Medical, 1998–. *Publications:* medical law reports. *Recreations:* novels of Elmore Leonard, digging up small trees. *Address:* 3 Serjeants' Inn, EC4Y 1BQ. *T:* (020) 7427 5000.

MOON, Richard John, PhD; HM Diplomatic Service; Ambassador to Latvia, since 2007; *b* 3 Jan. 1959; *s* of late John Frederick Moon and Caroline Bowden Moon; *m* 1987, Sandra Sheila Francis Eddis; one *s* one *d. Educ:* Chace Sch., Enfield; Wadham Coll., Oxford (MA); London Sch. of Econs (PhD 1994). Joined FCO, 1983; Second Sec., Jakarta, 1984–88; First Sec., FCO, 1988–93, Rome, 1993–97; FCO, 1997–99; UK Mission to UN, NY, 1999–2005; UK Delegn to OECD, Paris, 2005–07. *Recreations:* history of art, marathon running. *Address:* c/o Foreign and Commonwealth Office, King Charles Street, SW1A 2AH.

MOON, Sir Roger, 6th Bt *cr* 1887, of Copsewood, Stoke, Co. Warwick; retired; *b* 17 Nov. 1914; *s* of Jasper Moon (*d* 1975) (*g g s* of 1st Bt) and Isabel (*née* Logan); *S* brother,

1988, but his name does not appear on the Official Roll of the Baronetage; *m* 1950, Meg (*d* 2000), *d* of late Arthur Mainwaring Maxwell, DSO, MC; three *d. Educ:* Sedbergh. Coffee planter, Kenya, 1933–35; Rubber planter, Malaya, 1939–41 and 1946–63; Oil palms planter, Malaya, 1963–67. *Recreation:* gardening. *Heir: b* Humphrey Moon [*b* 9 Oct. 1919; *m* 1st, 1955, Diana Hobson (marr. diss. 1964); two *d*; 2nd, 1964, Elizabeth Anne (*d* 1994), *d* of late George Archibald Drummond Angus and *widow* of H. J. Butler; one *d*]. *Address:* The Barn House, Wykey, Ruyton-XI-Towns, Shropshire SY4 1JA. *T:* (01939) 260354.

MOONEY, Bel; writer and broadcaster; *b* 8 Oct. 1946; *d* of Edward and Gladys Mooney; *m* 1st, 1968, Jonathan Dimbleby, *qv* (marr. diss. 2006); one *s* one *d*; 2nd, 2007, Robin Allison-Smith. *Educ:* Trowbridge Girls' High School; University College London (1st cl. Hons, Eng. Lang. and Lit., 1969; Fellow 1994). Freelance journalist, 1970–79; columnist: Daily Mirror, 1979–80; Sunday Times, 1982–83; The Listener, 1984–86; The Times, 2005–07; Daily Mail, 2007–; Ed., Proof mag. (SW Arts), 2000–01; *television:* interview series: Mothers By Daughters, 1983; The Light of Experience Revisited, 1984; Fathers By Sons, 1985; Grief, 1995; various series for BBC Radio 4 (Sandford St Martin Trust award for Devout Sceptics, 1994) and films for BBC TV and Channel 4. Mem. Bd, Friends of Gt Ormond St, 1994–98. Governor, Bristol Polytechnic, 1989–91. Hon. Fellow, Liverpool John Moores Univ., 2002. Hon. DLitt Bath, 1998. *Publications: novels:* The Windsurf Boy, 1983; The Anderson Question, 1985; The Fourth of July, 1988; Lost Footsteps, 1993; Intimate Letters, 1997; The Invasion of Sand, 2005; *for children:* Liza's Yellow Boat, 1980; I Don't Want To!, 1985; The Stove Haunting, 1986; I Can't Find It!, 1988; It's Not Fair!, 1989; A Flower of Jet, 1990; But You Promised!, 1990; Why Not?, 1990; I Know!, 1991; The Voices of Silence, 1994; I'm Scared!, 1994; I Wish!, 1995; The Mouse with Many Rooms, 1995; Why Me?, 1996; The Green Man, 1997; Joining the Rainbow, 1997; I'm Bored, 1997; I Don't Want to Say Yes!, 1998; You Promised You Wouldn't be Cross, 1999; It's Not My Fault, 1999; So What?, 2002; Kitty's Big Ideas, 2002; Kitty's Friends, 2003; Mr Tubs is Lost, 2004; Who Loves Mr Tubs?, 2006; Big Dog Bonnie, 2007; Best Dog Bonnie, 2007; Bad Dog Bonnie, 2008; Brave Dog Bonnie, 2008; *miscellaneous:* The Year of the Child, 1979; Differences of Opinion (collected journalism), 1984; (with Gerald Scarfe) Father Kismass and Mother Claws, 1985; Bel Mooney's Somerset, 1989; From This Day Forward (Penguin Book of Marriage), 1989; Perspectives for Living, 1992; Devout Sceptics, 2003; (ed) Mothers and Daughters, 2006. *Recreations:* reading, riding pillion on a Harley-Davidson, playing with my dog. *Address:* c/o Conville and Walsh Ltd, 2 Ganton Street, W1F 7QL. *T:* (020) 7287 3030.

MOONIE, family name of **Baron Moonie.**

MOONIE, Baron *cr* 2005 (Life Peer), of Bennochy in Fife; **Lewis George Moonie;** *b* 25 Feb. 1947; *m* 1971, Sheila Ann Burt; two *s. Educ:* Grove Acad., Dundee; St Andrews Univ. (MB ChB 1970); Edinburgh Univ. (MSc 1981). MRCPsych 1979; MFCM 1984. Psychiatrist, Ciba-Geigy, Switzerland, and Organon Internat., Netherlands; Sen. Registrar (Community Medicine), subseq. Community Medicine Specialist, Fife Health Bd. Mem., Fife Regl Council, 1982–86. MP (Lab and Co-op) Kirkcaldy, 1987–2005. Opposition front bench spokesman on technology, 1990–92, on science and technol., 1992–97, and on industry, 1994–97; Parly Under-Sec. of State, 2000–03, and Minister for Veterans Affairs, 2001–03, MoD. Member: Social Services Select Cttee, 1987–89; Treasury Select Cttee, 1998–2000; H of C Commn, 1997; H of L Select Cttee on Econ. Affairs, 2007–. Chm., Finance and Services Cttee, 1997–2000. *Address:* House of Lords, SW1A 0PW.

MOONMAN, Eric, OBE 1991; Chairman, Essex Radio Group, 1991–2002; Visiting Professor of Management and Information, City University, since 1992; Adviser on Counter-Terrorism, Independent Television News and Independent Radio News, since 2001; *b* 29 April 1929; *s* of late Borach and Leah Moonman; *m* 1st, 1962, Jane (marr. diss. 1991); two *s* one *d*; 2nd, 2001, Gillian Louise Mayer. *Educ:* Rathbone Sch., Liverpool; Christ Church, Southport; Univ. of Liverpool (DipSocSc 1955; Sen. Hon. Fellow, 2005); Univ. of Manchester (MSc 1967). Human Relations Adviser, British Inst. of Management, 1956–62; Sen. Lectr in Industrial Relations, SW Essex Technical Coll., 1962–64; Sen. Research Fellow in Management Sciences, Univ. of Manchester, 1964–66. MP (Lab) Billericay, 1966–70, Basildon, Feb. 1974–1979; PPS to Minister without Portfolio and Sec. of State for Educn, 1967–68. Chairman: All-Party Parly Mental Health Cttee, 1967–70 and 1974–79; New Towns and Urban Affairs Cttee, Parly Labour Party, 1974–79. Dir, Centre for Contemporary Studies, 1979–90; Dir, Nat. Hist. Mus. Develt Trust, 1990–91. Sen. Vice-Pres., Bd of Deputies, 1985–91, 1994–99; Pres., Zionist Fedn, 2001– (Chm., 1975–80). Member: Stepney Council, 1961–65 (Leader, 1964–65); Tower Hamlets Council, 1964–67. Chm., Islington HA, 1981–90; Mem., Bloomsbury and Islington HA, 1990–92; Chair, City of Liverpool Continuing Health Care Rev., 1996–. Mem. Adv. Council, Centre for Counter-Terrorism, Washington, 1998–. Mem., Council, Toynbee Hall Univ. Settlement, 1960–95 (Chm., Finance Cttee); Governor, BFI, 1974–80. Consultant, Internat. Red Cross (Africa), 1991–95. Trustee: Balfour Diamond Jubilee Trust, 1985–; Winnicott Trust, 1990–93. FRSA. *Publications:* The Manager and the Organization, 1961; Employee Security, 1962; European Science and Technology, 1968; Communication in an Expanding Organization, 1970; Reluctant Partnership, 1970; Alternative Government, 1984; (ed) The Violent Society, 1987; Learning to Live in the Violent Society, 2006. *Recreations:* football (Chm., Everton Supporters' Club London Assoc., 1992–), theatre, music, cinema. *Address:* 1 Beacon Hill, N7 9LY.

MOOR, Jonathan Edward, FCA; Director of Airports Strategy, Department for Transport, since 2006; *b* 23 June 1964; *s* of late Rev. David Drury Moor and Evangeline Moor (*née* White); *m* 1990, Sara Louise Stratton; three *d. Educ:* Canford Sch.; Univ. of Kent at Canterbury (BA Hons (Geog.) 1985). ACA 1989, FCA 2000. Trainee, subseq. Audit Manager, Touche Ross & Co., 1985–91; Audit Manager, Dist Audit, 1991–94; Audit Commission: Resources Sen. Manager, 1994–97; Associate Dir of Finance and Corporate Planning, 1997–2000; Finance Dir, 2000–03; Finance Dir, 2003–04, Dir of Strategy and Resources, 2004–05, Driver, Vehicle and Operator Gp, DfT. *Recreations:* travel, golf, DIY, family. *Address:* Department for Transport, Great Minster House, 76 Marsham Street, SW1P 4DR. *T:* (020) 7944 4597, *Fax:* (020) 7944 2192; *e-mail:* jonathan.moor@dft.gsi.gov.uk.
See also P. D. Moor.

MOOR, Philip Drury; QC 2001; a Recorder, since 2002; *b* 15 July 1959; *s* of late Rev. David Drury Moor and Evangeline Moor (*née* White); *m* 1987, Gillian Stark; two *d. Educ:* Canford Sch., Pembroke Coll., Oxford (MA). Called to the Bar, Inner Temple, 1982, Bencher, 2004. Hd of Chambers, 2007–. Member: Cttee, Family Law Bar Assoc., 1987– (Actg Treas., 2000–01; Vice-Chm., 2002–03, Chm., 2004–05); Gen. Council of the Bar, 1987–89, 2004–05 (Mem., 2002–03, Vice-Chm., 2003, Professional Standards Cttee); Council of Legal Educn, 1988–91 (Mem. Bd of Examrs, 1989–92). *Recreations:* cricket, Association football, Rugby football. *Address:* 1 Hare Court, Temple, EC4Y 7BE. *T:* (020) 7797 7070, *Fax:* (020) 7797 7435; *e-mail:* moor@1hc.com. *Club:* MCC.
See also J. E. Moor.

MOOR, Dr Robert Michael, FRS 1994; Head of Protein Function Laboratory, Babraham Institute, 1996–99; *b* 28 Sept. 1937; *s* of Donald C. Moor and Gwendolen (*née* Whitby); *m* 1962, Felicia Alison Elizabeth Stephens; four *d*. *Educ:* Estcourt, Natal, S Africa; Gonville and Caius Coll., Cambridge Univ. (PhD 1965; ScD). Senior Scientist, ARC Unit of Reproductive Physiology and Biochemistry, 1965–86; Head, Dept of Molecular Embryology, AFRC Inst. of Animal Physiology and Genetics Res., 1986–93; Dep. Dir, Babraham Inst., 1993–97. Hon. Fellow, Italian Vet. Assoc., 1990. Hon. Dr Univ. of Milan, 1990. *Publications:* numerous contribs to learned jls. *Recreations:* mountaineering, music. *Address:* 19 Thornton Close, Cambridge CB3 0NF. *T:* (01223) 276669. *Club:* Alpino Italiano (Milan).

MOORBATH, Prof. Stephen Erwin, DPhil, DSc; FRS 1977; Professor of Isotope Geology, Oxford University, 1992–96, now Emeritus Professor; Professorial Fellow of Linacre College, 1990–96, now Emeritus Fellow (Fellow, 1970–90); *b* 9 May 1929; *s* of Heinz Moosbach and Else Moosbach; *m* 1962, Pauline Tessier-Varlêt; one *s* one *d*. *Educ:* Lincoln Coll., Oxford Univ. (MA 1957, DPhil 1959). DSc Oxon 1969. Asst Experimental Officer, AERE, Harwell, 1948–51; Undergrad., Oxford Univ., 1951–54; Scientific Officer, AERE, Harwell, 1954–56; Research Fellow: Oxford Univ., 1956–61; MIT, 1961–62; Sen. Res. Officer, 1962–78, Reader in Geology, 1978–92, Oxford Univ. Wollaston Fund, Geol Soc. of London, 1968; Liverpool Geol Soc. Medal, 1968; Murchison Medal, Geol Soc. of London, 1978; Steno Medal, Geol Soc. of Denmark, 1979. *Publications:* contribs to scientific jls and books. *Recreations:* music, philately, travel, linguistics. *Address:* 53 Bagley Wood Road, Kennington, Oxford OX1 5LY. *T:* (01865) 739507.

MOORCOCK, Michael John; author, since 1956; *b* 18 Dec. 1939; *s* of Arthur Moorcock and June Moorcock (*née* Taylor); *m* 1st, 1962, Hilary Bailey (marr. diss. 1978); one *s* two *d*; 2nd, 1978, Jill Riches (marr. diss. 1983); 3rd, 1983, Linda Mullens Steele. *Educ:* Michael Hall, Sussex; Pitman's Coll., Surrey. Ed., Tarzan Adventures, 1956–58; Asst Ed., Sexton Blake Liby, 1959–61; travelled as singer/guitarist in Scandinavia and W Europe, 1961–62; ed. and pamphlet writer for Liberal Party pubns dept, 1962–63; Ed., New Worlds, 1963–80 (Publisher, 1980–); writer and vocalist for Hawkwind, 1971–; writer, vocalist and fretted instruments for Deep Fix; vocalist and instrumentalist for Robert Calvert; writer for Blue Oyster Cult, and associated with various other bands. Has made recordings. *Publications:* books include: Byzantium Endures, 1981; The Laughter of Carthage, 1984; Mother London, 1988; Jerusalem Commands, 1992; Blood, 1994; Fabulous Harbours, 1995; The War Amongst the Angels, 1996; Tales from the Texas Woods, 1997; King of the City, 2000; (with Storm Constantine) Silverheart, 2000; London Bone, 2001; The Dreamthief's Daughter, 2001; Firing the Cathedral, 2002; The Skrayling Tree, 2003; The Life and Times of Jerry Cornelius, 2003; The Vengeance of Rome, 2006; The Metatemporal Detectives, 2007; various omnibus edns of novels; ed numerous anthologies, collections and short stories. *Recreations:* walking, mountaineering, travel. *Address:* c/o Morhaim, 30 Pierrepont Street, Brooklyn, NY 11201, USA. *T:* (718) 222 8400; c/o Nomads Association, 21 Honor Oak Road, Honor Oak, SE23 3SH; c/o Hoffman, 77 Boulevard St Michel, 75005 Paris, France. *Club:* Royal Over-Seas League.

MOORCRAFT, Dennis Harry; Under-Secretary, Inland Revenue, 1975–81; *b* 14 Aug. 1921; *s* of late Harry Moorcraft and Dorothy Moorcraft (*née* Simmons); *m* 1945, Ingeborg Utne (*d* 2000), Bergen, Norway; one *s* one *d*. *Educ:* Gillingham County Grammar Sch. Tax Officer, Inland Revenue, 1938. RNVR, 1940–46. Inspector of Taxes, 1948; Sen. Inspector of Taxes, 1956; Principal Inspector of Taxes, 1963. *Recreations:* gardening, garden construction, croquet, music.

MOORCROFT, David Robert, OBE 1999 (MBE 1983); Chief Executive, UK Athletics, 1997–2007; *b* 10 April 1953; *s* of Robert Moorcroft and Mildred Moorcroft (*née* Hardy); *m* 1975, Linda Ann, *d* of John Ward; one *s* one *d*. *Educ:* Woodlands Comp. Sch.; Tile Hill Coll. of Further Educn; Loughborough Univ. (BEd 1976). School teacher, 1976–81. Athlete: Olympic Games: finalist, 1,500m, Montreal, 1976; semi-finalist, 5,000m, Moscow, 1980; finalist, 5,000m, Los Angeles, 1984; Commonwealth Games: Gold Medal, 1,500m, Edinburgh, 1974, Edmonton, 1978; Gold Medal, 5,000m, Brisbane, 1982; European Championships: Bronze Medal, 1,500m, Prague, 1978; Bronze Medal, 5,000m, Athens, 1982; Europa Cup: Gold Medal, 5,000m, Zagreb, 1981; set world record for 5,000m, Oslo, 1982, European record for 3,000m, Crystal Palace, 1982. Commentator, BBC TV and radio, 1983–. Chief Executive: British Athletic Federation Ltd, 1997; UK Athletics 98, 1998.

MOORCROFT, Sir William, KBE 2008; Principal, Trafford College (formerly South Trafford College), since 2003; *b* Liverpool, 17 Feb. 1958; *s* of Robert and Diane Jane Moorcroft; *m* 1990, Wendy Anne Clarehugh; one *s*. *Educ:* Manchester Metropolitan Univ. (MA Mgt); Bolton Inst. (Cert Ed). MHCIMA 1992. Exec. Chef, Littlewoods Orgn, 1979–83; Lectr, Southport Coll., 1983–91; Nat. Chief Verifier, City & Guilds, 1991–94; Hd of Dept, 1994–98, Vice Prin., 1998–2004, South Trafford Coll., subseq. Trafford Coll. Mem. Bd, Learning and Skills Improvement Service, 2008–. *Recreation:* golf. *Address:* Trafford College, Manchester Road, Altrincham WA14 5PQ. *Club:* Southport and Ainsdale Golf.

MOORE, family name of **Earl of Drogheda** and **Barons Moore of Lower Marsh** and **Moore of Wolvercote**.

MOORE, Viscount; Benjamin Garrett Henderson Moore; *b* 21 March 1983; *s* and *heir* of Earl of Drogheda, *qv*. *Educ:* Pro Corda; Eton; Peterhouse, Cambridge; Universität der Kunste Berlin. *Address:* 40c Ledbury Road, W11 2AB.

MOORE OF LOWER MARSH, Baron *cr* 1992 (Life Peer), of Lower Marsh in the London Borough of Lambeth; **John Edward Michael Moore;** PC 1986; *b* 26 Nov. 1937; *s* of Edward O. Moore; *m* 1962, Sheila Sarah Tillotson (*d* 2008); two *s* one *d*. *Educ:* London Sch. of Economics (BSc Econ). Nat. Service, Royal Sussex Regt, Korea, 1955–57 (commnd). Chm. Conservative Soc., LSE, 1958–59; Pres. Students' Union, LSE, 1959–60. Took part in expedn from N Greece to India overland tracing Alexander's route, 1960. In Banking and Stockbroking instns, Chicago, 1961–65; Democratic Precinct Captain, Evanston, Ill, USA, 1962; Democratic Ward Chm. Evanston, Illinois, 1964; Dir, 1968–79, Chm., 1975–79, Dean Witter Internat. Ltd. An Underwriting Mem. of Lloyds, 1978–92. Councillor (C), London Borough of Merton, 1971–74; Chm., Stepney Green Cons. Assoc., 1968. MP (C) Croydon Central, Feb. 1974–1992. A Vice-Chm., Conservative Party, 1975–79; Parly Under-Sec. of State, Dept. of Energy, 1979–83; HM Treasury: Economic Sec., June–Oct. 1983; Financial Sec., 1983–86; Secretary of State: for Transport, 1986–87; for Social Services, 1987–88; for Social Security, 1988–89. Chairman: Credit Suisse Asset Mgt, 1991–2000; Energy Saving Trust Ltd, 1992–95 (Pres., 1995–2001); Director: Marvin & Palmer Associates Inc., 1989–; Monitor Inc., 1990–2006 (Chm., Monitor Europe, 1990–2006); Gartmore Investment Management, 1990–92; GTECH Corp., 1992–2001; Swiss American Inc., 1992–96; Blue Circle Industries, 1993–2001; Camelot PLC, 1994–96; Rolls-Royce plc, 1994–2005 (Dep. Chm., 1996–2003, Chm., 2003–05); BEA Associates, USA, 1996–98; Private Client Bank (formerly Private Client Partners), Zurich, 1999–2003; Chm. Trustees, Rolls-Royce Pension Fund, 1998–2007. Member: Adv. Bd, Sir Alexander Gibb & Partners, 1990–95; Supervisory Bd, ITT Automotive Europe GmbH (Germany), 1994–97. Mem. Council, Inst. of Dirs, 1991–2002. Mem. Ct of Governors, LSE, 1977–2002. *Address:* House of Lords, SW1A 0PW. *Club:* Royal Automobile.

MOORE OF WOLVERCOTE, Baron *cr* 1986 (Life Peer), of Wolvercote in the City of Oxford; **Philip Brian Cecil Moore,** GCB 1985 (KCB 1980; CB 1973); GCVO 1983 (KCVO 1976); CMG 1966; QSO 1986; PC 1977; Private Secretary to the Queen and Keeper of the Queen's Archives, 1977–86; a Permanent Lord-in-Waiting to the Queen, since 1990; *b* 6 April 1921; *s* of late Cecil Moore, Indian Civil Service; *m* 1945, Joan Ursula Greenop; two *d*. *Educ:* Dragon Sch.; Cheltenham Coll. (Scholar); Oxford Univ. Classical Exhibitioner, Brasenose Coll., Oxford, 1940. RAF Bomber Command, 1940–42 (prisoner of war, 1942–45). Brasenose Coll., Oxford, 1945–46 (Hon. Fellow 1981). Asst Private Sec. to First Lord of Admiralty, 1950–51; Principal Private Sec. to First Lord of Admiralty, 1957–58; Dep. UK Commissioner, Singapore, 1961–63; British Dep. High Comr in Singapore, 1963–65; Chief of Public Relations, MoD, 1965–66; Asst Private Secretary to the Queen, 1966–72, Dep. Private Secretary, 1972–77. Dir, General Accident, Fire and Life Assurance Corp., 1986–91. Chm., King George VI and Queen Elizabeth Foundn of St Catharine's, Cumberland Lodge, 1986–97. Vice-Pres., SPCK. *Recreations:* golf, Rugby football (Oxford Blue, 1945–46; International, England, 1951), hockey (Oxford Blue, 1946), cricket (Oxfordshire). *Address:* Hampton Court Palace, East Molesey, Surrey KT8 9AU. *Club:* MCC.

MOORE, Alan Edward, CBE 1980; Deputy Chairman: Lloyds TSB Group plc, 1998–2003 (Director, 1995–2003); Lloyds Bank Plc, 1998–2003 (Director, 1989–2003); TSB Bank plc, 1998–2003; *b* 5 June 1936; *s* of late Charles Edward and Ethel Florence Moore; *m* 1961, Margaret Patricia Beckley; one *s* one *d*. *Educ:* Berkhamsted Sch. FCIB, FCIS, FCT. Glyn Mills & Co., then Williams & Glyn's Bank, London, 1953–74; Dir Gen., Bahrain Monetary Agency, 1974–79; Dir and Treas., Lloyds Bank Internat., 1980–84; Dir of Treasury, Lloyds Bank, 1985–88; Dir of Corporate Banking and Treasury, Lloyds Bank, 1988–94; Dep. Chief Exec. and Treas., Lloyds Bank, 1994–98; Dep. Gp Chief Exec. and Treas., Lloyds TSB Gp plc, 1995–98. *Recreations:* photography, railway history, travel.

MOORE, Anthony Michael Frederick, (Anthony Michaels-Moore); baritone; *b* 8 April 1957; *s* of John Moore and Isabel (*née* Shephard); *m* 1980, Ewa Migocki; one *d*. *Educ:* Newcastle Univ. (BA Hons 1978); Royal Scottish Acad. of Music and Drama. First British winner, Pavarotti Comp., 1985. *Débuts:* Opera North, 1986; Royal Opera House, Covent Garden, 1987; Vienna State Opera, 1993; La Scala, Milan, 1993; Paris Opera, 1994; Buenos Aires, 1996; Metropolitan, NY, 1996; San Francisco, 1997; Chicago, 2000; Glyndebourne, 2001. *Rôles* include: Marcello, Belcore, Escamillo, Posa, Hamlet, Falke, Lescaut, Simon Boccanegra, Scarpia, Figaro, Orestes, Onegin, Rigoletto, Macbeth, Montforte, Ford, Ezio, Iago. Recordings incl. Carmina Burana, Lucia di Lammermoor, Falstaff, Aroldo, and La Favorite. Royal Philharmonic Soc. Award, 1997. *Recreations:* cricket, swimming, spicy food, computer action games. *Address:* c/o IMG Artists, The Light Box, 111 Power Road, Chiswick, W4 5PY. *T:* (020) 7957 5800.

MOORE, Prof. Brian Cecil Joseph, PhD; FMedSci; FRS 2002; Professor of Auditory Perception, University of Cambridge, since 1995; Fellow of Wolfson College, Cambridge, since 1983; *b* 10 Feb. 1946; *s* of Cecil George Moore and Maria Anna Moore. *Educ:* St Catharine's Coll., Cambridge (BA Nat. Sci. 1968; PhD Exptl Psychol. 1971). Lectr in Psychology, Reading Univ., 1971–77; Vis. Prof., Brooklyn Coll., NY, 1973–74; University of Cambridge: Lectr in Experimental Psychology, 1977–89; Reader in Auditory Perception, 1989–95. FMedSci 2001. Fellow, Acoustical Soc. of America, 1985; Hon. Fellow, Belgian Soc. of Audiology, 1997; Hon. Fellow, British Soc. of Hearing Aid Audiologists, 1999. *Publications:* An Introduction to the Psychology of Hearing, 1977, 5th edn 2003; Frequency Selectivity in Hearing, 1986; Perceptual Consequences of Cochlear Damage, 1995; Hearing, 1995; Cochlear Hearing Loss, 1998, 2nd edn 2007; The Perception of Speech: from sound to meaning, 2007. *Recreations:* music, playing the guitar, bridge, fixing things. *Address:* Department of Experimental Psychology, University of Cambridge, Downing Street, Cambridge CB2 3EB. *T:* (01223) 333574.

MOORE, Charles Hilary; journalist and author; Consulting Editor, The Telegraph Group, since 2004 (Editor, The Daily Telegraph, 1995–2003); *b* 31 Oct. 1956; *s* of Richard and Ann Moore; *m* 1981, Caroline Mary Baxter; twin *s* and *d*. *Educ:* Eton Coll.; Trinity Coll., Cambridge (BA Hons History). Joined editorial staff of Daily Telegraph, 1979, leader writer, 1981–83; Assistant Editor and political columnist, 1983–84, Editor, 1984–90, The Spectator; weekly columnist, Daily Express, 1987–90; Dep. Editor, Daily Telegraph, 1990–92; Editor, The Sunday Telegraph, 1992–95. Chm., Policy Exchange, 2005–. Trustee, Friends of the Union, 1993–. Mem. Council, Benenden Sch., 2000–. Hon. Dr Buckingham, 2006. *Publications:* (ed with C. Hawtree) 1936, 1986; (with A. N. Wilson and G. Stamp) The Church in Crisis, 1986; (ed with Simon Heffer) A Tory Seer: the selected journalism of T. E. Utley, 1989. *Recreation:* hunting. *Address:* c/o The Daily Telegraph, 111 Buckingham Palace Road, SW1W 0DT. *T:* (020) 7931 2000. *Clubs:* Beefsteak, White's.

MOORE, Cicely Frances, (Mrs H. D. Moore); *see* Berry, C. F.

MOORE, David James Ladd; Partnership Secretary, Freshfields, 1993–98; *b* 6 June 1937; *s* of James and Eilonwy Moore; *m* 1968, Kay Harrison; two *s*. *Educ:* King Edward VI Sch., Nuneaton; Brasenose Coll., Oxford (BA); Birkbeck Coll., Univ. of London (BA (History of Art) 2003; MA History 2005). PO, 1961–67 (Asst Principal 1961, Principal 1966); Cabinet Office, 1967–69; HM Treasury, 1969–80 (Asst Sec. 1973); Under Secretary: Cabinet Office, 1980–82; HM Treasury, 1982–83; Inland Revenue (Principal Finance Officer), 1983–85; HM Treasury, 1985–93. *Recreations:* cinema, tennis, history of art. *Address:* 183 Hampstead Way, NW11 7YB.

MOORE, Prof. David Robert, PhD; Director, MRC Institute of Hearing Research, since 2002; *b* 19 July 1953; *s* of William Leonard Moore and Joan Moore (*née* Kerr); *m* 1976, Victoria Dolouhgan; one *d*. *Educ:* Monash Univ., Victoria (BSc; PhD). NIH Internat. Fellow, Univ. of Calif, Irvine, 1983–84; University of Oxford: MRC Sen. Fellow, 1986–89; Res. Lectr, 1989–96; Reader, 1996–99; Prof. of Auditory Neurosci., 1999–2002. Vis. Prof., Univ. of Washington, Seattle, 1992; Vis. Schol., Center for Neural Sci., NY Univ., 1997. *Publications:* numerous peer-reviewed scientific contribs to internat. jls. *Recreations:* food and wine, cycling, family interests. *Address:* MRC Institute of Hearing Research, University Park, Nottingham NG7 2RD. *T:* (0115) 922 3431; *e-mail:* davem@ihr.mrc.ac.uk. *Club:* Yarragon Axe (Victoria, Australia).

MOORE, Prof. Derek William, FRS 1990; Professor of Applied Mathematics, Imperial College, London, 1973–96, now Professor Emeritus and Senior Research Fellow; *b* 19 April 1931; *s* of William McPherson Moore and Elsie Marjorie Moore (*née* Patterson). *Educ:* Jesus Coll., Cambridge (MA, PhD). Asst Lectr and Lectr in Maths, Bristol, 1958–64;

Sen. Postdoctoral Res. Fellow, Nat. Acad. of Scis, USA, 1964; Imperial College London: Sen. Lectr, Dept of Maths, 1967; Reader in Theoretical Fluid Mechanics, 1968. Sherman Fairchild Dist. Scholar, CIT, 1986. Foreign Hon. Mem., Amer. Acad. of Arts and Scis, 1985. Sen. Whitehead Prize, LMS, 2001. *Recreation:* jazz tenor saxophone. *Address:* 71 Boileau Road, W5 3AP. *T:* (020) 8998 8572.

MOORE, Derry; *see* Drogheda, Earl of.

MOORE, Most Rev. Desmond Charles, KBE 1996; former Bishop of Alotau, Papua New Guinea (RC); *b* Adelaide, 12 May 1926; *s* of Edwin John Moore and Margaret Mary Leahy. *Educ:* Christian Brothers Sch., Adelaide; Adelaide Univ.; Sacred Heart Monastery, Croydon, Vic. Entered novitiate, 1950, professed mem., 1951–, Congregation of Missionaries of the Sacred Heart of Jesus; ordained priest, 1957; Bursar and Assistant to Novice Master, St Mary's Towers Monastery, Douglas Park, 1958–61; Assistant to Parish Priest, Port Moresby, PNG, 1961–62; first Parish Priest, Boregaina Village, Rigo, 1962–67; Parish Priest, St Joseph's, Boroko, and Religious Superior, Missionaries of the Sacred Heart of Jesus, dio. of Port Moresby, 1967–70; cons. Bishop of Sideia, 1970, name of dio. changed to Alotau, 1977; retired, 2001. *Address:* Sacred Heart Monastery, 1 Roma Avenue, Kensington, NSW 2033, Australia. *T:* (2) 96627188, *T:* and *Fax:* (2) 93865206; *e-mail:* desmondmoore@gmail.com.

MOORE, (Douglas) Marks; His Honour Judge Marks Moore; a Circuit Judge, since 2007; *b* 31 Jan. 1950; *s* of Douglas Moore and Josephine Moore (*née* Ritchie); *m* 1983, Susan Clayton (separated); one *s* three *d*; partner, Maria Ketting-Paris. *Educ:* Regent House Sch., NI; Queen's Univ., Belfast (BA 1972; Dip. Soc. Anthropol. 1973). Irish Guards, 1974–76, Subaltern. Called to the Bar, 1979; Recorder, 1998–2007; Senior Trial Attorney: Internat. Criminal Tribunal for Rwanda, 2001–03, with responsibility: for prosecution of former Rwandan Govt; for the Special Investigation; Internat. Criminal Tribunal for Yugoslavia, The Hague, 2005–. *Recreations:* fishing, golf, squash. *Address:* Woolwich Crown Court, 2 Belmarsh Road, SE28 0EY. *Club:* Muthaiga Country (Kenya).

MOORE, Sir Francis Thomas, (Sir Frank), Kt 1983; AO 1991; Chairman, Taylor Byrne Tourism Group, since 1990; *b* 28 Nov. 1930; *m* 1972, Norma Shearer; two *s*. *Educ:* Nudgee Coll. Licensed Valuer, 1952–; Man. Dir, Radio Broadcasting Network of Queensland, 1957–78; Director: Universal Telecasters Qld Ltd, 1961–80; Trust Co. Australia Ltd, 1983–96; Chm., Nature Resorts Ltd, 1997–2002. Chairman: Queensland Tourist and Travel Corp., 1979–90; Tourism Council of Australia (formerly Australian Tourism Industry Assoc.), 1983–95; Nat. Centre for Studies in Travel and Tourism, 1987–94; Tourism Forecasting Council, 1996–2003; Co-op. Res. Centre for Sustainable Tourism, 1997–; Dir, Gold Coast Airport Ltd, 2001–04; Mem., World Travel and Tourism Council, 1992–. *Address:* GPO Box 1150, Brisbane, Qld 4001, Australia.

MOORE, George; Chairman, Grayne Marketing Co. Ltd, 1978–95; *b* 7 Oct. 1923; *s* of George Moore and Agnes Bryce Moore; *m* 1946, Marjorie Pamela Davies (*d* 1986); three *s*. *Educ:* University Coll. and Royal Technical Coll., Cardiff (Jt Engineering Diploma); Hull Univ. (Post Graduate Diploma in Economics). Served War, RN, 1942–46. Graduate Engineer, Electricity Authority, 1948–50; Development Engineer, Anglo-Iranian Oil Co., Abadan, 1950–52; Chief Electrical Engineer, Distillers' Solvents Div., 1952–58; Management Consultant, Urwick, Orr & Partners, 1958–64; Executive Dir, Burton Group, 1964–66; Group Managing Dir, Spear & Jackson International Ltd and Chm., USA Subsidiary, 1966–75; Dir of cos in Sweden, France, India, Australia, Canada, S Africa, 1966–75; Under Sec. and Regional Industrial Dir, NW Regional Office, DoI, 1976–78; Dir, Cordel Corporate Develt Ltd, 1978–95. FCMI (FBIM 1980); FInstD 1978; MIMC 1990. *Recreations:* golf, sailing. *Club:* Reform.

MOORE, George, OBE 1994; Member, South Yorkshire County Council, 1974–86 (Chairman, 1978–79); *b* 29 Jan. 1913; *s* of Charles Edward Moore and Edith Alice Moore; *m* 1943, Hannah Kenworthy; two *d*. *Educ:* Woodhouse, Sheffield. Started work in pit at 14 yrs of age, 1927; worked in hotel business, 1930; publican in own right for several yrs, after which went into fruit and vegetable business, first as retailer and eventually as wholesaler and partner in small co. Served in RAF for short period during war. Barnsley Bor. Council, then Barnsley MBC, 1961–94: served as Vice Chm., Health and Housing Cttee, and Vice Chm., Fire and Licensing Dept; Chairman: Barnsley and Dist Refuse Disposal Cttee, 1959–64; Sanitary Cttee, Barnsley, 1963–73; first Chm., Fire Service Cttee, S Yorks CC, 1974–78. Chm., Barnsley Community Health Council, 1974–92. Chm., Barnsley and Dist, Talking Newspaper for the Blind, 1978–94. *Recreation:* aviculture. *Address:* 34 Derwent Road, Athersley South, Barnsley, S Yorks S71 3QT. *T:* (01226) 206644.

MOORE, (Georgina) Mary; Principal, St Hilda's College, Oxford, 1980–90, Hon. Fellow, 1990; *b* 8 April 1930; *yr d* of late Prof. V. H. Galbraith, FBA, and late Georgina Rosalie Galbraith (*née* Cole-Baker); *m* 1963, Antony Ross Moore, CMG (*d* 2000); one *s*. *Educ:* The Mount Sch., York; Lady Margaret Hall, Oxford (BA Modern History 1951; MA; Hon. Fellow, 1981). Joined HM Foreign (later Diplomatic) Service, 1951; posted to Budapest, 1954; UK Permanent Delegn to United Nations, New York, 1956; FO, 1959; First Secretary, 1961; resigned on marriage. Mem., Council for Industry and Higher Educn, 1986–90. A Trustee: British Museum, 1982–92; Rhodes Trust, 1984–96; Pilgrim Trust, 1991–2005 (Chm., 1993–2005). JP Bucks, 1977–82. Hon. LLD Mount Holyoke Coll., 1991. Under the name Helena Osborne writes plays for television and radio. *Publications:* (as Helena Osborne): *novels:* The Arcadian Affair, 1969; Pay-Day, 1972; White Poppy, 1977; The Joker, 1979. *Recreations:* theatre, travel. *Address:* Touchbridge, Brill, Aylesbury, Bucks HP18 9UJ. *T:* and *Fax:* (01844) 238247. *Club:* University Women's.

See also J. H. Galbraith.

MOORE, Graham, QPM 1997; Chief Constable, West Yorkshire Police, 1998–2002; *b* 15 Jan. 1947; *s* of Graham and Kate Moore; *m* 1965, Susan Fletcher; one *s* one *d*. *Educ:* Brunts GS, Mansfield; Warwick Univ. (BA Hons Philosophy and Lit. 1975). Professional musician; Police Constable, Birmingham City Police, 1969–72; Inspector of Taxes, Inland Revenue, 1975–77; joined W Midlands Police, 1977; Asst Chief Constable, S Yorks Police, 1991–94; Dep. Chief Constable, Cambs Constabulary, 1994–98. *Recreations:* music, playing saxophone, collecting books, tennis, shooting.

MOORE, Prof. Henrietta Louise, PhD; FBA 2007; William Wyse Professor of Social Anthropology, University of Cambridge, since 2008; *b* Saunderton, 18 May 1957; *d* of Stephen Andrew Moore and Josephine Jane Mary Moore. *Educ:* Univ. of Durham (BA Archaeol. and Anthropol. 1979); Newham Coll., Cambridge (PhD 1983). Field Dir, UNA, Burkina Faso, 1983–84; Curatorial Asst for Anthropol., Univ. Mus. of Archaeol. and Anthropol., Cambridge, 1984–85; Lectr in Soc. Anthropol., Univ. of Kent, Canterbury, 1985–86; Lectr in Soc. Anthropol., 1986–88, Manager, African Studies Centre, 1987–90, Univ. of Cambridge; Lectr and Dir of Studies in Soc. Anthropol., Girton Coll., 1986–88; Fellow and Lectr in Anthropol. and Soc. and Pol Scis, Pembroke Coll., 1989–90; London School of Economics and Political Science: Lectr, 1990–93, Reader, 1993–97, in Soc. Anthropol.; Prof. of Soc. Anthropol., 1997–2008; Dir, Gender Inst., 1994–99; Dir, Culture and Globalization Prog., Centre for Global Governance, 2005–08; Gov., 1999–2005; Dep. Dir, 2002–05. Fellow: Centre for Globalization and Policy Res., Sch. of Public Affairs, UCLA, 2005–; Goodenough Coll., Univ. of London, 2005–; Maj. Res. Fellow, Leverhulme Trust, London, 2007–. Visiting Professor: Univ. of Bergen, 1988; Univ. of Bremen, 1990; Univ. of Calif, Berkeley, 1994, 1997; Univ. of Porto, 2004; Vis. Lectr, Univ. of Witwatersrand, 1992. Member: Adv. Bd for Global Coalition on Africa, Min. of For. Affairs, Netherlands, 1994–95; Educn Cttee, Catholic Inst. for Internat. Relns, 1995–98; Bd of Res. Counsellors, Foundn for Advanced Studies on Internat. Develt, Tokyo, 1996–99; Bd of Social Enterprise, London, 2002–04; Chm. Wkg Gp, Best Practice for Social Enterprise, DTI, 2001–02. FRAI 1981 (Mem. Council, 1989–92); Member: African Studies Assoc., 1986– (Mem. Council, 1986–89); Assoc. of Social Anthropologists of UK and Commonwealth, 1986– (Hon. Sec., 1991–94); Amer. Assoc. of Anthropologists, 2004–. FRSA 2000; AcSS 2001; MInstD 2002. *Publications:* Space, Text and Gender: an anthropological study of the Marakwet of Kenya, 1986, 2nd edn 1996; Feminism and Anthropology, 1988; (with M. A. Vaughan) Cutting Down Trees: gender, nutrition and change in the Northern Provinces of Zambia, 1890–1990, 1994 (Herskovits Prize, African Studies Assoc., USA, 1995); A Passion for Difference: essays in anthropology and gender, 1994; (ed) The Future of Anthropological Knowledge, 1996; (ed) Promoting the Health of Children and Young People: setting a research agenda, 1998; (ed jtly) Those Who Play with Fire: gender and fertility in Africa, 1999; (ed) Anthropological Theory Today, 1999; (ed with D. T. Sanders) Magical Interpretations, Material Realities: modernity, witchcraft and the occult in post colonial Africa, 2001; (with Ed Mayo) The Mutual State and How to Build It, 2001; (ed with D. T. Sanders) Anthropology in Theory: issues in epistemology, 2005; The Subject of Anthropology: gender, symbolism and psychoanalysis, 2007; (ed with David Held) Cultural Politics in a Global Age: uncertainty, solidarity and innovation, 2008. *Recreations:* relaxing, thinking, theatre, opera, walking. *Address:* Department of Social Anthropology, University of Cambridge, Free School Lane, Cambridge CB2 3RF. *Club:* Groucho.

MOORE, Rt Rev. Henry Wylie; General Secretary, Church Missionary Society, 1986–89, retired 1990; *b* 2 Nov. 1923; *m* 1951, Betty Rose Basnett; two *s* three *d*. *Educ:* Univ. of Liverpool (BCom 1950); Wycliffe Hall, Oxford; MA (Organization Studies) Leeds, 1972. LMS Railway Clerk, 1940–42. Served War with King's Regt (Liverpool), 1942–43; Rajputana Rifles, 1943–46. Curate: Farnworth, Widnes, 1952–54; Middleton, 1954–56; CMS, Khuzistan, 1956–59; Rector: St Margaret, Burnage, 1960–63; Middleton, 1963–74; Home Sec. and later Executive Sec., CMS, 1974–83; Bishop in Cyprus and the Gulf, 1983–86. *Recreation:* family life. *Address:* Fernhill Cottage, Hopesay, Craven Arms, Shropshire SY7 8HD.

MOORE, James Antony Axel Herring, OBE 1998; Executive Director, US-UK Educational Commission (Fulbright Commission), 1993–2002; *b* 26 April 1940; *s* of late Lieut A. D. W. Moore, RN (killed HMS Audacity, 1941) and Agneta Moore (*née* Wachtmeister); *m* 1964, Marianne Jerlström; two *s* one *d*. *Educ:* Wellington Coll.; Trinity Coll., Cambridge (MA); London Univ. Inst. of Educn (PGCE). Teacher: Norway, 1962–63; Thailand, 1964–67; British Council: Warsaw, 1967–70; Beirut, 1971–73; Ottawa, 1973–75; London, 1975–80; Chinese lang. trng, 1980–81; Director: Manila, 1981–85; Copenhagen, 1985–89; General Manager, Fellowships and Scholarships, 1990–93. *Recreations:* music, ski-ing, walking, sailing. *Address:* 7 Brook Lane, Haywards Heath RH16 1SF.

See also Vice-Adm. Sir M. A. C. Moore.

MOORE, John, (Jonathan Moore); actor; writer; director; *b* 25 Nov. 1963; *s* of Richard and Nora Moore. *Educ:* St Elpheges, Wallington; Roundshaw Sch., Wallington; Croydon Art Coll. *Writer: plays:* 1st play aged 11, Hornus' Poem; Sea Change, 1977; Obstruct the doors, cause delay and be Dangerous..., 1980; Street Captives, Edinburgh Fest., transf. Royal Exchange, 1981; Treatment, Donmar, 1982 (Edinburgh Fest. Fringe First award; filmed for TV); The Hooligan Nights (NT commn), 1985; Behind Heaven, Royal Exchange, transf. Donmar, 1986; Regeneration, 1989; This Other Eden, Soho Th., 1990; Fall From Light, 2002; The Bacchae (adaptation), 2003–05; *libretto:* Stewart Copeland's Horse Opera (televised, also actor), 1992; *directed:* Turnage's Greek (also writer of adaptation from play), Munich Biennale (Best Dir award), Edinburgh Fest., 1988–90 (dir. TV film, Royal Phil. Soc. Best Film award); Elegy for Young Lovers, La Fenice, Venice, 1989; 63 Dream Palace, Munich Biennale (Best Dir award) and German TV, 1990; Baa Baa Black Sheep, Opera North, Cheltenham Fest., 1993; Cask of Amontillado, Holders, Barbados, 1993; East and West (also writer of text), Almeida, 1994; Life with An Idiot, ENO, Scottish Opera, 1995; James MacMillan's Inez de Castro, Scottish Opera, Edinburgh Internat. Fest., 1996; Inkle and Yarico, Holders Easter Season, Barbados, 1997; Mottke the Thief (also writer of adaptation from novel by Schalom Asch), Bonn Opera, 1998; Nyman's Facing Goya, Santiago del Compostela, Perrelada Fest., 2001; Die Versicherung, State Th., Darmstadt, 2002; Magic Flute (also trans. of spoken text), Scottish Opera, 2003; Sex, Chips and Rock 'n' Roll, Royal Exchange, 2005; The Soldier's Tale (also actor), Savannah Fest., Georgia, 2006; The Ballad of Elizabeth Sulky Mouth, Greenwich, 2006; The Revenger's Tragedy, Royal Exchange, 2008; *actor: theatre* includes leading roles in: The Gorky Brigade, Royal Court, 1982; Venice Preserv'd, Almeida, 1985; Treatment, Gate, Donmar, Edinburgh Fest., 1986; Behind Heaven, Royal Exchange, Donmar, 1986; The Art of Success, RSC, 1987; The Idiot, Barbican, 1990; Dead Funny, Salisbury Playhouse, Th. Clwyd, 1998; Misalliance, 1998, The School of Night, 1999, Chichester Fest. Th.; A Midsummer Night's Dream, 2001, Macbeth, 2002, Arcola; Round the Horne, West End and No 1 UK tour, 2004; 2Graves (one-man play), Edinburgh Fest., transf. Arts Th., 2006; Holding Fire!, Shakespeare's Globe, 2007; *television* includes: Inside Story, 1986; Bleak House (series), 1986; Jack the Ripper (series), 1988; Roger Roger (two series), 1999, 2003; The People's Harry Enfield, 2001; Foyle's War, 2003; *films* include: My Beautiful Laundrette, 1985. Collaborated on theatre pieces with band Test Dept and mems of rock band Killing Joke and Jah Wobble; contrib. to BBC TV and radio arts discussion progs. Vis. Sen. Lectr, RCM, 2006; Guest Lectr, Drama Centre, London, 2006. *Publication:* Jonathan Moore: three plays, 2002. *Recreations:* thinking, hanging out with friends, reading, food, football, underwater knitting, plankton wrangling. *Address:* (writing) c/o Julia Kreitman, The Agency, 24 Pottery Lane, Holland Park, W11 4LZ. *T:* (020) 7727 1346; *e-mail:* info@theagency.co.uk; (acting) c/o Meg Poole, Richard Stone Partners, 2 Henrietta Street, WC2E 8PS. *T:* (020) 7497 0869; (opera) Performing Arts, 6 Windmill Street, W1T 2JB. *T:* (020) 7255 7362; *e-mail:* richard@performing-arts.co.uk; *web:* www.jonathanmooreuk.com. *Club:* Century.

MOORE, Hon. John Colinton, AO 2004; *b* Rockhampton, Qld, 16 Nov. 1936; *s* of Thomas R. Moore and Doris (*née* Symes); *m* 1st, 1965 (marr. diss.); two *s* one *d*; 2nd, 1980, Jacqueline Sarah, *d* of Hon. Sir William John Farquhar McDonald and Evelyn S. McDonald. *Educ:* Southport Jun. Sch., Qld; Armidale Sch., NSW; Univ. of Queensland (BCom; AAUQ). AASA. Stockbroker, 1960; Mem., Brisbane Stock Exchange, 1962–74. Former Director: Wm Brandt & Sons (Aust.); Phillips; First City; Brandt Ltd (PFCB Ltd); Merrill Lynch, Pierce, Fennell & Smith (Aust.) Ltd; Citi-national Ltd; Agricl Investments

Aust. Ltd. MP (L) Ryan, Qld, 1975–2001; Fed. Minister for Business and Consumer Affairs, 1980–82; Opposition spokesman: for Finance, 1983–84; for Communications, 1984–85; for Northern Develt and Local Govt, 1985–87; for Tspt and Aviation, 1987; for Business and Consumer Affairs, 1987–89; for Business Privatisation and Consumer Affairs, 1989–90; Shadow Minister for Industry and Commerce, and Public Admin, 1995–96; Minister for Industry, Sci. and Tourism, 1996–98; Vice-Pres., Exec. Council, 1996–98; Minister for Defence, 1998–2001. Member: various Govt cttees, 1984–96; various internat. delegns. Queensland Liberal Party: Vice-Pres. and Treas., 1967–73; Pres., 1973–76 and 1984–90; Mem., Qld State Exec., Liberal Party of Aust., 1966–91 and 1996–98. Mem. Council, Order of Australia., 1996–98. Mem., Anti-Cancer Council of Qld, 1972. *Recreations:* tennis, cricket, reading, golf. *Address:* 47 Dennis Street, Indooroopilly, Brisbane, Qld 4068, Australia. *Clubs:* Queensland, Brisbane, Tattersall's, Polo (Brisbane); Queensland Turf.

MOORE, John David; Headmaster, St Dunstan's College, Catford, 1993–97; *b* 16 Feb. 1943; *s* of John and Hilda Moore; *m* 1966, Ann Medora; one *s* one *d. Educ:* St John's Coll., Cambridge (BA Classics 1965; MA 1969); CertEd Cambridge Univ., 1966. Classics Master, Judd Sch., Tonbridge, 1966–69; trainee commodity trader, Gill and Duffus Ltd, 1969–70; English Master, Skinners' Sch., Tunbridge Wells, 1970–74; Head of General Studies and English Master, King's Sch., Macclesfield, Ches., 1974–80; Dep. Headmaster, Carre's Grammar Sch., Sleaford, Lincs, 1981–86; Headmaster, Ilford County High Sch. for Boys, London Borough of Redbridge, 1986–93. Member Committee: S Lakeland Carers, 1998–2001 (Chm., 1999–2001); Old Bradfordion Assoc., 1999– (Pres., 2003–06). Governor: Heron Hill Primary Sch., Kendal, 1998–2007; King's Sch., Macclesfield, 2000– (Mem., Govs' Educn Sub-Gp, 1998–; Chm., Educn Cttee, 2006–). Freeman, City of London, 1996. *Recreations:* cricket, walking, theatre, music. *Address:* 12 Undercliff Road, Kendal, Cumbria LA9 4PS.

MOORE, Captain John Evelyn, RN; Editor: Jane's Fighting Ships, 1972–87; Jane's Naval Review, 1982–87; *b* Sant Ilario, Italy, 1 Nov. 1921; *s* of William John Moore and Evelyn Elizabeth (*née* Hooper); *m* 1st, 1945, Joan Pardoe; one *s* two *d*; 2nd, Barbara (*née* Kerry) (*d* 2008). *Educ:* Sherborne Sch., Dorset. Served War: entered Royal Navy, 1939; specialised in hydrographic surveying, then submarines, in 1944. Commanded HM Submarines: Totem, Alaric, Tradewind, Tactician, Telemachus. RN Staff course, 1950–51; Comdr, 1957; attached to Turkish Naval Staff, 1958–60; subseq. Plans Div., Admty; 1st Submarine Sqdn, then 7th Submarine Sqdn in comd; Captain, 1967; served as: Chief of Staff, C-in-C Naval Home Command; Capt. DI3 (Navy), Defence Intell. Staff; retired list at own request, 1972. FRGS 1942. Hon. Professor: Aberdeen Univ., 1987–90; St Andrews Univ., 1990–92. *Publications:* Jane's Major Warships, 1973; The Soviet Navy Today, 1975; Submarine Development, 1976; (jtly) Soviet War Machine, 1976; (jtly) Encyclopaedia of World's Warships, 1978; (jtly) World War 3, 1978; Seapower and Politics, 1979; Warships of the Royal Navy, 1979; Warships of the Soviet Navy, 1981; (jtly) Submarine Warfare: today and tomorrow, 1986; (ed) The Impact of Polaris, 1999. *Recreation:* archaeology. *Address:* 1 Ridgelands Close, Eastbourne, East Sussex BN20 8EP. *T:* (01323) 638836.

MOORE, Prof. John Halstead Hardman, PhD; FBA 1999; George Watson's and Daniel Stewart's Professor of Political Economy, University of Edinburgh, since 2000; Professor of Economic Theory, London School of Economics, since 1990 (quarter-time since 2000); *b* 7 May 1954; *s* of Frank Moore, OBE and Audrey Jeanne Moore (*née* Halstead); *m* 1986, Dr Susan Mary Hardman; one *s* one *d. Educ:* Dorking County Grammar Sch.; Fitzwilliam Coll., Cambridge (BA 1st cl. Hons Maths 1976; MA 1983); LSE (MSc 1980; PhD 1984). Exec. Engr, Dundee Telephone Area, 1976–78; Temp. Lectr in Econs, LSE, 1980–81; Lectr, Birkbeck Coll., London Univ., 1981–83; Lectr, 1983–87, Reader, 1987–90, LSE. Vis. Asst Prof., MIT, 1986–87; Vis. Prof., Princeton Univ., 1991–92; Prof., St Andrews Univ., 1997–2000 (quarter-time); Leverhulme Personal Res. Prof., 1998–2003; ESRC Professorial Fellow, 2004–07. Ed., Rev. of Economic Studies, 1987–91. Lectures: Walras-Bowley, 1996, Marschak, 2002, Econometric Soc.; Clarendon, Oxford Univ., 2001; Schumpeter, European Econ. Assoc., 2006; Max Weber, European Univ. Inst., 2006; Bernoulli, Univ. of Basel, 2007; Keynes Lectr, British Acad., 2007. Fellow: Econometric Soc., 1989; Royal Soc. of Edinburgh, 2003. Foreign Hon. Member: Amer. Econ. Assoc., 2001; Amer. Acad. of Arts and Scis, 2002. Yrjö Jahnsson Award, European Econ. Assoc., 1999. *Publications:* articles on econs. *Recreations:* music, mountains. *Address:* University of Edinburgh, 50 George Square, Edinburgh EH8 9JY; London School of Economics, Houghton Street, WC2A 2AE.

MOORE, Sir John (Michael), KCVO 1983; CB 1974; DSC 1944; Chairman, Lymington Harbour Commission, 1993–99 (Deputy Chairman, 1990–93); Second Crown Estate Commissioner, 1978–83; *b* 2 April 1921; *m* 1986, Jacqueline Cingel, MBE. *Educ:* Whitgift Middle Sch.; Selwyn Coll., Cambridge. Royal Navy, 1940–46. Royal Humane Society Bronze Medal, 1942. Ministry of Transport, 1946; Joint Principal Private Sec. to Minister (Rt Hon. Harold (later Lord) Watkinson), 1956–59; Asst Sec., 1959; Under-Sec. (Principal Estabt Officer), 1966; Under-Sec., DoE, 1970–72; Dep. Sec., CSD, 1972–78. *Recreations:* sailing, remembering walking hills and mountains. *Address:* 38 Daniells Walk, Lymington, Hants SO41 3PN. *T:* (01590) 679963. *Club:* Royal Lymington Yacht.

MOORE, John Royston, CBE 1983; CChem, FRSC; Chairman, Bradford Health Authority, 1982–88; *b* 2 May 1921; *s* of late Henry Roland and Jane Elizabeth Moore; *m* 1947, Dorothy Mackay Hick, *d* of late Charles and Edith Mackay Hick; two *s. Educ:* Manchester Central Grammar Sch.; Univ. of Manchester (BSc Hons). War service, research and manufacture of explosives. Lecturer in schools and college, Manchester; Principal, Bradford Technical Coll., 1959–75; Sen. Vice Principal and Dir of Planning and Resources, Bradford Coll., 1975–80, retired. Chm., Wool, Jute and Flax ITB, 1981–83. Leader, Baildon Urban DC, 1965–68; Councillor, West Riding CC, until 1973; West Yorkshire MCC: Member, 1973–86; Leader, 1978–81; Leader of the Opposition, 1981–86. Dir, Yorkshire Enterprise Ltd, 1981–90. President, Yorks Conservative Adv. Cttee on Educn, 1975–89; past Chm., Conservative Nat. Adv. Cttee on Educn. Hon. Mem., and Councillor, City and Guilds of London Inst., 1977–92. Hon. MA Bradford, 1986. *Publication:* (as Royston Moore) Makere: the female Pharaoh-Queen of Sheba, 2008. *Recreations:* music, history, bridge. *Address:* Bicknor, 33 Station Road, Baildon, Shipley, West Yorkshire BD17 6HS. *T:* (01274) 581777.

MOORE, Jonathan; *see* Moore, John.

MOORE, Julian Keith; Head of Management Development Group, Office of Public Service and Science, Cabinet Office, 1992–93; *b* 18 Aug. 1945; *s* of late George H. D. Moore and Amy (*née* Ashwell); *m* 1970, Susan (*née* Dand); one *s* one *d. Educ:* St Paul's School; New College, Oxford (Open Scholar, MA). HM Treasury, 1968; Civil Service Dept, 1968–72; Private Sec. to Minister of State, N Ireland Office, 1972–73; Civil Service Dept, 1973–77; Private Sec. to Lord Privy Seal and Leader of House of Lords, 1977–79; Assistant Secretary: CSD, 1979–82; Home Office, 1982–85; Cabinet Office (MPO), 1985–87; Civil Service Comr, 1987–92; Dir, CSSB, 1987–91; Head, Office of Civil Service Comrs, 1991–92. Mem., Careers Adv. Bd, Univ. of London, 1988–92; UK Mem., Bd of Admin, Europ. Inst. of Public Admin, 1993. *Publications:* articles and reviews, Times Literary Supplement. *Recreations:* historical cryptography, walking. *Address:* 6 Priory Crescent, Lewes, E Sussex BN7 1HP. *Club:* Athenæum.

MOORE, Mark Jonathan, MA; Head of College, Clifton College, since 2005; *b* 25 April 1961; *s* of Dennis and Sheila Moore; *m* 1989, Joanna Hawley; two *s* two *d. Educ:* Wolverhampton Grammar Sch.; Downing Coll., Cambridge (BA Hons English 1983; PGCE 1984; MA 1987). Assistant Master: Marlborough Coll., 1984–87; Eton Coll., 1987–94; Hd of English, Radley Coll., 1994–2005. *Recreations:* ball games, reading, talking. *Address:* Clifton College, Bristol BS8 3JH. *T:* (0117) 315 7000, *Fax:* (0117) 315 7101. *Clubs:* Jesters; Hawks (Cambridge).

MOORE, Marks; *see* Moore, D. M.

MOORE, Martin Luke; QC 2002; *b* 25 April 1960; *s* of late Brig. Peter Neil Martin Moore, DSO (and two Bars), MC, and Enid Rosemary Moore; *m* 1985, Caroline Mary Mason; three *d. Educ:* Winchester Coll.; Lincoln Coll., Oxford (BA Hons). Called to the Bar, Lincoln's Inn, 1982; in practice, specialising in company law litigation and advice. *Address:* Inadown House, Newton Valence, Alton, Hants GU34 3RR. *T:* (01420) 588660; Erskine Chambers, 33 Chancery Lane, WC2A 1EN. *T:* (020) 7242 5532; *e-mail:* mmoore@erskine-chambers.co.uk.

MOORE, Mary; *see* Moore, G. M.

MOORE, Vice Adm. Sir Michael (Antony Claës), KBE 1997; LVO 1981; Chief Executive (formerly Director General), Institution of Mechanical Engineers, 1998–2007; *b* 6 Jan. 1942; *s* of Lieut A. D. W. Moore, RN (killed HMS Audacity, 1941) and Agneta Moore (*née* Wachtmeister); *m* 1969, Penelope Jane, JP, *d* of Rear-Adm. F. C. W. Lawson, *qv*; one *s* three *d. Educ:* Wellington Coll.; RNC Dartmouth. Swedish Naval Interpreter. Joined RN, 1960; served HM Ships Gurkha, Britannia and Ashton, 1963–67; Flag Lieut to Comdr FEF, Singapore, 1967–68; i/c HMS Beachampton, 1969; qualified as Navigator, 1970; HM Ships Tenby, Brighton, Plymouth and Tartar (i/c), 1970–77; Naval Ops, MoD, 1977–79; HMY Britannia, 1979–81; Captain, 1981; Naval Asst to Chief of Fleet Support, MoD, 1981–82; i/c HMS Andromeda, and Capt. 8th Frigate Sqn, 1983–84; i/c Ops, Northwood MHQ, 1985–87; Dir, Naval Warfare, MoD, 1988–90; Rear Adm., 1990; Maritime Advr to SACEUR, 1990–93; Vice Adm. 1994; C of S to Comdr Allied Naval Forces Southern Europe, 1994–97. Chm., Forces Pension Soc. (formerly Officers' Pension Soc.), 2006–. Hon. Fellow: Swedish Royal Soc. of Naval Scis, 1992; IMechE 2006. Younger Brother, Trinity House, 1988. *Address:* Churchill Cottage, Castle Street, Portchester, Hants PO16 9QW.

See also J. A. A. H. Moore.

MOORE, Prof. Michael Arthur, DPhil; FRS 1989; Professor of Theoretical Physics, University of Manchester, since 1976; *b* 8 Oct. 1943; *s* of John Moore and Barbara Atkinson; *m* 1967, Susan Eadington; three *s* one *d. Educ:* Huddersfield New Coll.; Oriel Coll., Oxford (BA 1964; DPhil 1967). Prize Fellow, Magdalen Coll., Oxford, 1967–71; Res. Associate, Univ. of Illinois, USA, 1967–69; Lectr in Physics, Univ. of Sussex, 1971–76. *Publications:* papers in scientific jls. *Recreation:* tennis. *Address:* The Schuster Laboratory, The University, Manchester M13 9PL.

MOORE, Rt Hon. Michael (Kenneth), ONZ 2000; PC 1990; Director-General, World Trade Organisation, 1999–2002; Adjunct Professor, Faculty of Law and Management, La Trobe University, since 2003; *b* 28 Jan. 1949; *m* 1975, Yvonne (*née* Dereany). *Educ:* Dilworth Sch.; Bay of Islands College (only Minister in Labour Govt without a degree). Worked as social worker, builder's labourer, meat freezing worker and printer; MP (Lab) Eden 1972–75 (youngest NZ MP ever elected); MP (Lab) Papanui, later named Christchurch North, then Waimakariri, 1978–99; spokesperson on housing, regional, small town and community development, the environment, tourism, recreation and sport, overseas trade and marketing, external relations and trade, finance; Minister of Foreign Affairs and Trade, 1990; trade missions led incl. Japan, Europe, Soviet Union, Pakistan, Turkey; Prime Minister of NZ, Sept.–Oct. 1990; Leader of the Opposition, 1990–93. *Publications:* On Balance, 1980; Beyond Today, 1981; A Pacific Parliament, 1982; The Added Value Economy, 1984; Hard Labour, 1987; Fighting for New Zealand, 1993; Children of the Poor, 1996; A Brief History of the Future, 1998; A World Without Walls, 2003. *Address:* Faculty of Law and Management, La Trobe University, Vic 3086, Australia.

MOORE, Michael Kevin; MP (Lib Dem) Berwickshire, Roxburgh and Selkirk, since 2005 (Tweeddale, Ettrick and Lauderdale, 1997–2005); *b* 3 June 1965; *s* of Rev. (William) Haisley Moore and Geraldine Anne, (Jill), Moore; *m* 2004, Alison Louise Hughes. *Educ:* Strathallan Sch.; Jedburgh Grammar Sch.; Univ. of Edinburgh (MA Jt Hons Politics and Modern Hist.). Research Asst to Archy Kirkwood, MP, 1987–88; with Coopers & Lybrand, Edinburgh, 1988–97 (a Manager, corporate finance). Lib Dem spokesman on defence, 2005–06; on foreign affairs, 2006–. Mem., Select Cttee on Scottish affairs, 1997–99. Gov. and Vice-Chm., Westminster Foundn for Democracy, 2002–05. Mem. Council, Chatham House, 2004–. Parly Vis. Fellow, St Antony's Coll., Oxford, 2003–04. CA 1991. *Recreations:* jazz, music, films, Rugby, hill-walking. *Address:* House of Commons, SW1A 0AA; *e-mail:* michaelmooremp@parliament.uk; (constituency) 11 Island Street, Galashiels TD1 1NZ. *T:* (01896) 663650.

MOORE, Michael Rodney Newton, CBE 1996; Chairman, Which? Ltd, since 1997; Director, HBOS Financial Services, since 2001; *b* 15 March 1936; *s* of Gen. Sir Rodney Moore, GCVO, KCB, CBE, DSO, PMN and Olive Marion (*née* Robinson); *m* 1986, Jan, *d* of Paul and Lilian Adorian; one *s. Educ:* Eton; Magdalen College, Oxford (MA); Harvard Business Sch. (MBA). Nat. Service Commission, Grenadier Guards, 1957–59, serving in Cyprus, Lebanon, UK. Called to the Bar, Gray's Inn, 1961; practised until 1964; joined Hill Samuel & Co., 1966 (Dir, 1970–71); subseq. Chm./Dir, various UK, USA & Swedish cos; Chairman: Tomkins, 1984–95; Quicks Gp, 1992–2002; Linx Printing Technologies, 1993–2005; London Internat. Gp, 1994–99; Warm Zones, 2001–04; Dir, Sir John Soane's Mus. Soc., 2004–05. Mem. Council of Mgt, Consumers' Assoc., 1997–2003. Trustee, Public Concern at Work, 1996–2003. Chm., NSPCC, 1988–95. *Recreations:* visiting ruins, opera, photography, reading. *Clubs:* Garrick, Pratt's, Boodle's.

MOORE, Michael S.; *see* Stuart-Moore.

MOORE, Miranda Jayne, (Mrs J. M. Haslam); QC 2003; *b* 4 Jan. 1961; *d* of Bryan John Moore and Anne Rosemary Janet Spokes Moore; *m* 1987, Jonathan Mark Haslam; one *s* one *d. Educ:* Univ. of Aston (BSc 1st Cl. Hons Business Studies). Called to the Bar, Lincoln's Inn, 1983; in practice as barrister, specialising in criminal law, 1984–. *Recreations:* dancing, theatre, shopping. *Address:* 5 Paper Buildings, Temple, EC4Y 7HB. *T:* (020) 7583 6117; *e-mail:* clerks@5pb.co.uk.

MOORE, (Sir) Norman Winfrid, (3rd Bt *cr* 1919; has established his claim but does not use the title); Senior Principal Scientific Officer, Nature Conservancy Council, 1965–83

(Principal Scientific Officer, 1958–65); Visiting Professor of Environmental Studies, Wye College, University of London, 1979–83; *b* 24 Feb. 1923; *s* of Sir Alan Hilary Moore, 2nd Bt; *S* father, 1959; *m* 1950, Janet, *o d* of late Mrs Phyllis Singer; one *s* two *d*. *Educ:* Eton; Trinity Coll., Cambridge (MA); Univ. of Bristol (PhD). Served War, 1942–45, Germany and Holland (wounded, POW). *Publications:* The Bird of Time, 1987; Oaks, Dragonflies and People, 2002; scientific papers and articles. *Heir: s* Peter Alan Cutlack Moore [*b* 21 Sept. 1951; *m* 1989, Pamela Edwardes; one *s* one *d*. *Educ:* Eton; Trinity Coll., Cambridge (MA); DPhil Oxon]. *Address:* The Farm House, 117 Boxworth End, Swavesey, Cambridge CB24 4RA.

MOORE, Sir Patrick (Alfred) Caldwell-, Kt 2001; CBE 1988 (OBE 1968); free-lance author, since 1968; *b* 4 March 1923; *s* of late Capt. Charles Caldwell-Moore, MC, and Gertrude Lilian Moore. *Educ:* privately (due to illness). Served with RAF, 1940–45: Navigator, Bomber Command. Concerned in running of a school, 1945–52; free-lance author, 1952–65; Dir of Armagh Planetarium, 1965–68. TV Series, BBC, The Sky at Night, 1957–; radio broadcaster. Composed and performed in Perseus and Andromeda (opera), 1975, Theseus, 1982, and Galileo, 2000. Pres., British Astronomical Assoc., 1982–84. Honorary Member: Astronomic-Geodetic Soc. of USSR, 1971; Royal Astronomical Soc. of New Zealand, 1983; Royal Astronomical Soc. of Canada, 1994. Editor, Year Book of Astronomy, 1962–. Lorimer Gold Medal, 1962; Goodacre Gold Medal, 1968; Arturo Gold Medal (Italian Astronomical Socs), 1969; Jackson-Gwilt Medal, RAS, 1977; Roberts-Klumpke Medal, Astronom. Soc. of Pacific, 1979. Fellow, QMW. Hon. FRS 2001. Hon. DSc: Lancaster, 1974; Hatfield Polytechnic, 1989; Birmingham, 1990; Leicester, Keele, 1995; Portsmouth, 1998; Glamorgan, 2001; TCD, 2002. *Publications:* More than 100 books, mainly astronomical, including The Amateur Astronomer, 1970, rev. edn 2006; Atlas of the Universe, 1970, rev. edn 2007; Guide to the Planets, 1976; Guide to the Moon, 1976; Can You Speak Venusian?, 1977; Guide to the Stars, 1977; Guide to Mars, 1977; (jtly) Out of the Darkness: the Planet Pluto, 1980; The Unfolding Universe, 1982; Travellers in Space and Time, 1983; (jtly) The Return of Halley's Comet, 1984; Stargazing, 1985; Exploring the Night Sky with Binoculars, 1986; The A–Z of Astronomy, 1986; TV Astronomer, 1987; Astronomy for the Under-Tens, 1987; Astronomers' Stars, 1987; (jtly) The Planet Uranus, 1988; The Planet Neptune, 1989; Space Travel for the Under Tens, 1989; Mission to the Planets, 1990; A Passion for Astronomy, 1991; The Earth for Under Tens, 1992; Fireside Astronomy, 1992; The Starry Sky, 1994; The Great Astronomical Revolution, 1994; Stars of the Southern Skies, 1994; Guinness Book of Astronomy, 1995; Teach Yourself Astronomy, 1995, 2008; Eyes on the Universe, 1997; Sun in Eclipse, 1999; West Country Eclipse, 1999; Patrick Moore on Mars, 1999; The Wandering Astronomer, 2000; Patrick Moore on the Moon, 2000, new edn 2006; The Star of Bethlehem, 2001; The Data Book of Astronomy, 2001; 80 Not Out (autobiog.), 2003; Patrick Moore: the autobiography, 2005; (with Arthur C. Clarke) Asteroid, 2005; Stars of Destiny, 2005; Venus, 2006; (jtly) Bang! The Complete History of the Universe, 2006. *Recreations:* cricket, chess, tennis, music, xylophone playing (composer of music in recordings The Ever Ready Band Plays Music by Patrick Moore, 1979, The Music of Patrick Moore, 1986, Moore Music, 1999). *Address:* Farthings, 39 West Street, Selsey, West Sussex PO20 9AD. *Clubs:* Athenæum, Lord's Taverners; Sussex County Cricket.

MOORE, Sir Patrick (William Eisdell), Kt 1992; OBE 1982; FRCS, FRACS; Consultant Surgeon, Honorary Staff, Auckland Hospital Board, now retired; *b* 17 March 1918; *m* 1942, Doris McBeth (Beth) Beedie; four *s*. *Educ:* Auckland Grammar Sch.; Otago Univ. (MB ChB); Univ. of London (DLO). Medical Officer, 28 Bn, 2 NZEF. Consultant Surgeon, Green Lane Hosp., 1951; Reader in Otolaryngology, Auckland Med. Sch., 1975–84. Vice-Pres., NZ League for Hard of Hearing, 1952–77; President: Deafness Res. Foundn, 1963–90; NZ Otolaryngological Soc., 1968–70; NZ Hunts Assoc., 1984–89; Founder and Patron, Hearing House of NZ, 1966; Master of Pakuranga Hunt, 1975–84; Auckland Cttee, NZ Racing Conf., 1976–84. Fellow, Selwyn Coll., Univ. of Otago, 2007. *Publications:* A Great Run, 1972; So Old So Quick (autobiog.), 2004. *Recreation:* writing. *Address:* Binswood, 229 Remuera Road, Auckland 1005, New Zealand. *T:* (9) 5202679. *Club:* Northern (Auckland).

MOORE, Prof. Peter Gerald, TD 1963; PhD; FIA; Principal, London Business School, 1984–89 (Professor of Statistics, 1965–93, now Emeritus; Fellow, 1993); *b* Richmond, Surrey, 5 April 1928; *s* of late Leonard and Ruby Moore; *m* 1958, Sonja Enevoldson Thomas, Dulwich; two *s* one *d*. *Educ:* King's College Sch., Wimbledon; University Coll. London (BSc (1st Cl. Hons Statistics), PhD; Rosa Morison Meml Medal 1949; Fellow, 1988). Served with 3rd Regt RHA, 1949–51, TA, 1951–65, Major 1963. Lectr, UCL, 1951–57; Commonwealth Fund (Harkness) Fellow, Princeton, NJ, 1953–54; Asst to Economic Adviser, NCB, 1957–59; Head of Statistical Services, Reed Paper Gp, 1959–65; Dep. Principal, London Business Sch., 1972–84. Director: Shell UK, 1969–72; Copeman Paterson Ltd, 1978–87; Martin Paterson Associates, 1984–88; Elf Petroleum UK plc, 1989–94; Partner, Duncan C. Fraser, 1974–77. Consultant, Pugh-Roberts Associates Inc., US, 1989–94. Gresham Prof. of Rhetoric, 1992–95. Member: Review Body on Doctors' and Dentists' Pay, 1971–89; Cttee on 1971 Census Security, 1971–73; UGC, 1979–84 (Vice-Chm., 1980–83); Cons. to Wilson Cttee on Financial Instns, 1977–80. Pres., Royal Statistical Soc., 1989–91 (Mem. Council, 1966–78, 1988–97; Hon. Sec., 1968–74; Guy Medal, 1970; Chambers Medal, 1995); Pres., Inst. of Actuaries, 1984–86 (Mem. Council, 1966–90; Vice-Pres., 1973–76); Member: Internat. Stat. Inst., 1972– (Council, 1985–91); Council, Internat. Actuarial Assoc., 1984–87; Industry and Employment Cttee, ESRC, 1983–88; Jarratt Cttee on Univ. Efficiency, 1984–85; Council, Hong Kong Univ. of Science and Technology, 1986–91; Acad. Council, China Europe Management Inst., Beijing, 1986–94; Univ. of London Senate, 1988–92; Council, UCL, 1989– (Vice-Chm., 1998–2000); Court, Cranfield Inst. of Technology, 1989–96; Court, City Univ., 1990–; Chm., Council of Univ. Management Schs, 1974–76; a Governor: London Business Sch., 1968–89; NIESR, 1985–; Sevenoaks Sch., 1984–90. Freeman, City of London, 1964; Mem., Court of Assts, 1987–, Master, 1994–95, Tallow Chandlers' Co. CCMI (CBIM 1986). Hon. DSc Heriot-Watt, 1985. J. D. Scaife Medal, Instn of Prodn Engrs, 1964. *Publications include:* Principles of Statistical Techniques, 1958, 2nd edn 1969; (with D. E. Edwards) Standard Statistical Calculations, 1965; Statistics and the Manager, 1966; Basic Operational Research, 1968, 3rd edn 1986; Risk and Business Decisions, 1972; (jtly) Case Studies in Decision Analysis, 1975; (with H. Thomas) Anatomy of Decisions, 1976, 2nd rev. edn 1988; Reason by Numbers, 1980; The Business of Risk, 1983; numerous articles in professional jls. *Recreations:* golf, opera, walking, travel. *Address:* London Business School, Sussex Place, Regent's Park, NW1 4SA. *T:* (020) 7262 5050; 3 Chartway, Sevenoaks, Kent TN13 3RU. *T:* (01732) 451936. *Clubs:* Athenæum, Ward of Cordwainer.

MOORE, Philip John, BMus; FRCO; Organist and Master of the Music, York Minster, 1983–2008; *b* 30 Sept. 1943; *s* of late Cecil and of Marjorie Moore; one *s* two *d*. *Educ:* Maidstone Grammar Sch.; Royal Coll. of Music (ARCM, GRSM); BMus Dunelm. FRCO 1965. Asst Music Master, Eton Coll., 1965–68; Asst Organist, Canterbury Cathedral, 1968–74; Organist and Master of the Choristers, Guildford Cathedral, 1974–83. Hon. FRSCM 2005; Hon. FGCM 2006. *Publications:* anthems, services, cantatas, organ music, song cycles, chamber music, orchestral music. *Recreations:* collecting fountain pens, collecting Imari, cooking, architecture. *Address:* Rectory Cottage, Barton-le-Street, Malton YO17 6PN.

MOORE, Philip Wynford, TD 1994; Interim Chief Finance Officer, HM Revenue and Customs, since 2008; *b* 5 Jan. 1960; *s* of Cecil Philip John Moore and Christine Margaret Moore; *m* 1995, Amanda Lawson; two *d*. *Educ:* St Albans Sch.; Clare Coll., Cambridge (BA Maths 1982). AIA 1986, FIA 1988. Life Dept, Commercial Union Insce Co., 1982–87; Managing Consultant, William M. Mercer, 1987–89; Coopers & Lybrand: leader of life actuarial practice, London, 1989–95; Partner, Financial Instns Gp, Coopers & Lybrand Consulting (East Asia), leader, E Asia Insce Consultancy practice, Hong Kong, 1995–98; Finance Dir and Actuary, National Provident Instn, 1998–2000; Corp. Dir of Finance and Hd of Mergers and Acquisitions, AMP (UK) plc, 2000–03; Gp Finance Dir, 2003–06, Gp Chief Exec., 2007, Friends Provident plc. Trustee, Childhood Eye Cancer Trust, 2007–. *Recreations:* family, flying (private pilot's licence), wine. *Address:* HM Revenue and Customs, 100 Parliament Street, SW1A 2BQ. *T:* (020) 7147 2247, *Fax:* (020) 7147 3310; *e-mail:* philip.moore@hmrc.gsi.gov.uk. *Club:* Honourable Artillery Company.

MOORE, Air Vice-Marshal Richard Charles, MBE 1989; Air Officer Administration, and Air Officer Commanding Directly Administered Units, 2003–05; *b* 5 Aug. 1950; *s* of Ernest William Moore and Hilda Margaret Moore (*née* Edwards); *m* 1977, Judith Ellen Owen; two *s*. *Educ:* Open Univ. (BSc Systems); RAF Staff Coll. Joined RAF, 1970; OC 16 Sqdn, 1983–85, 6 Wing, 1988–91, RAF Regt; MoD Staff appts, Regt 26 (RAF), 1985–88, Air Plans (LTC), 1991–95; Officer Commanding: Defence Nuclear Biol and Chem. Centre, 1995–97; RAF Honington, 1997–99; Comdt Gen., RAF Regt, 1999–2001; Team Leader, Ground Based Air Defence Integrated Project, Defence Procurement Agency, 2001–03. Chm., RAF Bobsleigh, Luge and Skeleton Bobsleigh Assoc., 1997–. *Recreation:* offshore sailing. *Address:* c/o RAF High Wycombe, Bucks HP14 4UE.

MOORE, Richard Hobart John de Courcy, FCA; Managing Partner, 1987–2004, and Senior Partner, since 1989, Moore Stephens; Chairman, Moore Stephens International Ltd, since 2005; *b* 31 Aug. 1949; *s* of late Hobart Harold de Courcy Moore and of Elizabeth Helen Moore; *m* 1977, Lucy Annabelle Sefton-Smith; one *s* one *d*. *Educ:* Stowe Sch. FCA 1979. Partner, Moore Stephens, 1975–. Comr, Royal Hospital Chelsea, 2006–. Treas., Shipwrights' Co., 1989–. *Recreations:* Real tennis, cricket. *Address:* 11 Chelsea Park Gardens, SW3 6AF. *T:* (020) 7352 7594. *Clubs:* Boodle's, MCC, Hurlingham, Queen's.

MOORE, Robert Jeffery; His Honour Judge Moore; a Circuit Judge, since 1995; Ethnic Minorities Liaison Judge for South Yorkshire and Humberside (formerly Sheffield), 1998–2004; *b* 1947; *s* of Jeffery Moore and Doreen Moore; *m* 1979, Susan Elaine Hatcliffe; two *s*. *Educ:* Loughborough Grammar Sch.; Univ. of Manchester (LLB Hons 1968). Called to the Bar, Gray's Inn, 1970; practised on North Eastern Circuit, from Sheffield, 1971–80 and from 11 Kings Bench Walk, Temple, 1980–95. Written Examinations and Interview Panel, Judicial Appts Commn, 2008. *Recreations:* my family, Leicester Tigers Rugby club, golf, Sheffield United FC. *Address:* The Law Courts, 50 West Bar, Sheffield S3 8PH. *Club:* Sickleholme Golf (Bamford).

MOORE, Sir Roger (George), KBE 2003 (CBE 1999); actor; *b* London, 14 Oct. 1927; *m* 1st, Doorn van Steyn (marr. diss. 1953); 2nd, 1953, Dorothy Squires (marr. diss. 1969; she *d* 1998); 3rd, Luisa Mattioli (marr. diss.); two *s* one *d*; 4th, 2002, Kristina Tholstrup. *Educ:* RADA. Special Ambassador for UNICEF, 1991–. Golden Globe World Film Favourite Award, 1980. Stage début, Androcles and the Lion. *TV series include:* Ivanhoe, 1958; The Alaskans, 1960–61; Maverick, 1961; The Saint, 1962–69 (dir some episodes); The Persuaders, 1972–73; The Man Who Woundn't Die, 1992; The Quest, 1995; *films include:* The Last Time I Saw Paris, 1954; The Interrupted Melody, 1955; The King's Thief, 1955; Diane, 1956; The Miracle, 1959; Rachel Cade, 1961; Gold of the Seven Saints, 1961; The Rape of the Sabine Women, 1961; No Man's Land, 1961; Crossplot, 1969; The Man Who Haunted Himself, 1970; Live and Let Die, 1973; The Man With The Golden Gun, 1974; Gold, 1974; That Lucky Touch, 1975; Street People, 1975; Shout at the Devil, 1975; Sherlock Holmes in New York, 1976; The Spy Who Loved Me, 1976; The Wild Geese, 1977; Escape to Athena, 1978; Moonraker, 1978; North Sea Hijack, 1979; The Sea Wolves, 1980; Sunday Lovers, 1980; For Your Eyes Only, 1980; The Cannonball Run, 1981; Octopussy, 1983; The Naked Face, 1983; A View to a Kill, 1985; Bed and Breakfast, 1989; Bullseye!, 1989; Fire, Ice and Dynamite, 1990; The Quest, 1997; Boat Trip, 2002. *Publication:* James Bond Diary, 1973. *Address:* Pinewood Studios, Iver Heath, Bucks SL0 0NH.

MOORE, Rear-Adm. Simon, CB 2000; Chief Executive, Action Medical Research (formerly Action Research), since 2001; *b* 25 Sept. 1946; *s* of Ronald and Christine Moore; *m* 1978, Catherine Sarcelet; three *d*. *Educ:* Brentwood Sch. Joined RN 1964; in command, HM Ships: Walkerton, 1974–75; Rhyl, 1983; Berwick, 1984–85; Asst Dir, Defence Policy, MoD, 1988–91; in command, HMS Fearless, 1991–93; Captain, BRNC, Dartmouth, 1993–95; Dir, Intelligence Regl Assessments, 1995–97; ACDS (Ops), MoD, 1997–2000. Pres., London Flotilla, 1999–2005. Gov., Hurstpierpoint Coll., 2001– (Chm. of Govs, 2003–). Liveryman, Curriers' Co., 2006–. *Recreations:* music, singing. *Address:* Action Medical Research, Vincent House, North Parade, Horsham, W Sussex RH12 2DP.

MOORE, Prof. Stuart Alfred; JP; DL; Chairman of the Bench, Manchester City Magistrates, since 2006; Robert Ottley Professor of Quantitive Studies, University of Manchester, 1992–97, now Emeritus Professor; *b* 9 Oct. 1939; *s* of Alfred Moore and Kathleen (*née* Dodd); *m* 1966, Diana Mary Connery; two *s* one *d*. *Educ:* Stockport Sch.; Manchester Univ. (MA Econs 1967). University of Manchester: Computer Asst, 1960–64; Lectr, then Sen. Lectr in Econ. Stats, 1964–92; Dean, Fac. of Econ. and Social Studies, 1980–83; Pro Vice-Chancellor, 1985–90, 1997–2000; Dep. Vice-Chancellor, 1990–96; Actg Vice-Chancellor, 1990–92; Chairman: Central Manchester Healthcare NHS Trust, 1992–2001; Stockport PCT, 2001–06. JP City of Manchester, 1996; DL Greater Manchester, 2007. Hon. DSocSc Manchester, 2001. *Publications:* various papers in learned jls. *Recreations:* gardening, photography, travel, thrillers, films. *Address:* Manchester City Magistrates' Court, Crown Square, Manchester M60 1PR. *T:* (0161) 830 4260; 2 Carisbrooke Avenue, Hazel Grove, Stockport SK7 5PL.

MOORE, Terence, CBE 1993; business consultant, since 1995; Group Managing Director and Chief Executive Officer, Conoco Ltd, 1987–95; *b* 24 Dec. 1931; *s* of Arthur Doncaster Moore and Dorothy Irene Gladys (*née* Godwin); *m* 1955, Tessa Catherine (*née* Wynne); two *s* one *d*. *Educ:* Strand Sch., London; BScEcon, Univ. of London; Harvard (AMP). ACII 1958; AICS 1959. Shell Internat. Petroleum Co., 1948–64; Locana Corp. Ltd (investment bank), 1964–65; Conoco Ltd, 1965–95: Dep. Man. Dir, Marketing and Operations, 1975; Man. Dir, Supply and Trading, Europe, 1979. Director: Conoco Pension Trustees Ltd, 1996–2003; James Fisher & Son plc, 1998–2004. Pres., Oil Industries Club, 2003–; Hon. Sec., Inst. of Petroleum, 1995–2001. Gov., Greenwich

Theatre, 1991–97 (Vice Chm. Govs, 1992–93). Chm., St Katherine and Shadwell Trust, 1999. *Publications:* articles in industry jls. *Recreations:* music, reading, walking, family and friends. *Address:* 67 Merchant Court, Thorpes Yard, 61 Wapping Wall, E1W 3SJ. *T:* and *Fax:* (020) 7481 0853; *e-mail:* t.moore@talktalk.net.

MOORE, Prof. Terry, PhD; FRAS, FRIN; Professor of Satellite Navigation, since 2001, and Director, Institute of Engineering Surveying and Space Geodesy, since 2003, University of Nottingham; *b* 3 May 1961; *s* of Colin Leonard and Edna Moore; *m* 1985, Ingrid Tamara Rejent; one *s* one *d*. *Educ:* Univ. of Nottingham (BSc 1st Cl. Civil Engrg 1982; PhD Space Geodesy 1986). FRAS 1983; FRIN 1995. University of Nottingham: Res. Fellow, 1985–88; Lectr, 1989–97; Reader in Satellite Navigation, 1997–2000; Dep. Hd, Sch. of Civil Engrg, 2008–. Special Prof., Chinese Acad. of Surveying and Mapping, 2004–. Vice Pres., Royal Inst. of Navigation, 2008–. Associate Fellow, Remote Sensing and Photogrammetry Soc., 2001. Member: NT; Caravan Club. *Publications:* chapters in: Sovereign Limits Beneath the Oceans: delimiting the new continental shelf, 1999; Guidelines for the use of GPS in Surveying and Mapping, 2003; contrib. papers to learned jls incl. Jl Navigation, Survey Rev., IEE Digest, GPS Solutions, Internat. Hydrographic Rev., Advances in Astronautical Scis, Hydro Internat., IALA Bulletin, Jl Surveying Engrg, Jl Satellite Positioning, Navigation and Communication, Jl British Interplanetary Soc., Navigation, Prequisas, Revista Brasileira de Cartografia, Space Communications Jl. *Recreations:* mountaineering, hill walking and other outdoor activities, travelling, camping and caravanning, music: listening, singing and playing guitar, reading, sport in general, Sheffield United FC in particular. *Address:* Institute of Engineering Surveying and Geodesy, University of Nottingham, University Park, Nottingham NG7 2RD. *T:* (0115) 951 3886, *Fax:* (0115) 951 3881; *e-mail:* terry.moore@nottingham.ac.uk. *Clubs:* Austrian Alpine (Section Britannia); Sheffield United Football.

MOORE, Maj. Gen. William Hewitt, CBE 2004; Director General Logistics, Support and Equipment, HQ Land Forces, 2007–08; *b* 24 Feb. 1958; *s* of Brian and Eileen Moore; *m* 1986, Jane Moore; two *s*. *Educ:* Univ. of Salford (BA Hons Pols and Hist. of Industrial Soc. 1979). Battery Comdr 1 Parachute Battery (Bull's Troop), RHA, 1992–94; Directing Staff, Army Staff Coll., 1994–96; CO 7th Parachute Regt, RHA, 1996–98; Col Force Develt, 1998–2001; Commander: Sierra Leone Armed Forces, 2001; 19 Mechanised Bde, 2001–03; Dir Equipment Capability (Ground Manoeuvre), MoD, 2004–07. Trustee, Malvern Coll., 2005–. FCMI. *Publications:* articles in RUSI, British Army Rev. *Recreations:* cricket, hill walking, ski-ing, mountain marathons, cricket coaching, scaring my family on holidays, rock music. *Address:* Headquarters Land, Erskine Barracks, Wilton, Salisbury, Wilts SP2 0AE.

MOORE, Sir William (Roger Clotworthy), 3rd Bt *cr* 1932; TD 1962; DL; *b* 17 May 1927; *s* of Sir William Samson Moore, 2nd Bt, and Ethel Cockburn Gordon (*d* 1973); *S* father, 1978; *m* 1954, Gillian, *d* of John Brown, Co. Antrim; one *s* one *d*. *Educ:* Marlborough; RMC, Sandhurst. Lieut Royal Inniskilling Fusiliers, 1945; Major North Irish Horse, 1956. Grand Juror, Co. Antrim, 1952–68. Prison visitor, 1968–72. Mem., Parole Bd for Scotland, 1978–80. High Sheriff, Co. Antrim, 1964; DL Co. Antrim, 1990. *Heir: s* Richard William Moore [*b* 8 May 1955. *Educ:* Portora; RMA. Lieut Royal Scots, 1974]. *Address:* Moore Lodge, Ballymoney, Co. Antrim, Northern Ireland BT53 7NT. *Club:* Kildare Street and University (Dublin).

MOORE-BICK, Maj. Gen. John David, CBE 1997 (OBE 1991); DL; FICE; FCIL; General Secretary, Forces Pension Society, since 2007; *b* 10 Oct. 1949; *s* of late John Ninian Moore-Bick and Kathleen Margaret Moore-Bick (*née* Beall); *m* 1973, Anne Horton; one *d*. *Educ:* Stonegate Sch.; Skinners'; St Catherine's Coll., Oxford (BA (Forestry), MA). Commissioned RA (V) 1969, regular commission, 1971; transf. to RE, 1972; served 45 Commando Gp, Junior Leaders' Regt RE and 23 Amphibious Engr Sqdn, 1972–79; Führungsakademie der Bundeswehr, 1979–82; HQ UKLF, 1982–84; Falkland Is, 1984–85; 26 Armd Engr Sqdn, 1985–86; Asst to Chm., NATO Mil. Cttee, 1986–88; 21 Engr Regt, Germany, and Gulf War, 1988–91; Chief Engr, Multi National Airmobile Div., 1991; Col Army Plans, MoD, 1991–94; Chief Engr, ARRC, 1994–95 and Implementation Force, Sarajevo, 1995–96; Dir, Army Staff Duties, MoD, 1996–99; Leader, MoD Study into Future of Shrivenham/Watchfield, 1999; MA to High Rep., Sarajevo, 2000; GOC UK Support Comd (Germany), 2001–03; Special Defence Advr, Serbia and Montenegro, 2003–04. Hon. Colonel: 39 (Skinners') Signal Regt, 2001–06; Sussex ACF, 2007–; Col Comdt, RE, 2002–. Chm., RE Assoc. Patron Eastbourne Scottish Pipe Band. Chm. Govs, Skinners' Sch. FICE 1997; FCIL (FIL 2003). Liveryman, Skinners' Co., 1988– (First Warden, 2007–08; Master, 2008–July 2009). DL E Sussex, 2006. 1st Cl. Service Order (Hungary), 1996. *Recreations:* Eastern Europe and Germany, Kent and Sussex Weald. *Address:* Castle Well, Ewhurst Green, E Sussex TN32 5TD. *Clubs:* Army and Navy; Royal Engineer Yacht (Commodore, 1997–99).

See also Rt Hon. Sir M. J. Moore-Bick.

MOORE-BICK, Rt Hon. Sir Martin (James), Kt 1995; PC 2005; **Rt Hon. Lord Justice Moore-Bick;** a Lord Justice of Appeal, since 2005; Deputy Head of Civil Justice, since 2007; *b* 6 Dec. 1946; *s* of late John Ninian Moore-Bick and Kathleen Margaret Moore-Bick (*née* Beall); *m* 1974, Tessa Penelope Gee; two *s* two *d*. *Educ:* The Skinners' Sch., Tunbridge Wells; Christ's Coll., Cambridge (MA). Called to the Bar, Inner Temple, 1969, Bencher, 1992; QC 1986; a Recorder, 1990–95; a Judge of the High Ct of Justice, QBD, 1995–2005. Chm., Legal Services Consultancy Panel, 2005–. *Recreations:* early music, gardening, reading. *Address:* Royal Courts of Justice, Strand, WC2A 2LL.

See also Maj. Gen. J. D. Moore-Bick.

MOORE-BRABAZON, family name of **Baron Brabazon of Tara**.

MOORE-BRIDGER, Timothy Peter, MA; Headmaster, King Edward VI Grammar School, Stratford-upon-Avon, since 1997; *b* 11 May 1945; *s* of Harry Charles and Winifred Jane Moore-Bridger; *m* 1980, Iwona Elzbieta Joanna (*née* Barycz); one *s* two *d*. *Educ:* Oswestry Sch., Shropshire; Queens' Coll., Cambridge (MA Mod. and Medieval Langs). Asst Master teaching French, Latin, Italian, Ancient History, St Paul's Sch., Barnes, 1967–88; Dep. Headmaster, Nottingham High Sch., 1988–97. Trustee: Shakespeare Birthplace Trust, 1997–; Hampton Lucy Grammar Sch. Trust, 2001–. *Recreations:* attending and supporting RSC productions, wine, gardening. *Address:* The Old Vicarage, Chapel Lane, Stratford-upon-Avon CV37 6BE. *T:* (01789) 267932, *Fax:* (01789) 293564; *e-mail:* head@kingedwardvi.warwickshire.sch.uk.

MOORE-GWYN, Alison Frances; Chief Executive Officer, Fields in Trust (National Playing Fields Association), since 2004; *b* 25 March 1950; *d* of late Clifford George White and Joyce Beatrice White (*née* Lawley); *m* 1974, David Moore-Gwyn; two *s* one *d*. *Educ:* Berkhamsted Sch. for Girls; Girton Coll., Cambridge (BA 1971). Admitted solicitor, 1976; served articles, Clifford Turner. Trustee, NPFA, 1990–2004 (Chm., 2000–04). Trustee: Orders of St John Care Trust, 2000–; St Endellion Easter Fest., 2004–. Gov., Berkhamsted Collegiate Sch., 1979–. *Recreations:* singing and enjoyment of music, fine art, travel, gardening, the family, sailing in fine weather only. *Address:* Fields in Trust, 2D Woodstock Studios, 36 Woodstock Grove, W12 8LE. *T:* (020) 8735 3380, *Fax:* (020) 8735 3397; *e-mail:* alison.moore-gwyn@fieldsintrust.org. *Club:* Beaulieu River Sailing.

See also D. C. S. White.

MOORE-WILTON, Maxwell William, AC 2001; Executive Director, Macquarie Bank, since 2006; Chairman and Director, Macquarie Airports Management Ltd, since 2006; Executive Chairman, Macquarie Media Group, since 2007; *b* 27 Jan. 1943; *s* of William Moore-Wilton and Cavell Little; *m* 1966, Janette Costin; one *s* one *d*. *Educ:* St Joseph's Coll., Qld; Univ. of Queensland (BEc). Commonwealth Department of Trade, Australia, 1964–78: Minister, Delegn for Trade Negotiations, Geneva, 1974–76; First Asst Sec., Policy Develt/Commodity Policy, 1976–78; Dep. Sec., Commonwealth Dept of Primary Industry, 1980–81; Gen. Manager, Australian Wheat Bd, Melbourne, 1981–84; Man. Dir, Australian Nat. Line, Melbourne, 1984–88; Chm., NSW Egg Corp., 1987–89; Chief Exec., Maritime Services Bd of NSW, 1989–91; Dir-Gen., NSW Dept of Transport, 1991–94; Chief Exec., Roads and Traffic Authy of NSW, 1994–95; Chm., Public Transport Corp., Vic, 1995–96; Nat. Dir, Policy Co-ordination and Priorities Rev., Australian Stock Exchange Ltd, 1995–96; Sec., Dept of Prime Minister and Cabinet, Australia, 1996–2002; Exec. Chm. and CEO, 2003–06, Chm., 2006–, Southern Cross Airports Corp. Hldgs (formerly Sydney Airport Corp.) Ltd. Centenary Medal, Aust., 2003. *Recreations:* reading, swimming. *Address:* 8 Beatrice Street, Clontarf, NSW 2093, Australia. *Club:* Union.

MOOREHEAD, Caroline Mary, OBE 2005; FRSL; writer; *b* 28 Oct. 1944; *d* of Alan Moorehead and Lucy (*née* Milner); *m* 1967, Jeremy Swift (marr. diss. 2001); one *s* one *d*. *Educ:* Sorbonne, Paris; University Coll. London (BA Hons 1965). Reporter, Time magazine, 1968–70; Feature Writer, Telegraph magazine, 1970–71; Feature Ed., TES, 1971–74; Feature Writer, The Times, 1973–85; Human Rights Columnist and Feature Writer, Independent, 1985–91; Associate Producer, BBC human rights TV series, 1988–99. Royal Literary Fund Fellow, 2003–05. Trustee: Council, PEN, 1992–97; London Liby, 1994–97; Index on Censorship, 1994–2005; British Inst. for Human Rights, 1995–2004; Soc. of Authors, 1996–99; RSL, 1996–2001; Helen Bamber Foundn, 2005–; Interrights, 2005; Mem., Eminent Persons Mission to USSR, 1994; Co-Founder, Africa and Middle East Refugee Assistance, 2003–. FRSL 1998. *Publications:* Fortune's Hostages, 1980; Sidney Bernstein: a biography, 1984; Freya Stark: a biography, 1987; (ed) Beyond the Rim of the World: the letters of Freya Stark, 1989; Troublesome People, 1991; (ed) Betrayed: children in today's world, 1994; Schliemann and the Lost Treasures of Troy, 1994; Dunant's Dream: war, Switzerland and the Red Cross, 1998; Iris Origo: Marchesa of the Val d'Orcia, 2000; Martha Gellhorn: a life, 2003; Human Cargo: a journey among refugees, 2005; (ed) Letters of Martha Gellhorn, 2006. *Recreations:* travel, music. *Address:* c/o Clare Alexander, Aitken Alexander Associates, 18–21 Cavaye Place, SW10 9PT.

MOORES, John, CBE 1993; Director, The Littlewoods Organisation, 1950–96; *b* 22 Nov. 1928; *s* of Sir John Moores, CBE; *m* 1st, 1949, Helen Sheila Moore; three *s* one *d*; 2nd, 1963, Jane Staveley-Dick; four *s* one *d*. *Educ:* Eton Coll.; Syracuse Univ., USA. Joined The Littlewoods Organisation, 1946, Dep. Chm., 1968–71; Chm., Medaillon Mode GmbH, 1968–71; Chm., Littlewoods Equal Opportunities, 1982–96. Mem. Council, Britain in Europe, 2000–. Chancellor, Liverpool John Moores Univ., 1994–99 (Sen. Pro-Chancellor, and Chm. Bd of Govs, 1992–94). Associated with the Liverpool Motorists' Annual Outing, 1956–; Pres., Roy Castle Lung Cancer Foundn, 1996–2001. DL Merseyside, 1993–2003. Hon. Freeman, City of Liverpool, 1994. *Recreations:* equal opportunities, languages, regionalisation, Europe, cattle breeding. *Address:* South Lodge, North Moss Lane, Formby, Liverpool L37 0AQ. *Club:* Boodle's.

See also Sir P. Moores.

MOORES, Sir Peter, Kt 2003; CBE 1991; DL; Director, The Littlewoods Organisation, 1965–93 (Chairman, 1977–80); *b* 9 April 1932; *s* of Sir John Moores, CBE; *m* 1960, Luciana Pinto (marr. diss. 1984); one *s* one *d*. *Educ:* Eton; Christ Church, Oxford; Wiener Akademie der Musik und darstellenden Kunst. Worked in opera at Glyndebourne and Vienna State Opera. Founded Peter Moores Foundn, 1964, to support opera, visual arts, educn, health, youth, social and envmtl projects; pioneer of opera recordings in English trans. incl. Der Ring des Nibelungen, Mary Stuart, Julius Caesar (all ENO), Carmen (new critical edn), Il Trovatore, Tosca, Der Rosenkavalier; rare 19th century Italian opera in original lang. with Opera Rara, incl. Maria Padilla, Emilia di Liverpool, Rosmonda d'Inghilterra, Ricciardo e Zoraide, Rossini's Otello, Zoraida di Granata; original English lang. recordings incl. Troilus and Cressida, Peter Grimes, Gawain (Royal Opera). Peter Moores Foundn Scholarships awarded to promising young opera singers. Estab. Transatlantic Slave Trade Gallery, Merseyside Maritime Mus., 1994. Endowed Faculty Dirship and Chair of Mgt Studies, 1992, and Lecturership in Chinese Business Studies, 2004, Oxford Univ. Benefactor, Chair of Tropical Horticulture, Univ. of WI, Barbados, 1995. Founded: Compton Verney House Trust, 1993 to house six perm. art collections and exhibns; Peter Moores Charitable Trust, 1998. Director: Singer & Friedlander, 1978–92; Scottish Opera, 1988–92; Trustee, Tate Gall., 1978–85; Governor of the BBC, 1981–83. DL Lancs, 1992. Hon. FRNCM, 1985. Hon. MA Christ Church, 1975. Gold Medal of the Italian Republic, 1974. *Recreations:* opera, shooting. *Address:* Parbold Hall, Parbold, near Wigan, Lancs WN8 7TG. *Club:* Boodle's.

See also John Moores.

MOORES, Dame Yvonne, DBE 1999; Chief Nursing Officer and Director of Nursing, Department of Health, 1992–99; *b* 14 June 1941; *d* of late Tom Abraham Quick and Phyllis Quick (*née* Jeremiah); *m* 1st, 1969, Bruce Holmes Ramsden; 2nd, 1975, Brian Moores. *Educ:* Itchen Grammar Sch., Southampton; Royal South Hampshire Hosp. (RGN); Southampton Gen. Hosp. (RM). Ward Sister, Whittington Hosp. and Royal Hampshire County Hosp., 1964–70; Principal Nursing Officer: N London HMC, 1971–72; W Manchester, 1973–74; Dist Nursing Officer, N Manchester, 1974–76; Area Nursing Officer, Manchester AHA, 1976–81; Chief Nursing Officer: Welsh Office, 1982–88; Scottish Office, Home and Health Dept, 1988–92. Vice-Chm., NHS Supply Council, 1979–82; Pres., Infection Control Nurses Assoc., 1987–90; Mem., WHO Global Adv. Gp for Nursing and Midwifery, 1992–97 (Chair, 1994–97); Vis. Prof., Sheffield Univ., 1996–99. Chm., Macmillan Cancer Unit Appeal, Calderdale, 2000–01. Dep. Chair, Cttee of Univ. Chairs, 2003–04. Bd Mem., Leadership Foundn for Higher Educn, 2005–07. Non-executive Director: NHBC, 2004– (Chm., Pensions Bd, 2007–); Poole Hosp. NHS Trust, 2006–. Mem. Council, Southampton Univ., 1994–2006 (Chm., 2000–06); Pro-Chancellor, Bournemouth Univ., 2006–. Mem., Internat. Award Cttee, Princess Srinagarindra Award, 2000–. Patron, Assoc. for Continence Advice, 2005–. Mem., Policy Steering Cttee, Ferndown Golf Club. Hon. Fellow, Coll. of Med., Univ. of Wales, 1995. Hon. FRSH; Hon. FFPHM 1996; Hon. FRCP. Hon. DSc: Portsmouth, 1993; Huddersfield, 1997; Bradford, 1998; DUniv: Central England, 2001; Southampton, 2006; Hon. DCL Northumbria, 1995; Hon. MA De Montfort, 1995. *Recreations:* bridge, golf, knitting. *Address:* The Chapter House, 43 Golf Links Road, Ferndown, Dorset BH22 8BT.

MOOREY, Adrian Edward; independent consultant, since 2003; *b* 4 May 1946; *s* of Edward Alfred Moorey and Lily Elizabeth Moorey; *m* 1st, 1969, Sandra Ann Jeffrey (marr.

diss.); one *s*; 2nd, 1987, Lesley Nicola Hancock; one *s* one *d*. *Educ:* Sir Joseph Williamson's Mathematical Sch., Rochester. Advertising and Marketing Asst, Lonsdale-Hands Orgn, 1964–67; Asst Information Officer, 1967–69, Inf. Officer, 1969–72, Home Office; Press Officer, PM's Office, 1973; Department of Employment: Sen. Press Officer, 1974–75; Chief Press Officer, 1976–81; Head of Inf., 1982–86; Director of Information: DTI, 1987–90; Home Office, 1990–94; Dir, Corporate and Govt Affairs, Cable and Wireless plc, 1995–99; Corporate Communications Dir, CAA, 1999–2001; Dir of Communications, NATS, 2001–03. *Recreations:* cricket, golf. *Address:* Ellesmere House, 56 Bloomfield Avenue, Bath BA2 3AE.

MOORHOUSE, Barbara Jane; Director General, Corporate Resources, Department for Transport, since 2007; *b* 21 Nov. 1958; *d* of Andre and Rosalind Moorhouse; *m* 2001, Mike Brittain. *Educ:* St Catherine's Coll., Oxford (BA Hons PPE 1981). FMCA 1990; ACT 1999. European Finance Dir, Courtaulds plc, 1986–90; Regulatory Dir, South West Water plc, 1991–95; Finance Dir, Johnson Controls Inc., 1995–96; Gp Finance Dir, Morgan Sindall plc, 1997–98; Interim Exec., Mondex Internat., Jigsaw plc and Energis plc, 1998–2000; Gp Finance Dir, Kewill Systems plc, 2000–02; Chief Financial Officer, Scala Business Solutions NV, 2003–04; Dir Gen., Finance, DCA, subseq. Finance and Commercial, MoJ, 2005–07. Non-exec. Dir, CSA, 2003–06; Mem., Financial Reporting Rev. Panel, 2004–. *Recreations:* horse-riding, ballroom dancing, walking, ski-ing. *Address:* Department for Transport, Great Minster House, 76 Marsham Street, SW1P 4DR.

MOORHOUSE, (Cecil) James (Olaf); *b* 1 Jan. 1924; *s* of late Captain Sidney James Humphrey Moorhouse and Anna Sophie Hedvig de Løvenskiold; *m* 1958, Elizabeth Clive Huxtable (marr. diss. 1995), Sydney, Aust.; one *s* one *d*; *m* 1997, Catherine Hamilton Peterson, New Mexico, USA. *Educ:* St Paul's School; King's Coll. and Imperial Coll., Univ. of London (BSc (Eng); DIC (Advanced Aeronautics)). CEng. Designer with de Havilland Aircraft Co., 1946–48; Project Engr, BOAC, 1948–53; Technical Advr 1953–68, and Environmental Conservation Advr 1968–72, Shell International Petroleum; Environmental Advr, Shell Group of Companies in UK, 1972–73; Group Environmental Affairs Advr, Rio-Tinto Zinc Corp., 1973–80, Consultant, 1980–84. Dir, Project Development International, 1985–90. Mem., Clean Air Council, 1974–80. Contested (C) St Pancras North, 1966 and 1970. MEP (C 1979–98, Lib Dem 1998–99), London S, 1979–84, London S and Surrey E, 1984–99. European Parliament: spokesman on transport for EDG, 1979–84 and 1987–89; spokesman on external economic relations for EDG, 1984–87 and 1989–92; Rapporteur, trade and economic relns between EU and Japan, 1985–99; dep. co-ordinator on external economic relations for EPP, 1992–94; co-ordinator on human rights for EPP and British Cons, 1994–98; spokesman on foreign affairs, defence and human rights for British Cons, 1997–98; Chm., delegn to N Europe and Nordic Council, 1979–84; First Vice-Chm., delegn to EFTA Parliamentarians, 1984–86; Vice-Pres., External Econ. Relations Cttee, 1989–92; Mem., EPP Bureau, 1994–98. Founder Mem., Bow Gp., 1950. Jt Founder, Lib Dem Human Rights Gp, 2001. Mem., Bd of Govs, ESU, 1952–59, 1981–87. Sir Evelyn Wrench Lectr, USA, 1999. Hon. Editor, Inst. of Petroleum, 1965–75. Polish Parlt Medal for work on human rights, 1997. *Publications:* (with Anthony Teasdale) Righting the Balance: a new agenda for Euro-Japanese trade, 1987; numerous articles and papers on aviation. *Recreations:* reading, travel, watching cricket, filmgoer. *Address:* 211 Piccadilly, W1J 9HF. *Clubs:* Sloane; University (Washington).

MOORHOUSE, Geoffrey, FRSL; writer; *b* Bolton, Lancs, 29 Nov. 1931; *s* of William Heald and Gladys Heald (*née* Hoyle, subseq. Moorhouse) and step *s* of Richard Moorhouse; *m* 1st, 1956, Janet Marion Murray; two *s* one *d* (and one *d* decd); 2nd, 1974, Barbara Jane Woodward (marr. diss. 1978); 3rd, 1983, Marilyn Isobel Edwards (marr. diss. 1996). *Educ:* Bury Grammar School. Nat. Service, Royal Navy (Coder), 1950–52; editorial staff: Bolton Evening News, 1952–54; Grey River Argus (NZ), Auckland Star (NZ), Christchurch Star-Sun (NZ), 1954–56; News Chronicle, 1957; (Manchester) Guardian, 1958–70 (Chief Features Writer, 1963–70). Rode camels 2000 miles across Sahara, 1972–73; deep-sea fisherman, Gloucester, Mass, 1976–77. FRGS 1972–95; FRSL 1982. Hon. DLitt Warwick, 2006. *Publications:* in numerous editions and translations: The Other England, 1964; The Press, 1964; Against All Reason, 1969; Calcutta, 1971; The Missionaries, 1973; The Fearful Void, 1974; The Diplomats, 1977; The Boat and The Town, 1979; The Best-Loved Game, 1979 (Cricket Soc. Award); India Britannica, 1983; Lord's, 1983; To the Frontier, 1984 (Thomas Cook Award, 1984); Imperial City: the rise and rise of New York, 1988; At the George (essays), 1989; Apples in the Snow, 1990; Hell's Foundations: a town, its myths and Gallipoli, 1992; Om: an Indian pilgrimage, 1993; A People's Game: the centenary history of Rugby League football 1895–1995, 1995; Sun Dancing: a medieval vision, 1997; Sydney, 1999; The Pilgrimage of Grace: the rebellion that shook Henry VIII's throne, 2002; Great Harry's Navy: how Henry VIII gave England seapower, 2005; The Last Office: 1539 and the dissolution of a monastery, 2008. *Recreations:* music, gardening, hill-walking, looking at buildings, watching cricket, and Bolton Wanderers FC. *Address:* Park House, Gayle, near Hawes, North Yorkshire DL8 3RT. *T:* and *Fax:* (01969) 667456. *Club:* Lancashire County Cricket.

MOORHOUSE, James; *see* Moorhouse, C. J. O.

MOORHOUSE, Judith Helen; Chair, General Teaching Council England, since 2004; *b* Eastleigh, Hants, 31 Oct. 1949; *d* of Edward and Joan Moorhouse. *Educ:* Coll. of Sarum St Michael, Salisbury (Cert Ed). Teacher of English: Fairoak Sch., Hants, 1971–72; Shackleton Sch., Fallingbostel, W Germany, 1972–73; Toynbee Sch., Eastleigh, 1973–74; Teacher of English, 1974–, Hd of Year, 1995–, Richmond Sch., N Yorks. National Union of Teachers: Exec. Mem., 1998–2004; Chm., Educn and Equal Opportunities Cttee, 2000–04; Pres., 2006–07. Mem., Governing Council, Nat. Coll. for Sch. Leadership, 2005–; Mem. Council, 2005–, Trustee, 2008–, Specialist Schs and Acads Trust. *Recreations:* basking on Greek beaches, far-flung travel, trade unionism and equal rights, singing - from blues to requiem masses, indiscriminate reading. *Address:* 67 Frenchgate, Richmond, N Yorks DL10 7AE. *T:* (01748) 825106, 07909 542283, *Fax:* (01748) 823740; *e-mail:* judy@moorhousegtc.fsnet.co.uk.

MOORHOUSE, (Kathleen) Tessa; a District Judge (formerly Registrar), Family Division of the High Court of Justice, 1982–2004; a Deputy District Judge, since 2004; *b* 14 Sept. 1938; *d* of late Charles Elijah Hall, MRCVS and Helen Barbara Hall; *m* 1959, Rodney Moorhouse. *Educ:* Presentation Convent, Derbyshire; Leeds Univ.; King's Coll., London. Called to the Bar, Inner Temple, 1971. Asst, Jardine's Bookshop, Manchester, 1953–56; student, Leeds Univ., 1956–59; teacher of educationally subnormal, 1959–61; student, King's Coll., London, 1961–62; Classifier, Remand Home, 1962–64; Lectr in Law, 1964–71; barrister in practice, 1971–82. *Address:* 1st Avenue House, 42–49 High Holborn, WC1V 6NP. *T:* (020) 7947 6000; Coram Chambers, Fulwood Place, WC1V 6HG.

MOORHOUSE, Michael George Currer; His Honour Judge Moorhouse; a Circuit Judge, since 2001; *b* 29 June 1946; *s* of Reginald Currer Moorhouse and Betty Moorhouse; *m* 1970, Jane Mary Ross; one *s* three *d*. *Educ:* Ampleforth Coll. Admitted solicitor, 1970; in private practice, 1970–2001; Partner, R. C. Moorhouse Co., subseq. Keeble Hawson Moorhouse, 1975–2001. *Recreations:* gardening, sport, walking. *Address:* Middlesbrough Combined Court, Russell Street, Middlesbrough TS1 2AE.

MOORHOUSE, Peter William; Chairman, Police Complaints Authority, 1996–99 (Deputy Chairman, 1991–96); *b* 25 Dec. 1938; *s* of Francis and Dorothy Moorhouse; *m* 1962, Jane Catton; two *s* one *d*. *Educ:* Stonyhurst Coll. Joined Schweppes Group, 1961, Divl Dir, 1980–87; Mem., Police Complaints Authy, 1988–2000. Mem., Local Review Cttee, Parole Bd, 1973–88 (Chm., 1977–79, 1986–88). Complaints Convenor, Beds and Herts HA, 2002–05. Gov., Stonyhurst Coll., 1991–94. FRSA 1995. *Recreations:* opera, art, walking, inland boating. *Address:* c/o HSBC, 1 High Street, Harpenden, Herts AL5 2RS.

MOORHOUSE, Tessa; *see* Moorhouse, K. T.

MOORTHY, Arambamoorthy Thedchana; Sri Lanka Foreign Service, retired; private academic research and writing, since 1984; *b* 10 Aug. 1928; *s* of late Mr Arambamoorthy and Mrs Nesamma Arambamoorthy; *m* 1959, Suseela T. Moorthy, *d* of Justice P. Sri Skanda Rajah; one *s* two *d*. *Educ:* BAEcon Hons (Sri Lanka). Called to Bar, Gray's Inn, 1965. Entered Foreign Service of Sri Lanka, 1953; Second Secretary: Indonesia, 1955–57; China, 1957–59; First Secretary: London, 1961–63; Federal Republic of Germany, 1964–66; Chargé d'Affaires, *ai*, Thailand, and Permanent Representative of Sri Lanka to Economic Commn for Asia and Far East, 1969; Chargé d'Affaires, *ai*, Iraq, 1970; Ambassador in Pakistan, 1978–Dec. 1980, and concurrently, Jan.–Dec. 1980, Ambassador to Iran with residence in Islamabad; High Comr in London, 1981–84. *Address:* 39 Gladstone Road, Wimbledon, SW19 1QU. *T:* (020) 8544 9537.

MOOSONEE, Archbishop of, since 2004; **Most Rev. Caleb James Lawrence;** Metropolitan of Ontario, since 2004; *b* 26 May 1941; *s* of James Otis Lawrence and Mildred Viola Burton; *m* 1966, Maureen Patricia Cuddy; one *s* two *d*. *Educ:* Univ. of King's College; BA Dalhousie Univ. 1962; BST 1964. Deacon 1963, priest 1965; Missionary at Anglican Mission, Great Whale River, Quebec, 1965–75; Rector of St Edmund's Parish, Great Whale River, 1975–79; Canon of St Jude's Cathedral, Frobisher Bay, Diocese of The Arctic, 1974; Archdeacon of Arctic Quebec, 1975–79; Bishop Coadjutor, Jan.–Nov. 1980, Bishop, 1980–, Diocese of Moosonee. Hon. DD, Univ. of King's Coll., Halifax, NS, 1980. *Recreations:* reading, photography. *Address:* The Diocese of Moosonee, Synod Office, Box 841, Schumacher, ON P0N 1G0, Canada. *T:* (705) 3601129.

MORAES, Claude Ajit; Member (Lab) London Region, European Parliament, since 1999; *s* of H. I. Moraes and Theresa (*née* Aranha); *m* Bharti Patel. *Educ:* St Modan's High Sch., Stirling; Univ. of Dundee (LLB 1988); Birkbeck Coll., Univ. of London (MSc 1989). Res. Asst to John Reid, MP and Paul Boateng, MP, 1987–89; postgrad. study in internat. law, LSE, 1990–91; Nat. Policy Officer, TUC, and TUC Rep. to ETUC, 1989–92; Dir, Jt Council for Welfare of Immigrants, 1992–98; Chief Exec., Immigrants' Aid Trust, 1994–98. Lab spokesperson on employment and social affairs, 2000–, Mem., Justice and Home Affairs Cttee, 2004–, EP. Comr, CRE, 1998–99. Mem., Council, Liberty, 1997–2005. Columnist, Tribune, 1998–2005. Trustee, Toynbee Hall Charity, 1997–2001. Patron: Naz Aids Proj., 1999–; Refugee Therapy Centre, 2005–. Contested (Lab) Harrow W, 1992. FRSA 1998. *Publications:* (jtly) Social Work and Minorities: European perspectives, 1998; (jtly) The Politics of Migration, 2003; (jtly) Immigratie Italiani: il futuro e convivenza, 2004; contributed: Full Employment and the Global Economy, 2004; Perspectives on Migration, 2005; European Civic Index, 2005; contrib. jls and nat. newspapers. *Recreations:* Scottish literature, chess, films, listening to Radio 4 and 5 and my MP3 player. *Address:* European Parliament, 13G 154 Rue Wiertz, 1047 Brussels. *T:* (Brussels) (2) 2845553, *T:* (020) 7609 5005; *e-mail:* mep@claudemoraes.net.

MORAHAN, Christopher Thomas; television, film and theatre director; *b* 9 July 1929; *s* of Thomas Hugo Morahan and Nancy Charlotte Morahan (*née* Barker); *m* 1st, 1954, Joan (*née* Murray) (decd); two *s* (one *d* decd); 2nd, 1973, Anna (*née* Wilkinson, acting name Anna Carteret); two *d*. *Educ:* Highgate; Old Vic Theatre School. Directing for ATV, 1957–61; freelance director in TV for BBC and ITV, 1961–71; Head of Plays, BBC TV, 1972–76; Associate, National Theatre, 1977–88; Director, Greenpoint Films, 1983–2003. Trustee, Cherub Theatre, 2005–. *Stage:* Little Murders, RSC, Aldwych, 1967; This Story of Yours, Royal Court, 1968; Flint, Criterion, 1970; The Caretaker, Mermaid, 1972; Melon, Th. Royal, Haymarket, 1987; A Letter of Resignation, Comedy, 1997; Quartet, Albery, 1999; The Importance of Being Earnest, Australia and NZ, 2000; Naked Justice, W Yorks Playhouse, 2001; The Dwarfs, Tricycle, 2003; Oldworld, tour, 2003; Hayfever, Clwyd Theatr Cymru, 2004; Daisy Miller, tour, 2005; The Rivals, Bath, 2005; The Linden Tree, Orange Tree Th., Richmond, 2006; Present Laughter, An Ideal Husband, Clwyd Theatr Cymru, 2006; Legal Fictions, tour, 2007, Savoy, 2008; Chichester Festival: Major Barbara, 1988; The Handyman, 1996; Racing Demon, 1998; The Importance of Being Earnest, Semi-Detached, The Retreat from Moscow, 1999; Heartbreak House, 2000; The Winslow Boy, Hock and Soda Water, 2001; for National Theatre: State of Revolution, 1977; Brand, Strife, The Philanderer, 1978; Richard III, The Wild Duck, 1979; Sisterly Feelings, 1980; Man and Superman, 1981; Wild Honey (London Standard, Olivier, British Theatre Assoc. and Plays and Players Awards for Best Dir of the Year), 1984; The Devil's Disciple, 1994; *films:* Clockwise, 1986; Paper Mask, 1990; *television: films:* The Gorge, 1967; In the Secret State, 1985; After Pilkington, 1987 (Special Jury Prize, San Francisco Film Fest., 1987, Prix Italia, 1987); Troubles, 1988; The Heat of the Day, 1989; Old Flames, 1990; Can You Hear Me Thinking?, 1990; Common Pursuit, 1992; The Bullion Boys, 1993 (Internat. Emmy Award, 1994); Summer Day's Dream, 1994; It Might Be You, 1995; Element of Doubt, 1996; The Dwarfs, 2003; HR, 2007; *series:* Emergency Ward 10; The Orwell Trilogy; Talking to a Stranger; Fathers and Families; Jewel in the Crown (Internat. Emmy Award, BAFTA Best Series Dir Award, BAFTA Desmond Davis Award, 1984; Primetime Emmy Award, 1985); Ashenden, 1991; Unnatural Pursuits, 1992 (Internat. Emmy Award, 1993); Peacock Spring, 1996; A Dance to the Music of Time, 1997. Best Play direction award, SFTA, 1969. *Recreations:* photography, bird watching. *Address:* c/o Sheperd Management, 45 Maddox Street, W1S 2PE. *T:* (020) 7495 7813. *Club:* Garrick.

MORAN, 2nd Baron *cr* 1943; **Richard John McMoran Wilson,** KCMG 1981 (CMG 1970); *b* 22 Sept. 1924; *er s* of 1st Baron Moran, MC, MD, FRCP, and Dorothy (*d* 1983), MBE, *d* of late Samuel Felix Dufton, DSc; *S* father, 1977; *m* 1948, Shirley Rowntree Harris; two *s* one *d*. *Educ:* Eton; King's Coll., Cambridge. Served War of 1939–45; Ord. Seaman in HMS Belfast, 1943; Sub-Lt RNVR in Motor Torpedo Boats and HM Destroyer Oribi, 1944–45. Foreign Office, 1945; Third Sec., Ankara, 1948; Tel-Aviv, 1950; Second Sec., Rio de Janeiro, 1953; First Sec., FO, 1956; Washington, 1959; FO 1961; Counsellor, British Embassy in S Africa, 1965; Head of W African Dept, FCO, 1968–73, concurrently Ambassador to Chad (non-resident), 1970–73; Ambassador to Hungary, 1973–76, to Portugal, 1976–81; High Comr in Canada, 1981–84. Cross Bencher, H of L, 1984–; Mem., Industry sub cttee, 1984–86, Envmt sub cttee, 1986–91, Agric. sub cttee, 1991–95, 1997–2000, EC Cttee; sub cttee on the 1996 Inter-governmental Conf., 1995–96; Mem. Science and Technol. Cttee sub cttees on scientific base of Nature Conservancy Council, 1990, on fish stocks, 1995; Chm., All Party Parly

Conservation Gp, 1992–2000 (Vice-Chm., 1989–92); elected Mem., H of L, 1999. Chm., Jt Fisheries Policy and Legislation Wkg Gp (Moran Cttee), 1997–. Vice-Chm., Atlantic Salmon Trust, 1988–95 (Mem. Management Cttee, 1984–; Vice-Pres., 1995–); Chm., Fisheries Adv. Cttee for Welsh Region, Nat. Rivers Authy, 1989–94; Mem., Regl Fisheries Adv. Cttee, Welsh Water Authority, 1987–89; Pres., Welsh Salmon and Trout Angling Assoc., 1988–95, 2000–; Chm., Salmon and Trout Assoc., 1997–2000 (Exec. Vice Pres., 2000–). Chm., Wildlife and Countryside Link, 1992–95; Pres., Radnorshire Wildlife Trust, 1993–; Vice-Pres., RSPB, 1997–98 (Mem. Council, 1989–94). Grand Cross, Order of the Infante (Portugal), 1978. *Publications:* (as John Wilson): C. B.: a life of Sir Henry Campbell-Bannerman, 1973 (Whitbread Award for biography, 1973); Fairfax, 1985; (with William and James Wilson) William Robert Grove: the lawyer who invented the fuel cell, 2007. *Recreations:* fishing, fly-tying, bird-watching. *Heir: s* Hon. James McMoran Wilson [*b* 6 Aug. 1952; *m* 1980, Hon. Jane Hepburne-Scott, *y d* of 10th Lord Polwarth, TD; two *s*]. *Address:* House of Lords, SW1A 0PW. *Clubs:* Beefsteak, Flyfishers' (Pres., 1987–88).

See also Baron Mountevans, Hon. G. H. Wilson.

MORAN, Andrew Gerard; QC 1994; a Recorder, since 1997; *b* 19 Oct. 1953; *s* of Francis Michael Moran and Winifrede Moran; *m* 1977, Carole Jane Sullivan; six *s* one *d*. *Educ:* West Park Grammar Sch., St Helens, Lancs; Britannia Royal Naval Coll., Dartmouth; Balliol Coll., Oxford (BA Law). Called to Bar, Gray's Inn, 1976, Bencher, 2005. *Recreations:* family, sport, travel. *Address:* St John's Building, 24A–28 St John Street, Manchester M3 4DJ. *T:* (0161) 214 1500, *Fax:* (0161) 835 3929; Stone Chambers, 4 Field Court, Gray's Inn, WC1R 5EF. *T:* (020) 7440 6900, *Fax:* (020) 7242 0197; 7 Harrington Street, Liverpool L2 9YH. *T:* (0151) 242 0707, *Fax:* (0151) 236 2800.

MORAN, Air Marshal Christopher Hugh, OBE 1997; MVO 1993; Deputy Commander, Allied Joint Force Command, Brunssum, since 2007; *b* 28 April 1956; *s* of late Edward Moran and Margaret Moran (*née* Hewitt); *m* 1980, Elizabeth Jane Goodwin; one *s* two *d*. *Educ:* Ullathorne Sch., Coventry; UMIST (BSc Hons 1977); KCL (MA 2000). Pilot Trng, RAF Coll., Cranwell, 1977–78; IV (Army Co-op.) Sqdn, Gütersloh, 1980–85; qualified Weapons Instructor (Harrier), 1983; Exchange Service, USMC, Sqdn VMA 542, 1985–87; 233 (Harrier) OCU, 1987–91; OC, IV (Army Co-op.) Sqdn, Laarbruch, 1994–96; acsc RAF Coll., Bracknell, 1991; Equerry to Duke of Edinburgh, 1992–93; OC, RAF Wittering, 1997–98; HCSC, JSCSC, Bracknell, 1999; Divl Dir, JSCSC, Bracknell, 1999–2000; Dir of Air Staff, MoD, 2000–02; AOC No 1 Gp, 2003–05; ACAS, 2005–07. *Recreations:* ski-ing, sailing, triathlon. *Address:* c/o RAF High Wycombe, Bucks HP14 4UE. *Clubs:* Royal Air Force; Yealm Yacht.

MORAN, Christopher John; Chairman, Christopher Moran Group of Companies, since 1970; *b* 16 Jan. 1948; *s* of late Thomas Moran and Iva Mary Moran (*née* Alcock); *m* 1981, Helen Elisabeth Taylor (marr. diss. 1999); two *s* (twins). *Educ:* Owen's Grammar Sch. Dir, C&UCO Properties Ltd, 2006–. Chairman: Finance Bd, LSO, 2004–; Co-operation Ireland (GB), 2004–; Co-operation Ireland, 2006–; Member: Consultative Cttee, Dulwich Picture Gall., 1993–96; Thames Adv. Bd, 1994–97. Trustee: UCL Hosps Charitable Foundn, 1999– (Chm., 2003–); Exec. Cttee, CCJ, 2003– (Vice Chm., 2008–); Mary Rose Trust, 2004–; LSO Endowment Trust, 2007–; Patron, ISS UK, 2007–. FRSA 2005. *Recreations:* architecture, opera, art, politics, country pursuits. *Address:* c/o Crosby Hall, Cheyne Walk, SW3 5AZ.

MORAN, David John; HM Diplomatic Service; on loan to Cabinet Office, since 2008; *b* 22 Aug. 1959; *s* of late Thomas Henry Moran and of Donna Lois Moran (*née* Zastrow); *m* 1993, Carol Ann Marquis. *Educ:* Stoke Brunswick Sch.; Tonbridge Sch.; Willamette Univ., Salem, Oregon (BA); Univ. of Sussex (MA). Oregon State Employment Div., 1979–80, 1982–83; DTI, 1985; ODA, 1985–88; Second Sec., E Africa Office, ODA, Nairobi, 1988–91; Hd of Section, Econ Relns Dept, FCO, 1991–93; First Sec., Moscow, 1993–96; Head: France and Switzerland Section, FCO, 1996–98; EU Charter of Rights Section, EU Dept (Internal), 1998–2000; Dep. UK Perm. Rep. to OECD, Paris, 2001–05; Ambassador to Uzbekistan, 2005–07; Counsellor, FCO, 2007–08. *Recreations:* writing and listening to music, theatre, swimming, football (Everton FC). *Address:* c/o Foreign and Commonwealth Office, King Charles Street, SW1A 2AH.

MORAN, Rt Rev. Mgr John, CBE 1985; Principal RC Chaplain and Vicar General (Army), 1981–85; *b* 3 Dec. 1929; *s* of Thomas Moran and Gertrude May (*née* Sheer). *Educ:* De La Salle Coll., Sheffield; Ushaw Coll., Durham. Ordained Priest, Leeds Diocese, 1956; Curate, Dewsbury, 1956–60; Prison Chaplain, Armley, 1960–61; commissioned Army Chaplain, 1961; service in BAOR, Singapore, Malaya, Hong Kong, UK; Chaplain, RMA Sandhurst, 1968–70, Staff Chaplain, 1970–71; Senior Chaplain, HQ BAOR, 1977–79, and HQ UKLF, 1979–80. *Recreations:* music, rivers, clocks.

MORAN, Air Vice-Marshal Manus Francis; Royal Air Force, retired; *b* 18 April 1927; *s* of John Thomas Moran and Katherine Mary (*née* Coyle); *m* 1955, Maureen Elizabeth Martin, *o d* of Martin Dilks; one *s* three *d* (and one *s* decd). *Educ:* Mount St Joseph Abbey, Roscrea; University College Dublin (MB ChB, BAO 1952; MCh 1964); DLO, RCP and RCS, 1963. St Vincent's Hosp., Dublin, 1952; GP, Lutterworth, 1953–54; joined RAF 1954; Department of Otorhinolaryngology: served London, 1955–56; Wroughton, 1956–58; Weeton, 1958–59; Akrotiri, 1959–61; Halton, 1963–65; Consultant in ORL, RAF, 1965; served Changi, Singapore, 1965–68; Vis. Consultant, Johore Bahru Gen. Hosp., 1966–68; Nocton Hall, 1968–75; Wegberg, 1975–78; Wroughton, 1978–83; Consultant Adviser in ORL (RAF), 1983–88; Dean of Air Force Medicine, 1988–90; Sen. Consultant, RAF, 1990–91; Civilian Consultant in ORL, RAF Hosp., Wroughton, 1991–95. QHP, 1988–91. Lectr in ORL, IAM Farnborough, for Dip. in Aviation medicine, RCP, 1983–88. Consultant: Nuffield Hosp., Leicester, 1992–2000; Met. Police, 1994–2003. Chm., Gen. Cttee, 8th British Acad. Conf. in ORL, 1987–91. Member: Irish Otological Soc.; Midland Inst. of Otology (Vice-Pres., 1971, 1975); Otology Section, RSM (Vice-Pres., Section of Laryngology, 1988–91, Pres., 1991–92); Council, British Assoc. of Otolaryngologists, 1983–88; Joseph Soc., BMA; BS Cttee on Auditory Alarms in med. monitoring equipment, 1983–88; Bd, Co-operation North, 1992–97. Chm., Marston Meysey Charitable Trust, 1989–91 (Vice-Chm., 1987–89); Special Trustee, Royal Nat. Throat, Nose and Ear Hosp., 1993–99. Mem. Editl Bd, Amer. ENT Jl, 1982–92. Hon. FRCSI 1991. Liveryman, Apothecaries' Soc. (Chm., Livery Cttee, 1994–96); Freeman, City of London. CStJ 1990. Med. Soc. (UCD) Gold Medal, 1951; Lady Cade Medal, RCS, 1980. *Publications:* Upper Respiratory Problems in Yellow Nail Syndrome (jtly), 1976; contribs to learned jls on ORL applied to aviation medicine, ureamic rhinitis, vestibular dysfunction, acoustic trauma and hearing conservation. *Recreations:* preservation of rural amenities, walking, poetry, theology, power boating. *Address:* The Old Forge House, Marston Meysey, Cricklade, Wilts SN6 6LQ. *T:* (01285) 810511. *Club:* Royal Air Force.

MORAN, Margaret; MP (Lab) Luton South, since 1997; *b* 24 April 1955; *d* of Patrick John, (Jack), Moran and Mary (*née* Murphy). *Educ:* Birmingham Univ. (BSocSc). Dir, Housing for Women, 1987–97. Mem., Lewisham BC, 1984–96 (Chairman: Housing Cttee, 1985–91; Direct Lab. Cttee, 1991; Leader, 1995–96). Dep. Chm., AMA, 1994 (Chm., Housing Cttee, 1992). Contested (Lab) Carshalton and Wallington, 1992. PPS to Minister for Cabinet Office, 1999–2003; an Asst Govt Whip, 2003–05. Member: NI Select Cttee, 1997–98; Public Admin. Select Cttee, 1999. *Address:* House of Commons, SW1A 0AA. *T:* (020) 7219 5049.

MORAN, Prof. Michael John, PhD; FBA 2004; W. J. M. Mackenzie Professor of Government, University of Manchester, since 1990; *b* 13 April 1946; *s* of Michael Moran and Bridget Moran (*née* Brennan); *m* 1967, Winifred Evaskitas; two *s*. *Educ:* Irish Christian Brothers, Kilrush; Cardinal Newman Secondary Mod. Sch., Birmingham; Univ. of Lancaster (BA 1967); Univ. of Essex (MA; PhD 1974). Lectr, Manchester Polytech., 1970–79; University of Manchester: Lectr, 1979–90; Dean, Faculty of Econ. and Social Studies, 1995–98. Ed., Political Studies, 1993–99; Co-Ed., Government and Opposition, 2000–06. *Publications:* scholarly monographs, student text books and contribs to learned jls. *Recreations:* operas, movies, mountains. *Address:* School of Social Sciences, University of Manchester, Manchester M13 9PL; *e-mail:* michael.moran@manchester.ac.uk.

MORAN, Rt Rev. Peter Antony; *see* Aberdeen, Bishop of, (RC).

MORAN, Terence Anthony, CB 2007; Chief Executive and Director General, Pension, Disability and Carers Service, since 2008; *b* Rotherham, 23 April 1960; partner, Stuart Hayes. *Educ:* St Joseph's Prim. Sch., Rawmarsh; Rawmarsh Comp. Sch.; Harvard Business Sch. (AMP 2006). Joined Civil Service, 1977; clerical asst, DHSS, 1977; Private Secretary: to Dir, Social Security Ops, 1990–91; to Chief Exec., Benefits Agency, 1992–96; Area Dir, Yorks, Benefits Agency, 2001–02; Dir, NW Reg., Jobcentre Plus, 2002–04; Chief Exec., Disability and Carers Service, 2004–07; Interim Chief Exec., Pension Service, 2007–08. Trustee, Nat. Bd, Victim Support, 2006–. *Recreations:* sports, music, gardening, walking. *Address:* Pension, Disability and Carers Service, Richmond House, 79 Whitehall, SW1A 2NS. *T:* (020) 7829 3067; *e-mail:* Terry.moran1@dwp.gsi.gov.uk.

MORATINOS CUYAUBÉ, Miguel Angel, Knight, Order of Civil Merit (Spain); Minister of Foreign Affairs, Spain, since 2004; *b* 8 June 1951; *m* Dominique Maunac; three *c*. *Educ:* Madrid (Law and Political Sci. degree); Diplomatic Sch. (Dip. Internat. Studies). Spanish Diplomatic Service: Dir-Hd, E Europe Co-ordination Desk, 1974–79; First Sec., 1979–80, Chargé d'affaires, 1980–84, Yugoslavia; Political Advr, Rabat, 1984–87; Dep. Dir Gen. for N Africa, 1987–91; Director General: Inst. for Co-operation with the Arab World, 1991–93; of Foreign Policy for Africa and ME, 1993–96; Ambassador, Israel, 1996; EU Special Rep. for the ME Peace Process, 1996–2003. Comdr, Order of Ouissam Alaouite (Morocco). *Publications:* The European Security and the Mediterranean, 1990; Mediterranean: a forgotten sea, 1990; Mediterranean and Middle East, 1995. *Recreations:* tennis, football. *Address:* Ministry of Foreign Affairs, Plaza Marqués de Salamanca 8, 28071 Madrid, Spain. *T:* (91) 3799966; *e-mail:* ministro@mae.es.

MORAUTA, Rt Hon. Sir Mekere, Kt 1991; MP Moresby North-West, Papua New Guinea, since 1997 (People's Democratic Movement, 1987–2002, Papua New Guinea Party, since 2002); Leader of the Opposition, since 2007; *b* 12 June 1946; *s* of Morauta Hasu and Morikoai Elavo; *m* Roslyn; two *s*. *Educ:* Univ. of Papua New Guinea (BEcon); Flinders Univ., SA. Res. Officer (Manpower Planning), Dept of Labour, 1971; Economist, Office of the Economic Advr, 1972; Sec. for Finance, Govt of PNG, 1973–82; Man. Dir, PNG Banking Corp., 1983–92; Gov., Bank of Papua New Guinea, 1993–94; Executive Chairman: Delta Seafoods, 1994–97; Morauta and Associates (Publishing), 1994–97. Minister: for Planning and Implementation, PNG, 1997–98; for Fisheries and Marine Resources, 1998–99; Prime Minister and Minister for Treasury, 1999–2002. Chm., Nat. Airline Commn, 1992–94. Mem. Bd, Angco; formerly Director: Highlands Gold (PNG); PNG Associated Industries; Thomas Nationwide Transport (PNG); James Barnes PNG; numerous public and commercial bodies. Former Mem. Fund Raising Cttees, Salvation Army and Red Cross. Hon. DTech Univ. of Technology, PNG, 1987; Hon. DEc PNG, 2001. *Publications:* numerous papers on economic and allied subjects.

MORAY, 20th Earl of, *cr* 1562; **Douglas John Moray Stuart;** Lord Abernethy and Strathearn, 1562; Lord Doune, 1581; Baron of St Colme, 1611; Baron Stuart (GB), 1796; *b* 13 Feb. 1928; *e s* of 19th Earl of Moray and Mabel Helen Maud Wilson (*d* 1968); *S* father, 1974; *m* 1964, Lady Malvina Murray, *er d* of 7th Earl of Mansfield and Mansfield; one *s* one *d*. *Educ:* Trinity Coll., Cambridge (BA), FLAS 1958. *Heir: s* Lord Doune, *qv*. *Club:* New (Edinburgh).

MORAY, ROSS AND CAITHNESS, Bishop of, since 2007; **Rt Rev. Mark Jeremy Strange;** *b* 2 Nov. 1961; *s* of Edward Strange and Dorothy Strange (*née* Tinker); *m* 1983, Jane Elizabeth; one *s* two *d*. *Educ:* Aberdeen Univ. (LTh); Lincoln Theol Coll. (Cert. in Ministry and Mission). Cathedral Verger, Worcester Cathedral, 1984–87; ordained deacon, 1989, priest, 1990; Curate, St Barnabas and Christchurch, Worcs, 1989–92; Vicar, St Wulstan, Warndon, Worcs, 1992–98; Rector, Holy Trinity, Elgin, 1998–2007; Priest-in-charge: St Margaret's, Lossiemouth, 1998–2007; St Michael's, Dufftown, 2004–07; St Margaret's, Aberlour, 2004–07. Canon, St Andrew's Cathedral, Inverness, 2000–07. Convenor, Scottish Episcopal Youth Network, 2002–; Synod Clerk, Moray, Ross and Caithness, 2003–07. Moray Scout Association: Area Comr, 1998–2001; Area Chaplain, 2001–; Chaplain, Elgin ATC, 2004–07. Chair, Elgin Community Planning Workers Gp, 2002–. *Recreations:* hill-walking, beach-combing, whisky-tasting. *Address:* Bishop's House, St John's Rectory, Arpafeelie, North Kessock, Inverness IV1 3XD; *e-mail:* bishop@moray.anglican.org.

MORAY, ROSS AND CAITHNESS, Dean of; *see* Black, Very Rev. L. A.

MORBY, Grainne; Manager and Family Advocate, Patient Advice and Liaison Service, Great Ormond Street Hospital for Children and UCL Institute of Child Health, since 2004; *b* 26 June 1951; *d* of Geoffrey and Dympna Morby. *Educ:* Essex Univ. (BA Hons). Dir, Community Information Project, LA, 1980–89; Dir of Communications, London Bor. of Hackney, 1989–95; acting Chief Exec., London Lighthouse, 1995–2001; Dir of London Services, Terrence Higgins Trust & Lighthouse, 2001–04. *Publication:* Knowhow: a guide to your rights, 1986. *Recreations:* gardening, Irish music. *Address:* Pals, Great Ormond Street Hospital for Children, Great Ormond Street, WC1N 3JH.

MORCOM, Christopher; QC 1991; *b* 4 Feb. 1939; *s* of late Dr Rupert Morcom and Mary Morcom (*née* Carslake); *m* 1966, Diane, *d* of late Jose Antonio Toledo and Winifred Anne (*née* Wardlaw); one *s* two *d*. *Educ:* Sherborne Sch.; Trinity Coll., Cambridge (BA Hons 1961; MA 1964). Called to the Bar, Middle Temple, 1963 (Cert. Honour, Astbury Scholar; Bencher, 1996); Barrister, Mauritius, 1979–. Member: Senate, Law Soc. Jt Wking Party on Intellectual Property Law, 1976–; Standing Adv. Cttee on Industrial Property, 1990–2001. Chm., Competition Law Assoc., 1985–99. Pres., Ligue Internationale du Droit de la Concurrence, 1996–98 (Vice Pres., 1994–96; Hon. Pres., 2000). Chm., Bar Musical Soc., 1991–. *Publications:* Service Marks: a guide to the new law, 1987; A Guide to the Trade Marks Act 1994, 1994; (jtly) The Modern Law of Trade Marks, 2000, 3rd edn 2008; legal articles in Law Soc. Gazette, Counsel, European Intellectual Property Rev.

Recreations: music, walking. *Address:* Hogarth Chambers, 5 New Square, Lincoln's Inn, WC2A 3RJ. *T:* (020) 7404 0404. *Club:* Athenæum.

MORDAUNT, Sir Richard (Nigel Charles), 14th Bt *cr* 1611; (does not use the title at present); documentary film producer; founder, Coolamon Media Australia; *b* 12 May 1940; *s* of Lt-Col Sir Nigel John Mordaunt, 13th Bt, MBE, and Anne (*d* 1980), *d* of late Arthur F. Tritton; *S* father, 1979; *m* 1964, Myriam Atchia (decd); one *s* one *d*; *m* 1995, Diana Barbara (*née* Davis); one step *d*. *Educ:* Wellington. Producer, award-winning documentaries, England and Australia, 1965–. *Heir: s* Kim John Mordaunt, *b* 11 June 1966. *Address: e-mail:* richardmordaunt@bigpond.com.

MORDEN, Jessica; MP (Lab) Newport East, since 2005; *b* 29 May 1968; *d* of Mick and Margaret Morden. *Educ:* Croesyceiliog Comp. Sch., Cwmbran; Univ. of Birmingham (BA Hons Hist. 1989). Researcher: to Huw Edwards, MP, 1991–92; to Llew Smith, MP, 1992–93; Organiser, SE Wales, Welsh Lab. Party, 1993–98; Elections Officer, Labour Party, 1998–99; Gen. Sec., Welsh Labour Party, 1999–2005. *Recreations:* gym, film. *Address:* House of Commons, SW1A 0AA. *T:* (020) 7219 6135, (constituency) (01633) 273111; *e-mail:* mordenj@parliament.uk. *Club:* Ringland Labour (Newport).

MORDUE, Jane Margaret; strategic management consultant and coach, since 2001; Chief Executive, Comparative Clinical Science Foundation, since 2005; Chairman, South East Area (formerly Region) Committee, Citizens Advice, since 2004; *b* 8 June 1953; *d* of late James Gibson Jones and Margaret Jones (*née* Finlayson); *m* 1990, Prof. Alan Osborn Betts (*d* 2005); *m* 2007, Howard James Mordue. *Educ:* Univ. of Leeds (BA); Cornell Univ. (EDP); INSEAD (AMP). MHSM. PA to Man. Dir, Fairclough Ltd, Leeds, 1976–79; University of London: PA to Principal and Information Officer, RVC, 1979–85; Admin. Assistant to Vice-Chancellor and Dep. Public Relations Officer, 1985–88; Sec., BPMF, 1988–96; Sec.-Gen., Law Soc., 1996–2000; Chm., Thames Valley Strategic HA, 2002–04. Vice-Chm., Gangmasters' Licensing Authy, 2005–. Mem., Bd of Trustees, Citizens Advice, 2008–. CDir 2003. FRSA 1996; FIHM 2003. *Recreations:* travel, music, photography. *Address:* Comparative Clinical Science Foundation, Clarissa House, High Street, Wappenham, Towcester, Northants NN12 8SN. *T:* and *Fax:* (01327) 860812. *Club:* Institute of Directors.

MORE, Michael, CBE 2008; PhD; Chief Executive, Westminster City Council, since 2008; *b* 21 May 1955; *s* of Norman More, *qv*; *m* 1982, Sue Jordan; two *s*. *Educ:* Univ. of Hull (BA 1st Cl. Hons; PhD 1982). CPFA 1985. Audit trainee, Nat. Audit Office, 1981–86; Cambridgeshire County Council: Audit Manager, 1986–90; Asst Dir, 1990–96; Hd of Finance, 1996–99; Dir of Resource Mgt, 1999–2002, Chief Exec., 2002–08, Suffolk CC; Clerk to Lord Lieut of Suffolk, 2002–08. Non-exec. Dir, Univ. Campus, Suffolk, 2005–. Chm., Prince's Trust, Suffolk, 2006–08. Trustee, Ipswich Town FC Sports and Educn Trust, 2004–08. *Publications:* articles in various academic philosophy jls. *Recreations:* reading, music, art, football. *Address:* Westminster City Council, Westminster City Hall, Victoria Street, SW1E 6QP.

MORE, Norman, FRICS; Managing Director, Redditch Development Corporation, 1979–85; *b* 20 Dec. 1921; *s* of Herbert and Anna More; *m* 1952, Kathleen Mary Chrystal; two *s* one *d*. *Educ:* Royal High Sch., Edinburgh; Edinburgh Univ. FRICS 1970 (ARICS 1951). Served in Royal Engineers, Middle East, N Africa, Italy, Greece and Germany, Major, 1941–48. Surveyor, Directorate of Lands and Accommodation, Min. of Works, 1948–58; Sen. Valuer, City Assessor's Office, Glasgow Corporation, 1958–63; Valuation and Estates Officer, East Kilbride Development Corp., 1963–65; Chief Estates Officer, Redditch Development Corp., 1965–79. Consultant Chartered Surveyor, to Grimley J. R. Eve, London and Birmingham, 1985–90. Mem., W Midlands Regl Bd, TSB Gp, 1984–89. Chairman, West Midlands Br., Royal Instn of Chartered Surveyors, 1974–75. Chm., Friendship Project for Children, 1992–99. Pres., Stratford-upon-Avon circle, Catenian Assoc., 1972–73. *Publications:* press articles and contribs to jls. *Recreations:* music, sport. *Address:* Mead Cottage, 192 Loxley Road, Stratford-upon-Avon, Warwickshire CV37 7DU. *T:* (01789) 293763. *Club:* East India, Devonshire, Sports and Public Schools.
See also M. More.

MORE-MOLYNEUX, James Robert, OBE 1983; DL; Vice Lord-Lieutenant of Surrey, 1983–96; *b* 17 June 1920; *s* of Brig. Gen. Francis Cecil More-Molyneux-Longbourne, CMG, DSO and Gwendoline Carew More-Molyneux; *m* 1948, Susan Bellinger; one *s*. *Educ:* Eton; Trinity Hall, Cambridge. War service in 4/7th Royal Dragoon Guards and 14th PWO The Scinde Horse, 1941–46; Founder Chm., Guildway Ltd, 1947–85 (introduced first manufactured timber frame houses with brick cladding to UK, 1960); founded Loseley Co-Partnership, 1950; Chm., Loseley Park Farms, 1950–92; opened Loseley House to public, 1950–; founded Loseley Dairy Products, 1967; part-time Dir, Seeboard, 1975–84. Founder: Loseley & Guildway Charitable Trust, 1973; Loseley Christian Trust, 1983. Mem. Exec. Cttee, Industrial Participation Assoc., 1952–77. Mem., Lambeth Partnership, 1992–2004. Lay Pastoral Asst, 1986–. High Sheriff of Surrey, 1974; DL Surrey 1976. Bledisloe Gold Medal for Landowners, RASE, 1984. *Publications:* The Loseley Challenge, 1995; The Spark of God, 2000. *Recreations:* countryside, Christian Healing Ministry, photography, writing. *Address:* Nursery Wing, Loseley Park, Guildford, Surrey GU3 1HS. *T:* (01483) 566090. *Club:* Farmers'.

MOREAU, Jeanne; Officier, Ordre National du Mérite, 1988 (Chevalier, 1970); Officier de la Légion d'Honneur, 1991 (Chevalier, 1975); actress; *b* 23 Jan. 1928; *d* of Anatole-Désiré Moreau and Kathleen Moreau (*née* Buckley); *m* 1949, Jean-Louis Richard (marr. diss.); one *s*; *m* 1977, William Friedkin (marr. diss.). *Educ:* Collège Edgar-Quinet; Conservatoire national d'art dramatique. *Theatre:* Comédie Française, 1948–52; Théâtre National Populaire, 1953; Le Récit de la Servante Zerline, 1986–89; La Celestine, 1989; co-dir, Attila, Paris Opera, 2001; *films* include: Les amants, 1958; Les liaisons dangereuses, 1959; Le dialogue des Carmelites, 1959; Moderato cantabile, 1960; Jules et Jim, 1961; La Baie des Anges, 1962; Journal d'une femme de chambre, 1963; Viva Maria, 1965; Mademoiselle, 1965; The Sailor from Gibraltar, 1965; The Immortal Story, 1966; Great Catherine, 1967; The Bride wore Black, 1967; Monte Walsh, 1969; Chère Louise, 1971; Nathalie Granger, 1972; La Race des Seigneurs, 1974; Mr Klein, 1976; Lumière (also Dir), 1976; Le Petit Théâtre de Jean Renoir, 1976; Madame Rosa, 1978; L'Intoxe, 1980; Querelle, La Truite, 1982; L'Arbre, 1983; Sauve-toi Lola, Le Paltoquet, Le Miracule, 1986; La Nuit de l'Ocean, 1987; Ennemonde, 1988; Jour après Jour, 1988; Nikita, 1989; La Comédie d'un Jour, 1989; Anna Karamazoff, 1989; La Femme Fardée, Until the End of the World, 1990; La Vielle Qui Marchait Dans La Mer, Le Pas Suspendu de la Cigogne, The Map of the Human Heart, L'Amant, 1991; A Demain, L'Absence, 1992; Je m'appelle Victor, 1992; I Love You I Love You Not, 1995; The Proprietor, 1997; Un amour de sorcière, 1997; A tout jamais, 1999; Time to Leave, 2006; *television* plays and series: Huis Clos, BBC, 1984; The Last Seance, Granada, 1984; Le Tiroir Secret, 1985; We Shall Meet Again, BBC, 1992; The Clothes in the Wardrobe, BBC, 1993; A Foreign Field, BBC, 1993; The Great Catherine, 1994. Chm. Jury, Cannes Film Festival, 1995. Commandeur des Arts et des Lettres, 1985 (Chevalier, 1966). *Recreation:* reading. *Address:* Spica Productions, 4 square du Roule, 75008 Paris, France.

MORELAND, Claire Josephine; *see* Hickman, C. J.

MORELAND, Robert John; management consultant; Member, Economic and Social Committee, European Community, 1986–98 (Chairman, Regional Policy and Town and Country Planning Section, 1990–98); *b* 21 Aug. 1941; *s* of late Samuel John Moreland and Norah Mary, (Molly) (*née* Haines). *Educ:* Glasgow Acad.; Dean Close Sch., Cheltenham; Univ. of Nottingham (BA Econs); Inst. of World Affairs, Conn, and Warwick Univ. (postgrad. work). Civil Servant, Govt of NS, Canada, 1966–67, Govt of NB, 1967–72; Sen. Economist, W Central Scotland Planning Study, 1972–74; Management Consultant, Touche Ross and Co., London, 1974–. Member (C): for Knightsbridge, Westminster CC, 1990–98 (Chief Whip, 1993–94; Chm. of Envmt, 1994–95; Chm., Planning and Envmt, 1995–97); Gloucester CC, 2001–02. Contested (C): Pontypool, Oct. 1974; GLA, 2000. Mem. (C) Staffs, European Parlt, 1979–84, contested same seat, 1984; Chm., Eur. Cttee, Bow Gp, 1977–78; Dep. Chm., Conservative Gp for Europe, 2006– (Vice-Chm., 1985–88, 2003–06; Treas., 2000–03). Dep. Chm., 1998–2000, Chm., 2000–, London Europe Soc. Treas., European Movement, 2003–08. Dir, Albert Meml Trust, 1997–2000. *Publications:* Climate Change, 2000; contrib. to Crossbow. *Recreations:* tennis, ski-ing, watching cricket and Rugby, golf. *Address:* 7 Vauxhall Walk, SE11 5JT. *T:* (020) 7582 2613. *Clubs:* MCC; Gloucestershire CC.

MORENO, Glen Richard; Chairman, Pearson plc, since 2005; *b* 24 July 1943; *s* of John Moreno and Ellen (*née* Oberg); *m* 1966, Cheryl Eschbach. *Educ:* Stanford Univ. (BA with Dist. 1965); Univ. of Delhi (Rotary Foundn Fellow 1966); Harvard Law Sch. (JD 1969). Gp Exec., Citigroup, 1969–87; Pres., 1987–92, Dir, 1987–, Fidelity Internat.; Sen. Ind. non-exec. Dir, Man Gp plc, 1994–. Trustee, Prince of Liechtenstein Foundn, 1998–. *Recreations:* reading, shooting, Angus cattle breeder, vintner. *Address:* Pearson plc, 80 Strand, WC2R 0RL. *T:* (020) 7010 2306, *Fax:* (020) 7010 6601; *e-mail:* glen.moreno@pearson.com. *Clubs:* Farmers', National Liberal.

MORENO RAZO, Alma-Rosa; Ambassador of Mexico to the Court of St James's, 2001–03; *b* 9 Jan. 1952; *d* of Alfredo Monreno-Ruiz and Eva Razo de Moreno; *m*; three *d*. *Educ:* Instituto Tecnológico Autónomo de México (BA Econs 1972); El Colegio de México (MEc 1977); Univ. of NY. Under-Dir-Gen. for Income Policy, Min. of Finance and Public Credit, 1986–87; Exec. Dir for Reconstruction and Syndicated Loans, Multibanco Comermex, 1987–88; Dir Gen. for Income Policy, Min. of Finance and Public Credit, 1988–93; Dep. Dir for Planning, Promotion and Tech. Assistance, Nat. Bank of Public Works and Services, 1993–95; Ministry of Finance and Public Credit: Adviser: to Minister of State for Income Matters, Feb.–Dec. 1995; to Sec. of State for Finance and Public Credit, 1996–97; Hd, Liaison Unit with Congress, 1997–98; Co-ordinator Gen. for Income and Tax Policy, 1998–99; Pres., Nat. Service for Tax Admin, 1999–2000. Vis. Prof., Centre for Res. and Econ. Studies, Mexico City, 2000–01.

MORETON, family name of **Earl of Ducie**.

MORETON, Lord; James Berkeley Moreton; *b* 6 May 1981; *s* and *heir* of 7th Earl of Ducie, *qv*.

MORETON, Sir John (Oscar), KCMG 1978 (CMG 1966); KCVO 1976; MC 1944; HM Diplomatic Service, retired; *b* 28 Dec. 1917; *s* of Rev. C. O. Moreton; *m* 1945, Margaret Katherine, *d* of late Sir John Fryer, KBE, FRS; three *d*. *Educ:* St Edward's Sch., Oxford; Trinity Coll., Oxford (MA). War Service with 99th (Royal Bucks Yeomanry) Field Regt RA, 1939–46: France, Belgium, 1940; India, Burma, 1942–45. Asst Master, Uppingham Sch., 1946; Colonial Office, 1948; Private Sec. to Perm. Under-Sec. of State, 1949–50; seconded to Govt of Kenya, 1953–55; Private Sec. to Sec. of State for Colonies (Rt Hon. Alan Lennox-Boyd), 1955–59; transf. to CRO, 1960; Counsellor, British High Commn, Lagos, 1961–64; IDC 1965; Asst Under-Sec. of State, CRO, 1965–66, CO 1966–68, FCO 1968–69; Ambassador to Vietnam, 1969–71; High Comr, Malta, 1972–74; Dep. Perm. Representative, with personal rank of Ambassador, UK Mission to UN, NY, 1974–75; Minister, British Embassy, Washington, 1975–77. Dir, Wates Foundn, 1978–87. Gentleman Usher of the Blue Rod, Order of St Michael and St George, 1979–92. Governor, St Edward's Sch., Oxford, 1980–92. Hon. DL Hanover Coll., Indiana, 1976. *Recreations:* most outdoor activities, formerly athletics (Oxford Blue and International, 880 yds, 1939). *Address:* Weston House, Leigh Place, Cobham, Surrey KT11 2HL. *Club:* Army and Navy.

MOREY, Anthony Bernard Nicholas, CBE 1993; HM Diplomatic Service, retired; *b* 6 Dec. 1936; *s* of late Bernard Rowland Morey and Madeleine Morey; *m* 1961, Agni Campbell Kerr; two *s* one *d*. *Educ:* Wimbledon Coll. Nat. service, 1955–57. FO, 1957–60; Kuwait, 1960–62; FO, 1962–65; Madras, 1965–66; FO, 1966; Tehran, 1967; Kabul, 1968–71; FCO, 1971–72; Washington, 1972–76; Zagreb, 1976–80; Lagos, 1980–83; seconded to Guinness Mahon, 1983–85; Counsellor and Consul General, Moscow, 1985–88; Dep. High Comr, Madras, 1989–91; Ambassador to Mongolia, 1991–93; Dep. High Comr, Calcutta, 1993–96. *Recreations:* gardening, music, cats. *Address:* Lattice House, Castleton, Sherborne, Dorset DT9 3SA. *Club:* Royal Calcutta Turf.

MORFEY, Dr Kathryn Margaret Victoria; Consultant, Warner Goodman & Streat, 2000–02 (Associate Solicitor, 1991–2000); *b* 26 May 1942; *d* of Sidney Charles Waterton and Catherine Margaret Waterton (*née* Lilley); *m* 1963, Christopher Leonard Morfey; one *d* (one *s* decd). *Educ:* Newnham Coll., Cambridge (BA 1963; MA 1968); Univ. of Southampton (PhD 1968; LLB 1977). Admitted Solicitor, 1980. Lecturer: Univ. of Bristol, 1963; Univ. of Southampton, 1967–69; Nat. Childbirth Trust Orgnr, 1970–75; solicitor in private practice, 1980–2002. Mem., Sch. Admission Appeal Panel, 2003–. Member: Gen. Synod, C of E, 1990–2000; Legal Adv. Commn, C of E, 1991–93; Cathedrals Fabric Commn for England, 1991–96; Cathedrals Statutes Commn, 1996–2000; Vice-Pres., Winchester Diocesan Synod, 1997–2003. Gov., King Alfred's Coll. of Higher Educn, 1992–99. *Recreations:* visiting other people's gardens, choral music.

MORGAN; *see* Elystan-Morgan.

MORGAN, family name of **Baron Morgan**.

MORGAN, Baron *cr* 2000 (Life Peer), of Aberdyfi in the co. of Gwynedd; **Kenneth Owen Morgan,** FBA 1983; FRHistS; Principal, then Vice-Chancellor, University College of Wales, Aberystwyth and Professor in the University of Wales, 1989–95, Emeritus Professor, 1999 (Research Professor, 1995–99); Vice-Chancellor, then Senior Vice-Chancellor, University of Wales, 1993–95; *b* 16 May 1934; *s* of David James Morgan and Margaret Morgan (*née* Owen); *m* 1973, Jane Keeler (*d* 1992); one *s* one *d*. *Educ:* University College School, London; Oriel College, Oxford (MA, DPhil 1958, DLitt 1985; Hon. Fellow, 2003). University College (later University of Wales), Swansea: Lectr in History Dept, 1958–66 (Sen. Lectr, 1965–66); Hon. Fellow, 1985; Hon. Prof., 1995; Fellow and Praelector, Modern Hist. and Politics, Queen's Coll., Oxford, 1966–89 (Hon. Fellow, 1992); Faculty Lectr, 1995–. Supernumerary Fellow, Jesus Coll., Oxford, 1991–92. Amer. Council of Learned Socs Fellow, Columbia Univ., 1962–63; Visiting Professor: Columbia Univ., 1965; Univ. of S Carolina, 1972; Univ. of Witwatersrand,

1997, 1998 and 2000; Vis. Benjamin Meaker Prof., Univ. of Bristol, 2000; Vis. Lectr, Univ. of Texas, 1994, 1999, and 2007. Lectures: Neale, UCL, 1986; Dodd, UCNW (Bangor), 1992, Univ. of Wales, Bangor, 2005; BBC (Wales), 1995; Prothero, RHistS, 1996; Merlyn-Rees, Univ. of Glamorgan, 2002; Presidential, Univ. of Rouen, 2003; Ford Special, Univ. of Oxford, 2005; London Guildhall, 2006; Gresham Coll., 2007. Member: Bd of Celtic Studies, 1972–2003; Council, Nat. Library of Wales, 1991–95. Mem., H of L Select Cttee on the Constitution, 2001–04. Chm., Fabian Soc. Commn on the Monarchy, 2002–03; Trustee, History of Parlt Trust, 2002–. Mem., Yr Academi Gymreig. FRHistS 1964 (Mem. Council, 1983–86). Editor, Welsh History Review, 1961–2003; Jt Editor, 20th Century British History, 1994–99. Hon. Mem., Gorsedd of Bards, Nat. Eisteddfod, 2008. Hon. Fellow: Univ. of Wales, Cardiff, 1997; Trinity Coll., Carmarthen, 1998. Hon. DLitt: Wales, 1997; Glamorgan, 1997; Greenwich, 2004. *Publications:* Wales in British Politics, 1963, 3rd edn 1980; David Lloyd George: Welsh radical as world statesman, 1963, 2nd edn 1982; Freedom or Sacrilege?, 1966; Keir Hardie, 1967; The Age of Lloyd George, 1971, 3rd edn 1978; (ed) Lloyd George: Family Letters, 1973; Lloyd George, 1974; Keir Hardie: radical and socialist, 1975 (Arts Council prize, 1976), 3rd edn 1997; Consensus and Disunity, 1979, 2nd edn 1986; (with Jane Morgan) Portrait of a Progressive, 1980; Rebirth of a Nation: Wales 1880–1980, 1981, new edn 1998 (Arts Council prize, 1982); David Lloyd George, 1981; Labour in Power 1945–1951, 1984, 2nd edn 1985; (ed jtly) Welsh Society and Nationhood, 1984; (ed) The Oxford Illustrated History of Britain, 1984, new rev. edn 2008; (ed) The Sphere Illustrated History of Britain, 1985; Labour People, 1987, new edn 1992; (ed) The Oxford History of Britain, 1988; The Red Dragon and the Red Flag, 1989; The People's Peace: British History 1945–1990, 1991, new edn as The People's Peace: British History since 1945, 2001; Academic Leadership, 1991; Modern Wales: politics, places and people, 1995; Britain and Europe, 1995; Steady As She Goes, 1996; (ed) The Young Oxford History of Britain & Ireland, 1996, rev. edn 2005; Callaghan: a life, 1997; (ed jtly) Crime, Protest and Police in Modern British Society, 1999; The Twentieth Century, 2000; The Great Reform Act, 2001; Universities and the State, 2002; Michael Foot: the life, 2007; many articles, reviews etc; contribs to Oxford DNB. *Recreations:* music, architecture, sport, travel. *Address:* The Croft, 63 Millwood End, Long Hanborough, Witney, Oxon OX29 8BP. *T:* (01993) 881341. *Clubs:* Reform, Middlesex County Cricket.

MORGAN OF DREFELIN, Baroness *cr* 2004 (Life Peer), of Drefelin in the County of Dyfed; **Delyth Jane Morgan;** a Baroness in Waiting (Government Whip), since 2007; Parliamentary Under-Secretary of State, Department for Children, Schools and Families, since 2008; *b* 30 Aug. 1961; *d* of late Julian Morgan and of Ann Morgan; *m* 1991, Jim Shepherd; one *d. Educ:* Bedford Coll., London, then UCL (BSc Physiol.; Fellow, 2005). Campaigns Co-ordinator, Shelter, 1986–88; Director: Workplace Nurseries Campaign, 1988–92; Commns, Nat. Asthma Campaign, 1992–96; Chief Exec., Breakthrough Breast Cancer, 1996–2005. Founding Mem., Long Term Conditions Alliance (Vice-Chm., 1996; Chm., 1996–98; Trustee, 1994–2000); Chm., DoH Primary Task Gp, Patient Choice, 2003; Member: NHS Nat. Cancer Taskforce, 2000–05; NHS Modernisation Bd, 2002–05. Parly Under-Sec. of State, DIUS, 2008. House of Lords: Member: Select Cttee on Merit of Statutory Instruments, 2005–07; Jt Cttee on Draft Children (contact) and Adoption Bill, 2005–; Vice Chair, All Party Gp on Breast Cancer, 2005–07. Mem. Exec. Council, Assoc. Med. Res. Charities, 1999–2004. Fellow, Cardiff Univ., 2005. *Address:* House of Lords, SW1A 0PW.

MORGAN OF HUYTON, Baroness *cr* 2001 (Life Peer), of Huyton in the County of Merseyside; **Sally Morgan;** non-executive Director: Carphone Warehouse plc, since 2005; Southern Cross Healthcare Plc, since 2005; Member, Board, Olympic Delivery Authority, since 2005; *b* 28 June 1959; *d* of Albert Edward Morgan and Margaret Morgan; *m* 1984, John Lyons; two *s. Educ:* Belvedere Girls' Sch., Liverpool; Durham Univ. (BA Geog. Hons); Univ. of London (PGCE, MA Educ.). Secondary Sch. Teacher, 1981–85; Labour Party: Student Organiser, 1985–87; Sen. Targetting Officer, 1987–93; Dir, Campaigns and Elecns, 1993–95; Head of Party Liaison for Leader of the Opposition, 1995–97; Pol Sec. to the Prime Minister, 1997–2001; Minister of State, Cabinet Office, 2001; Dir of Pol and Govt Relations, Prime Minister's Office, 2001–05. Advr to Bd, ARU, 2005–; Mem., Adv. Panel, Lloyds Pharmacy, 2005–. *Recreations:* relaxing with family and friends, cooking, gardening.

MORGAN, Rt Rev. Alan Wyndham, OBE 2005; Bishop Suffragan of Sherwood, 1989–2004; *b* 22 June 1940; *s* of A. W. Morgan; *m* 1965, Margaret Patricia, *d* of W. O. Williams; one *s* one *d. Educ:* Boys' Grammar School, Gowerton; St David's Coll., Lampeter (BA 1962); St Michael's Coll., Llandaff. Deacon 1964, priest 1965; Assistant Curate: Llangyfelach with Morriston, 1964–69; Cockett, 1969–72; St Mark with St Barnabas, Coventry, 1972–73; Team Vicar, St Barnabas, Coventry East, 1973–77; Bishop's Officer for Social Responsibility, Diocese of Coventry, 1978–83; Archdeacon of Coventry, 1983–89. Mem., Gen. Synod, 1980–89. Chairman: Dio. of Southwell Ministry Gp, 1989–97; Dio. of Southwell Social Housing Gp, 1990–97; Lay Training Partnership, Dio. of Southwell, 1998–2001; E Midlands Churches Forum, 1998–. Chm., 1986–89, Vice-Pres., 1989–93, NCVO; Chairman: Wkg Pty on Future of the Family, Bd of Social Responsibility, 1993–95; Notts Child Care Forum, 1993–99; Mansfield Social Strategy Gp, 1994–2003; Regl Awards Cttee, Nat. Lottery Charities Bd, 1999–2000 (Chm., E Midlands Regl Adv. Panel, 1995–99); Coalfields Regeneration Trust, 1999–; Notts Community Foundn, 2001–; Member: N Notts HA Local Res. Ethics Cttee, 1990–97; Governing Council, Family Policy Studies Gp, 1994–99; Dep. Prime Minister's Coalfield Task Force, 1997–98; Mansfield Area Strategic Partnership (formerly Mansfield Partnership Task Force), 1998–2002; President: Notts Help the Homeless, 1990–2001; Mansfield Disabled Inf. Advice Line, 1994–; Framework Housing, 2001–. Director: Greater Nottingham TEC, 1991–95; N Notts TEC, 1995–2001; Notts Enterprise, 2001–03. Trustee, Charities Aid Foundn, 1997–2002.

MORGAN, Alasdair Neil; Member (SNP) Scotland South, Scottish Parliament, since 2003 (Galloway & Upper Nithsdale, 1999–2003); *b* 21 April 1945; *s* of Alexander Morgan and Emily Morgan (*née* Wood); *m* 1969, Anne Gilfillan; two *d. Educ:* Breadalbane Acad., Aberfeldy; Univ. of Glasgow (MA Hons 1968); Open Univ. (BA Hons 1990). IT Project Manager, Lothian Reg., 1986–96; IT Consultant, W Lothian Council, 1996–97. Contested (SNP) Dumfries, 1992. MP (SNP) Galloway and Upper Nithsdale, 1997–2001. Mem., Select Cttee on Trade and Industry affairs, 1997–2001. Scottish Parliament: Mem., Rural Affairs Cttee, 1999–2000; Convenor, Justice I Cttee, 2000–01; Mem., Finance Cttee, 2001–03; Convenor, Enterprise and Culture Cttee, 2003–04; Vice Convenor, Finance Cttee, 2004–05; Mem., European and External Relations Cttee, 2007–; Dep. Presiding Officer, 2007–. Scottish National Party: Nat. Treas., 1983–90; Sen. Vice Convenor, 1990–91; Nat. Sec., 1992–97; Vice Pres., 1997–2004; Leader, Parly Gp, 1999–2001; Chief Whip, Scottish Parly Gp, 2005–. *Recreation:* hill walking. *Address:* Nether Cottage, Crocketford, Dumfries DG2 8RA. *T:* (office) (01556) 611956.

MORGAN, Anthony Hugh, CMG 1990; HM Diplomatic Service, retired; Consul-General, Zürich, Director of British Export Promotion in Switzerland and Consul-General, Liechtenstein, 1988–91; *b* 27 March 1931; *s* of late Cyril Egbert Morgan and late Muriel Dorothea (*née* Nash); *m* 1957, Cicely Alice Voysey; two *s* one *d. Educ:* King's Norton Grammar Sch.; Birmingham Univ. (BA 1952). Served HM Forces (RAF Educn Br.), 1952–55. Joined HM Foreign (later Diplomatic) Service, 1956; Cairo, then Cyprus, 1956; Khartoum, 1957; FO, 1959; Saigon, 1962; Second Sec., 1963; UK Delegn to NATO, 1965; First Sec., 1968; FCO, 1969; First Sec. and Head of Chancery, Calcutta, 1973; FCO, 1976; Dep. Head of Inf. Policy Dept, 1977; Counsellor: (Information), Brussels, 1977–79; (Commercial), Copenhagen, 1979–82; Vienna, 1982–88. Comdr, Order of Dannebrog, Denmark, 1979. *Recreations:* listening to music, looking at pictures. *Club:* Royal Air Force.

MORGAN, Arthur William Crawford, (Tony Morgan); Chief Executive, Industrial Society, 1994–2000; *b* 24 Aug. 1931; *s* of Arthur James and Violet Morgan; *m* 1955, Valerie Anne Williams; three *s. Educ:* Hereford High Sch.; Westcliff High Sch. Chm. and Chief Exec. Officer, Purle Bros Holdings, 1964–71; Dep. Chm., Wimpey Waste Management, 1974–81; Dir, Redland plc, 1971–73; Founder and Dir, Morgan Hemingway Investment Bank, 1973–78; working in California for non-profit organisations, incl. Hunger Project and Breakthrough Foundn, 1981–84; Chm., Wistech, 1984–90; Dir, Wraytech UK, 1996–99. Governor, BBC, 1972–77. Non-exec. Chm., Octopus Protected VCT plc, 2006–; non-executive Director: Alexander Corp., 1990–99; Quickheart Ltd, 2001–; Phoenix Venture Capital Trust, 2003–; Re-Energy plc, 2006–; Partner, Latitude Strategy Consulting, 2000–05. Sailed Olympic Games, Tokyo; Silver Medal, Flying Dutchman, 1964; Jt Yachtsman of the Year, 1965; Member: British Olympic Yachting Appeal, 1970; Royal Yachting Assoc. Council, 1968–72. Chairman: Hunger Project Trust, 1984–89; Youth at Risk, 1996–. FRSA. *Publications:* various technical papers. *Recreations:* squash, ski-ing, sailing, gardening, rowing. *Address:* Bovingdon, Marlow Common, Bucks SL7 2QR. *T:* (01628) 890654. *Club:* Royal Thames Yacht.

MORGAN, Most Rev. Barry Cennydd; *see* Wales, Archbishop of.

MORGAN, Bill; *see* Morgan, J. W. H.

MORGAN, Brian David Gwynne, FRCS, FRCOphth; Consultant Plastic Surgeon, University College Hospital, London and Mount Vernon Hospital, 1972–98; *b* 2 March 1935; *s* of Brig. John Gwynne Morgan and Ethel Lilian (*née* Bloomer); *m* 1962, Sally Ann Lewis; one *s* two *d. Educ:* Wycliffe Coll., Glos; University College Hosp., London (MB BS). FRCS 1963; FRCOphth 1995. University College Hospital: pre-registration house appts, 1959–61; Casualty Officer, 1961; Registrar in Surgery, St Richard's Hosp., Chichester, 1962–64; Registrar in Surgery, 1964–66, Sen. Registrar, 1967, UCH; Plastic Surgery Registrar and Sen. Registrar, Mt Vernon Hosp., 1967–70; Consultant Plastic Surgeon, Shotley Bridge, Durham, 1970–72. Mem. Council, 1991–99, Trustee, Hunterian Collection, RCS, 2000–. Fellow, UCL, 1992. *Publication:* Essentials of Plastic and Reconstructive Surgery, 1986. *Recreations:* water-colour painting, sailing, jazz trombone. *Address:* Stockers House, Stockers Farm Road, Rickmansworth, Herts WD3 1NZ. *T:* (01923) 773922, *Fax:* (01923) 773754; *e-mail:* bmorgan@mailbox.co.uk.

MORGAN, Rear-Adm. Brinley John, CB 1972; *b* 3 April 1916; *s* of Thomas Edward Morgan and Mary Morgan (*née* Parkhouse); *m* 1945, Margaret Mary Whittles; three *s. Educ:* Abersychan Grammar Sch.; University Coll., Cardiff (BSc 1937). Entered Royal Navy as Instr Lt, 1939. Served War of 1939–45: Cruisers Emerald and Newcastle, 1939–41; Aircraft Carrier Formidable, 1941–43; Naval Weather Service (Admty Forecast Section), 1943–45. Staff of C-in-C Medit., 1945–48; HQ, Naval Weather Service, 1948–50; Staff of Flag Officer Trg Sqdn in HM Ships Vanguard, Indefatigable and Implacable, 1950–52; Instr Comdr, 1951; Lectr, RN Coll., Greenwich, 1952–54; Headmaster, RN Schools, Malta, 1954–59; Instr Captain, 1960; Staff of Dir, Naval Educn Service, 1959–61 and 1963–64; Sen. Officers' War Course, 1961; HMS Ganges, 1961–63; Dean, RN Engineering Coll., Manadon, 1964–69; Instr Rear-Adm., 1970; Dir, Naval Educn Service, 1970–75, retired. Freeman, City of London, 1982. *Club:* Naval.

MORGAN, Bruce; District Judge (Magistrates' Courts), West Mercia, since 2003; *b* 30 March 1945; *s* of Francis William Morgan, DFC, and Phyllis Marie Morgan; *m* 1988, Sandra Joy Beresford; twin *d. Educ:* Oswestry School; Open Univ. (BA 1994). Solicitor of Supreme Court. Articled Clerk, Stourbridge, Worcs, 1964–69; Asst Solicitor, London, SE10, 1969–72; Partner with Lickfolds Wiley & Powles, 1973–86. Member: London Criminal Courts Solicitors Assoc. Cttee, 1971–73; Criminal Law Cttee, Westminster Law Soc., 1981–86; No 14 Area Regl Duty Solicitors Cttee, 1986–87; Metropolitan Stipendiary Magistrate, 1987–89; Stipendiary Magistrate, subseq. Dist Judge (Magistrates' Courts), W Midlands, 1989–2003. Member: Birmingham Magistrates' Court Cttee, 1990–93; Birmingham Magistrates' Bench Cttee, 1990–2003; Midland Mem., Nat., subseq. HM, Council of Dist Judges (Magistrates' Courts) (formerly Jt Council of Stipendiary Magistrates), 1995–2003; Member: W Mercia Area Judicial Forum, 2005–; W Mercia Judicial Issues Gp, 2005–. Member: British Acad. of Forensic Sci., 1970; Legal Medico Soc., 1970–; Our Soc., 1994–. Vice Chm., Cleobury North PCC, 1996–. Mem., Ludlow Rotary Club, 1969–98; Chm., Greenwich Round Table, 1983–84. Governor, Oswestry Sch., 1996– (Vice Chm., 1996–2000, 2007–). *Publications:* various articles in legal journals. *Recreations:* tennis, cricket, gardening, attending auctions, cooking. *Address:* c/o Worcester Magistrates' Court, Castle Street, Worcester WR1 3QZ. *Clubs:* Reform, Arts.

MORGAN, Vice-Adm. Sir (Charles) Christopher, KBE 1996; Director General, Chamber of Shipping, 1997–2003; Director, CM Shipping Consultants Ltd, since 2003; *b* 11 March 1939; *s* of late Captain Horace Leslie Morgan, CMG, DSO, RN and Kathleen Hilda Morgan; *m* 1970, Susan Caroline Goodbody; three *d. Educ:* Clifton College; BRNC Dartmouth. Joined RN, 1957; served Brunei, 1962–66; HMS Greatford in Comd, 1966; Specialist Navigation Course, 1967; HMS Eskimo in Comd, 1976; NDC 1978; Comdr Sea Training, 1979; MoD, 1981–83; RCDS, 1984; Captain 5th Destroyer Sqdn (HMS Southampton), 1985–87; Staff, Jt Service Defence Coll., 1987–89; Naval Sec., 1990–92; Flag Officer, Scotland, Northern England and NI, 1992–96. Younger Brother of Trinity House, 1977. Governor: Clifton Coll., 1994–; Sherborne Sch. for Girls, 2004–. Chm. Trustees, Royal Naval Benevolent Soc., 1996–2005; Gov., Tancred Soc., 1996–. Member, Council: King George's Fund for Sailors, 1997–2003; RNLI, 2002–; Chm., Bubbly charity, 2005–. Freeman, Co. of Master Mariners, 1999; Liveryman, Shipwrights' Co., 2000. FCMI; FRIN 1996; MInstD 1996. *Recreations:* family, golf, tennis, Rugby, wine, gardening. *Address:* c/o Lloyds TSB, 75 Cheap Street, Sherborne, Dorset. *Clubs:* Army and Navy; Royal North Devon Golf, Sherborne Golf.

MORGAN, Hon. Sir (Charles) Declan, Kt 2004; **Hon. Mr Justice Morgan;** a Judge of the High Court of Justice, Northern Ireland, since 2004; *b* 1952; *m*; three *c. Educ:* St Columb's Coll., Londonderry; Peterhouse, Cambridge (BA 1974); Queen's Univ., Belfast. Called to the Bar, NI, 1976; QC (NI) 1993; Sen. Crown Counsel, 2002–04. *Address:* Royal Courts of Justice, Chichester Street, Belfast BT1 3JF.

MORGAN, Charles Peter Henry; Director, Corporate Strategy, Morgan Motor Co. Ltd, since 2004; *b* 29 July 1951; *s* of Peter and Jane Morgan; *m* 2003, Kira Kopylova; one *s* one *d*, and one *s* two *d* from previous marriage. *Educ:* Sussex Univ. (BA Hons Hist. of Art 1971); Coventry Univ. (MBA Engrg Mgt 1994). News film cameraman, ITN, 1974–82; Co-founder and Dir, Television News Team Ltd, 1982–85; Marketing Dir, 1985–99, Man. Dir, 1999–2004, Morgan Motor Co. Ltd. Hon. DBA Coventry, 2003. Silver Nymph award for news TV film, Montreux Internat. TV Fest., 1978. *Recreations:* ski-ing, architecture and design, painting. *Address:* Morgan Motor Co. Ltd, Pickersleigh Road, Malvern Link, Worcs WR14 2LL. *T:* (01684) 573104; *e-mail:* charles.morgan@morgan-motor.co.uk. *Clubs:* Academy; British Racing Drivers'; St Moritz Tobogganing.

MORGAN, Christine Lesley; Executive Producer, Religion and Ethics, BBC Radio, since 2004; *b* 4 May 1958; *d* of Gerald Potts and Brenda Austin Potts (*née* Bell); *m* 1st, 1979, Christopher Harry Morgan (marr. diss. 1987); 2nd, 2000, Paul Vallely, *qv*; one *s*. *Educ:* Ormskirk Grammar Sch.; Southport Coll.; FE Teaching Dip. AEWVH 1987. Joined WRAF, 1976: HQ Strike Comd, 1976–78; Personal Staff of Chief of Air Staff, MoD, 1978–79; Design Team, Airmen's Comd Sch., Hereford, 1979–80; Personnel Asst to Purchasing Dir, H. P. Bulmer Ltd, 1980–83; Lectr in Business Studies, Royal Nat. Coll. for the Blind, 1983–87 (devised RNCB Nat. Work Experience Scheme, 1987); joined BBC Religious Broadcasting, 1987; Producer, Radio 4 Sunday, 1991–93; Producer, 1992–2004, Ed., 2004–, Thought for the Day; Series Producer: Sunday Radio 4, 1993–95; Heart and Soul, BBC TV, 1995; Producer: The Choice, 1995; File on 4, 1995–96; Heart of the Matter, BBC TV, 1998 (Series Producer, 1999–2001); Everyman, Letters to the Yorkshire Ripper, BBC TV, 2001; The Celibacy Debate, BBC TV; Exec. Producer, Music and Worship Progs, Religion and Ethics, 2002–04; Editor: Faith in Africa, 2005; Humphrys in Search of God, 2006. MA Lambeth, 2008. Sanford St Martin Award, 1992, 2007; Sony Bronze Award, 1995; Silver Award, Med. Radio of the Year, 1998; VLV New Prog. Award, 2007; Jerusalem Trust Award, 2007. *Recreation:* Thomas. *Address:* BBC, New Broadcasting House, Oxford Road, Manchester M60 1SJ. *Club:* Royal Commonwealth Society.

MORGAN, Rt Rev. Christopher Heudebourck; *see* Colchester, Area Bishop of.

MORGAN, Claire; *see* Durkin, C.

MORGAN, Clifford Isaac, CVO 1986; OBE 1977; Head of Outside Broadcasts Group, BBC Television, 1975–87; *b* 7 April 1930; *m* 1st, 1955, Nuala Martin (*d* 1999); one *s* one *d*; 2nd, 2001, Patricia Ewing. *Educ:* Tonyrefail Grammar School, South Wales. Played International Rugby Union for Wales, British Lions and Barbarians. Joined BBC, 1958, as Sports Organiser, Wales; Editor, Sportsview and Grandstand, 1961–64; Producer, This Week, 1964–66; freelance writer and broadcaster, 1966–72; Editor, Sport Radio, 1972–74; Head of Outside Broadcasts, Radio, 1974–75; Presenter, Sport on 4, 1987–98. President: London Glamorgan Soc., 1974–; Disability Wales (formerly Wales Council for the Disabled), 1990–; London Welsh Male Voice Choir, 1990–; Welsh Rugby Former Internat. Players' Assoc. (formerly Welsh Rugby Internats Benevolent Assoc.), 2001–; Welsh Pres., Cystic Fibrosis Res. Trust, 1987–97; Vice-President: Sequal, 1976–96; Welsh Sports Assoc. for Mental Handicap, 1988–92; NCH (formerly Nat. Children's Home), 1987–; London Welsh Trust, 1999–; Patron, Headline, Southampton head and neck cancer charity, 2006–. Chm., Saints and Sinners Club, 1984–85. Hon. Fellow, Polytechnic of Wales, 1989. Hon. MA Wales, 1988; DUniv: Keele, 1989; Central England, 1998; Hon. LLD Bristol, 1996. *Recreation:* music. *Address:* Glenford, Ducie Avenue, Bembridge, Isle of Wight PO35 5NE.

MORGAN, David; *see* Morgan, F. D.

MORGAN, (David) Dudley; retired from Theodore Goddard & Co., Solicitors, 1983; *b* 23 Oct. 1914; *y s* of Thomas Dudley Morgan; *m* 1948, Margaret Helene, *o d* of late David MacNaughton Duncan, Loanhead, Midlothian; two *d*. *Educ:* Swansea Grammar Sch.; Jesus Coll., Cambridge (MA, LLM). War Service with RAF in Intell. Br., UK, 1940–42 and Legal Br., India, 1942–46; Wing Comdr 1945. Admitted Solicitor, 1939, with Theodore Goddard & Co.; Partner 1948; Senior Partner, 1974–80; Consultant, 1980–83. *Recreation:* gardening. *Address:* St Leonard's House, St Leonard's Road, Nazeing, Waltham Abbey, Essex EN9 2HG. *T:* (01992) 892124. *Club:* Carlton.

MORGAN, David Gethin; County Treasurer, Avon County Council, 1973–94; *b* 30 June 1929; *s* of Edgar and Ethel Morgan; *m* 1st, 1955, Marion Brook (*d* 2001); 2nd, 2002, José Hall. *Educ:* Jesus Coll., Oxford (MA Hons English). CPFA, FInstAM(AdvDip). Accountant, Staffordshire CC, 1952–58; Computer Officer, Sen. O&M Officer, Cheshire CC, 1958–62; County Management Services Officer, Durham CC, 1962–65; Leicestershire CC: Asst County Treasurer, 1965–68; Dep. County Treasurer, 1968–73. Chm., Local Govt Finance Exec., CIPFA, 1991–92 (Vice Chm., 1987–91); Pres., Soc. of County Treasurers in England and Wales, 1988–89. Mem. Bd, UK Transplant Authy, 1996–2001. Hon. Freeman, City of London, 1989. Hon. MA UWE, 1994. *Publication:* Vol. XV Financial Information Service (IPFA). *Recreations:* local history, church architecture, tai chi. *Address:* 6 Wyecliffe Road, Henleaze, Bristol BS9 4NH. *T:* (0117) 962 9640.

MORGAN, His Honour David Glyn; a Circuit Judge, 1984–2001; *b* 31 March 1933; *s* of late Dr Richard Glyn Morgan, MC, and Nancy Morgan; *m* 1959, Ailsa Murray Strang; three *d*. *Educ:* Mill Hill Sch.; Merton Coll., Oxford (MA). Called to Bar, Middle Temple, 1958; practised Oxford Circuit, 1958–70; Wales and Chester Circuit, 1970–84. A Recorder of the Crown Court, 1974–84; Assigned Judge, Newport County Court, 1987; a Designated Family Judge and Dep. High Court Judge, 1990. 2nd Lieut, The Queen's Bays, 1955; Dep. Col, 1st The Queen's Dragoon Guards, 1976. An Hon. Pres., Royal Nat. Eisteddfod of Wales, Casnewydd, 1988. *Recreations:* fishing, Rugby football, opera. *Clubs:* Cavalry and Guards; Cardiff and County (Cardiff).

MORGAN, David Leslie; Chairman, M&G Group plc, 1997–98; *b* 23 Dec. 1933; *s* of Captain Horace Leslie Morgan, CMG, DSO, RN and Kathleen Hilda Morgan (*née* Bellhouse); *m* 1965, Clare Jean Lacy; one *s* one *d*. *Educ:* Clifton Coll., Bristol; University Coll., Oxford (BA Hons PPE 1957). Worked in FE, for Shell, and later stockbroking in Malaysia, 1957–65; banking and investment management, Deltec Internat., London and NY, 1965–70; Dir, E. D. Sassoon, 1970–72; M&G Group, 1972–98: Dir, 1973–91, Man. Dir, 1991–95, Chm., 1995–97, M&G Investment Management; Dep. Gp Man. Dir, 1991–94; Dep. Chm. and Man. Dir, 1994–97. MSI 1993. FRSA 1993. *Recreations:* walking, wine, theatre. *Address:* 2 Orme Square, W2 4RS. *Clubs:* Royal Automobile; Royal North Devon Golf; Royal Mid Surrey Golf.

MORGAN, David Thomas; land and development consultant; *b* 22 Jan. 1946; *s* of Janet Catherine and Noel David Morgan; *m* 1968, Quita Valentine; two *d*. *Educ:* Alleyne's Grammar School, Stevenage; Univ. of Newcastle upon Tyne (BA Hons Land Use Studies 1968). MRTPI 1971. Somerset CC, 1968–70; Worcs CC, 1970–71; Peterborough Develt Corp., 1971–81; Housing Develt Manager, 1981–85, Dir, Planning Services, 1985–87, LDDC; Chief Exec., Black Country Develt Corp., 1987–98. Mem., Inland Waterways Amenity Adv. Council, 1997–2006. *Recreations:* Rugby football, drama. *Address:* 3 Riverside Court, Caunsall, near Kidderminster, Worcs DY11 5YW. *T:* (01562) 851688.

MORGAN, Prof. David Vernon, PhD, DSc; FREng, FIET, FCGI; Professor of Microelectronics, since 1985, and Distinguished Research Professor, since 2003, University of Wales Cardiff; *b* 13 July 1941; *s* of late David Vernon Grenville Morgan and Isabel Lovina Benson Williams (formerly Morgan; *née* Emanuel); *m* 1965, Jean Anderson; one *s* one *d*. *Educ:* UCW, Aberystwyth (BSc; Hon. Fellow, 2006); Gonville and Caius Coll., Cambridge (PhD); Leeds Univ. (DSc). CPhys, FInstP; FREng (FEng 1966). Fellow, Univ. of Wales, at Cavendish Labs, Cambridge, 1966–68; Harwell Fellow, AERE, 1968–70; University of Leeds: Lectr, 1970–77; Sen. Lectr, 1977–80; Reader, 1980–85; Head of Electronics, 1988–94, Head, Cardiff Sch. of Engrg, 1995–2003, UWCC, subseq. Univ. of Wales Cardiff. Editor, Solid State Devices and Circuits series, 1975–; Founding Editor, Design and Measurement in Electronic Engineering series, 1986–. FCGI 1998. Papal Cross Pro Ecclesia et Pontifice, 2004. *Publications:* Channelling Theory Observation and Application, 1971; Solid State Electronics, 1972; An Introduction to Semiconductor Microtechnology, 1983, 2nd edn 1990; more than 200 papers in learned jls. *Recreations:* Rugby, golf, hill walking, yoga. *Address:* Cardiff School of Engineering, Cardiff University, Queen's Buildings, Newport Road, Cardiff CF24 3AA. *T:* (029) 2087 4424.

MORGAN, David Wynn; His Honour Judge David Wynn Morgan; a Circuit Judge, since 2000; *b* 18 April 1954; *s* of Arthur Islwyn Lewis Morgan and Mary Morgan (*née* Wynn); *m* 1982, Marian Eléna Lewis; one *s* one *d*. *Educ:* Kingswood Sch., Bath; Balliol Coll., Oxford (BA Jurisprudence). Called to the Bar, Gray's Inn, 1976; practised on Wales and Chester Circuit, 1977–2000; Asst Recorder, 1991–95, Recorder, 1995–2000. Mem., Parole Bd, 2002–. *Recreations:* music, reading, being in Pembrokeshire. *Address:* The Crown Court, Cathays Park, Cardiff CF1 3PG.

MORGAN, Hon. Sir Declan; *see* Morgan, Hon. Sir C. D.

MORGAN, Prof. Derec Llwyd, DPhil, DLitt; Vice-Chancellor and Principal, University of Wales, Aberystwyth, 1995–2004; Senior Vice-Chancellor, 2001–04, Professor Emeritus, since 2004, University of Wales; *b* 15 Nov. 1943; *s* of Ewart Lloyd Morgan and Margaret Morgan; *m* 1965, Jane Edwards; one *d*. *Educ:* Amman Valley GS; UCNW, Bangor (BA; Hon Fellow, 1996); Jesus Coll., Oxford (DPhil; Hon. Fellow, 1999); DLitt Wales, 1999. Res. Fellow, Univ. of Wales, 1967–69; Lectr, UCW, Aberystwyth, 1969–74; University College of North Wales, Bangor: Lectr, 1975–80, Sen. Lectr, 1980–83, Reader, 1983–89, Dept. of Welsh; Dir, Research Centre Wales, 1985–89; Prof. of Welsh, 1989–95, and Vice-Principal, 1994–95, UCW, Aberystwyth. Supernumerary Fellow, 1997–98, Welsh Supernumerary Fellow, 2003–04, Jesus Coll., Oxford. Member: Bd of Celtic Studies, Univ. of Wales, 1990–96; Court and Council, Nat. Library of Wales, 1995–2007; Governing Body, Inst. of Grassland and Environmental Res., 1995–2004. Member: Gen. Adv. Council, BBC, 1984–90; Broadcasting Council for Wales, 1990–95; ITC, 1999–2003. Chm., Rowntree Commn on Rural Housing in Wales, 2007–08. Royal National Eisteddfod of Wales: Chm. Council, 1979–82, 1985–86; Chm. Exec. Cttee, Ynys Môn, 1983; Pres. Court, 1989–93. Chairman: All-Wales Cultural Forum, 1999; Celtic Film and Television Festival, 2000; Sir Kyffin Williams Trust, 2006–. Non-executive Director: PO Bd, Wales and the Marches, 1996–2000; Menter a Busnes, 1997–2000. Trustee, James Pantyfedwen Foundn, 2004–. DUniv Wales, 2006. *Publications:* Y Tân Melys, 1966; Pryderi, 1970; Barddoniaeth Thomas Gwynn Jones: astudiaeth, 1972; Kate Roberts, 1974, 2nd edn 1991; (ed) Cerddi '75, 1975; Iliad Homer, 1976; (ed) Adnabod Deg, 1977; Gwna yn Llawen, Ŵr Ieuanc, 1978; Y Diwygiad Mawr, 1981 (trans., The Great Awakening in Wales, 1988); Williams Pantycelyn, 1983; Pobl Pantycelyn, 1986; (ed) Glas y Nef: cerddi ac emynau John Roberts Llanfwrog, 1987; Cefn y Byd, 1987; (ed) Emynau Williams Pantycelyn, 1991; (ed) Meddwl a Dychymyg Williams Pantycelyn, 1991; Ni cheir byth wir lle bo llawer o feirdd, 1992; Charles Edwards, 1994; Y Beibl a Llenyddiaeth Gymraeg, 1998; John Roberts Llanfwrog: pregethwr, bardd, emynydd, 1999; (contrib.) Gogoneddus Arglwydd, Henffych Well, 2000; Nid hwn mo'r llyfr terfynol: Hanes Llenyddiaeth Thomas Parry, 2004; (ed) Kyffin: a celebration, 2007. *Recreations:* cricket, gardening, fortunes and misfortunes of Swansea City AFC, reading. *Address:* Carrog Uchaf, Tregaian, Llangefni, Anglesey LL77 7UE. *Clubs:* Premier (Glamorgan County Cricket); Rygbi Llangefni.

MORGAN, Dianne; *see* Edwards, D.

MORGAN, Douglas, IPFA; County Treasurer, Lancashire County Council, 1985–92; *b* 5 June 1936; *s* of late Douglas Morgan and Margaret Gardner Morgan; *m* 1960, Julia (*née* Bywater); two *s*. *Educ:* High Pavement Grammar Sch., Nottingham. IPFA 1963 (4th place in final exam. and G. A. Johnston (Dundee) Prize). Nat. Service, RAF, 1954–56. Nottingham CBC, 1952–61; Herefordshire CC, 1961–64; Berkshire CC, 1964–67; Asst Co. Treas., W Suffolk CC, 1967–70; Asst, later Dep., Co. Treas., Lindsey CC, 1970–73; Dep. Co. Treas., Lancashire CC, 1973–85. Chm., NW & N Wales Region, CIPFA, 1985–86; Pres., NW & N Wales Region, Students' Soc., CIPFA, 1989–90. Treas., Lancs Cttee, Royal Jubilee & Prince's Trust, 1985–92; Hon. Treasurer: Lancs Playing Fields Assoc., 1985–92; NW Region Library System and NW Sound Archive, 1986–92; Mem., Exec. Cttee, Lancs Union of Golf Clubs, 1998–02. FRSA. *Publications:* articles for Public Finance & Accountancy and other local govt jls. *Recreations:* golf and "collecting" golf courses, jazz, playing "gypsy" in a motor caravan. *Address:* 8 Croyde Road, St Annes-on-Sea, Lancs FY8 1EX. *T:* (01253) 725808. *Club:* Fairhaven Golf (Centenary Captain, 1995–96).

MORGAN, Dudley; *see* Morgan, David D.

MORGAN, Prof. Edwin (George), OBE 1982; Titular Professor of English, University of Glasgow, 1975–80, now Emeritus; Poet Laureate for Glasgow, 1999–2005; National Poet for Scotland, since 2004; *b* 27 April 1920; *s* of Stanley Lawrence Morgan and Margaret McKillop Arnott. *Educ:* Rutherglen Academy; High Sch. of Glasgow; Univ. of Glasgow (MA 1st Cl. Hons, Eng. Lang. and Lit., 1947). Served War, RAMC, 1940–46. University of Glasgow: Asst, 1947, Lectr, 1950, Sen. Lectr, 1965, Reader, 1971, in English. Vis. Prof., Strathclyde Univ., 1987–90; Hon. Prof., UCW, 1991–95. Cholmondeley Award for Poets, 1968; Hungarian PEN Meml Medal, 1972; Scottish Arts Council Book Awards, 1968, 1973, 1975, 1977, 1978, 1983, 1985, 1991 and 1992; Soros Translation Award, NY, 1985; Queen's Gold Medal for Poetry, 2000. Visual/concrete poems in many internat. exhibns, 1965–. Opera librettos (unpublished): The Charcoal-Burner, 1969; Valentine, 1976; Columba, 1976; Spell, 1979. HRSA 1997. Hon. DLitt: Loughborough, 1981; Glasgow, 1990; Edinburgh, 1991; St Andrews, 2000; Heriot-Watt, 2000; DUniv: Stirling, 1989; Waikato, 1992; MUniv Open, 1992. Order of Merit (Republic of Hungary), 1997. *Publications: poetry:* The Vision of Cathkin Braes, 1952; The Cape of Good Hope, 1955; (ed) Collins Albatross Book of Longer Poems, 1963; Starryveldt, 1965; Emergent Poems, 1967; Gnomes, 1968; The Second Life, 1968; Proverbfolder, 1969; Penguin Modern Poets 15, 1969; Twelve Songs, 1970; The Horseman's Word, 1970; (co-ed) Scottish Poetry 1–6, 1966–72; Glasgow Sonnets, 1972;

Instamatic Poems, 1972; The Whittrick, 1973; From Glasgow to Saturn, 1973; The New Divan, 1977; Colour Poems, 1978; Star Gate, 1979; (ed) Scottish Satirical Verse, 1980; Poems of Thirty Years, 1982; Grafts/Takes, 1983; Sonnets From Scotland, 1984; Selected Poems, 1985; From the Video Box, 1986; Newspoems, 1987; Themes on a Variation, 1988; Tales from Limerick Zoo, 1988; Collected Poems, 1990; Hold Hands Among the Atoms, 1991; (ed) James Thomson, The City of Dreadful Night, 1993; Sweeping out the Dark, 1994; Virtual and Other Realities, 1997; Demon, 1999; New Selected Poems, 2000; Cathures, 2002; Love and a Life, 2003; Tales from Baron Munchausen, 2005; A Book of Lives, 2007; Beyond the Sun, 2007; *play:* A.D., a Trilogy, 2000; *prose:* Essays, 1974; East European Poets, 1976; Hugh MacDiarmid, 1976; Twentieth Century Scottish Classics, 1987; Nothing Not Giving Messages (interviews), 1990; Crossing the Border: essays in Scottish Literature, 1990; Language, Poetry, and Language Poetry, 1990; Evening Will Come They Will Sew the Blue Sail, 1991; *translations:* Beowulf, 1952; Poems from Eugenio Montale, 1959; Sovpoems, 1961; Mayakovsky, Wi the Haill Voice, 1972; Fifty Renascence Love Poems, 1975; Rites of Passage (selected poetic translations), 1976; Platen: selected poems, 1978; Master Peter Pathelin, 1983; Rostand, Cyrano de Bergerac: a new verse translation, 1992; Collected Translations, 1996; Doctor Faustus, 1999; Phaedra, 2000; Attila József, Sixty Poems, 2001. *Recreations:* photography, scrapbooks, walking in cities. *Address:* Clarence Court, 234 Crow Road, Glasgow G11 7PD. *T:* (0141) 357 7229.

MORGAN, Eluned; *see* Morgan, M. E.

MORGAN, (Evan) Roger; Senior Clerk, Science & Technology Committee, House of Lords, 1999–2003; *b* 18 April 1945; *s* of late Evan and of Stella Morgan; *m* 1st, 1967 (marr. diss.); one *s* one *d*; 2nd, 1997, Lesley Greene (*née* Smith). *Educ:* Whitgift Sch., South Croydon; Battersea Coll. of Advanced Technol. Main career spent within DES, then Dept for Educn, later Dept for Educn and Employment: Under Sec., Further Educn, 1991–94, Internat. Relns and Youth, 1994–95; Asst Dir, Internat. Dept for Educn and Employment, 1995–97. Various voluntary post-retirement positions, 2003–. *Recreations:* making music, cycling, gadgets. *Address: e-mail:* morgan.roger@btopenworld.com.

MORGAN, Francis Vincent; school governance consultant; Secretary, Association of Governing Bodies of Independent Schools (formerly Governing Bodies Association and Governing Bodies of Girls' Schools Association), 1998–2003; *b* 22 June 1936; *s* of Joseph Michael Morgan and Monica Morgan; *m* 1965, Annette Mary Tolhurst; one *s*. *Educ:* St Edward's Coll., Liverpool; Univ. of Liverpool (Oliver Lodge Prize; BSc 1958); St John's Coll., Cambridge (PGCE 1959); Chelsea Coll., Univ. of London (MEd 1974). Asst master, Stonyhurst Coll., 1959–62; various posts, Redrice Sch., Andover, 1962–68; Lectr in Physical Scis, Homerton Coll., Cambridge, 1968–70; Schs Advr, Borough of Southend-on-Sea, 1970–73; Head: Sacred Heart Sch., Tunbridge Wells, 1973–78; St Mary's Catholic Sch., Bishop's Stortford, 1978–84; Schs Officer, Archdio. Westminster, 1984–86; Dir of Educn, RC Dio. Brentwood, 1986–90; Dir, United Westminster Schs and Royal Foundn of Grey Coat Hosp., 1990–98. Mem., Indep. Schs Pension Scheme Cttee, 1996–2001. Governor: Stonyhurst Coll., 1986–91; New Hall Sch., Chelmsford, 1992–2001 (Chm., 1995–2001; Guardian, 2005–); Westminster Cathedral Choir Sch., 1998–; Sutton Valence Sch., 1998–2004; St Mary's Sch., Ascot, 2002–; Trustee: St Mary's Sch., Hampstead, 1992–2001; United Westminster Schs, 2000–06; Eastern Counties Educnl Trust (formerly Royal Eastern Counties Schs), 2002–. *Recreations:* books, music, chess, gardening. *Address:* Lowe's House, 1 Linton Road, Balsham, Cambs CB21 4HA. *T:* (01223) 894425. *Club:* Athenæum.
See also J. A. Morgan.

MORGAN, Prof. Frank; Vice-Chancellor, Bath Spa University (formerly Bath Spa University College), since 1996; *b* Stockport, 23 Nov. 1952; *s* of George Morgan and Hilda Morgan; *m* 1989, Gurcharan Kaur Dhillon; two *s*. *Educ:* Bridge Hall Sch., Stockport; Manchester Poly. and Preston Poly. (CPFA 1981). Greater Manchester Transport, 1976–80; Accountant, London Bor. of Southwark, 1980–83; Hd, Finance, North East London Poly., 1983–86; Dep. Dir, Bath Coll. of Higher Educn, subseq. Bath Spa University Coll., 1986–96. *Recreations:* studying seventeenth century French plays, watching Rugby League, exploring England's industrial heritage. *Address:* Bath Spa University, Newton Park, Bath BA2 7BN. *T:* (01225) 875619, *Fax:* (01225) 872646; *e-mail:* vc@bathspa.ac.uk.

MORGAN, (Frederick) David, OBE 2008; President, International Cricket Council, since 2008 (Director, since 2003); *b* 6 Oct. 1937; *s* of Frederick Barlow Morgan and Caroline Morgan (*née* Constable); *m* 1960, Ann Cruickshank; one *s*. *Educ:* Thomas Richards Technical Sch., Tredegar; Henley Management Coll. (Gen. Mgt Prog. 1975). British Steel: Works Manager, Hot Sheet Finishing and Cold Rolling, Llanwern, 1977–84; Regl Sales Manager, SW and Wales, Strip Products, 1984–85; Commercial Manager, Electricals, 1985–90; Commercial Dir, European Electrical Steels, 1991–2001. Dir, Newport Develt Bd, 1997–2002. Chm., Wkg Party on setting up ECB (reported 1996); Dep. Chm., 1997–2002, Chm., 2003–07, ECB. Chancellor's Medal, Univ. of Glamorgan, 2004. *Recreations:* music of the more serious kind, Church liturgy, wine, travel, Rugby, newspapers. *Address:* 49 Old Hill Crescent, Christchurch, Newport NP18 1JL. *T:* (01633) 420578, *Fax:* (01633) 420497; *e-mail:* FDM1@btconnect.com. *Clubs:* MCC; Glamorgan CC, Worcestershire CC.

MORGAN, Geoffrey Thomas, CB 1991; Under Secretary, Cabinet Office, 1985–91; *b* 12 April 1931; *s* of late Thomas Evan Morgan and Nora (*née* Flynn); *m* 1960, Heather, *d* of late William Henry Trick and of Margery Murrell Wells; two *d*. *Educ:* Roundhay Sch. National Service, Royal Signals, 1950–52; joined Civil Service, 1952; served in Mins of Supply and Aviation, 1952–65; HM Treasury, 1965–68 and 1981–83; CSD, 1968–81; seconded to Arthur Guinness Son & Co., 1970–72; Cabinet Office, 1983–91; Adviser to: World Bank in Washington, 1977–78; UN in NY, 1987–88; official missions to: People's Republic of China in Beijing, 1988, 1991; Govt of Hungary in Budapest, 1990–2000; Govt of Jamaica in Kingston, 1991; South Africa, 1991–95; Czech Republic, 1996–2000; Chile, 1998. Chm., Public Admin Cttee, WEU, 1990–91. Advr, Coopers & Lybrand, subseq. PricewaterhouseCoopers, 1991–2000. Panel Chm., CSSB, 1991–95; Chm., Internat. Adv. Panel, Civil Service Coll., 1998–2001. Trustee, Whitehall and Industry Gp, 1991–94. Trustee, Twickenham Mus., 2002–. FRSA 1996. *Recreation:* enjoying life with grandchildren. *Clubs:* Athenæum; Lensbury (Teddington).

MORGAN, George Lewis Bush; Chief Registrar, Bank of England, 1978–83; *b* 1 Sept. 1925; *s* of late William James Charles Morgan and Eva Averill Morgan (*née* Bush); *m* 1949, Mary Rose (*née* Vine); three *s*. *Educ:* Cranbrook Sch., Kent. Captain, Royal Sussex Regt, 1943–47. Entered Bank of England, 1947; Asst Chief Accountant, 1966; Asst Sec., 1969; Dep. Sec., 1973. Mem. Bd of Govs, Holmewood House Prep. Sch., Tunbridge Wells, 1983–98 (Chm., 1986–98). *Recreations:* golf, gardening. *Address:* Irvings Cottage, Fletching Street, Mayfield, East Sussex TN20 6TJ. *Club:* Piltdown Golf.

MORGAN, Dame Gillian (Margaret), DBE 2004; FRCP, FFPH; Permanent Secretary, Welsh Assembly Government, since 2008. *Educ:* University Coll. Hosp. Medical Sch. (MB BS). MRCGP 1976; DRCOG 1981; FFPH (FFPHM 1996); FRCP 1998. Leicestershire Health Authority: Dir of Quality and Contracts, 1989–91; Dir of Public Health, 1991–94; Chief Exec., North and East Devon HA, 1995–2002; Chief Exec., NHS Confederation, 2002–08. Hon. DSc City, 2006. *Recreation:* sailing. *Address:* Welsh Assembly Government, Cathays Park, Cardiff CF1 3NQ.

MORGAN, Sir Graham, Kt 2000; independent health care advisor, since 2007; *b* 20 Aug. 1947; *s* of Islwyn and Phyllis Morgan; partner 1967, Raymond Willetts. *Educ:* Treorchy Secondary Modern Sch.; Llandough Hosp. (RGN 1969). Staff Nurse: Llandough Hosp., Cardiff, 1969; Royal Marsden Hosp., 1970–72; Charge Nurse, St Mary's Hosp., Paddington, 1972–74; Nursing Officer, KCH, 1974–83; Asst Dir of Nursing, St Charles' Hosp., 1983–91; Special Nurse Advr, 1991–94, Dir of Nursing and Quality, 1994–99, Central Middlesex Hosp.; Exec. Dir of Nursing, 1999–2005, Dir of Clinical Strategy, 2005–07, NW London Hosps NHS Trust. Consultant in Health Care, Univ. of Nottingham, 1997. Ordained priest, 1984; NSM, St Michael and All Angels, Bedford Park, 2003–. *Publications:* (with Amanda Layton) Nuts and Bolts of Protocols, 1998; articles in various health care jls. *Recreations:* opera, dining out. *Address:* 24 Charleville Court, Charleville Road, W14 9JG. *Club:* National Liberal.

MORGAN, Gwyn; *see* Morgan, J. G.

MORGAN, Hugh Marsden; His Honour Judge Hugh Morgan; a Circuit Judge, since 1995; *b* 17 March 1940; *s* of late Hugh Thomas Morgan, Cyncoed, Cardiff and Irene Morgan (*née* Rees); *m* 1967, Amanda Jane Tapley; two *s* one *d*. *Educ:* Cardiff High Sch.; Magdalen Coll., Oxford (Demy; BCL; MA Jurisp.). Called to the Bar, Gray's Inn, 1964; in practice: Midland Circuit, 1965–71; SE Circuit, 1971–95; Asst Recorder, 1983–87; Recorder, 1987–95. Member: Matrimonial Causes Rule Cttee, 1989–91; Family Proceedings Rule Cttee, 1991–93; Fees and Legal Aid Cttee, Senate and Bar Council, 1976–82. Mem., Wine Cttee, SE Circuit, 1986–88. Mem. Cttee, Family Law Bar Assoc., 1976–89. *Recreations:* gardening, reading, travel, Roman remains. *Address:* c/o Kingston County Court, St James Road, Kingston upon Thames KT1 2AD.

MORGAN, Rt Hon. (Hywel) Rhodri; PC 2000; Member (Lab) Cardiff West, since 1999 and First Minister (formerly First Secretary) for Wales, since 2000, National Assembly for Wales; *b* 29 Sept. 1939; *s* of late Thomas John and Huana Morgan; *m* 1967, Julie Edwards (*see* Julie Morgan); one *s* two *d*. *Educ:* St John's College, Univ. of Oxford (Hons cl. 2, PPE 1961); Harvard Univ. (Masters in Govt 1963). Tutor Organiser, WEA, S Wales Area, 1963–65; Research Officer, Cardiff City Council, Welsh Office and DoE, 1965–71; Economic Adviser, DTI, 1972–74; Indust. Develt Officer, S Glamorgan County Council, 1974–80; Head of Bureau for Press and Inf., European Commn Office for Wales, 1980–87. MP (Lab) Cardiff West, 1987–2001. Opposition spokesman on: Energy, 1988–92; Welsh Affairs, 1992–97. Sec. for Economic Develt, Nat. Assembly for Wales, 1999–2000. *Publication:* Cardiff: half and half a capital, 1994. *Recreations:* long-distance running, wood carving, marine wildlife. *Address:* Lower House, Michaelston-le-Pit, Dinas Powys, South Glamorgan CF64 4HE. *T:* (home) (029) 2051 4262; (office) (029) 2022 3207; National Assembly for Wales, Cardiff Bay, Cardiff CF99 1NA. *T:* (029) 2089 8764.

MORGAN, Sir Ian Parry David H.; *see* Hughes-Morgan.

MORGAN, Ioan, CBE 2007; Principal, Warwickshire College, since 1997; *b* 4 April 1953; *s* of John and Marjorie Morgan; *m* 1976, Sandra Evans; two *s* one *d*. *Educ:* Univ. of Wales, Aberystwyth (BSc Hons 1975); London Univ. (CertEd). CBiol. Principal: Cambridgeshire Coll. of Agric. and Hort., 1985–89; Pembrokeshire Coll., 1989–97. Chm., 157 Gp of Colls, 2006. Mem., Commn for Skills and Employment, 2007–. FCGI. *Recreations:* dogs, countryside, Rugby, cricket, travel. *Address:* Warwickshire College, Warwick New Road, Leamington Spa, Warwicks CV32 5JE. *T:* (office) (01926) 318223, *Fax:* (01926) 318181; *e-mail:* imorgan@warkscol.ac.uk.

MORGAN, Janet; *see* Balfour of Burleigh, Lady.

MORGAN, Jeremy; *see* Morgan, T. J.

MORGAN, Sir John (Albert Leigh), KCMG 1989 (CMG 1982); HM Diplomatic Service, retired; Chairman: Celtic Development Co. (formerly East European Development Trust), since 1994; Ceiba Investments Ltd (formerly Beta Gran Caribe, then Ceiba Finance Ltd), Cuba, since 2002; Director and Company Secretary, Global Tote, since 1999; *b* 21 June 1929; *s* of late John Edward Rowland Morgan, Bridge, Kent; *m* 1st, 1961, Hon. Fionn Frances Bride O'Neill (marr. diss. 1975), *d* of 3rd Baron O'Neill, Shane's Castle, Antrim; one *s* two *d*; 2nd, 1976, Angela Mary Eleanor, *e d* of Patrick Warre Rathbone, MBE, Woolton, Liverpool; one *s* one *d*. *Educ:* Chingford County High Sch.; London School of Economics (BSc(Econ) Hons Econs and Law; Hon. Fellow, 1984). Served in Army, 1947–49: commnd 1948; interpreter with French Army, 1949. Entered Foreign Service, 1951; FO, 1951–53; 3rd Sec. and Private Sec. to HM Ambassador, Moscow, 1953–56; 2nd Sec., Peking, 1956–58; FO, 1958–63 (attended Geneva Conf. of Foreign Ministers on Berlin, 1959, and on Laos (interpreter in Russian and Chinese), 1961; interpreter for Mr Khrushchev's visit to UK, 1956, for Mr Macmillan's visit to Soviet Union, 1959, and for Summit Conf. in Paris, 1960); 1st Sec., 1960; Head of Chancery, Rio de Janeiro, 1963–64; FO, 1964–65; Chargé d'Affaires, Ulan Bator, 1965; Moscow, 1965–67; Dep. Hd, Econ. Relns Dept, subseq. Export Promotion Dept, FO, 1968; Head of Far Eastern Dept, FCO, 1970–72; Head of Cultural Relations Dept, FCO, 1972–80 (Member: Reviewing Cttee on Export of Works of Art; Fulbright Scholarship Commn; Selection Cttee, US Bicentennial Scholarships Prog.); Ambassador and Consul Gen. to Republic of Korea, 1980–83; Ambassador to Poland, 1983–86; Ambassador to Mexico, 1986–89. Man. Dir (Internat. Relations), Maxwell Communications Corp., 1989–90; Chairman: Invesco (formerly Drayton) Korea Trust plc, 1993–99 (Dir, 1991); Gulf Internat. Minerals (Vancouver), 1997–2003; Director: The European, 1990–91; Christies, 1993–95; Invesco Europe Ltd, 1994–99; Japan Discovery Trust, 1994–2005; Pres., Actions Asie Emergents, Paris, 1996–2001. Pres., IFPI, 1990–93. Served on Earl Marshal's Staff for State Funeral of Sir Winston Churchill, 1965, and for Investiture of Prince of Wales, 1969. Trustee, BM, 1991–99, now Emeritus (Trustee, BM Develt Trust, 1991–). Governor, LSE, 1971–94, 1997–2003; Chm., LSE Foundn, 1994–97. Chairman: Anglo-Korean Soc., 1990–96 (Hon. Pres., 2002–06); UK-Korea Forum for the Future, 1991–99; Member: Internat. Council, United World Colleges, 1990–; Internat. and Current Affairs Cttee, ESU, 1993–2000. Royal Philharmonic Orchestra: Dir, 1993–96; Hon. Life Mem. 1979; Chm., Development Trust, 1993–96; Vice Chm., South Bank Foundn Ltd, 1997–2003. FRSA; Fellow, Royal Asiatic Soc.; Hon. Life Mem., GB-China Centre. Hon. DSc (Politics) Korea Univ., 1983; Hon. LLD Mexico Acad. of Internat. Law, 1987. Order of the Aztec Eagle, 1st cl. (Mexico), 1994; Order of Diplomatic Merit, 1st cl. (Korea), 1999. *Publications:* (contrib.) Travellers' Tales, 1999; Martinis, Guns and Girls, 2002; (contrib.) More Tales from the Travellers, 2005; various works of French and Chinese literary criticism. *Recreations:* ornithology, oriental art. *Address:* 41 Hugh Street, SW1V 1QJ. *T:* (020) 7821 1037; Beaumont Cottage, South Brewham, near Bruton,

Somerset BA10 0JZ. *T:* (01749) 850606. *Club:* Travellers.
See also C. A. W. Gibson.

MORGAN, John Alfred; Director, Eleco Holdings plc, 1997–2001; *b* 16 Sept. 1931; *s* of late Alfred Morgan and Lydia Amelia Morgan; *m* 1959, Janet Mary Sclater-Jones; one *d.* *Educ:* Rugeley Grammar Sch.; Peterhouse, Cambridge (BA). Investment Research, Cambridge, 1953–59; Investment Manager, S. G. Warburg & Co. Ltd, 1959–67; Director: Glyn, Mills & Co., 1967–70; Williams & Glyn's Bank Ltd, 1970–76; Rothschild Asset Management, 1976–78; Central Trustee Savings Bank Ltd, 1982–86; Zurich Life Assce Co. Ltd, 1970–87; Sealink UK Ltd, 1983–85; Caviapen Investments Ltd, 1993–97; Yamaichi Bank (UK) plc, 1994–98. Gen. Manager, British Railways Pension Funds, 1978–86; Chief Exec., IMRO, 1986–93. Chm., Post Office Users' Nat. Council, 1978–82. *Recreations:* music, contemporary art, fell walking. *Club:* Reform.

MORGAN, His Honour John Ambrose; a Circuit Judge, 1990–2003; a Deputy Circuit Judge, since 2003; *b* 22 Sept. 1934; *s* of Joseph Michael Morgan and Monica Morgan; *m* 1970, Rosalie Mary Tyson; two *s.* *Educ:* St Edward's Coll., Liverpool; Univ. of Liverpool (Emmott Meml Scholar 1953; Alsopp Prizewinner 1953; LLB 1955). Law Soc. Finals 1957 (Local Govt Prize). Nat. Service, RAF, 1958–60. Admitted Solicitor, 1958; practised in local govt and private practice, 1960–70; called to the Bar, Gray's Inn, 1970; N Circuit, 1970–90; Dep. Stipendiary Magistrate, 1982; Asst Recorder, 1983; Recorder, 1988. Chm. of Govs, St Edward's Coll., Liverpool, 1987–95. *Recreations:* Rugby Union football (Pres., Liverpool RFU, 1980–82), golf, cricket, music, amateur operatics. *Address:* Tarnbrick, 80 Beech Lane, Liverpool L18 3ER. *Clubs:* Athenæum (Liverpool); Liverpool St Helen's RFC, Woolton Golf, Sefton Cricket (Pres., 2003–04).
See also F. V. Morgan.

MORGAN, John Christopher; Executive Chairman, Morgan Sindall plc, since 2000 (Chief Executive, 1994–99); *b* 31 Dec. 1955; *m* 1984, Rosalind Kendrew; two *s* one *d.* *Educ:* Peter Symonds Grammar Sch., Winchester; Univ. of Reading (BSc Estate Mgt 1977); Open Univ. (MBA 1994). Chairman: Morgan Lovell, 1977–94; Johnsons Freshly Squeezed Juice Ltd, 1985–96; Genetix plc, 2000–. Non-exec. Dir, Newfound NV, 2006–. *Address:* Morgan Sindall plc, 77 Newman Street, W1T 3EW. *T:* (020) 7307 9200.

MORGAN, (John) Gwyn(fryn), OBE 1999; private consultant; Head, South-East Asia, Directorate-General of External Relations, European Commission, 1995–99; Head, European Union Election Observation Team, Ivory Coast, 2000; *b* 16 Feb. 1934; *s* of Arthur G. Morgan, coal miner, and Mary Walters; two *s* two *d* from former marriages. *Educ:* Aberdare Boys' Grammar Sch.; UCW Aberystwyth; MA Classics 1957; Dip. Educn 1958. Senior Classics Master, The Regis Sch., Tettenhall, Staffs, 1958–60; Pres., National Union of Students, 1960–62; Sec.-Gen., Internat. Student Conf. (ISC), 1962–65; Head of Overseas Dept, British Labour Party, 1965–69; Asst Gen. Secretary, British Labour Party, 1969–72; Chef de Cabinet to Rt Hon. George Thomson, EC Comr, 1973–75; Head of Welsh Inf. Office, EEC, 1975–79; a Dir, Development Corp. for Wales, 1976–81, Hon. Consultant in Canada 1981–83; Head of EEC Press and Inf. Office for Canada, 1979–83; EEC Rep. in Turkey, 1983–86; Hd, Delgn of EEC to Israel, West Bank and Gaza, 1987–92; Ambassador-Head of Delegn of EC to Thailand, Vietnam, Laos, Cambodia, Myanmar and Malaysia, 1993–95. Vice-Chm., European Inst. for Asian Studies, Brussels, 2000–. Mem., Hansard Commn on Electoral Reform, 1975–76. Head, EU Election Observation Unit, Indonesia, 1999. *Publications:* contribs to numerous British and foreign political jls. *Recreations:* cricket, Rugby football, crosswords, wine-tasting. *Address:* 14 Ravenscroft Road, Chiswick, W4 5EQ. *T:* (020) 8994 4218, *Fax:* (office) (020) 7460 7091. *Clubs:* Reform, Royal Commonwealth Society, MCC; Cardiff and County.

MORGAN, John William Harold, (Bill), CBE 1998; FREng; Chairman, Trafford Park Urban Development Corporation, 1990–98; Director: AMEC plc, 1983–91 (Chairman, 1984–88); Hill Samuel & Co., 1983–89; *b* 13 Dec. 1927; *s* of John Henry and Florence Morgan; *m* 1952, Barbara (*née* Harrison); two *d.* *Educ:* Wednesbury Boys' High Sch.; Univ. of Birmingham (BScEng, 1st Cl. Hons). FIMechE, MIET. National Service commn with RAF, 1949–51. Joined English Electric Co., Stafford, as design engr, subseq. Chief Development Engr (Machines), 1953; Chief Develt Engr (Mechanical), 1957; Chief Engr (DC Machines), 1960; Product Div. Manager, 1962; Gen. Man., Electrical Machines Gp, 1965; Managing Director, English Electric-AEI Machines Gp (following merger with GEC/AEI), 1968; Asst Man. Dir and main board director, GEC plc, 1973–83. Chm., Staffordshire Cable, 1989–93; Dep. Chm., Petbow Holdings, 1983–86; Director: Simon Engineering, 1983–88; Pitney Bowes, 1989–92; Tekdata, 1989–99; UMIST Ventures, 1989–2001. Additional Mem., Monopolies and Mergers Commn (Electricity Panel), 1992–98. FREng (FEng 1978; Mem. Council, 1987–90). FRSA 1988. Hon. DSc Salford, 1997. S. G. Brown award for an outstanding contrib. to promotion and development of mechanical inventions, Royal Society, 1968. *Recreations:* craft activities, particularly woodworking. *Address:* Mullion, Whitmore Heath, near Newcastle, Staffs ST5 5HF. *T:* (01782) 680462.

MORGAN, Jonathan; Member (C) Cardiff North, National Assembly for Wales, since 2007 (South Wales Central, 1999–2007); *b* 12 Nov. 1974; *s* of Barrie and Linda Morgan. *Educ:* Bishop of Llandaff Church in Wales Sch., Cardiff; Cardiff Univ. (LLB Hons Law & Politics; MSc Econ European Policy). European Funding Officer, Cardiff Further Educn Coll., 1998–99. *Recreations:* theatre, golf, music. *Address:* National Assembly for Wales, Cardiff Bay, Cardiff CF99 1NA. *T:* (029) 2089 8734. *Clubs:* Merthyr Conservative (Merthyr Tydfil); County Conservative (Cardiff).

MORGAN, Julie; MP (Lab) Cardiff North, since 1997; *b* 2 Nov. 1944; *d* of late Jack Edwards and of Grace Edwards; *m* 1967, Rhodri Morgan, *qv*; one *s* two *d.* *Educ:* Howell's Sch., Llandaff; KCL (BA Hons); Manchester Univ.; Cardiff Univ. (DipSocAdmin, CQSW). Sen. Social Worker, Barry, S Glam. Social Services, 1980–83; Principal Officer and Develt Officer, W Glam. CC, 1983–87; Asst Dir, Child Care, Barnardo's, 1987–97. Member (Lab): S Glam. Council, 1985–96; Cardiff UA, 1996–97. Contested (Lab) Cardiff N, 1992. *Address:* House of Commons, SW1A 0AA; Cardiff North Constituency Office, 17 Plasnewydd, Whitchurch, Cardiff CF14 1NR; Lower House, Michaelston-le-Pit, Dinas Powys CF64 6HE.

MORGAN, Karen Jane, OBE 1999; DL; Chairman and Trustee, The Converging World, since 2007; Director, Wessex Water Services Ltd, 1998–2005; *b* 28 June 1945; *d* of Walter Anderson Caldwell and Jean Drummond Caldwell (*née* Hislop); *m* 1st, 1977, (Malcolm) John Methven (later Sir John Methven; he *d* 1980); three step *d*; 2nd, 1988, Andrew John Mantle Morgan; two step *s* two step *d.* *Educ:* St Leonard's Sch., St Andrews; Univ. of Edinburgh (BSc 1st Cl. Hons Chemistry). ICI Ltd, 1968–81. Director: Latchways Ltd, 1982–85; Southdown Bldg Soc., 1990–92 (Vice-Chm., 1991–92); Associate, Solomon Hare LLP, 1993–2005. Member: Bd, NRA, 1989–95; Bd, EA, 1995–98; Envmt Cttee, RSA, 1999–2005; Council, NERC, 2002–. Trustee, 1992–2007, Vice-Chm., 2001–07, Water Aid; Chm., EcoAlert Ltd, 2007–. Mem. Council, CNAA, 1982–88; Comr, Fulbright Commn, 1983–87; Mem., Bd of Govs, Bristol Poly., 1989–92; University of West of England: Mem., 1992–2003, Dep. Chm., 1994–97, Chm., 1998–2003, Bd of Govs; Pro Chancellor, 2004–; Mem., 1998–2003, Dep. Chm., 2000–02, Cttee of Univ. Chairmen; Member: Commn on Univ. Career Opportunity, 1999–2000; Jt Equality Steering Gp, 2001–03; Equality Challenge Unit Mgt Bd, 2003–06. Dir, At-Bristol, 2000–; Trustee, Plymouth Marine Lab., 2005–. Chm., Appeal Cttee, 2004–07, Vice Pres., 2007–, Penny Brohn Cancer Care (formerly Bristol Cancer Help Centre). Member: Governing Body, Colston's Collegiate Sch., 2004–; Governing Council, RAC, Cirencester, 2004– (Vice Chm., 2005–); Council, RSA, 2005–. Trustee, Bath Festivals Trust, 1993–98. FRSA 1998. Hon. DEd UWE, 2004. DL Glos, 2007. Freeman, 2001–03, Liveryman, 2003–, Co. of Water Conservators; Mem., Soc. of Merchant Venturers, 2003–; Mem. Court, Co. of Glos, 2008–. *Publication:* (contrib.) Time of Flight Mass Spectrometry, 1969. *Recreations:* music, sailing, ski-ing, travelling. *Address:* Little Skiveralls, Chalford Hill, Stroud, Glos GL6 8QJ. *Clubs:* Reform; Kandahar Ski; Royal Western Yacht, Clyde Cruising.

MORGAN, Prof. Keith John, DPhil; FRACI, FRSC; FAIM; Research Fellow, Research Institute for Higher Education, Hiroshima University, since 2003; *b* 14 Dec. 1929; *s* of C. F. J. Morgan and Winifred Burman (formerly Morgan, *née* Allen); *m* 1957, Hilary Chapman (marr. diss. 1999); one *d.* *Educ:* Manchester Grammar Sch.; Brasenose Coll., Oxford (MA, BSc, DPhil). Senior Research Fellow, Min. of Supply, 1955–57; ICI Res. Fellow, 1957–58; Lectr, Univ. of Birmingham, 1958–64; AEC Fellow, Purdue Univ., 1960–61; Lectr, Sen. Lectr, Prof., Dept. of Chemistry, Univ. of Lancaster, 1964–86 (Pro-Vice-Chancellor, 1973–78; Sen. Pro-Vice-Chancellor, 1978–86; Emeritus Prof.); Vice-Chancellor, Univ. of Newcastle, NSW, 1987–93 (Emeritus Prof.); Prof., Univ. of Electro-Communications, Tokyo, 1993–95. Visiting Professor: Hiroshima Univ., 1995–99, 2007–08; Nagoya Univ., 2002. Chm., Hunter Foundn for Cancer Res., 1992–93; Dep. Chm., Hunter Technol. Develt Centre, 1987–93; Member: Hunter Econ. Develt Council, 1989–93; Hunter Federal Task Force, 1991–93; Hunter Area Health Service Bd, 1992–93; Dir, Hunter Orch., 1991–93. Chm., Regl Council, AIM, 1989–93. Chm. of Govs, Newcastle Grammar Sch., 1991–93; Member: UCNS, 1980–86; Council, Lancashire Polytechnic, 1985–86. Mem., NSW Envmtl Res. Trust, 1990–93. Hon. DSc Newcastle, NSW, 1993. *Publications:* scientific and economic papers in various jls. *Recreations:* mountains, Mozart, cricket. *Address:* 9B Castle Hill, Lancaster LA1 1YS. *T:* (01524) 68619.

MORGAN, Kenneth, OBE 1978; journalist; consultant on Press ethics; Director: Press Council, 1980–90; Press Complaints Commission, 1991; *b* 3 Nov. 1928; *s* of Albert E. and Lily M. Morgan; *m* 1950, Margaret Cynthia, *d* of Roland E. Wilson; three *d.* *Educ:* Stockport Grammar School. Reporter, Stockport Express, 1944; Army, 1946, commissioned, 1947 (served Palestine, Egypt, GHQ MELF, British Army newspaper unit); journalism, 1949; Central London Sec., NUJ, 1962; Nat. Organiser, NUJ, 1966; Gen. Sec., NUJ, 1970–77, Mem. of Honour, 1978. Press Council: Consultative Mem., 1970–77; Jt Sec., 1977–78; Dep. Dir and Conciliator, 1978–79; Consultant, Press Complaints Commn, 1992. Director: Journalists in Europe Ltd, 1982–97; Reuters Founder's Share Co., 1984–99. Mem. Exec. Cttee: Printing and Kindred Trades Fedn, 1970–73; Nat. Fedn of Professional Workers, 1970–77; Fedn of Broadcasting Unions, 1970–77; Confedn of Entertainment Unions, 1970–77; Bureau, Internat. Fedn of Journalists, 1970–78. Member: NEDC for Printing and Publishing Industry, 1970; Printing Industries Cttee, TUC, 1974–77; Printing and Publishing Industries Trng Bd, 1975–77; Jt Standing Cttee, Nat. Newspaper Industry, 1976–77; British Cttee, Journalists in Europe, 1977–2003; C of E General Synod Cttee for Communications Press Panel, 1981–90; CRE Media Gp, 1981–85; Judge, Samuel Storey Editl Awards, 1981–98; Internat. Ombudsman Inst., 1983; Trustee, Reuters, 1984–99. Consultant: Nat. Media Commn, Ghana, 1995–99; Fiji Media Council, 1998; Media Trust Bd, Mauritius, 1998; Ind. Media Commn, Sierra Leone, 2003; Botswana Press Council, 2004; (with John Prescott Thomas) conducted Cabinet review of media legislation, Fiji, 1996–97; Advr, Minister of Information and Culture, Sierra Leone, 1998. Vice Pres. (former Chm.), Dulwich UNA, 1989–. Gov., 1992–99, Hon. Sec., 1993–99, ESU. Associate Mem. IPI, 1980; FRSA 1980. Methodist Recorder Lectr, 1989; British Council and Council of Europe lectures in Central and W Africa, Papua New Guinea, Fiji, Spain, Greece, Germany, Russia and Japan. Associate Press Fellow, Wolfson Coll., Cambridge, 1998–. *Publications:* Press Conduct in the Sutcliffe Case, 1983; (with David Christie) New Connexions: the power to inform, 1989; (jtly) Future Media Legislation and Regulation for the Republic of the Fiji Islands, 1996; A Press Council for Mauritius?: freedom, responsibility and redress for Mauritius and its media, 1999; *contributed to:* El Poder Judicial en le Conjunto de los Poderes del Estado y de la Sociedad, 1989; Media Freedom and Accountability, 1989; The Independence of the Journalist, Is de Klant of de Krant Koning, 1990; Beyond the Courtroom: alternatives for resolving press disputes, 1991; Sir Zelman Cowen: a life within the law, 1997; Arsenal for Democracy, 2002. *Recreations:* theatre, military history, inland waterways, travel. *Address:* 151 Overhill Road, Dulwich, SE22 0PT. *T:* (020) 8693 6585.

MORGAN, Loraine; District Judge (Magistrates' Courts) (formerly Metropolitan Stipendiary Magistrate), since 1995; *b* 2 Dec. 1953; *d* of late Enrico Bellisario and Elizabeth Bellisario (*née* Coyle); *m* 1976, Captain Dai Morgan, RN. *Educ:* St Augustine's Priory, Ealing; Univ. of Exeter; Coll. of Law, Guildford. Admitted Solicitor, 1981; Partner, Reynolds & Hetherington, Fareham, 1982–86, Allsworth & Spears, Fareham, 1986–88; Solicitor Advocate, 1988–95; Co-founder and Dir, Just Advocates Ltd, 1991–95; Plate Judge Advocate, 1996–2001; Asst Recorder, 1998–2000; a Recorder, 2000. Mem., Crown Court Rules Cttee, 1994. Vice-Pres., Bracton Law Soc., 1974–75; Cttee Mem., Hampshire Inc. Law Soc., 1990–94; Sec. and Chm., Southampton Criminal Courts Solicitors' Assoc., 1990–94; Vice-Chm., Criminal Law Solicitors' Assoc., 1991–94. *Recreations:* good wine, good food, the company of good friends. *Address:* c/o Southampton and New Forest Magistrates' Court, 100 The Avenue, Southampton SO17 1EY. *T:* (023) 8038 4200. *Club:* Lansdowne.

MORGAN, (Mair) Eluned; Member (Lab) Wales, European Parliament, since 1999 (Mid and West Wales, 1994–99); *b* 16 Feb. 1967; *d* of Rev. Bob Morgan and Elaine Morgan; *m* 1996, Dr Rhys Jenkins, one *s* one *d.* *Educ:* Atlantic Coll.; Univ. of Hull (BA). Stagiaire with Socialist Gp, Europe. Parlt, 1990; with S4C, 1991; researcher and reporter, Agenda TV, 1992; documentary researcher, BBC TV, 1993. Mem., Industry, Res. and Energy Cttee, EP, 2004–. *Recreations:* walking, reading. *Address:* Labour European Office, 1 Cathedral Road, Cardiff CF11 9SD; *e-mail:* emorgan@welshlabourmeps.org.uk.

MORGAN, Marilynne Ann, CB 1996; Solicitor to the Departments for Work and Pensions (formerly of Social Security) and of Health, and Head of Law and Special Policy Group, Department for Work and Pensions (formerly Department of Social Security), 1997–2004; *b* 22 June 1946; *d* of late J. Emlyn Williams and Roma Elizabeth Williams (*née* Ellis); *m* 1970, Nicholas Alan, *e s* of Rear-Adm. Sir Patrick Morgan, KCVO, CB, DSC. *Educ:* Gads Hill Place, Higham-by-Rochester; Bedford Coll., Univ. of London (BA Hons History). Called to the Bar, Middle Temple, 1972, Bencher, 2002. Res. Asst, Special Historical Sect., FCO, 1967–71; Department of Health and Social Security: Legal Asst, 1973; Sen. Legal Asst, 1978; Asst Solicitor, 1982; Under Sec. and Principal Asst Solicitor,

1985–91, DSS, 1988–91, DoE, 1991–92; Department of the Environment: Solicitor and Legal Advr, 1992–97; Chm., Departmental Task Force, 1994–95; Sen. Dir, Legal and Corporate Services Gp, 1996–97. Non-exec. Dir, Treasury Solicitor's Dept, 2004–. Vice-Chm. 1983–84, Chm. 1984–86, Legal Sect. of Assoc. of First Div. Civil Servants. Mem., General Council of the Bar, 1987–92. Hon. Legal Advr, CS Sports Council, 2006–. Trustee/Director: Alzheimer's Soc., 2003–; Ambache Orchestra, 2003–06; Alzheimer's Brain Bank UK, 2006–; Chm., Friends of Bucks Historic Churches, 2008–. *Publications:* contributor, Halsbury's Laws of England, 1982, 1986; articles in learned jls. *Recreations:* homely pursuits. *Clubs:* Royal Commonwealth Society, University Women's.

MORGAN, Martin Gerard; Senior Social Worker, Child Care Social Services, since 2005; *b* 25 Oct. 1966; *s* of Robert Morgan and Kathleen Morgan; *m* 2001, Dympna O'Hara. *Educ:* Queen's Univ., Belfast (BA Hons Inf. Mgt; MSW; DipSW). Child Protection Investigation Team, Child Care Social Services, 2002–03. Mem. (SDLP), Belfast City Council, 1993–2005; Lord Mayor of Belfast, 2003–04. *Recreations:* golf, athletics, reading political biographies. *Address: e-mail:* morganfdl2005@yahoo.co.uk.

MORGAN, Prof. Mary Susanna, PhD; FBA 2002; Professor of the History of Economics, London School of Economics and Political Science, University of London, since 1999. *Educ:* LSE (BSc 1978; PhD 1984). Res. Asst to Economist, Citibank, London, 1973–75; Exchange Control Dept, Bank of England, 1978–79; Res. Officer, Dept of Econs, LSE, 1979–82, 1983–84; Lectr, Dept of Econs and Related Studies, Univ. of York, 1984–87; Vis. Asst Prof., Dept of Econs, Duke Univ., 1987; Lectr, Dept of Econ. History, 1988–94, Reader in History of Econs, 1994–99, LSE. Prof. of History of Econ. Thought and Philosophy of Econ. Sci., Univ. of Amsterdam (part-time), 1992–. *Publications:* (ed jtly) The Probabilistic Revolution, vol. II: ideas in the sciences, 1987; The History of Econometric Ideas, 1990; (ed jtly) Higgling: transactors and their markets in the history of economics, 1994; (jtly) The Foundations of Econometric Analysis, 1995; (ed jtly) From Interwar Pluralism to Post-War Neoclassicism, 1998; (jtly) Methodology and Tacit Knowledge, 1999; (ed jtly) Models as Mediators, 1999; (ed jtly) Empirical Models and Policy Making, 2000; (ed jtly) The Age of Economic Measurement, 2001; articles in jls. *Address:* Department of Economic History, London School of Economics and Political Science, Houghton Street, WC2A 2AE.

MORGAN, Michael David; Development Director, Anglia Housing Association Group, 1993–98; *b* 19 Jan. 1942; *s* of Edward Arthur and Winifred Maud Morgan; *m* 1980, Ljiljana Radojcic; three *d. Educ:* Royal Liberty Sch., Romford; Prince Rupert Sch., Wilhemshaven, FRG; Coll. of Estate Management, London Univ. (BSc Est. Man.). FRICS. Sheffield City Council, 1964–67; Derby Borough Council, 1967–70; Telford Develt Corp., 1970–92 (Chief Exec. and Gen. Manager, 1986–92, retd). *Recreations:* cricket, jogging, gardening. *Address:* Red Roofs, Ashton Road, Kingsland, Shrewsbury SY3 7AP. *T:* (01743) 352800.

MORGAN, Michael Hugh, CMG 1978; HM Diplomatic Service, retired; *b* 18 April 1925; *s* of late H. P. Morgan; *m* 1957, Julian Bamfield; two *s. Educ:* Shrewsbury Sch.; Downing College, Cambridge; School of Oriental and African Studies, London Univ. Army Service 1943–46. HMOCS Malaya, 1946–56. Foreign Office, 1956–57; First Secretary, Peking, 1957–60; Belgrade 1960–64; attached to Industry, 1964; First Secretary, FCO, 1964–68; Counsellor and Head of Chancery, Cape Town/Pretoria, 1968–72; Counsellor, Peking, 1972–75; Inspector, FCO, 1975–77; High Comr, Sierra Leone, 1977–81; Ambassador to the Philippines, 1981–85. Consultant, British Rail Engrg, 1986–88; Dir, Swansea Overseas Trust, 1988–91. *Address:* 1 Silkmill Lane, Ludlow, Shropshire SY8 1BJ.

MORGAN, Prof. Michael John, PhD, ScD; FRS 2005; Professor of Visual Psychophysics, City University, since 2000; *b* 25 Aug. 1942; *m* 1996, Prof. Linda Partridge, *qv. Educ:* Queens' Coll., Cambridge (BA 1964; PhD 1969; ScD 1994). Asst in Res., 1965–71, Lectr, 1971–78, Univ. of Cambridge; Fellow, Queens' Coll., Cambridge, 1967–74; Professor of Psychology: Univ. of Durham, 1978–81; UCL, 1981–89; Professorial Fellow, Univ. of Edinburgh, 1989–93; Prof. of Visual Psychophysics, UCL, 1993–2000. *Publications:* Molyneux's Question: vision, touch and the philosophy of perception, 1977; The Space Between Our Ears, 2003; contrib. learned jls. *Address:* Department of Optometry and Visual Science, City University, Northampton Square, EC1V 0HB.

MORGAN, Patrick; HM Diplomatic Service, retired; Ambassador to El Salvador, 1999–2003; *b* 31 Jan. 1944; *s* of Matthew Morgan and Margaret (*née* Docherty); *m* 1966, Marlene Collins Beaton. *Educ:* St Columba's High Sch., Greenock. BoT, 1963–64; CRO, 1964–65; FCO, 1965–67; British Embassy: Bonn, 1967–69; Kuwait, 1969–71; La Paz, 1972–75; FCO, 1975–79; British Embassy: Washington DC, 1979–83; Jakarta, 1983–86; FCO, 1987–92; Ambassador to Honduras, 1992–95; Counsellor and Dep. Hd of Mission, Abu Dhabi, 1995–98; Counsellor, FCO, 1998–99. Governor, Al Khubairat Community Sch., Abu Dhabi, 1995–98. *Recreations:* swimming, squash, music, travel. *Address:* 4 Den Close, Beckenham, Kent BR3 6RP.

MORGAN, Hon. Sir Paul (Hyacinth), Kt 2007; **Hon. Mr Justice Morgan;** a Judge of the High Court, Chancery Division, since 2007; *b* 17 Aug. 1952; *s* of Daniel Morgan and Veronica Mary (*née* Elder); *m* 1980, Sheila Ruth Harvey; three *s. Educ:* St Columb's Coll., Londonderry; Peterhouse, Cambridge (BA 1974; MA 1979). Called to the Bar, Lincoln's Inn, 1975, Bencher, 2001. QC 1992; a Dep. High Court Judge, 2001–07. Dep. Chm., Agricl Land Tribunal, 1999–2007. *Publications:* (ed jtly) Megarry on Rent Acts, 11th edn, 1988; (ed jtly) Woodfall on Landlord and Tenant, 28th edn, 1990; (ed jtly) Gale on Easements, 17th edn, 2002. *Address:* Royal Courts of Justice, Strand, WC2A 2LL.

MORGAN, Peter John, PhD; FRSE, FIBiol; Director, Rowett Research Institute, since 1999; *b* 23 Feb. 1956; *s* of Dr John W. W. Morgan and Patricia M. Morgan; *m* 1991, Dr Denise Kelly; one *s* one *d. Educ:* Queen Mary Coll., London (BSc); Univ. of Aberdeen (PhD 1981). FIBiol 2001; FRSE 2002. AFRC post-doctoral res. asst, Dept of Zool., Univ. of Aberdeen, 1981–85; Rowett Research Institute, Aberdeen: SSO, 1985–89; PSO, 1989–; Leader, Molecular Neuroendocrinology Res. Gp, 1991–97; Head, Molecular Neuroendocrinology Unit and Mem., Sen. Mgt Gp, 1997–99. Hon. Prof., Dept of Zoology, Univ. of Aberdeen, 2000–. *Recreations:* music (pianist), squash, swimming, travel. *Address:* Rowett Research Institute, Greenburn Road, Bucksburn, Aberdeen AB21 9SB. *T:* (01224) 716663.

MORGAN, Peter William Lloyd, MBE 2003; External Member of Council, Lloyd's, since 2000; *b* 9 May 1936; *s* of late Matthew Morgan and of Margaret Gwynneth (*née* Lloyd); *m* 1964, Elisabeth Susanne Davis; three *d. Educ:* Llandovery Coll.; Trinity Hall, Cambridge. Joined IBM UK Ltd, 1959; Data Processing Sales Dir, 1971–74; Gp Dir of Marketing, IBM Europe, Paris, 1975–80; Director: IBM UK Ltd, 1983–87; IBM UK Holdings Ltd, 1987–89; Dir-Gen., Inst. of Dirs, 1989–94; National Provident Institution: Dir, 1990–94; Dep. Chm., 1995; Chm., 1996–99. Chairman: South Wales Electricity PLC, 1996 (Dir, 1989–95); Pace Micro Technology plc, 1996–2000; KSCL Ltd, 1999–2000; Technetix plc, 2002–; Strategic Thought Gp plc, 2004–; IXICO Ltd, 2006–; Director: Hyder Consulting (formerly Firth Holdings) plc, 1994–; Baltimore Technologies plc (formerly Zergo Holdings), 1994– (Dep. Chm., 1998–2000; Chm., 2000–03); Oxford Instruments plc, 2000–; Assoc. of Lloyd's Mems, 1997–. Mem., European Econ. and Social Cttee, 1994–2002, 2006–. Vice Pres., London Welsh Male Voice Choir, 1993–. Liveryman: Co. of Inf. Technologists, 1992– (Master, 2002–03); Welsh Livery Guild, 2005–. Radical of the Year, Radical Soc., 1990. *Publication:* Alarming Drum, 2005. *Recreations:* music, history, gardening, ski-ing, wine, dog walking. *Address:* Cleeves, Weydown Road, Haslemere, Surrey GU27 1DT. *Club:* Oxford and Cambridge.

MORGAN, Piers Stefan; Editor, Daily Mirror, 1995–2004; *b* 30 March 1965; *s* of Glynne and Gabrielle Pughe-Morgan; *m* 1991, Marion Elizabeth Shalloe; three *s. Educ:* Chailey Comprehensive Sch.; Lewes Priory Sixth Form Coll.; Harlow Journalism Coll. With Lloyd's of London, 1985–87; Reporter, Surrey and S London Newspapers, 1987–89; Showbusiness Editor, The Sun, 1989–94; Editor, News of the World, 1994–95. Editor of the Year, Newspaper Focus Awards, 1994. *Publications:* Private Lives of the Stars, 1990; Secret Lives of the Stars, 1991; Phillip Schofield: to dream a dream, 1992; Take That: our story, 1993; Take That: on the road, 1994; Va Va Voom: a fan's diary of Arsenal's invincible season, 2004; The Insider: the private diaries of a scandalous decade, 2005; Don't You Know Who I Am?, 2007. *Recreations:* cricket, Arsenal FC.

MORGAN, Rt Hon. Rhodri; *see* Morgan, Rt Hon. H. R.

MORGAN, Richard Martin, MA; Warden, Radley College, 1991–2000; *b* 25 June 1940; *s* of His Honour Trevor Morgan, MC, QC, and late Leslie Morgan; *m* 1968, Margaret Kathryn, *d* of late Anthony Agutter and of Mrs Launcelot Fleming; three *d. Educ:* Sherborne Sch.; Caius Coll., Cambridge (MA, DipEd); York Univ. Assistant Master, Radley Coll., 1963; Housemaster, 1969; Headmaster, Cheltenham College, 1978–90. Member, Adv. Council, Understanding British Industry, 1977–79. Pres., Mencap, S Wilts, 2004–; Chm., Prince's Trust, Salisbury, 2004–. JP Glos, 1978–90. *Recreations:* reading, music, Anthony Powell Soc. *Address:* Warmans, Bodenham, Salisbury, Wilts SP5 4EV. *T:* (01722) 333379. *Clubs:* Free Foresters', Jesters'.

MORGAN, Robin Milne; Principal: Daniel Stewart's and Melville College, Edinburgh, 1977–89; The Mary Erskine School, 1979–89; *b* 2 Oct. 1930; *o s* of Robert Milne Morgan and Aida Forsyth Morgan; *m* 1955, Fiona Bruce MacLeod Douglas; three *s* one *d. Educ:* Mackie Academy, Stonehaven; Aberdeen Univ. (MA); London Univ. (BA, External). Nat. Service, 2nd Lieut The Gordon Highlanders, 1952–54; Asst Master: Arden House Prep. Sch., 1955–60; George Watson's Coll., 1960–71; Headmaster, Campbell Coll., Belfast, 1971–76. *Recreations:* music, archaeology, fishing, entertaining my ten grandchildren. *Address:* Avernish House, Nostie, Kyle of Lochalsh, Ross-shire IV40 8EQ.

MORGAN, Robin Richard; Editor, The Sunday Times Magazine, since 1995; Contributing Editor, GQ Magazine, since 1999; *b* 16 Sept. 1953; *s* of Raymond Morgan and Jean Edith Bennett; *m*; two *s* one *d. Educ:* King Edward VI Grammar Sch., Stourbridge, W Midlands. County Express, Stourbridge, 1971–73; Evening Echo, Hemel Hempstead, 1973–79; Sunday Times, London, 1979–89: Reporter, 1979–83; Dep. News Editor, 1983–85; Insight Editor, 1985–87; Features Editor, Sunday Times, 1987–89; Editor, Sunday Express, 1989–91; Associate Editor, Sunday Times, 1991–92; Editor, Sunday Times Magazine, 1992–93; Editorial Dir designate, Reader's Digest, 1993–94. Campaigning Journalist of the Year: (commended) 1982; (winner) 1983. *Publications:* (jtly) The Falklands War, 1982; (jtly) Rainbow Warrior, 1986; (jtly) Bullion, 1988; (ed) Manpower, 1988; (jtly) Ambush, 1989; (jtly) The Book of Movie Biographies, 1997; (ed) Sinatra: Frank and friendly, 2007. *Recreations:* cinema, US politics, modern American fiction, travel. *Address:* The Sunday Times Magazine, 1 Pennington Street, Wapping, E98 1ST.

MORGAN, Prof. Rodney Emrys; Professor of Criminal Justice, University of Bristol, since 2007; Visiting Professor, London School of Economics, since 2007; *b* 16 Feb. 1942; *s* of William Emrys Morgan and Jessmine Lilian (*née* Reed); *m* 1966, Karin Birgitta Lang; three *s. Educ:* Haberdashers' Aske's Sch., Mill Hill; Paston Sch., N Walsham; Univ. of Southampton (BSc; Dip. Applied Social Studies). Lectr, Univ. of Southampton, 1971–72; Lectr, then Sen. Lectr, Univ. of Bath, 1972–89; University of Bristol: Reader, then Prof. of Criminal Justice, 1989–2001; Dean of Law, 1992–95; Emeritus Prof., 2001. HM Chief Inspector of Probation for England and Wales, 2001–04; Chm., Youth Justice Bd for England and Wales, 2004–07; Advr on criminal justice inspection, MoJ, 2007–. Vis. Fellow, Univ. of Oxford, 1985–87; Visiting Professor: Univ. of WA, 1991; Univ. of Freiburg, 1995; Univ. of Onati, 1996; Harvard Univ., 1996. Trustee: King's Coll. Centre for Criminol Res., 2003–; Police Foundn, 2006–; Dance Utd, 2006–; Bath Philharmonia, 2007–; Bath Alcohol and Drugs Adv. Service, 2007–; Pres., Mentoring Plus, 2007–. *Publications:* (ed jtly) Oxford Handbook of Criminology, 1994, 4th edn 2007; The Politics of Sentencing Reform, 1995; The Future of Policing, 1997; Preventing Torture, 1998; Protecting Prisoners, 1999; Crime Unlimited, 1999; Combating Torture in Europe, 2001; Handbook of Probation, 2007; contrib. numerous articles to law, social policy and criminology jls. *Recreations:* sailing, theatre, music, walking, gardening, taking risks. *Address:* Beech House, Lansdown Road, Bath BA1 5EG. *T:* (01225) 316676; *e-mail:* karin.rod@freeuk.com.

MORGAN, Roger; *see* Morgan, E. R.

MORGAN, Roger Hugh Vaughan Charles, CBE 1991; Librarian, House of Lords, 1977–91; *b* 8 July 1926; *s* of late Charles Langbridge Morgan, and Hilda Vaughan, both novelists and playwrights; *m* 1st, 1951, Harriet Waterfield (marr. diss. 1965), *d* of Gordon Waterfield; one *s* one *d* (and one *s* decd); 2nd, 1965, Susan Vogel Marrian, *d* of Hugo Vogel, Milwaukee, USA; one *s. Educ:* Downs Sch., Colwall; Phillips Acad., Andover, USA; Eton Coll.; Brasenose Coll., Oxford (MA). Grenadier Guards, 1944–47 (Captain, 1946). House of Commons Library, 1951–63; House of Lords Library, 1963–91. Burgess of Laugharne, 2004. *Recreations:* painting, photography, cooking. *Address:* 30 St Peter's Square, W6 9UH. *T:* (020) 8741 0267, *Fax:* (020) 8563 7881; Cliff Cottage, Laugharne, Carmarthenshire. *T:* (01994) 427398. *Clubs:* Garrick, Beefsteak.

See also Marchioness of Anglesey.

MORGAN, Prof. Roger Pearce; Professor, 1988–96, External Professor, 1996–2006, of Political Science, European University Institute, Florence; *b* 3 March 1932; *s* of Donald Emlyn Morgan and Esther Mary Morgan (*née* Pearce); *m* 1st, 1957, Annie-Françoise (Annette) Combes (marr. diss. 1988); three *s* one *d*; 2nd, 1988, Mrs Catherine Howell. *Educ:* Wolverton Grammar Sch.; Leighton Park Sch.; Downing Coll., Cambridge (MA 1957; PhD 1959); Univs of Paris and Hamburg. Staff Tutor, Dept of Extra-Mural Studies, London Univ., 1957–59; Asst Lectr and Lectr in Internat. Politics, UCW, Aberystwyth, 1959–63; Lectr in Hist. and Internat. Relations, Sussex Univ., 1963–67; Asst, then Dep. Dir of Studies, RIIA, 1968–74; Prof. of European Politics, 1974–78, and Dean, Sch. of Human and Environmental Studies, 1976–78, Loughborough Univ.; Head of European Centre for Political Studies, PSI, 1978–86; Vis. Fellow, Centre for Internat. Studies, LSE,

1987–88. Visiting Professor: Columbia Univ., 1965; Johns Hopkins Univ., 1969–70, 1988–89, 1995; Cornell Univ., 1972; Surrey Univ., 1980–84; UCLA, 1993, 2001; Univ. of Bonn, 1996–97; pt-time Prof., Dept of War Studies, KCL, 2000; Res. Associate, Center for Internat. Affairs, Harvard, 1965–66; Visiting Lecturer: Cambridge Univ., 1967; LSE, 1974, 1980–88; Associate Mem., Nuffield Coll., Oxford, 1980–83; Hon. Professorial Fellow, UCW, Aberystwyth, 1980–84, Hon. Prof., 1985–95; Sen. Associate Mem., St Antony's Coll., Oxford, 1996–97; Vis. Fellow, European Inst., LSE, 1998–2000. Lectr at RCDS, CS Coll., RNC, etc. Member: Council, RIIA, 1976–85, 1986–92 and 1997–2003; Academic Council, Wilton Park, 1982–83. Trustee, Gilbert Murray Trust, 1973–88. Officer's Cross, Order of Merit (Germany), 2002. *Publications:* The German Social Democrats and the First International 1864–72, 1965; Modern Germany, 1966; (ed jtly) Britain and West Germany: changing societies and the future of foreign policy, 1971 (German edn, 1970); West European Politics since 1945, 1972; (ed) The Study of International Affairs, 1972; High Politics, Low Politics: toward a foreign policy for Western Europe, 1973; The United States and West Germany 1945–1973: a study in alliance politics, 1974 (German edn 1975); West Germany's Foreign Policy Agenda, 1978; (ed jtly) Moderates and Conservatives in Western Europe, 1982 (Italian edn 1983); (ed jtly) Partners and Rivals in Western Europe: Britain, France and Germany, 1986; (ed) Regionalism in European Politics, 1986; (ed jtly) New Diplomacy in the Post-Cold War World, 1993; (ed jtly) The Third Pillar of the European Union, 1994; (ed jtly) Parliaments and Parties: the European Parliament in the political life of Europe, 1995; (ed jtly) New Challenges to the European Union: policies and policy-making, 1997; (ed jtly) Choice and Representation in the European Union, 2003; contribs to symposia and jls. *Recreations:* music, travel, watching cricket. *Address:* 10 John Spencer Square, N1 2LZ. *T:* (020) 7226 4702. *Clubs:* Reform; Middlesex County Cricket, Surrey County Cricket.

MORGAN, Shan Elizabeth; HM Diplomatic Service; Ambassador to Argentina and (non-resident) to Paraguay, since 2008; *b* 12 March 1955; *d* of Air Cdre Alun Morgan, CBE and Yvonne Morgan (*née* Davies). *Educ:* South Park High Sch., Lincoln; High Wycombe Grammar Sch.; Royal Latin Sch.; Univ. of Kent (BA Hons 1977). Manpower Services Commn, subseq. Employment Dept, then DfES, 1977–97; Eur. Commn DG V, 1984–87; Pvte Sec. to Perm. Sec., Dept of Employment, 1990–92; Govt Office for London, 1992–94; UK Govt Deleg. to ILO Governing Body, 1994–97; seconded to FCO, 1997; First Sec., Labour and Social Affairs, Paris, 1997–2001; Counsellor, Social, Envmtl and Regl Affairs, UK Perm. Repn, Brussels, 2001–06; transferred FCO, 2006; Dir, EU, FCO, 2006–08. FRSA. *Recreations:* walking, learning Welsh. *Address:* c/o Foreign and Commonwealth Office, King Charles Street, SW1A 2AH.

MORGAN, Stephen Peter, OBE 1992; Chairman: Bridgemere Group of Companies, since 1996; Harrow Estates plc, since 2002; *b* 25 Nov. 1952; *s* of Peter and Mary Morgan; *m* 1st, 1973, Pamela Borrett; one *s* one *d*; 2nd, 2002, Fiona Elspeth, (Didy), Boustead; one *s* one *d*. *Educ:* Colwyn High Sch.; Liverpool Poly. Founded Redrow Gp plc, 1974, Chm., 1974–2000. Owner, Carden Park Hotel, nr Chester, 2006–; owner and Chm., Wolverhampton Wanderers FC, 2007–. Chm., Morgan Foundn. FCIOB 2000. Hon. Fellow: John Moores Univ., 1993; NE Wales Inst. of Higher Educn, 1993; Cardiff Univ., 2005. *Publication:* The Redrow Way, 1999. *Recreations:* football, Rugby, ski-ing, walking, golf.

MORGAN, Terence Keith, FREng, FIET; Chief Executive Officer, Tube Lines Ltd, since 2002; *b* 28 Dec. 1948; *s* of Keith and Ivy Morgan; *m* 1970, Ann Jones; one *s* one *d*. *Educ:* Univ. of Birmingham (MSc 1977). FIET (FIEE 1990); FREng (FEng 1995). Leyland Bus Co., 1980–85; Production Dir, Land Rover, 1985–91; Man. Dir, Land Rover Vehicles, Rover Gp, 1991–95; BAE Systems: Man. Dir, Royal Ordnance, 1995–97; Gp HR Dir, 1997–2000; Gp Man. Dir Ops, 2000–02. *Recreations:* Rugby, golf. *Address:* Tube Lines Ltd, 15 Westferry Circus, Canary Wharf, E14 4HD. *Club:* Reform.

MORGAN, (Thomas) Jeremy; QC 2003; *b* 18 Aug. 1948; *s* of Thomas Morgan and Jean Morgan (*née* Campbell); *m* 1998, Delia Dumaresq; one *d*, and one step *s*. *Educ:* Loretto Sch.; Exeter Coll., Oxford (BA Greats); Univ. of Kent (BA Law). FCIArb 1998. Admitted solicitor, 1976; Solicitor: Garratt Lane Law Centre, Wandsworth, 1976–80; Southwark Law Project, 1980–82; sole practitioner, 1982–89; called to the Bar, Middle Temple, 1989; in practice as barrister, 1990–. Mem., Treasury Panel of Counsel, 1997–2003. *Recreations:* Italy, cinema, windsurfing, ballet. *Address:* 39 Essex Street, WC2R 3AT. *T:* (020) 7832 1111; *e-mail:* jeremy.morgan@39essex.com.

MORGAN, Most Rev. Thomas Oliver; Archbishop of Saskatoon and Metropolitan of the Ecclesiastical Province of Rupert's Land, 2000–03; *b* 20 Jan. 1941; *s* of Charles Edwin Morgan and Amy Amelia (*née* Hoyes); *m* 1963, Lillian Marie (*née* Textor); two *s* one *d*. *Educ:* Univ. of Saskatchewan (BA 1962); King's College, London (BD 1965); Tyndale Hall, Bristol (GOE 1966). Curate, Church of the Saviour, Blackburn, Lancs, 1966–69; Rector: Porcupine Plain, Sask, Canada, 1969–73; Kinistino, 1973–77; Shellbrook, 1977–83; Archdeacon of Indian Missions, Saskatchewan, 1983–85; Bishop of Saskatchewan, 1985–93; Bishop of Saskatoon, 1993–2003. Hon. DD Coll. of Emmanuel and St Chad, Saskatoon, 1986. *Address:* c/o PO Box 1965, Saskatoon, SK S7K 3S5, Canada.

MORGAN, Tony; see Morgan, A. W. C.

MORGAN, Rt Rev. Mgr Vaughan Frederick John, CBE 1982; Parish Priest, St Teresa's Charlbury, 1997–2007; *b* Upper Hutt, New Zealand, 21 March 1931; *o s* of late Godfrey Frederick Vaughan Morgan and Violet (Doreen) Vaughan Morgan. *Educ:* The Oratory Sch., S Oxon; Innsbruck Univ. Ordained, 1957; Archdiocese of St Andrews and Edinburgh, 1959–62; entered Royal Navy as Chaplain, 1962; Prin. RC Chaplain (Naval), and Vicar Gen. for RN, 1979–84; Chaplain, The Oratory Sch., 1984–97. Chaplain to High Sheriff of Oxfordshire, 2000–01. Prelate of Honour to HH Pope John Paul II, 1979. *Publications:* contribs to journals. *Recreations:* music, swimming, painting, heraldry. *Address:* Flat 28, Diamond Court, 153 Banbury Road, Oxford OX2 7AA. *T:* (01865) 516672. *Club:* Army and Navy.

MORGAN, Prof. William Basil; Professor of Geography, 1971–92, Professor Emeritus, since 1988, and Head of Geography Department, 1982–87, King's College London; *b* 22 Jan. 1927; *s* of William George Morgan and Eunice Mary (*née* Heys); *m* 1954, Joy Gardner (*d* 2004); one *s* one *d*. *Educ:* King Edward's Sch., Birmingham; Jesus Coll., Oxford (MA); PhD Glasgow. Assistant, Glasgow Univ., 1948; Lecturer: University Coll., Ibadan, Nigeria, 1953; Univ. of Birmingham, 1959; Reader in Geography, KCL, 1967. Participant in various UN university res. projects and conferences. *Publications:* (with J. C. Pugh) West Africa, 1969; (with R. J. C. Munton) Agricultural Geography, 1971; Agriculture in the Third World: a spatial analysis, 1978; (with R. P. Moss) Fuelwood and rural energy production and supply in the humid tropics, 1981; contribs to geographical and other learned jls and to various conf. collections. *Recreation:* development geography. *Address:* 57 St Augustine's Avenue, South Croydon, Surrey CR2 6JQ. *T:* (020) 8688 5687; *e-mail:* williammorgan@sky.com.

MORGAN-GILES, Rear-Adm. Sir Morgan (Charles), Kt 1985; DSO 1944; OBE 1943 (MBE 1942); GM 1941; DL; *b* 19 June 1914; *e s* of late F. C. Morgan-Giles, OBE, MINA, Teignmouth, Devon; *m* 1946, Pamela (*d* 1966), *d* of late Philip Bushell, Sydney, New South Wales; two *s* four *d*; *m* 1968, Marigold (*d* 1995), *d* of late Percy Lowe. *Educ:* Clifton Coll. Entered Royal Navy, 1932; served on China Station, and in destroyers. War Service: Atlantic convoys and Mediterranean; Tobruk garrison and Western Desert, 1941; with RAF, 1942; Sen. Naval Officer, Vis. (Dalmatia) and liaison with Commandos and Marshal Tito's Partisan Forces, 1943–44. Captain 1953; Chief of Naval Intelligence, Far East, 1955–56; Captain (D) Dartmouth Training Sqdn, 1957–58; HMS Belfast, in command, 1961–62; Rear-Adm. 1962; Adm. Pres., Royal Naval Coll., Greenwich, 1962–64; retd 1964. MP (C) Winchester, May 1964–79. Vice-Chm., Conservative Defence Cttee, 1965–75. Chm., HMS Belfast Trust, 1971–78; Life Vice-Pres., RNLI, 1989. Prime Warden, Shipwrights' Company, 1987–88. DL Hants, 1983. *Recreations:* sailing, country pursuits. *Address:* Anchor House, Little Sodbury Manor, Glos BS37 6QA. *T:* (01454) 327485. *Club:* Royal Yacht Squadron.
See also Baron Killearn.

MORGAN HUGHES, David; see Hughes.

MORGAN-WEBB, Dame Patricia, DBE 2000; Co-founder and Chief Executive, Morgan Webb Education Ltd, since 2003. Principal and Chief Exec., Clarendon Coll., 1991–98; Chief Exec., New Coll. Nottingham, 1998–2003. Member: Bd, QCA, 1997–2002; E Midlands Regl Cttee, FEFC; Derbys Learning and Skills Council, 2000–. Mem. Bd, E Midlands Develt Agency, 1998–2004; Dir, Gtr Nottingham TEC. *Address:* Morgan Webb Education Ltd, Church Hill Cottage, Church Hill, Longdon Green, WS15 4PU.

MORIARTY, Clare; Constitution Director, Ministry of Justice (formerly Department for Constitutional Affairs), since 2005; *b* 6 April 1963; *d* of Michael John Moriarty, *qv*; *m* 2001, James MacDonald; two *d*, and one step *s* two step *d*. *Educ:* North London Collegiate Sch.; Balliol Coll., Oxford (BA Hons Maths 1985). FCCA 1995. Joined DHSS, 1985; Cycle Internat., Ecole Nat. d'Admin, Paris, 1990–91; Prin. Private Sec. to Sec. of State for Health, 1994–97; Hon. Sen. Res. Fellow, Sch. of Public Policy, UCL, 1997–98; Hd, NHS Foundn Trust Unit, DoH, 2002–04; Whole Systems Dir, Portsmouth and SE Hampshire Health and Social Care Community, 2004–05. *Recreations:* family, singing, cycling, mountain walking, restoring and maintaining hill farm in Connemara, Ireland. *Address:* Ministry of Justice, Selborne House, 54 Victoria Street, SW1E 6QW. *T:* (020) 7210 1440; *e-mail:* clare.moriarty@justice.gsi.gov.uk.

MORIARTY, Gerald Evelyn; QC 1974; a Recorder of the Crown Court, 1976–98; *b* 23 Aug. 1928; *er s* of late Lt-Col G. R. O'N. Moriarty and Eileen Moriarty (*née* Moloney); *m* 1961, Judith Mary, *er d* of Hon. William Robert Atkin; four *s*. *Educ:* Downside Sch.; St John's Coll., Oxford (MA). Called to the Bar, Lincoln's Inn, 1951, Bencher, 1983. *T:* (020) 7727 4593. *Club:* Reform.

MORIARTY, Brig. Joan Olivia Elsie, CB 1979; RRC 1977; Matron-in-Chief and Director of Army Nursing Services, 1976–80; *b* 11 May 1923; *d* of late Lt-Col Oliver Nash Moriarty, DSO, RA, and Mrs Georgina Elsie Moriarty (*née* Moore). *Educ:* Royal Sch., Bath; St Thomas' Hosp. (nursing); Queen Charlotte's Hosp. (midwifery). SRN. VAD, Somerset, 1941–42; joined QAIMNS (R), 1947; Reg. QAIMNS (later QARANC), 1948, retired Jan. 1981; appts incl.: Staff Captain, WO; Instr, Corps Trng Centre; Liaison Officer, MoD; served in UK, Gibraltar, BAOR, Singapore, Malaya, Cyprus; Matron, Mil. Hosp., Catterick, 1973–76; Comdt, QARANC Trng Centre, Aldershot, 1976. Major 1960; Lt-Col 1971; Col 1973; Brig. 1977. QHNS, 1977–80. OStJ 1977.

MORIARTY, Prof. Michael, PhD; FBA 2006; Professor of French Literature and Thought, 1995–2005, Centenary Professor, since 2005, Queen Mary, University of London; *b* 27 May 1956; *s* of Martin Moriarty and Ellen Moriarty (*née* O'Connor); *m* 1992, Morag Elizabeth Shiach; two *s*. *Educ:* Warwick Sch.; St John's Coll., Cambridge (BA 1978, MA 1982; PhD 1984). University of Cambridge: Asst Lectr, 1986–90, Lectr, 1990–95, Dept of French; Res. Fellow, 1982–85, Lectr in French and Dir of Studies in Mod. Langs, 1985–95, Gonville and Caius Coll. Member: Panel 51 (French), RAE 2001; Sub-panel 52 (French), RAE 2008. *Publications:* Taste and Ideology in Seventeenth Century France, 1988; Roland Barthes, 1991; Early Modern French Thought: the age of Suspicion, 2003; Fallen Nature, Fallen Selves: Early Modern French Thought II, 2006; contrib. articles to French Studies, Romance Studies, etc. *Recreations:* walking, listening to music, crosswords. *Address:* School of Languages, Linguistics and Film, Queen Mary, University of London, Mile End Road, E1 4NS. *T:* (020) 7882 3210; *e-mail:* m.moriarty@qmul.ac.uk.

MORIARTY, Michael John, CB 1988; Deputy Chairman, Radio Authority, 1994–2000 (Member, 1991–2000); Deputy Under-Secretary of State and Principal Establishment Officer, Home Office, 1984–90; *b* 3 July 1930; *er s* of late Edward William Patrick Moriarty, OBE, and May Lilian Moriarty; *m* 1960, Rachel Milward, *d* of late J. S. Thompson and Isobel F. Thompson; one *s* two *d*. *Educ:* Reading Sch., Reading; St John's Coll., Oxford (Sir Thomas White schol.; MA Lit. Hum.). Entered Home Office as Asst Principal, 1954; Private Sec. to Parliamentary Under-Secretaries of State, 1957–59; Principal, 1959; Civil Service Selection Bd, 1962–63; Cabinet Office, 1965–67; Asst Sec., 1967; Private Sec. to Home Sec., 1968; Head of Crime Policy Planning Unit, 1974–75; Asst Under-Sec. of State, 1975–84; seconded to NI Office, 1979–81; Broadcasting Dept, 1981–84. UK Representative, 1976–79, and Chm., 1978–79, Council of Europe Cttee on Crime Problems. Sub-Treas., 1991–, Mem. Council, 2001–06, Chichester Cathedral; a Church Comr, 1996–98. Gov., Chichester Central C of E Jun. Sch., 2008– (Chm. of Govs, 2001–05). *Recreations:* music, walking, local interests. *Address:* 22 Westgate, Chichester, West Sussex PO19 3EU. *T:* (01243) 789985.
See also C. Moriarty.

MORIARTY, Stephen; QC 1999; *b* 14 April 1955; *s* of George William Moriarty and Dorothy Violet Moriarty (*née* Edwards); *m* 1988, Dr Susan Clare Stanford. *Educ:* Chichester High Sch. for Boys; Brasenose Coll., Oxford (BCL, MA; Vinerian Schol. 1978). Univ. Lectr in law, and Fellow and Tutor in Law, Exeter Coll., Oxford, 1979–86; called to the Bar, Middle Temple, 1986; in practice at the Bar, 1986–. *Recreations:* theatre, opera. *Address:* Fountain Court Chambers, Fountain Court, Temple, EC4Y 9DH. *T:* (020) 7583 3335. *Club:* Reform.

MORICE, Prof. Peter Beaumont, DSc, PhD; FREng, FICE, FIStructE; Professor of Civil Engineering, University of Southampton, 1958–91, now Emeritus; *b* 15 May 1926; *o s* of Charles and Stephanie Morice; *m* 1st, 1952, Margaret Ransom (marr. diss. 1986); one *s* two *d*; 2nd, 1986, Rita Corless (*née* Dunk) (*d* 2006). *Educ:* Barfield Sch.; Farnham Grammar Sch.; University of Bristol; University of London. Surrey County Council, 1947–48; Research Div., Cement and Concrete Assoc., 1948–57. Vis. Prof., Ecole Nat. des Ponts et Chaussées, Paris; Mem. Foundn Cttee, Sultan Qaboos Univ., Oman, 1980–86. FREng (FEng 1989). Compagnon du Beaujolais, 1987. Order of Sultan Qaboos

(Oman), 1986. *Publications:* Linear Structural Analysis, 1958; Prestressed Concrete, 1958; papers on structural theory in various learned journals. *Recreations:* sailing, DIY, reading, listening to music. *Address:* 12 Abbotts Way, Highfield, Southampton SO17 1QT. *T:* (023) 8055 7641; Au Village, La Sauvetat, 32500 Fleurance, France. *T:* 562652258.

MORISON, Hugh, CBE 2002; Chief Executive (formerly Director General), Scotch Whisky Association, 1994–2003; *b* 22 Nov. 1943; *s* of Archibald Ian Morison and Enid Rose Morison (*née* Mawer); *m* 1st, 1971, Marion Smithers (marr. diss. 1993); two *d*; 2nd, 1993, Ilona Bellos (*née* Roth). *Educ:* Chichester High School for Boys; St Catherine's Coll., Oxford (MA English Language and Literature; DipEd). Asst Principal, SHHD, 1966–69; Private Sec. to Minister of State, Scottish Office, 1969–70; Principal: Scottish Educn Dept, 1971–73; Scottish Economic Planning Dept, 1973–74; Offshore Supplies Office, Dept of Energy, 1974–75; Scottish Economic Planning Dept, 1975–82, Asst Sec., 1979; Gwilym Gibbon Res. Fellow, Nuffield Coll., Oxford, 1982–83; Scottish Development Dept, 1983–84; Under Secretary: SHHD, 1984–88; Industry Dept for Scotland, subseq. Scottish Office Industry Dept, 1988–93. Director: The Weir Gp, 1989–93; Praban na Linne Ltd, 2005–06. Member: Health Appts Adv. Cttee (Scotland), 1995–2000; Exec. Cttee, Barony Housing Assoc., 1996– (Chm., 2005–). Chm., Scottish Business and Biodiversity Gp, 1998–2003. Prés., 2001–03, Prés. d'honneur, 2003–, Confédn Eur. des Producteurs de Spiritueux. Gov., UHI, 2004–. Chm., Letterfearn Moorings Assoc., 2001–. FRSA 1990. *Publications:* The Regeneration of Local Economies, 1987; (with Ilona Bellos) Dauphiné, 1991. *Recreations:* hill walking, cycling, sailing, music, looking at ruins. *Address:* 12 Sunbury Place, Edinburgh EH4 3BY. *T:* (0131) 225 6568. *Clubs:* Royal Commonwealth Society; New (Edinburgh).

MORISON, Prof. John William Edgar, PhD; Professor of Jurisprudence, Queen's University, Belfast, since 1996; *b* 8 March 1958; *s* of John Edgar Morison and Ellen McCracken Morison; *m* 1984, Susan Royal; two *d*. *Educ:* Brackenber House; Campbell Coll.; University of Wales, Cardiff (LLB 1979; PhD 1985). Queen's University, Belfast: Lectr in Law, 1984–94; Reader in Law, 1994–96; Hd, Sch. of Law, 2003–07. Mem., NI Judicial Appointments Commn, 2003–. Dir, European Public Law Centre, Athens, 1996–. *Publications:* (with P. Leith) The Barrister's World and the Nature of Law, 1992; (with S. Livingstone) Reshaping Public Power: Northern Ireland and the British constitutional crisis, 1995; (ed jtly) Judges, Transition and Human Rights, 2007. *Recreations:* collecting art, dog walking. *Address:* School of Law, Queen's University, Belfast BT7 1NN; *e-mail:* j.morison@qub.ac.uk.

MORISON, Hon. Sir Thomas (Richard Atkin), Kt 1993; a Judge of the High Court of Justice, Queen's Bench Division, 1993–2007; *b* 15 Jan. 1939; *s* of Harold Thomas Brash Morison and Hon. Nancy Morison; *m* 1963, Judith Rachel Walton Morris (marr. diss. 1992); one *s* one *d*; *m* 1993, Caroline Yates. *Educ:* Winchester Coll.; Worcester Coll., Oxford, 1959–62 (MA). Passed final Bar examinations, 1959; called to the Bar, Gray's Inn, 1960, Bencher, 1987; pupil in Chambers, 1962–63; started practice, 1963; QC 1979; a Recorder, 1987–93. *Recreations:* reading, gardening, cooking. *Address:* c/o Royal Courts of Justice, Strand, WC2A 2LL. *Club:* Oriental.

MORLAND, Charles Francis Harold; Chairman, Refugee Legal Centre, since 2006; *b* 4 Sept. 1939; *s* of Sir Oscar Morland, GBE, KCMG, and Alice, *d* of Rt Hon. Sir Francis Oswald Lindley, GCMG, PC; *m* 1964, Victoria Longe (*d* 1998); two *s*. *Educ:* Ampleforth Coll.; King's Coll., Cambridge (MA). American Dept, FO, 1963–64; Local Dir, Oxford and Birmingham, Barclays Bank, 1964–79; on secondment as Under Sec. to Dept of Industry, 1979–81; Dir, Barclays Merchant Bank, then Barclays de Zoete Wedd, 1981–87; Man. Dir, Riggs AP Bank, 1987–89; Chm., Belmont Bank, 1991–93. Chm., Oxford Policy Inst., 1996–2005; Dir, British Inst. in Paris, 1997–2002. Chairman: Leonard Cheshire, 2000–05; Ryder Cheshire Foundn, 2005–07; Director: Centre for Accessible Environments, 2006–; Employment Opportunities for People with Disabilities, 2006–. *Recreations:* travel, cooking. *Address:* 2 Cottesmore Court, Stanford Road, W8 5QL. *T:* (020) 7937 4660. *Club:* Brooks's.
See also M. R. Morland.

MORLAND, Edward; Chief Executive, Health & Safety Laboratory, since 2005; *b* 23 June 1957; *s* of Albert Edward Morland and Eva Doris Morland; *m* 1977, Lynda Hockenhull; one *s* one *d*. *Educ:* Wade Deacon Grammar Sch.; Manchester Poly. (BSc 1st Cl. Hons Physics 1982); UMIST (MSc Mgt Sci. 1994). FInstP 2006. Res. Scientist, UKAEA, 1975–92; Mktg Manager, AEA Technology, 1992–97; Commercial Dir, then Ops Dir, 1997–2003, Chief Exec., 2003–05, AEA Rail. FRSA 2005; FRSocMed 2007. *Publication:* (jtly) Mechanical Testing, 1988. *Recreations:* reading history, supporting Manchester United, playing strategy games, hill walking with my wife. *Address:* Health & Safety Laboratory, Harpur Hill, Buxton, Derbyshire SK17 9JN. *T:* (01298) 218001; *e-mail:* eddie.morland@hsl.gov.uk.

MORLAND, Martin Robert, CMG 1985; HM Diplomatic Service, retired; consultant with Hardcastle and Co. Ltd, 1996–2002; *b* 23 Sept. 1933; *e s* of Sir Oscar Morland, GBE, KCMG and late Alice, *d* of Rt Hon. Sir Francis Oswald Lindley, PC, GCMG; *m* 1964, Jennifer Avril Mary Hanbury-Tracy; two *s* one *d*. *Educ:* Ampleforth; King's Coll., Cambridge (BA). Nat. Service, Grenadier Guards, 1954–56; British Embassy, Rangoon, 1957–60; News Dept, FO, 1961; UK Delegn to Common Market negotiations, Brussels, 1962–63; FO, 1963–65; UK Disarmament Delegn, Geneva, 1965–67; Private Sec. to Lord Chalfont, 1967–68; European Integration Dept, FCO, 1968–73; Counsellor, 1973–77, Rome (seconded temporarily to Cabinet Office to head EEC Referendum Information Unit, 1975); Hd of Maritime Aviation and Environment Dept, FCO, 1977–79; Counsellor and Head of Chancery, Washington, 1979–82; seconded to Hardcastle & Co. Ltd, 1982–84; Under-Sec., Cabinet Office, 1984–86; Ambassador to Burma, 1986–90; Ambassador and UK Perm. Rep. to Office of UN and other internat. orgns, Geneva, 1990–93; Dir, Public Affairs, BNFL, 1994–96. Mem. Cttee, Supporters of Nuclear Energy, 2005–. Chm. Govs, Westminster Cathedral Choir Sch., 2001–. Chm., Prospect Burma, 1994–. *Address:* 50 Britannia Road, SW6 2JP. *Club:* Garrick.
See also C. F. H. Morland.

MORLAND, Sir Michael, Kt 1989; a Judge of the High Court of Justice, Queen's Bench Division, 1989–2004; *b* 16 July 1929; *e s* of Edward Morland, Liverpool, and Jane Morland (*née* Beckett); *m* 1961, Lillian Jensen, Copenhagen; one *s* one *d*. *Educ:* Stowe; Christ Church, Oxford (MA). 2nd Lieut, Grenadier Guards, 1948–49; served in Malaya. Called to Bar, Inner Temple, 1953, Bencher 1979; Northern Circuit; QC 1972; a Recorder, 1972–89; Presiding Judge, Northern Circuit, 1991–95. Mem., Criminal Injuries Compensation Bd, 1980–89. Mem., Gardiner Cttee on measures to deal with terrorism in NI, 1974; Chairman: Cttee of Inquiry for DHSS in case of Paul Brown, 1980; Public Inquiry for NI Office into death of Rosemary Nelson, 2004. *Address:* c/o The Rosemary Nelson Inquiry, PO Box 50157, SW1E 6WW.

MORLAND, Sir Robert (Kenelm), Kt 1990; General Manager, Exports: Tate & Lyle Sugars, 1987–93; Tate & Lyle International, 1987–93; Director, Tate & Lyle Norway A/S, 1987–93; *b* 7 April 1935; *s* of late Kenelm and Sybil Morland; *m* 1st, 1960, Eve Charters (marr. diss. 1965); one *s*; 2nd, 1972, Angela Fraser; one *s*. *Educ:* Birkenhead Sch.; Rydal Sch., Colwyn Bay. Joined Tate & Lyle, 1953; held various managerial positions. Member: Cheshire Riverboard Authy, 1962–65; Birkenhead Nat. Assistance Bd, Adv. Cttee, 1962–65. Dir, 1996–98, Associate non-exec. Dir, 1999–2001, Kingston and Richmond HA; Bd Mem., Thames Health Primary Care Gp, 1999–2001; non-executive Director: Teddington, Twickenham and Hamptons PCT, 2001–02; Richmond and Twickenham PCT, 2002–04; Age Concern, Richmond upon Thames, 2004–05, Glos, 2005–. Member: Birkenhead CBC, 1959–65; Richmond upon Thames BC, 1968–71. Contested (C) Birkenhead, 1964. Chairman: Birkenhead Young Conservatives, 1955–58; Kew Conservatives, 1971–74; Richmond and Barnes (now Richmond Park) Cons. Assoc., 1975–79 (Dep. Pres., 1985–98); Cons. Docklands Action Cttee, 1990–92; Greenwich and Lewisham Cons. Action Gp, 1993–94; Dep. Chm., Nat. Trade and Industry Forum, Cons. Party, 1991–96; Vice-President: Gtr London Conservatives, 1990– (Dep. Chm., 1978–81; Jt Hon. Treas., 1981–87; Chm., 1987–90); Newham S Cons. Assoc., 1989–96; Member: Cons. Nat. Union Exec. Cttee, 1978–93; Cons. Bd of Finance, 1981–87. Ind. Mem., Standards Cttee, Cotswolds Conservation Bd, 2005–. Dir, Friends of the Cotswolds, 2007–. Chm., St Mary's Drama Gp, Hampton, 1999–2001 (Vice Chm., 1996–99). Vice Pres., Gloucestershire CCC, 2007–. *Recreations:* theatre, travel, cricket, horseriding. *Club:* Carlton.

MORLEY; *see* Hope-Morley, family name of Baron Hollenden.

MORLEY, 6th Earl of, *cr* 1815; **John St Aubyn Parker,** KCVO 1998; JP; Lt-Col, Royal Fusiliers; Lord-Lieutenant of Devon, 1982–98; Chairman, Plymouth Sound Ltd, 1974–94; *b* 29 May 1923; *e s* of Hon. John Holford Parker (*y s* of 3rd Earl), Pound House, Yelverton, Devon; *S* uncle, 1962; *m* 1955, Johanna Katherine, *d* of Sir John Molesworth-St Aubyn, 14th Bt, CBE; one *s* one *d*. *Educ:* Eton. 2nd Lt, KRRC, 1942; served NW Europe, 1944–45; Palestine and Egypt, 1945–48; transferred to Royal Fusiliers, 1947; served Korea, 1952–53; Middle East, 1953–55 and 1956; Staff Coll., Camberley, 1957; Comd, 1st Bn Royal Fusiliers, 1965–67. Director: Lloyds Bank Ltd, 1974–78; Lloyds Bank UK Management Ltd, 1979–86; Chm., SW Region, Lloyds Bank, 1989–91 (Chm., Devon and Cornwall Regl Bd, 1974–89). Mem., Devon and Co. Cttee, Nat. Trust, 1969–84; President: Plymouth Incorporated Chamber of Trade and Commerce, 1970–; Cornwall Fedn of Chambers of Commerce and Trader Assocs, 1972–79; West Country Tourist Bd, 1971–89. Governor: Seale-Hayne Agric. Coll., 1973–93; Plymouth Polytechnic, 1975–82 (Chm., 1977–82). Pres., Council of Order of St John for Devon, 1979–98. DL 1973, Vice Lord-Lieutenant, 1978–82, Devon. JP Plymouth, 1972. Hon. Colonel: Devon ACF, 1979–87; 4th Bn Devonshire and Dorset Regl, 1987–92. *Heir: s* Viscount Boringdon, *qv*. *Address:* Pound House, Yelverton, Devon PL20 7LJ. *T:* (01822) 853162.

MORLEY, Dame Carol Mary; *see* Black, Dame C. M.

MORLEY, Catherine; *see* Pepinster, C.

MORLEY, Prof. David Cornelius, CBE 1989; MD; FRCP; Founder and President, Teaching-aids At Low Cost (TALC), since 1964; *b* 15 June 1923; *s* of Rev. John Arthur Morley and Ruth Elwell Morley (*née* Potter); *m* 1952, Aileen Leyburn; two *s* one *d*. *Educ:* Marlborough Coll. (Foundn Schol.); Clare Coll., Cambridge (BA 1944; MB BChir 1947; MD 1955); St Thomas' Hosp. MRCS, LRCP 1947; DCH 1955; MRCP 1972, FRCP 1977. Nat. Service, Captain RAMC, Malaya, 1948–50. Gen. Practice, Yallourn, Vic, Australia, 1950–51; studied paediatrics, Newcastle-upon-Tyne, 1951–56; Paediatrician to Methodist Hosp., Ilesha, Nigeria, and Lectr, Univ. of Ibadan, 1956–61; Lectr, Dept of Human Nutrition, LSHTM, 1961–65; Institute of Child Health, London University: Sen. Lectr i/c UNICEF/WHO course for sen. paediatricians, 1965–72; Reader, 1972–78; Prof. of Tropical Child Health, 1978–88, then Prof. Emeritus. Initiated concept of Under Fives Clinics, 1961; with a colleague in Inst. of Educn, started Child-to-Child prog., 1978, which subseq. spread worldwide; designed Growth Charts for small children. Has lectured and travelled worldwide. Hon. MD Uppsala, 1986. King Faisal Award for Internat. Health, 1982; James Spence Medal, RCPCH, 1989; Leon Bernard Prize, WHO, 1992; Beacon Fellow for Lifetime in Philanthropy, 2003. *Publications:* Paediatric Priorities in the Developing World, 1978; See How They Grow, 1979; Practising Health for All, 1983; Reaching Health for All, 1993; My Name is Today, 1986 (French, Arabic and Thai edns); contribs to jls on Under Fives Clinics, Growth Charts, severe measles, diarrhoea and malnutrition. *Recreation:* gardening. *Address:* 51 Eastmoor Park, Harpenden, Herts AL5 1BN. *T:* and *Fax:* (01582) 712199; *e-mail:* david@morleydc.demon.co.uk.

MORLEY, David Howard; Senior Partner, Allen & Overy LLP, Solicitors, since 2008; *b* 21 Sept. 1956; *s* of Glyn and Yvonne Morley; *m* 1982, Sue (*née* Radcliffe); two *s* two *d*. *Educ:* St John's Coll., Cambridge (BA 1979). Admitted solicitor, 1982. Joined Allen & Overy, 1980: Partner, 1988; Hd, Banking Practice, 1998–2003; Worldwide Man. Partner, 2003–08. *Recreations:* cycling, ski-ing, sailing. *Address:* Allen & Overy, One Bishops Square, E1 6AO. *T:* (020) 3088 3000; *e-mail:* david.morley@allenovery.com.

MORLEY, Rt Hon. Elliot (Anthony); PC 2006; MP (Lab) Scunthorpe, since 1997 (Glanford and Scunthorpe, 1987–97); *b* 6 July 1952; *m* 1975; one *s* one *d*. *Educ:* St Margaret's C of E High Sch., Liverpool. Special needs teacher, comprehensive sch., Hull; head of individual learning centre, until 1987. Mem., Kingston upon Hull City Council, 1979–85; Chair, Hull City Transport Cttee, 1981–85. Contested (Lab) Beverley, 1983. Opposition front bench spokesman on food, agriculture and rural affairs, 1989–97; Labour spokesperson on animal welfare, 1992–97; Parly Sec., MAFF, then DEFRA, 1997–2003; Minister of State (Minister for the Envmt), DEFRA, 2003–06. Mem., Select Cttee for Agriculture, 1987–90; Dep. Chair, PLP Educn Cttee, 1987–90. Vice-Pres., Wildlife and Countryside Link, 1990–; Member of Council: RSPB, 1989–93; British Trust for Ornithology, 1992–95; Trustee, Birds of the Humber Trust. Hon. Pres., N Lincs RSPCA. Hon. Vice-Pres., Assoc. of Drainage Authorities. Hon. Fellow, Univ. of Lincoln (formerly Lincs and Humberside Univ.). Hon. FICE. *Recreations:* ornithology, the environment, the countryside. *Address:* House of Commons, SW1A 0AA; 9 West Street, Winterton, Scunthorpe, N Lincs DN15 9QG.

MORLEY, Herbert, CBE 1974; Director and General Works Manager, Samuel Fox & Co. Ltd, 1959–65; Director, United Steel Cos, 1966–70; *b* 19 March 1919; *s* of George Edward and Beatrice Morley; *m* 1st, 1942, Gladys Hardy (*d* 1991); one *s* one *d*; 2nd, 1994, Mrs Frances H. Suagee, Cincinnatti, Ohio. *Educ:* Almondbury Grammar Sch., Huddersfield; Sheffield Univ. (Assoc. Metallurgy); Univ. of Cincinnati (Post-Grad. Studies in Business Admin). Dir and Gen. Man., Steel Peech Tozer, 1965–68; British Steel Corporation: Dir, Northern Tubes Gp, 1968–70; Man. Dir, Gen. Steel Div., 1970–73; Man. Dir, Planning and Capital Develt, 1973–76. Chm., Templeborough Rolling Mills Ltd, 1977–82; Dep. Chm. and Dir, Ellison Circlips Gp Ltd, 1990–92; Director: Ellison-Morlock, 1985–92; Bridon Ltd, 1973–85. *Recreations:* music, cricket lover, weekend golfer. *Address:* 11120 Springfield Pike, Apt A211, Cincinnati, OH 45246, USA. *T:* (513) 7822557.

MORLEY, Leslie Sydney Dennis, DSc; FRS 1992; FREng, FIMA, FRAeS; Hon. Associate Professorial Research Fellow, Brunel University, 1985–94; *b* 23 May 1924; *s* of Sydney Victor Morley, RN (Chief Petty Officer (Gunnery), HMS Hood, killed in action with the Bismarck, 1941) and Doris May Huntley (*née* Evans); *m* 1951, Norma Baker; two *s* one *d*. *Educ:* Portsmouth Northern Secondary Sch.; Portsmouth Municipal Tech. Sch.; Southampton Univ. Coll. (HNC 1945); Coll. Aeronautics, Cranfield (DCAe 1948; DSc 1971); Univ. of Cambridge (Post-Grad. Dip. Structures and Materials 1959). FRAeS 1962; FIMA 1964; FREng (FEng 1982). Airspeed Ltd: apprentice toolroom fitter, Portsmouth, 1940–45; Stress Office, Christchurch, 1945–46; Res. Officer, Nat. Luchtvaartlab., Amsterdam, 1948–49; Tech. Asst, Bristol Aeroplane Co., Filton, 1949–50; Structures Dept, RAE, 1950–84, DCSO, 1976; Professorial Res. Fellow, Inst. of Computational Maths, Brunel Univ., 1985–98. *Publications:* Skew Plates and Structures, 1963; numerous articles on structural mechanics, esp. finite element method, plate and shell theory, in learned jls in Britain and abroad. *Recreations:* family, British heritage, gardening.

MORLEY, Malcolm A.; artist; *b* 7 June 1931. *Educ:* Camberwell Sch. of Arts and Crafts; Royal Coll. of Art (ARCA 1957). *One man exhibitions:* Kornblee Gall., NY, 1957, 1964, 1967, 1969; Galerie Gerald Piltzer, Paris, 1973; Stefanotty Gall., NY, 1973, 1974; Clocktower Gall., Inst. for Art & Urban Resources, 1976; Galerie Jurka, Amsterdam, 1977; Galerie Jollenbeck, Cologne, 1977; Nancy Hoffman Gall., NY, 1979; Suzanne Hilberry Gall., Birmingham, Mich, 1979; Xavier Fourcade, NY, 1981, 1982, 1984, 1986; Galerie Nicholine Pon, Zurich, 1984; Fabian Carlsson Gall., London, 1985; Pace Gall., NY, 1988, 1991; Anthony d'Offay Gall., London, 1990; Tate Gall., 1991; Mary Boone Gall., NY, 1993, 1995; Sperone Westwater, NY, 1999; retrospective: Whitechapel Art Gall., also shown in Europe and USA, 1983–84; Centre Georges Pompidou, Paris, 1993; Fundacio La Caixa, Madrid, 1995; Hayward Gall., 2001; *major exhibitions:* Wadsworth Atheneum, Hartford, Conn, 1980; Akron Art Mus., 1982; *work in collections:* Met. Mus. of Art, NY; Detroit Inst. of Art; Hirshhorn Mus. and Sculpture Gdn, Washington; Louisiana Mus., Humlebaek, Denmark; Neue Galerie der Stadt Aachen; Mus. of Contemp. Art, Chicago; Munson-Williams-Proctor Inst., Utica, NY; Mus. of Modern Art, NY; Mus. Moderner Kunst, Vienna; Nat. Gall. of Art, Washington; Mus. of Contemp. Art, LA; Wadsworth Atheneum, Hartford; Centre Georges Pompidou, Paris; Nelson-Atkins Mus., Kansas City; Ludwig Forum for Internat. Art, Aachen, Vienna, Budapest; Mus. van Hedendaagse Kunst, Utrecht. First Turner Prize, Tate Gall., 1984; Painting Award, Skowhegan Sch. of Painting and Sculpture, 1992. *Relevant publication:* Malcolm Morley, by Jean-Claude Lebensztejn, 2001. *Address:* Sperone Westwater, 415 West 13 Street, New York, NY 10014, USA.

MORNINGTON, Earl of; Arthur Gerald Wellesley; *b* 31 Jan. 1978; *s* and *heir* of Marquess of Douro, *qv*; *m* 2005, Jemma Madeleine, *d* of John Edward Aitken Kidd. *Educ:* Eton Coll.; Christ Church, Oxford. A Page of Honour to HM Queen Elizabeth the Queen Mother, 1993–95. *Address:* Stratfield Saye House, Hants RG7 2BZ.

MORPETH, Sir Douglas (Spottiswoode), Kt 1981; TD 1959; FCA; Senior Partner, Touche Ross & Co., 1977–85 (Partner, 1958–85); *b* 6 June 1924; *s* of late Robert Spottiswoode Morpeth and Louise Rankine Morpeth (*née* Dobson); *m* 1951, Anne Rutherford, *yr d* of Ian C. Bell, OBE, MC, Edinburgh; two *s* two *d*. *Educ:* George Watson's Coll., Edinburgh; Edinburgh Univ. (BCom). Commissioned RA; served 1943–47, India, Burma, Malaya. Mem., Inst. of Chartered Accountants in England and Wales, 1952, Fellow, 1957, Pres., 1972. Chm., Clerical Med. and Gen. Life Assce Soc., later Clerical Med. Investment Gp, 1978–94. Chairman: (of Trustees), British Telecom Staff Superannuation Scheme, 1983–92; British Borneo Petroleum Syndicate, 1985–95; Deputy Chairman: Brixton Estate plc, 1983–94; Leslie Langton Hldgs, 1987–91; Director: Allied-Irish Banks, 1986–91; First Ireland Investment Trust, 1992–99 (Chm., 1997–99). Mem., Investment Grants Advisory Cttee, 1968–71; Chm., Inflation Accounting Steering Gp, 1976–80; Vice-Chm., Accounting Standards Cttee, 1970–82. Chm., Taxation Cttee, CBI, 1973–76. Honourable Artillery Company: Member, 1949–; Lt-Col, comdg 1st Regt HAC (RHA), 1964–66; Master Gunner within the Tower of London, 1966–69. Master, Co. of Chartered Accountants in England and Wales, 1977–78. FRCM (Hon. Treasurer, RCM, 1983–96). *Recreations:* golf, gardening. *Clubs:* Athenæum, Caledonian.

MORPHET, David Ian; author; *b* 24 Jan. 1940; *s* of late Albert and Sarah Elizabeth Morphet; *m* 1968, Sarah Gillian Sedgwick; two *s* one *d*. *Educ:* King James's Grammar Sch., Almondbury, Yorks; St John's Coll., Cambridge (History Schol.; English Tripos, class I, Pts I and II). Foreign Office, 1961; Vice Consul, Taiz, 1963; Doha, 1963–64; FO, 1964–66; Asst Private Sec. to Foreign Secretary, 1966–68; First Sec., Madrid, 1969–72; Diplomatic Service Observer, CS Selection Board, 1972–74; transf. to Dept of Energy, 1974; Asst Sec., 1975; Dep. Chm., Midlands Electricity Board (on secondment), 1978–79; Under-Secretary: Electricity Div., 1979–83; Energy Policy Div., 1983–85; Atomic Energy Div., 1985–89; UK Governor: Internat. Energy Agency, Paris, 1983–85; IAEA, Vienna, 1985–89. Director: BICC Cables Ltd, 1981–89; Planning and Devélt, Balfour Beatty Ltd, 1989–91; Govt Affairs, BICC plc, 1992–95; Barking Power Ltd, 1993–2001; Dir Gen., Railway Forum, 1997–2000. Chm., Export Finance Cttee, CBI, 1992–96; Mem. Council, CBI, 1995–96 and 1997–2001. Founder Mem. and Chm., Nat. Schizophrenia Fellowship, 1977–83. *Publications:* Louis Jennings, MP: editor of The New York Times and Tory democrat, 2001; (ed) St John's College, Cambridge: excellence and diversity, 2007; *poetry:* Seventy-Seven Poems, 2002; The Angel and the Fox, 2003; Approaching Animals from A to Z, 2004; 39 Ways of Looking, 2005; The Silence of Green, 2007. *Recreations:* music, walking. *Address:* 11 Daisy Lane, SW6 3DD. *Club:* Athenæum.

MORPHET, Richard Edward, CBE 1998; Keeper, Modern Collection, Tate Gallery, 1986–96 (Keeper Emeritus, 1996–98); *b* 2 Oct. 1938; *s* of Horace Taylor Morphet and Eleanor Morphet (*née* Shaw); *m* 1965, Sarah Francis Richmond (*see* S. F. Morphet); two *d*. *Educ:* Bootham Sch., York; London Sch. of Economics (BA Hons History). Fine Arts Dept, British Council, 1963–66; Tate Gallery: Asst Keeper, 1966–73; Dep. Keeper, Modern Collection, 1973–86. Exhibitions (curator and author/editor of catalogue) include: Richard Hamilton, Tate, 1970; Bernard Cohen, Hayward, 1972; William Turnbull, Tate, 1973; Art in One Year: 1935, Tate, 1977; Meredith Frampton, Tate, 1982; Cedric Morris, Tate, 1984; The Hard-Won Image, Tate, 1984; Richard Hamilton, Tate, 1992; R. B. Kitaj, Tate, 1994; Encounters: New Art from Old, National Gallery, 2000; other exhibition catalogues include: Roy Lichtenstein, Tate, 1968; Andy Warhol, Tate, 1971; Howard Hodgkin, Arts Council, 1976; Leonard McComb, Serpentine, 1983; contribs to exhibn catalogues on Late Sickert, Hayward, 1981 and The Art of Bloomsbury, Tate, 1999. *Publications:* Jonathan Leaman, 2002; contrib. books on Eric Ravilious, 1983, and Anthony Gross, 1992; contrib. Apollo, Burlington Mag., Studio International, TLS, etc. *Fax:* (020) 7820 1610.

MORPHET, Sarah Frances, (Sally), CMG 2002; Research Counsellor, Foreign and Commonwealth Office, 1998–2000; *b* 8 July 1940; *d* of Sir John Christopher Blake Richmond and Diana Richmond (*née* Galbraith); *m* 1965, Richard Edward Morphet, *qv*; two *d*. *Educ:* Mayfield Convent, Sussex; Univ. of St Thomas, Houston, Texas; Newnham Coll., Cambridge (BA 1962, MA). COI, 1963–66; researcher, FCO, 1966–2000, covered major non-aligned meetings, 1979–2000. Vis. Prof., Univ. of Kent at Canterbury, 2001–06. *Publications:* contrib. chapters in books, including: United Nations, Divided World, 2nd edn 1993; The Conscience of the World, 1996; Human Rights and Comparative Foreign Policy, 2000; The United Nations at the Millennium, 2000; contrib. articles to Global Governance, Internat. Peacekeeping, Rev. of Internat. Studies, Security Dialogue. *Recreation:* riding. *T:* (020) 7820 1610; *e-mail:* sally.morphet@ntlworld.com.

MORPHY, Leslie Ann; Chief Executive, Crisis UK, since 2006; *b* 23 Jan. 1949; *d* of Hugh Webster Morphy and Grace Clara Morphy; *m* 1981, Bob Deffee; one *s* one *d* (and one *d* decd). *Educ:* London Sch. of Econs (BSc Econ); Birkbeck Coll., London (MSc). Researcher, Penguin, 1971–72; Mgr, NUS, 1972–78; freelance consultancy, 1983–89; Dir, Broadcasting Support Services, 1978–83; Hd, R&D, Basic Skills Agency, 1989–96; Dir, Prince's Trust, 1996–2006. Trustee: Bliss, 2004–; Inst. for Urban Information, 2007–. *Recreations:* being with my family, theatre, reading novels, growing things. *Address:* 4 West Park Road, Kew Gardens, Richmond, Surrey TW9 4DA. *T:* 07867 515541; *e-mail:* lmorphy@blueyonder.co.uk.

MORPURGO, Michael Andrew Bridge, OBE 2006 (MBE 1999); writer; Joint Founder Director, Farms for City Children, since 1976; Children's Laureate, 2003–05; *b* 5 Oct. 1943; *s* of Tony Valentine Bridge and late Catherine Noel Kippe (*née* Cammaerts), and step *s* of late Jack Eric Morpurgo; *m* 1963, Clare (MBE 1999), *d* of Sir Allen Lane, founder, Penguin Books; two *s* one *d*. *Educ:* King's Sch., Canterbury; RMA Sandhurst; King's Coll., London (AKC, BA 1967; FKC 2001). Primary school teacher, 1967–75; with Clare Morpurgo founded Farms for City Children and opened Nethercott House farm, 1976; opened Treginnis Isaf, 1989, Wick Court, Glos, 1998. Co-writer/presenter, The Invention of Childhood (series), BBC Radio 4, 2006. Hon. DEd: Plymouth, 2002; UCE, 2007; Hon. DLitt: Exeter, 2004; Herts, 2006; Hon. MA Worcester, 2007 (with Clare Morpurgo). Bookseller Assoc. Writer of the Year, 2005. Chevalier des Arts et des Lettres, 2004. *Publications:* over 100 books for children, including: Friend or Foe, 1978; (with Ted Hughes) All Around the Year, 1979; The Nine Lives of Montezuma, 1980; The White Horse of Zennor, 1982; War Horse, 1984 (performed NT, 2007–08); Twist of Gold, 1986; Mr Nobody's Eyes, 1989; Why the Whales Came (Silver Pencil award, Holland), 1989 (screenplay, When the Whales Came, 1991); My Friend Walter, 1990 (screenplay, 1994); Little Foxes, 1992; The Marble Crusher, 1992; King of the Cloud Forests, 1992 (Cercle d'Or, Montreuil, 1994; Prix Sorcière, 1995); The War of Jenkins Ear, 1992 (Best Book award, Amer. Liby Assoc., 1996); Blodin the Beast, 1993; Waiting for Anya, 1993; The Sandman and the Turtles, 1994; The Dancing Bear, 1995; The Wreck of the Zanzibar, 1995 (Whitbread Children's Award, and Children's Book Award, Fedn of Children's Books, 1996; IBBY Honour Book, 1998); Arthur High King of Britain, 1995; Sam's Duck, 1996; Muck and Magic, 1996; The Butterfly Lion, 1996 (Writers' Guild Award, 1996; Smarties Prize, 1997); The Ghost of Grania O'Malley, 1996; Robin of Sherwood, 1997; Farm Boy, 1997; Red Eyes at Night, 1997; Beyond the Rainbow Warrior, 1997; Escape from Shangri-la, 1998; Joan of Arc of Domrémy, 1998; Wartman, 1998; The Rainbow Bear, 1999 (Children's Book Award, Nat. Assoc. of Teachers of English); Kensuke's Kingdom, 1999 (Children's Book Award, Prix Sorcière, Prix Lire au Collège); Wombat Goes Walkabout, 1999 (Prix Sorcière); Animal Stories, 1999; Dear Olly, 2000; The Silver Swan, 2000; Black Queen, 2000; Tom's Sausage Lion, 2000; From Hereabout Hill, 2000; Billy the Kid, 2000; Classic Boys' Stories, 2000; Toro! Toro!, 2001; More Muck and Magic, 2001; Because a Fire was in my Head, 2001; Out of the Ashes, 2001 (Children's Book Award); The Last Wolf, 2002; The Sleeping Sword, 2002; Cool, 2002; Mr Skip, 2002; Gentle Giant, 2003; Private Peaceful, 2003 (Children's Book Award, Blue Peter Award, Prix Sorcière); Little Albatross, 2003; Dolphin Boy, 2004; It's a Dog's Life, 2004; Sir Gawain and the Green Knight, 2004; Aesop's Fables, 2004; Cockadoodle-doo Mr Sultana!, 2004; (with Jane Feaver) Cock Crow, 2004; The Best Christmas Present in the World, 2004; The Amazing Story of Adolphus Tips (Sheffield Book Award), 2005; I Believe in Unicorns, 2005; (with Michael Foreman) Beowulf, 2006; Singing for Mrs Pettigrew, 2006; Alone on a Wide Wide Sea, 2006 (Indep. Booksellers' Children's Book of Yr, 2007); (with Quentin Blake) On Angel Wings, 2006; (with Michael Foreman) The Mozart Question, 2007; Born to Run, 2007; (with Emma Chichester Clark) Hansel and Gretel, 2008; (with Michael Foreman) Kaspar, Prince of Cats, 2008; (with Christian Birmingham) This Morning I Met a Whale, 2008; libretti: Solar, 1981; Scarecrow (music by Phyllis Tate), 1982. *Recreation:* dreaming. *Address:* c/o David Higham Associates, 5–8 Lower John Street, Golden Square, W1R 4HA. *Club:* Chelsea Arts.

MORPURGO DAVIES, Anna Elbina; *see* Davies.

MORPUSS, Guy; QC 2008; barrister, since 1991; *b* Worcester, 13 March 1969; *s* of Richard and Rosemarie Morpuss; *m* 1999, Julie Davies; two *s*. *Educ:* Hillcrest High Sch., South Africa; Univ. of Birmingham (LLB 1st Cl. Hons). Called to the Bar, Lincoln's Inn, 1991; in practice as barrister specialising in commercial litigation. *Recreations:* running, travelling, ski-ing, music. *Address:* c/o 20 Essex Street, WC2R 3AL. *T:* (020) 7842 1200; *e-mail:* gmorpuss@20essexst.com.

MORRELL, Prof. David Cameron, OBE 1982; FRCP, FRCGP; Wolfson Professor of General Practice, United Medical and Dental Schools of Guy's and St Thomas' Hospitals, 1974–93, Emeritus Professor of General Practice, 1993; *b* 6 Nov. 1929; *s* of William and Violet Morrell; *m* 1953, Alison Joyce Morrell; three *s* two *d*. *Educ:* Wimbledon Coll.; St Mary's Hosp. Med. Sch. (MB BS). DObstRCOG; FFPH. Phys., RAF Med. Br., 1954–57; Principal in Gen. Practice, Hoddesdon, Herts, 1957–63; Lectr in Gen. Practice, Univ. of Edinburgh, 1963–67; Sen. Lectr, then Reader, in Gen. Practice, St Thomas's Hosp. Med. Sch., 1967–74. Pres., BMA, 1994–95. KSG 1982. *Publications:* The Art of General Practice, 1966, 4th edn 1991; An Introduction to Primary Medical Care, 1976, 2nd edn 1981; (with J. Cormack and M. Marinker) Practice: a handbook of general practice, 1976, 2nd edn 1987. *Recreations:* gardening, walking. *Address:* 14 Higher Green, Ewell KT17 3BA. *T:* (020) 8786 9270.

MORRELL, David William James; Scottish Legal Services Ombudsman, 1991–94; *b* 26 July 1933; *s* of Rev. W. W. Morrell, MBE, TD and Grace Morrell; *m* 1960, Margaret Rosemary Lewis; two *s* one *d*. *Educ:* George Watson's Coll., Edinburgh; Univ. of Edinburgh (MA Hons, LLB). Law Apprentice, Edinburgh, 1954–57; Admin. Asst, Univ. of Durham, 1957–60; Asst Registrar and Graduate Appts Officer, Univ. of Exeter, 1960–64; Sen. Asst Registrar, Univ. of Essex, 1964–66; Academic Registrar, 1966–73, Registrar, 1973–89, Univ. of Strathclyde; Lay Observer for Scotland, 1989–91. OECD Consultant on management in higher educn, 1990. Vice-Chm., Lomond Healthcare NHS Trust, 1995–99 (Chm., 1995–96); Mem., Argyll and Clyde Health Bd, 1999–2001. Governor: Univ. of Paisley (formerly Paisley Coll.), 1990–2002 (Vice-Chm., 1992–97, Chm., 1997–2002); Scottish Centre for Children with Motor Impairments, 1994–97; Chm., Conf. of Scottish Centrally-Funded Colls, 1997–2000. DUniv Paisley, 2005. *Publications:* papers on higher education and on provision of legal services. *Recreations:* hill-walking, fishing. *Address:* 29 Barclay Drive, Helensburgh, Dunbartonshire G84 9RA. *T:* (01436) 674875.

MORRELL, Frances Maine; Joint Chief Executive, Arts Inform, since 1997 (Chair, 1993–97); *b* 28 Dec. 1937; *d* of Frank and Beatrice Galleway; *m* 1964, Brian Morrell; one *d*. *Educ:* Queen Anne Grammar Sch., York; Hull Univ. (BA (Hons) English Lang. and Lit.); MA (Distinction) Goldsmiths Coll., Univ. of London 1995. Secondary Sch. Teacher, 1960–69; Press Officer, Fabian Soc. and NUS, 1970–72; Research into MPs' constituency role, 1973; Special Adviser to Tony Benn, as Sec. of State for Industry, then as Sec. of State for Energy, 1974–79. Dep. Leader, 1981–83, Leader, 1983–87, ILEA; Mem. for Islington S and Finsbury, GLC, 1981–86; Sec., Speaker's Commn on Citizenship, 1988–91; Exec. Dir, Inst. for Citizenship Studies, 1992–93; Dir of Studies, Practising Citizenship Project, 1994–98. Sen. Res. Fellow, Federal Trust for Educn and Res., 1993–; Mem., LSE Grad. Sch., 1996–. Member: Oakes Cttee, Enquiry into Payment and Collection Methods for Gas and Electricity Bills (report publ. 1976); Exec., Campaign for Labour Party Democracy, 1979–; Co Founder: Labour Co-ordinating Cttee, 1978; Women's Action Cttee, 1980–. Contested (Lab) Chelmsford, Feb. 1974. Chair: NCVQ Performing Arts Adv. Cttee, 1994–; London Schs Newspaper Project, 1994–; London Schs Arts Service, 2005–; Member: Bd of Dirs, Sadler's Wells Theatre, 1982–88; Bd, King's Head Theatre, 2000–; Bd, Islington Internat. Fest., 2000– (Dep. Chm., 2001–). Hon. FRIBA 2005. *Publications:* (with Tony Benn and Francis Cripps) A Ten Year Industrial Strategy for Britain, 1975; (with Francis Cripps) The Case for a Planned Energy Policy, 1976; From the Electors of Bristol: the record of a year's correspondence between constituents and their Member of Parliament, 1977; (jtly) Manifesto—a radical strategy for Britain's future, 1981; Children of the Future: the battle for Britain's schools, 1989; The Community Sphere, 2002. *Recreations:* reading, cooking, gardening. *Address:* 91 Hemingford Road, N1 1BY.

MORRELL, Leslie James, OBE 1986; JP; Chairman, Northern Ireland Water Council, 1982–93; *b* 26 Dec. 1931; *s* of James Morrell; *m* 1958, Anne Wallace, BSc; two *s* one *d*. *Educ:* Portora Royal Sch., Enniskillen; Queen's Univ., Belfast. BAgric 1955. Member: Londonderry CC, 1969–73; Coleraine Bor. Council, 1973–77; Mem. (U) for Londonderry, NI Assembly, 1973–75; Minister of Agriculture, NI Exec., 1973–74; Dep. Leader, Unionist Party of NI, 1974–80. Mem., BBC Gen. Adv. Cttee, 1980–86; Chm., BBC NI Agricl Adv. Cttee, 1986–91. Chm., NI Fedn of Housing Assocs, 1978–80; Member Board: Oaklee Homes, 2003–; Oaklee Housing Trust (NI), 2006–. Hon. Secretary: Oaklee Housing Assoc., 1992– (James Butcher Housing Assoc. (NI), 1981–92 (Chm., 1976–81)); James Butcher Retirement Homes Ltd, 1985–95. Mem. Exec., Assoc. of Governing Bodies of Voluntary Grammar Schs, 1978–84; Chm., Virus Tested Stem Cutting Potato Growers Assoc., 1977–88. JP Londonderry, 1966. *Address:* Dunboe House, Castlerock, Coleraine BT51 4UB. *T:* (028) 7084 8352.

MORRELL, Peter Richard; His Honour Judge Morrell; a Circuit Judge, since 1992; *b* 25 May 1944; *s* of Frank Richard Morrell and Florence Ethel Morrell; *m* 1970, Helen Mary Vint Collins; two *d*. *Educ:* Westminster Sch.; University, Coll., Oxford (MA). Admitted Solicitor, 1970; called to the Bar, Gray's Inn, 1974; a Recorder, 1990–92. C of E Reader, 2005–07, ordained Deacon, 2008, Peterborough Dio. *Recreations:* shooting, fishing, photography, Spain. *Address:* Leicester Crown Court, Wellington Street, Leicester LE1 6HG. *T:* (0116) 222 3434.

MORREY, Rev. William Reginald; Chair, Methodist Council, 2006–Sept. 2009; President of the Methodist Conference, 2004–05; Chair, Wales Synod, Methodist Church in Wales, since 2007; *b* 24 March 1953; *s* of Claude William Morrey and Joan Morrey; *m* 1976, Vicki Mountford; two *s*. *Educ:* Birmingham Univ. (BA Theol. 1974); Queen's Coll., Birmingham; Westhill Coll., Birmingham (Cert. in Community and Youth Work 1976). Minister: Bideford, 1976–79; Ecclesall, Sheffield, and Chaplain to Children's Hosp., 1979–84; Halifax, 1984–87; Supt Minister, Bangor and Chaplain to UCNW, Bangor, and to RAF Valley, 1987–94; Co-ordinator, Council for Methodism in Wales, 1994–97; Chm., S Wales Dist, Methodist Ch, 1997–2007. Foundn Trustee, N Wales Deaf Assoc., 1994–; Chm., NCH Cymru, 2005–07; Faith Communities Advr, Action for Children, 2008–. *Publication:* Seeing is Hearing: reflections on being deafened, 1995. *Recreations:* badminton, squash, walking. *Address:* c/o Methodist Church Conference Office, 25 Marylebone Road, NW1 5JR.

MORRICE, Jane, (Mrs Paul Robinson); Northern Ireland Member, European Economic and Social Committee, since 2006; Member, Northern Ireland Advisory Committee, Ofcom, since 2004; *b* 11 May 1954; *d* of George Eric Morrice and Irene (*née* Cleland); *m* 1988, Paul Robinson; one *s*. *Educ:* Univ. of Ulster (BA Hons W Eur. Studies 1977). Journalist, Brussels, specialising in internat. economy and Third World; business and labour relns corresp., 1980–87; BBC TV and Radio in NI, 1987–92; Head, Eur. Commn Office in NI, 1992–97; Mem., Eur. Commn Task Force preparing special support prog. for peace and reconciliation in NI and border counties of Ireland, 1992–97; Mem. (NI Women's Coalition) N Down, 1998–2003, and Dep. Speaker, 1999–2002, NI Assembly. Bd Mem., Laganside Corp., 1998–2007. *Publications:* North/South Dialogue, 1984; The Lomé Convention From Politics to Practice, 1985. *Recreations:* writing, swimming, tennis, photography. *Address:* 18 Ballyholme Esplanade, Bangor, Co. Down BT20 5LZ.

MORRICE, Philip; HM Diplomatic Service, retired; director and consultant, various companies in Australia and UK; *b* 31 Dec. 1943; *s* of late William Hunter Morrice and Catherine Jane Cowie; *m* 1988, Margaret Clare Bower; one *s* one *d*. *Educ:* Robert Gordon's College, Aberdeen. Entered HM Diplomatic Service, 1963; served Kuala Lumpur, 1964–67; CO, later FCO, 1967–69; Caracas, 1969–72; First Sec., UK Delegn to OECD, Paris, 1973–75; First Sec. (Energy), UK Perm. Rep. to EC, Brussels, 1975–78; FCO, 1978–81; First Sec. (Commercial), later Counsellor (Comm.), Rome, 1981–85; Counsellor (Econ. and Comm.), Lagos, 1986–88; Minister-Counsellor, Consul-Gen. and Dir of Trade Promotion, Brasilia, 1988–92; Director, Anglo-Taiwan Trade Cttee, subseq. British Trade and Cultural Office, Taipei (on secondment), 1992–95; Consul-Gen., Sydney, and Dir Gen. of Trade and Investment Promotion in Australia, 1995–99. Dir, KPMG Consulting, 1999–2001. *Publications:* The Schweppes Guide to Scotch, 1983; The Whisky Distilleries of Scotland and Ireland, 1987; The Teacher's Book of Whisky, 1993; numerous articles. *Recreations:* travel, tennis, golf. *Address:* TFG International Pty Ltd, Level 14, Norwich House, 6–10 O'Connell Street, Sydney, NSW 2000, Australia. *Clubs:* Royal Automobile; Union (Sydney); Royal Sydney Yacht Squadron; Royal Sydney Golf.

MORRILL, Rev. Prof. John Stephen, DPhil; FRHistS; FBA 1995; Professor of British and Irish History, University of Cambridge, since 1998; Fellow, Selwyn College, Cambridge, since 1975; *b* 12 June 1946; *s* of William Henry Morrill and Marjorie (*née* Ashton); *m* 1968, Frances Mead (*d* 2007); four *d*. *Educ:* Altrincham County Grammar Sch.; Trinity Coll., Oxford (BA 1967; MA, DPhil 1971; Hon. Fellow, 2006). FRHistS 1977. Keasbey Lectr in Hist., 1970–71, Jun. Res. Fellow, 1971–74, Trinity Coll., Oxford; Coll. Lectr in Hist., St Catherine's Coll., Oxford, 1973–74; Lectr in Mod. Hist., Univ. of Stirling, 1974–75; Cambridge University: Asst Lectr and Lectr, Faculty of History, 1975–92; Reader in Early Modern Hist., 1992–98; Dep. Dir, Centre for Arts, Humanities and Social Scis, 2001–04; Selwyn College, Cambridge: Dir of Studies in Hist., 1975–91; Tutor, 1979–91; Admissions Tutor, 1983–87; Sen. Tutor, 1987–91; Vice Master, 1994–2004. Vice-President: RHistS, 1993–97; British Acad., 2001–03; Mem., AHRB, 1999–2004 (Convenor, History Panel, 1999–2002; Chair, Res. Cttee, 2002–04). Ordained permanent deacon, RC Ch, 1996. Foreign Mem., Finnish Acad. of Arts and Scis, 2002. Centenary Fellow, Historical Assoc., 2006. FRSA 2008. Hon. DLitt UEA, 2002; DUniv Surrey, 2002. *Publications:* Cheshire 1630–1660, 1974; The Revolt of the Provinces 1630–1650, 1976, rev. edn 1980; The Cheshire Grand Jury 1625–1659, 1976; (with G. E. Aylmer) The Civil Wars and Interregnum: sources for local historians, 1979; Seventeenth-Century Britain, 1980; (ed) Reactions to the English Civil War, 1982; (ed) Land Men and Beliefs, 1985; Charles I, 1989; Oliver Cromwell and the English Revolution, 1990; (ed) The National Covenant in its British Context, 1990; (ed) The Impact of the English Civil War, 1991; (ed) Revolution and Restoration, 1992; The Nature of the English Revolution, 1993; (with P. Slack and D. Woolf) Public Men and Private Conscience in Seventeenth-Century England, 1993; (ed) The Oxford Illustrated History of Tudor and Stuart Britain, 1996; (with B. Bradshaw) The British Problem 1534–1707: state formation in the Atlantic Archipelago, 1996; Revolt in the Provinces: the English people and the tragedies of war, 1998; (jtly) Soldiers and Statesmen of the English Revolution, 1998; contribs to learned jls. *Recreations:* classical music, whisky and whiskey, cricket. *Address:* Selwyn College, Cambridge CB3 9DQ; 1 Bradford's Close, Bottisham, Cambs CB25 9DW. *T:* (01223) 811822.

MORRIS; *see* Temple-Morris, family name of Baron Temple-Morris.

MORRIS, family name of **Barons Killanin**, **Morris**, **Morris of Aberavon**, **Morris of Handsworth**, **Morris of Kenwood**, **Morris of Manchester** and **Naseby**.

MORRIS, 3rd Baron *cr* 1918; **Michael David Morris;** *b* 9 Dec. 1937; *er* twin *s* of 2nd Baron Morris and Jean Beatrice (later Lady Salmon; she *d* 1989), *d* of late Lt-Col D. Maitland-Makgill-Crichton; *S* father, 1975; *m* 1st, 1959, Denise Eleanor (marr. diss. 1962), *o d* of Morley Richards; 2nd, 1962, Jennifer (marr. diss. 1969), *o d* of Squadron Leader Tristram Gilbert; two *d*; 3rd, 1980, Juliet (marr. diss. 1996), twin *d* of Anthony Buckingham; two *s* one *d*; 4th, 1999, Nicola Mary, *o d* of Colin Morgan Watkins. *Educ:* Downside. *Heir:* *s* Hon. Thomas Anthony Salmon Morris, *b* 2 July 1982.

MORRIS OF ABERAVON, Baron *cr* 2001 (Life Peer), of Aberavon in the County of West Glamorgan and of Ceredigion in the County of Dyfed; **John Morris,** KG 2003; Kt 1999; PC 1970; QC 1973; Chancellor, University of Glamorgan, since 2001; Lord-Lieutenant of Dyfed, 2002–06; *b* Nov. 1931; *s* of late D. W. Morris, Penywern, Talybont, Cardiganshire and Mary Olwen Ann Morris (*née* Edwards, later Lewis); *m* 1959, Margaret M., *d* of late Edward Lewis, OBE, JP, of Llandysul; three *d*. *Educ:* Ardwyn, Aberystwyth; University Coll. of Wales, Aberystwyth; Gonville and Caius Coll., Cambridge (LLM; Hon. Fellow); Academy of International Law, The Hague; Holker Senior Exhibitioner, Gray's Inn. Commissioned Royal Welch Fusiliers and Welch Regt. Called to the Bar, Gray's Inn, 1954, Bencher, 1985; a Recorder, 1982–97. MP (Lab) Aberavon, Oct. 1959–2001. Parly Sec., Min. of Power, 1964–66; Jt Parly Sec., Min. of Transport, 1966–68; Minister of Defence (Equipment), 1968–70; Sec. of State for Wales, 1974–79; opposition spokesman on legal affairs and Shadow Attorney Gen., 1979–81 and 1983–97; Attorney General, 1997–99. Member: Cttee of Privileges, 1994–97; Select Cttee on Implementation of Nolan Report, 1995–97; Adv. Cttee on Business Appointments, 2002–. Dep. Gen. Sec. and Legal Adviser, Farmers' Union of Wales, 1956–58. Member: UK Delegn Consultative Assembly Council of Europe and Western European Union, 1963–64, 1982–83; N Atlantic Assembly, 1970–74. Chairman: Nat. Pneumoconiosis Jt Cttee, 1964–66; Joint Review of Finances and Management, British Railways, 1966–67; Nat. Road Safety Advisory Council, 1967. Mem. Council, Prince's Trust (Cymru), 2002–. Mem. Courts of University of Wales. Pres., London Welsh Trust, 2001–. Hon. Fellow: UCW, Aberystwyth; Trinity Coll., Carmarthen; UC, Swansea. Hon. LLD Wales, 1985. *Address:* House of Lords, SW1A 0PW.

See also D. W. Morris.

MORRIS OF BOLTON, Baroness *cr* 2004 (Life Peer), of Bolton in the County of Greater Manchester; **Patricia Morris,** OBE; DL; *b* 16 Jan. 1953; *d* of late James Sydney Whittaker, Bolton; *m* 1978, William Patrick Morris, *qv*; one *s* one *d*. *Educ:* Bolton Sch. Girls' Div.; Clifton and Didsbury Colls of Educn. Personal Assistant: to N Regl Dir, Slater Walker Ltd, 1974–75; to Chevalier Dr Harry D. Schultz, 1975; Fund Manager, PPS, 1975–77; Technical Analyst: Foster & Braithwaite, 1977–78; Charlton, Seal, Dimmock & Co., 1979–83; Policy and Political Advr to a Cons. MEP, 1999–2001. Mem., Cons. Women's Nat. Cttee, 1989; Vice-Chm., Cons. Party, 2001–05. Contested (C) Oldham Central and Royton, 1992. Opposition Whip, H of L, 2001–05; opposition spokesman on children, families and women, 2005–, on educn and skills, 2006–, H of L. Dep. Chm., Salford Royal Hosps NHS Trust, 1993–97; Advr to Abbot of Ampleforth, 1998–2004. Pres., Nat. Benevolent Instn, 2006–; Co-Chm., Women in Public Policy, 2007–; Patron, OXPIP, 2006–; Trustee, Disability Partnership, 2007–. Mem. Cttee, Patrons and Associates, Manchester City Art Galls, 1982–94; Mem., Manchester N Valuation and Community Charge Tribunal, 1988–92; Chm., Bolton Cancer Res. Campaign, 1992–95; Mem. Bd Mgt, 1994–97, Dir, 1997–2002, Bolton Lads' and Girls' Club. Gov. and Trustee, Bolton Sch., 1992–. DL Greater Manchester, 2008. *Address:* House of Lords, SW1A 0PW.

MORRIS OF HANDSWORTH, Baron *cr* 2006 (Life Peer), of Handsworth in the County of West Midlands; **William Manuel Morris,** Kt 2003; OJ 2002; DL; General Secretary, Transport and General Workers Union, 1992–2003 (Deputy General Secretary, 1986–92); a non-executive Director, Bank of England, 1998–2006; *b* 19 Oct. 1938; *s* of William and Una Morris; *m* 1957, Minetta (*d* 1990); two *s*. *Educ:* Mizpah Sch., Manchester, Jamaica; Handsworth Tech. Coll. Hardy Spicer Engineering, 1954. Joined TGWU, 1958: Shop Steward, 1962; Mem. Gen. Exec. Council, 1971–72; Dist Officer, Nottingham, 1973; Dist Sec., Northampton, 1976; Nat. Sec., Passenger Services, 1979–85. Mem., TUC Gen. Council, 1988–2003. Chm., Morris Inquiry, Metropolitan Police Authy, 2004. Member: Commn for Racial Equality, 1977–87; IBA Gen. Adv. Council, 1981–86; Bd, ITF, 1986–2003; Road Transport ITB, 1986–92; Prince's Youth Business Trust, 1987–90; BBC General Adv. Council, 1987–88; Employment Appeals Tribunal, 1988–; Economic and Social Cttee, EC, 1990–92; NEDC, 1992; ACAS, 1997–2003; Royal Commn on H of L reform, 1999; Commn for Integrated Transport, 1999–2005; Architects' Registration Bd, 2001–05; Panel on Takeovers and Mergers, 2005–. Chair, Midland Heart Housing Assoc., 2007–. Vis. Prof., Thames Valley Univ., 1997. Chancellor: Univ. of Technology, Jamaica, 2000–; Staffordshire Univ., 2004–. Member: Governing Body, Atlantic Coll., 1994–2004; Court: Luton Univ., 1994–; Univ. of Northampton (formerly Nene Coll., later UC Northampton), 1996–. Member: Bd of Govs, London South Bank (formerly S Bank) Univ., 1997–2005; Univ. Assembly, Greenwich Univ., 1997–; Trustee Bd, Open Univ. Foundn, 1997–. Mem., Cricket Bd for England and Wales, 2004–. DL Stafford, 2008. Hon. FRSA, 1992; Hon. FCGI, 1992.

Hon. LLD: South Bank, 1994; Teesside, 1997; Univ. of Technol., Jamaica, 2000; Luton, 2000; Birmingham, Warwick, 2002; Nottingham, 2005; DUniv: Leeds Metropolitan, 1996; Middlesex, Stafford, 2002; Hon. DLitt: Westminster 1997; Hull, 2007; Hon. DBA Greenwich, 1997; Hon. Dr Thames Valley, 1997; Hon. DLit, London South Bank, 2007; MUniv Open, 1995; Hon. MA UC Northampton, 2001. *Recreations:* walking, gardening, watching sports. *Address:* House of Lords, SW1A 0PW; *e-mail:* morrisw@parliament.uk.

MORRIS OF KENWOOD, 3rd Baron *cr* 1950, of Kenwood; **Jonathan David Morris;** company director; *b* 5 Aug. 1968; *s* of 2nd Baron Morris of Kenwood and of Hon. Ruth, *d* of Baron Janner; *S* father, 2004; *m* 1996, Melanie, *d* of Robin Klein; two *s*. *Heir: s* Hon. Benjamin Julian Morris, *b* 5 Nov. 1998.

MORRIS OF MANCHESTER, Baron *cr* 1997 (Life Peer), of Manchester in the co. of Greater Manchester; **Alfred Morris;** PC 1979; AO 1991; QSO 1989; *b* 23 March 1928; *s* of late George Henry Morris and Jessie Morris (*née* Murphy); *m* 1950, Irene (*née* Jones); two *s* two *d*. *Educ:* elem. and evening schs, Manchester; Ruskin Coll., Oxford; St Catherine's, Univ. of Oxford (MA); Univ. of Manchester (Postgrad. certif. in Educn). Employed in office of a Manchester brewing firm from age 14 (HM Forces, 1946–48); Teacher and Lectr, Manchester, 1954–56; Industrial Relations Officer, The Electricity Coun., London, 1956–64. Nat. Chm., Labour League of Youth, 1950–52; Observer, Coun. of Europe, 1952–53. Contested Liverpool, Garston, 1951. MP (Lab and Co-op) Manchester, Wythenshawe, 1964–97. PPS to Minister of Agric., Fisheries and Food, 1964–67, and to Lord President of the Council and Leader of House of Commons, 1968–70; Opposition front bench spokesman on social services, specialising in the problems of disabled people, 1970–74 and 1979–92; Parly Under-Sec. of State, DHSS, as Britain's first-ever Minister for Disabled People, 1974–79. Treasurer, British Gp, IPU, 1971–74; Mem., UK Delegn to UN Gen. Assembly, 1966; Chm., Food and Agriculture Gp of Parly Lab. Party, 1971–74; Representative of Privy Council on Council of RCVS, 1969–74; promoted Chronically Sick and Disabled Persons Act, 1970, Food and Drugs (Milk) Act, 1970, Police Act, 1972, as a Private Member; Parly Advr to the Police Fedn, 1971–74; Hon. Parly Advr to Royal British Legion, 1989–; Chm., Co-operative Parly Group, 1971–72 and 1983–85; Vice-Chm., All-Party Parly Retail Trade Gp, 1972–74; Vice-Pres., Parly and Scientific Cttee, 1991–95 (Chm., 1988–91); Chairman: Managing Trustees, Parly Pensions Fund, 1983–97 (Man. Trustee, 1980–83); Managing Trustees, H of C Members' Fund, 1983–97; Anzac Gp of MPs and Peers, 1982–97 (Pres., 1997–); Jt Treasurer, British-Amer. Parly Gp, 1983–97. Mem., US Congressional Cttee of Inquiry into Gulf War illnesses, 2002–; architect of indep. public Inquiry into Gulf War Illnesses (report 2004). Mem., Gen. Adv. Council, BBC, 1968–74, 1983–95; Patron: Disablement Income Group, 1970–; Motability, 1978–; Royal Schools for Deaf Children, 1995–; Life Patron, Rehabilitation International (RI), 1999; Mem., Exec. Cttee, Nat. Fund for Research into Crippling Diseases, 1970–74. Chm., World Cttees apptd to draft "Charter for the 1980s" for disabled people worldwide, 1980–81, and "Charter for the New Millennium", 2000; President: N of England Regional Assoc. for the Deaf, 1980–; Co-operative Congress, 1995–96; Soc. of Chiropodists and Podiatrists, 1997–; Haemophilia Soc., 1999–; Vice-Pres., Crisis at Christmas, 1995– (Trustee, 1982–95). Trustee, Hallé Orch., 2002. FABE 2000. Hon. Fellow, Manchester Metropolitan Univ. (formerly Poly.), 1990. Hon. MA Salford, 1997; Hon. LLD Manchester, 1998. Field Marshal Lord Harding Award, 1971, for services to the disabled; Grimshaw Meml Award of Nat. Fedn of the Blind, 1971; Paul Harris Fellowship, Rotary Internat., for services to the disabled internationally, 1992; AA Award, 1997; Earl Snowdon Award, 1998; Lifetime Achievement Award, People of the Year, 2000; Henry H. Kessler Award, Rehabilitation Internat., 2000. *Publications:* Value Added Tax: a tax on the consumer, 1970; The Growth of Parliamentary Scrutiny by Committee, 1970; (with A. Butler) No Feet to Drag, 1972; Ed. lectures (Human Relations in Industry), 1958; Ed. Jl (Jt Consultation) publ. Nat. Jt Adv. Coun. Elec. Supply Ind., 1959–61. *Recreations:* gardening, tennis, snooker, chess. *Address:* House of Lords, SW1A 0PW.

See also Rt Hon. C. R. Morris.

MORRIS OF YARDLEY, Baroness *cr* 2005 (Life Peer), of Yardley in the county of West Midlands; **Estelle Morris;** PC 1999; *b* 17 June 1952; *d* of Rt Hon. Charles Richard Morris, *qv* and Pauline Morris. *Educ:* Whalley Range High Sch., Manchester; Coventry Coll. of Educn (TCert); BEd Warwick Univ. Teacher, 1974–92. Councillor, Warwick DC, 1979–91 (Labour Gp Leader, 1981–89). MP (Lab) Birmingham, Yardley, 1992–2005. An Opposition Whip, 1994–95; opposition front-bench spokesman on educn, 1995–97; Parly Under-Sec. of State, 1997–98, Minister of State, 1998–2001, DFEE; Sec. of State for Educn and Skills, 2001–02; Minister of State (Minister for the Arts), DCMS, 2003–05. Hon. Fellow, St Martin's Coll., Lancaster, 2006. Hon. DLitt Warwick, 2002; Hon. DEd Wolverhampton, 2004; Hon. DArts Leeds Metropolitan, 2004; Hon. DLit Bradford, 2005; DUniv Birmingham, 2006; Hon. Dr Manchester Metropolitan, 2007. *Address:* House of Lords, SW1A 0PW.

MORRIS, Alan Douglas; Head of Performance Improvement Consulting—Gatwick Region, PricewaterhouseCoopers, since 2004; *b* 15 Sept. 1956; *s* of Leslie John Morris and Gladys Josephine Morris; *m* 1st, 1984, Barbara Caroline Alexandra Welsh (marr. diss. 1998); two *d*; 2nd, 1999, Anne Marie Stebbings. *Educ:* John Ruskin Grammar Sch., Croydon; Magdalene Coll., Cambridge (MA, LLM). FCMA. Joined Tate & Lyle, 1978; Esso Petroleum, 1981–84; Financial Controller: RBC Systems, 1984–87; MI Group, 1987–88; Simmons & Simmons: Finance Dir, 1988–96; Man. Dir, 1997–99; Hd of Operations—Legal, PricewaterhouseCoopers, 2000–04. *Recreations:* cricket, acting, singing, bridge, reading, airport lounges. *Address:* Spinningdale, Keymer Road, Burgess Hill, West Sussex RH15 0AH. *T:* (01444) 239830. *Club:* Oxford and Cambridge.

MORRIS, Albert, FCIB; Chairman, Inbucon Ltd, since 2007; Director, 1989–94, and Deputy Group Chief Executive, 1992–94, National Westminster Bank; *b* 21 Oct. 1934; *m* 1987, Patricia Lane (*d* 2005). *Educ:* Skerry's Coll., Liverpool; City of Liverpool Coll. of Commerce; Admin Staff Coll., Henley; MIT. National Westminster Bank: Head of Money Transmission, 1979–83; Dep. Gen. Manager, 1983–85, Gen. Manager, 1985–88, Management Services Div.; Chief Exec., Support Services, 1989–92. Director: NatWest Estate Management & Development Ltd, 1989–94; National Westminster Life Assce Ltd, 1992–94; Regent Associates, 1995–; Metroline plc, 1997– (Chm., 1997–2000); Chairman: BACS Ltd, 1985–94; Centre-file Ltd, 1988–94; Lorien plc, 1998–2007; Macro 4 plc, 2000–07. Founding Mem., 1985–87 and Mem. Council, 1990–94, UK Banking Ombudsman Scheme; Chm., APACS, 1993–94 (Dep. Chm., 1991–93; Dir, APACS Admin Ltd, 1987–94). Mem. Adv. Council, Sema Group, 1995–96; Special Advr, Ibos Ltd, 1995–96; non-exec. Mem., DSS Departmental Bd, 1993–97. Hon. Treas., Kingwood Trust, 1996–2000. CCMI; FCIB 1984 (Mem. Council, 1989–); FRSA 1989. Freeman, City of London, 1992; Liveryman, 1992–, Trustee, 2002–, Co. of Information Technologists. *Recreations:* golf, work, politics. *Address:* Stonebridge, 74 West Common, Harpenden, Herts AL5 2LD.

MORRIS, Air Marshal Sir Alec, KBE 1982; CB 1979; FREng; *b* 11 March 1926; *s* of late Harry Morris; *m* 1946, Moyna Patricia (*d* 2000), *d* of late Norman Boyle; one *s* one *d* (twins). *Educ:* King Edward VI Sch., East Retford; King's Coll., Univ. of London; Univ. of Southampton. Commnd RAF, 1945; radar duties, No 90 (Signals) Gp, 1945–50; Guided Weapons Dept, RAE, 1953–56; exchange duty, HQ USAF, 1958–60; space res., Min. of Supply, 1960–63; DS, RAF Staff Coll., 1963–65; OC Eng, No 2 Flying Trng Sch., Syerston, 1966–68; Asst Dir, Guided Weapons R&D, Min. of Tech., 1968–70; OC RAF Central Servicing Develt Estabt, Swanton Morley, 1970–72; SASO, HQ No 90 (Signals) Gp, 1972–74; RCDS, 1974; Dir of Signals (Air), MoD, 1975–76; Dir Gen. Strategic Electronic Systems, MoD (PE), 1976–79; Air Officer Engineering, RAF Strike Command, 1979–81; Chief Engineer, RAF, 1981–83. Exec., BAe, 1983–91, retd. FREng (FEng 1989). *Recreations:* tennis, gardening. *Address:* The Old Rectory, Church Street, Semington, Wilts BA14 6JW. *Clubs:* Royal Air Force; Bath and County (Bath).

MORRIS, Alfred Cosier, CBE 2003; DL; Vice Chancellor, University of the West of England, Bristol, 1992–2005 (Director, Bristol Polytechnic, 1986–92); *b* 12 Nov. 1941; *s* of late Stanley Bernard Morris, Anlaby, E Yorks, and Jennie Fletcher; *m* 1970, Annette, *er d* of Eamonn and May Donovan, Cork, Eire; one *d*. *Educ:* Hymers Coll., Hull (E Riding Scholar); Univ. of Lancaster (MA Financial Control 1970). FCA; FSS. Articled clerk to Oliver Mackrill & Co., 1958–63; Company Sec., Financial Controller and Dir, several cos, 1963–71; Sen. Leverhulme Res. Fellow in Univ. Planning and Orgn, Univ. of Sussex, 1971–74; Vis. Lectr in Financial Management, Univ. of Warwick, 1973; Group Management Accountant, Arthur Guinness Ltd, 1974–76; Management Consultant, Deloitte Haskins & Sells, 1976–77; Financial Adviser, subsids of Arthur Guinness, 1977–80; Dep. Dir, Polytechnic of the South Bank, 1980–85, Acting Dir, 1985–86. Adviser to H of C Select Cttee on Educn, Sci. and Arts, 1979–83. Chm., PCFC Cttee on Performance Indicators in Higher Educn, 1989–90; Member: CNAA, 1988–93; HEFCW, 1992–2000 (Chm., Audit Cttee, 1997–2000); Higher Educn Quality Council, 1992–94; South West Arts, 1994–2000; Bd, Westec, 1995–98; FEFCE, 1997–99 (Chm., Audit Cttee, 1997–99). Dir, Bristol and West, 1992–2002. Dir, SW Urban Regeneration Fund, 2003–08. Chairman: Bristol Old Vic Trust, 1992–94; Patrons of Bristol Old Vic, 1993–; Mem. Council, Bristol Old Vic Theatre Sch., 2006–; Chm., N Bristol NHS Trust, 2006–08; Mem., SW of England RDA, 1998–2002; Trustee: Bristol Cathedral Trust, 1988–2007; John Cabot's Matthew Trust, 1996–2002; Bristol Charities, 2006–; Mem. Exec. Cttee, Bristol Soc., 1992–. Pres., City Acad. Bristol, 2003–06; Dir, e-Univs Holding Co., 2002–04. Mem. Council, Clifton High Sch., 1995–2004. Patron: DAVAR, 1999–; Fast Track Trust, 2000–; Bristol Drugs Project, 2002–; Trustee: Quartet Community (formerly Gtr Bristol) Foundn, 1999–2004 (Chm., 1999–2000); Patrons of the RWA, 2000–06. Ringer, Antient Soc. of St Stephen's Ringers, 2007–; Mem., Soc. of Merchant Venturers of Bristol, 2004–; Pres., Dolphin Soc., 2008–09. DL, 2002, High Sheriff, 2006–07, Glos. Hon. Fellow: Humberside Univ., 1990; RWA, 2001. Hon. LLD: Bristol, 1993; UWE, 2006; Gloucestershire, 2007. *Publications:* (ed jtly and contrib.) Resources and Higher Education, 1982; articles and contribs to jls on higher educn. *Recreations:* sailing, wind-surfing. *Address:* Park Court, Sodbury Common, Old Sodbury BS37 6PX. *T:* (01454) 319900. *Club:* Salcombe Yacht.

MORRIS, Sir Allan Lindsay, 11th Bt *cr* 1806, of Clasemont, Glamorganshire; *b* 27 Nov. 1961; *o s* of Sir Robert Morris, 10th Bt and of Christine Morris (*née* Field); *S* father, 1999, but his name does not appear on the Official Roll of the Baronetage; *m* 1986, Cheronne Denise, *e d* of Dale Whitford; two *s* one *d*. *Heir: er s* Sennen John Morris, *b* 5 June 1995. *Address:* Georgetown, Halton Hills, ON, Canada.

MORRIS, Andrew Bernard; Chief Executive, NEC Group, since 2004; *b* 16 Oct. 1952; *s* of Sam and Golda Morris; *m* 1976, Jennifer Maizner; one *s* two *d*. *Educ:* Christ's Coll., London; Coll. for the Distributive Trades; Harvard Business Sch. Sales and Marketing Dir, City Industrial Ltd, 1980–84; Jt Man. Dir, 1984–86, Man. Dir, 1986–89, Sales and Mktg Dir, 1989–99, Business Design Centre; CEO, 1999–2004, non-exec. Chm., 2004, Earls Court & Olympia Gp Ltd. *Recreations:* tennis, cycling, reading. *Address:* National Exhibition Centre Ltd, Birmingham B40 1NT. *T:* (0121) 767 3334, *Fax:* (0121) 767 3865; *e-mail:* andrew.morris@necgroup.co.uk.

MORRIS, Andrew James; HM Diplomatic Service, retired; High Commissioner, Kingdom of Tonga, and Consul for Pacific Islands under American sovereignty South of the Equator, 1994–98; *b* 22 March 1939; *s* of late Albert Morris and of Clara Morris; *m* 1961, Ann Christine Healy; two *s*. Served Army, 1960–64. Entered FO, 1964; served Kuwait, Salisbury, Sofia, Muscat, and San Francisco, 1965–78; Consul, Los Angeles, 1978–82; FCO, 1982–86; First Sec., Kaduna, 1986–89; Dep. High Comr, Port Moresby, 1989–93; First Sec., FCO, 1993–94. *Recreations:* golf, travel.

MORRIS, Anne; *see* Molyneux, A.

MORRIS, Anthony Paul; QC 1991; **His Honour Judge Anthony Morris;** a Circuit Judge, since 2003; *b* 6 March 1948; *s* of late Isaac Morris Morris and Margaret Miriam Morris; *m* 1975, Jennie Foley; two *s*. *Educ:* Manchester Grammar Sch.; Keble Coll., Oxford (MA). Called to the Bar, Gray's Inn, 1970, Bencher, 2001; practising on Northern Circuit, 1970–2003. A Recorder of the Crown Court, 1988–2003. *Recreations:* travel, the arts, tennis, golf, gardening, Aldeburgh. *Address:* Central Criminal Court, Old Bailey, EC4M 7EH.

MORRIS, Air Marshal Sir (Arnold) Alec; *see* Morris, Air Marshal Sir Alec.

MORRIS, Carolyn; *see* Quinn, C.

MORRIS, Rt Hon. Charles Richard; PC 1978; DL; Chairman, Ponti's Group Ltd, 2001–05 (Deputy Chairman, 1987–2001); *b* 14 Dec. 1926; *s* of late George Henry Morris, Newton Heath, Manchester; *m* 1950, Pauline, *d* of Albert Dunn, Manchester; two *d*. *Educ:* Brookdale Park Sch., Manchester. Served with Royal Engineers, 1945–48. Pres., Clayton Labour Party, 1950–52. Mem. of Manchester Corporation, 1954–64: Chm. of Transport Cttee, 1959–62; Dep. Chm. of Establishment Cttee, 1963–64. Mem., Post Office Workers Union (Mem. Nat. Exec. Council, 1959–63). Contested (Lab) Cheadle Div. of Cheshire, 1959. MP (Lab) Manchester, Openshaw, Dec. 1963–1983; PPS to the Postmaster-General, 1964; Govt Asst Whip, 1966–67; Vice-Chamberlain, HM Household, 1967–69; Treasurer, HM Household (Deputy Chief Whip), 1969–70; PPS to Rt Hon. H. Wilson, MP, 1970–74; Minister of State: DoE, March–Oct. 1974; CSD, 1974–79; Dep. Shadow Leader of the House, 1980–83. Sec., NW Gp of Labour MPs, 1979–83. Chm., Oldham-Rochdale Groundwork Trust, 1984–99; Chm., Covent Garden Tenants' Adv. Gp, 1990–2005; Gov., Disley Sch., 1992–97. DL Greater Manchester, 1985. *Address:* Derwent Reach, Aston Lane, Oker, Matlock DE4 2JP. *T:* (01629) 732738.

See also Baron Morris of Manchester, Baroness Morris of Yardley.

MORRIS, Christopher; Senior Partner, Corporate Recovery, Deloitte & Touche, 1980–2000; *b* 28 April 1942; *s* of Richard Archibald Sutton Morris and Josephine Fanny Mary Morris (*née* Galliano); *m* 1968, Isabel Claire Ramsden Knowles (marr. diss.); two *s*. *Educ:* privately. FCA 1967. Partner, Touche Ross & Co., later Deloitte & Touche, 1970–2000; Nat. Dir, Corporate Special Services, 1975; Chm., 1992. Major insolvency assignments: Banco Ambrosiano; Laker Airways; Rush & Tomkins; Polly Peck, BCCI. Chm., Insolvency Management Ltd, subseq. IM Litigation Funding Ltd, 2002–; Dir, Begbies Traynor, 2004–. *Recreations:* racing, music, travel, food and wine, countryside. *Clubs:* Turf, Garrick.

MORRIS, Rev. Dr Colin; writer and broadcaster; Director, Centre for Religious Communication, Westminster College, Oxford, 1991–96; *b* 13 Jan. 1929; *o s* of Daniel Manley Morris and Mary Alice Morris, Bolton, Lancs; *m* 1985, Sandy James. *Educ:* Bolton County Grammar Sch.; Lincoln Coll., Oxford; Univ. of Manchester. Served RM, 1947–49. Student, Nuffield Coll., Oxford, 1953–56; ordained into Methodist ministry, 1956; Missionary, Northern Rhodesia, 1956–60; President: United Church of Central Africa, 1960–64; United Church of Zambia, 1965–68; Minister of Wesley's Chapel, London, 1969–73; Gen. Sec., Overseas Div., Methodist Church, 1973–78; Pres. of the Methodist Conference, 1976–77; Hd of Religious Programmes, BBC TV, 1978–84; Dep. Hd, 1978–79, Hd, 1979–87, Religious Broadcasting, BBC; Special Adviser to Dir-Gen., BBC, 1986–87; Controller, BBC NI, 1987–90. Chairman: Community and Race Relations Unit, BCC, 1974–76; Bd of Trustees, Refugee Legal Centre, 1993–95; Mem., Lord Chancellor's Adv. Cttee on Legal Educn and Conduct, 1991–94. Presenter, Sunday, BBC Radio 4, 1994–97. Lectures: Willson, Univ. of Nebraska, 1968; Cousland, Univ. of Toronto, 1972; Voigt, S Illinois Conf. United Methodist Church, 1973; Hickman, Duke University, North Carolina, 1974; Palmer, Pacific NW Univ., 1976; Heslington, Univ. of York, 1983; Hibbert, BBC Radio 4, 1986; William Barclay Meml, Glasgow, 1986; Univ. of Ulster Convocation, 1988; St Cuthbert's, Edinburgh, 1990; Studdert-Kennedy, Univ. of Leeds, 1994; Coll. of Preachers, 1995; Randall Preaching, Toronto, 1996; Hanna-Loane Lecture, 50th Anniversary Ulster Surgeon's Club, 2005. Select Preacher, Univ. of Cambridge, 1975, Oxford, 1976. Holds several hon. degrees. Officer-Companion, Order of Freedom (Zambia), 1966. *Publications:* Black Government (with President K. D. Kaunda), 1960; Hour After Midnight, 1961; Out of Africa's Crucible, 1961; End of the Missionary, 1961; Church and Challenge in a New Africa, 1965; Humanist in Africa (with President K. D. Kaunda), 1966; Include Me Out, 1968; Unyoung, Uncoloured, Unpoor, 1969; What the Papers Didn't Say, 1971; Mankind My Church, 1971; The Hammer of the Lord, 1973; Epistles to the Apostle, 1974; The Word and the Words, 1975; Bugles in the Afternoon, 1977; Get Through Till Nightfall, 1979; (ed) Kaunda on Violence, 1980; God-in-a-Box: Christian strategy in the TV age, 1984; A Week in the Life of God, 1986; Drawing the Line: taste and standards in BBC programmes, 1987; Starting from Scratch, 1990; Let God be God: TV sermons, 1990; Wrestling with an Angel, 1990; Start Your Own Religion, 1992; Raising the Dead: the art of preacher as public performer, 1996; God in the Shower: thoughts for the day, 2002; Bible Reflections Round the Year, 2005; Thing Shaken, Things Unshaken: reflections on faith and terror, 2006; Snapshots: episodes in a life, 2007; *relevant publications:* Spark in the Stubble, by T. L. Charlton, 1969; Bullet-Point Belief: the best of Colin Morris, by Rosemary Foxcroft, 2007. *Recreations:* writing, walking, music. *Address:* Tile Cottage, 8 Houndean Rise, Lewes, E Sussex BN7 1EG; *e-mail:* colinmmorris@aol.com.

MORRIS, Rev. Prof. Colin, FBA 2007; Professor of Medieval History, University of Southampton, 1969–92, now Emeritus; *b* 16 Sept. 1928; *s* of Henry Morris and Catherine Victoria Morris; *m* 1956, Brenda Gale; two *s* one *d. Educ:* Queen's College, Oxford (BA Modern Hist. 1st cl. 1948; BA Theol. 1st cl. 1951); Lincoln Theol Coll. Ordained deacon, 1953, priest, 1954. Fellow and Chaplain, Pembroke Coll., Oxford, 1953–69, now Emeritus. Pres., Ecclesiastical Hist. Soc., 1998–2000. FRHistS 1970. *Publications:* The Discovery of the Individual, 1972; The Papal Monarchy: the Western Church from 1050 to 1250, 1989; (ed with P. Roberts) Pilgrimage: the English experience from Becket to Bunyan, 2002; The Sepulchre of Christ and the Medieval West, 2005. *Recreations:* travel, liturgy, family and friends. *Address:* 12 Bassett Crescent East, Southampton SO16 7PB. *T:* (023) 8076 8176; *e-mail:* cm5@soton.ac.uk.

MORRIS, David; *see* Morris, W. D.

MORRIS, David Elwyn; a District Judge (formerly Registrar) of the Principal Registry of the Family Division of the High Court of Justice, 1976–91; *b* 22 May 1920; *s* of Rev. S. M. Morris and K. W. Morris; *m* 1st, 1947, Joyce Hellyer (*d* 1977); one *s* one *d*; 2nd, 1978, Gwendolen Pearce (*d* 1988), *widow* of Dr John Pearce; 3rd, 1990, Mrs C. M. Tudor. *Educ:* Mill Hill Sch.; Brasenose Coll., Oxford (Hulme Exhibnr; MA). With Friends' Ambulance Unit in China, 1942–44; served British Army in India, 1944–46. Called to Bar, Inner Temple, 1949; admitted Solicitor of the Supreme Court, 1955; Mem., Matrimonial Causes Rule Cttee, 1967–75. Partner, Jaques & Co. until 1975. Adv. Editor, Atkin's Encyclopaedia of Court Forms in Civil Proceedings, 1982–88. *Publications:* China Changed My Mind, 1948; The End of Marriage, 1971; contrib. Marriage For and Against, 1972; Pilgrim through this Barren Land, 1974. *Recreation:* reading. *Address:* 42 Frenchay Road, Oxford OX2 6TG. *T:* (01865) 558390. *Club:* Oxford and Cambridge.

MORRIS, David Griffiths; His Honour Judge David Morris; a Circuit Judge, since 1994; *b* 10 March 1940; *s* of Thomas Griffiths Morris and Margaret Eileen Morris; *m* 1971, Carolyn Mary (*née* Miller); one *s* one *d. Educ:* Abingdon Sch.; King's Coll., Univ. of London (LLB Hons). Called to the Bar, Lincoln's Inn, 1965, Bencher, 1999. Pupillage in London (Temple and Lincoln's Inn), 1965–67; Tenant in London Chambers (Temple), 1967–72; Tenant in Cardiff Chambers, 1972–94; Asst Recorder, 1979–84; Local Junior for Cardiff Bar, 1981–87; Head of Chambers, 1984–94, a Recorder, 1984–94. Judicial Member: Gwent Probation Bd, 1998–; Gwent Courts Bd, 2004–07; SE Wales Courts Bd, 2007–. Founder Member: Llantwit Major Round Table and 41 Clubs; Llantwit Major Rotary Club (Pres., 1984–85); Llanmaes Community Council, 1982–84. *Recreations:* Rugby Union football, cricket, swimming, theatre, reading, gardening, family. *Address:* Bryn Hafren, Newport Road, Castleton, Cardiff CF3 2UN. *T:* (01633) 681244. *Clubs:* Cardiff and County, United Services Mess (Cardiff); Pontypool Rugby Football (Past Pres.).

MORRIS, David Richard, CEng, FIMechE; Chairman, Northern Electric plc, 1989–97; *b* 25 July 1934; *s* of Frederick George Morris and Marjorie Amy (*née* Brown); *m* 1961, (Ann) Carole Birch; two *s* one *d. Educ:* Imperial College (BScEng). ACGI. Graduate Engrg apprenticeship, D. Napier & Son, Divl Chief Develt Engr and Gen. Manager, 1956–69, English Electric; Divl Gen. Manager and Divl Dir, General Electric Co., 1969–75; Subsid. Co. Man. Dir, Sears Holdings plc, 1975–80; Delta Group plc: Divl Man. Dir, 1980–84; Gp Exec. Dir, 1984–88. *Recreations:* sailing, golf, tennis, gardening.

MORRIS, Capt. David Simon, RN; Clerk to the Salters' Company, since 2006; *b* 4 Feb. 1951; *s* of late Basil Charles Owen Morris and Alice Joan Morris (*née* Crump); *m* 1987, Susie Turner; two *d. Educ:* Sedbergh Sch.; BRNC, Dartmouth. Joined RN, 1971; specialised in submarines and navigation; served in HM Ships Albion, Norfolk, Olympus, Repulse, Resolution, Osiris, Ocelot, 1972–81; Flag Lieut to Flag Officer Submarines, 1978–80; qualified Submarine Commnd, 1983; Exec. Officer, HMS Churchill, 1983–85; Defence Intelligence, MoD, 1985–87; commanded: HMS Onyx, 1987–89; HMS Revenge, 1991; HMS Renown (P), 1992–94; Dir, UK Strategic Targeting Centre, 1994–96; Cabinet Office, 1996–99; Dep. ACOS (Progs and Policy) to C-in-C Fleet, 1999–2001; Asst Dir, Directorate of Naval Ops and Strategic Plans, MoD, 2001–04; Navy Job Evaluation Judge, 2004–05. FCMI 2004; MNI 2004. Technical Deleg. (Alpine, Constitutent), 1995–; Chm., Combined Services Winter Sports Assoc. (Alpine), 1999–2004; Dir, Kandahar Ski Club, 2001–06. Freeman, Master Mariners' Co., 2004. Friend of RN Submarine Mus., 1999–. *Recreations:* ski-ing, relearning violin and piano with children, riding by proxy (through older daughter's interest), vintage cars and boats (owned both once but on hold until horses and education end), sailing, tennis, countryside. *Address:* Salters' Hall, 4 Fore Street, EC2Y 5DE. *T:* (020) 7588 5216, *Fax:* (020) 7638 3679; *e-mail:* clerk@salters.co.uk. *Clubs:* Hurlingham, Royal Navy of 1765 and 1785; Kandahar Ski.

MORRIS, Prof. David William, PhD; FRAgS; sheep farmer, since 1983; agricultural consultant, since 1986; *b* 7 Dec. 1937; *s* of late David William Morris and Mary Olwen Ann Lewis; *m* 1966, Cynthia Cooper; one *s* one *d. Educ:* Ardwyn Grammar Sch.; UC of Wales (BSc Agric.); Univ. of Newcastle upon Tyne (PhD). FRAgS 1974. Develt Officer, Agric. Div., ICI, 1963–64; Asst Dir, Cockle Park Exptl Farm, Newcastle upon Tyne Univ., 1964–68; Farms Manager for Marquis of Lansdowne, Bowood, Wilts, 1968–70; Principal, Welsh Agric. Coll., Aberystwyth, 1970–83; Prof. of Agric., UC Wales, Aberystwyth, 1979–83. Churchill Fellowship, 1973. Chm., Lleyn Sheep Soc., 2005–; Hon. Life Mem., British Charollais Sheep Soc., 2001. *Publications:* Practical Milk Production, 1976, 3rd edn 1977; (with M. M. Cooper) Grass Farming, 5th edn 1984. *Recreation:* farming. *Address:* Yr Ostrey, St Clears, Carmarthen, Carmarthenshire SA33 4AJ. *T:* (01994) 230240.

See also Baron Morris of Aberavon.

MORRIS, Sir Derek (James), Kt 2003; DPhil; Provost of Oriel College, Oxford, since 2004 (Fellow and Tutor in Economics, 1970–98, now Emeritus Fellow); *b* 23 Dec. 1945; *s* of Denis William and Olive Margaret Morris; *m* 1975, Susan Mary Whittles; two *s. Educ:* Harrow County Grammar Sch.; St Edmund Hall, Oxford (MA; Hon. Fellow); Nuffield Coll., Oxford; DPhil. Research Fellow, Centre for Business and Industrial Studies, Warwick Univ., 1969–70; Tutor and Sen. Tutor, Oxford University Business Summer Sch., 1970–78; Visiting Fellow, Oxford Centre for Management Studies, 1977–81; Economic Dir, Nat. Economic Develt Office, 1981–84; Oxford University: Sir John Hicks Res. Fellow, 1991–92; Chm., Social Studies Bd, 1993–94; Reader in Econs, 1996–98; Chm., Competition (formerly Monopolies and Mergers) Commn, 1998–2004 (Mem., 1991–2004; Dep. Chm., 1995–98). Vis. Lectr, Univ. of Calif, Irvine, 1986–87. Mem., Cttee of Inquiry into the Future of Cowley, 1990; Chm., Morris Review of Actuarial Profession, 2004–05; Mem., Cttee on Standards in Public Life, 2008–. Gov., NIESR, 1997–. Chm., Oxford Economic Forecasting, 1984–98; Dir, Oxford China Economics Ltd, 1993–97; Chm., Trustees, OUP Pension Fund, 2006–. Member Editorial Board: Oxford Economic Papers, 1984–97; Annual Register of World Events, 1985–97; Asst Editor, Jl of Industrial Economics, 1984–87; Associate Editor, Oxford Review of Economic Policy, 1985–98. Hon. Fellow, TCD, 2004. Hon. DCL: UC Dublin, 2004; UEA, 2005; Hon. DSc Cranfield, 2006. *Publications:* (ed) The Economic System in the UK, 1977, 3rd edn 1985; (with D. Hay) Industrial Economics, Theory and Evidence, 1979, 2nd edn 1991; (with D. Hay) Unquoted Companies, 1984; (ed jtly) Strategic Behaviour and Industrial Competition, 1987; (with D. Hay) State-Owned Enterprises and Economic Reform in China 1979–87, 1993; articles on unemployment, trade policy and performance, productivity growth, industrial policy, macroeconomic policy, the Chinese economy, exchange rates, profitability, the stock market and corporate control. *Recreations:* ski-ing, badminton, Rugby, reading history. *Clubs:* Reform, Oxford and Cambridge.

MORRIS, Desmond John, DPhil; writer on animal and human behaviour; *b* 24 Jan. 1928; *s* of late Capt. Harry Howe Morris and Dorothy Marjorie Fuller Morris (*née* Hunt); *m* 1952, Ramona Baulch; one *s. Educ:* Dauntsey's Sch.; Birmingham Univ. (BSc); Magdalen Coll., Oxford (DPhil). Postdoctoral research in Animal Behaviour, Dept of Zoology, Oxford Univ., 1954–56; Head of Granada TV and Film Unit at Zool. Soc. of London, 1956–59; Curator of Mammals, Zool. Soc. of London, 1959–67; Dir, Inst. of Contemp. Arts, London, 1967–68; Research Fellow, Wolfson Coll., Oxford, 1973–81. Chm. of TV programmes: Zootime (weekly), 1956–67; Life (fortnightly), 1965–68; TV series: The Human Race, 1982; The Animals Roadshow, 1987–89; The Animal Contract, 1990; Animal Country, 1991–95; The Human Animal, 1994; The Human Sexes, 1997. Hon. FLS 2006. Hon. DSc Reading, 1998. *Publications:* (Jt Ed.) International Zoo Yearbook, 1959–62; The Biology of Art, 1962; The Mammals: A Guide to the Living Species, 1965; (with Ramona Morris) Men and Snakes, 1965; (with Ramona Morris) Men and Apes, 1966; (with Ramona Morris) Men and Pandas, 1966; The Naked Ape, 1967; (ed) Primate Ethology, 1967; The Human Zoo, 1969; Patterns of Reproductive Behaviour, 1970; Intimate Behaviour, 1971; Manwatching: a field guide to human behaviour, 1977; (jtly) Gestures: their origins and distribution, 1979; Animal Days (autobiog.), 1979; The Giant Panda, 1981; The Soccer Tribe, 1981; Inrock (novel), 1983; The Book of Ages, 1983; The Art of Ancient Cyprus, 1985; Bodywatching: a field guide to the human species, 1985; The Illustrated Naked Ape, 1986; Catwatching, 1986; Dogwatching, 1986; The Secret Surrealist, 1987; Catlore, 1987; The Human Nest-builders, 1988; The Animals Roadshow, 1988; Horsewatching, 1988; The Animal Contract, 1990; Animal-Watching, 1990; Babywatching, 1991; Christmas Watching, 1992; The World of Animals, 1993; The Human Animal, 1994; The Naked Ape Trilogy, 1994; Bodytalk: a world guide to gestures, 1994; The Illustrated Catwatching, 1994; Illustrated Babywatching, 1995; Catworld: a feline encyclopedia, 1996; Illustrated Dogwatching, 1996; The Human Sexes, 1997; Illustrated Horsewatching, 1998; Cool Cats: the 100 cat breeds of the world, 1999; Body Guards: protective amulets and charms, 1999; The Naked Eye: travels in search of the human species, 2000; Dogs: the ultimate dictionary of over 1,000 dog breeds, 2001; Peoplewatching, 2002; The Nature of Happiness, 2004; The Naked Woman: a study of the female body, 2004; Watching: encounters with humans and other animals, 2006; The Naked Man: a study of the male body, 2008; numerous papers in zoological jls. *Recreations:* book-collecting, archæology. *Address:* c/o Jonathan Cape, Random Century House, 20 Vauxhall Bridge Road, SW1V 2SA; *web:* desmond-morris.com.

MORRIS, Desmond Victor; HM Diplomatic Service, retired; *b* 26 June 1926; *s* of late John Walter Morris and Bessie (*née* Mason); *m* 1st, 1951, Peggy Iris Mumford; two *d*; 2nd, 1961, Patricia Irene Ward, *d* of Charles Daniel and Emma Camwell; one *d. Educ:* Portsmouth Southern Secondary Sch. for Boys; Durham Univ. Served RAF, 1945–48. Joined HM Diplomatic Service, 1948; served at Seattle, Budapest, Saigon, Addis Ababa, Berne, Ankara and Pretoria; Dep. High Comr, Georgetown, 1973–78; Dep. Head of Accommodation and Services Dept, FCO, 1979–82; Consul-Gen. and Counsellor (Administration), Washington, 1982–86. *Recreations:* gardening, music, art. *Address:* Grayshott, Green Lane, Axminster, Devon EX13 5TD.

MORRIS, Frances Mary; Head of Collections, International Art, Tate, since 2007; *b* London, 13 Jan. 1959; *d* of Alan Croft Faulkner Morris and Elizabeth Villar; *m* 1989, Martin Caiger-Smith; two *s* one *d. Educ:* King's Coll., Cambridge (BA 1st cl. 1982); Courtauld Inst. of Art (MA Hist. of Art 1983). Curator, Tate Gall., 1987–97; Art Prog.

Curator, Tate Gall. of Modern Art, 1997–2000; Hd of Displays, and Curator, Modern and Contemp. Art, Tate Modern, 2000–07. Mem., Internat. Cttee for Mus and Collections of Modern Art, ICOM, 2000–. *Publications:* Paris Post War: art and existentialism, 1993; (with S. Morgan) Rites of Passage, 1995; (with R. Flood) Zero to Infinity: Arte Povera 1962–72, 2001; (with Christopher Green) Jungles in Paris, 2005; Tate Modern: the handbook, 2006; Louise Bourgeois, 2007. *Recreations:* sailing, walking. *Address:* 35 Aldebert Terrace, SW8 1BH. *T:* (020) 7735 2459; *e-mail:* frances.morris@tate.org.uk.

MORRIS, Hon. Frederick Reginald; President of the High Court, Republic of Ireland, 1998–2001; *b* 1 Dec. 1929; *s* of Michael Archdale Morris and Mary Archdale Morris (*née* Guiry); *m* 1965, Valerie Rose Farrell; two *d. Educ:* Glenstall Abbey Sch.; University Coll., Dublin; King's Inns, Dublin. Called to the Irish Bar, 1959 (Bencher, 1990), Inner Bar, 1973, Hon. Bencher, King's Inns, 2001; called to the Bar, Middle Temple, 1969, Hon. Bencher, 1999; Judge, High Court in Ireland, 1990–98; Mem., Council of State, 1998–2001. Chm., Tribunal of Inquiry into allegations of misconduct by mems of An Garda Siochana. Trustee, Acad. of Eur. Law, Trier. Freeman, City of Waterford, 1963. *Recreations:* sailing, golf, Rugby. *Address:* 17 Leeson Village, Upper Leeson Street, Dublin 4, Republic of Ireland; Four Courts, Dublin 7, Republic of Ireland. *Clubs:* Royal Irish Yacht (Dun Laoghaire); Milltown Golf (Dublin), Blainroe Golf (Co. Wicklow); University College Dublin Rugby.

MORRIS, Gareth; *see* Morris, John G.

MORRIS, Prof. Gillian Susan, PhD; Professor Associate, Brunel University, since 2003; barrister in private practice; *b* 30 March 1953; *d* of late Edgar and Eve Morris; partner, David Millett. *Educ:* Univ. of Bristol (LLB Hons 1974); Churchill Coll., Cambridge (PhD 1978). Lectr in Law, Nottingham Univ., 1977–79; Sen. Lectr in Law, Poly. of N London, 1980–88; Lectr, 1988–91, Reader, 1991–93, Prof. of Law, 1993–2003, Brunel Univ. Hon. Prof., Univ. of Warwick, 2007–. Called to the Bar, Inner Temple, 1997. Labour Law Expert for ILO, 1990–; Legal Expert Advr to EC, later EU, 1991–. Chair, Rev. Body for Nursing and Other Health Professions, later NHS Pay Rev. Body, 2005–; Deputy Chair: Central Arbitration Cttee, 2000–; Police Negotiating Bd and Police Adv. Bd for England and Wales, 2005–; Mem., Panel of Arbitrators, ACAS, 2007–. *Publications:* Strikes in Essential Services, 1986; (with S. Fredman) The State as Employer: labour law in the public services, 1989; (with T. J. Archer) Trade Unions, Employers and the Law, 1992, 2nd edn 1993; (with S. Deakin) Labour Law, 1995, 4th edn 2005; (with T. J. Archer) Collective Labour Law, 2000; contrib. articles to legal jls. *Recreations:* walking, swimming, travel, the arts. *Address:* Matrix Chambers, Griffin Building, Gray's Inn, WC1R 5LN.

MORRIS, Grant, OBE 1994; RCNC; Commercial Director, NATO Eurofighter and Tornado Management Agency, since 2008; *b* 28 May 1951; *s* of Lesley and Gena Morris; *m* 1975, Amanda Morgan; two *s* one *d. Educ:* Univ. of Bath (BSc Hons Engrg 1974). RCNC 1976; CEng, MIMechE 1979; MCIPS 2003. Proj. Manager, HMS Ocean, 1994–96; MoD, 1996; HQ QMG, 1997; Internat. Relns, MoD, 1997–2000; RCDS, 2001; Dir Commercial, 2002–06, Dir Gen. Commercial, 2006–07, Defence Logistics Orgn; Dir Gen. Commercial, Defence Equipment and Support, MoD 2007–08. Member: RYA; RNSA. *Recreations:* sailing, diving, cookery, travel, ski-ing, martial arts. *Address:* 5B Markweg, Ottering 83624, Germany; *e-mail:* foxys@ukgateway.net.

MORRIS, Prof. Howard Redfern, FRS 1988; Professor of Biological Chemistry, Imperial College, University of London, 1980–2001, now Professor Emeritus and Senior Research Investigator; *b* 4 Aug. 1946; *s* of Marion Elizabeth and Herbert Morris, Bolton, Lancs; *m* 1st, 1969, Lene Verny Jensen (marr. diss.); two *d*; 2nd, 1988, Maria Panico; one *s* one *d. Educ:* Univ. of Leeds (BSc 1967; PhD 1970). SRC Fellow, Cambridge, 1970–72; Scientific Staff, MRC Lab. of Molecular Biol., Cambridge, 1972–75; Imperial College: Lectr, Dept of Biochem., 1975–78; Reader in Protein Chem., 1978–80; Hd, Dept of Biochem., 1985–88; Chm., Div. of Life Sciences, 1985–88. Founder Chm., M-Scan Ltd, analytical chem. consultants, 1979–. Visiting Professor: Univ. of Virginia, 1978; Soviet Acad. of Scis, 1982; Univ. of Naples, 1983; Life Scis Div., E. I. Dupont, USA, 1984–85; Dow Lectr in Analytical Chem., Univ. of British Columbia, 1989–90. Royal Soc. Rep. to Council, Inst. of Cancer Res., 1994–98 (Council Mem. and Trustee, 1994–2004). Mem., EMBO, 1979–. BDH Gold Medal and Prize for analytical biochem., Biochem. Soc., 1978; Medal and Prize for macromolecules and polymers, RSC, 1982; Gold Medal for contribs to biopolymer sequencing and mass spectroscopy, Univ. of Naples/CNR Italy, 1989. *Publications:* (ed) Soft Ionisation Biological Mass Spectrometry, 1981; some 350 contribs to learned jls, on mass spectrometry, protein and glycoprotein structure elucidation, enkephalin, SRS-A leukotrienes, interleukin and calcitonin gene related peptide. *Recreations:* fell walking, gardening, guitar. *Address:* Department of Biological Sciences, Wolfson Laboratories, Imperial College, Prince Consort Road, SW7 2AZ. *T:* (020) 7594 5221, *Fax:* (020) 7225 0458; *e-mail:* h.morris@imperial.ac.uk, h.morris@m-scan.com.

MORRIS, Ian; *see* Morris, James I.

MORRIS, James; *see* Morris, Jan.

MORRIS, Air Vice-Marshal James, CBE 1984 (OBE 1977); Chief Executive, Scottish Society for the Prevention of Cruelty to Animals, 1991–2001; *b* 8 July 1936; *s* of late James and Davina Swann Morris; *m* 1959, Anna Wann Provan; three *s. Educ:* Kirkcaldy High Sch.; Edinburgh Univ. (BSc). Commnd RAF, 1957; Flying/Staff Duties, RAF, USN, RN, 1960–72; Sqn Comdr 201 Sqdn, 1975–77; psc 1978; Station Comdr RAF Kinloss, 1981–84; Dir Operational Requirements (Air), MoD, 1986–89; AO Scotland and NI, 1989–91. President: Scottish Area, RAFA, 1991–2006; Scottish Union Jack Assoc., 1995–2006. Regl Chm., Scottish and NI Air Cadets, 1995–97. HM Comr, Queen Victoria Sch., Dunblane, 1995–2005. Mem., Governing Bd, Scottish Food Quality Certification Ltd, 1998–2001; Chm., Mgt Bd, RAF Benevolent Fund Home, Alastrean House, 2001–05. *Recreation:* golf. *Address:* 22 The Inches, Dalgety Bay, Fife KY11 9YG. *Club:* Royal Air Force.

MORRIS, His Honour (James) Ian; a Circuit Judge, 1994–2007; *b* 6 Feb. 1944; *s* of late Thomas Orlando Morris and of Pearl Morris; *m* 1st, 1966, Maureen Burton (marr. diss. 1978); one *s* one *d*; 2nd, 1979, Christine Dyson (*d* 1980); 3rd, 1982, Alison Turner (marr. diss. 1988); 4th, 1998, Jane Boddington. *Educ:* King Henry VIII Grammar Sch., Coventry; Corpus Christi Coll., Oxford (BA Jurisp. 1967; MA 1970). Called to the Bar, Inner Temple, 1968; Asst Recorder, 1984, Recorder, 1988–94, Midland and Oxford Circuit. Chairman: Sandwell AHA Enquiry, 1979; Bromsgrove Hosp. Enquiry, 1982; RHA Counsel, Cttee of Enquiry, Legionnaires' Disease, Stafford, 1985. Founder and first Chm., Birmingham Cancer Support Gp, 1984. Hon. Pres., Council of Valuation Tribunal Members in England, 2006–. *Publications:* Just a Grain of Sand (poetry), 2004; contrib. Internat. Jl of Child Abuse and Neglect. *Recreations:* writing, music, walking. *Address:* c/o Worcester Crown Court, Foregate Street, Worcester.

MORRIS, Jan, CBE 1999; MA Oxon; FRSL; writer; *b* 2 Oct. 1926. Commonwealth Fellow, USA, 1953; Editorial Staff, The Times, 1951–56; Editorial Staff, The Guardian, 1957–62. Fellow, Yr Academi Gymreig; Mem., Gorsedd of Bards, Nat. Eisteddfod of Wales. Hon. FRIBA 1998. Hon. Fellow: UCW, 1992; UCNW, 2003; Hon. Student, Christ Church, Oxford, 2002. Hon. DLitt: Wales, 1993; Glamorgan, 1996. PEN Lifetime Award, 2005; Wales World-Wide Award, 2007. *Publications:* (as James Morris or Jan Morris): Coast to Coast, 1956; Sultan in Oman, 1957; The Market of Seleukia, 1957; Coronation Everest, 1958; South African Winter, 1958; The Hashemite Kings, 1959; Venice, 1960, 3rd edn 1993; The Upstairs Donkey, 1962 (for children); The World Bank, 1963; Cities, 1963; The Presence of Spain, 1964, rev. edn (as Spain), 1988; Oxford, 1965, 2nd edn 1986; Pax Britannica, 1968; The Great Port, 1970; Places, 1972; Heaven's Command, 1973; Conundrum, 1974; Travels, 1976; Farewell the Trumpets, 1978; The Oxford Book of Oxford, 1978; Destinations, 1980; My Favourite Stories of Wales, 1980; The Venetian Empire, 1980, 2nd edn 1988; The Small Oxford Book of Wales, 1982; A Venetian Bestiary, 1982; The Spectacle of Empire, 1982; (with Paul Wakefield) Wales, The First Place, 1982; (with Simon Winchester) Stones of Empire, 1983; The Matter of Wales, 1984, revd edn as Wales, 1998; Journeys, 1984; Among the Cities, 1985; Last Letters from Hav, 1985; (with Paul Wakefield) Scotland, The Place of Visions, 1986; Manhattan '45, 1987; Hong Kong, 1988, 3rd edn 1996; Pleasures of a Tangled Life, 1989; (with Paul Wakefield) Ireland, Your Only Place, 1990; Sydney, 1992; O Canada!, 1992; Locations, 1992; (ed) Travels with Virginia Woolf, 1993; (with Twm Morys) A Machynlleth Triad, 1994; Fisher's Face, 1995; Fifty Years of Europe: an album, 1997; Lincoln: a foreigner's quest, 1999; (with Twm Morys) Our First Leader, 2000; Trieste and the Meaning of Nowhere, 2001; A Writer's House in Wales, 2002; A Writer's World, 2003; Hav, 2006; Europe, 2006. *Address:* Trefan Morys, Llanystumdwy, Gwynedd, Cymru/Wales LL52 0LP. *T:* (01766) 522222; *e-mail:* janmorris1@msn.com.

MORRIS, Prof. Jeremy Noah, CBE 1972; FRCP; Professor of Public Health, University of London, at London School of Hygiene and Tropical Medicine, 1967–78, Hon. Research Officer, since 1978; *b* 6 May 1910; *s* of Nathan and Annie Morris; *m* 1939, Galina Schuchalter (*d* 1997); one *s* one *d. Educ:* Hutcheson's Grammar Sch., Glasgow; Univ. of Glasgow; University Coll. Hosp., London; London School of Hygiene and Tropical Medicine (Hon. Fellow 1979). MA, DSc, DPH. Qual., 1934; hosp. residencies, 1934–37; general practice, 1937–38; Asst MOH, Hendon and Harrow, 1939–41; Med. Spec., RAMC, 1941–46 (Lt-Col 1944–46); Rockefeller Fellow, Prev. Med., 1946–47; Dir, MRC Social Med. Unit, 1948–75; Prof., Social Med., London Hosp., 1959–67. Visiting Professor: Yale, 1957; Berkeley, 1963; Jerusalem, 1968, 1980; Adelaide, 1983. Consultant, Cardiology, WHO, 1960–2003. Lectures: Ernestine Henry, RCP London; Chadwick Trust; Gibson, RCP Edinburgh; Fleming, RCPS Glasgow; Carey Coombs, Univ. of Bristol; Brontë Stewart, Univ. of Glasgow; St Cyres, Nat. Heart Hosp.; Alumnus, Yale; Delamar, Johns Hopkins Univ.; Wade Hampton Frost, APHA; George Clarke, Univ. of Nottingham. Member: Royal Commission on Penal Reform; Cttee, Personal Social Services, Working Party Med. Admin, 1964–72; Health Educn Council, 1978–80; Chairman: Nat. Adv. Cttee on Nutrition Educn, 1979–83; Fitness and Health Adv. Gp, Sports Council and Health Educn Authority, 1980–. Hon. Member: Amer. Epid. Soc., 1976; Soc. for Social Medicine, 1978; British Cardiac Soc., 1982; Swedish Soc. for Sports Medicine, 1984. JP Middx, 1956–66. Hon. FFPH (Hon. FFCM 1977); Hon. FRSocMed 1991. Hon. MD Edinburgh, 1974; Hon. DSc: Hull, 1982; Loughborough, 2002. Bisset Hawkins Medal, RCP, 1980; Honor Award, Amer. Coll. of Sports Medicine, 1985; Jenner Medal, RSM, 1987; Alwyn Smith Medal, FPHM, 1996; Internat. Olympic Gold Medal and Prize in Exercise Sci., 1996; Chadwick Medal, LSHTM, 2002. *Publications:* Uses of Epidemiology, 1957, 3rd edn 1975 (trans. Japanese, Spanish); papers on coronary disease and exercise, and in social medicine. *Recreations:* walking, swimming, piano music. *Address:* 3 Briardale Gardens, NW3 7PN. *T:* (020) 7435 5024; *e-mail:* Jerry.Morris@LSHTM.ac.uk.

MORRIS, John Cameron; QC (Scot.) 1996; Sheriff of South Strathclyde, Dumfries and Galloway at Airdrie, since 1998; *b* 11 April 1952; *s* of Thomas and Louise Morris. *Educ:* Alan Glens Sch., Glasgow; Strathclyde Univ. Solicitor, Scotland, 1976–84; admitted Advocate, Scottish Bar, 1985; called to the Bar, Inner Temple, 1990. Crown Counsel, Scotland, 1989–92. Temp. Sheriff, 1992–98. *Recreations:* golf, music, reading. *Address:* Sheriff Court House, Graham Street, Airdrie ML6 6EE. *T:* (01236) 751121.

MORRIS, John Evan A.; *see* Artro Morris.

MORRIS, Prof. (John) Gareth, CBE 1994; FRS 1988; FIBiol; Professor of Microbiology, University of Wales, Aberystwyth, 1971–2000, now Emeritus; *b* 25 Nov. 1932; *s* of Edwin Morris and Evelyn Amanda Morris (*née* Griffiths); *m* 1962, Áine Mary Kehoe; one *s* one *d. Educ:* Bridgend Grammar Sch.; Univ. of Leeds; Trinity Coll., Oxford. DPhil; FIBiol 1971. Guinness Res. Fellow, Univ. of Oxford, 1957–61; Rockefeller Fellow, Univ. of Calif at Berkeley, 1959–60; Tutor in Biochem., Balliol Coll., Oxford, 1960–61; Lectr, subseq. Sen. Lectr, Univ. of Leicester, 1961–71. Vis. Associate Prof., Purdue Univ., USA, 1965. Member: UGC, 1981–86; Royal Commn on Environmental Pollution, 1991–99. *Publications:* A Biologist's Physical Chemistry, 1968, 2nd edn 1974; contribs on microbial biochemistry and physiology. *Recreations:* gardening, walking. *Address:* Cilgwyn, 16 Lôn Tyllwyd, Llanfarian, Aberystwyth, Dyfed SY23 4UH. *T:* (01970) 612502.

MORRIS, John Michael Douglas; General Secretary, 1986–99, and Company Secretary, 1990–99, Hon. Consultant, since 2000, British Boxing Board of Control; *b* 10 Aug. 1935; *s* of Charles Edward Douglas Morris and Mary Kathleen (*née* Murphy); *m* 1958, Jill Margaret Walker; two *s* two *d. Educ:* John Fisher Sch.; Dulwich Coll. Reporter, Northampton Chronicle & Echo, 1953–60; Sports sub-editor, Evening Standard, 1960–67; Gp Sports Editor, United Newspapers, 1967–77; freelance writer and publican, 1977–79; John Morris Sports Agency, Northampton, 1979–86. Co. Sec., European Boxing Union, 1991–99; Mem., Bd of Govs, World Boxing Council, 1986–99 (Consultant, 2000–). Commissioner of the Year: World Boxing Council, 1987, 1989, 1994, and 1997; World Boxing Assoc., 1988. Pres., Nat. Schs Amateur Boxing Assoc., 2002–. Chair, Towcester and Dist Local History Soc., 2007–. *Publications:* Play Better Tennis (instructional booklet), 1969; Come in No 3: biography of cricketer David Steele, 1977; Box On: biography of boxing referee Harry Gibbs, 1981. *Recreations:* amateur drama, reading, all sport. *Address:* 44 Alchester Court, Towcester, Northants NN12 6RT. *T:* (01327) 358590; *e-mail:* john@morris.2736.fsnet.co.uk.

MORRIS, Sir Keith (Elliot Hedley), KBE 1994; CMG 1988; HM Diplomatic Service, retired; *b* 24 Oct. 1934; *m* Maria del Carmen Carratala; two *s* two *d.* Entered Foreign Office, 1959; served Dakar, Algiers, Paris, Bogota; First Sec., FCO, 1971–76; Counsellor (Commercial), Warsaw, 1976–79; Minister-Counsellor, Mexico City, 1979–84; Head of Personnel Policy Dept, FCO, 1984–85; rcds, 1986; Minister (Commercial) and Consul-Gen., Milan, 1987–90; Ambassador to Colombia, 1990–94. Mem., Internat. Adv. Bd, Parra, Rodriguez & Cavelier, Bogota. Dir, British and Colombian Chamber of

Commerce. Mem., Comité des Sages, Network of European Foundns. *Recreations:* history, hill walking. *Address:* 72 Farquhar Road, SE19 1LT. *Club:* Polish Hearth.

MORRIS, Kenneth; Managing Director, Nirvana Europe Ltd, since 1999; *b* 17 April 1947; *s* of Thomas and Phyllis Morris; *m* 1988, Veronica Ann Young; two *s*. *Educ:* George Stephenson Grammar Sch., West Moor, Newcastle upon Tyne. Group Accountant, Newcastle upon Tyne CBC, 1972; Management Accountant, Tyne and Wear CC, 1974; Chief Accountant, 1976, Dep. Dir of Finance, 1982, Gateshead MBC; County Treasurer, 1988, Man. Dir, 1992–99, Northumberland CC. *Recreations:* sport, reading, music. *Address:* 3 Bank Top, Earsdon, Whitley Bay, Tyne and Wear NE25 9JS. *T:* (0191) 253 4907; (office) Saville Exchange, Howard Street, North Shields, Tyne and Wear NE30 1SE. *T:* (0191) 293 6592.

MORRIS, Mark William; American choreographer, director and dancer; Founder and Artistic Director, Mark Morris Dance Group, since 1980; *b* Seattle, 29 Aug. 1956; *s* of William Morris and Maxine Crittenden Morris. Dir of Dance, Théâtre Royal de la Monnaie, 1988–91; Jt Founder, White Oak Dance Project, 1990; has choreographed more than 120 modern dance works for Mark Morris Dance Gp, including: L'Allegro, il Penseroso ed il Moderato, 1988; Dido and Aeneas (opera), 1988; The Hard Nut, 1991; Four Saints in Three Acts, 2000; V, 2001; All Fours, 2003; Mozart Dances, 2007; choreography for other companies includes: ballets: Drink to Me Only With Thine Eyes, Amer. Ballet Theatre, 1988; Ein Herz, Paris Opera Ballet, 1990; Gong, Amer. Ballet Th., 2001; Sylvia, San Fransisco Ballet, 2004; operas: Nixon in China, Houston Grand Opera, 1987; Orfée et Euridice, Seattle Opera, 1988; The Death of Klinghoffer, Théâtre de la Monnaie, 1991; dir, Die Fledermaus, Seattle Opera, 1990; dir and choreographed, Platée, Royal Opera, 1997; King Arthur, ENO, 2006. Fellow, MacArthur Foundn. *Address:* Mark Morris Dance Group, 3 Lafayette Avenue, Brooklyn, NY 11217, USA.

MORRIS, Michael Clough; a District Judge (Magistrates' Courts), since 2002; *b* 28 Dec. 1946; *s* of Alfred Morris and Mary Morris, MBE, JP; *m* 1973, Hilary; three *s* one *d*. *Educ:* Calday Grange Grammar Sch., W Kirby; Univ. of Leeds (LLB Hons). Admitted solicitor, 1972; Partner, Wilkes Partnership, Birmingham, 1977–2002; Dep. Stipendiary Magistrate, 1995–2002. Birmingham Law Society: Chm., Criminal Law Cttee, 1994–2001; Dep. Vice Pres., 2001–. *Recreations:* fell-walking, golf. *Address:* Walsall Magistrates' Court, Stafford Street, Walsall WS2 8HA.

MORRIS, Michael Jeremy; Director, Cultural Industry Ltd, since 1988; Co-Director, Artangel, since 1991; *b* 30 March 1958; *s* of Lawrence and Monica Morris; *m* 1991, Sarah Culshaw; one *s* one *d*. *Educ:* Oundle Sch.; Keble Coll., Oxford (BA Hons). Dir, Performing Arts, ICA, 1984–88. Director: Artangel Media Ltd, 2000–; Shockheaded Peter Ltd, 2000–02. Mem., Arts Adv. Panel, British Council, 1983–86. Artistic Associate: Lyric Th., 1999–2004; RNT, 2003–. Trustee, Longplayer Trust, 2001–. Chevalier, Ordre National du Québec, 2002. *Publication:* (with J. Lingwood) Off Limits: 40 Artangel projects, 2002. *Recreations:* collecting unusual stringed instruments, accordions and cookery books, table tennis. *Address:* Artangel, 31 Eyre Street Hill, EC1R 5EW. *T:* (020) 7833 4974; *e-mail:* info@artangel.org.uk. *Club:* Two Brydges.

MORRIS, Michael Sachs; Director-General, British Insurance Brokers' Association, 1980–85; *b* 12 June 1924; *s* of late Prof. Noah Morris, MD, DSc, and Hattie Michaelis; *m* 1952, Vera Leonie, *er d* of late Paul and Lona Heller; one *s* one *d*. *Educ:* Glasgow Acad.; St Catharine's Coll., Cambridge. Wrangler, 1948. Scientific Officer, Admty Signals Estabt, 1943–46; Asst Principal, BoT, 1948; idc 1970; Under Secretary: Insurance Div., DoT, 1973; Shipping Policy Div., DoT, 1978–80. Chm., Consultative Shipping Gp, 1979–80. Mem., Barnet Health Authy, 1985–90. *Recreation:* sitting in the sun. *Address:* 5 Sunrise View, The Rise, Mill Hill, NW7 2LL. *T:* (020) 8959 0837. *Club:* Oxford and Cambridge.

MORRIS, Norma Frances, PhD; Research Fellow, University College London, since 1995; *b* 17 April 1935; *d* of Henry Albert Bevis and Lilian Eliza Bevis (*née* Flexon); *m* 1960, Samuel Francis Morris; one *s* two *d*. *Educ:* Ilford County High Sch. for Girls; University College London (BA, MA); Univ. of Twente, Netherlands (PhD). Assistante Anglaise, Paris, 1956–57; Asst Lectr, Univ. of Hull, 1959–60; MRC, 1960–95, Admin. Sec., 1989–95. Member: Nat. Biol Standards Bd, 1990–98; Gen. Chiropractic Council, 2002–04 (Chm., 1998–2002); Brit. Acupuncture Accreditation Bd, 2004–; Compass Collaborative Adv. Gp, 2007–. Trustee, Patients' Assoc., 2004–06. *Publications:* contribs science policy and medical sociology jls. *Recreations:* canoeing, opera, edible fungi. *Address:* Department of Science and Technology Studies, University College London, Gower Street, WC1E 6BT. *T:* (020) 7696 3703.

MORRIS, Peter Christopher West; solicitor; consultant with Morris and Warren, since 2005 (Partner, 2003–05); *b* 24 Dec. 1937; *s* of C. T. R. and L. B. Morris; *m* 1st, 1959, Joy (marr. diss.); two *s* one *d*; 2nd, 1987, Terese; one step *s* two step *d*. *Educ:* Seaford Coll.; Christ's Coll., Cambridge, 1958–61 (MA, LLB). Hockey Blue, 1959, 1960, 1961; Hockey for Wales, 1962–65. National Service, 1956–58. Admitted Solicitor, 1965; Partner with Wild Hewitson & Shaw, 1967; a Recorder of the Crown Court, 1980–84; voluntary removal from Roll of Solicitors, 1982; Barrister, Middle Temple, 1982–84; company dir, 1985–93; name restored to Roll of Solicitors, 1993; Partner with Morris and Rogers, 1998–2003. *Recreations:* golf, Arsenal Football Club. *Address:* 162 Church Road, Hove BN3 2DL. *Club:* Hawks (Cambridge).

MORRIS, Sir Peter (John), AC 2004; Kt 1996; FRS 1994; President, Royal College of Surgeons of England, 2001–04; Nuffield Professor of Surgery, Chairman, Department of Surgery and Director, Oxford Transplant Centre, Oxford University, 1974–2001, now Emeritus Professor; Fellow of Balliol College, 1974–2001, now Emeritus Fellow; Director, Centre for Evidence in Transplantation, Royal College of Surgeons of England and London School of Hygiene and Tropical Medicine, and Hon. Professor, University of London, since 2005; *b* 17 April 1934; *s* of Stanley Henry and Mary Lois Morris; *m* 1960, Mary Jocelyn Gorman; three *s* two *d*. *Educ:* Xavier Coll., Melbourne; Univ. of Melbourne (MB, BS, PhD). FRCS, FRACS, FACS, FRCP, FRCSGlas. Jun. surg. appts at St Vincent's Hosp., Melbourne, Postgrad. Med. Sch., London, Southampton Gen. Hosp. and MGH Boston, 1958–64; Research Fellow, Harvard Med. Sch., 1965–66; Asst Prof. in Surgery, Med. Coll. of Virginia, 1967; 2nd Asst in Surgery, Univ. of Melbourne, 1968–69, 1st Asst 1970–71; Reader in Surgery, Univ. of Melbourne, 1972–74. WHO Consultant, 1970–84; Cons. to Walter and Eliza Hall Inst. of Med. Res., 1969–74. Chairman: Nat. Kidney Res. Fund, 1986–90; Council, British Heart Foundn, 2003–; Inst. of Health Scis, Oxford Univ., 2000–04; Member: MRC, 1983–87; Oxford RHA, 1988–90; Council, RCS, 1991–2004 (Vice Pres., 2000–01); Council, ICRF, 1995–2001. President: Transplantation Soc., 1984–86; British Soc. for Histocompatibility and Immunogenetics, 1993–95; Eur. Surgical Assoc., 1996–98; Internat. Surgical Soc., 2001–03; Medical Protection Soc., 2007–. Hunterian Prof., RCS, 1972. Lectr, Coll. de France, 1982; Rudin Prof., Columbia Univ., NY, 1983; USA Nat. Kidney Foundn Prof., 1986; Nimmo Vis. Prof., Univ. of Adelaide, 1993; Ho Tam Kit Hing Vis. Prof., Univ. of Hong Kong, 1994; Waltman Walters Vis. Prof., Mayo Clinic, 1994; G. T. Diethelm Prof., Univ. of Alabama, 2002; Hon. Prof., LSHTM, 2005. Lectures: Champ Lyons, Univ. of Alabama, 1989; Fraser Meml, Univ. of Edinburgh, 1990; Bennett, TCD, 1991; Graham, Washington Univ., 1991; Murdoch Meml, Aberdeen Univ., 1991; Shaw, RCPE, 1991; Pybus Meml, N of Eng. Surg. Soc., 1992; Gallie, Royal Coll. of Physicians and Surgeons, Canada, 1992; Agnew, Univ. of Penn, 1993; Grey Turner, Internat. Surg. Soc., 1993; Belzer, Univ. of Wisconsin, 1998; Martin, Emory Univ., 1999; Cepellini, Eur. Foundn for Immuno-Genetics, 1999; Paul Russell, Harvard Med. Sch., 2000; Rienhoff, Johns Hopkins Med. Sch., 2003; Dist. Lectr, Stanford Univ., 2002; Syme Oration, RACS, 2002; Hunterian Oration and Medal, RCS, 2005; Pehr Edman, St Vincent's Med. Res. Inst., Melbourne Univ., 2005; Dunphy, UCSF, 2008; Raj Yadav Oration, Delhi, 2008. Governor: PPP Foundation (formerly PPP Healthcare Med. Trust), 1998–2003; Garfield Weston Foundn, 1998–; Trustee, Roche Organ Transplantation Res. Foundn, 1998–2004. Chm., Order of Australia Assoc., UK/Europe. Founder FMedSci 1998. Hon. Fellow: Amer. Surgical Assoc., 1982; Asian Surg. Soc., 1989; German Surgical Soc., 2003; Acad. of Med., Singapore, 2004; RCSI, 2006; Hon. FACS 1986; Hon. FRACS, 1995; Hon. FRCSE 1995; Hon. FDSRCS 2003; Hon. Mem., Amer. Soc. of Transplant Surgeons, 1993; Foreign Member: Inst. of Medicine, Nat. Acad. of Sci., 1997; Amer. Phil Soc., 2002. Hon. DSc: Hong Kong, 1999; Imperial Coll. London, 2003. Selwyn Smith Prize, Univ. of Melbourne, 1971; Cecil Joll Prize, RCS, 1988; Lister Medal, RCS, RCSE, Irish Coll. of Surgeons and Royal Soc., 1997; Neil Hamilton Fairley Medal, RCP, 2005; Medawar Prize, Transplantation Soc., 2006; Pioneer Award, Amer. Soc. of Transplant Surgeons, 2006; Internat. Surgical Soc. Prize, 2007. Editor, Transplantation, 1979–. *Publications:* Kidney Transplantation: principles and practice, 1979, 6th edn 2008; Tissue Transplantation, 1982; Transient Ischaemic Attacks, 1982; (ed jtly) Progress in Transplantation, vol. 1 1984, vol. 2 1985, vol. 3 1986; (ed) Oxford Textbook of Surgery, 1994, 2nd edn 2000; (ed) Transplantation Reviews, 1987–2002; numerous sci. articles and chapters in books concerned mainly with transplantation and surgery. *Recreations:* golf, tennis, cricket. *Address:* 19 Lucerne Road, Oxford OX2 7QB. *Clubs:* Oxford and Cambridge, MCC; Frilford Heath Golf (Oxford); Oxfordshire County Cricket; North Oxford Lawn Tennis; Melbourne Cricket (Melbourne); Barwon Heads Golf (Barwon Heads, Vic.).

MORRIS, Reyahn; *see* King, R.

MORRIS, Richard Francis Maxwell; Chief Executive, Associated Board of the Royal Schools of Music, since 1993; *b* 11 Sept. 1944; *s* of late Maxwell Morris and Frederica (*née* Abelson); *m* 1st, 1974, Sarah Quill (marr. diss. 1978); 2nd, 1983, Marian Sperling; two *d*. *Educ:* Eton Coll.; New Coll., Oxford (MA); Coll. of Law, London. Solicitor, Farrer & Co., 1967–71; Legal Advr and Banker, Grindlay Brandts, 1971–75; Corporate Finance Manager, S. G. Warburg & Co., 1975–79; Hodder and Stoughton: Group Finance Dir, 1979; Man. Dir, Educnl and Acad. Publishing, 1987; Jt Man. Dir, 1989–91; Dir, The Lancet, 1986–91; Man. Dir, Edward Arnold, 1987–91. Director: Invicta Sound, 1984–91; Southern Radio, 1991–92. Mem. Council, Kent Opera, 1985–90; Founder, Almaviva Opera, 1989–. Chm., Music Educn Council, 1998–2001 (Mem. Exec. Cttee, 1995–). Trustee: Council for Dance Educn and Trng, 1999–2005; Kent Music Sch., 2001–; Yehudi Menuhin Sch., 2004–. Hon. RCM 1994; Hon. RNCM 2001; Hon. FRAM 2007. *Recreations:* poetry, visual arts, golf. *Address:* Holdfast House, Edenbridge, Kent TN8 6SJ. *T:* (01732) 862439. *Club:* Athenæum.

MORRIS, Prof. Richard Graham Michael, CBE 2007; FRS 1997; Professor, since 1993, Royal Society Wolfson Professor, since 2006, of Neuroscience, Edinburgh University (Chairman, Department of Neuroscience, 1998–2002); *b* 27 June 1948; *s* of Robert Walter and Edith Mary Morris; *m* 1985, Hilary Ann Lewis; two *d*. *Educ:* Trinity Hall, Cambridge (BA 1969; MA 1971); Univ. of Sussex (DPhil 1973). FRSE 1994. Addison Wheeler Fellow, Univ. of Durham, 1973–75; BM (Nat. History), 1975–76; BBC Science and Features Dept, 1977; Lectr, Univ. of St Andrews, 1977–86; Reader, Dept of Pharmacology, Univ. of Edinburgh, 1986–93. Vis. Prof., MIT, 1991; Royal Society Leverhulme Fellow, 1996; Gatsby Res. Fellow, 1997. Member: Neuroscis Grants Cttee, MRC, 1981–85; Neuroscis and Mental Health Bd, MRC, 1993–97; Innovation Bd, MRC, 1997–2000; Strategy Develt Gp, MRC, 2000–04. Chm., Brain Res. Assoc., 1990–94; Hon. Sec., Exptl Psychol. Soc., 1985–89. Mem., RYA. Founder FMedSci 1998. Zotterman Medal, Swedish Physiol. Soc., 1999. *Publications:* contrib. to academic jls and books. *Recreation:* sailing. *Address:* Centre for Cognitive and Neural Systems, University of Edinburgh College of Medicine, 1 George Square, Edinburgh EH8 9JZ. *T:* (0131) 650 3520; *e-mail:* r.g.m.morris@ed.ac.uk.

MORRIS, Richard Keith, OBE 2003; FSA; archaeologist, writer, composer; Director, Institute for Medieval Studies, University of Leeds, since 2003; *b* 8 Oct. 1947; *s* of John Richard Morris and Elsie Myra (*née* Wearne); *m* 1972, Jane Whiteley; two *s* one *d*. *Educ:* Denstone Coll., Staffs; Pembroke Coll., Oxford (MA); Univ. of York (BPhil). FSA 1982; MIFA 1986. Musician, 1971–72; Res. Assistant, York Minster Archaeol. Office, 1972–75; Churches Officer, 1975–77, Res. Officer, 1978–88, Council for British Archaeol.; Hon. Lectr, Sch. of History, Univ. of Leeds, 1986–88; Lectr, Dept of Archaeol., Univ. of York, 1988–91; Dir, Council for British Archaeology, 1991–99 (Hon. Vice-Pres., 2001). Comr, English Heritage, 1996–2005; Chairman: Ancient Monuments Adv. Cttee for England, 1996–2000; Historic Settlements and Landscapes Adv. Cttee, 2001–03; Bede's World, 2001–; English Heritage Adv. Cttee, 2003–; Heritage Lottery Fund Expert Panel, 2005–. Pres., Soc. for Church Archaeol., 2001–05. Hon. Vis. Prof., Univ. of York, 1995. Hon. MIFA 2001. Frend Medal, Soc. of Antiquaries of London, 1992. *Publications:* Cathedrals and Abbeys of England and Wales, 1979; The Church in British Archaeology, 1983; Churches in the Landscape, 1989; (jtly) Guy Gibson, 1994; Cheshire, VC, OM, 2000; The Triumph of Time, 2007. *Recreations:* aviation history, natural history, dog walking. *Address:* 13 Hollins Road, Harrogate HG1 2JF. *T:* (01423) 504219.

MORRIS, Air Vice-Marshal Richard Vaughan, CBE 2000; AFC 1991; Chief of Staff and Deputy Commander-in-Chief, HQ Personnel and Training Command, Innsworth, 2000–01; *b* 24 Sept. 1949; *s* of Edgar Morris and Iona Morris (*née* Clement); *m* 1969, Sheena Blundell; two *s*. *Educ:* John Bright Grammar Sch., Llandudno. XV Sqn, Laarbruch, 237 OCU, Honington, 16 Sqn, Laarbruch, 1971–80; Tri-Nat. Tornado Trng Estabt, Cottesmore, 1980–82; PSO to ACAS, MoD, 1984–87; OC 14 Sqn, Bruggen, 1988–91; Comdr, British Forces Op. Jural, 1992; Station Comdr, Honington, 1993–94; Policy HQ Allied Forces Northwestern Europe, 1994; rcds, 1995; Comdt, Air Warfare Centre, Waddington, 1996–98; SASO, HQ 1 Gp, High Wycombe, 1998–2000; Comdr, British Forces Op. Desert Fox, 1998, Op. Allied Force, 1999; retired 2002. *Recreations:* golf, hill walking. *Address:* c/o Lloyds TSB, 65 High Street, Stamford PE9 2AT. *Club:* Royal Air Force.

MORRIS, Robert Matthew, CVO 1996; Assistant Under Secretary of State, Home Office, 1983–97; *b* 11 Oct. 1937; *s* of late William Alexander Morris and of Mary Morris (*née* Bryant); *m* 1965, Janet Elizabeth Gillingham; two *s* one *d*. *Educ:* Handsworth Grammar Sch.; Christ's Coll., Cambridge; Open Univ. (PhD 2004). S Staffords Regt, 1956–58. Joined Home Office, 1961; Asst Private Sec. to Home Sec., 1964–66; CSD, 1969–71; Principal Private Sec. to Home Sec., 1976–78; Sec. to UK Prison Services

Inquiry (May Cttee), 1978–79; Head of Crime Policy Planning Unit, 1979–81; Asst Under Sec. of State, Fire and Emergency Planning, 1983, Immigration Policy, Nationality and Passports, 1986, Criminal Justice and Constitutional, 1991; Registrar, Baronetage, 1991–96. Mem. Council, Internat. Social Service UK, 1998–2005. Sec. to (Hurd) Review of See of Canterbury, 2000–01. Hon. Sen. Res. Fellow, Constitution Unit, Sch. of Public Policy, subseq. Dept. of Political Sci., UCL, 1999–. *Address:* 4 Desenfans Road, SE21 7DN.

MORRIS, Ven. Roger Anthony Brett; Archdeacon of Worcester, since 2008; *b* Hereford, 18 July 1968; *s* of Anthony Edward Morris and Eirwen Morris; *m* 1991, Sally Jane; two *d*. *Educ:* Imperial Coll. London (BSc; ARCS 1989); Trinity Coll., Cambridge (BA 1992); Ridley Hall Theol Coll. Ordained deacon, 1993, priest, 1994; Asst Curate, Northleach Gp of Parishes, 1993–96; Rector, Coln River Gp of Parishes incl. Sevenhampton, 1996–2003; Dir of Parish Develt and Evangelism, Dio. of Coventry, 2003–08. *Recreations:* supporting Bristol Rovers, music, films, running a VW Camper Van. *Address:* The Archdeacon's House, Walkers Lane, Whittington, Worcester WR5 2RE; *e-mail:* roger.morris@me.com.

MORRIS, Rear-Adm. Roger Oliver, CB 1990; Hydrographer of the Navy, 1985–90; *b* 1 Sept. 1932; *s* of Dr Oliver N. Morris and H. S. (Mollie) Morris (*née* Hudson). *Educ:* Mount House School, Tavistock; Royal Naval College, Dartmouth. Entered Royal Navy, 1946, commissioned 1952; specialized in Hydrographic Surveying, 1956; commanded HM Ships Medusa, Beagle, Hydra, Fawn, Hecla, Hydra, 1964–80; RCDS 1978; Director of Hydrographic Plans and Surveys, 1980–81; Asst Hydrographer, 1982–84. Chm. of Council, Soc. for Nautical Res., 1989–94; Vice-Pres., Royal Inst. of Navigation, 1991–92; Pres., World Ship Soc., 1997–2000. *Publication:* Charts and Surveys in Peace and War, 1995. *Recreations:* heraldry, opera, bird watching. *Address:* Orchard House, Quantock View, Bishops Lydeard, Somerset TA4 3AW.

MORRIS, Simon C.; *see* Conway Morris.

MORRIS, Stephen Nathan; QC 2002; a Recorder, since 2000; a Deputy High Court Judge, since 2004; *b* 18 May 1957; *s* of late Jack Ellis Morris and June Audrey Morris (*née* Livingstone). *Educ:* Bradford Grammar Sch.; Christ's Coll., Cambridge (BA 1979, MA 1982). Called to the Bar, Lincoln's Inn, 1981; in private practice at the Bar, 1983–; Jun. Counsel to the Crown (A Panel), 1999–2002; Asst Recorder, 1998–2000. *Publications:* (contrib.) Plender: European Court Practice and Precedent, 1998; (contrib.) Bar Council Practitioners' Handbook of EC Law, 1998; (contrib.) Bellamy & Child: European Community Law of Competition, 5th edn 2001. *Recreations:* ski-ing, theatre, gardening, cooking. *Address:* 20 Essex Street, WC2R 3AL. *T:* (020) 7842 1200. *Club:* Royal Automobile.

MORRIS, Prof. Terence Patrick Michael; JP; Emeritus Professor of Criminology and Criminal Justice, University of London, since 1994 (Professor of Social Institutions, 1981–94); *b* 8 June 1931; *s* of Albert and Norah Avis Morris; *m* 1973, Penelope Jane, *y d* of Stanley and Alexandra Tomlinson. *Educ:* John Ruskin Grammar Sch., Croydon; LSE, Univ. of London (Leverhulme Schol.; BSc (Soc) 1953, PhD (Econ) 1955). Lectr in Sociology, LSE, 1955–63; Reader, 1963–69, Prof., 1969–81, Sociology (with special ref. to Criminology), London Univ.; Founder Dir, Mannheim Centre for Criminology and Criminal Justice, LSE, 1990. Visiting Professor of Criminology: Univ. of California, 1964–65; Univ. of Manitoba, 1996. Mem., Adv. Mission on Treatment of Offenders (Western Pacific, British Honduras, Bahamas), 1966. Vice-Pres., Howard League for Penal Reform, 1986–2004; Mem., Magistrates' Assoc. Treatment of Offenders Cttee (co-opted), 1969–77; Founder Mem., Inst. for Study of Drug Dependence. Man. Editor, British Jl of Sociology, 1965–74. JP Inner London, 1967. *Publications:* The Criminal Area, 1957; (with Pauline Morris) Pentonville: a sociological study of an English prison, 1963; (with L. J. Blom-Cooper) A Calendar of Murder, 1964; Deviance and Control: the secular heresy, 1976; Crime and Criminal Justice since 1945, 1989; (with L. J. Blom-Cooper) With Malice Aforethought: a study of the crime and punishment for homicide, 2004; contribs to Brit. Jl Criminology, Brit. Jl Sociology, Encycl. Britannica, Crim. Law Review. *Recreations:* cycling, photography. *Address:* Christmas Cottage, Lower Road, South Wonston, Winchester, Hants SO21 3ER. *Club:* Cyclists' Touring.

MORRIS, Timothy Colin; HM Diplomatic Service; Ambassador to Morocco, and concurrently (non-resident) to Mauritania, since 2008; *b* 17 Sept. 1958; *s* of late Maj. Charles Anthony Morris and of Sheila Ann Margaret Morris (*née* Watson); *m* 1996, Patricia Tena; three *s*. *Educ:* Winchester Coll.; Queen's Coll., Oxford (BA 1st Cl. Hons Modern Langs (French and Spanish) 1981). Joined HM Diplomatic Service, 1981; Japanese lang. trng, 1982–84; Second Sec., Commercial, Tokyo, 1984–87; FCO, 1987–89; Hd, Exports to Japan Unit, DTI, 1989–91; First Sec. and Hd, Political Section, Madrid, 1991–95; Dep. Hd, UN Dept, FCO, 1996–98; Counsellor, Trade and Investment, Tokyo, 1998–2002; Dep. Hd of Mission, Lisbon, 2003–04; Hd, Internat. Orgns Dept, FCO, 2005–08. *Recreations:* music, literature. *Address:* c/o Foreign and Commonwealth Office, King Charles Street, SW1A 2AH. *Club:* Oxford and Cambridge.

MORRIS, Rev. Canon Timothy David; Rector, Church of the Good Shepherd, Murrayfield, since 2002; Priest, St Salvador's Church, Stenhouse, since 2003; *b* 17 Aug. 1948; *s* of Joseph Ernest and Mabel Elizabeth Morris; *m* 1st, 1972, Dorothy Helen Ralph (marr. diss. 1987); one *d*; 2nd, 1988, Irene Elizabeth Lyness. *Educ:* King Edward's Grammar Sch., Bath; Coll. of Estate Management, London Univ. (BSc Econs); Trinity Coll., Bristol and Bristol Univ. (DipTh). Asst Estate Surveyor, Min. of Public Building and Works, Edinburgh, 1969–72; Curate, St Thomas's Church, Edinburgh, 1975–77; Rector: St James's Episcopal Church, Leith, Edinburgh, 1977–83; St Ninian's, Troon, Ayrshire, 1983–85; St Peter's, Galashiels, 1985–2002; Dean, Dio. Edinburgh, Episcopal Ch in Scotland, 1992–2001. Hon. Canon, St Mary's Cathedral, Edinburgh, 2002–. HM Lay Inspector of Educn, 2003–. Chm., Bd of Mgt, Positive Help, Edinburgh, 2003–. *Recreations:* music, Rugby Union, cricket, gardening. *Address:* The Rectory, 9 Upper Coltbridge Terrace, Edinburgh EH12 6AD. *T:* (0131) 337 2698.

MORRIS, Prof. Timothy John, PhD; Professor of Management Studies, Saïd Business School, Oxford University, and Fellow, Green Templeton College (formerly Templeton College), Oxford, since 2002; *b* 21 Jan. 1953; *s* of Ernest Joseph Morris and Dorothy Beatrice Morris; *m* 1999, Dr Helen Margaret Lydka; one *s* one *d* (and one *d* decd). *Educ:* Eltham Coll., London; Jesus Coll., Cambridge (BA Hons 1975); London Sch. of Econs (MSc 1980; PhD 1984); Nuffield Coll., Oxford; MA Oxon 2002. Faculty, London Business Sch., 1988–2000; Prof. of Organisational Behaviour, Imperial Coll. London, 2000–02; Dir, Clifford Chance Centre for Mgt of Professional Service Firms, Oxford Univ., 2003–05 and 2007–. *Publications:* (jtly) The Car Industry: labour relations and industrial adjustment, 1985; Innovations in Banking: business strategies and employee relations, 1986; (jtly) Union Business, 1993; (jtly) Career Frontiers: new conceptions of working lives, 2000; numerous articles in scholarly jls. *Recreations:* cycling, squash, cinema. *Address:* Saïd Business School, Oxford OX1 1HP. *T:* (01865) 288954, *Fax:* (01865) 288805; *e-mail:* tim.morris@sbs.ox.ac.uk.

MORRIS, Sir Trefor (Alfred), Kt 1996; CBE 1992; QPM 1985; HM Chief Inspector of Constabulary, 1993–96; Chairman, Police Information Technology Organisation, 1996–2000; Adviser, British Transport Police Committee, 1996–2001; *b* 22 Dec. 1934; *s* of late Kenneth Alfred Morris and Amy Ursula (*née* Burgess); *m* 1958, Martha Margaret (*née* Wroe); two *d*. *Educ:* Ducie Technical High School, Manchester; Manchester University (Dip. Criminology); Nat. Exec. Inst., USA. Constable to Chief Superintendent, Manchester City Police, Manchester and Salford Police, Greater Manchester Police, 1955–76; Asst Chief Constable, Greater Manchester Police, 1976–79; Dep. Chief Constable, 1979–84, Chief Constable, 1984–90, Herts; HM Inspector of Constabulary, 1990–93. Trustee, Police Foundn, 1993–96. Pres., Police Mutual Assurance Soc., 1994–97. Member: St Albans Diocesan Synod, 1989–96; PCC, St Mary's Church, Abergavenny, 1997–; Governing Body, Church in Wales, 2003–. Chm., St Mary's Priory Develt Trust, 1999–. Vice President: Herts Scouts, 1989–; Police Athletics Assoc.; Pres., Luton, N Herts Inst. of Mgt. Chm., Bryn-y-Cwm Community Forum, 2004–08. Mem. Bd, Abergavenny Food Fest., 1999–. Trustee, Hospice of the Valleys, 1997–2005. CCMI (CBIM 1986). FRSA 1993. OStJ 1984. *Recreations:* music, golf, wine, walking, gardening, medieval history. *Clubs:* Royal Over-Seas League; Monmouthshire Golf (Captain, 2005–06).

MORRIS, Prof. Trevor Raymond; Professor of Animal Production, University of Reading, 1984–95, now Professor Emeritus; *b* 11 April 1930; *s* of Ivor Raymond Morris and Dorothy May Morris; *m* 1st, 1954, Elisabeth Jean (*née* Warren) (*d* 1992); three *s* two *d*; 2nd, 1994, Mary (*née* Gillett). *Educ:* Rendcomb Coll., Glos; Reading Univ. (BSc, PhD, DSc). University of Reading: Asst Lectr, 1952–54, 1956–57; Lectr in Agric., 1957–69; Reader in Agric., 1969–81; Prof. of Agriculture, 1981–84; Hd of Dept of Agriculture, 1984–91. *Publications:* over 200 articles in sci. jls. *Recreations:* music, gardening. *Address:* Rowan Trees, Beech Road, Tokers Green, Oxfordshire RG4 9EH. *T:* (0118) 9470758.

MORRIS, Ulrike Luise; *see* Tillmann, U. L.

MORRIS, Warwick; HM Diplomatic Service, retired; Ambassador to South Korea, 2003–08; *b* 10 Aug. 1948; *e s* of late Clifford Morris and Patricia Morris (*née* O'Grady), JP; *m* 1972, Pamela Jean Mitchell, MBE; one *s* two *d*. *Educ:* Bishop's Stortford Coll. VSO, Cameroon, 1967–68; entered Diplomatic Service, 1969; Third Sec., Paris, 1972–74; Korean lang. trng, Yonsei Univ., Seoul, 1975–76; Second Sec., Seoul, 1977–79; FCO, 1979–83; First Sec., 1982; First Sec. (Commercial), Mexico City, 1984–87; Head of Chancery, Seoul, 1988–91; Dep. Head, Far Eastern Dept, FCO, 1991–93; Counsellor, 1993, Head, 1994, Permanent Under Sec.'s Dept, FCO; Econ. and Commercial Counsellor, New Delhi, 1995–98; RCDS, 1999; Ambassador to Vietnam, 2000–03. *Recreations:* sport, travel, philately. *Address:* Rosewood, Stonewall Park Road, Langton Green, Kent TN3 0HD. *Club:* Royal Commonwealth Society.

MORRIS, Prof. (William) David, PhD, DSc(Eng); Professor of Mechanical Engineering, University of Wales, Swansea (formerly University College of Swansea), 1985 (Head of Department, 1985–91 and 1995); *b* 14 March 1936; *s* of late William Daniel and Elizabeth Jane Morris; *m* 1959, Pamela Eira Evans; two *s* one *d*. *Educ:* Queen Mary College, London (1st Cl. Hons BSc Eng); UC of Swansea, Wales (PhD); Univ. of London (DSc(Eng)). CEng, FIMechE, FIET. Bristol Siddeley Engine Co., 1958–60; James Clayton Res. Fellow, Univ. of Wales, Swansea, 1960–63; Lectr, Dept of Mech. Engrg, Univ. of Liverpool, 1963–67; Lectr, 1967–72, Reader, 1972–79, Sch. of Engrg, Univ. of Sussex; J. H. Fenner Prof. of Mech. Engrg and Head, Dept of Engrg Design, Univ. of Hull, 1979–85; Vice Principal, UC Swansea, 1991–93. *Publications:* Differential Equations for Engineers and Applied Scientists, 1979; Heat Transfer and Fluid Flow in Rotating Coolant Channels, 1981. *Recreations:* oil painting, DIY, walking.

MORRIS, Very Rev. William James, KCVO 1995; JP; Minister of Glasgow Cathedral, 1967–2005; a Chaplain to the Queen in Scotland, 1969–96, an Extra Chaplain, since 1996; Dean of the Chapel Royal in Scotland, 1991–96; *b* Cardiff, 22 Aug. 1925; *o s* of William John Morris and Eliza Cecilia Cameron Johnson; *m* 1952, Jean Daveena Ogilvy Howie, CBE, LLD (*d* 2005), *o c* of Rev. David Porter Howie and Veena Christie, Kilmarnock; one *s*. *Educ:* Cardiff High Sch.; Univ. of Wales; Edinburgh Univ. BA 1946, BD 1949, Wales; PhD Edinburgh, 1954. Ordained, 1951. Asst, Canongate Kirk, Edinburgh, 1949–51; Minister, Presbyterian Church of Wales, Cadoxton and Barry Is, 1951–53; Buckhaven (Fife): St David's, 1953–57; Peterhead Old Parish, 1957–67; Chaplain to the Lord High Comr to the General Assembly of the Church of Scotland, 1975–76; Chaplain: Peterhead Prison, 1963–67; Glasgow DC, 1967; Trades House of Glasgow, 1967–2005; W of Scotland Engrs Assoc., 1967–2005; The High Sch. of Glasgow, 1974–76; Glasgow Acad., 1976–2005; Strathclyde Police, 1977–2005; Queen's Body Guard for Scotland, Royal Co. of Archers, 1994–2007; Soc. of Friends of Glasgow Cathedral, 2002–05 (Chm. Council, 1967–2002); Hon. Chaplain, The Royal Scottish Automobile Club; Moderator, Presbytery of Deer, 1965–66; Convener Adv. Bd, Church of Scotland, 1977–80; Vice-Chm., Bd of Nomination to Church Chairs, Church of Scotland, 1978–81. Mem. IBA, 1979–84 (Chm. Scottish Adv. Cttee). President: Rotary Club of Peterhead, 1965–66; Peterhead and Dist Professional and Business Club, 1967; St Andrew's Soc., Glasgow, 1992–2005 (Vice-Pres., 1967–82); Chairman: Iona Cath. Trust, 1976–2005 (Trustee, 1967); Club Service Cttee, Dist 101, RIBI, 1964–66; Prison Chaplaincies Bd (Church of Scotland Home Bd), 1969–83; Member: Scottish Cttee, British Sailors' Soc., 1967–83; Bd of Management, W of Scotland Convalescent Home, 1967–75; Gen. Convocation, Strathclyde Univ., 1967–2005; Council of Management, Quarriers' Homes, 1968–88; Bd of Management, Glasgow YMCA, 1973–88; Scottish Council on Crime, 1974–76; Church of Scotland Bd of Practice and Procedure, 1981–85; Bd of Governors, Jordanhill Coll. of Educn, Glasgow, 1983–91; Hon. Pres., Glasgow Soc. of Social Services Inc., 1984–. Hon. Member: Scottish Ambulance Assoc., 1981; Royal Faculty of Procurators in Glasgow, 1997. JP: Co. of Aberdeen, 1963–71; Co. of City of Glasgow, 1971. ChStJ 1991. FRCPS(Hon) 1983. Hon. LLD Strathclyde, 1974; Hon. DD Glasgow, 1979; Hon. DLitt Glasgow Caledonian, 2003. Lord Provost's Award, Glasgow, 1996; Paul Harris Fellow, Rotary Internat., 1997. *Publications:* A Walk Around Glasgow Cathedral, 1986; Amazing Graces, 2001. *Recreations:* fishing, gardening. *Address:* 1 Whitehill Grove, Newton Mearns, Glasgow G77 5DH. *T:* (0141) 6396327. *Clubs:* New (Edinburgh); RNVR (Scotland) (Hon.); University of Strathclyde Staff (Hon.); Rotary of Dennistoun (Hon.); Rotary of Glasgow (Hon.).

MORRIS, William Patrick; His Honour Judge William Morris; a Circuit Judge, since 1995; Resident Judge, Bolton Crown Court, since 2002; Honorary Recorder of Bolton, since 2008; *b* 17 March 1947; *s* of His Honour Sir William Gerard Morris and of Mollie Morris; *m* 1978, Patricia Whittaker (*see* Baroness Morris of Bolton); one *s* one *d*. *Educ:* Ampleforth Coll.; Gonville and Caius Coll., Cambridge (BA 1968, MA). Called to the Bar, Lincoln's Inn, 1970; a Recorder, 1988–95. *Recreations:* fishing, gardening, walking, watching Bolton Wanderers. *Address:* Bolton Crown Court, Blackhorse Street, Bolton BL1 1SU. *T:* (01204) 392881.

MORRIS, Wyn, FRAM; conductor; Principal Conductor, New Queen's Hall Orchestra; *b* 14 Feb. 1929; *s* of late Haydn Morris and Sarah Eluned Phillips; *m* 1962, Ruth Marie

McDowell; one *s* one *d.* *Educ:* Llanelli Grammar Sch.; Royal Academy of Music; Mozarteum, Salzburg. August Mann's Prize, 1950; Apprentice Conductor, Yorkshire Symph. Orch., 1950–51; Musical Dir, 17th Trg Regt, RA Band, 1951–53; Founder and Conductor of Welsh Symph. Orch., 1954–57; Koussevitsky Memorial Prize, Boston Symph. Orch., 1957; (on invitation George Szell) Observer, Cleveland Symph. Orch., 1957–60; Conductor: Ohio Bell Chorus, Cleveland Orpheus Choir and Cleveland Chamber Orch., 1958–60; Choir of Royal National Eisteddfod of Wales, 1960–62; London debut, Royal Festival Hall, with Royal Philharmonic Orch., 1963; Conductor: Royal Choral Society, 1968–70; Huddersfield Choral Soc., 1969–74; Ceremony for Investiture of Prince Charles as Prince of Wales, 1969; Royal Choral Soc. tour of USA, 1969; former Chief Conductor and Musical Dir, Symphonica of London. FRAM 1964. Specialises in conducting of Mahler; has recorded Des Knaben Wunderhorn (with Dame Janet Baker and Sir Geraint Evans), Das Klagende Lied, Symphonies 1, 2, 5, 8 and 10 in Deryck Cooke's final performing version. Mahler Memorial Medal (of Bruckner and Mahler Soc. of Amer.), 1968. *Recreations:* chess, Rugby football, climbing, cynghanedd and telling Welsh stories.

MORRISON, family name of **Viscount Dunrossil** and of **Baron Margadale**.

MORRISON, Alasdair; Chairman, MG Alba, since 2008; *b* 18 Nov. 1968; *m*; one *s* one *d*. Former Western Isles correspondent, BBC; former Editor, New Gael newspaper. Mem. (Lab) Western Isles, Scottish Parlt, 1999–2007. Dep. Minister for Enterprise in the Highlands and Islands and Gaelic, 1999–2001, for Enterprise and Lifelong Learning and Gaelic, 2001, Scottish Exec.

MORRISON, Sir (Alexander) Fraser, Kt 1998; CBE 1993; Deputy Chairman, Clydesdale Bank plc, 1999–2004 (Director, 1994–2004); Chairman: Teasses Capital Ltd, since 2003; Ramco Holdings Ltd, since 2005; *b* 20 March 1948; *s* of late Alexander Ferrier Sharp Morrison and of Catherine Colina (*née* Fraser); *m* 1972, Patricia Janice Murphy; one *s* two *d*. *Educ:* Tain Royal Acad.; Univ. of Edinburgh (BSc Hons Civil Engrg). CEng, FICE 1993; Eur Ing 1993; MIHT 1982; FCIOB 1995. Morrison Construction Gp, subseq. Morrison: Dir, 1970; Man. Dir, 1976–96; Chm., 1984–96; Exec. Chm., 1996–2000. Director: Shand Ltd, 1978–89; Alexander Shand Holdings Ltd, 1982–86. Chm., Highlands & Islands Enterprise, 1992–98. Federation of Civil Engineering Contractors: Chm., Scottish Sect., 1991–92; Chm., Nat. Fedn, 1993–94; Vice Pres., 1994–96. Chairman: Bd of Governors, Univ. of Highlands and Is Project, 1998–2001; Council St Leonard's Sch., St Andrews, 1999–2007. Dir, Chief Execs Orgn, 2003–. FRSA 1990; FScotvec 1994. Hon. DTech: Napier, 1995; Glasgow Caledonian, 1997; DUniv Open, 2000. *Recreations:* golf, ski-ing, shooting, opera, art. *Address:* Teasses House, near Ceres, Leven, Fife KY8 5PG. *T:* (01334) 828048.

MORRISON, His Honour Alexander John Henderson; a Circuit Judge, 1980–98; *b* 16 Nov. 1927; *yr s* of late Dr Alexander Morrison and Mrs A. Morrison; *m* 1978, Hon. Philippa, *y d* of 1st Baron Hives. *Educ:* Derby Sch.; Emmanuel Coll., Cambridge (MA, LLB). Called to the Bar, Gray's Inn, 1951. Mem. of Midland Circuit; Dep. Chm., Derbyshire QS, 1964–71; Regional Chm. of Industrial Tribunals, Sheffield, 1971–80; a Recorder of the Crown Court, 1971–80. A Pres., Mental Health Review Tribunals, 1983–98. Pres., Derbys Union of Golf Clubs, 1977–79. *Recreations:* golf, schools football. *Address:* c/o Derby Combined Court, Morledge, Derby DE1 2XE.

MORRISON, (Andrew) Neil, CBE 1997; QFSM 1989; HM Chief Inspector of Fire Services for Scotland, 1994–99; *b* 8 Sept. 1937; *e s* of late Andrew Steel Morrison and Margueritta Wilkin Caird; *m* 1963, Kathleen Rutherford; one *s*. *Educ:* Arbroath High Sch.; Dundee Coll. of Technol. FIFireE 1991. Angus Fire Brigade: Fireman, 1962–70; Leading Fireman, 1970–71; Sub-officer, 1971–74; Station Officer, 1974–75; Tayside Fire Brigade: Station Officer, 1975–76; Asst Divl Officer, 1976; Divl Officer, Grade III, 1976–79; Divl Officer, Grade I, 1979–80; Grampian Fire Brigade: Dep. Firemaster, 1980–85; Firemaster, 1985–93. Hon. DTech Robert Gordon Univ., 1994. *Recreations:* curling, golf, hill-walking, swimming. *Address:* 18 Slateford Gardens, Edzell, Angus DD9 7SX. *T:* (01356) 648768.

MORRISON, Rev. Angus, PhD; Minister, St Columba's Old Parish Church, Stornoway, since 2000; Convener, Church of Scotland Mission and Discipleship Council, since 2005; Chaplain to the Queen in Scotland, since 2006; *b* 30 Aug. 1953; *s* of Norman Morrison, MBE and Mary Ann Morrison; *m* 1983, Marion Jane Matheson; three *s* one *d*. *Educ:* Glasgow Univ. (MA Hons 1976); London Univ. (BD Hons 1993 ext.); Edinburgh Univ. (PhD 2001). Minister, Free Presbyterian Church of Scotland: Oban, 1979–86; Edinburgh, 1986–89; Minister, Associated Presbyterian Chs, Edinburgh, 1989–2000. Moderator: Gen. Assembly, Associated Presbyterian Chs, 1998–99; C of S Presbytery of Lewis, 2003–04; Chaplain, Nicolson Inst., Stornoway, 2003–; Chaplain to Lord High Comr to Gen. Assembly of C of S, 2005, 2006. *Publications:* (contrib.) Dictionary of Scottish Church History and Theology, 1993; (contrib.) Oxford DNB; (ed) Tolerance and Truth: the spirit of the age or the spirit of God?, 2007; (contrib.) Dizionario di Teologia Evangelica, 2007. *Recreations:* walking the dog, swimming, music, reading. *Address:* St Columba's Manse, Lewis Street, Stornoway, Isle of Lewis HS1 2JF. *T:* (01851) 703350/701546, *Fax:* (01851) 701546; *e-mail:* morrisonangus@btconnect.com.

MORRISON, Anne Catherine; Controller, Network Production, BBC TV, since 2006; *b* 18 Aug. 1959; *d* of late George Charles Morrison and of Persis Mae Morrison (*née* Ross); *m* 1989, Robert John Jarvis Johnstone; one *d*. *Educ:* Richmond Lodge Sch., Belfast; Churchill Coll., Cambridge (MA Eng. Lit). Gen. Trainee, BBC, 1981–83; Researcher and Dir, Documentary Features, BBC TV, 1983–87; Prod., Holiday, 1987–88; Series Prod., Crimewatch UK, 1988–90; Chief Assistant, Documentary Features, 1990–92; Exec. Prod., Taking Liberties, and Rough Justice, 1992; Dep. Head, 1992–94, Hd, 1994–96, Features, BBC TV; BBC Production: Head of Consumer and Leisure, 1996–98; Head of Features and Events, 1998–2000; Controller, Leisure and Factual Entertainment, 2000–01, General Factual Gp, 2001–02, Documentaries and Contemp. Factual, 2002–06, BBC TV. *Recreations:* reading, running, genealogy, gardening. *Address:* BBC, The Media Centre, 201 Wood Lane, W12 7TQ. *T:* (020) 8008 2871.

MORRISON, Blake; *see* Morrison, P. B.

MORRISON, Chloe Anthony, (Toni); writer; *b* 18 Feb. 1931; *d* of George Wofford and Ella Ramah Wofford (*née* Willis); *m* 1958, Harold Morrison (marr. diss. 1964); two *s*. *Educ:* Howard Univ.; Cornell Univ. (MA 1955). Lectr in English and Humanities: Texas Southern Univ., 1955–57; Howard Univ., 1957–64; Associate Prof. of English, NY State Univ. Coll., Purchase, 1971–72; Professor of Humanities: SUNY, Albany, 1984–89; Princeton Univ., 1989–. An Editor, Random House, NY, 1965. Numerous literary awards, incl Pulitzer Prize for Fiction, 1988; Nobel Prize for Literature, 1993. *Publications:* The Bluest Eye, 1970; Sula, 1974; Song of Solomon, 1977; Tar Baby, 1983; Beloved, 1987; Jazz, 1992; Playing in the Dark: whiteness and the literary imagination, 1992; (ed) Race-ing Justice, En-gendering Power, 1993; (ed jtly) Birth of a Nationhood, 1997; Paradise, 1998; Love, 2003; A Mercy, 2008. *Address:* c/o Suzanne Gluck, International Creative Management, 40 W 57th Street, New York, NY 10019, USA.

MORRISON, Dennis John; Regional Director, Government Office for the East Midlands, 1998–2002; Special Professor, Faculty of the Built Environment, University of Nottingham, since 2000; *b* 20 May 1942; *s* of Leonard Tait Morrison and Alice Morrison; *m* 1967, Frances Joan Pollard; one *s* one *d*. *Educ:* Ashton-upon-Mersey Boys' School; Lymm Grammar School; Manchester Univ. (BA, DipT&CP). MRTPI. Planning appointments: Lancs CC, 1966–70; Welsh Office, Cardiff, 1970–75; NW Region, DoE, Manchester, 1975–81; Regional Controller, NW Enterprise Unit, DoE, 1981–84; Regional Controller (Urban and Economic Affairs), Merseyside Task Force, Liverpool, 1984–89; Regl Dir, Depts of Envmt and Transport, E Midlands Region, 1989–94; Dir, Envmt and Transport, Govt Office for E Midlands, 1994–97; Regl Dir, Govt Office for Merseyside, 1997–98. Mem., Adv. Bd, Highways Agency, 1999–2003; Bd Mem., Industrial Trust E Midlands, 2000–. Non-exec. Dir, Independent Decision Makers Ltd, 2002–. Mem., Exec. Cttee, Liverpool Cathedral, 1986–. Vice Pres. and Trustee, Arkwright Soc., 2005–. FRGS. *Recreations:* antiquarian book collecting, horology, antique barometer restoration, hill walking, gardening, cooking, people watching. *Address:* Bowdon, Cheshire.

MORRISON, Donald Alexander Campbell; Assistant Under-Secretary of State, Home Office, 1972–76; *b* 30 Nov. 1916; *s* of late George Alexander Morrison, sometime MP for Scottish Univs, and late Rachel Brown Morrison (*née* Campbell); *m* 1st, 1951, Elma Margaret Craig (*d* 1970); one *s* one *d* (and one *s* decd); 2nd, 1973, Jane Margaret Montgomery (*d* 2006); one step *s*. *Educ:* Fettes Coll.; Christ Church, Oxford (BA). Home Office, 1939; Asst Sec., 1955. A Senior Clerk (acting), House of Commons, 1976–81. War Service, 1940–45: 79th (Scottish Horse) Medium Regt, RA, 1942–45. *Publications:* Haps and Such (poems), 1986; *children's operas:* The Granite and the Heather, 1990 (perf. Aboyne, 1990); Little Jenny Nobody, 1991 (perf. Aboyne, 1990, Canterbury Fest., 1992); The Golden Slave, 1992 (perf. Aboyne, 1992); Afternoon in Jericho, 1993 (perf. Wingham Fest., 1993); Smugglers at Bay, 1993 (perf. Canterbury Fest., 1993); Remember David, 1995 (perf. Wingham Fest., 1995). *Recreation:* music. *Address:* 27 High Street, Wingham, near Canterbury, Kent CT3 1AW. *T:* (01227) 720774.

MORRISON, Sir Fraser; *see* Morrison, Sir A. F.

MORRISON, Sir Garth; *see* Morrison, Sir W. G.

MORRISON, George Ivan, (Van), OBE 1996; singer and songwriter; *b* Belfast, 31 Aug. 1945; *s* of George Morrison and Violet Morrison; *m* 1967, Janet Planet (marr. diss. 1973); one *d*. Singer with Them, 1964–67; solo singer, 1967–. *Albums include:* with Them: Them, 1965; Them Again, 1966; solo: Blowin' Your Mind, 1967; Astral Weeks, 1968; Moondance, 1970; His Band and Street Choir, 1970; Tupelo Honey, 1971; St Dominic's Preview, 1972; Hard Nose the Highway, 1973; Veedon Fleece, 1974; A Period of Transition, 1977; Wavelength, 1978; Into the Music, 1979; Common One, 1980; Beautiful Vision, 1982; Inarticulate Speech of the Heart, 1983; A Sense of Wonder, 1985; No Guru, No Method, No Teacher, 1986; Poetic Champion Compose, 1987; Irish Heartbeat, 1988; Avalon Sunset, 1989; Enlightenment, 1990; Hymns to the Silence, 1991; Bang Master, 1991; Too Long in Exile, 1993; A Night in San Francisco, 1994; Days Like This, 1995; How Long Has This Been Going On, 1995; The Healing Game, 1996; Tell Me Something, 1996; The Philosopher's Stone, 1998; The Masters, 1999; Back on Top, 1999; Down the Road, 2002; What's Wrong with this Picture, 2003; Magic Time, 2005. *Address:* c/o Polydor Records Ltd, 72 Black Lion Lane, W6 9BE.

MORRISON, Graham, RIBA; Partner, Allies and Morrison, Architects, since 1983; *b* 2 Feb. 1951; *s* of Robert Morrison and Robina Sandison Morrison; *m* 1st, 1973 (marr. diss. 1993); one *s* one *d*; 2nd, 2001, Michelle Lovric, novelist. *Educ:* Brighton Coll.; Jesus Coll., Cambridge (MA; DipArch 1975). RIBA 1976. *Projects completed* include: Clove Bldg, London, 1990 (RIBA Award 1991); Sarum Hall Sch., London, 1995 (RIBA Award, Civic Trust Award, 1996); Nunnery Square, Sheffield, 1995 (RIBA Award 1996); British Embassy, Dublin, 1995 (RIBA Award 1997); Rosalind Franklin Bldg, Newnham Coll., Cambridge, 1995 (RIBA Award 1996); Abbey Mills Pumping Station, Stratford (RIBA Award), 1997; Rutherford Information Services Bldg, Goldsmiths Coll., London, 1997 (RIBA Award 1998); Blackburn Hse, London, 1999 (RIBA Award 2000); Blackwell, Cumbria, 2003 (RIBA Award, Civic Trust Award, 2003); extension to Horniman Mus., 2004 (RIBA Award, Civic Trust Award, 2004); 85 Southwark Street, London, 2004 (London Civic Trust Award, Bldg of Year Award, RIBA London, Nat. Winner for Corporate Workplace Bldg, British Council for Offices Awards, 2004); BBC Media Village, White City (RIBA Award 2005; Civic Trust Award 2006); Fitzwilliam Coll. Gatehouse and Auditorium (RIBA Award 2005; Civic Trust Award 2007); Girton Coll. Liby, Cambridge (RIBA Award 2006; Civic Trust Award 2007); City Lit (Civic Trust Award 2006); The Finlay Bldg, Merton Coll. (Civic Trust Award 2007); Farnborough Business Park, Hants (RIBA Award 2007); WWT Vis. Centre and Footbridge, Welney (Civic Trust Award 2007). *Exhibitions* include: New British Architecture, Japan, 1994; Allies and Morrison Retrospective, USA Schs of Architecture, 1996–98, Helsinki, Delft and Strasbourg, 1999. Architects to Royal Fest. Hall, 1994–. Lectures in Canada, Finland, India, Ireland, Japan, S Africa, UK, USA. Special Prof. of Architecture, Univ. of Nottingham, 2004–05. Member: RIBA Council, 1991–94; Architecture Adv. Cttee, Arts Council, 1996–97; Royal Fine Art Commn, 1998–99; Design Review Cttee, CABE, 2000–04; London Adv. Cttee, English Heritage, 2001–. External Examiner: Univ. of Cambridge, 1994–97; Univ. of Portsmouth, 2003–05. Dir, RIBA Jl, 1993–97. Masterplanning Architect of the Year and Public Bldg Architect of the Year, Bldg Design Awards, 2007. *Recreations:* Blues music, Venice. *Address:* 5 Winchester Wharf, 4 Clink Street, SE1 9DL; Palazzo Falier, Calle Fallier o Vitturi, San Marco 2905/6, Venice, Italy.

MORRISON, Howard Andrew Clive, CBE 2007 (OBE 1988); QC 2001; **His Honour Judge Morrison;** a Circuit Judge, since 2004; *b* 20 July 1949; *s* of Howard Edward Morrison and Roma Morrison (*née* Wilkinson); *m* 1980, Kathryn Margaret Moore; one *s* one *d*. *Educ:* London Univ. (LLB); Inns of Court Sch. of Law. Volunteer, Ghana, 1968–69, Desk Officer, Zambia and Malawi, 1975–76, VSO. Subaltern, Queen's Regt, 1970–74; Parachute Regt, TAVR and RARO, 1977–99. Called to the Bar: Gray's Inn, 1977; Fiji, 1988; Eastern Caribbean, 1990; in practice on Midland and Oxford Circuit, 1977–85; Resident Magistrate, then Chief Magistrate, Fiji, 1985–87; concurrently Sen. Magistrate for Tuvalu and locum Attorney Gen. of Anguilla, 1988–89; in practice on Midland and Oxford Circuit, 1989–2004; a Recorder, 1994–2004; engaged in defending in UN War Crime Tribunals, The Hague and Arusha, 1998–2004; Sen. Judge, Sovereign Base Areas, Cyprus, 2007–. Advocacy Teacher/Trainer, Gray's Inn, 1994–. Holding Redlich Dist. Vis. Fellow, Monash Univ., 2007. Lectures on internat. humanitarian law, Europe, Africa, Middle East, USA and Australia. Member: Race Relations Cttee, 1996–2002, Equal Opportunities Cttee, 2002–03, Bar Council; IBA; Commonwealth Judges and Magistrates Assoc.; Justice; British Inst. for Internat. and Comparative Law. Member, Bar: Fiji; E Caribbean. FRGS 1991. *Publications:* numerous legal articles, mainly on internat. criminal law. *Recreations:* travel, scuba diving, flying, sailing. *Address:* c/o 36 Bedford Row, WC1R 4JH.

MORRISON, Sir Howard (Leslie), Kt 1990; OBE 1976; entertainer, self-employed, since 1957; Youth Development Director for Maori Affairs, 1978–91; *b* 18 Aug. 1935; *s* of late Temuera Leslie Morrison and Gertrude Harete Morrison (*née* Davidson); *m* 1957, Rangiwhata Anne (*née* Manahi); two *s* one *d. Educ:* Huiarau Primary Sch.; Rotorua Primary Sch.; Rotorua High Sch.; Te Aute College. Surveyor's Asst, 1954–59; performer with Maori concert party groups since childhood; formed Howard Morrison Quartet, 1957 (part-time, later full-time); numerous recordings, TV, national tours; quartet disbanded 1965; solo entertainer, 1965–; tours in NZ, S Pacific, SE Asia; TV and films; Royal Command perfs, 1963, 1974, 1981. Patron, Life Educn Trust, NZ, 1996. Hon. Dr Waikato. Entertainer of the Year, 1966, 1990; Life Achievement Award, Entertainer of the Year, 1996. *Recreations:* golf, swimming. *Address:* Korokai Street, Ohinemutu Village, Rotorua, New Zealand. *T:* (7) 3485735, *Fax:* (7) 3480910; *e-mail:* Sir.H@xtra.co.nz. *Club:* Carbine (Auckland, NZ).

MORRISON, James, RSA 1992 (ARSA 1973); RSW 1968; painter in oil and water colours; *b* 11 April 1932; *s* of John Morrison and Margaret Thomson; *m* 1955, Dorothy McCormack; one *s* one *d. Educ:* Hillhead High Sch., Glasgow; Glasgow Sch. of Art (DA). Vis. Artist, Hospitalfield House, 1962, 1963; Duncan of Jordanstone College of Art, Dundee: Member of Staff, 1965–87; Head of Dept, 1978–87; Mem. Board, 1988–. Council Mem., Soc. of Scottish Artists, 1964–67; Keeper of the Collection, Royal Scottish Acad., 1992–. Mem., Inst. of Contemporary Scotland, 2000. Painting in Europe, USA and Canada, 1968–; painting in the High Arctic, 1990–96; painting in Africa, 1998; one-man exhibns, Scotland, London, Italy, Germany, Canada, 1956–; numerous works in public and private collections, UK and overseas. Torrance Award, RGI, 1958; Arts Council Travelling Award, 1968. DUniv Stirling, 1986. *Publications:* Aff the Squerr, 1976, 2nd edn 1990; Winter in Paris, 1991. *Recreation:* playing recorder in a chamber music group. *Address:* Craigview House, Usan, Montrose, Angus DD10 9SD. *T:* (01674) 672639.

MORRISON, Janet Rachel; Chief Executive, IndependentAge, since 2007; *b* 13 April 1964; *d* of Alastair and Jennifer Morrison; *m* 1997, Prof. Matthew Craven; one *s* one *d. Educ:* Univ. of Nottingham (BA Hons Pols 1985); Virginia State Univ. (MA Pol Sci. 1986). Dir, Policy and Res., NCVO, 1995–97; Sen. Policy Advr, BBC, 1997–99; Dep. Chief Exec., NESTA, 1999–2007. Member: Deregulation Task Force for Charities, 1994; Deakin Commn Charity Law Cttee, 1995. *Recreation:* family. *Address:* 27 Muswell Road, N10 2BS. *T:* (020) 8374 1728; IndependentAge, 6 Avonmore Road, W14 8RL. *T:* (020) 7605 4205.

MORRISON, Jasper, RDI 2001; designer; *b* 11 Nov. 1959; *s* of Alec and Dinah Morrison; *m* 1988, Ruth Donaghey. *Educ:* Kingston Polytechnic; RCA (MA Design). Established Office for Design, 1986. *Publications:* Jasper Morrison: designs, projects and drawings 1981–1989, 1990; A World Without Words, 1992, 2nd edn 1998; A New Tram for Hanover, 1997; Everything But the Walls, 2002. *Address:* 51 Hoxton Square, N1 6PB. *T:* (020) 7739 2522.

MORRISON, Ven. John Anthony; Archdeacon of Oxford, 1998–2005, now Archdeacon Emeritus; a Residentiary Canon of Christ Church, Oxford, 1998–2005, now Canon Emeritus; *b* 11 March 1938; *s* of late Major Leslie Claude Morrison and Mary Sharland Morrison (*née* Newson-Smith); *m* 1968, Angela, *d* of late Major Jonathan Eric Bush; two *s* one *d. Educ:* Haileybury; Jesus Coll., Cambridge (BA 1960; MA 1964); Lincoln Coll., Oxford (MA 1968); Chichester Theol Coll. Deacon 1964, priest 1965; Curate: St Peter, Birmingham, 1964–68; St Michael-at-the-Northgate, Oxford, 1968–74; Chaplain, Lincoln Coll., Oxford, 1968–74; Vicar, Basildon, Berks, 1974–82; RD Bradfield, 1978–82; Vicar, Aylesbury, Bucks, 1982–89; Team Rector, 1989–90; RD Aylesbury, 1985–89; Archdeacon of Buckingham, 1990–98. Examining Chaplain to Bishop of Oxford, 1972–78. Mem., Gen. Synod, 1980–90, 1998–2000. Sen. Treas., Corp. of Sons of the Clergy, 2005–08 (Treas., 2002–08). County Chaplain: Bucks, 1990–98, Oxon, 1998–2007, RBL; Bucks, 1990–98, Oxon, 1998–2007, St John Ambulance. Hon Chaplain, 007 Past Masters Assoc., 2007–. Master, Spectacle Makers' Co., 2006–07. *Address:* 39 Crown Road, Wheatley, Oxford 0X33 1UJ. *T:* (01865) 876625; *e-mail:* john.morrison@chch.ox.ac.uk. *Clubs:* Leander (Henley-on-Thames); Vincent's (Oxford).

MORRISON, Sir Kenneth (Duncan), Kt 2000; CBE 1990; Chairman, 1956–2008, and Managing Director, 1956–97 and 2002–08, William Morrison Supermarkets plc; *b* 20 Oct. 1931; *m* 1st, Edna (decd); one *s* two *d;* 2nd, Lynne; one *d.* Career in grocery retailing; co. now has over 100 stores. *Address:* c/o William Morrison Supermarkets plc, Hilmore House, Thornton Road, Bradford BD8 9AX.

MORRISON, Leslie; Chief Executive Officer, Invest Northern Ireland, since 2001; *b* 29 Jan. 1948. *Educ:* Queen's Univ., Belfast (BA Hons Mod. Languages 1971). Man. Dir, J. P. Morgan & Co., 1983–2001. *Address:* Invest Northern Ireland, Bedford Square, Bedford Street, Belfast BT2 7ES. *T:* (028) 9023 9090; *e-mail:* leslie.morrison@investni.com.

MORRISON, Hon. Mary Anne, DCVO 1982 (CVO 1970); Woman of the Bedchamber to the Queen, since 1960; *b* 17 May 1937; *o d* of 1st Baron Margadale, TD. *Educ:* Heathfield School. *Address:* The Old Rectory, Fonthill Bishop, Salisbury, Wilts SP3 5SF.

MORRISON, Murdo; Editor, Flight International, since 2001 (Managing Editor, 2001); *b* 22 June 1964; *s* of late John and of Mairi Morrison; *m* 1994, Juliet Parish; one *s* one *d. Educ:* Nicolson Inst., Stornoway; Glasgow Univ. (MA Hons Politics 1986); University Coll., Cardiff (Dip. Journalism 1987). Journalist, Commercial Motor, 1987–92; Editor, Car & Accessory Trader, 1992–94; Dep. Editor, Printweek, 1994–95; Editor: Planning Week, 1995; Motor Trader, 1995–2001. Governor, Middle Street Primary Sch., Brighton, 1998–2006 (Chm. of Govs, 2001–06). *Recreations:* football, spending time with my children, music. *Address:* Reed Business Information, Quadrant House, The Quadrant, Sutton, Surrey SM2 5AS. *T:* (020) 8652 4395, *Fax:* (020) 8652 3850; *e-mail:* murdo.morrison@flightglobal.com.

MORRISON, Neil; *see* Morrison, A. N.

MORRISON, Nigel Murray Paton; QC (Scot.) 1988; Sheriff of Lothian and Borders at Edinburgh, since 1996; *b* 18 March 1948; *o s* of late David Paton Morrison, FRICS, FLAS and Dilys Trenholm Pritchard or Morrison. *Educ:* Rannoch School. Called to the Bar, Inner Temple, 1972; admitted Scottish Bar, 1975; Asst Editor, Session Cases, 1976–82; Asst Clerk, Rules Council, 1978–84; Clerk of Faculty, Faculty of Advocates, 1979–87; Standing Junior Counsel to Scottish Develt Dept (Planning), 1982–86; Temporary Sheriff, 1982–96; Second (formerly Junior) Counsel to Lord President of Court of Session, 1984–89; First Counsel to Lord President, 1989–96; Counsel to Sec. of State under Private Legislation Procedure (Scotland) Act 1936, 1986–96. Chairman: Social Security Appeal Tribunals, 1982–91; Medical Appeal Tribunals, 1991–96. Dir of Judicial Studies, Judicial Studies Cttee, 2000–04. Trustee, Nat. Library of Scotland, 1989–98. Editor: Greens Civil

Practice Bulletin, 1995–2003; Greens Litigation Styles, 1998–2003. *Publications:* (jtly) Greens Annotated Rules of the Court of Session, 1994; (ed jtly) Sentencing Practice, 2000; contribs to Stair Memorial Encyclopaedia of the Laws of Scotland, Macphail on Sheriff Court Practice, 2nd edn. *Recreations:* music, riding, being taken for walks by my dogs. *Address:* Sheriff Court House, 27 Chambers Street, Edinburgh EH1 1LB. *T:* (0131) 225 2525. *Club:* New (Edinburgh).

MORRISON, (Philip) Blake, FRSL; poet, novelist and critic; *b* 8 Oct. 1950; *s* of Arthur Blakemore Morrison and Agnes O'Shea; *m* 1976, Katherine Ann Drake; two *s* one *d. Educ:* Ermysteds Grammar Sch., Skipton; Nottingham Univ. (BA); McMaster Univ. (MA); University College London (PhD; Fellow, 2006). FRSL 1988. Poetry and fiction editor, TLS, 1978–81; Dep. Literary Editor, 1981–86, Literary Editor, 1987–89, Observer; Literary Editor, 1990–94, Staff writer, 1994–95, Independent on Sunday. Prof. of Creative and Life Writing, Goldsmiths Coll., London Univ., 2003–. Writer: of plays, The Man with Two Gaffers, 2006, Lisa's Sex Strike, 2007; of opera libretto, Elephant and Castle, 2007. Eric Gregory Award, 1980; Somerset Maugham Award, 1984; Dylan Thomas Meml Prize, 1985; E. M. Forster Award, 1988. *Publications:* The Movement: English poetry and fiction of the 1950s, 1980; (ed jtly) The Penguin Book of Contemporary British Poetry, 1982; Seamus Heaney, 1982; Dark Glasses, 1984; The Ballad of the Yorkshire Ripper, 1987; The Yellow House, 1987; And When Did You Last See Your Father, 1993 (Waterstone's/Volvo/Esquire Non-Fiction Award, 1993; J. R. Ackerley Award, 1994); The Cracked Pot, 1995; (ed jtly) Mind Readings, 1996; As If, 1997; Too True, 1998; Dr Ox's Experiment (opera libretto), 1998; Selected Poems, 1999; The Justification of Johann Gutenberg, 2000; Things My Mother Never Told Me, 2002; Oedipus and Antigone (translations), 2003; South of the River, 2007. *Recreations:* football, tennis, running. *Address:* c/o Peters, Fraser & Dunlop, Drury House, 34–43 Russell Street, WC2B 5HA. *T:* (020) 7344 1000.

MORRISON, Richard Duncan; Columnist, since 1999, Chief Music Critic, since 2001, The Times; *b* 24 July 1954; *s* of Donald and Mary Morrison; *m* 1977, Marian Plant; two *s* one *d. Educ:* University Coll. Sch.; Magdalene Coll., Cambridge (MA). Asst Editor, Classical Music magazine, 1977–83; Dep. Editor, Early Music magazine, 1984–88; The Times: Music Critic, 1984–89; Dep. Arts Editor, 1989–90; Arts Editor, 1990–99. Dir of Music, St Mary, Hendon, 1976–. FRSA 1995. *Publication:* Orchestra: the LSO: a century of triumphs and turbulence, 2003. *Recreations:* walking, organ-playing. *Address:* 11 Sunningfields Crescent, NW4 4RD. *T:* (020) 8202 8028.

MORRISON, Hon. Sara Antoinette Sibell Frances, (Hon. Mrs Sara Morrison); *b* 9 Aug. 1934; *d* of 2nd Viscount Long and of Laura, Duchess of Marlborough; *m* 1954, Hon. Charles Andrew Morrison (marr. diss. 1984; he *d* 2005); one *s* one *d. Educ:* in England and France. Gen. Electric Co., 1975–98 (Dir 1980–98); Non-Executive Director: Abbey National plc (formerly Abbey Nat. Building Soc.), 1979–95; Carlton TV, 1992–98; Kleinwort Charter Trust, 1993–2002. Chairman: Nat. Council for Voluntary Orgns (formerly Nat. Council of Social Service), 1977–81; Nat. Adv. Council on Employment of Disabled People, 1981–84. County Councillor, then Alderman, Wilts, 1961–71; Chairman: Wilts Assoc. of Youth Clubs, 1958–63; Wilts Community Council, 1965–70; Vice-Chairman: Nat. Assoc. Youth Clubs, 1969–71; Conservative Party Organisation, 1971–75; Member: Governing Bd, Volunteer Centre, 1972–77; Annan Cttee of Enquiry into Broadcasting, 1974–77; Nat. Consumer Council, 1975–77; Bd, Fourth Channel TV Co., 1980–85; Video Appeals Cttee (Video Recordings Act, 1984), 1985–; Governing Council, Family Policy Studies Centre, 1983–99; Nat. Radiological Protection Bd, 1989–97; Council, PSI, 1980–93; Governing Body, Imperial Coll., London, 1986–2002 (Hon. Fellow 1993); UK Round Table on Sustainable Develt, 1995–98; Chm., WWF UK, 1998–2002; Dep. Chm., 2000–05, Vice Pres. Emeritus, 2005–, WWF Internat.; Chm., Council, Univ. of Bath, 2004–06. Life FRSA 1986; FCGI 2005. Hon. DBA Coventry, 1994; Hon. LLD De Montfort, 1998; Hon. DSc Buckingham, 2000. *Address:* Wyndham's Farm, Wedhampton, Devizes, Wilts SN10 3RR. *T:* (01380) 840221; 16 Groom Place, SW1X 7BA. *T:* (020) 7245 6553.

MORRISON, Stephen Roger; Chief Executive, All3Media, since 2003; *b* 3 March 1947; *s* of Hyman Michael Morrison and Rebecca (*née* Zolkwer); *m* 1979, Gayle Valerie Broughall; three *d. Educ:* High Sch., Glasgow; Edinburgh Univ. (MA Hons); Nat. Film Sch., Beaconsfield (ANFS). BBC Scotland (Radio and TV), 1970; Granada Television: Producer/Dir, Northern Documentary Unit, 1974; Ed., Granada Regl Progs, 1977; Hd of Arts and Features, 1981; Dir of Programmes, 1987–92; Man. Dir, Broadcasting, 1992–94; Man. Dir, 1993–94; Man. Dir, LWT, 1994–96; Chief Exec., Granada Media Gp, 1996–2002. Feature Films Producer: The Magic Toyshop, 1986; The Fruit Machine, 1988; (Exec. Producer) My Left Foot, 1989 (2 Acad. Awards); (Exec. Producer) The Field, 1990; Jack and Sarah, 1995; August, 1996. *Recreations:* walking, reading, films and theatre, talking and dining, touring delicatessens. *Address:* All3Media, Berkshire House, 168–173 High Holborn, WC1V 7AA. *T:* (020) 7845 4377. *Club:* Garrick.

MORRISON, Toni; *see* Morrison, C. A.

MORRISON, Van; *see* Morrison, G. I.

MORRISON, William Charles Carnegie, CBE 1993; CA; UK Deputy Senior Partner, Peat Marwick McLintock, later KPMG Peat Marwick, 1987–93; *b* 10 Feb. 1938; *s* of late William and Grace Morrison; *m* 1st; two *d;* 2nd, 1977, Joceline Mary (*née* Saint). *Educ:* Kelvinside Acad., Lathallan; Merchiston Castle Sch. Thomson McLintock & Co., subseq. KMG Thomson McLintock: qual. CA (with distinction), 1961; Partner, 1966; Jt Sen. Partner, Glasgow and Edinburgh, 1974–80; UK managing partner, 1980–87. Director: Thomas Cook & Son Ltd, 1971–72; Scottish Amicable Life Assce Soc., 1973–87, 1993–97; Securities Trust of Scotland, 1976–80; Brownlee & Co., 1978–80; Bank of Scotland, 1993–97; Chm., British Linen Bank Group Ltd, 1994–97; Mem. Bd, Scottish Amicable, 1997–2008. Pres., Inst. of Chartered Accountants of Scotland, 1984–85 (Vice-Pres., 1982–84). Chairman: Auditing Practices Bd of UK and Ireland, 1991–94; Exec. Cttee, The Accountants' Jt Disciplinary Scheme, 1993–; Mem., Financial Reporting Council, 1991–95. Vice Pres., Scottish Council (Develt and Industry), 1982–93 (mem. various cttees; Fellow, 1993); Member: Scottish Telecommunications Bd, 1978–80; Scottish Cttee, Design Council, 1978–81. Vis. Prof. in Accountancy, Univ. of Strathclyde, 1983. Governor, Kelvinside Acad., 1967–80 (Chm. of Governors, 1975–80); Hon. Treasurer, Transport Trust, 1982–88; Trustee, Indep. Living Funds, 1993–2002. FRSA 1990. *Publications:* occasional professional papers. *Recreations:* vintage transport, model railways. *Address:* 87 Campden Hill Court, Holland Street, W8 7HW. *T:* (020) 7937 2972. *Club:* Caledonian.

MORRISON, Sir (William) Garth, KT 2007; CBE 1994; Lord-Lieutenant, East Lothian, since 2001; *b* 8 April 1943; *s* of late Walter Courtenay Morrison and Audrey Elizabeth Morrison (*née* Gilbert); *m* 1970, Gillian Cheetham; two *s* one *d. Educ:* Pangbourne Coll.; Pembroke Coll., Cambridge (BA 1966). CEng 1973; MIET (MIEE 1973). Service in RN, retiring as Lieut, 1961–73; farming in family partnership, 1973–. Scouting: Area Comr, E Lothian, 1973–81; Chief Comr of Scotland, 1981–88; Chief

Scout, 1988–96; Mem., World Scout Cttee, 1991–2002. Chairman: East and Midlothian NHS Trust, 1994–97; Royal Infirmary of Edinburgh NHS Trust, 1997–99; Lothian Primary Care NHS Trust, 1999–2004. Member: Lothian Region Children's Panel, 1976–83; Scottish Community Educn Council, 1988–95 (Fellow, 1995); Nat. Lottery Charities Bd, 1995–99. Chm., SE Regl Cttee, 1996–2000, Pres., 2001–04, Scottish Landowners' Fedn. Vice-Pres., Commonwealth Youth Exchange Council, 1997–. Trustee: The MacRobert Trusts, 1998– (Chm., 2007–); Lamp of Lothian Collegiate Trust, 1978– (Chm., 2001–). DL E Lothian, 1984. Hon. DBA Napier, 2001. Argentine Gold Medal, 1962. *Publication:* chapter in The Scottish Juvenile Justice System, 1982. *Recreations:* golf, sailing, scouting. *Address:* West Fenton, North Berwick, East Lothian EH39 5AL. *T:* (01620) 842154.

MORRISON-BELL, Sir William (Hollin Dayrell), 4th Bt *cr* 1905; solicitor; *b* 21 June 1956; *s* of Sir Charles Reginald Francis Morrison-Bell, 3rd Bt and of Prudence Caroline, *d* of late Lt-Col W. D. Davies, 60th Rifles (she *m* 2nd, Peter Gillbanks); *S* father, 1967; *m* 1984, Cynthia Hélène Marie White; one *s* one *d. Educ:* Eton; St Edmund Hall, Oxford. *Heir: s* Thomas Charles Edward Morrison-Bell, *b* 13 Feb. 1985. *Address:* Highgreen, Tarset, Hexham, Northumberland NE48 1RP. *T:* (01434) 240223; 28 Batoum Gardens, W6 7QD. *T:* (020) 7602 1363.

MORRISON-LOW, Sir James; *see* Low.

MORRISSEY, Gerry Anthony; General Secretary, Broadcasting, Entertainment, Cinematograph and Theatre Union, since 2007; *b* 12 April 1960; *s* of Jimmy and Peggy Morrissey; *m* 1996, Susan Caird; one *s* one *d. Educ:* Christian Brothers Secondary Sch., Tipperary Town. Storeman, BBC, 1976–88; Broadcasting and Entertainments Trade Alliance, subseq. Broadcasting, Entertainment, Cinematograph and Theatre Union: full-time Union Official, 1988–91; Supervisory Official, 1991–99; Asst Gen. Sec., 1999–2007. Mem. Council, Broadcasting Standards Adv. Council, 2007–. Exec. Mem., Union Network Internat., 2002–. *Recreations:* tennis, badminton, running, Arsenal Football Club, National Hunt racing. *Address:* (office) Broadcasting, Entertainment, Cinematograph and Theatre Union, 373–377 Clapham Road, SW9 9BT. *T:* (020) 7346 0900; *e-mail:* gmorrissey@bectu.org.uk.

MORRITT, Rt Hon. Sir (Robert) Andrew, Kt 1988; CVO 1989; PC 1994; Chancellor of the High Court, since 2005; Vice-President of the Court of Protection, since 2005; *b* 5 Feb. 1938; *s* of Robert Augustus Morritt and Margaret Mary Morritt (*née* Tyldesley Jones); *m* 1962, Sarah Simonetta Merton, *d* of John Ralph Merton, *qv*; two *s. Educ:* Eton Coll.; Magdalene Coll., Cambridge (BA 1961). 2nd Lieut Scots Guards, 1956–58. Called to the Bar, Lincoln's Inn, 1962 (Bencher, 1984; Treas., 2005); QC 1977. Junior Counsel: to Sec. of State for Trade in Chancery Matters, 1970–77; to Attorney-Gen. in Charity Matters, 1972–77; Attorney General to HRH The Prince of Wales, 1978–88; a Judge of High Court of Justice, Chancery Div., 1988–94; a Lord Justice of Appeal, 1994–2000; Vice-Chancellor of the Supreme Court, 2000–05. Vice-Chancellor of Co. Palatine of Lancaster, 1991–94. Member: Gen. Council of the Bar, 1969–73; Adv. Cttee on Legal Educn, 1972–76; Top Salaries Review Body, 1982–87. Pres., Council of the Inns of Court, 1997–2000. *Recreations:* fishing, shooting. *Address:* Royal Courts of Justice, Strand, WC2A 2LL. *Club:* Garrick.

MORROW, Baron *cr* 2006 (Life Peer), of Clogher Valley in the county of Tyrone; **Maurice George Morrow;** Member (DemU) Fermanagh and South Tyrone, Northern Ireland Assembly, since 1998; Chairman, Democratic Unionist Party; *s* of Ernest and Eliza Jane Morrow; *m* 1976, Jennifer Reid; two *d. Educ:* Drumglass High Sch.; East Tyrone Coll. of Further and Higher Educn. Minister for Social Develt, NI, 2000–01. Mem. (DemU) Dungannon and S Tyrone BC. *Address:* House of Lords, SW1A 0PW.

MORROW, Cdre Anthony John Clare, CVO 1997; RN; Clerk to the Butchers' Company, since 2003; Extra Equerry to the Queen, since 1998; *b* 30 March 1944; *s* of late Capt. John Geoffrey Basil Morrow, CVO, DSC, RN and Dorothy April Bettine (*née* Mather); *m* 1st, 1969 (marr. diss. 1979); two *d*; 2nd, 1982, Julie, *d* of late R. M. Philips and Mrs M. Philips; one *s* one *d. Educ:* Summerfields, Oxford; Nautical Coll., Pangbourne; BRNC, Dartmouth. Entered RN, 1962: qualified Signals Officer, HMS Mercury, 1971; Lt-Comdr 1972; on staff of C-in-C Fleet, Signals Officer, HM Yacht Britannia, 1976–78; commanded HMS Lindisfarne, 1978–79; Comdr 1979; on staff, UK Mil. Rep. to NATO, 1980–83; commanded HMS Active, 1983–85; RN Exchange to CNO, US Navy, Washington, 1985–87; MoD, 1987–88; Capt. 1988; Captain, HMS Mercury, 1988–91; commanded Fourth Frigate Sqdn, HMS Active, 1991–93; ACOS, Plans and Policy, CINCHAN, Eastern Atlantic, 1993–94; Commodore Royal Yachts, 1995–98; retired 1998. Gen. Manager, W. & F. C. Bonham & Sons Ltd, 1999. Chm., Assoc. of Royal Yachtsmen, 1998–. Younger Brother, Trinity House, 1996. *Recreations:* outdoor activities, sports. *Clubs:* Royal Yacht Squadron, Royal London Yacht; Bosham Sailing; Imperial Poona Yacht.

MORROW, Graham Eric; QC 1996; **His Honour Judge Morrow;** a Circuit Judge, since 2006; *b* 14 June 1951; *s* of George Eric Morrow and Freda Morrow; *m* 1987, Rosalind Nola Ellis; one *s*, and two step *d. Educ:* Liverpool Coll. (Foundation Mem.); Univ. of Newcastle upon Tyne (LLB). Called to the Bar, Lincoln's Inn, 1974; Asst Recorder, 1990; a Recorder, 1997–2006. Trustee, Royal Sch. for the Blind, Liverpool. *Recreations:* cycling, swimming, ski-ing.

MORSE, Prof. Christopher George John, (Robin); Professor of Law, King's College London, since 1992; *b* 28 June 1947; *s* of John Morse and Margaret Gwenllian Morse (*née* Maliphant); *m* 1983, Louise Angela Stott; one *s. Educ:* Malvern Coll.; Wadham Coll., Oxford (MA, BCL). Called to the Bar, Middle Temple, 1971; King's College London: Lectr in Law, 1971–88; Reader, 1988–92; Hd and Dean, Sch. of Law, 1992–93, 1997–2001; FKC 2000. Visiting Professor: John Marshall Law Sch., Chicago, 1979–80; Univ. of Leuven, 1982; Dir of Studies, Hague Acad. of Internat. Law, 1990. *Publications:* Torts in Private International Law, 1978; (ed jtly) Dicey and Morris on the Conflict of Laws, 11th edn 1987 to 14th edn 2006; (ed jtly) Benjamin's Sale of Goods, 3rd edn 1987 to 7th edn 2006; Public Policy in Transnational Relationships, 1991; (ed jtly) Chitty on Contracts, 27th edn 1994 to 30th edn 2009; articles in learned jls and contribs to books. *Recreations:* Swansea City Association Football Club, travel. *Address:* School of Law, King's College London, Strand, WC2R 2LS. *T:* (020) 7848 5454.

MORSE, Sir Christopher Jeremy, KCMG 1975; Warden, Winchester College, 1987–97 (Fellow, 1966–82); Chancellor, Bristol University, 1989–2003; *b* 10 Dec. 1928; *s* of late Francis John Morse and Kinbarra (*née* Armfield-Marrow); *m* 1955, Belinda Marianne, *d* of Lt-Col R. B. Y. Mills; three *s* one *d* (and one *d* decd). *Educ:* Winchester; New Coll., Oxford (Hon. Fellow, 1979). 1st Class Lit. Hum. 1953. 2nd Lt KRRC, 1948–49. Fellow, All Souls Coll., Oxford, 1953–68, 1983–. Trained in banking at Glyn, Mills & Co., and made a director in 1964; Executive Dir, 1965–72, non-exec. Dir, 1993–97, Bank of England; Lloyds Bank: Dep. Chm., 1975–77; Chm., 1977–93; Lloyds Bank International: Chm., 1979–80; Dep. Chm., 1975–77 and 1980–85; Chm., Lloyds Merchant Bank Hldgs, 1985–88. Alternate Governor for UK of IMF, 1966–72; Chm. of Deputies of Cttee of Twenty, IMF, 1972–74; Chm., Cttee of London Clearing Bankers, 1980–82 (Dep. Chm., 1978–80); Mem., Council of Lloyd's, 1987–98; President: London Forex Assoc., 1978–91; Institut Internat. d'Etudes Bancaires, 1982–83; British Overseas Bankers' Club, 1983–84; BBA, 1984–91 (Vice-Pres., 1991–92); Internat. Monetary Conf., 1985–86; Banking Fedn of EC, 1988–90; CIB, 1992–93 (Vice-Pres., 1991–92); Vice-Pres., BITC, 1992–98. Mem., NEDC, 1977–81. Chm., City Communications Centre, 1985–87; non-executive Director: Alexanders Discount Co. Ltd, 1975–84; Legal & General Assce Soc., 1964 and 1975–87; ICI, 1981–93; Zeneca, 1993–99. Hon. Mem., Lombard Assoc., 1989. Governor, Henley Management Coll., 1966–85. Chairman: Per Jacobsson Foundn, 1987–99; Trustees, Beit Meml Fellowships for Med. Res., 1976–2003; GBA, 1994–99; Mem., British Selection Cttee, Harkness Fellowships, 1986–90. Pres., Classical Assoc., 1989–90. Freeman, City of London, 1978; Chm., City Arts Trust, 1976–79. FIDE Internat. Judge for chess compositions, 1975–; Pres., British Chess Problem Soc., 1977–79; Hon. Life Mem., British Chess Fedn, 1988; Hon. Master of Chess Composition, Perm. Commn for Chess Composition, FIDE, 2006. Pres., Crown and Manor Boys' Club, Hoxton, 2002–. Hon. DLitt City, 1977; Hon. DSc Aston, 1984; Hon. LLD Bristol, 1989. *Publication:* Chess Problems: tasks and records, 1995, 2nd edn 2001. *Recreations:* poetry, problems and puzzles, coarse gardening, golf. *Address:* 102a Drayton Gardens, SW10 9RJ. *T:* (020) 7370 2265. *Club:* Athenæum.

MORSE, Sir Jeremy; *see* Morse, Sir C. J.

MORSE, Robin; *see* Morse, C. G. J.

MORSON, Basil Clifford, CBE 1987; VRD 1963; MA, DM Oxon; FRCS; FRCPath; FRCP; Civilian Consultant in Pathology to the Royal Navy, 1976–86, now Emeritus; Consulting Pathologist and Research Consultant to St Mark's Hospital, since 1986 (Consultant Pathologist, 1956–86); Director, WHO International Reference Centre for Gastrointestinal Cancer, 1969–86; *b* 13 Nov. 1921; *s* of late A. Clifford Morson, OBE, FRCS; *m* 1st, 1950, Pamela Elizabeth Gilbert (marr. diss. 1982); one *s* two *d*; 2nd, 1983, Sylvia Dutton, MBE. *Educ:* Beaumont Coll.; Wadham Coll., Oxford; Middlesex Hosp. Medical Sch. House Surg., Middlesex Hosp., 1949; House Surg., Central Middlesex Hosp., 1950; Asst Pathologist, Bland-Sutton Institute of Pathology, Middlesex Hosp., 1950. Sub-Lt RNVR, 1943–46; Surgeon-Comdr RNR (London Div.), retd 1972. President: Sect. of Proctology, RSocMed, 1973–74; British Soc. of Gastroenterology, 1979–80 (Hon. Mem., 1987); British Div., Internat. Acad. of Pathology, 1979–81; Treas., RCPath, 1983–88 (Vice-Pres., 1978–81). Vis. Prof. of Pathology, Univ. of Chicago, 1959; Sir Henry Wade Vis. Prof., RCSE, 1970; Vis. Prof of Pathology, Univ. of Texas System Cancer Center, 1980 (Joanne Vandenberg Hill Award); Lectures: Lettsomian, Med. Soc., 1970; Sir Arthur Hurst Meml, British Soc. of Gastroenterology, 1970; Richardson, Massachusetts Gen. Hosp., Boston, 1970; Skinner, RCR, 1983; Shelley Meml, Johns Hopkins Univ., 1983; Kettle, RCPath, 1987. FRCS 1972; FRCP 1979 (MRCP 1973); Hon. Fellow: Amer. Soc. of Colon and Rectal Surgeons, 1974; Amer. Coll. of Gastroenterology, 1978; French Nat. Soc. of Gastroenterology, 1982; RSM, 1989; RACS, 1990. Hon. Mem., Pathological Soc. of GB and Ireland, 2006. John Hunter Medal, RCS, 1987; Frederick Salmon Medal, Sect. of Coloproctology, RSM, 1991; President's Award, British Div., Internat. Acad. of Pathol., 2005. *Publications:* Pathology of Alimentary Tract, in Systemic Pathology, ed W. St C. Symmers, 1966, 3rd edn 1987; (ed) Diseases of the Colon, Rectum and Anus, 1969; Textbook of Gastrointestinal Pathology, 1972, 4th edn 2003; Histological Typing of Intestinal Tumours, 1976; The Pathogenesis of Colorectal Cancer, 1978; Pathology in Surgical Practice, 1985; Colour Atlas of Gastrointestinal Pathology, 1988; numerous articles in medical journals. *Recreations:* gardening, ornithology, travel. *Address:* 14 Crossways Park, West Chiltington, W Sussex RH20 2QZ. *T:* (01798) 813528.

MORT, Rev. (Margaret) Marion; Non-Stipendiary Curate, St Barnabas, Swanmore, 1997–2007; *b* 10 May 1937; *d* of Rev. Ivan H. Whittaker and Margaret Whittaker; *m* 1959, Colin James Mort; one *s* two *d. Educ:* St Mary's Sch., Wantage; Queen's Coll., Harley St; Edinburgh Univ.; Southern Dios MTS. Nat. Sec., World Development Movement, 1970–72; Licensed Lay Reader, 1983–97; Mem. Gen. Synod, 1985–90 (rep. in Partners in Mission consultation for Church in Kenya, 1988). World Develt Educn Adviser, Dio. Portsmouth, 1984–91; Co-ordinator, then Officer, Decade of Evangelism (C of E), 1990–93; Mission and Evangelism Sec., Bd of Mission, Gen. Synod, 1993–94; ordained deacon, 1997, priest, 1998; permission to officiate, dio. Portsmouth, 2007–. Dir, Ocean Sound (ILR), 1985–92; Member: Bd of Christian Aid, 1987–90; Gen. Cttee, British and Foreign Bible Soc., 1993–95; Convenor, World Church Forum, dio. of Portsmouth, 2004–. Hon. Canon, Portsmouth Cathedral, 2001–07, now Emeritus. *Publications:* (jtly) Mission Audit, 1983; (jtly) Called to Order, 1988; (jtly) Building Bridges, 1995; (jtly) A Time for Sharing, 1995; church educnl papers; contribs to Church press. *Recreations:* gardening, good beer, good conversation. *Address:* Rivendell, High Street, Shirrell Heath, Southampton SO32 2JN. *T:* and *Fax:* (01329) 832178.

MORT, Timothy James; His Honour Judge Mort; a Circuit Judge, since 1996; *b* 4 March 1950; *s* of Dr Philip Mort and Sybil Mort; *m* 1979, Philippa Mary Brown; one *s* three *d. Educ:* Clifton Coll., Bristol; Emmanuel Coll., Cambridge (Schol.; MA Law Tripos 1971). Called to the Bar, Middle Temple, 1972; in practice, Northern Circuit, 1972–96. *Recreations:* tennis, Real tennis, music. *Address:* c/o Minshull Street Crown Court, Manchester M1 3FS. *Club:* Manchester Tennis & Racquet.

MORTENSEN, Prof. Neil James McCready, MD; FRCS; Professor of Colorectal Surgery, University of Oxford, since 1999; Fellow, Green Templeton College (formerly Green College), Oxford, since 2005; Consultant Colorectal Surgeon, John Radcliffe Hospital, Oxford, since 1986; *b* 16 Oct. 1949; *s* of late Peter Mortensen and of Rhoda Mortensen; *m* 1973, Jane Baker; one *s* two *d. Educ:* Hampton Sch.; Univ. of Birmingham Medical Sch. (MB ChB 1973); Univ. of Bristol (MD 1977). FRCS 1977. Consultant Sen. Lectr, Univ. of Bristol and Bristol Royal Infirmary, 1981–86; Reader in Colorectal Surgery, Univ. of Oxford, 1994–99. Treas. and Dir, 1996–2004, Chm., 2004–, British Jl of Surgery Soc.; President: Assoc. of Coloproctology, GB and Ire., 2002–03; Coloproctology Sect., RSocMed, 2003–04. *Publications:* An Atlas of Rectal Endosonography, 1991; Restorative Proctocolectomy, 1993; Ulcerative Colitis and Crohn's Disease, 1993; Controversies in Inflammatory Bowel Disease, 2001; original articles on all aspects of colorectal surgery and colorectal disease. *Recreations:* Real tennis, opera, farming. *Address:* Department of Colorectal Surgery, John Radcliffe Hospital, Oxford OX3 9DU. *T:* (01865) 220926, *Fax:* (01865) 741301.

MORTIMER, Hon. Barry; *see* Mortimer, Hon. J. B.

MORTIMER, Clifford Hiley, DSc, DrPhil; FRS 1958; Distinguished Professor in Zoology, University of Wisconsin-Milwaukee, 1966–81, now Distinguished Professor Emeritus; *b* Whitchurch, Som, 27 Feb. 1911; *er s* of Walter Herbert and Bessie Russell; *m* 1936, Ingeborg Margarete Closs (*d* 2000), Stuttgart, Germany; two *d. Educ:* Sibford and Sidcot Schs; Univ. of Manchester. BSc (Manchester) 1932, DSc (Manchester) 1946; Dr

Phil (Berlin) 1935. Served on scientific staff of Freshwater Biological Assoc., 1935–41 and 1946–56. Seconded to Admiralty scientific service, 1941–46. Sec. and Dir, Scottish Marine Biological Assoc., 1956–66; Dir, Center for Great Lakes Studies, Univ. of Wisconsin-Milwaukee, 1966–79. Hon. DSc Wisconsin-Milwaukee, 1985; DèsSc *hc* Ecole Polytechnique Fédérale de Lausanne, 1987. *Publications:* Lake Michigan in Motion, 2004; scientific papers on lakes and the physical and chemical conditions which control life in them. *Recreation:* music. *Address:* Milwaukee Catholic Home, 2462 N Prospect Avenue, Milwaukee, WI 53211, USA.

MORTIMER, Hugh Roger, LVO 1992; HM Diplomatic Service; Minister and Deputy Head of Mission, Berlin, since 2005; *b* 19 Sept. 1949; *s* of Phillip Roger Mortimer and Patricia Henley Mortimer (*née* Moreton); *m* 1974, Zosia Rzepecka (marr. diss. 2000); one *d* (and one *d* decd). *Educ:* Cheltenham Coll.; Univ. of Surrey (BSc Linguistics and Regl Studies); King's Coll., London (MA War Studies). Joined HM Diplomatic Service, 1973: Third Sec., Rome, 1975–78; Third, later Second Sec., Singapore, 1978–81; FCO, 1981–83; Second, later First Sec., UK Mission to UN, NY, 1983–86; FCO, 1986–89; on attachment to German Foreign Ministry, 1990; Dep. Head of Mission, Berlin, 1991–94; FCO, 1994–95; rcds 1996; Dep. Head of Mission, Ankara, 1997–2000; Ambassador to Slovenia, 2001–05. *Recreations:* jogging, squash, sailing, guitar playing. *Address:* c/o Foreign and Commonwealth Office, King Charles Street, SW1A 2AH.

MORTIMER, James Edward; General Secretary of the Labour Party, 1982–85; *b* 12 Jan. 1921; *m;* two *s* one *d*. *Educ:* Junior Techn. Sch., Portsmouth; Ruskin Coll., Oxford; London Sch. of Economics. Worked in Shipbuilding and Engrg Industries as Ship Fitter Apprentice, Machinist and Planning Engr; TUC Schol., Oxford, 1945–46; TUC Economic Dept, 1946–48; full-time Trade Union Official, Draughtsmen's and Allied Technicians' Assoc., 1948–68. Dir, London Co-operative Soc., 1968–71. Mem., NBPI, 1968–71; Mem., Bd, LTE, 1971–74. Chm., ACAS (formerly Conciliation and Arbitration Service), 1974–81. Member: Wilberforce Ct of Inquiry into the power dispute, 1970; Armed Forces Pay Review Body, 1971–74; EDC for Chemical Industry, 1973–74; Chm. EDC for Mechanical and Electrical Engineering Construction, 1974–82. Vis. Fellow, Admin. Staff Coll., Henley, 1976–82; Sen. Vis. Fellow, Bradford Univ., 1977–82; Vis. Prof., Imperial Coll. of Sci. and Technol., London Univ., 1981–83; Ward-Perkins Res. Fellow, Pembroke Coll., Oxford, 1981. Chm. Editl Cttee, Socialist Campaign Group News, 1987–; Mem. Exec. Cttee, Inst. of Employment Rights, 1989–2002, Vice-Pres., 2002–. Hon. DLitt Bradford, 1982. *Publications:* A History of Association of Engineering and Shipbuilding Draughtsmen, 1960; (with Clive Jenkins) British Trade Unions Today, 1965; (with Clive Jenkins) The Kind of Laws the Unions Ought to Want, 1968; Industrial Relations, 1968; Trade Unions and Technological Change, 1971; History of the Boilermakers' Society, vol. 1, 1973, vol. 2, 1982, vol. 3, 1993; (with Valerie Ellis) A Professional Union: the evolution of the Institution of Professional Civil Servants, 1980; In Defence of Trade Unionism, 1998; A Life on the Left, 1999; The Formation of the Labour Party: lessons for today, 2000; The Trade Disputes Act 1906, 2005. *Address:* 19 Northweald Lane, Kingston-upon-Thames, Surrey KT2 5GL. *T:* (020) 8547 1885.

See also J. E. Mortimer.

MORTIMER, James Edward; Deputy Director and Treasury Officer of Accounts, 1995–2000; *b* 9 Nov. 1947; *s* of James Edward Mortimer, *qv* and Renee Mabel Mortimer (*née* Horton); *m* 1969, Lesley Patricia Young. *Educ:* Latymer Upper Sch.; Wadham Coll., Oxford (MA, BPhil). HM Treasury, 1971–2000: Economic Advr, 1974–81; Principal, 1981–83; Grade 5, 1983–91; Under Sec., 1991–2000; Head of Aid and Export Finance Gp, 1991–95. *Recreations:* football, golf, cricket, birdwatching, cinema. *Address:* 21 Hogarth Way, Hampton, Middlesex TW12 2EL. *Clubs:* Royal Automobile; Old Latymerians Association.

MORTIMER, Hon. (John) Barry, GBS 1999; QC 1971; mediator and arbitrator; a Non-Permanent Judge, Court of Final Appeal, Hong Kong, since 1997; a Judge, Court of Appeal, Brunei Darussalam, since 2005; *b* 7 Aug. 1931; *s* of late John William Mortimer and Maud (*née* Snarr) Mortimer; *m* 1958, Judith Mary (*née* Page); two *s* two *d*. *Educ:* St Peter's School, York (Headmasters' Exhibitioner 1945); Emmanuel College, Cambridge; BA 1955, MA 1959. Commissioned into 4 RTR, 1951; served in Egypt, 1951–52; 45/51 RTR (TA), 1952–57. Called to the Bar, Middle Temple, 1956 (Bencher, 1980; Master Reader, 2003); Harmsworth Law Scholar 1957; Prosecuting Counsel on NE Circuit: to Post Office, 1965–69; to Inland Revenue, 1969–71; a Recorder, 1972–87; Judge, Supreme Court of Hong Kong, 1985–93; a Justice of Appeal, Court of Appeal, Supreme (later High) Court of Hong Kong, 1993–99 (a Vice-President, 1997–99). Chancellor, Dio. of Ripon, 1971–85. Chairman: Mental Health Review Tribunal, 1983–85; Overseas Trust Bank (Compensation) Tribunal, 1986–87; Member: Bar Council, 1970–75; Senate, 1979–85; Law Reform Commn, Hong Kong, 1990–99 (Chm., Sub-cttee on Privacy and Data Protection); Judicial Studies Bd, 1996–99; Vice Chm., Advocacy Inst. of Hong Kong, 1997–99; Chm., Criminal Court Users Cttee, 1998–99; Dir of Advocacy, Middle Temple, 2004–. Chm., Envmtl Impact Assessment Appeal Bd, Kowloon Canton Railway Corp. Spur Line Appeal, 2001. Dir, City Disputes Panel Ltd, 2000–. Hon. Diplomate, Amer. Bd of Trial Advocates, 1994. *Recreations:* reading, shooting, tennis. *Address:* The Grange, Staveley, Knaresborough, N Yorks HG5 9LD; 3/4 South Square, Gray's Inn, WC1R 5HP. *Club:* Hong Kong.

MORTIMER, Sir John (Clifford), Kt 1998; CBE 1986; QC 1966; FRSL; barrister; playwright and author; *b* 21 April 1923; *s* of Clifford Mortimer and Kathleen May (*née* Smith); *m* 1st, 1949, Penelope Ruth Fletcher (marr. diss. 1972; she *d* 1999); one *s* one *d*; 2nd, Penelope (*née* Gollop); two *d*; one *s*. *Educ:* Harrow; Brasenose Coll., Oxford (Hon. Fellow, 2006). Called to the Bar, 1948; Master of the Bench, Inner Temple, 1975. Mem. Nat. Theatre Bd, 1968–88. Chm. Council, RSL, 1989–99; Chm., 1990–2000, Vice-Pres., 2004–, Royal Court Theatre. Pres., Howard League for Penal Reform, 1991–2003. Pres., Berks, Bucks and Oxon Naturalists' Trust, 1984–90. Chm., Cttee to advise on vacant plinth, Trafalgar Square, 1999–2001. FRSL 1973. Hon. DLitt: Susquehanna Univ., 1985; St Andrews, 1987; Nottingham, 1989; Hon. LLD: Exeter, 1986; Brunel, 1990. Won the Italia Prize with short play, The Dock Brief, 1958; another short play What Shall We Tell Caroline, 1958. Full-length plays: The Wrong Side of the Park, 1960; Two Stars for Comfort, 1962; (trans.) A Flea in Her Ear, 1966; The Judge, 1967; (trans.) Cat Among the Pigeons, 1969; Come as You Are, 1970; A Voyage Round My Father, 1970 (filmed, 1982); (trans.) The Captain of Köpenick, 1971; I, Claudius (adapted from Robert Graves), 1972; Collaborators, 1973; Mr Luby's Fear of Heaven (radio), 1976; Heaven and Hell, 1976; The Bells of Hell, 1977; (trans.) The Lady from Maxim's, 1977; (trans.) A Little Hotel on the Side, 1984; opera (trans.) Die Fledermaus, 1988; A Christmas Carol (adapted from Dickens), 1994; Summer of a Dormouse (radio), 1999; Naked Justice, 2001; Hock and Soda Water, 2001; Full House, 2002; The Hairless Diva (adapted from Ionesco), 2002; Legal Fictions, 2008. Film Scripts: John and Mary, 1970; Brideshead Revisited (TV), 1981; Edwin (TV), 1984; Cider with Rosie (TV), 1998; Tea with Mussolini, 1999. British Acad. Writers Award, 1979; Life Achievement Award, Banff Television Fest., 1998; Lifetime Achievement Award, British Book Awards, 2005. *Publications: novels:* Charade, 1947; Rumming Park, 1948; Answer Yes or No, 1950; Like Men Betrayed, 1953, reissued

1987; Three Winters, 1956; Will Shakespeare: an entertainment, 1977; Rumpole of the Bailey, 1978 (televised; BAFTA Writer of the Year Award, 1980); The Trials of Rumpole, 1979; Rumpole's Return, 1980 (televised); Regina v Rumpole, 1981; Rumpole for the Defence, 1982; Rumpole and the Golden Thread, 1983 (televised); Paradise Postponed, 1985 (televised 1986); Rumpole's Last Case, 1987 (televised); Rumpole and the Age of Miracles, 1988 (televised); Summer's Lease, 1988 (televised 1989); Titmuss Regained, 1990 (televised 1991); Rumpole à la Carte, 1990; Dunster, 1992; Rumpole on Trial, 1992; Under the Hammer, 1994 (televised); Rumpole and the Angel of Death, 1995; Felix in the Underworld, 1997; The Sound of Trumpets, 1998; Rumpole Rests His Case, 2001; Rumpole and the Primrose Path, 2002; Rumpole and the Penge Bungalow Murders, 2004; Quite Honestly, 2005; Rumpole and the Reign of Terror, 2006; The Anti-Social Behaviour of Horace Rumpole, 2007; *travel:* (in collab. with P. R. Mortimer) With Love and Lizards, 1957; *plays:* The Dock Brief and Other Plays, 1959; The Wrong Side of the Park, 1960; Lunch Hour and Other Plays, 1960; Two Stars for Comfort, 1962; (trans.) A Flea in Her Ear, 1965; A Voyage Round My Father, 1970; (trans.) The Captain of Köpenick, 1971; Five Plays, 1971; Collaborators, 1973; Edwin and Other Plays, 1984; (trans.) Die Fledermaus, 1989; Naked Justice, 2001; Hock and Soda Water, 2001; *interviews:* In Character, 1983; Character Parts, 1986; *autobiography:* Clinging to the Wreckage (Book of the Year Award, Yorkshire Post), 1982; Murderers and Other Friends, 1994; Summer of a Dormouse, 2000; Where There's a Will, 2003; writes TV plays (incl. six Rumpole series); contribs to periodicals. *Recreations:* working, gardening, going to opera. *Address:* United Agents, 12–26 Lexington Street, W1F 0LE. *Club:* Garrick.

MORTIMORE, Prof. Peter John, OBE 1994; PhD; FBPsS; independent educational consultant; Director, Institute of Education, London University, 1994–2000 (Professor of Education, 1990–2000, now Emeritus); Pro-Vice-Chancellor, London University, 1999–2000; *b* 17 Jan. 1942; *s* of late Claude Mortimore and Rose Mortimore; *m* 1965, Jo Hargaden; three *d*. *Educ:* Chiswick County Grammar Sch.; St Mary's Coll., Strawberry Hill; Birkbeck Coll., London Univ. (BSc; Fellow 2001); Inst. of Education (MSc); Inst. of Psychiatry (PhD). CPsychol 1989; FBPsS 1989. Teacher, Sacred Heart Sch., SE5, 1964–66; Teacher and Head of Dept, Stockwell Manor Sch., SW9, 1966–73; Res. Officer, Inst. of Psychiatry, 1975–78; Mem., HM Inspectorate, 1978; Inner London Education Authority: Dir, Res. and Stats Br., 1979–85; Asst Educn Officer (Secondary Schs), 1985–87; Prof. of Educn, Lancaster Univ., 1988–90; Dep. Dir, London Univ. Inst. of Educn, 1990–94. Member: Educn Res. Bd, SSRC, 1981–82; Educn and Human Develt Cttee, ESRC, 1982–85; Univ. of London Exams and Assessment Council, 1991; Trustee, VSO, 1992–2002. Governor: SOAS, 1993–98; Birkbeck Coll., 1998–2000. Monthly columnist, Guardian Education, 2006–. Hon. FCP 1994; AcSS 2000. FRSA 1990. Hon. DLitt Heriot-Watt, 1998. *Publications:* (jtly) Fifteen Thousand Hours: secondary schools and their effects on children, 1979; (jtly) Behaviour Problems in Schools, 1984; (jtly) Secondary School Examinations, 1986; (jtly) School Matters: the junior years, 1988; (jtly) The Primary Head: roles, responsibilities and reflections, 1991; The Secondary Head: roles, responsibilities and reflections, 1991; (jtly) Managing Associate Staff, 1994; (jtly) Planning Matters, 1995; (jtly) Living Education, 1997; (jtly) Forging Links, 1997; Road to Improvement, 1998; (jtly) Understanding Pedagogy, 1999; (jtly) Culture of Change, 2000; (jtly) Improving School Effectiveness, 2001. *Recreations:* theatre, art, music, walking.

MORTIMORE, Simon Anthony; QC 1991; *b* 12 April 1950; *s* of late Robert Anthony Mortimore and Katherine Elizabeth Mackenzie Mortimore (*née* Caine); *m* 1983, Fiona Elizabeth Jacobson; one *s* one *d*. *Educ:* Westminster School; Exeter Univ. (LLB). Called to the Bar, Inner Temple, 1972. CEDR accredited mediator, 1997–. Mem., ACCA Disciplinary Panel, 2003–07. *Publications:* contribs to Bullen and Leake and Jacobs Precedents of Pleading, 13th edn 1990; Insolvency of Banks, 1996. *Recreations:* opera, general cultural interests, travel, golf. *Address:* 3/4 South Square, Gray's Inn, WC1R 5HP. *T:* (020) 7696 9900. *Clubs:* Hurlingham; Royal St George's Golf, Rye Golf.

MORTON, 22nd Earl of, *cr* 1458 (*de facto* 21st Earl, 22nd but for the Attainder); **John Charles Sholto Douglas;** Lord Aberdour, 1458; Lord-Lieutenant of West Lothian, 1985–2001; *b* 19 March 1927; *s* of Hon. Charles William Sholto Douglas (*d* 1960) (2nd *s* of 19th Earl) and Florence (*d* 1985), *er d* of late Major Henry Thomas Timson; *S* cousin, 1976; *m* 1949, Sheila Mary, *d* of late Rev. Canon John Stanley Gibbs, MC, Didmarton House, Badminton, Glos; two *s* one *d*. Director: Quickwing, 2001–; B-Fuel-Wise, 2003–. DL West Lothian, 1982. *Recreation:* polo. *Heir: s* Lord Aberdour, *qv*. *Address:* Dalmahoy, Kirknewton, Midlothian EH27 8EB. *Clubs:* Farmers'; Edinburgh Polo, Dalmahoy Country.

MORTON, Alison Margaret; *see* Kinnaird, A. M.

MORTON, Rev. Andrew Queen; Minister of Culross Abbey, 1959–87; *b* 4 June 1919; *s* of Alexander Morton and Janet Queen; *m* 1948, Jean, *e d* of George Singleton and late Jean Wands; one *s* two *d*. *Educ:* Glasgow Univ. MA 1942, BD 1947, BSc 1948. Minister of St Andrews, Fraserburgh, 1949–59. Dept of Computer Science, Univ. of Edinburgh, 1965–86. Hon. Res. Fellow, Glasgow Univ., 1990. FRSE 1973. *Publications:* The Structure of the Fourth Gospel, 1961; Authorship and Integrity in the New Testament, 1963; (with G. H. C. Macgregor) The Structure of Luke and Acts, 1965; Paul the Man and the Myth, 1965; (with S. Michaelson) The Computer in Literary Research, 1973; Literary Detection, 1979; (with S. Michaelson and N. Hamilton-Smith) Justice for Helander, 1979; (with James McLeman) The Genesis of John, 1980; (with S. Michaelson) The Cusum Plot, 1990; (with M. G. Farringdon) Fielding and the Federalist, 1990; Proper Words in Proper Places, 1992; The Authorship and Integrity of the New Testament Epistles, 1993; The Making of Mark, 1995; Gathering the Gospels, 1997; A Fresh Look at Matthew, 1998; Revelation, 1998; The Codex Sinaiticus Revisited, 2002; A Gospel Made to Measure, 2004; contrib. ALLC Jl; TLS. *Recreations:* thinking, talking. *Address:* 4A Manse Street, Aberdour, Burntisland, Fife KY3 0TT. *T:* (01383) 860131; *e-mail:* aqmorton@btinternet.com.

MORTON, Christopher; *see* Morton, D. C.

MORTON, (David) Christopher; His Honour Judge Morton; a Circuit Judge, since 1992; *b* 1 Dec. 1943; *s* of Rev. Alexander Francis Morton and Esther Ann Morton; *m* 1970, Sandra Jo Kobes; three *s* one *d*. *Educ:* Worksop Coll., Notts; Fitzwilliam Coll., Cambridge (BA, LLB). Called to the Bar, Inner Temple, 1968; Wales and Chester Circuit; practised in Swansea, 1969–92. *Recreations:* Welsh affairs, railways, family. *Address:* The Crown Court, St Helens Road, Swansea SA1 4PF. *T:* (01792) 510200. *Club:* Royal Overseas League.

MORTON, George Martin; Principal (formerly Senior) Planner, Trafford Borough Council, 1986–99; *b* 11 Feb. 1940; *s* of Rev. Thomas Ralph Morton, DD, and Janet Maclay MacGregor Morton (*née* Baird). *Educ:* Fettes Coll. Edinburgh; Edinburgh Coll. of Art; Glasgow Univ. Member: Manchester City Council, 1971–74; Greater Manchester Council, 1973–77. Sec., Tameside and Glossop CHC, 1984–86. MP (Lab) Manchester,

Moss Side, July 1978–1983; an Opposition Whip, 1979–83. *Address:* 4 St Annes Road, Manchester M21 8TD. *T:* (0161) 881 8195.

MORTON, Prof. John, OBE 1998; PhD; FBPsS; Director, Cognitive Development Unit, Medical Research Council, 1982–98; Hon. Professor, University College London, since 1998; *b* 1 Aug. 1933; *s* of late Winston James Morton and Mary Winifred Morton (*née* Nutter); *m;* one *d; m* 3rd, 1985, Guinevere Tufnell. *Educ:* Nelson Grammar Sch.; Christ's Coll., Cambridge (BA, MA); Reading Univ. (PhD 1961). FBPsS 1974 (Hon. FBPsS 1997). Scientist, MRC Applied Psychology Unit, Cambridge, 1960–82. Res. Fellow, Univ. of Michigan, 1967; Res. Associate and Lectr, Yale Univ., 1967–68; Vis. Scientist, MSH Paris, 1974–75; Max Planck Ges., Nijmegen, 1977–80; Visiting Professor: Cornell Univ., 1980; UCL, 1982–98; Vis Fellow, Tokyo Metropolitan Inst. of Gerontology, 1981. Pres., EPsS, 1998–2000 (Hon. Mem., 2001). MAE 1990. President's Award, BPsS, 1988; Ipsen Prize in neural plasticity, Ipsen Foundn, 2001. *Publications:* (ed) Biological and Social Factors in Psycholinguistics, 1971; (ed jtly) Psycholinguistics: Developmental and Pathological, Series I, 1977, Series II, 1979; (with M. Johnson) Biology and Cognitive Development, 1991; (ed jtly) Development Neurocognition, 1993; (ed jtly) The Acquisition and Dissolution of Language, 1994; (ed jtly) Cognitive Science: an introduction, 1996; Understanding Developmental Disorders: a causal modelling approach, 2004; articles in sci. jls. *Recreations:* theatre, cooking, song writing, chocolate, Burnley FC. *Address:* (office) Institute of Cognitive Neuroscience, University College London, Alexandra House, 17–19 Queen Square, WC1N 3AR. *T:* (020) 7679 1156.

MORTON, John, DPhil; Chief Executive, Engineering and Technology Board, since 2005; *b* Gateshead, 11 Dec. 1949; *s* of John Morton and Emiline Morton (*née* Watson); *m* 1977, Maria Rosario Larrarte; two *s. Educ:* Grammar Sch. for Boys, Gateshead; St Catharine's Coll., Cambridge (BA 1971); Exeter Coll., Oxford (DPhil 1975); Stanford Graduate Sch. of Business. CEng 1978. Lectr, Dept of Aeronautics, Imperial Coll. London, 1979–85; Sen. Res. Associate, NASA Langley Res. Center, USA, 1986; Prof., Dept of Engrg Sci. and Mechanics, 1986–93, Dir, Center for Composite Materials and Structures, 1991–93, Virginia Tech.; Defence Research Agency, subseq. Defence Evaluation and Research Agency: Dir, Structural Materials Centre, 1993–97; Dir, Mechanical Scis Sector, 1998–2001; Chief Operating Officer, Future Systems and Technol., QinetiQ, 2001–05. Vis. Prof., Dept of Aeronautics, Imperial Coll. London, 1995–. Chm., Women into Sci., Engrg and Construction, 2007–. Mem. Council, IMMM, 2004–. FIMMM 1992; FRAeS 1998. Liveryman, Co. of Engineers, 2006. *Publications:* articles on fracture mechanics, structural mechanics and the mechanics of composite materials. *Recreations:* tennis, gardening. *Address:* Engineering and Technology Board, 246 High Holborn, WC1V 7EX. *T:* (020) 3206 0438, *Fax:* (020) 3206 0490; *e-mail:* jmorton@etechb.co.uk. *Club:* Farmers'.

MORTON, Kathryn Mary Stuart, CB 2002; Solicitor and Director General, Legal Services, Department for Environment, Food and Rural Affairs, 2001–02; *b* 2 June 1946; *d* of late Samuel Stuart Morton and Joan Alice Bessie Morton (*née* Tapscott). *Educ:* Ealing Grammar Sch. for Girls; Univ. of Sussex (BA). Admitted Solicitor, 1980. Leverhulme Res. Scholarship, India, 1967–68; Res. Asst, Lancaster Univ., 1969–71; Res. Officer, ODI, 1971–74; Res. Associate, ODI, and free-lance economist, 1974–80; with Bird & Bird, 1978–82; OFT, 1982–85; DTI, 1985–97, Under Sec. (Legal), subseq. Dir, 1992–97; Legal Advr and Solicitor, MAFF, 1997–2001. *Publications:* Aid and Dependence, 1975; (with Peter Tulloch) Trade and Developing Countries, 1977. *T:* (020) 7226 2332; *e-mail:* kmsmorton@waitrose.com.

MORTON, Prof. Keith William; Professor of Numerical Analysis, and Professorial Fellow of Balliol College, Oxford University, 1983–97, now Emeritus Professor, Oxford University and Emeritus Fellow, Balliol College; Professor of Mathematics (part-time), University of Bath, 1998–2005; *b* 28 May 1930; *s* of Keith Harvey Morton and Muriel Violet (*née* Hubbard); *m* 1952, Patricia Mary Pearson; two *s* two *d. Educ:* Sudbury Grammar Sch.; Corpus Christi Coll., Oxford (BA 1952; MA 1954); New York Univ. (PhD 1964). Theoretical Physics Div., AERE, Harwell, 1952–59; Res. Scientist, Courant Inst. of Mathematical Sci., NY Univ., 1959–64; Head of Computing and Applied Maths, Culham Lab., UKAEA, 1964–72; Prof. of Applied Maths, Reading Univ., 1972–83. IMA Gold Medal, 2002. *Publications:* (with R. D. Richtmyer) Difference Methods for Initial-value Problems, 1967; (ed with M. J. Baines) Numerical Methods for Fluid Dynamics, Vol. I 1982, Vol. II 1986, Vol. III 1988, Vol. IV 1993, Vol. V 1995; (with D. F. Mayers) Numerical Solution of Partial Differential Equations: an introduction, 1994, 2nd edn 2005; Numerical Solution of Convection-Diffusion Problems, 1996; numerous articles on numerical analysis and applied maths in learned jls. *Recreations:* reading, Real tennis, walking, gardening, listening to music. *Address:* Roscarrock, 48 Jack Straw's Lane, Headington, Oxford OX3 0DW. *T:* (01865) 768823; *e-mail:* morton@comlab.ox.ac.uk.

MORTON, Patricia Ann; *see* Jacobs, P. A.

MORTON JACK, His Honour David; a Circuit Judge, 1986–2008; *b* 5 Nov. 1935; *o s* of late Col W. A. Morton Jack, OBE, and late Mrs Morton Jack (*née* Happell); *m* 1972, Rosemary, *o d* of F. G. Rentoul; four *s. Educ:* Stowe (scholar); Trinity Coll., Oxford (Cholmeley Schol., MA). 2nd Lieut, RIrF, 1955–57. Called to the Bar, Lincoln's Inn, 1962; a Recorder of the Crown Court, 1979–86. *Recreations:* country pursuits, sheep-keeping, reading, music, gardens.

MOSDELL, Lionel Patrick; Judge of the High Court of Kenya, 1966–72, Tanganyika, 1960–64; *b* 29 Aug. 1912; *s* of late William George Mosdell and late Sarah Ellen Mosdell (*née* Gardiner); *m* 1945, Muriel Jean Sillem; one *s* one *d. Educ:* Abingdon Sch.; St Edmund Hall, Oxford (MA). Solicitor, England, 1938. Served War of 1939–45, Gunner, Sussex Yeomanry RA, 1939–41; Commnd Rifle Bde, 1941; Libyan Arab Force; Force 133; No 1 Special Force; Egypt, Cyrenaica, Eritrea, Abyssinia, Italy (Capt.). Registrar of Lands and Deeds, N Rhodesia, 1946; Resident Magistrate, 1950; Senior Resident Magistrate, 1956; Barrister, Gray's Inn, 1952; Asst Solicitor, Law Soc., 1964–66. Part-time Chairman: Surrey and Sussex Rent Assessment Panel, 1972–82; Nat. Insce Local Tribunal, London S Region, 1974–84; Immigration Appeal Tribunal, 1975–84; Pensions Appeal Tribunals, 1976–86. Volunteer, SSAFA, 1988–2002. *Recreation:* reading. *Clubs:* Special Forces, Royal Commonwealth Society.

MOSELEY, Elwyn Rhys, CBE 2003; Commissioner for Local Administration in Wales (Ombudsman), 1991–2003; *b* 6 Aug. 1943; *s* of late Rev. Luther Moseley and Megan Eiluned Moseley (*née* Howells); *m* 1968, Annick Andrée Guyomard; two *s* one *d. Educ:* Caterham Sch.; Queens' Coll., Cambridge (MA). Solicitor. Asst Solicitor, Newport CBC, 1969–72; Sen. Asst Solicitor, Cardiff CBC, 1972–74; Cardiff City Council: City Solicitor, 1974–91; Dep. Chief Exec., 1979–91; Dir of Admin. and Legal Services, 1987–91.
See also T. H. Moseley.

MOSELEY, Sir George (Walker), KCB 1982 (CB 1978); Chairman, British Cement Association, 1987–96; *b* 7 Feb. 1925; *o c* of late William Moseley, MBE, and Bella Moseley; *m* 1st, 1950, Anne Mercer (*d* 1989); one *s* one *d;* 2nd, 1990, Madge James. *Educ:* High Sch., Glasgow; St Bees Sch., Cumberland; Wadham Coll., Oxford (MA). Pilot Officer, RAF Levies, Iraq, 1943–48. Asst Principal, Min. of Town and Country Planning, 1950; Asst Private Sec. to Minister of Housing and Local Govt, 1951–52; Private Sec. to Parly Sec., 1952–54; Principal Private Sec. to Minister of Housing and Local Govt, 1963–65; Asst Sec. 1965; Under-Sec. 1970–76; Dep. Sec., DoE, 1976–78, CSD, 1978–80; Second Permanent Sec., DoE, 1980–81, Perm. Sec., 1981–85. Chm., Cement Makers' Fedn, 1987–88. Member: Adv. Council on Public Records, 1989–91; Ancient Monuments Adv. Cttee, 1986–91; Historic Buildings and Monuments Commn for England, 1986–91. Trustee, Civic Trust, 1987–2000 (Chm. Trustees, 1990–2000). *Address:* Churchmead, Church Lane, Widdington, Saffron Walden, Essex CB11 3SF. *Club:* Royal Air Force.

MOSELEY, Joyce, OBE 2007; Chief Executive, Rainer, since 1999; *b* 12 Jan. 1947; *d* of late Harry Moseley and Kathleen Moseley (*née* Dalton); *m* 1995, Anthony Allen. *Educ:* Manchester High Sch. for Girls; Bedford Coll., Univ. of London (BScSoc Hons 1968 and Applied Social Studies 1970); Univ. of Surrey (MSc Social Res. 1984). Social worker and Sen. Social Worker, London Borough of Ealing, Sen. Social Worker and Area Manager, London Borough of Islington, 1974–86; Asst Dir, Herts CC, 1986–91; Dir of Social Services, London Borough of Hackney, 1991–97; consultancy, 1997–99. Mem., Youth Justice Bd for England and Wales, 1998–2004. *Publications:* Other People's Children, 1976; contrib. articles and chapters to social care pubns. *Recreations:* theatre, walking, food and wine. *Address:* Rainer, Rectory Lodge, High Street, Brasted, Kent TN16 1JF. *T:* (01959) 578218. *Club:* Two Brydges.

MOSELEY, His Honour (Thomas) Hywel; QC 1985; a Circuit Judge, 1989–2004; *b* 27 Sept. 1936; *s* of late Rev. Luther Moseley and Megan Eiluned Moseley; *m* 1960, Monique Germaine Thérèse Drufin; three *d. Educ:* Caterham Sch.; Queens' Coll., Cambridge (MA, LLM). Called to the Bar, Gray's Inn, 1964; in private practice, Cardiff, 1965–89, and London, 1977–89; a Recorder, 1981–89. Lectr in Law, 1960–65, Prof. of Law, 1970–82, UCW, Aberystwyth. Mem., Insolvency Rules Cttee, 1993–97. *Publication:* (with B. Rudden) Outline of the Law of Mortgages, 4th edn 1967. *Recreation:* bee-keeping. *Address:* Nantceiro, Llanbadarn Fawr, Aberystwyth, Ceredigion SY23 3HW. *T:* (01970) 623532.
See also E. R. Moseley.

MOSER, family name of **Baron Moser**.

MOSER, Baron *cr* 2001 (Life Peer), of Regents Park in the London Borough of Camden; **Claus Adolf Moser,** KCB 1973; CBE 1965; FBA 1969; Chairman, British Museum Development Trust, 1993–2003, now Trustee Emeritus; Chancellor, Open University of Israel, 1994–2004 (Hon. Fellow, 2002; Member Council, since 2004); Chairman, Askonas Holt (formerly Harold Holt) Ltd, 1990–2002; *b* Berlin, 24 Nov. 1922; *s* of late Dr Ernest Moser and Lotte Moser; *m* 1949, Mary Oxlin; one *s* two *d. Educ:* Frensham Heights Sch.; LSE, Univ. of London. RAF, 1943–46. London Sch. of Economics: Asst Lectr in Statistics, 1946–49; Lectr, 1949–55; Reader in Social Statistics, 1955–61; Prof. of Social Statistics, 1961–70; Vis. Prof. of Social Statistics, 1970–75; Oxford University: Vis. Fellow, Nuffield Coll., 1972–80; Warden, Wadham Coll., 1984–93 (Hon. Fellow, 1993); Pro-Vice Chancellor, 1991–93. Dir, Central Statistical Office and Hd of Govt Statistical Service, 1967–78. Statistical Adviser, Cttee on Higher Educn, 1961–64. Chm., Economist Intelligence Unit, 1979–83; Director: N. M. Rothschild & Sons, 1978–90 (Vice-Chm., 1978–84); The Economist Newspaper, 1979–93; Equity & Law Life Assurance Soc., 1980–87; International Medical Statistics Inc., 1982–88; Octopus Books Ltd, 1982–87; Property & Reversionary Investments plc, 1983–86. Mem., Nat. Commn on Educn, 1991–95; Chm., Basic Skills Agency, 1997–2002. Chairman: Royal Opera House, 1974–87; Adv. Bd, Music at Oxford, 1985–; Oxford Playhouse, 1992–2004 (Pres., 2004–); Member: Governing Body, Royal Academy of Music, 1967–79; BBC Music Adv. Cttee, 1971–83; Adv. Bd, LSO, 1996–; Pilgrim Trust, 1982–99; Wigmore Hall Develt Cttee, 2007–. Trustee: BM, 1988–2001; LPO, 1988–94; Glyndebourne Opera Arts Trust, 1989–93; Paul Hamlyn Foundn, 1991–; Soros Foundn, 1993–99; Rayne Foundn, 1995–. President: Royal Statistical Soc., 1978–80; BAAS, 1989–90; British Fedn of Fests for Music, Dance and Speech, 1990–99. Chancellor, Univ. of Keele, 1986–2002. Gov., Yehudi Menuhin Sch., 2000–. Hon. FRAM 1970. Hon. Fellow: LSE, 1976; Inst. of Educn, Univ. of London, 1997; Birkbeck Coll., 1998; RIBA, 2005. Hon. DSocSci Southampton, 1975; Hon. DSc: Leeds, 1977; City, 1977; Sussex, 1980; Wales, 1990; Liverpool, 1991; South Bank, 1994; Hon. DSc(Econ) London, 1991; Hull, 1994; DUniv: Surrey, 1977; Keele, 1979; York, 1980; Open, 1992; Hon. DTech Brunel, 1981; Dr *hc* Edinburgh, 1991; Heriot-Watt, 1995; Hon. DLitt: W of England, 1993; Brighton, 1994; Hon. DCL Northumbria, 1995. Albert Medal, RSA, 1996. Comdr de l'Ordre National du Mérite (France), 1976; Commander's Cross, Order of Merit (FRG), 1985. *Publications:* Measurement of Levels of Living, 1957; Survey Methods in Social Investigation, 1958; (jtly) Social Conditions in England and Wales, 1958; (jtly) British Towns, 1961; papers in statistical jls. *Recreation:* music. *Address:* 3 Regent's Park Terrace, NW1 7EE. *T:* (020) 7485 1619; 7 Ethelred Court, Old Headington, Oxford OX3 9DA. *T:* (01865) 761028. *Club:* Garrick.

MOSER, Dr Michael Edward; specialist international advisor on environment, UN Development Programme, Iran and The Maldives, and other international organisations; *b* 16 July 1956; *s* of late Roger Michael Moser and Noreen Moser (*née* Wane); *m* 1983, Joanna Jocelyn Stewart-Smith; three *d. Educ:* Shrewsbury Sch.; Durham Univ. (1st cl. Hons Ecol.; PhD). David Lack Studentship, BOU, 1980–82; British Trust for Ornithology: Estuaries Officer, 1983–86; Dir of Develt, 1986–88; Dir, Internat. Waterfowl and Wetlands Res. Bureau, then Wetlands Internat., 1988–99; English Nature: Mem., Council, 1999–2006; Dep. Chm., 2004–05; Acting Chm., 2005–06; Mem., UK Jt Nature Conservation Cttee, 2001–06. Mem. Council, RSPB, 2001–06; Chm., N Devon UNESCO Biosphere Reserve Partnership, 2007–. *Publication:* (with C. M. Finlayson) Wetlands, 1991. *Recreations:* natural history, travel, fly fishing. *Address:* West Week Farm, Week, Chulmleigh, Devon EX18 7EE.

MOSES, Rev. Alan; *see* Moses, Rev. L. A.

MOSES, Rt Hon. Sir Alan (George), Kt 1996; PC 2005; **Rt Hon. Lord Justice Moses;** a Lord Justice of Appeal, since 2005; *b* 29 Nov. 1945; *s* of late Eric George Rufus Moses, CB and of Pearl Moses (*née* Lipton); *m* 1992, Dinah Victoria Casson, *qv;* two *s* one *d* by a previous marriage. *Educ:* Bryanston Sch.; University Coll., Oxford (Quondam Exhibnr; BA). Called to the Bar, Middle Temple, 1968, Bencher, 1994; Mem., Panel of Junior Counsel to the Crown, Common Law, 1981–90; Junior Counsel to Inland Revenue, Common Law, 1985–90; a Recorder, 1986–96; QC 1990; a Judge of the High Ct, QBD, 1996–2005; Presiding Judge, SE Circuit, 1999–2002. Prof of Law, RA, 2006–. Mem. Cttee, London Library, 2003–06. Trustee: Koestler Award Trust, 2004–06 (Advr, 2006–); Pilgrim Trust, 2006–. *Address:* c/o Royal Courts of Justice, Strand, WC2A 2LL. *Club:* Union Socialista La Serra (Italy).

MOSES, Dinah Victoria, (Lady Moses); *see* Casson, D. V.

MOSES, Very Rev. Dr John Henry, KCVO 2006; Dean of St Paul's, 1996–2006, now Emeritus; Dean, Order of St Michael and St George, and Dean, Order of the British Empire, 1996–2006; *b* 12 Jan. 1938; *s* of late Henry William Moses and Ada Elizabeth Moses; *m* 1964, Susan Elizabeth; one *s* two *d*. *Educ:* Ealing Grammar School; Nottingham Univ. (Gladstone Meml Prize 1958; BA History 1959; PhD 1965); Trinity Hall, Cambridge (Cert. in Education 1960); Lincoln Theological Coll. Deacon 1964, priest 1965; Asst Curate, St Andrew, Bedford, 1964–70; Rector of Coventry East Team Ministry, 1970–77; Examining Chaplain to Bishop of Coventry, 1972–77; Rural Dean of Coventry East, 1973–77; Archdeacon of Southend, 1977–82; Provost of Chelmsford, 1982–96. Vis. Fellow, Wolfson Coll., Cambridge, 1987. Mem., Gen. Synod, 1985–2005; Church Comr, 1988–2006; Mem., ACC, 1997–2005. Chm. Council, Centre for Study of Theology, Essex Univ., 1987–96; Rector, Anglia Poly. Univ., 1992–96. Select Preacher, Oxford Univ., 2004–05. Vice-Pres., City of London Fest., 1997–2006. Freeman, City of London, 1997; Liveryman: Feltmakers' Co., 1998–; Plaisterers' Co., 1999–; Masons' Co., 2005–; Hon. Freeman, Water Conservators' Co., 2000–. Hon. Dr Anglia Poly. Univ., 1997; Hon. DD Nottingham, 2007. OStJ 2003. Order of Al Istiqlal of Hashemite (Jordan), 2002. *Publications:* The Sacrifice of God, 1992; A Broad and Living Way, 1995; The Desert, 1997; One Equall Light: an anthology of the writings of John Donne, 2003; The Language of Love, 2007. *Address:* Chestnut House, The Burgage, Southwell, Notts NG25 0EP. *T:* (01636) 814880; *e-mail:* johnandsusanmoses@btinternet.com. *Club:* Athenæum.

MOSES, Rev. (Leslie) Alan; Vicar of All Saints', Margaret Street, London, since 1995; Priest-in-Charge, The Annunciation, Bryanston Street, since 2006; *b* 3 Nov. 1949; *s* of Leslie Moses and Edna (*née* Watson); *m* 1971, Theresa Frances O'Connor; one *s* one *d*. *Educ:* Univ. of Hull (BA Hons History); Univ. of Edinburgh (BD Hons); Edinburgh Theol. Coll.; King's Coll., London (MA Systematic Theol. 2001). Ordained deacon 1976, priest 1977; Asst Curate, Old St Paul's, Edinburgh, 1976–79; Rector, St Margaret of Scotland, Leven, 1979–85; Priest-in-Charge, St Margaret of Scotland, Edinburgh, 1986–92; Rector, Old St Paul's, Edinburgh, 1985–95. Area Dean of Westminster-St Marylebone, 2001–. Mem., Gen. Synod of C of E, 2001–05. Chm., USPG: Anglicans in World Mission (formerly USPG), 2006– (Trustee, (formerly Gov.), 1997–). *Recreations:* reading, visiting museums, galleries, churches and other buildings, exploring places. *Address:* The Vicarage, 7 Margaret Street, W1W 8JQ. *T:* (020) 7636 1788, *Fax:* (020) 7436 4470.

MOSEY, Roger; Director of Sport, BBC, since 2005; *b* 4 Jan. 1958; *s* of late Geoffrey Mosey and of Marie Mosey (*née* Pilkington). *Educ:* Bradford Grammar Sch.; Wadham Coll., Oxford (MA Mod. Hist. & Mod. Langs); INSEAD (AMP 1999). Producer, Pennine Radio, 1979; Reporter, BBC Radio Lincolnshire, 1980; Producer: BBC Radio Northampton, 1982; Today programme, BBC Radio Four, 1984; BBC New York office, 1986; Editor: PM prog., 1987; World At One, 1989; Today prog., BBC Radio Four, 1993 (Sony Radio Gold Awards, 1994, 1995); Controller, BBC Radio Five Live, 1996–2000; Acting Dir, BBC Continuous News, 1999; Hd of TV News, BBC, 2000–05. Dir, Parly Broadcasting Unit Ltd, 1999–2003. Bd Mem., Union Dance, 2001–05. Member: Sony Radio Awards Cttee, 1999, 2000; Adv. Cttee, Edinburgh TV Fest., 2006. Fellow, Radio Acad., 1999. Sony Radio Gold Award for Radio 5 Live, 1998. *Publications:* contrib. The Business, Guardian. *Recreations:* American political history, music, football, exploring Italy. *Address:* BBC Television Centre, W12 7RJ. *T:* (020) 8225 6644; *e-mail:* roger.mosey@bbc.co.uk.

MOSHINSKY, Elijah; Associate Producer, Royal Opera House, since 1979; *b* 8 Jan. 1946; *s* of Abraham and Eva Moshinsky. *Educ:* Melbourne Univ. (BA); St Antony's Coll., Oxford. Apptd to Royal Opera House, 1973: work includes original productions of: Peter Grimes, 1975; Lohengrin, 1978, 1997; The Rake's Progress, 1979; Macbeth, 1981; Samson et Dalila, 1981; Tannhäuser, 1984; Otello, 1987; Die Entführung aus dem Serail, 1987; Attila, 1990; Simon Boccanegra, 1991; Stiffelio, 1993; Aida, 1994; I Masnadieri, 1997; Il Trovatore, 2002; for ENO: Le Grand Macabre, 1982; The Mastersingers of Nuremberg, 1984; The Bartered Bride, 1985, 1986; for Australian Opera: A Midsummer Night's Dream, 1978; Boris Godunov, 1980; Il Trovatore, 1983; Werther, Rigoletto, 1990; Les Dialogues des Carmélites; for Metropolitan Opera, NY: Un Ballo in Maschera, 1980; Samson, 1987; Ariadne auf Naxos, 1993; Otello, 1994; The Makropulos Case, 1996; The Queen of Spades; Samson et Dalila, 1998; other opera productions include: Wozzeck, 1976; Antony and Cleopatra, Chicago, 1990; I Vespri Siciliani, Grand Théâtre, Geneva; La Bohème, 1989, La Forza del Destino, 1990, Scottish Opera; Beatrice and Benedict, 1994, Cavalleria Rusticana and Pagliacci, 1996, WNO; Die Meistersinger von Nürnberg, Holland Fest.; Benvenuto Cellini, 50th Maggio Musicale, Florence, 1987; The Turn of the Screw, Broomhill Opera, 2000. Producer: Three Sisters, Albery, 1987; Light up the Sky, Globe, 1987; Ivanov, Strand, 1989; Much Ado About Nothing, Strand, 1989; Another Time, Wyndham's, 1989; Shadowlands, Queen's, 1989; Cyrano de Bergerac, Theatre Royal, Haymarket, 1992; Lord of the Flies, 1995, Richard III, 1998, RSC; productions at National Theatre: Troilus and Cressida, 1976; The Force of Habit, 1976; productions for the BBC: All's Well That Ends Well, 1980; A Midsummer Night's Dream, 1981; Cymbeline, 1982; Coriolanus, 1984; Love's Labour's Lost, 1985; Ghosts, 1986; The Rivals, 1987; The Green Man, 1990; Genghis Cohn, 1993; Danton, 1994. Director: Matador, Queen's, 1991; Beckett, Haymarket, 1991; Reflected Glory, Vaudeville, 1992; Old Wicked Songs, Gielgud, 1996; The Female Odd Couple, Apollo, 2001; Sleuth, Apollo, 2002. *Recreations:* telephone conversation, writing film scripts. *Address:* B5, Albany, W1J 0AN. *Club:* Garrick.

MOSIEWICZ, Muriel Anita; *see* Robinson, M. A.

MOSIMANN, Anton, OBE 2004; Owner, Mosimann's (formerly Belfry Club), since 1988; Principal, Mosimann Academy, London, since 1996; *b* 23 Feb. 1947; *s* of Otto and Olga Mosimann; *m* 1973, Kathrin Roth; two *s*. *Educ:* private school in Switzerland; youngest Chef to be awarded Chef de Cuisine Diplome; 3 degrees. Served apprenticeship in Hotel Baeren, Twann; worked in Canada, France, Italy, Japan, Sweden, Belgium, Switzerland, 1962–; cuisinier at: Villa Lorraine, Brussels; Les Près d'Eugénie, Eugénie-les-Bains; Les Frères Troisgros, Roanne; Paul Bocuse, Collonges au Mont d'Or; Moulin de Mougins; joined Dorchester Hotel, 1975, Maître Chef des Cuisines, 1976–88. Channel Four TV series: Cooking with Mosimann, 1989; Anton Mosimann Naturally, 1991; Swiss TV series: Healthy Food, 1997; Swiss Regional Cooking, 1998. World Pres., Les Toques Blanches Internationales, 1989–93; Hon. Mem., Chefs' Assoc., Canada, Chicago, Japan, Switzerland, S Africa. Freeman, City of London, 1999. Royal Warrant Holder to the Prince of Wales, 2000; Pres., Royal Warrant Holders' Assoc., 2006–07. Hon. Prof., Thames Valley Univ., 2004. Johnson & Wales University, RI: Dr of Culinary Arts *hc*, 1990; Hon. DSc Bournemouth Univ., 1998. Restaurateur of the Year, 2000. Numerous Gold Medals in Internat. Cookery Competitions; Chef Award, Caterer and Hotelkeeper, 1985; Personnalité de l'année award, 1986; Glenfiddich Awards Trophy, 1986; Chevalier, Ordre des Coteaux de Champagne, 1990; Grand Cordon Culinaire, Conseil Culinaire Français de Grande Bretagne, 1994; Swiss Culinary Ambassador of the Year, Hotel & Restaurant Assoc. of Switzerland, 1995; Catey Lifetime Achievement Award for Catering, Caterer and Hotelkeeper, 2004. Officier, Ordre Nat. du Mérite Agricole (France), 2006 (Chevalier, 1988). *Publications:* Cuisine à la Carte, 1981; A New Style of Cooking, 1983; Cuisine Naturelle, 1985; Anton Mosimann's Fish Cuisine, 1988; The Art of Anton Mosimann, 1989; Cooking with Mosimann, 1989; Anton Mosimann Naturally, 1991; The Essential Mosimann, 1993; Mosimann's World, 1996; Mosimann's Fresh, 2006. *Recreations:* classic cars (completed centennial Peking-Paris Rally, 2007), collecting antiquarian cookery books, enjoying fine wine, passionate about food and travelling, especially to the food markets of the Far East. *Address:* c/o Mosimann's, 11B West Halkin Street, SW1X 8JL. *T:* (020) 7235 9625. *Clubs:* Garrick, Reform.

MOSLEY, family name of **Baron Ravensdale**.

MOSLEY, Max Rufus; President, Fédération Internationale de l'Automobile, 1993–Oct. 2009; *b* 13 April 1940; *s* of Sir Oswald Mosley, 6th Bt and Hon. Diana (*d* 2003), *d* of 2nd Baron Redesdale; *m* 1960, Jean Taylor; two *s*. *Educ:* abroad; Christ Church, Oxford (MA Natural Sciences). Sec., Oxford Union Society, 1961. Called to the Bar, Gray's Inn, 1964; Dir, March Cars, 1969–79; Legal Adviser, Formula One Constructors' Assoc., 1971–82; Pres., Fédn Internat. du Sport Automobile, 1991–93 (Pres., Manufacturers' Commn, FISA, 1986–91). Chm., Eur. New Car Assessment Prog., 1997–2004; EU Commission: Co-founder, e-Safety Forum, 2003; Mem., High Level Gp, CARS 21 (Competitive Automotive Regulatory System for the 21st century), 2005–. Pres. and spokesperson, ERTICO Intelligent Transport Systems Europe, 2004–07 (Vice-Chm., 1999–2001, Chm., 2001–04, Supervisory Bd). Patron, eSafety Aware, 2006–. Hon. President: Automobile Users' Intergroup, EP, 1994–99; Nat. Road Safety Council NGO, Armenia, 2005. Founder Mem., Inst du Cerveau et de la Moelle Epinière, 2005. Hon. DCL Northumbria, 2005. Gold Medal, Castrol/Inst. of Motor Industry, 2000; Quattroruote Premio Speciale per la Sicurezza Stradale (Italy), 2001; Goldene VdM-Dieselring (Germany), 2001. Grande Ufficiale dell' Ordine al Merito (Italy), 1994; Order of Madarski Konnik, 1st degree (Bulgaria), 2000; Order of Merit (Romania), 2004; Huesped Ilustre de Quito (Ecuador), 2005; Chevalier de la Légion d'Honneur (France), 2005; Commandeur de l'Ordre de Saint Charles (Monaco), 2006. *Recreations:* snow-boarding, walking. *Address:* c/o Fédération Internationale de l'Automobile, 8 place de la Concorde, 75008 Paris, France.

MOSLEY, Nicholas; *see* Ravensdale, 3rd Baron.

MOSS, Ann; *see* Moss, J. A.

MOSS, Charles James, CBE 1977; Director, National Institute of Agricultural Engineering, 1964–77; *b* 18 Nov. 1917; *s* of James and Elizabeth Moss; *m* 1939, Joan Bernice Smith; two *d*. *Educ:* Queen Mary Coll., London Univ. (BSc 1938, Sir John William Lubbock Meml Prize 1938). Rotol Ltd, Gloucester, 1939–43; RAE Farnborough, 1943–45; CIBA Ltd, Cambridge, 1945–51; ICI Ltd, Billingham, 1951–58; Central Engineering Estabt, NCB, Stanhope Bretby, 1958–61; Process Develt Dept, NCB, London, 1961–63; Vis. Prof., Dept of Agric. Engrg, Univ. of Newcastle upon Tyne, 1972–75; Head of Agr. Engineering Dept, Internat. Rice Res. Inst., Philippines, 1977–80; Liaison scientist and agr. engineer, Internat. Rice Res. Inst., Cairo, 1980–81. *Publications:* papers in learned jls, confs., etc. *Recreations:* gardening, walking. *Address:* 1 Laurel Court, Endcliffe Vale Road, Sheffield, South Yorks S10 3DU.

MOSS, Christopher John; QC 1994; **His Honour Judge Moss;** a Circuit Judge, since 2002; *b* 4 Aug. 1948; *s* of John (Jack) Gordon Moss and Joyce (Joy) Mirren Moss (*née* Stephany); *m* 1st, 1971, Gail Susan Pearson (marr. diss. 1987); one *s* two *d*; 2nd, 1988, Tracy Louise Levy (marr. diss. 1997); one *s* one *d*; 3rd, 1999, Lisa Annette O'Dwyer; two *d*. *Educ:* Bryanston Sch.; University Coll. London (LLB). Called to the Bar, Gray's Inn, 1972, Bencher, 2002; a Recorder, 1993–2002. *Recreation:* playing the piano and accordion. *Address:* Central Criminal Court, Old Bailey, EC4M 7EH.

MOSS, Dr Christopher Michael; Astronomer, Liverpool John Moores University, since 2000; *b* 6 Nov. 1946; *s* of Joseph Moss and Hilda Moss (*née* Wilder). *Educ:* Heythrop Coll. (Bacc Phil 1969); MA Oxon 1972; BD London 1979; MA Cantab; DPhil Sussex 1976. Entered Jesuit Order, 1964; ordained priest, 1979; Staff Mem., Vatican Observatory, Rome and Vatican Observatory Res. Gp, Univ. of Arizona, 1980–85; Dean, 1986–92, Fellow, 1986–97, St Edmund's Coll., Cambridge; Postdoctoral Staff Mem., Inst. of Astronomy, Univ. of Cambridge, 1986–97; Principal, Heythrop Coll., London Univ., 1997–98; Associate Faculty Mem., Univ. of Arizona, 1998–2000; resigned from SJ, 2003. *Publications:* papers in astrophysical and astronomical jls. *Recreations:* walking, sketching, foreign travel. *Address:* Astrophysics Research Institute, Twelve Quays House, Egerton Wharf, Birkenhead CH41 1LD.

MOSS, David Christopher, FCILT; Chairman, Bradford on Avon Preservation Trust Ltd, since 2004; *b* 17 April 1946; *s* of Charles Clifford Moss and Marjorie Sylvia Moss (*née* Hutchings); *m* 1971, Angela Mary Wood; one *s*. *Educ:* King's Sch., Chester; Magdalene Coll., Cambridge (BA). Asst Principal, MPBW, 1968; Principal, 1972, DoE, and subseq. Dept of Transport and HM Treasury; Asst Sec., 1980, Dept of Transport and DoE; Under Sec., Internat. Aviation, Dept of Transport, 1988–93; Railtrack: Commercial Dir, 1993–95; European Affairs Dir, 1995–98; Dir Gen. (Europe), 1998–2001. Pres., European Civil Aviation Conf., 1990–93; Bd Chm., Jt Aviation Authorities, 1990–93. FCIT 1998. *Recreations:* opera, ecclesiastical architecture, wine. *Club:* Oxford and Cambridge.

MOSS, David John; Deputy Director, Workforce (formerly Programme Director, NHS Pay Reform), Department of Health, 2003–07; *b* 23 May 1947; *s* of late John Henry Moss and of Doris (*née* Fenna); *m* 1975, Susan Elizabeth Runnalls; three *s*. *Educ:* Sevenoaks Sch.; St John's Coll., Cambridge (MA); Poly. of Central London (Dip. Management Studies). IPFA; MHSM; FCMA. Management Trainee and Management Accounting, Philips Lamps, 1968–73; Asst Finance Officer, St Thomas' Hosp., 1973–74; Dist Finance Officer, Enfield Health Dist, 1974–79; Dist. Treasurer, E Dorset HA, 1979–86; General Manager: Poole Gen. Hosp., 1986–88; Southampton Gen. Hosp., 1988–91; Southampton Univ. Hosps, 1991–93; Chief Exec., Southampton Univ. Hosps Trust, 1993–2004. Chm., UK Univ. Hosp. Forum, 2001–03; Mem., Audit Commn, 2001–07. FRSA 1994; FCMI. *Publications:* (jtly) Managing Nursing, 1984; articles in professional jls. *Recreations:* cricket, golf, tennis, Rugby, history, opera, walking.

MOSS, (Sir) David John E.; *see* Edwards-Moss.

MOSS, Sir David Joseph, KCVO 1998; CMG 1989; HM Diplomatic Service, retired; High Commissioner in Kuala Lumpur, 1994–98; *b* 6 Nov. 1938; *s* of Herbert Joseph and Irene Gertrude Moss; *m* 1961, Joan Lillian Moss; one *d* (one *s* decd). *Educ:* Hampton Grammar Sch.; BA Hons. CS Commn, 1956; FO, 1957; RAF, 1957–59; FO, 1959–62; Third Sec., Bangkok, 1962–65; FO, 1966–69; First Sec., La Paz, 1969–70; FCO, 1970–73; First Sec. and Head of Chancery, The Hague, 1974–77; First Sec., FCO, 1978–79, Counsellor, 1979–83; Counsellor, Hd of Chancery and Dep. Perm. Rep., UK

Mission, Geneva, 1983–87; Asst. Under-Sec. of State, FCO, 1987–90; High Comr, New Zealand, 1990–94. *Recreations:* reading, listening to music. *Club:* Royal Over-Seas League.

MOSS, Elaine Dora; Children's Books Adviser to The Good Book Guide, 1980–86; *b* 8 March 1924; *d* of Percy Philip Levy and Maude Agnes Levy (*née* Simmons); *m* 1950, John Edward Moss, FRICS, FAI; two *d*. *Educ:* St Paul's Girls' Sch.; Bedford Coll. for Women (BA Hons); Univ. of London Inst. of Educn (DipEd); University College London Sch. of Librarianship (ALA). Teacher, Stoatley Rough Sch., Haslemere, 1945–47; Asst Librarian, Bedford Coll., 1947–50; freelance journalist and broadcaster (Woman's Hour, The Times, TES, TLS, The Spectator, Signal, etc.), 1956–; Editor and Selector, NBL's Children's Books of the Year, 1970–79; Librarian, Fleet Primary Sch., ILEA, 1976–82. Eleanor Farjeon Award, 1976. *Publications:* texts for several picture books, incl. Polar, 1976; catalogues for Children's Books of the Year, 1970–79; Picture Books for Young People 9–13, 1981, 3rd edn 1992; Part of the Pattern: a personal journey through the world of children's books 1960–1985, 1986; (with Nancy Chambers) The Signal Companion, 1996. *Recreations:* walking, art galleries, reading, ballet. *Address:* 19/1 View Road, N6 4DJ.

MOSS, Gabriel Stephen; QC 1989; *b* 8 Sept. 1949; *m* 1979, Judith; one *d*. *Educ:* University of Oxford (Eldon Schol. 1975; BA Jurisprudence 1971; BCL 1972; MA). Lectr, Univ. of Connecticut Law Sch., 1972–73; called to the Bar, Lincoln's Inn, 1974 (Hardwicke Schol., 1971; Cassel Schol., 1975; Bencher, 1998); admitted to the Bar of Gibraltar. Jt DTI Inspector, Bestwood plc, 1989. Formerly (part-time) Lectr/Tutor, Oxford, LSE, Council of Legal Educn. Member: Bd, Insolvency Res. Unit, Univ. of Sussex (formerly at KCL), 1991–; Insolvency Law Sub-Cttee, Consumer and Commercial Law Cttee, Law Soc., 1991–; Insolvency Cttee, Justice, 1993–; Insolvency Lawyers Assoc., 1999–. Fellow, Soc. of Advanced Legal Studies, 1998. Chm. Editl Bd, Insolvency Intelligence, 1994– (Mem., 1992–); Mem. Adv. Editl Bd, Receivers, Administrators and Liquidators Qly, 1993–. *Publications:* (ed with David Marks) Rowlatt on Principal and Surety, 4th edn 1982, 5th edn 1999; (with Gavin Lightman) The Law of Receivers of Companies, 1986, 4th edn 2007; (ed jtly) Insolvency, 1996–; (with Ian Kawaley *et al*) Cross-Frontier Insolvency of Insurance Companies, 2001; (with Ian Fletcher and Stuart Isaacs) The EC Regulation on Insolvency Proceedings, 2002; (with Bob Wessels) EU Banking and Insurance Insolvency, 2006. *Recreations:* classical music, foreign travel, tennis. *Address:* 3–4 South Square, Gray's Inn, WC1R 5HP. *T:* (020) 7696 9900, *Fax:* (020) 7696 9911; *e-mail:* clerks@southsquare.com.

MOSS, (James) Richard (Frederick), OBE 1955; FRINA; RCNC; Founder, Chairman, 1978–94, and President, since 1994, Polynous, Cambridge; Chief Executive, Balaena Structures (North Sea), 1974–77, retired; *b* 26 March 1916; *s* of late Lt-Cdr J. G. Moss, RN, and late Kathleen Moss (*née* Steinberg); *m* 1941, Celia Florence Lucas (*d* 2008); three *d*. *Educ:* Marlborough College; Trinity Coll., Cambridge (1st Cl. Hons Mech. Sci. Tripos and Maths Pt I, MA); RCNC, 1941. Constructor Comdr to C-in-C, Far East Fleet, 1949–52; Chief Constructor, HM Dockyard, Singapore, 1955–58; Supt, Naval Construction Research Estab., Dunfermline, 1965–68; Dir, Naval Ship Production, 1968–74. *Recreations:* yachting, music, bell ringing. *Address:* 13 Beaufort Place, Thompsons Lane, Cambridge CB5 8AG. *T:* (01223) 328583. *Club:* Royal Naval Sailing Association.

MOSS, Jane Hope; *see* Bown, J. H.

MOSS, Prof. (Jennifer) Ann, PhD; FBA 1998; Professor of French, University of Durham, 1996–2003, now Emeritus; *b* 21 Jan. 1938; *d* of John Shakespeare Poole and Dorothy Kathleen Beese (*née* Sills); *m* 1960, John Michael Barry Moss (marr. diss. 1966); two *d*. *Educ:* Barr's Hill Grammar Sch., Coventry; Newnham Coll., Cambridge (MA; PhD 1975). Asst Lectr, UCNW, 1963–64; Resident Tutor and part-time Lectr, Trevelyan Coll., Durham, 1966–79; University of Durham: Lectr in French, 1979–85; Sen. Lectr, 1985–88; Reader, 1988–96. Licensed Reader, C of E, 2005–. *Publications:* Ovid in Renaissance France, 1982; Poetry and Fable, 1984; Printed Commonplace-Books and the Structuring of Renaissance Thought, 1996; Latin Commentaries on Ovid from the Renaissance, 1998; Les Recueils de lieux communs: apprendre à penser à la Renaissance, 2002; Renaissance Truth and the Latin Language Turn, 2003. *Recreation:* daughters and grandchildren. *Address:* 7 Mountjoy Crescent, Durham DH1 3BA. *T:* (0191) 383 0672.

MOSS, (John) Michael, CB 1996; Command Secretary to Second Sea Lord and Commander-in-Chief Naval Home Command, 1994–96, and Assistant Under-Secretary of State (Naval Personnel), 1989–96, Ministry of Defence; *b* 21 April 1936; *s* of late Ernest and Mary Moss. *Educ:* Accrington Grammar Sch.; King's Coll., Cambridge (Foundn Scholar; MA Math. Tripos, Pt I Cl. I, Pt II Wrangler, Pt III Hons with Dist.). National Service, RAF Educn Branch: Pilot Officer 1958; Flying Officer 1959; Flt Lieut 1960; RAF Technical Coll., Henlow, 1959–60. Asst Principal, Air Min., 1960–63; Private Sec. to Air Member for Supply and Orgn, 1962–63; Principal, Air Min., 1963–64, and MoD, 1964–70; Private Sec. to Parly Under-Sec. of State for Defence for the RAF, 1969–70; Asst Sec., MoD, 1971–72; Estab. Officer, Cabinet Office, 1972–75; Sec., Radcliffe Cttee of Privy Counsellors on Ministerial Memoirs, 1975; returned to MoD as Asst Sec., 1976–83; RCDS, 1983; Asst Under-Sec. of State (Air), MoD (PE), 1984–88; Fellow, Center for Internat. Affairs, Harvard Univ., 1988–89. Chm., Greenwich Hosp. Adv. Panel, 1989–96. Choirman, 1968–2000, Sen. Sidesman, 2000–, St Bartholomew the Gt, Smithfield; Hon. Steward, Westminster Abbey, 1996–. *Recreations:* travel, photography, choral singing. *Address:* c/o Royal Bank of Scotland, Admiralty Arch, 49 Charing Cross, SW1A 2DX. *Clubs:* Royal Air Force, Oxford and Cambridge.

MOSS, John Ringer, CB 1972; adviser to companies in Associated British Foods Group, 1980–98; *b* 15 Feb. 1920; 2nd *s* of late James Moss and Louisa Moss; *m* 1946, Edith Bland Wheeler; two *s* one *d*. *Educ:* Manchester Gram. Sch.; Brasenose Coll., Oxford (MA). War Service, mainly India and Burma, 1940–46; Capt., RE, attached Royal Bombay Sappers and Miners. Entered Civil Service (MAFF) as Asst Princ., 1947; Princ. Private Sec. to Minister of Agric., Fisheries and Food, 1959–61; Asst Sec., 1961; Under-Sec., Gen. Agricultural Policy Gp, 1967–70; Dep. Sec., 1970–80. Mem., Economic Develt Cttee for Agriculture, 1969–70. Specialist Adviser to House of Lords' Select Cttee on European Communities, 1982–90. Chm. Council, RVC, 1983–90. *Recreations:* music, travel. *Address:* 16 Upper Hollis, Great Missenden, Bucks HP16 9HP. *T:* (01494) 862676.

MOSS, Katherine Ann, (Kate); fashion model; *b* 16 Jan. 1974; *d* of Peter Edward Moss and Linda Rosina Moss (*née* Shephard); one *d* by Jefferson Hack. *Educ:* Riddlesdown High Sch., Purley. Modelling contracts with Calvin Klein, 1992–2000, 2006–; campaigns incl. Burberry, Chanel, Dior, Dolce & Gabbana, Gucci, Katherine Hamnett, Rimmel, H. Stern, Versace, Louis Vuitton, Yves Saint Laurent; fashion design collaboration with Topshop, 2007. Fashion Personality of the Year, 1995, Model of the Year, 2001, 2006, British Fashion Awards. *Publication:* Kate, 1995. *Address:* c/o Storm Model Management, 5 Jubilee Place, SW3 3TD.

MOSS, Ven. Leonard Godfrey; Archdeacon of Hereford and Canon Residentiary of Hereford Cathedral, 1991–97, now Archdeacon Emeritus; *b* 11 July 1932; *s* of Clarence Walter Moss and Frances Lilian Vera Moss; *m* 1954, Everell Annette (*née* Reed); one *s* one *d* (and one *s* decd). *Educ:* Regent St Poly., London; King's Coll., London and Warminster (BD, AKC 1959). Quantity Surveyor's Asst, L. A. Francis and Sons, 1948–54; RE (National Service), 1954–56. Ordained: deacon, 1960; priest, 1961; Assistant curate: St Margaret, Putney, 1960–63; St Dunstan, Cheam, 1963–67; Vicar: Much Dewchurch with Llanwarne and Llandinabo, 1967–72; Marden with Amberley and Wisteston, 1972–84; Hereford Diocesan Ecumenical Officer, 1969–83; Prebendary of Hereford Cathedral, 1979–97; Bishop of Hereford's Officer for Social Responsibility and Non-Residentiary Canon of Hereford Cathedral, 1984–91; Priest-in-charge, Marden with Amberley and Wisteston, 1992–94. Proctor in Convocation, 1970–97. *Publications:* (contrib.) The People, the Land and the Church, 1987; articles and reviews in theol jls. *Recreations:* adult education, reading, listening to music, theatre. *Address:* 10 Saxon Way, Ledbury, Hereford HR8 2QY.

MOSS, Malcolm Douglas; MP (C) Cambridgeshire North East, since 1987; *b* 6 March 1943; *s* of late Norman Moss and Annie Moss (*née* Gay); *m* 1965, Vivien Lorraine (*née* Peake) (*d* 1997); two *d*; *m* 2000, Sonya Alexandra McFarlin (*née* Evans); one step *s* one step *d*. *Educ:* Audenshaw Grammar Sch.; St John's Coll., Cambridge (BA 1965, MA 1968). Teaching Cert 1966. Asst Master, 1966–68, Head of Dept, 1968–70, Blundell's Sch.; Insurance Consultant, 1970–72, Gen. Manager, 1972–74, Barwick Associates; Chairman: Mandrake Gp plc, 1986–88; Mandrake Associates Ltd (formerly Mandrake (Insurance and Finance Brokers)), 1986–93 (Dir, 1974–94); Fens Business Enterprise Trust, 1983–87 (Dir, 1983–94). Mem., Cambs CC, 1985–88. PPS to Minister of State, FO, 1991–93, to Sec. of State for NI, 1993–94; Parly Under-Sec. of State, NI Office and Minister for Health and Envmt, 1994–97; opposition front bench spokesman on NI, 1997–99; on MAFF, 1999–2001; opposition spokesman, for local govt and regions, 2001–02, for aviation and rural transport, 2002, for arts and tourism, 2002–03, for home and constitutional affairs, 2003–05, for tourism, licensing and gambling, 2005–06. Mem., Foreign Affairs Select Cttee, 2006–; Treas., Swiss All Party Parly Gp. 1987–89; Sec., Anglo-Bermuda All Party Parly Gp, 1989–91; Sec., 1988–91, Vice Chm., 1991–93, Cons. Backbench Energy Cttee. *Recreations:* tennis, ski-ing, amateur dramatics, gardening. *Address:* House of Commons, SW1A 0AA.

MOSS, Michael; *see* Moss, J. M.

MOSS, Peter Jonathan; His Honour Judge Peter Moss; a Circuit Judge, since 2004; *b* 29 March 1951; *s* of John Cottam Moss and Joyce Alison Moss (*née* Blunn); *m* (marr. diss.); three *s*. *Educ:* Charterhouse. Called to the Bar, Lincoln's Inn, 1976. Legal Mem., Mental Health Review Tribunal, 1994–; Asst Recorder, 1999–2000, Recorder, 2000–04. Liveryman, Clockmakers' Co. *Recreations:* golf, cricket, ski-ing, fishing. *Address:* Guildford Crown Court, Bedford Road, Guildford, GU1 4ST. *Clubs:* MCC; New Zealand Golf.

MOSS, Richard; *see* Moss, J. R. F.

MOSS, Ronald Trevor; His Honour Judge Moss; a Circuit Judge, since 1993; *b* 1 Oct. 1942; *s* of Maurice and Sarah Moss; *m* 1971, Cindy (*née* Fiddleman); one *s* one *d*. *Educ:* Hendon County Grammar School; Nottingham University (Upper Second BA; Hons Law). Admitted Solicitor, 1968; Partner, Moss Beachley, solicitors, 1973–84; Metropolitan Stipendiary Magistrate, 1984–93; Asst Recorder, 1986–90; Recorder, 1990–93; Luton Crown Court, 1993–2005, Resident Judge, 2001–05. Chm., Inner London Juvenile Courts, subseq. Inner London Youth and Family Panel, 1986–93. Mem. Cttee, London Criminal Courts Solicitors' Assoc., 1982–84. *Recreations:* golf, bridge, Watford Football Club. *Address:* c/o Harrow Crown Court, Hailsham Drive, Harrow, Middlesex HA1 4TU. *Club:* Moor Park Golf.

MOSS, Sir Stephen (Alan), Kt 2006; Chief Executive, Queen's Medical Centre, Nottingham, 2003–05; *b* 15 May 1947; *s* of George Ernest Moss and Dorothy May Moss. *Educ:* Kingsmead Sch., Hednesford; Wolverhampton Sch. of Nursing (RN; OND); Univ. of London (DN). Nursing Officer: Royal Hosp., Wolverhampton, 1973–75; Dudley Rd Hosp., Birmingham, 1975–77; Sen. Nursing Officer, subseq. Dir of Nursing, Derbys Royal Infirmary, 1977–84; Dir of Nursing, Queen's Med. Centre, Nottingham, 1984–2003. Member: Sheffield HA, 1987–91; Commn for Health Improvement, 1999–2004. Chm., Trust Nurses Assoc., subseq. Nurse Dirs Assoc., 1997–2003. *Recreations:* walking, pottering, antiques, theatre, travel. *Address:* 7 Hall Lane, Nether Hedge, Belper, Derbys DE56 2JW. *T:* (01773) 856170; *e-mail:* StephenM0109@aol.com.

MOSS, Stephen Raymond; writer with The Guardian; *b* 30 July 1957; *s* of Raymond Moss and Catherine Moss (*née* Croome); *m* 1984, Helen Bonnick; one *s*. *Educ:* Balliol Coll., Oxford (BA Modern Hist. 1978); Birkbeck Coll., London (MA in Victorian Studies 1986). Editor with Kogan Page Publishers Ltd, 1979–81; Editor: Managing Your Business, 1981–83; Marketing and Direction, 1983–89; joined The Guardian, 1989: Dep. Arts Ed., 1991–93; Dep. Features Ed., 1994–95; Literary Ed., 1995–98. *Publication:* (ed) Wisden Anthology 1978–2006: cricket's age of revolution, 2006. *Recreations:* chess, cricket, music. *Address:* c/o The Guardian, Kings Place, 90 York Way, N1 9AG; *e-mail:* stephen.moss@guardian.co.uk.

MOSS, Sir Stirling, Kt 2000; OBE 1959; FIE; racing motorist, 1947–62, retired; Managing Director, Stirling Moss Ltd; Director, Stirling Products Ltd; *b* 17 Sept. 1929; *m* 1st, 1957, Kathleen Stuart (marr. diss. 1960), *y d* of F. Stuart Molson, Montreal, Canada; 2nd, 1964, Elaine (marr. diss. 1968), 2nd *d* of A. Barbarino, New York; one *d*; 3rd, 1980, Susan, *y d* of Stuart Paine, London; one *s*. *Educ:* Haileybury and Imperial Service Coll. Brit. Nat. Champion, 1950, 1951, 1952, 1954, 1955, 1956, 1957, 1958, 1959, 1961; Tourist Trophy, 1950, 1951, 1955, 1958, 1959, 1960, 1961; Coupe des Alpes, 1952, 1953, 1954; Alpine Gold Cup (three consecutive wins), 1954. Only Englishman to win Italian Mille Miglia, 1955. Competed in 529 races, rallies, sprints, land speed records and endurance runs, finished in 387 and won 211. Successes include Targa Florio, 1955; Brit. Grand Prix, 1955, 1957; Ital. GP, 1956, 1957, 1959; NZ GP, 1956, 1959; Monaco GP, 1956, 1960, 1961; Leguna Seca GP, 1960, 1961; US GP, 1959, 1960; Aust. GP, 1956; Bari GP, 1956; Pescara GP, 1957; Swedish GP, 1957; Dutch GP, 1958; Argentine GP, 1958; Morocco GP, 1958; Buenos Aires GP, 1958; Melbourne GP, 1958; Villareal GP, 1958; Caen GP, 1958; Portuguese GP, 1959; S African GP, 1960; Cuban GP, 1960; Austrian GP, 1960; Cape GP, 1960; Watkins Glen GP, 1960; German GP, 1961; Modena GP, 1961. Twice voted Driver of the Year, 1954 and 1961. *Publications:* Stirling Moss's Book of Motor Sport, 1955; In the Track of Speed, 1957; Stirling Moss's Second Book of Motor Sport, 1958; Le Mans, 1959; My Favourite Car Stories, 1960; A Turn at the Wheel, 1961; All But My Life, 1963; Design and Behaviour of the Racing Car, 1964; How to Watch Motor Racing, 1975; Motor Racing and All That, 1980; My Cars, My Career, 1987; (with D. Nye) Fangio: a Pirelli album, 1991; Great Drives in the Lakes and Dales, 1993; (with C. Hilton) Stirling Moss's Motor Racing Masterpieces, 1994; *relevant publications:* Stirling Moss, by Robert Raymond, 1953; Racing with the Maestro, by Karl Ludvigsen, 1997; Stirling Moss: the authorised biography, by Robert Edwards, 2001. *Recreations:* historic racing, designing, model making. *Address:* (business) Stirling Moss Ltd, 46 Shepherd Street, W1J 7JN; (residence) 44 Shepherd Street, W1J 7JN. *Clubs:* Royal Automobile; British Racing Drivers' (Silverstone); British Automobile Racing

(Thruxton); British Racing and Sports Car (W Malling, Kent); Road Racing Drivers of America, 200 mph (Bonneville, USA); Internationale des Anciens Pilotes des Grand Prix (Bergamo); Chm. or Pres. of 36 motoring clubs.

MÖSSBAUER, Rudolf L., PhD; Professor of Experimental Physics, Technische Universität München, 1977–97, now Emeritus; *b* Munich, 31 Jan. 1929; *m*; one *s* two *d*. *Educ:* High Sch. and Technische Hochschule, München (equiv. Bachelor's and Master's degrees). PhD (München) 1958. Thesis work, Max Planck Inst., Heidelberg, 1955–57; Research Fellow: Technische Hochschule, München, 1958–59, and at Caltech, 1960–61; Prof. of Physics, CIT, 1962–64; Prof. of Experimental Physics, München, 1965–71; Dir, Institut Max von Laue-Paul Langevin, and French-German-British High-Flux-Reactor at Grenoble, 1972–77. Member: Bavarian Acad. of Sci.; Nat. Acad. of Scis, Washington; Amer. Acad. of Arts and Scis; Pontifical Acad.; Soviet Acad. of Sci.; Acad. Leopoldina, etc. Hon. degrees Oxford, Leeuwen, Madrid, Grenoble, etc. Nobel Prize for Physics (jtly), 1961, and numerous other awards. Bavarian Order of Merit, 1962; Order of Merit for Scis and the Arts (Germany), 1996. *Publications:* on gamma resonance spectroscopy (Mössbauer effect) and on neutrino physics. *Recreations:* photography, music, mountaineering. *Address:* Technische Universität München, Physik-Department E 15, James-Franck-Strasse, 85748 Garching, Germany.

MOSSE, Katharine Louise, (Kate); novelist and broadcaster; *b* 20 Oct. 1961; *d* of Richard and Barbara Mosse; *m* 2001, Gregory Charles Mosse (*né* Dunk); one *s* one *d*. *Educ:* New Coll., Oxford (BA Hons 1984, MA 1994). Publisher, 1984–92; Exec. Dir, Chichester Fest. Th., 1998–2001; presenter, BBC 4 and BBC2 TV and BBC Radio 4, 2000–. Dir, Mosse Associates Ltd, 2003–. Co-founder and Hon. Dir, Orange Prize for Fiction, 1996–. Hon. MA UC Chichester, 2006. *Publications:* Becoming a Mother, 1993, rev. 7th edn 2007; The House: behind the scenes at the Royal Opera House, Covent Garden, 1995; Eskimo Kissing, 1996; Crucifix Lane, 1998; Labyrinth, 2005; Sepulchre, 2007. *Recreations:* family, swimming, walking, reading, theatre. *Address:* c/o Lucas Alexander Whitley Agency, 14 Vernon Street, W14 0RT; *e-mail:* mark@lawagency.co.uk.

MOSSELMANS, Carel Maurits, TD 1961; Chairman: Rothschild International Asset Management, 1989–96; Janson Green Holdings Ltd, 1993–96; Janson Green Ltd, 1993–96 (non-executive Director, 1993–98); *b* 9 March 1929; *s* of Adriaan Willem Mosselmans and Jonkvrouwe Nancy Henriette Mosselmans (*née* van der Wyck); *m* 1962, Hon. Prudence Fiona McCorquodale, *d* of 1st Baron McCorquodale of Newton, KCVO, PC; two *s*. *Educ:* Stowe; Trinity Coll., Cambridge (MA Modern Langs and Hist.). Queen's Bays 2nd Dragoon Guards, 1947–49; City of London Yeomanry (Rough Riders), TA, 1949; Inns of Court and City Yeomanry, 1961; Lt-Col comdg Regt, 1963. Joined Sedgwick Collins & Co., 1952 (Dir, 1963); Director: Sedgwick Forbes Hldgs, 1978; Sedgwick Forbes Bland Payne, 1979; Chm., Sedgwick Ltd, 1981–84; Dep. Chm., 1982–84, Chm., 1984–89, Sedgwick Group plc; Chairman: Sedgwick Lloyd's Underwriting Agents (formerly Sedgwick Forbes (Lloyd's Underwriting Agents)), 1974–89; The Sumitomo Marine & Fire Insurance Co. (Europe), 1981–90 (Dir, 1975–81); Rothschild Asset Management, 1990–93 (Dir, 1989–99); Exco plc, 1991–96; Director: Coutts & Co., 1981–95; Tweedhill Fisheries, 1990–; Chm., Cttee of Mgt, Lionbrook Property Fund 'B' (formerly Five Arrows Property Unit Trust Managers Ltd), 1993–2003; Mem. Investors' Cttee, Lionbrook Property Partnership, 1997–2003; Chm., Indoor Golf Clubs plc, 1998–2004. Vice-Pres., BIIBA, 1987–89. *Recreations:* shooting, fishing, golf, music. *Address:* 15 Chelsea Square, SW3 6LF. *T:* (020) 7352 0621, *Fax:* (020) 7351 2489. *Clubs:* White's, Cavalry and Guards; Royal St George's Golf; Sunningdale Golf; Swinley Forest Golf; Royal & Ancient Golf (St Andrews).

MOSSON, Alexander Francis; Member (Lab), Glasgow City Council, since 1984; Lord Provost and Lord-Lieutenant of Glasgow, 1999–2003; *b* 27 Aug. 1940; *m* 1971, Maureen Sweeney; four *s* three *d*. *Educ:* St Patrick's Primary Sch.; St Mungo's Acad. Glasgow Corporation, 1955; apprentice boilermaker, Barclay Curle, 1956; plater, Alexander Stephens, 1959; insulating engineer, 1963. Active Trade Unionist from age of 17; Glasgow City Council: Convener, Environmental Services, 1995–99; Bailie, 1992–99; Dep. Lord Provost, 1996–99. Chm., Glasgow City Mktg Bureau, 2003–. Hon. FRCPSGlas 2003; Hon. FCLIP Scotland, 2003. Hon. LLD: Glasgow, 2001; Caledonian, 2002; Strathclyde, 2003. OStJ 2000. Golden Jubilee Medal, 2002. *Recreations:* painting with water colours and oils, watching football, researching Scottish and Middle East politics and history. *Address:* Glasgow City Council, City Chambers, George Square, Glasgow G2 1DU. *T:* (0141) 287 4001; 1 Danes Drive, Glasgow G14 9HZ.

MÖST, Franz W.; *see* Welser-Möst.

MOSTYN, 6th Baron *cr* 1831, of Mostyn, co. Flint; **Llewellyn Roger Lloyd Mostyn;** Bt 1778; *b* 26 Sept. 1948; *o s* of 5th Baron Mostyn, MC and of Yvonne Margaret (*née* Johnson); *S* father, 2000; *m* 1974, Denise Suzanne Duvanel; one *s* one *d*. *Educ:* Eton Coll. Directorate of Army Legal Services, 1974. Called to the Bar, Middle Temple, 1973; in practice, 1975–76 and 1985–89; with Kingsbury and Turner, Solicitors, 1976–78; part-time teacher, Bromley Coll. of Technology, 1981–85. *Recreations:* sport, cinema, theatre, classical music, Rugby, tennis. *Heir:* *s* Hon. Gregory Philip Roger Lloyd Mostyn, *b* 31 Dec. 1984. *Address:* 9 Anderson Street, SW3 3LU. *Club:* Lansdowne.

MOSTYN, Nicholas Anthony Joseph Ghislain; QC 1997; a Recorder, since 2000; *b* 13 July 1957; *s* of Jerome John Joseph Mostyn and Mary Anna Bridget Mostyn (now Learoyd); *m* 1981, Lucy Joanna Willis; three *s* one *d*. *Educ:* Ampleforth; Bristol Univ. (LLB). Called to the Bar, Middle Temple, 1980, Bencher, 2005; Asst Recorder, 1997–2000; a Dep. High Court Judge, 2000–. Kt of Honour and Devotion, SMO Malta, 2003. *Publications:* Child's Pay, 1993, 3rd edn 2002; At a Glance, annually, 1992–. *Recreations:* Wagner, Southampton FC, ski-ing. *Address:* 1 Hare Court, Temple, EC4Y 7BE. *T:* (020) 7797 7070. *Club:* MCC.

MOSTYN, Sir William Basil John, 15th Bt *cr* 1670, of Talacre, Flintshire; *b* 15 Oct. 1975; *s* of Sir Jeremy John Anthony Mostyn, 14th Bt and of Cristina, *o d* of Marchese Orengo, Turin; *S* father, 1988. *Heir:* *uncle* Trevor Alexander Richard Mostyn [*b* 23 May 1946; *m* 1st, 1986, Elizabeth Dax (marr. diss. 1988); 2nd, 2001, Hon. Julia Hamilton, *d* of Lord Belhaven and Stenton, *qv*]. *Address:* The Coach House, Church Lane, Lower Heyford, Oxon OX6 3NZ.

MOTE, Ashley; Member (UK Ind, then Ind) South East Region, European Parliament, since 2004; *b* 25 Jan. 1936; *m* 1972, Anna-Nicola Goddard; one *s* one *d*. *Educ:* City of London Freeman's Sch. Army, 1954–56. Journalist, Picture Post, then Farmers' Weekly, 1956–61; communications specialist, 1961–68; Unilever, 1968–72; founder, internat. marketing co., 1972–90. Writer and broadcaster; columnist, Compass, 2004–07. Pres., Hambledon Club, 1998–2007. *Publications:* The Glory Days of Cricket: biography of Broadhalfpenny Down, 1998; (jtly) The Winning Edge: the secrets and techniques of the world's best cricketers, 2001; Vigilance: a defence of British liberty, 2001; OverCrowded Britain: our immigration crisis exposed, 2003; J'Accuse..!, 2008. *Address:* PO Box 216, Alton, Hants GU34 4WY; European Parliament, Rue Wiertz, 1047 Brussels, Belgium.

MOTHERWELL, Bishop of, (RC), since 1983; **Rt Rev. Joseph Devine;** *b* 7 Aug. 1937; *s* of Joseph Devine and Christina Murphy. *Educ:* Blairs Coll., Aberdeen; St Peter's Coll., Dumbarton; Scots Coll., Rome. Ordained priest in Glasgow, 1960; postgraduate work in Rome (PhD), 1960–64; Private Sec. to Archbishop of Glasgow, 1964–65; Assistant Priest in a Glasgow parish, 1965–67; Lecturer in Philosophy, St Peter's Coll., Dumbarton, 1967–74; a Chaplain to Catholic Students in Glasgow Univ., 1974–77; Titular Bishop of Voli and Auxiliary to Archbishop of Glasgow, 1977–83. Papal Bene Merenti Medal, 1962. *Recreations:* general reading, music, Association football. *Address:* 22 Wellhall Road, Hamilton ML3 9BG. *T:* (01698) 423058.

MOTHERWELL, Prof. William Branks, PhD, DSc; FRS 2004; FRSE 2007; Alexander Williamson Professor of Chemistry (first incumbent), University College London, since 1993; *b* 10 May 1947; *s* of James Motherwell, BEM and Mary Motherwell (*née* Jarvie); *m* 1977, Dr Robyn Suzanne Hay; one *d*. *Educ:* Univ. of Glasgow (BSc 1st cl. 1969; PhD 1972; Carnegie Schol.); Univ. of London (DSc 1999). CChem; FRSC 1999. ICI Fellow, Univ. of Stirling, 1972–75; Schering-Plough Fellow, Imperial Coll., London, 1975–77; chargé de recherche, Inst. de Chimie des Substances Naturelles, CNRS, Gif-sur-Yvette, 1977–83; Lectr, 1983–90, Reader, 1990–93, Imperial Coll., London. Visiting Professor: Univ. of Paris, 1993; Univ. of Auckland, 1996; Université Bordeaux, 1998; Univ. of Rouen, 2002. Mem., Exec. Editl Bd, Tetrahedron, 1993–. Corday-Morgan Medal, 1983, Bader Award, 1991, Tilden Medal, 1999, Royal Soc. of Chemistry. *Publications:* over 170 scientific papers in learned jls. *Recreations:* music, walking, golf. *Address:* Department of Chemistry, Christopher Ingold Laboratories, University College London, 20 Gordon Street, WC1H 0AJ. *T:* (020) 7679 7533, *Fax:* (020) 7679 7524; *e-mail:* w.b.motherwell@ucl.ac.uk.

MOTION, Prof. Andrew; writer; Professor of Creative Writing, Royal Holloway, University of London, since 2003; Poet Laureate, 1999–2009; *b* 26 Oct. 1952; *s* of late Andrew Richard Motion and Catherine Gillian Motion; *m* 1st, 1973, Joanna Jane Powell (marr. diss. 1983); 2nd, 1985, Janet Elisabeth Dalley; two *s* one *d*. *Educ:* Radley Coll.; University Coll., Oxford (BA 1st Cl. Hons, MLitt; Hon. Fellow, 1999). Lectr in English, Univ. of Hull, 1977–81; Editor of Poetry Review, 1981–83; Poetry Editor, 1983–89, Editl Dir, 1985–87, Chatto & Windus; Prof. of Poetry, UEA, 1995–2003. Mem., Arts Council of England, subseq. Arts Council England, 1996–99 (Chm., Literature Adv. Panel, 1996–2003); Chm., MLA, 2008–. FRSL 1982; FRSA 2000. Hon. DLitt: Hull, 1996; Exeter, 1999; Brunel, 2000; Anglia, 2001; Sheffield Hallam, 2003; Sheffield, 2005; Aberdeen, 2006; Chester 2008; DUniv Open, 2002. *Publications:* *poetry:* The Pleasure Steamers, 1978, 4th edn 1999; Independence, 1981; The Penguin Book of Contemporary British Poetry (anthology), 1982; Secret Narratives, 1983; Dangerous Play, 1984 (Rhys Meml Prize); Natural Causes, 1987 (Dylan Thomas Award); Love in a Life, 1991; The Price of Everything, 1994; Salt Water, 1997; Selected Poems, 1998; Public Property, 2002; *criticism:* The Poetry of Edward Thomas, 1981; Philip Larkin, 1982; (ed) William Barnes: selected poems, 1994; Thomas Hardy: selected poems, 1994; *biography:* The Lamberts, 1986 (Somerset Maugham Award, 1987); Philip Larkin: a writer's life, 1993 (Whitbread Award, 1993); Keats, 1997; Wainewright the Poisoner, 2000; In the Blood (autobiog.), 2006; *novels:* The Pale Companion, 1989; Famous for the Creatures, 1991; The Invention of Dr Cake, 2003. *Address:* c/o Faber & Faber, 3 Queen Square, WC1N 3AU.

MOTO, Dr Francis; High Commissioner of Malawi to the United Kingdom and Republic of Ireland, since 2006; *b* 28 Feb. 1952; *s* of Bwanali and Rufina Moto; *m* 1982, Elizabeth Inglis; three *s* one *d*. *Educ:* Univ. of Malaŵi (DipEd; BEd); SOAS, Univ. of London (MA); PhD University Coll. London 1989. Chancellor College, University of Malaŵi: Staff associate, 1977–80; Lectr, 1980–90; Sen. Lectr, 1990–99; Associate Prof., 1999–2006; Hd of Dept and Dean of Faculty, 1985–2006; Vice Principal, 1994–98, Principal, 1998–2005, Univ. of Malaŵi. Mem. Bd, Malawi Privatisation Commn, 2003–05. Chm., Women and Law in Southern Africa (Trustee, Regl Bd), 1998–2005. Mem. Bd, Malawi Inst. of Educn, 1998–2005. Chm., Malawi Nat. Day of Educn, 2000–04. Malaŵi Govt Scholarship Award, 1972, 1978; Commonwealth Scholarship Award, 1986. *Publications:* Nzeru Umati Zako Nzokuuza, 1987; Gazing at the Setting Sun, 1994; Trends in Malawian Literature, 2001; Topics in Language, Power and Society, 2007; contribs to Studies in African Linguistics, Jl Contemporary African Studies, Jl Humanities, Jl Social Sci., Nordic Jl African Studies. *Recreations:* football, golf, lawn tennis, squash, dancing, table tennis. *Address:* Kwacha House, 70 Winnington Road, N2 0XT. *Clubs:* Gymkhana (Zomba); Blantyre Sports; Lilongwe Golf, Limbe Country.

MOTSON, John Walker, OBE 2001; BBC TV Sports Commentator, since 1971; *b* 10 July 1945; *s* of late William and Gwendoline Motson; *m* 1976, Anne Jobling; one *s*. *Educ:* Culford Sch., Bury St Edmunds. Barnet Press, 1963–67; Morning Telegraph, Sheffield, 1967–68; BBC Radio Sport, 1968–71 and 2001–; BBC TV Sport, 1971–. Commentator: 28 FA Cup Finals, 1977–; 8 World Cup Final Series, including 6 Finals, 1974–; 8 European Championships, 1976–2004. Commentator of the Year, RTS, 2004. *Publications:* Second to None: great teams of post-war soccer, 1972; (with J. Rowlinson) History of the European Cup, 1980; Motty's Diary: a year in the life of a commentator, 1986; Match of the Day: the complete record, 1992, 1994; Motty's Year, 2004; Motson's National Obsession, 2004; Motson's FA Cup Odyssey, 2005; Motson's World Cup Extravaganza, 2006. *Recreation:* running half-marathons. *Address:* c/o Jane Morgan Management, Thames Wharf Studios, Rainville Road, W6 9HA. *T:* (020) 7386 5345. *Club:* Cricketers'.

MOTT, Gregory George Sidney, CBE 1979; Managing Director, Vickers Shipbuilding and Engineering Ltd, 1979–84, retired; *b* 11 Feb. 1925; *s* of Sidney Cyril George Mott and Elizabeth Rolinda Mott; *m* 1949, Jean Metcalfe. *Educ:* Univ. of Melbourne (BMechE Hons). Trainee Manager, Vickers Armstrong Ltd Naval Yard, 1948–49; Supervising Engr, A. E. Turner and John Coates, London, 1950–52; Sen. Draughtsman, Melbourne Harbour Trust Comrs, 1952–56; joined Vickers Armstrong Ltd, Barrow, trng on submarine construction, 1956; seconded to Naval Section Harwell, for shielding design DS/MP1 (specialised in computer technol.), 1957–59; returned to Barrow as Project Manager, Dreadnought, 1959–61; Technical Manager, Nuclear, 1961–64; Projects Controller, 1964–67; Local Dir, Vickers Ltd Shipbuilding Gp, 1966; responsible for Special Projects Div., incl. Oceanics Dept, 1968–72; Man. Dir, Vickers Oceanics Ltd, on formation of company, 1972–75; Dir, Vickers Ltd Shipbuilding Gp, and Gen. Manager, Barrow Shipbuilding Works (retained directorship, Vickers Oceanics Ltd, resigned later), 1975–77; Dir, Vickers Shipbuilding Gp Ltd, 1977; Gen. Manager and Dir, Barrow Engrg Works, Vickers Shipbuilding Gp Ltd, 1978.

MOTT, John Charles Spencer, FREng; Chairman, William Sindall plc, 1990–94 (Director, 1989–94); *b* Beckenham, Kent, 18 Dec. 1926; *m* 1953, Patricia Mary (*née* Fowler); two *s*. *Educ:* Balgowan Central Sch., Beckenham, Kent; Brixton Sch. of Building; Battersea Polytechnic; Rutherford Coll. of Technology, Newcastle upon Tyne; Wolfson

Coll., Cambridge (BA English 1999; MA English 2004). FICE, FIStructE. Served war, Lieut, Royal Marines, 1943–46. Indentured as Engr with L. G. Mouchel & Partners, 1949–52; joined Kier Ltd, 1952; Agent on heavy civil engrg contracts, 1952–63; Chairman: French Kier Holdings plc, 1974–86 (Dir, on merger, 1973, Chief Exec., 1974–84); May Gurney Hldgs Ltd, 1986–89. Director: Kier Ltd, 1963; J. L. Kier & Co. Ltd (Holding Co.), 1968; RMC plc, 1986–94. Mem. Council, Fellowship of Engrg, 1983–86; Mem. Council, 1973–75, 1986–87, and Vice Pres., 1986–87, ICE; Mem., Bragg Cttee on Falsework, 1972–74. *Address:* 91 Long Road, Cambridge CB2 2HE. *Club:* Danish.

MOTT, Sir John (Harmar), 3rd Bt *cr* 1930; Regional Medical Officer, Department of Health and Social Security, 1969–84; *b* 21 July 1922; *s* of Sir Adrian Spear Mott, 2nd Bt and Mary Katherine (*d* 1972), *d* of late Rev. A. H. Stanton; *S* father, 1964; *m* 1950, Elizabeth, *d* of late Hugh Carson, FRCS; one *s* two *d*. *Educ:* Radley Coll.; New Coll., Oxford (MA 1948; BM, BCh, 1951). MRCGP 1958. Served War of 1939–45: Pilot, Royal Air Force, 1943–46. Middlesex Hospital: House Physician, 1951; House Surgeon, 1952; GP, Southport, Merseyside, 1952–69. *Recreation:* photography. *Heir: s* David Hugh Mott [*b* 1 May 1952; *m* 1980, Amanda Jane (marr. diss. 2007), *d* of Lt-Comdr D. W. P. Fryer, RN; two *s*]. *Address:* Staniford, Brookside, Kingsley, Cheshire WA6 8BG. *T:* (01928) 788123.

MOTT, Prof. Martin Gerard, FRCP, FRCPCH; Cancer and Leukemia in Children Professor of Paediatric Oncology, 1990–2000, now Emeritus, and Dean of Clinical Medicine and Dentistry, 1997–2000, University of Bristol; *b* 30 Nov. 1941; *s* of Mervyn Gerard Mott and Frances Emily Davis; *m* 1964, Patricia Anne Green; one *s* two *d*. *Educ:* Wimbledon Coll.; Univ. of Bristol (BSc 1963; MB ChB 1966; DSc 1991). FRCP 1983; FRCPCH 1996. Research Fellow, Univ. of Texas (M. D. Anderson Hosp.), 1972; Vis. Asst Prof., Stanford Univ., 1974–76; Sen. Lectr, then Reader, Univ. of Bristol, 1976–90. Founder Mem., UK Children's Cancer Study Gp, 1977–. International Society of Paediatric Oncology: Hon. Sec., 1979–82; Pres., Eur. Continental Branch, 1999–2000; Mem., GMC, 1999–2000. *Publications:* numerous contribs to learned jls on topics relating to childhood cancer. *Recreations:* music, ornithology. *Address:* 50 Downs Park West, Bristol BS6 7QL. *T:* (0117) 962 1476.

MOTT, His Honour Michael Duncan; a Circuit Judge, 1985–2006; a Deputy Circuit Judge, since 2006; *b* 8 Dec. 1940; *s* of late Francis J. Mott and Gwendolen Mott; *m* 1970, Phyllis Ann Gavin; two *s*. *Educ:* Rugby Sch.; Caius Coll., Cambridge (Exhibnr, MA). Called to Bar, Inner Temple, 1963; practised Midland and Oxford Circuit, 1964–69; Resident Magistrate, Kenya, 1969–71; resumed practice, Midland and Oxford Circuit, 1972; a Deputy Circuit Judge, 1976–80; a Recorder, 1980–85. *Recreations:* tennis, ski-ing, travel, music. *Address:* c/o Regional Director, Midland Circuit, Priory Court, 33 Bull Street, Birmingham B4 6DW. *Club:* Cambridge Union Society.

MOTT, Philip Charles; QC 1991; a Recorder of the Crown Court, since 1987; a Deputy High Court Judge, since 1998; *b* 20 April 1948; *s* of Charles Kynaston Mott and Elsie (*née* Smith); *m* 1977, Penelope Ann Caffery; two *d*. *Educ:* King's Coll., Taunton; Worcester Coll., Oxford (MA). Called to the Bar, Inner Temple, 1970, Bencher, 2006; in practice on Western Circuit, 1970–, Leader, 2004–07. Chm., Mental Health Review Tribunal (Restricted Patients Panel), 2000–. Bar Council: Member: Legal Services Cttee, 2004–05; Advocacy Trng Council, 2004–; Carter Response Gp, 2005–07; Vice-Chm., 2006, Gen. Mgt Cttee, 2007–08, Bar Policy and Res. Gp. *Recreations:* the countryside, growing trees, sailing. *Address:* Outer Temple Chambers, 222 Strand, WC2R 1BA. *T:* (020) 7353 6381. *Clubs:* Bar Yacht, Percuil Sailing.

MOTTELSON, Prof. Ben R., PhD; Danish physicist; Professor, Nordic Institute for Theoretical Atomic Physics, Copenhagen, since 1957; *b* Chicago, Ill, USA, 9 July 1926; *s* of Goodman Mottelson and Georgia Mottelson (*née* Blum); *m* 1948, Nancy Jane Reno; three *c*; became a Danish citizen, 1971. *Educ:* High Sch., La Grange, Ill; Purdue Univ. (officers' trng, USN, V12 program; BSc 1947); Harvard Univ. (grad. studies, PhD 1950). Sheldon Trav. Fellowship from Harvard at Inst. of Theoretical Physics, Copenhagen (later, the Niels Bohr Inst.), 1950–51. His Fellowship from US Atomic Energy Commn permitted continuation of work in Copenhagen for two more years, after which he held research position in CERN (European Organization for Nuclear Research) theoretical study group, formed in Copenhagen. Visiting Prof., Univ. of Calif at Berkeley, Spring term, 1959. Mem., Royal Danish Acad. of Scis and Letters, 1958. Nobel Prize for Physics (jtly), 1975; awarded for work on theory of Atomic Nucleus, with Dr Aage Bohr (3 papers publ. 1952–53). *Publications:* Nuclear Structure, vol. I, 1969; vol. II, 1975 (with A. Bohr); (jtly) The Principle Behind Quantum Mechanics, 2004; contrib. Rev. Mod. Phys (jt), etc. *Address:* Nordisk Institut for Teoretisk Fysik, Blegdamsvej 17, 2100 Copenhagen, Denmark.

MOTTISTONE, 4th Baron *cr* 1933, of Mottistone; **David Peter Seely,** CBE 1984; Lord Lieutenant for Isle of Wight, 1986–95; Governor of the Isle of Wight, 1992–95; *b* 16 Dec. 1920; 4th *s* of 1st Baron Mottistone; *S* half brother, 1966; *m* 1944, Anthea, *er d* of T. V. W. McMullan, Cultra, Co. Down, N Ireland; two *s* two *d* (and one *d* decd). *Educ:* RN Coll., Dartmouth. Convoy escorting, Atlantic and Mediterranean, 1941–44; qualified in Communications, 1944; Served in Pacific, 1945; in comd HMS Cossack, FE Flt, 1958–59; in comd HMS Ajax and 24th Escort Sqdn, FE Flt (offensive ops against Indonesian confrontation) (despatches), 1963–65; Naval Advr to UK High Comr, Ottawa, 1965–66; retired at own request as a Captain, 1967. Dir of Personnel and Training, Radio Rentals Gp, 1967–69; Director: Distributive Industry Trng Bd, 1969–75; Cake and Biscuit Alliance, 1975–81; Export Secretary: Biscuit, Cake, Chocolate and Confectionery Alliance, 1981–83. FIET; FIPD. DL Isle of Wight, 1981. Hon. DLitt Bournemouth, 1993. KStJ 1989. *Recreation:* yachting. *Heir: s* Hon. Peter John Philip Seely [*b* 29 Oct. 1949; *m* 1st, 1972, Joyce Cairns (marr. diss. 1975); one *s*; 2nd, 1982, Linda (marr. diss. 2001), *d* of W. Swain, Bulphan Fen, Essex; one *s* three *d*]. *Address:* The Old Parsonage, Mottistone, Isle of Wight PO30 4EE. *Clubs:* Royal Commonwealth Society, House of Lords Yacht (Cdre, 1985–98); Royal Yacht Squadron, Royal Cruising, Island Sailing, Royal Navy Sailing Association.

MOTTRAM, Lesley Anne; a District Judge (Magistrates' Courts), since 2005; *b* 3 May 1952; *d* of Fred and Peggy Pugh; *m* 1981, Michael Martin; one *s*. *Educ:* Priory Sch. for Girls, Shrewsbury; LLB Hons. Admitted solicitor, 1976; solicitor, specialising in criminal advocacy, West Midlands, 1977–2005. *Address:* Victoria Law Courts, Corporation Street, Birmingham B4 6QA. *T:* (0121) 212 6600.

MOTTRAM, Sir Richard (Clive), GCB 2006 (KCB 1998); Permanent Secretary, Intelligence, Security and Resilience and Chairman, Joint Intelligence Committee, Cabinet Office, 2005–07; *b* 23 April 1946; *s* of John Mottram and Florence Yates; *m* 1971, Fiona Margaret Erskine; three *s* one *d*. *Educ:* King Edward VI Camp Hill Sch., Birmingham; Univ. of Keele (1st Cl. Hons Internat. Relns). Entered Home Civil Service, 1968, assigned to Ministry of Defence: Asst Private Sec. to Sec. of State for Defence, 1971–72; Cabinet Office, 1975–77; Ministry of Defence: Private Sec. to Perm. Under Sec., 1979–81; Private Sec. to Sec. of State for Defence, 1982–86; Asst. Under Sec. of State, 1986–89; Dep. Under Sec. of State (Policy), 1989–92; Permanent Secretary: Office of Public Service and Sci., 1992–95; MoD, 1995–98; DETR, then DTLR, 1998–2002; DWP, 2002–05. Pres., Commonwealth Assoc. for Public Admin and Mgt, 2000–02. Governor: Ditchley Foundn; Ashridge Business Sch. (formerly Ashridge Mgt Coll.). AcSS 2000. Hon. DLitt Keele, 1996. *Recreations:* cinema, theatre. *Address:* e-mail: rcmottram@googlemail.com.

MOTYER, Rev. John Alexander; Minister of Christ Church, Westbourne, Bournemouth, 1981–89, retired; *b* 30 Aug. 1924; *s* of Robert Shankey and Elizabeth Maud Motyer; *m* 1948, Beryl Grace Mays; two *s* one *d*. *Educ:* High Sch., Dublin; Dublin Univ. (MA, BD); Wycliffe Hall, Oxford. Curate: St Philip, Penn Fields, Wolverhampton, 1947–50; Holy Trinity, Old Market, Bristol, 1950–54; Tutor, Clifton Theol Coll., Bristol, 1950–54, Vice-Principal, 1954–65; Vicar, St Luke's, Hampstead, 1965–70; Dep. Principal, Tyndale Hall, Bristol, 1970–71; Principal and Dean of College, Trinity Coll., Bristol, 1971–81. Vis. Prof. in OT, Reformed Theol Seminary, Jackson, Mississippi, 1999; Jean Alexander Bernhardt Lectr, Lenoir, NC, 2000. DD Lambeth, 1997. *Publications:* The Revelation of the Divine Name, 1959; After Death, 1965, repr. 1997; The Richness of Christ (Epistle to the Philippians), 1966; The Tests of Faith (Epistle of James), 1970, 2nd edn 1975; (Old Testament Editor) New Bible Commentary Revised, 1970, New Bible Commentary 21st Century Edition, 1994; The Day of the Lion (Amos), 1975; The Image of God: Law and Liberty in Biblical Ethics (Laing Lecture), 1976; The Message of Philippians, 1984; The Message of James, 1985; The Prophecy of Isaiah, 1993; A Scenic Route Through the Old Testament, 1994; Look to the Rock: an Old Testament background to our understanding of Christ, 1996; (contrib.) An Exegetical & Expository Commentary: the Minor Prophets, vol. 3, 1998; Isaiah (Tyndale Old Testament Commentaries), 1999; The Story of the Old Testament, 2001; The Message of Exodus: the days of our pilgrimage, 2005; Discovering the Old Testament, 2006; Treasures of the King: psalms from the life of David, 2007; Life 2: The Sequel: what happens when you die, 2008; contributor: New Bible Dictionary; Expositor's Bible Commentary; Law and Life (monograph); New International Dictionary of New Testament Theology; Evangelical Dictionary of Theology. *Recreations:* reading, odd-jobbing. *Address:* 27 Georges Road West, Poynton, Cheshire SK12 1JY. *T:* (01625) 267461.

MOUATT, (Richard) Brian, CBE 1997; Chief Dental Officer, Department of Health, 1991–96; *b* 4 Sept. 1936; *m* 1962, Ursula Wälti; one *s* one *d*. *Educ:* Blundell's Sch.; Edinburgh Univ. (BDS 1960). MGDS RCS 1979; FFGDP (UK) 2001. RAF Dental Branch, 1960–65 (to Sqn Leader); Dept of Public Health, Bournemouth, 1965–68; FCO, Chief Dental Officer to Republic of Zambia under Overseas Aid Scheme contract, 1968–72; gen. dental practice, Dorset, 1972–84; Dept of Health, 1984–96. Hon. Sen. Res. Fellow, Eastman Inst. of Dental Surgery, 1990–2005; Hon. Sen. Lectr, King's Coll. Sch. of Medicine and Dentistry, 1992–2000; Hon. Sen. Advr, Internat. Child Oral Health, Dept of Dental Public Health, KCL, 2006–. Chairman: FDI Developing Countries Fund, 1999–2001; FDI World Dental Develt, 1999–2006; Dental Protection Ltd, 2001–06. Mem. Bd, Medical Protection Soc., 1998–2006. Pres., Commonwealth Dental Assoc., 2000–04 (Vice-Pres., 1996–2000). Advr to Sec. of State for Educn and Skills (formerly Educn and Employment) on educnl matters for GCC, 1997–2005. *Recreations:* travel, water colour painting, sailing. *Address:* 30 Crescent Walk, West Parley, Dorset BH22 8PZ. *T:* (01202) 875139; *e-mail:* Mouatt@msn.com. *Club:* Athenæum.

MOULD, Timothy James; QC 2006; barrister; *b* 22 May 1960; *s* of John and Dorothy Mould; partner, Debbie Field; one *s* one *d*. *Educ:* Blueboys Sch., Minchinhampton; Wycliffe Coll. Jun. Sch.; Rugby Sch.; Queen's Coll., Oxford (BA Hons Lit. Hum. 1982); Poly. of Central London (Dip. Law 1986). Called to the Bar, Gray's Inn, 1987; in practice as a barrister, 1987–, specialising in planning and administrative law. *Publication:* (ed) Encyclopedia of Rating and Local Taxation, 2007. *Recreations:* music, cricket, keeping calm, travel, food and wine in Italy. *Address:* Landmark Chambers, 180 Fleet Street, EC4A 2HQ. *T:* (020) 7430 1221; *e-mail:* tmould@landmarkchambers.co.uk.

MOULDEN, Peter Ronald; a Senior Immigration Judge, Asylum and Immigration Tribunal (formerly a Vice-President, Immigration Appeal Tribunal), since 2000; Resident Senior Immigration Judge, Field House, London, since 2006; *b* 31 Jan. 1945; *s* of Ronald Charles and Kathleen Norah Bell Moulden; *m* 1970, Elaine Williams; one *s* one *d*. *Educ:* Cranleigh Sch. In practice as solicitor, 1969–99; Adjudicator, Immigration Appeal Tribunal, 1999–2000. Liveryman, Glass Sellers Co., 1980–; Craft-owning Freeman, Co. of Watermen and Lightermen, 2006–. *Recreation:* boating. *Address:* Asylum and Immigration Tribunal, Field House, 15 Bream's Buildings, EC4A 1DZ.

MOULTON, Alexander Eric, CBE 1976; RDI; FREng; Managing Director, Moulton Developments Ltd, since 1956; *b* 9 April 1920; *s* of John Coney Moulton, DSc, The Hall, Bradford-on-Avon, and Beryl Latimer Moulton. *Educ:* Marlborough Coll.; King's Coll., Cambridge (MA). Bristol Aeroplane Co., 1939–44: Engine Research Dept; George Spencer, Moulton & Co. Ltd, 1945–56; became Techn. Dir; estab. Research Dept (originated work on rubber suspensions for vehicles, incl. own design Flexitor); formed Moulton Developments Ltd, 1956 to do develt work on own designs of rubber suspensions for BLMC incl. Hydrolastic and Hydragas (Queen's Award to Industry, 1967); formed Moulton Bicycles Ltd to produce own design Moulton Bicycle, 1962 (Design Centre Award, 1964); designer of Moulton Coach, 1968–70; Chm., Moulton report on engrg design educn, Design Council, 1975–76; launched Alex Moulton Bicycle, 1983. Dir, SW Regional Bd, National Westminster Bank, 1982–87. RDI 1968 (Master, 1982–83); FRSA 1968; FREng (FEng 1980). Hon. Dr: RCA, 1967; Cranfield, 1994; Loughborough, 2006; Hon. DSc Bath, 1971. SIAD Design Medal, 1976; (jointly): James Clayton Prize, Crompton-Lanchester Medal, and Thomas Hawksley Gold Medal, IMechE, 1979; MacRobert Award (mem., jt winning team), FEng, 1991. *Publications:* numerous articles and papers on engineering and education. *Recreations:* cycling, canoeing, shooting. *Address:* The Hall, Bradford-on-Avon, Wilts BA15 1AJ. *T:* (01225) 862991. *Club:* Brooks's.

MOULTON, Jonathan Paul; Founder and Managing Partner, Alchemy Partners LLP, since 1997; *b* 15 Oct. 1950; *s* of Cecil Moulton and Elsie Moulton (*née* Pointon); *m* 1974, Pauline Dunn; one *s* one *d*. *Educ:* Univ. of Lancaster (BA Chem.). FCA 1977. Coopers & Lybrand: Manager, Liverpool, 1972–78; Manager in M&A gp, NY, 1978–80; Citicorp Venture Capital: NY, 1980–81; Man. Dir, London, 1981–85 (Mem., French and German Investment Cttees); Founder and Managing Partner, Schroder Ventures, London, 1985–94 (Mem., French and German Investment Cttees); Dir in Charge of Leveraged Buy-outs, Apax Partners, London, 1994–97 (Mem., Internat. Operating Cttee). Fellow, Soc. of Turnaround Professionals, 2000. *Recreations:* tennis, running, bridge, chess. *Address:* Alchemy Partners, 20 Bedfordbury, WC2N 4BL. *T:* (020) 7240 9596, *Fax:* (020) 7240 9594; *e-mail:* jmoulton@alchemypartners.co.uk.

MOUND, Laurence Alfred, DSc; FRES; Hon. Research Fellow, CSIRO Entomology (formerly Division of Entomology, Commonwealth Scientific and Industrial Research Organisation), since 1996; Research Associate, Natural History Museum (formerly British

Museum (Natural History)), since 1992 (Keeper of Entomology, 1981–92); *b* 22 April 1934; *s* of John Henry Mound and Laura May Cape; *m* 1st, 1958, Agnes Jean Solari (marr. diss. 1985); one *s* two *d*; 2nd, 1987, Sheila Helen Halsey (marr. diss. 1994); 3rd, 2004, Alice Wells. *Educ:* Warwick Sch.; Sir John Cass Coll., London; Imperial Coll., London (DIC); DSc London; Imperial Coll. of Tropical Agriculture, Trinidad (DipTropAgric). Nigerian Federal Dept of Agricl Research, 1959–61; Rockefeller Studentship, Washington and Calif, 1961; Empire Cotton Growing Corp., Republic of Sudan, 1961–64; Sen. Scientific Officer, BM (NH), 1964–69; Australian CSIRO Research Award, 1967–68; PSO, 1969–75, Dep. Keeper, Dept of Entomology, BM (NH), 1975–81. Sec., 1976–88, Vice-Chm., 1988–92, Council for Internat. Congresses of Entomology; Consultant Dir, Commonwealth Inst. of Entomology, 1981–92. Hon. Prof., Sch. of Pure and Applied Biology, Univ. of Wales at Cardiff, 1990–96; McMaster Res. Fellow, CSIRO, 1995–96. Editor, Jl of Royal Entomological Soc. of London, 1973–81 (Vice-Pres., RES, 1975–76). Numerous expedns studying thrips in tropical countries. *Publications:* over 260 technical books and papers on biology of thrips and whitefly, particularly in Bull. of BM (NH), incl. Whitefly of the World (with S. H. Halsey), Thrips of Central and South America (with R. Marullo), and Evolution of Ecological and Behavioural Diversity (with B. Crespi and D. Morris). *Recreations:* thrips with everything. *Address:* c/o CSIRO Entomology, GPO Box 1700, Canberra, ACT 2601, Australia. *T:* (2) 62464280, *Fax:* (2) 62464264; *e-mail:* laurence.mound@csiro.au.

MOUNT, Ferdinand; *see* Mount, W. R. F.

MOUNT, Peter William, CBE 2007; CEng; Chairman, Central Manchester and Manchester Children's University Hospitals NHS Trust, since 2001; *b* 14 Jan. 1940; *s* of William J. and Bridie Mount; *m* Margery; three *c*. *Educ:* De La Salle Sch., Manchester; UMIST (BSc Tech); Univ. of Vienna (short prog.). MIMechE. Prodn Engr, Rolls Royce Ltd, 1961–66; Mgt Consultant, PriceWaterhouseCoopers, 1966–72; Project Dir, Chloride Industrial Batteries, 1972–78; Man. Dir, Chloride Ireland, 1978–81; various Bd appts then CEO, Thorn EMI Fire Protection Ltd and Dir, Thorn Security Ltd, 1984–93. Chairman: Salford Royal Hosps NHS Trust, 1983–2001; Greater Manchester NHS Workforce, 1993–2004; NHS Confederation, 2003–07. Member: Audit Cttee, DoH, 2002–; Bd, Sector Skills Develt Agency, 2002–06 (Chm., Audit Cttee, 2002–06). Dep. Chm., Oldham TEC, 1987–93. Mem. Court, subseq. Gen. Assembly, Univ. of Manchester, 1995–. Founder and Chm. Trustees, charity working with Uganda schs. Co-holder of patent relating to gold processing. *Publication:* (jtly) Absenteeism in Industry, 1980. *Recreations:* walking, ski-ing, cars, computers, making and fixing things, music, good food, taking grandchildren for walks in the park. *Address:* 6 The Ceal, Compstall, Stockport, Cheshire SK6 5LQ. *T:* (0161) 427 4260; *e-mail:* pwmount@btinternet.com. *Club:* Royal Over-Seas League.

MOUNT, (William Robert) Ferdinand, (3rd Bt *cr* 1921, of Wasing Place, Reading, Berks, but does not use the title); author and journalist; Editor, Times Literary Supplement, 1991–2002; *b* 2 July 1939; *s* of Robert Francis Mount (*d* 1969), 2nd *s* of Sir William Arthur Mount, 1st Bt, CBE and his 1st wife, Lady Julia Pakenham (*d* 1956), *d* of 5th Earl of Longford; *S* uncle, 1993; *m* 1968, Julia Margaret, *d* of late Archibald Julian and Hon. Mrs Lucas; two *s* one *d* (and one *s* decd). *Educ:* Eton; Christ Church, Oxford. Has worked for Sunday Telegraph, Conservative Research Dept, Daily Sketch, National Review, Daily Mail, The Times; Political Columnist: The Spectator, 1977–82 and 1985–87; The Standard, 1980–82; Daily Telegraph, 1984–90; Sunday Times, 1997–2004; Head of Prime Minister's Policy Unit, 1982–83. Vice-Chm., Power Commn, 2005–. FRSL 1991 (Mem. Council, 2002–). *Publications:* Very Like a Whale, 1967; The Theatre of Politics, 1972; The Man Who Rode Ampersand, 1975; The Clique, 1978; The Subversive Family, 1982; The Selkirk Strip, 1987; Of Love and Asthma, 1991 (Hawthornden Prize, 1992); The British Constitution Now, 1992; Umbrella, 1994; The Liquidator, 1995; Jem (and Sam): a revenger's tale, 1998; Fairness, 2001; Mind the Gap, 2004; Heads You Win, 2004; The Condor's Head, 2007; Cold Cream: my early life and other mistakes, 2008. *Heir: s* William Robert Horatio Mount [*b* 12 May 1969; *m* 1997, Deborah Grey; two *s*]. *Address:* 17 Ripplevale Grove, N1 1HS. *T:* (020) 7607 5398.

MOUNT CHARLES, Earl of; Henry Vivian Pierpoint Conyngham; *b* 23 May 1951; *s* and *heir* of 7th Marquess Conyngham, *qv*; *m* 1st, 1971, Juliet Ann, *yr d* of Robert Kitson (marr. diss. 1985); one *s* one *d*; 2nd, 1985, Lady Iona Grimston, *yr d* of 6th Earl of Verulam; one *d*. *Educ:* Harrow; Harvard Univ. Irish Rep., 1976–78, Consultant, 1978–84, Sotheby's; Chairman: Slane Castle Ltd; Slane Castle Productions. Dir, Grapevine Arts Centre, Dublin. Trustee, Irish Youth Foundn. *Heir: s* Viscount Slane, *qv*. *Address:* Slane Castle, Co. Meath, Eire; Beau Parc House, Navan, Co. Meath, Eire. *Club:* Kildare Street and University (Dublin).

MOUNT EDGCUMBE, 8th Earl of, *cr* 1789; **Robert Charles Edgcumbe;** Baron Edgcumbe, 1742; Viscount Mount Edgcumbe and Valletort, 1781; Farm Manager, for Lands and Survey, New Zealand, 1975–84; *b* 1 June 1939; *s* of George Aubrey Valletort Edgcumbe (*d* 1977) and of Meta Blucher, *d* of late Robert Charles Lhoyer; *S* uncle, 1982; *m* 1960, Joan Ivy Wall (marr. diss. 1988); five *d*. *Educ:* Nelson College. Career from farm worker to farm manager, managing first farm, 1960; taking up family seat in Cornwall, 1984. *Recreations:* hunting game, restoring classic cars. *Heir: half-b* Piers Valletort Edgcumbe [*b* 23 Oct. 1946; *m* 1971, Hilda Warn (marr. diss.); two *d*]. *Address:* Empacombe House, Cremyll, Cornwall PL10 1HZ.

MOUNTAIN, Sir Edward (Brian Stanford), 4th Bt *cr* 1922, of Oare Manor, Co. Somerset, and Brendon, Co. Devon; Divisional Partner, Bidwells Property Consultants, Inverness, since 2004; *b* 19 March 1961; *er s* of Sir Denis Mortimer Mountain, 3rd Bt and Hélène Fleur Mary Mountain (*née* Kirwan-Taylor); *S* father, 2005, but his name does not appear on the Official Roll of the Baronetage; *m* 1987, Charlotte Sarah Jesson, *d* of His Honour Henry Pownall, QC; two *s* one *d*. *Educ:* King's School, Bruton; RMA Sandhurst; Sparshott Coll. (Dip. Farm Mgt); RAC, Cirencester (BSc Rural Land Mgt 1995); Commnd Army, 1981, Blues and Royals; Captain, 1983; Major, 1991. Joined Bidwells, 1995. *Recreations:* shooting, fishing. *Heir: s* Thomas Denis Edward Mountain, *b* 14 Aug. 1989. *Address:* Delfur Lodge, Orton, Morayshire IV32 7QQ. *T:* (01542) 860274; *e-mail:* emountain@delfur.com.

MOUNTBATTEN, family name of **Marquess of Milford Haven**.

MOUNTBATTEN OF BURMA, Countess (2nd in line) *cr* 1947; **Patricia Edwina Victoria Knatchbull,** CBE 1991; MSc 2007; CD; JP; DL; Viscountess Mountbatten of Burma, 1946; Baroness Romsey, 1947; Vice Lord-Lieutenant of Kent, 1984–2000; *b* 14 Feb. 1924; *er d* of Admiral of the Fleet 1st Earl Mountbatten of Burma, KG, GCB, OM, GCSI, GCIE, GCVO, DSO, PC, FRS, and Countess Mountbatten of Burma, CI, GBE, DCVO, LLD (*d* 1960) (Hon. Edwina Cynthia Annette Ashley, *e d* of 1st and last Baron Mount Temple, PC); *S* father, 1979; *m* 1946, 7th Baron Brabourne, CBE (*d* 2005); four *s* two *d* (and one *s* decd). *Educ:* Malta, England and New York City. Served War in WRNS, 1943–46. Colonel-in-Chief, Princess Patricia's Canadian Light Infantry, 1974–2007. Chm., Edwina Mountbatten Trust. President: Friends of Cassel Hosp.; Friends of William Harvey Hosp.; Shaftesbury Homes and Arethusa; Kent Branches of Save the Children and Relate; Kent Community Housing Trust; Dep. Pres., BRCS; Vice-President: NSPCC; FPA; Nat. Childbirth Trust; SSAFA; RLSS; Shaftesbury Soc.; Nat. Soc. for Cancer Relief; Kent Voluntary Service Council; The Aidis Trust; RCN; Royal Nat. Coll. for Blind; Mountbatten Community Trust. Hon. President: Soc. for Nautical Research; British Maritime Charitable Foundn; Patron: Commando Assoc.; Royal Naval Commando Assoc.; Legion of Frontiersmen of the Commonwealth; HMS Kelly Reunion Assoc.; Safer World Project; VADs (RN); Compassionate Friends; Nurses' Welfare Trust; SOS Children's Villages (UK); Sir Ernest Cassel Educational Trust; Vice-Patron, Burma Star Assoc. JP 1971 and DL 1973, Kent. Hon. DCL Kent, 2000. DStJ 1981. *Heir: s* Baron Brabourne, *qv*. *Address:* Newhouse, Mersham, Ashford, Kent TN25 6NQ. *T:* (01233) 503636.

MOUNTEVANS, 3rd Baron *cr* 1945, of Chelsea; **Edward Patrick Broke Evans;** *b* 1 Feb. 1943; *s* of 2nd Baron Mountevans and Deirdre Grace (*d* 1997), *d* of John O'Connell, Cork; *S* father, 1974; *m* 1973, Johanna Keyzer, *d* of late Antonius Franciscus Keyzer, The Hague. *Educ:* Rugby; Trinity Coll., Oxford. Reserve Army Service, 1961–66; 74 MC Regt RCT, AER; Lt 1964. Joined management of Consolidated Gold Fields Ltd, 1966; British Tourist Authority, 1972: Manager, Sweden and Finland, 1973; Head of Promotion Services, 1976; Asst Mkting Mgr, 1982–89; Advr, 1989. *Heir: b* Hon. Jeffrey Richard de Corban Evans [*b* 13 May 1948; *m* 1972, Hon. Juliet, *d* of Baron Moran, *qv*; two *s*].

MOUNTFIELD, Peter; Executive Secretary, Development Committee, World Bank, 1991–95; *b* 2 April 1935; *s* of late Alexander Stuart Mountfield and Agnes Elizabeth (*née* Gurney); *m* 1958, Evelyn Margaret Smithies; three *s*. *Educ:* Merchant Taylors' Sch., Crosby; Trinity Coll., Cambridge (BA); Graduate Sch. of Public Admin, Harvard. RN, 1953–55. Asst Principal, HM Treasury, 1958; Principal, 1963; Asst Sec., 1970; Under Secretary: Cabinet Office, 1977; HM Treasury, 1980–91. *Recreations:* reading, walking, looking at buildings. *Address:* Marchants, Church Street, Seal, Sevenoaks, Kent TN15 0AR. *T:* (01732) 761848.

See also Sir R. Mountfield.

MOUNTFIELD, Sir Robin, KCB 1999 (CB 1988); Permanent Secretary, Cabinet Office, 1998–99; *b* 16 Oct. 1939; *s* of late Alexander Stuart Mountfield and Agnes Elizabeth (*née* Gurney); *m* 1963, Anne Newsham; three *c*. *Educ:* Merchant Taylors' Sch., Crosby; Magdalen Coll., Oxford (BA). Assistant Principal, Ministry of Power, 1961, Principal, 1965; Private Sec. to Minister for Industry, 1973–74; Asst Sec., Dept of Industry, 1974, seconded to Stock Exchange, 1977–78; Under Sec., DoI, later, DTI, 1980–84; Deputy Secretary: DTI, 1984–92; HM Treasury, 1992–95; Permanent Sec., OPS, Cabinet Office, 1995–98. Non-exec. Dir, 2000–02, Consultant, 2002–, Innogy Hldgs plc, subseq. RWE, then RWE npower; Ind. Nat. Dir, Times Newspapers Hldgs Ltd, 2001–; non-exec. Dir, Medical Defence Union Ltd, 2004–06. Non-exec. Dir, Banking Code Standards Bd, 2006–; Lloyd's Members' Ombudsman, 2007–. Chairman: St Katharine and Shadwell Trust, 1999–; Property Trustees, CS Benevolent Fund, 2000–. Mem. Council, 1999–2008, Hon. Fellow 2008, Univ. of Essex; Mem. Council, BHF, 2000–. *T:* (020) 8293 0359; *e-mail:* rmountfield@hotmail.com.

See also P. Mountfield.

MOUNTFORD, Carol Jean, (Kali); MP (Lab) Colne Valley, since 1997; *b* 12 Jan. 1954; *m*; one *s* one *d*; *m* 1995, Ian Leedham. *Educ:* Crewe and Alsager Coll. (BA SocSc ext.). Civil Service posts, Dept of Employment, 1975–96. Mem., Dept of Employment Exec. Cttee, CPSA, 1986. Mem. (Lab) Sheffield CC, 1992–96. Parliamentary Private Secretary: to Minister for Work, 2003–04; to Immigration Minister, 2004–05; to Chief Sec. to Treasury, 2005–06; to Sec. of State for Defence, 2006–. Mem., Treasury Select Cttee, 2001–03. *Address:* House of Commons, SW1A 0AA. *T:* (020) 7219 4507.

MOUNTGARRET, 18th Viscount *cr* 1550 (Ire.); **Piers James Richard Butler;** Baron (UK) 1911; *b* 15 April 1961; *s* of 17th Viscount Mountgarret and Gillian Margaret (*née* Buckley); *S* father, 2004; *m* 1st, 1995, Laura Brown Gary (marr. diss. 2000); two *d*; 2nd, 2006, Fenella Mary, *d* of David and Mary Fawcus. *Educ:* Eton; St Andrews Univ. *Heir: b* Hon. Edmund Henry Richard Butler [*b* 1 Sept. 1962; *m* 1988, Adelle Lloyd (marr. diss. 1989)].

MOUSLEY, Timothy John; QC 2003; a Recorder, since 1998; *b* 29 April 1956; *s* of late James and Patricia Mousley; *m* 1981, Dianne (marr. diss. 2008); two *d*. *Educ:* Peter Symonds Sch., Winchester; Univ. of Keele (BA Hons Law and Econs). Called to the Bar, Middle Temple, 1979; barrister on Western Circuit, 1980–. *Recreations:* sport (watching), gardening. *Address:* 2 King's Bench Walk, Temple, EC4Y 7DE. *T:* (020) 7353 1746. *Clubs:* Southampton Football; Hampshire County Cricket; West Tytherley Wine.

MOUTRAY, Stephen; Member (DemU) Upper Bann, Northern Ireland Assembly, since 2003; *b* 25 Feb. 1959; *s* of William and Lena Moutray; *m* 1985, Myrtle Taylor; two *s* one *d*. *Educ:* Kingspark Primary Sch.; Lurgan Jun. High Sch.; Lurgan Coll. Company dir (retail); sub postmaster. Mem. (DemU), Craigavon BC, 2001–. *Recreations:* walking, swimming, collecting autographed biographies, travelling. *Address:* 50A High Street, Lurgan, Co. Armagh BT66 8AU. *T:* (028) 3831 0088, *Fax:* (028) 3831 0099; *e-mail:* stephenmoutray@btinternet.com.

MOVERLEY, John, OBE 2004; FRAgS, FIAgrE; Chief Executive, Royal Agricultural Society of England, since 2005; *b* Thornton, Yorks, 13 Feb. 1950; *s* of Robert John and Elsie Maria Moverley; *m* 1973, Elizabeth Ann; two *s*. *Educ:* Pocklington Sch.; St Catharine's Coll., Cambridge (Scholar; BA 1971; Wood Prize for Agric. 1971). FRAgS 2006; FIAgrE 2006. Mgt consultant, 1971–74; Lectr and Res. Fellow, Univ. of Nottingham, 1974–77; Sen. Lectr in Mgt, Bishop Burton and Shuttleworth Colls, 1977–86; Dep. Principal, Bicton Coll., 1986–88; Principal, Lincolnshire Coll. of Agric. and Hortic., 1988–97; Principal and Chief Exec., Myerscough Coll., 1997–2005. Pro Vice Chancellor, De Montfort Univ., 1994–97. Hon. Fellow: Univ. of Central Lancashire, 2005; Myerscough Coll., 2005. *Publications:* Microcomputers and Agriculture, 1984; numerous papers and articles. *Recreations:* sport, garden. *Clubs:* Farmers'.

MOVERLEY SMITH, Stephen Philip; QC 2002; *b* 10 Jan. 1960; *s* of Philip Smith and Carol Smith (*née* Moverley); *m* 1990, Caroline Topping; three *s*. *Educ:* Reading Sch.; Pembroke Coll., Oxford (MA). Called to the Bar, Middle Temple, 1985; in practice, specialising in international company and commercial litigation. *Recreations:* sailing, tennis. *Address:* 24 Old Buildings, Lincoln's Inn, WC2A 3UP. *T:* (020) 7404 0946, *Fax:* (020) 7405 1360; *e-mail:* sms@xxiv.co.uk.

MOWAT, Ashley; *see* Mowat, N. A. G.

MOWAT, David McIvor; JP; consultant, business columnist and commentator; Managing Director, Iatros Ltd, since 1994; Director, St Andrews Golf Club Manufacturing Ltd, since 1994; *b* 12 March 1939; *s* of Ian M. Mowat and Mary I. S. Steel; *m* 1964, Elinor Anne Birtwistle (*d* 2008); three *d*. *Educ:* Edinburgh Academy; University of Edinburgh (MA); BA Open Univ., 1984. Chief Executive: Edinburgh Chamber of

Commerce and Manufactures, 1967–90; Chamber Developments Ltd, 1971; Edinburghs Capital Ltd, 1986; Who's Who in Business in Scotland Ltd, 1989–90. Dep. Chm., Edinburgh Tourist Gp, 1985–90. Pres., British Chambers of Commerce Execs, 1987–89. JP Edinburgh, 1969. FRSA. *Address:* 37 Orchard Road South, Edinburgh EH4 3JA. *T:* (0131) 332 6865.

MOWAT, Mary Jane Stormont; Her Honour Judge Mowat; a Circuit Judge, since 1996; *b* 7 July 1948; *d* of late Duncan McKay Stormont Mowat and Jane Archibald Mowat (*née* Milne); *m* 1973, Prof. the Hon. Nicholas Michael John Woodhouse, *qv*, 2nd *s* of 5th Baron Terrington, DSO, OBE; one *s*. *Educ:* Sherborne Sch. For Girls; Lady Margaret Hall, Oxford (MA). Called to the Bar, Inner Temple, 1973. *Recreations:* music, walking, reading, riding.

MOWAT, Prof. (Norman) Ashley (George), FRCP, FRCPE, FRCPGlas; Consultant Physician and Gastroenterologist, Aberdeen Royal Infirmary, since 1975; Professor in Medicine, Aberdeen University Medical School, since 2002; Physician to the Queen in Scotland, since 2001; *b* 11 April 1943; *s* of William Mowat and Isabella Parker Mowat; *m* 1966, Kathleen Mary Cowie; one *s* two *d*. *Educ:* Fordyce Acad.; Aberdeen Univ. (MB ChB). MRCP 1971, FRCP 1984; FRCPE 1991; FRCPGlas 2002. Hse Officer, SHO, then Registrar, Trng, Aberdeen Teaching Hosps, 1966–72; Lecturer: in Medicine, Aberdeen Univ., 1972–73; in Gastroenterol., and Res. Fellow, St Bartholomew's Hosp., London, 1973–74; Clinical Sen. Lectr in Medicine, Aberdeen Univ. Med. Sch., 1975–2002. Vis. Physician to Shetland Is, 1975–94. President: Scottish Soc. of Gastroenterology, 2002–04; Scottish Soc. of Physicians, 2004–05. *Publications:* (ed jtly) Integrated Clinical Sciences: Gastroenterology, 1985; numerous contribs to med. and gastroenterol. jls. *Recreations:* sailing, photography, golf, reading. *Address:* Gastrointestinal Unit, Aberdeen Royal Infirmary, Foresterhill, Aberdeen AB25 2ZN. *T:* (01224) 681818, ext. 52570; York House, York Place, Cullen, Buckie AB56 4UW.

MOWBRAY, 27th Baron *cr* 1283, **SEGRAVE,** 28th Baron *cr* 1283, **AND STOURTON,** 24th Baron *cr* 1448, of Stourton, co. Wilts; **Edward William Stephen Stourton;** *b* 17 April 1953; *s* of Charles Edward Stourton, CBE, 26th Baron Mowbray, 27th Baron Segrave and 23rd Baron Stourton, and Hon. Jane de Yarburgh Bateson, *o c* of 5th Baron Deramore; *S* father, 2006; *m* 1980, Penelope Lucy, *e d* of Dr Peter Brunet; one *s* four *d*. *Educ:* Ampleforth. *Heir:* *s* Hon. James Charles Peter Stourton, *b* 12 Dec. 1991.

MOWBRAY, John; *see* Mowbray, W. J.

MOWBRAY, Sir John Robert, 6th Bt *cr* 1880; DL; *b* 1 March 1932; *s* of Sir George Robert Mowbray, 5th Bt, KBE, and of Diana Margaret, *d* of Sir Robert Heywood Hughes, 12th Bt; *S* father, 1969; *m* 1957, Lavinia Mary, *d* of late Lt-Col Francis Edgar Hugonin, OBE, Stainton House, Stainton in Cleveland, Yorks; three *d*. *Educ:* Eton; New College, Oxford. DL Suffolk, 1993. *Address:* The Hill House, Duffs Hill, Glemsford, Suffolk CO10 7PP. *T:* (01787) 281930.

MOWBRAY, (William) John; QC 1974; *b* 3 Sept. 1928; *s* of James Mowbray, sugar manufr and Ethel Mowbray; *m* 1960, Shirley Mary Neilan; one *s* three *d*. *Educ:* Upper Canada Coll.; Mill Hill Sch.; New Coll., Oxford. BA 1952. Called to Bar, Lincoln's Inn, 1953 (Bencher, 1983); called to Bahamian Bar, 1971, to Eastern Caribbean Bar, 1992. Chairman: Chancery Bar Assoc., 1985–94; Westminster Assoc. for Mental Health, 1981–88, 1999–2005; Westminster Christian Council, 1986–87 (Vice-Chm., 1984–85). Trustee, IMPACT, 2002–. *Publications:* Lewin on Trusts, 16th edn 1964, 18th edn 2007; Estate Duty on Settled Property, 1969; articles in jls. *Recreations:* music, observing nature in Sussex garden. *Club:* Travellers.

MOWL, Colin John, CB 2004; Executive Director, Macroeconomics and Labour Market, Office for National Statistics, since 2002; *b* 19 Oct. 1947; *s* of late Arthur Sidney and Ada Mowl; *m* 1980, Kathleen Patricia Gallagher; one *s* one *d*. *Educ:* Lawrence Sheriff Sch., Rugby; LSE (BSc Econs, MSc). Econ. Asst, MoT, 1970–72; Sen. Econ. Asst, Econ. Advr, HM Treasury, 1972–83; Res. Manager, Forex Research Ltd, 1983; HM Treasury: Sen. Econ. Advr, 1983–90; Grade 3, and Hd, Econ. Analysis and Forecasting Gp, later Dep. Dir, Macroecon. Policy and Prospects, 1990–95; Dep. Dir, subseq. Dir, Budget and Public Finances, 1995–2002. *Publications:* various Treasury working papers. *Recreations:* family, visiting France, sport. *Address:* Office for National Statistics, Drummond Gate, SW1V 2QQ.

MOWLL, Rev. (John) William (Rutley); Chaplain to the Queen, since 2000; Vicar, Boughton-under-Blean with Dunkirk, 1983–2007, and also Hernhill, 1989–2007; *b* 24 March 1942; *s* of Wilfred Rutley Mowll and Mary Gifford (*née* Holden); *m* 1966, Susan Frances Lisle Bullen; two *s*. *Educ:* Canterbury Cathedral Choir Sch.; King's Sch., Canterbury; Sarum Theol Coll. Ordained deacon, 1966, priest, 1967; Curate: Church of the Ascension, Oughtibridge, dio. Sheffield, 1966–69; St James, Hill, dio. Birmingham, 1969–72; Industrial Chaplain and Vicar, Upper Arley, 1973–78; Priest-in-Charge, 1978–81, Rector, 1981–83, Upton Snodsbury; Rural Dean, Ospringe, Faversham, 1995–2001; Hon. Minor Canon, Canterbury Cathedral, 1995–; Chaplain to High Sheriff of Kent, 2001–02. Occasional Lectr, Nat. Maritime Mus. Member: Guild of Master Craftsmen, 1984–; Soc. for Nautical Res. (South); Life Mem., HMS Warrior 1860. *Publications:* SS Great Britain: the model ship, 1982; HMS Warrior 1860: building a working model warship, 1997; (contrib.) Building Model Warships of the iron and steel era (ed P. Beisheim), 2002. *Recreations:* practising musician, amateur playwright, engineer in miniature craftwork, specialising in model ships. *Address:* Holly Cottage, Water Lane, Ospringe, Faversham, Kent ME13 8TS. *T:* (01795) 597597. *Club:* Faversham Farmers'.

MOWSCHENSON, Terence Rennie; QC 1995; a Recorder, since 2000; a Deputy High Court Judge, since 2003; *b* 7 June 1953; *s* of Henry and Hanny Mowschenson; *m* 1992, Judith Angela Strang. *Educ:* Eagle Sch., Umtali, Rhodesia; Peterhouse, Marandellas, Rhodesia; Queen Mary Coll., London (LLB Hons 1975); Exeter Coll., Oxford (BCL Hons 1976). FCIArb. Called to the Bar, Middle Temple, 1977, Bencher, 2003; Asst Recorder, 1997–2000. Chairman: Claims Mgt Tribunal, 1996–; Financial Services and Markets Act Tribunal, 2002–; Pension Regulator Tribunal, 2005–. Chm., Barristers' Benevolent Assoc., 1999– (Hon. Sec., 1995–97, Hon. Treas., 1997–99). *Recreations:* opera, reading, travel. *Address:* Wilberforce Chambers, 8 New Square, Lincoln's Inn, WC2A 3QP. *T:* (020) 7306 0102. *Club:* Royal Automobile.

MOXHAM, Prof. John, MD; FRCP; Professor of Respiratory Medicine, King's College London School of Medicine; Consultant Physician, since 1982, Medical Director, since 2003, King's College Hospital; *b* 9 Dec. 1944; *s* of late Wilson Moxham and Marie Moxham (*née* Bland), Evesham, Worcs; *m* 1978, Nicola Seaman; three *d*. *Educ:* Prince Henry's Grammar Sch., Evesham; LSE (BSc (Econ) 1967); UCH Med. Sch. (MB BS 1973; MD 1982). MRCP 1975, FRCP 1987. Lectr in Medicine, UCH, 1978–80; Sen. Registrar, Brompton and St James' Hosp., London, 1980–82. King's College School of Medicine and Dentistry, then Guy's, King's and St Thomas' School of Medicine, King's College London, subseq. King's College London School of Medicine: Prof. of Respiratory Medicine, 1990–; Dean: for Med. Student Admissions, 1991–96, Faculty of Clin. Medicine, 1997–98; KCH Campus, 1998–2000; Vice-Dean, 2000–03. Chm., Consultants' Cttee, KCH, 1995–97; non-exec. Dir, KCH NHS Trust, 2000–03. Chm., Doctors for Tobacco Law, 1991–97; Chm., 1996–98, Mem. Bd, 2006–, ASH; Mem., Ind. Inquiry into Access to Healthcare for People with Learning Disabilities, 2007–08. Thoracic Society: Scientific Meetings Sec., 1988–90; Mem. Exec., 1988–93; Chm., Tobacco Cttee, 1990–93. Bertram Louis Abrahams Lect., RCP, 2007. Gov., James Allen's Girls' Sch., 2004–. *Publications:* (ed jtly) Textbook of Medicine, 1990, 4th edn 2002; res. papers on clinical physiol., particularly ventilatory failure and respiratory muscle function. *Recreations:* family, art, walking the dogs, good beer, mooching around London. *Address:* 17 Maude Road, Camberwell, SE5 8NY. *T:* (020) 7703 4396; *e-mail:* john.moxham@kcl.ac.uk.

MOXON, Rt Rev. David John; *see* Waikato, Bishop of.

MOXON, Prof. (Edward) Richard, FMedSci; FRS 2007; Action Research Professor of Paediatrics, University of Oxford, 1984–2008, then Emeritus Professor; Fellow, Jesus College, Oxford, since 1984; Head, Molecular Infectious Diseases Group, Institute of Molecular Medicine, John Radcliffe Hospital, Oxford, 1988–2008; Founder and Chairman, Oxford Vaccine Group, 1994–2008; *b* 16 July 1941; *s* of late Gerald Richard Moxon and of Margaret Forster Mohun; *m* 1973, Marianne Graham; two *s* one *d*. *Educ:* Shrewsbury Sch.; St John's Coll., Cambridge (Keasby Award, 1961; BA 1963); St Thomas' Hosp. (MB, BChir 1966); MA Oxon 1984. MRCP 1968, FRCP 1984; FRCPCH 1997. Surgical House Officer, Kent and Canterbury Hosp., 1966; Medical House Officer, Peace Meml Hosp., Watford, 1966; Pathologist, St Thomas' Hosp., 1967; Sen. House Officer in Paediatrics: Whittington Hosp., 1968; Hosp. for Sick Children, Gt Ormond St, 1969; Children's Hosp. Medical Center, Boston, Mass, USA: Asst Resident in Pediatrics, 1970; Res. Fellow in Infectious Diseases Div., 1971–74; Johns Hopkins Hosp., Baltimore, Md, USA: Asst Prof. in Pediatrics, 1974–80; Associate Prof. in Pediatrics, 1980–84; Chief, Eudowood Div. of Pediatric Infectious Diseases, 1982–84. Vis. Scientist, Washington Univ., St Louis, 1990–91; Burroughs-Wellcome Vis. Prof., Allegheny Univ. of Health Scis, Philadelphia, 1999. Lectures: Mitchell, RCP, 1992; Blackfan, Children's Hosp. Med. Center, Boston, Mass, 1994; Teale, RCP, 1998; Dolman, Univ. of BC, 1999; Hattie Alexander Meml, Columbia, 2005; Award, Europ. Soc. of Clin. Microbiol. and Infectious Diseases, 2007; Fred Griffith Review, Soc. for Gen. Microbiol., 2007. Convenor, BPA Immunology and Infectious Diseases Gp, 1984–89; Chm., MRC Sub-Cttee, Polysaccharide Vaccines, 1986–90; Member: Steering Gp, Encapsulated Bacteria, WHO, 1987–93. Amer. Soc. Clinical Investigation. Founder FMedSci 1998; Fellow: Amer. Soc. of Microbiol., 2001; Infectious Diseases Soc. of America, 2002. Bill Marshall Award, ESPID, 2005. *Publications:* (with D. Isaacs): Neonatal Infections, 1991; A Practical Approach to Pediatric Infectious Diseases, 1996; Longman Handbook of Neonatal Infections, 1999; contribs to: Mandell's Principles and Practice of Infectious Diseases, 2nd edn 1985, 4th edn 1995; Forfar and Arneil's Textbook of Paediatrics, 4th edn 1992, 5th edn 1998; Oxford Textbook of Medicine, 3rd edn 1996, 4th edn 2000; editorial adviser: Lancet's Modern Vaccines, 1991; Lancet's Vaccine Octet, 1997; Yu, Merigan, Barrière, Antimicrobial Therapy and Vaccines, 1998; Stearns' Evolution in Health and Disease, 1998; many articles in learned jls on molecular microbiol., paediatric vaccines and infectious diseases, esp. relating to *Haemophilus influenzae* and *Neisseria meningitidis*. *Recreations:* tennis, music. *Address:* 9A North Parade Avenue, Oxford OX2 6LX.

MOXON, Rev. Michael Anthony, LVO 1998; Dean and Rector of St Mary's Cathedral, Truro, 1998–2004; *b* 23 Jan. 1942; *s* of Rev. Canon Charles Moxon and Phyllis Moxon; *m* 1969, Sarah-Jane Cresswell; twin *s* one *d*. *Educ:* Merchant Taylors' Sch., Northwood, Middx; Durham Univ.; Salisbury Theol Coll.; Heythrop Coll., London (BD 1978; MA 1996). Deacon, 1970; priest, 1971; Curate, Lowestoft gp of parishes, 1970–74; Minor Canon, St Paul's Cathedral, 1974–81; Sacrist of St Paul's, 1977–81; Warden of Coll. of Minor Canons, 1979–81; Vicar of Tewkesbury with Walton Cardiff, 1981–90; Canon, 1990–98, Canon Steward, 1994–97, Canon Treas., 1997–98, St George's Chapel, Windsor; Chaplain in Windsor Great Park, 1990–98. Chaplain to the Queen, 1986–98. Member: Gen. Synod of C of E, 1985–90; Council for the Care of Churches, 1986–90; C of E Bd of Educn, 2001–04. Chaplain, HQ Cornwall County Fire Brigade, 1998–2004. *Recreations:* music, reading, cricket. *Address:* 36 Trelawney Avenue, Treskerby, Redruth, Cornwall TR15 1RH.

MOXON BROWNE, Robert William; QC 1990; a Recorder, since 1991; a Deputy Judge of the Technology and Construction Court (formerly Deputy Official Referee), since 1992; a Deputy Judge of the High Court, since 1999; *b* 26 June 1946; *s* of late Kendall Edward Moxon Browne and Sheila Heron Moxon Browne; *m* 1968, Kerstin Elizabet Warne; one *s* one *d*. *Educ:* Gordonstoun School; University College, Oxford (BA). Called to the Bar, Gray's Inn, 1969; specialises in commercial and insurance law in London and on Western Circuit. Dir, Sirius Projects Ltd, 2005–. *Recreations:* walking, gardening, wine. *Address:* 2 Temple Gardens, EC4Y 9AY. *T:* (020) 7822 1200.

MOYERS, Bill D.; journalist; Founder and Executive Editor, Public Affairs Television Inc., since 1987; *b* 5 June 1934; *s* of John Henry Moyers and Ruby Moyers (*née* Johnson); *m* 1954, Judith Suzanne Davidson; two *s* one *d*. *Educ:* High Sch., Marshall, Texas; Univ. of Texas; Univ. of Edinburgh; Southwestern Theological Seminary. BJ 1956; MDiv 1959. Personal Asst to Senator Lyndon B. Johnson, 1959–60; Executive Asst, 1960; US Peace Corps: Associate Dir, 1961–63; Dep. Dir, 1963. Special Asst to President Johnson, 1963–66; Press Sec., 1965–67; Publisher of Newsday, Long Island, 1967–70; Exec. Ed., Bill Moyers' Jl, Public Broadcasting Service, 1971–76, 1978–81; editor and chief reporter, CBS Reports, 1976–79; Sen. News Analyst, CBS Evening News, 1981–86. Contributing Editor, Newsweek Magazine. Pres., Florence and John Schumann Foundn. Over thirty Emmy Awards, incl. most outstanding broadcaster, 1974; Lowell Medal, 1975; ABA Gavel Award for distinguished service to American system of law, 1974; ABA Cert. of Merit, 1975; Awards for The Fire Next Door: Monte Carlo TV Festival Grand Prize, Jurors Prize and Nymph Award, 1977; Robert F. Kennedy Journalism Grand Prize, 1978, 1988; Christopher Award, 1978; Sidney Hillman Prize for Distinguished Service, 1978, 1981, 1987; Distinguished Urban Journalism Award, Nat. Urban Coalition, 1978; George Polk Award, 1981, 1987; Alfred I. du Pont—Columbia Univ. Award, 1981, 1987, 1988, 1991, 2000; Peabody Award, 1977, 1981, annually 1986–89, 1999, 2000; Overseas Press Award, 1986; Regents Medal of Excellence, 1992; Walter Cronkite Award for Excellence in Journalism, 1995; Nelson Mandela Award for Health and Human Rights, 1996; Charles Frankel Prize in the Humanities, NEH, 1996; Peabody Award for Lifetime Achievement, 2004. *Publications:* Listening to America, 1971; Report from Philadelphia, 1987; The Secret Government, 1988; Joseph Campbell and the Power of Myth, 1988; A World of Ideas, 1989, 2nd edn 1990; Healing and the Mind, 1993; Language of Life, 1995; Genesis, 1996; Fooling With Words, 1999; Moyers on America, 2004. *Address:* (office) 450 West 33rd Street, New York, NY 10001, USA.

MOYES, James Christopher; Founder and Director, Momart Ltd, Fine Arts Services and Shipping Co., 1971–2000; working artist in all media; *b* 29 April 1943; *s* of Albert Jack Moyes and Catherine Louise Moyes; *m* 1st, 1969, Elizabeth McKee (marr. diss. 1981); one *d*; 2nd, 1987, Joanna Margaret Price (marr. diss. 2000); two *d*; 3rd, 2006, Alison Jane Winfield-Chislett. *Educ:* Univ. of Kent (BA); Slade Sch. of Art (MA 1999). Visiting Lecturer: Essex Univ., 1988–; UEA, 1988–98; Associate Vis. Lectr in Mus. Studies, Leicester Univ., 1990–2000. Vice Chm., Contemporary Arts Soc., 1996–99. Royal Warrant Holder, 1993 (re-assigned to Momart 1999). *Recreation:* rowing. *Address:* Studio #4, Ropewalk Mews, 118 Middleton Road, E8 4LP. *Club:* Quintin Boat.

MOYES, Lt-Comdr Kenneth Jack, MBE (mil.) 1960; RN retd; Under-Secretary, Department of Health and Social Security, 1975–78; *b* 13 June 1918; *s* of Charles Wilfrid and Daisy Hilda Moyes; *m* 1943, Norma Ellen Outred Hillier; one *s* two *d*. *Educ:* Portsmouth Northern Grammar Sch. FCIS. Royal Navy, 1939–63. Principal, Dept of Health and Social Security, 1963; Asst Secretary, 1970. *Recreations:* gardening, bridge. *Address:* Garden House, Darwin Road, Birchington, Kent CT7 9JL. *T:* (01843) 842015.

MOYES, Dr William; Chairman, Monitor, Independent Regulator of NHS Foundation Trusts, since 2004; *b* 18 Sept. 1949; *s* of William Moyes and Catherine (*née* Brannan); *m* 1971, Dr Barbara Ann Rice; one *s*. *Educ:* Lawside Acad., Dundee; Univ. of Edinburgh (BSc Chem. 1971; PhD Theoretical Chem. 1975); London Business Sch. (Public Sector Mgt Prog. 1988). DoE, 1974–76; Dept of Transport, 1976–80; Cabinet Office and Econ. Secretariat, 1980–83; Finance Div., Scottish Office, 1983–85; Scottish Educn Dept, 1985–87; Dept of Agric. and Fisheries for Scotland, 1987–90; Dir, Strategic Planning and Performance Mgt, Mgt Exec., NHS in Scotland, 1990–94; Hd, Infrastructure Finance, Bank of Scotland, 1994–2000; Dir-Gen., British Retail Consortium, 2000–04. Director: British Linen Investments Ltd, 1996–2000; Catalyst Healthcare Gp, 1996–2000; Summit Healthcare Gp, 1997–2000; Community Health Facilities (Oxford) Ltd, 1998–2000; Eurocommerce, 2001–04 (also Mem., Steering Cttee); BRC Trading Ltd, 2002–04; Skills Mart Ltd, 2002–04. Mem. Council, Univ. of Surrey, 2004–08. Dir, BLISS (Nat. Charity for Newborn), 2002–04. *Publications:* contrib. papers to scientific jls. *Recreations:* good food, gardening, theatre, hill walking. *Address:* Monitor, 4 Matthew Parker Street, SW1H 9NL. *T:* (020) 7340 2424, *Fax:* (020) 7340 2401; *e-mail:* William.Moyes@monitor-nhsft.gov.uk.

MOYLAN-JONES, Rear-Adm. Roger Charles, CEng, FIMechE; Director General Aircraft (Navy), 1992–95; *b* 18 April 1940; *s* of Brian Percy Jameson Moylan-Jones and Louie-Mae (*née* Brown); *m* 1961, Mary Howells; two *s* one *d*. *Educ:* King Edward VI Grammar Sch., Totnes; BRNC, Dartmouth; RNEC, Manadon (BSc Eng 1964). CEng, FIMechE 1990. Joined BRNC Dartmouth, 1958; service in 766, 890, 360 Sqdns and HMS Ark Royal, 1965–69; HMS Ganges, 1969–71; Air Engineering Officer, 706 Sqdn and 819 Sqdn; Staff of Flag Officer Carriers and Amphibious Ships, 1971–77; ndc 1978; Staff of: Flag Officer, Naval Air Comd, 1978–80; Dep. Chief of Defence Staff (OR), 1981–82; CSO to FONAC, 1983–84; Capt., HMS Daedalus, 1984–86; RCDS 1987; Director: Aircraft Support Policy (Navy), 1988–89; Naval Manning and Trng (Engrg), 1989–91. Capt., RN and Combined Services CC, 1969–73, 1982, 1983; Pres., RNCC, 1993–95 (Chm., 1985–89; Life Vice Pres., 1995). Chairman: Devon CCC, 1997–; Devon Cricket Bd, 1997–2003; Mem., ECB Mgt Bd, 2000–05; Dir, ECB Ltd, 2000–05. Trustee and Dir, England and Wales Cricket Trust, 2006–. *Recreations:* cricket, golf, travel. *Clubs:* Army and Navy, MCC; I Zingari, Free Foresters, Forty.

MOYLE, Rt Hon. Roland (Dunstan); PC 1978; barrister-at-law; Deputy Chairman, Police Complaints Authority, 1985–91; *b* 12 March 1928; *s* of late Baron Moyle, CBE; *m* 1956, Shelagh Patricia Hogan; one *s* one *d*. *Educ:* Infants' and Jun. Elem. Schs, Bexleyheath, Kent; County Sch., Llanidloes, Mont.; UCW Aberystwyth (LLB); Trinity Hall, Cambridge (MA, LLM). Called to the Bar, Gray's Inn, 1954. Commnd in Royal Welch Fusiliers, 1949–51. Legal Dept, Wales Gas Bd, 1953–56; Industrial Relations Executive with Gas Industry, 1956–62, and Electricity Supply Industry, 1962–66. MP (Lab) Lewisham N, 1966–74, Lewisham E, 1974–83; PPS to Chief Secretary to the Treasury, 1966–69, to Home Secretary, 1969–70; opposition spokesman on higher educn and science, 1972–74; Parly Sec., MAFF, 1974; Minister of State, NI Dept, 1974–76; Minister for Health, 1976–79; opposition spokesman on health, 1979–80; deputy foreign affairs spokesman, 1980–83; opposition spokesman on defence and disarmament, 1983. Mem., Select Cttee on Race Relations and Immigration, 1968–72; Vice-Chm., PLP Defence Group, 1968–72; Sec., 1971–74, Mem. Exec. Cttee, 1971–83, British Amer. Parly Gp; Treas., British S Amer. Gp, 1970–74. Pres., Montgomeryshire Soc., 2003–04. *Recreation:* pottering. *Address:* 139 Lee Park, Blackheath, SE3 9HE.

MOYNE, 3rd Baron *cr* 1932, of Bury St Edmunds; **Jonathan Bryan Guinness;** *b* 16 March 1930; *s* of 2nd Baron Moyne and Hon. Diana (*née* Mitford, later Hon. Lady Mosley) (*d* 2003); *S* father, 1992; *m* 1st, 1951, Ingrid Wyndham (marr. diss. 1962); two *s* one *d*; 2nd, 1964, Suzanne Phillips (*née* Lisney); one *s* one *d*. *Educ:* Eton; Oxford (MA, Mod. Langs). Journalist at Reuters, 1953–56. Merchant Banker: trainee at Erlangers Ltd, 1956–59, and at Philip Hill, 1959–62; Exec. Dir, 1962–64, non-exec. Dir, 1964–91, Leopold Joseph; Dir, Arthur Guinness Son & Co. Ltd, 1961–88. CC Leicestershire, 1970–74; Chairman, Monday Club, 1972–74. *Publications:* (with Catherine Guinness) The House of Mitford, 1984; Shoe: the Odyssey of a Sixties Survivor, 1989; Requiem for a Family Business, 1997. *Heir: s* Hon. Jasper Jonathan Richard Guinness [*b* 9 March 1954; *m* 1985, Camilla Alexandra, *d* of Robie David Corbett Uniacke; two *d*]. *Address:* The South Wing, Rodmarton Manor, Cirencester, Glos GL7 6PF.

See also Hon. D. W. Guinness, Lord Neidpath.

MOYNIHAN, family name of **Baron Moynihan.**

MOYNIHAN, 4th Baron *cr* 1929, of Leeds, co. York; **Colin Berkeley Moynihan;** Bt 1922; Founding Partner, CMA Consultants, since 1994; Director, Rowan Companies Inc., since 1996; Chairman: Pelamis Wave Power, since 2005; British Olympic Association, since 2005; *b* 13 Sept. 1955; *s* of 2nd Baron Moynihan, OBE, TD, and of June Elizabeth (who *m* 1965, N. B. Hayman), *d* of Arthur Stanley Hopkins; *S* half-brother, 1997; *m* 1992, Gaynor-Louise Metcalf; two *s* one *d*. *Educ:* Monmouth Sch. (Music Scholar); University Coll., Oxford (BA PPE 1977, MA 1982). Pres., Oxford Union Soc., 1976. Personal Asst to Chm., Tate & Lyle Ltd, 1978–80; Manager, Tate & Lyle Agribusiness, resp. for marketing strategy and develt finance, 1980–82; Chief Exec., 1982–83, Chm., 1983–87, Ridgways Tea and Coffee Merchants; external consultant, Tate & Lyle PLC, 1983–87. Chm. and CEO, Consort Resources Ltd, 2000–03; Exec. Chm., Clipper Windpower Marine Ltd, 2005–07. Dir, Inst. of Petroleum, 2001–03. MP (C) Lewisham East, 1983–92; contested (C) Lewisham East, 1992. Political Asst to the Foreign Sec., 1983; PPS to Minister of Health, 1985, to Paymaster General, 1985–87; Parly Under Sec. of State (Minister for Sport), DoE, 1987–90; Parly Under-Sec. of State, Dept of Energy, 1990–92. Chm., All-Party Parly Gp on Afghanistan, 1986; Vice Chm., Cons. Food and Drinks Sub-Cttee, 1983–85; Sec. Cons. Foreign and Commonwealth Affairs Cttee, 1983–85. Member: Paddington Conservative Management Cttee, 1980–81; Bow Group, 1978–92 (Mem., Industry Cttee, 1978–79, 1985–87); Chm., Trade & Industry Standing Cttee, 1983–87. Elected Mem., H of L, 1999. Sen. Opposition spokesman on foreign affairs, H of L, 1999–2002; Chm., Cons. Campaigning Bd, 2004–05; special advr to Leader of the Opposition, 2003–05 (Treas., Leadership Campaign Fund, 2003). Chm., Sydney Olympic UK Business Task Force, 1995–97; Member: Sports Council, 1982–85; Major Spectator Sports Cttee, CCPR, 1979–82; CCPR Enquiry into Sponsorship of Sport, 1982–83; Exec. Cttee, Assoc. Nat. Olympic Cttees, 2006–; IOC Internat. Relations Cttee, 2008–; Dir, LOCOG, 2005–; Steward, British Boxing Bd of Control, 1979–87. Trustee: Oxford Univ. Boat Club, 1980–84; Sports Aid Trust, 1983–87; Governor, Sports Aid Foundn (London and SE), 1980–82. Pres., British Water Ski, 2006–. Mem. Council, Royal Commonwealth Soc., 1980–82. Hon. Sec., Friends of British Council. Freeman, City of London, 1978; Liveryman, Worshipful Co. of Haberdashers, 1981. Patron: Land & City Families Trust; British Wind Energy Assoc. Oxford Double Blue, Rowing and Boxing, 1976 and 1977; World Gold Medal for Lightweight Rowing, Internat. Rowing Fedn, 1978; Olympic Silver Medal for Rowing, 1980; World Silver Medal for Rowing, 1981. *Recreations:* collecting Nonesuch Books, music, sport. *Heir: s* Hon. Nicholas Ewan Berkeley Moynihan, *b* 31 March 1994. *Address:* CMA Consultants, 9th Floor, Prince Consort House, 27–29 Albert Embankment, SE1 7TJ. *T:* (020) 7820 1078; *e-mail:* c.moynihan@cmagroup.org.uk. *Clubs:* Brooks's, Kandahar Ski; Leander (Henley-on-Thames); Vincent's (Oxford).

MPALANYI-NKOYOYO, Most Rev. Livingstone; Archbishop of Uganda, 1994–2003; *b* 1937. *Educ:* Buwalasi Coll., Uganda; Legon Trinity Coll., Ghana; East Bond Coll., England. Car mechanic; chauffeur to Bishop Lutaaya, dio. of W Buganda; ordained deacon, 1969, priest, 1970; served in parish: Kasubi, 1969–75; Nsangi, 1975–77; Archdeacon of Namirembe, 1977–79; Suffragan Bishop: dio. of Namirembe, 1980–81; dio. of Mukono, 1981–94. *Address:* c/o PO Box 14123, Kampala, Uganda.

MPUCHANE, Samuel Akuna; in business in Botswana, since 1991; *b* 15 Dec. 1943; *s* of Chiminya Thompson Mpuchane and Motshidiemang Phologolo; *m* Sisai Felicity Mokgokong; two *s* one *d*. *Educ:* Univ. of Botswana, Lesotho and Swaziland (BA Govt and Hist.); Southampton Univ. (MSc Internat. Affairs). External Affairs Officer, 1969–70; First Secretary: Botswana Mission to UN, 1970–71; Botswana Embassy, Washington, 1971–74; Under Sec., External Affairs, 1974–76; on study leave, 1976–77; Dep. Perm. Sec., Min. of Mineral Resources and Water Affairs, 1977–79; Admin. Sec., Office of Pres., 1979–80; Perm. Sec., Min. of Local Govt and Lands, 1980–81; High Comr for Botswana in UK, 1982–85; Perm. Sec. for External Affairs, 1986–90. Director, 1991–: Builders World; Building Materials Supplies; Royal Wholesalers; Parts World; Trade World; Blue Chip Investments; Continental Star Caterers; Minaras Investments (Pty) Ltd; Keystone Investments (Pty) Ltd; 21st Century Hldgs (Pty) Ltd; Kan Bw (Pty) Ltd. Mem. Bd Trustees, Univ. of Botswana Foundn, 2000–. *Recreations:* playing and watching tennis, watching soccer.

MSAKA, Bright; Chief Secretary for the President and Cabinet, Malaŵi, since 2004; *m* Primrose; three *c*. NP; Practised law, specialising in commercial litigation and tort; Lectr in Law, Univ. of Malaŵi; Examr of Co. Law, ACCA; High Comr of Malaŵi in UK, and concurrently Ambassador to Finland, Iceland, Norway, Portugal, Spain, Sweden, 1998–2003. *Address:* Office of the President and Cabinet, Private Bag 301, Lilongue 3, Malaŵi.

MSIMANG, Mendi; Order for Meritorious Service (Silver Class), South Africa, 1999; Treasurer-General, African National Congress, since 1998; *b* 1928, Johannesburg; *m* Mantombazana Tshabalala; four *c* from previous *m*. *Educ:* University Coll. of Roma, Lesotho. Rand Steam Laundries and Organizer, Laundry Workers' Union; Asbestos Assayer, Costa Rican Consulate. Joined ANC; Personal Sec. to Sec.-Gen. Walter Sisulu; with Nelson Mandela and Oliver Tambo's law practice, until 1960; left for UK, 1960; Rep., ANC Mission to UK and Ireland; Co-Founder, S Africa in Fact (ANC newsletter); Editor, Spotlight on S Africa (ANC jl); Admin. Sec., ANC Nat. Exec. Cttee in Exile, E Africa Br.; collaborated with Oliver Tambo to establish Solomon Mahlangu Freedom Coll., Tanzania; ANC Educn Officer; Admin. Sec. and Treas.-Gen., ANC's Office, Zambia; ANC Chief Rep. to India, 1969, to UK, 1988; returned to SA, 1990; elected Mem., ANC Parly Caucus, 1990; High Comr for S Africa in London, 1995–98. Mem., S African Adv. Council on Nat. Orders, 1998–. *Address:* PO Box 25929, Monument Park, Pretoria 0105, South Africa.

MTESA, Love; Ambassador of Zambia to United Nations, Geneva, since 2002; *b* 9 July 1942; *s* of late William Mutesa and Olive Mutesa; *m* Marie Madeleine; two *s* two *d*. *Educ:* Inst. of Public Relations, Paris (Dip. Internat. Relations 1974); Mercy Coll., NY (BSc Pol Sci 1985); Univ. of Westminster (MA Diplomatic Studies). Teacher, Ndola, Zambia, 1962–64; 2nd Sec., Zambian Embassy, Kinshasa, 1966–70; 1st Sec., Addis Ababa, 1970–73; Counsellor, Kinshasa, 1974–75; Dir, Africa and Middle East, Foreign Affairs, Lusaka, 1975–79; Dep. High Comr, Harare, 1980–82; Dep. Perm. Rep., UN, NY, 1982–85; resigned from Govt, June 1986; Chm. of Opposition Party, Movement for Multi-Party Democracy for Lusaka Dist, 1990–92; Sec., Internat. Relations Cttee, MMD, 1991–92; High Comr for Zambia in London, 1992–97; Chm., Inf. and Publicity, United Party for Nat. Develt, Zambia, 2001–02. Hon. Fellow, Univ. of Westminster, 1997. *Recreations:* table tennis, watching soccer.

MTETEMELA, Most Rev. Donald Leo; Bishop of Ruaha, since 1990; Archbishop of Tanzania, 1998–2008; *b* Nov. 1947; *s* of Weston Mtetemela and Anjendile Mtetemela; *m* 1990, Gladys Matonya; three *s* four *d*. *Educ:* Dodoma Secondary Sch.; St Philip's Theol Coll., Kongwa (LTh); Wycliffe Hall, Oxford; DipTh London Univ. Ordained, 1971; Pastor, 1971–82; Asst Bishop, Central Tanganyika, 1982–90. Chancellor, St John's Univ. of Tanzania. Mem., Windsor Continuation Gp, 2008–.

MUBARAK, (Mohammed) Hosny, Hon. GCMG 1985; President of Egypt, since 1981 (Vice President, 1975–81; Prime Minister, 1981–82); *b* 4 May 1928; *m* Suzanne; two *s*. *Educ:* Military Acad.; Air Force Acad. Joined Egyptian Air Force, 1950; Flight Instr., 1952–59, Dir Gen., 1967–69, Air Force Acad.; COS, 1969–72, C-in-C, 1972–75, Air Force; Lt Gen. 1973. Chm., OAU, 1989–90. National Democratic Party: Vice Chm., 1976–81; Sec. Gen., 1981–82; Chm., 1982–. *Address:* Presidential Palace, Abdeen, Cairo, Egypt.

MUCH, Ian Fraser Robert; Chief Executive, De La Rue plc, 1998–2004; *b* 8 Sept. 1944; *s* of Alan Fraser Much and Helen Isabella Much (*née* Barker); *m* 1978, Perena Amanda Richards; two *d*. *Educ:* Haileybury and ISC; Lincoln Coll., Oxford (MA Jurisp.). The Metal Box Co., 1966–73; Selkirk Metalbestos, 1974–78; Household International Inc., 1978–84; Factory Manager, Nampa, Idaho, 1978–80; Vice-Pres., Gen. Manager, Greensboro, N Carolina, 1980–84; BTR: Man. Dir, Dunlop Aviation Div., 1985–87; Gp Chief Exec., 1987–88; Dir, BTR Industries; T & N: Exec. Dir, 1988–98; Man. Dir, Engineering & Industrial, 1990–91, Bearings and Industrial, 1991–95; Chief Exec., Ops, 1995–96; Chief Exec., 1996–98. Non-executive Director: Manchester United plc, 2000–05; Chemring, 2004–; Simplyhealth (formerly HSA) Gp, 2005–; Senior plc, 2005–.

Governor, Haileybury and ISC, 2005–. Chm., Campaign Cttee, Lincoln Coll., Oxford, 2005–. *Recreations:* ski-ing, tennis, squash, golf, swimming, bridge, theatre.

MUCHLINSKI, Prof. Peter Thomas; Professor of International Commercial Law, School of Oriental and African Studies, University of London, since 2005; *b* 18 Oct. 1957; *s* of late Franciszek Ksawery Muchlinski and Maria Irena Muchlinska. *Educ:* London Sch. of Econs (LLB); Christ's Coll., Cambridge (LLM). Called to the Bar, Lincoln's Inn, 1981; Res. Officer, British Inst. of Human Rights, 1979–80; Lectr in Law, Univ. of Kent at Canterbury, 1981–83; Lectr in Law, 1983–96, Sen. Lectr, 1996–98, LSE; Drapers Prof. of Law, QMW, Univ. of London, 1998–2001; Prof. of Law and Internat. Business, Kent Law Sch., Univ. of Kent, 2001–05. Principal Advr on investment law, Div. of Investment Technol. and Enterprise Develt, UNCTAD, 1997–. FRSA 1999. *Publications:* Multinational Enterprises and the Law, 1995, 2nd edn 2007; contrib. articles to jls incl. Modern Law Rev., Internat. and Comparative Law Qly, Internat. Affairs. *Recreations:* gardening, history. *Address:* School of Law, School of Oriental and African Studies, Thornhaugh Street, Russell Square, WC1H 0XG. *T:* (020) 7898 4751.

MUDD, (William) David; consultant on tourism, transport and communications; cruise lecturer; *b* 2 June 1933; *o s* of Capt. W. N. Mudd and Mrs T. E. Mudd; *m;* one *s* one *d* (and one step *d*). *Educ:* Truro Cathedral Sch. Journalist, Broadcaster, TV Commentator; work on BBC and ITV (Westward Television). Editor of The Cornish Echo, 1952; Staff Reporter: Western Morning News, 1952–53 and 1959–62; Tavistock Gazette, 1963. Mem., Tavistock UDC, 1963–65. MP (C) Falmouth and Camborne, 1970–92. PPS, Dept of Energy, 1979–81; Mem., Transport Select Cttee, 1982–92. Secretary: Conservative West Country Cttee, 1973–76; Conservative Party Fisheries Sub-Cttee, 1974–75, 1981–82. Contested (Ind.) Falmouth and Camborne, 2005. Patron, Court Interpreters' Assoc., Supreme Court of Hong Kong, 1979–97. *Publications:* Cornishmen and True, 1971; Murder in the West Country, 1975; Facets of Crime, 1975; The Innovators, 1976; Down Along Camborne and Redruth, 1978; The Falmouth Packets, 1978; Cornish Sea Lights, 1978; Cornwall and Scilly Peculiar, 1979; About the City, 1979; Home Along Falmouth and Penryn, 1980; Around and About the Roseland, 1980; The Cruel Cornish Sea, 1981; The Cornish Edwardians, 1982; Cornwall in Uproar, 1983; Around and About the Fal, 1989; Around and About the Smugglers' Ways, 1991; Strange Stories of Cornwall, 1992; Dartmoor Reflections, 1993; The Magic of Dartmoor, 1994; Let the Doors be Lock'd, 2000; Better with a Pinch of Salt, 2003; Sugar 'n' Spice, 2005; The Sign of the Balloon, 2006; Clarence the Cornish Chough, 2008. *Recreations:* jig-saw puzzles, walking, cycling. *Address:* The Retreat, Down Park Drive, Tavistock, Devon PL19 9AH.

MUDDIMAN, Noel, CBE 1992 (OBE 1985); Director: CF Solutions, since 2004; Motability, 1995–2004 (Member of Council, since 2004); *b* 17 Dec. 1943; *s* of Flora Muddiman (*née* Holdsworth), and step *s* of late Arthur George Muddiman; *m* 1969, Patricia Anne Sevage; two *s*. *Educ:* Borden Grammar Sch.; RMA, Sandhurst. Commnd RCT, 1965; regtl posts in Germany, UK, Singapore; Staff Coll., Camberley, 1975; ndc, 1981; CO, 25 Transport and Movements Regt, RCT, 1983–85; Head of Personnel and Logistics, Falkland Islands, 1985–86; Principal Logistic Planner, British Forces Germany, 1987–90; Commander: Transport and Movements, BAOR, 1990–92; Logistic Support Gp (ME), 1991; rcds, 1992; Comdt, Army Sch. of Transport, 1993–95, retd. Vice Chm., Charity Investors Gp, 2002–; Chairman, Advisory Board: Charinco, 2007– (Mem., 2002–); Charishare, 2007– (Mem., 2002–). Norwegian Gulf War Medal, 1995. *Publication:* (jtly) Blackadder's War, 1995. *Recreations:* gardening, walking, photography.

MUDDIMER, Robert Michael; Deputy Chairman, Tomkins plc, 1996–97 (Director, 1986–97); Chairman, Gates Rubber Co., 1996–97; *b* 30 Jan. 1933; *m* 1959, Marguerite Conroy; two *s* one *d*. *Educ:* Kibworth Grammar Sch.; Univ. of Nottingham (BSc Mech. Eng 1956). FIET (FIMfgE 1966). Materials Mgt, Lansing Bagnall, 1965–68; Director: BTR Ind. Ltd, 1969–80; Molins Tobacco Ind. Ltd, 1981–86; Chm., Rank Hovis McDougall, 1992–96. *Recreations:* golf, sailing, wooden clockmaking.

MUDIE, Colin Crichton, RDI 1995; CEng; FRINA, FRIN; Principal Partner, Colin Mudie, Naval Architects and Yacht Designers, since 1958; *b* 11 April 1926; *s* of John Mudie and Janet Somerville Mudie (*née* Jack); *m* 1954, Rosemary Horder; one *s*. *Educ:* George Watson's, Edinburgh; Whitgift Sch.; University Coll., Southampton. CEng 1971; FRINA 1971; FRIN 1972 (Hon. FRIN 2004). Design apprentice: British Power Boat Co., Southampton, 1942–46; Laurent Giles & Partners Ltd, 1946–49; various marine projects incl. Sopranino voyage, 1951–52 and Small World transatlantic balloon flight, 1958–59. Winston Churchill Fellowship, 1968. Design work includes sail trng vessels, reproduction, expedition and exploration boats, power boats, sailing yachts, motor cruisers, etc; designer of sail trng ship, Young Endeavour, GB's gift to Australia for 1988 Bicentennial. Member: Cttee of Mgt, RNLI, 1987–2001 (Vice-Pres., 1997–2001, now Life Vice-Pres.); Council, RINA, 1988–97. Associate Mem., Acad. de Marinha, Portugal, 1995. FRSA 1996. Award for sail trng brig Royalist, Lloyd's Register of Shipping, 1971; Small Craft Medal, RINA, 1984; Award for sail trng barque Lord Nelson, British Design Council, 1993. *Publications:* Sopranino (with P. Ellam), 1954; Motor Boats and Boating, 1972; Power Boats, 1975; with Rosemary Mudie: The Story of the Sailing Ship, 1975; Power Yachts, 1977; The Sailing Ship, 1984; Sailing Ships, 2000; contrib. papers at various symposia, and articles and illustrations to professional, yachting and other jls. *Recreations:* sailing, motor boating, model making. *Address:* Bywater Lodge, Undershore Road, Lymington, Hants SO41 5SB. *T:* (01590) 672047. *Clubs:* Royal Ocean Racing; Royal Lymington Yacht, Lymington Town Sailing; Ocean Cruising.

MUDIE, George Edward; MP (Lab) Leeds East, since 1992; *b* 6 Feb. 1945. *Educ:* state schs. Former Mem. (Lab) Leeds CC, and Leader of Council. Treasurer of HM Household (Dep. Chief Govt Whip), 1997–98; Parly Under-Sec. of State, DfEE, 1998–99. *Address:* House of Commons, SW1A 0AA.

MUELLBAUER, Prof. John Norbert Joseph, PhD; FBA 1997; Professor of Economics, University of Oxford, since 1997; Official Fellow in Economics, Nuffield College, Oxford, since 1981; *b* 17 July 1944; *s* of late Prof. Norbert J. Muellbauer and Edith Heinz. *Educ:* King's Coll., Cambridge (MA 1965); Univ. of Calif at Berkeley (PhD 1975). Lectr in Economics, Univ. of Warwick, 1969–72; Lectr., 1972–75, Reader, 1975–77, Prof., 1977–81, in Economics, Birkbeck Coll., London Univ. Member: Gp of Outside Ind. Economists advising the Chancellor of the Exchequer, 1989; Retail Price Index Adv. Cttee, 1993–95; Fellow, Econometric Soc., 1976. Medal, Helsinki Univ., 1980. *Publications:* (with Angus Deaton) Economics and Consumer Behaviour, 1980; articles in Financial Times, Amer. Econ. Review, Econometrica, Econ. Jl, etc. *Recreations:* music, tennis. *Address:* Nuffield College, Oxford OX1 1NF. *T:* (01865) 278583.

MUELLER, Rudolf Gottfried, Hon. CBE 1997; Chairman, Chiltern Participations UK Ltd, 2004–06; *b* 28 May 1934; Swiss national; *m* Christiane Béroud; two *s*. *Educ:* primary and secondary schools, St Gallen, Switzerland; Internat. Management Inst., Geneva. Swiss Fed. Commercial Dip. 1953; grad. 1969 from Univ. of Geneva with dip. equivalent to MBA. James Capel & Co., 1969–77; joined Union Bank of Switzerland, 1977: Chm. and Chief Exec., UBS UK, 1989–96; Mem., Exec. Bd, UBS Gp, 1991–96; non-exec. Chm., UBS UK, 1996–98; Chairman: WJB Chiltern Gp plc (formerly Chiltern Gp plc), 1998–2003; WJB Chiltern Wealth Mgt Services Ltd, 2004–06. Non-executive Director: Lend Lease Corp. Ltd, 1996–2002; TI Gp, 1996–2000. Chm., Swiss Options Financial Futures Exchange, Zürich, 1986–88; Dir, London Stock Exchange, 1991–95. Chm., Bd of Trustees, Rix Centre, 2004–. Member of Board: Internat. Mgt Inst., Kiev, 1993–2005; Royal Opera House Trust, 1992–97; Dir, Royal Opera House, 1996–98. Hon. DBA East London, 2005. *Recreations:* golf, ski-ing, hiking, oenology. *Address:* (office) Linen Hall, Suite 321, 162 Regent Street, W1B 5TD.

MUFF, family name of **Baron Calverley**.

MUGABE, Robert Gabriel; President of Zimbabwe, since 1988; President, Zimbabwe African National Union-Patriotic Front, since 1988; *b* Kutama, 21 Feb. 1924; *m* 1961, Sarah Francesca Hayfron (*d* 1992); one *s* decd; *m* 1996, Grace Marufu; two *s* one *d*. *Educ:* Kutama Mission School; Fort Hare Univ. (BA (Educ), BSc (Econ)); London Univ. (by correspondence: BSc(Econ); BEd; LLB; LLM; MSc(Econ)); Univ. of S Africa (by correspondence BAdm). Teacher, 1942–58: Kutama, Mapanzure, Shabani, Empandeni Mission, Hope Fountain Mission, Driefontein Mission, Mbizi Govt Sch., Mambo Sch., Chalimbana Trng Coll., Zambia; St Mary's Teacher Trng Coll., Ghana. Publ. Sec. of Nat. Dem. Party, 1960–61; Publicity Sec. and acting Sec.-Gen., Zimbabwe African People's Union, 1961–62. Political detention, 1962; co-founded and became Sec.-Gen. ZANU, Aug. 1963, but in detention in Rhodesia, 1964–74; escaped to Mozambique and led armed struggle from there, 1975–79. Prime Minister 1980–87, Minister of Defence and of Public Service, 1980–84, First Sec. of Politburo, 1984–87, Zimbabwe. Jt Leader (with Joshua Nkomo) of the Patriotic Front, Oct. 1976; Pres., ZANU, 1977–87. Attended Confs: Geneva Constitutional Conf. on Rhodesia, 1976; Malta Conf., 1978; Lancaster House Conf., 1979. Holds hon. degrees from many instns. *Address:* Office of the President, Private Bag 7700, Causeway, Harare, Zimbabwe.

MUGGERIDGE, Sara Ann, (Sally), (Mrs R. D. Williams); Chief Executive, Industry and Parliament Trust, since 2003; *b* 10 Sept. 1949; *d* of John Raymond Muggeridge, MBE and Sylvia Barbara Ann (*née* Jenkins); *m* 1969, Richard David Williams; one *s* two *d*. *Educ:* Aida Foster Stage Sch.; S Hampstead High Sch.; Guildhall Sch. of Music and Drama (Cert. Acting); Westfield Coll., London (BA Hons); Henley Mgt Coll. (Co. of Marketors Award 1992; MBA). Mktg Manager, British Telecom plc, 1985–91; Cable & Wireless plc: Mktg Dir, Mercury Communications, 1991–93; Mgt Develt Dir, 1993–96; HR Dir, Asia, 1996–99; Mgt Develt Dir, Pearson plc, 1999–2003. Chartered Institute of Marketing: Mem. Council, 1985–95; Pres., CIM Singapore, 1996–98; Exec. Vice-Pres., 1999–2004; Mem., Academic Senate, 2007–. Member: Bd, Southern Arts, 1992–96; Council for Excellence in Mgt and Leadership, 2000–02; Professional Accreditation Cttee, IoD, 2006–. Trustee: Pearson Gp Pensions Ltd, 1999–2003; Tutu Foundn UK, 2003–; Foundn for Church Leadership, 2003–. Internat. Pres., Malcolm Muggeridge Soc., 2003–. Mem. Council, Univ. of Kent, 2006–. Fellow, Industry and Parlt Trust, 1995; FCIM 1988; FCIPD 1996; FRSA 1995; MInstD 1993. President's Award, CIM, 1999; Voluntary Sector Achiever of the Yr, Woman of the Yr Awards, 2007. *Films:* acted in The Hallelujah Handshake, 1970, and The Yes Girls, 1971; contrib. Timeshift: Malcolm Muggeridge (TV), 2003. *Publications:* contributor: The Laterite Road, 2005; Conversion: the spiritual journey of a twentieth century pilgrim, 2005; Seeing Through the Eye, 2005. *Recreations:* choral singing, running, dog walking, theatre and the arts. *Address:* Industry and Parliament Trust, 3 Whitehall Court, SW1A 2EL. *T:* (020) 7839 9400; *e-mail:* sallymuggeridge@ipt.org.uk. *Club:* Farmers.

MUHEIM, Franz Emmanuel; President, Swiss Red Cross, 1996–2001; Vice-President, International Federation of Red Cross and Red Crescent Societies, 1996–2001; Swiss Ambassador to the Court of St James's, 1989–94; *b* 27 Sept. 1931; *s* of Hans Muheim and Hélène (*née* Ody); *m* 1962, Radmila Jovanovic. *Educ:* Univs of Fribourg (LèsL), Geneva and Paris (arts degree). Joined Swiss Federal Dept of Foreign Affairs, 1960; served successively in Belgrade, Rabat and London, 1961–70; Council of Europe, UN and Internat. Orgns Sect., Dept of Foreign Affairs, Berne, 1971–77; Dep. Head of Mission, Minister Plenipotentiary, Washington, 1978–81; Dep. Dir of Political Affairs and Head of Political Div. Europe and N America, with rank of Ambassador, Berne, 1982–83; Dir, Internat. Orgns, Dept of Foreign Affairs, 1984–89. Head of Swiss delegns to internat. confs, *inter alia* UNESCO, ESA, Red Cross, Non-Aligned Movement. Fellow, Center for Internat. Affairs, Harvard Univ., 1981–82; Prof., Bologna Center, Johns Hopkins Univ., 1995–96. *Publication:* (ed jtly) Einblick in die Schweizerische Aussenpolitik: festschrift für Staatssekretär Raymond Probst, 1984; Multilateralism Today: festchrift zum 70. Geburtstag von a. Ständerat Franz Muheim, 1993. *Recreations:* walking, mountaineering, ski-ing, photography, music. *Address:* Es Chesaux, 1646 Echarlens, Switzerland. *T:* (026) 9152474, *Fax:* (026) 9152450.

MUIR, Prof. Alexander Laird, MD; FRCPE, FRCR, FRCSE; Professor of Postgraduate Medicine, University of Edinburgh, 1990–99; Honorary Consultant Physician, Edinburgh Royal Infirmary, 1974–99; Honorary Physician to the Army in Scotland, 1986–99; *b* 12 April 1937; *s* of Andrew Muir and Helena Bauld; *m* 1968, Berenice Barker Snelgrove, FRCR; one *s* one *d*. *Educ:* Morrisons Acad.; Fettes Coll.; Univ. of Edinburgh. MB ChB; MD 1970; FRCPE 1975 (MRCPE 1967); FRCR 1986; FRCSE 1994. MO, British Antarctic Survey, 1963–65; MRC Fellow, McGill Univ., 1970–71; Consultant Physician, Manchester Royal Infirmary, 1973–74; Edinburgh University: Sen. Lectr in Medicine, 1974; Reader in Medicine, 1981–89; Postgrad. Dean of Medicine, 1990–99. Physician to the Queen in Scotland, 1985–96. Canadian MRC Vis. Scientist, Univ. of British Columbia, 1982. Chm. and Med. Dir, Jt Cttee for Higher Med. Trng, 1998–2001; Mem., Admin of Radioactive Substances Adv. Cttee, 1986–91. Vice-Pres., RCPE, 1994–97. Founder FMedSci 1998. Member Editorial Board: Thorax, 1981–86; British Heart Jl, 1986–90. *Publications:* contribs on physiology and diseases of heart and lungs to medical books, symposia and jls. *Recreations:* gardening, reading, ski-ing, golf. *Address:* Tigh na Darroch, St Fillans, Perthshire PH6 2NG.

MUIR, Sir Laurence (Macdonald), Kt 1981; VRD 1954; company director; Deputy Chairman, National Science and Technology Centre Advisory Committee, 1986–96; Founding Chairman, Canberra Development Board, 1979–86; *b* 3 March 1925; *s* of Andrew Muir and Agnes Campbell Macdonald; two *s* two *d*. *Educ:* Yallourn State Sch.; Scotch Coll., Melbourne; Univ. of Melbourne (LLB). Served RAN, 1942–46 (Lieut); Lt-Comdr, RANR, 1949–65. Admitted Barrister and Solicitor, Supreme Court of Victoria, 1950. Sharebroker, 1950–80; Mem., Stock Exchange of Melbourne, 1960–80; Partner, 1962–80, Sen. Partner, 1976–80, Potter Partners. Director: ANZ Banking Gp, 1980–91; ACI Internat. Ltd (formerly ACI Ltd), 1980–88; Nat. Commercial Union Assce Co. of Aust. Ltd (formerly Commercial Union Assce Co. of Aust.), 1979–91; Wormald Internat. Ltd, 1980–88; Herald and Weekly Times Ltd, 1982–87; ANZ Pensions Ltd, 1982–91; Alcoa of Australia Ltd, 1982–96; Hudson Conway Ltd (formerly Australian Asset Management Ltd), 1987–2000; Templeton Global Growth Fund, 1987–99; Greening Australia, 1985–90; Australian Consolidated Press Group, subseq. Publishing and Broadcasting Ltd, 1992–2006; Member Board: Focus Books Pty Ltd, 1990–2006; Crown

Ltd, 2003–; Chairman: Aust. Biomedical Corp. Ltd, 1983–87; Liquid Air Australia Ltd, 1982–95; Elders Austral Chartering Pty Ltd, 1984–90; University Paton Ltd, 1986–90; State Development Fund Ltd, 2002–06. Chm., John Curtin Sch. of Medical Res. Adv. Bd, 1982–88; Member: Parlt House Construction Authority (Chm., Artworks Adv. Cttee), 1979–89; Council, Gen. Motors, Aust., 1977–94; L'Air Liquide World Adv. Cttee, 1983–95; Victoria Garden State Cttee; Vic. Appeals Cttee, Anti-Cancer Council; Commn for the Future, 1991–; Bd, Royal Soc. of Victoria Foundn, 2006–; Consultant, Alfred Hosp. Bd, 1983–88. Patron: Baker Med. Res. Inst.; Microsurgery Foundn; Earthwatch Australia; Trustee and Bd Mem., Sir Robert Menzies Meml Trust, 1984–96; Founder and Trustee, Delta Soc. Aust.; Trustee, Aust. Scout Educn & Trng Foundn; Life Trustee, Cttee for Economic Develt of Aust. Mem. Exec. Cttee, World Athletic Cup 1985; Council Mem., HRH Duke of Edinburgh's 6th Commonwealth Study Conf. (Chm., Aust. Finance Cttee). Fellow: Securities Inst. of Australia, 1962; Australian Inst. of Dirs, 1967; FAIM 1965. Centenary Medal Australia, 2003. *Recreations:* gardening, walking. *Address:* Unit 3, 61 Black Street, Brighton, Vic 3186, Australia. *Clubs:* Melbourne, Melbourne Cricket (Melbourne); Frankston Golf.

MUIR, (Sir) Richard James Kay, (4th Bt *cr* 1892, of Deanston, Perthshire); *S* father, 1994, but does not use the title and his name is not on the Official Roll of the Baronetage; *b* 25 May 1939; *s* of Sir John Harling Muir, 3rd Bt, TD and of Elizabeth Mary, *e d* of Frederick James Dundas; *m* 1st, 1965, Susan Elizabeth (marr. diss. 1974), *d* of George A. Gardener; two *d*; 2nd, 1975, Lady Linda Mary Cole, *d* of 6th Earl of Enniskillen, MBE; two *d*. *Heir:* *b* Ian Charles Muir [*b* 16 Sept. 1940; *m* 1967, Fiona Barbara Elspeth, *d* of Major Stuart Mackenzie; three *d*].

MUIR, Richard John Sutherland, CMG 1994; HM Diplomatic Service, retired; *b* 25 Aug. 1942; *s* of John Muir and Edna (*née* Hodges); *m* 1966, Caroline Simpson; one *s* one *d*. *Educ:* The Stationers' Co.'s Sch.; Univ. of Reading (BA Hons). Entered HM Diplomatic Service, 1964; FO, 1964–65; MECAS, Lebanon, 1965–67; Third, then Second Sec. (Commercial), Jedda, 1967–70; Second Sec., Tunis, 1970–72; FCO, 1972–75; First Sec., Washington, 1975–79; seconded to Dept of Energy, 1979–81; Dir-Gen., British Liaison Office, Riyadh, 1981–85; FCO 1985–94: Hd of Information Dept, 1987–90; Principal Finance Officer and Chief Inspector, 1991–94; Ambassador: to Oman, 1994–99; to Kuwait, 1999–2002. Chairman: Anglo-Omani Soc., 2004–; Sir William Luce Meml Fund, 2007–; Dir, Altajir Trust, 2007–.

MUIR, Tom; Inquiry Secretary, Competition Commission, since 1999; Under Secretary, Textiles and Retailing Division, Department of Trade and Industry, 1992–94; *b* 15 Feb. 1936; *s* of late William and Maria Muir; *m* 1968, Brenda Dew; one *s* one *d*. *Educ:* King Edward VI Sch., Stafford; Leeds Univ. (BA Econs 1962). FCIS 1994. English Electric Co. Ltd, 1954–59; BoT, 1962–68; UK Perm. Delegn to OECD (on secondment to HM Diplomatic Service), 1968–71; DTI, 1972–75; UK Perm. Repn to EC, 1975–79 (on secondment); DoI, 1979–81; Dept of Trade, 1981–83; DTI, 1983–94: Under Sec., Insce Div., 1982–87, Overseas Trade Div. 4, 1987–89, Internat. Trade Policy Div., 1989–92. Dir, British Retail Consortium, 1995–97. Chm., Fedn of British Artists (Mall Galls), 1998–2001. *Recreations:* walking, reading, looking at buildings and pictures, opera.

MUIR MACKENZIE, Sir Alexander (Alwyne Henry Charles Brinton), 7th Bt *cr* 1805; *b* 8 Dec. 1955; *s* of Sir Robert Henry Muir Mackenzie, 6th Bt and Charmian Cecil de Vere (*d* 1962), *o d* of Col Cecil Charles Brinton; *S* father, 1970; *m* 1984, Susan Carolyn, *d* of John David Henzel Hayter; one *s* one *d*. *Educ:* Eton; Trinity Coll., Cambridge. *Heir:* *s* Archie Robert David Muir Mackenzie, *b* 17 Feb. 1989.

MUIR WOOD, Sir Alan (Marshall), Kt 1982; FRS 1980; FREng, FICE; Consultant, Halcrow Group (Partner, 1964–84, Senior Partner, 1979–84, Sir William Halcrow & Partners); *b* 8 Aug. 1921; *s* of Edward Stephen Wood and Dorothy (*née* Webb); *m* 1943, Winifred Leyton Lanagan, (Dr W. L. Wood, mathematician); three *s*. *Educ:* Abbotsholme Sch.; Peterhouse, Cambridge Univ. (MA; Hon. Fellow 1982). FICE 1957. Engr Officer, RN, 1942–46. Asst Engr, British Rail, Southern Reg., 1946–50; Res. Asst, Docks and Inland Waterways Exec., 1950–52; Asst Engr, then Sen. Engr, Sir William Halcrow & Partners, 1952–64. Principally concerned with studies and works in fields of tunnelling, geotechnics, coastal engrg, energy, roads and railways; major projects include: (Proj. Engr) Clyde Tunnel and Potters Bar railway tunnels; (Partner) Cargo Tunnel at Heathrow Airport, and Cuilfail Tunnel, Lewes; studies and works for Channel Tunnel (intermittently, 1958–98); Dir, Orange-Fish Consultants, resp. for 80 km irrigation tunnel. Member: ACARD, 1980–84; SERC, 1981–84; Governing Body, Inst. of Development Studies, 1981–87; Council, ITDG, 1981–84; Chairman: SERC/ESRC Jt Cttee, 1983–85; Res. Councils Individual Merit Promotion Panel, 1989–94. Mem. Council, Royal Soc., 1983–84, a Vice-Pres., 1983–84; President: Internat. Tunnelling Assoc., 1975–77 (Hon. Life Pres., 1977); ICE, 1977–78; FREng (FEng 1977; a Vice-Pres., 1984–87). FIC 1981. Foreign Member, Royal Swedish Acad. of Engrg Sci., 1980; Hon. Fellow, Portsmouth Polytech., 1984. Hon. DSc: City, 1978; Southampton, 1986; Hon. LLD Dundee, 1985; Hon. DEng Bristol, 1991. Telford Medal, ICE, 1976; James Alfred Ewing Medal, ICE and Royal Soc., 1984; Gold Medal, ICE, 1998. *Publications:* Coastal Hydraulics, 1969, (with C. A. Fleming) 2nd edn 1981; Tunnelling: management by design, 2000; Civil Engineering in Context, 2004; papers, mainly on tunnelling, coastal engrg and wider aspects of engrg, in Proc. ICE and elsewhere. *Address:* Franklands, Bere Court Road, Pangbourne, Berks RG8 8JY. *T:* (0118) 984 2833. *Club:* Athenæum.

See also D. Muir Wood.

MUIR WOOD, Prof. David, PhD; FREng; Professor of Civil Engineering, University of Bristol, since 1995 (Head, Department of Civil Engineering, 1997–2002; Dean, Faculty of Engineering, 2003–07); *b* 17 March 1949; *s* of Sir Alan Muir Wood, *qv*; *m* 1978, Helen Rosamond Piddington; two *s*. *Educ:* Royal Grammar Sch., High Wycombe; Peterhouse, Cambridge (BA 1970, MA 1974; PhD 1974). FICE 1992; FREng (FEng 1998). University of Cambridge: res. student, Engrg Dept, 1970–73; William Stone Res. Fellow, Peterhouse, 1973–75; Fellow, Emmanuel Coll., 1975–87; Demonstrator/Lectr in Soil Mechanics, Engrg Dept, 1975–87; University of Glasgow: Cormack Prof. of Civil Engrg, 1987–95; Hd, Dept of Civil Engrg, 1991–93; Dean, Faculty of Engrg, 1993–94. Royal Soc. Res. Fellow, Norwegian Geotechnical Inst., Oslo, 1975; Royal Soc. Industry Fellow, Babtie Gp, 1995–96. Hon. Editor, Géotechnique, 1991–93. Associate, Geotechnical Consulting Gp, 1983–. Chm., Scottish Geotechnical Gp, 1991–93. Elder, Cairns Ch of Scotland, Milngavie, 1993–98. (Jtly) British Geotechnical Soc. Prize, 1978. *Publications:* (with R. J. Mair) Pressuremeter Testing: methods and interpretation, 1987; Soil Behaviour and Critical State Soil Mechanics, 1990; (jtly) Piled Foundations in Weak Rock, 1999; Geotechnical Modelling, 2004; contrib. numerous papers to professional jls and confs. *Recreations:* hill-walking, music, opera, travel. *Address:* University of Bristol, Department of Civil Engineering, Queen's Building, University Walk, Bristol BS8 1TR. *T:* (0117) 928 7706, *Fax:* (0117) 928 7783; *e-mail:* d.muir-wood@bristol.ac.uk; Leigh Lodge, Church Road, Abbots Leigh, Bristol BS8 3QP. *T:* (01275) 375563.

MUIRHEAD, Geoffrey, CBE 2004; FCILT, FICE; Group Chief Executive, Manchester Airports Group, since 2001; *b* 14 July 1949; *s* of John Thomas Muirhead and Irene Clarke; *m* 1972, Clare Elizabeth Parker; one *d*. *Educ:* Teesside Polytechnic. FCIT 1994; FICE 1998. Started career with British Steel; subseq. senior positions with William Press, Simon Carves, Fluor and Shand, incl. posts in Saudi Arabia, Belgium, Eire; Manchester Airport: Dir, Develt, 1988; Dir, Business Develt, 1992; Chief Exec., 1993–2001. Bd Member: ACI Europe, 1994– (Past Pres.); ACI World, 2001–; Mem., NW Business Leadership Team, 1993– (Dep. Chm., 2006–). Mem., NW Regl Council, CBI (Dep. Chm., 2002–05); Associate Mem., Greater Manchester Chamber of Commerce and Industry, 2001– (Past Pres.). Exec. Mem., NW Regl Assembly, 2006–. Mem. Bd, Manchester Metropolitan Univ. FRSA 1996. Hon. DBA: Manchester Metropolitan, 2003; Teesside, 2005; Hon. DSc Salford, 2004. *Recreations:* golf, travel. *Address:* Manchester Airports Group, Manchester M90 1QX.

MUIRHEAD, Dame Lorna (Elizabeth Fox), DBE 2000; Lord-Lieutenant of Merseyside, since 2006; Midwifery Sister, Liverpool Women's Hospital (formerly Liverpool Maternity Hospital), 1966–69 and 1974–2005; President, Royal College of Midwives, 1997–2004; *b* 13 Sept. 1942; *d* of Donald Fox and Joan Mary (*née* Harper); *m* 1966, Ronald A. Muirhead; one *s* one *d*. *Educ:* in Shropshire and Warwickshire. SRN 1963; SCM 1965; MTD 1970; FRCOG 2001. Nurse trng, Hallam Hosp., W Bromwich, 1960–63; midwifery trng, Hallam Hosp. and Marston Green Maternity Hosp., 1964–65; Staff Midwife, Liverpool Maternity Hosp., 1965–66; Midwifery Sister Tutor, 1969–71; part-time Lectr, Liverpool Poly., 1975–80; Sen. Lectr, British Shipping Fedn med. course, 1975–85; frequent Lectr at Univ. and Royal Coll. Midwives seminars and study days, 1980–. DL Merseyside, 2003. Fellow, Royal Coll. Midwives, 2005. Hon. Fellow, Liverpool John Moores Univ., 2001. CStJ 2008. *Publication:* chapter on A Midwife's Role in Epidural Analgesia, in Epidural Analgesia in Obstetrics, ed A. Doughty, 1980. *Recreations:* choral singing, music, poetry, restoration of old furniture. *Address:* 15 Ullet Road, Sefton Gate, Liverpool L17 3BL. *T:* (0151) 733 8710.

MUIRHEAD, Oona Grant, CBE 2000 (OBE 1992); Director of Strategy and Communications, Local Government Association, since 2005; *b* 29 Jan. 1956; *d* of Michael and Marian Muirhead. *Educ:* Univ. of Birmingham (BA Hons Russian; Dip. Vocational Techniques for Prof. Linguist). Ministry of Defence, 1979–2003: Defence Intelligence Service, 1979; various policy and operational posts, 1985–95; (first) Pol Advr to Chief of Jt Ops, 1995–97; Dir, Inf. Strategy and News, 1997–2000; rcds, 2000; DG, Mgt and Orgn, 2001–03; Prog. Dir for Modernising Rural Delivery, DEFRA, 2003–05. *Recreations:* gardening, golf, walking, decorating/DIY, opera, the Archers omnibus, reading mental chewing-gum. *Address:* Local Government Association, Local Government House, Smith Square, SW1P 3HZ; *e-mail:* oona.muirhead@lga.gov.uk.

MUIRHEAD, William Donald; Sheriff of Lothian and Borders at Linlithgow, since 2000; *b* 21 March 1948; *s* of William Ingram Muirhead and Phyllis Jessie Muirhead; *m* 1976, Maria de los Angeles Cabieces; one *s* two *d*. *Educ:* Melville Coll.; Edinburgh Univ. (LLB Hons). Solicitor, Aitken Nairn WS, 1972–2000. Pt-time Sheriff, 1993–99. *Recreations:* golf, music, hill walking. *Club:* Bruntsfield Links Golf.

MUIRHEAD, William Mortimer; Agent General for South Australia in London, since 2007; Founding Partner, M&C Saatchi, since 1995; *b* Adelaide, 11 July 1946; *s* of Denis and Lorna Muirhead; *m* 1971, Jeanne Elizabeth Meins; three *s*. *Educ:* Armidale Sch., Armidale, NSW; St Dunstan's Coll., London. Jackson Wain/Leo Burnett, 1966–70; Account Exec., Ogilvy & Mather, 1970–72; Account Dir, subseq. Gp Account Dir, Saatchi & Saatchi, 1972–89; Chm. and Chief Exec., Saatchi & Saatchi Advertising UK, 1989–92; Chm., Saatchi & Saatchi Europe, 1992–94; Chief Exec. and Pres., Saatchi & Saatchi Advertising Worldwide, 1994–95. *Recreations:* tennis, ski-ing, golf, music, travel. *Address:* Australia Centre, Strand, WC2B 4LG. *T:* (020) 7520 9100; *e-mail:* Bill.muirhead@south-aus.au. *Clubs:* Royal Automobile, Thirty.

MUIRHEAD-ALLWOOD, Sarah Kathryn, FRCS; Consultant Orthopaedic Surgeon: Royal National Orthopaedic Hospital, since 1991; King Edward VII's Hospital for Officers, since 1993; *b* 4 Jan. 1947; *c* of late Maj. W. R. Muirhead and of Joyce Muirhead (*née* Forster); *m* 1983; two *s*. *Educ:* Wellington; St Thomas' Hosp. Med. Sch. (BSc, MB BS). MRCS, FRCS, LRCP. St Thomas' Hospital: House Surg., 1971–72; Sen. House Officer, 1972–73; Anatomy Demonstrator, 1973; Sen. House Officer, Stoke Mandeville Hosp., 1973–74; Registrar: UCH, 1974–77; Charing Cross Hosp., 1977–78; Sen. Registrar, Queen Mary's Hosp., Roehampton, Westminster Hosp., Royal Nat. Orthopaedic Hosp., UCH, 1978–84; Consultant Orthopaedic Surgeon, Whittington Hosp., 1984–2004. Hon. Sen. Clin. Lectr, UCL, 1984; Hon. Consultant: St Luke's Hosp. for the Clergy, 1984; Hosp. of St John and St Elizabeth. Member: British Orthopaedic Assoc., 1980; BMA, 1983; British Hip Soc., 1989; European Hip Soc., 1993. *Publications:* contributions to: Joint Replacement—State of the Art, 1990; Recent Advances in Orthopaedic Surgery, 1991; Gray's Anatomy, 1995. *Recreations:* golf, sailing. *Address:* The London Hip Unit, 4th Floor, 30 Devonshire Street, W1G 6PU. *T:* (020) 7908 3709; *e-mail:* sarahmuirheada@aol.com.

MUIRHEAD-ALLWOOD, William Forster Gillespie; *see* Muirhead-Allwood, S. K.

MUKARJI, Dr (Satyanand) Daleep, OBE 2008; Director, Christian Aid, since 1998; *b* 22 Feb. 1946; *m* Azra Latifi; one *s* two *d*. *Educ:* Christian Med. Coll., Vellore, India (MB BS); London Sch. of Hygiene and Tropical Med. (DTPH); LSE (MSc). Med. Superintendent, Mission Hosp., Andhra Pradesh, India, 1972; MO and Project Dir, Leprosy Hosp., Dichpalli, 1973; Programme Dir, Rural Unit for Health and Social Affairs, Christian Med. Coll., Vellore, 1977–85; Gen. Sec., Christian Med. Assoc. of India, 1985–94; Exec. Sec., Urban Rural Mission, 1994–96, Health, Community and Justice, 1997–98, WCC, Geneva. *Recreations:* music, theatre, cinema. *Address:* Christian Aid, PO Box 100, SE1 7RT; 7 Torrington Grove, N12 9NA.

MUKHAMEDOV, Irek Javdatovich, OBE 2000; ballet dancer; Artistic Director, Greek National Opera Ballet, since 2007 (Artistic Co-ordinator, 2006–07); *b* 1960; *s* of Djavdat Rasulievich Mukhamedov and Rashida Nizamovna; *m* 1990, Maria Zubkhova; one *s* one *d*. *Educ:* Moscow Choreographic Inst. Soloist, Moscow Classical Co., 1978–81; Bolshoi Ballet, 1981–90; Principal, 1990–99, Guest Artist, 1999–2001, Royal Ballet Co.; founded Mukhamedov & Co., 1991. Vice Pres., Arts Educnl Sch., Tring, 2002–. *Leading rôles* in ballets including: Spartacus, Ivan the Terrible, Raymonda, La Bayadère, La Fille mal gardée, Manon, Giselle, Mr Worldly Wise, Mayerling, Different Drummer, Fearful Symmetries, Nutcracker, Les Biches, Prodigal Son, Othello, Cheating, Lying, Stealing, L'Après-midi d'un faune, The Crucible; musical: On Your Toes; *rôles created* include: Boris in The Golden Age; Vershinin in Winter Dreams; the foreman in the Judas Tree. *Address:* c/o Greek National Opera Ballet, 199 Piraeus and Alkminis 68 str, 118 53 Athens, Greece.

MUKHERJEE, Pranab Kumar; Member, and Leader of the House, Lok Sabha, since 2004; Minister of External Affairs, India, 1995–96 and since 2006; *b* 11 Dec. 1935; *s* of Kamda Kinkar Mukherjee, of an illustrious family which was involved actively in the Freedom Movement of India; *m* 1957, Suvra Mukherjee; two *s* one *d*. *Educ:* Vidyasagar Coll., Suri; Calcutta Univ. (MA (Hist. and Pol Sci.); LLB). Elected Mem., W Bengal,

Rajya Sabha, 1969, re-elected 1975, 1981, 1993, 1999; Leader, Rajya Sabha, 1980–85; Dep. Minister, Mins of Industrial Develt and of Shipping and Transport, 1973–74; Minister of State, Finance Min., 1974–77; Cabinet Minister i/c of Mins of Commerce, Steel and Mines, 1980–82; became youngest Minister to hold Finance Portfolio in Independent India, 1982–85; Dep. Chm., Planning Commn, 1991–93; Commerce Minister, 1993–95; Minister of Defence, 2004–06. Spokesman, All India Congress Cttee, 1991; Chm., Central Election Campaign Cttee of Congress Party, 1984, 1991, 1996, 1998. *Publications:* Crisis in Democracy; An Aspect of Constitutional Problems in Bengal, 1967; Mid-Term Poll, 1969; Beyond Survival: an emerging dimension of Indian economy, 1984; Off the Track: an analysis of Indian economy, 1987; Saga of Struggle and Sacrifice, 1992; Challenges before the Nation, 1992. *Recreations:* music, gardening, reading. *Address:* S-22, Greater Kailash, Part II, New Delhi 110048, India.

MUKHERJEE, Shiv Shankar; High Commissioner for India in the United Kingdom, since 2008; *b* Bihar, India, 1 Aug. 1949; *s of* Ananga Mukherjee and Sumita Devi Mukherjee (*née* Chakravarti); *m* 1972, Nalini Kapoor; one *s* one *d. Educ:* St Stephen's Coll., Univ. of Delhi (Postgrad. Chemistry 1970). Attaché, then Under Sec., Bangladesh, Min. of External Affairs, India, 1973–75; Second Sec., then First Sec., Damascus, 1975–79; First Sec., Brussels, 1979–82; Dep. High Comr, Lusaka, 1982–85; Counsellor (Press), Washington, 1985–88; Dir (Ext. Publicity), Min. of External Affairs, 1988–89; Hd, India Observer Mission, 1989–90, High Comr, 1990–92, Windhoek; Jt Sec. (Ext. Publicity), Min. of External Affairs, 1992–94; Dir Gen., Indian Council for Cultural Relns, 1994–95; Minister (Press Inf. and Culture), Washington, 1995–98; Ambassador, Cairo, 1998–2000; High Comr, Pretoria, 2000–04; Ambassador, Kathmandu, 2004–08. Member: India Habitat Centre, 1993–; India Internat. Centre, 1993–. *Recreations:* reading, golf, chess. *Address:* High Commission of India, India House, Aldwych, WC2B 4NA. *T:* (020) 7836 2556, *Fax:* (020) 7240 4688; *e-mail:* hc.london@mea.gov.in. *Clubs:* Delhi Press, Delhi Gymkhana.

MUKHERJEE, Tara Kumar, FLIA; Managing Director: Owl Financial Services Ltd, since 1988; Greater London Translation Unit, since 1993; President, Confederation of Indian Organisations (UK), since 1975; Chairman, European Multicultural Foundation, since 1996; *b* 20 Dec. 1923; *s of* Sushil Chandra Mukherjee and Sova Moyee Mukherjee; *m* 1951, Betty Patricia Mukherjee; one *s* one *d. Educ:* Scottish Church Collegiate Sch., Calcutta, India; Calcutta Univ. (matriculated 1939). Shop Manager, Bata Shoe Co. Ltd, India, 1941–44; Buyer, Brevitt Shoes, Leicester, 1951–56; Sundries Buyer, British Shoe Corp., 1956–66; Prodn Administrator, Priestley Footwear Ltd, Great Harwood, 1966–68; Head Stores Manager, Brit. Shoe Corp., 1968–70; Save & Prosper Group: Dist Manager, 1970–78; Br. Manager, 1978–84; Senior Sales Manager, 1984–85; Br. Manager, Guardian Royal Exchange PFM Ltd, 1985–88. Pres., India Film Soc., Leicester, 1958–70. Chairman: Leicester Community Centre Project, 1962–66; Charter 90 for Asians, 1990–; Mem., Brit. Europ. Movt, London, 2004–; Pres., EC Migrants Forum, Brussels, 1990–96. Dir, Coronary Prevention Gp, 1986–. Patron: London Community Cricket Assoc., 1987–; Asha Foundn, 1999–. FRSA. DUniv Middx, 2003. *Recreation:* cricket (1st Cl. cricketer; played for Bihar, Ranji Trophy, 1941; 2nd XI, Leics CCC, 1949). *Address:* Tallah, 51 Viking Way, Pilgrims Hatch, Brentwood, Essex CM15 9HY. *T:* (01277) 263207, *Fax:* (01277) 229946. *Club:* (Gen. Sec.) Indian National (Leicester).

MULCAHY, Sir Geoffrey (John), Kt 1993; Chairman: Javelin Group Ltd, since 2004; British Retail Consortium, since 2006; *b* 7 Feb. 1942; *s of* Maurice Frederick Mulcahy and Kathleen Love Mulcahy; *m* 1965, Valerie Elizabeth; one *s* one *d. Educ:* King's Sch., Worcester; Manchester Univ. (BSc); Harvard Univ. (MBA). Esso Petroleum, 1964–74; Norton Co., 1974–77; British Sugar, 1977–83; Woolworth Holdings, subseq. Kingfisher, 1983–2002: Gp Man. Dir, 1984–86; Chief Exec., 1986–93; Chm., 1990–95; Chief Exec., 1995–2002. *Recreations:* sailing, squash. *Address:* Javelin Group Ltd, 71 Victoria Street, SW1H 0HW. *Clubs:* Lansdowne, Royal Automobile, Royal Thames Yacht; Royal Southern Yacht.

MULDER, (Robert) Frederick, PhD; Senior Partner, Frederick Mulder, dealers in European original prints, since 1972; *b* 24 June 1943; *s of* William Eldred Bowman and Kathleen Elsie Delarue; *m* 1971, Valerie Ann Townsend (marr. diss. 2000); one *s* one *d* (and one *s* decd); one *s. Educ:* Eston High Sch., Sask.; Univ. of Saskatchewan (BA Hons Eng. 1965); Brown Univ., Providence, RI (MA Philos. 1967; PhD Philos. 1971); Linacre Coll., Oxford. Dir, P. and D. Colnaghi, 1972–75. Chm. of Trustees, Prairie Trust (formerly Frederick Mulder Trust), 1986–; Founding Chm., The Funding Network, 2002–; Trustee: Gaia Foundn, 1988–91; Network for Social Change, 1995–98; Oxford Res. Gp, 2000–06. *Recreation:* hill-walking. *Address:* e-mail: fm@frederickmulder.com.

MULDOON, Bristow Cook; Member (Lab) Livingston, Scottish Parliament, 1999–2007; *b* 19 March 1964; *s of* late Bristow Cook Muldoon and of Annie McKenzie Muldoon (*née* McCallum); *m* 1988, Catherine Sloan McMillan; three *s. Educ:* Cumbernauld High Sch.; Univ. of Strathclyde (BSc Hons Chem.); Open Univ. (BA Hons). Manager in rail industry, 1986–99; business analyst, Great North Eastern Rly, 1997–99. Member (Lab): Lothian Regl Council, 1994–96 (Vice-Chm., Econ. Develt); West Lothian Council, 1995–99 (Convener, Community Services). Non-exec. Dir, West Lothian NHS Trust, 1997–99. Member: Labour Party; Co-Op Party; TSSA. *Recreations:* golf, music, football, reading. *Club:* Uphall Golf.

MULDOON, Prof. Paul; Howard G. B. Clark Professor in the Humanities, Princeton University, since 1998; *b* Portadown, NI, 20 June 1951; *s of* late Patrick Muldoon and Brigid (*née* Regan); *m* 1987, Jean Hanff Korelitz; one *s* one *d. Educ:* St Patrick's Coll., Armagh; Queen's Univ., Belfast (BA Eng. Lang. and Lit. 1973). BBC Northern Ireland: Producer, Arts Progs (Radio), 1973–78; Sen. Producer, 1978–85; TV Producer, 1985–86; Judith E. Wilson Vis. Fellow, Cambridge Univ., 1986–87; Creative Writing Fellow, UEA, 1987; Lecturer: Sch. of the Arts, Columbia Univ., 1987–88; Creative Writing Program, Princeton Univ., 1987–88; Writer-in-residence, 92nd Street Y, NY, 1988; Roberta Holloway Lectr, Univ. of Calif, Berkeley, 1989; Vis. Prof., Univ. of Mass, Amherst, 1989–90; Princeton University: Lectr, 1990–95; Prof., 1995–98; Dir, Creative Writing Program, 1993–2002; Vis. Prof., Bread Loaf Sch. of English, Middlebury, Vt, 1997–; Prof. of Poetry, Univ. of Oxford, 1999–2004; Fellow, Hertford Coll., Oxford, 1999–2004, now Hon. Fellow. Pres., Poetry Soc. of GB, 1996–2005. Mem., Aosdana, 1980–. FRSL 1981; John Simon Guggenheim Meml Fellow, 1990. Readings of work throughout Europe, USA and Canada, Japan and Australia. Eric Gregory Award, 1972; Sir Geoffrey Faber Meml Award, 1980 and 1991; T. S. Eliot Prize for Poetry, 1994; Award in Literature, AAAL, 1996; Poetry Prize, Irish Times, 1997; Shakespeare Prize, 2004. *Publications: poetry:* Knowing My Place, 1971; New Weather, 1973; Spirit of Dawn, 1975; Mules, 1977; Names and Addresses, 1978; Immram, 1980; Why Brownlee Left, 1980; Out of Siberia, 1982; Quoof, 1983; The Wishbone, 1984; Selected Poems 1968–83, 1986; Meeting the British, 1987; Selected Poems 1968–86, 1987; Madoc: a mystery, 1990; Incantata, 1994; The Prince of the Quotidian, 1994; The Annals of Chile, 1994; Kerry Slides, 1996; New Selected Poems 1968–94, 1996; Hopewell Haiku, 1997; The Bangle (Slight Return), 1998; Hay, 1998; Poems 1968–1998, 2001; Moy Sand and Gravel, 2002

(Pulitzer Prize, 2003); Horse Latitudes, 2006; *drama:* Monkeys (TV play), 1989; Shining Brow (opera), 1993; Six Honest Serving Men (play), 1995; Bandanna (opera), 1999; *essays:* Getting Round: notes towards an Ars Poetica, 1998; To Ireland, I, 2000; The End of the Poem, 2006; *for children:* The O-O's Party, 1981; The Last Thesaurus, 1995; The Noctuary of Narcissus Batt, 1997; *translations:* The Astrakan Cloak, by Nuala Ni Dhomhnaill, 1993; (with R. Martin) The Birds, by Aristophanes, 1999; *edited:* The Scrake of Dawn, 1979; The Faber Book of Contemporary Irish Poetry, 1986; The Essential Byron, 1989; The Faber Book of Beasts, 1997; contribs to poetry anthologies; works trans. into numerous langs. *Recreations:* tennis, electric guitar. *Address:* c/o Faber & Faber, 3 Queen Square, WC1N 3AU. *Clubs:* Athenæum, Groucho.

MULDOON, Dame Thea (Dale), DBE 1993; QSO 1986; *b* 13 March 1927; *d of* Stanley Arthur and Annie Eveleen Flyger; *m* 1951, Rt Hon. Sir Robert David Muldoon, GCMG, CH, PC (*d* 1992); one *s* two *d. Educ:* Takapuna Grammar Sch. Associated with many charities. Chairman: North Shore sub-gp, Auckland Br., Govt Superannuitants Assoc., 2006–; Friends of Couldrey House Charitable Trust, 2006–. Founding Patron, North Shore Hospice; Patron: Hibiscus Coast Br., NZ Red Cross Soc.; several horticultural orgns; Vice Patron, NZ Foundn for Conductive Educn. *Recreations:* walking, gym.

MULDOWNEY, Diane Ellen, (Mrs Dominic Muldowney); see Trevis, D. E.

MULDOWNEY, Dominic John; composer; Music Director, Royal National (formerly National) Theatre, 1976–97; *b* 19 July 1952; *s of* William and Barbara Muldowney; *m* 1986, Diane Ellen Trevis, *qv;* one *d. Educ:* Taunton's Grammar School, Southampton; York Univ. (BA, BPhil). Composer in residence, Southern Arts Association, 1974–76; composer of chamber, choral, orchestral works, including work for theatre, ballet and TV. *Compositions include:* Piano Concerto, 1983, 2002; The Duration of Exile, 1984; Saxophone Concerto, 1985; Sinfonietta, 1986; Ars Subtilior, 1987; Lonely Hearts, 1988; Violin Concerto, 1989; Three Pieces for Orchestra, 1990; Percussion Concerto, 1991; Oboe Concerto, 1992; Trumpet Concerto, 1993; Concerto for 4 Violins, 1994; The Brontës (ballet), 1995; Trombone Concerto, 1996; Clarinet Concerto, 1997; Irish Love Songs, 1998; The Fall of Jerusalem (oratorio), 1999; War Oratorio (film), 2007; Tsunami (song cycle), 2008. *Recreation:* driving through France and across America.

MULFORD, Dr David Campbell; United States Ambassador to India, since 2004; *b* Rockford, Ill, 27 June 1937; *s of* Robert Lewis Mulford and Theodora Henie Moellenhauer Mulford; *m* 1985, Jeannie Louise Simmons; two *s. Educ:* Lawrence Univ., Wisconsin (BA Econs *cum laude* 1959); Univ. of Cape Town; Boston Univ. (MA Pol Sci. 1962; Dist. Alumni Award, 1992); St Antony's Coll., Oxford (DPhil 1966). Special Asst to Sec. and Under Sec., US Treasury, 1965–66; Man. Dir and Head, Internat. Finance, White, Weld & Co., Inc., 1966–74; Sen. Investment Advr, Saudi Arabian Monetary Agency, 1974–84, on secondment; Under Sec. and Asst Sec. for Internat. Affairs, US Treasury, 1984–92 (sen. advr on financial assistance to former Soviet Union states; head of internat. debt strategy; led US delegn to negotiate estabt of EBRD); Mem. Exec. Bd, 1992–2003, Chm. Europe, 1993–99, Chm. Internat., 1999–2003, Credit Suisse First Boston. Mem., Council on Foreign Relations, 1972–; Affiliate, Center for Strategic and Internat. Studies, Washington, 1992–. Hon. LLD Lawrence, Wisconsin, 1984. Alexander Hamilton Award, USA, 1992. Légion d'Honneur (France), 1990; Order of May (Argentina), 1993; Officer's Cross, Medal of Merit (Poland), 1995. *Publications:* Northern Rhodesia General Election, 1962; Zambia: the politics of independence, 1967. *Recreations:* golf, running, canoeing. *Address:* US Embassy, Shantipath, Chanakyapuri, New Delhi 110021, India. *Club:* Metropolitan (Washington).

MULGAN, Geoffrey John, CBE 2004; PhD; Director, The Young Foundation (formerly Institute of Community Studies), since 2004; *b* 28 Aug. 1961; *s of* Anthony Philip Mulgan and Catherine Mulgan (*née* Gough); *m* 1998, Rowena Young; one *s* one *d. Educ:* Balliol Coll., Oxford (MA 1982); Central London Poly. (PhD 1990). Investment Exec., Greater London Enterprise, 1984–86; Harkness Fellow, MIT, 1986–87; Consultant, and Lectr in Telecommunications, Central London Poly., 1987–90; Special Advr to Gordon Brown, MP, 1990–92; Fellow, BFI, 1992–93; Co-Founder and Dir, Demos, 1993–97 (Chm., Adv. Council, 1998–); Mem., Prime Minister's Policy Unit, 1997–2000; Director: Perf. and Innovation Unit, Cabinet Office, 2000–02; Prime Minister's Forward Strategy Unit, 2001–02; Strategy Unit, Cabinet Office, 2002–04; Head of Policy, Prime Minister's Office, 2003–04. Member: Health Innovation Council, 2008–; Prime Minister's Council on Social Action, 2008–. Visiting Professor: UCL, 1996–; LSE, 2004–; Melbourne, 2006–. Mem., Design Council, 2006–. Chm., Involve, 2005–; Trustee: Political Qly, 1995–; Work Foundn, 2005–. *Publications:* Saturday Night or Sunday Morning, 1987; Communication and Control, 1990; Politics in an Antipolitical Age, 1994; (ed) Life After Politics, 1997; Connexity, 1997; Good and Bad Power: the ideals and betrayals of government, 2006; The Art of Public Strategy, 2008. *Recreation:* making music. *Address:* 27 Lothair Road South, N4 1EN.

MULGRAVE, Earl of; John Samuel Constantine Phipps; *b* 26 Nov. 1994; *s* and *heir* of Marquis of Normanby, *qv.*

MULHOLLAND, family name of **Baron Dunleath.**

MULHOLLAND, Clare, OBE 1998; Vice Chairman of Council, Communications Regulatory Agency (formerly Independent Media Commission), Bosnia and Herzegovina, 1998–2005; *b* 17 June 1939; *d of* James Mulholland and Elizabeth (*née* Lochrin). *Educ:* Notre Dame High Sch., Glasgow; Univ. of Glasgow (MA Hons). Gen. trainee, then Press Officer, ICI, 1961–64; Press Officer: Granada Television, 1964–65; TWW, 1965–68; Press Officer, then Educn Officer, HTV, 1968–71; Independent Broadcasting Authority, later Independent Television Commission, 1971–97: Reg. Exec., Bristol, 1971–77; Reg. Officer, Midlands, 1977–82; Chief Asst, Television, 1982–83; Dep. Dir of Television, 1983–91; Dir of Programmes, 1991–96; Dep. Chief Exec., 1996–97; internat. broadcasting consultant, 1998–2008. Member: Arts Council of GB, 1986–94; Scottish Film Prodn Fund, 1984–90; Lottery Film Panel, Arts Council of England, 1997–2000. FRTS 1988. *Recreations:* travel, theatre, cinema.

MULHOLLAND, Frank; QC (Scot.) 2005; Solicitor General for Scotland, since 2007; *b* 18 April 1959; *s of* Charles and Jean Mulholland; *m* 1988, Marie Quinn; one *s. Educ:* Columba High Sch., Coatbridge; Univ. of Aberdeen (LLB Hons; DipLP); Univ. of Edinburgh (MBA 1997). Trainee solicitor, Bird Semple & Crawford Heron, 1982–84; Procurator Fiscal Depute: Greenock, 1984–87; Glasgow, 1987–91; NP 1992; SSC 1993; Crown Office: Solicitor: High Court Unit, 1991–94; Appeals Unit, 1994–97; Advocate Depute, 1997–2000; Asst Procurator Fiscal, 2000–01, Procurator Fiscal, 2001–03, Edinburgh; Sen. Advocate Depute, 2003–06; Area Procurator Fiscal, Lothian and Borders, 2006–07. *Recreations:* football, golf, military history. *Address:* Crown Office, 29 Chambers Street, Edinburgh EH1 1LD.

MULHOLLAND, Gregory Thomas; MP (Lib Dem) Leeds North West, since 2005; *b* 31 Aug. 1970; *m* 2004, Raegan Melita Hatton; one *d. Educ:* St Ambrose Coll., Altrincham;

Univ. of York (BA 1991; MA 1995). Account handler, several marketing and sales promotion agencies, 1997–2002. Mem. (Lib Dem), Leeds CC, 2003–05 (Lead Mem., Corp. Services and Metro (W Yorks PTA)). *Address:* (office) 427 Otley Road, Leeds LS16 6AJ; House of Commons, SW1A 0AA.

MULKEARNS, Most Rev. Ronald Austin, DD, DCL; Former Bishop of Ballarat (RC); *b* 11 Nov. 1930. *Educ:* De La Salle Coll., Malvern; Corpus Christi Coll., Werribee; Pontifical Lateran Univ., Rome. Ordained, 1956; Coadjutor Bishop, 1968–71; Bishop of Ballarat, 1971–97. *Address:* PO Box 411, Aireys Inlet, Vic 3231, Australia.

MULKERN, John, CBE 1987; JP; international airport and aviation consultant, since 1987; *b* 15 Jan. 1931; *s* of late Thomas Mulkern and Annie Tennant; *m* 1954, May Egerton (*née* Peters); one *s* three *d*. *Educ:* Stretford Grammar Sch.; Dip. Govt Admin of Local Govt Exam. Bd, London; Harvard Business Sch. (AMP 1977). Ministries of Supply and Aviation, Civil Service, 1949–65: Exec. Officer, finally Principal, Audit, Purchasing, Finance, Personnel and Legislation branches; British Airports Authority, 1965–87: Dep. Gen. Man., Heathrow Airport, 1970–73; Dir, Gatwick Airport, 1973–77; Man. Dir and Mem. of Bd, 1977–87. Chairman: British Airports International Ltd, 1978–82; Manchester Handling Ltd, 1988–94; Granik Ltd, 1990–91 (Pres., 1992–94); Director: London Luton Airport Ltd, 1991–2000; Reliance Aviation Security Ltd, 1992–94. President: Western European Airports' Assoc., 1981–83; Internat. Civil Airports Assoc. (Europe), 1986; Chm., Co-ordinating Council, Airports Assocs, 1982; Mem. Bd, Airport Operators Council Internat., 1978–81. Mem., Surrey Probation Cttee, 1996–2001. Trustee: Surrey Springboard, 1997–2001; BAA Pension Trust Co. Ltd, 1997–2000. Mem., Middlesex and Surrey Soc., 1995–. FCILT 1973 (Mem. Council, 1979–82); CCMI (CBIM 1981); FInstD 1982. JP Surrey, 1988. *Recreations:* family pursuits, opera, classical recorded music.

MULL, Very Rev. Gerald S.; *see* Stranraer-Mull.

MULLALLY, Rev. Dame Sarah Elisabeth, DBE 2005; Team Rector, Sutton, Surrey, since 2006; *b* 26 March 1962; *d* of Michael Frederick Mills Bowser and Ann Dorothy Bowser; *m* 1987, Eamonn James Mullally; one *s* one *d*. *Educ:* Nightingale Sch. of Nursing; S Bank Poly. (BSc Hons Nursing and RGN 1984); MSc Interprofessional Health and Welfare, S Bank Univ., 1992; DipTh Kent 2001; MA Pastoral Theol., Heythrop Coll., London Univ., 2006. Staff Nurse: St Thomas' Hosp., 1984–86; Royal Marsden Hosp., 1986–88; Ward Sister, Westminster Hosp., 1988–90; Sen. Nurse, Riverside HA, 1990–92; Asst Chief Nurse, Riverside Hosps, 1992–94; Dir of Nursing and Dep. Chief Exec., Chelsea and Westminster Healthcare Trust, 1994–99; Chief Nursing Officer, DoH, 1999–2004. Ordained deacon, 2001; NSM, Battersea Fields, 2001–04; Asst Curate, St George, St Saviour and All Saints, Battersea Fields, 2004–06. Non-exec. Dir, Royal Marsden NHS Foundn Trust, 2005–. Indep. Gov., S Bank Univ., 2005–. Hon. Fellow: S Bank Univ., 2000; Christ Church, Canterbury, 2006. Hon. Dr Health Sci.: Bournemouth, 2001; Wolverhampton, 2004; Hon. DSc Herts, 2005.

MULLALY, Terence Frederick Stanley; art historian and critic; *b* 14 Nov. 1927; *s* of late Col B. R. Mullaly (4th *s* of Maj.-Gen. Sir Herbert Mullaly, KCMG, CB, CSI) and Eileen Dorothy (*née* Stanley); *m* 1949, Elizabeth Helen (*née* Burkitt). *Educ:* in India, England, Japan and Canada; Downing Coll., Cambridge (MA). FSA 1977; FRNS 1981 (Mem. Council, 1993–95); FSAScot 1995. Archæological studies in Tripolitania, 1948, and Sicily, 1949; has specialised in study of Italian art, particularly Venetian and Veronese painting of 16th and 17th centuries; lecturer and broadcaster; Art Critic, Daily Telegraph, 1958–86. Vis. Prof., Finch Coll., NY, 1967–72. President: Brit. Section, Internat. Assoc. of Art Critics, 1967–73; British Art Medal Soc., 1986–98 (Vice Chm., 1982–86; Vice-Pres., 1998–); Member: Adv. Cttee, Cracow Art Festival, 1974, Palermo Art Festival, 1976; UK Delgn, Budapest Cultural Forum, 1985; Cttee, FIDEM Congress, 1992; Council: Attingham Summer Sch. Trust, 1984–90; Derby Porcelain Internat. Soc., 1985–; Friends, Univ. of Cyprus, 1995– (Vice Chm., 1998–); Artistic Adviser, Grand Tours, 1974–90; Director: Grand Tours, 1980–90; Specialtours, 1986. Editor, Jl of British-Italian Soc., 1995–. FRSA 1969. Commendatore, Ordine Al Merito, Italy, 1974 (Cavaliere Ufficiale, 1964); l'Ordre du Mérite Culturel, Poland, 1974; Order of Merit of Poland (Silver Medal), 1978; Bulgarian 1300th Anniversary Medal, 1981; Sacro Militare Ordine Costantiniano di S Giorgio (Silver Medal), 1982; Premio Pietro Torta per il restauro di Venezia, 1983; Socio Straniero, Ateneo Veneto, 1986. *Publications:* Ruskin a Verona, 1966; catalogue of exhibition, Disegni veronesi del Cinquecento, 1971; contrib. to catalogue of exhibition Cinquant' anni di pittura veronese: 1580–1630, 1974; ed and contrib. to catalogue of exhibition, Modern Hungarian Medal, 1984; contrib. to Affreschi del Rinascimento a Verona: interventi di restauro, 1987; Caterina Cornaro, Queen of Cyprus, 1989; catalogue of exhibn, Zofia Demkowska, 1997; (jtly) Cyprus: the legacy, 1999; contribs to DNB and on history of art, to Burlington Magazine, Master Drawings, Arte Illustrata, Arte Documento, Antologia di Belle Arti, The Minneapolis Inst. of Arts Bulletin, Bull. Univ. of New Mexico Art Mus., British Numismatic Jl, Numismatic Chronicle, Jl of British Art Medal Soc., Apollo, etc. *Recreations:* numismatics, Eastern Europe. *Address:* Waterside House, Pulborough, Sussex RH20 2BH. *T:* (01798) 872104.

MULLARD, Prof. Christopher Paul, CBE 2005; PhD; DL; Chairman and Chief Executive Officer, Focus Consultancy Ltd, since 1994; *b* 23 Nov. 1944; *m* 1989, Mike-Madelaine Elmont; one *s* two *d*. *Educ:* Park House Secondary Modern Sch., Newbury; Westminster City Coll., London; Univ. of Durham (MA 1975; PhD 1980). Northern Sec., CARD, 1964–68; Principal Community Relns Officer, Tyne and Wear, 1968–73; researcher and pt-time Lectr in Sociol., Univ. of Durham, 1973–76; Sen. Lectr in Sociol., King Alfred's Coll., Winchester, 1976–77; Lectr, Dept of Sociol. of Educn, Univ. of London Inst. of Educn, 1977–80; Dir, Race Relns Policy and Practice Res. Units, Univ. of London Inst. of Educn and LSE, 1980–86; University of Amsterdam: Royal Prof. in Ethnic Studies and Educn, and Dir, Centre for Race and Ethnic Studies, 1984–91; Advr to Senate, 1991–94. Vis. Prof., Royal Agriculture Coll., Cirencester, 2007–. Foundn Dir, Focus Inst. on Rights and Social Transformation, 2004–. Chairman: Bernie Grant Trust, 2000–; London Notting Hill Carnival Ltd, 2002–; Mem., Dep. Prime Minister's Bicentenary Adv. Gp on Commemorating the Abolition of the Slave Trade, 2006–; Patron: Caribbean Women Equality and Diversity Forum, 2001–; Caribbean Develt Trust (UK), 2005–. Hon. Consul for South Africa, 2006–. FRSA 2005; MInstD 1998. DL Wilts, 2007. *Publications:* Black Britain, 1973; Aborigines in Australia Today, 1974; Race, Power and Resistance, 1985; De Plurale Kubus, 1990; Antirassistiche Erziehung, 1991. *Recreations:* gardening, theatre, golf, travel. *Address:* Focus Consultancy, Elmsgate House, Steeple Ashton, Trowbridge, Wilts BA14 6HP. *Clubs:* Reform, Commonwealth, Royal Commonwealth Society.

MULLARKEY, Thomas, MBE 1996; Chief Executive, Royal Society for the Prevention of Accidents, since 2006; *b* 1 April 1957; *s* of James and Delia Mullarkey; *m* 1982, Sue Hamilton; two *s*. *Educ:* Maidstone Grammar Sch.; Univ. of Lancaster (BA Orgn Studies 1978); Indian Defence Services Staff Coll. (MSc Defence Studies 1992). Army officer, RA, 1975–95, service in UK, Germany, NI, Canada, India and Rwanda (co-ordinated UN restoration plan); Gen. Manager Projs, SBC Warburg, 1995–96; Gen. Manager, then Dir, Special Projs, XVII Commonwealth Games, Manchester, 1996–2001; Chief Exec., Nat. Security Inspectorate, 2002–06. Non-exec. Dir, Housing Solutions Gp (Maidenhead), 2005–. Hon. Vis. Fellow, Manchester Business Sch., 2005. *Publication:* A Thousand Hills: a story of crisis in Rwanda, 2001. *Recreations:* sailing, the hills, Daimlers, writing, holding forth. *Address:* Royal Society for the Prevention of Accidents, Edgbaston Park, Birmingham B5 7ST. *T:* (0121) 248 2000. *Clubs:* Royal Commonwealth Society, Special Forces.

MULLENS, Lt-Gen. Sir Anthony (Richard Guy), KCB 1989; OBE 1979 (MBE 1973); Associate, Varley Walker & Partners, since 1992; *b* 10 May 1936; *s* of late Brig. Guy John de Wette Mullens, OBE, and Gwendoline Joan Maclean; *m* 1964, Dawn Elizabeth Hermione Pease. *Educ:* Eton; RMA Sandhurst. Commnd 4th/7th Royal Dragoon Guards, 1956; regtl service, BAOR, 1956–58; ADC to Comdr 1st British Corps, 1958–60; Adjt 1962–65; sc 1967, psc; MA to VCGS, MoD, 1968–70; regtl service, 1970–72; Bde Major, 1972–73; Directing Staff, Staff Coll., 1973–76; CO 4/7 DG, BAOR, 1976–78; HQ BAOR, 1978–80; Comdr 7th Armd Bde, 1980–82; MoD (DMS(A)), 1982–85; Comdr 1st Armoured Div., 1985–87; ACDS (Operational Requirements), Land Systems, MoD, 1987–89; DCDS (Systems), MoD, 1989–92, retd. Consultant, BR, 1992–95. Col, Royal Dragoon Guards, 1994–99; Hon. Col, Eton Coll. CCF, 2001–07. Trustee, Army Museums Ogilby Trust, 1997–2007; President: 7th Armoured Div. Thetford Forest Meml Assoc., 1999–; 7th Armoured Div. Officers Club, 2000–05. Liveryman: Armourers' and Braziers' Co., 1974 (Mem., Ct of Assts, 1993–97; Renter Warden, 1996–97); Coachmakers' and Coachharness Makers' Co., 1976. Member: Alpheton Parish Council, 2000–03; Alpheton PCC, 1989–2006; Church Warden, St Peter and St Paul, Alpheton, 1997–2003. MInstD 1992–2002. Niedersachsen Verdienstkreuz am Bande, 1982, Erste Klasse, 1987. *Recreations:* travel, shooting. *Address:* 138 Cranmer Court, Sloane Avenue, SW3 3HE. *Club:* Cavalry and Guards.

MÜLLER, Alex; *see* Müller, K. A.

MULLER, Billie, (Mrs Robert Muller); *see* Whitelaw, Billie.

MULLER, Franz Joseph; QC 1978; a Recorder of the Crown Court, since 1977; *b* England, 19 Nov. 1938; *yr s* of late Wilhelm Muller and Anne Maria (*née* Ravens); *m* 1985, Helena, *y d* of Mieczyslaw Bartosz; two *s*. *Educ:* Mount St Mary's Coll.; Univ. of Sheffield (LLB). Called to the Bar, Gray's Inn, 1961, Bencher, 1994; called to NI Bar, 1982. Graduate Apprentice, United Steel Cos, 1960–61; Commercial Asst, Workington Iron and Steel Co. Ltd, 1961–63. Commenced practice at the Bar, 1964. Non-Executive Director: Richards of Sheffield (Holdings) PLC, 1969–77; Satinsteel Ltd, 1970–77; Joseph Rodgers and Son Ltd and Rodgers Wostenholm Ltd, 1975–77. Mem., Sen. Common Room, UC Durham, 1981. *Recreations:* the Georgians, fell walking, being in Greece, listening to music. *Address:* Slade Hooton Hall, Laughton en le Morthen, Yorks S25 1YQ; KBW, 3 Park Court, off Park Cross Street, Leeds LS1 2QH. *T:* (0113) 297 1200.

MÜLLER, Prof. (Karl) Alex, PhD; physicist at IBM Zurich Research Laboratory, since 1963; *b* 20 April 1927. *Educ:* Swiss Federal Institute of Technology, Zürich (PhD 1958). FInstP 1998. Battelle Inst., Geneva, 1958–63; Lectr, 1962, Titular Prof., 1970, Prof., 1987–, Univ. of Zürich; joined IBM Res. Lab., Zurich, 1963; Manager, Physics Dept, 1973; IBM Fellow, 1982–85; researcher, 1985–. Hon. degrees from twenty European and American univs. Prizes and awards include Nobel Prize for Physics (jtly), 1987. *Publications:* over 500 papers on ferroelectric and superconducting materials. *Address:* Physik-Institut, Universität Zürich-Irchel, Winterthurerstrasse 190, 8057 Zürich, Switzerland.

MULLIGAN, Christopher James; Director General, Passenger Transport Executive, Greater Manchester, 1991–2007; *b* 24 Feb. 1950; *s* of James Frederick Mulligan and Dorothy Mulligan (*née* Kneill); *m* 1989, Rowena May Burns. *Educ:* Hull Univ. (BA Hons 1971). Mem., CIPFA. Manchester CC, 1971–73; Gtr Manchester CC, 1973–77; Greater Manchester Passenger Transport Executive, 1977–2007: Dir of Finance, 1987–91. *Recreations:* reading, walking, good food. *Address:* 2 Piccadilly Place, Manchester M1 3BG.

MULLIGAN, (Margaret) Mary; Member (Lab) Linlithgow, Scottish Parliament, since 1999; *b* Liverpool, 12 Feb. 1960; *m* 1982, John Mulligan; two *s* one *d*. *Educ:* Notre Dame High Sch., Liverpool; Manchester Univ. (BA Hons Econs and Social Studies 1981). Retail and personnel mgt, 1981–86. Member (Lab): Edinburgh DC, 1988–95 (Chm., Housing Cttee, 1992–97; City of Edinburgh Council, 1995–99. Scottish Executive: PPS to First Minister, 2000–01; Dep. Minister for Health and Community Care, 2001–03, for Communities, 2003–04. Chm., Educn, Sports and Culture Cttee, Scottish Parlt, 1999–2000. *Recreations:* music, theatre, watching sports. *Address:* Scottish Parliament, Edinburgh EH99 1SP; (constituency office) 62 Hopetoun Street, Bathgate, West Lothian EH48 4PD.

MULLIGAN, Prof. William, FRSE; Professor of Veterinary Physiology, 1963–86, and Vice-Principal, 1980–83, University of Glasgow, now Professor Emeritus; *b* 18 Nov. 1921; *s* of John Mulligan and Mary Mulligan (*née* Kelly); *m* 1948, Norah Mary Cooper one *s* one *d* (and one *d* decd). *Educ:* Banbridge Academy; Queen's Univ. of Belfast (BSc); PhD London. FIBiol 1988. Assistant, Dept of Chemistry, QUB, 1943–45; Demonstrator/Lectr, St Bartholomew's Med. Coll., London, 1945–51; Sen. Lectr, Veterinary Biochemistry, Univ. of Glasgow, 1951–63; McMaster Fellow, McMaster Animal Health Laboratory, Sydney, Aust., 1958–60; Dean of Faculty of Veterinary Medicine, Univ. of Glasgow, 1977–80. Dr med. vet. *hc* Copenhagen, 1983. *Publications:* (jtly) Isotopic Tracers, 1954, 2nd edn 1959; numerous contribs to scientific jls on immunology and use of radiation and radioisotopes in animal science. *Recreations:* golf, tennis, gardening, pigeon racing, theatre. *Address:* 25 Woodland Way, Wivenhoe, Colchester, Essex CO7 9AT.
See also J. S. Pitt-Brooke.

MULLIN, Christopher John, (Chris); MP (Lab) Sunderland South, since 1987; *b* 12 Dec. 1947; *s* of Leslie and Teresa Mullin; *m* 1987, Nguyen Thi Ngoc, *d* of Nguyen Tang Minh, Kontum, Vietnam; two *d*. *Educ:* Univ. of Hull (LLB). Freelance journalist, travelled extensively in Indo-China and China; sub editor, BBC World Service, 1974–78; Editor, Tribune, 1982–84. Executive Member: Campaign for Labour Party Democracy, 1975–83; Labour Co-ordinating Cttee, 1978–82. Contested (Lab): Devon N, 1970; Kingston upon Thames, Feb. 1974. Parliamentary Under-Secretary of State: DETR, 1999–2001; DFID, 2001; FCO, 2003–05. Chm., Home Affairs Select Cttee, 1997–99, 2001–03; Mem., Standards and Privileges Cttee, 2007–. Chm., All Party Vietnam Gp, 1988–99; Sec., British Cambodia All Party Gp, 1992–99; Hon. Sec., British Tibet All Party Gp; Chm., PLP Civil Liberties Gp, 1992–97. Mem. Council, Royal African Soc., 2006–; Trustee, Prison Reform Trust, 2006–. Hon. LLD City, 1992. Editor: Arguments for Socialism, by Tony Benn, 1979; Arguments for Democracy, by Tony Benn, 1981. *Publications: novels:* A Very British Coup, 1982 (televised 1988); The Last Man Out of Saigon, 1986; The Year of the Fire Monkey, 1991; *non-fiction:* Error of Judgement—the truth about the Birmingham bombings, 1986, rev. edn 1997; pamphlets: How to Select or Reselect your MP, 1981; The Tibetans, 1981. *Address:* House of Commons, SW1A 0AA.

MULLIN, John; Editor, Independent on Sunday, since 2008; *b* Bellshill, 22 March 1963; *s* of John and Helen Mullin; *m* 1995, Maggie O'Kane; one *s* two *d*. *Educ:* Seafar Primary Sch., Cumbernauld; Hutchesons' Grammar Sch.; Glasgow Univ. (MA Politics and Econs 1984); City Univ., London (Dip. Newspaper Journalism 1985). The Guardian: reporter, 1990–96; Night Ed., 1996–97; Ireland corresp., 1997–2000; Dep. Ed., The Scotsman, 2000–03; Exec. Ed., The Independent, 2003–07; Dep. Ed., Independent on Sunday, 2007–08. *Recreation:* praying for a Scottish miracle. *Address:* The Independent, Independent House, 191 Marsh Wall, E14 9RS. *T:* (020) 7005 2000.

MULLIN, Rt Rev. Mgr (John Raymond) Noel, VG 1993; Chaplain, Plater College, 1998–2005; *b* 21 Dec. 1947; *s* of James Joseph Mullin and Mary Gertrude Mullin (*née* McLaughlin). *Educ:* Underley Hall Sch., Kirkby Lonsdale; Upholland Coll., Lancs; Univ. of London (MA); RM Commando Course, 1979. Ordained priest, 1972; joined RN as Chaplain, 1978; Prin. RC Chaplain (Naval) and Dir, Naval Chaplaincy Services (Trng and Progs), MoD, 1993–98; served at home and abroad, afloat and ashore, at peace and in conflict. QHC, 1996–98. *Recreations:* Rugby, cricket, fell walking, performing arts, food.

MULLIN, Prof. John William, DSc, PhD; FREng, FRSC, FIChemE; Ramsay Memorial Professor of Chemical Engineering, University College London, 1985–90, now Emeritus Professor; Hon. Research Fellow, University College London, since 1990; *b* Rock Ferry, Cheshire, 22 Aug. 1925; *er s* of late Frederick Mullin and Kathleen Nellie Mullin (*née* Oppy); *m* 1952, Averil Margaret Davies, Carmarthen; one *s* one *d*. *Educ:* Hawarden County Sch.; UCW Cardiff (Fellow, 1981); University Coll. London (Fellow, 1981). Served RAF, 1945–48. 8 yrs in organic fine chemicals industry; University College London: Lectr, 1956; Reader, 1961; Prof., 1969; Dean, Faculty of Engrg, 1975–77; Vice-Provost, 1980–86; Crabtree Orator, 1993; Dean, Faculty of Engrg, London Univ., 1979–85. Vis. Prof., Univ. New Brunswick, 1967. Chm. Bd of Staff Examrs, Chem. Engrg, Univ. London, 1965–70. Hon. Librarian, IChemE, 1965–77 (Mem. Council, 1973–76); Mem., Materials Sci. Working Gp, European Space Agency, 1977–81; Founder Mem., Brit. Assoc. for Crystal Growth; Chairman: Process Engrg Gp, SCI, 1996–99; BS and ISO cttees on industrial screens, sieves, particle sizing, etc. Mem., Parly Gp for Engrg Devel, 1994–2004. Member: Cttee of Management, Inst. of Child Health, 1970–83; Court of Governors, University Coll., Cardiff, 1982–99; Council, Sch. of Pharmacy, Univ. of London, 1983–2000 (Vice-Chm., 1988–2000; Hon. Fellow, 1998). Liveryman, Engineers' Co., 1984–. Moulton Medal, IChemE, 1970; Kurnakov Meml Medal, Inst. of Gen. and Inorganic Chem., USSR Acad. of Scis, 1991. Dr *hc* Inst Nat. Polytechnique de Toulouse, 1989. *Publications:* Crystallization, 1961, 4th edn 2001; (ed) Industrial Crystallization, 1976; papers in Trans IChemE, Chem. Engrg Sci., Jl Crystal Growth, etc. *Address:* 12 Church Place, Ickenham, Middx UB10 8XB. *T:* (01895) 634950. *Club:* Athenæum.

MULLIN, Rt Rev. Mgr Noel; *see* Mullin, Rt Rev. Mgr J. R. N.

MULLINS, Rt Rev. Daniel Joseph; Bishop of Menevia, (RC), 1987–2001, now Emeritus; *b* 10 July 1929; *s* of Timothy Mullins. *Educ:* Mount Melleray; St Mary's, Aberystwyth; Oscott Coll.; UC of S Wales and Mon, Cardiff (Fellow, University Coll., Cardiff). Priest, 1953; Curate at: Barry, 1953–56; Newbridge, 1956; Bargoed, 1956–57; Maesteg, 1957–60; Asst Chaplain to UC Cardiff, 1960–64; Sec. to Archbp of Cardiff, 1964–68; Vicar General of Archdiocese of Cardiff, 1968; Titular Bishop of Stowe and Auxiliary Bishop in Swansea, 1970–87. Pres., Catholic Record Soc. Hon. Fellow, St David's University Coll., Lampeter, 1987. *Recreations:* golf, walking. *Address:* 8 Rhodfa Gwendraeth, Kidwelly, Carms SA17 4SR.

MULLINS, Edwin Brandt; author, journalist and film-maker; *b* 14 Sept. 1933; *s* of late Claud Mullins and Gwendolen Mullins, OBE; *m* 1st, 1960, Gillian Brydone (*d* 1982); one *s* two *d*; 2nd, 1984, Anne Kelleher. *Educ:* Midhurst Grammar Sch.; Merton Coll., Oxford (BA Hons, MA). London Editor, Two Cities, 1957–58; Sub-editor and Art Correspondent, Illustrated London News, 1958–62; Art Critic: Sunday Telegraph, 1962–69; Telegraph Sunday Magazine, 1964–86; contributor, 1962–, to The Guardian, Financial Times, Sunday Times, Director, Apollo, Art and Artists, Studio, Radio Times, TV Times, Country Living. Scriptwriter and presenter of numerous TV documentaries for BBC, Channel 4 and RM Arts, Munich, incl. 100 Great Paintings, The Pilgrimage of Everyman, Gustave Courbet, Fake?, Prison, The Great Art Collection, A Love Affair with Nature, Masterworks, Paradise on Earth, Montparnasse Revisited, Dürer, Out of the Dark Ages—a tale of four Emperors, Georges de la Tour—Genius Lost and Found. *Publications:* Souza, 1962; Wallis, 1967; Josef Herman, 1967; Braque, 1968; The Art of Elisabeth Frink, 1972; The Pilgrimage to Santiago, 1974, repr. 2001; (ed) Great Paintings, 1981; (ed) The Arts of Britain, 1983; The Painted Witch, 1985; A Love Affair with Nature, 1985; The Royal Collection, 1992; Alfred Wallis: Cornish Primitive, 1994; In Search of Cluny—God's Lost Empire, 2006; Avignon of the Popes: city of exiles, 2007; *novels:* Angels on the Point of a Pin, 1979; Sirens, 1983; The Golden Bird, 1987; The Lands of the Sea, 1988; Dear Venus, 1992; With Much Love, 1993; All My Worldly Goods, 1994; The Outfit, 1995; The Devil's Work, 1996. *Recreations:* everything except football. *Address:* 25 The Crescent, Barnes, SW13 0NN.

MULLIS, Dr Kary Banks; American biochemist; Founder and Chief Executive Officer, Altermune LLC; *b* 28 Dec. 1944; *s* of Cecil Banks Mullis and Bernice Alberta Fredericks (*née* Barker); *m* 1963, Richards Train Haley (marr. diss.); one *d*; *m* 1975, Cynthia Gibson (marr. diss.); two *s*; *m* 1998, Nancy Cosgrove. *Educ:* Georgia Inst. of Technol. (BS Chemistry 1966); Univ. of Calif, Berkeley (PhD Biochemistry 1973). Lectr in Biochemistry, Univ. of Calif, Berkeley, 1972; Postdoctoral Fellow: Kansas Med. Sch., 1973–76; Univ. of Calif, San Francisco, 1977–79; Scientist, Cetus Corp., Calif, 1979–86; Dir of Molecular Biology, Xytronyx, Inc., San Diego, 1986–88; Consultant, Specialty Labs Inc., and Amersham Inc., 1988–. Member: American Chemistry Soc.; Inst. of Further Study (Dir, 1983–). Preis Biochemische Analytik, German Soc. Clin. Chemistry, 1990; Allan Award, American Soc. of Human Genetics, 1990; Nat. Biotechnology Award, 1991; Robert Koch Award, 1992; Japan Prize, Japanese Inst. for Sci. and Technology, 1993; (jtly) Nobel Prize for Chemistry, 1993. *Publications:* Dancing Naked in the Mind Field, 1999; articles in prof. jls. *Address:* Apartment 5, 6767 Neptune Place, La Jolla, CA 92031–5924, USA.

MULLIS, Marjorie; *see* Allthorpe-Guyton, M.

MULLOVA, Viktoria; violinist; *b* 27 Nov. 1959; *d* of Juri Mullov and Raisa Mullova; one *s* two *d*. *Educ:* Central Music Sch., Moscow; Moscow Conservatory. First prize, Sibelius Competition, Helsinki, 1980; Gold Medal, Tchaikovsky Competition, Moscow, 1982; left USSR, 1983. Has performed with most major orchestras; many festival appearances. Recordings include: violin concertos: Bach, Brahms, Tchaikovsky, Sibelius, Mendelssohn, Stravinsky, Bartok No 2, Shostakovich No 1, Prokoviev No 2, Paganini No 1; Bach partitas; sonatas for violin and piano: Bach, Janacek, Prokofiev, Debussy, Brahms; Vivaldi, Four Seasons; Through the Looking Glass (arrangements of works by Miles Davis, Weather Report and Youssou N'Dour). *Address:* c/o Askonas Holt, Lincoln House, 300 High Holborn, WC1V 7JH.

MULREADY, Rt Rev. David Gray; *see* Australia, North West, Bishop of.

MULRONEY, Rt Hon. (Martin) Brian; PC 1984; CC 1998; Senior Partner, Ogilvy, Renault, since 1993; *b* 20 March 1939; *s* of Benedict Mulroney and Irene O'Shea; *m* 1973, Mila Pivnicki; three *s* one *d*. *Educ:* St Francis Xavier Univ. (BA); Université Laval (LLL). Partner, Ogilvy, Renault (Montreal law firm), 1965–76; Pres., Iron Ore Co. of Canada, 1976–83. MP (Progressive Conservative): Central Nova, 1983–84; Manicouagan, 1984–88; Charlevoix, 1988–93. Leader of the Opposition, 1983–84; Prime Minister of Canada, 1984–93. Royal Comr, Cliche Commn investigating violence in Quebec construction industry, 1974. Director: Barrick Gold Corp.; Trizec Properties Inc. (formerly TrizecHahn Corp.); Archer Daniels Midland Co.; Cendant Corp.; Quebecor Inc.; Quebecor World Inc. Member, International Advisory Council: China Internat. Trust and Investment Corp.; J P Morgan Chase & Co.; Independent News and Media plc. Trustee, Montreal Heart Inst. Hon. LLD: St Francis Xavier Univ., 1979; Meml Univ., 1980. *Publication:* Where I Stand, 1983. *Recreations:* tennis, swimming.

MULRYNE, Prof. (James) Ronald, PhD; Professor of English, University of Warwick, 1977–2004, now Emeritus; *b* 24 May 1937; *s* of Thomas Wilfred Mulryne and Mary Mulryne; *m* 1964, Eithne Wallace; one *s* one *d*. *Educ:* St Catharine's Coll., Cambridge (BA 1958; MA 1960; PhD 1962). Fellow, Shakespeare Inst., Univ. of Birmingham, 1960–62; University of Edinburgh: Lectr, 1962–72; Reader in English Lit., 1972–77; Hd, Dept of English Lit., 1976–77; University of Warwick: Pro-Vice-Chancellor, 1982–87; Director: Centre for Study of Renaissance, 1993–2003; AHRB Centre for Study of Renaissance Elites and Court Cultures, 2000–03. Vis. Associate Prof., Univ. of Calif, San Diego, 1970–71; Sen. Vis. Res. Fellow, Jesus Coll., Oxford, 1987; Vis. Fellow, Magdalen Coll., Oxford, 1991. General Editor: Revels Plays, 1979–; Shakespeare's Plays in Performance, 1984–2004. Dir, Digitisation of Festival Books in the Collections of the British Library (on-line pubn), 2005. Founder Dir, Mulryne & Shewring Ltd, Publishers, 1989–. Chm., Drama and Theatre Bd, CNAA, 1972–78; Member: Council of Mgt, UCCA, 1984–87; Drama Panel and Chm., Drama Projects Cttee, Arts Council of GB, 1987–91; Drama and Dance Adv. Cttee, British Council, 1991–97 (Chm., 1993–97); Arts and Humanities Research Council (formerly Board): Convener, English Lang. and Lit. Panel, 2000–04; Mem., Res. Cttee, 2000–04; Mem. Bd of Mgt, 2002–04. Mem. Bd of Dirs, Birmingham Rep. Theatre, 1987–95; Governor, RSC, 1998–2003, 2004–. Trustee, Shakespeare's Birthplace Trust, 1985–2004. Gov., 1987–, Trustee, 1998–, King Edward VI Sch., Stratford-upon-Avon (Dep. Chm., 1998–99, Chm., 1999–, of Govs). Chm. Community Forum, World Class Stratford proj., 2007–. FEA 2002. Chevalier, Ordre des Palmes Académiques (France), 1992. *Publications include:* edited: Thomas Middleton, Women Beware Women, 1975; John Webster, The White Devil, 1970; Thomas Kyd, The Spanish Tragedy, 1970, 2nd edn 1989; edited with Margaret Shewring: Theatre of the English and Italian Renaissance, 1991; Italian Renaissance Festivals and their European Influence, 1992; Theatre and Government Under the Early Stuarts, 1993; Making Space for Theatre, 1995; Shakespeare and the Japanese Stage, 1998; The Cottesloe at the National, 1999; (ed with Elizabeth Goldring) Court Festivals of the European Renaissance, 2002; (ed with Takashi Kozuka) Shakespeare, Marlowe, Jonson: new directions in biography, 2006; (Gen. Ed.) Europa Triumphans: festivals of the European Renaissance, 2004; numerous books and articles, mainly on Shakespeare, Elizabethan Drama and W. B. Yeats. *Recreation:* theatre. *Address:* 3 Benson Road, Stratford-upon-Avon CV37 6UU. *T:* (01789) 205774.

MULVANEY, Prof. Derek John, AO 1991; CMG 1982; Professor of Prehistory, Australian National University, 1971–85, now Emeritus; *b* 26 Oct. 1925; *s* of Richard and Frances Mulvaney; *m* 1954, Jean Campbell (*d* 2004); four *s* two *d*. *Educ:* Univ. of Melbourne (MA); Clare Coll., Univ. of Cambridge (BA, MA 1959, PhD 1970). FAHA 1970; FSA 1977; Corresp. FBA 1983; FRAI 1996. Navigator, RAAF, 1943–46 (Flying Officer); Lectr and Senior Lectr in History, Univ. of Melbourne, 1954–64; Senior Fellow, ANU, 1965–70; Vis. Prof., Cambridge, 1976–77; Chair of Australian Studies, Harvard, 1984–85; Mem. Council, Aust. Inst. of Aboriginal Studies, 1964–80 (Chm., 1982–84); Australian Heritage Commissioner, 1976–82; Mem., Cttee of Inquiry, Museums and National Collections, 1974–75; Sec., Australian Acad. of Humanities, 1989–96. Hon. DLitt Melbourne, 2005. ANZAAS medal, 1988; Grahame Clark Medal, British Acad., 1999. *Publications:* Cricket Walkabout, 1967, 2nd edn 1988; The Prehistory of Australia, 1969, 2nd edn 1975; Australians to 1788, 1987; Encounters in Place, 1989; Commandant of Solitude, 1992; (ed jtly) My Dear Spencer: the letters of F. J. Gillen to Baldwin Spencer, 1997; (with J. Kamminga) Prehistory of Australia, 1999; Paddy Cahill of Oenpelli, 2004; numerous excavation reports and historical articles. *Recreation:* gardening. *Address:* 128 Schlich Street, Yarralumla, ACT 2600, Australia. *T:* (2) 62812352.

MULVEY, Prof. Laura Mary Alice, FBA 2000; Professor of Film and Media Studies, Birkbeck College, University of London, since 1999; *b* 15 Aug. 1941. *Educ:* St Paul's Girls' Sch.; St Hilda's Coll., Oxford (BA). Teacher of film studies and film practice; responsible for Birkbeck Coll. MA in Film and TV History and Theory. Co-director: six films with Peter Wollen; (with Mark Lewis) Disgraced Monuments, 1994. *Publications:* Visual and Other Pleasures, 1989; Citizen Kane, 1993; Fetishism and Curiosity, 1996; Death Twenty-four Times a Second: stillness and the moving image, 2006; articles and chapters in books. *Address:* School of History of Art, Film and Visual Media, Birkbeck College, 43 Gordon Square, WC1H 0PD.

MULVILLE, James Thomas; Managing Director, Hat Trick Productions, since 1985; *b* 5 Jan. 1955; *s* of James Lawrence Mulville and June Mulville; *m* 1st, 1974, Julia Kelly; 2nd, 1987, Denise O'Donoghue, *qv* (marr. diss. 1998); 3rd, 1999, Karen Page; three *s* one *d*. *Educ:* Alsop Comprehensive Sch., Liverpool; Jesus Coll., Cambridge (BA Hons; Pres., Cambridge Footlights, 1976–77). With BBC Light Entertainment as writer and producer, 1978–82; Jt Founder, Hat Trick Prodns, 1985; co-writer and performer: Who Dares Wins (series), Channel 4, 1983–88; Chelmsford 123, Channel 4, 1987–90; actor: That's Love, 1987–91; GBH, 1991. FRTS 2001. Hon. DLit Liverpool. *Publication:* (jtly) Who Dares Wins, 1986. *Recreations:* my children, family, friends, films, Everton Football Club. *Address:* c/o Hat Trick Productions, 10 Livonia Street, W1F 8AF. *T:* (020) 7434 2451. *Club:* Royal Automobile.

MUMBENGEGWI, Hon. Simbarashe Simbanenduku; MP, Republic of Zimbabwe, since 2005; Minister of Foreign Affairs, since 2005; *b* Chivi, Zimbabwe, 20 July 1945; *s* of late Chivandire Davis Mumbengegwi and Dzivaidzo Shuvai Mumbengegwi; *m* 1983, Emily; one *s* four *d*. *Educ:* Fletcher High Sch., Gweru, Zimbabwe; Monash Univ., Melbourne (BA Gen., BA Combined Hons, DipEd, MEd). Teacher, Dadaya Secondary Sch., Zvishavane, and schools in Melbourne, then Tutor in Politics at colls in Melbourne, 1966–78; MP: Midlands Province, 1980–85; Shurugwi Constituency, Midlands Province, 1985–90; Dep. Speaker and Chm. of Cttees, House of Assembly, Parlt of Zimbabwe, 1980–81; Dep. Minister of Foreign Affairs, 1981–82; Minister: of Water Resources and Devel, 1982; of Nat. Housing, 1982–84; of Public Construction and Nat. Housing, 1984–88; of Transport, 1988–90; Ambassador and Perm. Rep. of Zimbabwe to UN, NY, 1990–95; Vice-Pres., UN Gen. Assembly, 1990–91; Mem., UN Security Council, 1991–92 (Pres. at height of Gulf War, 1991, and 1992); Ambassador to Belgium,

Netherlands, Luxembourg and Perm. Rep. to EU, Brussels, 1995–99; Perm. Rep. to Orgn for Prohibition of Chem. Weapons, The Hague, 1997–99 (Mem. Council, 1997–99); High Comr, later Ambassador, to UK, and Ambassador to Ireland, 1999–2005. Participated in numerous ministerial confs and Heads of State summits of OAU, 1981–94; Hd of delegns to all annual confs of UN Commn for Human Settlements, 1983–88; served on numerous UN and ACP cttees. Mem., Youth Leagues of Nat. Democratic Party, ZAPU and ZANU, 1960–64; ZANU activist in exile, 1966–72; Zimbabwe African National Union: Dep. Chief Rep., 1973–76, Chief Rep., 1976–78, Australia and Far East; Chief Rep. to Zambia, 1978–80; ZANU-Patriotic Front: Provincial Treas., Midlands Province, 1981–84; Mem., Central Cttee, 1984–94, 2006– (Dep. Sec. for Publicity and Inf., 1984–89). *Recreations:* reading, photography, jogging, tennis, golf, swimming. *Address:* Ministry of Foreign Affairs, PO Box 4240, Harare, Zimbabwe.

MUMFORD, Lady Mary (Katharine), DCVO 1995 (CVO 1982); Lady-in-Waiting to HRH Princess Alexandra, since 1964; *b* 14 Aug. 1940; 2nd *d* of 16th Duke of Norfolk, KG, GCVO, GBE, TD, PC and Lavinia, Duchess of Norfolk, LG, CBE; *heir presumptive* to Lordship of Herries of Terregles; *m* 1986, Gp Captain Anthony Mumford, CVO, OBE (*d* 2006). *Address:* North Stoke Cottage, North Stoke, Arundel, West Sussex BN18 9LS. *T:* (01798) 831203; Lantonside, Glencaple, Dumfries DG1 4RQ. *T:* (01387) 770260.
See also Lady Herries of Terregles.

MUMFORD, Peter Taylor; theatre lighting and stage designer; television director; *b* 12 Dec. 1946; *s* of John and Doreen Mumford; *m* 1st, 1969, Mary Davida Becket (*d* 1992); three *s*; 2nd, 1995, Tana Marge Lester; one *d*. *Educ:* Central Sch. of Art (DipAD Theatre Design). Founding Mem., exptl theatre gp, Moving Being, late 1960s; freelance theatre artist, lighting and designing operas, plays and ballets, worldwide, 1978–; lighting designs for numerous productions, including: Fearful Symmetries, Royal Ballet, 1994; The Glass Blew In, Siobhan Davies Dance Co., 1995 (Olivier Award for Outstanding Achievement in Dance (for lighting design)); Bacchai, NT, 2003 (Olivier Award for Best Lighting Designer); Peter Pan, Northern Ballet Th., 2005; Midsummer Marriage, Lyric Opera, Chicago, 2005; Cinderella, for Scottish Ballet, 2005; Madame Butterfly, for ENO, 2005–06, and Metropolitan Opera, NY, 2006; Eugene Onegin, Royal Opera House, 2006; also set and lighting designs for Northern Ballet; dir, dance and music films for TV, incl. adaptations of Matthew Bourne's Swan Lake, and series of short films, 48 Preludes and Fugues (J. S. Bach). *Recreations:* fly fishing, occasionally getting on a horse! *Address:* Studio 4, Pickwick House, Ebenezer Street, N1 7NP; Domaine de la Villotte, 24560 Plaisance, France; *e-mail:* peter.mumford@virgin.net.

MUMMERY, Christopher John L.; *see* Lockhart-Mummery.

MUMMERY, Rt Hon. Sir John Frank, Kt 1989; PC 1996; **Rt Hon. Lord Justice Mummery;** DL; a Lord Justice of Appeal, since 1996; *b* 5 Sept. 1938; *s* of late Frank Stanley Mummery and Ruth Mummery (*née* Coleman), Coldred, Kent; *m* 1967, Elizabeth Anne Lamond Lackie, *d* of Dr D. G. L. Lackie and Ellen Lackie (*née* Easterbrook), Edinburgh; one *s* one *d*. *Educ:* Oakleigh House, Dover; Dover County Grammar Sch.; Pembroke Coll., Oxford, 1959–63 (MA, BCL; Winter Williams Prize in Law; Hon. Fellow, 1989). National Service, The Border Regt and RAEC, 1957–59. Called to Bar, Gray's Inn (Atkin Schol.), 1964 (Bencher, 1985; Treas., 2005). Treasury Junior Counsel: in Charity Matters, 1977–81; Chancery, 1981–89; a Recorder, 1989; a Judge of the High Court, Chancery Div., 1989–96. President: Employment Appeal Tribunal, 1993–96; Security Services Tribunal, 2000–; Intelligence Services Tribunal, 2000–; Investigatory Powers Tribunal, 2000–; Clergy Discipline Tribunals, 2003–; Chm., Clergy Discipline Commn, 2003–; Mem., Court of Ecclesiastical Causes Reserved, 2006–. Member, Senate of Inns of Court and Bar, 1978–81; President: Council of Inns of Court, 2000–03; Employment Law Bar Assoc., 2003–. Member: Justice Cttee on Privacy and the Law, 1967–70; Legal Adv. Commn, Gen. Synod of C of E, 1988–; Council of Legal Educn, 1989–92. Chm. Trustees, CAB, Royal Courts of Justice, 2003–. Gov., Inns of Court Sch. of Law, 1996–2001; Mem. Council, Pegasus Scholarship Trust, 1997–; Mem. Adv. Bd, British Inst. of Internat. and Comparative Law, 2001–. DL Kent, 2008. Hon. Fellow, Soc. for Advanced Legal Studies, 1997; Hon. Mem., Soc. of Legal Scholars, 1998; Hon. Pres., Charity Law Assoc., 2004–. Hon. LLD De Montfort, 1998; Hon LLD City, 2002. *Publication:* (co-ed) Copinger and Skone James on Copyright, 12th edn 1980, 13th edn 1991. *Recreation:* walks with family, friends and alone. *Address:* Royal Courts of Justice, Strand, WC2A 2LL.

MUNBY, Hon. Sir James (Lawrence), Kt 2000; **Hon. Mr Justice Munby;** Judge of the High Court of Justice, Family Division, since 2000; *b* 27 July 1948; *s* of Denys Lawrence Munby and Mary Munby (*née* Dicks); *m* 1977, Jennifer Anne Lindsay Beckhough; one *s* one *d*. *Educ:* Magdalen College Sch., Oxford; Wadham Coll., Oxford (BA). Called to the Bar, Middle Temple, 1971 (Bencher, 2000); QC 1988. *Address:* c/o Royal Courts of Justice, Strand, WC2A 2LL.

MUNBY, Dr John Latimer, CMG 1997; OBE 1984; Director, British Council, Greece, 1990–97; *b* 14 July 1937; *s* of late Lawrence St John Munby and Jennie Munby; *m* 1961, Lilian Cynthia Hogg; two *s*. *Educ:* King's Sch., Bruton; Lincoln Coll., Oxford (BA Jurisp., MA); Inst. of Educn, London Univ. (PGCE); Univ. of Essex (MA Applied Linguistics, PhD). Nat. service, 2nd Lieut, 1955–57. Educn Officer, Govt of Tanzania, 1961–68; joined British Council, 1969; seconded to Advanced Teachers' Coll., Zaria, then Ahmadu Bello Univ., Nigeria, 1969–72; Director: English Teaching Inf. Centre, 1974–76; English Lang. Consultancies Dept, 1976–78; Representative: Kuwait, 1978–81; Singapore, 1981–85; Dep. Controller, Home Div., 1985–87; Controller, Libraries, Books and Information Div., 1987–90. FRSA 1982. *Publications:* Read and Think, 1968; Communicative Syllabus Design, 1978; contrib. various jls. *Recreations:* music, sport, wine. *Address:* c/o CPS Registry, The British Council, 10 Spring Gardens, SW1A 2BN. *T:* (020) 7930 8466.

MUNDAY, Janice Margaret; Director, Business Support Simplification Project, Department for Business, Enterprise and Regulatory Reform, since 2007; *d* of late Richard Munday and of Margaret Elliott (*née* Rogers); partner, Martin Edward Stanley, *qv*; one *s* (and one *s* decd). Public Service Delivery, Cabinet Office, 1989–92; Accountancy Policy, DTI, 1992–95; Dir of Policy, Charity Commn, 1995–96; Department of Trade and Industry: Dir of Policy, Consumer Affairs, 1999–2000; Dir, Participation and Skills, then Head, Employment Relns, 2000–07 (Dir, Employment Relns, 2003–07). *Recreations:* enjoying London, gardening. *Address:* Department for Business, Enterprise and Regulatory Reform, 1 Victoria Street, SW1H 0ET. *T:* (020) 7215 5702, *Fax:* (020) 7215 6768; *e-mail:* janice.munday@berr.gsi.gov.uk.

MUNDAY, John, FSA; Keeper of Weapons and Antiquities, National Maritime Museum, Greenwich, 1976–84, now Keeper Emeritus; *b* 10 Aug. 1924; *s* of Rodney H. J. Munday and Ethel Emma Cutting; *m* 1953, Brenda Warden; two *s*. *Educ:* Portsmouth Northern Grammar Sch.; King's Coll., Newcastle; Durham Univ. (BA 1950; MA 1961). FSA 1972. Assistant, Portsmouth Public Libraries and Museums Dept, 1940–42. Served RN, 1942–46; Sub Lieut (Ex. Sp.), RNVR. National Maritime Museum, Greenwich: Asst Keeper, Librarian, 1951; Curator of Presentation, 1964; Dep. Keeper, 1969; Curator of Weapons and Antiquities, 1971. Hon. Vice Pres., Soc. for Nautical Res., 1985 (Hon. Sec., 1979–84); Member: Develt Cttee, SS Great Britain Project, 1980–86; HMS Victory Adv. Technical Cttee, 1985–2003. Chm. Trustees, Deal Maritime & Local Hist. Mus., 1997–2003. *Publications:* For Those in Peril… lifesaving, then and now, 1963; Oar Maces of Admiralty, 1966; Dress of the British Sailor, rev. edn 1977; Heads & Tails—the Necessary Seating (with drawings), 1978; Naval Cannon, 1987; E. W. Cooke, RA, FRS: a man of his time, 1996. *Recreations:* painting, collecting, considering. *Address:* 8 Langtons Court, Sun Lane, Alresford, Hants SO24 9UE. *T:* (01962) 736 393; *e-mail:* jb_munday@yahoo.co.uk.

MUNDELL, David Gordon; MP (C) Dumfriesshire, Clydesdale and Tweeddale, since 2005; *b* 27 May 1962; *s* of Dorah Mundell; *m* 1987, Lynda Jane Carmichael (separated); two *s* one *d*. *Educ:* Lockerbie Acad.; Edinburgh Univ. (LLB Hons 1984); Univ. of Strathclyde Business Sch. (MBA 1991). Trainee Solicitor, Tindal Oatts, Glasgow, 1985–87; Solicitor, Maxwell Waddell, Glasgow, 1987–89; Sen. Corporate Lawyer, Biggart Baillie & Gifford, Glasgow, 1989–91; Group Legal Advr Scotland, BT, 1991–98; Head of Nat. Affairs, BT Scotland, 1998–99. MSP (C) S of Scotland, 1999–2005. Shadow Sec. of State for Scotland, 2005–. Member: Law Soc. of Scotland, 1986–; Law Soc., 1992–. *Recreations:* family and friends, travel. *Address:* House of Commons, SW1A 0AA.

MUNDELL, Prof. Robert Alexander, CC 2003; PhD; Professor of Economics, Columbia University, since 1974; *b* 24 Oct. 1932; *s* of William Campbell Mundell and Lila Teresa Mundell; *m* 1st, 1957, Barba Sheff (*d* 1972); 2nd, 1998, Valerie S. Natsios; one *s*. *Educ:* Univ. of BC; MIT (PhD); London Sch. of Econs; Univ. of Chicago. Instructor, Univ. of BC, 1957–58; economist, Royal Commn on Price Spreads of Food Products, Ottawa, 1958; Asst Prof. of Econs, Stanford Univ., 1958–59; Prof. of Econs, Johns Hopkins Univ., Sch. of Advanced Internat. Studies, Bologna, 1959–61; Sen. Economist, IMF, 1961–63; Prof. of Internat. Econs, Grad. Inst. Internat. Studies, Geneva, 1965–75; Professor of Economics: Univ. of Chicago, 1966–71; Univ. of Waterloo, Ont., 1972–74. Vis. Prof. of Econs, McGill Univ., 1963–64, 1989–90; First Rockefeller Vis. Res. Prof. of Internat. Econs, Brookings Inst., 1964–65; Guggenheim Fellow, 1971; Annenburg Dist. Schol. in Residence, Univ. of Southern Calif, 1980; Richard Fox Vis. Prof. of Econs, Univ. of Penn, 1990–91. Ed., Jl Pol. Econ., 1966–71. Pres., N American Econ. and Financial Assoc., 1974–78. Hon. Dr: Paris, 1992; People's Univ. of China, 1995. Nobel Prize for Econs, 1999. *Publications:* The International Monetary System: conflict and reform, 1965; Man and Economics, 1968; International Economics, 1968; Monetary Theory: interest, inflation and growth in the world economy, 1971; contrib. learned jls. *Recreations:* painting, tennis, hockey, ski-ing, history. *Address:* 35 Claremont Avenue #5N, New York, NY 10027, USA. *T:* (212) 7490630; Palazzo Mundell, Strada di Santa Columba 2–4, Santa Columba, Siena 53100, Italy. *Club:* Reform.

MUNDY, Prof. Anthony Richard, FRCP, FRCS; Professor of Urology, University of London, since 1991; Director, Institute of Urology (formerly Institute of Urology and Nephrology), University College London, since 1996; *b* 25 April 1948; *s* of Peter Gordon Mundy and Betty (*née* Hall); *m* 1st, 1970, Sheila Peskett; 2nd, 1975, Marilyn Ashton; one *s* one *d*; partner, Debra Hendley; one *d*. *Educ:* Mill Hill Sch.; Université de Paris; St Mary's Hosp. Medical Sch., London (MB BS Hons 1971); MS London 1982. MRCP 1974, FRCP 1996; FRCS 1975. House Surgeon, St Mary's Hosp., London, 1971; House Physician, Barnet General Hosp., 1972; Casualty Officer, St Mary's Hosp., London, 1973; Surgical Registrar, Orsett Hosp., 1973–75; Guy's Hospital: Sen. Registrar, Surgery, 1975–78, Urology, 1978–81; Consultant Urologist, 1981–99; Consultant Urologist, St Peter's Hosps and UCL Hosps, 1986–. Vis. Consultant Urologist, St Luke's Hosp., Malta, 1984–; Hon. Civilian Consultant Urologist, RN, 1994–. Lectures: Pradke, Pune, India, 1992; Sir Ernest Finch, Sheffield, 1994; Bodo von Garrelts, Stockholm, 1995; Ballenger, Puerto Rica, 1996; Ian Aird, Imperial Coll., 1999; Grey Turner, Newcastle, 1999; C. E. Alken, Dusseldorf, 1999; Rovsing, Copenhagen, 2000; British Assoc. of Urol Surgeons, 2001; Hunterian Oration, RCS, 2007. Pres., British Assoc. of Urol Surgeons, 2006–08 (Mem. Council, 1990–93, 1995–2001; Vice-Pres., 2003–06); Member: Exec. Cttee, Eur. Assoc. of Urol., 1994–2000 (Mem., Acad., 2000–); Council, RCS, 2000–; Founder Mem., Genito-Urinary Reconstructive Surgeons, 1984–; Convenor, Urol Res. Soc., 1984–. Hon. Member, Urological Society: of Australasia, 1986; of HK, 1989; of Singapore, 1990; of Malaysia, 1994; of S Africa, 1998; of Holland, 1990. St Peter's Medal, British Assoc. of Urol Surgeons, 2002. *Publications:* Urodynamics: principles, practice and application, 1984, 2nd edn 1994; Current Operative Surgery: Urology, 1987; Neuropathic Bladder in Childhood, 1991; Urodynamic and Reconstructive Surgery of the Lower Urinary Tract, 1994; Scientific Basis of Urology, 1999, 2nd edn 2004; Succeeding as a Hospital Doctor, 2000, 3rd edn 2007; articles on reconstructive urology in various urological jls. *Recreations:* home, wine, history. *Address:* Emblem House, Tooley Street, SE1 2PR. *T:* (020) 7403 1221, *Fax:* (020) 7403 1664; *e-mail:* tony.mundy1@btinternet.com.

MUNDY, Jo A.; *see* Shapcott, J. A.

MUNGLANI, Rajesh, FRCA; Consultant in Pain Management, West Suffolk Hospital, Bury St Edmunds, since 2000; *b* 31 Aug. 1962; *s* of Balwani Rai Munglani and Krishna Gulati; *m* 1989, Dr Jane Bolland; four *d*. *Educ:* St George's Hosp., Univ. of London (MB BS 1985); DCH 1989. FRCA 1990. Clin Lectr, 1993–96, Lectr in Anaesthesia and Pain Mgt, 1997–2000, Univ. of Cambridge; Consultant in Anaesthesia and Pain Mgt, Addenbrooke's Hosp., Cambridge, 1997–2000. John Farman Prof., RCAnaes, 1997. Mem., St Barnabas' Ch, Cambridge. *Publications:* Pain: current understanding, emerging therapies and novel approaches to drug discovery, 2001; contrib. numerous papers and chapters on scientific basis of chronic pain, spinal pain incl. whiplash and complex regional pain syndromes. *Recreations:* walking in the Lake District, reading. *Address:* BUPA Cambridge Lea Hospital, 30 New Road, Impington, Cambridge CB4 9EL. *T:* (01223) 266927; *e-mail:* rajesh@munglani.com.

MUNIR, (Ashley) Edward, PhD; Barrister; Under Secretary, Ministry of Agriculture, Fisheries and Food, 1982–92; *b* 14 Feb. 1934; *s* of late Hon. Sir Mehmed Munir Bey, Kt, CBE, and late Lady (Vessime) Munir; *m* 1960, Sureyya S. V. Dormen; one *s*. *Educ:* Brentwood Sch.; St John's Coll., Cambridge (MA 1957); King's Coll., London (PhD 1992). Called to the Bar, Gray's Inn, 1956. Practised as barrister, 1956–60, 1992–; Crown Counsel, 1960–64; entered Govt Legal Service, 1964; Asst Solicitor, MAFF, 1975–82. *Publications:* Perinatal Rights, 1983; Fisheries after Factortame, 1991; Mentally Disordered Offenders, 1993. *Recreations:* walking, music. *Address:* (chambers) 5 St Andrew's Hill, EC4V 5BY. *T:* (020) 7332 5400. *Club:* Oxford and Cambridge.

MUNN, Sir James, Kt 1985; OBE 1976; MA; *b* 27 July 1920; *s* of Douglas H. Munn and Margaret G. Dunn; *m* 1946, Muriel Jean Millar Moles; (one *d* decd). *Educ:* Stirling High Sch.; Glasgow Univ. (MA (Hons)). Entered Indian Civil Service, 1941; served in Bihar, 1942–47. Taught in various schools in Glasgow, 1949–57; Principal Teacher of Modern Languages, Falkirk High Sch., 1957–62, Depute Rector, 1962–66; Rector: Rutherglen Acad., 1966–70; Cathkin High Sch., Cambuslang, Glasgow, 1970–83. Univ. Comr,

1988–95; Chairman: Manpower Services Cttee for Scotland, 1984–88; MSC, subseq. Training Commn, 1987–88; Scottish Adv. Bd, Open Coll., 1989–91; Pres., Inst. of Trng and Devel t, 1989–92 (Fellow, 1989). Member: Consultative Cttee on Curriculum, 1968–80 (Chm., 1980–87); University Grants Cttee, 1973–82; Chm., Cttee to review structure of curriculum at SIII and SIV, 1975–77. Mem. Court, Strathclyde Univ., 1983–91. Fellow: Paisley Coll. of Technology, 1988; SCOTVEC, 1989; FIPD 1995. Chevalier des Palmes Académiques, 1967. DUniv Stirling, 1978; Hon. LLD Strathclyde, 1988; Hon. DEd Napier Polytechnic, 1989. *Address:* 4 Kincath Avenue, High Burnside, Glasgow G73 4RP. *T:* (0141) 634 4654.

MUNN, Margaret Patricia, (Meg); MP (Lab) Sheffield, Heeley, since 2001; *b* 24 Aug. 1959; *d* of late Reginald Edward Munn and of Lillian Seward; *m* 1989, Dennis Clifford Bates. *Educ:* Univ. of York (BA Hons Language); Univ. of Nottingham (MA Social Work; CQSW); Open Univ. (Dip. Mgt Studies). Social Work Assistant, Berkshire, 1981–84; Social Worker, 1986–90, Sen. Social Worker, 1990–92, Nottinghamshire; Dist Manager, Barnsley, 1992–96; Children's Service Manager, Wakefield, 1996–99; Asst Dir of Children's Services, Social Services, York, 1999–2000. Parliamentary Under-Secretary of State: DCLG, 2006–07; FCO, 2007–08. Mem., Mgt Cttee, Wortley Hall Ltd, 1994–2000; Chm. Cttee, Barnsley Br., CRS Ltd, 1997–2001. PPS, DFES, 2003–05; Parly Under-Sec. of State, DTI, 2005–06. *Recreations:* tennis, swimming, gardening. *Address:* House of Commons, SW1A 0AA. *T:* (020) 7219 8316; Barkers Pool House, 2nd Floor, Burgess Street, Sheffield S1 2HF. *T:* (0114) 263 4004.

MUNNS, Victor George; Counsellor (Labour), Washington, 1983–86; *b* 17 June 1926; *s* of Frederick William Munns and Lilian Munns; *m* 1952, Pamela Ruth Wyatt; two *s*. *Educ:* Haberdashers' Aske's, Hatcham; University Coll., London (BA). Served HM Forces (Army Intell.), 1945–48. Min. of Labour Employment Service, 1951–61; ILO, Trinidad and Belize, 1962–63; Sec., Shipbldg Industry Trng Bd, 1964–66; Res. Staff, Royal Commn on Trade Unions, 1966; Principal, Dept of Employment (Indust. Trng and Indust. Relations), 1967–72; Dep. Chief Officer, Race Relations Bd, 1973–74; Sec., Health and Safety Commn, 1974–77; Asst Sec., Health and Safety Exec., 1977–82. Dir, Nailsworth Festival, 1992–96. *Club:* Royal Over-Seas League.

MUNRO, Sir Alan (Gordon), KCMG 1990 (CMG 1984); HM Diplomatic Service, retired; *b* 17 Aug. 1935; *s* of late Sir Gordon Munro, KCMG, MC and Lilian Muriel Beit; *m* 1962, Rosemary Grania Bacon; twin *s* two *d*. *Educ:* Wellington Coll.; Clare Coll., Cambridge (MA). MIPM. Mil. Service, 4/7 Dragoon Guards, 1953–55; Middle East Centre for Arab Studies, 1958–60; British Embassy, Beirut, 1960–62; Kuwait, 1961; FO, 1963–65; Head of Chancery, Benghazi, 1965–66 and Tripoli, 1966–68; FO, 1968–73; Consul (Commercial), 1973–74, Consul-Gen., 1974–77, Rio de Janeiro; Head of E African Dept, FCO, 1977–78; Head of Middle East Dept, FCO, 1979; Head of Personnel Ops Dept, FCO, 1979–81; Regl Marketing Dir (ME), MoD, 1981–83; Ambassador to Algeria, 1984–87; Dep. Under-Sec. of State, ME/Africa, FCO, 1987–89; Ambassador to Saudi Arabia, 1989–93. Director: Schroder Asseily & Co. Ltd, 1993–2000; Middle East Internat., 1997–2006; Dabbagh Gp (Jedda), 1998–2001; Internat. Trade & Investment Missions Ltd, 1998–2002; Advr, Tate and Lyle; Vice-Chm., Arab-British Chamber of Commerce, 1993–. Gov., Imperial Coll., 1994–2001. President: Soc. for Algerian Studies; Saudi-British Soc.; Chm., Beit Trust for Central Africa; Vice Chm., BRCS, 1994–2001; Chm., Jt Cttee, Red Cross and St John. *Publication:* An Arabian Affair (Arab Storm): politics and diplomacy behind the Gulf War, 1996, 2006. *Recreations:* historic buildings, gardening, music, history. *Club:* Travellers.

MUNRO, Dr Alan James; Fellow, since 1962, and Master, 1995–2002, Christ's College, Cambridge; *b* 19 Feb. 1937; *s* of John Bennet Lorimer Munro, CB, CMG and Gladys, (Pat), Maie Forbes Munro (*née* Simmons); *m* 1960, Mary, *d* of John Gibson Robertson, Dumfries; two *s*. *Educ:* Edinburgh Acad.; Christ's Coll., Cambridge (BA 1960; MA; PhD 1964). Nat. Service, 2nd Lt Queen's Own Cameron Highlanders, 1955–57; Demonstrator, 1963–67, Lectr, 1967–68, Dept of Biochemistry, Cambridge Univ.; Scientific Officer, MRC Lab. of Molecular Biology, Cambridge, 1968–71; Lectr, 1971–80, Reader, 1980–89, in Immunology, Dept of Pathology, Cambridge Univ.; Jt Founder and Scientific Dir, Cantab Pharmaceuticals plc, 1989–95. Director: Babraham Inst. Ltd, 1996–2002; Blackwell Science Ltd, 1997–2001; Genome Research Ltd, 1997–2001; Blackwell Publishing Ltd, 2001–07; Paradigm Therapeutics Ltd, 2002–07; Chm., Lorantis Holdings Ltd, 2000–03. Fulbright Travel Schol. and Vis. Scientist, Salk Inst., La Jolla, Calif, 1965–66; Boerhaave Prof., Univ. of Leiden, 1976–77. Chm., Link Cttee on Cell Engrg, DTI, 1994–2002. Gov., Lister Inst. of Preventive Medicine, 1996–2002. *Publications:* (jtly) The Immune System, 1981; papers in scientific jls on immunology and molecular biology. *Address:* Christ's College, Cambridge CB2 3BU.

MUNRO of Lindertis, Sir Alasdair (Thomas Ian), 6th Bt *cr* 1825; *b* 6 July 1927; *s* of Sir Thomas Torquil Alfonso Munro, 5th Bt and Beatrice Maude (*d* 1974), *d* of Robert Sanderson Whitaker; *S* father, 1985; *m* 1954, Marguerite Lillian, *d* of late Franklin R. Loy, Dayton, Ohio, USA; one *s* one *d*. *Educ:* Georgetown Univ., Washington, DC (BSS 1946); Univ. of Pennsylvania (MBA 1951); IMEDE, Lausanne. 2nd Lieut, USAF (previously US Army), 1946–53. Senior Vice-Pres., McCann-Erickson, New York, 1952–69; Pres., Jennings Real Estate, Waitsfield, Vermont, 1970–83. Founder, Dir (and Past Pres.), St Andrew's Soc. of Vermont, 1972–; Vice-Chm., Assoc. Bd of Directors, Howard Bank, Waitsfield, 1974–84; Founder, sometime Dir and Pres., Valley Area Assoc., Waitsfield, 1972–80. Chairman: Munro, Jennings & Doig, 1983–90; Highland Devel t Gp, 1987–91. *Publication:* Scottish Antiques, 2004. *Recreations:* gardening, travel, collector/dealer in Scottish antiques, Scottish heritage matters. *Heir: s* Keith Gordon Munro [*b* 3 May 1959; *m* 1989, Jada Louise Elwell; one *s* one *d*]. *Address:* RiverRidge, Box 940, Waitsfield, VT 05673, USA.

MUNRO, Colin Andrew, CMG 2002; HM Diplomatic Service, retired; Consultant to Organisation for Security and Co-operation in Europe and to International Organisation for Migration, since 2008; *b* 24 Oct. 1946; *s* of Capt. Frederick Bertram Munro and Jane Eliza (*née* Taylor); *m* 1967, Ehrengard Maria Heinrich; two *s*. *Educ:* George Watson's Coll., Edinburgh; Edinburgh Univ. (MA Hons Mod. Langs 1968); King's Coll., London (MA Internat Studies 2002). Asst Principal, Bd of Inland Revenue, 1968–69; FCO, 1969–71; Third, later Second, Sec., Bonn, 1971–73; Second, later First, Sec., Kuala Lumpur, 1973–77; FCO, 1977; Private Sec. to Minister of State, 1979–80; Hd of Chancery, Bucharest, 1981–82; FCO, 1983; Asst Head of W European Dept, 1985–87; Dep. Hd of Mission, E Berlin, 1987–90; Consul Gen., Frankfurt, 1990–93; Hd of OSCE and Council of Europe Dept, FCO, 1993–97; Ambassador to Republic of Croatia, 1997–2000; Dep. High Rep., Mostar, 2001; rcds, 2002; UK Perm. Rep. to OSCE, Vienna, 2003–07. Trustee, Accord Internat. (Mostar Sinfonietta). *Publications:* contrib. Jl of Prince Albert Soc., Jl of Inst. of Contemp. British Hist., Jl of Vienna Inst. for Peace Research. *Recreations:* sports especially hockey, cricket, ski-ing, golf, history, music. *Clubs:* Reform, Royal Automobile; Royal Selangor (Kuala Lumpur); Rotary (Vienna North East).

MUNRO, Colin William Gordon R.; *see* Ross-Munro.

MUNRO, Graeme Neil, CVO 2005; FSAScot; Director and Chief Executive, Historic Scotland, 1991–2004; *b* 28 Aug. 1944; *s* of Daniel Munro and Nancy Kirkwood (*née* Smith); *m* 1972, Nicola Susan Wells (*see* N. S. Munro); one *s* one *d*. *Educ:* Daniel Stewart's Coll., Edinburgh; Univ. of St Andrews (MA Hons 1967). FSAScot 1990. Joined Scottish Office as Asst Principal, 1968; Scottish Development Department: Housing, 1968; Planning, 1968–70; Private Sec. to Head of Dept, 1971; Principal, Roads, 1972–74; Scottish Home and Health Department: Hosp. Services, 1974–76; Criminal Justice, 1976–79; Assistant Secretary: Dept of Agriculture and Fisheries for Scotland (Fisheries), 1979–83; NHS Funding, Scottish Home and Health Dept, 1983–87; Management and Orgn, Scottish Office Central Services, 1987–90; Dir, Historic Buildings and Monuments, Scotland, 1990–91. Member: Council and Cases Cttee, Cockburn Assoc. (Edinburgh Civic Trust), 2005–; Mgt Cttee, Rosslyn Chapel Trust, 2005– (Dep. Chm. 2007–); Trustee, Historic Scotland Foundn, 2007–. FRSA. *Recreations:* gardening, walking, travel, reading, voluntary work in conservation and Third World fields. *Address:* 15 Heriot Row, Edinburgh EH3 6HP. *T:* (0131) 556 3201; *e-mail:* gandnmunro@hotmail.com.

MUNRO, Sir Ian Kenneth, 17th Bt *cr* 1634, of Foulis-Obsdale, Ross-shire; *b* 5 April 1940; *s* of Sir Kenneth Munro, 16th Bt and of Olive Freda (*née* Broome); *S* father, 2004. *Heir: cousin* Godfrey Roland Munro [*b* 1 July 1938; *m* 1985, Julie Pamela Gosling; two *s* one *d*].

MUNRO, John Farquhar; JP; Member (Lib Dem) Ross Skye and Inverness West, Scottish Parliament, since 1999; *b* 26 Aug. 1934; *m* 1962, Cecilia; one *s* one *d*. *Educ:* Plockton High Sch.; Sea Trng Coll., Gloucester. Merchant Marine Service, 1951–61; Plant Fitter, Kings Road Construction, 1961–65; Manager, contracting co., 1965–75; heavy haulage, bus operation, civil engrg, and quarrying contractor, 1975–93; crofter, 1971–97. Member: Local Council, 1966–74; Skye and Lochalsh DC, 1974–90 (Convenor, 1984–95); Highland Regl Council, 1978–82 (Chair, Gaelic Cttee, 1978–82); Highland Council, 1995–99. Chair, Ross, Cromarty and Skye Scottish Liberal Democrats, 1984–98. Non-executive Director: Highland Opportunities Ltd; Acair Publishing; Skye and Lochalsh Enterprise; former Mem., Electricity Consultative Council; Chair: Rail Devel t Partnership; Fishery Harbours Mgt; Shipping Service Adv. Cttee, Caledonian MacBrayne. Trustee, Gaelic Coll., Skye. *Recreations:* sailing, fishing, the company of my grandchildren. *Address:* Glomach House, Aultnachruinne, Glenshiel, Kyle of Lochalsh, Wester Ross IV40 8HN. *T:* (01599) 511222.

MUNRO, Julia Henrietta; University Librarian, University of Reading, since 2001; *b* 21 Dec. 1952; *d* of Leslie H. and Joan B. Tebbitt; *m* 1975, Dr Peter M. G. Munro; one *s* one *d*. *Educ:* Imperial Coll., London (BSc 1975); City Univ. (MSc 1977); Univ. of Reading (MBA 2000). ARCS 1975; MCLIP 2002. Grad. trainee liby asst, Poly. of Central London, 1975–76; Assistant Librarian: Paediatric Res. Unit, Guy's Hosp. Med. Sch., 1977–79; Centre for Envmtl Technol., Imperial Coll., London, 1979–84; UCL, 1984–93; Dep. Librarian, Univ. of Reading, 1993–2001. Mem., Lifelong Learning UK Sector Skills Council, 2005–. *Recreation:* family life with a neurotic Weimaraner and a punk cat. *Address:* University of Reading, Whiteknights, PO Box 223, Reading, Berks RG6 6AE. *T:* (0118) 378 8774, *Fax:* (0118) 378 6636; *e-mail:* j.h.munro@reading.ac.uk.

MUNRO, Kenneth Alexander; Member, Royal Commission on Reform of the House of Lords, 1999; *b* 17 Dec. 1936; *s* of James Gibb Munro and Jean Ralston (*née* McKay); *m* 1961, Elizabeth Coats Forrest McCreanor; two *d*. *Educ:* Hutchesons' Boys' Grammar Sch., Glasgow; Univ. of Glasgow (MA 1963). Served Intelligence Corps, 1955–57. Worked in family business, 1957–59; Scottish American Investment Co. Ltd, 1963–66; Electrical Trades Union, 1966–67; NEDO, 1967–69; Ford Motor Co. Ltd, 1969–74 (on secondment to Pay Bd, 1973–74); European Commission, 1974–98: responsible for employment policy in transport and Asst to Dir Gen. for Transport, Brussels, 1974–82; Press Officer and Dep. Head of Office, London, 1982–88; Head of Commn Office, Edinburgh, 1988–98. Chm., Centre for Scottish Public Policy, 1997–2008. Member: Equal Opportunities Adv. Cttee for Scotland, 1993–2006; BP (formerly BP-Amoco) Adv. Bd for Scotland, 1997–2003. Mem. (Lab), Brentwood DC, Essex, 1971–74. Convenor, Children in Scotland, 1999–2003. Hon. Sec., 1991–2000, Vice Chm., 2000–04, Chm., 2004–07, Scottish Council, Eur. Movement; Convenor, Scotland in Europe, 2000–06. Hon. Fellow, Faculty of Law, Univ. of Edinburgh, 1998. Contested: (Lab) W Aberdeenshire, 1964; (New Scottish Lab) Lothian, Scottish Parlt elecns, 1999. Vice-Chm., John Smith Meml Trust, 1994–2005 (Vice-Chm., Adv. Bd, 2005–07). Convenor, Internat. Cttee, Saltire Soc., 2005–08. Mem., Campaigns Cttee, Queen Margaret UC, 1999–2003. Mem., Scotch Malt Whisky Soc. FRSA. *Recreations:* theatre, cinema, swimming, walking. *Address:* 23 Greenhill Gardens, Edinburgh EH10 4BL. *T:* (0131) 447 2284. *Club:* New (Edinburgh).

MUNRO, Neil Christopher, CBE 2003; Head, Customer Contact Transformation Programme, HM Revenue and Customs, 2006–07; *b* 25 July 1947; *s* of late Alan and of Jean Munro; *m* 1987, Caroline Anne Virginia Smith; two *d*. *Educ:* Wallasey Grammar Sch.; St John's Coll., Oxford (BA Hons Mod. Hist., MA). MCIPD (MIPD 1993). Board of Inland Revenue, subsequently HM Revenue and Customs, 1970–2007: various posts in tax policy and mgt work; seconded to CBI as Head, Taxation Dept, 1978–80; Dep. Dir of Personnel, 1991–94; Director: Mgt Services, 1994–96; Tax Law Rewrite Project, 1996–2001; Revenue Policy: Corporate Services, 2001–05; Better Guidance Prog., 2005–06. *Recreations:* modern literature, music, cricket, cooking. *Address:* 66 Lavington Road, Ealing, W13 9LS. *Club:* MCC.

MUNRO, Nicola Susan, CB 2006; Head of Scottish Executive Development Department, 2001–07; *b* 11 Jan. 1948; *d* of Ernest Derek Wells and Barbara Gurney Wells; *m* 1972, Graeme Neil Munro, *qv*; one *s* one *d*. *Educ:* Harrogate Grammar Sch.; Univ. of Warwick (BA Hons History). Scottish Office, later Scottish Executive, 1970–2007: Head of Div. (hosp. services, food, med. educn), Scottish Home and Health Dept, 1986–89; Head of Div. (urban and local economic policy), Scottish Office Industry Dept, 1989–92; Head of Div. (curriculum, assessment, careers service, educn industry links), Scottish Office Educn Dept, 1992–95; Under-Sec., Public Health Policy, Scottish Office, then Scottish Exec., Dept of Health, 1995–2000; Hd of Envmt Gp, Scottish Exec. Rural Affairs Dept, 2000–01. Member: Council, Fairbridge in Scotland, 2007–; Scottish Consumer Council, 2008–; Scottish Refugee Council, 2008–. FRSA 1996. *Recreations:* reading, travel, gardening, family, friends. *Address:* 15 Heriot Row, Edinburgh EH3 6HP.

MUNROE-BLUM, Prof. Heather Anne Elise Lilian, OC 2003; PhD; Principal and Vice-Chancellor, and Professor of Epidemiology and Biostatistics, McGill University, since 2003; *b* 25 Aug. 1950; *d* of Donald Munroe and late Dorothy Munroe; *m* 1970, Leonard Blum, screenwriter; one *d*. *Educ:* McMaster Univ. (BA, BSW 1974); Wilfrid Laurier Univ. (MSW 1975); Univ. of NC, Chapel Hill (PhD with Dist. 1983). Psychiatric Social Worker and Social Work Supervisor, McMaster Univ. Med. Centre and St Joseph's Hosp., 1975–79; McMaster University: Clinical Lectr, 1976–79, Asst Clinical Prof., 1979–84, Dept of Psychiatry; Asst Prof., Depts of Psychiatry and Clinical Epidemiol. and Biostatistics, 1984–89; University of Toronto: Prof., and Dean, Faculty of Social Work, 1989–93; Prof., and Vice-Pres., Res. and Internat. Relns, 1994–2002. Asst Prof., Dept of

Social Work, Atkinson Coll., York Univ., 1982–84; Associate Sen. Fellow, Massey Coll., 1998 (Associate Fellow, 1990–93). Director: Neurosci. Canada Partnership, 2001–05 (Hon. Mem., 2005–); Neurosci. Canada Foundn, 2001–; McGill Univ. Health Centre, 2003–. Member: Assoc. of Univs and Colls of Canada, 2003– (Chair., Standing Adv. Cttee on Univ. Res.; Mem., Exec. Cttee, 2007–); Assoc. of Amer. Univs, 2003–; Conf. des recteurs et des principaux des Univs de Québec, 2003– (Vice Pres., 2005; Pres., 2007–). Fellow, Assoc. for Clinical Psychosocial Res., 1991; Specially Elected Fellow, Acad. of Sci., RSC, 2002. Hon. DSc Montréal, 2004; Hon. LLD: Toronto, 2005; McMaster, 2007; Dr *hc* Edinburgh, 2005. Outstanding Alumni Award, Sch. of Public Health, Univ. of NC, Chapel Hill, 1992; Dist. Alumni Award, McMaster Univ., 1995. *Publications:* (jtly) Schizophrenia in Focus: a psychosocial approach to treatment and rehabilitation, 1983; (jtly) PDQ Epidemiology, 1989; (ed jtly) Borderline Personality Disorder: an empirical perspective, 1992; (with E. Marziali) Interpersonal Group Psychotherapy for Borderline Personality Disorder, 1994; Growing Ontario's Innovation System: the strategic role of university research, 1999; contribs to books and numerous articles in learned jls. *Address:* James Administration Building, Room 506, 845 Sherbrooke Street West, Montreal, QC H3A 2T5, Canada. *T:* (514) 3984180, *Fax:* (514) 3984768; *e-mail:* heather.munroe.blum@mcgill.ca. *Clubs:* Mount Royal, University, St-Denis, 357C (Montreal); University (Toronto).

MUNROW, Roger Davis, CB 1993; Chief Master of the Supreme Court of Judicature (Chancery Division), 1986–92, retired (Master, 1985–86); *b* 20 March 1929; *s* of late William Davis Munrow, CBE and Constance Caroline Munrow (*née* Moorcroft); *m* 1st, 1957, Marie Jane Beresford (*d* 2001); three *d*: 2nd, 2001, Norma Eileen Boucher. *Educ:* Bryanston School; Oriel College, Oxford (MA). Solicitor. Entered Treasury Solicitor's Dept as Legal Assistant, 1959; Senior Legal Assistant, 1965; Assistant Treasury Solicitor, 1973; Principal Asst Treasury Solicitor, 1981. *Recreation:* swimming. *Address:* 5 Mallard Close, Harnham, Salisbury, Wilts SP2 8JB.

MURAD, Prof. Ferid, MD, PhD; Professor and Chairman, Department of Integrative Biology, Pharmacology and Physiology, Houston Medical School, since 1997 and Director, Institute of Molecular Medicine, Houston, since 1999, University of Texas; *b* 14 Sept. 1936; *s* of John Murad and Josephine Bowman; *m* 1958, Carol A. Leopold; one *s* four *d*. *Educ:* DePauw Univ. (BA 1958); Sch. of Medicine, Western Reserve Univ. (MD 1965; PhD 1965). University of Virginia: Dir, Clin. Res. Center, Sch. of Medicine, 1971–81; Prof., Depts of Internal Medicine and Pharmacology, 1975–81; Stanford University: Prof., Depts of Internal Medicine and Pharmacology, 1981–88; acting Chm., Dept of Medicine, 1986–88; Adjunct Prof., Dept of Pharmacology, Northwestern Univ., 1988–96. Albert and Mary Lasker Foundn Award for Basic Research, 1996; Nobel Prize in Medicine or Physiology, 1998. *Publications:* papers, published lecture. *Recreations:* golf, carpentry. *Address:* Department of Integrative Biology, Pharmacology and Physiology, University of Texas Medical School-Houston, Institute of Molecular Medicine, 1825 Pressler, Suite 530, Houston, TX 77225, USA. *Fax:* (713) 5002498; *e-mail:* ferid.murad@uth.tmc.edu.

MURAKAMI, Takashi; artist; *b* Tokyo, 1 Feb. 1962. *Educ:* Tokyo National Univ. of Fine Arts and Music (BFA 1986; MFA 1988; PhD 1993). Works include fine art pieces, design collaborations and curatorial projects. *Solo exhibitions* include: Bard Coll. Center for Curatorial Studies, NY, 1999; Mus. of Contemp. Art, Tokyo, and Mus. of Fine Arts, Boston, 2001; Fondation Cartier pour l'art contemporain, Paris, 2002; Rockefeller Center, NY, 2003; Fondazione Sandretto Re Rebaudengo, Turin, 2005; (retrospective) Mus. of Contemp. Art, LA, 2007. *Publications:* Superflat, 2000; (jtly) My Reality: contemporary art and the culture of Japanese animation, 2001; (ed) Little Boy: the arts of Japan's exploding subculture, 2004. *Recreation:* cactus growing. *Address:* Kaikai Kiki Co. Ltd, Marunuma Art Residence, 493 Kamiuchimagi, Asaka-city, Saitama 351–0001, Japan.

MURDIN, Paul Geoffrey, OBE 1988; PhD; FInstP; Senior Fellow, Institute of Astronomy, Cambridge University, since 2002; *b* 5 Jan. 1942; *s* of Robert Murdin and Ethel Murdin (*née* Chubb); *m* 1964, Lesley Carol Milburn; two *s* one *d*. *Educ:* Trinity School of John Whitgift; Wadham Coll., Oxford (BA Physics); Univ. of Rochester, NY (PhD Physics and Astronomy). FRAS 1970; FInstP 1992. Res. Associate, Univ. of Rochester, 1970–71; Sen. Res. Associate, Royal Greenwich Observatory, 1971–74; Sen. Res. Scientist, Anglo-Australian Observatory, NSW, 1975–78; Royal Greenwich Observatory: Prin. Sci. Officer, 1979–81; Hd of La Palma Operations, 1981–87; Hd of Astronomy Div., 1987–90; Dir, Royal Observatory, Edinburgh, 1991–93; Head of Astronomy, PPARC, and Dir of Sci., BNSC, 1994–2001. Sen. Mem., Wolfson Coll., Cambridge, 1990–; Vis. Prof., Liverpool John Moores Univ., 2002–. Mem. Bd of Trustees, Nat. Maritime Museum, 1990–2001. Pres., Faulkes Telescope Corp., 1999–2005. Member: Royal Astronomical Soc., 1963– (Councillor, 1997–99; Vice-Pres., 2000–01; Treas., 2001–); European Astronomical Soc., 1991– (Vice-Pres., 1991–93; Pres., 1993–97). *Publications:* The Astronomer's Telescope (with Patrick Moore), 1963; Radio Waves from Space, 1969; (with L. Murdin) The New Astronomy, 1974; (with D. Allen and D. Malin) Catalogue of the Universe, 1980; (with D. Malin) Colours of the Stars, 1985; End in Fire, 1989; Encyclopedia of Astronomy & Astrophysics, 2001; Firefly Encyclopedia of Astronomy, 2004; Full Meridian of Glory, 2009; Cosmic Discoveries, 2009; over 150 pubns in astronom. and other sci. jls, principally Monthly Notices of RAS. *Recreations:* writing, music, natural history, history of art. *Address:* Institute of Astronomy, Madingley Road, Cambridge CB3 0HA; *e-mail:* paul@murdin.com.

MURDOCH, Prof. Alison Pamela, MD; FRCOG; Professor of Reproductive Medicine, University of Newcastle upon Tyne, since 2003; Consultant Gynaecologist, Newcastle Hospitals NHS Trust, since 1991; *b* 12 Feb. 1951; *d* of John Peter Smith and Ruby Smith (*née* Easton); *m* 1972, Ian James Murdoch; two *s* two *d*. *Educ:* Univ. of Edinburgh (BSc 1972; MB ChB 1975; MD 1987). MRCOG 1982, FRCOG 2001. Early career researching in field of reproductive endocrinology; estabd clinic for infertility treatment, NE England, leading to regl clin. service, Newcastle Fertility Centre at Life. Founder Mem., Newcastle Embryonic Stem Cell Gp, 2001–; Chm., British Fertility Soc., 2002–06. *Address:* Newcastle Fertility Centre at Life, International Centre for Life, Times Square, Newcastle upon Tyne NE1 4EP. *T:* (0191) 219 4740.

MURDOCH, Elisabeth, (Mrs M. R. Freud); Chairman and Chief Executive, Shine Ltd, since 2001; *b* 22 Aug. 1968; *d* of Keith Rupert Murdoch, *qv* and Anna Murdoch Mann (*née* Torv); *m* 1st, 1994, Elkin Kwesi Pianim; two *d*; 2nd, 2001, Matthew Rupert Freud, *qv*; one *s* one *d*. *Educ:* Vassar Coll., NY (BA). Dir of Programming, KSTU-TV, 1994–95; Pres. and CEO, EP Communications, 1995–96; Man. Dir, BSkyB Plc, 1996–2001. Trustee, Tate, 2008–. *Address:* Shine Ltd, 140–142 Kensington Church Street, W8 4BN. *T:* (020) 7985 7000.

MURDOCH, Dame Elisabeth (Joy), AC 1989; DBE 1963 (CBE 1961); *b* 8 Feb. 1909; *d* of Rupert Greene and Marie (*née* de Lancey Forth); *m* 1928, Sir Keith (Arthur) Murdoch (*d* 1952); one *s* three *d*. *Educ:* Clyde Sch., Woodend, Victoria. Mem., 1933–65, Pres., 1953–65, Mgt Cttee, Royal Children's Hospital, Melbourne. Trustee: National Gallery, Victoria, 1968–76, now Emeritus Trustee; McClelland Regl Art Gall., 1972. Founding Mem., Bd of Mgt, Victorian Tapestry Workshop, 1976– (Chm., 1986–88). Patron, Murdoch Children's Res. Inst., 1962–. Fellow, Trinity Coll., Univ. of Melbourne, 2000. Freeman, Victorian Coll. of the Arts, 1986. Hon. LLD Melbourne, 1982. *Recreation:* gardening. *Address:* Cruden Farm, Langwarrin, Victoria 3910, Australia. *Clubs:* Alexandra, Lyceum (Melbourne).

See also K. R. Murdoch.

MURDOCH, Gordon Stuart; QC 1995; **His Honour Judge Murdoch;** a Circuit Judge, since 2002; *b* 7 June 1947; *s* of late Ian William Murdoch and Margaret Henderson McLaren Murdoch; *m* 1976, Sally Kay Cummings; two *s*. *Educ:* Falkirk High Sch.; Sidney Sussex Coll., Cambridge (MA, LLB). Called to the Bar, Inner Temple, 1970; a Recorder, 1995–2002. *Recreations:* music, walking. *Address:* Canterbury County Court, The Law Courts, Chaucer Road, Canterbury, Kent CT1 1ZA.

MURDOCH, John Derek Walter; Director of Art Collections, The Huntington Library, Art Collections and Botanical Gardens, California, since 2002; *b* 1 April 1945; *s* of James Duncan and Elsie Elizabeth Murdoch; *m* 1st, 1967, Prue Smijth-Windham (marr. diss. 1986); two *s* three *d*; 2nd, 1990, Susan Barbara Lambert, *qv* (marr. diss. 2007); 3rd, Allison Browne Freeman. *Educ:* Shrewsbury Sch.; Magdalen Coll., Oxford (BA); King's Coll., London (MPhil). Asst Keeper, Birmingham City Art Gall., 1969–73; Victoria & Albert Museum: Asst, then Dep. Keeper, Dept of Paintings, 1973–86; Keeper of Prints, Drawings, Photographs and Paintings, 1986–89; Asst Dir in charge of Collections, 1989–93; Dir, Courtauld Inst. Gall., 1993–2002. Vis. Fellow, British Art Center, Yale Univ., 1979. Trustee: William Morris Gall., Walthamstow, 1975–2002 (Dep. Chm., 1997–2002); Dove Cottage, Grasmere, 1982–2002. *Publications:* David Cox, 1970; Byron, 1974; English Watercolours, 1977; The English Miniature, 1981; Discovery of the Lake District, 1984; A Sort of National Property, 1985; Painters and the Derby China Works, 1986; Seventeenth Century Portrait Miniatures in the Collection of the Victoria and Albert Museum, 1997; contrib. to Rev. of English Studies, Jl of Warburg and Courtauld Insts, Burlington Magazine, Apollo. *Address:* The Huntington Library, Art Collections and Botanical Gardens, 1151 Oxford Road, San Marino, CA 91108, USA.

MURDOCH, (Keith) Rupert, AC 1984; publisher; Chairman, since 1991 and Chief Executive Officer, since 1979, News Corporation, United States; Director, News International plc, UK, since 1969 (Chairman, 1969–87 and 1994–95; Chief Executive, 1969–81; Managing Director, 1982–83); *b* 11 March 1931; *s* of late Sir Keith Murdoch and of Dame Elisabeth (Joy) Murdoch, *qv*; *m* Patricia Booker (marr. diss.); one *d*; *m* 1967, Anna Torv (marr. diss. 1999); two *s* one *d*; *m* 1999, Wendi Deng; two *d*. Chm., News America Publishing Inc.; Dir, Times Newspapers Hldgs Ltd, 1981– (Chm., 1982–90 and 1994–); Chm. and Chief Exec. Officer, Fox Entertainment Gp Inc., 1998–; Chm., British Sky Broadcasting, 1999–2007. KSG 1998. *Address:* 1211 Avenue of the Americas, New York, NY 10036, USA; 1 Virginia Street, E1 9XY.

See also E. Murdoch.

MURDOCH, Susan Barbara; *see* Lambert, S. B.

MURE, Kenneth Nisbet; QC (Scot.) 1989; *b* 11 April 1947; *o s* of late Robert and Katherine Mure. *Educ:* Cumbernauld Jun. Sch.; Glasgow High Sch.; Glasgow Univ. (MA, LLB). CTA (Fellow). Admitted to Scots Bar, 1975; called to English Bar, Gray's Inn, 1990. Lectr, Faculty of Law, Glasgow Univ., 1971–83. Temp. Sheriff, 1983–99. Member: CICAP, 2000–; VAT Tribunal, 2003–. *Address:* Advocates' Library, Edinburgh EH1 1RF.

MURERWA, Dr Herbert Muchemwa; MP (Zanu PF) Goromonzi, Zimbabwe; Minister of Finance, Zimbabwe, 2002–07; *b* 31 May 1941; *m* 1969, Ruth Chipo; one *s* four *d*. *Educ:* Harvard Univ.; EdD (Educational Planning). Economic Affairs Officer, UN Economic Commission for Africa, Addis Ababa, 1978–80; Permanent Sec., Min. of Manpower Planning, 1980–81; Permanent Sec., Min. of Labour and Social Services, 1982–84; High Comr for Zimbabwe in UK, 1984–90; Minister: for the Envmt and Tourism, 1990–95; of Industry and Commerce, 1995–96; of Finance, 1996–2000; of Higher Educn and Technol., 2000–01; of Internat. Trade and Technol., 2001–02; of Higher and Tertiary Educn, 2004.

MURFIN, Dr David Edward; Principal in general medical practice, Ammanford, 1974–2006; *b* 15 June 1946; *s* of Leslie Walter Murfin and Elizabeth Ann Murfin; *m* 1972, Ann Margaret Lewis; one *s* one *d*. *Educ:* Gowerton Boys' Grammar Sch.; King's Coll. London; St George's Hosp., London. Adviser to ABPI, 1991–2006. Mem. Council, RCGP, 1984–90 and 1993–96 (Vice Chm., 1994–96); Mem., Standing Cttee on Medicines, RCPCH, 1996–2001. *Recreations:* reading, walking, cycling. *Address:* Longmeadow, 30 Llandeilo Road, Llandybie, Ammanford, Carmarthen SA18 3JB. *T:* (01269) 850914.

MURFITT, Catriona Anne Campbell; Her Honour Judge Murfitt; a Circuit Judge, since 2007; *b* London, 16 Jan. 1958; *d* of Dr A. Ian Campbell Murfitt and Anne Murfitt (*née* Ritchie); partner, Iain Hutton-Jamieson. *Educ:* St Mary's Sch. Ascot; Leicester Poly. Sch. of Law (BA Hons Law). Called to the Bar, Gray's Inn, 1981; practised at Family Bar in London chambers, 1981–2007; Asst Recorder, 1998–2000; Recorder, 2000–07. Mem. Cttee, Family Law Bar Assoc., 1997–2003; Mem., Professional Complaints and Conduct Cttee, Bar Council, 2001–04. *Recreations:* creating a garden, art, landscapes, architecture, sacred choral music, textiles, ski-ing. *Address:* c/o Chelmsford County Court, Priory Place, New London Road, Chelmsford, Essex CM2 0PP. *T:* (01245) 264670; *e-mail:* catriona.murfitt@btinternet.com.

MURGATROYD, Prof. Walter, PhD; Professor of Thermal Power, Imperial College of Science and Technology, 1968–86, now Professor Emeritus; Rockefeller International Fellow, Princeton University, 1979; *b* 15 Aug. 1921; *m* 1952; one *s* one *d* (and one *s* decd). *Educ:* St Catharine's Coll., Cambridge. BA 1946, PhD 1952. Hawker Aircraft Ltd, 1942–44; Rolls Royce Ltd, 1944–46; Univ. of Cambridge, 1947–54; UK Atomic Energy Authority, Harwell, 1954–56; Head of Dept of Nuclear Engineering, Queen Mary Coll., Univ. of London, 1956–67, and Dean of Engineering, 1966–67. Member: British-Greek Mixed Commn, 1963–78; British-Belgian Mixed Commn, 1964–78; British-Austrian Mixed Commn, 1965–78. Specialist Adviser to H of C Select Cttee on Energy, 1980–90. *Publications:* contrib. to various scientific and technical journals. *Recreation:* music.

MURIA, Sir (Gilbert) John Baptist, Kt 1995; Chief Justice, Solomon Islands, 1993–2003; Supreme Court Justice, Belize, since 2007; *b* 2 Feb. 1953; *s* of late John Baptist Manumate and of Adriana Gala; *m* 1982, Rosemary Kekealu; one *s* three *d*. *Educ:* Univ. of Papua New Guinea (LLB). Called to the Bar: PNG, 1980; Solomon Is, 1981. Sen. Crown Counsel, Solomon Is, 1980; Sen. Legal Officer, 1981–83; Chief Legal Officer, 1984–87; Dep. Public Solicitor, 1987–89; Public Solicitor, 1989–91; Actg Attorney Gen., 1989; Puisne Judge, High Court of Solomon Is, 1991–93.

MURIE, John Andrew, MD; FRCSGlas, FRCSE; Consultant Vascular Surgeon, Royal Infirmary of Edinburgh, since 1989; *b* 7 Aug. 1949; *s* of John Andrew Murie and Jessie Murie (*née* Sutherland); *m* 1977, Edythe Munn; one *d*. *Educ:* Univ. of Glasgow (BSc 1st

Cl. Hons Biochem. 1971; MB ChB Hons 1975; MD 1984); MA Oxon 1984. FRCSGlas 1979; FRCSE 1993. Clin. Reader in Surgery, Nuffield Dept of Surgery, Univ. of Oxford and Fellow, Green Coll., Oxford, 1984–89; Hon. Consultant Surgeon, John Radcliffe Hosp., Oxford, 1984–89; Clin. Dir, Gen. and Vascular Surgery, Royal Infirmary of Edinburgh, 1995–2000; Hon. Sen. Lectr, Univ. of Edinburgh, 1989–. British Journal of Surgery: Mem. Editl Team, 1989–96; Jt Sen. Ed., 1996–2002; Editor in Chief, 2002–. Mem., Nat. Panel of Specialists, NHS Scotland, 2000–05. Member of Council: Assoc. of Surgeons of GB and Ireland, 1994–99 (Hon. Editl Sec., 1996–99); Vascular Surgical Soc. of GB and Ireland, 1998–2001; RCPSG, 1998–2006. *Publications:* (ed with J. J. Earnshaw) The Evidence for Vascular Surgery, 1999, 2nd edn 2006; contrib. numerous chapters in textbooks and papers in learned jls on general theme of surgery (particularly vascular surgery). *Recreations:* golf, reading, food and wine. *Address:* Department of Surgery, Royal Infirmary of Edinburgh, Old Dalkeith Road, Edinburgh EH16 4SA. *T:* (0131) 536 1000; 8 Dalhousie Crescent, Eskbank, Edinburgh EH22 3DP. *T:* (0131) 663 5676.

MURLEY, John Tregarthen, CB 1988; DPhil; *b* 22 Aug. 1928; *s* of John Murley and Dorothea Birch; *m* 1954, Jean Patricia Harris; one *d. Educ:* University College, London (BA 1st Cl. Hons History); St Antony's Coll., Oxford (DPhil). Entered FO, 1955; Counsellor, Washington, 1976–80. *Publication:* The Origin and Outbreak of the Anglo-French War of 1793, 1959. *Recreations:* tennis, golf, piano.

MURLEY, Richard Andrew; Managing Director, N. M. Rothschild & Sons Ltd, since 2006; *b* 7 Jan. 1957; *s* of Alan and Anne Murley; *m* 1986, Penelope Wiseman; two *s* one *d. Educ:* Christ Church, Oxford (MA). Admitted solicitor, 1981; with Linklaters & Paines, 1979–81; Dir, Kleinwort Benson Ltd, subseq. Dresdner Kleinwort Benson, 1981–98; Man. Dir, Goldman Sachs Internat., 1998–2006; Dir Gen., Panel on Takeovers and Mergers, 2003–05. Mem., Financial Reporting Review Panel, 2003–. *Recreations:* golf, sailing, ski-ing. *Address:* N. M. Rothschild & Sons Ltd, New Court, St Swithin's Lane, EC4P 4DU. *T:* (020) 7280 5000.

MURNAGHAN, Dermot John; Presenter, Sky News Today, since 2008; *b* 26 Dec. 1957; *s* of Vincent Murnaghan and Wendy Murnaghan (*née* Bush); *m* 1989, Maria Keegan; three *d. Educ:* Sussex Univ. (BA 1979, MA History 1980); City Univ. (Postgrad. Dip. Journalism, 1983). Presenter, Business Prog., Channel 4, 1984–88; correspondent, EBC Switzerland, 1988–89; presenter: Channel 4 Daily, 1989–92; Lunchtime News, ITN, 1992–99; ITV Nightly News, 1999–2001; ITV Evening News, 2001–02; BBC Breakfast, 2002–07; presenter: The Big Story, ITV, 1993–97; Britain's Most Wanted, ITV, 1997–2002. Interview of the Year Award, RTS, 1998; Newscaster of the Year Award, TRIC, 2000. *Recreations:* running, film, football, sailing, chess. *Address:* Sky News, British Sky Broadcasting, Grant Way, Isleworth, Middx TW7 5QD.

MURPHY, Baroness *cr* 2004 (Life Peer), of Aldgate in the City of London; **Elaine Murphy,** MD, PhD; FRCPsych; Chairman, Council, St George's, University of London, since 2006; *b* Nottingham, 16 Jan. 1947; *d* of Roger Lawson and Nell Lawson (*née* Allitt); *m* 1st, 1969, John Matthew Murphy (marr. diss. 2001); 2nd, 2001, Michael Alfred Robb, *qv. Educ:* Univ. of Manchester Med. Sch. (MB, ChB 1971; MD 1979); PhD UCL 2000. FRCPsych 1986. Prof. of Psychiatry of Old Age, UMDS of Guy's and St Thomas' Hosps, 1983–96; Res. Fellow, Wellcome Inst. for History of Medicine, 1996–2005; Dist Gen. Manager, Lewisham and N Southwark HA, 1988–90; Chairman: City and Hackney NHS Trust, 1996–99; E London and the City HA, 1999–2002; NE London Strategic HA, 2002–06. Vice-Chm., Mental Health Act Commn, 1988–94. Hon. Prof. of Old Age Psychiatry, QMW, 1995–2006. *Publications:* Dementia and Mental Illness in Older People, 1986, 2nd edn 1993; Affective Disorders in the Elderly, 1986; After the Asylums, 1991; papers on mental disorder, social policy and social history. *Recreations:* Italy, social history research. *Address:* House of Lords, SW1A 0PW.

MURPHY, Andrew John; Sheriff of Tayside Central and Fife at Falkirk, 1991–2005; *b* 16 Jan. 1946; *s* of Robert James Murphy and Robina Murphy (*née* Scott); *m* 1980, Susan Margaret Thomson; two *s* two *d. Educ:* Allan Glen's School, Glasgow; Edinburgh Univ. (MA, LLB). 2nd Lieut RA (V), 1971–73; Flt Lieut RAF, 1973–75. Admitted to Faculty of Advocates, Scottish Bar, 1970; called to Bar, Middle Temple, 1990; Crown Counsel, Hong Kong, 1976–79; Standing Junior Counsel to Registrar General for Scotland, 1982–85; Temporary Sheriff, 1983–85; Sheriff of Grampian, Highland and Islands at Banff and Peterhead, 1985–91. *Address:* c/o Sheriff's Chambers, Court House, Main Street, Camelon, Falkirk FK1 4AR.

MURPHY, Brian Gordon; Building Societies' Ombudsman, 1992–99; *b* 18 Oct. 1940; *s* of Albert and Doris Murphy; *m* 1973, Judith Ann Parkinson. *Educ:* Mill Hill Sch. Articled Smiles & Co.; admitted Solicitor, 1966; with Roythorne & Co. and Russell & Dumoulin, Canada; Partner: Knapp Fishers, 1968–87; Farrer & Co., 1987–92. Pt-time Chm., Employment (formerly Industrial) Tribunals, 1991–92 and 2000–03. Vice-Chm., Incorp. Council of Law Reporting for Eng. and Wales, 1992–96; Mem. Council, Law Soc., 1982–93 (Chm., Employment Law Cttee, 1987–90); Pres., Westminster Law Soc., 1983–84. *Recreations:* golf, theatre, photography, travel. *Club:* Phyllis Court (Henley).

MURPHY, Christopher Philip Yorke; political lecturer; *b* 20 April 1947; *s* of Philip John and Dorothy Betty Murphy; *m* 1969, Sandra Gillian Ashton. *Educ:* Devonport High Sch.; The Queen's Coll., Oxford (MA). Formerly Associate Dir, D'Arcy MacManus & Masius. President, Oxford Univ. Conservative Assoc., 1967; held number of Conservative Party offices, 1968–72. Parish Councillor, Windlesham, Surrey, 1972–76. Contested (C): Bethnal Green and Bow, Feb. 1974, Oct. 1974. MP (C) Welwyn Hatfield, 1979–87. Vice-Chairman: Parly Urban and New Town Affairs Cttee, 1980–87; Parly Arts and Heritage Cttee, 1981–86; Mem., Select Cttee on Statutory Instruments, 1980–87 (rep of cttee on Commonwealth Delegated Legislation Cttee, 1980–87); UK Delegate to Council of Europe/WEU, 1983–87 (Hon. Associate, 1988). Vice-President: C of E Artistic Heritage Commn, 1984–87; C of E Youth & Drugs Commn, 1986–87. Member: Nat. Cttee for 900th Anniversary of Domesday Book, 1986; Chief Pleas of Sark (Parlt), 1989–90 (Vice-Pres., Internat. Cttee of Chief Pleas, 1989–90); Arts Council of Bailiwick of Guernsey, 1988–90; Council, Société Guernésiaise, 1988–90. Life Mem., CPA, 1987. Hon. Sec., Société Sercquiaise, 1988–90. Sec., Sodor & Man Diocesan Synod, and Bishop's Advr, 1991–2000; Chapter Clerk, St German's Cathedral, 1992–2000; Diocesan Sec., Dio. of Sodor and Man, 1993–2000; Secretary: Diocesan Bd of Finance, 1993–2000; Church Comrs for IOM, 1993–2000; Legislative Cttee, 1997–2000; DAC for Care of Churches, 1997–2000. FRSA. Freeman, City of London, 1984. Hon. Citizen, Cork, 1985. *Recreations:* arts, heritage, travel, conservation, walking. *Address:* 7 Charles Street, Peel, Isle of Man IM5 1AF. *Club:* Oxford Union Society.

MURPHY, Conor Terence; MP (SF) Newry and Armagh, since 2005; Member (SF) Newry and Armagh, Northern Ireland Assembly, since 1998; Minister for Regional Development, Northern Ireland, since 2007; *b* 10 July 1963; *m* Catherine; one *s* one *d. Educ:* St Colman's Coll., Newry; Univ. of Ulster; Queen's Univ., Belfast (MA). Mem. (SF), Newry and Mourne DC, 1989–97. Contested (SF) Newry and Armagh, 2001. *Address:* (office) Main Street, Camlough, Newry, Co. Down BT35 7TG; House of Commons, SW1A 0AA.

MURPHY, Cornelius McCaffrey, (Neil Murphy), MBE 1982; Chairman, New Life Venues Ltd, 1992–95, retired; *b* 31 May 1936; 2nd *s* of Edward and Annie Murphy, Glasgow; *m* 1992, Carmel Murphy; two *s* two *d* by previous *m*, and two step *d. Educ:* Holyrood Sch.; Univ. of Glasgow (MA 1958). Joined The Builder Group, 1962, following spells of teaching and management trng: Editor, 1974–83, Editor-in-Chief, 1983–87, Building Magazine; Dir, 1979–92; Man. Dir, Building (Publishers) Ltd, 1981–90, Group Man. Dir, 1990–92. *Recreations:* reading, golf.

MURPHY, Denis; MP (Lab) Wansbeck, since 1997; *b* 2 Nov. 1948; *s* of late John Murphy and of Josephine Murphy; *m* 1969, Nancy, *d* of Robert and Annie Moffat; one *s* one *d. Educ:* St Cuthbert's Grammar Sch., Newcastle upon Tyne; Northumberland Coll. Apprentice electrician, 1965–69; underground electrician, Ellington Colliery, 1969–94. Mem. (Lab) Wansbeck DC (Leader, 1994–97). *Address:* House of Commons, SW1A 0AA.

MURPHY, Dervla; writer; *b* 28 Nov. 1931; *d* of Fergus Murphy and Kathleen Rochfort-Dowling; one *d. Educ:* Ursuline Convent, Waterford. American Irish Foundn Literary Award, 1975; Christopher Ewart-Biggs Meml Prize, 1978; Irish Amer. Cultural Inst. Literary Award, 1985. *Publications:* Full Tilt, 1965, 11th edn 1995; Tibetan Foothold, 1966, 5th edn 2000; The Waiting Land, 1967, 7th edn 1998; In Ethiopia with a Mule, 1968, 7th edn 1994; On a Shoe String to Coorg, 1976, 7th edn 1995; Where the Indus is Young, 1977, 7th edn 1995; A Place Apart, 1978, 4th edn 1987; Wheels Within Wheels, 1979, 6th edn 2001; Race to the Finish?, 1981, 2nd edn 1982; Eight Feet in the Andes, 1983, 7th edn 1994; Muddling Through in Madagascar, 1985, 6th edn 1998; Ireland, 1985; Tales from Two Cities, 1987, 5th edn 1999; (ed) Embassy to Constantinople, the Travels of Lady Mary Wortley Montague, 1988; In Cameroon with Egbert, 1989; Transylvania and Beyond, 1992, 4th edn 1993; The Ukimwi Road, 1993, 3rd edn 1994; South from the Limpopo, 1997, 3rd edn 1998; Visiting Rwanda, 1998; One Foot in Laos, 1999, 2nd edn 2000; Through the Embers of Chaos: Balkan journeys, 2002, 2nd edn 2003; Through Siberia by Accident, 2005, 2nd edn 2006; Silverland: beyond the Urals, 2006, 2nd edn 2007; The Island that Dared: Cuban journeys, 2008. *Recreations:* reading, music, cycling, swimming, walking. *Address:* The Old Market, Lismore, Co. Waterford, Ireland.

MURPHY, Foster; *see* Murphy, R. S. F.

MURPHY, Gerard Martin, PhD; Senior Managing Director, Blackstone Group International Ltd, since 2008; *b* 6 Nov. 1955; *m*; two *s. Educ:* University Coll., Cork (BSc, PhD 1980); University Coll., Dublin (MBS). Various exec. posts in Ireland, UK and USA, Grand Metropolitan plc, 1978–91; Chief Executive Officer: Greencore Group plc, 1991–95; NFC plc, subseq. Exel plc, 1995–2000; Carlton Communications plc, 2000–03; Kingfisher plc, 2003–08. Non-executive Director: Novar plc (formerly Caradon plc), 1997; Abbey Nat. plc, 2004–05; Reckitt Benckiser plc, 2005–. *Address:* Blackstone Group International Ltd, 40 Berkeley Square, W1J 5AL.

MURPHY, Rev. Canon Gervase; *see* Murphy, Rev. Canon J. G. M. W.

MURPHY, Prof. Gillian, PhD; Professor of Cancer Cell Biology, Department of Oncology, University of Cambridge, since 2002; Fellow of Wolfson College, Cambridge, since 2003; *b* 25 May 1946; *d* of Donald Ralph Emery and Joan Edwina Emery; *m* 1968, George Johnstone Park Murphy (*d* 2002). *Educ:* Univ. of Birmingham (BSc Biochem.; PhD Biochem. 1971). Nato Sci. Fellow, 1972–74; Res. Fellow, 1974–87, Arthritis Res. Campaign Sen. Fellow, 1987–97, Strangeways Res. Lab., Cambridge; Prof. of Cell Biol., Dept of Biol Sci., UEA, 1995–2002 (Hon. Prof., Biol Scis, 2002). Hon. Vis. Prof. of Biochem., Univ. of Hong Kong, 2000. Member: Biochem. Soc., 1975; Amer. Soc. for Biochem. and Molecular Biol. FMedSci 2005. *Recreations:* gardening, walking, handicrafts, music. *Address:* Cambridge Institute for Medical Research, Box 139, Hills Road, Cambridge CB2 2XY. *T:* (01223) 763342; *e-mail:* gm290@cam.ac.uk.

MURPHY, Ian Patrick; QC 1992; a Recorder, since 1990; *b* 1 July 1949; *s* of Patrick Murphy and Irene Grace (*née* Hooper); *m* 1974, Penelope Gay; two *d. Educ:* St Illtyd's Coll., Cardiff; LSE (LLB). Chartering Clerk, Baltic Exchange, 1970–71; called to the Bar, Middle Temple, 1972, Bencher, 2001; Asst Recorder, 1986–90. *Recreations:* golf, ski-ing, cricket. *Address:* Farrar's Building, Temple, EC4Y 7BD. *T:* (020) 7583 9241; 3 Llandaff Chase, Llandaff, Cardiff CF5 2NA. *Clubs:* Cardiff County; Royal Porthcawl Golf.

MURPHY, Rt Hon. James; PC 2008; MP (Lab) Renfrewshire East, since 2005 (Eastwood, 1997–2005); Secretary of State for Scotland, since 2008; *b* 23 Aug. 1967; *s* of Jim Murphy and Anne Murphy. *Educ:* Bellarmine Secondary Sch., Glasgow; Milnerton High Sch., Cape Town. Dir, Endsleigh Insurance, 1994–96; Project Manager, Scottish Lab. Party, 1996–97. PPS to Sec. of State for Scotland, 2001–02; an Asst Govt Whip, 2002–03; a Lord Comr of HM Treasury (Govt Whip), 2003–05; Parly Sec., Cabinet Office, 2005–06; Minister of State: DWP, 2006–07; (Minister for Europe), FCO, 2007–08. Parly Spokesman, Scottish PFA. Chm., Labour Friends of Israel, 2001–02. Pres., NUS, 1994–96. *Address:* House of Commons, SW1A 0AA.

MURPHY, James Patrick; Sheriff of Glasgow and Strathkelvin, 1989–2001; *b* 24 Jan. 1932; *s* of Henry Francis Murphy and Alice (*née* Rooney); dual British/Irish citizenship; *m* 1956, Maureen Coyne; two *s* one *d. Educ:* Notre Dame Convent; St Aloysius' Coll., Glasgow; Univ. of Glasgow (BL 1953). RNVR, 1952–57. Admitted Solicitor, 1953; assumed partner, R. Maguire Cook & Co., Glasgow, 1959; founded, with J. Ross Harper, firm of Ross Harper & Murphy, Glasgow, 1961; Sheriff of N Strathclyde, 1976–89. President: Glasgow Juridical Soc., 1962–63; Glasgow Bar Assoc., 1966–67; Sheriffs' Assoc., 1991–92; Mem. Council, Law Soc. of Scotland, 1974–76. Examnr, Glasgow Univ., 1990–94. Governor, St Aloysius' Coll., Glasgow, 1978–86. *Publications:* contribs to Bench Books, other people's books and legal jls. *Recreations:* cycling, books, book binding, history, calligraphy, footering. *Address:* 8 Kirklee Gate, Glasgow G12 0SZ.

MURPHY, Rev. Canon (John) Gervase (Maurice Walker), LVO 1987; MA; Chaplain of the Chapel Royal of St Peter ad Vincula, Tower of London, 1991–96; a Chaplain to the Queen, 1987–96, an Extra Chaplain, since 1996; *b* 20 Aug. 1926; *s* of William Stafford and Yvonne Iris Murphy; *m* 1957, Joy Hilda Miriam Livermore; five *d. Educ:* Methodist Coll., Belfast; Trinity Coll., Dublin (BA 1952, MA 1955; Rugby football team, 1947–52 (Capt., 1951–52); cricket colours); Birkbeck Coll., Univ. of London (BA Hons Classics, 2000). Guardsman, Irish Guards, 1944–45; commissioned Royal Ulster Rifles, 1945–47. TCD, 1947–52 and Divinity Sch., TCD, 1949–52. Ordained, deacon, 1952, priest, 1953; Curate, Shankill Parish, Lurgan, 1952–55; Royal Army Chaplains' Dept, 1955; served: Korea, 1955–57; Woolwich, 1957–59; Aden, 1959–62; Infantry Junior Leaders, Oswestry, 1962–64; Bagshot, 1964–65; Worthy Down, 1965; Commonwealth Bde Sen. Chaplain, 1965–67; Sen. Chaplain, Guards Depot, Pirbright, 1967–69; DACG, Rhine Area, 1969–72; Sen. Chaplain, RMA Sandhurst, 1972–74; Asst Chaplain General: BAOR, 1974–75; South East, 1975–77; Vicar of Ranworth and RD of Blofield, 1977–79; Chaplain for Holidaymakers on Norfolk Broads, 1977–79; Domestic Chaplain to the Queen, Rector of Sandringham and Leader of Sandringham Group of Parishes, 1979–87; RD of Heacham and Rising, 1985–87; Hon. Canon of Norwich Cathedral, 1986, Emeritus, 1987–; Rector, Christ Church Cathedral, Falkland Is, 1987–91; Chaplain, Lord Mayor of London, 1993–94. Vice-Pres., British Assoc. for Physical Trng, 1988– (Hon. Fellow, 1988). Played: Internat. Rugby football for Ireland, 1952, 1954 and 1958; Rugby football for British Army 1957, and for Barbarians, 1958. *Publication:* Christ Church Cathedral, Falkland Islands: its life and times 1892–1992, 1992; The Very Reverend Dean Lowther Edward Brandon 1846–1933, 2005. *Recreations:* sport, walking, gardening, interior decorating. *Address:* Saffron Close, 17 Ringstead Road, Heacham, Norfolk PE31 7JA. *T:* (01485) 572351. *Clubs:* East India (Hon. Chaplain Emeritus, 2007–), London Irish RFC, Public School Wanderers RFC; Leprechauns Cricket (Ireland); Mid-Ulster Cricket.

MURPHY, (John) Philip; Head of Policy and Corporate Affairs - Europe and Central Asia, BG Group, since 2006; *b* 3 June 1958; *s* of Robert Anthony Murphy and Cecily Vaughan Murphy (*née* Nicholson); *m* 1st, 1983, Elizabeth McManus (marr. diss. 1988); 2nd, 1991, Sophie Annabel Davies; one *s* one *d. Educ:* St Cuthbert's Grammar Sch., Newcastle upon Tyne; Hertford Coll., Oxford (BA 2nd Cl. Hons French and Latin); City Univ. (Postgrad. Dip. in Practical Journalism); LSE (Dip. Macro- and Micro-Econs). Reporter: Southern Evening Echo, Southampton, 1981–83; and local govt corresp., The Journal, Newcastle upon Tyne, 1983–86; Lobby Corresp., Thomson Newspapers, 1986–87; Political Editor: Yorkshire Post, 1987–96; Press Assoc., 1996–98; Exec. Dir (Communications), Arts Council of England, 1998–99; Asst Gen. Sec. and Dir of Media Communications, Labour Party, 1999–2000; Special Advr to Prime Minister, 2000–01; BG Group: Govt Affairs Manager, 2001–02; Hd of Govt and Public Affairs, and Dep. Hd of Policy and Corporate Affairs Dept, 2003–06. *Publication:* (with R. Caborn) Regional Government for England: an economic imperative, 1995. *Recreations:* football, golf, literature, late 19th and 20th century art, music. *Address:* BG Group, 100 Thames Valley Park Drive, Reading RG6 1PT. *Clubs:* Wisley Golf; Old Thorns Golf.

MURPHY, Laurence; QC (Scot.) 2000; *b* 12 April 1958; *s* of William John Murphy and Alison Boyd Spindlow or Murphy; *m* 1989, Christine Marie Cecile Germaine Boch; one *s* one *d. Educ:* Univ. of Glasgow (MA (Hons) 1980; LLB 1982). Solicitor, 1983–89; Advocate, 1990–. *Recreations:* golf, tennis, walking, music, travel. *Address:* Advocates' Library, Parliament House, Edinburgh EH1 1RF. *T:* (0131) 226 2881.

MURPHY, Michael James, (Mick); Member (SF) South Down, Northern Ireland Assembly, 1998–2003; *b* Banbridge, 6 Feb. 1942; *s* of Michael and Mary Theresa Murphy; *m* 1965, Carole Trainor; six *d. Educ:* Legannay Sch., Leitrim, Co. Down. Publican in Rostrevor, 1978–91. Elected Mem. (SF) Newry and Mourne DC, 1996–; Mem. (SF) NI Forum, 1996–98. Contested (SF) S Down, 2001. *Recreations:* Gaelic games, Irish culture.

MURPHY, Prof. Michael Joseph, FBA 2002; Professor of Demography, London School of Economics and Political Science, since 1997; *b* 19 March 1947. *Educ:* Trinity Coll., Cambridge (BA 1969); Univ. of York (BPhil). Statistician, CSO, 1971–78; Res. Fellow, LSHTM, 1978–80; Lectr, LSE, 1980–97. *Publications:* contrib. learned jls. *Address:* Department of Social Policy, London School of Economics and Political Science, Houghton Street, WC2A 2AE.

MURPHY, Michael Joseph Adrian; QC 1993; **His Honour Judge Murphy;** a Circuit Judge, since 1999; *b* 1 Oct. 1949; *s* of Patrick Joseph Murphy, Hirwaun, Mid-Glam., and late Frances Murphy; *m* 1973, Rosemary Dorothy Aitken; three *s* one *d. Educ:* Aberdare Grammar Sch., Mid-Glam.; Sheffield Univ. (LLB, MA). Called to the Bar, Inner Temple, 1973. A Recorder, 1989–99. *Address:* The Law Courts, 50 West Bar, Sheffield S3 8PH. *T:* (0114) 281 2400.

MURPHY, Neil; *see* Murphy, C. McC.

MURPHY, Dame Olwen; *see* Hufton, Dame O.

MURPHY, Patrick James, CMG 1985; HM Diplomatic Service, retired; Adviser on Central Europe, British Consultancy Charitable Trust, since 2005; *b* 11 March 1931; *e s* of late Dr James Murphy and Cicely Mary (*née* Crowley); *m* 1st, 1959, Barbara May Healey-Purse (marr. diss. 1969); two *s*; 2nd, 1974, Jutta Ulrike Oehlmann; one *s. Educ:* Cranbrook School; Gonville and Caius College, Cambridge (BA; Geography Tripos). Served RAF, 1950–52. Oxford and Cambridge Far Eastern Expedition, 1955–56; BBC Gen. Overseas Service, 1956; Joined FO, 1957; Frankfurt, 1958; Berlin, 1959; FO, 1962; Second Sec. (Commercial), Warsaw, 1962; First Sec., FO, 1965; First Sec. (Commercial) and Consul, Phnom Penh, 1966; Consul, Düsseldorf, 1969; Consul, Hamburg, 1971; FCO, 1974; First Sec., Vienna, 1977; Counsellor, FCO, 1981–87. Advr, Sultanate of Oman, 1987–90; Consultant, HM Diplomatic Service, 1990–95; Regl Dir for Poland and the Baltic States, 1995–2005, Czech and Slovak Republics, 1997–2005, and Belarus, 2000–05, BESO. Mem. Council, Polish Corps of Volunteer Experts, 2006–. Officer's Cross, Order of Merit (Poland), 2000. *Recreations:* history, travel, wine, Irish life. *Address:* 260 Dacre Park, SE13 5DD. *T:* (020) 8852 2483. *Club:* Royal Air Force.

MURPHY, Patrick Wallace; agricultural consultant, since 1996; Under Secretary, Land Use, Conservation and Countryside Group, Ministry of Agriculture, Fisheries and Food, 1994–96; *b* 16 Aug. 1944; *s* of Lawrence Vincent Murphy and Agnes Dunn; *m* 1972, Denise Lillieth Fullarton-Fullarton; two *s. Educ:* St Chad's College, Wolverhampton; Trinity Hall, Cambridge (BA Hons). Joined MAFF, 1966; Asst Private Sec. to Minister of Agriculture, Fisheries and Food, 1970; First Sec. (Agriculture and Commercial), British Embassy, Washington, 1974–78; Controller of Plant Variety Rights, 1978–82; Head, Land Use and Tenure Div., 1982–86; Under Sec., 1986; Head, Milk and Potatoes Gp, 1986–89; Hd of Pesticides, Vet. Medicines, Emergencies and Biotechnol. Gp, 1989–93; Hd of EC Gp, 1993–94. Non-exec. Dir, IDV (UK), 1985–88. *Recreations:* cricket, tennis, gardening.

MURPHY, Rt Hon. Paul (Peter); PC 1999; MP (Lab) Torfaen, since 1987; Secretary of State for Wales, since 2008; *b* 25 Nov. 1948; *s* of late Ronald and Marjorie Murphy. *Educ:* St Francis RC Primary Sch., Abersychan; West Monmouth Sch., Pontypool; Oriel Coll., Oxford (MA; Hon. Fellow, 2000). Management Trainee, CWS, 1970–71; Lectr in History and Govt, Ebbw Vale Coll. of Further Education, 1971–87. Mem., Torfaen Borough Council, 1973–87 (Chm., Finance Cttee, 1976–86); Sec., Torfaen Constituency Labour Party, 1974–87. Opposition front bench spokesman for Wales, 1988–94; on NI, 1994; on for. affairs, 1994–95; on defence, 1995–97; Minister of State, NI Office, 1997–99; Secretary of State: for Wales, 1999–2002; for NI, 2002–05. Chm., Intelligence and Security Cttee, 2005–08. Vis. Parly Fellow, St Antony's Coll., Oxford, 2006–07. *Recreation:* music. *Address:* House of Commons, SW1A 0AA. *T:* (020) 7219 3463, (office) (01495) 750078; *e-mail:* paulmurphymp@parliament.uk. *Clubs:* Oxford and Cambridge; St Joseph's (St Dials).

MURPHY, Peter John; QC 2002; a Recorder, since 2000; *b* 20 May 1958; s of John James Murphy and Joan Murphy; *m* 1997, Ceri Louise Phillips; two *s* three *d. Educ:* Leicester Univ. (LLB Hons). Joined chambers, Cardiff, 1980; called to the Bar, Gray's Inn, 1980; an Asst Recorder, 1997–2000. *Recreations:* amateur dramatics and singing, numerous sporting activities incl. swimming, football and squash, avid reader. *Address:* 30 Park Place, Cardiff CF10 3BS. *T:* (029) 2039 8421.

MURPHY, Peter William; His Honour Judge Peter Murphy; a Circuit Judge, since 2007; *b* Boston, Lincs, 10 Feb. 1946; *s* of William Joseph Murphy and Rhiannon Murphy (*née* Rees); *m* 1992, Christine Service; one *s*, and one step *s. Educ:* Queen Elizabeth's Grammar Sch., Blackburn; Downing Coll., Cambridge (BA 1966; LLB 1967). Called to the Bar: England and Wales, 1968; Calif, 1981; Texas, 1985; private practice, London, 1970–78; Principal Lectr, Inns of Court Sch. of Law, 1978–80; private practice, San Francisco, 1980–84; Prof. of Law, South Texas Coll. of Law, 1984–2007; Trial and Appellate Counsel, Internat. Criminal Tribunal for Former Yugoslavia, 1998–2007. Trustee, Amer. Inns of Court Foundn, 1985–99, now Emeritus. Founding Editor-in-Chief, 1991–2007, Emeritus Ed., 2008–, Blackstone's Criminal Practice. *Publications:* A Practical Approach to Evidence, 1980, 10th edn as Murphy on Evidence, 2007; Evidence Proof and Facts: a book of sources, 2003. *Recreations:* theatre, music, watching sports (Blackburn Rovers and Harlequins), chess. *Club:* Oxford and Cambridge.

MURPHY, Philip; *see* Murphy, J. P.

MURPHY, (Robert Somerville) Foster; Principal, Charitable Futures, since 2002; Chief Executive, Abbeyfield Society, 1992–2002; *b* 1 June 1940; *s* of Robert Somerville Foster Murphy and Eva Constance (*née* Harvey); *m* 1964, Patricia Mary Hamilton; one *s* one *d. Educ:* Dublin Univ. (MA); Downing Coll., Cambridge (MA); London Univ. (Dip. SocScis (ext.)). Irish Sec., SCM, 1965–67; Youth Sec., BCC, 1967–72; Youth Sec., subseq. Head of Div., then Dep. Dir, NCVO, 1972–81; Dir, Volunteer Centre, UK, 1981–92. Board Member: Innisfree HA, 1993–99; Internat. Assoc. for Homes & Services for the Aging, 1994–2003; Centre for Policy on Ageing, 1997–2002 (Chm., 2000–02); Citizen's Advice Notes Trust, 2002–05; Abbeyfield Internat., 2002– (Vice Chm., 2005–); Vegetarian Housing Assoc., 2004–07. Voluntary Advr, Officers' Assoc., 2003–. *Publication:* (jtly) Integrating Care, Housing and Community, 1998. *Recreations:* opera, orchids, keeping fit. *Address:* 64 Callander Road, SE6 2QE; *e-mail:* foster.murphy@ukgateway.net.

MURPHY, Rory; Head of Commercial Health and Wellbeing, First Assist; *b* 23 April 1955; *s* of Philip Murphy and Noreen Murphy (*née* Sheahan); *m* 1976, Catherine Deane; two *s. Educ:* Bishop Bright RC Grammar Sch., Leamington Spa. Photographer, Pitt Rivers Mus., Oxford, 1972–84 (on secondment as Union Official, 1979–84); Nat. Sec., ASTMS, Ireland, 1984–87; Asst Gen. Sec., ASTMS, later MSF, 1987–89; Chief Exec., Finers, Solicitors, 1989–90; Dir of Industrial Relations, Royal Coll. of Midwives, 1990–95; Gen. Sec., NatWest Staff Assoc., 1995–99; Jt Gen. Sec., UNIFI, 1999–2004; Asst Gen. Sec., Amicus, 2004–05. Mem. Adv. Bd, Good Corp. Trustee: Officers Assoc.; Community Foundn Network. *Recreations:* football (Arsenal), theatre, art, archaeology. *Address:* First Assist, 32 High Street, Purley CR8 2PP. *Club:* Poole Labour.

MURPHY, Dr Simon Francis; City Region Director, Urban West Midlands, since 2006; non-executive Chairman, Sandwell Local Improvement Finance Trust Company Ltd, since 2005; *b* 24 Feb. 1962; *s* of Patrick Joseph Murphy and Mary Frances Murphy; *m* 1992, Bridget Lee Brickley; one *s* one *d* (and one *s* decd). *Educ:* Sacred Heart Coll., Droitwich; N Worcs Coll., Bromsgrove; UCW, Aberystwyth (BSc Econ 1983; PhD 1986). Tutor, Dept of Political Sci., UCW, Aberystwyth, 1984–86; Asst to Leader of Labour Gp, Wolverhampton MBC, 1986–89; Head of Research, Office of John Bird, MEP, 1989–94. MEP (Lab) Midlands W, 1994–99, W Midlands Reg., 1999–2004. Whip, 1996–98, Leader, 2000–02, European PLP; Vice-President: Socialist Gp, EP, 2000–02; Eurogroup for Animal Welfare & Conservation, 1997–99. Contested (Lab) Wolverhampton SW, 1992. Chief Exec., Birmingham Forward, 2004–06. Dir, W Midlands Develt Agency, 1997. Dir, Capital Ventures Mgt Ltd, 2004–06; non-exec. Dir, Eur. Bd, iSoft Gp plc, 2003–06. Member: Better Regulation Commn (formerly Task Force), 2005–06; MG Rover Task Force, 2005–06; Technol. Transfer Fund Investment Gp, Advantage W Midlands, 2005–06. Gov., Univ. of Wolverhampton, 1996–99. *Publication:* (contrib.) Contemporary Minority Nationalisms, ed M. Watson, 1990; (contrib.) European Governance, 2002; Views from the Ukon: democracy, participation and policy-making in the EU; articles in Waterlog Mag. *Recreations:* running, reading, cooking, fishing, watching sport.

MURPHY, Stuart Neil Luke; Creative Director, Twofour Broadcast, since 2006; *b* 6 Nov. 1971; *s* of David Francis Murphy and Patricia Mary Murphy (*née* Downing); *m* 2002 (marr. diss. 2005); two *s. Educ:* St Mary's RC Sch., Ilkley; Clare Coll., Cambridge (MA Pol Geog.). Joined BBC as runner, youth progs, 1993; worked on progs incl. Sunday Show, Lifeswaps, Heart and Soul (BBC Religion), reportage, 1994–95; comedy documentaries on Marty Feldman and Tony Hancock, 1996; Asst Prod., Great Railway Journeys in Zimbabwe, Zambia and Tanzania, 1996; Producer: various shows, MTV Europe, 1997; Big Breakfast, Channel 4, 1997; BBC: Strategic Develt Exec., TV, 1998; Broadcast Develt Exec., 1999–2002; launched UK Play, music and comedy channel, 1999; Hd of Programming, 1999–2001, Channel Controller, 2001–03, BBC Choice; developed BBC 3, 2003, Controller, 2003–05; commissioned Little Britain, Nighty Night, Bodies, Casanova, The Mighty Boosh, Torchwood, Rock Profile, Gavin and Stacey, Early Doors, Monkeydust, Shirley Ghostman, Little Angels, House of Tiny Tearaways, Honey We're Killing the Kids, Who Rules the Roost; Creative Dir, RDF Media, 2006. *Recreations:* political biographies, theme parks, hiding from tigers and pirates in the garden with the kids. *Address:* Twofour, 5th Floor, 6–7 St Cross Street, EC1N 8AU. *Club:* Century.

MURPHY, Thomas, CBE 1991; Managing Director, Civil Aviation Authority, 1987–95; *b* 13 Nov. 1928; *s* of Thomas Murphy and Elizabeth Gray Murphy (*née* Leckie); *m* 1962, Sheila Jean Dorothy Young; one *s* three *d. Educ:* St Mirin's Acad., Paisley; Glasgow Univ. (MA Hons). Served Royal Artillery, 1951–53. Marks and Spencer, 1953–55; British Petroleum, 1955–86: appts in Territory of Papua New Guinea, Trinidad, Scotland, Algeria, USA, 1955–68; Asst Gen. Man., BP Tanker Co., 1968–76; Gen. Man., Gp Personnel, 1976–81; Advr, Organisation Planning, 1981–86. Non-executive Director: CAA, 1986–87; Parity plc, 1997–2001; Oriel Gp plc, 1998. Internat. Sen. Managers Programme, Harvard Business Sch., 1973. *Recreations:* walking, coarse golf, destructive gardening. *Address:* Woodruffe, Onslow Road, Sunningdale, Berks SL5 0HW. *T:* (01344) 623261. *Club:* Wentworth.

MURPHY, Thomas James; journalist, The Times, since 1990; singer and actor; *b* 26 June 1956; *s* of James Murphy and Beatrice Murphy (*née* Strand); *m* 1976, Janet Sallis; four *s. Educ:* Salesian Sch., Chertsey; Sussex Univ. (BA History); Warwick Univ. (MBA); Royal Acad. of Music (Cert.). Kitchen porter and factory labourer, 1977; trainee journalist, Slough Observer, 1978; Sports editor, Buckinghamshire Advertiser, 1981; Editor: Staines Informer, 1983; East Grinstead Courier, 1984; Sub-editor, The Independent, 1986; Dep. Chief sub-editor, London Evening News, 1987; Editor, The Universe, 1988–90. *Recreation:* swimming. *Address:* 21 Clarke Court, Walsingham Road, Hove, East Sussex BN3 4FW. *T:* (01273) 230436.

MURPHY-O'CONNOR, His Eminence Cardinal Cormac; *see* Westminster, Archbishop of, (RC).

MURRAY; *see* Erskine-Murray.

MURRAY, family name of **Duke of Atholl**, of **Earl of Dunmore**, and of **Earl of Mansfield and Mansfield**.

MURRAY, Rt Hon. Lord; Ronald King Murray; PC 1974; a Senator of the College of Justice in Scotland, 1979–95; *b* 15 June 1922; *s* of James King Murray, MIEE, and Muriel (*née* Aitken), Glasgow; *m* 1950, Sheila Winifred Gamlin; one *s* one *d*. *Educ:* George Watson's Coll., Edinburgh; Univ. of Edinburgh (MA (1st cl. hons Phil) 1948; LLB 1952); Jesus Coll., Oxford (Hon. Fellow, 1999). Served HM Forces, 1941–46; commnd in REME, 1942; India and SEAC, 1943–46. Asst in Moral Philosophy, Edinburgh Univ., 1949–52; called to Scottish Bar, 1953; QC (Scotland) 1967; Advocate-Depute, 1964–67; Senior Advocate-Depute, 1967–70. MP (Lab) Leith, Edinburgh, 1970–79; Lord Advocate, 1974–79. Vice-Chm., Edinburgh Univ. Court, 1990–93. Mem., Scottish Records Adv. Council, 1987–93. Hon. Pres., Leith Boys' Brigade, 1984–98. Dr *hc* Edinburgh, 1996. *Publications:* contrib. various jls and books. *Recreations:* sailing, astronomy. *Address:* 1 Inverleith Grove, Edinburgh EH3 5PB. *T:* and *Fax:* (0131) 551 5330. *Clubs:* Royal Scots (Edinburgh); Royal Forth Yacht, Forth Corinthian Yacht.

MURRAY, Bishop of The, since 2002; **Rt Rev. Ross Owen Davies;** *b* 4 Feb. 1955; *s* of Rex John Davies and Margaret June Cooper; *m* 1983, Christine Fyfield; two *s* twin *d*. *Educ:* Melbourne Univ. (BA 1977, LLB 1979); St Barnabas Coll., ACT (ThL 1981). Ordained deacon, 1981, priest, 1982; Assistant Curate: St Peter's, Ballarat, 1981–83; St Lucia, Brisbane, 1984–85; Rector, Camperdown, Vic, 1985–91; Parish Priest, England: Mundford, 1991–93; Kingsdon, 1993–97; Rector, Hindmarsh, Vic, 1997–2000; Archdeacon of The Murray, 2000–02. *Recreations:* singing, gardening, reading. *Address:* PO Box 394, Murray Bridge, SA 5253, Australia. *T:* (office) (8) 85322270; *e-mail:* r.davies@murray.anglican.org.

MURRAY, Alan James; Chief Executive Officer, Hanson plc, 2002–07; *b* 12 May 1953; *s* of James and Elsie Murray; *m* 2002, Pamela Clark. *Educ:* Lancaster Univ. (BA Hons Econ.). FCMA 1988. Finance Dir, Burton Gp, 1985–88; Hanson plc, 1988–: Finance Director: ARC General Products and S Region, 1993–94; Hanson Brick UK, 1994–95; Asst Finance Dir, 1995–97; Finance Dir, 1997–98; Chief Exec., Hanson Building Materials America, 1998–2002. *Recreations:* cinema, music, travel.

MURRAY, Alexander, FRHistS; FBA 1995; Fellow and Praelector in Modern History, University College, Oxford, 1980–2001, now Emeritus Fellow; *b* 14 May 1934; second *s* of late Stephen Hubert Murray and Margaret (*née* Gillett). *Educ:* Bedales Sch., Petersfield; New Coll., Oxford (BA Mod. Hist.; BPhil European Hist.). FRHistS 1971. Served RA, 1953–55. Asst Lectr in Medieval Hist., Univ. of Leeds, 1961–63; University of Newcastle upon Tyne: Lectr, 1963–77; Sen. Lectr, 1977–80; Public Orator, 1973–76; Chm., Faculty of Modern Hist., Univ. of Oxford, 1992–93. Directeur des Études Associé, École des Hautes Études en Sciences Sociales, Paris, 1986; Vis. Prof. of Medieval Hist., Harvard Univ., 1989–90. Mem., NYO, 1951–53. *Publications:* Reason and Society in the Middle Ages, 1978; The Violent Against Themselves, 1998; The Curse on Self-Murder, 2000; Doubting Thomas in Medieval Exegesis and Art, 2006; contrib. learned jls and collections. *Recreations:* music, walking. *Address:* University College, Oxford OX1 4BH.

MURRAY, Andrew Robin; HM Diplomatic Service, retired; Ambassador to Uruguay, 1998–2001; *b* 21 Sept. 1941; *s* of Robert Alexander Murray and Jean Agnes Murray (*née* Burnett); *m* 1965, Irene Dorothy Foy; one *s* one *d*. *Educ:* Glenalmond; Edinburgh Univ. (MA Hons 1965). Economist with Govt of Ontario, Canada, 1966; investment analyst, ICFC, 1969; joined HM Diplomatic Service, 1973; First Sec., Islamabad, 1975–78; Head of Chancery, Buenos Aires, 1979–81; FCO, 1982–84; Counsellor, UKMIS to UN, 1984–88; Counsellor and Dep. Head of Mission, Caracas, 1988–91; FCO, 1991–93; Counsellor (Econ. and Commercial), Stockholm, 1993–97. *Recreation:* sporadic sport. *Club:* New (Edinburgh).

MURRAY, Ann, Hon. DBE 2002; mezzo-soprano; *b* Dublin, 27 Aug. 1949; *m* 1981, Philip Langridge, *qv*; one *s*. *Educ:* Royal Manchester Coll. of Music. Roles include: *for English National Opera:* Ariodante; Beatrice; Charlotte; Rosina; Xerxes; *for Royal Opera:* Cherubino; Composer; Donna Elvira; Dorabella; Idamante; Oktavian; *other roles:* Cecilio; Cenerentola; Iphigénie; Nicklausse; Sextus. Many recitals and concerts (European recital tours, 1990, 1993, 1994); festival appearances incl. Aldeburgh, Edinburgh, Munich, Salzburg. *Address:* c/o Askonas Holt Ltd, Lincoln House, 300 High Holborn, WC1V 7JH.

MURRAY, Athol Laverick, PhD; FRHistS; Keeper of the Records of Scotland, 1985–90; *b* Tynemouth, Northumberland, 8 Nov. 1930; *s* of late George Murray and Margery Laverick; *m* 1958, Irene Joyce Cairns; one *s* one *d*. *Educ:* Royal Grammar Sch., Lancaster; Jesus Coll., Cambridge (BA, MA); Univ. of Edinburgh (LLB, PhD). Research Assistant, Foreign Office, 1953; Assistant Keeper, Scottish Record Office, 1953–83; Deputy Keeper, 1983–84. Consultant Archivist, Jersey Archives Steering Gp, 1990–92. Vice-Pres., Soc. of Antiquaries of Scotland, 1989–92; Chm., Scottish Records Assoc., 1997–2000. FRHistS 1971. *Publications:* The Royal Grammar School, Lancaster, 1951; Castle Tioram: the historical background, 1998; *Fasti Ecclesiae Scoticanae Medii Aevi*, 2003; articles in Scottish Historical Review, etc. *Address:* 33 Inverleith Gardens, Edinburgh EH3 5PR. *T:* (0131) 552 4465. *Club:* Civil Service.

MURRAY, Craig John; writer and broadcaster; *b* 17 Oct. 1958; *s* of Robert Cameron Brunton Murray and Poppy Katherine Murray (*née* Grice); *m* 1984, Fiona Ann Kennedy; one *s* one *d*. *Educ:* Paston Grammar Sch.; Univ. of Dundee (MA Hons). HM Diplomatic Service, 1984–2004: Second Sec., Lagos, 1986–89; FCO, 1990–94; First Sec., Warsaw, 1994–98; FCO, 1998–99; Dep. High Commr, Ghana, 1999–2002; Ambassador to Republic of Uzbekistan, 2002–04. Rector, Dundee Univ., 2007–. Contested (Ind.) Blackburn, 2005. *Publications:* Murder in Samarkand, 2006; Dirty Diplomacy, 2007; Influence Not Power, 2007. *Recreations:* drinking, gossiping, reading, Celtic music, football, cricket. *Address:* 31 Sinclair Gardens, West Kensington, W14 0AU. *Clubs:* National Liberal; Gin Dobry (Poznan).

MURRAY, Sir David (Edward), Kt 2007; Chairman, Murray International Holdings Ltd, since 1981; director of companies; *b* 14 Oct. 1951; *s* of late David Ian Murray and of Roma Murray; *m* 1972, Louise V. Densley (*d* 1992); two *s*. *Educ:* Fettes Coll.; Broughton High Sch. Formed: Murray International Metals Ltd, 1976; Murray International Holdings Ltd, 1981; Murray Foundn, 1997. Young Scottish Businessman of the Year, 1984. Chairman: UK2000 (Scotland), 1987; Rangers FC, 1988–2002, 2004–. Gov., Clifton Hall Sch., 1987. DUniv Heriot-Watt, 1986. *Recreations:* watching sport, collecting and producing wine (Chevalier du Taste Vin, 2006). *Address:* Murray International Holdings, 9 Charlotte Square, Edinburgh EH2 4DR. *T:* (0131) 317 7000.

MURRAY, David Edward, FRICS; management consultant, since 1997; Deputy Chief Executive (Property), Crown Estate, 1993–97; *b* 22 Jan. 1944; *s* of late Thomas and Emily Murray; *m* 1968, Barbara Collins, *d* of late Sir Geoffrey and Lady Collins, Dorset; two *s*. *Educ:* Abbotsholme Sch., Derbys; Manor Park Sch., Hants; Hammersmith Sch. of Art & Building. AIQS 1970; Dip. Constr. Econs 1975; FRICS 1983. Sir Robert McAlpine & Sons, 1962–67; Planning & Transportation Dept, GLC, 1968–72; Royal County of Berkshire: Gp Quantity Surveyor, 1972–77; Co. Quantity Surveyor, 1977–88; Dir of Property, 1988–93. External Examiner: Coll. of Estate Mgt, 1978–92; Univ. of Portsmouth, 1994–98. Pres., Soc. of Chief Quantity Surveyors in Local Govt, 1979; Royal Institution of Chartered Surveyors: Chm., Quantity Surveyor's R&D Cttee, 1983–84; Mem., Divl Council, 1975–; Trng Advr, 1998–; Mem., several panels and wkg parties. *Publications:* Cost Effectiveness in Property Management, 1984; Artificial Intelligence in Property Portfolio Management, 1988; papers on property mgt and procurement to various UK confs. *Recreations:* sport (especially sailing), reading, music. *Address:* Highcroft, 18 Highclere Drive, Camberley, Surrey GU15 1JY. *T:* (01276) 24345. *Club:* Parkstone Yacht (Dorset).

MURRAY, Rt Rev. David Owen; an Assistant Bishop of Perth, Western Australia, 1991–2006; Director, Centre for Spirituality, St George's Cathedral, Perth, since 2007; *b* 23 Dec. 1940; *s* of George Lawrence Murray and Winifred Eva (*née* Morgan); *m* 1971, Janet Mary Chittleborough; two *s*. *Educ:* Swanbourne State Sch.; Claremont High Sch.; St Michael's House, Crafers, SA (Kelham, Aust.) (ThL 1968). Jun. Postal Officer, 1955; Postal Clerk, 1957–65. Ordained deacon, 1968, priest, 1969; Asst Curate, Bunbury, 1968–70; Rector: Lake Grace, 1970–74; Jerramungup, 1974–79; Mt Barker, 1979–83; Chaplain to the Bishop of Bunbury, 1978–83; Rector: S Perth, 1983–88; Fremantle, 1988–94; Archdeacon of Fremantle, 1988–91; Administrator during Abp's absences, Dio. of Perth, 1995–2006; Supervisor of Spiritual Dirs, Dio. of Perth, 2007–. Perth Diocesan Trustee, 1992–2006. Episcopal Rep. for Australia and NZ, Adv. Council to Anglican Religious Communities, 1993–2006; Mem., ANZ Regl Cttee, St George's Coll., Jerusalem, 2000–06. Member: Governance Cttee and Mgt Council, St Hilda's Anglican Sch. for Girls, Mosman Park, WA, 2002–04; Council of Mgt, Peter Carnley Anglican Community Sch., 2007– (Chair, Bldgs and Grounds Cttee, 2008–). *Recreations:* bagpipe playing, walking, swimming, cycling, caravanning, theatre, concerts, reading, entertaining, motorcycling, sailing. *Address:* The Mallee Hut, 29 Charnley Gardens, Waikiki, WA 6169, Australia.

MURRAY, Denis James, OBE 1997; Ireland Correspondent, BBC, since 1988; *b* 7 May 1951; *s* of late James and Helen Murray; *m* 1978, Joyce Linehan; two *s* two *d*. *Educ:* St Malachy's Coll., Belfast; Trinity Coll., Dublin (BA Respondency 1993); Queen's Univ., Belfast (HDipEd). Grad. Trainee, then Reporter, Belfast Telegraph, 1975–77; Belfast Reporter, RTE, 1977–82; BBC: Dublin Correspondent, 1982–84; NI Political Correspondent, 1984–88. *Publication:* (contrib.) BBC Guide to 1997 General Election, 1997. *Recreations:* music, reading, sport, family! *Address:* c/o BBC, Ormeau Avenue, Belfast BT2 8HQ. *T:* (028) 9033 8000.

MURRAY, Diana Mary, FSA; FSAScot; Secretary, Royal Commission on the Ancient and Historical Monuments of Scotland, since 2004; *b* 14 Sept. 1952; *d* of Keith and Mary Collyer; *m* 1987, Robin Murray; two *d*. *Educ:* King Edward VI Camp Hill Sch. for Girls, Birmingham; Univ. of Cambridge (MA 1974). MIFA 1984; FSAScot 1977; FSA 1986. Royal Commission on the Ancient and Historical Monuments of Scotland: Res. Asst, 1976–83; Hd, NMRS recording section, 1983–90; Curator of Archaeology Record, 1990–95; Curator Depute, NMRS, 1995–2004. Chm., Inst. of Field Archaeologists, 1995–96. JP E Lothian, 2000–07. *Recreations:* choral singing, gardening. *Address:* Royal Commission on the Ancient and Historical Monuments of Scotland, John Sinclair House, 16 Bernard Terrace, Edinburgh EH8 9NX. *T:* (0131) 662 1456, *Fax:* (0131) 662 1477; *e-mail:* diana.murray@rcahms.gov.uk; The Rowans, 15 Manse Road, Dirleton, East Lothian EH39 5EL; *e-mail:* diana.murray@rowanberry.co.uk.

MURRAY, Rt Hon. Sir Donald (Bruce), Kt 1988; PC 1989; a Lord Justice of Appeal, Supreme Court of Northern Ireland, 1989–93; a Judge of the Restrictive Practices Court, 1987–93; *b* 24 Jan. 1923; *y s* of late Charles Benjamin Murray and late Agnes Mary Murray, Belfast; *m* 1953, Rhoda Margaret (*d* 2005), *o c* of late Thomas and Anna Parke, Londonderry; two *s* one *d*. *Educ:* Belfast Royal Acad.; Queen's Univ. Belfast (LLB Hons); Trinity Coll. Dublin (BA). 1st Cl., Certif. of Honour, Gray's Inn Prize, English Bar Final Exam., 1944; Called to Bar, Gray's Inn, 1945, Hon Bencher, 1987. Asst Parly Draftsman to Govt of NI, 1945–51; Asst Lectr, Faculty of Law, QUB, 1951–53. Called to NI Bar, 1953, and to Inner Bar, NI, 1964; Bencher, Inn of Court, NI, 1971; Chm., Gen. Council of Bar of NI, 1972–75; Judge of the High Court of Justice, NI, 1975–89. Dep. Chm., Boundary Commn for NI, 1976–84. Chairman: Incorporated Council of Law Reporting for NI, 1974–87 (Mem., 1971); Bd, SLS Legal Publications (NI), 1988–94. Member: UK Delegn to Commn Consultative des Barreaux des Pays des Communautés Européennes, 1972–75; Jt Standing Cttee of Bars of UK and Bar of Ireland, 1972–75; Deptl Cttee on Registration of Title to Land in N Ireland. Chm., Deptl Cttee on Reform of Company Law in NI; Inspector apptd to report on siting of new prison in NI. Mem., Ct of the General Synod of Church of Ireland. Chm., Opera Review Gp, Arts Council of NI, 1998. Hon. LLD QUB, 1996. *Publications:* articles in various legal periodicals. *Recreations:* playing the piano, DXing.

MURRAY, Duncan Law; Partner, Morton Fraser, Solicitors, since 2002; Part-time Sheriff, since 2006; *b* 5 May 1959; *s* of James Duncan Murray and Catherine Margaret Law or Murray; *m* 1988, Ianthe Elizabeth Lee Craig; two *s* one *d*. *Educ:* Aberdeen Grammar Sch.; Aberdeen Univ. (LLB Hons 1980). Robson McLean Paterson: apprentice, 1980–82; Asst, 1982–85; Partner, Robson McLean, 1985–2002. Pres., Law Soc. of Scotland, 2004–05. *Recreations:* golf, ski-ing, hill-walking, family. *Address:* Morton Fraser, 30–31 Queen Street, Edinburgh EH2 1JX. *T:* (0131) 247 1000, *Fax:* (0131) 247 1004; *e-mail:* duncan.murray@morton-fraser.com. *Club:* Luffness New Golf.

MURRAY, Elaine Kildare, PhD; Member (Lab) Dumfries, Scottish Parliament, since 1999; *b* 22 Dec. 1954; *d* of Kenneth and Patricia Murray; *m* 1986, Jeffrey Leaver; two *s* one *d*. *Educ:* Edinburgh Univ. (BSc 1st Cl. Hons Chemistry); Cambridge Univ. (PhD Physical Chemistry 1980). Res. Fellow, Cavendish Lab., Cambridge, 1979–82; Researcher, Royal Free Hosp., London, 1982–84; SSO, Inst. of Food Res., Reading, 1984–87; Asst to Alex Smith, MEP, 1990–93; Associate Lectr, Open Univ., 1992–99. Dep. Minister for Tourism, Culture and Sport, 2001–03, Shadow Minister for Enterprise, 2007, Scottish Exec. Vice Convener, Finance Cttee, Scottish Parlt. *Recreations:* horseriding, spending time with my family and pets, exercise, music, reading, gardening. *Address:* 5 Friars' Vennel, Dumfries DG1 2RQ. *T:* (constituency office) (01387) 279205; *e-mail:* elaine.murray.msp@scottish.parliament.uk.

MURRAY, Gordon; *see* Murray, I. G.

MURRAY, Prof. Gordon Cameron, RIBA; PPRIAS; Joint Senior Partner, Gordon Murray + Alan Dunlop Architects, since 1999; Professor of Architecture and Urban

Design, and Head, School of Architecture and Building Science, University of Strathclyde, since 2007 (Visiting Professor, 2002–07); *b* 26 July 1952; *s* of James and Jessie Murray; *m* 1975, Sharon Boyle; two *d*. *Educ:* Univ. of Strathclyde (BSc, BArch). MCIArb; RIBA 1988; FRIAS. Assistant Architect: Richard Moira, Betty Moira & James Wann, 1974; Dept of Architecture and Related Services, 1975–77; Project Architect, Sinclair and Watt Architects, 1978–87; Partner: Cunningham Glass Murray Architects, 1987–92; Glass Murray Architects, 1992–99. Ext. Examr, Univ. of Ulster, 2004–08. President: Glasgow Inst. of Architects, 1998–2000; RIAS, 2003–05. Mem. Bd, Lighthouse Trust, 2003–. *Publications:* An Integrated Transport System for Greater Glasgow, 1977; (with A. Sloan) James Miller, Architect: a monograph, 1990; (contrib.) Challenging Contextualism: the work of gm+ad architects, 2002; Curious Rationalism, 2006; contribs to Herald, Scotsman, Architects' Jl, Prospect, Architectural Rev., Architectural Res. Qly. *Recreations:* cinema, art, saxophone, jazz, travel. *Address:* Breckenridge House, 274 Sauchiehall Street, Glasgow G2 3EH. *T:* (0141) 331 2926, *Fax:* (0141) 332 6790; *e-mail:* gordonm@murraydunloparchitects.com.

MURRAY, Iain Richard, OBE 1991; HM Diplomatic Service, retired; Consul-General, Houston, 2001–04; *b* 13 Aug. 1944; *s* of William Potts Murray and Barbara (*née* Beard); *m* 1st, 1967, Victoria Crew Gee (marr. diss.); one *s* one *d*; 2nd, 1984, Judith Wilson (marr. diss. 1991); 3rd, 1993, Norma Wisden (*née* Hummel). *Educ:* King Alfred's Grammar Sch., Wantage; Univ. of Kent at Canterbury (BA Hons 1968); Univ. of London (BSc Hons Econs (ext.)). Exec. Officer, CRO, 1963–65; re-joined FCO, 1968: Econ./Commercial Attaché, Accra, 1970–72; Second Sec., Addis Ababa, 1972–75; Vice-Consul (Commercial), Rio de Janeiro, 1975–79; Consul, Oporto, 1979–83; on secondment to Press Office, 10 Downing Street, 1983–85; FCO, 1985–87; Chargé d'Affaires, San Salvador, 1987–91; Asst Hd, Jt Export Promotion Directorate, FCO/DTI, 1992–94; Commercial/Econ. Counsellor, Kuala Lumpur, 1994–96; Consul-Gen., São Paulo, and Dir, Trade Promotion, Brazil, 1997–2000. Man. Dir, Q Publications Ltd, 2005–08; Dir, Pathfinder Search Oil and Gas, 2008–; Mem., Energy Adv. Bd (formerly Dir, Energy Practice), Norman Broadbent, 2005–07. Mem., Keepers of the Quaich, 2000–. Hon. FEI 2004. *Recreations:* hill-walking, history through travel and reading, losing golf balls. *Club:* Farmers.

MURRAY, Rt Rev. Ian; *see* Argyll and the Isles, Bishop of, (RC).

MURRAY, (Ian) Gordon; Chief Executive Officer and Technical Director, Gordon Murray Design Ltd, since 2007; *b* 18 June 1946; *s* of William and Roma Murray; *m* 1970, Stella Gane; one *s*. *Educ:* Natal Tech. Coll., SA. Moved to England, 1969, to work in motor racing; joined Brabham, 1970: design draughtsman, 1970–73; Chief Designer, 1973–74; Technical Dir, 1974–86 (design innovations incl. fan car, 1978, and hydro-pneumatic suspension, 1981; 22 Grand Prix wins; 2 World Drivers' Formula 1 Championships, first turbo-powered World Championship, 1983); Technical Dir, McLaren Internat., 1986–90 (29 Grand Prix wins; 2 World Drivers' Formula 1 Championships; 2 World Formula 1 Constructors' Championships); Technical Dir, McLaren Cars Ltd, 1990–2004: designed and prod McLaren F1 road car (Fastest Road Car, 1992; GTR version won 2 championships, and Le Mans 1995). Hon. Prof., Durban Inst. of Technology, 2003–. *Recreations:* motor-cycles, music, food and fine wine, architecture. *Address:* Gordon Murray Design Ltd, Wharfside, Broadford Park, Shalford, Surrey GU4 8EP.

MURRAY, Irena, (Mrs Eric Ormsby), PhD; Director and Sir Banister Fletcher Librarian, British Architectural Library, Royal Institute of British Architects, since 2004; *b* 3 July 1946; *d* of Jiri and Hana Žantovský; *m* 1995, Dr Eric Ormsby; two step *s*. *Educ:* Charles Univ., Prague (BA 1968); Univ. of Western Ontario, London (MLS 1970); McGill Univ., Montreal (MArch 1991; PhD 2003). Bibliographer, Nat. Liby of Canada, 1972; Curator, Nat. Archives of Canada, 1973; McGill University: Librarian, 1973–80; Dir, Art and Arch. Liby, 1981–96; Chief Curator, Rare Books and Special Collections, 1996–2004. *Publications:* (ed) Moshe Safdie: buildings and projects 1967–1992, 1996; (trans.) Karel Teige, Modern Architecture in Czechoslovakia, 2000; (ed) Looking at European Architecture, 2007; (ed) Le Corbusier and Britain, 2008; over a dozen archival guides to Canadian architects, etc. *Recreations:* reading, writing. *Address:* Royal Institute of British Architects, 66 Portland Place, W1B 1AD. *T:* (020) 7307 3644, *Fax:* (020) 7307 3719; *e-mail:* irena.murray@inst.riba.org.

MURRAY, Prof. James Dickson, FRS 1985; FRSE 1979; Professor of Mathematical Biology, 1986–92, now Emeritus Professor, and Director, Centre for Mathematical Biology, 1983–92, University of Oxford; Professorial Fellow, 1986–92, Hon. Fellow, 2001, Corpus Christi College, Oxford; *b* 2 Jan. 1931; *s* of Peter and Sarah Murray; *m* 1959, Sheila (*née* Campbell); one *s* one *d*. *Educ:* Dumfries Acad.; Univ. of St Andrews (BSc 1953; Carstairs Medal; Miller Prize; PhD 1956); Univ. of Oxford (MA 1961; DSc 1968). CBiol, FIBiol 1988. Lectr, Applied Maths, King's Coll., Durham Univ., 1955–56; Gordon MacKay Lectr and Res. Fellow, Tutor in Applied Maths, Leverett House, Harvard, 1956–59; Lectr, Applied Maths, UCL, 1959–61; Fellow and Tutor in Maths, Hertford College, Oxford, 1961–63; Res. Associate, Harvard, 1963–64; Prof. of Engineering Mechanics, Univ. of Michigan, 1964–67; Prof. of Maths, New York Univ., 1967–70; Fellow and Tutor in Maths, 1970–85, Sen. Res. Fellow, 1985–86, Corpus Christi Coll., Oxford; Reader in Maths, Univ. of Oxford, 1972–86. Vis. Fellow, St Catherine's Coll., Oxford, 1967; Guggenheim Fellow, Pasteur Inst., Paris, 1968; Visiting Professor: Nat. Tsing Hua Univ., 1975; Univ. of Florence, 1976; MIT, 1979; Winegard Prof., Univ. of Guelph, 1979; Univ. of Utah, 1979, 1985; Ida Beam Prof., Univ. of Iowa, 1980; Univ. of Heidelberg, 1980; CIT, 1983; Univ. of Angers, 1993; La Chaire Européenne, Univ. of Paris, 1994, 1995, 1996; Stan Ulam Vis. Schol., Univ. of Calif. Berkeley's Los Alamos Nat. Lab., 1985; Philip Prof., 1988–94, Boeing Prof., 1997–2000, Prof. Emeritus, 2000, James D. Murray Prof. of Applied Maths and Neuropathol., 2007, Univ. of Washington; Lectures: Scott Hawkins, Southern Methodist Univ., Dallas, 1984; Landsdowne, Univ. of Victoria, 1990; Pinkham, Swedish Hosp., Seattle, 1992 and 1998; Curle, Univ. of St Andrews, 1994; Smith, St Catherine's Coll., Oxford, 1994; Faculty, Univ. of Washington, 1998. Math. Comr, SERC, 1985–88; Founding Pres., European Soc. for Mathematical and Theoretical Biol., 1991–94; Member: Bd of Dirs, Soc. for Mathematical Biol., USA, 1986–89; ESF Network Cttee, 1991–94. For. Mem., Acad. des Scis, France, 2000; Hon. Mem., Edinburgh Mathematical Soc., 2008. Hon. DSc: St Andrews, 1994; Strathclyde, 1999; Hon. Dr Math: Milan, 2004; Waterloo, 2006. Naylor Lect. and Prize in Applied Math., London Math. Soc., 1989. *Publications:* Asymptotic Analysis, 1974, 3rd edn 1996; Nonlinear Differential Equation Models in Biology, 1977 (Russian trans. 1983); (ed with S. Brenner and L. Wolpert) Theories of Biological Pattern Formation, 1981; (ed with W. Jäger) Modelling of Patterns in Space and Time, 1984; Mathematical Biology, 1989, 3rd edn in 2 vols, vol. I 2002 (Polish trans. 2006), vol. II 2003; (ed with H. G. Othmer and P. K. Maini) Experimental and Theoretical Advances in Biological Pattern Formation, 1993; (jtly) The Mathematics of Marriage, 2002; several hundred articles in learned jls on the application of maths in biomed. scis.

MURRAY, Jennifer Susan, (Jenni), OBE 1999; Presenter, Woman's Hour, since 1987, The Message, since 2001, BBC Radio 4; *b* 12 May 1950; *d* of Alvin Bailey and Win Bailey (*née* Jones); *m* 1971, Brian Murray (marr. diss. 1978); partner, David Forgham-Bailey; two *s*. *Educ:* Barnsley Girls' High Sch.; Hull Univ. (BA Hons French/Drama). BBC Radio Bristol, 1973–78; BBC TV South, 1978–82; BBC Newsnight, 1982–85; BBC Radio 4 Today, 1985–87. Vis. Prof., London Inst., 2000–. TV documentaries include: Everyman: Stand By Your Man, 1987, Breaking the Chain, 1988, As We Forgive Them, 1989; The Duchy of Cornwall, 1985, Women in Politics, 1989; Here's Looking At You, 1991; Presenter: Points of View, 1993; This Sunday, 1993–; Dilemmas, 1994; The Turning World, 1998–2001. Weekly columnist, The Express, 1998–2000. Pres., Fawcett Soc., 2001–; Patron, FPA, 2002–. Hon. DLitt Bradford, 1994; DUniv Open, 1999. *Publications:* The Woman's Hour Book of Humour, 1993; The Woman's Hour: a history of British women 1946–1996, 1996; Is It Me Or Is It Hot In Here, 2001; That's My Boy!, 2003; Memoirs of a Not So Dutiful Daughter, 2008; contrib. to newspapers and periodicals. *Recreations:* reading, theatre, riding. *Address:* c/o Woman's Hour, BBC, Broadcasting House, Portland Place, W1A 1AA. *T:* (020) 7765 4314.

MURRAY, John; *see* Dervaird, Hon. Lord.

MURRAY, Prof. John Joseph, CBE 1997; PhD; FDSRCS; FMedSci; Dean of Dentistry, University of Newcastle upon Tyne, 1992–2002, now Professor Emeritus; Clinical Director, Dental Hospital, Royal Victoria Infirmary NHS Trust, Newcastle upon Tyne, 1995–2002; *b* 28 Dec. 1941; *s* of late John Gerald Murray, Bradford, and Margaret Sheila (*née* Parle); *m* 1967, Valerie (*d* 2002), *d* of late Harry and Lillie Allen; two *s*. *Educ:* St Bede's Grammar Sch., Bradford; Univ. of Leeds (BChD 1966; MChD 1968; PhD 1970); FDSRCS 1973; MCCDRCS 1989. Res. Fellow in Children's and Preventive Dentistry, Leeds Univ., 1966–70; Sen. Lectr in Children's Dentistry, 1970–75, Reader, 1975–77, Inst. of Dental Surgery, London; University of Newcastle upon Tyne: Prof. of Child Dental Health, 1977–92; Dental Postgrad. Sub-Dean, 1982–92. Chm., Cleft Lip and Palate Cttee, Clinical Standards Adv. Gp, 1998. Chm., Educn Cttee, GDC, 1999–2003. Mem., Children's Task Force, DoH, 2002–05. Founder FMedSci 1998. Hon. MFPHM 1998. John Tomes Medal, BDA, 1993; H. Trendley Dean Award, Internat. Assoc. Dental Res., 1997; Colyer Gold Medal, RCS, 1999. *Publications:* (jtly) The Acid Etch Technique in Paedodontics and Orthodontics, 1985; Fluorides in Caries Prevention, 1976, 3rd edn (jtly) 1991; Appropriate Use of Fluorides for Human Health, 1985; The Prevention of Dental Disease, 1983, 4th edn 2003 as The Prevention of Oral Disease. *Recreations:* golf, photography. *Address:* 6 Regency Way, Darras Hall, Ponteland, Newcastle upon Tyne NE20 9AU. *T:* (01661) 871035. *Club:* Ponteland Golf (Capt. 2006; Chm., 2007–).

MURRAY, John Loyola; Hon. Mr Justice Murray; Chief Justice of Ireland, since 2004; *b* 27 June 1943; *s* of Cecil Murray and Catherine (*née* Casey); *m* 1969, Gabrielle Walsh; one *s* one *d*. *Educ:* Crescent Coll.; Rockwell Coll.; University Coll. Dublin and King's Inns (Barrister-at-Law). Called to the Bar, Supreme Court, Ireland, 1967, Bencher, 1985; called to the Inner Bar, 1981; Attorney Gen. of Ireland, Aug.–Dec. 1982; in private practice at the Bar of Ireland, 1982–87; Attorney Gen., 1987–91; Judge of Court of Justice of European Communities, 1991–99; Judge, Supreme Court of Ireland, 1999–2004. Mem., Council of State, 1982, 1987–91, 2004–. Vis. Lectr, Georgetown Univ. Summer Sch., Heidelberg and Florence, 1994–2002; Vis. Prof. of Law, Univ. of Louvain, 1997–2000; Hon. Co-chair, Internat. Law Inst., Washington, 1996–. Chairman: Bd, Courts Service, 2004–; Judicial Appts Adv. Bd, 2004–. Chairperson: Anti-Fraud Cttee, Eur. Central Bank, 2000–03; Ethical Cttee, EC, 2004–07. Governor: Marsh's Liby, Dublin, 2004–; St Patrick's Hosp., Dublin, 2004–. Hon. LLD: Limerick, 1993; New England Sch. of Law, 2006. Grand Cross, OM (Luxembourg), 1991. *Publications:* legal articles in law jls and other pubns. *Address:* The Supreme Court, Four Courts, Dublin 7, Ireland. *Clubs:* Athenæum; Stephen's Green, Fitzwilliam Lawn Tennis (Dublin); Royal Irish Yacht.

MURRAY, Prof. Joseph Edward, MD, DSc; plastic surgeon; Professor of Surgery, Harvard University, 1970–86, now Emeritus; *b* 1 April 1919; *s* of William Andrew Murray and Mary Murray (*née* DePasquale); *m* 1945, Virginia Link; three *s* three *d*. *Educ:* Holy Cross Coll., Worcester, Mass (AB 1940); Harvard Univ. (MD 1943). US Army, 1944–47. Chief Plastic Surgeon: Peter Bent Brigham Hosp., 1951–86, Surgeon Emeritus, 1986; Children's Hosp., Boston, 1972–85. Hon. FRCS; Hon. FRCSI; Hon. FRACS. Hon. DSc: Holy Cross Coll., 1965; Rockford Coll., 1966; Roger Williams Coll., 1986. Numerous honours and awards from US sci. instns; (jtly) Nobel Prize for Medicine, 1990. *Publication:* Surgery of the Soul: reflections on a curious career (autobiog.), 2001. *Address:* 108 Abbott Road, Wellesley Hills, MA 02481–6104, USA.

MURRAY, Sir Kenneth, Kt 1993; PhD; FRCPath; FRS 1979; FRSE; Biogen Professor of Molecular Biology, University of Edinburgh, 1984–98; *b* 30 Dec. 1930; *yr s* of Allen and Elizabeth Ann Murray; *m* 1958, Noreen Elizabeth Parker (*see* N. E. Murray). *Educ:* Birmingham Univ. FRCPath 1991. Dept of Molecular Biology, Univ. of Edinburgh: Sen. Lecturer, 1967–73; Reader, 1973–76; Prof., 1976–. Member: Biochemical Soc.; European Molecular Biology Organisation; Academia Europaea. Chm., Darwin Trust, Edinburgh, 1984– (Founder, 1983). FRSE 1989. *Publications:* papers on nucleic acid biochem., molecular genetics, genetic engineering and viral hepatitis. *Address:* c/o Institute of Cell and Molecular Biology, University of Edinburgh, Edinburgh EH9 3JR. *Clubs:* Athenæum; New (Edinburgh).

MURRAY, Kenneth Alexander George, CB 1977; MA, EdB; Special Adviser to the Home Office on Police Service, Prison Service, and Fire Service selection, 1977–80; Director, Civil Service Selection Board, and Civil Service Commissioner, 1964–77; *b* 16 June 1916; *s* of late George Dickie Murray and Isabella Murray; *m* 1942, Elizabeth Ward Simpson (*d* 1999); one *d*. *Educ:* Skene Street and Central Schools, Aberdeen; Aberdeen Univ. (MA English (1st Cl. Hons), EdB Psychol. (1st Cl. Hons)). RAMC and War Office Selection Bd, 1940–45, Captain. Psychological Adviser, Govt of India, 1945–47; Lectr in Psychology, Univ. of Hull, 1948–50; Principal Psychologist and Chief Psychologist, CS Selection Bd, 1951–63. Adviser to Police Service in high-grade selection, 1963–, also to Fire and Prison Services, to Church of Scotland and C of E; Adviser (earlier) to Govts of Pakistan and Western Nigeria through their Public Service Commns. FBPsS 1984. *Recreations:* reading, walking, bridge, watching cricket and Rugby League. *Address:* 15 Melvinshaw, Leatherhead, Surrey KT22 8SX. *T:* (01372) 372995. *Clubs:* MCC, Royal Commonwealth Society.

MURRAY, Prof. Leo Gerard; Director, Cranfield School of Management, 1986–2003; *b* 21 May 1943; *s* of Patrick and Teresa Murray; *m* 1970, Pauline Ball; one *s* one *d*. *Educ:* St Aloysius' Coll., Glasgow; Univ. of Rennes; Glasgow Univ. (MA Hons 1965). British Petroleum Co., 1965–67; Courtaulds Gp, 1968–75; A. T. Kearney Ltd, 1975–79; Rothmans International Ltd, 1979–86: Man. Dir, Murray Sons & Co. Ltd, 1979–82; Dir, Overseas Mfg and Licensing, 1982–85; Dir, ME Region, 1985–86. Pro Vice-Chancellor, Cranfield Inst. of Technology, then Univ., 1992–95. Mem., Textile Sector Gp, NEDO, 1987–88. Chairman: ICL Cranfield Business Games Ltd, 1987–92; Cranfield Conference Centre, 1993–2003; Man. Dir, Cranfield Management Develt Ltd, 1993–2003; Chm.,

Fairmays Solicitors, 2001–03. Board Member: E of England Develt Agency, 2000–06; E of England Internat., 2004–06. Non-exec. Dir, Spectris plc, 2003–06. Director and Treasurer: Council of Univ. Management Schs, 1987–92; Assoc. of Business Schs, 1992–93 and 1999–2003; Bd Mem., Eur. Foundn for Mgt Develt, 2000–03; Membre: Conseil d'Orientation, Ecole Internat. d'Affaires, Marseilles, 1988–91; Conseil d'Admin, Univ. Technique de Compiègne, 1996–99. Vice-Pres., Strategic Planning Soc., 1992–99. Chairman: Bd, Euro-Arab Management Sch., Granada, Spain, 2003–06; Govs, Nat. Centre for Languages, 2004–05. Trustee: Blind in Business, 1992–2005; Macintyre Charitable Trust, 2003–. FCIM 1988; FRSA 1989; CCMI 2000. *Recreations:* family, work, golf. *Address:* The Beeches, 2 Church Lane, Lathbury, Bucks MK16 8JY. *T:* (01908) 615574. *Club:* Woburn Golf and Country.

MURRAY, Leo Joseph, CB 1986; QC (Aust.) 1980; legislation consultant, since 1989; Parliamentary Counsel, Queensland, Australia, 1975–89; *b* 7 April 1927; *s* of William Francis Murray and Theresa Agnes Murray (*née* Sheehy); *m* 1957, Janet Barbara Weir (marr. diss. 1987); two *d. Educ:* St Columban's Coll., Brisbane; Univ. of Queensland (BA, LLB). Admitted Barrister, Supreme Court, Queensland, 1951; Asst Crown Prosecutor, 1958; Asst Parly Counsel, 1963. *Recreations:* golf, ski-ing. *Address:* 99 Red Hill Road, Nudgee, Qld 4014, Australia. *T:* (7) 32675786. *Clubs:* Irish, Nudgee Golf (Brisbane); Southern Alps Ski (Sydney).

MURRAY, Leslie Allan, (Les), AO 1989; poet; *b* 17 Oct. 1938; *s* of late Cecil Allan Murray and Miriam Pauline Murray (*née* Arnall); *m* 1962, Valerie Gina Morelli; three *s* two *d. Educ:* Univ. of Sydney (BA 1969). Acting Editor, Poetry Australia, 1973–80; Editor, New Oxford Book of Australian Verse, 1985–97; Literary Editor, Quadrant, 1987–. Hon. doctorates from univs of New England, Stirling, NSW, ANU and Sydney. Petrarca Prize, Germany, 1995; T. S. Eliot Prize, 1997; Queen's Gold Medal for Poetry, 1998. *Publications:* Collected Poems, 1976, rev. edn 1998, US edn as The Rabbiters Bounty, 1992; The Boys Who Stole the Funeral (verse novel), 1980; The Paperbark Tree (selected prose), 1991; (ed) Fivefathers, 1995; Subhuman Redneck Poems, 1996; A Working Forest (prose), 1997; Fredy Neptune (verse novel), 1998 (Mondello Prize, Italy, 2004) (trans. Dutch, 2000, Italian and German, 2004); Conscious & Verbal (verse), 1999; Learning Human: selected poems (NY Times and Amer. Nat. Liby Assoc. Notable Book award), 2001, updated edn 2003; Poems the Size of Photographs, 2002; New Collected Poems, 2002; Hell and After: the first important Australian poets, 2004; The Biplane Houses (verse), 2006. *Recreations:* work, gossip, fine coffee, ruminative driving, film-going. *Address:* c/o Margaret Connolly & Associates, 16 Winton Street, Warrawee, NSW 2074, Australia.

MURRAY, Michael Thomas; HM Diplomatic Service, retired; Member, Advisory Board, Tynedale Enterprise Project, since 2007; *b* 13 Oct. 1945; *s* of late Robert Murray and Anne Clark Murray (*née* Leech); *m* 1968, Else Birgitta Margareta Paues; one *s* one *d. Educ:* Bedlington Grammar Sch. Joined FO, 1964; DSAO, 1964; Prague, 1967; Vienna, 1971; Vice-Consul (Commercial), Frankfurt, 1973; Second Sec. (Develt), Khartoum, 1977; FCO, 1980; First Sec. and Hd of Chancery, Banjul, 1983; FCO, 1988; First Sec. (Develt/Econ.), Lusaka, 1995; on loan to DFID, Lusaka, 1998; Dep. Consul Gen., Chicago, 1999; Ambassador to Eritrea, 2002–06. Member: Cttee, Friends of Bellingham Surgery, 2007–; New Leader Project, Northumberland Uplands Local Action Gp, 2008–. *Recreations:* living lightly; coarse, chemical-free horticulture; my logpile, golf, arts and crafts. *Address:* The Old Rectory, Falstone, Hexham, Northumberland NE48 1AE. *Club:* Laholms Golf (Sweden).

MURRAY of Blackbarony, Sir Nigel Andrew Digby, 15th Bt *cr* 1628; farmer; *b* 15 Aug. 1944; *s* of Sir Alan John Digby Murray of Blackbarony, 14th Bt, and of Mabel Elisabeth, *d* of late Arthur Bernard Schiele, Arias, Argentina; *S* father, 1978; *m* 1980, Diana Margaret, *yr d* of Robert C. Bray, Arias, Argentina; one *s* two *d. Educ:* St Paul's School, Argentina; Salesian Agricl Sch., Argentina; Royal Agricultural Coll., Cirencester. Farms dairy cattle, store cattle, crops and bees. Holds a private pilot's licence. *Heir: s* Alexander Nigel Robert Murray [*b* 1 July 1981. *Educ:* Univ. of Buenos Aires]. *Address:* Establecimiento Tinamú, cc 67, 2624 Arias, Provincia de Córdoba, Argentina. *T:* (03468) 441231, 449801.

MURRAY, Prof. Noreen Elizabeth, (Lady Murray), CBE 2002; PhD; FRS 1982; FRSE; Professor of Molecular Genetics, Institute of Cell and Molecular Biology (formerly Department of Molecular Biology), University of Edinburgh, 1988–2001, now Emeritus; *b* 26 Feb. 1935; *d* of John and Lilian Grace Parker; *m* 1958, Sir Kenneth Murray, *qv. Educ:* King's College London (BSc; FKC 2006); Univ. of Birmingham (PhD). Research Associate: Stanford Univ., California, 1960–64; Univ. of Cambridge, 1964–67; Mem., MRC Molecular Genetics Unit, Edinburgh, 1968–74; Lectr, 1974, later Sen. Lectr, Reader, 1978–88, Dept. of Molecular Biology, Univ. of Edinburgh; scientist in European Molecular Biol. Lab., Heidelberg, 1980–82. Member: Sci. Scholarships Cttee, Royal Commn for 1851, 2002–; Sci. and Technol. Hons Cttee, Cabinet Office, 2005–. Mem., BBSRC, 1994–97; Pres., Genetical Soc., 1987–90. Mem., EMBO, 1981. Trustee, Darwin Trust of Edinburgh, 1990–. FRSE 1989. Hon. DSc: UMIST, 1995; Birmingham, 1995; Warwick, 2001. Gabor Medal, Royal Soc., 1989; AstraZeneca Award, Biochem. Soc., 2005. *Publications:* original research papers and reviews in field of genetics and molecular biology. *Recreation:* gardening. *Address:* c/o Institute of Cell Biology, University of Edinburgh, Mayfield Road, Edinburgh EH9 3JR. *T:* (0131) 650 5374.

MURRAY, Norman Loch, CA; Chairman, Cairn Energy plc, since 2002 (Director, since 1999); President, Institute of Chartered Accountants of Scotland, 2006–07; *b* 17 March 1948; *s* of Thomas Loch Murray and May Fox Murray (*née* Davidson); *m* 1973, Pamela Anne Low; two *s. Educ:* George Watson's Coll., Edinburgh; Heriot-Watt Univ. (BA 1971); Harvard Business Sch. (PMD 1987). CA 1976. Grad. trainee, Scottish & Newcastle Breweries, 1971–73; CA apprentice, Arthur Young McLelland Moores & Co., Edinburgh, 1973–76; Dep. Manager, Peat Marwick Mitchell & Co., Hong Kong, 1976–80; Asst Lectr, Accountancy and Finance, Heriot-Watt Univ., 1980; Manager, Royal Bank Develt Capital Ltd, 1980–84; Dir, Charterhouse Develt Capital Ltd, 1984–89; Dep. Chief Exec., 1989–96, Chief Exec., 1996–97, Chm., 1998, Morgan Grenfell Private Equity Ltd; Dir, Morgan Grenfell Asset Mgt Ltd, 1997–98. Non-executive Director: Taunton Cider Co. Ltd, 1991–93; Bristow Helicopter Gp Ltd, 1991–96; Penta Capital Partners Hldgs Ltd, 1999–2007; Robert Wiseman Dairies plc, 2003–; Greene King plc, 2004–. Mem. Council, 1992–97, Chm., 1997–98, British Venture Capital Assoc. Mem. Council, 1992–98, Sen. Vice-Pres., 2005–06, ICAS. Chm., Governing Council, George Watson's Coll., 2004– (Gov., 1994–2004). Gov., St Columba's Hospice, 1998– (Chm., Investment Cttee, 1998–2003). FRSA. Hon. Prof., Heriot-Watt Univ., Edinburgh, 2008–. *Publication:* (jtly) Making Corporate Reports Valuable, 1988. *Recreations:* climbing and hill walking, classic cars, golf, squash, travel. *Address:* Ettrick, 8 Pentland Avenue, Colinton, Edinburgh EH13 0HZ. *Clubs:* Harvard Business School of London; New (Edinburgh); Luffness New Golf; Royal Hong Kong Yacht.

MURRAY, Sir Patrick (Ian Keith), 12th Bt *cr* 1673; *b* 22 March 1965; *s* of Sir William Patrick Keith Murray, 11th Bt, and of Susan Elizabeth (who *m* 1976, J. C. Hudson, PhD), *d* of Stacey Jones; *S* father, 1977. *Educ:* Christ College, Brecon, Powys; LAMDA. *Heir: kinsman* Major Peter Keith-Murray, Canadian Forces [*b* 12 July 1935; *m* 1960, Judith Anne, *d* of late Andrew Tinsley; one *s* one *d*].

MURRAY, Rev. Paul B.; *see* Beasley-Murray.

MURRAY, Peter Gerald Stewart; Chairman, Wordsearch, since 2004 (Managing Director, 1983–2004); Founder Director, London Architecture Biennale, 2004, 2006; Exhibition Director, New London Architecture, since 2005; Director, London Festival of Architecture, 2008; *b* 6 April 1944; *s* of Stewart and Freda Murray; *m* 1967, Jane Wood; two *s* two *d. Educ:* King's Coll., Taunton; Sch. of Architecture, Royal West of England Acad., Bristol; Dept of Architecture, Univ. of Bristol; Architectural Assoc. Sch. of Architecture. Editor, Building Design, 1974–79; Editor, RIBA Jl, and Man. Dir, RIBA Magazines Ltd, 1979–84; founded Wordsearch Ltd and launched Blueprint mag., 1983. Editor, Pidgeon Digital, 2007–. Mem. Council, 1987–90, Hon. Sec., 1989–90, AA; Mem. Architecture Cttee, RA, 2000–06. Exhibition Co-organiser: New Architecture: the work of Foster, Rogers and Stirling, RA, 1986; Living Bridges: the inhabited bridge, past, present and future, RA, 1996; New City Architecture, Broadgate, 2004. Trustee, Bannister Fletcher, 1984–86. Hon. Sec. and Dep. Chm., Bedford Park Soc., 1998–. Dir, Cycle to Cannes, charity cycle ride, 2006–. FRSA 1990. Hon. FRIBA 2000. Liveryman, Co. of Architects, 2008. *Publications:* Modern Architecture in Britain, 1984; Contemporary British Architects, 1995; Living Bridges (exhibn catalogue), 1996; New Urban Environments, 1997; The Saga of Sydney Opera House, 2004; Architecture and Commerce, 2005. *Recreations:* cycling, tennis, looking at buildings, sketching, London. *Address:* 31 Priory Avenue, Bedford Park, W4 1TZ; *e-mail:* pgsmurray@mac.com. *Clubs:* Athenæum, Architecture (Hon. Sec., 1978–), Hurlingham.

MURRAY, Prof. Robin MacGregor, MD; Professor of Psychiatry, University of London, at Institute of Psychiatry, King's College London, since 1999; *b* 31 Jan. 1944; *s* of James Alistair Campbell Murray and Helen Murray; *m* 1970, Shelagh Harris; one *s* one *d. Educ:* Royal High Sch., Edinburgh; Glasgow Univ. (MB, ChB 1968; MD 1974). MRCP 1971; MRCPsych 1976; MPhil London, 1976; DSc London, 1989. Registrar, Dept of Medicine, Univ. of Glasgow/Western Infirmary, 1971; Sen. House Officer, successively Registrar and Sen. Registrar, Maudsley Hosp., 1972–76; Vis. Fellow, National Inst. of Health, Washington, DC, 1977; Institute of Psychiatry, 1978–: Sen. Lectr, 1978–82; Dean, 1982–89; Prof. of Psychol Medicine, KCL, 1989–99. Pres., Assoc. of European Psychiatrists, 1995–96. For. Mem., Inst. of Medicine, USA, 2004. Founder FMedSci 1998. *Publications:* (jtly) Essentials of Postgraduate Psychiatry, 1979; (jtly) Misuse of Psychotropic Drugs, 1981; Lectures on the History of Psychiatry, 1990; Schizophrenia, 1996; Neurodevelopment and Adult Psychopathology, 1997; Psychosis in the Inner City, 1998; (jtly) First Episode Psychosis, 1999; (ed jtly) Comprehensive Care of Schizophrenia, 2000; (jtly) An Atlas of Schizophrenia, 2002; Marijuana and Madness, 2004; articles on schizophrenia, depression, brain imaging and psychiatric genetics. *Recreations:* Scottish and Jamaican music, swimming.

MURRAY, Roger; Chairman, Fuerst Day Lawson Holdings, 1997–2007; *b* 8 June 1936; *s* of Donald Murray and Nancy (*née* Irons); *m* 1960, Anthea Mary (*née* Turnbull); one *s* three *d. Educ:* Uppingham Sch.; Brasenose Coll., Oxford (MA). RNVR (Sub-Lieut), 1954–56. Joined Cargill Inc., Minneapolis, 1959; President: Cargill Canada, 1973; Cargill Europe Ltd, 1982–97; Chm., Cargill plc, 1982–97; Mem., Management Cttee, Cargill Inc., 1986–97. Chairman: JP Morgan Fleming Emerging Markets IT, 1994–2003; Pacific Rim Palm Oil Ltd (Mauritius), 2001–05. Canadian and British citizen. *Recreations:* sailing, ski-ing, mountaineering, golf. *Address:* 11 Pembridge Place, W2 4XB. *T:* (020) 7243 0026.

MURRAY, Ronald King; *see* Murray, Rt Hon. Lord.

MURRAY, Sir Rowland William, 15th Bt *cr* 1630, of Dunerne, Fifeshire; *b* 22 Sept. 1947; *s* of Sir Rowland William Patrick Murray, 14th Bt and Josephine Margaret Murray (*née* Murphy) (*d* 1989); *S* father, 1994, but his name does not appear on the Official Roll of the Baronetage; *m* 1970, Nancy Diane, *d* of George C. Newberry; one *s* one *d. Educ:* Georgia State Univ. (SB 1974). General Manager, Beverly Hall Furniture Galleries, retail furniture and accessories. *Recreations:* golf, gardening, travel. *Heir: s* Rowland William Murray IV, *b* 31 July 1979. *Address:* 1187 Brookhaven Park Place, Atlanta, GA 30319, USA. *T:* (404) 2662408. *Clubs:* Midtown Atlanta Rotary, Atlanta High Museum of Art, Atlanta Botanical Gardens.

MURRAY, Ruth Hilary; *see* Finnegan, R. H.

MURRAY, Simon Anthony, CEng; consultant; Chairman, Geoffrey Osborne Ltd, since 2003; *b* 31 Aug. 1951; *s* of Frank Murray and Barbara (*née* Williams); *m* 1st, 1974, Anne Humphrey (marr. diss. 1982); 2nd, 1983, Lindsay Maxwell (marr. diss. 2004); two *s* one *d. Educ:* Welbeck Coll.; Imperial Coll., London (BSc). CEng 1978; MICE 1978; FCGI 1999. Ove Arup & Partners: S Africa, 1975–77; Kenya, Zimbabwe, Hong Kong and London, 1977–89; Dir, 1990–94; Man. Dir, Gp Technical Services, BAA plc, 1995–98; Dir, Major Projects and Investment, Railtrack plc, 1999–2001. Non-executive Director: Ascot Authority (Hldgs) Ltd, 2000–06; Manchester Airport Develts Ltd, 2002–04. Mem., EPSRC, 1998–2001. *Recreations:* jogging, wine, windsurfing. *Address:* 150 Langton Way, Blackheath, SE3 7JS.

MURRAY, Susan Elizabeth, (Mrs M. Weston); non-executive Director: Imperial Tobacco Group plc, since 2004; Enterprise Inns plc, since 2004; SSL International plc, since 2005; Wm Morrison Supermarkets plc, since 2005; Compass Group plc, since 2007; non-executive Chairman, Farrow and Ball, since 2007; *b* 16 Jan. 1957; *d* of Jesse and Irene Murray; *m* 1989, Michael Weston; one step *d. Educ:* Communications, Advertising and Mktg Dip. 1978. Colgate-Palmolive, 1979–82; General Foods, then Kraft General Foods, 1982–89; Duracell, 1989–92; Worldwide Pres. and CEO, Pierre Smirnoff Co., 1992–98; Chief Exec., Littlewoods Stores, Littlewoods, 1998–2004. Council Mem. and Dir, ASA, 2003–. *Recreations:* cycling, walking, theatre. *Address: e-mail:* info@susan-murray.com. *Clubs:* Forum UK, Women's Advertising Club of London.

MURRELL, Geoffrey David George, CMG 1993; OBE 1987; HM Diplomatic Service, retired; *b* 19 Dec. 1934; *s* of Stanley Hector Murrell and Kathleen Murrell (Martin); *m* 1962, Kathleen Ruth Berton; one *s* three *d. Educ:* Minchenden Grammar School, Southgate; Lincoln Coll., Oxford (BA French and Russian, MA). FCO Research Dept, 1959–61; Moscow, 1961–64; FCO, 1964–68; Moscow, 1968–70; Head, Soviet Section, FCO Research Dept, 1970–75; First Sec., Belgrade, 1975–78; Regional Dir, Soviet and East European Region, Research Dept, 1978–83; Counsellor, Moscow, 1983–87; Counsellor, Res. Dept, FCO, 1987–91; Minister-Counsellor, Moscow, 1991–94. *Publication:* Russia's Transition to Democracy, 1996. *Recreations:* tennis, guitar. *Club:* Oxford and Cambridge.

MURRELL, Prof. John Norman, PhD; FRS 1991; FRSC; Professor of Chemistry, University of Sussex, 1965–99, now Emeritus (Pro-Vice-Chancellor (Science), 1985–88); *b* London, 2 March 1932; *m* 1954, Dr D. Shirley Read; two *s* two *d. Educ:* Univ. of

London (BSc); Univ. of Cambridge (PhD). University of Sussex: Dean, Sch. of Molecular Scis, 1979–84; Acad. Dir of Univ. Computing, 1984–85; Dean, Chemistry, Physics and Envmtl Sci., 1996–99. Chm., Science Bd Computing Cttee, SERC, 1981–84. Hon. DSc Coimbra, Portugal, 1992. *Publications:* Theory of Electronic Spectra of Organic Molecules, 1960; (jointly): Valence Theory, 1965; Semi-empirical Self-consistent-field-molecular Theory of Molecules, 1971; Chemical Bond, 1978; Properties of Liquids and Solutions, 1982; Molecular Potential Energy Surfaces, 1985; Introduction to the Theory of Atomic and Molecular Scattering, 1989; Grow and Eat Something Different: some less common vegetables and fruit, 2007. *Address:* Department of Chemistry, University of Sussex, Falmer, Brighton BN1 9QJ.

MURRIN, Orlando Richard Charles; journalist and hôtelier; Editorial Director, Food Group, BBC Magazines, since 2004; Proprietor (with Peter Steggall), Le Manoir de Raynaudes, a gastronomic maison d'hôtes, since 2004; *b* 1 April 1958; *s* of Patrick John Murrin and Patricia Mary, *d* of W. J. Skardon, OBE, MI5. *Educ:* Blundell's Sch., Devon; Magdalene Coll., Cambridge (Exhibnr; BA Hons English). Radio 3 Sub-Editor, Radio Times, 1980–83; Chief Sub Ed., Living mag., 1983–85; Asst Ed., Country Homes and Interiors, 1985–87; advertising copywriter, 1987–90; Dep. Ed., Living mag., 1990–93; Ed., Woman and Home, 1993–96; Ed., BBC Good Food mag., 1997–2004. Clever Cook column, Daily Express, 1997–2002. Pianist, Kettners Restaurant, 1983–2002. *Publications:* The Clever Cookbook, 1999; The Can't Go Wrong Cookbook, 2002; The No-cook Cookbook, 2003; A Table in the Tarn, 2008. *Recreations:* cookery, 19th and early 20th century piano music, gardening (especially poisonous plants). *Address:* Le Manoir de Raynaudes, 81640 Monestiès, France. *Club:* Soho House.

MURRISON, Dr Andrew William; MP (C) Westbury, since 2001; *b* 24 April 1961; *s* of William Gordon Murrison, RD and Marion Murrison (*née* Horn); *m* 1994, Jennifer Jane Munden; five *d. Educ:* Harwich High Sch.; The Harwich Sch.; Bristol Univ. (MB ChB 1984; MD 1996); Hughes Hall, Cambridge (DPH 1996). MFOM 1994. Med. Officer, RN, 1981–2000, 2003 (Surg. Comdr); Consultant Occupational Physician, 1996–2001. Opposition front bench spokesman: on health, 2003–05; on defence, 2005–. Vice Chm., All Party Parly Gp on Morocco, 2006–. *Publications:* contribs to various biomed. pubns. *Recreations:* sailing, ski-ing. *Address:* House of Commons, SW1A 0AA.

MURSELL, Rt Rev. (Alfred) Gordon; *see* Stafford, Bishop Suffragan of.

MURTA, Prof. Kenneth Hall, FRIBA; Professor of Architecture, University of Sheffield, 1974–94, now Emeritus; *b* 24 Sept. 1929; *s* of John Henry Murta and Florence (*née* Hall); *m* 1955, Joan Wilson; two *s* two *d. Educ:* Bede Collegiate GS, Sunderland; King's Coll., Univ. of Durham (BArch, DipArch). Architect in private practice and public service, 1954–59; Sen. Lectr, Nigerian Coll. of Arts, Science and Technology, then Ahmadu Bello Univ., 1959–62; University of Sheffield: Lectr, then Sen. Lectr, 1962–74; Dean, Faculty of Architectural Studies, 1974–77, 1984–88. Major designs: Anglican Cathedral, Kaduna, Nigeria; St John, Sheffield Park; All Saints, Denaby Main; St Laurence, Heanor; St Lawrence, Frodingham; Christ Church, Pitsmoor; St Mary the less, St John's Coll., Univ. of Durham; Christ Church, Stannington; St Luke, Lodge Moor, Sheffield; St Leonard, Thrybergh, Rotherham; All Saints, Totley, Sheffield; All Saints, Breadsall, Derbys; St Edward the Confessor, Barnsley; Pilgrims, Fordcombe, Kent; Turangi, West Malvern; Clowance, Praze, Cornwall; Stable Block, Brodsworth Hall, Doncaster. Chm., Working Commn 88, Building Pathology, Internat. Council for Bldg Studies and Res., 1973–94. Council Mem., Inst. of Liturgy and Architecture, Univ. of Birmingham, 1972–86; Mem., Sheffield Cathedral Fabric Adv. Cttee, 2007– (Chm., 1992–2007). Mem. and Hon. Officer, ARCUK, 1991–97 (Mem., 1986–97, Vice-Chm., 1990–91, Chm., 1991–97, Bd of Architectural Educn); Chm., RIBA Yorks Reg., 1984–85. Gov., Sheffield Teaching Hospital NHS Foundn Trust, 2004–. Hon. Sec., Ecclesiological Soc., 1991–2000. Editor, The Ecclesiologist, 1991–97. *Publications:* contribs to Architectural Rev., Ecclesiologist, Churchbuilding, Trans RIBA, Architects' Jl, RIBA Jl. *Recreations:* cricket, soccer, churchwatching, travel, walking in cities on Sundays. *Address:* Underedge, Back Lane, Hathersage, Derbyshire S32 1AR. *T:* (01433) 650833. *Clubs:* Royal Over-Seas League; Ford & Hylton Lane Working Men's (Sunderland).

MURTHY, Krishnan G.; *see* Guru-Murthy.

MURTON, family name of **Baron Murton of Lindisfarne**.

MURTON OF LINDISFARNE, Baron *cr* 1979 (Life Peer), of Hexham in the County of Northumberland; **(Henry) Oscar Murton,** OBE 1946; TD 1947 (Clasp 1951); PC 1976; JP; a Deputy Chairman of Committees, 1981–2004 and a Deputy Speaker, 1983–2004, House of Lords; *b* 8 May 1914; *o s* of late H. E. C. Murton, and of E. M. Murton (*née* Renton), Hexham, Northumberland; *m* 1st, 1939, Constance Frances (*d* 1977), *e d* of late F. O'L. Connell; one *s* (one *d* decd); 2nd, 1979, Pauline Teresa (Freeman, City of London, 1980), *y d* of late Thomas Keenan, JP, Johannesburg. *Educ:* Uppingham Sch. Commissioned, TA, 1934; Staff Capt., 149 Inf. Bde, TA, 1937–39; Staff Coll., Camberley, 1939; tsc; active service, Royal Northumberland Fusiliers, 1939–46; Lt-Col, Gen. Staff, 1942–46 (C-in-C's commendation for special service, 1942, 1944). Managing Dir, Henry A. Murton Ltd, Departmental Stores, Newcastle-upon-Tyne and Sunderland, 1949–57. MP (C) Poole, 1964–79; Sec., Cons. Parly Cttee for Housing, Local Government and Land, 1964–67, Vice-Chm., 1967–70; Chm., Cons. Parly Cttee for Public Building and Works, 1970; PPS to Minister of Local Government and Development, 1970–71; an Asst Govt Whip, 1971–72; a Lord Comr, HM Treasury, 1972–73; Second Dep. Chm., 1973–74, First Dep. Chm., 1974–76, Dep. Speaker and Chm. of Ways and Means, House of Commons, 1976–79. Member: Exec. Cttee, Inter-Parliamentary Union British Group, 1970–71; Panel of Chairmen of Standing Cttees, 1970–71; Jt Select Cttee of Lords and Commons on Private Bill Procedure, 1987–88. Introduced: The Highways (Amendment) Act 1965; The Access to Neighbouring Land Act, 1992. Mem., Poole BC, 1961–63; Pres., Poole Cons. Assoc., 1983–95; a former Vice-Pres., Assoc. of Municipal Corporations; Mem. Herrison (Dorchester) Hosp. Group Management Cttee, 1963–74. Governor, Canford Sch., 1972–76. Chancellor, Primrose League, 1983–88. Freeman, City of London, 1977; Freeman, Wax Chandlers' Co.; Past Master, Clockmakers' Co. JP, Poole, 1963. *Recreations:* sailing, painting. *Address:* 49 Carlisle Mansions, Carlisle Place, SW1P 1HY. *T:* (020) 7834 8226.

MURTON, Dr John Evan; HM Diplomatic Service; High Commissioner, Mauritius, and Ambassador to Madagascar and The Comoros, since 2007; *b* 18 March 1972; *s* of Stewart Anthony Murton and Marion Elizabeth Murton; *m* 1998, Sarah Elizabeth Harvey; two *s* one *d. Educ:* Sidney Sussex Coll., Cambridge (BA Geog. 1994); Darwin Coll., Cambridge (PhD 1997). Entered FCO, 1997; UN Dept, FCO, 1997; Japanese lang. trng, 1998; Second Sec., Global Issues, 2000–03, First Sec., Energy and Envmt, 2003–04, Tokyo; Dep. Dir, NATO Sec. Gen.'s Private Office, 2004–07. *Recreations:* hiking, ski-ing, playing guitar badly. *Address:* Westminster House, John Kennedy Avenue, Floreal, Mauritius. *T:* 6865872; *e-mail:* john.murton@fco.gov.uk. c/o Foreign and Commonwealth Office, King Charles Street, SW1A 2AH.

MUSCATELLI, Prof. (Vito) Antonio, PhD; FRSE; Principal and Vice-Chancellor, Heriot-Watt University, since 2007; *b* 1 Jan. 1962; *s* of Ambrogio and Rosellina Muscatelli; *m* 1986, Elaine Flood; one *s* one *d. Educ:* High Sch., Glasgow; Univ. of Glasgow (MA Hons; PhD). University of Glasgow: Lectr, then Sen. Lectr, 1984–92; Daniel Jack Prof. of Pol Economy, 1992–2007; Dean, Fac. of Soc. Scis, 2000–04; Vice-Principal (Strategy and Budgeting, then Strategy and Advancement), 2004–07. Visiting Professor: Univ. of Parma, 1989; Catholic Univ. of Milan, 1991–97; Univ. of Bari, 1995. Adv. Panel of Econ. Consultants, Sec. of State for Scotland, 1998–2000; Special Advr, H of C Treasury Select Cttee, 2007–. Member: Res. and Knowledge Transfer Cttee, SFC, 2005–; HEFCE RAE Panel, 2001, 2008; Chair, Res. and Commercialisation Cttee, 2007–08, Convener, 2008–, Universities Scotland. Council, Royal Econ. Soc., 2002–06. FRSE 2003; AcSS 2004; FRSA. Editor, Scottish Jl of Political Economy, 1989–2003. *Publications:* (jtly) Macroeconomic Theory and Stabilisation Policy, 1988; (ed) Economic and Political Institutions in Economic Policy, 1996; Monetary Policy; Fiscal Policies and Labour Markets; Macroeconomic Policy Making in the EMU, 2004. *Recreations:* music, literature, football, strategic games. *Address:* Heriot-Watt University, George Heriot Wing, Riccarton, Edinburgh EH14 4AS. *T:* (0131) 451 3360, *Fax:* (0131) 451 3330; *e-mail:* principal@hw.ac.uk.

MUSEVENI, Lt-Gen. Yoweri Kaguta; President of the Republic of Uganda, since 1986; *b* 1944; *s* of Amos and Esteri Kaguta; *m* 1973, Janet Kataaha; one *s* three *d. Educ:* primary and secondary schs in Uganda; Univ. of Dar-es-Salaam, Tanzania (BA). Asst Sec. for Research in President's Office, 1970–71; Hd of Front for National Salvation and anti-Idi Amin armed gp, 1971–79; Minister of Defence, 1979–80, and Vice Chm. of ruling Military Commn; Chm., Uganda Patriotic Movement; Chm., High Comd of Nat. Resistance Army, 1981–. *Publications:* What is Africa's Problem? (essays), 1992; Sowing the Mustard Seed: the struggle for freedom and democracy in Uganda (autobiog.), 1997. *Recreations:* karate, football. *Address:* Office of the President, Parliamentary Buildings, PO Box 25497, Kampala, Uganda. *T:* (41) 234522/234503.

MUSGRAVE, Sir Christopher John Shane, 8th Bt *cr* 1782, of Tourin, Waterford; *b* 23 Oct. 1959; *er s* of Sir Richard Musgrave, 7th Bt and of Maria (*née* Cambanis); *S* father, 2000. *Educ:* Cheltenham. *Heir: b* Michael Shane Musgrave, *b* 30 Jan. 1968.

MUSGRAVE, Sir Christopher (Patrick Charles), 15th Bt *cr* 1611; *b* 14 April 1949; *s* of Sir Charles Musgrave, 14th Bt and of Olive Louise Avril, *o d* of Patrick Cringle, Norfolk; *S* father, 1970; *m* 1st, 1978 (marr. diss. 1992); two *d*; 2nd, 1995, Carol, *d* of Geoffrey Lawson. *Recreations:* drawing, painting, model-making, animals, gardening. *Heir: b* Julian Nigel Chardin Musgrave, *b* 8 Dec. 1951. *Address:* Barn Farm, Bunns Lane, Hambledon, Hants PO7 4QH.

MUSGRAVE, Rosanne Kimble, MA; educational consultant, 2000–08; Headmistress, Blackheath High School (GDST), 1989–2000; *b* 31 Jan. 1952; *d* of Gp Captain John Musgrave, DSO, and late Joanne Musgrave. *Educ:* Cheltenham Ladies' Coll.; St Anne's Coll., Oxford (MA); MA Reading Univ.; PGCE London Univ. Assistant teacher of English: Latymer Grammar Sch., 1976–79; Camden School for Girls (ILEA), 1979–82; Head of English: Channing Sch., Highgate, 1982–84; Haberdashers' Aske's School for Girls, Elstree, 1984–89. Dir, Heron Educn, 2005–. Pres., GSA, 1999; Dir of Member Support, ASCL, 2008–. Corporate Mem., Cheltenham Ladies' Coll., 1989; Gov., St Albans High Sch., 1996–. FRSA 1994. Freeman, City of London, 1993. *Recreations:* letterpress printing, DIY. *Address:* 14 Fortis Green, N2 9EL.

MUSGRAVE, Thea, CBE 2002; composer; *b* 27 May 1928; *d* of James P. Musgrave and Joan Musgrave (*née* Hacking); *m* 1971, Peter Mark, conductor, *s* of Irving Mark, NY. *Educ:* Moreton Hall, Oswestry; Edinburgh Univ.; Paris Conservatoire; privately with Nadia Boulanger. Dist. Prof., Queens Coll., CUNY, 1987–2002. *Works include:* Cantata for a summer's day, 1954; The Abbot of Drimock (Chamber opera), 1955; Triptych for Tenor and orch., 1959; Colloquy for violin and piano, 1960; The Phoenix and the Turtle for chorus and orch., 1962; The Five Ages of Man for chorus and orch., 1963; The Decision (opera), 1964–65; Nocturnes and arias for orch., 1966; Chamber Concerto No. 2, in homage to Charles Ives, 1966; Chamber Concerto No 3 (Octet), 1966; Concerto for orchestra, 1967; Music for Horn and Piano, 1967; Clarinet Concerto, 1968; Beauty and the Beast (ballet), 1968; Night Music, 1969; Memento Vitae, a concerto in homage to Beethoven, 1970; Horn concerto, 1971; From One to Another, 1972; Viola Concerto, 1973; The Voice of Ariadne (opera), 1972–73; Rorate Coeli, for chorus, 1974; Space Play, 1974; Orfeo I and Orfeo II, 1975; Mary, Queen of Scots (opera), 1976–77; Christmas Carol (opera), 1979; An Occurrence at Owl Creek Bridge (radio opera), 1981; Peripeteia (orchestral), 1981; Harriet, the Woman called Moses (opera), 1984; Black Tambourine for women's chorus and piano, 1985; Pierrot, 1985; For the Time Being for chorus, 1986; The Golden Echo, 1987; Narcissus, 1988; The Seasons (orchestral), 1988; Rainbow (orchestral), 1990; Simón Bolivar (opera), 1993; Autumn Sonata, 1993; Journey through a Japanese Landscape (marimba concerto), 1993; Wild Winter, 1993; On the Underground (vocal), 1994; Helios (oboe concerto), 1995; Phoenix Rising (orchestral), 1997; Lamenting with Ariadne, 2000; Pontalba (opera), 2003; Turbulent Landscapes (orchestral), 2004; Wood, Metal and Skin (percussion concerto), 2004; Journey Into Light (soprano and orch.), 2005; Voices of Power and Protest, 2006; Two's Company (concerto for percussion and oboe), 2007. Performances and broadcasts: UK, France, Germany, Switzerland, Scandinavia, USA, USSR, etc, Edinburgh, Cheltenham, Aldeburgh, Zagreb, Venice and Warsaw Festivals. Hon. MusDoc, CNAA. *Address:* c/o Novello & Co. Ltd, 14–15 Berners Street, W1T 3LJ.

MUSGRAVE, Prof. William Kenneth Rodgerson, PhD, DSc (Birmingham); Professor of Organic Chemistry, 1960–83, now Emeritus, and Head of Department of Chemistry, 1968–71, 1974–77, 1980–81, University of Durham; *b* 16 Sept. 1918; *s* of late Charles Musgrave and late Sarah Alice Musgrave; *m* 1944, Joyce Cadman; two *s. Educ:* Stanley Grammar Sch., Co. Durham; Univ. of Birmingham. Mem., Tube Alloys, Birmingham Univ., 1940–44; British-Canadian Atomic Energy Project, 1944–45; Univ. of Durham: Lecturer in Chemistry, 1945–56; Senior Lecturer, 1956–60; Personal Readership in Organic Chem., 1960; Second Pro-Vice-Chancellor, 1970–73; Pro-Vice-Chancellor and Sub-Warden, 1973–78; Acting Vice-Chancellor, 1979. *Publications:* (joint) Advances in Fluorine Chemistry, vol. I, edited by Stacey, Tatlow and Sharpe, 1960; Rodd's Chemistry of Carbon Compounds, vols Ia and IIIa, edited by Coffey; scientific papers in chemical journals. *Recreations:* gardening, rough shooting. *Address:* Apt 14, Pegasus Court, 61–63 Broad Road, Sale, Greater Manchester M33 2ES.

MUSGROVE, Prof. Frank, DLitt; Sarah Fielden Professor of Education, University of Manchester, 1970–82, now Emeritus; Dean of the Faculty of Education, 1976–78; *b* 16 Dec. 1922; *e s* of late Thomas and Fanny Musgrove; *m* Dorothy Ellen (*née* Nicholls); one *d. Educ:* Henry Mellish Grammar Sch., Nottingham; Magdalen Coll., Oxford (MA); Univ. of Nottingham (PhD); Univ. of Manchester (MEd); Open Univ. (DLitt 1982). Served War, RAFVR, 1941–45; Navigator, Bomber Command (commnd), Ops 149 Sqdn (tour of bombing missions completed 1944). Educational appts in England and in the Colonial Educn Service, E Africa, 1947–57; Lectureships in Univs of Leicester and Leeds, 1957–65; Foundn Chair of Research in Educn, Univ. of Bradford, 1965–70. Visiting Professor: of Educn, Univ. of BC, 1965; of Sociology, Univ. of California (Davis), 1969; Guest lectr, Inst. of Sociology, Univ. of Utrecht, 1968; The Chancellor's Lectr, Univ. of Wellington, NZ, 1970. Hon. Prof., Univ. of Hull, 1985–88. Co-editor, Research in Education, 1971–76. FRSA 1971. *Publications:* The Migratory Elite, 1963; Youth and the Social Order, 1964; The Family, Education and Society, 1966; Society and the Teacher's Role (with P. H. Taylor), 1969; Patterns of Power and Authority in English Education, 1971; Ecstasy and Holiness, 1974, new edn 1994; Margins of the Mind, 1977; School and the Social Order, 1979; Education and Anthropology, 1982; The North of England: from Roman to present times, 1990; Dresden and the Heavy Bombers, 2005; research papers in: Africa; Sociological Review; Brit. Jl of Sociology; Brit. Jl of Educational Psychology; Economic History Review; Brit. Jl of Social and Clinical Psychology, etc. *Recreation:* fly fishing. *Address:* Dib Scar, The Cedar Grove, Beverley, E Yorks HU17 7EP. *T:* (01482) 868799.

MUSGROVE, Harold John; Chairman, Worcester Acute Hospitals NHS Trust, 1999–2003; *b* 19 Nov. 1930; *s* of Harold Musgrove; *m* 1959, Jacquelin Mary Hobbs; two *s* two *d. Educ:* King Edward Grammar Sch., Birmingham; Birmingham Tech. Coll. Nat. Cert. of Mech. Eng. Apprentice, Austin Motor Co., 1945; held various positions, incl. Chief Material Controller (Commission as Navigator, RAF, during this period); Senior Management, Truck and Bus Group, Leyland Motor Corp., 1963–78; Austin Morris: Dir of Manufacturing, 1978–79; Man. Dir, 1979–80; Chm. and Man. Dir, 1980–81; Chm., Light Medium Cars Group, 1981–82; Chm. and Chief Exec., Austin Rover Gp, 1982–86; Chloride plc: Dir, 1989–92; Chm., Industrial Battery Sector, 1989–91; Chm., Power Supplies and Lighting Gp, 1991–92. Non-exec. Dir, Metalrax plc, 1986–2003. Chairman: W Midlands Ambulance Service, 1992–94; Birmingham Heartlands Hosp. NHS Trust, 1994–96; Birmingham Heartlands and Solihull (Teaching) NHS Trust, 1996–99. Pres., Birmingham Chamber of Industry and Commerce, 1987–88. Pres., Aston Villa FC, 1986–98. FIMI 1985. DUniv Birmingham, 2000. Midlander of the Year Award, 1980; IProdE Internat. Award, 1981; Soc. of Engineers Churchill Medal, 1982. *Recreations:* golf, soccer. *Address:* The Lodge, Laverton, Broadway, Worcs WR12 7NA.

MUSHARRAF, Gen. Pervez; President of Pakistan, 2001–08; Chief of Army Staff, 1998–2007; *b* 11 Aug. 1943; *s* of late Syed Musharraf Uddin; *m* 1968, Sehba Farid; one *s* one *d. Educ:* St Patrick's High Sch., Karachi; Forman Christian Coll., Lahore. Pakistan Mil. Acad., 1961; commnd Artillery Regt, 1964; Dir Gen., Mil. Ops, 1993–95; Chm., Jt Chiefs of Staff Cttee, 1999–2001; Chief Exec. of Pakistan, 1999–2002. *Publication:* In the Line of Fire (autobiog.), 2006.

MUSKERRY, 9th Baron *cr* 1781 (Ire.); **Robert Fitzmaurice Deane;** Bt 1710 (Ire.); *b* 26 March 1948; *s* of 8th Baron Muskerry and Betty Fairbridge, *e d* of George Wilfred Reckless Palmer; *S* father, 1988; *m* 1975, Rita Brink, Pietermaritzburg; one *s* two *d. Educ:* Sandford Park School, Dublin; Trinity Coll., Dublin (BA, BAI). *Heir: s* Hon. Jonathan Fitzmaurice Deane, *b* 7 June 1986. *Address:* 725 Ridge Road, Berea, Durban 4001, South Africa.

MUSONDA, Dr Moses; Dean, School of Education, Zambian Open University; *b* 10 March 1937; *s* of William Musonda and Margaret (*née* Mulenga); *m* 1972, Lucy Kawandami; three *s* two *d. Educ:* Kent State Univ., Ohio (BA 1967; MA 1968); Bryn Mawr Coll., Penn (PhD 1983). Lectr, then Associate Prof., Univ. of Zambia, 1968–94; on secondment as Dep. Dir-Gen., CICIBA (Internat. Centre for Bantu Civilisations), Gabon, 1986–90; Ambassador of Zambia to China, 1995–97; High Commissioner for Zambia: in UK, 1997–2001; in India, 2001; Perm. Sec., Min. of Educn, 2004. *Publications:* contrib. papers to jls and reviews on educn, language and literature. *Address:* Zambian Open University, PO Box 31925, Lusaka, Zambia.

MUSSON, Rear Adm. (John Geoffrey) Robin, CB 1993; Senior Naval Directing Staff, Royal College of Defence Studies, 1990–93; Chief Naval Supply and Secretariat Officer, 1991–93; *b* 30 May 1939; *s* of late Geoffrey William Musson and Winifred Elizabeth Musson (*née* Whyman); *m* 1965, Joanna Marjorie Ward; two *s* one *d. Educ:* Luton Grammar Sch.; BRNC, Dartmouth. Entered RN, 1957; served HM Ships: Bulwark, 1960–61; Decoy, 1961–62; 2nd Frigate Sqdn, 1964–65; HM Ships: Cavalier, 1966–67; Forth, 1967–69; Kent, 1975–76; NDC, 1979; MA, VCDS (Personnel and Logistics), 1980–81; Sec. to Chief of Fleet Support, 1982–83; CSO (Personnel and Admin), FONAC, 1984–86; Dir, Naval Officer Appts (Supply and WRNS), 1986–88; Captain, HMS Cochrane, 1988–90; retd, 1993. Admiralty Bd Gov., Royal Naval Benevolent Trust, 1995–2002. Gov. (formerly Mem. Cttee of Mgt), Royal Hosp. Sch., Holbrook, 1995–2002. Sec., Salisbury Dio. Sudan Link, 1995–2001. Freeman, City of London, 1993. *Recreations:* Scottish country dancing, mending things, history, hedge laying.

MUSSON, John Nicholas Whitaker; Warden of Glenalmond College (formerly Trinity College, Glenalmond), 1972–87; *b* 2 Oct. 1927; *s* of late Dr J. P. T. Musson, OBE and Gwendoline Musson (*née* Whitaker); *m* 1953, Ann Preist (*d* 2004); one *s* three *d. Educ:* Clifton; Brasenose Coll., Oxford (MA). Served with Welsh Guards and Lancs Fusiliers, 1945–48 (commnd); BA Hons Mod. Hist., Oxford, 1951; HM Colonial Service, later HM Overseas Civil Service, 1951–59: District Officer, N Nigeria; Lectr, Inst. of Administration, N Nigeria; Staff Dept, British Petroleum, London, 1959–61; Asst Master and Housemaster, Canford Sch., 1961–72. Chm., Scottish Div. HMC, 1981–83; Scottish Dir (formerly Scottish Sec.), ISCO, 1987–93. Governor: Clifton Coll., 1989– (Mem. Council, 1989–95); George Watson's Coll., Edinburgh, 1989–98. Mercy Corps Europe/Scottish European Aid: Dir and Trustee, 1996–2000; Country Dir (Bosnia and Herzegovina), resident in Sarajevo, 1998–99; Vice-Chm., Mercy Corps Scotland (Aid Internat.), 2000–07. *Recreations:* travel, art, Egyptology, swimming. *Address:* 47 Spylaw Road, Edinburgh EH10 5BP. *T:* (0131) 337 0089. *Club:* New (Edinburgh).

MUSSON, Rear Adm. Robin; *see* Musson, Rear Adm. J. G. R.

MUSTHAPHA, (Mohamed) Faisz; High Commissioner for Sri Lanka in the United Kingdom, 2002–05; *b* 5 Dec. 1940; *s* of Seyed Mohamed Musthapha and Masooda Musthapha; *m* 1967, Fathima Fatheena; one *s* one *d. Educ:* Trinity Coll., Kandy; Univ. of Ceylon (LLB); Sri Lanka Law Coll. Advocate of the Supreme Court of Sri Lanka, 1965–; President's Counsel, 1988; Dep. DPP, 1976–78. Chairman: and Mem., Finance Commn of Sri Lanka, 1987–90; Human Rights Commn, Sri Lanka, 1998–2000; Mem., Law Commn of Sri Lanka, 1997–2000. Dir, Amana Investments Ltd, 1996; Chm., Amana Thakaful Ltd (Risk Mgt Co.), 1998–. Mem., Council of Legal Educn, 1997–2000. Legal Advr, All Party Conf., 1987. Member: Sri Lanka Delegn to Thimpu Talks, Bhutan, 1987; Sri Lankan Gp, Internat. Court of Arbitration, The Hague, 1996. Mem., Bar Assoc. of Sri Lanka (Dep. Pres., 1986–98). Chm., Amal Internat. Sch., 1990–2000. *Publications:* contribs on Islam and law. *Recreations:* reading, bird watching, badminton. *Address:* 35 Kaviratne Place, Colombo 6, Sri Lanka. *T:* (11) 2586963, *Fax:* (11) 5555048; *e-mail:* faiszmusthapha@sltnet.lk.

MUSTILL, family name of **Baron Mustill**.

MUSTILL, Baron *cr* 1992 (Life Peer), of Pateley Bridge in the County of North Yorkshire; **Michael John Mustill,** Kt 1978; PC 1985; FBA 1996; a Lord of Appeal in Ordinary, 1992–97; *b* 10 May 1931; *o s* of late Clement William and Marion Mustill; *m* 1st, Beryl Reid Davies (marr. diss.); 2nd, Caroline Phillips; two *s*, and one step *d. Educ:* Oundle Sch.; St John's Coll., Cambridge (Hon. Fellow, 1992); LLD Cantab 1992. Royal Artillery, 1949–51 (commissioned, 1950). Called to Bar, Gray's Inn, 1955, Bencher, 1976. QC 1968. Dep. Chm., Hants QS, 1971; a Recorder of the Crown Court, 1972–78; Judge of High Court, QBD, 1978–85; a Lord Justice of Appeal, 1985–92. Presiding Judge, NE Circuit, 1981–84. Chairman: Civil Service Appeal Tribunal, 1971–78; Judicial Studies Board, 1985–89; Deptl Cttee on Law of Arbitration, 1985–90; Adv. Bd, Inst. of Criminology, Cambridge Univ., 1992–99. Hon. Prof. of Law, Birmingham Univ., 1995–; Yorke Dist. Vis. Fellow, 1996–, Arthur Goodhart Vis. Prof. of Legal Sci., and Fellow of St John's Coll., 2003–04, Cambridge Univ; Sen. Fellow, Lauterpacht Centre for Internat. Law, 2006–. President: British Maritime Law Assoc., 1995–2003; CIArb, 1995–98; Assoc. of Average Adjusters, 1996–97; London Shipping Law Centre, 1996–; Seldon Soc., 1997–2000; Expert Witness Inst., 1997–2002; Internat. Law Assoc., 2000–02 (Pres., British Br., 1997–2004); Vice-Pres., Court of Arbitration, Internat. Chamber of Commerce, 1997–2005. Member: Comité Maritime Internat., 1996–; Amer. Law Inst. Hon. LLD Birmingham; DUniv Leeds Metropolitan. *Publications:* The Law and Practice of Commercial Arbitration in England (with S. C. Boyd, QC), 1982, 2nd edn 1989, 2001 Companion; Anticipatory Breach of Contract, 1990; Joint Editor: Scrutton on Charterparties and Bills of Lading; Arnould on Marine Insurance; articles in legal periodicals. *Address:* 42 Laurier Road, NW5 1SJ. *Club:* Travellers.

MUSTOE, Mrs Anne, MA; travel writer and lecturer; *b* 24 May 1933; *d* of H.W. Revill; *m* 1960, Nelson Edwin Mustoe, QC (*d* 1976). *Educ:* Girton Coll., Cambridge (BA Classical Tripos 1955, MA 1958). DipIPM 1959. Guest, Keen & Nettlefolds Ltd, 1956–60; Head of Classics, Francis Holland School, NW1, 1965–69; independent travel agent, 1969–73; Dep. Headmistress, Cobham Hall, Kent, 1975–78; Headmistress, St Felix School, Southwold, 1978–87. Chm., ISIS, 1986–87; President, Girls' Schools Assoc., 1984–85; Mem., Board of Managers of Girls' Common Entrance Examinations, 1983–86. Mem., CS Final Selection Bd, 1980–92. Chm. Trustees, National Byway, 2005–. Governor: Hethersett Old Hall Sch., 1981–86; Cobham Hall, 1986–99; James Allen's Girls' Sch., 1991–97; Thornton Coll., 1992–97. FRGS 1996. JP Suffolk, 1981–85. *Publications:* A Bike Ride: 12,000 miles around the world, 1991; Escaping the Winter, 1993, 2nd edn 2003; Lone Traveller, 1998; Two Wheels in the Dust, 2001; Cleopatra's Needle, 2003; Amber, Furs and Cockleshells, 2005; Che Guevara and the Mountain of Silver, 2007. *Recreations:* music, cycling (world cycling tours, 1987–88, 1994–95). *Address:* 12 Melcombe Court, Dorset Square, NW1 6EP. *T:* (020) 7262 1701.

MUSTON, Rt Rev. Gerald Bruce; Bishop of North-West Australia, 1981–92; *b* 19 Jan. 1927; 3rd *s* of Stanley John and Emily Ruth Muston; *m* 1951, Laurel Wright; one *s* one *d. Educ:* N Sydney Chatswood High School; Moore Theological College, Sydney. ThL (Aust. Coll. of Theology). Rector, Wallerawang, NSW, 1951–53; Editorial Secretary, Church Missionary Society (Aust.), 1953–58; Rector, Tweed Heads, NSW, 1958–61; Vicar, Essendon, Vic, 1961–67; Rural Dean of Essendon, 1963–67; Rector of Darwin, NT, and Archdeacon of Northern Territory, 1967–69; Federal Secretary, Bush Church Aid Society of Aust., 1969–71; Bishop Coadjutor, dio. Melbourne (Bishop of the Western Region), 1971–81. *Recreations:* golf, reading. *Address:* 17/27 Beddi Road, Duncraig, WA 6023, Australia.

MUSTOW, Stuart Norman, CBE 1995; FREng, FICE; consulting engineer, since 1986; Director, W. S. Atkins International, 1986–95; *b* 26 Nov. 1928; *s* of Norman Eric Mustow and Mabel Florence Mustow (*née* Purcell); *m* 1964, Sigrid Hertha Young; two *s* one *d. Educ:* Aston Univ. (BSc). FIHT; FREng (FEng 1982). Mil. service, RA; Local Govt Engineering, 1949–69; City Engineer and Surveyor, Stoke on Trent, 1969–74; County Surveyor, W Midlands, responsible for roads, transport planning and Birmingham Airport, 1974–86. Chm., Hazards Forum, 1999–2003. Mem., Engineering Council, 1995–97. President: Inst. Municipal Engrs, 1980–81; ICE, 1993–94; Vice-Pres., Royal Acad. of Engrg, 1995–99. Hon. DSc Aston, 1994; Hon. DEng Birmingham, 2000. *Publications:* papers in learned jls. *Recreations:* outdoor life, church, social work.

MUTCH, Dr William Edward Scott, OBE 1989; FRSE; forestry and land use consultant, 1989–99; Member of Board and Chairman, South East Region, Scottish Natural Heritage, 1992–94; *b* 14 Aug. 1925; *s* of Wilfred Ernest Mutch and Helen Anderson Mutch (*née* Bannerman); *m* 1950, Margaret Isobel McKay; one *d. Educ:* Royal High Sch., Edinburgh; Edinburgh Univ. (BSc Forestry, PhD); St John's Coll., Oxford. FICFor. Colonial Service Forest Dept, Nigeria, 1946–52; University of Edinburgh: Lectr in Forestry, 1953; Sen. Lectr, 1963; Head of Dept of Forestry and Natural Resources, 1981–87. Dir, Central Scotland Woodlands Ltd, subseq. Central Scotland Countryside Trust, 1989–97. Member: Countryside Commn for Scotland, 1988–92; Nat. Forestry Res. Adv. Cttee, 1982–96; Nature Conservancy Council, 1989–91; Nature Conservancy Council for Scotland, 1991–92. Institute of Chartered Foresters: Pres., 1982–84; Inst. Medal, 1986. Editor, Scottish Forestry, 1957–62. *Publications:* Public Recreation in National Forests, 1967; The Interaction of Forestry and Farming, 1980; Farm Woodland Management, 1987; Tall Trees and Small Woods, 1998, rev. edn 2008; Steal me a Duchess, 2001; Eskdale Shoot, 2006; contribs to professional jls. *Recreations:* cabinet making, travel, painting. *Address:* Coulmony, West Netherton, Milnathort, Kinross KY13 0SB. *T:* (01577) 864608.

MUTHALAGAPPAN, Kumar Periakaruppan, FCA; Managing Director, Pearl Hotels and Restaurants Group Ltd, since 1997; *b* India, 2 June 1960; *s* of Muthu and Meena Muthalagappan; *m* 1988, Kannahi Sivanantham; two *s* one *d. Educ:* Univ. of Warwick (BSc Hons Accounting and Financial Analysis). FCA 1996. Senior Manager, KPMG, 1983–97. Member Board: Heart of England Tourist Bd, 2000–04; Visit Britain, 2002–. Mem. Bd, Olympic Delivery Authy, 2006–. Mem. Council, Univ. of Warwick, 2007–. Dep. Chm., City of Birmingham Symphony Orch., 2007–; Mem. Bd, Belgrade Th., 2000–04. *Recreations:* music, history, sport, gardening. *Address:* Pearl Hotels and Restaurants Group, 57 Warwick Road, Kenilworth, Warwicks CV8 1HN. *T:* (01926) 863648, *Fax:* (01926) 854420; *e-mail:* kumar@muthalagappan.com.

MUTI, Riccardo, Hon. KBE 2000; Conductor Laureate, Philadelphia Orchestra, 1992–2003 (Principal Guest Conductor, 1977–80; Principal Conductor and Music

Director, 1980–92); Music Director, La Scala, Milan, 1986–2005; *b* 28 July 1941; *m* 1969, Cristina Mazzavillani; two *s* one *d. Educ:* Diploma in pianoforte, Conservatorio di Napoli; Diploma in conducting and composition, Milan. Principal Conductor, 1973–82, Music Dir, 1979–82, New Philharmonia, later Philharmonia Orchestra, London; Principal Conductor, Orchestra Maggio Musicale Fiorentino, 1969–81. Concert tours in USA with Philadelphia Orch.; concerts at Salzburg, Edinburgh, Lucerne, Flanders, Vienna and Ravenna Festivals; concerts with Berlin Philharmonic, Vienna Philharmonic, Concertgebouw Amsterdam, NY Philharmonic, Bayerisches Rundfunk SO, Filarmonica della Scala, Israel Philharmonic, Boston SO, Chicago SO; opera in Florence, Salzburg, Vienna, Munich, Covent Garden, Milan, Ravenna. Hon. degrees from Univs of Bologna, Urbino, Milan, Lecce and Tel Aviv, and univs in England and USA. Recording prizes from France, Germany, Italy, Japan and USA. Accademico: dell'Accademia di Santa Cecilia, Rome; dell'Accademia Luigi Cherubini, Florence. Hon. Citizen: Milan; Florence; Sydney; Ravenna. Grande Ufficiale, Repubblica Italiana; Cavaliere, Gran Croce (Italy), 1991; Verdienstkreuz, 1st class (Germany), 1976; KM; Ehrenkreuz (Austria).

MUTTER, Anne-Sophie; violinist. *Educ:* studied with Prof. Aida Stucki in Switzerland. Début with Herbert von Karajan, Salzburg, 1977; soloist with major orchestras of the world; also plays with string trio and quartet; has given first performances and recorded many works for violin by contemporary composers incl. Lutosławski, Moret, Penderecki, Gubaidulina, Rihm, Dutilleux, Currier and Previn. Guest teacher, RAM, 1985. Founder: Rudolf Eberle Foundn, 1987; Anne-Sophie Mutter Foundn, 1997. Hon. Pres., Univ. of Oxford Mozart Soc., 1983. Hon. Mem., Beethoven Soc., 1996. Prizes and awards include: Jugend Musiziert Prize (FRG) for: violin, 1970 and 1974; piano, 1970; Künstler des Jahres Deutscher Schallplattenpreis, 1979; Grand Prix Internat. du Disque, Record Acad. Prize, Tokyo, 1982; Internat. Schallplattenpreis, 1993; Grammy, 1994, 1999, 2000, 2004; Siemens Music Prize, 2008. Bundesverdienstkreuz (1st Cl.), 1987; Cross of Honour for Sci. and Art (Austria), 2001. *Recreations:* graphic arts, sport.

MUTTRAM, Roderick Ian, FREng; Vice-President, Bombardier Transportation (UK) Ltd, since 2003; *b* 15 Jan. 1952; *s* of late Wilfred Reginald Muttram, DSC, RN and Dorothy May Muttram (*née* Best); *m* 1974, Jane Elisabeth Sinkinson; four *d. Educ:* St Bartholomew's Grammar Sch., Newbury; Victoria Univ. of Manchester (BSc Hons); Manchester Metropolitan Univ. (DMS). Gp Engrg and Quality Dir, Ferranti Instrumentation Gp, 1986–90; Dir and Gen. Manager, Defence Systems Div., Thorn EMI Electronics, 1990–93; Railtrack plc: Director: Electrical Engrg and Control Systems, 1994–97; Safety and Standards, 1997–2000; Dir, Railtrack Gp plc, 1997–2000; CEO, Railway Safety, 2000–03; indep. engrg and safety consultant, 2003. Chm., Rail Industry Trng Council, 2001–03. Chm. Supervisory Bd, Eur. Rail Res. Inst., Netherlands, 1994–2003; Vice-Chm., Eur. Rail Res. Adv. Council, 2004–05; Dir, Assoc. Européenne pour l'Intéroperabilité Ferroviaire, 2004–06. Freedom, City of London, 2004; Liveryman, Co. of Engineers, 2005. FREng 2002; MInstD 1994. *Publications:* (contrib.) The Yellow Book on Engineering Safety Management, 1996; numerous conf. papers in UK, Japan, Australia, USA; contrib. numerous papers to Jl Rail and Rapid Transit (IMechE), Japan Railway Tech. Rev., IEE Summer Schs. *Recreations:* small bore rifle shooting, motor vehicle restoration. *Address:* Bombardier Transportation (UK) Ltd, St Giles House, 10 Church Street, Reading, Berkshire RG1 2SD; The Cottage, The Street, Ewhurst, Cranleigh, Surrey GU6 7QA. *T:* (01483) 277218; *e-mail:* rod.muttram@ uk.transport.bombardier.com.

MUTTUKUMARU, Christopher Peter Jayantha, CB 2006; Legal Services Director, since 2001, and Legal Adviser, since 2003, Department for Transport (formerly Legal Director (Transport), Department for Transport, Local Government and the Regions); *b* 11 Dec. 1951; *y s* of late Maj. Gen. Anton Muttukumaru, OBE and of Margaret Muttukumaru; *m* 1976, Ann Elisabeth Tutton; two *s. Educ:* Xavier Coll., Melbourne; Jesus Coll., Oxford (BA, MA). Called to the Bar, Gray's Inn, 1974; in practice at the Bar, 1976–83; Treasury Solicitor's Dept, 1983–88; Law Officers' Dept, 1988–91; Head of Employment Litigation Sect., Treasury Solicitor's Dept, 1991–92; Sec., Scott Inquiry into Export of Defence and Defence-related Equipment to Iraq, 1992–96; Treasury Solicitor's Department: Dep. Legal Advr, MoD, 1996–98; Legal Advr to DCMS, 1998–99; Dir, Legal (Commercial, Envmt, Housing and Local Govt), DETR, 1999–2001. Mem. Adv. Bd, Law Sch., City Univ., 2008–. Gov., Eltham Coll., London, 1998– (Vice-Chm., Govs, 2006–). Mem., Editl Adv. Bd, Nottingham Law Jl. *Recreations:* reading, running, cricket (mostly watching), photography, sunflowers. *Address:* (office) Great Minster House, 76 Marsham Street, SW1P 4DR. *T:* (020) 7944 4770.

MWINYI, Ndugu Ali Hassan; President, United Republic of Tanzania, 1985–95; *b* 8 May 1925; *s* of late Hassan Mwinyi Chande and Asha Mwinyishehe; *m* 1960, Siti A. Mwinyi (*née* Abdulla); five *s* four *d. Educ:* Mangapwani Sch. and Dole Sch., Zanzibar; Teachers' Training Coll., Zanzibar; Durham Univ. Inst. of Education. Primary sch. teacher, head teacher, Tutor, Principal, Zanzibar, 1945–64; Acting Principal Sec., Min. of Educn, 1964–65; Dep. Gen. Manager, State Trading Corp., 1965–70; Minister of State, President's Office, Dar es Salaam, 1970–72; Minister for Health, 1972–75; Minister for Home Affairs, 1975–77; Ambassador to Egypt, 1977–81; Minister for Natural Resources and Tourism, 1982–83; Minister of State, Vice-President's Office, 1983; Vice-Pres., Union Govt, 1984. Chama Cha Mapinduzi (Revolutionary Party): Member, 1977; Nat. Exec. Cttee, 1982; Central Cttee, 1984; Vice-Chm., 1984–90; Chm., 1990–96; Mem., Afro-Shirazi Party, 1964. Chairman: Zanzibar Film Censorship Bd, 1964–65; E African Currency Bd, Zanzibar, 1964–67; Nat. Kiswahili Council, 1964–77; Tanzania Food and Nutrition Council, 1974–76. Mem., Univ. Council of Dar es Salaam, 1964–65. *Address:* c/o State House, Dar es Salaam, United Republic of Tanzania.

MYER, Sidney Baillieu, AC 1990; MA Cantab; Chairman, Myer Emporium Ltd, 1978–86 (Director, since 1955); Deputy Chairman, Coles Myer Ltd, 1985–94; Director: Myer Foundation, since 1959 (President, 1992–95; Vice-President, 1959–92); N. M. Rothschild Australia Holdings (formerly N. M. Rothschild & Son (Australia)), 1993–2003; *b* 11 Jan. 1926; *s* of late Sidney Myer and late Dame (Margery) Merlyn Baillieu Myer, DBE; *m* 1955, Sarah J., *d* of late S. Hordern; two *s* one *d. Educ:* Geelong Grammar Sch.; Pembroke Coll., Cambridge (MA). Sub-Lieut, RANVR, 1944–46. Joined Myer Emporium, 1953. Director: Elders IXL Ltd, 1972–82 and 1986–90; Cadbury Schweppes Aust. Ltd, 1976–82; Commonwealth Banking Corp., 1979–83; Network Ten Holdings Ltd and associated Cos, 1985–87; Chm., Nat. Mutual Life Assoc. of Australasia, 1988–92 (Dir, 1978–92). Dir, Howard Florey Inst. of Experimental Physiology and Medicine, 1971–2002 (Pres., 1992–96); Part-time Mem. Executive, CSIRO, 1981–85. Pres., French Chamber of Commerce (Vic), 1962–64; Rep. Chm., Aust.-Japan Foundn, 1976–81; Member: Consultative Cttee on Relations with Japan, 1978–81; Aust.-China Council, 1979–81; Nat. Bicentennial Sci. Centre Adv. Cttee, 1986–89; Nat. Adv. Cttee on Ageing, 2002–04. Councillor: Aust. Conservation Foundn, 1964–73; Vic. Coll. of Arts, 1973–78; Chm., Art Foundn of Vic., 1986–88; Vice-Pres., Nat. Gall. Soc. of Vic., 1964–68; Dir, Tasman Inst., 1990–98; Trustee: Sidney Myer Fund, 1958–2001 (Chm. Trustees, 1997–2001); Nat. Gall. of Vic., 1973–83 (Vice-Pres., 1977–83); Victorian Tapestry

Foundn, 1995–; Chm., Commonwealth Research Centres of Excellence Cttee, 1981–82. Hon. LLD Melbourne, 1993. Chevalier de la Légion d'Honneur, 1976. *Address:* Level 18, 8 Exhibition Street, Melbourne, Victoria 3000, Australia. *Fax:* (3) 98268051. *Clubs:* Naval and Military; Leander (Henley-on-Thames); Australian (Melbourne).

MYERS, David; Director, Shared Services Programme, Cabinet Office, 2005–07; *b* 28 March 1965; *s* of Frederick Myers and Beryl Adelaide Myers; *m* 1991, Janice Adele Harrison; three *d. Educ:* Highfield Sch., Liverpool; Univ. of Lancaster (BA Hons Econ 1st Cl 1987). British Gas plc, 1988–90; Rolls-Royce plc, 1990–92; KPMG, 1992; ICI Pharmaceuticals, 1993–96; Change Prog. Manager, Mil. Aircraft, BAe, 1996–98; Dir of IT, BAe Regl Aircraft, 1998–2000; Dir of IT and Business Change, BAE SYSTEMS Avionics, 2000–02; e-Business Dir, DEFRA, 2003–05. *Recreations:* landscape gardening, following St Helens Rugby League, exploring West Indies.

MYERS, (Denis) Kevin; Director, Hazardous Installations, Health and Safety Executive, since 2005; *b* 30 Sept. 1954; *s* of Stephen Myers and Bridget Myers (*née* McSweeney); *m* 1976, Jan Hannan; four *s* one *d. Educ:* St Bonaventure's Sch., Forest Gate; Luton Coll. of Technol. (BSc Hons Biochem. and Envmtl Biol.). Joined Health and Safety Exec., 1976, various posts in London, E Anglia and SW, 1976–93; Policy Officer, DG XI, Eur. Commn, 1993–95; Regl Dir, Home Counties Reg., 1997–2002; Chief Inspector of Construction, 2000–05, HSE. *Recreations:* family, Italy, football (West Ham United FC), cricket, opera. *Address:* Health and Safety Executive, Redgrave Court, Merton Road, Bootle, Merseyside L20 7HS. *T:* (0151) 951 4701, *Fax:* (0151) 951 4575.

MYERS, Derek John; Town Clerk and Chief Executive, Royal Borough of Kensington and Chelsea, since 2000; *b* 15 Aug. 1954; *s* of Alfred and Elsie Myers; *m* 1992, Anne Mercer; one *s* one *d. Educ:* Univ. of Manchester (BA Econs 1976; Dip. Social Work 1977); Univ. of London (LLB 1988). Social Services: Essex CC, 1977–86; Hillingdon LBC, 1986–92; Dir of Social Services, 1992–97, Chief Exec., 1997–2000, London Borough of Hounslow. Non-exec. Dir, DoH, 2005–. *Recreations:* tennis, cooking, hill-walking. *Address:* The Town Hall, Hornton Street, W8 7NX. *T:* (020) 7361 2299; *e-mail:* chiefex@ rbkc.gov.uk.

MYERS, Geoffrey, CBE 1984; CEng; FCILT; Chairman, TRANSAID, 1988–95; Vice-Chairman, British Railways Board, 1985–87 (Member, 1980–87); *b* 12 July 1930; *s* of Ernest and Annie Myers; *m* 1959, Patricia Mary (*née* Hall); two *s. Educ:* Belle Vue Grammar Sch.; Bradford Technical Coll. (BScEng London). CEng, MICE 1963; FCILT (FCIT 1973). RE, 1955–57. British Rail: civil engrg positions, 1957–64; Planning Officer, N Eastern Reg., 1964–66; Divl Movements Manager, Leeds Div., 1966–68; Dir of Studies, British Transport Staff Coll., 1968–70; Divl Man., Sheffield, 1970–76; Dep. Gen. Man., Eastern Reg., 1976–77, Gen. Man., 1977–78; Dir of Strategic Develt, 1978–80; Dep. Chief Exec. (Railways), 1983; Jt Managing Dir (Railways), 1984–85. Pres. Council, CIT, 1986–87. Bd Mem., TRANSAID Worldwide, 1998–2000. Mem. Council, Save the Children (UK), 1993–2000; Pres., White Rose Children's Charity, 1995–. Mem., Carmen's Co., 1983. Hon. DEng Bradford, 1988. OStJ 1979. *Recreations:* golf, walking. *Address:* The Spinney, Lands Lane, Knaresborough, N Yorks HG5 9DE. *T:* (01423) 863719.

MYERS, Geoffrey Morris Price; Under-Secretary, Agricultural and Food Research Council, 1973–87; *b* 8 May 1927. *Educ:* Reigate Grammar Sch.; King's Coll., London. Civil Service, 1950; UKAEA, 1959–67; Nat. Econ. Develt Office, 1967–69; Agric. Research Council, 1970. Chm., Croydon Soc., 2003–07. *Address:* 56 Northampton Road, Croydon CR0 7HT. *T:* (020) 8655 3158.

MYERS, Gordon Elliot, CMG 1979; Under-Secretary, Arable Crops, Pigs and Poultry Group, Ministry of Agriculture, Fisheries and Food, 1984–89, retired; *b* 4 July 1929; *s* of William Lionel Myers and Yvonne (*née* Arthur); *m* 1963, Wendy Jane Lambert; two *s* one *d. Educ:* Kilburn Grammar Sch.; University Coll., Oxford (BA 1st Cl. Hons Modern History). Asst Principal, MAFF, 1951; Principal, 1958; Asst Sec., 1966; Head successively of Land Drainage Div., Sugar and Tropical Foods Div., and EEC Div., 1966–74; Under-Sec., MAFF, 1975; Minister (Agriculture), Office of UK Perm. Rep. to EEC, 1975–79; Under-Sec., Food Policy Gp, 1980–85, Cereals and Sugar Gp, 1985–86, MAFF. Mem., Cttee on Simplification of Common Agricl Policy, EEC, 1990–94. Sec., Caribbean Banana Exporters Assoc., 1993–. *Publication:* Banana Wars: the price of free trade, 2004. *Address:* Woodlands, Nugents Park, Hatch End, Pinner, Middx HA5 4RA. *Club:* Oxford and Cambridge.

MYERS, John David; Chairman of Industrial Tribunals, 1982–97 (Regional Chairman for Newcastle, 1994–97); part-time Chairman of Employment Tribunals, 1998–2005; *b* 30 Oct. 1937; *s* of Frank and Monica Myers; *m* 1974, Anne McGeough (*née* Purcell), *widow* of J. T. McGeough; one *s. Educ:* Marist College, Hull; Hull University. LLB Hons. Called to the Bar, Gray's Inn, 1968. Schoolmaster, 1958–64; University, 1964–67; pupillage with J. D. Walker (later Judge Walker); practice at Hull, 1969–82 (Junior, NE Circuit, 1975–76). *Recreations:* cooking, oenology, bridge. *Club:* Alnmouth Golf.

MYERS, Kevin; *see* Myers, D. K.

MYERS, Martin Trevor, FRICS; Chairman, Mountgrange Capital plc, since 2002; Senior Partner, Mountgrange Real Estate Opportunity Fund, since 2007; *b* 24 Sept. 1941; *s* of Bernard Myers and Sylvia Marjorie Myers (*née* Pearman); *m* 1981, Nicole Josephine Yerna; one *s* one *d. Educ:* Arnold House, St John's Wood; Latymer Upper Sch.; Coll. of Estate Management, London Univ. (BSc). FRICS 1975. Jones Lang Wootton, 1965–83: Partner, 1969; Proprietary Partner, 1972; Chm. and Chief Exec., Arbuthnot Properties, 1983; merged with Imry Property Holdings, 1987, and with City Merchant Developers, 1988; Chief Exec. and Man. Dir, Imry Holdings Ltd, 1989–97; Exec. Dep. Chm., Trillium Gp, 1998–2001. Trustee, Royal Marsden Cancer Campaign, 2003–. Gov., South Bank Centre, 2003–. *Recreations:* golf, shooting, exercise. *Clubs:* Turf; Wisley Golf (Ripley).

MYERS, Dr Norman, CMG 1998; Managing Director, Norman Myers' Scientific Consultancy, since 1982; *b* 24 Aug. 1934; *s* of John Myers and Gladys Myers (*née* Haworth); *m* 1965, Dorothy Mary Halliman (separated 1992); two *d. Educ:* Keble Coll., Oxford (BA 1957; MA 1963); Univ. of Calif, Berkeley (PhD 1973). Dist Officer, Kenya Colonial Admin, 1958–61; high sch. teacher, Nairobi, 1961–65; freelance writer, professional photographer and lectr on African wildlife, Kenya, 1966–69; consultant in envmt and develt, 1972–: projects for develt orgns and res. bodies, incl. World Bank, UN agencies, OECD, EC, US Depts of State and Energy, NASA, US Nat. Acad. of Scis. Hon. Vis. Fellow, Green Coll., Oxford, 1992; Adjunct Prof., Duke Univ., 1997–; Prof. at Large, Univ. of Vermont, 2007–; Vis. Prof., Univs of Kent, Utrecht, Cape Town, Calif, Texas, Michigan, Cornell, Harvard and Stanford. For. Associate, US NAS, 1994; FWAAS 1989; FAAAS 1990; FRSA 1993; FLS 1993; Fellow, Royal Instn, 1997; Ext. Fellow, Saïd Business Sch., Oxford Univ., 2005. Hon. DSc Kent, 2003. Numerous awards for work in environment and development, including Volvo Envmt Prize, 1992; Pew Fellowship in Envmt, 1994; UNEP Sasakawa Envmt Prize, 1995; Blue Planet Prize, Asahi Glass Foundn, Japan, 2001. *Publications:* The Long African Day, 1972; The Sinking Ark, 1979 (trans. Japanese and Hungarian); Conversion of Tropical Moist Forests, 1980; A Wealth of Wild Species, 1983; The Primary Source: tropical forests and our future, 1984, rev. edn 1992; The Gaia Atlas of Planet Management, 1984 (trans. 11 langs), 2nd edn 2005; (ed jtly) Economics of Ecosystem Management, 1985; Future Worlds: challenge and opportunity in an age of change, 1990; Population, Resources and the Environment: the critical challenges, 1991; (ed) Tropical Forests and Climate, 1992; Ultimate Security: the environmental basis of political stability, 1993, 2nd edn 1996; Scarcity or Abundance: a debate on the environment, 1994 (trans. Italian); Environmental Exodus: an emergent crisis in the global arena, 1995; (jtly) Biodiversity Hotspots, 1999; Towards a New Greenprint for Business and Society, 1999; Food and Hunger in Sub-Saharan Africa, 2001; (jtly) Perverse Subsidies: how tax dollars can undercut the environment and the economy, 2001; New Consumers: the influence of affluence on the environment, 2004; contrib. numerous professional papers in scientific jls incl. Science, Nature, Population and Develt Rev., Jl Envmtl Econs & Mgt, Internat. Jl Social Econs. *Recreations:* professional photography, marathon running, mountaineering. *Address:* Upper Meadow, Douglas Downes Close, Headington, Oxford OX3 8FS. *T:* (01865) 750387. *Club:* Achilles.

MYERS, Sir Philip (Alan), Kt 1985; OBE 1977; QPM 1972; DL; one of Her Majesty's Inspectors of Constabulary, 1982–93; *b* 7 Feb. 1931; *s* of John and Catherine Myers; *m* 1951, Hazel Gittings; two *s. Educ:* Grove Park, Wrexham. RAF, 1949–50. Shropshire Constabulary, 1950–67; West Mercia Police, 1967–68; Dep. Chief Constable, Gwynedd Constabulary, 1968–70; Chief Constable, North Wales Police, 1970–81. OStJ 1972. DL Clwyd, 1983.

MYERS, Sir Rupert (Horace), KBE 1981 (CBE 1976); AO 1995; FTSE, FAA; Professor Emeritus; Vice-Chancellor and Principal, University of New South Wales, 1969–81; *b* 21 Feb. 1921; *s* of Horace Alexander Myers and Dorothy (*née* Harris); *m* 1944, Io Edwina King (*d* 2001); one *s* three *d*; *m* 2002, Nancy Marguerite Besley. *Educ:* Melbourne High Sch.; Univ. of Melbourne (BSc 1942; MSc 1943; PhD 1947). FTSE (FTS 1979); FAA 1997; CPEng, FIMMA, FRACI; FAIM; FAusIMM; FAICD. Commonwealth Res. Fellow, Univ. of Melbourne, 1942–47; Principal Res. Officer, CSIRO, AERE Harwell, 1947–52; University of New South Wales: Foundn Prof. of Metallurgy, 1952–81; Dean, Faculty of Applied Science, 1956–61; Pro-Vice-Chancellor, 1961–69. Chairman: NSW State Pollution Control Commn, 1971–89; Aust. Vice-Chancellors' Cttee, 1977–79; Cttee of Inquiry into Technol Change in Australia, 1979–80; Commonwealth Cttee of Review of Nat. Capital Develt Commn, 1982–83; Consultative Cttee for Nat. Conservation Strategy for Australia, 1983–85; Coastal Council of NSW, 1982–85; Cttee of Review of NZ Univs, 1987–88; Cttee of Review of Aust. Sci. and Technology Council, 1993; Cttee of Review, Co-operative Res. Centres Prog., 1995; Co-operative Res. Centre for Greenhouse Accounting, 1999–2003. Pres., Aust. Acad. of Technol Scis and Engrg, 1989–94 (Vice-Pres., 1985–88). Director: CSR Ltd, 1982–93; Energy Resources of Australia Ltd, 1982–97; IBM Australia Ltd, 1988–91. Member: Nat. Energy Adv. Cttee, 1980–82; Australian Manufacturing Council, 1980–82. Mem., Sydney Opera House Trust, 1976–83; Foundn Pres., Friends of Royal Botanic Gdns, Sydney, 1982–85. Hon. FIEAust, 1992. Hon. LLD Strathclyde, 1973; Hon. DSc Wollongong, 1976; Hon. DEng Newcastle, 1981; Hon. DLitt NSW, 1981. Centenary Medal, Australia, 2003. *Publications:* Technological Change in Australia, 1980; numerous on metallurgy and atomic energy (also patents). *Recreations:* bowls, music, working with silver. *Address:* 1303/30 Glen Street, Milsons Point, NSW 2061, Australia. *T:* and *Fax:* (2) 89203108.

MYERSON, His Honour Arthur Levey; QC 1974; a Circuit Judge, 1978–99; *b* 25 July 1928; *o s* of Bernard and Eda Myerson; *m* 1960, (Elaine) Shirley Harris; two *s. Educ:* Blackpool Grammar Sch.; Queens' Coll., Cambridge (BA 1950; LLB 1951); BA (Open Univ.) 1985. RAF, 1946–48. Called to the Bar, 1952; a Recorder of the Crown Court, 1972–78; Resident Judge, York Crown Court, 1996–99. Pres., HM Council of Circuit Judges, 1991. *Recreations:* walking, reading, fishing. *Address:* 20 Sandmoor Lane, Leeds LS17 7EA. *Club:* Moor Allerton Golf (Leeds).

See also D. S. Myerson.

MYERSON, (David) Simon; QC 2003; a Recorder, since 2001; *b* 22 Oct. 1962; *s* of His Honour Arthur Levey Myerson, *qv*; *m* 1987, Nicole Maurice; four *d. Educ:* Carmel Coll.; Downing Coll., Cambridge (MA). Called to the Bar, Middle Temple, 1986. *Recreations:* walking, reading, sailing. *Address:* Park Court Chambers, 16 Park Place, Leeds LS1 2SJ. *T:* (0113) 243 3277, *Fax:* (0113) 242 1285; *e-mail:* simon.myerson@netserv.net.

MYERSON, Prof. Jeremy; Royal College of Art: Professor of Design Studies, since 2003; Co-Director, Helen Hamlyn Research Centre, since 1999; Director, Innovation, since 2004; *b* 6 Aug. 1956; *s* of Alexander and Maxine Myerson; *m* 1986, Wendy Smith; two *s. Educ:* Hull Univ. (BA Hons); Royal Coll. of Art (MA). Editor: Creative Rev., 1984–86; Design Week, 1986–89; freelance writing and consultancy, 1989–95; Prof. of Contemporary Design, De Montfort Univ., 1995–98. Trustee: Gordon Russell Trust, 1994–; Audi Design Foundn, 2004–. *Publications:* IDEO: masters of innovation, 2001; Rewind: 40 years of design and advertising, 2002; The 21st Century Office, 2003; Space to Work: new office design, 2006. *Recreations:* architecture, jazz, football. *Address:* Royal College of Art, Kensington Gore, SW7 2EU. *T:* (020) 7590 4249, *Fax:* (020) 7590 4244; *e-mail:* jeremy.myerson@rca.ac.uk.

MYERSON, Simon; *see* Myerson, D. S.

MYKURA, Janey Patricia Winifred; *see* Walker, J. P. W.

MYLAND, Howard David, CB 1988; Deputy Comptroller and Auditor General, National Audit Office, 1984–89; *b* 23 June 1929; *s* of John Tarrant and Frances Grace Myland; *m* 1951, Barbara Pearl Mills; two *s* one *d. Educ:* Fairfields Schs; Queen Mary's Sch., Basingstoke. Served Intelligence Corps, 1948–50. Entered Exchequer and Audit Dept, 1948; Dep. Dir of Audit, 1972; Dir of Audit, 1977; Dep. Sec. of Dept, 1979; an Asst Auditor Gen., National Audit Office, 1984. Mem., CIPFA, 1979–. Mem., Basingstoke Round Table, 1962–70. *Publication:* Public Audit Law—Key Development Considerations, 1992. *Recreations:* travel, contract bridge.

MYLES, David Fairlie, CBE 1988; tenant hill farmer; *b* 30 May 1925; *s* of Robert C. Myles and Mary Anne S. (*née* Fairlie); *m* 1951, Janet I. (*née* Gall); two *s* two *d. Educ:* Edzell Primary Sch.; Brechin High Sch. National Farmers Union of Scotland: Mem. Council, 1970–79; Convenor of Organisation and Publicity Cttee, 1976–79. MP (C) Banff, 1979–83; Sec., Cons. backbench Cttees on European Affairs and on Agriculture, Fisheries and Food (Jt Sec.); Mem., Select Cttees on Agriculture and on European Legislation. Contested (C) Orkney and Shetland, 1983. Councillor, Angus DC, 1984–96 (Leader, Cons. Gp, 1992–96). Chm., Dairy Produce Quota Tribunal for Scotland, 1984–97; Member: Exec., Angus Tourist Bd, 1984–92; North of Scotland Hydro-Electric Bd,

1985–88; Extra-Parly Panel (Scotland), 1986–95; Potato Marketing Bd, 1988–97. Dean, Guildry of Brechin, 1993–95; Lord Pres., Ct of Deans of Scotland, 1995–96; Session Clerk, Edzell/Lethnot Parish Church, 1996–2001. *Recreations:* curling, Scottish fiddle music. *Address:* Dalbog, Edzell, Brechin, Angus DD9 7UU; (home) The Gorse, Dunlappie Road, Edzell, Brechin, Angus DD9 7UB. *Clubs:* Farmers'; Brechin Rotary.

MYLES, Lynda Robbie; independent film producer, Pandora Productions, since 1991; Head, Fiction Direction, National Film and Television School, since 2004; *b* 2 May 1947; *d* of late Alexander Watt Myles and Kathleen Kilgour Myles (*née* Polson); *m* 1972, Dr David John Will (marr. diss. 1978). *Educ:* Univ. of Edinburgh (MA Hons Mental Philosophy). Dir, Edinburgh Internat. Film Fest., 1973–80; Curator of Film, Pacific Film Archive, Univ. of Calif, Berkeley, 1980–82; Film Consultant, Channel Four TV, 1982–83; Producer, Enigma Films, 1983–86; Sen. Vice-Pres., Creative Affairs (Europe), Columbia Pictures, 1986–88; Commng Ed. for Drama, BBC TV, 1989–91. Co-Exec. Dir, East-West Producers' Seminar, 1990–94. Producer: Defence of the Realm, 1986; The Commitments, 1991; The Snapper, 1993; The Van, 1995; The Life of Stuff, 1997; When Brendan Met Trudy, 2000; (jtly) Killing Me Softly, 2001. Chair (first), Women in Film and TV, 1990–91; Mem. Bd, Ateliers du Cinéma Européen, 1998–. Gov., BFI, 1993–96. BFI Award, 1981. *Publication:* (with M. Pye) The Movie Brats, 1978. *Address:* Pandora Productions, 20 Ossington Street, W2 4LY. *T:* (020) 7243 3013. *Club:* Groucho.

MYLNE, Nigel James; QC 1984; a Recorder, since 1985; *b* 11 June 1939; *s* of late Harold James Mylne and Dorothy Evelyn Mylne (later D. E. Hogg); *m* 1st, 1967, Julie Phillpotts (marr. diss. 1977); two *s* one *d*; 2nd, 1979, Judith Hamilton (marr. diss. 1997); one *s. Educ:* Eton College. National Service, 10th Royal Hussars, 1957–59. Called to the Bar, Middle Temple, 1963, Bencher, 1995. Immigration Judge, 1997–; Pres., Mental Health Review Tribunals, 1999–. *Recreation:* beekeeping. *Address:* Langleys, Brixton Deverill, Wiltshire BA12 7EJ. *T:* (01985) 840992; *e-mail:* nmylneswalker@aol.com. *Clubs:* White's, Pratt's.

MYLREA, (Anthony) Paul; Director, Communications, Department for International Development, since 2007; *b* 21 March 1956; *s* of late Thomas Aloysius Mylrea and of Joan Mylrea (*née* Wilcox, now Taylor); *m* 1986, Frances Lowndes; one *s* two *d. Educ:* St Bede's Coll., Manchester; Univ. of Birmingham (BA Hons French 1978); Open Univ. (MBA 2003). Reuters: Corresp., London, Germany, Luxembourg, Belgium and Brazil, 1982–90; Chief Corresp., Chile, Bolivia and Peru, 1990–94; UK Political Corresp., 1994–97; Dep. Editor, 1997–99, Editor, 1999–2002, www.alertnet.org; Hd, Media, Oxfam GB, 2002–04; Dir, Gp Media, Transport for London, 2004–07. Associate Lectr, OU Business Sch., 2005–. *Recreations:* tying flies, fishing badly, folding bikes. *Address:* c/o Department for International Development, 1 Palace Street, SW1E 5HE. *T:* (020) 7023 1949; *e-mail:* p-mylrea@dfid.gov.uk. *Club:* Frontline.

MYNERS, Paul, CBE 2003; Financial Services Secretary, HM Treasury, since 2008; *b* 1 April 1948; adopted *s* of late Thomas Russell Myners and of Caroline Molly Myners; *m* 1995, Alison Macleod; one *s* one *d*, and three *d* by a previous marriage. *Educ:* Truro Sch., Cornwall; Univ. of London Inst. of Educn (BEd); Stanford Sch. of Business (SEP 1995). Daily Telegraph, 1970–74; N. M. Rothschild & Sons Ltd, 1974–85 (Dir, 1979); Gartmore plc: Chief Exec., 1985–93, 1999–2000; Chm., 1987–2001; Chairman: Guardian Media Gp plc, 2000–08; Land Securities PLC, 2006–08. Dep. Chm., PowerGen plc, 1999–2001; Exec. Dir, Nat. Westminster Bank, 1997–2000; non-executive Director: Orange plc, 1996–99; Coutts Group, 1997–2000; Guardian Newspapers Ltd, 2001–; mmO2 plc (formerly BT Wireless), 2001–04; Marks and Spencer, 2002–06 (Chm., 2004–06); Bank of New York, 2002–06; Mem., Ct of Dirs, Bank of England, 2005–; Advr, Govt of Singapore Investment Corp., 2006–; Chm., Personal Accounts Delivery Authy, DWP, 2007–08. Member: Financial Reporting Council, 1995–2004; Company Law Review Consultative Cttee, 1998–2000; Commn on English Prisons, 2007–; Commn on Vulnerable Employment, 2007–; Chm., Low Pay Commn, 2006–. Vis. Fellow, Nuffield Coll., Oxford, 2007–. Mem., Adv. Council, LSO, 1993–2003. Trustee: Nat. and Cornwall Maritime Mus. Trust, 1998–2004; Royal Acad. Trust, 2000–03; Tate Gall., 2003– (Chm., 2004–08; Chm. Council, Tate St Ives, 2001–); Glyndebourne, 2003–; Smith Inst., 2003–; Charities Aid Foundn, 2003–04; Nat. Gallery, 2007–08. FRSA 1994. Hon. LLD Exeter, 2003. Freeman, City of London, 1996. *Publications:* Developing a Winning Partnership, 1995; Creating Quality Dialogue, 1999; Institutional Investment in the UK: a review for HM Treasury, 2001. *Recreations:* family, contemporary art, opera, Rugby football. *Address:* House of Lords, SW1A 0PW. *Clubs:* City of London, Oriental; Hong Kong; Royal Cornwall Yacht.

[Created a Baron (Life Peer) 2008 but title not gazetted at time of going to press.]

MYNORS, Sir Richard (Baskerville), 2nd Bt *cr* 1964, of Treago, Co. Hereford; landowner; *b* 5 May 1947; *s* of Sir Humphrey Charles Baskerville Mynors, 1st Bt and Lydia Marian (*d* 1992), *d* of Sir Ellis Minns, LittD, FSA, FBA; *S* father, 1989; *m* 1970, Fiona Bridget, *d* of late Rt. Rev. G. E. Reindorp; three *d. Educ:* Marlborough; Royal College of Music (ARCM, ARCO); Corpus Christi Coll., Cambridge (MA). Asst Director of Music, King's School, Macclesfield, 1970–73; Director of Music: Wolverhampton Grammar School, 1973–81; Merchant Taylors' School, Crosby, 1981–88; Belmont Abbey Sch., Hereford, 1988–89. *Heir:* none. *Address:* Treago, St Weonards, Hereford HR2 8QB. *T:* (01981) 580208.

MYNOTT, Adam Robert John; East Africa Correspondent, BBC, since 2004; *b* 21 Oct. 1957; *s* of Michael J. Mynott and Rosalind S. Mynott; *m* 1987, Carol Elizabeth Schug; two *s* one *d. Educ:* Eastbourne Coll.; Univ. of Exeter (BA Hons Philos. 1980); London Coll. of Printing (Postgrad. Dip. Radio Journalism 1982). BBC: Producer, Today Prog., 1986–90; gen. news reporter, 1990–94; Sports Corresp., 1994–2001; S Asia Corresp., Delhi, 2001–04. *Publication:* The Battle for Iraq, 2003. *Recreations:* news and current affairs, starting DIY projects. *Address:* PO Box 58621, 00200 Nairobi, Kenya; *e-mail:* adam.mynott@bbc.co.uk. *Clubs:* Free Foresters, Sou'westers.

MYNOTT, Dr (Roger) Jeremy; Chief Executive of the Press, Secretary of the Press Syndicate and University Printer, Cambridge University Press, 1999–2002; Fellow, Wolfson College, Cambridge, since 1999; *b* 15 Feb. 1942; *s* of Clifford Harry Mynott and Margaret Mynott (*née* Ketley); *m* 2000, Diane Speakman. *Educ:* Colchester Royal Grammar Sch.; Corpus Christi Coll., Cambridge (BA 1964; MA 1968; PhD 1968). Schoolmaster, Magdalen Coll. Sch., Oxford, 1964–65; Cambridge University Press, 1968–2002: sub-editor, 1968–69; editor, 1969–73; sen. editor, 1973–75; Associate Dir, 1975–79; Editl Dir, Humanities and Social Scis, 1979–81; Dir, Publishing Develt, 1981–85; Press Editl Dir Worldwide, 1985–92; Man. Dir, Publishing Div. and Dep. Chief Exec., 1992–99. FRSA 1990. *Publications:* Little Thurlow 2000, 1999; Walks Round the Thurlows, 2005. *Recreations:* natural history (especially ornithology), walking, philosophy, vegetable gardening. *Address:* (office) Pitt Building, Trumpington Street, Cambridge CB2 1RP. *T:* (01223) 330828.

MYRES, Rear-Adm. John Antony Lovell, CB 1993; Hydrographer of the Navy, 1990–94; *b* 11 April 1936; *yr s* of late Dr John Nowell Linton Myres, CBE and Joan Mary Lovell Myres (*née* Stevens); *m* 1965, Alison Anne, *d* of late Lieut David Lawrence Carr, RN (killed in action 1941) and Mrs James Pertwee; three *s*. *Educ:* Winchester College. FRICS 1975–95; FRGS 1993–97; FRIN 1994–97. Entered RN 1954; specialised Hydrographic Surveying, 1959; CO HM Ships Woodlark, 1969–71, Fox, 1972–73, Hecla, 1974, 1978–79, 1981–82; Hydrographer, RAustN, 1982–85. Sec., UK Polar Medal Assessment Cttee, 1994–. Pres., Orders and Medals Res. Soc., 1997–2001. Vice Pres., RNLI, 2006–. Younger Brother of Trinity House, 1990. Freeman, City of London, 1990; Liveryman, Chartered Surveyors' Co., 1990–97. Guild Burgess of Preston, 1952. *Publications:* (jtly) British Polar Exploration and Research: a historic and medallic record with biographies, 2000; articles in professional jls. *Recreations:* naval and medallic history, gardening. *Club:* Antarctic.

MYRTLE, Brig. Andrew Dewe, CB 1988; CBE 1979 (MBE 1967); Chief Executive and Secretary, Tennis and Rackets Association, 1989–2001; *b* 17 Dec. 1932; *s* of Lt-Col John Young Elphinstone Myrtle, DSO, KOSB (killed in action in World War II) and late Doreen May Lake; *m* 1973, Mary Rose Ford; two *d*. *Educ:* Horris Hill Prep. Sch.; Winchester Coll.; RMA, Sandhurst (Sword of Honour); Army Staff Coll. Co. Comdr, 1 KOSB, 1964–66; Bde Major, 24 Infantry Bde, 1966–68; Co. Comdr, 1 KOSB, 1968–69, CO, 1969–71; MA to Adjt Gen., 1971–74; Comdt, Jun. Div., Staff Coll., 1974–77; Comd 8 Infantry Bde, 1977–79; student, RCDS, 1979; DDMO, MoD, 1980–83; Asst Comdt, RMA, Sandhurst, 1983–85; Comdr Land Forces, Cyprus, 1986–88. Col, KOSB, 1980–85. ADC to the Queen, 1985–88. *Recreations:* golf, fly-fishing. *Address:* Pen Guen, Stonor, Henley-on-Thames, Oxon RG9 6HB. *Clubs:* MCC; Huntercombe Golf; Queen's.

N

NAAS, Lord; Richard Thomas Bourke; *b* 7 Dec. 1985; *s* and *heir* of Earl of Mayo, *qv.*

NADER, Ralph; author, lecturer, lawyer; *b* Winsted, Conn, USA, 27 Feb. 1934; *s* of Nadra Nader and Rose (*née* Bouziane). *Educ:* Gilbert Sch., Winsted; Woodrow Wilson Sch. of Public and Internat. Affairs, Princeton Univ. (AB *magna cum laude*); Harvard Univ. Law Sch. (LLB). Admitted to: Bar of Conn, 1958; Bar of Mass, 1959; US Supreme Court Bar, 1963. Served US Army, 1959. Law practice in Hartford, Conn, 1959–; Lectr in History and Govt, Univ. of Hartford, 1961–63; Lectr, Princeton Univ., 1967–68. Member: Amer. Bar Assoc., 1959–; AAAS, 1964–; Phi Beta Kappa. Has pursued actively better consumer protection and improvement in the lot of the American Indian; lobbied in Washington for safer food, drugs, air, water and against nuclear reactors; played very important role in work for passing of: National Traffic and Motor Vehicle Safety Act, 1966; Wholesome Meat Act, 1967; Occupational Safety and Health Act, 1970; Safe Drinking Water Act, 1974; Freedom of Information Act, 1974; National Cooperative Bank Act, 1978. Nieman Fellows Award, 1965–66; named one of the Ten Outstanding Young Men of the Year by US Jun. Chamber of Commerce, 1967. *Publications:* Unsafe at Any Speed: the designed-in dangers of the American automobile, 1965, rev. edn 1991; (jtly) What to do with Your Bad Car, 1971; Working on the System: a manual for citizen's access to federal agencies, 1972; (jtly) Action for a Change, 1972; (jtly) Whistleblowing, 1972; (jtly) You and Your Pension, 1973; (ed) The Consumer and Corporate Accountability, 1973; (co-ed) Corporate Power in America, 1973; (jtly) Taming the Giant Corporation, 1976; (co-ed) Verdicts on Lawyers, 1976; (jtly) Menace of Atomic Energy, 1977; (co-ed) Who's Poisoning America?, 1981; (jtly) The Big Boys: power and position in American business, 1986; (jtly) Winning the Insurance Game, 1990; (jtly) No Contest, 1996; contrib. articles to many magazines; has weekly syndicated newspaper column. *Address:* PO Box 19367, Washington, DC 20036–9367, USA.

NADESAN, Pararajasingam, CMG 1955; OBE 1954; Governor, Rotary International, District 321; Member, Legislative Council, Rotary International; Director: National Development Bank, since 1995; Cargills (Ceylon) Ltd; Associated Hotels Co. Ltd; Past Chairman: Low Country Products Association; Air Ceylon; *b* 20 Dec. 1917; *s* of Sir Sangarapillai Pararajasingam, and Padmavati, *d* of Sir Ponnambalam Arunachalam; *m* 1st, 1941, Gauri Nair (decd); one *s* one *d*; 2nd, 1953, Kamala Nair; three *d*. *Educ:* Royal College, and Ceylon Univ. Coll.; Univ. of London (BA Hons). Tutor, Ceylon Univ. Coll., 1940; entered Ceylon Civil Service, 1941; held various appts in sphere of provincial administration, 1941–47; Asst Permanent Sec., Min. of Transport and Works, 1948–53; Dir of Civil Aviation in addition to duties as Asst Sec. Min. of Transport and Works, 1954–56; Sec. to the Prime Minister and Information Officer, Ceylon, 1954–56; Member: Ceylon Delegation to the Bandung Conf.; Commonwealth Prime Minister's Conf.; ICAO Gen. Assembly; ILO Cttee on Plantations. Past Mem., Nat. Planning Council. Pres. Emeritus and Life Mem., Ceylon Hotels Assoc.; FIH; FCIT. Past President: Orchid Circle of Ceylon; Sri Lanka Horticultural Soc. Officer Order of Merit (Italy), 1954; Knight Comdr Order of the Crown, Thailand, 1955; Comdr Order of Orange Nassau, Netherlands, 1955; Defence Medal, 1947; Coronation Medal, 1953; Ceylon Armed Services Inauguration Medal, 1956. *Recreations:* golf, tennis, gardening, collecting antiques, stamps and coins. *Address:* 52/1 Flower Road, Colombo 3, Sri Lanka. *T:* 573687. *Clubs:* Colombo, Orient, Rotary (Colombo); Gymkhana.

NAGAI, Kiyoshi, PhD; FRS 2000; Member, MRC Laboratory of Molecular Biology, since 1981; Fellow, Darwin College, Cambridge, since 1993; *b* 25 June 1949; *s* of Prof. Otoji Nagai and Naoko Nagai (*née* Matsumoto); *m* 1974, Yoshiko Majima; one *s* one *d*. *Educ:* Toin High Sch.; Osaka Univ. (BSc 1972; MSc 1974; PhD 1978). Thomas Usher Res. Fellow, Darwin Coll., Cambridge, 1981–83. Mem., EMBO, 2000. Novartis Medal and Prize, Biochem. Soc., 2000. *Publications:* (jtly) RNA: protein interactions, 1994; res. pubns and reviews in scientific jls. *Recreations:* playing cello in chamber groups, reading. *Address:* MRC Laboratory of Molecular Biology, Hills Road, Cambridge CB2 0QH; 100 Mowbray Road, Cambridge CB1 7TG. *T:* (01223) 402292.

NAGANO, Kent George; conductor; Music Director: Bayerische Staatsoper, since 2006; Montréal Symphony Orchestra, since 2006; *b* 22 Nov. 1951; *s* of George Kimiyoshi Nagano and Ruth Okamoto; *m* Mari Kodama; one *d*. *Educ:* Univ. of Calif. Music Director: Opéra de Lyon, 1988–98; Hallé Orch., 1991–2000; Artistic Dir, Deutsches Symphonie-Orchester Berlin, 2000–06; Music Dir, LA Opera, 2001–06. Has performed with: Boston Symphony Orch., 1984; Paris Opera (World Première, St François d'Assise, by Messiaen); Metropolitan Opera; Salzburg Fest.; Vienna Philharmonic; Berlin Philharmonic; NY Philharmonic; also World Premières: Death of Klinghoffer by John Adams, Brussels, Lyon and Vienna; L'Amour de loin by Saariaho; A White House Cantata by Bernstein; Das Gehege by Wolfgang Rihm; Alice in Wonderland by Unsuk Chin. Gramophone Record of Year, 1990; Gramophone Opera Award, 1993; Grammy Award, 1995, 2001. *Address:* c/o Van Walsum Management Ltd, The Tower Building, 11 York Road, SE1 7NX. *T:* (020) 7902 0520.

NAGDA, Kanti; Manager, Sangat Advice Centre, Harrow, since 1998; *b* 1 May 1946; *s* of Vershi Bhoja Nagda and Zaviben Nagda; *m* 1972, Bhagwati Desai; two *s*. *Educ:* City High Sch., Kampala, Uganda; Coll. of Further Educn, Chippenham, Wilts; E African Univ., Uganda; Cassio Coll., Watford. Sec.-Gen., Confedn of Indian Organisations (UK), 1975–98; Manager, Sancroft Community Centre, 1982–98. Pres., Nat. Congress of Gujarati Orgns, 1992–95; Vice Chair, NW London Community Foundn. Exec. Cttee Member: Harrow Community Relations Council, 1974–76; Gujarati Literary Acad. (GB), 1976–82. President: Uganda Art Circle, 1968–71; Anglo Indian Circle, 1973–82 and 1985–88; Indian Cricket Club, Harrow, 1976–80; Greenford (Willow Tree) Lions Club, 1988–89. Hon. Editorial Consultant, International Asian Guide & Who's Who, 1975–95; Asst Editor, Oshwal News, 1977–84. *Publications:* Muratiyo Ke Nokar (Gujarati novel), Kenya 1967; stories and articles in newspapers and jls. *Recreations:* cricket, photography. *Address:* 170 Tolcarne Drive, Pinner, Middx HA5 2DR. *T:* (020) 8863 9089. *Club:* Greenford Lions.

NAGEL, William, CMG 2002; Chairman, W. Nagel (International Diamond Brokers), since 1955; *b* 17 Jan. 1925; *m* 1960, Ruth Marion Josephine Yvonne Tand; one *s* three *d*. *Educ:* University Coll. London (LLB Hons 1949). Called to the Bar, Lincoln's Inn, 1949; post-grad. res. in Public Internat. Law, Fitzwilliam House, Cambridge Univ., 1950–53; Public Internat. Law Course, Internat. Court of Justice, The Hague, 1954; apptd Official Broker, De Beers, 1959. Special Advr to Minister of Foreign Affairs, Romania, 1992. Member: ESU; Foreign Press. Assoc.; RIIA. Freeman, City of London, 1988. Comdr, Order of the Crown (Belgium), 1996; Officer's Cross, Order of Merit (Germany), 2000; Comdr, Nat. Order Serviciul Credincios (Romania), 2002. *Address:* 10 Ely Place, EC1N 6RY. *T:* (020) 7242 9636, *Fax:* (020) 7430 0990; *e-mail:* wn@wnagel.net.

NAGLE, Terence John, FRICS; Director, Wynnstay Properties plc, since 1998; *b* 10 Nov. 1942; *s* of Richard and Bridget Nagle; *m* 1974, Elizabeth Mary Millett; two *s* two *d*. *Educ:* Ottershaw Sch.; St John's Seminary, Wonersh (BTh). FRICS 1964. Property Dir, 1984–93, Man. Dir, 1993–97, Brixton Estate plc. *Recreations:* gardening, tennis. *Address:* Pitch Place House, Worplesdon, Guildford, Surrey GU3 3LQ. *T:* (01483) 232036.

NAGLER, Neville Anthony; Executive Director, Taxation Disciplinary Board, since 2007; *b* 2 Jan. 1945; *s* of late Gerald and Sylvia Nagler; *m* 1971, Judy Mordant; one *s* one *d*. *Educ:* Christ's Coll., Finchley; Jesus Coll., Cambridge (MA); Cert. in Public Services Mgt, 2000. Asst Principal, HM Treasury, 1967–70; Private Sec. to Chancellor of Exchequer, 1970–71; Principal, 1972; transferred to Home Office, 1975; Asst Sec., Race Relations and Equal Opportunities, 1980–83; Head, Drugs and Extradition Div., 1983–88; Asst Sec., Home Office Finance Div., 1988–91; Chief Exec., subseq. Dir Gen., 1991–2004, Interfaith Consultant, 2005–07, Bd of Deputies of British Jews; Dir, Sternberg Foundn, 2005–06. Vice Chm., Inter Faith Network for UK, 2005–07. Lay Mem., Disciplinary Tribunals, Guild of Inns of Ct, 2005–; Mem., Lord Chancellor's Adv. Cttee for JPs in NW London, 2006–. UK Rep. to UN Commn on Narcotic Drugs, 1983–88; Chm., Council of Europe Pompidou Gp, 1984–88. Haldane Essay Prize, Haldane Soc., 1979; Cert. of Appreciation, US Drug Enforcement Admin, 1988. *Publications:* articles in Public Administration and UN Jl of Narcotic Drugs. *Recreations:* wine-making, listening to music, theatre, walking. *Address:* 24 Dawlish Drive, Pinner, Middx HA5 5LN. *T:* (020) 8868 3103.

NAHORSKI, Prof. Stefan Ryszard, PhD; FMedSci; Professor of Pharmacology, 1984–2006, now Emeritus, and Head of Department of Cell Physiology and Pharmacology, 1993–2006, University of Leicester; *b* 10 Dec. 1945; *s* of Stanislaw Nahorski and Linda Nahorska; *m* 1969, Catherine Mary Gower; one *s* two *d*. *Educ:* St Boniface's Coll., Plymouth; Univ. of Southampton (BSc Hons); Portsmouth Sch. of Pharmacy (PhD 1971). Research Asst, Portsmouth, 1968–71; MRC Fellow, Sheffield, 1971–75; University of Leicester: Lectr in Pharmacology, 1976–81; Reader, 1981–84. Founder FMedSci 1998. John Vane Medal, British Pharmacological Soc., 2004. *Publications:* Pharmacology of Adrenoceptors, 1985; Transmembrane Signalling, 1990; numerous research papers to learned jls. *Recreations:* tennis, walking, watching (supporting) soccer, sea angling.

NAHUM, Peter John; art dealer, Leicester Galleries, London, since 1984; *b* 19 Jan. 1947; *s* of Denis E. Nahum and Allison Faith Nahum (*née* Cooke); *m* 1987, Renate Angelika Meiser. *Educ:* Sherborne. Peter Wilson's Sotheby's, 1966–84; British Paintings Dept, Sotheby's, Belgravia, 1971–84, Sen. Dir, 1977–84; regular contributor to Antiques Road Show, BBC TV, 1980–2003. FRSA 2005. *Publications:* Prices of Victorian Paintings, Drawings and Watercolours, 1976; Monograms of Victorian and Edwardian Artists, 1976; Cross Section, British Art in the 20th Century, 1988; British Art in the Twentieth Century, 1989; Burne-Jones, The Pre-Raphaelites & Their Century, 1989; Burne-Jones: a quest for love, 1993; Fairy Folk in Fairy Land, 1997; Pre-Raphaelite . Symbolist . Visionary, 2001; Medieval to Modern, 2003. *Recreations:* sailing, photography, gardening, theatre, travel, walking. *Address:* 5 Ryder Street, SW1Y 6PY. *T:* (020) 7930 6059, *Fax:* (020) 7930 4678; *e-mail:* peternahum@leicestergalleries.com.

NAILATIKAU, Brig.-Gen. Hon. Ratu Epeli, LVO 1977; OBE 1979; CSM 1995; MSD 1988; Minister for Foreign Affairs and External Trade, Interim Government, Fiji, since 2007; *b* 5 July 1941; *s* of Ratu Sir Edward Cakobau, KBE, MC, ED and Adi Lady Vasamaca Tuiburelevu; *m* 1981, Adi Koila Nailatikau (*née* Mara), *d* of Ratu Sir Kamisese Mara, GCMG, KBE, CF, MSD, PC; one *s* one *d*. *Educ:* Levuka Public Sch.; Queen Victoria Sch., Fiji; Wadham Coll., Oxford. Enlisted in Royal Fiji Military Forces, 1962; commnd Fiji Infantry Regt, 1963; seconded to First Bn, Royal NZ Infantry Regt, Malaysia and Borneo, 1966; ADC to Governor of Fiji, 1968–69; Foreign Service Course, Oxford Univ., 1969–70; Second Secretary: Fiji High Commn, Canberra, 1970–72; Fiji Mission to UN, 1973–74; Australian Army Staff Coll., Queenscliffe, 1976 (psc); CO Fiji Bn, Fiji Infantry Regt serving with UNIFIL, 1978–79; Jt Services Staff Coll., Canberra, Australia, 1980 (jssc); Sen. Plans Officer, UNIFIL HQ, 1981; CS, 1981–82, Comdr, 1982–87, Royal Fiji Mil. Forces; Ambassador of Fiji to UK, and concurrently Ambassador to Denmark, Germany, Israel, the Holy See and Egypt, 1988–96; Roving Ambassador to Pacific Island countries, 1998; Perm. Sec. for Foreign Affairs and External Trade, Fiji, 1999; Mem., Military Council, May–July 2000; Deputy Prime Minister and Minister for Fijian Affairs: Interim Govt, July 2000–March 2001; Caretaker Govt, March–Sept. 2001; Speaker, House of Reps, Fiji, 2001–06. Fiji Equerry: to the Prince of Wales during Fiji Independence visit, 1970; to the Queen during Jubilee visit, 1977. Hon. Col 1st Bn Fiji Infantry Regt, 1996. OStJ 1985. Civil Service Medal (Fiji), 1995. *Recreations:* golf, tennis.

Address: Ministry for Foreign Affairs and External Trade, PO Box 2220, Government Buildings, Suva, Fiji. *T:* 3309628, *Fax:* 3301741.

NAIPAUL, Sir Vidiadhar Surajprasad, (Sir Vidia), Kt 1990; author; *b* 17 Aug. 1932; *m* 1st, 1955, Patricia Ann Hale (*d* 1996); 2nd, 1996, Nadira Khannum Alvi. *Educ:* Queen's Royal Coll., Trinidad; University Coll., Oxford (Hon. Fellow, 1983). Hon. Dr Letters Columbia Univ., NY, 1981; Hon. LittD: Cambridge, 1983; London, 1988; Oxford, 1992. British Literature Prize, 1993; Nobel Prize for Literature, 2001. *Publications:* The Middle Passage, 1962; An Area of Darkness, 1964; The Loss of El Dorado, 1969; The Overcrowded Barracoon, and other articles, 1972; India: a wounded civilization, 1977; The Return of Eva Perón, 1980; Among the Believers, 1981; Finding the Centre, 1984; A Turn in the South, 1989; India: a million mutinies now, 1990; Beyond Belief: Islamic excursions, 1998; Letters between a Father and Son, 1999; Reading & Writing: a personal account, 2000; The Writer and the World (collected essays), 2002; Literary Occasions (essays), 2003; A Writer's People, 2007; *novels:* The Mystic Masseur, 1957 (John Llewelyn Rhys Memorial Prize, 1958); The Suffrage of Elvira, 1958; Miguel Street, 1959 (Somerset Maugham Award, 1961); A House for Mr Biswas, 1961; Mr Stone and the Knights Companion, 1963 (Hawthornden Prize, 1964); The Mimic Men, 1967 (W. H. Smith Award, 1968); A Flag on the Island, 1967; In a Free State, 1971 (Booker Prize, 1971); Guerrillas, 1975; A Bend in the River, 1979; The Enigma of Arrival, 1987; A Way in the World, 1994; Half a Life, 2001; Magic Seeds, 2004. *Address:* c/o Aitken Alexander Associates Ltd, 18–21 Cavaye Place, SW10 9PT.

NAIRN, Margaret, RGN, SCM; Chief Area Nursing Officer, Greater Glasgow Health Board, 1974–84, retired; *b* 20 July 1924; *d* of James R. Nairn and Anne G. Nairn. *Educ:* Aberdeen Academy. Nurse Training: general: Aberdeen Royal Infirmary, to 1945 (RGN); midwifery: Aberdeen Maternity Hosp., until 1948 (State Certified Midwife); Health Visitors: Aberdeen Coll. for Health Visitors, until 1952 (Health Visitors Cert.); administrative: Royal Coll. of Nursing, London, to 1959 (Nursing Admin. Cert.); 6 months study in USA as British Commonwealth and Empire Nurses Scholar, 1956. Ward Sister and Night Supt, Aberdeen Maternity Hosp., 1945–52; Director of Nursing Services in Aberdeen and Glasgow, 1952–74. *Publications:* articles in medical and nursing press: A Study of 283 Families with Rent Arrears; Liaison Services between Hospital and Community Nursing Services; Health Visitors in General Practice. *Recreations:* reading, gardening, swimming, travel. *Address:* 12 Countesswells Terrace, Aberdeen AB1 8LQ.

NAIRN, Martin John L.; see Lambie-Nairn.

NAIRN, Sir Michael, 4th Bt *cr* 1904; DL; *b* 1 July 1938; *s* of Sir Michael George Nairn, 3rd Bt, TD, and Helen Louise, *yr d* of Major E. J. W. Bruce, Melbourne, Aust.; *S* father, 1984; *m* 1st, 1972, Diana (*d* 1982), *er d* of Leonard Bligh, NSW; two *s* one *d*; 2nd, 1986, Sally Jane, *d* of Major W. P. S. Hastings. *Educ:* Eton; INSEAD. DL Perth and Kinross, 1996. *Heir:* *s* Michael Andrew Nairn, *b* 2 Nov. 1973. *Club:* Caledonian.

NAIRN, Sir Robert Arnold S.; see Spencer-Nairn.

NAIRN, Prof. Tom C.; Professor of Nationalism and Global Diversity, Royal Melbourne Institute of Technology, since 2002; *b* 2 June 1932; *s* of David Robertson Nairn and Katherine Herd Cunningham; partner, Millicent Petrie. *Educ:* Dunfermline High Sch.; Univ. of Edinburgh (MA Philosophy 1956); Scuola Normale Superiore, Pisa; Univ. de Dijon. Lectr in Social Philosophy, Univ. of Birmingham, 1962–64; Lectr in Gen. Studies, Hornsey Coll. of Art, 1966–69; Fellow, Transnational Inst., Amsterdam, 1972–75; Dir, Scottish Internat. Inst., Edinburgh, 1976–80; work in commercial TV, Glasgow, 1992–94; Researcher with Ernest Gellner, Centre for Nationalism Studies, Prague Coll. of the Central European Univ., 1994–95; Lectr in Nationalism Studies, Grad. Sch., Univ. of Edinburgh, 1994–99. *Publications:* The Beginning of the End (with Angelo Quattrocchi), 1968; The Left Against Europe, 1975; The Break-up of Britain, 1977, new edn 2003; The Enchanted Glass: Britain and Monarchy, 1988; Faces of Nationalism, 1998; Pariah: misfortunes of the British kingdom, 2001; (with Paul James) Global Matrix, 2005. *Address:* Globalism Institute, Royal Melbourne Institute of Technology, 411 Swanston Street, GPO Box 2476V, Melbourne, Vic 3001, Australia.

NAIRN-BRIGGS, Very Rev. George Peter; DL; Dean (formerly Provost) of Wakefield, 1997–2007, now Dean Emeritus; *b* 5 July 1945; *s* of Frederick and Gladys Nairn-Briggs; *m* 1968, Candida Vickery; one *s* one *d*. *Educ:* Slough Tech. High Sch.; King's Coll., London (AKC 1969); St Augustine's Coll., Canterbury. Local authority housing, 1963–64; Press Officer, MAFF, 1964–66; ordained deacon, 1970, priest, 1971; Curate: St Laurence, Catford, 1970–73; St Saviour, Raynes Park, 1973–75; Vicar: Christ the King, Salfords, 1975–81; St Peter, St Helier, dio. Southwark, 1981–87; Bishop's Advr for Social Responsibility, Wakefield, 1987–97; Canon Residentiary, Wakefield Cathedral, 1992–97. A Church Comr, 2004–07. Mem., Gen. Synod of C of E, 1980–2007. DL W Yorks, 2006. *Publications:* Love in Action, 1986; Serving Two Masters, 1988; It Happens in the Family, 1992; contrib. to magazines and jls. *Recreations:* reading, buying antiques, travel. *Address:* Abbey House, 2 St James Court, Park Avenue, Wakefield WF2 8DN. *T:* (01924) 291029.

NAIRNE, Alexander Robert, (Sandy); Director, National Portrait Gallery, since 2002; *b* 8 June 1953; *s* of Rt Hon. Sir Patrick Nairne, *qv*; partner since 1981, Sylvia Elizabeth (Lisa) Tickner; one *s* one *d*. *Educ:* Radley Coll.; University Coll., Oxford (BA Modern History and Economics 1974; MA; Hon. Fellow 2006). Asst Dir, Museum of Modern Art, Oxford, 1974–76; Research Asst and Asst Keeper, Tate Gallery, 1976–79; Dir of Exhibitions, Inst. of Contemporary Arts, 1980–83; writer and associate producer, State of the Art, TV series, Channel 4, 1985–87; Dir of Visual Arts, Arts Council, 1987–92; Sen. Res. Fellow, Getty Grant Prog., 1992–93; Dir, Public and Regl Services, 1994–98, Dir, Nat. Progs, 1998–2002, Tate Gall. Mem., Fabric Adv. Cttee, St Paul's Cathedral, 1996–. Trustee, Artangel, 1993–2006. Vis. Fellow, Clark Art Inst., Mass, 2007. Gov., Middx Univ., 1994–2003 (Dep. Chm., 1999–2000); Member Council: RCA, 2001–; British Sch. in Rome, 2001–; Museums Assoc., 2005– (Vice Pres., 2006–). Hon. DArts Middx, 2005. *Publications:* State of the Art, 1987; Thinking about Exhibitions, 1996; The Portrait Now, 2006. *Recreation:* racing punting. *Address:* National Portrait Gallery, St Martin's Place, WC2H 0HE. *Clubs:* Chelsea Arts; Leander (Henley).
See also A. Nairne.

NAIRNE, Andrew; Executive Director, Arts Strategy, Arts Council England, since 2008; *b* 10 Feb. 1960; *s* of Rt Hon. Sir Patrick Nairne, *qv*; *m* 1995, Nicola Dandridge; two *s*. *Educ:* Radley Coll.; Univ. of St Andrews (MA Art Hist. 1983). Asst Curator, Kettle's Yard, Cambridge, 1984–85; Dep. Dir, Ikon Gall., Birmingham, 1985–86; Exhibns Dir, Centre for Contemp. Arts, Glasgow, 1986–92; Visual Arts Dir, Scottish Arts Council, Edinburgh, 1992–97; Dir, Dundee Contemp. Arts, 1997–2001; Dir, Modern Art Oxford, 2001–08. Vis. Fellow, Nuffield Coll., Oxford, 2002–. Chm., Visual Arts and Galls Assoc., 2005–07. FRSA 1997. *Recreation:* running. *Address:* 61 Southmoor Road, Oxford OX2 6RF. *T:* (01865) 554220.
See also A. R. Nairne.

NAIRNE, Rt Hon. Sir Patrick (Dalmahoy), GCB 1981 (KCB 1975; CB 1971); MC 1943; PC 1982; Master, St Catherine's College, Oxford, 1981–88 (Hon. Fellow, 1988); Chancellor, Essex University, 1983–97; *b* 15 Aug. 1921; *s* of late Lt-Col C. S. and Mrs E. D. Nairne; *m* 1948, Penelope Chauncy Bridges, *d* of late Lt-Col R. F. and Mrs L. C. Bridges; three *s* three *d*. *Educ:* Radley Coll.; University Coll., Oxford (Exhibr; Hon. Fellow, 1981). Seaforth Highlanders, 1941–45 (Capt.). 1st cl. hons Mod. Hist. (Oxon), 1947; MA 1947. Entered Civil Service and joined Admty, Dec. 1947; Private Sec. to First Lord of Admty, 1958–60; Asst Sec., 1960; Private Sec. to Sec. of State for Defence, 1965–67; Assistant Under-Sec. of State (Logistics), MoD, 1967–70; Dep. Under-Sec. of State, MoD, 1970–73; Second Perm. Sec., Cabinet Office, 1973–75; Perm. Sec., DHSS, 1975–81. Mem., Falkland Isles Review Cttee, 1982; Govt Monitor, Hong Kong, 1984; Chm., Commn on Conduct of Referendums, 1996. Central Independent TV: Mem. Bd, 1990–92; Dep. Chm., 1986–90. Chm., 1990–92, W Regl Bd. Church Comr, 1993–98; Chairman: Irene Wellington Educnl Trust, 1987–2002; Nuffield Council on Bioethics, 1991–96; President: Oxfordshire Craft Guild, 1993–97; Modern Art Oxford (formerly Oxford Mus. of Modern Art), 1998– (Chm. Adv. Bd, 1988–98); Vice-President: Soc. for Italic Handwriting, 1987– (Chm., 1981–87); Oxford Art Soc., 1990–; Trustee: Nat. Maritime Museum, 1981–91; Joseph Rowntree Foundn, 1983–96; Nat. AIDS Trust, 1987–95; Oxford Sch. of Drama, 1998–; Member: Radley Coll. Council, 1975–99; Council, Ditchley Foundn, 1988–2004; President: Assoc. of CS Art Clubs, 1976–89 (Vice-Pres., 1999–); Radleian Soc., 1980–83; Seamen's Hosp. Soc., 1982–2002. FRSA 1978–2000. Hon. LLD: Leicester, 1980; St Andrews, 1984; DU Essex, 1983. *Recreations:* watercolour painting, calligraphy. *Address:* Yew Tree, Chilson, Chipping Norton, Oxon OX7 3HU. *Club:* Oxford and Cambridge (Trustee, 1989–95).
See also A. Nairne, A. R. Nairne.

NAIRNE, Sandy; see Nairne, A. R.

NAISH, Sir (Charles) David, Kt 1994; DL; FRAgS; Director, 1998–2007, Chairman, 2002–07, Arla Foods UK (formerly Express Dairies plc); *b* 28 July 1940; *s* of Charles Naish and Muriel (*née* Turner); *m* 1966, Victoria Cockburn Mattock; two *s* one *d*. *Educ:* Worksop Coll.; RAC, Cirencester (MRAC). Jt Man. Dir, J. B. Eastwood Ltd, 1969–73; Chm., Thornhill Country Produce Ltd, 1982–85. Chm., Aubourn Farming Ltd, 1998–2003; Director: Assured British Meat Ltd, 1997–2001; Dalgety Gp Ltd, 1998–2003; Wilson Gp Ltd, 1997–; Caunton Investments Ltd, 2002–; Hilton Food Gp plc, 2007–. Chm., Silsoe Res. Inst., 1998–2006. President: NFU, 1991–98 (Dep. Pres., 1985–91); COPA, 1995–97. FRAgS 1986; FRSA 1992; FIGD 1996. DL Notts, 1991. Hon. DSc De Montfort, 1996; DUniv Essex, 1998. *Recreations:* shooting, vintage motor cars, golf. *Address:* Edwinstowe, Notts NG21 9QE. *Club:* Farmers' (Chm., 1980).

NAISH, Peter; Chief Executive, Wood Green Animal Shelter, 1997–2000; *b* 24 Jan. 1945; *s* of Frederick and Ida Naish; *m* 1970, Janet Kemp (marr. diss. 1996); one *s* two *d*. *Educ:* Hampton Grammar Sch.; King's Coll., London. Area Manager, Notting Hill Housing Trust, 1970–73; Chief Executive: Irwell Valley Housing Assoc., 1973–77; English Churches' Housing Gp 1971–89; Research and Development for Psychiatry, 1989–91; CLS Care Services, 1991–94; Chief Exec., EOC, 1994–97. *Recreations:* walking, music, poetry.

NAKAJIMA, Hiroshi, MD, PhD; Director-General of the World Health Organization, 1988–98, now Director-General Emeritus; President, International Research Institute of Health and Welfare, 1998–2001; *b* Japan, 16 May 1928; *m* Martha Ann (*née* De Witt); two *s*. *Educ:* Nat. Sen. High Sch., Urawa; Tokyo Med. Coll. (MD 1955; PhD 1960); Faculty of Medicine, Univ. of Paris. Research, Nat. Inst. of Health and Med. Res., Paris, 1958–67; Dir of Res. and Admin, Nippon Roche Res. Centre, Tokyo, 1967–73; Scientist, Evaluation and Control of Drugs, 1973–76, Chief, Drug Policies and Management, 1976–79, WHO HQ, Geneva; Regional Dir, Western Pacific Region, WHO, 1979–88. Perm. Hon. Advr, World Fedn of Acupuncture and Moxybustion Socs, Beijing, 1998–. Vis. Prof. in Public Health, Tokyo Med. Coll., 1987; Vis. Prof., Univ. of Tokyo, 1991; Hon. Prof., Universidad Nacional Mayor de San Marcos, Peru, 1992. Corresp. Mem., Acad. de Pharmacie, France, 1988; Assoc. Foreign Mem., Acad. Nat. de Médecine de France, 1989; Hon. Member: Japanese Pharmacological Soc., 1990; Amer. Urological Assoc., 1995; Foreign Mem., Russian Acad. of Med. Scis, 1995; Hon. Foreign Mem., Acad. Royale de Médecine de Belgique, 1991. FCPS(Pak) 1990; Hon. FRCP 1992. DM (*hc*): Med. Univ., Ulan Bator, Mongolia, 1991; Univ. Nat. du Benin, 1997; Hon. DSc Mahidol Univ., Bangkok, 1994; Dr *hc* Bucharest, 1994. Kojima Prize, Japan, 1984; Okamoto Award, Japan, 1989; Polio Eradication Champion Award, Rotary Internat., 1999. First Order of Merit (Japan), 2000; Order of Merit (Poland), 1990; Chevalier de la Légion d'Honneur (France), 1991; Commandeur, Ordre Nat. du Lion (Senegal), 1991; Equestrian Order of St Agatha (San Marino), 1995. *Publications:* articles and reviews in Japanese, French and English pubns. *Address:* La Cognaquerie, 86800 Pouillé, France. *T:* (5) 49565950.

NAKASONE, Yasuhiro; Prime Minister of Japan, 1982–87; Chairman, Institute for International Policy Studies (formerly International Institute for Global Peace), since 1988; Founder and President, Asia Pacific Parliamentary Forum, 1993–2003 (Hon. President, since 2004); *b* 27 May 1918; 2nd *s* of Matsugoroh Nakasone; *m* 1945, Tsutako Kobayashi; one *s* two *d*. *Educ:* Faculty of Law, Imperial Univ. (graduate). Joined Min. of Home Affairs, 1941; commd as Lt-Comdr, 1945. Mem., House of Representatives (elected 20 consecutive times), 1947–2003; Minister of State, Dir-Gen. of Science and Technology Agency, 1959–60; Minister of Transport, 1967–68; Minister of State, Dir-Gen. of Defence Agency, 1970–71; Minister of Internat. Trade and Industry, 1972–74; Minister of State for Admin. Management Agency, 1980–82. Chm. Exec. Council, 1971–72, Sec. Gen., 1974–76, Liberal Democratic Party. Hon. DHL, Johns Hopkins, 1984. Médaille de la Chancellerie, Univs of Paris. *Publications:* The Ideals of Youth, 1947; Japan Speaks, 1954; The New Conservatism, 1978; Human Cities—a proposal for the 21st century, 1980; Tenchiyujou (autobiography), 1996; The Making of the New Japan, 1999; Japan: a state strategy for the twenty-first century, 2002; Meditations, 2004. *Address:* Takada 2-18-6, Toshima-ku, Tokyo 171–0033, Japan.

NALL, Sir Edward William Joseph, 3rd Bt *cr* 1954, of Hoveringham, co. Nottingham; *b* 24 Oct. 1952; *er s* of Sir Michael Joseph Nall, 2nd Bt and of Angela Loveday Hanbury (*née* Coryton); *S* father, 2001; *m* 2004, Helen Fiona Batterbury (*née* Fergusson); one *d*. *Educ:* Eton. Commnd 13th/18th Royal Hussars (QMO), subseq. Light Dragoons, 1973; Major, 1985; retd, 1993. *Heir:* *b* Alexander Michael Nall [*b* 3 July 1956; *m* 1982, Caroline Jane Robinson; one *s* one *d*]. *Address:* Hoveringham Hall, Hoveringham, Nottingham NG14 7JR.

NALL-CAIN, family name of **Baron Brocket**.

NALLY, Edward; Partner, Fieldings Porter, Bolton, since 1982; *b* 18 Jan. 1956; *s* of Edward and Sarah Nally; *m* 1977, Julie Fagan; one *s* one *d*. *Educ:* De La Salle Grammar Sch., Salford; Nottingham Univ. (LLB Hons). Solicitor. Diocesan Solicitor, Salford RC Dio., 1983–. Dep. Vice-Pres., 2002–03, Vice-Pres., 2003–04, Pres., 2004–05, Law Soc.

Mem., Judicial Appts Commn, 2006–. Chm. of Governors, Pendleton Sixth Form Coll., Salford, 2000–07. *Recreations:* golf, walking, avid Bolton Wanderers football supporter. *Address:* Fieldings Porter, Silverwell House, Silverwell Street, Bolton BL1 1PT. *T:* (01204) 540900, *Fax:* (01204) 397254; *e-mail:* edward.nally@fieldingsporter.co.uk. *Club:* Royal Automobile.

NAMALIU, Rt Hon. Sir Rabbie (Langanai), KCMG 1996 (CMG 1979); PC 1989; MP for Kokopo (Pangu Pati), Papua New Guinea, 1982–2007; Minister of Finance, 2006–07; *b* 3 April 1947; *s* of Darius Namaliu and Utul Ioan; *m* 1978, Margaret Nakikus (*d* 1993); two *s*, and one step *d*; *m* 1999, Kelin Tavul (marr. diss. 2004); one *s* two *d*; *m* 2005, Darusila Watangia. *Educ:* Univ. of Papua New Guinea (BA); Univ. of Victoria, BC (MA). Senior Tutor, later Lectr in History, Univ. of Papua New Guinea, 1973; Principal Private Sec. to Chief Minister (Hon. Michael Somare), 1974–75; Vis. Pacific Fellow, Centre for Pacific Studies, Univ. of California, Santa Cruz, 1975; Provincial Comr, East New Britain Province, 1976; Chm., Public Services Commn, 1976–79; Exec. Officer to Leader of the Opposition (Rt Hon. Michael Somare), 1980–81; Minister for Foreign Affairs and Trade, 1982–84, for Primary Industry, 1985; Dep. Leader, 1985–88, Leader, 1988–92, Pangu Pati; Prime Minister, PNG, 1988–92; Leader of the Opposition, and Parly Leader of Pangu Pati, 1992–94; Speaker of Nat. Parlt, 1994–97; Senior Minister of State, 1997–98; Minister: for Petroleum and Energy, 1998–99; for Foreign Affairs and Immigration, 2002–06. Hon. LLD Univ. of Victoria, BC, 1983. *Recreations:* swimming, walking, reading, golf. *Address:* PO Box 6655, Boroko, National Capital District, Papua New Guinea.

NANDY, Dipak; Head of Equal Opportunities, Social Services Department, Nottinghamshire County Council, 1992–2000; *b* 21 May 1936; *s* of B. C. Nandy and Leela Nandy; *m* 1st, 1964, Margaret Gracie (decd); 2nd, 1972, Hon. Luise Byers (marr. diss. 1991); two *d*. *Educ:* St Xavier's Coll., Calcutta; Univ. of Leeds (BA 1st Cl. Hons English Literature, 1960; C. E. Vaughan Research Fellowship, 1960–62). Lectr, English Literature, Univ. of Leicester, 1962–66; Lectr and Fellow of Rutherford College, Univ. of Kent at Canterbury, 1966–68; founder-Director, The Runnymede Trust, 1968–73; Vis. Fellow, Adlai Stevenson Inst. of International Affairs, Chicago, 1970–73; Research Fellow, Social and Community Planning Research, 1973–75; Dep. Chief Exec., Equal Opportunities Commn, 1976–86; Chief Exec., Intermediate Technology Develt Gp, 1986–88; Hon. Lectr in Social Policy, Univ. of Birmingham, 1989–95; Financial and Admin. Dir, RSP, Queen Elizabeth House, Oxford, 1991. Member: Cttee of Inquiry into Future of Broadcasting, 1974–77; Council, Nat. Assoc. Citizens' Advice Bureaux, 1983–86; BBC: Chm., Asian Programmes Adv. Cttee, 1983–88; Mem., General Adv. Council. Member: Council, Northern Chamber Orch., 1980–84; Royal Nat. Theatre Bd, 1991–97; Governor, BFI, 1984–87. Mem. Ct, Leicester Univ., 2002–08. Trustee, CSV, 1981–91. Hon. Liaison, Employment and Labour Law Sect., Amer. Bar Assoc., 1980–. *Publications:* numerous essays in books, periodicals and newspapers on literature, political thought, race relations, urban problems, equality for women, broadcasting policy and development issues. *Recreations:* collecting records, opera, computing. *Address:* 8 Woodhedge Drive, Thorneywood, Nottingham NG3 6LU. *T:* (0115) 948 1631.

NANKIVELL, Owen; JP; economic and business consultant; Director, Hinksey Network (formerly Hinksey Centre), since 1982 (Executive Director, 1982–2002); *b* 6 April 1927; *s* of John Hamilton Nankivell and Sarah Ann Mares; *m* 1956, Mary Burman Earnshaw; one *s* two *d*. *Educ:* Torquay Grammar Sch.; Univ. of Manchester. BA (Econ) 1951, MA (Econ) 1963. FRSS. Admty, 1951–52; Colonial Office, 1952–55; Central Statistical Office, 1955–65; DEA, 1965–69; HM Treasury, 1969–72; Asst Dir, Central Statistical Office, 1972–79; Gp Chief Economist, Lucas Industries, 1979–82. JP Worcester, 1983–89, Torbay, 1989. *Publications:* All Good Gifts, 1978; Economics, Society and Values, 1995. *Recreations:* Christian, tennis, choral music, singing. *Address:* 3 Thorne Park Road, Torquay TQ2 6RX. *T:* and *Fax:* (01803) 690147; *e-mail:* owenmary@blueyonder.co.uk.

NAPIER, family name of **Lord Napier and Ettrick** and **Baron Napier of Magdala**.

NAPIER, 14th Lord *cr* 1627 (Scotland), **AND ETTRICK,** 5th Baron *cr* 1872 (UK); **Francis Nigel Napier,** KCVO 1992 (CVO 1985; LVO 1980); DL; a Bt of Nova Scotia, 1666, 11th Bt of Thirlestane, 22nd of Merchiston; Chief of the Name of Napier; Major, Scots Guards (Reserve of Officers); Private Secretary, Comptroller and Equerry, 1973–98, then Treasurer, 1998–2002, to HRH the Princess Margaret, Countess of Snowdon; *b* 5 Dec. 1930; *e s* of 13th Baron Napier and 4th Ettrick, TD, and Muir (*d* 1992), *e d* of Sir Percy Newson, Bt; *S* father, 1954; *m* 1958, Delia Mary, *yr d* of late A. D. B. Pearson; two *s* two *d*. *Educ:* Wellesley House; Eton; RMA, Sandhurst. Commissioned, 1950; served Malaya, 1950–51 (invalided); Adjt 1st Bn Scots Guards, 1955–57. Equerry to His late Royal Highness The Duke of Gloucester, 1958–60, retd, 1960. Deputy Ceremonial and Protocol Secretary, CRO, 1962–66; Purple Staff Officer at State Funeral of Sir Winston Churchill, 1966. Sat in House of Lords, 1954–99 (a Cons. Whip, 1970–71). On behalf of HM The Queen, handed over Instruments of Independence to Tuvalu (formerly Ellice Is), 1978. Member: Royal Co. of Archers (Queen's Body Guard for Scotland), 1953–; Exec. Cttee, Standing Council of the Baronetage, 1985–98. Standing Council of Scottish Chiefs. Mem., Rolls-Royce Enthusiasts Club. Pres., St John Ambulance Assoc. and Brigade for County of London, 1975–83. DL Selkirkshire, 1974, Ettrick and Lauderdale, 1975–94. Freeman, City of London; Liveryman, Worshipful Company of Grocers. Hon. DLitt Napier Univ., 1993. KStJ 1991 (CStJ 1988). *Heir: s* Master of Napier, *qv*. *Address:* Down House, Wylye, Wilts BA12 0QN. *Clubs:* Turf, Pratt's, Pitt.

NAPIER OF MAGDALA, 6th Baron *cr* 1868; **Robert Alan Napier;** *b* 6 Sept. 1940; *s* of 5th Baron Napier of Magdala, OBE, and Elizabeth Marian, *y d* of E. H. Hunt, FRCS; *S* father, 1987; *m* 1964, Frances Clare, *d* of late Alan Frank Skinner; one *s* one *d*. *Educ:* Winchester College; St John's Coll., Cambridge (BA 1st cl. Hons 1962; MA 1966). *Heir: s* Hon. James Robert Napier, *b* 29 Jan. 1966. *Address:* The Coach House, Kingsbury Street, Marlborough, Wilts SN8 1HU. *T:* (01672) 512333. *Club:* Leander (Henley-on-Thames).

NAPIER, Master of; Hon. Francis David Charles Napier; established Napier Garden Planning, 1999; *b* 3 Nov. 1962; *s* and *heir* of 14th Lord Napier (and 5th Baron Ettrick), *qv*; *m* 1993, Zara Jane, *o d* of Hugh McCalmont, Newmarket, Suffolk; one *s* one *d*. *Educ:* Stanbridge Earls School; South Thames Coll., Wandsworth, 1986–87 (City and Guilds Computer Diploma); Otley Coll., Ipswich (Nat. Cert. Hort. Garden Design and Construction, 1999). With a Lloyd's agency, 1984–92; with Heath Bloodstock Ltd, 1992–97. *Recreations:* travelling, horse-racing, squash. *Address:* Gowan Cottage, Westley Waterless, Newmarket, Suffolk CB8 0RQ. *Club:* Pratt's.

NAPIER, Brian William; QC (Scot.) 2002; PhD; *b* 9 Jan. 1949; *s* of George Napier and Isobella Ramsey Ross Napier; *m* 1st, 1971, Helen Marjorie Mercer (marr. diss. 2001); one *s* one *d*; 2nd, 2007, Elizabeth Clarke; one *s*. *Educ:* George Watson's Coll., Edinburgh; Univ. of Edinburgh (LLB 1971); Queens' Coll., Cambridge (MA 1974; PhD 1976). Res. Fellow, 1974, Fellow, 1974–89, Queens' Coll., Cambridge; Asst Lectr, 1975–79, Lectr, 1979–89, Univ. of Cambridge; Prof. of Law, Queen Mary and Westfield Coll., Univ. of London, 1989–96, Vis. Prof., 1996–; called to the Bar, Middle Temple, 1990 and Gray's Inn. Prof. Associé, Univs of Paris 1 and 2, 1980–81. Joint Editor: Harvey on Industrial Relations and Employment Law, 1988–; Transfer of Undertakings, 1999–. *Recreations:* walking, music. *Address:* c/o Faculty of Advocates, Parliament House, Edinburgh EH1 1RF. *T:* (0131) 260 5654.

NAPIER, Sir Charles Joseph, 6th Bt *cr* 1867, of Merrion Square, Dublin; *b* 15 April 1973; *o s* of Sir Robin Surtees Napier, 5th Bt and of Jennifer Beryl (who *m* 2001, Major Donald Black, MC), *d* of H. Warwick Daw; *S* father, 1994; *m* 2003, Imelda Blanche Elisabeth, *d* of late John Trafford and of Amanda Trafford; two *s*. *Educ:* Eton; Univ. of Edinburgh (MA Hons; Fencing Blue). Internat. student fencer (2 caps for Scottish Univs, foil and sabre). Scottish European Aid, 1995–96; Corporate Fundraiser, MIND, 1997–98; Appeal Dir, 1998–99, and Mem. Mgt Cttee, 2001–, Downside Settlement, Bermondsey; public affairs, The Policy Partnership, 1999–2006; Account Dir, PPS Gp, 2006; Associate Dir, Quintus Public Affairs, 2006–. Mem. (Lab), Hammersmith and Fulham LBC, 2002–06. Gov., Peterborough Primary Sch., Fulham, 2000–08. *Recreations:* watching and playing most sports, motorbikes, fishing. *Heir: s* Finnian John Lennox Napier, *b* 14 Feb. 2006. *Address:* 35 Warbeck Road, W12 8NS. *Club:* Flyfishers'.

NAPIER, Iain John Grant; Chairman: Imperial Tobacco Group plc, since 2007 (non-executive Director, since 2000; Joint Vice Chairman, 2004–07); McBride plc, since 2007; *b* 10 April 1949. *Educ:* Eastwood High Sch., Newton, Mearns. FCMA. Whitbread plc; Ford Motor Co.; joined Bass plc, 1989; Mktg and Commercial Dir, Bass Leisure Retail, 1989–93; Gp HR Dir, 1993–94; Chief Exec., Bass Leisure Div., 1994–96; Chm., Chateaux Lascombes wine estate, Bordeaux; Chief Exec., Bass Brewers and Bass International Brewers, 1996–2000; Chm., Bass Ireland; Dir, Bass plc, until 2000; Mem. Exec. Mgt Cttee, Interbrew SA, until 2001; Chief Exec., Taylor Woodrow plc, 2002–07. Former non-executive Director: BOC Gp plc; Perry Gp; Henderson Investors plc; St Modwens Properties plc; Tomkins plc; non-exec. Dir, Collins-Stewart plc, 2007–. *Address:* Imperial Tobacco Group plc, PO Box 244, Upton Road, Bristol BS99 7UJ. *T:* (0117) 933 7286.

NAPIER, John, RDI 1996; stage designer; *b* 1 March 1944; *s* of James Edward Thomas Napier and Lorrie Napier (*née* Godbold); *m* 1st, Andreane Neofitou; one *s* one *d*; 2nd, Donna King; one *s* one *d*. *Educ:* Hornsey Coll. of Art; Central Sch. of Arts and Crafts. Designed 1st production, A Penny for a Song, Phoenix, Leicester, 1967; *London productions:* Fortune and Men's Eyes, 1968; The Ruling Class, The Fun War, Muzeeka, George Frederick (ballet), La Turista, 1969; Cancer, Isabel's a Jezebel, 1970; Mister, The Foursome, The Lovers of Viorne, Lear, 1971; Jump, Sam Sam, Big Wolf, 1972; The Devils (ENO), Equus, The Party, 1973; Knuckle, 1974; Kings and Clowns, The Travelling Music Show, 1978; The Devils of Loudon, Lohengrin (Covent Garden); King John, Richard II, Cymbeline, Macbeth, Richard III, 1974; Hedda Gabler, 1975; Much Ado About Nothing, The Comedy of Errors, King Lear, Macbeth, 1976; A Midsummer Night's Dream, As You Like It, 1977; The Merry Wives of Windsor, Twelfth Night, Three Sisters, Once in a Lifetime, 1979; The Greeks, Nicholas Nickleby (SWET award, Tony Award), 1980; Cats (Tony award), 1981; Henry IV Parts I and II, Peter Pan, 1982; Macbeth (Covent Garden), 1983; Starlight Express, 1984 (Tony Award, 1987); Les Misérables, 1985 (Tony Award, 1987); Time, 1986; Miss Saigon, 1989; Children of Eden, 1990; Trelawny of the 'Wells', 1993; Sunset Boulevard, 1993 (Tony Award, 1995); Burning Blue, 1995 (Olivier award, 1996); The Tower, 1995; Jesus Christ Superstar, 1996; Who's Afraid of Virginia Woolf?, 1996; An Enemy of the People, 1997; Peter Pan, 1997; Martin Guerre, 1998; Candide, 1999; South Pacific, 2001; Skellig, 2003; Aladdin, 2004, 2005; Equus, 2007; *Glyndebourne:* Idomeneo, 1983; *USA:* Siegfried & Roy Show (Las Vegas; also co-dir), 1990; Jane Eyre (NY), 2000; Nabucco (Met. Opera), 2001; film designs incl. Hook, 1991; numerous designs for stage productions in Europe, Japan, Australia, USA and for TV. Cameron Mackintosh Vis. Prof. of Contemporary Theatre, Univ. of Oxford, 2001. Hon. Fellow, London Inst., 2001. American Acad. of Achievement, 1994. *Recreation:* photography. *Address:* c/o Macnaughton Lord Representation, Unit 10, The Broomhouse Studios, 50 Sullivan Road, SW6 3DX.

NAPIER, John Alan; Chairman: Kelda Group plc, since 2000; Royal & Sun Alliance Insurance Group plc, since 2003; *b* 22 Aug. 1942; *s* of late William Napier and Barbara Napier (*née* Chatten); *m* 1st, 1961, Gillian Reed (marr. diss. 1977); two *s* one *d*; 2nd, 1992, Caroline Denning; one *d*, and two step *s* one step *d*. *Educ:* Colchester Royal Grammar Sch.; Emmanuel Coll., Cambridge (MA Econs). Jun. and middle mgt, Internat. Publishing Corp. and Reed Internat., 1960–69; Managing Director: Index Printers, 1969–72; QB Newspapers, 1972–76; Exec. Dir (Australia), James Hardie Industries, 1976–86; Group Managing Director: AGB plc, 1986–90; Hays plc, 1991–98; Chm., Booker plc, 1998–2000. Mem. Bd, Yorkshire Forward, 2002–. *Recreations:* rural matters, outdoor activities, people, philosophy. *Address:* Kelda Group plc, Western House, Halifax Road, Bradford BD6 2SZ. *Clubs:* Oxford and Cambridge.

NAPIER, Sir John Archibald Lennox, 14th Bt *cr* 1627 (NS), of Merchistoun; *b* 6 Dec. 1946; *s* of Sir William Archibald Napier, 13th Bt and of Kathleen Mabel, *d* of late Reginald Greaves; *S* father, 1990; *m* 1969, Erica, *d* of late Kurt Kingsfield; one *s* one *d*. *Educ:* St Stithians; Witwatersrand Univ., Johannesburg. MSc(Eng); PhD. *Heir: s* Hugh Robert Lennox Napier, *b* 1 Aug. 1977. *Address:* Merchistoun, PO Box 65177, Benmore 2010, Republic of South Africa.

NAPIER, Maj.-Gen. Lennox Alexander Hawkins, CB 1983; OBE 1970; MC 1957; Vice Lord-Lieutenant of Gwent, 1995–2004; Inspector of Public Inquiries, 1983–98; *b* 28 June 1928; *s* of Major Charles McNaughton Napier and D. C. Napier; *m* 1959, Jennifer Dawn Wilson; one *s* two *d*. *Educ:* Radley; RMA Sandhurst. Joined Army, 1946; commnd into South Wales Borderers, 1948; commanded 1st Bn S Wales Borderers and 1st Bn Royal Regt of Wales, 1967–70; Instructor, JSSC, 1970–72; served Min. of Defence, 1972–74; Brigade Commander, Berlin Infantry Bde, 1974–76; Prince of Wales's Division: Divisional Brigadier, 1976–80; Col Commandant, 1980–83; GOC Wales, 1980–83. Col, The Royal Regt of Wales, 1983–89; Hon. Col, Cardiff Univ. OTC, 1985–92. Chm., Central Rail Users Cttee, 1985–95. Gwent: DL 1983; High Sheriff 1988. OStJ 1969. *Recreations:* shooting, gardening. *Address:* Osbaston Farm, Monmouth, NP25 5DL.

NAPIER, Michael; *see* Napier, T. M.

NAPIER, Sir Oliver John, Kt 1985; Senior Partner, Napier & Sons, Solicitors, 1976–2000; Chairman, Standing Advisory Commission on Human Rights, 1988–92; *b* 11 July 1935; *e s* of James J. and Sheila Napier; *m* 1961, Brigid (*née* Barnes); three *s* five *d* (and one *s* decd). *Educ:* Ballycruttle Public Elem. Sch., Downpatrick; St Malachy's Coll., Belfast; Queen's Univ., Belfast (LLB). Qual. Solicitor, NI, 1959; Lectr and Mem. Bd of Examrs, Incorp. Law Soc. of NI, 1965–71. Mem. Exec., Ulster Liberal Party, 1962–69; Founder Mem., New Ulster Movt, 1969; Founder Mem., Alliance Party, 1970, Leader 1973–84, Pres., 1989–92. Mem. (Alliance), E Belfast, NI Assembly, 1973–75; Minister of Legal Affairs, NI Executive, Jan.–May 1974; Mem. (Alliance), N Ireland Constitutional Convention for E Belfast, 1975–76; Mem. (Alliance) Belfast E, NI Assembly, 1982–86.

Contested (Alliance): E Belfast, 1979, 1983; N Down, 1997. Councillor for E Belfast, Belfast CC, 1977–89; Mem. for N Down, NI Forum, 1996–98. Mem. (Alliance), Negotiation Team for Good Friday Agreement, 1996–98. Member: Lawyers Insolvency Assoc., 1991–2000; Council, Soc. of Practitioners of Insolvency, 1993–2000. *Recreations:* many and varied. *Address:* 83 Victoria Road, Holywood, Co. Down BT18 9BG.

NAPIER, Paul James; Editor, Yorkshire Evening Post, since 2006; *b* 3 Oct. 1966; *s* of Dennis Napier and Brenda Napier (*née* Duthie); *m* 1996, Lara Katya Balmforth; one *s* one *d.* *Educ:* Kettering Boys' Sch.; Univ. of York (BA Hons English and Related Lit. 1989); Heriot-Watt Univ. (MBA 2000). Ed., Banbury Guardian, 1997–2001; Ed.-in-Chief, Bucks Herald, 2001; Editor: Scarborough Evening News, 2001–03; Hartlepool Mail, 2003–06. *Recreations:* family, reading, running. *Address:* Yorkshire Evening Post, Wellington Street, Leeds LS1 1RF. *T:* (0113) 238 8984, *Fax:* (0113) 238 8325; *e-mail:* paul.napier@ypn.co.uk.

NAPIER, Robert Stewart; Chairman, Met Office, since 2006; *b* 21 July 1947; *s* of Andrew Napier and Lilian V. Napier (*née* Ritchie); *m* 1977, Patricia Stewart; one *d.* *Educ:* Sedbergh School; Sidney Sussex College, Cambridge (BA 1969; MA 1971); Harvard Business School (AMP 1987). RTZ Corp., 1969–73; Brandts, 1973–75; Fisons, 1975–81; Redland: Finance Dir, 1981–87; Man. Dir, 1987–97; Chief Exec., 1991–97; Chief Exec., WWF-UK, 1999–2007. Director: United Biscuits (Hldgs), 1992–2000; Rentokil Initial plc, 1996–99; Anglian Water Services Ltd, 2002–; English Partnerships, 2004– (Chm., 2008–). Pres., Nat. Council of Building Material Producers, 1996–97; Chairman: CBI Transport Policy Cttee, 1995–97; Alliance of Construction Product Suppliers, 1996–97. Chm., Green Fiscal Commn, 2007–. Trustee: World in Need, 1988–91; ACET, 1991–94; CRASH, 1994–99 (Chm., 1998–99); Baynards Zambia Trust, 1996–; Carbon Disclosure Project, 2005– (Chm., 2008–); Watts Gall., 2006–; World Conservation Monitoring Centre 2000, 2007– (Chm., 2008–); S Georgia Heritage Trust, 2007–. Governor: Reigate Grammar Sch., 1995–2002; Sedbergh Sch., 1998– (Chm., 2000–). Hon. Organist, Grytviken Church, S Georgia. *Recreations:* hill walking, escaping to Scotland, the works of John Buchan. *Address:* *e-mail:* r.s.napier@btinternet.com.

NAPIER, (Thomas) Michael, CBE 2005; Senior Partner, Irwin Mitchell, solicitors, since 1983; President, Law Society, 2000–01; Attorney-General's pro bono envoy, since 2002; *b* 11 June 1946; *s* of late Montague Keith Napier and Mary Napier; *m* 1969, Denise Christine Willey; one *s* two *d.* *Educ:* Loughborough GS; Manchester Univ. (LLB 1967). Articled clerk, Moss Toone & Deane, Loughborough, 1968–70; admitted Solicitor, 1970; Asst Solicitor, W. H. Thompson, Manchester, 1970–72; Partner, Irwin Mitchell, 1973–; Jt Sen. Partner, Pannone Napier, 1985–94. Mem., Mental Health Act Commn, 1983–92 (Jt Vice-Chm., 1985–88; Chm., NE Reg., 1985–90). Vis. Prof., Nottingham Law Sch., 1992–. Jt Founder, 1990, Pres., 1994–96, Assoc. of Personal Injury Lawyers; Member: Council, Law Soc., 1993–2005; Council, Justice, 1995–; Civil Justice Council, 1998–2008. Bd Mem., Galleries of Justice, 2001–04. Chm., Adv. Cttee, Rampton Hosp., 1992–96. Trustee, Thalidomide Trust, 2001–. Editorial Consultant: Personal Injury Compensation (formerly Personal Medical Injuries Law Letter), 1985–; Med. Law Rev., 1994–; Ind. Lawyer, 2002–08. Hon. Bencher, Gray's Inn, 2005; Hon. QC 2006. Freeman, Co. of Cutlers in Hallamshire, 1992. FICPD 2004; FRSA 2005. Hon. LLD: Nottingham Trent, 2001; Sheffield, 2002. *Publications:* (jtly) Conditional Fees: a survival guide, 1995, 2nd edn 2001; (jtly) Recovering Damages for Psychiatric Injury, 1995; (Consulting Ed.) Litigation Funding, 1999; (contrib.) Blackstones Civil Practice, 2004; contrib. legal books and jls. *Recreation:* mountain biking in Norfolk. *Address:* Irwin Mitchell, 150 Holborn, EC1N 2NS. *T:* (020) 7421 3950, *Fax:* (020) 7242 6038; Windmill Hill, Great Walsingham, Norfolk NR22 6DR. *T:* (01328) 820213. *Club:* Athenæum.

NAPOLITAN, Leonard, CB 1970; Director of Economics and Statistics, Ministry of Agriculture, Fisheries and Food, 1965–77; *b* 9 April 1919; *s* of Domenic and Rose G. Napolitan; *m* 1945, Dorothy Laycock; two *d.* *Educ:* Univ. of London (BSc Econ. 1944); LSE (MSc Econ. 1946). Asst Agric. Economist, Univ. of Bristol, 1947–48; joined Min. of Agric. and Fisheries as Agric. Economist, 1948. Pres., Agric. Econs Soc., 1974–75. FRSA. *Address:* 4 Rectory Gardens, Burway Road, Church Stretton, Shropshire SY6 6DP.

NARAIN, Sase, OR 1976; CMG 1969; SC (Guyana) 1985; JP (Guyana); solicitor/attorney-at-law; Speaker of the National Assembly, Guyana, 1971–92; Chairman, National Bank of Industry and Commerce (Guyana), 1986–93; *b* 27 Jan. 1925; *s* of Oudit and Sookdai Naraine; *m* 1952, Shamshun Narain (*née* Rayman); four *s.* *Educ:* Modern Educational Inst.; Gibson and Weldon Law Tutors. Solicitor, admitted in England and Guyana, 1957. Town Councillor, City of Georgetown, 1962–70; Member: History and Arts Council, 1969–; Republic Cttee of Guyana, 1969; Pres., Guyana Sanatan Dharma Maha Sabha, 1963–94. Comr for Oaths to Affidavits, 1961; Notary Public, 1968. Dep. Chm., Public Service Commn, Guyana, 1966–71; Mem., Police Service Commn, 1966–71. Chm., Berger Paints (Guyana), 1966–78; Dir, Pegasus Hotels of Guyana, 1987–90. Member: Nat. Awards Cttee of Guyana, 1970–92; Bd of Governors, President's Coll., Guyana, 1985–88. JP 1962. *Recreations:* golf, cricket, swimming. *Address:* 14b New Garden Street, Queenstown, Georgetown, Demerara, Guyana. *T:* (2) 261409. *Clubs:* Georgetown Cricket, Everest Cricket (Guyana).

NARASIMHA, Prof. Roddam, FRS 1992; Chairman, Engineering Mechanics (formerly Fluid Dynamics) Unit, Jawaharlal Nehru Centre for Advanced Scientific Research, since 1990 (INSA Golden Jubilee Research Professor, 1991–94; Professor Ramanathan Distinguished Professor, 1995–2000); *b* 20 July 1933; *s* of Prof. R. L. Narasimhaiya and Smt R. N. Leela Devi; *m* 1965, Dr Neelima S. Rao; two *d.* *Educ:* University Coll. of Engineering, Bangalore (BE 1953); Indian Inst. of Science (DIISc 1955; AIISc 1957); California Inst. of Technology (PhD 1961). Res. Fellow, CIT, 1961–62; Indian Institute of Science: Asst and Associate Prof., 1962–70; Prof., 1970–98, and Chm., 1982–84, Dept of Aerospace Engrg; Dean of Engrg Faculty, 1980–82; Chm., 1982–89, Prof., 1982–98, Centre for Atmospheric Scis; Dir, Nat. Aeronautical Lab., subseq. Nat. Aerospace Labs, Bangalore, 1984–93; Dir, Nat. Inst. of Advanced Studies, Bangalore, 1997–2004. Chief Project Co-ordinator, Hindustan Aeronautics Ltd, 1977–79. Clark B. Millikan Vis. Prof., CIT, 1985–; Jawaharlal Nehru Vis. Prof., Cambridge, 1989–90. Member: Sci. Adv. Council to the Prime Minister, 1985–89, to the Cabinet, 1997–99, to Govt of India, 2000–03; Space Commn, Govt of India, 1989–. Pres., Indian Acad. of Scis, 1992–94. Fellow: Indian Nat. Sci. Acad., 1979; Third World Acad. of Scis, Italy, 1989; Foreign Associate: US Nat. Acad. of Engrg, 1989; US Nat. Acad. of Sci., 2000; Hon. Fellow, Aer. Soc. of India, 1985; Foreign Hon. Mem., Amer. Acad. Arts and Scis, 1999; Distinguished Alumnus: CIT, 1986; Indian Inst. of Sci., 1988. Bhatnagar Prize in Engrg, CSIR, India, 1976; Gujar Mal Modi Award for Sci., 1990; Srinivasa Ramanujan Medal, Indian Sci. Congress, 1998; Fluid Dynamics Award, Amer. Inst. Aeronautics and Astronautics, 2000; Lifetime Contribution in Engrg Award, Indian Nat. Acad. of Engrg, 2003. Kannada Rajyotsava Award, Karnataka, 1986; Padmabhushan, India, 1987. *Publications:* (ed) Computer Simulation, 1979; (ed) Turbulence Management and Relaminarisation, 1987; (ed) Developments in Fluid Mechanics and Space Technology, 1988; Surveys in Fluid Mechanics, vol. III, 1993; The Monsoon Trough Boundary Layer, 1997; Verses for the Brave, 2000; (ed) The Dynamics of Technology; numerous sci. papers in learned jls. *Recreations:* history, walking, music. *Address:* Jawaharlal Nehru Centre for Advanced Scientific Research, Jakkur, Bangalore 560064, India. *T:* (80) 23622750, ext. 2219, *Fax:* (80) 23622766.

NARASIMHAN, Prof. Mudumbai Seshachalu, PhD; FRS 1996; *b* 7 June 1932; *s* of Seshachalu Iyengar and Padmasani; *m* 1962, Sakuntala Raman; one *s* one *d.* *Educ:* Madras Univ. (BA Hons); Bombay Univ. (PhD 1960). Tata Institute, Bombay: Associate Prof., 1963–65; Prof., 1965–75; Sen. Prof., 1975–90; Prof. of Eminence, 1990–93; Hon. Fellow, 1994; Dir of Maths, Internat. Centre, subseq. Abdus Salam Internat. Centre, for Theoretical Physics, Trieste, 1992–98; Prof. of Geometry, Scuola Internazionale Superiore di Studi Avanzati, Trieste, 2000. S. S. Bhatnagar Prize in Mathematical Scis, CSIR, 1975; Meghnad Saha Award, Univ. Grants Commn, 1978; Award for Maths, Third World Acad. of Scis, 1987; Srinivasa Ramanujan Medal, INSA, 1988; C. V. Raman Birth Centenary Award, Indian Sci. Congress, 1994; King Faisal Internat. Prize for Sci., 2006. Chevalier, Ordre National du Mérite (France), 1989; Padma Bhushan (India), 1990. *Address:* TIFR Centre, PO Box 1234, IISc Campus, Bangalore 560012, India.

NARAYAN, Prof. Ramesh, FRS 2006; Thomas Dudley Cabot Professor of the Natural Sciences, Harvard-Smithsonian Center for Astrophysics, Harvard University; *s* of Prof. Gopalasamudram Narayana Ramachandran, FRS. *Educ:* St Patrick's Sch., Adyar; Madras Christian Coll.; National Aeronautical Labs, Bangalore; Calif Inst. of Technol. Arizona Univ., 1986–91; joined Harvard Univ., 1991. *Publications:* articles in jls. *Address:* Harvard-Smithsonian Center for Astrophysics, 60 Garden Street, Cambridge, MA 02138, USA.

NARAYANAN, Ravi; Director and Chief Executive, WaterAid, 1999–2005; *b* 20 June 1943; *s* of Vaidyanatha and Kanti Narayanan; *m* 1973, Geetha Subramanan; one *s* one *d.* *Educ:* Delhi Univ. (BSc Hons); Peterhouse, Cambridge (BA 1966, MA 1968). Dir, ActionAid India, 1985–92; Hd, Internat Ops, 1992–94, Dir, Asia Progs, 1994–99, ActionAid. Sen. Associate, Nat. Inst. of Advanced Studies, Bangalore, India. Mem., UK Delegn to Second World Water Forum, The Hague, 2000; NGO Advr to EC Delegn to World Summit of Sustainable Develt, Johannesburg, 2002. Member: World Panel on Financing Water Infrastructure, 2002–03; Millennium Project UN Taskforce on Water and Sanitation, 2004–05; Water Supply and Sanitation Collaborative Council, Geneva. Life Mem., Internat. Water Acad., Norway, 2005. *Address:* c/o WaterAid, Prince Consort House, 27–29 Albert Embankment, SE1 7UB.

NAREY, Martin James; Chief Executive, Barnardo's, since 2005; *b* 5 Aug. 1955; *s* of John and Ellenor Narey; *m* 1978, Jan Goudy; one *s* one *d.* *Educ:* Sheffield Poly. (BA Public Admin). Assistant Governor: HM Young Offender Inst. Deerbolt, 1982–86; Frankland, 1986–90; Gov. IV, Prison Service HQ, 1990–91; Home Office: Private Sec. to Minister of State, 1991–92; Criminal Policy, 1992–94; Head, Co-ordination of Computerisation in the Criminal Justice System Unit, 1994–96; Head of Crime Prevention Agency, 1996; Reviewer of Delay in the Criminal Justice System, 1996–97; HM Prison Service: Head of Security Policy, 1997–98; Dir of Regimes, 1998–99; Dir-Gen., 1999–2003; Perm. Under-Sec. of State, Home Office, 2003–05 (Comr for Correctional Services, 2003–04, Chief Exec., Nat. Offender Mgt Service, 2004–05). Hon. Prof., Sheffield Hallam Univ., 2006–; Hon. Dr: Sheffield Hallam; Teesside. Chartered Mgt Inst. Gold Medal for Leadership, 2003. *Publications:* review of delay in criminal justice system, report into security at the Maze Prison. *Recreations:* planning holidays, watching Middlesbrough FC. *Address:* Barnardo's, Tanners Lane, Barkingside, Ilford, Essex IG6 1QG.

NARJES, Karl-Heinz; Member, Commission of the European Communities, 1981–89 (Vice-President, 1985–89); *b* 30 Jan. 1924; *s* of Heinrich Narjes; *m* 1951, Eva-Maria Rahe; one *s* one *d.* *Educ:* Hamburg Univ. Entered Foreign Service, 1955; Chef du Cabinet, Pres. of EEC, 1963; Dir-Gen., Press and Inf. Directorate, EEC, 1968–69; Minister of Econs and of Transport, Schleswig-Holstein, 1969–73. Mem., Bundestag, 1972–81; Mem., For. Affairs Cttee, 1976–80; Pres., Econ. Affairs Cttee, 1972–76.

NARUEPUT, Owart S.; *see* Suthiwart-Narueput.

NASEBY, Baron *cr* 1997 (Life Peer), of Sandy in the co. of Bedfordshire; **Michael Wolfgang Laurence Morris;** PC 1994; *b* 25 Nov. 1936; *m* 1960, Dr Ann Appleby (Dr Ann Morris, MB, BS, MRCS, MRCP); two *s* one *d.* *Educ:* Bedford Sch.; St Catharine's Coll., Cambridge (BA Hons Econs; MA). Trainee to Marketing Manager, UK, India and Ceylon, Reckitt & Colman Gp, 1960–63; Service Advertising Ltd, 1964–68; Marketing Exec. to Account Supervisor, Horniblow Cox-Freeman Ltd, 1968–71, Dir 1969–71; Dir, Benton & Bowles Ltd, 1971–81; Proprietor: A. M. International, 1980–92; Julius International Consultants, 1997–2008. Non-executive Director: Tunbridge Wells Equitable Friendly Soc., 1992–2005 (Chm., 1998–2005); Mansell plc, 1998–2003; Invesco Recovery Trust 2005 plc, 1998–2005 (Chm., 2003–05); Chm., Invesco Recovery Trust 2011 plc, 2005–. Contested (C) Islington North, 1966. Islington Council: Councillor, 1968–70; Alderman, 1970–74; Chm. of Housing, 1968; Leader, 1969–71. MP (C) Northampton South, Feb. 1974–1997; contested (C) same seat, 1997. PPS to Minister of State, NI Office, 1979–81; Chm. of Ways and Means and Dep. Speaker, H of C, 1992–97. Member: Public Accounts Cttee, 1979–92; Select Cttee on Energy, 1982–85; Chairman's Panel, 1984–92; Mem. Council, Europe and Western European Union, 1983–91; Chairman: British Singapore Cttee, 1985–92 (Vice-Chm., 1997–); British Malaysia Cttee, 1987–92; British Burma Cttee, 1989–92; British Sri Lanka Cttee, 1997–; British Maldives Cttee, 2004–; formerly: Vice-Chm., British Indonesia Cttee; Treas., British ASEAN and Thai Cttees; Secretary: British Venezuela Cttee; Cons. Housing and Local Govt Cttee, 1974–76; Cons Trade Cttee, 1974–76; Cons. Environment Cttee, 1977–79; Vice-Chm., Cons. Energy Cttee, 1981–92; Founder, Parly Food and Health Forum. Captain, Parly Golf Soc., 1988–91. Chm. Trustees, Victoria County History for Northamptonshire, 1994–2008. Chm., Govs, Bedford Sch., 1989–2002 (Governor, 1982–2002). Hon. Fellow, Univ. of Northampton, 2007. Ratna (Sri Lanka), 2005. *Publications:* (jtly) Helping the Exporter, 1967; (contrib.) Marketing below the Line: Studies in Management, 1972; The Disaster of Direct Labour, 1978. *Recreations:* restoration work, cricket, tennis, golf, budgerigars, forestry. *Address:* Caesar's Camp, Sandy, Beds SG19 2AD. *T:* (01767) 680388. *Clubs:* Carlton, MCC, Lord's Taverners; All England Lawn Tennis and Croquet; George Row, Conservative, Billing Road (Northampton); Royal St George's Golf (Sandwich); John O'Gaunt Golf; Northamptonshire CC (Patron, 2006–).

NASH, Prof. Anthony Aubrey, PhD; Professor of Veterinary Pathology, since 1994, and Head, Centre for Infectious Diseases, University of Edinburgh; *b* 6 March 1949; *s* of Alfred Nash and Mabel Evelyn Nash (*née* Garrett); *m* 1979, Marion Eileen Bazeley; four *d.* *Educ:* Queen Elizabeth Coll., London (BSc Hons 1970); Univ. of Birmingham (MSc 1971; PhD 1976). Lecturer: in Immunology, Dept of Pathology, Univ. of Cambridge, 1984–94; in Pathology, Newnham Coll., Cambridge, 1987–94. Eleanor Roosevelt Fellow, Dept of Immunology, Scripps Clinic and Res. Foundn, Calif, 1989–90. Member Council: Soc. for Gen. Microbiology, 2000–04; BBSRC, 2002–05. FMedSci 1999; FRSE 2005. *Publications:* (jtly) Mims' Pathogenesis of Infectious Disease, 5th edn, 1999; over 100 articles in learned jls. *Recreations:* family, Leicester City Football Club. *Address:* Division of Biomedical Sciences, University of Edinburgh, Summerhall, Edinburgh EH9 1QH. *T:* (0131) 650 6164.

NASH, David John, OBE 2004; RA 1999; sculptor, primarily in wood; Research Fellow, University of Northumbria, since 1999; *b* 14 Nov. 1945; *s* of Lt-Col William Charles Nash and Dora Lillian Nash; *m* 1972, Claire Langdown; two *s*. *Educ:* Brighton Coll.; Kingston Sch. of Art (Higher DipAD); Chelsea Sch. of Art. Has worked in Blaenau Ffestiniog, 1967–; over 100 solo shows world wide; 80 works in internat. public collections incl. Tate Gall., Guggenheim, NY, Nat. Mus. of Wales and Metropolitan Mus., Japan. Hon. Dr: Art and Design, Kingston, 1998; Humanities and Letters, W Glamorgan, 2002. *Publications:* Wood Primer, 1987; Forms into Time, 1996; Black and Light, 2001; The Return of Art to Nature, 2003. *Address:* Capel Rhiw, Blaenau Ffestiniog, Gwynedd, N Wales LL41 3NT.

NASH, David Percy, FCA; *b* 24 May 1940; *s* of Percy and Kathleen Nash; *m* 1987, Susan Elizabeth Long (marr. diss. 2006); two *s*. *Educ:* Enfield Grammar Sch. FCA 1962. ICI plc, 1965–87; Gp Finance Dir, Cadbury Schweppes plc, 1987–89; Gp Finance Dir, 1989–93, Chm. and CEO, Food and Retailing Sector, 1993–95, Grand Metropolitan plc. Chairman: Kenwood Appliances plc, 1996–2001; Amicus Healthcare Gp Ltd, 1996–97; Niceopen Ltd, 1997; General Healthcare Gp Ltd, 1998–2000; Cable & Wireless Communications plc, 1998–2000; non-executive Director: IMRO, 1993–98; Cable and Wireless plc, 1995–2002 (Dep. Chm., 2002); Energy Gp plc, 1996–98; AXA UK plc, 1996–2001. Hon. Treas., Prince of Wales's Internat. Business Leaders' Forum, 1990–2007. *Recreations:* horseracing, cycling. *Club:* Royal Ascot Racing.

NASH, Ellison; *see* Nash, T. M. E.

NASH, Frances Clare; Head of European Division, Treasury Solicitor's Department, since 2004; *b* 29 Dec. 1960; *d* of Prof. Walter Nash and late Doreen Mary Nash (*née* Richardson). *Educ:* Forest Fields Coll., Nottingham; Jesus Coll., Oxford (BA 1982, MA); University Coll. London (LLM 1994). Admitted solicitor, 1986; private practice, 1986–87; Legal Dept, MAFF, 1987–93; Legal Secretariat to Law Officers, 1993–95; Legal Dept, MAFF, 1995–99; Dep. Legal Advr, MoD, 1999–2002; Dir, Legal Services, DEFRA, 2002–04. *Recreations:* gardening, tropical fishkeeping, international travel. *Address:* Treasury Solicitor's Department, One Kemble Street, WC2B 4TS. *T:* (020) 7210 3202; *e-mail:* Frances.Nash@Tsol.gsi.gov.uk.

NASH, John Edward; Member, Supervisory Board, Bank Winter AG, Vienna, since 1996; Chairman, S. G. Warburg Bank AG, 1980–87 (Director, 1977–87; Deputy Chairman, 1977–80); *b* 25 June 1925; *s* of Joseph and Madeleine Nash; *m* 1947, Ralda Everard Herring; two *s* two *d*. *Educ:* Univ. of Sydney (BEc); Balliol Coll., Oxford (BPhil). Teaching Fellow in Economics, Sydney Univ., 1947. Exec. Dir, Samuel Montagu & Co. Ltd, 1956; also Director, 1960–73: British Australian Investment Trust; Montagu Trust Ltd; Midland Montagu Industrial Finance Ltd; Capel Court Corp. (in Melb.); resigned all directorships on appt to Brussels, 1973; Dir of Monetary Affairs, EEC, 1973–77; Director: Reckitt & Colman plc, 1966–73 and 1977–86; S. G. Warburg & Co. Ltd, 1977–86; Mem. Adv. Bd, Bank S. G. Warburg Soditic AG, 1987–94. Dir Oxford Univ. Business Summer Sch., 1965; Research Fellow, Nuffield Coll., Oxford (part-time), 1966–69. Hon. Treasurer, PEP, 1964–73. Mem. Bd of Trustees, WWF Internat., 1979–92, 1993–94 (Hon. Treas., 1985–92). *Recreations:* golf, horse-racing, music. *Address:* Chalet Gstelli, 3785 Gsteig bei Gstaad, Switzerland. *T:* (33) 7551162, *Fax:* (33) 7551132. *Clubs:* Turf, MCC; University (Sydney).

NASH, Jonathan Scott; QC 2006; *b* 16 Oct. 1962; *s* of Bryan Whatmore Nash and Jean Nash (*née* Cowie); *m* 1995, Constance Chanteux (marr. diss. 2003); two *s*. *Educ:* Reigate Grammar Sch.; St John's Coll., Oxford (BA Modern Hist. 1984). Called to the Bar, Gray's Inn, 1986; in practice at the Bar, 1987–, specialising in commercial law. *Recreations:* music, tennis, books. *Address:* 3 Verulam Buildings, Gray's Inn, WC1R 5NT. *T:* (020) 7269 1106; *e-mail:* jnash@3vb.com. *Club:* Travellers.

NASH, Peter Philip, DPhil; Director, Transmissable Spongiform Encephalopathies and Zoonoses, Department for Environment, Food and Rural Affairs, 2002–06; *b* 18 May 1948; *s* of late Harold and Joan Nash; *m* 1977, June Mobbs; one *s* one *d*. *Educ:* Grove Park Grammar Sch., Wrexham; Jesus Coll., Oxford (MA, DPhil 1972). MAFF, subseq. DEFRA, 1972–: Head: Envmtl Protection Div., 1988–93; Financial Policy Div., 1993–97; Milk, Pigs, Eggs and Poultry Div., 1997–99; BSE Div., 1999–2002. *Recreations:* country walking, birdwatching, watching football. *T:* (020) 8349 2318.

NASH, Philip; Commissioner of Customs and Excise, 1986–90; *b* 14 March 1930; *s* of late John Hollett Nash and Edith Grace Nash (*née* Knee); *m* 1953, Barbara Elizabeth Bangs; one *s*. *Educ:* Watford Grammar School. National Service, RAF, 1949–50. HM Customs and Excise, 1950–90; on loan to Civil Service College, 1970–73; Asst Sec. and Head of Management Services, 1978–81; Asst Sec., Customs Directorate, 1981–86; Director, Customs, 1986–90. *Recreation:* family history. *Address:* Nutwood, 37 Lower Golf Links Road, Broadstone, Dorset BH18 8BQ. *T:* (01202) 601898.

NASH, Ronald Peter, CMG 2004; LVO 1983; HM Diplomatic Service, retired; High Commissioner, Trinidad and Tobago, 2004–06; *b* 18 Sept. 1946; *s* of John Henry Nash and Jean Carmichael Nash (*née* McIlwraith); *m* 1976, Annie Olsen; three *s*. *Educ:* Harefield Secondary Modern Sch.; Southall Tech. Sch.; Southall Grammar Tech. Sch.; Manchester Univ. (BA Hons). MCIL (MIL 1991). FCO, 1970; Moscow, 1974–76; UK Delegn to MBFR, Vienna, 1976–79; FCO, 1979–83; New Delhi, 1983–86; FCO, 1986–87; Dep. Hd of Mission, Vienna, 1988–92; Dep. High Comr, Colombo and (non-res.) Malé, 1992–95; Co-ordinator, Peace Implementation Conf. for Bosnia, 1995; Review of Africa Develt Prog., ODA, 1996; Hd, Human Rights Policy Dept, FCO, 1996–99; Ambassador: to Nepal, 1999–2002; to Afghanistan, 2002–03. Chm. Bd Dirs, Overseas Children's Sch., Colombo, Sri Lanka, 1994–95. *Address:* Ryecroft, 175 Hivings Hill, Chesham, Bucks HP5 2PN. *Club:* Berkhamsted Lawn Tennis and Squash.

NASH, Stephen Thomas, CMG 2000; HM Diplomatic Service, retired; Chairman, British Georgian Society, since 2004; *b* 22 March 1942; *s* of Thomas Gerald Elwin Nash and Gwendolen Selina Nash (*née* Osmaston); *m* 2004, Rusudan Benashvili; one *d*; two *s* two *d* from former marriages. *Educ:* Cheltenham Coll.; Pembroke Coll., Cambridge (MA Econs and History); Sch. of Oriental and African Studies (Arabic Studies); Queen's Coll., Oxford (MA Ethnology). Asst Dir, British Council, Baghdad, 1965–67; FCO 1967; served Caracas, Bogotá, Bangkok (SEATO), Guatemala; Dep. High Comr, Belmopan, 1981–82; Head, Indo-China Section, FCO, 1984–86; Chargé d'Affaires, Managua, 1986–88; seconded to British Aerospace, 1989–91; EC Monitor Mission to former Yugoslavia, Zagreb, 1991; Chargé d'Affaires, Tirana, 1993–95; Ambassador: to Georgia, 1995–98; to Albania, 1998–99; to Latvia, 1999–2002. Dir-Gen., Canning House, 2002–03. OSCE Election Observation Missions: to Latvia, 2002, and 2006 (Dep. Head); to Serbia (Head of Mission), 2004; to USA (Dep. Head), 2004; to Romania (Head), 2004. Dir, London

Inf. Network on Conflicts and State-building, 2002–06; Sen. Consultant, MEC Internat./Windsor Energy Gp, 2006–. Vice-Chm., Friends of Academic Res. in Georgia, 2003–; Board Member: Britain Estonia Latvia Lithuania Legal Assoc., 2002–07; British Latvian Assoc., 2004–; Anglo-Albanian Assoc., 2006–. Gov., Dulwich Village C of E Infant Sch., 2008–. *Recreations:* spending time with my children, choral singing, ski-ing, hill walking, gardening, viola-playing. *Club:* Arts.

NASH, (Timothy Michael) Ellison; His Honour Judge Nash; a Circuit Judge, since 1994; *b* 10 Dec. 1939; *s* of late Denis Frederick Ellison Nash, OBE, AE, FRCS and Joan Mary Andrew; *m* 1965, Gael Nash; one *s* one *d* (and two *s* decd). *Educ:* Dulwich Coll.; St Bartholomew's Hosp. Called to the Bar, Gray's Inn, 1964; Standing Counsel: DHSS, 1974–79; DTI, 1976–91; Asst Recorder, 1987–89; Recorder, 1990–94. Legal Assessor, GMC and Royal Dental Council, 1989–94; Chm., Home Office Police Appeal Tribunals, 1988–94. Metropolitan Police Special Constabulary, 1961–83. Examr, Dio. of Canterbury, 1990–94. *Recreation:* walking round in ever-increasing circles. *Address:* The Law Courts, Chaucer Road, Canterbury, Kent CT1 1ZA.

NASH, Ven. Trevor Gifford; Executive Co-ordinator, Advisers for Churches' Ministry of Healing in England, 1990–97 (Adviser, 1973–97); Hon. Chaplain, Winchester Cathedral, since 1998; *b* 3 May 1930; *s* of Frederick Walter Gifford Nash and Elsie Violet Louise Nash; *m* 1957, Wanda Elizabeth (*née* Freeston); four *d*. *Educ:* Haileybury College, Hertford; Clare Coll., Cambridge (MA); Cuddesdon Coll., Oxford. Curate: Cheshunt, 1955–57; Kingston-upon-Thames, 1957–61; Priest-in-Charge, Stevenage, 1961–63; Vicar, Leagrave, Luton, 1963–67; Senior Chaplain, St George's Hosp. Gp, London, 1967–73; Rector, St Lawrence with St Swithun, Winchester, 1973–82; Priest-in-Charge, Holy Trinity, Winchester, 1977–82; RD of Winchester, 1978–82; Archdeacon of Basingstoke, 1982–90, Archdeacon Emeritus, 1990; Hon. Canon of Winchester, 1980–. Pres., Guild of Health, 1993–97; Warden, Guild of St Raphael, 1995–98. RAChD (TA), 1956–61. *Recreations:* painting, music, walking. *Address:* The Corner Stone, 50B Hyde Street, Winchester, Hants SO23 7DY. *T:* (01962) 861759.

NASHA, Margaret Nnananyana, (Mrs Lawrence Nasha); MP (Democratic Party), Botswana, since 1994; Minister of Local Government; *b* 6 Aug. 1947; *d* of Sadinyana and Motlatshiping Ramontshonyana; *m* 1975, Lawrence Nasha; four *s*. *Educ:* Univ. of Botswana (BA 1976). Several posts as broadcaster, 1968–84; Dir of Information and Broadcasting, Botswana, 1985–89; High Comr in UK, 1989–93; Government of Botswana: Dep. Minister, 1994–97, Minister, 1997–98, of Local Govt, Lands and Housing; Minister: of Minerals, Energy and Water Affairs, 1998–99; of Local Govt, 1999–2002; of Lands and Housing, 2003. *Recreations:* leisure walks, tennis. *Address:* PO Box 917, Gaborone, Botswana.

NASMITH, Sir James Duncan D.; *see* Dunbar-Nasmith.

NASMYTH, Prof. Kim Ashley, PhD; FRS 1989; Whitley Professor of Biochemistry, since 2006, and Head, Department of Biochemistry, since 2007, University of Oxford; Fellow, Trinity College, Oxford, since 2006; *b* 18 Oct. 1952; *s* of James Nasmyth and Jenny Hughes; *m* 1982, Anna Dowson; two *d*. *Educ:* Eton Coll.; York Univ. (BA); Edinburgh Univ. (PhD). Jane Coffin Childs Postdoctoral Fellow, Dept of Genetics, Univ. of Washington, 1978–80; Robertson Fellow, Cold Spring Harbor Lab., NY, 1980–81; Staff Mem., MRC Lab. of Molecular Biol., Cambridge, 1982–87; Unofficial Fellow, King's Coll., Cambridge, 1984–87; Sen. Scientist, 1987–96, Dir, 1997–2005, Inst. of Molecular Pathology, Vienna. Hon. Prof., Univ. of Vienna, 1995–. MAE 1993; Member: EMBO, 1985; Austrian Acad. of Scis, 1999; Foreign Hon. Mem., Amer. Acad. of Arts and Scis, 1999. *Recreations:* climbing, ski-ing. *Address:* Department of Biochemistry, University of Oxford, South Parks Road, Oxford OX1 3QU. *T:* (01865) 275263.

NASON, Justin Patrick Pearse, OBE 1980; HM Diplomatic Service, retired; *b* 29 March 1937; *s* of John Lawrence Nason and Catherine Agnes (*née* McFadden); *m* 2000, Jeannine Dubois. *Educ:* Ampleforth; University Coll., Oxford. National Service, RAF, 1956–58. BICC, 1962–63; entered HM Foreign Service, 1963; FO, 1964–65; Prague, 1965–67; FCO, 1967–71; First Sec., Pretoria and Cape Town, 1971–74; Head of Chancery, Saigon, 1974–75; FCO, 1975–79; Head of Chancery, Kampala, 1979–81; Nat. Defence Coll. of Canada, 1981–82; Dep. High Comr, Colombo, 1982–85; Barclays Bank (on secondment), 1986–87; Minister Counsellor, Mexico City, 1988–90; temp. duty, Accra, 1990–91; Ambassador to Guatemala, 1991–95. *Recreation:* golf. *Club:* Oxford and Cambridge.

NASSAR, Mohamed Mouafak; Assistant Secretary General, League of Arab States, since 2004; *b* 15 Nov. 1940; *s* of Mohamad Nadim and Wanda Nassar; *m* 1974, Hanan Kniefati; one *s* one *d*. *Educ:* Coll. of Law, Damascus Univ. (LLB). Dep. Dir, Cultural Centre, Aleppo, 1965–66; Min. of Tourism, 1966–74; Min. of Foreign Affairs, 1974; Third Sec., London, 1975–81; Dep. Dir, Protocol Dept, Min. of Foreign Affairs, 1981–84; Chargé d'Affaires, Dar-es-Salaam, 1984–87; Hd, Syrian Interests Section, London, 1987–90; Dir, Western Europe Dept, Min. of Foreign Affairs, 1990–94; Chargé d'Affaires, Islamabad, 1994–2000; Chief of Cabinet, Min. of Foreign Affairs, 2001–02; Ambassador of Syria to UK, 2002–04. *Address:* League of Arab States, Midan El-Tahrir, Cairo, Egypt.

NASSAU, Bishop of; *see* West Indies, Archbishop of.

NATALEGAWA, (Raden Mohammad) Marty (Muliana), DPhil; Permanent Representative of the Republic of Indonesia to the United Nations, since 2007; *b* 22 March 1963; *s* of Raden Sonson Natalegawa and Siti Komariyah Natalegawa; *m* 1987, Sranya Bamrungphong; two *s* one *d*. *Educ:* Corpus Christi Coll., Cambridge (MPhil 1986); London Sch. of Econs (BSc Hons 1989); Australian National Univ. (DPhil 1993). Agency for Policy Analysis and Develt, Dept of For. Affairs, 1986–90; Indonesian Perm. Mission to UN, NY, 1994–99, Hd of Political Sect., 1999; Department of Foreign Affairs: Dep. Dir, 1999–2000, Dir, 2001–02, for Internat. Orgns; Spokesperson of Dept, 2002–05; Chief of Staff, Office of Minister of For. Affairs, 2002–04; Dir Gen. for ASEAN Co-operation, 2003–05; Ambassador to UK and to Ireland, 2005–07. Foreign Service Award, 1996, 2006; Public Relns Soc. Award, 2004. *Recreations:* classic cars, football, walks. *Address:* Permanent Mission of Indonesia to UN, 325 East 38th Street, New York, NY 10016, USA. *T:* (212) 972 8333, *Fax:* (212) 972 9780; *e-mail:* rm3n@yahoo.com.

NATHAN, family name of **Baron Nathan**.

NATHAN, 3rd Baron *cr* 1940, of Churt, Surrey; **Rupert Harry Bernard Nathan**; *b* 26 May 1957; *o s* of 2nd Baron Nathan and of Philippa Gertrude (*née* Solomon); *S* father, 2007; *m* 1st, 1987, Ann Hewitt (marr. diss. 1997); 2nd, 1997, Jane, *d* of D. Cooper; one *s*. *Educ:* Charterhouse; Durham Univ. (BA). *Heir:* *s* Alasdair Harry St John Nathan.

NATHAN, David Brian; QC 2002; *b* 29 Nov. 1948; *s* of Ephraim and Jenny Nathan; *m* Susan Mary Hayes; two *d*; one *s* one *d* from previous marriage. *Educ:* City of London Sch.; Manchester Univ. (LLB Hons). Called to the Bar, Middle Temple, 1971; in practice as barrister, specialising in all areas of criminal defence work, 1971–; Hd of Chambers, 2002–.

Recreations: reading, watching old movies. *Address:* (chambers) 9 Lincoln's Inn Fields, WC2A 3BP.

NATHAN, Peter Joseph; His Honour Judge Nathan; a Circuit Judge, since 2005; *b* 20 Dec. 1949; *s* of Laurence Nathan and Julia Nathan; *m* 1974, Denise Pomper; three *s*. *Educ:* Homefield Prep. Sch., Sutton; Wallington Independent Grammar Sch.; London Sch. Economics (LLB Hons 1971, LLM 1972). Called to the Bar, Inner Temple, 1973; admitted solicitor, 1981; founder Mem., One Garden Court Family Law Chambers, 1989; Dep. Dist Judge, 1993–2005; a Recorder of the Crown Court, 2000–05. *Recreations:* walking, reading history, travel, gardening.

NATHAN, Sara Catherine; freelance journalist, since 1997; *b* 16 Feb. 1956; *d* of Derek Nathan and Mary Nathan (*née* Lavine); *m* 1984, Malcolm John Singer; one *s* one *d*. *Educ:* New Hall, Cambridge (BA Hons); Stanford Univ., Calif. (Harkness Fellow). News trainee, 1980–82; with BBC news and current affairs, incl. Results Ed., Election prog., 1992, Newsnight, Breakfast Time/News, Money Prog., 1982–93; Editor: The Magazine, BBC Radio 5, 1993–95; Channel 4 News, 1995–97; columnist, The Scotsman, 1999–2000. Chm., Animal Procedures Cttee, 2006–. Lay Member: Professional Conduct Cttee, Bar Council, 1998–2004; Judicial Appts Commn, 2006–; Member: HFEA, 1998–2005; Radio Authy, 1999–2003; Criminal Injuries Compensation Appeals Panel, 2000–06; Gambling Rev. Body, 2000–01; Regulatory Decisions Cttee, FSA, 2001–; OFCOM, 2002–07 (Dep. Chm., Content Bd, 2003–06); Cttee, ICSTIS (Phonepay Plus), 2002–08. Chm., Children's First Commn, Lambeth, 2000–02; Marshall Scholarship Comr, 2000–07. Mem., BAFTA. *Recreations:* cinema, embarrassing my children. *Address:* 29 Goldsmith Avenue, W3 6HR.

NATHAN, Sellapan Ramanathan; *see* Sellapan, R.

NATHAN, Stephen Andrew; QC 1993; a Recorder, since 2000; *b* 30 April 1947; *s* of Frederick Emil Nathan and Margot Sophie Jeanette Nathan (*née* Welch); *m* 1999, Colleen Toomey; one *s*; one *d*. *Educ:* Hall Sch., Hampstead; Cranleigh Sch., Surrey (Schol.); New Coll., Oxford (BA Law 1968; MA 1972). Called to the Bar, Middle Temple, 1969, Bencher, 2005; in practice at the Bar, 1970–; Asst Recorder, 1989–2000. Mem. Cttee, London Common Law and Commercial Bar Assoc., 1999–. Dep. Chm., Guild of Guide Lectrs, 1975–76; Chm., Ponsonby Residents' Assoc., 1995–99. *Publication:* (jtly) Employee Competition: covenants, confidentiality and garden leave, 2007. *Recreations:* tennis, swimming, fine cooking. *Address:* Blackstone Chambers, Blackstone House, Temple, EC4Y 9BW. *T:* (020) 7583 1770. *Club:* Royal Automobile.

NATHANSON, Vivienne Hilary; Director of Professional Activities (formerly Head, Professional Resources and Research Group), British Medical Association, since 1996; *b* 9 March 1955; *d* of Norman Eric Nathanson and Margaret Nathanson (*née* Milman). *Educ:* Birkenhead High Sch., GDST; Middx Hosp. Med. Sch., Univ. of London (MB BS 1978). Med. Registrar, Glan Clwyd Hosp., 1981–84; British Medical Association: mgt trainee, 1984–86; Hd, Med. Ethics and Internat. Affairs, 1987–90; Scottish Sec., 1990–95. Prof., Sch. for Health, Univ. of Durham, 2004–. Hon. DSc Strathclyde, 2004. *Recreations:* bridge, opera. *Address:* British Medical Association, BMA House, Tavistock Square, WC1H 9JP. *T:* (020) 7383 6111; 214 Princess Park Manor, Royal Drive, N11 3FS.

NATKIEL, Rod; Managing Director and Head of Production, Rod Natkiel Associates, since 1999; *b* 30 Jan. 1952; *s* of late Daniel Natkiel and Marjorie Jessie (*née* Pinkham); *m* 1976, Janet Ruth Sawtell; two *s*. *Educ:* Kingston Grammar Sch.; Univ. of Bristol (BA Drama); Univ. of Birmingham (MBA Dist.). Associate Dir and Resident Musical Dir, Contact Th., Manchester, 1975–78; Dir/Producer, TV Light Entertainment, BBC Scotland, 1978–84; freelance Exec. Producer/Producer/Dir in Entertainment, Drama, News and Current Affairs, 1984–92; Prodn Exec., Birmingham Media Develt Agency, 1992–93; Hd of Network Television, BBC Midlands and E, 1992–96; Hd of Network Prodn, BBC Birmingham, 1996–99. Vis. Prof. in TV Studies, Univ. of Central England, 1993–99. Mem., Arts Council of England, 1997–98; Chair: W Midlands Arts Bd, 1997–2001; Screen W Midlands, 2001–03. Chm., Variety Club Midlands, 1997–2000. *Recreations:* squash, cricket, theatre, cinema, DIY. *Address:* 5 Vesey Road, Sutton Coldfield, W Midlands B73 5NP. *T:* (0121) 355 2197, *Fax:* (0121) 355 8033; *e-mail:* rod@rodnatkiel.co.uk.

NATTRASS, Michael Henry, FRICS; Member (UK Ind) West Midlands Region, European Parliament, since 2004; *b* 14 Dec. 1945. Property mgt; co-founder and Sen. Partner, Nattrass Giles, chartered surveyors, 1980–. Dep. Leader, UK Independence Party. *Address:* Nattrass Giles, 123 New John Street, Birmingham B6 4LD; European Parliament, Rue Wiertz, 1047 Brussels, Belgium.

NATWAR-SINGH, Kanwar; Padma Bhushan, 1984; MP (Congress Party) Bharatpur: Lok Sabha, 1984–89 and 1998–99; Rajya Sabha, 2002–08; Union Minister for External Affairs, India, 2004–05; *b* 16 May 1931; *s* of Govind Singhji and Prayag Kaur; *m* 1967, Princess Heminder Kumari, *e d* of late Maharaja Yadvindra Singhji of Patiala; one *s* (one *d* decd). *Educ:* St Stephen's Coll., Delhi Univ. (BA 1st cl. hons History 1951); Corpus Christi Coll., Cambridge, 1952–54 (Fellow 2005); Peking Univ. Joined Indian Foreign Service, 1953; 3rd Sec., Peking, 1956–58; Under Sec., Ministry of External Affairs, and Private Sec. to Sec. General, 1958–61; Adviser, Indian Delegn to UN, NY, 1961–66; Rapporteur, UN Cttee on Decolonisation, 1962–66; Rapporteur, UN Trusteeship Council, 1965; Alt. Deleg. of India to UN Session for 1962; Rep. of India on Exec. Bd of UNICEF, NY, 1962–66; Dep. Sec. to Prime Minister of India, 1966–67; Dir, Prime Minister's Secretariat, New Delhi, 1967–70; Jt Sec. to Prime Minister, 1970–71; Ambassador to Poland, 1971–73; Dep. High Comr in London, 1973–77; High Comr for India in Zambia and Botswana, 1977–80; Ambassador to Pakistan, 1980–82; Sec., Min. of External Affairs, India, 1982–84; Minister of State for Steel, 1984–85, for Fertilizers, 1985–86; Union Minister of State for Foreign Affairs, 1986–89. Attended Commonwealth Heads of Govt Meetings: Jamaica, 1975; Lusaka, 1979; Member: Commonwealth Cyprus Cttee, 1977; Indian Delegn to Zimbabwe Indep. Celebrations, 1980; Sec.-Gen., 7th Non-Aligned Summit, New Delhi, 1983; Chief Co-ordinator, Commonwealth Heads of State and Govt Meeting, New Delhi, 1983; Pres., UN Conf. on Disarmament and Develt, 1987; Leader, Indian Delegn to 42nd Session of UN Gen. Assembly, 1987. Dir, Air India, 1982–84. Exec. Trustee, UNITAR, 1981–86. Pres., All India Tennis Fedn, 1988–92. Hon. Res. Fellow, UCL. Hon. Dr Pol Sci. Seoul, 2005. E. M. Forster Literary Award, 1989. Comdr, Ordre Nat. du Lion (Senegal), 2005. *Publications:* E. M. Forster: A Tribute, 1964; The Legacy of Nehru, 1965; Tales from Modern India, 1966; Stories from India, 1971; Maharaja Suraj Mal, 1707–1763, 1981; Curtain Raisers, 1984; Profiles and Letters, 1997; The Magnificent Maharaja Bhupinder Singh of Patiala 1891-1938, 1997; Heart to Heart, 2003; Yours Sincerely, 2008; writes and reviews for national and international newspapers and magazines. *Recreations:* tennis, watching cricket, reading, writing, collecting books and reading them, good conversation followed by prolonged periods of reflective uninterrupted silence. *Address:* (home) 19 Teen Murti Lane, New Delhi 110011, India. *Clubs:* Garrick, Royal Over-Seas League (Life Mem.); India International Centre (Life Mem.), Gymkhana (Life Mem; Pres., 1984) (Delhi).

NATZLER, David Lionel; Principal Clerk, Table Office, House of Commons, since 2006; *b* 16 Aug. 1952; *o s* of Pierre Jean Natzler and late Brenda Agnes Natzler (*née* Wrangham); *m* 1988, Hilary Joan Gauld Thompson; two *s* one *d*. *Educ:* Eton Coll.; Trinity Coll., Cambridge (BA 1973): Harvard Univ. (Kennedy Schol.). House of Commons: Clerk of Select Committee: on Social Services, 1981–85; on Defence, 1989–95; on Procedure, 1995–97; on Trade and Industry, 1997–2001; Principal Clerk, Select Cttees, 2001–04; Sec., H of C Commn, 2004–06. *Address:* House of Commons, SW1A 0AA. *T:* (020) 7219 3312; *e-mail:* natzlerdl@parliament.uk.

NAUGHTIE, (Alexander) James; journalist and broadcaster; Presenter, Today, BBC Radio 4, since 1994; *b* 9 Aug. 1951; *s* of Alexander and Isabella Naughtie; *m* 1986, Eleanor Updale; one *s* two *d*. *Educ:* Keith Grammar Sch.; Aberdeen Univ. (MA Hons); Syracuse Univ., New York (MA). The Press and Journal, 1975–77; The Scotsman, 1977–84; The Guardian, 1984–88; Presenter: The World at One, BBC Radio 4, 1988–94; Opera News, BBC Radio 3, 1990–93; BBC Proms, 1992–2004; Bookclub, BBC Radio 4, 1998–. Laurence M. Stern Fellow, Washington Post, 1981. Chancellor, Stirling Univ., 2008–; Mem. Council, Gresham Coll., 1997–. Member: Edinburgh Internat. Festival Trust, 2003–; Marshall Aid Commemoration Commn, 2005–. Patron: Southbank Sinfonia, 2003–; Prince of Wales Arts and Kids Foundn, 2005–. Trustee, Gulbenkian Prize for Museums and Galls, 2004–. Hon. LLD: Aberdeen, 1990; St Andrews, 2001; DUniv Stirling, 2001; Hon. DLitt: Glasgow Caledonian, 2002; Napier, 2002. Personality of the Year, Sony Radio Awards, 1991. *Publications:* (ed) Playing the Palace: a Westminster collection, 1984; The Rivals: the intimate story of a political marriage, 2001; The Accidental American, 2004; The Making of Music: a journey with notes, 2007; contribs to newspapers, magazines, journals. *Recreations:* books, opera. *Address:* BBC News Centre, W12 8QT. *Clubs:* Travellers, Garrick.

NAUGHTON, Philip Anthony; QC 1988; *b* 18 May 1943; *s* of late Francis and Madeleine Naughton; *m* 1968, Barbara, *d* of Prof. F. E. Bruce; two *s* one *d*. *Educ:* Wimbledon Coll.; Univ. of Nottingham (LLB). Called to the Bar, Gray's Inn, 1970, Bencher, 1997. Marketing and public relations posts with BP Chemicals Ltd and Air Products Ltd, 1964–71; commenced practice as barrister, 1971. *Recreations:* walking, sailing. *Address:* 3 Serjeants' Inn, EC4Y 1BQ. *T:* (020) 7427 5000.

NAVARRETE, Jorge Eduardo; Ministry of Foreign Affairs, Mexico, since 2003 (with rank of Ambassador); Member of South Commission; *b* 29 April 1940; *s* of late Gabriel Navarrete and Lucrecia López; *m* 1st, 1962, María Antonieta Linares (marr. diss. 1973); one *s*; 2nd, 1976, María de Navarrete (*d* 1985); 3rd, 1987, Angeles Salceda (marr. diss. 1994); 4th, 1996, Martha López. *Educ:* Nat. Sch. of Economics, Nat. Autonomous Univ. of Mexico (equivalent BA Econ.); post-graduate studies in internat. economy. Center for Latin American Monetary Studies, Mexico, 1963–65; Nat. Foreign Trade Bank, Mexico, 1966–72; joined Mexican Foreign Service, 1972; Ambassador to: Venezuela, 1972–75; Austria, 1976–77; Yugoslavia, 1977–79; Dep. Perm. Rep. to UN, NY, 1979; Under Sec. (Economics), Min. of Foreign Affairs, Mexico, 1979–85; Ambassador: to UK and Republic of Ireland, 1986–89; to China, 1989–93; to Chile, 1993–95; Under Sec. for Energy, 1995–97; Ambassador to Brazil, 1997–2000; Perm. Rep. to UN, NY, 2000–02; Ambassador to Germany, 2002–03. Holds decorations from Argentina, Brazil, Dominican Republic, Ecuador, Federal Republic of Germany, Italy, Panama, Poland, Sweden, Venezuela. *Publications:* The International Transfer of Technology (with G. Bueno and M. S. Wionczeck), 1969; Mexico's Economic Policy, 2 vols, 1971, 1972; Cancun 1981: the international meeting on co-operation and development, 1982; The External Debt of Latin America: issues and policies, 1987; numerous essays on Mexican and Latin American economic issues, in Mexican and foreign jls. *Recreation:* chess. *Address:* Farallón 121-A, 01900 Mexico City, Mexico.

NAVRATILOVA, Martina; tennis player; *b* Prague, 18 Oct. 1956; *d* of late Jana Navratilova. Left Czechoslovakia, 1975; adopted American nationality, 1981. Professional player, 1975–94. Has won 167 singles and over 170 doubles titles, including 18 Grand Slam singles titles (a record 9 Wimbledon singles wins) and 41 Grand Slam doubles titles. Pres., Women's Tennis Assoc., 1979–80, 1994–95. *Publications:* Martina (autobiog.), 1985; The Total Zone (novel), 1994; Breaking Point, 1996. *Address:* c/o International Management Group, 1 Erieview Plaza, Cleveland, OH 44114, USA.

NAYAR, Kuldip; syndicated columnist; Mem., Rajya Sabha, 1997–2003; President: Citizens for Democracy; Transparency International; *b* 14 Aug. 1924; *m* 1949, Bharti; two *s*. *Educ:* Northwestern Univ., USA (BA Hons, LLB, MSc in journalism; Hon. PhD(Phil.) 1998; Alumni Award, 1999). Press Officer to Home Minister, India, 1954–64; Editor and General Manager, United News of India, 1964–67; Delhi Editor, The Statesman, 1967–75; Editor, Indian Express News Service, 1975–81; syndicated columnist, 1981–; correspondent, The Times, London, 1968–89; High Comr in UK, 1990. Mem., Indian delegn to UN Gen. Assembly. Prof. Emeritus, Symbiosis Inst. of Mass Communication, Pune Univ., 2001. Numerous journalism and public service awards. *Publications:* Between the Lines, 1967; India: the critical years, 1968; India, the critical years, 1971; Distant Neighbours, 1972; The Supersession of Judges, 1974; India After Nehru, 1975; The Judgement, 1977; In Jail, 1978; A report on Afghanistan, 1980; The Tragedy of Punjab, 1985; India House, 1992; The Martyr Bhagat Singh's Experiments in Revolution, 2000; Wall at Wagah: Indo-Pak relations, 2003. *Recreations:* music (Indian and Western); cricket, hockey. *Address:* D7/2 Vasant Vihar, New Delhi 110057, India. *T:* 26142388.

NAYLER, Georgina Ruth; Director, Pilgrim Trust, since 1996; *b* 16 March 1959; *d* of Dennis Nayler and Yvonne (*née* Loader); partner, Simon Stillwell; one *s* one *d*. *Educ:* Brentwood County High Sch. for Girls; Univ. of Warwick (BA). Joined Nat. Heritage Meml Fund, 1982: Asst Dir, 1987–88; Dep. Dir, 1988–89; Dir, 1989–95. Mem., Historic Bldgs Council for Scotland, 1990–96. Mem., Adv. Bd, Faculty of Arts, Univ. of Warwick, 2003–. *Recreations:* gardening, activities with my children. *Address:* c/o The Pilgrim Trust, Cowley House, 9 Little College Street, SW1P 3SH.

NAYLOR, (Andrew) Ross; MD; FRCSE, FRCS; Consultant Vascular Surgeon, since 1995, and Professor of Vascular Surgery, since 2003, Leicester Royal Infirmary; *b* 22 March 1958; *s* of Robert Charles Naylor and Patricia Mary Naylor; *m* 1982, May Bruce MacPherson; one *s* one *d*. *Educ:* Merchiston Castle Sch., Edinburgh; Univ. of Aberdeen (MBChB (commendation) 1981; MD 1990). FRCSE 1986; FRCS 1994. House Officer, Aberdeen Hosps, 1981–82; Lectr in Pathology, Aberdeen Royal Infirmary, 1982–83; Sen. House Officer, Surgery, Aberdeen Hosps, 1983–85; Surgical Registrar, Edinburgh Hosps, 1985–88; Res. Fellow in Surgery, Edinburgh Univ., 1988–90; Lectr in Surgery, Leicester Univ., 1991–93; Consultant Vascular Surgeon, Aberdeen Royal Infirmary, 1993–95. Hon. Reader in Surgery, Leicester Royal Infirmary, 1995–2003. Hunterian Prof., RCS, 2002. Mem. Council, Vascular Soc. of GB and Ireland, 2007–. *Publications:* (ed jtly) Carotid Artery Surgery: a problem based approach, 2001; 290 pubns in peer reviewed jls, esp. relating to carotid artery disease. *Recreations:* ski-ing, gardening. *Address:* 9 Dalby Avenue, Bushby, Leicester LE7 9RE. *T:* (0116) 252 3252, *Fax:* (0116) 252 3179; *e-mail:* arnaylor@hotmail.com.

NAYLOR, Bernard; University Librarian, Southampton University, 1977–2000; President, Library Association, 2001–02; *b* 7 May 1938; *s* of William Edward Naylor and Lilian Naylor (*née* Oakes); *m* 1967, Frances Gemma Trenaman; four *s* one *d*. *Educ:* Balliol Coll., Oxford (BA 1963; MA 1965); Sch. of Librarianship and Archive Administration, University Coll. London (Dip. Lib. 1966). MCLIP (ALA 1969). Asst, Foreign Accessions Dept, Bodleian Liby, 1964–66; Librarian and Bibliographer, Univ. of London Inst. of Latin American Studies, 1966–74; Sec., Library Resources Co-ordinating Cttee, Univ. of London, 1974–77; Co-ordinator of Inf. Services, 1988–93, of Acad. Support Services, 1998–2000, Southampton Univ. Member: British Liby Adv. Cttee on Lending Services, 1978–86 (Chm., 1981–85); Council, Standing Conf. of Nat. and Univ. Libraries, 1979–82, 1984–90 (Vice-Chm., 1984–86; Chm., 1986–88); British Council Libraries Adv. Cttee, 1982–96 (Chm., 1986–95); British Liby Bd, 1995–2001. Chm., Hants Area Tech. Res. Indust. Commercial Service Exec., 1981–2000. Trustee: Nat. MSS Conservation Trust, 1995–; Hansard Trust, 2002–; Liby Assoc. Benevolent Fund, 2002– (Chm., 2008–). Chm., Laser Foundn, 2003–05. Gov., La Sainte Union Coll., Southampton, 1996–97. FRSA 1997. Mem., British Council, 1995. Hon. DLitt Southampton, 2006. *Publications:* Accounts of Nineteenth Century South America, 1969; Directory of Libraries and Special Collections on Latin America and the West Indies, 1975; articles in liby jls. *Recreations:* playing the piano (in private), learning foreign languages. *Address:* 12 Blenheim Avenue, Highfield, Southampton SO17 1DU. *T:* (023) 8055 4697.

NAYLOR, (Charles) John, OBE 1993; Secretary and Treasurer, then Chief Executive, Carnegie United Kingdom Trust, 1993–2003; Chair, Office of Scottish Charity Regulator, since 2006; *b* 17 Aug. 1943; *s* of late Arthur Edgar Naylor, MBE and Elizabeth Mary Naylor; *m* 1968, Margery Thomson; two *s*. *Educ:* Royal Grammar Sch., Newcastle upon Tyne; Haberdashers' Aske's Sch., Elstree; Clare Coll., Cambridge (MA History). Jun. and sen. exec. posts in industry, 1965–75; Dir, YMCA National Centre, Lakeside, Cumbria, 1975–80; Dep. National Sec., 1980–82, Nat. Sec., 1982–93, National Council of YMCAs; mem. and chm. of YMCA European and world cttees, 1976–92. Vice-Chm., Nat. Council for Voluntary Youth Services, 1985–88; Mem., Nat. Adv. Council for Youth Service, 1985–88. Chairman: Assoc. of Heads of Outdoor Educn Centres, 1979–80; MSC and DES Working Party on Residential Experience and Unemployment, 1980–81; DES Adv. Cttee for Innovation in Youth Work, 1986–92; Mem., Scottish Charity Law Review Commn, 2000–01. Member: Community Fund Scottish Cttee, 2003–04 (Chm., 2004–06); UK Bd, Big Lottery Fund, 2004–06. Chm., 1995–2000, Trustee, 2000–06, Brathay Exploration Gp; Trustee and Treas., The Tomorrow Project, 2000–. Trustee, Med. Res. Scotland (formerly Scottish Hosps Endowment Res. Trust), 2005–. Mem., subseq. Chair, UK Scout Assoc. Develt Grants Bd, 2003–. Kirk Elder, 1998–. CCMI; FRSA. *Publications:* contribs on youth, outdoors and grant making to UK periodicals and books. *Recreations:* the outdoors (partic. mountains), theatre, golf. *Address:* Orchard House, 25b Cramond Glebe Road, Edinburgh EH4 6NT.

NAYLOR, Prof. David, OC 2006; MD, DPhil; FRCP, FRSC 2004; President, since 2005, and Professor of Medicine, since 1996, University of Toronto; *b* 26 Oct. 1954; *s* of Thomas Naylor and Edna (*née* Aziz); *m* 1985, Ilse Treurnicht, DPhil; two *s* two *d*. *Educ:* Univ. of Toronto (MD 1978); Hertford Coll., Oxford (Rhodes Schol. 1979; DPhil 1983). FRCP (Canada) 1986. Resident in internal medicine, Univ. of Western Ontario teaching hosps, 1983–86; MRC Res. Fellow, Clinical Epidemiol., Toronto Gen. Hosp., 1987–88; University of Toronto: Asst Prof., 1988–92, Associate Prof., 1992–96, of Medicine; Dean of Medicine and Vice Provost, Relns with Health Care Instns, 1999–2005; Founding Dir, Clinical Epidemiology Prog., Sunnybrook Health Scis Centre, Toronto, 1990–96; Founding CEO, Inst. for Clinical Evaluative Scis, 1991–98; Sen. Scientist, MRC of Canada, 1998–99. Chm., Nat. Adv. Cttee on SARS and Public Health, 2003. Fellow, Canadian Acad. of Health Scis, 2005; For. Associate, Inst. of Medicine, NAS, 2005. Hon. Life Mem., Canadian Public Health Assoc., 2005. Member Editorial Board: BMJ, 1996–98; Jl of American Med. Assoc., 1998–; Canadian Med. Assoc. Jl, 1998–2000. *Publications:* co-author of numerous books and chapters, and over 250 jl articles. *Recreation:* golf. *Address:* Simcoe Hall 206, University of Toronto, 27 King's College Circle, Toronto, ON M5S 1A1, Canada. *T:* (416) 9782121, *Fax:* (416) 9711360; *e-mail:* president@utoronto.ca. *Club:* Scarboro Golf.

NAYLOR, Maj.-Gen. (David) Murray, CB 1992; MBE 1972; DL; Director-General, Territorial Army and Organisation, Ministry of Defence, 1989–92; *b* 5 March 1938; *s* of Thomas Humphrey Naylor and Dorothy Isobel Durning Naylor (*née* Holt); *m* 1965, Rosemary Gillian Hicks Beach; three *s*. *Educ:* Eton Coll. psc, rcds. Joined Scots Guards, 1956; commnd as National Service and later as Regular Officer; commanded: 2nd Bn Scots Guards, 1976–79; 22nd Armoured Bde, 1982–83; Dep. Mil. Sec. (A), 1985–87; GOC NE Dist and Comdr 2nd Inf. Div., 1987–89. Chm., N Yorks Ambulance Service NHS Trust, 1992–97. Mem. (C), N Yorks CC, 1997–2005. DL N Yorks, 1994. Mem., Merchant Adventurers Co. of York, 1998. Gov., St Peter's Sch., York, 1991–2005 (Chm. of Govs, 2000–05). *Publication:* Among Friends: Scots Guards 1956–1993, 1995. *Recreations:* shooting, walking, tennis, travel. *Address:* Minster Hill, Huttons Ambo, York YO60 7HJ. *T:* (01653) 695008. *Club:* Cavalry and Guards.

NAYLOR, Prof. Ernest, OBE 1998; PhD, DSc; Lloyd Roberts Professor of Marine Zoology (formerly Lloyd Roberts Professor of Zoology), 1982–96, now Professor Emeritus, and Head of School of Ocean Sciences, 1992–96, University College of North Wales, Bangor; *b* 19 May 1931; *s* of Joseph and Evelyn Naylor; *m* 1956, Carol Gillian Bruce; two *d*. *Educ:* Swanwick Hall Grammar Sch.; Univ. of Sheffield (BSc); Univ. of Liverpool (PhD, DSc). FIBiol 1972–96. Commnd RAF, 1954–56 (Educn Br.). Successively Asst Lectr, Lectr, Sen. Lectr and Reader in Zoology, University Coll. of Swansea, Wales, 1956–71; Prof. of Marine Biology, Univ. of Liverpool, 1971–82; Dean of Sci., UCNW, Bangor, 1989–91. Visiting Professor: Duke Univ., USA, 1969, 1970; Univ. of Otago, NZ, 1982. Mem., NERC, 1976–82 (Mem., Marine Sci. and Technol. Bd, 1994–96); Specialist Adviser to H of L Select Sub-Cttee on Marine Sci. and Technology, 1985; Indep. Mem., Co-ordinating Cttee on Marine Sci. and Technology, 1988–91; Indep. Assessor, Inter-Agency Cttee on Marine Sci. and Technol., 1991–98; UK Rep., EC Adv. Cttee for Marine Science and Technol., 1989–96. President: Sect. D (Zoology), BAAS, 1982; Estuarine and Coastal Sciences Assoc., 1986–89 (Hon. Life Mem. 2001); Soc. for Expmtl Biology, 1989–91 (Hon. Life Mem. 1997); Member Council: Marine Biol Assoc. of UK, 1977–80, 1982–85; Challenger Soc. for Marine Sci. (Hon. Life Mem. 2007). Founding Ed., Estuarine, Coastal and Shelf Science, 1972–2000. *Publications:* British Marine Isopods, 1972; (co-ed with R. G. Hartnoll) Cyclic Phenomena in Marine Plants and Animals, 1979; over 160 papers in learned jls. *Recreations:* travel, gardening. *Address:* School of Ocean Sciences, Bangor University, Menai Bridge, Anglesey LL59 5EY. *T:* (01248) 382842; *e-mail:* e.naylor@bangor.ac.uk.

NAYLOR, John; *see* Naylor, C. J.

NAYLOR, Maurice; *see* Naylor, W. M.

NAYLOR, Maj.-Gen. Murray; *see* Naylor, Maj.-Gen. D. M.

NAYLOR, Peter Brian, CBE 1987; Representative, British Council, Greece, 1983–86; *b* 10 July 1933; *s* of late Eric Sydney Naylor and Phyllis Marian Jolly; *m* 1st, 1958, Barbara Pearson (*d* 1995); two *s* one *d* (and one *s* decd); 2nd, 2005, Heather Margaret Fibbens (*née* White). *Educ:* Grange High Sch., Bradford; Selwyn Coll., Cambridge (Open Exhibnr; BA 1957). Wool Top Salesman, Hirsch, Son & Rhodes, Bradford, 1957; British Council: Asst Rep., Bangkok, 1959; Courses Dept and E Europe Dept, London, 1962; Asst Rep., Warsaw, 1967; Reg. Rep., Dacca, E Pakistan, 1969; Actg Rep., Athens, 1971; Rep., Argentina, 1972, Brazil, 1975; Controller, European Div., 1978–83. *Publication:* contrib. Blood Sweat and Tears, 1992. *Recreations:* reading, writing, drawing, salukis. *Address:* 3 Farmadine Court, Saffron Walden, Essex CB11 3HT. *T:* (01799) 527708. *Club:* Saffron Walden Golf.

NAYLOR, Sir Robert (Antony), Kt 2008; Chief Executive, University College London Hospitals NHS Trust, since 2000; b 13 Nov. 1949; *s* of Francis Thomas Naylor and Kathleen Mary (*née* Donellan); *m* 1974, Jane Karen Evans; one *s* one *d*. *Educ:* Presentation Coll., Reading; Thames Poly. (BSc Hons Chem. London). Grad. mgt trainee, King's Fund, 1972–74; Hosp. Sec., National Hosp., Queen Sq., 1974–77; Dist Administrator, Enfield HA, 1977–84; Chief Exec., Birmingham Heartlands and Solihull NHS Trust, 1984–2000. Proprietor, Henley Hotel, 1988–2001. Hon. Sen. Fellow, Univ. of Warwick. *Recreations:* golf, scuba diving. *Address:* 4 Chester Terrace, Regent's Park, NW1 4ND. *T:* (office) (020) 7380 9890; *e-mail:* robert.naylor@uclh.nhs.uk.

NAYLOR, Ross; *see* Naylor, A. R.

NAYLOR, (William) Maurice, CBE 1973; FIHM; JP; Director, National Association of Health Authorities, 1981–84; *b* 20 Dec. 1920; *s* of Thomas and Agnes Naylor; *m* 1948, Maureen Ann, *d* of John and Mary Walsh; one *s* two *d*. *Educ:* St Joseph's Coll., Market Drayton; Manchester Univ. (BA Admin). FIHM (FHSM 1956, Hon. FHSM 1987). War service, 1941–46, RA (FE, POW, 1942–45). Parly Asst, Town Clerk's Office, Manchester, 1950–55; Asst Sec., Manchester RHB, 1955–57; Dep. Sec., 1957–63, Sec., 1963–73, Sheffield RHB; Regl Administrator, Trent RHA, 1973–81. Institute of Health Services Management: Mem., Nat. Council, 1966–86; Chm., 1974; Pres., 1975–76; Chm. Educn Cttee, 1980–86. Member: Cttee on Hosp. Supplies Orgn, 1969; Steering Cttee on Reorgn of NHS, 1973–74; Cornwall AHA, 1982–84; Chm., Patient Transport Services Working Party, 1981. Trustee, NHS Pensioners Trust, 1991–99. Hon. MBA Sheffield, 1982. *Publications:* (contrib.) Challenges for Change, 1971; Organisation of Area Health Services, 1972; (contrib. and Chm., Editl Cttee) Health Care in the United Kingdom: its organisation and management, 1982; contrib. to professional jls. *Address:* 7 Hewitt Drive, Kirby Muxloe, Leicester LE9 2EB. *T:* (0116) 239 2606.

NAYLOR-LEYLAND, Sir Philip (Vyvian), 4th Bt *cr* 1895, of Hyde Park House; Chairman, Milton (Peterborough) Estates Co.; *b* 9 Aug. 1953; *s* of Sir Vivyan Edward Naylor-Leyland, 3rd Bt and Hon. Elizabeth Anne Fitzalan-Howard, *yr d* of 2nd Viscount FitzAlan of Derwent, OBE (she *m* 2nd, Sir Stephen Hastings, MC, and *d* 1997); *S* father, 1987; *m* 1980, Lady Isabella Lambton, *d* of Viscount Lambton (*d* 2006); four *s* two *d*. *Educ:* Eton; RMA Sandhurst; NY Univ. Business Sch.; RAC Cirencester. 2nd Lieut, Life Guards, 1973, Lieut, 1975–76. Chm., Peterborough Royal Foxhound Show Soc., 1995– (Vice-Chm., 1988–95); Pres., Nat. Coursing Club, 1988–. Jt Master, Fitzwilliam (Milton) Hunt, 1987–. *Heir:* *s* Thomas Philip Naylor-Leyland, *b* 22 Jan. 1982. *Address:* Milton, Peterborough, Cambs PE6 7AA; Nantclwyd Hall, Ruthin, Denbighshire LL15 2PR. *Clubs:* White's; Air Squadron; Sunningdale Golf.

NAYSMITH, (John) Douglas, PhD; MP (Lab and Co-op) Bristol North West, since 1997; *b* 1 April 1941; *s* of late James Naysmith and Ina (*née* Vass); *m* 1966, Caroline (separated), *d* of Sidney Hill and late Kate Hill; one *s* one *d*. *Educ:* Musselburgh Burgh Sch.; George Heriot's Sch., Edinburgh; Edinburgh Univ. (BSc, PhD). CBiol 1989, FIBiol 1999. Res. Asst, Edinburgh Univ., 1966–69; Fellow, Yale Univ., 1969–70; Res. Immunologist, Beecham Res. Labs, 1970–72; University of Bristol: Res. Associate, 1972–76; Fellow, 1976–81; Lectr in Immunology, Dept of Pathology, 1981–95; Administrator, Registrar's Office, 1995–97. FRSocMed 1980. *Address:* House of Commons, SW1A 0AA.

NAZARETH, Gerald Paul, GBS 2000; CBE 1985 (OBE 1976); Non-Permanent Judge, Hong Kong Court of Final Appeal, since 1997; Justice, Bermuda Court of Appeal, since 2001; *b* 27 Jan. 1932; *m* 1959, Elba Maria Fonseca; three *d*. *Educ:* Nairobi; St Xavier's College, Bombay; LLB Bombay Univ. Called to the Bar, Lincoln's Inn, 1962. Public Prosecutor, and Senior Crown Counsel, Kenya, 1954–63; Solicitor General, British Solomon Islands, 1963–73; Attorney General and Legal Advisor, Western Pacific High Commn, 1973–76; Hong Kong: Law Draftsman, 1976–84; MLC, 1979–84; QC, 1982; Judge of the High Court, 1985–91; Justice of Appeal, 1991–2000 and Vice-Pres., 1994–2000, Court of Appeal. Comr, Supreme Court, Brunei, 1989–93. Member: Law Reform Commn, Hong Kong, 1982–84 (Chm., Sub-Cttee on Copyright Law, 1987–92); Wkg Gp on Sino-British Jt Declaration on Hong Kong, Beijing, 1984. Vis. Fellow, ANU, 1972. Vice-Pres., Commonwealth Assoc. of Legislative Counsel, 1983–90. *Recreations:* music, reading, gardening, walking. *T:* (020) 8274 0730.

NAZARETH, Prof. Irwin, PhD; FRCGP; Professor of Primary Care and Population Sciences, since 2002, and Vice Dean, Primary Care, since 2007, University College London; Director, General Practice Research Framework, General Medical Council, since 2005; *b* Bombay, 12 Oct. 1958; *s* of Ignatius Nazareth and Caroline Rodrigue-Nazareth. *Educ:* Topiwala Nat. Medical Coll., Bombay (MB BS 1984); London (PhD 1987). LRCPE 1986; LRCSE 1986; LRCPSGlas 1986; DRCOG 1988; MRCGP 1989, FRCGP 2004. SHO, 1984–89; University College London: Sir Jules Thorne Res. Fellow, 1990–93; Lectr in Primary Care, 1994–95; Sen. Lectr in Primary Care Medicine, 1995–2002. *Publications:* contrib. key chapters in six books on med. practice and res.; over 100 original res. papers in scientific med. jls. *Recreations:* running, travel, music. *Address:* Department of Primary Care and Population Health, University College London Medical School, Rowland Hill Street, NW3 2NF.

NAZIR-ALI, Rt Rev. Dr Michael; *see* Rochester, Bishop of.

NDUNGANE, Most Rev. (Winston Hugh) Njongonkulu; President and Founder, African Monitor; Archbishop of Cape Town and Metropolitan of Southern Africa, 1996–2008; *b* Kokstad, 2 April 1941; *s* of Foster Tunyiswa Ndungane and Tingaza (*née* Gcanca); *m* 1st, 1972, Nosipho Ngcelwane (*d* 1986); one *s* one *d*; 2nd, 1987, Nomahlubi Vokwana. *Educ:* Lovedale High Sch., Alice, E Cape; Federal Theol Seminary, Alice (Associate, 1973); King's Coll., London (AKC, BD 1978; MTh 1979; FKC 1997). Ordained deacon, 1973, priest, 1974; Assistant Priest: St Mark's, Athlone, Cape Town, 1973–75; St Mark, Mitcham, 1975–76; St Peter's, Hammersmith, 1976–77; St Mary the Virgin, Primrose Hill, 1977–79; Asst Chaplain, St George's, Paris, 1979; Rector, St Nicholas, Elsies River, Cape Town, 1980–81; Provincial Liaison Officer, CPSA, 1981–84; Principal, St Bede's Coll., Umtata, 1985–86; Provincial Canon, 1987; Chief Exec. Officer, CPSA, 1987–91; Bishop of Kimberley and Kuruman, 1991–96. Vis. Scholar, Ch Divinity Sch. of the Pacific, Berkeley, 1990–91. Chairman: SACC Church

Leaders' Forum, 1997–98; Nat. Poverty Hearings, 1998; Member: Budget Gp, USPG, 1981–86; ACC, and its Standing Cttee, 1981–90; Bd, SABC, 1993– (Chm., Religious Broadcasting Panel, 1995–). Hon. DD: Rhodes Univ., 1997; Protestant Episcopal Seminary, Va, 2000; Hon. DHL Worcester State Coll., Mass, 2000; Hon. DSocSc Natal, 2001. *Publications* include: The Commuter Population for Claremont, Cape, 1973; Human Rights and the Christian Doctrine of Man, 1979; A World with a Human Face: a voice from Africa, 2003; contributions to: Peace and Peacemaking, 1984; Open to the Spirit, 1987; Doing Ethics in Context, 1994; Ethics and Values: a global perspective, 1997; Change and Challenge, 1998; articles in periodicals. *Address:* African Monitor, PO Box 44986, Claremont, Cape Town 7735, South Africa.

NEAGLE, Lynne; Member (Lab) Torfaen, National Assembly for Wales, since 1999; *b* Merthyr Tydfil, 18 Jan. 1968; *m* 1996, Huw George Lewis, *qv*; one *s*. *Educ:* Cyfartha High Sch., Merthyr Tydfil; Reading Univ. (BA Hons French and Italian). Vol. Housing Rights Worker, Shelter Cymru, 1991–93; Inf. Project Officer, Mid Glam Assoc. of Voluntary Orgns, 1993–94; Res. Asst to Glenys Kinnock, MEP, 1994–97; Carers Develt Officer, Voluntary Action Cardiff, 1997–99. *Recreations:* cinema, reading, swimming. *Address:* (office) 73 Upper Trosnant Street, Pontypool, Torfaen NP4 8AU.

NEAL, Prof. Bernard George, MA, PhD, ScD; FREng; Emeritus Professor, since 1982 and Fellow, since 1986, Imperial College, London University (Professor of Applied Science, 1961–72, of Engineering Structures, 1972–81, of Civil Engineering, 1981–82, and Head of Civil Engineering Department, 1976–82); *b* 29 March 1922; *s* of late Horace Bernard Neal, Wembley, and Hilda Annie Webb; *m* 1948, Elizabeth Ann, *d* of late William George Toller, Woodbridge, and Bertha Catharine Toller; one *s* one *d*. *Educ:* Merchant Taylors'; Trinity College, Cambridge (Schol.). MA Cantab, 1947; PhD Cantab 1948; ScD Cantab 1965; FInstCE 1960; FIStructE 1966; FREng (FEng 1980). Temp. Experimental Officer, Admiralty, 1942–45; Research Student, Univ. of Cambridge, 1945–48; Research Associate, Brown University, USA, 1948–49; Demonstrator, 1949–51, Lecturer, 1951–54, Univ. of Cambridge; Research Fellow, 1947–50, Staff Fellow, 1950–54, Trinity Hall, Cambridge; Prof. of Civil Engineering, University Coll. of Swansea, 1954–61. Pro-Rector, Imperial Coll., London, 1972–74. Dean of City and Guilds Coll., 1964–67; Visiting Prof., Brown Univ., USA, 1959–60. Pres., Welding Inst., 1998–2000 (Chm., Res. Bd, 1974–98; Hon. FWeldI 1996). Vice-Pres., 1995–2004, Pres., 2004–, Croquet Assoc. Telford Premium, 1951, Manby Premium, 1952, Instn Civil Engineers. *Publications:* The Plastic Methods of Structural Analysis, 1956; Structural Theorems and their Applications, 1964; technical papers on theory of structures, strength of materials. *Recreations:* lawn tennis, croquet. *Address:* 41 Asquith Road, Cheltenham GL53 7EJ. *T:* (01242) 510624. *Clubs:* All England Lawn Tennis and Croquet (Mem. Cttee, 1982–96; Vice-Pres., 1996–), Hurlingham; Cheltenham Croquet (Pres., 1995–).

NEAL, Prof. David Edgar, FRCS; Professor of Surgical Oncology, University of Cambridge, since 2002; *b* 9 March 1951; *s* of Norman and Beth Neal; *m* 1972, Deborah Mary Heyworth; three *d*. *Educ:* University Coll. London (BSc 1st Cl. Hons Anatomy; MB BS, MS). FRCS 1980. Tutor and Lectr in Surgery, Univ. of Leeds, 1981–83; First Asst in Urology, 1983–87, Sen. Lectr in Urological Surgery, 1988–92, Consultant Urologist, 1992–, Freeman Hosp., Newcastle upon Tyne; Prof. of Surgery, 1992–2002 and Dir, Med. Res., 1997–2002, Univ. of Newcastle upon Tyne. Mem., King's Fund Mgt Cttee, 1996–. Member: Council, RCS, 2002–; Postgraduate Medical Educn and Trng Bd, 2003–; Council, Acad. of Medical Scis, 2006–. Hon. Mem., Urological Soc. Australia, 1999; Corresp. Mem., Amer. Assoc. Genito-urinary Surgeons, 1999. St Peter's Medal, Brit. Assoc. of Urological Surgeons, 2001. *Publications:* Tumours in Urology, 1994; (jtly) Basic Science in Urology, 1999; contrib. articles to The Lancet, Annals Oncol. *Recreations:* playing the classical guitar, maintenance of classic motor cycles. *Address:* Department of Oncology, Addenbrooke's Hospital, Cambridge CB2 2QQ.

NEAL, Sir Eric (James), AC 1988; Kt 1982; CVO 1992; Governor, South Australia, 1996–2001; Chancellor, Flinders University, since 2002; *b* 3 June 1924; *s* of James and May Neal; *m* 1950, Thelma Joan, *d* of R. E. Bowden; two *s*. *Educ:* South Australian Sch. of Mines. CEng; FIGEM, FAIM. Boral Ltd: Dir, 1972–92; Chief Exec., 1973–87; Man. Dir, 1982–87; Chairman: Atlas Copco Australia Pty Ltd, 1989–96; Metal Manufacturers Ltd, 1990–96 (Dir, 1987–96); Director: Westpac Banking Corp., 1985–92 (Dep. Chm., 1987–88; Chm., 1989–92); John Fairfax Ltd, 1987–88; BHP Co. Ltd, 1988–94; Coca Cola Amatil Ltd, 1987–96. Mem., Australian Adv. Council, Gen. Motors, 1987–94. Mem., Cttee apptd by Fed. Govt to advise on Higher Defence Orgn, 1982. Mem., Amer. Bureau of Shipping, 1976–90; first Nat. Pres., Aust. Inst. of Co. Dirs, 1990–92. Chm. Exec. Cttee, Duke of Edinburgh's Sixth Commonwealth Study Conf. 1986; Nat. Chm., Duke of Edinburgh's Award Scheme in Australia, 1984–92; Internat. Trustee, Duke of Edinburgh's Award Internat. Assoc., 1986–97. Chief Comr, City of Sydney, 1987–88. Mem., Co. of Engineers, 2004. Hon. FIEAust 1985; Hon. Fellow, Aust. Inst. of Building, 1998; Emeritus Mem., Aust. Inst. of Mgt, 1998. Hon. DEng Sydney, 1989; DUniv: S Australia, 1996; Flinders, 2001. US Dept of Defense Medal for Dist. Public Service, 1992. *Recreations:* naval history, travel, reading, shipping. *Address:* Flinders University, GPO Box 2100, Adelaide, SA 5001, Australia. *Clubs:* Adelaide (Adelaide); Melbourne (Melbourne); Union (Sydney).

NEAL, Frederick Albert, CMG 1990; FCIL; aviation consultant; UK Representative on Council of International Civil Aviation Organization, Montreal, 1983–93; *b* 22 Dec. 1932; *s* of Frederick William George Neal and Frances Elizabeth (*née* Duke); *m* 1958, Gloria Maria Moirano. *Educ:* Royal Grammar Sch., High Wycombe; Sch. of Slavonic Studies, Cambridge; Birkbeck Coll., London (BA). FCIL (FIL 1965). Min. of Supply, 1953; Asst Defence Supply Attaché, Bonn, 1958–64; Principal, Min. of Technology (subseq. DTI), 1967; Asst Sec., DTI, 1974; Counsellor (Economic and Commercial), Ottawa, 1975–80; Asst Sec., Dept of Trade, 1980–83. *Recreations:* golf, bridge, music. *Address:* 2 Hambledon Court, 19B Crescent East, Hadley Wood, Herts EN4 0EY. *Clubs:* Royal Over-Seas League; Hadley Wood Golf.

NEAL, (Harry) Morton, CBE 1991; FIC; Chairman, Harry Neal Ltd, since 1985; *b* 21 Nov. 1931; *s* of late Godfrey French Neal and Janet Bryce Morton; *m* 1954, Cecilia Elizabeth Crawford, *d* of late Col M. Crawford, DSO; one *s* three *d*. *Educ:* Uppingham Sch.; London Univ. (BSc(Eng)); City and Guilds Coll. (ACGI). Flying Officer, RAF, 1953. Chm., Connaught Hotel Ltd, 1980–94 (Dir, 1966–97); Dir, Savoy Hotel Ltd, 1982–93. Chm., St Anselm Develt Co. Ltd, 1985–. Member of Lloyd's. Chm., City and Guilds of London Inst., 1979–91 (Vice Pres., 1999–2004); Member: TEC, then BTEC, 1982–94; Court of City Univ., 1982–91; Delegacy, St Mary's Hosp. Med. Sch., 1993–98; Board of Governors: Imperial Coll., London, 1988–2001; Willesden Tech. Coll., 1983–86; Francis Holland Sch., 1988–2006 (Vice-Chm., 1996–2005); Mgt Cttee, Courtauld Inst. of Art, 1983–99; Council, Univ. of Herts, 2006–. Trustee: Buckminster Estate, 1969–2005; Samuel Courtauld Trust, 1989–2006; Prince of Wales Inst. of Architecture, 1991–99 (Mem., Bd of Advrs, 1993–99). President: Greater London Middx W County (formerly NW County) Scout Council, 1983–2007; City and Guilds Coll. Assoc., 1994–95; Herts Agricl Soc., 2004; City and Guilds Assoc., 2006–08. Liveryman, Carpenters' Co., 1955– (Master, 1997–98). High Sheriff, Herts, 1999–2000. FCIOB, FRSA; FCGI 1983. Hon. Fellow, Courtauld Inst. of Art, 2007. Chevalier de Tastevin, 1981. *Recreations:* gardening, shooting. *Address:* Great Sarratt Hall, Sarratt, Rickmansworth, Herts WD3 4PD.

NEAL, Michael David; Headmaster, Cranborne Chase School, 1969–83; *b* 27 Jan. 1927; *s* of David Neal, FCA; *m* 1952, Barbara Lisette, *d* of late Harold Carter, MA; two *s* two *d*. *Educ:* Winchester; University Coll., Oxford (BA); BSc Open Univ. 1996. Rifle Bde, 1945–48 (Captain); Asst Master, RNC Dartmouth, 1952–54; Eton Coll., 1954–69 (Housemaster, 1963–69). Mem., Eton UDC, 1960–63. *Address:* Wegnall's Mill, Presteigne, Powys LD8 2LD. *T:* (01544) 267012.

NEAL, Morton; *see* Neal, H. M.

NEALE, Sir Gerrard Anthony, (Sir Gerry), Kt 1990; *b* 25 June 1941; *s* of Charles Woodhouse Neale and Phyllis Muriel Neale; *m* 1965, Deirdre Elizabeth McCann; one *s* two *d*. Councillor, Borough of Milton Keynes, 1973–79, Mayor, 1976–77. Chm., Buckingham Constituency Cons. Assoc., 1974–76. Contested (C) N Cornwall, Oct. 1974, 1992; MP (C) N Cornwall, 1979–92. PPS to Minister for Consumer Affairs, 1981–82, to Minister of State for Trade, 1981–83, to Sec. of State for Transport, 1985–86, to Sec. of State for the Environment, 1986–87, to Sec. of State for Defence, 1987–89. *Recreations:* sailing, golf, painting.

NEALE, Gordon William, OBE 2002; Chief Executive, Disability Sport England, since 1998; *b* 10 April 1945; *s* of William and Lily Neale; *m* 2000, Elizabeth (*née* Irvine); one *s* one *d*. *Educ:* Beechfield Secondary Sch.; North London Univ. HM Forces, 1960–86 (GSM, Borneo, Malaya, NI; UN medal); Sport Develt Officer: Lee Valley Regl Park, 1986–88; English Volleyball Assoc., 1988–90; Disability Sport England, 1990–. Co-ordinator, London Wheelchair Marathon, 1993–. Mem., Commonwealth Games Cttee, 2001–. Trustee, Swimathon Foundn, 2000–. Silver Jubilee Medal, 1977. *Recreations:* volleyball, swimming, cycling, disability sport. *Address:* 30 Holly Avenue, Whitley Bay, Tyne and Wear NE26 1ED. *T:* (0191) 252 0165, *Fax:* (0191) 251 3303; *e-mail:* mrgneale@btinternet.com. *Club:* Marden Bridge Volleyball.

NEALE, Gregory David; Editor at large, BBC History Magazine, since 2004 (Founding Editor, 2000–04); *b* 1 May 1954; *s* of Laurence Edwin Neale and Jean Alicia Neale (*née* Gilbert). *Educ:* Birkbeck Coll., London (BA Hons Hist.); Pembroke Coll., Oxford (MSt Modern Hist.). Work on newspapers, including: The Times, 1982–86; Daily Telegraph, 1987–89; Sunday Telegraph, 1989–99. Editor of the Year, BSME, 2000, 2002. *Publication:* The Green Travel Guide, 1998, 2nd edn 1999. *Recreations:* reading, walking, thinking about gardening. *Clubs:* BBC; Sutton United Supporters.

NEALE, Rt Rev. John Robert Geoffrey, AKC; Hon. Assistant Bishop, Dioceses of Bath and Wells, and of Bristol, since 1991; *b* 21 Sept. 1926; *s* of late Geoffrey Brockman Neale and Stella Beatrice (*née* Wild). *Educ:* Felsted Sch.; King's Coll., London Univ. Served War of 1939–45: Lieut RA; Army, 1944–48. Business, G. B. Neale & Co. Ltd, EC2, 1948–51. King's Coll. London, 1951–55 (Jelf Prize, 1954). Deacon, 1955, priest, 1956; Curate, St Peter, St Helier, Dio. of Southwark, 1955–58. Chaplain, Ardingly Coll., Sussex, 1958–63; Recruitment Sec., CACTM (ACCM), 1963–67; Archbishops' Rep. for ordination candidates, 1967–68; Canon Missioner, Dio. of Guildford, Hon. Canon of Guildford Cath. and Rector of Hascombe, Surrey, 1968–74; Suffragan Bishop (later Area Bishop) of Ramsbury, 1974–88; Hon. Canon of Salisbury Cathedral, 1974–88; Archdeacon of Wilts, 1974–80; Sec., Partnership for World Mission, 1989–91; Hon. Asst Bishop, Dio. of Gloucester, 1996–2004. FIC 1991. *Publication:* Ember Prayer, 1965. *Recreation:* horticulture. *Address:* 26 Prospect, Corsham, Wilts SN13 9AF. *T:* (01249) 712557.

NEALE, Keith Douglas; Chairman, Privatised Pension Trust, since 1997; independent adviser to pension funds, since 2002; *b* 27 March 1947; *s* of Douglas Jeffrey and Dorothy Neale; *m* 1969, Mary Williamson; one *s* one *d*. East Midlands Electricity Board, 1964; Trainee Accountant, Blackwell RDC, 1965; County Treasurer's Dept, Lindsey CC, Lincs, 1968; Asst Dir of Finance, Humberside CC, 1974; Dep. County Treasurer, 1982–87, County Treasurer, 1987–2002, Essex; Treasurer: Essex Police Authy, 1995–2002; Essex Fire Authy, 1998–2002. Treasurer: E Anglia Tourist Bd, 1987–96; E of England Tourist Bd, 1996–2006. Pres., Soc. of County Treasurers, 1998–99 (Hon. Sec., 1991–97; Vice-Pres., 1997–98); Advr, Policy Cttee, ACC, 1993–97. Member: CIPFA (Mem., Pensions (formerly Superannuation) Panel, 1994–); UK Steering Cttee on Local Govt Pensions (formerly Superannuation), 1991–2002; Cttee, Nat. Assoc. of Pension Funds Investment, 1995–2000; Public Sector and Not-for-Profit Cttee, Accounting Standards Bd, 1999–2002. Freeman, City of London, 1999. *Address:* Moorfield House, 14 Hay Green, Danbury, Essex CM3 4NU. *T:* (01245) 221497.

NEALE, Kenneth James, OBE 1959; FSA; consultant; author and lecturer; Assistant Under Secretary of State, Home Office, 1976–82; *b* 9 June 1922; *s* of late James Edward and Elsie Neale; *m* 1943, Dorothy Willett; three *s* one *d*. *Educ:* Hackney Downs (Grocers') Sch., London. Entered Civil Service as Clerical Officer, Tithe Redemption Commn, 1939. Lieut, RNVR, 1941–46. Exec. Officer, Min. of Nat. Insce, 1947–51; Asst Princ., 1951–55, Principal, 1955–64, Colonial Office; Sec. for Interior and Local Govt, Cyprus, 1957; Dep. Admin Sec., Cyprus, 1958–59; Central African Office, 1962–64; Asst Sec., Commonwealth Office, and Counsellor, Diplomatic Service, 1964–67; Home Office: Asst Sec., 1967–70; Dir, Industries and Supply, 1970–75; Controller, Planning and Develt, 1976–80; Dir, Regimes and Services, 1980–82. Member: Prisons Bd, 1967–69, 1976–82; European Cttee on Crime Problems, 1976–84; Council of Europe Steering Gp on Reform of the Russian Prison System, 1995–2001; Chairman: Council of Europe Select Cttee on Standard Minimum Rules for Treatment of Prisoners, 1978–80; Council of Europe Cttee for Co-operation in Prison Affairs, 1981–84; Consultant: Prison Service Coll., 1982–90; Council of Europe, 1984–2001; Open Univ., 1990–93. Chairman: Essex Archaeol and Historical Congress, 1984–87 (Pres., 1987–90); Sampfords Soc., 1984–2004; Friends of Historic Essex, 1986–2002 (Vice Pres., 2002–); Member: Council, Essex Soc. for Archaeol. and Hist. (formerly Essex Archaeol Soc.), 1984–87; Library, Museum and Records Cttee, Essex CC, 1986–96; Essex Adv. Bd, Victoria County Hist., 2002–; President: Chingford Hist. Soc., 1971–89; Saffron Walden Hist. Soc., 2000–. Mem. Editl Bd, Essex Jl, 1989–2002. *Publications:* Discovering Essex in London, 1970, 2nd edn 1986; Victorian Horsham, 1975; Work in Penal Institutions, 1976; Essex in History, 1977, 2nd edn 1997; Her Majesty's Commissioners, 1978; (ed) Strategies for Education within Prison Regimes, 1986; (ed) An Essex Tribute, 1987; (contrib.) Imprisonment: European perspectives, 1991; (ed) Essex Heritage, 1992; (ed) Prison Service People, 1993; (ed jtly) Essex Wills 1558–1603, vols 8–12, 1993–2000; (ed) Essex: 'full of profitable thinges', 1996; Heritage Sampford: community archaeology, historical research and landscape evaluation, 2007; various articles and papers on local history, archaeology, natural history, penology. *Recreations:* reading, local history, archaeology, natural history. *Address:* Honeysuckle Cottage, Great Sampford, Saffron Walden, Essex CB10 2RW. *T:* (01799) 586304.

NEALE, Mark Frost; Managing Director, Budget, Tax and Welfare, HM Treasury, since 2005; *b* 7 July 1957; *s* of Sir Alan (Derrett) Neale, KCB, MBE and Joan Neale (*née* Frost); *m* 1988, Xanthe Waddington Lunghi; one *s* one *d*. *Educ:* Queen's Coll., Oxford (BA 1st Cl. Hons Modern Hist. 1979). CSD, 1980–83; DES, then DFE, 1983–95; HM Treasury, 1995–98; Head, Structural Unemployment Policy Div., DFEE, 1998–2000; Dir, Finance and Commercial and Corporate Services, Employment Service, 2000–01; Dir, Children, Poverty and Housing Costs, then Children and Housing, DWP, 2001–03; Dir Gen., Security, Internat. and Organised Crime, Home Office, 2003–05. *Recreation:* playing with the children. *Address:* HM Treasury, 1 Horseguards Road, SW1A 2HQ. *Club:* Reform.

NEALE, Michael Cooper, CB 1987; FIMechE, FRAeS; *b* 2 Dec. 1929; *s* of late Frank and Edith Kathleen Neale; *m* 1956, Thelma Weare; one *s* two *d*. *Educ:* West Bridgford Grammar Sch., Nottingham; Queen Mary Coll., Univ. of London (BScEng 1st cl. Hons; MScEng). Postgraduate research on fuel injection in diesel engines, 1951–53; Engr Officer, Royal Air Force, 1953–56; joined Civil Service, 1956; Aeroplane and Armament Experimental Estabt, Boscombe Down, 1956–58; joined Nat. Gas Turbine Estabt, Pyestock, 1958; Asst Director of Engine Develt, MoD Headquarters, 1971; Dep. Director (R&D), Nat. Gas Turbine Estabt, 1973–80; Dir Gen. Engines (PE), MoD, 1980–87; Sec., Royal Commn for Exhibn of 1851, 1987–94; non-exec. dir of cos and industrial consultant, 1988–96. Hon. Treas., Castleton Church, Dorset, 2002–08. Silver medallist, RAeS, 1987. *Publications:* papers in Aeronautical Research Council reports and memoranda series and elsewhere in the technical press, mainly concerning engines. *Recreations:* old railways, cricket. *Address:* Quill Cottage, 32 Hound Street, Sherborne, Dorset DT9 3AA. *T:* (01935) 814332. *Clubs:* Athenæum, Royal Over-Seas League; Somerset CC, Dorset CC.

NEAME, Robert Harry Beale, CBE 1999; DL; President, Shepherd Neame Ltd, brewers, since 2006 (Chairman, 1971–2005); *b* 25 Feb. 1934; *s* of Jasper Beale Neame and Violet Evelyn Neame; *m* 1st, Sally Elizabeth Corben; one *s* two *d* (and one *s* decd); 2nd, 1974, Yvonne Mary Mackenzie; one *d*. *Educ:* Harrow (Head of School). Joined Shepherd Neame, 1956; Dir, 1957–2006. SE Regl Dir, National Westminster Bank, 1982–92; Dir, SE Adv. Bd, Royal Insurance Co., 1988–2000; Director: Folkestone Racecourse, 1985– (Chm., 1988–99); Marr Taverns PLC, 1992–96; non-executive Director: Mendocino Brewing Co. (USA), 1998–2004; Merrydown plc, 1998–2004. Chairman: SE England Tourist Bd, 1979–90 (Vice-Pres., 1990–2003); Gatwick Airport Consultative Cttee, 1990–95; Member: SE RHA, 1977–78; Canterbury and Thanet RHA, 1990–94; Inland Waterways Amenities Adv. Council, 1992–98. Chairman, British Section: IULA, 1986–89; CEMR, 1986–89; Vice Chm., Consultative Council of Regl and Local Authorities, 1989. Mem. (C) for Faversham, Kent CC, 1965–89 (Leader, 1982–84). Pres., Kent CCC, 2003–04. DL 1992, High Sheriff, 2001, Kent. *Recreations:* cricket, squash, rackets (Army Rackets Champion, 1954), golf, shooting, ski-ing. *Address:* Dane Court Farmhouse, Kits Hill, Selling, Faversham, Kent ME13 9QP. *T:* (01227) 752284. *Clubs:* Press; MCC, Free Foresters, I Zingari, Band of Brothers, Butterflies; Kandahar Ski; Escorts, Jesters; Royal St George's Golf (Sandwich).

NEAME, Ronald, CBE 1996; film producer and director; *b* 23 April 1911; *s* of Elwin Neame and Ivy Close; *m* 1933, Beryl Yolanda Heanly (marr. diss. 1992; she *d* 1999); one *s*; *m* 1993, Donna Bernice Friedberg. *Educ:* University College School; Hurstpierpoint College. Entered film industry, 1928; became Chief Cameraman, 1934. In charge of production on: In Which We Serve, This Happy Breed, Blithe Spirit, Brief Encounter, 1942–45; produced: Great Expectations, Oliver Twist, The Magic Box; directed: Take My Life, The Card, 1945–51; The Million Pound Note, 1953; The Man Who Never Was, 1954; Windom's Way, 1957; The Horse's Mouth, 1958; Tunes of Glory, 1960; I Could Go On Singing, 1962; The Chalk Garden, 1963; Mr Moses, 1964; Gambit, 1966; The Prime of Miss Jean Brodie, 1968; Scrooge, 1970; The Poseidon Adventure, 1972; Odessa File, 1973; Meteor, 1978; Hopscotch, 1979; First Monday in October, 1980; Foreign Body, 1985; The Magic Balloon, 1989. *Publication:* Straight from the Horse's Mouth: an autobiography, 2003. *Address:* 2317 Kimridge, Beverly Hills, CA 90210, USA.

NEARS, Colin Gray, CBE 1998; television producer; Member of Council, and Chairman of Advisory Panel on Dance, Arts Council of Great Britain, 1982–90; *b* 19 March 1933; *s* of William Charles Nears and Winifred Mildred Nears (*née* Gray). *Educ:* Ipswich Sch.; King's Coll., Cambridge (MA). Admin. Asst, RIBA, 1956; BBC, 1958–87; Producer: Schools Television, 1960; Music and Arts, 1967; Editor, Review, 1971–72. Author and director of programmes on literature, the visual arts, music and dance. Director: Royal Opera House, 1995–98 (Mem., 1990–98, Dep. Chm., 1991–98, Ballet Bd); Birmingham Royal Ballet Bd, 1993–2002 (Chm., 1993–99); Gov., Royal Ballet Sch., 1993–2000; Trustee: Royal Ballet Benevolent Fund, 1992–; Dancers' Resettlement Fund, subseq. Dancers' Career Develt, 1991–; Member Board: Riverside Trust, 1991–93; Rambert Dance Co., 1993–2001. FRSA. BAFTA award for Best Specialised Programme, 1973; Prix Italia music prize, 1982. *Recreations:* reading, gardening, painting. *Address:* 16 Ashchurch Terrace, W12 9SL. *T:* (020) 8749 3615.

NEARY, Ian James, DPhil; Lecturer in Japanese Politics, Nissan Institute of Japanese Studies, University of Oxford, since 2004; Fellow, St Antony's College, Oxford, since 2004; *b* 9 July 1951; *s* of Kenneth and Joan Neary; *m* 1979, Suzuko Anai; one *s* one *d*. *Educ:* King Edward VII Grammar Sch., Sheffield; Sheffield Univ. (BA); Kyushu Univ.; Sussex Univ. (DPhil). Lecturer: Dept of Hist. and Politics, Huddersfield Poly., 1979–84; Dept of Politics, Newcastle Univ., 1984–89; Prof. of Japanese Politics, Dept of Government, Essex Univ., 1989–2004. Pres., British Assoc. Japanese Studies, 1991–94. *Publications:* Politics, Protest and Social Control: origins of Buraku liberation, 1989; (with J. Howells) Intervention and Technological Innovation: government and the pharmaceutical industry in the UK and Japan, 1995; Human Rights in Japan, S Korea and Taiwan, 2002; The State and Politics in Japan, 2002; articles on Japan and human rights in Japan Forum, Social Res., etc. *Recreations:* running, brewing and drinking beer, gardening. *Address:* Nissan Institute of Japanese Studies, 27 Winchester Road, Oxford OX2 6NA. *T:* (01865) 274570, *Fax:* (01865) 274574.

NEARY, Prof. (James) Peter, DPhil; FBA 2008; Professor of Economics, University of Oxford, since 2006; Fellow, Merton College, Oxford, since 2006; *b* Drogheda, Ireland, 11 Feb. 1950; *s* of late Peter Austin Neary and of Anne Rosemary Neary (*née* Loughran); *m* 1st, 1972, Frances Ruane (marr. diss. 1997); two *s*; 2nd, 1997, Mairéad Hanrahan; two *d*. *Educ:* Christian Brothers, Drogheda; Clongowes Wood Coll.; University Coll., Dublin (BA 1970; MA 1971); Univ. of Oxford (MPhil 1976; DPhil 1978). Res. Asst, Econ. and Soc. Res. Inst., Dublin, 1970–72; Trinity College, Dublin: Asst Lectr, 1972–74; Lectr, 1978–80; Fellow, 1980; Heyworth Res. Fellow, Nuffield Coll., Oxford, 1976–78; Prof. of Political Economy, University Coll., Dublin, 1980–2006. Visiting Scholar: MIT, 1978; Inst. for Internat. Econ. Studies, Stockholm, 1979; Internat. Inst. for Applied Systems Analysis, Laxenburg, 1981; Visiting Professor: Princeton Univ., 1980; Univ. of Calif, Berkeley, 1982; Queen's Univ., Ont., 1986–88; Univ. of Ulster, Jordanstown, 1992–93; Ecole Polytechnique, Paris, 1999–2000. Co-Editor, Jl of Internat. Economics, 1980–83; Associate Editor: Economic Jl, 1981–85; Econometrica, 1984–87; Rev. of Economic Studies, 1984–93; Economica, 1996–2000; Ed., European Economic Rev., 1986–90. Fellow: Centre for Econ. Policy Res., 1983; Econometric Soc., 1987 (Mem. Council, 1994–99); Member: Council, Royal Econ. Soc., 1984–89, 1992–97; Eur. Econ. Assoc., 1985–92 (Pres., 2002; Fellow, 2004); President: Irish Econ. Assoc., 1990–92 Internat. Trade and Finance Soc., 1999–2000; Econs Section, BAAS, 2005. MAE 1989; Mem., RIA, 1997. Gold Medal in Soc. Scis, RIA, 2006. *Publications:* Measuring the Restrictiveness of International Trade Policy (with J. E. Anderson), 2005; (ed jtly) Natural Resources and the Macroeconomy, 1986; (ed jtly) Theory, Policy and Dynamics in International Trade, 1993; (ed) Readings in International Trade, 1995; over 100 articles, mainly on internat. economics. *Recreations:* family, travel, reading, music. *Address:* Department of Economics, Manor Road Building, Oxford OX1 3UQ.

NEARY, Martin Gerard James, LVO 1998; conductor and organist; Organist and Master of the Choristers, Westminster Abbey, 1988–98; Conductor, Millennium Consort Singers, since 2007; *b* 28 March 1940; *s* of late Leonard Walter Neary and of Jeanne Marguerite (*née* Thébault); *m* 1967, Penelope Jane, *d* of Sir Brian Warren and Dame Josephine Barnes, DBE; one *s* two *d*. *Educ:* HM Chapels Royal, St James's Palace; City of London Sch.; Gonville and Caius Coll., Cambridge (Organ Schol.; MA Theol. and Music). FRCO. Organist, St Mary's, Hornsey Rise, 1958; St Margaret's, Westminster: Asst Organist, 1963–65; Organist and Master of Music, 1965–71; Prof. of Organ, Trinity Coll., London, 1963–72; Organist and Master of Music, Winchester Cathedral, 1972–87. Organ Advr to dio. of Winchester, 1975–87. Conductor, Twickenham Musical Soc., 1966–72; Founder and Conductor: St Margaret's Westminster Singers, 1967–71; English Chamber Singers; Conductor, Waynflete Singers, 1972–88; Dir, Southern Cathedrals Festival, 1972, 1975, 1978, 1981, 1984, 1987; Conductor, Aspen Music Festival, 1980; Artistic Dir, Paulist Choristers of California, 1999–2003; Dir of Music, First Congregational Ch of LA, 2001–02; Guest Conductor: Australian Youth Choir, 1999–; BBC Singers; Netherlands Chamber Choir. Consultant, Millennium Youth Choir, RSCM, 1999–2001. President: Cathedral Organists' Assoc., 1985–88; RCO, 1988–90, 1996–98 (Mem. Council, 1982–; a Vice-Pres., 1990–96); Organists' Benevolent League, 1988–; John Carpenter Club, 1997–98; Chairman: Church Services Cttee, Musicians Benevolent Fund, 1993–99; Herbert Howells Soc., 1993–. Many organ recitals and broadcasts in UK, incl. Royal Festival Hall; has conducted many premières of music by British composers incl. John Tavener's Ultimos Ritos, 1979, and Akathist, 1988, Jonathan Harvey's Hymn, 1979, and Passion and Resurrection, 1981; conducted John Tavener's Veil of the Temple, Holland Fest., 2005; with Martin Neary Singers perf. madrigals and graces at 10 Downing Street, 1970–74. Toured US and Canada, 1963, 1968, 1971, 1973, 1975, 1977, 1979, 1982, 1984, 1986, 1988, 1992, 1996, appearances incl. Carnegie Hall, Lincoln Center, Kennedy Center, Roy Thomson Hall; many European tours, including Russia, 1994, Ukraine, 1996; BBC Promenade Concerts, incl. organ soloist on First Night, 2004; sometime Conductor with: ECO; LSO; BBCSO; Bournemouth SO and Sinfonietta; Acad. of Ancient Music; Winchester Baroque Ensemble; Orch. of the Age of Enlightenment; Arts Council Contemporary Music Network Tour, 1993; many recordings, incl. Purcell, Music for Queen Mary, and Tavener, Akathist. FRSCM 1997. Hon. FTCL 1969; Hon. RAM 1988. Hon. DMus Southampton, 1997. Hon. Citizen of Texas, 1971. Prizewinner, St Alban's Internat. Organ Festival, 1963; Conducting Scholarship, Berkshire Music Center, USA, 1963; Diploma, J. S. Bach Competn, Leipzig, 1968; UK/USA Bicentennial Fellow, 1979–80; Artist-in-residence, Univ. of California at Davis, 1984, 2007. *Compositions* include: What is Man?; May the grace of Christ (Nat. Anthem arr.); All Saints Mass, 2004; responses, descants, carol and hymn arrangements, incl. Make me a channel of your peace. *Publications:* edns of early organ music; contribs to organ jls. *Recreation:* watching cricket. *Address:* 44 Radipole Road, Fulham, SW6 5DL. *T:* and *Fax:* (020) 7736 5268; *e-mail:* martin@mneary.co.uk. *Club:* Garrick.

NEARY, Most Rev. Michael; *see* Tuam, Archbishop of, (RC).

NEARY, Peter; *see* Neary, J. P.

NEATH, Gavin Ellis, CBE 2007; Senior Vice President, Global Communications, Unilever plc, since 2008; *b* 5 April 1953; *s* of Ronald William Neath and Frances Gillian Neath; *m* 2006, Ann; three *d*. *Educ:* Univ. of Manchester; Univ. of Warwick; Stanford Univ. BA American Studies; MSc Mgt Scis. Unilever: graduate trainee, 1977; Mktg Dir, Lever France, 1985–90; Category Dir Laundry, Lever Europe, 1990–94; Man. Dir, Lever Ponds (SA), 1994–98; Chm., Unilever Bestfoods UK, 1998–2004; Chm., 2004–06, Nat. Manager, 2006–08, Unilever UK. Pres., Food and Drink Fedn, 2005–07. Mem. Develt Bd, Royal Court Th., 2005–08. FIGD. Dep. Chm., St Margaret's Film Club. *Recreations:* theatre, cinema, cricket, Rugby. *Address:* Unilever plc, 100 Victoria Embankment, Blackfriars, EC4Y 0DY. *T:* (020) 7822 5252; *e-mail:* gavin.neath@unilever.com.

NEAVE, Julius Arthur Sheffield, CBE 1978 (MBE (mil.) 1945); JP; DL; General Manager, since 1966, Director since 1977, Mercantile & General Reinsurance Co. Ltd (Managing Director, 1980–82); *b* 17 July 1919; *s* of Col Richard Neave and Helen Mary Elizabeth (*née* Miller); *m* 1951, Helen Margery, *d* of Col P. M. Acton-Adams, DSO, Clarence Reserve, Marlborough, NZ; three *d*. *Educ:* Sherborne School. Joined Mercantile & General Reinsurance Co. Ltd, 1938. Served War, 1939–46: called as Territorial, commnd 13th/18th Royal Hussars, Adjt 3 years, final rank Major (despatches 1945). Returned to Mercantile & General, 1946; Asst Gen. Manager, 1964. Dir, Prudential Corp., 1982–92. (First) Chairman, Reinsurance Offices Assoc., 1969–74, Hon. Pres., 1974–82; Chm., Reinsurance Panel, British Insce Assoc., 1971–82; representative, Gt Britain: Cttee, annual internat. meeting of reinsurers, Monte Carlo, 1969–82; Vice-Pres., Assoc. Internat. pour l'Etude de l'Assurance, Geneva, 1976–83, Pres., 1983. Dir and Governor, Internat. Insce Seminars, 1977–82 (Founder's Gold Medal, 1977); President: Insce Inst. of London, 1976–77, 1983–84; Chartered Insce Inst., 1983–84 (Mem. Council, 1975–); Mem. Court, Insurers' Co., 1979– (Master, 1984–85). Hon. Fellow, RSA, 1975. Essex: JP (Brentwood), 1975; DL, 1983; High Sheriff, 1987–88. OStJ 1988. *Publications:* Speaking of Reinsurance, 1980; Still Speaking of Reinsurance, 1983. *Recreations:* shooting, fishing, golf, needlework. *Address:* Mill Green Park, Ingatestone, Essex CM4 0JB. *T:* (01277) 353036. *Club:* Cavalry and Guards.

NEAVE, Sir Paul (Arundell), 7th Bt *cr* 1795, of Dagnam Park, Essex; Divisional Director, Carr Sheppards Crosthwaite; *b* 13 Dec. 1948; *s* of Sir Arundell Thomas Clifton Neave, 6th Bt and Richenda Alice Ione (*d* 1994), *d* of Sir Robert Joshua Paul, 5th Bt; *S* father, 1992; *m* 1976, Coralie Jane Louise, *e d* of Sir Robin Kinahan, ERD; two *s*. *Educ:* Eton. Mem., Stock Exchange, 1980; formerly Dir, Henderson Crosthwaite Ltd. *Heir:* *s* Frederick Paul Kinahan Neave, *b* 25 Jan. 1981. *Address:* Queen's House, Monk Sherborne, Hants RG26 5HH.

NEBHRAJANI, Sharmila; Chief Operating Officer, BBC Future Media and Technology, since 2000; *b* 30 March 1966; *d* of Vir and Jayantee Nebhrajani. *Educ:* City of London Sch. for Girls; St Anne's Coll., Oxford (BA 1st Cl. Physiolog. Scis 1988). Mem. ICAEW 1991. Mgt Consultant, Coopers & Lybrand, 1988–93; Strategic Planning Manager, Cable & Wireless, 1993–95; Asst Dir, Corporate Finance, Price Waterhouse, 1995–96; Hd, Corporate Planning, BBC, 1996–2000. Vice Chm., Human Fertilisation and Embryology Authy, 1998–; Mem., Olympic Lottery Distributor, 2006–; a Charity Comr, 2007–. Yale World Fellow, 2007. FRSA 2006. *Address:* BBC Broadcast Centre, 201 Wood Lane, W12 7TP.

NEEDHAM, family name of **Earl of Kilmorey**.

NEEDHAM, Phillip; Chief Executive, ADAS Group (formerly ADAS Agency), 1995–2000; *b* 21 April 1940; *s* of Ephraim and Mabel Jessie Needham; *m* 1962, Patricia Ann (*née* Farr); two *s* two *d*. *Educ:* Dunstable Grammar Sch.; Univ. of Birmingham (BSc); Imperial Coll., London Univ. (MSc, DIC). National Agricultural Advisory Service, subseq. Agricultural Development and Advisory Service, MAFF: Soil Scientist, 1961; Regional Soil Scientist, Reading, 1979; Hd of Soil Science, London, 1982; Sen. Agricl Scientist, 1985; Dep. Dir of R&D, 1987; Dir, Farm and Countryside Service and Commercial Dir, 1988–92; Dir of Ops, 1992–95. *Publications:* contribs to books and jls on various aspects of crop nutrition and soil science. *Address:* 58 Harpsden Road, Henley-on-Thames, Oxon RG9 1EG.

NEEDHAM, Rt Hon. Sir Richard; *see* Kilmorey, Earl of.

NEEDLE, Clive John; independent public policy advisor, since 1999; Director, EuroHealthNet (formerly European Network of Health Promoting Agencies), Brussels, since 2000. *Educ:* Southend High Sch.; Aston Univ. MEP (Lab) Norfolk, 1994–99; contested (Lab) Eastern Region, 1999, 2004. Chm., EU/EC Mental Health Platform, 2005–. Columnist, Eastern Daily Press, 2004–. *Address:* 37 Kingsey Road, Norwich, Norfolk NR1 3RB.

NEEL, Janet; *see* Baroness Cohen of Pimlico.

NEELY, William Robert Nicholas; International Editor, ITN, since 2002; *b* 21 May 1959; *s* of late William John Neely and of Patricia (*née* Larney); *m* 1988, Marion Kerr; two *d*. *Educ:* St Malachy's Coll., Belfast; Queen's Univ., Belfast (BA Jt Hons Eng. Lit. and Hist.). Reporter: BBC NI, 1981–86; BBC Network, 1987–88; Sky News, Jan.–June 1989; ITN, 1989–90; Washington Correspondent, 1991–97, Europe Correspondent, 1997–2002, ITN. *Address:* c/o ITN, 200 Gray's Inn Road, WC1X 8XZ.

NEESON, Liam; *see* Neeson, W. J.

NEESON, Séan; Member (Alliance) Antrim East, Northern Ireland Assembly, since 1998; *b* 6 Feb. 1946; *s* of Patrick and Mary Neeson; *m* 1978, Carol Henderson; two *s* two *d*. *Educ:* Queen's Univ., Belfast (BA); St Joseph's Coll. of Educn, Belfast (Postgrad. Dip. in Educn 1968); Univ. of Ulster, Jordanstown (Postgrad. Dip. in Mktg 1988). Teacher, Head of History Dept, St Comgall's High Sch., Larne, 1968–85; marketing and PR consultant, 1988–98. Mem. (Alliance) Carrickfergus Council, 1977–; Mayor of Carrickfergus, 1993–94; Mem., NI Assembly, 1982–86. Leader, Alliance Party of NI, 1998–2001. Representative for NI: on Congress of Local and Regl Authorities in Europe, 2002; on Nat. Adv. Cttee on Historic Ships, 2007. Mem. Bd, Nat. Museums and Galleries (NI), 1998–2008. *Publications:* articles on maritime heritage in jls. *Recreation:* study of British and Irish maritime heritage. *Address:* 44 Milebush Park, Carrickfergus, Co. Antrim BT38 7QR. *T:* (028) 9336 4105, (office) (028) 9052 1314.

NEESON, William John, (Liam), OBE 2000; actor; *b* Ballymena, NI, 7 June 1952; *s* of late Barney Neeson and of Katherine Neeson; *m* 1994, Natasha Jane Richardson, *qv*; two *s*. Winner, NI Youth Heavyweight Boxing Championship. *Theatre* includes: The Risen, Lyric Players' Theatre, Belfast, 1976; Of Mice and Men, Abbey Theatre, Dublin; The Informer, Dublin Theatre Fest.; Translations, NT; The Plough and the Stars, Royal Exchange, Manchester; Anna Christie, Broadway, 1993; The Judas Kiss, Playhouse Theatre, 1998; The Crucible, Broadway, 2002; *films* include: Excalibur, 1981; Krull, 1983; The Bounty, 1984; Duet for One, Lamb, The Mission, 1986; A Prayer for the Dying, Suspect, 1987; The Dead Pool, The Good Mother, 1988; Darkman, Crossing the Line (retitled The Big Man, 1991), 1990; Shining Through, Under Suspicion, Leap of Faith, Husbands and Wives, 1992; Ethan Frome, 1993; Schindler's List, Nell, 1994; Rob Roy, 1995; Before and After, Michael Collins (Best Actor Award, Venice Film Fest.), 1996; Les Misérables, 1998; Star Wars Episode One: the Phantom Menace, The Haunting, 1999; Gangs of New York, K-19: The Widowmaker, 2002; Love Actually, 2003; Kinsey, Kingdom of Heaven, Batman Begins, 2005; Breakfast at Pluto, 2006; Seraphim Falls, 2007; *television* includes: Arthur the King; Miami Vice; A Woman of Substance; Hold the Dream; Next of Kin; Sweet As You Are.

NEGARA BRUNEI DARUSSALAM, HM Sultan of; Hassanal Bolkiah Mu'izzaddin Waddaulah, DKMB, DK, PSSUB, DPKG, DPKT, PSPNB, PSNB, PSLJ, SPMB, PANB; Hon. GCMG; DMN, DK (Kelantan), DK (Johor), DK (Negeri Sembilan), DK (Pahang); Ruler of Negara Brunei Darussalam (formerly Brunei), since 1967; Prime Minister, Negara Brunei Darussalam, since its independence, Jan. 1984; Minister of Defence, since 1986 (Finance and Home Affairs Minister, 1984–86); *b* 15 July 1946; *s* of Sultan Sir Muda Omar 'Ali Saifuddien Sa'adul Khairi Waddien, DKMB, DK, GCVO, KCMG, PSSUB, PHBS, PBLI (*d* 1986); *m* 1st, 1965, Rajah Isteri Anak Saleha; two *s* four *d*; *m* 1981, Pengiran Isteri Hajjah Mariam (marr. diss. 2003); two *s* two *d*; *m* 2005, Azrinaz Mazhar Hakim. *Educ:* Victoria Inst., Kuala Lumpur; RMA Sandhurst (Hon. Captain, Coldstream Guards, 1968; Hon. General 1984). Collar of the Supreme Order of the Chrysanthemum; Grand Order of Mugunghwa. *Address:* Istana Nurul Iman, Bandar Seri Begawan, Negara Brunei Darussalam.

NEGUS, Her Honour Norma Florence, (Mrs D. J. Turner-Samuels); a Circuit Judge, 1990–97; *b* 31 July 1932; *d* of late George David Shellabear and Kate (*née* Calvert); *m* 1st, 1956, Richard Negus (marr. diss. 1960); 2nd, 1976, David Jessel Turner-Samuels, *qv*. *Educ:* Malvern Girls' Coll., Malvern, Worcs. Fashion promotion and advertising in UK, Canada and USA, 1950–61; Merchandise Editor, Harper's Bazaar, 1962–63; Asst Promotion Manager, Vogue and House & Garden, 1963–65; Unit Manager, Trends Merchandising and Fashion Promotion Unit, 1965–67; Export Marketing Manager and Advertising Manager, Glenoit (UK) Ltd, 1967–68. Called to the Bar, Gray's Inn, 1970; Mem., Middle Temple, 1984. In practice on SE Circuit, 1971–84; a Metropolitan Stipendiary Magistrate, 1984–90; a Recorder, 1987–90. Member: Parole Bd, 1991–94; Mental Health Review Tribunal, 1996–97. Mem., Central Criminal Court Bar Mess, 1978–84. *Recreations:* reading, writing, theatre, music, travel, swimming. *Address:* c/o Cloisters, 1 Pump Court, Temple, EC4Y 7AA.

NEGUS, Richard; consultant designer; Senior Partner, Negus & Negus, 1967–87; *b* 29 Aug. 1927; *s* of Bertie and Kate Negus; *m* 1949, Pamela Wheatcroft-Hancock (*d* 2000); two *s* one *d*. *Educ:* Battersea Grammar Sch.; Camberwell Sch. of Arts and Crafts. FSTD. Staff designer, Festival of Britain, 1948–51; Partner, Negus & Sharland, 1951–67; Lecturer, Central Sch. of Art, 1951–53. Consultant to: Cotton Board Design Centre, 1960–67; BNEC, 1969–75; British Airways, 1973–84, 1990–; Pakistan Airlines, 1975–79 and 1989–92; Rank Organisation, 1979–86; City of Westminster, 1973–75; National Exhibition Centre, 1974–77; Lloyds Bank, 1972–75; Godfrey Davis, 1971–80; John Laing, 1970–73; Andry Montgomery, 1967–; Celltech, 1980–83; Vickers Ltd, 1980–83; SDP, 1981–88; Historic Buildings and Monuments Commn, 1984–93; Nat. Maritime Mus., 1984–; Royal Armouries, 1984–; The Emirates (Airline), 1985–88; Tower of London, 1986–91; Science Museum, 1987–92; Northern Foods, 1986–91; Waterford/Wedgwood, 1987; DoE Royal Parks, 1987–88; Nature Conservation Council, 1987–89; John Lewis Partnership, 1987–89; Nat. Theatre, 1989–91; Internat. Youth Hostels, 1989; Dubai Tourist Bd, 1990–95; Blue Circle Properties, 1990–92. Member: Design Council Poster Awards Cttee, 1970–72; PO Stamps Adv. Cttee, 1977–2002; CNAA, 1980–85; Design Council, 1981–86; Art and Design Cttee, Technician Educn Council, 1981–86. Advisor, Norwich Sch. of Art, 1969–71; External Assessor: Birmingham and Bradford Colls of Art, 1969–73; Medway Coll. of Design, 1989–95; Governor: Camberwell Sch. of Art, 1964–78; Chelsea Sch. of Art, 1977–85; Mem. Court, RCA, 1979–82. PPCSD (Pres., SIAD, 1977–79, Vice Pres. 1966–68). Hon. RCM 1995. *Publications:* Designing for Export Printing, 1972; Display of Text in Museums, 1989; contribs to: Design Mag., The Designer, Graphis, Gebrauchgraphick, Architectural Review, Rolls Royce Mag., Creative Review, Art and Artists. *Recreations:* painting, the countryside, sailing. *Address:* 73 Hemingford Road, N1 1BY. *T:* (020) 7607 8642.

NEHER, Prof. Dr Erwin; Research Director, Max-Planck-Institut für biophysikalische Chemie, Göttingen, since 1983; *b* 20 March 1944; *s* of Franz Xaver Neher and Elisabeth Neher; *m* 1978, Dr Eva-Maria Ruhr; three *s* two *d*. *Educ:* Technical Univ., Munich (PhD); Univ. of Wisconsin. Research Associate: Max-Planck-Inst. für Psychiatrie, Munich, 1970–72; Max-Planck-Inst. für biophysikalische Chemie, 1972–75 and 1976–83; Yale Univ., 1975–76; Fairchild Scholar, CIT, 1988–89. For. Mem., Royal Soc., 1994. Nat. and internat. sci. awards: (jtly) Nobel Prize in Physiology or Medicine, 1991. *Publications:* Elektronische Messtechnik in der Physiologie, 1974; (ed) Single Channel Recording, 1983. *Address:* Max-Planck-Institut für biophysikalische Chemie, Am Fassberg, 37077 Göttingen, Germany. *T:* (551) 2011675.

NEIDLE, Prof. Stephen, PhD, DSc, CChem, FRSC; Professor of Chemical Biology, since 2002, Cancer Research UK Professorial Fellow, since 2002 and Director of Research, Centre for Cancer Medicines, since 2004, School of Pharmacy, University of London; *b* 1 July 1946; *e s* of Michael and Hetty Neidle; *m* 1971, Andrea Anne Finn; two *s* one *d*. *Educ:* Hendon County Sch.; Imperial Coll., London (BSc 1967; PhD 1970; DSc 1995). CChem, FRSC 1999. ICI Research Fellow, Univ. of London, 1970–72; Mem., Scientific Staff, Dept of Biophysics, KCL, 1972–85; Institute of Cancer Research, University of London: Reader, 1986–90; Prof. of Biophysics, 1990–2002; Dean, 1997–2002. Vis. Prof., Univ. of Rome, 2006. Guggenheim Lect., Univ. of Reading, 2005. Cancer Research Campaign: career develt awardee, 1979–85; Life Fellow, 1985–; Dir, Biomolecular Structure Unit, 1985–. Bristol-Myers Squibb Lectr, SUNY, 1993; Paul Ehrlich Lectr, Société de Chimie Thérapeutique, France, 2004. Chm., Chemical Biol. Forum and Mem. Council, RSC, 2002–. Hon. Fellow, Sch. of Pharmacy, Univ. of London, 2007. Award in Bio-organic and Medicinal Chem., 1999, Interdisciplinary Award, 2002, RSC; Aventis Prize in Medicinal Chem., Aventis Pharma, France, 2004. *Publications:* DNA Structure and Recognition, 1994; (ed) Oxford Handbook of Nucleic Acid Structure, 1999; Nucleic Acid Structure and Recognition, 2002; Principles of Nucleic Acid Structure, 2007 (ed) Cancer Drug Design and Discovery, 2007; numerous papers on nucleic acid structure and on design of anti-cancer drugs. *Recreations:* film noir, theatre. *Address:* School of Pharmacy, University of London, 29–39 Brunswick Square, WC1N 1AX. *T:* (020) 7753 5800.

NEIDPATH, Lord; Hon. James Donald Charteris, Lord Douglas of Neidpath, Lyne and Munard; DL; *b* 22 June 1948; *s* and *heir* of 12th Earl of Wemyss and March, *qv*; *m* 1st, 1983, Catherine Ingrid (marr. diss. 1988), *d* of Baron Moyne, *qv*, and of Mrs Paul Channon; one *s* one *d*; 2nd, 1995, Amanda Claire, *y d* of late Basil Feilding. *Educ:* Eton; University College, Oxford (BA 1969, MA 1974); St Antony's Coll., Oxford (DPhil 1975); Royal Agricultural Coll., Cirencester (Diploma, 1978); MRICS (ARICS 1983). Page of Honour to HM Queen Elizabeth the Queen Mother, 1962–64. Mem., Royal Co. of Archers (Queen's Body Guard for Scotland), 1978–. Mem. Council, Nat. Trust for Scotland, 1987–92; Chm., Heart of England Reg., Hist. Houses Assoc., 1991–96. DL Glos, 2005. *Publication:* The Singapore Naval Base and the Defence of Britain's Eastern Empire 1919–42, 1981. *Heir: s* Hon. Francis Richard Percy Charteris, *b* 15 Sept. 1984. *Address:* Stanway, Cheltenham, Glos GL54 5PQ. *T:* (01386) 584469. *Clubs:* Brooks's, Pratt's, Ognisko Polskie; Puffin's, New (Edinburgh).

NEIGHBOUR, Oliver Wray, FBA 1982; Music Librarian, Reference Division of the British Library, 1976–85; *b* 1 April 1923; *s* of Sydney William Neighbour, OBE, TD, and Gwenydd Joyce (*née* Prentis). *Educ:* Eastbourne Coll.; Birkbeck Coll., London (BA 1950). Entered Dept of Printed Books, BM, 1946; Asst Keeper in Music Room, 1951; Dep. Keeper, 1976. *Publications:* (with Alan Tyson) English Music Publishers' Plate Numbers, 1965; The Consort and Keyboard Music of William Byrd, 1978; (ed) Music and Bibliography: essays in honour of Alec Hyatt King, 1980; article on Schoenberg in New Grove Dictionary of Music and Musicians, 1980, rev. edn 2001; editor of first publications of works by Schumann, Schoenberg and Byrd. *Recreations:* walking, ornithology. *Address:* 12 Treborough House, 1 Nottingham Place, W1U 5LA. *T:* (020) 7935 1772.

NEIGHBOUR, Roger Harvey, FRCGP; President, Royal College of General Practitioners, 2003–06; *b* 9 June 1947; *s* of late Kenneth George Neighbour and Eileen Nora Neighbour (*née* Roberts). *Educ:* Watford Grammar Sch.; King's Coll., Cambridge (BA 1968, MA 1972); St Thomas' Hosp. (MB BChir 1971). MRCGP 1975, FRCGP 1987; DObstRCOG 1975. GP, Abbots Langley, Herts, 1974–2003. Trainer, 1977–94, and Course Organiser, 1979–86, Watford Vocational Trng Scheme. Mem., 1984–2004, and Convener, 1997–2002, Panel of MRCGP Examrs. Hon. FRCP 2004; Hon. FRACGP 2006. Hon. DSc Hertfordshire, 2004. *Publications:* The Inner Consultation, 1987, 2nd edn 2004; The Inner Apprentice, 1992, 2nd edn 2004; (jtly) The Successful GP Registrar's Companion, 2003; I'm Too Hot Now, 2005; papers on med. assessment and educn, psychotherapy and Franz Schubert; contribs to British Jl of Gen. Practice, Educn for Primary Care. *Recreations:* playing the violin, music of Schubert, France, writing, armchair philosophy, trying to give up golf. *Address:* Argowan, Bell Lane, Bedmond, Herts WD5 0QS; Appt 26, La Falaise d'Hacqueville, 52 rue Saint Gaud, 50400 Granville, France.

NEIL, Alexander; Member (SNP) Central Scotland, Scottish Parliament, since 1999; *b* 22 Aug. 1951; *s* of late Alexander Neil and Margaret Gunning Neil; *m* Isabella Kerr; one *s*. *Educ:* Dundee Univ. (MA Hons Econs 1973). Marketing Manager: Digital Equipment Corp., 1979–83; Future Technology Systems, 1983–84; Dir, Cumnock and Doon Enterprise Trust, 1983–88; Economic and Business Advr, 1988–. Dir, Prince's Scottish Youth Business Trust, 1988–90; non-exec. Dir and Chm., Network Scotland Ltd, 1989–96. *Recreations:* reading, travel. *Address:* 26 Overmills Road, Hazelbank, Ayr KA7 3LQ. *T:* (01292) 286675.

NEIL, Andrew Ferguson; publisher, broadcaster and company chairman; Editor-in-Chief, since 1996, and Chief Executive, since 1999, Press Holdings Media Group (formerly European Press Holdings; owner of The Spectator, Spectator Business and Apollo magazines), since 2004; Chairman: World Media Rights, London, since 2005; ITP, Dubai, since 2006; b Paisley, 21 May 1949; s of James and Mary Neil. Educ: Paisley Grammar Sch.; Univ. of Glasgow (MA Hons Politics and Economics, 1971). Conservative Res. Dept, 1971–72; joined The Economist, 1973; Correspondent in Belfast, London, NY and Washington, covering politics and business, 1973–82; UK Editor, London, 1982–83; Editor, The Sunday Times, 1983–94; Exec. Editor and Chief Correspondent, Fox Network News, NY, 1994; columnist, The Sunday Times and Daily Mail, 1995–96; Contributing Editor, Vanity Fair, NY, 1995–; Ed.-in-Chief, 1996–2006, Publisher, 1999–2006, The Scotsman, Scotland on Sunday and Edinburgh Evening News. Exec. Chm., Sky TV, 1988–90; Co-Proprietor and Dir, CGA and Country Magazine, 1990–97. Appears regularly on various current affairs television and radio programmes in Britain and America; presenter, television: formerly of The Midnight Hour, Westminster On-Line, Is This Your Life?, The Andrew Neil Show, Despatch Box, Thursday Night Live; currently of The Daily Politics, This Week with Andrew Neil, Straight Talk with Andrew Neil; formerly presenter, radio, Sunday Breakfast. Lord Rector, St Andrews Univ., 1999–2002. FRSA 1997. Publications: The Cable Revolution, 1982; Britain's Free Press: Does It Have One?, 1988; Full Disclosure, 1996; British Excellence, 1998. Recreations: dining out in London, New York, Aspen and the Côte d'Azur. Address: Glenburn Enterprises Ltd, PO Box 584, SW7 3QY. Club: Royal Automobile.

NEIL, Matthew, CBE 1976; Secretary and Chief Executive, Glasgow Chamber of Commerce, 1954–83; b 19 Dec. 1917; er s of John Neil and Jean Wallace. Educ: John Neilson High Sch., Paisley; Glasgow Univ. (MA, LLB). Served War, 1939–46: Far East, ME, Mediterranean and Western Europe; RHA, RA and Air Observation Post; RAuxAF, 1950–57. Admitted solicitor, 1947; Hon. Sheriff, Renfrew and Argyll, now N Strathclyde, 1973–. Mem., British Overseas Trade Adv. Council, 1975–82. Hon. LLD Glasgow, 1983. Recreations: golf, music. Address: 39 Arkleston Road, Paisley PA1 3TH. T: (0141) 889 4975. Clubs: East India, Devonshire, Sports and Public Schools; Lamlash Golf, Prestwick Golf.

NEIL, Ronald John Baille, CBE 1999; Chief Executive, BBC Production, 1996–98; b 16 June 1942; s of John Clark Neil and Jean McMillan Taylor; m 1967, Isobel Anne Clark. Educ: High Sch. of Glasgow. Reporter, Daily Express, 1961; BBC, 1967–98: Newsreader/Reporter, Reporting Scotland, 1967; Producer, Nationwide and 24 Hours, 1969; Output Editor, Nationwide, 1973; Dep. Editor, Newsnight, 1979; Editor: That's Life, 1981; Newsnight, 1981; Breakfast Time, 1983; Six O'Clock News, 1984; TV News, 1985; Dep. Dir, 1987–88, Dir, 1988–89, News and Current Affairs; Man. Dir, Regl Broadcasting, BBC, 1989. Recreations: food, wine. Club: Reform.

NEIL-DWYER, Glenn, FRCS, FRCSE; Consultant Neurosurgeon, Southampton University Hospitals NHS Trust, 1987–2002; b 17 May 1938; s of Glen Shamrock Neil-Dwyer and Violet Agatha Hussey; m 1966, Jennifer Susan Edith Taylor; three s. Educ: Ruthin Sch.; St Mary's Hosp., London (MB BS; MS 1974). FRCSE 1967; FRCS 1968. Sen. House Officer, Neurosurgery, Addenbrooke's Hosp., 1968–69; Registrar, then Sen. Registrar, Wessex Neurol Centre, Southampton, 1969–74; Consultant Neurosurgeon: Cornwall Regl Hosp. and UCH (Jamaica), 1974–75; Brook Gen. Hosp., London, 1975–87; Consultant Advr in Neurosurgery to the Army, 1992–2005. Pres., Soc. of British Neurol Surgeons, 1998–2000; Member, Council: RCS 1998–2000; Med. Defence Union, 2000–; Sec., Eur. Assoc. Neurosurgical Socs, 1999–2003. Publications: contrib. numerous papers to peer-reviewed jls on neurosurgical topics. Recreations: golf, sport, walking, travel, opera. Address: Annesley Glade, Bank, Lyndhurst, Hants SO43 7FD. T: (023) 8028 3352. Club: MCC.

NEILAND, Prof. Brendan Robert; Gallery Artist, Redfern Gallery, since 1992; Keeper of the Royal Academy, 1998–2004; b 23 Oct. 1941; s of Arthur Neiland and Joan Agnes Bessie Whiley; m 1970, Hilary Vivienne Salter; two d. Educ: Birmingham Sch. of Art (DipAD Hons); Royal Coll. of Art (MA). RE 1988–92 (Hon. RE 1998). Prof. of Painting, Univ. of Brighton, 1996–98. Vis. Prof. of Fine Art, Loughborough Univ., 1999. Exhibited: Angela Flowers Gall., 1970–78; Fischer Fine Art, 1978–92; Redfern Gall., 1993; retrospective exhibition, Turlej Gall., Crakow, Poland and Sharjah Art Museum, UAE, 2006. Scholar, Crabtree Foundn, 1982. FRSA 1996. Silver Medal, RCA, 1969; John Moores XI Prize, 1978; Daler Rowney Award, RA Summer Exhibn, 1989. Publication: Upon Reflection, 1997. Recreations: listening to the cricket commentary on Radio 4, drinking fine wines. Address: 2 Granard Road, SW12 8UL. T: and Fax: (020) 8673 4597; Crepe, La Grévé sur le Mignon, 17170 Courçon, France. T: 546016297. Clubs: Chelsea Arts, Arts, Garrick.

NEILD, Prof. Robert Ralph; Professor of Economics, University of Cambridge, 1971–84, now Emeritus; Fellow of Trinity College, Cambridge, since 1971; b 10 Sept. 1924; o s of Ralph and Josephine Neild, Letchmore Heath, Hertfordshire; m 1st, 1957, Nora Clemens Sayre (marr. diss. 1961); 2nd, 1962, Elizabeth Walton Griffiths (marr. diss. 1986); one s four d (incl. twin d); 3rd, 2004, Virginia Matheson. Educ: Charterhouse; Trinity Coll., Cambridge. Royal Air Force, 1943–44; Operational Research, 1944–45. Secretariat of United Nations Economic Commission for Europe, Geneva, 1947–51; Economic Section, Cabinet Office and Treasury, 1951–56; Lecturer in Economics, and Fellow, Trinity College, Cambridge, 1956–58; National Institute of Economic and Social Research: at first as Editor of its Quarterly Economic Review; then as Deputy Director of the Institute, 1958–64; MIT Center for International Studies, India Project, New Delhi, 1962–63; Economic Adviser to HM Treasury, 1964–67; Dir, Stockholm Internat. Peace Research Inst., 1967–71. Vis. Fulbright Prof., Hampshire Coll. and Five Colls, Amherst, Mass, USA, 1985. Mem., Fulton Cttee on Reform of CS, 1966–68; Vice-Chm., Armstrong Cttee on Budgetary Reform in UK, Inst. for Fiscal Studies, 1979–80. Director: Nat. Mutual Life Assce Soc., 1959–64; Investing in Success Equities Ltd, 1961–64, 1972–87. Publications: Pricing and Employment in the Trade Cycle, 1964; (with T. S. Ward) The Measurement and Reform of Budgetary Policy, 1978; Tax Policy in Papua New Guinea, 1980; How to Make Up Your Mind about the Bomb, 1981; An Essay on Strategy, 1990; (ed with A. Boserup) The Foundations of Defensive Defence, 1990; The English, the French and the Oyster, 1995; Public Corruption: the dark side of social evolution, 2002; Riches and Responsibility: the financial history of Trinity College, Cambridge; various articles. Recreations: oysters, painting. Address: Trinity College, Cambridge CB2 1TQ.

NEILL, family name of **Baron Neill of Bladen.**

NEILL OF BLADEN, Baron cr 1997 (Life Peer), of Briantspuddle in the co. of Dorset; **Francis Patrick Neill,** Kt 1983; QC 1966; Chairman, Committee on Standards in Public Life, 1997–2001; Warden of All Souls College, Oxford, 1977–95; Vice-Chancellor, Oxford University, 1985–89; b 8 Aug. 1926; s of late Sir Thomas Neill, JP, and Lady (Annie Strachan) Neill (née Bishop); m 1954, Caroline Susan, d of late Sir Piers Debenham, 2nd Bt, and Lady (Angela) Debenham; three s two d (and one s decd). Educ: Highgate Sch.; Magdalen College, Oxford (Hon. Fellow, 1988). Gibbs Law Scholar, 1949; Eldon Law Scholar, 1950. BA 1950; BCL 1951; MA 1972. Served Rifle Brigade, 1944–47 (Captain);

GSO III (Training), British Troops Egypt, 1947. Fellow of All Souls Coll., Oxford, 1950–77, Sub-Warden 1972–74, Hon. Fellow, 1997; Lectr in Air Law, LSE, 1955–58. Called to the Bar, Gray's Inn, 1951; Bencher, 1971; Vice-Treas., 1989; Treas., 1990; Member, Bar Council, 1967–71, Vice-Chm., 1973–74, Chm., 1974–75; Chm., Senate of the Inns of Court and the Bar, 1974–75; a Recorder of the Crown Court, 1975–78; a Judge, Cts of Appeal of Jersey and Guernsey, 1977–94. Chm., Justice—All Souls Cttee for Rev. of Admin. Law, 1978–87. Chairman: Press Council, 1978–83; DTI Cttee of Inquiry into Regulatory Arrangements at Lloyd's, 1986–87; Feltrim Loss Review Cttee at Lloyd's, 1991–92; first Chm., Council for the Securities Industry, 1978–85; Vice-Chm., CVCP, 1987–89. Independent Nat. Dir, Times Newspaper Hldgs, 1988–97. Hon. Prof. of Legal Ethics, Birmingham Univ., 1983–84. Hon. LLD: Hull, 1978; Buckingham, 1994; Hon. DCL Oxon, 1987. Publication: Administrative Justice: some necessary reforms, 1988. Recreations: music and forestry. Address: 20 Essex Street, WC2R 3AL. Clubs: Athenæum, Garrick, Beefsteak, Oxford and Cambridge.
    See also Rt Hon. C. Geidt, Rt Hon. Sir Brian Neill.

NEILL, Alistair, FFA, FIA; General Manager, Scottish Widows' Fund & Life Assurance Society, 1988–92; President, Faculty of Actuaries in Scotland, 1990–92; b 18 Nov. 1932; s of Alexander Neill and Marion Wilson; m 1958, Mary Margaret Hunter; one s two d. Educ: George Watson's Coll., Edinburgh; Univ. of Edinburgh (John Welsh Math. Bursar; MA 1953); Univ. of Wisconsin (Fulbright Grantee; MS 1954); BSc Open Univ. 2001. Instructor Lieut, RN, 1958–60. Actuarial management posts in Scottish Widows' Fund, 1961–92. Chm., Pensions Cttee, ABI, 1986–92. Publication: Life Contingencies, 1977, 5th edn 1989. Recreations: golf, model railways. Address: 24 Bonaly Crescent, Edinburgh EH13 0EW. T: (0131) 441 2038.

NEILL, Alistair Klaas; Chief Executive, Merthyr Tydfil County Borough Council, since 2003; b 5 Nov. 1956; s of John and Woutertje Neill; m 1992, Kathryn Shapland; one s two d. Educ: Glasgow Univ. (MA English and Philos.; DMS in Business, distn). Marketing Manager, Unilever, 1985–88; Marketing Dir and Strategy Dir, BP, 1988–94; Pres. Internat. Ops, LFI, 1994–2002; Chief Operating Officer, Northants CC, 2003. Lectr in Mgt, Warwick, Cardiff and HK Univs. MInstD 1992. Two Leading Wales Awards, 2005. Publication: Sick Pay Schemes, and Causes of Malingering, 1979. Recreations: my wife, my children, our dog, our parrot, cycling in Monmouthshire, playing guitar and singing woefully. Address: Merthyr Tydfil County Borough Council, Civic Centre, Castle Street, Merthyr Tydfil CF47 8AN. T: (home) (01873) 832275; e-mail: aneill@onetel.com. Club: Cardiff Business.

NEILL, Rt Hon. Sir Brian (Thomas), Kt 1978; PC 1985; a Lord Justice of Appeal, 1985–96; a Justice of Appeal, 1997–98, and President, 1998–2003, Court of Appeal for Gibraltar; b 2 Aug. 1923; s of late Sir Thomas Neill and Lady (Annie Strachan) Neill (née Bishop); m 1956, Sally Margaret, d of late Sydney Eric and Marguerite Backus; three s. Educ: Highgate Sch.; Corpus Christi Coll., Oxford (Hon. Fellow 1986). Rifle Brigade, 1942–46 (Capt.). MA Oxford. Called to the Bar, Inner Temple, 1949, Bencher, 1976. QC 1968; a Recorder of the Crown Court, 1972–78; a Judge of the High Court, Queen's Bench Div., 1978–84. A Judge of the Commercial and Admiralty Courts, 1980–84; a Judge of Employment Appeal Tribunal, 1981–84. Mem., Departmental Cttee to examine operation of Section 2 of Official Secrets Act, 1971; Chairman: Adv. Cttee on Rhodesia Travel Restrictions, 1973–78; IT and the Courts Cttee, 1985–96; Supreme Court Procedure Cttee, 1986–90; Civil Mediation Council, 2003–06. Mem., Ct of Assts, 1972–, Master, 1980–81, Turners' Co. Chm. of Trustees, Lord Slynn of Hadley European Law Foundn, 2003–. Governor, Highgate Sch., 1969–90. Publication: (with Colin Duncan) Defamation, 1978, 2nd edn (ed with R. Rampton), 1984. Clubs: MCC, Hurlingham.
    See also Baron Neill of Bladen.

NEILL, Rev. Bruce Ferguson; Church of Scotland Minister, Maxton and Mertoun: with St Boswells, 1996–2007; with Newtown, 2006–07; b 9 Jan. 1941; s of Thomas Ferguson Neill and Jane (née Bruce); m 1966, Ishbel Macdonald; two s one d. Educ: Lesmahagow Primary; Hamilton Academy; Glasgow Univ. and Trinity Coll., Glasgow (MA, BD). Probationer Asst, Drumchapel Old Parish Church, 1964–66; Minister, Dunfermline Townhill Parish Church, 1966–71; commnd as Chaplain, RN, 1971; Naval appts include: HMS Drake, 1972; RM, 1972; HMS Seahawk, 1974; HMS Cochrane, 1976; ships of 1st and 2nd Flotillas, 1979; HMS Dryad, 1981; Britannia RNC, 1983; HMS Cochrane, 1986; ships of Minor War Vessels Flotilla, 1989–91; Prin. Naval Chaplain, Church of Scotland and Free Churches, 1991–96. QHC, 1991–96. Recreations: gardening, hill walking, off-shore sailing, woodwork, music, model making.

NEILL, Sir (James) Hugh, KCVO 1996; CBE 1969; TD 1950; JP; Lord-Lieutenant for South Yorkshire, 1985–96; Chairman, James Neill Holdings, 1963–89; b 29 March 1921; o s of Col Sir Frederick Neill, CBE, DSO, TD, DL, JP, and Lady (Winifred Margaret) Neill (née Colver); m 1st, 1943, Jane Margaret Shuttleworth (d 1980); two d; 2nd, 1982, Anne O'Leary; one s. Educ: Rugby School. War service with RE and Royal Bombay Sappers and Miners, UK, Norway, India, Burma and Germany, 1939–46 (despatches, Burma, 1945). Mem., British Overseas Trade Bd, 1973–78; Pres., European Tool Cttee, 1972–76; Mem., Trent Regional Health Authority, 1974–80; Chm. Exec. Cttee, Sheffield Council for Voluntary Service, 1953–87; Mem. Council, CBI, 1965–83; Chm., E and W Ridings Regional Council, FBI, 1962–64; Pres., Nat. Fedn of Engrs Tool Manufrs, 1963–65; Pres., Fedn of British Hand Tool Manufrs, 1960–61. Pres., Sheffield Chamber of Commerce, 1984–85. FCMI. Hon. Col, 3rd Bn Yorks Vol., subseq. 3rd/4th Bn Yorks Vol., later 3rd Bn Duke of Wellington's, 1988–93. Chm., Yorks & Humberside TAVRA, 1991–94. Hon. Fellow, Sheffield City Polytechnic, 1978; Hon. LLD Sheffield, 1982. Master Cutler of Hallamshire, 1958; High Sheriff of Hallamshire, 1971; DL South Yorkshire, 1974, JP 1985. KStJ 1996. Recreation: golf. Address: Barn Cottage, Lindrick Common, near Worksop S81 8BA. T: (01909) 562806. Clubs: East India; Lindrick (Worksop); Royal and Ancient (St Andrews); Hon. Co. of Edinburgh Golfers (Muirfield).

NEILL, John Mitchell, CBE 1994; Chief Executive, Unipart Group of Companies, since 1987; b 21 July 1947; s of Justin Bernard Neill and Johanna Elizabeth Neill; m 1975, Jacquelyn Anne, d of late Philip Brown; two s. Educ: George Heriot's Sch., Edinburgh; Univ. of Strathclyde (BA, MBA, DBA). Europe AC Delco: Planning Manager, 1969–71; Marketing Manager, 1972–73; British Leyland: Merchandising Manager, 1974–75, Sales and Marketing Dir, 1976, Parts Div.; Managing Director: Car Parts Div., 1977–78; BL Components, 1979–80; Unipart Gp, 1981–82; Gp Man. Dir, Unipart Gp Ltd, 1983–86. A Dir, Bank of England, 1996–2003. Dir, Charter plc, 1994–. Dir, BITC, 1992–. Vice President: Inst. of Mktg, 2002– (Pres., 2000–01; Dep. Pres., 2001–02); Inst. of Motor Industry; BEN; Pres., SMMT, 2000–01. Trustee, Nat. Motor Mus. Address: Unipart Group of Companies Ltd, Unipart House, Cowley, Oxford OX4 2PG.

NEILL, Most Rev. John Robert Winder; see Dublin, Archbishop of, and Primate of Ireland.

NEILL, Nigel John Dermot, (Sam), DCNZM 2007; OBE 1992; actor; b 14 Sept. 1947; s of Dermot Neill and Priscilla Beatrice Neill (Ingham); m 1989, Noriko Watanabe; two s two *d.* *Educ:* Christ's Coll., Canterbury, NZ; Canterbury Univ., NZ (BA 1971). Director, NZ Nat. Film Unit, 1973–78; freelance actor, 1978–. *Films* include: My Brilliant Career, 1979; A Cry in the Dark, 1988; Dead Calm, 1989; Death in Brunswick, 1991; The Piano, Jurassic Park, 1993; In the Mouth of Madness, 1995; Restoration, 1996; The Event Horizon, 1997; Dish, 2000; Jurassic Park III, 2001; Dirty Deeds, 2003; Angel, 2007; *television* includes: Reilly: the Ace of Spies (series), 1983; Jessica, 2004; Mary Bryant (series), 2005; Merlin, 2006; The Tudors (series), 2007. Wine producer, Two Paddocks Wine, Queenstown, NZ, 1973–. Hon. DLitt. *Recreations:* drinking, idling, farming, dogs, ski-ing, fly fishing, reading, ukelele, conviviality and isolation. *Address:* c/o Shanahan Management, Level 3 Berman House, 91 Campbell Street, Surry Hills, Sydney, NSW 2010, Australia.

NEILL, Robert James Macgillivray; MP (C) Bromley and Chislehurst, since June 2006; *b* 24 June 1952; *s* of John Macgillivray Neill and Elsie May Neill (*née* Chaston). *Educ:* London Sch. of Econs (LLB Hons 1973). Called to the Bar, Middle Temple, 1975; barrister in private practice, 1975–2006. Member (C): Havering BC, 1974–90 (Chm., Envmt and Social Services Cttees); Romford, GLC, 1985–86; Greater London Authority: Mem. (C) Bexley and Bromley, London Assembly, 2000–08; Leader, Cons. Gp, 2000–02, 2004–06; Chair, Planning and Spatial Develt Cttee, 2002–04. Shadow Minister for Local Govt, and Deputy Chm., Cons. Party, 2007–. Mem., Select Cttee on Justice and Constitutional Affairs. Dep. Chm., Commn on London Governance, 2004–06. Leader, London Fire and Civil Defence Authy, 1985–87. Mem., Metropolitan Police Authy, 2004–08. Regl Chm., Gtr London Cons. Party, 1996–99 (Dep. Chm., 1993–96). Contested (C) Dagenham, 1983 and 1987. Mem., UK Delegn, Cttee of Regions of EU, 2002–08. Non-exec. Dir, NE London HA, 2002–06. *Recreations:* opera, travel, sailing. *Address:* House of Commons, SW1A 0AA. *Club:* St Stephen's.

NEILL, Sam; *see* Neill, N. J. D.

NEILSON, Ian (Godfrey), DFC 1944; TD 1951; *b* 4 Dec. 1918; *er s* of James Wilson Neilson, solicitor, Glasgow; *m* 1945, D. Alison St Clair Aytoun, Ashintully; one *s* one *d.* *Educ:* Glasgow Acad.; Glasgow Univ. (BL). Legal Trng, Glasgow, 1935–39; Territorial Army, 1938; War Service, 1939–45: Field Artillery; Air Observation Post, 1941; RA Staff, HQ 21 Army Gp, 1944; Lt-Col comdg War Crimes Investigation Unit, Germany, 1945–46; formed and commanded No 666 (Scottish) Sqdn, RAuxAF, 1948–53. Enrolled Solicitor, 1946. Royal Institution of Chartered Surveyors: Scottish Sec., Edinburgh, 1946–53; Asst Sec., London, 1953–61; Under-Sec., 1961–65; The Boys' Brigade: Brigade Sec., 1966–74; Officer, 5th Mid-Surrey Co., 1972–78; Nat. Hon. Vice-Pres., 1982–; Hon. Vice-Pres., W of England Dist, 1983–; Hon. Vice-Pres., Wilts Bn, 1985–. Clerk to Governors of the Cripplegate Foundn, Cripplegate Educnl Foundn, Trustees of St Giles and St Luke's Jt Parochial Charities, and Governors of the Cripplegate Schs Foundn, 1974–81. Hon. Treasurer, Thames Youth Venture Adv. Council (City Parochial Foundn), 1968–76. Vice-Chm., British Council of Churches Youth Dept, 1971–74; Trustee: St George's Chapel, London Airport, 1978–97 (Chm., 1983–96); Douglas Haig Meml Homes, 1979–96; Mem., Nat. Council for Voluntary Youth Services, 1966–74; Pres., London Br., Glasgow Academical Club, 1977–79; Chm. of Governors, Lucas-Tooth Leadership Training Fund for Boys, 1976–83; Governor, Kingsway-Princeton Coll. of Further Educn, 1977–83. Elder, United Reformed Church, St Andrew's, Cheam, 1972–83; Lay Mem., Provincial Ministerial Cttee, URC, 1974–83; Dir and Jt Sec., URC Trust, 1982–95; Mem. Council: Christchurch, Marlborough, 1984–90, 1992–97; St Peter's and St Paul's Trust, Marlborough, 1985–. BIM: Hon. Sec., City of London Branch, 1976–79, Chm., 1979–81, Vice Pres., 1981–87; Chm., Inner London Branches Area Cttee, 1981–83; FCMI (FBIM 1980). Sen. Instr, Royal Yachting Assoc., 1977–87; Vice-Pres. and Vice-Chm., Air Observation Post Officers Assoc., 1978–; Chm., Epsom Choral Soc., 1977–81; Mem., Marlborough Coll. Choral Soc., 1985–2003. Mem., Marlborough Probus Club, 1993 (Chm. 1998–99). Member: Soc. for Army Histl Res., 1997–; Air-Britain (Historians), 2006–. Freeman, City of London, 1975; Freeman, GAPAN, 1976–78, Liveryman, 1978–2004; Chm., Queenhithe Ward Club, 1977–78. Hon. Editor, Tower and Town, Marlborough, 1984–95; Compiler and Reader, Talking Newspaper for the Blind, Marlborough, 1987–2003. *Recreations:* golf, music, gardening. *Address:* The Paddock, Kingsbury Street, Marlborough, Wilts SN8 1HZ. *T:* (01672) 515114. *Clubs:* Marlborough Golf; Chartered Surveyors' Golfing Society (Hon. Mem.).

NEILSON, John Stuart; Group Director, Research Base, Department for Innovation, Universities and Skills (formerly Science and Engineering Base Group, Office of Science and Technology, then Research Base, Office of Science and Innovation, Department of Trade and Industry), since 2005; *b* 31 May 1959; *s* of late Ian Neilson, ISO, and Dr Betty Neilson (*née* Harley); *m* 1985, Alison Christine Green; one *s* one *d.* *Educ:* St Paul's Sch.; Corpus Christi Coll., Cambridge (BA 1st Cl. Hons 1980; Prize for Mgt Studies, ICE, 1980). Joined Department of Energy, 1980: Second Private Sec. to Sec. of State for Energy, 1983–85; Principal, 1985; on secondment to Econ. Secretariat, Cabinet Office, 1988–89; Principal Private Sec. to Sec. of State for Energy, 1989–92; Department of Trade and Industry: Private Sec. to Minister for Energy, 1992–93; Asst Sec., 1993; Director: UK Communications Policy, 1993–97; Aerospace and Defence Industries Policy, 1997–2000; Man. Dir, Customers and Supply, Ofgem, 2000–05. *Address:* Department for Innovation, Universities and Skills, Kingsgate House, 66–74 Victoria Street, SW1E 6SW. *T:* (020) 3300 8761.

NELDER, John Ashworth, DSc; FRS 1981; Visiting Professor, Imperial College of Science, Technology and Medicine (formerly Imperial College of Science and Technology), since 1971; Head of Statistics Department, 1968–84, and of Division of Biomathematics, Jan.–Oct. 1984, Rothamsted Experimental Station; *b* 8 Oct. 1924; *s* of Reginald Charles and Edith May Ashworth Nelder; *m* 1955, Mary Hawkes; one *s* one *d.* *Educ:* Blundell's Sch., Tiverton; Cambridge Univ. (MA); DSc Birmingham. Head, Statistics Section, National Vegetable Research Station, 1950–68. Pres., Royal Statistical Soc., 1985–86. Hon. DSc Paul Sabatier, Toulouse, 1981. *Publications:* Computers in Biology, 1974; (with P. McCullagh) Generalized Linear Models, 1983, 2nd edn 1989; (jtly) Generalized Linear Models with Random Effects, 2006; responsible for statistical programs (computer), Genstat and GLIM; numerous papers in statistical and biological jls. *Recreations:* piano-playing, music, natural history. *Address:* Cumberland Cottage, 33 Crown Street, Redbourn, St Albans, Herts AL3 7JX. *T:* (01582) 792907.

NELIGAN, John Oliver; His Honour Judge John Neligan; a Circuit Judge, since 1996; *b* 21 June 1944; *yr s* of late Desmond Neligan, OBE and Penelope Anne Stabb; *m* 1971, Mary Brigid Daniel; one *s* two *d.* *Educ:* Brickwall Sch., Northiam. Admitted Solicitor, 1969; called to the Bar, Middle Temple, 1975; practised on Western Circuit; Recorder, 1994–96. Asst Comr, Boundary Commn for England, 1992–95. Mem., Mental Health Review Tribunal, 2001–. *Recreations:* walking, painting, gardening. *Address:* Cuttisbeare, Butterleigh, Cullompton, Devonshire EX15 1PL.
See also M. H. D. Neligan.

NELIGAN, His Honour Michael Hugh Desmond; a Circuit Judge, 1990–2005; *b* 2 Dec. 1936; *s* of late Desmond West Edmund Neligan, OBE and Penelope Anne, *d* of Henry Mason; *m* 1965, Lynn (*née* Maidment); three *d.* *Educ:* Bradfield College; Jesus College, Cambridge. Commissioned Royal Sussex Regt, 1960–62; served East Africa with 23rd and 4th Bns, King's African Rifles. Called to the Bar, Middle Temple, 1965; Prosecuting Counsel to the Crown, 1972; Metropolitan Stipendiary Magistrate, 1987–90. *Recreations:* cabinet making, gardening, dog-walking.
See also J. O. Neligan.

NELIS, Mary Margaret; Member (SF) Foyle, Northern Ireland Assembly, 1998–2004; *b* 27 Aug. 1935; *d* of Denis Elliott and Catherine Coyle Elliott; *m* 1955, William Nelis; eight *s* one *d* (and one *s* decd). *Educ:* Inch Island Nat. Sch.; St Eugene's Convent Sch., Derry; Univ. of Ulster; Magee Adult Educn Faculty. Factory worker, 1949–56; Teacher, NW Coll. of Technol., Derry, then Derry Youth & Community Workshop, 1975–83. Mem., Sinn Féin, 1980–. Mem. (SF) Derry CC, 1994. Community develt, 1960–: Literacy trainee and Soc. Mem., Derry Reading Workshop, Cornhill High Sch., Derry, 1974–75; Founder Member: Foyle Hills Tenants' Assoc., 1968–73; Dove House, 1985–90; Founder Mem. and Man. Dir, Templemore Co-op., Derry, 1988–91. *Recreations:* painting, writing, music, children. *Address:* 35 Westland Avenue, Derry City, Co. Londonderry BT48 9JE. *T:* (028) 7128 6453.

NELL, family name of **Baroness O'Neill of Bengarve.**

NELLIST, David; caseworker, Citizens Advice Bureau, since 1997; *b* 16 July 1952; *m* 1984, Jane Warner; one *s* three *d.* Mem., Unite (formerly Amicus). Welfare Rights Advr, Robert Zara & Co., 1992–97. Member: (Lab) W Midlands CC, 1982–86; (Socialist) Coventry CC, 1998– (Leader, Socialist Gp, 1999–). MP (Lab, 1983–91, Ind. Lab, 1991–92) Coventry SE; contested: (Ind. Lab) Coventry SE, 1992; (Socialist) Coventry S, 1997; (Socialist) Coventry NE, 2001; (Socialist Alternative) Coventry NE, 2005. Mem. Nat. Cttee, Socialist Party, 1997–; Chairman: Socialist Alliance, 1998–2001; Campaign for a New Workers' Party, 2006–. *Address:* 33 Coundon Road, Coventry CV1 4AR. *T:* (024) 7622 9311; *e-mail:* dave@nellist.net.

NELMES, Dianne Gwenllian, (Mrs I. McBride); Director, Daytime and Lifestyle Programming, ITV Productions (formerly Director, Daytime and Regional Programming, Granada Media, then Director, Lifestyle Programming, Granada), since 2003; *b* Windlesham; *d* of late James Allen Nelmes and Celandine Nelmes (*née* Kimber); *m* 1986, Ian McBride. *Educ:* Holt Co. Girls' Sch., Wokingham; Newcastle upon Tyne Univ. (BA Hons Econs/Politics 1973; Pres., Students' Union, 1973–74). Professional Cert. NCTJ 1978. Thomson grad. trainee journalist, 1974–78; journalist, on-screen reporter/presenter, BBC TV NE, 1978–83; News Ed., journalist, World in Action, Granada TV, 1983–87; Producer/Dir, Brass Tacks, BBC TV, 1987–88; Granada TV, 1988–98: Launch Ed., This Morning, 1988–89; Exec. Producer, Entertainment, 1989–92; Ed., World in Action, 1992–93; Controller: Factual Progs, 1993–96; Lifestyle Progs (launched 5 satellite-digital channels), 1996–98; Daytime, ITV Network Ltd, 1998–2000; Documentaries and Features, ITV Network, 2000–03. Trustee, Refuge, 2006–. Mem., BAFTA. FRTS 1996; FRSA 2002. *Recreations:* canal boating, walking, cooking. *Address:* ITV Productions, London Television Centre, Upper Ground, SE1 9LT. *T:* (020) 7620 1620.

NELMES, Prof. Richard John, OBE 2001; ScD, PhD; FRS 2003; FRSE; FInstP; Professor of Physical Crystallography, since 1992 and Chairman, Centre for Science at Extreme Conditions, since 2003, University of Edinburgh; Senior Visiting Fellow, ISIS Facility, Rutherford Appleton Laboratory, since 1994; *b* 14 Oct. 1943; *s* of Arthur John Nelmes and Mabel Alice Nelmes (*née* Knell); *m* 1994, Patricia Ann Baldwin. *Educ:* Whitgift Sch., Croydon; St John's Coll., Cambridge (MA; ScD); Univ. of Edinburgh (PhD). FInstP 2001. University of Edinburgh: SRS Postdoctoral Fellow, 1969–71; Postdoctoral Res. Fellow, 1971–76; Lectr, 1976–85; Sen. Lectr, 1985–89; Reader and Professorial Fellow, 1989–92; EPSRC Sen. Fellow, 1989–94. FRSE 1995. Duddell Medal and Prize, Inst. of Physics, 2007. *Publications:* articles in scientific jls. *Recreations:* driving remote northern roads, reverie, music. *Address:* ISIS Facility, Rutherford Appleton Laboratory, Chilton, Didcot, Oxon OX11 0QX. *T:* (01235) 445285; SUPA, School of Physics, University of Edinburgh, Mayfield Road, Edinburgh EH9 3JZ; *e-mail:* r.j.nelmes@ed.ac.uk.

NELSON, family name of **Earl Nelson** and **Baron Nelson of Stafford.**

NELSON, 9th Earl *cr* 1805, of Trafalgar and of Merton; **Peter John Horatio Nelson;** Baron Nelson of the Nile and of Hilborough, Norfolk, 1801; Viscount Merton, 1805; *b* 9 Oct. 1941; *s* of Captain Hon. John Marie Joseph Horatio Nelson (*d* 1970) (*y s* of 5th Earl) and of Kathleen Mary, *d* of William Burr, Torquay; *S* uncle, 1981; *m* 1st, 1969, Maureen Diana (marr. diss. 1992), *d* of Edward Patrick Quinn, Kilkenny; one *s* one *d*; 2nd, 1992, Tracy Cowie; one *s.* Chm., Retainacar Ltd, 1988–94. Vice-Pres., Jubilee Sailing Trust; Hon. Life Member: Royal Naval Assoc.; Royal Naval Museum. *Heir: s* Viscount Merton, *qv.*

NELSON OF STAFFORD, 4th Baron *cr* 1960; **Alistair William Henry Nelson;** Bt 1955; Design Engineer, Farm Force Engineering Ltd, 2000–07; *b* 3 June 1973; *o s* of 3rd Baron Nelson of Stafford and of Dorothy Irene Nelson; *S* father, 2006. *Educ:* Ampleforth Coll.; Loughborough Univ. (BEng Hons Manufacturing, Engrg and Mgt). Mech. Applications Engr, European Gas Turbines, 1995–2000. *Recreations:* horse trials, horse racing, shooting, ski-ing. *Heir: uncle* Hon. James Jonathan Nelson [*b* 17 June 1947; *m* 1977, Lucy Mary Brown; three *d*]. *Address:* Eastlands, Eastlands Road, Tibthorpe, Driffield, N Humberside YO25 9LD.

NELSON (NZ), Bishop of, since 2007; **Rt Rev. Richard Ellena;** *b* 15 Jan. 1951; *s* of Victor Albert Ellena and Helen Mae Ellena; *m* 1972, Hilary Geoghegan; one *s* one *d.* *Educ:* Canterbury Univ. (BMus); St John's Coll., Auckland (LTh). Head, Dept of Music, Rangiora High Sch., Christchurch, 1976–82; ordained priest, 1985; Vicar: St Peter's, Kensington-Otipua, 1986–91; Blenheim Anglican Parish, 1992–2006; Archdeacon, Nelson and Marlborough, 2001–06; Vicar-Gen., Dio. of Nelson, 2002–06. *Recreations:* reading, walking, sailing. *Address:* PO Box 100, Nelson, New Zealand. *T:* (3) 5483124; *e-mail:* bprichard@nelsonanglican.org.nz.

NELSON, Anthony; *see* Nelson, R. A.

NELSON, Hon. Brendan John; MP (L) Bradfield, NSW, since 1996; Leader, Parliamentary Liberal Party, and Leader of the Opposition, Australia, since 2007; *b* Coburg, Vic, 19 Aug. 1958; *s* of Desmond John and Patricia Anne Nelson; *m* 1st, 1980, Deanna (marr. diss. 1981); 2nd, 1983, Kathleen (marr. diss. 1999); one *s* one *d*; 3rd, 1999, Gillian Adamson; one step *d.* *Educ:* Modbury High Sch.; St Ignatius Coll.; Univ. of Adelaide; Flinders Univ. (BM BS 1983). FAMA 1995. Gen. med. practitioner, 1985–95, private gen. practice, Hobart, 1991–95; Dir, Hobart and Launceston After Hours Med. Service Pty Ltd, 1987–91; med. columnist, Woman's Day mag., 1995–97. Fed. Pres., AMA, 1993–95 (Fed. Vice Pres., 1991–93; Pres., Tasmanian Br., 1990–92). Parly Sec. to Minister of Defence, 2001; Minister: for Educn, Sci. and Trng, 2001–06; for Defence,

2006–07. Chm., House of Reps Standing Cttee for Employment, Educn and Trng, 1997–98, for Employment, Educn and Workplace Relns, 1998–2001. Chm., Sydney Airport Community Forum, 1998–2001. Hon. FRACP 1995. Gold Medal, AMA, 1995; Centenary Medal, 2003. *Recreations:* fishing, tennis, motorcycles, music, guitars. *Address:* Suite 8, 12–16 Tryon Road, Lindfield, NSW 2070, Australia.

NELSON, David Brian; Senior Executive and Joint Head of Design, Foster + Partners, since 2007; *b* 15 April 1951; *s* of Victor Henry Nelson and Edna Mary (*née* Elliot); *m* 1977, Caroline Georgette Evans; two *d. Educ:* Loughborough Coll. of Art; Hornsey Coll. of Art; Royal Coll. of Art (MA). Joined Foster Associates, 1976; Dir, 1984; Partner, 1991; Dep. Chm., 2004–05. Projects, in Asia, Europe, Australia and USA, include: Century Tower, Tokyo, 1991; Amer. Air Mus., Duxford, 1997; New German Parlt, Reichstag, Berlin, 1999; Stanford Univ. Labs, Calif, 2003; Petronas Univ. of Technol., Malaysia, 2004; McLaren Technology Centre for McLaren, 2005; new Supreme Court, Singapore, 2006; Deutsche Bank Place, Sydney, Australia, 2006; transport projects: Bilbao Metro, Spain, 1995; Canary Wharf Underground Stn, 1999; N Greenwich Transport Interchange, London, 2000. Hon. FRIBA 2002. *Recreations:* motorsport, aviation, travel. *Address:* Foster + Partners, Riverside Three, 22 Hester Road, SW11 4AN. *T:* (020) 7738 0455, *Fax:* (020) 7738 1107; *e-mail:* dnelson@fosterandpartners.com. *Club:* Architecture.

NELSON, Eric Victor, LVO 1975; HM Diplomatic Service, retired; *b* 11 Jan. 1927; *s* of Victor H. H. and E. Vera B. Nelson (*née* Collingwood); *m* 1960, Maria Teresa (Marité) Paul (*d* 2008); one *d* (and one *d* decd). *Educ:* Western High School; George Washington University, Washington DC. Royal Air Force, 1945–48. Board of Trade, 1949; served FO, later FCO: Athens, Belgrade, Haiphong, Caracas; First Sec., Saigon, 1962; First Sec. and Consul, Bujumbura, 1964 (Chargé d'Affaires *ai*, 1966–67); FO 1968; First Sec. and Consul, Asunçión, 1971; First Sec., Mexico City, 1974; FCO, 1978; seconded to Brunei Govt Service as Special Adviser to HM Sultan of Brunei, for Establishment of Brunei Diplomatic Service, 1981–84; Consul-Gen., Bordeaux, 1984–87. Order of the Aztec Eagle, Mexico, 1975. *Recreations:* photography, giving illustrated talks, tourism, cartooning, sculpture. *Address:* 8 Purberry Grove, Ewell, Surrey KT17 1LU.

NELSON, Sir Jamie (Charles Vernon Hope), 4th Bt *cr* 1912, of Acton Park, Acton, Denbigh; *b* 23 Oct. 1949; *s* of Sir William Vernon Hope Nelson, OBE and Hon. Elizabeth Ann Bevil Cary, *er d* of 14th Viscount Falkland; *S* father, 1991, but his name does not appear on the Official Roll of the Baronetage; *m* 1983, Maralyn Beverly Hedge (*née* Pyatt); one *s. Heir: b* Dominic William Michael Nelson [*b* 13 March 1957; *m* 1981, Sarah, *e d* of late John Neil Hylton Jolliffe; three *s* one *d*].

NELSON, Dame Janet Laughland, (Dame Jinty Nelson), DBE 2006; PhD; FBA 1996; Professor of Medieval History, King's College, London, since 1993; *b* 28 March 1942; *d* of William Wilson Muir and Elizabeth Barnes Muir (*née* Laughland); *m* 1965, Howard George Horatio Nelson; one *s* one *d. Educ:* Keswick Sch., Cumbria; Newnham Coll., Cambridge (BA 1964; PhD 1967). King's College, London: Lectr, 1970–87; Reader, 1987–93; Dir, Centre for Late Antique and Medieval Studies, 1994–2000; FKC 2001. Chm., Adv. Bd, Inst. of Histl Res., Univ. of London, 1998–2001. Vice-Pres., British Acad., 1999–2001; FRHistS 1982 (Pres., 2000–04); Corresp. Fellow, Medieval Acad. of Amer., 2000. Hon. DLitt: UEA, 2004; St Andrews, 2007. *Publications:* Politics and Ritual in Early Medieval Europe, 1986; The Annals of St-Bertin, 1991; Charles the Bald, 1992; The Frankish World, 1996; Rulers and Ruling Families, 1999; (ed jtly) Rituals of Power, 2000; (ed jtly) The Medieval World, 2001; Courts, Elites, and Gendered Power in the Earlier Middle Ages, 2007; (ed jtly) Lay Intellectuals in the Carolingian World, 2007. *Recreations:* music, walking, looking after grandchildren Elias, Ruth, Martha and Miriam. *Address:* 71 Oglander Road, SE15 4DD. *T:* (020) 8693 7252.

NELSON, John Frederick, FCA; Chairman, since 2005, Director, since 2004, Hammerson plc; *b* 26 July 1947; *s* of George Frederick Nelson and Betty Violet Roddick; *m* 1976, Caroline Vivien Hannam; two *s* one *d.* FCA 1970. Kleinwort Benson, 1971–86, Dir, 1980–86; Lazard Brothers: Man. Dir, 1986–99; Vice Chm., 1990–99; Chm., Credit Suisse First Boston Europe, 1999–2002. Non-executive Director: Woolwich plc, 1998–2000; BT Gp plc, 2002–08; Kingfisher plc, 2002– (Dep. Chm., 2002–06; Jt Dep. Chm., 2006–07). Senior Advr, Charterhouse Capital Partners LLP, 2006–. Dir, ENO, 2002–. *Recreations:* sailing, opera, ski-ing, tennis. *Clubs:* Hurlingham; Bosham Sailing.

NELSON, John Graeme; Management Consultant, since 1997, Chairman, since 1999, First Class Partnerships; *b* 19 June 1947; *s* of late Charles and of Jean Nelson; *m* 1971, Pauline Dickinson; two *s* one *d. Educ:* Aylesbury and Slough Grammar Schs; Univ. of Manchester (BA Econ Hons). Management trainee, BR Western Reg., 1968; Asst Station Man., Liverpool Street, 1971; Area Passenger Man., Shenfield, 1973; Passenger Sales Officer, Leeds, 1977; Passenger Man., Sheffield Div., 1979; Personal Asst, Chief Exec. BRB, 1981; Parcels Man., Southern Reg., 1982; Nat. Business Man., Red Star Parcels, 1984; Gen. Man., BR Eastern Reg., 1987; Man. Dir, Network SouthEast, 1991; Gp Man. Dir, S and E, BR, 1994–97; Dir, London Develt, Railtrack, 1997. Director: First Class Insight Ltd, 1997–2003; Renaissance Trains Ltd, 1999–; Hull Trains, 1999–; Laing Rail, 2002–06; Wrexham, Shropshire & Marylebone Railway Ltd, 2006–; Tracsis plc, 2007–; YourRail Ltd, 2008–; Member, Board: M40 Trains Ltd, 1998–2002; SE Trains (Hldgs) Ltd, 2003–06. Chm., Tees, E and N Yorks Ambulance Service NHS Trust, 1997–2002. Member, Advisory Board: Nat. Railway Mus., 2006–; Yorks Rail Acad., 2007–. *Recreations:* piano, football, painting, psephology. *Address:* First Class Partnerships, 32 St Paul's Square, York YO24 4BD. *T:* (01904) 638659; *e-mail:* fcp@easynet.co.uk.

NELSON, Marjorie J.; *see* Jackson-Nelson.

NELSON, Michael Edward; Chairman, Reuter Foundation, 1982–90; General Manager, 1976–89, and Deputy Managing Director, 1981–89, Reuters Ltd; *b* 30 April 1929; *s* of late Thomas Alfred Nelson and Dorothy Pretoria Nelson; *m* 1960, Helga Johanna (*née* den Ouden); two *s* one *d. Educ:* Latymer Upper School; Magdalen College, Oxford (MA). Joined Reuters, London, as trainee financial journalist, 1952; assignments Asia, 1954–57; returned to London; Manager, Reuters Economic Services, 1962; Chairman, 1987–88: Reuters Asia; Reuters Europe; Reuters Overseas. Trustee: Visnews, 1990–92 (Chm., 1985–89); Internat. Inst. of Communications, 1989–95 (Chm., UK Chapter, 1989–92); Chm. Adv. Council, World Link, 1990–92. Mem., Newspaper Panel, MMC, 1989–95. External examiner, Journalism MA, Sheffield Univ., 1999–2001. Mem. Council, Internat. Assoc. for Media and Hist., 2001–. Trustee, St Bride's Church, 1989–. Vice-Pres., Music Fest. of Beaulieu-sur-Mer, 2005. Hon. Res. Fellow, Univ. of Kent, 1997–. *Publications:* War of the Black Heavens: the battles of western broadcasting in the cold war, 1997; Queen Victoria and the Discovery of the Riviera, 2001; Americans and the Making of the Riviera, 2007. *Recreations:* walking, music, history. *Address:* 21 Lansdowne Road, W11 3AG. *T:* (020) 7727 8533; Domaine de la Rose, 2 Chemin des Restanques, 06650 Opio, France. *T:* 493773232. *Club:* Garrick.

NELSON, Nicholas; Teacher, Newlands Girls' School, Maidenhead, since 2001; *b* 20 Jan. 1947; *s* of late Peter Nelson and Margaret Nelson; *m* 1972, Charmian Alice (*née* Bell); one *s* two *d. Educ:* Pudsey Grammar Sch., Yorkshire; Reading Univ. (BA (Hons) History; CertEd 1992). BOAC/British Airways air cargo mgt in Japan/UK, 1969–81; DHL International (UK) Ltd: Gen. Man., 1981; Man. Dir, 1982; Regional Dir (Europe), 1987; Man. Dir, Parcels, PO, then Royal Mail Parcelforce, 1987–91; teacher, 1992–95, Head Teacher, 1995–2000, Queens' Sch., Bushey; Dir, Resources and Planning, Design Council, 2001. *Recreation:* cricket. *Address:* Newlands Girls' School, Farm Road, Maidenhead, Berks SL6 5JB.

NELSON, Philip Raymond, CMG 2005; JP; HM Diplomatic Service, retired; *b* 7 April 1950; *s* of David George Nelson and Marjorie Lilian Nelson (*née* Roberts); *m* 1st, 1971, Cynthia Lesley Elson (marr. diss. 1978); 2nd, 1992, Lyndsay Ann Halper; two *s. Educ:* Collyers Sch., Horsham; Lincoln Coll., Oxford (BA Hons 1971); Fletcher Sch. of Law and Diplomacy, Tufts Univ. (AM 1972). Joined HM Diplomatic Service, 1972; Budapest, 1974–76; Private Sec. to Sir Nicholas Henderson, 1976–79; First Secretary: Rome, 1980–83; Manila, 1990; Budapest, 1991–94; Counsellor, FCO, 1994–2005. JP Ealing, 2007. *Recreations:* ski(mountaineer)ing, sailing. *Address:* *e-mail:* ravenscourt@compuserve.com. *Clubs:* Oriental, Royal Ocean Racing.

NELSON, (Richard) Anthony; Vice Chairman, Citi; Chairman, Gateway To London, since 2002; *b* 11 June 1948; *o s* of late Gp Captain R. G. Nelson, BSc, CEng, FRAeS, MICE, and of Mrs J. M. Nelson; *m* 1974, Caroline Victoria Butler; one *s* one *d. Educ:* Harrow Sch. (State scholarship; Head of School; Rothschild Scholar, 1966); Christ's Coll., Cambridge (MA (Hons) Economics and Law). N. M. Rothschild & Sons Ltd, 1969–73; Man. Dir, Salomon Smith Barney, 1997–2000; Vice-Chm., Citigroup Corporate and Investment Bank, then Citigroup Global Capital Markets, subseq. Citigroup Global Markets, now Citi, 2000–; Chairman: Southern Water, 2002–04; Britain in Europe, 2005–07; ifs Proshare, 2007–; Dir, Internat. Financial Services London, 2007–. Contested (C) E Leeds, Feb. 1974. MP (C) Chichester, Oct. 1974–97. PPS to Minister for Housing and Construction, 1979–83, to Minister of State for the Armed Forces, 1983–85; Economic Sec., 1992–94, Minister of State, 1994–95, HM Treasury; Minister of State, DTI, 1995–97. Member: Select Cttee on Science and Technology, 1975–79; Select Cttee on Televising of Proceedings of the House, 1988–92. Dir, Chichester Fest. Th., 1983–92. Mem., Governing Body, ICC (UK), 2005–. FRSA 1979. *Recreations:* Rugby, music. *Address:* The Old Vicarage, Easebourne, near Midhurst, W Sussex GU29 0AL.

NELSON, Richard Campbell; Deputy Chairman, Intertek Group plc (formerly Intertek Testing Services), since 2005 (Executive Chairman, 1996–2001; Chief Executive, 1996–2005); *b* 11 Feb. 1943; *s* of Campbell Louis Nelson and Pauline (*née* Blundell); *m* 1971, Rosemary Eleanor Sterling; one *s* three *d. Educ:* Rugby Sch.; London Business Sch. (MSc Econs). Chartered Accountant. Dir, 1972–84, Chief Exec., 1982–84, Esperanza Ltd, subseq. Transcontinental Services Ltd; Chief Exec., Inchcape Testing Services, 1984–96. *Recreations:* golf, tennis, bridge. *Address:* 8 Pembridge Place, W2 4XB. *T:* (020) 7221 7778; *e-mail:* richard@richardcnelson.com. *Club:* Turf.

NELSON, Dr (Richard) Stuart, FInstP; Consultant, β Technology Ltd, 1996–2001; *b* 1 May 1937; *s* of Richard and Winifred Emily Nelson; *m* 1965, Veronica Mary Beck; one *s* two *d. Educ:* Univ. of Reading (BSc 1st Cl. Hons Physics, 1958; DSc 1969). FInstP 1968. Joined UKAEA, Harwell, 1958; Div. Head, Materials Develt Div., 1981; Dir, Nuclear Power Res., 1984; Dir, Northern Res. Labs, 1987–90 (including Risley, Springfield and Windscale Labs); Memb. Bd, UKAEA, 1991–96; Man. Dir, Industrial Business Gp, 1991–94, Exec. Dir, Ops, 1994–96, AEA Technology. Vis. Prof., Univ. of Sussex, 1970–. *Publications:* The Observation of Atomic Collisions in Crystalline Solids, 1968; Ion Implantation, 1973; Innovation Business, 1999; 200 papers in scientific jls. *Recreations:* hockey (played for Berkshire), golf (Club Captain, 1998), tennis. *Address:* 5 Whitehills Green, Goring, Reading, Berks RG8 0EB.

NELSON, Hon. Sir Robert (Franklyn), Kt 1996; a Judge of the High Court of Justice, Queen's Bench Division, 1996–2008; *b* 19 Sept. 1942; *s* of late Clarence William and Lucie Margaret Nelson; *m* 1968, Anne-Marie Sabina Hall; two *s. Educ:* Repton; St John's Coll., Cambridge (MA). Called to the Bar, Middle Temple, 1965 (Harmsworth Entrance Exhibn, 1963), Bencher, 1993; QC 1985; a Recorder, 1986–96. *Recreations:* cricket, opera, golf.

NELSON, Stephen Keith James; Chief Executive Officer, BAA Ltd, 2006–08; *b* 5 Jan. 1963; *s* of late Bertram James Nelson, OBE and of Constance Nelson (*née* Dangerfield); *m* 1991, Catherine; one *s* one *d. Educ:* Tonbridge Sch. (Scholar); St John's Coll., Oxford (Open Scholar; MA 1st cl. Lit. Hum.). Diageo: Man. Dir, Guinness GB, 1999–2000; CEO, Guinness World Records, 2000–01; Pres., Diageo N America (SW), 2001–03; J Sainsbury plc: Trading Dir, 2003–04; Mktg Dir, 2004–05; Gp Retail Dir, BAA plc, 2005–06. *Recreations:* family, cycling, guitar, reading, museums, galleries.

NELSON, Stuart; *see* Nelson, R. S.

NEOPTOLEMOS, Prof. John P., MD; FRCS, FMedSci; Professor of Surgery and Head, Division of Surgery and Oncology, since 1996, and The Owen and Ellen Evans Chair of Cancer Studies and Head, School of Cancer Studies, since 2005, University of Liverpool; Hon. Consultant Surgeon, Royal Liverpool University Hospital, since 1996; *b* 30 June 1951; *m* 1974, Linda Joan Blaylock; one *s* one *d. Educ:* Owen's Grammar Sch., N London; Churchill Coll., Cambridge (MA); Guy's Hosp., London (MB BChir); Univ. of Leicester (MD 1985). FRCS 1981. Guy's Hosp., London, 1976–77; Leicester Royal Infirmary, 1978–84 and 1986–87; UCSD, 1984–85; Sen. Lectr, then Reader, Dept of Surgery, Univ. of Birmingham, and Consultant Surgeon, City Hosp., Birmingham, 1987–94; Prof. of Surgery, Queen Elizabeth Hosp., Birmingham, 1994–96. Hunterian Prof. of Surgery, RCS, 1987–88; Moynihan Travelling Fellow, Assoc. of Surgeons of GB and Ireland, 1988. Has made scientific contribs to aetiology, diagnosis and treatment of diseases of the pancreas and biliary tree. Pres., Pancreatic Soc. of GB and Ireland, 1994–95 (Mem. Cttee, 1987–90). Mem. Cttee, Surgical Res. Soc., 1994–98. Chairman: Eur. Study Gp for Pancreatic Cancer, 1991–; Pancreas Cancer Sub Group, NCRI, 2004–; Treas., Eur. Digestive Surgery, 1997–2004; Member Council: Eur. Pancreatic Club, 1995–2002 (Sec., 1996–2002); United Eur. Gastroenterol. Fedn, 1997–2002 (Mem., Scientific Cttee, 2002–06); Member, World Council: Internat. Hepato-Pancreato-Biliary Assoc., 1995–98; Internat. Assoc. of Pancreatology, 1996–2004 (Pres., 2000–02). FMedSci 2007. Rodney Smith Prize, RCS, 1987. *Publications:* Cancer of the Pancreas, 1990, 2006; Cancer: a molecular approach, 1993; Pancreatic Cancer: molecular and clinical advances, 1996; The Pancreas, 2 vols, 1998; Acute Pancreatitis, 1999; Exocrine Pancreas Cancer, 2005; contrib. numerous scientific papers in peer-reviewed jls, incl. New England Jl of Medicine, Lancet, GUT, Amer. Jl Physiology, British Jl Cancer, British Jl Surgery, Annals of Surgery, Gene Therapy, Cancer Res., Digestive Surgery, Gastroenterol., Proc. NAS, USA, Internat. Jl Cancer, Oncogene, Jl Nat. Cancer Inst. *Recreations:* squash, Latin and ballroom dancing. *Address:* Division of Surgery and Oncology, Royal Liverpool University Hospital, 5th Floor, UCD Building, Daulby Street, Liverpool L69 3GA. *T:* (0151) 706 4175, *Fax:* (0151) 706 5798; *e-mail:* j.p.neoptolemos@liv.ac.uk. *Club:* Heswall Squash (Trustee, 2005–).

NERINA, Nadia, (Mrs Charles Gordon); Prima Ballerina; Ballerina with Royal Ballet, 1951–69; *b* Cape Town, Oct. 1927; *née* Nadine Judd; *m* 1955, Charles Gordon. Joined Sadler's Wells Sch., 1946; after two months joined Sadler's Wells Theatre Ballet; transferred Sadler's Wells Ballet, Royal Opera House (now Royal Ballet), as soloist, 1967. *Rôles:* Princess Aurora in The Sleeping Beauty; Ondine; Odette-Odile in Swan Lake; Swanhilda in Coppelia; Sylvia; Giselle; Cinderella; Firebird; Can Can Dancer in La Boutique Fantasque; Ballerina in Petrushka; Colombine in Carnaval; Mazurka, Little Waltz, Prelude, in Les Sylphides; Mam'zelle Angot; Ballet Imperial; Scènes de Ballet; Flower Festival of Genzano; Les Rendezvous; Polka in Façade; The Girl in Spectre de la Rose; Casse Noisette; Laurentia; Khadra; Vagabonds; The Bride in A Wedding Bouquet; *creations:* Circus Dancer in Mardi Gras; Fairy Spring in Cinderella; Queen of the Earth in Homage to the Queen; Faded Beauty in Noctambules; Variation on a Theme; Birthday Offering; Lise in La Fille Mal Gardée; Electra; The Girl in Home; Clorinda in Tancredi. Appeared with Royal Ballet: Europe; South Africa; USA; Canada; USSR; Bulgaria; Romania. Recital Tours with Alexis Rassine: South Africa, 1952–55; England, 1956–57; concert performances, Royal Albert Hall and Royal Festival Hall, 1958–60. *Guest appearances include:* Turkish Nat. Ballet, 1957; Bolshoi Ballet, Kirov Ballet, 1960; Munich Ballet, 1963; Nat. Finnish Ballet, Royal Danish Ballet, 1964; Stuttgart Ballet, 1965; Ballet Theatre, Opera House Chicago, 1967; Royal Command Variety Performances, 1963–66. Mounted, dir. and prod three Charity Gala performances, London Palladium, 1969, 1971, 1972. Many TV appearances, UK and USA. Hon. Consultant on Ballet, Ohio Univ., 1967–69. British Jury Member: 3rd Internat. Ballet Competition, Moscow, 1977; Benois de la Danse Competition, Moscow, 1993, Paris, 1996. Fellow, 1959, Patron, 1964, Cecchetti Soc. Mem. Council, RSPCA, 1969–74. *Publications:* contrib.: La Fille Mal Gardée, 1960; Ballet and Modern Dance, 1974; *relevant publication:* Ballerina, ed Clement Crisp, 1975.

NESBITT, Dermot William Gibson; Member (UU) South Down, Northern Ireland Assembly, 1998–2007; *b* 14 Aug. 1947; *s* of William Cromwell Nesbitt and Georgina Nesbitt; *m* 1970, Margaret Oriel Patterson; one *s* one *d. Educ:* Queen's Univ., Belfast (BSc 1st cl. Hons Econs). School Teacher, 1969–74; Lectr, Ulster Poly., 1976; Queen's Univ., Belfast, 1976–98 (Sen. Lectr and Head, Dept of Accounting and Finance). Mem., NI Forum for Political Dialogue, 1996–98. Jun. Minister, assisting David Trimble, 1999–2002, Minister of the Envmt, 2002, NI. Contested (UU) S Down, 1997, 2001, 2005. *Publications:* over 20 academic publications. *Recreations:* gardening, family. *Address:* 21 Downpatrick Road, Crossgar, Downpatrick, Co. Down BT30 9EQ. *T:* (028) 4483 1561.

NESBITT, Judith; Chief Curator, Tate Britain, since 2001; *b* 24 March 1962; *d* of Thomas Robert Cecil Nesbitt and Joan Nesbitt (*née* Fleming); partner, Prof. Guy Lennox Claxton. *Educ:* Univ. of York (BA Hons Eng./Hist. of Art 1983); Courtauld Inst., London (MA Hist. of Art 1985). Sen. Asst Keeper, City Art Gall., Leeds, 1986–91; Exhibns Curator, Tate Gall. Liverpool, 1991–95, curated: Roy Lichtenstein, Robert Gober, 1993; Ann Hamilton, 1994; Sigmar Polke, 1995; Dir, Chisenhale Gall., 1995–98, curated shows of: Michael Landy, Pipilotti Rist, Gillian Wearing, Sam Taylor-Wood, Wolfgang Tillmans, Yukinori Yanagi, Paul Noble, Thomas Hirshhorn; Hd of Programming, Whitechapel Art Gall., 1998–2000, curated with Francesco Bonami, Examining Pictures, 1999; Hd of UK Content, Eyestorm.com, 2000–01; Tate Britain, 2001–, co-curated with Jonathan Watkins: Days Like These, 2003; Michael Landy Semi-Detached, 2004. Mem., Adv. Panel, Platform for Art, 2004–. Hon. FRCA 1998. *Recreations:* ski-ing, gardening, hymn singing. *Address:* Tate Britain, Millbank, SW1P 4RG. *T:* (020) 7887 8960, *Fax:* (020) 7887 8091; *e-mail:* judith.nesbitt@tate.org.uk.

NESS, Air Vice-Marshal Charles Wright, CEng, FRAeS; Director General, Combat Air, Defence Equipment and Support Organisation, since 2007; *b* 6 Nov. 1957; *s* of Air Marshal Sir Charles Ernest Ness, KCB, CBE and Audrey Ness; one *d. Educ:* Mill Hill Sch.; Liverpool Univ. (BEng). CEng 1986; FRAeS 1998. Joined RAF, 1975; Sen. Engrg Officer, 111 Sqn, 1986–88; OC, Engrg and Supply Wing, RAF Coningsby, 1993–95; Dep. Dir, Logistics Policy (RAF), 1995–97; Hd, Aero Engines Multi-Disciplinary Gp, 1997–99; Air Cdre, Communications and Inf. Systems, 1999; COS, Equipment Support (Air), 2000–02; Harrier Integrated Project Team Leader, 2003–04; Dir, Logistics No 1 Gp, 2004–05; Cluster Leader, No 1 Gp Integrated Project Team, 2004–05; Hd, RAF Process and Orgn Review, 2005–06; COS, Strategy, Policy and Plans, RAF High Wycombe, 2006–07. *Address:* RAF Wyton, Huntingdon, Cambs PE28 2EA. *Club:* Royal Air Force.

NESS, Robert; Director UK, British Council, since 2005; *b* 30 March 1953; *s* of late Robert Mitchell Ness and of Mary Ness (*née* Connor); *m* 1985, Geraldine McKendrick; two *s* one *d. Educ:* Arbroath High Sch.; Edinburgh Univ. (MA Hons; DipEd); Moray House Coll. of Educn (PGCE). Teacher, Madrid, 1978–80; joined British Council, 1981: English Tuition Co-ordinating Unit, 1981–83; Overseas Educnl Appts Dept, 1983–86; Asst Rep., Austria, 1987–89; English Lang. Div., 1989–92; Dep. Dir, SA, 1992–97; Dir, Cyprus, 1997–2000; Dir, Portugal, and Cultural Counsellor, Lisbon, 2000–03; Regl Dir, E Europe, 2003–05. *Recreations:* music, especially jazz, running, travel. *Address:* The British Council, 10 Spring Gardens, SW1A 2BN. *Clubs:* Royal British, Gremio Literario (Lisbon).

NESSLING, Paul William Downs; HM Diplomatic Service; High Commissioner, Kingdom of Tonga, 2002–06; *b* 26 Sept. 1945; *s* of late Herbert William Nessling and Mary Alice Nessling (*née* Perry); *m* 1975, Kathryn Lynne Freeman; one *d. Educ:* Latymer Upper Sch., Hammersmith. Mgt trainee, Midland Bank, 1962–63; buyer, BAT, 1965–66; Department of Trade and Industry, 1967–75: on secondment as Third Sec., Chicago, 1970; Asst Private Sec. to Sec. of State, 1972–75; Private Sec. to Minister of Prices, 1974–75; on secondment as Second Sec., Bahrain, 1975–79; HM Diplomatic Service, 1979–: Second Secretary: FCO, 1979–81; Lisbon, 1981–82; and Consul, Warsaw, 1982–84; Hd of Chancery, Aden, 1984; First Secretary: (Aid) and Dep. UK Perm. Rep. to UNEP, Nairobi, 1984–87; FCO, 1987–89; (Commercial), Harare, 1989–93; (Commercial), Muscat, 1993–96; Sarajevo, 1996–97; Dep. Dir, Jt Export Promotion Directorate, FCO, 1997–98; Dep. High Comr, Lusaka, 1998–2001. *Recreations:* current affairs, tennis, travelling, reading, walking. *Address:* c/o Foreign and Commonwealth Office, King Charles Street, SW1A 2AH.

NETANYAHU, Binyamin; Member, Knesset, since 1988; Leader of the Opposition, since 2006; *b* 21 Oct. 1949; *s* of Cela and Benzion Netanyahu; *m* (marr. diss.); one *d*; *m* 3rd, 1991, Sara; two *s. Educ:* MIT (BA 1976; MBA). Man. Consultant, Boston Consulting Gp, 1976–78; Exec. Dir, Jonathan Inst., Jerusalem, 1978–80; Sen. Manager, Rim Industries, Jerusalem, 1980–82; Dep. Chief of Mission, Washington, 1982–84; Perm. Rep. to UN, 1984–88; Deputy Minister: Ministry of Foreign Affairs, 1988–91; Prime Minister's Office, 1991–92; Prime Minister of Israel and Minister of Housing and Construction, 1996–99; Foreign Minister, 2002–03; Finance Minister, 2003–05. Leader, Likud, 1993–99 and 2005–. *Publications:* (ed) Self-Portrait of a Hero: the letters of Jonathan Netanyahu, 1981; Terrorism: how the West can win, 1986; A Place Among the Nations: Israel and the world, 1993; Fighting Terrorism, 1996. *Address:* The Knesset, Kiryat Ben-Gurion, Jerusalem 91950, Israel.

NETHERCOT, Prof. David Arthur, OBE 2006; PhD, DSc; FREng, FIStructE, FICE; Professor of Civil Engineering, and Head of Department of Civil and Environmental Engineering, Imperial College London (formerly Imperial College of Science, Technology and Medicine, University of London), since 1999; *b* 26 April 1946; *s* of late Arthur Owen Martin Nethercot and Dorothy May Nethercot; *m* 1968, Hedd Dwynwen Evans; two *d. Educ:* Univ. of Wales Coll. of Cardiff (BSc, PhD, DSc). FIStructE 1989; FICE 1994; FREng (FEng 1993); FCGI 2001. ICI Fellow, Univ. of Wales, 1970–71; Lectr, 1971–81, Sen. Lectr, 1981–86, Reader, 1986–89, Univ. of Sheffield; Prof. of Civil Engrg, 1989–99, Hd of Dept, 1994–99, Univ. of Nottingham. Visiting Professor: Japan Soc. for Promotion of Science, Univ. of Nagoya, 1980; Swiss Federal Inst. of Tech., Lausanne, 1990. Pres., IStructE, 2003–04 (Mem. Council, 1986–89, 1991–97; Vice-Pres., 2001–03); Member: Cttee on Structural Use of Steel in Building, BSI, 1986–2006 (Chm., 1995–2006); Joint Bd of Moderators, 1993–2000 (Chm., 1996–98); Standing Cttee on Structural Safety, 1996–2001; Council, Royal Acad. of Engrg, 2000–03. FRSA 2002. *Publications:* (jtly) Design for Structural Stability, 1979, 2nd edn 1985; Limit States Design of Structural Steelwork, 1986, 3rd edn 2001; (jtly) Design of Members Subject to Combined Bending and Torsion, 1989; (jtly) Lateral Stability of Steel Beams and Columns: common causes of restraint, 1992; about 400 sci. papers on structural engrg. *Recreation:* sport. *Address:* Department of Civil and Environmental Engineering, Imperial College London, South Kensington Campus, SW7 2AZ. *T:* (020) 7594 6097, *Fax:* (020) 7594 6042.

NETHERTHORPE, 3rd Baron *cr* 1959, of Anston, W Riding; **James Frederick Turner;** *b* 7 Jan. 1964; *s* of 2nd Baron Netherthorpe, and of Belinda, *d* of F. Hedley Nicholson; *S* father, 1982; *m* 1989, Elizabeth Curran Fahan, *d* of Edward Fahan, Connecticut; two *s* two *d. Educ:* Heatherdown Prep. Sch.; Harrow Sch. *Heir: s* Hon. Andrew James Edward Turner, *b* 24 March 1993. *Address:* Boothby Hall, Boothby Pagnell, Grantham, Lincs NG33 4DQ. *T:* (01476) 585482.

NETHSINGHA, Andrew Mark, FRCO; Director of Music, and Fellow, St John's College, Cambridge, since 2007; *b* 16 May 1968; *s* of Lucian Nethsingha and Jane (*née* Symons); *m* 1996, Lucy Kathleen Sellwood; one *s* two *d. Educ:* Exeter Cathedral Sch.; Clifton Coll.; Royal Coll. of Music (ARCM); St John's Coll., Cambridge (Organ Student; BA 1990; MA). FRCO 1987. Chorister, Exeter Cathedral, 1976–81; Organ Schol., St George's Chapel, Windsor Castle, 1986–87; Asst Organist, Wells Cathedral, 1990–94; Master of Choristers and Organist, Truro Cathedral, 1994–2002; Dir of Music, Gloucester Cathedral, 2002–07. Musical Director: Three Spires Singers and Orch., 1994–2002; Gloucester Choral Soc., 2002–07; Artistic Dir, Gloucester Three Choirs Fest., 2002–07. Pres., Cathedral Organists' Assoc., 2007–May 2009. Hon. Fellow, N and Midlands Sch. of Music, 2006. *Recreations:* walking, travel. *Address:* St John's College, Cambridge CB2 1TP. *T:* (01223) 338683, *Fax:* (01223) 338762; *e-mail:* an323@cam.ac.uk.

NETTEL, Caroline Gillian; *see* Mawhood, C. G.

NETTEL, Julian Philip; Chief Executive, Barts and The London NHS Trust, since 2007; *b* 23 Oct. 1953; *s* of Leopold and Clare Nettel; *m* 1980, Caroline Gillian Mawhood, *qv*; two *s. Educ:* Univ. of Bristol (BA Hons Philosophy). DipHSM, MHSM 1977. Hosp. Sec., Westminster Hosp., 1983–86; General Manager, Whittington and Royal Northern Hosps, 1986–90; Ops Dir, KCH and Dulwich Hosp., 1990–92; Exec. in Residence, Faculty of Admin, Univ. of Ottawa, 1992–93; Chief Executive: Ealing Hosp. NHS Trust, 1994–99; St Mary's NHS Trust, London, 1999–2007. Mem., Expert Reference Gp on Renal Nat. Service Framework, DoH, 2001–03. Gov., Wimbledon Sch. of Art. *Recreations:* painting, cycling, bridge, keeping fit, gardening, golf, jazz. *Address:* 35 Skeena Hill, SW18 5PW. *T:* (020) 8788 2017; *e-mail:* julian@jnettel.freeserve.co.uk. *Clubs:* Roehampton, Royal Anglo-Belgian.

NETTLETON, Catherine Elizabeth, OBE 1999; HM Diplomatic Service; Ambassador to Peru, since 2006; *b* 13 March 1960; *d* of late Kenneth Arthur Nettleton and Olga Nettleton (*née* Musgrave). *Educ:* Exeter Univ. (BA Hons); Manchester Univ. (MA). Inland Revenue, 1982; FCO, 1983; full-time Mandarin lang. training, 1984; Vice Consul, Beijing, 1987–89; Second Sec., FCO, 1989–91; First Sec. (Political/Economic), Mexico City, 1991–95; First Sec., 1995–99, Counsellor, 1999–2000, FCO; Political/Economic Counsellor, Beijing, 2000–03; rcds, 2004; Hd, FCO Services: Presidencies, FCO, 2004–06. *Recreations:* walking, mountaineering, ski mountaineering, theatre. *Address:* c/o Foreign and Commonwealth Office, King Charles Street, SW1A 2AH.

NEUBERGER, family name of **Baroness Neuberger** and **Baron Neuberger of Abbotsbury**.

NEUBERGER, Baroness *cr* 2004 (Life Peer), of Primrose Hill in the London Borough of Camden; **Rabbi Julia Babette Sarah Neuberger,** DBE 2004; Chief Executive, The King's Fund, 1997–2004; a Civil Service Commissioner, 2001–02; *b* 27 Feb. 1950; *d* of late Walter and Alice Schwab; *m* 1973, Anthony John Neuberger; one *s* one *d. Educ:* South Hampstead High Sch.; Newnham Coll., Cambridge (BA, MA); Leo Baeck Coll., London (Rabbinic Dip.). Lectr and Associate Fellow, Leo Baeck Coll., 1979–97; Associate, Newnham Coll., Cambridge, 1983–96; Harkness Fellow, Harvard Univ., 1991–92; Associate Fellow, King's Fund Coll., 1993–97; Bloomberg Prof. of Philanthropy and Public Policy, Divinity Sch., Harvard Univ., 2006. Rabbi, South London Liberal Synagogue, 1977–89; Chm., Rabbinic Conf., Union of Liberal and Progressive Synagogues, 1983–85. Chm., Camden and Islington Community Health Services NHS Trust, 1993–97; Member: Council, N London Hospice Gp, 1984–91; Ethics Adv. Gp, RCN, 1986–93; BMA Ethics Cttee, 1992–94; NHS Health Adv. Service, 1993–97; Council, St George's Hosp. Med. Sch., 1987–93; Chairman: Patients' Assoc., 1988–91; RCN Commn on the Health Service, 1988; Adv. Cttee, UK Clearing House on Health Outcomes, Nuffield Inst., 1992–95; Sainsbury Centre for Mental Health review of training needs of mental health workers; Chair, Commn on the Future of Volunteering, 2006–08; Prime Minister's Champion for Volunteering, 2007–. Member: Cttee on Standards in Public Life, 2001–04; Interim (formerly Voluntary) Licensing Authority for IVF, 1987–91; Human Fertilization and Embryology Authority, 1990–95; GMC, 1993–2001; MRC, 1995–2000; Exec., Anchor Housing Assoc. and Trust, 1985–87; Exec., NCVO, 1988–89; Exec., Unicef UK, 1989–91; Council, SCF, 1994–96; Bd, Citizenship Foundn, 1989–92; Council, St George's House, Windsor, 1989–94; Council, Runnymede Trust, 1989–97; Library and Information Commn, 1995–97; Bd, Inst. for Jewish Policy Res., 2006–; DCMS Mem., Review of Funding of BBC, 1999; Governor, British Inst. of Human Rights, 1989–93; Trustee: Imperial War Mus., 1999–2006; Multifaith Secondary School Trust, 2001–; Booker Prize Foundn, 2002–; Walter and Liesel Schwab Charitable Trust, 2003–; Urban Village, 2004–; Jewish Care, 2004–07; British Council, 2004–07; Liberal Democrats, 2005–; New Philanthropy Capital, 2008–. Member: Nat. Cttee, SDP, 1982–88; Policy Cttee, SDP, 1983–85; Convenor, SDP/Liberal Lawyers' Working Party on Legal Services, 1985–87; Mem., Editorial Bd, Political

Qly, 1987–93. Presenter, Choices, BBC TV, 1986 and 1987. Chancellor, Univ. of Ulster, 1993–2000. Member Council: RHBNC, 1991–93; UCL, 1993–97; Mem. Visiting Cttee, Meml Church, Harvard Univ., 1994–2000; Governor: James Allen's Girls' Sch., 1994–97; Dulwich Coll. Prep. Sch., 1995–97. Booker Prize Judge, 1994. Hon. FCGI 1997; Hon. Fellow, Mansfield Coll., Oxford, 1998. DUniv: Humberside, 1992; Stirling, 1995; Open, 1997; Hon. DSc: Ulster, 1994; Oxford Brookes, 1995; London, 2006; Hon. DLitt: City, 1994; Teesside, 1995; Hon. LLD: Nottingham, 1996; QUB, 2000; Aberdeen 2002; Hon. Dr Sheffield Hallam, 2001. *Publications:* The Story of Judaism (for children), 1986, 2nd edn 1988; (ed) Days of Decision (4 in series), 1987; Caring for Dying Patients of Different Faiths, 1987, 3rd edn 2004; (ed with John A. White) A Necessary End, 1991; Whatever's Happening to Women?, 1991; Ethics and Healthcare: the role of Research Ethics Committees in the UK, 1992; (ed) The Things That Matter (anthology of women's spiritual poetry), 1993; On Being Jewish, 1995; Dying Well: a guide to enabling a better death, 1999, 2nd edn 2004; (ed with Bill New) Hidden Assets: values and decision-making in the NHS today, 2002; The Moral State We're In, 2005; Not Dead Yet, 2008; contribs to various books on cultural, religious and ethical factors in nursing, reviews for variety of jls and newspapers. *Recreations:* sailing, Irish life, opera, setting up the old girls' network, children. *Address:* House of Lords, SW1A 0PW.

NEUBERGER OF ABBOTSBURY, Baron *cr* 2007 (Life Peer), of Abbotsbury in the county of Dorset; **David Edmond Neuberger,** Kt 1996; PC 2004; a Lord of Appeal in Ordinary, since 2007; *b* 10 Jan. 1948; *s* of Prof. Albert Neuberger, CBE, FRS and Lilian Ida (*née* Dreyfus); *m* 1976, Angela, *d* of Brig. Peter Holdsworth; two *s* one *d*. *Educ:* Westminster; Christ Church, Oxford (MA). N. M. Rothschild & Sons, 1970–73; called to the Bar, Lincoln's Inn, 1974, Bencher, 1993; QC 1987; a Recorder, 1990–96; a Judge of the High Ct of Justice, Chancery Div., 1996–2004; Supervisory Chancery Judge, Midland, Wales and Chester, and Western Circuits, 2001–04; a Lord Justice of Appeal, 2004–06. Chm., Adv. Cttee on Spoliation of Art, 1999–. Chm., Schizophrenia Trust, 2003–. Gov., Univ. of the Arts, London (formerly London Inst.), 2000–. *Address:* House of Lords, SW1A 0PW. *Club:* Garrick.

See also M. S. Neuberger.

NEUBERGER, Michael Samuel, PhD; FRS 1993; Member, Scientific Staff, since 1980, and Joint Head, Division of Protein and Nucleic Acid Chemistry, since 2002, Medical Research Council Laboratory of Molecular Biology, Cambridge; Fellow, Trinity College, Cambridge, since 1985; *b* 2 Nov. 1953; *s* of Prof. Albert Neuberger, CBE, FRS and Lilian Ida (*née* Dreyfus); *m* 1991, Gillian Anne, *d* of late James and Anne Pyman; two *s* two *d*. *Educ:* Westminster Sch.; Trinity Coll., Cambridge (BA 1974; MA); Imperial Coll., University of London (PhD 1978). Res. Fellow, Trinity Coll., Cambridge, 1977–81; SRC Postdoctoral Fellow, Imperial Coll., London, 1977–79; EMBO Postdoctoral Fellow, Inst. of Genetics, Cologne, 1979–80. Internat. Res. Scholar, Howard Hughes Med. Inst., 1992–97. Mem., EMBO, 1989; Founder FMedSci 1998. Hon. Prof., Univ. of Cambridge, 2002. Novartis Medal, Biochem. Soc., 2001; William Bate Hardy Prize, Cambridge Philos. Soc., 2001; Prix J.-P. Lecocq, Acad. des Scis, Inst de France, 2002; GlaxoSmithKline Prize, Royal Soc., 2003; Dannie-Heineman Prize, Akad. der Wissenschaften zu Göttingen, 2003. *Publications:* articles in learned jls on molecular biol. and immunology. *Address:* Medical Research Council Laboratory of Molecular Biology, Hills Road, Cambridge CB2 0QH. *T:* (01223) 248011; Trinity College, Cambridge CB2 1TQ. *T:* (01223) 338400.

See also Baron Neuberger of Abbotsbury.

NEUBERT, Sir Michael (Jon), Kt 1990; *b* 3 Sept. 1933; *s* of Frederick Henry and Mathilda Marie Louise Neubert; *m* 1959, Sally Felicity Bilger; one *s*. *Educ:* Queen Elizabeth's Sch., Barnet; Bromley Grammar Sch.; Royal Coll. of Music; Downing Coll., Cambridge (MA (Cantab) Modern and Medieval Langs). Travel and industrial consultant. Councillor, Borough of Bromley, 1960–63; London Borough of Bromley: Councillor, 1964–68; Alderman, 1968–74; Leader of the Council, 1967–70; Mayor, 1972–73. Contested (C): N Hammersmith, 1966; Romford, 1970. MP (C) Havering, Romford, Feb. 1974–1983, Romford, 1983–97; contested (C) same seat, 1997. PPS to: Minister for Social Security and for the Disabled, 1980; Ministers of State, NI Office, 1981; Minister of State for Employment, 1981–82; Sec. of State for Trade, 1982–83; Asst Govt Whip, 1983–86; a Lord Comr of HM Treasury, 1986–88; Vice-Chamberlain of HM Household, 1988; Parly Under-Sec. of State for the Armed Forces, 1988–89, for Defence Procurement, 1989–90, MoD. Chm., Cons. Back bench Employment Cttee, 1992–95; Joint Chm., Cons. Back bench Educn and Employment Cttee, 1995–97; Mem., 1922 Exec. Cttee, 1992–97. Chm., Bromley Conservative Assoc., 1968–69. Rector's Warden, St Margaret's, Westminster, 1997–2007 (Parly Warden, 1995–97). Chm., IoW Internat. Oboe Competition, 1997–2002. *Publication:* Running Your Own Society, 1967. *Recreations:* music, literature, cinema, theatre, the countryside. *Club:* Carlton.

NEVILL, family name of **Marquess of Abergavenny.**

NEVILL, Amanda Elizabeth; Director, British Film Institute, since 2003; *b* 21 March 1957; *d* of John Henry Howard King and Jill King (*née* Livett); *m* 1980, Dominic John Nevill (marr. diss. 1986); two *d*. *Educ:* Bar Convent, York; British Inst., Paris. Rowan Gall., London, 1978–79; Francis Kyle Gall., London, 1979–80; Bath Internat. Fest. Contemporary Art Fair, 1980–84; Adminr, 1985–90, Sec., 1990–94, Royal Photographic Soc.; Head, Nat. Mus. of Photography, Film and TV, 1994–2003. FRSA. Hon. FRPS 1994. Hon. DLit Bradford, 2000. *Address:* British Film Institute, 21 Stephen Street, W1T 1LN. *T:* (020) 7957 8903.

NEVILL, Prof. Bernard Richard, FCSD; designer; Professor of Textile Design, Royal College of Art, 1984–89 (Fellow, since 1984); Director, Bernard Nevill Ltd (own furnishing collections), since 1990; *b* 24 Sept. 1934; *s* of R. G. Nevill. *Educ:* privately; St Martin's Sch. of Art; Royal Coll. of Art. FSIA 1970. Designed exhibn, Opera and Ballet, for Cotton Bd, Manchester, 1950; lectured in art, fashion, history of costume, textile design and fashion drawing, Shoreditch Coll., 1954–56 (resp. for first dress show staged at GLC Chm's annual reception, County Hall); Lectr, St Martin's Sch. of Art and RCA, 1959–74 (liaised between Fashion and Textile Schs, devising projs and themes for finale to RCA annual diploma show; lectured in theatre design and book illustration, Central Sch. of Art and Design, 1957–60; freelance illustrator, Good Housekeeping, Woman's Jl, Vogue, Harper's Bazaar, incl. covers for Queen and Sketch, 1956–60; freelance journalist, Vogue, Sketch and textile and fashion periodicals, 1956–66; Art Critic, Vogue, 1965–66; Designer (later Design Dir), Liberty Prints, 1961: for next decade, produced collections which became fashion landmarks and re-estabd Liberty's as major source of fashion textiles worldwide; collections designed: Islamic, 1963 (anticipated Eastern revival in fashion); Jazz, 1964 (first re-appraisal of Art Deco); Tango, 1966; Renaissance, 1967; Chameleon, 1969 (co-ordinated prints); Designer and Design Dir, Ten Cate, Holland, 1969–71; Design Consultant in dress fabrics to Cantoni (founders of cotton industry in Italy), 1971–84: printed velvets and cottons have placed Cantoni in forefront of internat. ready-to-wear; designed printed sheet collection for Cantoni Casa, 1977; textile consultant and designer of dress fabrics, Unitika Ltd, Japan, 1990–; dress fabric collections for KBC,

Germany, 1993–; furnishing textile designs commnd by Pierre Frey, France, 1991–; furnishing collections produced by DMC Texunion, France, 1992–; designing own-label home textile and furniture collections, with Hodsoll McKenzie, 1999–2001; redesign and supervision of restoration of interiors: Lennoxlove Castle, 1988–89; Eastnor Castle, 1989. Designed: two collections for Internat. Wool Secretariat, 1975–77; English Country House Collection for Sekers Internat., 1981–82 (used this collection when redesigning Long Gall., Lutyen's British Embassy, Washington); Collections for Romanex de Boussac, France, 1982–87, including English Gardens, Botanic, Figurative Porcelain Prints and Printed Damasks; furnishing collection for restored Château de Bagnole, France. Designed costumes: films: Genevieve, 1953; Next To No Time, 1955; The Admirable Crichton, 1957; musical: Marigold, 1958; opera: Così fan tutte (Glyndebourne), 1962. Engaged in restoration of Fonthill Abbey and woodlands, 1976–. Mem., Adv. Panel, National Dip. of Design, 1964–66; Governor, Croydon Coll. of Art, 1966–67. FRSA 1966, resigned 1977. Book reviewer, TLS, 1987–. Illustrated articles on his work have appeared in the Press. *Recreations:* looking at large well-built walls and buildings; passionate conservationist and environmentalist, collector, bibliophil; tree-worship, chamber music. *Address:* West House, 35 Glebe Place, SW3 5JP; Fonthill Abbey, Fonthill Gifford, near Salisbury, Wilts SP3 6PX.

NEVILLE, family name of **Baron Braybrooke.**

NEVILLE, Prof. Adam Matthew, CBE 1994; TD 1963; FREng; FRSE; arbitrator and consultant on concrete and structural design and failures; Partner (formerly Director), A & M Neville Engineering, since 1975; Principal and Vice-Chancellor, University of Dundee, 1978–87; *b* 5 Feb. 1923; *m* 1952, Dr Mary Hallam Cousins; one *s* one *d*. *Educ:* Queen Mary Coll., London Univ. (BSc 1st cl. Hons; Hon. Fellow, QMW, 1997); MSc, PhD, DSc (Eng) London; DSc Leeds. FICE, FIStructE; FREng (FEng 1986); FRSE 1979. Served War, Polish Forces under British comd, MC; Major RE (TA), 1950–63. Lectr, Southampton Univ., 1950–51; Engr, Min. of Works, NZ, 1951–54; Lectr, Manchester Univ., 1955–60; Prof. of Civil Engrg, Nigerian Coll. of Technology, 1960–62; Foundn Dean of Engrg, Calgary Univ., 1963–67, also Foundn Dean of Graduate Studies, 1965–66; Vis. Prof., Swiss Federal Inst. of Technology, 1967–68; Prof. and Head of Dept of Civil Engineering, Univ. of Leeds, 1968–78. Chm., Cttee of Principals of Scottish Univs, 1984–86. Former Chm., Permanent Concrete Commn, RILEM (Internat. Union of Testing and Res. Labs for Materials and Structures); Dir, Petroleum Recovery Res. Inst.; Advr to Canadian Govt on management of concrete research. Member Council: Concrete Soc., 1968–77, (Pres., 1974–75); IStructE, 1976–79; Faculty of Building, 1976–80; Royal Acad. (formerly Fellowship) of Engrg, 1989–95 (Vice-Pres., 1991–95); Open University, 1979–87; Council of Europe Standing Conference on Univ. Problems, 1980–87 (Pres., 1984–86); Member: Bd, Architectural Educn, ARC, 1980–87; Exec. Cttee, IUPC, 1979–90 (Vice-Chm., 1983–85); British Library Adv. Council, 1989–94; SERC Envmt Cttee, 1988–91; Athlone-Vanier Fellowships Bd, 1990–96; NAPAG, 1992–97. Trustee, Carnegie Trust for Univs of Scotland, 1978–87. Mem. Editorial Boards of various technical jls. Fellow: Amer. Concrete Inst., 1973 (Hon. Mem., 1986); Concrete Soc., 1994 (Hon. Mem., 2000); Hon. Fellow: Inst. of Concrete Technology, 1976; Singapore Concrete Inst., 1987; Hon. Mem., Brazilian Concrete Inst., 2007; Hon. For. Mem., Académie Royale des Sciences d'Outre-Mer, Belgium, 1974. Hon. LLD: St Andrews, 1987; Dundee, 1998; Hon. DAppSci Sherbrooke, Quebec, 1999. IStructE Research Award, 1960; Reinforced Concrete Assoc. Medal, 1961; Senior Research Fellowship, Nat. Research Council of Canada, 1967; Stanton Walker Award (US) 1968; Medal of Univ. of Liège (Belgium), 1970; Arthur R. Anderson Award, 1972, Turner Medal, 2001, Amer. Concrete Inst.; President's Medal, Soc. of Engrs, 1985; Silver Medal, Inst. of Concrete Technology, 1993; Gold Medal, Concrete Soc., 2007; Sustained Achievement Medal, RAEng. OStJ 1983. *Publications:* Properties of Concrete, 1963, 4th edn 1995, trans. into 13 languages; (with J. B. Kennedy) Basic Statistical Methods, 1964, 3 edns; Creep of Concrete: plain, reinforced and prestressed, 1970; (with A. Ghali) Structural Analysis: a unified classical and matrix approach, 1971, 6th edn 2008 (trans. Chinese, Japanese); Hardened Concrete: physical and mechanical aspects, 1971; High Alumina Cement Concrete, 1975; (with W. H. Dilger and J. J. Brooks) Creep of Plain and Structural Concrete, 1983; (with J. J. Brooks) Concrete Technology, 1987; Neville on Concrete, 2003, 2nd edn 2007; Concrete: Neville's insights and issues, 2006; numerous research papers on concrete and concrete structures. *Recreations:* ski-ing (reminiscing), travel (Travelers' Century Club Plaque, 1990). *Clubs:* Athenæum; New (Edinburgh).

See also Dame E. L. Neville.

NEVILLE, Prof. (Alexander) Munro, MD; FRCPath; Professor of Medical Oncology, Imperial College London, since 2006; *b* 24 March 1935; *s* of Alexander Munro and Georgina Neville; *m* 1961, Anne Margaret Stroyan Black; one *s* one *d*. *Educ:* Hillhead High Sch.; Univ. of Glasgow (MB ChB 1959; PhD 1965; MD 1969); Harvard Med. Sch.; DSc London, 1985. MRCPath 1969, FRCPath 1981. Med. appts, Glasgow Royal and Victoria Infirmaries, 1960–65; Res. Fellow, Harvard Med. Sch., 1965–67; Sen. Lectr in Pathology, Univ. of Glasgow, 1967–70; Hon. Consultant Pathologist, Royal Marsden Hosp., 1970–85; Prof. of Experimental Pathology, Univ. of London, 1972–85; Dean, Inst. of Cancer Research, 1982–84; Dir, Ludwig Inst. for Cancer Research, London Branch, 1975–85; Administrator, subseq. Associate Dir. and Res. Sec., Ludwig Inst. for Cancer Res., NY and London, 1985–2005. Vis. Prof. of Pathol., RPMS, 1992–2006. Hon. Treas., RCPath, 1993–98. *Publications:* The Human Adrenal Cortex, 1982; numerous papers on oncology and pathology in primary jls. *Recreations:* golf, gardening. *Address:* 6 Woodlands Park, Tadworth, Surrey KT20 7TL. *T:* (01737) 844113; Department of Medical Oncology, Hammersmith Hospital, Du Cane Road, W12 0HS; *e-mail:* munroneville@f2s.com. *Clubs:* Athenæum; Banstead Downs.

NEVILLE, Prof. Brian George Richard, FRCP, FRCPCH; Prince of Wales's Professor of Childhood Epilepsy, Institute of Child Health, University College London, Great Ormond Street Hospital for Children NHS Trust and National Centre for Young People with Epilepsy, since 2004; *b* 13 Feb. 1939; *s* of George Edward Neville and Louisa Nellie Neville; *m* 1964, Heather Maureen Gemmell; one *s* three *d*. *Educ:* St Dunstan's Coll., Catford; Guy's Hosp. Med. Sch., London (MB BS 1964). MRCP 1966, FRCP 1980; FRCPCH 1997. Consultant Paediatric Neurologist, Guy's Hosp., 1973–89; Prof. of Paediatric Neurology, Inst. of Child Health, UCL, 1989–2004; Hon. Consultant Paediatric Neurologist, Great Ormond St Hosp. for Children, Nat. Centre for Young People with Epilepsy and Nat. Hosp. for Neurology and Neurosurgery, 1989–. Hon. Paediatric Neurologist: Jersey, 1989–2004; Malta, 1992–. Sec., 1980–83 and Pres., 1986–89, British Paediatric Neurology Assoc.; Founder and Chm., Europ. Acad. of Childhood Disability, 1989–2002; Co-Founder and Chm., Europ. Soc. of Movt Analysis in Children, 1993–96. *Publications:* (ed jtly) Congenital Hemiplegia, 2000; (ed jtly) The Management of Spasticity Associated with the Cerebral Palsies in Children or Adults, 2000; articles in paediatric neurology, particularly epilepsy and disability. *Recreations:* music, church organist, cycling, walking. *Address:* UCL Institute of Child Health, Neurosciences Unit, The Wolfson Centre, Mecklenburgh Square, WC1N 2AP. *T:* (020) 7837 7618, *Fax:* (020) 7833 9469; *e-mail:* bneville@ich.ucl.ac.uk. *Club:* Royal Society of Medicine.

NEVILLE, Dame Elizabeth (Louise), DBE 2003; QPM 1996; PhD; Chief Constable, Wiltshire Constabulary, 1997–2004; *b* 5 Dec. 1953; *d* of Prof. Adam Matthew Neville, *qv*; *m* 2003, Nicholas David Cox; one *s* one *d* from previous marriage. *Educ:* St Hilda's Coll., Oxford (MA; Hon. Fellow, 2006); University Coll. London (PhD). Metropolitan Police, 1973–86; Thames Valley Police, 1986–91; Asst Chief Constable, Sussex Police, 1991–94; Dep. Chief Constable, Northamptonshire, 1994–97. Non-exec. Dir, Serious Fraud Office, 2004–. Member: Police Appeals Tribunal, 2004–08; Ind. Complaints Assessor, DVO Gp, subseq. Safety, Service Delivery and Logistics Gp, DfT, 2004–; Complaints Adjudicator, Assets Recovery Agency, 2004–08; Civil Nuclear Police Authy, 2005–; Ind. Adjudicator, Companies House, 2007–. Sen. Advr, Olive Gp, 2006–07. Dir, Ajay Shopfit Maintenance Ltd. Trustee: Cumberland Lodge (formerly King George VI and Queen Elizabeth Foundn of St Catharine's), 2002–; Wiltshire Bobby Van. Patron, Swindon Sanctuary, 2004–. Mem., Bd of Govs, Stonar Sch., Wilts, 2005–. Hon. Fellow, Univ. of Northampton, 2004. Hon. LLD Southampton Solent, 2004. *Recreations:* ski-ing, riding, sailing. *Club:* Reform.

NEVILLE, John, CM 2006; OBE 1965; actor, stage and film; Hon. Professor in Drama, Nottingham University, since 1967; Artistic Director, Festival Theatre, Stratford, Ontario, 1985–89; *b* Willesden, 2 May 1925; *s* of Reginald Daniel Neville and Mabel Lillian (*née* Fry); *m* 1949, Caroline Hooper; three *s* three *d*. *Educ:* Willesden and Chiswick County Schools; Royal Academy of Dramatic Art. Worked as a stores clerk before studying at RADA. First appearance on stage, walking-on part in Richard II; subseq. parts at Open Air Theatre, in repertory at Lowestoft, and with Birmingham Repertory Co.; Bristol Old Vic Co., 1950–53; Old Vic Co., London, 1953–61; Nottingham Playhouse, 1961–63; Theatre Director, Nottingham Playhouse, 1963–68; Dir, Park Theatre Co., Fortune, 1969; Theatre Director: Citadel Theatre, Edmonton, Canada, 1973–78; Neptune Theatre, Halifax, NS, 1978–83. Parts with Old Vic include: Ferdinand in The Tempest, Macduff, Richard II, Orlando in As You Like It, Henry Percy in Henry IV, Part I, Mark Antony; during Old Vic tour of Europe, 1958, Hamlet, Sir Andrew Aguecheek. Played lead in Irma La Douce, Lyric, 1959–60; produced Henry V, Old Vic, 1960; The Lady From the Sea, Queen's, 1961; The School for Scandal, Haymarket, 1962; Alfie, Mermaid and Duchess, 1963. Acted in: The Chichester Festival Theatre, 1962; Beware of the Dog, St Martin's, 1967; Iago in Othello, Nottingham Playhouse, 1967; Mr and Mrs, Palace, 1968; The Apple Cart, Mermaid, 1970; The Beggar's Opera, The Doctor's Dilemma, Chichester, 1972; Sherlock Holmes, NY, 1975; Happy Days, Nat. Theatre, 1977; Grand Theatre, London, Ontario: acted in Dear Antoine and Arsenic and Old Lace, directed Hamlet, 1983; Stratford, Ontario: acted in Loves Labours' Lost, 1983, Merchant of Venice, 1984, Intimate Admiration, 1987, My Fair Lady, 1988; directed Mother Courage, and Othello, 1987, Three Sisters, 1989; acted in: The School for Scandal, NT, 1990; The Dance of Death, Almeida, 1995; Beethoven's Tenth, Chichester, 1996; Krapp's Last Tape, Nottingham Playhouse, 1999. Tour W Africa (Jt Dir and acting), 1963. *Films:* Oscar Wilde; Topaze; Billy Budd; A Study in Terror; Adventures of Baron Munchausen; The X-Files. Has appeared on television, incl. The First Churchills, series for BBC 2. Hon. Dr Dramatic Arts Lethbridge Univ., 1979; Hon. DFA Nova Scotia Coll. of Art and Design, 1981; Hon. LLD Ryerson Univ., 1999. *Address:* 24 Wellesley Street West, #511, Toronto, ON M4Y 2X6, Canada. *Clubs:* Royal Over-Seas League; Arts and Letters (Toronto).

NEVILLE, (John) Oliver, MA, PhD; Principal, Royal Academy of Dramatic Art, 1984–93; *b* 14 Aug. 1929; *s* of Frederick and Ethel Neville; *m* 1st, 1952, Shirley Hall; one *s* one *d*; 2nd, 1964, Pat Heywood. *Educ:* Price's Sch., Fareham; King's Coll., Cambridge (Le Bas Student; BA Eng. Lit., MA, PhD). After National Service, engaged in following with ultimate aim of becoming a theatre director: studied theatre design under Reginald Leefe, 1949–51; joined Old Vic Co., walking on in Tyrone Guthrie's Tamburlaine, with Donald Wolfit, 1951; studied singing with Clive Carey and Frank Titterton; seasons of rep. at York, Scarborough, Worthing, Bristol, Birmingham and Manchester, 1952–58; re-joined Old Vic Co., 1958 (roles included Warwick in Henry VI Trilogy and Claudius in Hamlet); toured America, Poland, Russia, India, Pakistan, Ceylon, with Old Vic and Bristol Old Vic, as stage dir, actor and dir; Associate Dir, Old Vic Co., 1960–62 (directed Macbeth and The Tempest); Director: Library Theatre, Manchester, 1963–66; Arts Theatre, Ipswich, 1966–69; Mature Student, Cambridge, 1969–76 (PhD on Ben Jonson's Masques and Poetry); Caroline Spurgeon Res. Fellow, Bedford Coll., London, 1977–79; Sen. Lectr in Drama, Univ. of Bristol, 1979–84. *Recreations:* mediaeval church architecture and stained-glass, gardening. *Address:* c/o Peters, Fraser & Dunlop, Drury House, 34–43 Russell Street, WC2B 5HA.

NEVILLE, Munro; *see* Neville, A. M.

NEVILLE, Air Vice-Marshal Patrick, CB 1988; OBE 1976; AFC 1960; Chief of Air Staff, Royal New Zealand Air Force, 1986–89, retired; *b* 23 Sept. 1932; *s* of Patrick Joseph Neville and Helena Neville; *m* 1954, Barbara Howell; one *s* one *d*. *Educ:* Purbrook Park County High Sch. (SchCert). Commnd 1951; Navigator: RAF, 1951–55; RNZAF, 1955; CO No 14 Sqdn RNZAF, 1966–69; Base Comdr, RNZAF Base Ohakea, NZ, 1969–70; Hon. ADC to Gov. Gen., 1972; Sen. ASO, Air HQ, ANZUK Force Singapore; later, Dep. Comdr NZ Force SE Asia in Singapore, 1973–75; RNZAF Air Staff, 1975–77; Base Comdr, RNZAF Base Auckland, 1978–79; AOC RNZAF Support Gp, 1980–82; Asst CDS for Operations and Plans, Defence HQ, Wellington, 1982–83; Hd of NZ Defence Liaison Staff, London, 1984–86. Gp Captain 1973, Air Cdre 1980, Air Vice-Marshal 1986. FNZIM; FRAeS. *Recreations:* golf, fishing. *Address:* 12 Mark Place, Lynmore, Rotorua 3010, New Zealand. *T:* (7) 3459650. *Club:* Rotorua Golf.

NEVILLE-JONES, Baroness *cr* 2007 (Life Peer), of Hutton Roof in the County of Cumbria; **(Lilian) Pauline Neville-Jones,** DCMG 1996 (CMG 1987); Shadow Security Minister and National Security Adviser to the Leader of the Opposition, since 2007; *b* 2 Nov. 1939; *d* of Roland Neville-Jones and Dr Cecilia Emily Millicent Winn. *Educ:* Leeds Girls' High Sch.; Lady Margaret Hall, Oxford (BA Hons Mod. History). Harkness Fellow of Commonwealth Fund, USA, 1961–63; HM Diplomatic Service, 1963–96: Third Sec., Salisbury, Rhodesia, 1964–65; Third, later Second Sec., Singapore, 1965–68; FCO, 1968–71; First Sec., Washington, 1971–75; FCO, 1975–77; Mem. Cabinet, later Chef de Cabinet to Christopher Tugendhat, European Comr for Budget, Financial Control, Financial Instns and Taxation, 1977–82; Vis. Fellow, RIIA, and Inst. français des relations internationales, 1982–83; Head of Planning Staff, FCO, 1983–87; Minister (Econ.), 1987–88, Minister, 1988–91, Bonn; Dep. Sec., Cabinet Office (on secondment), 1991–94; Chm., Jt Intelligence Cttee, Cabinet Office, 1993–94; Political Dir and Dep. Under-Sec. of State, FCO, 1994–96; Sen. Advr to High Rep. for Bosnia (on secondment), 1996. Man. Dir, and Hd of Global Business Strategy, NatWest Markets, 1996–98; Vice Chm., Hawkpoint Partners Ltd, 1998–2000; Chm., QinetiQ Group plc, 2002–05. Chm., Information Assurance Adv. Council, 2002–07. A Gov., BBC, 1998–2004. Mem. Council, Oxford Univ., 2004–06; Mem. Adv. Council, City Univ., 2006–. FRSA 1986. DUniv Open, 1998; Hon. DSc (Econ) London, 1999; Hon. DSc City, 2007. Légion d'Honneur, 2007. *Recreations:* antiques, cooking, gardening. *Address:* House of Lords, SW1A 0PW.

NEVILLE-ROLFE, Lucy Jeanne, (Lady Packer), CMG 2005; Executive Director, Corporate and Legal Affairs, Tesco plc, since 2006; *b* 2 Jan. 1953; *d* of Edmund and late Margaret Neville-Rolfe; *m* Sir Richard John Packer, *qv*; four *s*. *Educ:* Somerville Coll., Oxford (BA PPE; MA; Hon. Fellow, 2003). Joined MAFF, 1973; Pvte Sec. to Minister of Agric., Fisheries and Food, 1977–79; EC Sheepmeat and Milk, 1979–86; Land Use, 1986–88; Food Safety Act, 1988–90; Head of Personnel, 1990–92; Mem., Prime Minister's Policy Unit, 1992–94; Under Sec., 1994; Dir, Deregulation Unit, DTI, then Better Regulation Unit, Cabinet Office, 1995–97; Gp Dir of Corporate Affairs, 1997–2006, and Company Sec., 2003–06, Tesco plc. Non-executive Director: John Laing Construction, 1991–92; Bd of Mgt, FCO, 2000–05; Carbon Trust, 2008–; Chm., Dobbies Garden Centres plc, 2007–. Member: Dep. Prime Minister's Local Govt Funding Cttee, 2003–04; ESRC Panel on Cultures of Consumption, 2003–07; Corporate Leaders Gp on Climate Change, 2005–. British Retail Consortium: Bd of Mgt, 1998–; Dep. Chair, 2003; Chm., Confederation of British Industry: Mem., Econs and Eur. Cttees, 1998–; Vice Pres., Euro Commerce, 1998–; Mem., UNICE Task Force on Enlargement, 1999–2004. *Recreations:* cricket, racing, gardening, art, architecture, theatre. *Address:* Tesco plc, Tesco House, Delamare Road, Cheshunt, Herts EN8 9SL. *T:* (01992) 632222, *Fax:* (01992) 623371.

See also M. T. Neville-Rolfe.

NEVILLE-ROLFE, Marianne Teresa, CB 2000; Executive Director, South East England Development Agency, 2001–04; *b* 9 Oct. 1944; *d* of Edmund Neville-Rolfe and late Margaret (*née* Evans); *m* 1st, 1972, David William John Blake (marr. diss. 1992); 2nd, 2001, Peter Andrew Hill. *Educ:* St Mary's Convent, Shaftesbury; Lady Margaret Hall, Oxford (BA). CBI, 1965–73 (Head, Brussels Office, 1971–72); Principal, DTI, 1973, Asst Sec., 1982, Under Sec., Internal European Policy Div., 1987; Chief Exec., CS Coll., and Dir, Top Management Prog., OMCS, then OPSS, Cabinet Office, 1990–94; Regl Dir, Govt Office for NW, 1994–99; Chief Exec., New East Manchester Ltd, 2000. Mem., ESRC, 2000–03. *Recreations:* travel, opera. *Address:* Angle Croft, Somerford Booths, Congleton, Cheshire CW12 2JU.

See also L. J. Neville-Rolfe.

NEVIN, Prof. Norman Cummings, OBE 2003; MD; FRCP, FRCPE, FRCPath, FFPH; Professor of Medical Genetics, Queen's University of Belfast, 1975–2000, now Emeritus (Personal Chair, 1975–78); Consultant Clinical Geneticist and Head, Northern Ireland Regional Genetics Service, Belfast City Health Trust, 1968–2000; *b* 10 June 1935; *s* of Joseph and Sarah Nevin; *m* 1961, Jean Hamilton; one *s* one *d*. *Educ:* Queen's Univ. of Belfast (BSc 1957; MB BCh; BAO 1960; MD 1964). FRCPE 1976; FFPH (FFPHM 1981); FRCPath 1981; FRCP 1990. House physician and surgeon, Royal Victoria Hosp., Belfast, 1960–61; John Dunville Fellow in Pathology, QUB, 1961–64; Registrar in Medicine, Royal Victoria Hosp., 1964–65; MRC Fellow, MRC Clinical Genetics Unit, Inst. of Child Health, London and MRC Population Genetics Res. Unit, Oxford, 1965–67; Lectr in Human Genetics, QUB, 1967–75. Mem., Gene Therapy Adv. Cttee, 1993–2006 (Chm., 1996–2006). Mem., Assoc. Physicians of GB and Ireland, 1986–. President: Clinical Genetics Soc., 1991–92; Ulster Paediatric Soc., 1989. *Publications:* numerous contribs on congenital abnormalities in learned medical jls. *Recreations:* walking (hill), painting, medical ethics. *Address:* 17 Ogles Grove, Hillsborough, Co. Down, Northern Ireland BT28 6RS.

NEW, Maj.-Gen. Sir Laurence (Anthony Wallis), Kt 1990; CB 1986; CBE 1980; Lieutenant Governor of the Isle of Man, and President of the Tynwald Court, 1985–90; International President, Association of Military Christian Fellowships, 1991–2002; *b* 25 Feb. 1932; *s* of Lt-Col S. W. New, MBE and Mrs C. M. New; *m* 1956, Anna Doreen Verity (CStJ); two *s* two *d*. *Educ:* King William's College, Isle of Man. RMA Sandhurst, 1950–52; commissioned, RTR, 1952; service in Hong Kong, Germany, Malaya, Borneo; CO 4 RTR, 1971–73; Bde Major, 20th Armd Bde, 1969–70; Sec., Defence Policy Staff, 1970–71; Defence and Military Attaché, Tel Aviv, 1974–77; Col GS, MoD, 1977–79; Brig. GS, MoD, 1981–82; ACGS (Op. Reqs), 1983–84; ACDS (Land Systems), MoD, 1984–85; graduate Staff Coll., JSSC, RCDS. Col Comdt, RTR, 1986–93; Vice Pres., TA&VRA, 1985–90; Hon. Col I of M ACF, 1998–2002. Gen. Sec., Officers' Pensions Soc., 1990–95; Campaign Dir, War and Service Widows Pensions Campaign, 1994–95. Consultant, Lagan Gp of Cos, 1998–; Director: Charles Brand (IOM) Ltd, 1999–2006; Lagan Construction (IOM) Ltd, 2006–. Lectr, Sir John Cass Business Sch., City of London (formerly City Univ. Business Sch.), 1992–2002; Instructor, 2003–05, Team Dir, 2005–, Pointman Leadership Inst. Licenced Reader, C of E, 1974–; Local Preacher, Methodist Church, IOM Dist, 2004–; Church Warden, St Peter upon Cornhill, 1986–95; Pres., Soldiers' and Airmen's Scripture Readers Assoc., 1985–99; Vice Pres., Officers' Christian Union, 1988–93. President: Manx Music Fest., 1985–90; Mananan Internat. Fest. of Music and the Arts, 1987–; Manx Nat. Youth Band, 1995–; Mannin Art Gp, 1996–2007; Friends of the Gaiety Theatre, 1996–2006. County Pres., St John Ambulance Brigade and Assoc., 1985–90, and 1999–2007; Patron: I of M Red Cross, 1985–90; Burma Star Assoc. (I of M), 1995–; Pres., Normandy Veterans Assoc. (I of M), 1997–; Vice-Pres., 4/7th RTR Old Comrades, 1997–. Pres., Fishermen's Mission, 1998–2007; Vice Patron, Royal Nat. Mission to Deep Sea Fishermen, 1999–; Patron: Ramsey Life Boat, 1999–; Choice of Living in Community Homes, 1999–; Friends of Chernobyl's Children, 1999–. Chairman: Bishop Barrow's Trustees, 1985–90; Royal Jubilee and Prince's Trust (I of M), 1986–90; Pres., White House School, Wokingham, 1985–. Freeman, City of London, 1985. CCMI 2004 (FBIM 1979; CBIM 1986). KStJ 1986. Internat. Centurion Award, Washington, 2000. *Recreations:* family, music, water colour painting. *Address:* The Granary, Ballaquark Farm, Laxey, Isle of Man IM4 7PH. *Fax:* 08700 941434; *e-mail:* generalnew@manx.net. *Club:* Army and Navy.

NEW SOUTH WALES, Metropolitan of; *see* Sydney, Archbishop of.

NEW WESTMINSTER, Bishop of, since 1994; **Rt Rev. Michael Ingham;** *b* 25 Aug. 1949; *s* of Herbert and Dorothy Ingham; *m* 1982, Gwen Robbins; two *d*. *Educ:* Univ. of Edinburgh (MA 1970; BD 1973 (First Class Hons)). Ordained deacon and priest, 1974; Asst Curate, St John the Evangelist, Ottawa, Ontario, 1974–76; Rector: Christ the King, Burnaby, BC, 1976–80; St Francis-in-the-Wood, W Vancouver, 1980–89; Principal Sec. to the Primate, Toronto, 1989–92; Dean of Christ Church Cathedral, Vancouver, 1992–94. Hon. DD Vancouver Sch. of Theol., 1998. *Publications:* Rites for a New Age, 1985, 2nd edn 1990; Mansions of the Spirit, 1997. *Recreations:* sailing, golf. *Address:* #580–401 West Georgia Street, Vancouver, BC V6B 5A1, Canada. *T:* (604) 6846306.

NEWALL, family name of **Baron Newall**.

NEWALL, 2nd Baron *cr* 1946; **Francis Storer Eaton Newall;** DL; former company director and chairman of several companies; Chairman, British Greyhound Racing Board, 1985–97; *b* 23 June 1930; *o s* of 1st Baron (Marshal of the RAF Lord) Newall, GCB, OM, GCMG, CBE, AM; *S* father, 1963; *m* 1956, Pamela Elizabeth, *e d* of E. H. L. Rowcliffe, Pinkney Park, Malmesbury, Wilts; two *s* one *d*. *Educ:* Eton College; RMA Sandhurst. Commissioned into 11th Hussars (Prince Albert's Own), 1950; served in: Germany, 1950–53; Malaya, 1953–55; on staff of GHQ FarELF, Singapore, 1955–56; Adjt Royal

Gloucestershire Hussars, 1956–58; retired 1961. Introduced Farriers Registration Acts and Betting Gaming and Lotteries Amendment Acts (Greyhound Racing) in House of Lords. Cons. Whip and front bench spokesman, 1976–79; Founder Mem., House of Lords all party Defence Study Group; official visits to NATO, SHAPE, Norway, Morocco, Bonn, Cyprus, BAOR, Qatar, Oman, Bahrain and Romania; Deleg. to Council of Europe and WEU, 1983–97. Mem., Select Cttee on Laboratory Animals Protection Bill. Pres., Soc. for Protection of Animals Abroad. Chm., British Moroccan Soc., 2000–05. Mem., Merchant Taylors' Co. (Master, 1985–86). DL Greater London, 1988. *Recreations:* sport, travel, meeting people. *Heir: s* Hon. Richard Hugh Eaton Newall [*b* 19 Feb. 1961; *m* 1996, Keira, *d* of Robert Glen; two *d*]. *Address:* Wotton Underwood, Aylesbury, Bucks HP18 0RZ. *Club:* Cavalry and Guards.

NEWALL, Sir Paul (Henry), Kt 1994; TD 1967; JP; DL; Lord Mayor of London, 1993–94; *b* 17 Sept. 1934; *s* of late Leopold Newall and Frances Evelyn Newall (*née* Bean); *m* 1969, Penelope Moyra (MBE 2008), *o d* of Sir Julian (Errington) Ridsdale, CBE and of Lady Ridsdale (*see* V. E. P. Ridsdale); two *s*. *Educ:* Harrow; Magdalene Coll., Cambridge (MA Econs). Nat. Service, commnd Royal Fusiliers, 1953–55; TA 1955–70, Major. Partner, Loeb Rhoades & Co. (mem., NY Stock Exchange), 1971; Overseas Director: Shearson Loeb Rhoades Inc., 1978; Shearson Lehman American Express (UK) Hldgs, 1981; Exec. Dir, Lehman Brothers Securities, 1990; Dir, Lehman Brothers Ltd (formerly Shearson Lehman International Ltd), 1985–94 (Sen. Advr, 1993–98); non-exec. Dir, Guardian Royal Exchange plc, 1995–99. Member: Adv. Cttee, Energy Internat. NV, 1978–98; Korea Advisers Gp, 1997–, Asia Pacific Advisers Gp, 2000–02, Trade Partners UK; UK-Japan 21st Century Gp., 1997–. Vice-Pres., Inst. of Export, 1995–2002. City of London: Mem., Court of Common Council (Ward of Cripplegate), 1980–81; Alderman, Ward of Walbrook, 1981–2005; Sheriff, 1989–90; Chm., City of London TAVRA, 1986–89; Vice-Chm., TA&VRA for Gtr London, 1989–95; Hon. Col, The London Regt, 1995–2001; Master, Bakers' Co., 1990–91; Founder Master, Guild of Internat. Bankers, 2001; Member: Guild of Freemen, 1988– (Court, 1988–91); Court, HAC, 1980–2005; Incorp. of Bakers of Glasgow, 1995–; Hon. Liveryman, Marketors' Co., 1995; Hon. Freeman, Fuellers' Co., 1995. Vice-Pres., City of London Sector, British Red Cross, 1986–; Member: Friends of St Paul's Cathedral; City Heritage Soc.; Samuel Pepys Club; Pro-Chancellor and Chm. Council, City Univ., 1997–2003; Governor: MENCAP City Foundn, 1982–97; City of London Freemen's Sch., 1987–88; City of London Girls' Sch., 1997–98; City of London Boys' Sch., 1999–2001; Trustee: Morden Coll., 1991–2004; City of London Endowment Trust for St Paul's Cathedral, 1996–2004; Temple Bar Trust, 1996–2004; Internat. Bankers Charitable Trust, 1992–2008; Exec. Trustee, Army Benevolent Fund, 1998–2007; Pres., Fedn of Old Comrades Assocs of London Territorial and Auxiliary Units, 2003–; Patron: Samaritans Nat. Appeal, 1989–98; Internat. Centre for Child Studies, 1989–93. Hon. Rep., City of Seoul, 1996–; Chm., UK-Korea Forum for the Future, 1999–2008. Churchwarden, St Stephen's, Walbrook, 1981–2005. Burgess, City of Glasgow, 1995. One of HM Lieutenants of City of London, 1975–; DL Gtr London, 1977; JP City of London, 1981; Hon. Vis. Magistrate, HM Tower of London, 1988–. Hon. DLitt City, 1993. KStJ 1993. Hon. Citizen, Georgia, USA, 1994. Order of Diplomatic Merit (First Class) (Korea), 1999. *Publication:* Japan and the City of London, 1996. *Recreations:* fencing, fly fishing, shooting, water-ski-ing, tennis, trees. *Address:* Grove Park, Yoxford, Suffolk IP17 3HX. *Clubs:* East India, City Livery, United Wards, Walbrook Ward, MCC, Pilgrims.

NEWALL, Peter; HM Diplomatic Service, retired; Ambassador to Senegal and, concurrently, to Mali, Guinea-Bissau and Cape Verde, 2004–07; *b* 20 March 1947; *s* of Bobbie and Clio Newall; *m* 1969, Marina (*née* McHugh); one *s* two *d*. *Educ:* Kent Coll., Canterbury. Joined HM Diplomatic Service, 1966; Attaché, Tehran, 1970–72; Entry Clearance Officer, New Delhi, 1972–75; Finance Dept, FCO, 1975–79; 2nd Sec. (Commercial), Belgrade, 1979–82; 1st Sec. (Commercial), Kuwait, 1982–85; Nuclear Energy Dept, FCO, 1985–89; HM Consul, Marseilles, 1989–90; Jt Mgt Officer, Geneva, 1990–95; Counter Terrorism Policy Dept, FCO, 1995–97; Non-Proliferation Dept, FCO, 1997–99; Jt Mgt Officer, Brussels, 1999–2004. *Recreations:* golf, ski-ing, tennis, cinema, fixing things.

NEWARK, Archdeacon of; *see* Peyton, Ven. N.

NEWBERRY, Raymond Scudamore, OBE 1989; Director, Brazil, British Council, 1990–93; *b* 8 Feb. 1935; *s* of late James Henry Newberry and Doris Ada Newberry; *m* 1967, Angelina Nance (*d* 2007); one *s* one *d*. *Educ:* Bristol Grammar Sch.; Selwyn Coll., Cambridge (BA); Univ. of Leeds (DipESL); Univ. of Bristol (DipEd). National Service, 1953–55. Lectr, Coll. of Arts, Baghdad Univ., 1959–62; British Council posts, 1962–94: Lectr, Teheran, 1963–64; Educn Officer, Calcutta, 1964–66; Head of English Dept, Advanced Teacher Trng Coll., Winneba, Ghana, 1966–70; Advr on English Lang., Min. of Educn, Singapore, 1970–74; Rep., Colombia, 1975–80; Director: North and Latin American Dept, 1980–82; America and Pacific Dept, 1982–84; Rep., Australia, 1984–89. Consultant, London Film Commn, 1996–99. Conf. organiser, Soc. of Bookbinders, 2003–07. *Publication:* (with A. Maley) Between You and Me, 1974. *Recreations:* bookbinding, golf. *Address:* Silverwood, Wildwood Close, Woking, Surrey GU22 8PL. *T:* (01932) 341826.

NEWBERY, Prof. David Michael Garrood, FBA 1991; Professor of Economics, University of Cambridge, since 1988; Fellow, Churchill College, Cambridge, since 1966; *b* 1 June 1943; *s* of late Alan James Garrood Newbery, OBE, RN, and of Betty Amelia Newbery; *m* 1975, Dr Terri Eve Apter; two *d*. *Educ:* Portsmouth Grammar Sch.; Trinity Coll., Cambridge (BA, MA); PhD 1976, ScD 2001, Cantab. Economist, Treasury, Tanzania, 1965–66; Cambridge University: Asst Lectr, 1966–71; Lectr, 1971–86; Reader, 1986–88; Dir, Dept of Applied Econs, 1988–2003. Associate Prof., Stanford Univ., 1976–77; Div. Chief, World Bank, Washington, 1981–83; Fellow, Centre for Economic Policy Res., 1984–; Vis. Prof., Princeton, 1985; Vis. Scholar, IMF, 1987; Ford Vis. Prof., Univ. of California, Berkeley, 1987–88; Sen. Res. Fellow, Inst. for Policy Reform, Washington, DC, 1990–96. Mem. (Competition (formerly Monopolies and Mergers) Commn, 1996–2003. Pres., European Economic Assoc., 1996 (Vice-Pres., 1994); Mem. Council, REconS, 1984–89; Fellow, Econometric Soc., 1989 (Frisch Medal, 1990). Bd Mem., Review of Economic Studies, 1968–79; Associate Editor: Economic Jl, 1977–2000; European Economic Review, 1988–93. *Publications:* Project Appraisal in Practice, 1976; (with J. E. Stiglitz) The Theory of Commodity Price Stabilization, 1981; (with N. H. Stern) The Theory of Taxation for Developing Countries, 1987; (with I. P. Székely) Hungary: an economy in transition, 1992; Tax and Benefit Reform in Central and Eastern Europe, 1995; Privatization, Restructuring and Regulation of Network Utilities, 2000; articles in learned jls. *Recreation:* ski-ing. *Address:* 9 Huntingdon Road, Cambridge CB3 0HH. *T:* (01223) 360216.

NEWBIGGING, David Kennedy, OBE 1982; DL; Chairman, Council of Trustees, Cancer Research UK, since 2004 (Deputy Chairman, 2002–04); *b* 19 Jan. 1934; *s* of late David Locke Newbigging, CBE, MC, and Lucy Margaret; *m* 1968, Carolyn Susan (*née* Band); one *s* two *d*. *Educ:* in Canada; Oundle Sch., Northants. Joined Jardine Matheson

& Co. Ltd, Hong Kong, 1954; Dir, 1967; Man. Dir, 1970; Chm. and Sen. Man. Dir, 1975–83; Chairman: Hongkong & Kowloon Wharf & Godown Co. Ltd, 1970–80; Jardine Matheson & Co. Ltd, 1975–83; Jardine Fleming Holdings Ltd, 1975–83; Hongkong Land Co. Ltd, 1975–83; Hongkong Electric Holdings Ltd, 1982–83 (Dir, 1975–83); Rentokil Gp plc, 1987–94 (Dir, 1986–94); Redfearn PLC, 1988; NM UK Ltd 1990–93; Ivory & Sime plc, 1992–95 (Dir, 1987–95); Maritime Transport Services Ltd, 1993–95; Faupel plc (formerly Faupel Trading Gp plc), 1994–2005 (Dir, 1989–2005); Equitas Holdings Ltd, 1995–98; Thistle Hotels plc, 1999–2003; Friends Provident Life Office, subseq. plc, 1998–2005 (Dir, 1993–2005); Dep. Chm., 1996–98); Talbot Hldgs Ltd, 2003–07; Synesis Life Ltd, 2006–; Deputy Chairman: Provincial Gp plc, 1985–91 (Dir, 1984–91); Benchmark Gp plc, 1996–2004; Director: Hongkong & Shanghai Banking Corp., 1975–83; Hong Kong Telephone Co., 1975–83; Safmarine and Rennies Holdings Ltd (formerly Rennies Consolidated Holdings), 1975–85; Provincial Insurance, 1984–86; Provincial Life Insurance Co., 1984–86; CIN Management, 1985–87; PACCAR (UK) Ltd, 1986–97; Internat. Financial Markets Trading Ltd, 1986–93; United Meridian Corp., USA, 1987–98; Wah Kwong Shipping Hldgs Ltd (Hong Kong), 1992–99; Market Bd, Corp. of Lloyd's, 1993–95; Merrill Lynch & Co. Inc., USA, 1997–2007; Ocean Energy Inc., USA, 1998–2003; PACCAR Inc., USA, 1999–2006. Dir, British Coal Corp. (formerly NCB), 1984–87. Mem., Internat. Council, Morgan Guaranty Trust Co. of NY, 1977–85; Mem. Supervisory Bd, DAF Trucks NV, 1997–2000. Chm., Council of Trustees, Mission to Seafarers (formerly Missions to Seamen), 1993–2006. Chm. of Trustees, Wilts Community Foundn, 1991–97; Trustee, UK Trust for Nature Conservation in Nepal (formerly King Mahendra UK Trust for Nature Conservation), 1988–. Member: Hong Kong Exec. Council, 1980–84; Hong Kong Legislative Council, 1978–82. Chairman: Hong Kong Tourist Assoc., 1977–82; Hong Kong Gen. Chamber of Commerce, 1980–82; Steward, Royal Hong Kong Jockey Club, 1975–84. JP (unofficial) Hong Kong, 1971; DL Wilts, 1993; High Sheriff, Wilts, 2003–04. *Recreations:* most outdoor sports; Chinese art. *Address:* 4th Floor, 61 Lincoln's Inn Fields, WC2A 3PX. *T:* (020) 7061 8178. *Clubs:* Boodle's; Hongkong (Hong Kong); Bohemian (San Francisco).

NEWBIGIN, John Lesslie; cultural entrepreneur; consultant, since 2005; *b* Liverpool, 13 Oct. 1947; *s* of Rt Rev. James Edward Lesslie Newbigin and Helen Stewart Newbigin (*née* Henderson); *m* 1978, Juliet Grimshaw (marr. diss. 1994); two *d*. *Educ:* Queens' Coll., Cambridge (BA Hons 1970). Youth worker, ILEA, 1972–73; writer in residence, Common Stock Th., 1973–74; community worker, Avenues Unlimited, 1975–81; Manager, Brixton Young Families Housing Aid Assoc., 1981–84; Dir, London Youth Fest., 1984–85; Policy Advr, Office of the Leader of the Opposition, 1986–92; Asst to Chm., Enigma Prodns, 1992–97; Special Advr, DCMS, 1997–2000; Hd, Corporate Relns, Channel 4 TV, 2000–05. Vis. Prof., UEL, 2006–. Member Board: Keen Students Sch., 2000–; First Light Movies Ltd, 2004–; Cultural Industries Develt Agency, 2005–; Mediabox, 2006–; Becta, 2008–; Member Advisory Board: BT Connected Earth, 2003–; John Smith Meml Trust, 2006–; Aluna, 2007–. Chm. of Trustees, Culture 24, 2006–; Trustee: Whitechapel Art Gall., 2002–; Theatre Royal Stratford East, 2004–; Big Art Proj., 2007–. *Recreations:* walking, talking, cycling, recycling. *Address:* 50 Cephas Avenue, E1 4AT. *T:* (020) 7790 4012; *e-mail:* john@newbigin.co.uk.

NEWBOLD, Yvette Monica, (Yve); Chair, Ethical Trading Initiative, 2000–02; *b* 6 July 1940; *d* of late Thomas Peter Radcliffe and of Anne Gertrude Radcliffe (*née* Flynn); *m* 1958, Anthony Patrick Newbold; three *s* one *d*. *Educ:* Blessed Sacrament Convent, Brighton; LLB London; Solicitor, 1970. Staff Counsel: IBM, 1968–71; Rank Xerox, 1972–79; Internat. Counsel, Xerox (USA), 1979–82; European Counsel, Walt Disney Productions, 1983–85; Co. Sec., Hanson, 1986–95; Chief Exec., Pro-Ned, 1995–97; Partner, Heidrick & Struggles, 1998–2000. Non-executive Director: BT, 1991–97; Coutts & Co., 1994–98. Chair, Inst. for Global Ethics, 2005– (Mem., Adv. Bd, 1997–2004); Member: Royal Commn on Criminal Justice, 1991–93; Sen. Salaries Rev. Body, 1994–97; BT Social Report Panel, 2002–05; Adv. Bd, FTSE4Good, 2003–. Governor, London Business Sch., 1990–97. *Address:* 6 Park Village West, NW1 4AE.

NEWBOROUGH, 8th Baron *cr* 1776 (Ire.), of Bodvean; **Robert Vaughan Wynn;** Bt 1742; landowner and organic farmer; *b* 11 Aug. 1949; *o s* of 7th Baron Newborough, DSC and Rosamund Lavington Wynn (*née* Barbour); *S* father, 1998; *m* 1st, 1981, Sheila Christine Massey (marr. diss. 1988); one *d*; 2nd, 1988, Susan Elizabeth Hall (*née* Lloyd); one step *s*. *Educ:* Milton Abbey. Chm. and Man. Dir, Wynn Electronics, 1982–89; Dir, Country Wide Communications, 1992–. *Recreations:* ski-ing, sailing, golf, tennis. *Heir: uncle* Hon. Charles Henry Romer Wynn [*b* 25 May 1923; *m* 1947, Hon. Angela Hermione Ida Willoughby, *er d* of 11th Baron Middleton, KG, MC, TD; two *s*]. *Address:* Peplow Hall, Peplow, Market Drayton, Shropshire TF9 3JP. *T:* (01952) 840230.

NEWBURGH, 12th Earl of, *cr* 1660 (Scot.); **Don Filippo Giambattista Francesco Aldo Maria Rospigliosi;** Viscount Kynnaird, Baron Levingston, 1660; 11th Prince Rospigliosi (Holy Roman Empire), 11th Duke of Zagarolo, 14th Prince of Castiglione, Marquis of Giuliana, Count of Chiusa, Baron of La Miraglia and Valcorrente, Lord of Aidone, Burgio, Contessa and Trappeto, and Conscript Roman Noble, Patrician of Venice, Genoa and Pistoia; *b* 4 July 1942; *s* of 11th Earl of Newburgh and of Donna Giulia, *d* of Don Guido Carlo dei Duchi Visconti di Mondrone, Count of Lonate Pozzolo; *S* father, 1986; *m* 1972, Baronessa Donna Luisa, *d* of Count Annibale Caccia Dominioni; one *d*. *Heir: d* Princess Donna Benedetta Francesca Maria Rospigliosi, *b* 4 June 1974. *Address:* Piazza Sant'Ambrogio 16, 20123 Milan, Italy.

NEWBY, family name of **Baron Newby.**

NEWBY, Baron *cr* 1997 (Life Peer), of Rothwell in the co. of West Yorkshire; **Richard Mark Newby;** OBE 1990; Chairman, Live Consulting Ltd, since 2001; *b* 14 Feb. 1953; *s* of Frank and Kathleen Newby; *m* 1978, Ailsa Ballantyne Thomson; two *s*. *Educ:* Rothwell Grammar Sch.; St Catherine's Coll., Oxford (MA). HM Customs and Excise: Administration trainee, 1974; Private Sec. to Permanent Sec., 1977–79; Principal, Planning Unit, 1979–81; Sec. to SDP Parly Cttee, 1981; joined SDP HQ Staff, 1981; Nat. Sec., SDP, 1983–88; Exec., 1988–90, Dir of Corporate Affairs, 1991, Rosehaugh plc; Director: Matrix Public Affairs Consultants, subseq. Matrix Communications Consultancy Ltd, 1992–99; Flagship Gp, 1999–2001; non-exec. Dir, Elmwood Design Ltd, 2004–. Chair, Internat. Develt through Sport, UK, 2007–. Dep. Chm., Lib Dem Gen. Election Team, 1995–97; Chief of Staff to Rt Hon. Charles Kennedy, 1999–2006. Lib Dem spokesman on Treasury affairs, H of L, 1998–. Member: Select Cttee on Monetary Policy Cttee of Bank of England, 1998–2000; Select Cttee on Economic Affairs, 2001–03; Ecclesiastical Cttee, 2002–; Dep. Chm., All Party Social Enterprise Gp, 2003–. Sec., Yorks and Humber Peers' Gp, 2002–. FRSA 2006. *Recreations:* family, football, cricket. *Address:* 179 Fentiman Road, SW8 1JY. *Club:* MCC.

NEWBY, Sir Howard (Joseph), Kt 2000; CBE 1995; Vice Chancellor, University of Liverpool, since 2008; *b* 10 Dec. 1947; *s* of Alfred Joseph Newby and Constance Annie (*née* Potts); *m* 1st, 1970, Janet Elizabeth (*née* Craddock) (marr. diss. 2003); two *s*; 2nd, 2005, Sheila Mary Watt (*née* Mann); one step *s* one step *d*. *Educ:* John Port Grammar Sch.,

Etwall, Derbyshire; Atlantic Coll., St Donat's, Glamorgan; Univ. of Essex (BA, PhD). University of Essex: Lectr in Sociology, 1972–75; Sen. Lectr, 1975–79; Reader, 1979–83; Prof. of Sociology, 1983–88; Dir, Data Archive, 1983–88, Chm. and Chief Exec., 1988–94, ESRC; Vice-Chancellor, Southampton Univ., 1994–2001; Chief Exec., HEFCE, 2001–06; Vice Chancellor, UWE, 2006–08. Prof. of Sociology and Rural Sociology, Univ. of Wisconsin-Madison, 1980–83; visiting appointments: Univ. of NSW, 1976; Sydney, 1976; Newcastle upon Tyne, 1983–84. Chm., CEST, 1995–99; Pres., CVCP, 1999–2001. Sen. non-exec. Dir, Carter & Carter plc, 2007–. Member: UFC, 1991–93; Rural Develt Commn, 1991–99; South and West RHA, 1994–96; ESTA, 1997–98; Railway Heritage Cttee, 1999–. Trustee, Nat. Mus. of Sci. and Industry, 2007–. Hon. Fellow, Univ. of Wales, Cardiff, 1996. Hon. DLitt: City of London Poly., 1991; South Bank Univ., 1992; Surrey, 1992; Portsmouth, 1992 (Hon. Fellow, Portsmouth Poly., 1991); Ulster, 1994; Stirling, 2002; DU: Essex, 2000; Leicester, 2002; Hon. DSocSci Southampton, 2002. *Publications:* (jtly) Community Studies, 1971; The Deferential Worker, 1977; (jtly) Property, Paternalism and Power, 1978; Green and Pleasant Land?, 1979, 2nd edn 1985; (jtly) The Problem of Sociology, 1983; (jtly) Approximación Teoretica a la Sociologia Rural, 1983; Country Life, 1987; The Countryside in Question, 1988; (jtly) Social Class in Modern Britain, 1988; *edited jointly:* The Sociology of Community, 1974; Doing Sociological Research, 1977; International Perspectives in Rural Sociology, 1978; The Rural Sociology of the Advanced Societies, 1980; Political Action and Social Identity, 1985; Restructuring Capital, 1985; The National Trust: the next hundred years, 1995; over 50 papers in learned jls. *Recreations:* sharing everything in married life, especially time with our family, walks and cycle rides, Derby County and railway interests. *Address:* University of Liverpool, Liverpool L69 3BX. *Club:* Athenæum.

NEWCASTLE, Bishop of, since 1997; **Rt Rev. (John) Martin Wharton;** *b* 6 Aug. 1944; *s* of John and Marjorie Wharton; *m* 1970, Marlene Olive Duckett; two *s* one *d*. *Educ:* Van Mildert Coll., Durham (BA 1969); Linacre Coll., Oxford (BA 1971; MA 1976); Ripon Hall, Oxford, 1969. Ordained: deacon, 1972, priest, 1973; Assistant Curate: St Peter, Birmingham, 1972–75; St John the Baptist, Croydon, 1975–77; Dir of Pastoral Studies, Ripon Coll., Cuddesdon, 1977–83; Asst Curate, Cuddesdon, 1979–83; Exec. Sec., Bd of Ministry and Training, dio. of Bradford, 1983–91; Hon. Canon, Bradford Cathedral, 1984; Bishop's Officer for Ministry and Training, 1992; Residentiary Canon, Bradford Cathedral, 1992; Area Bishop of Kingston-upon-Thames, 1992–97. *Recreation:* sport. *Address:* Bishop's House, 29 Moor Road South, Newcastle upon Tyne NE3 1PA.

NEWCASTLE, NSW, Bishop of, since 2005; **Rt Rev. Brian George Farran;** *b* 15 Dec. 1944; *s* of George Farran and Dorothy Barnes; *m* 1971, Robin Jeanne Marsden; one *s* two *d*. *Educ:* ANU (BA); St John's Theol Coll., Morpeth (ThL); Deakin Univ. (BLitt). Ordained deacon, 1967, priest, 1968; Curate: St Phillips, O'Connor, 1968; St Alban's, Griffith, 1969–71; Rector: Ch of the Epiphany, Lake Cargelligo, 1972–75; St Barnabas, N Rockhampton, 1975–79; St Saviour's, Gladstone, 1979–82; Dean of St Paul's Cathedral, Rockhampton, Queensland, 1983–89; Regl Dir, Australian Bd of Missions, Province of Victoria, 1989–92; an Asst Bp of Perth, WA, 1992–2005 (Bp of Goldfields Region, 1992–98, of Northern Region, 1998–2005). Vice-Chm., Gen. Bd of Religious Educn, Anglican Church of Australia, Vic, 1984–2000. Chm., Commn on Ministry, 2001–; Mem., Standing Cttee, Gen. Synod, 1998–. Chm. Council, Peter Moyes Anglican Community Sch., Mindarie, Perth, WA, 2000–. Fellow, Guildford Grammar Sch., Guildford, Perth, WA, 2001. DMin Studies, MCD, 2005. *Recreations:* gardening, music, films, reading. *Address:* (home) Bishopscourt, 34 Brown Street, Newcastle, NSW 2300, Australia; (office) 51 Newcommen Street, PO Box 517, Newcastle, NSW 2300, Australia.

NEWCASTLE, Dean of; *see* Dalliston, Very Rev. C. C.

NEWCOME, Rt Rev. James William Scobie; *see* Penrith, Bishop Suffragan of.

NEWDEGATE; *see* FitzRoy Newdegate, family name of Viscount Daventry.

NEWELL, Christopher William Paul; Principal Legal Advisor to Director of Public Prosecutions, since 2005; *b* 30 Nov. 1950; *s* of Nicolas Gambier Newell and Edith Alice Newell (*née* Edgill); *m* 1998, Teresa Mary Martin; one *d*. *Educ:* Wellington College; Southampton Univ. (LLB Hons). Called to the Bar, Middle Temple, 1973; Department of Director of Public Prosecutions: Legal Asst, 1975–78; Sen. Legal Asst, 1978–79; Law Officers' Dept, 1979–83; Sen. Legal Asst, DPP, 1983–86; Asst DPP, 1986; Branch Crown Prosecutor, Crown Prosecution Service, 1986–87; Asst Legal Sec., Law Officers' Dept, 1987–89; Crown Prosecution Service: Dir of HQ Casework, 1989–93; Dir (Casework), 1993–96; Dir, Casework Evaluation, 1996–98; Dir, Casework, 1998–2005. Sen. Vice-Chm., Criminal Law Cttee, IBA, 2002–06 (Vice-Chm., 2000–02). Trustee: Nat. Deaf Children's Soc., 2001–; Centre for Accessible Envmts, 2001–08 (Vice-Chm., 2004–08); Crime Reduction Initiatives, 2001–. *Recreations:* sport, travel. *Address:* Crown Prosecution Service, 50 Ludgate Hill, EC4M 7EX. *T:* (020) 7796 8553.

NEWELL, David Richard; Director: Newspaper Society, since 1997; Newspaper Publishers Association, since 2007; *b* 21 Sept. 1951; *s* of late Dick Newell and Davida Newell (*née* Juleff); *m* 1978, Cora Sue Feingold; one *d*. *Educ:* Shrewsbury Sch.; Birmingham Univ. (LLB Hons 1973); Southampton Univ. (MPhil 1976). US, UK and British Council res. grants, 1974–81. Admitted Solicitor, 1978; Lawford & Co., 1976–78; Lectr in Law, Leicester Univ., 1978–86 (Postgrad. Tutor, 1979–84; Dir, Employment Law Postgrad. prog., 1983–86); Hon. Legal Advr, Leicester Legal Advice Centre, 1979–84; Hd of Govt and Legal Affairs, 1984–96, Dep. Dir, 1992–97, Newspaper Soc. Sec., Parly and Legal Cttee, Guild of Editors, 1984–97; Member: Cttee of Advertising Practice, 1984–; Advertising Assoc. Cttees, 1984–; Council, Campaign for Freedom of Information, 1990– (Award for campaigning against official secrecy, 1989); Employment and Media Cttees, Law Soc., 1990–97; Advertising Law Gp, 1995–; UK Assises Gp, 1995–; Confedn of Communication and Inf. Industries, 1984–; CPU, 1997–; Council, World Assoc. of Newspapers, 1997–; Chm., Legal Framework Cttee, 1995–98, Bd Mem., 1996–, European Newspaper Publishers' Assoc. Director: ABC, 1997–; Press Standards Bd of Finance, 1997–; Advertising Standards Bd of Finance, 1998–; Publishers' NTO, 2001–; Digital Content Forum, 2001–. Mem., CBI Council, 1999–. Press Awards Judge, 1999–. Special Award, UK Press Gazette, 1988. *Publications:* The New Employment Legislation: a guide to the Employment Acts 1980 and 1982, 1983; Understanding Recruitment Law, 1984; (jtly) How to Study Law, 1986, 5th edn 2005; (jtly) Financial Advertising Law, 1989; (jtly) Aspects of Employment Law, 1990; (jtly) Law for Journalists, 1991; (jtly) Tolleys Employment Law, 1994, 2nd edn 2000; (jtly) The Law of Journalism, 1995; (contrib.) Copinger on Copyright, 1998; research papers and articles on employment law, media and legal policy issues. *Recreations:* country and seaside walks, sailing, tennis. *Address:* Newspaper Society, St Andrew's House, 18–20 St Andrew Street, EC4A 3AY. *T:* (020) 7636 7014; *e-mail:* ns@newspapersoc.org.uk.

NEWELL, Donald, FRICS; Co-Chairman, Europe Middle East Africa Division, CB Richard Ellis Services Inc., USA, 1998–2000; *b* 31 Aug. 1942; *s* of Stephen Newell and Ida Laura Newell (*née* Hatch); *m* 1968, Rosemary Litler-Jones; one *s* two *d*. *Educ:* Cheshunt Grammar Sch. FRICS 1968. Lander Bedells & Crompton, 1961–68; Hillier Parker May & Rowden, Chartered Surveyors, 1968–98: Partner, 1973–98; Man. Partner, 1986–90; Sen. Partner, 1990–98. Director: Oncor Internat., USA, 1995–98; CB Hillier Parker, 1998–2000; non-executive Director: London Merchant Securities PLC, 1998–2007; Derwent London plc, 2007–. Dir, Paddington Business Improvement Dist Ltd, 2005–. Pres., Brit. Council for Offices, 1991–92. Liveryman, Co. of Pattenmakers, 1979 (Master, 2004–05); Chartered Surveyors, 1993–. *Recreation:* sport. *Address:* 21 Chelwood House, Gloucester Square, W2 2SZ. *Clubs:* Buck's, MCC.

NEWELL, Rev. Canon Edmund John, DPhil; Residentiary Canon and Sub Dean, Christ Church, Oxford, since 2008; *b* 9 Sept. 1961; *s* of Kenneth Ernest Newell and late Mary Newell (*née* James); *m* 1989, Susan Georgina Greer; one *d*. *Educ:* Ilfracombe Sch.; University Coll. London (BSc(Econ) 1983); Nuffield Coll., Oxford (DPhil 1988; MA 1989); Oxford Ministry Course; Ripon Coll., Cuddesdon. Prize Res. Fellow, 1987, British Acad. Postdoctoral Fellow, 1989–92, Nuffield Coll., Oxford. Ordained deacon, 1994, priest, 1995; Curate, Deddington with Barford, Clifton and Hempton, 1994–98; Domestic Chaplain and Res. Asst to Bp of Oxford, 1998–2001; Chaplain, Headington Sch., Oxford, 1998–2001; Canon Residentiary, 2001–08, Chancellor, 2003–08, St Paul's Cathedral. Dir, St Paul's Inst., 2003–08. FRHistS 1998. *Publications:* (ed) Seven Words for the 21st Century, 2002; (ed with Claire Foster) The Worlds We Live In, 2005; (with Sabina Alkire) What Can One Person Do?, 2005; (ed) Seven Words for Three Hours: a Good Friday meditation in words and music, 2005; contribs to books, articles in learned jls and newspapers. *Recreations:* cricket, running, badminton, music. *Address:* Christ Church, Oxford OX1 1DP.

NEWELL, Michael Cormac; film director; *b* 28 March 1942; *s* of Terence William Newell and Mollie Louise Newell; *m* 1979, Bernice Stegers; one *s* one *d*. *Educ:* St Albans Sch.; Magdalene Coll., Cambridge (MA). Television dir, Granada TV, 1964–70: Ready When You Are Mr Magill; Baa Baa Black Sheep; Charm; freelance television dir, 1970–80: Melancholy Hussar; Just Your Luck; Destiny; Mr and Mrs Bureaucrat; Gift of Friendship; *films* include: Man in the Iron Mask, 1976; The Awakening, 1979; Dance with a Stranger, 1984 (Prix de la Jeunesse, Cannes); Good Father, 1986 (Prix Italia); Sweet and Sour, 1988; Into the West, 1992; Four Weddings and a Funeral, 1994 (Best Dir, BAFTA Awards, 1995); An Awfully Big Adventure, 1995; Donnie Brasco, 1997; Pushing Tin, 1999; Mona Lisa Smile, 2004; Harry Potter and the Goblet of Fire, 2005; Love in the Time of Cholera, 2008; executive producer, Photographic Fairies, 1997; Best Laid Plans, 200 Cigarettes, 1999; High Fidelity, Traffic, 2000. Hon. DA Herts, 2005. *Recreations:* walking, reading (anything but fiction). *Address:* Fifty Cannon Entertainment, c/o Independent Talent Group Ltd, Oxford House, 76 Oxford Street, W1D 1BS.

NEWELL, Rt Rev. Phillip Keith, AO 1993; Bishop of Tasmania, 1982–2000; *b* 30 Jan. 1930; *s* of Frank James and Ada Miriam Newell; *m* 1959, Merle Edith Callaghan; three *s*. *Educ:* Univ. of Melbourne; Trinity Coll., Melbourne. BSc 1953; DiplEd(Hons) 1954; ThL(Hons) 1959; BEd 1960; MEd 1969; FACE 1990. Mathematics Master: Melbourne High School, 1954–56; University High School, 1957–58; Tutor in Physics, Secondary Teachers' Coll., 1957; Assistant Curate: All Saints, East St Kilda, Melbourne, 1960–61; S Andrew's, Brighton, Melbourne, 1962–63; Asst Priest, S James, King Street, Sydney, 1963–67; Chaplain, Sydney Hosp., 1963–67; Rector, Christ Church, St Lucia, Brisbane, 1967–82; Residentiary Canon, S John's Cathedral, Brisbane, 1973–82; Archdeacon of Lilley, Brisbane, 1976–82. GCSJ 1979; KStJ 1981; OMLJ 2004 (ChLJ 1992). *Publications:* Body Search, 1993; A Pocket Lent Book, 1996. *Recreations:* education, music (classical and light opera), singing, choral conducting, wine making, travel, cricket (spectator), tennis (occasional game). *Address:* 4 Howley Court, Howrah, Tas 7018, Australia. *T:* and *Fax:* (3) 6247 1706.

NEWELL, Robert Fraser, LVO 2000; Director-General, Royal Over-Seas League, since 1991; *b* 3 May 1943; *s* of late Horace and Henrietta Newell; *m* 1969, Shahnaz Bakhtiar; two *d*. *Educ:* University Coll. Sch. FIH (MHCIMA 1986, FHCIMA 1997). Hotel mgt positions in London, Iran and Kenya, 1965–75; Dir of Admin, Kenya Utalii Coll., Nairobi, 1975–79; Gen. Manager, Royal Over-Seas League, 1979–91. Vis. Lectr in Hotel Financial Mgt, Ecole Hotelière de Lausanne, 1983–2001. Chm., Assoc. of London Clubs, 1992–95; Member: Club Secs and Managers Assoc., 1982–; Council of Commonwealth Socs Cttee (formerly Jt Commonwealth Socs Council), 1991–; Cttee, Eur. Atlantic Gp, 1993–; Cttee, Kenya Soc., 1996–; Council, Mayfair St James's Assoc., 2001–. Fellow, Brit. Assoc. Hotel Accountants, 1997; FCMI (FIMgt 1983). *Recreations:* tennis, music, gardening. *Address:* Royal Over-Seas League, Over-Seas House, Park Place, St James's Street, SW1A 1LR. *T:* (020) 7408 0214.

NEWENS, (Arthur) Stanley; *b* 4 Feb. 1930; *s* of Arthur Ernest and Celia Jenny Newens, Bethnal Green; *m* 1st, 1954, Ann (*d* 1962), *d* of J. B. Sherratt, Stoke-on-Trent; two *d*; 2nd, 1966, Sandra Christina, *d* of J. A. Frith, Chingford; one *s* two *d*. *Educ:* Buckhurst Hill County High Sch.; University Coll., London (BA Hons History); Westminster Training Coll. (Post-Graduate Certificate of Education). Coal face worker in N Staffs mines, 1952–55. Secondary Sch. Teacher, 1956–65, 1970–74. MP (Lab) Epping, 1964–70 (NUT sponsored); MP (Lab and Co-op) Harlow, Feb. 1974–1983; contested (Lab) Harlow, 1983 and 1987; MEP (Lab and Co-op) London Central, 1984–99. Chairman: Eastern Area Gp of Lab. MPs, 1974–83; Tribune Gp of MPs, 1982–83 (Vice-Chm., 1981–82); PLP Foreign Affairs Gp, 1982–83 (Vice-Chm., 1976–77); Dep. Leader, British Lab. Gp of MEPs, 1988–89 (Chm., 1985–87); Pres., EP Central Amer. and Mexico Delegn, 1994–96; Vice-Chm., Labour Action for Peace. Active Member: Labour Party, holding numerous offices, 1949–; NUM, 1952–55; NUT, 1956–. Pres., Liberation (Movement for Colonial Freedom), 1992– (Chm., 1967–92). Dir, London Co-operative Soc., 1971–77 (Pres., 1977–81); Mem., Central Exec., Co-op. Union, 1974–80. Sec., Harlow Council for Voluntary Service, 1983–84. Mem., Harlow Health Centres Trust, 1984–. Chairman: Harlow Civic Soc., 1999–; Gibberd Garden Trust, 1999–; Pres., Waltham Abbey Historical Soc., 1998–; Vice-President: Friends of Historic Essex, 1982–; Socialist History Soc., 2005–; Member: Adv. Bd, Modern Record Centre, 1974–85, 1999–2008; Council, London Record Soc., 2001–05; Council, Essex Soc. for Archaeol. and Hist., 2002– (Pres., 2005–08). *Publications:* The Case Against NATO (pamphlet), 1972; Nicolae Ceausescu, 1972; Third World: change or chaos, 1977; A History of North Weald Bassett and its People, 1985; A Short History of the London Co-op Society Political Committee, 1988; (with Ron Bill) Leah Manning, 1991; The Kurds, 1994; Pathfinders, 1998; A Brief History of 100 Years of the Labour Party in the Eastern Region, 2000; Chris Morris: a landworker's struggle, 2003; A History of Struggle: 50th anniversary of Liberation (Movement for Colonial Freedom), 2004; (ed) A. E. Newens, The Memoirs of an Old East-Ender, 2006; pamphlets and articles. *Recreations:* local historical research, family, reading, gardening. *Address:* The Leys, 18 Park Hill, Harlow, Essex CM17 0AE. *T:* (01279) 420108.

NEWEY, Guy Richard; QC 2001; a Deputy High Court Judge, since 2006; *b* 21 Jan. 1959; *s* of His Honour John Henry Richard Newey, QC and of Mollie Patricia Newey (*née* Chalk); *m* 1986, Angela Clare Neilson; one *s* three *d*. *Educ:* Tonbridge Sch.; Queens'

Coll., Cambridge (MA 1st Cl., LLM 1st Cl.); Council of Legal Educn (1st Cl. in Bar Exams). Called to the Bar, Middle Temple, 1982; in practice at Chancery Bar, 1983–; Jun. Counsel to the Crown, Chancery, and A Panel, 1990–2001; Jun. Counsel to Charity Comrs, 1991–2001. Inspector into affairs of MG Rover, 2005–. An Acting Deemster, Isle of Man, 2003–. Gov., New Beacon Educnl Trust Ltd, 2001–. *Publications:* (contrib.) Directors' Disqualification, 2nd edn 1998; (contrib.) Civil Court Service, 1999. *Address:* Maitland Chambers, 7 Stone Buildings, Lincoln's Inn, WC2A 3SZ. *T:* (020) 7406 1200.

NEWEY, Sidney Brian; consultant in transport; Assistant to Chief Executive, Railways, British Rail, 1990–93, retired; *b* 8 Jan. 1937; *s* of Sidney Frank Newey and Edith Mary Newey; *m* 1967, Margaret Mary Stevens (*d* 1996); one *s*. *Educ:* Burton upon Trent Grammar Sch.; Worcester Coll., Oxford (MA Mod. History). British Rail: Traffic apprentice, Western Region, 1960; Stationmaster, Southall, Middx, 1964; Freight Marketing Manager, Western Region, 1971; Divl Manager, Birmingham, 1978; Dep. General Manager, London Midland Region, 1980; Gen. Manager, Western Region, 1985–87; Director, Provincial, 1987–90. Chm., Oxford Diocesan Bd of Finance, 2001–. *Recreations:* fell walking, history, reading, village and church affairs. *Address:* Chestnut Cottage, The Green South, Warborough, Oxon OX10 7DN. *T:* (01865) 858322.

NEWFOUNDLAND, CENTRAL, Bishop of, since 2005; **Rt Rev. David Torraville;** *b* 29 May 1953; *s* of Rev. Canon Arnold Torraville and Nita Marie Torraville; *m* 1979, Karen Flemming; one *s* one *d*. *Educ:* Meml Univ. of Newfoundland (BA, BEd); Queen's Coll., St John's, Newfoundland (MDiv). Fellow in Pastoral Leadership Develt, Princeton Theol Seminary. Rector: Twillingate, 1985–89; Cathedral of St Martin, Gander, 1989–2000; Exec. Officer, Dio. Central Newfoundland, 2001–05. *Recreation:* flyfishing. *Address:* 34 Fraser Road, Gander, NL A1V 2E8, Canada. *T:* (office) (709) 2562372, *Fax:* (709) 2562396; *e-mail:* bishopcentral@nfld.net. *Club:* Kiwanis Internat.

NEWFOUNDLAND, EASTERN, AND LABRADOR, Bishop of, since 2004; **Rt Rev. Cyrus Clement James Pitman;** *b* 24 March 1944; *s* of John and Ella Pitman; *m* 1968, Mary (*née* Lee); three *s* one *d*. *Educ:* Newfoundland Meml Univ. (BA); Queen's Coll., Newfoundland (LTh). Ordained deacon, 1967, priest, 1968; Curate, Channel, 1967–70; Incumbent, Flower's Cove, 1970–75; Rector, Meadows, 1975–80; Dir of Prog., Dio. W Newfoundland, 1980–82; Curate, St Mary the Virgin, St John's, 1982–87; Rector: Petty Harbour, 1987–90; St Paul, Goulds, Kilbride, 1990–93; All Saints, Conception Bay S, 1993–2000; St Mary the Virgin, St John's, 2000–03; Archdeacon, Avalon E and W, 2002–03; Exec. Archdeacon and Admin. Asst to Bishop of Eastern Newfoundland and Labrador, 2003–04. Regl Dean, Avalon W, 1990; Canon, Stall of St Columba, 1997. *Address:* Synod Office, 19 King's Bridge Road, St John's, NL A1C 3K4, Canada. *T:* (709) 5766697, *Fax:* (709) 5767122; *e-mail:* cpitman@anglicanenl.nf.net.

NEWHAM, Prof. Dianne Jane, PhD; Professor of Physiotherapy, since 1993, and Director, Centre for Applied Biomedical Research, since 2000, King's College, London; *b* 31 July 1949; *d* of Geoffrey Newham and Denise Millicent Newham; partner, Terry N. Williams; one *s*. *Educ:* Nairobi Convent Sch., Kenya; Ockbrook Moravian Sch.; Prince of Wales Sch. of Physiotherapy (MCSP, SRP 1976); UCL (MPhil 1982); North London Poly. (PhD 1985). Lab. Asst, Boots Co. Ltd, 1967–70; VSO, Nigeria, 1970–72; University College London: Physiotherapist, 1976–79; Res. Physiotherapist, Dept of Medicine, 1979–82; Associate Res. Fellow, Medicine and Surgery, 1985–87; Lectr in Physiology, 1987–89; King's College, London: Reader, 1989–93; Hd of Physiotherapy, 1989–2000. Mem., Working Gp on estabt of UK Acad. of Med. Scis, 1996–98. *Publications:* chapters on human muscle pain, skeletal muscle function and fatigue; original research papers in jls of physiology, physiotherapy and rehabilitation. *Recreations:* travel, gardening, food and wine. *Address:* Division of Applied Biomedical Research, King's College London, Shepherd's House, Guy's Campus, SE1 1UL. *T:* (020) 7848 6320.

NEWING, John Frederick, CBE 1999; QPM 1988; DL; Chief Constable, Derbyshire Constabulary, 1990–2000; *b* 1 March 1940; *s* of Frederick George Newing and Emily Beatrice Newing (*née* Bettles); *m* 1963, Margaret May Kilborn (*d* 2007); two *s* one *d*. *Educ:* Kettering Grammar Sch.; Leeds Univ. (BA Hons Social and Public Administration). Joined Metropolitan Police, 1963; Police Staff Coll., 1967–68; Bramshill Scholarship, Leeds Univ., 1969–72; Community Relations Br., 1974; Staff Officer to Commissioner, 1977; Chief Supt i/c Marylebone Div., 1980; Senior Command Course, Police Staff Coll., 1981; Comdr, Community Relations, 1982, Public Order Branch, 1984; Dep. Asst Comr i/c W London Area, 1985–87; seconded to Home Office Science and Technology Gp, 1987–90. Pres., ACPO, 1998–99. Chm., E Midlands Regl Bd, Crimestoppers, 2001–06. DL Derbyshire, 2000. *Publications:* articles in Policing and other professional jls. *Recreations:* reading, walking, voluntary youth work, such sports as age allows. *Address:* Glapwell, Derbys.

NEWING, Rt Rev. Dom Kenneth Albert, OSB; *b* 29 Aug. 1923; *s* of Albert James Pittock Newing and Nellie Louise Maude Newing; unmarried. *Educ:* Dover Grammar School; Selwyn College, Cambridge (MA); Theological College, Mirfield, Yorks. Deacon, 1955; priest, 1956; Assistant Curate, Plymstock, 1955–63; Rector of Plympton S Maurice, Plymouth, 1963–82; Archdeacon of Plymouth, 1978–82; Bishop Suffragan of Plymouth, 1982–88; joined Order of St Benedict, 1988; solemn (life) profession, 1989. *Address:* Elmore Abbey, Church Lane, Speen, Newbury, Berks RG14 1SA. *T:* (01635) 33080.

NEWINGTON, Sir Michael (John), KCMG 1993 (CMG 1982); HM Diplomatic Service, retired; Ambassador to Brazil, 1987–92; *b* 10 July 1932; *er s* of late J. T. Newington, Spalding, Lincs; *m* 1956, Nina Gordon-Jones; one *s* one *d*. *Educ:* Stamford Sch.; St John's Coll., Oxford. MA. RAF, 1951–52, Pilot Officer. Joined Foreign Office, 1955; Economic Survey Section, Hong Kong, 1957–58; resigned 1958. ICI, 1959–60. Rejoined FO, 1960; Second, later First Sec. (Economic), Bonn, 1961–65; First Sec., Lagos, 1965–68; Asst Head of Science and Technology Dept, FCO, 1968–72; Counsellor (Scientific), Bonn, 1972–75; Counsellor and Consul-Gen., Tel Aviv, 1975–78; Head of Republic of Ireland Dept, FCO, 1978–81; Consul-Gen., Düsseldorf, 1981–85; Ambassador to Venezuela and concurrently (non-resident) to Dominican Republic, 1985–87. *Recreations:* gardening, cultivating olives. *Address:* Mas Bomuré, 83460 Taradeau, France; 2 Church Street, St Clements, Sandwich, Kent CT13 9EH.

NEWLAND, Prof. Adrian Charles, FRCP, FRCPath; Professor of Haematology, Barts and the London School of Medicine and Dentistry, Queen Mary (formerly St Bartholomew's and Royal London School of Medicine and Dentistry, Queen Mary and Westfield College), University of London, since 1992; Director of Pathology, Barts and the London NHS Trust, since 2004; President, Royal College of Pathologists, since 2005; *b* 26 Aug. 1949; *m* 1973, Joanna Mary Shaw; one *s* one *d*. *Educ:* City of Norwich Sch.; Downing Coll., Cambridge (MA 1975); London Hospital Med. Coll. (MB BCh 1975). MRCP 1976, FRCP 1992; FRCPath 1992. Hon. Consultant, Barts and the London (formerly Royal Hosps) NHS Trust, 1981–; Dir of R and D, Barts and the London NHS Trust, 1997–2001; Dir, NE Thames Cancer Network, 2001–. Pres., British Soc. for Haematology, 1998–99. Hon. Sec., Acad. of Medical Royal Colleges, 2007–. Ed. in Chief, Hematology, 1995–. *Publications:* (jtly) Pocket Consultant Haematology, 1986; (ed jtly) Cambridge Medical Reviews, vols 14, 1991; numerous contribs in field of haematology incl. chapters in books; over 250 papers in learned jls. *Recreations:* good literature, fine wine, walking, foreign travel. *Address:* Department of Haematology, The Royal London Hospital, Whitechapel, E1 1BB. *T:* (020) 3246 0338, *Fax:* (020) 3246 0351; *e-mail:* a.c.newland@qmul.ac.uk; 41 Elmwood Road, Dulwich, SE24 9NS. *Clubs:* Athenæum, MCC.

NEWLAND, Prof. David Edward, MA; ScD; FREng, FIMechE, FIET; Professor of Engineering (1875), 1976–2003, now Emeritus, Head, Engineering Department, 1996–2002, and a Deputy Vice-Chancellor, 1999–2003, University of Cambridge; Fellow, Selwyn College, Cambridge, since 1976; consulting engineer; *b* 8 May 1936; *s* of late Robert W. Newland and Marion A. Newland (*née* Dearman); *m* 1959, Patricia Frances Mayne; two *s*. *Educ:* Alleyne's Sch., Stevenage; Selwyn Coll., Cambridge (Lyttleton Scholar, 1956; Mech. Sciences Tripos: Rex Moir Prize, 1956, Ricardo Prize, 1957; MA 1961; ScD 1990); Massachusetts Inst. of Technol. (ScD thesis on nonlinear vibrations, 1963). English Electric Co., 1957–61; Instr and Asst Prof. of Mech. Engrg, MIT, 1961–64; Lectr and Sen. Lectr, Imperial Coll. of Science and Technol., 1964–67; Prof. of Mech. Engrg, Sheffield Univ., 1967–76. Mem., Royal Commn on Envmtl Pollution, 1984–89. Visitor, Transport and Road Res. Lab., 1990–92; non-exec. Dir, Cambridge-MIT Inst., 2000–02. Past or present mem., cttees of IMechE, DTI, BSI, SERC, Design Council, Engrg Council and Royal Academy (formerly Fellowship) of Engineering, including: Mem., Editorial Panel, 1968–82 and Consultant Editor, 1983–87, Jl Mech. Engrg Sci., Proc. IMechE, Part C; Engrg Awards Panel, Design Council, 1977–79; Council, Fellowship of Engrg, 1985–88; Working Party on Engineers and Risk Issues, Engrg Council, 1990–94; Member: SRC Transport Cttee, 1969–72; Mech. Engrg and Machine Tools Requirements Bd, 1977, 1978; Chm., BSI Tech. Cttee on bellows expansion jts, 1976–85. Technical witness, Flixborough Inquiry, 1974–75, and other engrg and patents cases; investigations following Piper Alpha, Potters Bar and other accidents; Engrg Advr, London Millennium Bridge Trust, 2000–01. Governor, St Paul's Schs, 1978–93. Freeman, City of London, 2000; Liveryman, Engrs' Co., 2001. Churchwarden, Ickleton, 1979–87. Distinguished Alumni Lectr, MIT, 1999. FREng (FEng 1982). Hon. DEng Sheffield, 1997. Charles S. Lake award, 1975, and T. Bernard Hall prize, IMechE, 1991, for papers in IMechE Procs; Applied Mechanics Award for dist. contributors, ASME, 2002. *Publications:* An Introduction to Random Vibrations and Spectral Analysis, 1975, 3rd edn, as Random Vibrations, Spectral and Wavelet Analysis, 1993; Mechanical Vibration Analysis and Computation, 1989; Discover Butterflies, 2006; technical papers, mostly in British and Amer. engrg jls. *Recreations:* music, jogging, bell ringing, photography. *Address:* c/o University Engineering Department, Trumpington Street, Cambridge CB2 1PZ. *T:* (home) (01799) 530268. *Club:* Athenæum.

NEWLAND, Martin; Editor and Launch Editor, The National, Abu Dhabi, since 2008; *b* 26 Oct. 1961; *s* of Edward and Elena Newland; *m* 1987, Bénédicte Smets; three *s* one *d*. *Educ:* Downside Sch.; Goldsmiths Coll., London Univ. (BA Hons (Hist.) 1984); Heythrop Coll., London Univ. (MTh 1986). News Editor, Catholic Herald, 1986–88; Daily Telegraph: reporter, 1989–93; Home Ed., 1993–98; Dep. Ed. and Launch Ed., National Post, Canada, 1998–2003; Ed., The Daily Telegraph, 2003–05. *Recreations:* music, fitness, martial arts.

NEWLANDS, David Baxter; Chairman: Paypoint plc, since 1998; Prospect Investment Management, since 1999; Tomkins plc, since 2000 (Director, since 1999); KESA Electricals plc, since 2003; OB10 (formerly Oxford Business Exchange), since 2004; Impress Coöperative UA, since 2007; *b* 13 Sept. 1946; *s* of George Frederick Newlands and Helen Frederica Newlands; *m* 1973, Susan Helena Milne; two *s* two *d*. *Educ:* Edinburgh Acad. FCA 1969. Deloitte & Touche, 1963–86, Partner, 1977–86; Gp Finance Director: Saatchi & Saatchi, 1986–89; General Electric Co. plc, 1989–97. Non-executive Director: Weir Gp, 1997–2003; Global Software Services, 1998–2004; Standard Life Assce Co., 1999–2006 (Dep. Chm., 2004–06); London Regl Transport, 1999–2001; Britax Internat. plc, 1999–2001 (Chm., 2000–01). Chm. Trustees, SeeAbility, 2001–07. *Recreations:* golf, Rugby, bridge. *Address:* Lane End, Chucks Lane, Walton-on-the-Hill, Surrey KT20 7UB. *T:* (01737) 812582. *Clubs:* Caledonian, Royal Automobile; Walton Heath Golf (Dir, 2001–); Sutton and Epsom Rugby (Cheam); Golf House (Elie).

NEWLANDS, Rev. Prof. George McLeod, PhD, DLitt; Professor of Divinity, University of Glasgow, 1986–2008; Principal, Trinity College, Glasgow, 1991–97 and 2002–07; *b* 12 July 1941; *s* of George and Mary Newlands; *m* 1967, Mary Elizabeth Wallace; three *s*. *Educ:* Perth Acad.; Univ. of Edinburgh (MA 1st Cl. Classics (Vans Dunlop Scholar, 1963); BD 1st Cl. Eccles. Hist. (Cunningham Fellow, 1966); PhD 1970; DLitt 2005); Univ. of Heidelberg; Univ. of Zürich; Churchill Coll., Cambridge (MA). Ordained minister, C of S, 1970, and priest, C of E, 1982. Asst Minister, Muirhouse, Edinburgh, 1969–70; Lectr in Divinity, Univ. of Glasgow, 1969–73; Cambridge University: Lectr in Divinity, 1973–86; Fellow, Wolfson Coll., 1975–82; Fellow and Dean, Trinity Hall, 1982–86; Glasgow University: Dean, Faculty of Divinity, 1988–90; Dir, Centre for Theol., Lit. and the Arts, 1999–2002. Hensley Henson Lectr, Oxford, 1995. Vis. Prof., Univ. of Mainz, 1999; Vis. Scholar: Claremont Sch. of Theol., Calif, 2002; Princeton Theol Seminary, 2005, 2009. Member: Doctrine Commn, C of E, 1983–86; Convener, Panel on Doctrine, C of S, 1995–. Member: Eur. Cttee, World Alliance of Reformed Churches, 1987–95; Church and Nation Cttee, C of S, 1992–96; Unity, Faith and Order Commn, Action for Churches Together in Scotland, 1995–; Scottish Churches Initiative for Unity, 1995–2003; HEFCE RAE Panel for Theology and Religious Studies, 1996, 2001, 2008 (Chm.); Center of Theol Inquiry, Princeton, 1998; Netherlands RAE Panel, 1999. FRSA 2005; FRSE 2008. Mem. Editl Bd, Theology in Scotland, 1996–. *Publications:* Hilary of Poitiers, 1978; Theology of the Love of God, 1980; (ed) Explorations in Theology 8, 1981; The Church of God, 1984; Making Christian Decisions, 1985; God in Christian Perspective, 1994; Generosity and the Christian Future, 1997; (ed jtly) Scottish Christianity in the Modern World, 2000; John and Donald Baillie: transatlantic theology, 2002; The Transformative Imagination, 2004; (ed jtly) Fifty Key Christian Thinkers, 2004; (ed jtly) Believing in the Text, 2004; Traces of Liberality, 2006; Christ and Human Rights, 2006; (jtly) Faith and Human Rights, 2008; *festschrift:* The God of Love and Human Dignity: essays for George Newlands, by P. Middleton, 2007; contribs to theol pubns. *Recreations:* music, walking, commuting. *Address:* School of Divinity, University of Glasgow, Glasgow G12 8QQ; 49 Highsett, Cambridge CB2 1NZ. *Club:* New (Edinburgh).

NEWLING, Caro; Joint Founder and Director, Neal Street Productions Ltd, since 2003; *b* London, 12 April 1957; adopted *d* of John and Evelyn Newling; partner, Gary Hamilton Powell. *Educ:* Brighton and Hove High Sch.; Roedean Sch.; Warwick Univ. (BA Hons Th. Studies); Webber-Douglas Acad. of Dramatic Art. Sen. Press Officer, RSC, 1986–91; Co-Founder and Exec. Producer, Donmar Warehouse Th., 1992–2002; over 70 prodns for Donmar Warehouse, W End and NY; prodns for Neal Street Productions, London and NY, incl. The Bridge Project, Shrek The Musical. Mem. Bd, National Th., 2002–. *Recreation:* walking the Sussex Downs and the Scottish hills with friends and dogs. *Address:*

Neal Street Productions Ltd, 26–28 Neal Street, First Floor, Covent Garden, WC2H 9QQ. *T*: (020) 7240 8890; *e-mail*: cnewling@nealstreetproductions.com.

NEWMAN, Very Rev. Adrian; Dean of Rochester, since 2005; *b* 21 Dec. 1958; *s* of John Henry Newman and Ruth Doreen Newman; *m* 1981, Gillian Ann Hayes; three *s*. *Educ*: Univ. of Bristol (BSc (Econ.) 1980); Trinity Theol Coll., Bristol (DipHE (Theol.) 1985; MPhil (Theol.) 1989). Ordained deacon, 1985, priest, 1986; Curate, St Mark's, Forest Gate, 1985–89; Vicar, Hillsborough and Wadsley Bridge, Sheffield, 1989–96; Rector, St Martin-in-the-Bull-Ring, Birmingham, 1996–2004. *Recreations*: sport, music, reading. *Address*: The Deanery, Priors Gate House, Rochester, Kent ME1 1SR. *T*: (01634) 202183; *e-mail*: dean@rochestercathedral.org.

NEWMAN, Catherine Mary; QC 1995; a Recorder, since 2000; a Deputy High Court Judge, since 2008; Lieutenant-Bailiff (Judge) of the Royal Court of Guernsey, since 2001; *b* 7 Feb. 1954; *d* of Dr Ernest Newman and Josephine (*née* McLaughlin); *m* 1982, Ian James Gouldsbrough (marr. diss. 2008); one *s* one *d*. *Educ*: University Coll. London (LLB 1st Cl. Hons 1978). Called to the Bar, Middle Temple, 1979 (Harmsworth Schol.), Bencher, 2002; in practice in business and commercial fields, Chancery Div., 1980–; Dep. Registrar in Bankruptcy, 1991–2000; an Asst Recorder, 1998–2000. Member: Bar Council, 1987–90; Public Interest Adv. Panel, Legal Services Commn, 2000–04; Council, UCL, 2008–. Chm., Inns of Ct and Bar Educnl Trust, 2005–. *Publications*: Bar Finals Guide, 1980, 3rd edn 1987; Insolvency Issues, 1999; (consulting ed.) French on Winding Up, 2008. *Recreation*: eating with friends. *Address*: Maitland Chambers, 7 Stone Buildings, Lincoln's Inn, WC2A 3SZ. *T*: (020) 7406 1200.

NEWMAN, Charles William Frank; a District Judge, since 1991; *b* 30 May 1946; *s* of John Leonard Newman and Enid Mary Newman; *m* 1st, 1970, Clare Willatt (decd) one *d*; 2nd, 1986, Anna Elizabeth Meacock; two *s*. *Educ*: Hawthorne Road Primary Sch., Kettering; Kimbolton Sch.; Queen Mary Coll., London (LLB Hons 1968). Admitted solicitor, 1972; Registrar of Co. Court, 1987. Mem., Judicial Appts Commn, 2006–. Gov., Queen's Sch., Chester, 2003–. *Recreations*: cooking, reading, walking in the Lakes. *Club*: Army and Navy.

NEWMAN, Edward; Member for Neighbourhood Services (formerly Housing), Executive Committee, Manchester City Council, since 2004; *b* 14 May 1953; *m* three *c*. Formerly in light engineering, cable making; postal worker, Manchester. Mem. (Lab), Manchester CC, 1979–85, 2002–. MEP (Lab) Greater Manchester Central, 1984–99. Chm., Willow Park Housing Trust. *Publication*: (contrib.) The European Ombudsman: origins, establishment, evolution, 2005. *Address*: 234 Ryebank Road, Chorlton cum Hardy, Manchester M21 1LU.

NEWMAN, Sir Francis (Hugh Cecil), 4th Bt *cr* 1912, of Cecil Lodge, Newmarket; *b* 12 June 1963; *s* of Sir Gerard Robert Henry Sigismund Newman, 3rd Bt and of Caroline Philippa, *d* of late Brig. Alfred Geoffrey Neville, CBE, MC; *S* father, 1987; *m* 1990, Katharine, *d* of Timothy Edwards; three *s* one *d*. *Educ*: Eton; Univ. of Pennsylvania (BA Econs). *Recreations*: family, collecting, field sports. *Heir*: *s* Thomas Ralph Gerard Newman, *b* 7 Jan. 1993. *Address*: Burloes Hall, Royston, Herts SG8 9NE. *Clubs*: Turf, Penn; Eton Vikings.

NEWMAN, Frederick Edward Fry, CBE 1986; MC 1945; Chairman: Dan-Air Services, 1953–89; Davies & Newman Holdings, 1971–90; *b* 14 July 1916; *s* of Frank Newman and Katharine Newman; *m* 1947, Margaret Helen (*née* Blackstone) (*d* 2002); two *s* one *d*. *Educ*: The Leys School, Cambridge. Joined Davies & Newman, 1937; served HAC and 9th Field Regt, RA, 1939–46; formed Dan-Air Services, 1953. *Address*: Cranstone, Hook Heath Road, Woking, Surrey GU22 0DT. *T*: (01483) 772605.

NEWMAN, Sir Geoffrey (Robert), 6th Bt *cr* 1836; Director, Blackpool Sands (Devon) Utilities Co. Ltd, since 1970; *b* 2 June 1947; *s* of Sir Ralph Alured Newman, 5th Bt, and of Hon. Ann Rosemary Hope, *d* of late Hon. Claude Hope-Morley; *S* father, 1968; *m* 1980, Mary, *y d* of Colonel Sir Martin St John Valentine Gibbs, KCVO, CB, DSO, TD; one *s* three *d*. *Educ*: Heatherdown, Ascot; Kelly Coll., Tavistock. 1st Bn, Grenadier Guards, 1967–70; Lt, T&AVR, until 1979. Daniel Greenaway & Sons Ltd, 1973–75; Mem., Transglobe Expedition, 1977–79; Prodn Controller, Wadlow Grosvenor Internat., 1980–90. Vice Chm. and Dir, Dartmouth Tourist Inf. Centre, 1995–2003; Mem., Devon Assoc. of Tourist Attractions, 1995–. Chm., Dartmouth Swimming Pool, 1999–. Walk Leader/Guide, The Wayfarers, 1991–. Pres., Dartmouth and Kingswear Soc., 2001–; Chm., Marine Conservation Soc., 2002–. Trustee, Britannia Mus., Britannia RNC, 2007–. FRGS. *Recreations*: sub-aqua, sailing, all sports. *Heir*: *s* Robert Melvil Newman, *b* 4 Oct. 1985.

NEWMAN, Hon. Sir George (Michael), Kt 1995; a Judge of the High Court of Justice, Queen's Bench Division, 1995–2007; a Deputy High Court Judge, since 2007; arbitrator and mediator; *b* 4 July 1941; *s* of late Wilfred James Newman and Cecilia Beatrice Lily Newman; *m* 1966, Hilary Alice Gibbs (*née* Chandler); two *s* one *d*. *Educ*: Lewes County Grammar Sch.; St Catharine's Coll., Cambridge (Squire Schol.; BA Law). Called to the Bar, Middle Temple, 1965 (Blackstone Scholar; Bencher, 1989), Trinidad and Tobago, 1979, St Kitts and Nevis, 1989. QC 1981; a Recorder, 1985–95. Counsel and Constitutional Advr to Gov. Gen. of Fiji, 1987; Constitutional Advr to Pres. of Fiji, 1988–90. Fellow, Inst. of Advanced Legal Studies, 1999. FRSA 1991. *Publication*: (jtly) contribs to Halsbury's Laws of England, 4th edn. *Recreations*: tennis, golf, ski-ing, the countryside. *Address*: 3 Hare Court, Temple, EC4Y 7BJ. *Club*: Royal Ashdown Forest.

NEWMAN, Jeremy Steven, FCA; Chief Executive Officer, BDO International, since 2008; *b* 30 Sept. 1959; *s* of Harold and Marilyn Newman; *m* 1987, Judi Levy; one *s* one *d*. *Educ*: Haberdashers' Aske's Sch., Elstree; City of London Poly. (Dip. Accountancy with Dist.); Harvard Business Sch. (AMP; ISMP). FCA 1982. Joined Stoy Hayward & Co., subseq. BDO Stoy Hayward LLP, 1978; Partner, 1986; Man. Partner, 2001–07. Hon. Treasurer: Community Security Trust, 2000–; Labour Friends of Israel, 2004–05; Trustee, various charitable trusts. Chm. of Trustees, Morasha Jewish Primary Sch., 2007–; Founder Mem. and Gov., Leigh City Technology Coll. *Recreations*: opera, cinema, reading, spending time with my wife and children. *Address*: 55 Baker Street, W1U 7EU. *T*: (020) 7893 2318, *Fax*: (020) 7935 2257; *e-mail*: jeremy.newman@bdo.co.uk.

NEWMAN, John Arthur, FSA; Reader, Courtauld Institute of Art, University of London, 1987–2001; *b* 14 Dec. 1936; *s* of late Arthur Charles Cecil Newman and Wynifred Kate Newman (*née* Owles); *m* 1965, Margaret Banner; two *d*. *Educ*: Dulwich Coll.; University Coll., Oxford (MA); Courtauld Inst. of Art, London Univ. (Academic Dip. 1965). Lectr, Courtauld Inst. of Art, 1966–87. Mem., Historic Buildings Council for England, 1977–84; Comr, English Heritage, 1986–89; Chm., Adv. Bd for Redundant Churches, 2000–05; Mem., Royal Commn on Ancient and Historical Monuments of Wales, 2000–. Pres., Soc. of Architectural Historians of GB, 1988–92. *Publications*: Buildings of England series: Kent (2 vols), 1969; (with Nikolaus Pevsner) Dorset, 1972; Shropshire, 2nd edn 2006; (contrib.) The History of the King's Works, vol. V, 1975; (ed

with Howard Colvin) Roger North on Architecture, 1981; (contrib.) The History of the University of Oxford, vol. III, 1986, vol. IV, 1997; Buildings of Wales series: Glamorgan, 1995; Gwent/Monmouthshire, 2000. *Address*: 31 Gordon Road, Sevenoaks, Kent TN13 1HE.

NEWMAN, Prof. Judith Alice, PhD; Professor of American Studies, University of Nottingham, since 2000; *b* 9 May 1950; *d* of Ellis Edward Newman and Alice Dorothy Elizabeth Newman (*née* Herringshaw); *m* 1978, Ian Revie (marr. diss. 1999); one *s*, and one step *s*. *Educ*: Univ. of Edinburgh (MA English, MA French); Clare Coll., Cambridge (PhD 1982). University of Newcastle upon Tyne: Lectr, 1976–91; Reader, 1991–95; Prof. of American and Postcolonial Literature, 1995–2000. Chairman: British Assoc. for American Studies, 1995–98 (Sec., 1993–95); American Studies Panel, 2001 RAE; Main Panel L, 2008 RAE; Member: AHRC Res. Panel for English, 2004–07 (Convenor, 2007–); AHRC Peer Review Coll., 2004. Founding FEA 1999; AcSS 2000. *Publications*: Saul Bellow and History, 1984; John Updike, 1988; Nadine Gordimer, 1988; (ed) Dred: a tale of the Great Dismal Swamp, 1992, 2nd edn 1998; The Ballistic Bard, 1995; Alison Lurie, 2000; Nadine Gordimer's Burger's Daughter (critical essays), 2003; Fictions of America, 2007; 60 scholarly essays in learned jls and collections. *Recreations*: family, gardening, genealogy, trips home to Caithness. *Address*: School of American and Canadian Studies, University of Nottingham, University Park, Nottingham NG7 2RD. *T*: (0115) 951 4351, *Fax*: (0115) 951 4270; *e-mail*: Judith.Newman@nottingham.ac.uk.

NEWMAN, Sir Kenneth (Leslie), GBE 1987; Kt 1978; QPM 1982; Commissioner of the Metropolitan Police, 1982–87; non-executive director of various companies; *b* 15 Aug. 1926; *s* of John William Newman and Florence Newman; *m* 1949, Eileen Lilian. *Educ*: London Univ. (LLB Hons). Served War, RAF, 1942–46. Palestine Police, 1946–48; Metropolitan Police, 1948–73; Comdr, New Scotland Yard, 1972; Royal Ulster Constab., 1973–79; Sen. Dep. Chief Constable, 1973; Chief Constable, 1976–79; Comdt, Police Staff Coll., and HM Inspector of Constabulary, 1980–82. Vis. Prof. of Law, Bristol University, 1987–88. Registrar, Imperial Soc. of Knights Bachelor, 1991–98. Chairman: Disciplinary Cttee, Security Systems Inspectorate, British Security Industry Assoc., 1987–97; Assoc. for Prevention of Theft in Shops, 1987–91; Pres., Assoc. of Police and Public Security Suppliers, 1993–2000; Vice Pres., Defence Manufacturers Assoc., 1987–2000. Trustee: Police Foundn, 1982– (Chm., Res. Cttee, 1991–98); Community Action Trust (Crime Stoppers), 1987–2003; World Humanity Action Trust, 1993–98. CCMI (FBIM 1977). Freeman of the City of London, 1983. KStJ 1987 (CStJ 1984). Communicator of the Year, BAIE, 1984. Order of: Bahrain, Class 2, 1984; the Aztec Eagle, Cl. 2, Mexico, 1985. King Abdul Aziz, Cl. 1, Saudi Arabia, 1987; Grand Officer: Order of Orange-Nassau, Netherlands, 1982; Grand Order of the Lion, Malaŵi, 1985; Order of Ouissam Alouite, Morocco, 1987; Commander: National Order of Legion of Honour, France, 1984; Order of Military Merit, Spain, 1986; Kt Comdr, Order of Merit, West Germany, 1986; Medal of Merit, Cl. 1, Qatar, 1985. *Recreations*: walking, reading, bridge.

NEWMAN, Kevin; Senior Executive Vice President and Head of Personal Financial Services, HSBC Bank USA, since 2003; *b* 28 June 1957; *s* of John and Valerie Newman; *m* 1983, Catherine Stewart-Murray; two *s* one *d*. *Educ*: Keele Univ. (BA Amer. Studies and Politics); Essex Univ. (US Govt and Politics). Mars Gp Services, 1981–85; Inf. Centre Manager, Business Systems Manager and Management Inf. Systems Dir, Woolworth, 1985–89; First Direct: joined 1989; Ops Dir, 1990; Chief Exec., 1991–97; Global Delivery Dir, Citibank, 1997–2000; Hd, HSBC.com, 2001–03. *Recreations*: squash, tennis, ski-ing, golf, gym workout, American football, family.

NEWMAN, Dr Lotte Therese, (Mrs N. E. Aronsohn), CBE 1998 (OBE 1991); general practitioner since 1958; President, Royal College of General Practitioners, 1994–97; *b* 22 Jan. 1929; *d* of Dr George Newman and Dr Tilly Newman; *m* 1959, Norman Edward Aronsohn; three *s* one *d*. *Educ*: North London Collegiate Sch.; Univ. of Birmingham; King's College London and Westminster Hosp. Med. Schs BSc 1951, MB BS 1957; LRCP, MRCS 1957; FRCGP 1977. Casualty Officer, Westminster Hosp.; Paediatric House Officer, Westminster Children's Hosp.; gen. medicine, St Stephen's Hosp. Director: Private Patients Plan, 1983–96; Private Patients Plan (Lifetime) plc, 1991–96; Gov., PPP Medical Trust, 1997–99. Mem. Council, 1980–94, Vice-Chm., 1987–89, former Provost, NE London Faculty and former Examr, RCGP; Hon. Sec., 1981–86, Pres. elect, 1986–87, Pres., 1987–88, Medical Women's Fedn; Pres., Internat. Soc. of Gen. Practice, 1988–90; Europ. Regl Vice-Pres., World Orgn of Nat. Colls, Acads and Academic Assocs of GPs/Family Physicians, 1992–94; Member: GMC, 1984–99 (Chm., Registration Cttee, 1997–99); Council, BMA, 1985–89 (Member: Med. Ethics Cttee; General Med. Services Cttee, 1983–86 and 1988–91; Private Practice and Prof. Fees Cttee, 1985–89; Forensic Medicine Sub-Cttee, 1985–89; Visitor to Council, 1996–97); Adv. Cttee on Breast Cancer Screening, 1988–97; Home Office Misuse of Drugs Tribunal, 1993–; Disability Benefits Forum, 1998–99; Ind. Practice Forum, Acad. of Medical Royal Colls, 2002–03; Chm., Camden and Islington Local Med. Cttee, 1986–89 (Vice-Chm., 1983–86); Chm., Regional Co-ordinating Cttee of Area Local Med. Cttees, 1985–87; Lectr, Royal Army Med. Coll., 1976–89 (first woman to give Sir David Bruce Lecture in Gen. Practice, 1989); temp. Adviser, WHO; formerly UK rep., OECD and Mem., Expert Cttees studying Primary Health Care in Germany, Switzerland, Sweden. Med. Advr, St John Ambulance, 1999–2003. Mem., Parole Bd, 1992–94. Mackenzie Lectr, RCGP, 1991; Dame Hilda Rose Lectr, Med. Women's Fedn, 1994. Member: Hunterian Soc.; Hampstead Medical Soc.; Assurance Med. Soc., 1987–2006. FRSocMed 1977; Fellow: BMA, 1998; Royal NZ Coll. of Gen. Practitioners, 1998. Freeman, City of London; Liveryman, Apothecaries' Soc. of London. Sir David Bruce Medal, RAMC, 1990; Purkinje Medal for Services to Medicine, Czech Soc. of Gen. Practice, 1985; Jewish Women's Distinction Award, 1994. *Publications*: papers on: women doctors; multidisciplinary training and courses of Primary Health Care Team; breast feeding; ENT conditions and management of mental health handicap in gen. practice. *Recreations*: listening, music, boating. *Address*: The White House, One Ardwick Road, NW2 2BX. *T*: (020) 7435 6630, *Fax*: (020) 7435 6672; *e-mail*: JH44@dial.pipex.com. *Clubs*: Royal Automobile, City Livery, Little Ship.

NEWMAN, Malcolm, CPFA; Director, Carlisle Partnerships, since 1997; *b* 2 April 1946; *s* of John George and Elizabeth Newman; *m* 1980, Marilyn Wilson; one *s* one *d*. *Educ*: Jarrow Grammar Sch. Clerk, Hebburn UDC, 1962–66; Newcastle upon Tyne City Council: various positions, 1966–71; Sen. Audit Asst, 1971–72; Sen. Management Accountant, 1972–73; Chief Accountant, 1973–77; Asst City Treas. (Accounting), 1977–79; Man. (Cons.) and Gen. Man., Wilson Johnson, 1979–80; Asst Finance Officer (Audit and Tech.), Sefton MDC, 1980–82; Hd of Financial Services 1982–85, Bor. Treas. 1985–87, London Borough of Southwark; City Treas., 1987–97, Dep. Chief Exec., 1990–97, Sheffield City Council. Director: Hallamshire Investments plc, 1988–; Northern Gen. Hosp. NHS Trust, 1997–; Chm., START Fedn, 1994–. Governor: Sheffield Hallam Univ. (formerly Sheffield Poly.), 1989–94; Silverdale Sch., 1993–97. *Recreations*: outdoors, jogging, Newcastle United, learning about myself. *Address*: The Coach House, 9 Whalton Park, Morpeth, Northumberland NE61 3TU.

NEWMAN, Nanette, (Mrs Bryan Forbes); actress and writer; *b* 29 May 1934; *d* of Sidney and Ruby Newman; *m* 1955, Bryan Forbes, *qv*; two *d*. *Educ:* Sternhold Coll., London; Italia Conti Stage Sch.; RADA. Appeared as a child in various films for Children's Film Foundn; other film appearances include: The L-Shaped Room, 1962; The Wrong Arm of the Law, 1962; Seance on a Wet Afternoon, 1963; The Wrong Box, 1965; The Whisperers, 1966; Deadfall, 1967; The Madwoman of Chaillot, 1968; The Raging Moon, 1971 (Variety Club Best Film Actress Award); The Stepford Wives, 1974; International Velvet, 1978 (Evening News Best Film Actress Award); The Mystery of Edwin Drood, 1992; *television:* Call My Bluff, What's My Line, London Scene, Stay with me till Morning, Jessie (title role), Let There Be Love, A Breath of Fresh Air, Late Expectations, The Endless Game, The Mixer; own series: The Fun Food Factory, 1977; Newman Meets, 2000–01; Celebrations, 2001; Patten on a Plate, 2001. *Publications:* God Bless Love, 1972 (repr. 16 times); Lots of Love, 1973 (repr. 7 times); Vote for Love, 1976 (repr. 4 times); All Our Love, 1978; Fun Food Factory, 1976 (repr. twice); Fun Food Feasts, 1978; The Root Children, 1978; The Pig Who Never Was, 1979; Amy Rainbow, 1980; The Facts of Love, 1980; That Dog, 1980; Reflections, 1981; The Dog Lover's Coffee Table Book, 1982; The Cat Lover's Coffee Table Book, 1983; My Granny was a Frightful Bore, 1983, repr. 2003; A Cat and Mouse Love Story, 1984; Nanette Newman's Christmas Cook Book, 1984; Pigalev, 1985; The Best of Love, 1985; The Summer Cookbook, 1986; Archie, 1986; Small Beginnings, 1987; Bad Baby, 1988; Entertaining with Nanette Newman and her Daughters Sarah and Emma, 1988; Sharing, 1989; Charlie the Noisy Caterpillar, 1989; ABC, 1990; 123, 1991; Cooking for Friends, 1991; Spider the Horrible Cat, 1992; There's a Bear in the Bath, 1993; There's a Bear in the Classroom, 1996; The Importance of Being Ernest the Earwig, 1996; Take 3 Cooks, 1996; Up to the Sky and Down Again, 1999; To You With Love, 1999; Bedtime Stories, 2002; Good Baby, Bad Baby, 2003; Small Talk, 2004; Ben's Book, 2005; Eating In, 2005. *Recreation:* painting. *Address:* c/o Lloyds Private Banking, 50 Grosvenor Street, W1X 9FH. *Fax:* (01344) 845174.

NEWMAN, Paul; American actor and director; *b* 26 Jan. 1925; *s* of Arthur Newman and Theresa (*née* Fetzer); *m* 1st, 1949, Jacqueline Witte; two *d* (one *s* decd); 2nd, 1958, Joanne Woodward; three *d*. *Educ:* Kenyon Coll. (BA); Yale Drama Sch. Mil. Service, USNR, 1943–46. Chairman: Newman's Own; Salad King. Team owner, and formerly driver, IndyCar racing. *Stage appearances include:* Picnic, 1953–54; Sweet Bird of Youth, 1959; Our Town, NY, 2002; *films include:* Somebody Up There Likes Me, 1956; Cat on a Hot Tin Roof, 1958; The Hustler, 1961; Sweet Bird of Youth, 1962; Hud, 1963; Torn Curtain, 1966; Cool Hand Luke, 1967; Butch Cassidy and the Sundance Kid, 1969; The Sting, 1973; Drowning Pool, 1975; Quintet, 1979; Fort Apache, the Bronx (also dir), 1980; Absence of Malice, 1981; The Verdict, 1982; Harry and Son (also wrote and directed), 1984; The Color of Money, 1986 (Academy Award, 1987); Blaze, 1990; Shadow Makers, 1990; Mr and Mrs Bridge, 1991; The Hudsucker Proxy, 1994; Nobody's Fool, 1995; Twilight, 1998; Message in a Bottle, 1999; Where the Money Is, 2000; Road to Perdition, 2002; *films directed include:* Rachel, Rachel, 1968; When Time Ran Out, 1980; The Glass Menagerie, 1987; *TV mini-series:* Empire Falls, 2005. Hon. Academy Award for career achievement, 1986. *Address:* Newman Haas Racing, 500 Tower Parkway, Lincolnshire, IL 60069, USA.

NEWMAN, Prof. Ronald Charles, PhD; FRS 1998; FInstP; Professor of Physics, University of London, 1989–99, now Emeritus; Senior Research Fellow, Centre for Semiconductor Materials and Devices, Department of Physics, Imperial College, London, 1999–2006; *b* 10 Dec. 1931; *s* of Charles Henry Newman and Margaret Victoria May Newman (*née* Cooper); *m* 1956, Jill Laura Weeks; two *d*. *Educ:* Imperial Coll. of Sci. and Technol. (BSc 1st Cl. Hons, ARCS; DIC 1954; PhD 1955). FInstP 1971. Research scientist, AEI Central Res. Lab., Aldermaston Court, 1955–63; Sen. Res. Scientist, AEI Rugby, 1963–64; University of Reading: Lectr, Dept of Physics, 1964–69; Reader, 1969–75; Prof., 1975–89; Vis. Prof., 1989–Sept. 2009; Associate Dir, IRC for Semiconductor Materials, ICSTM, 1989–99. Vis. Prof., Dept of Electrical Engrg and Electronics, UMIST, 2000–05. Has held numerous consultancies. *Publications:* Infra-Red Studies of Crystal Defects, 1973; (contrib.) Semiconductors and Semimetals, 1993; (contrib.) Handbook on Semiconductors, 1994; numerous contribs to learned jls. *Recreations:* music, foreign travel. *Address:* 23 Betchworth Avenue, Earley, Reading, Berks RG6 7RH. *T:* (0118) 966 3816.

NEWMAN, Vice Adm. Sir Roy (Thomas), KCB 1992 (CB 1991); JP; DL; Flag Officer Plymouth, and Commander Central Sub Area Eastern Atlantic, 1992–96; *b* 8 Sept. 1936; *s* of Mr and Mrs T. U. Newman; *m* 1960, Heather (*née* Macleod); four *s*. *Educ:* Queen Elizabeth's Grammar Sch., Barnet, Herts. Joined RN, 1954; specialised in anti-submarine warfare, 1963; joined Submarine Service, 1966; Comdr 1971, Captain 1979; commanded: HMS Onyx, 1970–71; HMS Naiad, 1978–79; First Submarine Sqn and HMS Dolphin, 1981–83; Seventh Frigate Sqn and HMS Cleopatra, 1984–85; Dir of Naval Warfare, 1986–88; Flag Officer Sea Trng, 1988–89; COS to C-in-C Fleet and Dep. Comdr Fleet, 1990–92. Pres., Royal Naval Assoc., 1996–2001 (Vice Patron, 2001–). Chm., Trustees, RN Submarine Mus., 1998–2005. Younger Brother, Trinity House, 1997. Freeman, Shipwrights' Co., 1996. JP SE Hants, 1996; DL Hants, 2001. *Recreations:* cricket, golf, music, reading. *Club:* Army and Navy.

NEWMAN TAYLOR, Sir Anthony John, Kt 2008; CBE 2003 (OBE 1992); FRCP; FFOM, FMedSci; Consultant Physician, Royal Brompton Hospital, since 1977; Professor of Occupational and Environmental Medicine, since 1992, and Head, National Heart and Lung Institute, Faculty of Medicine, since 2006, Imperial College London; *b* 11 Dec. 1943; *s* of Reginald John Newman Taylor and Violet Anne (*née* Hilliard); *m* 1st, 1968, Gillian Frances Crick (marr. diss.); two *s* one *d*; 2nd, 1986, Frances Victoria Costley; one *s*. *Educ:* Radley Coll.; St Bartholomew's Hosp. Med. Coll. (MB BS 1970; MSc 1979). FRCP 1986; FFOM 1987; FMedSci 1999. Postgrad. trng, St Bartholomew's and Brompton Hosps, 1970–77; Royal Brompton Hospital: Med. Dir, 1994–2005; Dir of Research, 1997–2006; Acting Chief Exec., 1996, July–Oct. 2002 and June 2004–March 2005; Dep. Chief Exec., 2003–06. Civilian Advr in Chest Medicine to RAF, 1983–. Chm., Industrial Injuries Adv. Council, 1996–2008 (Mem., 1983–; Chm., Res. Wkg Gp, 1984–96); Mem., MRC Cttee on toxic hazards in envmt and workplace, 1982–90. Advr in occupational medicine, Nat. Asthma Campaign, subseq. Asthma UK, 1994–. WHO Advr to Minister of Health, India on long term consequences of methyl isocyanate exposure to population of Bhopal, 1985; Advr to Dept of Health, Valencia on epidemic of lung disease in textile spray workers, 1994. Chm., Coronary Artery Disease Res. Assoc., 1998–. Trustee, Colt Foundn, 2005– (Chm., 2008–). Gov., Royal Brompton Hosp., 1994–2005; non-exec. Dir, Royal Brompton Harefield Trust, 2006–. Gov., Chislehurst C of E Primary Sch., 1995–99. *Publications:* chapters in textbooks on respiratory disease and occupational and environmental lung disease; papers in Lancet, BMJ, Thorax, Amer. Jl of Respiratory Disease and Critical Care Medicine; Jl of Allergy and Clinical Immunology, etc. *Recreations:* history and politics, cricket. *Address:* 11 Waldegrave Road, Bickley, Kent BR1 2JP. *Clubs:* Athenæum, MCC.

NEWMARCH, Michael George, (Mick); Chief Executive, Prudential Corporation plc, 1990–95; *b* 19 May 1938; *s* of late George Langdon Newmarch and Phyllis Georgina Newmarch; *m* 1959, Audrey Clarke; one *s* two *d*. *Educ:* Univ. of London (BSc (Econs) external). Joined Prudential, 1955, Econ. Intelligence Dept; Exec. Dir, Prudential Corp., 1985–95; Chairman: Prudential Money Funds, 1983–95; Prudential Holborn, 1986–89; Prudential Financial Services, 1987–95 (Chief Exec., 1987–89); Prudential Currency Fund, 1987–95; Prudential Assce Co., 1990–95; Prudential Portfolio Managers, 1990–95 (Chief Exec., 1982–89); Prudential Nominees, 1990–95; Prudential Services, 1990–95; Mercantile and Gen. Gp., 1990–95. Non-executive Chairman: Transacsys, 2000–02; Weston Medical, 2001–03; non-exec. Dir, Celltech Gp (formerly Celltech plc), 1996–2004. Chm., Princess Royal Trust for Carers, 2004– (Vice-Chm., 1989); Trustee, Berks Community Foundn, 1998–2002 (Chm. Trustees, 1999–2002). Member: Adv. Bd, Orchestra of the Age of Enlightenment, 1992–2005; Council, Univ. of Reading, 1999–. *Recreations:* salmon and trout fishing, flytying, bridge, theatre, concerts. *Club:* Flyfishers'.

NEWMARK, Brooks Phillip Victor; MP (C) Braintree, since 2005; *b* 8 May 1958; *s* of late Howard Newmark and of Gilda Newmark (now Gourlay); *m* 1985, Lucy Keegan; four *s* one *d*. *Educ:* Bedford Sch.; Harvard Coll. (AB); Worcester Coll., Oxford (res. grad.); Harvard Business Sch. (MBA). Vice Pres., Shearson Lehman Brothers Inc., 1984–87; Director: Newmark Brothers Ltd, 1987–92; Stellican Ltd, 1992–98; Partner, Apollo Mgt LP, 1998–2005. Contested (C): Newcastle Central, 1997; Braintree, 2001. Opposition Treasury Whip, 2007–. *Recreations:* football (Newcastle United supporter), running, skiing. *Address:* House of Commons, SW1A 0AA. *Clubs:* Beefsteak, Boodle's, White's; St Moritz Tobogganing.

NEWPORT, Viscount; Alexander Michael Orlando Bridgeman; *b* 6 Sept. 1980; *s* and *heir* of 7th Earl of Bradford, *qv*.

NEWPORT, Dr Ronald William; Head of Daresbury Laboratory, Council for the Central Laboratory of the Research Councils, 1995–96; *b* 3 Nov. 1933; *s* of Thomas Prescott Newport and Elsie Newport; *m* 1959, Joan Margaret Williams; one *s* one *d*. *Educ:* Nantwich and Acton County Grammar Sch.; Univ. of Liverpool (BSc 1955; PhD 1960). Res. Physicist, British Nat. Hydrogen Bubble Chamber, 1960–62; Science Research Council, subseq. Science and Engineering Council, later Engineering and Physical Sciences Research Council: Rutherford High Energy Laboratory, later Rutherford Appleton Laboratory: Res. Physicist, 1962–79; Div. Manager, Technol. Dept, 1979–81; Dep. Div. Head, Instrumentation Div., 1981–84; Project Manager, James Clerk Maxwell Telescope, 1981–87; Associate Dir for Technol., 1987–88; Head of Science Div., 1988–91, Associate Dir Progs, 1991–94, SERC; Dep. Dir, Daresbury and Rutherford Appleton Lab., 1994–95. Member: Steering Cttee, Institut Laue Langevin, 1989–92; Council, European Synchrotron Radiation Facility, 1989–92 (Chm., 1993–95). MRI 1995; FRSA 1997; FRAS 2004. MacRobert Award, for James Clerk Maxwell Telescope, Fellowship of Engineering, 1988. *Publications:* various papers, mainly on instrumentation. *Recreations:* reading, walking, photography, travel. *Address:* 5 Chapel Lane, Sutton Courtenay, Abingdon, Oxon OX14 4AN. *T:* (01235) 848424.

NEWRY AND MORNE, Viscount; Robert Francis John Needham; Director, Newfield Information Technology (formerly Collabra Net Solutions) Ltd, since 2000; *b* 30 May 1966; *s* and *heir* to Earl of Kilmorey, *qv*; *m* 1991, Laura Mary, *o d* of Michael Tregaskis; one *s* one *d*. *Educ:* Sherborne Prep. School; Eton College; Lady Margaret Hall, Oxford (BA); Imperial Coll., London (MBA 1993). Management trainee, Benjamin Priest, 1988–90; Sales Man., Lewmar Marine Ltd, 1991–92; Asst Man., Business Develt, Inchcape Pacific Ltd, 1994–95; Business Develt Manager, Inchcape NRG, 1995–97; Dir, Ops, Inchcape NRG HK, 1998–2000; Exec. Dir, NRG Solutions, 1997–2000; Dir, Morne Consultancy Ltd, 2000; Associate Dir, Ricoh UK Ltd, 2001–03. Non-exec. Dir, Fenix Media Ltd, 2001–. *Recreations:* squash, theatre, travelling. *Heir:* *s* Hon. Thomas Francis Michael Needham, *b* 25 Sept. 1998. *Address:* Lattimer Place, Chiswick, W4 2UA.

NEWSAM, Sir Peter (Anthony), Kt 1987; Chairman, Central London Connexions Board, 2002–05; Director, University of London Institute of Education, 1989–94; *b* 2 Nov. 1928; *s* of late W. O. Newsam and of Mrs D. E. Newsam; *m* 1st, 1953, Elizabeth Joy Greg (marr. diss. 1987); four *s* one *d*; 2nd, 1988, Sue Addinell; one *d*. *Educ:* Clifton Coll.; Queen's Coll., Oxford (MA, DipEd). Asst Principal, BoT, 1952–55; teacher, 1956–63; Asst Educn Officer, N Riding of Yorks, 1963–66; Asst Dir of Educn, Cumberland, 1966–70; Dep. Educn Officer: W Riding of Yorks, 1970–72; ILEA, 1972–76; Educn Officer, ILEA, 1977–82; Chm., CRE, 1982–87; Sec., ACC, 1987–89; Dep. Vice-Chancellor, Univ. of London, 1992–94; Chief Adjudicator, Sch. Orgn and Admissions, 1999–2002. *Address:* Greenlea, Church Lane, Thornton le Dale, Pickering, N Yorks YO18 7QL.

NEWSON, Prof. Linda Ann, PhD; FBA 2000; Professor of Geography, King's College, London, since 1994; *b* 2 Aug. 1946; *d* of Donald George Newson and Evelyn Maud Newson (*née* Lee). *Educ:* Grey Coat Hosp., Westminster; University Coll. London (BA 1967; PhD 1972). King's College, London: Lectr, 1971–87; Reader, 1987–94; Hd, Sch. of Humanities, 1997–2000; FKC 2001. Vis. Prof., Univ. of Calif, Berkeley, 1989. Fellow, Newberry Liby, Chicago, 1985 and 2000. C. O. Sauer Award, Conf. of Latin Americanist Geographers, USA, 1992; Back Award, RGS, 1993. *Publications:* Aboriginal and Spanish Colonial Trinidad: a study in culture contact, 1976; The Cost of Conquest: Indian societies in Honduras under Spanish rule, 1986; Indian Survival in Colonial Nicaragua, 1987; Patterns of Life and Death in Early Colonial Ecuador, 1995; (with S. Minchin) From Capture to Sale: the Portuguese slave trade to Spanish America in the early seventeenth century, 2007. *Address:* Department of Geography, King's College London, Strand, WC2R 2LS. *T:* (020) 7848 2364.

NEWSON, Marc Andrew, RDI 2006; designer; *b* Sydney, Australia, 20 Oct. 1963; *s* of Carol Conomos. *Educ:* Sydney Coll. of the Arts. Solo exhibitions include: Design Works, Powerhouse Mus., Sydney, 2001; Kelvin 40, Fondation Cartier pour l'art contemporain, Paris, 2004; Groningen Mus., Netherlands, 2004; Design Mus., London, 2004–05; Gagosian Gall., NY, 2007. Designer of Year Award, Design Miami, 2006. *Recreation:* gardening. *Address:* Marc Newson Ltd, 175–185 Gray's Inn Road, WC1X 8EU. *T:* (020) 7287 9388, *Fax:* (020) 7287 9347; *e-mail:* pod@marc-newson.com. *Club:* Groucho.

NEWSON-SMITH, Sir Peter (Frank Graham), 3rd Bt *cr* 1944, of Totteridge, co. Hertford; Director of Music, Clayesmore Preparatory School, 1979–2003; *b* 8 May 1947; *s* of Sir John Newson-Smith, 2nd Bt and of Vera, Lady Newson-Smith; *S* father, 1997; *m* 1974, Mary Ann Owens (*née* Collins); one *s* one *d*, and two step *s*. *Educ:* Dover Coll.; Trinity Coll. of Music, London. GTCL; LT (MusEd). Asst Dir of Music, Dover Coll. Jun. Sch., 1969–73; Director of Music: Westbourne House, Chichester, 1973–78; Hazelwood, Limpsfield, 1978–79. Hon. Treas., Music Masters' Assoc., 2002–06. Chm., Young Musicians of Muscat, 2002–. Freeman, City of London, 1969; Liveryman, Musicians' Co., 1969–. *Recreations:* travel, DIY, gardening. *Heir:* *s* Oliver Nicholas Peter Newson-Smith, *b* 12 Nov. 1975. *Address:* Lovells Court, Marnhull, Sturminster Newton, Dorset DT10 1JJ.

NEWSUM, Jeremy Henry Moore, FRICS; Group Chief Executive, Grosvenor (formerly Chief Executive, Grosvenor Estate Holdings), 1989–2008 (non-executive Director, since 2008); *b* 4 April 1955; *s* of Neill Henry Hillas Newsum and late Jane Ridsdale Newsum (*née* Moore); *m* 1979, Gillian Lucy Ratcliff; three *d. Educ:* Rugby; Reading Univ. (BSc Estate Mgt). With: Grosvenor Estate Holdings, 1976–78; Savills, 1979–85; London Partner, Bidwells, 1985–87; with Grosvenor (formerly Grosvenor Estate Hldgs), 1987–. Non-exec. Dir, TR Property Investment Trust, 2002–. Pres., British Property Fedn, 2001–02. A Church Comr, 1993–2000. Mem. Council, Imperial Coll. London, 2004–. Exec. Trustee, Grosvenor Estate, 1993–. *Recreation:* any sport. *Address:* Priory House, Swavesey, Cambs CB24 4QJ. *T:* (01954) 232084.

NEWTON, family name of **Baron Newton of Braintree**.

NEWTON, 5th Baron *cr* 1892, of Newton-in-Makerfield, Co. Lancaster; **Richard Thomas Legh;** *b* 11 Jan. 1950; *er s* of 4th Baron Newton and of Priscilla Egerton-Warburton; *S* father, 1992; *m* 1978, Rosemary Whitfoot, *yr d* of Herbert Clarke; one *s* one *d. Educ:* Eton; Christ Church, Oxford (MA). Solicitor, May May & Merrimans, 1976–79. General Comr for Income Tax, 1983–. Mem., Wealden DC, 1987–99. Mem., Sussex Downs Conservation Bd, 1992–95, 1997–98. *Recreation:* bridge. *Heir: s* Hon. Piers Richard Legh, *b* 25 Oct. 1979. *Address:* Laughton Park Farm, Laughton, Lewes, East Sussex BN8 6BU. *T:* (01825) 840627. *Clubs:* Pratt's, MCC.

NEWTON OF BRAINTREE, Baron *cr* 1997 (Life Peer), of Coggeshall in the co. of Essex; **Antony Harold Newton,** OBE 1972; PC 1988; DL; economist; Chairman, Royal Brompton and Harefield NHS Trust, since 2001; *b* Aug. 1937; *m* 1st, 1962, Janet Huxley (marr. diss. 1986); two *d*; 2nd, 1986, Mrs Patricia Gilthorpe; one step *s* two step *d. Educ:* Friends' Sch., Saffron Walden; Trinity Coll., Oxford. Hons PPE. President: OU Conservative Assoc., 1958; Oxford Union, 1959. Formerly Sec. and Research Sec., Bow Group. Head of Conservative Research Dept's Economic Section, 1965–70; Asst Dir, Conservative Research Dept, 1970–74. Chm. Coningsby Club, 1965–66. Contested (C) Sheffield, Brightside, 1970. MP (C) Braintree, Feb. 1974–1997; contested (C) same seat, 1997. An Asst Govt Whip, 1979–81; a Lord Comr of HM Treasury, 1981–82; Parly Under-Sec. of State for Social Security, 1982–84, and Minister for the Disabled, 1983–84, Minister of State (Minister for Social Security and the Disabled), 1984–86, Minister of State (Minister for Health) and Chm., NHS Management Bd, 1986–88, DHSS; Chancellor of Duchy of Lancaster and Minister of Trade and Industry, 1988–89; Sec. of State for Social Security, 1989–92; Lord Pres. of the Council and Leader of H of C, 1992–97. Vice-Chm., Fedn of Univ. Conservative and Unionist Assocs, 1959. Mem., FEFC, 1998– (Chm., E Region Cttee, 1998–). Professional Standards Dir, Inst. of Dirs, 1998–. Chair, Standing Conf. on Drug Abuse, 1997–; Chairman: NE Essex Mental Health NHS Trust, 1997–2001; E Anglia's Children's Hospices, 1998–. Gov., Felsted Sch. Interested in taxation and social services. DL Essex, 2002. *Address:* House of Lords, SW1A 0PW.

NEWTON, Air Vice-Marshal Barry Hamilton, CB 1988; CVO 2002; OBE 1975; an Extra Gentleman Usher to The Queen, since 2002 (a Gentleman Usher, 1989–2002); Hon. Inspector-General, Royal Auxiliary Air Force, since 2000; *b* 1 April 1932; *s* of Bernard Hamilton Newton, FCA and Dorothy Mary Newton; *m* 1959, Constance Lavinia, *d* of Col J. J. Aitken, CMG, DSO, OBE and Constance Marion Aitken (*née* Drake); one *s* one *d. Educ:* Highgate; RAF College Cranwell. Commissioned 1953; flying and staff appointments including: 109 (Pathfinder Sqn); 76 Sqn (nuclear trials Australia and Christmas Island); psc 1966; Personal Staff Officer to C-in-C RAF Germany/Comdr, 2 ATAF, 1967; OC Ops Wing, RAF Cottesmore, 1969; Defence Policy Staff, 1972, 1978; ndc 1974; Cabinet Office, 1975, 1979; Air Cdre Flying Trng, HQ RAF Support Comd, 1982; ADC to the Queen, 1983–84; Sen. Directing Staff (Air), RCDS, 1984; Comdt, JSDC, 1986–88. Vice-Chm., Council of TAVRAs, 1989–99; (First) Hon. Air Cdre, No 606 (Chiltern) Sqn, RAuxAF, 1996–2007; Pres., UK Reserve Forces Assoc., 2005–. Hon. Freeman, Lightmongers' Co., 2002; Freeman, City of London, 2002; Liveryman, GAPAN, 2007–. *Recreations:* military history, walking, philately. *Address:* c/o National Westminster Bank, Blue Boar Row, Salisbury, Wilts SP1 1DF. *Club:* Royal Air Force.

NEWTON, Sir (Charles) Wilfrid, Kt 1993; CBE 1988; Chairman and Chief Executive, London Regional Transport, 1989–94; Chairman, London Underground Ltd, 1989–94; *b* 11 Dec. 1928; *s* of late Gore Mansfield Newton and Catherine Knox Newton; *m* 1954, Felicity Mary Lynn Thomas; two *s* two *d. Educ:* Orange Prep. Sch., Johannesburg; Highlands North High Sch., Johannesburg; Univ. of Witwatersrand, Johannesburg. FCILT (FCIT 1989). Chartered Accountant (South Africa). Articled clerk, 1947–52, Audit Senior, 1952–55, Saml Thomson & Young, Chartered Accountants, Johannesburg; Territory Accounting Manager, Vacuum Oil Co. Ltd, SA, 1955–58; Territory Accounting and Finance Manager, Mobil Oil Ltd, S Africa, 1958–62; Actg Controller, Mobil Sekiyu KK, Tokyo, 1962–63; Finance Manager and Dep. Gen. Manager, Mobil, E Africa, Nairobi, 1963–65; Finance Dir, Mobil Sekiyu KK, Tokyo, and Chief Financial Officer, Mobil Interests in Japan, 1965–68; Turner & Newall plc: Finance Dir, 1968–71; Man. Dir of Finance and Planning, 1971–75; Gp Man. Dir, Mining, Plastics and Chemicals, 1975–82; Gp Chief Exec., 1982–83; Chm. and Chief Exec., Mass Transit Railway Corp., Hong Kong, 1983–89; Chm., Hong Kong Futures Exchange Ltd, 1986–89; non-executive Chairman: Jacobs Hldgs plc, 1992–99; Mountcity Investments Ltd, 1992–; Raglan Properties plc, 1994–98; Guy Maunsell Internat. Ltd, 1994–2001; non-executive Director: Hongkong & Shanghai Banking Corp. Ltd, Hong Kong, 1989–92; Sketchley plc, 1990–99; HSBC Hldgs plc, 1992–99; Midland Bank plc, subseq. HSBC Bank plc, 1992–99. CCIM (CBIM 1977); FRSA 1986. Hon. FREng (Hon. FEng 1993); Hon. FHKIE 1994. JP Hong Kong, 1994–89. *Recreations:* sailing, reading. *Address:* Newtons Gate, 12 Ramley Road, Pennington, Lymington, Hants SO41 8GQ. *T:* (01590) 679750; 7A Balmoral House, Windsor Way, Brook Green, W14 0UF. *T:* (020) 7602 4996. *Clubs:* Carlton; Wanderers (Johannesburg); Hong Kong, Aberdeen Yacht, Royal Hong Kong Yacht (Hong Kong); Royal Lymington Yacht.

NEWTON, Clive Richard; QC 2002; *b* 11 Sept. 1944; *s* of Henry Newton and Winifred Newton; *m* 1986, Robin Jeanne Williams (marr. diss. 1999); two *s. Educ:* Harrow Co. Grammar Sch. for Boys; Wadham Coll., Oxford (maj. schol.; BA First Cl. Hons; MA; BCL). Called to the Bar, Middle Temple, 1968 (Major Harmsworth Entrance Exhibnr; Astbury Law Schol.; Archibald Safford Prizeman; (jtly) Criminal Law Prize, 1967); *ad eundem* Lincoln's Inn, 1978, Inner Temple, 1984; Lecturer: Wadham Coll., Oxford, 1969–76 and 1980–82; Oriel Coll., Oxford, 1985–. Mem., Anglo-American Real Property Institute, 1992. *Publications:* General Principles of Law, 1972, 3rd edn 1983; (with R. S. Parker) Cases and Statutes on General Principles of Law, 1980; (ed jtly) Jackson's Matrimonial Finance and Taxation, 5th edn 1992, to 7th edn 2002. *Recreations:* walking, swimming, cricket, theatre. *Address:* 1 King's Bench Walk, Temple, EC4Y 7DB. *T:* (020) 7936 1500, *Fax:* (020) 7936 1590; *e-mail:* cnewton@1kbw.co.uk.

NEWTON, Clive Trevor, CB 1991; Independent Chairman, Disciplinary Committee, National Association of Funeral Directors, since 1995; *b* 26 Aug. 1931; *s* of late Frederick Norman and Phyllis Laura Newton; *m* 1961, Elizabeth Waugh Plowman; one *s* one *d. Educ:* Hove Grammar School for Boys. LLB London. Called to Bar, Middle Temple, 1969; certified accountant, 1962–. Examiner, Insolvency Service, Board of Trade, 1952, Sen. Examiner, 1963, Asst Official Receiver, 1967; Principal, Marine Div., BoT, 1969; Sen. Principal, Marine Div., Dept of Trade, 1973; Asst Director of Consumer Credit, Office of Fair Trading, 1974; Asst Sec., Regional Development Grants Div., Dept of Industry, 1978; Dir of Consumer Affairs, OFT, 1980; Under Sec., Head of Consumer Affairs Div., DTI, 1986–91. Member: Legislation Cttee, Nat. Fedn of Consumer Gps, 1991–2001 (Vice Chm., 1993–96); E Sussex Valuation Tribunal, 1998–2003. Chartered Association of Certified Accountants, subseq. Association of Chartered Certified Accountants: Mem., 1983–92, Chm., 1987–91, and 1997–99, Disciplinary Cttee; Chm., Authorisation Appeal Cttee, 1994–97, 1998–2001. Lay Performance Assessor, GMC, 1997–2001; Ind. Chm. Disciplinary Cttee, Nat. Assoc. for Pre-Paid Funeral Plans, 1995–2001; Chm., Compliance Cttee, Funeral Planning Authy Ltd, 2001–. Director: Concordia (YSV) Ltd, 1994–99; Kennington Oval Ltd, 2003–. Vice Chm., Sussex Area Cttee, Sanctuary Housing Assoc., 1999–2002. *Recreations:* golf, watching cricket. *Clubs:* Royal Automobile; Surrey County Cricket (Mem. Gen. Cttee, 2000–; Treas., 2003–), East Brighton Golf.

NEWTON, David Alexander; Chairman, Carr's Milling Industries, 1997–2005 (Director, 1996–2005); *b* 6 Oct. 1942; *s* of Alexander and Hazel Newton; *m* 1965, Kathleen Mary Moore; one *s* one *d. Educ:* Morecambe Grammar Sch.; Wyvern Coll. Mgt trainee, J. Bibby & Sons Ltd, UK, 1964–67; Area Manager, Cobb Breeding Co., 1967–69; Gen. Manager and Dir, Anglian Food Gp, 1969–72; Agricl Dir, Sovereign Chicken Ltd, 1972–82; Ops Dir, Ross Poultry Ltd, 1982–84; Chief Exec. Officer and Dir, Buxted Poultry Ltd, 1984–85; Hillsdown Holdings: Dir, 1985–96; Chief Operating Officer, 1992–93; Chief Exec. Officer, 1993–96; Chm., Maple Leaf Mills Ltd, Toronto, 1987–90; Pres. and Chief Exec. Officer, Canada Packers Inc., 1990–92. Director: Bernard Matthews Hldgs Ltd, 1996–; Bodfari, 1996–2005; MRCT, 1997–2005; Chm., Firstan Ltd. FCMI (FBIM 1984); FInstD 1984. *Recreations:* golf, music, watching sports. *Club:* Diss Golf (Norfolk).

NEWTON, Derek Henry; Chairman, C. E. Heath plc, 1984–87; *b* 14 March 1933; *s* of Sidney Wellington Newton and Sylvia May Newton (*née* Peacock); *m* 1957, Judith Ann (*d* 1995), *d* of Roland Hart, Kingston, Surrey; two *d. Educ:* Emanuel School. FCII. Commissioned Royal Artillery, 1952–54 (Lieut). Clerical, Medical & General Life Assurance Society, 1954–58; C. E. Heath Urquhart (Life & Pensions), 1958–83, Chm., 1971–84; Dir. C. E. Heath, 1975, Dep. Chm., 1983–84; Director: Glaxo Insurance (Bermuda), 1980–93; Glaxo Trustees, 1980–92; Clarges Pharmaceutical Trustees, 1985–92. Governor, BUPA Med. R&D, 1981–94. *Recreations:* cricket, golf. *Address:* Pantiles, Meadway, Oxshott, Surrey KT22 0LZ. *T:* (01372) 842273. *Clubs:* Royal Automobile, MCC; Surrey County Cricket (Chm., 1979–94; Pres., 2004).

NEWTON, Rev. Sir George (Peter Howgill), 4th Bt *cr* 1900, of The Wood, Sydenham Hill; Vicar, Holy Trinity, Aldershot, since 2003 (Priest-in-charge, 1999–2003); *b* 26 March 1962; *s* of Sir (Harry) Michael (Rex) Newton, 3rd Bt and Pauline Jane Newton; *S* father, 2008; *m* 1988, Jane Louise Rymer; two *d. Educ:* Sherborne; Pembroke Coll., Cambridge (MA Maths; Sen. Optimae); Oak Hill Coll. (BA Theol and Pastoral Studies 1993). Ordained deacon, 1993, priest, 1994. Curate, St Thomas', Blackpool, 1993–99. Liveryman, Girdlers' Co. *Recreations:* cricket, bridge. *Heir: uncle* Rev. Canon Christopher Wynne Newton [*b* 23 July 1925; *m* 1950, Margaret Ormerod; two *s*]. *Address:* 2 Cranmore Lane, Aldershot, Hants GU11 3AS. *T:* (01252) 320618; *e-mail:* vicar@htca.org.uk.

NEWTON, Gillian Mary; Chief Executive, Fire Service College, Department for Communities and Local Government (formerly Office of the Deputy Prime Minister), since 2004; *b* 13 Oct. 1952; *d* of late Thomas Frank Newton and of Florence Elizabeth Newton (*née* Johnston). *Educ:* Trinity Grammar Sch., Northampton; Univ. of Hull; St Thomas' Hosp., London (RGN 1975); South Bank Poly., London (DipEd 1984); Univ. of Surrey (MSc Educnl Studies 1988). Various posts incl. Ward Sister, and Asst Dir of Nurse Educn, NHS, 1975–93; Dir, Professional Develt, Frances Harrison Coll., Guildford, 1991–93; Head: Sch. of Health Studies, Univ. of Portsmouth, 1993–95; Educn, NHS Exec., DoH, 1995–2000; Trng and Develt, HM Prison Service, 2000–04. *Publication:* (with C. Andrewes) Medical Nursing, 1984. *Recreations:* hill and fell walking, cycling, classical music, jazz, gardening. *Address:* Fire Service College, Moreton-in-Marsh, Glos GL56 0RH. *T:* (01608) 812001; *e-mail:* gnewton@fireservicecollege.ac.uk.

NEWTON, Ian; *see* Newton, R. E. I.

NEWTON, Prof. Ian, OBE 1999; FRS 1993; FRSE; Head, Avian (formerly Vertebrate) Ecology Section, NERC Institute of Terrestrial Ecology, 1989–99, now Fellow, NERC Centre for Ecology and Hydrology; *b* 17 Jan. 1940; *s* of Haydn Edwin Newton and Nellie Newton (*née* Stubbs); *m* 1962, Halina Teresa Bialkowska; two *s* one *d. Educ:* Bristol Univ. (BSc Zoology 1961); Worcester Coll., Oxford (DPhil Ornithology 1964; DSc 1982). FRSE 1994. Dept of Zoology, Oxford, 1964–67; Nature Conservancy, Edinburgh, 1967–73; Institute of Terrestrial Ecology, Natural Environment Research Council: Edinburgh, 1973–79; Huntingdon, 1979–99; research on avian population ecology, incl. finches, waterfowl, birds of prey, impact of pesticides. President: BOU, 1999–2003 (Vice-Pres., 1989–93); British Ecological Soc., 1994–95; Chairman: Council, RSPB, 2003–; Bd, Peregrine Fund, 2005–. Hon. Fellow, Amer. Ornith. Union, 1983. Union Medal, BOU, 1988; President's Medal, British Ecological Soc., 1989; Gold Medal, RSPB, 1991; Elliot Coue's Award, Amer. Ornith. Union, 1995; Marsh Award in Conservation Biology, Zool Soc. of London, 1995. *Publications:* Finches, 1972; Population Ecology of Raptors, 1979; The Sparrowhawk, 1986; (ed) Lifetime Reproduction in Birds, 1989; Population Limitation in Birds, 1998; The Speciation and Biogeography of Birds, 2003; The Ecology of Bird Migration, 2008; papers in sci. jls. *Recreations:* apple growing, walking. *Address:* NERC Centre for Ecology and Hydrology, Monks Wood, Abbots Ripton, Huntingdon, Cambs PE28 2LS. *T:* (01487) 772552.

NEWTON, Jeremy; Managing Director, Royal Academy of Dramatic Art, since 2007; *b* 14 June 1955; *s* of Arthur James Newton and Dorothy Burton Newton; *m* 1978, Mary Rose Colleran; one *s* one *d. Educ:* Manchester GS; St John's Coll., Cambridge (MA Hons Mod. and Medieval Langs). FCA 1989. Audit Supervisor, Coopers & Lybrand, 1976–80; Dep. Dir, 1980–84, Dir, 1984–90, Chief Exec., 1990–94, Eastern Arts Assoc., then Eastern Arts Bd; Nat. Lottery Dir, Arts Council of England, 1994–98; Chief Exec., NESTA, 1998–2005; Dir, Louise T. Blouin Foundn, 2005–07. Chair, Youth Dance England, 2005–. DUniv Loughborough, 2006. *Recreations:* theatre, cinema, chess, lacrosse, stand-up comedy. *Address: e-mail:* jeremynewton@rada.ac.uk.

NEWTON, Rev. Dr John Anthony, CBE 1997; Associate Tutor, Wesley College, Bristol, since 1995; *b* 28 Sept. 1930; *s* of late Charles Victor Newton and of Kathleen Marchant; *m* 1963, Rachel, *d* of late Rev. Maurice H. Giddings and of Hilda Giddings, Louth, Lincs; four *s. Educ:* Grammar School, Boston, Lincs; University Coll., Hull; London Univ.; Wesley House, Cambridge. BA, PhD (Lond), MA (Cantab). Research Fellow, Inst. of Historical Research, London Univ., 1953–55; Housemaster and actg

Chaplain, Kent Coll., Canterbury, 1955–56; trained for Methodist Ministry, Wesley House, 1956–58; Asst Tutor, Richmond Coll., Surrey, 1958–61, having been ordained, 1960; Circuit Minister at Louth, Lincs, 1961–64, and Stockton-on-Tees, 1964–65; Tutor at Didsbury Coll. (from 1967, Wesley Coll.), Bristol, 1965–72; taught Church History, St Paul's United Theolog. Coll., Limuru, Kenya, and Univ. of Nairobi, 1972–73; Principal of Wesley Coll., Bristol, 1973–78; Superintendent Minister, London Mission (W London) Circuit, 1978–86; Chm., Liverpool Dist of Methodist Church, 1986–95; Warden, John Wesley's Chapel, Bristol, 1995–2000. President of the Methodist Conference, 1981–82; Jt Pres., Merseyside and Region Churches' Ecumenical Assembly, 1987–95; Moderator, Free Church Federal Council, 1989–90 and 1993–94; a Pres., Churches Together in England, 1990–94. Hon. Canon, Lincoln Cathedral, 1988. Chm. of Governors, Westminster Coll., Oxford, 1979–88; Trustee, Wesley House, Cambridge, 1979–88. President: Chesterton Soc., 1991–; Wesley Historical Soc., 1996–. Governor, Rydal School, Colwyn Bay, 1986–95. Hon. Fellow, Liverpool John Moores Univ., 1993. Hon. DLitt Hull, 1982; DD Lambeth, 1995. *Publications:* Methodism and the Puritans, 1964; Susanna Wesley and the Puritan Tradition in Methodism, 1968; The Palestine Problem, 1972; Search for a Saint: Edward King, 1977; The Fruit of the Spirit in the Lives of Great Christians, 1979; A Man for All Churches: Marcus Ward, 1984; The Wesleys for Today, 1989; Heart Speaks to Heart: ecumenical studies in spirituality, 1994. *Recreations:* music, walking, book-collecting. *Address:* 3 College Road, Westbury-on-Trym, Bristol BS9 3EJ. *T:* (0117) 959 3225.

NEWTON, Sir John Garnar, 4th Bt *cr* 1924, of Beckenham Kent; *b* 10 July 1945; *s* of Sir Kenneth Garnar Newton, 3rd Bt, OBE, TD and Margaret Isabel, *d* of Rev. Dr George Blair, Dundee; *S* father, 2008, but his name does not appear on the Official Roll of the Baronetage; *m* 1972, Jacynth Anne Kay Miller; three *s* (incl. twins). *Educ:* Reed's Sch., Cobham. Church Warden, Throcking PCC. Trustee, Barnet Almshouses. Master, Leathersellers' Co., 2005–06. *Heir: er twin s* Timothy Garnar Newton [*b* 4 Sept. 1973; *m* 2004, Sarah Jane Howat].

NEWTON, Prof. (John) Michael, DSc; Professor of Pharmaceutics, School of Pharmacy, University of London, 1984–2001, now Emeritus (Fellow, School of Pharmacy, 2000); Hon. Professor, Department of Mechanical Engineering, University College London, since 2001; *b* 26 Dec. 1935; *s* of Richard and Dora Newton; *m* 1st, 1959, Janet Hinninghan (marr. diss. 1986); one *s* two *d*; 2nd, 2003, Fridrun Podzeck. *Educ:* Leigh Grammar Sch., Lancs; Sch. of Pharmacy, Univ. of London (BPharm; DSc 1990); Univ. of Nottingham (PhD). FRPharmS. Apprentice pharmacist, Royal Albert Edward Infirmary, Wigan, 1953–55; Demonstrator, Univ. of Nottingham, 1958–62; Sen. Lectr, Sunderland Polytechnic, 1962–64; Lectr, Univ. of Manchester, 1964–67; Sen. Scientist, Lilly Research Centre Ltd, 1968–71; Lectr, Univ. of Nottingham, 1972–78; Prof. of Pharmaceutics, Univ. of London, at Chelsea College, 1978–83. Mem., Medicines Commn, 1996–2000. Dist. Lectr, Nagai Foundn, Tokyo, 1997. Hon. Dr Uppsala, 1995. Harrison Meml Medal, RPSGB, 1996. *Publications:* numerous articles in sci. jls associated with pharmaceutical technology. *Recreations:* fell walking, long distance running (Belgrave Harriers), gardening.

NEWTON, (John) Nigel; Founder, and Chief Executive, Bloomsbury Publishing Plc, since 1986 (Chairman, 1986–2007); *b* 16 June 1955; *s* of late Peter Leigh Newton and Anne St Aubyn Newton; *m* 1981, Joanna Elizabeth Hastings-Trew; one *s* two *d*. *Educ:* Deerfield, Mass; Selwyn Coll., Cambridge (BA 1976; MA). Asst to Sales Dir, Macmillan Ltd, 1976–78; Dep. Man. Dir, Sidgwick & Jackson Ltd, 1978–86. Campaign mem., Rescue The Cuckmere Valley, 2002–. *Recreations:* walking, great views. *Address:* (office) 36 Soho Square, W1D 3QY. *T:* (020) 7494 2111; *e-mail:* nigel.newton@bloomsbury.com. *Clubs:* Garrick, Beefsteak, MCC, Hurlingham.

NEWTON, Rt Rev. Keith; *see* Richborough, Bishop Suffragan of.

NEWTON, Lesley; Her Honour Judge Newton; a Circuit Judge, since 2001; *b* 4 April 1955; *d* of Archie Newton and Joan Newton (*née* Robinson); *m* 1987, David Anthony Hernandez, *qv*; one *s* one *d*. *Educ:* Univ. of Manchester (LLB 1976). Called to the Bar, Middle Temple, 1977; barrister on N Circuit, 1979–2001; Head, Young Street Chambers, Manchester, 1997–2001. Mem., Family Justice Council, 2004–. *Address:* The Courts of Justice, Crown Square, Manchester M60 9FD. *T:* (0161) 954 1800.

NEWTON, Margaret; Schools Officer, Diocese of Oxford, 1984–88, retired; *b* 20 Dec. 1927; 2nd *d* of F. L. Newton, KStJ, MB, ChB, and Mrs A. C. Newton, MBE, BA. *Educ:* Sherborne School for Girls; St Andrews Univ.; Oxford University. MA Hons St Andrews, 1950; Educn Dip. Oxon 1951. Asst Mistress, King Edward VI Grammar School, Handsworth, Birmingham, 1951–54; Classics Mistress, Queen Margaret's Sch., York, 1954–60 (House Mistress, 1957); House Mistress, Malvern Girls' College, 1960–64 (Head of Classics Dept, 1962); Headmistress, Westonbirt Sch., 1965–80; Gen. Sec., Friends of the Elderly, 1981–83. *Address:* 14 Lygon Court, Fairford, Glos GL7 4LX.

NEWTON, Michael; *see* Newton, J. M.

NEWTON, Nigel; *see* Newton, J. N.

NEWTON, Peter Marcus; HM Diplomatic Service, retired; Executive Director, Canada UK Chamber of Commerce, 2000–02; *b* 16 Sept. 1942; *s* of Leslie Marcus Newton and Edith Mary Newton; *m* 1972, Sonia Maria; two *s* one *d*. *Educ:* Hamilton Academy; Glasgow Univ. (MA Hons); McGill Univ. (postgrad. studies). Third Sec., CRO, later CO, 1965; Kinshasa, 1967; Lima, 1968; First Sec., FCO, 1972; First Sec. (Econ.), Tokyo, 1975; First Sec. and Head of Chancery, Caracas, 1979; FCO, 1981; Counsellor, FCO, 1985–87; Consul-Gen., Montreal, 1987–89; Dep. High Comr, Ottawa, 1989–92; Head of S Atlantic and Antarctic Dept, FCO, 1992–95; Ambassador to Guatemala, 1995–98. *Address:* 81 Highlands Heath, Portsmouth Road, SW15 3TX.

NEWTON, Richard James; Chairman, National and Provincial Building Society, 1988–93; *b* 17 Nov. 1927; *s* of Alfred Richard Newton and Rosamond Newton (*née* Tunstill); *m* 1961, Elizabeth Seraphine Meuwissen (*d* 1986); four *s*. *Educ:* Clifton; St John's College, Cambridge (MA). Managerial positions at: Courtaulds, 1951–58; Midland Silicones, 1959–62; Chemstrand, 1963–66; Keith Shipton & Co., 1967–69; Man. Dir, Bury & Masco (Holdings), 1970–77; non-executive Director: Sketchley, 1978–87 (Chm., 1983–87); National & Provincial Building Soc., 1985–93. Fellow and Bursar, Trinity Hall, Cambridge, 1977–89. Gov., Clifton Coll., 1990– (Mem. Council, 1993–98). *Recreations:* music, fell-walking, playing the piano. *Address:* 15 Valiant House, Vicarage Crescent, Battersea, SW11 3LU.

NEWTON, (Robert Edward) Ian; school inspector and educational consultant, since 1995; *b* 4 Aug. 1946; *o s* of John Newton and Ethel Albiston; *m* 1969, Rev. Fiona Olive Pallant; one *s* one *d*. *Educ:* Dulwich Coll.; Oriel Coll., Oxford (BA Hons Nat. Sci. (Physics) 1967; MA 1973); Inst. of Education, London Univ. (Postgrad. CertEd 1968). Rugby School: Physics Teacher, 1968; Sixth Form girls' housemaster, 1976; Head of Physics, 1991; Headmaster, Bedales Sch., 1992–94. Admin. Officer, HMC/GSA Wkg Party on Univ. Admission, 1996–98; Charter Mark Award assessor, 1996–97; Reporting Inspector, Ind. Schs Inspectorate, 2000–. Qualified Yachtmaster Ocean, 2000–. Chm., Edward Barnsley Educnl Trust and Workshop Co., 1997–2000. Governor: Coventry Sch. Foundn, 1999–2003; Laxfield Sch., 2005–. FRGS 2001. CFM 1983. *Publication:* Wave Physics, 1990. *Recreations:* sailing, playing the bassoon, walking. *Address:* The Vicarage, 15 Noyes Avenue, Laxfield, Suffolk IP13 8EB. *T:* (01986) 798998. *Club:* Royal Naval Sailing Association.

NEWTON, Roderick Brian; His Honour Judge Newton; a Circuit Judge, since 2005; *b* 15 April 1958; *s* of Brian Newton and June Newton; *m* 1978, Clare Augusta Swanzy; two *s* two *d*. *Educ:* Bishop's Stortford Coll.; City of London Poly. (BA Hons 1980). Called to the Bar, Middle Temple, 1982; Asst Recorder, 1998–2000; Recorder, 2000–05. *Recreations:* gardening, horses, livestock, classical music. *Address:* Chelmsford Crown Court, New Street, Chelmsford CM1 1EL. *T:* (01245) 603000.

NEWTON, Trevor, OBE 1991; Deputy Chairman 1990–96, and Group Managing Director 1991–96, Yorkshire Water plc; *b* 22 Sept. 1943; *m* 1968, Christine Diane Bingham. *Educ:* Acklam Hall Grammar Sch., Middlesbrough; Manchester Univ. (BA Hons Econs). CIPFA 1970. Local Government Finance: Middlesbrough, 1966–71; Coventry, 1971–73; Bradford, 1973–76; Yorkshire Water Authority: Asst Finance Dir, 1976–83; Finance Dir, 1983–89; Finance Dir, Yorks Water plc, 1989–90. *Publication:* Cost-Benefit Analysis in Administration, 1971. *Recreation:* gardening.

NEWTON, Sir Wilfrid; *see* Newton, Sir C. W.

NEWTON DUNN, William Francis; Member, East Midlands Region, European Parliament (C, 1999–2000; Lib Dem, since 2000); *b* 3 Oct. 1941; *s* of late Lt-Col Owen Newton Dunn, OBE, and Barbara (*née* Brooke); *m* 1970, Anna Terez Arki; one *s* one *d*. *Educ:* Marlborough Coll. (scholar); Gonville and Caius Coll., Cambridge (MA); INSEAD Business Sch., Fontainebleau (MBA). With Fisons Ltd (Fertilizer Division), 1974–79. MEP (C) Lincolnshire, 1979–94; contested (C) Lincolnshire and Humberside S, 1994. European Parliament: Cons. Spokesman: on Transport, 1984–87; on Rules of Procedure, 1987–89; on Political Affairs, 1989–91; Chm., 1979 Cttee (Cons. backbench MEPs), 1983–88; Mem. Bureau, Cons. MEP Gp, 1988–94; Dep. Leader, EDG, 1991–93; Chm. and Jt Leader, British Cons. MEP Sect., EPP, 1993–94; Chm., 2000–; Whip, 2004–, Lib Dem MEPs. Contested (C): Carmarthen, Feb. 1974; Cardiff W, Oct. 1974. *Publications:* Greater in Europe, 1986; Big Wing: biography of Air Chief Marshal Sir Trafford Leigh-Mallory, 1992; The Man Who Was John Bull: biography of Theodore Hook, 1996; The Devil Knew Not (novel), 2000; Europe Needs an FBI, 2004; several pamphlets on the EU's democratic deficit. *Recreations:* walking, writing. *Address:* 10 Church Lane, Navenby, Lincoln LN5 0EG. *T:* (01522) 810812; *e-mail:* bill.newtondunn@europarl.europa.eu.

NEYROUD, Peter William, QPM 2004; Chief Constable and Chief Executive, National Policing Improvement Agency, since 2007 (Chief Constable and Chief Executive designate, 2006–07); *b* 12 Aug. 1959; *s* of John Arthur Lucien Neyroud and Penelope Mary Anne (*née* Edwards); *m* 1986, Sarah Longman; two *s* two *d*. *Educ:* Winchester Coll.; Oriel Coll., Oxford (MA Mod. Hist.); Portsmouth Univ. (MSc Prof. Studies); Wolfson Coll., Cambridge (Dip Applied Criminology). Joined as Constable, Hampshire Constabulary, 1980; Sergeant, Southampton and Basingstoke, 1984–86; Inspector, Southampton, 1987–91; Chief Inspector, E Hampshire, 1991–93; Staff to Pres., ACPO, 1993–95; Detective Supt and Dir of Intelligence, 1995–97; West Mercia Constabulary: Asst Chief Constable (Support), 1998–2000; Dep. Chief Constable, 2000–02; Chief Constable, Thames Valley Police, 2002–06. Member: Sentencing Guidelines Council, 2004–08; Ind. Review Panel, Parole Bd, 2006–. Vis. Fellow, Nuffield Coll., Oxford; Leon Radzinowicz Vis. Fellow, Cambridge Univ. Hon. LLD Portsmouth, 2006. *Publications:* Policing, Ethics and Human Rights, 2001; Participation in Policing, 2001; Police Ethics for the 21st Century, 2003; Dictionary of Policing, 2008. *Recreations:* running, reading, writing, gardening, four children. *Address:* National Policing Improvement Agency, 10–18 Victoria Street, SW1H 0NN; *e-mail:* peter.neyroud@npia.pnn.police.uk.

NGAIZA, Christopher Pastor; Chairman and Managing Director, Kamachumu Inn Ltd, Tanzania, since 2001; *b* 29 March 1930; parents decd; *m* 1952, Thereza; three *s* two *d* (and one *s* decd). *Educ:* Makerere University Coll.; Loughborough Co-operative College. Local Courts Magistrate, 1952–53; Secretary/Manager, Bahaya Co-operative Consumer Stores, 1955–57; Loughborough Co-operative Coll., 1957–59; Auctioneer and Representative of Bukoba Native Co-operative Union, Mombasa, 1959–61; joined Tanzanian Foreign Service, 1961; Counsellor, Mission to UN, 1961–62; Counsellor, Tanganyika High Commn, London, 1962–63; High Commissioner for United Republic of Tanganyika and Zanzibar in London, 1964–65; Tanzanian Ambassador: to Netherlands, 1965–67, to Arab Republic of Egypt, 1972–77; Mem., E African Common Market Tribunal, 1968–69; Tanzania's first High Comr to Zambia, 1969–72; Special Personal Assistant to Pres. of Tanzania, 1977–83; Comr for Kagera River Basin Orgn, 1978–83. Chm. and Man. Dir, PES Consultants Ltd, 1986–2000. *Recreations:* music, tennis. *Address:* Kamachumu Inn Ltd, PO Box 59, Kamachumu, Tanzania.

NGALI, Mwanyengela; Permanent Secretary, Ministry of Energy, Kenya, 1999–2001; Chairman, Kenya Pipeline Co. Ltd, since 2005; *b* 1 Jan. 1947; *s* of Ngali Maganga and Ruth Mkandoo; *m* 1970, Elizabeth Wuganga; two *s* three *d*. *Educ:* Alliance High Sch., Kikuyu, Kenya; Univ. of Nairobi (BCom). Sales exec., Voice of Kenya, 1971–72; sales rep., Esso Standard Kenya Ltd, 1972–73; joined Kenyan Diplomatic Service, 1974: Commercial Attaché: Washington, 1974–81; London, 1981–82; First Sec. and Actg High Comr, Kampala, 1983–84; Counsellor, Jeddah and Riyadh, 1984–87; Under-Sec., Min. of Commerce, 1987–92; Dir, Political Affairs, Min. of Foreign Affairs and Internat. Co-operation, 1992; Counsellor and Actg High Comr, London, 1992–93; High Comr, Canada, 1993–95; High Comr, London, and Ambassador to Republic of Ireland and Switzerland, 1996–99. Contested (Kanu) Wundanyi, Kenya, 2002. Director: Nat. Oil Corp. of Kenya, 2003–05; Investment Promotion Centre, 2004–05; Africa Online Ltd, 2001– (Dep. Chm.); Chm., Taskforce on Internally Displaced People, 2004–. *Publication:* Mwana Taabu na Michezo Mingine ya Kuigiza, 1970. *Recreations:* walking, tennis, cycling, reading. *Address:* POB 11048, 00100 Nairobi, Kenya. *T:* (2) 575850.

NGATA, Sir Henare Kohere, KBE 1982 (OBE); chartered accountant, retired; *b* Waiomatatini, 19 Dec. 1917; *s* of Sir Apirana Ngata and Arihia, *d* of Tuta Tamati; *m* 1940, Rora Lorna, *d* of Maihi Rangipo Mete Kingi; one *s*. *Educ:* Waiomatatini Sch.; Te Aute Coll., Victoria Univ. of Wellington, BA; BCom; FCA (NZ Soc. of Accountants). Served 28th Maori Bn, 1939–45: POW, Greece; Germany, 1941–45. Director: Fieldair Ltd, 1960–79; Gisborne Sheepfarmers Mercantile Co. Ltd; Gisborne Sheepfarmers Freezing Co. Ltd. Member: Gisborne Reg. Commn, NZ Historic Places Trust, 1962–70; NZ Maori Council, 1962–85; C of E Provincial Commn on Maori Schs, 1964–66; Gisborne/East Coast Regional Develt Council, 1973–78; Finance Cttee, Bishopric of Aotearoa. Nat. Pres., 28th Maori Bn Assoc., 1964–66. Vice-Pres., NZ Nat. Party, 1967–69. JP Gisborne, 1965. Hon. LLD, Victoria Univ. of Wellington, 1979. *Address:* 10 Grant Road, Gisborne, New Zealand.

NIBLETT, Anthony Ian; His Honour Judge Niblett; a Circuit Judge, since 2002; *b* 11 June 1954; *s* of late A. W. Niblett and of J. A. Niblett (*née* McMickan); *m* 1991, Valerie Ann Ranger; one *s* one *d*. *Educ:* Varndean Grammar Sch., Brighton; Univ. of Birmingham (LLB Hons); Coll. of Law. Called to the Bar, Inner Temple, 1976; Barrister, SE Circuit, 1977–2002; Asst Recorder, 1993–98; a Recorder, 1998–2002. Member: Professional Conduct Cttee, Bar Council, 1993–97; S Eastern Circuit Cttee, 1995–98 and 2000–02; Sussex Probation Bd, 2007–. Jun. (Sec.), Sussex Bar Mess, 1986–95. Gov., Varndean Coll., Brighton, 1997–2003. *Recreations:* travel, history, gardening. *Address:* Lewes Combined Court Centre, The Law Courts, High Street, Lewes, E Sussex BN7 1YB. *Club:* Travellers.

NIBLETT, Robin, DPhil; Director, Royal Institute of International Affairs (Chatham House), since 2007; *b* 20 Aug. 1961; *s* of Alan and Christine Niblett; *m* 1990, Trisha de Borchgrave; two *d*. *Educ:* Cottesmore Sch.; Charterhouse; New Coll., Oxford (BA Mod. Langs 1984; MPhil 1993; DPhil Internat. Relns 1995). Musician, 1985–87; Center for Strategic and International Studies, Washington, DC: Res. Associate, 1988–91; Eur. Rep., 1992–97; Dir, Strategic Planning, 1997–2000; Exec. Vice Pres. and Chief Operating Officer, 2001–06. *Publication:* (ed with W. Wallace) Rethinking European Order: West European responses, 1989–97, 2001. *Recreations:* tae kwon do, tennis, electric guitar. *Address:* Royal Institute of International Affairs, Chatham House, 10 St James's Square, SW1Y 4LE. *T:* (020) 7957 5702.

NICE, Sir Geoffrey, Kt 2007; QC 1990; a Recorder, since 1987; Commissioner, Royal Court, Jersey, 2006–07; *b* 21 Oct. 1945; *s* of William Charles Nice and Mahala Anne Nice (*née* Tarryer); *m* 1974, Philippa Mary Gross; three *d*. *Educ:* St Dunstan's College, Catford; Keble College, Oxford. Called to the Bar, Inner Temple, 1971, Bencher, 1996. Member: CICB, 1995–2002; Bd, Indict, 2001–04. Sen. Trial Attorney, 1998–2001, Principal Trial Attorney, Milosevic prosecution, 2002–06, Internat. Criminal Tribunal for Former Yugoslavia. Contested (SDP/Liberal Alliance) Dover, 1983, 1987. Hon. LLD Kent, 2005. *Address:* 1 Temple Gardens, Temple, EC4Y 9BB. *T:* (020) 7583 1315. *Club:* Reform.

NICHOL, Comdt (Daphne) Patricia, CBE 1986; Director, Women's Royal Naval Service, 1982–86; *b* 25 Sept. 1932; *d* of Captain Ralph Geoffrey Swallow, RN and Daphne Lucy Regina Swallow (*née* Parry); *m* 1991, Capt. Peter Dale Nichol, RN. *Educ:* St George's Sch., Ascot; Portsmouth Polytechnic (Hon. Fellow, 1983). Joined WRNS as Signal Wren, 1950; qualified as WRNS Communications Officer, 1955; served in HMS Drake and Malta, 1956–58; Oslo, Portsmouth, HMS Mercury, Northwood and Gibraltar, 1958–67; HMS Pembroke and HMS Heron, 1968–71; passed Naval Staff Course, 1972; HMS Dauntless, 1973–74; Staff of C-in-C Naval Home Comd and MoD, 1974–76; National Defence College Latimer Course, 1976–77; Staff of Naval Secretary, 1977; Command Personnel Officer to C-in-C Naval Home Comd, 1977–79; Dep. Dir, WRNS, 1979–81; Staff Officer Training Co-ordination and Comd WRNS Officer to C-in-C Naval Home Comd, 1981–82; Hon. ADC to the Queen, 1982–86. Asst Sec., Benevolent Dept, Officers' Assoc., 1987–89; Case Sec., DGAA, 1989–90. Member: Nat. Exec. Cttee, Forces Help Soc. and Lord Roberts Workshops, 1986–95; Council and Exec. Cttee, Shipwrecked Fishermen and Mariners Royal Benevolent Soc., 1991–96, 1998–2002; Council, Soc. of Friends of RN Mus. and HMS Victory, Portsmouth, 1994–97. Hon. Fellow, Univ. of Portsmouth, 1993. *Recreations:* tennis, dressmaking and needlework, reading, theatre, opera, music. *Address:* c/o Lloyds TSB, 23 Elm Grove, Hayling Island, Hants PO11 9EA.

NICHOL, Sir Duncan (Kirkbride), Kt 1993; CBE 1989; Hon. Professorial Fellow, Manchester Centre for Healthcare Management, University of Manchester, 1999–2004 (Professor and Director, Health Services Management Unit, 1994–98); *b* 30 May 1941; *s* of James and Mabel Nichol; *m* 1972, Elizabeth Wilkinson; one *s* one *d*. *Educ:* Bradford Grammar Sch.; St Andrews Univ. (MA Hons). FHSM 1987; Hon. FFPHM 1991. Asst Gp Sec. and Hosp. Sec. to Manchester Royal Infirmary, 1969–73; Dep. Gp Sec. and Actg Gp Sec., Univ. Hosp. Management Cttee of S Manchester, 1973–74; Dist Administrator, Manchester S Dist, 1974–77; Area Administrator, Salford AHA(T), 1977–81; Regional Administrator, 1981–84, Regional Gen. Manager, 1984–89, Mersey RHA; Chief Exec., NHS Management Executive, 1989–94. Chairman: Parole Bd of England and Wales, 2004–08; QC Selection Panel, 2005–08; HM Courts Service Bd, 2008–; Comr for Judicial Appts, 2001–06. Non-executive Director: HM Prisons Bd/Correctional Services Strategy Bd, 1994–2005; BUPA, 1994–2002; Primary Group, 2001–08; Synergy Healthcare, 2002–; Deltex Medical, 2004–; Christie Hospital NHS Trust, 2008–; Chairman: B Plan Information Systems, 1999–2001; Clinical Pathology Accreditation (UK) Ltd, 2000–. Member: Central Health Services Council, 1980–81; NHS Training Authy, 1983–85; Chm., Jt Prison and Probation Services Accreditation Panel for Offending Behaviour Progs, 1999–2005. Pres., Inst. of Health Services Management, 1984–85; Chm., Educn Cttee, King Edward's Hosp. Fund for London, 1987–94. Hon. DLitt Salford, 1990. *Publications:* contributed: Health Care in the United Kingdom, 1982; Management for Clinicians, 1982; Working with People, 1983; Managers as Strategists, 1987. *Recreations:* walking, golf. *Club:* Athenæum.

NICHOL, Prof. Lawrence Walter, DSc; FAA; Vice-Chancellor, Australian National University, 1988–93; *b* 7 April 1935; *s* of Lawrence Gordon Nichol and Mavis Lillian Nichol (*née* Burgess); *m* 1963, Rosemary Esther (*née* White); three *s*. *Educ:* Univ. of Adelaide (BSc 1956, Hons 1957; PhD 1962; DSc 1974). Postdoctoral Fellow, Clark Univ., Mass, 1961–62; Res. Fellow, ANU, 1963–65; Sen. Lectr, then Reader, Univ. of Melbourne, 1966–70; Prof. of Phys. Biochem., ANU, 1971–85; Vice-Chancellor, Univ. of New England, 1985–88. FRACI 1971–94; FAA 1981; Fellow, Royal Soc. of NSW, 1986. David Syme Res. Prize, 1966; Lemberg Medal, Aust. Biochem. Soc., 1977. *Publications:* Migration of Interacting Systems, 1972; Protein-Protein Interactions, 1981; over 100 papers in internat. sci. jls. *Recreations:* philately, cinema, art, Spanish language. *Address:* Unit 36, 171 Walker Street, North Sydney, NSW 2060, Australia.

NICHOL, Comdt Patricia; see Nichol, Comdt D. P.

NICHOLAS, (Angela) Jane (Udale), OBE 1990; Dance Director, Arts Council of Great Britain, 1979–89, retired; *b* 14 June 1929; *d* of late Bernard Alexander Royle Shore, CBE; *m* 1964, William Alan Nicholas. *Educ:* Norland Place Sch.; Rambert Sch. of Ballet; Arts Educnl Trust; Sadler's Wells Ballet Sch. Founder Mem., Sadler's Wells Theatre Ballet, 1946–50; Mem., Sadler's Wells Ballet at Royal Opera House, 1950–52; freelance dancer, singer, actress, 1952–60; British Council Drama Officer, 1961–70; Arts Council of Great Britain: Dance Officer, 1970–75; Asst Dance Dir, 1975–79. Member: Exec. Cttee, Dance UK, 1989–98; Creative Dance Artists Trust, 1990–93; Riverside Arts Trust, 1991–97; Benesh Inst. Endowment Fund, 1992–; Bd, Birmingham Royal Ballet, 1993–2002. FRSA 1990. *Recreations:* pruning, weeding, collecting cracked porcelain. *Address:* 21 Stamford Brook Road, W6 0XJ. *T:* (020) 8741 3035.

NICHOLAS, Sir David, Kt 1989; CBE 1982; Editor and Chief Executive, 1977–89, Chairman, 1989–91, Independent Television News; *b* 25 Jan. 1930; *m* 1952, Juliet Davies; one *s* one *d*. *Educ:* Neath Grammar School; University Coll. of Wales, Aberystwyth. BA (Hons) English. National Service, 1951–53. Journalist with Yorkshire Post, Daily Telegraph, Observer; joined ITN, 1960; Deputy Editor, 1963–77. Produced ITN General Election Results, Apollo coverage, and ITN special programmes. Dir, Channel Four TV, 1992–97. Chm., Sports News TV, 1996–2003. Visiting Editor: Graduate Sch. of Journalism, Berkeley, Calif, 1993; Sch. of Journalism, Univ. of Boulder, Colorado, 1994. Chm., Deptford Challenge Trust, 1996–2005. Mem. Council, Goldsmiths Coll., 1996–2003 (Hon. Fellow, 2004). FRTS 1980. Fellow, UC Aberystwyth, 1990. Hon. LLD Wales, 1990; Hon. DHL Southern Illinois, 2000. Producers' Guild Award 1967, on return of Sir Francis Chichester; Cyril Bennett Award, RTS, 1985; Judges' Award, RTS, 1991; News World Lifetime Achievement Award, 2001. *Recreations:* walking, sailing, golf. *Clubs:* Garrick, Reform (Chm., Media Gp, 1998–2003).

NICHOLAS, Prof. David, PhD; Director, School of Library, Archive and Information Studies, University College London, since 2004; *b* 14 March 1947; *s* of Roy and Rita Nicholas; *m* 1976, Kay Reeves; one *s* one *d*. *Educ:* Huish's Grammar Sch., Taunton; Poly. of N London (MPhil 1986); PhD City Univ. 1995. MCLIP (ALA 1968). Asst Librarian, Hackney Public Libraries, 1971; Librarian, Middleton St George Coll. of Educn, Co. Durham, 1972; Res. Fellow, Univ. of Bath and Poly. of N London, 1973–76; Res./Inf. Asst, Time-Life International, 1976–77; Poly., later Univ. of N London, 1978–97, Sen. Res. Tutor, 1990–97; Hd, Dept of Inf. Sci., City Univ., 1998–2004; Dir, UCL Centre for Publishing, 2005–. *Publications:* Immunology: an information profile, 1985; Online Searching: its impact on information users, 1987; Assessing Information Needs, 2000; Digital Consumers, 2008. *Recreations:* cycling, gardening, travelling by train. *Address:* University College London, Gower Street, WC1E 6BT; *e-mail:* david.nicholas@ucl.ac.uk.

NICHOLAS, Jane; see Nicholas, A. J. U.

NICHOLAS, Sir John (William), KCVO 1981; CMG 1979; HM Diplomatic Service, retired; *b* 13 Dec. 1924; *m* 1st, 1944, Rita Jones (*d* 2000); two *s*; 2nd, 2002, Diana Grigson. *Educ:* Birmingham Univ. Served 7th Rajput Regt, Indian Army, 1944–47; joined Home Civil Service, 1949; War Office, 1949–57; transf. to CRO 1957; First Sec., Brit. High Commn, Kuala Lumpur, 1957–61; Economic Div., CRO, 1961–63; Dep. High Comr in Malawi, 1964–66; Diplomatic Service Inspector, 1967–69; Dep. High Comr and Counsellor (Commercial), Ceylon, 1970–71; Dir, Establishments and Finance Div., Commonwealth Secretariat, 1971–73; Hd of Pacific Dependent Territories Dept, FCO, 1973–74; Dep. High Comr, Calcutta, 1974–76; Consul Gen., Melbourne, 1976–79; High Comr to Sri Lanka and (non-resident) to Republic of the Maldives, 1979–84.

NICHOLAS, Mark Charles Jefford; commentator, Five (formerly Channel 5) cricket, since 2006; *b* 29 Sept. 1959; *s* of late Peter Jefford Nicholas and of Anne Evelyn Nicholas (stage name Loxley; she later *m* Brian Widlake). *Educ:* Bradfield Coll. Professional cricketer, Hampshire CCC, 1977–95: county cap, 1982; captain, 1984–95; winning team: John Player Sunday League, 1986; Benson & Hedges Cup, 1988, 1992; NatWest Trophy, 1992. Advertising dept, The Observer, 1980; PR consultant, Hill & Knowlton (UK) Ltd, 1987–88; TV and radio commentator; presenter and commentator: Sky TV, 1999; Channel 4 cricket, 1999–2005. Former journalist, Daily Telegraph. *Address:* c/o Five, 22 Long Acre, WC2E 9LY.

NICHOLAS, Michael Bernard, FRCO; organist, choral director and composer; *b* 31 Aug. 1938; *s* of Bernard Victor Herbert Nicholas and Dorothy (*née* Gilfillan); *m* 1975, Heather Grant Rowdon; two *s*. *Educ:* City of London Sch.; Jesus Coll., Oxford (MA). FRCO 1958 (CHM 1964). Organist and Choirmaster: Louth Parish Church, Lincs, 1960–64; St Matthew's Ch., Northampton, 1965–71; Organist and Master of Choristers, Norwich Cathedral, 1971–94 (Organist Emeritus, 2005); (part-time) Lectr in Music, UEA, 1971–94; Chief Exec., RCO, 1994–97. Conductor: Louth Choral and Orchestral Soc., 1960–64; Northampton Bach Choir and Orch., 1965–71; Norwich Philharmonic Chorus, 1972–94; Musical Dir, Allegri Singers, 1994–2000; Organist and Dir of Music, All Saints' Church, Blackheath, 1995–99; Dir of Music, St Mary-le-Tower, Ipswich, 1999–. Chief Examr, Guild of Church Musicians, 2005–. A Vice-President: Organ Club, 1995–; Church Music Soc., 2002–; Mem., Cathedral Organists' Assoc., 1971– (Pres., 1975–77). Hon. FGCM 1995. Hon. DMus UEA, 1995. *Publications:* Sightsinging, 1966; Muse at St Matthew's, 1968; various choral and organ compositions. *Recreations:* bridge, walking, reading. *Address:* Cansell Grove Farmhouse, Poy Street Green, Rattlesden, Bury St Edmunds, Suffolk IP30 0SR. *Clubs:* Athenæum; Ipswich and Suffolk (Ipswich).

NICHOLAS, Shân; Director, Taprobane Management Services Ltd, since 2007; Interim Chief Executive, YWCA (England and Wales), since 2007; *b* 24 Oct. 1952; *d* of Kenneth Nicholas and Jane Nicholas (*née* Selliam); one *d* with Pal Luthra. *Educ:* London Sch. of Econs and Pol Sci. (BSc Econ 1974); London Sch. of Hygiene and Tropical Medicine (MSc Med. Demography 1977). Asst Dir, Runnymede Trust, 1978–85; Hd, Human Resource Develt, London Bor. of Hackney, 1986–94; Exec. Dir Corp. Develt and Co. Secretary, Stonham Housing, 1998–2005; Chief Exec., Princess Royal Trust for Carers, 2005–07. *Publications:* (contrib.) Britain's Black Population, 1980; articles for British and French jls on race and immigration. *Recreations:* arts, theatre, music, reading, food, day dreaming. *Address:* e-mail: Shan.nicholas1@btopenworld.com.

NICHOLL, His Honour Anthony John David; a Circuit Judge, 1988–2003; *b* 3 May 1935; *s* of late Brig. and Mrs D. W. D. Nicholl; *m* 1961, Hermione Mary (*née* Landon); one *s* two *d*. *Educ:* Eton; Pembroke Coll., Oxford; Wycliffe Hall, Oxford (DBTS). Called to Bar, Lincoln's Inn, 1958. Practised in London, 1958–61, in Birmingham, 1961–88; Head of Chambers, 1976–87; Chm., Fountain Court Chambers (Birmingham) Ltd, 1984–88. A Recorder, 1978–88. Reader, Coventry Dio., 2003–. *Recreations:* history, theology, music, gardening and other rural pursuits. *Address:* Black Martin Farm, Ettington, Straford-on-Avon, Warwicks CV37 7PD.

NICHOLL, Air Vice-Marshal Steven Mark, CB 2001; CBE 1991; AFC 1981; FRAeS; Director, Military Requirements, MASS, BAE SYSTEMS, since 2002; *b* 15 Nov. 1946; *s* of late Capt. Jack Nicholl, BOAC and Berry Nicholl; *m* 1974, Suzanne Tucker; two *s* one *d*. *Educ:* Abingdon Sch.; Pembroke Coll., Oxford (BA Eng.). FRAeS 1993. RAF university cadetship, 1965; flying/staff duties, 1970–88; Gp Capt. Plans, HQ RAF Germany, 1989–91; OC RAF Leuchars, 1992–93; rcds 1994; Dir Air Ops, Dir Air Plans, 1995–98, ACDS OR Air, subseq. Capability Manager (Strike), 1998–2001, MoD. *Recreations:* family, golf, ski-ing, hang-gliding, reading. *Address:* 1 Tythe Close, Stewkley, Bucks LU7 0HD. *Clubs:* Royal Air Force; Leighton Buzzard Golf.

NICHOLLS, family name of **Baron Nicholls of Birkenhead.**

NICHOLLS OF BIRKENHEAD, Baron *cr* 1994 (Life Peer), of Stoke D'Abernon in the County of Surrey; **Donald James Nicholls,** Kt 1983; PC 1986; a Lord of Appeal in Ordinary, 1994–2007; Second Senior Lord of Appeal, 2002–07; *b* 25 Jan. 1933; *yr s* of late William Greenhow Nicholls and Eleanor Jane; *m* 1960, Jennifer Mary, *yr d* of late W. E. C. Thomas, MB, BCh, MRCOG, JP; two *s* one *d*. *Educ:* Birkenhead Sch.; Liverpool Univ. (LLB 1st cl. hons); Trinity Hall, Cambridge (Foundn Schol.; BA 1st cl. hons with dist., Pt II Law Tripos, LLB 1st cl. hons with dist.; Hon. Fellow, 1986). 2nd Lieut, RAPC, 1951–53. Certif. of Honour, Bar Final, 1958; called to Bar, Middle Temple, 1958, Bencher, 1981, Treas., 1997; in practice, Chancery Bar, 1958–83; QC 1974; Judge of High Court of Justice, Chancery Div., 1983–86; a Lord Justice of Appeal, 1986–91; Vice-Chancellor, Supreme Court, 1991–94; a Non-permanent Judge, Hong Kong Court of Final Appeal, 1998–2004. Chairman: Lord Chancellor's Adv. Cttee on Legal Educn and Conduct, 1996–97; Jt Parly Cttee on Parly Privilege, 1997–99. Mem., Senate of Inns of Court and the Bar, 1974–76. Patron, Cayman Is Law Sch., 1994–2006. Pres., Birkenhead Sch., 1986–. Hon. LLD Liverpool, 1987. *Recreations:* walking, history, music. *Address:* House of Lords, SW1A 0PW. *Club:* Athenæum (Trustee, 1998–).

See also Hon. J. P. Nicholls.

NICHOLLS, Brian; Director, John Brown Engineering, 1979–91; *b* 21 Sept. 1928; *s* of late Ralph and Kathleen Nicholls; *m* 1961, Mary Elizabeth Harley; one *s* two *d. Educ:* Haberdashers' Aske's Sch., Hampstead; London Univ. (BSc Econ); Harvard Business Sch. George Wimpey & Co., 1951–55; Constructors John Brown Ltd, 1955–75; Director: CJB Projects Ltd, 1972–75; CJB Pipelines Ltd, 1974–75; Dep. Chm., CJB Mohandessi Iran Ltd, 1974–75; Industrial Adviser, Dept of Trade, 1975–78; Director: John Brown Engrg Gas Turbines, 1979–91; Rugby Power Co., 1990–91; Vice Pres., John Brown Power Ltd, 1987–90; consultant, Scottish Enterprise, 1991–98. Member: Council, British Rly Industry Export Gp, 1976–78; Overseas Projects Bd, 1976–78; BOTB, 1978. Member: Council, British Chemical Engineering Contractors Assoc., 1973–75; Trade and Industry Cttee, British Algerian Soc., 1974–75; Scottish Council (Develt and Industry), 1983–98 (Vice Pres., 1991–98; Fellow 1998). Columnist, Jazz Jl, 1952–58; Ed., Jazz News, 1957–59. Dep. Chm., Nat. Jazz Fedn, 1954–59; Dir, Scottish Opera, 1993–99. Freeman Mem., Incorp. of Coopers of Glasgow, 1991; Mem., Trades House of Glasgow, 1990. *Recreations:* writing, walking, music. *Address:* Blairlogie Park, Hillfoots Road, Blairlogie, by Stirling FK9 5PY. *T:* (01259) 761497. *Club:* Western (Glasgow).

NICHOLLS, Christine Stephanie, DPhil; writer; *b* 23 Jan. 1943; *d* of Christopher James Metcalfe, Mombasa, Kenya, and Olive Metcalfe (*née* Kennedy); *m* 1966, Anthony James Nicholls, *s* of Ernest Alfred Nicholls, Carshalton; one *s* two *d. Educ:* Kenya High School; Lady Margaret Hall, Oxford (BA); St Antony's Coll., Oxford (MA, DPhil). Henry Charles Chapman Res. Fellow, Inst. of Commonwealth Studies, London Univ., 1968–69; freelance writer for BBC, 1970–74; res. asst, 1975–76; Jt Editor, 1977–89, Editor, 1989–95, DNB; Editor, Sutton Pocket Biographies, 1996–. *Publications:* The Swahili Coast, 1971; (with Philip Awdry) Cataract, 1985; Power: a political history of the 20th Century, 1990; The Dictionary of National Biography: 1961–70, 1981; 1971–80, 1986; 1981–85, 1990; Missing Persons, 1993; 1986–90, 1996; (ed) The Hutchinson Encyclopedia of Biography, 1996; David Livingstone, 1998; The History of St Antony's College, Oxford, 1950–2000, 2000; Elspeth Huxley: a biography, 2002; Red Strangers: the white tribe of Kenya, 2005. *Recreations:* reading novels, playing the flute. *Address:* 27 Davenant Road, Oxford OX2 8BU. *T:* (01865) 511320.

NICHOLLS, Clive Victor; QC 1982; a Recorder, 1984–99; *b* 29 Aug. 1932; twin *s* of late Alfred Charles Victor Nicholls and of Lilian Mary (*née* May); *m* 1960, Alison Virginia, *d* of late Arthur and Dorothy Oliver; three *s* three *d. Educ:* Brighton Coll.; Trinity Coll., Dublin (MA, LLB); Sidney Sussex Coll., Cambridge (BA *ad eund*; LLM). Called to the Bar: Gray's Inn, 1957 (Bencher, 1990); Australian Capital Territories, 1991. Trustee, Bob Champion Cancer Trust, 1994– (Chm. Trustees, 1982–94). *Publication:* (jtly) The Law of Extradition and Mutual Assistance: international practice and procedure, 2002, 2nd edn 2007. *Recreations:* sailing, fishing. *Address:* 3 Raymond Buildings, Gray's Inn, WC1R 5BH. *T:* (020) 7400 6400. *Clubs:* Garrick; Royal Western Yacht (Plymouth).

See also C. A. A. Nicholls.

NICHOLLS, Colin Alfred Arthur; QC 1981; a Recorder, 1984–99; *b* 29 Aug. 1932; twin *s* of late Alfred Charles Victor Nicholls and of Lilian Mary (*née* May); *m* 1976, Clarissa Allison Spenlove, *d* of late Clive and of Theo Dixon; two *s. Educ:* Brighton Coll.; Trinity Coll., Dublin. MA, LLB. Called to the Bar, Gray's Inn, 1957 (Albion Richardson Schol.), Bencher, 1989. Auditor, 1956, and Hon. Mem., 1958–, TCD Historical Soc. Commonwealth Lawyers Association: Mem. Council, 1987–; a Vice Pres., 1990–96; Hon. Treas., 1996–; Hon. Sec., 1999–2003; Pres., 2003–05; Hon. Life Pres., 2007. Fellow, Soc. of Advanced Legal Studies, 1998. Gov., FBA, 2001–07. Trustee: Commonwealth Human Rights Initiative, 1998–2007; Commonwealth Law Conf. Foundn, 2003–07. *Publication:* (jtly) Corruption and Misuse of Public Office, 2006. *Recreation:* painting (exhib. RHA and ROI). *Address:* 3 Raymond Buildings, Gray's Inn, WC1R 5BH. *T:* (020) 7400 6400. *Clubs:* Garrick, Royal Commonwealth Society.

See also C. V. Nicholls.

NICHOLLS, David Alan, CB 1989; CMG 1984; Senior Political-Military Associate, Institute for Foreign Policy Analysis, Cambridge, Mass, USA, since 1991; *s* of Thomas Edward and Beatrice Winifred Nicholls; *m* 1955, Margaret (*née* Lewis); two *d. Educ:* Cheshunt Grammar School; St John's Coll., Cambridge (Schol., Wright's Prizeman 1952, 1953; BA Hons 1954; MA 1989). Served RAF (Flying Officer), 1950–51. Admiralty, 1954–64; Asst Principal, 1954; Private Sec. to Parliamentary Sec., 1958–59; Principal, 1959; MoD, 1964–75; Private Sec. to Minister of Defence for Admin, 1968–69; Asst Sec., 1969; Cabinet Office, 1975–77; Asst Under-Sec. of State, MoD, 1977–80; Asst Sec., Gen. for Defence Planning and Policy, NATO, 1980–84; Dep. Under Sec. of State (Policy), MoD, 1984–89. Vis. Fellow, Magdalene Coll., Cambridge, 1989–90; Associate Fellow, RIIA, 1990–93; Hon. Fellow, Graduate Sch. of Internat. Studies, Univ. of Birmingham, 1992–. Chm., Defence and Security Cttee, London Chamber of Commerce and Industry, 1994–2004 (Mem., 1991–). Chm., Soc. for Italic Handwriting, 1987–97. Mem., Visiting Cttee, RCA, 1991–92. *Recreations:* sketching, printmaking. *Address:* c/o HSBC, Church Stretton, Shropshire SY6 6BT. *Club:* National Liberal.

NICHOLLS, Rt Rev. John; Bishop of Sheffield, 1997–2008; *b* 16 July 1943; *s* of late James William and Nellie Nicholls; *m* 1969, Judith Dagnall; two *s* two *d. Educ:* Bacup and Rawtenstall Grammar School; King's Coll., London (AKC); St Boniface Coll., Warminster. Curate, St Clement with St Cyprian, Salford, 1967–69; Curate, 1969–72, Vicar 1972–78, All Saints and Martyrs, Langley, Manchester; Dir of Pastoral Studies, Coll. of the Resurrection, Mirfield, 1978–83; Canon Residentiary of Manchester Cathedral, 1983–90; Suffragan Bishop of Lancaster, 1990–97. Hon. Fellow, Univ. of Central Lancashire, 1997. *Publication:* (jtly) A Faith Worth Sharing? a Church Worth Joining?, 1995. *Recreations:* music (listening and singing), reading, films. *Address:* 77 Rowton Grange Road, Chapel-en-le-Frith, High Peak, SK23 0LD. *Club:* Royal Over-Seas League.

NICHOLLS, John; see Nicholls, R. J.

NICHOLLS, Prof. John Graham, FRS 1988; Professor of Biophysics, International School for Advanced Studies, Trieste, since 1998; *b* 19 Dec. 1929; *s* of late Dr Nicolai and of Charlotte Nicholls; *m* (marr. diss.); two *s. Educ:* Berkhamsted Sch.; Charing Cross Hosp.; King's Coll. and University Coll., London. BSc (1st cl. Hons); PhD; MB, BS. Research and teaching in Neurobiology at: Oxford, 1962; Harvard, 1962–65; Yale,

1965–68; Harvard, 1968–73; Stanford, 1973–83; Biocenter, Basel, 1983–98. *Publications:* From Neuron to Brain (with S. Kuffler), 1976, 3rd edn 1992; The Search for Connections, 1987. *Recreations:* Latin American history, music. *Address:* Scuola Internazionale Superiore di Studi Avanzati, via Beirut 2, Trieste 34014, Italy.

NICHOLLS, Hon. John (Peter); QC 2006; barrister; *b* 30 Nov. 1963; *s* of Baron Nicholls of Birkenhead, *qv; m* 1991, Divya Bhatia, *d* of Captain and Mrs Rajindar Bhatia; one *s* one *d. Educ:* Winchester Coll.; Trinity Hall, Cambridge (BA 1st Cl. Law 1985). Called to the Bar, Middle Temple, 1986; in practice as a barrister, specialising in business and commercial fields, Maitland Chambers, 1987–. *Recreations:* sport, travel. *Address:* Maitland Chambers, 7 Stone Buildings, Lincoln's Inn, WC2A 3SZ. *T:* (020) 7406 1200, *Fax:* (020) 7406 1300; *e-mail:* jnicholls@maitlandchambers.com. *Clubs:* Aula; Hawks' (Cambridge); Lensbury; Bombay Gymkhana.

NICHOLLS, Jonathan William Nicholas, PhD; Registrary, University of Cambridge, since 2007; Fellow of Emmanuel College, Cambridge, since 2007; *b* Chelmsford, 16 June 1956; *s* of Arthur John Nicholas Nicholls and Cecily Mary Nicholls (*née* Cosgrove); *m* 1998, Susan Catherine Rasmussen; one step *s* one step *d. Educ:* Univ. of Bristol (BA 1st Cl. Hons Eng. 1978); Emmanuel Coll., Cambridge (PhD 1984); Harvard Univ. (Herchel Smith Scholar, 1981–82). University of Warwick: Admin. Officer, Asst Registrar, Sen. Asst Registrar then Academic Registrar, 1982–99; Registrar, 1999–2003; Registrar and Sec., Univ. of Birmingham, 2004–07. Dep. Chm., Assoc. of Heads of Univ. Admin, 2006–. *Publication:* The Matter of Courtesy: medieval courtesy books and the Gawain-poet, 1984. *Recreations:* football, cricket, birds, books, music. *Address:* University of Cambridge, The Old Schools, Cambridge CB2 1TN. *T:* (01223) 332294; *e-mail:* Registrary@admin.cam.ac.uk. *Club:* Oxford and Cambridge.

NICHOLLS, Michael John Gadsby; QC 2006; barrister, author and mediator; *b* 29 April 1948; *s* of late Ronald Harry Nicholls and Betty Jean Nicholls (*née* Gadsby); *m* 1st, 1970, Marian Howe (marr. diss. 2006); 2nd, 2007, Debbie Taylor. *Educ:* Whitley Abbey Sch., Coventry; BRNC, Dartmouth; Inns of Court Sch. of Law. Served RN, 1967–72 (specialist in hydrographic survey), Lieut 1971. Called to the Bar, Middle Temple, 1975; Army Legal Services, 1975–80, Major 1979; Dep. Dir, Army Legal Services, BAOR (GSO2), 1979; admitted solicitor, 1980, and in private practice, 1980–83; on staff of Official Solicitor to Supreme Court, 1983–98; specialist in internat. and domestic family law. *Publications:* (contrib.) Principles and Practice of Forensic Psychiatry, 1990; (jtly) The Human Rights Act 1998: a special bulletin, 1998; (contrib.) The Legal Aspects of Munchausen's Syndrome by Proxy, 2001; (jtly) International Movement of Children: law, practice and procedure, 2004; contribs on internat. family law to learned jls. *Recreations:* riding, painting, fly-fishing. *Address:* 1 Hare Court, Temple, EC4Y 7BE. *T:* (020) 7797 7070. *Clubs:* Guards Polo, Honourable Artillery Company Saddle.

NICHOLLS, Michael William Newbery, FRCPath; Vice-President, 1998–2007, and Hon. Treasurer, 2000–08, Fellowship of Postgraduate Medicine (President, 1993–98); *b* 22 May 1931; *s* of William Stanley Nicholls, MBE and Florence May (*née* King); *m* 1957, Pamela Winifred Hemer (*d* 1997); two *s. Educ:* Xaverian Coll., London; UCL; UCH Med. Sch. (MB, BS). MRCS, LRCP; FRCPath 1980. Resident hosp. posts and general practice, 1955–61; Asst Microbiologist and Registrar, UCH, 1961–70; Consultant Microbiologist, Chichester and Worthing HAs, 1972–90; Dean of Postgrad. Medicine, SE Thames Reg., Univ. of London, 1990–95; Chief Exec., Centre for Educn R and D, 1990–94; Hon. Sen. Lectr in Med. Microbiology, UMDS, 1991–95. Mem., Worthing HA, 1982–90. Freeman, City of London, 1984; Mem., Livery Cttee, Soc. of Apothecaries, 1994. *Publications:* various contribs, usually of new or creatively provocative material on med. microbiol., med. educn and the needed reforms in postgrad. and continuing med. educn. *Recreations:* sailing, singing, chamber music. *Address:* Creekside, Greenacres, Birdham, Chichester, W Sussex PO20 7HL. *T:* (01243) 512937. *Clubs:* Athenæum; Offshore Cruising (Southampton).

NICHOLLS, Sir Nigel (Hamilton), KCVO 1998; CBE 1982; Clerk of the Privy Council, 1992–98; *b* 19 Feb. 1938; *s* of late Bernard Cecil Hamilton Nicholls and Enid Kathleen Nicholls (*née* Gwynne); *m* 1967, Isobel Judith, *d* of Rev. Canon Maurice Dean; two *s. Educ:* King's School, Canterbury; St John's College, Oxford (BA 1962; MA 1966). Asst Principal, Admiralty, 1962, MoD, 1964; Asst Private Sec. to Minister of Defence for RN, 1965–66; Principal, 1966; Directing Staff, RCDS, 1971–73; Asst Private Sec. to Sec. of State for Defence, 1973–74; Asst Sec., 1974; Defence Counsellor, UK Delegation to MBFR Talks, Vienna, 1977–80; Asst Under-Sec. of State, MoD, 1984; Under Sec., Cabinet Office, 1986–89; Asst Under-Sec. of State (Systems), MoD, 1989–92. Mem. Council, Malvern St James (formerly Malvern Girls' Coll.), 1999–2007 (Chm., 2003–07). Chm., Malvern Hills DFAS, 2003–06. Freeman, City of London, 1999; Liveryman, Woolmen's Co., 1999–. Companion, IMM, 1999. *Recreations:* choral singing, genealogy, walking. *Address:* Loddiswell, 28 Avenue Road, Great Malvern, Worcs WR14 3BG. *Club:* Oxford and Cambridge.

NICHOLLS, Patrick Charles Martyn; Consultant: Dunn & Baker, solicitors, 1987–2001; Foresight Communications, since 2002; CVS, solicitors, since 2003; *b* 14 Nov. 1948; *s* of late Douglas Charles Martyn Nicholls and Margaret Josephine Nicholls; *m* 1976, Bridget Elizabeth Fergus Owens; one *s* two *d. Educ:* Redrice Sch., Andover. Qualified solicitor, 1974; Partner, Dunn & Baker, 1976–87. Mem., E Devon District Council, 1980–84. MP (C) Teignbridge, 1983–2001; contested (C) same seat, 2001. PPS to Ministers of State: Home Office, 1984–86; MAFF, 1986–87; Parliamentary Under-Secretary of State: Dept of Employment, 1987–90; DoE, 1990; Opposition spokesman on health, 1997–98, on agric., 1998–99. Vice Chm., Social Security Select Cttee, 1990–93. Vice-Chm., Cons. Party, 1993–94. Vice Chm., Soc. of Cons. Lawyers, 1986–87. Steward, British Boxing Bd of Control, 1985–87. Freeman, City of London, 1996. *Recreations:* theatre, opera, historical research, ski-ing. *Address:* Whitehall Manor, Whitehall, Hemyock, Devon EX15 3UQ. *T:* (01823) 680100; CVS, solicitors, 17 Albemarle Street, W1S 4HP; Foresight Communications, 1 Northumberland Avenue, WC2N 5BW. *Club:* Carlton.

NICHOLLS, Philip, CB 1976; *b* 30 Aug. 1914; *yr s* of late W. H. Nicholls, Radlett; *m* 1955, Sue, *yr d* of late W. E. Shipton; two *s. Educ:* Malvern; Pembroke Coll., Cambridge. Asst Master, Malvern, 1936; Sen. Classical Master, 1939; resigned, 1947. Served in Army, 1940–46: 8th Bn, The Worcestershire Regt; HQ, East Africa Command; Allied Commn for Austria. Foreign Office (German Section), 1947; HM Treasury, 1949; a Forestry Commissioner (Finance and Administration), 1970–75, retired. Mem. Council, Malvern Coll., 1960–90 (Vice-Chm., 1963–88). *Address:* Barnards Green House, Barnards Green, Malvern, Worcs WR14 3NQ. *T:* (01684) 574446.

NICHOLLS, Prof. (Ralph) John; Consultant Surgeon, St Mark's Hospital, London, 1978–2006, now Emeritus; Visiting Professor, Imperial College London, since 2006; *b* 20 May 1943; *s* of Clifton Wilson Nicholls and Muriel Morten Nicholls (*née* Heathcote); *m* 1966, Stella Mary McBride; two *s* one *d* (and one *d* decd). *Educ:* Felsted Sch., Essex; Gonville and Caius Coll., Cambridge (BA 1964; MB 1968, BChir 1967, MChir 1978;

MA 1999); London Hosp. Med. Coll. London Hosp. trng posts, 1966–78; MRC Res. Fellow, 1971–72; Alexander von Humboldt Fellow, 1976–77; Consultant Surgeon, St Thomas' Hosp., 1982–93; Clin. Dir, St Mark's Hosp., London, 1997–2001; Associate Med. Dir, NW London Hosps NHS Trust, 2005–06; Hon. Prof. of Colorectal Surgery, ICSM, 1997–. Hon. Civilian Consultant in Surgery to RAF, 1999–; Consultant, Policlinico de Monza, Italy, 2006–. Ed., Colorectal Disease, 1999–. Mem., Specialist Adv. Cttee in Gen. Surgery, Jt Cttee for Higher Surgical Trng, 1997–2003. President: Assoc. of Coloproctology of GB and Ireland, 1999–2000; Eur. Assoc. of Coloproctology, 2004; Sec., Div. of Coloproctology, Sect. of Surgery, Union Européene des Médecins Specialistes, 1997–2003. Fellow, Amer. Soc. Colon and Rectal Surgeons, 1993. Hon. FRCPSGlas 1992; Hon. FRCSE 2007; Hon. Fellow: Brazilian Soc. Surgery, 1982; Swiss Soc. Gastroenterol., 1990. Membre d'Honneur: Assoc. Française de Chirurgie, 1997; Academie Nationale de Chirurgie, 2005; Hon. Member, Society of Surgery: of Yugoslavia, 2002; of Chile, 2003; of Italy, 2004; of Spain, 2004. *Publications:* (ed jtly) Restorative Proctocolectomy, 1993; (ed with R. R. Dozois) Colorectal Surgery, 1997; contribs to learned jls incl. Lancet, BMJ, British Jl Surgery, Annals of Surgery. *Recreations:* languages, travel, history. *Address:* 24 St Mark's Crescent, NW1 7TU. *T:* (020) 7267 4433. *Club:* Athenæum.

NICHOLLS, Robert Michael, CBE 1995; Regional Health Commissioner, London, Appointments Commission, since 2007 (non-executive Director, 2007–08); *b* 28 July 1939; *s* of late Herbert Edgar Nicholls and Bennetta L'Estrange (*née* Burges); *m* 1961, Dr Deírín Deirdre (*née* O'Sullivan); four *s*. *Educ:* Hampton Sch.; University Coll. of Wales (BA 1961); Univ. of Manchester (DSA 1962). FHSM (AHA 1963; FHA 1993). Asst Sec., Torbay Hosp., 1964; House Governor, St Stephen's Hosp., Chelsea, 1966; Asst Clerk to the Governors, St Thomas' Hosp., 1968; Dep. Gp Sec., Southampton Univ. Hosp. Management Cttee, 1972; Dist Administrator, Southampton and SW Hampshire Health Dist, 1974; Area Administrator, Newcastle upon Tyne AHA(T), 1977; Regl Administrator, SW RHA, 1981; Dist Gen. Man., Southmead DHA, 1985; Regl Gen. Man., later Chief Exec., Oxford RHA, 1988–93; Exec. Dir, London Implementation Gp, NHS Mgt Exec., 1993–96; health care mgt consultant, 1996–2005; Chm., Nat. Clinical Assessment Authy, 2003–05; Regl Comr, London, NHS Appts Commn, 2005–07. Non-exec. Dir, Nestor Healthcare Gp plc, 1997–2003 (Sen. non-exec. Dir, 2001–03). Health Sector Reform Advr, British Council, 1997–2003. Member: Health Educn Council, 1984–87; CMO's Med. Educn Wkg Pty, 1992–93; GMC, 1996–2005 (Chm., Preliminary Proceedings Cttee, 2000–03). Mem. Clinical Adv. Bd, Oxford Univ. Med. Sch., 2001–. National Council, Inst. of Health Service Management (formerly IHA): Mem., 1976–86; Pres., 1983–84. Associate Fellow, Templeton Coll., Oxford, 1996–2001. *Publications:* (contrib.) Resources in Medicine, 1970; (contrib.) Working with People, 1983; (contrib.) Rationing of Healthcare in Medicine, 1993; (contrib.) Doctors in Society, 2005. *Recreations:* bird-watching, jazz, opera, sport. *Address:* Thame, Oxon.

NICHOLS, Rt Rev. Anthony Howard, PhD; Lecturer in Biblical Studies, Trinity Theological College, Perth, since 2003; *b* 29 March 1938; *m* 1968, Judith Margaret Ross; two *s* two *d*. *Educ:* Univ. of Sydney (BA; MEd); Univ. of London (BD Hons); Macquarrie Univ. (MA Hons); Moore Coll., ACT (Theol. scholar); PhD Univ. of Sheffield 1997. Latin and history teacher, 1960–63. Assistant Curate: St Paul's Chatswood, 1966; St Bede's, Drummoyne, 1967; Lectr, Biblical Studies, Moore Coll., Sydney, 1968–72; Lectr, Biblical Studies and Educn, 1972–81, Dean of Faculty of Theology, 1977–81, Satya Wacana Christian Univ., Salatiga, Indonesia; Principal: Nungalinya Coll., Darwin (Training Coll. for Aboriginal theol students), 1982–87; St Andrew's Hall, Melbourne (CMS Training Coll.), 1988–91; Bishop of NW Australia, 1992–2003. Vis. Lectr, Anglican Inst., Bandung, Indonesia, 2004–. Stephen Bayne Scholar, Univ. of Sheffield, 1985–86. *Publications:* jl articles on Bible translation, missiology, Indonesian religions, Aboriginal culture, and philosophy of educn. *Address:* Unit 6, 56 Matheson Road, Applecross, WA 6153, Australia.

NICHOLS, Dinah Alison, CB 1995; Director: Shires Smaller Companies plc, since 1999; Pennon Group plc, since 2003; a Crown Estate Commissioner, since 2003; Chair, National Forest Company, since 2005; *b* 28 Sept. 1943; *d* of late Sydney Hirst Nichols and Freda Nichols. *Educ:* Wyggeston Girls' Grammar Sch., Leicester; Bedford Coll., Univ. of London (Reid Arts Schol.; BA Hons History, 1965; Hon. Fellow, RHBNC, 1997). Ministry of Transport: Asst Principal, 1965–69; Asst Private Sec. to Minister, 1969–70; Principal, 1970–74; Cabinet Office, 1974–77; Asst Sec., DoE, 1978–83; Principal Private Sec. to Sec. of State for Transport, 1983–85; Under Sec., DoE, 1985–91; Dep. Sec., DoE, later DETR, then DEFRA, 1991–2002; Dir Gen., Envmt, 1996–2002. Director: John Laing ETE, 1987–90; Anglian Water plc, 1992–95. Sec. of State for the Envmt's Rep., Commonwealth War Graves Commn, 1993–97. Dir, Cities in Schs, 1996–2000; Mem. Bd, Toynbee Housing Assoc., 1996–; Chairman: Toynbee Partnership Housing Assoc., 2002–; Groundwork N London (formerly Groundwork Camden & Islington), 2004–. Trustee: Travel Foundn, 2003–; Envmtl Campaigns (ENCAMS), 2005–. Winston Churchill Meml Fellow, 1969. FRSA. *Recreations:* fell walking, choral singing (Goldsmiths Choral Union), classical music, theatre. *Clubs:* Arts; Swiss Alpine.

NICHOLS, Jeremy Gareth Lane, MA; Headmaster, Stowe School, 1989–2003; Interim Headmaster, Aiglon College, Switzerland, 2007; *b* 20 May 1943; *yr s* of late Derek Aplin Douglas Lane Nichols and of Ruth Anne Baiss (formerly Nichols); *m* 1972, Patricia Anne, *d* of Cdre Alan Swanton, DSO, DFC and bar, RN; one *s* three *d*. *Educ:* Lancing Coll., Sussex; Fitzwilliam Coll., Cambridge (BA English Lit. 1966; MA); Perugia Univ. Assistant Master: Livorno Naval Acad., 1965; Rugby Sch., 1966–67; Eton Coll., 1967–89, House Master, 1981–89; Gilman Sch., Baltimore, USA, 1979–80. Chm., Assoc. of Educnl Guardians for Internat. Students. Founding Mem. Bd and Pres., Model EP, 1994–2000. Advr Trustee, Manor Charitable Trust, 1989–2003. Governor: Wellesley House Sch., 1985–2004; Papplewick Sch., 1988–2003; Aysgarth Sch., 1990–2004. FCT (FCollP 1997); FRSA. *Recreations:* outdoor pursuits, sport, music, old cars. *Address:* Tresithick House, St Erme, Truro, Cornwall TR7 9AU. *Clubs:* East India, Lansdowne; Hawks (Cambridge); I Zingari, Free Foresters, Corinthian Casuals.

NICHOLS, John Roland; HM Diplomatic Service; Ambassador to Switzerland and (non-resident) to Liechtenstein, since 2008; *b* 13 Nov. 1951; *s* of Richard Alan Nichols and Katherine Louisa Nichols (*née* Barham); *m* 1983, Suzanne, *d* of James Harry Davies, MBE, RA retd, and Helen Christine Davies, JP (*née* Berry); one *s* one *d*. *Educ:* Latymer Upper Sch., Hammersmith; Univ. of Surrey (BSc Hons). Admitted as solicitor, 1977; entered FCO, 1977: First Secretary: Budapest, 1979–82; FCO, 1982–85; Brasilia, 1985–89; FCO, 1989–93; Counsellor and Dep. High Comr, Dhaka, 1993–95; Consul-Gen., Geneva, 1995–97; Dep. Hd of Mission, Dir of Trade Promotion and Consul-Gen., Berne, 1997–2000; Dep. Chief Exec., and Dir of Communications, Internat. Financial Services, London (on secondment), 2000–03; Ambassador to Hungary, 2003–07. *Recreations:* trying hard to be more than a Sunday painter, travel, cycling, gardening, opera, music, theatre. *Address:* c/o Foreign and Commonwealth Office, King Charles Street, SW1A 2AH.

NICHOLS, John Winfrith de Lisle, BSc (Eng); CEng; FIET; retired; Director: National Maritime Institute, 1976–79; Computer Aided Design Centre, Cambridge, 1977–79; *b* 7 June 1919; *er s* of late John F. Nichols, MC, PhD, FRHistS, FSA, Godalming; *m* 1942, Catherine Lilian (*d* 1984), *er d* of Capt. A. V. Grantham, RNR, Essex; two *s* two *d*. *Educ:* Sir Walter St John's Sch., Battersea; London Univ. Royal Navy, 1940–46; GPO, Dollis Hill, 1946–47; RN Scientific Service, 1947–55; Chief Research Officer, Corp. of Trinity House, 1955–59; UKAEA, 1959–65; Min. of Technology, later DTI and Dept of Industry, 1965–76; Under-Sec., and Chm., Requirement Bd for Computers, Systems and Electronics, 1972–74; Under Sec., Research Contractors Div., DoI, 1974–76. *Recreations:* gardening, sailing, caravanning.

NICHOLS, Judith Elaine; Senior Immigration Judge, Asylum and Immigration Tribunal, since 2006; a Recorder, since 2007; *b* 7 Jan. 1959; *d* of Anthony John Banks and Avrielle Doreen Mary Banks; *m* 1986, Timothy William Nichols (*d* 1999). *Educ:* Bridlington High Sch. for Girls; Liverpool Poly. (BA Hons); Christleton Coll. of Law, Chester. Admitted solicitor, 1983; Asst Solicitor, London Bor. of Sutton, 1983–85; Prosecuting Solicitor, Cambs CC, 1985–87; Principal Legal Advr, Richmond upon Thames Magistrates' Court, 1987–93; Hd of Legal Services, Uxbridge Magistrates' Court, 1993–2000; Dep. Dist Judge (Magistrates' Courts), 1997–2007; pt-time Immigration Adjudicator, 1997–2000; Immigration Judge, 2000–05, Designated Immigration Judge, 2005–06. Pres., Council of Immigration Judges, 2004–05. *Recreations:* gardening, walking, theatre, ballet, prevaricating. *Address:* Asylum and Immigration Tribunal, Field House, 15 Bream's Buildings, EC4A 1DZ. *T:* (020) 7073 4165; *e-mail:* judith.nichols@judiciary.gsi.gov.uk.

NICHOLS, Peter Richard, FRSL 1983; playwright since 1959; *b* 31 July 1927; *s* of late Richard George Nichols and Violet Annie Poole; *m* 1960, Thelma Reed; one *s* two *d* (and one *d* decd). *Educ:* Bristol Grammar Sch.; Bristol Old Vic Sch.; Trent Park Trng College. Actor, mostly in repertory, 1950–55; worked as teacher in primary and secondary schs, 1958–60. Mem., Arts Council Drama Panel, 1973–75. Playwright in residence, Guthrie Theatre, Minneapolis, 1976. *TV plays:* Walk on the Grass, 1959; Promenade, 1960; Ben Spray, 1961; The Reception, 1961; The Big Boys, 1961; Continuity Man, 1963; Ben Again, 1963; The Heart of the Country, 1963; The Hooded Terror, 1963; The Brick Umbrella, 1964; When the Wind Blows, 1964 (later adapted for radio); Daddy Kiss It Better, 1968; The Gorge, 1968; Hearts and Flowers, 1971; The Common, 1973; Greeks Bearing Gifts (Inspector Morse series), 1991; *films:* Catch Us If You Can, 1965; Georgy Girl, 1967; Joe Egg, 1971; The National Health, 1973; Privates on Parade, 1983; *stage plays:* A Day in The Death of Joe Egg, 1967 (Evening Standard Award, Best Play; Tony Award, Best Revival, 1985); The National Health, 1969 (Evening Standard Award, Best Play); Forget-me-not Lane, 1971; Chez Nous, 1973; The Freeway, 1974 (radio broadcast, 1991); Privates on Parade, 1977 (Evening Standard Best Comedy, Soc. of West End Theatres Best Comedy and Ivor Novello Best Musical Awards); Born in the Gardens, 1979 (televised 1986); Passion Play, 1980 (Standard Best Play award, 1981); A Piece of My Mind, 1986; Blue Murder, 1995; So Long Life, 2000; Nicholodeon (revue), 2000; *musical:* Poppy, 1982 (SWET Best Musical Award). *Publications:* Feeling You're Behind (autobiog.), 1984; Diaries 1969–1977, 2000; some TV plays in anthologies; all above stage plays published separately and in 2 vols, Nichols: Plays One and Two, 1991. *Recreations:* listening to jazz, looking at cities. *Address:* c/o Alan Brodie Representation, 6th Floor, Fairgate House, 78 New Oxford Street, WC1A 1HB.

NICHOLS, Sir Richard (Everard), Kt 1998; Senior Partner, Sedgwick Kelly Solicitors, 2000–02 (Partner, 1996–2000); Lord Mayor of London, 1997–98; *b* 26 April 1938; *s* of late Guy Everard Nichols and of Patricia Mary (*née* Hurst); *m* 1966, Shelagh Mary Loveband; two *s* one *d*. *Educ:* Christ's Hosp., Horsham. Nat. Service, commnd RE, 1956–58. Admitted solicitor, 1963; Asst Solicitor, Gunston & Smart, Hong Kong, 1963–64; Sen. Partner, 1976–96, Kelly Nichols & Blayney. Chancellor, Univ. of Ulster, 2002–. Almoner, Christ's Hosp., 1984–2004; Gov., City Literary Inst., 1990–95. Alderman, Ward of Candlewick, 1984–; Sheriff, City of London, 1994–95. Master, Salters' Co., 1988. KStJ 1997. *Recreations:* wine, travel, coarse gardening. *Address:* Newhall Farm, Bucks Hill, Kings Langley, Herts WD4 9AH. *T:* (01923) 269882. *Club:* East India.

NICHOLS, Most Rev. Vincent Gerard; *see* Birmingham, Archbishop of, (RC).

NICHOLSON OF WINTERBOURNE, Baroness *cr* 1997 (Life Peer), of Winterbourne in the Royal County of Berkshire; **Emma Harriet Nicholson;** Member (Lib Dem) South East Region, England, European Parliament, since 1999; *b* 16 Oct. 1941; *d* of Sir Godfrey Nicholson, 1st Bt and late Lady Katharine Constance Lindsay, 5th *d* of 27th Earl of Crawford; *m* 1987, Sir Michael Harris Caine (*d* 1999); one adopted *s* two step *c*. *Educ:* St Mary's School, Wantage; Royal Academy of Music. LRAM, ARCM. Computer Programmer, Programming Instructor, Systems Analyst, ICL, 1962–66; Computer Consultant, John Tyzack & Partners, 1967–69; Gen. Management Consultant and Computer Consultant, McLintock Mann and Whinney Murray, 1969–74; joined Save the Children Fund, 1974, Dir of Fund Raising, 1977–85, Pres., Hatherleigh Dist Br. Contested (C) Blyth Valley, 1979. MP Devon West and Torridge (C, 1987–95, Lib Dem, 1995–97). PPS to Minister of State, Home Office, 1992–93, MAFF, 1993–95, to Financial Sec. to HM Treasury, 1995–97. Mem., Select Cttee on Employment, 1990–91; Founder and Jt Chm., All Party Parly Gp for Romanian Children; Vice Chm., All Party Gp on Penal Affairs, 1992; Mem., Parly Panel, RCN, 1990–92; Sec. then Chm., Cons. Backbench Envmt Cttee, 1990–91; Vice-Chm., Cons. Party, 1983–87. Alternate Mem., UK Delegn to WEU and Council of Europe, 1990–92. European Parliament: Vice Pres., Cttee on For. Affairs, Human Rights, Common Defence and Security Policy; Member: Cttee on Women's Rights and Equal Opportunities; Delegns to Mashreq countries and Gulf States, and to Euro-Mediterranean Partnership; Rapporteur for Iraq and Romania; Jt Chm., High Level Gp for Romanian Children. Fellow, Industry and Parlt Trust. Vis. Parly Fellow, St Antony's Coll., Oxford, 1995–96 (Sen. Associate Mem., 1997–98, 1998–99). WHO Envoy on Health, Peace and Develt, E Mediterranean Reg., 2002. Vice-Moderator, Movement for Ordination of Women, 1991–93. Founder and Pres., Caine Prize for African Writing; Founder and Mem., Parly Appeal for Romanian Children; Trustee: Africa '95; Booker Prize Foundn. Dir, Shelter; Chm., AMAR Internat. Charitable Foundn, 1991–; Jt Chm., Children's High Level Gp, 2006–; Member: Exec. Bd, UNICEF UK; MRC; Mgt Bd, European Movement (Vice-Chm.); POW Adv. Trust on Disability; Council, PITCOM; Centre for Policy Studies; RIIA; Adv. Bd, Women of Tomorrow Awards; RAM Appeal Cttee; Courts of Reading, Southampton, Exeter and Sussex Univs; Editl Panel, 300 Gp Newsletter. Vice President: Small Farmers' Assoc.; ADC; ADAPT (Founder and Chm.); Methodist Homes for the Aged; LEPRA; Farms for City Children; Local Govt Gp for Europe. Deputy Chairman: Duke of Edinburgh's Award 30th Anniv. Tribute Project, 1986–88; Duke of Edinburgh's Internat. Project '87, 1987–88. President: Plymouth and W Devon Cassette, Talking Newspaper; W Regl Assoc. for the Deaf; Vice Pres., Little Foundn; Co-Patron, Manningford Trust; Patron: Hospice Care Trust, N Devon; CRUSAID; Devon Care Trust; Blind in Business; Wilsford Trust; Chm. Adv. Cttee, Carnegie UK Trust Venues Improvement Programmes. Mem., Co. of Inf. Technologists. FRSA. Hon. Dr: N London, 1998; Timisoara, Romania, 2002; Acad. of Econ. Studies, Bucharest. *Publications:* Why does the

West forget?, 1993; Secret Society, 1996; (ed jtly) The Iraqi Marshlands, 2002; contrib. various periodicals. *Recreations:* music, chess, reading, walking. *Address:* House of Lords, SW1A 0PW. *Club:* Reform.

NICHOLSON, Air Vice-Marshal Antony Angus, CBE 1997; LVO 1980; FRAeS; defence consultant, since 2004; *b* 27 June 1946; *s* of late Air Cdre Angus Archibald Norman Nicholson, CBE, AE and of Joan Mary, *d* of Ernest Beaumont, MRCVS, DVSM; *m* 1980, Fenella Janet Fraser; one *s* one *d*, and one step *s*. *Educ:* Eton Coll.; Churchill Coll., Cambridge (MA). FRAeS 1998. Joined RAF, 1968: helicopter pilot, 28 Sqn (Hong Kong), 3 Sqn SOAF (Oman), and 230 Sqn (UK), 1970–75; OC 3 Sqn SOAF, 1975–77; Equerry to HRH Duke of Edinburgh, 1978–80; OC 72 Sqn, 1981–83; MoD, 1984–86; RAF Instr, Army Staff Coll., 1986–88; Stn Comdr, RAF Shawbury, 1988–90; rcds 1991; Air Cdre Flying Trng, 1993–96; Dir, Operational Requirements (Air), 1996–98; Dir Gen. Air Systems 1, Defence Procurement Agency, 1998–2000. Eurofighter Internat. Ltd, 2000–01; Dir, Babcock Defence, 2001–04. DSM (Oman), 1977. *Recreations:* squash, hill walking, Gloucester RFC. *Address:* c/o Barclays Bank, High Street, Odiham, Hants RG29 1LL. *Club:* Army and Navy.

NICHOLSON, Brian Thomas Graves, CBE 1998; Chairman, Advertising Standards Board of Finance, 1989–99; *b* 27 June 1930; *s* of late Ivor Nicholson, CBE, and Mrs Alan McGaw; *m* Henrietta, *d* of late Nevill Vintcent, OBE, DFC, and Mrs Ralph Dennis; two *s* (and one *s* decd). *Educ:* Charterhouse. Reporter, Newcastle Evening Chronicle, 1949–53; Montreal Star, Toronto Telegram, and Victoria Times, 1953–54; Manchester Evening Chronicle, 1954–56; Sunday Graphic, 1956–57; Advertisement Manager, Sunday Times, 1957–65; Director: Sunday Times, 1963–65; Beaverbrook Newspapers plc, 1967–77; Man. Dir, Evening Standard, 1972–77; Jt Man. Dir, Observer, 1977–84; Hd of Public Affairs, Lloyd's of London, 1990–92; Director: CompAir, 1977–85; Center for Communication (USA), 1981–95; Lloyd's of London Press, 1982–93; London Broadcasting Co., 1983–90; Royal Opera House Covent Garden, 1984–89; Royal Ballet, 1984–92 (Mem., Bd of Govs, 1995–2006); News (UK), 1985–87; CCA Galleries plc, 1986–89; Logie Bradshaw Media, 1986–97; Messenger Newspapers Gp, 1986–89; Aurora Productions, 1987–91; Messenger Television Ltd, 1989–2000; Whitespace Software Ltd, 1990–2004; Home Counties Newspaper Holdings plc, 1991–98; Messenger Leisure Ltd, 1994–2003; Benesh Inst., 1995–98; Birmingham Royal Ballet, 2001–06; Chairman: Audit Bureau of Circulation, 1975–77; Marlar Internat. Ltd, 1985–90; Carthusian Trust, 1987–2000; SE Arts Bd (formerly Assoc.), 1989–95; Publicitas Hldg (UK) Ltd, 1989–99; Adv. Cttee on Advertising, COI, 1993–98; Charterhouse Sports Centre Ltd, 1995–2001; Dance Teachers' Benevolent Fund, 1999–2003. Vice President: CAM Foundn, 1975–2000; Royal Theatrical Fund (formerly Royal Gen. Theatrical Fund Assoc.), 1986– (Vice-Chm., 1996–2000); Pres., History of Advertising Trust, 2000–; Member: Council of Commonwealth Press Union, 1975–99; Adv. Bd, New Perspective Fund (USA), 1984–97; Trustee, Glyndebourne Opera Co., 1977–2000; Gov., British Liver Foundn, 1989–99. Mem., Editorial Adv. Bd, Focus in Education Ltd, 1986–90. Churchwarden, St Bride's Church, Fleet Street, 1978–2002. Mackintosh Medal, Advertising Assoc., 2000. *Recreations:* travelling, listening, playing games. *Address:* 6 Laxford House, Cundy Street, SW1W 9JU. *Clubs:* Beefsteak, Brooks's, Pratt's, MCC.

NICHOLSON, Sir Bryan (Hubert), GBE 2005; Kt 1987; Chairman, Financial Reporting Council, 2001–05 (Director and Deputy Chairman, 1993–96; Member, 1996–98); Senior Advisor, Penfida Partners LLP, since 2006; *b* 6 June 1932; *s* of late Reginald Hubert and Clara Nicholson; *m* 1956, Mary Elizabeth, *er d* of A. C. Harrison of Oxford; one *s* one *d* (and one *s* decd). *Educ:* Palmers School, Grays, Essex; Oriel College, Oxford (MA PPE; Hon. Fellow, 1989). 2nd Lieut, RASC, 1950–52; Unilever Management Trainee, 1955–58; Dist. Manager, Van den Berghs, 1958–59; Sales Manager, Three Hands/Jeyes Group, 1960–64; Sperry Rand: Sales Dir, UK, Remington Div., 1964–66; Gen. Manager, Australia, Remington Div., 1966–69; Managing Dir, UK and France, Remington Div., 1969–72; Dir, Ops, Rank Xerox (UK), 1972–76; Dir, Overseas Subsidiaries, Rank Xerox, 1976; Exec. Main Bd Dir, Rank Xerox, 1976–84; Chm., Rank Xerox (UK) and Chm., Rank Xerox GmbH, 1979–84; Chm., MSC, 1984–87; Chm. and Chief Exec., PO, 1987–92; Chairman: BUPA, 1992–2001 (Vice Pres., 2001–05; Pres., 2005–); Varity Hldgs, later Varity Europe Ltd, 1993–96; Cookson Gp, 1998–2003; Accountancy Foundn, 2003–04 (Dir, 2000–03). Non-executive Director: Rank Xerox, 1984–87; Baker Perkins Holdings, 1982–84; Evode, 1981–84; Internat. Post Corp. SA, 1988–92; GKN, 1991–2000; Varity Corp., USA, 1993–96; LucasVarity, 1996–99; Equitas Hldgs Ltd, 1996–2005; Action Centre for Europe Ltd, 1996–2004; Newsquest plc, 1997–99; non-executive Chairman: GOAL plc, 2001–02; EDI plc, 2004– (Dep. Chm., 2002–04); Member: Adv. Bd, Active Internat., 2001–; Europ. Adv. Bd, Proudfoot Consulting, 2006–. Confederation of British Industry: Mem. Council, 1987–2002; Mem., President's Cttee, 1990–98; Dep. Pres., 1993–94, 1996–97; Pres., 1994–96; Chairman: Task Force on Vocational Educn and Training, 1988–89; Educn and Training Affairs Cttee, 1990–93; Global Counsellor, Conf. Bd, 1994–2007 (Emeritus, 2007); Chairman: CNAA, 1988–91; NICG, 1988–90; NCVQ, 1990–93; Interchange Panel, 1996–97; Pres., N of England Educn Conf., 1996. Department of Employment: Member: Adv. Cttee on Women's Employment, 1985–87; Women's Issues Wkg Gp, 1992–93; Race Relns Adv. Gp, 1985–87. Member: NEDC, 1985–92; Council, Inst. of Manpower Studies, 1985–93; Governing Council, Business in the Community, 1985–93; Council, Prince's Youth Business Trust, 1986–2002; Council, Industrial Soc., 1988–2002 (Chm., 1990–93); Adv. Council, Economic and Regional Analysis, 1998–; Prime Minister's Adv. Cttee on Business Appointments, 1998–; Editl Bd, European Business Jl, 1988–2005; Adv. Bd, Britain in Europe, 1999–2004; Council, Atlantic Coll., 1999–2002; Adv. Gp, Higher Educn Policy Inst., 2002–05. President: Involvement and Participation Assoc., 1990–94; ACFHE, 1992–93; AFC, 1993–94; Nat. Centre for Young People with Epilepsy, 2005–; Vice President: SRHE, 1992–; Re-Solv (Soc. for Prevention of Solvent Abuse), 1985–; NCH Action for Children (formerly Nat. Children's Home), 1989–2002. Observer, Public Interest Oversight Bd, Internat. Fedn of Accountants, 2006–. Chancellor, Sheffield Hallam Univ., 1992–2001; Pro Chancellor and Chm. Council, Open Univ., 1996–2004. President: Oriel Soc., 1988–92; Open Univ. Foundn, 2004–. Patron, Rathbone Community Industry (formerly Rathbone Soc.), 1987–; Vice Pres., Industrial Trust, 1999–; Trustee: Babson Coll., Mass, USA, 1990–96; Buxton Fest. Foundn, 2003–; Internat. Accounting Standards Cttee Foundn, 2006–. President: Wakefield Trinity Wildcats, 2000–; Nomad Th., E Horsley, 2002–. UK Hon. Rep. for W Berlin, 1983–84. CCMI (CBIM 1985); Hon. CIPD 1994. FCGI (CGIA 1988); FCIM 1990; FRSA 1985. Freeman, City of London, 1988. Hon. Fellow: Manchester Metropolitan Univ. (formerly Polytechnic), 1990; SCOTVEC, 1994; Scottish Qualifications Authy, 1997; Open Univ., 2006. Hon. DEd CNAA, 1992; DUniv Open, 1994; Hon. DLitt Glasgow Caledonian, 2000. *Recreations:* tennis, bridge, opera, political history. *Club:* Oxford and Cambridge (Chm., 1995–97).

NICHOLSON, Sir Charles (Christian), 3rd Bt *cr* 1912, of Harrington Gardens, Royal Borough of Kensington; *b* 15 Dec. 1941; *s* of Sir John Norris Nicholson, 2nd Bt, KBE, CIE and Vittoria Vivien (*d* 1991), *y d* of Percy Trewhella; *S* father, 1993; *m* 1975, Martha Don, *d* of Stuart Warren Don and *widow* of Niall Anstruther-Gough-Calthorpe; one step *s* one step *d*. *Educ:* Ampleforth; Magdalen Coll., Oxford. *Heir: b* James Richard Nicholson [*b* 24 Oct. 1947; *m* 1980, Sarah Hazel, *d* of Richard Alan Budgett; one *s* one *d*]. *Address:* Turners Green Farm, Elvetham, Hartley Wintney, Hants RG27 8BE. *Clubs:* Brooks's, Pratt's; Royal Yacht Squadron.

See also Sir E. H. Anstruther-Gough-Calthorpe.

NICHOLSON, (Charles) Gordon (Brown), CBE 2002; QC (Scot.) 1982; Temporary Judge of the High Court and Court of Session, since 2002; Sheriff Principal of Lothian and Borders and Sheriff of Chancery, 1990–2002; *b* 11 Sept. 1935; *s* of late William Addison Nicholson, former Director, Scottish Tourist Board, and Jean Brown; *m* 1963, Hazel Mary Nixon; two *s*. *Educ:* George Watson's Coll., Edinburgh; Edinburgh Univ. (Hon. Fellow, Faculty of Law, 1988). MA Hons (English Lit.) 1956, LLB 1958. 2nd Lieut Queen's Own Cameron Highlanders, 1958–60. Admitted Faculty of Advocates, Edinburgh, 1961; in practice at Bar; Standing Junior Counsel, Registrar of Restrictive Trading Agreements, 1968; Advocate-Depute, 1968–70; Sheriff of: South Strathclyde, Dumfries and Galloway, 1970–76; Lothian and Borders, 1976–82; Mem., Scottish Law Commn, 1982–90. Vice-Pres., Sheriffs' Assoc., 1979–82 (Sec., 1975–79); Convener, Sheriffs Principal, 1991–2002. Member: Scottish Council on Crime, 1972–75; Dunpark Cttee on Reparation by Offenders, 1974–77; May Cttee of Inquiry into UK Prison Service, 1978–79; Kincraig Review of Parole in Scotland, 1988–89; Judicial Studies Cttee, 1997–2002; Criminal Justice Forum, 2000–02; Chm., Cttee on Licensing Law in Scotland, 2001–03. Hon. President: Victim Support Scotland (formerly Scottish Assoc. of Victim Support Schemes), 1989–2005 (Chm., 1987–89); Scottish Assoc. for Study of Delinquency, 1988–2002 (Chm., 1974–79; Hon. Vice-Pres., 1982–88); Jt Patron, Children Law UK (formerly British Juvenile and Family Courts Soc.), 1995–2003. Chm., Edinburgh CAB, 1979–82. Comr, Northern Lighthouse Bd, 1990–2002 (Vice Chm., 1993–94; Chm., 1994–95). *Publications:* The Law and Practice of Sentencing in Scotland, 1981, 2nd edn 1992; (ed jtly) Sheriff Court Practice by I. Macphail, 2nd edn 1999; contrib. to legal periodicals. *Recreation:* music. *Address:* Back o'Redfern, 24C Colinton Road, Edinburgh EH10 5EQ. *T:* (0131) 447 4300. *Club:* New (Edinburgh).

NICHOLSON, David John; public affairs consultant, Butler-Kelly Ltd, since 1998; *b* 17 Aug. 1944; *s* of late John Francis Nicholson and Lucy Warburton Nicholson (*née* Battrum); *m* 1981, Frances Mary, *d* of late Brig. T. E. H. Helby, MC; two *s* one *d*. *Educ:* Queen Elizabeth's Grammar School, Blackburn; Christ Church, Oxford (MA Hons Mod. Hist.). Dept of Employment, 1966; Research Fellow, Inst. of Historical Res., 1970; Cons. Res. Dept, 1972 (Head, Political Section, 1974–82); Assoc. of British Chambers of Commerce, 1982–87 (Dep. Dir-Gen., 1986–87). Contested (C) Walsall S, 1983; MP (C) Taunton, 1987–97; contested (C) same seat, 1997. PPS to Minister for Overseas Develt, 1990–92. Member: Select Cttee on Parly Comr for Admin, 1992–97; Public Accounts Cttee, 1992–94; Select Cttee on Employment, 1994–96; Select Cttee on Educn and Employment, 1996–97; Jt Sec., All-Party Parly Gp for Population and Develt, 1990–94; Treasurer: All-Party Parly Gp on Water, 1993–97; All-Party Parly Gp on Waste Management, 1995–97; Sec., Cons. Backbench Social Services Cttee, 1988–90; Chm., Cons. W Country Mems Cttee, 1994–95 (Vice-Chm., 1992–93); Sec., Cons. Backbench Agriculture Cttee, 1995–97. Pres., Taunton Horticultural and Floricultural Soc., 1992–. *Publication:* (ed with John Barnes) The Diaries of L. S. Amery: vol. I, 1896–1929, 1980; vol. II, The Empire at Bay, 1929–45, 1988. *Recreations:* travel, gardening, music, old buildings. *Address:* Allshire, East Anstey, Tiverton, Devon EX16 9JG.

NICHOLSON, Rev. Prof. Ernest Wilson, DD; FBA 1987; Provost of Oriel College, Oxford, 1990–2003; Pro-Vice-Chancellor, University of Oxford, 1993–2003; *b* 26 Sept. 1938; *s* of Ernest Tedford Nicholson and Veronica Muriel Nicholson; *m* 1962, Hazel (*née* Jackson); one *s* three *d*. *Educ:* Portadown Coll.; Trinity Coll., Dublin (Scholar; BA 1960; MA 1964; Hon. Fellow, 1992); Glasgow Univ. (PhD 1964); MA (by incorporation) 1967, BD 1971, DD 1978, Cambridge; DD Oxford (by incorporation) 1979. Lectr in Hebrew and Semitic Languages, TCD, 1962–67; Univ. Lectr in Divinity, Cambridge Univ., 1967–79; Fellow: University Coll. (now Wolfson Coll.), Cambridge, 1967–69 (Hon. Fellow, 1992); Pembroke Coll., Cambridge, 1969–79; Chaplain, Pembroke Coll., Cambridge, 1969–73, Dean, 1973–79; Oriel Prof. of the Interpretation of Holy Scripture, and Fellow of Oriel Coll., Oxford Univ., 1979–90. At various times vis. prof. at univs and seminars in Europe, USA, Canada and Australia. Pres., SOTS, 1988. Chm., Jardine Foundn, 1993–2000. Hon. Fellow: St Peter's Coll., Oxford, 1994; Oriel Coll., Oxford, 2003. Comdr, Order of Merit (Italian Republic), 1990. *Publications:* Deuteronomy and Tradition, 1967; Preaching to the Exiles, 1971; Exodus and Sinai in History and Tradition, 1973; (with J. Baker) The Commentary of Rabbi David Kimḥi on Psalms 120–150, 1973; Commentary on Jeremiah 1–25, 1973; Commentary on Jeremiah 26–52, 1975; God and His People: covenant and theology in the Old Testament, 1986; The Pentateuch in the Twentieth Century: the legacy of Julius Wellhausen, 1997; (ed) A Century of Theological and Religious Studies in Britain, 2003; articles in biblical and Semitic jls. *Recreations:* music, the English countryside. *Address:* 39A Blenheim Drive, Oxford OX2 8DJ.

NICHOLSON, Frank; DL; Managing Director, Vaux Breweries Ltd, 1984–99; Director, Swallow Group plc (formerly Vaux Group), 1987–99; *b* 11 Feb. 1954; 5th *s* of late Douglas Nicholson, TD and Pauline Nicholson; *m* 1986, Lavinia Stourton; three *s*. *Educ:* Harrow Sch.; Magdalene Coll., Cambridge (MA). FRICS 1977. Assistant, Debenham, Tewson and Chinnocks, 1976–81; Tied Trade Dir, Vaux Breweries Ltd, 1981–84. Dir, Washington Develt Corp., 1985–88; Chairman: Sunderland Youth Enterprise Trust, 1986–; Wearside Opportunity, 1988–92; City of Sunderland Partnership, 1992–99. Dep. Chm., Sunderland Univ. (formerly Poly.), 1991–2002 (Hon. Fellow, 1991). Gov., Durham Sch., 1999–. DL 1995, High Sheriff, 1999–2000, Co. Durham. Prince of Wales Community Ambassador's Award, 1995. *Recreation:* country sports. *Address:* Cocken House, Chester-le-Street, Co. Durham DH3 4EN. *T:* (0191) 388 0505. *Clubs:* Royal Automobile; Northern Counties (Newcastle); Pallion Workingmen's (Co. Durham).

See also Sir P. D. Nicholson.

NICHOLSON, Gordon; *see* Nicholson, C. G. B.

NICHOLSON, Dr Howard, FRCP; Physician, University College Hospital, since 1948; Physician, Brompton Hospital, 1952–77, retired; Fellow of University College, London, since 1959; *b* 1 Feb. 1912; *s* of Frederick and Sara Nicholson; *m* 1941, Winifrid Madeline Piercy (*d* 2001). *Educ:* University Coll., London, and University Coll. Hospital. MB, BS, London, 1935; MD London 1938; MRCP 1938, FRCP 1949. House appointments and Registrarship, UCH, 1935–38; House Physician at Brompton Hosp., 1938. Served War, 1940–45, RAMC; Physician to Chest Surgical Team and Officer i/c Medical Div. (Lt-Col). Registrar, Brompton Hosp., and Chief Asst, Inst. of Diseases of Chest, 1945–48. Goulstonian Lecturer, RCP, 1950. *Publications:* sections on Diseases of Chest in The Practice of Medicine (ed J. S. Richardson), 1961, and in Progress in Clinical Medicine, 1961; articles in Thorax, Lancet, etc. *Recreations:* reading, going to the opera. *Address:* Chelwood, Laughton, Lewes, E Sussex BN8 6BE.

NICHOLSON, Jack; American film actor, director and producer; *b* 22 April 1937; *s* of John and Ethel May Nicholson; *m* 1961, Sandra Knight (marr. diss. 1966); one *d*. *Films* *include:* Cry-Baby Killer, 1958; Studs Lonigan, 1960; The Shooting (also produced); Easy Rider, 1969; Five Easy Pieces, 1970; The Last Detail, 1973; Chinatown, 1974; One Flew Over the Cuckoo's Nest, 1975 (Acad. Award for Best Actor, 1976); The Passenger, 1975; The Shining, 1980; The Postman Always Rings Twice, 1981; Reds, 1981; Terms of Endearment (Acad. Award for Best Supporting Actor), 1984; Prizzi's Honor, 1985; Heartburn, 1986; The Witches of Eastwick, 1986; Ironweed, 1987; Batman, 1988; The Two Jakes, 1991 (also dir.); A Few Good Men, 1992; Man Trouble, 1993; Hoffa, 1993; Wolf, 1994; The Crossing Guard, 1996; Mars Attacks!, 1997; Blood & Wine, 1997; As Good as it Gets (Acad. Award for Best Actor), 1998; The Pledge, 2001; About Schmidt, 2003; Anger Management, 2003; Something's Gotta Give, 2004; The Departed, 2006; The Bucket List, 2008. *Address:* c/o Bresler Kelly & Associates, 11500 West Olympic Boulevard, Suite 510, Los Angeles, CA 90064–1529, USA.

NICHOLSON, James Frederick; farmer; Member (UU), Northern Ireland, European Parliament, since 1994 (OUP, 1989–94); *b* 29 Jan. 1945; *s* of Thomas and Matilda Nicholson; *m* 1968, Elizabeth Gibson; six *s*. *Educ:* Aghavilly Primary Sch. Member: Armagh Dist Council, 1975–97 (Chm., 1994–95; Mayor of Armagh, March–June 1995); Southern Health and Social Services Bd, 1977–. Mem. (OU) Newry and Armagh, NI Assembly, 1982–86. Contested (OUP) Newry and Armagh, 1987. MP (OU) Newry and Armagh, 1983–85. *Address:* European Office, Cunningham House, 429 Hollywood Road, Belfast BT4 2LN. *T:* (028) 9076 5504; *e-mail:* j_nicholson@uup.org.

NICHOLSON, Rt Hon. Sir (James) Michael (Anthony), Kt 1988; PC 1995; a Lord Justice of Appeal, Supreme Court of Judicature, Northern Ireland, 1995–2007; *b* 4 Feb. 1933; *s* of late Cyril Nicholson, QC, DL and late Eleanor Nicholson (*née* Caffrey); *m* 1973, Augusta Mary Ada, *d* of late Thomas F. Doyle and of Mrs Elizabeth Doyle, Co. Cork; one *s* two *d*. *Educ:* Downside; Trinity College, Cambridge (MA). Called to the Bar of N Ireland, 1956; to English Bar, Gray's Inn, 1963 (Hon. Bencher, 1995); to Bar of Ireland, 1975; QC (NI), 1971; Bencher, Inn of Court of NI, 1978; Chm., Exec. Council of Inn of Court of NI and of Bar Council, 1983–85; High Court Judge, NI, 1986–95. Chm., Mental Health Review Tribunal (NI), 1973–76; Mem., Standing Adv. Commn for Human Rights (NI), 1976–78. High Sheriff, Co. Londonderry, 1972. President: Irish Cricket Union, 1978; NW ICU, 1986–93. *Recreations:* cricket, chess. *Address:* c/o Royal Courts of Justice, Chichester Street, Belfast, Northern Ireland BT1 3JF. *Club:* MCC.

NICHOLSON, Jeremy Mark; QC 2000; *b* 21 March 1955; *s* of Eric Day Nicholson and Joy Nicholson; *m* 1987, Elizabeth Brooke-Smith; two *s*. *Educ:* Rugby Sch.; Trinity Hall, Cambridge (MA). Called to the Bar, Middle Temple, 1977 (Harmsworth Schol.); in practice at the Bar, 1978–. *Recreations:* sailing, travelling, walking, pursuing superficial interests. *Address:* 4 Pump Court, Temple, EC4Y 7AN. *T:* (020) 7842 5555. *Club:* Royal Automobile.

NICHOLSON, Lindsay, (Mrs Mark Johansen), FRAS; Editorial Director, National Magazine Company, since 2006; *b* 7 Aug. 1956; *d* of late Anthony Cuthbertson-Nicholson and of Sheila (*née* Pigram); *m* 1st, 1981, John Merritt (*d* 1992); one *d* (and one *d* decd); 2nd, 2004, Mark Johansen. *Educ:* University Coll. London (BSc Hons Astronomy and Physics). Editl trng scheme, Mirror Gp Newspapers, 1978–80; worked on magazines: Woman's Own, 1981–83; Honey, 1983–84; Living, 1984–85; Best, 1987–89; Woman, 1992–95; Editor-in-Chief: Prima (incl. Launch of Prima Baby and Your Home), 1995–99; Good Housekeeping mag., 1999–2006. Chairman: BSME, 1997; Women in Journalism, 2002–04; Editl Trng Cttee, PPA, 2002–05; Press Complaints Comr, 2007–. Trustee, Home-Start, 2000–; Patron, The Way (Widowed and Young) Foundn, 2007–. FRAS 2003. Hon. Vis. Prof., City Univ., 2007–. Editor of Year, 1999, Chairman's Award, 2005, PPA; Mark Boxer Award, BSME, 2007. *Publication:* Living on the Seabed, 2005. *Recreations:* dance, riding, theatre. *Address:* National Magazine Company, 72 Broadwick Street, W1F 9EP. *T:* (020) 7439 5247. *Club:* Groucho.

NICHOLSON, Margaret Beda; *see* Yorke, M.

NICHOLSON, Maria Bernadette; *see* Maguire, M. B.

NICHOLSON, Martin Buchanan, CMG 1997; HM Diplomatic Service, retired; Associate Fellow, Royal Institute of International Affairs, 1999–2002; *b* 12 Aug. 1937; 2nd *s* of late Carroll and Nancy Nicholson; *m* 1964, Raili Tellervo Laaksonen; one *s* one *d*. *Educ:* Oundle Sch.; St Catharine's Coll., Cambridge (BA 1961; MA 1964); Moscow Univ. (Post-grad.). Entered Foreign Office, 1963; served Moscow, 1965–68 and 1971; Prague, 1972–75; Research Dept, FCO, 1975–78 and 1981–86; Mem., UK Delegn to MBFR, Vienna, 1978–81; Advr on Soviet, later Russian, Affairs, Cabinet Office (on secondment), 1987–94; Minister-Counsellor, Moscow, 1994–97. Res. Associate, IISS, 1998–99. *Publications:* Towards a Russia of the Regions, 1999; articles on Soviet and Russian affairs in The World Today and Internat. Affairs. *Recreations:* gardening, playing the flute, family history. *Address:* 13 Riverdale Gardens, Twickenham TW1 2BX. *T:* (020) 8892 8214.
See also Sir Robin Nicholson.

NICHOLSON, Rt Hon. Sir Michael; *see* Nicholson, Rt Hon. Sir J. M. A.

NICHOLSON, Michael Thomas, OBE 1992; reporter and presenter, Tonight programme, ITV, since 1998; *b* 9 Jan. 1937; *s* of Major Allan Nicholson and Doris Alice (*née* Reid); *m* 1968, Diana Margaret Slater; two *s*, and two adopted *d*. *Educ:* Leicester Univ. (BA). Joined ITN, 1963: News Editor, 1965–66; War Correspondent, 1968–94: Nigeria, Biafra, Beirut, Jordan, Cyprus, Congo, Israel, Indo-Pakistan, Rhodesia, Angola, Falklands, Gulf, Bosnia, Croatia; Southern Africa Corresp., 1977–81; Newscaster, 1982–86; Washington Corresp., Channel 4, 1989–90; Sen. Foreign Correspondent, ITN, 1991–98. Campaign Medals: Falklands War, 1982; Gulf War, 1991; Baghdad, Gulf War II, 2003. *Publications:* Partridge Kite, 1976; Red Joker, 1978; December Ultimatum, 1981; Pilgrims Rest, 1983; Across the Limpopo, 1986; A Measure of Danger, 1991; Natasha's Story, 1993 (filmed as Welcome to Sarajevo, 1996). *Recreations:* sailing, walking. *Address:* Grayswood, Surrey.

NICHOLSON, Sir Paul (Douglas), Kt 1993; Chairman, Vaux Group, 1976–99 (Managing Director, 1971–92); Lord-Lieutenant, County Durham, since 1997; *b* 7 March 1938; *s* of late Douglas Nicholson, TD and Pauline Nicholson; *m* 1970, Sarah, *y d* of Sir Edmund Bacon, Bt, KG, KBE, TD; one *d*. *Educ:* Harrow; Clare College, Cambridge (MA). FCA. Lieut, Coldstream Guards, 1956–58; joined Vaux Breweries, 1965. Chm., Northern Investors Co., 1984–89; Director: Tyne Tees Television, then Yorkshire-Tyne Tees Television Hldgs, 1981–97; Northern Development Co., 1986–2000; Northern Electric, 1990–97; Scottish Investment Trust plc, 1998–2005; Steelite International plc, 2000–02. Chm., Urban Develt Corp. for Tyne and Wear, 1987–98. Chm., N Region, CBI, 1977–79; Chm., N Regional Bd, British Technology Group, 1979–84. Chm., Brewers and Licensed Retailers Assoc. (formerly Brewers' Soc.), 1994–96; Pres., NE Chamber of Commerce, 1995–96. High Sheriff, Co. Durham, 1980–81; DL Co. Durham, 1980. *Publication:* Brewer At Bay (memoirs), 2003. *Recreations:* deerstalking, driving horses (Pres., Coaching Club, 1990–97). *Address:* Quarry Hill, Brancepeth, Durham DH7 8DW. *T:* (0191) 378 0275. *Clubs:* Boodle's, Pratt's; Northern Counties (Newcastle upon Tyne).
See also F. Nicholson.

NICHOLSON, Ralph Lambton Robb; Secretary, United Kingdom Atomic Energy Authority, 1984–86; *b* 26 Sept. 1924; *s* of Ralph Adam Nicholson and Kathleen Mary Nicholson (*née* Robb); *m* 1951, Mary Kennard; one *s* two *d*. *Educ:* Sherborne School; Cambridge Univ.; Imperial College, London (BSc; ACGI). FIChemE. Royal Engineers, 1943–47. Chemical engineer, Distillers Co., 1950–51; Wellcome Foundation, 1951–54; Fisons, 1954–58; planning and commercial manager, UKAEA, 1958–67; Dir, Min. of Technology Programmes Analysis Unit, 1967–71; Principal Programmes and Finance Officer, UKAEA, 1971–84. *Publications:* contribs to energy and management jls. *Recreations:* gardening, music, canals. *Address:* The Garth, Midgham, Reading, Berks RG7 5UJ. *T:* (0118) 971 2211.

NICHOLSON, Robin Alaster, CBE 1999; Director, Edward Cullinan Architects, since 1989 (Partner, 1979–89); *b* 27 July 1944; *s* of late Gerald Hugh Nicholson and Margaret Evelyn Nicholson (*née* Hanbury); *m* 1969, Fiona Mary Bird; three *s*. *Educ:* Eton Coll.; Magdalene Coll., Cambridge (MA); University Coll. London (MSc 1969). RIBA 1989. Architect: Evan Walker Associates, Toronto, 1966; James Stirling, Chartered Architects, 1969–76; Boza Lührs Muzard, Santiago, Chile, 1973; Tutor in Architecture: UCL, 1974–76; Poly of N London, 1976–79. Vis. Fellow, Univ. of Wales, 1984. Dir, RIBA Journals Ltd, 1993–97. Mem. Council, 1991–97, Vice Pres., 1992–94, RIBA; Chm., Construction Industry Council, 1998–2000; Mem. Bd, Movement for Innovation, 1998–2002; Mem., DETR, subseq. DTLR, then ODPM, Urban Sounding Bd, 2001–03; Comr, Commn for Architecture and the Built Envmt, 2002–; Dir, NHBC, 2007–. FRSA 1995. Hon. FIStructE 2002. *Recreations:* gardening, making things. *Address:* (office) 1 Baldwin Terrace, N1 7RU. *T:* (020) 7704 1975. *Club:* The Edge.

NICHOLSON, Sir Robin (Buchanan), Kt 1985; PhD; FRS 1978; FREng; *b* 12 Aug. 1934; *s* of late Carroll and Nancy Nicholson; *m* 1st, 1958, Elizabeth Mary Caffyn (*d* 1988); one *s* two *d*; 2nd, 1991, Yvonne, *d* of late Arthur and Gwendoline Appleby. *Educ:* Oundle Sch.; St Catharine's Coll., Cambridge (BA 1956; PhD 1959; MA 1960). FIMMM; MInstP; FREng (FEng 1980). University of Cambridge: Demonstrator in Metallurgy, 1960; Lectr in Metallurgy, 1964; Fellow of Christ's Coll., 1962–66, Hon. Fellow 1984; Prof. of Metallurgy, Univ. of Manchester, 1966. Inco Europe Ltd: Dir of Research Lab., 1972; Dir, 1975; Man. Dir, 1976–81; Co-Chm., Biogen NV, 1979–81. Chief Scientific Advr to Cabinet Office, 1983–85 (Central Policy Review Staff, 1981–83). Director: Pilkington Brothers, then Pilkington, plc, 1986–96; Rolls-Royce plc, 1986–2005; BP plc, 1987–2005. Chairman: CEST, 1987–90; ACOST, 1990–93. Member: SERC (formerly SRC), 1978–81; Council for Sci. and Technol., 1993–2000. Mem. Council: Royal Soc., 1983–85; Fellowship of Engrg, 1986–89; Exeter Univ., 2005–. Pres., Inst. of Materials, 1997–98. Foreign Associate, Nat. Acad. of Engrg, USA, 1983. CCMI. MAE. Hon. FIChemE; Hon. Fellow UMIST, 1988. Hon. DSc: Cranfield, 1983; Aston, 1983; Manchester, 1985; Hon. DMet Sheffield, 1984; Hon. DEng Birmingham, 1986; DUniv Open, 1987. Rosenhain Medallist, Inst. of Metals, 1971; Platinum Medal, Metals Soc., 1982. *Publications:* Precipitation Hardening (with A. Kelly), 1962; (jtly) Electron Microscopy of Thin Crystals, 1965; (ed and contrib. with A. Kelly) Strengthening Methods in Crystals, 1971; numerous papers to learned jls. *Recreations:* family life, gardening, music. *Club:* MCC.
See also M. B. Nicholson.

NICKELL, Prof. Stephen John, CBE 2007; FBA 1993; Warden, Nuffield College, Oxford, since 2006; *b* 25 April 1944; *s* of John Edward Hilary Nickell and Phyllis Nickell; *m* 1976, Susan Elizabeth (*née* Pegden); one *s* one *d*. *Educ:* Merchant Taylors' Sch.; Pembroke Coll., Cambridge (BA; Hon. Fellow 2006); LSE (MSc). Maths teacher, Hendon County Sch., 1965–68; London School of Economics: Lectr, 1970–77; Reader, 1977–79; Prof. of Economics, 1979–84; Dir, Inst. of Econs and Stats, Prof. of Econs, and Fellow of Nuffield Coll., Oxford Univ., 1984–98; Sch. Prof. of Econs, LSE, 1998–2005. Member: Academic Panel, HM Treasury, 1981–89; ESRC, 1990–94; Monetary Policy Cttee, Bank of England, 2000–06; Bd, UK Statistics Authy, 2008–; Chairman: Nat. Housing and Planning Advice Unit, 2007–; Adv. Cttee on Civil Costs, 2007–. President: Eur. Assoc. of Labour Economists, 1999–2002; REconS, 2001–04 (Mem. Council, 1984–94). Fellow, Econometric Soc., 1980. Hon. Member: Amer. Economic Assoc., 1997; Amer. Acad. Arts and Scis, 2006. Hon. Fellow, Nuffield Coll., Oxford, 2003. Hon. DSc Warwick, 2008. *Publications:* The Investment Decisions of Firms, 1978; (with R. Layard and R. Dornbusch) The Performance of the British Economy, 1988; (with R. Jackman and R. Layard) Unemployment, 1991; (with R. Jackman and R. Layard) The Unemployment Crisis, 1994; The Performance of Companies, 1995; articles in learned jls. *Recreations:* reading, cricket, cooking. *Address: e-mail:* steve.nickell@nuffield.ox.ac.uk.

NICKERSON, Rachel; *see* Campbell-Johnston, R.

NICKLAUS, Jack William; professional golfer, 1961–2000; *b* 21 Jan. 1940; *s* of Louis Charles Nicklaus and Helen (*née* Schoener); *m* 1960, Barbara Jean Bash; four *s* one *d*. *Educ:* Upper Arlington High Sch.; Ohio State Univ. Won US Amateur golf championship, 1959, 1961; became professional golfer, 1961; designs golf courses in USA, Europe, and Far East; Chm., Golden Bear Internat. Inc. Captained US team which won 25th Ryder Cup, 1983. *Major wins include:* US Open, 1962, 1967, 1972, 1980; US Masters, 1963, 1965, 1966, 1972, 1975, 1986; US Professional Golfers' Assoc., 1963, 1971, 1973, 1975, 1980; British Open, 1966, 1970, 1978, and many other championships in USA, Europe, Australia and Far East. Hon. Dr Athletic Arts Ohio State, 1972; Hon. LLD St Andrews, 1984. Presidential Medal of Freedom (USA), 2005. *Publications:* My 55 Ways to Lower Your Golf Score, 1962; Take a Tip from Me, 1964; The Greatest Game of All, 1969 (autobiog.); Lesson Tee, 1972; Golf My Way, 1974; The Best Way to Better Your Golf, vols 1–3, 1974; Jack Nicklaus' Playing Lessons, 1976; Total Golf Techniques, 1977; On and Off the Fairway, 1979 (autobiog.); The Full Swing, 1982; My Most Memorable Shots in the Majors, 1988; Jack Nicklaus: my story, 1997. *Address:* (office) 11780 US Highway #1, North Palm Beach, FL 33408, USA.

NICKLESS, Edmund Francis Paul, CSci, CGeol, FGS; Executive Secretary, Geological Society of London, since 1997; *b* 25 Jan. 1947; *e s* of Philip Wilfred Nickless and Gabrielle Frances Nickless (*née* Hughes); *m* 1970, Elisabeth Deborah Pickard; two *d*. *Educ:* Salvatorian Coll., Harrow; Queen Mary Coll., Univ. of London (BSc). FGS 1971; CGeol 1990; EurGeol 2002; CSci 2004. Various posts with British Geol Survey, London and Edinburgh, 1968–83; Sec., Earth Scis Directorate, NERC, Swindon, 1983–89; Envmtl Advr, Sci. and Technol. Secretariat, Cabinet Office, 1989–91; Asst Dir, British Geol Survey, 1991–97. FRSA 1998. *Publications:* various papers on geology in learned jls and official pubns of British Geol Survey. *Recreations:* listening to music, gardening, walking. *Address:* Ringrose House, Main Street, Belton-in-Rutland LE15 9LB. *T:* (01572) 717324; Geological Society of London, Burlington House, Piccadilly, W1J 0BG. *Club:* Athenæum.

NICKLIN, Susanna; Director of Literature, British Council, since 2005; *b* 26 June 1964; *d* of Philip and Hilary Nicklin; *m* 1997, Paul Marsh; one *s* one *d*. *Educ:* Exeter Coll., Oxford (MA). Literary Agent, 1987–2002; Dir, English PEN, 2002–05. FRSA. *Recreations:* singing with the Bach choir, travelling, reading, family meals. *Address:* c/o British Council, 10 Spring Gardens, SW1A 2BN. *T:* (020) 7389 3169, *Fax:* (020) 7389 3175; *e-mail:* susanna.nicklin@britishcouncil.org. *Clubs:* Athenæum, Royal Automobile.

NICKOLS, Herbert Arthur; Headmaster, Westonbirt School, Tetbury, Gloucestershire, 1981–86; *b* 17 Jan. 1926; *s* of Herbert and Henrietta Elizabeth Nickols; *m* 1953, Joyce Peake; two *s* one *d*. *Educ:* Imperial Coll., Univ. of London (BSc). ACGI. Res. Demonstrator, Imperial Coll., 1947–49; Housemaster, Sen. Science Master and later Dep. Headmaster, St Edmund's Sch., Canterbury, Kent, 1949–81. *Recreations:* music, travel, cricket. *Address:* 39 Carlton Leas, The Leas, Folkestone, Kent CT20 2DJ. *T:* (01303) 254749.

NICKSON, family name of **Baron Nickson**.

NICKSON, Baron *cr* 1994 (Life Peer), of Renagour in the District of Stirling; **David Wigley Nickson,** KBE 1987 (CBE 1981); FRSE; Vice Lord-Lieutenant of Stirling and Falkirk, 1997–2005; *b* 27 Nov. 1929; *s* of late Geoffrey Wigley Nickson and Janet Mary Nickson; *m* 1952, Helen Louise Cockcraft; three *d*. *Educ:* Eton; RMA, Sandhurst. Commnd Coldstream Guards, 1949–54. Joined Wm Collins, 1954; Dir, 1961–85; Jt Man. Dir, 1967; Vice Chm., 1976–83; Gp Man. Dir, 1979–82; Chm., Pan Books, 1982. Director: Scottish United Investors plc, 1970–83; General Accident plc, 1971–98 (Dep. Chm., 1993–98); Scottish & Newcastle (formerly Scottish & Newcastle Breweries) plc, 1981–95 (Dep. Chm., 1982–83; Chm., 1983–89); Clydesdale Bank, 1981–89 (Dep. Chm., 1990–91; Chm., 1991–98); Radio Clyde PLC, 1982–85; Edinburgh Investment Trust plc, 1983–94; Hambro's PLC, 1989–98; National Australia Bank Ltd, 1991–96. Chm., Top Salaries, then Sen. Salaries, Rev. Body, 1989–95; Chairman: SDA, 1989–90, Scottish Enterprise, 1990–93; CBI in Scotland, 1979–81; Pres., CBI, 1986–88 (Dep. Pres., 1985–86). Member: Scottish Indust. Develt Adv. Bd, 1975–80; Scottish Econ. Council, 1980–94; NEDC, 1985–88; Scottish Cttee, Design Council, 1978–81; Nat. Trng Task Force, 1989–91. Chairman: Countryside Commn for Scotland, 1983–85; Scottish Adv. Cttee, ICRF, 1994–2001; Atlantic Salmon Trust, 1989–96 (Mem., Council of Management, 1982–; Vice-Pres., 1996–); Conon Dist Salmon Fishery Bd, 1994–2005; Sec. of State for Scotland's Atlantic Salmon Task Force, 1996; Pres., Assoc. of Scottish Dist Salmon Fishery Bds, 1996– (Vice Chm., 1989–92); Dir, Countryside Alliance, 1998–2000. Chm., Loch Lomond Shores Trust, 1999–2002. Trustee: Game Conservancy, 1988–91; Prince's Youth Business Trust, 1987–90; Princess Royal's Trust for Carers, 1990–94. Chancellor, Glasgow Caledonian Univ., 1993–2002. Capt., Queen's Body Guard for Scotland, Royal Co. of Archers. Freeman, City of London, 1999; Hon. Freeman, Fishmongers' Co., 1999. DL Stirling and Falkirk, 1982. CCMI (CBIM 1980); FRSE 1987. Hon. Fellow, Paisley Coll., subseq. Univ. of Paisley, 1992. DUniv Stirling, 1986; Hon. DBA Napier Polytechnic, 1990; DUniv Glasgow Caledonian, 1993. *Recreations:* fishing, shooting, bird watching, the countryside. *Address:* The River House, Doune, Perthshire FK16 6DA. *T:* (01786) 841614. *Clubs:* Boodle's, Flyfishers'.

NICOL, family name of **Baroness Nicol**.

NICOL, Baroness *cr* 1982 (Life Peer), of Newnham in the County of Cambridgeshire; **Olive Mary Wendy Nicol;** *b* 21 March 1923; *d* of James and Harriet Rowe-Hunter; *m* 1947, Alexander Douglas Ian Nicol (CBE 1985); two *s* one *d*. Civil Service, 1943–48. Opposition Whip, 1983–87, Opposition Dep. Chief Whip, 1987–89, Dep. Speaker, 1995–2002, H of L; Member: H of L Science and Technol. Select Cttee, 1990–93; Envmt and Social Affairs sub-cttee, European Communities Cttee, 1993–95; Sustainable Develt Select Cttee, 1994–95; Select Cttee on Animals in Scientific Procedures, 2001–02; Member: Ecclesiastical Cttee, 1989–95; Sci. and Technol. Subcttee on Disposal of Nuclear Waste, 1998–99; Bd Mem., Parly OST, 1998–99. Trustee, Cambridge United Charities, 1967–86; Director, Cambridge and District Co-operative Soc., 1975–81, Pres. 1981–85; Member: Supplementary Benefits Tribunal, 1976–78; Cambridge City Council, 1972–82; Assoc. of District Councils, Cambridge Branch, 1974–76 and 1980–82; various school Governing Bodies, 1974–80; Council, Granta Housing Soc., 1975–; Careers Service Consultative Group, 1978–81. JP Cambridge City, 1972–86. *Recreations:* reading, walking. *Address:* c/o House of Lords, SW1A 0PW.

NICOL, Andrew George Lindsay; QC 1995; a Recorder, since 2000; a Deputy High Court Judge, since 2003; *b* 9 May 1951; *s* of late Duncan Rennie Nicol and Margaret (*née* Mason); *m* 2005, Camilla Palmer; two *s*. *Educ:* Selwyn Coll., Cambridge (BA, LLB); Harvard Law Sch. (LLM). Harkness Fellow, 1973–75; Special Assistant: to Dir of Housing and Community Develt, California, 1975–76; Allen Allen and Hemsley, solicitors, Sydney, NSW, 1976–77; Lectr in Law, LSE, 1977–87; called to the Bar, Middle Temple, 1978, Bencher, 2004; barrister, 1979–; an Asst Recorder, 1998–2000. Chm., Immigration Law Practitioners' Assoc., 1997–2000. *Publications:* (with G. Robertson) Media Law, 1984, rev. edn 2007; (with A. Dummett) Subjects, Citizens, Aliens and Others, 1990; (with G. Millar and A. Sharland) Media Law and Human Rights, 2001. *Recreations:* family, sailing, walking. *Address:* Doughty Street Chambers, 10 Doughty Street, WC1N 2PL. *T:* (020) 7404 1313, *Fax:* (020) 7404 2283.

NICOL, (Andrew) William; JP; BSc; FICE, FIMechE, FIET; Chairman, 1987–93, and Chief Executive, 1990–93, South Western Electricity plc; *b* 29 April 1933; *s* of Arthur Edward Nicol and Ethel Isabel Gladstone Nicol (*née* Fairley); *m* 1960, Jane Gillian Margaret Mann; one *s*. *Educ:* King's College School, Wimbledon; Durham Univ. (BSc). W. S. Atkins & Partners, 1960–67; Electricity Council, 1967–69; London Electricity Board, 1969–81; Dep. Chm., SE Electricity Board, 1981–87. Chairman: Trustees, NICEIC Pension Fund, 1986–93; South Western Enterprises, 1992–93. JP Surrey 1976. *Recreation:* Honourable Artillery Company. *Club:* Caledonian.

NICOL, Angus Sebastian Torquil Eyers; barrister; a Recorder of the Crown Court, 1982–98; *b* 11 April 1933; *s* of late Henry James Nicol and Phyllis Mary Eyers; *m* 1968, Eleanor Denise Brodrick; two *d*. *Educ:* RNC, Dartmouth. Served RN, 1947–56. Called to the Bar, Middle Temple, 1963. A Chairman: Disciplinary Cttee, Potato Marketing Bd, 1988–96; VAT and Duties (formerly VAT) Tribunal, 1988–2005; Adjudicator and Special Adjudicator, Immigration Appellate Authy, 1998–2002; Mem., Appeals Cttee, Taxation Disciplinary Bd, 2006–. Founder Vice-Chm. and Mem. Council, Monday Club, 1961–68. Lectr in Gaelic, Central London Adult Educn Inst., 1983–96; Sen. Steward, Argyllshire Gathering, 1983, 1998; Dir, 1981–, and Jt Sec., 1984–, Highland Soc. of London; Conductor, London Gaelic Choir, 1985–91; Chieftain of Clan MacNicol and Comr for all Territories of GB south of River Tweed, 1988–; President: Scottish Piping Soc. of London, 2006–; Coisir Lumainn (London Gaelic Choir), 2007–. Piping Correspondent, The Times, 1979–. FSA (Scot.). *Publications:* Gaelic poems and short stories in Gairm, etc. *Recreations:* music, Gaelic language and literature, shooting, fishing, sailing, gastronomy. *Address:* 5 Paper Buildings, Temple, EC4Y 7HB. *T:* (020) 7612 3200.

NICOL, Dr Richard Charles, FREng, FIET; Director and Chief Executive Officer, Fynntek Ltd, research consulting, since 2001; Director, Cambridge-MIT Institute, Adastral Park, 2003–06; *b* 14 July 1948; *s* of George Nicol and Alice (*née* Ardley); *m* 1974, Rosemary Jane Greaves; one *s* one *d*. *Educ:* University Coll. London (BSc Eng; PhD 1976). FIET (FIEE 1994). Joined Post Office Res., 1970; British Telecommunications, 1976–88; Manager, Univ. Res. Prog., 1988–92; BT Laboratories, then BTexact Technologies: Divl Manager, Visual Telecomms, 1992–95; Hd, Centre for Human Communications, 1995–98; Hd of Res., 1998–2001. Dir, Suffolk Develt Agency, 2000–; Mem. Bd, Suffolk Learning and Skills Council, 2001–08. Vice-Chm. Corp., Suffolk Coll., 1995–; Mem. Council, Univ. of Essex, 2006–. FREng 2000. *Recreations:* sailing, football (Ipswich Town). *Club:* Ipswich and Suffolk.

NICOL, William; *see* Nicol, A. W.

NICOLI, Eric Luciano, CBE 2006; Executive Chairman, 1999–2007, and Chief Executive Officer, 2007, EMI Group plc; Chairman, Tussauds Group, 2001–07 (Director, 1999–2007); *b* 5 Aug. 1950; *s* of Virgilio and Ida Nicoli; *m* 1977, Rosalind West (marr. diss. 2005); one *s* one *d*; *m* 2006, Lucy Caldwell; two *d*. *Educ:* Diss Grammar Sch.; King's College London (BSc Hons 1st class Physics). Marketing, Rowntree Mackintosh, 1972–80; United Biscuits: Marketing, 1980–83; Business Planning, 1984; Managing Dir, Frozen Food Div., 1985, Biscuit and Confectionery Div., 1986–88; Chief Exec., Europe, 1989–90; Gp Chief Exec., 1991–99; Chm., HMV Gp plc, 2001–04 (Dir, 2000–04); Dir, Thorn EMI plc, then EMI Gp plc, 1993–2007; Chm., Vue Entertainment Ltd, 2006–. Dep. Chm., BITC, 1991–2003. Chm., Per Cent Club, 1995–2007. Trustee, Comic Relief, 1999–2004; Chm., EMI Music Sound Foundn, 2003– (Trustee, 2001). *Recreations:* music, sport, food.

NICOLL, Alison Jane; *see* Watt, A. J.

NICOLL, Prof. Angus Gordon, CBE 2002; FRCP, FRCPCH, FFPH; Consultant, Communicable Disease Surveillance Centre, Health Protection Agency Centre for Infections, since 1991 (Director, 2000–05); on secondment as National Expert, European Centre for Disease Prevention and Control, 2005–Aug. 2009; *b* 5 Aug. 1950; *s* of James Nicoll and Mary Laugharne; *m* 1982, Mary Grizel Braham; one *s* two *d*. *Educ:* Trinity Coll., Cambridge (MA; BChir 1976, MB 1977); Middlesex Hosp., LSHTM (MSc Epidemiol. 1985). Paediatric trng, London, Scotland and Nottingham; trng in public health, London and Africa; Sen. Lectr in HIV Epidemiol., LSHTM and in E Africa, 1987–91. Hon. Sen. Lectr, Inst. of Child Health, London, 1996–; Hon. Prof., LSHTM, 2001–. *Publication:* (ed jtly) Manual of Childhood Infections, 1987, 2001. *Recreations:* family, running and other outdoor pursuits, theatre, social history. *Address:* (until Aug. 2009) European Centre for Disease Prevention and Control, 17183 Stockholm, Sweden. *T:* (8) 58601213. *Clubs:* John Snow Society; St Albans Striders.

NICOLL, Douglas Robertson, CB 1980; retired; *b* 12 May 1920; *s* of James George Nicoll and Mabel Nicoll (*née* Styles); *m* 1st, 1949, Winifred Campion (*d* 1987); two *s*; 2nd, 1992, Mrs Cathryn Sansom. *Educ:* Merchant Taylors' School; St John's College, Oxford (MA 1946). FO (Govt Code & Cipher Sch., Bletchley Pk, deciphering German Enigma machine), 1941–45; FCO (GCHQ), 1946–80; Joint Services' Staff College, 1953; Under Secretary, 1977–80; Cabinet Office, 1980–81. *Publications:* contrib. to DNB and Oxford DNB. *Recreations:* chess, bridge, National Hunt racing, politics. *Address:* c/o National Westminster Bank, 31 The Promenade, Cheltenham, Glos GL50 1LH. *Club:* Travellers.

NICOLL, Sir William, KCMG 1992 (CMG 1974); a Director General, Council of European Communities, 1982–91; *b* 28 June 1927; *s* of Ralph Nicoll and Christina Mowbray Nicoll (*née* Melville); *m* 1954, Helen Morison Martin; two *d*. *Educ:* Morgan Acad., Dundee; St Andrews Univ. Entered BoT, 1949; British Trade Comr, India, 1955–59; Private Sec. to Pres. of BoT, 1964–67; Commercial Inspector, FCO, 1967–69; DTI, 1969–72; Office of UK Perm. Rep. to European Communities, 1972–75; Under Sec., Dept of Prices and Consumer Protection, 1975–77; Dep. UK Rep. to EEC, 1977–82. Fulbright Fellow, George Mason Univ., Va, USA, 1991–92. Editor, European Business Jl, 1993–2002. Hon. LLD Dundee, 1983. *Publications:* (ed and contrib.) Competition Policy Enquiry, 1988; (with T. C. Salmon) Understanding the European Communities, 1990; (with T. C. Salmon) Understanding the New European Community, 1993; (ed jtly) Perspectives on European Business, 1995, 2nd edn 1998; (ed jtly) Europe 2000, 1996; Building European Union, 1997; Europe Beyond 2000, 1998; (with T. C. Salmon) Understanding European Union, 2000, Polish edn 2003; contributed to: Government and Industry, ed W. Rodgers, 1986; Britain and Europe, 1988; The State of the EC, ed G. Rosendahl, 1993; Margaret Thatcher, Prime Minister Indomitable, ed W. Thompson, 1994; Maastricht and Beyond, ed A. N. Duff, 1994; The Council of the EU, ed M. Westlake, 1996, 3rd edn 2006; Britain, the Commonwealth and Europe, ed A. May, 2001; The EU Today, 2001; contribs to various jls on European subjects and to local hist. studies. *Address:* Outback, Nackington Road, Canterbury, Kent CT4 7AX. *T:* (01227) 456495.

NICOLLE, Frederick Villeneuve, FRCSCan; Consultant Plastic Surgeon, Hammersmith Hospital, since 1970; Senior Lecturer, University of London and Royal Postgraduate Medical School, since 1970; *b* 11 March 1931; *s* of Arthur Nicolle and Alice Nicolle (*née* Cobbold); *m* 1957, Helia Immaculata Stuart-Walker; one *s* two *d*. *Educ:* Eton; Trinity Coll., Cambridge (BA; MB BChir 1956; MChir 1970). FRCSCan 1963. McLaughlin Travelling Fellow, Canada, 1964; Consultant Plastic Surgeon, Montreal Gen. Hosp. and Montreal Children's Hosp., 1964–69; Lectr, McGill Univ., 1964–69; returned to UK, 1970; in private practice in aesthetic and reconstructive plastic surgery, 1970–. Vis. Prof. in Plastic Surgery, China, Syria, S America, SA, Australia, NZ and guest lectr in many countries. President: Brit. Assoc. Aesthetic Plastic Surgery, 1984–86 (Mem., 1980–); Chelsea Clinical Soc., 1986; Internat. Alpine Surgical Soc., 1996, 1997; Treas., Internat. Soc. Aesthetic Plastic Surgery, 1986–94 (Trustee, 1992–94); Member: Brit. Assoc. Plastic Surgery, 1966; Internat. Soc. Plastic Surgery, 1971; Amer. Soc. Aesthetic Plastic Surgery, 1982. *Publications:* The Care of the Rheumatoid Hand, 1975; Aesthetic Rhinoplasty, 1996; chaps in numerous text books of plastic and reconstructive surgery; contrib. British Jl Plastic Surgery and Jl Aesthetic Surgery. *Recreations:* painting, ski-ing, shooting, fishing, tennis. *Address:* Stud House, Chilton Foliat, Hungerford, Berks RG17 0TE. *T:* (01488) 680930. *Club:* White's.

NICOLLE, Stéphanie Claire; QC (Jersey) 1995; HM Solicitor General for Jersey, 1994–2008; *b* 11 March 1948; *d* of Walter Arthur Nicolle and Madeleine Claire Nicolle (*née* Vitel). *Educ:* Convent of the Faithful Companions of Jesus, Jersey; St Aidan's Coll., Univ. of Durham. Called to the Bar, Gray's Inn, 1976; called to the Jersey Bar, 1978; Crown Advocate, 1986–94. *Publications:* (with P. Matthews) The Jersey Law of Property, 1991; The Origin and Development of Jersey Law, 1998.

NICOLSON, family name of **Baron Carnock**.

NICOLSON, Roy Macdonald; Chief Executive, Scottish Amicable Life plc, 1997–2000; *b* 12 June 1944; *s* of Alan Neil Nicolson and Mary Nicolson; *m* 1972, Jennifer Margaret Miller; one *s* one *d*. *Educ:* Paisley Grammar School. FFA. Joined Scottish Amicable, 1960; Asst London Secretary, 1971; Asst Actuary, 1973; Pensions Manager (Operations), 1976; Asst Gen. Manager (Pensions), 1982; Gen. Manager (Systems), 1985; Dep. Chief Gen. Manager, then Man. Dir, 1990. Director: J. Rothschild Assurance Hldgs, 1991–99; St James's Place Capital, 1997–2000; Prudential Assurance Co., 1997–2000; Nat. Australia WM (Europe), 2001–; Nat. Australia WM Hldgs, 2003–; Nat. Australia Gp (Europe), 2004–; Chairman: Advice First Ltd, 2002–; BDO Stoy Hayward Wealth Mgt, 2004–. *Recreations:* golf, bridge. *Address:* Ardgarten, Doune Road, Dunblane, Perthshire FK15 9HR. *T:* (01786) 823849.

NIEDUSZYŃSKI, Anthony John; Secretary to Monopolies and Mergers Commission, 1993–96; *b* 7 Jan. 1939; *er s* of Tadeusz Adolf Antoni Nieduszyński, LLD and Madaleine Gladys Lilian (*née* Huggler); *m* 1980, Frances, *yr d* of Wing Comdr Max Oxford, OBE; one *d*. *Educ:* St Paul's School (Foundation Scholar); Merton College, Oxford (Postmaster; 1st cl. Hon. Mods 1959; 1st cl. Lit Hum 1961; MA). Board of Trade, 1964; Private Sec. to Pres. of BoT, 1967–68; Principal Private Sec. to Minister for Trade and Consumer Affairs, 1972–74 and to Sec. of State for Trade, 1974; Asst Sec., Dept of Prices and Consumer Protection, 1974, Dept of Industry, 1977, Home Office, 1982; Under Sec., DTI, 1985–93; Head: of Radiocommunications Div., 1985; of Air Div., 1988; of Business Task Forces Div. 2, 1990; of Aerospace Div., 1992. *Recreations:* fell walking, growing olives and vines in Italy, language, opera. *Address:* Clarendon House, 33 Strand, Topsham, Exeter, Devon EX3 0AY.

NIELSEN, Aksel Christopher W.; *see* Wiin-Nielsen.

NIELSEN, Hon. Erik H., DFC; PC (Can.) 1984; QC (Can.) 1962; Principal, Solar Electric Engineering Distributors, Canada, since 1992; President: Solar Electric Engineering Hawaii Inc., since 1993; Electricycle Inc., since 1994; *b* 24 Feb. 1924; *m* 1st, Pamela Hall (*d* 1969); three *c*; 2nd, 1983, Shelley Coxford. *Educ:* Dalhousie Univ. (LLB). Royal Canadian Air Force, 1942–51; flew Lancaster bombers, War of 1939–45. Called to the Bar of Nova Scotia, 1951; legal practice in Whitehorse, Yukon, 1952–. MP (PC) Yukon, 1957–87; Minister of Public Works, 1979–80; Dep. Opposition House Leader, Opposition House Leader, Leader of the Opposition, and Dep. Leader of the Opposition, 1980–84; Dep. Leader, Progressive Cons. Party, 1983; Dep. Prime Minister and Pres. of the Queen's Privy Council for Canada, 1984–85; Minister of Nat. Defence, 1985–86. Pres., Canadian Transport Commn, 1987; Chm., Nat. Transportation Agency of Canada, 1987–92. Dep. House Leader, 1980–81; Opposition appts, 1981–83. Caucus Chm., Cttee on Govt Planning and Orgn, 1983–84. Chm., Ministerial Task Force on Program Review (report published, 1985). Member: Canadian Bar Assoc; Yukon Law Soc.; NS Barristers' Soc.; Hon. Mem., Whitehorse Chamber of Commerce; Hon. Life Mem., Yukon Chamber of Mines, 1987. Hon. Fellow, Canadian Sch. of Mgt, 1984. Hon. Life Mem., Royal Canadian Mounted Police Veterans' Assoc., 1990. *Publication:* The House is Not a Home, 1989. *Address:* MSPO PO Box 31024, Whitehorse, YT Y1A 5P7, Canada.

NIELSON, Poul; Member, European Commission, 1999–2004; *b* 11 April 1943; *s* of Svend and Esther Nielson; *m* 1967, Anne-Marie Jørgensen; one *s* two *d*. *Educ:* Århus Univ. (Masters degree in Political Sci. 1972). Nat. Chm., Social Democratic Student Movt, 1966–67; Chm., Foreign Affairs Cttee, SDP, 1974–79. MP (SDP) Denmark, 1971–73, 1977–84, 1986–99; Minister of Energy, 1979–82; Minister for Develt Co-operation, 1994–99. Head of Section, Min. of Foreign Affairs, 1974–79, 1984–85; Cons. in Public Mgt, Danish Admin. Sch., 1985–86; Investment Cons., Danish Wage Earner Pensions Fund, 1985–88; Man. Dir, LD Energi A/S, 1988–94; Mem., Bd of Dirs, Denerco, Danop, Vestas and other cos, 1986–94. Polio Eradication Champion Award, Rotary Internat., 1999. *Publications:* Power Play and Security, 1968; The Company Act and the Wage Earners, 1974; Politicians and Civil Servants, 1987. *Recreations:* photography, literature, music, gardening.

NIEMEYER, Oscar; architect; *b* Rio de Janeiro, 15 Dec. 1907; *s* of Oscar Niemeyer Soares; *m* Anita Niemeyer; one *d*. *Educ:* Escola Nacional de Beles Artes, Univ. of Brazil. Joined office of Lúcio Costa, 1935; worked on Min. of Education and Health Building, Rio de Janeiro, Brazilian Pavilion, NY World Fair, etc., 1936–41. Has designed more than 500 buildings; major projects include: Pamphulha, Belo Horizonte, 1941–43; also Quitandinha, Petrópolis; Exhibition Hall, São Paulo, 1953; Brasilia (Dir of Architecture), 1957–60; French Communist Party HQ, Paris, 1971; Mus. of Contemporary Art, Niteroi, Brazil, 1996; summer pavilion, Serpentine Gall., 2003. Brazilian Rep., UN Bd of Design Consultants, 1947. Lenin Peace Prize, 1963; Prix Internat. de l'Architecture Aujourd'hui, 1966; Royal Gold Medal for Architecture, RIBA, 1998; Praemium Imperiale, Japan Art Assoc., 2004. *Publication:* The Curves of Time: the memoirs of Oscar Niemeyer, 2001. *Address:* 3940 Avenida Atlântica, CEP 22070–002, Rio de Janeiro, Brazil.

NIENOW, Prof. Alvin William, FREng; Professor of Biochemical Engineering, University of Birmingham, 1989–2004, now Emeritus; *b* 19 June 1937; *o s* of late Alvin William Nienow and Mary May Nienow (*née* Hawthorn); *m* 1959, Helen Mary Sparkes; two *s* one *d*. *Educ:* St Clement Danes Grammar Sch.; University Coll. London (BSc Eng, 1st Cl. Hons; PhD; DSc Eng). FIChemE; CEng, FREng (FEng 1985); CSci 2003. Industry, 1958–61; Lectr and Sen. Lectr, 1963–80, Hon. Res. Fellow, 1980–, Dept of Chem. and Biochem. Engineering, UCL; University of Birmingham: Prof. of Chem. Engineering, 1980–89; Dir, SERC, later BBSRC, Centre for Biochem. Engrg, 1989–2000. Vis. Prof., Fellow and Lectr, China and Japan; Eminent Speaker, Chemical Coll., IEAust, 1999. Member: AFRC, 1987–90; Biotechnol. Directorate, SERC, 1990–93; Engrg Bd, SERC, then EPSRC, 1991–94; Planning and Resources Bd, BBSRC, 1994–96; Council, IChemE, 1984–89; Scientific Adv. Cttee, EFCE, 1987–94; Standing Cttee for Engrg, Royal Acad. of Engrg, 1996–98; Internat. Adv. Bd, Inst. of Chemical Process Fundamentals, Acad. of Scis, Czech Republic, 1996–; numerous other scientific and engrg bodies. Consultant: BHR Gp Fluid Mixing Processes, 1985–; Rhône-Poulenc Conseil Technologique, 1988–2000 (Pres., 1998–2000). Mem., Governing Body, Silsoe Res. Inst., 1996–98. Hon. Mem., Czech Soc. of Chemical Engrg, 2008. Ed. (Europe and Africa), Jl Chem. Engrg, Japan, 2001–05. Moulton Medal, 1984, Donald Medal, 2000, IChemE; Jan E. Purkyne Medal, Czech Acad. of Science, 1993; Lifetime Contribution Award, Eur. Fedn of Chemical Engrg Wkg Party on Mixing, 2003. *Publications:* (jtly) Mixing in the Process Industries, 1985, 2nd edn revised 1997; (ed) 3rd International Conference on Bioreactor and Bioprocess Fluid Dynamics, 1993, 4th International Conference, 1997; numerous papers on mixing, fluidisation and biochem. engrg in learned jls. *Recreations:* sport, travel, dancing, music, real ale. *Address:* Department of Chemical Engineering, University of Birmingham, Edgbaston, Birmingham B15 2TT. *T:* (0121) 414 5325. *Clubs:* Athenæum, MCC; Edgbaston Priory, Reading Cricket.

NIGHTINGALE, Anne, MBE 2000; presenter, BBC Radio 1, since 1970; *b* Osterley, W London; one *s* one *d*. *Educ:* Lady Eleanor Holles Sch., Hampton; Poly. of Central London (Dip. Journalism). Columnist, Cosmopolitan, 1975–78; Presenter, The Old Grey Whistle Test, BBC TV, 1978–82; regular broadcaster on BBC Radio 4; regular appearances as DJ at major music festivals, UK, Europe, USA and Asia. Music albums: Annie on One, 1995; y4K Presents: Annie Nightingale, 2007. *Publications:* How to Form a Beat Group, 1965; Chase the Fade (autobiog.), 1982; Wicked Speed (autobiog.), 2000; contrib. The Guardian, Punch, Radio Times, etc. *Recreation:* studying architecture and tall buildings. *Address:* BBC Radio 1, W1W 6AJ; *e-mail:* annienightingale@gmail.com.

NIGHTINGALE, Benedict; *see* Nightingale, W. B. H.

NIGHTINGALE, Caroline Ann; *see* Slocock, C. A.

NIGHTINGALE, Sir Charles (Manners Gamaliel), 17th Bt *cr* 1628; Grade 7, Department of Health, 1996–2007; *b* 21 Feb. 1947; *s* of Sir Charles Athelstan Nightingale, 16th Bt, and Evelyn Nadine Frances (*d* 1995), *d* of late Charles Arthur Diggens; *S* father, 1977. *Educ:* St Paul's School. BA Hons Open Univ., 1990. Entered DHSS as Executive Officer, 1969; Higher Executive Officer, 1977; Sen. Exec. Officer, DoH, 1989. *Heir:* *cousin* Edward Lacy George Nightingale, *b* 11 May 1938. *Address:* 16 Unity Grove, Harrogate HG1 2AQ.

NIGHTINGALE, Mary; Newscaster, ITV Evening News, since 2001; *b* 26 May 1963; *d* of David Trewyn Nightingale and Jennifer Constance Mary Nightingale (*née* Tetley); *m* 2000, Paul Fenwick; one *s* one *d*. *Educ:* Oakdene Sch., Beaconsfield; St Margaret Sch., Exeter; King Edward VI Sch., Totnes; Bedford Coll., London (BA Hons English 1985). Presenter: World Business Satellite, TV Tokyo, 1990–94; World Business Report, BBC World Service TV, 1991–93; London Tonight and London Today, ITV, 1993–99; Reuters Financial Television, 1994; BBC Radio Five Live, 1994–97; Rugby World Cup, ITV, 1995; Newscaster, ITN World News, 1995; Presenter: Ski Sunday, BBC, 1996; Holiday, BBC, 1997–98; Wish You Were Here?, ITV, 1999–2001. Newscaster of the Year, TRIC, 2002, 2004. *Recreations:* travel, family. *Address:* c/o ITN, 200 Gray's Inn Road, WC1X 8XZ.

NIGHTINGALE, Neil; Head, BBC Natural History Unit, since 2003; *b* 6 Feb. 1960; *s* of Ivor and Ann Nightingale; *m*. *Educ:* Wadham Coll., Oxford (BA (Zool.) 1982). Freelance journalist; BBC: researcher; producer, 1989–95, credits include: The Natural World; Wildlife on One; Lost Worlds Vanished Lives; The Private Life of Plants; The Restless Year; Editor: The Natural World, 1995–2001; The Wildlife Specials, 1997–2001; Executive Producer, 2001–03: Wild Africa; Wild Down Under; Congo; Wild New World; Wild Battlefields. *Publications:* New Guinea: an island apart, 1992; Wild Down Under, 2003. *Recreations:* sailing, diving, wildlife, travel. *Address:* BBC Natural History Unit, Whiteladies Road, Bristol BS8 2LR; *e-mail:* neil.nightingale@bbc.co.uk.

NIGHTINGALE, Nicholas John; Secretary General, World Alliance of YMCAs, 1999–2002; *b* 29 Aug. 1942; *s* of late Christopher, (Toby), and of Muriel, (Buster), Nightingale; *m* 1968, Sue Lyth (Rev. Dr Sue Nightingale); one *s* two *d* (and one *d* decd). *Educ:* Brighton, Hove and Sussex GS; Trinity Coll., Dublin (BA, LLB 1964); Harvard Business Sch. (AMP 1983). Qualified as solicitor, 1968; Solicitor, Slaughter & May, 1970–74; Partner, Patterson Glenton & Stracey, 1974; Solicitor and Co. Sec., Rowntree Mackintosh, 1975–85; Exec. Dir, Rowntree plc, 1985–89; Co. Sec., Tate & Lyle, 1989–93; Nat. Sec., YMCA England (formerly Nat. Council, YMCAs), 1993–98. Director: Tom Smith Crackers, 1983–85; Original Cookie Co., 1985–89; Cookie Jar, 1989–98; Ellis Patents, 1990–. Chm., Service 9, Bristol Council of Social Service, 1966–70; Treas., YMCA Metropolitan Reg., 1992–93. Vice Chm., Yorks Rural Community Council, 1985–89. Member: Ecumenical Advocacy Cttee, Ecumenical Advocacy Alliance, 2000–02; Council, Assoc. for Prevention of Torture, 2001–. Mem., York Merchant Adventurers, 1986–. Co-ordinator: York Rethink Carers Gp, 2002–; Yorks Churches Trade Justice Campaign, 2004–. Chm. Govs, Easingwold Sch., 2004–. *Recreations:* family life, walking, singing, gardening, tennis. *Address:* Westfield Farm, Sheriff Hutton, York YO60 6QQ. *T:* (01347) 878423.

NIGHTINGALE, Roger Daniel; economist and strategist; *b* 5 June 1945; *s* of Douglas Daniel John Nightingale and Edna Kathleen Vincent; one *s* four *d*. *Educ:* Welwyn Garden City Grammar Sch.; Keele Univ. (BA double hons Maths and Econs); University Coll. London (MSc Stats). Economist, Hoare & Co., 1968; Datastream, 1972, Dir, 1975; Hoare Govett, 1976, Dir, 1980; Head of Economics and Strategy Dept, Smith New Court, 1988–90; founded Roger Nightingale & Associates Ltd, consultancy firm, 1990. *Publications:* articles in financial magazines and newspapers. *Recreations:* snooker, collecting dictionaries, European history. *Club:* Reform.

NIGHTINGALE, (William) Benedict (Herbert); theatre critic, The Times, since 1990; *b* 14 May 1939; *s* of late Ronald Nightingale and Hon. Evelyn Nightingale, *d* of 1st Baron Burghclere; *m* 1964, Anne Bryan Redmon; two *s* one *d*. *Educ:* Charterhouse Sch.; Magdalene College, Cambridge (BA Hons); Univ. of Pennsylvania. General writer and northern drama critic, The Guardian, 1963–66; Literary Editor, New Society, 1966–68; theatre critic, New Statesman, 1968–86; Sunday theatre critic, New York Times, 1983–84; Prof. of English, Theatre and Drama, Univ. of Michigan, 1986–89. Mem., Drama Panel, and New Writing Cttee, Arts Council, 1975–80. Gov., Goldsmiths' Coll., 1978–81. *Publications:* Charities, 1973; Fifty Modern British Plays, 1981; Fifth Row Center, 1985; The Future of the Theatre, 1998. *Address:* 40 Broomhouse Road, SW6 3QX. *Club:* Garrick.

NIGHY, William Francis, (Bill); actor; *b* 12 Dec. 1949; *s* of Alfred Martin Nighy and Catherine Josephine (*née* Whittaker); partner, Diana Quick; one *d*. *Educ:* St Francis of Assisi Primary Sch., Caterham; John Fisher Grammar Sch., Purley; Guildford Sch. of Dance and Drama. *Theatre includes:* acting debut in The Milk Train Doesn't Stop Here Anymore, Watermill Th., Newbury; Everyman Th., Liverpool, 1972–75; Landscape, Silence, Gateway Th., Chester; The Warp, ICA, 1979; Betrayal, Almeida, 1991; A Kind of Alaska, Donmar Warehouse, 1998; The Vertical Hour, NY, 2006; National Theatre: Illuminatus!, 1977; A Map of the World, 1984; Pravda, 1985; King Lear, 1986; Mean Tears, 1987; Arcadia, 1993; The Seagull, 1994; Skylight, 1997; Blue/Orange, 2000–01; *television includes:* Easter 2016, 1982; The Last Place on Earth, 1985; Antonia and Jane, The Men's Room, 1991; The Maitlands, 1993; Longitude, 2000; Auf Wiedersehen, Pet (series 3), 2002; State of Play (Best Actor award, BAFTA, 2004), The Lost Prince, The Canterbury Tales, Ready When You are Mr McGill, The Young Visiters, 2003; He Knew He Was Right, 2004; The Girl in the Café, 2005; Gideon's Daughter, 2006; extensive work on BBC radio, inc. Lord of the Rings; *films include:* Fairy Tale, 1997; Still Crazy, 1998 (Peter Sellers Comedy Award, Evening Standard British Film Awards); Blow Dry, The Lawless Heart, Lucky Break, 2001; AKA, 2002; I Capture the Castle, Underworld, Love Actually, 2003 (Best Supporting Actor awards: Los Angeles Film Critics, 2003; BAFTA, and London Film Critics' Circle, 2004; Peter Sellers Comedy Award, Evening Standard British Film Awards, 2004); Shaun of the Dead, Enduring Love, 2004; The Hitchhiker's Guide to the Galaxy, The Constant Gardener, 2005; Pirates of the Caribbean: Dead Man's Chest, Stormbreaker, 2006; Notes on a Scandal, 2007. *Recreations:* reading, rhythm and blues, walking the dog. *Address:* c/o Markham & Froggatt Ltd, 4 Windmill Street, W1T 2HZ. *Club:* Garrick.

NIKOLAJEVA, Prof. Maria, PhD; Professor of Education, University of Cambridge, since 2008; *b* Moscow, 16 May 1952; *d* of Alexei Nikolajev and Natalia Nikolajeva (*née* Tiain); *m* 1981, Staffan Skott; two *s* one *d*. *Educ:* Moscow Linguistic Univ. (MA 1973); Stockholm Univ. (PhD 1988). Jun. Researcher, Film Research Inst., Moscow, 1974–81; Stockholm University: Post-doctoral Researcher, 1991–94; Sen. Lectr, 1994; Associate Prof., 1995–99; Prof., 1999–2008; Associate Prof., Åbo Akademi Univ., 1997– (Vis. Prof., 1998–99). Visiting Professor: Univ. of Massachusetts, Amherst, 1993; San Diego State Univ., 1999–2001; Hon. Prof., Univ. of Worcester, 2007. *Publications:* Den förlorade tiden och andra fantastiska berättelser, 1985; Masjas ryska kokbok, 1986; (with Bo Dellensten) Upptäck datorn!, 1987; The Magic Code: the use of magical patterns in fantasy for children, 1988; Selma Lagerlöf ur ryskt perspektiv, 1991; (ed) Modern litteraturteori och metod i barnlitteraturforskningen, 1992; (ed) Voices from Far Away: current trends in international children's literature research, 1995; (ed) Aspects and Issues in the History of Children's Literature, 1995; (ed) Återkommande mönster i Selma Lagerlöfs författarskap, 1995; När Sverige erövrade Ryssland: en studie i kulturernas samspel, 1996; Children's Literature Comes of Age: toward a new aesthetic, 1998; Barnbokens byggklossar, 1998, 2nd edn 2004 (trans. Danish); (with Ulla Bergstrand) Läckergommarnas kungarike, 1999; From Mythic to Linear: time in children's literature, 2000; Bilderbokens pusselbitar, 2000 (trans. Danish); (with Carole Scott) How Picturebooks Work, 2001; The Rhetoric of Character in Children's Literature, 2002; The Aesthetic Approach to Children's Literature, 2005; (ed with Sandra Beckett) Beyond Babar: the European tradition in children's literature, 2006; *fiction:* Var är solen?, 1987 (trans. Finnish, Danish, Dutch); Vem sa det först?, 1989; Nedräkningen, 1993 (trans. Danish, Lithuanian); Det finns inga kungar, 1994; contribs to essay collections; articles in academic jls incl. Children's Lit. Assoc. Qly, Children's Lit. in Educn, The Lion and the Unicorn, Canadian Children's Lit., Marvels & Tales, Papers, Style, Para*doxa, Compar(a)ison, Neohelikon. *Recreations:* travel, nature, animal and bird watching, gardening, papermaking, doll-house decoration. *Address:* University of Cambridge, Faculty of Education, 184 Hills Road, Cambridge CB2 2PQ. *T:* (01223) 767600; *e-mail:* mn351@cam.ac.uk.

NIKOLAYEVA-TERESHKOVA, Valentina Vladimirovna; *see* Tereshkova.

NIMMO, Very Rev. Dr Alexander Emsley; Dean of Aberdeen and Orkney, since 2008; *b* Glasgow, 28 Feb. 1953; *s* of Alexander Emsley Nimmo and Christina Agnes Nimmo (*née* Roff). *Educ:* Univ. of Aberdeen (BD 1976; PhD 1997); Univ. of Edinburgh (MPhil 1983). FSA (Scot.) 1993. Edinburgh Theol Coll., 1976–78; ordained deacon, 1978, priest 1979; Precentor, Inverness Cathedral, 1978–81; Priest-in-Charge, 1981–83, Rector, 1984, St Peter's, Stornoway; Rector: St Michael and All Saints, Edinburgh, 1984–1990; St Margaret's, Aberdeen, 1990–. Canon, St Andrew's Cathedral, Aberdeen, 1996; Synod Clerk, 2001. Chaplain: Saughton Prison, Edinburgh, 1987–90; HM Theatre, Aberdeen, 1990–; Episcopal Vis. Chaplain, Peterhead Prison, 2004–07. Mem., 1745 Assoc. *Publications:* (contrib.) Dictionary of Scottish Church History and Theology, 1993; (contrib.) After Columba - after Calvin, 1999. *Recreations:* music, hill-walking, cooking, gardening, languages. *Address:* The Clergy House, St Margaret of Scotland, Gallowgate, Aberdeen AB25 1EA. *T:* (01224) 644969; *e-mail:* alexander306@btinternet.com. *Club:* Aberdeenshire Theological.

NIMMO SMITH, Rt Hon. Lord; William Austin Nimmo Smith; PC 2005; a Senator of the College of Justice in Scotland, since 1996; *b* 6 Nov. 1942; *s* of late Dr Robert Herman Nimmo Smith and Mrs Ann Nimmo Smith; *m* 1968, Jennifer Main; one *s* one *d*. *Educ:* Eton Coll. (King's Scholar, 1956); Balliol Coll., Oxford (BA Hons Lit. Hum. 1965); Edinburgh Univ. (LLB 1967). Admitted to Faculty of Advocates, 1969; Standing Junior Counsel to Dept of Employment, 1977–82; QC (Scot.) 1982; Advocate-Depute, 1983–86; Temp. Judge, Court of Session, 1995–96. Chairman: Medical Appeal Tribunals, 1986–91; Vaccine Damage Tribunals, 1986–91; Mem. (part-time), Scottish Law Commn, 1988–96. Chm. Council, Cockburn Assoc. (Edinburgh Civic Trust), 1996–2001. *Recreations:* mountaineering, music. *Address:* Parliament House, Parliament Square, Edinburgh EH1 1RQ.

NINEHAM, Rev. Prof. Dennis Eric, DD (Oxon); BD (Cantab); Hon. DD (Birmingham); Hon. DD (BDS Yale); Professor of Theology and Head of Theology Department, Bristol University, 1980–86, now Emeritus; Honorary Canon of Bristol Cathedral, 1980–86, now Emeritus; *b* 27 Sept. 1921; *o c* of Stanley Martin and Bessie Edith Nineham, Shirley, Southampton; *m* 1946, Ruth Corfield, *d* of Rev. A. P. Miller; two *s* one *d* (and one *d* decd). *Educ:* King Edward VI Sch., Southampton; Queen's Coll., Oxford (Hon. Fellow, 1991). Asst Chaplain of Queen's Coll., 1944; Chaplain, 1945; Fellow and Praelector, 1946; Tutor, 1949; Prof. of Biblical and Historical Theology, Univ. of London (King's Coll.), 1954–58; Prof. of Divinity, Univ. of London, 1958–64; Regius Prof. of Divinity, Cambridge Univ., and Fellow, Emmanuel Coll., 1964–69; Warden of Keble Coll., Oxford, 1969–79, Hon. Fellow, 1980. FKC 1963. Examining Chaplain: to Archbishop of York and to Bishop of Ripon; to Bishop of Sheffield, 1947–54; to Bishop of Norwich, 1964–73; to Bishop of Bristol, 1981–. Select Preacher to Univ. of Oxford, 1954–56, 1971, 1990, 1992, 1994, and to Univ. of Cambridge, 1959; Proctor in Convocation of Canterbury: for London Univ., 1955–64; for Cambridge Univ., 1965–69. Mem. General Synod of Church of England for Oxford Univ., 1970–76; Mem., C of E Doctrine Commn, 1968–76. Roian Fleck Resident-in-Religion, Bryn Mawr Coll., Pa, 1974; Provost's Visitor, Trinity Coll., Toronto, 1992; Vis. Prof., Rikkyo Univ., Tokyo, 1994. Governor of Haileybury, 1966–93. *Publications:* The Study of Divinity, 1960; A New Way of Looking at the Gospels, 1962; Commentary on St Mark's Gospel, 1963; The Use and Abuse of the Bible, 1976; Explorations in Theology, no 1, 1977; Christianity Mediaeval and Modern, 1993; (Editor) Studies in the Gospels: Essays in Honour of R. H. Lightfoot, 1955; The Church's Use of the Bible, 1963; The New English Bible Reviewed, 1965; contrib. to: Studies in Ephesians (editor F. L. Cross), 1956; On the Authority of the Bible, 1960; Religious Education, 1944–1984, 1966; Theologians of Our Time, 1966; Christian History and Interpretation, 1967; Christ for us To-day, 1968; Christian Believing, 1976; The Myth of God Incarnate, 1977; Imagination and the Future, 1980; God's Truth, 1988; A Dictionary of Biblical Interpretation, 1990; Resurrection, 1994; Jesus in History, Thought and Culture, 2004. *Recreation:* reading. *Address:* 9 Fitzherbert Close, Iffley, Oxford OX4 4EN. *T:* (01865) 715941.
See also Very Rev. J. H. Drury.

NINIS, Ven. Richard Betts; Archdeacon of Lichfield (formerly Stafford) and Treasurer of Lichfield Cathedral, 1974–98; *b* 25 Oct. 1931; *s* of late George Woodward Ninis and Mary Gertrude Ninis; *m* 1967, Penelope Jane Harwood; two *s* one *d*. *Educ:* Lincoln Coll., Oxford (MA); Bishop's Hostel, Lincoln (GOE). Curate, All Saints, Poplar, 1955–62; Vicar of: St Martins, Hereford, 1962–71; Bullinghope and Dewsall with Callow, 1966–71. Diocesan Missioner for Hereford, 1971–74. Chm., USPG, 1988–91. Chm., Derbyshire Coll. of Higher Educn, 1978–90; Vice Chm., Univ. of Derby, 1992–98. Hon. Dr Derby, 1999. *Recreations:* gardening, travel. *Address:* Hillview, 32 Robert Street, Williton, Taunton, Som TA4 4QL.

NIRENBERG, Dr Marshall Warren; Research Biochemist; Chief, Laboratory of Biochemical Genetics, National Heart, Lung and Blood Institute, National Institutes of Health, Bethesda, Md, since 1966; *b* New York, 10 April 1927; *m* 1961, Perola Zaltzman; no *c*. *Educ:* Univs of Florida (BS, MS) and Michigan (PhD). Univ. of Florida: Teaching Asst, Zoology Dept, 1945–50; Res. Associate, Nutrition Lab., 1950–52; Univ. of Michigan: Teaching and Res. Fellow, Biol Chemistry Dept, 1952–57; Nat. Insts of Health, Bethesda: Postdoctoral Fellow of Amer. Cancer Soc., Nat. Inst. Arthritis and Metabolic Diseases, 1957–59, and of Public Health Service, Section of Metabolic Enzymes, 1959–60; Research Biochemist, Section of Metabolic Enzymes, 1960–62 and Section of Biochem. Genetics, 1962–66. Member: Amer. Soc. Biol Chemists; Amer. Chem. Soc.; Amer. Acad. Arts and Sciences; Biophys. Soc.; Nat. Acad. Sciences; Washington Acad. Sciences; Sigma Xi; Soc. for Study of Development and Growth; (Hon.) Harvey Soc.; Leopoldina Deutsche Akademie der Naturforscher; Neurosciences Research Program, MIT; NY Acad. Sciences; Pontifical Acad. Science, 1974. Robbins Lectr, Pomona Coll., 1967; Remsden Mem. Lectr, Johns Hopkins Univ., 1967. Numerous awards and prizes, including Nobel Prize in Medicine or Physiology (jtly), 1968. Hon. Dr Science: Michigan, Yale, and Chicago, 1965; Windsor, 1966; Harvard Med. Sch., 1968; Hon. PhD, Weitzmann Inst. of Science, Israel, 1978. *Publications:* numerous contribs to learned jls and chapters in symposia. *Address:* NIH Laboratory of Biochemical Genetics, 10 Center Drive, Building 10, Bethesda, MD 20892–1654, USA; 7001 Orkney Parkway, Bethesda, MD 20817, USA.

NISBET, Prof. Hugh Barr; Professor of Modern Languages, University of Cambridge, 1982–2007, now Emeritus; Fellow, Sidney Sussex College, since 1982; *b* 24 Aug. 1940; *s* of Thomas Nisbet and Lucy Mary Hainsworth; *m* 1st, 1962, Monika Luise Ingeborg Uecker (marr. diss. 1981); two *s*; 2nd, 1995, Angela Maureen Parker (*née* Chapman). *Educ:* Dollar Acad.; Univ. of Edinburgh. MA, PhD 1965. University of Bristol: Asst Lectr in German, 1965–67; Lectr, 1967–72; Reader, 1972–73; Prof. of German Lang. and Lit., Univ. of St Andrews, 1974–81. Mem., Gen. Teaching Council for Scotland, 1978–81. Pres., British Soc. for Eighteenth Century Studies, 1986–88. Governor, Dollar Acad., 1978–81. Jt Editor, Cambridge Studies in German, 1983–; Germanic Editor, 1973–80, Gen. Editor, 1981–84, Modern Language Rev. *Publications:* Herder and the Philosophy and History of Science, 1970; (ed with Hans Reiss) Goethe's Die Wahlverwandtschaften, 1971; Goethe and the Scientific Tradition, 1972; (ed) German Aesthetic and Literary Criticism: Winckelmann to Goethe, 1985; (ed with Claude Rawson) Cambridge History of Literary Criticism, 9 vols, 1989–; (ed with John Hibberd) Texte, Motive und Gestalten der Goethezeit, 1989; (ed with D. E. D. Beales) Sidney Sussex College, Cambridge: historical essays, 1996; (ed with Laurence Dickey) Hegel's Political Writings, 1999; Gotthold Ephraim Lessing: Leben, Werk, Zeit, 2008; *translations:* Kant, Political Writings, 1970, 2nd edn 1991; Hegel, Lectures on the Philosophy of World History, 1975, 2nd edn 1980; Hegel, Elements of the Philosophy of Right, 1991; Hegel, Political Writings, 1999; (and ed) Lessing, Philosophical and Theological Writings, 2005; articles and reviews on German literature and thought. *Recreations:* music, art history. *Address:* Sidney Sussex College, Cambridge CB2 3HU. *T:* (01223) 338877.

NISBET, Prof. John Donald, OBE 1981; MA, BEd, PhD; FEIS; Professor of Education, Aberdeen University, 1963–88; *b* 17 Oct. 1922; *s* of James Love Nisbet and Isabella Donald; *m* 1952, Brenda Sugden; one *s* one *d*. *Educ:* Dunfermline High Sch.; Edinburgh Univ. (MA, BEd); PhD (Aberdeen); Teacher's Certif. (London). Royal Air Force, 1943–46. Teacher, Fife, 1946–48; Lectr, Aberdeen Univ., 1949–63. Editor: British Jl of Educnl Psychology, 1967–74; Studies in Higher Education, 1979–84; Chairman: Educnl Research Bd, SSRC, 1972–75; Cttee on Primary Educn, 1974–80; Scottish Council for Research in Educn, 1975–78; President: British Educnl Research Assoc., 1975; Scottish Inst. of Adult and Continuing Educn, 1991. FEIS 1975. Hon. DEd Edinburgh, 2004. *Publications:* Family Environment, 1953; Age of Transfer to Secondary Education, 1966; Transition to Secondary Education, 1969; Scottish Education Looks Ahead, 1969; Educational Research Methods, 1970; Educational Research in Action, 1972; Impact of Research, 1980; Towards Community Education, 1980; (ed) World Yearbook of Education, 1985; Learning Strategies, 1986; Curriculum Reform: assessment in question, 1993; Educational Disadvantage, 1994; Pipers and Tunes: a decade of educational research in Scotland, 1995; Thirty Years On, 2005; papers in jls on educnl psychology and curriculum develt. *Recreation:* golf. *Address:* 7 Lawson Avenue, Banchory AB31 5TW. *T:* (01330) 823145.

NISBET, Prof. Robin George Murdoch, FBA 1967; Corpus Christi Professor of Latin, Oxford, 1970–92; Fellow of Corpus Christi College, Oxford, 1952–92, Hon. Fellow 1992; *b* 21 May 1925; *s* of R. G. Nisbet, Univ. Lecturer, and A. T. Husband; *m* 1969, Anne (*d* 2004), *d* of Dr J. A. Wood. *Educ:* Glasgow Academy; Glasgow Univ.; Balliol Coll., Oxford (Snell Exhibitioner; Hon. Fellow, 1989). Tutor in Classics, Corpus Christi College, Oxford, 1952–70. Kenyon Medal, British Acad., 1997. *Publications:* Commentary on Cicero, *in Pisonem*, 1961; (with M. Hubbard) on Horace, *Odes I*, 1970; *Odes II*, 1978; Collected Papers on Latin Literature, 1995; (with N. Rudd) Commentary on Horace, *Odes III*, 2004. *Recreation:* 20th century history. *Address:* 80 Abingdon Road, Cumnor, Oxford OX2 9QW. *T:* (01865) 862482.

NISBET-SMITH, Dugal, CBE 1996; Director, Newspaper Society, 1983–97; *b* 6 March 1935; *s* of David and Margaret Homeward Nisbet-Smith; *m* 1959, Dr Ann Patricia Taylor; one *s* two *d*. *Educ:* Southland Boys' High Sch., Invercargill, NZ. Journalist on Southland Daily News, NZ, 1952–56; Features writer and reporter, Beaverbrook Newspapers, London, 1956–60; variously Asst Editor, Gen. Manager and Man. Dir, Barbados Advocate Co., Barbados, WI, Gen. Manager, Sierra Leone Daily Mail Ltd, W Africa, Dep. Gen. Manager, Trinidad Mirror Co., 1960–66; Sen. Industrial Relations Manager, Mirror Gp Newspapers, London, 1966–68; Develt Manager, 1969–71, Production Dir, 1971–73, Man. Dir, 1974–78, Scottish Daily Record and Sunday Mail Ltd, Glasgow; joined Bd, Mirror Gp Newspapers, 1976; Dir/General Manager, 1978–80, Man. Dir, 1980–81, Times Newspapers Ltd; Publishing Advr to HH the Aga Khan, Aiglemont, France, 1981–83. *Recreations:* travel, sculpture, painting. *Address:* 2 Middleton Place, Langham Street, W1W 7TA. *T:* (020) 7636 6403.

NISSAN, Gwyneth; *see* Williams, G.

NISSEN, Alexander David; QC 2006; a Recorder, since 2007; *b* 30 Aug. 1963; *s* of Charles Nissen and Jillian Nissen (*née* Moss); *m* 1995, Sally Daniel. *Educ:* Mill Hill Sch.; Manchester Univ. (LLB Hons 1984). Called to the Bar, Middle Temple, 1985; in practice as barrister, specialising in construction and engrg law and related professional negligence disputes, 1989–. FCIArb 2000; Chartered Arbitrator, 2003. *Publications:* (contrib.) Keating on Building Contracts, 5th edn 1991 to 8th edn 2006; contrib. articles in Construction Law Jl. *Recreations:* theatre, escaping exercise, Coronation Street, dreaming about good food. *Address:* Keating Chambers, 15 Essex Street, WC2R 3AA. *T:* (020) 7544 2600, *Fax:* (020) 7544 2700; *e-mail:* anissen@keatingchambers.com.

NISSEN, David Edgar Joseph, CB 1999; Solicitor and Director General Legal Services, Department of Trade and Industry, 1997–2002; *b* 27 Nov. 1942; *s* of Tunnock Edgar

Nissen and Elsie Nissen (*née* Thorne); *m* 1969, Pauline Jennifer (*née* Meaden); two *d*. *Educ:* King's School, Chester; University College London (LLB). Solicitor, admitted 1969. Asst Solicitor, W Midlands Gas Board, 1969–70; Prosecuting Solicitor, Sussex Police Authority, 1970–73; HM Customs and Excise, 1973–90: Asst Solicitor, 1983–87; Principal Asst Solicitor, 1987–90; Legal Advr to Dept of Energy (Principal Asst Treasury Solicitor), 1990–92; Solicitor to HM Customs and Excise, 1992–95; Legal Advr to Home Office, 1995–97. *Recreations:* photography, music, gardening.

NISSEN, George Maitland, CBE 1987; Chairman, Chiswick House Friends, since 2001; *b* 29 March 1930; *s* of Col Peter Norman Nissen, DSO, and Lauretta Maitland; *m* 1956, Jane Edmunds, *d* of late S. Curtis Bird, New York; two *s* two *d*. *Educ:* Eton; Trinity Coll., Cambridge (MA). National Service, KRRC, 1949–50, 2/Lieut. Sen. Partner, Pember & Boyle, Stockbrokers, 1982–86; Chairman: Foreign & Colonial Emerging Markets Trust (formerly CDFC Trust) plc, 1987–99; Liberty Syndicate Management Ltd, 1997–2002; Director: Morgan Grenfell Gp, 1984–87 (Advr, 1987–92); Festiniog Rly, 1993–2003. Mem., Stock Exchange, 1956–92 (Dep. Chm., 1978–81; Mem. Council, 1973–91); Chairman: Gilt-Edged Market Makers Assoc., 1986–92; IMRO, 1989–92; Dir, The Securities Assoc., 1986–89; Mem., Inflation Accounting Steering Gp, 1976–80. Non-exec. Dir, Ealing, Hammersmith and Hounslow HA, 1993–96. Mem. Council, GDST (formerly GPDST), 1993–. Gov., Godolphin and Latymer School, Hammersmith, 1987–97; Trustee, Lucy Cavendish Coll., Cambridge, 1994–97; Pres., Reed's Sch., Cobham, 1995–. Chm. of Trustees, CPRW, 1991–; Trustee, Chiswick House and Gardens Trust, 2005–. Chm., Book Guild, 1993–. Hon. FRAM 1994. *Recreations:* railways, music. *Address:* Swan House, Chiswick Mall, W4 2PS. *T:* (020) 8995 8306.

NITTVE, (Arvid) Lars (Olov); Director, Moderna Museet, Stockholm, since 2001; *b* 17 Sept. 1953; *s* of Bengt and Ulla Nittve; *m* 1988, Anna Olsson (marr. diss. 1999); one *s*. *Educ:* Stockholm Univ. (MA 1978). Res. Asst and Lectr, Dept of Art History, Stockholm Univ., 1978–85; Art Critic, Svenska Dagbladet, Stockholm, 1979–85; Sen. Curator, Moderna Museet, Stockholm, 1986–90; Director: Rooseum-Center for Contemporary Art, Malmö, 1990–95; Louisiana Mus. of Modern Art, Humlebæk, Denmark, 1995–98; Tate Gall. of Modern Art, subseq. Tate Modern, 1998–2001. *Publications* include: Svenska Valaffischer, 1979; Ola Billgren, 1985; Jan Håfström: grammaticus, 1990; Ulrik Samuelson: exit, 1987; Landskapet i nytt ljus, 1987; The Sublime - Walter De Maria, 1992; Truls Melin, 1992; Rolf Hanson, 1995. *Address:* Moderna Museet, Skeppsholmen, Box 16382, 103 27 Stockholm, Sweden. *T:* (8) 51956259.

NIVEN, Alastair Neil Robertson, OBE 2001; PhD; Principal, King George VI and Queen Elizabeth Foundation of St Catharine's, Cumberland Lodge, since 2001; *b* 25 Feb. 1944; *s* of late Harold Robertson Niven and Elizabeth Isobel Robertson Niven (*née* Mair); *m* 1970, Helen Margaret Trow; one *s* one *d*. *Educ:* Dulwich Coll.; Gonville and Caius Coll., Cambridge (MA); Univ. of Ghana (Commonwealth Schol.; MA); Univ. of Leeds (PhD). Lecturer in English: Univ. of Ghana, 1968–69; Univ. of Leeds, 1969–70; Lectr in English Studies, Univ. of Stirling, 1970–78; Dir Gen., Africa Centre, London, 1978–84; Chapman Fellow 1984–85, Hon. Fellow 1985, Inst. of Commonwealth Studies; Special Asst to Sec. Gen., ACU, 1985–87; Lit. Dir, Arts Council of GB, then of England, 1987–97; Dir of Literature, British Council, 1997–2001. Visiting Professor: Univ. of Aarhus, 1975–76; Sheffield Hallam Univ., 1998–2002; Vis. Fellow, Aust. Studies Centre, Univ. of London, 1985; Hon. Lectr, SOAS, 1979–85; Hon. Fellow, Univ. of Warwick, 1988. Editor, Jl of Commonwealth Literature, 1979–92. Chairman: Public Schools Debating Assoc. of Eng. and Wales, 1961–62; Literature Panel, GLAA, 1981–84; Welfare Policy Cttee, 1983–87, Exec. Cttee, 1987–92, UK Council for Overseas Student Affairs; Southern Africa Book Develt Educn Trust, 1997–2003; Soc. of Bookmen, 2003–04; Sec. and Treas., Assoc. for Commonwealth Lit. and Lang. Studies, 1986–89; Member: Public Affairs Cttee, Royal Commonwealth Soc., 1979–99; Laurence Olivier Awards Theatre Panel, 1989–91; British Library Adv. Cttee for the Centre for the Book, 1990–97; Home Office Standing Cttee on Arts in Prisons, 1995–97. Trustee, Millennium Liby Trust, 1998–. President: Windsor WEA, 2003–; English PEN, 2003–07. Judge: Booker Prize, 1994; Forward Poetry Prizes, 1996; David Cohen British Literature Prize, 2000 (deviser of Prize, 1992); The Independent Foreign Fiction Prize, 2001; Chairman of Judges: Eurasia Reg., 1994, 1995, Adv. Cttee, 1996–2006, Commonwealth Writers' Prize; Stakis Prize for Scottish Writer of Year, 1998; ESU Marsh Prize for Biography, 1999–2007. Chm. of Govs, Royal Sch., Windsor, 2004–08. Mem. Editorial Bd, Annual Register, 1988–. *Publications:* The Commonwealth Writer Overseas (ed), 1976; D. H. Lawrence: the novels, 1978; The Yoke of Pity: the fiction of Mulk Raj Anand, 1978; D. H. Lawrence: the writer and his work, 1980; (with Sir Hugh W. Springer) The Commonwealth of Universities, 1987; (ed) Under Another Sky: the Commonwealth Poetry Prize anthology, 1987; (ed jtly) Enigmas and Arrivals: an anthology of Commonwealth writing, 1997; articles in Afr. Affairs, Ariel, Brit. Book News, Jl of Commonwealth Lit., Jl of Indian Writing in English, Jl of RSA, Lit. Half-Yearly, Poetry Review, TES, THES, World Lit. Written in English, etc; study guides on Elechi Amadi, Wm Golding, R. K. Narayan, Raja Rao. *Recreations:* theatre, travel. *Address:* Cumberland Lodge, The Great Park, Windsor, Berks SL4 2HP. *T:* (01784) 497786. *Clubs:* Athenæum, Royal Commonwealth Society.

See also C. H. R. Niven, P. A. R. Niven.

NIVEN, Dr Colin Harold Robertson, OBE 2007; Master of Schools (Shanghai, Beijing, Suzhou), for Dulwich College International, China, 2003–06; *b* 29 Sept. 1941; *s* of late Harold Robertson Niven and Elizabeth Isobel Robertson Niven (*née* Mair). *Educ:* Dulwich Coll. (Capt. of School); Gonville and Caius Coll., Cambridge (MA); Brasenose Coll., Oxford (DipEd); Nancy Univ. (LèsL); Lille Univ. (Dr de l'Univ.). Lycée Mixte, Châlons-sur-Marne, 1963–64; Samuel Pepys Comprehensive Sch., 1964; Sedbergh Sch., 1964; Fettes Coll., 1965–73 (Housemaster, 1971–73); Head of Mod. Langs, Sherborne Sch., 1973–83; Principal: Island Sch., Hong Kong, 1983–87; St George's English Sch., Rome, 1988–91; Vis. Fellow, Westminster Coll., Oxford, 1991; Dir of Internat. Liaison, Sherborne Internat. Study Centre, 1992; Headmaster, Alleyn's Sch., Dulwich, 1992–2002; Master, Dulwich Coll. Internat. Sch., Shanghai, 2003–05. Hon. Res. Fellow, Exeter Univ., 1981–83. Dir, West Heath Ltd, 2003–. Chm., European Div., 1990–91, Chm., London Div., 1998, HMC. Sen. Consultant, CfA (Charity Fundraising Appts), 2002–06. Pres., Marlowe Soc., 1996–2003; Chm., Friends of E. H. Shepard, 2002–. Trustee, Dulwich Picture Gall., 1996–99. Vice-Pres., Rugby Fives Assoc., 2001–. Governor: Portsmouth GS, 1999–2003; Sherborne Sch. Internat. Col., 2001–; Blackheath Nursery and Prep. Sch., 2006–; Trustee, Campion Sch., Athens, 2002–; Member: Council, King's Coll., Madrid, 1999–2004; Educn Cttee, 1999–, Cttee, London Branch, 2006–, ESU. Patron, Ind. Schs MLA, 1998–. Pres., Edward Alleyn Club, 2005–06 (Vice-Pres., 2003). FRSA. Freeman, City of London, 1999. CCF Medal 1983. Officier, Ordre des Palmes Académiques (France), 2002. *Publications:* Voltaire's Candide, 1978; Thomas Mann's Tonio Kröger, 1980; Vailland's Un jeune homme seul (critical edn), 1983; Island School: the first twenty years, 1987. *Recreations:* theatre, sport, foreign travel, cats, opera (Mem. choir, Dorset Opera, 1978–91). *Address:* 9 Oakfield Gardens, Dulwich Wood Avenue, SE19 1HF. *T:* (020) 8670 6957. *Clubs:* Royal Over-Seas League, Royal Commonwealth Society, English-Speaking Union.

See also A. N. R. Niven, P. A. R. Niven.

NIVEN, Peter Ashley Robertson, FRCS, FRCOG; Consultant Obstetrician and Gynaecologist, United Bristol Hospitals, 1976–2003; *b* 3 March 1938; *s* of late Harold Robertson Niven and Elizabeth Isobel Robertson Niven (*née* Mair); *m* 1964, Sarah Peta Callaway; three *s*. *Educ:* Dulwich Coll.; Gonville and Caius Coll., Cambridge (Open Exhibnr 1955; BA 1959; MA 1963); St Bartholomew's Hosp. (MB BChir 1962). FRCS 1966; MRCOG 1969, FRCOG 1981. Eden Travelling Fellow, RCOG, 1972; Purdue Frederick Award, Amer. Coll. of Obstetricians and Gynecologists, 1975; Sen. Registrar, St Bartholomew's Hosp., 1971–74; Consultant, Newcastle Gen. and Hexham Gen. Hosps, 1975–76. Chm., Higher Trng Cttee, and Mem. Council, RCOG, 1992–95; Pres., SW Obstetrical and Gynaecol Soc., 1997–98; Mem., Gynaecol Vis. Soc. of GB and Ireland, 1978. FRSocMed 1971. *Recreations:* ski-ing, golf, Rugby, cricket, history, travel, long distance walking. *Address:* 21 Clifton Park, Clifton, Bristol BS8 3BZ. *T:* (0117) 973 8446. *Club:* Royal Over-Seas League.

See also A. N. R. Niven, C. H. R. Niven.

NIVISON, family name of **Baron Glendyne**.

NIX, Prof. John Sydney; Emeritus Professor, University of London, since 1989 (Professor of Farm Business Management, 1982–89, and Head, Farm Business Unit, 1974–89, Wye College); *b* 27 July 1927; *s* of John William Nix and Eleanor Elizabeth (*née* Stears); *m* 1st, 1950, Mavis Marian (*née* Cooper) (*d* 2004); one *s* two *d*; 2nd, 2005, Susan Marie (*née* Clement). *Educ:* Brockley County Sch.; University Coll. of the South-West. BSc Econ (London), MA Cantab. Instr Lieut, RN, 1948–51. Farm Economics Branch, Sch. of Agriculture, Univ. of Cambridge, 1951–61; Wye College: Farm Management Liaison Officer and Lectr, 1961–70; Sen. Tutor, 1970–72; Sen. Lectr, 1972–75; Reader, 1975–82; apptd to personal chair, the first in Farm Business Management in UK, 1982; Fellow, 1995. Founder Mem., Farm Management Assoc., 1965; formerly Member: Study Groups etc. for Natural Resources (Tech.) Cttee; Agric. Adv. Council; ARC Tech. Cttee; ADAS Exptl and Develt Cttee; Meat and Livestock Commn; Countryside Commn. Programme Advr, Southern Television, 1966–81; Specialist Advr, Select Cttee on Agric., 1990–91. British Institute of Management: Chm., Jl Cttee of Centre of Management of Agric., 1971–96; Chm., Bd of Farm Management, 1979–81; Nat. Award for outstanding and continuing contrib. to advancement of management in agric. industry, 1982 (1st recipient). President: Agricl Economics Soc., 1990–91; Kingshay Farming Trust, 1991–96; Assoc. of Indep. Crop Consultants, 1993–97; Guild of Agricl Journalists., 2000–02. CCMI (CBIM 1983). FRSA 1984; FRAgS 1985; FIAgrM 1993. Hon. Fellow, RASE, 2007. Liveryman, Farmers' Co., 1999–. Agricl Communicators Award (1st recipient), Hydro Agri (UK), 1999; Farmers' Club Cup, 2005; Lifetime Achievement Award, NFU, 2006. *Publications:* Farm Management Pocketbook, 1966, 38th edn 2007; (with C. S. Barnard) Farm Planning and Control, 1973, 2nd edn 1979, Spanish edn 1984; (with W. Butterworth) Farm Mechanisation for Profit, 1983; (with G. P. Hill and N. T. Williams) Land and Estate Management, 1987, 4th edn 2003; articles in Jl of Agricl Econs, Jl of RASE, Farm Management, etc. *Recreations:* Rugby, cricket, old films, reading the papers. *Address:* Imperial College London, Wye Campus, Ashford, Kent TN25 5AH. *T:* (020) 7594 2855. *Club:* Farmers'.

NIXON, Anthony; Business and Management Consultant, A. & M. Nixon Enterprises, since 1992; *b* 25 Nov. 1932; *s* of late Aitzad and Hydray Nixon; *m* 1975, Marion Audrey Farr; one *s* four *d*. *Educ:* Univ. of Peshawar (BA 1955); Univ. of Karachi (DipM 1959; MA Econ. 1960); UCW, Aberystwyth (MSc Pol Econ. 1986); Leeds Poly. (Dip. Liby and Inf. Sci., 1966); Salford Univ.; Manchester Univ. ACP 1958. Local Govt Officer, Lancs CC, 1968–71; Chief College Librarian and Lectr, Burnley Coll. of Further and Higher Educn, 1972–93 (Mem., Acad. Bd and Bd Cttees); Chairman and Managing Director: A. & M. Nixon Enterprises Ltd, 1990–91; Costcutter Nixon Supermkt, 1993–96. Columnist, New Life (London weekly mag.), 1987–88. Probation Officer Volunteer and Exec. Cttee Mem., Rossendale Probation and Aftercare Service, 1975–81; Chairman: NHS Exec. Complaints Procedure, NW Reg., DoH, 1999–2003; Complaints Procedure, Cumbria and Lancs NHS Strategic HA, 2003; East Lancashire Hospitals NHS Trust: Mem., Patient and Public Involvement Forum, 2005–07; Mem., Develt Cttee for Rossendale, 2006–. Lancashire Probation Board: Mem., 2001–07; Chairman: Audit and Assessment Cttee, 2002–04 (Mem., 2001–02); Complaints Appeal Panel, 2002–; Member: Performance Cttee, 2003–04; Information Security Gp, 2003–05; Risk Mgt Cttee, 2003–. Lay Assessor, Lancs Reg., Nat. Care Standards Commn (formerly Inspection Unit, Social Services, Lancs CC), 2000–06; Mem., Local Involvement Network (LINKS), NHS Health & Social Care, Lancs CC, 2007–. Mem., Community Relns Council, 1980–92, Chm., Employment Panel, 1987–88, Hyndburn and Rossendale. Ind. Mem., Standards and Ethics Cttee, 2004– and Mem., Rossendale Strategic Partnership Cttee, 2004–06, Rossendale BC. Dir, Exec. Trustee and Sec., Bd of Dirs, BHAF Ltd, Manchester, 1998–2001 (Chm., Finance Cttee); non-exec. Dir and Trustee, Burnley, Pendle and Rossendale Crossroads Ltd, 2005–06. Cttee Mem., Rossendale Dist, CPRE, 2005–. Business Advr and Mentor, Prince's Business Trust, 1999–. Chm., E Lancs Reg., CS Fellowship, 2002–. Mem. Ct, Univ. of Manchester, 2002–04. Gov., Lancashire County Sch., Rossendale, 1980–93, 2004–. Travelled extensively in Russian Fedn and Republics of Latvia, Estonia and Lithuania and met prominent govt and religious leaders, industrialists, trade union officials, etc in order to promote goodwill between Britain and former Soviet Union, 1987; organised exchange visits between British and Soviet families for first time during Soviet rule, 1987–91. Consultant: Collective Farm, Piraviena, Rumsiskes, Lithuania, 1988–90; Pedagogical Univ., Vilnius, Lithuania, 1997. Has given talks on local radio in Lancs on various Russian, Lithuanian, Estonian and Latvian radio and TV stations. *Publications:* South Asia: detente and co-operation or confrontation?, 1982; (contrib.) Day of Peace 1917–87, 1987; Meeting People through Russia to the Baltics, 1990; contrib. articles to Sunday Times, New Scientist and British and foreign jls. *Recreations:* discussing politics and philosophising on national and international economic and social issues; travelling, reading, country walks, picnics, futurologist. *Address:* Rose & Oak, 7 Flax Close, Helmshore, Rossendale, Lancs BB4 4JL; *e-mail:* anthonynixon96@yahoo.co.uk. *Club:* Inter-Varsity (Manchester).

NIXON, Prof. John Forster, FRS 1994; Professor of Chemistry, 1986–2003, Research Professor of Chemistry, since 2003, University of Sussex; *b* 27 Jan. 1937; *s* of late Supt Edward Forster Nixon, MBE and Mary Nixon (*née* Lytton); *m* 1960, Dorothy Joan (Kim) Smith; one *s* one *d*. *Educ:* Univ. of Manchester (BSc 1st Cl. Hons Chem. 1957, MSc 1958; PhD 1960; DSc 1973). Research Associate in Chem., Univ. of Southern Calif., LA, 1960–62; ICI Fellow, Inorganic Chem. Dept, Univ. of Cambridge, 1962–64; Lectr in Inorganic Chem., Univ. of St Andrews, 1964–66; University of Sussex: Lectr in Chem., 1966–76; Reader, 1976–86; Subject Chm. in Chem., 1981–84; Dean, Sch. of Chem. and Molecular Scis, 1989–92. Vis. Associate Prof. in Chem., Univ. of Victoria, BC, Canada, 1970–71; Visiting Professor: Simon Fraser Univ., BC, 1976; IIT, Bangalore, 2005; Vis. Fellow, ANU, 2004. Mem., Editl Bd, Phosphorus, Sulfur and Silicon, 1989–2006. Mem. Bd of Dirs, Internat. Council for Main Gp Chem., 2000–06. Member: Internat. Cttee on

Phosphorus Chem., 1983, 2000–; IUPAC Commn on Inorganic Nomenclature, 1985–87; Inorganic Chem. Panel, SERC Cttee, 1986–89; EPSRC Cttee, 1997–98. Royal Soc. Leverhulme Trust Sen. Res. Fellow, 1993. Mem. Council, Dalton Div., RSC, 1994–99. Corday-Morgan Medal and Prize, Chem. Soc., 1973; Main Gp Element Medal, 1985, Tilden Lectr and Medal, 1992, Ludwig Mond Lectr and Medal, 2003, RSC; Geza Zemplen Medal, Budapest Technical Inst., 2003; Alexander von Humboldt Prize, 2004. FRSA 1992. *Publications:* (jtly) Phosphorus: the carbon copy, 1998; numerous papers in various learned jls. *Recreations:* walking, playing squash, tennis, badminton, watching cricket, theatre. *Address:* Department of Chemistry, School of Life Sciences, University of Sussex, Brighton, Sussex BN1 9QJ. *T:* (01273) 678536.

NIXON, Patrick Michael, CMG 1989; OBE 1984; HM Diplomatic Service, retired; Regional Coordinator for Coalition Provisional Authority, Southern Iraq, 2004; *b* 1 Aug. 1944; *s* of John Moylett Gerard Nixon and late Hilary Mary (*née* Paterson); *m* 1968, Elizabeth Rose Carlton; four *s*. *Educ:* Downside; Magdalene Coll., Cambridge. Joined HM Diplomatic Service, 1965; MECAS, Lebanon, 1966; Cairo, 1968; Lima, 1970; FCO, 1973; Tripoli, Libya, 1977; British Inf. Services, New York, 1980; Asst, later Hd, Near East and N Africa Dept, FCO, 1983; Ambassador and Consul-Gen. at Doha, Qatar, 1987–90; Counsellor, FCO, 1990–93; High Comr to Zambia, 1994–97; Dir, FCO, 1997–98; Ambassador to UAE, 1998–2003. Governor: All Hallows Sch., Cranmore Hall, 2003– (Chm., 2005–); Downside, 2005–. *Address:* The Old Vicarage, Church Street, Maiden Bradley, Warminster, Wilts BA12 7HN; *e-mail:* patricknixon@onetel.com.

NIXON, Rev. Rosemary Ann; Vicar of Cleadon, 1999–2007; *b* 25 May 1945; *d* of Edwin Nixon and Dorothy Hall. *Educ:* Bishop Grosseteste Coll. of Educn (CertEd); Trinity Coll., Bristol (DipTh (London); BD Hons (London)); Durham Univ. (MA); Edinburgh Univ. (MTh). School teacher, Denton, Manchester, 1966–69; Parish Worker, St Luke's, West Hampstead, 1973–75; Tutor, St John's Coll., Durham and Dir of St John's Coll. Extension Prog., 1975–89; ordained deacon, 1987, priest, 1994; Team Vicar and Dir of the Urban Studies Unit, Parish of Gateshead, 1990–92; Staff Mem., Edinburgh Theol Coll., 1992–95; Principal, Theol Inst., Scottish Episcopal Church, 1995–99. Hon. Canon, St Mary's Cathedral, Edinburgh, and Pantonian Prof. of Theol., Edinburgh, 1996–99. Mem., SOTS, 1981–. *Publications:* Who's the Greatest?: Sunday schools today, 1984; Jonah: working with the word, 1986; The Message of Jonah, 2003; articles in theol dictionaries and periodicals. *Recreations:* music, hill walking, photography, friends. *Address:* Charisholme, 6 Wearside Drive, Durham DH1 1LE. *T:* (0191) 384 6558.

NIXON, Sir Simon (Michael Christopher), 5th Bt *cr* 1906, of Roebuck Grove, Milltown, co. Dublin and Merrion Square, City of Dublin; *b* 20 June 1954; *s* of Major Cecil Dominic Henry Joseph Nixon, MC (*d* 1994), and of Brenda Nixon (*née* Lewis); *S* uncle, 1997; *m* 2002, Pauline Julia Jones. *Heir: b* Michael David Hugh Nixon, *b* 19 May 1957.

NIZAMI, Farhan Ahmad, CBE 2007; DPhil; Founder Director, Oxford Centre for Islamic Studies, since 1985; Prince of Wales Fellow, Magdalen College, Oxford, since 1997; *b* 25 Dec. 1956; *s* of late Prof. Khaliq Nizami and Razia Nizami; *m* 1983, Farah Deba Ahmad; one *s* one *d*. *Educ:* Aligarh Muslim Univ., India (BA Hons History, 1st cl., 1977; Univ. Medal, 1977; Begam Khursheed Nurul Hasan Gold Medal, 1977; Nat. Schol., 1977–79; MA, 1st cl., 1979; Univ. Medal, 1979); Wadham Coll., Oxford (Oxford Overseas Schol.; Frere Exhibnr; DPhil 1983). Rothman's Fellow in Muslim Hist., 1983–85, Fellow, 1985–97, Emeritus Fellow, 1997, St Cross Coll., Oxford. Secretary: Bd of Trustees, Islamic Trust, 1985–; Bd of Dirs, Oxford Trust for Islamic Studies, 1998–; Dir, Oxford Inspires, 2002–03; Chm., Oxford Endeavours Ltd, 2003–. Scholar Consultant to Christian-Muslim Forum, 2005–. Member: Council, Al-Falah Prog., Univ. of Calif, Berkeley, 1997–2004; Adv. Council, Wilton Park, 2000–04 (Chm., 2004–); Court, Oxford Brookes Univ., 2000–; Adv. Bd, Dialogues Project, World Policy Inst., New York Univ., 2003–. Member: Archbp of Canterbury's Ref. Gp for Christian-Muslim Relations, 2001–04; Academic Consultative Cttee, Cumberland Lodge, 2003–; Steering Cttee C-100, World Econ. Forum, Davos, 2003–07; Internat. Adv. Panel, Business Forum, Organisation of the Islamic Conf., Malaysia, 2004–. Gov., Magdalen Coll. Sch., Oxford, 2005–. Patron, Oxford Amnesty Lectures, 2003–. Founder Editor, Jl of Islamic Studies, 1990–; Series Editor, Makers of Islamic Civilization, 2004–. Class IV, Order of Crown (Brunei), 1992. *Recreations:* reading, cricket. *Address:* Oxford Centre for Islamic Studies, George Street, Oxford OX1 2AR. *T:* (01865) 278731.

NKOYOYO, Most Rev. Livingstone M.; *see* Mpalanyi-Nkoyoyo.

NOAKES, Baroness *cr* 2000 (Life Peer), of Goudhurst in the co. of Kent; **Sheila Valerie Masters,** DBE 1996; Opposition spokesman, House of Lords, on work and pensions, since 2001, on HM Treasury, since 2003 (on health, 2001–03); company director; *d* of Albert Frederick Masters and Iris Sheila Masters (*née* Ratcliffe); *m* 1985, Colin Barry Noakes. *Educ:* Eltham Hill Grammar Sch.; Univ. of Bristol (LLB). FCA. Joined Peat Marwick Mitchell & Co., 1970; seconded to HM Treasury, 1979–81; seconded to Dept of Health as Dir of Finance, NHS Management Exec., 1988–91; Partner, Peat Marwick Mitchell & Co., subseq. KPMG Peat Marwick, then KPMG, 1983–2000; a Dir, Bank of England, 1994–2001 (Chm., Cttee of non-exec. Dirs, 1998–2001). Non-executive Director: Hanson plc, 2001–07; Carpetright plc, 2001–; SThree (formerly Solutions in Staffing and Software) plc, 2001–07; John Laing plc, 2002–04; ICI plc, 2004–08; Severn Trent plc, 2008–. Comr, Public Works Loan Bd, 1995–2001; Member: Council, ICAEW, 1987–2002 (Pres., 1999–2000); Inland Revenue Management Bd, 1992–99; NHS Policy Bd, 1992–95; Chancellor of Exchequer's Private Finance Panel, 1993–97; Bd of Companions, Inst. of Mgt, 1997–2002; Public Services Productivity Panel, 1998–2000; Adv. Council, Inst. of Business Ethics, 1998–2003. Trustee, Reuters Founders Share Co., 1998–. Mem. Bd, ENO, 2000–. Governor: London Business Sch., 1998–2001; Eastbourne Coll., 2000–04; Marlborough Coll., 2000–02. Hon. DBA London Guildhall, 1999; Hon. LLD Bristol, 2000; Hon. DSc Buckingham, 2001. *Recreations:* ski-ing, horse racing, opera, early classical music. *Address:* House of Lords, SW1A 0PW. *T:* (020) 7219 5230. *Club:* Farmers'.

NOAKES, John Edward, OBE 1993; FRCGP; Partner, group medical practice in Harrow, 1961–99; *b* 27 April 1935; *s* of Edward and Mary Noakes; *m* 1960, Margaret Ann Jenner; two *s* one *d*. *Educ:* Wanstead County High Sch.; Charing Cross Hospital Medical Sch. (MB BS); DObstRCOG. Trainer, Gen. Practice Vocational Trng Scheme, Northwick Park Hosp., 1974–82. Member: Brent Harrow Local Med. Cttee, 1972–97; Harrow HA, 1982–90; CMO's Wkg Gp on Health of Nation, 1990–98; Chm., Brent Harrow Med. Audit Adv. Gp, 1992–95. Non-exec. Director: HEA, 1995–2000; HDA, 2000–03. Mem. Council, RCGP, 1989–94 (Vice-Chm., 1990–92; Chairman: NW London Faculty, 1989–91; Maternity Care Task Gp, 1994). *Recreations:* music (mainly opera), horticulture (Alpine plants), exploring Britain's canal system in own Narrow Boat. *Address:* Old Church Cottage, Chapel Lane, Long Marston, Herts HP23 4QT.

NOAKES, Michael, RP; portrait and landscape painter; *b* 28 Oct. 1933; *s* of late Basil and Mary Noakes; *m* 1960, Vivien Noakes (*née* Langley), DPhil, FRSL, writer; two *s* one *d*. *Educ:* Downside; Royal Academy Schs, London. Nat. Dipl. in Design, 1954; Certificate of Royal Academy Schools, 1960. Commnd: National Service, 1954–56. Has broadcast and appeared on TV on art subjects in UK and internationally; Art Correspondent, BBC TV programme Town and Around, 1964–68; subject of BBC films: (with Eric Morley) Portrait, 1977, 1978; (with JAK) Changing Places, 1989. Member Council: ROI, 1964–78 (Vice-Pres. 1968–72; Pres., 1972–78; Hon. Mem. Council, 1978–; Fellow, 1996–); RP, 1969–71, 1972–74, 1978–80, 1993–95, 2004, 2006–07; NS, 1962–76 (Hon. Mem., 1976–); Chm., Contemp. Portrait Soc., 1971; a Dir, Fedn of British Artists, 1981–83 (a Governor, 1972–83). Freeman, City of London; Liveryman, Co. of Woolmen. *Exhibited:* Nat. Portrait Gall. Permt Collection; Christie's (one man show); Royal Soc. of Portrait Painters; Royal Acad.; many other mixed exhibns with socs in UK and abroad. Judge, Miss World Contest, 1976. Platinum disc, 1977 (record sleeve design Portrait of Sinatra). *Portraits include:* The Queen and most other members of the Royal family, sometimes being commissioned several times; Margaret Thatcher when Prime Minister and again currently, Bill Clinton when President, Pope Benedict XVI (commissioned by the Vatican); other leading figures from academic life, the arts, the services, the City and numerous private commns for families. *Represented in collections:* the Queen and Royal Collection Windsor; Prince of Wales; British Mus.; Nat. Portrait Gall. (incl. Hugill Fund Purchase, RA, 1972); numerous Oxford and Cambridge colleges; County Hall, Westminster; various livery companies and Inns of Court; House of Commons; Univs of London, Nottingham, East Anglia; City Univ.; Frank Sinatra. Designed £5 coin for 50th birthday of the Prince of Wales, 1998. *Publications:* A Professional Approach to Oil Painting, 1968; (with Vivien Noakes) The Daily Life of The Queen, 2000; contributions to various art journals. *Recreation:* idling. *Address:* Eaton Heights, Eaton Road, Malvern WR14 4PE. *T:* (01684) 575530; *e-mail:* mail@michael-noakes.co.uk. *Club:* Garrick.

NOBAY, Prof. (Avelino) Robert, PhD; Senior Research Associate, Financial Markets Group, London School of Economics and Political Science, since 1996; Brunner Professor of Economic Science, University of Liverpool, 1980–96; *b* 11 July 1942; *s* of Theodore Anastasio Nobay and Anna Gracia D'Silva; *m* 1st, 1965; two *s*; 2nd, 1987, Carole Ann McPhee. *Educ:* Univ. of Leicester (BA); Univ. of Chicago; PhD Southampton. Jun. Economist, Electricity Council, London, 1964–66; Res. Officer, NIESR, 1966–70; Sen. Lectr, Univ. of Southampton, 1970–80. Vis. Associate Prof., Univ. of Chicago, 1977–79; Adjunct Prof., Centre for Internat. Econ. Studies, Univ. of Adelaide, 2001–. *Publications:* (with H. G. Johnson) The Current Inflation; (with H. G. Johnson) Issues in Monetary Economics. *Recreations:* sailing, golf, music.

NOBBS, David Gordon; writer; *b* 13 March 1935; *s* of Gordon and Gwen Nobbs; *m* 1st, 1968, Mary Blatchford (marr. diss. 1998); two step *s* one step *d*; 2nd, 1998, Susan Sutcliffe; one step *d*. *Educ:* Marlborough; St John's Coll., Cambridge (BA English). Wrote scripts for: That Was the Week That Was, BBC TV, 1963; The Frost Report, The Two Ronnies, The Fall and Rise of Reginald Perrin, 1976–78; BBC TV: The Hello Goodbye Man, 1984; Dogfood Dan and The Carmarthen Cowboy, 1988; Love on a Branch Line, 1994; Gentlemen's Relish, 2000; Yorkshire TV: Sez Les; Cupid's Darts, 1981; A Bit of a Do, 1989, 1990; Rich Tea and Sympathy, 1991; Stalag Luft, 1993; Granada: Our Young Mr Wignall, 1976; The Glamour Girls, 1980, 1982; Channel 4: Fairly Secret Army, 1984, 1986; The Life and Times of Henry Pratt, 1992. *Publications:* The Itinerant Lodger, 1965; Ostrich Country, 1968; A Piece of the Sky is Missing, 1969; The Fall and Rise of Reginald Perrin, 1975; The Return of Reginald Perrin, 1977; The Better World of Reginald Perrin, 1978; Second From Last in the Sack Race, 1983; A Bit of a Do, 1986; Pratt of the Argus, 1988; Fair Do's, 1990; The Cucumber Man, 1994; The Legacy of Reginald Perrin, 1995; The Reginald Perrin Omnibus, 1999; Going Gently, 2000; I Didn't Get Where I Am Today: an autobiography, 2003; Sex and Other Changes, 2004; Pratt à Manger, 2006; Cupid's Dart, 2007. *Recreations:* cricket, football, bird-watching, travel, food, drink, bridge, theatre. *Address:* c/o Jonathan Clowes, Iron Bridge House, Bridge Approach, NW1 8BD. *Club:* Hereford United Football.

NOBES, (Charles) Patrick; retired Headmaster and teacher of English; *b* 17 March 1933; *o c* of Alderman Alfred Robert Nobes, OBE, JP, and Marguerite Violet Vivian (*née* Fathers), Gosport, Hants; *m* 1958, Patricia Jean (*née* Brand) (marr. diss. 2004); three *s*. *Educ:* Price's Sch., Fareham, Hants; University Coll., Oxford. MA. With The Times, reporting and editorial, 1956–57; Head of English Dept, King Edward VI Grammar Sch., Bury St Edmunds, 1959–64; Head of English and General Studies and Sixth Form Master, Ashlyns Comprehensive Sch., Berkhamsted, 1964–69; Headmaster: The Ward Freman Sch., Buntingford, Herts, 1969–74; Bedales Sch., 1974–81; Weymouth Grammar Sch., 1981–85, later The Budmouth Sch., 1985–86; St Francis' Coll., Letchworth, 1986–87. Chairman: HMC Co-ed Schs Gp, 1976–80; Soc. of Headmasters of Independent Schs, 1978–80; Mem., SHA Council, 1985–86. Pres., Soc. of Old Priceans, 1999–. General Editor and adapter, Bulls-Eye Books (series for adults and young adults with reading difficulties), 1972–. *Recreations:* writing, cricket and hockey, King Arthur, Hampshire, music, First World War.

NOBLE, Adam; *see* Noble, R. A.

NOBLE, Adrian Keith; freelance director; Artistic Director, Royal Shakespeare Company, 1991–2003; *b* 19 July 1950; *s* of late William John Noble and Violet Ena (*née* Wells); *m* 1991, Joanne Elizabeth Pearce; one *s* one *d*. *Educ:* Chichester High Sch. for Boys; Bristol Univ. (BA); Drama Centre, London. Associate Dir, Bristol Old Vic, 1976–79; Resident Dir, RSC, 1980–82; Guest Dir, Royal Exchange Theatre, Manchester, 1980–81; Associate Dir, RSC, 1982–90. *Stage productions include:* Ubu Rex, A Man's A Man, 1977; A View from the Bridge, Titus Andronicus, The Changeling, 1978; Love for Love, Timon of Athens, Recruiting Officer (Edinburgh Fest.), 1979; Duchess of Malfi, 1980, Paris 1981 (Critics Award for Best Dir, 1982); Dr Faustus, The Forest, A Doll's House, 1981 (Critics Awards for Best Dir and Best Revival, 1982); King Lear, Antony and Cleopatra, 1982; A New Way to Pay Old Debts, Comedy of Errors, Measure for Measure, 1983; Henry V, The Winter's Tale, The Desert Air, 1984; As You Like It, 1985; Mephisto, The Art of Success (and NY, 1989), Macbeth, 1986; Kiss Me Kate, 1987; The Plantagenets, 1988; The Master Builder, 1989; The Three Sisters, 1990; Henry IV, parts 1 and 2, 1991; The Thebans, 1991; Hamlet, Winter's Tale (Globe Award for Best Dir, 1994), 1992; King Lear, Travesties, Macbeth, 1993; A Midsummer Night's Dream, 1994; Romeo and Juliet, The Cherry Orchard, 1995; Little Eyolf, 1996; Cymbeline, Twelfth Night, 1997; The Tempest, The Lion, the Witch and the Wardrobe, 1998; The Family Reunion, 1999; The Seagull, The Secret Garden, 2000; Chitty Chitty Bang Bang (also NY, 2005), Pericles, 2002; Brand, A Woman of No Importance, 2003; The Home Place, Gate, Dublin, 2005; Summer and Smoke, 2006, Kean, 2007, Apollo; *opera:* Don Giovanni, Kent Opera, 1983; The Fairy Queen (Grand Prix des Critiques), 1989, Il Ritorno d'Ulisse in Patria (Grand Prix des Critiques), 2000, Aix-en-Provence Fest.; The Magic Flute, Glyndebourne, 2004; Falstaff, Gothenburg, 2005; Così fan Tutti, 2006, Marriage of Figaro, 2007, Lyon; *film:* A Midsummer Night's Dream, 1996. Vis. Prof., London Inst., 2001–. Hon. Bencher, Middle Temple, 2001. Hon. DLitt:

Birmingham, 1994; Bristol, 1996; Exeter, 1999; Warwick, 2001. *Address:* c/o Duncan Heath, Independent Talent Group Ltd, Oxford House, 76 Oxford Street, W1N 0AX.

NOBLE, Alison; *see* Noble, J. A.

NOBLE, Alistair William; Sheriff of Glasgow and Strathkelvin, since 1999; *b* 10 Jan. 1954; *s* of late William Alexander Noble and Alexanderina Noble (*née* Fraser); *m* 1986, Olga Helena Marr Wojtas. *Educ:* Aberdeen Grammar Sch.; Aberdeen Univ. (LLB). Admitted Advocate, 1978; Temporary Sheriff, 1986; Sheriff of N Strathclyde at Dunoon, 1992–99. *Recreation:* reading. *Address:* Sheriff's Chambers, Sheriff Court House, 1 Carlton Place, Glasgow G5 9DA. *T:* (0141) 429 8888.

NOBLE, Amelia Anne Doris, (Mrs S. Manchipp); designer; Partner, Kerr/Noble, since 1997; *b* 5 May 1973; *d* of David and Antonia Noble; *m* 2000, Simon Manchipp; one *s*. *Educ:* Bedgebury Sch., Goudhurst; London Guildhall Univ. (Foundn Course in Art and Design); Central St Martin's Coll. of Art and Design (BA Hons); Royal Coll. of Art (MA). Vis. Lectr, Central St Martins Coll. of Art and Design, 1997–2002. Clients include Liberty, V&A Mus., British Council, Design Mus., David Chipperfield Architects, and Tate Modern. *Recreation:* connecting with my plants. *Address:* Kerr/Noble, 2nd Floor, 74 Great Eastern Street, EC2A 3JL. *T:* (020) 7739 5777; *e-mail:* amelia@kerrnoble.com. *Club:* Typographic Circle.

NOBLE, Andrew James, LVO 1995; HM Diplomatic Service; Director, Security and Estates (formerly Head, Security Strategy Unit, later Security Director), Foreign and Commonwealth Office, since 2005; *b* 22 April 1960; *s* of Kenneth John Noble and late Rosemary Noble; *m* 1992, Helen Natalie Pugh; two *s* two *d*. *Educ:* Honley High Sch., Huddersfield; Gonville and Caius Coll., Cambridge (BA Hons Modern and Medieval Langs 1982). Entered HM Diplomatic Service, 1982; Third Sec., Bucharest, 1983–86; Federal Foreign Ministry, Bonn, 1986–87 (on secondment); Second Sec., Bonn, 1987–89; FCO, 1989–94; First Sec., Cape Town/Pretoria, 1994–98; Dep. Hd, Security Policy Dept, FCO, 1998–2001; Dep. Hd of Mission and Consul Gen., Athens, 2001–05. *Recreations:* choral singing, cooking, my family. *Address:* c/o Foreign and Commonwealth Office, King Charles Street, SW1A 2AH; *e-mail:* Andrew.Noble@fco.gov.uk.

NOBLE, Barrie Paul; Chairman, 2004–08, Vice President, since 2008, West Oxfordshire Conservative Association; *b* 17 Oct. 1938; *s* of late Major and Mrs F. A. Noble; *m* 1965, Alexandra Helene Giddings; one *s*. *Educ:* Hele's, Exeter; New Coll., Oxford (BA Jurisprudence); Univ. of Dakar. RAF, 1957–59. HM Diplomatic Service, 1962–93: Third, later Second Sec., (Leopoldville) Kinshasa, 1965–67; Second Sec. (Commercial), Kaduna, 1967–69; FCO, 1969–72; First Sec., 1972–75 and Head of Chancery, 1975, Warsaw; FCO, 1976–80; Counsellor, UK Mission to UN, Geneva, 1980–84; Counsellor: FCO, 1984–89; Paris, 1989–93; Chm., CSSB Panel, 1993–97; Chm. and Assessor, CSSB Preliminary (Disabled) Interview Bd, 1997–99. *Publication:* Droit Coutumier, Annales Africaines, 1965. *Recreations:* grass cutting, bridge, ski-ing. *Clubs:* Royal Air Force, Ski Club of Great Britain.

NOBLE, Rt Rev. Brian Michael; *see* Shrewsbury, Bishop of, (RC).

NOBLE, David, CBE 1989; Under Secretary and Head of Administrative Division, Medical Research Council, 1981–89, retired; *b* 12 June 1929; *s* of late William Ernest Noble and Maggie (*née* Watt); *m* 1969, Margaret Patricia Segal. *Educ:* Buckhurst Hill County High Sch., Essex; University Coll., Oxford (BA Hons English, 1952). Admin. Assistant, UCH, 1952–58; Mem., Operational Res. Unit, Nuffield Provincial Hosps Trust, 1958–61; Project Sec., Northwick Park Hosp. and Clinical Res. Centre, NW Thames RHA and MRC, 1961–68; Medical Research Council: Principal, 1968–72; Asst Sec., 1972–81. Member: Nat. Biological Standards Bd, 1983–90; PHLS Bd, 1990–97 (Dep. Chm., 1996–97). *Publications:* contribs to literature on operation and design of hosps and res. labs. *Recreations:* music, reading, travel. *Address:* 173 Bittacy Hill, NW7 1RT. *T:* (020) 8346 8005.

NOBLE, Sir David (Brunel), 6th Bt *cr* 1902, of Ardmore and Ardadan Noble, Cardross, Co. Dunbarton; sales consultant, Allied Maples Group Ltd, 1989–97; *b* 25 Dec. 1961; *s* of Sir Marc Brunel Noble, 5th Bt, CBE and of Jennifer Lorna, *d* of late John Mein-Austin; *S* father, 1991; *m* 1st, 1987, Virginia Ann (marr. diss. 1993), *yr d* of late Roderick Wetherall; two *s*; 2nd, 1993, Stephanie (*née* Digby); two *s* one *d* (and one *s* decd). *Educ:* Eton Coll.; Cambridge Tutors, Croydon; Canterbury Coll.; Greenwich Univ. (BA). Sales Exec., Gabriel Communications Ltd, 1986–88. Patron, Special Needs Children, 1997–. *Recreations:* golf, photography, gardening. *Heir: s* Roderick Lancaster Brunel Noble, *b* 12 Dec. 1988. *Address:* Meridian Court, 4 Wheelers Lane, Linton, Maidstone, Kent ME17 4BL. *Club:* HAC.

NOBLE, David Clive; Director General, Finance, Defence Equipment and Support, Ministry of Defence, since 2007; *b* 11 Nov. 1955; *s* of Keith and Dorothy Noble; *m* 1982, Jennifer Bainbridge; two *s* one *d*. *Educ:* King Edward VI Sch., Southampton; Queen's Coll., Oxford (BA 1978). ACMA 1986. Finance Director: Rolls-Royce and Associates, 1995–98; Rolls-Royce Energy Ops, 1998–2001; Gp Finance Dir, Nedalo, 2002–03; Finance Dir, Defence Procurement Agency, 2003–07. *Recreation:* reality television. *Address:* Defence Equipment and Support, Ministry of Defence, Abbey Wood, Bristol BS34 8JH; *e-mail:* davidcnoble@yahoo.com.

NOBLE, David Jonathan; Chief Parliamentary Counsel and Compiler of Statutes, New Zealand, since 2007 (on secondment); Legal Adviser, Department for Children, Schools and Families (formerly Department for Education and Skills), since 2004; *b* 19 April 1955; *s* of Kevin Charles Noble and Dr Prudence Mary Noble (*née* Proudlove); *m* 1986, Diana Stuart Jeffery; one *s* one *d*. *Educ:* Wallington Grammar Sch. for Boys, Surrey; Univ. of Birmingham (MSocSc); Univ. of Warwick (LLB Hons; Lord Rootes Scholar.). Res. Asst, Faculty of Laws, UCL, 1978–81; called to the Bar, Gray's Inn, 1981; Sen. Asst Solicitor, London Bor. of Camden, 1983–86; Solicitor, Nabarro Nathanson, 1986; Principal Solicitor, London Bor. of Camden, 1986–87; Sen. Principal Legal Asst, DoE, 1987–91; Nat. Expert, DG XI, EC, 1991–94; Asst Solicitor, DoE, 1994–96; Sen. Principal Jurist, DG XI, EC, 1996–98; Principal Estabt Officer, Legal Secretariat to Law Officers, 1998–2000; Dir of Legal Services, Food Standards Agency, 2000–01; Dep. Legal Advr, Home Office, 2001–04. Mem. Editl Bd, Environmental Law Rev. *Publications:* (contrib.) Discretion and Welfare, 1981; (contrib.) Protecting the European Environment: enforcing EC environmental law, 1996; (contrib.) Perspectivas de Derecho Communitario Ambiental, 1997; articles pubd in Urban Law and Policy and Jl of Planning and Environmental Law. *Recreations:* swimming, ski-ing, shopping. *Address:* (office) Level 12, Reserve Bank Building, 2 The Terrace, PO Box 18070, Wellington, New Zealand. *T:* (4) 4729639, *Fax:* (4) 4991724; *e-mail:* david.noble@parliament.govt.nz. *Club:* Royal Over-Seas League.

NOBLE, Prof. Denis, CBE 1998; FMedSci; FRS 1979; Burdon Sanderson Professor of Cardiovascular Physiology, Oxford University, 1984–2004, now Professor Emeritus; Tutorial Fellow, 1963–84, Professorial Fellow, 1984–2004, now Emeritus, Balliol College, Oxford; *b* 16 Nov. 1936; *s* of George and Ethel Noble; *m* 1965, Susan Jennifer Barfield, BSc, BA, DPhil; one *s* one *d*. *Educ:* Emanuel Sch., London; University Coll. London (BSc, MA, PhD; Fellow 1985). Asst Lectr, UCL, 1961–63; Tutor in Physiology, Balliol Coll., and Univ. Lectr, Oxford Univ., 1963–84; Praefectus of Holywell Manor (Balliol Graduate Centre), 1971–89; Vice-Master, Balliol Coll., 1983–85. Founder Dir, Physiome Scis Inc., 1994–2003. Visiting Professor: Alberta, 1969–70; Univs of BC, Calgary, Edmonton, and SUNY at Stonybrook, 1990; Univ. of Auckland, 1990; Osaka Univ., 2005; Adjunct Prof., Xian Jiaotong Univ., China, 2003–07. Lectures: Darwin, British Assoc., 1966; Nahum, Yale, 1977; Bottazzi, Pisa, 1985; Ueda, Tokyo, 1985; Lloyd Roberts, London Med. Soc., 1987; Allerdale Wyld, Northern Industrial and Technical Soc., 1988; Bowden, UMIST, 1988; Annual, Internat. Science Policy Foundn, 1993; Rijlant, Internat. Congress of Electrocardiology, Japan, 1994; Frank May, Leicester Univ., 1996; Conf. Claude Bernard, Soc. de Physiologie, Lille, 1996; Stevenson, Univ. of Western Ontario, 1996; Larmor, Belfast, 2003; Magnes, Jerusalem, 2003; Conway, UCD, 2004. Chm., Jt Dental Cttee (MRC, SERC, Depts of Health), 1985–90. Hon. Sec., 1974–80, Foreign Sec., 1986–92, Hon. Mem., 1997, Physiol Soc.; Founder Mem., Save British Science; Pres., Med. Section, BAAS, 1991–92; Sec. Gen., IUPS, 1994–2001 (Chm., IUPS Congress, Glasgow, 1993). Member: Partnership Korea, DTI, 1995–2000; Korea Adv. Gp, UK Trade & Investment (formerly Trade Partners UK), DTI, 2000–06. Editor, Progress in Biophysics, 1967–; Cons. Ed., Jl of Experimental Physiology, 2004–; Chief Ed., Disease Models, 2004–07; Head, Physiol. Faculty, Faculty of 1000, 2004–. Founder FMedSci 1998; Hon. MRCP 1988; Hon. FRCP 1994; Hon. FIPEM 2001. MAE 1989; Hon. Member: Amer. Physiol. Soc., 1996; Japanese Physiol Soc., 1998; Hon. Foreign Mem., Acad. Royale de Médicine de Belgique, 1993. Hon. DSc: Sheffield, 2004; Bordeaux 2, 2005; Warwick, 2008. Scientific Medal, Zoolog. Soc., 1970; Gold Medal, British Heart Foundn, 1985; Pierre Rijlant Prize, Belgian Royal Acad., 1991; Baly Medal, RCP, 1993; Hodgkin-Huxley-Katz Prize, Physiol Soc., 2004; Mackenzie Prize, British Cardiac Soc., 2005. *Publications:* Initiation of the Heartbeat, 1975, 2nd edn, 1979; Electric Current Flow in Excitable Cells, 1975; Electrophysiology of Single Cardiac Cells, 1987; Goals, No Goals and Own Goals, 1989; Sodium-Calcium Exchange, 1989; Ionic Channels and the Effect of Taurine on the Heart, 1993; The Logic of Life, 1993; (ed with J.-D. Vincent) Ethics of Life, 1997 (trans. French 1998); The Music of Life, 2006 (trans. French 2007, Spanish 2008, Italian 2009, Japanese 2009); papers mostly in Jl of Physiology; contribs on sci. res. and funding to New Scientist, nat. press, radio and TV. *Recreations:* Indian and French cooking, Occitan language and music, classical guitar. *Address:* 49 Old Road, Oxford OX3 7JZ. *T:* (office) (01865) 272533.

NOBLE, Gillian Mae, CB 1999; Director (formerly Deputy Director) (Law and Order, Health and Local Government), HM Treasury, 1995–2001; *b* Edinburgh, 18 Nov. 1947; *d* of John Noble and Jessie Mae Noble (*née* Bonnington). *Educ:* Aberdeen Univ. (MA Hons Econ. Sci. 1969); University Coll. London (MSc Public Sector Econs 1974). Joined MoT, subseq. DoE, as econ., 1969; transf. to HM Treasury, 1976; various posts dealing with: planning and control of public expenditure, 1976–84; pensions and social security, 1984–87; Asst Sec., 1986; Head: Banking Div., 1987–92; Educn Sci. and Nat. Heritage Div., 1992; Under Sec., 1993; Hd, Health, Social Services and Territorial Depts Gp, 1993–95. Lay Mem., Nat. Biol Standards Bd, 2002–. Trustee: Meningitis Trust, 1996–; St George's Hospital Charity (formerly Charitable Foundn), 2001– (Chm., 2002–). *Recreations:* listening to music, visiting heritage properties.

NOBLE, Sir Iain (Andrew), 3rd Bt *cr* 1923, of Ardkinglas and Eilean Iarmain; OBE 1988; businessman and entrepreneur, historian and writer; Proprietor, Fearann Eilean Iarmain estate, Isle of Skye, since 1972, and Hotel Eilean Iarmain; Chairman, Pràban na Linne Ltd (The Gaelic Whiskies), since 1976; Chairman and Chief Executive, Sir Iain Noble & Partners Ltd, since 2000; *b* 8 Sept. 1935; *s* of Sir Andrew Napier Noble, 2nd Bt, KCMG and Sigrid, 2nd *d* of Johan Michelet, Norwegian Diplomatic Service; *S* father, 1987; *m* 1990, Lucilla Charlotte James, *d* of late Col H. A. C. Mackenzie, OBE, MC, TD, DL, JP, Dalmore. *Educ:* China; Argentina; Eton; University Coll., Oxford (MA 1959). Matthews Wrightson, London, 1959–64; Scottish Council (Develt and Industry), Edinburgh, 1964–69; Jt Founder and Jt Man. Dir, Noble Grossart Ltd, merchant bankers, Edinburgh, 1969–72; Jt Founder and Chm., Seaforth Maritime Ltd, Aberdeen, 1972–78; Founder and Chairman: Lennox Oil Co. plc, Edinburgh, 1980–85; Noble Gp Ltd, merchant bankers, 1980–2000; non-exec. Chm., Skye Bridge Ltd, 1994–96; Founder and Dir, Adam and Co. plc, Edinburgh, 1983–93; Dir, Premium Investment Trust, 1993–2002. Dep. Chm., Traverse Theatre, Edinburgh, 1966–68; Mem., Edinburgh Univ. Court, 1970–73; Founder, first Chm., 1973–74, and Trustee, 1974–84, College of Sabhal Mor Ostaig, Isle of Skye; Trustee, Nat. Museums of Scotland, 1987–91 (Trustee, Charitable Trust, 1991–). Founder, and Chm., Scots Australian Council, 1991–99; Pres., Saltire Soc., 1992–96. Keeper of the Quaich, 2000–. Visits to Faroe Isles, 1969–75. Hotel Eilean Iarmain awarded Hotel of the Year, Relais Routier, 2001. Scotsman of the Year Award, 1981. *Publication:* (ed) Sources of Finance, 1968. *Recreations:* Comhradh, beul-aithris is ceol le deagh chompanaich. *Heir: b* Timothy Peter Noble [*b* 21 Dec. 1943; *m* 1976, Elizabeth Mary, *d* of late Alexander Wallace Aitken; two *s* one *d*]. *Address:* An Lamraig, Eilean Iarmain, An t-Eilean Sgitheanach IV43 8QR; 20 Great Stuart Street, Edinburgh EH3 7TN. *T:* (offices) (01471) 833266 and (0131) 220 2400. *Club:* New (Edinburgh).

NOBLE, Rt Rev. John Ashley; Bishop of North Queensland, 2002–07; *b* 30 March 1944; *s* of Mowbray Lloyd Noble and Norma June (*née* Shucksmith); *m* 1969, Lorene May Christine Wardrop; one *s* one *d*. *Educ:* St Francis Theological Coll., Brisbane (ThL 1965); Univ. of Queensland (BA 1973); Mt Gravatt Teachers' Coll., Brisbane (Cert. in Teaching, Secondary 1973). Deacon 1965, priest 1968; Asst Curacies, 1965–69; History Subject Master, Queensland Dept of Educn, 1974–78; Asst Chaplain, St Peter's Coll., Adelaide, 1979–81; Chaplain, St Paul's Sch., Brisbane, 1981–82; Diocese of Brisbane: Rector, St John's, Dalby, 1982–84; Rector, St Barnabas', Sunnybank, 1984–88; Lectr, St Francis Theol Coll., 1989–93; an Asst Bishop, 1993–2002; Bishop of the Northern Region, 1993–99; Dir, Ministries Develt and Theol Educn, 1999–2002. *Recreations:* reading, music, computers. *Address:* 59 Scotchmer Street, Fitzroy North, Vic 3068, Australia.

NOBLE, Prof. (Julia) Alison, DPhil; CEng; FIET; Professor of Engineering Science, University of Oxford, since 2002; Fellow of Wolfson College, Oxford, since 2005; *b* Nottingham, 28 Jan. 1965; *d* of James Bryan Noble and Patricia Ann Noble; *m* 2001, Mark Louis Durand; two *d*. *Educ:* St Hugh's Coll., Oxford (BA Hons 1st Cl. Engrg Sci. 1986; DPhil Engrg Sci. 1989). CEng 1995; FIET 2001. Res. Scientist, GE Corporate R&D Center, Schenectady, NY, 1989–94; Lectr, 1995–2000, Reader, 2000–02, in Engrg Sci., Univ. of Oxford. Sen. MIEEE 2006. *Publications:* articles in professional jls. *Recreations:* pilates, attending live concerts and sports events. *Address:* Institute of Biomedical Engineering, Department of Engineering Science, University of Oxford, Old Road Campus Research Building, off Roosevelt Drive, Headington, Oxford OX3 7DQ. *T:* (01865) 617690; *e-mail:* alison.noble@eng.ox.ac.uk.

NOBLE, (Richard) Adam; Head of Research Analysts, Foreign and Commonwealth Office, 2007–08; *b* 9 June 1962; *s* of John Alfred Noble and Susan Vera Noble (*née* Thornton); *m* 1994, Katrina Johnson; two *s*. *Educ:* Bolton Sch. (Boys' Div.); SSEES, Univ.

of London (BA Hons); Moscow State Univ.; St Antony's Coll., Oxford (MPhil). Joined FCO, 1987; Third, then Second Sec. (Chancery), Moscow, 1987–89; Second, then First Sec., FCO, 1989–93; First Sec., The Hague, 1993–95; FCO, 1995–98; First Sec. (Political) New Delhi, 1998–2001; Hd, Res. Analysts, FCO, 2001–02; Dep. Consul-Gen. and Dep. Hd of Mission, Hong Kong, 2004–06; Chief Exec., Wilton Park, 2006–07.

NOBLETT, Ven. William Alexander; Chaplain-General and Archdeacon to HM Prisons, since 2001; Chaplain to the Queen, since 2005; *b* Dublin, 16 April 1953; *s* of Joseph Henry and Hilda Florence Noblett; *m* 1986, Margaret Armour; one *s*. *Educ:* High Sch., Dublin; Salisbury and Wells Theol Coll.; Univ. of Southampton (BTh 1978); MTh Oxford 1999. Ordained deacon, 1978, priest, 1979; Curate, Sholing, Southampton, 1978–80; Rector, Ardamine Union, 1980–82; Chaplain, RAF, 1982–84; Vicar, Middlesbrough St Thomas, 1984–87; Chaplain of HM Prison: Wakefield, 1987–93; Norwich, 1993–97; Full Sutton, 1997–2001. Canon and Prebend, York Minster, 2001–. *Publication:* Prayers for People in Prison, 1998. *Recreations:* reading, music. *Address:* Room 410, Abell House, John Islip Street, SW1P 4LH.

NODDER, Timothy Edward, CB 1982; Deputy Secretary, Department of Health and Social Security, 1978–84; *b* 18 June 1930; *s* of Edward Nodder; *m* 1952, Sylvia Broadhurst; two *s* two *d*. *Educ:* St Paul's Sch.; Christ's Coll., Cambridge. Under-Sec., DHSS, 1972. *Recreation:* natural history. *Address:* 83 Oakley Street, SW3 5NP.
See also L. A. McLaughlin.

NOEL, family name of **Earl of Gainsborough**.

NOEL, Geoffrey Lindsay James; Metropolitan Stipendiary Magistrate, 1975–93; *b* 19 April 1923; *s* of Major James Noel and Maud Noel; *m* 1st, 1947; two *d*; 2nd, 1966, Eileen Pickering (*née* Cooper); two step *s*. *Educ:* Crewkerne Sch., Somerset. Enlisted Royal Regt of Artillery, 1941; commnd, 1942; attached 9th Para Bn, 6 Airborne Div., 1944, Captain; POW Oflag 79; RWAFF, 1952–55; Major 1957; retd 1960. Called to Bar, Middle Temple, 1962; practised London and SE circuit. Chm., Juvenile Courts, 1977–79; Dep. Circuit Judge, 1980–82. *Recreations:* gardening, golf. *Address:* Loja, Albourne Road, Hurstpierpoint, Hassocks, W Sussex BN6 9ES.

NOEL, Hon. Gerard Eyre Wriothesley, FRSL; author and lecturer; Editorial Director, Catholic Herald, 1976–81 and since 1984 (Editor, 1971–76 and 1982–84); *b* 20 Nov. 1926; *s* of 4th Earl of Gainsborough, OBE, TD, and Alice (*née* Eyre); *m* 1958, Adele, *d* of Major V. N. B. Were and Dr Josephine Were (*née* Ahern), OBE; two *s* one *d*. *Educ:* Georgetown, USA; Exeter Coll., Oxford (MA, Modern History). Called to Bar, Inner Temple, 1952. Director: Herder Book Co., 1959–66; Search Press Ltd, 1972–. Literary Editor, Catholic Times, 1958–61; Asst Editor, Catholic Herald, 1968–71. Sen. Res. Fellow, St Anne's Coll., Oxford, 1993–. Lects and lect. tours, UK, USA, Ireland and Spain; Vis. Lectr, Oxford Centre for Jewish Studies, 1992–93. Mem. Exec. Cttee, 1974–, Hon. Treasurer, 1979–81, Vice Chm., 2004–, Council of Christians and Jews. Contested (L) Argyll, 1959. FRSL 1999. Liveryman, Co. of Stationers and Newspapermakers. Freeman, City of London. Gold Staff Officer at Coronation, 1953. *Publications:* Paul VI, 1963; Harold Wilson, 1964; Goldwater, 1964; The New Britain, 1966; The Path from Rome, 1968; Princess Alice: Queen Victoria's Forgotten Daughter, 1974; contrib. The Prime Ministers, 1974; The Great Lock-Out of 1926, 1976; The Anatomy of the Roman Catholic Church, 1980; Ena: Spain's English Queen, 1984; Cardinal Basil Hume, 1984; (jtly) The Anatomy of the Catholic Church: before and after Pope John Paul II, 1994; Stranger than Truth: life and its fictions, 1996; A Portrait of the Inner Temple, 2002; Sir Gerard Noel, MP and the Noels of Chipping Campden, 2004; Miles: a portrait of the 17th Duke of Norfolk, 2004; (contrib.) Here is Chelsea, 2004; (contrib.) Anglicanism and the Western Christian Tradition, 2004; A Volume on Vermouth, 2006; The Catholic Herald: 1966–2006, a scrapbook, 2006; The Renaissance Popes, 2006; New Light on Lourdes, 2008; Pius XII: the hound of Hitler, 2008; *translations:* The Mystery of Love, 1960; The Way to Unity after the Council, 1967; The Holy See and the War in Europe (Official Documents), 1968; contrib. Oxford DNB; articles in: Church Times, Catholic Times, Jewish Chronicle, Baptist Times, Catholic Herald, Literary Review, European, International Mind. *Recreations:* Romance languages, Renaissance popes, old films. *Address:* (office) Herald House, Lamb's Passage, EC1Y 8TQ; Westington Mill, Chipping Campden, Glos GL55 6EB. *Clubs:* Pratt's, Garrick, White's.
See also R. J. B. Noel.

NOEL, Lynton Cosmas; barrister, retired 1994; *b* 25 Oct. 1928; *m* 1962, Teresa Angela Diamonda; one *s* one *d*. *Educ:* St Joseph's RC Sch., Grenada; Polytechnic/Holborn Coll. of Law, Languages and Commerce; Inns of Court Sch. of Law (LLB). Called to the Bar, Lincoln's Inn, 1976. Asst Head Teacher, 1956–60; Telephone Engr, GPO, 1960–67; practised law, 1976–84; Lectr in Law, Coll. of Law Studies, 1984; 1st Sec., Grenada High Commn, London, 1984–85; Chargé d'Affaires, Caracas, 1985–90; High Comr for Grenada in London, 1990–92; returned to practice at the Bar, 1992. *Recreations:* music, chess.

NOEL, Robert John Baptist; Lancaster Herald of Arms, since 1999; *b* 15 Oct. 1962; *s* of Hon. Gerard Eyre Wriothesley Noel, *qv*. *Educ:* Ampleforth; Exeter Coll., Oxford (MA Hebrew); St Edmund's Coll., Cambridge (MPhil Internat. Relns). Baltic Exchange, 1984–85; Christie's, 1988–91; Bluemantle Pursuivant, 1992–99. Vice-Chm., White Lion Soc., 1998–. Fellow, Purchase Soc., 1998. Officer of Arms Attendant, Imperial Soc. of Kts Bach., 2001–. *Address:* College of Arms, 130 Queen Victoria Street, EC4V 4BT. *T:* (020) 7332 0414, *Fax:* (020) 7248 6448. *Clubs:* Brooks's, Beefsteak, Garrick, Pratt's, Chelsea Arts.

NOEL-BAKER, Hon. Francis Edward; Director, North Euboean Enterprises Ltd, since 1973; *b* 7 Jan. 1920; *o s* of Baron Noel-Baker, PC, and late Irene, *o d* of Frank Noel, British landowner, of Achmetaga, Greece; *m* 1957, Barbara Christina (*d* 2004), *yr d* of late Joseph Sonander, Sweden; four *s* one *d* (and one *s* decd). *Educ:* Westminster Sch.; King's Coll., Cambridge (Exhibitioner; 1st cl. hons History). Founder and Chm., CU Lab. Club, 1939; left Cambridge to join Army, summer 1940, as Trooper, Royal Tank Regt; Commissioned in Intelligence Corps and served in UK, Force 133, Middle East (despatches). Editor, United Nations World/World Horizon, 1945–47, Go! magazine, 1947–48; BBC European Service, 1950–54. MP (Lab) Brentford and Chiswick Div. of Middx, 1945–50; PPS Admiralty, 1949–50; MP (Lab) Swindon, 1955–68; sent by Prime Minister to mediate in Cyprus, 1956; Sec., 1955–64, Chm., 1964–68, UN Parly Cttee; resigned from Lab. Party, 1969; Vice-Chm., Lab. Cttee for Europe, 1976–78; Member: SDP 1981–83; NUJ, 1946–81. Chm., Advertising Inquiry Council, 1951–68. Chairman: North Euboean Foundation Ltd, 1965–; Candili Craft Centre, Philip Noel-Baker Centre, Euboea, 1983–; Dir, Fini Fisheries, Cyprus, 1976–90; Founder Pres., European Council for Villages and Small Towns, 1984–; Hon. Pres., Union of Forest Owners of Greece, 1968–. Member: Parochial Church Council, St Martin in the Fields, 1960–68; Freedom from Hunger Campaign UK Cttee Exec. Cttee, 1961; Ecology Party, 1978–; Soil Assoc., 1979–. Governor, Campion Sch., Athens, 1973–78. Archives Fellow Commoner, Churchill Coll., Cambridge, 1989. Wine Constable, Guyenne, 1988–. *Publications:* Greece, the Whole Story, 1946; Spanish Summary, 1948; The Spy Web, 1954; Land and People of Greece, 1957; Nansen, 1958; Looking at Greece, 1967; My Cyprus File, 1985; Book Eight: a taste of hardship, 1987; Three Saints and Poseidon, 1988. *Recreation:* gardening. *Address:* Achmetaga Estate, 340–04 Procopi, Greece. *T:* (22270) 41204, *Fax:* (22270) 41190. *Club:* Special Forces.
See also M. E. F. Chance.

NOEL-BUXTON, family name of **Baron Noel-Buxton**.

NOEL-BUXTON, 3rd Baron *cr* 1930; **Martin Connal Noel-Buxton;** *b* 8 Dec. 1940; *s* of 2nd Baron Noel-Buxton and Helen Nancy (*d* 1949), *yr d* of late Col K. H. M. Connal, CB, OBE, TD; *S* father, 1980; *m* 1st, 1964, Miranda Mary (marr. diss. 1968), *er d* of H. A. Chisenhale-Marsh; 2nd, 1972, Sarah Margaret Surridge (marr. diss. 1982), *o d* of N. C. W. Barrett, TD; one *s* one *d*; 3rd, 1986, Abigail Marie, *yr d* of E. P. R. Clent; one *d*. *Educ:* Bryanston School; Balliol College, Oxford (MA). Admitted a Solicitor, 1966. *Heir: s* Hon. Charles Connal Noel-Buxton, *b* 17 April 1975.

NOEL-PATON, Hon. (Frederick) Ranald; Chairman, Murray Global Return plc, 2000–05 (Director, 1998–2005); *b* 7 Nov. 1938; *s* of Baron Ferrier, ED and Joane Mary, *d* of Sir Gilbert Wiles, KCIE, CSI; *m* 1973, Patricia Anne Stirling; four *d*. *Educ:* Rugby School; McGill Univ. (BA). Various posts, British United Airways, 1965–70; various sen. exec. posts, British Caledonian Airways, 1970–86; John Menzies Plc: Gp Man. Dir, 1986–97; Dep. Chm., 1997–98. Dir, 1986–98, Chm., 1998–2004, Pacific Assets Trust plc; Director: General Accident plc, 1987–98; Macallan-Glenlivet plc, 1990–96; Royal Bank of Scotland Gp, 1991–93. Hon. DBA Napier, 1992. *Recreations:* fishing, walking, golf, gardening, bird watching, the arts. *Address:* Pitcurran House, Abernethy, Perthshire PH2 9LH. *Clubs:* Royal Perth Golfing Soc. and County and City (Perth); Royal and Ancient Golf (St Andrews); Shek-O Country, Hong Kong (Hong Kong).

NOEST, Peter John, FRICS; Managing Director: P. H. Gillingham (Investments) Ltd, since 1987; Capital Consultancy Group, since 1993; Cotswold Land and Estates Ltd, since 2000; Chairman, P. H. Gillingham Group Ltd, since 2003; *b* 12 June 1948; *s* of Major A. J. F. Noest and Mrs M. Noest-Gerbrands; *m* 1st, 1972, Lisabeth Penelope Moody (marr. diss. 1993); one *s* one *d*; 2nd, 1993, Jocelyn Claire (*d* 2003), *yr d* of late A. D. Spencer; one *s*. *Educ:* St George's Coll., Weybridge; Royal Agricl Coll., Cirencester. FRICS 1978 (ARICS 1973). Joined Knight Frank & Rutley, 1971; Partner i/c Dutch office, Amsterdam, 1972; London Partner, 1977; full equity Partner, 1981; Consultant, 1983, full equity Partner, 1984, Hampton & Sons; Dir, Hampton & Sons Holdings, 1987 (subseq. merged with Lambert Smith to form Lambert Smith Hampton); Dir, Lambert Smith Hampton, 1988–92. *Publication:* contrib. Estates Gazette. *Recreations:* hunting, shooting, photography, travel. *Address:* Manor Farmhouse, Withington, Cheltenham, Glos GL54 4BG. *Club:* Turf.

NOGAMI, Yoshiji; Ambassador of Japan to the Court of St James's, 2004–08; *b* 19 June 1942; *s* of Hiroshi Nogami and Masako Nogami; *m* 1978, Geraldine Ann Woods McDermott; three *s*. *Educ:* Univ. of Tokyo (BA American Studies). Joined Min. of Foreign Affairs, Japan, 1966; Econ. Counsellor, Washington, 1985–88; Actg Dir, Japan Inst. for Internat. Affairs, Tokyo, 1988–91; Deputy Director-General: ME and African Affairs Bureau, 1991–93, Foreign Policy Bureau, 1993–94, Min. of Foreign Affairs; Consul Gen., Hong Kong, 1994–96; Dir Gen., Econ. Affairs Bureau, Min. of Foreign Affairs, 1996–97; Ambassador to OECD, 1997–99; Dep. Minister for Foreign Affairs, 1999–2001; Vice-Minister for Foreign Affairs, 2001–02; Sen. Vis. Fellow, RIIA, 2002–04. Officier de la Légion d'Honneur (France), 2001. *Recreations:* golf, cookery. *Address:* c/o Embassy of Japan, 101–104 Piccadilly, W1J 7JT. *Clubs:* Athenæum, Travellers, Royal Automobile; Brocket Hall.

NOGUEIRA, Albano Pires Fernandes; Ambassador of Portugal; *b* 8 Nov. 1911; *m* 1937, Alda Maria Marques Xavier da Cunha (*d* 1998). *Educ:* Univ. of Coimbra. 3rd Sec., Washington, 1944; 2nd Sec., Pretoria, 1945; 1st Sec., Pretoria, 1948; Head of Mission, Tokyo, 1950; Counsellor, London, 1953; Consul-Gen., Bombay, 1955; Consul-Gen., NY, 1955; Dep. Perm. Rep. UN, NY, 1955; Asst Dir-Gen., Econ. Affairs, Lisbon, 1959; Dir Gen., Econ. Affairs, Lisbon, 1961; Ambassador to: European Communities, Brussels, 1964; NATO, 1970; Court of St James's, 1974–76; Sec.-Gen., Ministry for Foreign Affairs, 1977. Vis. Prof., Univ. of Minho, Braga, 1979, 1980. Mem., Internat. Assoc. of Literary Critics, 1981–. Grand Cross: Merito Civil (Spain), 1961; Order of Infante Dom Henrique (Portugal), 1964; Isabel la Católica (Spain), 1977; Merit (Germany), 1977; St Olav (Norway), 1978; Christ (Portugal), 1981; the Flag with golden palm (Yugoslavia), 1978; Grand Officer: Cruzeiro do Sul (Brazil), 1959; White Elephant (Thailand), 1960. *Publications:* Imagens em Espelho Côncavo (essays); Portugal na Arte Japonesa (essay); Uma Agulha no Céu (novel); contribs to: NATO and the Mediterranean, 1985; NATO's Anxious Birth—the Prophetic Vision of the 1940s, 1985; contrib. leading Portuguese papers and reviews. *Recreations:* reading, writing. *Address:* Avenida Gaspar Corte-Real 18, Apt 4D, 2750–164 Cascais, Portugal. *T:* (21) 4868264; Rua Alberto de Oliveira 5–3–Esc., 3000–016 Coimbra, Portugal. *T:* (239) 715035. *Clubs:* Grémio Literário, Automóvel de Portugal (Lisbon).

NOKES, Prof. David Leonard, PhD; FRSL; Professor of English, King's College, London, since 1998; *b* 11 March 1948; *s* of Anthony John Nokes and Ethel Murray Nokes; *m* 1997, Margaret Andrée Marie Denley (*née* Riffard); one *d*. *Educ:* King's Coll., Wimbledon; Christ's Coll., Cambridge (BA 1st Cl. 1969; MA 1972; PhD 1974). Lectr, 1973–86, Reader, 1986–98, King's Coll., London. FRSL 1994. Mem., Johnson Club. *Adaptations for television:* Clarissa, 1991; The Count of Solar, 1992; The Tenant of Wildfell Hall, 1996; *radio play:* The Man on the Heath, 2005. *Publications include:* Jonathan Swift: a hypocrite reversed (James Tait Black Meml Prize), 1985; Raillery and Rage, 1987; John Gay, 1995; Jane Austen, 1997; The Nightingale Papers (novel), 2005. *Recreations:* reading, writing, painting. *Address:* 3 Hobson's Acre, Great Shelford, Cambridge CB2 5XB; *e-mail:* DavidLNokes@aol.com.

NOKES, Stephen Anthony; Headmaster, John Hampden Grammar School, High Wycombe, since 2000; *b* Portsmouth, 31 Aug. 1952; *s* of Alan and Sheila Nokes; *m* 1984, Diana Rose; two *s*. *Educ:* St John's Coll., Southsea; University Coll. Swansea (MA); St John's Coll., Oxford (PGCE 1978); Univ. of Hertfordshire (AdvDip 1982). Teacher of Hist., Chiswick Sch., 1978–86; Hd of Hist. and Pols, Chesham High Sch., 1986–89; Hd of Humanities, 1989–92, Sen. Teacher, 1992–96, Dep. Hd, 1996–99, Beaconsfield High Sch. Chm., Bucks Sch. Forum, 2008–; founder Mem., Professional Assoc. of Selective Schs, 2007–; Member: High Achieving Sports Schs, 2007–; Internat. Boys' Schs Coalition, 2007–. Chm., Thames Valley Politics Assoc., 1997–2000. Governor: Davenies Sch., Beaconsfield, 2005–; Westfield Sch., Bourne End, 2005–. *Publication:* (jtly) Guide to First World War Battlefield Sites, 1987. *Recreations:* watching, analysing, discussing sport especially Rugby; theatre, ballet and travel (with wife); collecting and driving sports and classic cars (with sons); watching movies, playing with techno gadgets (middle-aged male). *Address:* John Hampden Grammar School, Marlow Hill, High Wycombe, Bucks HP11

1SZ. *T*: (01494) 529589, *Fax*: (01494) 447714; *e-mail*: office@ johnhampdengrammar.bucks.sch.uk.

NOLAN, Benjamin; QC 1992; a Recorder, since 1989; a Deputy High Court Judge; *b* 19 July 1948; *s* of Benjamin Nolan and Jane Nolan (*née* Mercer); two *d. Educ*: St Joseph's Coll., Blackpool; Newcastle upon Tyne Polytechnic; LLB London, 1970. Called to the Bar, Middle Temple, 1971, Bencher, 2004. *Recreations*: travel, cooking, walking, swimming, gardening. *Address*: Broad Chare Chambers, 33 Broad Chare, Newcastle upon Tyne NE1 3DQ. *T*: (0191) 232 0541.

NOLAN, Dominic Thomas; QC 2006; a Recorder, since 2005; *b* 16 Jan. 1963; *s* of Dennis Nolan and Patricia Nolan; *m* 1988, Catherine Lucy, (Kate), Allen; three *s. Educ*: St Teresa's Jun. Boys' Sch., Norris Green; St Edward's Coll., Liverpool; Univ. of Nottingham (LLB Hons 1984). Called to the Bar, Lincoln's Inn, 1985 (Hardwicke Scholar, Buchanan Prizeman, Student of the Yr, 1985). Special Lectr, Sch. of Law, Univ. of Nottingham, 2003–. *Recreations*: family, friends, music, National Hunt racing, running slowly. *Address*: Ropewalk Chambers, 24 The Ropewalk, Nottingham NG1 5EF. *T*: (0115) 947 2581.

NOLAN, Prof. Peter Hugh, PhD; Sinyi Professor of Chinese Management, Judge Business School (formerly Judge Institute of Management Studies), University of Cambridge, since 1997; Fellow, Jesus College, Cambridge, since 1979; *b* 28 April 1949; *s* of Charles Patrick Nolan and Barbara Vere Nolan; *m* 1975, Siobáin Suzanne Mulligan; one *s* one *d. Educ*: St Boniface's Coll., Plymouth; Fitzwilliam Coll., Cambridge (Open Schol.; BA 1970); SOAS, Univ. of London (MSc 1971; PhD 1981). Res. Fellow, Contemporary China Inst., SOAS, Univ. of London, 1971–75; Lectr, Dept of Economic History, Univ. of NSW, 1976–78; Res. Officer, Inst. of Commonwealth Studies, Oxford Univ., 1978–79; Cambridge University: Asst Lectr, 1979–84, Lectr, 1984–97, Faculty of Econs and Politics; Dir of Studies in Econs, Jesus Coll., 1980–97; Chair, Develt Studies Cttee, 1995–. *Publications*: (jtly) Inequality: India and China compared 1950–1970, 1976; Growth Processes and Distributional Change in a South Chinese Province: the case of Guangdong, 1983; (ed jtly) Re-thinking Socialist Economics, 1986; The Political Economy of Collective Farms: an analysis of China's post-Mao rural economic reforms, 1988; (ed jtly) Market Forces in China: competition and small business—the Wenzhou debate, 1989; (ed jtly) The Chinese Economy and Its Future, 1990; State and Market in the Chinese Economy: essays on controversial issues, 1993; (ed jtly) China's Economic Reforms in the 1980s: the costs and benefits of incrementalism, 1994; (ed jtly) The Transformation of the Communist Economies: against the mainstream, 1995; China's Rise, Russia's Fall: politics and economics in the transition from Stalinism, 1995; Indigenous Large Firms in China's Economic Reforms: the case of Shougang Iron and Steel Corporation, 1998; Coca-Cola and the Global Business Revolution, 1999; China and the Global Economy, 2001; China and the Global Business Revolution, 2001; (in Chinese) Looking at China's Enterprises, 2002; China at the Crossroads, 2003; Transforming China, 2003; (jtly) The Global Business Revolution and the Cascade Effect, 2007; Integrating China, 2007; Capitalism and Freedom: the contradictory character of globalisation, 2007. *Recreations*: swimming, music, playing recorder. *Address*: Jesus College, Cambridge CB5 8BL. *T*: (01223) 339477.

NOLAN, Philip Michael Gerard, PhD; Chairman, Infinis Limited, since 2007; *b* 15 Oct. 1953; *m* 1978, Josephine Monaghan; two *s. Educ*: Queen's Univ., Belfast (BSc Geol. 1976; PhD 1980); London Business Sch. (MBA 1991). Lectr in Geol., Ulster Poly., 1979–81; joined BP, 1981: geologist, holding posts in exploration, appraisal and develt, in UK, US and Australia, 1981–87; BP Exploration, London: commercial and planning posts, Head Office, 1987–93; Manager, Acquisitions and Disposals, 1993–95; on secondment as Man. Dir, Interconnector (UK) Ltd, 1995–96; joined BG, 1996: Dir, East Area, 1996–97, Man. Dir, 1997–99, Chief Exec., 1999–2001, Transco; Dir, BG, 1999–2000; Chief Executive: Lattice Gp plc, 2000–01; eircom Ltd, 2002–06. Non-exec. Dir, De la Rue plc, 2000–. *Recreations*: golf, watching football and Rugby, walking, listening to music, reading. *Address*: Infinis Limited, 500 Pavilion Road, Northampton Business Park, Northampton NN4 7YJ.

NOON, Sir Gulam (Kaderbhoy), Kt 2002; MBE 1996; Founder, Noon Products Ltd, 1989 (Chairman, 1989–2005, non-executive Chairman, since 2005); Chairman, Noon Group, since 1995; *b* Bombay, 24 Jan. 1936; *s* of Kaderbhoy Ebrahimjee and Safiabai Kaderbhoy; *m* 1998, Mohini Kent; two *d*. Joined family business, Royal Sweets, Bombay, 1953; Man. Dir, Bombay Halwa Ltd, London, 1972–. Mem. Bd, Transport for London, 2004–. Founder, Asian Business Assoc., 1995 (Chm.); Mem. Bd, 1998–, Pres., 2002–; London Chamber of Commerce and Ind.; Chm., London Internat. Trade Forum, 2002–. Mem. Adv. Council, Prince's Trust, 1996–; Founder Mem., Cancer Res. UK, 2002–; Mem. Bd, Care Internat. UK, 2002–06; Trustee: Noon Foundn, 1995–; Arpana Charitable Trust UK, 1996–2006; Memorial Gates Trust, 1998–; British Food Trust, 1999–; Maimonides Foundn, 2002–. MUniv Surrey, 1998; Hon. DBA: London Guildhall, 2001; DUniv: Middlesex, 2002; UCE, 2002. Asian of the Year, 1994; Outstanding Lifetime Achievement Award, Asian Business Network, 1998; Multicultural Achievement Award, Carlton TV, 2002; Best Business Leader, Sage Business Awards, 2003; Asian Jewel Award, 2003. *Recreations*: cricket, current affairs, cinema. *Address*: 25 Queen Anne's Gate, St James's Park, SW1H 9BU. *Clubs*: Reform, MCC.

NOON, Paul Thomas; General Secretary, Prospect, since 2002 (Joint General Secretary, 2001–02); *b* 1 Dec. 1952; *s* of Thomas Noon and Barbara Noon (*née* Grocott); *m* 1977, Eileen Elizabeth Smith; two *d*. MoD, 1971–74; Institution of Professional Civil Servants: Asst Negotiations Officer, 1974–77; Negotiations Officer, 1977–81; Asst Sec., 1981–89; Asst Gen. Sec., 1989–99; Gen. Sec., Instn of Professionals, Managers and Specialists, 1999–2001. Mem., Gen. Council, 2001–, Exec. Cttee, 2002–, TUC. Board Member: Unions Today, 1999–2002; Trade Union Fund Managers, 2001–; Chairman: CCSU, 2001–03; Civil Service Housing Assoc., (Vice-Chm., 1999–2002). Mem. Bd, ETM Placements, 2006–07. *Recreations*: reading, politics, family. *Address*: 3 Warwick Close, Bexley, Kent DA5 3NL. *T*: (01322) 550968, *Fax*: (01322) 550309; Prospect, 8 Leake Street, SE1 7NN. *T*: (020) 7902 6704, *Fax*: (020) 7902 6667.

NOONEY, David Matthew; Director, Civil Justice and Legal Services, Department for Constitutional Affairs, 2003–04; *b* 2 Aug. 1945; *m* 1973, Maureen Georgina Revell; one adopted *d. Educ*: St Joseph's Acad., Blackheath. FICMA. HM Treasury, 1965–86; on loan to Lord Chancellor's Dept as Management Accounting Advr, 1986–88, transf. to the Dept, 1989; Head, Resources Div., 1988–91; Head, Civil Business, 1991–93; Head, Legal Services and Agencies Div., 1993; Prin. Estabt and Finance Officer, then Dir, Corporate Services, CPS, 1993–98; on secondment to Welsh Office, 1998–99; Dir, Modernising Govt Prog., LCD, 1999–2003. *Recreations*: sport, theatre, crosswords, poetry.

NOORDHOF, Jennifer Jane; *see* Eady, J. J.

NORBROOK, Prof. David Gordon Ellis, DPhil; Merton Professor of English Literature, University of Oxford, since 2002; Fellow of Merton College, Oxford, since 2002; *b* 1 June 1950. *Educ*: Univ. of Aberdeen (MA 1972); Balliol Coll., Oxford;

Magdalen Coll., Oxford (Prize Fellow 1975; DPhil 1978). Oxford University: Lectr in English, 1978–98; Fellow and Tutor in English, Magdalen Coll., 1978–98, Emeritus Fellow, 1999; Prof. of English, Univ. of Maryland, 1999–2002. Vis. Prof., Graduate Center, CUNY, 1989. *Publications*: Poetry and Politics in the English Renaissance, 1984, 2nd edn 2002; (with Henry Woudhuysen) The Penguin Book of Renaissance Verse, 1992; Writing the English Republic: poetry, rhetoric and politics 1627–1660, 1999 (James Holly Hanford Prize, Milton Soc. of America, 2000); (ed) Lucy Hutchinson's Order and Disorder, 2001; numerous articles and reviews. *Recreation*: (armchair) travel. *Address*: Merton College, Oxford OX1 4JD.

NORBURN, Prof. David, PhD; Director, The Management School, Imperial College of Science, Technology and Medicine, and Professor of Management, University of London, 1987–2003; *b* 18 Feb. 1941; *s* of late Richard Greville and Constance Elizabeth Norburn; *m* 1st, 1962, Veronica Ellis (marr. diss. 1975); one *s* one *d*; 2nd, 1975, Prof. Susan Joyce Birley, *qv. Educ*: Bolton Sch.; LSE (BSc); City Univ. (PhD). Salesman, Burroughs Corp., 1962–66; Management Consultant, Price Waterhouse, 1966–67; Sen. Lectr, Regent Street Polytechnic, 1967–70; Sen. Res. Fellow, City Univ., 1970–72; Lectr, Sen. Lectr, Dir, MBA programme, London Business Sch., 1972–82; Inaugural Chairholder, Franklin D. Schurz Prof. in Strategic Management, Univ. of Notre Dame, Indiana, 1982–85; Prof. of Strategic Management, Cranfield Inst. of Technology, 1985–87. Director: Newchurch & Co., 1985–97; Whurr Publishing Co. Ltd, 1994–2002; Com. Medica Ltd, 1999–2003; Management Diagnostics Ltd, 2001–08; Mainstream Hldgs (US), 2005–. Director: Strategic Mgt Soc., 1993–2002; Bd of Companions, Inst. of Mgt, 1994–97. Freeman, Clockmakers' Co. CCMI; FRSA. Editor, European Business Journal, 1988–2003. *Publications*: British Business Policy (with D. Channon and J. Stopford), 1975; (jtly) Globalisation of Telecommunications, 1994; (jtly) Fusion in Home Automation, 1994; (with Sir William Nicoll and R. Schoenberg) Perspectives on European Business, 1995; articles in professional jls. *Recreations*: antiquarian horology, competitive tennis, carpentry. *Address*: The Mill House, Benham Park, Marsh Benham, Newbury, Berks RG20 8LX.

NORBURN, Susan Joyce, (Mrs David Norburn); *see* Birley, S. J.

NORBURY, 7th Earl of, *cr* 1827 (Ire.); **Richard James Graham-Toler;** Baron Norwood 1797; Baron Norbury 1800; Viscount Glandine 1827; *b* 5 March 1967; *o s* of 6th Earl of Norbury and of Anne, *d* of Francis Mathew; *S* father, 2000.

NORBURY, Brian Martin; Member, Independent Monitoring Board (formerly Board of Visitors), Pentonville Prison, since 1994 (Chairman, 1999–2003 and 2005–06); *b* 2 March 1938; *s* of Robert Sidney Norbury and Doris Lilian (*née* Broughton). *Educ*: Churcher's Coll., Petersfield; King's Coll., London (BA; AKC 1959). National Service, RAEC, 1959–61. Asst Principal, WO, 1961; Private Sec. to Under Sec. of State for War, 1962; Asst Private Sec. to Dep. Sec. of State for Defence, 1964; Principal, MoD, 1965, Cabinet Office, 1969; Private Sec. to Sec. of the Cabinet, 1970–73; Asst Sec., MoD, 1973; Principal Private Sec. to Sec. of State for Defence, 1979–81; Under Sec., MoD, 1981, DES, later Dept for Educn, 1984–94. Lay Mem., Special Educnl Needs Appeals Tribunal, 1994–2003. Trustee, Choice Support, 1999–. FRSA 1992. *Recreation*: remembering riding on top of Routemaster buses. *Address*: 6 The Red House, 49–53 Clerkenwell Road, EC1M 5RS. *Club*: Reform.

NORCROSS, Lawrence John Charles, OBE 1986; Headmaster, Highbury Grove School, 1975–87; *b* 14 April 1927; *s* of Frederick Marshall Norcross and Florence Kate (*née* Hedges); *m* 1958, Margaret Wallace; three *s* one *d. Educ*: Ruskin Coll., Oxford; Univ. of Leeds (BA Hons English). Training Ship, Arethusa, 1941–42; RN, 1942–49 (E Indies Fleet, 1944–45); clerical asst, 1949–52; Asst Teacher: Singlegate Sch., 1957–61; Abbey Wood Sch., 1961–63; Housemaster, Battersea County Sch., 1963–74; Dep. Headmaster, Highbury Grove Sch., 1974–75. Member: NAS/UWT, 1970–86; Secondary Heads' Assoc., 1975–87; HMC, 1985–87; Trustee and Mem. Exec. Cttee, Nat. Council for Educnl Standards, 1976–89; Trustee: Educnl Res. Trust, 1986–; Ind. Primary and Secondary Educn Trust, 1987–93; Grant Maintained Schools Trust, 1988–94; Nat. Cttee for Educnl Standards, 1997–; Director: Choice in Educn, 1989–94; Grant-Maintained Schs Foundn, 1994–97; Member: Educn Study Gp, Centre for Policy Studies, 1980–; Univ. Entrance and Schs Examinations Council, Univ. of London, 1980–84; Steering Cttee, Campaign for a Gen. Teaching Council. Mem., Adv. Council, Educn Unit, IEA, 1986–90. Founder and Hon. Sec., John Ireland Soc., 1960–; former Chm., Contemp. Concerts Co-ordination. *Publications*: (with F. Naylor) The ILEA: a case for reform, 1981; (with F. Naylor and J. McIntosh) The ILEA after the Abolition of the GLC, 1983; (contrib.) The Wayward Curriculum, 1986; GCSE: the Egalitarian Fallacy, 1990; occasional articles. *Recreations*: talking to friends, playing bridge badly, watching cricket, listening to music. *Address*: Amberley, Cotswold Close, Tredington, Shipston-on-Stour, Warwicks CV36 4NR. *T*: (01608) 661628. *Club*: Surrey County Cricket.

NORDEN, Denis, CBE 1980; scriptwriter and broadcaster; *b* 6 Feb. 1922; *s* of George Norden and Jenny Lubell; *m* 1943, Avril Rosen; one *s* one *d. Educ*: Craven Park Sch., London; City of London Sch. Theatre Manager, 1939–42; served RAF, 1942–45; staff-writer in Variety Agency, 1945–47. With Frank Muir, 1947–64: collaborated for 17 years writing comedy scripts, including: (for radio): Take It From Here, 1947–58; Bedtime with Braden, 1950–54; (for TV): And So To Bentley, 1956; Whack-O!, 1958–60; The Seven Faces of Jim, 1961, and other series with Jimmy Edwards; resident in TV and radio panel-games; collaborated in film scripts, television commercials, and revues; joint Advisors and Consultants to BBC Television Light Entertainment Dept, 1960–64; jointly received Screenwriters Guild Award for Best Contribution to Light Entertainment, 1961; together on panel-games My Word!, 1956–93, and My Music, 1967–. Since 1964, solo writer for television and films; Looks Familiar (Thames TV), 1973–87; It'll Be Alright on the Night (LWT), 1977–2005; It'll be Alright on the Day, 1983; In On The Act, 1988; Pick of the Pilots, 1990; Denis Norden's Laughter File, 1991–2005; Denis Norden's Trailer Cinema, 1992; Laughter by Royal Command, 1993; 40 Years of ITV Laughter, 1995; Legends of Light Music, 1995. Film Credits include: The Bliss of Mrs Blossom; Buona Sera, Mrs Campbell; The Best House in London; Every Home Should Have One; Twelve Plus One; The Statue; The Water Babies. Variety Club of GB Award for Best Radio Personality (with Frank Muir), 1978; Male TV Personality of the Year, 1980; Lifetime Achievement Award: Writers' Guild of GB, 1999; RTS, 2000. *Publications*: (with Frank Muir): You Can't Have Your Kayak and Heat It, 1973; Upon My Word!, 1974; Take My Word for It, 1978; The Glums, 1979; Oh, My Word!, 1980; The Complete and Utter My Word Stories, 1983; Coming to You Live! behind-the-screen memories of 50s and 60s Television, 1986; You Have My Word, 1989. *Recreations*: reading, loitering. *Club*: Saturday Morning Odeon.

NORDMANN, François; Swiss Ambassador to France, since 2002, and to Monaco, since 2006; *b* 13 May 1942; *s* of Jean and Bluette Nordmann; *m* 1980, Miriam Bohadana. *Educ*: Univ. de Fribourg (licencié en droit). Private Sec. to Foreign Minister, Switzerland, 1975–80; Counsellor and Perm. Observer, Mission to UN, NY, 1980–84; Ambassador to Guatemala, El Salvador, Honduras, Nicaragua, Costa Rica and Panama, 1984–87;

Ambassador and Head of Swiss Perm. Delegn to UNESCO, Paris, 1987–92; Ambassador and Dir, Directorate of Internat. Orgns, Swiss Foreign Min., Berne, 1992–94; Ambassador to UK, 1994–99; Mission to Internat. Orgns, Geneva, 2000–02. *Recreations:* reading, theatre, walking, golf. *Address:* Swiss Embassy, 142 rue de Grenelle, 75007 Paris, France. *Club:* Cercle de l'Union Interalliée (Paris).

NORFOLK, 18th Duke of, *cr* 1483; **Edward William Fitzalan-Howard;** DL; Earl of Arundel, 1139; Baron Beaumont, 1309; Baron Maltravers, 1330; Earl of Surrey, 1483; Baron FitzAlan, Clun, and Oswaldstre, 1627; Earl of Norfolk, 1644; Baron Howard of Glossop, 1869; Earl Marshal and Hereditary Marshal and Chief Butler of England; Premier Duke and Earl; *b* 2 Dec. 1956; *er s* of 17th Duke of Norfolk, KG, GCVO, CB, CBE, MC and Anne Mary Teresa, CBE (*née* Constable-Maxwell); *S* father, 2002; *m* 1987, Georgina, *y d* of Jack and Serena Gore; three *s* two *d*. *Educ:* Ampleforth Coll., Yorks; Lincoln Coll., Oxford. Chairman: Sigas Ltd, 1979–88; Parkwood Group Ltd, 1989–2002. DL W Sussex, 2002. *Recreations:* ski-ing, motor-racing, shooting. *Heir: s* Earl of Arundel and Surrey, *qv*. *Address:* Arundel Castle, West Sussex BN18 9AB. *T:* (01903) 883400. *Club:* British Racing Drivers (Silverstone).

NORFOLK, Archdeacon of; *see* Hayden, Ven. D. F.

NORFOLK, Ven. Edward Matheson; Archdeacon of St Albans, 1982–87, Emeritus since 1987; *b* 29 Sept. 1921; *s* of Edward and Chrissie Mary Wilson Norfolk; *m* 1947, Mary Louisa Oates; one *s* one *d* (and one *s* decd). *Educ:* Latymer Upper School; Leeds Univ. (BA); College of the Resurrection, Mirfield. Deacon, 1946; priest, 1947; Assistant Curate: Greenford, 1946–47; King Charles the Martyr, South Mymms, 1947–50; Bushey, 1950–53; Vicar: Waltham Cross, 1953–59; Welwyn Garden City, 1959–69; Rector, Great Berkhamsted, 1969–81; Vicar, King's Langley, 1981–82. Hon. Canon of St Albans, 1972–82. *Recreations:* walking, bird-watching. *Address:* 5 Fairlawn Court, Sidmouth, Devon EX10 8UR.

NORFOLK, Lawrence William; writer, since 1988; *b* 1 Oct. 1963; *s* of Michael Norfolk and Shirley Kathleen (*née* Blake); *m* 1994, Vineeta Rayan; two *s*. *Educ:* KCL (BA Hons (English) 1986; AKC 1986). *Publications:* Lemprière's Dictionary, 1991 (Somerset Maugham Award, 1992); The Pope's Rhinoceros, 1996; In the Shape of a Boar, 2001; (with Neal White) Ott's Sneeze, 2002. *Recreations:* swimming, skydiving, reading. *Address:* c/o Blake Friedmann Literary Agency, 122 Arlington Road, NW1 7HP.

NORFOLK, Leslie William, CBE 1973 (OBE 1944); TD 1946; CEng; Chief Executive, Royal Dockyards, Ministry of Defence, 1969–72; *b* 8 April 1911; *e s* of late Robert and Edith Norfolk, Nottingham; *m* 1944, A. I. E. W. (Nancy) Watson (then WRNS), *d* of late Sir Hugh Watson, IFS (retd); two *s* one *d*. *Educ:* Southwell Minster Grammar Sch., Notts; University Coll., Nottingham (BSc). MICE; MIMechE; MIEE. Assistant and later Partner, E. G. Phillips, Son & Norfolk, consulting engineers, Nottingham, 1932–39. 2nd Lieut 1931, 5 Foresters TA, transferred and served with RE, France, Gibraltar, Home Forces, 1939–45, Lt-Col. Engineer, Dyestuffs Div., ICI Ltd, 1945–53; Resident Engineer, ICI of Canada, Kingston, Ont., 1953–55; Asst Chief Engr, Metals Div., ICI Ltd, 1955–57; Engineering Manager, Severnside Works, ICI Ltd, 1957–59; Engineering Director, Industrias Quimicas Argentinas Duperial SAIC, Buenos Aires, 1959–65; Director, Heavy Organic Chemicals Div., ICI Ltd, 1965–68; retired from ICI, 1968. *Recreations:* home workshop, industrial archaeology. *Club:* Bath & County (Bath).

NORGARD, John Davey, AO 1982; Chairman, Australian Broadcasting Commission, 1976–81; retired as Executive General Manager, Operations, BHP Co. Ltd, and as Chairman, Associated Tin Smelters, 1970; *b* 3 Feb. 1914; *s* of John Henry and Ida Elizabeth Norgard; *m* 1943, Irena Mary Doffkont; one *s* three *d*. *Educ:* Adelaide Univ. (BE); SA Sch. of Mines (FSASM). Part-time Chm., Metric Conversion Bd, Australia, 1970–81; Chairman: Commonwealth Employment Service Review, 1976–77; Pipeline Authority, 1976–81; Mem., Nat. Energy Adv. Cttee, 1977–80. Dep. Chancellor, La Trobe Univ., 1972–75. Chm., Grad. Careers Council of Australia, 1979–86. *Address:* 29 Montalto Avenue, Toorak, Victoria 3142, Australia. *T:* (3) 98274937. *Clubs:* Australian, Royal Melbourne Golf (Melbourne).

NORGROVE, David; Chairman, The Pensions Regulator, since 2005; *b* 23 Jan. 1948; *s* of Douglas and Ann Norgrove; *m* 1977, Jenny Stoker; one *s* two *d*. *Educ:* Christ's Hosp.; Exeter Coll., Oxford (BA); Emmanuel Coll., Cambridge (Dip. Econs); London Sch. of Econs (MSc). HM Treasury, 1972–78 and 1980–85; First Nat. Bank of Chicago, 1978–80; Private Sec. to the Prime Minister, 1985–88; Marks and Spencer, 1988–2004, Exec. Dir, 2000–04. Non-exec. Dir, Strategic Rail Authy, 2002–04. Trustee, BM, 2004– (Chm., British Mus. Co., 2004–05). Trustee: Hanover Trust, 1993–2003; Media Trust, 1998–2003; Mencap, 2000–03. *Recreations:* music, walking, ski-ing. *Address:* The Pensions Regulator, Napier House, Trafalgar Place, Brighton BN1 4DW. *T:* (01273) 627612, *Fax:* (01273) 627630; *e-mail:* david.norgrove@thepensionsregulator.gov.uk.

NORGROVE, Michael William; Director, Central Compliance, HM Revenue and Customs, since 2006; *b* 16 Dec. 1952; *s* of Walter and Nell Norgrove; *m* 1977, Lalita (*née* Shiner); one *s* one *d*. *Educ:* Palmer's Boys' Sch., Grays, Essex; Bedford Coll., London (BA 1974); King's Coll. London (MA 1975); St John's Coll., Oxford (PGCE 1978). Joined HM Customs and Excise as Exec. Officer, 1978, Admin trainee, 1981; seconded to HM Treasury, 1985–87; Principal, 1986; seconded to UK Permanent Repn, Brussels, 1988–93; Asst Sec., 1992; Head, Financial Mgt Div., 1993–98; apptd Comr, HM Bd of Customs and Excise, 1998; Comr, Ops (Compliance), 1998–2001; Dir, Large Business Gp, 2001–02; Exec. Dir, Intelligence, HM Customs and Excise, subseq. HMRC, 2002–06. *Recreations:* Real tennis, golf, jazz. *Address:* HM Revenue and Customs, 100 Parliament Street, SW1A 2BQ.

NORLAND, Otto Realf; Director, Northern Navigation International Ltd, USA, 1991–2006; London representative, Deutsche Schiffsbank (formerly Deutsche Schiffahrtsbank) AG, 1984–2000; Chairman, Otto Norland Ltd, 1984–2000; *b* 24 Feb. 1930; *s* of Realph I. O. Norland and Aasta S. Sæther; *m* 1955, Gerd Ellen Andenæs; two *d* (one *s* decd). *Educ:* Norwegian University College of Economics and Business Administration, Bergen. FCIB. Hambros Bank Ltd, 1953–84, Dir, 1964–84. Director: Alcoa of Great Britain Ltd, 1968–84 (Chm., 1978–84); Banque Paribas Norge A/S, Oslo, 1986–88. Dir, Aluminium Fedn Ltd, 1979–84 (Pres., 1982). Freeman, City of London, 2005; Freeman, 2004, Liveryman, 2006, Shipwrights' Co. *Recreations:* tennis, ski-ing, books (polar explorations). *Clubs:* Naval and Military, Den Norske; Norske Selskab (Oslo).

NORMAN, Rear-Adm. Anthony Mansfeldt, CB 1989; Bursar and Fellow, St Catharine's College, Cambridge, 1989–97; *b* 16 Dec. 1934; *s* of Cecil and Jean Norman; *m* 1961, Judith Pye; one *s* one *d*. *Educ:* Royal Naval Coll., Dartmouth. Graduate ndc. Various sea/shore appts, 1952–73; Staff of Dir Underwater Weapons, 1973–74; student ndc, 1974–75; CO HM Ships Argonaut and Mohawk, 1975–76; Fleet Anti-Submarine Warfare Officer, 1976–78; CO (Captain), HMS Broadsword, 1978–80; Asst Dir Naval Plans, MoD, 1980–83; Captain: 2nd Frigate Sqdn, HMS Broadsword, 1983–85; Sch. of Maritime Ops, HMS Dryad, 1985–86; Dir Gen., Naval Personal Services, MoD (Navy), 1986–89. *Recreations:* tennis, hill walking, travel. *Address:* c/o National Westminster Bank, 208 Piccadilly, W1A 2DG. *Club:* Army and Navy.

NORMAN, Archibald John; Chairman, Aurigo Management Partners LLP, since 2007; *b* 1 May 1954; *s* of Dr Archibald Percy Norman, *qv*; *m* 1983, Vanessa Mary Peet; one *d*. *Educ:* Univ. of Minnesota; Emmanuel Coll., Cambridge (BA Hons Econs, MA); Harvard Business Sch. (MBA 1979). Citibank NA, 1975–77; McKinsey & Co. Inc., 1979–86, Principal 1984; Gp Finance Dir, Woolworth Holdings plc, later Kingfisher plc, 1986–91; Gp Chief Exec., 1991–96, Chm., 1996–99, Asda Group plc. Chairman: Chartwell Land plc, 1987–91; Energis plc, 2002–05; HSS, 2007–; non-exec. Chm., French plc, 1999–2001; non-exec. Dir, Geest plc, 1988–91; Member: British Railways Bd, 1992–94; Railtrack Gp Bd, 1994–2000. Sen. Advr, Lazard & Co., 2004–; Advr to Coles Supermarkets, Australia, 2007–. Member: DTI Deregulation Taskforce, 1993–97; Anglo-German Deregulation Taskforce, 1995. MP (C) Tunbridge Wells, 1997–2005. Chief Exec. and Dep. Chm., Cons. Party, 1998–99 (a Vice-Chm., 1997–98); Opposition front bench spokesman on the envmt, transport and the regions, 2000–01. Gov., NIESR, 1997–. Fellow, Marketing Soc. Hon. Dr Leeds Metropolitan, 1995. Yorkshire Business Man of the Year, 1995; NatWest Retailer of the Year, 1996. *Recreations:* farming, opera, music, fishing, ski-ing, tennis. *Address:* Davies House, 33 Davies Street, W1K 4LR.

NORMAN, Archibald Percy, MBE 1945; MD; FRCP, FRCPCH, FRCPI; Physician, Hospital for Sick Children, 1950–77, then Hon. Physician; Paediatrician, Queen Charlotte's Maternity Hospital, 1951–77, then Hon. Paediatrician; *b* 19 July 1912; *s* of Dr George Percy Norman and Mary Margaret MacCallum; *m* 1950, Aleida Elisabeth M. M. R. Bisschop; five *s*. *Educ:* Charterhouse; Emmanuel Coll., Cambridge. FRCP 1954; FRCPI 1995; FRCPCH 1996. Served War of 1939–45, in Army, 1940–45. Chairman: Med. and Res. Cttee, Cystic Fibrosis Res. Trust, 1976–84; E Surrey Cttee, Mencap Homes Foundn, 1987–92; Mem., Attendance Allowance Appeals Bd, 1978–84. Mem., Bd of Trustees, Children's Trust, 1987–98 (Chm., 1991–93). *Publications:* (ed) Congenital Abnormalities, 1962, 2nd edn 1971; (ed) Moncreiff's Nursing and Diseases of Sick Children, 1966; (ed) Cystic Fibrosis, 1983; contributions to medical journals. *Address:* White Lodge, Heather Close, Kingswood, Surrey KT20 6NY. *T:* (01737) 832626.

See also A. J. Norman.

NORMAN, Sir Arthur (Gordon), KBE 1969 (CBE 1966); DFC 1943 (and Bar 1944); Chairman, The De La Rue Company, 1964–87; *b* N Petherton, Som, 18 Feb. 1917; *m* 1944, Margaret Doreen Harrington (*d* 1982); three *s* two *d*. *Educ:* Blundell's Sch. Joined Thomas De La Rue & Co., 1934. RAF, 1939–45; Wing-Comdr, 1943. Rejoined Thomas De La Rue & Co., 1946; Director, 1951; Managing Director, 1953–77. Vice-Chm., Sun Life Assurance Society, 1984–87 (Dir, 1966–87); Director: SKF (UK) Ltd, 1970–87; Kleinwort, Benson, Lonsdale plc, subseq. Kleinwort Benson Gp, 1985–88. Pres., CBI, 1968–70. Bd mem., Internat. Inst. for Environment and Develt, 1982–92; Chairman: WWF UK, 1977–84, 1987–90; UK CEED, 1984–96; Mem., Nature Conservancy Council, 1980–86. *Recreations:* golf, country life. *Address:* Fir Tree Cottage, Hammoon, Sturminster Newton, Dorset DT10 2DB.

NORMAN, Barry (Leslie), CBE 1998; author, journalist and broadcaster; *b* 21 Aug. 1933; *s* of late Leslie and Elizabeth Norman; *m* 1957, Diana, *o d* of late A. H. and C. A. Narracott; two *d*. *Educ:* Highgate Sch. Entertainments Editor, Daily Mail, 1969–71, then made redundant; writer and presenter of Film 1973–81, and Film 1983–98, BBC1; presenter of: Today, Radio 4, 1974–76; Going Places, Radio 4, 1977–81; Breakaway, Radio 4, 1979–80; Omnibus, BBC1, 1982; The Chip Shop, Radio 4, 1984; How Far Can You Go?, Radio 4, 1990; writer and presenter of: The Hollywood Greats, BBC1, 1977–79, 1984, 1985; The British Greats, 1980; Talking Pictures (series), BBC1, 1988; Barry Norman's Film Night, BSkyB, 1998–2001. Dir, Nat. Film Finance Corp., 1980–85. Weekly columnist: The Guardian, 1971–80; Radio Times. Gov., BFI, 1996–2001. Hon. LittD: UEA, 1991; Hertfordshire, 1996. Richard Dimbleby Award, BAFTA, 1981; Columnist of the Year, 1991; Special Award: London Film Critics' Circle, 1995; Guild of Regl Film Writers, 1995. *Publications:* The Matter of Mandrake, 1967; The Hounds of Sparta, 1968; Tales of the Redundance Kid, 1975; End Product, 1975; A Series of Defeats, 1977; To Nick a Good Body, 1978; The Hollywood Greats, 1979; The Movie Greats, 1981; Have a Nice Day, 1981; Sticky Wicket, 1984; The Film Greats, 1985; Talking Pictures, 1988; The Birddog Tape, 1992; 100 Best Films of the Century, 1993; The Mickey Mouse Affair, 1995; Death on Sunset, 1998; And Why Not? (memoirs), 2002. *Recreation:* playing village cricket. *Address:* c/o Curtis Brown Ltd, Haymarket House, 28–29 Haymarket, SW1Y 4SP. *T:* (020) 7396 6600.

NORMAN, David Mark; Chairman, Norlan Resources Ltd, since 1998; *b* 30 Jan. 1941; *s* of late Mark Richard Norman, CBE and of Helen Norman (*née* Bryan); *m* 1966, Diana Sheffield; one *s* three *d*. *Educ:* Eton Coll.; McGill Univ. (BA); Harvard Business Sch. (MBA). Norcros Ltd, 1967–77, Dir of Ops and Main Bd Dir, 1975–77; Russell Reynolds Associates Inc., 1977–82: Exec. Dir, 1977–78; Man. Dir, 1978–82; Chairman: Norman Resources Ltd, 1982–83; Norman Broadbent Internat. Ltd, 1983–98; Chm. and Chief Exec., 1987–97, non-exec. Chm., 1997–98, BNB Resources plc. Chm., Royal Ballet Sch., 2000–; Gov., Royal Ballet, 1996–. Trustee, Royal Botanic Gardens, Kew 2002–. *Recreations:* golf, tennis, rackets, classical music, opera, ballet. *Address:* Norlan Resources Ltd, 11 Eaton Place, SW1X 8BN. *T:* (020) 7285 5031, *Fax:* (020) 7235 5036; Burkham House, Alton, Hants GU34 5RS. *T:* (01256) 381211; *e-mail:* dmnorman2@aol.com. *Clubs:* Boodle's; Queen's, All England Lawn Tennis.

NORMAN, Rev. Dr Edward Robert; Canon Residentiary, 1995–2004, and Chancellor, 1999–2004, York Minster; *b* 22 Nov. 1938; *o s* of Ernest Edward Norman and Yvonne Louise Norman. *Educ:* Chatham House Sch.; Monoux Sch.; Selwyn Coll., Cambridge (MA, PhD, DD). FRHistS. Lincoln Theological Coll., 1965. Deacon, 1965; Priest, 1971. Asst Master, Beaconsfield Sec. Mod. Sch., Walthamstow, 1957–58; Fellow of Selwyn Coll., Cambridge, 1962–64; Fellow of Jesus Coll., Cambridge, 1964–71; Lectr in History, Univ. of Cambridge, 1965–88; Dean of Peterhouse, Cambridge, 1971–88 (Emeritus Fellow); Dean of Chapel, Christ Church Coll., Canterbury, 1988–95. Wilkinson Prof. of Church History, Wycliffe Coll., Univ. of Toronto, 1981–82; Associated Schol., Ethics and Public Policy Center, Washington, 1986–; Hon. Prof., Univ. of York, 1996–2004. NATO Res. Fellow, 1966–68. Asst Chaplain, Addenbrooke's Hosp., Cambridge, 1971–78. Hon. Curate, St Andrew-by-the Wardrobe, and St James Garlickhythe, City of London, 2005–. Lectures: Reith, 1978; Prideaux, 1980; Suntory-Toyota, LSE, 1984. Six Preacher in Canterbury Cathedral, 1984–90. FRSA. *Publications:* The Catholic Church and Ireland, 1965; The Conscience of the State in North America, 1968; Anti-Catholicism in Victorian England, 1968; The Early Development of Irish Society, 1969; A History of Modern Ireland, 1971; Church and Society in Modern England, 1976; Christianity and the World Order, 1979; Christianity in the Southern Hemisphere, 1981; The English Catholic Church in the Nineteenth Century, 1983; Roman Catholicism in England, 1985; The Victorian Christian Socialists, 1987; The

House of God: church architecture, style and history, 1990; Entering the Darkness: Christianity and its modern substitutes, 1991; An Anglican Catechism, 2001; Out of the Depths, 2001; Secularisation, 2002; Anglican Difficulties, 2004; The Mercy of God's Humility, 2004; The Roman Catholic Church, 2007. *Recreation:* watching television. *Address:* 2 St Anne's Court, Burlington Street, Kemp Town, Brighton BN2 1AA. *T:* (01273) 679952. *Club:* Athenæum.

NORMAN, Gailene Patricia S.; *see* Stock-Norman.

NORMAN, Ven. Garth; Archdeacon of Bromley and Bexley (formerly Bromley), 1994–2003, now Emeritus; *b* 26 Nov. 1938; *s* of Harry and Freda Norman; *m* 1977, Jacqueline Elisabeth (*née* Junge-Bateman); one *s*. *Educ:* Henry Mellish Grammar Sch., Nottingham; Univ. of Durham (BA Hons Theol, DipTh, MA); Univ. of East Anglia (MEd); Univ. of Cambridge (PGCE). Deacon 1963, priest 1964; Curate, St Anne's, Wandsworth, 1963–66; Team Vicar, Trunch, Norfolk, 1966–71; Rector of Gimingham, 1971–77; Team Rector of Trunch, 1977–83; RD, Repps, 1975–83; Principal, Chiltern Christian Trng Scheme, Dio. of Oxford, 1983–88; Dir of Training, Dio. of Rochester, 1988–94; Hon. Canon of Rochester Cathedral, 1991–2003. *Recreations:* walking, music. *Address:* 5 Riverside, Southwell, Notts NG25 0HA. *T:* (01636) 815209.

NORMAN, George Alfred B.; *see* Bathurst Norman.

NORMAN, Geraldine Lucia; UK Representative, State Hermitage Museum, St Petersburg, since 2001; Secretary, Friends of The Hermitage, since 2003; *b* 13 May 1940; *d* of Harold Hugh Keen and Catherine Eleanor Lyle Keen (*née* Cummins); *m* 1971, Frank Norman (*d* 1980). *Educ:* St Mary's Sch., Calne; St Anne's Coll., Oxford (MA). Teaching Asst, UCLA, 1961–62; Statistician, The Times, 1962–66; Econ. Writer, FAO, Rome, 1966–67; Sale Room Corresp., The Times, 1969–87; Art Market Corresp., The Independent, 1987–95. Exec. Dir, Hermitage Develt Trust, 1999–2001; Exec. Ed., Hermitage Mag., 2003–05. Medal in memory of 300 years of St Petersburg (Russian Fedn), 2005. News Reporter of Year, British Press Awards, 1976. *Publications:* (as Geraldine Keen) The Sale of Works of Art, 1971; Nineteenth Century Painters and Painting: a dictionary, 1977; (with Tom Keating and Frank Norman) The Fake's Progress, 1977; (as Florence Place) Mrs Harper's Niece, 1982; Biedermeier Painting, 1987; (with Natsuo Miyashita) Top Collectors of the World, 1993; The Hermitage: the biography of a great museum, 1997. *Recreations:* transcendental meditation, reading detective stories. *Address:* 5 Seaford Court, 220 Great Portland Street, W1W 5QR. *T:* (020) 7387 6067.
See also M. H. Keen.

NORMAN, Gregory John, AO 1999 (AM 1987); golfer; *b* 10 Feb. 1955; *s* of M. Norman; *m* 1981, Laura Andrassy (marr. diss. 2007); one *s* one *d*; *m* 2008, Christine Marie Evert, *qv*. *Educ:* Townsville Grammar Sch.; High Sch., Aspley, Queensland. Professional golfer, 1976–; tournament wins include: Open, Turnberry, 1986; Open, Royal St George's, 1993; Australian Open, 1980, 1985, 1987, 1995, 1996; US PGA, 1993, 1994; Players' Championship, 1994; numerous awards and other wins in Australia, S Africa, USA. *Publications:* My Story, 1983; Shark Attack, 1988; Greg Norman's Better Golf, 1994. *Address:* Great White Shark Enterprises Inc., 501 North A1A, Jupiter, FL 33477, USA.

NORMAN, (Herbert) John (La French), FIMIT, FISOB; writer and organ consultant; *b* 15 Jan. 1932; *s* of late Herbert La French Norman, Hon. RCO, FRSA, and Hilda Caroline (*née* West); *m* 1956, Jill Frances Sharp; one *s* two *d*. *Educ:* Tollington Sch.; Imperial Coll., London (BSc 1953). ARCS 1953. Wm Hill & Son and Norman & Beard Ltd (organbuilders by appt to HM Queen), 1953–74; Dir, 1960–74; Man. Dir, 1970–74; Exec., IBM UK Ltd, 1974–90. Work on organs in cathedrals in Gloucester, Norwich, Lichfield, Southwell Minster, Chelmsford and Brisbane, Australia; also Bath Abbey and RCO. Organ Advr, Dio. London, 1975–; Organ Consultant to: Harrow Sch.; Lancing Coll.; Mill Hill Sch.; English and American Ch, Den Haag; Gibraltar Cathedral; Liberal Jewish Synagogue, St John's Wood; St Margaret's, Westminster; St Mary's Pro-cathedral, Dublin; St Helen's, Bishopsgate; St Mary's, Twickenham; Chapel of St Mary Undercroft, Houses of Parliament; Mullingar Cathedral, Ireland; St Lawrence, Whitchurch (Handel organ); Parish Churches of Oakham, Westbourne, Ashton-on-Ribble, Baldock, Bolton, Farnham, Coulsdon and Donaghadee (NI); Armenian Ch, Kensington; St Botolph, Aldersgate; Worcester Cathedral; St Mary-le-Bow, City of London. Founding Editor: Musical Instrument Technol., 1969–2002; The Organbuilder, 1983–2000; In Sight, 1991–95; Columnist, Organists' Rev., 1980–. Member: St Albans Diocesan Synod, 1980–86; Organs Cttee, Council for Care of Churches, 1987–2001; London DAC for Care of Churches, 1989–; Cathedrals Fabric Commn for England, 1991–2001. Chm., British Inst. of Organ Studies, 2006–; Past Pres., Inst. of Musical Instrument Technol. Freeman, City of London; Liveryman, Musicians' Co., 1972–. *Publications:* (with Herbert Norman) The Organ Today, 1966, 2nd edn 1980; The Organs of Britain, 1984; (with Jim Berrow) Sounds Good, 2002; The Box of Whistles, 2007. *Recreations:* writing, music, architecture, travel. *Address:* 15 Baxendale, Whetstone, N20 0EG. *T:* (020) 8445 0801.

NORMAN, Jessye; soprano, concert and opera singer; *b* Augusta, Ga, USA, 15 Sept. 1945; *d* of late Silas Norman Sr and Janie King Norman. *Educ:* Howard Univ., Washington, DC (BM *cum laude*). Peabody Conservatory, 1967; Univ. of Michigan, 1967–68 (MMus). Operatic début, Deutsche Oper, Berlin, 1969; La Scala, Milan, 1972; Royal Opera House, Covent Garden, 1972; NY Metropolitan Opera, 1983; American début, Hollywood Bowl, 1972; Lincoln Centre, NYC, 1973. Tours include North and South America, Europe, Middle East, Australia, Israel, Japan. Many international festivals, including Aix-en-Provence, Aldeburgh, Berlin, Edinburgh, Flanders, Helsinki, Lucerne, Salzburg, Tanglewood, Spoleto, Hollywood, Ravinia. Hon. Fellow: Newnham Coll., Cambridge, 1989; Jesus Coll., Cambridge, 1989. Hon. DMus: Howard Univ., 1982; Univ. of the South, Sewanee, 1984; Boston Conservatory, 1984; Univ. of Michigan and Brandeis Univ., Mass, 1987; Harvard Univ., 1988; Cambridge, 1989; Hon. DHL Amer. Univ. of Paris, 1989. Hon. RAM 1987. Musician of the Year, Musical America, 1982; prizes include: Grand Prix du Disque (Acad. du Disque Français), 1973, 1976, 1977, 1982, 1984; Grand Prix du Disque (Acad. Charles Cros), 1983; Deutscher Schallplattenpreis, 1975, 1981; Cigale d'Or, Aix-en-Provence Fest., 1977; IRCAM record award, 1982; Grammy, 1984, 1988. Commandeur de l'Ordre des Arts et des Lettres, France, 1984. *Address:* L'Orchidée, PO Box 710, Crugers, NY 10521, USA. *T:* (914) 2712037, *Fax:* (914) 2712038.

NORMAN, John; *see* Norman, H. J. La F.

NORMAN, Prof. Kenneth Roy, FBA 1985; Professor of Indian Studies, University of Cambridge, 1990–92, Emeritus Professor 1992; *b* 21 July 1925; *s* of Clement and Peggy Norman; *m* 1953, Pamela Raymont; one *s* one *d*. *Educ:* Taunton School; Downing College, Cambridge (MA 1954). Fellow and Tutor, Downing College, Cambridge, 1952–64; Lectr in Indian Studies (Prakrit), 1955–78, Reader, 1978–90, Univ. of Cambridge. Foreign Mem., Royal Danish Acad. of Sciences and Letters, 1983. *Publications:* Elders' Verses I (Theragāthā), 1969; Elders' Verses II (Therīgāthā), 1971; (trans.) Jain Cosmology, 1981; Pāli Literature, 1983; The Group of Discourses (Suttanipāta), Vol. I, 1984, Vol. II, 1992, 2nd edn 2001; Collected Papers: Vol. I, 1990, Vol. II, 1991, Vol. III, 1992, Vol. IV, 1993, Vol. V, 1994, Vol. VI, 1996, Vol. VII, 2001, Vol. VIII, 2007; Poems of Early Buddhist Monks, 1997; The Word of the Doctrine (Dhammapada), 1997; A Philological Approach to Buddhism, 1997; (with W. Pruitt) The Pātimokkha, 2001; (with W. Pruitt) Kaṅkhāvitaraṇī, 2003; (ed) Pāli Tipitakam Concordance, Vol. II 4–9, 1963–73; (ed) Critical Pāli Dictionary Vol. II 11–17, 1981–90. *Recreations:* pottery, reading. *Address:* 6 Huttles Green, Shepreth, Royston, Herts SG8 6PR. *T:* (01763) 260541.

NORMAN, Sir Mark (Annesley), 3rd Bt *cr* 1915; DL; farmer; *b* 8 Feb. 1927; *s* of Sir Nigel Norman, 2nd Bt, CBE, and Patricia Moyra (*d* 1986) (who *m* 2nd, 1944, Sir Robert Perkins), *e d* of late Colonel J. H. A. Annesley, CMG, DSO; *S* father, 1943; *m* 1953, Joanna Camilla, *d* of late Lt-Col I. J. Kilgour; two *s* one *d*. *Educ:* Winchester Coll.; RMA. Coldstream Guards, 1945–47; Flying Officer, 601 (County of London) Sqdn, RAuxAF, 1953–56. Hon. Air Cdre, No 4624 (County of Oxford) Movements Sqdn, RAuxAF, 1984–2000. Chm., Anglo-US Cttee, RAF Upper Heyford, 1984–91. Director: Gotaas-Larsen Shipping Corp., 1979–88. Chm., IU Europe Ltd, 1973–87. Mem., Council, St Luke's, Oxford, 1985–91 (Chm., 1986–88). Patron and Churchwarden, St Peter's, Wilcote, 1972–2006. High Sheriff, 1983–84, DL 1985, Oxon. *Recreations:* gardening, workshop, offshore cruising. *Heir:* *s* Nigel James Norman, late Major 13/18th Royal Hussars (Queen Mary's Own) [*b* 5 Feb. 1956; *m* 1994, Mrs Juliet Marriott, *e d* of R. Baxendale; three *s* one *d*]. *Address:* Wilcote Manor, Wilcote, Chipping Norton, Oxon OX7 3EB. *T:* (01993) 868357, *Fax:* (01993) 868032. *Clubs:* Royal Air Force; St Moritz Tobogganing; Royal Southern Yacht.
See also Sir T. P. A. Norman.

NORMAN, Philip Frank William; author and journalist; *b* 13 April 1943; *s* of Clive and Irene Norman; *m* 1990, Sue Summers; one *d*. *Educ:* Ryde Sch., Isle of Wight. Trainee reporter, Hunts Post, Huntingdon, 1961–64; Reporter: Cambridge News, 1965; Northern Despatch, 1965; Northern Echo, 1965–66; Feature Writer, Sunday Times Mag., 1966–75; Atticus Columnist and Feature Writer, Sunday Times, 1976–82. Writer, musical, This is Elvis: Viva Las Vegas, 2006 (2 national tours). *Publications:* Slip on a Fat Lady, 1970; Plumridge, 1971; Wild Thing, 1972; The Skaters' Waltz, 1979 (one of 20 Best Young British Novelists, 1983); Shout!: the true story of the Beatles, 1981, 4th edn 2003; The Road Goes on For Ever, 1982; The Stones, 1984, 4th edn 2001; Tilt the Hourglass and Begin Again, 1985; Your Walrus Hurt the One You Love, 1985; Awful Moments, 1986; Pieces of Hate, 1987; The Life and Good Times of the Rolling Stones, 1989; Words of Love, 1989; Days in the Life: John Lennon remembered, 1990; The Age of Parody, 1990; Elton, 1991, 3rd edn, as Sir Elton, 2000; Everyone's Gone to the Moon, 1995; Buddy: the biography, 1996; Babycham Night, 2003; John Lennon: the life, 2008; contrib. Times, Guardian, Daily Mail, New York Times, Vanity Fair, Playboy, Cosmopolitan, GQ, Spectator, New Statesman etc. *Recreations:* literature, cinema, running. *Address:* 46 Willoughby Road, NW3 1RU; *e-mail:* philip@philipnorman.com. *Club:* Groucho.

NORMAN, Sir Ronald, Kt 1995; OBE 1987; DL; CEng; Chairman, Priority Sites, 1997–2001; *b* 29 April 1937; *s* of Leonard William Norman and Elsie Louise Norman (*née* Cooke); *m* 1st, 1961, Jennifer Mansfield (marr. diss. 1972); two *s* one *d*; 2nd, 1975, Joyce Lyons. *Educ:* Dulwich Coll.; King's Coll., London (BSc Eng.). CE; CEng, MICE 1966. Man. Dir, then Chm., Cecil M. Yuill Ltd, Developers, Hartlepool, 1965–86; Chm., R. Norman Ltd, Developers, Durham, 1986–93. Chm., Teesside Develt Corp., 1987–98. Pres., Cleveland Community Foundn, 1998–; Vice-Pres., Trincomalee Trust, 1998–. Pres., Durham Co. Scouts Assoc., 2006–. DL Cleveland, 1996. *Recreations:* mountain climbing, book collecting. *Address:* Sparrow Hall, Dalton-Piercy, Cleveland TS27 3HY. *T:* (01429) 273857.

NORMAN, Susan Elizabeth, (Mrs J. C. Sheridan); Chief Executive and Registrar, United Kingdom Central Council for Nursing, Midwifery and Health Visiting, 1995–2002; *b* 9 Aug. 1946; *d* of late Dr J. M. Norman and of Betty Norman (*née* Colyer); *m* 1983, John Christopher Sheridan. *Educ:* St Nicholas Sch., Fleet, Hants; Dartington Hall, Devon; St Thomas' Hosp. (RGN); Bedford Coll., London (RNT); South Bank Univ. (BEd Hons). Student nurse, St Thomas' Hosp., 1965–69; Dist Nurse, RBK&C, 1969–71; Staff Nurse, Royal Marsden Hosp., 1972; Nursing Officer (Dist Nursing), Kensington and Chelsea, 1972–73; Staff Nurse, Montreal Gen. Hosp., 1974–75; Tutor Student, London Univ., 1975–77; Tutor and Sen. Tutor, Nightingale Sch., 1977–87; Principal Nursing Officer (Asst Sec.), DoH, London and Leeds, 1988–95. Vis. Prof., London South Bank (formerly S Bank) Univ., 2002–. President: Nat. Assoc. of Theatre Nurses, 2002–04; Nightingale Fellowship, 2007–; Chair, in touch Support, 2006–. FRSA 1997. Hon. DSc Plymouth, 2002. *Publication:* Nursing Practice and Health Care, 1989, 5th edn 2008. *Recreations:* music (singing and opera), walking, UK and France, eating out.

NORMAN, Sir Torquil (Patrick Alexander), Kt 2007; CBE 2002; Chairman, Roundhouse Trust, since 1996; *b* 1933; *s* of Sir Henry Nigel St Valery Norman, 2nd Bt, CBE and Patricia Moyra Norman; *m* 1961, Lady (Elizabeth) Anne, *d* of Alexander Victor Edward Paulet Montagu; three *s* two *d*. *Educ:* Eton; Trinity Coll., Cambridge (BA 1957). Served RAF. Investment banker, NY; Man. Dir, Berwick Timpo, toy co., until 1979; former Chm., Bluebird Toys. Set up Norman Trust; bought Roundhouse, 1996, re-launched as arts venue, 2006. *Address:* Roundhouse Trust, Chalk Farm Road, NW1 8EH.
See also Sir M. A. Norman, Bt.

NORMANBY, 5th Marquis of, *cr* 1838; **Constantine Edmund Walter Phipps;** Baron Mulgrave (Ire.) 1767; Baron Mulgrave (GB) 1794; Earl of Mulgrave and Viscount Normanby 1812; *b* 24 Feb. 1954; *e s* of 4th Marquis of Normanby KG, CBE and of Hon. Grania Guinness (OBE 2000), *d* of 1st Baron Moyne; *S* father, 1994; one *d* by Ms Sophie McCormick; *m* 1990, Mrs Nicola St Aubyn (*see* Marchioness of Normanby); two *s* one *d*. *Educ:* Eton; Worcester Coll., Oxford; City Univ. *Publications:* Careful with the Sharks, 1985; Among the Thin Ghosts, 1989. *Heir:* *s* Earl of Mulgrave, *qv*. *Address:* Mulgrave Castle, Whitby, N Yorks YO21 3RJ. *Clubs:* Travellers, Garrick.

NORMANBY, Marchioness of; Nicola Phipps; journalist, author; *b* 15 Feb. 1960; *d* of late Milton Shulman and of Drusilla Beyfus, *qv*; *m* 1st, 1987, Edward St Aubyn (marr. diss. 1990); 2nd, 1990, Earl of Mulgrave (*see* Marquis of Normanby); two *s* one *d*. *Educ:* St Paul's Girls' Sch.; Corpus Christi Coll., Oxford (BA Hons). Trustee, Nat. Gall., 2004–. *Publication:* (as Nicola Shulman) A Rage for Rock Gardening, 2002, 3rd edn 2004. *Recreations:* singing, Latin, gardening. *Address:* Mulgrave Castle, Whitby, N Yorks YO21 3RJ.
See also A. Shulman.

NORMAND, Andrew Christie, CB 2001; SSC; FSAScot; Sheriff at Glasgow, since 2006; *b* 7 Feb. 1948; *m* 1975, Barbara Jean Smith; two *d*. *Educ:* George Watson's Coll., Edinburgh; Univ. of Edinburgh (MA 1968; LLB 1970); Queen's Univ., Kingston, Ont (LLM 1972). Admitted solicitor, 1974. Crown Office: Legal Asst, Edinburgh, 1974–76, 1977; seconded to Scottish Law Commn, 1976; Sen. Legal Asst, Edinburgh, 1977–78,

Perth, 1978–81; Asst Solicitor, 1981–87; Procurator Fiscal, Airdrie, 1987–88; Dep. Crown Agent for Scotland, 1988–90; Regl Procurator Fiscal, Glasgow, 1990–96; Crown Agent for Scotland, 1996–2003; an all-Scotland Sheriff, 2003–06. *Address:* Sheriff Court of Glasgow and Strathkelvin, 1 Carlton Place, Glasgow G5 9DA.

NORMANTON, 6th Earl of, *cr* 1806; **Shaun James Christian Welbore Ellis Agar;** Baron Mendip, 1794; Baron Somerton, 1795; Viscount Somerton, 1800; Baron Somerton (UK), 1873; Royal Horse Guards, 1965; Blues and Royals, 1969; left Army, 1972, Captain; *b* 21 Aug. 1945; *er s* of 5th Earl of Normanton; *S* father, 1967; *m* 1970, Victoria Susan (marr. diss. 2000), *o d* of late J. H. C. Beard; one *s* two *d*. *Educ:* Eton. *Recreations:* shooting, ski-ing, scuba diving, motor boating. *Heir: s* Viscount Somerton, *qv*. *Address:* Somerley, Ringwood, Hants BH24 3PL. *T:* (01425) 473253. *Clubs:* White's; Royal Yacht Squadron.

NORMINGTON, Sir David (John), KCB 2005 (CB 2000); Permanent Secretary, Home Office, since 2006; *b* 18 Oct. 1951; *s* of late Ronald Normington and of Kathleen Normington (*née* Towler); *m* 1985, Winifred Anne Charlotte Harris, *qv*. *Educ:* Bradford Grammar Sch.; Corpus Christi College, Oxford (BA Hons Mod. Hist.). Department of Employment, subseq. Department for Education and Employment: joined 1973; Private Sec. to Perm. Sec., 1976–77; Principal Private Sec. to Sec. of State for Employment, 1984–85; Employment Service Regional Dir for London and SE Region, 1987–89; Hd of Strategy and Employment Policy Div., 1990–92; Dir of Personnel and Develt, 1992–95, of Personnel and Support Services, 1995–97; Dir Gen., Strategy, Internat. and Analytical Services, 1997–98; Dir Gen. for Schs, 1998–2001; Permanent Sec., DfEE, then DfES, 2001–05. *Recreations:* gardening, ballet, walking, cricket. *Address:* Home Office, 2 Marsham Street, SW1P 4DF; *e-mail:* Davidnormington.submissions@homeoffice.gsi.gov.uk.

NORMINGTON, Winifred Anne Charlotte, (Lady Normington); *see* Harris, W. A. C.

NORREY, Philip Julian, PhD; Chief Executive, Devon County Council, since 2006; *b* 9 July 1963; *s* of Harold and Dorothy Norrey; *m* 2003, Stephanie Ann Sloman. *Educ:* Colchester Royal Grammar Sch.; Univ. of Bristol (BA Hons Hist. 1984; PhD Hist. 1988). Audit Examiner, District Audit, 1989; graduate trainee, Somerset CC, 1990; Asst Dir of Educn, N Somerset DC, 1996–98; Dep. Dir, 1998–2003, Dir, 2003–06, of Educn, Devon CC. Hon. Fellow, Univ. of Exeter, 2003. *Publication:* contrib. Historical Jl. *Recreations:* cycling, food and wine, historical research, Burnley Football Club, railways, classical music, 70s and 80s TV drama. *Address:* c/o Devon County Council, County Hall, Topsham Road, Exeter EX2 4QD. *T:* (01392) 383201; *e-mail:* phil.norrey@devon.gov.uk.

NORREYS, Lord; Henry Mark Willoughby Bertie; *b* 6 June 1958; *s* and *heir* of the Earl of Lindsey (14th) and Abingdon (9th), *qv*; *m* 1989, Lucinda, *d* of Christopher Moorsom; two *s*. *Educ:* Eton; Univ. of Edinburgh. Kt of Honour and Devotion, SMO Malta, 1995; Kt of Justice, Constantinian Order of St George, 1998; Kt, Order of St Maurice and St Lazarus, 1999. *Heir: s* Hon. Willoughby Henry Constantine St Maur Bertie, *b* 15 Jan. 1996. *Address:* The Old Dairy, Gilmilnscroft, Sorn, Mauchline, Ayrshire KA5 6ND. *Clubs:* Pratt's; Puffin's (Edinburgh).

NORRIE, family name of **Baron Norrie**.

NORRIE, 2nd Baron *cr* 1957; **George Willoughby Moke Norrie;** *b* 27 April 1936; *s* of 1st Baron Norrie, GCMG, GCVO, CB, DSO, MC, and Jocelyn Helen (*d* 1938), *d* of late R. H. Gosling; *S* father, 1977; *m* 1st, 1964, Celia Marguerite, JP (marr. diss. 1997), *d* of John Pelham Mann, MC; one *s* two *d*; 2nd, 1997, Mrs Pamela Ann McCaffry, *d* of Sir Arthur Ralph Wilmot, 7th Bt. *Educ:* Eton College; RMA Sandhurst. Commissioned 11th Hussars (PAO), 1956; ADC to C-in-C Middle East Comd, 1960–61; GSO 3 (Int.) 4th Guards Brigade, 1967–69; retired, 1970. Underwriting Mem. of Lloyd's, 1977–97. Director: Fairfield Nurseries (Hermitage) Ltd, 1976–89; International Garden Centre (British Gp) Ltd, 1984–86; Conservation Practice Ltd, 1989–91; Hilliers (Fairfield) Ltd, 1989–97; Advisor to: S Grundon (Waste) Ltd, 1991–2001; CH2M Hill Ltd (London), 1994–96. Non-exec. Dir, Philip T. English Internat. Financial Services Ltd. Mem., EC Cttee, Sub Cttee F (Environment), H of L, 1988–92. President: British Trust for Conservation Volunteers, 1987–; Internat. Cultural Exchange, 1988–2000; Commercial Travellers Benevolent Instn, 1992–; Royal British Legion (Newbury Branch), 1971–96; Nat. Kidney Fedn, 1994–2001; Vice President: Tree Council, 1990–; Council for Nat. Parks, 1990–. Mem. Council, Winston Churchill Meml Trust, 1993–. Patron: Age Resource, 1991–2004; Faure-Alderson Romanian Appeal, 1993–2001; Janki Foundn, 1997–; UK Patron, RLSS, 1994– (Mem., Commonwealth Council, 1999–). Gov., Dunstan Park Sch., Thatcham, 1989–94. Mem., British Soc. of Dowsers, 1999–. Sponsored: Swimming and Water Safety Bill, 1993 (enacted under statutory order, 1994); Nat. Parks Bill, 1993 (incorp. in Envmt Act, 1995). Freeman, City of London, 1999. Green Ribbon Political Award for services to the envmt, H of L, 1993. *Recreations:* fishing, golf, Real tennis. *Heir: s* Hon. Mark Willoughby John Norrie [*b* 31 March 1972; *m* 1998, Carol, *e d* of Michael Stockdale; two *s*]. *Address:* Holehouse, Penpont, Thornhill, Dumfriesshire DG3 4AP. *T:* (01848) 600243. *Clubs:* Cavalry and Guards, White's, MCC.

NORRIE, Marian Farrow, (Mrs W. G. Walker); Her Honour Judge Norrie; a Circuit Judge, since 1986; *b* 25 April 1940; *d* of Arthur and Edith Jackson; *m* 1st, 1964; two *d*; 2nd, 1983, (William) Guy Walker, CBE (*d* 2007); one step *s* two step *d*. *Educ:* Manchester High Sch. for Girls; Nottingham Univ. (LLB). Admitted Solicitor of Supreme Court, 1965; a Recorder, 1979–86. Consultant, Norrie, Bowler & Wrigley, Solicitors, Sheffield, 1983–86 (Sen. Partner, 1968–83). Member: Parole Bd, 1983–85; Appts Commn, Press Council, 1985. *Address:* The Family Centre, Brighton County Court, 1 Edward Street, Brighton BN2 2JD.

NORRINGTON, Humphrey Thomas, OBE 2001; Vice Chairman, Barclays Bank, 1991–93; *b* 8 May 1936; *s* of Sir Arthur Norrington and Edith Joyce, *d* of William Moberly Carver; *m* 1963, Frances Guenn Bateson; two *s* two *d*. *Educ:* Dragon School, Oxford; Winchester; Worcester College, Oxford (MA). Barclays Bank: joined, 1960; general management, 1978–87; Dir, 1985–93; Exec Dir, Overseas Ops, 1987–91. Chm., Exec. Cttee, British Bankers' Assoc., 1990–91. Chm., Southwark Cathedral Develt Trust, 1986–93; Director: City Arts Trust, 1988–93; Mildmay Mission Hosp., 1992–2007 (Vice Pres., 2007–); World Vision UK, 1991–2005. Member, Archbishops' Commission: on Rural Areas, 1988–90; on Orgn of the C of E, 1994–95. Chm., Premier Christian Media Trust, 1999–; Trustee, Stewards' Trust, 2007–. Hon. Treas., RSPB, 1996–2003; Hon. Treas., 1997–2004, Vice Pres., 2005–, RCM. *Recreations:* music, countryside. *Address:* Hill House, Frithsden Copse, Berkhamsted, Herts HP4 2RQ. *T:* (01442) 871855. *Club:* Oxford and Cambridge.
See also Sir R. A. C. Norrington.

NORRINGTON, Sir Roger (Arthur Carver), Kt 1997; CBE 1990 (OBE 1980); Chief Conductor: Radio Sinfonie Orchester Stuttgart, since 1998; Camerata Academica Salzburg, since 1997; *b* 16 March 1934; *s* of late Sir Arthur Norrington and Edith Joyce, *d* of William Moberly Carver; *m* 1st, 1964, Susan Elizabeth McLean May (marr. diss. 1982); one *s* one *d*; 2nd, 1986, Karalyn Mary Lawrence; one *s*. *Educ:* Dragon Sch., Oxford; Westminster; Clare Coll., Cambridge (BA; Hon. Fellow, 1991); Royal Coll. of Music. Freelance singer, 1962–72. Principal Conductor: Kent Opera, 1966–84; Bournemouth Sinfonietta, 1985–89; Music Director: Orch. of St Luke's, NY, 1990–94; Schütz Choir of London, 1962–82; London Classical Players, 1978–98. Prince Consort Prof., RCM, 1997. Guest conducts many British, European and American orchestras, appears at Covent Garden, Coliseum, Proms and festivals; broadcasts regularly at home and abroad. Débuts: British, 1962; BBC Radio, 1964; TV 1967; Germany, Austria, Denmark, Finland, 1966; Portugal, 1970; Italy, 1971; France and Belgium, 1972; USA, 1974; Holland, 1975; Switzerland, 1976. Many gramophone recordings. Hon. RAM 1988. FRCM 1992. DUniv York, 1991; Hon. DMus Kent, 1994. Cavaliere, Orden al Merito (Italy), 1981; Ehrenkreuz, 1st cl. (Austria), 1999. *Publications:* occasional articles in various musical journals. *Recreations:* gardening, reading, walking.
See also H. T. Norrington.

NORRIS, Brig. His Honour (Alaric) Philip, OBE 1982; a Circuit Judge, 1995–2008; *b* 20 Sept. 1942; *yr s* of late Charles Henry Norris and Maud Frances Norris (*née* Neild); *m* 1967, Pamela Margaret Parker; three *s*. *Educ:* Sir William Turner's Sch., Coatham, Redcar; Queens' Coll., Cambridge (MA); Dip. in Law and Amer. Studies, Univ. of Virginia, USA, 1979. Admitted Solicitor, 1968; commnd Army Legal Services, 1970; served MoD, SHAPE, BAOR, Berlin, NEARELF, NI, UKLF/Land Comd, USA and Geneva; retired, in rank of Brig., 1995. Asst Recorder, 1988–92, Recorder of the Crown Court, 1992–95. Liveryman, Fruiterers' Co., 2005–. *Recreations:* a bit of all sorts, but not golf.

NORRIS, Hon. Sir Alastair Hubert, Kt 2007; FCIArb; **Hon. Mr Justice Norris;** a Judge of the High Court, Chancery Division, since 2007; *b* 17 Dec. 1950; *s* of Hubert John Norris and Margaret Murray (*née* Savage); *m* 1982, Patricia Lesley Rachel White; one *s* two *d*. *Educ:* Pate's Grammar Sch., Cheltenham; St John's Coll., Cambridge (MA). FCIArb 1991. Called to the Bar, Lincoln's Inn, 1973, Bencher, 2005; QC 1997; an Asst Recorder, 1998–2000; a Recorder 2000–01; a Circuit Judge, 2001–07. *Recreation:* sailing. *Address:* Royal Courts of Justice, Strand, WC2A 2LL. *Clubs:* Gloucestershire County Cricket; Marlow Sailing, Teifi Boating.

NORRIS, Dan; MP (Lab) Wansdyke, since 1997; *b* 28 Jan. 1960; *s* of David Norris and June Norris (*née* Allen). *Educ:* Chipping Sodbury Comprehensive Sch.; Univ. of Sussex (MSW). Researcher and author. Member (Lab): Bristol CC, 1989–92, 1995–97; Avon CC, 1994–96. Contested (Lab): Northavon, 1987; Wansdyke, 1992. Member: Lab. Leadership Campaign Team, 1998–2000; Lab. Parly Campaign Team, 2000–01. An Asst Govt Whip, 2001–03; PPS to Sec. of State for NI, 2005–07, to Sec. of State for Foreign and Commonwealth Affairs, 2007–. Founder, Kidscape SW, 2000. Hon. Fellow, Sch. of Cultural and Community Studies, Univ. of Sussex, 1989. Mem., GMB. Ed., Liberal Demolition (qly jl), 2000–. *Publications:* Violence Against Social Workers: the implications for practice, 1990; contribs to learned jls and newspaper articles. *Recreation:* photography. *Address:* House of Commons, SW1A 0AA. *Club:* Radstock Working Men's.

NORRIS, Rt Rev. Mgr David Joseph; Protonotary Apostolic to the Pope; Vicar General of Westminster Diocese, 1972–99; General Secretary to RC Bishops' Conference of England and Wales, 1967–83; *b* 17 Aug. 1922; *s* of David William and Anne Norris. *Educ:* Salesian Coll., Battersea; St Edmund's Coll., Ware; Christ's Coll., Cambridge (MA). Priest, 1947; teaching at St Edmund's Coll., Ware, 1948–53; Cambridge, 1953–56; Private Secretary to Cardinal Godfrey, 1956–64; National Chaplain to Catholic Overseas Students, 1964–65; Private Secretary to Cardinal Heenan, 1965–72. *Recreations:* reading, music, sport. *Address:* Cathedral Clergy House, 42 Francis Street, SW1P 1QW. *T:* (020) 7798 9055.

NORRIS, David Owen, FRAM, FRCO; pianist and broadcaster; *b* 16 June 1953; *s* of Albert Norris and Margaret Norris (*née* Owen); two *s*. *Educ:* Royal Academy of Music (FRAM 1986); Keble Coll., Oxford (MA; Hon. Fellow, 2006). FRCO 1972. Repetiteur, Royal Opera House, 1977–80; Asst Mus. Dir, RSC, 1977–79; Prof., Royal Acad. of Music, 1977–89; Dir, Petworth Fest., 1986–92; Artistic Dir, Cardiff Fest., 1992–95; Gresham Prof. of Music, 1993–97; Prof., 1999–2007, Vis. Prof., 2007–, RCM; AHRC (formerly AHRB) Fellow in Performing Arts, 2000–04, Prof., 2007–, Southampton Univ. Chm., Steans Inst. for Singers, Chicago, 1992–98. Concerts world-wide; tours of Australia, USA, Canada; radio and TV progs in GB and N America. Gilmore Artist, 1991. Has made numerous recordings incl. Elgar Concerto, Lambert Concerto, Elgar complete piano music, Dyson complete piano and chamber music, Quilter duets and piano music, Schubert Kosegarten Liederspiel. *Address:* 17 Manor Road, Andover, Hants SP10 3JS. *Club:* Savile.

NORRIS, Geoffrey; Chief Music Critic, Daily Telegraph, since 1995; *b* 19 Sept. 1947; *s* of Leslie and Vera Norris. *Educ:* Univ. of Durham (BA); Inst. Teatra, Muzyki i Kinematografii, Leningrad; Univ. of Liverpool. ARCM 1967. Lectr in Music History, RNCM, 1975–77; Commning Editor, Scholarly Music Books, OUP, 1977–83; Music Critic: The Times, 1983; Daily Telegraph, 1983–95. Prof., Rachmaninoff Music Inst., Tambov, 2005–. Mem., Critics' Circle. *Publications:* Rakhmaninov, 1976, 2nd edn, Rachmaninoff, 1993; (with Robert Threlfall) A Catalogue of the Compositions of S. Rachmaninoff, 1982; contribs to New Grove Dictionary of Music and Musicians, Oxford Companion to Music. *Recreation:* Italy. *Address:* The Daily Telegraph, 111 Buckingham Palace Road, SW1W 0DT. *Club:* Arts.

NORRIS, Gilbert Frank; Chief Road Engineer, Scottish Development Department, 1969–76; *b* 29 May 1916; *s* of Ernest Frank Norris and Ada Norris; *m* 1941, Joan Margaret Catherine Thompson; one *s*. *Educ:* Bemrose Sch., Derby; UC Nottingham. FICE. Served with Notts, Bucks and Lindsey County Councils, 1934–39; Royal Engineers, 1939–46; Min. of Transport: Highways Engr in Nottingham, Edinburgh and Leeds, 1946–63; Asst Chief Engr, 1963–67; Dep. Chief Engr, 1967; Dir, NE Road Construction Unit, 1967–69. *Address:* Woodhead Lee, Lamlash, Isle of Arran KA27 8JU.

NORRIS, Col Graham Alexander, OBE (mil.) 1945; JP; Vice Lord-Lieutenant of County of Greater Manchester, 1975–87; *b* 14 April 1913; *er s* of late John O. H. Norris and Beatrice H. Norris (*née* Vlies), Manchester; *m* 1st, 1938, Frances Cicely, *d* of late Walter Gorton, Minchinhampton, Glos; one *d*; 2nd, 1955, Muriel, *d* of late John Corris, Manchester. *Educ:* William Hulme's Grammar Sch.; Coll. of Technology, Manchester; Regent St Polytechnic, London; Merchant Venturers Techn. Coll., Bristol. CEng, FIMechE. Trng as automobile engr, Rolls Royce Ltd, Bristol Motor Co. Ltd; Joseph Cockshoot & Co. Ltd: Works Man., 1937, Works Dir 1946, Jt. Man. Dir 1964, Chm. and Man. Dir, 1968; Dir, Lex Garages Ltd, 1968–70; Dir, Red Garages (N Wales) Ltd, 1973–88. War service, RAOC and REME, UK, ME and Italy, 1940–46 (Lt-Col); Comdr

REME 22 (W) Corps Tps (TA), 1947–51; Hon. Col, 1957–61. Mem., NEDC for Motor Vehicle Distrib. and Repair, 1966–74; Pres., Motor Agents Assoc., 1967–68; Vice-Pres., Inst. of Motor Industry, 1973–76; Mem., Industrial Tribunal Panel, 1976–82. Pres., Manchester and Dist Fedn of Boys' Clubs, 1968–74; Vice-Pres., NABC, 1972–98; Chm. Council, UMIST, 1971–83; Member Court: Univ. of Manchester; UMIST. Master, Worshipful Co. of Coachmakers and Coach Harness Makers, 1961–62; Freeman, City of London, 1938. JP, Lancashire 1963; DL Co. Palatine of Lancaster, 1962. *Recreations:* walking, social service activities. *Address:* c/o Croft of Greenbog, Glenkindle, Alford, Aberdeenshire AB33 8SE.

NORRIS, John Hallam Mercer, CBE 1987; Crown Estate Commissioner, 1991–99; Vice Lord-Lieutenant of Essex, 1992–2003; *b* 30 May 1929; *s* of late William Hallam Norris and Dorothy Edna Norris (*née* Mercer); *m* 1954, Maureen Joy Banyard; two *d*. *Educ:* Brentwood School. Mem., BSES Expedn, Newfoundland, 1947. Partner, W. H. Norris & Sons, 1963–. Chm., Essex River Authy, 1971–74; Member: Anglian Water Authy, 1974–85; Adv. Cttee, 1988, Board, 1989–94, NRA; Adv. Cttee, Envmt Agency, 1994–96; Founder Mem., Envmt Agency Bd, 1996–97; Chairman: Essex Land Drainage Cttee, 1974–89; Crouch Harbour Authy, 1981–88. President: CLA, 1985–87 (Mem., Exec. Cttee, 1973–; Chm., 1983–85); Essex Agricl Soc., 1989; Soc. of Old Brentwood, 2003–04. Chm., Chelmsford Cathedral Council, 2000–. FRAgS 1992; Hon. FIWEM 1992. DL Essex, 1989. *Recreations:* fishing, sailing. *Address:* Mountnessing Hall, Brentwood, Essex CM13 1UN. *T:* (01277) 352152. *Clubs:* Boodle's, Farmers'.

NORRIS, John Robert, CBE 1991; PhD, DSc; Director, Group Research, Cadbury Schweppes Ltd, 1979–90; *b* 4 March 1932; *s* of Albert Norris and Winifred May Perry; *m* 1st, 1956, Barbara Jean Pinder (*d* 1994); two *s* one *d* (and one *s* decd); 2nd, 1998, Pauline Mary Corrigan. *Educ:* Depts of Bacteriology and Agriculture, Univ. of Leeds (BSc 1st Cl. Hons 1954, PhD 1957, DSc 1987). Lectr in Bacteriology, Univ. of Glasgow, 1957–63; Microbiologist, Shell Research Ltd, 1963–73 (Dir, Borden Microbiol Lab., 1970–73); Dir, Meat Res. Inst., ARC, 1973–79. Editor, Methods in Microbiology, 1969–92. *Publications:* papers in microbiol jls. *Recreations:* walking, wood carving, Yoga. *Address:* Langlands, 10 Langley Road, Bingley, West Yorks BD16 4AB. *T:* (01274) 406973. *Club:* Farmers'.

NORRIS, Philip; *see* Norris, A. P.

NORRIS, Rufus; theatre director; *b* 16 Jan. 1965; *s* of Malcolm and Lauriston Norris; *m* 1994, Tanya Ronder; two *s*. *Educ:* North Bromsgrove High Sch.; Kidderminster Coll. of Further Educn; RADA (Dip.). Actor, 1989–92; director, 1992–; Artistic Dir, Arts Threshold, 1992–95; Asst Dir, Royal Court Th., 1996–97; Associate Dir, Young Vic Th., 2002–. Director: Afore Night Come, 2001, Sleeping Beauty, 2002, Young Vic; Festen, Lyric, 2004; Tintin, Barbican, 2005, Playhouse, 2007; Cabaret, Lyric, 2006; Vernon God Little, Young Vic, 2007. Arts Foundn Fellow, 2001. *Recreations:* pride, self-doubt, harassing my wife, being harassed by my children, talking incessantly to myself in extreme dialects. *Address:* c/o Nick Marston, Curtis Brown, Haymarket House, 28–29 Haymarket, SW1Y 4SP.

NORRIS, Stephen Anthony; Managing Director, Film, Framestore CFC, since 2006; *b* 14 June 1959; *s* of Roy Anthony Norris and Brenda Winifred Norris; *m* 1986, Susan Jennifer Boyle; two *s* one *d*. *Educ:* St Nicholas Grammar Sch. Warner Bros Productions, London, 1979–82; European Production, Warner Bros, LA, 1982–84; Dir of Ops, Enigma Productions, 1984–86; Sen. Vice Pres., Columbia Pictures, LA, 1986–88; Man. Dir, Enigma Productions Ltd, 1989–97; British Film Comr, 1998–2006. Dir, British Film and TV Producers Assoc., 1989–91; Vice Chm., Producers Alliance for Cinema and TV, 1991–93; Council Member: British Screen Adv. Council, 1998–2006; BAFTA, 1999–2005. Associate Producer/Producer: Memphis Belle, 1990; Being Human, 1993; War of the Buttons, 1994; Le Confessional (Best Film, Canadian Acad., 1995); My Life So Far, 1998. *Recreations:* cinema, Rugby, my family. *Address:* (office) 9 Noel Street, W1F 8GH.

NORRIS, Steven John; Senior Partner, Park Place Communications, since 2001; Chairman: Jarvis plc, since 2003; AMT-Sybex Ltd, since 2005; Agio Global, since 2007; *b* 24 May 1945; *s* of John Francis Birkett Norris and Eileen Winifred (*née* Walsh); *m* 1969, Peta Veronica Cecil-Gibson (marr. diss.); two *s*; *m* 2000, Emma Courtney; one *s*. *Educ:* Liverpool Institute; Worcester College, Oxford. MA. Private company posts, 1967–90; Dir-Gen., Road Haulage Assoc., 1997–2000. Bd Mem., Transport for London, 2000–01. Mem., Berks CC, 1977–85. Mem., Berks AHA, 1979–82; Vice-Chm., W Berks District HA, 1982–85. Contested (C) Oxford E, 1987. MP (C): Oxford E, 1983–87; Epping Forest, Dec. 1988–1997. PPS to Hon. William Waldegrave, MP, Minister of State, DoE, 1985–87, to Rt Hon. Nicholas Ridley, Sec. of State for Trade and Industry, 1990, to Rt Hon. Kenneth Baker, Home Sec., 1991–92; Parly Under-Sec. of State, Dept of Transport, 1992–96. Vice Chm., Cons. Party, 2000–01. Chairman: Grant Maintained Schools Trust, 1988–89; Crime Concern Trust, 1988–91; Alcohol and Drug Addiction Prevention and Treatment, 1990–92; Prince Michael Road Safety Awards Scheme, 1997–2004. FCILT (FCIT 1997); FIHT 1997; Hon. CompICE 1996. Freeman, City of London, 1985; Liveryman: Coachmakers' and Coach-Harness Makers' Co., 1985–; Watermen and Lightermen's Co., 1997–; Co. of Carmen, 1998–. *Publication:* Changing Trains, 1996. *Recreations:* reading, not walking. *Address:* Park Place Communications, 4th Floor, Denman House, 20 Piccadilly, W1J 0DG. *Clubs:* Brooks's, Royal Automobile, Garrick.

NORRIS, Sydney George, CB 1996; Director of Finance, Prison Service, Home Office, 1996–97; *b* 22 Aug. 1937; *s* of late George Samuel Norris, FCA and Agnes Rosa Norris; *m* 1965, Brigid Molyneux FitzGibbon; two *s* one *d*. *Educ:* Liverpool Inst. High Sch. for Boys; University Coll., Oxford (MA); Trinity Hall and Inst. of Criminology, Cambridge (Dip. in Criminology); Univ. of California, Berkeley (MCrim). Intelligence Corps, 1956–58; Home Office, 1963–97; Private Sec. to Parly Under Sec. of State, 1966; Harkness Fellow, 1968–70; Sec., Adv. Council on Penal System, 1970–73; Principal Private Sec. to Home Sec., 1973–74; Asst Sec., 1974; seconded to HM Treasury, 1979–81; Asst Under Sec. of State, 1982; seconded to NI Office as Principal Estabt and Finance Officer, 1982–85; Dir of Operational Policy, Prison Dept, 1985–88; Police Dept, 1988–90; Principal Finance Officer, 1990–96. Parish Warden, Mortlake with East Sheen, 2002–06. *Recreations:* running, fell walking, gardening, ski-ing, choral singing, piano. *Address:* 58 East Sheen Avenue, SW14 8AU. *Club:* Thames Hare and Hounds.

NORRIS, William John; QC 1997; *b* 3 Oct. 1951; *s* of Dr John Phillips Norris, QGM and late Dr Joan Hattersley Norris; *m* 1987, Lesley Jacqueline Osborne; two *d*. *Educ:* Sherborne Sch.; New Coll., Oxford (MA). Called to the Bar, Middle Temple, 1974 (Benefactors' Scholarship; Bencher, 2007). Chm., Personal Injury Bar Assoc., 2006–08. Trustee, Injured Jockeys Fund, 2006–. Gen. Ed., Kemp and Kemp, The Quantum of Damages, 2004–. *Publication:* Perhaps It Will Brighten Up Later, 2004. *Recreations:* sailing, cricket, shooting, racing. *Address:* 39 Essex Street, WC2R 3AT. *T:* (020) 7832 1111. *Clubs:* Royal Cruising, Royal Lymington Yacht.

NORRISS, Air Marshal Sir Peter (Coulson), KBE 2000; CB 1996; AFC 1977; defence consultant; Chairman, Turbomeca UK Ltd (formerly Microturbo Ltd), since 2002; Non-executive Director, Chemring Group plc, since 2004; *b* 22 April 1944; *s* of Arthur Kenworthy Norriss and Marjorie Evelyn Norriss; *m* 1971, Lesley Jean McColl; two *s* one *d*. *Educ:* Beverley Grammar Sch.; Magdalene Coll., Cambridge (MA 1970); Harvard Business Sch. Joined RAF, 1966; Flying Instruction RAF Coll., Cranwell, 1969–71; Buccaneer Pilot, 1972–76; RAF Staff Coll., 1977; on Staff of RAF Minister, 1977–79; OC, No 16 Sqn, 1980–83; Head, RAF Presentation Team, 1984; Station Comdr, RAF Marham, 1985–87; ADC to the Queen, 1985–87; Higher Comd and Staff Course, 1988; on Staff, Operational Requirements, 1988–91; Dir Gen. Aircraft 2, 1991–95; Dir Gen. Air Systems 1, MoD (PE), 1995–98; Controller Aircraft, 1996–2000, and Dep. Chief of Defence Procurement (Ops), 1998–2000, MoD (PE, subseq. Defence Procurement Agency). Non-exec. Dir, DERA, 1998–2000. Pres., RAeS, 2003–04. *Recreations:* golf, ski-ing. *Club:* Royal Air Force.

NORTH, family name of **Earl of Guilford.**

NORTH, Lord; Frederick Edward George North; *b* 24 June 2002; *s* and *heir* of Earl of Guilford, *qv*.

NORTH, Alan; *see* North, R. A.

NORTH, Prof. Douglass Cecil, PhD; Professor of Economics, Washington University, since 1983; *b* 5 Nov. 1920; *s* of Henry North and Edith Saitta; *m* 1st, 1944, Lois Heister; three *s*; 2nd, 1972, Elisabeth Case. *Educ:* Univ. of California at Berkeley (BA, PhD). Acting Asst Prof., Asst Prof. and Associate Prof., Univ. of Washington, Seattle, 1950–83; University of Washington, St Louis: Henry R. Luce Prof. of Law and Liberty and Prof. of Econs and of History, 1983–; Spencer T. Olin Prof. in Arts and Scis, 1995–. Peterkin Prof. of Political Economy, Rice Univ., 1979; Pitt Prof. of American Instns, Cambridge, 1981–82. Fellow, Amer. Acad. of Arts and Scis.; Corresp. FBA, 1996. Hon. degrees: Cologne 1988; Zürich 1993; Stockholm 1994. (Jtly) Nobel Prize for Economics, 1993. *Publications:* The Economic Growth of the United States 1790–1860, 1961; Growth and Welfare in the American Past, 1966; (with Roger Miller) The Economics of Public Issues, 1971; (with Lance Davis) Institutional Change and American Economic Growth, 1971; (with Robert Thomas) The Rise of the Western World, 1973; Structure and Change in Economic History, 1981; Institutions, Institutional Change and Economic Performance, 1990; Understanding the Process of Economic Change, 2004. *Recreations:* tennis, hiking, music, photography. *Address:* Economics Department, Washington University, Campus Box 1208, 1 Brookings Drive, St Louis, MO 63130–4899, USA.

NORTH, Prof. John David, FBA 1992; Senior Research Associate, Museum of the History of Science, University of Oxford, since 2003; Professor of History of Philosophy and the Exact Sciences, University of Groningen, Netherlands, 1977–99, now Emeritus; *b* 19 May 1934; *s* of late J. E. and G. A. North, Cheltenham; *m* 1957, Marion Pizzey; one *s* two *d*. *Educ:* Grammar Sch., Batley; Merton Coll., Oxford (BA 1956, MA 1960, DPhil 1964, DLitt 1993); London Univ. (BSc 1958). University of Oxford: Nuffield Foundn Res. Fellow, 1963–68; Asst Curator, Mus. of Hist. of Sci., 1968–77; University of Groningen, 1977–: Dean, Central Inter-Faculty, 1981–84; Dean of Faculty, 1991–93. Vis. Prof., Univs in Germany, Denmark and USA. Member: Council, Mus. Boerhaave, Leiden, 1986–94; Comité Scientifique, CNRS, Paris, 1985–99; Acad. internat. d'histoire des scis, 1967– (Hon. Permanent Sec., 1983–); IAU, 1977 (Pres., Hist. Commn, 1988–92). Member: Royal Netherlands Acad., 1985 (Mem Council, 1990–93); Acad. Leopoldina, 1992; Foreign Mem., Royal Danish Acad., 1985. Editor: Archives internat. d'hist. des scis, 1971–84; Travaux de l'Académie, 1984–97. Kt, Order of Netherlands Lion, 1999. *Publications:* The Measure of the Universe, 1965, 2nd edn 1990; Isaac Newton, 1967; (ed) Mid-Nineteenth Century Scientists, 1969; Richard of Wallingford, 3 vols, 1976; (ed with J. Roche) The Light of Nature, 1985; Horoscopes and History, 1986; Chaucer's Universe, 1988, 2nd edn 1990; Stars, Minds and Fate, 1989; The Universal Frame, 1989; Fontana History of Astronomy and Cosmology, 1994; Stonehenge, 1996; The Ambassadors' Secret, 2002, 2nd edn 2004; God's Clockmaker: Richard of Wallingford and the invention of time, 2005; Cosmos: an illustrated history of astronomy and cosmology, 2008. *Recreation:* archaeology. *Address:* 28 Chalfont Road, Oxford OX2 6TH. *T:* (01865) 558458.

NORTH, John Joseph; Associate, Department of Land Economy, University of Cambridge, since 1992 (Senior Visiting Fellow, 1985–92); *b* 7 Nov. 1926; *s* of Frederick James North and Annie Elizabeth North (*née* Matthews); *m* 1958, Sheila Barbara Mercer; two *s*. *Educ:* Rendcomb College; Univ. of Reading (BSc, DipAgric); Univ. of California (MS). FIBiol 1972. Agricultural Adviser, Nat. Agricultural Advisory Service, 1951; Kellogg Fellowship, USA, 1954–55; Regional Agricultural Officer, Cambridge, 1972; Senior Agricultural Officer, 1976; Chief Agricl Officer, ADAS, MAFF, 1979. *Recreations:* golf, gardening. *Address:* 28 Hauxton Road, Little Shelford, Cambridge CB22 5HJ. *T:* (01223) 843369.

NORTH, Sir Jonathan; *see* North, Sir W. J. F.

NORTH, Sir Peter (Machin), Kt 1998; CBE 1989; DCL; FBA 1990; Principal of Jesus College, Oxford, 1984–2005; Pro-Vice-Chancellor, University of Oxford, 1988–93, and 1997–2005 (Vice-Chancellor, 1993–97); *b* Nottingham, 30 Aug. 1936; *o s* of late Geoffrey Machin North and Freda Brunt (*née* Smith); *m* 1960, Stephanie Mary (OBE 2000; JP, DL), *e d* of T. L. Chadwick; two *s* one *d*. *Educ:* Oakham Sch.; Keble Coll., Oxford (BA 1959, BCL 1960, MA 1963, DCL 1976; Hon. Fellow, 1984). National Service, Royal Leics Regt, 2nd Lieut, 1955–56. Teaching Associate, Northwestern Univ. Sch. of Law, Chicago, 1960–61; Lecturer: University Coll. of Wales, Aberystwyth, 1961–63; Univ. of Nottingham, 1963–65; Tutor in Law, 1965–76, Fellow, 1965–84, Keble Coll., Oxford. Mem., Hebdomadal Council, 1985–99. A Law Comr, 1976–84; called to the Bar, Inner Temple, 1992 (Hon. Bencher, 1987). Vis. Professor: Univ. of Auckland, 1969; Univ. of BC, 1975–76; Dir of Studies, Hague Acad. of Internat. Law, 1970 (general course in private internat. law, 1990); Lectures: Hague Acad. of Internat. Law, 1980; Horace Read Meml, Dalhousie Univ., 1980; Colston, Bristol Univ., 1984; Frances Moran Meml, TCD, 1984; Philip James, Leeds Univ., 1985; James Smart, 1988; MacDermott, QUB, 1991; Graveson, KCL, 1992; Douglas McK. Brown, Univ. of BC, 1998; F. A. Mann, 2000. Chairman: Road Traffic Law Review, 1985–88; Conciliation Project Adv. Cttee, 1985–88; Management Cttee, Oxford CAB, 1985–88; Appeal Cttee, Assoc. of Certified Accountants, 1990–93 (Mem., 1987–93); Ind. Review of Parades and Marches in NI, 1996–97; Ind. Cttee for Supervision of Standards of Telephone Inf. Services, 1999–2006; Standing Adv. Cttee on Private Internat. Law, 2004–; Member: Lord Chancellor's Adv. Cttee on Legal Educn, 1973–75; Social Scis and the Law Cttee, ESRC (formerly SSRC), 1982–85; Govt and Law Cttee, ESRC, 1985–87; Adv. Devlt Council, Nat. Fisheries Mus., 1996–2000; Sen. Salaries Review Body, 2004–; Accountancy Investigation and Disciplinary Bd Tribunal, 2005–. Council Member: British Inst. of Internat. and Comparative Law, 1986– (Chm., Private Internat. Law Section, Adv. Bd, 1986–92); Univ. of Reading, 1986–89; British Acad., 1996–99; Mem., Academic Council, and

Internat. Adv. Bd, Univ. Canada West, 2004–. Oxford University Press: Delegate, 1993–; Chm., Finance Cttee, 2005– (Mem., 1993–2005); Vice-Chm., Visitors, Ashmolean Mus., Oxford, 2006–07 (Visitor, 2004–07). Pres., Oxford Inst. of Legal Practice, 1999–; Mem., Inst. of Internat. Law, 1985; Mem., Internat. Acad. of Comparative Law, 1990. Hon. QC 1993. Hon. Fellow: UCNW, Bangor, 1988; Trinity Coll., Carmarthen, 1995; Univ. of Wales, Aberystwyth, 1996; Jesus Coll., Oxford, 2005. Hon. LLD: Reading, 1992; Nottingham, 1996; Aberdeen, 1997; New Brunswick, 2002; DHL Arizona, 2005. Mem., Editorial Cttee, British Yearbook of Internat. Law, 1983–; General Editor, Oxford Jl of Legal Studies, 1987–92. *Publications:* (ed jtly) Chitty on Contracts, 23rd edn 1968 to 26th edn 1989; Occupiers' Liability, 1971; The Modern Law of Animals, 1972; Private International Law of Matrimonial Causes, 1977; Cheshire and North's Private International Law, 13th edn 1999; Contract Conflicts, 1982; (with J. H. C. Morris) Cases and Materials on Private International Law, 1984; Private International Law Problems in Common Law Jurisdictions, 1993; Essays in Private International Law, 1993; articles and notes in legal jls. *Recreations:* children, grandchildren, gardening, cricket (both playing and sleeping through). *Address:* 34 Woodstock Close, Oxford OX2 8DB. *T:* (01865) 557011; 5 Coln Manor, Coln St Aldwyns, Cirencester, Glos GL7 5AD. *T:* (01285) 750400.

NORTH, Prof. (Richard) Alan, PhD; FRS 1995; Vice-President and Dean, Faculty of Life Sciences, since 2004, and Faculty of Medical and Human Sciences, since 2006, University of Manchester; *b* 20 May 1944; *s* of Douglas Abram North and Constance (*née* Ramsden); *m* 1st, 1969, Jean Valerie Aitken Hall (marr. diss. 1982); two *d*; 2nd, 1991, Annmarie Surprenant; two *s*. *Educ:* Univ. of Aberdeen (BSc; MB, ChB 1969; PhD 1973). Asst and Associate Prof., Dept of Pharmacol., Loyola Univ., Chicago, 1975–81; Massachusetts Institute of Technology: Associate Prof., Dept of Nutrition and Food Sci., 1981–84; Prof. of Neuropharmacol., Dept of Applied Biol Scis, 1984–86; Sen. Scientist, Vollum Inst., Oregon Health Scis Univ., Portland, 1987–93; Prin. Scientist, Geneva Biomedical Res. Inst., Glaxo Wellcome R&D (formerly Glaxo Inst. for Molecular Biol.), 1993–98; Prof. of Molecular Physiol., Inst. of Molecular Physiol., Univ. of Sheffield, 1998–2004. Visiting Professor: Flinders Univ., 1983; Bogomoletz Inst., 1984; Frankfurt Univ., 1988. Gaddum Lecture, British Pharmacol Soc., 1988. Mem., MRC, 2001–06. Pres., Physiol Soc., 2003–06. Ed.-in-Chief, British Jl of Pharmacol., 2000–04. FMedSci 2004. *Publications:* original res. papers in jls of physiol., pharmacol., neuroscience and biochem. *Recreation:* mountaineering. *Address:* University of Manchester, Michael Smith Building, Oxford Road, Manchester M13 9PT. *T:* (0161) 275 1499, *Fax:* (0161) 275 1498; *e-mail:* r.a.north@manchester.ac.uk.

NORTH, Richard Conway; Chairman, Woolworths Group plc, since 2007 (non-executive Director, 2006); *b* 20 Jan. 1950; *s* of John and Megan North; *m* 1978, Lindsay Jean Buchanan; three *d*. *Educ:* Marlborough Coll.; Sidney Sussex Coll., Cambridge (BA 1971). FCA 1976; FCT 1993. Coopers & Lybrand, 1971–91: qualified as accountant, 1974; seconded to: NY, 1976–78; Midland Bank, 1981–82; Partner, 1983–91; Group Finance Director: Burton Gp plc, 1991–94; Bass, subseq. Six Continents, plc, 1994–2003; CEO, Hotel Div., Six Continents, subseq. InterContinental Hotels Gp plc, 2002–04. Non-executive Director: ASDA Gp plc, 1997–99; Bristol Hotel Company Inc., 1997–98; Leeds United plc, 1998–2002; Felcor Lodging Trust Inc., 1998–2004; LogicaCMG (formerly Logica) plc, 2002–04; Majid Al Fatteim Gp LLC, 2006–; Mecom plc, 2007–. Member: Cttee, 100 Gp, 1996–2000; Exec. Cttee, World Travel and Tourism Council, 2004. Mem. Senate, ICAEW, 1991–2000. *Recreations:* golf, soccer, rock 'n' roll, history. *Clubs:* Athenæum, Hurlingham; Burhill Golf (Walton on Thames); Huntercombe Golf.

NORTH, Robert, (Robert North Dodson); freelance choreographer; Professor and Director, Ballett Akademie, Munich, Germany; Ballet Director, Krefeld and Mönchengladbach Theatres, Germany, since 2007; *b* 1 June 1945; *s* of Charles Dodson and Elizabeth Thompson; *m* 1st, 1978, Janet Smith (marr. diss.); 2nd, 1999, Sheri Cook. *Educ:* Pierrepont Sch. (A levels in Maths, Physics and Art); Central Sch. of Art; Royal Ballet Sch. Dancer and choreographer, London Contemporary Dance Co., 1966–81 (Jt Artistic Dir, 1980–81); seasons with Martha Graham Dance Co., 1967 and 1968; Teacher of Modern Dance, Royal Ballet Sch., 1979–81; Artistic Dir, Ballet Rambert, 1981–86; freelance work, Europe and USA, 1986–90; Ballet Dir, Teatro Regio, Turin, 1990–91; Artistic Dir, Gothenburg Ballet, 1991–96; Dir, Corps de Ballet, Arena di Verona, 1997–99; Artistic Dir, Scottish Ballet, 1999–2002. Has choreographed ballets for dance companies throughout the world, including: Royal Ballet; English National Ballet; Dance Theatre of Harlem; Royal Danish Ballet; San Francisco Ballet; Oakland Ballet; Finnish Nat. Ballet; Batsheva; Janet Smith and Dancers; La Scala, Milan; Rome Opera; Staatsoper Dresden; Györ Ballett; *ballets choreographed* include: Troy Game; Death and the Maiden; The Annunciation; A Stranger I Came; Running Figures; Pribaoutki; Colour Moves; Entre dos Aguas; full-length ballets: Carmen; Elvira Madigan; Romeo & Juliet; Living in America; Prince Rama and the Demons; Life, Love & Death; The Russian Story; The Snowman; The Cradle Will Rock; Eva; Ragazzi Selvaggi; Orlando; Carmina Burana; Bach; Wie Ihr's Wollt; also choreography for films, television (incl. Lonely Town, Lonely Street, and For My Daughter (Golden Prague Award)), theatre, musicals and opera (Carmen, Royal Albert Hall). *Address:* c/o Val West, 49 Springcroft Avenue, N2 9JH.

NORTH, Sir Thomas (Lindsay), Kt 1982; FAIM, FRMIA; Chairman, G. J. Coles & Coy Limited, Melbourne, Australia, 1979–83, Hon. Chairman, 1983–84; *b* 11 Dec. 1919; *s* of John North and Jane (*née* Irwin); *m* 1944, Kathleen Jefferis; two *d*. *Educ:* Rutherglen, Vic. FAIM 1972. Joined G. J. Coles & Co. Ltd, 1938; Gen. Man., 1966; Dep. Man. Dir, 1969; Man. Dir, 1975–79; Dir, various G. J. Coles subsid. cos. Dep. Chm., KMart (Australia) Ltd, 1975–; Chairman: Island Cooler Pty Ltd, 1985–; Smurfit Australia Pty Ltd. 1986–. *Recreations:* horse racing, swimming. *Address:* Chiltern, 5/627 Toorak Road, Toorak, Vic 3142, Australia. *T:* (3) 98223161. *Clubs:* Athenæum, Royal Automobile of Victoria (Melbourne); Australian Armoured Corps (Sydney); Victorian Amateur Turf (Dep. Chm.), Victoria Racing, Moonee Valley Race; Melbourne Cricket.

NORTH, Sir (William) Jonathan (Frederick), 2nd Bt *cr* 1920; *b* 6 Feb. 1931; *s* of Muriel Norton (*d* 1989), 2nd *d* of Sir William Hicking, 1st Bt, and Hon. John Montagu William North (marr. diss. 1939; he *d* 1987), 2nd *s* of 8th Earl of Guilford; *S* grandfather, 1947 (under special remainder); *m* 1956, Sara Virginia, *d* of Air Chief Marshal Sir Donald Hardman, GBE, KCB, DFC; one *s* two *d*. *Educ:* Marlborough Coll. *Heir:* *s* Jeremy William Francis North [*b* 5 May 1960; *m* 1986, Lucy, *d* of G. A. van der Meulen, Holland; two *s* two *d*]. *Address:* Frogmore, Weston-under-Penyard, Herefordshire HR9 5TQ.

NORTHAM, Jeremy Philip; actor; *b* 1 Dec. 1961; *s* of late Prof. John and Rachel Northam. *Educ:* King's Coll. Sch., Cambridge; Bristol Grammar Sch.; Bedford Coll., London (BA Hons English); Old Vic Theatre Sch. *Theatre* includes: National Theatre, 1989–91: Hamlet, School for Scandal, The Voysey Inheritance (Olivier Award for Outstanding Newcomer); Royal Shakespeare Co., 1992–94: Loves Labour's Lost, The Country Wife, The Gift of the Gorgon; Old Times, Donmar Warehouse, 2004; *television* includes: Journey's End, Piece of Cake, 1988; Martin of Lewis, 2003; The Tudors, 2007; Fiona's Story, 2008; *films* include: Wuthering Heights, Soft Top Hard Shoulder, 1992; Carrington, The Net, Voices, 1995; Emma, 1996; Mimic, Amistad, 1997; The Misadventures of Margaret, 1998; Gloria, The Winslow Boy, An Ideal Husband, Happy Texas, 1999; The Golden Bowl, 2000; Enigma, Gosford Park, 2001; Possession, 2002; Cypher, The Singing Detective, 2003; The Statement, Stroke of Genius, 2004; Guy X, 2005; A Cock and Bull Story, 2006. Best Actor, Evening Standard Awards, 2000; Best Film Actor, Variety Club, 2000; Best British Actor, Critics Circle Award, 2000. *Address:* c/o ARG, 4 Great Portland Street, W1W 8PA. *T:* (020) 7436 6400.

NORTHAMPTON, 7th Marquess of, *cr* 1812; **Spencer Douglas David Compton;** DL; Earl of Northampton, 1618; Earl Compton, Baron Wilmington, 1812; *b* 2 April 1946; *s* of 6th Marquess of Northampton, DSO, and Virginia (*d* 1997), *d* of Lt-Col David Heaton, DSO; *S* father, 1978; *m* 1st, 1967, Henriette Luisa Maria (marr. diss. 1973), *o d* of late Baron Bentinck; one *s* one *d*; 2nd, 1974, Annette Marie (marr. diss. 1977), *er d* of C. A. R. Smallwood; 3rd, 1977, Hon. Mrs Rosemary Dawson-Damer (marr. diss. 1983); one *d*; 4th, 1985, Hon. Mrs Michael Pearson (marr. diss. 1988); one *d*; 5th, 1990, Pamela Martina Raphaela Kyprios. *Educ:* Eton. DL Northants 1979. *Recreation:* freemasonry (Pro Grand Master, United Grand Lodge of England, 2001–). *Heir:* *s* Earl Compton, *qv*. *Address:* Compton Wynyates, Tysoe, Warwicks CV35 0UD. *Club:* Turf.

NORTHAMPTON, Bishop of, (RC), since 2005; **Rt Rev. Peter John Haworth Doyle;** *b* 3 May 1944; *s* of John Robert Doyle and Alice Gertrude Doyle (*née* Haworth). *Educ:* St Ignatius Coll., Stamford Hill; Allen Hall Seminary. Ordained priest, 1968; Asst Priest, Portsmouth and Windsor, 1968–75; Adminr, St John's Cathedral, Portsmouth, 1975–87; Parish Priest: St Joseph's, Maidenhead, 1987–91; St Peter's, Winchester, 1991–2005. Canon, Portsmouth Cathedral, 1983–2005; VG, Dio. Portsmouth, (RC), 2001–05. Mem., Old Brotherhood, 1994–2005. *Recreations:* Rugby (played for Windsor and Portsmouth RFCs, now a spectator), golf, ski-ing. *Address:* Bishop's House, Marriott Street, Northampton NN2 6AW. *T:* (01604) 715635, *Fax:* (01604) 792186; *e-mail:* admin@northamptondiocese.com.

NORTHAMPTON, Archdeacon of; *see* Allsopp, Ven. C.

NORTHARD, John Henry, CBE 1987 (OBE 1979); FREng; Hon. FIMMM; Director of Operations, 1985–88, Deputy Chairman, 1988–92, British Coal Corporation; Chairman, British Coal Enterprise Ltd, 1991–93; *b* 23 Dec. 1926; *s* of William Henry Northard and Nellie Northard; *m* 1952, Marian Josephine Lay; two *s* two *d*. *Educ:* St Bede's Grammar School, Bradford; Barnsley Mining and Technical College (Certificated Colliery Manager, first class). CEng, FREng (FEng 1983). Colliery Manager, Yorks, 1955–57, Leics, 1957–63; Group Manager, Leics Collieries, 1963–65; Dep. Chief Mining Engineer, NCB, Staffs Area, 1965–70; Area Dep. Dir (Mining), NCB, N Derbyshire Area, 1970–73; Area Dir, NCB, N Derbyshire Area, 1973–81, Western Area, 1981–85; Bd Mem., NCB, 1986–92. Pres., IMinE, 1982. CCMI. SBStJ 1981. *Publications:* contribs to mining engineering instns and tech. jls.

NORTHBOURNE, 5th Baron *cr* 1884; **Christopher George Walter James,** DL; FRICS; Bt 1791; Chairman: Betteshanger Farms Ltd, since 1975; Betteshanger Investments Ltd; *b* 18 Feb. 1926; *s* of 4th Baron Northbourne and Katherine Louise (*d* 1980), *d* of late George A. Nickerson, Boston, Mass; *S* father, 1982; *m* 1959, Aliki Louise Hélène Marie Sygne, *e d* of Henri Claudel, Chatou-sur-Seine, and *g d* of late Paul Claudel; three *s* one *d*. *Educ:* Eton; Magdalen Coll., Oxford (MA). Director: Anglo Indonesian Corp., 1971–96; Plantation & General (formerly Chillington Corp.) PLC, 1986–96; Center Parcs PLC, 1988–96 (Dep. Chm., 1988–96). Elected Mem., H of L, 1999. DL Kent, 1996. *Heir:* *s* Hon. Charles Walter Henri James [*b* 14 June 1960; *m* 1987, Catherine Lucy, *d* of Ralph Burrows; two *s* one *d*]. *Address:* 11 Eaton Place, SW1X 8BN. *T:* (020) 7235 6790; Coldharbour, Northbourne, Deal, Kent CT14 0NT. *T:* (01304) 611277. *Clubs:* Brooks's, Royal Yacht Squadron.

NORTHBROOK, 6th Baron *cr* 1866; **Francis Thomas Baring;** Bt 1793; Trustee, Fortune Forum, since 2006; *b* 21 Feb. 1954; *s* of 5th Baron Northbrook and of Rowena Margaret, 2nd *d* of Brig.-Gen. Sir William Manning, GCMG, KBE, CB; *S* father, 1990; *m* 1987, Amelia Sarah Elizabeth (marr. diss. 2006), *er d* of Dr Reginald Taylor; three *d*. *Educ:* Winchester Coll.; Bristol Univ. (BA Hons 1976). Trainee accountant, Dixon Wilson & Co., 1976–80; Baring Brothers and Co. Ltd, 1981–89; Sen. Investment Man., Taylor Young Investment Management Ltd, 1990–93; Investment Man., Smith and Williamson Securities, 1993–95; Dir, Mars Asset Mgt Ltd, 1996–2006. Chm., Dido Films Ltd, 2002–07. Elected Mem., H of L, 1999; an Opposition Whip, 1999–2000. Trustee, Winchester Medical Trust, 1991–96. *Heir:* (to baronetcy) *kinsman* Peter Baring [*b* 12 Sept. 1939; *m* 1973, Rose, *d* of George Nigel Adams; one *s*]. *Address:* House of Lords, SW1A 0PW. *Clubs:* White's, Pratt's, Beefsteak.

NORTHCOTE, family name of **Earl of Iddesleigh**.

NORTHCOTE, His Honour Peter Colston; a Circuit Judge 1973–89; *b* 23 Oct. 1920; *s* of late William George Northcote and late Edith Mary Northcote; *m* 1947, Patricia Bickley; two *s*. *Educ:* Ellesmere Coll.; Bristol Univ. Called to Bar, Inner Temple, 1948. Chm., Nat. Insce Tribunal; Chm., W Midland Rent Tribunal; Dep. Chm., Agric. Land Tribunal. Commnd KSLI, 1940; served 7th Rajput Regt, Far East (Major). *Recreations:* music, travel, ski-ing. *Address:* Pendil House, Pendil Close, Wellington, Salop TF1 2PQ. *T:* (01952) 641160.

NORTHERN, Richard James, MBE 1982; HM Diplomatic Service; Assistant Director, Human Resources, Foreign and Commonwealth Office, since 2006; *b* 2 Nov. 1954; *s* of James Wilfred Northern and Margaret Northern (*née* Lammie); *m* 1981, Linda Denise Gadd; two *s* one *d*. *Educ:* Bedford Sch.; Jesus Coll., Cambridge (BA 1976; MA 1979). Joined HM Diplomatic Service, 1976: FCO, 1976–78; MECAS, Beirut and London, 1978–80; Third Sec. and Vice Consul, Riyadh, 1980–83; Second, later First, Sec. (Political/Inf.), Rome, 1983–87; First Secretary: FCO, 1987–92; (Economic), Ottawa, 1992–94; Dep. Consul Gen. and Dep. Dir for Trade and Investment, Toronto, 1994–97; Counsellor (Econ./Commercial), Riyadh, 1997–2000; Counsellor, FCO, 2000–01; Dir Gen. for Trade and Investment in Italy, and Consul Gen., Milan, 2001–06. *Recreations:* tennis, music, languages. *Address:* c/o Foreign and Commonwealth Office, King Charles Street, SW1A 2AH. *Club:* Royal Over-Seas League.

NORTHESK, 14th Earl of, *cr* 1647; **David John MacRae Carnegie;** Lord Rosehill and Inglismaldie 1639; estate manager/owner; *b* 3 Nov. 1954; *s* of 13th Earl of Northesk, and Jean Margaret (*d* 1989), *yr d* of Captain (John) Duncan George MacRae; *S* father, 1994; *m* 1979, Jacqueline Reid, *d* of Mrs Elizabeth Reid, Sarasota, Florida, USA; three *d* (one *s* decd). *Educ:* West Hill Park, Titchfield; Eton; Brooke House, Market Harborough; UCL. Elected Mem., H of L, 1999; an Opposition Whip, 1999–2002. *Heir:* *kinsman* Patrick Charles Carnegy, *b* 23 Sept. 1940. *Address:* House of Lords, SW1A 0PW.

NORTHFIELD, Baron *cr* 1975 (Life Peer), of Telford, Shropshire; **(William) Donald Chapman;** Chairman: Telford Development Corporation, 1975–87; Consortium Developments Ltd, 1986–92; *b* 25 Nov. 1923; *s* of Wm H. and Norah F. E. Chapman, Barnsley. *Educ:* Barnsley Grammar Sch.; Emmanuel Coll., Cambridge (Sen. Schol.; BA 1st

Cl. Hons (Economics) 1945, MA 1948, also degree in Agriculture; Hon. Fellow, 2003). Research in Agric. Economics, Cambridge, 1943–46. Cambridge City Councillor, 1945–47; Sec., Trades Council and Labour Party, 1945–57; MP (Lab) Birmingham (Northfield), 1951–70. Research Sec. of the Fabian Soc., 1948–49, Gen. Sec., 1949–53. Gwilym Gibbon Fellow, Nuffield Coll., Oxford, 1971–73; Vis. Fellow, Centre for Contemporary European Studies, Sussex Univ., 1973–79. Special Adviser to EEC Commn, 1978–84; Chairman: Rural Develt Commn, 1974–80; Inquiry into recent trends in acquisition and occupancy of agric. land, 1977–79. *Publications:* The European Parliament: the years ahead, 1973; The Road to European Union, 1975; articles and Fabian pamphlets. *Recreation:* travel. *Address:* House of Lords, SW1A 0PW.

NORTHLAND, Viscount; courtesy title of heir to Earldom of Ranfurly, not used by current heir.

NORTHOLT, Archdeacon of; *see* Treweek, Ven. R.

NORTHOVER, Baroness *cr* 2000 (Life Peer), of Cissbury in the co. of West Sussex; **Lindsay Patricia Northover,** PhD; Liberal Democrats' spokesperson on international development, House of Lords, since 2002; *b* 21 Aug. 1954; *d* of Maurice Charles Colin Granshaw and Patricia Winifred Granshaw (*née* Jackson); *m* 1988, Prof. John Martin Alban Northover, *qv*; two *s* one *d*. *Educ:* Brighton and Hove High Sch.; St Anne's Coll., Oxford (exhibitioner; MA Modern History); Bryn Mawr Coll. (ESU schol.); Univ. of Pennsylvania (MA History and Philosophy of Sci. 1978; PhD 1981). Res. Fellow, UCL and St Mark's Hosp., 1980–83; Fellow, St Thomas's Hosp. Med. Sch., 1983–84; Lectr, Wellcome Inst. for the History of Medicine and UCL, 1984–91. Mem., cttee negotiating Liberal and SDP merger, 1987–88; Chair: SDP Health and Welfare Assoc., 1987–88; SDP Parly Cands' Assoc., 1987–88; Lib Dem Parly Cands' Assoc., 1988–91; Chair, Women Liberal Democrats, 1992–95. House of Lords: Lib Dem spokesperson on health, 2001–02; Member: Select Cttee on Embryonic Stem Cell Res., 2001–02; Sub-Cttee on Foreign Affairs, Defence and Internat. Develt, Select Cttee on EU, 2003–04. Sec., All-Party Gp on Overseas Develt, 2003–; Mem. Council, Overseas Develt Inst., 2005–; Vice-Chair, All-Party Gp on Debt, Aid and Trade, 2005–. Mem. Exec., CPA, 2006–. Contested: (SDP/Alliance) Welwyn, Hatfield, 1983 and 1987; (Lib Dem) Basildon, 1997. Trustee, Tropical Health and Educn Trust, 2007–. Patron, Breast Cancer Campaign, 2002–. Trustee, Bryn Mawr Coll. Assoc. (GB). *Publications:* St Mark's Hospital, London: a social history of a specialist hospital 1835–1985, 1985; academic books and contribs to learned jls. *Address:* House of Lords, SW1A 0PW.

NORTHOVER, Prof. John Martin Alban; Professor of Intestinal Surgery, Imperial College, London, since 2001; Director, Colorectal Cancer Unit, Cancer Research UK (formerly Imperial Cancer Research Fund), 1985–2005; *b* 17 June 1947; *s* of William Joseph Northover and Peggy Vesta Northover (*née* Jacobs); *m* 1st, 1974, Sheila Ann Scott (marr. diss. 1987); two *s*; 2nd, 1988, Lindsay Patricia Granshaw (*see* Baroness Northover); two *s* one *d*. *Educ:* Southern Grammar Sch., Portsmouth; King's Coll. Hosp., London (MB BS Hons 1970; MS 1980). KCH and Middlesex Hosp. trng posts, 1970–84; Consultant Surgeon, St Mark's Hosp., 1984–. Res. Fellow, Univ. of Cape Town, 1976–77. Arris and Gale Lectr, RCS, 1979. Hon. Civilian Consultant Advr in Colorectal Surgery to the Army, 1998–. Chm., MRC Colorectal Cancer Trials Data Monitoring and Ethics Cttee, 1995–. Mem., Adv. Cttee on Distinction Awards, NW London, 2001–03. Vice-Pres., Internat. Soc. of Univ. Colon and Rectal Surgeons, 1998–99; Mem., James IV Assoc. of Surgeons, 2001–; Corresp. Mem., Surgical Res. Soc. of Southern Africa, 1989; Hon. Mem., Sect. of Colon and Rectal Surgery, RACS, 1992. *Publications:* (ed jtly) Pocket Examiner in Surgery, 1984, 2nd edn 1992; (ed with J. Kettner) Bowel Cancer: the facts, 1992; (ed with R. Phillips) Modern Coloproctology, 1993; (ed jtly) Current Surgical Practice, Vol. 8, 1998; (ed with W. Longo) Re-operative Colon and Rectal Surgery, 2003; book chapters; numerous contribs to learned jls incl. Lancet, BMJ, British Jl Surgery, British Jl Cancer. *Address:* St Mark's Hospital, Northwick Park, Watford Road, Middx HA1 3UJ. *T:* (020) 8235 4250, *Fax:* (020) 8235 4277; 149 Harley Street, W1G 6DE. *T:* (020) 7486 1008.

NORTHUMBERLAND, 12th Duke of, *cr* 1766; **Ralph George Algernon Percy;** DL; Bt 1660; Earl of Northumberland, Baron Warkworth 1749; Earl Percy 1766; Earl of Beverley 1790; Lord Lovaine, Baron of Alnwick 1784; Chairman, since 1992, and President, since 1995, Northumberland Estates; *b* 16 Nov. 1956; 2nd *s* of 10th Duke of Northumberland, KG, GCVO, TD, PC, FRS and of Lady Elizabeth Diana Montagu-Douglas-Scott, *er d* of 8th Duke of Buccleuch and Queensberry, KT, GCVO, PC; *S* brother, 1995; *m* 1979, Isobel Jane Miller, *d* of John W. M. M. Richard; two *s* two *d*. *Educ:* Eton; Oxford Univ. MRICS (ARICS 1986). Land Agent with: Cluttons, 1979–82; Humberts, 1982–86; Northumberland Estates, 1986–96. DL Northumberland, 1997. *Recreations:* tennis, fishing, shooting, painting. *Heir: s* Earl Percy, *qv*. *Address:* Alnwick Castle, Alnwick, Northumberland NE66 1NG. *T:* (01665) 602456; Syon House, Brentford, Middlesex TW8 8JF. *T:* (020) 8560 2353.

NORTHUMBERLAND, Archdeacon of; *see* Miller, Ven. G. V.

NORTHWAY, Eileen Mary, CBE 1990; RRC 1982 (ARRC 1969); Principal Nursing Officer and Matron-in-Chief, Queen Alexandra's Royal Naval Nursing Service, 1986–90, retired; *b* 22 July 1931; *d* of Ernest and Margaret Northway. *Educ:* St Michael's Convent, Newton Abbot. SRN 1952, SCM 1954; joined QARNNS 1956. QHNS, 1986–90. OStJ 1985. *Recreations:* gardening, reading.

NORTON, family name of **Barons Grantley** and **Rathcreedan**.

NORTON, 8th Baron *cr* 1878; **James Nigel Arden Adderley;** *b* 2 June 1947; *er s* of 7th Baron Norton, OBE and of Betty Margaret, *o d* of James McKee Hannah; *S* father, 1993; *m* (marr. diss.); one *s* one *d*; *m* 1997, Frances Elizabeth Prioleau, *yr d* of George Frederick Rothwell; one *d*. *Educ:* Downside. FCA 1970. *Heir: s* Hon. Edward James Arden Adderley, *b* 19 Oct. 1982. *Address:* Chalet Petrus, rue de Patier 24, 1936 Verbier, Switzerland.

NORTON OF LOUTH, Baron *cr* 1998 (Life Peer), of Louth in the co. of Lincolnshire; **Philip Norton,** PhD; Professor of Government, since 1986, Director, Centre for Legislative Studies, since 1992, and Head, Department of Politics and International Studies, 2002–07, University of Hull; *b* 5 March 1951; *y s* of late George E. Norton and Ena D. Norton. *Educ:* Univ. of Sheffield (BA 1st cl. Hons; Nalgo Prize 1972; PhD); Univ. of Pennsylvania (MA; Thouron Scholar). Lectr, 1977–82, Sen. Lectr, 1982–84, Reader, 1984–86, Univ. of Hull. Member: Exec. Cttee, Study of Parlt Gp, 1981–93 (Acad. Sec., 1981–85); Exec. Cttee, British Politics Gp (USA), 1982–95 (Pres., 1988–90); Exec. Cttee, Political Studies Assoc. of UK, 1983–89; Society and Politics Res. Develt Gp, ESRC, 1987–90; Council, Hansard Soc., 1997– (Dir of Studies, 2002–). Chm., H of L Select Cttee on the Constitution, 2001–04. Chairman: Cons. Pty Commn to Strengthen Parlt, 1999–2000; Standards Cttee, Kingston-upon-Hull City Council, 1999–2003. Co-Chm., Res. Cttee of Legislative Specialists, Internat. Political Sci. Assoc., 1994–2003. Pres., Politics Assoc., 1993–2008; Vice-Pres., Political Studies Assoc., 2002–. Trustee, Hist. of Parlt Trust, 1999–. Governor, King Edward VI Grammar Sch., Louth, 1988– (Warden, 1990–93). FRSA 1995; AcSS 2001. Assoc. Ed., Political Studies, 1987–93; Ed., Jl of Legislative Studies, 1995–. *Publications:* Dissension in the House of Commons 1945–74, 1975; Conservative Dissidents, 1978; Dissension in the House of Commons 1974–79, 1980; The Commons in Perspective, 1981; (jtly) Conservatives and Conservatism, 1981; The Constitution in Flux, 1982; The British Polity, 1984, 4th edn 2001; Law and Order and British Politics, 1984; (ed) Parliament in the 1980s, 1985; (ed jtly) The Political Science of British Politics, 1986; (ed) Legislatures, 1990; (ed) Parliaments in Western Europe, 1990; (ed) New Directions in British Politics, 1991; (jtly) Politics UK, 1991, 6th edn 2006; (ed jtly) Parliamentary Questions, 1993; (jtly) Back from Westminster, 1993; Does Parliament Matter?, 1993; (ed) National Parliaments and the European Union, 1996; (ed jtly) The New Parliaments of Central and Eastern Europe, 1996; (ed) The Conservative Party, 1996; (ed) Legislatures and Legislators, 1998; (ed) Parliaments and Governments in Western Europe, 1998; (ed) Parliaments and Pressure Groups in Western Europe, 1999; (ed jtly) Parliaments in Asia, 1999; (ed) Parliaments and Citizens in Western Europe, 2002; Parliament in British Politics, 2005; (ed jtly) Post-Communist and Post-Soviet Parliaments: the initial decade, 2007; (ed jtly) The Internet and Parliamentary Democracy in Europe, 2008. *Recreations:* table-tennis, walking. *Address:* Department of Politics, University of Hull, Hull, East Yorkshire HU6 7RX. *T:* (01482) 465863. *Clubs:* Royal Over-Seas League, Royal Commonwealth Society.

NORTON, Donald; Regional Administrator, Oxford Regional Health Authority, 1973–80, retired; *b* 2 May 1920; *s* of Thomas Henry Norton and Dora May Norton (*née* Prentice); *m* 1945, Miriam Joyce, *d* of Herbert and Florence Mann; two *s* one *d*. *Educ:* Nether Edge Grammar Sch., Sheffield; Univs of Sheffield and London. LLB, DPA; FHA. Senior Administrator Sheffield Regional Hosp. Bd, 1948–51; Sec. Supt, Jessop Hosp. for Women and Charles Clifford Dental Hosp., Sheffield, 1951–57; Dep. Sec., Archway Gp of Hosps, London, 1957–60; Gp Sec., Dudley Road Gp of Hosps, Birmingham 1960–70; Sec., Oxford Regional Hosp. Bd, 1970–73. *Recreations:* marriage, gardening. *Address:* Room 108, Sunrise of Edgbaston, 5 Church Road, Birmingham B15 3SH.

NORTON, Dame Hilary Sharon Braverman; *see* Blume, Dame H. S. B.

NORTON, Hugh Edward; non-executive Director: Inchcape plc, 1995–2004; Standard Chartered plc, 1995–2006; *b* 23 June 1936; *s* of late Lt-Gen. Edward F. Norton, CB, DSO, MC and I. Joyce Norton; *m* 1965, Janet M. Johnson (*d* 1993); one *s*; *m* 1998, F. Joy Harcup; one *s* one *d*. *Educ:* Winchester Coll.; Trinity Coll., Oxford (BA Hons Lit.Hum.). British Petroleum Co., 1959–95: Chief Exec., BP Exploration Co., 1986–89; Man. Dir, 1989–95. *Recreations:* painting, ornithology, tennis, travel, chess.

NORTON, James, FCIS; General Secretary, Arthritis and Rheumatism Council for Research, 1981–98; *b* 12 July 1931; *s* of James and May Norton; *m* 1956, Dora Ashworth; one *s*. *Educ:* West Hill Sch., Stalybridge; Open Univ. (BA Hons 2002); Univ. of Sheffield (MA Historical Res. 2005). FCIS 1972. Stalybridge, Hyde, Mossley and Dukinfield Tspt Bd, 1947–60; Wing Comdr, RAF, 1961–81. *Recreations:* walking, cricket, Manchester United. *Address:* 665 Chatsworth Road, Chesterfield S40 3PA. *T:* (01246) 566160. *Club:* Royal Air Force.

NORTON, Jim; *see* Norton, M. J.

NORTON, John Lindsey; Chairman, National Society for Prevention of Cruelty to Children, 1995–2001 (Hon. Treasurer, 1991–95); *b* 21 May 1935; *s* of Frederick Raymond Norton and Doris Ann Norton; *m* 1959, Judith Ann Bird; three *d*. *Educ:* Winchester College; Cambridge Univ. (MA). Blackburn Robson Coates & Co., 1959–63; BDO Binder Hamlyn, later Binder Hamlyn, 1963–96: Nat. Man. Partner, 1983–88; Chm., BDO Binder, 1988–92; Sen. Partner, Binder Hamlyn, 1993–96. Chairman: Barking Power Ltd, 1995–; Thames Valley Power Ltd, 1995– (Dir, 1995–). *Recreations:* walking, gardening, golf. *Address:* Knowle Cottage, 1 Shorts Lane, Beaminster, Dorset DT8 3BD. *Clubs:* Army and Navy, Sloane.

NORTON, Michael Aslan, OBE 1998; social entrepreneur; author; *s* of Richard and Helene Norton; *m* 1977, Hilary Sharon Braverman Blume, *qv*; one *d*, and two step *s*. *Educ:* Charterhouse; King's Coll., Cambridge (MA Natural Scis). Investment Manager, Samuel Montagu & Co., 1964–67; Exec., New Enterprises, IPC, 1968; Publishing Exec., BPC Publishing, 1969–71; freelance writer, lectr, OU tutor and activist, 1971–75; Founder and Director: Directory of Social Change, 1975–94; Centre for Innovation in Voluntary Action, 1995–. Creator of first lang. teaching prog. in UK for non-English speaking immigrant families and children, 1965–70; Co-ordinator, Save Piccadilly Campaign, 1972–74; Co-Founder: Soho Housing Assoc., 1974; Changemakers, 1994 (Chm., 1994–); UnLtd, the Foundn for Social Entrepreneurs, 2001; Founder: Books for Change, 1996; YouthBank UK, 1998; Booksline (India), 2000; Young Achievers Trust, 2006; Otesha Proj. UK, 2007; Sponsor, Children's Develt Bank prog. for street banking in S Asia, 2004; Initiator, MyBnk children's banking and financial literacy prog. in UK, 2006. *Publications:* The Community Newspaper Kit, 1975; The Mural Kit, 1976; Colour in your Environment, 1979; A Guide to the Benefits of Charitable Status, 1981; A Guide to Company Giving, 1984; The WorldWide Fundraisers Handbook, 1996; The Non-Profit Sector in India, 1997; Getting Started in Fundraising (India), 2000; (with Nina Botting) The Complete Fundraising Handbook, 4th edn 2001 to 5th edn 2007; Getting Started in Communication (India), 2003; 365 Ways to Change the World, 2005; Need to Know? Fundraising, 2007; The Everyday Activist, 2007. *Recreations:* cycling, bridge, crosswords, dreaming up ideas to change the world, mentoring and supporting emerging social entrepreneurs.

NORTON, Michael James, (Jim), DEng; Senior Policy Adviser, e–Business and e–Government, Institute of Directors, since 2004; *b* 15 Dec. 1952; *s* of Christopher Stephen Norton and Lilian Ivy Norton; *m* 1976, Barbara Foster; one *s*. *Educ:* Roan Sch., Blackheath; Sheffield Univ. (BEng Hons (Electronic Engrg) 1974; Mappin Medal, 1974). AMIEE 1974, FIET (FIEE 1997). Post Office (Telecommunications), later British Telecommunications, 1970–87 (lastly, Sen. Man., Internat. Business); Practice Dir, Butler Cox plc, 1987–90; Marketing Dir, Cable & Wireless (Europe), 1990–93; Chief Exec., Radiocoms Agency, DTI, 1993–98; Dir, Electronic Commerce Team, Performance and Innovation Unit, Cabinet Office, 1999; Hd of Electronic Business Policy, IoD, 1999–2001; Chm., Deutsche Telekom Ltd, 2001–02. Non-executive Director: Securicor plc, 2000–02; 3i European Technology Trust, 2000–04; Zetex (formerly Telemetrix) plc, 2000– (Sen. Indep. Dir, 2003–08); F & C Capital & Income (formerly F & C PEP & ISA) Trust plc, 2001–. Mem., Commn on Nat. Security in 21st Century, IPPR, 2007–. Ext. Bd Mem., POST, 2001–; Strategic Stakeholder Gp Mem., Nat. Hi-Tech Crime Unit, 2005–06; Council Mem., PITCOM, 2005–. Vis. Prof. of Electronic Engrg, Univ. of Sheffield, 1998–. FRSA 1993; FInstD 2001. Hon. DEng Sheffield, 2003. *Recreations:* reading, music, amateur radio. *Address:* Institute of Directors, Policy Unit, 116 Pall Mall, SW1Y 5ED. *T:* (020) 7451 3279; *web:* www.profjimnorton.com.

NORTON, Hon. Sir Nicholas John H.; *see* Hill-Norton.

NORTON, Capt. Peter Allen, GC 2006; *b* 10 Dec. 1962; *m* 1994, Susan Ann Chapman; two *s*. Enlisted RAOC, 1983; trained as Ammunition Technician; Instr, Improvised Explosive Device Disposal, Army Sch. of Ammunition, 1993–95; loan service, Royal Army of Oman, 1995–98; Sen. Ammunition Technician, RLC, 1998; commnd RLC, 2002; 2nd i/c Combined Explosives Exploitation Cell, Iraq, 2005 (GC for outstanding bravery and leadership). MIExpE 1991. *Recreations:* family, photography, Open University studies, learning to walk!

NORTON-GRIFFITHS, Sir John, 3rd Bt *cr* 1922; FCA; *b* 4 Oct. 1938; *s* of Sir Peter Norton-Griffiths, 2nd Bt, and Kathryn (*d* 1980), *e d* of late George F. Schrafft; *S* father, 1983; *m* 1964, Marilyn Margaret, *er d* of late Norman Grimley. *Educ:* Eton. FCA 1966. *Heir: b* Michael Norton-Griffiths [*b* 11 Jan. 1941; *m* 1965, Ann, *o d* of late Group Captain Blair Alexander Fraser; one *s*].

NORWICH, 2nd Viscount *cr* 1952, of Aldwick; **John Julius Cooper,** CVO 1993; FRSL, FRGS, FSA; writer and broadcaster; *b* 15 Sept. 1929; *s* of 1st Viscount Norwich, PC, GCMG, DSO, and Lady Diana Cooper (*d* 1986), *d* of 8th Duke of Rutland; *S* father, 1954; *m* 1st, 1952, Anne (Frances May) (marr. diss. 1985), *e d* of late Hon. Sir Bede Clifford, GCMG, CB, MVO; one *s* one *d*; 2nd, 1989, Mollie Philipps, *e d* of 1st Baron Sherfield, GCB, GCMG, FRS. *Educ:* Upper Canada Coll., Toronto, Canada; Eton; University of Strasbourg; New Coll., Oxford. Served 1947–49 as Writer, Royal Navy. Entered Foreign Office, 1952; Third Secretary, British Embassy, Belgrade, 1955–57; Second Secretary, British Embassy, Beirut, 1957–60; worked in Foreign Office (First Secretary from 1961) and in British Delegation to Disarmament Conference, Geneva, from 1960 until resignation from Foreign Service 1964. Chairman: British Theatre Museum, 1966–71; Venice in Peril Fund, 1970–; Colnaghi, 1992–96; Chm., World Monuments Fund in Britain; Member: Exec. Cttee, National Trust, 1969–95 (Properties Cttee, 1970–87); Franco-British Council, 1972–79; Bd, English Nat. Opera, 1977–81. Curator, Sovereign Exhibn, London, 1992. Has made some thirty documentary films for television, mostly on history and architecture. Commendatore, Ordine al Merito della Repubblica Italiana, 1995; Stella della Solidarietà Italiana, 2001. *Publications:* (as John Julius Norwich): Mount Athos (with Reresby Sitwell), 1966; The Normans in the South (as The Other Conquest, US), 1967, new edn as The Normans in Sicily, 1992; Sahara, 1968; The Kingdom in The Sun, 1970; (ed) Great Architecture of the World, 1975; A History of Venice: vol. I, The Rise to Empire, 1977: vol. II, The Greatness and the Fall, 1981; Christmas Crackers: being ten commonplace selections, 1970–79, 1980; (ed) Britain's Heritage, 1982; (ed) The Italian World: history, art and the genius of a people, 1983; Fifty Years of Glyndebourne, 1985; A Taste for Travel (anthology), 1985; The Architecture of Southern England, 1985; Byzantium: vol. 1, The Early Centuries, 1988; vol. 2, The Apogee, 1991; vol. 3, The Decline and Fall, 1995; More Christmas Crackers 1980–89, 1990; Venice: a traveller's companion, 1990; (ed) The Oxford Illustrated Encyclopaedia of the Arts, 1990; (with H. C. Robbins Landon) Five Centuries of Music in Venice, 1991; (with C. Miles) Love in the Ancient World, 1997; (with Quentin Blake) The Twelve Days of Christmas, 1998; Shakespeare's Kings, 1999; Still More Christmas Crackers, 2000; Paradise of Cities: Venice in the 19th century, 2003; (ed) The Duff Cooper Diaries, 2005; The Middle Sea: a history of the Mediterranean, 2006; Trying to Please (memoirs), 2008; (ed) Seventy Cities of History, 2008. *Recreations:* sight-seeing, nightclub piano, walking at night through Venice. *Heir: s* Hon. Jason Charles Duff Bede Cooper, *b* 27 Oct. 1959. *Address:* 24 Blomfield Road, W9 1AD. *T:* (020) 7286 5050, *Fax:* (020) 7266 2561. *Club:* Beefsteak.

See also A. J. Beevor, Baron Milford.

NORWICH, Bishop of, since 1999; **Rt Rev. Graham Richard James;** *b* 19 Jan. 1951; *s* of late Rev. Lionel Dennis James and Florence Edith May James (*née* James); *m* 1978, Julie Anne Freemantle; one *s* one *d* (and one *d* decd). *Educ:* Northampton Grammar Sch.; Univ. of Lancaster (BA 1972); Univ. of Oxford (DipTh 1974); Cuddesdon Theological Coll. Deacon 1975, priest 1976; Asst Curate, Christ the Carpenter, Peterborough, 1975–78; Priest-in-charge, later Team Vicar, Christ the King, Digswell, 1979–83; Selection Sec. and Sec. for Continuing Ministerial Educn, ACCM, 1983–85; Sen. Selection Sec., ACCM, 1985–87; Chaplain to Archbishop of Canterbury, 1987–93; Bishop Suffragan of St Germans, 1993–99. Hon. Canon: St Matthew's Cathedral, Dallas, Texas, 1989–; Truro Cathedral, 1993–99. Vice-Moderator, Churches Commn on Inter-Faith Relations, 1993–99; Chm., Rural Bishops Panel, C of E, 2001–06; Member: Gen. Synod of C of E, 1995–; Archbps' Council, 2006– (Chm., Ministry Div., 2006–). Chm., Central Religious Adv. Cttee, BBC and Ofcom, 2004–. Mem. Bd, Countryside Agency, 2001–06; Chm., Norfolk Community Foundn, 2005–; Pres., Royal Norfolk Agricl Assoc., 2005. *Publications:* (contrib.) Say One for Me, 1992; (ed) New Soundings, 1997; A Fallible Church, 2008; contribs to Theology. *Recreations:* theatre, discovering secondhand bookshops. *Address:* Bishop's House, Norwich NR3 1SB. *T:* (01603) 629001, *Fax:* (01603) 761613; *e-mail:* bishop@bishopofnorwich.org. *Clubs:* Athenæum; Norfolk.

NORWICH, Dean of; *see* Smith, Very Rev. G. C. M.

NORWICH, Archdeacon of; *see* McFarlane, Ven. J. E.

NORWOOD, Mandi, (Mrs M. Norwood-Kelly); Editor-in-Chief, Shop Etc., since 2004; *b* 9 Oct. 1963; *m* 1995, Martin Kelly; two *d*. Sub-editor, Look Now, 1983–84; Features Editor, Clothes Show, 1986; Dep. Editor, More!, 1986–90; Editor: Looks, 1989–90; Company, 1990–95; Cosmopolitan, 1995–2000; Ed.-in-Chief, Mademoiselle, 2000–01. Ed. of Year, British Press Awards, 1993. *Publication:* Sex and the Married Girl, 2003. *Address:* (office) Hearst Corp., 959 8th Avenue, New York, NY 10019, USA. *Club:* Groucho.

NORWOOD, Her Honour Suzanne Freda, (Mrs John Lexden Stewart); a Circuit Judge, 1973–95; *b* 24 March 1926; *d* of late Frederic Francis Norwood and of Marianne Freda Norwood (*née* Thomas); *m* 1954, John Lexden Stewart (*d* 1972); one *s*. *Educ:* Lowther Coll., Bodelwyddan; St Andrews Univ. MA English, MA Hons History. Called to Bar, Gray's Inn, 1951; practised at Bar, SE Circuit. Member: Parole Bd, 1976–78; Mental Health Review Tribunal, 1983–98 (Chm., Oxford and Anglia Area, 1994–98). Member: Greenwich and Bexley AHA, 1979–82; Greenwich DHA, 1982–85; Bexley DHA, 1985–90. Pres., Medico-Legal Soc., 1990–92. Hon. LLD St Andrews, 1996. *Recreations:* walking, housekeeping, opera. *Address:* 69 Lee Road, SE3 9EN.

NORWOOD-KELLY, Mandi; *see* Norwood, M.

NOSS, Celia Mary; *see* Hoyles, C. M.

NOSS, John Bramble; HM Diplomatic Service, retired; *b* 20 Dec. 1935; *s* of John Noss and Vera Ethel (*née* Mattingly); *m* 1957, Shirley May Andrews; two *s* one *d*. *Educ:* Portsmouth Grammar School. Foreign Office, 1954; RAF, 1955–57; served FO, Beirut, Copenhagen, FCO; Russian language training, 1965; Moscow, 1965–68; Santiago, 1968–70; FCO, 1970–73; First Sec. (Economic), Pretoria, 1974–77; First Sec. (Commercial), Moscow, 1977–78; FCO, 1978–81; Consul (Inward Investment), New York, 1981–85; High Comr, Solomon Is, 1986–88; Dep. Hd of Mission and Commercial Counsellor, Helsinki, 1988–91; Consul-Gen., Perth, 1991–93; Internat. Primary Aluminium Inst., 1994–97 (Dep. Sec. Gen., 1996–97). *Recreations:* photography, reading, golf. *Address:* 8 Hither Chantlers, Langton Green, Tunbridge Wells, Kent TN3 0BJ. *T:* (01892) 862157.

NOSSAL, Sir Gustav (Joseph Victor), AC 1989; Kt 1977; CBE 1970; FRS 1982; FAA; Director, The Walter and Eliza Hall Institute of Medical Research, Melbourne, 1965–96; Professor of Medical Biology, University of Melbourne, 1965–96, now Professor Emeritus; *b* Austria, 4 June 1931; *m* 1955, Lyn B. Dunnicliff; two *s* two *d*. *Educ:* Sydney Univ. (1st Cl. Hons BScMed (Bacteriology), 1952; 1st Cl. Hons MB, BS 1954 (Mills Prize)); Melbourne Univ. (PhD 1960). FAA 1967; FRACP 1967; Hon. FRCPA 1971; FRACMA 1971; FRCP 1980; FTS 1981; Hon. FRSE 1983. Jun., then Sen. Resident Officer, Royal Prince Alfred Hosp., Sydney, 1955–56; Res. Fellow, Walter and Eliza Hall Inst. of Med. Res., 1957–59; Asst Prof., Dept of Genetics, Stanford Univ. Sch. of Medicine, Calif, 1959–61; Dep. Dir (Immunology), Walter and Eliza Hall Inst. of Med. Res., 1961–65. Vis. scientist and vis. professor to several univs and res. insts; has given many lectures to learned societies, assocs and univs. Dir, CRA Ltd, 1977–97. World Health Organisation: Member: Expert Adv. Panel on Immunology, 1967; Adv. Cttee Med. Res., 1973–80; Special Consultant, Tropical Disease Res. Prog., 1976; Chm., Global Programme for Vaccines and Immunization, 1993–2002. Chm., West Pac Adv. Co. Med. Res., 1976–80; Member: Aust. Science and Technol. Council, 1975–83; Bd, CSIRO, 1987–94; Prime Minister's Sci. and Engrg Council, 1989–98. Chairman: Felton Bequests' Cttee, 1977–; Vic. Health Promotion Foundn, 1987–96. President: Internat. Union of Immunological Socs, 1986–89; Australian Acad. of Science, 1994–98. Mem., Aust. Soc. of Immunology; Hon. Mem., Amer. (1975), French (1979), Indian (1976), Soc. of Immunology; Foreign Hon. Mem., Amer. Acad. of Arts and Scis, 1974. For. Associate, US Nat. Acad. of Scis, 1979; Fellow, New York Acad. of Scis, 1977; For. Fellow, Indian Nat. Sci. Acad., 1980. Hon. MD Johannes Gutenberg Univ., Mainz, 1981. Emil von Behring Prize, Philipps Univ., Marburg, Germany, 1971; Rabbi Shai Shacknai Memorial Prize, Univ. of Jerusalem, 1973; Ciba Foundn Gold Medal, 1978; Burnet Medal, Aust. Acad. of Sci., 1979; Robert Koch Gold Medal, Univ. of Bonn, 1996. Mem. Editorial Bd of several med. jls. *Publications:* Antibodies & Immunity, 1968 (rev. edn 1977); Antigens Lymphoid Cells & The Immune Response, 1971; Medical Science & Human Goals, 1975; Nature's Defences (Boyer Lectures), 1978; Reshaping Life: key issues in genetic engineering, 1984. *Recreations:* golf, literature. *Address:* Department of Pathology, University of Melbourne, Parkville, Vic 3052, Australia. *T:* (3) 93446946. *Clubs:* Melbourne (Melbourne); National, Cape Schanck.

NOTLEY, Maj.-Gen. Charles Roland Sykes, CB 1994; CBE 1991; President of the Ordnance Board, 1992–94; *b* 5 May 1939; *s* of late Major Henry Sykes Notley, 3rd Carabiniers, and Mrs Stephanie Paterson-Morgan; *m* 1965, Katherine Sonia Bethell; two *d*. *Educ:* Winchester Coll. Commnd 3rd Carabiniers, 1959; Command, Royal Scots Dragoon Guards, 1979–82; Dir, Op. Requirements (Land), MoD, 1986–89; Dir, Logistic Ops (Army), MoD, 1989–90; Vice-Pres., Ordnance Board, 1991–92. *Recreations:* equitation, sailing. *Address:* c/o Royal Bank of Scotland, 62 Threadneedle Street, EC2R 8LA. *Clubs:* Royal Ocean Racing; Royal Yacht Squadron (Cowes).

NOTT, Rt Hon. Sir John (William Frederic), KCB 1983; PC 1979; Farmer, Trewinnard Farms Ltd; *b* 1 Feb. 1932; *s* of late Richard Nott, Bideford, Devon, and Phyllis (*née* Francis); *m* 1959, Miloska Sekol Vlahovic, Maribor, Slovenia; two *s* one *d*. *Educ:* King's Mead, Seaford; Bradfield Coll.; Trinity Coll., Cambridge. Lieut, 2nd Gurkha Rifles (regular officer), Malayan emergency, 1952–56; Trinity Coll., Cambridge, 1957–59 (BA Hons Law and Econs); Pres., Cambridge Union, 1959; called to the Bar, Inner Temple, 1959; Gen. Manager, S. G. Warburg & Co. Ltd, Merchant Bankers, 1959–66. MP (C) Cornwall, St Ives, 1966–83; Minister of State, HM Treasury, 1972–74; Cons. front bench spokesman on: Treasury and Economic Affairs, 1974–76; Trade, 1976–79; Sec. of State for Trade, 1979–81; Sec. of State for Defence, 1981–83. Chm. and Chief Executive, Lazard Brothers & Co. Ltd, 1985–90 (Dir, 1983–90); Chm., Hillsdown Hldgs plc, 1993–99 (Dir, 1991–99). Chairman: Etam plc, 1991–95; Maple Leaf Foods Inc., Canada, 1993–95; Dep. Chm., Royal Insurance PLC, 1986–91 (Dir, 1985–91); Director: AMEC plc, 1991–93; Apax Partners & Co. Capital Ltd, 1996–; Altium Capital Hldgs, 1996–; Chiswell Associates Ltd, 1999–2002; 30 St James Square Investments, 2001–; Adviser: Apax Partners, 1990–98; Freshfields, 1991–95. *Publications:* Here Today, Gone Tomorrow (autobiog.), 2002; Mr Wonderful Takes a Cruise, 2004; Haven't We Been Here Before? Afghanistan to the Falklands: a personal connection, 2007. *Recreations:* farming, fishing, shooting. *Address:* 31 Walpole Street, SW3 4QS. *T:* (020) 7730 2351, *Fax:* (020) 7730 9859. *Clubs:* Pratt's, Beefsteak, Buck's.

See also H. G. W. Swire.

NOTT, Rt Rev. Peter John; Bishop of Norwich, 1985–99; Hon. Assistant Bishop, Diocese of Oxford, since 1999; *b* 30 Dec. 1933; *s* of Cecil Frederick Wilder Nott and Rosina Mabel Bailey; *m* 1961, Elizabeth May Maingot; one *s* three *d*. *Educ:* Bristol Grammar School; Dulwich Coll.; RMA Sandhurst; Fitzwilliam House, Cambridge; Westcott House, Cambridge (MA). Curate of Harpenden, 1961–64; Chaplain of Fitzwilliam Coll., Cambridge, 1964–69; Fellow of Fitzwilliam Coll., 1967–69, Hon. Fellow, 1993; Chaplain of New Hall, Cambridge, 1966–69; Rector of Beaconsfield, 1969–77; Bishop Suffragan of Taunton, 1977–85. Archbishop's Adviser to HMC, 1980–85; President: SW Region, Mencap, 1978–84; Somerset Rural Music Sch., 1981–85; Royal Norfolk Agricl Assoc., 1996. Vice-Chm., Archbishops' Commn for Rural Areas, 1988–90. Trustee, Nat. Army Mus., 2001–. Dean, Priory of England, Order of St John of Jerusalem, 1999–2003. KStJ 1999. *Publications:* Moving Forward in Prayer, 1991; Bishop Peter's Pilgrimage: his diary and sketchbook, 1996. *Address:* Westcot House, Westcot, Wantage, Oxon OX12 9QA. *T:* (01993) 850688.

NOTT, Roger Charles L.; *see* Lane-Nott.

NOTTAGE, Raymond Frederick Tritton, CMG 1964; Chairman, Bobath Centre for Children with Cerebral Palsy, 1987–2002; Deputy Chairman, Association of Lloyd's Members, 1985–91; Treasurer, Arkwright Arts Trust, Hampstead, 1975–92; *b* 1 Aug. 1916; *s* of Frederick and Frances Nottage; *m* 1941, Joyce Evelyn, *d* of Sidney and Edith Philpot; three *d*. *Educ:* Hackney Downs Secondary Sch. Civil servant, Post Office Headquarters, 1936–49; Editor of Civil Service Opinion, and Member Exec. Cttee, Soc. of Civil Servants, 1944–49; Dir-Gen., RIPA, 1949–78. Mem. Hornsey Borough Council, 1945–47. Mem. Cttee on Training in Public Admin. for Overseas Countries, 1961–63; Vice-Pres. Internat. Inst. of Admin. Sciences, 1962–68; Mem. Governing Body, Inst. of Development Studies, Univ. of Sussex, 1966–76; travelled abroad as Consultant and Lectr. *Publications:* Sources of Local Revenue (with S. H. H. Hildersley), 1968; Financing Public Sector Pensions, 1975; (with Gerald Rhodes) Pensions: a plan for the future, 1986; articles on public administration. *Recreations:* music, reading.

NOTTINGHAM, Bishop of, (RC), since 2000; **Rt Rev. Malcolm Patrick McMahon,** OP; *b* 14 June 1949; *s* of Patrick McMahon and Sarah McMahon (*née* Watson). *Educ:* St Aloysius Coll., Highgate; Univ. of Manchester Inst. of Sci. and Technol. (BSc); Blackfriars, Oxford; Heythrop Coll., London Univ. (BD; MTh). Pres., Students' Union, UMIST, 1970–71; contracts engr, London Transport, 1971–76; joined Dominican Order, 1976; ordained priest, 1982; Student Chaplain, Leicester Univ., 1984–85; Asst Priest, 1985–89, Prior and Parish Priest, 1989–92, St Dominic's Priory, NW5; Prior Provincial, English Province of Order of Preachers (Dominican Order), 1992–2000; Prior of Blackfriars, Oxford, 2000. John Hopton Fellow, Blackfriars Hall, Oxford, 2001–. *Publications:* contrib. articles and reviews in New Blackfriars, Dominican Ashram and Signum. *Recreations:* walking, golf, reading thrillers. *Address:* Bishop's House, 27 Cavendish Road East, The Park, Nottingham NG7 1BB.

NOTTINGHAM, Archdeacon of; *see* Hill, Ven. P.

NOULTON, John David; transport consultant; *b* 5 Jan. 1939; *s* of John Noulton and Kathleen (*née* Sheehan); *m* 1961, Anne Elizabeth Byrne; three *s* one *d*. *Educ:* Clapham Coll. ComplCE 1994. Asst Principal, Dept of Transport, 1970–72; Principal, DoE, 1972–78; Pvte Sec. to Minister of State, DoE, 1976–78; Asst Sec., Depts of the Environment and of Transport, 1978–85; Under Sec., Dept of Transport, 1985–89. British Co-Chm., Channel Tunnel Intergovtl Commn, 1987–89; Director: Transmanche Link, 1989–92; Public Affairs, Eurotunnel, 1992–2004. Special Advr to Chm., London Olympic Develt Authy, 2006. Chm., Council for Travel and Tourism, 2001–03. Trustee and Treas., Franco-British Council, 2004–. *Recreations:* boating, swimming, walking, writing, Mediterranean gardening. *Address:* 74 Garricks House, Wadbrook Street, Kingston upon Thames, Surrey KT1 1HS. *T:* (020) 8546 3855.

NOURRY, Arnaud; Chairman and Chief Executive Officer, Hachette Livre, since 2003; *b* 7 Jan. 1961; *s* of Claude Nourry and Marie Paule Boiron; *m* 1996, Danielle Belforti; two *s* one *d*. *Educ:* Ecole Supérieure de Commerce, Paris (MBA 1982); Paris Univ. (3rd degree Sociology 1983). Consultant, Mensia, 1986–90; Hachette Livre: Project Manager, 1990–95; Dep. CFO, 1995–97; Gen. Manager, Hatier textbook div., 1998–2002. Ordre National du Mérite (France), 2006. *Recreations:* classical music, tennis, wine. *Address:* Hachette Livre, 43 quai de Grenelle, 75905 Paris Cedex 15, France. *T:* (1) 43923543, *Fax:* (1) 43923532; *e-mail:* anourry@hachette-livre.fr.

NOURSE, Rt Hon. Sir Martin (Charles), Kt 1980; PC 1985; a Lord Justice of Appeal, 1985–2001; Vice-President, Court of Appeal (Civil Division), 2000–01; Acting Master of the Rolls, 2000; *b* 3 April 1932; *yr s* of late Henry Edward Nourse, MD, MRCP, of Cambridge, and Ethel Millicent, *d* of Rt Hon. Sir Charles Henry Sargant, Lord Justice of Appeal; *m* 1972, Lavinia, *yr d* of late Comdr D. W. Malim; one *s* one *d*. *Educ:* Winchester (Fellow, 1993–2006); Corpus Christi Coll., Cambridge (Hon. Fellow, 1988). National Service as 2nd Lieut, Rifle Bde, 1951–52; Lieut, London Rifle Bde Rangers (TA), 1952–55. Called to Bar, Lincoln's Inn, 1956, Bencher, 1978, Treas., 2001; Mem., General Council of the Bar, 1964–68; a Junior Counsel to BoT in Chancery matters, 1967–70; QC 1970; Attorney Gen., Duchy of Lancaster, 1976–80; a Judge of the Courts of Appeal of Jersey and Guernsey, 1977–80; Judge of the High Court of Justice, Chancery Div., 1980–85. Pres., Council of Inns of Court, 1992–95. Dep. Chm., Takeover Panel Appeal Bd, 2006–. *Address:* Dullingham House, Dullingham, Newmarket, Cambs CB8 9UP.

NOUSS, Hunada, FCA; Director-General, Finance and Corporate Services, Department for Communities and Local Government, since 2007; *b* 19 Jan. 1959. *Educ:* Lady Margaret Hall, Oxford (BA Hons PPE, MA). FCA 1984; ATII 1985. Arthur Andersen, 1980–90; Dir of Tax and Treasury, Lowe Gp plc, 1990–92; Dir, Financial Planning, Diageo plc, and other roles, 1993–2001; Finance Dir, Burger King, 2001–05. *Recreations:* photography, travel. *Address:* Department for Communities and Local Government, Eland House, Bressenden Place, SW1E 5DU; *e-mail:* hunada.nouss@communities.gsi.gov.uk.

NOUVEL, Jean Henri; architect, since 1966; *b* 12 Aug. 1945; *s* of Roger Nouvel and Renée Nouvel (*née* Barlangue); *m* 1992, Catherine Richard; one *d*; two *s* by Odile Fillion. *Educ:* Ecole Nationale Supérieure des Beaux Arts, Paris. Founder: Jean Nouvel and Associates, 1984–89; Jean Nouvel and Emmanuel Cattani, 1989–94; Ateliers Jean Nouvel, 1994–. Projects include: residential, educational, office and retail buildings in France; Institut du Monde Arabe, Paris, 1987; Hôtel de Saint-James, Bordeaux; Lyon Opera House, 1993; Fondation Cartier, Paris, 1994; Palais de Justice, Nantes, 2000; Cultural and Congress Centre, Lucerne, 2000; Gasometer, Vienna, 2001; Andel, Prague, 2001; Reina Sofia Mus. extension, Madrid, 2005; Guthrie Theater, Minneapolis, 2006; Musée du quai Branly, Paris, 2006. Silver Medal, 1983, Gold Medal, 1998, French Acad. of Architecture; Grand Prix National d'Architecture, France, 1987; Praemium Imperiale, Japan Art Assoc., 2001; Royal Gold Medal, RIBA, 2001. Commandeur, Ordre des Arts et des Lettres (France), 1997 (Chevalier, 1983); Chevalier: Ordre du Mérite (France), 1987; Légion d'Honneur, 2002. *Address:* Ateliers Jean Nouvel, 10 Cité d'Angoulême, 75011 Paris, France.

NOYER, Christian; Governor, Bank of France, since 2003; *b* 6 Oct. 1950. *Educ:* Univ. of Rennes (lic. en droit 1971); Univ. of Paris (DèS droit 1972); Inst d'Etudes Politiques, Paris (Dip. 1972); Ecole Nat. d'Admin. Entered Treasury, Min. of Finance, France, 1976; Financial Attaché, Perm. Repn to EEC, Brussels, 1980–82; French Treasury: Chief of Banking Office and of Export Credit Office, 1982–85; Advr to Minister for Econ. Affairs and Finance, 1986–88; Dep. Dir in charge of internat. multilateral issues, 1988–90; Dep. Dir in charge of debt mgt, monetary and banking issues, 1990–92; Dir responsible for public hldgs and public financing, 1992–93; Chief of Staff to Minister for Economic Affairs, 1993; Dir, Treasury, 1993–95; Chief of Staff to Minister for Econ. Affairs and Finance, 1995–97; Dir, Min. of Econ. Affairs, Finance and Industry, 1997–98; Vice-Pres., European Central Bank, 1998–2002; Special Advr, Min. of Economy, Finance and Industry, France, 2002–03. Member: European Monetary Cttee, 1993–95, 1998 (Alternate Mem., 1988–90); Econ. and Financial Cttee, 1999–; OECD Working Party, 1993–95; Alternate Mem., G7 and G10, 1993–95. Alternate Gov., IMF and World Bank, 1993–95. Chm., Paris Club of Creditor Countries, 1993–97. Chevalier, Ordre Nat. du Mérite (France), 1994; Officier, Légion d'Honneur (France), 2007 (Chevalier, 1998); Comdr, Ordre Nat. du Lion (Senegal), 1995; Grand Cross, Order of Civil Merit (Spain), 2002. *Publications:* Banks: the rules of the game, 1990; articles in jls. *Address:* Banque de France, 39 rue Croix des Petits Champs, 75001 Paris, France.

NOYES, Dr Peter, CPsychol; Vice Chancellor, University of Wales, Newport, since 2007; *b* 4 Aug. 1956; *s* of Alfred and Nora Noyes; *m* 1980, Prof. Janet Martin; two *s* one *d*. *Educ:* Loughborough Univ. (BSc Hons Social Psychol. 1977; PGCE Primary Educn 1981); PhD Educnl Psychol. London Univ. 1984. CPsychol 1989. Child Care Officer, Marchant-Holliday Sch., 1981–82; teacher: Wadebridge Jun. Sch., 1982–83; Saltash Jun. Sch., 1983–86; Res. Associate, Univ. of Bristol, 1986–88; Cheltenham and Gloucester College of Higher Education: Hd, Dept of Community and Social Studies, Res. Dir and Hd of Psychol., 1988–92; Dean: Educn and Health, 1992–93; Business and Social Studies, 1993–96; University of Wales College, Newport, subsequently University of Wales, Newport: Dean, Educn, Humanities and Sci., 1996–97; Asst Principal, 1997–99; Dep. Vice Chancellor, 1999–2006. Mem. Council, Univ. of Wales, 2005–. Member: Assoc. Sci. Educn, 1986–; British Educnl Res. Assoc., 1986–. FRSA 2002. *Publications:* articles in educn and psychol. jls. *Recreations:* supporter of Brighton and Hove Albion FC, Rugby, horse racing, theatre. *Address:* University of Wales, Newport, Caerleon Campus, Lodge Road, Newport NP18 3QT. *T:* (01633) 432000, *Fax:* (01633) 432002; *e-mail:* peter.noyes@newport.ac.uk.

NOYORI, Prof. Ryoji, DEng; President, RIKEN, and University Professor, Nagoya University, since 2003; *b* Kobe, Japan, 3 Sept. 1938; *s* of Kaneki and Suzuko Noyori; *m* 1972, Hiroko Oshima; two *s*. *Educ:* Univ. of Kyoto (BSc 1961; MSc 1963; DEng 1967); Harvard Univ. Res. Associate, Dept of Industrial Chemistry, Univ. of Kyoto, 1963–68; Nagoya University: Associate Prof. of Chemistry, 1968–72; Prof. of Chemistry, 1972–2003; Dir, Chemical Instrument Centre, 1979–91; Dean, Graduate Sch. of Sci., 1997–99; Dir, Res. Centre for Materials Sci., 2000. Adjunct Prof., Kyushu Univ., 1993–96. Sci. Advr, 1992–96, Mem., Scientific Council, 1996–, Min. of Educn, Sci. and Culture, subseq. Educn, Culture, Sports, Sci. and Technol., Japan. For. Mem., Royal Soc., 2005. Numerous awards, incl. (jtly) Nobel Prize for Chemistry, 2001. *Publications:* Asymmetric Catalysis in Organic Synthesis, 1994; articles in scientific jls. *Address:* RIKEN, 2–1 Hirosawa, Wako, Saitama 351–0198, Japan; Department of Chemistry, Graduate School of Science, Nagoya University, Chikusa, Nagoya, Aichi 464–8602, Japan; (home) Luxembourg House 1105, 8–9 Yonban-cho, Chiyoada-ku, Tokyo 102–0081, Japan.

NSUGBE, Oba Eric; QC 2002; a Recorder, since 1999; Senior Advocate, Nigeria, 2005; *b* 23 Dec. 1962; *s* of Philip O. Nsugbe and Patricia Nsugbe; *m* 1994, Ambereen Laila (*née* Salamat); one *s* one *d*. *Educ:* St Edward's Sch., Oxford; Univ. of Hull (LLB Hons); Inns of Court Sch. of Law; Nigerian Law Sch. Called to the Bar, Gray's Inn, 1985, Bencher, 2005; barrister and solicitor, Nigeria, 1986. Mem., Judicial Studies Bd of England and Wales, 1996–2002. Bar Council: Member: Professional Conduct Cttee, 2001–; Pupillage and Trng Cttee, 2000–02; Response Cttee on Carter Reform of Legal Aid, 2006–07. Member: Glidewell Cttee on Judicial Appts and Silk, 2002–03; Cttee on reform of Silk, DCA, 2004–05. Gray's Inn Advocacy Trainer, 2004–07. *Recreations:* squash, football, jazz, travel, African art. *Address:* (chambers) 3 Pump Court, Temple, EC4Y 7AJ. *T:* (020) 7353 0711, *Fax:* (020) 7353 3319; *e-mail:* oba.nsugbe@virgin.net.

NUGEE, Christopher George; QC 1998; a Recorder, since 2002; a Deputy High Court Judge, since 2003; *b* 23 Jan. 1959; *s* of Edward George Nugee, *qv* and Rachel Elizabeth Nugee, *qv*; *m* 1991, Emily Thornberry, *qv*; two *s* one *d*. *Educ:* Radley Coll.; Corpus Christi Coll., Oxford (BA 1st Cl. Hons Lit. Hum 1981); City Univ. (Dip. Law (Distinction) 1982). Called to the Bar, Inner Temple, 1983 (Queen Elizabeth Schol., 1983; Eldon Law Schol., 1984), Bencher, 2003; in practice at the Bar, 1984–. Member: Bar Council, 1991–93 (Mem., Professional Conduct Cttee, 1992–96); Cttee, Assoc. of Pension Lawyers, 1998–2002. *Recreations:* cycling, my family. *Address:* Wilberforce Chambers, 8 New Square, Lincoln's Inn, WC2A 3QP. *T:* (020) 7306 0102.

NUGEE, Edward George, TD 1964; QC 1977; *b* 9 Aug. 1928; *o s* of late Brig. George Travers Nugee, CBE, DSO, MC, RA, and Violet Mary (*née* Richards, later Brooks); *m* 1955, Rachel Elizabeth Makower (*see* R. E. Nugee); four *s*. *Educ:* Brambletye; Radley Coll. (Open Scholar); Worcester Coll., Oxford (Open Exhibnr; Law Mods, Distinction, 1950; 1st Cl. Hons Jurisprudence, 1952; Eldon Law Scholar, 1953; MA 1956). National Service, RA, 1947–49 (Office of COS, GHQ, FARELF); service with 100 Army Photographic Interpretation Unit, TA, 1950–64 (retd Captain, Intell. Corps, 1964). Read as pupil with Lord Templeman and Lord Brightman; called to the Bar, Inner Temple, 1955, Bencher 1976, Treas. 1996; *ad eundem* Lincoln's Inn, 1968. Jun. Counsel to Land Commn (Chancery and Conveyancing), 1967–71; Counsel for litigation under Commons Registration Act, 1965, 1968–77; Conveyancing Counsel to Treasury, WO, MAFF, Forestry Commn, MoD (Admiralty), and DoE, 1972–77; Conveyancing Counsel of Court, 1976–77. Poor Man's Lawyer, Lewisham CAB, 1954–72. Member: CAB Adv. Cttee, Family Welfare Assoc., 1969–72; Management Cttee, Greater London Citizens Advice Bureaux Service Ltd, 1972–74; Man. Cttee, Forest Hill Advice Centre, 1972–76; Bar Council, 1962–66 (Mem., External Relations Cttee, 1966–71); Council of Legal Educn, 1967–90 (Vice-Chm. 1976–82, and Chm. of Bd of Studies, 1976–82); Adv. Cttee on Legal Educn, 1971–90; Common Professional Exam. Bd, 1976–89 (Chm., 1981–87); Lord Chancellor's Law Reform Cttee, 1973–; various working parties and consultative groups of Law Commn, 1966–; Inst. of Conveyancers, 1971– (Pres., 1986–87); Chm., Cttee of Inquiry into Management Problems of Privately Owned Blocks of Flats, 1984–85. Church Comr, 1990–2001 (Mem., Bd of Govs, 1993–2001); Mem., C of E Legal Adv. Commn, 2001–. Trustee, Temple Music Trust, 1997–. Chm. Governors, Brambletye Sch., 1972–77; Mem. Council, Radley Coll., 1975–95. *Publications:* (jtly) Nathan on the Charities Act 1960, 1962; (ed jtly) Halsbury's Laws of England, titles Landlord and Tenant (3rd edn 1958), Real Property (3rd edn 1960 to 4th edn reissue 1998); contribs to legal jls. *Recreations:* travel, cooking, church and family life. *Address:* Wilberforce Chambers, 8 New Square, Lincoln's Inn, WC2A 3QP. *T:* (020) 7306 0102; 35 The Panoramic, 12 Pond Street, Hampstead, NW3 2PS. *T:* (020) 7435 9204.
See also C. G. Nugee.

NUGEE, Emily; *see* Thornberry, E.

NUGEE, Rachel Elizabeth, MA; *b* 15 Aug. 1926; *d* of John Moritz Makower and Adelaide Gertrude Leonaura Makower (*née* Franklin); *m* 1955, Edward George Nugee, *qv*; four *s*. *Educ:* Roedean Sch., Brighton; Lady Margaret Hall, Oxford; MA (Eng. Lang. and Lit.); Reading Univ. (Dip. Soc. Studies). FO, Bletchley Park (Station X), 1944–45. Joined Mothers' Union, 1956; Diocesan Pres., London Dio., 1974–76; Internat. Pres., 1977–82; MU rep. on Women's Nat. Commn, 1983–88. Chm., Edmonton Area Social Responsibility Policy Cttee, 1987–90; Member: Royal Free Hosp. (Hampstead Gen. Hosp.) House Cttee and Patients' Services Cttee, 1961–72; London Diocesan Bd for Social Responsibility, 1984–85, 1987–90; Law of Marriage Gp, General Synod, 1985–88; Lord Chancellor's Adv. Cttee on Conscientious Objectors, 1986–2000. Trustee: One plus One – the Marriage and Partnership res. charity, subseq. One plus One Marriage and Partnership Research, 1984–94; King's Cross Furniture Project, 1996–98; Grandparents' Assoc., 2001–07; Mothers' Union, London Dio., 2002–. Voluntary Worker: Witness Service, CCC, Old Bailey, 1997–2000; Personal Support Unit, Royal Cts of Justice, 2001–03. JP Inner London (Thames), 1971–96; Dep. Chm. of Bench, 1985–91; Court Chm., Inner London Family Panel, 1991–96. *Publications:* several religious articles and booklets. *Recreations:* active support of Church and family life, reading, especially history, visiting friends, criminal and family law. *Address:* Flat 35 The Panoramic, 12 Pond Street, Hampstead, NW3 2PS. *T:* (020) 7435 9204.
See also C. G. Nugee.

NUGENT, family name of **Earl of Westmeath**.

NUGENT, Sir Christopher George Ridley, 6th Bt *cr* 1806, of Waddesdon, Berks; *b* 5 Oct. 1949; *er s* of Sir Robin George Colborne Nugent, 5th Bt and Ursula Mary, *d* of Lt-

Gen. Sir Herbert Fothergill Cooke, KCB, KBE, CSI, DSO; *S* father, 2006, but his name does not appear on the Official Roll of the Baronetage; *m* 1985, Jacqueline Vagba; three *s*. *Educ:* Eton; Univ. of East Anglia. *Heir: s* Terence Nugent, *b* 1 March 1986.

NUGENT, Adm. Sir James Michael B.; *see* Burnell-Nugent.

NUGENT, Sir John (Edwin Lavallin), 7th Bt *cr* 1795; *b* 16 March 1933; *s* of Sir Hugh Charles Nugent, 6th Bt, and Margaret Mary Lavallin, *er d* of late Rev. Herbert Lavallin Puxley; *S* father, 1983; *m* 1959, Penelope Anne, *d* of late Brig. Richard Nigel Hanbury, CBE, TD; one *s* one *d*. *Educ:* Eton. Short service commn, Irish Guards, Lieut, 1953–56. PA to William Geoffrey Rootes (later 2nd Baron Rootes), Chm. of Rootes Gp, 1957–59; joined board of Lambourn group of cos, 1959, Chm., 1980–90. High Sheriff of Berks, 1981–82; JP Berks, 1962–87. *Recreations:* garden and fishing. *Heir: s* Nicholas Myles John Nugent [*b* 17 Feb. 1967; *m* 1999, Alice, *d* of Peter Player; two *d*]. *Address:* The Steward's House, Ballinlough Castle, Clonmellon, Navan, Co. Meath, Ireland. *T:* (046) 9433135.

NUGENT, Sir (Walter) Richard (Middleton), 6th Bt *cr* 1831, of Donore, Westmeath; *b* 15 Nov. 1947; *er s* of Sir Peter Walter James Nugent, 5th Bt and of Anne Judith, *o d* of Major Robert Smyth; *S* father, 2002; *m* 1985, Kayoko Okabe. *Educ:* Headfort; Downside. FCA 1970. Deloitte, Plender, Griffiths & Co., 1967–74; Gp Tax Mgr, Europe, Carrier Corp., 1974–76; Chief Accountant, Swire Pacific Ship Mgt, 1977–79; Corporate Accountant, Asia Pacific, Everett Steamship Corp., SA, 1980–84; Dir of Finance, IMS Japan KK, 1986–2003. *Heir:* none. *Address:* 61–6 Yaguchi-dai, Naka-ku, Yokahama-shi 231–0831, Kanagawa-ken, Japan. *T:* (45) 6219283; *e-mail:* nugentwr@gol.com. *Clubs:* Lansdowne; Kildare Street and University (Dublin).

NUNAN, Manus; lecturer; *b* 26 March 1926; *s* of Manus Timothy Nunan, Dist Justice, and Nan (*née* FitzGerald); *m* 1987, Valerie (*née* Robinson); one *s* one *d* by previous marriages. *Educ:* St Mary's Coll., Dublin; Trinity Coll., Dublin (BA, LLB). Called to the Irish Bar, King's Inns, 1950; called to the English Bar, Gray's Inn, 1956. Asst d'Anglais, Lycée Masséna, Nice, 1949–50; practised at Irish Bar, 1950–53; entered Colonial Legal Service, 1953; Crown Counsel, Nigeria, 1953–59; legal draftsman, Northern Nigeria, 1959–62; Solicitor-Gen., Northern Nigeria, 1962–64; Minister of Govt, Northern Nigeria, 1962; QC (Nigeria) 1962; practised at English Bar, 1965–85; a Recorder, 1978–84; since 1985 has lectured throughout English-speaking world on the life and trials of Oscar Wilde, Dr Samuel Johnson and his circle, Talleyrand, Bernard Shaw, Oliver Gogarty; autobiog. lect., Never Listen to an Irishman; Evelyn Wrench Lectr, E-SU of USA, 1988; Vis. Lectr, Broward Community Coll., Fla, 1989; Lecturer: Amer. Irish Historical Soc., NY, 1990; Nat. Portrait Gall., 1991–94; Bournemouth Internat. Festival, QE2, Oxford Univ. E-SU Soc., and Mus. of Modern Art, Oxford, 1992; Shirley Soc., Cambridge Univ., 1993; Centre Culturel Irlandais, Paris, 1994. Hon. Mem., Univ. Philos. Soc., TCD, 1987. *Address:* 53 Stonecrop, Colchester, Essex CO4 5UG. *Club:* Kildare Street and University (Dublin).

NUNBURNHOLME, 6th Baron *cr* 1906; **Stephen Charles Wilson;** *b* 29 Nov. 1973; *o s* of 5th Baron Nunburnholme and of Linda Kay (*née* Stephens); S father, 2000; *m* 2002, Chie Mannami, MA (RCA); two *s*. *Educ:* Nottingham Univ.; Univ. of Westminster. *Heir: s* Hon. Charles Taiyo Christobal Wilson, *b* 14 Sept. 2002.

NUNES, Prof. Terezinha, PhD; Professor of Educational Studies, University of Oxford, since 2005; Fellow, Harris Manchester College, Oxford, since 2005; *b* 3 Oct. 1947; *d* of Luiz Conzaga Nunes and Semíramis Oliveira Nunes; *m* 1st, 1973, David W. Carraher (marr. diss. 1990); one *s* one *d*; 2nd, 1995, Prof. Peter Elwood Bryant, *qv*. *Educ:* Univ. Federal de Minas Gerais (BS Psychol); City Univ. of New York (MA Psychol. 1975; PhD 1976). Accredited Psychologist. Res. asst, NY Infant Day Care Study, 1973–75; Adjunct Lectr, Dept of Psychol., Brooklyn Coll., NY, 1975; Hd, Inst. of Child Develt, Belo Horizonte, Brazil, 1976–77; Associate Prof., 1976–78, and Hd, Centre of Applied Psychol., 1977, Dept of Psychol., Univ. Federal de Minas Gerais; University of Pernambuco: Associate Prof. and Course Tutor, Masters prog. in Psychol., 1978–90; Hd, Pedagogical Centre, 1981–84; Res. Fellow, Sch. of Educn, Open Univ., 1990–91; Institute of Education, University of London: Lectr, 1991–93; Sen. Lectr, 1993–96; Course Tutor for Masters in Child Develt, 1993–98; Prof. of Educn, Child Develt and Learning, 1996–2000; Res. Tutor and Hd, Child Develt and Learning Acad. Gp, 1998–2000; Prof. of Psychol. and Hd of Dept, Oxford Brookes Univ., 2000–05. Fulbright Fellow, 1971–76; Vis. Fellow, Wolfson Coll., Oxford, 1988–89; British Acad. Res. Reader, 2003–04. *Publications:* as Terezinha Carraher: O Método Clínico: usando os exames de Piaget, 1982; (jtly) Na Vida, Dez; Na Escola, Zero: os contextos culturais da aprendizagem de matemática, 1988; Sociedade e Inteligência, 1989; as Terezinha Nunes: (jtly) Dificuldades de aprendizagem da leitura: teoria e prática, 1992; (jtly) Street Mathematics and School Mathematics, 1993; (with P. E. Bryant) Children Doing Mathematics, 1996 (trans. Portuguese, Spanish and Greek); Developing Children's Minds Through Literacy and Numeracy: an inaugural lecture, 1998; (jtly) Introdução à Educação Matemática: os números e as operações numéricas, 2001, 2nd edn 2005; Teaching Mathematics to Deaf Children, 2004; (with P. E. Bryant) Improving Literacy Through Teaching Morphemes, 2006; (with P. E. Bryant) Children's Reading and Spelling: beyond the first steps, 2008; papers in acad. jls on research on child develt, maths educn, literacy learning and deaf children's learning. *Recreations:* travelling, reading, cooking. *Address:* Department of Education, University of Oxford, 15 Norham Gardens, Oxford OX2 6PY. *T:* (01865) 284892, *Fax:* (01865) 274027; *e-mail:* terezinha.nunes@education.ox.ac.uk.

NUNN, Imogen Mary, (Lady Nunn); *see* Stubbs, I. M.

NUNN, John Francis, PhD, DSc, MD; FRCS, FRCA; FGS; Head of Division of Anaesthesia, Medical Research Council Clinical Research Centre, 1968–91; *b* 7 Nov. 1925; *s* of late Francis Nunn, Colwyn Bay; *m* 1949, Sheila, *d* of late E. C. Doubleday; one *s* two *d*. *Educ:* Wrekin Coll.; Birmingham Univ. (MD (Hons) 1970; PhD 1959; DSc 1992). FRCA (FFARCS 1955); FRCS 1983. MO, Birmingham Univ. Spitzbergen Expedition, 1948; Colonial Med. Service, Malaya, 1949–53; University Research Fellow, Birmingham, 1955–56; Leverhulme Research Fellow, RCS, 1957–64; Part-time Lectr, Postgrad. Med. Sch., Univ. of London, 1959–64; Consultant Anæsth., Hammersmith Hosp., 1959–64; Prof. of Anaesthesia, Univ. of Leeds, 1964–68. Member: Council, RCS, 1977–82 (Mem. Board, Faculty of Anaesthetists, Vice-Dean, 1977–79, Dean, 1979–82); Council, Assoc. of Anaesthetists, 1973–76 (Vice Pres., 1988–90); Pres., Sect. Anaesthesia, RSM, 1984–85. Hunterian Professor, RCS, 1960; Visiting Professor to various American Universities, 1960–98; British Council Lecturer: Switzerland, 1962; USSR, 1963; Czechoslovakia, 1969; China, 1974. Joseph Clover Lectr, RCS, 1968. Mem., Egypt Exploration Soc. FGS 2001. Hon. FFARCSI 1985; Hon. FRSocMed 1992; Hon. FANZCA 1993 (Hon. FFARACS); Hon. FRCA 1993. Hon. Dr: Turin, 1993; Uppsala, 1996. (1st) Sir Ivan Magill Gold Medal, Assoc. of Anaesthetists of GB and Ireland, 1988; Richardson Award, Geologists' Assoc., 1999. *Publications:* Applied Respiratory Physiology, 1969, 4th edn as Nunn's Applied Respiratory Physiology, 1993; (ed jtly) General Anaesthesia, 3rd edn 1971, 5th edn 1989; Ancient Egyptian Medicine, 1996; (jtly) The Tale of Peter Rabbit (in ancient Egyptian hieroglyphs), 2005; several chapters in medical text-books, and publications in Journal Appl. Physiol., Lancet, Nature, British Journal Anæsth., etc. *Recreations:* Egyptology, model engineering. *Address:* 3A Dene Road, Northwood, Middx HA6 2AE. *T:* (01923) 826363.

NUNN, Rear-Adm. John Richard Danford, CB 1980; Bursar and Official Fellow, Exeter College, Oxford, 1981–88, retired; *b* 12 April 1925; *s* of Surg. Captain Gerald Nunn and Edith Florence (*née* Brown); *m* 1951, Katharine Mary (*née* Paris); three *d*. *Educ:* Epsom Coll. CEng, FIMechE; MPhil Cantab, 1981; MA Oxon, 1982. Entered RN, 1943; RN Engrg Coll., Keyham, 1943–47; HMS Devonshire, Second Cruiser Sqdn, 1945; HMS Vengeance, 1947; Advanced Engineering Course, RNC Greenwich, 1949–51. HMS Amethyst, Korea, 1952–53; HMS Tiger, 1957–59; Commander, 1960; HMS Glamorgan, 1967–68; Captain, 1969; Sea Dart and Seaslug Chief Engineer, 1970–72; Cabinet Office, 1973–74; Staff of SACLANT, 1975–77; Rear-Adm., 1978; Port Adm., Rosyth, 1977–80. Fellow Commoner, Downing Coll., Cambridge, 1980–. Vice Chm. of Govs, Peter Symonds VI Form Coll., Winchester, 1996–99. Editor, The Naval Review, 1980–83. *Recreations:* sailing, tennis, gliding, travel. *Address:* No 4 Godfrey Pink Way, Bishops Waltham, Hants SO32 1PB. *Club:* Royal Naval Sailing Association (Portsmouth).

NUNN, Sir Trevor (Robert), Kt 2002; CBE 1978; director; Artistic Director, Royal National Theatre, 1997–2003; *b* 14 Jan. 1940; *s* of late Robert Alexander Nunn and of Dorothy May (*née* Piper); *m* 1st, 1969, Janet Suzman, *qv* (marr. diss. 1986); one *s*; 2nd, 1986, Sharon Lee Hill (marr. diss. 1991); two *d*; 3rd, 1994, Imogen Stubbs, *qv*; one *s* one *d*. *Educ:* Northgate Grammar Sch., Ipswich; Downing Coll., Cambridge (BA). Producer, Belgrade Theatre, Coventry; Royal Shakespeare Company: Chief Exec., 1968–86; Artistic Dir, 1968–78; Jt Artistic Dir, 1978–86; Dir Emeritus, 1986–. Mem., Arts Council of England, 1994–96. Hon. MA: Newcastle upon Tyne, 1982; Warwick. *Address:* 49B British Grove, W4 2NL.

NUNNELEY, Sir Charles (Kenneth Roylance), Kt 2003; CA; Chairman: Nationwide Building Society, 1996–2002 (Director, 1994–2002; Deputy Chairman, 1995–96); National Trust, 1996–2003; *b* 3 April 1936; *s* of late Robin Michael Charles Nunneley and Patricia Mary (*née* Roylance); *m* 1961, Catherine Elizabeth Armstrong Buckley; one *s* three *d*. *Educ:* Eton Coll. CA 1961. Robert Fleming (merchant bankers), 1962–96: Dir, 1968–96; Dep. Chm., 1986–96; Chairman: Save & Prosper Gp, 1989–96; JP Morgan Income & Capital Investment Trust (formerly Fleming, then JP Morgan Fleming, Income & Capital Investment Trust) plc, 1992–2007; IMRO Ltd, 1992–97 (Dir, 1986–97); Monks Investment Trust plc, 1996–2005 (Dir, 1977–2005); Edinburgh Fund Managers Gp plc, 2003; Dep. Chm., Clerical Medical & General Life Assurance Soc., 1978–96 (Dir, 1974–96); Dir, Macmillan Ltd, 1982–96. Chm., Instnl Fund Managers' Assoc., 1989–92. National Trust: Member: Council, 1992–2003; Exec. Cttee, 1991–2003; Chm., Finance Cttee, 1991–96. Chm. Council, N Wessex Downs Area of Outstanding Natural Beauty, 2004–. Mem. Court, Grocers' Co., 1975– (Master, 1982–83). Governor, Oundle Schs, 1975–99. *Recreations:* walking, theatre, photography. *Address:* 4 Grenville Place, SW7 4RU.

NUNNELEY, John Hewlett, MBE 2001; Chairman, AMF Microflight Ltd, 1987–93; *b* Sydney, NSW, 26 Nov. 1922; *o s* of Wilfrid Alexander Nunneley and Audrey Mary (*née* Tebbitt); *m* 1945, Lucia, *e d* of Enrico Ceruti, Milan, Italy; one *s* one *d*. *Educ:* Lawrence Sheriff Sch., Rugby. Served War of 1939–45: Somerset LI, seconded KAR; Abyssinia, Brit. Somaliland, 1942; Burma campaign, 1944 (wounded, despatches); Captain and Adjt. Various management posts in aircraft, shipping, printing and publishing industries, 1946–55. Exec., Beaverbrook Newspapers, 1955–62; joined BTC, 1962: Chief Publicity Officer, 1962–63; Chief Development Officer (Passenger) BR Bd, 1963–64; Chief Passenger Manager, 1964–69; Pres. and Chm., BR-Internat. Inc., New York, USA, 1966–69; Man. Dir, British Transport Advertising Ltd, 1969–87. Principal Advertising Consultant, Hong Kong Govt, 1981–83. Member: Passenger Co-ordination Cttee for London, 1964–69; Outdoor Advertising Council, 1969–88. Pres., European Fedn of Outdoor Advertising (FEPE), 1984–87. Introduced BR Corporate Identity, 1964 and Inter-City concept, 1965. Hon. Mem., All-Burma Veterans Assoc. of Japan, 1991; Chm., Burma Campaign Fellowship Gp, 1996–2002. Freeman, GAPAN, 1990. City of Paris Medal, 1986. *Publications:* Tales from the King's African Rifles, 1997; (ed) Tales from the Burma Campaign 1942–1945, 1998; (with K. Tamayama) Tales by Japanese Soldiers, 2000; numerous articles on aviation, transport and advertising subjects. *Recreations:* gliding (FAI Gold C and Two Diamonds), powered flight. *Address:* 6 Ashfield Close, Petersham, Surrey TW10 7AF.

NURSAW, Sir James, KCB 1992 (CB 1983); QC 1988; HM Procurator General and Treasury Solicitor, 1988–92; *b* 18 Oct. 1932; *s* of William George Nursaw (*d* 1994); *m* 1959, Eira, *yr d* of late E. W. Caryl-Thomas, MD, BSc, Barrister-at-law; two *d*. *Educ:* Bancroft's School; Christ's Coll., Cambridge (Schol.; MA, LLB). Called to Bar, Middle Temple, 1955 (Blackstone Entrance Schol. and Prize, Harmsworth Schol.), Bencher, 1989. Senior Research Officer, Cambridge Univ. Dept of Criminal Science, 1958. Joined Legal Adviser's Branch, Home Office, 1959; Principal Asst Legal Advr, HO and NI Office, 1977–80; Legal Secretary, Law Officers' Dept, 1980–83; Legal Adviser, Home Office and NI Office, 1983–88. Counsel to Chm. of Cttees, H of L, 1993–2002. Liveryman, Loriners' Co. *Clubs:* Oxford and Cambridge, MCC.

NURSE, Sir Paul (Maxime), Kt 1999; PhD; FRS 1989; President, Rockefeller University, New York, since 2003; *b* 25 Jan. 1949; *s* of Maxime Nurse and Cissie Nurse (*née* White); *m* 1971, Anne Teresa (*née* Talbott); two *d*. *Educ:* Harrow County Grammar Sch.; Univ. of Birmingham (BSc): Univ. of East Anglia (PhD). Research Fellow, Univ. of Edinburgh, 1973–79; SERC Advanced Fellow and MRC Sen. Fellow, Univ. of Sussex, 1979–84; Hd of Cell Cycle Control Laboratory, Imp. Cancer Res. Fund, London, 1984–87; Oxford University: Fellow, 1987–93, Hon. Fellow, 1993–, Linacre Coll.; Iveagh Prof. of Microbiology, 1987–91; Royal Soc. Napier Res. Prof., 1991–93; Dir of Lab. Res., 1993–96, Dir Gen., 1996–2002, ICRF; Chief Exec., Cancer Res. UK, 2002–03. MAE 1992; Foreign Associate US NAS, 1995. Fleming Lectr, 1984, Marjory Stephenson Lectr, 1990, Soc. of Gen. Microbiology; Florey Lectr, Royal Soc., 1990; Wenner-Gren Lectr, Stockholm, 1993; Dunham Lectr, Harvard, 1994. Pres., Genetical Soc., 1990–94. Founder FMedSci 1998. Ciba Medal, Biochemical Soc., 1991; Feldberg Foundn Prize, 1991; (jtly) Louis Jeantet Prize for Medicine, Geneva, 1992; Gairdner Foundn Internat. Jt Award, 1992; Royal Soc. Wellcome Medal, 1993; Jimenez Diaz Meml Award, Madrid, 1993; Rosenstiel Award, Brandeis Univ., 1993; Pezcoller Award for Oncology Res., Trento, 1995; Royal Soc. Royal Medal, 1995; Dr Josef Steiner Prize, Steiner Cancer Foundn, Bern, 1996; Dr H. P. Heineken Prize, Netherlands, 1996; Alfred P. Sloan Jr Prize and Medal, General Motors Cancer Res. Foundn, 1997; Judd Award, Meml Sloan-Kettering Cancer Center, NY, 1998; Lasker Award, Albert and Mary Lasker Foundn, NY, 1998; (jtly) Nobel Prize for Physiology or Medicine, 2001. *Publications:* numerous, in sci. jls, concerned with cell and molecular biology. *Recreations:* gliding, astronomy, talking. *Address:* Rockefeller University, 1230 York Avenue, New York, NY 10021–6399, USA.

NURSTEN, Prof. Harry Erwin, PhD, DSc; CChem, FRSC; FIFST; FSLTC; Professor of Food Science, Reading University, 1976–92, Professor Emeritus 1992; *s* of Sergius Nursten and Helene Nursten; *m* 1950, Jean Patricia Frobisher. *Educ:* Ilkley Grammar Sch.; Leeds Univ. (BSc 1st Cl. Hons Colour Chemistry, 1947; PhD 1949; DSc 1973). FRIC 1957; FIFST 1972; FSLTC 1986. Bradford Dyers Assoc. Res. Fellow, Dept of Colour Chem. and Dyeing, Leeds Univ., 1949–52; Lectr in Textile Chem. and Dyeing, Nottingham and Dist Tech. Coll., 1952–54; Lectr 1955–65, Sen. Lectr 1965–70, and Reader 1970–76, Procter Dept of Food and Leather Science, Leeds Univ.; Head of Dept of Food Sci., 1976–86, Head of Dept of Food Science and Technology, 1986–89, Head of Sub-Dept of Food Sci., 1989–91, Reading Univ. Res. Associate, Dept of Nutrition, Food Science and Technol., MIT, 1961–62; Visiting Professor: Univ. of Calif, Davis, 1966; Univ. of Zimbabwe, 1994. Chief Examiner, Mastership in Food Control, 1982–90. Pres., Soc. of Leather Technologists and Chemists, 1974–76. Bill Littlejohn Memorial Medallion Lectr, Brit. Soc. of Flavourists, 1974; Sen. Medal, Food Chemistry Gp, RSC, 1996. *Publications:* (ed jtly) Progress in Flavour Research, 1979; (contrib.) Rothe and Kruse, Aroma, Perception, Formation, Evaluation, 1995; (contrib.) Schubert and Spiro, Chemical and Biological Properties of Tea Infusions, 1997; (ed jtly) The Maillard Reaction in Foods and Medicine, 1998; (contrib.) Caffeinated Beverages: health benefits, physiological effects, and chemistry, 2000; (jtly) Capillary Electrophoresis for Food Analysis: method development, 2000; (contrib.) Rothe, Flavour 2000: perception, release, evaluation, formation, acceptance, nutrition/health, 2001; The Maillard Reaction: chemistry, biochemistry, and implications, 2005; (contrib.) Bredie and Petersen, Flavour Science: recent advances and trends, 2006; papers mainly in Jl Sci. Food Agric. and Jl Chromatog. *Address:* Department of Food Biosciences, School of Chemistry, Food Biosciences and Pharmacy, University of Reading, Whiteknights, PO Box 226, Reading RG6 6AP. *T:* (0118) 931 6725.

NUSSBAUM, David Simon Matthew; Chief Executive, WWF-UK, since 2007; *b* Stoke on Trent, 13 July 1958; *s* of Gerald and Enid Nussbaum; *m* 1983, Kathleen Kinderman; two *s* two *d*. *Educ:* Queens' Coll., Cambridge (BA Theol. 1980). Univ. of Edinburgh (MTh 1981); Heriot-Watt Univ. (Dip. Accounting 1982); London Business Sch. (MSc Finance (Distn) 1998). CA 1985; CTA 1985. Audit Sen./Asst, 1982–86, Asst Manager, 1986–87, Price Waterhouse; Investment Controller, 3i plc, 1987–90; Commercial and Business Develt Manager, Reedpack Ltd, 1990–91; Corporate Develt Dir, 1991–92, Finance Dir, 1992–97, Field Group plc; Dir, Finance, Inf. and Planning, and a Dep. Chief Exec., Oxfam, 1997–2002; Man. Dir, 2002–03, Chief Exec., 2003–07, Transparency International. Non-executive Director: Traidcraft plc, 1991–2006 (Chm., 1999–2006); Shared Interest, 2006–; Low Carbon Accelerator, 2006–. FRSA. MInstD. *Publications:* (contrib.) Christianity and the Culture of Economics, 2001; (contrib.) Charities, Governance and the Law: the way forward, 2003. *Recreation:* Post-Christendom orthopraxis. *Address:* WWF-UK, Panda House, Weyside Park, Godalming, Surrey GU7 1XR. *T:* (01483) 412202, *Fax:* (01483) 418401; *e-mail:* dnussbaum@wwf.org.uk, dsmnussbaum@aol.com.

NÜSSLEIN-VOLHARD, Christiane, PhD; Director, since 1985, and Director of Department of Genetics, since 1990, Max Planck Institute for Developmental Biology; *b* 20 Oct. 1942; *d* of Rolf Volhard and Brigitte Volhard (*née* Haas). *Educ:* Univ. of Tübingen. Res. Associate, Max Planck Institute for Virus Research, 1972–74; EMBO Fellow: Biozentrum Basel Lab., 1975–76; Univ. of Freiberg, 1977; Head of Gp, European Molecular Biology Lab., Heidelberg, 1978–80; Gp Leader, Friedrich Miescher Lab., 1981–85, Scientific Mem., 1985–90, Max Planck Ges. Sec.-Gen., EMBO. Mem., Nat. Ethics Council of Germany, 2001–. (Jtly) Nobel Prize for Physiology or Medicine, 1995. *Publications:* Coming to Life: how genes drive development, 2006; articles in learned jls. *Address:* Max-Planck-Institut für Entwicklungsbiologie, Spemannstraße 35/III, 72076 Tübingen, Germany.

NUTBEAM, Prof. Donald, PhD; FFPH; Provost and Deputy Vice-Chancellor, University of Sydney, Australia, since 2006 (Pro-Vice-Chancellor, 2003–06); *b* 18 May 1955; *s* of late Walter Charles Nutbeam and of Ada Rose Nutbeam; *m* 1978, Sarah Choules; one *s* one *d*. *Educ:* St Bartholomew's Grammar Sch., Newbury; Univ. of Southampton (MA; PhD 1988). FFPH 2003. Health Educn Officer, Portsmouth Health Dist, 1978–81; Res. Assistant, Wessex RHA, 1981–83; Res. Fellow in Health Promotion, Southampton Univ., 1983–85; Hd of Res., Welsh Heart Prog., Univ. of Wales Coll. of Medicine, 1985–88; Dir, Res. and Policy, Health Promotion Authy, Wales, 1988–90; University of Sydney, Australia: Prof. of Public Health, 1990–2001; Hd, Dept. of Public Health and Community Medicine, 1997–2000; Associate Dean of Medicine, 1999–2000; Hd of Public Health, DoH, 2000–03. Vis. Prof., LSHTM, 2001–. *Publications:* numerous contribs to scientific jls and texts. *Recreations:* sport, singing. *Address:* Room L2.22, Main Quadrangle (A14), University of Sydney, NSW 2006, Australia. *Club:* Athenæum.

NUTT, Prof. David John, DM; FRCP, FRCPsych, FMedSci; Director, Psychopharmacology Unit, since 1988, Professor of Psychopharmacology, since 1994, and Head of Community Based Medicine, since 2004, University of Bristol; *b* 16 April 1951; *s* of R. J. (Jack) Nutt and Eileen M. (*née* Baber); *m* 1979, Diana Margaret Sliney; two *s* two *d*. *Educ:* Bristol GS; Downing Coll., Cambridge (MB BChir); Guy's Hosp.; Lincoln Coll., Oxford (DM 1983). MRCP 1977, FRCP 2002; MRCPsych 1983, FRCPsych 1994. Oxford University: Clinical Scientist, MRC Clinical Pharmacology Unit, 1978–82; Lectr, Dept of Psychiatry, 1982–84; Wellcome Sen. Fellow in Clinical Sci., 1985–86; Head, Section of Clinical Sci., Nat. Inst. of Alcohol Abuse and Alcoholism, NIH, 1986–88; Bristol University: Head: Div. of Psychiatry, 1995–97; Dept of Clinical Medicine, 1997–2003; Dean of Clinical Medicine and Dentistry, 1999–2003. Chm., Adv. Council on the Misuse of Drugs, 2008– (Chm., Technical Cttee, 2000–08); Member: Ind. Inquiry into Misuse of Drugs Act 1971, 1997–2000 (reported, 2000); Cttee on the Safety of Medicines, 2001–; Lead Scientist, DTI Foresight Prog., Brain Science Addiction and Drugs, 2005–06. FMedSci 2002. *Publications:* Inverse Agonists, 1994; jointly: Hypnotics and Anxiolytics, 1995; Depression, Anxiety and the Mixed Conditions, 1997; Panic Disorder: clinical diagnosis, management and mechanisms, 1998; Generalized anxiety disorder: diagnosis, treatment and its relationship to other anxiety disorders, 1998; Atlas of Psychiatric Pharmacotherapy, 1999, rev. edn 2006; Milestones in Drug Therapy: anxiolytics, 2000; Post Traumatic Stress Disorder: diagnosis, management and treatment, 2000; Clinician's Manual on Anxiety Disorder and Comorbid Depression, 2000; Anxiety Disorders: an introduction to clinical management and research, 2001; Mood and Anxiety Disorders in Children and Adolescents, 2001; Anxiety Disorders Comorbid with Depression: panic disorder and agoraphobia, 2002; Generalised Anxiety Disorder: symptomatology, parthogenesis and management, 2002; Anxiety Disorders, 2003; Calming the Brain, 2003; (jtly) Treating Depression Effectively, 2004, 2nd edn 2007; (jtly) Drugs and the Future: brain science, 2006; (jtly) Serotonin and Sleep: molecular, functional and clinical aspects, 2007; (jtly) Handbook of Fear and Anxiety, 2008; (jtly) Addiction, 2008; (with S. J. Wilson) Sleep Disorders, 2008. *Recreations:* golf, gardening, Austin Healeys. *Address:* Dorothy Hodgkin Building, Whitson Street, Bristol BS1 3NY. *T:* (0117) 331 3178.

NUTTALL, Christopher Peter; consultant to Government of Barbados on criminal justice research, information and policy, since 2000; Director of Research and Statistics, Home Office, 1989–99; *b* 20 April 1939; *s* of Barbara Goodwin and David Nuttall; *m* 1966, Caryn Thomas; two *s*. *Educ:* Queen Elizabeth Grammar Sch., Wakefield; Univ. of Keele (BA); Univ. of California at Berkeley (MA). Home Office Res. Unit, 1963–75 (Principal Res. Officer, 1971–75); Dir of Res., 1975–80, Dir Gen., Res. and Stats, 1980–82, Min. of Solicitor Gen., Ottawa; Asst Dep. Solicitor Gen. of Canada, 1982–89; Asst Under-Sec. of State, Home Office, 1989. UN Human Rights Fellow, 1967–68. *Publications:* Parole in England and Wales, 1977; The Barbados Crime Survey, 2002; Sentencing in Barbados, 2003; articles on parole, deterrence, crime prevention and imprisonment. *Recreations:* The United States, photography, taking baths, books. *Address:* The Cottage, The Hill, Polstead, Suffolk CO6 5AH.

NUTTALL, Rev. Derek, MBE 1990; Minister, United Reformed Church, Windsor, 1990–2003; *b* 23 Sept. 1937; *s* of Charles William Nuttall and Doris Nuttall; *m* 1965, Margaret Hathaway Brown (*d* 1993); two *s* one *d*; *m* 2000, Doreen Margaret Fox. *Educ:* Ironville Sch.; Somercotes Sch.; Overdale Coll., Selly Oak (Diploma). Semi-skilled worker in industry, 1953–60; office clerk, 1960–61; college, 1961–65; ministry in Falkirk, 1965–67; Vice Chm., Central Scotland Br., The Samaritans, 1966–67; ordained, 1967; ministry and community work in Aberfan, 1967–74: Gen. Sec., Community Assoc.; mem., church and community cttees; Nat. Organiser, 1974–78, Dir, 1978–90, Cruse—the Nat. Orgn for the widowed and their children, subseq. Cruse—Bereavement Care. Member: Exec., Internat. Fedn of Widow/Widower Orgns, 1980–90; Internat. Workgroup on Death and Dying, 1980–90; Internat. Liaison Gp on Disasters, 1986–90; Sec., Wkg Party on Social and Psychological Aspects of Disasters, 1989–91. Chm., Churches Together in Windsor, 1992–95; Convenor, Reading and Oxford Dist URC Pastoral Cttee, 1995–98. Chaplain: King Edward VII Hosp., Windsor, 1991–2003; Thames Valley Hospice, Windsor, 1993–2003. *Publications:* The Early Days of Grieving, 1986, rev. and expanded edn 2006; (contrib.) Interpreting Death, 1997; articles and papers on bereavement and on needs of widows, widowers and bereaved children. *Recreations:* music, reading, writing, keeping up with the family's activities, enjoying East Sussex. *Address:* Lymewood, Tilsmore Road, Heathfield, East Sussex TN21 0XT. *T:* (01435) 866026.

NUTTALL, Sir Harry, 4th Bt *cr* 1922, of Chasefield, Bowdon, Chester; *b* 2 Jan. 1963; *s* of Sir Nicholas Keith Lillington Nuttall, 3rd Bt and Rosemary Caroline (*née* York); *S* father, 2007; *m* 1st, 1996, Kelly Marie Allen (marr. diss. 1999); 2nd, 2002, Dalit, *o d* of late Isaac Cohen, Stockholm; one *s* one *d*. Heir: *s* James Isaac Nuttall, *b* 2 Nov. 2005. *Clubs:* White's; British Racing Drivers'.

NUTTALL, Rt Rev. Michael; Bishop of Natal, 1982–2000; *b* 3 April 1934; *s* of Neville and Lucy Nuttall; *m* 1959, Dorris Marion Meyer; two *s* one *d*. *Educ:* Maritzburg Coll. (matric. 1951); Univ. of Natal (BA 1955); Rhodes Univ. (BA Hons in History 1956); MA (Cantab); MA, DipEd (Oxon); BD Hons (London). Teacher at Westville High Sch., Natal, 1958; Lectr in History, Rhodes Univ., 1959–62; Theological Student, St Paul's Coll., Grahamstown, 1963–64; ordained deacon, 1964; priest, 1965; Assistant Priest, Cathedral of St Michael and St George, Grahamstown, 1965–68; Lectr in Ecclesiastical History, Rhodes Univ., 1969–74; Dean of Grahamstown, 1975; Bishop of Pretoria, 1976–81. Pemberton Fellow, University Coll. Durham, 2001. Hon. DTheol Western Cape, 1998; Hon. DLitt Natal, 2000. *Publications:* Prayerfulness in the Spirit, 2002; chapters in: Better Than They Knew, Volume 2 (ed R. M. de Villiers), 1974; Authority in the Anglican Communion (ed Stephen W. Sykes), 1987; Change and Challenge (ed J. Suggit and M. Goedhals), 1998; Number Two to Tutu – a memoir, 2003; articles in Dictionary of S African Biography. *Recreations:* walking, bird watching. *Address:* 5 River Glen, 124 Chase Valley Road, Pietermaritzburg, 3201, South Africa.

NUTTALL, Prof. Patricia Anne, OBE 2000; PhD; Professor of Virology, University of Oxford, since 1996; Fellow of Wolfson College, Oxford, 1974–77 and since 1990; Director: NERC Centre for Ecology & Hydrology, since 2001; CEH Oxford, since 1997; *b* 21 Jan. 1953; *m*; twin *d*. *Educ:* Univ. of Bristol (BSc 1974); Univ. of Reading (PhD 1978); MA Oxon 1995. Worked in Australia and Slovakia; joined NERC Inst. for Virology and Envmtl Microbiol., subseq. CEH Oxford, 1980; acting Dir, 1995–97. Ivanovsky Medal for Virology, Russian Acad. of Scis, 1996. *Address:* NERC Centre for Ecology & Hydrology, Maclean Building, Crowmarsh Gifford, Wallingford, Oxon OX10 8BB.

NUTTALL, Peter Francis; a District Judge (Magistrates' Courts) (formerly Stipendiary Magistrate), Nottinghamshire, since 1991; *b* 20 Feb. 1944; *s* of Francis Nuttall and Dorothy May Nuttall (*née* Horning); *m* 1965, Wendy Anna Ida Griffiths; one *s* two *d*. *Educ:* Lewes County Grammar Sch. for Boys; Coll. of Law, Guildford and London. Articled Clerk, Uckfield, 1961, Harrow, 1964; Asst to Justices' Clerk, 1964–68; Dep. Clerk to Justices, Watford, 1968–73; Clerk to Justices, Pendle and Ribble Valley, 1973–85; Clerk to Bradford Justices, 1985–90. Chm., Yorks Region Mental Health Review Tribunal, 1986–90. *Recreations:* dinghy sailing, fruit growing, photography, painting, committed francophile. *Address:* c/o Westminster City Magistrates' Court, 70 Horseferry Road, SW1P 2AX. *T:* (020) 7205 1044.

NUTTALL, Simon James; Visiting Professor, 1995–2006, and Member of the Academic Council, 1997–2006, College of Europe, Bruges; *b* 6 Oct. 1940; *s* of John C. Nuttall and Amy L. Nuttall. *Educ:* Glossop Grammar Sch.; St John's Coll., Oxford (MA). HM Diplomatic Service, 1963–71; Office of Clerk of the Assembly, Council of Europe, 1971–73; Eur. Commn, 1973–95. Vis. Fellow, 1995–97, Acad. Visitor, 2000–04, LSE. *Publications:* European Political Co-operation, 1992; European Foreign Policy, 2000; articles on European foreign policy. *Recreations:* reading, writing. *Address:* Duck House, South Street, Sherborne, Dorset DT9 3LT; 14 Lesley Court, Strutton Ground, SW1P 2HZ. *Club:* Oxford and Cambridge.

NUTTER, Most Rev. Harold Lee, CM 1997; DD; Archbishop of Fredericton and Metropolitan of the Ecclesiastical Province of Canada, 1980–89, retired (Bishop of Fredericton, 1971, Bishop Emeritus, 1992); Vice-Chairman, New Brunswick Police Commission, 1988–98; *b* 29 Dec. 1923; *s* of William L. Nutter and Lillian A. Joyce; *m* 1946, Edith M. Carew; one *s* one *d*. *Educ:* Mount Allison Univ. (BA 1944); Dalhousie Univ. (MA 1947); Univ. of King's College (MSLitt 1947). Rector: Simonds and Upham, 1947–51; Woodstock, 1951–57; St Mark, Saint John, NB, 1957–60; Dean of Fredericton, 1960–71. Co-Chairman, NB Task Force on Social Development, 1970–71; Mem., Adv. Cttee to Sec. of State for Canada on Multi-culturalism, 1973. Member: Bd of Governors, St Thomas Univ., 1979–89; Bd of Regents, Mount Allison Univ., 1978–84; Vice-Chm., Bd of Governors, Univ. of King's Coll., 1971–89. Pres., Atlantic Ecumenical Council, 1972–74, 1984–86. Co-Chm., Dialogue New Brunswick, 1989–90. Hon. DD: Univ. of King's College, 1960; Montreal Diocesan Coll., 1982; Wycliffe Coll., 1983; Trinity Coll., Toronto, 1985; Hon. LLD, Mount Allison Univ., 1972. Golden Jubilee Medal, 2002. *Publication:* (jointly) New Brunswick Task Force Report on Social Development, 1971. *Address:* Apt 248, 200 Reynolds Street, Fredericton, NB E3A 0A3, Canada.

NUTTING, Diane Patricia, (Lady Nutting), OBE 1998; Chairman: Georgian Group, since 1999; Prince of Wales's Drawing School, since 2003; *b* 8 Sept. 1941; *d* of Duncan and Patricia Kirk; *m* 1st, 1959, 2nd Earl Beatty, DSC (*d* 1972); one *s* one *d*; 2nd, 1973, John Nutting (*see* Sir John Nutting, Bt); one *s* one *d*. *Educ:* Moira House, Eastbourne. Director: Anglia Television, 1980–95; Chiltern Radio, 1985–95. Member: Council, Nat. Trust, 1985–2000 (Chm., Thames and Chiltern Region, 1984–97; Mem., Properties Cttee, 1991–); Royal Fine Art Commn, 1985–2000; Cathedrals Fabric Commn, 1990–2000; St Albans Fabric Commn, 1993–; Churches Preservation Trust, 1997–. Trustee: Nat. Heritage Meml Fund and Heritage Lottery Fund, 1991–97; British Architectl Liby Trust, 2002–. Mem., Westminster CC, 1968–78 (Mem. Town Planning Cttee). JP Inner London, 1978. *Recreations:* history, architectural history. *Address:* Chicheley Hall, Newport Pagnell, Bucks MK16 9JJ. *T:* (01234) 391252, *Fax:* (01234) 391388; *e-mail:* enquiries@chicheleyhall.co.uk; K3 Albany, Piccadilly, W1V 9RQ.

NUTTING, Sir John (Grenfell), 4th Bt *cr* 1903, of St Helens, Booterstown, co. Dublin; QC 1995; a Recorder of the Crown Court, since 1986; a Judge, Courts of Appeal of Jersey and Guernsey, since 1995; a Deputy High Court Judge, since 1998; *b* 28 Aug. 1942; *s* of Rt Hon. Sir Anthony Nutting, 3rd Bt, PC and of Gillian Leonora (*née* Strutt); *S* father, 1999; *m* 1973, Diane Patricia, Countess Beatty (*see* D. P. Nutting); one *s* one *d*, and one step *s* one step *d*. *Educ:* Eton Coll.; McGill Univ. (BA 1964). Called to the Bar, Middle Temple, 1968, Hon. Bencher 1991; Jun. Treasury Counsel, 1981–86; First Jun. Treasury Counsel, 1987–88; Sen. Treasury Counsel, 1988–93; First Sen. Treasury Counsel, 1993–95. Mem., Bar Council, 1976–80, 1986–87; Chm., Young Bar, 1978–79; Vice Chm., Criminal Bar Assoc., 1995. Member: Lord Chancellor's Adv. Cttee on Legal Educn and Conduct, 1997–99; Appts Panel, Ind. Supervisory Authy for Hunting, 2001–05; Commissioner: for Interception of Communications (Jersey and Guernsey), 1999–2004; for Regulation of Investigatory Powers (Jersey and Guernsey), 2004–. Chm., Helmsdale River Bd, and Helmsdale Dist Salmon Fishery Bd, 2001–. Pres., NE Milton Keynes Conservative Assoc., 1990–93. A Patron, Philharmonia Orch., 2001–. FRPSL 1970. *Recreations:* shooting, stalking, fishing, stamp collecting. *Heir: s* James Edward Sebastian Nutting [*b* 12 Jan. 1977; *m* 2007, Antonia, *d* of Eugen von Boch]. *Address:* Chicheley Hall, Newport Pagnell, Bucks MK16 9JJ; K3 Albany, Piccadilly, W1V 9RQ; Achentoul, Kinbrace, Sutherland KW11 6UB; (chambers) 3 Raymond Buildings, Grays Inn, WC1R 5BH. *Clubs:* White's, Pratt's, Mark's, The Other.

NUTTON, Prof. Vivian, PhD; FBA 2008; Professor of the History of Medicine, University College London, since 1993; *b* Halifax, Yorks, 21 Dec. 1943; *s* of Eli and Constance Nutton; *m* 1973, Christine Clements; one *s* two *d*. *Educ:* Elland C of E Prim. Sch.; Bradford Grammar Sch.; Selwyn Coll., Cambridge (BA 1965; PhD 1970). Res. Fellow, 1967–69, Fellow and Dir of Studies in Classics, 1969–77, Selwyn College, Cambridge; Historian (Ancient), Wellcome Inst., and Hon. Lectr, UCL, 1977–93. Visiting Professor: Johns Hopkins Univ., Baltimore, 1988; Russian Peoples' Friendship Univ., Moscow, 1998; Vis. Fellow, Inst. for Advanced Study, Princeton, 2000; Hooker Dist. Vis. Prof., McMaster Univ., 2007. Corresp. Mem., Internat. Acad. of Hist. of Medicine, 1985; Member: Acad. Internat. d'Histoire des Scis, 1993; Academia Europaea, 2000; Deutsche Akademie der Wissenschaften (formerly Deutsche Akademie der Naturforscher Leopoldina), 2002; Fellow, Studio Firmano per la Storia della Medicina, 2003. Hon. FRCP 1999. *Publications:* Galen, On Prognosis: text, translation, commentary, 1979; (ed) Galen: problems and prospects, 1981; (ed jtly) Theories of Fever from Antiquity to the Enlightenment, 1981; John Caius and the Manuscripts of Galen, 1987; From Democedes to Harvey: studies in the history of medicine, 1988; (ed) Medicine at the Courts of Europe, 1500–1837, 1990; (jtly) The Western Medical Tradition, 800 BC to AD 1800, 1995 (Histoire de la lutte contre la maladie, 1999); (ed jtly) The History of Medical Education in Britain, 1995; Galen, On My Own Opinions: text, translation and commentary, 1999; (ed) The Unknown Galen, 2002; Ancient Medicine, 2004; (ed) Pestilential Complexities: understanding medieval plague, 2008; (trans. and ed) Girolamo Mercuriale, De arte gymnastica, 2008. *Recreations:* bellringing, singing, playing piano and organ. *Address:* Wellcome Trust Centre for the History of Medicine, 183 Euston Road, NW1 2BE. *T:* (020) 7679 8146; *e-mail:* ucgavnu@ucl.ac.uk.

NYAKYI, Anthony Balthazar; Tanzanian Ambassador to Burundi, 1998; *b* 8 June 1936; *m* 1969, Margaret Nyakyi; two *s* two *d*. *Educ:* Makerere Coll., Univ. of E Africa (BA Gen.). Admin. Office, Prime Minister's Office and Min. of Educn, Tanzania, 1962–63; Head of Political Div., Foreign Service Office, 1963–68; Ambassador for Tanzania: to the Netherlands, 1968–70; to Fed. Republic of Germany, 1970–72; Principal Sec., Foreign Affairs, 1972–78; Principal Sec., Defence, 1978–80; High Comr to Zimbabwe, 1980–81, in London, 1981–89; Permanent Tanzanian Rep. to UN, 1989–94; Special Rep. of UN Sec. Gen. in Liberia, 1994–98. *Address:* c/o Ministry of Foreign Affairs, POB 9000, Dar es Salaam, Tanzania.

NYE, Prof. John Frederick, FRS 1976; Melville Wills Professor of Physics, University of Bristol, 1985–88 (Professor of Physics, 1969–88), now Professor Emeritus; *b* 26 Feb. 1923; *s* of Haydn Percival Nye and Jessie Mary, *d* of Anderson Hague, painter; *m* 1953, Georgiana Wiebenson; one *s* two *d*. *Educ:* Stowe; King's Coll., Cambridge (Maj. Schol.; MA, PhD 1948). Research, Cavendish Laboratory, Cambridge, 1944–49; Univ. Demonstrator in Mineralogy and Petrology, Cambridge, 1949–51; Bell Telephone Laboratories, NJ, USA, 1952–53; Lectr, 1953, Reader, 1965, Univ. of Bristol; Visiting Professor: in Glaciology, California Inst. of Technol., 1959; of Applied Sciences, Yale Univ., 1964; of Geophysics, Univ. of Washington, 1973. President: Internat. Glaciological Soc., 1966–69; Internat. Commn of Snow and Ice, 1971–75. For. Mem., Royal Swedish Acad. of Scis, 1977. Kirk Bryan Award, Geol. Soc. of Amer., 1961; Seligman Crystal, Internat. Glaciol Soc., 1969; Antarctic Service Medal, USA, 1974; NPL Metrology Award, 1986; Charles Chree Medal, Inst. of Physics, 1989. *Publications:* Physical Properties of Crystals, 1957, rev. edn 1985; Natural Focusing and Fine Structure of Light, 1999; papers on physics of crystals, glaciology, optics, microwaves, and applications of catastrophe theory in scientific jls. *Address:* 45 Canynge Road, Bristol BS8 3LH. *T:* (0117) 973 3769.

See also P. H. Nye.

NYE, Peter Hague, FRS 1987; Reader in Soil Science, University of Oxford, 1961–88; Fellow of St Cross College, Oxford, 1966–88 (Senior Fellow, 1982–83), now Emeritus Fellow; *b* 16 Sept. 1921; *s* of Haydn Percival Nye and Jessie Mary (*née* Hague); *m* 1953, Phyllis Mary Quenault; one *s* one *d* (and one *d* decd). *Educ:* Charterhouse; Balliol Coll., Oxford (MA, BSc (Domus Exhibnr)); Christ's Coll., Cambridge. Agricl Chemist, Gold Coast, 1947–50; Lectr in Soil Science, University Coll. of Ibadan, Nigeria, 1950–52; Sen. Lectr in Soil Science, Univ. of Ghana, 1952–60; Res. Officer, Internat. Atomic Energy Agency, Vienna, 1960–61. Vis. Professor, Cornell Univ., 1974, 1981, Messenger Lectures, 1989; Commonwealth Vis. Prof., Univ. of Western Aust., 1979; Vis. Prof., Royal Vet. and Agricl Univ., Copenhagen, 1990; Hon. Res. Prof., Scottish Crops Res. Inst., 1995–2000. Pres., British Soc. Soil Science, 1968–69; Mem. Council, Internat. Soc. Soil Science, 1968–74. Governor, Nat. Vegetable Res. Station, 1972–87. *Publications:* (with D. J. Greenland) The Soil under Shifting Cultivation, 1961; (with P. B. Tinker) Solute Movement in the Soil-Root System, 1977, 2nd edn as Solute Movement in the Rhizosphere, 2000; articles, mainly in Jl of Soil Science, Plant and Soil, Jl of Agricl Science. *Recreations:* formerly cycling, cricket, tennis, squash. *Address:* 15 Stourwood Road, Southbourne, Bournemouth BH6 3QP. *T:* and *Fax:* (01202) 269092.

See also J. F. Nye.

NYE, Rick; *see* Nye, R. C.

NYE, Robert; writer; *b* 15 March 1939; *s* of Oswald William Nye and Frances Dorothy Weller; *m* 1st, 1959, Judith Pratt (marr. diss. 1967); three *s*; 2nd, 1968, Aileen Campbell; one *d*, and one step *s* one step *d*. *Educ:* Southend High School, Essex. Freelance writer, 1961–. FRSL 1977. *Publications: poetry:* Juvenilia 1, 1961; Juvenilia 2, 1963 (Eric Gregory Award, 1963); Darker Ends, 1969; Agnus Dei, 1973; Two Prayers, 1974; Five Dreams, 1974; Divisions on a Ground, 1976; A Collection of Poems 1955–1988, 1989; 14 Poems, 1994; Henry James and Other Poems, 1995; Collected Poems, 1995; The Rain and the Glass: 99 poems, new and selected, 2005 (Cholmondeley Award, 2007); Sixteen Poems, 2005; *fiction:* Doubtfire, 1967; Tales I Told My Mother, 1969; Falstaff, 1976 (The Guardian Fiction Prize, 1976; Hawthornden Prize, 1977); Merlin, 1978; Faust, 1980; The Voyage of the Destiny, 1982; The Facts of Life and Other Fictions, 1983; The Memoirs of Lord Byron, 1989; The Life and Death of My Lord Gilles de Rais, 1990; Mrs Shakespeare: the complete works, 1993; The Late Mr Shakespeare, 1998; *plays:* (with Bill Watson) Sawney Bean, 1970; The Seven Deadly Sins: A Mask, 1974; Penthesilea, Fugue and Sisters, 1976; *children's fiction:* Taliesin, 1966; March Has Horse's Ears, 1966; Wishing Gold, 1970; Poor Pumpkin, 1971; Out of the World and Back Again, 1977; Once Upon Three Times, 1978; The Bird of the Golden Land, 1980; Harry Pay the Pirate, 1981; Three Tales, 1983; Lord Fox and Other Spine-Chilling Tales, 1997; *translation:* Beowulf, 1968; *editions:* A Choice of Sir Walter Ralegh's Verse, 1972; William Barnes: Selected Poems, 1973; A Choice of Swinburne's Verse, 1973; The English Sermon 1750–1850, 1976; The Faber Book of Sonnets, 1976; PEN New Poetry 1, 1986; (jtly) First Awakenings: the early poems of Laura Riding, 1992; A Selection of the Poems of Laura Riding, 1994; Some Poems by Ernest Dowson, 2006; Some Poems by Thomas Chatterton, 2007; Some Poems by Clere Parsons, 2008; contribs to British and American periodicals. *Recreation:* gambling. *Address:* Thornfield, Kingsland, Ballinhassig, Co. Cork, Ireland.

NYE, Roderick Christopher, (Rick); Director, Populus, since 2003; *b* 28 Feb. 1967; *s* of late Bertram Edward Nye and of Elsie Doreen Nye; *m* 1994, Diana Grace, *d* of John and Priscilla Douglas. *Educ:* Norton Knatchbull Sch., Ashford; American Univ., Washington; Univ. of Leeds (BA Hons 1989). Policy Advr to David Owen, 1989–90; Journalist, VNU Business Publications, 1990–92; Dep. Dir, 1992–95, Dir, 1995–99, Social Market Foundn; Dir, Cons. Res. Dept, 1999–2003. Mem. (C), Westminster CC, 1998–2002. *Publications:* Welfare to Work: the 'America Works' experience, 1996; (ed) The Future of Welfare, 1997. *Recreations:* United States, reading, sport (watching), Chelsea FC. *Address:* (office) 10 Northburgh Street, EC1V 0AT. *Club:* Sam's.

NYE, Simon Beresford; writer; *b* 29 July 1958; *s* of Dennis Beresford Nye and Sheila Elizabeth Nye; partner, Claudia Stumpfl; two *s* two *d*. *Educ:* Collyer's Sch., Horsham; Bedford Coll., London (BA French and German 1980). Writer: *television series*: Men Behaving Badly, 1992–99; Frank Stubbs Promotes, 1993–95; Is It Legal?, 1995–98; My Wonderful Life, 1997–98; How Do You Want Me?, 1998–99; Beast, 2000–01; The Savages, 2001; Wild West, 2002–03; Hardware, 2003–04; Carrie and Barry, 2004–05; *television films:* True Love, 1996; The Railway Children, 2000; Pollyanna, 2003; Pride, 2004; Beauty, 2004; Tunnel of Love, 2004; Open Wide, 2005; My Family and Other Animals, 2005; *translations* of plays: Don Juan, 2002; Accidental Death of an Anarchist, 2003. *Publications:* Men Behaving Badly, 1989; Wideboy, 1991; The Best of Men Behaving Badly, 2000; Catwalk Dogs, 2007; various translations. *Recreation:* avoiding the heat. *Address:* c/o Rod Hall Agency, 6th Floor, Fairgate House, 78 New Oxford Street, WC1A 1HB. *T:* (020) 7079 7987.

NYMAN, Michael, CBE 2008; composer; *b* 23 March 1944; *s* of Mark and Jeanette Nyman; *m* 1970; two *d*. *Educ:* Royal Academy of Music; King's College London (BMus); Conservatorul Ciprian Porumbescu, Bucharest. FRAM 1991. Music critic, Spectator, New Statesman, The Listener, 1968–78; formed: Michael Nyman Band, 1977; MN Records, 2005. *Film scores include:* The Draughtsman's Contract, 1982; Drowning by Numbers, 1988; The Cook, The Thief, His Wife and Her Lover, 1989; Monsieur Hire, 1989; The Hairdresser's Husband, 1990; Prospero's Books, 1991; The Piano, 1992; Carrington, 1994; The Diary of Anne Frank, 1995; The Ogre, 1996; Gattaca, 1997; Ravenous, 1998; Wonderland, The End of the Affair, 1999; Act Without Words, 2000; The Claim, 2001; 24 Hours in The Life of a Woman, The Actors, 2002; Natalie, 2003; Detroit: Ruin of a City, 9 Songs, A Cock and Bull Story, The Libertine, 2005; Man on Wire, 2008; *other compositions:* A Broken Set of Rules, Royal Ballet, 1983; The Man Who Mistook his Wife for a Hat (opera), 1986; String Quartets, 1985, 1988, 1990, 1995; Six Celan Songs, 1990–91; Noises, Sounds and Sweet Airs (opera), 1991; Where the Bee Dances, for saxophone and orch., 1991; Songs for Tony, 1993; The Piano Concerto, 1993; MGV (Musique à Grand Vitesse), 1993; Harpsichord Concerto, 1995; Trombone Concerto, 1995; After Extra Time, 1996; Double Concerto for Saxophone and Cello, 1997; Cycle of Disquietude, 1998; The Commissar Vanishes, 1999; Facing Goya (opera), 2000, revised 2002; Concerto for Saxophone Quartet and Orch., 2001; a dance he little thinks of, for orch., 2001; Violin Concerto, 2003; Man and Boy: Dada (opera), For John Peel (trio), Acts of Beauty (chamber ensemble), 2004; Love Counts (opera), Melody Waves, 2005; ballet scores. *Publication:* Experimental Music: Cage and Beyond, 1974, 2nd edn 1999. *Recreation:* QPR. *Address:* Michael Nyman Ltd, 5 Milner Place, N1 1TN. *Club:* Groucho.

NZIMBI, Most Rev. Benjamin Mwanzia; *see* Kenya, Archbishop of.

O

OAKDEN, Edward Anthony, CMG 2006; HM Diplomatic Service; Ambassador to the United Arab Emirates, since 2006; *b* 3 Nov. 1959; *s* of Richard Ralph Oakden and Patricia Jeanne Oakden; *m* 2001, Ana Romero Galán; two *d*. *Educ:* Repton Sch.; Cambridge Univ. (BA Hons Hist.). Entered FCO 1981; Second Secretary: Baghdad, 1984–85; Khartoum, 1985–88; Private Sec. to Ambassador and First Sec., Washington, 1988–92; Deputy Head: EU Dept (Ext.), 1992–94; Eastern Adriatic Dept, 1994; Private Sec. to Prime Minister, 1995–97; Deputy Head: EU Dept (Internal), 1994–98; of Mission, Madrid, 1998–2002; Hd, Security Policy Dept, 2002; Dir, Internat. Security, 2002–04; Dir, Defence and Strategic Threats, and Ambassador for Counter-terrorism, 2004–06. *Recreations:* family, running, swimming, history, classical music. *Address:* c/o Foreign and Commonwealth Office, King Charles Street, SW1A 2AH.

OAKELEY, Sir John (Digby Atholl), 8th Bt *cr* 1790, of Shrewsbury; Director, Dehler Yachts UK, 1988, retired; *b* 27 Nov. 1932; *s* of Sir Atholl Oakeley, 7th Bt and of Mabel, (Patricia), *d* of Lionel H. Birtchnell; *S* father, 1987; *m* 1958, Maureen Frances, *d* of John and Ellen Cox; one *s* one *d*. *Educ:* private tutor. Own charter business, 1958–61; Contracts Manager, Proctor Masts, 1961–72; Managing Director: Freedom Yachts Internat. Ltd, 1981–88; Miller & Whitworth, 1972–81. *Publications:* Winning, 1968; Sailing Manual, 1980; Downwind Sailing, 1981. *Recreation:* yachting (holder of national, international, European and world titles; twice represented Great Britain in Olympic Games). *Heir:* *s* Robert John Atholl Oakeley [*b* 13 Aug. 1963; *m* 1989, Catherine Amanda, *d* of late William Knowles; one *s* one *d*]. *Address:* 10 Bursledon Heights, Long Lane, Bursledon, Hants SO3 8DB. *Club:* Royal Air Force Yacht (Hamble).

OAKES, Sir Christopher, 3rd Bt *cr* 1939; *b* 10 July 1949; *s* of Sir Sydney Oakes, 2nd Bt, and Greta (*d* 1977), *yr d* of Gunnar Victor Hartmann, Copenhagen, Denmark; *S* father, 1966; *m* 1978, Julie Dawn, *d* of Donovan Franklin Cowan, Regina, Canada; one *s* one *d*. *Educ:* Bredon, Tewkesbury; Georgia Mil. Acad., USA. *Heir:* *s* Victor Oakes, *b* 6 March 1983.

OAKES, Joseph Stewart; barrister-at-law; *b* 7 Jan. 1919; *s* of Laban Oakes and Mary Jane Oakes; *m* 1950, Irene May Peasnall (*d* 1995). *Educ:* Royal Masonic Sch., Bushey; Stretford Grammar Sch.; Manchester Univ., 1937–40 (BA Hons). Royal Signals, 1940–48, Captain. Called to Bar, Inner Temple, 1948; practised on Northern Circuit, 1948–91; a Recorder, 1975–82. Presiding Legal Mem., Mental Health Review Tribunal, 1971–91. *Recreations:* horticulture, photography, music, freemasonry. *Address:* 38 Langley Road, Sale, Greater Manchester M33 5AY. *T:* (0161) 962 2068.

OAKESHOTT, family name of **Baron Oakeshott of Seagrove Bay**.

OAKESHOTT OF SEAGROVE BAY, Baron *cr* 2000 (Life Peer), of Seagrove Bay in the co. of Isle of Wight; **Matthew Alan Oakeshott;** Joint Managing Director: OLIM Ltd, since 1986; Value and Income Trust plc, since 1986; *b* 10 Jan. 1947; *o s* of Keith Robertson Oakeshott, CMG and of Jill Oakeshott; *m* 1976, Dr Pippa Poulton; two *s* one *d*. *Educ:* Charterhouse (Sen. Foundn Scholar); University Coll. and Nuffield Coll., Oxford (BA 1st cl. Hons PPE). ODI/Nuffield Fellow, Kenya Ministry of Finance and Planning, 1968–70; Special Advr to Rt Hon. Roy Jenkins, MP, 1972–76; Investment Mgr, then Dir, Warburg Investment Management, 1976–81; Investment Mgr, Courtaulds Pension Fund, 1981–85; founded OLIM Ltd (Independent Investment Managers), 1986. Mem. (Lab) Oxford City Council, 1972–76. Member: SDP Nat. Cttee, 1981–82; SDP Nat. Economic Policy Cttee, 1981–83. Contested: (Lab) Horsham and Crawley, Oct. 1974; (SDP/Alliance) Cambridge, 1983. A Lib Dem spokesman on Treasury, 2001–, and on Work and Pensions, 2003–, H of L; Mem., Select Cttee on Economic Affairs, H of L, 2001–. *Publication:* (contrib.) By-Elections in British Politics, 1973. *Recreations:* music, elections, watching Arsenal FC. *Address:* Pollen House, 10–12 Cork Street, W1S 3NP. *T:* (020) 7439 4400.

OAKHAM, Archdeacon of; *see* Painter, Ven. D. S.

OAKLEY, Brian Wynne, CBE 1981; *b* 10 Oct. 1927; *s* of Bernard and Edna Oakley; *m* 1953, Marian Elizabeth (*née* Woolley); one *s* three *d*. *Educ:* Exeter Coll., Oxford (MA). FInstP, FBCS. Telecommunication Res. Establishment, 1950; Head, Industrial Applications Unit, RRE, 1966–69; Head, Computer Systems Branch, Min. of Technology, 1969–72; Head, Res. Requirements Div., DTI, 1972–78; Sec., SRC, later SERC, 1978–83; Dep. Sec., DTI, and Dir, Alvey Programme, 1983–87. Dir, Logica (Cambridge) Ltd. Pres., BCS, 1988. DUniv York, 1988. *Publication:* (with Kenneth Owen) Alvey, 1990. *Recreations:* theatre, sailing. *Address:* 120 Reigate Road, Ewell, Epsom, Surrey KT17 3BX. *T:* (020) 8393 4096.

OAKLEY, Christopher John, CBE 1999; Chief Executive, Comm VA MEF, since 2003; *b* 11 Nov. 1941; *s* of late Ronald Oakley and Joyce Oakley; *m* 1st, 1962, Linda Margaret Viney (marr. diss. 1986); one *s* two *d*; 2nd, 1990, Moira Jean Martingale (marr. diss. 2003); one *s*, and two adopted *d*; 3rd, 2004, Lisa Hanson; one step *d*. *Educ:* Skinners' School, Tunbridge Wells. Kent and Sussex Courier, 1959; Bromley and Kentish Times, 1963; Kent and Sussex Courier, 1963; Evening Argus, Brighton, 1966; Evening Echo, Basildon, 1969; Evening Post, Leeds, 1970; Dep. Editor, Yorkshire Post, 1976; Editor, Lancashire Evening Post, 1981; Dir, Lancashire Evening Post, 1981–83; Editor, Liverpool Echo, 1983–89; Dir, Liverpool Daily Post and Echo Ltd, 1984–89; Editor-in-Chief, 1989–91, Man. Dir, 1990–93, Chm., 1993–97, Birmingham Post & Mail; Gp Chief Exec., Midland Ind. Newspapers plc, 1991–97; Man. Dir, Mirror Regl Newspapers, 1997–98; Chief Exec., Regl Ind. Media, 1998–2002; Exec. Chm., HRM Partnership Ltd, 2002–03. Chairman: Coventry Newspapers, 1991–97; Midland Weekly Media, 1997. Pres., Newspaper Soc., 1997–98; Hon. Vice Pres., Soc. of Editors. Nat. Appeals Chm., Newspaper Press Fund, 2000–. Trustee, Royal Armouries, 2002–. Hon. Fellow, Univ. of Central Lancashire, 1998. *Address:* Comm VA MEF, Dreve des Pins 40, 1420 Braine-l'Alleud, Belgium.

OAKLEY, Ven. Mark David; Priest-in-charge, Grosvenor Chapel, Mayfair, since 2008; Deputy Priest in Ordinary to the Queen, since 1996; *b* 28 Sept. 1968; *s* of David Oakley and Sheila (*née* Cupples). *Educ:* Shrewsbury Sch.; King's Coll., London (BD 1st cl. 1990; AKC 1990); St Stephen's House, Oxford. Ordained deacon, 1993, priest, 1994; Asst Curate, St John's Wood Ch, 1993–96; Chaplain to the Bp of London, 1996–2000; Priest-in-charge, subseq. Rector, St Paul's, Covent Garden, 2000–05; Archdeacon of Germany and Northern Europe, and Chaplain of St Alban's, Copenhagen, 2005–08. Area Dean, Westminster St Margaret, 2004–05. Eric Abbott Meml Lectr, Eric Abbott Meml Trust, Westminster Abbey and Keble Coll., Oxford, 2002. Governor: St Clement Danes Sch., 2000–05; City Literary Inst., 2002–05. Freeman, City of London, 1999. FRSA 1998. *Publications:* The Collage of God, 2001; (ed) John Donne: selected poetry and prose, 2004; (ed) Readings for Weddings, 2004. *Recreations:* theatre, contemporary fiction, travelling around the Baltic, reading in the bath. *Club:* Garrick.

OAKLEY, Robin Francis Leigh, OBE 2001; European Political Editor, CNN, since 2000; *b* 20 Aug. 1941; *s* of Joseph Henry Oakley, civil engineer and Alice Barbara Oakley; *m* 1966, Carolyn Susan Germaine Rumball; one *s* one *d*. *Educ:* Wellington College; Brasenose College, Oxford (MA). Liverpool Daily Post, 1964–70; Sunday Express, 1970–79; Assistant Editor: Now! magazine, 1979–81; Daily Mail, 1981–86; Political Editor: The Times, 1986–92; BBC, 1992–2000. Presenter, The Week in Westminster, BBC Radio, 1987–92, 2000–05. Turf columnist: Spectator, 1995–; FT, 2003–. Trustee, Thomson Foundn, 2001–. *Publications:* Valley of the Racehorse: a year in the life of Lambourn, 2000; Inside Track: the political correspondent's life, 2001. *Recreations:* theatre, horse racing, sports, bird watching. *Address:* 17 West Square, Kennington, SE11 4SN. *Club:* Royal Automobile.

OAKLEY, Prof. Stephen Phelps, PhD; FBA 2008; Kennedy Professor of Latin, and Fellow of Emmanuel College, University of Cambridge, since 2007; *b* 20 Nov. 1958; *s* of Julian Oakley and Jillian Oakley (now Marshallsay); *m* 1998, Ruth Mary Otway; two *s*. *Educ:* Bradfield Coll., Berks; Queens' Coll., Cambridge (BA Hons Classics 1980; MA 1983; PhD 1985). Res. Fellow, 1984–86, Official Fellow, 1986–98, Emmanuel Coll., Cambridge; Reader in Classics, 1998–2002, Prof. of Latin, 2002–07, Univ. of Reading. *Publications:* The Hill Forts of the Samnites, 1995; A Commentary on Livy, books 6–10, Vol. 1 1997, Vol. 2 1998, Vol. 3 2005, Vol. 4 2005; contrib. learned jls. *Recreations:* gardening, exploring Dorset. *Address:* Emmanuel College, Cambridge CB2 3AP. *T:* (01223) 334200; *e-mail:* spo23@cam.ac.uk.

OAKLEY, Dame Susan (Elizabeth Anne); *see* Devoy, Dame S. E. A.

OAKS, Agnes; freelance ballerina; Resident Guest Artist with English National Ballet, since 1997; *b* 29 May 1970; *d* of Juhan Oks and Valentina Oks; *m* 1990, Thomas Edur, *qv*. *Educ:* Estonian State Ballet Sch.; Bolshoi Ballet Sch., Moscow; Royal Ballet Sch. (PDTC 2007). Principal Ballerina with: Estonian Opera Ballet, 1989–90; English Nat. Ballet, 1990–96; Birmingham Royal Ballet, 1996–97; has danced most classical ballets, inc. Swan Lake, Cinderella, Sleeping Beauty, The Nutcracker, Giselle, Coppélia, Romeo and Juliet, Don Quixote, and many others. Patron (with Thomas Edur): British Ballet Orgn, 2004–; English Nat. Ballet Sch., 2008–. 2001 Year Award, Achievements in Dance, Estonia, 2002; Unique Partnership Award (with Thomas Edur), Critics Circle, 2003; Olivier Award, Achievements in Dance (with Thomas Edur), 2004. Third Class Order of the White Star (Estonia), 2001.

OAKSEY, 2nd Baron *cr* 1947 (properly **TREVETHIN,** 4th Baron *cr* 1921, **AND OAKSEY); John Geoffrey Tristram Lawrence,** OBE 1985; Racing Correspondent to Daily Telegraph, 1957–94; racing commentator: ITV, since 1970; Channel Four Racing, since 1984; *b* 21 March 1929; *o s* of 1st Baron Oaksey and 3rd Baron Trevethin and Marjorie (*d* 1984), *d* of late Commander Charles N. Robinson, RN; *S* father, 1971; *m* 1st, 1959, Victoria Mary (marr. diss. 1987), *d* of late Major John Dennistoun, MBE; one *s* one *d*; 2nd, 1988, Rachel Frances Crocker, *d* of late Alan Hunter. *Educ:* Horris Hill; Eton; New College, Oxford (BA); Yale Law School. Racing Correspondent: Horse and Hound, 1959–88; Sunday Telegraph, 1960–88; columnist, Racing Post, 1988–90. Director: HTV, 1980–91; Elite Racing Club, 2000–. JP Malmesbury, 1978–99. *Publications:* History of Steeplechasing (jointly), 1967; The Story of Mill Reef, 1974; Oaksey on Racing, 1991; Mince Pie for Starters (autobiog.), 2003. *Recreations:* ski-ing, riding. *Heir:* *s* Hon. Patrick John Tristram Lawrence, *qv*. *Address:* Hill Farm, Oaksey, Malmesbury, Wilts SN16 9HS. *T:* (01666) 577303, *Fax:* (01666) 577962. *Club:* Brooks's.

OATEN, Mark; MP (Lib Dem) Winchester, since 1997; *b* 8 March 1964; *s* of Ivor Condell Oaten and Audrey Oaten; *m* 1992, Belinda Fordham; two *d*. *Educ:* Hatfield Poly. (BA Hons 1986); Hertfordshire Coll. of FE, Watford (Dip in Public Relns 1989). Consultant, Shandwick Public Affairs, 1990–92; Consultant, 1992–95, Man. Dir, 1995–97, Westminster Public Relations. Dir, Oasis Radio, 1995–96. Mem. (Lib Dem) Watford BC, 1986–94. Contested (Lib Dem) Watford, 1992. PPS to Leader of Liberal Democrat Party, 1999–2001. Lib Dem spokesman: on disabilities, 1997–99; on foreign affairs and defence, 1999–2001; on Cabinet Office, 2001–02; on home affairs, 2003–. Mem., Select Cttee on Public Admin, 1999–2001. Chm., All-Pty Prisoners of War Gp, 1998–2000; Sec., All-Pty EU Accession Gp, 2000–05; Co-Chm., All-Pty Adoption Gp, 2000–05; Treas., All-Pty Human Rights Gp, 2000–05. Chm., Lib Dem Parly Pty, 2001–03. Mem., Council of Europe, 2008–. Director: British Healthcare Trades Assoc., 2008–; Unlock, 2008–. *Publication:* Coalition, 2007. *Recreations:* gardening, cinema, swimming, football. *Address:*

House of Commons, SW1A 0AA. *T:* (020) 7219 3000, *Fax:* (020) 7219 2389; *e-mail:* oatenm@parliament.uk.

OATES, Joan Louise, PhD; FBA 2004; Fellow, Girton College, Cambridge, 1971–95, Life Fellow, since 1995; Fellow, McDonald Institute for Archaeological Research, Cambridge, since 1995; *b* 6 May 1928; *d* of Harold Burdette Lines and Beatrice Naomi Lines; *m* 1956, (Edward Ernest) David (Michael) Oates, FBA (*d* 2004); one *s* two *d*. *Educ:* Syracuse Univ., Syracuse, NY (BA 1950); Girton Coll., Cambridge (Fulbright Schol., Wenner-Gren Schol.; PhD 1953). Asst Curator, Metropolitan Mus. of Art, NYC, 1954–56; Lectr in Hist. and Archaeol. of Ancient Near East, Univ. of Cambridge, 1989–95. Guggenheim Fellow, 1966–67. *Publications:* Babylon, 1976 (trans. German, Italian, Spanish, Polish, Lithuanian, Turkish), rev. edn 2005; (ed jtly) Of Pots and Plans, 2002; with David Oates: The Rise of Civilization, 1976 (trans. Japanese, Hungarian, Arabic); Nimrud: an Assyrian City revealed, 2001, 2nd edn 2004; Excavations at Tell al Rimah: the pottery, 2001; Excavations at Tell Brak, vol. 1, Mitanni and Old Babylonian, 1997, vol. 2, Nagar in the 3rd Millennium BC, 2001; over 100 papers in jls and chapters in books. *Recreations:* snorkelling, walking, bird watching, painting. *Address:* 86 High Street, Barton, Cambridge CB23 7BG. *T:* (01223) 262273.

OATES, Rev. Canon John; Rector of St Bride's Church, Fleet Street, 1984–2000; Prebendary, St Paul's Cathedral, 1997–2001, now Prebendary Emeritus; *b* 14 May 1930; *s* of John and Ethel Oates; *m* 1962, Sylvia Mary, *d* of Herbert Charles and Ada Harris; three *s* one *d*. *Educ:* Queen Elizabeth School, Wakefield; SSM, Kelham. Curate, Eton College Mission, Hackney Wick, 1957–60; Development Officer, C of E Youth Council and mem. staff, Bd of Education, 1960–64; Development Sec., C of E Council for Commonwealth Settlement, 1964–65, Gen. Sec. 1965–70; Sec., C of E Cttee on Migration and Internat. Affairs, Bd for Social Responsibility, 1968–71; Vicar of Richmond, Surrey, 1970–84; RD, Richmond and Barnes, 1979–84; Area Dean, City of London, 1997–2000; permission to officiate, dios of London and Southwark, 2000–. Commissary: of Archbishop of Perth and Bishop of NW Australia, 1968–; to Archbishop of Jerusalem, 1969–75; to Bishop of Bunbury, 1969–. Hon. Canon, Bunbury, 1969–. Mem., Unilever Central Ethical Compliance Gp, 1991–97; Consultant, Creative Visions, USA, 2001–. Chapter Clerk, London City Deanery, 1994–97; Mem., Coll. of Canons, St Paul's Cathedral, 2001–. Chaplain: Inst. of Journalists, 1984–2000 (Life FCIJ 1995); Inst. of Public Relations, 1984–2000; Publicity Club of London, 1984–2000; London Press Club, 1984–2000; Co. of Marketors, 1984–2000; Co. of Stationers and Newspapermakers, 1989–2000; Co. of Turners, 1995–2001. Freeman, City of London, 1985; Hon. Liveryman: Marketors' Co., 1999–; Turners' Co., 2000–. *Recreations:* broadcasting, walking, exploring. *Address:* 27 York Court, The Albany, Kingston upon Thames KT2 5ST. *T:* (020) 8974 8821; *e-mail:* john@joates.co.uk. *Clubs:* Athenæum, Garrick.

OATES, (John) Keith; Deputy Chairman, 1994–99 and Managing Director, 1991–99, Marks and Spencer plc; a Governor of the BBC, 1988–93; *b* 3 July 1942; *s* of late John Alfred Oates and Katherine Mary (*née* Hole); *m* 1968, Helen Mary (*née* Blake); one *s* three *d*. *Educ:* King's Sch., Chester; Arnold Sch., Blackpool; London School of Economics (BScEcon); Univ. of Manchester Inst. of Sci. and Technology (DipTech Industrial Admin); Bristol Univ. (MSc Management Accounting). FCT 1982. Work Study trainee, Reed Paper Gp, 1965–66; Budgets and Planning Man., IBM (UK) Ltd, 1966–73; Gp Financial Controller, Rolls Royce (1971) Ltd, 1973–74; Controller, Black and Decker Europe, 1974–78; Vice Pres., Finance, Thyssen Bornemisza NV, 1978–84; Finance Dir, Marks and Spencer plc, 1984–91 (Founder Chm., Marks and Spencer Financial Services). Chm., Phaunos Timber Fund Ltd, 2006–; non-executive Director: John Laing plc, 1987–89; British Telecom, 1994–2000; Guinness, 1995–97; MCI Communications Corp., 1996–97; Diageo, 1997–2004; FSA, 1998–2001; Coutts Bank, Monaco, 2002–05; English Cttee, Forestry Commn, 2007–. Member: Council, CBI, 1988–2000; Bd, London First, 1993–96; Sports Council of GB, 1993–97; English Sports Council, 1997–99; Chm., Quality, Efficiency and Standards Team, 1999–2000. Chm., Europ. Council of Financial Execs, 1984; Mem., 100 Gp Chartered Accountants, 1985–93. Pres., UMIST Assoc., 1996–97. Mem. Council, Wycombe Abbey Sch., 1995–. Patron: Campaign for Resource, Bristol Univ., 1996–2002; London Christies Against Cancer, 1999–2001. DTI Innovation Lecture, 1997. CCMI (CIMgt 1992). FRSA 1993. Hon. LLD Bristol, 1998; Hon. DSc UMIST, 1998. *Recreations:* music, travel, fly fishing, ski-ing, spectator sports (esp. Association Football, athletics and cricket). *Club:* MCC.

OATES, Laurence Campbell, CB 2006; Official Solicitor to the Supreme Court, 1999–2006; Public Trustee, 2001–06; *b* 14 May 1946; *s* of Stanley Oates and late Norah Christine Oates (*née* Meek); *m* 1968, Brenda Lilian Hardwick; one *s* one *d*. *Educ:* Beckenham and Penge Grammar School; Bristol Univ. (LLB 1967). Called to the Bar, Middle Temple, 1968; Dept. of Employment, 1976–80; Law Officers' Dept, 1980–83; Asst Treasury Solicitor, Dept of Transport, 1983–88; Lord Chancellor's Department: Under Sec. and Hd of Legislation Gp, 1988–92; Circuit Administrator, Midland and Oxford Circuit, 1992–94; Assoc. Head of Policy Gp, 1995–96; Dir, Magistrates' Courts' Gp, 1996–99. *Recreations:* music, golf. *Address:* Cedar Waters, White Rose Lane, Woking, Surrey GU22 7JY.

OATES, Sir Thomas, Kt 1972; CMG 1962; OBE 1958 (MBE 1946); Governor and Commander-in-Chief of St Helena, 1971–76; *b* 5 Nov. 1917; *er s* of late Thomas Oates, Wadebridge, Cornwall; unmarried. *Educ:* Callington Grammar School, Cornwall; Trinity College, Cambridge (Mathematical Tripos (Wrangler); MA). Admiralty Scientific Staff, 1940–46; HMS Vernon, Minesweeping Section, 1940–42; British Admiralty Delegn, Washington, DC, 1942–46; Temp. Lieut, RNVR. Colonial Administrative Service, Nigeria, 1948–55; seconded to HM Treasury, 1953–55; Adviser to UK Delegn to UN Gen. Assembly, 1954. Financial Sec. to Govt of: British Honduras, 1955–59, Aden, 1959–63; Dep. High Comr, Aden, 1963–67; Permanent Sec., Gibraltar, 1968–69; Dep. Governor, Gibraltar, 1969–71. *Recreation:* reading. *Address:* Tristan, Trevone, Padstow, Cornwall PL28 8QX. *Clubs:* East India, Devonshire, Sports and Public Schools, Royal Commonwealth Society.

OATLEY, Brian; Chairman, Invicta Community Care NHS Trust, 1997–2001; *b* 1 June 1935; *s* of Arnold and Vivian Oatley. *Educ:* Bolton School; King's College, Cambridge (BA, PGCE). Teacher, North Manchester Grammar School, 1959–64; Assistant, Senior Assistant and Deputy County Education Officer, Kent County Council, 1964–84, County Educn Officer, 1984–88. Chm., Maidstone Priority Care NHS Trust, 1991–97. Member: RHS; Kent Trust for Nature Conservation; Camden Choir. Gov., Kent Inst. of Art and Design, 1989–98. *Recreations:* music, travel, gardening. *Address:* 6A Arundel Square, N7 8AT.

OATLEY, Michael Charles, CMG 1991; OBE 1975; international intelligence consultant; *b* 18 Oct. 1935; *s* of Sir Charles Oatley, OBE, FRS and Lady Oatley (*née* Enid West); *m* 1st, Pippa Howden; two *s* one *d*; 2nd, Mary Jane Laurens; one *s*. *Educ:* The Leys Sch.; Trinity Coll., Cambridge. Served RN, 1953–55. HM Foreign, later Diplomatic, Service, 1959–91; a Man. Dir, Kroll Associates, 1991–94; Man. Dir, 1994–98, Chm., 1998–2001, Ciex Ltd. Director: Ovag Ltd, 2002–; ICT Cambridge Ltd, 2004–06. *Address:* Manor Farmhouse, Caundle Marsh, Sherborne, Dorset DT9 5LX. *Clubs:* Chelsea Arts, Naval.

OBAMA, Barack Hussein, Jr, JD; US Senator from Illinois, since 2005; *b* Honolulu, 4 Aug. 1961; *s* of Barack Obama and Ann Dunham; *m* 1992, Michelle Robinson; two *d*. *Educ:* Columbia Univ. (BA Pol Sci. 1983); Harvard Univ. (JD *magna cum laude* 1991). Ed.-in-Chief, Harvard Law Review. Writer and financial analyst, Business Internat. Corp., 1984–85; Dir, Developing Communities Project, Chicago, 1985–88; Exec. Dir, Project Vote, Illinois, 1992; Associate, Miner, Barnhill & Galland, PC, Chicago, 1993–96, Of Counsel, 1996–2004; Sen. Lectr, Law Sch., Univ. of Chicago, 1993–2004. Mem., Illinois Senate, Dist 13, Springfield, 1997–2005; US Senate: Member: Envmt and Public Works Cttee, 2005–06; Foreign Relns Cttee; Veterans' Affairs Cttee. Democratic Candidate for Presidency of USA, 2008. *Publications:* Dreams from My Father: a story of race and inheritance, 1995; Audacity of Hope: thoughts on reclaiming the American dream, 2006. *Address:* United States Senate, 713 Hart Senate Office Building, Washington, DC 20510, USA.

OBAN (St John's Cathedral), Provost of; *see* MacCallum, Very Rev. N. D.

OBASANJO, Gen. Olusegun; President of Nigeria, 1999–2007; Nigerian Head of State, Head of the Federal Military Government and Commander-in-Chief of the Armed Forces, Nigeria, 1976–79; Member, Advisory Council of State, 1979–2007; farmer; *b* Abeokuta, Ogun State, Nigeria, 5 March 1937; *m*; two *s* three *d*. *Educ:* Abeokuta Baptist High Sch.; Mons Officers' Cadet Sch., England. Entered Nigerian Army, 1958; commission, 1959; served in Zaire (then, the Congo), 1960. Comdr, Engrg Corps, 1963; Comdr of 2nd (Rear) Div. at Ibadan; GOC 3rd Inf. Div., 1969; Comdr, 3rd Marine Commando Div.; took surrender of forces of Biafra, in Nigerian Civil War, 1969–70; Comdr Engrg Corps, 1970–75. Political post as Federal Comr for Works and Housing, Jan.–July 1975. Chief of Staff, Supreme HQ, July 1975–Feb. 1976. Mem., Internat. Indep. Commn on Disarmament and Security; Mem., Africa Progress Panel, 2006–. Part-time Associate, Univ. of Ibadan. *Publications:* My Command (autobiog.), 1980; Africa in Perspective: myths and realities, 1987; Nzeognu, 1987; Africa Embattled, 1988; Constitution for National Integration and Development, 1989; Not My Will, 1990; Challenge of Leadership in African Development, 1990; Impact of Europe in 1992 on West Africa, 1990; Leadership Challenge of Economic Reforms in Africa, 1991; Challenge of Agricultural Production and Food Security in Africa, 1992. *Recreations:* squash, table tennis, billiards, snooker.

O'BEIRNE RANELAGH, John, (John Ranelagh), PhD; Director, Nordic World, since 2006 (Executive Chairman, 2006–08); Consultant, TV 2 Norway, since 1991; Member, Independent Television Commission, 1994–99; *b* 3 Nov. 1947; *o s* of late James O'Beirne Ranelagh and Elaine Lambert O'Beirne Ranelagh; *m* 1974, Elizabeth Grenville, *y d* of Prof. Sir William Hawthorne, *qv*. *Educ:* St Christopher's Sch.; Cambridgeshire Coll. of Arts and Technology; Christ Church, Oxford (MA); Eliot Coll., Univ. of Kent (PhD). Chase Manhattan Bank, 1970; Campaign Dir, Outset Housing Assoc., 1971; Univ. of Kent Studentship, 1972–74; BBC TV, 1974; Conservative Res. Dept, 1975–79; Associate Producer, Ireland: a television history, BBC TV, 1979–81; Commissioning Editor, Channel Four TV Co., 1981–88 (Sec. to the Bd, 1981–83); Dep. Chief Exec. and Dir of Programmes, TV2 Denmark, 1988; Exec. Producer and writer, CIA, BBC TV/NRK/Primetime, 1989–92; Associate, Hydra Associates, 1989–91; Consultant, TVI Portugal, 1992–94; Director: Kanal Kaks, Estonia, 1995–97; TMS Ltd, 1999–2002; Barnimagen, 2000–01; Exec. Producer, Lykkelandet, 2003–04 (Gullruten Prize winner). Dir, Broadcasting Research Unit, 1988–90 (Mem., Exec. Cttee, 1984–87). Mem., Political Cttee, UNA, 1978–90. Governor, Daneford Sch., 1977–81. *Publications:* Science, Education and Industry, 1978; (with Richard Luce) Human Rights and Foreign Policy, 1978; Ireland: an illustrated history, 1981; A Short History of Ireland, 1983, 2nd edn 1995; The Agency: the rise and decline of the CIA, 1986 (Nat. Intelligence Book Award, and New York Times Notable Book of the Year, 1987); (contrib.) Freedom of Information, ed by Julia Neuberger, 1987; (contrib.) The Revolution in Ireland 1879–1923, ed D. G. Boyce, 1988; Den Anden Kanal, 1989; Thatcher's People, 1991; CIA: a history, 1992; (contrib.) In the Name of Intelligence: essays in honor of Walter Pforzheimer, 1994. *Recreations:* Bentley motor cars, reading. *Address:* The Garner Cottages, Mill Way, Grantchester, Cambridge CB3 9NB. *Clubs:* Travellers, Chelsea Arts, Groucho; Metropolitan (Washington).

OBORNE, Peter Alan; Political Columnist, Daily Mail, since 2006; Contributing Editor, The Spectator, since 2006; *b* 11 July 1957; *s* of Brig. John Oborne and Margaret Oborne; *m* 1986, Martine Karmock; two *s* three *d*. *Educ:* Sherborne Sch.; Christ's Coll., Cambridge (BA Hist. 1978). N. M. Rothschild & Sons Ltd, 1981–84; Financial Weekly, 1985–86; Daily Telegraph, 1986; Reporter, Evening Standard, 1987–96; Asst Ed., Sunday Express, 1996–2001; Political Ed., Spectator, 2001–06. Presenter, films (all for Channel 4) including: Mugabe's Secret Famine, 2003; Afghanistan: here's one we invaded earlier, 2003; Dirty Race for the White House, 2004; Iraq: the reckoning, 2005; Spinning Terror, 2006. *Publications:* Alastair Campbell: New Labour and the rise of the media class, 1999, revd edn (with Simon Walters), 2004; Basil D'Oliveira: cricket and conspiracy, 2004; The Rise of Political Lying, 2005; The Use and Abuse of Terror, 2006; The Triumph of the Political Class, 2007; (with James Jones) Muslims Under Siege, 2008. *Recreations:* reading, cricket, horse-racing. *Address:* c/o Daily Mail, Northcliffe House, 2 Derry Street, W8 5TT. *T:* (020) 7938 6000; *e-mail:* peter.oborne@btinternet.com.

O'BRIEN, family name of **Baron Inchiquin**.

O'BRIEN, Anthony John; Director, Poland, British Council, since 2006; *b* 17 Jan. 1951; *s* of Padraig and Sheila O'Brien; *m* 1975, Yolanda Lange; three *d*. *Educ:* Jesus Coll., Cambridge (BA Law 1971); Univ. of Manchester (DipTEO, PGCE 1975); Inst. of Educn, London (MA Educn 1986). Volunteer teacher of English, VSO, Aswan, Egypt, 1971–73; Lectr in ESP, Univ. of Tabriz, Iran, 1975–77; British Council: Dir of Studies, Morocco, 1978–82; Consultant, London, 1982–85; Dir, English Language Centre, Singapore, 1986–90, Hong Kong, 1990–94; Dir, Morocco, 1994–97; Dir, English Lang. Teaching, London, 1997–2002; Dir, Sri Lanka, 2002–06. *Publications:* Nucleus: medicine, 1980; Teacher Development: evaluation and teacher profiles in TESOL, 1984; numerous articles for professional jls. *Recreations:* learning other cultures, travel, bird watching. *Address:* British Council, Al. Jerozolimskie 59, 00-697 Warsaw, Poland. *T:* (22) 6955920, *Fax:* (22) 6955999; *e-mail:* tony.obrien@britishcouncil.org.

O'BRIEN, Basil Godwin, CMG 1996; High Commissioner of the Bahamas to the United Kingdom, 1999–2007, and Ambassador to the European Union, Belgium, France, Germany and Italy, 1999; *b* 5 Dec. 1940; *s* of late Cyril O'Brien and Kathleen O'Brien (*née* Brownrigg); *m* 1967, Marlene Devika Chand; two *s*. *Educ:* St John's Coll., Nassau; Univ. Tutorial Coll., London; London Inst. of World Affairs (Dip. Internat. Affairs, London Univ.). HEO, Min. of Ext. Affairs, Bahamas, 1969–70; Asst Sec., later Dep. Perm. Sec., Cabinet Office, 1970–78; Permanent Secretary: Min. of Tourism, 1978–86; Min. of

Foreign Affairs, 1986–89; Min. of Agriculture, Trade and Ind., 1989–93; Min. of Educn, 1993–94; Sec. to Cabinet and Hd, Public Service, 1994–99. Permanent Representative: to IMO, London; to Internat. Orgn for Migration and WTO, Geneva; to Bureau of Internat. Expositions, Paris. Formerly: Director: Bahamas Hotel Trng Coll.; Bahamasair Hldgs Co. Past Chm., Bd of Govs, St John's Coll., Nassau. Past Mem., Anglican Central Educn Authy. *Recreations:* walking, swimming, gardening. *Clubs:* Royal Automobile, Royal Over-Seas League, Royal Commonwealth Society; Skal.

O'BRIEN, Most Rev. Brendan; *see* Kingston (Ontario), Archbishop of, (RC).

O'BRIEN, Brian Murrough Fergus; Deputy Special Commissioner of Income Tax, 1991–2006; *b* 18 July 1931; *s* of late Charles Murrough O'Brien, MB, BCh and Elizabeth Joyce O'Brien (*née* Peacocke). *Educ:* Bedford Sch.; University Coll., Oxford (BA 1954, MA 1959). Nat. Service, Royal Inniskilling Fusiliers, 1950–51. Called to the Bar, Lincoln's Inn, 1955; Office of Solicitor of Inland Revenue, 1956–70; Asst Solicitor, Law Commn, 1970–80; Secretary, Law Commn, 1980–81. Special Comr of Income Tax, 1981–91. Mem., Senate of Inns of Court and Bar Council, 1977–80; Hon. Gen. Sec., 1962–67 and Chm., 1974–76, CS Legal Soc.; Chm., Assoc. of First Div. Civil Servants, 1979–81. Lay Chm., Westminster (St Margaret's) Deanery Synod, 1978–82. Trustee, St Mary's, Bourne St, 1968–2005. *Recreations:* music, travel. *Address:* Rathkeale Cottage, Castlematrix, Rathkeale, Co. Limerick, Ireland. *T:* (69) 64234. *Clubs:* Reform; Kildare Street and University (Dublin).

O'BRIEN, Charles Michael, MA; FIA, FPMI; General Manager (formerly Manager), and Actuary, 1957–84, Council Member, 1984–99, Royal National Pension Fund for Nurses; *b* 17 Jan. 1919; *s* of late Richard Alfred O'Brien, CBE, MD, and Nora McKay; *m* 1950, Joy, *d* of late Rupert Henry Prebble and Phyllis Mary Langdon; two *s. Educ:* Westminster Sch.; Christ Church, Oxford (MA). Commissioned, Royal Artillery, 1940 (despatches, 1945). Asst Actuary, Equitable Life Assce Soc., 1950; Asst Manager, Royal National Pension Fund for Nurses, 1953–57. Director: M & G Assurance Gp Ltd, 1984–91; M & G Life Assurance Co. Ltd, 1991–94. Institute of Actuaries: Fellow, 1949; Hon. Sec., 1961–62; Vice-Pres., 1965–68; Pres., 1976–78. Mem., Governing Body, 1970–95, Hon. Fellow, 1998, Westminster Sch. *Address:* The Boundary, Goodley Stock, Crockham Hill, Edenbridge, Kent TN8 6TA. *T:* (01732) 866349.

O'BRIEN, Conor Cruise; Contributing Editor, The Atlantic, Boston; Editor-in-Chief, The Observer, 1979–81; Pro-Chancellor, University of Dublin, 1973; *b* 3 Nov. 1917; *s* of Francis Cruise O'Brien and Katherine Sheehy; *m* 1st, 1939, Christine Foster (marr. diss. 1962); one *s* one *d* (and one *d* decd); 2nd, 1962, Máire Mac Entee; one adopted *s* one adopted *d. Educ:* Sandford Park School, Dublin; Trinity College, Dublin (BA, PhD). Entered Department of External Affairs of Ireland, 1944; Counsellor, Paris, 1955–56; Head of UN section and Member of Irish Delegation to UN, 1956–60; Asst Sec., Dept of External Affairs, 1960; Rep. of Sec.-Gen. of UN in Katanga, May-Dec. 1961; resigned from UN and Irish service, Dec. 1961. Vice-Chancellor, Univ. of Ghana, 1962–65; Albert Schweitzer Prof. of Humanities, New York Univ., 1965–69. TD (Lab) Dublin North-East, 1969–77; Minister for Posts and Telegraphs, 1973–77. Mem. Senate, Republic of Ireland, 1977–79. Vis. Fellow, Nuffield Coll., Oxford, 1973–75; Fellow, St Catherine's Coll., Oxford, 1978–81; Vis. Prof. and Montgomery Fellow, Dartmouth Coll., USA, 1984–85; Sen. Res. Fellow, Nat. Humanities Center, N Carolina, 1993–94. Member: Royal Irish Acad.; Royal Soc. of Literature. Hon. DLitt: Bradford, 1971; Ghana, 1974; Edinburgh, 1976; Nice, 1978; Coleraine, 1981; QUB, 1984. Valiant for Truth Media Award, 1979. *Publications:* Maria Cross (under pseud. Donat O'Donnell), 1952 (reprinted under own name, 1963); Parnell and his Party, 1957; (ed) The Shaping of Modern Ireland, 1959; To Katanga and Back, 1962; Conflicting Concepts of the UN, 1964; Writers and Politics, 1965; The United Nations: Sacred Drama, 1967 (with drawings by Felix Topolski); Murderous Angels, 1968; (ed) Power and Consciousness, 1969; Conor Cruise O'Brien Introduces Ireland, 1969; (ed) Edmund Burke, Reflections on the Revolution in France, 1969; Camus, 1969; A Concise History of Ireland, 1972; (with Máire Cruise O'Brien) The Suspecting Glance, 1972; States of Ireland, 1972; Herod, 1978; Neighbours: the Ewart-Biggs memorial lectures 1978–79, 1980; The Siege: the saga of Israel and Zionism, 1986; Passion and Cunning, 1988; God Land: reflections on religion and nationalism, 1988; The Great Melody: a thematic biography and commented anthology of Edmund Burke, 1992; Ancestral Voices, 1994; On the Eve of the Millennium, 1996; The Long Affair: Thomas Jefferson and the French Revolution, 1996; Memoir: my life and themes, 1998. *Recreation:* travelling. *Address:* Whitewater, Howth Summit, Dublin, Ireland. *T:* (1) 8322474. *Club:* Athenæum.

O'BRIEN, David P.; Chairman: EnCana Corporation, since 2002 (Director, since 1990); Royal Bank of Canada, since 2004 (Director, since 1996); *b* 9 Sept. 1941; *s* of John L. O'Brien and Ethel (*née* Cox); *m* 1968, Gail Baxter Corneil; one *s* two *d. Educ:* Loyola Coll. (BA Hons Econs 1962); McGill Univ. (BCL 1965). Associate and Partner, Ogilvy Renault (law firm), 1967–77; various mgt posts, 1978–85, Exec. Vice Pres., 1985–89, Petro-Canada; Pres. and CEO, Noverco Inc., 1989; Dir, 1990–, Chm., 1992–, PanCanadian Petroleum Ltd (Pres. and CEO, 1990–95); Dir, 1995–2001, Pres. and Chief Operating Officer, 1995–96, Chm., Pres. and CEO, 1996–2001, Canadian Pacific Ltd; Chm. and CEO PanCanadian Energy Corp., 2001–02. Director: TransCanada Pipelines Ltd, 2001–; Molson Inc., 2002–. Dir, C. D. Howe Inst. *Recreations:* tennis, biking. *Clubs:* Calgary Petroleum, Calgary Golf and Country, Glencoe Golf and Country (Calgary).

O'BRIEN, Prof. Denis Patrick, FBA 1988; Professor of Economics, University of Durham, 1972–97, now Emeritus; *b* Knebworth, Herts, 24 May 1939; *s* of Patrick Kevin O'Brien and Dorothy Elizabeth Crisp; *m* 1st, 1961, Eileen Patricia O'Brien (*d* 1985); one *s* two *d*; 2nd, 1993, Julia Stapleton; one *d. Educ:* Douai Sch.; University Coll. London (BSc (Econ) 1960); PhD Queen's Univ., Belfast, 1969. In industry, 1960–62; Queen's University, Belfast: Asst Lectr, 1963–65; Lectr, 1965–70; Reader, 1970–72. Dist. Fellow, History of Econs Soc., 2003. *Publications:* (with D. Swann) Information Agreements, 1969; J. R. McCulloch, 1970; Correspondence of Lord Overstone, 3 vols, 1971; (jtly) Competition in British Industry, 1974; (ed) J. R. McCulloch: Treatise on Taxation, 1975; The Classical Economists, 1975; Competition Policy, Profitability and Growth, 1979; (with J. Presley) Pioneers of Modern Economics in Britain, 1981; (with A. C. Darnell) Authorship Puzzles in the History of Economics, 1982; (with J. Creedy) Economic Analysis in Historical Perspective, 1984; Lionel Robbins, 1988; Thomas Joplin and Classical Macroeconomics, 1993; Methodology, Money and the Firm, 2 vols, 1994; The Classical Economists Revisited, 2004; History of Economic Thought as an Intellectual Discipline, 2007; The Development of Monetary Economics, 2007. *Recreation:* the violin.

O'BRIEN, Dermod Patrick; QC 1983; a Recorder of the Crown Court, 1978–2005; *b* 23 Nov. 1939; *s* of Lieut D. D. O'Brien, RN, and Mrs O'Brien (*née* O'Connor); *m* 1974, Zoë Susan Norris (marr. diss. 2003); two *s. Educ:* Ampleforth Coll., York; St Catherine's Coll., Oxford. BA (Jurisprudence); MA. Called to Bar, Inner Temple, 1962, Bencher, 1993; joined Western Circuit, 1963. Head of Chambers, 1999–2003. Governor, Milton Abbey Sch., 1992–. *Recreations:* fishing, shooting, ski-ing. *Address:* Rodwell Manor, West Lambrook, Kingsbury Episcopi, Somerset TA13 5HA; (chambers) 2 Temple Gardens, Temple, EC4Y 9AY. *T:* (020) 7822 1200. *Club:* Boodle's.

O'BRIEN, Edna; writer; *b* Ireland; marr. diss.; two *s. Educ:* Irish convents; Pharmaceutical Coll. of Ireland. Yorkshire Post Novel Award, 1971; Ulysses Medal, UCD, 2006. *Publications:* The Country Girls, 1960 (screenplay for film, 1983); The Lonely Girl, 1962; Girls in Their Married Bliss, 1963; August is a Wicked Month, 1964; Casualties of Peace, 1966; The Love Object, 1968; A Pagan Place, 1970; A Pagan Place (play), 1971; Night, 1972; A Scandalous Woman (short stories), 1974; Mother Ireland, 1976; Johnnie I hardly knew you, 1977; Mrs Reinhardt and other stories, 1978; Virginia (play), 1979; The Dazzle, 1981; Returning, 1982; A Christmas Treat, 1982; A Fanatic Heart (selected stories), 1985; Tales for the Telling, 1986; Flesh and Blood (play), 1987; Madame Bovary (play), 1987; The High Road, 1988; Lantern Slides (short stories), (Los Angeles Times Award) 1990; Time and Tide, 1992 (Writers' Guild Award, 1993); House of Splendid Isolation, 1994; Down by the River, 1997; James Joyce, 1999; Wild Decembers, 1999; In The Forest, 2002; Iphigenia (play), 2003; Triptych (play), 2003; The Light of Evening, 2006. *Recreations:* walking, reading, meditating. *Address:* c/o Independent Books, 4/6 Soho Square, W1D 3PZ. *T:* (020) 7240 9992; MacNaughton Lord Entertainment and Theatre, 19 Margravine Gardens, W6 8RL. *T:* (020) 8741 0606.

O'BRIEN, Sir Frederick (William Fitzgerald), Kt 1984; QC (Scotland) 1960; Sheriff Principal of Lothian and Borders, 1978–89; Sheriff of Chancery in Scotland, 1978–89; Hon. Sheriff at Edinburgh and Paisley, since 1990; *b* 19 July 1917; *s* of Dr Charles Henry Fitzgerald O'Brien and Helen Jane; *m* 1950, Audrey Muriel Owen; two *s* one *d. Educ:* Royal High Sch.; Univ. of Edinburgh; MA 1938; LLB 1940. Admitted Faculty of Advocates, 1947. Comr, Mental Welfare Commission of Scotland, 1962–65; Home Advocate Depute, 1964–65; Sheriff-Principal of Caithness, Sutherland, Orkney and Shetland, 1965–75; Interim Sheriff-Principal of Aberdeen, Kincardine and Banff, 1969–71; Sheriff Principal of N Strathclyde, 1975–78. Hon. Mem., Sheriffs' Assoc., 1990–. Member: Scottish Medical Practices Cttee, 1973–76; Scottish Records Adv. Council, 1974–83; Convener of Sheriffs Principal, 1972–89; Chm., Sheriff Court Rules Council, 1975–81. Chm., Northern Lighthouse Bd, 1983–84 and 1986–87. Convener, Gen. Council Business Cttee, Edinburgh Univ., 1980–84. Hon. Pres., Royal High Sch. Former Pupils Club, 1982–92 (Pres. 1975–76); Chm., Edinburgh Sir Walter Scott Club, 1989–92. *Recreations:* golf, music. *Address:* 22 Arboretum Road, Edinburgh EH3 5PN. *T:* (0131) 552 1923. *Clubs:* New, Scottish Arts (Edinburgh); Bruntsfield Golf (Hon. Mem.); Scottish Bench and Bar Golf (former Captain).

See also S. J. O'Brien.

O'BRIEN, John Gerard; Chief Executive, London Councils, since 2007; *b* 18 Jan. 1960; *s* of Patrick and Bridget O'Brien; *m* 1990, Anne-Marie Boyce; one *s. Educ:* St Martin's Sch., Brentwood; Univ. of Warwick (BA Hons Hist. and Politics 1982). Grad. trainee, Basildon DC, 1982–84; Principal Asst, Westminster CC, 1984–88; Mgt Consultant, KPMG, 1988–99; Dir (Solutions), Improvement and Develt Agency for Local Govt, 1999–2003; Dir, Local Govt Perf. and Practice, ODPM, subseq. DCLG, 2003–06; Dir, Ind. Commn, LGA (on secondment), 2006–07. *Publication:* (with K. Ennals) The Enabling Role of Local Authorities, 1990. *Recreations:* family, friends, sport. *Address:* London Councils, 59½ Southwark Street, SE1 0AL. *Club:* Essex County Cricket.

O'BRIEN, Prof. John W., PhD; Rector Emeritus, Concordia University (incorporating Loyola College and Sir George Williams University, Montreal), since 1984 (Rector and Vice-Chancellor, 1969–84; Professor of Economics, 1965–96); *b* 4 Aug. 1931; *s* of Wilfred Edmond O'Brien and Audrey Swain; *m* 1956, Joyce Helen Bennett; two *d. Educ:* McGill Univ., Montreal, Que; BA 1953, MA 1955, PhD 1962. Sir George Williams Univ.: Lectr in Economics, 1954; Asst Prof. of Economics, 1957; Associate Prof. of Economics and Asst Dean, 1961; Dean, Faculty of Arts, 1963; Vice-Principal (Academic), 1968–69. Hon. DCL Bishop's, 1976; Hon. LLD: McGill, 1976; Concordia, 2004. *Publication:* Canadian Money and Banking, 1964 (2nd edn, with G. Lermer, 1969). *Address:* 38 Holton Avenue, Westmount, QC H3Y 2E8, Canada.

O'BRIEN, His Eminence Cardinal Keith Michael Patrick; *see* St Andrews and Edinburgh, Archbishop of, (RC).

O'BRIEN, Margaret Anne; Director of Midwifery, since 2000, and General Manager, since 2002, Queen Charlotte's and Chelsea Hospital, London; President, Royal College of Midwives, 2004–08; *b* 18 March 1955; *d* of Eric James Hues and Enid Dorothy Hues; *m* 1st, 1977, Malcolm Richard Elliott (marr. diss. 2006); one *s*; 2nd, 2007, Jarrard Micheal O'Brien. *Educ:* Steyning Grammar Sch. Registered Nurse, 1976; Registered Midwife, 1979. Midwife, Southlands Hosp., Shoreham, 1979–95; Regl Officer, Royal Coll. of Midwives, 1995–97; Hd of Midwifery, Southampton Gen. Hosp., 1997–2000. *Recreation:* exploring the different and unusual. *Address:* Queen Charlotte's and Chelsea Hospital, Du Cane Road, W12 0HS. *T:* (020) 8383 5094, *Fax:* (020) 8383 3997; *e-mail:* maggie.o'brien@imperial.nhs.uk.

O'BRIEN, Michael; QC 2005; MP (Lab) Warwickshire North, since 1992; Minister of State, Department of Energy and Climate Change, since 2008; *b* 19 June 1954; *s* of Timothy Thomas and Mary O'Brien; *m* 1987, Alison Munro; two *d. Educ:* Worcester Tech. Coll.; North Staffs Poly. (BA Hons Hist. and Pol.). Lectr in Law, Colchester Inst., 1981–87; solicitor, 1987–92. Opposition spokesperson: HM Treasury, 1995–96; City, 1996–97; Parly Under-Sec. of State, Home Office, 1997–2001, FCO, 2002–03; Minister of State: (Minister for Trade, Investment and Foreign Affairs), FCO and DTI, 2003–04; (Minister for Energy, e-Commerce and Postal Services), DTI, 2004–05; Solicitor General, 2005–07; Minister of State, DWP, 2007–08. Member: Home Affairs Select Cttee, 1992–94; Treasury Select Cttee, 1994–95. Chm., Lab. Home Affairs Cttee, 1995–96. Parly Advr, Police Fedn, 1993–96. *Address:* House of Commons, SW1A 0AA. *Clubs:* Bedworth Ex-Service Men's (Bedworth); Wood End Social (Kingsbury, N Warwicks).

O'BRIEN, Prof. Michael, PhD; FBA 2008; Professor of American Intellectual History, University of Cambridge, since 2005; Fellow, Jesus College, Cambridge, since 2002; *b* Plymouth, 13 April 1948; *s* of John McCarthy O'Brien and Lilian Isabella O'Brien; *m* 1969, Patricia Caroline Mary Bacon. *Educ:* Trinity Hall, Cambridge (BA 1969; PhD 1976); Vanderbilt Univ. (MA). Jun. Fellow, Michigan Soc. of Fellows, 1976–79; University of Arkansas: Asst Prof., 1980–82; Associate Prof., 1982–85; Prof., 1985–87; Shriver Prof., Miami Univ., Ohio, 1987–2002; University of Cambridge: Sen. Mellon Schol., 1993–2002; Lectr, 2002–03; Reader in American Intellectual Hist., 2003–05; Fellow Commoner, Jesus Coll., 1993–2002. Visiting Professor: Univ. of S Carolina, 1980; Univ. of Alabama, 1985. Fellow: Huntington Liby, 1987; Liguria Study Center, 2008. *Publications:* The Idea of the American South, 1920–1941, 1979; (ed) All Clever Men, Who Make Their Way: critical discourse in the Old South, 1982; A Character of Hugh Legaré, 1985; (ed with D. Moltke-Hansen) Intellectual Life in Antebellum Charleston, 1986; Rethinking the South: essays in intellectual history, 1988; (ed) An Evening When Alone: four journals of single women in the South, 1827–67, 1993; Conjectures of Order: intellectual life and the American South, 1810–1860, 2 vols, 2004 (Bancroft Prize,

Columbia Univ.; Merle Curti Award, Orgn of American Historians; Hugh Holman Award, Soc. for the Study of Southern Lit.; Owsley Award, Southern Historical Soc.; Amer. Studies Network Book Prize, Eur. Assoc. for American Studies); Henry Adams and the Southern Question, 2005; Cosmopolitismo e Località, 2006; Placing the South, 2007. *Recreations:* golf, squash, supporting Tottenham Hotspur. *Address:* Jesus College, Cambridge CB5 8BL. *T:* (01223) 339317, *Fax:* (01223) 324910; *e-mail:* mo10003@cam.ac.uk. *Club:* Gog Magog Golf.

O'BRIEN, (Michael) Vincent; racehorse trainer, 1943–94, retired; *b* 9 April 1917; *s* of Daniel P. O'Brien and Kathleen (*née* Toomey); *m* 1951, Jacqueline (*née* Wittenoom), Perth, Australia; two *s* three *d. Educ:* Mungret Coll., Ireland. Started training in Co. Cork, 1944; moved to Co. Tipperary, 1951. Champion trainer: Nat. Hunt, 1952–53 and 1954–55; Flat, 1966 and 1967. Won all major English and Irish hurdle and steeple-chases, incl. 3 consecutive Grand Nationals, Gold Cups and Champion Hurdles. From 1959 concentrated on flat racing and trained winners of 44 Classics, incl. 6 Epsom Derbys, 6 Irish Derbys and 1 French Derby; also 3 Prix de l'Arc de Triomphe, Breeders Cup Mile, and Washington International; trainer of Nijinsky, first triple crown winner since 1935. Hon. LLD NUI, 1983; Hon. DSc Ulster, 1995. *Relevant publication:* Vincent O'Brien, the Official Biography, by Jacqueline O'Brien and Ivor Herbert, 2005. *Recreations:* fishing, golf. *Address:* Ballydoyle House, Cashel, Co. Tipperary, Ireland. *T:* (62) 62615, *Fax:* (62) 61217.

O'BRIEN, Prof. Patrick Karl, DPhil; FBA 1990; Professor of Economic History, University of London, 1990–98; Centennial Professor of Economic History, London School of Economics, since 1999; *b* 12 Aug. 1932; *s* of William O'Brien and Elizabeth Stockhausen; *m* 1959, Cassy Cobham; one *s* two *d. Educ:* London Sch. of Economics (Lilian Knowles Schol.; BSc 1958); Nuffield Coll., Oxford (DPhil). London University: Res. Fellow, 1960–63; Lectr, 1963–70; Reader in Econs and Econ. Hist., 1967–70; Oxford University: Univ. Lectr in Econ. Hist., 1970–84; Reader, 1984–90; Faculty Fellow, 1970–84, Professorial Fellow, 1984–90, Emeritus Fellow, 1991, St Antony's Coll.; Dir, Inst. of Historical Res., Univ. of London, 1990–98 (Hon. Fellow, 2000). Pres., Econ. Hist. Soc., 1999–2001. Hon. Dr: Carlos III, Madrid, 1998; Uppsala, 1999. *Publications:* The Revolution in Egypt's Economic System, 1966; The New Economic History of the Railways, 1977; (with C. Keyder) Economic Growth in Britain and France 1780–1914, 1978; (ed jtly) Productivity in the Economies of Europe in the 19th and 20th Centuries, 1983; (ed) Railways and the Economic Development of Western Europe 1830–1914, 1983; (ed) International Productivity Comparisons 1750–1939, 1986; The Economic Effects of the Civil War, 1988; (ed jtly) The Industrial Revolution and British Society, 1993; (ed) Industrialization: perspectives on the international economy, 1998; (ed) Philips Atlas of World History, 2000; Imperialism and Industrialization of Britain and Europe, 2000; (ed) Urban Achievement in Early Modern Europe, 2001; (ed) The Political Economy of British Historical Experience, 2002; (ed) Two Hegemonies: Britain 1846–1914 and the United States 1941–2001, 2002; contribs to many learned jls. *Recreations:* theatre, Western art, walking. *Address:* 66 St Bernards Road, Oxford OX2 6EJ. *T:* (01865) 512004.

O'BRIEN, Prof. (Patrick Michael) Shaughn, MD; DSc; FRCOG; Foundation Professor of Obstetrics and Gynaecology, Keele University Medical School, since 1989; Consultant Obstetrician and Gynaecologist, University Hospital North Staffordshire, since 1989; *b* 1 April 1948; *s* of late Patrick O'Brien and Joan O'Brien (*née* Edleston); *m* 1985, Sandie Louise Norman; one *s* one *d. Educ:* Boys' Grammar Sch., Pontypridd; Welsh Nat. Sch. of Medicine, Univ. of Wales (MB BCh 1972; MD 1979); DSc Keele, 2008. MRCOG 1979, FRCOG 1991. Res. Fellow, Univ. of Nottingham, 1974–76; Sen. House Officer, John Radcliffe Hosp., Oxford, 1976–77; Registrar: Brighton Sussex Co. Hosp., 1977–78; Middlesex Hosp., 1978–79; Clin. Lectr and Sen. Registrar, Univ. of Nottingham, 1979–84; Sen. Lectr and Consultant, Royal Free Hosp. Med. Sch., 1984–89. Postgrad. Clin. Tutor, N Staffs Hosp., 1996–2000; Chm., N Staffs Med. Inst., 2002–05. Vice Pres., 2004–07, Internat. Fellow, Council, 2008–, RCOG. Founder and Foundn Editor-in-Chief, The Obstetrician and Gynaecologist, 1998–2004; Editor-in-Chief, Map of Medicine (Gynaecol.), 2008–. FRSocMed. *Publications:* Premenstrual Syndrome, 1987; The Year Book of Obstetrics and Gynaecology, vol. 5, 1997, vol. 6, 1998, vol. 7, 1999, vol. 8, 2000; Problems of Early Pregnancy, 1997; Evidence Based Fertility, 1998; Gene Identification, Manipulation and Therapy, 1998; Fetal Programming, 1999; Hormones and Cancer, 1999; Introduction to Research Methodology, 1999; Placenta, 2000; Disorders of the Menstrual Cycle, 2000; Psychological Disorders in Obstetrics and Gynaecology, 2006; Introduction to Research Methodolgy, 2007; The Premenstrual Syndromes: PMS and PMDD, 2007; over 300 pubns inc. 40 chapters and numerous orig. res. papers, abstracts and revs on premenstrual syndrome, menopause, menstrual disorders, pre-eclampsia, GnRH analogues, gynaecological endocrinology. *Recreations:* classical music, jazz, play clarinet and saxophone, travel, ski-ing, sailing, windsurfing holidays. *Address:* Cardington House, Shrewsbury SY1 1ES. *T:* (01782) 552472.

O'BRIEN, Patrick William; His Honour Judge O'Brien; a Circuit Judge, since 1991; *b* 20 June 1945; *s* of William C. O'Brien and Ethel M. O'Brien; *m* 1970, Antoinette Wattebot; one *s* two *d. Educ:* St Joseph's Academy, Blackheath; Queens' College, Cambridge (MA, LLM). Called to the Bar, Lincoln's Inn, 1968, Bencher, 2003; practised SE Circuit; a Recorder, 1987. *Publication:* (contrib. jtly) Great Oxford: essays on the life and work of Edward de Vere, 17th Earl of Oxford, 2004. *Recreations:* cricket, choral singing, musical theatre. *Address:* Cambridge County Court, 197 East Road, Cambridge CB1 1BA. *Clubs:* MCC; Norfolk (Norwich).

O'BRIEN, Prof. Paul, PhD; CChem, FRSC; CEng, FIMMM; Professor of Inorganic Materials Chemistry, Manchester Materials Science Centre and School of Chemistry, University of Manchester, since 1999; *b* 22 Jan. 1954; *s* of Thomas O'Brien and Maureen O'Brien (*née* Graham); *m* 1979, Kym Evans. *Educ:* Cardinal Langley Grammar Sch., Middleton, Manchester; Univ. of Liverpool (BSc 1975); University Coll., Cardiff (PhD 1978). CChem, FRSC 1993; CEng, FIMMM (FIMM 2001). Lectr, Chelsea Coll., Univ. of London, 1978–84; Lectr, 1984–91, Reader in Inorganic Chem., 1991–94, QMC; Professor of Inorganic Chemistry: QMW, 1994; Imperial Coll., London, 1995–99; Res. Dean, Faculty of Sci. and Engrg, 2000–02, Hd, Dept of Chem., 2002–, Univ. of Manchester. Vis. Prof. and Dist. MDI Schol., Molecular Design Inst., Dept of Chem., Georgia Inst. of Technol., 1997–99; Sumitomo Prof. of Materials Chem., Imperial Coll., London, 1997–99; Royal Soc. Amersham Internat. Res. Fellow, 1997–98. A. G. Evans Meml Medal Lectr, Cardiff Univ., 2005. Corresp. Fellow, Worldwide Innovation Foundn, 2006. Hon. DSc Zululand, Kwa Zulu, Natal, 2006. Potts Medal (Dist. Alumnus Award), Univ. of Liverpool, 2001; Kroll Medal and Prize, IMMM, 2007. *Publications:* (with A. C. Jones) CVD of Compound Semiconductors: precursor synthesis, development and applications, 1997; (ed jtly) Advanced Chemistry Texts, 2003–; (ed jtly) Nanoscience and Nanotechnology series, 2005–; numerous contribs to learned jls. *Recreations:* hill-walking, camping with my family and dog, reading, maintaining my elderly farmhouse/land, theatre, travel. *Address:* University of Manchester, School of Chemistry, Oxford Road, Manchester M13 9PL. *T:* (0161) 275 4653, *Fax:* (0161) 275 4616; *e-mail:* paul.obrien@manchester.ac.uk.

O'BRIEN, Raymond Francis, CBE 2000; Chairman, Liverpool Land Development Co., 2002–05; *b* 13 Feb. 1936; *s* of late Ignatius and Anne O'Brien; *m* 1959, Mary Agnes, (Wendy), *d* of late James and Agnes Alcock; two *s* two *d. Educ:* St Mary's Coll., Great Crosby, Liverpool; St Edmund Hall, Oxford (BA Hons 1959; MA 1962). IPFA. Accountant, Cheshire CC, 1959–65; Head of Data Processing, Staffs CC, 1965–67; Asst County Treas., Notts CC, 1967–70; Dep. Clerk, Notts CC, 1970–73; Clerk of CC and Chief Executive, Notts, 1973–77; Chief Exec., Merseyside MCC, and Clerk to Lord Lieut, Merseyside, 1978–86; Chief Exec. and Bd Mem., Severn-Trent Water Authy, 1986–87; Chief Exec., FIMBRA, 1987–90. Chm., Speke/Garston Development Co., 1995–2003. Consultant, Information Corp. (UK) Ltd, 1993. Mem., Merseyside Area Bd, MSC, 1980–86; Director: Merseyside Economic Development Co. Ltd, 1981–86; Merseyside Cablevision Ltd, 1982–86; Anfield Foundation, 1983–92. Chm., Midlands Reg. Electricity Consumers Cttee, 1996–2000. DL Merseyside, 1980–86. *Recreations:* sports critic, gardening, music, reading. *Address:* Cornerways, 12 Selworthy Road, Birkdale, Southport, Merseyside PR8 2NS. *T:* and *Fax:* (01704) 551780.

O'BRIEN, Sir Richard, Kt 1980; DSO 1944, MC 1942 (Bar 1944); Chairman, Manpower Services Commission, 1976–82; *b* 15 Feb. 1920; *s* of late Dr Charles O'Brien and of Marjorie Maude O'Brien; *m* 1951, Elizabeth M. D. Craig; two *s* three *d. Educ:* Oundle Sch.; Clare Coll., Cambridge (MA). Served, 1940–45, with Sherwood Foresters and Leicesters, N Africa, ME, Italy and Greece; Personal Asst to Field Marshal Montgomery, 1945–46. Develt Officer, Nat. Assoc. of Boys' Clubs, 1946–48; Richard Sutcliffe Ltd, Wakefield (latterly Prodn Dir), 1948–58; Dir and Gen. Man., Head Wrightson Mineral Engrg Ltd, 1958–61; Dir, Industrial Relns, British Motor Corp., 1961–66; Industrial Adviser (Manpower), DEA, 1966–68; Delta Metal Co. Ltd (subseq. Dir of Manpower, and Dir 1972–76), 1968–76. Chairman: CBI Employment Policy Cttee, 1971–76; Crown Appointments Commn, 1979; Engineering Industry Trng Bd, 1982–85; Archbishop's Commn on Urban Priority Areas, 1983–85; Industrial Participation Assoc., 1983–86; Policy Studies Inst., 1984–90 (Jt Pres., 1991–98); Employment Inst. and Charter for Jobs, 1985–87; Community Educn Develt Centre, 1989–94; People for Action, 1991–98 (Pres., 1994–); Deputy Chairman: AMARC, 1988–91; Church Urban Fund, 1988–94. Member: NEDC, 1977–82; Engrg Council, 1985–88; President: British Inst. of Industrial Therapy, 1982–87; Inst. of Trng and Develt, 1983–84; Nat. Assoc. of Colls of Further and Higher Educn, 1983–85; Concordia (Youth Service Volunteers), 1987–91 (Chm., 1981–87); Campaign for Work, 1988–92; Employment Policy Inst., 1992–95. Mem. Bd, Community Industry, 1991–96; Member Council: Industrial Soc., 1962–86; Univ. of Birmingham, 1969–88; Hymns Ancient & Modern, 1984–2000. Mem. Ct of Governors, ASC, 1977–83. Chm., Chiswick House Friends, 1997–2000. Hon. DSc Aston, 1979; Hon. LLD: Bath, 1981; Liverpool, 1981; Birmingham, 1982; Hon. DLitt: Warwick, 1983; CNAA (Coll. of St Mark and St John), 1988; DCL Lambeth, 1987; Hon. Fellow Sheffield City Polytech., 1980. JP Wakefield, 1955–61. *Publications:* contrib: Conflict at Work (BBC pubn), 1971; Montgomery at Close Quarters, 1985; Seekers and Finders, 1985; articles in various jls. *Recreations:* reading, theatre, cinema. *Address:* 54 Abbotsbury Close, W14 8EQ. *T:* (020) 7371 1327.

O'BRIEN, Air Vice-Marshal Robert Peter, CB 1997; OBE 1983; Air Secretary, 1994–97, and Chief Executive, RAF Personnel Management Agency, 1997–98; *b* 1 Nov. 1941; *s* of Major Thomas Joseph O'Brien, MC, RE and Doris Winifred O'Brien; *m* 1964, Carole Evelyn Anne Wallace; two *s. Educ:* Salesian College, Farnborough; RAF College, Cranwell. BA (External) London. Commissioned 1962; Pilot 31 Sqn (Canberras), 1963–66; Central Flying Sch./4FTS (Gnats), 1966–67; ADC to AOC 38 Gp, 1967–70; Flt Comdr, 15 Sqn (Buccaneers), 1970–73; Army Staff Coll., 1974; HQ RAF Germany, 1975–77; OC London UAS (Bulldogs), 1977–79; Chief Instr/TTTE (Tornados), 1980–83; Stn Comdr, RAF Marham, 1983–85; Air Staff, MoD, 1985–87; Dep. Comdr/COS HQ BF Cyprus, 1988–91; Dir of Infrastructure (RAF), MoD, 1991–92; Comdt, JSDC, 1992–94. ADC to the Queen, 1983–85. *Recreations:* flying No. 3 Air Experience Flight, hill walking. *Address:* c/o Lloyds TSB, Cox's and King's Branch, PO Box 1190, 7 Pall Mall, SW1Y 5NA. *Club:* Royal Air Force.

O'BRIEN, (Robert) Stephen, CBE 1987; Joint President, London First, since 2005 (Chief Executive, 1992–2002; Chairman, 2002–05); Chairman: International Health Partners, since 2005; Tower Hamlets Primary Care Trust, since 2005; *b* 14 Aug. 1936; *s* of Robert Henry and Clare Winifred O'Brien; *m* 1st, 1958, Zoë T. O'Brien (marr. diss. 1989); two *s* two *d;* 2nd, 1989, Meriel Barclay. *Educ:* Sherborne Sch., Dorset. Joined Charles Fulton & Co. Ltd, 1956; Dir, 1964; Chm., 1973–82; Chief Exec., 1983–92, Vice-Chm., 1992–, BITC. Chm., Cranstoun, 1969–83 (Pres., 1983–88); Dir, Kirkland-Whittaker Co. Ltd, 1980–82. Chief Exec., London Forum, 1993–94; Vice-Chm., 1993–2005, Chief Exec., 1995–99, London First Centre, subseq. Think London. Chairman: Foreign Exchange and Currency Deposit Brokers Assoc., 1968–72; Project Fullemploy, 1973–91; Home Sec.'s Adv. Bd on Community Radio, 1985–86. Ordained Deacon, 1971; Hon. Curate St Lawrence Jewry, 1973–80; Chm., Christian Action, 1976–88. Vice-Chm., Church Urban Fund, 1994–2002. Pres., Esher Assoc. for Prevention of Addiction, 1979–90. Chm., UK 2000, 1988–92 (Mem. Bd, 1986–92); Director: Cities in Schools, 1989–95; Prince of Wales' Business Leaders Forum, subseq. Internat. Business Leaders Forum, 1990–; Member: Admin. Council, Royal Jubilee Trusts, 1984–89; Mgt Cttee, Action Resource Centre, 1986–91; Council, RSA, 1987–91; Trustee: Learning from Experience Trust, 1986–94; Immigrants Aid Trust, 1997–2007; PYBT, 1987–99; Chm., Prince's Trust Regl Council for London, 2000–06. Chm., Unicorn Children's Th., 2006–. Chm. Govs, UEL, 1999–2005. Hon. LLD Liverpool, 1994; Hon DSc City, 2000; DUniv: Middx, 2001; UEL 2005. *Recreations:* classical music, gardening, cooking. *Address:* 170 Pierpoint, 16 Westferry Road, E14 8NQ.

O'BRIEN, Prof. Sean Patrick, FRSL; freelance writer, since 1989; Professor of Creative Writing, University of Newcastle, since 2006 (Visiting Professor, 2003–06); *b* 19 Dec. 1952; *s* of Patrick Francis O'Brien and Mary Irene O'Brien; partner, Ms Gerry Wardle. *Educ:* Selwyn Coll., Cambridge (BA 1974); Birmingham Univ. (MA 1977); Leeds Univ. (PGCE 1981). Teacher of English, Beacon Community Coll., Crowborough, 1981–89; Fellow in Creative Writing, Univ. of Dundee, 1989–91; Northern Arts Literary Fellow, Univs of Durham and Newcastle upon Tyne, 1992–94; Lectr on Writing (MA course), 1998, and Prof. of Poetry, 2003–06, Sheffield Hallam Univ. British Council Visiting Writer: Univ. of Odense, 1996; Hokudai Univ., Sapporo, 1997; Writer in Residence: South Bank Centre Poetry Internat., 1998; Univ. of Leeds, 1999; (with Julia Darling) Live Theatre Newcastle, 2001–03. Ext. Examnr, MLitt, Univ. of St Andrews, 2003–06. Specialist Advr to Scottish Arts Council, 2003–05. Vice Pres., Poetry Soc., 2006. Mem., Newcastle Lit. and Philosophical Soc., 1990. Mem., Vujonistas. FRSL 2007. Hon. DCL Northumbria, 2003. Gregory Award, 1979; Somerset Maugham Award, 1984; Cholmondeley Award, 1988; E. M. Forster Award, AAAL, 1993; Northern Writer of the Year, Northern Arts and New Writing North, 2001; Northern Rock Foundn Award, 2007. *Publications:* The Indoor Park, 1983; The Frighteners, 1987; HMS Glasshouse, 1991;

Ghost Train (Forward Prize for Best Collection), 1995; (jtly) Penguin Modern Poets 5, 1995; The Deregulated Muse: essays on contemporary poetry in Britain and Ireland, 1998; (ed) The Firebox: poetry in Britain and Ireland after 1945, 1998; Downriver (Forward Prize for Best Collection), 2001; Cousin Coat: selected poems 1976–2001, 2002; The Birds, 2002; (jtly) Rivers, 2002; Keepers of the Flame, 2003; Laughter When We're Dead, in Live Theatre: six plays from the North East, 2003; (ed jtly) Ten Hallam Poets, 2005; (contrib.) Elipsis 1 (short stories), 2005; The Inferno, a New Verse Version, 2006; The Drowned Book, 2007 (Forward Prize for Best Collection, 2007; T. S. Eliot Prize, 2007); The Silence Room (short stories), 2008; Afterlife (novel), 2009. *Recreations:* reading, listening to music, writing a novel. *Address:* c/o Triple PA, 15 Connaught Gardens, Forest Hall, Newcastle upon Tyne NE12 8AT. *T:* and *Fax:* (0191) 266 2225; *e-mail:* triplepa@blueyonder.co.uk.

O'BRIEN, Shaughn; *see* O'Brien, P. M. S.

O'BRIEN, Stephen Rothwell; MP (C) Eddisbury, since July 1999; *b* Tanzania, 1 April 1957; *s* of David and Rothy O'Brien; *m* 1986, Gemma Townshend; two *s* one *d.* *Educ:* Sedbergh Sch.; Emmanuel Coll., Cambridge (MA); Chester Coll. of Law. Solicitor, Freshfields, 1981–88; Gp Internat. Dir, then Gp Sec., Redland plc, 1988–98. PPS to Opposition spokesman on foreign affairs, 2000, to Chm. of Cons. Pty, 2000–01; an Opposition Whip, 2001–02; Shadow Financial Sec. to the Treasury, 2002; Shadow Paymaster Gen., 2002–03; Shadow Sec. of State for Industry, 2003–05; Shadow Minister for Skills and Higher Educn, 2005; Shadow Minister for Health, 2005–. Member, Select Committee: on Educn and Employment, 1999–2001; on Envmt, Food and Rural Affairs, 2001. All Party Groups: Chairman: Malaria; Tanzania; Primary Headache Disorders; Roofing; Jt Chm., Minerals; Vice-Chairman: Aid, Trade and Debt; Member: Africa; British-American; Hong Kong. Introduced Private Members Bill on Honesty in Food Labelling, 2001 and 2003. Mem., Cons. Nat. Membership Cttee, 1999–2001; Secretary: Cons. Trade and Industry Cttee, 1999–2001; Cons. NI Cttee, 1999–2001. Associate Mem., British-Irish Inter-Parly Body, 2000–. Mem., Internat. Investment Panel and SE Regl Council, CBI, 1995–98. UK Building Materials Producers, then Construction Products Association: Chm., Public and Parly Affairs Cttee, 1995–99; Member: Cttee of Mgt; Pres.'s Strategy Cttee; Econ. and Market Forecasting Panel, 1989–95; Parly Advr, Manufg Technologies Assoc., 2005–. FCIS 1997 (Parly Advr, 2000–). Director: Cambridge Univ. Careers Service, 1992–99; City of London Sinfonia, 2001–; Small Business Res. Trust, 2006–07. Chm., Malaria Consortium, 2006–. Trustee, Bd, Liverpool Sch. of Tropical Medicine, 2006–. Chm., Chichester Cons. Assoc., 1998–99 (Vice-Pres., 1999–). *Recreations:* music (piano, conducting), fell-walking, golf, historic vehicles. *Address:* House of Commons, SW1A 0AA. *T:* (020) 7219 6315. *Club:* Winsford Constitutional and Conservative (Cheshire).

O'BRIEN, Susan Joyce; QC (Scot.) 1998; Chairman, Faculty Services Ltd, 2005–07; *b* 13 Aug. 1952; *d* of Sir Frederick O'Brien, *qv*; *m* 1978, Peter Ross, Professor of Evolutionary Computing, Napier Univ.; two *d.* *Educ:* St George's Sch., Edinburgh; Univ. of York (BA Hons 1973; BPhil 1976); Univ. of Edinburgh (LLB 1978). Admitted Solicitor, Scotland, 1980; Asst Solicitor, Shepherd & Wedderburn WS, 1980–86; WS 1983; admitted to Faculty of Advocates, 1987; Standing Junior Counsel to: Registrar Gen., 1991; Home Office, 1992–97; Keeper of the Registers, 1998; Temp. Sheriff, 1995–99. Chair, Caleb Ness Inquiry for Edinburgh and the Lothians Child Protection Cttee, report pubd 2003. Part-time Employment Judge (formerly Chm., Employment Tribunal), 2000–. Member: Panel, Disciplinary Appeal Bd, Faculty of Actuaries, 2002–; Panel of Legal Assessors for Gen. Teaching Council for Scotland, 2005–. Reporter, Scottish Legal Aid Bd, 1999–2005. *Recreation:* gardening. *Address:* 21 Nile Grove, Edinburgh EH10 4RE. *T:* (0131) 446 9210.

O'BRIEN, Timothy Brian, RDI 1991; designer; Hon. Associate Artist, Royal Shakespeare Company, since 1988 (Associate Artist, 1966–88); *b* 8 March 1929; *s* of Brian Palliser Tiegue O'Brien and Elinor Laura (*née* Mackenzie). *Educ:* Wellington Coll.; Corpus Christi, Cambridge (MA); Yale Univ. Design Dept, BBC TV, 1954; Designer, Associated Rediffusion, 1955–56; Head of Design, ABC Television, 1956–66 (The Flying Dutchman, 1958); partnership in stage design with Tazeena Firth, 1961–79; output incl.: The Bartered Bride, The Girl of the Golden West, 1962; West End prodns of new plays, 1963–64; London scene of Shakespeare Exhibn, 1964; Tango, Days in the Trees, Staircase, RSC, and Trafalgar at Madame Tussaud's, 1966; All's Well that Ends Well, As You Like It, Romeo and Juliet, RSC, 1967; The Merry Wives of Windsor, Troilus and Cressida (also Nat. Theatre, 1976), The Latent Heterosexual, RSC, 1968; Pericles (also Comédie Française, 1974), Women Beware Women, Bartholomew Fair, RSC, 1969; 1970: Measure for Measure, RSC; Madame Tussaud's in Amsterdam; The Knot Garden, Royal Opera; 1971: Enemies, Man of Mode, Merchant of Venice, RSC; 1972: La Cenerentola, Oslo; Lower Depths, The Island of the Mighty, RSC; As You Like It, OCSC; 1973: Richard II, Love's Labour's Lost, RSC; 1974: Next of Kin, NT; Summerfolk, RSC; The Bassarids, ENO; 1975: John Gabriel Borkman, NT; Peter Grimes, Royal Opera (later in Göteborg, Paris); The Marrying of Ann Leete, RSC; 1976: Wozzeck, Adelaide Fest.; The Zykovs, RSC; The Force of Habit, NT; 1977: Tales from the Vienna Woods, Bedroom Farce, NT; Falstaff, Berlin Opera; 1978: The Cunning Little Vixen, Göteborg; Evita, London (later in Australia, Austria, USA); A Midsummer Night's Dream, Sydney Opera House; 1979: The Rake's Progress, Royal Opera; 1981: Lulu, Royal Opera; 1982: La Ronde, RSC; Le Grand Macabre, ENO; 1983: Turandot, Vienna State Opera; 1984: The Mastersingers of Nuremberg, ENO; Tannhäuser, Royal Opera; 1985: Samson, Royal Opera; Sicilian Vespers, Grande Théâtre, Geneva; Old Times, Haymarket; Lucia di Lammermoor, Köln Opera; 1986: The Threepenny Opera, NT; Die Meistersinger von Nürnberg, Netherlands Opera; The American Clock, NT; 1987: Otello, and Die Entführung aus dem Serail, Royal Opera; 1988: Three Sisters, RSC; 1989: Cymbeline, RSC; Exclusive, Strand; 1990: King, Piccadilly; Love's Labours Lost, RSC; 1991: Twelfth Night, Tartuffe, Playhouse; War and Peace, Kirov, Leningrad; Beauty and the Beast, City of Birmingham Touring Opera; 1992: Christopher Columbus, RSC; 1993: Eugene Onegin, Royal Opera; Misha's Party, RSC; 1994: On Approval, Playhouse; The Clandestine Marriage, Queen's; 1995: The Merry Wives of Windsor, NT; The Merry Wives of Windsor, Oslo; 1996: Outis, La Scala, Milan; 1997: A Christmas Carol, Clwyd; 1998: Evita, US tour; 1999: Twelfth Night, Macbeth, Clwyd; 2001: Bedroom Farce, Clwyd; 2002: Romeo and Juliet, Clwyd; 2004: Werther, Lisbon; 2005: Ulysses Comes Home, Birmingham Opera Co.; 2006: Das Rheingold, Lisbon; 2007: Die Walküre, Lisbon; 2008: Siegfried, Lisbon; Macbeth, Clwyd. Chm., Soc. of British Theatre Designers, 1984–91; Master, Faculty of RDI, 1999–2001. (Jtly) Gold Medal for Set Design, Prague Quadriennale, 1975; (jtly) Golden Triga, for Best Nat. Exhibit, Prague Quadriennale, 1991. *Address:* The Level, Blackbridge Road, Freshwater Bay, Isle of Wight PO40 9QP; *e-mail:* all@highwaterjones.com.

O'BRIEN, Sir Timothy John, 7th Bt *cr* 1849; *b* 6 July 1958; *s* of John David O'Brien (*d* 1980) and of Sheila Winifred, *o d* of Sir Charles Arland Maitland Freake, 4th Bt; *S* grandfather, 1982, but his name does not appear on the Official Roll of the Baronetage; *m* 2000, Susannah, *yr d* of Bryan Farr; three *d.* *Educ:* Millfield; Univ. of Hartford, Conn. *Heir:* *b* James Patrick Arland O'Brien [*b* 22 Dec. 1964; *m* 1992, Lianna Mace; two *s*].

O'BRIEN, Una; Director General, Policy and Strategy, Department of Health, since 2007; *b* Solihull, 23 Dec. 1957; *d* of Patrick O'Brien and Margaret O'Brien (*née* Langtry). *Educ:* Convent HCJ, Birmingham; St Anne's Coll., Oxford (BA Hons Modern Hist.); Harvard Univ. (Kennedy Schol.); London Sch. of Econs (MSc Econ Internat. Relns). Parly res. asst to Lab. frontbench spokesmen on NI, 1980–82; Res. Officer, Inst. of Educn, Univ. of London, 1984–86; Corporate Services Manager, London Lighthouse, 1987–90; Department of Health, 1990–: Policy Manager, for people with physical disability, 1990–92; Performance Manager, NHS W Midlands, NHS Mgt Exec., 1992–93; Private Sec., Minister of State for Health, 1993–94; Principal Private Sec., Sec. of State for Transport, 1994–95; Dep. Dir, Prime Minister's Efficiency Unit, Cabinet Office, 1996–98; Sec., Public Inquiry into Paediatric Cardiac Surgery in Bristol (Kennedy Inquiry), 1998–2001; on secondment to NHS as Dir, Develt and Clin. Governance, UCL NHS Foundn Trust, 2002–05; Dir, Provider Reform, Policy and Strategy Directorate, 2005–07. Non-exec. Dir, Govt Legal Service. Gov., Jack Tizard Sch., Hammersmith, 2006–. *Recreations:* travel, theatre, walking, the River Thames. *Address:* Department of Health, Richmond House, 70 Whitehall, SW1A 2NS. *T:* (020) 7210 5258, *Fax:* (020) 7210 5685; *e-mail:* una.obrien@dh.gsi.gov.uk.

O'BRIEN, Vincent; *see* O'Brien, M. V.

O'BRIEN, William; JP; *b* 25 Jan. 1929; *m* Jean; three *d.* *Educ:* state schools; Leeds Univ. Coalminer, 1945–83. Wakefield DC: Mem., 1973–83; former Dep. Leader and Chm., Finance and Gen. Purposes Cttee. Mem., NUM, 1945–; Local Branch Official, 1956–83. MP (Lab) Normanton, 1983–2005. Opposition front bench spokesman on the Environment, 1987–92, for Northern Ireland, 1992–96. Member: Public Accounts Cttee, 1983–88; Energy Select Cttee, 1986–88; Envmt, Transport and Regions Select Cttee, 1997–2005; Public Accounts Commn, 1997–2005. JP Wakefield, 1979. *Recreations:* reading, organising. *Address:* 29 Limestrees, Ferrybridge Road, Pontefract WF8 2QB.

O'BRIEN, Adm. Sir William (Donough), KCB 1969 (CB 1966); DSC 1942; Commander-in-Chief, Western Fleet, Feb. 1970–Sept. 71, retd Nov. 1971; Vice-Admiral of the United Kingdom and Lieutenant of the Admiralty, 1984–86; *b* 13 Nov. 1916; *s* of late Major W. D. O'Brien, Connaught Rangers and I. R. Caroe (*née* Parnis); *m* 1943, Rita Micallef, Sliema, Malta; one *s* two *d.* *Educ:* Royal Naval Coll., Dartmouth. Served War of 1939–45: HM Ships Garland, Wolsey, Witherington, Offa, 1939–42; Cottesmore i/c, 1943–44; Arakan Coast, 1945. HMS Venus i/c, 1948–49; Commander 1949; HMS Ceylon, 1952; Admiralty, 1953–55; Captain, 1955; Captain (D) 8th DS in HMS Cheviot, 1958–59; HMS Hermes i/c, 1961–64; Rear-Admiral 1964; Naval Secretary, 1964–66; Flag Officer, Aircraft Carriers, 1966–67; Comdr, Far East Fleet, 1967–69; Admiral 1969. Rear-Admiral of the UK, 1979–84. Chairman: Kennet and Avon Canal Trust, 1974–91; King George's Fund for Sailors, 1974–86. Pres., Assoc. of RN Officers, 1973–88. *Address:* 16/17 Hays Park, near Shaftesbury, Dorset SP7 9JR. *T:* (01747) 830989. *Club:* Army and Navy.

O'BRIEN QUINN, James Aiden; *see* Quinn.

OBRIST, Hans Ulrich; Co-Director, Exhibitions and Programmes, and Director, International Projects, Serpentine Gallery, since 2006; *b* Zurich, 21 May 1968; *s* of Fritz Obrist and Ella Obrist (*née* Bernegger). *Educ:* Univ. of Gallen (Economy and Soc. Scis). Curator in Residence, Cartier Foundn, Paris, 1991; Founder and Head, Migrateurs prog., 1993–2006, Curator, 2000–06, Musée d'Art Moderne de la Ville de Paris; Curator, Museum in Progress, Vienna, 1993–2000. Lectr, Univ. of Lüneburg, 1993–2000; Prof., Univ. of Venice, 2000–. Founder and Ed. in Chief, Point d'Ironie, 1997–; special correspondent, Domus, Milan, 2003–. Has curated of over 150 exhibitions. *Publications include:* (ed) Gerhard Richter's Sils, 1992; (ed) Gerhard Richter's Text: schriften und interviews, 1993; (ed) Paul-Armand Gette's Nymphaeum, 1993; (ed) Bertrand Lavier's Argo, 1994; (ed) Christian Boltanski's Les Vacances à Berck-Plage (About 1975), 1995; (ed) Annette Messager's Nos Témoignages, 1995; (ed) Gerhard Richter's The Daily Practice of Painting: writings and interviews 1962–93, 1995; Do It, 1995; (ed) Gilbert & George's Oh, the Grand Old Duke of York, 1996; (ed jtly) The Words of Gilbert & George, with Portraits of the Artists from 1968 to 1997, 1997; (ed jtly) Unbuilt Roads, 107 Unrealised Projects, 1997; (ed jtly) Sogni/Dreams, 1999; (ed jtly) Weltwissen Wissenwelt: Das globale Netz von Text und Bild, 2000; (ed jtly) Interarchive: archival practices and sites in the contemporary art field, 2002; (ed jtly) Bridge the Gap?, 2002; Hans Ulrich Obrist: interviews, vol. 1, 2003; (ed) Do It, 2004; (ed jtly) Prefaces by Hans Ulrich Obrist 1989–2005, 2005; (ed jtly) Smithson Time: a dialogue, 2005; (ed jtly) Matthew Barney: drawing restraint 1987–2002 v.1, 2006; (jtly) Anri Sala, 2006; (with Pedro Reyes) El Aire Es Azul/The Air is Blue, 2006; (jtly) doststopdontstopdontstopdontstop, 2006; (with Robert Violette) The Words of Gilbert & George, 2006; (ed jtly) Barry Flanagan: sculpture 1965–2005, 2006; Hans Ulrich Obrist: everything you always wanted to know about curating but were afraid to ask, 2007; (with Nicolas Trembley) The Secret Files of Gilbert and George, 2007; (with Pedro Reyes) The Air is Blue—Art Meets Architecture: Luis Barragan revisited, 2007; The Future Will Be..., 2007; (jtly) Ryan Gander: intellectual colours, 2007; (with Adrian Notz) Merz World: processing the complicated order, 2007; (ed jtly) Rirkrit Tiravanija—A Retrospective, 2007; (jtly) Olafur Eliasson: the Goose Lake Trail (Southern Route), 2007; (jtly) Thomas Bayrle: 40 years of Chinese rock 'n' roll, 2007; Formulas for Now, 2008; (jtly) Susan Hefuna: Pars Pro Toto, 2008; (jtly) Victor Man, 2008; The Conversation Series: Rem Koolhaas, 2007; Yona Friedman, 2007; Wolfgang Tillmans, 2007; Gilbert and George, 2007; Zaha Hadid, 2007; Thomas Demand, 2007; John Chamberlain, 2007; Olafur Eliasson, 2008; Nancy Spero, 2008; Philippe Parreno, 2008; Rosemarie Trockel, 2008; Dominique Gonzalez-Foerster, 2008; contributing editor for internat. art magazines incl. Artforum, Atlantica, Flash Art Internat., der Freund, Paradis Mag., Numero d and Trans. *Address:* Serpentine Gallery, Kensington Gardens, W2 3XA. *T:* (020) 7402 6075, *Fax:* (020) 7402 4103; *e-mail:* information@serpentinegallery.org.

O'BYRNE, Andrew John Martin; QC 2006; *b* 23 April 1950; *s* of late Andrew John O'Byrne and Winifred O'Byrne; *m* 1977, Anne Victoria Roby; two *s.* *Educ:* St Joseph's Coll., Blackpool; Univ. of Liverpool (LLB). Called to the Bar, Gray's Inn, 1978; in practice, specialising in criminal law, incl. serious fraud. *Recreations:* family, reading, good wine, good company. *Address:* Peel Court Chambers, Sunlight House, Quay Street, Manchester M3 3JZ. *T:* (0161) 832 3791, *Fax:* (0161) 835 3054.

O'CATHAIN, Baroness *cr* 1991 (Life Peer), of The Barbican in the City of London; **Detta O'Cathain,** OBE 1983; Managing Director, Barbican Centre, 1990–95; *b* 3 Feb. 1938; *d* of late Caoimhghin O'Cathain and Margaret O'Cathain; *m* 1968, William Bishop (*d* 2001). *Educ:* Laurel Hill, Limerick; University College, Dublin (BA). Aer Lingus, Dublin, 1961–66; Group Economist, Tarmac, 1966–69; Economic Advr, Rootes Motors, 1969–72; Sen. Economist, Carrington Vyella, 1972–73; Economic Advr, British Leyland, 1973–74; Dir, Market Planning, Leyland Cars, 1974–76; Corporate Planning Exec.,

Unigate, 1976–81; Milk Marketing Board: Head of Strategic Planning, 1981–83; Dir and Gen. Manager, 1984; Man. Dir Milk Marketing, 1985–88. Advr on Agricl Marketing to Minister of Agriculture, 1979–83. Non-executive Director: Midland Bank, 1984–93; Channel 4, 1985–86; Tesco, 1985–2000; Sears, 1987–94; British Airways, 1993–2004; BET, 1994–96; BNP Paribas (formerly BNP) UK Holdings Ltd, 1995–2005; Thistle Hotels, 1996–2003; South East Water plc, 1998–2008; William Baird Plc, 2000–02; Allders plc, 2000–03. FCIM 1987 (Pres., 1998–2001); FRSA 1986. Hon. Fellow, Harris Manchester Coll., Oxford, 2008. Mem., Brooklands Mus. Trust, 2006– (Chm., Appeal Bd, 2007–). *Recreations:* music, reading, walking, gardening. *Address:* House of Lords, SW1A 0PW. *T:* (020) 7219 3000.

O'CEALLAIGH, Dáithí; Ambassador of Ireland to the United Nations, Geneva, since 2007; *b* 24 Feb. 1945; *m* 1968, Antoinette Reilly; one *s* one *d.* *Educ:* University College Dublin (BA). Teacher, Zambia, 1968–71; entered Diplomatic Service, Ireland, 1973; Third Sec., 1973, First Sec., 1974, Dept of Foreign Affairs; First Sec., Moscow, 1975–77, London, 1977–82; First Sec., 1982–85, Counsellor, 1985, Anglo-Irish Div., Dublin; Counsellor, Anglo-Irish Secretariat, Maryfield, 1985–87; Consul General, New York, 1987–93; Ambassador, Finland and Estonia, 1993–98; Asst Sec., Admin Div., 1998–2000; Second Sec. General, Anglo-Irish Div., 2000–01, Dublin; Ambassador to UK, 2001–07. *Recreations:* bird-watching, cinema, history, theatre, jazz. *Address:* c/o Permanent Mission of Ireland to the United Nations, 45–47 rue de Lausanne, 1202 Geneva 2, Switzerland.

OCEAN, Humphrey; *see* Butler-Bowdon, H. A. E.

OCKELTON, (Christopher) Mark (Glyn); Deputy President, Asylum and Immigration Tribunal (formerly Immigration Appeal Tribunal), since 2000; a Recorder, since 2003; a Deputy High Court Judge, since 2008; *b* 11 July 1955; *s* of Denis William Ockelton and Elvire Mabel Louise Jeanne (*née* May); *m* 1992, Brigid Joan Oates; one step *s* one step *d.* *Educ:* Winchester Coll.; Peterhouse, Cambridge (BA 1976; MA 1980); BD London 1989. Called to the Bar, Lincoln's Inn, 1977 (Bencher, 2001); Lectr in Law, 1979–93, Sen. Lectr, 1993–96, Hon. Fellow, 1996–2003, Vis. Fellow, 2003–, Univ. of Leeds; Immigration Adjudicator, 1992–96; Chm., 1996–2000, Vice-Pres., Jan.–May 2000, Immigration Appeal Tribunal. Vis. Prof. of Law, Univ. of Louisville, 1984–85; Vis. Lectr, Univ. du Maine, France, 1989. Parish Clerk: St Mary's Ch, Whitby, 1994–; St Mary's Ch, Rotherhithe, 2004–. Mem., Ancient Soc. of Coll. Youths, 1974–. Parish Clerks' Co., 2005. Hon. Col, Commonwealth of Ky, 1985. *Publications:* The Tower, Bells and Ringers of Great St Mary's, Cambridge, 1981; Trusts for Accountants, 1987; Heydon and Ockelton's Evidence: cases and materials, 3rd edn 1991, 4th edn 1996; contrib. articles and reviews in legal, philosophical, antiquarian and campanological jls. *Recreations:* books, bells, ecclesiology, looking at architecture. *Address:* Asylum and Immigration Tribunal, Field House, 15–25 Bream's Buildings, EC4A 1DZ. *Club:* Athenæum.

OCKENDON, Dr John Richard, FRS 1999; Research Director, Oxford Centre for Industrial and Applied Mathematics, 1989–Sept. 2009, and Director, Oxford Centre for Collaborative Applied Mathematics, since 2008, University of Oxford; Fellow, St Catherine's College, Oxford, since 1965;; *b* 13 Oct. 1940; *s* of George and Doris Ockendon; *m* 1967, Hilary Mason; one *d.* *Educ:* Dulwich Coll.; St John's Coll., Oxford (MA; DPhil 1965). Lecturer: Christ Church, Oxford, 1963–65; in Applicable Maths, Univ. of Oxford, 1975–2008. Adv. Prof., Fudan Univ., Shanghai, 1999. Chair, Scientific Cttee, Smith Inst. Knowledge Trng Network, 2006–. Gold Medal, IMA, 2006. *Publications:* (with C. Elliott) Free Boundary Problems, 1981; (with H. Ockendon) Viscous Flow, 1997; (jtly) Applied Partial Differential Equations, 1999; (with H. Ockendon) Waves and Compressible Flow, 2003; (jtly) Applied Solid Mechanics, 2008. *Recreations:* mathematical modelling, bird watching, Hornby-Dublo, old sports cars. *Address:* St Catherine's College, Oxford OX1 3UJ. *T:* (01865) 270513.

O'CONNELL, Sir Bernard, Kt 2004; management consultant, since 2004; Principal and Chief Executive Officer, Runshaw College, Lancashire, 1984–2004; *b* 16 April 1945; *s* of Richard and Brigid O'Connell; *m* 1966, Jane; one *s* one *d.* *Educ:* London Univ. (BSc Econ.); Liverpool Univ. (MA, MEd); Manchester Univ. (Teacher's Cert.). Millbank Coll. of Commerce, 1968–79; Vice-Principal, Old Swan Tech. Coll., 1979–84. *Publications:* Creating an Outstanding College, 2005; college manuals. *Recreations:* watching Liverpool FC, travel, reading. *Address:* 28 Magazine Brow, Wallasey, Merseyside CH45 1HP. *T:* (0151) 639 1556; *e-mail:* o'connellbernard@yahoo.co.uk.

O'CONNELL, Desmond Henry, Jr; Group Managing Director, BOC Group, 1986–90; *b* 22 Feb. 1936; *s* of Desmond H. and Rosemary O'Connell; *m* 1964, Roberta M. Jaeger; two *s* one *d.* *Educ:* University of Notre Dame, Indiana; Harvard Business School. BS Elec. Eng., MBA. McKinsey & Co., Chicago, 1962–69; Walsh, Killian & Co., 1969–70; Baxter Travenol Labs, Deerfield, 1970–80; Airco, Montvale, NJ, 1980–86. Non-exec. Dir, Lucas Industries, 1988. *Recreations:* golf, ski-ing. *Address:* 971 Lagoon Lane South, Mantoloking, NJ 08738, USA. *Clubs:* East India; Leander; Indian Hill Country (Winnetka, Ill); Ridgewood Country (Ridgewood, NJ); Harvard (New York); Bay Head Yacht (Bay Head, NJ).

O'CONNELL, Enda; *see* O'Connell, P. E.

O'CONNELL, Sir Maurice (James Donagh MacCarthy), 7th Bt *cr* 1869, of Lakeview, Killarney and Ballybeggan, Tralee; *b* 10 June 1958; *s* of Sir Morgan Donal Conail O'Connell, 6th Bt and of Elizabeth, *o d* of late Major John MacCarthy O'Leary; *S* father, 1989; *m* 1993, Francesca, *d* of late Clive Raleigh; one *s.* *Heir:* *s* Morgan Daniel Clive MacCarthy O'Connell, *b* 17 Nov. 2003. *Address:* Lakeview House, Killarney, Co. Kerry, Ireland.

O'CONNELL, Prof. (Patrick) Enda, PhD; CEng, FREng; FICE; Professor of Water Resources Engineering, and Director of Water Resource Systems Research Laboratory, School of Civil Engineering and Geosciences, since 1984, Director of Earth Systems Engineering, since 2003, University of Newcastle upon Tyne; *b* 3 April 1945; *s* of Patrick and Cecilia O'Connell; *m* 1974, Jane Rosemary; one *s* two *d.* *Educ:* University Coll., Galway (BEng 1st Cl. Hons (Civil)); Imperial Coll., London (DIC; PhD). Asst Lectr, 1968–69, Lectr, 1969–76, Dept of Civil Engrg, Imperial Coll., London; Section/Div. Hd, NERC Inst. of Hydrol., 1976–84. FREng 2005. *Publications:* contrib. internat. jls incl. Jl Hydrol., Hydrological Processes, Hydrological Scis, Hydrol., Earth Systems Scis, Sci. of the Total Envmt, Water Resources Mgt, Water Resources Res. *Recreations:* walking in the Yorkshire Dales, ski-ing, salmon angling in the West of Ireland, enjoying the food and wines of Tuscany. *Address:* School of Civil Engineering and Geosciences, University of Newcastle upon Tyne, Newcastle upon Tyne NE1 7RU. *T:* (0191) 222 6405, *Fax:* (0191) 222 6669; *e-mail:* p.e.oconnell@ncl.ac.uk.

O'CONNELL, Stephen; Member (C) Croydon and Sutton, London Assembly, Greater London Authority, since 2008; *b* Dulwich, 9 Sept. 1956; *s* of Ronald John and Phyllis Jean O'Connell; *m* 1999, Michele Cook; two *s.* *Educ:* Brockley Co. Grammar Sch. CeMAP 2000; CeFA 2001. Barclays Bank, 1976–2005. Mem. (C) Croydon Council, 2002– (Cabinet Mem., Safety and Cohesion, 2006; Dep. Leader, 2006–08). Mem., Metropolitan Police Authy, 2008– (Chm., Finance Cttee, 2008–). *Recreations:* dog walking, real ale, political literature, Crystal Palace Football Club. *Address:* Greater London Authority, City Hall, The Queen's Walk, SE1 2AA. *T:* (020) 7983 4405, *Fax:* (020) 7983 4419; *e-mail:* Steve.O'Connell@london.gov.uk.

O'CONNOR, Rev. Canon (Brian) Michael (McDougal); Dean of Auckland, New Zealand, 1997–2000; *b* 20 June 1942; *s* of Brian McDougal O'Connor and Beryl O'Connor; *m* 1968, Alison Margaret Tibbutt (marr. diss. 2004); two *s.* *Educ:* Lancing Coll.; St Catharine's Coll., Cambridge (BA, MA); Cuddesdon Coll., Oxford. Admitted Solicitor, 1964; Asst Curate, St Andrew, Headington, 1969–72; Sec., Oxford Dio. Pastoral Cttee, 1972–79; Vicar, Rainham, Kent, 1979–97; Rural Dean of Gillingham, 1981–88; Priest-in-charge, Little Missenden, 2002–04. Hon. Canon: of Rochester Cathedral, 1988–97; of Auckland Cathedral, 2000–. Church Comr, 1995–97. Member: General Synod, 1975–90 (Mem., Standing Cttee, 1985–90); Crown Appointments Commn, 1987–90; ACC, 1988–92. Deleg., WCC Assembly, Canberra, 1991. Commissary for Bishop: of Auckland, NZ, 1996–97; of Newcastle, NSW, 1996–. Exec. Officer, Ecclesiastical Law Soc., 2001–07. *Address:* 1 Steadys Lane, Stanton Harcourt, Witney, Oxon OX29 5RL. *T:* (01865) 882776; *e-mail:* canonmichaeloc@aol.com.

O'CONNOR, His Eminence Cardinal Cormac M.; *see* Murphy-O'Connor.

O'CONNOR, Prof. Daniel John; Professor of Philosophy, University of Exeter, 1957–79, now Emeritus; *b* 2 April 1914; *m* 1st, 1948, Kathleen Kemsley (*d* 2000); no *c*; 2nd, 2003, Maureen Castle. *Educ:* Birkbeck Coll., University of London. Entered Civil Service, 1933; Commonwealth Fund Fellow in Philosophy, University of Chicago, 1946–47; Professor of Philosophy, University of Natal, SA, 1949–51; Professor of Philosophy, University of the Witwatersrand, Johannesburg, 1951–52; Lecturer in Philosophy, Univ. Coll. of North Staffordshire, 1952–54; Professor of Philosophy, University of Liverpool, 1954–57. Visiting Professor, University of Pennsylvania, 1961–62. *Publications:* John Locke, 1952; Introduction to Symbolic Logic (with A. H. Basson), 1953; Introduction to the Philosophy of Education, 1957; A Critical History of Western Philosophy (ed), 1964; Aquinas and Natural Law, 1968; Free Will, 1971; (ed jtly) New Essays in the Philosophy of Education, 1973; The Correspondence Theory of Truth, 1975; various papers in philosophical journals. *Address:* 101a Pennsylvania Road, Exeter EX4 6DT.

O'CONNOR, Hon. Deirdre Frances; Judge, Federal Court of Australia, 1990–2002; President, Administrative Appeals Tribunal, 1990–94 and 1999–2002; *b* 5 Feb. 1941; *d* of D. A. Buff; *m* 1974, Michael John Joseph, SC; five *s.* *Educ:* Bethlehem Coll., Ashfield; Sydney Univ. (BA; LLB 1st Cl. Hons); DipEd New England. Lectr in Law, Univ. of NSW, 1974–75; Sen. Lectr in Law, Macquarie Univ., 1975–78; part-time Lectr on media and law, Aust. Film and TV Sch., 1975–80; admitted NSW Bar, 1980; Comr, NSW Law Reform Commn, 1983–85; Chm., Aust. Broadcasting Tribunal, 1986–90. President: Nat. Native Title Tribunal, 1993–94; Aust. Industrial Relns Commn, 1994–97. Mediator, NSW Workers Compensation Commn, 2002–; Judicial Mem., NSW Parole Bd, 2003– (Alternate Chm.). Mem., Aust. Inst. Judicial Admin, 1992–. Trustee, Internat. Inst. of Communications, 1989–92. Member, Council: Order of Australia, 1990–96; Univ. of Canberra, 1992–95. *Recreations:* reading, antiques.

O'CONNOR, Denis Francis, CBE 2002; QPM 1996; HM Inspector of Constabulary, since 2004; *b* 21 May 1949; *m* 1972, Louise (*née* Harvey); one *s* two *d.* *Educ:* Le Sante Union Coll.; Southampton Univ. (BEd Hons 1974); Cranfield Inst. of Tech. (MSc 1985). Chief Supt, Notting Hill, 1990; Asst Chief Constable, Surrey Police, 1991; Dep. Chief Constable, Kent Constabulary, 1993; Asst Comr, SW Area, later S London, Metropolitan Police, 1997–2000; Chief Constable, Surrey Police, 2000–04. Former Member: Criminal Justice Wkg Gp, Adv. Council on Misuse of Drugs; DoH Task Force on Effectiveness of Drugs Services; Mem., Indep. Inquiry into the Misuse of Drugs Act 1971, 1997–2000. Vice-Pres., ACPO, 2002–04. *Publications:* Developing a Partnership Approach for Drugs Education, 1992; Management by Objectives on Trial, 1992; Community Policing: are good intentions enough?, 1994; Increasing Community Safety from Drug Related Crime, 1995; Criminal Justice: what works?, 1995; Drugs: partnerships for policy, prevention and education, 1998; article in Criminal Justice Jl. *Recreations:* reading, running, gardening. *Address:* HM Inspectorate of Constabulary, National Agencies and Police Forces, Allington Towers, 19 Allington Street, SW1E 5EB. *T:* (020) 7035 5713.

O'CONNOR, Desmond Bernard, (Des), CBE 2008; entertainer and singer; *b* 12 Jan. 1932; *m* 1st, Phyllis; one *d*; 2nd, Gillian Vaughan; two *d*; 3rd, Jay; one *d*; 4th, Jodie Brooke Wilson; one *s.* Served RAF. Former Butlin's Red Coat, Filey; professional début, Palace Theatre, Newcastle upon Tyne, 1953; one-man shows, UK, Canada and Australia, 1980–; Royal Variety Show appearances, incl. compère, 1997. *Television includes:* Spot the Tune, 1958; Sunday Night at the London Palladium; Kraft Music Hall Presents: The Des O'Connor Show, 1970–71; Take Your Pick, 1992, 1994, 1996; Pot of Gold, 1993, 1995; Countdown, 2007–08; own shows: Des O'Connor Tonight, 1977–2003; The Des O'Connor Show; Des O'Connor Now, 1985; Fame in the Family, 2000–; Today with Des and Mel, 2002–06. Has made over 1,000 appearances at the London Palladium. No 1 single, I Pretend, 1968. Male TV Personality, TV Times, annually 1969–73; Lifetime Achievement Award, Nat. TV Awards, 2001. *Publication:* Bananas Can't Fly (autobiog.), 2001. *Address:* c/o Lake-Smith Griffin Associates, 418 Strand, WC2R 0PT; *e-mail:* info@lakesmithgriffin.co.uk.

O'CONNOR, Gillian Rose; mining correspondent, Financial Times, 1999–2001; *b* 11 Aug. 1941; *d* of Thomas McDougall O'Connor and Kathleen Joan O'Connor (*née* Parnell). *Educ:* Sutton High School for Girls; St Hilda's College, Oxford. Editor, Investors Chronicle, 1982–94; Personal Finance Ed., FT, 1994–98. *Publication:* A Guide to Stockpicking, 1996. *Address:* Phlox Cottage, Wroxton Lane, Horley, Banbury OX15 6BB.

O'CONNOR, Rev. Canon Michael; *see* O'Connor, Rev. Canon B. M. McD.

O'CONNOR, Patrick Michael Joseph; QC 1993; *b* 7 Aug. 1949; *s* of Denis Bellew O'Connor and Ingelore Biegel; *m* 1986, Gillian Denise Brasse; two *d.* *Educ:* St Francis Xavier's Grammar Sch., Liverpool; UCL (LLB Hons). Called to the Bar, Inner Temple, 1970. *Publications:* articles in Criminal Law Review and other academic and professional jls. *Address:* Doughty Street Chambers, 10–11 Doughty Street, WC1N 2PL. *T:* (020) 7404 1313.

O'CONNOR, Ronald; Executive Director (Education, Training and Young People), Glasgow City Council, since 2004; *b* 1 Dec. 1950; *s* of John O'Connor and Mary O'Connor (*née* McDermott); *m* 1992, Marie Harvey Milne; one *s.* *Educ:* Stirling Univ. (BA (Hons), Dip Ed). Teacher, modern langs, Belmont Acad., Ayr, 1977–81; Principal Teacher, modern langs, 1981–83, Asst Head, 1983–88, Garnock Acad.; Educn Officer, 1988–93, Asst Dir of Educn, 1993–95, Strathclyde Regl Council; Glasgow City Council:

Sen. Depute Dir of Educn, 1995–99; Dir of Social Work Services, 1999–2002; Dir of Educn Services, 2002–04. *Recreations:* golf, football, reading. *Address:* Wheatley House, 25 Cochrane Street, Glasgow G1 1HL. *T:* (0141) 287 4551.

O'CONNOR, Rory, CBE 1991; Member, Gibraltar Court of Appeal, 1991–97; Judge of the High Court of Hong Kong, 1977–90; *b* Co. Down, 26 Nov. 1925; *s* of late James O'Connor and Mary (*née* Savage); *m* 1963, Elizabeth, *d* of late Frederick Dew; one *s* two *d. Educ:* Blackrock Coll., Dublin; Univ. Coll., Dublin (BCom). Called to Irish Bar, King's Inns, 1949. Resident Magistrate, Kenya, 1956–62; Hong Kong: Magistrate, 1962–70; District Judge, 1970–77. *Address:* 12 Windermere Crescent, Bangor, Co. Down, N Ireland BT20 4QH.

O'CONNOR, Sandra Day; Associate Justice of the Supreme Court of the United States, 1981–2006; retired; *b* 26 March 1930; *d* of Harry and Ada Mae Day; *m* 1952, John Jay O'Connor III; three *s. Educ:* Stanford Univ. (BA 1950; LLB 1952). Legal appts in Calif and Frankfurt, 1952–57; in private practice, 1959–60; Asst Attorney-Gen., Arizona, 1965–69; Judge: Maricopa County Superior Ct, 1975–79; Arizona Ct of Appeals, 1979–81. Mem. Senate, Arizona, 1969–75 (majority leader, 1972–75). Director: Nat. Bank of Arizona, Phoenix, 1971–74; Blue Cross/Blue Shield, Arizona, 1975–79. American Bar Association: Member: Exec. Bd, Central Eur. and Eurasian Law Initiative, 1990–; Exec. Cttee, Mus. of Law, 2000–; Adv. Commn, Standing Cttee on Law Library of Congress, 2002–; Commn on Civic Educn and Separation of Powers, 2005–; Mem., Adv. Cttee, Judicial, Amer. Soc. of Internat. Law, 2001–; Hon. Mem., Adv. Cttee for Judiciary Leadership Develt Council. Chm., Maricopa County Juvenile Detention Home, 1963–64; Pres., Heard Museum, Phoenix, 1968–74, 1976–81; Member: Nat. Bd, Smithsonian Assocs, 1981; Selection Cttee, Oklahoma City Nat. Meml and Mus., 2005–; Adv. Bd, Stanford Center on Ethics, 2005–; Adv. Bd, Smithsonian Nat. Mus. of Natural History, 2006–; Bd of Trustees, Rockefeller Foundn, 2006–; Co-Chm., Nat. Adv. Council, Campaign for Civic Mission of Schs, 2005–. Trustee, Stanford Univ., 1976–81; Chancellor, Coll. of William and Mary, 2005–. Hon. Bencher, Gray's Inn, 1982.

O'CONNOR HOWE, Mrs Josephine Mary; HM Diplomatic Service, retired; *b* 25 March 1924; *d* of late Gerald Frank Claridge and late Dulcie Agnes Claridge (*née* Waldegrave); *m* 1947, John O'Connor Howe (decd); one *d. Educ:* Wychwood Sch., Oxford; Triangle Coll. (course in journalism). Inter-Allied Information Cttee, later, United Nations Information Office, 1942–45; Foreign Office: The Hague, 1945–46; Internat. News Service and freelance, 1946–50; FO, 1952; Counsellor, FCO, 1974–1979. Reader's Digest, 1979–83; Dir, Council for Arms Control, 1983–84; Exec. Editor, Inst. for the Study of Conflict, 1985–89; Freelance Editor specialising in internat. affairs, arms control, etc., 1985–. *Publication:* (ed) Armed Peace—the search for world security, 1984. *Recreations:* theatre, gardening, grandchildren. *Address:* 56 High Street, Charing, Kent TN27 0LS. *T:* (01233) 714762.

ODDIE, Bill; *see* Oddie, W. E.

ODDIE, His Honour Christopher Ripley; a Circuit Judge, 1974–94, sitting at Mayor's and City of London Court, 1989–94; *b* Derby, 24 Feb. 1929; *o s* of Dr and Mrs J. R. Oddie, Uttoxeter, Staffs; *m* 1957, Margaret Anne, *d* of Mr and Mrs J. W. Timmis; one *s* three *d. Educ:* Giggleswick Sch.; Oriel Coll., Oxford (MA). Called to Bar, Middle Temple, 1954, Oxford Circuit. Contested (L) Ludlow, Gen. Election, 1970. A Recorder of the Crown Court, 1972–74. Chm., County Court Rule Cttee, 1985–87 (Mem., 1981–87). Member: Judicial Studies Bd, 1989–91; Cttee, Council of Her Majesty's Circuit Judges, 1989–91. Mem. Council, St Mary's Hosp. Med. Sch., 1980–88. Gen. Editor, Butterworth's County Court Precedents and Pleadings, 1988–92. *Recreations:* reading, opera, walking. *Address:* 89 The Vineyard, Richmond, Surrey TW10 6AT. *T:* (020) 8940 4135.

ODDIE, Prof. Guy Barrie; Robert Adam Professor of Architecture, 1968–82, now Emeritus, and Head of Department of Architecture, 1968–80, University of Edinburgh; *b* 1 Jan. 1922; *o s* of Edward Oddie and Eleanor Pinkney; *m* 1952, Mabel Mary Smith (*d* 1990); two step *d. Educ:* state schools in London and Co. Durham; King's Coll., Univ. of Durham (later Univ. of Newcastle upon Tyne) (BArch Dunelm). Local Defence Volunteer, later Home Guard, 1939–45; commnd Univ. OTC. Demonstrator, Univ. of Newcastle upon Tyne, 1944–45; Asst, public offices, Glasgow and Coventry, 1945–47; Research Architect, Building Res. Stn, 1947–50; Sen. Lectr, Birmingham Sch. of Architecture, 1950–52; Develt Gp, Min. of Educn, 1952–58; Staff architect, UGC, 1958–63 (designed innovative hall of residence, Reading Univ.); Consultant to OECD, 1963–66; Dir, Laboratories Investigation Unit, DES, 1966–68. Sen. Res. Advr to OECD Prog. on Educnl Bldg, 1972–84. Participant in and advocate for 1950's architectural movement led by school-designers and aimed at producing quality buildings on time, in the number needed and at a politically acceptable cost; involved in campus develt for new univs recommended by Robbins report, 1963. *Publications:* School Building Resources and their Effective Use, 1966; Development and Economy in Educational Building, 1968; Industrialised Building for Schools, 1975; contrib. Architects Jl, Architectural Rev., RIBA Jl. *Recreations:* slamming political correctness, writing light verse while anticipating publication of my memoirs in 2009, yet still revelling in the company of friends. *Address:* 29 The Causeway, Edinburgh EH15 3QA.

ODDIE, William Edgar, (Bill), OBE 2003; writer, actor and broadcaster; *b* 7 July 1941; *m* 1st, Jean Hart (marr. diss.); two *d*; 2nd, Laura Beaumont; one *d. Educ:* Halesowen Grammar Sch.; King Edward's Sch., Birmingham; Pembroke Coll., Cambridge (BA 1963; MA 1967). Mem. Council, RSPB. *Theatre* includes: writer and performer, Cambridge Circus (revue), Cambridge Footlights, transf. London, then NZ and Australia; performer: Tommy; Mikado, Coliseum, 1988; The Ghost Train, Lyric, Hammersmith, 1992; *television* includes: joint writer: Doctor in the House; Doctor at Large; Astronauts; writer and actor: TW3; BBC3; The Goodies (eight series), 1970–81; presenter: Ask Oddie; Who Do You Think You Are? (one prog. of series), 2004; The Truth About Killer Dinosaurs, 2005; wildlife programmes incl. Birding With Bill Oddie (three series); Bill Oddie Goes Wild; Britain Goes Wild; Springwatch (series), 2005, 2006 and 2007; Autumnwatch, 2006; Bill Oddie: Back in the USA, 2007; Bill Oddie's Wild Side (series), 2008; *radio* includes: jt writer, I'm Sorry I'll Read That Again; presenter, Breakaway. *Publications:* Little Black Bird Book, 1982; Gone Birding, 1983; (jtly) Big Bird Race, 1983; (jtly) The Toilet Book, 1986; Bird Watching With Bill Oddie, 1988; Bird Watching for Under Tens; Bill Oddie's Colouring Guides, 1991–92; Follow That Bird!, 1994; (jtly) Bird in the Nest, 1995; (jtly) Birding With Bill Oddie, 1997; Bill Oddie's Gripping Yarns: tales of birds & birding, 2000; One Flew into the Cuckoo's Egg, 2008; articles in jls. *Address:* c/o All Electric Productions, PO Box 1805, Andover, Hants SP10 3ZN. *T:* (01264) 771726; *e-mail:* info@allelectricproductions.co.uk.

ODDIE, Dr William John Muir; Editor, Catholic Herald, 1998–2004; *b* 1 June 1939; *s* of John Male and Irene Oddie; *m* 1969, Cornelia; one *s* two *d. Educ:* Silcoates Sch., Yorks; Trinity Coll., Dublin (BA 1964; MA 1980); Leicester Univ. (PhD 1970); St Stephen's House, Oxford (MA Oxon 1981). Sec., Ancient Monuments Soc., 1970–72; ordained deacon, 1977, priest 1978; Asst Curate, Holy Trinity, Westbury on Trym, Bristol, 1978–80; Bp's Chaplain to Graduates, Oxford Univ., 1980–85; Librarian, Pusey House, Oxford, 1980–85; Fellow, St Cross Coll., Oxford, 1981–85; Rector, St Andrew's, Romford, 1985–87; received into RC Church, 1991; freelance journalist, Sunday Telegraph, Daily Telegraph, Daily Mail, Sunday Times, etc, 1987–98. Chm., G. K. Chesterton Soc., 2008–. *Publications:* Dickens and Carlyle: the question of influence, 1972; After the Deluge: essays towards the desecularisation of the Church, 1987; What will Happen to God? feminism and the reconstruction of Christian belief, 1989; The Crockford's File: Gareth Bennett and the death of the Anglican mind, 1989; The Roman Option: crisis and the realignment of English-speaking Christianity, 1996; John Paul the Great: maker of the post-conciliar Church, 2003; Chesterton and the Romance of Orthodoxy: the making of GKG, 1874–1908, 2008. *Recreations:* reading, music, travel, domestic pursuits. *Address:* 6 Sunningwell Road, Oxford OX1 4SX. *T:* (01865) 439473.

ODDSSON, Hon. Davíd, Hon. KBE 1990; Chairman, Board of Governors, Central Bank of Iceland, since 2005; *b* 17 Jan. 1948; *s* of Oddur Ólafsson and Ingibjörg Kristín Lúdvíksdóttir; *m* 1970, Ástrídur Thorarensen; one *s. Educ:* Univ. of Iceland (grad. Lawyer). Reykjavík Theatre Co., 1970–72; Morgunbladid Daily, 1973–74; Almenna Bókafélagid Publishing House, 1975–76; Office Manager, 1976–78, Man. Dir. 1978–82, Reykjavík Health Fund; Mayor of Reykjavík, 1982–91; MP (Ind) Reykjavik, 1991–2005; Prime Minister of Iceland, 1991–2004; Foreign Minister, 2004–05. Leader, Independent Party, 1991–2005. Hon. LLD Manitoba, 2000. Grand Cross, Order of Merit (Luxembourg). *Publications:* (trans.) Estonia: a study of imperialism, by Anders Küng, 1973; Róbert Elíasson Returns from Abroad (TV drama), 1977; A Policy of Independence, 1981; Stains on the White Collar (TV drama), 1981; Everything's Fine (TV drama), 1991; A Couple of Days without Gudny (short stories), 1997; Stolen from the Author of the Alphabet (short stories), 2002. *Recreations:* bridge, forestry, angling. *Address:* Central Bank of Iceland, Kalkofnsvegi 1, 150 Reykjavík, Iceland.

ODDY, Andrew; *see* Oddy, W. A.

ODDY, Christine Margaret; consultant; Lecturer (part-time): in European Union and International Political Economy, Warwick University Open Studies, since 2000; in Financial Studies, London Metropolitan (formerly London Guildhall) University, since 2000; *b* 20 Sept. 1955; *d* of Eric Lawson Oddy and Audrey Mary Oddy. *Educ:* Stoke Park Sch., Coventry; University Coll. London (LLB Hons); Licence Spéciale en droit européen, Inst. d'Etudes européennes, Brussels; Birkbeck Coll., London (MSc (Econ)). Stagiaire (grad. trainee) in EC, 1979–80; Articled Clerk, Clifford Turner, 1980–82; admitted Solicitor, 1982; Lectr in Law, City of London Poly., 1984–89. MEP (Lab) Midlands Central, 1989–94, Coventry and N Warwicks, 1994–99; European Parliament: Member: Legal Affairs Cttee, 1989–99; Social Affairs Cttee, 1989–99; Women's Rights Cttee, 1989–99; Central America Delegn, 1989. Sec., Anti-Racism Wkg Gp, 1989–99, and Treas., Eur. Parly Labour Pty, 1994–99. Contested (Ind.) Coventry NW, 2001. Non-executive Director: Coventry Univ., 2002–; Coventry Refugee Centre, 2002–. Law Soc. rep., Home Office Adv. Gp on Rehabilitation of Offenders Act, 2001–02. Member: RIIA, 1990; Law Soc., 1982 (Mem., Employment Law Cttee); ESU, 1987; Inst. for Employment Rights. Co-Chair, S Asia Assoc. for Regl Co-operation, 1998 (Chair, Saving Sight in S Asia, 1998). Vice Patron, Vocaleyes, 2003–. FRSA 1992. *Recreations:* travel, wine, theatre, cinema. *Address:* 33 Longfellow Road, Coventry CV2 5HD. *T:* (024) 7645 6856.

ODDY, Revel, FSA; Keeper, Department of Art and Archaeology, Royal Scottish Museum, Edinburgh, 1974–83; *b* 11 April 1922; *s* of Sidney Oddy and Muriel Barnfather; *m* 1949, Ariadne Margaret, *d* of late Sir Andrew Gourlay Clow, KCSI, CIE; two *s* two *d. Educ:* Worksop Coll.; Pembroke Coll., Cambridge (MA). FSA 1982. Served War, Loyal Regt and King's African Rifles, 1941–46. Mod. langs master, Dr Challoner's Grammar Sch., Amersham, 1949; Res. Asst, V&A Mus., London, 1950–55; Asst Keeper, Royal Scottish Mus., Edinburgh, 1955–74. *Recreations:* mild gardening, reading. *Address:* 44 Findhorn Place, Edinburgh EH9 2NT. *T:* (0131) 667 5815. *Club:* Civil Service.

ODDY, (William) Andrew, OBE 2002; DSc; FSA; Keeper of Conservation, British Museum, 1985–2002; *b* 6 Jan. 1942; *s* of late William T. Oddy and Hilda F. Oddy (*née* Dalby); *m* 1965, Patricia Anne Whitaker; one *s* one *d. Educ:* Bradford Grammar Sch.; New Coll., Oxford (BA 1964; BSc 1965; MA 1969; DSc 1994). FSA 1973; FIIC 1974. Joined British Museum Research Lab., 1966, research into conservation and ancient technology; Head of Conservation, 1981. Member: Scientific Cttee, Internat. Congress on Deterioration and Preservation of Stone, 1976–91; Dept of Transport Adv. Cttee on Historic Wrecks, 1981–91; Council, Textile Conservation Centre, 1985–99; Cons. Cttee, Council for Care of Churches, 1985–90; Cons. Cttee, Cons. Unit, Mus. and Gall. Commn, 1987–92; Science-based Archaeol. Cttee, SERC, 1990–93; Council, Internat. Inst. for Conservation of Historic and Artistic Works, 1990–96 (Pres., 2001–07); Fabric Adv. Cttee, Cathedral and Abbey Church of St Alban, 1991–. Member: Council, RNS, 1975–78 and 2007–; Res. Cttee, Soc. of Antiquaries of London, 2001–05. Trustee: Anna Plowden Trust, 1998–2006; Gabo Trust, 2002–. Hon. Res. Fellow, UCL, 1992–2001. Lectures: Chester Beatty, RSA, 1982; Leventritt, Harvard Univ. Art Mus., 1996; Forbes Prize, Internat. Inst. for Conservation, 1996. Freeman, Goldsmiths' Co., 1986. *Publications:* editor: Problems in the Conservation of Waterlogged Wood, 1975; Aspects of Early Metallurgy, 1980; Scientific Studies in Numismatics, 1980; Metallurgy in Numismatics II, 1988; The Art of the Conservator, 1992; Restoration: is it acceptable?, 1994; joint editor: Conservation in Museums and Galleries, 1975; Metallurgy in Numismatics I, 1980; Aspects of Tibetan Metallurgy, 1981; A Survey of Numismatic Research 1978–1984, 1986; Metallurgy in Numismatics IV, 1998; Reversibility: does it exist?, 1999; Past Practice - Future Prospects, 2001; (jtly) Romanesque Metalwork: copper alloys and their decoration, 1986; papers in learned jls. *Recreation:* travel. *Address:* 6 Ashlyns Road, Berkhamsted, Herts HP4 3BN.

O'DEA, Sir Patrick Jerad, KCVO 1974; retired public servant, New Zealand; Extra Gentleman Usher to the Queen, since 1981; *b* 18 April 1918; 2nd *s* of late Patrick O'Dea; *m* 1945, Jean Mary, *d* of Hugh Mulholland; one *s* three *d. Educ:* St Paul's Coll. and Univ. of Otago, Dunedin, NZ; Victoria Univ., Wellington, NZ. Joined NZ Public Service, 1936; served in Agriculture Dept, 1936–47. Served War in Royal New Zealand Artillery of 2 NZEF, 1941–45. With Industries and Commerce Dept, 1947–49; subseq. served with Dept of Internal Affairs in various posts interrupted by 2 years' full-time study at Victoria Univ. of Wellington (DPA). Group Exec. Officer, Local Govt, 1959–64; Dep. Sec., 1964–67; Sec. for Internal Affairs, NZ, 1967–78; formerly Sec. for: Local Govt; Civil Defence; Sec. of Recreation and Sport; Clerk of the Writs; NZ Sec. to the Queen, 1969–78, reapptd 1981, for visit of Queen and Duke of Edinburgh to NZ. Nat. Co-ordinator and Chm., Duke of Edinburgh Award in NZ, 1975–90; Chm., Duke of Edinburgh NZ Foundn, 1988–92; Mem., Vicentian Foundn. *Publications:* several papers on local govt in New Zealand. *Recreations:* gardening, golf, bowls. *Address:* 8 Cranbrook Grove, Waikanae, Kapiti Coast, New Zealand. *T:* (4) 2931235. *Club:* Waikanae Golf.

O'DELL, Mrs June Patricia, OBE 1990; Chair, Probus Women's Housing Society Ltd, 1998–2006 (Member Board, since 1993); *b* 9 June 1929; *d* of Leonard Vickery, RN and Myra Vickery; *m* 1951 (marr. diss. 1963); one *s* two *d*. *Educ:* Edgehill Girls College; Plymouth Technical College. Estate Agent; Sen. Partner, Chesney's, Estate Agents, 1965–88; Dir, Eachdale Developments Ltd, 1988–98. Nat. Pres., Fedn of Business and Professional Women, 1983–85; Chm., Employment Cttee, Internat. Fedn of Business Professional Women, 1983–87; Dep. Chm., EOC, 1986–90; Member: Women's Nat. Commn, 1983–85; European Adv. Cttee for Equal Treatment between Women and Men, 1986–90; Authorised Conveyancing Practitioners Bd, 1991–95; Legal Aid Adv. Cttee, 1993–94. Non-exec. Dir, Aylesbury Vale Community Healthcare NHS Trust, 1991–98. Gov., Sir William Ramsay Sch., 2002–05. FRSA 1986 (Mem. Council, 1992–97). *Recreations:* music, particularly opera and choral; writing, literature, the countryside, equestrian events. *Address:* Gable End, High Street, Great Missenden, Bucks HP16 9AA.

ODELL, Prof. Peter Randon; Professor Emeritus, Erasmus University, Rotterdam (Director, Centre for International Energy Studies, 1981–91); *b* 1 July 1930; *s* of late Frank James Odell and late Grace Edna Odell; *m* 1957, Jean Mary McKintosh; two *s* two *d*. *Educ:* County Grammar Sch., Coalville; Univ. of Birmingham (BA, PhD); Fletcher Sch. of Law and Diplomacy, Cambridge, Mass (AM). FInstPet 1973. RAF 1954–57. Economist, Shell International Petroleum Co., 1958–61; Lectr, LSE, 1961–65; Sen. Lectr, LSE, 1965–68; Prof. of Economic Geography, Erasmus Univ., 1968–81. Visiting Professor: LSE, 1983–2001; College of Europe, Bruges, 1983–90; Plymouth Univ., 1996–2003; Scholar in Residence, Rockefeller Centre, Bellagio, 1984; Killam Vis. Scholar, Univ. of Calgary, 1989; Vis. Scholar, Univ. of Cambridge, 1996–99. Stamp Meml Lectr, London Univ., 1975. Canadian Council Fellow, 1978. Adviser, Dept of Energy, 1977–79; Special Advr, Trade and Industry Select Cttee, H of C, 2001–02. Contested (Lib Dem) Suffolk, EP elecns, 1989. European Editor, Energy Jl, 1988–90. FRSA 1983; FRGS 1995; FEI 2003. Internat. Assoc. for Energy Econs Prize, for outstanding contribns to energy econs and its literature, 1991; RSGS Centenary Medal, 1993; OPEC Lifetime Achievement Award for outstanding contrib. to petroleum industry, 2006. *Publications:* An Economic Geography of Oil, 1963; Natural Gas in Western Europe, 1969; Oil and World Power, 1970, 8th edn 1986; (with D. A. Preston) Economies and Societies in Latin America, 1973, 2nd edn 1978; Energy: Needs and Resources, 1974, 2nd edn 1977; (with K. E. Rosing) The North Sea Oil Province, 1975; The West European Energy Economy: the case for self-sufficiency, 1976; (with K. E. Rosing) The Optimal Development of the North Sea Oilfields, 1976; (with L. Vallenilla) The Pressures of Oil: a strategy for economic revival, 1978; British Oil Policy: a Radical Alternative, 1980; (with K. E. Rosing) The Future of Oil, 1980–2080, 1980, 2nd edn 1983; (ed with J. Rees) The International Oil Industry: an interdisciplinary perspective, 1986; Global and Regional Energy Supplies: recent fictions and fallacies revisited, 1991; Europe's Energy: resources and choices, 1998; Fossil Fuel Resources in the 21st Century, 1999; Oil and Gas: crises and controversies 1961–2000, Vol. 1, Global Issues, 2001, Vol. 2, Europe's Entanglement, 2002; Why Carbon Fuels will Dominate the 21st Century's Global Energy Economy, 2004; A New World Energy Order, 2007. *Address:* 7 Constitution Hill, Ipswich IP1 3RG. *T:* (01473) 253376; *e-mail:* peterodell2@btinternet.com.

ODELL, Sir Stanley (John), Kt 1986; *b* 20 Nov. 1929; *s* of George Frederick Odell and Florence May Odell; *m* 1952, Eileen Grace Stuart; four *d*. *Educ:* Bedford Modern School. Chairman: Mid Beds Young Conservatives, 1953–59; Mid Beds Cons. Assoc., 1964–69 (Pres., 1991–); Beds Cons. European Constituency Council, 1979; E of England Provincial Council, Cons. Party, 1983–86 (Pres., 1991–93); Nat. Union of Cons. and Unionist Assocs, 1989–90 (Vice Chm., 1986–89); Pres., Bedford & Kempston Cons. Assoc., 2005–. Chairman: S Beds Community Health Care NHS Trust, 1994–99; Beds and Luton Community Health Care NHS Trust, 1999–2001; Mary Seacole Homes for the Homeless in Luton, 1999–. Chm., Anglo-American Cttee, RAF Chicksands, 1987–96. Member of Court: Bedfordshire (formerly Luton) Univ., 1994–; Intelligence Corps, 2002–. Chm., Biggleswade and Dist Young Farmers' Club, 1949–51; Founder Playing Mem., Biggleswade Rugby Club, 1949. Patron: Friends of Chicksands Priory, 1984–; Camphill, Beds, 1998–; John Bunyan Museum, Bedford, 1999–; Churchwarden, Campton Parish Church, 1993–. Hon. Fellow, Luton Univ., 2002. *Recreations:* politics, shooting. *Address:* Woodhall Farm, Campton, Shefford, Beds SG17 5PB. *T:* (01462) 813230. *Club:* Farmers'.

ODGERS, Sir Graeme (David William), Kt 1997; DL; Chairman, Kent Economic Board (formerly Kent and Medway Economic Board), since 2001; *b* 10 March 1934; *s* of late William Arthur Odgers and Elizabeth Minty (*née* Rennie); *m* 1957, Diana Patricia Berge; one *s* two *d* (and one *d* decd). *Educ:* St John's Coll., Johannesburg; Gonville and Caius Coll., Cambridge (Mech. Scis Tripos); Harvard Business Sch. (MBA, Baker Scholar). Investment Officer, Internat. Finance Corp., Washington DC, 1959–62; Management Consultant, Urwick Orr and Partners Ltd, 1962–64; Investment Executive, Hambros Bank Ltd, 1964–65; Director: Keith Shipton and Co. Ltd, 1965–72; C. T. Bowring (Insurance) Holdings Ltd, 1972–74; Chm., Odgers and Co. Ltd (Management Consultants), 1970–74; Dir, Industrial Develt Unit, DoI, 1974–77; Assoc. Dir (Finance), General Electric Co., 1977–78; Gp Finance Dir, 1979–86, Gp Man. Dir, 1983–86, Tarmac; British Telecommunications: pt-time Mem. Bd, 1983–86; Govt Dir, 1984–86; Dep. Chm. and Chief Finance Officer, 1986–87; Gp Man. Dir, 1987–90; Chief Exec., Alfred McAlpine plc, 1990–93; Chm., Monopolies and Mergers Commn, 1993–97. Non-executive Director: Dalgety, 1987–93; Nat. & Provincial Bldg Soc., 1990–93; Scottish and Southern Energy, 1998–2004. Chm., Locate in Kent, 1998–2006; Dep. Chm., Kent Partnership, 2001–. Chm., New Marlowe Th. Develt Trust, 2007–. Mem., Kent Ambassadors, 1998–. DL Kent, 2002. Hon. DLaws Greenwich, 2004; Hon. DCL Kent, 2005. *Recreation:* golf. *Address:* 5 The Coach House, Springwood Park, Tonbridge, Kent TN11 9LZ. *Clubs:* Carlton; Wildernesse (Sevenoaks).

ODITAH, Dr Fidelis Hilary Izuka; QC 2003; Senior Advocate of Nigeria, since 2004; *b* 27 March 1964; *s* of Augustine and Vera Oditah; *m* 1992, Precilla Osondu; two *s* two *d*. *Educ:* Univ. of Lagos (LLB); Magdalen Coll., Oxford (MA, BCL; DPhil 1989). Called to the Bar, Lincoln's Inn, 1992; Fellow and Tutor in Law, Merton Coll., Oxford, and Travers Smith Braithwaite Lectr in Corporate Finance Law, Univ. of Oxford, 1989–97. Vis. Prof., Univ. of Oxford, 2000–. Mem., London Court of Internat. Arbitration, 2004–. *Publications:* Legal Aspects of Receivables Financing, 1991; The Future for the Global Securities Markets, 1996; Insolvency of Banks, 1996; contrib. learned jls. *Recreations:* golf, tennis, table tennis. *Address:* 3–4 South Square, Gray's Inn, WC1R 5HP. *T:* (020) 7696 9900, *Fax:* (020) 7696 9911; *e-mail:* fidelisoditah@southsquare.com.

ODLING-SMEE, John Charles, CMG 2005; Director, European II Department, International Monetary Fund, 1992–2003; *b* 13 April 1943; *s* of late Rev. Charles William Odling-Smee and Katharine Hamilton Odling-Smee (*née* Aitchison); *m* 1996, Carmela Veneroso. *Educ:* Durham School; St John's College, Cambridge (BA 1964); MA Oxon 1966. Junior Research Officer, Dept of Applied Economics, Cambridge, 1964–65; Asst Research Officer, Inst. of Economics and Statistics, Oxford, 1965–66; Fellow in Economics, Oriel College, Oxford, 1966–70; Research Officer, Inst. of Economics and Statistics, Oxford, 1968–71 and 1972–73; Economic Research Officer, Govt of Ghana, 1971–72; Senior Research Officer, Centre for Urban Economics, LSE, 1973–75; Economic Adviser, Central Policy Review Staff, Cabinet Office, 1975–77; Senior Economic Adviser, HM Treasury, 1977–80; Senior Economist, IMF, 1981–82; Under-Sec., HM Treasury, 1982–89; Dep. Chief Economic Advr, HM Treasury, 1989–90; Sen. Advr, IMF, 1990–91. *Publications:* (with A. Grey and N. P. Hepworth) Housing Rents, Costs and Subsidies, 1978, 2nd edn 1981; (with R. C. O. Matthews and C. H. Feinstein) British Economic Growth 1856–1973, 1982; articles in books and learned jls. *Address:* 3506 Garfield Street NW, Washington, DC 20007, USA. *T:* (202) 3383471.

O'DOHERTY, Patrick; Principal, Lumen Christi College, Derry, since 2003 (Vice Principal, 1997–2003); *b* Londonderry, 10 Nov. 1956; *s* of Gerard and Agnes O'Doherty; *m* 1977, Darina; two *d*. *Educ:* St Columb's Coll., Derry; Queen's Univ., Belfast (BEd 1979); Univ. of Ulster (MSc Educn Mgt 1996). Professional Qual. for Headship NI 2001. St Columb's College: Teacher of English, 1979–82; Hd of Latin, 1982–88; Hd of English, 1988–97. *Recreations:* visiting Italy, classical civilizations.

ODONE, Cristina; writer and broadcaster; Deputy Editor, The New Statesman, 1998–2004; *b* 11 Nov. 1960; *d* of Augusto and Ulla Odone; *m* 2005, Edward Lucas; one *d*. *Educ:* Worcester Coll., Oxford (MA). Freelance journalist, 1983–84; journalist: Catholic Herald, 1985–86; The Times diary, 1987; Vice-Pres., Odone Associates, Washington, 1988–92; Editor, The Catholic Herald, 1992–96 (Mem., Bd of Dirs, 2007–); television reviewer, The Daily Telegraph, 1996–98. Member: Adv. Bd, Citizens' Service Scheme, 1995–; Bd of Dirs, Longford Trust, 2003–. FRSA 1996. *Publications:* novels: The Shrine, 1996; A Perfect Wife, 1997; The Dilemmas of Harriet Carew, 2008; non-fiction: In Bad Faith, 2008. *Recreations:* walking, travelling. *Address:* c/o Curtis Brown Ltd, 5th Floor, Haymarket House, 28–29 Haymarket, SW1Y 4SP.

O'DONNELL, Sir Augustine Thomas, (Gus), KCB 2005 (CB 1994); Secretary of the Cabinet and Head of the Home Civil Service, since 2005; *b* 1 Oct. 1952; *s* of Helen O'Donnell (*née* McClean) and James O'Donnell; *m* 1979, Melanie Joan Elizabeth Timmis; one *d*. *Educ:* Univ. of Warwick (BA Hons); Nuffield Coll., Oxford (MPhil). Lectr, Dept of Political Economy, Univ. of Glasgow, 1974–79; Economist, HM Treasury, 1979–85; First Sec. (Econ.), British Embassy, Washington, 1985–88; Sen. Economic Adviser, 1988–89, Press Sec., 1989–90, HM Treasury; Press Sec. to Prime Minister, 1990–94; Under Sec., Monetary Gp, 1994–95, Dep. Dir, Macroeconomic Policy and Prospects Directorate, 1995–96, HM Treasury; Minister (Economic), British Embassy, Washington, and UK Exec. Dir, IMF and World Bank, 1997–98; HM Treasury: Dir, Macroeconomic Policy and Prospects Directorate, 1998–2000; Man. Dir, Macroeconomic Policy and Internat. Finance, 2000–02; Hd of Govt Econ. Service, 1998–2003; Permanent Sec., 2002–05. *Publications:* articles in economic jls. *Recreations:* football, cricket, golf, tennis. *Address:* Cabinet Office, 70 Whitehall, SW1A 2AS. *Club:* Old Salesians FC.

O'DONNELL, Prof. Barry, FRCS, FRCSI; President, Royal College of Surgeons of Ireland, 1998–2000; Professor of Paediatric Surgery, Royal College of Surgeons in Ireland, 1986–93, now Professor Emeritus; Consultant Paediatric Surgeon, Our Lady's Hospital for Sick Children, Dublin, 1957–93; *b* 6 Sept. 1926; *e s* of Michael J. O'Donnell and Kathleen O'Donnell (*née* Barry); *m* 1959, Mary Leydon, BA, BComm, BL, *d* of John Leydon, LLD, KCSG; three *s* one *d*. *Educ:* Christian Brothers College, Cork; Castleknock College, Dublin; University College, Cork (MB Hons 1949). MCh NUI, 1954. FRCS 1953, FRCSI 1953; FRCSEd *ad hominem* 1992; FRCPSGlas *qua surgeon* 1999. Ainsworth Travelling Scholar, Boston (Lahey Clinic and Boston Floating Hosp., 1955–56); Sen. Registrar, Hosp. for Sick Children, London, 1956–57. Vis. Prof. at many US univs, incl. Harvard, Columbia, Johns Hopkins, Michigan, Pennsylvania; Hunterian Prof., RCS, 1986. Jt Pres., British, Canadian and Irish Med. Assocs, 1976–77; President: British Assoc. of Paediatric Surgeons, 1980–82; Surgical Sect., Royal Acad. of Medicine of Ireland, 1990–92; Mem. Council, RCSI, 1972–77 and 1993–96 (Vice Pres., 1996–98); Chm., Jl Cttee, BMA, 1982–88. Director: Standard Chartered Bank, Ireland, 1977–90; West Deutsche Landesbank, 1990–96. Hon. FRCS 2007. Hon. Fellow: Amer. Acad. of Pediatrics, 1974; New England Surgical Assoc., 1996; Amer. Surgical Assoc., 1998; Coll. of Medicine of S Africa, 2001; Hon. FACS 1999; Hon. Mem., Boston Surgical Soc., 2000. People of the Year Award, New Ireland Insce Co., 1984; Denis Browne Gold Medal, British Assoc. of Paediatric Surgeons, 1989; Urology Medal, American Acad. of Pediatrics, 2003; Dist. Alumnus Award, UC, Cork, 2004. *Publications:* Essentials of Paediatric Surgery, 1961, 4th edn 1992; Abdominal Pain in Children, 1985; (ed jtly) Paediatric Urology, 3rd edn 1997; Terence Millin, 2003; Irish Surgeons and Surgery in the Twentieth Century, 2008. *Recreations:* repeating myself, incompetent golf. *Address:* 28 Merlyn Road, Ballsbridge, Dublin 4, Ireland. *T:* and *Fax:* 2694000; *e-mail:* bodonnel@indigo.ie. *Clubs:* Royal Irish Yacht; Portmarnock Golf.

O'DONNELL, Sir Christopher (John), Kt 2003; Chief Executive, Smith & Nephew plc, 1997–2007; *b* 30 Oct. 1946; *s* of Anthony John O'Donnell and Joan Millicent O'Donnell; *m* 1971, Maria Antonia Wallis; three *s* one *d*. *Educ:* Imperial Coll., London (BSc Eng Hons); London Business Sch. (MSc Econ). Man. Dir, Vickers Ltd Medical Engineering, 1974–79; Area Vice Pres., Europe, C. R. Bard, Inc., 1979–88; Man. Dir, Smith & Nephew Medical Ltd, 1988–93; Gp Dir, Smith & Nephew plc, 1993–97. Non-exec. Dir, BOC Gp, 2001–06. *Recreations:* tennis, golf. *Address:* Wetherby, W Yorks.

O'DONNELL, Sir Gus; *see* O'Donnell, Sir A. T.

O'DONNELL, Hugh Bede Butler; Member (Lib Dem) Scotland Central, Scottish Parliament, since 2007; *b* 1 May 1952; *s* of late Hugh O'Donnell and Christina O'Donnell; *m*; one *s* one *d*. *Educ:* Queen Margaret Coll., Edinburgh (BA Hons 1996); Southern Connecticut State Univ. Civil Servant, 1969–72; manager, Tesco Plc, 1972–85; agent, Prudential Portfolio Managers, 1985–95; support worker, Quarriers, 1995–99; Party Aide to Donald Gorrie, MSP, 1999–2007. Non-exec. Dir, Social Enterprise, RECAP, 2003–. Election Supervisor, UN Mission to Kosovo, 2001. *Recreations:* relaxing on island of Kos, failing to learn Greek, TV crime fiction, bad DIY, olive picking, the life of Alexander the Great, reading historical fiction, raging at the world. *Address:* Scottish Parliament, Edinburgh EH99 1SP. *T:* (0131) 348 5795; *e-mail:* Hugh.ODonnell.msp@scottish.parliament.uk.

O'DONNELL, James Anthony, FRCO, FRSCM; Organist and Master of the Choristers, Westminster Abbey, since 2000; *b* 15 Aug. 1961; *s* of late Dr (James Joseph) Gerard O'Donnell and of Dr Gillian Anne O'Donnell. *Educ:* Westcliff High Sch., Essex; Jesus Coll., Cambridge (Organ Scholar and Open Scholar in Music; BA 1982, MA). Westminster Cathedral: Asst Master of Music, 1982–88; Master of Music, 1988–99. Prof. of Organ, 1997–2004, Vis. Prof., 2004–, RAM. FRCO 1983 (Performer of the Year, 1987; Mem. Council, 1989–2003); FRSCM 2000. Hon. RAM 2001; Hon. FGCM 2001. Has made many recordings with Westminster Cathedral Choir and Choir of Westminster Abbey. Gramophone Record of the Year and Best Choral Recording awards, 1998 for masses by Martin and Pizzetti; Royal Philharmonic Soc. award, 1999. KCSG 1999. *Recreations:* opera, food, wine. *Address:* c/o The Chapter Office, 20 Dean's Yard,

Westminster Abbey, SW1P 3PA. *Club:* Athenæum.
See also D. K. Womersley.

O'DONNELL, Dr Michael; author and broadcaster; *b* 20 Oct. 1928; *o s* of late Dr James Michael O'Donnell and Nora (*née* O'Sullivan); *m* 1953, Catherine Dorrington Ward (*d* 2007); one *s* two *d*. *Educ:* Stonyhurst; Trinity Hall, Cambridge (Lane Harrington Schol.); St Thomas's Hosp. Med. Sch., London (MB, BChir). FRCGP 1990. Editor, Cambridge Writing, 1948; Scriptwriter, BBC Radio, 1949–52. General Medical Practitioner, 1954–64. Editor, World Medicine, 1966–82. Member: GMC, 1971–97 (Chm., Professional Standards Cttee, 1995–97); Longman Editorial Adv. Bd, 1978–82. Mem., Alpha Omega Alpha Honor Med. Soc., 1995. Inaugural lecture, Green Coll., Oxford, 1981. John Rowan Wilson Award, World Medical Journalists Assoc., 1982; John Snow Medal, Assoc. of Anaesthetists of GB and Ireland, 1984. Scientific Adviser: O Lucky Man (film), 1972; Inside Medicine (BBC TV), 1974; Don't Ask Me (Yorkshire TV), 1977; Don't Just Sit There (Yorkshire TV), 1979–80; Where There's Life (Yorkshire TV), 1981–83. *Television plays:* Suggestion of Sabotage, 1963; Dangerous Reunion, 1964; Resolution, 1964; *television documentaries:* You'll Never Believe It, 1962; Cross Your Heart and Hope to Live, 1975; The Presidential Race, 1976; From Europe to the Coast, 1976; Did History Really Happen?, 1977, 1998; Chasing the Dragon, 1979; Second Opinion, 1980; Judgement on Las Vegas, 1981; Is Your Brain Really Necessary, 1982; Plague of Hearts, 1983; Medical Express, 1984; Can You Avoid Cancer?, 1984; O'Donnell Investigates…booze, 1985; O'Donnell Investigates…food, 1985; O'Donnell Investigates…the food business, 1986; O'Donnell Investigates…age, 1988; Health, Wealth and Happiness, 1989; What is this thing called health, 1990; The Skin Trade, 1991; Whose Blue Genes?, 1992; Out of Town, Out of Mind, 1993; Beyond belief, 1994; Way beyond belief, 1995; Dads, 1995; Still Beyond Belief, 1996; New Age Superstition, 1999; *radio:* contributor to Stop the Week (BBC), 1976–92; Chm., My Word (BBC), 1983–92; Presenter: Relative Values (BBC), 1987–97; The Bhamjee Beat, 1995; Utopia and Other Destinations, 1996–98; Murder, Magic and Medicine, 1998–2001. Medical Journalists Assoc. Award, 1973, 1982, 1990, 1996, Lifetime Achievement Award, 2007; British Science Writers' Award, 1979. *Publications:* Cambridge Anthology, 1952; Europe Tomorrow, 1971; My Medical School, 1978; The Devil's Prison, 1982; Doctor! Doctor! an insider's guide to the games doctors play, 1986; The Long Walk Home, 1988; Dr Michael O'Donnell's Executive Health Guide, 1988; A Sceptic's Medical Dictionary, 1997; Medicine's Strangest Cases, 2002; Madness and Creativity in Literature and Culture, 2004; Dr Donovan's Bequest, 2006; The Age-old Dilemma, 2007; contrib. Punch, New Scientist, The Listener, The Times, The Guardian, Daily Telegraph, Daily Mail. *Recreations:* walking, listening to music, loitering (with and without intent). *Address:* Handon Cottage, Markwick Lane, Loxhill, Godalming, Surrey GU8 4BD. *T:* (01483) 208295. *Club:* Garrick.

O'DONNELL, Rt Hon. Turlough; PC 1979; Lord Justice of Appeal, Supreme Court of Northern Ireland, 1979–89; *b* 5 Aug. 1924; *e s* of Charles and Eileen O'Donnell; *m* 1954, Eileen McKinley; two *s* two *d*. *Educ:* Abbey Grammar Sch., Newry; Queen's Univ., Belfast (LLB). Called to Bar of Northern Ireland, 1947; called to Inner Bar, 1964; Puisne Judge, NI, 1971–79. Chairman: NI Bar Council, 1970–71, Council of Legal Educn, NI, 1980–90. *Recreations:* golf, folk music. *Address:* c/o Royal Courts of Justice (Ulster), Belfast BT1 3JF.

O'DONNELL BOURKE, Patrick Francis John; Group Chief Executive, Viridian Group Ltd, since 2007; *b* 22 March 1957; *m* 1992, Jane; three *s*. *Educ:* Stonyhurst Coll.; Trinity Coll., Cambridge (BA 1979). ACA 1983. KPMG, 1979–86; Hill Samuel, 1986–87; Barclays de Zoete Wedd, 1987–95; Powergen: Hd of M&A, 1995–98; Gp Treas., 1998–2000; Gp Finance Dir, Viridian Gp, 2000–07. *Address:* Viridian Group Ltd, 120 Malone Road, Belfast BT9 5HT.

O'DONOGHUE, Denise, OBE 1999; Managing Director, Hat Trick Holdings, until 2006; *b* 13 April 1955; *d* of late Micheal O'Donoghue and Maura O'Donoghue; *m* 1987, James Mulville, *qv* (marr. diss. 1998); *m* 2006, Michael Holland. *Educ:* St Dominic's Girls' Sch.; York Univ. (BA Hons). Coopers & Lybrand, 1979–81; Dir, IPPA, 1981–83; Holmes Associates, 1983–86; Man. Dir, Hat Trick Films, 1995–2006. FRTS 1998; CCMI (CIMgt 1998). Awards from RTS, BAFTA, and Broadcasting Press Guild; Emmy Awards. *Address:* c/o Hat Trick Productions, 10 Livonia Street, W1V 8AF. *T:* (020) 7432 2907.

O'DONOGHUE, Gen. Sir Kevin, KCB 2005; CBE 1996; Chief of Defence Materiel, Ministry of Defence, since 2007; Chief Royal Engineer, since 2004; *b* 9 Dec. 1947; *s* of late Phillip James O'Donoghue and Winifred Mary O'Donoghue; *m* 1973, Jean Monkman; three *d*. *Educ:* Eastbourne Coll.; UMIST (BSc 1st Cl. Hons). Commnd RE, 1969; 23 Engr Regt, BAOR; Adjt 21 Engr Regt, 1974; Instructor, RMA Sandhurst, 1976; Staff Coll., Canada, 1978; Mil. Ops, MoD, 1979; MA to CGS, 1980; OC 4 Field Sqdn, 1982; Directing Staff, Staff Coll., Camberley, 1984; Comdr, 25 Engr Regt, BAOR, 1986–88; Dep. ACOS, HQ UKLF, 1988; Higher Comd and Staff Course, 1990; Comdr Corps RE, 1 (BR) Corps, 1990; Comd Engr, ACE Rapid Reaction Corps, 1992; NATO Defence Coll., 1993; Dir, Staff Ops, SHAPE, 1993; COS HQ QMG, 1996–99; ACGS, 1999–2001; UK Mil. Rep. to NATO and EU, 2001–02; DCDS (Health), 2002–04, Chief of Defence Logistics, 2004–07, MoD. Col, Royal Glos, Berks and Wilts Regt, 2001–07; Col Comdt, RE, 2002–. Hon. Col Comdt, RLC, 2008–. *Recreations:* military history, furniture restoration, gardening. *Address:* Defence Equipment and Support, MoD Abbey Wood, Bristol BS34 8JH. *Clubs:* National Liberal, Army and Navy.

O'DONOGHUE, His Honour Michael; a Circuit Judge, 1982–94; *b* 10 June 1929; *s* of late Dr James O'Donoghue, MB, ChB and Vera O'Donoghue (*née* Cox). *Educ:* Rhyl Grammar School; Univ. of Liverpool (LLB (Hons) 1950). Called to the Bar, Gray's Inn, 1951; National Service as Flying Officer, RAF, 1951–53; practised at the Chancery Bar, 1954–82; Lectr in Law (part time), Univ. of Liverpool, 1966–82. Mem. (part-time), Lands Tribunal, 1990–94. *Recreations:* music, sailing, photography. *Club:* Royal Welsh Yacht (Caernarfon) (Commodore, 1980–82; Pres., 1994–).

O'DONOGHUE, Rt Rev. Patrick; *see* Lancaster, Bishop of, (RC).

O'DONOGHUE, Philip Nicholas, CBiol, FIBiol; General Secretary, Institute of Biology, 1982–89; *b* 9 Oct. 1929; *s* of Terence Frederick O'Donoghue and Ellen Mary (*née* Haynes); *m* 1955, Veronica Florence Campbell; two *d*. *Educ:* East Barnet Grammar Sch.; Univ. of Nottingham (BSc; MSc 1959). FIBiol 1975. Experimental Officer, ARC's Field Stn, Compton, 1952–55 and Inst. of Animal Physiology, Babraham, 1955–61; Scientific Officer, National Inst. for Res. in Dairying, Shinfield, 1962–66; Lectr in Exptl Vet. Science and later Sen. Lectr in Lab. Animal Science, Royal Postgrad. Med. Sch., Univ. of London, 1966–82. Hume Meml Lect., UFAW, 1990. Vice-Pres., Inst. of Animal Technicians, 1969–2001; Hon. Sec., Inst. of Biology, 1972–76; Member: TEC, 1973–79 (Chm., Life Sciences Cttee, 1973–80); Council, Section of Comparative Medicine, RSM, 1983–96 (Pres., 1985–86); President: Lab. Animal Sci. Assoc., 1989–91; Fedn of European Lab. Animal Sci. Assocs, 1990–95. Editor, Laboratory Animals, 1967–82. Lab. Animal Sci. Assoc. Award, 1994. *Publications:* (with V. F. O'Donoghue) Georgian Cookery: recipes and remedies from 18th century Totteridge, 2007; editor of books and author of articles chiefly on the law relating to and the effective use and proper care of laboratory animals. *Recreations:* music, local history, talking, limited gardening. *Address:* 21 Holyrood Road, New Barnet, Herts EN5 1DQ. *T:* (020) 8449 3692. *Clubs:* Athenæum, Royal Society of Medicine.

O'DONOHOE, Stephanie Nicola; *see* Barwise, S. N.

O'DONOVAN, Kathleen Anne; Member of Court, Bank of England, 1999–2005 (Chairman, Audit Committee); *b* Warwicks, 23 May 1957. *Educ:* University Coll. London (BSc Econs). Joined Turquands Barton Mayhew, subseq. Ernst & Young, 1975; Partner, 1989–91; Finance Dir, BTR, then BTR Siebe, subseq. Invensys plc, 1991–2002. Non-executive Director: EMI Gp, 1997–2007 (Chm., Audit Cttee, 1999–2007); Prudential plc, 2003– (Chm. Audit Cttee, 2006–); Great Portland Estates, 2003–; O_2, 2005–07; Trinity Mirror plc, 2007–.

O'DONOVAN, Michael; Chief Executive, Multiple Sclerosis Society, 2002–06; *b* 26 Sept. 1946; *s* of James and Mary O'Donovan; *m* 1969, Susan Mary (*née* O'Brien); three *s*. *Educ:* St Ignatius Coll., N15; Durham Univ. (BA Hons Mod. Hist.). Beecham Group: Gen. Manager, then Man. Dir, Toiletries and Household Div., 1981–85; Regl Man. Dir, Far East, 1985–89; SmithKline Beecham, subseq. GlaxoSmithKline: Vice-Pres., Over-the-Counter Medicine Develt, 1990–92; Vice-Pres., Strategic Planning, 1993–2001. Non-executive Director: Adler Europe, 2005–07; Eur. MS Platform, 2007–; Treas., Eur. Patients' Forum, 2006–. Vice-Chm., Neurol Alliance, 2003–06 (Mem., 2003–06); Mem. Adv. Cttee, Inst. of Complex Neurodisability, 2003–. Trustee, Long Term Conditions (formerly Medical Conditions) Alliance, 2005– (Chm., 2008–). MInstD 1994. *Recreations:* keeping fit, modern history. *Club:* Windsor.

O'DONOVAN, Rev. Canon Oliver Michael Timothy, DPhil; FBA 2000; Professor of Christian Ethics and Practical Theology, University of Edinburgh, since 2006; *b* 28 June 1945; *s* of Michael and Joan M. O'Donovan; *m* 1978, Joan Elizabeth Lockwood; two *s*. *Educ:* University Coll. Sch., Hampstead; Balliol Coll., Oxford (MA, DPhil); Wycliffe Hall, Oxford; Princeton Univ. Ordained deacon 1972, priest 1973, dio. of Oxford. Tutor, Wycliffe Hall, Oxford, 1972–77; Prof. of Systematic Theology, Wycliffe Coll., Toronto, 1977–82; Regius Prof. of Moral and Pastoral Theology, Univ. of Oxford, 1982–2006; Canon of Christ Church, Oxford, 1982–2006. McCarthy Vis. Prof., Gregorian Univ., Rome, 2001. Member: C of E Bd for Social Responsibility, 1976–77, 1982–85; ARCIC, 1985–90; Anglican-Orthodox Jt Doctrinal Discussions, 1982–84; Gen. Synod of C of E, 2005–. Pres., Soc. for the Study of Christian Ethics, 1997–2000. Hulsean Lectr, Cambridge Univ., 1993–94; Bampton Lectr, Oxford Univ., 2003. Hon. DD Wycliffe Coll., Toronto, 2002. *Publications:* The Problem of Self-Love in Saint Augustine, 1980; Begotten or Made?, 1984; Resurrection and Moral Order, 1986; On the Thirty Nine Articles, 1986; Peace and Certainty, 1989; The Desire of the Nations, 1996; (with Joan Lockwood O'Donovan) From Irenaeus to Grotius, 1999; Common Objects of Love, 2002; The Just War Revisited, 2003; (with Joan Lockwood O'Donovan) Bonds of Imperfection, 2004; The Ways of Judgment, 2005; contrib. Jl of Theol Studies, Jl of Religious Ethics, Ethique and Studies in Christian Ethics. *Address:* The University of Edinburgh, School of Divinity, New College, Mound Place, Edinburgh EH1 2LX.

O'DONOVAN, Prof. Peter Joseph, FRCS, FRCOG; Consultant Gynaecologist, since 1990, Lead Gynaecological Cancer, since 2006, Lead Intellectual Property, since 2007, Bradford Teaching Hospitals NHS Trust; Professor of Medical Innovation, since 2003, Director, Institute of Pharmaceutical Innovation, since 2008, University of Bradford; *b* 13 Dec. 1954; *s* of Patrick Joseph O'Donovan and Sheila Doreen O'Donovan; *m* 1988, Carmel Beirne; two *s* two *d*. *Educ:* Presentation Brothers' Coll., Cork; UC Cork, Nat. Univ. Ireland (MB BCh BAO). FRCS 1982; MRCOG 1986, FRCOG 1998. Bradford Teaching Hospitals NHS Trust: Dir, Post Grad. Med. Educn, 1997–2003; Dir, Merit Centre, 1997–. Mem., Medical Devices Agency, DoH, 2001–. Dir, Medipex (NHS Innovation), 2004–. Dir, Eur. Acad. Gynaecol Surgery, 2007–. Pres., British Soc. for Gynaecological Endoscopy, 2002–04; Treas., Eur. Soc. Gynaecol Endoscopy, 2006–. Ed. in Chief, Reviews in Gynaecological Practice, 2001–05; Ed., Gynecol Surgery, 2003–06. *Publications:* Recent Advances in Gynaecological Surgery, 2002; Conservative Surgery for Menorrhagia, 2003; Preserving Your Womb: alternatives to hysterectomy, 2005; Ambulatory Gynaecological Surgery, 2006; Complications in Gynaecological Surgery, 2007; Conservative Surgery for Abnormal Uterine Bleeding, 2007; Modern Management of Abnormal Uterine Bleeding, 2008. *Recreations:* food, wine, tennis, Rugby Union (as spectator), reading tabloid newspapers, writing, travel. *Address:* Cotswold, 3 Creskeld Crescent, Bramhope, Leeds LS16 9EH. *T:* (0113) 2614259, (office) (01274) 364888; *e-mail:* podonovan@hotmail.com.

O'DOWD, Sir David (Joseph), Kt 1999; CBE 1995; QPM 1988; DL; law enforcement consultant; HM Chief Inspector of Constabulary, 1996–2001; *b* 20 Feb. 1942; *s* of late Michael Joseph O'Dowd and Helen (*née* Merrin); *m* 1963, Carole Ann Watson; one *s* one *d*. *Educ:* Gartree High Sch.; Oadby, Leics; Univ. of Leicester (Dip. Social Studies); Open Univ. (BA); Univ. of Aston (MSc); FBI Nat. Acad., USA. Sgt, Inspector and Chief Inspector, CID, Leicester City Police, 1961–77; Supt, W Midlands Police, Coventry and Birmingham, 1977–84; Hd, Traffic Policing, Dir, Complaints and Discipline Investigation Bureau and Hd, Strategic Planning and Policy Analysis Unit, Metropolitan Police, 1984–86; Chief Constable, Northants Police, 1986–93; HM Inspector of Constabulary, 1993–96. British Chief Constables' Rep., Nat. Exec. Inst., FBI Acad., Washington, 1988. Dir, police extended interview scheme, 1992–93. Vis. Teaching Fellow, Mgt Centre, Univ. of Aston, Birmingham, 1988; Vis. Prof., UWE, 2002. Fellow, 1994, Gov., 2002–, Univ. of Northampton (formerly Nene Coll., then UC Northampton). CCMI (CIMgt 1988). DL 2002, High Sheriff, 2006–07, Northants. Hon. DSc Aston, 2003. OStJ 1999. *Recreations:* golf, ski-ing. *Club:* Northampton Golf (Harlestone, Northants).

O'DOWD, John Fitzgerald; Member (SF) Upper Bann, Northern Ireland Assembly, since 2003; *b* Banbridge, Co. Down, 10 May 1967; *s* of Vincent and Bridie O'Dowd; *m* 1998, Mary; one *s* one *d*. *Educ:* Lismore Comp. Sch. Mem., Craigavon Council, 1997–. *Address:* Sheena Campbell House, 77 North Street, Lurgan, Co. Armagh BT67 9AH. *T:* (028) 3834 9675; *e-mail:* johnodowd@sinn-fein.ie.

O'DRISCOLL, Most Rev. Percival Richard; Archbishop of Huron and Metropolitan of Ontario, 1993–2000; Bishop of Huron, 1990–2000; *b* 4 Oct. 1938; *s* of T. J. O'Driscoll and Annie O'Driscoll (*née* Copley); *m* 1965, Suzanne Gertrude Savignac; one *s* one *d*. *Educ:* Bishop's Univ., Lennoxville, Quebec (BA, STB); Huron Coll., London, Ont. (DD). Ordained deacon 1964, priest 1966; Assistant Curate: St Matthias, Ottawa, 1965–67; St John Evan, Kitchener, 1967–70; Religious Educn Dir, St Paul's Cathedral and Bishop Cronyn Memorial, London, 1970; Rector: St Michael & All Angels, London, 1970–75; St Batholomew's, Sarnia, 1975–80; Rector, St Paul's Cathedral, and Dean of Huron, 1980–87; Suffragan Bishop of Huron, 1987–89; Coadjutor Bishop, 1989–90. *Recreations:* camping, hiking, photography. *Address:* 4–1241 Beaverbrook Avenue, London, Ontario, N6H 5P1, Canada. *Club:* London (Ontario).

ÖE, Kenzaburo; Japanese writer; *b* 31 Jan. 1935; *m* 1960, Yukari Itami; two *s* one *d. Educ:* Tokyo Univ. (BA French Lit. 1959). Visited Russia and Western Europe to research and write series of essays on Youth in the West, 1961. Shinchosa Lit. Prize, 1964; Tanizaka Prize, 1967; Nobel Prize for Literature, 1994. *Publications* include: The Catch, 1958 (Akutagawa Prize); Nip the Buds, Shoot the Kids, 1958; Our Age, 1959; Screams, 1962; The Perverts, 1963; Hiroshima Notes, 1963; Adventures in Daily Life, 1964; A Personal Matter, 1964; The Silent Cry (original title, Football in the First Year of the Man'en Era), 1967; Teach us to Outgrow our Madness: four short novels, 1978; (ed) Fire from the Ashes: short stories about Hiroshima and Nagasaki, 1985; The Treatment Tower, 1990; Japan, the Ambiguous and Myself (lectures), 1995; A Quiet Life, 1998; Rouse Up O Young Men of the New Age!, 2002; Somersault, 2003; A Healing Family (biog. and autobiog.), 2007. *Address:* Marion Boyars Publishers Ltd, 24 Lacy Road, SW15 1NL; 585 Seijo-Machi, Setagaya-Ku, Tokyo, Japan.

OEHLERS, Maj.-Gen. Gordon Richard, CB 1987; Director, Corps of Commissionaires, 1994–99; *b* 19 April 1933; *s* of late Dr Roderic Clarke Oehlers and Hazel Ethne Oehlers (*née* Van Geyzel); *m* 1956, Doreen, (Rosie), Gallant; one *s* one *d. Educ:* St Andrews School, Singapore. CEng, FIET. Commissioned Royal Corps of Signals, 1958; UK and Middle East, 1958–64; Adjutant, 4th Div. Signals Regt, 1964–66; Instructor, School of Signals, 1966–68; OC 7th Armd Bde HQ and Signals Sqdn, 1968–70; GSO2 (Weapons), 1970–72; CO 7th Signal Regt, 1973–76; Commander Corps Royal Signals, 1st (British) Corps, 1977–79; Dir, Op. Requirements 4 (Army), 1979–84; ACDS (Comd Control, Communications and Inf. Systems), 1984–87. Dir of Security and Investigation, British Telecom, 1987–94. Col Comdt, RCS, 1987–93; Hon. Col 31st (Greater London) Signal Regt (Volunteers), 1988–94. Chm., Royal Signals Instn, 1990–93. Pres., British Wireless Dinner Club, 1986–87. *Recreations:* interested in all games esp. badminton (Captain Warwicks County Badminton Team, 1954–56), lawn tennis (Chm., Army Lawn Tennis Assoc., 1980–86), golf. *Address:* c/o National Westminster Bank, 4 High Street, Petersfield, Hants GU32 3JF. *Club:* Liphook Golf (Captain, 1998–99).

OESTERHELT, Dr Jürgen; Ambassador of Germany to the Holy See, 1997–2000; *b* 19 Aug. 1935; *s* of Dr Egon Oesterhelt and Trude (*née* Pfohl); *m* 1964, Katharina Galeiski; one *s* one *d. Educ:* Munich Univ. (LLD 1959); State Bar Exam. 1962; Columbia Univ., NY (Master of Comparative Law 1963). Internat. lawyer in Paris, 1963–64; joined German Diplomatic Service, 1964; Moscow, 1965–66; UN, NY, 1967–71; Sofia, 1971–74; German Foreign Office, 1974–77; Athens, 1977–80; Foreign Office: Hd of Div., Legal Dept, 1980–85; Dir, Political Dept, 1985–86; Dir Gen., Legal Dept and Legal Advr to Foreign Minister, 1986–92; Ambassador to Turkey, 1992–95; Ambassador to the UK, 1995–97. Mem., Bd of Trustees, Anglo-German Foundn, 2003–. Commander's Cross: Order of Merit (Germany), 1997 (Cross, 1988); Order of Phoenix (Greece), 1982; Order of White Rose (Finland), 1989; Grand Cross, Order of Merit (Austria), 1990. *Recreations:* music, reading. *Address:* Auf der Königsbitze 4, 53639 Königswinter, Germany; *e-mail:* juergen@oesterhelt.de.

OESTREICHER, Rev. Canon Paul; Hon. Consultant, Centre for International Reconciliation, Coventry Cathedral, 1997–2005 (Director of the International Ministry of Coventry Cathedral, 1986–97); Canon Residentiary of Coventry Cathedral, 1986–97, now Canon Emeritus; Member of the Society of Friends (Quakers), since 1982; Quaker Chaplain to the University of Sussex, since 2004; journalist; *b* Germany, 29 Sept. 1931; *s* of Paul Oestreicher and Emma (*née* Schnaus); *m* 1st, 1958, Lore Feind (*d* 2000); one *s* two *d* (and one adopted *s* decd); 2nd, 2002, Dr Barbara Einhorn. *Educ:* King's High Sch., Dunedin; Otago and Victoria Univs, NZ; Lincoln Theol College. BA Mod. Langs Otago 1953; MA Hons Polit. Sci. Victoria 1955. Fled to NZ with refugee parents, 1939; Editor, Critic (Otago Univ. newspaper), 1952–53; subseq. free-lance journalist and broadcaster; returned to Europe, 1955. Humboldt Res. Fellow, Bonn Univ., 1955–56, Free Univ. of Berlin, 1992–93; fraternal worker with German Lutheran Church at Rüsselsheim, trng in problems of industrial soc. (Opel, Gen. Motors), 1958–59; ordained 1959; Curate, Dalston, E London, 1959–61; Producer, Relig. Dept, BBC Radio, 1961–64; Assoc. Sec., Dept of Internat. Affairs, Brit. Council of Churches with special resp. for East-West Relations, 1964–69; Vicar, Church of the Ascension, Blackheath, 1968–81; Asst Gen. Sec. and Sec. for Internat. Affairs, BCC, 1981–86; Dir of (Lay) Trng, Dio. Southwark, 1969–72; Hon. Chaplain to Bp of Southwark, 1975–81; Public Preacher in Dio. Southwark, 1981–86; Hon. Canon of Southwark Cathedral, 1978–83, Canon Emeritus 1983–86. Member: Gen. Synod of C of E, 1970–86, 1996–97; Internat. Affairs Cttee, C of E, 1965–2001. Member: Brit. Council of Churches working parties on Southern Africa and Eastern Europe; Anglican Pacifist Fellowship, 1960– (Counsellor, 1998–); Exec. Cttee, Christian Peace Conf., Prague, 1964–68; Exec. Mem., Christian Concern for Southern Africa, 1978–81; Chm. of Trustees, Christian Inst. (of Southern Africa) Fund, 1984–95; Chairman: British Section, Amnesty International, 1974–79; Christians Aware, 1999–2000; Pres., Action by Christians against Torture, 2005–. Mem. Council, Keston Coll. (Centre for the Study of Religion and Communism), 1976–82. Vice-Chm., Campaign for Nuclear Disarmament, 1980–81, Vice-Pres. 1983–; Mem. Alternative Defence Commn, 1981–87; Vice-Chm., Ecumenical Commn for Church and Society in W Europe (Brussels), 1982–86. Trustee, Dresden Trust, 1993–2005. Companion, Community of the Cross of Nails, 2007–. Shelley Lectr, Radio NZ, 1987. Freeman, Meiningen, Germany, 1995. Hon. DLitt Coventry Polytechnic, 1991; Hon. LLD Sussex, 2005; DD Lambeth, 2008; Hon. DD Otago, 2009. Prize for Promotion of European Unity, Wartburg Foundn, 1997; Award of Merit, City of Coventry, 2002. Order of Merit, 1st Cl. (Germany), 1995; Order of Merit, Free State of Saxony, 2004. *Publications:* (ed English edn) Helmut Gollwitzer, The Demands of Freedom, 1965; (trans.) H. J. Schultz, Conversion to the World, 1967; (ed, with J. Klugmann) What Kind of Revolution: A Christian-Communist Dialogue, 1968; (ed) The Christian Marxist Dialogue, 1969; (jtly) The Church and the Bomb, 1983; The Double Cross, 1986. *Recreations:* addicted to newsprint, active and passive, Mozart, Bach and the cry of seagulls. *Address:* 97 Furze Croft, Furze Hill, Hove, E Sussex BN3 1PE. *T:* (01273) 728033; *e-mail:* paulo@reconcile.org.uk.

O'FARRELL, Declan Gerard, CBE 2000; FCCA; Chief Executive Officer, Castletown Corporation Limited, since 2003; Chairman, West Herts College, since 2004; *b* 10 Feb. 1949; *s* of Bartholomew and Mary Carmel O'Farrell; *m* 1971, Jennie; one *s* three *d. Educ:* Finchley Catholic Grammar Sch. FCCA 1973. With British Tissues, 1967–81 (mgt trainee to Gp Mgt Accountant); financial analyst, Express Dairies, 1981; various financial posts with Express Foods Gp (Financial Controller, Distribn Div., until 1986); joined LT bus operations, 1986; Dir, 1989–2004, Man. Dir, 1989–94, Chief Exec., 1994–2003, Metroline (new bus co. subsid.), subseq. Metroline plc. Dir, NW London TEC, 1990–2001 (Chm., 1993–96); Founder Mem., London TEC Council. Chm., Business Link London, 1997–2001. CCMI (CIMgt 2001); FRSA 2000. *Recreations:* gardening, golf.

O'FARRELL, Finola Mary Lucy, (Mrs S. Andrews); QC 2002; a Recorder, since 2006; *b* 15 Dec. 1960; *d* of John Stephen O'Farrell and Rosaleen Mary O'Farrell; *m* 1993, Stuart Andrews; one *d. Educ:* St Philomena's Sch., Carshalton; Durham Univ. (BA Hons).

Called to the Bar, Inner Temple, 1983; in practice, specialising in construction law. Mem., editl team, Keating on Building Contracts, 5th edn 1991, 6th edn 1995; Jt Ed., Construction Law Yearbook, 4th edn, 1999. *Publication:* (contrib.) Engineers' Dispute Resolution Handbook, 2006. *Recreations:* horse riding, contemporary dance and art, theatre. *Address:* Keating Chambers, 15 Essex Street, Outer Temple, WC2R 3AA. *T:* (020) 7544 2600, *Fax:* (020) 7544 2700; *e-mail:* fofarrell@keatingchambers.com.

O'FERRALL, Rev. Patrick Charles Kenneth, OBE 1989; Hon. Assistant Priest, SS Peter and Paul, Godalming, since 2007 (Curate (Ordained Local Minister), 2000–07); *b* 27 May 1934; *s* of late Rev. Kenneth John Spence O'Ferrall and Isoult May O'Ferrall; *m* 1st, 1960, Mary Dorothea (*d* 1997), 4th *d* of late Maj. C. E. Lugard and Mrs K. I. B. Lugard; one *s* two *d*; 2nd, 1999, Wendy Elizabeth Barnett (*née* Gilmore). *Educ:* Winchester Coll.; New Coll., Oxford (BA Lit.Hum. 1958; MA); Harvard Business Sch. (AMP 1983). Nat. Service, 1952–54, 2nd Lieut, Royal Fusiliers. Iraq Petroleum and associated cos, 1958–70; BP, 1971–73; Total CFP Paris (Total Moyen Orient), 1974–77; Total Oil Marine, London: Commercial Manager, 1977–82; Dir, Gas Gathering Pipelines (N Sea) Ltd, 1977–78; Project Co-ordination Manager, Alwyn N, 1983–85; Projects Co-ordination Manager, 1985–90; Dep. Chm., 1991–93, Chm., 1993–99, Lloyd's Register of Shipping. Mem., Offshore Industry Adv. Bd, 1992–94. Chm., City of London Outward Bound Assoc., 1993–97. Mem., Court of Common Council, Corp. of London, 1996–2001. Liveryman, Co. of Shipwrights, 1992–; Master, Coachmakers' and Coach Harness Makers' Co., 1993–94. FRSA 1993; CCMI (CIMgt 1994). Hon. FREng 2000. Lay Reader, 1961–2000; ordained deacon, 2000, priest, 2001. *Recreations:* music (playing violin and singing), tennis, wine, crosswords, travel. *Address:* Catteshall Grange, Catteshall Road, Godalming, Surrey GU7 1LZ. *T:* (01483) 410134, *Fax:* (01483) 414161; *e-mail:* patrick@oferrall.co.uk. *Clubs:* MCC, Aldgate Ward (Pres., 1998).

OFFER, Prof. Avner, DPhil; FBA 2000; Chichele Professor of Economic History, University of Oxford, since 2000; Fellow, All Souls College, Oxford, since 2000; *b* 15 May 1944; *s* of Zvi and Ivriyah Offer; *m* 1966, Leah Koshet; one *s* one *d. Educ:* Western Valley Sch., Yif'at, Israel; Hebrew Univ. (BA 1973); St Antony's Coll., Oxford; Merton Coll., Oxford (MA 1976; DPhil 1979). Mil. service, Israel, 1962–65; Kibbutz mem., 1965–67; Conservation Officer, Israel, 1967–69; Jun. Res. Fellow, Merton Coll., Oxford, 1976–78; Lectr in Econ. and Social Hist., 1978–90, Reader, 1990–91, Univ. of York; Reader in Recent Social and Econ. Hist., Univ. of Oxford, and Fellow, Nuffield Coll., 1992–2000. Hartley Fellow, Univ. of Southampton, 1981–82; Vis. Associate, Clare Hall, Cambridge, 1984; Res. Fellow, Inst. Advanced Study, ANU, 1985–88; Sen. Fellow, Rutgers Univ., 1991–92; Sen. Vis. Fellow, Remarque Inst., NY Univ., 1999. *Publications:* Property and Politics 1870–1914: landownership, law, ideology and urban development in England, 1981; The First World War: an agrarian interpretation, 1989; (ed) In Pursuit of the Quality of Life, 1996; The Challenge of Affluence: self-control and well-being in the United States and Britain since 1950, 2006; articles on land, law, empire, consumption and quality of life. *Recreations:* reading, classical music, visual arts. *Address:* 15 Hamilton Road, Oxford OX2 7PY. *T:* (01865) 553380.

OFFER, Ven. Clifford Jocelyn; Archdeacon of Norwich and Canon Residentiary (Canon Librarian) of Norwich Cathedral, 1994–2008; *b* 10 Aug. 1943; *s* of late Rev. Canon Clifford Jesse Offer and Jocelyn Mary Offer; *m* 1980, Dr Catherine Mary Lloyd; two *d. Educ:* King's Sch., Canterbury; St Peter's Coll., Oxford (sent down); Exeter Univ. (BA 1967); Westcott House, Cambridge. Ordained deacon, 1969, priest, 1970; Curate, St Peter and St Paul, Bromley, 1969–74; Team Vicar, Southampton City Centre, 1974–83; Team Rector, Hitchin, 1983–94. Vice Chm., then Chm., St Albans ABM, 1989–94; Chairman: Norwich Diocesan Adv. Bd for Mission and Ministry (formerly ABM), 1994–99, 2000–03; Norwich Course Mgt Cttee, 1999–2003; Norwich Bd of Ministry, 2003–08; Warden of Readers, dio. Norwich, 1994–2008; Bishops' Selector, 1995–2008; Mem., Gen. Synod of C of E, 1999–2005. Mem., Council for E Anglia Studies, 2000–08. FRSA 1997. *Publications:* King Offa in Hitchin, 1992; In Search of Clofesho, 2002. *Recreations:* collecting naval buttons, ship-modelling, growing chrysanthemums. *Address:* Chase House, Peterstow, Herefordshire HR9 6JX. *T:* (01989) 567874.

OFFMANN, Karl Auguste; President, Republic of Mauritius, 2002–03; *b* 25 Nov. 1940; *s* of Laurent Wilford Offmann and Liliane Armoorgum; *m* 1969, Marie-Rose Danielle Mouton; two *s. Educ:* Mech. Engrg Apprenticeship Scholar 1956; Claver House, London (Dip. Social and Political Sci. 1975). Plant and Personnel Manager, L'Express, daily newspaper, 1963–79. Leader, Internat. Young Christian Workers Movement, 1957–79; politician, 1976–2002 (full-time, 1982–2002). Founder Mem., Africa Forum, 2006–. Grand Commander, Order of Star and Key of the Indian Ocean (Republic of Mauritius); Grand Croix 1st class, l'Ordre National à Madagascar. *Address:* P18 Cité Jules Koenig–Vuillemin, Beau–Bassin, Mauritius. *T:* 4542880, 4549634; *e-mail:* offmann@intnet.mu.

OFFNER, Gary John; Director, New South Wales Department of State and Regional Development, since 2003; *b* 26 Oct. 1961; *s* of John Frederick Offner and Dorothy Offner; *m* 1993, Beth Frances Hickey. *Educ:* Christian Brothers Coll., Sutherland; Barristers' Admission Board (Dip. Law 1988); Univ. of Technology, Sydney (MBA 1993). Joined NSW Public Sector, 1980; admitted to NSW Bar, 1988; Advr to Minister for Natural Resources, 1988–89; Manager, Internat. Div., NSW Dept of State and Regl Develt, 1990–97; Official Rep. of NSW Govt in UK and Europe and Dir, NSW Govt Trade and Investment Office, 1997–2001; Dir, Strategic Markets, NSW Govt, 2001–03; Review Dir, NSW Premier's Dept, 2003. *Recreations:* golf, cricket, Rugby. *Address:* L49 MLC Centre, 19 Martin Place, Sydney, NSW 2000, Australia. *Club:* Sydney Cricket Ground.

OFILI, Christopher; artist; *b* Manchester, 1968. *Educ:* Tameside Coll. of Technol.; Chelsea Sch. of Art (Christopher Head drawing scholarship 1989; BA); Hochschule der Kunst, Berlin; Royal Coll. of Art (MA). British Council Travel Scholarship, Zimbabwe, 1992. Trustee, Tate, 2000–05. Solo exhibitions include: Kepler Gall., London, 1991; Victoria Miro Gall., London, 1996, 2000, 2002; Contemporary Fine Art, Berlin, 1997, 2005; Southampton City Art Gall., 1998; Serpentine Gall., London, 1998; Whitworth Art Gall., Manchester, 1998–99; Gavin Browns Enterprise, NY, 1999; Gall. Side 2, Japan, 2001; (as GB rep.) Venice Biennale, 2003; Studio Mus., Harlem, 2005; Tate Britain, 2005–07; Kestnergesellschaft, Hanover, 2006; David Zwirner, NY, 2007. Group exhibitions include: Cornerhouse Gall., Manchester, 1993; MOMA, Oxford, 1995; ICA, 1997; Mus. of Contemp. Art, Sydney, 1997; RA, 1997; Walker Art Gall., Liverpool, 1997; British Council touring exhibn, incl. Finland, Sweden and Czech Republic, 1997–2000; Tate Gall., 1998–99; 6th Internat. Biennale, Istanbul, 1999; Carnegie Mus. of Art, Pittsburgh, 1999–2000; Brooklyn Mus. of Art, NY, 1999; Saatchi Gall., 2000; South Bank Centre, 2000; Mus. of Contemp. Art, LA, 2001; Bronx Mus. of the Arts, NY, 2002 (and touring); Santa Monica Mus. of Art, Calif, 2002; MOMA, NY, 2002; Nat. Gall. and UK tour, 2003; Joslyn Art Mus., Omaha, 2004; Palais de Tokyo, 2005; ICA, Boston, 2005; MOMA, NY, 2005; MOMA, NY, V&A, Hayward Gall., London, 2006; MIMA, Middlesbrough, Gary Tatinsian Gall., Moscow, 2007. Hon. Fellow, Univ. of the Arts,

London, 2004. Turner Prize, 1998; Southbank Award, Visual Arts, London, 2004. *Address:* c/o Victoria Miro Gallery, 16 Wharf Road, N1 7RW.

O'FLAHERTY, Prof. Coleman Anthony, AM 1999; Deputy Vice-Chancellor, University of Tasmania, Australia, 1991–93, Professor Emeritus 1993; *b* 8 Feb. 1933; *s* of Michael and Agnes O'Flaherty; *m* 1957, Nuala Rose Silke (*d* 1999). *Educ:* Nat. Univ. of Ireland (BE); Iowa State Univ. (MS, PhD). FICE; FIEI; FIE(Aust); FIHT; FCILT. Engineer: Galway Co. Council, Ireland, 1954–55; Canadian Pacific Railway Co., Montreal, 1955–56; M. W. Kellogg Co., USA, 1956–57; Asst Prof., Iowa State Univ., 1957–62; Leeds University: Lectr, 1962–66; Prof. of Transport Engineering, Inst. for Transport Studies and Dept of Civil Engineering, 1966–74; First Asst Comr (Engineering), Nat. Capital Develt Commn, Canberra, 1974–78; Dir and Principal, Tasmanian Coll. of Advanced Educn, subseq. Tasmanian State Inst. of Technology, 1978–90. Vis. Prof., Univ. of Melbourne, 1973. Chairman: Tasmanian Liby Adv. Bd, 1997–2006; Tasmania State Liby and Archives Trust, 1997–2006. Trustee, Tasmanian Mus. and Art Gall., 1993–2000. Pres., Tasmanian Div., Assoc. Independent Retirees, 2005–07. Hon. LLD Tasmania, 1994. *Publications:* Highways, 1967, vol. I of 4th edn (Transport Planning and Traffic Engineering), 1997, vol. II of 4th edn (Highway Engineering), 2001; (jtly) Passenger Conveyors, 1972; (jtly) Introduction to Hovercraft and Hoverports, 1975; contribs to professional jls. *Recreation:* walking. *Address:* 22 Beach Road, Legana, Tasmania 7277, Australia. *T:* (3) 63301990, *Fax:* (3) 63301204. *Club:* Launceston.

O'FLAHERTY, Stephen John, CMG 2003; Managing Director, Goldman Sachs International, since 2005; *b* 15 May 1951; *s* of late Brig. Denis O'Flaherty, CBE, DSO and of Jill O'Flaherty; *m* 1975, (Sarah) Louise Gray; one *s* two *d*. *Educ:* Douai Sch.; Jesus Coll., Oxford (BA). HM Diplomatic Service, 1975–2004: entered FCO, 1975; Second Sec., New Delhi, 1977–80; First Secretary: FCO, 1980–81; Prague, 1981–84; FCO, 1984–88; Vienna, 1988–92; Counsellor, FCO, 1992–2004. *Address:* (office) Peterborough Court, 133 Fleet Street, EC4A 2BB; *e-mail:* stephen.oflaherty@gs.com.

of MAR, family name of **Countess of Mar**.

OGATA, Prof. Sadako; President, Japan International Co-operation Agency, since 2003; Co-Chair, Commission on Human Security, 2001–03; *b* 16 Sept. 1927; *m*; one *s* one *d*. *Educ:* Univ. of the Sacred Heart, Tokyo (BA); Georgetown Univ. (MA); PhD California (Berkeley). Prof., 1980–90, Director of Internat. Relations, 1987–88, Dean, Faculty of Foreign Studies, 1989–90, Sophia Univ., Japan. Minister, Perm. Mission of Japan to UN, 1976–78; Chm. Exec. Bd, UNICEF, Japanese Rep. to UN Commn on Human Rights, 1982–85; UN High Comr for Refugees, 1991–2000. Hon. DCL Oxon, 1998; Hon. LLD Cantab, 1999. *Address:* Japan International Co-operation Agency, 6th–13th Floors, Shinjuku Maynds Tower Building, 2–1–1 Yoyogi, Shibuya-ku, Tokyo 151–8558, Japan.

OGDEN, Sir Peter (James), Kt 2005; Founder and Chairman, The Ogden Trust, since 1994; *b* 26 May 1947; *s* of James Platt Ogden and Frances Ogden (*née* Simmonds); *m* 1970, Catherine Rose Blincoe; two *s* one *d*. *Educ:* Rochdale Grammar Sch.; Univ. of Durham (BSc 1968; PhD 1971); Harvard Business Sch. (MBA 1973). Man. Dir, Morgan Stanley & Co., 1985; Chairman: Computacenter Ltd, 1985–97 (non-exec. Dir, 1997–); Dealogic Ltd, 1985–. Gov., Westminster Sch., 2002–. Hon. DCL Durham, 2002. *Recreation:* sailing. *Address:* The Ogden Trust, Hughes Hall, Cambridge CB1 2EW. *T:* (01223) 518164, *Fax:* (01223) 518173; *e-mail:* ogdentrust@hughes.cam.ac.uk. *Club:* Royal Yacht Squadron (Cowes).

OGDEN, Prof. Raymond William, PhD; FRS 2006; George Sinclair Professor of Mathematics, University of Glasgow, since 1984; *b* 19 Sept. 1943; *s* of Arthur and Norah Ogden; *m* 1969, Susanne Thomas; two *s* two *d*. *Educ:* Gonville and Caius Coll., Cambridge (BA 1966; PhD 1970). SRC Postdoctoral Res. Fellow, UEA, 1970–72; Lectr, 1972–76, Reader, 1976–80, in Maths, Univ. of Bath; Prof. of Maths, Brunel Univ., 1981–84. *Publications:* Non-linear Elastic Deformations, 1984, 2nd edn 1997; more than 150 articles in internat. scientific jls. *Recreations:* music, wine, learning languages, absorbing the sun in the Mediterranean. *Address:* Department of Mathematics, University of Glasgow, Glasgow G12 8QW. *T:* (0141) 330 4550, *Fax:* (0141) 330 4111; *e-mail:* rwo@maths.gla.ac.uk.

OGG, Derek Andrew; QC (Scot.) 1999; Senior Advocate Depute, since 2007; *b* 19 Sept. 1954; *s* of Alec and Elsie Ogg. *Educ:* Edinburgh Univ. (LLB 1978). Dip. in Master Advocacy, Nat. Inst. for Trial Advocacy, USA, 1996. Asst Solicitor, Ross & Connel Solicitors, Dunfermline, 1978–80; Partner and Founder, Hunter Burns & Ogg Solicitors, Edinburgh, Perth and Dunfermline, 1980–89; Standing Jun. Counsel, Scottish Office, 1983–88; called to the Scottish Bar, 1989; Jun. Counsel, 1989–99; Reserve Counsel, UN *Ad Hoc* Tribunal for War Crimes in Former Republic of Yugoslavia, The Hague, 1998–2004. Chm. (*ad hoc*), Discipline Tribunal, ICAS, 2001–. Chm., Faculty of Advocates Criminal Bar Assoc., 2003–05. Founder and Chm., Scottish Aids Monitor, 1983–93; Trustee, Nat. Aids Trust, 1987–90. Mem., Royal Philosophical Soc., Glasgow. Founding Fellow (FFCS) 2002, Hon. Fellow, 2004, Inst. for Contemporary Scotland. *Recreations:* hill-walking in Scotland, collecting and competing classic cars, supporter of Celtic Football Club, reading history. *Address:* 2/2, 18 Lanark Street, Glasgow G1 5PY. *T:* (0141) 572 4843; *e-mail:* derekandrewogg@hotmail.com.

OGILVIE, (Dame) Bridget (Margaret), (Dr Bridget Ogilvie), AC 2007; DBE 1997; FRCPath, FMedSci; FRS 2003; FAA; FIBiol; Director: Wellcome Trust, 1991–98; AstraZeneca (formerly Zeneca Group plc), 1997–2006; High Steward of University of Cambridge, since 2001; *b* 24 March 1938; *er d* of late John Mylne Ogilvie and Margaret Beryl (*née* McRae). *Educ:* New England Girls' Sch., Armidale, NSW; Univ. of New England, Armidale (BRurSc 1960; Distinguished Alumni Award, 1994); PhD 1964, ScD 1981, Cambridge. FIBiol 1985; FRCPath 1992. Parasitology Div., Nat. Inst. for Med. Res., London, 1963–81; Ian McMaster Fellow, CSIRO Div. of Animal Health, Australia, 1971–72; with Wellcome Trust, 1979–98: Co-ordinator, Tropical Med. Prog., 1979–81; Dep. Sec. and Asst Dir, 1981–84; Dep. Dir, Science, 1984–89; Dir, Science Progs, 1989–91. Director: Lloyds Bank, 1995; Lloyds TSB Gp, 1996–2000. Visiting Professor: Dept of Biology, Imperial Coll., London, 1985–92; UCL, 1998–. Member: Council for Science and Technol., 1993–2000; Commonwealth Scholarship Commn, 1993–2000; Adv. Council for Chemistry, Univ. of Oxford, 1997–2001; Australian Health and Med. Res. Strategic Review, 1998–99; Chairman: COPUS, 1998–2002; AstraZeneca Sci. Teaching Trust, 1998–2006; Medicines for Malaria Venture, 1999–2006; Adv. Cttee for Sci., Technol., Business, British Liby, 2000–02. Non-executive Director: Scottish Sci. Trust, 1999–2002; Manchester Technol. Fund, 1999–2004. Chm., Assoc. of Med. Res. Charities, 2002–07. Trustee: Sci. Mus., London, 1992–2003; RCVS Trust Fund, 1998–2001; NESTA, 1998–2002; Cancer Res. UK (formerly CRC), 2001–; Sense about Science, 2002–; Centre of the Cell, UK, 2005–. Chairman, Governing Body: Inst. for Animal Health, 1997–2003; Lister Inst., 2002–. Founder FMedSci 1998. Hon. Member: British Soc. for Parasitology, 1990; Amer. Soc. of Parasitologists, 1992; BVA, 1998; BAAS, 2005; Hon. FRCP 1996 (Hon. MRCP 1992); Hon. FRACP 1998; Hon. ARCVS 1993. Hon. Fellow: UCL, 1993; Girton Coll., Cambridge, 1993; St Edmund's Coll.,

Cambridge, 1999; Hon. FRVC 1994; Hon. FIBiol 1998; Hon. FRSocMed 1999. Hon. DSc: Nottingham, Salford, Westminster, 1994; Glasgow, Bristol, ANU, 1995; Buckingham, Dublin, Trent, Oxford Brookes, 1996; Greenwich, 1997; Auckland, NZ, Durham, Kent, 1998; Exeter, Imperial Coll., London, 1999; Leicester, 2000; Manchester, St Andrews, 2001; Wollongong, 2005; Hon. LLD: TCD, 1996; Dundee, 1998; Hon. MD Newcastle, 1996; Dr *hc* Edinburgh, 1997. Lloyd of Kilgerran Prize, Foundn for Sci. and Technology, 1994; Wooldridge Meml Medal, BVA, 1998; Australian Soc. for Medical Res. Medal, 2000; Kilby Award, Kilby Awards Foundn, USA, 2003; Duncan Davies Meml Medal, Res. and Develt Soc., 2004; Ralph Doherty Meml Medal, Qld Inst. of Medical Res., 2006. *Publications:* contrib. scientific papers to parasitological and immunological jls. *Recreations:* the company of friends, looking at landscapes, music, gardening. *Address:* 79 Brondesbury Road, NW6 6BB. *Clubs:* Reform; Oxford and Cambridge; Queen's (Sydney).

OGILVIE, Ven. Gordon; Archdeacon of Nottingham, 1996–2006; *b* 22 Aug. 1942; *s* of late Gordon and Eliza J. Ogilvie (*née* Cullen); *m* 1967, Sylvia Margaret, *d* of late Rankin and Jessie Weir; one *s* one *d*. *Educ:* Hillhead High Sch., Glasgow; Glasgow Univ. (MA 1964); London Coll. of Divinity (ext. BD London Univ., 1967). Ordained deacon, 1967, priest, 1968; Asst Curate, Ashtead, 1967–72; Vicar, St James, New Barnet, 1972–80; Dir, Pastoral Studies, Wycliffe Hall, Oxford, 1980–87; Priest-in-charge, 1987–89, Team Rector, 1989–96, Harlow Town Centre with Little Parndon; Chaplain, Princess Alexandra Hosp., Harlow, 1988–96. Hon. Canon, Chelmsford Cathedral, 1993–96. *Recreations:* cricket, piano, photography. *Address:* 49 Argyle Street, St Andrews, Fife KY16 9BX. *T:* (01334) 470185.

OGILVIE, Prof. Sheilagh Catheren, PhD; FBA 2004; Professor of Economic History, University of Cambridge, since 2004; *b* 7 Oct. 1958; *d* of Robert Townley Ogilvie and Sheilagh Stuart Ogilvie. *Educ:* Queen Elizabeth Sch.; Univ. of St Andrews (MA 1st cl. Hons 1979); Trinity Coll., Cambridge (PhD 1985); Univ. of Chicago (MA 1992). Res. Fellow, Trinity Coll., Cambridge, 1984–88; Univ. Asst Lectr, 1989–92, Univ. Lectr, 1992–99, Reader in Econ. History, 1999–2004, Faculty of Econs, Univ. of Cambridge. Series Ed. (with Bob Scribner), Germany: a new social and economic history, 1450–present, 3 vols, 1995–2003. *Publications:* The Park Buffalo: the history of the conservation of the North American bison, 1979; (ed) Proto-Industrialization in Europe, 1993; (ed with Markus Cerman) Protoindustrialisierung in Europa: Industrielle Produktion vor dem Fabrikszeitalter, 1994; Germany: a new social and economic history, (ed) vol. 2, 1630–1800, 1996, (ed with Richard Overy) vol. 3, Since 1800, 2003; (ed with Markus Cerman) European Proto-Industrialization, 1996; State Corporatism and Proto-Industry: the Württemberg Black Forest 1590–1797, 1997; A Bitter Living: women, markets and social capital in Early Modern Germany, 2003; articles in Amer. Historical Rev., Bohemia, Continuity and Change, Econ. Hist. Rev., Histoires et sociétés rurales, Historical Jl, Historická Demografie, Jahrbuch für Wirtschaftsgeschichte, Jl of Econ. Hist., Past & Present, Social Hist. and Trans of RHistS. *Recreations:* indiscriminate reading, walking in Central European mountains, thinking, talking, counting. *Address:* Faculty of Economics, University of Cambridge, Sidgwick Avenue, Cambridge CB3 9DD. *T:* (01223) 335222, *Fax:* (01223) 335475; *e-mail:* sco2@econ.cam.ac.uk.

OGILVIE-GRANT, family name of **Earl of Seafield**.

OGILVIE-LAING of Kinkell, Gerald, NDD; FRBS 1993 (ARBS 1987); sculptor; *b* 11 Feb. 1936; *s* of Gerald Francis Laing and Enid Moody (*née* Foster), and *g s* of Capt. Gerald Ogilvie Laing; adopted name of Ogilvie-Laing by Deed Poll, 1968; *m* 1st, 1962, Jenifer Anne Redway; one *d*; 2nd, 1969, Galina Vassilovna Golikova; two *s*; 3rd, 1988, Adaline Havemeyer Frelinghuysen; two *s*. *Educ:* Berkhamsted Sch.; RMA, Sandhurst; St Martin's Sch. of Art, London (NDD) 1964. Served Royal Northumberland Fusiliers, 1955–60, resigned; lived in NYC, 1964–69; Pop painting, 1962–65, abstract sculpture, 1965–73; Artist in Residence, Aspen Inst., 1966; restored Kinkell Castle, Scotland, 1969–70 (Civic Trust Award, 1971); established Tapestry Workshop, 1970–74; changed to figurative sculpture, 1973. Vis. Prof. of Painting and Sculpture, Univ. of New Mexico, 1976–77; Prof. of Sculpture, Columbia Univ., 1986–87. Installed: Callanish sculpture, Strathclyde Univ., 1971; Frieze of Wise and Foolish Virgins, Edinburgh, 1979; Fountain of Sabrina, Bristol, 1980; Conan Doyle Meml, and Axis Mundi, Edinburgh, 1991; Bank Station Dragons, 1995; four figures on Rowland Hill Gate, Twickenham Rugby Stadium, 1996; St George and Dragon sequence, Harrow, 1996; Cricketer, Wormsley, Bucks, 1998; Fire Icon, Bluewater, Kent, 1999; Glass Virgins, Edinburgh, and Fifth Fusilier Meml, Badajoz, Spain, 2000; Batsman, MCC, Lord's Ground, 2001; Wormsley Sundial, 2001; Falcon Square, Mercat Cross, Inverness, 2003; series of anti-war paintings inspired esp. by Iraq conflict, exhibited King's Coll., Cambridge, NY and Paris, 2005, London, 2007 and 2008; exhibits frequently; work in many public and private collections worldwide, including Tate Gall., V&A, Nat. Portrait Gall., London and Edinburgh, Nat. Gall. (portrait bust of Sir Paul Getty, 1997), Nat. Army Mus., London, Scottish Nat. Gall. of Modern Art, Mus. of Modern Art, NY, Whitney Mus., NY, and Smithsonian Instn. Member: Art Cttee, Scottish Arts Council, 1978–80; Royal Fine Art Commn for Scotland, 1987–95. Chm., Black Isle Civic Trust, 1991–93. *Publication:* Kinkell—the Reconstruction of a Scottish castle, 1974, 2nd edn 1984. *Address:* Kinkell Castle, Ross and Cromarty IV7 8AT. *T:* (01349) 861485; *e-mail:* kinkell@btinternet.com. (London studio) Flat 9, 22 Leathermarket Street, SE1 3HP. *T:* (020) 7378 8538. *Clubs:* Chelsea Arts, Academy, Frontline, Ivy.

OGILVIE THOMPSON, Julian; Director: De Beers Consolidated Mines Ltd, 1966–2006 (Deputy Chairman, 1982–85 and 1998–2001; Chairman, 1985–97); De Beers SA, 2002–08; *b* 27 Jan. 1934; *s* of late Hon. N. Ogilvie Thompson, formerly Chief Justice of S Africa, and of Eve Ogilvie Thompson; *m* 1956, Hon. Tessa Mary Brand, *yr* surv. *d* of 4th Viscount Hampden, CMG and Leila, Viscountess Hampden; two *s* two *d*. *Educ:* Diocesan Coll., Rondebosch; Univ. of Cape Town; Worcester Coll., Oxford. MA. Diocesan Coll. Rhodes Scholar, 1953. Joined Anglo American Corp. of SA Ltd, 1956; Dir, 1970; Exec. Dir, 1971–82; Dep. Chm., 1983–90; Chm., 1990–2002; Anglo American plc: Chief Exec., 1999–2000; Chm., 1999–2002; Chairman: Anglo American Gold Investment Co. Ltd, 1976–90; Minorco SA (formerly Minerals and Resources Corp. Ltd), 1982–99; Vice Chairman: First Nat. Bank Ltd, 1977–90; Urban Foundn, 1986–95. Rhodes Trustee, 2002–; Trustee, Mandela Rhodes Foundn, 2003–. Hon. LLD Rhodes, 1986. Comdr, Order of the Crown (Belgium), 1993; Grand Official, Order of Bernardo O'Higgins (Chile), 1996; Presidential Order of Honour (Botswana), 1997. *Recreations:* shooting, fishing, golf. *Address:* Froome, Froome Street, Athol Extension 3, Sandton, 2196, S Africa. *T:* (11) 8843925. *Clubs:* White's; Rand (Johannesburg); Kimberley (Cape Province); The Brook (NY).

See also Baroness Dacre.

OGILVY, family name of **Earl of Airlie**.

OGILVY, Lord; David John Ogilvy; *b* 9 March 1958; *s* and *heir* of 13th Earl of Airlie, *qv; m* 1st, 1981, Hon. Geraldine Harmsworth (marr. diss. 1991), *d* of 3rd Viscount Rothermere; one *d*; 2nd, 1991, Tarka Kings; three *s*. *Educ:* Eton and Oxford (MA). Man.

Dir, Richard L. Feigen UK Ltd, art dealers, 1982–2002. *Heir: s* Master of Ogilvy, *qv*. *Address:* Airlie Castle, Kirriemuir, Angus DD8 5NG.

OGILVY, Master of; David Huxley Ogilvy; *b* 11 Dec. 1991; *s* and *heir* of Lord Ogilvy, *qv*.

OGILVY, Sir Francis (Gilbert Arthur), 14th Bt *cr* 1626 (NS), of Inverquharity, Forfarshire; Chartered Surveyor; *b* 22 April 1969; *s* of Sir David John Wilfrid Ogilvy, 13th Bt and of Penelope Mary Ursula, *d* of Captain Arthur Lafone Frank Hills, OBE; *S* father, 1992; *m* 1996, Dorothy, *e d* of Rev. Jock Stein and Rev. Margaret Stein; three *s* one *d*. *Educ:* Edinburgh Acad.; Glenalmond; RAC, Cirencester (BSc Hons). MRICS. *Heir: s* Robert David Ogilvy, *b* 8 July 1999. *Address:* Winton House, Pencaitland, E Lothian EH34 5AT.

OGILVY, Hon. James (Donald Diarmid); Chairman, Foreign & Colonial Management Ltd, 1998–99 (Chief Executive, 1988–97); *b* 28 June 1934; *y s* of 12th Earl of Airlie, KT, GCVO, MC and Lady Alexandra Marie Bridget Coke, *d* of 3rd Earl of Leicester, GCVO, CMG; *m* 1st, 1959, June Ducas (marr. diss. 1978; she *d* 2001); two *s* two *d*; 2nd, 1980, Lady Caroline (*née* Child-Villiers), *d* of 9th Earl of Jersey. *Educ:* Eton Coll. Served 1st Bn, Scots Guards, Egypt, 1953–55 (2nd Lieut). Partner, Rowe & Pitman, 1959–86; Vice Chm., Mercury Asset Management plc, 1986–88. Chairman: Sutherlands (Holdings), 1998–2000; Off Plan Fund, 2004–05. Director: Foreign and Colonial Investment Trust, 1990–97; Foreign & Colonial Emerging Markets, 1995–98; Berkshire Capital Corp. UK, 1998–2006; Lord North Street Holdings Ltd, 2005–; Black Sea Fund, 2005–06. Dir, 1974–76, Chm., 1976–83, Inst. for Obstetrics and Gynaecology; Gov., Queen Charlotte's and Chelsea Hosp. for Women, 1974–80. Chm., Museum of Garden History, 2002–. Mem., Queen's Body Guard for Scotland, Royal Co. of Archers. Grand Official, Nat. Order of the Southern Cross (Brazil), 1993. *Recreations:* shooting, golf. *Address:* Sedgebrook Manor, Sedgebrook, Grantham, Lincs NG32 2EN. *T:* (01949) 842337; Flat 20, Stack House, Cundy Street, SW1W 9JS. *Clubs:* White's, Pratt's.

OGILVY-WEDDERBURN, Sir Andrew John Alexander, 13th and 7th Bt *cr* 1704 and 1803; *b* 4 Aug. 1952; *s* of Sir (John) Peter Ogilvy-Wedderburn, 12th and 6th Bt, and late Elizabeth Katharine, *e d* of John A. Cox, Drumkilbo; *S* father, 1977; *m* 1984, Gillian Meade, *yr d* of Richard Adderley, Pickering, N Yorks; two *s* (twins) one *d* (and one *s* decd). *Educ:* Gordonstoun. *Heir: s* Peter Robert Alexander Ogilvy-Wedderburn, *b* 20 April 1987. *Address:* Silvie, Alyth, Perthshire PH11 8NA.

OGLESBY, Michael John; DL; Vice Lord-Lieutenant, Greater Manchester, since 2008; Chairman, Bruntwood Ltd, since 2000; *b* Scunthorpe, 5 June 1939; *s* of George Oglesby and Alice Oglesby; *m* Jean; one *s* one *d*. *Educ:* De Aston Sch., Market Rasen; Aston Univ., Birmingham (BSc Building). Founder, 1978, CEO, 1980–2000, Bruntwood Estates Ltd. Chairman: MIDAS, 2004–; RNCM, 2004–; MCRC, 2005–. High Sheriff, Gtr Manchester, 2007. Hon. LLD Manchester, 2006; Hon. DSc Aston, 2007. *Recreations:* sailing, ski-ing, theatre, music. *Address:* Bruntwood Ltd, City Tower, Piccadilly Plaza, Manchester M1 4BD.

OGLESBY, Peter Rogerson, CB 1982; *b* 15 July 1922; *s* of late Leonard William Oglesby and late Jessie Oglesby (*née* Rogerson); *m* 1947, Doreen Hilda Hudson (*d* 2006); three *d*. *Educ:* Woodhouse Grove Sch., Apperley Bridge. Clerical Officer, Admlty, 1939–47; Exec. Officer, Min. of Nat. Ins., 1947–56; Higher Exec. Officer, MPNI, 1956–62, Principal 1962–64; Principal Private Secretary: to Chancellor of Duchy of Lancaster, 1964–66; to Minister without Portfolio, 1966; to First Sec. of State, 1966–68; to Lord President, 1968; Asst Sec., Cabinet Office, 1968–70, Asst Sec., DHSS, 1970–73; Sec., Occupational Pensions Bd, 1973–74; Under Sec., 1974–79; Dep. Sec., 1979–82, DHSS. Dir, Regency Final Gp, 1983–91. *Address:* 7 Roebuck Heights, North End, Buckhurst Hill, Essex IG9 5RF. *T:* (020) 8504 9104.

OGLEY, William David; Chief Executive, States of Jersey, since 2003; *b* 26 May 1955; *s* of Thomas William and Olive Ogley; *m* 1976, Anne Dolores Walker; two *d*. *Educ:* Manchester Univ. (BA Hons Physics and Psych.); CIPFA (prize winner). Derbyshire CC, 1976–83 (to Principal Accountant, 1980–83); Group Accountant, Oxfordshire CC, 1983–85; Hertfordshire County Council: Sen. Asst. County Treasurer, 1985–88 (Educn and Social Services); Dep. County Treasurer, 1988–90; Dir, Inf. Systems, 1990–91; Dir of Finance, 1991–93; Dep. Controller and Dir of Resources, Audit Commn, 1993–96; Chief Exec., 1996–2003. *Recreations:* tennis, gardening, sailing, family, reading. *Address:* PO Box 140, St Helier, Jersey, Channel Islands JE4 8QT.

OGMORE, 3rd Baron *cr* 1950, of Bridgend; **Morgan Rees-Williams;** *b* 19 Dec. 1937; *s* of 1st Baron Ogmore, PC, TD and (Alice Alexandra) Constance Rees-Williams (*née* Wills); *S* brother, 2004; *m* 1990, Beata Ewa Solska; two *s*. *Educ:* Mill Hill Sch. Lieut, The Welch Regt, 1956–58. *Heir: s* Hon. Tudor David Rees-Williams, *b* 11 Dec. 1991. *Address:* 50 Novello Street, SW6 4JB. *T:* (020) 7736 2734.

OGNALL, Hon. Sir Harry Henry, Kt 1986; DL; a Judge of the High Court of Justice, Queen's Bench Division, 1986–2000; *b* 9 Jan. 1934; *s* of Leo and Cecilia Ognall; *m* 1977, Elizabeth Young; two step *s* and two *s* one *d* of former marriage. *Educ:* Leeds Grammar Sch.; Lincoln Coll., Oxford (MA (Hons)); Univ. of Virginia, USA (LLM; Fulbright Scholar, 1956). Called to Bar (Gray's Inn), 1958; Bencher, 1983. Joined NE Circuit; a Recorder, 1972–86; QC 1973. Member: Criminal Injuries Compensation Bd, 1976; Planning Cttee, Senate of Inns of Court and Bar, 1980–83; Professional Conduct Cttee, 1985; Judicial Studies Bd (Chm., Criminal Cttee), 1986–89; Parole Bd, 1989–91 (Vice-Chm., 1990–91); a Judicial Mem., Proscribed Orgns Appeal Commn, 2001–. Arbitrator, Motor Insurers' Bureau Agreement, 1979–85. Chm., eWitness Ltd, 2000–05. Trustee, Martin House Hospice, 2002–. DL W Yorks, 2000. *Recreations:* golf, photography, music, travel. *Clubs:* Ganton Golf, Ilkley Golf, Ilkley Bowling.

O'GRADY, Frances Lorraine Maria; Deputy General Secretary, Trades Union Congress, since 2003; *b* 9 Nov. 1959; *d* of James and Margaret O'Grady; one *s* one *d*. *Educ:* Milham Ford Comprehensive Sch., Oxford; Manchester Univ. (BA Pols and Mod. Hist.); Middlesex Polytechnic (Dip Ind Relns and Trade Union Studies). Employment Rights Officer, Women and Employment Project, 1982–87; Health and Safety Officer, City Centre, London, 1987–88; Campaigns Officer, Health Rights, 1988–89; Sen. Researcher, TGWU, 1989–94; Trades Union Congress: Campaigns Officer, 1994–96; Dir, New Unionism, 1996–98; Hd, Orgn, 1998–2003. Member: Unite (TGWU); NUJ. *Publication:* (with Heather Wakefield) Women, Work and Maternity: the inside story, 1989. *Recreations:* labour history, cinema, Arsenal FC. *Address:* Trades Union Congress, Congress House, Great Russell Street, WC1B 3LS. *T:* (020) 7636 4030, *Fax:* (020) 7636 0632; *e-mail:* fogrady@tuc.org.uk.

O'GRADY, Prof. Francis William, CBE 1984; TD 1970; MD, MSc; FRCP, FRCPath, FFPM; Foundation Professor of Microbiology, University of Nottingham, 1974–88, now Emeritus; *b* 7 Nov. 1925; *s* of Francis Joseph O'Grady and Lilian Maud Hitchcock; *m* 1951, Madeleine Marie-Thérèse Becquart; three *d*. *Educ:* Middlesex Hosp. Med. Sch., London (BSc 1st Cl. Hons; MB, BS Hons; MSc; MD). FRCP 1976; FRCPath 1972; FFPM 1989. House Physician, Middx and North Middx Hosps, 1951; Asst Pathologist, Bland-Sutton Inst. of Pathol., Middx Hosp., 1952–53, 1956–58 and 1961–62; Pathologist, RAMC, 1954–55, AER, 1956–72; Asst Prof. of Environmental Medicine, Johns Hopkins Univ., Baltimore, 1959–60; Reader, 1962–66, and Prof. of Bacteriology, 1967–74, Univ. of London; Bacteriologist, St Bartholomew's Hosp., 1962–74; Chief Scientist, DHSS, subseq. DoH, 1986–90. Hon. Consultant Microbiologist, PHLS, 1974–96. Mem., MRC, 1980–84, 1986–90; Chm., MRC Physiol Systems and Disorders Bd, 1980–82 (Mem., 1977–80; Mem., Grants Cttee, 1975–76); Chm., MRC Cttee on Hosp. Infection, 1977–80 (Mem., 1967–77). Member: Antibiotics Panel, Cttee on Med. Aspects of Food Policy, 1968–72; Sub-Cttee on Toxicity, Clin. Trials and Therapeutic Efficacy, 1971–75, and Sub-Cttee on Biol Substances, 1971–81, Cttee on Safety of Medicines; Jt Sub-Cttee on Antimicrobial Substances, Cttee on Safety of Medicines and Vet. Products Cttee, 1973–80; Cttee on Rev. of Medicines, 1975–81; Public Health Lab. Service Bd, 1980–86, 1993–96; Nat. Biological Standards Bd, 1983–87. Hon. Consultant Microbiologist to the Army, 1982–91. William N. Creasy Vis. Prof. of Clin. Pharmacology, Duke Univ., NC, 1979. Erasmus Wilson Demonstrator, RCS, 1967; Foundn Lectr, Univ. of Hong Kong, 1974; Sydney Watson Smith Lectr, RCPE, 1975; Jacobson Vis. Lectr, Univ. of Newcastle upon Tyne, 1979; Berk Lectr, British Assoc. of Urol Surgeons, 1980; Garrod Lectr, British Soc. for Antimicrobial Chemotherapy, 1983; Jenner Lectr, St George's Hosp. Med. Sch., 1988. Pres. Council, British Jl of Exper. Pathol., 1980–91 (Mem., 1968–80); Mem. Editorial Boards: Jl of Med. Microbiol., 1970–75; Pathologie Biologie, 1973–78; British Jl of Clin. Pharmacol., 1974–84; Drugs, 1976–88; Gut, 1977–83; Jl of Infection, 1978–83; Revs of Infectious Diseases, 1979–88. *Publications:* Airborne Infection: transmission and control, 1968; Antibiotic and Chemotherapy, 1968, 7th edn 1997; (ed) Urinary Tract Infection, 1968; (ed) Microbial Perturbation of Host Defences, 1981; papers on clin. and exper. infection and on antimicrobial chemotherapy. *Address:* 32 Wollaton Hall Drive, Nottingham NG8 1AF.

O'GRADY, Michael Gerard; QC (Scot.) 1999; Sheriff of Lothian and Borders at Edinburgh, since 2007; Temporary Judge, since 2004; *b* 19 Aug. 1954; *s* of Thomas Anthony O'Grady and Margaret Imelda O'Grady (*née* King); *m* 1996, Sheena Margaret McDougall. *Educ:* Univ. of Glasgow (MA, LLB). Solicitor in private practice, 1977–88; admitted to Faculty of Advocates, 1988; Advocate Depute, 1993–97; Standing Junior to FCO, 1997–99; Chm., Advocates' Criminal Law Gp, 1999–2000; Floating Sheriff of Glasgow and Strathkelvin, 2000–07. Examiner, Glasgow Graduate Law Sch., 2002–. *Recreations:* guitar, travel, reading, art. *Address:* Sheriff Court House, 27 Chambers Street, Edinburgh EH1 1LB. *Club:* Scottish Arts (Edinburgh).

OGSTON, Prof. Derek, CBE 1995; MD, PhD, DSc; FRCP; FRSE 1982; Professor of Medicine, 1983–97, and Vice Principal, 1987–97, University of Aberdeen; *b* 31 May 1932; *s* of Frederick John Ogston and Ellen Mary Ogston; *m* 1963, Cecilia Marie Clark; one *s* two *d*. *Educ:* King's Coll. Sch., Wimbledon; Univ. of Aberdeen (MA, PhD 1962; MD 1969; DSc 1975; MLitt 1999; BTh 2005). FRCP Edin. 1973; FRCP 1977; FIBiol 1987. University of Aberdeen: Res. Fellow, 1959–62; Lectr in Medicine, 1962–69; Sen. Lectr in Med., 1969–75; Reader in Med., 1975–76; Regius Prof. of Physiology, 1977–83; Dean, Faculty of Medicine, 1984–87. MRC Trav. Fellow, 1967–68. Vice-Chm., Grampian Health Bd, 1993–97 (Mem., 1991–97); Mem., GMC, 1984–94. Member: Governing Body, Rowett Res. Inst., 1977–92; Court, Univ. of Aberdeen, 1998–2002. Hon. LLD Aberdeen, 2007. *Publications:* Physiology of Hemostasis, 1983; Antifibrinolytic Drugs, 1984; Venous Thrombosis, 1987; The Life and Work of George Smith, RSA, 2000; George Leslie Hunter 1877–1931, 2002; Working Children, 2003; Leslie Hunter: drawings and paintings of France and Italy, 2004; Children at School, 2005; scientific papers on haemostasis. *Recreations:* music, travel. *Address:* 64 Rubislaw Den South, Aberdeen AB15 4AY. *T:* (01224) 316587.

OGUS, Prof. Anthony Ian, CBE 2002; FBA 2007; Professor of Law, University of Manchester, 1987–2008, now Emeritus; *b* 30 Aug. 1945; *s* of Samuel Joseph Ogus and Sadie Phyllis Ogus (*née* Green); *m* 1st, 1980, Catherine Klein (*d* 1998); 2nd, 2001, Helen Margaret Legard Owens. *Educ:* St Dunstan's Coll.; Magdalen Coll., Oxford (BA 1966; BCL 1967; MA 1970). Asst Lectr in Law, Univ. of Leicester, 1967–69; Tutorial Fellow in Law, Mansfield Coll., Oxford, 1969–75; Sen. Res. Fellow, Centre for Socio-Legal Studies, Wolfson Coll., Oxford, 1975–78; Prof. of Law, Univ. of Newcastle, 1978–87. Res. Prof., Univ. of Maastricht, 1997–2008. Mem., Social Security Adv. Cttee, 1994–. Hamlyn Trustee, 1979–2001. *Publications:* Law of Damages, 1973; (jtly) Law of Social Security, 1978, 5th edn 2002; (jtly) Policing Pollution, 1983; (jtly) Readings in the Economics of Law and Regulation, 1984; Regulation: legal form and economic theory, 1994; (jtly) Controlling the Regulators, 1998; (jtly) Economie du droit: le cas français, 2002; Costs and Cautionary Tales: economic insights for the law, 2006; articles in legal periodicals. *Recreations:* theatre, opera, concerts, cycling, reading, walking. *Address:* Woodland House, Midgeley Lane, Goldsborough HG5 8NN. *T:* (01423) 864099. *Club:* Oxford and Cambridge.

O'HAGAN, 4th Baron *cr* 1870; **Charles Towneley Strachey;** *b* 6 Sept. 1945; *s* of Hon. Thomas Anthony Edward Towneley Strachey (*d* 1955; having assumed by deed poll, 1938, the additional Christian name of Towneley, and his mother's maiden name of Strachey, in lieu of his patronymic) and Lady Mary (who *m* 1981, St John Gore, *qv*; she *d* 2000), *d* of 3rd Earl of Selborne, PC, CH; *S* grandfather, 1961; *m* 1995, Mrs Elizabeth Lesley Eve Macnamara (*née* Smith); two *d* from previous marriages. *Educ:* Eton; (Exhibitioner) New College, Oxford. Page to HM the Queen, 1959–62. Independent Member, European Parliament, 1973–75; Junior Opposition Whip, House of Lords, 1977–79; MEP (C) Devon, 1979–94. *Heir: brother* Hon. Richard Towneley Strachey [*b* 29 Dec. 1950; *m* 1983, Sally Anne, *yr d* of Frederick Cecil Cross]. *Address:* The Granary, Beaford, Winkleigh, Devon EX19 8AB. *Club:* Pratt's.

O'HAGAN, Dr Dara; Member (SF) Upper Bann, Northern Ireland Assembly, 1998–2003; *b* 29 Aug. 1964; *d* of Joseph and Bernadette O'Hagan. *Educ:* Univ. of Ulster (BA Hons Hist. and Politics 1991); Queen's Univ., Belfast (MSSc 1994; PhD 1998). Contested (SF) Upper Bann, 2001.

O'HALLORAN, Sarah Jane; *see* Vaughan Jones, S. J.

O'HANLON, Michael David Peter, PhD; Director, Pitt Rivers Museum, Oxford, since 1998; Professorial Fellow, Linacre College, Oxford, since 1998; *b* 2 July 1950; *s* of late Michael Charles O'Hanlon, Kitale, Kenya, and of Rosemary Alice Sibbald; *m* 1981, Linda Helga Elizabeth, *d* of (Anthony) Noble Frankland, *qv*; one *d*. *Educ:* Kenya; Plymouth Coll., Devon; Pembroke Coll., Cambridge (MA); University Coll. London (PhD 1985). Field res., Wahgi Valley, PNG Highlands, 1979–81; Curator, Pacific collections, Ethnography Dept, BM, 1983–98. Visitor: Mus. of Hist. of Sci., Oxford Univ., 1998–; Oxford Univ. Mus. of Nat. Hist., 2002–; Mem., Overseers' Cttee, Peabody Mus., Harvard, 2003–. Mem. Council, 1994–97, Hon. Sec., 1997–98, RAI. Reviews Editor, MAN, 1988–90; Mem., Editl Bd, Jl Material Culture, 1996–. *Publications:* Reading the Skin, 1989; Paradise: portraying the New Guinea Highlands, 1993; (ed with E. Hirsch)

The Anthropology of Landscape, 1995; (ed with Robert L. Welsch) Hunting the Gatherers: ethnographic collectors, agents and agency in Melanesia 1870s–1930s, 2000; (ed with E. Ewart) Body Arts and Modernity, 2007; contrib. articles and reviews in professional jls. *Address:* c/o Pitt Rivers Museum, South Parks Road, Oxford OX1 3PP.

O'HARA, Bill; JP; National Governor of the BBC for Northern Ireland, 1973–78; *b* 26 Feb. 1929; *s* of William P. O'Hara and Susanna Agnes O'Hara (*née* Gill); *m* 1953, Anne Marie Finn; two *s* two *d. Address:* Summer Cottage, 12 Raglan Road, Bangor, Co. Down, N Ireland BT20 3TL. *Clubs:* Royal Ulster Yacht, Royal Belfast Golf.

O'HARA, Edward; MP (Lab) Knowsley South, since Sept. 1990; *b* 1 Oct. 1937; *s* of Robert Edward O'Hara and Clara O'Hara (*née* Davies); *m* 1962, Lillian Hopkins (separated); two *s* one *d. Educ:* Magdalen Coll., Oxford (MA 1962); PGCE 1966, DipED (Adv.) 1970, London. Assistant Teacher: Perse Sch., Cambridge, 1962–65; Birkenhead Sch., 1966–70; Lectr and Principal Lectr, C. F. Mott Coll. of Educn, 1970–74; Principal Lectr and Sen. Tutor, Dean of Postgrad. Studies, City of Liverpool Coll. of Higher Educn, 1974–83; Head of Curriculum Studies, Sch. of Educn and Community Studies, Liverpool Polytechnic, 1983–90. Knowsley Borough Council: Mem., 1975–91; Mem., all Standing Cttees; Chairman: Youth Cttee, 1977–79 and 1981–82; Educn Cttee, 1978–79 and 1987–90; Econ. Develt and Planning Cttee, 1990–91. Mem., Speaker's Panel of Chairmen, 1993–. Co-Chm., All Pty Gp on Ageing and Older People, 1997–; Chairman: All Pty MV Derbyshire Gp, 1997–2005; British-Greek Gp, IPU, 1997–; Argentine Gp, IPU, 2005–. Member: Bd of Management, NFER, 1986–90; European Assoc. of Teachers; Socialist Educn Assoc.; Hon. Mem. and Parly Advr, Assoc. of Chief Educn Social Workers, 1992–93; Member: Labour Movement in Europe; Perm. Cttee of Assembly of European Regions, 1989–90; Merseyside Rep., Régions Européennes de Tradition Industrielle, 1989–90; Deleg., Council of Europe and WEU, 1997–: Gen. Rapporteur for Cultural Heritage and Museums Rapporteur, Council of Europe; Chair, Technol. and Aerospace Cttee, and Mem., Presidential Cttee, WEU. Member: Fabian Soc.; Co-op Party; Socialist Educn Assoc. Mem., Bd of Management, Royal Liverpool Philharmonic Soc., 1987–90; Corresp. Mem., Foundn for Hellenic Culture. Trustee, Community Develt Foundn (Chm., 1997–); Vice-Chm., Develt Trust Bd, Nat. Wildflower Centre, 1996–. Vice-Pres., TS Iron Duke, Huyton. Governor: Knowsley Community Coll.; Prescot Co. Primary Sch. Pres., Knowsley South Jun. FC. *Recreations:* music (classical, jazz, folk, esp. Rembetiko), reading, theatre, travel, Greek language and culture. *Address:* 69 St Mary's Road, Huyton, Merseyside L36 5SR. *T:* (0151) 489 8021. *Club:* Halewood Labour.

O'HARA, Prof. Michael John, PhD; FRS 1981; FRSE 1969; Professor of Geology, 1978-93, Hon. Professor, 2004, University of Wales, Aberystwyth; *b* 22 Feb. 1933; *s* of Michael Patrick O'Hara, OBE, and Winifred Dorothy O'Hara; *m* 1st, 1962, Janet Tibbits; one *s* two *d*; 2nd, 1977, Susan Howells; two *s* one *d. Educ:* Dulwich Coll. Prep. Sch.; Cranleigh; Peterhouse, Cambridge (MA, PhD). Asst, Lectr, Reader and Prof. (1971), Edinburgh Univ., 1958–78; Dist. Res. Prof., UWCC, 1994–2003. Principal Investigator, NASA Lunar Science Prog., 1968–75; Prof. of Geology, Sultan Qaboos Univ., Oman, 1988–90. Sherman-Fairchild Vis. Scholar, Calif Inst. of Technology, 1984–85; Visiting Professor: Harvard Univ., 1986; North West Univ., Xi'an, 2004; Concurrent Prof., Nanjing Univ., 2004; Honorary Professor: China Inst. of Geoscis, Beijing, 2004; Durham Univ., 2005. Member: Council, NERC, 1986–88; UGC, 1987–89. Associate Mem., Geol Soc. of France; Geochemistry Fellow, Geochemical Soc. and Eur. Assoc. for Geochem., 1997; Fellow, Amer. Geophys. Union, 2004. Murchison Medal, Geol Soc., 1983; Bowen Award, Amer. Geophys. Union, 1984. *Publications:* numerous in learned jls. *Recreation:* mountaineering.

O'HARE, John Edward; Master of Supreme Court Costs (formerly Taxing) Office, since 1995; *b* 26 Feb. 1949; *s* of Kevin Mark Plunkett O'Hare and Kathleen Mary O'Hare; *m* 1st, 1970, Vivien Eleanor Harwood; one *s*; 2nd, 1993, Alison Jane Springett; one *s. Educ:* Bromley Boys' GS; Leicester Univ. (LLB). Called to the Bar, Lincoln's Inn, 1972; College of Law: Lectr, 1974–78; Sen. Lectr, 1978–85; Principal Lectr, 1985–95. *Publications:* Civil Litigation, 1980, 14th edn 2009; White Book Service, 2007, 2009. *Recreations:* bridge, cycling. *Address:* Supreme Court Costs Office, Clifford's Inn, Fetter Lane, EC4A 1DQ.

O'HARE, Peter, PhD; Director, Marie Curie Research Institute, since 2002 (Group Leader, since 1986); *b* 9 Dec. 1956; *s* of Eugene and Sinéad O'Hare; *m* 1983, Jane Hillier; two *d. Educ:* St Columb's Coll., Derry; Sheffield Univ. (BSc 1978); NIMR, London (PhD 1981). Res. Fellow, NIMR, London, 1981–83; Damon-Runyon Res. Fellow, Johns Hopkins Univ. Medical Sch., 1983–86. *Publications:* numerous articles on molecular and cell biology, virology and field of gene delivery, in learned jls, Nature, Cell etc. *Recreations:* passionate (though untalented) photographer, hiking, canoeing, vociferous supporter of Irish Rugby, history of science. *Address:* Marie Curie Research Institute, The Chart, Oxted, Surrey RH8 0TL. *T:* (01883) 722306, *Fax:* (01883) 714375; *e-mail:* P.OHare@mcri.ac.uk.

O'HEAR, Prof. Anthony, PhD; Professor of Philosophy (formerly Garfield Weston Professor of Philosophy), and Head of Department of Education, University of Buckingham, since 2003; Director, Royal Institute of Philosophy, since 1994; *b* 14 Jan. 1942; *s* of Hugo O'Hear and Ann Margery Hester O'Hear (*née* Gompertz); *m* 1981, Patricia Catherine Mary Patterson (Patricia Linton, in ballet); one *s* two *d. Educ:* St Ignatius' Coll., Tottenham; Heythrop Coll.; Warwick Univ. (MA 1968; PhD 1971). Lecturer in Philosophy: Univ. of Hull, 1971–75; Univ. of Surrey, 1975–84; Prof. of Philosophy, Univ. of Bradford, 1985–2003. Vis. Res. Fellow, LSE, 2002–; Calouste Gulbenkian Vis. Prof., Catholic Univ. of Portugal, 2004–05. Ed., Philosophy, 1995–. Member: CATE, 1990–94; SCAA, 1993–97; TTA, 1994–97. *Publications:* Karl Popper, 1980; Education, Society and Human Nature, 1981; Experience, Explanation and Faith, 1984; What Philosophy Is, 1985; The Element of Fire, 1988; Introduction to the Philosophy of Science, 1989; Jesus for Beginners, 1993; Beyond Evolution, 1997; After Progress, 1999; Philosophy in the New Century, 2001; Plato's Children, 2006; The Great Books, 2007; The Landscape of Humanity, 2008. *Recreations:* music, visual arts, ski-ing, tennis, Rugby. *Address:* University of Buckingham, Hunter Street, Buckingham MK18 1EG. *T:* (01280) 820219; *e-mail:* anthony.ohear@buckingham.ac.uk. *Club:* Athenæum.

OHLSON, Sir Brian (Eric Christopher), 3rd Bt *cr* 1920; money broker, retired; *b* 27 July 1936; *s* of Sir Eric James Ohlson, 2nd Bt, and Marjorie Joan, *d* of late C. H. Roosmale-Cocq; *S* father, 1983. *Educ:* Harrow School; RMA Sandhurst. Commissioned into Coldstream Guards, 1956–61. Started money broking, 1961. *Recreations:* sport of kings, cricket, bowls, safaris, bridge, Real tennis. *Heir: b* Peter Michael Ohlson [*b* 18 May 1939; *m* 1968, Sarah, *o d* of Maj.-Gen. Thomas Brodie, CB, CBE, DSO]. *Address:* 1 Courtfield Gardens, SW5 0PA. *Clubs:* MCC, Hurlingham, Queen's.

OISTRAKH, Igor Davidovich; violinist, violist and conductor; Professor, Royal Conservatoire, Brussels, since 1996; *b* Odessa, 27 April 1931; *s* of late David Oistrakh; *m* 1960, Natalia Nikolaevna Zertsalova, pianist, Hon. Artist of Russia; one *s. Educ:* Music Sch. and State Conservatoire, Moscow. FRCM. Many foreign tours (USSR, Europe, the Americas, Japan, Aust.); Prof., Internat. Summer Acad., Belgium, 1997–. Many gramophone recordings. Mem. jury of major violin competitions. Hon. President: César Franck Soc., Liège; Russian Br., Europ. String Teachers Assoc.; Hon. Member: Beethoven Soc., Bonn; Ysaye Foundn, Liège; Wieniawski Soc., Poznan; Heifetz Soc., USA; Mendelssohn and Schumann Foundns, Leipzig. 1st prize: Violin Competition, Budapest, 1949; Wieniawski Competition, Poznan, 1952; Igor Oistrakh internat. violin competition estabd Iserlohn, Germany, 1993. People's Artist of USSR, 1989.

OKA, Prof. Takeshi, PhD; FRS 1984; FRSC 1977; Professor of Chemistry, Astronomy and Astrophysics, 1981–2003, and Robert A. Millikan Distinguished Service Professor, 1989–2003, University of Chicago, now Emeritus Professor; *b* 10 June 1932; *s* of Shumpei and Chiyoko Oka; *m* 1960, Keiko Nukui; two *s* two *d. Educ:* University of Tokyo. BSc, PhD. Fellow, Japanese Soc. for Promotion of Science, 1960–63; National Research Council of Canada: Postdoctorate Fellow, 1963–65; Asst Research Physicist, 1965–68; Associate Research Physicist, 1968–71; Senior Research Physicist, 1971–75; Herzberg Inst. of Astrophysics, 1975–81. Centenary Lectr, Royal Soc., 1982; Chancellor's Distinguished Lectr, Univ. of California, 1985–86. Fellow, Amer. Acad. of Arts and Scis, 1987. Hon. DSc: Waterloo, 2001; London, 2004. Steacie Prize, Steacie Fund, NRSC, 1972; Earle K. Plyler Prize, Amer. Physical Soc., 1982; William F. Meggers Award, 1997, Ellis R. Lippincott Award, 1998, Optical Soc. of America; E. Bright Wilson Award in Spectroscopy, ACS, 2002; Davy Medal, Royal Soc., 2004. *Address:* Department of Chemistry, University of Chicago, 5735 S Ellis Avenue, Chicago, IL 60637, USA.

OKALIK, Hon. Paul; MLA for Iqaluit West, Nunavut, since 1999; Premier, Minister of Executive and Intergovernmental Affairs, since 1999 and Minister of Justice, since 2000, Nunavut, Canada; *b* 26 May 1964; one *s* one *d. Educ:* Iqaluit High Sch.; Carleton Univ. (BA); Univ. of Ottawa (LLB 1997). Called to the Bar, 1999. *Address:* Office of the Premier, Government of Nunavut, Box 2410, 2nd Floor Legislative Building, Iqaluit, Nunavut X0A 0H0, Canada.

O'KEEFE, John Harold; TV consultant; *b* 25 Dec. 1938; *s* of Terence Harold O'Keefe and Christian Frances (*née* Foot); *m* 1959, Valerie Anne Atkins; two *s* two *d. Educ:* Acton County Grammar School. Dir, Newspaper Publishers Assoc., 1974; Hd of Industrial Relations, 1974–81, Production Dir, Central London, 1981, Thames TV, 1982; Man. Dir, Limehouse Studios, 1982–86. *Address:* Prospect Cottage, Kempley, Dymock, Glos GL18 2BN.

O'KENNEDY, Michael E., Hon. CMG 2004; SC; TD (FF) Tipperary North, 1969–80, 1982–93 and 1997–2002; *b* Nenagh, Co. Tipperary, 21 Feb. 1936; *s* of Éamonn and Helena O'Kennedy; *m* 1965, Breda, *d* of late Andrew Heavey and of Mary Heavey; one *s* two *d. Educ:* St Flannan's College, Ennis, Co. Clare; St Patrick's Coll., Maynooth, Co. Kildare; Univ. Coll., Dublin. MA 1957. Called to Irish Bar, 1961; Bencher, King's Inns, Dublin, 1998; Senior Counsel 1973. Mem., Irish Senate, 1965–69, 1993–97; Mem., Oireachtas Select Constitutional Cttee, 1966; Parly Sec. to Minister for Educn, 1970–72; Minister without Portfolio, Dec. 1972–Jan. 1973; Minister for Transport and Power, Jan.–March 1973; Opposition spokesman on Foreign Affairs (incl. Anglo-Irish Affairs), 1973–77; Minister for Foreign Affairs, 1977–79; Pres., Council of Ministers of the European Communities, July–Dec. 1979; Minister for Finance, 1979–81; Pres., Bd of Govs, EIB, 1979; opposition spokesman on finance, 1983–87; Minister for Agriculture and Food, 1987–91; Minister for Labour, 1991–92; Pres., Council of Agriculture Ministers, EC, Jan.–June 1990. Mem., Commn of the European Communities, 1981–82. Personal Rep. of An Taoiseach, Eur. Convention for Charter of Fundamental Human Rights, 1999. Co-Chm., British-Irish Parly Body, 1997. Non-executive Director: Hanzard Europe Ltd; Tradewise Underwriting Agencies Ltd.

OKEOVER, Sir Andrew Peter Monro W.; *see* Walker-Okeover.

OKINE, Most Rev. Robert Garshong Allotey; Archbishop of West Africa, 1993–2003; Bishop of Koforidua-Ho, Ghana, 1981–2003; *b* 12 July 1937; *s* of late Robert Cudjoe Okine and Miriam Naadjah Decker; *m* 1967, Juliana Sakai (*née* Nerquaye-Tetteh); two *s* two *d. Educ:* Anglican Church schs, Gold Coast and Gambia; Methodist Boys' High Sch., Bathurst, The Gambia; Adisadel Coll., Cape Coast, Ghana; Theol Coll., SSM, Kelham (GOE 1964); Inst. of Pastoral Educn, London, Ont. (CertCPE 1972); Huron Coll., Univ. of W Ontario, Canada (BMin 1973); Vanderbilt Univ., Nashville, USA (MA 1975); George Peabody Coll. for Teachers, Nashville, USA (EdS 1975); Haggai Inst. for Advanced Leadership Trng, Singapore (Cert. Completion 1990). Ordained deacon 1964, priest 1965; Asst Curate, St Andrew's, Sekondi, 1964–66; Chaplain and teacher, Adisadel Coll., Cape Coast, 1966–68; Rector: St James, Agona-Swedru, 1968–69; Bishop Aglionby Meml Parish, Tamale, 1969–71; Assistant Priest: St Anne's, Byron, and St George's, London, Ont., Canada, 1971–73; Holy Trinity Episcopal Church, Nashville, USA, 1973–75; Christ Church Parish, Cape Coast, 1975–81; Headmaster, Acad. of Christ the King, 1976–81; Principal, St Nicholas Theol Coll., 1976–81; Archdeacon of Koforidua and Rector, St Peter's, Koforidua, Feb.–Oct. 1981. Hon. Canon, Cathedral Church of Most Holy Trinity, Accra, 1979–81. Chairman: Provincial Liturgical Commn, 1984–2003; Bd of Educn, Anglican Educn Unit, 1991–2003; Human Resources Develt Desk, Jt Anglican Diocesan Council, 1991–2003; Council, Anglican Provinces of Africa, 1999–2003; Mem., Anglican Peace and Justice Network, Global Anglican Consultative Council, 1996–2002. Founder, Kwabeng Anglican Secondary Technical Sch., 1983; Gov., Adisadel Coll., 1987–97. Patron, YMCA (Eastern), 1984–2003. Hon. DD W Ontario, 1982. Order of the Volta (Ghana), 2008. *Recreations:* entertaining, watching good movies, listening to all brands of music. *Address:* 10 Lizam Road (off ECOMOG), Haatso, Accra, Ghana, West Africa.

OKOGIE, His Eminence Cardinal Anthony Olubunmi; *see* Lagos, Archbishop of, (RC).

OKRI, Ben, OBE 2001; FRSL; novelist and poet; *b* 15 March 1959; *s* of Silver and Grace Okri. *Educ:* Univ. of Essex. Poetry Editor, West Africa, 1983–86; broadcaster and presenter, BBC, 1983–85; Fellow Commoner in Creative Arts, Trinity Coll., Cambridge, 1991–93. Mem. Bd, RNT, 1999–2006. Member: Soc. of Authors, 1986–; Council, RSL, 1999–2004. FRSL 1998; FRSA 2003. Hon. DLitt: Westminster, 1997; Essex, 2002; Exeter, 2004. Crystal Award, World Econ. Forum, Switzerland, 1995. *Publications:* Flowers and Shadows, 1980; The Landscapes Within, 1982; Incidents at the Shrine, 1986 (Commonwealth Prize for Africa, 1987; Paris Review Aga Khan Prize for fiction, 1987); Stars of the New Curfew, 1988; The Famished Road, 1991 (Booker Prize, 1991; Premio Letterario Internazionale Chianti-Ruffino-Antico Fattore, 1993; Premio Grinzane Cavour, 1994); An African Elegy, 1992; Songs of Enchantment, 1993; Astonishing the Gods, 1995; Birds of Heaven, 1995; Dangerous Love, 1996 (Premio Palmi, 2000); A Way of Being Free, 1997; Infinite Riches, 1998; Mental Fight, 1999; In Arcadia, 2002; Starbook, 2007. *Recreations:* music, chess, theatre, art, good conversation, walking, silence. *Address:* c/o Orion Books Ltd, Orion House, 5 Upper St Martin's Lane, WC2H 9EA. *Club:* PEN International (Vice-Pres., English Centre, 1997).

OLAH, Prof. George Andrew, PhD; Distinguished Professor of Chemistry and Director, Loker Hydrocarbons Research Institute, University of Southern California, since 1977; *b* 22 May 1927; *s* of Julius Olah and Magda Krasznai; *m* 1949, Judith Lengyel; two *s. Educ:* Technical Univ. of Budapest (PhD Chemistry 1949). Faculty Mem., Technical Univ. of Budapest, 1950–55; Associate Dir for Organic Chem., Central Res. Inst., Hungarian Acad. of Scis, 1955–56; Res. Scientist, Dow Chemical Co., 1957–65; Prof. and Chm., Dept of Chem., Case Western Reserve Univ., Cleveland, Ohio, 1965–77. For. Mem., Royal Soc., 1997. Numerous hon. doctorates. Nobel Prize in Chemistry, 1994; numerous awards. *Publications:* Theoretical Organic Chemistry, 2 vols, 1954; (ed) Friedel–Crafts and Related Reactions, 4 vols, 1963–65; (ed jtly) Carbonium Ions, 5 vols, 1968–75; Friedel–Crafts Chemistry, 1973; Carbocations and Electrophilic Reactions, 1973; Halonium Ions, 1975; (jtly) Superacids, 1985; (jtly) Hypercarbon Chemistry, 1987; (jtly) Nitration: methods and mechanism, 1989; (ed) Cage Hydrocarbons, 1990; (ed jtly) Electron Deficient Boron and Carbon Clusters, 1991; (ed jtly) Chemistry of Energetic Materials, 1991; (ed jtly) Synthetic Fluorine Chemistry, 1992; (jtly) Hydrocarbon Chemistry, 1994; A Life of Magic Chemistry (autobiog.), 2001; (jtly) Beyond Oil and Gas: the methanol economy, 2006; numerous scientific papers and 100 patents. *Address:* Loker Hydrocarbons Research Institute, University of Southern California, Los Angeles, LA 90089, USA. *T:* (213) 7405976.

OLAZÁBAL, José Maria; golfer; *b* Fuenterrabia, Spain, 5 Feb. 1966; *s* of Gaspar and Julia Olazábal. Professional golfer, 1985–; wins include: European Masters, 1986; Benson and Hedges Internat. Open, 1990, 2000; NEC World Series, 1990, 1994; The Internat. (USA), 1991; Grand Prix of Europe, 1991; Mediterranean Open, 1992, 1994; Volvo PGA Championship, 1994; US Masters, 1994, 1999; Dubai Desert Classic, 1998; French Open, 2001; Buick Invitational, 2002; Member: European Ryder Cup Team, 1987, 1989, 1991, 1993, 1997, 1999, 2006, 2008 (Vice-Captain); Spanish Team, Alfred Dunhill Cup, 1999, 2000. *Address:* c/o 112 PGA Tour Boulevard, Ponte Vedra Beach, FL 32082, USA.

OLDENBURG, Claes Thure; artist; *b* Stockholm, 28 Jan. 1929; *s* of Gosta Oldenburg and Sigrid Elisabeth (*née* Lindfors); *m* 1st, 1960, Pat Muschinski (marr. diss. 1970); 2nd, 1977, Coosje van Bruggen. *Educ:* Yale Univ. (BA 1951); Art Inst. Chicago. Apprentice reporter, City News Bureau, Chicago, 1950–52; became American citizen, 1953. First gp exhibn at Club St Elmo, Chicago, 1953; subseq. at local shows, Chicago and Evanston, 1953–56; moved to NY, 1956; has participated in numerous gp exhibns of contemp. art in USA and Europe, including: Dallas Mus. Contemp. Art, 1961, 1962; ICA, 1963; Mus. Mod. Art, NY, 1963, 1988, 1990, 1991; Washington Gall. Mod. Art, 1963; Tate Gall., 1964; Metropolitan Mus. Art, NY, 1969; one-man shows in USA and Europe, including: Reuben Gall., NY, 1960; Sidney Janis Gall., NY, 1964–70; travelling exhibitions: Tate Gall. and other European galls, 1970; Musée d'Art Moderne, Paris, 1977; Nat. Gall. of Art, Washington, 1995; Solomon R. Guggenheim Mus., NY, and galls in London, LA and Bonn, 1995–96; numerous commnd works in permanent collections in USA and Europe, incl. Centre Georges Pompidou, Paris, Museums of Contemp. Art, Chicago and LA, Tate Gall.; numerous outdoor works in corporate and private collections. Member: AAIL, 1975; Amer. Acad. Arts and Scis, 1978. Awards include: Brandeis Award for Sculpture, 1971; Medal, Amer. Inst. Architects, 1977; Wilhelm-Lehmbruck Sculpture Award, Duisburg, 1981; Wolf Foundn Prize, Israel, 1989; Lifetime Achievement Award, Internat. Sculpture Centre, 1994. *Publications:* Spicy Ray Gun, 1960; Ray Gun Poems, 1960; More Ray Gun Poems, 1960, 2nd edn 1973; Injun and Other Histories, 1960; Store Days, 1967; Notes, 1968; Constructions, Models and Drawings, 1969; Notes in Hand, 1971; Raw Notes, 1973; Log, May 1974–August 1976, 1976; (jtly) Il Corso del Coltello: Menu, 1985 (trans. Italian 1985); (jtly) Sketches and Blottings toward the European Desktop, 1990 (trans. Italian 1990); Multiples in Retrospect, 1991; (with Coosje van Bruggen) Large-Scale Projects, 1994; exhibn catalogues; contribs to books and jls. *Address:* c/o Pace Wildenstein Gallery, 32 E 57th Street, New York, NY 10022–2513, USA.
See also R. E. Oldenburg.

OLDENBURG, Richard Erik; Hon. Chairman, Sotheby's North and South America, since 2000 (Chairman, 1995–2000); *b* 21 Sept. 1933; *s* of Gösta Oldenburg and Sigrid Elisabeth (*née* Lindforss); *m* 1st, 1960, Harriet Lisa Turnure (*d* 1998); 2nd, 2003, Mary Ellen Meehan. *Educ:* Harvard Coll. (AB 1954). Manager, Design Dept, Doubleday & Co., NYC, 1958–61; Man. Editor, Trade Div., Macmillan Co., NYC, 1961–69; Dir, Publications, 1969–72, Dir, 1972–94, Museum of Modern Art, NYC. *Address:* c/o Sotheby's, 1334 York Avenue, New York, NY 10021, USA.
See also C. T. Oldenburg.

OLDFATHER, Irene; Member (Lab) Cunninghame South, Scottish Parliament, since 1999; *b* 6 Aug. 1954; *d* of Campbell and Margaret Hamilton; *m* 1978, Rodrick Oldfather; one *s* one *d. Educ:* Univ. of Strathclyde (BA Hons Politics 1976; MSc Res. 1983). Lectr in US Politics, Univ. of Arizona, 1978–79; Policy Planner, Glasgow CC, 1980–90; Political Researcher, MEP, 1990–97; freelance journalist, European affairs, 1994–98; part-time Lectr, Paisley Univ., 1996–98. Scottish Parliament: Convenor, Cross Party Gp on Tobacco Control; Member: Eur. Cttee, 1999– (Convenor, 2001–03; Vice-Convenor, 2003–); Health and Community Care Cttee, 1999–2001. Alternate Mem., European Cttee of Regions, 1997–. *Publication:* res. paper for Scotland Europa. *Recreations:* going to ballet, reading, children, pets. *Address:* Scottish Parliament, Edinburgh EH99 1SP. *T:* (0131) 348 5769; (constituency office) Sovereign House, Academy Road, Irvine KA12 8RL. *T:* (01294) 313078, *Fax:* (01294) 313605.

OLDFIELD, Bruce, OBE 1990; designer; *b* 14 July 1950; parents unknown; brought up by Dr Barnardo's, Ripon, Yorks. *Educ:* Ripon Grammar School; Sheffield City Polytechnic (Hon. Fellow 1987); Ravensbourne College of Art; St Martin's College of Art. Established fashion house, 1975; produced designer collections of high fashion clothes for UK and overseas; began exporting clothes worldwide, 1975; began making couture clothes for individual clients, 1981; opened first Bruce Oldfield retail shop, selling ready to wear and couture to international clientèle, 1984. Exhibitor: British Design Exhibn, Vienna, 1986; Australian Bicentennial Fashion Show, Sydney Opera House, 1988. Lectures: Fashion Inst., NY, 1977; Los Angeles County Museum, 1983; Internat. Design Conf., Aspen, Colorado, 1986 (Speaker and show). Vice Pres., Barnardo's. Trustee, Royal Acad., 2000–02. Gov., London Inst., 2000–02. Hon. Fellow RCA, 1990. Hon. DCL Northumbria at Newcastle, 2001; DUniv UCE, 2005. Designed for films: Jackpot, 1974; The Sentinel, 1976. *Publications:* (with Georgina Howell) Bruce Oldfield's Season, 1987; Bruce Oldfield: Rootless: an autobiography, 2004. *Recreations:* music, reading, driving, working. *Address:* 27 Beauchamp Place, SW3 1NJ. *T:* (020) 7584 1363; *e-mail:* hq@bruceoldfield.com; *web:* www.bruceoldfield.com.

OLDFIELD, Michael Gordon, (Mike); musician and composer; *b* 15 May 1953; *s* of Dr Raymond Henry Oldfield and Maureen Bernadine Liston; five *s* two *d. Educ:* St Edward's, Reading; Presentation Coll., Reading. Records include: Tubular Bells, 1973 (over 16 million copies sold to date); Hergest Ridge; Ommadawn; Incantations; Platinum; QE2, 1980; Five Miles Out, 1982; Crises, 1983; Discovery, 1984; The Killing Fields (film sound track), 1984; Islands, 1987; The Wind Chimes (video album), 1988; Earthmoving, 1989;

Amarok, 1990; Heaven's Open, 1991; Tubular Bells II, 1992; The Songs of Distant Earth, 1994; Voyager, 1996; Tubular Bells III, 1998; Music of the Spheres, 2008. Extensive world wide concert tours, 1979–. Mem., Assoc. of Professional Composers. Freeman, City of London, 1982. Hon. Pict. *Publication:* Changeling (autobiog.), 2007. *Recreations:* helicopter pilot, squash, ski-ing, cricket. *Club:* Jacobs Larder (Ealing).

OLDHAM, Prof. (Charles Herbert) Geoffrey, CBE 1990; Professorial Fellow, Science Policy Research Unit, University of Sussex, 1966–97, now Hon. Professor (Director, 1980–92); Science Adviser to President, International Development Research Centre, Ottawa, on secondment, 1992–96; *b* 17 Feb. 1929; *s* of Herbert Cecil Oldham and Evelyn Selina Oldham (*née* Brooke); *m* 1951, Brenda Mildred Raven; two *s* one *d* (and one *s* decd). *Educ:* Bingley Grammar Sch.; Reading Univ. (BSc Hons); Toronto Univ. (MA, PhD). Research geophysicist, Chevron Research Corp., 1954–57; Sen. Geophysicist, Standard Oil Co. of California, 1957–60; Fellow, Inst. of Current World Affairs, studying Chinese lang. and sci., 1960–66; Scientific Directorate, OECD, 1965–66; Dep. Dir, Science Policy Res. Unit, 1966–80; Associate Dir, Internat. Develt Res. Centre, Ottawa, 1970–80. Vis. Prof., Stanford Univ., 1979; Vis. Researcher, Aust. Sci. and Tech. Adv. Council, 1988. Chm., UN Adv. Cttee on Sci. and Tech. for Develt, 1991–92; UK Mem., UN Commn on Sci., Technol. and Develt, 1993–97; Mem., WHO Adv. Cttee, Health Res., 1995–99. Chm. Bd, SciDev.Net, 2001–08. Hon. LLD York, Canada, 2006. *Publications:* articles in jls on science, technology and Chinese development. *Recreations:* travel, esp. long distance train journeys, golf. *Address:* 7 Martello Mews, Seaford, E Sussex BN25 1JT.

OLDHAM, Sir John, Kt 2003; OBE 2001; FRCGP; Senior Partner, Manor House Surgery, Glossop, since 1987; Executive Chairman, Quest4Quality Ltd, since 2007; *b* 17 Aug. 1953; *s* of Kenneth and Marian Oldham; *m* 1987, Julia Robinson. *Educ:* Manchester Univ. (MB ChB 1977); Manchester Business Sch. (MBA Dist. 1992); DCH London 1980. FRCGP 2002. House Officer, Manchester Royal Infirmary, 1978–79; SHO, Royal Manchester Children's Hosp., 1979–80; GP trainee, Darbishire House, Manchester, 1980–81; SHO, St Mary's Hosp., Manchester, 1981–84; Principal GP, Glossop, 1984–. Hd, Nat. Primary Care Develt Team, 2000–06; Advisor (part-time): Mersey RHA, 1989–91; Primary Care Div., DoH, 1996–99; Med. Advr (pt-time), Derbys FHSA and N Derbys HA, 1990–96. Non-exec. Bd Mem., School Food Trust, 2005–. *Publications:* Sic Evenit Ratio Ut Componitur: the small book about large system change, 2004; contribs to BMJ. *Recreations:* hiking, cooking, blues music. *Address:* Manor House Surgery, Manor Street, Glossop, Derbys SK13 8PS. *T:* (01457) 892606; *e-mail:* john.oldham@quest4quality.co.uk.

OLDMAN, Gary; actor; *b* 21 March 1958; *m* 1st, Lesley Manville (marr. diss.); one *s*; 2nd, 1991, Uma Thurman (marr. diss. 1993); 3rd, Donya Fiorentino (marr. diss. 2001); two *s. Educ:* South East London Sch. for Boys; Rose Bruford Coll. of Speech and Drama (BA Theatre Arts 1979). *Theatre* includes: Greenwich Young People's Theatre; Theatre Royal, York; Glasgow Citizens' Theatre: Massacre at Paris, A Waste of Time, Desperado Corner, Chinchilla, 1980 (toured Europe and S America); Royal Court Theatre: Rat in the Skull, 1984; The Pope's Wedding, 1984; Women Beware Women, 1986; Serious Money, 1987; Royal Shakespeare Company: The Desert Air, 1985; The War Plays, 1985; Real Dreams, 1986; The Country Wife, Royal Exchange, Manchester, 1986; Entertaining Mr Sloane, Oldham Rep. Co., 1987; *films* include: Sid and Nancy, 1986; Prick Up Your Ears, 1987; Track 29, 1988; Paris By Night, 1989; State of Grace, 1990; JFK, Chattahoochee, 1991; Bram Stoker's Dracula, 1992; True Romance, 1993; Romeo is Bleeding, Immortal Beloved, The Professional, 1994; Murder in the First, The Scarlet Letter, 1995; The Fifth Element, Air Force One, 1997; Lost in Space, Nil By Mouth, 1998 (writer and dir; BAFTA Award for best original screenplay); Hannibal, The Contender, 2001; Harry Potter and the Prisoner of Azkaban, 2004; Batman Begins, 2005; Harry Potter and the Goblet of Fire, 2005; Backwoods, 2006; Harry Potter and the Order of the Phoenix, 2007; The Dark Knight, 2008; *television* includes: Remembrance, 1982; Meantime, 1984; Heading Home, 1991; Fallen Angels: dead end for Delia, 1993.

O'LEARY, (Michael) John; Editor, The Times Higher Education Supplement, 2002–07; *b* 11 Dec. 1951; *s* of Captain Daniel Joseph O'Leary, RN, and Sylvia Jane O'Leary; *m* 1977, Susan Berenice Whittingham; two *s* one *d. Educ:* Taunton Sch.; Sheffield Univ. (BA Politics 1973; Pres., Students' Union, 1973–74). Reporter, Evening Chronicle, Newcastle upon Tyne, 1975–78; Reporter/news editor, 1978–85, Dep. Editor, 1985–90, THES; Educn Corresp., 1990–93, Educn Editor, 1993–2002, The Times. Mem., Govt Inquiry into Primary Sch. Test Standards, 1999. *Publication:* The Times Good University Guide, annually 1993–. *Recreations:* squash, tennis, travel, watching Arsenal. *Club:* Woodford Wells (Woodford).

O'LEARY, Peter Leslie; Under-Secretary, Inland Revenue, 1978–84; *b* 12 June 1929; *s* of Archibald and Edna O'Leary; *m* 1960, Margaret Elizabeth Debney; four *d. Educ:* Portsmouth Southern Grammar Sch.; University Coll., London (BA). Joined Inland Revenue as Inspector, 1952; Sen. Principal Inspector, 1974. *Recreations:* horology, gardening. *Address:* 17 Sleaford Road, Heckington, Sleaford, Lincs NG34 9QP. *T:* (01529) 461213.

OLINS, Wallace, (Wally), CBE 1999; MA Oxon; FCSD; Founder, Wolff Olins; Chairman, Saffron Brand Consultants, Madrid and London, since 2001; *b* 19 Dec. 1930; *s* of Alfred Olins and Rachel (*née* Muscovitch); *m* 1st, 1957, Maria Renate Olga Laura Steinert (marr. diss. 1989); two *s* one *d*; 2nd, 1990, Dornie Watts; one *d. Educ:* Highgate Sch.; St Peter's Coll., Oxford (Hons History, MA). National Service, Army, in Germany, 1950–51. S. H. Benson Ltd, London, 1954–57; Benson, India, 1957–62; Caps Design Group, London, 1962–65; Wolff Olins, London, 1965–2001. Vis. Lectr, Design Management, London Business Sch., 1984–89; Visiting Professor, Management School: Imperial Coll., 1987–89; Lancaster Univ., 1992–; Visiting Professor: Copenhagen Business Sch., 1993–; DUXX (formerly Centro de Excelencia Empresarial), Mexico, 1995–2002; Saïd Business Sch., Oxford Univ., 2002–. Non-exec. Dir, HEA, 1996–99; Dir, Glasgow Year of Design and Architecture, 1999. Vice-Pres., SIAD, 1982–85. Chm., Design Dimension Educnl Trust, 1987–93; Mem. Develt Trust, RPO, 1994–99. Mem., Council, RSA, 1989–95. Bicentenary Medal, RSA, 2000; D&AD President's Award, 2003. *Publications:* The Corporate Personality, 1978; The Wolff Olins Guide to Corporate Identity, 1983; The Wolff Olins Guide to Design Management, 1985; Corporate Identity, 1989; International Corporate Identity, vol. 1, 1995; The New Guide to Identity, 1996; Trading Identities, 1999; On Brand, 2003; numerous articles in Design and Management publications. *Recreations:* looking at buildings, shopping for books, theatre. *Address:* 1–10 Praed Mews, W2 1QY. *Club:* Groucho.

OLIPHANT, Tuelonyana Rosemary D.; *see* Ditlhabi Oliphant.

OLIVE, Prof. David Ian, CBE 2002; FRS 1987; Research Professor of Physics, University of Wales Swansea (formerly University College of Swansea), 1994–2002, now Emeritus Professor; *b* 16 April 1937; *s* of Ernest Edward Olive and Lilian Emma Olive (*née* Chambers); *m* 1963, Jenifer Mary Tutton; two *d. Educ:* Royal High Sch., Edinburgh;

Univ. of Edinburgh (MA); Univ. of Cambridge (BA, PhD). Fellow of Churchill Coll., 1963–70; Lectr, Univ. of Cambridge, 1965–71; Staff Mem., CERN, 1971–77; Imperial College: Lectr, 1977; Reader, 1980; Prof. of Theoretical Physics, 1984–92; Res. Prof. of Maths, Univ. Coll. of Swansea, 1992–94. Visiting Professor: Univ. of Virginia, 1982–83; Univ. of Geneva, 1986; Inst. for Advanced Studies, Princeton, 1987–88; Newton Inst. for Math. Scis, Cambridge, 1992, 1997; Kramers Prof., Univ. of Utrecht, 2000. Dirac Medal and Prize, Abdus Salam Internat. Centre for Theoretical Physics, Trieste, 1997. *Publications:* (jtly) The Analytic S-Matrix, 1966; (jtly) Kac-Moody and Virasoro Algebras, 1988; (jtly) Paul Dirac: the man and his work, 1998; many articles on theoretical physics in learned jls. *Recreations:* listening to music, golf. *Address:* 4 Havergal Close, Caswell, Swansea SA3 4RL. *Club:* Pennard Golf.

OLIVENNES, Kristin; *see* Scott Thomas, K.

OLIVER, Prof. (Ann) Dawn (Harrison), PhD; FBA 2005; Professor of Constitutional Law, University College London, 1993–2008, now Emeritus; *b* 7 June 1942; *d* of Gordon and Mieke Taylor; *m* 1967, Stephen John Lindsay Oliver (*see* Sir S. J. L Oliver); one *s* two *d. Educ:* Newnham Coll., Cambridge (BA 1964; MA 1967; PhD 1993; Associate Fellow, 1996–99). Called to the Bar, Middle Temple, 1965 (Harmsworth Schol.; Bencher, 1996); in practice at the Bar, 1965–69; Consultant, Legal Action Gp, 1971–76; University College London: Lectr in Law, 1976–87; Sen. Lectr, 1987–90; Reader in Public Law, 1990–93; Dean, Faculty of Laws, and Head of Law Dept, 1993–98; Dean, 2007; Hon. Fellow, 2001. Hon. Fellow, Soc. of Advanced Legal Studies, 1997–. Member: Commn on Election Campaigns, Hansard Soc., 1990–91; Wkg Party on Noise, DoE, 1990–91; Study of Parlt Gp, 1991–; Labour and Liberal Democrats Jt Consultative Cttee on Constitutional Reform, 1996–97; Royal Commn on Reform of the H of L, 1999; Fabian Commn on the future of the Monarchy, 2002–03; Animal Procedures Cttee, Home Office, 2003–. Mem., Bar Vocational Course Rev., Bar Standards Cttee, 2008. Chm., Advertising Adv. Cttee, ITC, 1999–2003. Trustee, Citizenship Foundn, 1990–94. Editor, Public Law, 1993–2001. *Publications:* (ed jtly) The Changing Constitution, 1985, 6th edn 2007; (ed jtly) New Directions in Judicial Review, 1988; (ed jtly) Economical with the Truth: the press in a democratic society, 1990; Government in the United Kingdom: the search for accountability, effectiveness and citizenship, 1991; (jtly) The Foundations of Citizenship, 1994; (jtly) Public Service Reform: issues of accountability and public law, 1996; (ed jtly) Halsbury's Laws of England on Constitutional Law and Human Rights, 1996; (ed jtly) The Law and Parliament, 1998; Common Values and the Public-Private Divide, 1999; Constitutional Reform in the UK, 2003; (ed jtly) Human Rights and the Private Sphere, 2008; articles on constitutional and admin. law. *Recreations:* walking, London, Aldeburgh, travel. *Address:* Faculty of Laws, University College London, Bentham House, Endsleigh Gardens, WC1H 0EG. *T:* (020) 7679 1409.

OLIVER, Benjamin Rhys; Stipendiary Magistrate for Mid-Glamorgan, 1983–95; a Recorder of the Crown Court, 1972–93; *b* 8 June 1928; *m* 1955; one *s* one *d. Educ:* Llandovery and Aberystwyth. Called to the Bar, Inner Temple, 1954. An Asst Recorder, Swansea, Cardiff and Merthyr Tydfil QS, 1967–71. A Chm., Med. Appeal Tribunals and Vaccine Damage Tribunals, 1981–83. *Recreation:* golf.

OLIVER, Hon. David Keightley Rideal; QC 1986; *b* 4 June 1949; *o s* of Baron Oliver of Aylmerton, PC; *m* 1st, 1972, Marisa Mirasierras (marr. diss. 1987); two *s;* 2nd, 1988, Judith Britannia Caroline Powell; two *s. Educ:* Westminster School; Trinity Hall, Cambridge; Institut d'Etudes Européennes, Brussels. Called to the Bar, Lincoln's Inn, 1972, Bencher, 1994; Junior Counsel to Dir-Gen. of Fair Trading, 1980–86. *Recreations:* gardening, bird watching, shooting. *Address:* Erskine Chambers, 33 Chancery Lane, WC2A 1EN. *T:* (020) 7242 5532.

OLIVER, Dawn, (Lady Oliver); *see* Oliver, A. D. H.

OLIVER, Dame Gillian (Frances), DBE 1998; Independent Consultant and Advisor for Nursing and Allied Health Professionals, Macmillan Cancer Relief, 2004–06 (Director of Service Development, 2000–04); *b* 10 Oct. 1943; *d* of Frank Joseph Power and Ethel Mary Power; *m* 1966, Martin Jeremy Oliver; three *d. Educ:* Brentwood County High Sch., Essex; Middlesex Hosp., London (RN); Open Univ. (BA 1979). Night Sister and Ward Sister, Clatterbridge Centre for Oncology, 1978–87; Advr in Oncology Nursing, RCN, 1987–89; Regl Nurse, Cancer Services, Mersey RHA, 1989–90; Dir of Patient Services, Clatterbridge Centre for Oncology, 1990–2000. Hon. Fellow, Liverpool John Moores Univ., 2006. *Recreations:* travel, music, literature. *Address:* 1 Well Close, Ness, Neston, Cheshire CH64 4EE.

OLIVER, Comdr James Arnold, RN; Clerk, Ironmongers' Company, 1990–2005 (Deputy Clerk, 1989–90); *b* 10 Aug. 1941; *s* of Capt. Philip Daniel Oliver, CBE, RN and Audrey Mary Oliver (*née* Taylor); *m* 1973, Anne Elise de Burgh Sidley. *Educ:* Sedbergh Sch.; BRNC. Joined RN, 1959; seaman officer, 1959–88; navigation specialist, 1969; Divl Officer, Dartmouth, 1971–73; served in minesweepers, frigates and HM Ships Ark Royal, 1973–74, Sheffield, 1976–78, and Fearless, 1984–86; CO, Barbados Coastguard, 1981–83. Clerk and Trust Manager, Ewelme Almshouse Charity, 2006–. Mem. Court, Ironmongers' Co., 2006–. FCMI (FIMgt 1994). *Recreations:* cruising under sail, country life, carriage driving.
    See also Sir S. J. L. Oliver.

OLIVER, Sir (James) Michael (Yorrick), Kt 2003; DL; Chairman: Zirax plc, since 2005; Europa Oil & Gas, since 2007; Hampden Underwriting plc, since 2007; Lord Mayor of London, 2001–02; *b* 13 July 1940; *s* of George Leonard Jack Oliver and Patricia Rosamund Oliver (*née* Douglas); *m* 1963, Sally Elizabeth Honor Exner; two *d. Educ:* Brunswick Sch.; Wellington Coll. FSI (MSI 1992). Rediffusion Ltd, 1959–63; Manager, Helios Ltd, 1965–70; Kitcat & Aitken, 1970–86 (Partner, 1977–86); Dir, Kitcat & Aitken & Co., 1986–90; Man. Dir, Carr Kitcat & Aitken, 1990–93; Dir, Lloyds Investment Managers Ltd, 1994–96; Dir, Investment Funds, Hill Samuel Asset Management Ltd, subseq. Scottish Widows Investment Partnership, 1996–2001. Director: Garbhaig Hydro Power Co., 1988–; German Investment Trust, 1994–97; German Smaller Cos Investment Trust, 1994–2001; Euro Spain Fund Ltd, 1996–2005; Portugal Growth Fund, 1996–2000; Hill Samuel UK Emerging Cos Investment Trust plc, 1996–2000; European Growth Fund, 2001–08; Chm., Central and Eastern European Fund Ltd, 2003–. Dir, Centrepoint Soho, 1992–96. Trustee: UK Growth & Income Fund; Income Plus Fund, 1992–2004. Chm., St John Ambulance, City of London Centre, 1998–99, 2003–. Governor: Bishopsgate Foundn, 1983– (Chm., 1985–88); King Edward's Sch., Witley, 1992–2007; Univ. of East London, 1999–2003; Chancellor, City Univ., 2001–02. Chm., Steering Cttee for Mus. of Port of London and Docklands, 1993– (Chm., Trustees, 1996–98); Mem., Mus. of London Develt Council, 1991–96; Trustee: Geffrye Mus., 1992–97; Mus. of London, 2003–. Common Councilman, City of London Corp., 1980–87; Alderman, Ward of Bishopsgate, 1987–; Sheriff, City of London, 1997–98. Liveryman, Ironmongers' Co., 1962– (Master, 1991–92). JP City of London, 1987; DL Cambs, 2004. FRGS 1962. Hon. LLD UEL, 1999; Hon. DLitt City, 2001. KStJ 2001. *Recreations:* archaeology, travel.

Address: Paradise Barns, Bucks Lane, Cambridge CB23 1HL. *T:* (01223) 263303. *Clubs:* City of London, East India, City Livery.

OLIVER, Jamie Trevor, MBE 2003; chef; *b* May 1975; *s* of Trevor and Sally Oliver; *m* 2000, Juliette Norton; two *d. Educ:* Westminster Catering Coll. Began cooking at parents' pub, The Cricketers, Clavering, Essex; worked in France; head pastry chef, The Neal Street Restaurant, London; sous chef, River Café, London; consultant chef, Monte's, London, until 2002; established restaurants: Fifteen, London, 2002; Fifteen, Amsterdam, 2004; Fifteen, Cornwall, 2006. Presenter, TV series: The Naked Chef (3 series), 1999–2001; Jamie's Kitchen, 2002; Return to Jamie's Kitchen, 2003; Jamie's School Dinners, 2005; Jamie's Great Escape, 2005; Jamie's Return to School Dinners, 2006; Jamie's Chef, 2007; Jamie at Home, 2007, 2008; Jamie's Ministry of Food, 2008. *Publications:* The Naked Chef, 1999; The Return of the Naked Chef, 2000; Happy Days with the Naked Chef, 2001; Jamie's Kitchen, 2002; Jamie's Dinners, 2004; Jamie's Italy, 2005; Jamie at Home: cook your way to the good life, 2007; Jamie's Ministry of Food: anyone can learn to cook in 24 hours, 2008. *Address:* c/o Outside Organisation, 177–178 Tottenham Court Road, W1T 7NY.

OLIVER, Rt Rev. John Keith; Bishop of Hereford, 1990–2003; Hon. Assistant Bishop, diocese of Swansea and Brecon, since 2004; *b* 14 April 1935; *s* of Walter Keith and Ivy Oliver; *m* 1961, Meriel Moore; two *s* (and one *d* decd). *Educ:* Westminster School; Gonville and Caius Coll., Cambridge (MA, MLitt); Westcott House. Asst Curate, Hilborough Group of Parishes, Norfolk, 1964–68; Chaplain and Asst Master, Eton College, 1968–72; Team Rector: South Molton Group of Parishes, Devon, 1973–82; Parish of Central Exeter, 1982–85; Archdeacon of Sherborne, 1985–90. Chm., ABM, 1993–98. Chaplain, 2003–, Trustee, 2005–, RABI; Trustee, Marches Energy Agency, 2004–. ARAgS 2007. *Publications:* The Church and Social Order, 1968; contribs to Theology, Crucible. *Recreations:* railways, music, architecture, motorcycling. *Address:* The Old Vicarage, Glascwm, Powys LD1 5SE. *Clubs:* Farmers, Oxford & Cambridge.

OLIVER, Ven. John Michael; Archdeacon of Leeds, 1992–2005; *b* 7 Sept. 1939; *s* of Frederick and Mary Oliver; *m* 1964, Anne Elizabeth Barlow; three *d. Educ:* Ripon Grammar Sch.; St David's Coll., Lampeter (BA 1962); Ripon Hall, Oxford. Ordained deacon, 1964, priest 1965; Asst Curate, St Peter, Harrogate, 1964–67; Senior Curate, Bramley, Leeds, 1967–72; Vicar: St Mary, Harrogate, 1972–78; St Mary with St David, Beeston, Leeds, 1978–92. Ecumenical Officer for Leeds, 1980–86; Rural Dean of Armley, 1986–92; Hon. Canon of Ripon, 1987–92. *Recreations:* cricket, theatre, cooking, a reluctant gardener. *Address:* 42A Chapel Lane, Barwick in Elmet, Leeds LS15 4EJ. *T:* (0113) 393 5019; *e-mail:* olivers@barwickelmet.wanadoo.co.uk.

OLIVER, Kaye Wight, CMG 2001; OBE 1994; HM Diplomatic Service, retired; High Commissioner to Lesotho, 1999–2002; *b* 10 Aug. 1943. Joined Dept of Customs and Excise, 1962; entered Diplomatic Service, 1965; served FCO, Kuala Lumpur, Lilongwe and Paris; First Sec., Nairobi, 1983–84; Head of Chancery and Consul, Yaoundé, 1984–87; FCO, 1987–90; Consul and Dep. Head of Mission, later Chargé d'Affaires, Kinshasa, Burundi and Rwanda, 1990–94; on secondment to ODA, 1994–95; Ambassador to Rwanda, 1995–98 and (non-resident) to Burundi, 1996–98. *Address:* 7 Elliott Road, Chiswick, W4 1PF.

OLIVER, Sir Michael; *see* Oliver, Sir J. M. Y.

OLIVER, Prof. Michael Francis, CBE 1985; MD; FRCP, FRCPEd, FFPH; FRSE; Professor Emeritus, University of Edinburgh, since 1990; *b* 3 July 1925; *s* of late Captain Wilfrid Francis Lenn Oliver, MC (DLI), and Cecilia Beatrice Oliver (*née* Daniel); *m* 1st; two *s* one *d* (and one *s* decd); 2nd, Helen Louise Daniel. *Educ:* Marlborough Coll.; Univ. of Edinburgh (MB, ChB 1947, MD (Gold Medal) 1957). FRSE 1987. Edinburgh University: Consultant Physician, Royal Infirmary and Sen. Lectr in Medicine, 1961; Reader in Medicine, 1973; Personal Prof. of Cardiology, 1977; Duke of Edinburgh Prof. of Cardiology, 1979–89; Dir, Wynn Inst. for Metabolic Res., 1989–93; Hon. Prof., Nat. Heart and Lung Inst., 1989–93. Dist. Res. Fellow, Imperial Coll., London, 2000–. Sen. Ed., European Jl Clin. Investigation, 1967–72. Mem., Cardiovascular Panel, Govt Cttee on Medical Aspects of Food Policy, 1971–74, 1982–84; UK Rep. Mem., Adv. Panel for Cardiovascular Disease, WHO, 1972–2001; Chm., BBC-Medical Adv. Gp in Scotland, 1975–81; Mem. Scientific Bd, Internat. Soc. of Cardiology, 1968–78 (Chm., Council on Atherosclerosis and Ischaemic Heart Disease, 1968–75); Chairman: Brit. Atherosclerosis Gp, 1970–75; Science Cttee, Fondation Cardiologique Princess Lilian, Belgium, 1976–85; MoT Panel on driving and cardiovascular disease, 1985–90; Jt Cttee on Higher Medical Training, 1987–90. Convener, Cardiology Cttee, Scottish Royal Colls, 1978–81; Council Mem., Brit. Heart Foundn, 1976–85. Pres., British Cardiac Soc., 1981–85; Pres., RCPEd, 1986–88. FESC 1986. Hon. FRCPI 1988. Hon. FRACP 1988. Hon. Fellow, Amer. Coll. of Cardiology, 1973. Hon. MD: Karolinska Inst., Stockholm, 1980; Univ. Bologna, 1985. Purkinje Medal, 1981; Polish Cardiac Soc. Medal, 1984. *Publications:* Acute Myocardial Infarction, 1966; Intensive Coronary Care, 1970, 2nd edn 1974; Effect of Acute Ischaemia on Myocardial Function, 1972; Modern Trends in Cardiology, 1975; High-Density Lipoproteins and Atherosclerosis, 1978; Coronary Heart Disease in Young Women, 1978; Strategy for Screening of Coronary Heart Disease, 1986; contribs to sci. and med. jls on causes of coronary heart disease, biochemistry of fats, myocardial metabolism, mechanisms of sudden death, clinical trials of drugs, and population studies of vascular diseases. *Recreations:* living in Italy, art history. *Address:* Keepier Wharf, 12 Narrow Street, E14 8DH. *T:* (020) 7790 4203; Apecolle, Spedalicchio, 06019 Umbertide (Pg), Italy. *Clubs:* Athenæum, Garrick; Medical Pilgrims.

OLIVER, Pauline Ann, (Mrs D. D. Walker); Director of Social Services, Lancashire County Council, 1990–2003; *b* 17 Nov. 1947; *d* of Percy Leonard Parsons and Doreen Maud Parsons; *m* 1991, David Douglas Walker. *Educ:* Rosebery County Grammar Sch., Epsom; Univ. of Surrey (BSc Hons Human Relns); Goldsmiths' Coll., Univ. of London (CQSW 1972, Dip. Applied Social Studies 1972). Asst Housemother, London Borough of Wandsworth, 1966–67; Social Worker, Surrey CC, 1970–73; social work and managerial posts, London Borough of Lewisham, 1973–83; London Borough of Bexley: Asst Chief Social Services Officer, 1983–87; Chief Social Services Officer, 1987–88; Dep. Dir of Social Services, Lancs CC, 1988–90. Member: Social Care Assoc.; British Agencies for Adoption and Fostering; Assoc. of Women Sen. Managers (Personal Social Services). MCMI. *Recreations:* reading, antiques, gardening.

OLIVER, Maj.-Gen. Richard Arthur, CB 1999; OBE 1986; Chief Executive, Year Out Group, since 2000; *b* 16 July 1944; *s* of late Arthur R. L. and Betty Oliver; *m* 1972, Julia Newsum; three *s. Educ:* Repton Sch.; RMA, Sandhurst; RMCS (psc†). GSO2, Exercise Planning Staff, HQ BAOR, 1977–79; OC, 25 Field Sqdn Regt, 1979–81; GSO2, Exercise Planning Staff, HQ 3rd Armoured Div., 1981; Chief Logistic Plans, HQ 1st (Br.) Corps, 1982–83; CO, 36 Engr Regt, 1983–85; Col, Army Staff Duties 2, MoD (Army), 1985–88; hcsc, Army Staff Coll., 1988; Comdr, Berlin Infantry Bde, 1988–90; rcds 1991; Brig., AQ, HQ 1st (Br.) Corps, 1992; Deputy Chief of Staff: G1/G4 HQ Allied Comd Europe, Rapid Reaction Corps, 1992–94; HQ Land Comd, 1994–96; COS HQ Adjutant

Gen. (PTC), 1996–99. Business Develt Advr, Granada Food Services, 1999–2000. Member: Nat. Bd, Race for Opportunity, BITC, 1998–99; Bd of Trustees (formerly Council), Cranstoun Drug Services, 2000– (Chm., 2001–); Pilot Bd, Young Volunteer Challenge, DfES, 2003–05; Travel Advice Review Gp, FCO, 2004–06; Consular Stakeholders Panel, FCO, 2007–. FInstD 1998. *Publications:* (contrib.) The British Army and the Operational Level of War, 1989; articles in RUSI Jl and various educnl and travel mags. *Recreations:* gardening, fishing, shooting, indoor rowing, reading, water colours. *Address:* Queensfield, 28 Kings Road, Easterton, Devizes, Wilts SN10 4PX. *T:* (01380) 812368. *Club:* Army and Navy.

OLIVER, Prof. Roland Anthony, MA, PhD (Cantab); FBA 1993; Professor of the History of Africa, London University, 1963–86; *b* Srinagar, Kashmir, 30 March 1923; *s* of late Major D. G. Oliver and Lorimer Janet (*née* Donaldson); *m* 1st, 1947, Caroline Florence (*d* 1983), *d* of late Judge John Linehan, KC; one *d*; 2nd, 1990, Suzanne Doyle, *widow* of Brig. Richard Miers. *Educ:* Stowe; King's Coll., Cambridge. Attached to Foreign Office, 1942–45; R. J. Smith Research Studentship, King's Coll., Cambridge, 1946–48; Lecturer, School of Oriental and African Studies, 1948–58, Hon. Fellow, 1992; Reader in African History, University of London, 1958–63. Francqui Prof., University of Brussels, 1961; Visiting Professor: Northwestern Univ., Illinois, 1962; Harvard Univ., 1967; travelled in Africa, 1949–50 and 1957–58; org. international Conferences on African History and Archæology, 1953–61. President: African Studies Assoc., 1967–68; British Inst. in Eastern Africa, 1981–93. Vice-Pres., Royal African Soc., 1965– (Mem. Council, 1959–65); Mem., Perm. Bureau, Internat. Congress of Africanists, 1973–78; Chm., Minority Rights Group, 1973–91. Corresp. Member, Académie Royale des Sciences d'Outremer, Brussels. Editor (with J. D. Fage) Jl of African History, 1960–73. Haile Selassie Prize Trust Award, 1966; Distinguished Africanist Award, American African Studies Assoc., 1989. *Publications:* The Missionary Factor in East Africa, 1952; Sir Harry Johnston and the Scramble for Africa, 1957; (ed) The Dawn of African History, 1961; (with J. D. Fage) A Short History of Africa, 1962; (ed with Gervase Mathew) A History of East Africa, 1963; (with A. E. Atmore) Africa since 1800, 1967; (ed) The Middle Age of African History, 1967; (with B. M. Fagan) Africa in the Iron Age, 1975; (with A. E. Atmore) The African Middle Ages, 1400–1800, 1981; The African Experience, 1991; In the Realms of Gold: pioneering in African history, 1997; (with A. E. Atmore) Medieval Africa, 2001; Gen. Editor (with J. D. Fage), Cambridge History of Africa, 8 vols, 1975–86. *Address:* Frilsham Woodhouse, Thatcham, Berks RG18 9XB. *T:* (01635) 201407.

OLIVER, Dr Ronald Martin, CB 1989; RD 1973; FRCP; Deputy Chief Medical Officer (Deputy Secretary), Department of Health and Social Security, 1985–89, retired; *b* 28 May 1929; *s* of late Cuthbert Hanson Oliver and Cecilia Oliver; *m* 1957, Susanna Treves Blackwell; three *s* one *d*. *Educ:* King's Coll. Sch., Wimbledon; King's Coll., London; St George's Hosp. Med. Sch. (MB, BS 1952). MRCS, LRCP 1952; DCH 1954; DPH 1960; DIH 1961; MD London 1965; MFOM 1978; FRCP 1998 (MRCP 1987); MFCM 1987. Served RNR: Surg. Lieut, 1953–55; Surg. Lt-Comdr, retd 1974. St George's Hosp., London: House Surgeon and Physician, 1952–53; Resident Clin. Pathologist, 1955–56; trainee asst, gen. practice, 1956–57; Asst County MO, Surrey CC, 1957–59; MO, London Transport Exec., 1959–62; MO, later SMO, Treasury Med. Service (later CS Med. Adv. Service), 1962–74; seconded Diplomatic Service as Physician, British Embassy, Moscow, 1964–66; SMO, 1974–79, SPMO, 1979–85, DHSS; Chief Med. Advr, ODA, 1983–85. Gov., Manor House Sch., Little Bookham, 1991–99 (Chm., 1995–99). *Publications:* papers in med. jls on epidemiology of heart disease, public health, toxicology, and health service admin. *Recreations:* golf, sailing, gardening, bad bridge. *Address:* Greenhill House, 5 Mayfield, Leatherhead, Surrey KT22 8RS. *T:* (01372) 362323. *Club:* Effingham Golf.

OLIVER, Prof. Stephen George, PhD; FMedSci; Professor of Systems Biology and Biochemistry, University of Cambridge, since 2007; *b* 3 Nov. 1949; *s* of late Anthony George Oliver and Ivy Florence Oliver (*née* Simmons); *m* 1972, Rowena Philpott (marr. diss. 2008); one *d*. *Educ:* Univ. of Bristol (BSc Hons Microbiol. 1971); Nat. Inst. for Medical Research (PhD 1974). SRC Res. Fellow, Univ. of Calif, Irvine, 1974–77; Lectr in Microbiol., Univ. of Kent, Canterbury, 1977–81; University of Manchester Institute of Science and Technology, subseq. University of Manchester: Sen. Lectr in Applied Molecular Biol. 1981–87; Prof. of Biotechnol., 1987–99; Prof. of Genomics, 1999–2007. Ed.-in-Chief, Yeast, 1985–. Chairman: MRC Bioinformatics and Mathematical Biol. Fellowships Panel, 2001–04; Wellcome Trust Molecules, Genes and Cells Funding Cttee, 2004–08. FMedSci 2002. Fellow, Amer. Acad. for Microbiol., 2000; Mem. EMBO 2004. Hon. Mem., Hungarian Acad. of Scis, 1998. *Publications:* (ed with K. Gull) The Fungal Nucleus, 1981; (with T. A. Brown) Microbial Extrachromosomal Inheritance, 1985; (with J. M. Ward) A Dictionary of Genetic Engineering, 1985; (ed with M. F. Tuite) Biotechnology Handbooks—Saccharomyces, 1991; (jtly) The Eukaryotic Genome: organisation and regulation, 1997; (ed jtly) Encyclopedia of Microbiology, vols 1–4, 2000; articles in scientific jls. *Recreations:* music, the outdoors, searching for hills to walk or bike up in East Anglia. *Address:* Department of Biochemistry, University of Cambridge, Cambridge CB2 1GA.

OLIVER, Rt Rev. Stephen John; *see* Stepney, Area Bishop of.

OLIVER, Sir Stephen (John Lindsay), Kt 2007; QC 1980; Presiding Special Commissioner, and President, VAT and Duties (formerly Value Added Tax) Tribunals, since 1992; President: Financial Services and Markets Tribunal, since 2001; Pensions Regulator Tribunal, since 2005; *b* 14 Nov. 1938; *s* of late Philip Daniel Oliver and Audrey Mary Oliver; *m* 1967, Anne Dawn Harrison Taylor (*see* A. D. H. Oliver); one *s* two *d*. *Educ:* Rugby Sch.; Oriel Coll., Oxford (MA Jurisprudence). National Service, RN, 1957–59: served submarines; Temp. Sub-Lieut. Called to the Bar, Middle Temple, 1963; Bencher, 1987; a Recorder, 1989–91; Circuit Judge, 1991–92. Asst Boundary Comr, Parly Boundary Commn, 1977. Chm. Blackheath Concert Halls Charity, 1986–92; Mem. Council, London Sinfonietta, 1993–. Trustee: Britten-Pears Foundn, 2001–; TaxAid, 2007–. *Recreations:* music, golf. *Address:* 15–19 Bedford Avenue, WC1B 3AS. *T:* (020) 7612 9662, *Fax:* (020) 7323 9156; *e-mail:* Stephen.Oliver@judiciary.gsi.gov.uk.

See also J. A. Oliver.

OLIVER-JONES, Stephen; QC 1996; **His Honour Judge Oliver-Jones;** a Circuit Judge, since 2000; *b* 6 July 1947; *s* of Arthur William Jones and Kathleen Jones; *m* 1972, Margaret Anne Richardson; one *s* one *d*. *Educ:* Marling Sch., Stroud; UC, Durham Univ. (BA Hons). Lectr in Law, Durham Tech. Coll., 1968–70. Called to the Bar, Inner Temple, 1970; Mem., Oxford, later Midland and Oxford, Circuit; an Asst Recorder, 1988–93; a Recorder, 1993–2000; Designated Civil Judge for W Midlands and Warwicks, 2002–. Pres., Mental Health Rev. Tribunal, 2000–. Mem., Civil Procedure Rule Cttee, 2002–. *Recreations:* fly fishing, postal history. *Address:* Coventry Combined Court, 140 Much Park Street, Coventry CV1 2SN.

OLIVIER, Lady; *see* Plowright, Dame J. A.

OLIVIER, Joan Sheila Ross; JP; Headmistress, Lady Margaret School, Parsons Green, 1984–2006; *b* 30 April 1941; *m* 1966, John Eric Hordern Olivier; one *s*. *Educ:* Queen Mary Coll., Univ. of London (BA Hons); Hughes Hall, Cambridge (PGCE). Hd of History, Camden Sch. for Girls, 1965–73; Dep. Hd, Lady Margaret Sch., 1973–84. JP Wimbledon, 1993. *Recreation:* bad bridge.

OLLERENSHAW, Eric, OBE 1991; Member (C), Hackney London Borough Council, 1990 (Leader, Conservative Group, 1996); *b* 26 March 1950; *s* of Eric and Barbara Ollerenshaw. *Educ:* London Sch. of Economics and Political Science (BSc Econs). History teacher, Northumberland Park Sch., Tottenham, Hendon Sch., Barnet, and Tom Hood Sch., Leytonstone, 1973–2000. Member (C): ILEA, 1986–90 (Leader, Conservative Gp, 1988–90); London Assembly, GLA, 2000–04 (Dep. Leader, 2000–02, Leader, 2002–04, Conservative Gp). Mem. Bd, London Develt Agency, 2004–. *Recreations:* reading, listening to music.

OLLERENSHAW, Dame Kathleen (Mary), DBE 1971; DL; MA, DPhil; FIMA, FCP, CMath; Freeman of the City of Manchester, 1984; Chairman, Council for St John Ambulance in Greater Manchester, 1974–89; Member, Manchester City Council, 1956–81, Leader of Conservative Opposition, 1977–80; Alderman, 1970–74, Hon. Alderman since 1981; Lord Mayor, 1975–76, Deputy Lord Mayor, 1976–77; *b* 1 Oct. 1912; *d* of late Charles Timpson, JP, and late Mary Elizabeth Timpson (*née* Stops); *m* 1939, Robert Ollerenshaw (*d* 1986); (one *s* decd one *d* decd). *Educ:* Ladybarn House Sch., Manchester; St Leonards Sch., St Andrews; (open schol. in maths) Somerville Coll., Oxford (BA (Hons) 1934, MA 1943, DPhil 1945; Hon. Fellow, 1978). Foundation Fellow, Institute of Mathematics and its Applications (FIMA), 1964 (Mem. Council, 1973–94, Vice-Pres., 1976–77, Pres., 1978–79; Hon. Fellow 1986). Research Assistant, Shirley Institute, Didsbury, 1937–40. Hon. Res. Fellow, Dept of Computer Sci., Univ. of Manchester, 1999–2003. Chairman: Educn Cttee, Assoc. of Municipal Corporations, 1968–71; Assoc. of Governing Bodies of Girls' Public Schs, 1963–69; Manchester Educn Cttee, 1967–70 (Co-opted Mem., 1954–56); Manchester Coll. of Commerce, 1964–69; Council, Science and Technology Insts, 1980–81; first Chm., Court, Royal Northern Coll. of Music, Manchester, 1971–86 (CRNCM 1978); Member: Central Adv. Council on Educn in England, 1960–63; CNAA, 1964–74; SSRC, 1971–75; Tech. Educn Council, 1973–75; (Vice-Pres.) British Assoc. for Commercial and Industrial Educn (Mem. Delegn to USSR, 1963); Exec., Assoc. of Educn Cttees, 1967–71; Nat. Adv. Council on Educn for Industry and Commerce, 1963–70; Gen. Adv. Council of BBC, 1966–72; Schools Council, 1968–71; Management Panel, Burnham Cttee, 1968–71; Nat. Foundn of Educnl Res., 1968–71; Layfield Cttee of Inquiry into Local Govt Finance, 1974–76; Court, Univ. of Salford, 1967– (Mem. Council, 1967–89; a Pro-Chancellor, 1983–89); Court, Univ. of Manchester, 1964–; Manchester Polytechnic, 1968–86 (first Chm., 1969–72; Dep.-Chm., 1972–75; Hon. Fellow, 1979); Court, UMIST, 1971–87 (Vice-Pres., 1976–86; Hon. Fellow, 1987); Court, Lancaster Univ., 1991– (Mem. Council, 1975–91; a Dep. Pro-Chancellor, 1978–91); Council, CGLI, 1972–84 (Hon. Fellow, 1978; Vice-Pres., 1979–84); Rep. Governor, Royal Coll. of Advanced Technol., Salford, 1959–67; Governor: St Leonard's Sch., St Andrews, 1950–72 (Pres., 1980–2003); Manchester High Sch. for Girls, 1959–69; Ladies' Coll., Cheltenham, 1966–68; Chetham's Hosp. Sch., Manchester, 1967–77; Further Educn Staff Coll., Blagdon, 1960–74. Sen. Res. Fellow (part-time), 1972–75, Hon. Res. Fellow, 1975–77, Lancaster Univ.; Hon. Res. Fellow, Dept of Computer Science, Univ. of Manchester, 1998–2001. Member: Manchester Statistical Soc., 1950– (Mem. Council, 1977–; Vice-Pres., 1977, Pres., 1981–83); Manchester Astronomical Soc., 1990– (Hon. Vice-Pres., 1994–); Hon. Member: Manchester Technology Assoc., 1976– (Pres., 1982); Manchester Literary and Philosophical Soc., 1982–; Hon. Col, Manchester and Salford Univs OTC, 1977–81; Mem., Mil. Educn Cttee, 1979–. Dir, Greater Manchester Independent Radio, Ltd, 1972–83. Winifred Cullis Lecture Fellow to USA, 1965; Fourth Cockroft Lecture, UMIST and Manchester Tech. Assoc., 1977. DL Greater Manchester, 1987. Hon. LLD CNAA, 1975; Hon. DSc Salford, 1975; Hon LLD Manchester, 1976; Hon. DSc Lancaster, 1992; Hon. LLD Liverpool, 1994. Mancunian of the Year, Jun. Chamber of Commerce, 1977; Pick of the Year, BBC Woman's Hour, 2004. DStJ 1983 (CStJ 1978) (Mem., Chapter Gen., 1974–96). Catherine Richards Award, IMA, 2006. *Publications:* Education of Girls, 1958; Education for Girls, 1961; The Girls' Schools, 1967; Returning to Teaching, 1974; The Lord Mayor's Party, 1976; First Citizen, 1977; (with Prof. David Brée) Most-Perfect Pandiagonal Magic Squares: their construction and enumeration, 1998; To Talk of Many Things (autobiog.), 2004; Constructing Magic Squares of Arbitrarily Large Size, 2006; papers in mathematical journals, 1945–54 and 1977–, incl. Proc. RI 1981 (on form and pattern), Phil. Trans Royal Soc. 1982 (on magic squares), and Proc. Royal Soc. 1986 (on pandiagonal magic squares); articles on education and local govt in national and educational press. *Recreations:* research mathematics, astronomy. *Address:* 2 Pine Road, Didsbury, Manchester M20 6UY. *T:* (0161) 445 2948. *Club:* English-Speaking Union.

OLLILA, Jorma Jaakko; Chairman, Board of Directors, Nokia Corporation, since 2006 (Chief Executive Officer, 1992–2006; and Chairman, Group Executive Board, 1999–2006); Chairman, Royal Dutch Shell, since 2006; *b* Seinäjoki, Finland, 15 Aug. 1950; *m* Liisa Annikki Metsola; two *s* one *d*. *Educ:* Univ. of Helsinki (MSc Political Sci. 1976); LSE (MSc Econ 1978); Helsinki Univ. of Technology (MSc Eng 1981). Citibank: Account Manager, Corporate Bank, Citibank NA, London, 1978–80; Account Officer, 1980–82, Mem. Bd of Mgt, 1983–85, Citibank Oy; Nokia: Mem., Gp Exec. Bd, 1985–2006; Vice-Pres., Internat. Operations, 1985–86; Sen. Vice-Pres., Finance, 1986–89; Dep. Mem., Bd of Dirs, 1989–90; President: Nokia Mobile Phones, 1990–92; Nokia, 1992–99. Chm., Bd, MTV Oy, 1993–97; Member Board: ICL plc, 1992–2000; Otava Books and Magazines Gp Ltd, 1996–; UPM-Kymmene, 1997–; Ford Motor Co., 2000–; Member Supervisory Board: Tietotehdas Oy, 1992–95; Pohjola Insurance Co. Ltd, 1992–97; NKF Holding NV, 1992–99; Oy Rastor Ab, 1992–93; Sampo Insurance Co. Ltd, 1993–2000; Merita Bank Ltd, 1994–2000. Chm. Supervisory Bd, Finnish Foreign Trade Assoc., 1993–98; Vice Chm. Bd, Finnish Sect., ICC, 1993–97; Member: Planning Bd for Defence Economy, 1992–96; Technol. Delegn, Ministry of Trade and Industry, 1992–95; Bd and Exec. Cttee, Confedn of Finnish Industry and Employers, 1992–2002 (Dep. Chm. Bd, 1995–2002); Council, State Technical Res. Centre, 1992–93; Bd, Econ. Inf. Bureau, 1993–97; Council, Centre for Finnish Business and Policy Studies, 1993–2001; Supervisory Bd, Foundn for Pediatric Res., 1993–98; Sci. and Technology Policy Council of Finland, 1993–2002; Council of Supervisors, Res. Inst. of Finnish Economy, 1993–2000; Exec. Bd, Assoc. for Finnish Cultural Foundn, 1993–99; Delegn, Finnish-Swedish Chamber of Commerce, 1993–; Supervisory Bd, WWF Finland, 1995–97; Competitiveness Adv. Gp, EC, 1995–96; European Round Table of Industrialists, 1997–; GBDe Business Steering Cttee, 1999–. Overseas Adv. Trustee, American-Scandinavian Foundn, 1994–. Chm. Adv. Cttee, Helsinki Univ. of Technology, 1996– (Vice-Chm., 1993–95); Member: Council, Helsinki Sch. of Econs and Business Admin, 1993–98; Dean's Council, John F. Kennedy Sch. of Govt, Harvard, 1995–; Internat. Bd, United World Colls, 1995–. Hon. PhD Helsinki, 1995; Hon. DSc Helsinki Univ. of Technol., 1998. Comdr 1st Cl., Order of White Rose (Finland), 1996;

Order of White Star (Estonia), 1995; Comdr, Order of Orange (Nassau), 1995; Officer's Cross, Order of Merit (Hungarian Republic), 1996; Commander's Cross, Order of Merit, Germany, 1997, Poland, 1999. *Address:* Nokia, Keilalahdentie 4, PO Box 226, 00045 Helsinki, Finland.

OLMERT, Ehud; Prime Minister of Israel, 2006–08 (Acting, Jan.–April 2006, Interim Prime Minister, April–May 2006); Member, Knesset, 1973–98 and since 2003; *b* Nahlat Jabotinsky, Binyamina, 30 Sept. 1945; *s* of Mordechai and Bella Olmert; *m* Aliza Richter; two *s* two *d*. *Educ:* Hebrew Univ. of Jerusalem (BA Psychol. and Philos. 1968; BA Law 1973). Military service, 1963, 13th Regt, Golani Bde, wounded, completed service at Hamahane newspaper, 1971. Started practising law, private law firm, 1975; Sen. Partner, Ehud Olmert and Associates Law Firm, 1978. Volunteer, Israel Defence Forces, 1979–82, completed officers' course, volunteered for reserve service in Lebanon. Knesset: Member, 1981–88: For. Affairs and Defence Cttee; Finance Cttee; Educn and Culture Cttee; Defence Budget Cttee; Minister: of Minority Affairs, 1988–90; of Health, 1990–92; of Industry, Trade and Labour, 2003–06; of Communications, 2003–05; of Finance, 2005 and 2007; of Welfare and Social Services, 2006–07; Vice Prime Minister, 2003. Mayor of Jerusalem, 1993–2003. *Address:* Knesset, Kiryat Ben Gurion, Jerusalem 91950, Israel.

OLNER, William John; MP (Lab) Nuneaton, since 1992; *b* 9 May 1942; *s* of Charles William Olner, miner and Lillian Olner; *m* 1962, Gillian Everitt. *Educ:* Atherstone Secondary Modern Sch.; North Warwicks Tech. Coll. Engineer, Rolls Royce, 1957–92. Nuneaton and Bedworth Borough Council: Cllr, 1972–92; Leader, 1982–87; Mayor, 1987–88; Chm., Envmtl Health Cttee, 1990–92. Member: Envmt, Transport and the Regions (formerly Envmt) Select Cttee, 1995–2001; Foreign Affairs Select Cttee, 2001–05; DCLG (formerly ODPM) Select Cttee, 2005–. Chm., Industry and Parlt Trust, 2007–. *Recreations:* hospice movement, walking, current affairs. *Address:* c/o House of Commons, SW1A 0AA.

O'LOAN, Declan; Member (SDLP) North Antrim, Northern Ireland Assembly, since 2007; *b* Ballymena, 5 Aug. 1951; *s* of Charles and Elizabeth O'Loan; *m* 1975, Nuala Patricia (*see* Dame N. P. O'Loan); five *s*. *Educ:* Imperial Coll., London (BSc 1973); Fitzwilliam Coll., Cambridge (PGCE 1974); Univ. of Ulster (MBA 1989). Teacher of Maths: Ramsden Sch. for Boys, 1974–76; Rainey Endowed Sch., Magherafelt, Co. Derry, 1976–80; St Mary's Yala, Kenya, 1980–82; St Patrick's Iten, Kenya, 1982–83; Methodist Coll., Belfast, 1983–87; Teacher of Maths, 1987–2005, Hd of Maths, 1990–2005, St Louis Grammar Sch., Ballymena. Mem., Ballymena BC, 1993–. *Address:* (constituency office) 64 William Street, Ballymena, Co. Antrim BT43 6AW. *T:* (028) 2565 6841, *Fax:* (028) 2565 6844; *e-mail:* declanoloanmla@hotmail.com.

O'LOAN, Dame Nuala (Patricia), DBE 2008; Roving Ambassador and Special Envoy for Conflict Resolution, Ireland, 2008; *b* 20 Dec. 1951; *m* 1975, Declan O'Loan, *qv*; five *s*. *Educ:* King's College, London (LLB Hons); Coll. of Law. Solicitor of Supreme Ct of England and Wales. Articled Clerk, Stephenson Harwood, London, 1974–76; Law Lectr, Ulster Poly., 1976–80; University of Ulster: Law Lectr, 1985–92; Sen. Lectr, 1992–2000; Jean Monnet Chair in European Law, 1992–99; Police Ombudsman for NI, 2000–07. Special Comr, CRE, 2004–05. Chm., Formal Investigation into Human Rights, Equality and Human Rights Commn, 2008; Mem., Indep. Gp for Dialogue and Peace, 2007. Lay Visitor, RUC Stations, 1991–97; Chm., NI Consumer Council for Electricity, 1997–2000; Member: Gen. Consumer Council for NI, 1991–96 (Convenor, Energy and Transport Gp, 1994–96); UK Domestic Coal Consumers' Council, 1992–95; Ministerial Working Gp on Green Economy, 1993–95; Northern HSS Bd, 1993–97 (Convenor for Complaints, 1996–97); Police Authy for NI, 1997–99; Legal Expert Mem., EC Consumers' Consultative Council, 1994–95. *Publications:* articles on European law, policing and consumer law, and faith issues. *Recreations:* music, reading. *Address:* 48 Old Park Avenue, Ballymena, Northern Ireland, BT42 1AX. *T:* (028) 2564 9636; *e-mail:* nuala_oloan@yahoo.com.

O'LOGHLEN, Sir Colman (Michael), 6th Bt *cr* 1838; *b* 6 April 1916; *s* of Henry Ross O'Loghlen (*d* 1944), 6th *s* of 3rd Bt, and of Doris Irene, *d* of late Major Percival Horne, RA; *S* uncle, 1951; *m* 1939, Margaret, *d* of Francis O'Halloran, Melbourne, Victoria; six *s* two *d*. *Educ:* Xavier Coll., Melbourne; Melbourne Univ. (LLB). Formerly Captain AIF. Sometime Magistrate and Judge of Supreme Court, PNG. *Heir: s* Michael O'Loghlen, *b* 21 May 1945. *Address:* Qld 4078, Australia.

OLSEN, Hon. John Wayne, AO 2007; Consul General for Australia in New York, since 2006; *b* 7 June 1945; *s* of S. J. Olsen; *m* 1968, Julie, *d* of G. M. Abbott; two *s* one *d*. *Educ:* Kadina Memorial High Sch.; Sch. of Business Studies, SA. Managing Dir, J. R. Olsen & Sons Pty Ltd, 1968–79. Pres., S Australia Liberal Party, 1976–79; South Australia Government: MP (L): Rocky River, 1979–85; Custance, 1985–90; Kavel, 1992–2002; Chief Sec. and Minister of Fisheries, 1982; Leader of the Opposition, 1982–90; Senator for SA, 1990–92; Shadow Minister of Industry, Trade, Regl Develt, Public Works and Small Business, 1992–93; Minister for Industry, Mfrg, Small Business, Regl Develt and Minister for Infrastructure, 1993–96; Minister for State Develt, and for Multicultural and Ethnic, then Multicultural, Affairs, 1996–2001; Premier of SA, 1996–2001; Consul Gen. for Australia in LA, 2002–06. Fellow, Nat. Inst. of Accts. *Recreation:* barefoot water ski-ing. *Address:* PO Box 135, Belair, SA 5052, Australia. *Club:* West Adelaide Football.

OLSEN, Noel David Lyche, FRCP, FFPH; independent consultant public health physician, since 1996; Chairman, Alcohol Education and Research Council, UK, since 2002; *b* 20 Jan. 1946; *s* of Frank Olsen and late Dora (*née* Wyatt); *m* 1982, Nicky Tewson; two *d*. *Educ:* Mill Hill Sch.; St George's Hosp. Med. Sch. (MB BS 1969); London Sch. of Hygiene and Tropical Medicine (MSc 1978); Henley Mgt Coll. MRCP 1972, FRCP 1993; MFPHM 1979, FFPH (FFPHM 1986). Instructor, Outward Bound Trust, and Watch Officer, Sail Trng Schooner, Malcolm Miller, (intermittent periods) 1966–75; jun. med. posts at St George's Hosp., the Brompton Hosp., Edinburgh Univ. and Royal Free Hosp., 1969–74; Consultant Chest Physician, Barking, London, 1974–76; Sen. Registrar and Lectr, LSHTM and KCH Med. Sch., 1977–79; Dist Community Physician, Cambridge, 1979–82; Dist MO, Hampstead HA, 1982–91; Dir, Public Health, Plymouth, 1991–95. Hon. Associate Lectr, Univ. of Cambridge, 1979–82; Hon. Sen. Lectr, Royal Free Hosp. Sch. of Medicine, 1982–92; Sen. Vis. Res. Fellow, Plymouth Univ., 1994–96. Temp. Consultant Advr, Poverty and Health, WHO, Geneva and Bangladesh, 1999. Member: Nat. Taskforce for Physical Activity, DoH, 1993–96; Air Quality Strategy Forum, DEFRA, 1998–; Fuel Poverty Adv. Gp, DEFRA/DTI, 2002–. Chm., Public Health Medicine Consultative Cttee, UK, 1994–98; Mem., Jt Consultants' Cttee, 1994–98. Hon. Sec., Internat. Agency on Tobacco and Health, 1991–. Mem. Council, 1993–98, Mem., Bd of Sci., 1994–, BMA; Mem. Cttee, BMJ, 1995–2002. Chm., WaterVoice SW, 2001–. Nat. Hon. Sec., ASH, 1975–94; Chm., Policy Cttee, Alcohol Concern, 1987–90; Trustee, Nat. Heart Forum, 1988– (Nat. Hon. Sec., 1988–94). Ind. Gov., Univ. of Plymouth, 2006–. *Publications:* Smoking Prevention: a health promotion guide for the NHS, 1980; contrib. articles on medical audit, preventive medicine, social, envmtl and health policy, fuel poverty and health effects of inequality. *Recreations:* sailing, ski-ing. *Address:* Oakdale, Courtwood, Newton Ferrers, Devon PL8 1BW. *T:* (01752) 873054, *Fax:* (01752) 872653. *Clubs:* Royal Ocean Racing; Yealm Yacht (Newton Ferrers).

OLSSON, Curt Gunnar; Chairman, Skandinaviska Enskilda Banken, 1984–96; *b* 20 Aug. 1927; *s* of N. E. and Anna Olsson; *m* 1954, Asta Engblom; two *d*. *Educ:* Stockholm Sch. of Econs (BSc Econs 1950). Managing Director, Stockholm Group: Skandinaviska Banken, 1970–72; Skandinaviska Enskilda Banken, 1972–76; Man. Dir and Chief Exec., Head Office, 1976–82, and first Dep. Chm., 1982–84, Skandinaviska Enskilda Banken. Dir, Fastighets AB Hufvudstaden, 1983–2003. Hon. Consul Gen. for Finland, 1989–99. Hon. DEcon, Stockholm, 1992. Kt Order of Vasa, Sweden, 1976; King Carl XVI Gustaf's Gold Medal, Sweden, 1982; Comdr, Royal Norwegian Order of Merit, 1985; Comdr, Order of the Lion, Finland, 1986.

OLSWANG, Simon Myers; Senior Partner, 1981–98, Chairman, 1998–2002, Olswang, solicitors (formerly Simon Olswang & Co.); *b* 13 Dec. 1943; *s* of Simon Alfred Olswang and Amelia Olga Olswang; *m* 1969, Susan Jane Simon; one *s* two *d*. *Educ:* Bootham Sch., York; Newcastle upon Tyne Univ. (BAEcon). Admitted solicitor, 1968; Attorney at Law, California State Bar, 1978. Trainee, Asst Solicitor, then Partner, Brecher & Co., 1966–81; Founder, Simon Olswang & Co., 1981. Member: Entertainments Symposium Adv. Bd, UCLA, 1982–88; British Screen Adv. Council, 1985– (Chm., Wkg Party on Convergence, 1994–99); non-exec. Director: Press Assoc., 1995–97; Amdocs Ltd, 2004–; DIC Entertainment Inc., 2005–. Member: Council, BFI, 1998–99; Bd, BL, 2001–08; Bd, Intellectual Property Inst., 2004–06. Chm. Govs and Trustee, Langdon Coll. of Further (Special) Educn, 1992–; Mem., Bd of Trustees, Council of Christians and Jews, 2006–. *Publications:* (contrib.) Accessright: an evolutionary path for copyright into the digital era, 1995; (contrib.) Masters of the Wired World, 1988. *Recreations:* family, friends, sailing, ski-ing, theatre, travel. *Address:* c/o Olswang, 90 High Holborn, WC1V 6XX. *T:* (020) 7067 3000. *Clubs:* Garrick; Royal Motor Yacht (Poole).

OLSZEWSKI, Jan; MP Poland 1991–93 and since 1997; Chairman, Movement for Reconstruction of Poland, since 1995; *b* Warsaw, 20 Aug. 1930. *Educ:* Warsaw Univ. Mem., underground Boy Scouts during German occupation. Res. Asst, Legal Scis Dept, Polish Acad. Scis, 1954–56; Mem., editorial staff, Po Prostu, 1956–57 (periodical then closed down by authorities); subseq. banned from work as journalist; apprenticeship in legal profession, 1959–62; practised as trial lawyer, specialising in criminal law; served as defense counsel in political trials; suspended from the Bar, 1968, for defending students arrested for anti-communist demonstrations; returned as attorney, 1970. Co-Founder: (with Zdzisław Najder), Polish Independence Alliance, 1975–80; Workers' Defense Cttee, 1976–77; co-author of statute of Free Trade Unions, 1980, which he personally delivered to Gdansk shipyard; involved in formation of Solidarity, and legal advr, 1980; defense counsel at trials of Solidarity activists (incl. Lech Wałęsa), 1980–89; attorney for family of Fr Jerzy Popiełuszko at trial of his assassins, 1985; Mem., President Lech Wałęsa's Adv. Cttee, Jan.–Nov. 1991; Prime Minister of Poland (first non-communist govt), 1991–92. *Address:* Ruch Odbudowy Polski, ul. Piekna 22 M 7, 00549 Warsaw, Poland.

OLVER, Richard Lake, FREng; Chairman, BAE SYSTEMS, since 2004; *b* 2 Jan. 1947; *s* of Graham Lake Olver and Constance Evelyn Olver; *m* 1968, Pamela Kathleen Larkin; two *d*. *Educ:* City Univ. (BSc 1st Cl., Civil Eng); Univ. of Virginia Business Sch. MICE; FREng 2005. British Petroleum: joined Engineering Dept, 1973, UK and overseas; Vice-Pres., BP Pipeline Inc., 1979; Divl Manager, New Technology, 1983; Divl Manager, Corporate Planning, 1985; Man. Dir, Central North Sea Pipelines, 1988; Gen. Manager, BP Gas Europe, 1988; Chief of Staff, BP, and Head, Corporate Strategy, 1990; Chief Exec., BP Exploration, USA, and Exec. Vice-Pres., BP America, 1992; Dep. CEO, 1995, CEO, 1998, BP Exploration; Chm., BP Amer. Adv. Bd, 1998; Man. Dir, BP Exploration and Production, 1998–2003; Dep. Gp Chief Exec., BP plc, 2003–04; Dep. Chm., TNK-BP (Russia), 2004–06. Mem., Trilateral Commn, 2005–. Non-executive Director: Reuters, 1997–2008; Thomson-Reuters, 2008–. Hon. DSc: City, 2004; Cranfield, 2006. *Recreations:* sailing, downhill ski-ing, ballet, fine art. *Address:* BAE SYSTEMS, Stirling Square, 6 Carlton Gardens, SW1Y 5AD.

OLVER, Sir Stephen (John Linley), KBE 1975 (MBE 1947); CMG 1965; HM Diplomatic Service, retired; *b* 16 June 1916; *s* of late Rev. S. E. L. Olver and Mrs Madeleine Olver (*née* Stratton); *m* 1953, Maria Morena, Gubbio, Italy; one *s*. *Educ:* Stowe. Indian Police, 1935–44; Indian Political Service, Delhi, Quetta, Sikkim and Bahrain, 1944–47; Pakistan Foreign Service, Aug.–Oct. 1947; Foreign Service, Karachi, 1947–50; Foreign Office, 1950–53; Berlin, 1953–56; Bangkok, 1956–58; Foreign Office, 1958–61; Washington, 1961–64; Foreign Office, 1964–66; The Hague, 1967–69; High Comr, Freetown, 1969–72; High Comr, Nicosia, 1973–75. *Recreations:* photography, painting. *Address:* 6 Saffrons Court, Compton Place Road, Eastbourne, Sussex BN21 1DX.

O'MAHONY, Patrick James Martin; His Honour Judge O'Mahony; a Circuit Judge, since 2004; *b* 18 April 1951; *s* of Patrick Noel and Elizabeth Nora O'Mahony; *m* 1979, Jane Tayler; one *s* two *d*. *Educ:* Stonyhurst Coll.; UCL (LLB (Laws) 1972). Called to the Bar, Inner Temple, 1973; in practice as barrister, London, 1973–83 and 1988–2004; Sen. Crown Counsel, Attorney Gen.'s Chambers, Hong Kong, 1983–88. Hon. Recorder of Margate, 2002–. *Recreations:* long distance running, horse racing, literary criticism. *Address:* c/o Circuit Secretariat, 2 Southwark Bridge, SE1 9HS. *Clubs:* Hong Kong Football; Red and Yellow Racing.

O'MALLEY, Stephen Keppel; His Honour Judge O'Malley; DL; a Circuit Judge, since 1989; *b* 21 July 1940; *s* of late D. K. C. O'Malley and Mrs R. O'Malley; *m* 1963, Frances Mary, *e d* of late James Stewart Ryan; four *s* two *d*. *Educ:* Ampleforth Coll.; Wadham Coll., Oxford (MA). Called to Bar, Inner Temple, 1962; Mem. Bar Council, 1968–72; Co-Founder, Bar European Gp, 1977; a Recorder, Western Circuit, 1978–89. Wine Treasurer, Western Circuit, 1986–89. DL Somerset, 1998. *Publications:* Legal London, a Pictorial History, 1971; European Civil Practice, 1989. *Address:* The Crown Court, Shire Hall, Taunton TA1 4EU.

OMAND, Sir David (Bruce), GCB 2004 (KCB 2000); Visiting Professor, King's College London, since 2006; Security and Intelligence Co-ordinator and Permanent Secretary, Cabinet Office, 2002–05; *b* 15 April 1947; *s* of late J. Bruce Omand, JP, and of Esther Omand; *m* 1971, Elizabeth, *er d* of late Geoffrey Wales, RE, ARCA; one *s* one *d*. *Educ:* Glasgow Acad.; Corpus Christi Coll., Cambridge (BAEcon); Open Univ. (BSc Maths/Physics 2007). Ministry of Defence: Asst Principal, 1970; Private Sec. to Chief Exec. (PE), 1973; Asst Private Sec. to Sec. of State, 1973–75, 1979–80; Principal, 1975; Asst Sec., 1981; Private Sec. to Sec. of State, 1981–82; on loan to FCO as Defence Counsellor, UK Delegn to NATO, Brussels, 1985–88; Asst Under Sec. of State (Management Strategy), 1988–91, (Programmes), 1991–92; Dep. Under Sec. of State (Policy), MoD, 1992–96; Dir, GCHQ, 1996–97; Permanent Under-Sec. of State, Home Office, 1998–2001; Chm., Centre for Mgt and Policy Studies, Cabinet Office, 2001–02. Trustee, Natural History Mus., 2006–. *Recreations:* opera, hill-walking. *Club:* Reform.

O'MARA, Margaret; Director, Human Resources, National Offender Management Service, Home Office, 2006–07; *b* 10 May 1951; *d* of Thomas Patrick and Madge O'Mara. *Educ:* St Hilda's Coll., Oxford (1st Cl. Hons Lit.Hum.); University Coll. London (MSc Econs of Public Policy). Entered HM Treasury, 1973; Private Sec. to Chancellor of Exchequer, 1982–85; Head: Economic Briefing Div., 1985–87; Monetary Policy Div., 1987–90; Public Expenditure Div., monitoring Dept of Employment, 1990–92; Arts Gp, then Libraries, Museums and Galls Gp, Dept of Nat. Heritage, 1992–95; Dir, Personnel and Support, then Personnel, HM Treasury, 1995–2000; Associate Dir, Policing and Security, NIO, 2000–03; Director: Organised Crime, 2003–04, Crime Reduction, 2004–06, Home Office. *Recreations:* walking, cooking, Irish history.

O'MORCHOE, David Nial Creagh, CB 1979; CBE 2007 (MBE 1967); (The O'Morchoe); Chief of O'Morchoe; *b* 17 May 1928; *s* of Nial Creagh O'Morchoe and Jessie Elizabeth, *d* of late Charles Jasper Joly, FRS, FRIS, MRIA, Astronomer Royal of Ireland; *S* father as Chief of the Name (O'Morchoe, formerly of Oulartleigh and Monamolin), 1970; *m* 1954, Margaret Jane, 3rd *d* of George Francis Brewitt, Cork; two *s* one *d*. *Educ:* St Columba's Coll., Dublin (Fellow 1983–2007; Chm. of Fellows, 1989–99); RMA Sandhurst. Commissioned Royal Irish Fusiliers, 1948; served in Egypt, Jordan, Gibraltar, Germany, Kenya, Cyprus, Oman; psc 1958, jssc 1966; CO 1st Bn RIrF, later 3rd Bn Royal Irish Rangers, 1967–68; Directing Staff, Staff Coll., Camberley, 1969–71; RCDS 1972; Brigade Comdr, 1973–75; Brig. GS, BAOR, 1975–76; Maj.-Gen. 1977; Comdr, Sultan of Oman's Land Forces, 1977–79, retired. Dep. Col, 1971–76, Col 1977–79, The Royal Irish Rangers. Pres., Republic of Ireland Dist, RBL, 1999–; SSAFA Forces Help (formerly SSAFA/Forces Help Society): Chm., Rep. of Ireland Br., 1987–2008; Council Mem., 2002–; Mem. Council, Concern, Dublin, 1984–2004 (Sec., 1989–98). Member: Church of Ireland Gen. Synod, 1993–2005; Rep. Church Body, 1994–2004. Founder Mem., Standing Council of Irish Chiefs and Chieftains, 1992 (Chm., 1994–98). Mem., Order of Friendly Brothers of St Patrick, 1980– (Grand Pres., 2002–08). *Recreations:* sailing and an interest in most sports. *Heir:* *s* Dermot Arthur O'Morchoe, *b* 11 Aug. 1956. *Address:* c/o Bank of Ireland, Gorey, Co. Wexford, Ireland; *e-mail:* omor@esatclear.ie. *Clubs:* Kildare Street and University, Friendly Brothers (Dublin); Irish Cruising.

OÑATE, Santiago; Legal Adviser, Organisation for the Prohibition of Chemical Weapons, since 2004; *b* 24 May 1949; *s* of Santiago Oñate and Clara Laborde; *m* 1981, Laura Madrazo; three *d*. *Educ:* Universidad Nacional Autónoma de México (LLB 1972); postgrad. studies at Università degli Studi di Pavia, LSE and Univ. of Wisconsin-Madison. Prof. of Law, Universidad Autónoma Metropolitana-Azcapotzalco, Mexico, 1976–81; Vis. Prof., Law Sch., Univ. of Wisconsin-Madison, 1981–82. Mem. Congress, Chamber of Deputies, Mexico, 1985–88; Mem., Representative Assembly of Federal Dist, Mexico, 1988–91; Ambassador, Permanent Rep. to OAS, Washington, 1991–92; Attorney Gen. for Protection of Envmt, 1992–94; COS, President's Office, 1994; Sec. of State for Labour, 1994–95; Pres., Nat. Exec. Cttee, Partido Revolucionario Institucional, 1995–96; Ambassador for Mexico: to UK, 1997–2001; to the Netherlands, 2001–03. *Publications:* La Acción Procesal en la Doctrina y el Derecho Positivo Mexicano, 1972; El Estado y el Derecho, 1977; Legal Aid in Mexico, 1979; Los Trabajadores Migratorios Frente a la Justicia Norteamericana, 1983. *Recreations:* theatre, music, walking, nature protection. *Address:* (office) Johan de Wittlaan 32, 25 17 JR The Hague, Holland. *Club:* University (Mexico).

ONDAATJE, Sir Christopher; *see* Ondaatje, Sir P. C.

ONDAATJE, Michael; writer; *b* 12 Sept. 1943; *s* of Philip Mervyn Ondaatje and Enid Doris Gratiaen. *Educ:* Dulwich Coll.; Univ. of Toronto; Queen's Univ., Canada. *Publications: poetry:* The Dainty Monsters, 1967; The Man with Seven Toes, 1968; There's a Trick I'm Learning to Do, 1979; Secular Love, 1984; The Cinnamon Peeler, 1991; (ed) The Long Poem Anthology, 1979; Handwriting, 1998; *prose:* Leonard Cohen (criticism), 1968; The Collected Works of Billy the Kid (poetry and prose), 1970; (ed) The Broken Ark, 1971; How to Train a Bassett, 1971; Rat Jelly, 1973; Coming Through Slaughter, 1976; Running in the Family (autobiog.), 1982; In the Skin of a Lion, 1987 (Trillium Award); (ed) From Ink Lake: an anthology of Canadian stories, 1990; Elimination Dance, 1991 (trans. French); The English Patient, 1992 (jt winner, Booker Prize; Trillium Award; filmed, 1997); Anil's Ghost, 2000; The Conversations: Walter Murch and the art of editing film, 2002; Divisadero, 2007. *Address:* 2275 Bayview Avenue, Toronto, ON N4N 3M6, Canada.

See also Sir P. C. Ondaatje.

ONDAATJE, Sir (Philip) Christopher, OC 1993; Kt 2003; CBE 2000; President, Ondaatje Foundation, since 1975; *b* 22 Feb. 1933; *s* of Philip Mervyn Ondaatje and Enid Doris Gratiaen; *m* 1959, Valda Bulins; one *s* two *d*. *Educ:* Blundell's Sch., Tiverton; LSE. National and Grindlays Bank, London, 1951–55; Burns Bros, & Denton, Toronto, 1955–56; Montrealer Mag. and Canada Month Mag., 1956–57; Maclean-Hunter Publishing Co. Ltd, Montreal, 1957–62; Financial Post, Toronto, 1963–65; Pitfield Mackay, Ross & Co. Ltd, Toronto, 1965–69; Founder: Pagurian Corp. Ltd, 1967–89; Loewen, Ondaatje, McCutcheon & Co. Ltd, 1970–88. Mem. Adv. Bd, Royal Soc. of Portrait Painters, 1998–; Mem. Council, RGS, 2001–05. Trustee, Nat. Portrait Gall., 2002–. Mem., Canada's Olympic Bob-Sled Team, 1964. FRGS 1992. Hon. LLD Dalhousie, 1994; Hon. DLitt: Buckingham, 2002; Exeter, 2003. *Publications:* Olympic Victory, 1964; The Prime Ministers of Canada (1867–1967), 1967, rev. edn (1867–1985), 1985; Leopard in the Afternoon, 1989; The Man-Eater of Punanai, 1992; Sindh Revisited: a journey in the footsteps of Sir Richard Francis Burton, 1996; Journey to the Source of the Nile, 1998; Hemingway in Africa, 2003; The Power of Paper, 2007; The Glenthorne Cat, 2008. *Recreations:* tennis, golf, adventure, photography. *Address:* Glenthorne, Countisbury, near Lynton, N Devon EX35 6NQ. *Clubs:* Travellers, MCC; Somerset County Cricket (Life Mem.); Chester Golf; Lyford Cay (Bahamas).

See also M. Ondaatje.

O'NEIL, Roger; non-executive Board Member: Clearvision International Ltd, since 1997; Norwegian Energy Co. AS, since 2006; *b* 22 Feb. 1938; *s* of James William O'Neil and Claire Kathryn (*née* Williams); *m* 1976, Joan Mathewson; one *s* one *d*. *Educ:* Univ. of Notre Dame (BS Chemical Engrg, 1959); Cornell Univ. (MBA 1961). Joined Mobil Corp., New York, 1961; Various staff and exec. positions in Japan, Hong Kong, Australia, Paris, Cyprus, London and New York, 1963–73; Chm., Mobil cos in SE Asia, Singapore, 1973–78; Manager, Planning, Mobil Europe Inc., London, 1978–81; Manager, Corporate Econs and Planning, Mobil Corp., New York, 1981–82; Gp Vice Pres., Container Corp. of America, Chicago, 1982–84; Pres., Mobil Oil Italiana SpA, Rome, 1984–87; Chm. and Chief Exec., Mobil Oil Co., London, 1987–91; Dir and Vice Pres., Mobil Europe, 1991–92; Exec. Vice Pres. and Mem. Exec. Cttee, Statoil, 1992–97. Sen. Oil and Gas Advr, Dresdner Kleinwort Benson, 1997–2003. Non-exec. Bd Mem., Enterprise Oil plc, 1997–2002. Vice-Pres., Inst. of Petroleum, 1989–93 (FInstPet 1988). Mem., Adv. Bd, Johnson Business Sch., Cornell Univ., 1990–. FRSA 1988. *Recreations:* archæology, skiing, tennis. *Address:* 3 Ormonde Gate, SW3 4EU. *Clubs:* Royal Automobile, Hurlingham; Royal Mid-Surrey Golf.

O'NEIL, William Andrew, CM 1995; CMG 2004; Secretary-General, International Maritime Organization, 1990–2003; *b* Ottawa, 6 June 1927; *s* of Thomas Wilson and Margaret O'Neil (*née* Swan); *m* 1950, Dorothy Muir; one *s* two *d*. *Educ:* Carleton Univ.; Univ. of Toronto (BASc Civil Engrg 1949). Engrg posts with Fed. Dept of Transport, 1949–55; Div. Engr, Regl Dir and Dir of Construction, St Lawrence Seaway Authy, 1955–71; Federal Department of Transport: Dep. Administrator, Marine Services, 1971–80; also Comr, Canadian Coast Guard, 1975–80; St Lawrence Seaway Authority, 1980–90: Pres. and Chief Exec. Officer; Dir, Canarctic Shipping Co.; Pres., Seaway Internat. Bridge Corp. Council of International Maritime Organization: Canadian Rep., 1972–90; Chm., 1980–90. Chm., Canadian Cttee, Lloyd's Register of Shipping, 1987–88; Mem. Bd, Internat. Maritime Bureau, 1991–. Chm., Governing Bd, Internat. Maritime Law Inst., Malta, 1991–. Chancellor, World Maritime Univ., 1991–. Member: Assoc. of Professional Engrs of Ont; ASCE; Engrg Alumni Hall of Dist., Univ. of Toronto, 1996. Hon. Freeman, Shipwrights' Co., 2002. FILT (FCIT 1994); FRSA 1992; Foreign Mem., Royal Acad. of Engrg, 1994. Hon. Titulary Mem., Comité Maritime Internat., 2001. Hon. LLD: Univ. of Malta, 1993; Meml Univ. of Newfoundland, Canada, 1996; Korea Maritime, 2002; Hon. DSc Nottingham Trent, 1994. Engrg Medal, 1972, Gold Medal, 1995, Assoc. of Professional Engrs of Ont; Distinguished Public Service Award, USA, 1980; Admirals' Medal, Admirals' Medal Foundn, Canada, 1994; NUMAST Award, 1995; Seatrade Personality of the Year Award, 1995; Silver Bell Award, Seamen's Church Inst., NY, 1997; Cdre Award, Conn Maritime Assoc., USA, 1998; Dioscuri Prize, Italian Naval League, 1998; Vice-Adm. Jerry Land Medal, Soc. of Naval Architects and Marine Engrs, USA, 1999; Halert C. Shepheard Award, Chamber of Shipping of America, 2000; Dist. Servs Medal, Directorate Gen. for Maritime Affairs, Colombia, 2001; Lifetime Achievement Award, Communications and IT in Shipping, 2002; 15 Nov. 1817 Medal, Uruguay, 2002. Ordre Nat. des Cèdres (Lebanon), 1995; Grand Cross, Order of Vasco Nuñez de Balboa (Panama), 1998; Golden Jubilee Medal, 2002. *Address:* 15 Ropers Orchard, SW3 5AX.

O'NEILL, family name of **Barons O'Neill, O'Neill of Clackmannan** and **Rathcavan**.

O'NEILL, 4th Baron *cr* 1868; **Raymond Arthur Clanaboy O'Neill,** TD 1970; Lord-Lieutenant of County Antrim, 1994–2008; *b* 1 Sept. 1933; *s* of 3rd Baron and Anne Geraldine (she *m* 2nd, 1945, 2nd Viscount Rothermere, and 3rd, 1952, late Ian Fleming, and *d* 1981), *e d* of Hon. Guy Charteris; *S* father, 1944; *m* 1963, Georgina Mary, *er d* of Lord George Montagu Douglas Scott; three *s*. *Educ:* Eton; Royal Agricultural Coll. 2nd Lieut, 11th Hussars, Prince Albert's Own; Major, North Irish Horse, AVR; Lt-Col, RARO; Hon. Colonel: NI Horse Sqn, RYR, 1986–91; 69 Signal Sqn, NI Horse, 1988–93. Chairman: Ulster Countryside Cttee, 1971–75; NI Museums Council, 1993–98; Vice-Chm., Ulster Folk and Transport Mus., 1987–90 (Trustee, 1969–90); Member: NI Tourist Bd, 1973–80 (Chm., 1975–80); NI Nat. Trust Cttee, 1980–91 (Chm., 1981–91); Museums and Galleries Commn, 1987–94; President: Youth Action (formerly NI Assoc. of Youth Clubs), 1965–2007; Royal Ulster Agricl Soc., 1984–86 (Chm. Finance Cttee, 1974–83). DL Co. Antrim, 1967. *Recreations:* vintage motoring, railways, gardening. *Heir:* *s* Hon. Shane Sebastian Clanaboy O'Neill [*b* 25 July 1965; *m* 1997, Celia, *e d* of Peter Hickman; three *s*]. *Address:* Shanes Castle, Antrim, N Ireland BT41 4NE. *T:* (028) 9446 3264. *Club:* Turf.

See also Sir J. A. L. Morgan.

O'NEILL OF BENGARVE, Baroness *cr* 1999 (Life Peer), of The Braid in the County of Antrim; **Onora Sylvia O'Neill,** CBE 1995; PhD; FBA 1993; FMedSci; Principal, Newnham College, Cambridge, 1992–2006; President, British Academy, 2005–July 2009; *b* 23 Aug. 1941; *d* of Hon. Sir Con O'Neill, GCMG and of Rosemary Margaret (*née* Pritchard) (now Lady Garvey); *m* 1963, Edward John Nell (marr. diss. 1976); two *s*. *Educ:* St Paul's Girls' Sch.; Somerville Coll., Oxford (BA, MA; Hon. Fellow, 1993); Harvard Univ. (PhD). Asst, then Associate Prof., Barnard Coll., Columbia Univ., 1970–77; University of Essex: Lectr, 1977–78; Sen. Lectr, 1978–83; Reader, 1983–87; Prof. of Philosophy, 1987–92. Hon. Prof. of Ethics and Political Philos., Faculty of Philos., Univ. of Cambridge, 2003. Member: Animal Procedures Cttee, 1990–94; Nuffield Council on Bioethics, 1991–98 (Chm., 1996–98); Human Genetics Adv. Commn, 1996–99. Chm., Nuffield Foundn, 1998– (a Trustee, 1997–). Fellow, Wissenschaftskolleg, Berlin, 1989–90. President: Aristotelian Soc., 1988–89; Mind Assoc., 2003–04. FMedSci 2002; Fellow, Austrian Acad. Sci., 2003. Mem., Amer. Philos. Soc., 2003. Foreign Hon. Mem., Amer. Acad. of Arts and Scis, 1993; Hon. FRS 2007; Hon. MRIA 2003. Hon. Bencher, Gray's Inn, 2002. Hon. DLitt: UEA 1995; Dublin, 2002; Ulster, 2003; Bath, 2004; DU Essex, 1996; Hon. LLD: Nottingham, 1999; Aberdeen, 2001; Hon. DLit London, 2003; Hon. DCL Oxford, 2003. *Publications:* Acting on Principle, 1976; Faces of Hunger, 1986; Constructions of Reason, 1989; Towards Justice and Virtue, 1996; Bounds of Justice, 2000; Autonomy and Trust in Bioethics, 2002; A Question of Trust, 2002; (with N. Manson) Rethinking Informed Consent in Bioethics, 2007; numerous articles on philosophy, esp. political philosophy and ethics in learned jls. *Recreations:* walking, talking. *Address:* British Academy, 10 Carlton House Terrace, SW1Y 5AH. *T:* (020) 7969 5200.

O'NEILL OF CLACKMANNAN, Baron *cr* 2005 (Life Peer), of Clackmannan in Clackmannanshire; **Martin John O'Neill;** *b* 6 Jan. 1945; *s* of John and Minnie O'Neill; *m* 1973, Elaine Marjorie Samuel; two *s*. *Educ:* Trinity Academy, Edinburgh; Heriot Watt Univ. (BA Econ.); Moray House Coll. of Education, Edinburgh. Insurance Clerk, Scottish Widows Fund, 1963–67; Asst Examiner, Estate Duty Office of Scotland, 1971–73; Teacher of Modern Studies: Boroughmuir High School, Edinburgh, 1974–77; Craigmount High School, Edinburgh, 1977–79; Social Science Tutor, Open Univ., 1976–79. MP (Lab): Stirlingshire E and Clackmannan, 1979–83; Clackmannan, 1983–97; Ochil, 1997–2005. Opposition spokesman on Scottish affairs, 1980–84, on defence matters, 1984–88, on energy, 1992–95; chief opposition spokesman on defence, 1988–92. Mem., Select Cttee, Scottish Affairs, 1979–80; Chm., Select Cttee on Trade and Industry, 1995–2005. Member: GMB; EIS. FRSA. *Recreations:* watching football, reading, listening to jazz, the cinema. *Address:* House of Lords, SW1A 0PW.

O'NEILL, Aidan Mark Sebastian; QC (Scot.) 1999; *b* 27 Jan. 1961; *s* of John Joseph, (Jack), O'Neill and Teresa Josephine Birt; civil partnership 2006, Douglas Edington. *Educ:* St Francis Xavier Coll., Coatbridge; Holy Cross High Sch., Hamilton; Langside Coll., Glasgow; Univ. of Edinburgh (LLB Hons 1st cl. 1982); Univ. of Sydney (LLM Hons 1st cl. 1987); European Univ. Inst., Florence (LLM 1993). Admitted Faculty of Advocates, 1987; called to the Bar, Inner Temple, 1996; Standing Jun. Counsel to Educn Dept, Scottish Office, 1997–99; Associate Mem., Matrix Chambers, Gray's Inn, 2000. Inaugural Univ. Center for Values, Law and Public Affairs Fellow in Law and Normative Inquiry, Princeton Univ., 2007–08. *Publications:* (jtly) EU Law for UK Lawyers: the domestic impact of EU law within the UK, 1994, 2nd edn 2008; Decisions of the European Court of Justice and their Constitutional Implications, 1994; Judicial Review in Scotland: a practitioner's guide, 1999; articles in jls incl. Modern Law Rev., European Human Rights

Law Rev., Public Law, Northern Ireland Legal Qly, Edinburgh Law Rev., Legal Studies, Common Market Law Rev., Scots Law Times, The Tablet. *Address:* Advocates' Library, Parliament House, Edinburgh EH1 1RF. *T:* (0131) 226 5071, *Fax:* (0131) 225 3642.

O'NEILL, Alan Dennis; Chairman, Hertfordshire Learning and Skills Council, 2003–08; *b* 2 March 1945; *s* of Dennis O'Neill and Audrey Florence O'Neill; *m* 1969, Susan Fearnley; one *s* two *d. Educ:* King George V Sch., Southport; Bishopshalt Sch., Hillingdon; Univ. of Birmingham (BSc Hons Physics 1966). Joined Kodak Ltd as res. scientist, 1966; Dir and Manager, Manufacturing Ops, 1991–96; Chief Purchasing Officer and Vice-Pres., Eastman Kodak Co., 1996–98; Chm. and Man. Dir, 1998–2001. *Recreations:* bee-keeping, running, golf. *Address:* St Michael's Croft, Woodcock Hill, Berkhamsted, Herts HP4 3TR.

O'NEILL, Brendan Richard, PhD; FCMA; Chief Executive, ICI plc, 1999–2003 (Chief Operating Officer, 1998–99; Director, 1998–2003); *b* 6 Dec. 1948; *s* of John Christopher O'Neill and Doris O'Neill (*née* Monk); *m* 1979, Margaret Maude; one *s* two *d. Educ:* West Park GS, St Helens; Churchill Coll., Cambridge (MA Nat. Sci. 1972); Univ. of East Anglia (PhD Chemistry 1973). FCMA (FCIMA 1983). Ford Motor Co., 1973–75; British Leyland, 1975–81; BICC plc, 1981–83; Gp Financial Controller, Midland Bank, 1983–87; Guinness plc: Dir of Financial Control, 1987; Finance Dir, 1988–90, Man. Dir, Internat. Reg., 1990–92, United Distillers; Man. Dir, Guinness Brewing Worldwide, 1993–97; Chief Exec., Guinness, Diageo plc, 1997–98. Director: Guinness plc, 1993–97; EMAP plc, 1995–2002; Diageo plc, 1997–98; Tyco International, 2003–; Rank Gp plc, 2004–07; Endurance Specialty Hldgs Ltd, 2004–; Informa plc, 2008–. Mem. Council, 2000–07, Finance Cttee, 1994–2000, Cancer Res. UK (formerly ICRF). *Recreations:* music, reading, family.

O'NEILL, Dennis James, CBE 2000; operatic tenor; Director (and Founder), Cardiff International Academy of Voice, Cardiff University, since 2007; *b* 25 Feb. 1948; *s* of late Dr William P. O'Neill and of Eva A. O'Neill (*née* Rees); *m* 1st, 1970, Ruth Collins (marr. diss. 1987); one *s* one *d;* 2nd, 1988, Ellen Folkestad. *Educ:* Gowerton Boys' Grammar Sch. FTCL 1969; ARCM 1971. Specialist in Italian repertoire and works of Verdi in particular; Début: Royal Opera House, Covent Garden, 1979; Vienna State Opera, 1981; Hamburg State Opera, 1981; San Francisco Opera, 1984; Chicago Lyric Opera, 1985; Paris Opera, 1986; Metropolitan Opera, NY, 1986; Bayerische Staatsoper, Munich, 1992; has performed worldwide in opera and concerts. Many recordings. Presenter, Dennis O'Neill, BBC TV, 1987, 1988, 1989. Vis. Prof., RAM, 2005 (Hon. RAM, 2006). Dir, Wexford Fest. Artists Develt prog., 2005–. Hon. Fellow, Univ. of Cardiff, 1997; Hon. FRWCMD (Hon. FWCMD, 1993). Hon. DMus Glamorgan, 2003. Verdi medal, Amici di Verdi, 2005; Golden Jubilee Award, Welsh Music Guild, 2005. OStJ 2008 (SBStJ 2006). *Recreations:* dinner parties, Verdi. *Address:* c/o Ingpen & Williams, 7 St George's Court, 131 Putney Bridge Road, SW15 2PA. *T:* (020) 8874 3222.

O'NEILL, Jonjo; racehorse trainer, since 1986; *b* 13 April 1952; *s* of Thomas and Margaret O'Neill; *m* 1997, Jacqueline Bellamy; three *s* two *d. Educ:* Castletownroche Nat. Sch. National Hunt jockey, 1969–87: winner, 901 races; Champion Jockey, 1977–78, 1979–80; broke record for number of winners in one season, 149 in 1977–78; winner: Cheltenham Gold Cup: 1979 on Alverton; 1986 on Dawn Run; Champion Hurdle: 1980 on Sea Pigeon; 1984 on Dawn Run; has trained over 1,000 winners incl. Gipsy Fiddler, Windsor Castle Stakes, Royal Ascot; also 14 winners at Cheltenham National Hunt Fest., 16 winners at Aintree Fest. and 3 winners at Punchestown Fest. Ireland's People of Year Award, 1986. *Address:* Jackdaws Castle, Temple Guiting, Cheltenham, Glos GL54 5XU. *T:* (01386) 584209, *Fax:* (01386) 584219; *e-mail:* jonjo@jonjooneillracing.com.

O'NEILL, Mark William Robert; Head, Glasgow Arts and Museums, since 2005; *b* 10 Nov. 1956; *s* of Michael O'Neill and Greta (*née* Desmond). *Educ:* University Coll., Cork (BA Hons 1976; HDipEd 1977); Leicester Univ. (Grad. Cert. Mus. Studies 1985); Getty Leadership Inst. (Mus. Mgt Inst. 1993). Curator, Springburn Mus., 1985–90; Glasgow Museums, 1990–2005: Keeper of Social Hist., 1990–92; Sen. Curator of Hist., 1992–97; Hd, Curatorial Services, 1997–98; Head, 1998–2005. FMA 1997. *Publications:* contrib. numerous articles on philosophy and practice of museums. *Recreations:* classical music, fiction, psychology. *Address:* Glasgow Arts and Museums, Cultural and Sport Glasgow, Glasgow City Council, 20 Trongate, Glasgow G1 5ES. *T:* (0141) 287 0446, *Fax:* (0141) 287 5151; *e-mail:* mark.o'neill@csglasgow.org.

O'NEILL, Martin Hugh Michael, OBE 2004 (MBE 1983); Manager, Aston Villa Football Club, since 2006; *b* Kilrea, NI, 1 March 1952; *m* Geraldine; two *d.* Professional footballer: Nottingham Forest, 1971–81 (League Champions, 1978; European Cup winners, 1979 and 1980); Norwich City, 1981, 1982–83; Manchester City, 1981–82; Notts Co., 1983–85; Mem., NI team, 1971–84 (64 caps); Manager: Grantham Town, 1987–89; Shepshed Charterhouse, 1989; Wycombe Wanderers, 1990–95 (Vauxhall Conf. winners, promoted to Football League, 1992–93); Norwich City, 1995; Leicester City, 1995–2000; Celtic, 2000–05. *Address:* c/o Aston Villa Football Club, Villa Park, Trinity Road, Birmingham B6 6HE.

O'NEILL, Michael Angus; HM Diplomatic Service; UK Special Representative for Sudan, Foreign and Commonwealth Office, since 2007; *b* 25 May 1965; *s* of Capt. Shane O'Neill and Jean O'Neill (*née* Macintosh Mayer); *m* 1991, Claire Naomi, *d* of Sir David (Gordon) Bannerman, *qv;* three *s* one *d. Educ:* Manchester Grammar Sch.; Brasenose Coll., Oxford (MA); LSE (MSc). MoD, 1988–91; Second Sec., UK Delegn to NATO, 1991–94; joined HM Diplomatic Service, 1994; Second, later First, Sec., FCO, 1994–98; Vis. Fellow, Inst. for Nat. Security Studies, Washington, DC, 1998–99; First Sec., Washington, 1999–2002; Counsellor, UK Mission to UN, NY, 2002–06; Counsellor, UK Perm. Repn to EU, Brussels, 2006–07. *Recreations:* travel, watching football, walking a chocolate labrador. *Address:* c/o Foreign and Commonwealth Office, King Charles Street, SW1A 2AH.

O'NEILL, Prof. Michael Stephen Charles, DPhil; Professor of English Literature, since 1995, and Director (Arts and Humanities), Institute of Advanced Study, since 2005, University of Durham; *b* 2 Sept. 1953; *s* of Peter and Margaret O'Neill; *m* 1977, Rosemary McKendrick; one *s* one *d. Educ:* Exeter Coll., Oxford (BA 1st Cl. English 1975; MA 1981; DPhil 1981). University of Durham: Lectr, 1979–91; Sen. Lectr, 1991–93; Reader, 1993–95. Founding FEA 2000; FRSA 2006. Eric Gregory Award for Poetry, 1983; Cholmondeley Award, 1990. *Publications:* The Human Mind's Imaginings: conflict and achievement in Shelley's poetry, 1989; Percy Bysshe Shelley: a literary life, 1989; The Stripped Bed (poems), 1990; (with Gareth Reeves) Auden, MacNeice, Spender: the Thirties poetry, 1992; (ed and introd) Shelley, 1993; (ed) The Bodleian Shelley Manuscripts, vol. XX, The 'Defence of Poetry' Fair Copies, 1994; Romanticism and the Self-Conscious Poem, 1997; (ed with D. H. Reiman) Fair-Copy Manuscripts of Shelley's Poems in European and American Libraries, 1997; (ed) Keats: bicentenary readings, 1997; (ed) Literature of the Romantic Period: a bibliographical guide, 1998; (ed with Zachary Leader) Percy Bysshe Shelley: the major works, 2003; The Poems of W. B. Yeats: a sourcebook, 2004; (ed with Mark Sandy) Romanticism, 4 vols, 2006; (ed with C.

Mahoney) Romantic Poetry: an annotated anthology, 2007; The All-Sustaining Air: romantic legacies and renewals in British, American and Irish poetry since 1900, 2007; (jtly) Dante Rediscovered: from Blake to Rodin, 2007; contrib. The Wordsworth Circle, Essays in Criticism, The Charles Lamb Bulletin, Romanticism etc. *Recreations:* running, swimming, listening to music. *Address:* Department of English Studies, University of Durham, Hallgarth House, 77 Hallgarth Street, Durham DH1 3AY. *T:* (0191) 334 2582, *Fax:* (0191) 334 2501; *e-mail:* m.s.o'neill@dur.ac.uk.

O'NEILL, Prof. Patrick Geoffrey, BA, PhD; Professor of Japanese, School of Oriental and African Studies, University of London, 1968–86, now Emeritus; *b* 9 Aug. 1924; *m* 1951, Diana Howard; one *d. Educ:* Rutlish Sch., Merton; Sch. of Oriental and African Studies, Univ. of London. Lectr in Japanese, Sch. of Oriental and African Studies, Univ. of London, 1949. Vis. Prof., Univ. of Michigan, 1961–62. Chm., Organizing Cttee, Eur. Assoc. for Japanese Studies, 1973 (Sec., 1974–79); Pres., British Assoc. for Japanese Studies, 1980–81. First Sakura Award, Nihon Zenkoku Gakushikai, 1976. Order of the Rising Sun (Japan), 1987. *Publications:* A Guide to Nō, 1954; Early Nō Drama, 1958; (with S. Yanada) Introduction to Written Japanese, 1963; A Programmed Course on Respect Language in Modern Japanese, 1966; Japanese Kana Workbook 1967; A Programmed Introduction to Literary-style Japanese, 1968; Japanese Names, 1972; Essential Kanji, 1973; (ed) Tradition and Modern Japan, 1982; (with H. Inagaki) A Dictionary of Japanese Buddhist Terms, 1984; A Reader of Handwritten Japanese, 1984; (trans.) Japan on Stage, by T. Kawatake, 1990; annotated plate supplement, in H. Plutschow, Matsuri, 1996; P. G. O'Neill—Collected Writings, 2001.

O'NEILL, Paul Henry; Senior Advisor, The Blackstone Group, since 2003; Chairman (non-executive), Value Capture LLC, since 2005; *b* 4 Dec. 1935; *m* 1955, Nancy Jo Wolfe; one *s* three *d. Educ:* Fresno State Coll., Calif (BA Econs); Indiana Univ. (MPA). Computer analyst, Veterans Admin, 1961–66; Asst Dir, Associate Dir and Dep. Dir, Office of Mgt and Budget, 1967–77; Vice-Pres., 1977–85, Pres., 1985–87, Internat. Paper Co.; Chm. and CEO, 1987–99, Chm., 1999–2000, Alcoa; Sec., US Treasury, 2001–02. Director: Eastman Kodak, 2003–06; TRW Automotive Hldgs, 2003–; Nalco Co., 2003–; Qcept, 2004–; Celanese Corp., 2004–. Director: Inst. for Internat. Econs, 2003–; Center for Global Develt, 2004–07; Microcredit Enterprises Fund, Inc., 2006–. Mem. Bd of Trustees, RAND Corp., 2003– (formerly Chm.). *Recreation:* painting. *Address:* Suite 100, One North Shore Center, 12 Federal Street, Pittsburgh, PA 15212, USA.

O'NEILL, Robert James, CMG 1978; HM Diplomatic Service, retired; *b* 17 June 1932; *m* 1958, Helen Juniper; one *s* two *d. Educ:* King Edward VI Sch., Chelmsford; Trinity Coll., Cambridge (Schol.; 1st cl. English Tripos Pts I and II). Entered HM Foreign (now Diplomatic) Service, 1955; FO, 1955–57; British Embassy, Ankara, 1957–60; Dakar, 1961–63; FO, 1963–68, Private Sec. to Chancellor of Duchy of Lancaster, 1966, and to Minister of State for Foreign Affairs, 1967–68; British Embassy, Bonn, 1968–72; Counsellor Diplomatic Service, 1972; seconded to Cabinet Office as Asst Sec., 1972–75; FCO, 1975–78; Dep. Governor, Gibraltar, 1978–81; Under Sec., Cabinet Office, 1981–84; Asst Under-Sec. of State, FCO, 1984–86; Ambassador to Austria, and concurrently Head of UK Delegn, MBFR, Vienna, 1986–89; Ambassador to Belgium, 1989–92; EC Presidency Rep. for Macedonia, 1992. EU Rep., OSCE Bosnia elections Task Force, 1995. Mem., Chelmsford Diocesan Synod, 2003–. *Publication:* (with N. Weaver) Edward Bawden in the Middle East, 2008. *Recreations:* diplomatic history, hill-walking. *Address:* 4 Castle Street, Saffron Walden, Essex CB10 1BP. *T:* (01799) 520291. *Clubs:* Travellers, Royal Anglo-Belgian.

O'NEILL, Prof. Robert John, AO 1988; FASSA; Director, Lowy Institute for International Policy, since 2003; Chairman, Australian Strategic Policy Institute, Canberra, 1999–2005; Deputy Chairman of Board, Graduate School of Government, University of Sydney, 2003–05; Chichele Professor of the History of War, and Fellow of All Souls College, University of Oxford, 1987–2001, now Emeritus Fellow; *b* 5 Nov. 1936; *s* of Joseph Henry and Janet Gibbon O'Neill; *m* 1965, Sally Margaret Burnard; two *d. Educ:* Scotch Coll., Melbourne; Royal Military Coll. of Australia; Univ. of Melbourne (BE); Brasenose Coll., Oxford (MA, DPhil 1965; Hon. Fellow, 1990). FASSA 1978; FIE(Aust) 1981–96; FRHistS 1990–2004. Served Australian Army, 1955–68; Rhodes Scholar, Vic, 1961; Fifth Bn Royal Australian Regt, Vietnam, 1966–67 (mentioned in despatches); Major 1967; resigned 1968. Sen. Lectr in History, Royal Military Coll. of Australia, 1968–69; Australian National University: Sen. Fellow in Internat. Relations, 1969–77, Professorial Fellow, 1977–82; Head, Strategic and Defence Studies Centre, 1971–82 (Adjunct Prof., 2001–); Dir, IISS, 1982–87; Dir of Graduate Studies, Modern History Faculty, Univ. of Oxford, 1990–92. Official Australian Historian for the Korean War, 1969–82. Dir, Shell Transport and Trading, 1992–2002. Chairman: Management Cttee, Sir Robert Menzies Centre for Australian Studies, Univ. of London, 1990–95; Bd, Centre for Defence Studies, KCL, 1990–95; Chm. Council, IISS, 1996–2001 (Mem. Council, 1977–82, 1992–94, Vice-Chm. Council, 1994–96). Governor: Ditchley Foundn, 1989–2001; Internat. Peace Acad., 1990–2001; Salzburg Seminar, 1992–97; Trustee: Imperial War Museum, 1990–98 (Chm. Trustees, 1998–2001); Commonwealth War Graves Commn, 1991–2001; Mem., Rhodes Trust, 1995–2001. Mem., Adv. Bd, Investment Co. of America, 1988–; Dir, two Mutual Funds, Capital Group, LA, 1992–. Pres., Rylstone and Dist Historical Soc., 2003–07. Chm., Round Table Moot, 1986–92. Hon. Col 5th (Volunteer) Royal Green Jackets, 1993–99. Hon. DLitt ANU, 2001. *Publications:* The German Army and the Nazi Party 1933–1939, 1966; Vietnam Task, 1968; General Giap: politician and strategist, 1969; (ed) The Strategic Nuclear Balance, 1975; (ed) The Defence of Australia: fundamental new aspects, 1977; (ed) Insecurity: the spread of weapons in the Indian and Pacific Oceans, 1978; (ed jtly) Australian Dictionary of Biography, Vols 7–14, 1979–97; (ed with David Horner) New Directions in Strategic Thinking, 1981; Australia in the Korean War 1950–1953, Vol. 1, Strategy and Diplomacy, 1981, Vol. II, Combat Operations, 1985; (ed with David Horner) Australian Defence Policy for the 1980s, 1982; (ed) Security in East Asia, 1984; (ed) The Conduct of East-West Relations in the 1980s, 1985; (ed) New Technology and Western Security Policy, 1985; (ed) Doctrine, the Alliance and Arms Control, 1986; (ed) East Asia, the West and International Security, 1987; (ed) Security in the Mediterranean, 1989; (ed with R. J. Vincent) The West and the Third World, 1990; (ed with Beatrice Heuser) Securing Peace in Europe 1945–62, 1992; (ed jtly) War, Strategy and International Politics, 1992; (ed with John Baylis) Alternative Nuclear Futures, 1999; articles in many learned jls. *Recreations:* local history, walking.

O'NEILL, Sally Jane; QC 1997; a Recorder, since 2000; *b* 30 Sept. 1953; *d* of late Maj. John O'Neill, RA retd and of Frances Agnes O'Neill (*née* Riley); *m* 1986, David Bloss Kingsbury. *Educ:* St Joseph's Convent, Stafford; Alleyne's Grammar Sch., Uttoxeter; Mid-Essex Technical Coll. (LLB 1975). Called to the Bar, Gray's Inn, 1976, Bencher, 2002; in practice at the Bar, 1976–. An Asst Recorder, 1997–2000. *Recreations:* gardening, tennis, ski-ing, sailing, bull dogs. *Address:* Furnival Chambers, 32 Furnival Street, EC4A 1JQ. *T:* (020) 7405 3232.

O'NEILL, William Alan; Executive Vice President, News Corporation, 1990–2002; Director, News International plc, 1995–2002; *b* 22 May 1936; *s* of John O'Neill and Martha O'Neill (*née* Kitson); *m* 1962, Alene Joy Brown; one *s* one *d*. *Educ:* Sydney Tech. Coll. Gp Employee Relns Manager, News Ltd (Australia), 1977–80; Gen. Manager, 1981, Dir, 1981–90, Times Newspapers Ltd; Vice-Pres. (Personnel), News America Publishing, 1984–85; Exec. Vice-Pres., and Gen. Manager, New York Post, 1985–86, and Vice-Pres. (Human Resources), News Corp., 1986; Man. Dir, News Internat. Newspapers, 1987–90; Director: News Corp., 1987–90; News Gp Newspapers Ltd, 1987–90; Director and Executive Vice-President: News America Inc., 1990–2002; News America Publishing Inc., 1990–2002; CEO, News Internat. plc, 1995. Chm., Convoys Ltd, 1987–89; Dep. Chm., Townsend Hook, 1987–89; Director: Sky TV; Eric Bemrose Ltd. *Recreations:* travelling, genealogy. *Address:* 31 Wolfeton Way, San Antonio, TX 78218–6035, USA. *T:* (210) 8058871.

ONIONS, Jeffery Peter; QC 1998; *b* 22 Aug. 1957; *s* of late Derrick and Violet Onions; *m* 1987, Sally Louise Hine; one *d*. *Educ:* St Alban's Sch.; St John's Coll., Cambridge (BA 1979, MA 1983; LLM (LLB 1980); hockey blue 1977–79). Called to the Bar, Middle Temple, 1981 (Astbury Schol.); in practice at the Bar, 1981–. Mem., Bar Council, 1987–89. *Recreations:* cricket, wine, opera. *Address:* 1 Essex Court, Temple, EC4Y 9AR. *T:* (020) 7583 2000. *Clubs:* MCC, Middlesex CC, Surrey CC; Hawks (Cambridge); 1890.

O'NIONS, Sir (Robert) Keith, Kt 1999; PhD; FRS 1983; Director, Institute for Security Science and Technology, Imperial College London, since 2008; Visiting Professor, University of Oxford, and Fellow, Wolfson College, Oxford, since 2004; *b* 26 Sept. 1944; *s* of William Henry O'Nions and Eva O'Nions; *m* 1967, Rita Margaret Bill; three *d*. *Educ:* Univ. of Nottingham (BSc 1966); Univ. of Alberta (PhD 1969). Post-doctoral Fellow, Oslo Univ., 1970; Demonstr in Petrology, Oxford Univ., 1971–72, Lectr in Geochem., 1972–75; Associate Prof., then Prof., Columbia Univ., NY, 1975–79; Royal Soc. Res. Prof., 1979–95, and Fellow, Clare Hall, 1980–95, Cambridge Univ.; Oxford University: Prof. of Physics and Chemistry of Minerals, 1995–2004 (on leave of absence, 2000–04); Head, Dept of Earth Scis, 1995–99; Fellow, St Hugh's Coll., 1995–2004, now Hon. Fellow; Chief Scientific Advr, MoD, 2000–04; Dir Gen. of Res. Councils, Office of Sci. and Technol., later Dir Gen., Sci. and Innovation, DTI, subseq. DIUS, 2004–08. Trustee, Natural History Mus., 1996–2006 (Chm., 2003–06). Hon. FREng 2005. Hon. Fellow, Indian Acad. of Scis, 1998; For. Fellow, Nat. Indian Sci. Acad., 2000; Mem., Norwegian Acad. of Sciences, 1980. Hon. doctorates from Univs of Abertay, Alberta, Cardiff, Edinburgh, Glasgow, Heriot-Watt, Paris, RHBNC and Loughborough. Macelwane Award, Amer. Geophys. Union, 1979; Bigsby Medal, Geol. Soc. London, 1983; Holmes Medal, Eur. Union of Geosciences, 1995; Lyell Medal, Geol Soc. of London, 1995; Urey Medal, Eur. Assoc. Geochemistry, 2001. *Publications:* contrib. to jls related to earth and planetary sciences. *Address:* Institute for Security Science and Technology, Imperial College, Faculty Building, SW7 2AZ.

ONIONS, Robin William; His Honour Judge Onions; a Circuit Judge, since 2000; *b* 12 April 1948; *s* of late Ernest Onions, DFC, and Edith Margaret Onions; *m* 1970, Catherine Anne Graham; two *s*. *Educ:* Prestfelde Sch., Shrewsbury; Priory Grammar Sch., Shrewsbury; London Sch. of Econs (LLB 1970). Articled clerk, Royal Borough of Kingston upon Thames, 1971–73; admitted solicitor, 1973; J. C. H. Bowdler & Sons, Shrewsbury, subsequently Lanyon Bowdler: solicitor, 1974–76; Partner, 1977–2000; Sen. Partner, 1993–2000. *Recreations:* football, cricket, travel, gardening, keeping fit? *Address:* Shrewsbury Crown Court, The Shirehall, Abbey Foregate, Shrewsbury, Shropshire SY2 6LU.

ONSLOW, family name of **Earl of Onslow**.

ONSLOW, 7th Earl of, *cr* 1801; **Michael William Coplestone Dillon Onslow;** Bt 1660; Baron Onslow, 1716; Baron Cranley, 1776; Viscount Cranley, 1801; *b* 28 Feb. 1938; *s* of 6th Earl of Onslow, KBE, MC, TD, and Hon. Pamela Louisa Eleanor Dillon (*d* 1992), *o d* of 19th Viscount Dillon, CMG, DSO; *S* father, 1971; *m* 1964, Robin Lindsay, *o d* of Major Robert Lee Bullard III, US Army, and of Lady Aberconway; one *s* two *d*. *Educ:* Eton; Sorbonne. Life Guards, 1956–60, served Arabian Peninsula. Farmer. Governor, Royal Grammar Sch., Guildford; formerly Governor, University Coll. at Buckingham. High Steward of Guildford. Elected Mem., H of L, 1999. *Heir: s* Viscount Cranley, *qv*. *Address:* Temple Court, Clandon Park, Guildford, Surrey GU4 7RQ. *Clubs:* White's, Garrick, Beefsteak.

ONSLOW, Andrew George; QC 2002; *b* 10 Feb. 1957; *s* of late John Onslow and of Susan Margaret Ursula Onslow; *m* 1991, Elizabeth Jane Owen; three *s* two *d*. *Educ:* Lancing Coll.; Corpus Christi Coll., Oxford (Open Schol.; BA 1st Cl. Hons Lit.Hum. 1979); City Univ. (Dip. Law 1981). Called to the Bar, Middle Temple, 1982; in practice, specialising in commercial law. *Address:* 3 Verulam Buildings, Gray's Inn, WC1R 5NT. *T:* (020) 7831 8441, *Fax:* (020) 7831 8479; *e-mail:* aonslow@3vb.com.

ONSLOW, Sir John (Roger Wilmot), 8th Bt *cr* 1797; Captain, Royal Yacht of Saudi Arabia; *b* 21 July 1932; *o s* of Sir Richard Wilmot Onslow, 7th Bt, TD, and Constance (*d* 1960), *o d* of Albert Parker; *S* father, 1963; *m* 1955, Catherine Zoia (marr. diss. 1973), *d* of Henry Atherton Greenway, The Manor, Compton Abdale, near Cheltenham, Gloucestershire; one *s* one *d*; *m* 1976, Susan Fay (*d* 1998), *d* of E. M. Hughes, Frankston, Vic, Australia. *Educ:* Cheltenham College. *Heir: s* Richard Paul Atherton Onslow [*b* 16 Sept. 1958; *m* 1984, Josephine Anne Dean; one *s* one *d*].

ONTARIO, Metropolitan of; *see* Moosonee, Archbishop of.

ONTARIO, Bishop of, since 2002; **Rt Rev. George Lindsey Russell Bruce;** *b* 20 June 1942; *s* of late Harold George Bruce and Helen Florence (*née* Wade); *m* 1965, Theodora Youmatoff; three *s* two *d*. *Educ:* Coll. Militaire Royal de St Jean; Royal Military Coll., Kingston (BA Hons 1964); Canadian Land Forces Command and Staff Coll., Kingston (psc 1970); Montreal Diocesan Coll. (LTh, Dip. Min. 1987; Hon. DD, 2003). Served in staff appts, Canadian Army, 1959–86; retd with rank of Colonel. Ordained deacon, 1987, priest, 1987; Diocese of Ottawa: Asst Curate, St Matthew's, Ottawa, 1987–90; Rector: Parish of Winchester, 1990–96; St James, Perth, 1996–2000; Dean of Ontario, Rector of Kingston, and Incumbent, St George's Cathedral, Ontario, 2000–02. Regional Dean: Stormont, 1994–96; Lanark, 1998–2000. Regtl Chaplain to Gov. Gen.'s Foot Guards (Militia), 1988–97. *Recreations:* golf, coaching soccer. *Address:* (office) 90 Johnson Street, Kingston, ON K7L 1X7, Canada. *T:* (613) 5444774; (home) 855 Gainsborough Place, Kingston, ON K7P 1E1, Canada; *e-mail:* gbruce@ontario.anglican.ca.

OPENSHAW, Hon. Dame Caroline Jane, (Lady Openshaw); *see* Swift, Hon. Dame C. J.

OPENSHAW, Hon. Sir (Charles) Peter (Lawford), Kt 2005; DL; **Hon. Mr Justice Openshaw;** a Judge of the High Court of Justice, Queen's Bench Division, since 2005; a Presiding Judge, North Eastern Circuit, since 2009; *b* 21 Dec. 1947; *s* of late Judge William Harrison Openshaw and Elisabeth Joyce Emily Openshaw; *m* 1979, Caroline Jane Swift (*see* Hon. Dame C. J. Swift); one *s* one *d*. *Educ:* Harrow; St Catharine's College, Cambridge (MA). Called to the Bar, Inner Temple, 1970, Bencher, 2003; practised on Northern Circuit, Junior 1973; Assistant Recorder, 1985; a Recorder, 1988–99; QC 1991; Hon. Recorder of Preston, 1999–2005; a Sen. Circuit Judge, 1999–2005. DL Lancs, 2000. *Recreations:* fishing, gardening, village life. *Address:* Royal Courts of Justice, Strand, WC2A 2LL.

OPENSHAW, Prof. Peter John Morland, PhD; FRCP; Professor of Experimental Medicine and Head, Department of Respiratory Medicine, National Heart and Lung Institute, since 1997, and Director, Centre for Respiratory Infections, since 2008, Imperial College London; *b* Glastonbury, 11 Nov. 1954; *s* of William Arthur Openshaw and Susan Elizabeth (*née* Scott Stokes); *m* 1st, 1979, Clare Patricia Vaughan (*d* 1996); two *s* one *d*; 2nd, 2001, Evelyn Samuels Welch; one step *s* two step *d*. *Educ:* Sidcot and Bootham Quaker Schs; Guy's Hosp., Univ. of London (BSc 1976; Paediatric Prize, 1978; MB BS 1979; Gold Medal in Medicine 1979); PhD NIMR 1988. MRCP 1982, FRCP 1994. SHO, Brompton Hosp., 1981–82; Medical Registrar and Lectr, RPMS, 1983–85; Wellcome Trust Sen. Fellow in Clin. Sci., 1988–98; Hon. Physician, St Mary's Hosp., 1990–. Mem., Adv. Gp on pandemic influenza, DoH, 2007–. Mem., various Wellcome Trust funding panels, 1997–. Mem. Council, British Soc. for Immunol., 2006–. FMedSci 1999. Mem., Med. Res. Club, 1989– (Sec., 2004–). *Publications:* contrib. papers on viral immunology and respiratory medicine to jls incl. Nature Medicine, Jl Exptl Medicine. *Recreations:* fresh air, odd music, tying knots. *Address:* Respiratory Medicine, St Mary's Campus, Imperial College, Norfolk Place, Paddington, W2 1PG. *T:* (020) 7594 3853, *Fax:* (020) 7262 8913; *e-mail:* p.openshaw@imperial.ac.uk.

OPIE, Alan John; baritone; *b* 22 March 1945; *s* of Jack and Doris Winifred Opie; *m* 1970, Kathleen Ann Smales; one *s* one *d*. *Educ:* Truro Sch.; Guildhall Sch. of Music (AGSM); London Opera Centre. Principal rôles include: Papageno in The Magic Flute, Sadler's Wells Opera, 1969; Tony in the Globolinks, Santa Fé Opera, 1970; Officer in the Barber of Seville, Covent Garden, 1971; Don Giovanni, Kent Opera, and Demetrius, English Opera Gp, 1972; Prin. Baritone with ENO, 1973–96; *English National Opera:* Figaro; Papageno; Guglielmo; Beckmesser; Valentin; Lescaut in Manon; Eisenstein and Falke in Die Fledermaus; Danilo; Silvio; Junius in Rape of Lucretia; Cecil in Gloriana; Faninal in Der Rosenkavalier; Germont in La Traviata; Marcello and Schaunard in La Bohème; Kovalyov in The Nose; Strephon in Iolanthe; Grosvenor in Patience; Tomsky in Queen of Spades; Paolo in Simon Boccanegra; Harlequin in Ariadne auf Naxos; Dr Faust by Busoni; Sharpless in Madame Butterfly; Fiddler in Königskinder; Sancho in Don Quixote, 1994; Alfonso in Cosí fan Tutte, 1997; Falstaff, 1997 and 2004; Don Carlo in Ernani, 2000; title rôle in Rigoletto, 2003; *Royal Opera, Covent Garden:* Hector in King Priam, 1985; Ping in Turandot, 1986; Mangus in The Knot Garden, 1988; Falke in Die Fledermaus, 1989; Paolo in Simon Boccanegra; rôles in Death in Venice, 1992; Sharpless in Madame Butterfly, 1993; Faninal in Der Rosenkavalier, 1995; Germont in La Traviata, 2001, 2002; Balstrode in Peter Grimes, 2004; *Glyndebourne Festival Opera:* Sid in Albert Herring, 1985, 1990; rôles in Death in Venice, 1989; Figaro in Le Nozze di Figaro, 1991; Balstrode in Peter Grimes, 1992; Dr Falke in Die Fledermaus, 2006; *Scottish Opera:* Baron in La Vie Parisienne, 1985; Storch in Intermezzo, 1986; Forester in Cunning Little Vixen, 1991; *Opera North:* Diomede in Troilus and Cressida, 1995; *Metropolitan Opera, NY:* Balstrode in Peter Grimes, 1994; Sharpless in Madama Butterfly, 1997; Fieramosca in Benvenuto Cellini, 2003; *La Scala, Milan:* title role, Outis, by Berio, world première 1996; Forester in Cunning Little Vixen, 2003; Germont in La Traviata, Berlin, 2001; Balstrode in Peter Grimes, Florence, Japan, Paris Bastille, 2002; Sharpless in Madame Butterfly, China, 2002, Los Angeles, 2004; Mao in Madame Mao (world première), Santa Fe, 2003; has also appeared at Bayreuth Fest., Berlin (Unter den Linden, Berlin Staatsoper, 1990) and in Amsterdam and Munich (rôles include Beckmesser), and at Buxton Fest. and in Brussels, Chicago, Vienna, Paris, Strasbourg, Dallas, Toronto and Sydney. *Address:* Chartwood Lodge, Punchbowl Lane, Dorking, Surrey RH5 4ED.

OPIE, Geoffrey James; freelance lecturer on 19th and 20th century art and design, 1989–2005, now retired; *b* 10 July 1939; *s* of Basil Irwin Opie and Florence Mabel Opie (*née* May); *m* 1st, 1964, Pamela Green; one *s* one *d*; 2nd, 1980, Jennifer Hawkins; one *s*. *Educ:* Humphry Davy Grammar School, Penzance; Falmouth Sch. of Art (NDD); Goldsmiths' Coll., London (ATC). Asst Designer, Leacock & Co., 1961; Curator, Nat. Mus. of Antiquities of Scotland, 1963; Designer, Leacock & Co., 1967; Curator, Victoria and Albert Mus., 1969, Educn Dept, 1978–89, Head of Educn Services, 1983–89. *Publications:* The Wireless Cabinet 1930–1956, 1979; (contrib.) Encyclopedia of Interior Design, 1997; contribs to various jls. *Recreations:* painting, literature, music, motorcycling.

OPIE, Iona Margaret Balfour, CBE 1999; FBA 1998; folklorist; *b* 13 Oct. 1923; *d* of late Sir Robert Archibald, CMG, DSO, MD, and of Olive Cant; *m* 1943, Peter Mason Opie (*d* 1982); two *s* one *d*. *Educ:* Sandecotes Sch., Parkstone. Served 1941–43, WAAF meteorological section. Hon. Mem., Folklore Soc., 1974. Coote-Lake Medal (jtly with husband), 1960. Hon. MA: Oxon, 1962; OU, 1987; Hon. DLitt: Southampton, 1987; Nottingham, 1991; DUniv Surrey, 1997. *Publications:* (with Peter Opie or using material researched with him): I Saw Esau, 1947, 2nd edn (illus. Maurice Sendak), 1992; The Oxford Dictionary of Nursery Rhymes, 1951, 2nd edn 1997; The Oxford Nursery Rhyme Book, 1955; The Lore and Language of Schoolchildren, 1959; Puffin Book of Nursery Rhymes, 1963 (European Prize City of Caorle); Children's Games in Street and Playground, 1969 (Chicago Folklore Prize); The Oxford Book of Children's Verse, 1973; Three Centuries of Nursery Rhymes and Poetry for Children (exhibition catalogue), 1973, enl. edn 1977; The Classic Fairy Tales, 1974; A Nursery Companion, 1980; The Oxford Book of Narrative Verse, 1983; The Singing Game, 1985 (Katharine Briggs Folklore Award; Rose Mary Crawshay Prize; Children's Literature Assoc. Book Award); Babies: an unsentimental anthology, 1990; Children's Games with Things, 1997; edited jointly: The Treasures of Childhood, 1989; A Dictionary of Superstitions, 1989; sole author: Tail Feathers from Mother Goose, 1988; The People in the Playground, 1993; My Very First Mother Goose (illus. Rosemary Wells), 1996; Here Comes Mother Goose (illus. Rosemary Wells), 1999. *Recreation:* opsimathy.

OPIE, Julian Gilbert; artist; *b* 12 Dec. 1958; *s* of Roger and Norma Opie. *Educ:* Magdalen Coll. Sch., Oxford; Chelsea Coll. of Art; Goldsmiths' Sch. of Art. Trustee, Tate Gall., 2002–06. *Solo exhibitions include:* Lisson Gall., London, 1983, 1985, 1986, 2001, 2004, 2008; Hayward Gall., 1993; Ikon Gall., Birmingham, 2001; Galerie Barbara Thumm, Berlin, 2002, 2007; Barbara Krakow Gall., Boston, 2002, 2007; K21, Dusseldorf, 2003; Neues Mus., Nuremberg, 2003; MCA, Chicago, 2003; ICA, Boston, 2005; Scai The Bathhouse, Tokyo, 2005; Alan Cristea Gall., London, 2006; Centro de Arte Contemporáneo, Malaga, 2006; Arts Council of Indianapolis, 2006; Walking on the Vltava, Mus. Kampa, Prague, 2007; MAK, Vienna, 2008; Krobath Wimmer, Vienna, 2008; Art Tower, Mito, 2008; numerous group exhibitions; *works in collections include:* British Council, Contemp. Arts Soc., Tate Gall., Cincinnati Mus. of Modern Art, Stedelijk Mus., Amsterdam; *commissions include:* perimeter wall paintings, HM Prison Wormwood Scrubs, 1994; Imagine You Are Moving, Heathrow Airport, 1997; outdoor installation, Public Art Fund, City Hall Park, NYC, 2004. *Publication:* (jtly) Julian Opie Portraits, 2003. *Address:* c/o Lisson Gallery, 66–68 Bell Street, NW1 6SP.

OPIE, Lisa Moreen; Managing Director, Content, Five, since 2006; *b* 27 Feb. 1960; *d* of Ivan and Lucille Opie; *m* 1991, Julian Meres; one *s* one *d*. *Educ:* Welsh Coll. of Music and Drama; Univ. of Wales (Grad. Dip.); Indiana Univ. Actress, various theatre cos, 1982–88; Researcher Presenter, BBC Radio Wales, 1988–90; Flextech, 1993–2006: a Promotions Producer, 1993–94, Dep. Hd of Programming, 1994–97, Children's Channel; Hd of Programming, Trouble, 1997–99; Exec. Vice Pres., Flextech Channels, 1999–2003; Man. Dir, Flextech Television, 2003–06. Gov., Nat. Film and TV Sch., 2007–. Member: BAFTA; RTS; FRSA. *Recreations:* pottery, ski-ing, music, cooking, reading. *Address:* Channel Five Broadcasting Ltd, 22 Long Acre, WC2E 9LY.

ÖPIK, Lembit; MP (Lib Dem) Montgomeryshire, since 1997; *b* 2 March 1965; *s* of Uno and Liivi Öpik. *Educ:* Royal Belfast Academical Instn; Bristol Univ. (BA Hons Philosophy). Pres., Univ. of Bristol Students' Union, 1985–86; Mem., Nat. Exec., NUS, 1987–88. Procter and Gamble Ltd, 1988–97: Brand Asst, 1988–89; Asst Brand Manager, 1989–91; Corporate Trng and Orgn Develt Manager, 1991–96; Global Human Resources Trng Manager, 1996–97. Mem., Newcastle upon Tyne CC, 1992–97. Mem., Lib Dem Federal Exec., 1991–. Lib Dem spokesman for Young People, 1997–2002, for NI, 1997–2007, for Wales, 2001–07, for Business, Enterprise and Regulatory Reform, 2007; for Housing, 2007–; Mem., Welsh Affairs team, 1997–2007. Leader, Welsh Liberal Democrats, 2001–07. *Recreations:* aviation, astronomy, motorcycling, cinema. *Address:* House of Commons, SW1A 0AA. *T:* (020) 7219 1144; *e-mail:* opikl@parliament.uk; Montgomeryshire Liberal Democrats, 3 Park Street, Newtown, Powys SY16 1EE. *T:* (01686) 625527.

OPPENHEIM, Prof. Charles, PhD, DSc; FCLIP; Professor of Information Science, since 1998, and Head, Department of Information Science, Loughborough University, since 2006; *b* 25 April 1946; *s* of Georg Oppenheim and Eva Henrietta Oppenheim (*née* Stein); *m* 1st, 1968, Pauline Jeanette Kirwan (marr. diss. 1994); two *d*; 2nd, 1996, Adrienne Muir. *Educ:* Orange Hill Boys' Grammar Sch.; UMIST (BSc; PhD); City Univ. (Dip Inf Sci); London Univ. (Cert Ed); DSc Loughborough, 2006. FCLIP 1981, hon. FCLIP 1995. Patent Inf. Officer, Glaxo Holdings, 1970–73; Lecturer: Plymouth Polytechnic, 1973–76; City Univ., 1976–80; Dir, R & D, Derwent Publications, 1980–84; Product Develt Manager, Pergamon Infoline, 1984–87; Business Develt Manager, Reuters, 1987–92; Prof. of Inf. Sci., Strathclyde Univ., 1992–96; Prof., De Montfort Univ., 1996–98. FRSA 2000. *Publications:* The Legal and Regulatory Environment for Electronic Information, 1992, 4th edn 2001; more than 300 articles in jls. *Recreations:* chess, philately, collecting interesting T-shirts. *Address:* Department of Information Science, Loughborough University, Loughborough, Leics LE11 3TU. *T:* (01509) 223065, *Fax:* (01509) 223053; *e-mail:* c.oppenheim@lboro.ac.uk. *Club:* Market Harborough Chess.

OPPENHEIM, Jeremy; Director, Organisational Design and Development, since 2008, Children's Champion, since 2005, UK Border (formerly Border and Immigration) Agency, Home Office; *b* 6 June 1955; *s* of Ian and Doryene Oppenheim; *m* 1985, Karen J. Tanner; two *d*. *Educ:* Lancaster Univ. (BA Hons); London Univ. (CQSW; Dip. Social Work). Qualified Youth and Community Worker. Social Worker, Jewish Welfare Bd, 1977–79; part-time Detached Youth Worker, ILEA, 1978–81; Social Worker, 1982–85; Team Manager, 1985–89; Service Manager, 1989–93, Haringey; Asst Dir, Social Services, Barking and Dagenham, 1993–97; Dir, Social Services, Hackney, 1997–99; Chief Exec., Jewish Care, 1999–2003; Home Office: Dir, Nat. Asylum Support Service, 2004–06; Dir, Social Policy, 2006–07; Dir, Regionalisation and Stakeholders, Border and Immigration Agency, 2007–08. *Recreations:* family, friends, cooking, reading. *Address:* UK Border Agency, Apollo House, 36 Wellesley Road, Croydon CR9 3RR. *T:* (020) 8604 6883; *e-mail:* Jeremy.Oppenheim@homeoffice.gsi.gov.uk.

OPPENHEIM, Hon. Phillip Anthony Charles Lawrence; author, broadcaster; Managing Director, Cubana Ltd; *b* 20 March 1956; *s* of late Henry Oppenheim and of Baroness Oppenheim-Barnes, *qv*; *m* 2003, Dr Susie Morris. *Educ:* Harrow; Oriel College, Oxford. BA Hons. MP (C) Amber Valley, 1983–97; contested (C) same seat, 1997. PPS to Sec. of State for Health, 1988–90, to Sec. of State for Educn and Sci., 1990–92, to Home Sec., 1992–93, to Chancellor of the Exchequer, 1993–94; Parliamentary Under-Secretary of State: Dept of Employment, 1994–95; DTI, 1995–96; Exchequer Sec. to HM Treasury, 1996–97. Co-editor, What to Buy for Business, 1980–85. Columnist, The Sunday Times, 1998–2000. *Publications:* A Handbook of New Office Technology, 1982; Telecommunications: a user's handbook, 1983; A Word Processing Handbook, 1984; The New Masters: can the West match Japan?, 1991; Trade Wars: Japan versus the West, 1992. *Recreations:* Rugby, tennis, travel, ski-ing, tropical plants. *Address:* 29 Redburn Street, SW3 4DA.

OPPENHEIM-BARNES, Baroness *cr* 1989 (Life Peer), of Gloucester in the county of Gloucestershire; **Sally Oppenheim-Barnes;** PC 1979; *b* 26 July 1930; *d* of Mark and Jeanette Viner; *m* 1st, 1949, Henry M. Oppenheim (*d* 1980); one *s* two *d*; 2nd, 1984, John Barnes (*d* 2004). *Educ:* Sheffield High Sch.; Lowther Coll., N Wales. Formerly: Exec. Dir, Industrial & Investment Services Ltd; Social Worker, School Care Dept, ILEA. Trustee, Clergy Rest House Trust. MP (C) Gloucester, 1970–87. Vice Chm., 1971–73, Chm., 1973–74, Cons. Party Parly Prices and Consumer Protection Cttee; Opposition Spokesman on Prices and Consumer Protection, 1974–79; Mem. Shadow Cabinet, 1975–79; Min. of State (Consumer Affairs), Dept of Trade, 1979–82. Chairman: Nat. Consumer Council, 1987–89; Council of Management, Nat. Waterways Museums Trust, 1988–89. Non-executive Director: and Mem., Main Bd, Boots Co., 1982–93; Fleming High Income Trust, 1989–97; HFC Bank, 1989–98. *Recreations:* tennis, bridge. *Address:* c/o House of Lords, Westminster, SW1A 0AA.

See also Hon. P. A. C. L. Oppenheim.

OPPENHEIMER, (Lætitia) Helen, (Lady Oppenheimer); writer on moral and philosophical theology; *b* 30 Dec. 1926; *d* of Sir Hugh Lucas-Tooth (later Munro-Lucas-Tooth), 1st Bt; *m* 1947, Sir Michael Oppenheimer, Bt, *qv*; three *d*. *Educ:* Cheltenham Ladies' Coll.; Lady Margaret Hall, Oxford (Schol.; BPhil, MA). Lectr in Ethics, Cuddesdon Theological Coll., 1964–69. Served on: Archbp of Canterbury's Gp on the law of divorce (report, Putting Asunder, 1966); C of E Marriage Commn (report, Marriage, Divorce and the Church, 1971); Wkg Party, ACCM (report, Teaching Christian Ethics, 1974); C of E Wkg Party on Educn in Personal Relationships (Chm.), 1978–82; Inter-Anglican Theol and Doctrinal Commn (report, For the Sake of the Kingdom, 1986); General Synod Wkg Party on the law of marriage (report, An Honourable Estate, 1988). Pres., Soc. for the Study of Christian Ethics, 1989–91. Lectures: John Coffin Meml, London Univ., 1977; First Mary Sumner, Mothers' Union, 1978; Larkin-Stuart, Trinity Coll., Toronto, 1997; Fourth Leveson, Leveson Centre for the Study of Ageing, 2005; preached University Sermon, Oxford, 1979, Cambridge, 1983. DD Lambeth, 1993. *Publications:* Law and Love, 1962; The Character of Christian Morality, 1965, 2nd edn 1974; Incarnation and Immanence, 1973; The Marriage Bond, 1976; The Hope of Happiness: a sketch for a Christian humanism, 1983; Looking Before

and After: The Archbishop of Canterbury's Lent Book for 1988; Marriage, 1990; Finding and Following, 1994; Making Good: creation, tragedy and hope, 2001; Profitable Wonders (anthology), 2003; What A Piece of Work: on being human, 2006; contributor: New Dictionary of Christian Theology, 1983; New Dictionary of Christian Ethics, 1986; Companion Encyclopedia of Theology, 1996; Dictionary of Ethics, Theology and Society, 1996; articles in Theology, Religious Studies, Studies in Christian Ethics, etc, and in various collections of essays. *Address:* L'Aiguillon, Grouville, Jersey, Channel Islands JE3 9AP. *Club:* Victoria (Jersey).

OPPENHEIMER, Michael Anthony; His Honour Judge Oppenheimer; a Circuit Judge, since 1991; *b* 22 Sept. 1946; *s* of Felix Oppenheimer and Ingeborg Hanna Oppenheimer; *m* 1973, Nicola Anne Brotherton (*see* N. A. Oppenheimer); one *s* one *d*. *Educ:* Westminster Sch.; LSE (LLB). Called to the Bar, Middle Temple, 1970 (Blackstone Exhibnr 1970); Asst Recorder, 1985–89; Recorder, 1989–91. Chm., Bar Disciplinary Tribunal, 1999–. *Recreations:* cinema, theatre, wine and food, performing and listening to music. *Club:* Athenæum.

OPPENHEIMER, Sir Michael (Bernard Grenville), 3rd Bt *cr* 1921; *b* 27 May 1924; *s* of Sir Michael Oppenheimer, 2nd Bt, and Caroline Magdalen (who *m* 2nd, 1935, Sir Ernest Oppenheimer; she *d* 1972), *d* of Sir Robert G. Harvey, 2nd Bt; *S* father, 1933; *m* 1947, Laetitia Helen Lucas-Tooth (*see* L. H. Oppenheimer); three *d*. *Educ:* Charterhouse; Christ Church, Oxford (BLitt, MA). Served with South African Artillery, 1942–45. Lecturer in Politics: Lincoln Coll., Oxford, 1955–68; Magdalen Coll., Oxford, 1966–68. *Publication:* The Monuments of Italy, 6 vols, 2002. *Heir:* none. *Address:* L'Aiguillon, Grouville, Jersey, Channel Islands JE3 9AP. *Club:* Victoria (Jersey).

OPPENHEIMER, Nicholas Frank; Chairman, De Beers Consolidated Mines Ltd, since 1998; *b* Johannesburg, 8 June 1945; *s* of late Harry Frederick Oppenheimer, and Bridget (*née* McCall); *m* 1968, Orcillia Lasch; one *s*. *Educ:* Harrow Sch.; Christ Church, Oxford (BA PPE, MA). Joined Anglo-American Corp., 1968; Dir, 1974; non-exec. Dir, Anglo-American plc, 1999–; Deputy Chairman: Anglo-American Corp. of SA Ltd; De Beers Consolidated Mines Ltd, 1985–97; Dep. Chm., 1990, subseq. Chm., De Beers Centenary AG; Chairman: Central Selling Orgn, 1985–; Anglogold, 1997–2000. Director: De Beers Hldgs Ltd, 1983–; De Beers Industrial Corp. Ltd; E. Oppenheimer & Son (Pty) Ltd. *Address:* PO Box 61631, Marshalltown 2107, South Africa.

OPPENHEIMER, Nicola Anne; Partner, Odgers Ray & Berndtson, since 2001; *b* 30 Sept. 1950; *d* of Basil Vincent Brotherton and Joan Pamela Brotherton; *m* 1973, Michael Anthony Oppenheimer, *qv*; one *s* one *d*. *Educ:* St Margaret's Sch., Bushey; Queen's Coll., London; Queen Mary Coll., London Univ. (LLB). Called to the Bar, Middle Temple, 1972. Lord Chancellor's Department, 1973–96: Judicial Appts Div., 1985; Head of Personnel Management, 1987; Head of Legal Services and Agencies Div., 1991; Prin. Estabt and Finance Officer, 1993–96; Cabinet Office: Prin. Estabt and Finance Officer, 1996–2000; Fellow, Knowledge Mgt Centre for Mgt and Policy Studies, 2000–01. Chairman, Trustees: King's Consort, 1998–2000; Orchestra of St John, 2000–01; Trustee: Classical Opera Co., 1999–2005; The English Concert, 2001–; Early Opera Co., 2005–; Member, Development Board: RAM, 1996–; LAMDA, 1999–2007. *Recreations:* early music, theatre, ski-ing, walking. *Address:* Odgers Ray & Berndtson, 11 Hanover Square, W1S 1JJ. *T:* (020) 7529 1111; *e-mail:* nicky.oppenheimer@odgers.com.

OPPENHEIMER, Peter Morris; Student of Christ Church, Oxford, 1967–2008, now Emeritus; President, Oxford Centre for Hebrew and Jewish Studies, 2000–08; *b* 16 April 1938; *s* of late Friedrich Rudolf and Charlotte Oppenheimer; *m* 1964, Catherine, *er d* of late Dr Eliot Slater, CBE, FRCP, and Dr Lydia Pasternak; two *s* one *d*. *Educ:* Haberdashers' Aske's Sch.; The Queen's Coll., Oxford (BA 1961). National Service, RN, 1956–58. Bank for International Settlements, Basle, 1961–64; Research Fellow, Nuffield Coll., Oxford, 1964–67; Univ. Lectr in Econs, 1967–2000; on secondment as Chief Economist, Shell Internat. Petroleum Co., 1985–86. Vis. Prof., London Graduate Sch. of Business Studies, 1976–77; Temp. Econ. Attaché, British Embassy, Moscow, 1991. Mem., Gen. Bd of Faculties, Oxford Univ., 1989–97. Director: Panfida plc (formerly Investing in Success Equities Ltd), 1975–92; Target Hldgs, 1982–84; J. Rothschild Investment Management, 1982–86; Jewish Chronicle Ltd, 1986–2006 (Chm., 2001–04); Delbanco, Meyer and Co. Ltd, 1986–2001; Dixons Group plc, 1987–93 (Chm., Audit Cttee, 1987–92); OAO Purneftegaz, Russia, 1998–2001; OAO Tomskueft of VNK, Russia, 1999; Far Eastern Shipping Co., Russia, 1999–2000; VSMPO, Russia, 1999–2001. Chm., Caminus Energy Ltd, 1991–93. Delegate, OUP, 1987–97 (Mem., Finance Cttee, 1989–97). Specialist Advr, H of C Expenditure Cttee, 1975–76. Mem., Royal Commn on Legal Services, 1976–79. Mem. Council, Trade Policy Research Centre, 1976–89, and co-Editor, The World Economy, 1977–89; Member: Internat. Econs Steering Gp and Energy and Envmt Steering Gp, RIIA, 1989–; Editl Bd, International Affairs, 1989–; Mem. Bd, Jewish Policy Res. (formerly Inst. of Jewish Affairs), 1991–2001; Renewable Energy Adv. Gp, Dept of Energy, 1991–92; Academic Adv. Council, World ORT Union, 1992–; Spoliation Adv. Panel, DCMS, 2000–. Governor: St Edward's Sch., Oxford, 1979–; St Clare's, Oxford, 1985– (Chm., 1993–2006); Haberdashers' Monmouth Schs, 1987–2003. Hon. Freeman, Haberdashers' Co., 1987. Presenter: (BBC radio): File on 4, 1977–80; Third Opinion, 1983; Poles Apart, 1984; (BBC TV) Outlook, 1982–85; (Granada TV) Under Fire, 1988; (participant) Round Britain Quiz, Radio 4, 1979–96. *Publications:* (ed) Issues in International Economics, 1980; (ed with B. Granville and contrib.) Russia's Post-Communist Economy, 2001; contribs to symposia, conference procs, prof. jls, bank reviews, etc. *Recreations:* music, opera, amateur dramatics, swimming, ski-ing. *Address:* 6 Linton Road, Oxford OX2 6UG. *T:* (01865) 558226.

O'PREY, Prof. Paul Gerard, PhD; Vice-Chancellor and Professor of Modern Literature, Roehampton University, since 2004; *b* 2 April 1956; *s* of Desmond Alexander O'Prey and Ada Dorothy O'Prey (*née* Reid); *m* 1984, Maria del Pilar Garcia Navarro; one *s* one *d*. *Educ:* St George Sch., Southampton; King Edward VI Sch., Southampton; Keble Coll., Oxford; Univ. of Bristol (PhD). Sec. to Robert Graves, 1977–81; writer, translator and researcher, 1981–88; University of Bristol: Tutor in English, 1989–93; Warden of Goldney, 1989–2004; Sen. Warden, 1993–95; Director: Res. Develt, 1995–99; Res. and Enterprise Develt, 1999–2002; Academic Affairs, 2002–04. *Publications:* In Broken Images: selected letters of Robert Graves 1914–1946, 1982; (ed) Joseph Conrad, Heart of Darkness, 1983; Between Moon and Moon: selected letters of Robert Graves 1946–1972, 1984; (ed) Robert Graves Selected Poems, 1986; The Reader's Guide to Graham Greene, 1988; (with Lucia Graves) Emilia Pardo Bazán, The House of Ulloa, 1990; (ed) Robert Graves: collected writings on poetry, 1995; chapters in books and articles in jls. *Address:* Roehampton University, Roehampton Lane, SW15 5PH. *T:* (020) 8392 3101, *Fax:* (020) 8392 3029; *e-mail:* vice-chancellor@roehampton.ac.uk. *Club:* Athenæum.

O'RAHILLY, Prof. Stephen, MD; FRCP, FRCPI, FMedSci, FRCPath; FRS 2003; Professor of Clinical Biochemistry and Medicine (formerly Professor of Metabolic Medicine), Departments of Medicine and Clinical Biochemistry, University of Cambridge, since 1996; Fellow of Pembroke College, Cambridge, since 2007; Hon. Consultant Physician, Addenbrooke's Hospital, since 1994; *b* 1 April 1958; *s* of Patrick

Francis O'Rahilly and Emer (*née* Hyland); *m* 1990, Suzy Oakes. *Educ:* Beneavin Coll., Finglas, Dublin; University Coll., Dublin (MB BCh BAO 1981; MD 1987; Hon. Fellow, Faculty of Medicine, 2000). FRCP 1996; FRCPI 1996; FRCPath 2002. House Officer, Mater Hosp., Dublin, 1981–82; Senior House Officer: St Bartholomew's Hosp., London, 1982–83; Hammersmith Hosp., 1983–84; Res. Fellow, Nuffield Dept of Medicine, Diabetes Res. Lab., Univ. of Oxford, 1984–87; Registrar in Diabetes and Endocrinology, Oxford HA, 1987–89; MRC Travelling Fellow, Harvard Med. Sch., Boston, 1989–91; Wellcome Trust Sen. Fellow in Clinical Sci., Univ. of Cambridge, 1991–96; Fellow, Churchill Coll., Cambridge, 1992–2006. British Diabetic Association: Redcliffe-Maud Fellow, 1986–87; R. D. Lawrence Lectr, 1996. Lectures: Clinical Endocrinology Trust, 1999; Rufus Cole, Rockefeller Univ., 2000; McCallum, Univ. of Toronto, 2000; Andrew Marble, Joslin Clinic, Boston, USA, 2001; Linacre, St John's Coll., Cambridge, 2004; H. C. Jacobaeus, Novo Nordic Foundn, 2005; Kroc Lectr, Univ. of Mass, 2007. FMedSci 1999. Hon. Member: Assoc. of American Physicians, 2004; Assoc. of Physicians, 2004. Medal, Soc. of Endocrinology, 2000; Graham Bull Prize, RCP, 2000; Novartis Award for diabetes research, 2001; European Jl of Endocrinology Prize, 2001; Heinrich Wieland Prize, 2002; Carl W. Gottschalk Award, Univ. of N Carolina, 2003; Rolf Luft Award, Karolinska Inst., 2005; Solomon Berson Award, Mt Sinai Med. Sch., NY, 2007; Clinical Investigator Award, Endocrine Soc., USA, 2007; Feldberg Prize, 2007. *Publications:* papers on: pathophysiol. and genetics of non-insulin-dependent diabetes; mechanism of insulin action; molecular and cell biol. of human fat cells; molecular basis for human obesity. *Recreations:* reading, food and wine, tennis. *Address:* University of Cambridge, Institute of Metabolic Science, Box 289, Addenbrooke's Hospital, Hills Road, Cambridge CB2 0QQ.

ORAMO, Sakari; Chief Conductor and Artistic Adviser, Royal Stockholm Philharmonic Orchestra, since 2008; Chief Conductor, Finnish Radio Symphony Orchestra, since 2003; *b* Finland, 1965; *m* Anu Komsi, soprano; two *s*. *Educ:* musical training as violinist; Sibelius Acad., Helsinki (conducting, under Jorma Panula). Formerly violinist, Avanti! Chamber Orch.; Concert Master, 1992–94, Co-Principal Conductor, 1994, Finnish Radio SO (professional conducting début, 1993); Artistic Dir, Finland 75 SO, 1995–98; Principal Conductor and Artistic Adviser, 1998–99, Music Dir, 1999–2008, Principal Guest Conductor, 2008–, City of Birmingham SO; Principal Conductor, Kokkola Opera, 2006–. Débuts include: CBSO, 1995; Henry Wood Promenade Concert, 1999. Guest Conductor: LA Philharmonic Orch.; NY Philharmonic Orch.; Berlin Philharmonic; NHK SO, Japan; Oslo Philharmonic Orch. *Address:* c/o Harrison Parrott Ltd, 12 Penzance Place, W11 4PA.

ORANMORE and BROWNE, 5th Baron *cr* 1836 (Ire.); **Dominick Geoffrey Thomas Browne;** Baron Mereworth (UK) 1926; *b* 1 July 1929; *e s* of 4th Baron Oranmore and Browne (*s* of 3rd Baron and Lady Verena Ponsonby, *d* of 8th Earl of Bessborough) and his 1st wife, Mildred Helen, *d* of Hon. Thomas Egerton (3rd *s* of 3rd Earl of Ellesmere and Lady Bertha Anson, *e d* of 3rd Earl of Lichfield); *S* father, 2002; *m* 1957, Sara Margaret Wright (marr. diss. 1974). Poet and playwright. *Heir: b* Hon. Martin Michael Dominick Browne [*b* 27 Oct. 1931; *m* 1958, Alison Margaret Bradford; one *s* one *d*].

ORCHARD, Rev. Prof. Stephen Charles, PhD; Principal, Westminster College, Cambridge, 2001–07; Moderator, General Assembly of United Reformed Church, 2007–08; *b* 30 March 1942; *s* of Ronald and Evelyn Orchard; *m* 1965, Linda Irene Smith; one *s* two *d*. *Educ:* Derby Sch.; Trinity Coll., Cambridge (BA 1965; PhD 1969); Cheshunt Coll., Cambridge. Ordained, Congregational Ch, 1968; Minister: Abercarn, S Wales, 1968–70; Sutton, Surrey, 1970–77; Free Ch, Welwyn Gdn City, 1977–82; Asst Gen. Sec. (Community Affairs), BCC, 1982–86; Gen. Sec. and Dir, Christian Educn Movt, 1986–2001. Chair, British and Foreign Sch., 1996–2007. Associate Prof., Sch. of Educn, Brunel Univ., 1999; Sen. Mem., St Edmund's Coll., Cambridge, 2004–. Ed., REToday, 1990–2001. Chm., RE Council of England and Wales, 1999–2001. Templeton Prize judge, 1996–99. Chm., URC Hist. Soc., 1997–; Pres., Cambridge Theol Fedn, 2005–07. Chair: Alliance House Foundn, 2001–; Westhill Endowment Trust, 2006–; Trustee, Dr Williams's Liby, 1999–. Hon. DHum Brunel, 2000. *Publications:* History of Cheshunt College, 1968; A Christian Appreciation of the Welfare State, 1985; Our Commonwealth: a Christian view of taxation, 1987; The Pursuit of Truth in Community: a Christian view of education, 1992; (with W. L. H. Smith) The History of the Post Office in Lewes, 1992; A Human Jesus, 2006; (ed) The Sunday School Movement, 2007; contrib. Oxford DNB, British Jl Religious Educn, Jl URC History Soc., Derbys Family Hist. Soc. *Recreations:* music, walking, cricket. *Address:* c/o Westminster College, Madingley Road, Cambridge CB3 0AA.

ORCHARD, Stephen Michael, CBE 1999; Chief Executive, 1989–2003, and Member, 1992–2003, Legal Services Commission (formerly Legal Aid Board); *b* 5 Aug. 1944; *s* of Stephen Henry Orchard and Ellen Frances Orchard; *m*; one *s* one *d*. *Educ:* Swanage Grammar School. Lord Chancellor's Dept, 1961–89. *Recreations:* walking, food and wine. *Address:* 28 Cow Lane, Wareham, Dorset BH20 4RE.

ORCHARD, Susan Kathleen; *see* Doughty, S. K.

ORCHARD-LISLE, Brig. Paul David, CBE 1988; TD 1961; DL; Chairman, Falcon Property Trust, since 2003; *b* 3 Aug. 1938; *s* of late Mervyn and Phyllis Orchard-Lisle. *Educ:* Marlborough College; Trinity Hall, Cambridge (MA; Hon. Fellow, 1999). FRICS. Nat. Service, RA, 1956–58. Joined Healey & Baker, 1961; Sen. Partner, 1988–99; Chm., Healey & Baker Investment Advisers Inc., 1999–2001. RA (TA), 1958–88; ADC (TA), 1985–87; Brig. (TA), UKLF, 1985; Chm., TAVRA Greater London, 1988–91. Pres., RICS, 1986–87; Chm., RICS Foundn, 2003–05. Hon. Fellow, Coll. of Estate Management, 1985. Chm., Slough Estates plc, 2005–06 (non-exec. Dir, 1984–2006; Dep. Chm., 1993–2005); Director: Europa Capital Partners, 2000–06; Standard Life Property Income Trust, 2004–; Trinity Capital plc, 2006–. Commonwealth War Graves Comr, 1998–2003. Chm., RA Mus., 2000–06. Member Council: Union Jack Club, 1997–; SSAFA, 2001–07. Property Advr, RBL, 2007–. Pres. of Council, Reading Univ., 1994–2003 (Mem. Council, 1989–94); Mem. Council, Marlborough Coll., 1991–2006 (Chm., 2001–06); Governor: West Buckland Sch., 1986–2005 (Chm., 2000–05; Pres., 2006–); Harrow Sch., 1988–99; Nottingham Trent Univ., 1992–94. Trustee: Church Schs Foundn, 2001–; Crafts Council, 2004–06. Chm., Crown Golf (UK), 2008–; Dir, Powerleague, 2008–. Hon. DSc City, 1998; Hon. LLD Reading, 2003. DL Gtr London, 1987 (Representative DL Westminster, 2007). *Recreations:* golf, squash. *Address:* 6a Aria House, 23 Craven Street, WC2 5NT. *Club:* Athenæum.

ORD, Andrew James B.; *see* Blackett-Ord.

ORD, Jeffrey, CBE 2004; QFSM 1995; HM Chief Inspector of Fire Services for Scotland, since 2004; *b* 22 June 1949; *s* of Stanley and Alice Ord; *m* 1970, Beryl Dobinson; one *s*. *Educ:* Realby Sch., Sunderland. Joined Fire Service, 1967: Sunderland Fire Bde, 1967–86; on secondment as Tutor and Course Dir, Fire Service Coll., 1983–86; Comdr, N Div., 1986–87, Hd of Ops (Asst Chief Officer), 1987–88, Kent Fire Bde; Northumberland Fire and Rescue Service: Chief Fire Officer, 1988–92; Dir, Protective Services, Chief Fire Officer and Co. Emergency Planning Officer, 1992–96; Chief Fire Officer, S Yorks Fire and Rescue Service, 1996–99; Firemaster, Strathclyde Fire Bde, 1999–2004. JP Kent, 1971. DUniv Glasgow, 2001. OStJ 1994. *Recreations:* walking, tennis, avid Sunderland Football supporter. *Address:* (office) St Andrew's House, Regent Road, Edinburgh EH1 3DG.

ORDE, His Honour Denis Alan; a Circuit Judge, 1979–2001; *b* 28 Aug. 1932; *s* of late John Orde, CBE, Littlehoughton Hall, Northumberland, and Charlotte Lilian Orde, County Alderman; *m* 1961, Jennifer Jane, *d* of late Dr John Longworth, Masham, Yorks; two *d*. *Educ:* Oxford Univ. (MA Hons). Served Army, 1950–52, 2nd Lieut 1951; TA, 1952–64 (RA), Capt. 1958. Pres., Oxford Univ. Conserv. Assoc., 1954; Mem. Cttee, Oxford Union, 1954–55; Vice-Chm., Fedn of Univ. Conserv. Assocs., 1955. Called to Bar, Inner Temple, 1956; Pupil Studentship, 1956; Profumo Prize, 1959; Bencher, 1998; Hd of Chambers, 1979. Assistant Recorder: Kingston upon Hull, 1970; Sheffield, 1970–71; a Recorder of the Crown Court, 1972–79; Liaison Judge to Magistrates, 1983–97; Dep. High Court Judge (Civil), 1983–2005; Resident Judge, Crown Court, 1986–2001; sat in NE and London. A Pres., Mental Health Review Tribunal (Restricted Cases), 2001–05. Chairman: Criminal Justice Liaison Cttee, Cos of Northumberland, Tyne and Wear and Durham, 1995–2000; Criminal Justice Strategy Cttee for Durham Co., 2000–01; Mem., Lord Chancellor's County Adv. Cttee, 1987–2001. Contested (C): Consett, 1959; Newcastle upon Tyne West, 1966; Sunderland South, 1970. Rep. for NE, Bow Gp, 1962–70. Mem., Chollerton PCC, 1980–91. Life Vice-Pres., Northumberland LTA, 1982–. Gov., Christ's Hospital, Sherburn, 1993–98. *Publications:* Nelson's Mediterranean Command, 1997; In the Shadow of Nelson: the life of Admiral Lord Collingwood, 2008; contrib. Oxford DNB. *Recreations:* writing naval history, cricket, family history, biography. *Address:* Chollerton Grange, Chollerton, near Hexham, Northumberland NE46 4TG; Aristotle Court, 75 Plater Drive, Oxford Waterside, Oxford OX2 6QU. *Clubs:* Northern Counties (Newcastle); Oxford Univ. Cricket.

ORDE, Sir Hugh (Stephen Roden), Kt 2005; OBE 2001; Chief Constable, Police Service of Northern Ireland, since 2002; *b* 27 Aug. 1958; *s* of Thomas Henry Egil Orde and Stella Mary Orde; *m* 1985, Kathleen Helen; one *s*. *Educ:* Univ. of Kent at Canterbury (BA Hons Public Admin and Mgt). Joined Metropolitan Police, 1977; Sergeant, Brixton, 1982; Police Staff Coll., 1983; Inspector, Greenwich, 1984–90 (Bramshill Schol., 1984–87); Staff Officer to Dep. Asst Comr, SW London, as Chief Inspector, 1990; Chief Inspector, Hounslow, 1991–93; Superintendent, Territorial Support Gp, 1993–95; Detective Chief Superintendent, Major Crimes, SW Area, 1995–98; Comdr, Crime, S London, 1998; Dep. Asst Comr (Comr's Comd), 1999–2002. *Recreations:* marathon running, wine, gardening. *Address:* Police Service of Northern Ireland, Knock Road, Belfast BT5 6LE.

ORDE, Sir John (Alexander) Campbell-, 6th Bt *cr* 1790, of Morpeth; *b* 11 May 1943; *s* of Sir Simon Arthur Campbell-Orde, 5th Bt, TD, and Eleanor (*d* 1996), *e d* of Col Humphrey Watts, OBE, TD, Haslington Hall, Cheshire; *S* father, 1969; *m* 1973, Lacy Ralls (marr. diss. 1991), *d* of Grady Gallant, Nashville, USA; one *s* three *d*. *Educ:* Gordonstoun. *Heir: s* John Simon Arthur Campbell-Orde, *b* 15 Aug. 1981. *Address:* PO Box 22974, Nashville, TN 37202, USA. *Club:* Caledonian.

ORDE-POWLETT, family name of **Baron Bolton**.

ORDIDGE, Prof. Roger John, PhD; FMedSci; Joel Professor of Physics Applied to Medicine, since 1994, and Vice Dean for Research, Faculty of Engineering Sciences, since 2006, University College London; *b* 22 Aug. 1956; *s* of John Ordidge and Margaret Ordidge; *m* 1978, Claire Page; one *s* two *d*. *Educ:* Univ. of Nottingham (BSc Phys 1977; PhD Phys 1981). Develt Scientist, 1982–83, Sen. Develt Scientist, 1983–86, Oxford Research Systems; Lectr in Phys, Univ. of Nottingham, 1986–89; Prof. of Phys, Oakland Univ., Mich, 1989–93; Co-Dir, MR Research Lab., Henry Ford Hosp., Detroit, 1989–93. Institute of Neurology: Hon. Sen. Fellow, 1996–; Dir, Wellcome Trust High Field MR Res. Lab., 1999–. Fellow, Internat. Soc. of Magnetic Resonance in Medicine, 2001–. FMedSci 2006. *Publications:* approx. 150 res. papers on MRI and its applications in learned jls; eight patents on design of MRI scanners. *Recreations:* tennis, racquet sports in general, golf, travel. *Address:* Department of Medical Physics and Bioengineering, Malet Place Engineering Building, University College London, Gower Street, WC1E 6BT. *T:* (020) 7679 0256, *Fax:* (020) 7679 0255; *e-mail:* ordidge@mpb.ucl.ac.uk.

O'REGAN, Sister Pauline Margaret, DCNZM 2001; CBE 1990; writer; *b* 28 June 1922; *d* of John Joseph O'Regan and Mary Margaret O'Regan (*née* Barry). *Educ:* Cronadun Primary Sch., W Coast, NZ; St Mary's High Sch., Greymouth; Univ. of Canterbury, Christchurch (MA Hist.). Entered Order of Sisters of Mercy, 1942; professed as Sister of Mercy, 1944; teacher, St Mary's Coll., Christchurch, 1945–49; Principal: Villa Maria Coll., Christchurch, 1950–66; Mercy Coll., Timaru, 1967–68; teacher, Aranui High Sch., Christchurch, 1973–77; community worker, Aranui, 1978–. Winston Churchill Fellow, 1979. Mem., Winston Churchill Meml Trust Bd, NZ, 1985–90. *Publications:* A Changing Order, 1986, 2nd edn 1995; (jtly) Community, 1989; Aunts and Windmills, 1991; There is Hope for a Tree, 1995; Miles to Go, 2004. *Recreations:* walking, films, reading. *Address:* Christchurch, New Zealand.

O'REGAN, Sir Stephen Gerard, (Sir Tipene), Kt 1994; Ngai Tahu tribal leader; company director; *b* 23 Sept. 1939; *s* of Rolland O'Regan and Rena Ruhia O'Regan (*née* Bradshaw); *m* 1963, Sandra Ann McTaggart; one *s* four *d*. *Educ:* Marist Brothers Primary Sch.; St Patrick's Coll.; Victoria Univ. (BA (Hons) Pol Sci. and Hist.); Wellington Teachers' Coll. Sen. Lectr and Head of Dept of Social Studies and Maori, Wellington Teachers' Coll., 1968–83; founded Aoraki Consultant Services, 1983, now Principal Dir. Maori Fisheries Negotiator with Crown, 1987–92. Chairman: Mawhera Incorp., 1976–88; Sealord Group (formerly Sealord Products) Ltd, 1993–2002; Ngai Tahu Hldg Corp. Ltd, 1996–2000; Te Tapuae o Rehua Ltd, 1997–; Escorial Co. Ltd, 1999–; Dep. Chm., Transit NZ Authy, 2000–06; Director: Ngai Tahu Fisheries Ltd, 1986–90; Broadcasting Corp. of NZ, 1986–88; Television NZ Ltd, 1988–95; Whale Watch Kaikoura Ltd, 1988–; Moana Pacific Fisheries Ltd, 1990–95; Ngai Tahu Property Group Ltd, 1993–2000; Meridian Energy Ltd, 2000–05; Clifford Bay Marine Farms Ltd, 2000–. QEII Postgrad. Schol. in Maori, 1977–78; Lansdowne Fellow, Univ. of Victoria, BC, 1994; Canterbury University: Ngai Tahu Fellow (History), 1977–78; Vis. Lectr, NZ History, 1989–2000; Sen. Res. Fellow, 2001–; Asst Vice-Chancellor (Maori), 2004–. Chairman: Ngai Tahu Maori Trust Bd, 1983–96 (Mem., 1974–96); Ngai Tahu Charitable Trust, 1983–97; Ngai Tahu Negotiating Gp, 1990–99; Maori Fisheries Commn, 1990–93; Treaty of Waitangi Fisheries Commn, 1993–2000; Dep. Chm., Fedn of Maori Authorities, 1986–88 (Exec. Mem., 1988–97); Member: Maori Adv. Cttee, NZ Historic Places Trust, 1977–90; NZ Geographic Bd, 1983–; Bd of Trustees, Nat. Mus. of NZ, 1984–94; NZ Conservation Authy, 1990–96; Bd, Law of the Sea Inst., 1995–2001; Bd of Trustees, Marine Stewardship Council, 2000–05. Patron: Foundn for Res. on Marine Mammals, 2001–; Christchurch Ark Fest., 1998–. Writer and presenter, Manawhenua: the Natural World of the Maori (TV documentary series), 1987. Dist. Fellow, Inst. of Dirs, NZ, 2001. Hon. DLitt Canterbury, 1992. New Zealander of the Year, Nat. Business

Review, 1993; Supreme Award, NZ Seafood Industry Council, 2002. *Publications:* contribs to numerous books, articles in jls, reports, etc.

O'REILLY, Sir Anthony (John Francis), Kt 2001; PhD; Chief Executive, Independent News & Media, since 2004 (Executive Chairman, 2000–04); Chairman: Independent Newspapers PLC, since 1980; Waterford Wedgwood PLC, since 1993; *b* Dublin, 7 May 1936; *o c* of J. P. O'Reilly, former Inspector-General of Customs; *m* 1962, Susan (marr. diss.), *d* of Keith Cameron, Australia; three *s* three *d* (of whom two *s* one *d* are triplets); *m* 1991, Chryss Goulandris. *Educ:* Belvedere Coll., Dublin; University Coll., Dublin (BCL 1958); Bradford Univ. (PhD 1980). Admitted Solicitor, 1958. Industrial Consultant, Weston Evans UK, 1958–60; PA to Chm., Suttons Ltd, Cork, 1960–62; Chief Exec. Officer, Irish Dairy Bd, 1962–66; Man. Dir, Irish Sugar Bd, 1966–69; Man. Dir, Erin Foods Ltd, 1966–69; Jt Man. Dir, Heinz-Erin, 1967–70; Man. Dir, H. J. Heinz Co. Ltd, UK, 1969–71; H. J. Heinz Co.: Sen. Vice-Pres., N America and Pacific, 1971–72; Exec. Vice-Pres. and Chief Op. Off., 1972–73; Pres. and Chief Operating Officer, 1973–79; Pres., 1979–96; CEO, 1979–98; Chm., 1987–2000. Lectr in Business Management, UC Cork, 1960–62. Director: Robt McCowen & Sons Ltd, 1961–62; Agricl Credit Corp. Ltd, 1965–66; Nitrigin Eireann Teoranta, 1965–66; Allied Irish Investment Bank Ltd, 1968–71; Thyssen-Bornemisza Co., 1970–72; Independent Newspapers (Vice Chm., 1973–80); Nat. Mine Service Co., 1973–76; Mobil, 1979–88; Bankers Trust Co., 1980–90; Allegheny Internat. Inc., 1982–87; Washington Post, 1987–94; GEC, 1990–92; Chairman: Fitzwilliam Securities Ltd, 1971–77; Fitzwilton Ltd, 1978– (Dep. Chm., 1972–78); Atlantic Resources PLC, 1981–. Member: Incorp. Law Soc.; Council, Irish Management Inst.; Hon. LLD: Wheeling Coll., 1974; Rollins Coll., 1978; Trinity Coll., 1978; Allegheny Coll., 1983. *Publications:* Prospect, 1962; Developing Creative Management, 1970; The Conservative Consumer, 1971; Food for Thought, 1972. *Recreations:* Rugby (played for Ireland 29 times), tennis. *Address:* Independent News & Media, 2023 Bianconi Avenue, City West, Dublin 24, Ireland; Castlemartin, Kilcullen, Co. Kildare, Ireland. *Clubs:* Reform, Annabel's; Stephen's Green (Dublin); Duquesne, Allegheny, Fox Chapel, Pittsburgh Golf (Pittsburgh); Carlton (Chicago); Lyford Cay (Bahamas).

O'REILLY, Most Rev. Colm; *see* Ardagh and Clonmacnoise, Bishop of, (RC).

O'REILLY, Francis Joseph; Chancellor, University of Dublin, Trinity College, 1985–98 (Pro-Chancellor, 1983–85; Hon. Fellow, 1999); Chairman, Ulster Bank Ltd, 1982–89 (Deputy Chairman, 1974–82; Director, 1961–90); Director, National Westminster Bank, 1982–89; *b* 15 Nov. 1922; *s* of Lt-Col Charles J. O'Reilly, DSO, MC, MB, KSG and Dorothy Mary Martin; *m* 1950, Teresa Mary, *e d* of Captain John Williams, MC; three *s* seven *d*. *Educ:* St Gerard's Sch., Bray; Ampleforth Coll., York; Trinity Coll., Dublin (BA, BAI). Served HM Forces, RE, 1943–46. John Power & Son, 1946–66 (Dir, 1952–66, Chm., 1955–66); Chm., Player & Wills (Ire.) Ltd, 1964–81; Chm., 1966–83, Dir, 1983–88, Irish Distillers Gp. President: Marketing Inst. of Ireland, 1983–85; Inst. of Bankers in Ireland, 1985–86. President: Equestrian Fedn of Ireland, 1963–79; Royal Dublin Soc., 1986–89 (Mem. Cttees, 1959–80; Chm. of Soc., 1980–86); Chm., Collège des Irlandais, Paris, 1987–2000. Hon. Life Delegate, Fédn Equestre Internationale, 1979–. MRIA 1987–. LLD *hc:* Univ. of Dublin, 1978; NUI, 1986. GCLJ 1992. KCSG 2001. *Recreations:* fox-hunting, racing, gardening. *Address:* Rathmore, Naas, Co. Kildare, Ireland. *T:* (45) 862136. *Clubs:* Kildare Street and University (Dublin); Irish Turf (The Curragh, Co. Kildare).

O'REILLY, Prof. Sir John (James), Kt 2007; DSc, PhD; CEng, FREng; FIET; CPhys, CSci, FInstP, FBCS; Vice-Chancellor, Cranfield University, since 2007; *b* 1 Dec. 1946; *s* of Patrick William and Dorothy Ann O'Reilly; one *s* one *d*. *Educ:* Brunel Univ. (BTech 1969; DSc 1991); Essex Univ. (PhD 1982). CSci 2004. Student apprentice, RRE, Malvern, 1963–69; Lectr, then Sen. Lectr, Univ. of Essex, 1972–85; Prof. of Electronic Engrg, 1985–94, Hd, Sch. of Electronic Engrg and Computer Systems, 1985–93, UCNW, later Univ. of Wales, Bangor; Principal Res. Fellow, BT Labs, 1993–94; Prof. of Telecommunications, 1994–2001, Hd, Dept of Electronic and Electrical Engrg, 1997–2001, UCL; Chief Exec., EPSRC, 2001–06. Chief Exec., IDB Ltd, 1986–94. Pres., IEE, 2004–05 (Vice-Pres., 2000–02; Dep. Pres., 2002). FREng 1993; FBCS 2004. Hon. FIChemE 2004. *Publications:* Telecommunication Principles, 1984; Optimisation Methods in Electronics and Communications, 1984; (ed with K. W. Cattermole) Problems of Randomness in Communication Engineering, 1984; contrib. numerous jl and conf. papers. *Recreations:* music, theatre, running, cooking. *Address:* Cranfield University, Cranfield, Beds MK43 0AL. *T:* (01234) 754014, *Fax:* (01234) 752853; *e-mail:* john.oreilly@cranfield.ac.uk.

O'REILLY, Most Rev. Leo; *see* Kilmore, Bishop of.

O'REILLY, Air Vice-Marshal Patrick John, CB 1999; CEng, FIET, FRAeS; Director of Military Support, Claverham Ltd, 2000–06; *b* 26 April 1946; *s* of John Francis O'Reilly and Elizabeth O'Reilly (*née* Hammond); *m* 1974, Christine Adair Williamson; two *s*. *Educ:* Ryland Bedford Sch., Sutton Coldfield; Aston Univ. (BSc). Joined RAF 1969; numerous aircraft engrg appts in UK, Germany and the Falkland Is involving fast-jet and rotary aircraft; rcds 1991; Air Officer Wales, 1992–94; Dir Gen. Technical Services, and Pres. of Ordnance Bd, 1996–98, retd 1999. Pres., Wales, Midlands and SW Area, RAFA. Liveryman, Engineers' Co., 2004. *Recreation:* shooting. *Address:* Seend, Wilts. *Clubs:* Royal Air Force; Bath and County.

O'REILLY, William John, CB 1981; OBE 1971; FCPA; Commissioner of Taxation, Australian Taxation Office, 1976–84, retired; *b* 15 June 1919; *s* of William O'Reilly and Ruby (*née* McCrudden). *Educ:* Nudgee Coll., Brisbane, Qld; Univ. of Queensland (AAUQ 1950). FCPA 1990 (FASA 1983). Served RAAF, 1942–44. Joined Australian Public Service, 1946; Australian Taxation Office: Brisbane, 1946–55; Melbourne, 1955–61; Canberra, 1961–84; Asst Comr of Taxation, 1963; First Asst Comr of Taxation, 1964; Second Comr of Taxation (Statutory Office), 1967. *Recreations:* reading, walking. *Address:* 258/42 Ridley Road, Bridgeman Downs, Qld 4035, Australia. *T:* (7) 38632421. *Clubs:* Commonwealth, Canberra (Canberra).

OREJA AGUIRRE, Marcelino; Member, European Commission, 1994–99; President, Institute of European Studies, San Pablo-CEU University, since 2000; *b* 13 Feb. 1935; *m* 1967, Silvia Arburua; two *s*. *Educ:* Univ. of Madrid (LLD). Prof. of Internat. Affairs, Diplomatic Sch., Madrid, 1962–70; Dir of Internat. Service, Bank of Spain, 1970–74; Minister of Foreign Affairs, 1976–80; Governor-Gen., Basque Country, 1980–82; Sec. Gen., Council of Europe, 1984–89; Mem. (Partido Popular) European Parlt, 1989–94 (Chm., Institutional Affairs Cttee, 1989–94). *Address:* 81 Nunez de Balboa, 28006 Madrid, Spain. *T:* (1) 5759101.

ORFORD, Julia Amanda; *see* Dias, J. A.

ORGAN, Diana Mary; Chief Executive, Young Gloucestershire, since 2006; *b* 21 Feb. 1952; *d* of Jack Stanley Pugh and Vera Lillian Pugh; *m* 1975, Richard Thomas Organ; two *d*. *Educ:* Church of England Coll., Edgbaston; St Hugh's Coll., Oxford (BA Hons 1973); Bath Univ. (CertEd 1974). Special Needs Teacher, High Heath Special Sch., 1975; Remedial Teacher, Cardiff, 1976; Special Needs Teacher, Plymouth, 1977–78; Dep. Head, St German's Primary Sch., 1978–79; Head, Special Needs Units, Shepton Mallet, 1979–82; special needs posts, Somerset, 1982–92; Lab Gp policy researcher, Oxfordshire CC, 1993–95. MP (Lab) Forest of Dean, 1997–2005. Director: Glos Envmtl Trust Co., 2005–; Community Foster Care, 2005–; UK Youth, 2006–. *Recreations:* gardening, cinema, sailing, swimming. *Address:* Young Gloucestershire, West Quay, The Docks, Gloucester GL1 2LG. *T:* (01452) 501008, *Fax:* (01452) 501007; *e-mail:* diana.organ@younggloss.org.uk.

ORGAN, (Harold) Bryan; painter; *b* Leicester, 31 Aug. 1935; *o c* of late Harold Victor Organ and Helen Dorothy Organ; *m* (marr. diss. 1981); *m* 1982, Sandra Mary Mills. *Educ:* Wyggeston Sch., Leicester; Coll. of Art, Loughborough; Royal Academy Schs, London. Lectr in Drawing and Painting, Loughborough Coll. of Art, 1959–65. One-man exhibns: Leicester Museum and Art Gallery, 1959; Redfern Gallery, 1967, 1969, 1971, 1973, 1975, 1978, 1980; Leicester 1973, 1976; New York, 1976, 1977; Turin, 1981. Represented: Kunsthalle, Darmstadt, 1968; Mostra Mercato d'Arte Contemporanea, Florence, 1969; 3rd Internat. Exhibn of Drawing, Germany, 1970; Sao Paolo Museum of Art, Brazil; Baukunst Gallery, Cologne, 1977. Works in public and private collections worldwide. Portraits in National Portrait Gallery include: Dr Roy Strong, 1971; Lester Piggott, 1973; Harold Macmillan, 1980; Prince of Wales, 1981; Lady Diana Spencer, 1981; Lord Denning, 1982; Jim Callaghan, 1983; Duke of Edinburgh, 1983; other portraits include: Malcolm Muggeridge, 1966; Sir Michael Tippett, 1966; Mary Quant, 1969; Princess Margaret, 1970; Elton John, 1973; Lester Piggott, 1973; President Mitterrand, 1985; Richard Attenborough, 1985, 2003; Colin Cowdrey, 1996; Lord Woolf, 2002; Roy Jenkins, 2002; Martin Johnson, 2004. Hon. MA Loughborough, 1974; Hon. DLitt: Leicester, 1985; Loughborough, 1992. *Address:* c/o Redfern Gallery, 20 Cork Street, W1X 2HL. *T:* (020) 7734 1732.

ORGILL, Richard Michael James; Global Head of Corporate and Institutional Banking, HSBC Holdings plc, 1998–2001; *b* 14 Oct. 1938; *m* 1968, Anne Whitley; two *s* one *d*. *Educ:* Bryanston Sch. FCIB 1989. Gen. Manager and Chief Exec. Officer, Hongkong and Shanghai Banking Corp., Malaysia, 1985–89; Gen. Manager Internat., Hongkong and Shanghai Banking Corp., Hong Kong, 1989–90; Gen. Manager and Chief Exec. Officer, Hongkong Bank of Australia Ltd, 1990–93; Chief Operating Officer, 1993–94, Dir and Dep. Chief Exec., 1994–98, Midland Bank plc. Director: HSBC (formerly Midland) Bank plc, 1994–2001; Hongkong and Shanghai Banking Corp. Ltd, 1999–2001; HSBC Investment Bank Hldgs plc, 1999–2001; ICICI Bank UK Ltd, 2002–.

ORHNIAL, Anthony Joseph Henry, CB 2007; Director, Personal Tax and Welfare Reform, HM Treasury, 2005–07; *b* 31 Oct. 1947; *s* of Antoine Orhnial and Hilda Orhnial (now Mell); *m* 1982, Gertrud Wienecke; one *d*. *Educ:* St Edward's Coll., Malta; St Benedict's Sch., Ealing; London Sch. of Economics (BSc (Econ), MSc (Econ)). Research Asst, RTZ Services Ltd, 1970–71; Kingston Polytechnic, Kingston on Thames: Lectr, 1971–74; Sen. Lectr, 1974–84; Principal Lectr in Economics, 1984–88; Principal: Inland Revenue, 1988–91; HM Treasury, 1991–93; Asst Dir, 1993–2000, Dir, 2000–05, Personal Tax, Inland Revenue. Vis. Lectr in Economics, Konstanz Univ., Germany, 1979–80. *Publications:* Limited Liability and the Modern Corporation, 1982; articles in Economica, Jl of Accounting Research, British Review of Economics. *Recreations:* travel, reading, cookery, carpentry. *Address:* 32 Marjorie Grove, SW11 5SJ.

O'RIORDAN, Rear-Adm. John Patrick Bruce, CBE 1982; DL; Chief Executive, St Andrew's Group of Hospitals, Northampton, 1990–2000; *b* 15 Jan. 1936; *yr s* of Surgeon Captain Timothy Joseph O'Riordan, RN and Bertha Carson O'Riordan (*née* Young); *m* 1959, Jane, *e d* of John Alexander Mitchell; one *s* two *d*. *Educ:* Kelly College. Nat. Service and transfer to RN, 1954–59; served in submarines, Mediterranean, Home and Far East; HM Ships Porpoise (i/c) and Courageous, NDC, HMS Dreadnought (i/c), MoD, 1960–76; Captain (SM), Submarine Sea Training, 1976–78; RCDS, 1979; HMS Glasgow (i/c), 1980–81; ACOS (Policy), Saclant, USA, 1982–84; Dir, Naval Warfare, MoD, 1984–86; Mil. Dep. Comdt, NATO Defence Coll., Rome, 1986–89. Consultant, Spencer Stuart and Associates, 1989. Director: Workbridge Enterprises Ltd, 1990–2000; Indep. Healthcare Assoc., 1993–2000; NXD O'Riordan Bond, 1999–. Chairman: SSAFA Forces Help (formerly SSAFA) Northants, 1996–2000; SSAFA Forces Help, Dumfriesshire and the Stewartry, 2000–08 (Chm., Scottish Resources Cttee, 2006–08). JP Northants, 1991–2000; DL Northants, 1997. *Recreations:* sailing, Rugby football, stalking, fishing, painting. *Address:* Nether Crae, Mossdale, Kirkcudbrightshire DG7 2NL. *T:* (01644) 450644. *Clubs:* Army and Navy, Royal Navy of 1765 and 1785; Royal Yacht Squadron, Royal Naval Sailing Association.

See also Lt Gen. A. J. N. Graham.

O'RIORDAN, Marie; Editor, Marie Claire, since 2001; *b* 3 April 1960; *d* of Michael and Maura O'Riordan. *Educ:* University Coll. Dublin (BA English and Hist.; MA Modern English and American Lit.). More! magazine: Prodn Editor, 1990–92; Dep. Editor, 1992–94; Editor, 1994–96; Editor, Elle magazine, 1996–99; Gp Publishing Dir, EMAP Elan, 1999–2001. EMAP Editor of Year, 1996; IPC Media Editor of Year, 2003 and 2005. *Recreations:* reading, movies, walking, travelling, partying! *Address:* Marie Claire, IPC Media, 7th Floor, Blue Fin Building, 110 Southwark Street, SE1 0LS. *Clubs:* Soho House, Groucho.

O'RIORDAN, Prof. Timothy; DL; FBA 1999; Professor of Environmental Sciences, University of East Anglia, 1980–2006, now Emeritus; *b* 21 Feb. 1942; *s* of late Kevin Denis O'Riordan and Norah Joyce O'Riordan (*née* Lucas); *m* 1967, Ann Morison Philip (*d* 1992); two *d*. *Educ:* Univ. of Edinburgh (MA 1963); Cornell Univ. (MS 1965); Univ. of Cambridge (PhD 1967). Asst Prof. and Associate Prof., Dept of Geography, Simon Fraser Univ., Canada, 1967–74; Reader, Sch. of Environmental Scis, UEA, 1974–80. Chm., Envmt Cttee, Broads Authy, 1989–98; Mem., UK Sustainable Develt Commn, 2000–; Adviser: Envmtl Res. Directorate, EC, 1996–97; Accounting for Sustainability Project, 2007; Member, Environmental Advisory Council: Dow Chemicals, 1992–98; Eastern Group plc, 1995–; Asda plc, 2004–. Pres., CPRE Norfolk, 2002–. FRSA. DL Norfolk, 1998. Gill Meml Award, RGS, 1982. *Publications:* Environmentalism 1976, 2nd edn 1981; (jtly) Countryside Conflicts, 1986; (jtly) Sizewell B: an anatomy of the inquiry, 1987; (ed) Environmental Science for Environmental Management, 1994, 2nd edn 1999; (ed jtly) Interpreting the Precautionary Principle, 1994; (ed) The Politics of Climate Change in Europe, 1996; (ed) Ecotaxation, 1997; (ed jtly) The Transition to Sustainability, 1998; Globalism, Localism and Identity, 2000; (ed jtly) Reinterpreting the Precautionary Principle, 2001; (ed jtly) Biodiversity, Human Livelihoods, and Sustainability, 2002. *Recreation:* classical double bass playing. *Address:* Wheatlands, Hethersett Lane, Colney, Norwich NR4 7TT. *T:* (01603) 810534; *e-mail:* t.oriordan@uea.ac.uk.

ORITA, Masaki; Professor of International Law, Chuo University, since 2007; Chairman, Institute of Foreign Studies, since 2005; *b* 29 July 1942; *s* of Saburo Orita and Saeko Orita; *m* 1967, Masako Okami; one *s*. *Educ:* Univ. of Tokyo (LLB 1965); St Catherine's Coll.,

Oxford (Dip. Econ. and Pol Sci.). Entered Ministry of Foreign Affairs, Japan, 1965; First Secretary: USSR, 1975–77; Japanese Delegn to OECD, 1977–79; Dep. Budget Examiner, Min. of Finance, Tokyo, 1979–81; Dir, Treaties Div., Min. of Foreign Affairs, 1981–84; Pol Counsellor, USA, 1984–87; Dir, Overseas Estabts Div., Minister's Secretariat, 1987–89; Dep. Dir-Gen., ME and African Affairs Bureau, 1989; Exec. Asst to Prime Minister of Japan, 1989–91; Consul-Gen., Hong Kong, 1992–94; Dir-Gen., Treaties Bureau, 1994–95, N American Bureau, 1995–97, Min. of Foreign Affairs; Ambassador to Denmark (and concurrently to Lithuania), 1997–2001; Ambassador to UK, 2001–04; Sen. Advr to Minister of Foreign Affairs, 2005–06; Ambassador and Special Envoy for UN Reform, 2005–06. Comdr, Order of Orange Nassau (Netherlands), 1991; Grand Cross, Order of Danneborg (Denmark), 1998. *Address:* 1–29–5–203 Daizawa, Setagaya-ku, Tokyo 155–0032, Japan. *Club:* Kojunsha (Tokyo).

ORKNEY, 9th Earl of, *cr* 1696; **Oliver Peter St John;** Lord Dechmont, Viscount Kirkwall, 1696; Professor of Political Studies, University of Manitoba, since 1998 (Associate Professor, 1972–98); *b* Victoria, BC, 27 Feb. 1938; *s* of Lt-Col Frederick Oliver St John, DSO, MC (*d* 1977; *g s* of 5th Earl of Orkney) and of Elizabeth, *d* of E. H. Pierce; *S* kinsman, 1998; *m* 1st, 1963, Mary Juliet (marr. diss. 1985), *d* of W. G. Scott-Brown, CVO, MD, FRCS, FRCSE; one *s* three *d* (and one *d* decd); 2nd, 1985, Mrs Mary Barbara Huck (*née* Albertson); one step *s* three step *d*. *Educ:* Woodbridge Sch.; Univ. of British Columbia (BA 1960); LSE (MSc 1963); PhD London Univ. 1972. Lecturer: UCL, 1963–64; Univ. of Manitoba, 1964–66; Asst Prof., Univ. of Manitoba, 1966–72. Visiting Professor: Carleton Univ., 1981–82; Canadian Armed Forces, W Germany, 1985 and 1990–91; Univ. of Victoria, 1986; USAF Special Ops Sch., Florida, 1993–. Member: RIIA, 1962; Canadian Inst. of Internat. Affairs, 1964–. Regular radio and TV commentaries, Canada and USA. Outreach Award, Univ. of Manitoba, 1996; Stanton Award for Excellence in Teaching, 1997. *Publications:* Fireproof House to Third Option, 1977; Mackenzie King to Philosopher King, 1984; Air Piracy, Airport Security and International Terrorism: winning the war against hijackers, 1991; numerous contribs to jls. *Recreations:* swimming, squash, tennis, photography, touring, farming. *Heir: s* Oliver Robert St John [*b* 19 July 1969; *m* 1997, Consuela Hazel Davies]. *Address:* 595 Gertrude Avenue, Winnipeg, MB R3L 0M9, Canada. *T:* (204) 2841089, *Fax:* (204) 4533615; *e-mail:* hrtland@mts.net.

ORMAN, Stanley, PhD; Chief Executive Officer, Orman Associates, Maryland, since 1996; *b* 6 Feb. 1935; *s* of Jacob and Ettie Orman; *m* 1960, Helen (*née* Hourman); one *s* two *d*. *Educ:* Hackney Downs Grammar School; King's College London. BSc (1st Cl. Hons) 1957; PhD (Organic Chem.) 1960. MICorr; FRIC 1969. Research Fellowship, Brandeis Univ., 1960–61; AWRE Aldermaston, research in corrosion and mechano-chemical corrosion, 1961–74, project work, 1974–78; Director Missiles, 1978–81, Chief Weapon System Engineer Polaris, 1981–82, MoD; Minister-Counsellor, Hd of Defence Equip. Staff, British Embassy, Washington, 1982–84; Dep. Dir, AWRE, MoD, 1984–86; Dir Gen., SDI Participation Office, MoD, 1986–90; Chief Exec. Officer, General Technology Systems Inc., 1990–95. Founder Chm., Reading Ratepayers' Assoc., 1974; Pres., Reading Hebrew Congregation, 1970–74. *Publications:* Faith in G.O.D.S.: stability in the nuclear age, 1991; numerous papers on free radical chemistry, materials science, mechano-chemical corrosion and ballistic missile defence, in learned jls. *Recreations:* sporting—originally athletics, now tennis; designing bow ties, woodwork, embroidery. *Address:* 11420 Strand Drive #104, Rockville, MD 20852, USA; *e-mail:* stanleyo1@comcast.net.

ORME, Jeremy David, FCA; accountant; *b* 27 Dec. 1943; 2nd *s* of John Samuel Orme, CB, OBE, and of Jean Esther (*née* Harris); *m* 2001, Jennifer Anne Page, *qv*; two *s* from former marriage. *Educ:* Winchester Coll.; Christ Church, Oxford (MA). Robson Rhodes, chartered accountants, 1966–87, Man. Partner, 1982–87; Asst Sec. (on secondment), Dept of Transport, 1979–81; SIB, 1987–98 (investigations and enforcement roles); FSA, 1998–2001 (various roles concerned with financial crime). Member: National Bus Co., 1984–86 (Dep. Chm. 1985–86); Audit Commn for Local Authorities and NHS in England and Wales, 1989–2000 (Dep. Chm., 1997–2000); Chm., Financial Fraud Information Network, 1997–2000.

See also B. J. Coles.

ORME, Prof. Michael Christopher L'Estrange, MD; FRCP; Chairman, European Association for Clinical Pharmacology and Therapeutics, 2003–07 (Secretary, 1991–2003); Professor of Pharmacology and Therapeutics, Liverpool University, 1984–2001, now Emeritus; *b* 13 June 1940; *s* of Christopher Robert L'Estrange Orme and Muriel Evelyn Janet Orme; *m* 1967, Joan Patricia Abbott; one *s*. *Educ:* Sherborne Sch.; Sidney Sussex Coll., Cambridge (MB BChir 1964; MA 1965; MD 1975); King's Coll. Hosp. FRCP 1980; FFPM 1989; FFSRH (FFFP 1994); FFPH (FFPHM 2000). House Officer and Registrar posts, KCH, Hammersmith Hosp., Brompton Hosp. and St Mary's Hosp., 1965–69; Sen. Registrar, Hammersmith Hosp., 1970–73; Wellcome Fellowship, Karolinska Inst., Stockholm, 1973–74; Liverpool University: Sen. Lectr, 1975–81; Reader in Clinical Pharmacology, 1981–84; Dean, Faculty of Medicine, 1991–96. Hon. Consultant Physician, Royal Liverpool and Broadgreen Univ. Hosps NHS Trust, 1975–2001; Dir of Educn and Trng, NW Regl Office, NHS Exec., 1996–2001. Gov., Glos Hosp. NHS Foundn Trust, 2008–. Secretary: Clin. Sect., British Pharmacol Soc., 1982–88; Clin. Sect., Internat. Union of Pharmacol., 1987–93. Pres., Liverpool Medical Inst., 1994–95; Chm., Specialist Adv. Cttee on Clin. Pharmacol. and Therapeutics, 1991–93; Member: Internat. Adv. Bd, World Conf. on Clin. Pharmacol. and Therapeutics, 1989, 1992, 1996, 2000; WHO Scientific Working Gp on Drugs in Breast Milk, and on Filariasis, 1981–96. Gov., Birkenhead Sch., Wirral, 1990–2005. Founder FMedSci 1998. Hon. FRCGP 1998. Hon. Fellow, Univ. of Central Lancs, 2001. Hon. DSc Salford, 2000; Hon. MD Internat. Med. Univ., Malaysia, 2004. Paul Martini Prize, Paul Martini Stiftung, Germany, 1974. *Publications:* Self Help Guide to Medicine, 1988; (ed) Therapeutic Drugs, 1991; contribs to learned jls. *Recreations:* sailing, astronomy, cooking, walking. *Address:* Lark House, Clapton-on-the-Hill, Cheltenham, Glos GL54 2LG. *T:* (01451) 822238.

ORME, Prof. Nicholas Ian, DPhil, DD, DLitt; FSA, FRHistS; Professor of History, University of Exeter, 1988–2007, now Emeritus; *b* 3 June 1941; *s* of late Edward and Kathleen Orme; *m* 1981, Rona Jane Monro; one *d*. *Educ:* Bristol Cathedral Sch.; Magdalen Coll., Oxford (MA 1966, DPhil 1969, DLitt 1986). FRHistS 1973; FSA 1982. Lectr, Univ. of Exeter, 1964–88. Research Fellow: Nuffield Foundn, 1991; Leverhulme Trust, 1993; British Acad., 1998; Vis. Res. Fellow, Merton Coll., Oxford, 1982; Vis. Scholar, St John's Coll., Oxford, 1997; Vis. Prof., Univ. of Minnesota, 1998; Vis. Lectr, Arizona State Univ., 2002. Chm. Council, 1996–2000, and Vice-Pres., 1996–, Devon and Cornwall Record Soc.; President: Somerset Archaeol Soc., 1997; Bristol and Glos Archaeol Soc., 2003; Devon History Soc., 2003–06. Licensed Reader, Church of England, 1993–; Lay Canon, Truro Cathedral, 2005–. Corresp. Fellow, Medieval Acad. of America, 2003. *Publications:* English Schools in the Middle Ages, 1973; Education in the West of England 1066–1548, 1976; The Minor Clergy of Exeter Cathedral, 1980; Early British Swimming, 1983; From Childhood to Chivalry, 1984; Exeter Cathedral as it was 1050–1550, 1986; Education and Society in Medieval and Renaissance England, 1989; John Lydgate's Table Manners for Children, 1989; (ed) Unity and Variety: a history of the Church in Devon and Cornwall, 1991; (with M. Webster) The English Hospital: 1070 to 1570, 1995; White Bird Flying (children's stories), 1995; English Church Dedications, 1996; Education in Early Tudor England, 1998; The Saints of Cornwall, 2000; Medieval Children, 2001; (with David Lepine) Death and Memory in Medieval Exeter, 2003; (with John Chynoweth and Alexandra Walsham) Richard Carew's Survey of Cornwall, 2004; Medieval Schools, 2006; Cornish Wills 1342–1540, 2007; Cornwall and the Cross, 2007. *Recreations:* exercising, walking, church-crawling. *Address:* c/o Department of History, University of Exeter, Amory Building, Rennes Drive, Exeter EX4 4RJ.

ORME, Robert Thomas Neil; His Honour Judge Orme; a Circuit Judge, since 1992; *b* 25 Jan. 1947; *s* of Thomas Elsmore Orme and Iris Marguerita Orme; *m* 1971, Angela Mary Stokes; one *s* one *d*. *Educ:* Denstone Coll., Staffs; University Coll. London (LLB Hons). Called to the Bar, Gray's Inn, 1970; Midland and Oxford Circuit; Asst Recorder, 1984–88; Recorder, 1988–92. W Midlands Probation Cttee, 1996–2001; W Midlands Probation Bd, 2001–; a Pres., Mental Health Review Tribunals, 2001–. Gov., Denstone Coll., Staffs, 2000–. Chm., Moseley Soc., 1993–. *Recreations:* opera, theatre, keen interest in conservation. *Address:* Queen Elizabeth II Law Courts, Birmingham B4 7NA. *T:* (0121) 681 3300.

ORMEROD, Alec William; Deputy Judge and Prison Adjudicator, 2003–08; *b* 19 July 1932; *s* of William and Susan Ormerod; *m* 1976, Patricia Mary Large. *Educ:* Nelson Grammar Sch.; Christ's Coll., Cambridge (Major Scholar; MA, LLM). Solicitor. Mil. Service, Staff of GOC London Dist, 1956–58. Asst Lectr in Law, Burnley Coll., 1953–55; Local Govt Service, 1958–64; Sen. Partner, Boyle and Ormerod, Solicitors, Aylesbury, 1964–88; Metropolitan Stipendiary Magistrate then Dist Judge (Magistrates' Cts), 1988–2003; Chm., Family Ct, 1991–2003; AJAG, 1996–2003; Judge, Summary Appeals Ct, 2000–03. Councillor, Aylesbury Borough Council, 1966–72. Freeman, City of London, 1973. *Recreations:* travel, fine art, gardening. *Address:* 1 Miller Way, Sherborne, Dorset DT9 3SG. *Club:* Naval and Military.

ORMEROD, Prof. (Lawrence) Peter, MD, DSc; FRCP; Consultant General and Respiratory Physician, Royal Blackburn Hospital (formerly Blackburn Royal Infirmary), since 1981; Professor of Respiratory Medicine, Lancashire Postgraduate School of Medicine and Health, University of Central Lancashire, Preston, since 2000; *b* 28 Aug. 1950; *s* of Milton Blackburn Ormerod and Dorothy Ormerod; *m* 1970, Pauline Morris; one *s* one *d*. *Educ:* Bacup and Rawtenstall Grammar Sch.; Univ. of Manchester (BSc Hons Pharmacol. 1971; MB ChB Hons 1974; MD 1986; DSc Med 2000). FRCP 1990. Jun. doctor posts, Manchester, 1974–77; Registrar, Respiratory and Gen. Medicine, Birmingham, 1977–78; Sen. Registrar, N Manchester Gen. Hosp., 1978–80. Pres., British Thoracic Soc., 2008–. *Publications:* (with P. D. O. Davies) Case Presentations in Clinical Tuberculosis, 1999; over 100 articles, incl. over 80 on clinical, bacteriological and epidemiological aspects of tuberculosis, in learned jls. *Recreations:* league cricket player until 52, military history. *Address:* Chest Clinic, Royal Blackburn Hospital, Blackburn, Lancs BB2 3HH. *T:* (01254) 734523, *Fax:* (01254) 736077; *e-mail:* Lawrence.Ormerod@elht.nhs.uk.

ORMEROD, Mark Edward, CB 2007; Director, Access to Justice Policy, Ministry of Justice, since 2008; *b* 3 Aug. 1957; *s* of Dr Thomas Edward Ormerod and late Dr June Anne (*née* Vaux). *Educ:* Oundle Sch.; Leeds Univ. (BA); Univ. de Tours (MèsL). Trainee accountant, Whinney Murray, 1980–81; joined Lord Chancellor's Department, 1981: Inner London Crown Court, 1981–83; posts at HQ, 1983–93; Private Sec. to Lord Chancellor, 1993–96; Head: of Magistrates' Courts Div., 1996–97; of Criminal Justice Div., 1997–99; Dir, Criminal Justice, 1999–2001; career break, 2001–02; Director: Criminal Law and Policy, Home Office, 2002–04; Family Justice, DCA, 2004–05; Civil, Family and Customer Services, HMCS, DCA, subseq. MoJ, 2005–08. Sec., Sir Hayden Phillips' review of honours system, Cabinet Office, 2004. Gov., Aylwin Girls' Sch., 2002–06. *Recreations:* sailing, ski-ing, singing. *Address:* c/o Ministry of Justice, Selborne House, 54–60 Victoria Street, SW1E 6QW.

ORMEROD, Pamela Catherine; *see* Meadows, P. C.

ORMEROD, Peter; *see* Ormerod, L. P.

ORMESSON, Comte Jean d'; Chevalier des Palmes académiques, 1962; Commandeur des Arts et Lettres, 1973; Grand Officier de la Légion d'honneur, 2002 (Officier, 1988); Officier de l'Ordre national du Mérite, 1978; Membre Académie française 1973; President, International Council for Philosophy and Humanistic Studies (UNESCO), 1992–96 (Secretary-General, 1971–92; Deputy, 1950–71); writer and journalist; *b* 16 June 1925; 2nd *s* of Marquis d'Ormesson, French diplomat and Ambassador; *m* 1962, Françoise Béghin; one *d*. *Educ:* Ecole Normale Supérieure. MA (History), Agrégé de philosophie. Mem. French delegns to various internat. confs, 1945–48; Mem. staff of various Govt Ministers, 1958–66; Mem. Council ORTF, 1960–62; Mem. Control Cttee of Cinema, 1962–69; Mem. TV Programmes Cttee, ORTF, 1973–74. Mem., Brazilian Acad. of Letters, 1979. Diogenes: Dep. Editor, 1952–72; Mem. Managing Cttee, 1972–80; Editor, 1980–82; Editor-in-Chief, 1982–; Le Figaro: Dir, 1974–77; Editor-in-Chief, 1975–77. *Publications:* L'Amour est un plaisir, 1956; Du côté de chez Jean, 1959; Un amour pour rien, 1960; Au revoir et merci, 1966; Les Illusions de la mer, 1968; La Gloire de l'Empire, 1971 (Grand Prix du Roman de l'Académie française), Amer. edn (The Glory of the Empire), 1975, Eng. edn 1976; Au Plaisir de Dieu, 1974, Amer. edn (At God's Pleasure), 1977, Eng. edn 1978; Le Vagabond qui passe sous une ombrelle trouée, 1978; Dieu, sa vie, son œuvre, 1981; Mon dernier rêve sera pour vous, 1982; Jean qui grogne et Jean qui rit, 1984; Le Vent du soir, 1985; Tous les hommes en sont fous, 1986; Le Bonheur à San Miniato, 1987; Garçon de quoi écrire, 1989; Histoire du Juif errant, 1991; Tant que vous penserez à moi, 1992; La Douane de mer, 1994; Presque rien sur presque tout, 1996; Casimir mène la grande vie, 1997; Une autre histoire de la littérature française, vol. I 1997, vol. II 1998; Le rapport Gabriel, 1999; Voyez comme on danse, 2001; C'était bien, 2002; Et toi mon cœur, pourquoi bats-tu?, 2003; Une fête en larmes, 2005; Odeur du temps, 2007; La vie ne suffit pas, 2007; articles and essays, columns in Le Figaro, Le Monde, Le Point, La Revue des Deux Mondes, La Nouvelle Revue Française. *Recreation:* ski-navigation. *Address:* Académie française, 23 quai Conti, 75006 Paris, France.

ORMOND, Richard Louis, CBE 2001; Director, National Maritime Museum, 1986–2000 (Head of Picture Department, 1983–86); *b* 16 Jan. 1939; *s* of late Conrad Eric Ormond and Dorothea (*née* Gibbons); *m* 1963, Leonée Jasper; two *s*. *Educ:* Christ Church, Oxford (MA). Assistant Keeper, 1965–75, Dep. Director, 1975–83, Nat. Portrait Gallery. Kress Prof., Nat. Gall. of Art, Washington, 2001–02. *Publications:* J. S. Sargent, 1970; Catalogue of Early Victorian Portraits in the National Portrait Gallery, 1973; Lord Leighton, 1975; Sir Edwin Landseer, 1982; The Great Age of Sail, 1986; F. X. Winterhalter and the Courts of Europe, 1987; (jtly) Frederic, Lord Leighton, 1996; (jtly) Sargent Abroad, 1997; (jtly) John Singer Sargent: the early portraits, 1998; (jtly) John Singer Sargent (catalogue of exhibn at Tate Gallery), 1998; (jtly) John Singer Sargent:

portraits of the 1890s, 2002; (jtly) John Singer Sargent: the later portraits, 2003; The Monarch of the Glen: Landseer in the Highlands, 2005; (jtly) John Singer Sargent: figures and landscapes, 1874–1882, 2006; (jtly) Sargent's Venice, 2006. *Recreations:* cycling, opera, theatre. *Address:* 8 Holly Terrace, N6 6LX. *T:* (020) 8340 4684. *Club:* Garrick.

ORMONDROYD, Janet Eve Lynne; Chief Executive, Bristol City Council, since 2008; *b* Baildon, W Yorks, 4 Sept. 1954; *d* of Rowland and Elsie Briggs; *m* 1999, Doug Greenwood; one *s* one *d. Educ:* Salt Grammar Sch., Shipley; Bradford-Ilkley Coll. (BA Hons); Bradford Univ. (MA Managing Change). Dir, Bradford Council, 1988–2003; Dir, Local Govt Practice, ODPM, 2003–04; Chief Exec., Suffolk Coastal DC, 2004–05; Dep. Chief Exec., Hull CC, 2005–08. *Recreations:* swimming, gardening, travelling. *Address:* Bristol City Council, Council House, College Green, Bristol BS1 5TR.

ORMROD, Prof. (William) Mark, DPhil; FSA, FRHistS; Professor of Medieval History, University of York, since 1995; *b* 1 Nov. 1957; *s* of David F. Ormrod and Margaret S. Ormrod; partner, Richard M. Dobson. *Educ:* King's Coll., London (BA 1979; AKC 1979); Worcester Coll., Oxford (DPhil 1984). FRHistS 1990; FSA 2006. Lectr in Medieval Hist., Queen's Univ., Belfast, 1984–87; British Acad. Postdoctoral Res. Fellow, St Catharine's Coll., Cambridge, 1987–90; Lectr in Medieval Hist., Univ. of York, 1990–95. *Publications:* The Reign of Edward III, 1990, 2nd edn 2000; Political Life in Medieval England, 1995; (with Anthony Musson) The Evolution of English Justice, 1999; (ed) The Kings and Queens of England, 2001, 2nd edn 2004; (ed with Rosemary Horrox) A Social History of England, 2006; contrib. to English Histl Rev., Speculum, etc. *Recreations:* music, theatre, literature, travel. *Address:* Department of History, University of York, York YO10 5DD. *T:* (01904) 433913, *Fax:* (01904) 433918; *e-mail:* wmo1@york.ac.uk.

ORMSBY, Irena; *see* Murray, I.

ORMSBY GORE, family name of **Baron Harlech**.

OROMBI, Most Rev. Henry Luke; *see* Uganda, Archbishop of.

O'RORKE, Richard Charles Colomb; His Honour Judge O'Rorke; a Circuit Judge, since 1994; *b* 4 June 1944; *s* of late Charles Howard Colomb O'Rorke and Jacqueline O'Rorke; *m* 1966, Jane Elizabeth Phoebe Harding; one *s* three *d. Educ:* Blundell's Sch.; Exeter Coll., Oxford. Called to the Bar, Inner Temple, 1968; Recorder, Midland and Oxford Circuit, 1987–94. *Recreations:* Japanese literature and culture, gardening. *Address:* c/o Midland and Oxford Circuit Office, 33 Bull Street, Birmingham B4 6DW.

O'ROURKE, Andrew; Ambassador of Ireland, retired; *b* 7 May 1931; *s* of Joseph O'Rourke and Elizabeth (*née* O'Farrell); *m* 1962, Hanne Stephensen; one *s* two *d. Educ:* Trinity Coll., Dublin (BA, BComm). Joined diplomatic service, 1957; Third Sec., Berne, 1960; First Sec., London, 1964; First Sec., later Counsellor, Dept of Foreign Affairs, Dublin, 1969–73; Counsellor, later Dep. Perm. Rep., Perm. Rep. of Ireland to EEC, 1973–78; Sec.-Gen., Dept of For. Affairs, 1978–81; Perm. Rep. to EEC, 1981–86; Ambassador to: France, OECD and UNESCO, 1986–87; UK, 1987–91; Denmark, Norway and Iceland, 1991–96. Grand Cross: Order of Civil Merit, Spain, 1985; OM, Luxembourg, 1986; OM, Portugal, 1987. *Recreations:* walking, golf, European affairs. *Address:* 2 Sorrento Lawn, Dalkey, Co. Dublin, Ireland. *Club:* Kildare Street and University (Dublin).

O'ROURKE, Patrick Jake; journalist, since 1970; author; *b* 14 Nov. 1947; *s* of Clifford Bronson O'Rourke and Delphine O'Rourke (*née* Loy); *m* 1st, 1990, Amy Lumet (marr. diss.); 2nd, 1995, Christina Mallon; one *s* two *d. Educ:* Miami Univ. (BA); Johns Hopkins Univ. (MA). Free-lance writer and ed., miscellaneous small press publications, 1970–73; National Lampoon: writer/editor, 1973–75; Man. Editor, 1975–77; Editor-in-Chief, 1977–81; free-lance writer, 1981–85; Foreign Corresp., Rolling Stone, 1986–2001; Contributing Ed., Weekly Standard, 1996–; Corresp., Atlantic Monthly, 2001–06. *Publications:* Modern Manners, 1983; The Bachelor Home Companion, 1987; Republican Party Reptile, 1987; Holidays in Hell, 1988; Parliament of Whores, 1991; Give War a Chance, 1992; All the Trouble in the World, 1994; Age and Guile Beat Youth, Innocence and a Bad Haircut, 1995; Eat the Rich, 1998; The CEO of the Sofa, 2001; Peace Kills, 2004; On the Wealth of Nations, 2007. *Address:* c/o Grove/Atlantic Press, 841 Broadway, New York, NY 10003, USA.

ORR, Dr Andrew William, FRCGP; author; Vice Lord-Lieutenant of Kincardineshire, since 2008; *b* London, 12 July 1946; *s* of Lt Col Harold Arthur Orr, RA and Joan Margaret Newland Orr (*née* Glossop); *m* 1971, Antonia Sybilla Atkinson; two *s* one *d. Educ:* Haileybury Coll.; St Bartholomew's Hosp. (MB BS 1971); DRCOG 1974; DCH 1977. MRCS 1971; LRCP 1971; MRCGP 1977, FRCGP 1999. RAMC, 1970–78, Regtl Med. Officer, Scots Guards; Capt. 1973; Major 1977; GP, Montrose, 1978–2006. Trainer and Tutor in Gen. Practice, Univ. of Dundee, 1984–2006; Exec., Angus Div. of Gen. Practice, 1987–2006; Member: E Scotland Postgrad. Cttee, 1989–2004; Scottish Intercollegiate Guidelines Network, 2001–03. Designer and Partner, Rank & File Stationery Products, 1987–97. Consultant to offshore petroleum trng industries, 1993–2000. Founder, Montrose Day Care Centre, 1984; Chm., Montrose Bamse Proj., 2006–. Mem., Queen's Bodyguard for Scotland (Royal Co. of Archers), 1990–. DL Kincardineshire, 2004. *Publications:* Sea Dog Bamse: World War II canine hero (with Angus Whitson), 2008; various med. res. and rev. articles. *Recreations:* collecting and conserving paintings and antiques, historical research and writing, field sports, fishing vessel 'Sybilla'. *Address:* Kirkside, St Cyrus, Montrose, Angus DD10 0DA; *e-mail:* orrkirkside@btinternet.com.

ORR, Prof. Christopher John, MBE 2008; RA 1995; RE 1990; artist; Professor of Printmaking, and Director of Printmaking Department, Royal College of Art, since 1998; *b* 8 April 1943; *s* of Ronald Orr and Violet (*née* Townley); *m* 1984, Catherine Terris; one *s* one *d. Educ:* Royal Coll. of Art (MA; RCA 1967). Artist and teacher, 1967–. One man touring exhibitions: The Complete Chris Orr, 1976; Many Mansions, 1990. Work in public collections: British Council; Arts Council; V&A Mus.; Science Mus.; Govt Art Collection; BM. *Publications:* Many Mansions, 1990; The Small Titanic, 1994; Happy Days, 1999; Semi-Antics, 2001; The Disguise Factory, 2003; Cities of Holy Dreams, 2007. *Address:* *e-mail:* chrisorr@aol.com;; *web:* www.chrisorr-ra.com. *Club:* Chelsea Arts.

ORR, Craig Wyndham; QC 2006; barrister; *b* 8 Jan. 1962; *s* of late Joseph Leonard Orr and of Dawyne Orr; *m* 1998, Jane Lloyd-Sherlock; two *s* one *d. Educ:* St Andrew's Coll., Grahamstown, SA; Rugby Sch.; Downing Coll., Cambridge (BA Hons 1984); University Coll., Oxford (BCL 1985). Called to the Bar, Middle Temple, 1986 (Fox Scholar 1986); in practice as a barrister, 1988–, specialising in commercial litigation. Trustee, Safe Ground Charity, 2002–. *Publications:* (jtly) Fountain Court Chambers' Carriage by Air, 2001; (contrib.) Professional Negligence and Liability, 2006–. *Recreations:* travel, wine, food. *Address:* Fountain Court, Temple, EC4Y 9DH. *T:* (020) 7583 3335, *Fax:* (020) 7353 0329.

ORR, David Malcolm; Director, Department of Finance and Personnel, Northern Ireland, since 2006; President, Institution of Civil Engineers, 2007–08; *b* 19 Aug. 1953; *s* of James and Mabel Orr; *m* 1975, Vyvienne McKay; one *s* one *d. Educ:* Belfast Royal Acad.; Queen's Univ., Belfast (BSc 1974, MSc 1978). FICE 2002; FIEI 2006; FIAE 2007. Joined Roads Service, NI, 1974: Chartered Civil Engr, 1974–2008; Dir, Network Services, 2001–06. Vice Pres., ICE, 2004–07. *Recreations:* travel, cycling, local history. *Address:* Department of Finance and Personnel, Rathgael House, Balloo Road, Bangor, Co. Down BT19 7NA.

ORR, Deborah Jane, (Mrs W. W. Self); newspaper columnist, The Independent, since 1998; *b* 23 Sept. 1962; *d* of John Scott Orr and Winifred Meta Orr; *m* 1997, William Woodard Self, *qv*; two *s*, and one step *s* one step *d. Educ:* St Andrews Univ. (MA 1983). Dep. Editor, City Limits Magazine, 1988–90; Editor, Guardian Weekend Magazine, 1993–98. Columnist of the Year, What the Papers Say Awards, 1999. *Address:* The Independent, Independent House, 191 Marsh Wall, E14 9RS; *e-mail:* d.orr@independent.co.uk.

ORR, Iain Campbell; HM Diplomatic Service, retired; *b* 6 Dec. 1942; *s* of late Rev. David Campbell Orr and Hilda Dora Moore; *m* 1978, Susan Elizabeth Gunter; one *s* one *d. Educ:* Kirkcaldy High Sch.; St Andrews Univ. (MA); Linacre Coll., Oxford (BPhil). Asst Lectr, Dept of Politics, Glasgow Univ., 1967–68; entered HM Diplomatic Service, 1968; language student, Hong Kong, 1969–71; Second, later First Sec., Peking, 1971–74; FCO, 1974–78; Asst Political Adviser, Hong Kong, 1978–81; Dublin, 1981–84; FCO, 1984–87; Consul-Gen., Shanghai, 1987–90. Dep. High Comr, Wellington, 1991–94; Counsellor, FCO, 1994–98; Dep. High Comr, Ghana, 1998–2000. *Recreations:* natural history, islands, anthologies, reading poetry. *Address:* c/o Foreign and Commonwealth Office, SW1A 2AH.

ORR, Dr James Henry; consultant in forensic psychiatry, 1982–98; *b* 2 Feb. 1927; *s* of Hubert Orr and Ethel Maggs; *m* 1950, Valerie Elizabeth Yates; two *s* one *d. Educ:* Bristol Grammar Sch.; Bristol Univ. (MB, ChB 1955). DPM; FRCPsych. Enlisted, 1944; commnd RE, 1947; demobilised, 1949. Hosp. appts, 1955–56; gen. practice, 1956–58; Medical Officer, HM Prison: Leeds, 1958; Winchester, 1962; Lincoln, 1966; SMO, Leeds, 1967; Asst Dir, Prison Med. Services, 1973; Dir, Prison Med. Services, and Mem., Prisons Bd, 1976–82; Mem., Parole Bd, 1983–86. *Recreation:* gardening.

ORR, Prof. Jean Agnes, CBE 2004; Professor of Nursing, and Head, School of Nursing and Midwifery, Queen's University of Belfast, since 1991; *b* 10 Sept. 1943; *d* of E. Smyth; *m* 1968, I. Orr. *Educ:* Ulster Poly. (BA Hons Social Admin 1976); Manchester Univ. (MSc 1978). RN 1965; Registered Health Visitor 1971. Nursing Officer, Down and Lisburn Trust, NI, 1976–77; Lectr, Ulster Poly., 1978–81; Lectr, 1981–89, Sen. Lectr, 1989–91, Manchester Univ. Subject Specialist Reviewer, QAA, 1999–2002. Member: Council of Deans and Hds of UK Univ. Faculties for Nursing, Midwifery and Health Visiting, 1991–; Bd, IVINUR (Internat. Virtual Nursing Sch.), 2004–; Nursing and Midwifery Council, 2006–; Council, Pharmaceutical Soc. of NI, 2006–. Adjunct Faculty Mem., Univ. of Mass, 1995–; Mem. Bd, Univ. of Mass/Ghana Health Care Consortia, 1995–; Ext. Academic Advr, Univ. Teknologi MARA, Malaysia, 2006–. Patron, WAVE Trauma Centre, NI, 2001–; Trustee: Early Childhood Develt Prog., 1985–; Marie Curie Cancer Care UK, 2000–. *Publications:* Learning to Care in the Community, 1985, 2nd edn 1993; Health Visiting, 1985, 2nd edn 1992; Women's Health in the Community, 1987; A Community Health Profile, 1994. *Recreations:* travelling, music, good food. *Address:* School of Nursing and Midwifery, Queen's University, 97 Lisburn Road, Belfast BT9 7BL. *T:* (028) 9097 2079, *Fax:* (028) 9097 5878; *e-mail:* j.orr@qub.ac.uk.

ORR, Sir John, Kt 2001; OBE 1992; QPM 1997; DL; Chief Constable of Strathclyde Police, 1996–2001; *b* 3 Sept. 1945; *s* of late Samuel Orr and of Margaret Orr (*née* Walker); *m* 1966, Joan Underwood; two *s* one *d. Educ:* James Hamilton Acad., Kilmarnock; Open Univ. (BA 1983); Glasgow Univ. (DipFM 1987). Cadet, Renfrew & Bute Constab., 1961–64; Kilmarnock Burgh Police, 1964–66; Cumbria Constab., 1966–69; Ayrshire Constab., 1969–75; Strathclyde Police, 1975–87; Detective Chief Supt and Jt Head, Strathclyde Police CID, 1987–90; Dep. Chief Constable, Dumfries and Galloway Constab., 1990–94; Asst Insp. of Constab. for Scotland, 1994–95. Pres., ACPO in Scotland, 1997–98; Chm. Crime Cttee, ACPO, 1998–2001; Mem., Scottish Crime Prevention Council, 1997–2001. Trustee, Crimestoppers Trust, 2001–04; Patron, Craighalbert Centre, Cumbernauld, 2001–; Chm. of Trustees, Cash for Kids' Charity, Radio Clyde, Glasgow, 2002–. Chm., Kilmarnock FC, 2001–03 (Hon. Pres., 2003–). Advr, Royal Bank of Scotland Gp, 2001–. Graduate, FBI Nat. Exec. Inst., Washington, 1997. Honorary President: Glasgow Bn, Boy's Bde, 1997–2004; Football Safety Officers Assoc. (Scotland), 2007–. DL Dumfries, 2001. Hon. LLD Glasgow Caledonian, 1998; DUniv Glasgow, 2001. Paul Harris Fellow, Rotary Internat., 1997. Lord Provost of Glasgow's Award for Public Service, 1998. *Recreations:* football, reading. *Address:* c/o Adam & Co., 22 Charlotte Square, Edinburgh EH2 4DF.

ORR, John Carmichael; Chairman: Molins plc, 1991–99; Waddington plc, 1997–99; *b* 19 Aug. 1937; *s* of John Washington Orr and Nora Margaret Orr (*née* Carmichael); *m* 1967, Janet Sheila Grundy; one *s* one *d. Educ:* King Edward's Sch., Birmingham; Trinity Hall, Cambridge (MA). Industrial & Commercial Finance Corporation Ltd, 1960–68; S. G. Warburg & Co. Ltd, 1969–81 (Dir, 1972–81); Finance Dir, Grand Metropolitan plc, 1981–87; Man. Dir, Merrill Lynch Europe Ltd, 1987–90. Non-executive Director: Sketchley plc, 1990–99; Throgmorton Trust plc, 1990–2002; Marston, Thompson & Evershed plc, 1992–96; Govett Strategic Investment Trust plc, 1992–97; Granada plc, 1992–2004; W. H. Smith plc, 1993–2004; Lazard Brothers & Co. Ltd, 1993–2002. Trustee, Foundn for Liver Res. (formerly Liver Res. Trust), 1999– (Chm., 2003–). *Recreations:* tennis, golf, opera, theatre. *Address:* 7 Kitson Road, SW13 9HJ. *T:* (020) 8563 9616. *Clubs:* Roehampton; Royal Wimbledon.

ORR, John Douglas, FRCSEd; Consultant Paediatric Surgeon, Royal Hospital for Sick Children, Edinburgh, since 1984; President, Royal College of Surgeons of Edinburgh, 2006–Oct. 2009 (Vice-President, 2003–06); *b* 11 July 1945; *s* of Sir John Henry Orr, OBE, QPM and (Isobel) Margaret Orr; *m* 1971, Elizabeth Erica Yvonne Miklinska; two *s* one *d. Educ:* George Heriot's Sch., Edinburgh; High Sch., Dundee; St Andrews Univ. (MB ChB 1969); Univ. of Stirling (MBA). FRCSE 1975. Sen. Surgical Registrar, Aberdeen Royal Infirmary, 1978–80; Sen. Paediatric Surgical Registrar, Edinburgh and Gt Ormond St Hosps, 1980–84; Med. Dir, Royal Hosp. for Sick Children, Edinburgh, 1996–2000; Associate Med. Dir, Lothian Univ. Hosps NHS Trust, 2000–05. *Recreation:* golf. *Address:* 428 Lanark Road, Edinburgh EH13 0LT; Royal College of Surgeons of Edinburgh, Nicolson Street, Edinburgh EH8 9DW. *T:* (0131) 527 1635, *Fax:* (0131) 557 9771; *e-mail:* president@rcsed.ac.uk. *Club:* Royal & Ancient Golf (St Andrews).

ORR-EWING, Hon. Sir (Alistair) Simon, 2nd Bt *cr* 1963, of Hendon, co. Middlesex; *b* 10 June 1940; *e s* of Baron Orr-Ewing, OBE and of Joan Helen Veronica Orr-Ewing (*née* McMinnies); *S* to Btcy of father, 1999; *m* 1968, Victoria, *er d* of Keith Cameron; two *s* one *d. Educ:* Harrow; Grenoble Univ.; Trinity Coll., Oxford (BA Hons PPE). FRICS

1972. Trainee surveyor, 1968–72. Dir various private cos. Mem. (C), RBK&C Council, 1982–90 (Chm., Planning Cttee, 1986–88). *Recreations:* ski-ing, shooting, tennis. *Heir: er s* Archie Cameron Orr-Ewing [*b* 29 March 1969; *m* 1999, Nicola de Selincourt; three *s*]. *Address:* Fifield House, Fifield, Chipping Norton, Oxon OX7 6HJ. *T:* (01993) 830305. *Clubs:* Boodle's, Queen's, MCC.

ORR EWING, Sir Archibald Donald, 6th Bt *cr* 1886, of Ballikinrain, Stirlingshire, and Lennoxbank, co. Dunbarton; *b* 20 Dec. 1938; *er s* of Major Sir Ronald Archibald Orr Ewing, 5th Bt and Marion Hester, *yr d* of Col Sir Donald Walter Cameron of Lochiel, KT, CMG; *S father*, 2002; *m* 1st, 1965, Venetia Elizabeth Turner (marr. diss. 1972); 2nd, 1972, Nicola Jean-Anne Black; one *s*. *Educ:* Gordonstoun; Trinity Coll., Dublin (MA). Grand Master Mason of Scotland, 1999–2004. *Heir: s* Alistair Frederick Archibald Orr Ewing, *b* 26 May 1982. *Address:* Cardross House, Port of Menteith, Stirling FK8 3JY.

ORR EWING, Major Edward Stuart, CVO 2007; landowner and farmer, since 1969; Lord-Lieutenant of Wigtown, 1989–2006; *b* 28 Sept. 1931; *s* of late Captain David Orr Ewing, DSO, DL and of Mary Helen Stuart Orr Ewing (*née* Noaks), *m* 1st, 1958, Fiona Anne Bowman (*née* Farquhar) (marr. diss. 1981); one *s* two *d*; 2nd, 1981, Diana Mary Waters. *Educ:* Sherborne; Royal Military Coll. of Science. Regular soldier, The Black Watch, 1950–69. DL Wigtown, 1970. *Recreations:* country sports, ski-ing, painting. *Address:* Dunskey, Portpatrick, Wigtownshire DG9 8TJ. *T:* (01776) 810211. *Club:* New (Edinburgh).

ORR-EWING, Hamish; Chairman, Rank Xerox Ltd, 1980–86; *b* 17 Aug. 1924; *o s* of Hugh Eric Douglas Orr-Ewing and Esme Victoria (*née* Stewart), Strathgarry, Killiecrankie, Perthshire; *m* 1st, 1947, Morar Margaret Kennedy; one *s* (one *d* decd); 2nd, 1954, Ann Mary Teresa Terry. *Educ:* Heatherdown, Ascot; Eton. Served War, Captain Black Watch. Salesman, EMI, 1950; Ford Motor Co., 1954; Ford Light Car Planning Manager, 1959–63; Leyland Motor Corp. Ltd, 1963–65; joined Rank Xerox, 1965; apptd to Bd as Dir of Product Planning, 1968; Dir of Personnel, 1970; Man. Dir, Rank Xerox (UK) Ltd, 1971; Reg. Dir for Rank Xerox Ops in UK, France, Holland, Sweden and Belgium, 1977; Chairman: Jaguar plc, 1984–85; White Horse Hldgs, 1987–91; Dir, Tricentrol PLC, 1975–86. Chairman: Work and Society, 1982–85; European Govt Business Relations Council, 1980–84; Member: MSC, 1983–85; Engrg Council, 1984–87; Envmt Awards Panel, RSA, 1987–94; President: Inst. of Manpower Studies, 1986–89; Inst. of Training and Develt, 1987–89. CBI: Member: Bd, Educn Foundn (UBI), 1982–87; Council, 1985–87; Chm., Educn and Trng Cttee, 1985–87. Trustee: Shaw Trust, 1985– (Pres., 2003–); Roman Res. Trust, 1990–97. Governor: Interphil, 1985–94; New Coll., Swindon, 1984–95 (Chm. of Govs, 1986–92); Bradon Forest Sch., 1989–92. CCMI (CBIM 1981). *Recreations:* anything mechanical, country life, the Roman Empire. *Address:* Fox Mill Farm, Purton, near Swindon, Wilts SN5 4EF. *T:* (01793) 770496.

ORR-EWING, Hon. Sir Simon; *see* Orr-Ewing, Hon. Sir A. S.

ORREGO-VICUÑA, Prof. Francisco; Professor of International Law, School of Law and Institute of International Studies, University of Chile, since 1969; Judge, World Bank Administrative Tribunal, since 1992 (Vice-President, 1995–2001; President, 2001–04); *b* 12 April 1942; *s* of Fernando Orrego Vicuña and Raquel Vicuña Viel; *m* 1965, Soledad Bauzá; one *s* two *d*. *Educ:* Univ. of Chile (Degree in Law); LSE (PhD). Admitted to legal practice, 1965. Sen. Legal Advisor, OAS, 1965–69 and 1972–74; Dir, Inst. of Internat. Studies, Univ. of Chile, 1974–83; Ambassador of Chile to UK, 1983–85. Pres., Chilean Council on Foreign Relations, 1989–2000; Mem. Adv. Council on Foreign Policy, Min. of Foreign Affairs, 1997–. Mem. Panel of Arbitrators and Conciliators, ICSID, 1995–; Pres. Panel, UN Compensation Commn, 1998–2001; Arbitrator: Internat. Chamber of Commerce, 1999–; 20 Essex St Chambers, London, 2004–; Mem., London Court of Internat. Arbitration, 2001– (Vice-Pres., 2006–07). *Publications:* Derecho de la Integración Latinoamericana, 1969; Los Fondos Marinos, 1976; Antarctic Resources Policy, 1983; The Exclusive Economic Zone, 1984; Antarctic Mineral Exploration, 1988; The Exclusive Economic Zone in International Law, 1989; The Changing International Law of High Seas Fisheries, 1999; International Dispute Settlement in an Evolving Global Society, 2004; contrib. Amer. Jl of Internat. Law and Annuaire Français de Droit Internat. *Recreations:* golf, ski-ing. *Address:* Avenida El Golf 40, 6th Floor, Santiago 755–0107, Chile. *T:* (2) 4416325. *Club:* Athenæum.

ORRELL, James Francis Freestone; His Honour Judge Orrell; a Circuit Judge, since 1989; *b* 19 March 1944; *s* of late Francis Orrell and Marion Margaret Orrell; *m* 1970, Margaret Catherine Hawcroft; two *s*. *Educ:* Ratcliffe; Univ. of York (BA History). Called to the Bar, Gray's Inn, 1968; Recorder, Midland and Oxford Circuit, 1988. *Address:* c/o Derby Combined Court Centre, Morledge, Derby DE1 2XE.

ORRELL-JONES, Keith; Chairman, Smiths Group (formerly Smiths Industries) plc, 1998–2004; *b* 15 July 1937; *m* 1961, Hilary Kathleen Pegram; four *s*. *Educ:* Newcastle-under-Lyme High Sch.; St John's Coll., Cambridge (BA 1961; MA 1967). Tarmac Civil Engineering, 1961–64; RMC plc, 1964–70; Marley plc, 1970–72; Area Manager, ARC, 1972–81; Pres., ARC America, 1981–87; Chief Exec., ARC, 1987–89; Dir, Consolidated Gold Fields, 1989; Pres., Blue Circle America, and Dir, Blue Circle Industries plc, 1990–92; Gp Chief Exec., Blue Circle Industries, 1992–99; Chm., FKI plc, 1999–2004. Dir, Smiths Industries plc, 1992–98. FRSA 1989; CCMI (CIMgt 1992). *Address:* 6 Gerald Road, SW1W 9EQ. *Club:* Royal Automobile.

ORSON, Rasin Ward, CBE 1985; FIET; consultant; Member, The Electricity Council, 1976–89; *b* 16 April 1927; *s* of Rasin Nelson Orson and Blanche Hyre; *m* 1st, 1950, Marie Goodenough; two *s*; 2nd, 1979, Lesley Jean Vallance. *Educ:* Stratford Grammar Sch.; London School of Economics (BScEcon 1948). Asst Statistician, Min. of Civil Aviation, 1948, Statistician, 1953; Electricity Council: Head of Economics and Forecasting Branch, 1963; Dep. Commercial Adviser, 1968; Commercial Adviser, 1972. Dir, Chloride Silent Power, 1974–89. *Recreations:* music, photography. *Address:* The Old Garden, Dunorlan Park, Tunbridge Wells, Kent TN2 3QA. *T:* (01892) 524027.

ORTIZ DE ROZAS, Carlos; career diplomat, retired; Professor of International Relations, University of Belgrano, Buenos Aires, since 1995; *b* 26 April 1926; *m* 1952, María del Carmen Sarobe. *Educ:* School of Diplomacy, Min. of Foreign Affairs, Buenos Aires (grad. 1949). Lawyer, Faculty of Law, Univ. of Buenos Aires, 1950. Entered Argentine Foreign Service, 1948; served Bulgaria, Greece, UAR and UK (Minister); Ambassador to Austria, 1967–70; Permanent Rep. to UN, 1970–77; Pres. UN Security Council, 1971–72; Chairman: First (Polit. and Security) Cttee of 29th Gen. Assembly, 1974; Preparatory Cttee of Special Session on Disarmament, 1977–78; Cttee on Disarmament, Geneva, 1979; Mem. Adv. Bd on Disarmament Studies, New York, 1978–92; Ambassador to UK, 1980–82; Head, Argentine Special Mission to the Holy See, 1982–83; Ambassador to France, 1984–89; Dep. Foreign Minister, 1990; Ambassador to USA, 1991–93; retd Foreign Service, 1994. Universidad del Salvador, Buenos Aires: Prof. of History and Constitutional Law, and Prof. of Political Science, Faculty of Law, 1958–80; Prof. of Internat. Relations, School of Political Sciences, and at School of

Diplomacy, 1962–80. Mem. Bd of Dirs, Bunge and Born SA, 1995–99; President: Bunge and Born Foundn, 1994–99; Alliance Française, Buenos Aires, 2000–02. Mem., Nat. Acad. of Moral and Political Scis, 2005. Holds many foreign decorations incl. Grand Cross, Order of Pius IX, 1985, and Commandeur, Légion d'Honneur, 1985. *Address:* Gelly y Obes 2263, 1425 Buenos Aires, Argentina. *Clubs:* Jockey, Círculo de Armas (Buenos Aires).

ORWIN, Peter David, OBE 1991; MC 1966; HM Diplomatic Service, retired; Security and Business Risks Adviser, Syngenta (formerly Zeneca Agrochemicals), since 1999; *b* 20 Dec. 1944; *s* of late John Antony Arnold Orwin and of Catherine Mary Orwin (*née* Rutherford); *m* 1977, Pamela Jane Heath; one *s* two *d*. *Educ:* Peter Symonds Sch.; RMA, Sandhurst. Commnd into Prince of Wales's Own Regt of Yorkshire, 1964; served Berlin, 1965; Aden, 1965–67; UK, 1968–69; Cyprus, 1969–70; UK/MoD, 1970–74; retd 1975; entered HM Diplomatic Service, 1975: First Secretary: Athens, 1977–84; Brasilia, 1984–87; FCO, 1987–89; First Sec., then Counsellor, Tel Aviv, 1989–93; Counsellor, FCO, 1993–96; Counsellor, The Hague, 1996–99. Director: Drum-Cussac Ltd, 2001–02; PE-2 Ltd, 2004–. Dir, Welund Report, 2008. Associate MInstD. *Recreations:* country pursuits, travel, sailing, tennis. *Address:* 31 Molyneux Place, Tunbridge Wells, Kent TN4 8DQ. *Club:* Mayfield Tennis.

OSBALDESTON, Prof. Michael David, OBE 2008; Professor and Director, Cranfield School of Management, since 2003; *b* 12 Feb. 1949; *s* of Richard Grahame Osbaldeston and Betty Osbaldeston (*née* Mackenzie); *m* 1974, Valerie Davies; one *s* one *d*. *Educ:* Bishop Vesey's Grammar Sch.; Liverpool Univ. (BSc Hons); Liverpool Univ. Business Sch. (MBA). FCIPD (FIPD 1985). Consultant, Merrett Cyriax Associates, 1971–73; Researcher, Ashridge Res. Unit, 1973–76; Ashridge Management College, 1976–2000: Programme Dir, 1977–81; Dir, Ext. Relns, 1982–84; Dir of Studies, 1985–87; Dean, 1988–90; Chief Exec., 1990–2000; Dir of Global Learning, Shell Internat. Ltd, 2000–02. Non-executive Director: Chartwell Ltd, 1997–2001; Univ. of Stellenbosch Business Sch.-Exec. Develt Ltd, 2000–. Vice-President: Strategic Planning Soc., 1995–2000; Eur. Foundn for Mgt Develt, 1997–2000. CCMI (CIMgt 1991); FRSA 1991. *Publications:* The Way We Work: a European study of changing practice in job design, 1979; (contrib.) Redesigning Management Development in The New Europe, 1998; contrib. numerous articles and papers in mgt jls. *Recreations:* sailing, theatre, France. *Address:* 4 Nether Swell Manor, Nether Swell, Stow-on-the-Wold, Glos GL54 1JZ. *T:* (01451) 870774; Cranfield School of Management, Cranfield University, Cranfield, Bedford MK43 0AL. *Club:* Athenæum.

OSBORN, Alec; *see* Osborn, W. A.

OSBORN, Frederic Adrian, (Derek), CB 1991; Member, European Economic and Social Committee, since 2006 (Chairman, Sustainable Development Observatory, since 2006); Chairman, Stakeholder Forum for Sustainable Development, since 2004; *b* 14 Jan. 1941; *s* of late Rev. George R. Osborn and E. M. Osborn, MBE; *m* 1971, Caroline Niebuhr Tod (*d* 2003); one *d* one *s*. *Educ:* Leys School, Cambridge; Balliol College, Oxford (BA Maths 1963; BPhil 1965). Min. of Housing and Local Govt, 1965–75; Dept of Transport, 1975–77; Department of the Environment, 1977–95: Under Sec., Finance, 1982–86, Housing Gp, 1986–87; Dep. Sec., Local Govt and Finance, 1987–89; Dir Gen., Envmtl Protection, 1990–95. Chm., EEA, 1995–2000; Co-Chm., UN Special Session on sustainable develt, 1997; Bd Mem. for England and Wales, Envmt Agency, 1996–98; Special Advr, H of C Envmtl Audit Cttee, 1998–99, 2001–; Chairman: Internat. Inst. for Envmt and Develt, 1998–2004 (Vice-Chm., 2004–06); UK Round Table on Sustainable Develt, 1999–2000; Mem., Sustainable Develt Commn, 2000–06. Mem. Bd, Severn Trent Plc, 1998–2006; Chm., Jupiter Global Green Investment Trust, 2001–06. Vis. Fellow, Green Coll., Oxford, 1996–97; Vis. Prof., Sch. of Public Policy, UCL, 1998–. *Publications:* Earth Summit II, 1998; contribs to Jl of Envmtl Law, Pol Qly. *Recreations:* walking, piano, reading, bridge.

OSBORN, Sir John (Holbrook), Kt 1983; semi-retired scientist, soldier, industrialist and politician; *b* 14 Dec. 1922; *s* of late Samuel Eric Osborn and Aileen Decima, *d* of Colonel Sir Arthur Holbrook, KBE, MP; *m* 1st, 1952, Molly Suzanne (*née* Marten) (marr. diss.); two *d*; 2nd, 1976, Joan Mary MacDermot (*née* Wilkinson) (*d* 1989); 3rd, 1989, Patricia Hine (*née* Read). *Educ:* Rugby; Trinity Hall, Cambridge (Part 2 Tripos in Metallurgy; MA); Diploma in Foundry Technology, Nat. Foundry Coll., 1949. Served in Royal Corps of Signals, 1943–47 (West Africa, 1944–46; Captain); served in RA (TA) Sheffield, 1948–55, Major. Joined 1947, and Technical Dir, 1951–79, Samuel Osborn & Co. Ltd, and associated companies. Chairman, Hillsborough Divisional Young Conservative and Liberal Association, 1949–53. MP (C) Hallam Div. of Sheffield, 1959–87 (NL and U, 1959–64); PPS to the Secretary of State for Commonwealth Relations and for the Colonies, 1963–64. Chairman: Cons. Parly Transport Cttee, 1970–74; Anglo-Swiss Parly Gp, 1981–87; (or Vice-Chm.) Anglo-Soviet Parly Gp, 1968–87; Vice Chm., Parly and Scientific Cttee, 1963–66, 1982 (Officer, 1959–87; Life Mem., 1987); Jt Sec., 1922 Cttee, 1968–87; Member: Science and Technol. Select Cttee, 1970–73; Educn, Science and Arts Select Cttee, 1979–83; Chm., All Party Channel Tunnel Gp, 1985–87; Individual Mem., Parly Gp for Energy Studies, 1987– (Chm., 1985–87; Vice-Chm., Cons. Parly Energy Cttee, 1979–81). Mem., UK Delegn to Council of Europe and WEU, 1973–75, 1980–87 (Hon. Associate, Council of Europe, 1987–, WEU, 1990–); Council of Europe: Vice Chm., Science and Technol. Cttee, 1981–87; Chm., Eur. Scientific Contact Gp, 1982–87; Chm., Econ. Affairs and Develt Sub-Cttee (North/South: Europe's role), 1985–87. Mem., European Parlt, 1975–79. Life Member, British Branch: CPA, 1987 (Mem., 1959–87); IPU, 1987 (Mem. Exec., 1968–75, 1979–83). Mem. Cttee, European Atlantic Gp, 1990–. Mem., Interim (formerly Voluntary) Licensing Authy, MRC/RCOG, 1987–91. Chairman: Friends of Progress, 1989–95; Business and Develt Cttee, UK Chapter, Soc. for Internat. Develt, 1990–95. Mem., RIIA, 1985–. Freeman Co. of Cutlers in Hallamshire, 1987 (Asst Searcher, 1951–65; Searcher, 1965–70 and 1973–87). Fellow, Institute of British Foundrymen, 1948–72 (Member Council, Sheffield Branch, 1954–64); FIMMM (FIM 1986; MISI 1947); Fellow, Institute of Directors; Member Council: Sheffield Chamber of Commerce, 1956–89 (Hon. Life Mem., 1989); Assocs British Chambers of Commerce, 1960–62 (Hon. Secretary, 1962–64); British Iron and Steel Res. Association, 1965–68; CBI and Yorks and WR Br., CBI, 1968–79; Industrial Soc., 1963–79 (Life Mem.). Hon. Patron, Sheffield Inst. of Advanced Motorists, 1996– (Pres., 1960–96); Chm., H of C Motor Club, 1979–84. Mem., Court and Council Sheffield Univ., 1951–79. Trustee: Talbot Trust, 1950–98; Zackery Merton Trust, 1951–2002 (Chm., 1988–98). FRSA 1966. Travelled widely in business and politics. *Recreations:* golf, photography, gardening, walking. *Address:* Newlands, 147 Hawton Road, Newark, Notts NG24 4QG. *T:* (01636) 704480. *Club:* Carlton.

OSBORN, Sir Richard (Henry Danvers), 9th Bt *cr* 1662, of Chicksands Priory, Co. Bedford; fine art consultant; *b* 12 Aug. 1958; surv. *s* of Sir Danvers Lionel Rouse Osborn, 8th Bt, and Constance Violette, JP, OStJ (*d* 1988), *d* of late Major Leonard Frank Rooke, KOSB and RFC; *S father*, 1983; *m* 2006, Belinda Mary Elworthy; one *d*. *Educ:* Eton. Christie's, 1978–83; Consultant to P & D Colnaghi Ltd, 1984–86. Dir, Paul Mitchell Ltd (antique frames and picture conservation), 1991–2002. *Recreations:* cricket, tennis, squash, horse racing, Real tennis, golf. *Heir: kinsman* William Danvers Osborn [*b* 4 June 1909; *m* 1939, Jean Burns, *d* of R. B. Hutchinson, Vancouver; one *d*]. *Address:* 48 Lessar Avenue, SW4 9HQ. *Clubs:* Pratt's, MCC, Turf, Queen's; New Zealand Golf.

OSBORN, (Wilfred) Alec, MBE 2005; CEng, FIMechE; President, Institution of Mechanical Engineers, 2006–07; *b* 16 May 1939; *s* of Fredrick Osborn and Annie Osborn (*née* Wade); *m* 1963, Mary Jane Flanders; three *d*. *Educ:* Grantham Coll. for Further Educn. CEng 1969; FIMechE 1991. Student apprentice, Rubery Owen & Co., 1955–60; Design Engr, British Racing Motors, 1960–69; Perkins Engines: Design Engr, 1969–75; Chief Engineer: Applications Engrg, 1975–77; Test Ops, 1977–82; Product Engrg, 1982–2002; Consultant, 2002–04. Institution of Mechanical Engineers: Chm., Combustion Engines Gp, 1994–97; Vice Pres., 2002–04; Dep. Pres., 2004–06; Chm., Technical Strat. Bd, 2004–06. Industrial Advr, Sch. of Mechanical Engrg, Univ. of Leeds, 2008–. Freeman, City of London, 2002; Liveryman, Co. of Engineers, 2002–. Chairman: Govs, Deacon's Sch., Peterborough, 1997–2004; Interim Exec. Bd, Hereward Community Coll., Peterborough, 2002–04; Dir, Thomas Deacon City Acad., Peterborough, 2004–. Trustee, Maudslay Scholarship Foundn, Pembroke Coll., Cambridge, 2007–. *Recreations:* golf, cricket, gardening, walking. *Address:* 61 The High Street, Thurlby, Bourne, Lincs PE10 0ED. *Clubs:* Farmers, MCC; Rutland County Golf.

OSBORNE, Rt Hon. Lord; Kenneth Hilton Osborne; PC 2001; a Senator of the College of Justice in Scotland, since 1990; *b* 9 July 1937; *s* of Kenneth Osborne and Evelyn Alice (*née* Hilton); *m* 1964, Clare Ann Louise Lewis; one *s* one *d*. *Educ:* Larchfield Sch., Helensburgh; Merchiston Castle Sch., Edinburgh; Edinburgh Univ. (MA, LLB). Admitted to Faculty of Advocates in Scotland, 1962; QC (Scotland) 1976. Standing Junior Counsel to Min. of Defence (Navy) in Scotland, 1974–76; Advocate-Depute, 1982–84. Chairman: Disciplinary Cttee, Potato Marketing Bd, 1975–90; (part-time), VAT Tribunals, 1985–90; Medical Appeal Tribunals, 1987–90; Mem., Lands Tribunal for Scotland, 1985–87. Chm., Local Govt Boundary Commn for Scotland, 1990–2000. *Recreations:* ski-ing, fishing, gardening, music, cooking. *Address:* 42 India Street, Edinburgh EH3 6HB. *T:* (0131) 225 3094; Primrose Cottage, Bridgend of Lintrathen, by Kirriemuir, Angus. *T:* (01575) 560316. *Club:* New (Edinburgh).

OSBORNE, Rt Rev. Basil Alfred Herbert Ernst; *see* Amphipolis, Bishop of.

OSBORNE, Rev. Canon Brian Charles; Vicar of Holy Trinity, Skirbeck, Boston, Lincolnshire, 1980–2003; Chaplain to the Queen, 1997–2008; *b* 17 May 1938; *s* of Walter and Gweneth Osborne; *m* 1968, Kathryn Ruth Grant; two *d*. *Educ:* St Andrews Univ. (MA Hons Classics); DipTh London Univ. 1980; Clifton Theol Coll. Ordained deacon, 1963, priest, 1964; Asst Curate, Holy Trinity, Boston, 1963–68; Priest-in-charge, 1968–71, Incumbent, 1971–75, St John's, New Clee, Grimsby; Vicar, St Augustine's, Derby, 1975–80. Pt-time Chaplain, Pilgrim Hosp., Boston, 1984–88. Rural Dean, Holland East, 1985–94; Hon. Canon of Lincoln, 1992–2006, now Canon Emeritus. Retired Clergy Advr, 2004–. *Recreations:* golf, reading, photography. *Address:* 3 Newlands Road, Haconby, Bourne, Lincs PE10 0UT. *T:* (01778) 570818. *Club:* Kirton Holme Golf.

OSBORNE, Charles (Thomas), FRSL; author and critic; *b* 24 Nov. 1927; *s* of Vincent Lloyd Osborne and Elsa Louise Osborne; *m* 1970, Marie Korbelářová (marr. diss. 1975); civil partnership 2006, Kenneth Thomson. *Educ:* Brisbane State High Sch. Studied piano and voice, Brisbane and Melbourne; acted in and directed plays, 1944–53; wrote poetry and criticism, published in Aust. and NZ magazines; co-owner, Ballad Bookshop, Brisbane, 1947–51; actor, London, provincial rep. and on tour, also TV and films, 1953–57; Asst Editor, London Magazine, 1958–66; Asst Lit. Dir, Arts Council of GB, 1966–71, Lit. Dir, 1971–86; Chief Theatre Critic, The Daily Telegraph, 1987–91. Broadcaster, musical and literary progs, BBC, 1957–; Dir, Poetry International, 1967–74; Sec., Poetry Book Soc., 1971–84; opera critic, Jewish Chronicle, 1985–. Mem. Editorial Board: Opera, 1970–; Annual Register, 1971–87. Vice Pres., Richard Strauss Soc., 1994–. FRSL 1996. MInstD 2002. DUniv Griffith Univ., Australia, 1994. Gold Medal, Amici di Verdi, 1993. *Publications:* (ed) Australian Stories of Today, 1961; (ed) Opera 66, 1966; (with Brigid Brophy and Michael Levey) Fifty Works of English Literature We Could Do Without, 1967; Kafka, 1967; Swansong (poems), 1968; The Complete Operas of Verdi, 1969 (Italian trans. 1975, French trans. 1989); Ned Kelly, 1970; (ed) Australia, New Zealand and the South Pacific, 1970; (ed) Letters of Giuseppe Verdi, 1971; (ed) The Bram Stoker Bedside Companion, 1973; (ed) Stories and Essays by Richard Wagner, 1973; The Concert Song Companion, 1974; Masterpieces of Nolan, 1976; Masterpieces of Drysdale, 1976; Masterpieces of Dobell, 1976; Wagner and his World, 1977 (USA 1977; trans. Spanish 1985); Verdi, 1977 (trans. Spanish 1985); (ed) Dictionary of Composers, 1977; The Complete Operas of Mozart, 1978 (trans. Ital. 1982); (ed) Masterworks of Opera: Rigoletto, 1979; The Opera House Album, 1979 (trans. Dutch 1981); W. H. Auden: the Life of a Poet, 1980; (ed with Kenneth Thomson) Klemperer Stories, 1980 (trans. German 1981); The Complete Operas of Puccini, 1981; The Life and Crimes of Agatha Christie, 1982, 2nd edn 1999; The World Theatre of Wagner, 1982; How to Enjoy Opera, 1983 (trans. Spanish 1985); The Dictionary of Opera, 1983 (trans. Finnish 1984; trans. Portuguese 1987); Letter to W. H. Auden and Other Poems, 1984; Schubert and his Vienna, 1985 (trans. German 1986); Giving It Away (memoirs), 1986; (ed) The Oxford Book of Best-Loved Verse, 1986; Verdi: a life in the theatre, 1987; The Complete Operas of Richard Strauss, 1988; Max Oldaker: last of the matinée idols, 1988; The Complete Operas of Wagner, 1990; The Bel Canto Operas, 1993; The Pink Danube (novel), 1998; First Nights, Second Thoughts, 2001; The Yale Opera Guide, 2004; novels, adapted from plays by Agatha Christie: Black Coffee, The Unexpected Guest, 1998; Spider's Web, 2000; The Importance of Being Earnest (novel, adapted from play by Oscar Wilde), 1999; poems in: The Oxford Book of Australian Verse, 1956; Australian Poetry, 1951–52, etc; The Queensland Centenary Anthology, 1959; Australian Writing Today, 1968; various jls; contrib.: TLS, Observer, Sunday Times, Times, Guardian, New Statesman, Spectator, London Mag., Encounter, Opera, Chambers Encyc. Yearbook, and Enciclopedia dello spettacolo; also cassettes. *Recreations:* travelling, planning future projects. *Address:* 125 St George's Road, SE1 6HY. *T:* (020) 7928 1534.

OSBORNE, Christopher Wyndham; HM Diplomatic Service; Ambassador to Mongolia, since 2006; *b* 18 June 1946; *m* 1967, Gillian Mary; three *s*. Entered Commonwealth Office, later FCO, 1966; Attaché: Lusaka, 1968–70; Kampala, 1970–73; Third Sec., Bridgetown, 1973–76; Desk Officer for Falkland Is, FCO, 1976–79; Second Secretary: (Political), Dacca, 1979–81; (Commercial), Caracas, 1982–85; Press Officer, FCO, 1986–89; First Secretary: (Information), Hong Kong, 1989–94; Non Proliferation Dept, FCO, 1994–96; Hong Kong, 1996–97; Dep. Hd of Mission, Luanda, 1998–2000; Dep. Hd, Protocol Div. and Asst Marshal of Diplomatic Corps, FCO, 2001–05. *Address:* c/o Foreign and Commonwealth Office, King Charles Street, SW1A 2AH.

OSBORNE, Clive Maxwell Lawton; Legal Adviser, Serious Organised Crime Agency, since 2005; *b* 20 July 1955; *s* of Raymond Peter Osborne and Eileen Mary Osborne (*née* Lawton); *m* 1985, Ursula Frances Amanda Futcher; one *s* one *d*. *Educ:* Newcastle High Sch.; Christ Church, Oxford (MA). Called to the Bar, Gray's Inn, 1978; joined Home Office, 1980; Asst Legal Advr, 1991–97; Legal Dir, DTI, 1997–99; Asst Legal Advr, NI Office, 1999–2001; Dep. Legal Advr, Home Office and NI Office, 2001–05. *Address:* Serious Organised Crime Agency, PO Box 8000, SE11 5EN.

OSBORNE, David Allan; HM Diplomatic Service, retired; Ambassador to Honduras, 1998–2002; *b* 31 Aug. 1942; *s* of Donald Stewart Osborne and Caroline Susie Osborne (*née* Stanbury); *m* 1966, Joan Marion Duck; one *s* two *d*. *Educ:* St Albans Grammar Sch.; Central London Poly. (DMS). Joined Commonwealth Relations Office, 1961; Accra, 1963–65; FCO, 1966–68; Guatemala City, 1968–73; Bonn, 1973–74; Valletta, 1974–77; sabbatical, 1977–78; First Sec., FCO, 1978–79; Mexico City, 1979; San José (concurrently accredited to Managua and San Salvador), 1980–84; FCO, 1984–88; Dep. Consul Gen., São Paulo, 1988–91; EU Monitor, Croatia, 1991–92; FCO, 1992–94; Santiago, 1994–95; FCO, 1995–96; Chargé d'Affaires, Managua, 1997. EU Monitor Medal, 1992. *Recreations:* reading, walking, chess, indigenous cultures in Latin America, various sports. *Address:* Firlings, Firle Road, Seaford, East Sussex BN25 2HU.

OSBORNE, Denis Gordon, CMG 1990; adviser on governance and development, since 1992; *b* 17 Sept. 1932; *s* of A. Gordon Osborne and Frances A. Osborne (*née* Watts); *m* 1970, Christine Susannah, *d* of P. Rae Shepherd and C. Elaine Shepherd; two *d*. *Educ:* Dr Challoner's Grammar Sch., Amersham; University Coll., Durham (BSc 1st Cl. Hons Physics, PhD). FInstP 1966. Lectr in Physics, Univ. of Durham, 1957; Lectr, Fourah Bay Coll., Sierra Leone, 1957–58; Lectr, 1958–63, Sen. Lectr, 1963–64, Univ. of Ghana; Reader in Physics, 1964–66, Prof., 1966–71, Dean of Science, 1968–70, Univ. of Dar es Salaam; Res. Fellow, UCL, 1971–72; Cons. for World Bank missions to Malaysia and Ethiopia, 1971, 1972; Overseas Development Administration: Principal, 1972; Multilateral Aid Dept, 1972–75; Mediterranean and Near East Dept, 1975–77; Sci. and Technology Dept, 1977–80; Asst Sec., 1980; Hd of Dept in Natural Resources Div., 1980–84; Hd of E and W Africa Dept, 1984–87; HM Diplomatic Service, High Comr in Malaŵi, 1987–90; RIPA Internat., 1990–92. Reader, C of E, 1975–, at local parish church, 1980–. *Publications:* Way Out: some parables of science and faith, 1977; research papers on develt, corruption and governance, and until 1978 on geophysics, particularly the equatorial ionosphere. *Address:* The Arc, North Elham, Canterbury CT4 6NH; *e-mail:* do@governance.org.uk. *Club:* Athenæum.

OSBORNE, Douglas Leonard, FCIS; Chief Executive, Leukaemia Research Fund, 1989–2007; *b* 19 Oct. 1940; *s* of Leonard Osborne and Gladys Ellen (*née* Ward); *m* 1969, Barbara Helen Bartrop; one *s* one *d*. *Educ:* Royal Masonic Sch. ACIS 1967, FCIS 1985. London Association for the Blind: Asst Sec., 1965–75; Asst Dir, 1975–79; Dir, 1979–83; Administrator, Leukaemia Res. Fund, 1983–89. Mem. Council, Metropolitan Soc. for the Blind, 1979–. *Publication:* (ed jtly) Charities Administration, 1986, and Supplements, 1987–. *Recreations:* listening to music, cooking, travel. *Address:* 11 Thorpewood Avenue, SE26 4BU.

OSBORNE, George Gideon Oliver; MP (C) Tatton, since 2001; *b* 23 May 1971; *s* and *heir* of Sir Peter George Osborne, Bt, *qv*; *m* 1998, Hon. Frances Victoria, *d* of Baron Howell of Guildford, *qv*; one *s* one *d*. *Educ:* St Paul's Sch., London; Davidson Coll., N Carolina (Dean Rusk Schol.); Magdalen Coll., Oxford (MA Hons Mod. Hist.). Freelance journalist, 1993; Hd, Pol Sect., Cons. Res. Dept, 1994–95; Special Advr, MAFF, 1995–97; Pol Office, 10 Downing St, 1997; Pol Sec. to Leader of Opposition, 1997–2001; Sec. to Shadow Cabinet, 1997–2001. An Opposition Whip, 2003; Opposition frontbench spokesman on Treasury, 2003–04; Shadow Chief Sec. to HM Treasury, 2004–05; Shadow Chancellor of the Exchequer, 2005–. Member: Public Accounts Cttee, 2001–03, Public Accounts Commn, 2002–03, H of C; Select Cttee on Transport, 2003. Trustee, Arts and Business, 2006–. Vice-Pres., E Cheshire Hospice, 2001–. *Address:* House of Commons, SW1A 0AA. *T:* (020) 7219 8214.

OSBORNE, Georgiana Louise; Lord-Lieutenant of Angus, since 2001; *b* 24 Aug. 1944; *d* of Richard Douglas Moore and June Louise Moore (*née* Peachey); *m* 1968, James Carnegy Osborne; three *s* one *d*. *Educ:* Wellington Diocesan Sch. for Girls (Nga Tawa), Marton, NZ; Victoria Univ. of Wellington (BA); Lausanne Univ. (Philips Overseas Schol. 1964). Dep. Pres., Angus Br., 1991–98, Pres., Tayside Br., 1999–2004, BRCS. JP Angus, 2001–08. Patron, 2003, Trustee, 2004–, Angus Coll.; Trustee, Queen Mother's Memorial Fund for Scotland, 2003–08. Badge of Honour for Distinguished Service, 1996, for Outstanding Service, 2004, BRCS. *Recreations:* music and the arts in general, tennis, golf, ski-ing. *Address:* Balmadies, Guthrie, Forfar, Angus DD8 2SH. *T:* and *Fax:* (01307) 818242.

OSBORNE, Ven. Hayward John; Archdeacon of Birmingham, since 2001; Priest-in-charge, Allens Cross, since 2008; *b* 16 Sept. 1948; *s* of Ernest and Frances Joy Osborne; *m* 1973, Sandra Julie Hollander; two *s* three *d*. *Educ:* Sevenoaks Sch.; New Coll., Oxford (BA 1970, MA 1973); King's Coll., Cambridge (PGCE); Westcott House Theol Coll., Cambridge. Ordained deacon, 1973, priest, 1974; Curate, Bromley Parish Ch, 1973–77; Team Vicar, Halesowen, 1977–83; Team Rector, St Barnabas, Worcester, 1983–88; Vicar, St Mary, Moseley, Birmingham, 1988–2001; Area Dean, Moseley, 1994–2001. Mem., Gen. Synod of C of E, 1998–. Hon. Canon, Birmingham Cathedral, 2000. *Recreations:* music, theatre, computing. *Address:* Diocesan Office, 175 Harborne Park Road, Birmingham B17 0BH. *T:* (0121) 426 0441.

OSBORNE, Helena; *see* Moore, G. M.

OSBORNE, Jana; General Secretary, National Federation of Women's Institutes, since 1996; *b* 11 Jan. 1953; *d* of Jan Koutny' and Miloslava Koutna'; *m* 1978, Graeme Stephen Osborne. *Educ:* Charles Univ., Prague (BA Hons Modern Langs 1978); Poly. of Central London (Postgrad. Personnel Mgt Course); Kingston Univ. (LLM Employment Law, 2003). MIPD 1989. Journalist and interpreter, Nikon Denpa News, Prague, 1974–79; Personnel Officer, Bowater Industrial plc, 1987–88; Office Manager, Thorpac Gp plc, 1988–89; National Federation of Women's Institutes: Personnel Officer, 1989–92; Head of Personnel, 1992–95; Gen. Manager, 1995–96. *Recreations:* cycling, walking, classical music, literature, gardening. *Address:* (office) 104 New Kings Road, SW6 4LY. *T:* (020) 7371 9300.

OSBORNE, Very Rev. June; DL; Dean of Salisbury, since 2004; *b* 10 June 1953; *d* of Wilfred and Enid Osborne; *m* 1984, Paul Anthony Goulding, *qv*; one *s* one *d*. *Educ:* Manchester Univ. (BA Hons (Econ.) 1974); St John's Coll., Nottingham; Wycliffe Hall, Oxford; Birmingham Univ. (MPhil 1993). Lay Asst, St Aldate's, Oxford, 1975–77; ordained dss, 1980, deacon, 1987, priest, 1994; Curate, St Martin-in-the-Bullring, and Chaplain, Birmingham Children's Hosp., 1980–84; Minister-in-charge, St Paul with St Mark, Old Ford, 1984–95; Canon Treas., Salisbury Cathedral, 1995–2004. DL Wilts, 2006. *Recreations:* supporting Manchester City FC, reading novels, watching my children's activities. *Address:* The Deanery, 7 The Close, Salisbury, Wilts SP1 2EF. *T:* (01722) 555110, *Fax:* (01722) 555155; *e-mail:* thedean@salcath.co.uk.

OSBORNE, Kenneth Hilton; *see* Osborne, Rt Hon. Lord.

OSBORNE, Prof. Michael John, FAHA; FAIM; Foundation Distinguished Professor, Institute for Advanced Study, La Trobe University, Australia, since 2006; *b* 25 Jan. 1942; *s* of Samuel Osborne and Olive May Osborne (*née* Shove); *m* 1978, Dawn Brindle (marr. diss. 2005). *Educ:* Eastbourne Grammar Sch.; Christ Church, Oxford (MA); Catholic Univ. of Leuven (DPhil and Lett.). Lectr, Dept of Classics, Bristol, 1966–67; Lectr, then Sen. Lectr, Dept of Classics and Archaeology, Univ. of Lancaster, 1967–82; University of Melbourne: Prof. and Chm., Dept of Classical and Near Eastern Studies, 1983–90, now Prof. Emeritus; Dep./Associate Dean, Faculty of Arts, 1985–89; Pro-Vice-Chancellor and Vice-Pres., Academic Bd, 1989; Vice-Chancellor and Pres., La Trobe Univ., 1990–2006. Mem., Inst. for Advanced Study, Princeton, 1978–79; Visiting Professor: Maximilians Univ., Munich, 1973; Leuven, 1975, 1988; Vis. Fellow, other univs, 1972–85; Prof., Peking Univ., China, 2003–; Hon. Professor: Yunnan Univ., China, 1994; Kunming Med. Coll., China, 1995; Yunnan Normal Univ., China, 1997; Yunnan Agricl Univ., China, 2001; Harbin Med. Univ., China, 2001; Sichuan Univ., China, 2002. Chm., Victorian Vice-Chancellors' Cttee, 1993–94; Member: Bd of Dirs, Australian Vice-Chancellors' Cttee, 1994–96 (Chm., Students and Scholarships Cttee, 1995–96; Chm., Standing Cttee for Internat. Affairs, 1996–2004; Leader, delegn to Hungary, Czech and Slovak Republics, 1993, to S Africa, 1994, to China, 1998–); Business/Higher Educn Round Table (Mem., Task Force on Higher Educn, 1996–; Mem. Bd of Dirs, 1996–2003); Res. Cttee, Cttee for Econ. Develt of Australia, 1993–96; Bd of Dirs, Internat. Develt Program, 1996–99; Bd of Dirs, Grad. Careers Council of Australia, 1996–98; Co-Chm. Planning Cttee, Australian Educn Internat., 2000–02. President: Univ. Mobility in Asia Pacific Scheme, 2000–02; Internat. Network of Univs, 2000–06; Co-Pres., Peking Univ.-La Trobe Univ.-Beijing Foreign Studies Univ. Centre for China Studies, 2005–08; Chm., Nat. Centre for Hellenic Studies and Res., 2005–; Mem., Governing Bd, World Heritage Trng and Res. Inst. for Asia and Pacific Region. FAHA 1985; FAIM 2000. Laureate, Royal Acad. of Sci., Letters and Fine Arts, Belgium, 1980; Alexander S. Onassis Public Benefit Foundn Res. Fellow, 2001; Hon. Fellow, Hungarian Acad. of Engrg, 1998; Corresp. Mem., Acad. of Athens, 1998. Hon. DLitt: Athens, 2001; La Trobe, 2007. Aristotle Award, Greece, 1998; Hon. Distinction, Hellenic Republic of Cyprus, 2000; Centenary Medal, Australia, 2003; Niki Award, Australia, 2005; Gold Crown of World Congress of Greeks of the Diaspora, Greece, 2006. *Publications:* Naturalization in Athens, 4 vols, 1981–83; Lexicon of Greek Personal Names, vol. II: Attica, 1994; The Foreign Residents of Athens, Studia Hellenistica Vol. 33, 1995; Correspondence between China and Great Britain: vol. I, railways and mines, 2006, vol. II, education, 2007, vol. III, commerce and trade, 2008; numerous articles in learned jls on Greek history, Greek epigraphy and Greek archaeology. *Recreations:* tennis, travel, Australian Rules football. *Address:* Institute for Advanced Study, La Trobe University, Melbourne, Vic 3086, Australia. *T:* 0417 047942. *Club:* Essendon Football.

OSBORNE, Prof. Nigel, MBE 2003; composer; Reid Professor of Music, Edinburgh University; *b* 1948. *Educ:* St Edmund Hall, Oxford; studied at Warsaw Acad. and Polish Radio Exptl Studio. FRCM 1996. Staff of Music Dept, Nottingham Univ., 1978; Co-Editor-in-Chief, Contemporary Music Review. Initiator of programme of rehabilitation for refugee children in Balkans and Caucasus, 1992–. Queen's Award, Edinburgh Univ., 1997. *Compositions include:* Seven Words, 1971 (Radio Suisse Romande Prize); Heaventree, 1973 (Gaudeamus Prize); Kinderkreuzzug, 1974; I am Goya, 1977 (Radcliffe Award); Orlando Furioso, 1978; In Camera, 1979; Sinfonia, 1982; Sinfonia II, 1983; Zansa, 1985; The Electrification of the Soviet Union (opera), 1987; Violin Concerto, 1990; Terrible Mouth, 1991; The Sun of Venice, 1993; Art of Fugue, 1993; Sarajevo (opera), 1994; Evropa (first opera of war in Sarajevo), 1995; Oboe Concerto, 1998; String Quartet no 1, 1999; Widows (opera), 2000; Differences in Demolition (opera), 2007; orchestral, choral, instrumental, ballet and electronic music; numerous recordings. *Address:* c/o Faculty of Music, Edinburgh University, 12 Nicolson Square, Edinburgh EH8 9DF.

OSBORNE, Sir Peter (George), 17th Bt *cr* 1629; Chairman and Managing Director, Osborne & Little plc (design company), since 1967; *b* 29 June 1943; *s* of Lt-Col Sir George Osborne, 16th Bt, MC, and Mary (Grace) (*d* 1987), *d* of C. Horn; *S* father, 1960; *m* 1968, Felicity Alexandra, *d* of Grantley Loxton-Peacock; four *s*. *Educ:* Wellington Coll., Berks; Christ Church Coll., Oxford. *Heir: s* George Gideon Oliver Osborne, *qv*. *Address:* 67 Lansdowne Road, W11 2LG. *Club:* White's.

OSBORNE, Richard Ellerker; author and broadcaster; *b* 22 Feb. 1943; *s* of late William Harold Osborne and Georgina Mary Osborne (*née* Farrow); *m* 1985, Hailz-Emily Wrigley; one *s*. *Educ:* Worksop Coll.; Univ. of Bristol (BA, MLitt). Asst Master, Bradfield Coll., 1967–88 (Head of Sixth Form Gen. Studies, 1978–88; Head of English, 1982–88); presenter and contrib., BBC Radio 3, 1969–; Music Critic, The Oldie, 1991–. Mem., Critics' Panel, Gramophone, 1974–; Chm., Music Section, Critics' Circle, 1984–87. *Publications:* Rossini, 1985, 2nd edn 2007; Conversations with Karajan, 1989; Herbert von Karajan: a life in music, 1998; Till I End My Song: English music and musicians 1440–1940: a perspective from Eton, 2002; Karajan: Mensch und Mythos, 2008; contribs to newspapers, jls, music dictionaries and guides. *Recreations:* hill-walking, food and wine, reading in the garden, watching cricket. *Address:* 2 Vaughan Copse, Eton, Berks SL4 6HL. *T:* (01753) 671368.

OSBORNE, Col Robert; Director, Tree Council, 1991–2001; *b* 14 March 1936; *s* of Kenneth George Hulbert Osborne and Mary Irene (*née* Daymond); *m* 1st, 1961, Sybil Kathi Gisela Hudson (*née* von Knobloch) (marr. diss. 1988); two *s*; 2nd, 1988, Claudia Downing (*née* Radok); one step *d*. *Educ:* Cheltenham Coll.; RMA, Sandhurst. Commnd RTR, 1955; served BAOR and UK, 1956–72; Staff Coll., Camberley, 1968; US Army, 1972–75; UN Force in Cyprus, 1977–80; Defence and Military Attaché, Cairo, 1983–86; NATO Defence Coll., Rome, 1987; HQ NATO, Brussels, 1987–90, retd. Hon. Citizen, State of Texas, USA, 1974. *Recreations:* antiquities, the countryside, plain cookery. *Address:* Unwin's House, Waterbeach Road, Landbeach, Cambridge CB25 9FA. *T:* (01223) 861243.

OSBORNE, Prof. Robin Grimsey, PhD; FBA 2006; Professor of Ancient History, University of Cambridge, since 2001; Fellow, since 2001 and Senior Tutor, since 2009, King's College, Cambridge; *b* 11 March 1957; *s* of John Leonard Osborne and Joyce Elizabeth Osborne (*née* Warner); *m* 1979, Catherine Joanna Rowett; two *d*. *Educ:* Colchester Royal Grammar Sch.; King's Coll., Cambridge (BA 1979; PhD 1982; MA 1983). Jun. Res. Fellow, King's Coll., Cambridge, 1982–86; University of Oxford: Tutorial Fellow in Ancient Hist., Magdalen Coll., 1986–89; Univ. Lectr in Ancient Hist., 1989–96; Prof. of Ancient Hist., 1996–2001; Fellow and Tutor, 1989–2001, Emeritus Fellow, 2001–, Corpus Christi Coll. Chm., Council of Univ. Classical Depts, 2006–. Pres., Soc. for Promotion of Hellenic Studies, 2002–06. Member, Editorial Board: American Jl of Archaeology; Jl of Hellenic Studies; Omnibus; Past and Present; World Archaeology. *Publications:* Demos: the discovery of classical Attika, 1985; Classical Landscape with Figures: the ancient Greek city and its countryside, 1987; (ed jtly) Art and Text in Ancient Greek Culture, 1994; (ed jtly) Placing the Gods: sanctuaries and the sacred landscape of ancient Greece, 1994; (ed jtly) Ritual, Finance, Politics: Athenian democratic accounts presented to David Lewis, 1994; Greece in the Making 1200–479 BC, 1996 (trans. Spanish 1998, Greek 2000); Archaic and Classical Greek Art, 1998; (ed jtly) Performance Culture and Athenian Democracy, 1999; (ed) The Athenian Empire, 4th edn 2000; (ed) Classical Greece, vol. 1, Short Oxford History of Europe, 2000 (trans. Spanish 2001, Polish 2002); (ed jtly) Greek Historical Inscriptions 403–323 BC, 2003; (ed) Studies in Ancient Greek and Roman Society, 2004; Greek History, 2004; (ed) The Old Oligarch, 2nd edn 2004; (ed jtly) Mediterranean Urbanization 800–600 BC, 2005; (ed jtly) Poverty in the Roman World, 2006; (ed jtly) Rethinking Revolutions through Classical Greece, 2006; (ed jtly) Art's Agency and Art History, 2007; (ed jtly) Classical Archaeology, 2007; (ed) Debating the Athenian Cultural Revolution: art, literature, philosophy and politics 430–380 BC, 2007; numerous articles in learned jls. *Address:* King's College, Cambridge CB2 1ST; *e-mail:* ro225@cam.ac.uk.

OSBORNE, Roy Paul; HM Diplomatic Service; Director, Trade and Investment, Berne, since 2005; *b* 13 July 1951; *s* of Gilbert William Osborne and Jean Mary Osborne; *m* 1977, Vivienne Claire Gentry; two *d*. *Educ:* St Christopher's Junior Sch., Cowley; Magdalen Coll. Sch., Oxford. Entered FCO, 1970; served Oslo, Islamabad and Rome; FCO, 1981–85, Asst Private Sec. to Minister of State, 1983–85; Second Sec., Commercial/Aid, later First Sec., Head of Chancery and Consul, Yaoundé, 1985–89; First Sec., Press and Inf., Madrid, 1989–93; Section Head, Drugs and Internat. Crime, FCO, 1993–97; Ambassador to Nicaragua, 1997–2000; Dep. Hd, Overseas Territories Dept, 2001–04. *Recreations:* birdwatching, wild life conservation, gardening, tennis, jogging. *Address:* c/o Foreign and Commonwealth Office, SW1A 2AH.

OSBORNE, Sandra Currie; MP (Lab) Ayr, Carrick and Cumnock, since 2005 (Ayr, 1997–2005); *b* 23 Feb. 1956; *d* of Thomas Clark and Isabella Clark; *m* 1982, Alastair Osborne; two *d*. *Educ:* Camphill Sen. Secondary Sch., Paisley; Anniesland Coll.; Jordanhill Coll.; Strathclyde Univ. (MSc). Community Worker, Glasgow; Women's Aid. Mem. (Lab), S Ayrshire Council, 1991–97. *Address:* House of Commons, SW1A 0AA.

OSBORNE, Steven; classical pianist; *b* Broxburn, Scotland; *s* of Ian Osborne and Jean McNeil; *m* 2004, Jean Johnson. *Educ:* St Mary's Music Sch., Edinburgh; Univ. of Manchester (MusB 1st cl. Hons 1991); Royal Northern Coll. of Music (Postgrad. Dip.; MusM). Orchestral collaborations include: CBSO, NHK Symphony Orch., BBC SO, BBC Scottish SO, Scottish Chamber Orch., Munich Philharmonic, Berlin SO, Australian Chamber Orch.; performances at venues including: Carnegie Hall, Kennedy Center, Suntory Hall, Philharmonie, Berlin, Concertgebouw Amsterdam, Royal Albert Hall. Recordings include works by Debussy, Rachmaninov, Alkan, Tippett, Beethoven, Messiaen, Shostakovich, Liszt and Kapustin. Clara Haskil Prize, 1991; (jtly) First Prize, Naumburg Internat. Piano Competition, 1997. *Recreations:* hill walking, tennis, pool, reading, jazz. *Address:* c/o Sulivan Sweetland, 1 Hillgate Place, Balham Hill, SW12 9ER. *T:* (020) 8772 3470; *e-mail:* es@sulivansweetland.co.uk.

OSBORNE, Susan Edna, CBE 2005; Director of Nursing, Imperial College Healthcare NHS Trust, 2007–08; *b* 7 Dec. 1952; *d* of late John Gilbertson Osborne and Edna Joan Osborne (*née* Boughen). *Educ:* Dame Alice Harpur Sch. for Girls, Bedford; University Coll. Hosp. (SRN 1974); Queen Charlotte's Hosp. for Women (SCM 1976); London Univ. (DipN); South Bank Univ. (MSc). Staff Nurse, Orthopaedic/Surgery, UCH, 1974–75; pupil midwife, Queen Charlotte's Hosp., 1975–76; Staff Nurse, Medicine, Radcliffe Infirmary, 1976–77; Night Sister, UCH, 1977–78; Sister, Intensive Therapy Unit, then Nursing Officer, Whittington Hosp., London, 1979–83; Sen. Nurse, Central Middx Hosp., 1983–86; Dep. Dir, Nursing Service, 1986–87, Acute Service Manager, 1987–89, Homerton Hosp.; Actg Regl Nurse, 1989–90, NHS Trust Develt Officer, 1990–91, NE Thames RHA; Chief Exec., Royal London Homeopathic Hosp. NHS Trust, 1991–94; mgt and nursing consultant, 1994–98; Dir, Nursing and Quality, Luton & Dunstable Hosp. NHS Trust, 1998–2000; Dir of Nursing Services, St Mary's NHS Trust, 2000–07. FRSA 1994. *Publications:* numerous contribs to nursing and health services jls, incl. Jl Advanced Nursing, Nursing Times, Jl Nursing Mgt, Health Services Jl. *Recreations:* general socialising, theatre, the Archers, cats, golf, enjoying life.

OSBORNE, Trevor, FRICS; Chairman, Trevor Osborne Property Group Ltd, since 1973; *b* 7 July 1943; *s* of Alfred Osborne and Annie Edmondson; *m* 1st, 1969, Pamela Ann Stephenson (marr. diss. 1998); one *s* one *d*; 2nd, 2003, Barbara Jane Fitzpatrick. *Educ:* Sunbury Grammar School. South Area Estate Manager, Middx County Council, 1960–65; Partner, A. P. C., 1966–67; Principal, Private Property Interests, 1967–73; Chm., 1973–93, Chief Exec., 1981–93, Speyhawk plc; Chairman: St George, 1985–96; Hawk Development Management, 1992–98; Lucknam Park Ltd, 1991–95; Building & Property Management Services, 1993–96; non-exec. Dir, Redland, 1989–92. Pres., British Property Fedn, 1991–92 (Mem. Council, 1985–92); BPF Visiting Fellow: Land Management, Reading Univ., 1987–90; Oxford Brookes Univ., 2003. Founder Mem. and Chm., POW Urban Villages Forum, 1992–99; Member: Royal Opera House Develt Bd, 1987–94 (Chm., ROH Development Ltd, 1994); Council of Advrs, Prince of Wales Inst. of Architecture (Trustee, 1991–93); Council, City Property Assoc., 1987–94; Royal Fine Art Commn, 1994–99 (Trustee, 2003–); Council Mem., Georgian Group, 2002–; Chm., Adv. Bd, SE Excellence, 2006–. Formerly Mem., Wokingham DC (Leader, 1980–82); Trustee, Wokingham Cons. Assoc., 1982–91. Pres., Windsor Arts Centre; Chm., St Sebastian's Playing Field Trust; Dir, London First, 1992–95. Freeman, City of London; Liveryman, Chartered Surveyors' Co. Fellow, Duke of Edinburgh Award World Fellowship; FRSA. *Recreations:* travel, walking, art, theatre, opera, tennis. *Address:* Trevor Osborne Property Group Ltd, 85 Wimpole Street, W1G 9SB. *Clubs:* Athenæum, Arts.

OSEI, Isaac; Chief Executive, Ghana Cocoa Board, since 2006; *b* 29 March 1951; *s* of late Nana Osei Nkwantabisa I and of Eunice Rosina Osei; *m* 1980, Marian Fofo; two *s* two *d*. *Educ:* Achimota Sch.; Univ. of Ghana (BSc Hons Econs); Center for Develt Econs, Williams Coll., Mass (MA Develt Econs). Asst Econ. Planning Officer, Min. of Finance, Ghana, 1973–77; Chief, Commercial Ops, 1977–81, Projects, R&D, 1981–82, Ghana Tourist Develt Co.; Managing Consultant, Ghanexim Econ. Consultants, 1982–2000; High Comr for Ghana in UK, 2001–06. Chair, Bd of Govs, Commonwealth Secretariat, 2002–04. Director: E. K. Osei & Co. (Civil Eng. and Gen. Bldg Contractors), 1982–95; Kas Products Ltd (Quarry Masters), 1982–99; Intravenous Infusions Ltd, 1988– (Man. Dir, 1999–2001). *Recreations:* from a distance, football and American football, reading. *Address:* Ghana Cocoa Board, Kwame Nkrumah Avenue, PO Box 933, Accra, Ghana; *e-mail:* ikeosei@email.com.

OSGERBY, Jay, RDI 2007; Founding Director and Co-owner: BarberOsgerby, since 1996; Universal Design Studio, since 2001; *b* Oxford, 23 Oct. 1969; *s* of Paul Osgerby and Wendy Osgerby (*née* Hickman); *m* 2000, Helen Louise Smith; one *s* two *d*. *Educ:* Ravensbourne Coll. (BA 1st cl. Hons Furniture and Product Design); Royal Coll. of Art (MA Arch. and Interior Design). Tutor: Oxford Brookes Univ., 1993–97; Ravensbourne Coll., 1996–2000. Mem. Jury, workshop/conf., 2003, and Dip. and Masters course, Ecole cantonale d'art de Lausanne; Dir, workshop, Vitra Design Mus., 2004. Vis. Tutor, RCA, 2008–. FRSA. Jerwood Applied Arts Prize (jtly), Jerwood Foundn, 2004. *Address:* BarberOsgerby, 35–42 Charlotte Road, EC2A 3PG. *T:* (020) 7033 3884, *Fax:* (020) 7033 3882; *e-mail:* mail@barberosgerby.com.

O'SHEA, David Michael; Solicitor to the Metropolitan Police, 1982–87, retired; *b* 27 Jan. 1927; *s* of late Francis Edward O'Shea and Helen O'Shea; *m* 1953, Sheila Winifred Polkinghorne; two *s*. *Educ:* St Ignatius Coll., London; King's Coll., London Univ. (LLB). Served RN, 1946–48. Articled H. C. L. Hanne & Co., London, 1949–52; admitted solicitor, 1952; in practice with H. C. L. Hanne & Co., 1952–56; joined Solicitor's Dept, Metropolitan Police Office, 1956; Dep. Solicitor, 1976–82. *Recreation:* travel. *Address:* c/o Solicitor's Department, New Scotland Yard, SW1H 0BG.

O'SHEA, Michael Kent; Director, Export Control and Non-Proliferation, Department of Trade and Industry, 2002–04; *b* 12 March 1951; *s* of Donovan Henry Victor and Joan O'Shea; *m* 1988, Linda Beata Szpala (*d* 2005). *Educ:* Bristol Grammar Sch.; Corpus Christi Coll., Cambridge (BA 1st Cl. Hons History). Department of Trade and Industry, 1973–2004: Under Sec., Finance and Resource Mgt, 1992–96; Dir, Engrg Automotive and Metals, 1996–98; Dir, Engrg Industries, 1998–2002. *Recreations:* watching cricket and National Hunt racing, playing bridge, listening to Wagner, walking, drinking good beer and wine, cinema, theatre, opera. *Club:* Gloucestershire CC.

O'SHEA, Prof. Michael Roland, PhD; Director, BBSRC Sussex Centre for Neuroscience, University of Sussex, since 1991; *b* 5 April 1947; *s* of Capt. Jack Arthur O'Shea and Ellen O'Shea (*née* Hughes); *m* 1977, Barbara Moore (marr. diss. 1991); (one *d* decd). *Educ:* Forest Hill Sch., London; Univ. of Leicester (BSc 1st Cl. Hons Biol Scis 1968); Univ. of Southampton (PhD Neurobiol. 1971). University of California, Berkeley: NATO Fellow, 1971–73; NIH Fellow, 1973–75; SRC Fellow, Univ. of Cambridge, 1975–77; Asst Prof., Univ. of Southern Calif., LA, 1977–79; Associate Prof., Brain Research Inst., Univ. of Chicago, 1979–85; Professor of: Neurobiol., Univ. of Geneva, 1985–88; Molecular Cell Biol., RHBNC, Univ. of London, 1988–91. *Publications:* numerous papers on neuroscience in learned jls. *Recreations:* classical music, mountaineering, modern poetry, triathlons, restoration of classic Lotus. *Address:* 29 Eldred Avenue, Brighton BN1 5EB. *T:* (01273) 678508; Sussex Centre for Neuroscience, School of Biological Sciences, University of Sussex, Brighton BN1 9QG.

O'SHEA, Sir Timothy (Michael Martin), Kt 2008; PhD; Principal and Vice-Chancellor, University of Edinburgh, since 2002; *b* 28 March 1949; *s* of John Patrick O'Shea and Elisabeth Hedwig Oberhof; *m* 1982, Prof. Eileen Scanlon; two *s* two *d*. *Educ:* Royal Liberty Sch., Havering; Sussex Univ. (BSc); Leeds Univ. (PhD). Postgrad. res., Univs of Texas at Austin and Edinburgh; Open University: founder, Computer Assisted Learning Res. Gp, 1978; Lectr, 1980–82, Sen. Lectr, 1983–87, Inst. of Educnl Technol.; Prof. of IT and Educn, 1987–97; Pro-Vice-Chancellor for QA and Res., 1994–97; Vis. Res. Prof., 1997–; Master of Birkbeck Coll., and Prof. of Inf. and Communication Technologies, 1998–2002, Pro-Vice-Chancellor, 2001–02, Univ. of London. Vis. Scientist, Xerox PARC, and Vis. Schol., Univ. of Calif, Berkeley, 1986–87. Chm., NATO prog. on Advanced Educnl Technol., 1988–90. Chairman: London Metropolitan Network Ltd, 1999–2002; HERO Ltd, 2000–. Director: Edexcel Foundn, 1998–2001 (Mem., Exec. Cttee, 1998–2001); Univs and Colls Staff Develt Agency, 1999–2000. Chm., Inf. Systems Sector Gp, CVCP, 1999–. Member: HEFCE Cttee on Equal Opportunities, Access and Lifelong Learning, 1998–; Jt Inf. Systems Cttee, 2000–; Bd, UUK, 2001–. Pres., Psychol. Sect., BAAS, 1991–92; Chm., Artificial Intelligence Soc., 1979–82. Trustee, Eduserv, 1999–2000. Curator, Sch. of Advanced Study, London Univ., 1999–2002; Provost, Gresham Coll., 2000–02; Mem. Council, RCM, 2001–; Governor: City Lit. Inst., 1998–2000; SOAS, 1998–2002; St George's Med. Sch., London Univ., 2000–02. Presenter and author, The Learning Machine (TV series), 1985. *Publications:* include: Self-improving teaching systems, 1979; (jtly) Learning and Teaching with Computers, 1983; (jtly) Artificial Intelligence: tools, techniques and applications, 1984; (ed) Advances in Artificial Intelligence, 1985; (ed jtly) Intelligent Knowledge-based Systems: an introduction, 1987; (ed jtly) Educational Computing, 1987; (ed jtly) New Directions in Educnl Technology, 1992; contrib. learned jls. *Address:* University of Edinburgh, Old College, South Bridge, Edinburgh EH8 9YL.

OSHEROFF, Prof. Douglas Dean, PhD; Professor of Physics and Applied Physics, Stanford University, since 1987 (Chairman, Department of Physics, 1993–96 and 2001–04); *b* 1 Aug. 1945; *s* of William and Bessie Anne Osheroff; *m* 1970, Phyllis Shih-Kiang Liu. *Educ:* California Inst. of Technology (BSc Physics 1967); Cornell Univ. (PhD Physics 1973). AT&T Bell Laboratories: Mem., technical staff, 1972–81; Hd, Solid State and Low Temp. Physics Res., 1981–87. MNAS, 1987; Mem., Amer. Acad. Arts and Scis, 1982. Fellow, APS. Sir Francis Simon Meml Award, 1976; Oliver E. Buckley Condensed Matter Physics Prize, 1981; Macarthur Prize Fellow Award, 1981; (jtly) Nobel Prize for Physics, 1996. *Publications:* contrib. chapters in books; numerous papers and articles in jls incl. Phys Rev., Phys Rev. Letters, Jl Low Temp. Phys. *Recreations:* photography, hiking, travel, music. *Address:* Department of Physics, Stanford University, Stanford, CA 94305–4060, USA.

OSLER, Douglas Alexander, CB 2002; HM Senior Chief Inspector of Education (formerly of Schools), Scottish Executive (formerly Scottish Office), 1996–2002; *b* 11 Oct. 1942; *s* of Alexander Osler and Jane Brown; *m* 1973, Wendy Cochrane; one *s* one *d*. *Educ:* Univ. of Edinburgh (MA Hons Hist.); Moray House Coll. of Educn (Teaching Cert.). Teacher, Liberton High Sch., Edinburgh, 1965; Principal Teacher, History, Dunfermline High Sch., 1969; HM Inspector, Chief Inspector, Depute Sen. Chief Inspector of Schools, Scottish Office, 1974–95. Interim Scottish Prisons Complaints Comr, 2003; Reviewer, Parole Bd of Scotland, 2004; Indep. Reviewer, Scottish Courts Service, 2005. Chm., Inquiry into Child Abuse at Cabin Hill Sch., Belfast, 2004–05; Indep. Chm., Scottish Cons. Party Policy Adv. Gp, 2006; Chm. Comrs, S Eastern Educn and Liby Bd, NI, 2006–. ESU Fellowship, 1966; Internat. Vis. Fellowship, USA, 1989; Vis. Prof., Strathclyde Univ., 2003–05. KSG 2001. *Recreations:* golf, gardening, reading, Rotary International.

OSMAN, Dr Mohammad Kheir; Member of Foundation Committee, 1981–86, Professor and Dean of Students, 1985–98, and Educational Advisor to the Vice-Chancellor, 1994–98, Sultan Qaboos University, Muscat, Sultanate of Oman; *b* Gedarif, Sudan; *s* of Osman Khalifa Taha and Khadija Al Shareef; *m* 1953, Sara Ahmed. *Educ:* Khartoum Univ. (BA); London Univ. (PGCE; AcDip; MA); UCLA (PhD). Director: Educational Research and Planning, 1970–71; Sudan/ILO Mgt and Productivity Centre, Khartoum, 1972; Minister of Education, 1972–75; Mem., Sudan Nat. Assembly, 1972–75; Ambassador to UK, 1975–76; Manager, UNDP/UNESCO Educnl Project, Oman, 1977–84; Adviser to Min. of Educn, Oman, 1984–85. Professional interests include Western educnl experience and indigenous Afro/Arab conditions, and the problems of change through institutional educnl systems; keen interest in nature, and developing countries' adjustment of educn to globalization, information and technology. Constitution Decoration, 1973; Two-Niles Decoration for Public Service, 1979; Sultan Qaboos Decoration, 1986.

OSMOND, Prof. Charles Barry, PhD; FRS 1984; FAA; President and Executive Director, Biosphere 2 Center, Columbia University, 2001–03; Visiting Fellow, School of Biochemistry and Molecular Biology, Australian National University, since 2004; *b* 20 Sept. 1939; *s* of Edmund Charles Osmond and Joyce Daphne (*née* Krauss); *m* 1st, 1962, Suzanne Alice Ward; one *s* one *d* (and two *s* decd); 2nd, 1983, Ulla Maria Cornelia Gauhl (*née* Büchen). *Educ:* Morisset Central Sch.; Wyong High Sch.; Univ. of New England, Armidale (University Medal in Botany, 1961; BSc 1961, MSc 1963); Univ. of Adelaide (PhD 1965). FAA 1978. Post-doctoral Res. Associate, Botanical Sciences Dept, Univ. of Calif, LA, 1965; Royal Commn for Exhibn of 1851 and CSIRO Fellow, Botany Sch., Cambridge Univ., 1966; successively Res. Fellow, Fellow and Sen. Fellow, Dept of Environmental Biol., ANU, Canberra, 1967–78, Prof. of Biology, 1978–87; Exec. Dir, Biol Sciences Center, Desert Res. Inst., Reno, 1982–86; Arts and Scis Prof., Duke Univ., USA, 1987–91; Prof., 1991–2001, and Dir, 1991–98, Res. Sch. of Biol Scis, ANU, Canberra. Fulbright Sen. Scholar, Univ. of Calif, Santa Cruz, 1973–74; Carnegie Instn Fellow (Plant Biol.), Stanford, 1973–74; Richard Mereton Guest Prof., Technical Univ., Munich, 1974; Overseas Fellow, Churchill Coll., Cambridge, 1980. Mem., German Nat. Acad. Leopoldina, 2001. Goldacre Award, Aust. Soc. of Plant Physiologists, 1972; Edgeworth David Medal, Royal Soc. of NSW, 1974; Forschungspreis, Alexander von Humboldt Foundn, 1997; Clarke Medal, Royal Soc. of NSW, 1998. *Publications:* (ed jtly) Photosynthesis and Photorespiration, 1971; (ed jtly) Photorespiration in Marine Plants, 1976; (jtly) Physiological Processes in Plant Ecology, 1980; (ed jtly) Encyclopedia of Plant Physiology, Vols 12 A-D, Physiological Plant Ecology, 1981–83; (ed jtly) Photoinhibition, 1987; (ed jtly) New Vistas in Measurement of Photosynthesis, 1989; (ed jtly) Plant Biology of the Basin and Range, 1990; (ed jtly) Water and Life, 1992; (ed jtly) Nurturing Creativity in Research, 1997; articles on plant metabolic biology and its ecological implications in learned jls. *Recreations:* biological research, social cricket, music of romantic composers, confections of Continental Europe. *Address:* PO Box 3252, Weston Creek, ACT 2611, Australia. *T:* (2) 62871487.

OSMOND, Michael William Massy, CB 1977; Solicitor to the Department of Health and Social Security, and to the Office of Population Censuses and Surveys, and the General Register Office, 1974–78; *b* 1918; *s* of late Brig. W. R. F. Osmond, CBE, and Mrs C. R. E. Osmond; *m* 1943, Jill Ramsden (*d* 1989); one *s* one *d*. *Educ:* Winchester; Christ Church, Oxford. 2nd Lieut Coldstream Guards, 1939–40. Called to Bar, Inner Temple, 1941; Asst Principal, Min. of Production, 1941–43; Housemaster, HM Borstal Instn, Usk, 1943–45; Legal Asst, Min. of Nat. Insce, 1946; Sen. Legal Asst, 1948; Asst Solicitor, Min. of Pensions and Nat. Insce, 1958; Principal Asst Solicitor, DHSS, 1969. *Recreation:* music. *Address:* Hunters, Cherry Tree Lane, Cirencester, Glos GL7 5DT. *T:* (01285) 653707. *Club:* Oxford and Cambridge.

OSMOND, Richard George; Secretary, The Post Office, 1995–97; *b* 22 Jan. 1947; *s* of late Lt-Col Clifford George Osmond, OBE, RE and Florence Rose Osmond (*née* Baker). *Educ:* Merchant Taylors' Sch. (Exhibr); Univ. of Exeter. FCIPD (FIPD 1988). Post Office, 1967–97: Dep. Sec., 1985; Controller, Corporate Personnel, 1986; Head of Community Affairs, 1989; Dir, Group Personnel, 1993. Dir, Headteachers into Industry, 1990–96; Mem., Adv. Bd, Centre for Educn and Industry, Univ. of Warwick, 1992–98, Hon. Associate Fellow, 1998–2001; Chm., Policy Adv. Cttee, Sch. Curriculum and Industry Partnership, 1995–97. Vis. Fellow, Inst. of Educn, London Univ., 1997–99. Diocesan Gov., Univ. of Winchester (formerly King Alfred's Coll., Winchester), 1999–2008; Chm. of Governors, Peter Symonds' Coll., Winchester, 2000–04. Vice Pres., ACRE, 1997–2007. FRSA 1990 (Member: Early Learning Study, 1993–94; Educn Adv. Gp, 1996–2001). Mem. Council, Friends of Cathedral Music, 1977–83, 2003–. Freeman, City of London, 1989; Liveryman, Musicians' Co., 1990–. *Recreations:* church music, bird watching, bridge. *Address:* 10 Hazel Grove, Badger Farm, Winchester SO22 4PQ. *T:* and *Fax:* (01962) 850818. *Club:* Athenæum.

OSMOTHERLY, Sir Edward (Benjamin Crofton), Kt 2002; CB 1992; Clerk Adviser, European Scrutiny Committee, House of Commons, since 2003; *b* 1 Aug. 1942; *s* of Crofton and Elsie Osmotherly; *m* 1970, Valerie (*née* Mustill); one *d* one *s*. *Educ:* East Ham Grammar School; Fitzwilliam College, Cambridge (MA). Asst Principal, Ministry of Housing and Local Govt, 1963–68 (Private Sec. to Parly Sec., 1966–67, to Minister of State, 1967–68); Principal, 1968–76; Harkness Fellow, 1972–73 (Guest Scholar, Brookings Instn, Washington DC; Exec. Fellow, Univ. of California at Berkeley); Asst Sec., DoE, 1976–79; seconded to British Railways Bd, 1979; Head of Machinery of Govt Div., CSD, 1980–81; Under Sec. (Railways), Dept of Transport, 1982–85; Under Sec., Dir of Personnel, Management and Training, Depts of the Environment and of Transport, 1985–89; Dep. Sec., Public Transport and Res. Dept, 1989–92, Prin. Establishment and Finance Officer, 1992–93, Dept of Transport; Local Govt Ombudsman, 1993–2001; Chm., Commn for Local Admin in England, 1994–2001; Mem., Adjudication Panel for England, 2002–03. Chm., Ind. Review of Govt Business Statistics, 1996. Chm., British and Irish Ombudsman Assoc., 1998–2001. *Recreation:* reading.

OST, Michael Stuart; non-executive Chairman, Henlys Group plc, 2003–04 (non-executive Director, 2002); *b* 29 Oct. 1944; *s* of Peter Stuart Ost and Betty Constance Ost; *m* 1977, Judith Ann Latham; one *s*. *Educ:* Scarborough High Sch. for Boys; London School of Economics (BSc Econ). Univ. Apprentice, Rolls-Royce Aero Engines Ltd, 1963–67; Singer Co.: Corporate Auditor, NY, 1968–70; Financial Controller, Thailand, 1970–72; Mktg Dir, Brazil, 1972–75; Gen. Manager, Turkey, 1975–77; Vice Pres., Far East, Getz Corp., 1978–82; President: Singer Brazil, 1982–83; Latin America Div., Singer, 1983–84; Exec. Vice Pres., Carrier International, 1984–85; Pres., ETO Carrier, 1985–87; Group Chief Executive: McKechnie plc, 1987–97; Coats Viyella plc, 1997–99. Non-executive Director: Lex Service plc, 1993–2002; Porvair plc, 1999; non-exec. Dep. Chm., MG plc, 1999–2000. Chm., Pension Trustees, RAC plc, 2003–. FRSA 1993; CCMI (CIMgt 1994). *Recreations:* golf, bridge, reading. *Clubs:* Savile, Royal Automobile; Landings (Savannah, USA); Worplesdon Golf.

OSTERLEY, Robin Marius; Chief Executive, Making Music (formerly The National Federation of Music Societies), since 1997; Chairman, National Music Council, since 2001; *b* 22 Feb. 1957; *s* of Allan Osterley and Barbara Dora Osterley; two *s* two *d*. *Educ:* Monkton Combe Sch.; St Edmund Hall, Oxford (BA Hons 1979). Sen. Mktg Manager, ICL, 1982–93; Mktg Manager, Orch. of St John's, Smith Square, 1994; Man. Dir, Cala Records Ltd, 1994–96. Member: Live Music Forum, 2004–; Further Educn and Higher Educn Creative Industries Task Force, 2004–. Chm., Stevenage Fest., 2005–. Chm. Govs, Hunsdon JMI Sch., 2005–. *Recreations:* singing, conducting, bad piano playing, running slowly, never letting the grass grow under the feet. *Address:* *e-mail:* robin@makingmusic.org.uk. *T:* (office) 0870 909 2611.

OSTLERE, Dr Gordon; *see* Gordon, Richard.

OSTRIKER, Prof. Jeremiah Paul, PhD; Professor, Department of Astrophysical Sciences, since 1971, and Director, Princeton Institute for Computational Science and Engineering, since 2005, Princeton University; *b* 13 April 1937; *s* of Martin Ostriker and Jeanne (*née* Sumpf); *m* 1958, Alicia Suskin; one *s* two *d*. *Educ:* Harvard Univ. (AB Physics and Chem. 1959); Univ. of Chicago (PhD Astrophysics 1964). Postdoctoral Fellow, Univ. of Cambridge, 1964–65; Princeton University: Res. Associate and Lectr, 1965–66; Asst Prof., 1966–68; Associate Prof., 1968–71; Chm., Dept of Astrophysical Scis, and Dir,

Observatory, 1979–95; Charles A. Young Prof. of Astronomy, 1982–2002; Provost, 1995–2001; Plumian Prof. of Astronomy and Experimental Philosophy, Inst. of Astronomy, and Fellow of Clare Coll., Univ. of Cambridge, 2001–04. Mem., Editl Bd and Trustee, Princeton Univ. Press, 1982–84 and 1986. Trustee, 1997–2006, Hon. Trustee, 2007–, Amer. Mus. of Natural Hist. Foreign Mem., Royal Soc., 2007. Treas., NAS, 2008–. Hon. DSc Chicago, 1992. Henry Norris Russell Prize, AAS, 1980; Vainu Bappu Meml Award, INSA, 1993; Karl Schwarzschild Medal, Astronomische Ges., 1999; US Nat. Medal of Sci., 2000; Gold Medal for Astronomy, RAS, 2004. *Publications:* Development of Large-Scale Structure in the Universe, 1991; (ed with J. N. Bahcall) Unsolved Problems in Astrophysics, 1997; (ed with A. Dekel) Formation of Structure in the Universe, 1999; contribs to Astrophysical Jl and Nature on topics in theoretical astrophysics. *Recreations:* squash, bicycling. *Address:* Department of Astrophysical Sciences, Peyton Hall, Ivy Lane, Princeton, NJ 08544–1001, USA; *e-mail:* ostriker@princeton.edu.

OSTROWSKI, Joan Lorraine; *see* Walley, J. L.

O'SULLEVAN, Sir Peter (John), Kt 1997; CBE 1991 (OBE 1977); Racing Correspondent: Daily Express, 1950–86; Today, 1986–87; BBC Television Commentator, 1946–97; *b* 3 March 1918; *o s* of late Col John Joseph O'Sullevan, DSO, formerly Resident Magistrate, Killarney, and Vera, *o d* of Sir John Henry, DL, JP; *m* 1951, Patricia, *o d* of Frank Duckworth, Winnipeg, Manitoba, Canada. *Educ:* Hawtreys; Charterhouse; Collège Alpin, Switzerland. Specialised in ill-health in early life and not accepted for fighting forces in 1939–45 war, during which attached to Chelsea Rescue Services. Subsequently worked for John Lane, the Bodley Head, on editorial work and MSS reading. Joined Press Assoc. as Racing Correspondent, 1945, until appointed Daily Express, 1950, in similar capacity. Race-broadcasting 1946–97 (incl. Australia, S Africa, Italy, France, USA); in 1953 became first regular BBC TV and horse-racing commentator to operate without a race-reader; commentated: first television Grand National, 1960; world's first televised electronic horse race from Atlas computer at Univ. of London, transmitted by BBC TV Grandstand, 1967; first horse race transmitted live via satellite, from NY, to invited audience in London, 1980; completed 50th Grand National broadcast, 1997. Director: Internat. Racing Bureau, 1979–93; Racing Post Ltd, 1985–95. Mem., Jockey Club, 1986–. Chm., Osborne Studio Gall., 1999–. Patron: Brooke Hosp. for Animals; Internat. League for Protection of Horses; Thoroughbred Rehabilitation Centre. Derby Award for Racing Journalist of the Year, 1971 (with late Clive Graham), 1986; Racehorse Owner of the Year Award, Horserace Writers' Assoc., 1974; Clive Graham Meml Award for services to racing, Press Club, 1978, 1985; Evening News Sports Commentator of the Year, 1978; William Hill Golden Spurs for services to racing, 1985; Par Excellence Award, Racing Club of Ireland, 1993; Sport on TV Award, Daily Telegraph, 1994; Media Award, Variety Club of GB, 1995; Services to Racing Award, Daily Star, 1995; Lesters Award, Jockeys' Assoc., 1996; TV Sports Award, RTS, 1996; George Ennor Trophy, Horserace Writers and Photographers Assoc., 1997; Special Award, TRIC, 1998. *Publications:* Calling the Horses: a racing autobiography, 1989; Peter O'Sullevan's Horse Racing Heroes, 2004. *Recreations:* racehorse owning, in minor way (happiest broadcasting experience commentating success of own horses, Be Friendly, 1966–67, and Attivo, 1974); travel, reading, art, food and wine. *Address:* 37 Cranmer Court, SW3 3HW. *T:* (020) 7584 2781.

O'SULLIVAN, Alison Jane; Director of Children's Services, Kirklees Metropolitan Council, since 2006; *b* 25 March 1955; *d* of Kenneth Attenborough and Hazel (*née* Wain, now Hart); *m* 1983, Patrick Joseph O'Sullivan; two *s*. *Educ:* John Port Comprehensive Sch., Etwall, Derbys; Univ. of Bradford (BA Hons (Applied Social Studies), CQSW, 1978); Huddersfield Poly. (DMS 1990). Bradford Social Services: social worker, Manningham area of Bradford, 1978–83; Team Manager, 1983–92; Sen. Manager, Children's Services, 1992–97; Assistant Director: Learning Disability, Physical Disability, and Sensory Impairment and Mental Health Services, 1997–99; Adult Services, 1999–2000; on secondment to Bradford AHA, as Jt Comr for Older People's Services, 2000–02; Dir of Social Services, Bradford CC, 2002–05. *Recreations:* building extensions, gardening, narrowboating, watching romantic comedies. *Address:* Kirklees Metropolitan Council, Oldgate House, 2 Oldgate, Huddersfield HD1 6QF. *T:* (01484) 225242, *Fax:* (01484) 225237; *e-mail:* alison.o'sullivan@kirklees.gov.uk.

O'SULLIVAN, David; Director General for Trade, European Commission, since 2005; *b* 1 March 1953; *s* of Gerald and Philomena O'Sullivan; *m* 1984, Agnes O'Hare; one *s* one *d*. *Educ:* St Mary's Coll., Rathmines, Dublin; Trinity Coll. Dublin (MA 1975); Coll. of Europe, Bruges. Irish Diplomatic Service, 1977–79; entered European Commission, 1979: First Sec., Delegn to Tokyo, 1981–84; Mem., Cabinet of Comr Peter Sutherland, 1985–89; Hd, Educn and Trng Unit, 1989–93; Dep. Hd, Cabinet of Comr Padraig Flynn, 1993–96; Dir, Eur. Social Fund, 1996–99; Dir-Gen., Educn, Trng and Youth, Feb.–May 1999; Hd, Cabinet of Pres. Romano Prodi, 1999–2000; Sec.-Gen., 2000–05. Hon. DPhil Dublin Inst. of Technol., 2005. *Recreations:* tennis, music, cinema. *Address:* European Commission, rue de la Loi 200, Wetstraat, 1049 Brussels, Belgium.

O'SULLIVAN, Michael Joseph, CMG 2008; Director, Cambridge Commonwealth Trust and Cambridge Overseas Trust, since 2008; *b* 21 Dec. 1958; *s* of Patrick Joseph O'Sullivan and Mary Elizabeth O'Sullivan (*née* Herbert); *m* 1989, Moira Helen Grant; one *s* two *d*. *Educ:* Brasenose Coll., Oxford (BA Hons German and French); Wolfson Coll., Cambridge (MPhil Linguistics). VSO Teacher of English, Xiangtan, Hunan, China, 1982–84; joined British Council, 1985: E Europe and N Asia Dept, 1985–87; Asst Dir, China, 1987–90; UK planner, Corporate Affairs, 1991–93; Dir, S China (Hong Kong), 1993–95; Hd, Corporate Planning, 1995–97; Policy Dir, Asia Pacific, 1997–2000; Dir, China, 2000–05; Regl Dir, China, 2005–07; Sec. Gen., EU Chamber of Commerce, China, 2007–08. *Recreations:* music, travel. *Address:* Cambridge Overseas Trust, Trinity College, Cambridge CB2 1TQ.

O'SULLIVAN, Michael Neil; His Honour Judge O'Sullivan; a Circuit Judge, since 2004; *b* 5 Feb. 1943; *s* of Ernest George Patrick Sullivan (who changed family name to O'Sullivan by Deed Poll, 1967) and Dorothy Florence (*née* Piper); *m* 1972, Maria Colette Smith; one *s* two *d*. *Educ:* Beaumont Coll.; City of London Coll. Exporter, motor mechanic, asst works manager, advertiser, Co. Court Clerk and Trust Adminr, 1960–70; called to the Bar: Gray's Inn, 1970; King's Inns, Ireland, 1994. Asst Recorder, 1991–95, Recorder, 1995–2004. *Recreations:* Rugby Union (player, coach, club and internat. spectator), wood-turning, fly-fishing, reading and writing poetry, walking between interesting public houses. *Address:* The Law Courts, Chaucer Road, Canterbury, Kent CT1 1ZA. *Club:* Folkestone Rugby Football.

O'SULLIVAN, Prof. Patrick Edmund, OBE 1988; PhD; CEng; FInstE; Haden-Pilkington Professor of Environmental Design and Engineering, University College London, 1999–2002, now Emeritus; non-executive Director, Titon Holdings, since 2002; *b* 28 March 1938; *s* of Daniel O'Sullivan and Margaret Cecilia (*née* Mansfield); *m* 1963, Diana Grimshaw; three *s* one *d*. *Educ:* Finchley Catholic Grammar Sch.; Leeds Univ. (BSc); Durham Univ. (PhD). FCIBSE 1975. University of Newcastle upon Tyne: DSIR Post-Doctoral Res. Fellow, 1963–64; Sen. Res. Fellow in Bldg Sci., 1964–66; Lectr, 1966–70; Sen. Lectr, 1970; Prof. of Architectural Sci., UWIST, 1970–89; Dean, Faculty of the Built Envmt, and Head, Bartlett Sch., UCL, 1989–99. Chm., Bldg Regulation Adv. Cttee, DETR, 2000–01. Hon. FRIBA; Hon. FCIBSE 2000. MIOA 1975. Gold Medal, RSH, 1999. *Publications:* Insulation and Fenestration, 1967; articles in learned jls. *Recreations:* swimming, riding, walking, theatre, bridge. *Club:* Farmers.

O'SULLIVAN, Patrick Henry Pearse, FCA; Vice Chairman and Chief Growth Officer, Zurich Financial Services, since 2007 (Group Finance Director, 2002–07); *b* 15 April 1949; *s* of Cornelius J. O'Sullivan and Marie Slowey; *m* 1974, Evelyn Holohan; two *s* one *d*. *Educ:* Trinity Coll., Dublin (BBS 1971); London Sch. of Econs (MSc Accounting and Finance 1975). FCA 1985. Arthur Andersen & Co., 1971–74; with Bank of America, working in Germany, San Francisco, LA, Miami and London, 1975–87; Gen. Manager, BA Futures Inc., London, 1987–88; Exec. Dir and Financial Controller, Goldman Sachs, 1988–89; Man. Dir, Internat. Financial Guaranty Insce Co., 1990–93; Hd, Internat. Banking and Structured Finance, 1994–96, Chief Operating Officer, 1996–97, Barclays/BZW; Chief Exec., Eagle Star Insce Co. Ltd, 1997–2002. Non-exec. Dir, Collins Stewart plc, 2007–. *Recreation:* golf. *Address:* Zurich Financial Services, Mythenquai 2, 8022 Zurich, Switzerland. *T:* (44) 6252570, *Fax:* (44) 6250570; *e-mail:* patrick.o'sullivan@zurich.com. *Clubs:* Royal Automobile, Mark's; Wisley.

O'SULLIVAN, Ronnie; snooker player; *b* 5 Dec. 1975; *s* of Ronnie and Maria O'Sullivan. World Jun. Snooker Champion, Bangalore, 1991; turned professional, 1992; wins include: UK Championship, 1993 (youngest ever winner of a ranking event), 1997, 2001; British Open, 1994; Masters, 1995, 2005, 2007; Asian Classic, 1996; German Open, 1996; Regal Scottish Open, 1998, 2000; China Open, 1999, 2000; Regal Scottish Masters, 1998, 2000, 2002; Irish Masters, 2001, 2003, 2005; Embassy World Championship, 2001, 2004; Premier Snooker League, 2001, 2002; Welsh Open, 2004, 2005; Totesport Grand Prix, 2004. *Address:* c/o World Professional Billiards and Snooker Association, Ground Floor, Albert House, 111–117 Victoria Street, Bristol BS1 6AX.

O'SULLIVAN, Sally Angela; Chair, August Media, since 2005; *b* 26 July 1949; *d* of Lorraine and Joan Connell; *m* 1st, 1973, Thaddeus O'Sullivan (marr. diss.); 2nd, 1980, Charles Martin Wilson, *qv* (marr. diss. 2001); one *s* one *d*. *Educ:* Ancaster House Sch.; Trinity Coll., Dublin (BA). Dep. Editor, Woman's World, 1977–78; Women's Editor: Daily Record, 1980; Sunday Standard, 1981; Editor, Options, 1982–88; Launch Editor, Country Homes & Interiors, 1986; Editor: She, 1989; Harpers & Queen, 1989–91; Editor-in-Chief: Good Housekeeping, 1991–95; Ideal Home, Homes & Ideas, Woman & Home, Homes & Gardens, Country Homes & Interiors, Beautiful Homes, Living, etc, 1996–98; Chief Exec., Cabal Communications, 1998–2003; Gp Editorial Dir, Highbury House Communications, 2003–05. Non-executive Director: London Transport, 1995–2000; Anglian Water, 1996–2001. Member: Broadcasting Standards Council, 1994–2003; Foresight Retail and Consumer Services Panel, 1999–2001. Magazine Editor of the Year, 1986 and 1994. *Recreations:* family, horses, farming.

See also Sir M. B. Connell.

O'SULLIVAN, Hon. Victoria; *see* Glendinning, Hon. V.

OSWALD, Prof. Andrew John, DPhil; Professor of Economics, Warwick University, since 1996; *b* 27 Nov. 1953; *s* of Ian Oswald and late Joan Oswald (*née* Thomsett); *m* 1975, Coral Simpson (marr. diss. 2004); two *d*; partner, Amanda Goodall. *Educ:* Hollywood High Sch., Perth, Aust.; Currie High Sch., Edinburgh; Stirling Univ. (BA); Strathclyde Univ. (MSc); Nuffield Coll., Oxford (DPhil 1980). Lectr, Balliol Coll., Res. Officer at Inst. of Econs and Stats, and Jun. Res. Fellow, St John's Coll., Oxford Univ., 1979–82; Vis. Lectr, Princeton Univ., 1983–84; Jun. Res. Fellow, St John's Coll., Oxford, 1985–86; Sen. Res. Fellow, Centre for Lab Econs, LSE, 1987–98; De Walt Ankeny Prof. of Econs, Dartmouth Coll., USA, 1989–91; Sen. Res. Fellow, Centre for Econ. Performance, LSE, 1992–95; Jacob Wertheim Fellow, Harvard Univ., 2005; ESRC Professorial Fellow, 2006–09; Vis. Fellow, Cornell Univ., 2008. Tassie Medallion, Stirling Univ., 1975; Lester Prize, Princeton Univ., 1995; Medal, Univ. of Helsinki, 1996. *Publications:* (with A. Carruth) Pay Determination and Industrial Prosperity, 1989; (with D. Blanchflower) The Wage Curve, 1994; contrib. numerous articles to jls. *Recreations:* walking, racquet sports. *Address:* Economics Department, Warwick University, Coventry CV4 7AL. *T:* (024) 7652 3510.

OSWALD, Lady Angela Mary Rose, CVO 2001 (LVO 1993); Woman of the Bedchamber to HM Queen Elizabeth the Queen Mother, 1983–2002; *b* 21 May 1938; *d* of 6th Marquess of Exeter, KCMG, and Lady Mary Burghley, *d* of 7th Duke of Buccleuch, KT; *m* 1958, Sir (William Richard) Michael Oswald, *qv*; one *s* one *d*. *Educ:* Winceby House Sch., Bexhill. Extra Woman of the Bedchamber to HM Queen Elizabeth the Queen Mother, 1981–83. Freeman, City of London, 1995. *Address:* The Old Rectory, Weasenham St Peter, King's Lynn, Norfolk PE32 2TB. *T:* (01328) 838311.

OSWALD, Adm. of the Fleet Sir (John) Julian (Robertson), GCB 1989 (KCB 1987); Director, Marine and General Mutual Life Insurance (International), since 2004; *b* 11 Aug. 1933; *s* of George Hamilton Oswald and Margaret Elliot Oswald (*née* Robertson), Newmore, Invergordon; *m* 1958, Veronica Therese Dorette Thompson; two *s* three *d*. *Educ:* Beaudesert Park, Minchinhampton; Britannia RNC, Dartmouth. Junior Officer, 1951; served in HM Ships Devonshire, Vanguard, Verulam, Newfoundland, Jewel, Victorious, Naiad; specialised in Gunnery, 1960; Commanded HMS Yarnton, 1962–63, HMS Bacchante, 1971–72; MoD, 1972–75; RCDS, 1976; Commanded HMS Newcastle, 1977–79; RN Presentation Team, 1979–80; Captain, Britannia RNC, 1980–82; ACDS (Progs), 1982–84; ACDS (Policy and Nuclear), 1985; Flag Officer, Third Flotilla, and Comdr, Anti-Submarine Warfare, Striking Fleet, 1985–87; C-in-C, Fleet, Allied C-in-C, Channel, and C-in-C, E Atlantic, 1987–89; First Sea Lord and Chief of Naval Staff, and First and Principal Naval ADC to the Queen, 1989–93. Chairman: Aerosystems Internat., 1995–2005; Green Issues Communications, 1999–2008; non-exec. Dir, Marine and Gen. Mutual Life Insurance, 1994–2006. Vice-Chm., S and W RHA, 1993–96. Vice President: RUSI, 1992–; World Ship Trust, 1997–; Mem., European Atlantic Gp, 1988–. Chairman: Nat. Historic Ships Cttee, 1995–2004; Ends of the Earth, 1996–2004; Maritime Trust, 1994–2006; Naval Rev., 1999–2006. Trustee, Nat. Maritime Mus., 1995–2004. President: Jellicoe Sea Cadets, Newcastle, 1979–96; Invergordon Br., RBL, 1992–; Assoc. of Royal Naval Officers, 1993–2003; Sea Cadet Assoc., 1994–2003; Trident Trust, 1993–; Officers' Assoc., 1994–2003; Frinton Soc., 1993–99. Member: Mensa, 1964–; Catholic Union, 1987–. Book reviewer for various publications. FRSA 1995. Hon. Mem., Krewe Rex, New Orleans, 1990. Hon. DBA CNAA, 1992; Hon. LLD Portsmouth, 2000. *Publications:* The Royal Navy—Today and Tomorrow, 1993; articles on strategy and defence policy. *Recreations:* walking, stamp collecting, family, fishing. *Address:* c/o Naval Secretary, Fleet Headquarters, Whale Island, Portsmouth PO2 8BY.

OSWALD, Sir Michael; *see* Oswald, Sir W. R. M.

OSWALD, Richard Anthony; Deputy Health Service Commissioner, 1989–96; *b* 12 Jan. 1941; *s* of late Denis Geoffrey Oswald and Dorothy Lettice Oswald (*née* Shaw); *m* 1963,

Janet Iris Penticost; three *s* one *d* (and one *d* decd). *Educ:* The Leys School, Cambridge. DipHSM, MHSM, 1966. NHS admin. posts, 1961–77; Dist Administrator, Leeds West, 1977–84; Gen. Manager, Leeds Western HA, 1985–89. Trustee: CHASE Children's Hospice Service, 1998–2005 (Chm., 1999–2001); St Mary's Historic House and Gardens Charitable Trust, 2006–. *Recreations:* acting, bird-watching, painting. *Address:* Wymarks Cottage, Brighton Road, Shermanbury, Horsham, W Sussex RH13 8HQ. *T:* (01403) 711961.

OSWALD, Sir (William Richard) Michael, KCVO 1998 (CVO 1988 LVO 1979); National Hunt Advisor to the Queen, since 2003; Racing Manager for Queen Elizabeth the Queen Mother, 1970–2002; *b* 21 April 1934; *s* of Lt-Col William Alexander Hugh Oswald, ERD and Rose-Marie (*née* Leahy); *m* 1958, Lady Angela Mary Rose Cecil (*see* Lady A. M. R. Oswald); one *s* one *d*. *Educ:* Eton; King's College, Cambridge (MA). 2nd Lieut The King's Own Royal Regt, 1953; Captain, Royal Fusiliers (TA), 1957. Manager, Lordship and Egerton Studs, 1962–70; Manager, 1970–97, Dir, 1998–99, Royal Studs. Mem. Council, Thoroughbred Breeders' Assoc., 1964–2001 (Pres., 1996–2001); Chm., Bloodstock Industry Cttee, Animal Health Trust, 1989–2002; Trustee, British Equine Veterinary Assoc. Trust, 1998–2004. Mem., Jockey Club. Hon. Air Cdre, No 2620 (Co. of Norfolk) Sqdn, RAuxAF, 2001–. Hon. DSc De Montfort, 1997. *Recreations:* painting, military history. *Address:* The Old Rectory, Weasenham St Peter, King's Lynn, Norfolk PE32 2TB. *T:* (01328) 838311, *Fax:* (01328) 838264; The Royal Studs, Sandringham, Norfolk PE35 6EF. *T:* (01485) 540588. *Club:* Army and Navy.

See also Lt Col A. F. Matheson of Matheson, yr.

OTAKA, Tadaaki, Hon. CBE 1997; Music Advisor and Chief Conductor, Sapporo Symphony Orchestra, since 1998; Music Advisor and Principal Conductor, Kioi Sinfonietta, Tokyo, since 1995; *b* 8 Nov. 1947; *s* of Hisatada and Misako Otaka; *m* 1978, Yukiko. *Educ:* Toho Music Coll., Tokyo; Vienna Acad. Chief Conductor, Tokyo Philharmonic Orch., 1974–91, now Conductor Laureate; Conductor, Sapporo SO, 1981–86; Principal Conductor, BBC Nat. Orch. of Wales, 1987–95, now Conductor Laureate; Chief Conductor, Yomiuri Nippon SO, 1992–98; Dir, Britten Pears Orch., 1998–2001. Suntory Award (Japan), 1992. *Recreations:* fishing, cooking, computer. *Address:* c/o Askonas Holt Ltd, Lincoln House, 300 High Holborn, WC1V 7JH. *T:* (020) 7400 1700.

OTLEY, Prof. David Templeton, PhD; Distinguished Professor of Accounting and Management, Lancaster University Management School, since 2000; *b* 10 June 1944; *s* of late Frank Otley and of Catherine Otley; *m* 1971, Shelagh Elizabeth Gill; one *s* one *d*. *Educ:* Wellington Grammar Sch.; Churchill Coll., Cambridge (BA 1966, MA 1970); Brunel Univ. (MTech 1971); Manchester Business Sch. (PhD 1976). CDipAF 1980. OR Scientist, NCB, 1966–69; University of Lancaster: Lectr in Financial Control, 1972–83; Sen. Lectr, 1983–86; Prof. of Mgt Control, 1987–88; KPMG Prof. of Accounting, 1988–2000; Associate Dean, 2002–. Non-exec. Dir, Lancaster HA, 1992–94. Vice-Chm., Business and Mgt Panel, 1996 RAE; Chairman: Accounting and Finance Panel, 2001 RAE; Main Panel I, 2008 RAE. Mem. Mgt Bd, ICAEW Centre for Business Performance, 1999–; Sen. Moderator, ICAEW Advanced Stage Examinations, 2001–; Member: ESRC Res. Grants Bd, 1996–2001; ESRC Audit Cttee, 2002–. Chm., Mgt Control Assoc., 1983–88, 2005–. Pres., Mgt Accounting Sect., AAA, Aug. 2009–. Gen. Editor, British Jl of Mgt, 1989–98. Fellow, British Acad. of Mgt, 1994. *Publications:* (with C. R. Emmanuel) Accounting for Management Control, 1985, 2nd edn 1990; Accounting Control and Organizational Behaviour, 1987; (jtly) Accounting for the Human Factor, 1989; (jtly) Management Control: theories, issues and practices, 1995, 2nd edn 2005; numerous contribs to acad. and prof. jls. *Address:* Lancaster University Management School, Lancaster LA1 4YX. *T:* (01524) 593636, *Fax:* (01524) 847321; *e-mail:* d.otley@lancs.ac.uk. *Club:* Oxford and Cambridge.

O'TOOLE, Dr Barbara Maria; Managing Director, MOPA Public Affairs, since 2004; *b* 24 Feb. 1960. *Educ:* Convent of the Sacred Heart, Fenham, Newcastle upon Tyne; Newcastle upon Tyne Poly. (BA Hons 1983); Univ. of Newcastle upon Tyne (PhD 1994). Lecturer: Postgrad. Sch. for Advanced Urban Studies, Univ. of Bristol, 1991–94; in Politics, Univ. of Newcastle upon Tyne, 1994–97; Hd, Policy Promotion, Local Govt Internat. Bureau, 1997–99. MEP (Lab) NE Region, 1999–2004. Former Chm., Northern Film & Media. *Publications:* Prélèvement Obligatoire: a transitional comparison of European local taxation systems, 1991; Rebuilding the City: property led regeneration in the UK, 1992; An Evaluation of the Castlemilk Initiative for the Scottish Office, 1995; Regulation Theory and the British State, 1996.

O'TOOLE, (Seamus) Peter; actor; *b* 2 Aug. 1932; *s* of Patrick Joseph O'Toole; *m* 1960, Siân Phillips, *qv* (marr. diss. 1979); two *d*; *m* 1983, Karen Brown (marr. diss.); one *s*. *Educ:* Royal Academy of Dramatic Art. With Bristol Old Vic Company, 1955–58; first appearance on London stage as Peter Shirley in Major Barbara, Old Vic, 1956. Associate Dir, Old Vic Co., 1980. *Plays include:* Oh, My Papa!, Garrick, 1957; The Long and the Short and the Tall, Royal Court and New, 1959; season with Shakespeare Memorial Theatre Company, Stratford-on-Avon, 1960; Baal, Phœnix, 1963; Hamlet, National Theatre, 1963; Ride a Cock Horse, Piccadilly, 1965; Juno and the Paycock, Man and Superman, Pictures in the Hallway, Gaiety, Dublin, 1966; Waiting for Godot, Happy Days (dir.), Abbey, Dublin, 1969; Uncle Vanya, Plunder, The Apple Cart, Judgement, Bristol Old Vic, 1973; Uncle Vanya, Present Laughter, Chicago, 1978; Macbeth, Old Vic, 1980; Man and Superman, Haymarket, 1982; Pygmalion, Shaftesbury, 1984, Yvonne Arnaud, Guildford, and NY, 1987; The Apple Cart, Haymarket, 1986; Jeffrey Bernard is Unwell, Apollo, 1989, Shaftesbury, 1991, Old Vic, 1999; Our Song, Apollo, 1992. *Films include:* Kidnapped, 1959; The Day They Robbed the Bank of England, 1959; The Savage Innocents, 1960; Lawrence of Arabia, 1962; Becket, 1963; Lord Jim, 1964; What's New, Pussycat, 1965; How to Steal a Million, 1966; The Bible… in the Beginning, 1966; The Night of the Generals, 1967; Great Catherine, 1968; The Lion in Winter, 1968; Goodbye Mr Chips, 1969; Brotherly Love, 1970; Murphy's War, 1971; Under Milk Wood, 1971; The Ruling Class, 1972; Man of La Mancha, 1972; Rosebud, 1975; Man Friday, 1975; Foxtrot, 1975; The Stunt Man, 1977; Coup d'Etat, 1977; Zulu Dawn, 1978; Power Play, 1978; The Antagonists, 1981; My Favorite Year, 1981; Supergirl, 1983; Club Paradise, 1986; The Last Emperor, 1987; High Spirits, 1988; Creator, 1990; King Ralph, 1991; Wings of Fame, 1991; Rebecca's Daughters, 1992; Fairytale: the true story, 1997; Bright Young Things, 2003; Troy, 2004; Lassie, 2005; Venus, 2006; *television:* Rogue Male, 1976; Strumpet City, 1979; Masada, 1981; Svengali, 1982; Pygmalion, 1983; Kim, 1983; Banshee, 1986; The Dark Angel, 1989; Civvies, 1992; Coming Home (serial), 1998; Casanova, 2005. Hon. Academy Award, 2003. *Publications:* Loitering With Intent: the Child (autobiog.), 1992; Loitering With Intent: the Apprentice, 1996. *Address:* c/o Steve Kenis & Co., Royalty House, 72–74 Dean Street, W1D 3SG. *Club:* Garrick.

OTTAWAY, Richard Geoffrey James; MP (C) Croydon South, since 1992; *b* 24 May 1945; *s* of late Professor Christopher Ottaway, PhD, FRCVS and Grace Ottaway; *m* 1982, Nicola E. Kisch. *Educ:* Backwell Secondary Modern School, Somerset; Bristol University. LLB (Hons). Entered RN as an Artificer apprentice, 1961; commissioned and entered RNC, Dartmouth, 1966; served with Western Fleet, HM Ships Beechampton, Nubian and Eagle, 1967–70; Bristol Univ., 1971–74; articled to Norton Rose Botterell & Roche, 1974; admitted Solicitor, 1977; specialist in international, maritime and commercial law; Partner, William A. Crump & Son, 1981–87. Dir, Coastal Europe Ltd, 1988–95. MP (C) Nottingham N, 1983–87; contested (C) same seat, 1987. PPS to Ministers of State, FCO, 1985–87, to Pres. of BoT, 1992–95, to Dep. Prime Minister, 1995; an Asst Govt Whip, 1995–96; a Lord Comr of HM Treasury (Govt Whip), 1996–97; an Opposition Whip, 1997; Opposition front bench spokesman on: local govt and London, 1997–98; defence, 1999–2000; Treasury, 2000–01; the envmt, 2004–05. Member: Standards and Privileges Select Cttee, 2001–04; Foreign Affairs Select Cttee, 2003–04; Parly Intelligence and Security Cttee, 2005–. Vice-Chm., 1922 Cttee. Chm., All-Party Parly Gp on Population and Development, 1992–95. A Vice-Chm., 1998–99, Mem. Bd, 2006–, Cons. Party. *Publications:* (jtly) Road to Reform, 1987; (jtly) Privatisation 1979–1994, 1994; Has London lost its confidence?, 2002; papers on combating internat. maritime fraud, on financial matters and on the environment. *Recreations:* jazz, ski-ing, yacht racing. *Address:* c/o House of Commons, SW1A 0AA. *Club:* Royal Corinthian Yacht.

OTTER, Stephen; Chief Constable, Devon and Cornwall Constabulary, since 2007; *b* Bethnal Green, 24 May 1962; *s* of Tony and Rosemary Otter; *m* 2005, Sophie Hamer; three *s* one *d*. *Educ:* London Sch. of Econs (MSc(Econ) Criminal Justice Studies); Fitzwilliam Coll., Cambridge (Postgrad. Dip. Applied Criminol.). Patrol Constable, Maidenhead, Thames Valley Police, 1982–85; Patrol Inspector, 1985–87, Detective Inspector, 1987–88, Tsim Sha Tsui, Royal Hong Kong Police; Metropolitan Police: Constable, 1989; Bor. Comdr, 1999; Comdr, 2001; Asst Chief Constable, 2001–04, Dep. Chief Constable, 2004–07, Avon and Somerset Police. FRSA. *Recreations:* reading, listening to music, gardening. *Address:* Police Headquarters, Middlemoor, Exeter, Devon EX2 7HQ. *T:* (01392) 452011; *e-mail:* stephen.otter@devonandcornwall.pnn.police.uk. *Club:* Exeter Rowing.

OTTON, Sir Geoffrey (John), KCB 1981 (CB 1978); Second Permanent Secretary, Department of Health and Social Security, 1979–86, retired; *b* 10 June 1927; *s* of late John Alfred Otton and Constance Alma Otton; *m* 1952, Hazel Lomas (*née* White); one *s* one *d*. *Educ:* Christ's Hosp.; St John's Coll., Cambridge (MA). Home Office, 1950–71: (seconded to Cabinet Office, 1959–61; Principal Private Sec. to Home Sec., 1963–65); Dept of Health and Social Security, 1971–86. *Recreation:* music. *Address:* 72 Cumberland Road, Bromley, Kent BR2 0PW. *T:* (020) 8460 9610.

OTTON, Rt Hon. Sir Philip (Howard), Kt 1983; PC 1995; FCIArb; arbitrator and mediator; Surveillance Commissioner, since 2001; Judge of the Court of Appeal, Gibraltar, since 2003; Judge of Civil and Commercial Court, Qatar, 2007; a Lord Justice of Appeal, 1995–2001; *b* 28 May 1933; *o s* of late Henry Albert Otton and Leah Otton, Kenilworth; *m* 1965, Helen Margaret, *d* of late P. W. Bates, Stourbridge; two *s* one *d*. *Educ:* Bablake School, Coventry; Birmingham Univ. LLB 1954. 2nd Lieut, 3rd Dragoon Guards, 1955–57. Called to the Bar, Gray's Inn, 1955, Bencher 1983; QC 1975. Dep. Chm., Beds QS, 1970–72; Junior Counsel to the Treasury (Personal Injuries), 1970–75; a Recorder of the Crown Court, 1972–83; Judge of the High Court, QBD, 1983–95; Presiding Judge, Midland and Oxford Circuit, 1986–88; Judge in Charge of Official Referees Courts, 1991–95. Chairman: Royal Brompton and National Heart and Lung Hospitals SHA, 1991–94; Royal Brompton and Harefield (formerly Royal Brompton Hosp.) NHS Trust, 1994–2002; Nat. Heart and Lung Inst., 1991–95. Non-exec. Dir, Equitable Life Assurance Soc., 2001–03. President: Soc. of Construction Law, 1995–2004; Bar Disability Panel, 1996–2001; Professional Negligence Bar Assoc., 1997–2001; Personal Injury Bar Assoc., 2000–02. Mem., Transitional Med. Bd, Imperial Coll. Sch. of Medicine, 1995–2002. Governor, Nat. Heart and Chest Hosps, 1979–85. Trustee, Migraine Trust, 1992–98. Pres., Holdsworth Club, Birmingham Univ., 2000–01. Visitor, Univ. of Essex, 2001–05. Hon. Legal Advr, OStJ, 2001–. Convenor, FA Premier League, 2004–. Fellow: Inst. of Advanced Legal Studies, 1999; Amer. Law Inst., 2000; Hon. Fellow, Inst. of Judicial Admin, Birmingham Univ., 1995. Hon. Mem., Amer. Bar Assoc. FCIArb 1994; FRSocMed 1998. Hon. LLD: Nottingham Trent, 1997; Birmingham, 2007; DU Essex, 2006. Award of Merit, City of Coventry, 2005. *Recreations:* theatre, opera, music. *Address:* 20 Essex Street, WC2R 3AL. *T:* (020) 7583 9294, *Fax:* (020) 7583 1341; *e-mail:* clerks@20essexst.com. *Clubs:* Garrick, Pilgrims.

OTTON-GOULDER, Catharine Anne; QC 2000; a Recorder, since 2000; *b* 9 April 1955; *e d* of Prof. Michael Douglas Goulder, DD and Alison Clare (*née* Gardner). *Educ:* Somerville Coll., Oxford (BA 1st Cl. Hons Lit. Hum. 1977). Admitted as solicitor, 1980; called to the Bar, Lincoln's Inn, 1983; Mem., Brick Court Chambers, 1984–; Asst Recorder, 1997–2000. Reader, C of E, 1998–. *Address:* Brick Court Chambers, 7–8 Essex Street, WC2R 3LD.

OTTY, Timothy John; QC 2006; *b* 12 Aug. 1967; *s* of Neville and Jean Otty; *m* 1998, Gabriella Ricciardi. *Educ:* Tower House Prep. Sch.; St Paul's Sch.; Trinity Coll., Cambridge (exhibnr, BA 1989, MA 1992); Inns of Court Sch. of Law. Called to the Bar, Lincoln's Inn, 1990 (Tancred Schol.; European Bursary Award). Stagiaire, Eur. Commn of Human Rights, 1993; Legal Consultant, Kurdish Human Rights Project, 1995–; Vice Chm., Bar Human Rights Cttee of England and Wales, 2005–. Mem., Exec. Cttee, Commonwealth Lawyers' Assoc., 2005–. Trustee, Irene Taylor Music in Prisons Trust, 2007–. *Publication:* (contrib.) Sweet & Maxwell's Human Rights Practice, 1st edn. *Recreations:* marathon running, golf, Liverpool FC, Italy. *Address:* 20 Essex Street, WC2R 3AL. *T:* (020) 7842 1200, *Fax:* (020) 7842 1270. *Club:* Roehampton.

OUELLET, Hon. André; PC (Can.) 1972; QC (Can.) 1992; President and Chief Executive Officer, Canada Post Corporation, 1999–2004 (Chairman, 1996–99); *b* St Pascal, Quebec, 6 April 1939; *s* of Albert Ouellet and Rita Turgeon; *m* 1965, Édith Pagé; two *s* two *d*. *Educ:* Univ. of Ottawa (BA 1960); Univ. of Sherbrooke (LLL 1963). Called to the Bar. MP (L): Montreal-Papineau, 1967–88; Papineau-St-Michel, 1988–96; PMG, 1972–74; Minister: for Consumer and Corporate Affairs, 1974–76; of Urban Affairs, 1976–78; of Public Works, 1978–79; PMG 1980–84, and Minister for Consumer and Corporate Affairs, 1980–83; Minister of Labor, 1983–84; Minister of State for Regl Economic Develt, 1984; Pres., Privy Council and Govt Leader in H of C, 1984; Minister of Foreign Affairs, 1993–96. Hon. Dr Ottawa, 1995. *Recreations:* tennis, ski-ing, reading, theatre. *Address:* 17 Chase Court, Ottawa, ON K1V 9Y6, Canada.

OUELLET, His Eminence Cardinal Marc; *see* Quebec, Archbishop of, (RC).

OUGHTON, John Raymond Charles; non-executive Director, KMG Group, since 2008 (Managing Director, 2008); *b* 21 Sept. 1952. *Educ:* Reading Sch.; University Coll., Oxford (BA Mod. Hist. 1974). Joined MoD, 1974; Mem. UK Delegn, UN Law of Sea Conf., 1978; Asst Pvte Sec. to Minister of State for Defence, 1978–80; on secondment to Canadian Govt, 1980–81; Sales Policy, 1981–83; Office of Personal Advr to Sec. of State for Defence, 1984; Pvte Sec. to Minister for the Armed Forces, 1984–86; Sen. Principal, Directorate of Procurement Policy, 1986–87; Asst Sec., Dir of Procurement Policy, 1988–89; Head of Resources and Progs (Navy), 1990–93; Office of Public Service,

Cabinet Office: Under Sec. and Head, Govt Efficiency Unit, 1993–98; Dir, Efficiency and Effectiveness Gp, 1996–98; Ministry of Defence: Dep. Under-Sec. of State, 1998; Hd, Chief of Defence Logistics Implementation Team, 1998–99; Dep. Chief of Defence Logistics, 1999–2003; Dep. Chief Exec., 2003–04, Second Permanent Sec. and Chief Exec., 2004–07, OGC. FRSA; FCIPS. *Recreations:* squash, tennis, travel, watching cricket and football. *Address:* 1 Adderley Grove, SW11 6NA. *T:* (020) 7223 5793; *e-mail:* johnoughton@yahoo.co.uk. *Clubs:* Oxford and Cambridge; Tottenham Hotspur Football, Middlesex CC.

OULTON, Sir (Antony) Derek (Maxwell), GCB 1989 (KCB 1984; CB 1979); QC 1985; MA, PhD; Permanent Secretary, Lord Chancellor's Office, and Clerk of the Crown in Chancery, 1982–89; barrister-at-law; Life Fellow, Magdalene College, Cambridge, since 1995 (Fellow, 1990–95); *b* 14 Oct. 1927; *y s* of late Charles Cameron Courtenay Oulton and Elizabeth, *d* of T. H. Maxwell, KC; *m* 1955, Margaret Geraldine (*d* 1989), *d* of late Lt-Col G. S. Oxley, MC, 60th Rifles; one *s* three *d*. *Educ:* St Edward's Sch., Oxford; King's Coll., Cambridge (scholar; BA (1st Cl.), MA; PhD 1974). Called to Bar, Gray's Inn, 1952, Bencher, 1982–2002; in private practice, Kenya, 1952–60; Private Sec. to Lord Chancellor, 1961–65; Sec., Royal Commn on Assizes and Quarter Sessions, 1966–69; Asst Solicitor, 1969–75. Dep. Sec., 1976–82, and Dep. Clerk of the Crown in Chancery, 1977–82, Lord Chancellor's Office. Vis. Prof. in Law, Bristol Univ., 1990–91. Chm., Mental Health Foundn Cttee on the Mentally Disordered Offender, 1989–92. Trustee, Nat. Gallery, 1989–96. Pres., Electricity Arbitration Assoc., 1990–2001. *Publications:* (jtly) Legal Aid and Advice, 1971; (ed) Lewis, We the Navigators, 2nd edn 1994; contrib. Oxford DNB. *Address:* Magdalene College, Cambridge CB3 0AG. *T:* (01223) 332100.

OULTON, Claire Marion, MA; Headmistress, Benenden School, since 2000; *b* 23 July 1961; *d* of Prof. L. Zisman and S. Zisman; *m* 1986, Nicholas Oulton; two *d*. *Educ:* Somerville Coll., Oxford (BA Hons History 1983; MA 1994); KCL (PGCE 1984). Teacher of History, Benenden Sch., 1984–88; Head of History, Charterhouse, 1988–94; Headmistress, St Catherine's Sch., Guildford, 1994–2000. *Address:* Benenden School, Benenden, Cranbrook, Kent TN17 4AA. *T:* (01580) 240592.

OUSELEY, Baron *cr* 2001 (Life Peer), of Peckham Rye in the London Borough of Southwark; **Herman George Ouseley,** Kt 1997; President, Different Realities Partnership Ltd, since 2006 (Managing Director, 2000–06); non-executive Director, Focus Consultancy Ltd, since 2000; *b* 24 March 1945. Various public service posts, 1963–86; Race Relations Adviser: Lambeth BC, 1979–81; GLC, 1981–84; Dir of Educn, 1986–88, Chief Exec., 1988–90, ILEA; Chief Exec., London Borough of Lambeth, 1990–93; Chm., CRE, 1993–2000. Member: Council, Inst. of Race Relations, 1990–; Council, FA, 2008–; Chair: Kick It Out, 1994–; PRESET Educn and Employment Charitable Trust, 1997–; Patron: Presentation Housing Assoc., 1990–; Daneford Trust, 1998–; Helena Kennedy Foundn, 2003–. Non-exec. Dir, Brooknight Security, 1995–. Pres., LGA, 2001–04. Trustee, Manchester United Foundn, 2007–. *Publications:* The System, 1981; pamphlets and articles on local government, public services, employment, training and race equality issues. *Address:* (office) 439c London Road, Croydon, Surrey CR0 3PF.

OUSELEY, Hon. Sir Duncan (Brian Walter), Kt 2000; **Hon. Mr Justice Ouseley;** a Judge of the High Court, Queen's Bench Division, since 2000; *b* 24 Feb. 1950; *s* of late Maurice and Margaret Ouseley; *m* 1974, Suzannah Price; three *s*. *Educ:* Trinity Sch., Croydon; Fitzwilliam Coll., Cambridge (MA); University Coll. London (LLM). Called to the Bar, Gray's Inn, 1973 (Atkin Scholar 1972); Bencher 2000; Junior Counsel to the Crown, Common Law, 1986–92; QC 1992; a Recorder, 1994–2000; QC (NI) 1997; Jt Hd of Chambers, 2000. Pres., Immigration Appeal Tribunal, 2003–05; Chm., Special Immigration Appeal Commn, 2003–06. Chairman, Examination in Public Shropshire Structure Plan, 1985, Hampshire Structure Plan, 1991. Vice-Chm. Planning and Envmt, Bar Assoc., 2000. *Recreations:* family, sport, music, wine. *Address:* Royal Courts of Justice, Strand, WC2A 2LL. *Club:* Garrick.

OUSTON, Hugh Anfield; Head, Robert Gordon's College, Aberdeen, since 2004; *b* Dundee, 4 April 1952; *s* of Philip and Elizabeth Ouston; *m* 1988, Yvonne Caroline Young; two *s* two *d*. *Educ:* Glenalmond Coll.; Christchurch, Univ. of Oxford (BA Hons); Univ. of Aberdeen (DipEd). Teacher of History, N Berwick High Sch., 1977–84; Hd of History, Beeslack High Sch., 1984–92; Asst Hd, Dunbar Grammar Sch., 1992–97; Dep. Principal, George Watson's Coll., Edinburgh, 1997–2004. *Recreations:* bird watching, gardening, hill walking. *Address:* Robert Gordon's College, Schoolhill, Aberdeen AB10 1FE. *T:* (01224) 646346; *e-mail:* h.ouston@rgc.aberdeen.sch.uk. *Club:* Royal Northern and University (Aberdeen).

OUTRAM, Sir Alan James, 5th Bt *cr* 1858; MA; *b* 15 May 1937; *s* of late James Ian Outram and late Evelyn Mary Littlehales; *S* great-uncle, 1945; *m* 1976, Victoria Jean, *d* of late George Dickson Paton, Bexhill-on-Sea; one *s* one *d*. *Educ:* Spyway, Langton Matravers, Swanage; Marlborough College, Wilts; St Edmund Hall, Oxford. Harrow School: Asst Master, 1961–98; Housemaster, 1979–91; Under Master, 1992–96. Lt-Col TAVR. Pres., Dorset LTA, 1995–2005, now Life Vice-Pres. *Recreations:* golf, bridge, cycling. *Heir: s* Douglas Benjamin James Outram, *b* 15 March 1979. *Address:* Chase House, Moorside, Sturminster Newton, Dorset DT10 1HQ. *Club:* Vincent's (Oxford).

OVENDEN, Rev. Canon John Anthony, LVO 2007; Canon of Windsor, Chaplain in the Great Park and Chaplain, Cumberland Lodge, since 1998; Canon Chaplain, since 1998, and Canon Precentor, since 2007, St George's Chapel; Chaplain to the Queen, since 2002; *b* 26 May 1945; *s* of Edward and Marjorie Ovenden; *m* 1974, Christine Ann Broadhurst; two *s* one *d*. *Educ:* St Paul's Cathedral Choir Sch.; Ardingly Coll.; Borough Rd Coll. of Educn; Salisbury and Wells Theol Coll.; Open Univ. (BA 1980, 1993); KCL (MA 1996). Ordained deacon, 1974, priest, 1975; Assistant Curate: Handsworth, Sheffield, 1974–77; Uckfield, and Priest in Charge of Isfield, Sussex, 1977–80; Precentor and Sacrist, Ely Cathedral, 1980–85; Vicar, St Mary's, Primrose Hill, 1985–98. Golden Jubilee Medal, 2002. *Publication:* (contrib.) Christians and Muslims in the Commonwealth: a dynamic role in the future, ed Anthony O'Mahony and Ataullah Siddiqui, 2001. *Recreations:* theatre-going, music, walking, sport. *Address:* Chaplain's Lodge, The Great Park, Windsor SL4 2HP. *T:* (01784) 432434.

OVENDEN, John Frederick; County Councillor, Kent, 1985–2001 (Leader, Labour Group, 1994–97); *b* 17 Aug. 1942; *s* of late Richard Ovenden and Margaret Louise Ovenden (*née* Lucas); *m* 1963, Maureen (*née* White); one *d*. *Educ:* Salmestone County Primary Sch., Margate; Chatham House Grammar Sch., Ramsgate. Asst Exec. Engr, Post Office, 1961–74. MP (Lab) Gravesend, Feb. 1974–1979. Contested (Lab) Gravesham, 1983. Manager, Post Office, subseq. British Telecom, 1979–90. *Recreations:* football (Gillingham FC), cricket (Kent), gardening, books. *Club:* Gillingham Labour (Gillingham).

OVERBURY, (Henry) Colin (Barry), CBE 1993 (OBE (mil.) 1974); independent lecturer in EC Law, since 1993; Consultant in EC Law, Allen & Overy, Solicitors, since 1993; *b* 13 Jan. 1931; *s* of Stanley and Daisy Overbury; *m* 1st, 1954, Dawn Rhodes Dade (marr. diss. 1981); three *s*; 2nd, 1989, Louise Jane Rosewarne. *Educ:* Dragon Sch., Oxford; Eastbourne Coll.; Law Society's Coll. of Law. Admitted Solicitor of the Supreme Court, 1955. HM Army Legal Services, 1955–74: progressively, Captain, Major, Lt-Col; Retired List, Lt-Col, 1974. European Commission: Prin. Administrator, 1974–82; Adviser, 1982–84; Hd of Div., 1984–86; Dir, Directorate-Gen. for Competition, 1986–93, retd; Hon. Dir Gen., 1993. Sen. Fellow of the Salzburg Seminar, 1984. *Publications:* articles in Common Market Law Rev., 1977, Fordham Univ. Law Inst. Jl, 1984, 1989. *Recreations:* travel, boating, good living. *Clubs:* Lansdowne; Cercle Royal Gaulois (Brussels); Royal Harwich Yacht.

OVERBURY, Rupert Simon; His Honour Judge Overbury; a Circuit Judge, since 2007; *b* Aldershot, 26 Dec. 1957; *s* of Colin Overbury and Dawn Rhodes Overbury (*née* Dade, now Boyd); *m* 1996, Claire Elizabeth Brett; two *s*. *Educ:* Framlingham Coll.; Central London Poly. (BA Hons Law). Called to the Bar, Middle Temple, 1984; barrister, 3 New Square, Lincoln's Inn, 1984–93, 18 Red Lion Court, 1993–2007; Recorder, 2003–07. Chm., Trustee Bd, Saxmundham and Leiston CAB, 2006–. *Recreations:* fly-fishing, shooting, travel. *Address:* Basildon Crown Court, The Gore, Basildon, Essex SS14 2BU. *T:* (01268) 458000; *e-mail:* hhjudge.overbury@judiciary.gsi.gov.uk.

OVEREND, Prof. (William) George; Professor of Chemistry in the University of London, 1957–87, now Professor Emeritus; Master, Birkbeck College, 1979–87 (Vice-Master, 1974–79; Hon. Fellow, 1988); *b* 16 Nov. 1921; *e s* of late Harold George Overend, Shrewsbury, Shropshire; *m* 1949, Gina Olava, *y d* of late Horace Bertie Cadman, Birmingham; two *s* one *d*. *Educ:* Priory School, Shrewsbury; Univ. of Birmingham. BSc (Hons) 1943, PhD 1946, DSc 1954, Birmingham; CChem; FRSC (FRIC 1955); CSci 2004. Asst Lecturer, Univ. Coll., Nottingham, 1946–47; Research Chemist with Dunlop Rubber Co. Ltd and subsequently British Rubber Producers' Assoc., 1947–49; Hon. Research Fellow, 1947–49, Lecturer in Chemistry, 1949–55, Univ. of Birmingham; Vis. Associate Prof., Pennsylvania State Univ., 1951–52; Reader in Organic Chemistry, Univ. of London, 1955–57; Hd of Dept of Chem., Birkbeck Coll., London, 1957–79. Univ. of London: Mem., Academic Council, 1963–67, 1976–79 and 1984–87; Mem., Collegiate Council, 1979–87; Mem., University Entrance and Schools Examination Council, 1966–67 and 1985–87; Mem., F and GP Cttee, 1976–87; Mem., External Cttee, 1984–87; Chm., Bd of Studies in Chemistry, 1974–76; Mem., Senate, 1976–87; Mem., Jt Cttee of Court and Senate for collective planning, 1976–79; Dean, Faculty of Science, 1978–79; Chm., Acad. Adv. Bd in Sci., 1978–79; Mem., Extra-Mural Council, 1979–87, Chm., 1983–84; Chm., Cttee for Extra-Mural Studies, 1984–87. Mem. Council, Inst. of Educn, 1979–82; Leverhulme Emeritus Fellow, 1987–89. Mem., Lewisham Council for Tertiary Educn, 1980; Member Council: National Inst. of Adult Continuing Educn, 1983–88; London and E Anglian Gp for GCSE, 1986–87; Mem. Chem. Bd, 1981–84, Mem. Adv. Bd on Credit Accumulation and Transfer, 1986–87, CNAA. Rep. of South Bank Poly., Assoc. of Colls of Further and Higher Educn, 1981–91. Royal Institute of Chemistry: Examiner, 1958–62; Assessor, 1959–72; Mem., Institutions and Examinations Cttee, 1969–75 (Chm., 1976–85); Mem. Council, 1977–80; Mem. Qual. and Admissions Cttee, 1977–80; Mem. Qual. and Exam. Bd, RSC, 1980–85; Chemical Society (subseq. Royal Society of Chemistry): Mem. Council, 1967–70, 1972–77; Mem. Publications Bd, 1967–78; Hon. Sec. and Hon. Treasurer, Perkin Div., 1972–75; Vice-Pres., 1975–77; Mem., Interdivisional Council, 1972–75; Mem., Educn and Trng Bd, 1972–78; Soc. of Chemical Industry: Mem., Council, 1955–65; Mem., Finance Committee, 1956–65; Mem., Publications Cttee, 1955–65 (Hon. Sec. for publications and Chairman of Publications Committee, 1958–65); Member: Brit. Nat. Cttee for Chemistry, 1961–66, 1973–78; Brit. Nat. Cttee for Biochemistry, 1975–81; Chemical Council, 1960–63 and 1964–69 (Vice-Chm. 1964–69); European Cttee for Carbohydrate Chemists, 1970–85 (Chm.); Hon. Sec., Internat. Cttee for Carbohydrate Chemistry, 1972–75 (Pres., 1978–80); Mem., Jt IUPAC-IUB Commn on Carbohydrate Nomenclature, 1971–. Jubilee Memorial Lecturer, Society of Chemical Industry, 1959–60; Lampitt Medallist, Society of Chemical Industry, 1965; Member: Pharmacopœia Commission, 1963–81; Home Office Poisons Board, 1973–94. Governor: Polytechnic of the South Bank, 1970–91 (Chm., 1980–89; Chm., Audit Cttee, 1989–91; Hon. Fellow 1989); Thomas Huxley Coll., 1971–77; Mem., Council of Governors, Queen Elizabeth Coll., Univ. of London, 1983–85. Mem., Cttee of Management, Inst. of Archaeology, 1980–86. FCMI (FBIM 1988). Hon. FCollP 1986. DUniv Open, 1988. *Publications:* The Use of Tracer Elements in Biology, 1951; papers in Nature, and Jl of Chemical Soc. *Recreation:* gardening (rose grower). *Address:* The Retreat, Nightingales Lane, Chalfont St Giles, Bucks HP8 4SR. *Clubs:* Athenæum, Royal Automobile.

OVERY, Prof. Richard James, PhD; FRHistS; FBA 2000; Professor of History, Exeter University, since 2004; *b* 23 Dec. 1947; *s* of James Herbert Overy and Margaret Grace Overy (*née* Sutherland); *m* 1992, Kim Turner (marr. diss. 2004); two *d*, and one *s* two *d* from previous marriage. *Educ:* Sexey's Grammar Sch., Som; Gonville and Caius Coll., Cambridge (BA 1969; MA 1972; PhD 1977). Cambridge University: Res. Fellow, Churchill Coll., 1972–73; Lectr, Queens' Coll., 1973–79; Asst Univ. Lectr, 1976–79; King's College, London: Lectr, 1980–88; Reader, 1988–92; Prof. of Modern Hist., 1992–2004; FKC 2003. Trustee, RAF Mus., 1999–2003. FRHistS 1997; FRSA 2006. T. S. Ashton Prize, Econ. Hist. Soc., 1982; Cass Prize, Business Hist. Soc., 1987; Samuel Eliot Morison Prize, Soc., for Mil. Hist., 2001. *Publications:* William Morris, Viscount Nuffield, 1976; The Air War 1939–45, 1980; The Nazi Economic Recovery, 1982, 2nd edn 1996; Goering: the Iron Man, 1984, 2nd edn 2000; The Origins of the Second World War, 1987, 2nd edn 1998; The Road to War, 1989, 2nd edn 1999; War and Economy in the Third Reich, 1994; The Interwar Crisis 1919–1939, 1994; Why the Allies Won, 1995; The Penguin Atlas of the Third Reich, 1996, 2nd edn 2000; The Times Atlas of the Twentieth Century, 1996, 2nd edn 1999; Bomber Command 1939–45, 1997; Russia's War, 1998; (Gen. Ed.) The Times History of the World, 1999; The Battle, 2000; Interrogations: the Nazi elite in Allied hands 1945, 2001; The Dictators, 2004 (Wolfson Prize for History, Hessell Tiltman Prize for History, 2005); contrib. to Econ. Hist. Rev., Jl of Strategic Studies, Past and Present, English Histl Rev., etc. *Recreations:* tennis, running, opera. *Address:* Department of History, University of Exeter, Amory Building, Rennes Drive, Exeter EX4 4RJ; *e-mail:* r.overy@ex.ac.uk. *Club:* Academy.

OVEY, Rev. Dr Michael John; Principal, Oak Hill Theological College, London, since 2007; *b* Isle of Wight, 9 Dec. 1958; *s* of Kenneth John and Elizabeth Ruth Ovey; *m* 1987, Heather Elizabeth Jefferyes; two *s* one *d*. *Educ:* Balliol Coll., Oxford (BA 1981; BCL 1982); Trinity Coll. and Ridley Hall, Cambridge (BA 1991); Moore Coll., Sydney (MTh 2000); King's Coll. London (PhD 2005). Barrister, 1982–85; Parly Draftsman, 1985–88; ordained deacon, 1991, priest, 1992; Curate and Dir of Trng, All Saints, Crowborough, 1991–95; Junior Lectr, Moore Theol Coll., Sydney, 1995–98; Oak Hill Theological College, London: Kingham Hill Res. Fellow, 1998–2005; Lectr and College Dean, 2005–07. *Publications:* (with Dr S. Jeffery and Dr A. Sach) Pierced For Our Transgressions, 2007; articles in Oak Hill Sch. Theol. Papers, IVP Dictionary of Apologetics, IVP

Dictionary of Theology, Cambridge Papers, Churchman, Reformed Theol Rev. *Address:* Oak Hill Theological College, Chase Side, Southgate, N14 4PS. *T:* (020) 8449 0467, *Fax:* (020) 8441 5996.

OWEN, family name of **Baron Owen**.

OWEN, Baron *cr* 1992 (Life Peer), of the City of Plymouth; **David Anthony Llewellyn Owen,** CH 1994; PC 1976; European Union Co-Chairman, International Conference on Former Yugoslavia, 1992–95; *b* Plympton, South Devon, 2 July 1938; *s* of Dr John William Morris Owen and Mary Llewellyn; *m* 1968, Deborah Schabert; two *s* one *d*. *Educ:* Bradfield College; Sidney Sussex College, Cambridge (BA 1959; MB, BChir 1962; MA 1963; Hon. Fellow, 1977); St Thomas' Hospital. FRCP 2005. St Thomas' Hospital: house appts, 1962–64; Neurological and Psychiatric Registrar, 1964–66; Research Fellow, Medical Unit, 1966–68. Contested (Lab) Torrington, 1964; MP (Lab 1966–81, SDP, 1981–92) Plymouth Sutton, 1966–74, Plymouth Devonport, 1974–92. PPS to Minister of Defence, Administration, 1967; Parly Under-Sec. of State for Defence, for RN, 1968–70; Opposition Defence Spokesman, 1970–72, resigned over EEC, 1972; Parly Under-Sec. of State, DHSS, 1974; Minister of State: DHSS, 1974–76; FCO, 1976–77; Sec. of State for Foreign and Commonwealth Affairs, 1977–79; Opposition spokesman on energy, 1979–80. Sponsored 1973 Children's Bill; ministerially responsible for 1975 Children's Act. Co-founder, SDP, 1981; Chm., Parly Cttee, SDP, 1981–82; Dep. Leader, SDP, 1982–83; Leader, SDP, 1983–87, resigned over issue of merger with Liberal Party, re-elected, 1988–92. Chm., New Europe, 1999–2005. Chairman: Decision Technology Internat., 1970–72; Middlesex Hldgs, subseq. Global Natural Energy plc, 1995–2006; Yukos International, 2002–05; Europe Steel, 2002–; Director: New Crane Publishing, 1992–2005; Coats Viyella plc, 1994–2001; Abbott Laboratories Inc., 1996–; Intelligent Energy, 2003–05. Member: Indep. Commn on Disarmament and Security Issues, 1980–89; Indep. Commn on Internat. Humanitarian Issues, 1983–88; Carnegie Commn on Preventing Deadly Conflict, 1994–99; Eminent Persons Gp on Curbing Illicit Trafficking in Small Arms and Light Weapons, 1999–2003. Chm., Humanitas, 1990–2001. Governor, Charing Cross Hospital, 1966–68. Patron: Disablement Income Group, 1968–; Greenham Common Trust, 2004–; Pres., Enham Trust, 2004–. Pres., Nat. Marine Aquarium, 2006–. Chancellor, Liverpool Univ., 1996–. *Publications:* (ed) A Unified Health Service, 1968; The Politics of Defence, 1972; In Sickness and in Health, 1976; Human Rights, 1978; Face the Future, 1981; A Future That Will Work, 1984; A United Kingdom, 1986; Personally Speaking to Kenneth Harris, 1987; Our NHS, 1988; Time to Declare (autobiog.), 1991; (ed) Seven Ages (anthology of poetry), 1992; Balkan Odyssey, 1995; The Hubris Syndrome, 2007; In Sickness and in Power, 2008; articles in Lancet, Neurology, Clinical Science, Brain, Qly Jl Med., and Foreign Affairs. *Recreation:* sailing. *Address:* 78 Narrow Street, Limehouse, E14 8BP. *T:* (020) 7987 5441, (office) (01442) 872617, *Fax:* (01442) 876108.

OWEN, Albert; MP (Lab) Ynys Môn, since 2001; *b* 10 Aug. 1959; *s* of late William Owen and Doreen Owen (*née* Woods); *m* 1983, Angela Margaret Magee; two *d*. *Educ:* Holyhead Comprehensive Sch.; Coleg Harlech; Univ. of York (BA Hons Politics 1997). Merchant seafarer, 1975–92; full-time educn, 1992–97; Manager, Centre for the Unwaged (advice, trng and information centre), 1997–2001. *Recreations:* travel by train, cooking, gardening, walking, running, cycling. *Address:* House of Commons, SW1A 0AA; (constituency office) Ty Cledwyn, 18 Thomas Street, Holyhead, Anglesey LL65 1RR. *T:* (01407) 765750.

OWEN, (Alfred) David, OBE 1997; Group Chairman, Rubery Owen Holdings Ltd, since 1975; *b* 26 Sept. 1936; *m* 1966, Ethne (*née* Sowman); two *s* one *d*. *Educ:* Brocksford Hall; Oundle; Emmanuel Coll., Cambridge Univ. (MA). Joined Rubery Owen Gp, 1960; Gen. Man., Rubery Owen Motor Div., 1962–67; Dep. Man. Dir, Rubery Owen & Co. Ltd, 1967; Acting Chm. and Man. Dir, Rubery Owen Holdings Ltd, 1969; Director: Severn Valley Railways (Holdings) plc, 1984–; Blackwell Sci. Ltd, 1993–2003; Welconstruct Gp (formerly Grimmitt Hldgs) Ltd, 2001–07; Darlaston Housing Trust Ltd, 2001–; Walsall Housing Regeneration Community Agency, 2005–. Warden, Birmingham Assay Office, 1999–2005. Member: Council, Univ. of Aston, 1981–2001; Bd, British Library, 1982–90; Bd, Nat. Exhibn Centre, 1982–2006; Bd, Castle Vale Housing Action Trust, 1993–2000. President: Comité de Liaison Eur. de la Distrib. Ind. de Pièces de rechange et équipements pour Autos, 1988–90; Comité de Liaison de la Construction de Carrosseries et de Remorques, 1998–99; Commercial Trailer Assoc., 1992–2004. Treas., SMMT, 2001–. Chm., Charles Hayward Foundn, 2004–. Hon. DSc Aston, 1988; DUniv Central England, 2000. *Recreations:* walking, photography, music, industrial archaeology, local history, collecting books. *Address:* Mill Dam House, Mill Lane, Aldridge, Walsall, West Midlands WS9 0NB. *T:* (office) (0121) 526 3131. *Club:* National.

OWEN, Alun, MC 1945; retired; Under-Secretary, Land Use Planning Group, Welsh Office, 1975–79; *b* 14 March 1919; *m* 1946, Rhona Evelyn Griffiths; one *s* four *d*. *Educ:* West Monmouth Grammar Sch.; Bridgend Grammar Sch.; LSE (BScEcon). Mil. Service, 1939–46: Ches. Regt, 1940–46 (Captain) (despatches, Normandy, 1944); Civil Service, Min. of Labour NW Region, 1946–48; Min. of Fuel and Power, 1948–50; Customs and Excise, 1950–59; Welsh Office, Min. of Housing and Local Govt, 1959–62; Welsh Bd of Health, 1962–69; Welsh Office, 1969–79. *Address:* 12 Knowbury Avenue, Penarth, South Glam CF64 5RX.

OWEN, His Honour Aron, PhD; a Circuit Judge, 1980–92 (Resident Judge, Clerkenwell County Court, 1986–92); Deputy Judge, Clerkenwell County Court, and Family Division, Royal Courts of Justice, 1992–94; *b* 16 Feb. 1919; *m* 1946, Rose (*née* Fishman), JP; one *s* two *d*. *Educ:* Tredegar County Grammar Sch.; Univ. of Wales (BA Hons, PhD). Called to the Bar, Inner Temple, 1948. Freeman, City of London, 1963. *Recreations:* travel, gardening. *Address:* 44 Brampton Grove, Hendon, NW4 4AQ. *T:* (020) 8202 8151.

OWEN, Arthur Leslie, (Les); Group Chief Executive, AXA Asia Pacific Holdings, 2000–06 (Board Member, 1998–2006); *b* 6 Feb. 1949; *s* of Arthur Llewellyn Owen and Annie Louise Owen (*née* Hegarty); *m* 1972, Valerie Emmott; three *d*. *Educ:* Holt High Sch., Liverpool; Univ. of Manchester (BSc Hons Maths). FIA 1975; FIAA 2004. Joined Sun Life Corp., 1971: Chief Gen. Manager, 1992–95; Gp Man. Dir, 1995–97; Chief Exec., AXA Sun Life plc, 1997–99; Board Member: Sun Life & Provincial Hldgs plc, 1996–2000; AXA Nichidan, Japan, 1999–2002; Alliance Bernstein (formerly Alliance Capital Management) (Australia & NZ), 2000–06; AXA Minmetals, China, 2002–06; Computershare plc, 2006–; Football Fedn of Aust., 2007–; Discovery Hldgs, 2007–; Chm., AXA China Region, 2002–06. Member Board: Western TEC, 1994–98; PIA, 1997–99. *Recreations:* sport, soccer, cricket, golf, gardening, reading. *Address:* Broadway Lea, Broadway, Shipham, Somerset BS25 1UE.

OWEN, Bernard Laurence; a Chairman of Industrial Tribunals, 1982–95; *b* 8 Aug. 1925; *s* of Albert Victor Paschal Owen and Dorothy May Owen; *m* 1950, Elsie Yarnold; one *s* two *d*. *Educ:* King Edward's School, Birmingham; solicitor. Commissioned Royal Warwickshire Regt, 1945, service in Sudan, Eritrea, Egypt; staff appts in GHQs Middle East and Palestine, 1946–47; retired 1947 (Major); qualified as solicitor, 1950; a Senior Partner, C. Upfill Jagger Son & Tilley, 1952–82. *Recreations:* gardening, photography, bird watching.

OWEN, David; *see* Owen, A. D.

OWEN, David Christopher; QC 2006; barrister, mediator and arbitrator; *b* 21 June 1958; *s* of Kenneth and Barbara Owen; *m* 1985, Philippa Reid; one *s* one *d*. *Educ:* Marlborough Coll.; Merton Coll., Oxford (BA 1st Cl. Hons Hist.). Administrator, Defence Procurement and Overseas Finance Divs, HM Treasury, 1979–81; called to the Bar, Middle Temple, 1983; Mediator Accreditation, CEDR, 2003. Mem., Magic Circle, 1978–. *Publication:* (ed jtly) MacGillivray on Insurance Law, 9th edn, 10th edn 2003. *Recreations:* magic, music, travel. *Address:* 20 Essex Street, WC2R 3AL. *T:* (020) 7842 1200, *Fax:* (020) 7842 1270; *e-mail:* clerks@20essexst.com.

OWEN, David Harold Owen, OBE 1998; Registrar of the Privy Council, 1983–98; *b* 24 May 1933; *er* twin *s* of late Lloyd Owen Owen and Margaret Glyn Owen, Machynlleth, Powys; *m* 1st, 1961, Ailsa Ransome Wallis (*d* 1993); three *d*; 2nd, 1995, Julia (*née* Beck), *widow* of W. M. Lowe. *Educ:* Harrow Sch.; Gonville and Caius Coll., Cambridge. Called to the Bar, Gray's Inn, 1958. Served Royal Welch Fusiliers, 1951–53 (2nd Lieut). Campbell's Soups Ltd, King's Lynn, 1958–68; Lord Chancellor's Dept, 1969–80 (Private Sec. to Lord Chancellor, 1971–75); Chief Clerk, Judicial Cttee of Privy Council, 1980–83. *Recreations:* music, travel. *Address:* Whitelea, Stoney Lane, Bovingdon, Herts HP3 0DP. *Club:* Reform.

OWEN, Sir Geoffrey (David), Kt 1989; Senior Fellow, Department of Management, London School of Economics and Political Science, since 1998; *b* 16 April 1934; *s* of late L. G. Owen and Violet Owen (*née* Chamberlain); *m* 1st, 1961, Dorothy Jane (*d* 1991); two *s* one *d*; 2nd, 1993, Miriam Marianna Gross, *qv*. *Educ:* Rugby Sch.; Balliol Coll., Oxford (MA). Joined Financial Times, 1958, feature writer, industrial correspondent; US Correspondent, 1961; Industrial Editor, 1967; Executive, Industrial Reorganisation Corp., 1967–69; Dir of Admin, Overseas Div., 1969, Dir of Personnel and Admin, 1972, British Leyland Internat.; Dep. Editor, 1974–80, Editor, 1981–90, Financial Times; Dir, Business Policy Prog., Centre for Econ. Performance, LSE, 1991–98. Dir, Laird Gp, 2000–06. Chm., Wincott Foundn, 1998–. *Publications:* Industry in the USA, 1966; From Empire to Europe, 1999. *Address:* London School of Economics and Political Science, Houghton Street, WC2A 2AE.

OWEN, Gillian Frances, PhD; energy and environment policy consultant, since 1988; Senior Research Fellow, Centre for Management under Regulation, University of Warwick, since 2004; *b* 26 May 1954; *d* of Iorwerth Ellis Owen and Edith Maud Owen; *m* 1980, David Ian Green. *Educ:* Newcastle upon Tyne (BA Librarianship/Social Scis 1976); Birkbeck Coll., Univ. of London (PhD Public Policy 1994). Asst Cataloguer, Clwyd CC, 1976–77; Asst Librarian, Coll. of Librarianship, Wales, 1978; Energy Advice Officer, City of Newcastle upon Tyne, 1979–81; Information and Develt Officer, 1981–84, Chief Officer, 1984–88, Nat. Energy Action. Specialist Advr, Envmt Select Cttee, 1993–95; Mem., Monopolies and Mergers, subseq. Competition, Commn, 1996–2002; Expert Advr, Economic and Social Cttee, EC, 1996, 2002; Special Advr, Energy Services Assoc. Non-exec. Dir, Ofwat, 2007–. Member: Bedfordshire Police Authy, 1994–2003; Adv. Bd, Ofgem, 1999–2000; Fuel Poverty Adv. Gp, 2002–; DEFRA Regulation Task Force, 2003–05; European Competition and Consumer Gp, Competition Working Gp, 2004–; Vice Chm., Consumer Congress, 1987; Chm., Public Utilities Access Forum, 1995–. Trustee, Pilkington Energy Efficiency Trust, 2003–. *Publication:* Public Purpose or Private Benefit: the politics of energy conservation, 1999. *Recreations:* travel, walking, cycling, art, design and architecture, theatre, cinema. *Address:* Centre for Management under Regulation, Warwick Business School, University of Warwick, Coventry CV4 7AZ. *T:* (01234) 358163.

OWEN, Gordon Michael William, CBE 1991; Chairman, NXT plc, 2001–05; *b* 9 Dec. 1937; *s* of Christopher Knowles Owen and late Mrs Margaret Joyce Milward (*née* Spencer); *m* 1963, Jennifer Pearl, (Jane), Bradford (marr. diss. 2001); one *s* one *d*; *m* 2001, Tina Elizabeth (*née* Davies). *Educ:* Cranbrook Sch. Cable & Wireless, 1954–91: Dir, 1986–91; Jt Man. Dir, 1987–88; Dep. Chief Exec., 1988–90; Gp Man. Dir, 1990–91; Chairman: Mercury Communications Ltd, 1990–91 (Man. Dir, 1984–90); Peterstar Communications, St Petersburg, 1992–94; Energis Communications Ltd, subseq. Energis plc, 1993–2002; Utility Cable plc, 1994–98; Acorn (formerly Acorn Computer) Group, 1996–98; Yeoman Gp plc, 1996–2004; Director: Portals Gp, 1988–95; London Electricity, 1989–97; Waste Gas Technology, 1993–2002; Olivetti SpA, 1996–2001. Chm., MacIntyre Care, 1993–2003. Chm., Acad. of St Martin in the Fields Orch., 2002–04 (Vice-Chm., 1994–2002). Chm. Bd of Govs, St Michael's Sch., Otford, 1994–. *Recreations:* beekeeping, stamp collecting, sailing, bad golf. *Address:* Sutton End House, Sutton, W Sussex RH20 1PY.

OWEN, Griffith; *see* Owen, S. G.

OWEN, Sir Hugo Dudley C.; *see* Cunliffe-Owen.

OWEN, Ivor Henri, CBE 1992; CEng, FIMechE; Director General, Design Council, 1988–93; *b* 14 Nov. 1930; *s* of Thomas and Anne Owen; *m* 1954, Jane Frances Graves; two *s* one *d*. *Educ:* Liverpool College of Technology; Manchester College of Science and Technology. Engineering apprentice, later design engineer, Craven Bros (Manchester), Stockport, 1947–57; Manufacturing Develt Engr, Steam Turbine Div., English Electric, Rugby, 1957–62; Manager, Netherton Works, English Electric, Bootle, 1962–66 (hydro electric plant, steam turbine components, condensers, nuclear equipment); Manager, English Electric Computers, Winsford, 1966–69; Manager, Winsford Kidsgrove Works, ICL, 1969–70; Man. Dir, RHP Bearings, 1970–81; Thorn EMI: Chief Exec., Gen. Engineering Div., 1981–83; Chm., Appliance and Lighting Group, 1984–87; Dir, 1984–87. Chm., Ball Roller Bearing Manufrs Assoc., 1978–80; Vice-Pres., Fedn European Bearing Manufrs Assoc., 1978–80. Royal Acad. of Engrg Vis. Prof., Univ. of Bath, 1994–97. FRSA. *Recreations:* theatre, reading, running, gardening, motor cycling, silversmithing. *Address:* Linden House, Back Ends, Chipping Campden, Glos GL55 6AU.

OWEN, Jane Caroline; HM Diplomatic Service; Director of Trade and Investment, New Delhi, since 2006; *b* 15 April 1963; *d* of Thomas and Jeanne Owen; *m* 1998, David Donnelly; one *s* one *d*. *Educ:* Ellerslie Sch., Malvern; Trinity Coll., Cambridge (BA Hons 1986). English teacher, JET prog., Osaka, Japan, 1986; entered FCO, 1987; Mexico and Central American Dept, FCO, 1987; Japanese lang. trng, 1988–90; 2nd Sec., Commercial, Tokyo, 1990–93; Head: Exports to Japan Unit, DTI, 1993–96 (on secondment); Mediterranean and Asia Sect., EU Dept (External), FCO, 1996–98; Dep. Hd of Mission, Hanoi, 1998–2002; Dir of Trade Promotion, Tokyo, 2002–06. *Recreations:* theatre, calligraphy, travelling, scuba diving. *Address:* c/o Foreign and Commonwealth Office, King Charles Street, SW1A 2AH.

OWEN, Jennifer Ann; Director, Adults, Health and Community Wellbeing (formerly Adult Social Care), Essex County Council, since 2004; *b* 23 Aug. 1954; *d* of Col John Edward Owen and Jean Wardle Owen; *m* 2001, Jeff Jerome; one *s*. *Educ:* Sheffield Poly. (BA Hons Applied Soc. Studies; CQSW, CMS 1976). Regl Dir, Social Services Inspectorate, DoH, 2001–04. Pres., Assoc. of Dirs of Adult Social Services, April 2009– (Vice-Pres., 2008–April 2009); Bd Mem., Research in Practice for Adults, 2006–; Trustee, Bd, SCIE, 2007–. *Recreations:* theatre, country walks, travelling, company of friends.

OWEN, Hon. Sir John (Arthur Dalziel), Kt 1986; a Judge of the High Court of Justice, Queen's Bench Division, 1986–2000; Dean, Arches Court of Canterbury and Auditor, Chancery Court of York, and Master of the Faculty Office, 1980–2000; *b* 22 Nov. 1925; *s* of late R. J. Owen and Mrs O. B. Owen; *m* 1952, Valerie, *d* of W. Ethell; one *s* one *d*. *Educ:* Solihull Sch.; Brasenose Coll., Oxford (MA, BCL 1949); LLM Wales, 1996. RN, 1944; commnd 2nd King Edward VII's Own Goorkha Rifles, 1946. Called to Bar, Gray's Inn, 1951, Bencher, 1980. Dep. Chm., Warwickshire QS, 1967–71; QC 1970; a Recorder, 1972–84; Dep. Leader, Midland and Oxford Circuit, 1980–84; a Circuit Judge, CCC, 1984–86; a Presiding Judge, Midland and Oxford Circuit, 1988–92. Mem. Senate of the Inns of Court and the Bar, 1977–80. Chm., West Midlands Area Mental Health Review Tribunal, 1972–80. Mem., General Synod of Church of England, Dio. Coventry, 1970–80; Chancellor, Dio. Derby, 1973–80, Dio. Coventry, 1973–80, Dio. Southwell, 1979–80. DCL Lambeth, 1993. *Club:* Garrick.
See also Baroness Seccombe.

OWEN, John Aubrey; Senior Partner, Inside Advice, consultancy services, since 2001; *b* 1 Aug. 1945; *s* of late Prebendary Douglas Aubrey Owen and Patricia Joan Owen (*née* Griggs); *m* 1971, Julia Margaret Jones; one *s* one *d*. *Educ:* City of London Sch., St Catharine's Coll., Cambridge (MA). Joined Min. of Transport, 1969; Asst Private Sec. to Minister for Transport Industries, 1972; DoE, 1973–75; Dept of Transport, 1975–78; seconded to Cambridgeshire CC, 1978–80; DoE, 1980–2001: Regional Dir, Northern Regional Office, Depts of the Environment and Transport, 1987–91; Dir, Personnel Management, 1991–95. Dir, Regeneration, then Skills, Educn and Regeneration, later Skills, Enterprise and Communities, Govt Office for London, 1995–2001. Chm., Mosaic (formerly New Islington and Hackney) Housing Assoc., 2002–06; Dep. Chm., Family Mosaic Housing Assoc., 2006–. MInstD. *Recreations:* gardening, opera, reading, watching cricket. *Address:* 33 Valley Road, Welwyn Garden City, Herts AL8 7DH. *T:* (01707) 321768; *e-mail:* johna.owen@ntlworld.com. *Club:* Middlesex CC.

OWEN, Prof. John Joseph Thomas, FRS 1988; Sands Cox Professor and Head of Department of Anatomy, University of Birmingham, 1978–2001; *b* 7 Jan. 1934; *s* of Thomas and Alice Owen; *m* 1961, Barbara Schofield Forster (marr. diss. 1992); two *s*. *Educ:* Univ. of Liverpool (BSc, MD); MA Oxon 1963. Lecturer: Univ. of Liverpool, 1960–63; Univ. of Oxford, 1963–72; Fellow, St Cross Coll., Oxford, 1968–72; Sen. Scientist, Imperial Cancer Res. Fund's Tumour Immunology Unit, UCL, 1972–74; Prof. of Anatomy, Univ. of Newcastle upon Tyne 1974–78. Vis. Scholar, Stanford Univ., USA, 2000–01; Greenberg Scholar, Oklahoma Med. Res. Foundn, USA, 2001–02. Medical Research Council: Mem., Physiol Systems and Disorders Bd, 1978–83; Chm., Grants Cttee, B, 1980–83; Mem., Cell Bd, 1991–94; Member: Wellcome Trust's Biochemistry and Cell Biology Panel, 1987–90; Council, Nat. Kidney Res. Fund, 1987–90; Council, Royal Soc., 1991–93. Founder FMedSci 1998. *Publications:* numerous contribs to sci. literature. *Recreations:* sport, travel.

OWEN, Prof. John V.; *see* Vallance-Owen.

OWEN, John Wyn, CB 1994; Chairman, University of Wales Institute, Cardiff, since 2005; Member, Administrative Council, Madriaga European Foundation, since 2005; *b* 15 May 1942; *s* of late Idwal Wyn Owen and of Myfi Owen (*née* Hughes); *m* 1967, Elizabeth Ann (*née* MacFarlane); one *s* one *d*. *Educ:* Friars School, Bangor; St John's Coll., Cambridge (BA 1964, MA 1968); Hosp. Admin. Staff Coll. (DipHA 1967). Trainee, King Edward VII's Hosp. Fund for London, 1964–66; Dep. Hosp. Sec., West Wales Gen. Hosp., Carmarthen, 1966–67; Hosp. Sec., Glantawe HMC, Swansea, 1967–70; Staff Training Officer, Welsh Hosp. Bd, Cardiff, 1968–70; Divl Administrator, Univ. of Wales, Cardiff, HMC, 1970–72; St Thomas' Hospital: Asst Clerk, and King's Fund Fellow, 1972–74; Dist Administrator, St Thomas' Health Dist, Teaching, 1974–79; Trustee, Refresh, 1976–78; Hon. Tutor, Med. Sch., 1974–79; Praeceptor, Sch. of Health Administration, Univ. of Minnesota, 1974–79; Exec. Dir, United Medical Enterprises, London, 1979–85; Dir, NHS Wales, Welsh Office, 1985–94; Chm., Welsh Health Common Services Authy, 1985–94; Dir Gen., NSW Health Dept, Sydney, 1994–97; Sec., Nuffield Trust, 1997–2005. Chairman: Olympic Health and Med. Working Cttee, 1994–97; DoH Change Mgt Gp on Nurse Regulation, 1999–2001; Member: Strategic Planning and Evaluation Cttee, Nat. Health and MRC, 1994–97; Australian Health Ministers' Adv. Council, 1994–97 (Chm., 1995–97); Health Adv. Bd, 1994–97; Public Health Assoc., 1994; Mgt Cttee, Nat. Breast Cancer Centre, 1995–97. Mem. Bd, UK Health Protection Agency, 2006–; Vice-Chm., Nat. Heart Forum, 2007–. Sen. Associate, Judge Inst. of Mgt Studies, Univ. of Cambridge, 1997–; Adjunct Prof., Public Health, Univ. of Sydney, 2006–; Visiting Fellow: Univ. of NSW, 1979; LSE, 1997–. Trustee, Florence Nightingale Museum Trust, 1983–90; Chm., Health Bldg Educn Gp, British Consultants' Bureau, 1983–85; Mem. Adv. Forum, Personnel Lead Body, 1992–94. Chm., Europe in the World, European Foundn Centre, 2004–05. Founder Mem., Med. Chapter, Australian Opera, 1995–97; Mem., NSW Cambridge Soc. Cttee, 1996–97; Sec., London Cambridge Soc., 1997–2004 (Chm., 2004–). Member: Court, Univ. of Wales, 1998–; Council, Univ. of Wales Coll. of Medicine, 1997–2005. Mem., Inst. of Medicine, NAS, USA, 1998. FRGS 1968; FRSA 1998; FHSM 1992; FACHSE 1994; FRSocMed 1997; CCMI 2005. Hon. FFPHM 1991; Hon. MRCP 2002. Hon. Fellow: UCW, Aberystwyth, 1991; UCW, Bangor, 1992. Hon. Mem., Gorsedd of Bards, 2000. DUniv Glamorgan, 1999; Hon. DSc City, 2004. *Publications:* contribs to professional jls. *Recreations:* organ playing, opera, travel. *Address:* Newton Farm, Newton, Cowbridge CF71 7RZ. *T:* (01446) 775113. *Club:* Athenæum.

OWEN, John Wynne, CMG 1998; MBE 1979; DL; HM Diplomatic Service, retired; Chairman (non-executive): CLS Fabrication Ltd, since 1989; Autoport North America Inc., since 2004 (Director, since 2002); Iceman Capital Advisors Ltd, since 2006; *b* 25 April 1939; *s* of Thomas David Owen and Mair Eluned Owen; *m* 1st, 1962, Thelma Margaret Gunton (*d* 1987); one *s* two *d*; 2nd, 1988, Carol Edmunds; one step *d*. *Educ:* Gowerton Grammar Sch.; Westminster Coll., London. FO 1956; 2nd Lieut Royal Signals, 1958–60; served Djakarta, Saigon, Paris, San Salvador, to 1967; resigned 1967; business, 1967–70; reinstated 1970; FCO, 1970–73; Tehran, 1973–77; São Paulo, 1978–80; Peking, 1980–82; FCO, 1983; special leave, 1985; Chm., Gunham, Holdings Ltd, 1985–89; Counsellor, FCO, 1989–92; Consul Gen., Boston, 1992–95; Governor, Cayman Is, 1995–99. Non-executive Director: Scimitar Advrs, 1999–; Queensgate Bank and Trust Co., 2006–. Chairman: British Laminated Plastics Fabricators' Assoc., 1987–90; Isle of Wight Strategic Partnership, 2006–08. Trustee: Grandparents Fedn, 2000– (Dep. Chm., 2002–); Fidelity UK Foundn, 2006–; Fidelity Internat. Foundn, 2007–. Fellow, Univ. of Wales, Aberystwyth, 2006. FCMI. Freeman, City of London, 1978; Liveryman, Loriners' Co., 1978– (Mem., Ct of Assts, 1999–; Master, 2005). DL Isle of Wight, 2007. *Recreations:* walking, art, reading, fly-fishing.

OWEN, Les; *see* Owen, A. L.

OWEN, Lynette Isabel; Copyright Director, Pearson Education Ltd, since 2002; *b* 29 June 1947; *d* of Warwick Jack Burgoyne Owen and Betty Isabel Owen (*née* Drummond). *Educ:* Bedford Coll., London (BA Hons (English) 1968). Rights Asst, CUP, 1968–73; Rights Manager, Pitman Publishing Ltd, 1973–75; N American Sales Manager, Marshall Cavendish, 1975–76; Rights Manager, 1976–87, Rights Dir, 1988–94, Longman Gp UK; Rights and Contracts Dir, Addison Wesley, 1994–98; Rights Dir, Pearson Educn Ltd, 1998–2001. London Internat. Book Fair/British Council Lifetime Achievement Award for contribn to internat. publishing, 2003; (inaugural) Kim Scott Walwyn Prize, 2004. *Publications:* Selling Rights, 1991, 5th edn 2006; Publishing Agreements, contrib. 2nd and 3rd edns, gen. ed. and contrib. 4th edn 1993–7th edn 2007; handbooks on copyright and licensing for Eastern Europe, China, etc; numerous articles in Bookseller, Publishing News, Learned Publishing, etc. *Recreations:* theatre, music, art, reading. *Address:* 147B St Pancras Way, NW1 0SY. *T:* and *Fax:* (020) 7284 0470; *e-mail:* lynette@owen.e–books.org.uk.

OWEN, Michael James; professional footballer, since 2005, and Captain, since 2008, Newcastle United Football Club; *b* 14 Dec. 1979; *s* of Terence Owen and Janette Owen; *m* 2005, Louise Bonsall; one *s* one *d*. *Educ:* Hawarden High Sch.; Idsall Sch.; Lilleshall Sch. of Excellence. Liverpool Football Club, 1996–2004: member, winning team: Worthington Cup, 2001; FA Cup 2001; UEFA Cup, 2001; Charity Shield, 2001; European Super Cup, 2001; player, Real Madrid, 2004–05. Mem., England Football Team, 1998–; mem., World Cup team, 1998, 2002, 2006. Young Player of the Year, PFA, 1998; BBC Sports Personality of the Year, 1998; Ballon d'Or, France Football, 2001. *Publications:* (with Dave Harrison) Michael Owen: in person (autobiog.), 2000; Michael Owen's Soccer Skills, 2000; (with Paul Hayward) Michael Owen: off the record (autobiog.), 2004. *Address:* c/o Wasserman Media Group, 5th Floor, 33 Soho Square, W1D 3QU.

OWEN, Prof. Michael John, PhD; FRCPsych, FMedSci; Professor of Psychological Medicine, and Head, Department of Psychological Medicine, since 1998, Deputy Pro Vice-Chancellor for Research, since 2005, Cardiff University (formerly University of Wales College of Medicine, Cardiff); *b* 24 Nov. 1955; *s* of Dr John Robson Owen and Mary Gillian Owen (*née* Dowsett); *m* 1985, Dr Deborah Cohen; two *s* one *d*. *Educ:* Univ. of Birmingham (BSc Anatomical Studies 1977; PhD Neurosci. 1982; MB ChB 1983). MRCPsych 1987, FRCPsych 1997. University of Wales College of Medicine, Cardiff: Sen. Lectr, Dept of Psychological Medicine and Inst. of Med. Genetics, 1990–95; Prof. of Neuropsychiatric Genetics, 1995–98; Pro Vice-Chancellor for Res., 2001–04; Chm., Div. of Community Specialties, School of Medicine, Cardiff Univ., 2002–05. Hon. Consultant Psychiatrist, Cardiff and Vale NHS Trust, 1990–. FMedSci 1999. *Publications:* (jtly) Seminars in Psychiatric Genetics, 1994; (ed jtly) Psychiatric Genetics and Genomics, 2002; articles on psychiatric genetics and psychiatry. *Recreations:* walking, cycling, reading, sailing, fishing. *Address:* Department of Psychological Medicine, Cardiff University, Henry Wellcome Building for Biomedical Research in Wales, Heath Park, Cardiff CF14 3XN. *T:* (029) 2074 3058, *Fax:* (029) 2074 6554; *e-mail:* owenmj@cardiff.ac.uk.

OWEN, Dr Myrfyn; Director General, Wildfowl and Wetlands Trust, 1992–97; ecological consultant, since 1997; *b* 8 April 1943; *s* of William Owen and Anne Mary Owen; *m* 1967, Lydia Marian Vaughan (*née* Rees); two *d*. *Educ:* Sir Hugh Owen Grammar Sch.; University Coll., Aberystwyth (BSc 1964); Univ. of Leeds (PhD 1967). Wildfowl Trust, later Wildfowl and Wetlands Trust: Ecologist, 1967; Conservation Res. Officer, 1974; Asst Dir (Res.), 1979; Head of Res., 1988; Dir, 1991–92. *Publications:* Wildfowl of Europe, 1976; Wild Geese of the World, 1980; Wildfowl in Great Britain, 1986; Waterfowl Ecology, 1990; numerous scientific papers. *Recreations:* gardening, cookery, cycling, wildlife. *Address:* Woodleigh House, 62 Woodmancote, Dursley, Glos GL11 4AQ. *T:* (01453) 543244.

OWEN, Nicholas David Arundel; Presenter, BBC News, since 2007; *b* 10 Feb. 1947; *m* 1983, Brenda (*née* Firth); one *s* one *d*, and one step *s* one step *d*. Newspaper journalist, 1964–81; BBC TV, 1981–83; Presenter, ITN, 1984–2007. *Publications:* The Brighton Belle, 1972; History of the British Trolleybus, 1974; Diana, The People's Princess, 1997. *Recreations:* reading, walking, golf, bridge. *Address:* BBC News, Television Centre, Wood Lane, W12 7RJ.

OWEN, Patricia, (Mrs Peter Owen); *see* Hodge, P.

OWEN, Peter Francis, CB 1990; Secretary General, Institute of Chartered Accountants in England and Wales, 2002–03 (Executive Director, 1998–2002); *b* 4 Sept. 1940; *s* of Arthur Owen and Violet (*née* Morris); *m* 1963, Ann Preece; one *s* one *d*. *Educ:* The Liverpool Inst.; Liverpool Univ. (BA French). Joined MPBW, 1964; Cabinet Office, 1971–72; Private Sec. to successive Ministers of Housing and Construction, 1972–74; Asst Sec., Housing Policy Review, 1975–77, Local Govt Finance, 1977–80; Under Sec. and Regional Dir of Northern and Yorks and Humberside Regs, Depts of the Environment and of Transport, 1980–82; Under Secretary: Rural Affairs, DoE, 1983; Local Govt Finance Policy, DoE, 1984–86; Dep. Sec., Housing and Construction, DoE, 1986–90; Head of Econ. and Domestic Affairs Secretariat, Cabinet Office, 1990–94; Dep. Sec., Sch. Curriculum and Teachers, DFE, 1994–95; Dir Gen. for Schools, DfEE, 1995–98. *Recreations:* reading, gardening, French, classical guitar. *Address:* Oakmead, The Avenue, Hampton, Middlesex TW12 3RS.

OWEN, Philip W.; *see* Wynn Owen.

OWEN, Richard Wilfred, FCA; retired from Touche Ross, 1993; *b* 26 Oct. 1932; *s* of Wilfred Owen and Ivy (*née* Gamble); *m* 1966, Sheila Marie Kerrigan; three adopted *s* one adopted *d*, and one foster *s* one foster *d*. *Educ:* Gunnersbury Catholic Grammar Sch. Lloyds Bank, 1949–51; RAF Russian translator, 1951–53; accountancy articles, 1953–58; Thomson McLintock, 1958–62; Crompton Parkinson, 1962–64; Touche Ross & Co., Chartered Accountants and Management Consultants, 1964–93: admitted to Partnership, 1969; seconded to Treasury, 1971; Partner-in-Charge, Management Consultancy, 1974–87, Nat. Dir, Personnel, 1987–93; UK Chm., 1988–90; Europ. Dir, Management Consultancy, 1990–92. Pres., Management Consultancies Assoc., 1987. Chm., Cardinal Hume Centre, 1996–2002; Trustee, Isabel Hospice, 1994–2000. KSG 1997. *Address:* 25 Gainsborough House, Frognal Rise, NW3 6PZ.

OWEN, Robert Frank; QC 1996; a Recorder, since 2000; *b* 31 May 1953; *s* of Tudor Owen and Pat Owen; *m* 1980, Anna Shaw; three *s*. *Educ:* Prestatyn High Sch.; Poly. of Central London (LLB Hons). Called to the Bar, Gray's Inn, 1977. *Recreations:* coastal walking, sport. *Address:* 24 The Ropewalk, Nottingham NG1 5EF.

OWEN, Robert John Richard; Chairman, Crosby Asset Management Ltd (formerly Crosby Capital Partners Inc.), since 2002; *b* 11 Feb. 1940; *s* of Richard Owen and Margaret Owen (*née* Fletcher); *m* (marr. diss.); two *s* one *d*; *m* Margaret Helen. *Educ*: Repton School; Oxford University. Foreign Office, 1961–68, incl. HM Embassy, Washington, 1965–68; HM Treasury, 1968–70; Morgan Grenfell & Co., 1970–79 (Dir, 1974); Lloyds Bank International, 1979–85 (Dir); Chm. and Chief Exec., Lloyds Merchant Bank, 1985–88; Comr for Securities, Hong Kong, 1988–89; Chm., Securities and Futures Commn, Hong Kong, 1989–92. Chairman: Techpacific Capital Ltd, 1999–2004; Internat. Securities Consultancy Ltd, 2000–; IB Daiwa Ltd, 2005–; Sen. Advr, Nomura Internat. (Hong Kong) Ltd, 1993–2007; Dep. Chm., Nomura Asia Hldgs Ltd, 1994–97; Director: European Capital Co. Ltd, 1992–2001; Sunday Communications Ltd, 2000–07; Singapore Exchange Ltd, 2004–; Citibank (Hong Kong) Ltd, 2004–; Repton Dubai Ltd, 2007–. Mem. Council and Mem. Regulatory Bd, Lloyd's of London, 1993–95; Bd Mem., Dubai Financial Services Authority, 2002–. Gov., Repton Sch., 1994–. *Recreations*: oriental paintings, mountain walking. *Address*: c/o Crosby Asset Management Ltd, 2701 Citibank Tower, 3 Garden Road, Central, Hong Kong.

OWEN, Hon. Sir Robert (Michael), Kt 2000; **Hon. Mr Justice Owen**; a Judge of the High Court, Queen's Bench Division, since 2001; *b* 19 Sept. 1944; *s* of Gwynne Llewellyn Owen and Phoebe Constance Owen; *m* 1969, Sara Josephine Rumbold; two *s*. *Educ*: Durham Sch.; Exeter Univ. (LLB). Called to Bar, Inner Temple, 1968, Bencher, 1995; QC 1988. Judicial Mem., Transport Tribunal, 1985–97; Recorder, 1987–2000; Dep. High Court Judge, 1994–2000; Presiding Judge, Western Circuit, 2005–08. DTI Inspector, 1991–92. Chm., Gen. Council of the Bar, 1997. Chm., London Common Law and Commercial Bar Assoc., 1994–95. Chairman: vCJD Trust, 2002–; Fowey Harbour Commn Consultative Gp, 2006–. Gov., Coll. of Law, 1998–2004. FRSA 1997. Hon. LLD Exeter, 2007. *Address*: Royal Courts of Justice, Strand, WC2A 2LL. *T*: (020) 7797 7500. *Clubs*: Travellers, Les Six; Royal Yacht Squadron.

OWEN, (Samuel) Griffith, CBE 1977; MD, FRCP; Second Secretary, Medical Research Council, 1968–82, retired; *b* 3 Sept. 1925; *e s* of late Rev. Evan Lewis Owen and of Marjorie Lawton; *m* 1954, Ruth, *e d* of late Merle W. Tate, Philadelphia, Pa, USA; two *s* two *d*. *Educ*: Dame Allen's Sch.; Durham Univ. (MB, BS Dunelm 1948; MD 1954). MRCP 1951, FRCP 1965. Clinical and research appts at Royal Victoria Infirmary, Newcastle upon Tyne, 1948–49 and 1950–53; RAMC, SMO, HM Troopships, 1949–50; Med. Registrar, Nat. Heart Hosp., 1953–54; Instr in Pharmacology, Univ. of Pennsylvania Sch. of Med., 1954–56; Reader in Med., Univ. of Newcastle upon Tyne, 1964–68 (First Asst, 1956, Lectr, 1960, Sen. Lectr, 1961); Hon. Cons. Physician, Royal Victoria Infirmary, Newcastle upon Tyne, 1960–68; Clin. Sub-Dean of Med. Sch., Univ. of Newcastle upon Tyne, 1966–68 (Academic Sub-Dean, 1964–66); Examr in Med., Univ. of Liverpool, 1966–68; Examr in Membership, RCP, 1967–68 and Mem., Research Cttee, RCP, 1968–76; Member: Brit. Cardiac Soc., 1962–82; Assoc. of Physicians of GB, 1965–; European Molec. Biol. Conf., 1971–82; European Molec. Biol. Lab., 1974–82; Exec. Council, European Science Foundn, 1974–78; Comité de la Recherche Médicale et de la Santé Publique, EEC, 1977–82; Scientific Coordinating Cttee, Arthritis and Rheumatism Council, 1978–82; NW Thames RHA, 1978–82. Consultant to WHO, SE Asia, 1966 and 1967–68; Commonwealth Fund Fellow, Univ. of Illinois, 1966; Fellow, Hunterian Soc., 1978. Chm., Feldberg Foundn, 1974–78; Governor, Queen Charlotte's Hosp. for Women, 1979–82. Liveryman, Soc. of Apothecaries, 1976–. *Publications*: Essentials of Cardiology, 1961 (2nd edn 1968); Electrocardiography, 1966 (2nd edn 1973); contribs to med. jls on heart disease, cerebral circulation, thyroid disease, med. research, etc. *Recreations*: gastronomy, music, theatre. *Address*: Flat 17, 9 Devonhurst Place, Heathfield Terrace, Chiswick, W4 4JB. *T*: (020) 8995 3228. *Club*: Royal Society of Medicine.

OWEN, Susan Jane; Director General for Corporate Performance, Department for International Development, since 2006; *b* 3 June 1955; *d* of Glyn and Diana Owen; *m* 1987, Prof. Martin C. Albrow; one *s*. *Educ*: Lady Eleanor Holles Sch.; Newnham Coll., Cambridge (MA); University Coll. Cardiff (MSc Econ. 1977). Lectr, UC Cardiff, 1979–88; HM Treasury: Econ. Advr, 1989–95; Asst Sec./Grade 5, EU Co-ordination, 1995–98; on secondment: Econ. Advr, Work/Family Balance Policy, No 10 Policy Unit, 1998–99; Econ. Counsellor, Washington, 1999–2002; Dir, EMU Policy, Euro Preparations and Debt Mgt, 2002–05; Dir of Ops, 2005. *Publications*: contrib. articles to jls incl. Fiscal Studies, Work, Employment and Society, Jl Labour Economics. *Recreations*: family, friends, cooking, gardening. *Address*: Department for International Development, 1 Palace Street, SW1E 5HE. *T*: (020) 7023 0417. *Club*: Everton Football.

OWEN, Tim Wynn; QC 2000; a Recorder, since 2004; *b* 11 Jan. 1958; *s* of Meurig Wynn Owen and Thelma Owen (*née* Parry); *m* 1992, Jemma Redgrave; two *s*. *Educ*: Atlantic Coll.; London Sch. of Economics (BA 1st Cl. Hons History 1979); PCL (Dip. Law 1982). Campaign Co-ordinator, Radical Alternatives to Prison, 1979–81; called to the Bar, Middle Temple, 1983 (Bencher, 2005); in practice at the Bar, 1984–; called to the Bar of Antigua and Barbuda, 1994. *Publication*: (jtly) Prison Law, 1993, 3rd edn 2003. *Recreations*: film, travel. *Address*: Matrix Chambers, Griffin Building, Gray's Inn, WC1R 5LN. *T*: (020) 7404 3447.

OWEN, Trevor Bryan, CBE 1987; Chairman: Bethlem Royal and Maudsley Special Health Authority, 1988–94; Committee of Management, Institute of Psychiatry, 1990–97; *b* 3 April 1928; *s* of Leonard Owen, CIE and Dilys (*née* Davies Bryan); *m* 1955, (Jennifer) Gaie (*née* Houston); one *s* one *d*. *Educ*: Rugby Sch.; Trinity Coll., Oxford (Scholar; MA). Sch. Student, British Sch. of Archaeology, Athens, 1953–54; ICI, 1955–78: wide range of jobs culminating in, successively: Chm., J. P. MacDougall Ltd; Dir, Paints, Agricl and Plastics Divs; Co. Personnel Manager; Man. Dir, Remploy Ltd, 1978–88. Member: Higher Educn Review Gp, Govt of NI, 1979–81; CNAA, 1973–79; Continuing Educn Adv. Council, BBC, 1977–85; Council, CBI, 1982–88; Council, Industrial Soc., 1967–88; Council, Inst. of Manpower Studies, 1975–88 (Chm., 1977–78); Chm. Bd of Governors, Nat. Inst. for Social Work, 1985–91 (Mem., 1982–97; Mem., Working Party on Role and Tasks of Social Workers, 1981–82); Chm., Phab, 1988–91. *Publications*: Business School Programmes—the requirements of British manufacturing industry (with D. Casey and N. Huskisson), 1971; Making Organisations Work, 1978; The Manager and Industrial Relations, 1979; articles in jls. *Address*: 8 Rochester Terrace, NW1 9JN.

OWEN, Tudor Wyn, FRAeS; **His Honour Judge Owen**; a Circuit Judge, since 2007; *b* Aberdare, Glamorgan, 16 May 1951; *s* of late Abel Rhys Owen and Mair Owen (*née* Jenkins); *m* (marr. diss.). *Educ*: Aberdare Boys Grammar Sch.; King's Coll. London (LLB Hons 1973); Council of Legal Educn. Called to the Bar, Gray's Inn, 1974; in practice on SE Circuit, 1975–2007; DTI Inspector, 1987; Asst Recorder, 1990–93; Recorder, 1993–2007. Mem., SE Circuit Cttee, 1994–97. General Council of the Bar: Mem., 1988–94; Member: Bar Professional Conduct Cttee, 1989–91; Bar Professional Standards Cttee, 1991–93; Gen. Mgt Cttee, 1992–94; Vice-Chm., Bar Cttee, 1991–92. Mem., Criminal Bar Assoc. (Mem. Cttee, 1986–92; Treas., 1989–92). Panel Mem., Bar Disciplinary Tribunals, 1995–2007. Mem. Adv. Gp, Judicial Appts Commn, 2008–. UK

delegate to European Air Sports, 2005–06. FRAeS 2003. Freeman, City of London, 2004; Liveryman, GAPAN, 2005 (Mem. Court, 2006–). *Recreations*: flying helicopters and WWII aeroplanes, racing historic Formula 1 cars, riding the Cresta Run (St Moritz). *Address*: Chelsea, SW3; *e-mail*: HHJudge.TudorOwen@judiciary.gsi.gov.uk. *Clubs*: Garrick, Royal Air Force, Royal Aero; St Moritz Tobogganing.

OWEN, Ursula Margaret, OBE 2004; Editor and Chief Executive, Index on Censorship, since 1993; *b* 21 Jan. 1937; *d* of Emma Sophie Sachs (*née* Boehm) and Werner Sachs; *m* 1960, Edward Roger John Owen (marr. diss.); one *d*. *Educ*: Putney High Sch.; St Hugh's Coll., Oxford (BA Hons Physiol.); Bedford Coll., London (Dip. Soc. Studies). Lectr, English Lang., Amer. Univ. in Cairo, 1962–63; research work in mental health and physical disabilities, 1964–67; Editor, Frank Cass, 1971–73; Sen. Editor, Barrie & Jenkins, 1973–75; Virago Press: Co-founder, 1974; Editl Dir, 1974–90; Jt Man. Dir, 1982–90; Dir, Paul Hamlyn Fund, 1990–92. Cultural Policy Advr to Lab. Party, 1990–92. Dir, New Statesman and Society, 1983–90. Chm., Educn Extra, 1993–2002; Mem., Royal Literary Fund Cttee, 1989–94. Mem. Bd, English Touring Opera, 2007–. Governor: Parliament Hill School, 1991–93; South Bank Centre, 2003–. *Publications*: (ed) Fathers: Reflections by Daughters, 1983; (ed with Mark Fisher) Whose Cities?, 1991. *Recreations*: music, reading, film, travel. *Address*: Index, 6–8 Amwell Street, EC1R 1UQ. *T*: (020) 7278 2313. *Club*: Groucho.

OWEN-JONES, Sir Lindsay Harwood, KBE 2005 (CBE 2000); non-executive Chairman, L'Oréal, since 2006 (Chairman and Chief Executive Officer, 1988–2006); *b* 17 March 1946; *s* of Hugh A. Owen-Jones and Esmee Owen-Jones (*née* Lindsay); *m*; one *d*; *m* 1994, Cristina Furno. *Educ*: Worcester Coll., Oxford (BA; Hon. Fellow, 2006); European Inst. of Business Admin. Product Manager, L'Oréal, 1969; Head, Public Products Div., Belgium, 1971–74; Manager, SCAD (L'Oréal subsid.), Paris, 1974–76; Marketing Manager, Public Products Div., Paris, 1976–78; Gen. Manager, SAIPO (L'Oréal subsid.), Italy, 1978–81; Pres., 1981–83, Chm., 1991–, COSMAIR (L'Oreal agent), USA; Vice-Pres., L'Oréal Man. Cttee and Mem. Bd of Dirs, 1984; Pres. and Chief Operating Officer, 1984–88. Director: Air Liquide, 1994–; Sanofi-Aventis, 1999–; Ferrari, 2005–. Commandeur, Légion d'Honneur (France), 2005 (Officier, 1998). Hon. DSc Cranfield Sch. of Mgt, 2001. *Recreation*: private helicopter pilot. *Address*: L'Oréal, 41 rue Martre, 92117 Clichy, France. *T*: 47567000.

OWENS, Ann Rosemarie; see Easter, A. R.

OWENS, Prof. David Howard, PhD; Professor and Head of Department of Automatic Control and Systems Engineering, University of Sheffield, since 1999; *b* 23 April 1948; *s* of Maurice Owens and Joan Owens; *m* 1969, Rosemary Frost; one *s* one *d*. *Educ*: Imperial Coll., London (BSc 1st Cl. Hons Phys 1969; PhD 1973). CEng 1976; FIET (FIEE 1976); FIMechE 2001; CMath 1979; FIMA 1979. SO, UKAEA Winfrith, 1969–73; Lectr, Sen. Lectr, then Reader, Dept of Control Engrg, Univ. of Sheffield, 1973–84; Prof. of Engrg Maths, 1984–87; Prof. of Mechanical Engrg, 1987–90; Strathclyde Univ.; Prof. and Hd, Sch. of Engrg and Computer Sci., Univ. of Exeter, 1990–99; Dean of Engrg and Convener of Deans, Univ. of Sheffield, 2002–06. Dir and Chm., Exeter Enterprises Ltd, 1995–99; Dir, Iter8 Control Systems, 2007–. Chm., UK Automatic Control Council, 1999–2002; Ind. Mem., Nuclear Safety Adv. Cttee, HSE, 1995–2006. Freeman, Co. of Cutlers in Hallamshire, 2007. *Publications*: Feedback and Multivariable Systems, 1979; Multivariable and Optimal Systems, 1981; Analysis and Control of Multipass Processes, 1982; Stability Analysis for Linear Repetitive Processes, 1992; Control Systems Theory and Applications for Linear Repetitive Processes, 2007; over 500 technical articles in areas of control and systems engrg. *Recreations*: reading, guitar, entertaining. *Address*: Department of Automatic Control and Systems Engineering, University of Sheffield, Mappin Street, Sheffield S1 3JD. *T*: (0114) 222 5134, *Fax*: (0114) 222 5661; *e-mail*: d.h.owens@sheffield.ac.uk.

OWENS, Prof. Ian Peter Farrar, PhD; Professor of Evolutionary Ecology, since 2004, Deputy Director, NERC Centre for Population Biology, since 2004, and Head, Department of Life Sciences, since 2007, Imperial College London; *b* Sutton Coldfield, 1967; *s* of Peter and Sheila Owens; *m* 1992, Sally Ann Gibbins; two *s*. *Educ*: Univ. of Liverpool (BSc Zoology 1989); Univ. of Leicester (PhD Evolutionary Biol. 1992). Natural Hist. Mus. Scholar, Ornithological Section, Natural Hist. Mus., Tring, 1987; NERC Student, Univ. of Leicester, 1989–91; NERC Postdoctoral Res. Fellow, Inst. of Zool., Zool Soc. of London and UCL, 1992–95; Lectr in Ecol., 1995–98, Sen. Lectr in Ecol., 1998–2000, Univ. of Queensland; Imperial College London: Governors' Lectr in Biol., 2000–02; Reader in Evolutionary Ecol., Silwood Park, 2003–04; Hd, Ecol. and Evolution Section, 2006–; Hd, Div. of Biol., 2006–. Member: NERC Peer Rev. Coll., 2002–07; NERC Steering Panel on Post-genomics and proteomics, 2004–; DEFRA Peer Rev. Panel, 2006–. Ed., Behavioral Ecology, 2001–07; Member, Editorial Board: Jl of Evolutionary Biology, 2001–06; Series B Biol Scis, Procs of Royal Soc., 2002–08; Ecology Letters, 2003–06; BMC Evolutionary Biology, 2006–; BMC Ecology, 2006–. External Examiner: Univ. of Lancaster, 2005–08; UEA, 2007–09. Hon. Res. Fellow, Inst. of Zool., Zool. Soc. of London, 2004. Scientific Medal, Zool. Soc. of London, 2005. *Publications*: Evolutionary Ecology of Birds: life histories, mating systems and extinction (with P. M. Bennett), 2002; approx. 100 articles in scientific jls on ecology, evolution, animal behaviour and biodiversity. *Recreations*: bird watching, natural history, walking. *Address*: Department of Life Sciences, Imperial College London, Silwood Park Campus, Ascot, Berks SL5 7PY. *T*: (020) 7594 2215, *Fax*: (020) 7594 2339; *e-mail*: i.owens@imperial.ac.uk.

OWENS, John Ridland; Chairman: Owens Associates, independent consultancy specialising in strategic advice and government relations, 1993–2002; *b* 21 May 1932; *s* of Dr Ridland Owens and late Elsie Owens; *m* 1st, 1958, Susan Lilian (*née* Pilcher); two *s* one *d*; 2nd, 1985, Cynthia Rose (*née* Forbes); one *s*. *Educ*: Merchant Taylors' Sch.; St John's Coll., Oxford (MA). National Service, RA (Lieut), 1951–52. ICI, 1955–67; Managing Dir, Cape Asbestos Fibres, 1967–73; Dir Gen., Dairy Trade Fedn, 1973–83; Dep. Chm., Assilec, Paris, 1973–83; Exec. Dir, Nat. Dairy Council, 1975–83; Dep. Dir Gen., CBI, 1983–90; Dir Gen., Building Employers Confederation, 1990–92; Dir, UK Skills Ltd, 1990–92. Chm., Haringey Healthcare NHS Trust, 1993–99. Vice-Chm., EEC Adv. Cttee on Milk and Milk Products; Member: Food and Drink Industry Council, 1973–83; RSA Industry Cttee for Industry Year, 1986; Council, Assoc. of Business Sponsorship of the Arts, 1985–94; Exec. Cttee, PRO NED, 1983–90; Council, CBI, 1990–92; NHS Supplies Policy Steering Gp, 1995–97; Mem. Trust Council, 1995–97, Chm., Procurement and Facilities Mgt Gp, 1995–97, NAHAT, then NHS Confedn. Member: Council, CGLI, 1988–93; Court, City Univ., 1988–2005. Founder: Stokesley Soc.; Civic Trust for NE; Nat. Mus. of Dairying. FRSA (Mem. Council, 1995–2001). Mem. Court, Merchant Taylors' Co., 1982 (Master, 2002–03, First Upper Warden, 2007–08); Freeman, Painter Stainers' Co., 2005. Governor: Merchant Taylors' Sch., 1996–2005 (Vice-Chm. Govs, 1999–2005); Middx Univ., 1999–2002. Mem., Armed Forces Art Soc., 2005–. Practising painter-etcher. *Publications*: Marketing for the NHS—Putting Patients First,

1993; Strategic Procurement for the NHS: working with suppliers, 1996; articles for The Times Review of Industry. *Recreations:* painting, etching, walking. *Club:* Reform.

OWENS, Matthew, FRCO; Organist and Master of the Choristers, Wells Cathedral, since 2005; *b* 17 Jan. 1971; *s* of John Duncan Owens and Brenda Owens; *m* 2004, Alison Darragh. *Educ:* Chetham's Sch. of Music, Manchester; Queen's Coll., Oxford (BA Hons Music 1992); Royal Northern Coll. of Music (MusM 1994; PPRNCM 1994); Sweelinck Conservatorium, Amsterdam. FRCO 1994. Sub organist, Manchester Cathedral, 1996–99; Organist and Master of Music, St Mary's Episcopal Cathedral, Edinburgh, 1999–2004. Asst and Associate Dir, Nat. Youth Choir, 1993–2000; Organist, Musical Dir and Singer, BBC Daily Service, 1994–99; Artistic Dir and Conductor, Exon Singers, 1997–; Conductor, Wells Cathedral Oratorio Soc., 2005–. Tutor in Organ Studies: Chetham's Sch. of Music, 1994–99; RNCM, 1995–2000; Wells Cathedral Sch., 2006–. *Publications:* educational articles, and reviews in Organists' Rev., Choir and Organ. *Recreations:* reading, concerts, opera, cooking, travel, film, art, politics, chess, badminton, waving to cows. *Address:* c/o Wells Cathedral Music Office, Chain Gate, Cathedral Green, Wells, Somerset BA5 2UE. *T:* (01749) 674483; *e-mail:* musicoffice@wellscathedral.uk.net.

OWENS, Prof. Nicholas John Paul, PhD; CBiol; Director, British Antarctic Survey, since 2007; *b* 17 Jan. 1954; *s* of Michael John Joseph Benedict Owens and Christine Mary Theresa Owens; *m* 1982, Susan Mary Forster; four *s*. *Educ:* Univ. of Liverpool (BSc 1976); Univ. of Dundee (PhD 1981). MIBiol, CBiol 1983. Res. Scientist, Inst. for Marine Envmtl Res., 1979–92; University of Newcastle: Prof. of Marine Sci., 1992–2000; Hd, Dept of Marine Scis and Coastal Mgt, 1993–99; Dir, NERC Plymouth Marine Lab., 2000–07. Bd Dir, PML (formerly Plymouth Marine) Applications Ltd, 2001–07. Trustee, Nat. Marine Aquarium, 2002–. Hon. Prof., Univ. of Plymouth, 2006–. *Publications:* over 80 articles in learned marine sci. jls. *Recreations:* game fishing, yachting, running, mountaineering, gardening. *Address:* British Antarctic Survey, High Cross, Madingley Road, Cambridge CB3 0ET. *T:* (01223) 221524, *Fax:* (01223) 350456; *e-mail:* n.owens@bas.ac.uk.

OWENS, Prof. Susan Elizabeth, OBE 1998; Professor of Environment and Policy, Department of Geography, University of Cambridge, since 2004; Fellow of Newnham College, Cambridge, since 1981; *b* 24 Jan. 1954; *d* of Alfred Raymond Penrose and Patricia Mary Penrose (*née* Dorrell); *m* 1976. *Educ:* Stevenage Girls' Sch.; Univ. of East Anglia (BSc Hons, PhD). Res. Officer, Energy Panel, SSRC, 1979; Res. Fellow, Inst. of Planning Studies, Univ. of Nottingham, 1980–81; University of Cambridge: Asst Lectr in Geography, 1981–86; Lectr, 1986–2000; Reader in Envmt and Policy, 2000–04. Global Envmtl Change Programme Res. Fellow, ESRC, 1993–94. Member: UK Round Table on Sustainable Develt, 1995–98; Countryside Commn, 1996–99; Govt Adv. Panel on Integrated Transport Policy, 1997–98; Royal Commn on Envmtl Pollution, 1998–2008 (Special Advr, 1992–94); Steering Panel for OST review of Sci. in DEFRA, 2005–06; Strategic Res. Bd, ESRC, 2007–; Chm., Governance Working Gp, European Envmtl and Sustainability Adv. Councils, 2003–06. Mem., sub-panel H31, Town and Country Planning, 2008 RAE. AcSS 2002. Hon. MRTPI 2006. Back Award, RGS (with IBG), 2000. *Publications:* Energy, Planning and Urban Form, 1986; (jtly) Environment, Resources and Conservation, 1990; (ed jtly) Britain's Changing Environment from the Air, 1991; (jtly) Land Use Planning Policy and Climate Change, 1992; (jtly) Land and Limits: interpreting sustainability in the planning process, 2002; contrib. learned jls, incl. Trans Inst. of British Geographers, Land Use Policy, Town Planning Review, Political Qly, Jl of Risk Res., Envmt and Planning A, Govt and Policy (Envmt and Planning C), Envmtl Conservation, European Envmt. *Recreations:* walking, literature. *Address:* Department of Geography, University of Cambridge, Downing Place, Cambridge CB2 3EN. *T:* (01223) 333362, 333399.

OWER, Dr David Cheyne, TD 1975; Senior Principal Medical Officer, Department of Health and Social Security, 1976–87; *b* 29 July 1931; *s* of Ernest Ower and Helen Edith Cheyne (*née* Irvine); *m* 1954, June Harris; two *s* two *d*. *Educ:* King's Coll. Sch., Wimbledon; King's Coll., London; King's Coll. Hosp. Med. Sch. (MB, BS 1954). DObstRCOG 1959; FFPH (FFCM 1983; MFCM 1976). Jun. hosp. appts, King's Coll. Hosp. and Kingston Hosp., 1955; RAF Med. Br., 1956–58; gen. practice, 1959–64; DHSS (formerly Min. of Health) Med. Staff, 1965–87. T&AVR, and RAMC(V), 1962–; Lt-Col RAMC(V); CO 221 (Surrey) Field Amb., 1973–75. *Recreations:* music, bridge, thinking about playing golf. *Address:* 15 North Street, Winchcombe, Cheltenham, Glos GL54 5LH. *T:* (01242) 603379.

OWERS, Anne Elizabeth, CBE 2001; HM Chief Inspector of Prisons for England and Wales, since 2001; *b* 23 June 1947; *d* of William Spark and Anne Smailes Spark (*née* Knox); *m* 1st, 1968 (marr. diss.); two *s* one *d*; 2nd, 2005, Edmund Stephen Cook. *Educ:* Washington Grammar Sch., Co. Durham; Girton Coll., Cambridge (BA Hons 1968). Research and teaching in Zambia, 1968–71; work at JCWI, 1981–92 (Gen. Sec., 1986–92); Dir, Justice, 1992–2001. Chm. Bd of Trustees, Refugee Legal Centre, 1994–98; Member: Lord Chancellor's Adv. Cttee on Legal Educn and Conduct, 1997–99; Home Office Task Force on Human Rights, 1999–2001; Legal Services Consultative Panel, 2000–01. Chm., Christian Aid, 2008–. Hon. Fellow: South Bank Univ., 2005; Lucy Cavendish Coll., Cambridge, 2007. DUniv Essex, 2006. *Publications:* (ed jtly) Economic, Social and Cultural Rights, 1999; chapters and papers on immigration and nationality matters and on prisons. *Recreations:* music, walking, friends, family. *Address:* HM Inspectorate of Prisons, 1st Floor, Ashley House, 2 Monck Street, SW1P 2BQ.

OWUSU, Elsie Margaret Akua, OBE 2003; RIBA; Founder and Principal, Elsie Owusu Architects, since 1989; Partner, Feilden & Mawson LLP, architects, since 2006; *b* 9 Dec. 1953; *d* of Paul Kofi Owusu and Joyce Ophelia Owusu; one *d*. *Educ:* Demonstration Sch., Legon, Ghana; Streatham Hill and Clapham Girls' High Sch.; Architectural Association Sch. of Architecture. RIBA 1989. Design Team, Solon SE Housing Assoc., 1981–85; Women's Design Service, 1985–86; in private practice, Owusu and Teague, 1986–89. Founder Member: Soc. of Black Architects, 1990 (first Chm., 1990–92); Black Internat. Construction Orgn, 1996–; Sec., Fedn of Black Housing Orgns, 1994–96 (Mem., Exec. Cttee, 1994–96); Member: Educnl Vis. Bd, RIBA, 1995–96; Haringey Employment Commn, 1996–97; Trafalgar Square Plinth Cttee, 1999–2000; Building Regulations Adv. Cttee, 2001–03; Enabling Panel, CABE, 2002–; Board Member: Arts Council of England, subseq. Arts Council England, 2002–; NT, 2002–04. Acting Chair, Aduna, 2006–. Vice-Pres., Women's Transport Seminar, 2005. Member: Bd of Governors, Middlesex Univ., 1996–2000; Corp., Coll. of NE London, 1996–2001. FRSA. *Recreations:* reading, walking, drawing, dreaming. *Address:* 30 Chalfont Court, Baker Street, NW1 5RS. *T:* (020) 7387 3767, *Fax:* (020) 7387 1449.

OXBURGH, family name of **Baron Oxburgh**.

OXBURGH, Baron *cr* 1999 (Life Peer), of Liverpool in the county of Merseyside; **Ernest Ronald Oxburgh,** KBE 1992; PhD; FRS 1978; Chairman: D1 Oils plc, since 2007; 2OC, since 2007; Rector, Imperial College of Science, Technology and Medicine, 1993–2001; *b* 2 Nov. 1934; *m* Ursula Mary Brown; one *s* two *d*. *Educ:* Liverpool Inst.; University Coll., Oxford (BA 1957, MA 1960); Univ. of Princeton (PhD 1960). Departmental Demonstrator, 1960–61, Lectr in Geology, 1962–78, Univ. of Oxford; Fellow of St Edmund Hall, Oxford, 1964–78, Emeritus Fellow, 1978, Hon. Fellow, 1986; University of Cambridge: Prof. of Mineralogy and Petrology, 1978–91; Hd of Dept of Earth Scis, 1980–88; Fellow of Trinity Hall, 1978–82, Hon. Fellow, 1983; Queens' College: Pres., 1982–89; Professorial Fellow, 1989–91; Hon. Fellow, 1992; Chief Scientific Advr, MoD, 1988–93. Chm., Shell Transport & Trading plc, 2004–05. Chm., SETNET, 2001–05. Visiting Professor: CIT, 1967–68; Stanford and Cornell Univs, 1973–74; Sherman Fairchild Distinguished Vis. Scholar, CIT, 1985–86. Trustee, Natural History Mus., 1993–2002 (Chm. Trustees, 1999–2002). Chm., H of L Select Cttee on Sci. and Technol., 2001–05. Member: SERC, 1988–93; Hong Kong UGC, 1988–2002; Nat. Cttee of Inquiry into Higher Educn (Dearing Cttee), 1996–97. President: Eur. Union of Geosciences, 1985–87 (Hon. Fellow 1993); BAAS, 1995–96; Carbon Capture and Storage Assoc., 2005–. FGS (Pres., 2000–02); Fellow: Geol. Soc. of America; Amer. Geophys. Union. Hon. Mem., Geologists' Assoc.; Foreign Corresp., Geologische Bundesanstalt, Austria and of Geological Soc. of Vienna; Foreign Member: Venezuelan Acad. of Scis, 1992; Deutsche Akad. der Naturforscher Leopoldina, 1994; Corresp. Mem., Australian Acad. of Sci., 1999; For. Associate, US Acad. of Scis, 2001. FIC 2003. Hon. FIMechE 1993; Hon. FCGI 1996; Hon FREng 2000. Hon. Fellow, Univ. Coll., Oxford, 1983. DSc (*hc*): Univ. of Paris, 1986; Leicester, 1990; Loughborough, 1991; Edinburgh, 1994; Birmingham, 1996; Liverpool, 1996; Southampton, 2003; Liverpool John Moores, 2006; Lingnan, Hong Kong, 2006; Newcastle upon Tyne, 2007. Bigsby Medal, Geol Soc., 1979. Officier, Ordre des Palmes Académiques (France), 1995. *Publications:* contribs to Nature, Jl Geophys Res., Phil Trans Royal Soc., Annual Reviews, Science, Bull. Geol Soc. America, Jl Fluid Mechanics, Jl Geol Soc. London. *Recreations:* mountaineering, orienteering, reading, theatre. *Address:* c/o House of Lords, SW1A 0PW.

OXENBURY, Helen Gillian; children's writer and illustrator; *b* Suffolk, 2 June 1938; *d* of Thomas Bernard Oxenbury and Muriel (*née* Taylor); *m* 1964, John Burningham, *qv*; one *s* two *d*. *Educ:* Ipswich Sch. of Art; Central Sch. of Art. Stage designer, Colchester, 1960, Tel-Aviv, 1961; TV designer, London, 1963. *Publications: author and illustrator:* Number of Things, 1967; ABC of Things, 1971; Pig Tale, 1973; (with F. Maschler) A Child's Book of Manners: Verses, 1978; The Queen and Rosie Randall, 1979; 729 Curious Creatures, 1980; 729 Merry Mixips, 1980; 729 Puzzle People, 1980; 729 Animal Allsorts, 1980; Crazy Creatures, 1980; Assorted Animals, 1980; Bill and Stanley, 1981; Bedtime, 1982; Monkey See, Monkey Do, 1982; Holidays, 1982; Helping, 1982; Mother's Helper, 1982; Animals, 1982; Beach Day, 1982; Shopping Trip, 1982; Good Night, Good Morning, 1982; The Birthday Party, 1983; The Dancing Class, 1983; Eating Out, 1983; The Car Trip, 1983; The Drive, 1983; The Checkup, 1983; First Day of School, 1983; First Day at Playschool, 1983; Playschool, 1983; Grandma and Grandpa, 1984; Our Dog, 1984; The Important Visitor, 1984; Helen Oxenbury Nursery Story Book, 1985; Tom and Pippo Go Shopping, 1988; Tom and Pippo's Day, 1988; Tom and Pippo in the Garden, 1988; Tom and Pippo Go for a Walk, 1988; Tom and Pippo Make a Mess, 1988; Tom and Pippo Read a Story, 1988; Tom and Pippo See the Moon, 1988; Tom and Pippo and the Washing Machine, 1988; Pippo Gets Lost, 1989; Tom and Pippo and the Dog, 1989; Tom and Pippo in the Snow, 1989; Tom and Pippo Make a Friend, 1989; Tom and Pippo on the Beach, 1993; It's My Birthday, 1994; First Nursery Stories, 1994; *illustrator:* The Great Big Enormous Turnip, 1968; The Quangle-Wangle's Hat, 1969; Letters of Thanks, 1969; The Dragon of an Ordinary Family, 1969; The Hunting of the Snark, 1970; Meal One, 1971; Cakes and Custard: Children's Rhymes, 1974; Balooky Klujypop, 1975; Animal House, 1976; Tiny Tim: Verses for Children, 1981; We're Going on a Bear Hunt, 1989; Farmer Duck, 1992; The Three Little Wolves and The Big Bad Pig, 1993; So Much, 1994; Alice in Wonderland, 1999; Franny B. Kranny, 2001; Big Momma Makes the World, 2002; Alice Through the Looking Glass, 2005. *Address:* c/o Greene and Heaton Ltd, 37 Goldhawk Road, W12 8QQ.

OXENBURY, Dame Shirley (Ann), DBE 1992 (OBE 1987); Personal Assistant to Rt Hon. Christopher Patten, 1997–2000; *b* 4 July 1936. *Educ:* Ensham County Sch., London, SW17. PA to Harold Fielding, 1965–70; Personal Assistant (at Conservative Central Office) to Chairman of the Conservative Party: Katharine Macmillan, Sara Morrison, Baroness Young, 1970–75; Lord Thorneycroft, 1975–81; Cecil Parkinson, 1981–83; John Gummer, 1983–85; Norman Tebbit, 1985–87; Peter Brooke, 1987–89; Kenneth Baker, 1989–90; Christopher Patten, 1990–92; Norman Fowler, 1992–94; Jeremy Hanley, 1994–95; Brian Mawhinney, 1995–97. Women's Transport Service (FANY), 1979–87. *Recreations:* tennis, swimming, arts, learning languages. *T:* (020) 7798 8316.

OXFORD, Bishop of, since 2007; **Rt Rev. John Lawrence Pritchard;** *b* 22 April 1948; *s* of late Rev. Canon Neil Lawrence Pritchard and Winifred Mary Coverdale (*née* Savill); *m* 1972, Susan Wendy Claridge; two *d*. *Educ:* St Peter's Coll., Oxford (MA (Law) 1973; Hon. Fellow, 2007); St John's Coll., Durham (MLitt (Theol.) 1993). Ordained deacon, 1972, priest, 1973; Asst Curate, St Martin's-in-the Bull Ring, Birmingham, 1972–76; Diocesan Youth Chaplain and Asst Dir of Educn, dio. of Bath and Wells, 1976–80; Vicar, St George's, Wilton, Taunton, 1980–88; Dir of Pastoral Studies, 1989–93, Warden, 1993–96, Cranmer Hall, St John's Coll., Durham; Archdeacon of Canterbury, 1996–2001; Bishop Suffragan of Jarrow, 2002–07. Member: Gen. Synod of C of E, 1999–2001, 2007–; Bd, Church Army, 2003–; Min. Council, 2008–. Bishops' Inspector, 1999–2004. Pres., St John's Coll., Durham, 2008–. Pres., Guild of Health, 2003. *Publications:* Practical Theology in Action, 1996; The Intercessions Handbook, 1997; Beginning Again, 2000; Living the Gospel Stories Today, 2001; How to Pray, 2002; The Second Intercessions Handbook, 2004; Living Easter through the Year, 2005; Leading Intercessions, 2005; How to Explain your Faith, 2006; The Life and Work of a Priest, 2007. *Recreations:* photography, walking, travel, music, cricket, reading. *Address:* Diocesan Church House, North Hinksey Lane, Oxford OX2 0NB. *T:* (01865) 208222; *e-mail:* bishopoxon@oxford.anglican.org.

OXFORD, Archdeacon of; *see* Hubbard, Ven. J. R. H.

OXFORD AND ASQUITH, 2nd Earl of, *cr* 1925; **Julian Edward George Asquith,** KCMG 1964 (CMG 1961); Viscount Asquith, *cr* 1925; Governor and Commander-in-Chief, Seychelles, 1962–67; Commissioner, British Indian Ocean Territory, 1965–67; *b* 22 April 1916; *o s* of late Raymond Asquith and Katharine Frances (*d* 1976), *d* of late Sir John Horner, KCVO; *S* grandfather, 1928; *m* 1947, Anne Mary Celestine, CStJ (*d* 1998), *d* of late Sir Michael Palairet, KCMG; two *s* three *d*. *Educ:* Ampleforth; Balliol Coll., Oxford (Scholar), 1st Class Lit. Hum., 1938. Lieut, RE, 1941; Assistant District Commissioner, Palestine, 1942–48; Dep. Chief Secretary, British Administration, Tripolitania, 1949; Director of the Interior, Government of Tripolitania, 1951; Adviser to Prime Minister of Libya, 1952; Administrative Secretary, Zanzibar, 1955; Administrator of St Lucia, WI, 1958. KStJ. *Heir: s* Viscount Asquith, *qv*. *Address:* The Manor House, Mells, Frome, Somerset BA11 3PN. *T:* (01373) 812324. *Club:* Naval and Military.

See also Hon. D. A. G. Asquith, Baron Hylton.

OXFUIRD, 14th Viscount of, *cr* 1651; **Ian Arthur Alexander Makgill**, MA; Bt 1627 (NS); Lord Makgill of Cousland, 1651; Director, Ticon UK Ltd, management consultancy; *b* 14 Oct. 1969; *s* of 13th Viscount of Oxfuird, CBE and of Alison Campbell, *e d* of Neils Max Jensen, Randers, Denmark; *S* father, 2003. *Educ:* Canford Sch., Wimborne; Univ. of Plymouth (BA Hons Media); Univ. of Middlesex (MA Design for Computer Media). Project manager for business to consumer IT projects for Axon and Tesco; started mgt consultancy firm for public sector, Ticon UK Ltd, 2003. *Recreations:* boxing, ski-ing, contemporary art. *Heir:* twin *b* Hon. Robert Edward George Makgill, *b* 14 Oct. 1969. *Address:* 28b Prince of Wales Mansions, Prince of Wales Drive, Battersea, SW11 4BQ; *e-mail:* ian@oxfuird.com.

OXLEY, Julian Christopher; non-executive Director, Heatherwood and Wexham Park Hospitals NHS Trust, 1999–2006; *b* 23 Nov. 1938; *s* of Horace Oxley and Lilian Oxley (*née* Harris); *m* 1979, Carol (*née* Heath); one *d*, and two step *d*; one *s* two *d* from previous marr. *Educ:* Clifton Coll., Bristol; Oriel Coll., Oxford (Organ Scholar, MA). FCA. Dir and Sec., Williams & James plc, 1970–84; Guide Dogs for the Blind Association: Dir and Sec., 1984–89; Dir-Gen., 1989–96; Chm., Internat. Fedn of Guide Dog Schs, 1990–97. Mem. Council, Gloucester Civic Trust, 1972–75. Chm. of Govs, Selwyn Sch., Gloucester, 1980–84. Trustee, Nat. Confedn of PTAs, 2002– (Chm., 2004–). *Recreations:* music, old furniture, railway signalling. *Address:* Holden End, Lower Dawlish Water, Devon EX7 0QN. *T:* (01626) 866877; *e-mail:* julian.oxley@btinternet.com.

OXMANTOWN, Lord; Laurence Patrick Parsons; Marketing Director, Guohua Real Estate, since 2002; *b* 31 March 1969; *s* and *heir* of Earl of Rosse, *qv*; *m* 2004, Anna, *d* of Qicai Lin; one *s* one d. *Educ:* Aiglon Coll., Switzerland; Univ. of Beijing Language Inst. *Heir: s* Hon. William Charles Parsons, *b* 28 June 2008. *Address:* 1059 Le Leman Lake Villas, SE Baixing zhuang, Houshayou, Shunyi District, Beijing 101300, China.

OZ, Amos; Professor of Hebrew Literature, Ben-Gurion University of the Negev, since 1987 (Agnon Professor in Modern Hebrew Literature, 1993); *b* Jerusalem, 4 May 1939. *Educ:* Hebrew Univ. of Jerusalem (BA Hebrew Literature and Philosophy 1965). Teacher of Literature and Philosophy, Hulda High Sch. and Regl High Sch., Givat Brenner, 1963–86. Vis. Fellow, St Cross Coll., Oxford, 1969–70; Writer in Residence: Hebrew Univ. of Jerusalem, 1975–76, 1990; Tel Aviv Univ., 1996; Visiting Professor: Univ. of Calif at Berkeley, 1980; Oxford Univ., 1998; Writer in Residence and Visiting Professor of Literature: Boston Univ., 1987; Princeton Univ., 1997. Member: Peace Now, 1977–; Catalan Acad. of Mediterranean, 1989; Acad. of Hebrew Language, 1991. Hon. Dr: Hebrew Union Coll., Cincinnati and Jerusalem, 1988; Western New England Coll., Mass, 1988; Tel Aviv, 1992; Brandeis, 1998. Bernstein Prize, 1983; Bialik Prize, 1986; Internat. Peace Prize, German Publishers' Union, 1992; Israel Prize for Literature, 1998. Officier de l'Ordre des Arts et des Lettres, 1984, Chevalier de la Légion d'Honneur, 1997,

(France). *Publications: stories:* Where the Jackal Howls, 1965; *novels:* Elsewhere Perhaps, 1966; My Michael, 1968 (elected one of 100 masterpieces of the 20th century, Bertelsmann Club, Germany, 1999; elected one of best foreign bks in China, 1999); Touch the Water, Touch the Wind, 1973; A Perfect Peace, 1982; Black Box, 1987 (Prix Femina Etranger, Wingate Prize, 1988); To Know a Woman, 1989; The Third Condition, 1991; Don't Call it Night, 1994; Panther in the Basement, 1995; The Same Sea, 1999; *for children:* Soumchi, 1977 (Ze'ev Award, Hans Christian Andersen Medal, 1978; Luchs Prize, Germany, Hamore Prize, France, 1993); *novellas:* Unto Death, 1971; The Hill of Evil Counsel, 1976; *anthology:* Other People, 1974; *essays:* Under This Blazing Light, 1978; In the Land of Israel, 1983; The Slopes of Lebanon, 1987; Report of the Situation, 1992; The Silence of Heaven, 1993; Israel, Palestine and Peace, 1994; The Real Cause of My Grandmother's Death, 1994; The Story Begins, 1996; All Our Hopes, 1998; *memoir:* A Tale of Love and Darkness, 2004; work translated into 33 languages; articles on literary, political and ideological topics in jls.

OZAWA, Seiji; Japanese conductor; Music Director, Vienna State Opera, since 2002; Co-founder and Artistic Director, Tokyo Opera Nomori, since 2005; *b* Shenyang, China, 1 Sept. 1935; *m* 1st, Kyoko Edo; 2nd, Vera Ilyan; one *s* one d. *Educ:* Toho School of Music, Tokyo; studied with Hideo Saito, Eugène Bigot, Herbert von Karajan, Leonard Bernstein. Won Besançon Internat. Comp., 1959, Koussevitzky Meml Scholarship, 1960. Asst Conductor, NY Philharmonic Orch., 1961–62 and 1964–65; music dir, Ravinia Fest., Chicago, 1964–68; conductor, Toronto SO, 1965–69; music dir, San Francisco SO, 1970–76, music advisor, 1976–77; Artistic Advr, Tanglewood Fest., 1970–73; Music Dir, Boston SO, 1973–2002. Tours with Boston Symphony Orchestra: Europe, 1976, 1988, 1993; Japan, 1978; China (musical and cultural exchange), 1979; European music festivals, 1979, 1984, 1991; 14 USA cities (orchestra's hundredth birthday), 1982; Japan, 1982 and 1986; Far East, 1989, 1994; S America, 1992; tours with Vienna Philharmonic: Asia, 1993, 1996, 2000; Europe, 1997, 1998, 2000, 2001; Berlin Philharmonic: regular concerts; tours incl. US/Asia, 1993; Guest conductor with major orchestras in Canada, Europe, Far East and USA; Conductor: Saito Kinen Orch., Japan (European tours, 1987, 1989, 1991; Carnegie Hall, NY, 1991; Saito Kinen Fest., 1992–); Salzburg Fest. Opera highlights: La Scala, Milan; Covent Garden, London; Paris Opera (incl. world première of Messiaen's Saint François d'Assise); Vienna State Op. début, Eugene Onegin, 1988; many recordings (awards). Evening at Symphony, PBS television series with Boston Symphony Orch. (Emmy award). Hon. DMus: Univ. of Mass; New England Conservatory of Music; Wheaton Coll., Norton, Mass. Seiji Ozawa Hall inaugurated at Tanglewood, Mass, 1994. Inouye Award (first), for lifetime achievement in the arts, Japan, 1994. *Address:* Tokyo Opera Nomori, Jimbo-cho Mitsui Building 17F, Kanda Jimbo-cho 1–105, Chiyoda-ku, Tokyo 101–0051, Japan.

P

PACEY, Stephen James; Social Security and Child Support Commissioner, since 1996; *b* 5 July 1949; *s* of Randall Brown Pacey and May Pacey (*née* Oldknow); *m* 1978, Jessica Susan Turley; one *s*. *Educ:* Kimberley County Secondary Modern Sch.; Beeston Coll.; Trent Poly. (LLB 1971). Admitted Solicitor, 1975 (Wolverhampton Law Soc. Centenary Prizeman, 1975). Directorate of Legal Affairs, CBI, 1971–72; Lectr in Law, Isleworth Poly., 1972–73; solicitor in private practice, 1975–87; consultant planning inspector, 1989–91; Chm., Independent Tribunal Service, 1991–96; Dep. Social Security and Child Support Comr, 1993–96. Chairman (part-time): Social Security Appeal Tribunals, 1984–91; Med. Appeal Tribunals, 1987–91; Industrial Tribunals, 1988–91; Registered Homes Appeal Tribunals, 1992–96; pt-time Immigration Judge, 1998. Freeman, City of London, 1984. *Recreations:* photography, literature, performing arts. *Address:* Commissioners' Office, Third Floor, Procession House, 55 Ludgate Hill, EC4M 7JW.

PACINO, Alfredo James, (Al); actor; *b* New York, 25 April 1940; *s* of Salvatore Pacino and late Rosa Pacino; one *d* by Jan Tarrant; twin *s* and *d* by Beverly D'Angelo. *Educ:* High Sch. of Performing Arts, NY; Actors Studio, NY. Has worked as mail delivery boy, messenger, cinema usher and bldg supt; actor, dir and writer, NY theatres; appeared in première of The Indian Wants the Bronx, Waterford, Conn, 1966, and NY, 1968; Broadway début, Does a Tiger Wear a Necktie?, 1969 (Tony Award, best supporting actor); film début, Me, Natalie, 1969; *theatre includes:* Camino Real, Lincoln Center Rep. Theater, 1970; The Basic Training of Pavlo Hummel, 1972, (title rôle) Richard III, 1973, Boston Theater Co.; Arturo Ui, 1975; Jungle of Cities, 1979; American Buffalo, 1981, transf. UK, 1984; Julius Caesar, 1988; Salome, 1992; Circle in the Square, 1992; Hughie (also dir), 1996; The Resistible Rise of Arturo Ui, Michael Schimmel Centre, NY, 2002; *films include:* Panic in Needle Park, 1971; The Godfather, 1972 (Best Actor Award, Nat. Soc. of Film Critics, USA); Scarecrow, 1973; Serpico, The Godfather Part II, 1974; Dog Day Afternoon, 1975; Bobby Deerfield, 1977; And Justice for All, 1979; Cruising, 1980; Author! Author!, 1982; Scarface, 1983; Revolution, 1985; The Local Stigmatic, 1989 (also play, Actors Playhouse, NY, 1969); Sea of Love, The Godfather Part III, 1990; Frankie and Johnny, 1991; Glengarry Glen Ross, Scent of a Woman (Acad. Award for best actor, 1993), 1992; Carlito's Way, Two Bits, 1994; City Hall, Heat, 1995; Donny Brasco, Looking for Richard (also writer, prod. and dir), 1996; Devil's Advocate, 1997; Man of the People, 1999; Any Given Sunday, Insider, Chinese Coffee (also dir), 2000; Insomnia, Simone, 2002; The Recruit, 2003; People I Know, The Merchant of Venice, 2004; Two for the Money, 2006; Ocean's Thirteen, 2007; *television includes:* Angels in America, 2004. Co-artistic Dir, Actors Studio Inc., NY, 1982–83; Mem., Artistic Directorate, Globe Theatre, 1997–. Cecil B. DeMille award for lifetime achievement, Golden Globe Awards, 2001. *Address:* c/o CAA, 2000 Avenue of the Stars, Los Angeles, CA 90067, USA.

PACK, Prof. Donald Cecil, CBE 1978 (OBE 1969); MA, DSc; CMath, FIMA; FEIS, FRSE; Professor of Mathematics, University of Strathclyde, Glasgow, 1953–82, Hon. Professor, 1982–86, Professor Emeritus, 1986 (Vice-Principal, 1968–72); *b* 14 April 1920; *s* of late John Cecil and Minnie Pack, Higham Ferrers; *m* 1947, Constance Mary Gillam; two *s* one *d*. *Educ:* Wellingborough School; New Coll., Oxford. Lecturer in Mathematics, University College, Dundee, University of St Andrews, 1947–52; Visiting Research Associate, University of Maryland, 1951–52; Lecturer in Mathematics, University of Manchester, 1952–53. Guest Professor: Technische Universität, Berlin, 1967; Bologna Univ. and Politecnico Milano, 1980; Technische Hochschule Darmstadt, 1981; other vis. appts at Warsaw Univ., 1977, Kaiserslautern, 1980, 1984. Member: Dunbartonshire Educn Cttee, 1960–66; Gen. Teaching Council for Scotland, 1966–73; Chairman: Scottish Certificate of Educn Examn Bd, 1969–77; Cttee of Inquiry into Truancy and Indiscipline in Schools in Scotland, 1974–77; Member: various Govt Scientific Cttees, 1952–84; Defence Scientific Adv. Council, 1975–80; Consultant, MoD, 1984–2001. DERA Vis. Fellow, 1999. Member: British Nat. Cttee for Theoretical and Applied Mechanics, 1973–78; Internat. Adv. Cttee on Rarefied Gas Dynamics Symposia, 1976–88; Council, Gesellschaft für Angewandte Mathematik und Mechanik, 1977–83; Council, RSE, 1960–63; Scottish Arts Council, 1980–85; Hon. Mem., European Consortium for Mathematics in Industry, 1988. Founder Chm., NYO of Scotland, 1978–88 (Chm., Steering Cttee, 1978; Hon. Pres., 1988–); Mem., European Music Year UK Cttee (Chm., Scottish Sub-Cttee), 1982–86; Founder and First Hon. Treasurer, IMA, 1964–72; Governor, Hamilton Coll. of Education, 1977–81; Pres., Milngavie Music Club, 1983–93 (Hon. Pres., 1994–). *Publications:* papers on fluid dynamics. *Recreations:* music, gardening, golf. *Address:* 18 Buchanan Drive, Bearsden, Glasgow G61 2EW. *T:* (0141) 942 5764.

PACK, Maj.-Gen. Simon James, CB 1997; CBE 1994 (OBE 1990); Royal Marines, retired; Parnership Secretary, Gill Jennings & Every LLP, 2002–08; *b* 10 July 1944; *s* of late Captain A. J. Pack, OBE, RN and Eloise Pack; *m* 1970, Rosemary-Anne Fuller; one *s* one *d*. *Educ:* Fernden Prep. Sch.; Hurstpierpoint Coll.; Ecole de Commerce, Switzerland (Dip. French). Commnd into RM, 1962; served 3 Cdo Bde, Malaya, Sarawak, 1963–66; HMS Zulu, 1966–68; ADC to Governor of Queensland, 1969–70; Adjt, 41 Cdo, NI and Malta, 1970–72; Instructor, Officers Tactics Wing, Warminster, 1972–75; 42 Cdo, Norway, Hong Kong, 1976–79; Directorate of Naval Plans, MoD, 1979–81; Directing Staff, Army Staff Coll., 1981–83; MoD, 1984–87; CO 45 Cdo Gp, 1987–89; COS, HQ Cdo Forces, 1989–90; Dir, Defence Commitments Staff, MoD, 1990–94; Comdr, British Forces, Gibraltar and NATO Comdr, Western Mediterranean, 1994–97. Internat. Teams Dir, England and Wales Cricket Bd, 1997–2001. ADC to the Queen, 1990–94. Non-exec. Dir, Maritime Services Mgt Ltd, 1997–99. Dir, Friends of Gibraltar Heritage Soc., 2000–. Gov., Oratory Sch., Reading, 1991–2000. FCMI (FIMgt 1997). *Recreations:* cricket, golf, gardening, sailing, family bridge. *Address:* Littlecroft, Privett, Hants GU34 3NR; 13A Prince of Wales Mansions, Prince of Wales Drive, SW11 4BG.

PACKER, Jane, (Mrs G. Wallis); floral artist; Founder and Chair, Jane Packer Ltd, since 1982; *b* 22 Sept. 1959; *d* of Maurice and Brenda Packer; *m* 1990, Gary Wallis; one *s* one *d*. First Jane Packer Flowers shop opened James St, London W1, 1981; stores opened in NY, Seoul and Tokyo, 2001; estabd Jane Packer Flower Sch., London, 1989, sister sch. in Minato-ku, Tokyo, 1990. Consultant, M&S Horticulture, 1987–; designer Marks and Spencer Garden, Hampton Court Flower Show, 1991 (award from RHS), 1992 (award from RHS), 1993 (Gold Medal), 1994 (Gold Medal), 1995 (Gold Medal), 1996 (Gold Medal), 1997 (Gold Medal), 1998 (Silver Medal). Lecture tours in Europe, USA, Japan and UK. Prince Philip Medal, C&G, 2005. *Publications:* Celebrating with Flowers, 1986; Flowers For All Seasons, 4 books, Spring, Summer, Autumn, Winter, 1989; New Flower Arranging, 1993; Complete Guide to Flower Arranging, 1995, 10th edn 2005; Living With Flowers, 1996, 2nd edn 1997; Fast Flowers, 1998, 5th edn 2005; Flowers, Design, Philosophy, 2000, 3rd edn 2005; World Flowers, 2003, 2nd edn 2006; Colour, 2007. *Recreations:* family, garden, cooking. *Address:* Jane Packer Ltd, 32–34 New Cavendish Street, W1G 8UE. *T:* (020) 7935 0787.

PACKER, Rt Rev. John Richard; *see* Ripon and Leeds, Bishop of.

PACKER, Prof. Kenneth John, PhD; FRS 1991; CChem, FRSC; Research Professor in Chemistry, Nottingham University, 1993–2001, now Emeritus; *b* 18 May 1938; *s* of late Harry James Packer and Alice Ethel Packer (*née* Purse); *m* 1962, Christine Frances Hart; one *s* one *d*. *Educ:* Harvey Grammar Sch., Folkestone; Imperial Coll., London (BSc Hons Chemistry, 1st cl., 1959); Cambridge Univ. (PhD 1962). CChem 1985, FRSC 1985. Post-doctoral Res. Fellow, Central Res. Dept, E. I. duPont de Nemours, Wilmington, USA, 1962–63; University of East Anglia: SERC Res. Fellow, 1963–64; Lectr in Chemistry, 1964–71; Sen. Lectr, 1971–78; Reader, 1978–82; Prof., 1982–84; BP Research: Sen. Res. Associate, Spectroscopy, 1984–87; Prin. Res. Associate, 1987–90; Chief Res. Associate, Analytical Res. Div., 1990–92; Chief Scientist, Gp Res. and Engrg, BP Internat., 1992–93. Visiting Professor in Chemistry: Southampton Univ.; KCL; Imperial Coll., London, 1985–92; UEA, 2004–. Science and Engineering Research Council: Member: Physical Chem. Cttee, 1976–81; Chem. Cttee, 1979–82; Sci. Bd, 1988–91; Chm., Central Services Panel, 1980–82; Cttee Mem., Chm. and Sec., British Radiofrequency Spectroscopy Gp; Mem. Council, Faraday Div., 1988–91, Mem. Scientific Affairs Bd, 1992–, RSC; Hon. Sec., Royal Instn of GB, 1993–98. Gov., Hampton Sch., Hanworth, 1990–93. Ed., Molecular Physics, 1982–88. *Publications:* NMR Spectroscopy of Solid Polymers, 1993; contrib. approx. 150 papers on topics involving devlt and application of NMR spectroscopy to internat. jls. *Recreations:* fly-fishing, ski-ing, gardening, music. *Address:* The Beeches, 68 Cawston Road, Aylsham, Norwich NR11 6ED. *T:* (01263) 731728.

PACKER, Lucy Jeanne, (Lady Packer); *see* Neville-Rolfe, L. J.

PACKER, Sir Richard (John), KCB 2000; consultant; Permanent Secretary, Ministry of Agriculture, Fisheries and Food, 1993–2000; *b* 18 Aug. 1944; *s* of late George Charles Packer and Dorothy May Packer (*née* Reynolds); *m* 1st, Alison Mary Sellwood; two *s* one *d*; 2nd, Lucy Jeanne Blackett-Ord (*see* L. J. Neville-Rolfe); four *s*. *Educ:* City of London School; Manchester Univ. (BSc 1965, MSc 1966). Ministry of Agriculture, Fisheries and Food, 1967–2000: on secondment as 1st Sec., Office of Perm Rep. to EEC, 1973–76; Principal Private Sec. to Minister, 1976–78; Asst Sec., 1979; Under Sec., 1985–89; Dep. Sec. (Agricl Commodities, Trade and Food Prodn), 1989–93. Non-exec. Dir, Express Dairies plc, subseq. Arla Foods (UK), 2002–07. *Publication:* The Politics of BSE, 2006. *Recreations:* ideas, sport. *Address:* 113 St George's Road, SE1 6HY.

PACKER, William John; painter and critic; contributor, Financial Times, since 1974 (art critic, 1974–2004); *b* 19 Aug. 1940; *o s* of late Rex Packer and Evelyn Mary Packer (*née* Wornham); *m* 1965, Clare, *er d* of late Thomas Winn and Cecily Philip; three *d*. *Educ:* Windsor Grammar Sch.; Wimbledon Sch. of Art (NDD 1963); Brighton Coll. of Art (ATC 1964). Teaching full-time, 1964–67, part-time in art schs, 1967–77; external assessor, 1980–2000. First exhibited, RA, 1963 and continues to exhibit widely; one-man exhibn, Piers Feetham Gall., 1996, 2001, 2004, jt exhibn, 2005; jt exhibn, Chapel Row Gall., Bath, 2007. Member: Fine Art Board, CNAA, 1976–83; Adv. Cttee, Govt Art Collection, 1977–84; Crafts Council, 1980–87; Cttee, Nat. Trust Foundn for Art, 1986–98. Sole selector, first British Art Show, 1979–80; jt selector for exhibns and prizes, incl. Liverpool John Moores Exhibn, Hunting Prize, Discerning Eye. Curator, Elizabeth Blackadder Retrospective, Scottish Arts Council, 1982. London corresp., Art & Artists, 1969–74. Inaugural Henry Moore Lectr, Florence, 1986. Ballinglen Artist Fellow, Ballinglen Foundn, Co. Mayo, 1995. Mem., NEAC, 2005–. Hon. Fellow, RCA, 1988; Hon. RBA 1992; Hon. RBS; Hon. Mem., PS. *Publications:* The Art of Vogue Covers, 1980; Fashion Drawing in Vogue, 1983; Henry Moore: a pictorial biography, 1985; Carl Erickson, and René Bouët-Willaumez, 1989; John Houston, 2003; Tai-Shan Schierenburg, 2005; contribs to magazines, newspapers and exhibn catalogues. *Recreation:* Venice. *Address:* 60 Trinity Gardens, Brixton, SW9 8DR. *T:* (020) 7733 4012. *Clubs:* Garrick, Chelsea Arts, Academy.

PACKHAM, Christopher Gary; naturalist, author, and broadcaster; *b* 4 May 1961; *s* of Colin Harold Packham and Marion Rita Packham (*née* Smith); one *d*. *Educ:* Bitterne Park Schs; Richard Taunton Coll.; Southampton Univ. (BSc Hons Zoology 1983). Freelance camera assistant, 1983–86; freelance cameraman and photographer, 1985–89; wildlife presenter for TV, 1985–; programmes include: Really Wild Show, Go Wild, Watchout, X-Creatures, Postcards from the Wild; Inside Out; Hands on Nature; Nature's Calendar. President: London Wildlife Trust, 1996–; Hants Ornithological Soc., 2000–; Hants Water Fest., 2005–; Bat Conservation Trust, 2006–; Vice-President: The Wildlife Trusts, 2005–; Hants Wildlife Trust, 2005–; Butterfly Conservation, 2006–; RSPB; Trustee: Marwell

Zoo Trust, 1998–2003; Herpetological Conservation Trust, 1998–2005; Wildfowl and Wetland Trust, 2000–04; Hawk Conservancy Trust, 2002–. *Publications:* Chris Packham's Back Garden Nature Reserve, 2001; Chris Packham's Wild Side of Town, 2003. *Recreations:* travelling to horrible places to see beautiful things and photographing them, having no time to do anything, berating my dogs for barking. *Address:* All Electric Productions, PO Box 1805, Andover, Hants SP10 3ZN; *e-mail:* info@allelectricproductions.co.uk.

PACKSHAW, Robin David; Chairman, International City Holdings, Money and Securities Brokers, 1985–89; *b* 20 March 1933; *s* of late Savil Packshaw and Fay Mary Packshaw; *m*; three *s* one *d. Educ:* Diocesan Coll., Cape Town; Bradfield Coll., Berks. Served RM, 1951–53; commnd and served in Special Boat Service; RMFVR, 1953–58. Iraq Petroleum Co. Ltd, 1953–63; Long Till and Colvin Ltd, 1963–69; founded Packshaw & Associates Ltd, Sterling Money Brokers, 1969, became Fulton Packshaw Ltd, 1973; Chairman: Charles Fulton (UK) Ltd, Internat. For. Exch. and Currency Deposit Brokers, 1982; Manex Sterling Brokers Ltd, 1993; Consultant: BITC, 1990–92; London First, 1992–93; Sterling, then Sterling Internat., Brokers Ltd, 1993–99. Dep. Chm., Partners in the Countryside, 1996–2001. Chm., Radionic Assoc. 1991–99. Chm., Stours Br., N Dorset Conservation Assoc., 1989–95. Church Warden, All Saints, Stour Row, Dorset, 1984–95. Gov., Stour Provost Co. Primary Sch., 1992–95. Freeman, City of London, 1983; Life Mem., Guild of Freemen of City of London. FZS 1972; FRGS 1997; FRSA 1997. Hon. Fellow, Radionic Assoc., 1999. *Recreations:* travel, people, voluntary work. *Address:* 5 Hurlingham Court, Ranelagh Gardens, SW6 3SH. *T:* (020) 7736 6832.

PADFIELD, Nicholas David; QC 1991; a Recorder, since 1995; *b* 5 Aug. 1947; *s* of David Padfield and Sushila, *d* of Sir Samuel Runganadhan; *m* 1st, 1978, Nayana Parekh (*d* 1983); one *d*; 2nd, 1986, Mary Barran, JP, *d* of Sir Edward Playfair, KCB; two *s. Educ:* Dragon Sch., Charterhouse; University Coll., Oxford (Open Scholar, MA; hockey blue; England hockey internat.); Trinity Hall, Cambridge (LLM Internat Law). FCIArb. Called to the Bar, Inner Temple, 1972, Bencher, 1995; called to various overseas Bars. Mem., Panel of Lloyd's Arbitrators, 1991–. Dep. Chm., Cons. Party Ethics and Integrity Cttee. Chairman: Commonwealth and Ethnic Barristers' Assoc., 2003–04; London br., CIArb, 2007–. Member, Council of Advisors, Lord Slynn Eur. Law Foundn. Internat. Council for Capital Formation, Council of Advisors, 2005–. Mem. Cttee, London Oratory Appeal, 1990–95. Freeman: City of London, 2003; Scriveners' Co., 2003. *Address:* 2 Netherton Grove, Chelsea, SW10 9TQ. *T:* (020) 7351 1961. *Clubs:* Garrick, MCC; Vincent's (Oxford).

PADMORE, Elaine Marguirite; Director of Opera, Royal Opera House, Covent Garden, since 2000; *b* Haworth, Yorks, 3 Feb. 1947; *d* of Alfred and Florence Padmore. *Educ:* Newland High Sch., Hull; Arnold Sch., Blackpool; Birmingham Univ. (MA; BMus); Guildhall Sch. of Music; LTCL. Liberal Studies Lectr, Croydon and Kingston Colls of Art, 1968–70; Books Editor, OUP Music Dept, 1970–71; Producer, BBC Music Div., 1971–76; Announcer, Radio 3, 1982–90. Major BBC Radio 3 series include: Parade, Music of Tchaikovsky's Russia, England's Pleasant Land, Journal de mes Mélodies; Presenter of numerous programmes, incl. Festival comment, Edinburgh Fest., 1973–81; Chief Producer, Opera, BBC Radio, 1976–83: series incl. complete operas of Richard Strauss and first performances of works by Delius and Havergal Brian; formerly active as professional singer (soprano), particularly of opera; Lectr in Opera, RAM, 1979–87; Artistic Director: Classical Prodns, London, 1990–92; Wexford Festival Opera, 1982–94; DGOS Opera Ireland, 1989–90 and 1991–93; Artistic Consultant, 1992 London Opera Fest.; Dir, Royal Danish Opera, Copenhagen, 1993–2000. Hon. ARAM. Hon. FTCL. Hon. DMus Birmingham. Hungarian Radio Pro Musica Award for prog. Summertime on Bredon, 1973; Prix Musical de Radio Brno for prog. The English Renaissance, 1974; Sunday Independent Award for services to music in Ireland, 1985. Kt, Order of Dannebrog (Denmark), 1994. *Publications:* Wagner (Great Composers' Series), 1970; Music in the Modern Age: chapter on Germany, 1973; contributor to: New Grove Dict. of Music, Proc. of Royal Musical Assoc., Music and Letters, The Listener. *Recreations:* gardening, travel, art exhibitions. *Address:* Royal Opera House, Covent Garden, WC2E 9DD.

PADMORE, Mark Joseph; tenor; *b* 8 March 1961; *s* of Peter Francis Padmore and Sheila Mary (*née* Stoyles); *m* 1996, Josette Patricia Simon (marr. diss. 2004); one *d. Educ:* Simon Langton Grammar Sch. for Boys; King's Coll., Cambridge (BA (Hons), MA). Has performed at major festivals, incl. Aix-en-Provence, Edinburgh, BBC Proms, Salzburg, Spoleto, Tanglewood, Glyndebourne, Mostly Mozart, NY; opera house débuts: Teatro Comunale, Florence, 1992; Opéra Comique, Paris, 1993; Théâtre du Châtelet, 1995; Royal Opera House, Covent Gdn, 1995; Scottish Opera, 1996; Opéra de Paris, 1996; ENO, 1999; has also performed with WNO and Opera de Lausanne; concert appearances include: LSO; City of Birmingham Orch.; RPO; Les Arts Florissants; English Baroque Soloists; Czech Philharmonic Orch.; Berlin Phil.; Vienna Phil.; NY Phil.; Philadelphia Orch.; Royal Concertgebouw Orchs; Freiburg Baroque; Orch. of the Age of Enlightenment; English Concert; has given recitals in Barcelona, Brussels, Copenhagen, Madrid, Milan, Moscow, NY and Paris; in Lieder has appeared at: Wigmore Hall; Cheltenham Fest.; Queen Elizabeth Hall; de Singel Hall, Antwerp; has made more than 60 recordings, incl. As Steals the Morn (Vocal Recording of the Year, BBC Music Magazine, 2008), La Clemenza di Tito, St John and St Matthew Passions and The Creation and Messiah. *Recreation:* cycling and theatre. *Address:* c/o Maxine Robertson Management, 14 Forge Drive, Claygate, KT10 0HR. *T:* (020) 7993 2917; *e-mail:* info@maxinerobertson.com.

PADOA-SCHIOPPA, Tommaso; banker and economist; Minister of Economy and Finance, Italy, since 2006; *b* Belluno, Italy, 23 July 1940. *Educ:* Luigi Boccini Univ., Milan; Massachusetts Inst. Technol. (MSc). C. & A. Brenninkmeyer, 1966–68; Economist, Res. Dept, Banca d'Italia, 1970–79; Dir Gen. for Econ. and Financial Affairs, CEC, Brussels, 1979–83; Central Dir for Econ. Res., 1983, Dep. Dir Gen., 1984–97, Banca d'Italia; Pres., Commissione Nazionale per le Società e la Borsa, 1997–98; Mem., Exec. Bd, European Central Bank, 1998–2005. Mem., Bd of Dirs, EIB, 1979–83. Jt Sec., Delors Cttee for Study of Eur. Econ. and Monetary Union, 1988–89; Chm., Banking Adv. Cttee, CEC, 1988–91; Member: G-7 Deputies; G-10 Deputies; G-20 Deputies; Chairman: Eur. Regl Cttee, IOSCO, 1997–98; FESCO, 1997–98; Mem., Wkg Party 3, Econ. Policy Cttee, OECD. Hon. Prof., Univ. of Frankfurt am Main, 1999. Alternate Mem. Council, Eur. Monetary Inst., 1995–97; Member, Advisory Board: Inst. for Internat. Econs; Eur. Univ. Inst. Hon. Dr Trieste, 1999. *Publications:* include: (with F. Modigliani) The Management of an Open Economy with 100% plus Wage Indexation, 1978; (with F. Padoa-Schioppa) Agenda e Non-Agenda: limiti o crisi della politica economica?, 1984; Money, Economic Policy and Europe, 1985; Efficiency, Stability and Equity: a strategy for the evolution of the economic system of the European Community, 1987; La moneta e il sistema dei pagamenti, 1992; The Road to Monetary Union in Europe: The Emperor, the Kings and the Genies, 1994; Europe: the impossible status quo, 1997; Il governo dell'economia, 1997; Che cosa ci ha insegnato l'avventura europea, 1998. *Address:* Ministry of Economy and Finance, Via XX Settembre 97, 00187 Rome, Italy.

PADOVAN, John Mario Faskally; Chairman, Dawnay Day Property Finance Group, since 2004; *b* 7 May 1938; *s* of Umberto Mario Padovan and Mary Nina Liddon Padovan; *m* 1964, Sally Kay (*née* Anderson); three *s. Educ:* St George's College, Weybridge; King's College London (LLB; FKC 2003); Keble College, Oxford (BCL). FCA. County Bank, 1970–84: Dir, 1971; Dep. Chief Exec., 1974; Chief Exec., 1976; Chm., 1984; Dep. Chm., Hambros Bank and Dir, Hambros, 1984–86; Chm., Merchant Banking Div., Barclays de Zoete Wedd Gp, 1986–91; Dep. Chm., Barclays de Zoete Wedd, 1989–91; Dep. Chm., 1992, Chm., 1993–95, AAH; Dir, 1989–91, Chm., 1991–95, Mabey Hldgs. Chairman: Gardner Merchant, 1993–95; Evans of Leeds, 1997–99 (Dir, 1994–97); Furniture Village, 1998–2001; Schroder Split Fund, 2000– (Dir, 1992–); Williams Lea Gp, 2000–04 (Dir, 1992–2000); Director: Tesco, 1982–94; Whitbread, 1992–2002; Interserve (formerly Tilbury Douglas), 1996–2005 (Dep. Chm., 2003–05); HFC Bank, 1997–2003. Mem. Court, Drapers' Co., 1991– (Master, 1999–2000). *Recreations:* golf, walking, contemporary art. *Address:* 15 Lord North Street, SW1P 3LD. *T:* (020) 7222 3261. *Clubs:* Royal St George's Golf, West Surrey Golf.

PAGE, Adrienne May; QC 1999; a Recorder, 1999–2004; *b* 14 July 1952; *d* of late Gwythian Lloyd Page and of Betty Page (*née* Spring); *m* 1983, Anthony Crichton Waldeck (marr. diss. 2007); one step *s* one step *d. Educ:* Godolphin Sch., Salisbury; Univ. of Kent at Canterbury (BA Social Sci.). Called to the Bar, Middle Temple, 1974, Bencher, 2003; Asst Recorder, 1995–99. *Recreation:* gardening. *Address:* 5 Raymond Buildings, Gray's Inn, WC1R 5BP. *T:* (020) 7242 2902. *Club:* Beaulieu River Sailing.

PAGE, Annette, (Mrs Ronald Hynd); Ballerina of the Royal Ballet until retirement, 1967; Ballet Mistress, Ballet of the Bayerischestaatsoper, Munich, 1984–86; *b* 18 Dec. 1932; *d* of James Lees and Margaret Page; *m* 1957, Ronald Hynd, *qv*; one *d. Educ:* Royal Ballet School. Audition and award of scholarship to Roy. Ballet Sch., 1944. Entry into touring company of Royal Ballet (then Sadler's Wells Theatre Ballet), 1950; promotion to major Royal Ballet Co. (Sadler's Wells Ballet), 1955. Mem., Arts Council of GB, 1976–79. *Roles included:* The Firebird, Princess Aurora in Sleeping Beauty, Odette-Odile in Swan Lake, Giselle, Lise in La Fille Mal Gardée, Juliet in Romeo and Juliet, Cinderella, Swanilda in Coppelia, Nikiya in La Bayadère, Les Sylphides, Miller's Wife in Three Cornered Hat, Terpsichore in Apollo, Blue Girl in Les Biches, Mamzelle Angot, Ballerina in Petrouchka, Symphonic Variations, Les Rendezvous, Beauty and the Beast, La Capricciosa in Lady and the Fool, Queen of Hearts in Card Game, Agon, Polka in Solitaire, Ballerina in Scènes de Ballet, Queens of Fire and Air in Homage to the Queen, Blue Girl in Les Pâtineurs, Tango and Polka in Façade, Julia and Pepè in A Wedding Bouquet, Moon and Pas de Six in Prince of the Pagodas, Danses Concertantes, Faded Beauty and Young Lover in Noctambules, Flower Festival Pas de Deux, Ballerina in Ballet Imperial. *Recreations:* music, books, gardening.

PAGE, Anthony (Frederick Montague); stage, film and television director; *b* India, 21 Sept. 1935; *s* of Brig. F. G. C. Page, DSO, OBE, and P. V. M. Page. *Educ:* Oakley Hall, Cirencester; Winchester Coll. (Schol.); Magdalen Coll., Oxford (Schol., BA); Neighborhood Playhouse Sch. of the Theater, NY. Asst, Royal Court Theatre, 1958: co-directed Live Like Pigs, directed The Room; Artistic Dir, Dundee Repertory Theatre, 1962; The Caretaker, Oxford and Salisbury; Women Beware Women, and Nil Carborundum, Royal Shakespeare Co., 1963; BBC Directors' Course, then several episodes of Z-Cars, Horror of Darkness and 1st TV prodn Stephen D; Jt Artistic Dir, Royal Court, 1964–65; directed Inadmissible Evidence (later Broadway and film), A Patriot for Me, 1st revival of Waiting for Godot, Cuckoo in the Nest; Diary of a Madman, Duchess, 1966; Artistic Dir, two seasons at Royal Court: Uncle Vanya, 1970; Alpha Beta (also film); Hedda Gabler; Krapp's Last Tape; Not I; Cromwell; other plays transf. from Royal Court to West End: Time Present; Hotel in Amsterdam; revival, Look Back in Anger; West of Suez; directed Hamlet, Nottingham, 1970; Rules of the Game, Nat. Theatre; King Lear, Amer. Shakespeare Fest., 1975; Cowardice, Ambassadors, 1983; Heartbreak House, Broadway, 1984 (televised); Mrs Warren's Profession, RNT, 1985; Three Tall Women, Wyndham's, 1994; Absolute Hell, RNT, 1995; The Doll's House, Playhouse, 1996, NY, 1997 (Tony Award); A Delicate Balance, Theatre Royal, Haymarket, 1997; The Forest, Sleep With Me, 1999; Finding the Sun, Marriage Play, 2001, RNT; Cat on a Hot Tin Roof, Lyric, 2001, NY, 2003; The Master Builder, Albery, 2003; The Goat, or Who is Sylvia, Almeida, transf. Apollo, 2004; Who's Afraid of Virginia Woolf?, NY, 2005, Apollo, 2006; revival, The Night of the Iguana, Lyric, 2005; The Lady From Dubuque, Theatre Royal, Haymarket, 2007; *television:* The Parachute; Emlyn; Hotel in Amsterdam; Speaking of Murder; You're Free; The Changeling; Headmaster; Sheppey; Absolute Hell, 1991; Middlemarch, 1994; in USA: Missiles of October; Pueblo Incident; FDR, the Last Year; Bill (starring Mickey Rooney (Golden Globe Award); Johnny Belinda; Bill on His Own; The Nightmare Years; Patricia Neal Story; Murder by Reason of Insanity; Second Serve; Pack of Lies; Chernobyl: The Final Warning, 1990; Guests of the Emperor; The Human Bomb; *films:* Inadmissible Evidence; I Never Promised You a Rose Garden; Absolution; Forbidden. Directors' and Producers' Award for TV Dir of Year, 1966. *Recreations:* painting, reading, travelling. *Address:* 6 Arundel Gardens, W11 2LA.

PAGE, (Arthur) Hugo (Micklem); QC 2002; *b* 16 Sept. 1951; *s* of Sir (Arthur) John Page, *qv*; *m* 1992, Angélique, *d* of Marquis de Folin, Paris. *Educ:* Harrow Sch.; Magdalene Coll., Cambridge (MA). Called to the Bar, Inner Temple, 1977; in practice, specialising in commercial law. Contested (C) Pontefract and Castleford, Oct. 1978, 1979. *Publication:* (contrib.) Halsbury's Laws, 4th edn, 1991. *Recreations:* travel, book collecting. *Address:* 20 Brechin Place, SW7 4QA. *T:* (020) 7370 6826, *Fax:* (020) 7373 8834; Blackstone Chambers, Blackstone House, Temple, EC4Y 9BW. *T:* (020) 7583 1770, *Fax:* (020) 7822 7350; *e-mail:* hugopage@blackstonechambers.com.

PAGE, Sir (Arthur) John, Kt 1984; Chairman, Three Valleys Water, 1986–2001; *b* 16 Sept. 1919; *s* of Sir Arthur Page, QC (late Chief Justice of Burma), and Lady Page, KiH; *m* 1950, Anne, MA (Cantab), *d* of Charles Micklem, DSO, JP, DL, Longcross House, Surrey; four *s. Educ:* Harrow; Magdalene College, Cambridge. Joined RA as Gunner, 1939, commissioned, 1940; served War of 1939–45, Western Desert (wounded), France, Germany; demobilised as Major, comdg 258 Battery Norfolk Yeomanry, 1945; various positions in industry and commerce, 1946–. Chm. Bethnal Green and E London Housing Assoc., 1957–70; contested (C) Eton and Slough, Gen. Election, 1959. MP (C) Harrow W, March 1960–1987. PPS to Parly Under-Sec. of State, Home Office, 1961–63; Conservative Parly Labour Affairs Cttee: Sec., 1960–61, 1964–67, Vice-Chm., 1964–69, Chm., 1970–74; Sec., Conservative Broadcasting Cttee, 1974–76. Pres., Cons. Trade Unionists Nat. Adv. Council, 1967–69; Member: Parly Select Cttee on Race Relations and Immigration, 1970–71; British Delegn to Council of Europe and WEU, 1972–87 (Chm. Budget Cttee, 1973–74, Social and Health Cttee, 1975–78). Mem. Exec., IPU, British Gp, 1970 (Treasurer, 1974–77; Vice-Chm., 1977–79; Chm., 1979–82); Acting Internat. Pres., IPU, 1984 (Dep. Internat. Pres., 1982–84). Vice-Pres., British Insurance Brokers Assoc., 1980–; President: Water Companies Assoc., 1986–89 (Dep. Pres., 1984–86); Independent Schools Assoc., 1971–78; Chm., Council for Indep. Educn, 1974–80. *Recreations:* painting, politics, defending the Monarchy. *Address:* Hitcham Lodge,

Taplow, Maidenhead, Berks SL6 0HG. *T:* (01628) 605056. *Clubs:* Brooks's, MCC.
See also A. H. M. Page.

PAGE, Ashley, OBE 2006; Artistic Director, Scottish Ballet, since 2002; *b* 9 Aug. 1956; named Ashley Laverty; *s* of John Henry Laverty and Sheila Rachel Laverty; *m* Nicola Roberts; one *s* one *d. Educ:* St Andrew's Sch., Rochester; Royal Ballet Schs. Joined Royal Ballet at Covent Garden, 1976; Soloist, 1980, Principal Dancer, and choreographer, 1984–2002. Works choreographed for: Royal Ballet; Ballet Rambert, subseq. Rambert Dance Co.; Dutch Nat. Ballet; Dance Umbrella Fest. and other cos in GB and abroad; for Scottish Ballet: The Nutcracker; Cinderella; The Sleeping Beauty; The Pump Room; Nightswimming into Day. *Recreations:* interest in all the arts, travel. *Address:* Scottish Ballet, 261 West Princes Street, Glasgow G4 9EE.

PAGE, Benjamin Charles; Managing Director, Ipsos MORI Public Sector, since 2008; *b* Exeter, 9 Jan. 1965; *s* of Charles Page and Elizabeth Page (*née* Barrett); *m* 1994, Janet Pritchard; one *s. Educ:* St John's Coll., Oxford (BA Hons Modern Hist.). Researcher: MIL (NOP), 1986–87; MORI, 1988–94; Dir, Social Research, 1994–2000; Chm., Ipsos MORI Social Research Inst., 2000–. Mem., CABE, 2003–. Dir, Involve, 2006–. *Publications:* Blair's Britain, 2007; contribs to Municipal Jl, Health Service Jl, PR Week, Local Govt Chronicle. *Recreations:* Italy, history, restaurants, skateboarding, insomnia. *Address:* Ipsos MORI, 79–81 Borough Road, SE1 1FY. *T:* (020) 7347 3242; *e-mail:* ben.page@ipsos.com.

PAGE, Bruce; journalist; *b* 1 Dec. 1936; *s* of Roger and Beatrice Page; *m* 1969, Anne Louise Darnborough; one *s* one *d. Educ:* Melbourne High Sch.; Melbourne Univ. The Herald, Melbourne, 1956–60; Evening Standard, 1960–62; Daily Herald, 1962–64; Sunday Times, 1964–76; Daily Express, 1977; Editor, The New Statesman, 1978–82. Dir, Direct Image Systems and Communications Ltd, 1992–95. *Publications:* (jtly) Philby, 1968, 3rd edn 1977; (jtly) An American Melodrama, 1969; (jtly) Do You Sincerely Want to be Rich?, 1971, 2nd edn 2005; (jtly) Destination Disaster, 1976; contrib. Ulster, 1972; The Yom Kippur War, 1974; The British Press, 1978; The Murdoch Archipelago, 2003. *Recreations:* sailing, reading. *Address:* Beach House, Shingle Street, Shottisham, Suffolk IP12 3BE. *T:* (01394) 411427.

PAGE, Dr Christopher Howard; Senior Research Fellow, Sidney Sussex College, Cambridge, since 1985; Reader in Medieval Music and Literature, University of Cambridge, since 1997; Director, Gothic Voices, since 1982; *b* 8 April 1952; *s* of Ewart Lacey Page and Marie Victoria (*née* Graham); *m* 1st, 1975, Régine Fourcade (marr. diss. 2004); 2nd, 2004, Anne Dunan. *Educ:* Sir George Monoux Grammar Sch.; Balliol Coll., Oxford (BA English 1974; MA); Univ. of York (DPhil). Jun. Res. Fellow, Jesus Coll., Oxford, 1977–80; Lecturer in English: New Coll., Oxford, 1980–85; Univ. of Cambridge, 1989–97. Editor, Plainsong and Medieval Music, 1991–. Presenter, Spirit of the Age, Radio 3, 1992–. Fellow, Fellowship of Makers and Restorers of Historical Instruments, 1982. Former Chm., Plainsong and Medieval Music Soc. Dent Medal, Royal Musical Assoc., 1991. *Publications:* Voices and Instruments of the Middle Ages, 1987; The Owl and the Nightingale, 1989; the *Summa Musice*, 1991; Discarding Images, 1993; Songs of the Trouvères, 1995; Latin Poetry and Conductus Rhythm in Medieval France, 1997; articles in Early Music, Galpin Soc. Jl, Plainsong and Medieval Music, Musical Times. *Address:* Sidney Sussex College, Cambridge CB2 3HU. *T:* (01223) 338800.

PAGE, Prof. Clive Peter, PhD; Professor of Pharmacology, and Director, Sackler Institute of Pulmonary Pharmacology, King's College London, since 1995; *b* 14 Oct. 1958; *s* of Peter and Edna Page; *m* 2004, Clare O'Leary; two *s* one *d. Educ:* Grovelands Primary Sch., Hailsham; Bexhill Grammar Sch.; Chelsea Coll., Univ. of London (BSc Hons Pharmacol.); Cardiothoracic Inst., Imperial Coll., London (PhD Pharmacol. 1984). Sandoz Ltd, Basel, 1984–86; Lectr, 1986–89, Reader, 1989–95, in Pharmacol., KCL. Chairman, Board: Stirling Products Ltd, Perth, Australia, 2004–; Verona Pharma Ltd, 2006–; Director: Helperby Therapeutics plc, 2004–; Babraham Biosciences Ltd, 2007–. Chm., Animal Scis Gp, Biosciences Fedn, 2004–. *Publications:* (jtly) Integrated Pharmacology, 1997, 3rd edn 2006; over 200 scientific articles in learned jls. *Recreations:* travel, mountain walking, good food and wine. *Address:* Sackler Institute of Pulmonary Pharmacology, King's College London, Guy's Campus, London Bridge, SE1 9RT. *T:* (020) 7848 6096, *Fax:* (020) 7848 6097; *e-mail:* clive.page@kcl.ac.uk. *Club:* Naval and Military.

PAGE, David John, FCCA; Deputy Chief Executive, Leeds City Council, since 2001; *b* 24 Feb. 1954; *s* of Clifford Page and Evelyn Page (*née* Banks); *m* 1976, Carole Watson; one *s* one *d. Educ:* W Leeds Boys' High Sch.; Leeds Poly. FCCA 1976. Trainee accountant, CEGB, 1972–74; Leeds City Council, 1974–: Chief Accountant, 1985–88; Asst Dir of Finance, 1988–89; Sen. Asst Dir of Finance, 1989–92; Dir of Finance, 1992–99; Exec. Dir (Resources), 1999–2001. Chief Finance Officer, W Yorks PTA, 2000–; Dir, Educn Leeds, 2001–. Mem. Bd, Yorkshire CCC, 2006–. *Recreations:* music, all sports, caravanning, quizzes. *Address:* 3 Stonegate, Ossett, Wakefield, WF5 0JD. *T:* (01924) 279875; *e-mail:* davejpage@btinternet.com.

PAGE, David Michael; Chairman: The Clapham House Group PLC, since 2003; Clerkenwell Ventures plc, since 2005; *b* 20 June 1952; *s* of Edwin D. and N. M. E. Page; *m* 1980, Julia Hatts; three *s* one *d. Educ:* by Jesuits. Cartographer, 1970–71; waiter, PizzaExpress, 1973–76; primary sch. teacher, 1975–76; PizzaExpress: major-franchise, 1981–93; Man. Dir, 1993–96; Chief Exec., 1996–98, 2000–03, Chm., 1998–2002; non-exec. Dir, 2003–05. Non-exec. Dir, Singer and Friedlander AIM VCT Trust, 2005–. FRSA. *Recreations:* theatre, Royal Opera House, cricket, watching and playing. *Address:* Clerkenwell Ventures plc, 15 Frith Street, W1D 4RF; The Clapham House Group PLC, 1 Lyndsey Street, EC1A 9HP. *T:* 07836 346934; *e-mail:* david.page@claphamhousegroup.com.

PAGE, David Norman, ARSA; RIBA; Senior Partner, Page\Park Architects, since 1981; *b* 4 Sept. 1957; *s* of Catherine and Bernard Page. *Educ:* Strathclyde Univ. (BSc; BArch). ARIAS 1982. Lectr, Dept of Architecture and Bldg Sci., Strathclyde Univ., 1982–94. Mem., Royal Fine Art Commn for Scotland, 1995. Projects include: Mus. of Scottish Country Life; Maggie's Highland Cancer Care Centre, Inverness (Best Bldg in Scotland, RIAS Award, 2006). DUniv Strathclyde, 2004. *Publication:* (with Miles Glendinning) Clone City, 1999. *Recreation:* walking streets and landscapes. *Address:* Page\Park Architects, James Morrison Street, Glasgow; *e-mail:* d.page@pagepark.co.uk. *Club:* Adam Smith.

PAGE, Rt Rev. Dennis Fountain; *b* 1 Dec. 1919; *s* of Prebendary Martin Fountain Page and Lilla Fountain Page; *m* 1946; Margaret Bettine Clayton; two *s* one *d. Educ:* Shrewsbury Sch.; Gonville and Caius Coll., Cambridge (MA); Lincoln Theological Coll.; BSc Open Univ., 1996. Curate, Rugby Parish Church, 1943; Priest-in-Charge, St George's Church, Hillmorton, Rugby, 1945; Rector of Hockwold, Vicar of Wilton and Rector of Weeting, Norfolk, 1949; Archdeacon of Huntingdon and Vicar of Yaxley, 1965–75; Hon. Canon of Ely Cathedral, 1968; Bishop Suffragan of Lancaster, 1975–85. *Publication:* Reflections on the Reading for Holy Communion in the Alternative Service Book 1980, 1983. *Recreations:* music, astronomy, gardening. *Address:* Larkrise, Hartest Hill, Hartest, Bury St Edmunds, Suffolk IP29 4ES.

PAGE, Prof. Edward Charles, PhD; FBA 2001; Sidney and Beatrice Webb Professor of Public Policy, London School of Economics, since 2001; *b* London, 19 Oct. 1953; *s* of Edward Charles Page and Winifred Victoria Page; *m* 1975, Christine Mary Batty; one *s* two *d. Educ:* Kingston Poly. (BA (CNAA) German and Politics 1976); Univ. of Strathclyde (MSc Politics 1978; PhD Politics 1982). Lectr in Politics, Univ. of Strathclyde, 1978–81; University of Hull: Lectr, 1981–89; Sen. Lectr, 1989–92; Reader, 1992–95; Prof., 1995–2001. Vis. Associate Prof., Texas A&M Univ., 1986–87. Dir, ESRC Res. Prog. on Future Governance: Lessons from Comparative Public Policy, 1998–2003. Co-Ed., Eur. Jl Political Res., 2000–06; Associate Ed., Jl of Public Policy, 2006–. *Publications:* (ed with R. Rose) Fiscal Stress in Cities, 1982; Political Authority and Bureaucratic Power, 1985, 2nd edn 1992; (ed with M. Goldsmith) Central and Local Government Relations: a comparative analysis of West European Unitary States, 1987; Centralism and Localism in Europe, 1992; (ed with J. Hayward) Governing the New Europe, 1995; People Who Run Europe, 1997; (ed with V. Wright) Bureaucratic Elites in Western Europe, 1999; Governing by Numbers: delegated legislation and everyday policy making, 2001; (jtly) Policy Bureaucracy: government with a cast of thousands, 2005; (ed with V. Wright) From the Active to the Service State, 2006; contrib. to jls incl. British Jl Pol Sci., Eur. Jl Pol Res., Govt and Policy, W Eur. Politics, Jl Public Policy, Jl Theoretical Politics, Leviathan, Local Govt Studies, Pol Studies, Politique et Management Publique, Pouvoirs, Public Admin, Urban Affairs Qly. *Recreation:* jazz. *Address:* Department of Government, London School of Economics, Houghton Street, WC2A 2AE. *T:* (020) 7849 4629.

PAGE, Ewan Stafford, PhD, MA, BSc; Vice-Chancellor, University of Reading, 1979–93; *b* 17 Aug. 1928; *s* of late Joseph William Page and Lucy Quayle (*née* Stafford); *m* 1955, Sheila Margaret Smith; three *s* one *d. Educ:* Wyggeston Grammar Sch., Leicester; Christ's Coll., Cambridge (MA, PhD, Rayleigh Prize 1952); Univ. of London (BSc). Instr, RAF Techn. Coll., 1949–51; Lectr in Statistics, Durham Colls, 1954–57; Director: Durham Univ. Computing Lab., 1957–63; Newcastle Univ. Computing Lab., 1963–78; Visiting Prof., Univ. of N Carolina, Chapel Hill, USA, 1962–63; University of Newcastle upon Tyne: Prof. of Computing and Data Processing, 1965–78; Pro-Vice Chancellor, 1972–78 (Actg Vice-Chancellor, 1976–77). Member: Newcastle AHA, 1976–79; Berks AHA, 1980–82; Oxford RHA, 1982–84; West Berks DHA, 1984–93; Berks HA, 1993–96. Mem. Bd, Aycliffe and Peterlee Develt Corp., 1969–78. Chairman: Food Adv. Cttee, 1988–94; Univs' Authorities Panel, 1988–93. Pres., British Computer Soc., 1984–85 (Dep. Pres., 1983–84); Member: Gen. Optical Council, 1984–2001 (Vice-Chm., 1989–2001); Bd, Optical Consumer Complaints Service, 1999–; Vice-Pres., Assoc. of Optometrists, 2002–05; Hon. Treasurer, Royal Statistical Soc., 1983–89. CCMI (CBIM 1986); Hon. Fellow, Amer. Statistical Assoc., 1974; Hon. FBCS, 1976; Hon. Fellow, Northumbria Univ. (formerly Newcastle upon Tyne Poly.), 1979. Hon. DSc Reading, 1993. Chevalier, l'Ordre des Palmes Académiques (France), 1991. *Publications:* (jtly) Information Representation and Manipulation in a Computer, 1973, 2nd edn 1978; (jtly) Introduction to Computational Combinatorics, 1978; papers in statistical and computing jls. *Recreations:* golf, music, reading, Freemasonry. *Address:* High View, Charlcombe Lane, Bath BA1 5TT.

PAGE, Gordon Francis de Courcy, CBE 2000; FRAeS; DL; Chairman, Cobham plc, 2001–08; *b* 17 Nov. 1943; *s* of Sir Frederick William Page, CBE, FRS and late Kathleen (*née* de Courcy); *m* 1969, Judith Cecilia Mays; two *s* two *d. Educ:* Moffats Prep. Sch.; Cheltenham Coll.; St Catharine's Coll., Cambridge (BA; MA 1970). With Rolls-Royce plc, 1962–89; Cobham plc, 1990–2008, Chief Exec., 1992–2001. Mem., 2000–, Chm., 2004–, Industrial Develt Adv. Bd, DTI. Mem., Dorset LSC, 2001–; Pres., Dorset Chamber of Commerce and Industry, 2004–05; Mem., SW Innovation and Sci. Council, 2005–. Chairman: FKI plc, 2004–; Hamworthy plc, 2004–; PH Warr plc, 2008–. President: SBAC, 1997–98, 2002–03; Chartered Mgt Inst., 2003–04; Mem. Council, 2000–, Pres., 2006–07, RAeS. Pro-Chancellor, Cranfield Univ., 2007–. Gov., Canford Sch., 2003– (Dep. Chm., 2008–). FInstD 1990. DL Dorset, 2006. Hon. DSc Cranfield, 2003. *Recreations:* theatre, travel, classic cars. *Address:* Avon Reach, The Close, Avon Castle, Ringwood, Hants BH24 2BJ. *T:* (01425) 475365, *Fax:* (01425) 425680; *e-mail:* gordonpage@btinternet.com.

PAGE, Howard William Barrett; QC 1987; *b* 11 Feb. 1943; *s* of Leslie Herbert Barrett Page and Phyllis Elizabeth Page; *m* 1969, Helen Joanna Shotter (LVO 1996); two *s* one *d. Educ:* Radley Coll.; Trinity Hall, Cambridge (MA, LLB). Called to the Bar, Lincoln's Inn, 1967 (Mansfield Schol.); Bencher, 1994. Comr, Royal Ct of Jersey, 2000–; Dep. Pres., Lloyd's Appeal Tribunal, 2000–. *Recreations:* music, walking. *Address:* 6 New Square, Lincoln's Inn, WC2A 3QS.

PAGE, Hugo; *see* Page, A. H. M.

PAGE, Jennifer Anne, CBE 1994; Chief Executive, New Millennium Experience Company Ltd, 1997–2000; *b* 12 Nov. 1944; *d* of Edward and Olive Page; *m* 2001, Jeremy David Orme, *qv. Educ:* Barr's Hill Grammar School, Coventry; Royal Holloway College, Univ. of London (BA Hons). Entered Civil Service, 1968; Principal, DoE, 1974; Asst Sec., Dept of Transport, 1980; seconded BNOC, 1981; LDDC, 1983; Senior Vice-Pres., Pallas Invest SA, 1984–89; Chief Executive: English Heritage (Historic Buildings and Monuments Commn), 1989–95; Millennium Commn, 1995–97. Vice-Chair, Cathedrals Fabric Commn for England, 2006–. Member, Board: Railtrack Group, 1994–2001; Equitable Life Assurance Soc., 1994–2001.

PAGE, Sir John; *see* Page, Sir A. J.

PAGE, Maj.-Gen. John Humphrey, CB 1977; OBE 1967; MC 1952; *b* 5 March 1923; *s* of late Captain W. J. Page, JP, Devizes and late Alice Mary Page (*née* Richards); *m* 1956, Angela Mary Bunting; three *s* one *d. Educ:* Stonyhurst. Commnd into RE, 1942; served in NW Europe, India, Korea, Middle East and UK, 1942–60; Instr, Staff Coll., Camberley, 1960–62; comd 32 Armd Engr Regt, 1964–67; idc 1968; CCRE 1st Br. Corps, 1969–70; Asst Comdt, RMA Sandhurst, 1971–74; Dir of Personal Services (Army), MoD, 1974–78, retd. Col Comdt, RE, 1980–85. Dir, London Law Trust, 1979–88. Dir, RBM (Holdings), 1980–86. Member Council: REOWS, 1980–92 (Chm., 1990–92; Chm. Investment Cttee, 1990–95); Officers' Pension Soc., 1979–96; Vice-Chm., SSAFA, 1983–87. Chm. Trustees, Home-Start Consultancy, 1982–90; Mem., Management Cttee, Stackpole Trust, 1981–92; Chm. for Wilts, Winged Fellowship Trust, 1997–2000; Chm., The Trust For Devizes, 1999–2002. Chm., Bd of Governors, St Mary's Sch., Shaftesbury, 1985–93 (Trustee, St Mary Sch. Shaftesbury Trust, 1990–99); Mem., Bd of Governors, Stonyhurst Coll., 1980–90 (Trustee, Stonyhurst Charitable Fund, 1983–97). KSG 1993. *Recreations:* rough gardening, watercolour painting, military history, English cathedrals and churches, the family, including fifteen grandchildren. *Address:* c/o Lloyds TSB, Devizes, Wiltshire.

PAGE, Prof. John Kenneth; energy and environmental consultant; Professor of Building Science, University of Sheffield, 1960–84, now Emeritus; *b* 3 Nov. 1924; *s* of late Brig. E. K. Page, CBE, DSO, MC; *m* 1954, Anita Bell Lovell; two *s* two *d*. *Educ:* Haileybury College; Pembroke College, Cambridge. Served War of 1939–45, Royal Artillery, 1943–47. Asst Industrial Officer, Council of Industrial Design, 1950–51; taught Westminster School, 1952–53; Sen. Scientific Officer, Tropical Liaison Section, Building Research Station, 1953–56; Chief Research Officer, Nuffield Div. for Architectural Studies, 1956–57; Lecturer, Dept of Building Science, Univ. of Liverpool, 1957–60. Sen. Res. Fellow, Dept of Physics, UMIST, 2000–03; Fellow, Tyndall Centre for Climate Change, UMIST, subseq. Univ. of Manchester, 2002–05. Chm., Environmental Gp, and Mem., Econ. Planning Council, Yorks and Humberside Region, 1965–78; Regl Chm., Yorks and Humberside, CPRE, 2003–. Founding Chm., UK Section, Internat. Solar Energy Soc.; Initiating Dir, Cambridge Interdisciplinary Envmtl Centre, 1990–92. Consultant author working with UN internat. agencies on energy use in Third World and on environmental health in tropical bldgs; working with WMO on revision of internat. technical note on building climatology, 2005. Farrington Daniels Internat. Award, for distinguished contribs to solar energy studies, 1989. *Publications:* 200 papers on Energy policy, Environmental Design and Planning, Environmental Management, Building Climatology and Solar Energy. *Address:* 15 Brincliffe Gardens, Sheffield S11 9BG. *T:* (0114) 255 1570.

PAGE, Oliver, OBE 2004; financial services consultant, since 2006; *b* 29 April 1946; *s* of Sir Harry Robertson Page and Lady Elsie Page (*née* Dixon); *m* 1968, Jennifer Jane Murphy; one *d*. *Educ:* Trinity Coll., Cambridge (MA; DipEcon). Bank of England, 1968–98: posts included: Chief Manager, Reserves Management, 1984–90; Hd of Banking Supervision, 1996–98; Dir, Complex, then Financial, later Major Retail Gps Div., Sector Leader for Financial Stability and Dir responsible for ARROW2, FSA, 1998–2006. UK Alternate Dir, EIB, 1989–95. Non-executive Director: Mitsubishi UFJ Securities Internat. Ltd; HBOS; consultant, LTSB. Mem., Basel Cttee on Banking Supervision, 1998–2006 (Chm., Capital Gp, 1999–2005; Co-Chm., Jt Basel/IOSCO Trading Book Review, 2004–05). *Address: e-mail:* jennandoliver.page@ntlworld.com.

PAGE, Piers John B.; *see* Burton-Page.

PAGE, Prof. Raymond Ian, LittD; Fellow, Corpus Christi College, Cambridge, since 1962; Elrington and Bosworth Professor of Anglo-Saxon, University of Cambridge, 1984–91, now Professor Emeritus; *b* 25 Sept. 1924; *s* of Reginald Howard Page and Emily Louise Page; *m* 1953, Elin Benedicte Hustad, *d* of Tormod Kristoffer Hustad and Anne Margarethe Hustad, Oslo; two *d* (one *s* decd). *Educ:* King Edward VII Sch., Sheffield; Rotherham Technical Coll,; Univ. of Sheffield. LittD Cambridge 1974. Assistant Lecturer and Lecturer, Univ. of Nottingham, 1951–61; Cambridge University: successively Lectr, Reader and Professor, Dept of Anglo-Saxon, Norse and Celtic, 1961–91; Sandars Reader in Bibliography, 1989–90; Corpus Christi College: Librarian, 1965–91; Dir, Leverhulme Trust Res. Gp on MS Evidence, Parker Liby, 1989–94. Special Prof. in Anglo-Saxon Studies, Univ. of Nottingham, 1992–97; Hon. Sen. Res. Fellow, Dept of Eng. Lang., Univ. of Glasgow, 1993–; Hon. Res. Fellow, Dept of Anglo-Saxon, Norse and Celtic, Univ. of Cambridge, 2007–. Hon. LittD Sheffield, 1994; Hon. Dr philos Trondheim, 1996. Dag Strömbäck prize, Royal Gustav Adolfs Acad., Uppsala, 1995. *Address:* Ashton House, Newnham Road, Cambridge CB3 9EY.

PAGE, Richard Lewis; *b* 22 Feb. 1941; *s* of Victor Charles and Kathleen Page; *m* 1964, Madeleine Ann Brown; one *s* one *d*. *Educ:* Hurstpierpoint Coll.; Luton Technical Coll. Apprenticeship, Vauxhall Motors, 1959–64; HNC Mech. Engineering; Chm. of family co., 1964–95, 1997–. Young Conservatives, 1964–66; Councillor, Banstead UDC, 1968–71; contested (C) Workington, Feb. and Oct. 1974; MP (C): Workington, Nov. 1976–1979; Herts SW, Dec. 1979–2005; PPS: to Sec. of State for Trade, 1981–82; to Leader of the House, 1982–87; Parly Under-Sec. of State, DTI, 1995–97; opposition front-bench spokesman on trade and industry, 2000–01. Mem., Public Accounts Cttee, 1987–95, 1997–2000; Vice-Chairman: Cons. Trade and Industry Cttee, 1988–95; All Party Engrg Gp, 1997–2005; Jt Chm., All Party Racing and Bloodstock Industries Cttee, 1998–2005; Chm., All Party Parly Scientific Cttee, 2003–05. Chm., Internat. Office, Cons. Central Office, 1999–2000. Gov., Foundn for Western Democracy, 1998–2000. Vice Chm., Chemical Industry Council, 1997–. Chm. Investment Cttee, Leukaemia Res. Fund, 2005– (Hon. Treas., 1987–95; Mem., 1991–95, 1997–). Gov. and Trustee, Royal Masonic Sch., 1984–95, 1997–. *Recreation:* most sport. *Address:* Gomshall, Surrey.

PAGE, Roy Malcolm; Headmaster, Royal Grammar School, High Wycombe, since 2006; *b* 24 June 1950; *s* of Alec John Page and Janet Selina Page; *m* 1973, Marilyn Rose Dawson; one *s* one *d*. *Educ:* Portsmouth Poly. (BSc Maths 1971); Univ. of Reading (PGCE 1972); National Coll. for Sch. Leadership (NPQH 2001). Royal Grammar School, High Wycombe: Teacher of Maths, 1972–; Boarding Housemaster, 1982–84; Dep. Headmaster, 1989–2001; Sen. Dep. Headmaster, 2001–06. Member: NT; RSPB. *Recreations:* hockey, cricket, Rugby, golf, keeping fit, classic cars, bird watching, foreign travel. *Address:* Royal Grammar School, Amersham Road, High Wycombe, Bucks HP13 6QT. *T:* (01494) 551403, *Fax:* (01494) 551419; *e-mail:* rmp@rgshw.com. *Clubs:* Rotary (Princes Risborough); High Wycombe Sports; Knotty Green Cricket.

PAGE, Simon Richard; District Judge (formerly Registrar), Guildford, Epsom and Reigate County Courts, and High Court of Justice, 1980–2000; a Recorder of the Crown Court, 1980–99; *b* 7 March 1934; *s* of Eric Rowland Page and Vera (*née* Fenton); *m* 1st, 1963 (marr. diss. 1977); three *s* one *d*; 2nd, 1984. *Educ:* Lancing; LSE (LLB External, 1956). Admitted solicitor (hons), 1957. National Service, Second Lieut RA, 1957–59. Private practice as solicitor, 1959–75; Pres., West Surrey Law Soc., 1972–73; Registrar, Croydon County Court, 1975–80; Pres., Assoc. of County Court and District Registrars, 1983–84. *Recreations:* squash racquets, cricket, bridge. *Address:* c/o The Law Courts, Mary Road, Guildford GU1 4PS.

PAGE, Stephen Alexander; Chief Executive and Publisher, Faber & Faber Ltd, since 2001; *b* 17 Feb. 1965; *s* of James and Frances Page; *m* 1993, Caroline Hird; two *s*. *Educ:* Bristol Univ. (BA Hons History). Bookseller, 1986–88; Marketing Exec./Manager, Longman, 1988–90; variety of roles at Transworld Publishers, 1990–94; 4th Estate: Sales Dir, 1994–95; Dep. Man. Dir, 1995–2000, Man. Dir, 2000; Gp Sales and Mktg Dir, HarperCollins Publishers, 2000–01. Pres., Publishers Assoc., 2006–07. *Recreations:* music (listening and playing), film, reading, parenting, food. *Address:* Faber & Faber Ltd, 3 Queen Square, WC1N 3AU. *T:* (020) 7465 7603; *e-mail:* stephen.page@faber.co.uk.

PAGE WOOD, Sir Anthony John, 8th Bt *cr* 1837; *b* 6 Feb. 1951; *s* of Sir David (John Hatherley) Page Wood, 7th Bt and of Evelyn Hazel Rosemary, *d* of late Captain George Ernest Bellville; *S* father, 1955. *Educ:* Harrow. Dir, Société Générale, London, 1988–2001. *Heir: kinsman* Matthew Wakefield Drury Evelyn-Wood [*b* 9 July 1917; *m*; one *s*]. *Address:* 77 Dovehouse Street, SW3 6JZ.

PAGET, family name of **Marquess of Anglesey**.

PAGET DE BEAUDESERT, Lord; Benedict Dashiel Paget; *b* 11 April 1986; *s* and *heir* of Earl of Uxbridge, *qv*.

PAGET, David Christopher John; QC 1994; **His Honour Judge Paget;** a Circuit Judge, since 1997; a Permanent Judge, Central Criminal Court, since 1998; *b* 3 Feb. 1942; *s* of late Henry Paget and Dorothy Paget (*née* Colenutt), Johannesburg, S Africa; *m* 1968, Dallas Wendy (*née* Hill); two *d*. *Educ:* St John's Coll., Johannesburg; Inns of Court Sch. of Law. Called to Bar, Inner Temple, 1967, Bencher, 2003; Jun. Prosecuting Counsel to the Crown, 1982–89, Sen. Prosecuting Counsel, 1989–94, CCC; a Recorder, 1986–97. Freeman, City of London, 1999; Liveryman, Co. of Coopers, 1999–. *Recreations:* walking, bird watching, listening to music. *Address:* Central Criminal Court, Old Bailey, EC4M 7EH. *T:* (020) 7248 3277. *Club:* Garrick.

PAGET, Lt-Col Sir Julian (Tolver), 4th Bt *cr* 1871; CVO 1984; an Extra Gentleman Usher to the Queen, since 1991 (Gentleman Usher, 1971–91); author; *b* 11 July 1921; *s* of General Sir Bernard Paget, GCB, DSO, MC (*d* 1961) (*g s* of 1st Bt), and Winifred (*d* 1986), *d* of Sir John Paget, 2nd Bt; *S* uncle, Sir James Francis Paget, 3rd Bt, 1972; *m* 1954, Diana Frances, *d* of late F. S. H. Farmer; one *s* one *d*. *Educ:* Radley College; Christ Church, Oxford (MA). Joined Coldstream Guards, 1940; served North West Europe, 1944–45; retired as Lt-Col, 1968. Ed., Guards Magazine, 1976–93. *Publications:* Counter-Insurgency Campaigning, 1967; Last Post: Aden, 1964–67, 1969; The Story of the Guards, 1976; The Pageantry of Britain, 1979; Yeomen of the Guard, 1984; Discovering London's Ceremonial and Traditions, 1989; Wellington's Peninsular War: the battles and battlefields, 1990; Hougoument, The Key to Victory at Waterloo, 1992; No Problem Too Difficult, 1999; (ed) The Coldstream Guards 1650–2000, 2000; The Crusading General: the life of General Sir Bernard Paget, 2008. *Recreations:* fishing, shooting, travel, writing. *Heir: s* Henry James Paget [*b* 2 Feb. 1959; *m* 1993, Mrs Margrete Varvill (*née* Lynner); one *s* one *d*]. *Clubs:* Cavalry and Guards, Flyfishers'.

See also N. J. Cox.

PAGET, Sir Richard (Herbert), 4th Bt *cr* 1886, of Cranmore Hall, Co. Somerset; independent marketing consultant; *b* 17 Feb. 1957; *s* of Sir John Starr Paget, 3rd Bt and Nancy Mary, *d* of Lt-Col Francis Parish, DSO, MC; *S* father, 1992; *m* 1985, Richenda Rachel, *d* of Rev. Preb. J. T. C. B. Collins; three *d*. *Educ:* Eton Coll. AES, 1983–87; Nixdorf Computers, 1987–88; Inforem plc, 1988–89; Sales Manager, SAS Inst., 1989–95; Outplacement Councillor, Encos, 1995–97; Empathy Audit Manager, Harding and Yorke Ltd, 1997–99; Business Development Manager: UMTC, 1999–2001; Somersault Creative Marketing, 2001–; non-exec. Dir, SFM Technol. Ltd, 1999–. Mem. Ct, Russia Co. Pres., Paget Gorman Signed Speech Soc. *Recreations:* carriage driving, cricket, tennis. *Heir: b* David Vernon John Paget [*b* 26 March 1959; *m* 1990, Cluny Macpherson; one *s* two *d*]. *Address:* Burridge Heath Farm, Little Bedwyn, Marlborough, Wilts SN8 3JR; *e-mail:* richard@pagets.org.uk.

PAGET-WILKES, Ven. Michael Jocelyn James; Archdeacon of Warwick, since 1990; *b* 11 Dec. 1941; *s* of Arthur Hamilton Paget-Wilkes and Eleanor Bridget Paget-Wilkes; *m* 1969, Ruth Gillian Macnamara; one *s* two *d*. *Educ:* Harper Adams Agricultural Coll. (NDA); London Coll. of Divinity (ALCD). Agricultural Extension Officer, Tanzania, 1964–66; attended London Coll. of Divinity, 1966–69; Curate, All Saints', Wandsworth, 1969–74; Vicar: St James', Hatcham, New Cross, 1974–82; St Matthew's, Rugby, 1982–90. *Publications:* The Church and Rural Development, 1968; Poverty, Revolution and the Church, 1981. *Recreations:* squash, tennis, music, ski-ing, gardening. *Address:* 10 Northumberland Road, Leamington Spa, Warwicks CV32 6HA.

PAGETT, Nicola Mary; actress; *b* 15 June 1945; *d* of Barbara Scott and H. W. F. Scott; took stage name of Pagett; *m* 1977, Graham Swannell (marr. diss. 1999); one *d*. *Educ:* St Maurs Convent, Yokohama; The Beehive, Bexhill; RADA. *Stage:* Voyage Round My Father, Haymarket, 1971; Ophelia in Hamlet, Greenwich, 1974; Yahoo, Queen's, 1976; Taking Steps, Lyric, 1980; The Trojan War will not take place, NT, 1983; School for Scandal, Duke of York's, 1984; Aren't We All?, Haymarket, 1984; Old Times, Haymarket, 1985; The Light of Day, Hammersmith, 1987; The Rehearsal, Garrick, 1990; Party Time, Almeida, 1991; The Rules of the Game, Almeida, 1992; What the Butler Saw, NT, 1995; *films:* Seven Men at Daybreak, 1974; Oliver's Story, 1978; Privates on Parade, 1982; *television series:* Upstairs, Downstairs, 1972; Napoleon in Love, 1974; Anna Karenina, 1977; Scoop, 1987; A Bit of a Do, 1988–90; Ain't Misbehavin', 1994–95. *Publication:* Diamonds Behind My Eyes, 1997. *Address:* c/o Gavin Barker Associates, 2D Wimpole Street, W1G 0ED.

PAGLIARI, Paul; Director, Change and Corporate Services, Scottish Government (formerly Scottish Executive), 2006; *b* 31 March 1960; *s* of Luigi and Giovanna Pagliari. *Educ:* Univ. of Glasgow (MA 1981). FCIPD. Director of Human Resources: Scottish Power, 1999–2001; Scottish Water, 2002–05; Immigration and Nationality Directorate, Home Office, 2005–06. Mem., Employment Appeals Tribunal. *Recreations:* ski-ing, tennis, socialising, reading, cinema.

PAGNAMENTA, Peter John; television producer and writer; *b* 12 April 1941; *s* of Charles Francis Pagnamenta and Daphne Pagnamenta; *m* 1966, Sybil Healy; one *s* one *d*. *Educ:* Shrewsbury; Trinity Hall, Cambridge (MA). Joined BBC, 1965; Prodn Asst, Tonight and 24 Hours, 1965–67; Asst Editor, 24 Hours, 1967; New York office, 1968–71 (Producer, US Election coverage and Apollo flights); Editor: 24 Hours, 1971; Midweek, 1972–75; Panorama, 1975–77; Dir of News and Current Affairs, Thames Television, 1977–80; Exec. Producer, All Our Working Lives (eleven part series), BBC2, 1984; Editor, Real Lives (documentary strand), BBC 1, 1984–85; Head of Current Affairs Gp, BBC TV, 1985–87; Exec. Producer, BBC TV Documentary Dept, 1981–85, 1987–97; Executive Producer: Nippon (eight parts), BBC 2, 1990; People's Century (26 parts), BBC 1, 1995–99; Pagnamenta Associates Ltd: Bubble Trouble (three parts), BBC 2, 2000. *Publications:* (with Richard Overy) All Our Working Lives, 1984; (ed) The Hidden Hall, 2005; (with Momoko Williams) Falling Blossom, 2006. *Recreations:* walking, fishing. *Address:* 145 Elgin Crescent, W11 2JH. *T:* (020) 7727 9960.

PAHL, Prof. Raymond Edward, PhD; FBA 2008; Visiting Research Professor in Sociology, Institute of Social and Economic Research, University of Essex, since 1999; Professor, University of Kent, 1972–96, now Emeritus; *b* London, 17 July 1935; *s* of Ronald Herman Pahl and Jean Fleming Pahl (*née* Heron); *m* 1959, Janice Mary Cockburn (marr. diss. 1997); two *s* one *d*. *Educ:* St Albans Sch.; St Catharine's Coll., Cambridge (BA 1959); London Sch. of Econs (PhD 1964). Extra-Mural Tutor, Univ. of Cambridge, 1959–65; Lectr, 1965–68, Sen. Lectr, 1968–72, Univ. of Kent. Pt-time Prof. of Sociol., Univ. of Essex, 1994–99; Hon. Vis. Prof., Univ. of Keele, 1999–. Assessor to Gtr London Develt Plan Inquiry, 1970–72. Member: Social Studies Sub-Cttee, Univ. Grants Cttee, 1979–89; Archbishop of Canterbury's Commn on Urban Priority Areas, 1983–85. President: RC21, Internat. Sociological Assoc., 1974–78; Section N, BAAS, 1975. AcSS 2004. *Publications:* Whose City?, 1970; (with J. M. Pahl) Managers and Their Wives, 1971; Divisions of Labour, 1984 (trans. Spanish, 1991); After Success: fin-de-siècle anxiety and identity, 1995 (trans. Portuguese, 1997); On Friendship, 2000 (trans. Spanish, 2003); (with

L. Spencer) Rethinking Friendship, 2006. *Recreations:* collecting Italian and British art, choral singing, hill walking, pottering in house and garden. *Address:* Institute of Social and Economic Research, University of Essex, Wivenhoe Park, Colchester, Essex CO4 3SQ. *T:* (01206) 872645, *Fax:* (01206) 873151; *e-mail:* rpahl@essex.ac.uk.

PAIBA, His Honour Denis Anthony; a Circuit Judge, 1982–98; *b* 10 Dec. 1926; *e s* of late Geoffrey Paiba and Geraldine Paiba; *m* 1955, Lesley Patricia Dresden; two *s*. *Educ:* University Coll. Sch. (Junior); Magdalen Coll. Sch., Oxford; Jesus Coll., Cambridge. 44 Royal Marine Commando, 1945–47. Financial Times, 1957–58. Called to the Bar, Gray's Inn, 1958; a Dep. Circuit Judge and a Dep. Family Div. Judge, 1969–80; a Recorder of the Crown Court, 1980–82. *Recreations:* theatre, music, gardening, study of English ceramics up to 1850, watching Rugby and cricket, wining and dining. *Address:* 11 Angel Mews, Roehampton High Street, SW15 4HU. *T:* and *Fax:* (020) 8788 4674.

PAICE, Clifford, FCILT; Member and Group Director, Economic Regulation, Civil Aviation Authority, 1989–97; *b* 26 Feb. 1938; *s* of Owen Edward and Dorothy Paice; *m* 1968, Elisabeth Marlin (*see* E. W. Paice); one *s* two *d*. *Educ:* Cambridgeshire High Sch.; LSE (BSc Econ.). FCILT (FCIT 1990). Joined Civil Service, 1959: War Office, 1959–61; MoD, 1962–65; Min. of Econ. Affairs, 1965–68; Treasury, 1968–72; Head, Econ. Divs, CAA, 1972–89. FRSA 1997. *Address:* 142 Cromwell Tower, Barbican, EC2Y 8DD. *T:* (020) 7628 5228.

PAICE, Elisabeth Willemien, FRCP; Dean Director, London Deanery (formerly Department of Postgraduate Medical and Dental Education), University of London, since 2001; *b* 23 April 1945; *d* of Ervin Ross, (Spike), Marlin and Hilda van Stockum, HRHA; *m* 1968, Clifford Paice, *qv*; one *s* two *d*. *Educ:* Trinity Coll., Dublin (MB, BCh, BAO, MA); Dundee Univ. (Dip. Med. Ed.). FRCP 1989. Clinical training, Westminster Hosp.; Senior Registrar in Rheumatology: Stoke Mandeville Hosp., 1977–79; UCH, 1979–82; Consultant Rheumatologist, Whittington Hosp. NHS Trust, 1982–95; Associate Dean, N Thames E, 1992–95, Dean Dir, N Thames, 1995–2000, Postgrad. Medicine, Univ. of London. Vis. Prof., Faculty of Clinical Scis, UCL, 2003–. Chm., Conf. of Postgrad. Med. Deans, 2006–. *Publications:* Delivering the New Doctor, 1998; contrib. various articles on rheumatology and postgrad. med. educn. *Address:* London Deanery, Stewart House, 32 Russell Square, WC1B 5DN. *T:* (020) 7866 3237.

PAICE, James Edward Thornton; MP (C) Cambridgeshire South East, since 1987; *b* 24 April 1949; *s* of late Edward Paice and of Winifred Paice; *m* 1973, Ava Barbara Patterson; two *s*. *Educ:* Framlingham College, Suffolk; Writtle Agricultural College. Farm Manager, 1970–73; farmer, 1973–79; Framlingham Management and Training Services Ltd: Training Officer, 1979–82; Training Manager, 1982–85; Gen. Manager/Exec. Dir, 1985–87; non-exec. Dir, 1987–89; non-exec. Dir, United Framlingham Farmers, 1989–94. PPS to Minister of State, 1989–91, to Minister, 1991–93, MAFF, to Sec. of State for the Envmt, 1993–94; Parly Under-Sec. of State, DFE, then DFEE, 1994–97; opposition front bench spokesman on agriculture, 1997–2001, on home affairs, 2001–04; Shadow Minister for Agriculture and Rural Affairs, 2005– (Shadow Sec. of State, 2004–05). Mem., Select Cttee on Employment, 1987–89. Chm., All Party Racing and Bloodstock Cttee, 1992–94. Gov., Writtle Agricl Coll., 1991–94. *Recreations:* shooting, countryside issues. *Address:* House of Commons, SW1A 0AA.

PAIGE, Deborah Penrose; freelance theatre and television director; *b* 7 Feb. 1950; *d* of David and Barbara Dunhill; *m* 1969, John Paige (marr. diss. 1985); two *d*. *Educ:* Godalming County Grammar Sch.; Dartington Hall Sch.; Bristol Old Vic Theatre Sch. Actress, 1970–84; Asst Dir, Bristol Old Vic, 1986–87; Associate Dir, Soho Theatre Co., 1988–90; Artistic Director: Salisbury Playhouse, 1990–94, productions incl. A Midsummer Night's Dream, 1991, The Tempest, 1992, States of Shock (co-production with Nat. Th.), 1993, For Services Rendered (transf. Old Vic), 1993; Sheffield Theatres, 1995–2000, productions incl. The Merchant of Venice, 1996, King Lear, 1997, South Pacific, 1997, Brassed Off (transf. NT), 1999; Founder, Paigeworks, 2005. Regular guest dir, RADA and LAMDA. Director, television: Eastenders, 2001–02; Casualty, 2003, 2005; Judge John Deed, 2004; Holby City, 2006–07. *Recreations:* walking, music, reading.

PAIGE, Elaine, OBE 1995; actress and singer; *b* 5 March 1948; *d* of Eric Bickerstaff and Irene Bickerstaff. *Educ:* Southaw Sch. for Girls, Barnet. *Theatre:* The Roar of the Greasepaint, the Smell of the Crowd, UK tour, 1964; Rock Carmen, Maybe That's Your Problem, Alexandra, Birmingham, 1966; Nuts, Stratford East, 1967; Maybe That's Your Problem, Roundhouse; West End début, Hair, Shaftesbury, 1968; Jesus Christ Superstar, Palace, 1971; Sandy in Grease, New London, 1973; Rita in Billy, Drury Lane, 1974; Eva Perón in Evita, Prince Edward, 1978 (Best Actress in a Musical, SWET, 1978); Grizabella in Cats, New London, 1981; Carabosse in Abbacadabra, Lyric Hammersmith, 1983; Florence Vassey in Chess, Prince Edward, 1986; Reno Sweeney in Anything Goes, Prince Edward, 1989 (co-producer); Edith Piaf in Piaf, Piccadilly, 1993; Norma Desmond in Sunset Boulevard, Adelphi, 1994 and 1995, NY, 1996; Célimène in The Misanthrope, Piccadilly, 1998; Anna in The King and I, London Palladium, 2000–01; Angèle in Where There's a Will, UK tour, 2003; Mrs Lovett in Sweeney Todd, NY, 2004; Beatrice Stockwell in The Drowsy Chaperone, Novello, 2007; has appeared in four Royal Variety Performances; *television:* Phyllis Dixey, Ladykillers, 1980; Ladybirds, 1980; Elaine Paige in Concert, 1985; A View of Harry Clark (play), 1988; Showstoppers: In Concert at the White House, 1988; Unexplained Laughter (play), 1989; Elaine Paige in Concert, 1991; South Bank Show: the faces of Elaine Paige, 1996; Boston Pops Opening, 1997; Dora Bunner in A Murder is Announced, 2005; Where the Heart Is, 2005; opening of Winter Olympic Games, Salt Lake City, 2002; concert tours in UK, Europe, ME, Australia, NZ and FE. Has made numerous recordings (8 consecutive gold albums, incl. 4 multi-platinum). Variety Club Awards: Showbusiness Personality of Year, 1978; Recording Artiste of Year, 1986; Best Actress, 1995; Gold Badge of Merit, BASCA, 1993; Lifetime Achievement Award, HMV, 1996; Lifetime Achievement Award, NODA, 1999. *Recreations:* antiques, ski-ing, gardening, tennis, clay pigeon shooting. *Address:* E. P. Records, c/o Michael Storrs Music Ltd, 11 Maiden Lane, WC2E 7NA. *T:* (020) 7078 1458, *Fax:* (020) 7078 1456; *e-mail:* msm@css-stellar.com. *Clubs:* Mosimann's, Queen's.

PAIGE, Victor Grellier, CBE 1978; Chairman, National Health Service Management Board, and Second Permanent Secretary, Department of Health and Social Security, 1985–86; *b* 5 June 1925; *s* of Victor Paige and Alice (*née* Grellier); *m* 1948, Kathleen Winifred, 3rd *d* of Arthur and Daisy Harris; one *s* one *d*. *Educ:* East Ham Grammar Sch.; Univ. of Nottingham. CIPD, FCILT, FAIM. Roosevelt Mem. Schol. 1954. Dep. Personnel Manager, Boots Pure Drug Co. Ltd, 1957–67; Controller of Personnel Services, CWS Ltd, 1967–70; Dir of Manpower and Organisation, 1970–74, Exec. Vice-Chm. (Admin), 1974–77, Nat. Freight Corp.; Dep. Chm., Nat. Freight Corp., later Nat. Freight Co., 1977–82; Dir, 1977–88 (non-exec., 1985–88), and Dep. Chm., 1982–85, Nat. Freight Consortium; Chm., Iveco (UK), 1984–85. Chm., PLA, 1980–85; Member: Manpower Services Commn, 1974–80; Thames Water Authy, 1983–85. Member: Notts Educn Cttee, 1957–63; Secondary Schs Examn Council, 1960–63; UK Adv. Council for Educn in Management, 1962–65; Careers Adv. Bd, Univ. of Nottingham, 1975–81; Chairman: Regional Adv. Council for Further Educn, E Mids, 1967; Exec. Council, British Assoc. for Commercial and Industrial Educn, 1974 (Vice-Pres. 1980); Pres., Inst. of Admin. Management, 1984–90; Vice-Pres., Chartered Inst. of Transport, 1984–85 (Mem. Council, 1976–79); Mem. Council, CBI, 1983–85 (Chm., Educn and Trng Cttee, 1983–85). Mem. Court, Henley, The Management College, 1985–94. Governor, British Liver Trust, 1990–98. Vice-Pres., London Fedn of Boys' Clubs. Freeman, Co. of Watermen and Lightermen of the River Thames; Freeman, City of London, 1981. Commander, Order of Orange Nassau, The Netherlands, 1982. *Publications:* contrib. techn. press on management. *Recreations:* reading, sport generally, athletics in particular (Pres. Notts Athletic Club, 1962–67). *Address:* 7 Benningfield Gardens, Castle Village, Berkhamsted, Herts HP4 2GW. *T:* (01442) 865030. *Club:* MCC.

PAIN, Barry Newton, CBE 1979; QPM 1976; Commandant, Police Staff College, Bramshill, and HM Inspector of Constabulary, 1982–87, retired; *b* 25 Feb. 1931; *s* of Godfrey William Pain and Annie Newton; *m* 1952, Marguerite Agnes King; one *s* one *d*. *Educ:* Waverley Grammar Sch., Birmingham. Clerk to Prosecuting Solicitor, Birmingham, 1947–51; 2nd Lieut (Actg Captain) RASC, Kenya, 1949–51. Birmingham City Police, 1951–68; Staff Officer to HM Inspector of Constabulary, Birmingham, 1966–68; Asst Chief Constable, Staffordshire and Stoke-on-Trent Constabulary, 1968–74; Chief Constable of Kent, 1974–82; JSSC 1970. Adviser to Turkish Govt on Reorganization of Police, 1972. Pres., Assoc. of Chief Police Officers, 1981–82. *Recreations:* golf, shooting, boating.

PAIN, Gillian Margaret; Chief Reporter, Scottish Office Inquiry Reporters Unit, 1993–96; *b* 29 May 1936; *d* of late Geoffrey Ernest Pain and Florence Agnes Pain (*née* Marshall). *Educ:* Felixstowe Coll., Suffolk; Univ. of St Andrews (MA 1957); University Coll. London (DipTP 1965). MRTPI. Asst Teacher of Geography, Northfield Sch., Watford, 1957–58; Photogrammetrist, Hunting Aero Surveys, 1958–60; Asst Map Res. Officer, Directorate of Mil. Surveys, 1960–62; posts with Essex Co. Planning Dept, 1962–73, Asst Chief County Planning Adviser, 1970–73; Department of the Environment: Sen. Housing and Planning Inspector, 1973–77; Principal Planning Inspector, 1977–86; Asst Chief Planning Inspector, 1986–93. Pres., Town and Country Planning Summer Sch., 1992–94. *Publication:* Planning and the Shopkeeper, 1967. *Recreations:* sailing, ski-ing, classical music. *Club:* Blackwater Sailing (Past Commodore) (Essex).

PAIN, Jacqualyn Christina Mary; Headmistress, Northwood College, since 2009; *b* 31 Aug. 1957; *d* of J. K. and J. W. Pain. *Educ:* Sch. of St Helen and St Katharine, Abingdon; St David's UC, Lampeter (MA); Birkbeck Coll., London Univ. (MA); Univ. of Leicester (MBA); NPQH 2001. Teacher: Tiffin Girls' Sch., 1981–83; Old Palace Sch., 1983–84; James Allen's Girls' Sch., 1984–96 (on secondment to Inst. of Educn, Univ. of London, 1992–94); Dep. Head, Northwood Coll., 1996–2000; Head, Henrietta Barnett Sch., 2000–05; Headmistress, St Albans High Sch., 2005–08. *Recreations:* running, woodwork, philosophy, cooking. *Address:* Northwood College, Maxwell Road, Northwood, Middx HA6 2YE. *Clubs:* University Women's, International Rescue.

PAINE, Sir Christopher (Hammon), Kt 1995; DM; FRCP, FRCR; Consultant in Radiotherapy and Oncology, Churchill Hospital, Oxford, 1970–95; President, British Medical Association, 2000–01; *b* 28 Aug. 1935; *s* of late Major John Hammon Paine and Hon. Mrs Joan Frances Shedden, MBE; *m* 1959, Susan Martin; two *s* two *d*. *Educ:* Eton Coll.; Merton Coll., Oxford (BM, BCh 1961; DM 1981); St Bartholomew's Hosp. Med. Sch. FRCP 1976; FRCR (FFR 1969). Junior med. posts, Oxford, London, Paris, 1962–70; Oxford University: Lectr in Radiotherapy and Oncology, 1972–95; Dir of Clinical Studies (clinical dean), 1982–85; Dist Gen. Manager, Oxfordshire HA, 1984–88; Chm., Oxford Med. Staff Council, 1991–92. Med. Dir, Adv. Cttee for Distinction Awards, 1994–99. Pres., British Oncological Assoc., 1989–91; Royal College of Radiologists: Dean, Faculty of Clinical Oncology, 1990–92; Vice-Pres., 1991–92; Pres., 1992–95. Pres., RSocMed, 1996–98. Dir, MGT Capital Investments Inc., 2002–. Member: Med. Adv. Bd, Internat. Hosps Gp Ltd, 1996–; Adv. Bd, Weill Cornell Med. Coll., Qatar, 2001–. Trustee, London Clinic, 1999–. Hon. Fellow: HK Coll. of Radiologists, 1995; Faculty of Radiologists, RCSI, 1995; Hon. FRCSE, 2005. *Publications:* papers on health services and cancer. *Recreation:* gardening. *Address:* The Avenue, Wotton Underwood, Aylesbury, Bucks HP18 0RP. *T:* (01296) 770742; *e-mail:* northavenue@btinternet.com. *Club:* Farmers'.

PAINE, Surg. Rear Adm. Michael Patrick William Halden, FRCS; Medical Director General (Naval), 1997–99; *b* 18 March 1939; *s* of Comdr Geoffrey W. W. H. Paine, RN and Eileen Paine (*née* Irwin); *m* 1972, Thayer Clark. *Educ:* Downside Sch.; London Hosp. Med. Coll. (MB BS 1963); Southampton Univ.; Edinburgh Univ. FRCS 1976. Joined Royal Navy, 1963; HMS Plymouth, 1965–66; HMS Repulse (SSBN), 1967–68; surgical trainee, RN Hosp. Haslar, 1969–75; PMO, HMS Bulwark, 1975–76; RN Hosp. Plymouth, 1977–79; Orthopaedic Senior Registrar: Southampton Gen. and Lord Mayor Treloar's Hosps, 1979; RN Hosp. Haslar, 1980; Cons. Orth. Surg., RN Hosp. Plymouth, 1981–82; HMS Illustrious, 1982–84; Cons. Orth. Surg., RN Hosp. Haslar, 1984–88; RAMC Sen. Officers' Course (Course Medal), 1986; Defence Med. Services Directorate, MoD, 1988–90 (Mem., Thompson Rev. of Service Hosps); Fleet MO, 1990–92; ACOS (Med. and Dental), C-in-C Fleet, 1992–97. QHS 1994–99. *Recreation:* sailing. *Address:* 513 Canaan Street, Canaan, NH 03741, USA.

PAINE, Peter Stanley, CBE 1981; DFC 1944; Chairman, Oracle Teletext Ltd, 1984–93; *b* 19 June 1921; *s* of Arthur Bertram Paine and Dorothy Helen Paine; *m* 1st, 1942, Sheila Mary (*d* 1994), *d* of Frederick Wigglesworth, MA; two *s* two *d*; 2nd, 1999, Marion Dyason Strong (*née* Hunter). *Educ:* King's Sch., Canterbury. Served 1940–46, 2 Gp RAF (Flt-Lt). Worked in Punch Publishing Office, 1945–47; Sales Promotion Man., Newnes Pearson, 1948–52, Odhams Press, then Sales Dir and Dir of Tyne Tees Television, 1958–67; Sales Dir and Dir of Yorkshire Television, 1967–74; Managing Director: Tyne Tees Television, 1974–83; Tyne Tees Television Holdings, 1981–84. Director: Trident Television, 1970–81; Independent Television News Ltd, 1982–83; Independent Television Publications Ltd, 1977–83; Broadcasters Audience Res. Bd, 1980–86; Member: Council, Independent Television Companies Assoc., 1974–83 (4 yrs Chm. Marketing Cttee); Cable Authority, 1984–90. *Recreations:* golf, fishing, theatre, music, reading. *Address:* Briarfield, Ashwood Road, Woking, Surrey GU22 7JW. *T:* (01483) 773183. *Club:* Worplesdon Golf.

PAINE, Roger Edward; management coach and consultant; Vice President, Solace Enterprises Ltd, since 2001 (Executive Director, 1996–99; Managing Director, 1999–2001); *b* 20 Oct. 1943; *s* of Ethel May Jones and Edward Paine. *Educ:* Stockport Sch.; Univ. of Wales (BA Hons); Univ. of Manchester (part time; Dip TP); Univ. of Birmingham (MSocSci). Town Planner: Lancs CC, 1964–66; Stockport CB, 1966–68; Lancs CC, 1968–70; Salford City, 1970; Stockport Borough: Corporate Planner, 1971–73; Head of Corporate Planning, 1973–75; Co-ordinator of Central Units, 1975–77; Dep. Chief Exec., Camden, 1977–80; Chief Executive: Wrekin Council, 1980–88; Cardiff CC, 1988–94. Pres., Solace, 1992–93. Chm., Coll. of Traditional Acupuncture, Leamington Spa. Dir of Music, Evesham Parish Church; Dir, Evesham Fest.

of Music. *Recreations:* music, travel, sport. *Address:* Pilgrims House, Barksdale, Winchcombe, Cheltenham, Glos GL54 5QW.

PAINES, Nicholas Paul Billot; QC 1997; a Recorder, since 2002; *b* 29 June 1955; *s* of late Anthony John Cooper Paines and of Anne Paines; *m* 1985, Alison Jane Sargent Roberts; one *s* three *d*. *Educ:* Downside Sch.; New Coll., Oxford (BA 1977; MA 1984); Université Libre de Bruxelles (Licence speciale en droit européen). Called to the Bar, Gray's Inn, 1978; in practice at the Bar, 1980–; called to the Bar, NI, 1996; Mem., Supplementary Panel of Jun. Counsel to the Crown (Common Law), 1993–97. A Dep. Social Security and Child Support Comr, 2001–. Mem., Bar Council, 1991–96; Treas., Bar European Gp, 2001– (Chm., 1996–98). Mem. Council, St Christopher's Fellowship, 1983–2002. Jt Editor, Common Market Law Reports, 1996–. *Publications: contributions to:* Halsbury's Laws of England, 3rd edn, 1986; Vaughan, Law of the European Communities, 1986; Bellamy and Child, Common Market Law of Competition, 4th edn, 1993. *Recreation:* family life. *Address:* Monckton Chambers, 1–2 Raymond Buildings, Gray's Inn, WC1R 5NR. *T:* (020) 7405 7211.

PAINTER, Ven. David Scott; Archdeacon of Oakham, since 2000; Canon Residentiary of Peterborough Cathedral, since 2000; *b* 3 Oct. 1944; *s* of Frank Painter and Winifred Ellen Painter (*née* Bibbings). *Educ:* Queen Elizabeth's Sch., Crediton; Trinity Coll. of Music (LTCL 1965); Worcester Coll., Oxford (BA 1968; MA 1972); Cuddesdon Theol Coll. Ordained deacon, 1970, priest, 1971; Curate, St Andrew, Plymouth, 1970–73; Chaplain, Plymouth Poly., 1971–73; Curate, All Saints, St Marylebone, 1973–76; Domestic Chaplain to Archbishop of Canterbury, 1976–80; Vicar, Holy Trinity, Roehampton, 1980–91; RD, Wandsworth, 1985–90; Canon Residentiary and Treas., Southwark Cathedral, and Dio. Dir of Ordinands, Southwark, 1991–2000. *Recreations:* music, country walking, crossword puzzles. *Address:* 7 Minster Precincts, Peterborough, Cambs PE1 1XS. *T:* (01733) 891360, *Fax:* (01733) 554524; *e-mail:* david.painter@peterborough-cathedral.org.uk.

PAINTER, Terence James, CB 1990; a Deputy Chairman and Director General, Board of Inland Revenue, 1986–93; *b* 28 Nov. 1935; *s* of late Edward Lawrence Painter and Ethel Violet (*née* Butler); *m* 1959, Margaret Janet Blackburn; two *s* two *d*. *Educ:* City of Norwich Sch.; Downing Coll., Cambridge (BA (History)). Nat. Service Commn, Royal Norfolk Regt, 1958–59. Entered Inland Revenue as Asst Principal, 1959; Principal, 1962; seconded to Civil Service Selection Bd, 1967–68; Asst Sec., 1969; seconded to HM Treasury, 1973–75; Under-Sec., 1975–86. *Recreations:* music, books, walking. *Club:* Reform.

PAISLEY, family name of **Baroness Paisley of St George's**.

PAISLEY OF ST GEORGE'S, Baroness *cr* 2006 (Life Peer), of St George's in the County of Antrim; **Eileen Emily Paisley;** Vice-President, Democratic Unionist Party, since 1994; *m* 1956, Ian Paisley (*see* Rev. and Rt Hon. Ian Paisley); twin *s* three *d*. Mem. (DemU) Belfast City Council, 1967–73. Member (DemU): East Belfast, NI Assembly, 1973–74; NI Constitutional Convention, 1975–76. *Address:* House of Lords, SW1A 0PW.
See also I. R. K. Paisley.

PAISLEY, Bishop of, (RC), since 2005; **Rt Rev. Philip Tartaglia,** STD; *b* 11 Jan. 1951; *s* of Guido and Annita Tartaglia. *Educ:* St Mungo's Acad., Glasgow; St Vincent's Coll., Langbank; St Mary's Coll., Blairs; Pontifical Scots Coll., Rome; Pontifical Gregorian Univ., Rome (PhB; STD 1980). Ordained priest, 1975; Dean of Studies, Pontifical Scots Coll., Rome, 1978–79; Asst Priest, Our Lady of Lourdes, Cardonald, 1980–81; Lectr, 1981–83, Dir of Studies, 1983–85, St Peter's Coll., Newlands, Glasgow; Vice-Rector, 1985–87, Rector, 1987–93, Chesters Coll., Bearsden, Glasgow; Asst Priest, St Patrick's, Dumbarton, 1993–95; Parish Priest, St Mary's, Duntocher, 1995–2004; Rector, Pontifical Scots Coll., Rome, 2004–05. *Address:* Diocesan Offices, Cathedral Precincts, Incle Street, Paisley PA1 1HR.

PAISLEY, Rev. and Rt Hon. Ian (Richard Kyle); PC 2005; MP (DemU) North Antrim, since 1974 (ProtU 1970–74) (resigned seat Dec. 1985 in protest against Anglo-Irish Agreement; re-elected Jan. 1986); Member (DemU) Antrim North, since 1998, and First Minister, 2007–08, Northern Ireland Assembly; Minister, Martyrs Memorial Free Presbyterian Church, Belfast, since 1946; *b* 6 April 1926; 2nd *s* of late Rev. J. Kyle Paisley and Mrs Isabella Paisley; *m* 1956, Eileen Emily Cassells (*see* Baroness Paisley of St George's); two *s* three *d* (incl. twin *s*). *Educ:* Ballymena Model Sch.; Ballymena Techn. High Sch.; S Wales Bible Coll.; Reformed Presbyterian Theol. Coll., Belfast. Ordained, 1946; Moderator, Free Presbyterian Church of Ulster, 1951–2008; Pres., Whitefield Coll. of the Bible, 1979–. Commenced publishing The Protestant Telegraph, 1966. Contested (Prot U) Bannside, NI Parlt, 1969; MP (Prot U), Bannside, Co. Antrim, NI Parlt, 1970–72; Leader of Opposition, 1972; Chm., Public Accounts Cttee, 1972. Co-Founder, Democratic Unionist Party, NI, 1972, Leader, 1972–2008. Mem. (Democratic Unionist), N Antrim, NI Assembly, 1973–75; Mem. (UUUC), N Antrim, NI Constitutional Convention, 1975–76; Mem. (DemU) N Antrim, NI Assembly, 1982–86. MEP (DemU) NI, 1979–2004. Hon. DD Bob Jones Univ., SC. FRGS. Mem., Internat. Cultural Soc., Korea, 1977. *Publications:* History of the 1859 Revival, 1959; Christian Foundations, 1960; Ravenhill Pulpit, Vol. 1, 1966, Vol. 2, 1967; Exposition of the Epistle to the Romans, 1968; Billy Graham and the Church of Rome, 1970; The Massacre of St Bartholomew, 1972; America's Debt to Ulster, 1976; (jtly) Ulster—the facts, 1981; No Pope Here, 1982; Dr Kidd, 1982; Those Flaming Tennents, 1983; Mr Protestant, 1985; Be Sure, 1986; Paisley's Pocket Preacher, 1987, vol. II, 1988, vol. III, 1989, vol. IV, 1990; Jonathan Edwards: the theologian of revival, 1987; Union with Rome, 1989; The Soul of the Question, 1990; The Revised English Bible: an exposure, 1990; What a Friend We Have in Jesus, 1994; Understanding Events in Northern Ireland: an introduction for Americans, 1995; Ian Paisley Library, 10 vols, 1997–99. *Address:* House of Commons, SW1A 0AA; The Parsonage, 17 Cyprus Avenue, Belfast BT5 5NT.
See also I. R. K. Paisley.

PAISLEY, Ian Richard Kyle; Member (DemU) Antrim North, Northern Ireland Assembly, since 1998; *b* 12 Dec. 1966; *s* of Rev. and Rt Hon. I. R. K. Paisley, *qv* and Baroness Paisley of St George's, *qv*; *m* 1990, Fiona Margaret Elizabeth Currie; two *s* two *d*. *Educ:* Shaftesbury House Coll.; Methodist Coll.; Queen's Univ., Belfast (BA Hons Modern History; MSSc Irish Politics 1995). Res. Asst for Dr Ian Paisley, MP, H of C, 1989–. Member: NI Forum for Political Dialogue, 1996–98; NI Police Bd, 2001–. Justice spokesman, DUP, 1992–2002. Jun. Minister, Office of First Minister and Dep. First Minister, NI, 2007–08. Fellow, Sch. of Leadership, Maryland State Univ., 1997. Royal Humane Soc. Testimonial, 1999. *Publications:* Reasonable Doubt: the case for the UDR Four, 1991; Echoes: Protestant identity in Northern Ireland, 1994; Peace Deal?, 1998; Ian Paisley: a life in photographs, 2004; articles in jls. *Recreations:* my children, Chinese food, cinema, Rugby, motorcycling. *Address:* Parliament Buildings, Stormont, Belfast BT4 3XX; 256 Ravenhill Road, Belfast BT6 8GJ; 46 Hill Street, Ballymena BT43 6BH.

PAISNER, Harold Michael; Senior Partner, Berwin Leighton Paisner LLP, since 2007; *b* 4 June 1939; *s* of Leslie and Suzanne Paisner; *m* 1967, Judith Rechtman; two *s*. *Educ:* St Paul's Sch., London; University Coll., Oxford (BA Hons); Coll. of Law, London. Investment and merchant banking, 1963; admitted Solicitor, 1971; registered with Paris Bar; former Sen. Partner, Paisner & Co. UK Nat. Pres., Union Internat. des Avocats, 2006– (former Pres., Foreign Investment Cttee); Member: Internat. Issues Cttee, Law Soc.; Internat. Bar Assoc.; British Baltic Lawyers Assoc. Hon. Mem., Lithuanian Bar. Non-executive Director: Think London, 2002–; FIBI Bank (UK) plc, 2005–; Interface Inc., 2007–. Dir, Inst. of Jewish Policy Res. Gov., Ben Gurion Univ. of the Negev. *Recreations:* music, reading history, biography and current affairs, ski-ing. *Address:* 16 Ilchester Place, W14 8AA. *T:* (office) (020) 7760 1000; *e-mail:* harold.paisner@blplaw.com. *Club:* Athenæum.

PAJARES, Ramón, OBE 2000; Director and Advisor, Como Hotels and Investments Co. Ltd, 2000–05; *b* 6 July 1935; *s* of Juan Antonio Pajares Garcia and Rosario Salazar; *m* 1963, Jean Kathleen Porter; one *s* two *d*. *Educ:* Madrid Inst. of Hotel and Tourism Studies. Nat. Service, Spanish Navy, 1955–57. Hotel posts: Ritz, Barcelona, 1954–55; San Jorge, Playa de Aro, 1957; Pargue, Llavaneras, 1957–59; Mansion, Eastbourne, 1959–61; Kleiner Reisen, Koblenz, Germany, 1961; Feldbergerhof, Feldberg, 1961–62; Le Vieux Manoir, Morat, Switzerland, 1962; Reina Isabel, Canary Is, 1963–69; Food and Beverage Dir, Inn on the Park, London, 1969–71; Gen. Manager, San Antonio, Lanzarote, Canary Is, 1972–74; Gen. Manager and Vice-Pres., Inn on the Park, later Four Seasons, 1975–94; Man. Dir, Savoy Gp of Hotels and Restaurants, 1994–99. Member: Assoc. Culinaire Française, 1971; Cookery and Food Assoc., 1973. Pres., BHA, 2000–06. FIH (FHCIMA 1982). Freeman, City of London, 1988. Hon. DEd Bournemouth, 2000. Hotelier of Year Award, Brit. Hotel and Catering Ind., 1984; Personalité de l'année for Hotel Ind., 1986; Catey Special Award, Caterer & Hotel Keeper Mag., 1997; Lifetime Achievement Award, Eur. Hotel Design and Develt Awards, 1998; British Travel Industry Hall of Fame, 1998; Hotelier of World, Hotels Mag., 1998; Spanish Govt Silver Medal, for services to tourism, 2000. Mérito Civil (Spain), 1984; Oficial de la Orden de Isabel la Católica (Spain), 1989. *Recreation:* classical music.

PAKENHAM, family name of **Earl of Longford**.

PAKENHAM, Henry Desmond Verner, CBE 1964; HM Diplomatic Service, retired; *b* 5 Nov. 1911; *s* of Hamilton Richard Pakenham and Emilie Willis Stringer; *m* 1st, 1946, Crystal Elizabeth Brooksbank (marr. diss., 1960); one *s* one *d* (and one *s* decd); 2nd, 1963, Venetia Maude; one *s* one *d*. *Educ:* Monkton Combe; St John Baptist College, Oxford. Taught modern languages at Sevenoaks School, 1933–40. Served in HM Forces, 1940–45. Entered Foreign Service, 1946; served in Madrid, Djakarta, Havana, Singapore, Tel Aviv, Buenos Aires and Sydney; retired 1971. Chm., Suffolk Preservation Soc., 1979–82. Asst Editor, Satow's Guide to Diplomatic Practice, 5th edn, 1979. *Address:* The Mill House, Lavenham, Suffolk CO10 9RD.

PAKENHAM, Hon. Sir Michael (Aidan), KBE 2003; CMG 1993; HM Diplomatic Service, retired; Senior Adviser, Access Industries, since 2004; *b* 3 Nov. 1943; *s* of 7th Earl of Longford, KG, PC, and Elizabeth, Countess of Longford, CBE; *m* 1980, Meta (Mimi) Landreth Doak, *d* of William Conway Doak of Maryland, USA; two *d* two step *d*. *Educ:* Ampleforth College (schol.); Trinity College, Cambridge (schol.; MA Classics); Rice University, Texas (exchange fellow). Washington Post, 1965; Foreign Office, 1965; Nairobi, 1966; Warsaw, 1967; FCO, 1970; Asst Private Sec., later Private Sec. to Chancellor of Duchy of Lancaster (European Community Affairs), on secondment to Cabinet Office, 1971–74; Geneva (CSCE), 1974; New Delhi, 1974; Washington, 1978; Head of Arms Control and Disarmament Dept, FCO, 1983–87; Counsellor (External Relations), UK Perm. Rep. to EC, Brussels, 1987–91; Ambassador and Consul-Gen., Luxembourg, 1991–94; Minister, Paris, 1994–97; Cabinet Office (on secondment): Dep. Sec. (Overseas and Defence), 1997–99; Chm., Jt Intelligence Cttee, 1997–2000 and Intelligence Co-ordinator, 1999–2000; Ambassador to Poland, 2001–03. Chm., Pakenvest International Ltd, 2004–; Consultant, Thales International, 2004–06; Dir, Westminster Gp, 2008–. Trustee, Chevening House, 2005–. Mem. Council, KCL, 2005–. Freeman of City of London, 1992. *Recreations:* tennis, golf, reading history, museums, Arsenal FC. *Address:* Cope House, 15B Kensington Palace Gardens, W8 4QG. *T:* (020) 7908 9966. *Clubs:* Garrick, Beefsteak, Pitt, Pilgrims, MCC; High Post Golf, Sunningdale Golf.

PAKENHAM, Thomas Frank Dermot; writer; *b* 14 Aug. 1933; *e s* of 7th Earl of Longford, KG, PC, and Elizabeth, Countess of Longford, CBE; *S* father, 2001, but does not use the title; *m* 1964, Valerie, *d* of Major R. G. McNair Scott; two *s* two *d*. *Educ:* Dragon School, Oxford; Belvedere Coll., Dublin; Ampleforth Coll., York; Magdalen Coll., Oxford (BA Greats 1955). Travelled, Near East and Ethiopia, 1955–56 (discovered unrecorded medieval Ethiopian church at Bethlehem, Begemdir, 1956). Free-lance writing, 1956–58. Editorial staff: Times Educational Supplement, 1958–60; Sunday Telegraph, 1961; The Observer, 1961–64. Founder Mem. 1958, and Member Cttee 1958–64, Victorian Soc.; Founder Mem., and Mem. Cttee 1968–72, Historic Irish Tourist Houses and Gardens Assoc. (HITHA); Treas., 1972–2002, Chm., 2002–05, British-Irish Assoc.; Sec. (co-founder), Christopher Ewart-Biggs Memorial Trust, 1976–; Founder and Chm., Irish Tree Soc., 1990–. Chm., Ladbroke Assoc., 1988–91. Sen. Associate Mem., St Antony's Coll., Oxford, 1979–81. Hon. DLitt: Ulster, 1992; TCD, 2000; QUB, 2004. *Publications:* The Mountains of Rasselas: an Ethiopian adventure, 1959, 1998; The Year of Liberty: the story of the Great Irish Rebellion of 1798, 1969; The Boer War, 1979 (Cheltenham Prize, 1980); (selected and introd with Valerie Pakenham) Dublin: a travellers' companion, 1988; The Scramble for Africa, 1991 (W. H. Smith Prize, 1992; Alan Paton Meml Prize, 1992); Meetings with Remarkable Trees, 1996; Remarkable Trees of the World, 2002; The Remarkable Baobab, 2004; In Search of Remarkable Trees: on safari in southern Africa, 2007. *Recreation:* water. *Address:* 111A Elgin Crescent, W11 2JF. *T:* (020) 7727 7624; Tullynally, Castlepollard, Westmeath, Ireland. *T:* (044) 9661159. *Club:* Beefsteak.

PAKENHAM-WALSH, John, CB 1986; Standing Counsel to General Synod of Church of England, 1988–2000; *b* 7 Aug. 1928; *s* of late Rev. W. P. Pakenham-Walsh, formerly ICS, and Guendolen (*née* Elliott); *m* 1951, Deryn, *er d* of late Group Captain R. E. G. Fulljames, MC, and Mrs Muriel Fulljames; one *s* four *d*. *Educ:* Bradfield Coll.; University Coll., Oxford (MA). Called to the Bar, Lincoln's Inn, 1951. Crown Counsel, Hong Kong, 1953–57; Parly Counsel, Fedn of Nigeria, 1958–61; joined Legal Adviser's Br., Home Office, 1961; Under Sec. (Legal), Home Office, 1980–87. Hon. QC 1992. *Address:* 2 Roberts Close, Burton Bradstock, Bridport, Dorset DT6 4ST. *T:* (01308) 897651.

PAKINGTON, family name of **Baron Hampton**.

PALACIO VALLELERSUNDI, Ana; Senior Vice-President and General Counsel, World Bank, 2006–08; *b* Madrid, 22 July 1948. *Educ:* French Lycée, Madrid; Univ. Complutense, Madrid (degrees in Law, Pol. Sci., Sociol.). Non-practising lawyer; lectr. MEP, 1994–2002 (Chm., Legal Affairs and Internal Market Cttee, 1999–2002); Mem. for Toledo, Congress of Deputies, Spain; Minister of Foreign Affairs, 2002–04. Mem. Bd

Governors, Law Soc. of Madrid; Dep. Chm. Council, European Law Socs; Pres. Exec. Council, Europäische Rechtsakademie (Acad. of European Law), Trier. Mem. Editorial Bd, Revue du Droit de l'Union Européene. Hon. Mem., Law Soc. of England and Wales; Mem., Inner Temple. Cruz de San Raimundo de Peñafort; Gran Cruz: Orden Piana (Vatican), 2002; Orden del Mérito (Germany), 2002; Placa de Plata de la Orden Nacional José Matias Delgado (El Salvador), 2003.

PALADE, Prof. George Emil; scientist, USA; Professor, Department of Cellular and Molecular Medicine and Dean for Scientific Affairs, School of Medicine, University of California at San Diego, 1990–2000, Emeritus Professor and Emeritus Dean for Scientific Affairs, since 2001; *b* Iassy, Romania, 19 Nov. 1912; *s* of Emil Palade and Constanta Cantemir; *m* 1st, 1941, Irina Malaxa (decd); one *s* one *d*; 2nd, 1970, Dr Marilyn Farquhar. *Educ:* Liceul Al. Hasdeu, Buzau, Romania; Med. Sch., Univ. of Bucharest (MD). Arrived in US, 1946; naturalized US citizen, 1952. Instructor, Asst Prof., then Lectr in Anatomy, Sch. of Med., Univ. of Bucharest, 1940–45; Visiting Investigator, Rockefeller Inst. for Med. Research, 1946–48; continuing as an Assistant (later the Inst. became Rockefeller Univ., NYC); promoted to Associate, 1951, and Associate Mem., 1953; Prof. of Cell Biology, Rockefeller Univ. and full Member of Rockefeller Inst., 1956; Prof. of Cell Biology, Yale Univ. Med. Sch., 1973; Sen. Res. Scientist, Yale Univ., 1983–90. Fellow, Amer. Acad. of Arts and Sciences; Member: Nat. Acad. of Sciences; Pontifical Acad. of Sciences; Leopoldina Acad.; Romanian Acad.; For. Mem., Royal Soc., 1984. Awards include: Albert Lasker Basic Research, 1966; Gairdner Award, 1967; Hurwitz Prize, 1970; Nobel Prize for Medicine, 1974; Nat. Medal of Science, USA, 1986. *Publications:* Editor: Annual Review of Cell Biology, 1985–95; Jl of Cell Biology (co-founder); Jl of Membrane Biology; numerous contribs med. and sci. jls on structure, biochemistry and function of sub-cellular components. *Address:* School of Medicine, University of California, San Diego, 9500 Gilman Drive, La Jolla, CA 92093–0602, USA. *T:* (858) 5347708, *Fax:* (858) 5346573.

PALETHORPE-TODD, Richard Andrew; *see* Todd.

PALEY, Maureen; Founder and Director, Maureen Paley (formerly Interim Art), since 1984; *b* New York, 17 Sept. 1959; *d* of Alfred and Sylvia Paley. *Educ:* Sarah Lawrence Coll., Bronxville, NY; Brown Univ. (BA); Royal Coll. of Art (MA). Worked in photography and film, 1980–84; Lecturer: Bournemouth and Poole Coll. of Art, 1981–83; AA, 1981–82; curator: Antidotes to Madness?, Riverside Studios, London, 1986; Photography as Performance, Photographer's Gall., London, 1986; Wall Works, Cornerhouse, Manchester, 1987; Symptoms of Interference, Conditions of Possibility: Ad Reinhardt, Joseph Kosuth, Felix Gonzalez-Torres, Camden Art Centre, 1994; Wall to Wall, Serpentine Gall., Southampton City Art Gall., Leeds City Art Gall., 1995; The Cauldron, Henry Moore Sculpture Trust, Halifax. Vis. Lectr, RCA, Chelsea Coll. of Art and Design. *Publications:* Technique Anglaise, 1991; Gillian Wearing: signs, 1997; Art London, 1999, 2nd edn 2000; Paul P. When Ghost Meets Ghost, Peter Hujar, 2008; exhibition catalogues. *Address:* Maureen Paley, 21 Herald Street, E2 6JT. *T:* (020) 7729 4112, *Fax:* (020) 7729 4113; *e-mail:* info@maureenpaley.com. *Clubs:* Annabel's, Groucho, Soho House.

PALIN, Michael Edward, CBE 2000; actor, writer and traveller; *b* 5 May 1943; *s* of late Edward and Mary Palin; *m* 1966, Helen M. Gibbins; two *s* one *d*. *Educ:* Birkdale Sch., Sheffield; Shrewsbury; Brasenose Coll., Oxford (BA 2nd Cl. Hons Mod. Hist.). Pres., Transport 2000. Actor and writer: Monty Python's Flying Circus, BBC TV, 1969–74; Ripping Yarns, BBC TV, 1976–80; actor: Three Men in a Boat, BBC, 1975; GBH, Channel 4, 1991; writer: East of Ipswich, BBC TV, 1987; Number 27, BBC1, 1988; *stage play:* The Weekend, Strand, 1994. *Films:* actor and jt author: And Now for Something Completely Different, 1970; Monty Python and the Holy Grail, 1974; Monty Python's Life of Brian, 1978; Time Bandits, 1980; Monty Python's "The Meaning of Life", 1982; American Friends, 1991; actor, writer and co-producer: The Missionary, 1982; actor: Jabberwocky, 1976; A Private Function, 1984; Brazil, 1985; A Fish Called Wanda, 1988 (Best Supporting Film Actor, BAFTA Award, 1988); Fierce Creatures, 1997. *Television series:* contributor, Great Railway Journeys of the World, BBC, 1980, 1994; retraced Phileas Fogg's journey for Around the World in Eighty Days, BBC, 1989; travelled from North to South Pole for Pole to Pole, BBC, 1992; Palin's Column, 1994; circumnavigated the Pacific Ocean for Full Circle, BBC, 1995–96; Michael Palin's Hemingway Adventure, BBC, 1999; Sahara With Michael Palin, 2002; Himalaya, 2004 (Best Presenter Award, RTS, 2005); Michael Palin's New Europe, 2007; presenter: Palin on Redpath, 1997; The Bright Side of Life, 2000; The Ladies who Loved Matisse, 2003; Michael Palin and the Mystery of Hammershoi, 2005. Lifetime Achievement Award, British Comedy Awards, 2002; Special Award, BAFTA, 2005. *Publications:* Monty Python's Big Red Book, 1970; Monty Python's Brand New Bok, 1973; Dr Fegg's Encyclopeadia of *All* World Knowledge, 1984; Limericks, 1985; Around the World in Eighty Days, 1989; Pole to Pole, 1992 (Travel Writer of the Year, British Book Awards, 1993); Pole to Pole: the photographs, 1994; Hemingway's Chair (novel), 1995; Full Circle, 1997; Michael Palin's Hemingway Adventure, 1999; Sahara, 2002; (jtly) The Pythons Autobiography by The Pythons, 2003; Himalaya, 2004 (TV and Film Book of the Year, British Book Awards, 2005); Diaries 1969–1979: the Python years, 2006; New Europe, 2007; *for children:* Small Harry and the Toothache Pills, 1981; (with R. W. Seymour and Alan Lee) The Mirrorstone, 1986; The Cyril Stories, 1986. *Recreations:* reading, running, railways—preferably all three in a foreign country. *Address:* (office) Mayday Management Ltd, 34 Tavistock Street, WC2E 7PB. *Club:* Athenæum.

PALIN, Air Chief Marshal Sir Roger Hewlett, KCB 1989; OBE 1978; Controller, Royal Air Force Benevolent Fund, 1993–98; *b* 8 July 1938; *m* 1967, Kathryn Elizabeth Pye; two *d*. *Educ:* Canford Sch.; St John's Coll., Cambridge (BA 1967; MA 1979; Hon. Fellow, 2007); psc. FRAeS; FIPD. Commnd KRRC, 1958; served 3 Para. Bn, 1958–59, 10 Para. Bn (TA), 1959–62; Flight Lieut, 1964; Sqn Leader, 1970; Wing Comdr, 1975; Group Captain, 1980; ADC to the Queen, 1981–82; Air Cdre, 1984; Dir of Defence Policy, MoD, 1984–85; Air Vice-Marshal, 1986; ACDS (Progs), 1986–87; AOC No 11 Gp, 1987–89; Air Marshal, 1989; C-in-C, RAF Germany and Comdr Second Allied Tactical Air Force, 1989–91; Air Chief Marshal, 1991; Air Mem. for Personnel, 1991–93; Air ADC to the Queen, 1991–93; retired 1993. Guest Schol., Woodrow Wilson Internat. Center for Scholars, Washington, 1980; Res. Associate, IISS, 1993. *Recreations:* sport, travel, international relations, defence studies.

PALING, Her Honour Helen Elizabeth, (Mrs W. J. S. Kershaw); a Circuit Judge, 1985–2000; *b* 25 April 1933; *o d* of A. Dale Paling and Mabel Eleanor Thomas; *m* 1961, William John Stanley Kershaw, PhD; one *s* three *d*. *Educ:* Prince Henry's Grammar Sch., Otley; London Sch. of Economics. LLB London 1954. Called to Bar, Lincoln's Inn, 1955; a Recorder, 1972–85. *Address:* c/o Quayside Law Courts, Newcastle upon Tyne NE1 2LA. *T:* (0191) 201 2000.

PALIOS, Markos, FCA; corporate turnaround specialist; *b* 9 Nov. 1952; five *d*. *Educ:* Manchester Univ. (BSc). FCA 1995; MIPA. Professional footballer, Tranmere Rovers FC, and Crewe Alexandra FC, 1973–86; Partner, Arthur Young, 1986–89; Partner, 1989–2003, UK Leader for Business Regeneration, 1997–2003, Coopers & Lybrand, then PricewaterhouseCoopers; Chief Exec., Football Assoc., 2003–04; European Leader, FTI Palladium Partners, 2005–06. *Recreations:* family, football, flying. *Address:* *e-mail:* mark.palios@co-doc.com.

PALLEY, Dr Claire Dorothea Taylor, OBE 1998; Constitutional Adviser, Republic of Cyprus, 1980–94, 1999–2004 and 2005–08; Principal of St Anne's College, Oxford, 1984–91, Hon. Fellow, 1992; *b* 17 Feb. 1931; *d* of Arthur Aubrey Swait, Durban; *m* 1952, Ahrn Palley (marr. diss. 1985; he *d* 1993); five *s*. *Educ:* Durban Girls' Coll.; Univs of Cape Town and London. BA 1950, LLB 1952, Cape Town; PhD London 1965; MA Oxon 1984. Called to Bar, Middle Temple. Queen's University, Belfast: Lectr, 1966–67; Reader, 1967–70; Prof. of Public Law, 1970–73; Dean of Faculty of Law, 1971–73; Prof. of Law, 1973–84, and Master of Darwin Coll., 1974–82, Univ. of Kent. Member: Council, Minority Rights Group, 1975–94; UN Sub-Commn on Prevention of Discrimination and Protection of Minorities, 1988–98. Hon. LLD: QUB, 1991; Cape Town, 2008. *Publications:* The Constitutional History and Law of Southern Rhodesia, 1966; The United Kingdom and Human Rights, 1991; An International Relations Debacle: the UN Secretary-General's Mission of Good Offices in Cyprus 1999–2004, 2005; contrib. learned jls. *Address:* 13 Nikou Sophocleous Avenue, Pachna, 4700 Limassol, Cyprus.

PALLISER, Rt Hon. Sir (Arthur) Michael, GCMG 1977 (KCMG 1973; CMG 1966); PC 1983; HM Diplomatic Service, retired; Vice-Chairman, Board of Salzburg Global Seminar (formerly Board of Salzburg Seminar), 1995–2008; *b* 9 April 1922; *s* of late Admiral Sir Arthur Palliser, KCB, DSC, and Lady Palliser (*née* Margaret Eva King-Salter); *m* 1948, Marie Marguerite (*d* 2000), *d* of late Paul-Henri Spaak; three *s*. *Educ:* Wellington Coll.; Merton Coll., Oxford (Hon. Fellow 1987). Served with Coldstream Guards, 1942–47 (despatches); Capt. 1944. Entered HM Diplomatic Service, 1947; SE Asia Dept, Foreign Office, 1947–49; Athens, 1949–51; Second Sec., 1950; Foreign Office: German Finance Dept, 1951–52; Central Dept, 1952–54; Private Sec. to Perm. Under-Sec., 1954–56; First Sec., 1955; Paris, 1956–60; Head of Chancery, Dakar, 1960–62 (Chargé d'Affaires in 1960, 1961 and 1962); Counsellor, and seconded to Imperial Defence College, 1963; Head of Planning Staff, Foreign Office, 1964; a Private Sec. to PM, 1966; Minister, Paris, 1969; Ambassador and Head of UK Deleg. to European Communities, Brussels, 1971; Ambassador and UK Permanent Representative to European Communities, 1973–75; Permanent Under-Sec. of State, FCO and Head of Diplomatic Service, 1975–82. Fellow, Center for Internat. Affairs, Harvard, 1982; Chm., Samuel Montagu & Co., 1984–85, 1986–93 (Dir, 1983–96; Vice Chm., 1988, 1993–96); Deputy Chairman: Midland Montagu (Hldgs), 1987–93; Midland Bank, 1987–91. Director, 1983–92: BAT Industries plc; Booker plc; Eagle Star Hldgs; Shell Transport & Trading Co. plc; Director: United Biscuits (Hldgs), 1983–89; Arbor Acres Farm Inc., 1985–91; UK-Japan 2000 Gp, 1987–96; XCL Ltd, 1994–2000. Dep. Chm., BI (formerly BIEC), 1987–95. Pres., China-Britain Trade Gp, 1992–96; Member: Council, IISS, 1982–91 (Chm., 1983–90; Vice-Pres., 1999–); Trilateral Commn, 1982–96; Security Commn, 1983–92; Council, British N American Cttee and Res. Assoc., 1987–95 (British Chm., 1990–92); BOTB, 1993–96; Adv. Bd, RAND Europe, 1995–2003 (Chm., 1999–2003); Adv. Council, British Consultants Bureau, 1997–2002. Mem., Royal Nat. Theatre Bd, 1988–96. Pres., Internat. Social Service of UK, 1982–96; Chairman: City and E London Confedn of Medicine and Dentistry, 1989–95; Major Projects Assoc., 1994–98. Trustee, The Tablet, 1989–. Governor, Wellington Coll., 1982–92. FRSA 1983. Hon. Fellow, QMW, 1990. Chevalier, Order of Orange Nassau, 1944; Commandeur, Légion d'Honneur, 1996 (Chevalier, 1957). *Address:* 12B Wedderburn Road, NW3 5QG. *T:* (020) 7794 0440, *Fax:* (020) 7916 2163. *Club:* Buck's.

PALMER, family name of **Earl of Selborne**, **Baron Palmer** and **Baron Lucas of Crudwell**.

PALMER, 4th Baron *cr* 1933, of Reading; **Adrian Bailie Nottage Palmer;** Bt 1916; *b* 8 Oct. 1951; *s* of Col the Hon. Sir Gordon Palmer, KCVO, OBE, TD, MA, FRCM and the Hon. Lady Palmer, DL; *S* uncle, 1990; *m* 1st, 1977, Cornelia Dorothy Katherine (marr. diss. 2004), *d* of R. N. Wadham, DFC, Exning, Newmarket; two *s* one *d*; 2nd, 2006, Loraine, *d* of Jim McMurrey, Texas, USA. *Educ:* Eton; Edinburgh Univ. Mem., Exec. Council, HHA, 1981–99; Chm., HHA for Scotland, 1994–99 (Mem., Exec. Council, 1980–99; Vice Chm., 1993). Elected Mem., H of L, 1999. Mem., Queen's Body Guard for Scotland (Royal Company of Archers), 1992–96. Scottish Rep. to European Landowning Orgn, 1986–92. Pres., British Assoc. for Biofuels and Oils, 2000–. Sec., The Royal Caledonian Hunt, 1989–2005. *Recreations:* gardening, shooting, hunting. *Heir:* *s* Hon. Hugo Bailie Rohan Palmer, *b* 5 Dec. 1980. *Address:* Manderston, Duns, Berwickshire TD11 3PP. *T:* (01361) 883450. *Clubs:* Pratt's; New (Edinburgh).

PALMER, Adrian Oliver; QC 1992; a Recorder, since 1992; *b* 20 Aug. 1950; *s* of Richard Gilbert Palmer and Patricia Mary Palmer; *m* 1974, Rosemary Shaw; one *s* one *d*. *Educ:* Clifton Coll., Bristol; St John's Coll., Cambridge (MA). Called to the Bar, Middle Temple, 1972, Bencher, 2003. *Recreations:* gardens, sheep, walking. *Address:* Guildhall Chambers, 23 Broad Street, Bristol BS1 2HG. *T:* (0117) 927 3366.

PALMER, Prof. Andrew Clennel, PhD; FRS 1994; FREng, FICE; Managing Director, Bold Island Engineering Ltd, since 2005; Fellow, Churchill College, Cambridge, since 1996; *b* 26 May 1938; *s* of Gerald Basil Coote Palmer and Muriel Gertrude Palmer (*née* Howes); *m* 1963, Jane Rhiannon Evans; one *d*. *Educ:* Pembroke Coll., Cambridge (BA, MA); Brown Univ. (PhD). FICE 1986; FREng (FEng 1990). Lectr, Liverpool Univ., 1965–67; Cambridge University: Sen. Asst in Res., 1967–68; Lectr, 1968–75; Fellow, Churchill Coll., 1967–75; Chief Engr, R. J. Brown and Associates, 1975–79; Prof. of Civil Engrg, UMIST, 1979–82; Vice-Pres. Engrg, R. J. Brown and Associates, 1982–85; Man. Dir, Andrew Palmer and Associates, 1985–93; Technical Dir, SAIC Ltd, 1993–96; Jafar Res. Prof. of Petroleum Engineering, Cambridge Univ., 1996–2005. Vis. Professor: Harvard Univ., 2002–03; Nat. Univ. of Singapore, 2006–. Pres., Pipeline Industries Guild, 1998–2000. Hon. DSc Clarkson, 2007. *Publications:* Structural Mechanics, 1976; Subsea Pipeline Engineering, 2004; articles and papers in scientific and engrg jls. *Recreations:* travel, glass-blowing, cooking, languages. *Address:* 49 Ashley Gardens, Ambrosden Avenue, SW1P 1QF; *e-mail:* acp24@eng.cam.ac.uk. *Club:* Athenæum.

PALMER, Andrew Eustace, CMG 1987; CVO 1981; HM Diplomatic Service, retired; an Extra Equerry to the Duke of Kent, since 1996; *b* 30 Sept. 1937; *s* of late Lt-Col Rodney Howell Palmer, MC, and of Mrs Frances Pauline Ainsworth (*née* Gordon-Duff); *m* 1962, Davina, *d* of Sir Roderick Barclay, GCVO, KCMG; two *s* one *d*. *Educ:* Winchester Coll.; Pembroke Coll., Cambridge (MA). Second Lieut, Rifle Bde, 1956–58. Joined HM Foreign (later Diplomatic) Service, 1961; American Dept, FO, 1962–63; Third, later Second, Secretary (Commercial), La Paz, 1963–65; Second Sec., Ottawa, 1965–67; Treasury Centre for Administrative Studies, 1967–68; Central Dept, FO, later Southern European Dept, FCO, 1968–72; First Sec. (Information), Paris, 1972–76; Asst Head of Defence Dept, FCO, 1976–77; RCDS 1978; Counsellor, Head of Chancery and Consul-Gen., Oslo, 1979–82; Hd, Falkland Is Dept, FCO, 1982–85; Fellow, Harvard

Center for Internat. Affairs, 1985–86; Ambassador to Cuba, 1986–88; seconded as Pvte Sec. to the Duke and Duchess of Kent, 1988–90; Ambassador to the Holy See, 1991–95. Local organiser, Bilderberg Conf., Turnberry, 1998. Mem. Council, 1996–2008, Vis. Fellow, Politics and Internat. Relns, 2008–, Reading Univ.; Chm., Friends of Univ. of Reading, 2005–. Comdr, Order of St Olav (Norway), 1981. *Publication:* A Diplomat and his Birds, 2005. *Recreations:* fishing, following most sports, photography, ornithology. *Address:* Peasemore Manor, Newbury, Berks RG20 7JF. *Clubs:* Brooks's, MCC.

See also Viscount Garmoyle.

PALMER, Angela Silver, (Mrs J. D. F. Palmer); artist; *b* 27 March 1957; *m* 1988, Jeremy David Fletcher Palmer, *er s* of Maj.-Gen. Sir (Joseph) Michael Palmer, *qv*; two *s* one *d*. *Educ:* George Watson's Ladies' Coll., Edinburgh; Ruskin Sch. of Drawing and Fine Art, Oxford (BA 2005); RCA (MA 2007). Trainee, Evening News, Edinburgh, 1979–82; Peterborough Column, Daily Telegraph, 1982–84; Editor, PHS, The Times, 1984–86; News Editor, Observer, 1986–88; Editor: Observer Mag., 1988–92; Elle, 1992–93. Commissions: Wellcome Trust; Aberdeen Univ.; Pembroke Coll., Oxford; Exeter Coll., Oxford; exhibtd RA Summer Exhibn, 2005; solo exhibn, Waterhouse and Dodd Gall., London, 2008. FRSA 2003. Journalist of the Year, Scotland, 1980; Waugh Scholarship and Fitzgerald Prize, Exeter Coll., Univ. of Oxford, 2003; Polly Campbell Award, Jerwood Space, 2007; RCA Soc. and Thames and Hudson Award, 2007. *Recreation:* family.

PALMER, Lt-Gen. Anthony Malcolm Douglas, CB 2005; CBE 1995; Deputy Chief of Defence Staff (Personnel), 2002–05; *b* 13 March 1949; *s* of late Lt-Col A. G. D. Palmer and Joan Palmer (*née* Wintour); *m* 1972, Harriet Ann Jardine; two *s* one *d*. *Educ:* Woodcote House; Winchester Coll. Commnd RGJ, 1969; despatches, 1972, 1990; BAOR, 1969–70; NI, 1970–71; Shorncliffe, 1971–73; Catterick, 1973–74; Warminster, 1974–76; 2nd Bn RGJ, 1976, Ops Officer, 1978–80; Trng Co. Cmdr, Winchester, 1980–81; Staff Coll., Pakistan, 1981; Co. Cmdr, 3rd Bn RGJ, 1983–85; MoD, 1985–87; Directing Staff, Camberley, 1987–89; CO, 2nd Bn RGJ, 1989–91; Col, MoD, 1991; Comdr, 8 Inf. Bde, 1993; rcds 1995; Dir, Army Plans, 1996–99; Chief Exec., Army Trng and Recruiting Agency, 1999–2002. *Recreations:* music, bridge, golf, tennis, fishing. *Address:* c/o Army and Navy Club, 36–39 Pall Mall, SW1Y 5JN. *Clubs:* Army and Navy, Royal Green Jackets.

PALMER, Anthony Thomas Richard; *see* Palmer, Tony.

PALMER, Anthony Wheeler; QC 1979; a Recorder of the Crown Court, 1980–2002; *b* 30 Dec. 1936; *s* of late Philip Palmer and of Doris Palmer; *m* Jacqueline, *d* of Reginald Fortnum, Taunton; one *s* two *d*. *Educ:* Wrekin Coll., Salop. Called to the Bar, Gray's Inn, 1962. *Address:* 17 Warwick Avenue, Coventry CV5 6DJ.

PALMER, Arnold Daniel; professional golfer since 1954; golf course designer; *b* 10 Sept. 1929; *s* of Milfred J. and Doris Palmer; *m* 1954, Winifred Walzer (*d* 1999); two *d*; *m* 2005, Kathleen Gawthrop. *Educ:* Wake Forest Univ. Winner of numerous tournament titles, including: British Open Championship, 1961, 1962; US Open Championship, 1960; Masters Championship, 1958, 1960, 1962, 1964; Spanish Open Championship, 1975; Professional Golfers' Assoc. Championship, 1975; Canadian PGA, 1980; USA Seniors' Championship, 1981. Hon. Dr of Laws: Wake Forest; Nat. Coll. of Educn; Hon. DHum: Thiel Coll.; Florida Southern College; St Vincent Coll. Hon. Member: Royal and Ancient Golf Club, 1979; Troon Golf Club, 1982; Royal Birkdale Golf Club, 1983. *Publications:* (all jointly): Arnold Palmer Golf Book, 1961; Portrait of a Professional Golfer, 1964; My Game and Yours, 1965; Situation Golf, 1970; Go for Broke, 1973; Arnold Palmer's Best 54 Golf Holes, 1977; Arnold Palmer's Complete Book of Putting, 1986; Play Great Golf, 1987; Arnold Palmer, A Personal Journey, 1994; A Golfer's Life, 1999; Playing by the Rules, 2002; Memories, Stories and Memorabilia, 2004. *Recreations:* aviation (speed record for flying round world in twin-engine jet, 1976), bridge, hunting, fishing. *Address:* PO Box 52, Youngstown, PA 15696, USA. *T:* (724) 5377751. *Clubs:* (Owner and Pres.) Latrobe Country; (Pres. and Part-Owner) Bay Hill (Orlando, Fla); (Tournament Professional) Laurel Valley Golf; (Part-Owner) Pebble Beach Co.; (Hon. Life Mem., 1992–) Carnoustie Golf; numerous other country, city, golf.

PALMER, Bernard Harold Michael, OBE 1989; MA; Editor of the Church Times, 1968–89; *b* 8 Sept. 1929; *e s* of late Christopher Harold Palmer; *m* 1954, Jane Margaret (*d* 2006), *d* of late E. L. Skinner; one *s* one *d*. *Educ:* St Edmund's School, Hindhead; Eton (King's Scholar); King's College, Cambridge. BA 1952; MA 1956. Member of editorial staff, Church Times, 1952–89; Managing Director, 1957–89; Editor-in-Chief, 1960–68; Chm., 1962–89. DLitt Lambeth, 1988. *Publications:* Gadfly for God: a history of the Church Times, 1991; High and Mitred: a study of prime ministers as bishop-makers, 1992; Reverend Rebels: five Victorian clerics and their fight against authority, 1993; Men of Habit: the Franciscan ideal in action, 1994; A Class of Their Own: six public-school headmasters who became Archbishop of Canterbury, 1997; Imperial Vineyard: the Anglican church in India under the Raj from the Mutiny to Partition, 1999; Willingly to School: a history of St Edmund's, Hindhead, 2000; Serving Two Masters: parish patronage in the Church of England since 1714, 2003; Blue Blood on the Trail: Lord Peter Wimsey and his circle, 2004. *Recreations:* cycling, penmanship. *Address:* 151 Rickstones Road, Witham, Essex CM8 2PQ. *T:* (01376) 517577. *Club:* Royal Commonwealth Society.

PALMER, Brian Desmond; formerly Under Secretary, Northern Ireland Office; *b* 1 May 1939; *m* 1964, Hilary Eileen Latimer; one *s* one *d*. *Educ:* Royal Belfast Academical Instn; Queen's Univ. of Belfast (LLB 1962). Joined Northern Ireland Civil Service, 1957: Estate Duty Office, 1957–62; Min. of Home Affairs, 1962–65; Dept of the Environment, 1965–77; Head of Central Secretariat, 1977–81. *Recreation:* golf.

PALMER, Caroline Ann, (Cally), CBE 2006; Chief Executive, Royal Marsden NHS Foundation Trust (formerly NHS Trust), since 1998; *d* of Christopher and Ann Palmer; two *s* one *d* by a previous marriage; *m* 2004, Phil Yeates. *Educ:* Woking Girls Grammar Sch.; Westfield Coll., London Univ. (BA 1979); London Business Sch. (MSc 1995). MHSM, DipHSM 1983. Gen. mgt trng scheme, 1980–83; Asst Unit Adminr, St Luke's Hosp., 1983–85; Royal Free Hospital, subseq. Royal Free Hampstead NHS Trust: Associate Unit Adminr, 1985–87; Dep. Manager, 1987–90; Gen. Manager, 1990–94; Dep. CEO, 1994–98. *Recreations:* history of art, ballet. *Address:* Royal Marsden NHS Trust, Fulham Road, SW3 6JJ.

PALMER, Sir (Charles) Mark, 5th Bt *cr* 1886; *b* 21 Nov. 1941; *s* of Sir Anthony Frederick Mark Palmer, 4th Bt, and Henriette Alice (later Lady Abel Smith, DCVO); *S* father, 1941; *m* 1976, Hon. Catherine Elizabeth Tennant, *y d* of 2nd Baron Glenconner; one *s* one *d*. *Heir:* *s* Arthur Morris Palmer, *b* 9 March 1981. *Address:* Mill Hill Farm, Sherborne, Northleach, Glos GL54 3DU. *T:* (01451) 844395.

PALMER, David Erroll Prior, CBE 2003; Chairman, UK Hydrographic Office, since 2005; *b* 20 Feb. 1941; *s* of Sir Otho Prior-Palmer, DSO, and Sheila Peers (*née* Weller-Poley), OBE; *m* 1974, Elizabeth Helen Young; two *s* one *d*. *Educ:* Eton; Christ Church, Oxford (MA PPE). Joined Financial Times, 1964: New York Correspondent, 1967; Management Editor, 1970; News Editor, 1972; Foreign Editor, 1979; Dep. Editor, 1981; Gen. Manager and Dir, 1983; Dep. Chief Exec., 1989; Chief Exec., 1990–93; Independent Newspapers (Ireland): Man. Dir, 1994–98; Chm., 1999–2002; Chairman: South-West Sussex Radio, 1995–2004; Dedalo Grupo Grafico, 2004–06; Dir, Polestar Gp, 2003–06. Dir, The Mary Rose Trust, 2004–. First British finisher, seventh over-all, Observer Singlehanded Transatlantic Race, 1976; Nat. Dragon Champion, Edinburgh Cup, 2007. *Publication:* The Atlantic Challenge, 1977. *Recreations:* sailing, travelling. *Address:* 42 Lancaster Gate, W2 3NA. *Clubs:* Royal Yacht Squadron (Cowes); Itchenor Sailing (near Chichester); Royal St George Yacht (Dublin).

PALMER, David Vereker; DL; Chairman, 1982–88, and Chief Executive, 1978–88, Willis Faber plc; Chairman, Syndicate Capital Trust plc, 1993–96; *b* 9 Dec. 1926; *s* of late Brig. Julian W. Palmer and Lena Elizabeth (*née* Vereker); *m* 1950, Mildred Elaine O'Neal; three *d*. *Educ:* Stowe. ACII 1950. Commnd The Life Guards, 1944; served as regular officer in Europe and ME, 1944–49; joined Edward Lumley & Sons, 1949; Manager, New York office, 1953–59; joined Willis, Faber & Dumas Ltd, 1959; Dir, 1961. Mem. Lloyd's, 1953. Chm., British Insurance & Investment Brokers Assoc., 1987–90 (Dep. Chm., 1984–87); Pres., Insurance Inst. of London, 1985–86. Commissioner, Royal Hosp. Chelsea, 1982–88. Mem. Council, St George's House, Windsor, 2000–04. Pres., Henley and Dist Agricl Assoc., 2006. Trustee, Tower Hill Improvement Trust, 1978–2007. Master, Worshipful Co. of Insurers, 1982. High Sheriff, Bucks, 1993–94, DL Bucks, 1995. *Recreations:* farming, shooting. *Address:* Burrow Farm, Hambleden, near Henley-on-Thames, Oxon RG9 6LT. *T:* (01491) 571256. *Clubs:* City of London, Cavalry and Guards.

PALMER, Felicity Joan, CBE 1993; mezzo-soprano. *Educ:* Erith Grammar Sch.; Guildhall Sch. of Music and Drama. AGSM (Teacher/Performer), FGSM. Kathleen Ferrier Meml Prize, 1970; major appearances at concerts in Britain, America, Belgium, France, Germany, Italy, Russia and Spain, firstly as soprano and then as mezzo-soprano; début as soprano, Dido in Dido and Aeneas, Kent Opera, 1972; début in USA, Marriage of Figaro, Houston, 1973; soprano roles included: Pamina in The Magic Flute, ENO, 1975; Cleopatra in Julius Caesar, Herrenhausen Hanover, and Frankfurt Opera, 1978; title role, Alcina, Bern Opera, 1978; Elektra in Idomeneo, Zurich Opera, 1980; the Countess in The Marriage of Figaro, ENO; Elvira in Don Giovanni, Scottish Opera and ENO; Marguerite in Damnation of Faust, ENO; mezzo-soprano roles include: ENO: Tristan und Isolde, 1981; Rienzi, 1983; Mazeppa, 1984; Herodias in Salome, and The Witch in Hansel and Gretel, 1987; Orfeo, Opera North, 1984; King Priam, Royal Opera, 1985; Albert Herring, Glyndebourne, 1985; Tamburlaine, Opera North, 1985; Katya Kabanova, Chicago Lyric Opera, 1986; début at La Scala, Milan, as Marguerita in world première of Riccardo III by Flavio Testi, 1987; Last Night of the Proms, 1987; début, Netherlands Opera, as Kabanicha in Katya Kabanova, 1988, same role, Glyndebourne, 1988; Mistress Quickly in Falstaff, 1988 and 1990, Marcellina in The Marriage of Figaro, 1989, Glyndebourne; world première of Tippett's New Year, Houston, USA, 1989; The Marriage of Figaro and The Gambler (Prokofiev), Chicago, 1991; Klytemnestra in Elektra, WNO, 1992, La Scala, Milan and Japan, 1995, Royal Opera, 1997, Netherlands Opera, 2006; Orlando, Aix-en-Provence, 1993; Dialogue des Carmelites, Geneva, 1993, Metropolitan, NY, 2002; La Fille du Régiment, San Francisco, 1993, Royal Opera, 2007; Ariodante, WNO, 1994; The Rake's Progress, Chicago, 1994; Ballo in Maschera, Catania, 1995; Countess in The Queen of Spades, Glyndebourne, 1995; Juno/Ino in Semele, Royal Opera, 1996; Mahagonny, Paris, 1997, Chicago, 1998; Fricka in The Ring, Munich, 1997 and 1999, Canaries, 1999, Met. Opera House, NY, 2000; Sweeney Todd, Royal Opera, 2003; recitals in Amsterdam, Paris, Vienna, 1976–77, Tokyo, 1991; concert tours with BBC SO, Europe, 1973, 1977 and 1984, Australasia, Far East and Eastern Europe, 1977–; ABC tour of Australia, 1978. Recordings include: Poèmes pour Mi, with Pierre Boulez; Holst Choral Symphony, with Sir Adrian Boult; title role in Gluck's Armide; Elektra in Idomeneo, with Nikolaus Harnoncourt; Klytemnestra in Elektra, with Semyon Bychkov, Christoph von Dohnányi and James Levine; The Music Makers; Sea Pictures; Britten's Phaedra; recitals, with John Constable, of songs by Poulenc, Ravel and Fauré, and of Victorian ballads. *Address:* c/o Intermusica, 16 Duncan Terrace, N1 8BZ.

PALMER, Rev. Preb. Francis Harvey; Prebendary of Sawley in Lichfield Cathedral, 1986–89; Prebendary Emeritus since 1989; *b* 13 Jan. 1930; *s* of Harry Hereward North Palmer and Ada Wilhelmina Annie Utting; *m* 1955, Mary Susan Lockhart; three *d*. *Educ:* Nottingham High Sch.; Jesus Coll., Cambridge (Exhibr); Wycliffe Hall, Oxford. MA. Deacon, 1955; Priest, 1956. Asst Curate: Knotty Ash, Liverpool, 1955–57; St Mary, Southgate, Crawley, 1958–60; Chaplain, Fitzwilliam House, Cambridge, 1960–64; Vicar of Holy Trinity, Cambridge and Chaplain to Cambridge Pastorate, 1964–71; Principal, Ridley Hall, Cambridge, 1971–72; Rector of Worplesdon, Surrey, 1972–80; Diocesan Ecumenical Officer, Guildford, 1974–80; Diocesan Missioner, Lichfield, 1980–89. *Publication:* (contrib.) New Bible Dictionary, 1959. *Address:* The Old Vicarage, Claverley, Wolverhampton WV5 7DT.

PALMER, Prof. Frank Robert, FBA 1975; Professor and Head of Department of Linguistic Science, University of Reading, 1965–87; *b* 9 April 1922; *s* of George Samuel Palmer and Gertrude Lilian (*née* Newman); *m* 1948, Jean Elisabeth Moore; three *s* two *d*. *Educ:* Bristol Grammar Sch.; New Coll., Oxford (Ella Stephens Schol., State Schol.) 1942–43 and 1945–48; Merton Coll., Oxford (Harmsworth Sen. Schol.) 1948–49; MA Oxon 1948; Craven Fellow, 1948. Served war, E Africa, 1943–45. Lectr in Linguistics, Sch. of Oriental and African Studies, Univ. of London, 1950–60 (study leave in Ethiopia, 1952–53); Prof. of Linguistics, University Coll. of N Wales, Bangor, 1960–65; Dean of Faculty of Letters and Social Sciences, Univ. of Reading, 1969–72. Linguistic Soc. of America Prof., Buffalo, 1971; Distinguished Visiting Professor: Foreign Languages Inst., Beijung, 1981; Univ. of Delaware, 1983. Professional visits to Canada, USA, Mexico, Venezuela, Peru, Chile, Argentina, Uruguay, Brazil, India, Japan, China, Indonesia, Morocco, Tunisia, Uganda, Kuwait and most countries of Europe. MAE 1991. Hon. DLitt Reading, 1996. *Publications:* The Morphology of the Tigre Noun, 1962; A Linguistic Study of the English Verb, 1965; (ed) Selected Papers of J. R. Firth, 1968; (ed) Prosodic Analysis, 1970; Grammar, 1971, 2nd edn 1984; The English Verb, 1974, 2nd edn 1987; Semantics, 1976, 2nd edn 1981; Modality and the English Modals, 1979, 2nd edn 1990; Mood and Modality, 1986, 2nd edn 2001; (ed jtly) Studies in the History of Western Linguistics, 1986; Grammatical Roles and Relations, 1994; (ed) Grammar and Meaning, 1995; (ed jtly) Modality in Contemporary English, 2003; (ed jtly) English Modality in Perspective: genre analysis and cultural studies, 2004; articles and reviews on Ethiopian langs, English and linguistic theory, in learned jls. *Recreations:* gardening, crosswords. *Address:* Whitethorns, Roundabout Lane, Winnersh, Wokingham, Berks RG41 5AD. *T:* (0118) 978 6214.

PALMER, Geoffrey, OBE 2005; actor; *b* 4 June 1927; *m* 1963, Sally Green; one *s* one *d*. *Educ:* Highgate Sch. *Theatre* includes: Difference of Opinion, Garrick; West of Suez, Royal Court, 1971; Private Lives, Globe, 1973; Eden End, NT, 1974; St Joan, Old Vic,

1977; Tishoo, Wyndham's, 1979; Kafka's Dick, Royal Court, 1986; Piano, NT, 1990; *television* includes: The Fall and Rise of Reginald Perrin, 1976–78; Butterflies; The Last Song; Absurd Person Singular, 1984; Insurance Man, 1985; Fairly Secret Army, 1985; Seasons Greetings, 1986; As Time Goes By, 1992–2002; The Savages, 2001; He Knew He Was Right, 2004; *films* include: O Lucky Man!, 1973; The Honorary Consul, 1982; A Zed and Two Noughts, 1985; Clockwise, 1986; A Fish Called Wanda, 1988; The Madness of King George, 1994; Mrs Brown, 1997; Tomorrow Never Dies, 1998; Anna and the King, 1999; Peter Pan, 2002; Piccadilly Jim, 2003; Pink Panther II, 2007.

PALMER, Sir Geoffrey (Christopher John), 12th Bt *cr* 1660; *b* 30 June 1936; *er s* of Lt-Col Sir Geoffrey Frederick Neill Palmer, 11th Bt, and Cicely Katherine (who *m* 1952, Robert W. B. Newton; she *d* 1989), *o d* of late Arthur Radmall, Clifton, nr Watford; *S* father, 1951; *m* 1957, Clarissa Mary, *er d* of Stephen Villiers-Smith, Knockholt, Kent; four *d*. *Educ:* Eton. Agent for Burberrys, Norway, Sweden, Finland, 1971–94. *Recreations:* golf, crossword puzzles, shooting. *Heir: b* Jeremy Charles Palmer [*b* 16 May 1939; *m* 1968, Antonia, *d* of late Ashley Dutton; two *s*]. *Address:* Carlton Curlieu Hall, Leicestershire LE8 0PH. *T:* (0116) 259 2656. *Clubs:* MCC, I Zingari, Free Foresters, Eton Ramblers, Butterflies, Gentlemen of Leicestershire, Lincolnshire Gentlemen's Cricket, Derbyshire Friars, XL, Frogs, Old Etonian Golfing Society, Old Etonian Racquets and Tennis, Northants Amateurs' CC.

PALMER, Rt Hon. Sir Geoffrey (Winston Russell), AC 1991; KCMG 1991; PC 1985; President, Law Commission, New Zealand, since 2005; Professor of Law, Victoria University of Wellington, New Zealand, 1974–79, and since 1991; *b* 21 April 1942; *s* of Leonard Russell and Jessie Patricia Palmer; *m* 1963, Margaret Eleanor Hinchcliff; one *s* one *d*. *Educ:* Nelson Coll.; Victoria Univ. of Wellington (BA; LLB); Univ. of Chicago (JD). Barrister and Solicitor, High Court of New Zealand. Prof. of Law, Univ. of Iowa, 1969–73, and 1991–95. Vis. Professor of Law, Univ. of Virginia, 1972–73. MP (Lab) Christchurch Central, NZ, 1979–90; Dep. Prime Minister, 1984–89; Attorney-Gen., 1984–89; Minister of Justice, 1984–89; Minister for the Environment, 1987–90; Prime Minister, 1989–90. Partner, Chen Palmer & Partners (formerly Chen & Palmer), barristers and solicitors, Wellington, 1995–2004. *Publications:* Unbridled Power?—an interpretation of New Zealand's constitution and government, 1979, 2nd edn 1987; Compensation for Incapacity—a study of law and social change in Australia and New Zealand, 1979; Environmental Politics—a greenprint for New Zealand, 1990; New Zealand's Constitution in Crisis, 1992; Environment—the international challenge, 1995; Bridled Power, 1997, 3rd edn 2004; Constitutional Conversations, 2002. *Recreations:* cricket, golf, playing the trumpet. *Address:* 63 Roxburgh Street, Mount Victoria, Wellington, New Zealand. *T:* (4) 8015185; Law Commission, 10th Floor, Novell House, 89 The Terrace, Wellington, New Zealand.

PALMER, His Honour Henry; *see* Palmer, His Honour R. H. S.

PALMER, Horace Anthony, (Tony); Chairman, Meyer International, 1997–99 (Director, 1995–99); *b* 20 Feb. 1937; *s* of Horace Charles and Violet Victoria Palmer; *m* 1961, Beryl Eileen Freakley; two *d*. *Educ:* Pinner County Grammar School; Hammersmith Sch. of Building. FRICS; FCIOB. Trainee Quantity Surveyor, 1954; joined Taylor Woodrow, 1954; Contracts Manager, 1970; Subsidiary Dir, 1974; Subsidiary Man. Dir, 1987; Man. Dir, 1989; Chief Exec., 1990–97. Chairman: High Point Rendel Gp plc; Monacon Hldgs Ltd; Parker Plant Ltd; Pilkington Tiles, 1998–; Galliford, subseq. Galliford Try, 1999–2005; non-exec. Dir, Berkeley Gp, 1997–2007. *Recreations:* sports, reading biography.

PALMER, Howard William Arthur; QC 1999; a Recorder, since 2006; *b* 24 June 1954; *s* of William Alexander Palmer, CBE, DL and Cherry Ann Palmer (*née* Gibbs); *m* 1983, Catherine Margaret Jackson; one *s* three *d*. *Educ:* Eton Coll.; University Coll., Oxford (MA Juris). Called to the Bar, Inner Temple, 1977; Lectr, KCL, 1977–78; barrister in private practice, 1978–. *Recreations:* cricket, golf, fieldsports, theatre, enjoying the countryside. *Address:* 2 Temple Gardens, EC4Y 9AY. *T:* (020) 7822 1200. *Clubs:* MCC; Berkshire County Cricket.

PALMER, James Edwin; Partner, Herbert Smith LLP, since 1994; *b* 10 Sept. 1963; *s* of Malcolm John Frederick Palmer and Rachel Mary Palmer; *m* 1990, Nicola Jane Lister White; three *s*. *Educ:* Winchester Coll.; Queens' Coll., Cambridge (BA 1985). Joined Herbert Smith, 1986; admitted solicitor, 1988. Chairman: Company Law Sub-Cttee, City of London Law Soc., 2002–06; Law Soc./City of London Law Soc. Takeovers Jt Wkg Party, 2002–; Mem., Listing Authority Adv. Cttee, FSA, 2008–. *Publications:* (contrib.) Butterworths Takeovers: law and practice, 2005; (contrib.) Hannigan and Prentice: the Companies Act 2006—a commentary, 2007; (contrib.) Buckley on the Companies Acts, 2007–. *Recreations:* fly fishing, reading. *Address:* Herbert Smith LLP, Exchange House, Primrose Street, EC2A 2HS. *T:* (020) 7374 8000; *e-mail:* james.palmer@herbertsmith.com.

PALMER, Joe; *see* Palmer, T. J.

PALMER, John, CB 1986; Chairman, European Passenger Services, British Rail, 1990–94; *b* 13 Nov. 1928; 2nd *s* of late William Nathaniel Palmer and Grace Dorothy May Palmer (*née* Procter); *m* 1958, Lyliane Marthe Jeanjean; two *d*. *Educ:* Heath Grammar Sch., Halifax; The Queen's Coll., Oxford (Lit.Hum.) (MA). Entered Min. of Housing and Local Govt, 1952; Cabinet Office, 1963–65; Asst Sec., 1965; Under Secretary: DoE, 1971; Dept of Transport, 1976–82; Dep. Sec., Dept of Transport, 1982–89. Liveryman, Carmens' Co., 1987. *Address:* 72 College Road, SE21 7LY. *Club:* Oxford and Cambridge.

PALMER, Sir John (Edward Somerset), 8th Bt *cr* 1791; retired; Director, W. S. Atkins Agriculture, 1979–88; *b* 27 Oct. 1926; *e s* of Sir John A. Palmer, 7th Bt; *S* father, 1963; *m* 1956, Dione Catharine Skinner; one *s* one *d*. *Educ:* Canford School; Cambridge Univ. (MA); Durham Univ. (MSc). Colonial Service, Northern Nigeria, 1952–61. R. A. Lister & Co. Ltd, Dursley, Glos, 1962–63; Min. Overseas Develt, 1964–68. *Recreations:* fishing, sailing. *Heir: s* Robert John Hudson Palmer [*b* 20 Dec. 1960; *m* 1990, Lucinda Margaret Barker]. *Address:* Court Barton, Feniton, Honiton, Devon EX14 3BD. *T:* (01404) 851020.

PALMER, Maj.-Gen. Sir (Joseph) Michael, KCVO 1985; Defence Services Secretary, 1982–85; *b* 17 Oct. 1928; *s* of late Lt-Col William Robert Palmer, DSO, and late Joan Audrey Palmer (*née* Smith); *m* 1953, Jillean Monica Sherston; two *s* one *d*. *Educ:* Wellington College. Commissioned 14th/20th King's Hussars, 1948; Adjutant 14th/20th King's Hussars, 1953–55; Adjutant Duke of Lancaster's Own Yeomanry, 1956–59; psc 1960; jssc 1965; CO 14th/20th King's Hussars, 1969–72; Comdr RAC 1st (BR) Corps, 1974–76; Asst Chief of Staff, Allied Forces Central Europe, 1976–78; Director, Royal Armoured Corps, 1978–81. Col, 14th/20th King's Hussars, 1981–92; Hon. Col, Duke of Lancaster's Own Yeomanry, 1988–92. Chm., Copley Marshall & Co. Ltd, 1980–2004. Director: Alexanders, Laing & Cruickshank Service Co., 1986–89; Credit Lyonnais Construction Co., 1988–90. Chm. of Governors, Sandroyd Sch., 1984–99. Liveryman, Salters' Co., 1965 (Master, 1989–90). FCMI. *Recreations:* riding, shooting, music, reading. *Club:* Cavalry and Guards.

See also Angela Palmer.

PALMER, Prof. Marilyn, PhD; FSA 1991; Professor of Industrial Archaeology, Leicester University, since 2000; *b* 30 April 1943; *d* of Joseph Henry Allum and Mary Winifred Allum; *m* 1965, David Palmer (marr. diss. 1991). *Educ:* St Anne's Coll., Oxford (BA Hons Modern History 1965; MA 1969); Leicester Univ. (PGCE (Distinction) 1966; Postgrad. Cert. in British Archaeol. (Distinction) 1973; PhD 1976). History Teacher, Loughborough High Sch., 1966–69; Lectr, 1969–72, Sen. Lectr, 1972–77, Loughborough Coll. of Educn; Loughborough University: Lectr, 1977–80; Sen. Lectr, 1980–83; Head, History Dept, 1983–88; Leicester University: Sen. Lectr in History, 1988–98; Reader in Industrial Archaeol., and Hd, Archaeol. Div., 1998–2000; Head, Sch. of Archaeol. and Ancient Hist., 2000–06; adult educn lectr on indust. archaeology, 1973–. Gilder Lehrman Fellow, Colonial Williamsburg Foundn, 2006; Vis. Fellow, All Souls Coll., Oxford, 2007. Member: Royal Commn on Historical Monuments of England, 1993–99; Archaeol. Panel, 1999–, Industrial Archaeol. Adv. Cttee, 1999– (Chm., 2002–), NT; Industrial Archaeol. Adv. Panel, English Heritage, 2001– (Mem., Ancient Monuments Adv. Cttee, 1999–2001); Chm., Assoc. for Indust. Archaeology, 2004–08 (Mem. Council, 1980–2004; Pres., 1986–89). Jt Editor, Industrial Archaeology Review, 1984–2002. *Publications:* (with P. A. Neaverson) Industrial Landscapes of the East Midlands, 1992; Industry in the Landscape, 1994; Industrial Archaeology: principles and practice, 1998; South-West Textile Industry: a social archaeology, 2005; articles in jls. *Recreations:* hill walking, folk dancing, travelling—and industrial archaeology! *Address:* School of Archaeology and Ancient History, University of Leicester, Leicester LE1 7RH. *T:* (0116) 252 2821.

PALMER, Sir Mark; *see* Palmer, Sir C. M.

PALMER, Maj.-Gen. Sir Michael; *see* Palmer, Maj.-Gen. Sir J. M.

PALMER, Michael Julian Barham, CMG 1990; writer; Advisor to the Governor, Luxembourg Central Bank, since 2000; *b* 2 Feb. 1933; *s* of Cecil Barham Palmer and Phyllis Palmer; *m* 1983, Dr Karin Reichel. *Educ:* Corpus Christi College, Oxford (MA). Research Officer, Political and Economic Planning, 1957–61; Sec., Political Cttee, Council of Europe, 1961–66; Councillor for Defence and Armaments, WEU, 1966–68; Dir of Cttees, N Atlantic Assembly, 1968–72; Dir-Gen. of Research, European Parlt, 1972–90. Jean Monnet Prof., European Univ. Inst., Florence, 1989. Economic Consultant, Inst. for East-West Studies, NY and Prague, 1992–98. Chm., East-West Cttee, European League for Economic Co-operation, 1996–2006. Austrian Order of Merit, 1990; Order of Oak Leaf Crown (Luxembourg), 1990. *Publications:* European Organisations, 1959; European Unity, 1968; Prospects for a European Security Conference, 1971; The European Parliament, 1981; From Ensor to Magritte, 1994; Belgian paintings in the Simon collection, 1997; Liliane Heidelberger–Sculptrice, 1999; The Central Bank of Luxembourg, 2001; Belgian Art 1940–2000, 2002; 500 Belgian Masterpieces, 2006; Brief History of Belgian Art, 2007; articles in The World Today, Foreign Policy, The Times, Christie's International, EIU publications. *Recreations:* music, art, cooking, mountain walking. *Address:* 8 rue des Franciscaines, 1539 Luxembourg Grand Duchy.

PALMER, Monroe Edward, OBE 1982; FCA; chartered accountant; *b* 30 Nov. 1938; *s* of William and Sybil Polikoff; *m* 1962, Susette Sandra (*née* Cardash); two *s* one *d*. *Educ:* Orange Hill Grammar Sch. FCA 1963. Chm., Hendon CAB, 1981–83; Vice-Chm., Barnet CAB, 1986–88; Treasurer: Disablement Assoc., London Borough of Barnet, 1971–88; Liberal Parly Party, 1977–83; Jt Treasurer, Liberal Party, 1977–83; Chm., Lib Dem Friends of Israel, 1987–. Councillor (L, then Lib Dem) London Borough of Barnet, 1986–94 and 1998– (Leader, Lib Dem Gp, 1999–). Contested: (L) Hendon South, 1979, 1983, 1987; (Lib Dem) Hastings and Rye, 1992, 1997. Dir, Barnet Homes, 1994–. *Recreations:* politics, fishing, horse riding. *Address:* 31 The Vale, NW11 8SE. *T:* (020) 8455 5140. *Club:* National Liberal.

PALMER, Nicholas Douglas; MP (Lab) Broxtowe, since 1997; *b* 5 Feb. 1950; *s* of late Reginald Palmer and Irina Palmer (*née* Markin); *m* 2000, Fiona Hunter. *Educ:* Copenhagen Univ. (MSc equivalent); Birkbeck Coll., London (PhD Maths 1975). Computer scientist: Ciba-Geigy, Switzerland, 1977–82 and 1985–97; MRC London, 1982–85. PPS to DEFRA Ministerial team, 2003–05, to Energy Minister, DTI, 2005–07, to Sci. Minister, DTI, 2007, to Minister for Energy, BERR, 2007–08. Member: European Scrutiny Select Cttee, 1998–99; NI Select Cttee, 1999–2001; HM Treasury Select Cttee, 2001–03. Contested (Lab): Chelsea, 1983; E Sussex and S Kent, EP elecn, 1994. *Publications:* The Comprehensive Guide to Board Wargaming, 1973; The Best of Board Wargaming, 1980; Beyond the Arcade, 1985. *Recreation:* games played by post. *Address:* House of Commons, SW1A 0AA. *T:* (020) 7219 4197, (office) (020) 7219 2553; *e-mail:* palmern@parliament.uk.

PALMER, Prof. Nigel Fenton, DPhil; FBA 1997; Professor of German Medieval and Linguistic Studies, University of Oxford, since 1992; Professorial Fellow, St Edmund Hall, Oxford, since 1992; *b* 28 Oct. 1946; *s* of James Terence Palmer and Constance May Palmer (*née* Fenton); *m* 1974, Susan Patricia Aldred; one *s* one *d*. *Educ:* Hyde County Grammar Sch.; Worcester Coll., Oxford (MA, DPhil). Lectr in German, Durham Univ., 1970–76; University of Oxford: Univ. Lectr in Medieval German, 1976–90; Reader in German, 1990–92; Fellow, Oriel Coll., 1976–92. Fellow, Humboldt Foundn, 1982. *Publications:* Visio Tnugdali, 1976; Tondolus der Ritter, 1980; (with K. Speckenbach) Träume und Kräuter, 1990; Die Blockbücher der Berlin-Breslauer Sammelbandes, 1992; German Literary Culture in the Twelfth and Thirteenth Centuries, 1993; Zisterzienser und ihre Bücher, 1998. *Address:* St Edmund Hall, Oxford OX1 4AR. *T:* (01865) 510487.

PALMER, Prof. Norman Ernest, CBE 2006; barrister; Professor of the Law of Art and Cultural Property, University College London, 2001–04, now Emeritus; Visiting Professor of Law, King's College London, since 2005; President, Foundation for International Cultural Diplomacy, since 2006; *b* 16 Aug. 1948; *s* of Norman George Palmer and Muriel (*née* Walker); *m* 1970, Judith Ann Weeks (marr. diss.); one *d*; *m* 1994, Ruth Redmond-Cooper; one *d*. *Educ:* Palmer's Endowed Sch., Grays Thurrock; Magdalen Coll., Oxford (BA Jurisp. 1969; BCL 1971; MA 1974). Called to the Bar, Gray's Inn, 1973; Head of Chambers, 1992–99. Lectr and Sen. Lectr in Law, Univs of Liverpool, Tasmania and Manchester, 1971–81; Professor of Law: Univ. of Reading, 1981–84 (Head of Dept, 1982–84); Univ. of Essex, 1984–90 (Dean of Faculty, 1985–88); Prof. of English Law, Univ. of Southampton, 1990–91 (Dep. Dean of Faculty); Rowe & Maw Prof. of Commercial Law, subseq. Prof. of Commercial Law, UCL, 1991–2001. Standing Internat. Counsel, Nat. Gallery of Australia, 2001–. Sec. and a Dir, Internat. Cultural Property Soc., 1990–95 (Editor, Jl, 1991–95). Chairman: Treasure Valuation (formerly Treasure Trove Reviewing) Cttee, 2001– (Mem., 1996–); Ministerial Adv. Panel on Illicit Trade in Cultural Objects, 2000–05; Wkg Gp on Human Remains in Mus. Collections, 2001–03. Member: Standing Conf. for Portable Antiquities, 1995–; Spoliation Adv. Panel, 2000–;

Legal Sub-Cttee, Quinquennial Rev. of Reviewing Cttee on Export of Works of Art, 2001–04. Principal Academic Advr, Inst. of Art and Law, 1996–. Editor, Art, Antiquity and Law, 1996–. Dr hc Geneva, 2005. *Publications*: (ed with E. L. G. Tyler) Crossley Vaines on Personal Property, 5th edn, 1973; Bailment, 1979, 2nd edn 1991; (ed jtly) Emden's Construction Law, 1990; (with C. J. Miller) Business Law, 1992; (ed jtly) Interests in Goods, 1993, 2nd edn 1998; (with E. McKendrick) Product Liability in the Construction Industry, 1993; Art Loans, 1997; The Recovery of Stolen Art, 1998; Museums and the Holocaust, 2000; Halsbury's Laws of England, 4th edn and re-issue: (ed jtly) Titles on Tort; (ed with A. Powell) Bailment; (ed with W. J. Swadling) Carriers; (ed with A. H. Hudson) Confidence and Data Protection; (ed with N. Bamforth et al) Libraries and Other Scientific and Cultural Institutions; (ed jtly) Lien; (ed jtly) Damages. *Recreations*: literature, biography, travel, antique motor cars, collecting memorial verse. *Address*: 3 Stone Buildings, Lincoln's Inn, WC2A 3XL. *T*: (020) 7242 4937.

PALMER, Most Rev. Norman Kitchener, CMG 1981; MBE 1975; *b* 2 Oct. 1928; *s* of Philip Sydney and Annie Palmer; *m* 1960, Elizabeth Lucy Gorringe; three *s* one *d. Educ*: Kokeqolo, Pawa, Solomon Is; Te Aute, NZ; Ardmore, NZ (Teachers' Cert.); St John's Theological Coll., NZ (LTh; ordained deacon, 1964). Appts in Solomon Islands: Deacon/Teacher, Pawa Secondary (Anglican), 1966; priest, Pawa, 1966; Priest/Headmaster: Alanguala Primary, 1967–69; St Nicholas Primary, 1970–72; Dean, St Barnabas Cathedral, 1973–75; Bishop of Central Melanesia, 1975–87; Archbishop of Melanesia, 1975–87. Member, Public Service Advisory Bd, 1971–75. *Address*: Varei Village, Bauro District, General Post Office, Kira Kira, Makira Province, Solomon Islands.

PALMER, Penelope Jane; see Dash, P. J.

PALMER, Sir Reginald (Oswald), GCMG 1992; MBE 1973; Governor General, Grenada, 1992–96; *b* 15 Feb. 1923; *m* 1954, Judith Juliana Parke; two *s* five *d. Educ*: St George's RC Boys' Sch.; Govt Teachers' Trng Coll., Trinidad; Univ. of Birmingham (CertEd); Univ. of Calgary (BEd 1971). Pupil Teacher, 1939–41; pupil teacher scholarship, 1941; Asst Teacher, 1945–56; Headteacher, 1956–68; Tutor, Grenada Teachers' Coll., 1968–72; Asst Educn Officer, 1972–73; Principal, Grenada Teachers' Coll., 1973–74; Chief Educn Officer, 1974–80, retd. Manager, Grenada Teacher's Sch. Supplies Ltd, 1980–87; Pres., Grenada Employers' Fedn, 1987–89. Dir, Grenada Bank of Commerce, 1990–92. Foundn Mem., Grenada Teachers' Social Security and Welfare Assoc. (Sec. 1951–69); Pres., Grenada Union of Teachers, 1962–63. Member: Public Service Commn, 1983–87; Local Adv. Council, Sch. of Continuing Educn, 1978– (Pres. 1989–98). Chm., Grenada Drug Avoidance Cttee, 1988–92. Dir, Richmond Fellowship of Grenada, 1991–92. *Recreations*: reading, backyard gardening, walking, sea-bathing. *Address*: Mount Parnassus, PO Box 884, St George's, Grenada, West Indies.

PALMER, Richard William, CBE 2006 (OBE 1987); Executive Vice President, British Olympic Association, since 1997; *b* 13 April 1933; *s* of late Richard Victor Palmer and Mary Ellen Palmer (*née* Sambrook). *Educ*: Haverfordwest Grammar Sch.; Trinity Coll., Carmarthen; The College, Chester (Dip PE); Univ. of Leicester (MEd). Head, PE Dept, Windsor Grammar Sch., 1961–64; Sec., UAU, 1964–69; Gen. Sec., British Univs Sports Fedn, 1969–74; Dep. Sec. Gen., 1975–77, Sec. Gen., 1977–97, British Olympic Assoc. Vice Pres., European Olympic Cttees, 1993–97; Pres., British Inst. of Sports Administrators, 1997–2003; Chm., Confedn of British Sport, 1998–99; Mem., Sports Council of Wales, 2005–. Gen. Sec., Commonwealth Games Council for England, 1977–86; Dep. Chef de Mission, GB, 1976, Chef de Mission, GB, 1980, 1984, 1988, 1992, 1996, Olympic Games and Olympic Winter Games; Gen. Team Manager, England, Commonwealth Games, 1978, 1982, 1986. Technical Advr, London's 2012 Olympic Bid, 2004–05; Ind. Advr, Glasgow's 2014 Commonwealth Games Bid, 2006–07. Dir, Sports Coach UK, 1998–. FRSA 1998. Freeman of Pembroke, 1990. Prix de Merit, Assoc. of Nat. Olympic Cttees, 1990; J. L. Manning Award, Sports Journalists' Assoc., 1996; Olympic Order, IOC, 1998; Emlyn Jones Award, British Inst. of Sports Admin, 2003. *Recreations*: golf, sailing, Rugby Union, gardening, fishing. *Address*: British Olympic Association, 1 Wandsworth Plain, SW18 1EH. *T*: (020) 8871 2677. *Clubs*: Scribes, East India; Cardiff County; Haverfordwest and Fulwell Golf; Llangwm Boat.

PALMER, His Honour (Robert) Henry (Stephen); a Circuit Judge, 1978–93; *b* 13 Nov. 1927; *s* of Henry Alleyn Palmer and Maud (*née* Obbard); *m* 1955, Geraldine Elizabeth Anne Evens; one *s* two *d. Educ*: Charterhouse; University Coll., Oxford. Called to the Bar, 1950. Dep. Chm., Berks QS, 1970. A Recorder of the Crown Court, 1972–78. Resident Judge: Acton Crown Court, 1987–91; Harrow Crown Court, 1991–93; Pres., 1983–98, S Thames Regl Chm., 1993–99, Mental Health Rev. Tribunal. Dir of Appeals, Specialist Trng Authy, Med. Royal Colls, 1997–99. *Publications*: Harris's Criminal Law, 1960; Guide to Divorce, 1965. *Recreation*: self-sufficiency.

PALMER, Roy Newberry, FFFLM; HM Coroner, Greater London (South District), since 2001; Deputy Coroner, City of London, since 2002; Assistant Deputy Coroner, Greater London (Inner South District), since 1999; *b* Peterborough, 2 Aug. 1944; *s* of late George Joseph Palmer and Muriel Joyce Palmer (*née* Clarke); *m* 1967, Dr Celia Mountford; two *d. Educ*: St George's Coll., Salisbury, Southern Rhodesia; Mt St Mary's Coll., Spinkhill, Derbys; London Hosp. Med. Coll., Univ. of London (MB BS 1968); LLB London 1974. MRCS 1967; LRCP 1968; DObstRCOG 1970; FFFLM 2005. Called to the Bar, Middle Temple, 1977. GP, Sawbridgeworth, Herts, 1970–73; Medical Protection Society: Asst Sec., 1973–85; Dep. Sec., 1985–89; Sec. and Med. Dir, 1989–98; Dep. Coroner, Gtr London (W Dist), 2000–01. Vis. Sen. Res. Fellow, Sch. of Law (Centre of Med. Law and Ethics), 1999–2002. Gov., Expert Witness Inst., 2000–06 (Chm., Professional Bodies Adv. Gp, 1999–2006). President: Medico-Legal Soc., 2000–02; Sect. of Clin. Forensic and Legal Medicine, RSocMed, 2001–03; SE England Coroners' Soc., 2004–05 (Vice-Pres., 2003–04). Member: Council, Coroners' Soc. of England and Wales, 2003–; Exec. Council, British Acad. of Forensic Scis, 2004–06 (Pres., 2009–); Bd, Faculty of Forensic and Legal Medicine, RCP, 2006 (Mem., Fellowship Cttee). Pres., Soc. for Relief of Widows and Orphans of Medical Men, 1997–. Hon. Sec., 2005–07, Vice-Pres., 2007–Oct. 2009, Med. Soc. of London. Hon. Warden, Queen's Chapel of the Savoy, 1987–. Freeman, City of London, 1998; Liveryman, Apothecaries' Soc., 1998 (Hon. Sec., 2003–05; Chm., 2007–); Freeman, Barbers' Co., 2008. *Publications*: contrib. chapters on medico-legal topics in textbooks. *Recreations*: classical music, opera, theatre, art galleries, food and wine. *Address*: HM Coroner's Court, Barclay Road, Croydon CR9 3NE. *T*: (020) 8681 5019, *Fax*: (020) 8686 3491; *e-mail*: LondonCoroner@aol.com; City of London Coroner's Court, Milton Court, Moor Lane, EC2Y 9BJ. *Clubs*: Garrick, Royal Society of Medicine.

PALMER, Prof. Sarah Rosalind, (Mrs G. Williams), PhD; FRHistS; Director, Greenwich Maritime Institute, since 1998, and Professor of Maritime History, since 1999, University of Greenwich; *b* 16 Sept. 1943; *d* of Arthur Montague Frank Palmer and Marian Ethel Francis, (Jill), Palmer; *m* 1st, 1969, William David Walburn (marr. diss. 1978); one *s* one *d*; 2nd, 1979, Glyndwr Williams. *Educ*: Wimbledon High Sch. (GPDST); Univ. of Durham (BA); Univ. of Indiana (MA); London Sch. of Econs and Pol Sci. (PhD 1979). FRHistS 1980. Res. Asst, LSE, 1967–68; Queen Mary College, London: Lectr,

then Sen. Lectr in Econ. Hist., 1969–98; Hd, Dept of Hist., 1994–98. Chm., British Commn for Maritime Hist., 2003–. Trustee, Nat. Mus, Liverpool, 2000–. Member (Lab): Maidstone BC, 1970–73; Kent CC, 1985–93. Contested (Lab and Co-op): Weston-super-Mare, 1970; Bristol NW, 1983. Vice Pres., Marine Soc. and Sea Cadets, 2004–. Sen. Res. Fellow, Bahria Univ., Pakistan, 2008–. FRSA 1996. *Publications*: Shipping, Politics and the Repeal of the Navigation Laws, 1990; contrib. learned jls. *Recreations*: gardening, walking, cooking. *Address*: Russet Barn, 281 Broadwater Road, W Malling, Kent ME19 6HT.

PALMER, Rev. Canon Dr Stephen Charles; Vicar, Newport Minster, and St John's, Newport, Isle of Wight, since 2002; Chaplain to the Queen, since 2008; *b* Lowestoft, 13 May 1947; *s* of Thomas Clement Palmer and Joanna Edith Barbara Palmer (*née* Stoy); *m* 1968, Christine, *d* of Alan Tranah and Masie Tranah (*née* Owen); one *s* one *d. Educ*: RN Weapons Electrical Sch. (HMS Collingwood); Oak Hill Theol Coll. (Dip. Pastoral Studies 1974); Portsmouth Univ. (PhD 2004). FRGS 1998; FLS 2001. Served Royal Navy, 1963–71; RN Wireless Station Suara, Singapore, 1964; HMS Whitby, 1966; HMS Blake, 1969; ordained deacon, 1974, priest, 1975; Curate, Crofton Parish, 1974; Bishop of Portsmouth's Domestic Chaplain, 1977; Rector: Brighstone, Brook and Mottistone, IoW, 1980–91; Falkland Islands, 1991–96; Vicar, Christchurch Portsdown Hill, 1996–2002. Rural Dean, W Wight, 1986–91; Hon. Canon, Portsmouth Cathedral, 1991–; Bishop of Portsmouth's Advr on Envmt, 1998–2006. Chaplain: RN Reserve, 1979–91; IoW Council, 2003–. Member: Council, Royal Nat. Mission to Deep Sea Fisherman, 1998–2007; Exec. Council, British Beekeepers Assoc., 2003; Trustee, S Georgia Whaling Mus., 1992–96. *Publications*: (contrib.) The Falkland Islands Dictionary of Biography, 2008; numerous articles in Falkland Islands Jl, 1995–2008. *Recreations*: beekeeping, postal history, amateur radio. *Address*: Fintry Schoolhouse, Fintry, near Turriff, Aberdeenshire AB53 5RN; *e-mail*: palmers@fintry.plus.com. *Club*: Union Jack.

PALMER, Prof. Stuart Beaumont, PhD; FREng; Professor of Experimental Physics, since 1987, Deputy Vice-Chancellor, since 2001, University of Warwick; *b* 6 May 1943; *s* of Frank Beaumont Palmer and Florence Beryl Palmer (*née* Wilkinson); *m* 1966, Susan Mary Clay; two *s* one *d. Educ*: Ilkeston Grammar Sch.; Sheffield Univ. (BSc 1964; PhD 1968; DSc 1986). CPhys, FInstP, 1981; FInstNDT 1989; CEng, FIET (FIEE 1992). University of Hull: Asst Lectr, 1967–70; Lectr, 1970–78; Sen. Lectr, 1978–83; Reader, 1983–87; University of Warwick: Chair, Physics Dept, 1989–2001; Pro-Vice-Chancellor, 1995–99; Sen. Pro-Vice-Chancellor, 1999–2000; Actg Vice-Chancellor, 2001. Vis. Prof., Univ. of Grenoble, 1982–83; Vis. Scientist, Queen's Univ., Kingston, Canada, 1986. Chm., Standing Conf. of Profs of Physics, 2001–03; chm. and mem., various SERC and EPSRC cttees and working gps. FREng 2000. *Publications*: (with M. Rogalski) Advanced University Physics, 1995, 2nd edn 2005; (with M. Rogalski) Quantum Physics, 1999; (with M. Rogalski) Solid State Physics, 2000; over 250 contribs to learned scientific jls in magnetism, ultrasound and non destructive testing. *Recreations*: tennis, sailing, flying, skiing. *Address*: University of Warwick, Coventry CV4 7AL. *T*: (024) 7657 4004; Max Gate, Forrest Road, Kenilworth CV8 1LT. *Clubs*: Athenæum; Hull Sailing; Warwick Boat; Coventry Flying.

PALMER, Thomas Joseph, (Joe), CBE 1990; Chairman, Personal Investment Authority, 1993–2000; *b* 11 Sept. 1931; *m* 1955, Hilary Westrup; two *s* two *d. Educ*: King's School, Bruton; Trinity College, Cambridge. MA. Asst Gen. Man. (Planning), Legal and General Assurance Soc., 1969–72, Dir and Gen. Man. (Admin.), 1972–78; Legal & General Group plc: Dir, 1978–91; Gen. Man. (Internat.), 1978–83; Group Chief Exec., 1984–91. Chm., Laser Richmount, 1991–93; Director: SIB, 1991–93; Halifax BS, 1991–93; National Power plc, 1991–96; Sedgwick Gp, 1992–93; ProShare, 1992–94. Chairman: London Business Sch. Assoc., 1974–78; Assoc. of British Insurers, 1989–91; Pres., Insurance Inst. of London, 1982–83; Dir, Investors' Compensation Scheme, 1992–93. Gov., King's Sch., Bruton, 1989–2005 (Jun. Warden, 2001–03). Hon. Fellow, London Business Sch., 1990. *Recreations*: gardening, long-distance walking.

PALMER, Dr Timothy Noel, FRS 2003; Head, Predictability and Seasonal Forecast Division, European Centre for Medium-Range Weather Forecasts, since 2002; *b* 31 Dec. 1952; *s* of Alfred Henry Palmer and Anne Josephine Palmer; *m* 1978, Gill Dyer; three *s. Educ*: Wimbledon Coll.; Bristol Univ. (BSc 1974); Wolfson Coll., Oxford (DPhil 1977; DSc 1999). Vis. Scientist, Univ. of Washington, 1981; PSO, Meteorological Office, 1982–2002. Lead author, Third Assessment Report, Intergovtl Panel on Climate Change, 2001. Chm., Monsoon Numerical Experimentation Gp, UN WMO, 1989–96; Co-ordinator, EU Vth Framework Project: Development of a Multi-model Ensemble System for Interannual Prediction, 1999–2003; Co-Chm., World Climate Res. Prog. Climate Variability and Predictability Scientific Steering Gp, UN WMO, 2004–. *Publications*: contrib. to learned jls. *Recreations*: golf, cycling, ski-ing, playing guitar (folk, blues, rock and roll). *Address*: European Centre for Medium-Range Weather Forecasts, Shinfield Park, Reading RG2 9AX. *T*: (0118) 949 9600; *e-mail*: tim.palmer@ecmwf.int.

PALMER, Tony; see Palmer, H. A.

PALMER, Tony; film, television and theatre director; author; brought up by godparents, late Bert Spencer (railway engineer) and Elsie Spencer; *m* 2001, Michela Antonello; two *s* one *d. Educ*: Lowestoft Grammar Sch. Presenter, Night Waves, R3, 1994–98 (Sony Award, 1996). FRGS 1993. *Films*: over 100, including: All My Loving, 1968; Farewell Cream, 1968 (Platinum Record); 200 Motels, 1971 (Gold Record); Rory Gallagher Irish Tour, 1974 (Platinum Record); All This & World War Two, 1976 (Gold Record); All You Need is Love, 1977; A Time There Was, 1979 (Italia Prize); At the Haunted End of the Day, 1980 (Italia Prize); Once at a Border, 1981 (Special Jury Prize, San Francisco); Wagner, 1982 (Best Drama, NY Film and TV Fest.); Puccini, 1984; God Rot Tunbridge Wells, 1985 (Best Drama, NY); Maria, 1986 (Gold Medal, NY); Testimony, 1987 (Fellini Prize); The Children, 1989 (Best Director, NY); Menuhin, 1990 (Grand Award, NY); The Symphony of Sorrowful Songs, 1993 (platinum CD; Jury Prize, Chicago Film Fest.); England, My England, 1995 (Best Dir, NY); Parsifal, 1998 (1st prize, Casta Diva, Moscow; Golden Mask, Russia); The Harvest of Sorrow, 1999; Ladies and Gentlemen, Miss Renée Fleming, 2001; Hero – the Bobby Moore Story, 2002; Toward the Unknown Region – Malcolm Arnold, 2003; John Osborne and the Gift of Friendship, 2004; Margot, 2005; The Salzburg Festival, 2006; O Thou Transcendent: the life of Ralph Vaughan Williams, 2008; *theatre*: Billy Connolly's Great Northern Welly Boot Show, 1972; John Osborne's Deja Vu, Comedy, 1992; dir operas, Berlin, Karlsruhe, Munich, Hamburg, Zürich, Augsburg, St Petersburg, Savonlinna, Moscow, Ravello, Helsinki, Bonn. Numerous BAFTA and Emmy awards. *Publications*: Born Under a Bad Sign, 1970; Trials of Oz, 1971; Electric Revolution, 1972; Biography of Liberace, 1976; All You Need is Love, 1976; Charles II, 1979; A Life on the Road (biog. of Julian Bream), 1982; Menuhin: a family portrait, 1991. *Recreation*: walking. *Address*: Nanjizal, St Levan, Cornwall TR19 6JJ. *Club*: Garrick.

PALMES, Peter Manfred Jerome; Principal Assistant Director, Public Prosecutions Department, 1979–81; *b* 28 Feb. 1920; *s* of late Manfred Palmes and Gwendoline Robb; *m* 1st, 1945, Sylvia Theodor (decd); 2nd, 1969, Brenda Laban; one step *d. Educ*

Charterhouse; Worcester Coll., Oxford. Served War of 1939–45: Oxford and Bucks LI and 1/8th Gurkha Rifles, 1940–45. Called to Bar, Inner Temple, 1948. Public Prosecutions Dept: Legal Assistant, 1948; Sen. Legal Asst, 1958; Asst Solicitor, 1969; Asst Director, 1977. Jubilee Medal, 1977. *Address:* Chapel Lodge, Cross Colwood Lane, Bolney, West Sussex RH17 5RY.

PÁLSSON, Thorsteinn; Editor-in-Chief, Fréttablaðið, since 2006; *b* 29 Oct. 1947; *s* of Pall Sigurdsson and Ingigerdur Thorsteinsdottir; *m* 1973, Ingibjórg Rafnar; one *s* two *d.* *Educ:* Commercial Coll., Reykjavik; Univ. of Iceland (law degree). Journalist, Morgunbladid, 1974–75; Editor-in-Chief, Visir, 1975–79; Admin. Dir, Confedn of Icelandic Employers, 1979–83; MP (Independence) Southland, Iceland, 1983–99; Minister: of Finance, 1985–87; of Industry, 1987; Prime Minister, 1987–88; Minister: of Fisheries, 1991–99; of Justice and Ecclesiastical Affairs, 1991–99; Ambassador: to UK, 1999–2002; to Denmark, 2003–05. Chm., Independence Party, 1983–91.

PALTROW, Gwyneth; actress; *b* Los Angeles, 29 Sept. 1973; *d* of late Bruce W. Paltrow and of Blythe Katharine Danner; *m* 2003, Chris Martin; one *s* one *d.* *Educ:* Spence Sch., New York; Univ. of Calif, Santa Barbara. Williamstown Theater, Mass. Acting début, Picnic (with Blythe Danner); Rosalind, in As You Like It, 1999; Proof, Donmar Warehouse, 2002; other plays include: The Adventures of Huck Finn; Sweet Bye and Bye; The Seagull. Film début, Shout, 1991; films include: Moonlight and Valentino; Seven, 1995; Emma, 1996; Great Expectations, Sliding Doors (Best Actress, Golden Globe Awards, 1999), Hush, A Perfect Murder, 1998; Shakespeare in Love (Academy Award for Best Actress, 1999), The Talented Mr Ripley, 1999; Duets, 2000; Bounce, 2001; Shallow Hal, The Royal Tenenbaums, Possession, 2002; Sylvia, Sky Captain and the World of Tomorrow, 2004; Proof, Infamous, 2006; Running with Scissors, 2007; The Good Night, Iron Man, 2008. *Address:* c/o CAA, 2000 Avenue of the Stars, Los Angeles, CA 90067, USA.

PALUMBO, family name of **Baron Palumbo**.

PALUMBO, Baron *cr* 1991 (Life Peer), of Walbrook in the City of London; **Peter Garth Palumbo,** MA; Chairman, Arts Council of Great Britain, 1989–94; *b* 20 July 1935; *s* of late Rudolph and of Elsie Palumbo; *m* 1st, 1959, Denia (*d* 1986), *d* of late Major Lionel Wigram; one *s* two *d*; 2nd, 1986, Hayat, *er d* of late Kamel Morowa; one *s* two *d.* *Educ:* Eton College; Worcester College, Oxford. MA Hons Law. Governor, London School of Economics and Political Science, 1976–94; Chairman: Tate Gallery Foundn, 1986–87; Painshill Park Trust Appeal, 1986–96; Serpentine Gall., 1994–; Bd Mem. and Dir, Andy Warhol Foundn for the Visual Arts, 1994–97; Trustee: Mies van der Rohe Archive, 1977–; Tate Gallery, 1978–85; Whitechapel Art Gallery Foundation, 1981–87; Natural History Mus., 1994–2004; Design Mus., 1995–2005; Trustee and Hon. Treas., Writers and Scholars Educnl Trust, 1984–99; Mem. Council, Royal Albert Hall, 1995–99. Chm., Jury, Pritzker Architecture Prize, 2004–. Chancellor, Portsmouth Univ., 1992–2007; Gov., Whitgift Sch., 2002–. Liveryman, Salters' Co., 1965–. Hon. FRIBA 1986; Hon. FFB 1994; Hon. FIStructE 1994. Hon. DLitt Portsmouth, 1993. Patronage of the Arts Award, Cranbrook Acad. of Arts, Detroit, 2002. Nat. Order of Southern Cross (Brazil), 1993. *Recreations:* music, travel, gardening, reading. *Address:* 2 Astell Street, SW3 3RU. *T:* (020) 7351 7371. *Clubs:* Athenæum, White's, Pratt's, Garrick.

PAMPLIN, Elizabeth Ann, FCIPD; human resources and corporate ethics consultant, since 1999; Chief Executive, Liberal Democrats, 1998–99; *b* 13 April 1940; *d* of Richard Thomas Webb and Hilda Ethel Webb (*née* Teague); *m* 1969, Terence Michael Pamplin (*d* 2004); twin *d.* *Educ:* Rosebery GS; St Hugh's Coll., Oxford (BA PPE 1962; DPSA 1963). FCIPD (FIPD 1991). Clarks Ltd, 1963–66; Industrial Trng Service, 1966–71; Sen. Lectr, Personnel Mgt and Trng, Slough Coll. of HE, 1973–75; human resource management and consultancy: MSC, 1975–77; Petroleum Industry Trng Bd, 1977–82; RBK&C, 1983–91; P & L Associates, 1991–93; DoT, 1993–96; Cabinet Office, 1996–97. Examr in personnel mgt, PCL, then Univ. of Westminster, 1985–98; Nat. Examr, IPD, subseq. CIPD, 1996–2004. Governor: Lord Mayor Treloar Sch., 2000–; Wavell Sch., 2006–; Abbey Sch., 2006–. Contested (SDP), 1983, (SDP/L Alliance), 1987, Reigate. Freeman, City of London, 1997; Liveryman, Co. of Musicians, 1997–. FRGS 2000. *Publications:* reports and articles. *Recreations:* music, early dance, walking, countryside conservation. *Address:* Little Critchmere, Manor Crescent, Haslemere, Surrey GU27 1PB.

PANAYIDES CHRISTOU, Tasos, Hon. GCVO 1990; Chairman, ENESEL (formerly AVRA) Shipmanagement SA, since 1997; *b* 9 April 1934; *s* of Christos Panayides and Efrosini Panayides; *m* 1969, Pandora Constantinides; two *s* one *d.* *Educ:* Paphos Gymnasium; Teachers' Training Coll.; Univ. of London (Diploma in Education); Univ. of Indiana, USA (MA Political Science, Diploma in Public Administration). Teacher, 1954–59; First sec. to Pres., 1960–63; Director, President's Office, 1963–69; Ambassador of Cyprus to Federal Republic of Germany, Switzerland, Austria, and Atomic Energy organisation, Vienna, 1969–78; High Comr in UK, and Ambassador to Sweden, Norway, Denmark and Iceland, 1979–90; Doyen of the Diplomatic Corps in London and Sen. High Comr, 1988–90; Permanent Sec., Min. of Foreign Affairs, Cyprus, 1990–94; Ambassador to Sweden, Finland, Norway, Denmark, Latvia, Lithuania and Estonia, 1994–96. Rep., Exec. Cttee, Union of Greek Shipowners, 1997–2003; Pres., Cypriot Union of Shipowners, 2004–. Chairman: Commonwealth Foundn Grants Cttee, 1985–88; Commonwealth Fund Tech. Co-operation Bd of Reps, 1986–89; Commonwealth Steering Cttee of Sen. Officials, 1994–95. Hon. Fellow, Ealing Coll. of Higher Educn, 1983. Freeman, City of London, 1984. Hon. LLD Birmingham, 1991. 1st Cl., Grand Order and Grand Cross with Star and Sash, Federal Republic of Germany, 1978; Grand Cross in Gold with Star and Sash, Austria, 1979; Golden Cross of the Archdiocese of Thyateira and Great Britain, 1981; Grand Cross in Gold of Patriarchate of Antioch, 1984. *Publications:* articles in newspapers and magazines. *Recreations:* swimming, reading books. *Address:* ENESEL SA, Kolonaki International Centre, 23A Vas. Sofias Avenue, 10674 Athens, Greece.

PANDOLFI, Filippo Maria; a Vice-President of the Commission of the European Communities, 1989–92; *b* 1 Nov. 1927; *m* 1963, Carola Marziani; three *s* one *d.* *Educ:* Catholic Univ. of Milan (BA in philosophy). Member, Italian Parliament (Christian Democrats), 1968–88; Under Secretary of State, Min. of Finance, 1974–76; Minister of Finance, 1976–78; Minister of the Treasury, 1978–80; Chm. of Interim Cttee of IMF, 1979–80; Minister of Industry, 1980–82; Minister of Agriculture, 1983–88. *Recreations:* music, classical Greek, rock climbing. *Address:* Via Negri Giulio Enrico 3, 24128 Bergamo, Italy.

PANFORD, Frank Haig; QC 1999; *b* 23 Jan. 1949; *s* of Frank Essandoh Martin Panford and Susanna Panford (*née* Holdbrook-Smith); *m* 1st, 1979, Hilary Ann Luper (marr. diss. 1986); one *d*; 2nd, 1994, Najma Khanzada; two *s.* *Educ:* Holborn Coll. of Law (LLB Hons London 1971); Hague Acad. Internat. Law (Diplôme de Droit Privé 1976); Wolfson Coll., Cambridge (LLB 1979). Called to the Bar, Middle Temple, 1972; Lectr in Law, Poly. of Central London, 1974–92; Legal Advr and Sen. Film Examr, BBFC, 1984–90; in practice at the Bar, 1992–; called to Gibraltar Bar, 1994. Mem., Charter 88, 1998–99. *Recreations:* African politics, music, cooking, travel.

PANK, Dorian Christopher L.; *see* Lovell-Pank.

PANK, Maj.-Gen. (John) David (Graham), CB 1989; Chief Executive, Newbury Racecourse plc, 1990–98; *b* 2 May 1935; *s* of late Edward Graham Pank and Margaret Sheelah Osborne Pank; *m* 1st, 1963, Julia Letitia Matheson (*d* 2002); two *s* one *d*; 2nd, 2003, Jill Sarah Bevan (*née* Murrell). *Educ:* Uppingham Sch. Commnd KSLI, 1958; served in Germany, Borneo, Singapore and Malaya; commanded: 3rd Bn The Light Infantry, 1974–76; 33rd Armoured Bde, 1979–81; Comdr Land Forces, NI, 1983–85; Dir Gen. of Personal Services, Army, 1985–88; Dir of Infantry, 1988–90. Col, The LI, 1987–90. President: Army Cricket Assoc., 1987–89; Combined Services Cricket Assoc., 1988. Dir, Racecourse Assoc., 1994–98. *Recreations:* racing, fishing, cricket. *Address:* c/o Royal Bank of Scotland, London Drummonds Branch, 49 Charing Cross, SW1A 2DX. *Clubs:* Army and Navy, Victory Services; Mounted Infantry; Free Foresters, I Zingari, Mount Cricket.

PANKE, Dr Helmut; Chairman, Board of Management, BMW AG, 2002–06; *b* Storkow, 31 Aug. 1946. *Educ:* Phillips Exeter Acad., Exeter, NH (Dip.); Univ. of Munich (Masters degree in Physics 1972; Dr rer. nat. 1976). Res. at Swiss Inst. for Nuclear Res., and Lectr, Univ. of Munich, 1976–78; Consultant, McKinsey & Co., Inc., Düsseldorf and Munich, 1978–82; BMW AG, 1982–2006: Head: Planning and Controlling, R&D Div., 1982–85; Corporate Planning, 1985–88; Organization, 1988–90; Corporate Strategy and Co-ordination, 1990–93; Chm. and CEO, BMW (US) Hldg Corp., 1993–95; Exec. Dir, 1995–96; Member, Board of Management: Human Resources, IT, 1996–99; Finance, 1999–2002. *Address:* c/o BMW AG, Petuelring 130, 80788 Munich, Germany. *T:* (89) 3820.

PANKHURST, Julie Kathryn; Co-founder, Friendsreunited, 2000–05; *b* 16 Jan. 1967; *d* of John Victor Hill and Patricia May Hill; *m* 1998, Stephen Pankhurst, *qv*; two *d.* *Educ:* Queen Elizabeth's Girls' Sch., Barnet; Dehavilland Coll., Borehamwood; Luton Coll. of Higher Educn (HNC); Middlesex Poly. (HND Dist.). Software engr, GEC Avionics Ltd, 1985–88; Sen. Analyst Programmer, MFI Furniture Centres Ltd, 1988–2000. Patron, Plan UK, 2005–; Trustee, Happy Charitable Trust, 2006–. *Recreations:* photography, looking after my children, tennis.

PANKHURST, Stephen; Director and Co-founder, Friendsreunited, 2000–05; *b* 4 Jan. 1964; *s* of Nigil Frederick Pankhurst and Irene Pankhurst; *m* 1998, Julie Kathryn Hill (*see* J. K. Pankhurst); two *d.* *Educ:* Orange Hill Sch.; Imperial Coll., London (BSc Hons Maths). Software engr, GEC Avionics Ltd, 1985–87; developer, ITL, 1987–90; Develt Manager, Bovis Construction, 1990–93; freelance software consultant, 1993–2000; Dir/Co-founder, Happygroup, 2000–05. *Recreations:* football, cinema, walking, comic collecting, playing with my children. *Address:* *e-mail:* steve@scruffybeggars.co.uk.

PANNICK, David Philip; QC 1992; Fellow of All Souls College, Oxford, since 1978; a Recorder, 1995–2005; *b* 7 March 1956; *s* of late Maurice Pannick and of Rita Pannick; *m* 1st, 1978, Denise Sloam (*d* 1999); two *s* one *d*; 2nd, 2003, Nathalie Trager-Lewis; one *s* one *d.* *Educ:* Bancroft's Sch., Woodford Green, Essex; Hertford Coll., Oxford (MA, BCL; Hon. Fellow, 2004). Called to the Bar, Gray's Inn, 1979, Bencher, 1998. Jun. Counsel to the Crown (Common Law), 1988–92; Dep. High Court Judge, 1998–2005. Columnist, The Times, 1991–. Mem., Editl Bd, Public Law, 1990–. Hon. LLD Hertfordshire, 1998. *Publications:* Judicial Review of the Death Penalty, 1982; Sex Discrimination Law, 1985; Judges, 1987; Advocates, 1992; (ed with Lord Lester of Herne Hill) Human Rights Law and Practice, 1999, 2nd edn 2004. *Recreations:* travel, supporting Arsenal FC, musicals. *Address:* Blackstone Chambers, Blackstone House, Temple, EC4Y 9BW. *T:* (020) 7583 1770.

[Created a Baron (Life Peer) 2008 but title not gazetted at time of going to press.]

PANNONE, Rodger John; DL; Senior Partner, Pannone & Partners (formerly Pannone March Pearson), Solicitors, 1993–2003, now Consultant; President of the Law Society of England and Wales, 1993–94; *b* 20 April 1943; *s* of late Cyril John Alfred Pannone and Violet Maud (*née* Weeks); *m* 1966, Patricia Jane Todd; two *s* one *d.* *Educ:* St Brendan's Coll., Bristol; Coll. of Law, London; Law Sch., Manchester. Articled to Casson & Co., Salford, 1966–69; Asst Solicitor and Partner, W. H. Thompson, 1969–73; Partner, Pannone March Pearson, subseq. Pannone & Partners, 1973–2003; Chm., Renovo PLC, 2006–; Dir, Co-operation Legal Services Ltd, 2006–. Member: Lord Chancellor's Adv. Cttee on Civil Justice, 1986–89; Council, Law Soc., 1979–96 (Vice-Pres., 1992–93). Gov., Coll. of Law, 1990– (Chm., 1999–2005); Mem. Council, Manchester Univ., 1996– (Chm., 2000–04). Vice-Pres., British Acad. of Experts, 1994–. Chm., Manchester Concert Hall Ltd, 1993–2007. Regl Chm., Emmaus North West, 2005–. FRSA 1992. DL Greater Manchester, 1999. Hon. Life Mem., Canadian Bar, 1993. Hon. Fellow: Manchester Metropolitan Univ., 1994; Birmingham Univ., 1998. Hon. DLitt Salford, 1993; Hon. LLD Nottingham Trent, 1993; Hon. LittD Manchester, 2004. *Publications:* numerous legal pubns. *Recreations:* the Lake District, walking slowly, food and wine. *Address:* 17 Ballbrook Avenue, Didsbury, Manchester M20 6AB. *T:* (0161) 909 3000; 123 Deansgate, Manchester M3 2BU. *Clubs:* St James's (Manchester); Wyresdale Anglers.

PANTER, Howard Hugh; Joint Chief Executive and Creative Director, Ambassador Theatre Group Ltd, since 2000; *b* 25 May 1949; *s* of late Hugh Panter and of Hilary Panter (*née* Robinson); *m* 1994, Rosemary Anne Squire, *qv*; one *d*, and one step *s* one step *d.* *Educ:* Clayesmore Sch.; London Acad. of Music and Dramatic Art (Dip. Prodn and Stage Mgt). Producer: Knightsbridge Prodns, 1975–79; SRO Prodns, 1979–80; Man. Dir, Freedman Panter Prodns, 1980–86; Man. Dir, Turnstyle Gp Ltd, 1987–2000. *Recreations:* opera, contemporary dance, visual arts, cricket. *Address:* Ambassador Theatre Group, 39–41 Charing Cross Road, WC2H 0AR. *T:* (020) 7534 6112, *Fax:* (020) 7534 6109; *e-mail:* louisabell@theambassadors.com. *Club:* Garrick.

PANTER, Ven. Richard James Graham, (Ricky); Archdeacon of Liverpool, since 2002; Vicar, St John and St James, Orrell Hey, Bootle, since 1996; *b* 18 Sept. 1948; *s* of Rev. Ernest Downes Panter and Marjorie (*née* Lea); *m* 1974, Jane Christine Wilson; two *s* two *d.* *Educ:* Monkton Combe Sch., Bath; Worcester Coll. of Educn (Cert. Ed.); Oak Hill Theol Coll. Teacher, RE, Chatham Tech. High Sch. for Boys, 1970–71; Primary Teacher, St John's Boscombe C of E Primary Sch., 1971–73. Ordained deacon, 1976, priest, 1977; Curate, Holy Trinity, Rusholme, 1976–80; Asst Vicar, St Cyprian with Christchurch, Edge Hill, 1980–85; Vicar, St Andrews, Clubmoor, 1985–96; Area Dean of Bootle, 1999–2002. *Recreations:* singing (Royal Liverpool Phil. Choir), walking, caravanning. *Address:* St John and St James Vicarage, 2a Monfa Road, Bootle, Merseyside L20 6BQ. *T:* (0151) 922 3758, (office) (0151) 709 9722; *e-mail:* archdeaconricky@blueyonder.co.uk.

PANTER, Rosemary Anne; *see* Squire, R. A.

PANTLIN, Sir Dick (Hurst), Kt 1993; CBE 1977 (OBE 1970); Partner, 1946–52, Co-Managing Director, 1952–68, Henrijean International Insurance Brokers; *b* 8 Dec. 1919;

s of Albert Ralph Pantlin and Gwendolyn Clara Thomas; *m* 1946, Janine Henrijean; two *s*. *Educ:* Felsted; Alliance Française, Paris. ACIB. War service, Royal Marines, 1940–46, Major (despatches 1944). Founder and Chairman: British Sch., Brussels, 1969–95 (Hon. Pres., 1995–); Council of British Indep. Schs in EC, 1980–95 (Hon. Pres., 1995–); Trustee, St George's English Sch., Rome, 1988–97; Pres., British Chamber of Commerce, Belgium and Luxembourg, 1975–77; Vice-Pres., Royal Belgo-British Union, 1975–2000; Founder and first Pres., Council of British Chambers of Commerce in Continental Europe, 1975–78. Chevalier: Ordre de la Couronne (Belgium), 1959; Ordre de Léopold (Belgium), 1969. *Publications:* articles for expatriates on educn, British nationality and voting legislation. *Recreations:* golf, travel, politics, ancestral research. *Address:* Les Jardins de Longchamp, Avenue Winston Churchill 255, 1180 Brussels, Belgium. *T:* and *Fax:* (2) 3752721; *e-mail:* dpantlin@voo.be. *Clubs:* Army and Navy; Royal Golf de Belgique.

PANTLING, Mary; *see* Allen, M.

PANTON, (Elizabeth) Jane; Headmistress, Bolton School Girls' Division, 1994–2005, and Chairman of Executive Committee, Bolton School, 2002–05; *b* 20 June 1947; *d* of Richard Henry Panton and Constance Doreen Panton. *Educ:* Clayton Hall Grammar Sch., Newcastle; Merchant Taylors' Sch. for Girls, Liverpool; St Hugh's Coll., Oxford (MA Hons History); West Midlands Coll. of Educn, Walsall (PGCE). Teacher, Moreton Hall, near Oswestry, 1972–73; Third Mistress, Shrewsbury High Sch., 1973–83; Head of History and of Sixth Form, Clifton High Sch., Bristol, 1983–88; Headmistress, Merchant Taylors' Sch. for Girls, Crosby, Liverpool, 1988–94. Member: ISC (formerly HMC/GSA) Assisted Places Working Party, 1992–2000; GSA Professional Develt Cttee, 1992–96; ISIS North Cttee, 1993–99 (Chm., 1997–99); Chm., GSA NW, 2000–02. Mem., Sefton FHSA, 1990–92. Mem. Council, Liverpool Univ., 1990–94. Management Committee: Landscape Trust; Lake District Summer Music. Mem., Yealand Conyers Parish Council. Gov., Westholme Sch., Blackburn. *Recreations:* fell walking, UK and abroad, birdwatching, foreign travel, music, art, reading.

PANTON, Dr Francis Harry, CBE 1997 (MBE (mil.) 1948); Consultant, Ministry of Defence, 1984–99; Director, Royal Armament Research and Development Establishment, Ministry of Defence, 1980–83; *b* 25 May 1923; 3rd *s* of George Emerson Panton and Annie Panton; *m* 1st, 1952, Audrey Mary Lane (*d* 1989); two *s*; 2nd, 1995, Pauline Joyce Dean. *Educ:* City Sch., Lincoln; University College and Univ. of Nottingham; PhD (Chem.) Nottingham, 1952; PhD (History) Kent, 1999. Served War of 1939–45: commissioned, Bomb Disposal, Royal Eng., 1943–47. Pres., Univ. of Nottingham Union, 1950–51; Vice-Pres., Nat. Union of Students, 1952–54; Technical Officer, ICI, Billingham, 1952–53; Permanent Under-Secretary's Dept, FO, 1953–55; Office of Political Adviser, Berlin, 1955–57; Dep. Head, Technical Research Unit, MoD, 1957–58; Attaché, British Embassy, Washington, DC, 1958–59; Technical Adviser, UK Delegn to Conf. on Discontinuance of Nuclear Tests, Geneva, 1959–61; Permanent Under-Secretary's Dept, FO, 1961–63; Counsellor (Defence), British Embassy, Washington, DC, 1963–66; Head of Defence Science 6, MoD, 1966–68; Asst Chief Scientific Adviser (Nuclear), MoD, 1969–76; Dir Gen., Estabs, Resources and Programmes (B), MoD, April–Sept. 1976; Dir, Propellants, Explosives and Rocket Motor Estabt, and Head, Rocket Motor Exec., MoD, 1976–80. Consultant, Cabinet Office, 1985–97. Chairman: Mgt Cttee, Canterbury Archaeol Trust, 1985–2000; Dover Bronze Age Boat Trust, 1995–2006 (Hon. Pres., 2007–); Mem. Council, Kent Archaeol Soc., 1990– (Hon. Librarian, 1999–; Vice-Pres., 2005–). FRSC (FRIC 1961); FRSA 1973; FRAeS 1982. *Recreations:* archaeology, local history. *Address:* Grove End, Tunstall, Sittingbourne, Kent ME9 8DY. *T:* (01795) 472218. *Club:* Reform.

PANTON, Jane; *see* Panton, E. J.

PANUFNIK, Roxanna; composer of classical music; *b* 24 April 1968; *d* of Sir Andrzej Panufnik and Camilla Panufnik (*née* Jessel); *m* 2001, Stephen Macklow-Smith; one *s* two *d*. *Educ:* Royal Acad. of Music (GRSM Hons 1989; LRAM 1989; ARAM 1998). FRSA. Major *compositions:* Westminster Mass, 1998; The Music Programme (opera), 1999; Powers and Dominions (harp concerto), 2001; LEDA (ballet), 2003; Abraham (violin concerto), 2004; Love Abide (choir and orch.), 2006; major recordings: Westminster Mass; Angels Sing; The Upside Down Sailor; Beastly Tales. *Recreations:* food (eating and cooking), reading, aerobic exercise, playing with my children. *Address:* c/o Universal Edition (London) Ltd, 48 Great Marlborough Street, W1F 7BB. *T:* (020) 7292 9160; *e-mail:* uelpromotion@universaledition.com.

PAOLETTI, (Romano) Roland, CBE 2000. *Educ:* Manchester Univ. (DipArch 1958). RIBA 1970. Projects include: Metro, Hong Kong, 1988 (Chief Architect); Jubilee Line extension stations, London, 1999 (Head of Architecture and Station Design) (Millennium Bldg of Year Award, 2000).

PAPADEMOS, Lucas, PhD; Vice-President, European Central Bank, since 2002; Professor of Economics, University of Athens, since 1988; *b* Athens, 11 Oct. 1947. *Educ:* Athens Coll.; Massachusetts Inst. of Technol. (BSc Physics 1970; MSc Electrical Engrg 1972; PhD Econs 1977). Res. Asst and Teaching Fellow, MIT, 1973–75; Lectr in Econs, 1975–77, Asst and Associate Prof. of Econs, 1977–84, Columbia Univ., NY; Sen. Economist, Federal Reserve Bank of Boston, 1980; Vis. Prof. of Econs, Athens Sch. of Econs and Business, 1984–85; Bank of Greece: Econ. Counsellor (Chief Economist), 1985–93; Dep. Gov., 1993–94; Gov., 1994–2002. Gov., IMF for Greece, 1994–2002; Member: Monetary Cttee, EC, 1985–88, 1990; Gen. Council, 1999–, Governing Council, 2001–, European Central Bank; Committee of EC Central Bank Governors, subseq. Council of EMI: Mem., 1985–93, Chm., 1989, Cttee of Alternates; Chm., Monetary Policy Sub-Cttee, 1992–94; Council Mem., 1994–98. Chm., Adv. Bd, Hellenic Observatory, Eur. Inst., LSE, 1998–. Grand Comdr, Order of Honour (Greece), 1999. *Publications:* (jtly) Efficiency, Stability and Equity: a strategy for the evolution of the economic system of the European Community, 1987; (jtly) Stabilisation and Recovery of the Greek Economy, 1990; (with P. De Grauwe) The European Monetary System in the 1990s, 1990; (jtly) External Constraints on Macroeconomic Policy: the European experience, 1991; contrib. numerous articles and essays to books and learned jls, incl. Greek Econ. Rev., Eur. Econ. Rev. and Econ. Bulletin. *Address:* European Central Bank, Kaiserstrasse 29, 60311 Frankfurt am Main, Germany.

PAPADOPOULOS, Tassos; President of Cyprus, 2003–08; *b* 7 Jan. 1934; *m* Photini Michaelides; two *s* two *d*. Called to the Bar, Gray's Inn. Founder and Man. Partner, Tassos Papadopoulos & Co., law firm, Nicosia, until 2003. Mem., House of Reps, 1970–2003 (Pres., 1976). Former Minister: of the Interior; of Finance; of Labour and Social Insurance; of Health; of Agriculture and Natural Resources. Leader, Democratic Party, 2000. *Address:* c/o Presidential Palace, Dem. Severis Avenue, 1400 Nicosia, Cyprus.

PAPALOIZOU, Prof. John Christopher Baillie, DPhil; FRS 2003; Professor of Mathematical Physics, University of Cambridge, since 2005; *b* 4 May 1947; *s* of Michael and Sarah Papaloizou; *m* 1978, Elaine Joseph; one *s*. *Educ:* UCL (BSc 1st cl. Hons 1965); Univ. of Sussex (DPhil 1972). Research Fellow: Univ. of Sussex, 1971–73; Univ. of Oxford, 1973–74; Res. Associate, Culham Lab., 1974–76; Res. Fellow, Christ's Coll., Cambridge, 1976–80; Queen Mary College, London University: Lectr, 1980–86; Reader, 1986–88; Prof. of Mathematics and Astronomy, 1988–2004. *Publications:* monthly notices of RAS and papers in Astronomy and Astrophysics and Astrophysical Jl. *Club:* Royal Astronomical Society Dining.

PAPANDREOU, George Andreas; MP; President, Panhellenic Socialist Movement, since 2004; *b* St Paul, Minn, 16 June 1952; *m* 1989, Ada Papapanou; one *s* one *d*. *Educ:* King City Secondary Sch., Toronto; Amherst Coll., Massachusetts (BA Sociol.); Stockholm Univ. (undergrad. studies Sociol.); LSE (MSc Sociol. and Develt). Member of Parliament: Achaia (Patras) Dist, 1981–96; 1st Dist, Athens, 1996–2004; 1st Dist, Salonika, 2004–. Under Sec. for Cultural Affairs, Ministry of Culture, 1985–87; Minister of Educn and Religious Affairs, 1988–89, 1994–96; Dep. Minister of Foreign Affairs, 1993–94; Alternate Minister of Foreign Affairs, 1996–99; Minister of Foreign Affairs, 1999–2004. Chm., Parly Cttee of Educn, 1981–85; Vice-Chm., cross-party Parly Cttee for Free Radio, 1987; in charge, Parly Cttee for Culture and Educn, 1989–93; Panhellenic Socialist Movement: Member: Central Cttee, 1984–; Exec. Office, 1987–88, 1996–; Pol Bureau, 1996–; Sec., Cttee on Greek Diaspora, 1990–93. Founding Member: Helsinki Citizens Assembly, Prague, 1990; Lagonisi Initiative on Co-operation in Balkans, 1994; Member Board: Foundn of Mediterranean Studies (Mem., Res. Teams); Foundn for Res. and Self-Educn. Fellow, Center for Internat. Affairs, Harvard Univ., 1992–93. Hon. Dr Law Amherst Coll., 2002. Botsis's Foundn for the Promotion of Journalism Award, 1988; SOS against Racism, and Affiliated Orgns Cttee Award, 1996; Abdi Ipekci Special Award for Peace and Friendship, 1997; (jtly) Statesman of the Year, Peace Building Awards, Eastwest Inst., 2000. Comdr, Order of Yaroslav (Ukraine), 1996; Grand Commander: Order of Polish Republic (Poland), 1996; Order of Merit (Hungary), 2003; Grand Cross: Order of the Lion (Finland), 1996; Order of Civil Merit (Spain), 1998; Order of Polar Star (Sweden), 1999; Order of White Star (Estonia), 1999; Order of Honour, first class (Austria), 1999; Order of Merit, first class (Germany), 2000; Order of Isabella the Catholic (Spain), 2001; Order of the Crown (Belgium), 2001; Order of Infante Dom Henrique (Portugal), 2002; Order of Pius IX (Vatican), 2002; Order of Merit (Italy), 2003; Order of El Sol (Peru), 2003. *Address:* Panhellenic Socialist Movement, Harilaou Trikoupi 50, 10680 Athens, Greece.

PAPANDREOU, Vassiliki, (Vasso); MP (Pasok) Athens, since 1993; *d* of Andreas and Anastasia Papandreou. *Educ:* Athens Economic Univ. (BSc 1969); London Univ. (MSc 1971); Reading Univ. (PhD 1980). Economics Tutor, Exeter Univ., 1971–73; Res. Asst, Oxford Univ., 1973–74; Lectr, High Business and Econs Sch., Athens, 1981–85; MP, Greece, 1985–89; Dep. Minister, 1985–86; Alternate Minister: for Industry, Energy and Technology, 1986–87; for Trade, 1988–89; Minister: of Develt, 1996–99; of the Interior, Public Admin and Decentralisation, 1999–2001; of the Envmt, Physical Planning and Public Works, 2001–04. Mem., CEC, 1989–92. Vice President: Parly Assembly, Council of Europe, 1995–96; Parly Assembly, WEU, 1995–96. Panhellenic Socialist Movement: Mem., Central Cttee, 1974–; Mem., Exec. Bureau of Central Cttee, 1984–88, 1996–2006. Dir, Hellenic Orgn for Small and Medium Size Firms, 1981–85. Mem., Bd of Dirs, Commercial Bank of Greece, 1982–85. Hon. DEd CNAA, 1992; Hon. DLitt Sheffield, 1992; Dr *hc* Paul Sabatier Univ., Toulouse, 1993. Chevalier, Legion of Honour (France), 1993; Grand Cross, Order of Leopold II (Belgium), 1993. *Publications:* Multinational Companies and Less Developed Countries: the case of Greece, 1981; numerous papers and articles. *Address:* Academias 28, 10671 Athens, Greece.

PAPOULIAS, George Dimitrios; Commander, Order of Phoenix; Order of George I; Greek Ambassador to the Court of St James's and (non-resident) to Iceland, 1990–93; *b* 19 May 1927; *s* of Dimitrios G. Papoulias and Caterina Kontopoulou; *m* 1974, Emily Pilavachi; one *d*. *Educ:* Athens Univ. (Law degree; Econ. and Comm. Scis degree). Military service, 2nd Lieut, 1950–51. Entered Greek Diplomatic Service, 1955; served Athens, New Delhi, Bonn; Dep. Perm. Deleg. to UN and to Internat Orgns, Geneva, 1964–69; Counsellor, 1967; Dir, Political Affairs, Min. of N Greece, 1969–70; Minister, Paris and Perm. Rep. to Unesco, 1971–74; Mem., Bd of Dirs, Resettlement Fund, Council of Europe, 1971–74; Ambassador to UN, NY, 1975–79, to Turkey, 1979–83, to USA, 1983–89; Alternate Minister and Minister for Foreign Affairs, 1989, 1990; special envoy of Greek govt to UN talks on former Yugoslav Republic of Macedonia, 1993. Holds foreign orders and decorations. *Recreations:* archaeology, history. *Address:* Rigillis 16, Athens 10674, Greece. *T:* 7229888. *Club:* Athenian (Greece).

PAPOULIAS, Dr Karolos; President of the Hellenic Republic, since 2005; *b* 4 June 1929; *s* of Maj. Gen. Grigoris Papoulias and Vassilikh Papoulias; *m* May Panou; three *d*. *Educ:* Univ. of Athens (law degree); Univ. of Milan (Master of Law (Civil Law)); Univ. of Cologne (PhD Private Internat. Law). Sec., Socialist Democratic Union, 1967–74; Member: Central Cttee, PASOK, 1974–2004 (Sec., Internat. Relns Cttee, 1975–85); Co-ordination Council, 1974–2004; Exec. Bureau, 1974–2004; Political Secretariat, 1974–2004; Co-ordinating Cttee, Socialist and Progressive Parties of Mediterranean, 1975–85. MP (PASOK) Ioanina, 1977; Under-Sec., 1981–85; Dep. Minister of Foreign Affairs, 1981–85; Minister of Foreign Affairs, 1985–89; Dep. Minister of Defence, 1989–90; Minister of Foreign Affairs, 1993–96; Hd, Parly Delegn to OSCE, 1997–2003; Pres., Standing Cttee for Defence and Foreign Affairs, 1998–2004. Awarded numerous foreign decorations, including: Grand Cross, Order of Merit (Cyprus), 1984; Grand Cross, 1988, Grand Collar, 2005, Order of Makarios III (Cyprus); Grand Cross, Order of Redeemer (Hellenic Republic), 2005; Grand Cross, 1994, Collar, 2006, Order of Merit (Italy). *Publications:* monograph on the Greek Resistance 1941–1944; contrib. studies and articles to European newspapers and mags. *Recreations:* athletics, gardening, theatre, art, literature. *Address:* Presidential Mansion, Vassileos Georgiou B'st. No 2, Athens 10028, Greece. *T:* (210) 7283111, *Fax:* (210) 7232342; *e-mail:* publicrelations@presidency.gr. *Clubs:* Athenian, Hellenic Language Heritage; Ethnicos Gymnastikos Syllogos.

PAPOUTSIS, Christos D.; MP (Pasok) Athens, since 2000; economist; *b* 11 April 1953; *m* Lia Taliouri; one *d*. *Educ:* Univ. of Athens. Pres., Nat. Students' Orgn, Students of Greece, 1978–80. Special Advr, Min. of Presidency of Govt, Greece, 1981–84; European Parliament: Mem., 1984–95; Vice Chm., Socialist Gp; Mem. Cttees on Foreign Affairs, Security and Defence; Mem., Budgets and Budgetary Control Cttees, 1989–94; Vice-Chm., Canada Delegn, 1984–89; Mem., USA Delegn, 1989–94; Mem., EC, 1995–99; Minister for Merchant Shipping, Greece, 1999–2001. Mem., Central Cttee, Pan-Hellenic Socialist Movt, 1977– (PASOK) (Dep. Sec. Youth, 1978–81; Internat. Sec., 1988–94). *Publications:* European Destinations, 1994; The Colour of the Future, 1998; For Europe in the 21st Century, 1999. *Address:* Lykavittou 5, 10672 Athens, Greece; *e-mail:* papoutsi@otonet.gr.

PAPP, Helen Richenda; *see* Wallace, H. R.

PAPPANO, Antonio; conductor and pianist; Music Director, Royal Opera House, Covent Garden, since 2002; Principal Conductor, Academia Nazionale di Santa Cecilia, Rome, since 2005; *b* London, 30 Dec. 1959; *m* 1995, Pamela Bullock. *Educ:* studied under Norma Verrilli, Arnold Franchetti and Gustav Meier, USA. Has worked as pianist and assistant conductor with: NY City Opera; Gran Teatro del Liceo, Barcelona; Frankfurt Opera; Lyric Opera of Chicago; Bayreuth Fest.; Music Dir, Norwegian Opera, 1990–92; Music Dir, Th. Royal de la Monnaie, Brussels, 1992–2002. Principal Guest Conductor, Israel Philharmonic Orch., 1997–2000. Has conducted world-class orchestras in Europe and the USA, incl. Boston SO, Chicago SO, Cleveland Orch., LA Philharmonic, LSO, Berlin Philharmonic, Concertgebouw Orch. and Orch. de Paris; has also conducted at Metropolitan Opera and Bayreuth Fest. Recordings include: La Rondine; Il Trittico; Werther; The Turn of the Screw; Manon; Tosca; Don Carlos; Tristan und Isolde; Tchaikovsky Symphonies 4, 5, 6 and Respighi's Roman Trilogy. *Address:* c/o IMG Artists, The Light House, 111 Power Road, Chiswick, W4 5PY.

PAPPENHEIM, Karin; Chief Executive, Employment Opportunities for People with Disabilities, since 2004; *b* 11 Dec. 1954; *d* of Wolfgang and Joy Pappenheim; one *s* one *d*. *Educ:* St Paul's Girls' Sch.; Sussex Univ. (BA Hons Intellectual Hist.); London Coll. of Printing; Université de Toulouse; Goldsmiths' Coll. (Post grad. dip. in communicns). Weidenfeld & Nicolson, Publishers, 1977–79; Camden Social Services, 1980–82; Greater London Assoc. for Disabled People, 1982–84; Alcohol Concern, 1984–89; FPA, 1989–95; Dir, Nat. Council for One Parent Families, 1995–97; Chief Exec., Haemophilia Soc., 1998–2004. Trustee: Terrence Higgins Trust, 1998–2003; NCVO, 1999–2005. *Recreations:* family and friends, travel in France. *Address:* (office) Crystal Gate, 3rd Floor, 28-30 Worship Street, EC2A 2AH.

See also M. Pappenheim.

PAPPENHEIM, Mark; arts journalist; *b* 25 May 1956; *s* of Wolfgang and Joy Pappenheim; *m* 1988, Katie Tearle; two *s*. *Educ:* St Paul's Boys' Sch.; Merton Coll., Oxford (BA Hons Lit. Hum., MA); City Univ., London (Cert. Arts Admin). Box-office manager, Buxton Fest. and Opera Hse, 1979–80; Asst Hd of Educn, WNO, 1980–81; Fest. Administrator, Vale of Glamorgan Fest., 1982; Asst Administrator, Live Music Now, 1982–83; Pubns Ed., Opera North, 1983–84; Radio Ed., Radio Times, 1984–90; with The Independent, 1990–: Arts Editor, 1996–98; Classical Music Reviews Ed., 1998–; Opera Critic, The Daily Express, 1998–2002. Editor: BBC Proms programmes, 1998–2005; BBC Proms Guide, 2000–06; BBC Proms interactive television notes, 2006–; Lufthansa Festival of Baroque Music Programmes, 2008–. *Publications:* numerous articles; essays; programme notes, incl. BBC Proms, Edinburgh Internat. Fest., Royal Opera, Glyndebourne Fest. Opera, South Bank Centre, EMI Records, Decca Classics, Warner Classics; contrib. BBC Music Mag., Internat. Record Review. *Recreation:* beekeeping (editor, newsletter of Sussex Beekeepers' Assoc., Brighton & Lewes Div., 2006–). *Address:* 42 Ferrers Road, Lewes, E Sussex BN7 1PZ. *T:* (01273) 483546.

See also K. Pappenheim.

PAPPS, Alastair Harkness, CB 2002; Associate Director, Centre for Management and Policy Studies, Cabinet Office (on secondment from HM Prison Service), 1999–2002; *b* 28 April 1942; *s* of Osborne Stephen Papps and Helen Papps (*née* Harkness); *m* 1963, Marian Caroline Clayton; two *s* one *d*. *Educ:* King Edward's Sch., Birmingham; St Catharine's Coll., Cambridge (MA); Univ. of Newcastle upon Tyne (Dip. in Applied Social Studies 1970). Joined HM Prison Service, 1965; Prison Service Staff Coll., Wakefield, 1965–66; Asst Gov., Huntercombe Borstal, 1966–69; Tutor, Prison Service Staff Coll., Wakefield, 1970–73; Asst Gov., 1973–75, Dep. Gov., 1975–77, Wakefield Prison; Personnel Div., Prison Service HQ, 1977–80; Governor: Acklington Prison, 1980–83; Durham Prison, 1983–87; Frankland Prison, 1987–89; Dep. Dir, subseq. Dir, North Regl Office, 1989–90; Area Manager, North East, 1990–95; Dir of Ops–North, and Mem., Prisons Bd, 1995–99. Ed., Prison Service Jl, 1987–89. Vice-Chm., Standards Cttee, Rutland CC, 2006–. Chm., NICRO UK Trust for a Safer S Africa, 2000–; Expert Advr, Zahid Mubarek public judicial inquiry, 2004–06. Trustee, Prisons Video Trust, 2007–. Lay Mem., Professional Conduct Bd, BPsS, 2007–. *Publications:* articles in jls. *Recreations:* reading, theatre, cinema, travel, observing politics. *Address:* Wick House, 17 Well Cross, Edith Weston, Oakham, Rutland LE15 8HG. *Club:* Nottingham.

PAPUA NEW GUINEA, Archbishop of, since 1996; **Most Rev. James Simon Ayong;** Primate of the Anglican Church of Papua New Guinea, since 1996; Bishop of Aipo Rongo, since 1995; *b* 3 Sept. 1944; *s* of Julius and Margaret Ayong; *m* 1967, Gawali Susuwa (*d* 2003); one *d*, and one adopted *s*. *Educ:* Martyrs' Sch.; Newton Theol Coll. (DipTh); Martin Luther Seminary (BTh). Govt Administrative Officer, 1964–71; Church Purchasing Officer and Radio Operator, 1976–79. Ordained deacon, 1982, priest, 1984; asst priest, Resurrection parish, Popondetta, 1985–86; Lectr, 1987–88, Principal, 1989–93, Newton Theol Coll.; locum at Burgess Hill, Sussex, UK, and student at Chichester Theol Coll., 1993–94; Parish priest, Gerehu, Port Moresby, 1994–95. *Recreations:* reading, watching Rugby football. *Address:* PO Box 893, Mount Hagen, Western Highlands Province, Papua New Guinea. *T:* 5421131, *Fax:* 5421181.

PAQUET, Dr Jean-Guy, CC 1994 (OC 1984); FRSC; Chairman of Board, National Optics Institute (President and Chief Executive Officer, 1994); *b* Montmagny, Qué, 5 Jan. 1938; *s* of Laurent W. Paquet and Louisianne Coulombe. *Educ:* Université Laval (BSc Engrg Physics, 1959; DSc Elec. Engrg, 1963); Ecole Nat. Sup. de l'Aéronautique, Paris (MSc Aeronautics, 1960). FRSC 1978; FAAAS 1981. Université Laval: Asst Prof. of Elec. Engrg, 1962; Associate Prof., 1967; Head, Elec. Engrg Dept, 1967–69; Vice-Dean (Research), Faculty of Science, 1969–72; Prof. of Elec. Engrg, 1971; Vice-Rector (Academic), 1972–77; Rector, 1977–87; Pres., La Laurentienne Vie Inc., 1987–94. Fellowships: French Govt, 1959; NATO, 1962; Nat. Science Foundn, 1964; Québec Govt, 1965. Def. Res. Bd of Canada Grant, 1965–76. National Research Council of Canada: Fellowship, 1961; Grant, 1964–77; Mem., Associate Cttee on Automatic Control, 1964–70; Special Asst to Vice-Pres. (Scientific), 1971–72. Pres., Conf. of Rectors and Principals of Univs of Prov. of Québec, 1979–81. Member: Council, Univs of Prov. of Qué, 1973–77; Bd, Assoc. of Scientific, Engrg and Technol Community of Canada, 1970–77 (Pres., 1975–76); Bd, French Canadian Assoc. for Advancement of Science, 1969–71; Canadian Assoc. of Univ. Res. Administrators; Special Task Force on Res. and Develt, Science Council of Canada, 1976; Order of Engrs, Qué; Amer. Soc. for Engrg Educn; Amer. Management Assoc., 1980; Soc. for Res. Administrators. Member Board: Interamerican Univs Assoc., 1980–87; Assoc. des universités partiellement ou entièrement de langue française, 1981–87 (Vice-Pres., 1983); Assoc. of Commonwealth Univs, 1981–87; Founding Mem., Corporate Higher Educn Forum. Pres., Selection Cttee, Outstanding Achievement Awards, Canada, 1984 (Mem., 1983). DSc *hc* McGill Univ., 1982; DLaw *hc*, York Univ., 1983. *Publications:* (with P. A. Roy) Rapport d'études bibliographiques: l'automation dans la production et la distribution de l'énergie électrique, 1968; (with J. F. Le Maître) Méthodes pratiques d'étude des oscillations non-linéaires: application aux systèmes par plus-ou-moins, 1970; more than fifty pubns in scientific jls, on control systems engrg; articles on research, develt and scientific policy. *Recreations:* jogging, travels, golf. *Address:* National Optics Institute, 2740 rue Einstein, Sainte-Foy, Québec, QC G1P 4S4, Canada. *T:* (418) 6577006, *Fax:* (418) 6577088. *Clubs:* Cercle de la Garnison de Québec, Golf Royal Québec (Québec).

PARASKEVA, Janet; First Civil Service Commissioner, since 2006; Chairman, Child Maintenance and Enforcement Commission, since 2008 (Chairman designate, 2007–08); *b* 28 May 1946; *d* of Antonis Paraskeva and Doris Amanda Paraskeva (*née* Fowler); *m* 1967, Alan Richard Derek Hunt (marr. diss. 1983); two *d*, and two step *s*. *Educ:* Open Univ. (BA Social Scis 1983). HM Inspector of Schs, DES, 1983–88; Dir, Nat. Youth Bureau, 1988–91; Chief Exec., Nat. Youth Agency, 1991–95; Dir, England, Nat. Lotteries Charities Bd, 1995–2000; Chief Exec., Law Soc., 2000–06. Member: Nat. Bd for Crime Prevention, 1993–95; Youth Justice Bd, 1998–2000. Chair, Olympic Lottery Distributor, 2006–; non-executive Director: Fosse Community NHS Trust, 1992–99; Serious Organised Crime Agency, 2005–; Assets Recovery Agency, 2007–08. Ind. Mem., Consumer Council for Water, 2005–08. JP City of Leicester, 1993–2000. Hon. LLD Brighton, 2006. *Publications:* articles in youth, educn and law jls and periodicals and in TES. *Recreation:* gardening. *Address:* (office) 35 Great Smith Street, SW1P 3BQ.

PARAYRE, Jean-Paul Christophe; Officier de la Légion d'Honneur; Commandeur, l'Ordre National du Mérite, 1991; Chairman, Vallourec, since 2000 (Member, Supervisory Board, 1989–2000); Member, Supervisory Board, Peugeot SA, since 1984; *b* Lorient, 5 July 1937; *s* of Louis Parayre and Jehanne Malarde; *m* 1962, Marie-Françoise Chaufour; two *s* two *d*. *Educ:* Lycées in Casablanca and Versailles; Ecole Polytechnique, Paris; Ecole Nationale des Ponts et Chaussées. Engr, Dept of Highways, 1963–67; Technical Adviser: Min. of Social Affairs, 1967; Min. of Economy and Finance, 1968; Dir of Mech. Industries, Min. of Industry and Res., 1970–74; Manager of Planning, Automobile Div. of Peugeot, 1975; Manager, Automobile Div., Peugeot-Citroën, 1976; Chm. and CEO, Peugeot SA, 1977–84; Mem., Supervisory Bd, 1977–84, Dir-Gen., 1984–88, Chm. and Chief Exec. Officer, 1988–90, Dumez SA; Vice-Chm. and Chief Operating Officer, Bolloré, 1994–99 (Dir, 1994–2000); Chm. and CEO, Saga, 1996–99. Chm., GIE Trans-Manche Construction, 1986–92; Vice-Chm., Lyonnaise des Eaux-Dumez, 1990–92; Mem., Board of Directors: Crédit National, then Natexis, 1978–97; Valeo, 1986–91; GTM, 1986–92; LVMH, 1987–89; Jean Lefebvre, 1988–92; McAlpine, 1990–92; Inchcape plc, 1991–94; Indosuez, 1991–94; Bolloré (formerly Albatros) Investissement, 1994–; Coflexip, 1995–2000; Delmas, 1995–99; Stena International BV, 1995–; Tarmac plc, 1995–99; Sea Invest France, 1999–2004; Stena UK, 1999–2003; Carillion plc, 1999–2004; Suef, 1999–; Stena Line, 2001–. *Recreations:* tennis, golf. *Address:* 203 avenue Molière, 1050 Brussels, Belgium. *Clubs:* Polo de Paris, Golf de Morfontaine; Golf Country de Cannes-Mougins.

PARBO, Sir Arvi (Hillar), AC 1993; Kt 1978; non-executive Chairman, WMC (formerly Western Mining Corporation) Ltd, 1990–99 (Chairman and Managing Director, 1974–86; Executive Chairman, 1986–90); *b* 10 Feb. 1926; *s* of Aado and Hilda Parbo; *m* 1953, Saima Soots; two *s* one *d*. *Educ:* Clausthal Mining Acad., Germany; Univ. of Adelaide (BE Hons). Western Mining Corporation: Underground Surveyor, 1956; Underground Manager, Nevoria Mine, 1958–60; Techn. Asst to Man. Dir, 1960–64; Dep. Gen. Supt, WA, 1964–68; Gen. Manager, 1968–71 (Dir, 1970–); Dep. Man. Dir, 1971; Man. Dir, 1971. Director: Aluminium Co. of America, 1980–98; Hoechst Australia (formerly Hoechst Australian Investments Pty) Ltd, 1981–97; Chase AMP Bank Ltd, 1985–91; Sara Lee Corp., 1991–98; Chairman: Munich Reinsurance Company of Australia Ltd, 1984–98 (Dir, 1983–); Zurich Insurance Australian Group, 1985–98; Alcoa of Australia Ltd, 1978–96; The Broken Hill Pty Co. Ltd, 1989–92 (Dir, 1987–92). Member: Chase Internat. Adv. Bd; Degussa AG Supervisory Bd, 1988–93. Hon. DSc: Deakin, 1989; Curtin, 1989; Hon. DEng Monash, 1989; DUniv Flinders, 1991; Hon. DBusiness, Central Qld, 1999; Hon. LLD Sydney, 2000. Australian Achiever, 1990; Centenary Medal, Australia, 2003. Comdr, Order of Merit (Germany), 1979; Grand Cordon, Order of the Sacred Treasure (Japan), 1990; Order of White Star (Estonia), 2001. *Recreations:* reading, carpentry. *Address:* 737 Highbury Road, Vermont South, Vic 3133, Australia. *T:* (3) 98028264. *Clubs:* Melbourne, Australian (Melbourne); Hannans (Kalgoorlie).

PARDOE, Alan Douglas William; QC 1988; **His Honour Judge Pardoe;** a Circuit Judge, since 2003; a Chairman, Mental Health Review Tribunals (Restricted), since 2005; *b* 16 Aug. 1943; *s* of William Pardoe and Grace Pardoe, DSc, FRSC. *Educ:* Oldbury Grammar Sch.; St Catharine's Coll., Cambridge (MA, LLB). Called to the Bar, Lincoln's Inn, 1971, Bencher, 1998. Asst Lectr and Lectr in Law, Univ. of Exeter, 1965–70; Vis. Lectr in Law, Univ. of Auckland, NZ, 1970; Lectr in Law, Univ. of Sussex, 1970–74; in practice at the Bar, 1973–2003. A Recorder, 1990–2003. *Publications:* A Practical Guide to the Industrial Relations Act 1971, 1972; articles in legal periodicals. *Recreations:* mountain-walking, cooking. *Address:* Crown Court at Snaresbrook, 75 Hollybush Hill, E11 1QW. *Club:* Travellers.

PARDOE, John George Magrath, CBE 1975; FRAeS; Director-General, Airworthiness, Civil Aviation Authority, 1972–79. *Educ:* Coll. of Aeronautical Engineering. Entered design work in Aircraft Industry, 1935; joined Accidents Inspection Br. of Air Ministry, 1942; joined Staff, Air Registration Bd, 1945; Chief Technical Officer, 1969. Médaille de l'aéronautique, 1980.

PARDOE, John Wentworth; Chairman, Sight and Sound Education Ltd, 1979–89; *b* 27 July 1934; *s* of Cuthbert B. Pardoe and Marjorie E. W. (*née* Taylor); *m* 1958, Joyce R. Peerman; two *s* one *d*. *Educ:* Sherborne; Corpus Christi Coll., Cambridge (MA). Television Audience Measurement Ltd, 1958–60; Osborne Peacock Co. Ltd, 1960–61; Liberal News, 1961–66. MP (L) Cornwall N, 1966–79; Treasurer of the Liberal Party, 1968–69. Presenter, Look Here, LWT, 1979–81. Sen. Res. Fellow, PSI, 1979–81. Consultant to Nat. Assoc. of Schoolmasters, 1967–73. Director: William Schlackman Ltd, 1968–71; Gerald Metals, 1972–83; Mem. London Metal Exchange, 1973–83. Mem., Youth Trng Bd, 1985–89. *Recreations:* walking, reading, music, carpentry. *Address:* 18 New End Square, NW3 1LN.

PAREKH, family name of **Baron Parekh**.

PAREKH, Baron *cr* 2000 (Life Peer), of Kingston upon Hull, in the East Riding of Yorkshire; **Bhikhu Chhotalal Parekh,** FBA 2003; Professor of Political Philosophy, University of Westminster, since 2001; Professor of Political Theory, University of Hull, 1982–2001, now Emeritus; *b* 4 Jan. 1935; *s* of Chhotalal Parekh and Gajaraben Parekh; *m* 1959, Pramila (*née* Dalal); three *s*. *Educ:* Univ. of Bombay (BA 1954, MA 1956); Univ. of London (PhD 1966). Tutor, LSE, 1962–63; Asst Lectr, Univ. of Glasgow, 1963–64; Lectr, Sen. Lectr and Reader, Hull Univ., 1964–82. Vice-Chancellor, Univ. of Baroda, 1981–84. Visiting Professor: Univ. of BC, 1967–68; Concordia Univ., 1974–75; McGill Univ., 1976–77; Harvard Univ., 1996; Inst. of Advanced Study, Vienna, 1997; Univ. of Pompeu Fabra, Barcelona, 1997; Univ. of Pennsylvania, 1998; Ecole des Hautes Etudes en Sciences Sociales, Paris, 2000; Centennial Prof., LSE, 2001–03. Mem., Rampton/Swann Cttee of Inquiry into Educnl Problems of Ethnic Minority Children, 1978–82; Mem. Council, PSI, 1985–90; Vice Pres., UK Council for Overseas Students Affairs, 1989–94; Chm., British Assoc. of S Asia Scholars, 1989–91, 2004–. Dep. Chm., CRE, 1985–90; Member: Commn on Rise of Neo-Fascism in Europe, 1992–93; Nat. Commn on Equal Opportunities, CVCP, 1994–99; Chm., Commn on Future of Multi-Ethnic

Britain, 1998–2000. Trustee: Runnymede Trust, 1986–; Inst. for Public Policy Res., 1988–95; Gandhi Foundn, 1988– (Vice-Pres., 1996–2002); Anne Frank Educnl Trust, 1992–. AcSS 1999 (Pres., 2003–); FRSA 1988; Fellow, Asiatic Soc., Bombay, 2004. Holds 8 hon. doctorates. British Asian of the Year, Asian Who's Who, 1991; Special Lifetime Achievement Award for Asians, BBC, 1999; Sir Isaiah Berlin Prize, Pol Studies Assoc., 2003. Saraswat Gaurav Award, Gujarat, 2004; Pravasi Bharatiya Samman Award, India, 2005; Pride of India Award, 2006; Distinguished Global Thinker Award, New Delhi, 2006. Padma Bhushan (India), 2007. *Publications:* Politics and Experience, 1968; Dissent and Disorder, 1971; The Morality of Politics, 1972; Knowledge and Belief in Politics, 1973; Bentham's Political Thought, 1973; Colour, Culture and Consciousness, 1974; Jeremy Bentham: ten critical essays, 1974; The Concept of Socialism, 1975; Hannah Arendt and the Search for a New Political Philosophy, 1981; Karl Marx's Theory of Ideology, 1982; Contemporary Political Thinkers, 1982; Political Discourse, 1986; Gandhi's Political Philosophy, 1989; Colonialism, Tradition and Reform, 1989; Jeremy Bentham: critical assessments (4 vols), 1993; The Decolonisation of Imagination, 1995; Crisis and Change in Contemporary India, 1995; Gandhi, 1997; Rethinking Multiculturalism, 2000; A New Politics of Identity, 2008; articles in learned jls incl. Political Studies, British Jl of Political Science, Social Research, Jl of History of Ideas, Indian Jl of Social Science, Ethics, Hist. of Pol Thought, TLS, Canadian Jl of Philosophy, Radical Philosophy, THES, Transit, Les Temps Modernes, Constellations, Dialegs, Rev. of Internat. Studies, Internat. Relations. *Recreations:* reading, music, walking. *Address:* 211 Victoria Avenue, Hull HU5 3EF.

PARENT, Hon. Gilbert; PC (Can.) 2001; Ambassador for the Environment, Department of Foreign Affairs and International Trade, Canada, 2000–04; Vice Chairman, Protocol Energy International; *b* 25 July 1935; *s* of Joseph Nelson Parent and Marie Delina (*née* Boulanger); *m*; four *d*. *Educ:* St Joseph's Coll., Rensselear, Ind. (BSc); Niagara Univ., NY (MA); State Univ. of NY (MEd). French teacher: Notre Dame High Sch., Welland, Ont, 1957–59; Dennis Morris High Sch., St Catharines, Ont, 1959–70; Vice-Principal, Thorold Secondary Sch., 1970–74; history teacher, Niagara South Bd of Educn, 1985–89. MP (L) Welland-St Catharines-Thorold, 1974–85 and 1988–2001. Speaker of H of C, Canada, 1994–2000. Hon. LLD: St Joseph's Coll., Ind., 1995; Niagara Univ., NY, 1995; Brock Univ., Ont, 1996. *Recreations:* reading, playing golf, spending time with grandchildren, promoting greater awareness of Parliament among young people. *Address:* 110 Bloor Street West, Toronto, ON M5S 2W4, Canada.

PARFIT, Derek Antony, FBA 1986; Senior Research Fellow, All Souls College, Oxford, since 1984; *b* 11 Dec. 1942; *s* of Norman and Jessie Parfit. *Educ:* Eton; Balliol College, Oxford (BA Modern History, 1964). Fellow of All Souls Coll., Oxford, 1967–. *Publication:* Reasons and Persons, 1984. *Recreation:* architectural photography. *Address:* All Souls College, Oxford OX1 4AL. *T:* (01865) 279282.

PARFITT, Andrew John; Controller: BBC Radio 1, since 1998; BBC 1Xtra, since 2002; BBC Switch (formerly BBC Teens), since 2006; BBC Asian Network, since 2008; *b* 24 Sept. 1958; *s* of John Raymond Parfitt and Jeanne Parfitt; *m* 1996, Laura Druce; two *d*. *Educ:* Bristol Old Vic Theatre Sch.; Wharton Business Sch. Asst stage manager, Bristol Arts Centre, 1978; studio manager, BBC, 1979–84; programme presenter, British Forces Broadcasting Service, 1984; BBC: educn producer, 1985; producer, features and magazines, Radio 4, 1986–91; Breakfast Show Editor, Radio 5, 1991–93; Radio 1: Editor, 1993–95; Managing Editor, 1995–98. *Recreations:* running, painting, music, presenting radio programs. *Address:* BBC Radio 1, Yalding House, 152–156 Great Portland Street, W1N 4DJ.

PARFITT, David John; film producer; Director: Renaissance Theatre Company, since 1987; Trademark Films, since 1999; Trademark Theatre Company, since 2001; *b* 8 July 1958; *s* of late William Arnold Parfitt and of Maureen Parfitt (*née* Collinson); *m* 1st, 1988, Susan Coates (marr. diss. 1993); one *s*; 2nd, 1996, Elizabeth Barron; two *s*. *Educ:* Bede Grammar Sch., Sunderland; Barbara Speake Stage Sch., London. Actor, 1970–88; producer, 1985–: productions include: *theatre*: Tell Me Honestly, 1985, John Sessions at the 11th Hour, 1986, Donmar Warehouse; Romeo and Juliet, 1986, Public Enemy, 1987, Lyric Hammersmith; Napoleon, Albery, 1987; Much Ado About Nothing, As You Like It, and Hamlet, Phoenix, 1988; Look Back in Anger, Lyric, 1989; A Midsummer Night's Dream, King Lear, Dominion, 1990; Scenes from a Marriage, Wyndhams, 1990; Travelling Tales, Haymarket, 1991; Uncle Vanya, Lyric Hammersmith, 1991; Coriolanus, Chichester Fest. Th., 1992; Les Liaisons Dangereuses, Playhouse, 2004; Elling, Bush, 2007; *television*: Twelfth Night, 1988; Look Back in Anger, 1989; *films*: Henry V, 1988; Peter's Friends, 1992; Swan Song, 1992; Much Ado About Nothing, 1993; Mary Shelley's Frankenstein, 1994; The Madness of King George, 1995; Twelfth Night, 1996; The Wings of the Dove, 1997; Shakespeare in Love, 1998; (consultant) Gangs of New York, 2002; I Capture the Castle, 2003; Chasing Liberty, 2004; (exec. prod.) Dean Spanley, 2008; A Bunch of Amateurs, 2008. BAFTA: Mem. Bd of Trustees, 2000–; Chm., Film Cttee, 2004–07; Chm., 2008–. Trustee, Chicken Shed Th. Co., 1997–; Patron, Royalty Th., Sunderland, 1999–. Hon. DA Sunderland, 1999; Hon. Dr Drama RSAMD, 2001. *Address:* Trademark Films, 11 Trinity Rise, SW2 2QP. *T:* (020) 7240 5585; *e-mail:* mail@trademarkfilms.co.uk.

PARGETER, Rt Rev. Philip; Auxiliary Bishop of Birmingham, (RC), and Titular Bishop of Valentiniana, since 1989; *b* 13 June 1933; *s* of Philip William Henry Pargeter and Ellen Pargeter. *Educ:* St Bede's Coll., Manchester; Oscott Coll., Sutton Coldfield. Priest, 1959; on staff of Cotton College, 1959–85; Administrator, St Chad's Cathedral, Birmingham, 1985–90; Canon, 1986. *Recreations:* reading, listening to music, walking. *Address:* Grove House, 90 College Road, Sutton Coldfield B73 5AH. *T:* (0121) 354 4363.

PARHAM, Prof. Peter Robert, PhD; FRS 2008; Professor, Stanford University, since 1992; scientist and immunogeneticist, since 1977; *b* Stanmore, Middx, 15 Aug. 1950; *s* of Ronald and Hilda Parham; *m* 1978, Frances Brodsky. *Educ:* Stanburn Prim. Sch., Stanmore; Haberdashers' Aske's Sch., Elstree; St John's Coll., Cambridge (BA Natural Scis 1972); Harvard Univ. (PhD Biochem. and Molecular Biol.). Jun. Fellow, Soc. of Fellows, Harvard Univ., 1977–80; Asst Prof., 1980–88, Associate Prof., 1988–92, Stanford Univ. *Publication:* The Immune System, 2000, 3rd edn 2009. *Recreations:* seaside swimming, landmarks, watching bad birds. *Address:* Department of Structural Biology, 299 Campus Drive West, Stanford University, Stanford, CA 94305, USA. *T:* (650) 7237456, *Fax:* (650) 7238464; *e-mail:* peropa@stanford.edu.

PARHAM, Philip John; HM Diplomatic Service; High Commissioner to Tanzania, since 2006; *b* 14 Aug. 1960; *s* of John Carey Parham and Christian Mary Parham (*née* Fitzherbert); *m* 1985, Anna Catherine Astrid Louise, (Kasia), Giedroyc; five *s* two *d*. *Educ:* Eton Coll.; Christ Church, Oxford (MA Lit.Hum.). Morgan Grenfell, 1983–89 (Sen. Asst Dir, 1988); Barclays de Zoete Wedd Ltd, 1989–93 (Dir, 1993); joined FCO, 1993; FCO, 1993–96 (Private Sec. to Parly Under-Sec. of State, 1995); First Sec. (Chancery), Washington, 1996–2000; Dir, Trade and Investment Promotion, Saudi Arabia, 2000–03; FCO, 2003–04; Hd, Counter Terrorism Policy Dept, FCO, 2004–06. Liveryman, Skinners' Co. *Recreations:* children, theology, tennis, researching the parentage of Mary Anne Smythe. *Address:* c/o Foreign and Commonwealth Office, King Charles Street, SW1A 2AH. *Club:* Yacht (Dar es Salaam).

PARHAM, Richard David; Chairman: Coventry, Solihull and Warwickshire Partnerships, 2000; Dixi & Associates, since 2001; Coventry and Warwickshire Connexions, since 2001; Coventry and Warwickshire Regeneration Zone, since 2001; *b* 17 Nov. 1944; *s* of James Parham and Lily Elizabeth Parham; *m* 1967, Janet Burton; one *s* one *d*. *Educ:* Royal Liberty Sch., Romford; Barking Coll. of Technol. Ford Motor Co., 1961–67; Rootes Motors, 1967–69; Chrysler UK, then Chrysler UK/Talbot Motor Co., 1969–81: Profit Analysis Manager, then Finance Manager, Hills Precision Ltd, 1969–72; Manager, Product and Pricing Analysis, then Pricing and Investment, 1972–76; Co. Comptroller, 1976–77; Dir of Finance, 1977–80; Asst Man. Dir, 1981–94, Man. Dir, 1994–99, Peugeot Talbot, subseq. Peugeot, Motor Co. Mem. Council, Coventry and Warwicks LLSC. Chm. Bd of Govs, Coventry Univ., 2002–; Mem. Ct, Warwick Univ., 1998–. Hon. DBA Coventry 1999. *Recreations:* Rugby, cricket, music, reading, golf.

PARIS, Archbishop of, (RC), since 2005; **His Eminence Cardinal André Armand Vingt-Trois;** Chevalier de la Légion d'Honneur; Officier de l'Ordre National du Mérite; *b* 7 Nov. 1942; *s* of Armand Vingt-Trois and Laulette (*née* Vuillamy). *Educ:* Lycée Henri IV, Paris; St Sulpice Seminary, Issy-les-Moulineaux; Institut Catholique, Paris (BTh 1962). Military service, Germany, 1964–65; ordained priest, 1969; Asst Pastor, St Jeanne de Chantal, Paris, 1969–74; Dir and Prof. of Sacramental and Moral Theology, St Sulpice Seminary, Issy-les-Moulineaux, 1974–81; Vicar Gen., Archdiocese of Paris, 1981–99; ordained Aux. Bishop of Paris, 1988; Metropolitan Archbishop of Tours, 1999. Cardinal, 2007. French Bishops' Conference: Member: Episcopal Cttee for Charismatic Renewal, 1988–96; Permt Cttee for Information and Communications, 1988–97; Permt Cttee for Econ. Affairs, 1997–99; Pres., Cttee for the Family, 1998–2005. Mem., Presidency Cttee, Pontifical Council for the Family and Congregation of Bishops, 2006–. *Publications:* A Year of Blessings, 2000; To Know the Catholic Faith, 2000; Catecheses for the Jubilee Year, 2001; The Family: 15 questions to the Church, 2003. *Address:* c/o Diocese de Paris, 7 rue St Vincent, 75018 Paris, France.

PARIS, Andrew Martin Ingledew, FRCS; Consultant Urological Surgeon, The Royal London Hospital, 1976–2005, and St Bartholomew's Hospital, 1994–2005, now Emeritus Consulting Urological Surgeon; *b* 27 Nov. 1940; s of late Vernon Patrick Paris and of Heather Constance Ingledew Paris (*née* Dear); *m* 1975, Susan Philippa, *d* of Perys Goodwin Jenkins; one *d*. *Educ:* London Hosp. Med. Coll., Univ. of London (MB BS 1964). MRCS 1964, FRCS 1971; LRCP 1964; DObstRCOG 1967. Clinical Dir of Surgery and Urology, Royal London Hosp., then Barts and the London NHS Trust, 1979–2002; Consultant Paediatric Urological Surgeon, Newham Gen. Hosp., 1995–2005. Hon. Urological Surgeon, Italian Hosp., London, 1979–90. Regl Advr on Urology, NE Thames, 1982–87. Examr in Dental Surgery, RCS, 1983–89. Founder Mem., St John Ambulance Air Wing, Hon. Surgeon, 1971–92; Trustee, St John Travelling Fellowships in Transplantation, 1992–. FRSocMed (Vice Pres., Section of Urology, 1983–84). Sen. Mem., British Assoc. of Urological Surgeons, 2005; Mem., Urological Club of GB and Ire. Trustee: Marie Celeste Samaritan Soc., 1996– (Chm., 2006–); Long Shop Mus., 2004–. Freeman, City of London, 1984; Liveryman, Soc. of Apothecaries, 1967– (Chm. Livery Cttee, 1992–93; Mem. Ct of Assts, 1994–; Master, 2007–08). OStJ 1985. *Publications:* contribs on urology and transplantation to med. jls. *Recreations:* ski-ing just out of control, sailing too close to the wind, avoiding my bees' stings. *Address:* The Old Vicarage, Aldringham cum Thorpe, Suffolk IP16 4QF. *T:* (01728) 833673, (consulting rooms) (020) 7702 8818, *Fax:* (020) 7702 8868; *e-mail:* andrewparis@tiscali.co.uk. *Clubs:* Athenæum; Aldeburgh Yacht.

PARIS, Prof. Jeffrey Bruce, PhD; FBA 1999; Professor of Mathematics, Manchester University, since 1984; *b* 15 Nov. 1944; *s* of George William and Marie Eileen Paris; *m* 1st, 1967, Malvyn Loraine Blackburn (marr. diss. 1983); two *d*; 2nd, 1983, Alena Vencovská; three *s* one *d*. *Educ:* Manchester Univ. (BSc 1st Cl. Maths 1966; PhD Mathematical Logic 1969). Manchester University: Lectr, Dept of Maths, 1969–74; Reader, 1974–84. Junior Whitehead Prize, London Mathematical Soc., 1983. *Publications:* The Uncertain Reasoner's Companion, 1994; numerous research papers in learned jls. *Recreations:* football, angling, painting, pop music. *Address:* School of Mathematics, The University of Manchester, Manchester M13 9PL. *T:* (0161) 275 5880.

PARISH, Neil Quentin Gordon; Member (C) South West Region, England, European Parliament, since 1999; *b* 26 May 1956; *s* of Reginald Thomas Parish and Kathleen Susan Mary Parish; *m* 1981, Susan Gail; one *s* one *d*. *Educ:* Brymore Sch., Somerset. Left sch. at 16 to run farm of 100 acres; farm increased to 300 acres, dairy and arable, 1990. Member (C): Sedgemoor DC, 1983–95 (Dep. Leader, 1989–95); Somerset CC, 1989–93; Parish Council, 1985–. European Parliament: spokesman on agriculture and on fisheries; Chairman: Agric. Cttee, 1999–; Agric. and Rural Develt Cttee, 2007–; Animal Welfare Intergroup, 2007–; Member: Envmt Cttee, 2001–; Fisheries Cttee, 2002–; Mem., EU Australian and NZ delegn. Contested (C) Torfaen, 1997. *Recreations:* swimming, walking. *Address:* 9c Mill Park Industrial Estate, White Cross Road, Woodbury Salterton, Exeter, Devon EX5 1EL.

PARISH, Richard, CBiol; FFPH, FRSH, FRIPH; Chief Executive, Royal Society of Health, since 2005; *b* 11 Oct. 1951; *s* of Leslie Thomas Parish, FCCA and Winifred Alice Parish; *m* 1976, Joan Margaret Shepherd; one *s* one *d*. *Educ:* Univ. of London (BSc ext. 1975); South Bank Poly. (PDipHEd 1978); Huddersfield Univ. (MEd). CBiol 1989; MIBiol 1989; Hon. MFPHM 2001, FFPH 2006; FRIPH 2006. Dir of Health Promotion, Stockport HA, 1980–85; Head of Progs, 'Heartbeat Wales', and Sen. Lectr, Welsh Nat. Sch. of Medicine, 1985–87; Dir of Ops, Health Promotion Authy for Wales, 1987–90; Principal and Chief Exec., Humberside Coll. of Health, 1990–96; Dir, Health and Community Studies, and Prof. of Public Health, Sheffield Hallam Univ., 1996–97; Hd, Health Studies, and Prof., Univ. of York, 1997–99; Regl Dir, Educn and Trng, NHS Eastern Reg., 1999; Chief Exec., HDA, 2000–03; Consultant, WHO, 2003–05. Visiting Professor: Univ. of Wolverhampton, 2001–; Anglia Ruskin (formerly Anglia Poly.) Univ., 2003–. Chm., Nat. No-Smoking Day, 2005–. Exec. Bd Mem., Nat. Heart Forum, 2000–. Gov., Moggerhanger Primary Sch. FRSH 1988; MCIPR (MIPR 1989). *Publications:* contribs on health promotion and health policy, incl. for WHO. *Recreations:* photography, rambling, cycling. *Address:* (office) RSH House, 38a St George's Drive, SW1V 4BH. *T:* (020) 7630 0121; Gypsy Wood House, 2 St Johns Road, Moggerhanger, Bedford MK44 3RJ. *T:* (01767) 640516. *Club:* Bedford Boat.

PARISOT, Pierre Louis André; Chevalier de l'Ordre du Mérite; Chevalier de la Légion d'Honneur; Vice-President, Strategic Sourcing and Purchasing, Veolia Environnement, since 2002; Chairman, Transmanche-Link (TML), since 1991; *b* Ambacourt, France, 9 Jan. 1940; *s* of Louis Parisot and Marie (*née* Boye); *m* 1963, Evelyne Treilhou; two *s* two *d*. *Educ:* Ecole Polytechnique; Ecole Nationale des Ponts et Chaussées; Institut d'Etudes Politiques de Paris. Assistant to the Director, Civil Works Department: Réunion Island, 1966–72; Morbihan, Brittany, 1973–76; Dep. Dir, Personnel Policy and Mod. Management Methods, Min. of Civil Works, Transport and Envmt, 1976–77; Technical

Advr, French Home Office Cabinet, 1977–80; Internat. Dir, St Gobain subsid., SOBEA, 1980–84; Dir Gen., SOGEA (Gp Générale des Eaux), 1985–90; Chm., Supervisory Bd, Société des Tuyaux Bonna (Gp Générale des Eaux, subseq. Vivendi), 1990–; Dep. Man. Dir, Société Générale d'Entreprises, 1991–97; Chairman and Chief Executive: Consortium Stade de France SA, 1995–98; Omnium de Traitement et de Valorisation, 1997–2001. *Recreations:* sailing, ski-ing. *Address:* Veolia Environnement, 36–38 avenue Kléber, 75799 Paris Cedex 15, France. *T:* (1) 71750283.

PARIZEAU, Jacques, PhD; Member, Québec National Assembly (Parti Québécois) for Assomption, 1976–84 and 1989–96; Prime Minister of Québec, 1994–96; *b* Montreal, 9 Aug. 1930; *s* of Gerard Parizeau and Germaine Parizeau (*née* Biron); *m* 1st, 1956, Alicja Poznanska (decd); one *s* one *d*; 2nd, 1992, Lisette Lapointe. *Educ:* Ecole des Hautes Etudes Commerciales, Montreal; Institut d'Etudes Politiques, Paris (Dip. 1952); London Sch. of Econs (PhD 1955). Prof., Ecole des Hautes Etudes Commerciales, Montreal, 1955–65, 1967–76 and 1985–89 (Dir, Applied Econs Inst., 1973–75). Econs and financial advr to Prime Minister and Cabinet of Québec, 1961–69; Minister of Finance, 1976–84; also Pres., Treasury Bd and Minister of Revenue and of Financial Instns; Leader, Official Opposition, 1989–94. Parti Québécois: Mem., 1969–; Chm., Nat. Exec., 1970–73; Pres., 1988–96. Pres., Québec Financial Instns Task Force, 1967–69; Chm., Québec Municipalities Study Commn, 1985. *Publications:* The Terms of Trade of Canada, 1956; Initiation à l'économie du Québec, 1975; Pour un Québec souverain, 1997; numerous articles. *Recreations:* reading, music, gardening.

PARK, family name of **Baroness Park of Monmouth**.

PARK OF MONMOUTH, Baroness *cr* 1990 (Life Peer), of Broadway in the County of Hereford and Worcester; **Daphne Margaret Sybil Désirée Park,** CMG 1971; OBE 1960; HM Diplomatic Service, retired; Principal of Somerville College, Oxford, 1980–89; *b* England, 1 Sept. 1921; British parents; unmarried. *Educ:* Rosa Bassett Sch.; Somerville Coll., Oxford (Hon. Fellow, 1990). WTS (FANY), 1943–47 (Allied Commn for Austria, 1946–48). FO, 1948; UK Delegn to NATO, 1952; 2nd Sec., Moscow, 1954; FO, 1956; Consul and 1st Sec., Leopoldville, 1959; FO, 1961; Lusaka, 1964; FO, 1967; Consul-Gen., Hanoi, 1969–70; Hon. Res. Fellow, Univ. of Kent, 1971–72, on sabbatical leave from FCO; Chargé d'Affaires *ai*, Ulan Bator, Apr.–June 1972; FCO, 1973–79. Gov., BBC, 1982–87. Chm., Legal Aid Adv. Cttee to the Lord Chancellor, 1985–91. Chm., RCHME, 1989–94. Member: British Library Bd, 1983–89; Sheffield Develt Corp. Bd, 1989–92; RIIA; Royal Asiatic Soc.; Forum UK; Mem. Council, VSO, 1981–84; Mem. Council, GB-Sasakawa Foundn, 1994–2001 (Patron, 2002–); Dir, Zoo Develt Trust, 1989–90. Pro-Vice-Chancellor, Univ. of Oxford, 1985–89. Pres., Soc. for Promotion of Training of Women, 1995–2006. Mem., Thatcher Foundn, 1992–; Trustee: Royal Armouries Develt Trust, 1991–92; Jardine Educnl Trust, 1991–98; Phoenix-Zimbabwe Trust. Vice-Patron, Atlantic Council Appeal, 2001–. MRSA. Hon. LLD: Bristol, 1988; Mount Holyoke Coll., 1992. *Recreations:* good talk, politics, and difficult places. *Address:* House of Lords, SW1A 0PW. *Clubs:* Oxford and Cambridge, Naval and Military, Royal Commonwealth Society, Special Forces.

PARK, Hon. Sir Andrew (Edward Wilson), Kt 1997; a Judge of the High Court of Justice, Chancery Division, 1997–2006; *b* 27 Jan. 1939; *m* 1962, Ann Margaret Woodhead; two *s* one *d* (and one *s* decd). *Educ:* Leeds Grammar Sch.; University Coll., Oxford. Winter Williams Law Schol., 1959; BA (Jurisp.) 1960, MA 1964. FTII 1990. Various academic posts in UK and abroad, 1960–68. Called to the Bar, Lincoln's Inn, 1964, Bencher, 1986; QC 1978; QC (NI) 1992; a Recorder, 1989–94; practice at Revenue Bar, 1965–97. Chairman: Taxation and Retirement Benefits Cttee of the Bar Council, 1978–82; Revenue Bar Assoc., 1987–92; Treasurer, Senate of the Inns of Court and Bar, 1982–85. Mem. Editl Bd, Simon's Taxes, 2007–. Hon. Pres., London Br., 2007–, Hon. Fellow, 2008, Chartered Inst. of Taxation. *Publications:* The Sources of Nigerian Law, 1963; various articles, notes and reviews in legal periodicals, mainly concerning taxation. *Recreations:* tennis, golf. *Address:* Loseberry, 30 Hare Lane, Claygate, Surrey KT10 9BU.

PARK, David; *see* Park, W. D.

PARK, Gilbert Richard, TD 1985; FRCA; Consultant in Anaesthesia and Intensive Care, Addenbrooke's Hospital, Cambridge, since 1983; Secretary General, World Federation of Societies of Intensive and Critical Care Medicine, 2001–05; *b* 17 May 1950; *s* of Whyrill Heslop and Czeslawa Park; one *s* one *d*. *Educ:* Edinburgh Univ. (BSc; MB ChB; MD); MA Cantab. FRCA 1976. Training posts in Edinburgh, 1974–83; Associate Lectr, Univ. of Cambridge, 1984–; Dir, Intensive Care, Addenbrooke's Hosp., 1985–2000; Consultant in Anaesthesia and Resuscitation, RAMC, 1985–92. Hunterian Prof., RCS, 1986; Vis. Prof., Duke Univ., 1992. Non-exec. Dir, UK Transplant, 2001–05. Hon. Mem. Bulgarian Soc. of Anaesthetists, 2001; Academician, European Acad. of Anesthesiology, 2001. Hon. Dr of Med. Sci. Pleven, 1995. *Publications: jointly:* Intensive Care: a handbook, 1988; Anaesthesia and Intensive Care Information, 1989, 2nd edn 1995; The Management of Acute Pain, 1991, 2nd edn 2001; Sedation and Analgesia in the Critically Ill Patient, 1993; A Colour Atlas of Intensive Care, 1995; Fighting for Life, 1996; A Pocket Book of Pharmacology in the Critically Ill, 1996; Algorithms for Rational Prescribing in the Critically Ill, 1997; Handbook of drugs in intensive care: an A–Z guide, 2000; Anaesthesia and Intensive Care Information: key facts in anaesthesia and intensive care, 2002; (ed) Liver Disease, 1993; *edited jointly:* Anaesthesia and Intensive Care for Patients with Liver Disease, 1995; Sedation and Analgesia in the Critically Ill, 1995; Tricks and Traps, 1997; Sepsis in the Critically Ill, 1999; Beginners Guide to Fluid and Electrolyte Balance, 2000; Pharmacology in the Critically Ill, 2001; Top Tips in Intensive Care, 2001; 150 papers in learned jls; specialised educnl calendars. *Recreations:* landscape photography, hill walking, diving, motorcycling. *Address:* Malyons, 15 High Green, Great Shelford, Cambridge CB2 5EG. *T:* (01223) 217433, *Fax:* (01223) 216782; *e-mail:* gilbertpark@doctors.org.uk.

PARK, Graham; *see* Park, J. G.

PARK, Ian Grahame, CBE 1995; Chairman, Northcliffe Newspapers Group Ltd, 1995–2003 (Managing Director, 1982–95); Director, Daily Mail and General Trust plc, since 1994; *b* 15 May 1935; *s* of William Park and Christina (*née* Scott); *m* 1965, Anne Turner; one *s*. *Educ:* Lancaster Royal Grammar Sch.; Queens' Coll., Cambridge. 1st Bn Manchester Regt, Berlin (Nat. Service Commn), 1954–56. Trainee Journalist, Press and Journal, Aberdeen, 1959; Asst Lit. Editor, Sunday Times, 1960–63; various management posts, Thomson Newspapers, 1963–65; Liverpool Daily Post and Echo, 1965–82, Man. Dir and Editor in Chief, 1972–82; Dir, Associated Newspaper Holdings Ltd, 1983–95. Mem. Council, Newspaper Soc., 1967–95 (Pres., 1980–81); Dir, Press Assoc., 1973–83 (Chm., 1978–79 and 1979–80); Dir, Reuters, 1978–82, 1988–94. Mem. Newspaper Panel, Monopolies and Mergers Commn, 1986–95. Dir, Radio City (Sound of Merseyside Ltd), 1973–82; Dir, Liverpool Playhouse, 1973–80; Trustee, Blue Coat Soc. of Arts, Liverpool, 1973–82. FRSA. Gov. and Trustee, Dr Johnson's House Trust, 1996–. *Recreations:* eighteenth-century English pottery, twentieth-century English pictures.

Address: (office) Daily Mail and General Trust plc, 2 Derry Street, W8 5TT. *Club:* Reform.

PARK, (Ian) Michael (Scott), CBE 1982; Consultant, Paull & Williamsons, Advocates, Aberdeen, 1991–2000 (Partner, 1964–91); *b* 7 April 1938; *m* 1964, Elizabeth Mary Lamberton Struthers, MBE, BL; one *s* (and one *s* decd). *Educ:* Aberdeen Grammar Sch.; Aberdeen Univ. (MA, LLB). Admitted Mem. Soc. of Advocates, Aberdeen, 1962 (Treas., 1991–92; Pres., 1992–93). Temp. Sheriff, 1976–94; Hon. Sheriff at Aberdeen, 1997–. Law Society of Scotland: Mem. Council, 1974–85; Vice-Pres., 1979–80; Pres., 1980–81. A Chm., Med. Appeal Tribunals, 1991–96; Member: Criminal Injuries Compensation Bd, 1983–2000; Criminal Injuries Compensation Appeals Panel, 1996–2002. Chm., Aberdeen Citizens Advice Bureau, 1976–88. Frequent broadcaster on legal topics. *Recreations:* golf, gardening, cheating Parkinson's Disease. *Address:* Beechwood, 46 Rubislaw Den South, Aberdeen AB15 4AY. *T:* (01224) 313799. *Club:* New (Edinburgh).

PARK, (James) Graham, CBE 1995; solicitor; Consultant, H. L. F. Berry & Co. Solicitors, 2004–07 (Senior Partner, 1983–2003); Compliance Officer, Conservative Party, since 1999; *b* 27 April 1941; *s* of late Alderman James Park, OBE and Joan Park (*née* Sharp); *m* 1969, Susan Don; one *s*. *Educ:* Malvern Coll., Worcs; Manchester Univ. (LLB Hons). Articled, 1965; admitted as solicitor, 1968; Partner, H. L. F. Berry & Co. Solicitors, 1969–83. Member: Parole Bd, 1996–2002 and 2003–; Criminal Injuries Compensation Appeals Panel, 2000–; Mental Health Rev. Tribunal, 2003–. Chairman, Constituency Conservative Association: Knutsford, 1982–83; Altrincham and Sale, 1983–87; Chm., NW Area Cons. Assoc., 1992–95; Vice-Pres., 1996–98, Pres., 1998, Nat. Union of Cons. and Unionist Assocs; Pres., Nat. Cons. Convention and Mem., Bd of Mgt, 1998–99, Chm., Constitutional Cttee, 2000–06, Cons. Party; Chm., Cons. Party Conf., 1998. Contested (C): Crewe, Feb. and Oct. 1974; Middleton and Prestwich, 1979. Mem. Court, Salford Univ., 1989–97. *Recreations:* cricket, motor-racing, cycling. *Address:* (office) 758 Oldham Road, Failsworth, Manchester M35 9XB. *T:* (0161) 681 4005.

PARK, John William; Member (Lab) Scotland Mid and Fife, Scottish Parliament, since 2007; *b* 14 Sept. 1973; *s* of George and Elizabeth Park; *m*; two *d*. Electrical fitter, 1989–98, trade union convenor, 1998–2001, Rosyth Dockyard; Res. Officer, 2001–02, Nat. Industrial Campaigns Officer, 2002–03, AEEU, then Amicus; Hd, Employee Relns, Babcock Naval Services, 2003–04; Asst Sec., Scottish TUC, 2004–07. *Address:* Scottish Parliament, Edinburgh EH99 1SP. *T:* (0131) 348 6754; *e-mail:* John.Park.msp@scottish.parliament.uk.

PARK, Dame Merle (Florence), (Dame Merle Bloch), DBE 1986 (CBE 1974); Principal, Royal Ballet; Director, Royal Ballet School, 1983–98; *b* Salisbury, S Rhodesia, 8 Oct. 1937; *d* of P. J. Park, Eastlea, Salisbury, S Rhodesia, C Africa; *m* 1st, 1965, James Monahan, CBE (marr. diss. 1970; he *d* 1985); one *s*; 2nd, 1971, Sidney Bloch (*d* 2000). *Educ:* Elmhurst Ballet Sch. Founder, Ballet Sch., St Peter's Sq., W6, 1977–83. Joined Sadler's Wells Ballet, 1955; first rôle, a Mouse (Sleeping Beauty prologue); first solo, Milkmaid (Façzce); principal soloist, 1959. First danced: Blue Bird (Act III, Sleeping Beauty), 1956; Swanhilda (Coppelia), Mamzelle Angot (Mamzelle Angot), 1958; Lise (Fille Mal Gardée), 1960; Cinderella, 1962; Juliet (Romeo and Juliet), 1965; Giselle, Celestial (Shadow Play), 1967; Clara (Nutcracker), Aurora (Sleeping Beauty), 1968; Odette (Swan Lake), 1971; A Walk to Paradise Garden, 1972; Firebird, Odette/Odile (Swan Lake), Dances at a Gathering, 1973; Manon, Emilia (The Moor's Pavane), Aureole, Terpsichore (Apollo), Elite Syncopations, 1974; Lulu, 1976; Kate (The Taming of the Shrew), La Bayadère, Tuesday's Child (Jazz Calendar), Triad, Symphonic Variations, Waltzes of Spring (in Royal Opera Fledermaus), Le Papillon, 1977; Countess Larisch (Mayerling), 1978; La Fin du Jour, 1979; Mary Vetsera (Mayerling), Natalia (A Month in the Country), Adieu, 1980; Chloë (Daphnis and Chloë), Isadora, 1981; Raymonda, 1983. Queen Elizabeth Award, Royal Acad. of Dancing, 1982. *Recreations:* gardening, coaching professionals, reading. *Address:* c/o Royal Ballet School, 46 Floral Street, Covent Garden, WC2E 9DA.

PARK, Michael; *see* Park, I. M. S.

PARK, Nicholas Wulstan, CBE 1997; RDI 2006; director and animator of 3D stop motion films; Partner, Aardman Animations Ltd, since 1995; *b* 6 Dec. 1958. *Educ:* Sheffield Poly., Faculty of Art and Design; National Film and TV Sch. Films include: A Grand Day Out, 1989 (BAFTA award for Best Animated Short, 1990); Creature Comforts, 1990 (Acad. Award for Best Animated Short, 1990); The Wrong Trousers, 1993 (Acad. Award and BAFTA award for Best Animated Short Film, 1993); A Close Shave, 1995 (Acad. Award and BAFTA award for Best Animated Film, 1995; Emmy for Best Popular Arts Programme, 1996); Chicken Run, 2000; Cracking Contraptions, 2002; Wallace and Gromit: the curse of the Were-Rabbit, 2005 (BAFTA Alexander Korda award, 2006); TV series: Shaun the Sheep, BBC1, 2007. *Address:* Aardman Animations Ltd, 1410 Aztec West Business Park, Almondsbury, Bristol BS32 4RT. *T:* (01454) 859000.

PARK, Stephen, FCA, FCT; Managing Director, Ashley Interim Management, Ltd, since 2002; *b* 7 Aug. 1952; *m* Linda Susan; three *s* one *d*. FCA 1977; FCT 1992. Articled clerk, Alliott Peirson & Co., 1972–77; Audit Sen., Arthur Andersen & Co., 1977–80; Financial Planning and Analysis Manager, Data Gen. Ltd, 1980–81; Hanson plc, 1981–92 (Associate Dir and Asst to Chm. and Chief Exec.); Gp Finance Dir, Sears plc, 1992–94; Dep. Finance Dir, Allders plc, 1995–96; Finance Dir, DERA, 1997–2001. *Address: e-mail:* Park.Stephen@btinternet.com.

PARK, (William) David, FSA; Director, Conservation of Wall Painting Department, Courtauld Institute of Art, London, since 1985; *b* 23 May 1952; *s* of late Bill and Elizabeth Park; *m* 1984, Leslie Ross (marr. diss. 1985). *Educ:* Dorking County Grammar Sch.; Univ. of Manchester (BA 1973, MA 1974); Corpus Christi Coll., Cambridge. FSA 1986. Leverhulme Res. Fellow, Courtauld Inst., London, 1980–85. Co-ordinator, Nat. Survey of Medieval Wall Painting, 1980–; Mem. Council, British Archaeol. Assoc., 1993–96; Chm., Paintings Cttee, Council for the Care of Churches, 1996–2006. Visiting Professor: Univ. Paris 1, Panthéon-Sorbonne, 2001; Chubinashvili Inst., Tbilisi, 2003. *Publications:* (ed with C. Norton) Cistercian Art and Architecture in the British Isles, 1986; (with C. Norton and P. Binski) Dominican Painting in East Anglia: the Thornham Parva Retable and the Musée de Cluny Frontal, 1987; (ed jtly) Early Medieval Wall Painting and Painted Sculpture in England, 1990; (with S. Boldrick and P. Williamson) Wonder: painted sculpture from Medieval England, 2002; contrib. learned jls. *Recreation:* Paris. *Address:* Conservation of Wall Painting Department, Courtauld Institute of Art, Somerset House, Strand, WC2R 0RN. *T:* (020) 7848 2871.

PARKER, family name of **Earls of Macclesfield** and **Morley**.

PARKER, Alan; Founder and Chairman, Brunswick Group LLP, since 2004 (Senior Partner, 1987–2004); *b* 3 May 1956; *s* of Sir Peter Parker, KBE, LVO; *m* 1st, 1977, Caroline Louise (marr. diss. 2006), *d* of Thaddeus Gordon; one *s* three *d*; 2nd, 2007, Jane

Hardman; two *s*. Dep. Man. Dir, Broad St Associates, 1982–87. Chm., Save the Children, 2008–; Vice Chairman: China Now; Employment Opportunities; Vice Pres., Business Commitment to the Envmt; Trustee, Temenos; Mus. of Illustration. Gov., SOAS. *Recreation:* friends. *Address:* Brunswick Group LLP, 16 Lincoln's Inn Fields, WC2A 3ED. *T:* (020) 7404 5959, *Fax:* (020) 7831 2823.

PARKER, Alan Charles, CBE 2008; Chief Executive, Whitbread plc, since 2004; *b* 25 Nov. 1946; *s* of Charles and Kathleen Parker; *m* 1974, Pauline Howell; one *s* one *d*. *Educ:* West Buckland, Sch.; Univ. of Surrey (BSc Hotel Mgt); Harvard Business Sch. (AMP). Sales and Mktg Dir, Thistle Hotels, 1974–82; Sales and Mktg Dir, 1982–85, Man. Dir Europe, 1985–87, Crest Hotels; Sen. Vice Pres. for Europe, ME and Africa, Holiday Inn, 1987–92; Man. Dir, Whitbread Hotel Co., 1992–2004. Mem. Bd, VisitBritain, 2003–; non-exec. Dir, Jumeirah Group LLC, 2007–. Chm., British Hospitality Assoc., 2000–05; Dir, World Travel and Tourism Council, 2003–. Vis. Prof., Univ. of Surrey, 2000. Trustee, West Buckland Sch., 2005–. FIH (FHCIMA 1992). Business Leader of the Year, Hotel Report Awards, 2003. *Recreations:* golf, Rugby, opera, horseracing. *Address:* Whitbread plc, 130 Jermyn Street, 4th Floor, SW1Y 4UR. *T:* (020) 7806 5480, *Fax:* (020) 7806 5487; *e-mail:* alan.parker@whitbread.com.

PARKER, Alan Frank Neil; education consultant; Schools Adjudicator, since 2004; *b* 24 July 1953; *s* of Frank Parker, ISO and Joan Parker; *m* 1983, Valerie Shawcross, *qv* (marr. diss. 2002). *Educ:* Leicester Poly. (BA Hons 1977); Inst. of Education, London Univ. (MA Educn 1984). UK Council for Overseas Student Affairs, 1977–83; Sen. Adminr (Educn), ACC, 1984–85; Principal Officer (Colls) Surrey CC, 1986–89; Asst Sec. (Educn), 1990–92, Educn Officer, 1992–97, AMA; Dir of Educn, London Borough of Ealing, 1997–2002. Vice-Pres., 2001, Pres., 2002, ConfEd (formerly Soc. of Educn Officers); Mem. Council, Assoc. of Dirs of Children's Services. Dir and Trustee, NFER, 2002–. FRSA 1996. *Publications:* (contrib.) Visions of Post-Compulsory Education, 1992; (contrib. jtly) The Promises and Perils Facing Today's School Superintendent, 2002; Education and Inspections Act 2006: the essential guide, 2007; pamphlets. *Recreations:* outdoor activities, visual and performing arts. *Address:* c/o Office of the Schools Adjudicator, Mowden Hall, Staindrop Road, Darlington DL3 9BG.

PARKER, Sir Alan (William), Kt 2002; CBE 1995; film director and writer; Chairman, Film Council, 1999–2004; *b* 14 Feb. 1944; *s* of William and Elsie Parker; *m* 1st, 1966, Annie Inglis (marr. diss. 1992); three *s* one *d*; 2nd, 2001, Lisa Moran; one *s*. *Educ:* Owen's Sch., Islington. Advertising Copywriter, 1965–67; Television Commercials Director, 1968–78. Wrote screenplay, Melody, 1969; wrote and directed: No Hard Feelings, 1972; Our Cissy, 1973; Footsteps, 1973; Bugsy Malone, 1975; A Turnip Head's Guide to the British Cinema, 1985; Angel Heart, 1987; Come See the Paradise, 1990; The Road to Wellville, 1995; Evita, 1996; Angela's Ashes, 2000; directed: The Evacuees, 1974; Midnight Express, 1977; Fame, 1979; Shoot the Moon, 1981; The Wall, 1982; Birdy, 1984; Mississippi Burning, 1989; The Commitments, 1991; The Life of David Gale, 2003. Vice-Chm., Directors Guild of Great Britain, 1982–86; Chm., BFI, 1998–99. Hon. DLitt UEA, 1998; Hon. DArts Sunderland, 2005. BAFTA Michael Balcon Award for Outstanding Contribution to British Film, 1985. Officier, Ordre des Arts et des Lettres (France), 2005. *Publications:* novels: Bugsy Malone, 1976; Puddles in the Lane, 1977; The Sucker's Kiss, 2003; cartoons: Hares in the Gate, 1983; Making Movies, 1998; Will Write and Direct For Food, 2005; non-fiction: The Making of Evita, 1997.

PARKER, Ann; see Burdus, J. A.

PARKER, Anne Mary, CBE 1990; Chair, National Care Standards Commission, 2001–04; *b* 11 Oct. 1939; *d* of Daniel Morley and Mary Morley (*née* Waters); *m* 1968, Dr Andrew Parker (marr. diss. 2000). *Educ:* Notre Dame Grammar Sch., Blackburn; Univ. of Keele (BA Hons); Univ. of Manchester (AdvDip Social Admin; Hon. Fellow 1996). Berkshire County Council: Asst Co. Welfare Services Officer, 1967–71; Asst Dir, 1971–74, Dep. Dir, 1974–80, Dir, 1980–94, Social Services; Simon Fellow, Manchester Univ., 1994–95; freelance consultant, 1996–97; Indep. Case Examr, CSA, 1997–2001. Non-exec. Dir, Nestor Health Care, 1999–2001. Chair, Complaints Panel, Audit Commn, 2004–07; Member: Health Educn Council, 1984–91; Criminal Injuries Compensation Appeals Panel, 2000–; Ext. Reviewer, Office of Parly and Health Service Ombudsman, 2005–08. Board Member: Centre for Policy in Ageing, 1991–97 (Vice-Chm.); Carers Nat. Assoc., then Carers UK, 1995–2002 (Chm., 1998–2002). Hon. Sec., Assoc. of Dirs of Social Services, 1986–89. Mem. Bd, NISW, 1990–98 (Life Fellow, 1998). Mem. Bd, Anchor Trust, 1996–99; Trustee, Lloyds TSB Foundn, 2004–. *Address:* 7 Lingdale Court, Lingdale Road, West Kirby CH48 5DJ. *T:* and *Fax:* (0151) 632 1199; *e-mail:* anne@parker9866.freeserve.co.uk.

PARKER, Cameron Holdsworth, CVO 2007; OBE 1993; JP; Lord-Lieutenant of Renfrewshire, 1998–2007; Vice-Chairman, Lithgows Ltd, 1991–97 (Managing Director, 1984–92); *b* 14 April 1932; *s* of George Cameron Parker and Mary Stevenson Parker; *m* 1st, 1957, Elizabeth Margaret Thomson (*d* 1985); three *s*; 2nd, 1986, Marlyne Honeyman, JP, FSI. *Educ:* Morrison's Acad., Crieff; Glasgow Univ. (BSc Hons). John G. Kincaid & Co. Ltd, Greenock: Asst Manager, 1958; Asst Gen. Man., 1961; Dir, 1963; Man. Dir, 1967; Chm., 1976; Chm. and Chief Exec., Scott Lithgow Ltd, Port Glasgow, 1980–83. Bd Mem., British Shipbuilders, 1977–80, 1981–83. Director, 1984–94 (Chairman, 1984–92): Campbeltown Shipyard Ltd; J. Fleming Engrg Ltd; Glasgow Iron & Steel Co. Ltd; Landcatch Ltd; Lithgow Electronics Ltd; Malakoff & Wm Moore Ltd; McKinlay & Blair Ltd; Prosper Engrg Ltd; Director: Lithgows Pty Ltd, 1984–94; Scottish Homes, 1992–96; Clyde Shaw Ltd, 1992–94. Mem. Scottish Council, CBI, 1986–92. Mem., Argyll and Clyde Health Bd, 1991–95. Pres., SSAFA, Renfrewshire, 1998–2007. Hon. Pres., Accord Hospice, Paisley, 1998–2007. Freeman, City of London, 1981; Liveryman, Co. of Shipwrights, 1981–. DL 1993, JP 1998, Renfrewshire. DUniv Paisley, 2003. *Recreation:* golf. *Address:* Heath House, Rowantreehill Road, Kilmacolm, Renfrewshire PA13 4PE. *T:* (01505) 873197.

PARKER, Charles Herbert; Clerk to the Mercers' Company, since 1998; *b* 26 July 1953; *e s* of Capt. Herbert Blake Parker, RN and Diana Katharine Parker (*née* Barnwell); *m* 1977, Victoria Kathleen Scott; two *s* one *d* (and one *d* decd). *Educ:* Winchester Coll.; Trinity Coll., Oxford (MA 1979); Insead (MBA 1982). Commercial Dir, Charter plc, 1990–96. Director: Johnson Matthey plc, 1990–93; Cape plc, 1990–96. Governor: Royal Ballet Sch., 2000–; Thomas Telford Sch., 2002–; Walsall Acad., 2003–; Sandwell Acad., 2006–. *Recreations:* shooting, classical ballet, narrow boats. *Address:* Mercers' Hall, Ironmonger Lane, EC2V 8HE. *Club:* Boodle's.

See also N. R. Parker.

PARKER, Christopher James Francis; QC 2006; *b* 22 June 1958; *s* of Bernard James and Peta Jocelyn Parker; *m* 1988, Stevie Jenkinson; one *s* one *d*. *Educ:* Ampleforth; Univ. of Exeter (LLB 1979). RN, 1980–88. Called to the Bar, Gray's Inn, 1986. *Address:* 3 Paper Buildings, Temple, EC4Y 7EU.

PARKER, Christopher Roy; QC 2008; *b* Leeds, 13 Oct. 1958; *s* of Roy and Margaret Parker; *m* 2000, Caroline Wilkinson; two *s*. *Educ:* Univ. of Oxford (MA, BCL); Univ. of Illinois (LLM); Harvard Univ. (LLM). Called to the Bar: Lincoln's Inn, 1984; BVI, 2006; in practice as barrister specialising in company law, insolvency, commercial fraud and trusts. *Recreations:* sailing, football, tennis. *Address:* Maitland Chambers, 7 Stone Buildings, Lincoln's Inn, WC2A 3SZ. *T:* (020) 7406 1200, *Fax:* (020) 7406 1300; *e-mail:* cparker@maitlandchambers.com. *Club:* Queen's.

PARKER, Christopher Stuart, CBE 1999; Headmaster, Nottingham High School, 1995–2007; *b* 16 Feb. 1947; *s* of Gerald Stuart Parker and late Brenda Mary Parker (*née* Briggs); *m* 1969, Margaret, *er d* of late Charles Godfrey Hannant and Frances Hannant; two *s*. *Educ:* Windsor Grammar Sch.; Bristol Univ. (BA 1968); St Catharine's Coll., Cambridge (PGCE 1969). Asst Master, Bedford Modern Sch., 1969–72; Head of Geography, Bradford Grammar Sch., 1972–78; Dep. Head, Goffs Sch., 1978–86; Headmaster, Batley Grammar Sch., 1986–95. HMC-OFSTED Lead Insp., 1995–98; Member: Admiralty Interview Bd, 1990–97; Assisted Places Cttee, ISC, 1995–2004 (Chm., 2002–04); Jt Chair, HMC/GSA/Ind. Schs Bursars' Assoc. Assisted Places Wkg Party, 1996–98; Chairman: Assisted Places Cttee, 1996–2004, Bridges and Partnerships Cttee, 1998–99, HMC; Govt Adv. Gp on Independent/State Sch. Partnerships, 1997–2002; Jt Chm., LGA/ISC Cttee, 2001–; Mem., Permanent Forum on Independent/State Sch. Partnerships, 2002–04 (Chm., Evaluation Cttee, 2002–04). Governor: Nottingham Trent Univ., 1996–99; Bedford Modern Sch., 2007–; Trustee, Seckford Foundn, 2007–. FRSA 1994. *Publications:* articles in American Jl of Geography, Envmt and Planning. *Recreations:* watching sport, escaping to France when possible. *Address:* Mill End, 19 Mill Lane, Briston, Melton Constable, Norfolk NR24 2JG. *Club:* East India.

PARKER, Christopher William Oxley, MA; JP; DL; *b* 28 May 1920; *s* of late Lieut-Col John Oxley Parker, TD, and Mary Monica (*née* Hills); *m* 1947, Jocelyn Frances Adeline, *d* of late Colonel C. G. Arkwright, Southern Rhodesia; one *s* two *d*. *Educ:* Eton; Trinity Coll., Oxford. Served War of 1939–45, 147th Field Regt (Essex Yeomanry) RA, 1939–42. Director: Strutt and Parker (Farms) Ltd; Local Dir, Chelmsford Bd, Barclays Bank, 1951–83. Mem., Nat. Trust Properties Cttee, 1974–89; Mem. Exec. Cttee, CLA, 1959–73; Pres., Essex CLA, 1987–. JP Essex, 1952; High Sheriff of Essex, 1961; DL Essex 1972. *Address:* Faulkbourne Hall, Witham, Essex CM8 1SP. *T:* (01376) 513385.

PARKER, Prof. David, DPhil; FRS 2002; CChem, FRSC; Professor of Chemistry, Durham University, since 1992; *b* 30 July 1956; 2nd *s* of Joseph William Parker and late Mary Parker (*née* Hill); *m* 1979, Fiona Mary MacEwan; one *s* two *d*. *Educ:* Durham Johnston Sch.; King Edward VI Grammar Sch., Stafford; Christ Church, Oxford (BA, MA); Hertford Coll., Oxford (DPhil 1980). CChem 1989; FRSC 1992. NATO post-doctoral Fellow, Univ. Louis Pasteur, Strasbourg, 1980–81; Durham University: Lectr, 1982–89; Sen. Lectr, 1989–92; Hd, Dept of Chemistry, 1995–98 and 2003–06. Visiting Professor: Strasbourg, 1994; Monash, 1998 and 2006; Lectures: Iddles, Univ. of New Hampshire, 2003; Vielberth, Regensburg, 2004; Chem. Soc. Inaugural, UCD, 2006. Royal Society of Chemistry: Hickinbottom Fellowship, 1988–89; Tilden Lectr, 2003–04; Corday-Morgan Medal, 1987; Interdisciplinary Award, 1995; Supramolecular Chem. Award, 2002; ICI Prize in Organic Chem., 1991; IBC Supramolecular Sci. and Technol. Award, 2000; Wolfson Res. Merit Award, Royal Soc., 2004–. *Publications:* Macrocycle Synthesis, 1996; patents; contrib. numerous papers, res. and rev. articles to learned jls. *Recreations:* cricket, golf, hill-walking, soccer. *Address:* Department of Chemistry, University of Durham, South Road, Durham DH1 3LE. *T:* (0191) 334 2033, *Fax:* (0191) 384 4737; *e-mail:* david.parker@dur.ac.uk. *Clubs:* Durham City Cricket; Brancepeth Castle Golf.

PARKER, (Diana) Jean, CBE 1989; Director, Goldsborough Healthcare plc, 1994–97; *b* 7 June 1932; *d* of Lewis William Reeve Morley and Amy (*née* Southwood); *m* 1959, Dudley Frost Parker (*d* 1971); one *s* one *d*. *Educ:* Kesteven and Grantham Girls' Sch.; Birmingham Univ. (BCom). Director: Vacu-Lug Traction Tyres Ltd, 1957–; Central Independent Television Plc, 1982–97; British Steel (Industry) Ltd, 1986–90; Grantham and Dist Hosp. NHS Trust, 1995–98; Chm., Middle England Fine Food Ltd, 1995–2004. Mem. Bd, E Midlands Electricity, 1983–90; Mem., E Midlands, later Eastern Adv. Bd, National Westminster Bank, 1985–92. Chairman: Lincs Jt Develt Cttee, 1983–97; Chm., CBI Smaller Firms Council, 1986–88. Chm., N Lincs HA, 1987–90; non-exec. Dir, Lincs Ambulance and Health Service Trust, 1991–92; Chm., Lincs Community Council, 2000–03.

PARKER, Sir Eric (Wilson), Kt 1991; FCA; Chairman, Caradon plc, 1998–99 (Director, Metal Box plc, then MB-Caradon, later Caradon plc, 1985–99); *b* 8 June 1933; *s* of late Wilson Parker and Edith Gladys (*née* Wellings); *m* 1955, Marlene Teresa (*née* Neale); two *s* two *d*. *Educ:* The Priory Grammar Sch. for Boys, Shrewsbury. FCA 1967 (ACA 1956). Articled Clerk with Wheeler, Whittingham & Kent, Shrewsbury, 1950–55; National Service, Pay Corps, 1956–58; Taylor Woodrow Gp, 1958–64; Trafalgar House Gp, 1965–93: Finance/Admin Dir, 1969; Dep. Man. Dir, 1973; Gp Man. Dir, 1977; Chief Exec., 1983–92; Dep. Chm., 1988–93; Chm., Graham Consulting, 1993–97. Non-exec. Chm., Albert Goodwin plc, 2003–; non-executive Director: European Assets Trust NV, 1972–85; Sealink UK Ltd, 1979–81; British Rail Investments Ltd, 1980–84; Evening Standard Co. Ltd, 1982–85; Touche Remnant Hldgs Ltd, 1985–89; The Royal Automobile Club (formerly The Automobile Pty Ltd), 1986–95; Hardy Oil & Gas, later British Borneo, plc, 1989–2000; Internat. Real Estates (formerly Criterion Properties) plc, 1998–; Job Partners Ltd, 2000–02. Advr, Phoenix Develt Capital Fund, 1992–97; Mem. Adv. Bd, QMG, MoD, 1997–2000. Director: Kvaerner Trustee (KEPS) Ltd, 2001–; Trafalgar House Pension Trust Ltd (formerly Kvaerner Trustee (KPF) Ltd), 2001–. Director: British Horseracing Bd, 1999–2004; Horserace Betting Levy Bd, 2000–04; Horserace Totaliser Bd, 2002–; National Stud, 2005–; Pres., Race Horse Owners' Assoc., 1998–2001 (Dir, 1994–). Proprietor, Crimbourne Stud, 1991–. Patron, Teenage Cancer Trust. CCMI (CBIM 1983). *Recreations:* sports (including golf and horseracing), wines. *Address:* Crimbourne House, Crimbourne Lane, Wisborough Green, Billingshurst, W Sussex RH14 0HR. *Clubs:* Royal Automobile, MCC; West Sussex Golf.

PARKER, Frederick John, (Jack), FICE, FIStructE, FIHT; Chief Highway Engineer (Under Secretary), Department of Transport, 1988–91; *b* 6 Sept. 1927; *s* of Charles Fred Parker and Eleanor Emily (*née* Wright); *m* 1955, Ann Shirley Newnham; three *d*. *Educ:* Shene Grammar School; Univ. of Liverpool (BEng 1948; MEng 1951). Engineer with Scott, Wilson, Kirkpatrick & Partners in London, Hong Kong and elsewhere, 1952–65; Sen. Engineer, then Partner, with Husband & Co., 1965–78; Director, W. S. Atkins & Partners, 1978–88. Institution of Highways and Transportation: Chm., Greater London Br., 1975–77; Vice-Pres., 1985; Pres., 1988. Vice-Chm., Brit. Nat. Cttee of Permanent Internat. Assoc of Road Congresses, 1988–91. *Publications:* professional papers in engineering jls. *Recreations:* athletics (Olympics 1952 and 1956, European silver medallist 1954); local affairs, music. *Address:* 83A Temple Sheen Road, East Sheen, SW14 7RS. *T:* (020) 8876 1059. *Club:* South London Harriers.

PARKER, Geoffrey; *see* Parker, James G. and Parker, N. G.

PARKER, Prof. Geoffrey Alan, FRS 1989; Derby Professor of Zoology, School of Biological Sciences, University of Liverpool, since 1996; *b* 24 May 1944; *s* of late Dr Alan Parker and G. Ethel Parker (*née* Hill); *m* 1st, 1967, Susan Mary Wallis (*d* 1994); one *s* one *d*; 2nd, 1997, Carol Elizabeth Emmett; one step *d*. *Educ:* Stockton Heath Primary Sch.; Lymm Grammar Sch.; Univ. of Bristol (BSc (1st Cl. Hons Zoology; Rose Bracher Prize for Biology); PhD); Univ. of Cambridge (MA). University of Liverpool: Asst Lectr, 1968–69; Lectr, 1969–76; Sen. Lectr, 1976–80; Reader, 1980–89; Prof. in Dept of Envmtl and Evolutionary Biol., 1989–96. Fellow of King's Coll., Cambridge, 1978–79; Nuffield Sci. Res. Fellow, 1982–83; BBSRC (formerly SERC) Sen. Res. Fellow, 1990–95. Lectures: Niko Tinbergen, Assoc. for Study of Animal Behaviour, 1995; Hamilton, Internat. Soc. for Behavioural Ecology, 2006. Medal, Assoc. for Study of Animal Behaviour, 2002; Dist. Animal Behaviorist Award, Animal Behavior Soc., 2003; Spallanzani Medal, 8th Biology of Spermatozoa Conf., 2005; Frink Medal, Zool Soc. of London, 2005; Dist. Zoologist Award, Benelux Congress of Zoology, 2007. *Publications:* (jtly) Evolution of Sibling Rivalry, 1997; many scientific papers in learned jls. *Recreations:* playing jazz in local bands (clarinet), mainly Dixieland; breeding, showing and judging exhibition bantams (Hon. Sec./Treasurer, 1987–94, Pres., 2002–, Partridge & Pencilled Wyandotte Club; Mem. Council, 1986–90, 2004–, Pres., 2003–06, Poultry Club; Vice-Pres., Plymouth Rock Club, 2002–05; Supreme Champion, Nat. Poultry Club GB Show, 1997). *Address:* Saunton, The Runnel, Neston, South Wirral, Cheshire CH64 3TG. *T:* (0151) 336 4202.

PARKER, Geoffrey John, CBE 1985; Deputy Chairman, Maritime Transport Services Ltd, 1997–98 (Chief Executive, 1989–97); Chairman, Thamesport (London) Ltd, 1997–98; *b* 20 March 1937; *s* of Stanley John Parker and Alice Ellen Parker; *m* 1957, Hazel Mary Miall; two *s* two *d*. *Educ:* County Grammar Sch., Hendon. Commercial Dir, Townsend Car Ferries Ltd, 1972–74; Man. Dir, Atlantic Steam Navigation Co., 1974–87; Man. Dir, 1976–87, Chm., 1983–87, Felixstowe Dock & Rly Co.; Chairman: Larne Harbour Bd, 1983–87; European Ferries PLC, 1986–87; Chief Exec., Highland Participants, 1987–89. Mem., Nat. Bus Co., 1980–87. FCIT 1982. *Recreation:* golf. *Address:* 101 Valley Road, Ipswich, Suffolk IP1 4NF. *T:* (01473) 216003. *Clubs:* Ipswich and Suffolk (Ipswich); Ipswich Golf (Purdis Heath, Ipswich).

PARKER, Jack; *see* Parker, F. J.

PARKER, (James) Geoffrey, CBE 1996; High Master, Manchester Grammar School, 1985–94; Chairman, Teacher Training Agency, 1994–97; *b* 27 March 1933; *s* of late Ian Sutherland Parker and Kathleen Lilian Parker; *m* 1956, Ruth Major (*d* 2005); two *d*. *Educ:* Alderman Newton's Sch., Leicester; Christ's Coll., Cambridge (Exhibnr); Wadham Coll., Oxford. National Service, RA, 1954–56. Asst Master, Bedford Modern Sch., 1957–66; Head of History Dept, Tonbridge Sch., 1966–75; Headmaster, Queen Elizabeth Grammar Sch., Wakefield, 1975–85. Chairman: HMC, 1991; ISIS, 1994–97. Gov., Charterhouse, 1993–2005; Trustee: St George's English Sch., Rome, 1992–97; Berlin British Sch., 1994–2005. *Address:* Ty Mawr, Carno, Powys SY17 5LL. *T:* (01686) 420276.

PARKER, Dr James Gordon, OBE 2002; Registrar of Public Lending Right, since 1991; *b* 1 June 1952; *s* of James Frank Taylor Parker and Mary Hutchison Gordon; *m* 1975, Catherine Ann Hyndman; one *s* one *d*. *Educ:* Stranraer High Sch.; Edinburgh Univ. (MA 1st Cl. Hons History 1974; PhD 1977). Vans Dunlop Res. Schol., Edinburgh Univ., 1974–77; Carnegie Travelling Schol. to India, 1976;. Royal Commission on Historical Manuscripts: Res. Asst, 1977–87; Asst Keeper, resp. for Nat. Register of Archives, 1987–91. Mem., PLR Adv. Cttee, 1991–2006; Co-ordinator, Internat. PLR Network, 1995–; Editor, Writers Talk, 2007–. Patron, Laser Foundn, 2001–07. FRSA 2007. Benson Medal, RSL, 2004. *Publications:* (contrib.) The Scots Abroad, 1985; Bibliographies of British Statesmen No 5 (Lord Curzon), 1991; (contrib.) International Directory of Company Histories, vol. 4, 1991; (ed) Proceedings of the First International Conference on Authors' Lending Right, 1996; (ed) Whose Loan is it Anyway?: essays in celebration of PLR's 20th anniversary, 1999; contrib. New DNB; reviews and contribs to learned jls. *Recreations:* golf, squash, gardening, family. *Address:* Public Lending Right, Richard House, Sorbonne Close, Stockton-on-Tees TS17 6DA; *e-mail:* jim.parker@plr.uk.com; 14 Ash Grove, Kirklevington, Yarm, Stockton-on-Tees TS15 9NQ. *T:* (01642) 791445.

PARKER, James Mavin, (Jim Parker); composer and conductor; *b* Hartlepool, 18 Dec. 1934; *s* of James Robertson Parker and Margaret Mavin; *m* 1969, Pauline George; two *d*; one *d* by a previous marriage. *Educ:* various grammar schools; Guildhall Sch. of Music (AGSM 1959; Silver Medal; Hon. GSM 1986). LRAM 1959. Professional oboeist, 1959; joined the Barrow Poets, 1963. Wrote musical settings of Sir John Betjeman's poems, Banana Blush, 1973 (recorded these and subsequent settings with Sir John as speaker); wrote music for Chichester Theatre, 1974–77; music for television and films, 1977–, includes: Credo; Another Six English Towns; Good Behaviour; Wynne and Penkovsky; Mapp and Lucia; Time After Time; Betjeman's Britain; Late Flowering Love; The Miser; España Viva; The Blot (silent film made in 1921); Girl Shy (Harold Lloyd silent film); Wish Me Luck; House of Cards; Parnell and the Englishwoman; The House of Eliott; Soldier Soldier; Body and Soul; To Play the King (BAFTA award for best TV music, 1993); Goggle Eyes; Late Flowering Lust; Moll Flanders (BAFTA award, 1996); Tom Jones (BAFTA award, 1997); A Rather English Marriage (BAFTA award, 1998); The Midsomer Murders; Born and Bred; Foyle's War. *Compositions* include: with William Bealby-Wright: Moonshine Rock, 1972; Mister Skillicorn Dances, 1974; with Cicely Herbert: Mayhew's London, 1978; La Comédie Humaine, 1986; (with John Betjeman) Poems (ballet), 1981; In The Gold Room (words by Oscar Wilde), 1983; (with Jeremy Lloyd) The Woodland Gospels, 1984; (with John Edmunds) Pelican Five, 1986. Recordings with Barrow Poets, Keith Michell, Peter Sellers, Harry Secombe, Twiggy, etc. *Publications:* (with Wally K. Daly) Follow the Star, 1975; (with Jeremy Lloyd) Captain Beaky, 1977; with Tom Stanier: The Shepherd King, 1979; The Burning Bush, 1980; All Aboard, 1983; Blast Off, 1986; A Londoner in New York (suite for brass), 1986; (with Tom Stanier and Chris Ellis) BabylonTimes, 1988; English Towns (for flute and piano), 1988; Mississippi Five (woodwind quintet), 1991; Lullingstone (for concert band), 1986; The Golden Section (brass quintet), 1993; Concerto for clarinet and strings, 1994; (with Alan Platt) The Happy Prince (one act opera), 1995; Light Fantastic (for string sextet or ten brass), 2002; Boulevard (for woodwind quintet), 2006; Mexican Wildlife (for brass quintet), 2006; Fat Tuesday in New Orleans (for concert wind band), 2007. *Recreations:* literature, 20th Century art. *Address:* 16 Laurel Road, Barnes, SW13 0EE. *T:* (020) 8876 8442.

PARKER, James Roland Walter, CMG 1978; OBE 1968; HM Diplomatic Service, retired; Governor and Commander-in-Chief, Falkland Islands and Dependencies, and High Commissioner, British Antarctic Territory, 1976–80; *b* 20 Dec. 1919; *s* of late Alexander Roland Parker, ISM; *m* 1941, Deirdre Mary Ward (*d* 2001). Served War of 1939–45: 1st London Scottish, 1940–41. Ministry of Labour, 1938–57; Labour Attaché, Tel Aviv, 1957–60; Labour Adviser: Accra, 1960–62; Lagos, 1962–64; seconded to Foreign Office, 1965–66; Dep. High Comr, Enugu, 1966–67; Commonwealth Office (later FCO), 1968–70; Head of Chancery, Suva, Fiji, 1970–71; High Comr in The Gambia, 1972–75; Consul-Gen., Durban, 1976. *Address:* 7 Elliscombe Park, Higher Holton, Wincanton, Som BA9 8EA.

PARKER, Jean; *see* Parker, D. J.

PARKER, Sir John; *see* Parker, Sir T. J.

PARKER, Prof. John Stewart, DPhil; Director, Botanic Garden, and Professor of Plant Cytogenetics, since 1996, Curator, Herbarium, since 2001, University of Cambridge; Fellow, Clare Hall, Cambridge, since 2007; *b* 12 July 1945; *s* of George Parker and Helen Parker (*née* Teare); *m* 1970, Iris Veronica Berry (marr. diss.); two *s*; *m* 1999, Mary Elizabeth Edmunds. *Educ:* Birkenhead Sch.; Christ Church, Oxford (BA 1966; MA 1970; DPhil 1971). Lectr, 1969–90, Reader, 1990–92, QMC; Prof. of Botany, Univ. of Reading, 1992–96; Fellow, St Catharine's Coll., Cambridge, 1997–2007. Dir, NIAB, 2004– (Mem. Council, 1998–2001). Mem. Council, RHS, 1998–99. Trustee: Royal Botanic Gardens, Kew, 1996–2002; Brogdale Horticultural Trust, 1999–2004; Science and Plants for Schs, 1998–; Sci. Cttee, Mendel Mus., Brno, 2002–04 (Advr and Designer, Genetic Gdn). Hon. Res. Fellow, Natural History Mus., 1995–. Reina Victoria Eugenia Chair, Complutense Univ., Madrid, 2007–08. *Publications:* numerous papers in scientific jls. *Recreations:* church architecture, bird watching, landscape history, gardening, apples and cheese. *Address:* University of Cambridge Botanic Garden, 1 Brookside, Cambridge CB2 1JE. *T:* (01223) 336265.

PARKER, Rt Hon. Sir Jonathan (Frederic), Kt 1991; PC 2000; a Lord Justice of Appeal, 2000–07; *b* 8 Dec. 1937; *s* of late Sir (Walter) Edmund Parker, CBE and late Elizabeth Mary Butterfield; *m* 1967, Maria-Belen Burns; three *s* one *d*. *Educ:* Winchester College; Magdalene College, Cambridge (MA). Called to Bar, Inner Temple, 1962, Bencher, 1985; practising member of the Bar, 1962–91; QC 1979; a Recorder, 1989–91; Attorney Gen. of Duchy of Lancaster, 1989–91; Judge of the High Court of Justice, Chancery Div., 1991–2000; Vice Chancellor, Co. Palatine of Lancaster, 1994–98. *Recreations:* painting, gardening. *Address:* The Grange, Radwinter, Saffron Walden, Essex CB10 2TF. *Club:* Garrick.

PARKER, Hon. Dame Judith Mary Frances, DBE 2008; **Hon. Mrs Justice Parker;** a Judge of the High Court, Family Division, since 2008; *b* 19 June 1950. *Educ:* Univ. of Oxford (BA Juris. 1972). Called to the Bar, Middle Temple, 1973; QC 1991; Recorder, 2000–08. *Address:* Royal Courts of Justice, Strand, WC2A 2LL.

PARKER, Keith John, OBE 1993; Director, MNA Broadcasting Ltd, since 2005; *b* 30 Dec. 1940; *s* of late Sydney John Parker and Phyllis Mary Parker; *m* 1962, Marilyn Ann Edwards; one *s*. Various editorial appointments; Editor, Shropshire Star, 1972–77; Editor, 1977–95, Gen. Manager, 1995, Express & Star, Wolverhampton; Man. Dir, Shropshire Newspapers, 1996–2002; Ed., Shropshire Mag., 1997–2002; Man. Dir, Express & Star Ltd, Wolverhampton, 2002–05. Director: Midland News Assoc. Ltd, 1996–2005; Telford Radio Ltd, 1998–; Chairman: Kidderminster Radio Ltd, 2005–; Shrewsbury and Oswestry FM Ltd, 2005–. President: Guild of British Newspaper Editors, 1987–88 (Vice-Pres., 1986–87; Chm., Parly and Legal Cttee, 1991–94); Midland Newspaper Soc., 1999–2000; Chm., Newspaper Qualifications Council, 2004–07; Member: Press Complaints Commn, 1992–94; Data Protection Tribunal, 1996–2006; Parly, Editl and Regulatory Cttee (formerly Govt and Legal Affairs Cttee), 1997–2005, Council, 2002–04, Newspaper Soc. Director: Shropshire Chamber of Commerce, Trng and Enterprise, 2000–01; Black Country Consortium, 2004–05. Trustee, Ironbridge Gorge Mus. Develt Trust, 2000–02. *Recreations:* reading, travel. *Address:* 94 Wrottesley Road, Tettenhall, Wolverhampton, West Midlands WV6 8SJ. *T:* (01902) 758595.

PARKER, Kenneth Blades; QC 1992; a Law Commissioner, since 2006; a Recorder, since 2000; a Deputy High Court Judge, since 2006; *b* 20 Nov. 1945; *s* of Rudolph Parker, Capt., Argyll and Sutherland Highlanders and Catherine (*née* Boyd); *m* 1967, Margaretha Constance Beyerman; three *s* one *d*. *Educ:* Kettering Grammar Sch.; Exeter Coll., Oxford (Class. Schol.; 1st cl. Lit. Hum. 1968; 1st cl. BCL 1973; Vinerian Schol.). Lectr in Law, Univ. of Oxford and Fellow, Exeter Coll., Oxford, 1973–76; called to the Bar, Gray's Inn, 1975, Bencher, 2002. Specialist Advr, H of C Select Cttee for Trade and Ind., 1991. Mem., Information Tribunal, 2002–. *Publications:* (Asst Ed.) Chitty on Contracts, 23rd edn, 1972; (contrib.) Common Market Law of Competition, 1987. *Recreations:* tennis, skiing. *Address:* Law Commission, Steel House, 11 Tothill Street, SW1H 9LJ.

PARKER, Lyn; HM Diplomatic Service; Ambassador to the Netherlands, since 2005; *b* 25 Nov. 1952; *s* of Ronald Arthur Parker and Tjardina Torrenga; *m* 1991, Jane Elizabeth Walker; two *d*. *Educ:* King's Sch., Canterbury; Magdalen Coll., Oxford (BA Jurisprudence); Manchester Univ. (MA European Community Studies). Lectr in Law, Manchester Univ., 1975–78; joined HM Diplomatic Service, 1978; Second, later First, Sec., Athens, 1980–84; FCO, 1984–88; Cabinet Office, 1989–91; Head of Chancery and Political Counsellor, New Delhi, 1992–95; Counsellor (Political), UK Perm. Repn to EU, Brussels, 1995–99; Hd, Whitehall Liaison Dept, FCO, 1999–2001; High Comr to Cyprus, 2001–05. *Recreations:* music, sailing, cycling. *Address:* c/o Foreign and Commonwealth Office, King Charles Street, SW1A 2AH.

PARKER, (Lynda) Tanya; Chairman, Pensions Appeal Tribunal, since 2001; Deputy Social Security Commissioner for Northern Ireland, since 2006; Deputy Social Security and Child Support Commissioner, since 2008; *d* of Sidney Sansom and Olive May (*née* Hudson); *m* 1968, Prof. David Francis Parker; two *c*. *Educ:* Manchester Univ. (LLB); Univ. of Calif, Berkeley (LLM). Called to the Bar, Gray's Inn, 1966; Associate WS, 2002. Lecturer: Nottingham Univ., 1966–73; Univ. of WI, 1970–72 (on secondment). Regl Chm., Appeals Service, 1991–2000; Social Security and Child Support Commr, 2000–08. *Recreations:* friends, travel, performing and visual arts. *Address:* (office) George House, 126 George Street, Edinburgh EH2 4HH. *Club:* Royal Over-Seas League.

PARKER, Major Sir Michael (John), KCVO 2000 (CVO 1991); CBE 1996 (MBE (mil.) 1968); Producer: Royal Tournament, 1974–99; Edinburgh Tattoo, 1991–94; *b* 21 Sept. 1941; *s* of Capt. S. J. Wilkins and V. S. M. Wilkins (*née* Parker); name changed by Deed Poll, 1959; *m* 2005, Emma Bagwell Purefoy (*née* Gilroy). *Educ:* Dulwich Coll. Prep. Sch.; Hereford Cathedral Sch.; RMA Sandhurst. Captain, Queen's Own Hussars, 1961–71 (produced Berlin Tattoo, 1965, 1967 and 1971); Major, TA, Special List, attached QOH, 1973–. Producer of international events, 1972–: Berlin Tattoo, 1972–88, Bandanza, 1990; Last Tattoo, 1992; Aldershot Army Display, 1974–83; Queen's Bonfire, Windsor and others, Queen's Silver Jubilee, 1977; Wembley Musical Pageant, 1979, 1981, 1985; Great Children's Party for Internat. Year of the Child, 1979; Carols for the Queen, 1979; Royal Fireworks (Prince of Wales's wedding), 1981; Heart of the Nation, son et lumière, Horse Guards, 1983, 1985; America's Cup, Newport, 1983; Great St John Party (180,000 children), Hyde Park, 1985; King Hussein of Jordan's 50th Birthday Celebration, 1985; Finale, Christmas Horse Show, Olympia, 1986–; Jordanian Royal Wedding, 1987, 1993; Coronation Anniversary Celebration, Jordan, 1988; Joy to the World, Royal Albert Hall, 1988–97; Royal Equestrian Day, Oman, 1990; Fortress Fantasia, Gibraltar, 1990;

Queen Mother's 90th Birthday Celebration, Horse Guards, 1990; Opening Ceremony, World Equestrian Games, 1990; Economic Summit Spectacular, Buckingham Palace, 1991; British Nat. Day Expo '92, Seville, 1992; The Queen's 40th Anniversary Celebration, 1992; Memphis in May Internat. Tattoo, 1992–94; King Hussein of Jordan's 40th Anniversary Celebrations, Unveiling of Queen Elizabeth Gate in Hyde Park, 1993; Channel Tunnel Gala Fireworks Display, D-Day Celebrations in Portsmouth, Normandy Veterans, RAH, Army Benevolent Fund, Drumhead Service, Royal Hosp. Chelsea, Pavarotti, Internat. Horse Show Modena Italy, P&O ship naming, China, 1994; P&O ship naming, Portsmouth, VE Day 50th Anniversary Celebrations in Hyde Park and Buckingham Palace, VJ 50th Anniversary Celebrations on Horse Guards, Jersey Liberation Fireworks, Horse Show in Los Angeles, 1995; Oriana Gala, Sydney, 1996; Dawn Princess Naming, Fort Lauderdale, and The Countryside Rally, Hyde Park, 1997; Fireworks, Royal Windsor Horse Show, 1998–; re-opening of Albert Memorial, Hyde Park, 1998; Centenary Celebrations for King Abdul Aziz al Saud, Saudi Arabia, 1999; Royal Mil. Tattoo, Horse Guards, 2000; Queen Mother's 100th birthday celebrations, Horse Guards, 2000; All The Queen's Horses, Windsor, 2002; London Golden Jubilee Weekend Fest., June 2002, incl. nat. beacon, fireworks and nat. processions; Opening of Meml Gates, Constitution Hill, 2002; opening of Memphis SO, Canon Performing Arts Center, 2003; Centenary Celebration, Royal Welsh Agricl Show, 2004; Music on Fire!, RMA Sandhurst, 2004; 60th Anniv. Liberation Celebrations, Jersey, 2005; RYS Trafalgar 200th Anniv. Fireworks, 2005; Central Sch. of Speech and Drama Centenary, Old Vic, 2006; Not Forgotten Assoc. concert, Tower of London, and Christmas celebration, St James's Palace, 2006; Music on Fire!, RMA Sandhurst, 2006, 2008. Vice-President: Morriston Orpheus Choir, 1972–; Queen Elizabeth the Queen Mother's Meml Fund, 2001–; Support for Africa, 2002–; CiB; Patron: Chicken Shed Theatre Co., 2002–; Brooklands SLD Sch., 2002–. Evening Standard Ambassador for London, 1995; Walpole Gold Medal for Excellence, and Walpole Award for Best Cultural Achievement, 2002; CiB Communicator of the Year Award, 2002; Derek Harper Technol. Award, RTS, 2003. KStJ 1985 (OStJ 1982). Grand Officer, Order of al Istiqlal (Jordan), 1987. *Publication:* The Awful Troop Leaders Gunnery Crib, 1969. *Recreations:* painting, antiques.

PARKER, Michael Joseph Bennett; Managing Director, 1970–80, and Chairman, 1980–98, Favor Parker Ltd; *b* 22 June 1931; *s* of Henry Gordon Parker and Alice Rose Parker; *m* 1960, Tania Henrietta Tiarks; two *s* one *d.* *Educ:* Eton; Magdalene Coll., Cambridge (BA Agric., MA). Chm., Favor Parker Gp, 1977–98. Chm., Land Settlement Assoc., 1982–85; Mem., UKAEA, 1985–88. *Recreations:* country sports, wind-surfing, lying in the sun. *Address:* Gooderstone Manor, King's Lynn, Norfolk PE33 9BP. *T:* (01366) 328255.

PARKER, (Michael) Miles, PhD; Deputy Chief Scientific Adviser and Director for the Evidence Programme (formerly of Science), Department for Environment, Food and Rural Affairs, since 2002; *b* 20 Nov. 1948; *s* of Michael Rowton Parker and Anne Margaret Bodkin; *m* 1991, Claire Christine Nihoul; two *s*, and two step *d.* *Educ:* Ampleforth Coll., York; Trinity Coll., Dublin Univ. (BA Mod.; PhD). Asst Inspector of Fisheries, Dept for Agric. and Fisheries, Ireland, 1975–83; Ministry of Agriculture, Fisheries and Food: PSO, Directorate of Fisheries Res., 1983–87; Principal, Food Contamination and Safety Policy, 1987–89; Sci. Liaison Officer, Chief Scientist's Gp, 1989–92; Grade 6, Cabinet Office Sci. Secretariat, 1992; Hd, Sci. Div., MAFF, 1992–98; Dir of Food Res., Central Sci. Lab., 1998; Dir, Internat., OST, 1998–2002. Non-exec. Dir, Cadbury Ltd, 1993–95. Chm., Marine Pollution Working Gp, Internat. Council for Exploration of the Sea, 1983–85. *Publications:* (ed with P. Tett) Exceptional Plankton Blooms, 1987; articles on marine ecol. and marine pollution in scientific jls. *Recreation:* omnicuriosity. *Address:* Fairhaven, Long Lane, Fowlmere, Cambs SG8 7TG. *T:* (01763) 208063, *Fax:* (01763) 209066.

PARKER, Michael St J.; *see* St John Parker.

PARKER, Miles; *see* Parker, Michael M.

PARKER, Lt-Gen. Nicholas Ralph, CBE 2002; Commander Regional Forces, Land Forces Command, since 2007; *b* 13 Oct. 1954; *s* of Capt. Herbert Blake Parker, RN and Diana Katharine Parker (*née* Barnwell); *m* 1979, Rebecca Clare Wellings; two *s.* *Educ:* Sherborne Sch.; RMA Sandhurst. CO, 2nd Bn Royal Green Jackets, 1994–95; Comdr, 20 Armoured Bde, 1997–2000; Comdr, Jt Task Force, Sierra Leone, 2001; GOC 2nd Div., and Gov., Edinburgh Castle, 2002–04; Comdt, Jt Services Comd and Staff Coll., 2004–05; Dep. Comdg Gen., Multinat. Corps, Iraq, 2005–06; GOC NI, 2006–07. Officer, Legion of Merit (USA), 2007. *Recreations:* fishing, drawing, Coronation Street. *Club:* Army and Navy.
See also C. H. Parker.

PARKER, Prof. (Noel) Geoffrey, PhD, LittD; FBA 1984; Andreas Dorpalen Professor of History, since 1997 and Distinguished University Professor, since 2007, Ohio State University; *b* 25 Dec. 1943; *s* of late Derek Geoffrey Parker and Kathleen Betsy Symon; *m* 1st, Angela Maureen Chapman; one *s* one *d*; 2nd, Jane Helen Ohlmeyer; two *s.* *Educ:* Nottingham High Sch.; Christ's Coll., Cambridge (BA 1965; MA; PhD 1968; LittD 1981). Fellow of Christ's Coll., Cambridge, 1968–72; Lectr in Mod. Hist., 1972–78, Reader in Mod. Hist., 1978–82, and Prof. of Early Mod. Hist., 1982–86, St Andrews Univ. Charles E. Nowell Dist. Prof. of History, Univ. of Illinois at Urbana-Champaign, 1986–93 (Dept Chair, 1989–91); Robert A. Lovett Prof. of Military and Naval Hist., Yale Univ., 1993–96. British Acad. Exchange Fellow, Newberry Library, Chicago, 1981; J. S. Guggenheim Foundn Fellow, 2001–02; H. F. Guggenheim Sen. Fellow, 2002–03; Visiting Professor: Vrije Universiteit, Brussels, 1975 (Dr phil and letters *hc*, 1990); Univ. of BC, Vancouver, Canada, 1979–80; Keio Univ., Tokyo, 1984; Oxford Univ., 2004. Lees Knowles Lectr in Mil. Hist., Univ. of Cambridge, 1984. Television scripts and broadcasts. Corresp. Fellow, Spanish Royal Acad. of History, 1988–. Hon. Dr Letters, Katholieke Univ., Brussels, 2005. Samuel E. Morison Prize, Soc. for Mil. Hist., 1999; Alumni Assoc. Award for Distinguished Teaching, Ohio State Univ., 2006. Order of Isabel the Catholic (Spain), Kt Grand Cross, 1992 (Encomienda, 1988); Order of Alfonso the Wise (Spain), Kt Grand Cross, 1996. *Publications:* The Army of Flanders and the Spanish Road 1567–1659, 1972, 4th edn 2004; The Dutch Revolt, 1977, 3rd edn 1985; Philip II, 1978, 4th edn 2001; Europe in Crisis 1598–1648, 1979, 2nd edn 2001; Spain and the Netherlands 1559–1659, 1979, 2nd edn 1990; The Thirty Years' War, 1984, 2nd edn 1996; (ed) The World: an illustrated history, 1986, 3rd edn 1995; The Military Revolution: military innovation and the rise of the West 1500–1800, 1988, 3rd edn 1996 (Dexter Prize, 1987–90); (with Colin Martin) The Spanish Armada, 1988, 3rd edn 1999; (ed) Cambridge Illustrated History of Warfare, 1995, 2nd edn 2008; (ed) The Times Compact Atlas of World History, 1995, 5th edn 2008; (ed with Robert C. Cowley) The Reader's Companion to Military History, 1996; The Grand Strategy of Philip II, 1998; Success is Never Final: Empire, war and faith in early modern Europe, 2002, 2nd edn 2003; edited numerous other works; articles and reviews. *Recreations:* travel, archaeology. *Address:* History Department, Ohio State University, 230 West 17th Avenue, Columbus, OH 43210–1367, USA. *T:* (614) 2926721, *Fax:* (614) 2922282.

PARKER, Sir Peter; *see* Parker, Sir W. P. B.

PARKER, Peter Joseph Jacques, PhD; FMedSci; FRS 2006; Principal Scientist, Cancer Research UK (formerly Imperial Cancer Research Fund), since 1990; *b* 30 Sept. 1954; *s* of Philip Joseph Jacques Parker and Phyllis Joyce Eileen Jacques Parker; *m* 1976, Jennifer Jean Cave; one *s.* *Educ:* Brasenose Coll., Oxford (BA 1976; PhD 1979). Gp Leader, ICRF, 1985–86; Lab. Hd, Ludwig Inst., London, 1986–90. Hon. Prof., UCL, 1997–. *Publications:* over 260 res. and review articles in learned jls. *Recreations:* tennis, walking, theatre. *Address:* London Research Institute, Cancer Research UK, 44 Lincoln's Inn Fields, WC2A 3PX; *e-mail:* peter.parker@cancer.org.uk.

PARKER, Philip Laurence; QC 2000; **His Honour Judge Parker;** a Circuit Judge, since 2008; *b* 10 Aug. 1953; *s* of Robert Bernard Parker and Barbara Doherty Parker; *m* 1980, (marr. diss. 2002); three *d.* *Educ:* Prior Park Coll., Bath; King Edward's Sch., Birmingham; Matthew Boulton Tech. Coll., Birmingham; Univ. of Birmingham (LLB). Called to the Bar, Middle Temple, 1976. *Recreation:* golf. *Address:* Birmingham Crown Court, Queen Elizabeth II Law Courts, 1 Newton Street, Birmingham B4 7NA.

PARKER, Sir Richard (William) Hyde, 12th Bt *cr* 1681; DL; *b* 5 April 1937; *o s* of Sir William Stephen Hyde Parker, 11th Bt, and Ulla Ditlef (*d* 1998), *o d* of C. Ditlef Nielsen, PhD, Copenhagen; *S* father, 1951; *m* 1972, Jean, *d* of late Sir Lindores Leslie, 9th Bt; one *s* three *d* (incl. twin *d*). *Educ:* Millfield; Royal Agricultural College. High Sheriff and DL, Suffolk, 1995. *Heir: s* William John Hyde Parker, *b* 10 June 1983. *Address:* Melford Hall, Long Melford, Suffolk CO10 9AA.

PARKER, Robert Christopher Towneley, FBA 1998; DPhil; Wykeham Professor of Ancient History, and Fellow of New College, University of Oxford, since 1996; *b* 19 Oct. 1950; *s* of Geoffrey Parker and Janet Parker (*née* Chidley); *m* 1979, Joanna Hilary Martindale; one *d.* *Educ:* St Paul's Sch., London; New Coll., Oxford (MA, DPhil). CUF Lectr in Greek and Latin Languages and Literature, Oxford Univ., and Fellow of Oriel Coll., Oxford, 1976–96. Foreign Mem., Royal Danish Acad., 2007. *Publications:* Miasma, 1983; Athenian Religion: a history, 1996; Polytheism and Society in Athens, 2005 (Criticos Prize, London Hellenic Soc.). *Recreation:* gardening. *Address:* New College, Oxford OX1 3BN.

PARKER, Robert Stewart, CB 1998; Parliamentary Counsel, since 1992; *b* 13 Jan. 1949; *o s* of Robert Arnold Parker and Edna Parker (*née* Baines). *Educ:* Brentwood School; Trinity College, Oxford (Scholar; First in Mods; MA 1974). Called to the Bar, Middle Temple, 1975 (Harmsworth Exhibnr; Astbury Senior Law Scholarship); Lincoln's Inn *ad eundem*, 1977. Classics Master, Brentwood School, 1971–74; in practice at the Bar, 1975–80; Office of Parly Counsel, 1980; Law Commn, 1985–87; Dep. Parly Counsel, 1987–92. Freeman, City of London, 1984; Liveryman, Wheelwrights' Co., 1984. Member: Horatian Soc.; City of London Br., Royal Soc. of St George; Kipling Soc.; Edinburgh Walter Scott Club. MCMI (MBIM 1984); FRSA 2000. *Publications:* Cases and Statutes on General Principles of Law (with C. R. Newton), 1980; (contrib.) The Best of Days? (Brentwood School Millennium book), 2000. *Recreations:* the Livery, cricket, bridge, books, music. *Address:* Office of the Parliamentary Counsel, 36 Whitehall, SW1A 2AY. *Clubs:* Athenæum, City Livery, Langbourn Ward, Civil Service.
See also E. Blackburn.

PARKER, Rt Hon. Sir Roger (Jocelyn), Kt 1977; PC 1983; a Lord Justice of Appeal, 1983–92; *b* 25 Feb. 1923; *s* of Captain Hon. T. T. Parker, DSC, RN (Retired) and Marie Louise Leonie (*née* Kleinwort); *m* 1948, Ann Elizabeth Frederika (*née* White); one *s* three *d.* *Educ:* Eton; King's Coll., Cambridge. Served Rifle Bde, 1941–46. Called to Bar, Lincoln's Inn, 1948, Bencher, 1969; QC 1961. Dep. Chm., Herts QS, 1969–71; Judge of the Courts of Appeal, Jersey and Guernsey, 1974–83; a Judge of the High Court, QBD, 1977–83. Member, Bar Council, 1968–69, Vice-Chm., 1970–72, Chm., 1972–73. Vice-Pres., Senate of Four Inns of Court, 1972–73. Treas., Lincoln's Inn, 1990–91. Conducted Windscale Nuclear Fuel Reprocessing Inquiry, 1977. Chm., Court of Inquiry into Flixborough Explosion, 1974. *Clubs:* Lansdowne; Leander.

PARKER, Prof. Roger Leslie, PhD; FBA 2008; Thurston Dart Professor of Music, King's College London, since 2007; *b* 2 Aug. 1951; *m* 1972, Lynden Cranham; two *s* one *d.* *Educ:* Goldsmiths' Coll., London (BMus 1973); King's Coll., London (MMus 1975; PhD 1981). Associate Prof., Cornell Univ., 1982–93; Oxford University: Lectr in Music, 1994–97; Prof. of Music, 1997–99; Fellow, St Hugh's Coll., 1994–99; Prof. of Music, Cambridge Univ., 1999–2006; Fellow, St John's Coll., Cambridge, 1999–2006. Jt Gen. Ed., Donizetti Critical Edn, 1987–. Premio Giuseppe Verdi, Istituto nazionale di studi verdiani, 1985; Dent Medal, Royal Musical Assoc., 1991. *Publications:* (ed jtly) Reading Opera, 1988; (ed) Oxford Illustrated History of Opera, 1994; Leonora's Last Act, 1997; Remaking the Song, 2006. *Address:* Department of Music, King's College London, Strand, WC2R 2LS.

PARKER, Stephen; Legal Adviser to HM Treasury, since 2003; *b* 3 Oct. 1957; *s* of Fernley and Ann Parker; *m* 1987, Philippa Casimir-Mrowczynska; three *s.* *Educ:* Stockport Grammar Sch.; Emmanuel Coll., Cambridge (MA, LLB). Called to the Bar, Lincoln's Inn, 1982; Legal Asst, then Sen. Legal Asst and Lawyer, DTI, 1984–87; Law Officers' Dept, 1987–88; Lawyer: DTI, 1988–94; Home Office, 1994–2000; Dir, Legal Services A, DEFRA, 2001–03. *Recreations:* mineralogy, photography, history. *Address:* HM Treasury, 1 Horse Guards, SW1A 2HQ. *T:* (020) 7270 5666; *e-mail:* stephen.parker@hm-treasury.gsi.gov.uk. *Club:* Oxford and Cambridge.

PARKER, Tanya; *see* Parker, L. T.

PARKER, Sir (Thomas) John, Kt 2001; DSc; FREng; Chairman, National Grid (formerly National Grid Transco) plc, since 2002; Deputy Chairman, DP World, since 2007; Joint Chairman, Mondi plc and Mondi Ltd, since 2007; *b* 8 April 1942; *s* of Robert Parker and Margaret Elizabeth Parker (*née* Bell); *m* 1967, Emma Elizabeth (*née* Blair); one *s* one *d.* *Educ:* Belfast Coll. of Technology; Queen's Univ. Belfast (DSc (Eng)). FREng (FEng 1983); FRINA; FIMarE. Harland & Wolff, Belfast: Student Apprentice Naval Architect, 1958–63; Ship Design Staff, 1963–69 (Nat. Physical Lab. (Ship Hydrodynamics), 1964); Numerical Applications Manager, 1969–71; Prodn Drawing Office Manager, 1971–72; Gen. Manager, Sales and Projects, 1972–74; Man. Dir, Austin-Pickersgill Ltd, Sunderland, 1974–78; British Shipbuilders: Dir of Marketing, 1977–78; Bd Mem. for Shipbuilding, 1978–83; Dep. Chief Exec., 1980–83; Chm. and Chief Exec., Harland and Wolff, 1983–93; Dep. Chm. and Chief Exec., 1993–94, Chm., 1994–2000, Babcock Internat. Gp. Mem., British Coal Corp., 1986–93; Chairman: Lattice Gp plc, 2000–02; Firth Rixson, 2001–03; RMC Gp plc, 2002–05; Peninsular and Oriental Steam Navigation Co., 2005–06; non-executive Director: GKN, 1993–2002; BG plc, 1997–2000; P&O Princess Cruises, 2000–03 (Dep. Chm., 2001–03); Brambles Industries, 2001–03; Carnival plc, 2003–; Carnival Inc., 2003–; EADS, 2007–. Non-exec. Dir, 2004–, Sen. non-exec. Dir, 2005–, Bank of England. Chancellor, Univ. of Southampton, 2006–. Member: Council, RINA, 1978–80, 1982– (Pres., 1996–99); Bd of Governors,

Sunderland Polytechnic, 1976–81; Internat. Cttee, Bureau Veritas, Paris, 1979–83; Gen. Cttee, Lloyd's Register of Shipping, 1983– (Chm. Tech. Cttee, 1996–2001); Industrial Develt Bd of NI, 1983–87. Hon. ScD Trinity Coll. Dublin, 1986; Hon. DSc: Ulster, 1992; Abertay Dundee, 1997; Southampton, 2007; DUniv Surrey, 2001. *Publications:* papers to Trans IES, RINA, RAEng. *Recreations:* reading, ships, sailing, music. *Address:* National Grid plc, 1-3 Strand, WC2N 5EH.

PARKER, Timothy Charles; Partner, CVC Capital Partners, since 2007 (Member, Advisory Board, 2004–07); *b* 19 June 1955; *s* of Clifford and Eileen Parker; *m* 1984, Thérèse Moralis; two *s* two *d*. *Educ:* Pembroke Coll., Oxford (MA); London Business School (MSc). Chief Executive: Kenwood Appliances plc, 1986–95; C. & J. Clark Ltd, 1996–2002; CEO, 2002–04, Dep. Chm., 2004–, Kwik-Fit; Chief Exec., AA, 2004–07. Director: Kleeneze plc, 1998–2002; CDC Capital Partners, then CDC Gp plc, 2001–04; Legal & Gen. plc, 2002–04; Boots plc, 2004–; Compass Group plc, 2007–08; non-exec. Dir, PBL Media, 2007–; Chm., Emerging Africa Infrastructure Fund, 2007–08. First Dep. Mayor of London, 2008; Chief Exec., GLA Gp, 2008. Board Member: SW Regl Develt Agency, 1998–2001; Audit Commn, 2006–07. Vis. Fellow, Oxford Univ. Centre for Corporate Reputation, 2008. Gov., Bedales Sch. FRSA 1990. *Address:* CVC Capital Partners, 111 Strand, WC2R 0AG. *Clubs:* Reform, Travellers.

PARKER, Sir (William) Peter (Brian), 5th Bt *cr* 1844, of Shenstone Lodge, Staffordshire; FCA; Partner, Stephenson Nuttall & Co., chartered accountants, Newark, since 1988; *b* 30 Nov. 1950; *s* of Sir (William) Alan Parker, 4th Bt and Sheelagh Mary, *o d* of late Dr Sinclair Stevenson; *S* father, 1990; *m* 1976, Patricia Ann, *d* of R. Filtness and Mrs D. Filtness; one *d* (one *s* decd). *Educ:* Eton. FCA 1974. *Heir: cousin* Timothy John Parker, *b* 17 May 1959. *Address:* Apricot Hall, Sutton-cum-Beckingham, Lincoln LN5 0RE.

PARKER-BROWN, Hazel Christine; Director of Corporate Services, Commission for Social Care Inspection, since 2004; *m*; two *s* one *d*. Head, Finance Policy (formerly Public Expenditure) Div., 1990–94, Head, Finance, Strategy and Audit Div., 1994–95, PSA; Head, Office Services Div., DoE, 1995–97; Dir, Human Resource Services, Highways Agency, DETR, 1998–99; Dir, Human Resources, DETR, then DTLR, subseq. Dir of Human Resources and Corporate Services, DfT, 1999–2002; Dir, Business Delivery Services, DfT, 2002–04. *Address:* Commission for Social Care Inspection, 33 Greycoat Street, SW1P 2QF. *T:* (020) 7979 2000; *e-mail:* hazel.parkerbrown@csci.gsi.gov.uk.

PARKER-JERVIS, Roger; DL; Deputy Chairman, CGA plc, 1982–90; *b* 11 Sept. 1931; *s* of George Parker-Jervis and late Ruth, *d* of C. E. Farmer; *m* 1958, Diana, *d* of R. St V. Parker-Jervis; two *s* one *d*. *Educ:* Eton; Magdalene College, Cambridge. Served Rifle Brigade, 1950–51, Queen Victoria Rifles, 1951–54; ADC to Governor of Tasmania, 1954–56. Bucks County Council: Mem., 1967–93; Chm., 1981–85. Mem., Milton Keynes Develt Corp., 1975–92; Pres., Timber Growers of England and Wales, 1981–83; Vice-Chm., Forestry Cttee of GB, 1981–83. Chm., Bucks Historic Buildings Trust, 1983–98; Mem., Thames and Chiltern Regl Cttee, NT, 1987–94. High Sheriff of Bucks, 1973–74, DL Bucks, 1982. *Publication:* Down the Rhône, 1997. *Recreations:* barging and caravanning in France, painting. *Address:* The Old Schoolhouse, The Green, Brill, Bucks HP18 9RU. *T:* (01844) 238025. *Clubs:* Farmers', Rifles.

PARKER-SMITH, Jane Caroline Rebecca; international concert organist and recording artist, since 1970; *b* 20 May 1950; *m* 1996, John Gadney. *Educ:* Barton Peveril Grammar Sch., Eastleigh; Royal Coll. of Music, London (ARCM 1966); postgrad. study with Nicolas Kynaston, London, and Jean Langlais, Paris. LTCL 1969. Concerts include: Westminster Cathedral, 1970; RFH, 1975, 2003; BBC Prom. Concerts, 1972; Jyvaskyla Fest., Finland, 1977; Stockholm Concert Hall, 1980; Hong Kong Arts Fest., 1988; Roy Thomson Hall, Toronto, 1989; City of London Fest., 1992; Fest. Paris Quartier d'Été, 1995; Centennial Convention, NY, 1996, Nat. Convention, Philadelphia, 2002, American Guild of Organists; Sejong Cultural Centre, Seoul, 2004; Birmingham Symphony Hall, 2005; Esplanade Concert Hall, Singapore, 2005; Walt Disney Concert Hall, LA, 2006. Mem., ISM, 1995–. Hon. FGMS 1996; Hon. FNMSM 1997. *Recreations:* cooking, antiques, travel, Daily Telegraph cryptic crossword. *Address:* 141 The Quadrangle Tower, Cambridge Square, W2 2PL. *T:* and *Fax:* (020) 7262 9259; *e-mail:* jane@parker-smith.demon.co.uk.

PARKES, Sir Edward (Walter), Kt 1983; DL; FREng; Vice-Chancellor, University of Leeds, 1983–91; Chairman, Committee of Vice-Chancellors and Principals of the Universities of the United Kingdom, 1989–91 (Vice-Chairman, 1985–89); *b* 19 May 1926; *o s* of Walter Frederick Parkes; *m* 1950, Margaret Parr, CBE (*d* 2007); one *s* one *d*. *Educ:* King Edward's, Birmingham; St John's College, Cambridge; Scholar; 1st cl. hons Mech. Sci. Tripos, 1945; MA, PhD, ScD; FIMechE. At RAE and in the aircraft industry, 1945–48; research student and subsequently Univ. Lecturer, Cambridge, 1948–59; Fellow and Tutor of Gonville and Caius College; Vis. Prof., Stanford Univ., 1959–60; Head of the Department of Engineering, Univ. of Leicester, 1960–65; Prof. of Mechanics, Cambridge, and Professorial Fellow, Gonville and Caius Coll., 1965–74 (Mem. Gen. Bd, Dep. head of Dept of Engineering); Vice-Chancellor, City Univ., 1974–78; Chm., UGC, 1978–83. Member: Brynmor Jones Cttee, 1964–65; Adv. Bd for Res. Councils, 1974–83; University and Polytechnic Grants Cttee for Hong Kong, 1974–96; Chairman: Clinical Academic Staff Salaries Cttee, 1985–90; Academic Adv. Bd, Asian Univ. of Sci. and Technology, Thailand, 1994–98. Chm., Adv. Panel on Limestone Workings in the W Midlands, 1983–95. DL W Yorks, 1990. Hon. FIMechE 1992. Hon. DTech Loughborough, 1984; Hon. DSc: Leicester, 1984; City, 1988; Hon. LLD Wales, 1984. Silver Bauhinia Star (Hong Kong), 1999. *Publications:* Braced Frameworks, 1965, 2nd edn 1974; papers on elasticity, dynamic plasticity or thermal effects on structures in Proc. and Phil. Trans. Royal Society and other jls. *Address:* The Cottage, Headington Hill, Oxford OX3 0BT. *Club:* Athenæum.

PARKES, John Alan, CBE 1996; DL; financial consultant; Chief Executive, Humberside County Council, and Clerk to Humberside Lieutenancy, 1988–96; Director, EMIH Ltd, since 1998; *b* 18 Jan. 1939; *s* of Arthur and Alice Parkes; *m* 1963, Margaret Jill (*née* Clayton); two *d*. *Educ:* Nottingham High Sch.; Oriel Coll., Oxford (MA). IPFA 1965 (Gold Medal, 1965). Various posts from graduate traineeship, Council Finance, Derbyshire, 1961–68; Asst County Treasurer, Glos, 1968–71; Dep., then County Treasurer, Lindsey, 1971–74; Dir of Finance, Humberside, 1974–88. Member: Phildrew Ventures Adv. Cttee, 1986–96; Financial Reporting Council, 1990–95. Advr, ACC, 1976–96; Sec., 1980–86, Pres., 1987–88, Soc. of County Treasurers; Dir, Humberside TEC, 1990–96. A Public Works Loan Comr, 1996– (Dep. Chm., 2002–05; Chm., 2005–). Mem., ER and Hull HA, 2000–02. Mem. Council, Univ. of Hull, 1996–2007 (Treas. and Pro-Chancellor, 2001–07, Pro-Chancellor Emeritus, 2007). Freeman, City of London, 1988. Hon. Fellow, Univ. of Humberside, 1991. DL E Riding of Yorks, 1997. *Publications:* articles on local govt finance in prof. jls. *Recreations:* walking, cars, railways. *Address:* 2 Burton Road, Beverley HU17 7EH. *T:* (01482) 881228.

PARKES, John Hubert, CB 1984; Permanent Secretary, Department of Education, Northern Ireland, 1979–90; *b* 1 Oct. 1930; 2nd *s* of Frank Hubert Parkes and Mary Edith (*née* Barnes), Birmingham; *m* 1956, Elsie Griffiths Henderson; two *s*. *Educ:* George Dixon Sch., Birmingham; Magdalen Coll., Oxford (MA). Joined NI Civil Service, 1953; Asst Sec. 1966; RCDS 1972; Dep. Sec., 1973. Hon. DLitt Ulster, 1991. *Address:* The New House, Boreham Street, Hailsham, E Sussex BN27 4SF. *Club:* Oxford and Cambridge.

PARKES, Prof. Malcolm Beckwith, DLitt; FSA; FRHistS; FBA 1993; Professor of Palaeography, University of Oxford, 1996–97, now Emeritus; Lyell Reader in Bibliography, Oxford, 1998–99; Fellow, Keble College, Oxford, 1965–97, now Emeritus; *b* 26 June 1930; *s* of Edward James Lennard Parkes and Clara Parkes (*née* Beckwith); *m* 1954, Ann Winifred Dodman; two *s*. *Educ:* Colfe's Grammar Sch.; Strasbourg Univ.; Hertford Coll., Oxford (BA Eng. Lang. and Lit. 1953; MA 1957; BLitt 1959; Gordon-Duff Prize 1959; DLitt 1985). FSA 1971; FRHistS 1977. Archivist, Lambeth Palace Library, 1957–58; Lectr in English Lang., Keble and Mansfield Colls, Oxford, 1961–65; Tutor in Eng. Lang., Keble Coll., Oxford, 1965–97; Lectr, Faculty of English, 1964–71, Lectr in Palaeography, 1971–93, Reader, 1993–96, Univ. of Oxford. Vis. Prof., Universität Konstanz, 1974 and 1980; James J. Hill Prof., Univ. of Minn (Twin Cities), 1991; Vis. Prof. of Latin, Harvard, 1998; Vis. Fellow, Princeton Univ., 1996; Mem., Inst. for Advanced Study, Princeton, 1997. Special Lecturer: in Palaeography and Diplomatic, Univ. of Durham, 1972; in Palaeography, Univ. of London, 1976; Lectures: Jarrow, 1982; Mont Follick, Univ. of Manchester, 1986; Robert F. Metzdorf, Univ. of Rochester, NY, 1987; James L. Rosier, Univ. of Pennsylvania, 1995; Fellows', Medieval Acad. of America, 2000. Mem., Standing Conf. of Nat. and Univ. Libraries, Adv. Cttee on MSS, 1977–86. Member: Wolfenbütteler Mediävistischen Arbeitskreis, 1986–2004; Comité Internat. de Paléographie Latine, 1986–; Council, EETS, 1995–. Corresp. Fellow, Medieval Acad. of America, 1992. *Publications:* English Cursive Book Hands 1250–1500, 1969, rev. edn 1979; (ed with A. G. Watson) Medieval Scribes, Manuscripts and Libraries: essays presented to N. R. Ker, 1978; Medieval Manuscripts of Keble College, Oxford, a descriptive catalogue, 1979; Scribes, Scripts and Readers, 1991; Pause and Effect: an introduction to the history of punctuation in the West, 1992; Their Hands Before Our Eyes: a closer look at scribes, 2008; introductions to facsimile edns of various manuscripts; articles and chapters on topics in palaeography, book production and ownership, and history of reading in learned jls and series. *Recreation:* growing fuchsias. *Address:* Keble College, Oxford OX1 3PG. *T:* (01865) 559002.

PARKES, Richard John Byerley; QC 2003; a Recorder, since 2000; *b* 8 June 1950; *s* of Richard Byerley Parkes and Margaret Elizabeth Parkes (*née* Service); *m* 1981, Janet Oliver (marr. diss. 2006); three *s*. *Educ:* Westminster Sch. (Queen's Schol.); Peterhouse, Cambridge (Exhibnr in Classics, MA). Teacher, Latin and Greek: Shrewsbury Sch., 1972–73; Poole Grammar Sch., 1973–76; called to the Bar, Gray's Inn, 1977, Bencher, 2006; a Dep. High Court Judge, 2007–. A Pres., Restricted Patients Panel, Mental Health Review Tribunal, 2007–. A contributing editor, Civil Procedure (The White Book), 1999–. *Publications:* (contrib. and ed) Gatley on Libel and Slander, 9th edn 1997, 10th edn 2004; (contrib.) The Law of Privacy and the Media, 2002. *Recreations:* cricket, sailing, Real tennis, shooting, choral music. *Address:* 5 Raymond Buildings, Gray's Inn, WC1R 5BP. *T:* (020) 7242 2902, *Fax:* (020) 7831 2686; *e-mail:* richardparkes@5rb.com. *Club:* MCC.

PARKHOUSE, James, MD, FFARCS; Director, 1984–89, Hon. Assistant Director, 1989–2001, Medical Careers Research Group, Oxford; *b* 30 March 1927; *s* of Charles Frederick Parkhouse and Mary Alice Sumner; *m* 1952, Hilda Florence Rimmer; three *s* two *d*. *Educ:* Merchant Taylors' Sch., Great Crosby; Liverpool Univ. (MD 1955). MB ChB, 1950; MA Oxon 1960; MSc Manchester 1974. DA; FFARCS 1952. Anaesthetist, RAF Med. Br., 1953–55. Sen. Resident Anaesth., Mayo Clinic, 1957–58; First Asst, Nuffield Dept of Anaesths, Oxford, and Hon. Cons. Anaesth., United Oxford Hosps, 1958–66; Prof. and Head of Dept of Anaesths, Univ. of Manitoba, and Chief Anaesth., Winnipeg Gen. Hosp., 1967–68; Postgrad. Dean, Faculty of Med., Sheffield Univ., and Hon. Cons. Anaesth., United Sheffield Hosps, 1969–70; Prof. of Anaesths, Manchester Univ., and Hon. Cons. Anaesth., Manchester and Salford AHAs (Teaching), 1970–80; Prof. of Postgraduate Med. Educn, Univ. of Newcastle upon Tyne, and Postgrad. Dean and Dir, Northern Postgrad. Inst. for Medicine and Dentistry, 1980–84. Consultant, postgrad. med. trng, WHO, 1969–89; Specialist Adviser, H of C Social Services Cttee, 1980–81, 1984. Member: Sheffield Reg. Hosp. Bd, 1969–70; Bd, Faculty of Anaesthetists, 1971–82; Neurosciences Bd, MRC, 1977–80; GMC, 1979–89; Nat. Trng Council, NHS, 1981–84; North Tyneside HA, 1982–84. *Publications:* A New Look at Anaesthetics, 1965; Medical Manpower in Britain, 1979; Doctors' Careers, 1991; contrib. to The Lancet, BMJ and specialist jls. *Recreations:* music, golf. *Address:* 8 Toremil Close, Hartrigg Oaks, New Earswick, York YO32 4DP. *T:* (01904) 764575.

PARKHOUSE, Nicholas, DM; FRCS; Consultant Plastic Surgeon, King Edward VII Hospital Sister Agnes (formerly King Edward VII Hospital for Officers), since 1998; *b* 7 Aug. 1957; *s* of late David Parkhouse and of Eileen Croxford, 'cellist; *m* 1986, Helen, *d* of late Austin and of Margaret Fitzmaurice; two *s* two *d*. *Educ:* St Paul's Sch.; Oriel Coll., Oxford (Open Exhibnr; BA 1978); Middx Hosp. Med. Sch. (MB BS 1981); DM 1990, MCh 1991, Oxon. FRCS 1985. Surgical trng at John Radcliffe Hosp., Oxford, Wexham Park, Orsett and Basildon Hosp., E Grinstead, Mt Vernon and UCH, 1982–91; Consultant Plastic Surgeon: Mt Vernon Hosp., 1991–94; Queen Victoria Hosp., E Grinstead, 1994–2006. Director: Rainsford Burn Centre, 1991–94; McIndoe Burns Centre, E Grinstead, 1994–97; McIndoe Surgical Centre Ltd, 2002–. Hunterian Prof., RCS, 1989; Visiting Professor: USC, 2001; Mayo Clinic, Minn, 2001. Ed., British Jl Plastic Surgery, 1997–2002. Mem. Council, British Assoc. Plastic Surgeons, 1997–2002, 2005–. Plastic Surgery Advr to NICE. Fellow, Amer. Assoc. of Plastic Surgeons, 2004. Freeman, City of London, 1998; Liveryman, GAPAN, 1998. De Havilland Trophy, 1990. *Publications:* contrib. chapters on burn injury; contrib. scientific jls on reconstructive surgery and restoration of function. *Recreations:* flying, fishing, family. *Address:* The Cadogan Clinic, 120 Sloane Street, SW1X 9BW; The McIndoe Surgical Centre, E Grinstead, W Sussex RH19 3EB. *T:* 0870 428 0919; Chelworth House, Chelwood Gate, W Sussex RH17 7JZ. *T:* (01825) 740615. *Clubs:* Air Squadron; Vincent's (Oxford); Leander (Henley); Houghton (Stockbridge).

PARKHOUSE, Peter; Chairman, Severn NHS Trust, 1992–95; *b* 22 July 1927; *s* of late William Richard Parkhouse, MBE, and Alice Vera Parkhouse (*née* Clarke); *m* 1st, 1950, Mary Alison Holland (*d* 1987); one *s* one *d*; 2nd, 1994, Sally Isabel Squires. *Educ:* Blundell's Sch.; Peterhouse, Cambridge (organist, 1944–45; BA 1947; MA 1951). Instr Lieut, RN, 1947–50; Cologne Univ., 1950–51; Asst Master, Uppingham Sch., 1951–52; Asst Principal, Min. of Food, 1952; transf. to MAFF, 1955; served in private office of successive Ministers and Parly Secs, 1954–58; Principal 1958; Principal Private Sec. to Minister, 1966–67; Asst Sec. 1967; Under-Sec. 1973; Dir in Directorate-Gen. for Agriculture, Commn of European Communities, 1973–79; Under-Sec., 1979–84. Mem., EDC for Agriculture, 1982–84. Mem., Mgt Cttee, Cheltenham Internat. Fest. of Music, 1992–95. Mem., Tetbury Hosp. Action Gp, 1989–92; Trustee, Tetbury Hosp. Trust Ltd, 1992–93 and 1996–2004; Gov., Barnwood House Trust, 1996–2004. Vice-Pres., Nat.

Star Coll. (formerly Nat. Star Centre, Coll. of Further Educn), Cheltenham, 2002–07 (Dir, 1997–2002). *Recreations:* music (organist emeritus of Tetbury Parish Church), fishing. *Address:* Stafford House, The Chipping, Tetbury, Glos GL8 8ET. *T:* (01666) 502540. *Club:* Oxford and Cambridge.

PARKIN, Bernard Maurice Walcroft; artist and photographer; Racing Photographer to the Queen, since 2002 (Racing Photographer to Queen Elizabeth the Queen Mother, 1993–2002 (Royal Warrant, 1993–2007)); Official Photographer to Cheltenham Racecourse, 1972–2007; *b* 7 Jan. 1930; *s* of Horace Parkin and Dorothy Jane Parkin; *m* 1955, Pamela Edith Humphreys; one *s* one *d. Educ:* Cheltenham Dunalley; Cheltenham Central Boys' Sch.; Cheltenham Sch. of Art. Garrison cartographer, RA, Malta, 1948–49; estabd own business of photography, design artwork, calligraphy and cartooning, specialising in horseracing, 1953–; Spirax-Sarco Ltd: company artist, 1960–91; Ed. and Producer, Spirax News (worldwide engrg monthly), 1980–91. Press Officer, Stratford-upon-Avon Racecourse, 1968–75; Artist: to Jockeys Assoc. of GB, 1969–2007; to Stable Lads Welfare Trust, 1989–2000. Has compiled large liby of own racing photos, 1953–. Mem., Royal Warrant Holders Assoc., 1993–. Hon. Life Mem., Cheltenham Racecourse, 2007. Founder Mem., Cleeve Hill Round Table, 1965. *Publications:* many books illustrated with technical drawings, cartoons, caricatures or photographs including: Steam Trapping and Air Venting, by Lionel Northcroft, 1968; The History of Royal Ascot, by Dorothy Laird, 1974; Great Horsemen of the World, by Guy Wathen, 1990; The Book of Derby Quotations, by Laurie Brannan, 2004; by Stewart Peters: Festival Gold, 2004; Grand National, 2005; The Hennessy Gold Cup, 2006. *Recreations:* travel, gardening (including landscape), hill walking, illustrated short story writing, poetry, Jack Russell terriers and public speaking. *Address:* Beldon House, Bushcombe Lane, Woodmancote, Cheltenham GL52 9QQ. *T:* (01242) 672784. *Club:* Stratford-upon-Avon Race (Hon. Mem. 1976; Chm., 1976–83).

PARKIN, Prof. David John, PhD; FBA 1993; Professor of Social Anthropology, Oxford University, 1996–2008, now Emeritus; Fellow of All Souls College, Oxford, since 1996; *b* 5 Nov. 1940; *s* of Cecil Joseph Parkin and Rose May Parkin (*née* Johnson); *m* 1st, 1962, Monica Ann Lacey (marr. diss. 1998); two *s* one *d;* 2nd, 2003, Vibha Joshi; one *s. Educ:* London Univ. (BA 1st cl. Hons African Studies 1962); SOAS (PhD Social Anthropol. 1965). FRAI 1966. Res. Associate, E African Inst. of Social Res., Makerere Univ. Coll., Kampala, Uganda, 1962–64 and 1966–67; School of Oriental and African Studies, University of London: Asst Lectr, 1964–65; Lectr, 1965–71; Lecturer: Sussex Univ., 1971–72; SOAS, 1972–76; Reader in Anthropol., 1976–81; Prof. of Anthropology with ref. to Africa, 1981–96, SOAS. University of Nairobi: Sen. Res. Fellow, Lang. Survey Unit, 1968–69; Sen. Res. Associate, 1977–78; Vis. Prof., Univ. of Calif, Berkeley, 1980; Directeur d'études Associé, Ecole des Hautes Etudes en Sciences Sociales, Paris, 1986, 1987 and 1993; Chercheur Associé, CNRS, Paris, 1992–93. Hon. Dir, Internat. African Inst., 1992–95. Chm., Assoc. of Social Anthropologists of GB and Commonwealth, 1989–93. MAE 1993. Rivers Meml Medal, RAI, 1985. *Publications:* Neighbours and Nationals in an African City Ward, 1969; Palms, Wine and Witnesses, 1972; (ed) Town and Country in Central and Eastern Africa, 1975; The Cultural Definition of Political Response, 1978; The Sacred Void, 1991; edited: Semantic Anthropology, 1982; The Anthropology of Evil, 1985; Swahili Language and Society, 1985; Transformations of African Marriage, 1987; Social Stratification in Swahili Society, 1989; Bush, Base, Forest, Farm, 1992; Continuity and Autonomy in Swahili Communities, 1994; The Politics of Cultural Performance, 1996; Autorité et Pouvoir chez les Swahili, 1998; Islamic Prayer Across the Indian Ocean, 2000; Anthropologists in a Wider World, 2000; Holistic Anthropology, 2007. *Recreations:* music, voyaging, swimming, squash. *Address:* All Souls College, Oxford OX1 4AL.

PARKIN, John Mackintosh; Administrator, Royal Courts of Justice, 1982–85, retired; *b* 18 June 1920; *s* of Thomas and Emily Cecilia Parkin; *m* Biancamaria Giuganino, Rome; two *d. Educ:* Nottingham High Sch.; Emmanuel Coll., Cambridge (Sen. Schol.; MA). Royal Artillery, 1939–46 (Captain). Asst Principal, WO, 1949; Registrar, RMCS, 1957–60; Principal Private Sec. to Sec. of State for War, 1960–62; Asst Sec. 1962; Sen. Fellow, Harvard Univ., 1966–67; Comd Sec., BAOR, 1967–70; Asst Under-Sec. of State, MoD, 1974–80. Mem., Royal Patriotic Fund Corpn, 1977–80. *Recreation:* history of architecture and art. *Address:* 18 Dulwich Mead, 48–50 Half Moon Lane, SE24 9HS. *T:* (020) 7274 7581.

PARKIN, Sara Lamb, OBE 2001; Founder Director, since 1994, and Trustee, since 1996, Forum for the Future; *b* 9 April 1946; *d* of late Dr George Lamb McEwan and of Marie Munro Rankin; *m* 1969, Dr Donald Maxwell Parkin; two *s. Educ:* Barrs Hill School, Coventry; Edinburgh Royal Infirmary (RGN). Ward Sister, Royal Infirmary, Edinburgh, and Res. Asst, Nursing Res. Unit, Univ. of Edinburgh, 1973–74; Council Mem., Brook Adv. Centre, 1974–76; Family Planning Nurse, Leeds AHA, 1976–80. Green Party, UK: Internat. Liaison Sec., 1983–90; Speaker, 1989–92; Chair, Executive, 1992; Co-Sec., European Green Co-ordination, 1985–90. Member: Bd, Envmt Agency, 2000–06; NERC, 2003–; Sci. in Society Adv. Panel, Res. Councils UK. Member: Council of Head Teachers in Industry, 2002–06; Bd, Leadership Foundn for Higher Educn, 2003–; Trustee, Friends of the Earth Trust, 1995–2002. CompICE 1996; CompInstE 2002. Hon. FSE 2006. *Publications:* Green Parties: an international guide, 1989; Green Futures: agenda for the twenty first century, 1991; Green Light on Europe, 1991; The Life and Death of Petra Kelly, 1994; Positive Deviance: sustainability literate leadership for the 21st century, 2009. *Recreations:* reading, films, theatre, opera, walking. *Address:* (office) 19–23 Ironmonger Row, EC1V 3QN. *T:* (020) 7324 3676.

PARKIN, Stuart Stephen Papworth, PhD; FRS 2000; FInstP; IBM Fellow, IBM Almaden Research Center, San Jose, California, since 1983; *b* 9 Dec. 1955. *Educ:* Edinburgh Acad.; Trinity Coll., Cambridge (BA 1977; PhD 1980). Res. Fellow, Trinity Coll., Cambridge, 1979. FIEEE 2003; FAAAS 2003. Vis. Prof., Nat. Taiwan Univ., 2006; Distinguished Vis. Prof., Nat. Univ. of Singapore, 2007. Fellow, APS. C. V. Boys Prize, Inst. of Physics, 1991; Internat. Prize for new materials, American Physical Soc., 1994; Europhysics Prize, Hewlett Packard, 1997; IBM Master Inventor, 1997; Prize for Industrial Applications of Physics, American Inst. of Physics, 1999; Innovator of the Year, R&D Mag., 2001; Humboldt Res. Award for US Senior Scientists, 2004. *Address:* IBM Almaden Research Center, 650 Harry Road, San Jose, CA 95120–6099, USA; *e-mail:* parkin@almaden.ibm.com.

PARKINS, Graham Charles; QC 1990; a Recorder, since 1989; *b* 11 Nov. 1942; *s* of John Charles Parkins and Nellie Elizabeth Parkins; *m* 1st, 1964, Carole Ann Rowe (marr. diss. 1977); two *s* one *d;* 2nd, 1977, Susan Ann Poole (*d* 1994); two *d;* 3rd, 1995, Linda Smith. *Educ:* Harwich County High Sch.; Mid-Essex Coll. of Law; LLB Hons London. Called to the Bar, Inner Temple, 1972; an Asst Recorder, 1986–89. Mem., FB Soc., Norwich. *Recreations:* golf, relaxing. *Address:* 41 Tollgate Drive, Stanway, Colchester CO3 0PE. *Club:* North Countryman's (Colchester).

PARKINSON, family name of **Baron Parkinson.**

PARKINSON, Baron *cr* 1992 (Life Peer), of Carnforth in the County of Lancashire; **Cecil Edward Parkinson;** PC 1981; chairman and director of companies; *b* 1 Sept. 1931; *s* of Sidney Parkinson, Carnforth, Lancs; *m* 1957, Ann Mary, *d* of F. A. Jarvis, Harpenden, Herts; three *d. Educ:* Royal Lancaster Grammar Sch., Lancaster; Emmanuel Coll., Cambridge (BA 1955; MA 1961). Joined Metal Box Company as a Management Trainee; joined West, Wake, Price, Chartered Accountants, 1956; qualified 1959; Partner, 1961–71; founded Parkinson Hart Securities Ltd, 1967; Director of several cos, 1965–79, 1984–87, 1992–. Constituency Chm., Hemel Hempstead Conservative Assoc.; Chm., Herts 100 Club, 1968–69; contested (C) Northampton, 1970. MP (C) Enfield West, Nov. 1970–1974, Hertfordshire South, 1974–83, Hertsmere, 1983–92. PPS to Minister for Aerospace and Shipping, DTI, 1972–74; an Asst Govt Whip, 1974; an Opposition Whip, 1974–76; Opposition Spokesman on trade, 1976–79; Minister for Trade, Dept of Trade, 1979–81; Paymaster General, 1981–83; Chancellor, Duchy of Lancaster, 1982–83; Sec. of State for Trade and Industry, June-Oct. 1983, for Energy, 1987–89, for Transport, 1989–90. Sec., Cons. Parly Finance Cttee, 1971–72; Chm., Anglo-Swiss Parly Gp, 1979–82; Pres., Anglo-Polish Cons. Soc., 1986–98. Chm., Cons. Party, 1981–83 and 1997–98. *Publication:* Right at the Centre: an autobiography, 1992. *Recreations:* reading, opera, golf, ski-ing; ran for combined Oxford and Cambridge team against Amer. Univs, 1954 and 1955; ran for Cambridge against Oxford, 1954 and 1955. *Address:* House of Lords, SW1A 0PW. *Clubs:* Beefsteak, Garrick, Pratt's; Hawks (Cambridge).

PARKINSON, Ewart West, BSc, DPA; CEng, FICE, PPRTPI, FIMunE; OStJ; development adviser in urban regeneration; Director of Environment and County Engineer, County of South Glamorgan, 1973–85; *b* 9 July 1926; *s* of Thomas Edward Parkinson and Esther Lilian West Hammond; *m* 1948, Patricia Joan Wood; two *s* one *d. Educ:* Wyggeston Sch., Leicester; Coll. of Technology, Leicester (BSc, DPA). Miller Prize (bridge design), Instn CE, 1953. After working with Leicester, Wakefield, Bristol and Dover Councils, he became Dep. Borough Engr, Chelmsford, 1957–60; Dep. City Surveyor Plymouth, 1960–64; City Planning Officer, Cardiff, 1964–73, specialising in reconstruction of war damaged cities and urban regeneration. Mem. Council, RTPI, 1971–83 (Vice-Pres., 1973–75, Pres., 1975–76, Chm. Internat. Affairs Bd, 1975–80); Member: Sports Council for Wales, 1966–78 (Chm., Facilities Cttee); Internat. Soc. of City and Regional Planners, 1972; Govt Deleg. to UN Conf. on Human Settlements, 1976; Watt Cttee for Energy, 1977–83 (Chm., Working Gp on Energy and Envt, 1980–83); UK mem., Internat. Wkg Party on Urban Land Policy, Internat. Fedn for Housing and Planning, 1979–85; Chairman: Internat. Wkg Party on Energy and the Environment, Internat. Fedn for Housing and Planning, 1982–85 (Life Mem. 1986); Wkg Party on Land Policy, Royal Town Planning Inst., 1983–85; Development Advisor: to Mayor of Sanya Hainan, China, 1999–2001; to cities of Nanjing and Xiamen, China, 2001; to city of Huzhou, China, 2003; to province of Fujian, 2005; led Study Tours to Soviet Union, 1977, India and Bangladesh, 1979, China, 1980, Kenya, Zimbabwe and Tanzania, 1981; lecture visits to People's Republic of China at invitation of Ministry of Construction, 1982, 1986, 1989, 1990, 1991, 1996, 1997. Chm., Ind. Commn on Councillors' Allowances, Cardiff, 1999. Director: Moving Being Theatre Co., 1986–90; W. S. Atkins (Wales), 1988–2002; Pontypridd Market Co., 1988–. Chairman: STAR Community Trust Ltd, 1979–95; Intervol, 1985–89; Wales Sports Centre for the Disabled Trust, 1986–2003; Norwegian Church Preservation (formerly Rebuilding) Trust, 1992–2001 (Man. Trustee, 1988; Pres., 2001); Roald Dahl Arts Project Trust, 1995–; Dir, Cardiff Action for the Single Homeless, 1988–; Vice-Pres., Wales Council for the Disabled, 1982–2000; Patron, Touch Trust and Shopmobility Wales, 2005–; Diamond Jubilee Silver Medal, Nat. Housing and Town Planning Council, 1978; many urban design awards, from Prince of Wales Cttee, Civic Trust, Concrete Soc., and Cardiff 2000; RTPI Award for outstanding contribn to planning during long and distinguished career, 2004. OStJ 1980 (S Glamorgan Council, 1975–). St Olav's Medal (Norway), 2004. *Publications:* The Land Question, 1974; And Who is my Neighbour?, 1976; articles in prof. jls on land policy, energy and the environment, and public participation. *Recreations:* working, travelling, being with family, talking with friends. *Address:* 42 South Rise, Llanishen, Cardiff CF14 0RH. *T:* (029) 2075 6394.

PARKINSON, Graham Edward, CBE 2001; a District Judge (Magistrates' Courts) (formerly Metropolitan Stipendiary Magistrate), 1982–2002, Deputy District Judge, 2002–07; Chief Metropolitan Stipendiary Magistrate, 1997–2000; *b* 13 Oct. 1937; *s* of Norman Edward Parkinson and late Phyllis (*née* Jaquiss); *m* 1963, Dinah Mary Pyper; one *s* one *d. Educ:* Loughborough Grammar Sch. Admitted Solicitor of the Supreme Court, 1961. Articled to J. Tempest Bouskell, Leicester, 1955–60; Asst Solicitor: Slaughter & May, 1961–63; Amery Parkes & Co., 1963–67; Partner, Darlington and Parkinson, Ealing, 1967–82. A Recorder, 1989–2000; Chm., Inner London Magistrates' Courts Cttee, 1997–2001; a Chairman: Inner London Youth Court, 2000; City and Family Proceedings Court, 2001. Pres., Central and S Middx Law Soc., 1978–79; Mem. Cttee, London Criminal Courts Solicitors Assoc., 1978–80; Chm., Legal Cttee, Magistrates' Assoc., 1992–97; Mem., Lord Chancellor's Adv. Cttee for Inner London, 1997–99. *Recreations:* opera, reading, playing piano and church organ. *Address:* The Old Stables, Melchbourne Park, Melchbourne, Bedford, MK44 1BD.

PARKINSON, Howard, CVO 1998; HM Diplomatic Service, retired; High Commissioner, Republic of Mozambique, 2003–07; *b* 29 March 1948; *s* of Ronald Parkinson and Doris (*née* Kenyon); *m* 1974, Linda Wood; one *s* one *d. Educ:* Openshaw Tech. High Sch., Manchester. BoT, 1967–69; joined HM Diplomatic Service, 1969; Latin American Floater, 1972–74; Vice Consul: Tegucigalpa, 1974–75; Buenos Aires, 1975–78; Second Sec., Maputo, 1978–81; Second, later First Sec., FCO, 1981–85; First Sec. (Commercial), Lisbon, 1985–89; on loan to British Gas, 1989–91; Asst Hd, Migration and Visa Dept, FCO, 1991–94; Consul Gen., Washington, 1994–96; Commercial and Econ. Counsellor, Kuala Lumpur, 1997–2000; Dep. High Comr, Mumbai (Bombay), 2001–03. *Recreations:* travel, music, reading. *Address:* e-mail: howardparkinson@hotmail.com.

PARKINSON, Sir Michael, Kt 2008; CBE 2000; interviewer, television presenter, writer; *b* 28 March 1935; *m* Mary Heneghan; three *s. Educ:* Barnsley Grammar School. Journalist on local paper; The Guardian; Daily Express; columnist on Sunday Times; radio work; has written for Punch, The Listener, New Statesman; Columnist: Daily Mirror, 1986–90; Daily Telegraph, 1991–; Editor, Catalyst, 1988–; Producer and interviewer: Granada's Scene; Granada in the North; World in Action; What the Papers Say; reporter on 24 Hours (BBC); Exec. producer and presenter, London Weekend Television, 1968; Presenter: Cinema, 1969–70; Tea Break, Where in the World, The Movie Quiz, 1971; host of own chat show, Parkinson, 1971–82 and 1998–2007 (Most Popular Talk Show, Nat. TV Awards, 1998, 1999, 2000, 2001); TV-am, 1983–84; Parkinson in Australia, 1979–84; The Boys of '66, 1981 (documentary); Give Us a Clue, 1984–92; All Star Secrets, 1984–86; The Skag Kids, 1985; Parkinson One-to-One, 1987–88; Desert Island Discs, BBC Radio 4, 1986–88; LBC Radio, 1990; Help Squad, 1991–92; Ghostwatch, 1992; Surprise Party, 1993; A League Apart: 100 years of Rugby League, BBC2, 1995; Going for a Song, BBC1, 1995–99; Parkinson on Sport, R5, 1994–97; Parkinson's Sunday Supplement, R2, 1996–. Founder-Director, Pavilion Books, 1980–97. Chancellor, Nottingham Trent Univ., 2008–. Fellow, BFI, 1998. Hon. Dr: Lincs, 1999; Humberside,

1999. Sports Feature Writer of the Year, British Sports Journalism Awards, 1995; Sony Radio Award, 1998; Sports Writer of the Year, British Press Awards, 1998; Media Personality of the Year, Variety Club, 1998; Best Light Entertainment, BAFTA, 1999; Media Soc. annual award, 2000. *Publications:* Football Daft, 1968; Cricket Mad, 1969; (with Clyde Jeavons) Pictorial History of Westerns, 1972; Sporting Fever, 1974; (with Willis Hall) Football Classified, 1974; George Best: an intimate biography, 1975; (with Willis Hall) A-Z of Soccer, 1975; Bats in the Pavilion, 1977; The Woofits, 1980; Parkinson's Lore, 1981; The Best of Parkinson, 1982; Sporting Lives, 1992; Sporting Profiles, 1995; Michael Parkinson on Golf, 1999; Michael Parkinson on Football, 2001; Michael Parkinson on Cricket, 2002; Parky: my autobiography, 2008. *Address:* c/o CSS-Stella Management Ltd, 34–43 Russell Street, WC2B 5HA.

PARKINSON, Prof. Michael Henry, CBE 2007; PhD; Professor of Urban Affairs, and Director, European Institute for Urban Affairs, Liverpool John Moores University, since 1992; *b* 11 Aug. 1944; *s* of John Parkinson and Margaret Parkinson (*née* Corrin); *m* 1966, Fran Anderson; one *s* one *d. Educ:* Univ. of Liverpool (BA); Univ. of Manchester (MA (Econ) with Dist.); Liverpool John Moores Univ. (PhD 2002). Prof. of Political Sci., 1972–73, Dir, Urban Studies Prog., 1976–79, Washington Univ. in St Louis; Liverpool Univ., 1979–92. Director: CITIES Prog., ESRC, 2000–03; State of English Cities Prog., ODPM, 2004–06; Neighbourhoods, Cities and Regions Panel, DCLG, 2007–. City Advr, Birmingham CC, 2006–. Dir, Merseyside Develt Corp., 1992–97. Adviser to: EC; DCLG; ODPM; H of C Select Cttee; OECD; EUROCITIES; Core Cities; LGA. Mem., Living Landmarks Cttee, Big Lottery. Gov., Merseyside Further Educn Coll. and Special Sch. *Publications:* Liverpool on the Brink, 1985; Reshaping Local Government, 1987; Regenerating the Cities, 1988; Leadership and Urban Regeneration, 1990; Cultural Policy and Urban Regeneration, 1994; European Cities Towards 2000, 1994; Competitive European Cities, 2004; City Matters, 2004; State of English Cities, 2006. *Recreations:* suffering with Liverpool FC, good wine, the cinema, boxing, exploring Crete, looking after our Joe. *Address:* European Institute for Urban Affairs, Liverpool John Moores University, 51 Rodney Street, Liverpool L1 9AT. *T:* (0151) 231 5163; *e-mail:* m.h.parkinson@ljmu.ac.uk.

PARKINSON, Ronald Dennis; Assistant Curator, Victoria and Albert Museum, 1978–98; *b* 27 April 1945; *s* of Albert Edward Parkinson and Jennie Caroline Clara Meager. *Educ:* St Dunstan's Coll.; Clare Coll., Cambridge (MA). Res. Assistant: Paul Mellon Foundn for British Art, 1971–72; V&A Mus., 1972–74; Asst Keeper, Tate Gall., 1974–78. *Publications:* (ed jtly) Richard Redgrave, 1988; Catalogue of British Oil Paintings 1820–1860 in the Victoria and Albert Museum, 1990; British Watercolours at the Victoria and Albert Museum, 1998; Constable, the man and his art, 1998; articles in Apollo, Burlington Mag., Cambridge Res., Connoisseur, Country Life, Times Higher Educn Sup. *Recreations:* reading, shopping. *Address:* 13 Childebert Road, SW17 8EY. *Club:* Algonquin.

PARKINSON, Stephen Lindsay; Partner, since 2005, and Head of Criminal and Regulatory Litigation Department, since 2006, Kingsley Napley; *b* 15 June 1957; *s* of late Rev. Edward James Parkinson and of Dr Mary Vere Parkinson (*née* Young); *m* 1982, Penelope Jane Venvell; one *s* two *d. Educ:* Hampton Grammar Sch.; Chippenham Sch.; University Coll. London (LLB 1979). Called to the Bar, Lincoln's Inn, 1980; admitted solicitor, 2005; pupillage, 1980–82; sub-editor, Butterworths Legal Publishers, 1982–84; Legal Asst, Dept of DPP, 1984–86; Sen. Crown Prosecutor, then Asst Br. Crown Prosecutor, CPS, 1986–88; Law Officers' Dept, 1988–91; Hd, Internat. Co-operation Unit, CPS, 1991–92; Asst Solicitor, DTI, 1992–96; Hd, Company/Chancery Litigation Gp, Treasury Solicitor's Dept, 1996–99; Dep. Legal Sec. to Law Officers, 1999–2003; barrister, seconded to Kingsley Napley, 2003–05. *Publications:* (contrib.) Blackstone's Criminal Practice, 2009; (with David Corker) Disclosure in Criminal Proceedings, 2009. *Recreations:* life of Churchill, jogging, walking. *Address:* Kingsley Napley, Knight's Quarter, 14 St John's Lane, EC1M 4AJ.

PARKS, Timothy Harold; author; *b* 19 Dec. 1954; *s* of late Harold James Parks and of Joan Elizabeth Parks (*née* MacDowell); *m* 1979, Rita Maria Baldasarre; one *s* one *d. Educ:* Westminster City Sch.; Downing Coll., Cambridge (BA 1977). Harvard Univ. Mktg Exec., Tek Translation and Internat. Print, 1979–80; freelance teacher and translator, Verona, 1981–85; Lectr, Univ. of Verona, 1985–. Vis. Lectr, Istituto Universitario di Lingue Moderne, Milan, 1992–. Mem., Soc. of Authors, 1986–. *Publications:* fiction: Tongues of Flames, 1985 (Somerset Maugham Award, Betty Trask Award); Loving Roger, 1986 (John Llewellyn Rhys Award); Home Thoughts, 1987; Family Planning, 1989; Goodness, 1991; Shear, 1993; Mimi's Ghost, 1995; Europa, 1997; Destiny, 1999; Judge Savage, 2003; Rapids, 2005; Cleaver, 2006; Dreams of Rivers and Seas, 2008; as John MacDowell: Cara Massimina, 1990; essays: Adultery and Other Diversions, 1998; Hell and Back, 2001; The Fighter, 2007; *non-fiction:* Italian Neighbours, 1992; An Italian Education; Translating Style, 1997; A Season with Verona, 2002; Medici Money: banking, metaphysics and art in 15th-century Florence, 2005; translations from Italian of books by several authors, incl. Calasso, Calvino, Moravia, and Tabucchi; contribs to short story and essay collections, conf. proceedings and jls. *Address:* c/o Antony Harwood Ltd, 103 Walton Street, Oxford OX2 6EB. *T:* (020) 7384 9209.

PARMINTER, Kathryn Jane, (Kate); Chief Executive, Campaign to Protect Rural England (formerly Director, Council for the Protection of Rural England), 1998–2004; *b* 24 June 1964; *d* of James Henry Parminter and June Rose Parminter (*née* Cayless); *m* 1994, Neil Sherlock; two *d. Educ:* Millais Sch.; Collyer's Sixth Form Coll., Horsham; Lady Margaret Hall, Oxford (MA Theol.). Graduate trainee, Nestlé Co., 1986–88; Parly researcher for Simon Hughes, MP, 1988–89; Sen. Account Exec., Juliette Hellman Public Relns, 1989–90; Royal Society for the Prevention of Cruelty to Animals: Public Relations Officer, 1990–92; Head: Campaigns and Events, 1992–95; Public Affairs, 1995–96; Press and Public Affairs, 1996–98. Mem., Commn into Public Services, 2003–04, Adv. Bd, 2004–; NCC. Mem. (Lib Dem), Horsham DC, 1987–95. Member: Lib Dem Policy Review Gp, 2005–07; Lib Dem Reform Commn, 2008. Trustee, IPPR, 2007–. Chm., Campaign for Protection of Hunted Animals, 1997–98. *Publications:* (contrib.) Working For and against Government, in Pressure Group Politics in Modern Britain, 1996; (contrib.) The Progressive Century: the future of the Centre Left in Britain, 2001. *Recreations:* pre-Raphaelite paintings, walking. *Club:* National Liberal.

PARMLEY, Dr Andrew Charles, FRCO; Head of Senior School, Harrodian School, since 2001; *b* Manchester, 17 Oct. 1956; *s* of Granville and Betty Parmley; *m* 1980, Wendy Davina Calder Hodgson. *Educ:* Blackpool Grammar Sch.; Royal Acad. of Music (BMus); Manchester Univ. (MusM); Royal Holloway Coll., London (PhD 1987); Jesus Coll., Cambridge. FRCO (CHM) 1976; FTCL 1977. Director of Music: Forest Sch., 1983–92; S Hampstead High Sch., 1992–96; Grey Coat Hosp., Westminster, 1996–2001; St James' Garlickhythe, 1982–. Examr, adjudicator, composer, broadcaster, conductor, editor and writer. Chairman of Governors: City of London Sch. for Girls, 2001–03; GSMD, 2003–06. Chm., Montessori St Nicholas Charity; Patron: London Docklands Singers; Marcel Sinfonia; Thames Chamber Choir. Mem., Common Council, Vintry Ward,

1992–2001, Alderman, 2001; Past Master, Parish Clerks' Co.; Liveryman: Musicians' Co.; Glass Sellers' Co.; Vintners' Co. Hon. Liveryman: Joiners' Co.; Water Conservators' Co.; Hon. Freeman, Horners' Co. Comité d'Honneur, Les Editions des Abbesses. *Recreations:* fundraising for organ restoration, Leukaemia Research Fund, etc, fishing (Captain, Corp. of London Members' Fishing Team), marathons – running and walking. *Address:* 125 Marsham Court, Marsham Street, SW1P 4CB; *e-mail:* aparmley@btinternet.com. *Clubs:* Reform, Guildhall.

PARMOOR, Baron *cr* 1914, of Frieth, co. Bucks; **(Michael Leonard) Seddon Cripps; His Honour Judge The Lord Parmoor;** a Circuit Judge, since 1998; President, Immigration Services Tribunal, since 2000; *b* 18 June 1942; *s* of (Matthew) Anthony Leonard Cripps, CBE, DSO, TD, QC and Dorothea Margaret Cripps; *S* cousin, 2008; *m* 1971, Elizabeth Anne Millward Shennan; one *s* one *d* (and one *s* decd). *Educ:* Eton Coll. Called to the Bar, Middle Temple, 1965; Member *ad eundem,* Lincoln's Inn, 1969, Inner Temple, 1984; a Recorder, 1986–98; Standing Counsel to HM Customs and Excise, 1989–98. Chairman, Disciplinary Committee: Milk Mktg Bd, 1979–90; Potato Mktg Bd, 1979–90. Legal Mem., Immigration Appeal Tribunal, 1998–2000. Liveryman, Fuellers' Co., 1985; Freeman, City of London, 1986; Hon. Lt Col, Alabama State Militia, 1975. *Recreations:* family, walking slowly. *Heir: s* Hon. Henry William Anthony Cripps [*b* 2 Sept. 1976; *m* 2003, Katherine Helen Bernadette, *d* of Sir Michael Terence Wogan, *qv;* one *s* one *d*]. *Address:* Aylesbury Crown Court, Market Square, Aylesbury, Bucks HP20 1XD.

PARNABY, Dr John, CBE 1987; FREng; Chairman and Chief Executive Officer, BPSE Ltd, since 1998; Chairman, Aston Academy of Life Sciences Ltd, since 2003; *b* 10 July 1937; *s* of John Banks Parnaby and Mary Elizabeth Parnaby; *m* 1959, Lilian Armstrong; three *s* one *d. Educ:* Durham Univ. (BSc Mech. Engrg, 1961); Glasgow Univ. (PhD Control Systems Engrg, 1966). MIEE 1966, Hon. FIET (Hon. FIEE 1989); FIProdE 1978; FIMechE 1978 (Hon. FIMechE 1998); FREng (FEng 1986). Technical Apprentice, 1954–58, Ironworks Develt Engr, 1961–62, United Steel Co.; Res. Asst, Univ. of Durham, 1962–63; Lectr in Mech. Engrg, Univ. of Glasgow, 1963–66; Sen. Projects Engr, Albright & Wilson Ltd, 1966–67; Works Man., Solway Chemicals Ltd, 1967–70; University of Bradford: Sen. Lectr, 1970–73; Prof. of Manufg Systems Design, 1973–80 (Chm., Sch. of Manufacturing Systems Engrg, 1975–80); Technical and Marketing Dir, subseq. Jt Man. Dir, Rieter Scragg Ltd, 1980–82; Gen. Man., Dunlop Ltd, 1982–83; Gp Dir, Technology, Lucas Industries, 1983–90; Man. Dir and CEO, Lucas Electronic Systems Products (formerly Lucas Applied Technology Sector), 1990–96; Gp Dir, LucasVarity plc, 1996–98; Chairman: Lucas Metier, later Lucas Mgt Systems, 1990–96; Lucas Engrg and Systems Ltd, 1990; Lucas Gp Dir, Develt, 1995–96; Knowledge Process Software plc, 2000–05; Think Digital Solutions plc, 2001–04; Amchem Ltd, 2001–03. Dir and CEO, Geared Systems Inc., 1996–98; Director: Scottish Power plc, 1994–2001; Molins plc, 1998–2003; Jarvis plc, 1999–2001. Chm., Anglo-German Res. Cttee, British Council, 1990–. Chm., Link Bd, DTI/OST, 1993–96; Mem., DTI/EPSRC Innovative Manufrs Initiative Mgt Cttee, 1998–. Vis. Hon. Prof. of Manufacturing Systems Engrg, Univ. of Birmingham, 1984–2000; Vis. Hon. Prof. of Engrg, Univ. of Cambridge, 1999–. Pres., IProdE, 1989; Pres., IEE, 1995–96 (Dep. Pres., 1993–95); Mem. Council, Royal Acad. of Engrg, 1997–2001; Senator, Engrg Council, 1997–2001. Mem., Queen's Anniversary Award Cttee, 1996–2002. Aston University: Mem. Council, 1999–; Treas. and Chm. Finance Cttee, 2002–; Hon. DSc, 2002. Hon. Fellow: Coventry Poly., 1989; Sheffield Poly., 1991; Univ. of Wales, 1995. Hon. DTech: Liverpool Poly., 1990; CNAA 1990; Loughborough, 1991; Napier, 1997; Hon. DSc Hull, 1991; DUniv Open, 1992; Hon. DEng: Bradford, 1993; Newcastle, 2000; Aston, 2002. Gold Medal, Instn of Manufg Engrs, 1987; Silver Medal, 1990, Faraday Medal, 1994, IEE. *Publications:* Minicomputers and Microcomputers in Engineering and Manufacture, 1986; Manufacturing Systems Engineering Miniguide Handbook, 1989, 2nd edn 1992; Managing by Projects for Business Success, 1993; over 60 papers in engrg and management jls on manufg systems, control engrg, process engrg, business process systems engrg, organisation design and management and machinery design. *Recreations:* hockey, sailing, golf. *Address:* Crest Edge, Beechnut Lane, Solihull, W Midlands B91 2NN. *T:* (0121) 705 4348; *e-mail:* drjparnaby@aol.com.

PARNELL, family name of **Baron Congleton.**

PARNELL, Rowena; *see* Arshad, Rowena.

PARR, Donald; *see* Parr, T. D.

PARR, John Robert; an Hon. Director, General Secretariat, Council of Ministers of European Union (formerly Council of Ministers of European Communities), since 1989; *b* 25 Sept. 1934; *s* of Henry George Parr and Hilda Frances Parr (*née* Pattison); *m* 1993, Prof. Margaret Dolores O'Reilly; one *d. Educ:* Dulwich Coll.; Merton Coll., Oxford (Postmaster; MA). Joined British Iron and Steel Fedn as Admin. Asst, 1959, Dep. Sec., 1963–65; Principal, Industrial Policy Div., Dept of Economic Affairs, 1965–68; British Steel Corp., 1968–73; Co-ordinator, EC Affairs, 1972–73; Dir-Gen., British Footwear Manufacturers Fedn, 1973–76; Divl Hd, Gen. Secretariat, Council of Ministers of European Communities, 1976–89; Dir Gen., Air Transport Users Council, 1989–96. Chm., Airline-Consumer Forum, IATA, Geneva, 1995–99. Dir, Ulster Orch. Soc., 2007–; Chm., Friends of Ulster Orch., 2007–. *Recreations:* political history of 19th and 20th centuries, opera and other forms of classical music, Irish country life. *Address:* 7 Culmore Square, Derry BT48 8GF.

PARR, Martin; freelance photographer and film-maker; *b* 23 May 1952; *s* of Donald Parr and Joyce Parr (*née* Watts); *m* 1980, Susan P. Mitchell; one *d. Educ:* Manchester Poly. (1st cl. Creative Photography 1973). Freelance photographer, 1973–; Mem., Magnum, photo co-operative, 1994–; freelance TV film-maker, 1996–; Vis. Prof. of Photography, Univ. of Industrial Arts, Helsinki, 1990–92; Visiting Lecturer: Nat. Coll. of Art and Design, Dublin, and Chelsea Sch. of Art, 1975–82; Sch. of Documentary Photography, Newport, 1982–84; W Surrey Coll. of Art and Design, 1983–. Exhibitions worldwide, including: Photographer's Gall., 1977, 1981, 1982, 1987, 1995; Whitechapel Art Gall., 1978; Hayward Gall., 1979; Serpentine Gall., 1986; Nat. Centre of Photography, Paris, 1987, 1995; RA, 1989; RPS, 1989; Janet Borden Gall., NY, 1991, 1992, 1996; Nat. Mus. of Photography, Bradford, 1998; retrospective exhibn, Barbican Gall., 2002. Work in permanent collections incl. V&A Mus., MOMA, NY, Walker Art Gall., Liverpool. Arts Council of GB Photography Award, 1975, 1976, 1979. *Publications:* Bad Weather, 1982; A Fair Day, 1984; (with Ian Walker) The Last Resort: photographs of New Brighton, 1986, 2nd edn 1998; (jtly) The Actual Boot: the photographic postcard 1900–1920, 1986; The Cost of Living, 1989; Signs of the Times, 1992; Home and Abroad, 1993; From A to B, 1994; Small World, 1995; West Bay, 1997; Flowers, 1999; Common Sense, 1999; Boring Postcards, 1999; Auto Portrait, 2000; Think of England, 2000; Boring Postcards USA, 2000; Boring Postcards Germany, 2001; Martin Parr Retrospective, 2002; Phone Book, 2002; Bliss, 2003; 7 Communist Still Lives, 2003; Fashion Magazine, 2005; Mexico, 2006; Parking Spaces, 2007. *Recreation:* working! *Address:* c/o Magnum, 63 Gee Street, EC1V 3RS. *T:* (020) 7490 1771. *Club:* Clifton Poker.

PARR, (Thomas) Donald, CBE 1986; Chairman, William Baird PLC, 1981–98; *b* 3 Sept. 1930; *s* of Thomas and Elizabeth Parr; *m* 1954, Gwendoline Mary Chaplin; three *s* one *d*. *Educ*: Burnage Grammar Sch. Own business, 1953–64; Chm., Thomas Marshall Investments Ltd, 1964–76; Director: William Baird PLC, 1976–; Vendôme Luxury Gp (formerly Dunhill Holdings) PLC, 1986–98; Hepworth PLC, 1989–98; Kwik Save Group, 1991–98. Chm., British Clothing Industry Assoc., 1987–91; Member: NW Industrial Develt Bd, 1975–87; Ct of Governors, UMIST, 1984–2004. *Recreation*: sailing. *Address*: Mariners, 13 Queens Road, Cowes, Isle of Wight PO31 8BQ. *Clubs*: Boodle's, Royal Ocean Racing; Royal Yacht Squadron (Cowes).

PARRIS, Matthew Francis; author, journalist and broadcaster; *b* 7 Aug. 1949; *s* of late Leslie Francis Parris and of Theresa Eunice Parris (*née* Littler); civil partnership 2006, Julian Glover. *Educ*: Waterford School, Swaziland; Clare Coll., Cambridge (BA Hons; Hon. Fellow, 2006); Yale Univ., USA (Paul Mellon Fellowship). Foreign Office, 1974–76; Conservative Research Dept, 1976–79; MP (C) West Derbyshire, 1979–86; Presenter, Weekend World, LWT, 1986–88. Columnist, 1987–, Parly Sketch Writer, 1988–2001, The Times. Mem., Broadcasting Standards Council, 1992–97. Various journalistic awards. *Publications*: Inca-Kola: a traveller's tale of Peru, 1990; So Far So Good, 1991; Look Behind You!, 1993; (ed) Scorn, 1994; Great Parliamentary Scandals, 1995; (ed) Scorn with Added Vitriol, 1995; (ed jtly) Read My Lips: a treasury of things politicians wish they hadn't said, 1996; I Couldn't Possibly Comment: parliamentary sketches, 1997; The Great Unfrocked: two thousand years of church scandal, 1998; (ed) Scorn with Extra Bile, 1999; Off-Message, 2001; Chance Witness: an outsider's life in politics (autobiog.), 2002; Castle in Spain: a mountain ruin, an impossible dream, 2005; (ed jtly) Mission Accomplished!: a treasury of things politicians wish they hadn't said, 2007. *Address*: c/o The Times, Pennington Street, E98 1BD.

PARROTT, Andrew Haden; conductor and musicologist; Music Director: London Mozart Players, 2000–06; New York Collegium, since 2002; *b* 10 March 1947. *Educ*: Merton Coll., Oxford (schol.; BA 1969). Dir of Music, Merton Coll., Oxford, 1969–71; sometime musical assistant to Sir Michael Tippett. Founded Taverner Choir, 1973, then Taverner Consort and Taverner Players, for performance of music ranging from medieval to late 18th century. Débuts: BBC Prom. concerts, 1977; EBU, 1979; La Scala, 1985; Salzburg, 1987; Guest Conductor worldwide of symphony and chamber orchs, opera and contemporary music. Over 50 recordings. Hon. Res. Fellow, Royal Holloway, Univ. of London, 1995–; Hon. Sen. Res. Fellow, Univ. of Birmingham, 2000–. *Publications*: (ed jtly) New Oxford Book of Carols, 1992; The Essential Bach Choir, 2000, German edn 2003; contrib. learned jls. *Address*: c/o Allied Artists, 42 Montpelier Square, SW7 1JZ.

PARROTT, Brian Robert; consultant in social care, health and local government, since 2001; Chairman, Suffolk Family Carers, since 2006; Joint Chairman, Association of Directors of Adult Social Services Associates Network, since 2008; *b* 24 Sept. 1949; *s* of late Derek Parrott and Lilian Parrott (*née* Thoy); *m* 1974, Pamela Elizabeth Rigby; two *s*. *Educ*: Bedford Modern Sch.; Downing Coll., Cambridge (BA 1971; MA 1974); Univ. of Kent (CQSW 1973). Social Worker, Camden LBC, 1973–76; Sen. Social Worker, Notts CC, 1976–81; Area Officer, Haringey LBC, 1981–85; an Asst Dir, 1985–90, First Asst Dir, 1990–95, Social Services, Suffolk CC; Dir of Social Services, Surrey CC, 1995–2001. Chm., Central Suffolk NHS PCT, 2002–05. Dir, Verita (The Inquiry Consultancy), 2002–06. Chm., Resources Cttee, Assoc. of Dirs of Social Services, 2000–01. Trustee, In Control, 2008–. Vis. Fellow, UEA, 2002–05. FRSA 1999. *Publications*: (jtly) A Unitary Approach to Social Work: application in practice, 1981; contribs to social work and local govt publications and jls. *Recreations*: travel, mountain walking, running, sport, Ipswich Town FC. *Address*: 3 Jervis Close, Holbrook, Ipswich, Suffolk IP9 2RR. *T*: (01473) 327702.

PARROTT, Jasper William; Director, since 1969, Chairman and Managing Director, since 1987, HarrisonParrott Ltd; *b* 8 Sept. 1944; *s* of Sir Cecil Parrott, KCMG, OBE and of Lady (Ellen) Parrott; *m* 1974, Cristina Ortiz, pianist; two *d*. *Educ*: Tonbridge Sch.; Peterhouse, Cambridge (MA). With Ibbs and Tillett, concert mgt, 1965–69. Chm., 1983–84, Pres., 1986–89, British Assoc. of Concert Agents. Dir, The Japan Festival UK, 1991; Internat. Consultant and Advr, Sakip Sabanci Mus., Istanbul, 2005–07; Consultant, Reykjavik Concert and Conf. Centre, 2007–. Hon. Trustee, Royal Botanical Gardens, Kew, 1995–. *Publications*: Beyond Frontiers, 1984 (trans German, Japanese, French, Russian, Norwegian, Finnish and Icelandic). *Recreations*: books, tennis, languages, gardens. *Address*: c/o HarrisonParrott Ltd, 12 Penzance Place, W11 4PA. *T*: (020) 7229 9166.

PARROY, Michael Picton; QC 1991; a Recorder, since 1990; *b* 22 Oct. 1946; *s* of Gerard May and Elizabeth Mary Parroy; *m* 1978, Susan Patricia Blades (*née* Winter). *Educ*: Malvern College; Brasenose College, Oxford (MA). Called to the Bar, Middle Temple, 1969, Bencher, 2001; Head of Chambers, 3 Paper Bldgs, 1995–2004. Trustee, Wincanton Recreational Trust, 2000–. *Publication*: Road Traffic, in Halsbury's Laws of England, 4th edn, vol. 40, 1983. *Recreations*: gardening, food and wine, dog walking. *Address*: 3 Paper Buildings, Temple, EC4Y 7EU.

PARRY; *see* Jones Parry and Jones-Parry.

PARRY, Alan; President, Johnson & Higgins Ltd, 1989–97 (Chairman, 1987–89); *b* 30 Oct. 1927; *s* of George Henry James Edgar Parry and Jessica Cooke; *m* 1954, Shirley Yeoman; one *s* one *d*. *Educ*: Reedham School. Leonard Hammond Ltd, 1941; Sedgwick Collins Ltd, 1948, Dir, 1960; Dir, Man. Dir, Dep. Chm. and Chm., Sedgwick companies and subsidiaries, to 1981; Chm., Carter Brito e Cunha, 1982–87. Mem., Lloyd's Insurance Brokers' Assoc., 1961–64, 1970–73, 1975–78 (Chm., 1977); Mem. Council, BIBA, and LIBA and BIBA rep. on Cttee on Invisible Exports, 1977; Mem., Cttee of Lloyd's, 1979–82, 1985–88 (Dep. Chm., 1987–88). *Recreations*: flyfishing, drama. *Address*: 2 Mayfield Grange, Little Trodgers Lane, Mayfield TN20 6BF.

PARRY, Anthony Joseph, QFSM 1990; County Fire Officer, 1985–90, and Chief Executive, County Fire Service, 1986–90, Greater Manchester; *b* 20 May 1935; *s* of Henry Joseph Parry and Mary Elizabeth McShane; *m* 1959, Elizabeth Therese Collins; three *s* one *d*. *Educ*: St Francis Xavier's Coll., Liverpool. MIFireE. Liverpool Fire Bde, 1958; Fire Service Technical Coll., 1967; Gloucestershire Fire Service, 1969; Avon Fire Service, 1974; Lancashire County Fire Service, 1975. Long Service and Good Conduct Medal, 1978. *Address*: 10 Oakenclough Drive, Bolton BL1 5QY.

PARRY, Rear Adm. Christopher John, CBE 2004; Director, Merl House Ltd; *b* 29 Nov. 1953; *s* of Comdr John Jenkyn Parry, OBE, PhD, RN and Joan Elizabeth Parry (*née* Axford); *m* 1989, Jacqueline Margaret Nicholson; one *s* one *d*. *Educ*: Portsmouth Grammar Sch.; Jesus Coll., Oxford (BA 1975, MA 1980). HMS London, 1977–78; aviation appts in FAA, 1978–88: 826 Naval Air Sqdn, HMS Antrim, incl. Falklands War (despatches); HMS Hermione and Brazen; Staff of FO Sea Trng; Exec. Officer, HMS York, 1988–89; Central Staff, MoD, 1989–92; Staff of C-in-C Fleet, 1992–93; CO, HMS Gloucester, 1994–96; Captain, Maritime Warfare Centre, 1996–98; rcds 1999; CO, HMS Fearless, 2000–01; Dir, Operational Capability, MoD, 2001–03; Comdr, UK/Netherlands Amphibious Task

Gp, 2003–05; Dir-Gen., Jt Docrine and Concepts, subseq. Developments, Concepts and Doctrine, MoD, 2005–08. Pres., Combined Services and RN Rugby Leagues, 2001–08. FCMI; MInstD. *Publications*: (with J. M. Parry) The Isle of Wight, 2000, 4th edn 2006; numerous anonymous and occupational contribs to successive Govt Reviews, pubns and papers. *Recreations*: sport, walking, medieval and military history, being in Wales. *Clubs*: Vincent's (Oxford).

PARRY, His Honour David Johnston; a Circuit Judge, 1995–2002; a Deputy Circuit Judge, 2002–07; *b* 26 Aug. 1941; *s* of Kenneth Johnston Parry and Joyce Isobel Cooper (formerly Parry); *m* Mary Harmer; one *s* three *d*. *Educ*: Merchant Taylors' Sch., Northwood; St Catharine's Coll.; Cambridge (MA Hons). Admitted Solicitor, 1969; Partner, later Jt Sen. Partner, Dixon Ward, Richmond, 1969–95; Asst Recorder, 1986–91; Recorder, 1991–95. Co-Chm., Richmond Legal Advice Service, 1969–95; Administrator, Richmond Duty Solicitors' Scheme, 1990–95; part-time Chm., Independent Tribunal Service, 1993–96; a part-time Chm., Lord Chancellor's Adv. Cttee for SW London, 2006–. Member: Law Society; London Criminal Courts Solicitors' Assoc. Liveryman, Merchant Taylors' Co., 2001–. *Recreations*: family activities, reading, music, television, DIY, sport, lying on a beach, relaxing in the sun, travel. *Address*: c/o Court Service, 2nd Floor, Rose Court, 2 Southwark Bridge, SE1 9HS. *Club*: Old Merchant Taylors'.

PARRY, Prof. Eldryd Hugh Owen, OBE 1982; MD, FRCP; Chairman, Tropical Health and Education Trust, 1989–2007; *b* 28 Nov. 1930; *s* of Dr Owen Parry and Dr Constance Parry (*née* Griffiths); *m* 1960, Helen Madeline, *d* of Humphry and Madeline House; one *s* three *d*. *Educ*: Shrewsbury; Emmanuel Coll., Cambridge (Hon. Fellow 2007); Welsh Nat. Sch. of Medicine (BChir 1955; MA; MD). FWACP. Junior posts, Cardiff Royal Infirmary, Nat. Heart Hosp., Hammersmith Hosp., 1956–65; seconded to UCH, Ibadan, 1960–63; Associate Prof., Haile Selassie I Univ., Addis Ababa, 1966–69; Prof. of Medicine, Ahmadu Bello Univ., 1969–77; Foundn Dean, Faculty of Health Sciences, Univ. of Ilorin, Nigeria, 1977–80; Dean and Prof. of Medicine, Sch. of Med. Scis, Kumasi, 1980–85; Dir, Wellcome Tropical Inst., 1985–90; Sen. Res. Fellow, 1990–95, Vis. Prof., 1996–, Hon. Fellow, 1997, LSHTM. Special Prof., Dept of Med., Univ. of Nottingham, 1997–. Albert Cook Meml Lectr, Kampala, 1974. Member: Med. and Dental Council, Ghana, 1980–85; Council, All Nations Christian Coll., 1986–99; Founding Mem., Amoud Univ. Med. Faculty, Somaliland, 2006. Hon. FRSTM&H 1993 (Donald Mackay Medal, 1998); Hon. FRCS 2008; Hon. Fellow: Ghana Coll. of Physicians and Surgeons, 2003; UWCM, 2004. Hon. DSc Kwame Nkrumah Univ. of Sci. and Technol., Kumasi, Ghana, 2003. Frederick Murgatroyd Prize, RCP, 1973; Centenary Lifetime Achievement Medal, RSTM&H, 2007. *Publications*: Principles of Medicine in Africa, 1976, 3rd edn 2004 (RSM/Soc. of Authors prize, 2004; BMA first prize public health, 2005); papers on medicine in the tropics in med. jls. *Recreations*: tennis, Wales, old Welsh furniture. *Address*: 21 Edenhurst Avenue, SW6 3PD.
See also J. P. H. House.

PARRY, Emyr Owen; solicitor; a Recorder of the Crown Court, 1979–99; District Judge at the Caernarfon Group of County Courts and the District Registry of the High Court at Llangefni, Caernarfon and Rhyl, 1992–2003; *b* 26 May 1933; *s* of Ebenezer Owen Parry and Ellen Parry; *m* 1959, Enid Griffiths; one *s* one *d*. *Educ*: Caernarfon Grammar Sch.; University Coll. of Wales, Aberystwyth (LLB Hons Wales, 1954). Admitted solicitor, 1957. Estabd own practice in Llangefni, Anglesey, 1958; formed partnership (Emyr Parry & Davies) with Mrs Elinor C. Davies, 1964; Dep. Circuit Judge, 1975. Chairman: Social Security (formerly National Insurance) Appeals Tribunal, Holyhead Area, 1969–92; Medical Appeal Tribunal, 1986–92; Solicitor Mem., Lord Chancellor's County Court Rule Cttee, 1975–80. *Recreations*: cricket, music, theatre.

PARRY, Isabel Clare; Her Honour Judge Parry; a Circuit Judge, since 2002; *b* 29 Jan. 1957; *d* of Elwyn James Griffith Parry and Joyce McLean Parry (*née* Edwards); *m* 1983, Gareth Richard Llewellyn George; one *s* one *d*. *Educ*: St Clare's Convent Grammar Sch., Porthcawl; Girton Coll., Cambridge (MA); Inns of Court Sch. of Law. Called to the Bar, Gray's Inn, 1979; Asst Recorder, 1996–2000; a Recorder, 2000–02. *Recreations*: music, theatre, cooking.

PARRY, Jann Peta Olwen; writer and dance critic, The Observer, 1983–2006; *b* 12 Feb. 1942; *d* of John Hywel Parry and Evelyn Florence Upton; *m* 1994, Richard Ruegg Kershaw. *Educ*: Univ. of Cape Town (BA); Girton Coll., Cambridge (BA Hons 1965). Producer/writer, BBC World Service, 1970–89; Dance Critic: Listener, 1981; Spectator, 1982, 1995–96. Member: Dance Panel, Arts Council, 1988–90; Exec. Cttee, Dance UK, 1991–2001. Mem., Critics' Circle, 1983–. *Publications*: contrib. to Dance Now, Dance Mag. (US), Dancing Times, Dance & Dancers. *Recreations*: research, ballet classes—striving to appreciate technical perfection with no hope of achieving it. *Address*: 82 Prince of Wales Mansions, Prince of Wales Drive, SW11 4BL. *T: and Fax*: (020) 7738 8732.

PARRY, Prof. Jonathan Patrick, PhD; FBA 2001; Professor of Anthropology, London School of Economics and Political Science, since 1993; *b* 10 Sept. 1943; *s* of Dennis Arthur Parry and Kathleen Aroma Parry (*née* Forbes); *m* 1972, Margaret Dickinson; one *s* one *d*. *Educ*: King's Coll., Cambridge (BA 1965; PhD 1971). Lectr, Dept of Social Anthropol., Univ. of Edinburgh, 1971–74; Lectr, 1974–84, Sen. Lectr, 1984–86, Reader, 1986–93, Dept of Social Anthropol., subseq. Dept of Anthropol., LSE. *Publications*: Caste and Kinship in Kangra, 1979; (ed with M. Bloch) Death and the Regeneration of Life, 1982; (ed with M. Bloch) Money and the Morality of Exchange, 1989; Death in Banaras, 1994; (ed with J. Breman) The World of Indian Industrial Labour, 1999; (ed with R. Guha) Institutions and Inequalities, 1999. *Recreations*: reading novels, cinema. *Address*: Department of Anthropology, London School of Economics and Political Science, Houghton Street, WC2A 2AE.

PARRY, Rev. Canon Marilyn Marie, PhD; Canon Residentiary of Christ Church, Oxford and Diocesan Director of Ordinands, Oxford, since 2001; *b* 24 Aug. 1946; *d* of Robert Warren Fortey and Jane Carolyn (*née* Turner); *m* 1969, Rev. David Thomas Newton Parry; one *s* one *d*. *Educ*: Western Coll., Oxford, Ohio (BA Maths, Theol. and Philos. 1968). Univ. of Manchester (MA Theol. 1977, PhD 2000). Gilmore Scheme (IDC 1978). Diocese of Manchester: Accredited Lay Worker, 1978; ordained deaconess, 1979, deacon, 1987, priest, 1994; Curate, St Peter, Westleigh, 1978–85 and C of E Chaplain, Leigh Infirmary, 1983–85; Chaplain's Asst, N Manchester Gen. Hosp., 1985–90 and Chaplaincy Team Leader, Booth Hall Children's Hosp., 1989–90; Northern Ordination Course: New Testament Tutor, 1990–97; Dir of Studies, 1991–97; Nat. Advr for Pre-Theol Educn and Selection Sec., Ministry Div., Archbishops' Council, 1997–2001. Select Preacher, Oxford Univ., 2003–04. *Recreations*: playing clarinet (chamber music), walking, conversation with friends. *Address*: Diocesan Church House, North Hinksey, Oxford OX2 0NB. *T*: (01865) 208260.

PARRY, Prof. Martin Lewis, OBE 1998; PhD; Chairman, Working Group II, Intergovernmental Panel on Climate Change, since 2003; *b* 12 Dec. 1945; *s* of John Fyson Parry and Frances Joan (*née* Stewart); *m* 1968, Cynthia Jane Mueller; two *d*. *Educ*: Univ.

of Durham (BA Hons); Univ. of West Indies (MSc); Univ. of Edinburgh (PhD). Lectr, Univ. of Edinburgh, 1972–73; University of Birmingham: Lectr, 1973–86; Sen. Lectr, 1986–88; Reader, 1988–89; Prof. of Envmtl Management, 1989–91; Prof. of Envmtl Management, and IBM Dir, Envmtl Change Unit, Oxford Univ., 1991–94; Prof. of Envmtl Mgt, Dept of Geography, UCL, 1996–99; Dir, Jackson Envmt Inst., UCL, subseq. at UEA, 1996–2003; Prof. of Envmtl Scis, UEA, 1999–2003. Ed., Global Envmtl Change, 1992–2005. Peek Award, RGS, 1991; Gerbier-Mumm Internat. Award, WMO, 1993. *Publications:* Climatic Change, Agriculture and Settlement, 1976; The Impact of Climatic Variations on Agriculture, Vol. 1 1988, Vol. 2 1989; Climate Change and World Agriculture, 1990; Economic Implications of Climate Change in Britain, 1995; Climate Impact and Adaptation Assessment, 1998; (ed) Climate Change 2007: impacts, adaptation and vulnerability, 2007. *Recreations:* sailing, ski-ing.

PARRY, Richard Hawley Grey, PhD, ScD; FICE; civil engineering consultant, since 1967; Secretary General, International Society for Soil Mechanics and Geotechnical Engineering, 1981–99; *b* 27 April 1930; *s* of late Joseph Grey Parry and Ena Rachel (*née* Hawley); *m* 1954, Frances Irene McPherson; three *s* one *d*. *Educ:* Swinburne Technical Coll.; Melbourne Univ. (BCE 1951; MEngSc 1954; MEng 1963); Imperial Coll., London (PhD 1957); MA 1967, ScD 1983, Cantab. Res. Student and Sen. Demonstrator, Melbourne Univ., 1952–54; Shell Res. Student, Imperial Coll., London, 1954–56; Engr, Soil Mechanics Ltd, 1956–57; Res. Officer, CSIRO, 1957–60; Dir, Foundation Engineering (Aust.) Pty Ltd, 1960–67; Colombo Plan consultant on bridge sites, Sarawak, 1963–64; Lectr, Engrg Dept, Cambridge Univ., 1967–90; Fellow, Pembroke Coll., Cambridge, 1970–90, now Fellow Emeritus. MASCE (Life Mem.). British Geotech. Soc. Prize, 1978; Skempton Gold Medal, British Geotech. Soc., 1999. *Publications:* (ed) Stress-Strain Behaviour of Soils, 1971; Mohr Circles, Stress Paths and Geotechnics, 1995, 2nd edn 2004; Engineering the Pyramids, 2004; Engineering the Ancient World, 2005; technical papers in learned jls and proceedings. *Recreations:* archaeology, history of civil engineering, allotment, golf, family history, reading. *Address:* 5 Farm Rise, Whittlesford, Cambridge CB2 4LZ. *T:* (01223) 832024. *Club:* Gog Magog Golf.

PARRY, Richard James; Strategic Director (formerly Director) of Education, City and County of Swansea, since 1998; *b* 4 Oct. 1953; *s* of John and Margaret Parry; *m* 1st, 1981, Barbara Parish; one *s* one *d*; 2nd, 1991, Gwyneth Selby; one *d*. *Educ:* Emmanuel Coll., Cambridge (BA, MA). Teacher, 1976–88: Head of Maths, Hatfield Sch., 1979–82; Head of Maths, Fearnhill Sch., Letchworth, 1983–88; Maths Adv. Teacher, Herts, 1985–88; Maths Advr, 1988–93, Chief Advr, 1993–96, W Glam; Asst Dir of Educn, 1996–97, acting Chief Educn Officer, 1997–98, City and County of Swansea. *Recreations:* golf, distance running, sport generally. *Address:* c/o Education Department, County Hall, Swansea SA1 3SN. *T:* (01792) 636351.

PARRY, Roger George; Chairman: Johnston Press plc, since 2001; Future (formerly Future Network) plc, since 2001; Mobile Streams plc, since 2006; YouGov plc, since 2007; Media Square, since 2007; *b* 4 June 1953; *s* of George Parry and Margarita (*née* Mitchell); *m* 1990, Johanna Waterous; one *s*. *Educ:* Sutton Grammar Sch.; Bristol Univ. (BSc Hons); Jesus Coll., Oxford (MLitt). With Saatchi & Saatchi, 1976; freelance reporter: and producer, BBC, 1977–85; LBC, 1979–83; Thames TV, 1979–83; consultant, McKinsey & Co., 1985–88; Director: WCRS Gp plc, 1988–90; Aegis Gp plc, 1990–94; Advr, KPMG, 1993–95; Vice-Pres., Carat N America, 1995–98; CEO, More Gp plc, 1995–98; Chief Exec., 1998–2004, Chm., 2004–06, Clear Channel Internat. Director: Jazz FM plc, 1995–2002; iTouch plc, 2000–05. Trustee: Shakespeare's Globe, 1987– (Chm., 2005–); Liver Foundn, 2004–. *Publications:* People Businesses: managing professional service firms, 1991; Enterprise, 2003; Making Cities Work, 2003. *Recreations:* ski-ing, squash, sailing, tennis, backgammon, fishing, swimming, cinema, computer games, horse racing, NY Times crossword. *Clubs:* Garrick, Hurlingham, MCC; Ocean (Bahamas).

PARRY, Victor Thomas Henry, MA Oxon; FCLIP; Director of Central Library Services and Goldsmiths' Librarian, University of London, 1983–88; *b* 20 Nov. 1927; *s* of Thomas and Daisy Parry; *m* 1959, Mavis K. Russull; two *s* one *d*. *Educ:* St Julian's High Sch., Newport; St Edmund Hall, Oxford (MA); University College, London (DipLib). FCLIP (FLA 1959). Manchester Public Libraries, 1950–56; Colonial Office and CRO Library, 1956–60; Librarian, Nature Conservancy, 1960–63; British Museum (Natural History), 1963–74; Chief Librarian and Archivist, Royal Botanic Gdns, Kew, 1974–78; Librarian, SOAS, Univ. of London, 1978–83. Sen. Examiner, LA, 1959–68. Chm., Circle of State Librarians, 1966–68; Mem., Adv. Cttee, British Library Dept of Humanities and Social Scis (formerly Reference Div.), 1983–90; Council Member: Sir Anthony Panizzi Foundn, 1983–89; London Soc., 1984–88. Chm., Friends of Univ. of London Liby, 1998–2000. FRAS 1981; FRSA 1985. *Publications:* contrib. prof. books and jls. *Recreations:* ball games, books, bridge, railways. *Address:* 69 Redway Drive, Twickenham TW2 7NN. *T:* (020) 8894 0742. *Club:* Surrey CC.

PARRY, Vivienne Mary Hunt; writer and broadcaster; *b* 4 June 1956; *d* of late Michael Mills and of Mary Mills; *m* 1978, Paul Parry (marr. diss. 2007); two *s*. *Educ:* St Swithun's Sch., Winchester; Bedford Coll., London; University Coll. London (BSc Hons Zoology). Nat. Organiser, Birthright, 1979–94; Presenter, Tomorrow's World, 1994–97; Reporter, Panorama, How Safe is Beef?, and Test Tube Bodies, 1996; Presenter, Morning Surgery, 1997; Columnist: News of the World, 1998–2002; Guardian, 2004–05; Body & Soul supplement, The Times, 2005–; Presenter, Radio 4: Inside the Ethics Committee (3 series), 2005, 2006, 2007; Am I Normal? (4 series), 2006, 2007, 2008. Administrator, GUS Charitable Trust, 1997–2007; Trustee, Diana Meml Fund, 1998. Mem. Council, UCL, 2005–. *Publications:* The Real Pregnancy Guide, 1996; The Truth About Hormones, 2005. *Recreations:* gardening, swimming, walking. *Address:* 15 Duke's Avenue, Muswell Hill, N10 2PS.

PARRY-EVANS, Air Chief Marshal Sir David, GCB 1991 (KCB 1985); CBE 1978; Royal Air Force, retired; *b* 19 July 1935; *s* of late Group Captain John Parry-Evans, MRCS, LRCP, DLO, and Dorothy Parry-Evans; *m* 1960, Ann, 2nd *d* of late Charles Reynolds and Gertrude Reynolds; two *s*. *Educ:* Berkhamsted School. Joined RAF, 1956; served FEAF, Coastal Command, United States Navy, RN Staff Coll., 1958–70; Headquarters Strike Command, 1970–74; OC 214 Sqn, 1974–75; OC RAF Marham, 1975–77; MoD, 1977–81 (Director of Defence Policy, 1979–81); Comdt, RAF Staff Coll., 1981–82; AOC Nos 1 and 38 Groups, RAF Strike Comd, 1982–85; C-in-C RAF Germany, and Comdr, Second ATAF, 1985–87; Dep. Chief of Defence Staff (Progs and Personnel), 1987–89; Air Mem. for Personnel, 1989–91. Gov., Royal Star and Garter Home, 1991–99 (Chm., 1996–99). Chief Comdr, St John Ambulance, 1992–98. KStJ 1992. *Address:* c/o National Westminster Bank, 26 Spring Street, W2 1WE. *Club:* Royal Air Force.

PARRY EVANS, Mary Alethea, (Lady Hallinan); a Recorder of the Crown Court, 1978–97; *b* 31 Oct. 1929; *o c* of Dr Evan Parry Evans, MD, JP, and Dr Lilian Evans; *m* 1955, Sir (Adrian) Lincoln Hallinan (*d* 1997); two *s* two *d*. *Educ:* Malvern Girls' Coll.; Somerville Coll., Oxford (BCL, MA). Called to Bar, Inner Temple, 1953; Wales and Chester Circuit. Member: Cardiff City Council, 1961–70; S Glamorgan CC, 1972–81; S Glamorgan Health Authority, 1977–81. Lady Mayoress of Cardiff, 1969–70. *Address:* (chambers) 33 Park Place, Cardiff CF1 3BA. *T:* (029) 2023 3313.

PARRY JONES, Terence Graham; *see* Jones, Terry.

PARSLOE, Prof. Phyllida; Chairman, North Bristol NHS Trust, 1999–2003; Professor of Social Work, Bristol University, 1978–96, now Emeritus Professor; *b* 25 Dec. 1930; *d* of late Charles Guy Parsloe and Mary Zirphie (*née* Munro). *Educ:* Bristol Univ. (BA, PhD); London Univ. (Cert. in Mental Health). Probation Officer, Devon CC, 1954–59; Psychiatric Social Worker, St George's Hospital, 1959–65; Lectr, London Sch. of Economics, 1965–70; Associate Prof., Sch. of Law, Indiana Univ., 1970–73; Prof. of Social Work, Univ. of Aberdeen, 1973–78; Pro-Vice Chancellor, 1988–91, Warden of Wills Hall, 1991–97, Bristol Univ. Member: Central Council for Educn and Training in Social Work, 1986–92; Commonwealth Scholarships Commn. Mem., Thornbury Town Council, 2004–. *Publications:* The Work of the Probation and After Care Officer, 1967; Juvenile Justice in Britain and America, 1978; (with Prof. O. Stevenson) Social Service Teams: the practitioner's view, 1978; Social Service Area Teams, 1981; report to the Sec. of State for Scotland on Social Work in Prisons, 1987; (with S. Macara *et al*) Data Protection in Health and Social Services, 1988; Aiming for Partnership, 1990; (ed) Risk Assessment in Social Care and Social Work, 1999; contribs to: British Jl of Social Work, Community Care, Social Work Today, British Jl Criminology. *Recreations:* hill walking, crafts, gardening. *Address:* Lion House, 9 Castle Street, Thornbury, S Glos BS35 1HA.

PARSONS, family name of **Earl of Rosse**.

PARSONS, Adrian; *see* Parsons, C. A. H.

PARSONS, Alan; *see* Parsons, T. A.

PARSONS, Alfred Roy, AO 1986; High Commissioner for Australia in the UK, 1984–87, retired; *b* 24 May 1925; *s* of W. G. R. Parsons and R. E. Parsons; *m* 1958, Gillian Tryce Pigot; two *s* one *d*. *Educ:* Hobart High School; Univ. of Tasmania (postgraduate research; BCom); Canberra University College. Dept of Foreign Affairs, 1947; Djakarta, 1950–53, Rangoon, 1956–58, Berlin, 1961–62; Aust. Mission to UN, NY, 1962–64; Counsellor, Djakarta, 1964–66; High Comr, Singapore, 1967–70; First Asst Sec., Canberra, 1970–73; High Comr, Kuala Lumpur, 1973–76; Dep. Sec., periodically Acting Sec., Dept of Foreign Affairs, 1978–83. Chm., Commonwealth Observer Gp on Namibia, 1989. Member: Australia Japan Foundn, 1978–83; Australia China Council. Centenary Medal, Australia, 2003. *Recreations:* golf, reading. *Address:* 11 Hotham Crescent, Deakin, Canberra, ACT 2600, Australia. *Clubs:* Commonwealth (Canberra); Royal Canberra Golf, Canberra Wine and Food.

PARSONS, Prof. Barry Eaton, PhD; Professor of Geodesy and Geophysics, University of Oxford, since 2003; Fellow of St Cross College, Oxford, since 1986; *b* 24 May 1948; *s* of Ernest Harold Parsons and Olive Parsons (*née* Eaton). *Educ:* Downing Coll., Cambridge (BA Natural Scis 1969; PhD 1973). Res. Asst, Principal Res. Scientist and Associate Prof., Dept of Earth and Planetary Scis, MIT, 1973–86; Reader in Geodesy, Univ. of Oxford, 1986–; Dir, Centre for Observation and Modelling of Earthquakes and Tectonics, 2002–. *Publications:* articles in Geophysical Jl Internat., Geophysical Res. Letters, Jl of Geophysical Res., Nature, Science, Earth and Planetary Science Letters. *Address:* Department of Earth Sciences, University of Oxford, Parks Road, Oxford OX1 3PR.

PARSONS, (Charles) Adrian (Haythorne); consultant to solicitors on charity matters; *b* 15 June 1929; *s* of Dr R. A. Parsons and Mrs W. S. Parsons (*née* Haythorne); *m* 1951, Hilary Sharpe; one *d*. *Educ:* Bembridge Sch.; Wadham Coll., Oxford. Called to Bar, Gray's Inn, 1964. Coutts & Co., Bankers, 1952–64; joined Charity Commn, 1964; Dep. Comr, 1972; Comr, 1974–89; Head of Legal Staff, 1981; Unit Trust Ombudsman, 1989–90; National Solicitors Network Ombudsman, 1989–94. Complaints Convenor, Retained Organs Commn, 2003–04. *Address:* 6 Garrick Close, The Green, Richmond, Surrey TW9 1PF. *T:* (020) 8940 3731. *Club:* Oxford and Cambridge.

See also Sir R. E. C. F. Parsons.

PARSONS, (Christopher) Nicholas, OBE 2004; actor, presenter and solo performer; *b* 10 Oct. 1923; *s* of late Dr Paul Frederick Nigel Parsons and Nell Louise Parsons (*née* Maggs); *m* 1st, 1954, Denise Pauline Rosalie Bryer (marr. diss. 1989); one *s* one *d*; 2nd, 1995, Ann Reynolds. *Educ:* St Paul's Sch.; Univ. of Glasgow. *Theatre* includes: The Hasty Heart, Aldwych, 1945; Charley's Aunt, Palace, 1947; Arsenic and Old Lace (tour); in rep., Bromley, Kent, 1949–51; cabaret incl. Quaglino's, Ciros, The Colony, Society, Café de Paris, 1951–65; comedian, Windmill Th., 1952, Watergate Revue, Lyric Revue, 1954; Swing Along with Arthur Haynes, Palladium, 1963; Boeing Boeing, Duchess, 1967; Say Who You Are, Vaudeville, 1968; Uproar in the House, Whitehall, 1968; Charlie Girl, Victoria Palace and tour, 1986–87; Into the Woods, Phoenix, 1990; Rocky Horror Show, Duke of York's, 1994 and 1995 (tours 1996, 1998–99 and 2000); numerous pantomimes and one-man shows incl. Nicholas Parsons' Happy Hour, Edinburgh Fringe, 1999–; *television* includes: comedy partnership with Arthur Haynes, 1956–66; Last Train to Surbiton (series), 1966; Benny Hill Show, 1969–70; host: Sale of the Century, 1971–84; The All New Alphabet Game, 1988; Laughlines, 1990; Just a Minute, 1994, 1995 and 1999; *films* include: Brothers-in-Law, Carlton-Browne at the FO, Happy is the Bride, Upstairs Downstairs, Too Many Crooks, Eyewitness, Carry on Regardless; *radio* includes: host, Just a Minute, 1967–; Listen to This Space, 1967–73. Rector, St Andrews Univ., 1988–91. Barker, Variety Club of GB, 1975–; Mem., Lord's Taverners, 1965– (Pres., 1998–2000); Trustee, Aspire, Deaf-Blind UK; Gov., NSPCC, 1977; Ambassador, ChildLine, 2004–. Hon. LLD St Andrews, 1991; Hon. DA Lincoln, 2007. Radio Personality of Year, Variety Club, 1967. *Publications:* Egg on the Face, 1985; The Straight Man; my life in comedy, 1994. *Recreations:* golf, gardening, photography. *Address:* c/o Jean Diamond, Diamond Management, 31 Percy Street, W1T 2DA. *T:* (020) 7631 0400, *Fax:* (020) 7631 0500.

PARSONS, Colin James, FCA; Chairman, Trow Engineering (Canada), since 2003 (Director, 1999–2003); *b* Neath, Wales, 15 Jan. 1934; *m* 1960, Alice McAuley; two *s*. *Educ:* Haverfordwest and Neath Grammar Schs. CA 1955; FCA 1991. Peat Marwick Mitchell, Toronto, 1957–59; Monarch Development Corp., 1959–99: Pres., 1977–92; Chm., 1992–99; Taylor Woodrow plc: Dir, 1987–; Gp Chm., 1992–99; Chief Exec., 1997–98. Pres. and Chm., London Chamber of Commerce and Industry, 1998–2000; Pres., Canada-UK Chamber of Commerce, 1998–99. Dir, Foundn for Canadian Studies in UK, 1997–2000. *Recreations:* running, golf. *Address:* 154 Valley Road, Toronto, ON M2L 1G4, Canada. *Clubs:* Brooks's; Albany, Granite, Donalda (Toronto).

PARSONS, David; *see* Parsons, J. D.

PARSONS, David Huw; a District Judge (Magistrates' Courts), since 2004; *b* 11 May 1957; *s* of Dr D. Ll. Parsons and Margaret P. G. Parsons; *m* 1979, Siân Griffiths; three *d*. *Educ:* Duffryn High Sch., Newport; University Coll. of Wales, Aberystwyth (LLB Hons).

Admitted solicitor, 1981; Sen. Partner and Founding Partner, Hodson, Parsons Solicitors, Newport, S Wales, 1983–2004; Actg Stipendiary Magistrate, 2000–01; Dep. Dist Judge (Magistrates' Courts), 2001–04; Immigration Adjudicator, 2001–04. *Recreations:* my children, reading, motor-cycling, hill walking, cooking, ski-ing, staying on Lundy. *Address:* c/o Bristol Magistrates' Court, Nelson Street, Bristol BS1 2PZ. *T:* (0117) 943 5117.

PARSONS, Graham Colin; a District Judge (Magistrates' Courts), since 2004; *b* 8 May 1953; *s* of late Jack Rowland Parsons and of Davina Evelyn Parsons. *Educ:* Worthing High Sch. for Boys; Guildford Coll. of Law. Admitted solicitor, 1978; Prosecuting Solicitor, Hampshire Police Authy, 1979–85; private practitioner specialising in criminal defence work, 1985–2004; Actg Stipendiary Magistrate, 1998–2000, subseq. Dep. Dist Judge (Magistrates' Courts), 2000–04. *Recreations:* sailing, travel, choral music. *Address:* Brighton Magistrates' Court, Edward Street, Brighton, East Sussex BN2 2LG.

PARSONS, Sir John (Christopher), KCVO 2002 (CVO 1998; LVO 1992); Deputy Keeper of the Privy Purse and Deputy Treasurer to the Queen, 1988–2002; an Extra Equerry to the Queen, since 2002; *b* 21 May 1946; *s* of late Arthur Christopher Parsons and of Veronica Parsons; *m* 1982, Hon. Anne Manningham-Buller, *d* of 1st Viscount Dilhorne, PC; two *s* one *d*. *Educ:* Harrow; Trinity College, Cambridge (MA Mech. Scis). FCA, FIBC. Dowty Group Ltd, 1968–72; Peat, Marwick, Mitchell & Co., 1972–85; Asst Treas. to the Queen, 1985–87; Dep. Dir (Finance), Royal Collection, 1992–93. Lay Mem., Chapter, Peterborough Cathedral, 2001– (Treas., 2004–). Trustee and Treas., Music in Country Churches, 2006–; Trustee, Country Houses Foundn, 2006–. Gov., Elstree Sch., 1987– (Vice-Chm., 2002–). *Address:* The Old Rectory, Eydon, Daventry, Northants NN11 3QE. *Clubs:* Brooks's, Pratt's.

PARSONS, Prof. (John) David, DSc; FREng, FIET; independent consultant, since 1998; David Jardine Professor of Electrical Engineering, 1982–98, and Head, Department of Electrical Engineering and Electronics, 1983–86 and 1996–98, University of Liverpool; *b* 8 July 1935; *s* of Oswald Parsons and Doris Anita (*née* Roberts); *m* 1969, Mary Winifred Stella Tate. *Educ:* University College of Wales, Cardiff (BSc); King's College London (MSc (Eng), DSc (Eng)). FIET (FIEE 1986); FREng (FEng 1988). GEC Applied Electronics Labs, 1959–62; Regent Street Poly., 1962–66; City of Birmingham Poly., 1966–68; Lectr, Sen. Lectr and Reader in Electronic Engrg, Univ. of Birmingham, 1969–82; University of Liverpool: Dean, Faculty of Engrg, 1986–89; Pro-Vice-Chancellor, 1990–96. Vis. Prof., Univ. of Auckland, 1982; Vis. Res. Engr, NTT, Japan, 1987. UN Expert in India, 1977; Hon. SPSO, RSRE, Malvern, 1978–82. Member Council: IERE, 1985–88; IEE, 1988–89. *Publications:* Electronic and Switching Circuits, 1975; Mobile Communication Systems, 1989; The Mobile Radio Propagation Channel, 1992, 2nd edn 2000; many papers on radio communication systems and radio propagation in learned jls. *Recreations:* golf, bridge, ski-ing. *Address:* 70A Freshfield Road, Formby, Merseyside L37 7BQ.

PARSONS, Sir (John) Michael, Kt 1970; Deputy Chairman and Chief Executive, 1979–81, Senior Managing Director, 1976–81, Director, 1971–81, Inchcape & Co. Ltd; *b* 29 Oct. 1915; *s* of late Rt Rev. Richard Godfrey Parsons, DD, Bishop of Hereford; *m* 1st, 1946, Hilda Mary Frewen (marr. diss. 1964); one *s* two *d*; 2nd, 1964, Caroline Inagh Margaret Frewen. *Educ:* Rossall Sch.; University Coll., Oxford. Barry & Co., Calcutta, 1937. Served in Royal Garhwal Rifles (Indian Army), 1939–45: Bde Major, 1942; POW, Singapore, 1942. Macneill & Barry Ltd, Calcutta, 1946–70; Chm. & Managing Dir, 1964–70; Chm., Macdonald Hamilton & Co. Pty Ltd, 1970–72; Chairman and Director: Assam Investments, 1976–81; Paxall Investments Ltd, 1982–84; Dep. Chm. and Dir, Inchcape Insurance Hldgs Ltd, 1979–83; Dir, Commonwealth Develt Finance Co. Ltd, 1973–86. Vice-Chm., Indian Jute Mills Assoc., 1960–61; President: Bengal Chamber of Commerce, 1968–69; Associated Chambers of Commerce of India, 1969; Chm., UK Cttee, Fedn of Commonwealth Chambers of Commerce, 1974; Mem., Advisory Council on Trade, Bd of Trade, India, 1968–69. Chm. Council, Royal Commonwealth Soc., 1976–80, Vice Pres., 1980–; Pres., India, Pakistan and Bangladesh Assoc., 1973–78, Vice Pres., 1978. Dep. Chm., Internat. Bd, United World Colls, 1981–86. *Publication:* Room to Swing a Cat (autobiog.), 2003. *Recreation:* golf. *Address:* Garrett House, Park Road, Aldeburgh, Suffolk IP15 5EN. *T:* (01728) 452917. *Club:* Oriental.

PARSONS, Luke Arthur; QC 2003; *b* 3 March 1962; *s* of John Andrew Parsons and Frances Patricia Parsons; *m* 1989, Isabelle Jane Munro; five *s*. *Educ:* John Fisher Sch., Purley; Bristol Univ. (LLB 1984). Called to the Bar, Inner Temple, 1985; practising commercial barrister, 1986–. Gov., Lineacre Centre on Bioethics, 2002–. *Publication:* (jtly) Admiralty and Commercial Forms and Precedents, 1991. *Recreations:* castles, classical music, theatre. *Address:* Quadrant Chambers, Quadrant House, 10 Fleet Street, EC4Y 1AU. *T:* (020) 7583 4444, *Fax:* (020) 7583 4455; *e-mail:* luke.parsons@quadrantchambers.com.

PARSONS, Sir Michael; *see* Parsons, Sir J. M.

PARSONS, Nicholas; *see* Parsons, C. N.

PARSONS, Prof. Peter John, FBA 1977; Regius Professor of Greek, University of Oxford, 1989–2003; Student of Christ Church, Oxford, 1964–2003; *b* 24 Sept. 1936; *s* of Robert John Parsons and Ethel Ada (*née* Frary); *m* 2006, Barbara Montagna Macleod (*d* 2006). *Educ:* Raynes Park County Grammar Sch.; Christ Church, Oxford (MA 1961). Oxford University: Craven Scholar, 1955; 1st Cl. Hons Mods and de Paravicini Scholar, 1956; Chancellor's Prize for Latin Verse and Gaisford Prize for Greek Verse, 1st Cl. Lit. Hum., Derby Scholar, Dixon and Sen. Scholar of Christ Church, 1958; Passmore Edwards Scholar, 1959; Lectr in Documentary Papyrology, 1960–65; Lectr in Papyrology, 1965–89. J. H. Gray Lectr, Univ. of Cambridge, 1982; Heller Lectr, Univ. of Calif, Berkeley, 1988. Hon. PhD: Bern, 1985; Athens, 1995; Hon. DLitt Milan, 1994. *Publications:* (jtly) The Oxyrhynchus Papyri XXXI, 1966, XXXIII and XXXIV, 1968, LIV, 1987, LIX, 1992, LX, 1994, LXVI, 1999, LXVIII, 2003, LXXI, 2007; The Oxyrhynchus Papyri XLII, 1973; (with H. Lloyd-Jones) Supplementum Hellenisticum, 1983; City of the Sharp-Nosed Fish: Greek lives in Roman Egypt, 2007; articles in learned jls. *Recreations:* music, cinema, cooking and eating. *Address:* Christ Church, Oxford OX1 1DP. *T:* (01865) 422132.

PARSONS, Sir Richard (Edmund Clement Fownes), KCMG 1982 (CMG 1977); HM Diplomatic Service, retired; Ambassador to Sweden, 1984–87; *b* 14 March 1928; *s* of Dr R. A. Parsons; *m* 1960, Jenifer Jane Mathews (*d* 1981); three *s*. *Educ:* Bembridge Sch.; Brasenose Coll., Oxford. Served in Army, 1949–51; joined HM Foreign (subseq. Diplomatic) Service, 1951; FO, 1951–53; 3rd Sec., Washington, 1953–56; 2nd Sec., Vientiane, 1956–58; FO, 1958–60; 1st Sec., Buenos Aires, 1960–63; FO, 1963–65; 1st Sec., Ankara, 1965–67; FO, 1967–69; Counsellor, Lagos, 1969–72; Head of Personnel Ops Dept, FCO, 1972–76; Ambassador to: Hungary, 1976–79; Spain, 1980–84. Plays produced in London, Edinburgh and Brighton. Chm., W Norfolk Music Soc., 2004–. *Publications:* The Moon Pool, 1988; Mortmain and other plays, 1993; *as John Haythorne:* None of Us Cared for Kate, 1968; The Strelsau Dimension, 1981; Mandrake in Granada, 1984; Mandrake in the Monastery, 1985. *Recreations:* reading, writing, music, travel. *Address:* Lancaster House, Old Methwold Road, Whittington, King's Lynn, Norfolk PE33 9TN. *Club:* Garrick.

See also C. A. H. Parsons.

PARSONS, Roger, PhD, DSc; FRS 1980; FRSC; Professor of Chemistry, University of Southampton, 1985–92, now Emeritus; *b* 31 Oct. 1926; *s* of Robert Harry Ashby Parsons and Ethel Fenton; *m* 1953, Ruby Millicent Turner; three *s* one *d*. *Educ:* King Alfred Sch., Hampstead; Strathcona High Sch., Edmonton, Alta; Imperial Coll. of Science and Technol., (BSc, PhD). DSc Bristol 1962; ARCS 1946; FRIC 1962. Asst Lectr, Imp. Coll. of Science and Technol., 1948–50; Deedes Fellow, UC Dundee, St Andrews Univ., 1950–54; Lectr, then Reader in Electrochem., Bristol Univ., 1954–79; Dir, Lab. d'Electrochimie Interfaciale, Centre Nat. de la Recherche Scientifique, Meudon, France, 1977–84. Unesco Specialist, Buenos Aires, 1961; Vis. Prof., Calif Inst. of Technol., 1966–67. Editor, Jl of Electroanal. Chem., 1962–99. Royal Society of Chemistry: Pres., Faraday Div., 1991–93 (Vice-Pres., 1984–91, 1993–99); Liversidge Lectr, 1989–90. Hon. Fellow, Polish Chem. Soc., 1981. Palladium Medal, US Electrochem. Soc., 1979; Bruno Breyer Medal, Electrochem. Div., RACI, 1980; Prix Paul Pascal de l'Acad. des Scis, 1983; Galvani Medal, Electrochem. Div., Italian Chem. Soc., 1986; Frumkin Meml Medal, Internat. Soc. of Electrochem., 2000; Davy Medal, Royal Soc., 2003. DUniv Buenos Aires, 1997. *Publications:* Electrochemical Data, 1956; (ed with J. Lyklema) Electrical Properties of Interfaces, 1983; (ed jtly) Standard Potentials in Aqueous Solution, 1985; (ed with R. Kalvoda) Electrochemistry in Research and Development, 1985; *circa* 200 papers in scientific jls. *Recreations:* listening to music, going to the opera. *Address:* 16 Thornhill Road, Bassett, Southampton SO16 7AT.

PARSONS, Susie; Managing Director, Susie Parsons Management Solutions, since 2005; *b* 29 April 1950; *d* of Alfred and Dorothy Parsons; partner, Dave Perry; one *s*. *Educ:* E Grinstead Co. Grammar Sch.; Univ. of Lancaster (BA Hons French Studies); King's Coll. London (PGCE). Teacher of French, John Kelly Girls' High Sch., LB of Brent, 1973–74; Dir, Community Educn, Shelter, 1974–77; Housing Projects Officer, N Kensington Law Centre, 1977–81; Sec., Paddington and N Kensington CHC, 1981–84; Gen. Manager, London Energy and Employment Network, 1984–87; Hd, Press and Publicity, London Borough of Hackney, 1987–94; Exec. Dir, 1994–97, Chief Exec., 1997–99, London Lighthouse; Chief Exec., CRE, 1999–2001; ind. mgt consultant, 2001–02; Chief Exec., Campaign for Learning, 2002–05. *Publications:* (jtly) Workout, 1979; The Right Side of the Law, 1993; (jtly) Learning to Learn in Schools, 2005; (jtly) Learning to Learn for Life, 2005; (contrib.) Reinventing Education, 2005; numerous reports, pamphlets, articles etc on health, social care, quality, equality, women in mgt and lifelong learning. *Recreations:* friendship, swimming, voluntary work, the arts. *Address:* 171 Oxford Gardens, W10 6NE; *e-mail:* susie@spms.org.uk.

PARSONS, (Thomas) Alan, CB 1984; LLB; Chief Adjudication Officer, Department of Health and Social Security, 1984–86; *b* 25 Nov. 1924; *s* of late Arthur and Laura Parsons; *m* 1st, 1947, Valerie Vambeck; one *s*; 2nd, 1957, Muriel Lewis; two *s*. *Educ:* Clifton Coll.; Bristol Univ. (LLB). Called to the Bar, Middle Temple, 1950. Served, Royal Marines, 1943–46. Legal Asst, Min. of Nat. Insurance, 1950; Sen. Legal Asst, Min. of Pensions and Nat. Insurance, 1955; Asst Solicitor, 1968, Principal Asst Solicitor, 1977, DHSS. *Recreations:* walking, listening to music. *Address:* 18 Alpine Grove, E9 7SX. *T:* (020) 8986 0930.

PÄRT, Arvo; free-lance composer, since 1982; *b* Estonia, 11 Sept. 1935; *s* of August Pärt and Linda Anette Pärt (*née* Mäll); *m* 1st, 1959, Hille Aasmäe (marr. diss.); one *d*; one *d* by Marina Nestieva; 2nd, 1972, Nora Supina; two *s*. *Educ:* composition studies with Heino Eller, Conservatory of Music, Tallinn, Estonia. Sound Engr, Estonian broadcasting station, Tallinn, 1958–67; free-lance composer, Tallinn, 1967–80; emigrated to Vienna, 1980; became Austrian citizen, 1981; Scholar, Deutscher Akademischer Austauschdienst, Berlin, 1981. Hon. Member: Amer. Acad. of Arts and Letters, 1996; Royal Sch. of Church Music, 2003; Accad. Nazionale di Santa Cecilia, Rome, 2004; Associate Mem., Royal Acad. of Sci and Fine Arts, Belgium, 2001. Hon. PhD: Acad. of Music, Tallinn, 1990; Royal Swedish Music Acad., 1991; Hon. DMus: Sydney, 1996; Durham, 2002; Hon. Dr: Univ. of Tartu, Estonia, 1998; Univ. Nacional de Gen. San Martin Escuela de Humanidades, Argentina, 2003; Freiburg, 2007. Triumph award, Russia, 1997; Culture Prize, Estonia, 1998; Herder Award, Germany, 2000; Composition Trophy C. A. Seghizzi, Gorizia, Italy, 2003; Borderland Award, Sejny, Poland, 2003; Composer of the Year, Musical America, 2005; Eur. Award of Sacred Music, Germany, 2005; Internat. Brückepreis, Görlitz/Zgorzelec, Germany/Poland, 2007; Baltic Star Prize, St Petersburg, 2007; Sonning Music Prize, Denmark, 2008. Order of the Nat. Coat of Arms (Estonia), 2nd class 1998, 1st class 2006; Commandeur de l'Ordre des Arts et des Lettres (France), 2001; Cross of Honour for Sci. and Art, 1st class (Austria). *Compositions* include: Sinfonie No 1, 1963; Sinfonie No 2, 1966; Credo, 1968; Sinfonie No 3, 1971; Fratres (variations for ensembles, orchestra and various instruments), 1977, 1980, 1983, 1985, 1989, 1990, 1991, 1992; Tabula Rasa (double violin concerto), 1977; Sarah was Ninety Years Old, 1977, 1990; Passio, 1982; Stabat Mater, 1985; Te Deum, 1985; Miserere, 1989; Berliner Messe (choir, soloists and organ), 1990; Berliner Messe (choir, soloists and string orch.), 1991; Sieben Magnificat-Antiphonen, 1991; Litany (soloists, choir and orch.), 1994; Kanon Pokajanen (choir a cappella), 1997; Como anhela la Cierva (solo soprano and orch.), 1999; Cantique des Degrés (choir and orch.), 1999; Orient et Occident (orch.), 2000 (Classical Brit Contemp. Music Award, 2003); Cecilia, Vergine Romana (choir and orch.), 2000; Salve Regina (choir and organ), 2002; Lamentate (piano and orch.), 2003; In Principio (choir and orch.), 2003; Passacaglia (violin and piano), 2003; L'Abbé Agathon (soprano and 8 celli), 2004; Da Pacem Domine (choir and instruments), 2004; Vater Unser (voice and piano), 2005; Für Lennart (orch.), 2006; La Sindone (violin and orch.), 2006; Passacaglia (violin or two violins and orch.), 2007; These Words... (string orch.), 2008. *Address:* c/o Universal Edition Ltd, 48 Great Marlborough Street, W1V 2BN.

PARTHIER, Prof. Benno; Director, Institut für Pflanzenbiochemie, Halle, 1990–98, now Emeritus; President, Deutsche Akademie der Naturforscher Leopoldina, 1990–2003; *b* 21 Aug. 1932; *s* of Hermann and Helene Parthier; *m* 1967, Christiane Luecke; one *s* two *d*. *Educ:* Martin Luther Univ., Halle-Wittenberg (Dip. Biol. 1958; Dr rer. nat. 1961; Dr habil. 1967). Asst, Botanical Inst., Univ. Halle, 1958–65; Head, Dept of Molecular Biol., Inst. of Plant Biochemistry, Acad. of Scis, GDR, 1967–90. Mem., learned socs, Germany and overseas. Hon. Dr Würzburg, 2003. *Publications:* (with R. Wollgiehn) Von der Zelle zum Molekül, 1971 (Polish edn 1976); (with L. Nover and M. Luckner) Zell differenzierung, Molekulare Grundlagen und Probleme, 1978 (English edn 1982); numerous papers in sci. jls; Editor or co-Editor 10 sci. jls. *Recreations:* gardening, travelling. *Address:* Deutsche Akademie der Naturforscher Leopoldina, Emil Abderhalden-Strasse 37, 06108 Halle, Germany. *T:* (345) 4723915.

PARTINGTON, Adrian Frederick, FRCO; Director of Music, Gloucester Cathedral, since 2008; Artistic Director, BBC National Chorus of Wales, since 2000; *b* Nottingham,

1 Oct. 1958; *s* of Kendrick and Mary Partington; *m* 1981, Clare Diana Crane; four *s* one *d*. *Educ:* King's Sch., Worcester; Royal Coll. of Music; King's Coll., Cambridge (BA 1981). FRCO 1978. Organ Scholar: St George's Chapel, Windsor, 1976–78; King's Coll., Cambridge, 1978–81; Asst Organist, Worcester Cathedral, 1981–91; Dir of Music, Sch. of St Mary and St Anne, Abbots Bromley, 1991–95; Lectr, RWCMD, 1995–. Conductor: City of Birmingham Symphony Youth Chorus, 1995–2000; Bristol Choral Soc., 2000–. Jt Artistic Dir, Three Choirs Fest., 2008–. *Address:* 7 Millers Green, Gloucester GL1 2BN. *T:* (01452) 524764; *e-mail:* a.partington@gloucestercathedral.org.uk.

PARTINGTON, Ven. Brian Harold, OBE 2002; Archdeacon of Man, 1996–2005, now Emeritus; Vicar of St George's, Douglas, 1996–2004; *b* 31 Dec. 1936; *s* of Harold Partington and Edith (*née* Hall); *m* 1962, Valerie Nurton; two *s* one *d*. *Educ:* Burnage Grammar Sch., Manchester; St Aidan's Coll., Birkenhead. Nat. Service, RAF, 1955–57; local govt officer, Manchester Corp., 1953–59. Ordained deacon, 1963, priest, 1964; Assistant Curate: Emmanuel Church, Didsbury, Manchester, 1963–66; St Mary's, Deane, Bolton, 1966–68; Vicar: Kirk Patrick, Sodor and Man, 1968–96; Foxdale, 1977–96; St John's, 1977–96. Bishop's Youth Officer, 1968–77; Rural Dean of Peel, 1976–96; Canon of St Patrick, St German's Cathedral, 1985–96. Pres., Hospice Care, 2008– (Chm., 1988–96; Vice Pres., 1996–2008). Exec. Chm., IOM Sports Council, 1990–2002; Chm., Internat. Island Games Orgn, 2005–07 (Vice-Chm., 2001–05; Hon. Life Mem., 2007); Principal, RYA Trng Centre, IOM Yacht Club, 2006–; President: IOM Hockey Assoc., 1997–2006; IOM Cricket Assoc., 1998–2006; Pres. Elect, IOM Union, 2008. Mem., Douglas Rotary Club. *Recreations:* cricket, golf, travel. *Address:* Brambles, Kirk Patrick, Isle of Man IM5 3AH. *T:* (01624) 844173. *Clubs:* Royal Commonwealth Society; St John's Cricket; Peel Golf (Capt., 2006).

PARTINGTON, Gillian Doreen, (Mrs W. D. Partington); *see* Ruaux, G. D.

PARTINGTON, Prof. (Thomas) Martin, CBE 2002; Professor of Law, Bristol University, 1987–2006, now Emeritus; Special Consultant to the Law Commission, 2006–07 (a Law Commissioner, 2001–05); *b* 5 March 1944; *s* of Thomas Paulett Partington and Alice Emily Mary Partington; *m* 1st, 1970, Marcia Carol Leavey (marr. diss.); one *s*; 2nd, 1978, Daphne Isobel Scharenguivel; one *s* one *d*. *Educ:* King's Sch., Canterbury; Peterhouse, Cambridge (BA 1965; LLB 1966). Called to the Bar, Middle Temple, 1984, Bencher, 2006. Asst Lectr, Bristol Univ., 1966–69; Lectr, Warwick Univ., 1969–73, LSE, 1973–80; Prof. of Law, Brunel Univ., 1980–87 (Dean, Faculty of Soc. Scis, 1985–87); Dean, Faculty of Law, 1988–92, Pro-Vice-Chancellor, 1995–99, Bristol Univ. Visiting Professor: Osgoode Hall Law Sch., Canada, 1976; Univ. of NSW, 1983; Vis. Sen. Res. Fellow, Inst. of Advanced Legal Studies, 2006–. Academic Advr, Coll. of Law, 2006–. Chm., Cttee of Heads of Univ. Law Schools, 1990–92. Vice-Chm., Legal Action Gp, 1982–83; Member: Lord Chancellor's Adv. Cttee on Legal Aid, 1988–91; Law Society's Trng Cttee, 1989–92; Law Society's Academic Consultative Cttee, 1989–92; Judicial Studies Bd, 1992–95 (Mem., Tribunals Cttee, 1988–95); Trng Cttee, Indep. Tribunal Service, 1990–94; Council on Tribunals, 1994–2000; Civil Justice Council, 1998–2005; Bd, United Bristol Healthcare NHS Trust, 1998–2001; Adv. Cttee, Leverhulme Trust Res. Awards, 1999–2006; External Adviser, Educn and Trng Cttee, Inst. of Housing, 1985–89. Part time Chairman: Soc. Security Appeals Tribunal, 1990–94; Med. Appeals Tribunal, 1992–94; Disability Appeals Tribunal, 1992–94. Expert Consultant: Leggatt Review of Tribunals, 2000–01; Employment Tribunals Taskforce, 2001–02. Barrister, Chambers of A. Arden, QC, 1993–. Chm., Socio-Legal Studies Assoc., 1993–95. Gen. Editor, Anglo-American Law, now Common Law World, Review, 1984–2003. FRSA 1999. Hon. Fellow, Soc. of Advanced Legal Studies, 2001. Hon. QC 2008. *Publications:* Landlord and Tenant, 1975; Claim in Time, 1978; (with A. Arden) Housing Law, 1983; (with P. O'Higgins) Bibliography of Social Security Law, 1986; Secretary of State's Powers of Adjudication in Social Security Law, 1990; (with J. Hill) Housing Law: cases, materials and commentary, 1991; United Kingdom: Social Security Law, 1998; (with M. Harris) Administrative Justice in the 21st Century, 1999; English Legal System: an introduction, 2000, 4th edn 2008; articles on public law, housing law, social security law, legal educn, Legal Aid and Legal Services. *Recreations:* playing the violin, reading fiction, cooking. *Address:* First Floor Flat, 8/9 Clifton Hill, Bristol BS8 1BN. *T:* (0117) 973 6294.

PARTRIDGE, Bernard B.; *see* Brook-Partridge.

PARTRIDGE, Derek William, CMG 1987; HM Diplomatic Service, retired; *b* 15 May 1931; *o s* of late Ernest and Ethel Elizabeth Partridge (*née* Buckingham), Wembley. *Educ:* Preston Manor County Grammar Sch., Wembley. Entered Foreign Service (later Diplomatic Service), 1949. Royal Air Force, 1949–51. Served: Foreign Office, 1951–54; Oslo, 1954–56; Jedda, 1956; Khartoum, 1957–60; Sofia, 1960–62; Bangkok, 1962; Manila, 1962–65; Djakarta, 1965–67; FCO, 1967–70; Diplomatic Service Inspectorate, 1970–72; British Consul-General, Brisbane, 1972–74; First Sec. (Economic and Commercial), Colombo, 1974–77; FCO, 1977–86: Counsellor and Head of Migration and Visa Dept, 1981–83; Counsellor and Head of Nationality and Treaty Dept, 1983–86; High Comr, Sierra Leone, 1986–91. Mem. (Lib Dem) Southwark BC, 1994–2002. Mem., Royal African Soc. *Address:* 16 Wolfe Crescent, Rotherhithe, SE16 6SF. *T:* and *Fax:* (020) 7231 2759. *Club:* National Liberal.

PARTRIDGE, Ian Harold, CBE 1992; concert singer (tenor); *b* 12 June 1938; *s* of late Harold Partridge and Ena Stinson; *m* 1959, Ann Glover; two *s*. *Educ:* New Coll., Oxford (chorister); Clifton Coll. (music scholar); Royal Coll. of Music; Guildhall Sch. of Music (LGSM, singing and teaching). Began as piano accompanist, although sang tenor in Westminster Cath. Choir, 1958–62; full-time concert singer, 1963–; performs in England and all over the world, both in recitals (with sister Jennifer) and in concerts; has worked with many leading conductors, incl. Stokowski, Boult, Giulini, Boulez and Colin Davis. Opera debut at Covent Garden as Iopas in Berlioz, Les Troyens, 1969. Title role, Britten's St Nicolas, Thames Television (Prix Italia, 1977). Over 150 records, *including:* Bach, St John Passion; Handel, Chandos Anthems, and Esther; Schubert, Die Schöne Müllerin, Die Winterreise; Schumann, Dichterliebe; Beethoven, An die ferne Geliebte; Vaughan-Williams, On Wenlock Edge; Warlock, The Curlew; Fauré and Duparc Songs; Britten, Serenade and Winter Words; Lord Berners, Complete Songs; as conductor (of Pro Cantione Antiqua), The Triumphs of Oriana. Innumerable radio broadcasts, many TV appearances. Prof., RAM, 1996–. Chm., Royal Soc. of Musicians, 1999–2001 (Gov., 1995–99); Pres., ISM, 1996–97; Dir, Performing Artists' Media Rights Assoc., 1996–2002. Governor, Clifton Coll., 1981–. Sir Charles Santley Meml Gift, Musicians' Co., 1992. Hon. RAM 1996. Harriet Cohen Award, 1967. *Recreations:* bridge, horse racing, theatre, cricket. *Address:* 127 Pepys Road, SW20 8NP. *Club:* Garrick.

PARTRIDGE, John Albert, CBE 1981; RA; FRIBA; architect in private practice; a Senior and Founder Partner, Howell, Killick, Partridge & Amis (HKPA), 1959–95, now Consultant; *b* 26 Aug. 1924; *s* of George and Gladys Partridge; *m* 1953, Doris (*née* Foreman); one *s* one *d*. *Educ:* Shooter's Hill Grammar Sch., Woolwich; Polytechnic School of Architecture, Regent Street. FRIBA 1966 (ARIBA 1951); RA 1988 (ARA 1980). London County Council Housing Architects Dept, 1951–59; Design Tutor, Architectural Assoc., 1958–61. The work of HKPA includes universities, colleges, public buildings, housing and leisure buildings; principal commissions include: Wolfson, Rayne and Gatehouse building, St Anne's Coll., Oxford; New Hall and Common Room building, St Antony's Coll., Oxford; Wells Hall, Reading Univ.; Middlesex Polytechnic College of Art, Cat Hill; Medway Magistrates' Court; The Albany, Deptford; Hall of Justice, Trinidad and Tobago; Warrington Court House; Basildon Magistrates' Courthouse; Berlin Mineral Spa Project; Haywards Heath Magistrates' Courthouse; Japanese University Chaucer Coll., Univ. of Kent, Canterbury. RIBA: Vice-Pres., 1977–79; Hon. Librarian, 1977–81; Chm. Res. Steering Gp, 1977–84. Vice-Pres., Concrete Soc., 1979–81. External Examiner in Architecture: Bath Univ., 1975–78, 1992; Thames Polytechnic, 1978–86; Cambridge Univ., 1979–81; Manchester Univ., 1982; South Bank Polytechnic, 1982–86; Brighton Polytechnic, 1987–90; RCA, 1991–93. Governor, Building Centre Trust, 1982–96; Chm., Assoc. of Consultant Architects, 1983–85. Mem., NEDO Construction Res. Strategy Cttee, 1983–86; Architect Mem., FCO Adv. Bd on the Diplomatic Estate, 1985–92. Award for dist. services to archt., Assoc. of Consultant Architects, 2005. *Publications:* articles in technical press. *Recreations:* looking at buildings, travel, sketching and taking photographs. *Address:* Cudham Court, Cudham, near Sevenoaks, Kent TN14 7QF. *T:* (01959) 571294. *Club:* Arts.

PARTRIDGE, Prof. Linda, CBE 2003; FRS 1996; FRSE; Weldon Professor of Biometry, University College London, since 1994; *b* 18 March 1950; *d* of George and Ida Partridge; *m* 1st, 1983, Dr V. K. French (marr. diss. 1992); 2nd, 1996, Prof. Michael John Morgan, *qv*. *Educ:* Convent of the Sacred Heart, Tunbridge Wells; St Anne's Coll., Oxford (MA); Wolfson Coll., Oxford (DPhil 1974). Post-doctoral Fellow, York Univ., 1974–76; Edinburgh University: Lectr, 1976–87; Reader in Zoology, 1987–92; Prof. of Evolutionary Biol., 1992–93; NERC Res. Prof., 1997–2002, BBSRC Professorial Fellow, 2002–07, UCL. Mem. Council, BBSRC, 1998–2001. Trustee, Natural Hist. Mus., 2000–08. President: Internat. Soc. for Behavioural Ecology, 1990–92; Assoc. for Study of Animal Behaviour, 1995–97; Genetical Soc., 1999–2003. Member: Eur. Acad. of Scis, 2004; EMBO, 2005. FRSE 1992; FMedSci 2004. Hon. DSc St Andrews, 2004. Frink Medal, Zool Soc. of London, 2000; Sewall Wright Award, Amer. Soc. of Naturalists, 2002; Fondation IPSEN Longevity Prize, 2004; Lord Cohen Medal, British Soc. for Res. on Ageing, 2004; Medal, Assoc. for Study of Animal Behaviour, 2005. *Publications:* on ageing and evolutionary biology in scientific jls. *Recreations:* tennis, hill walking, gardening. *Address:* Department of Biology, University College London, Darwin Building, Gower Street, WC1E 6BT.

PARTRIDGE, Sir Michael (John Anthony), KCB 1990 (CB 1983); Permanent Secretary, Department of Social Security, 1988–95; *b* 29 Sept. 1935; *s* of late Dr John Henry Partridge, DSc, PhD, and Ethel Green; *m* 1968, Joan Elizabeth Hughes; two *s* one *d*. *Educ:* Merchant Taylors'; St John's Coll., Oxford (BA (1st Cl. Hons Mods and Lit Hum) 1960, MA 1963; Hon. Fellow, 1991). Entered Home Civil Service (Min. of Pensions and Nat. Insce), 1960; Private Sec. to Permanent Sec., 1962–64; Principal, 1964–71 (MPNI, Min. of Social Security and DHSS); DHSS: Asst Sec., 1971–76; Under Sec., 1976–81; Dep. Sec., 1981–83; Dep. Under-Sec. of State, Home Office, 1983–87; Second Permanent Sec., DHSS, 1987–88. Non-executive Director: Norwich Union, 1996–2000; Epworth Investment Mgt Ltd, 1996–; The Stationery Office, 1997–99; Aviva (formerly CGNU), 2000–03; Harefield Res. Foundn, 2001– (Vice-Chm., 2003–); Chm., The Stationery Office Pension Scheme, 2003–. Senior Treasurer, Methodist Ch Finance Div., 1980–96; Mem., Central Finance Bd and Council, Methodist Ch, 1980–. Trustee: Harefield Hosp. Heart Transplant Trust, 1991–2003; Methodist Ministers' Pensions Trust, 1993–. Member: Court, Univ. of York, 1991–95; Council, Univ. of Sheffield, 2001–03. Governor: Middlesex Univ., 1992– (Chm., 1997–2001; Pro-Chancellor, 2002–); Merchant Taylors' Sch., 1992–99; Chm. of Govs, Heathfield Sch., 2004–. Pres., Old Merchant Taylor's Soc., 2002–03. CCMI (CBIM 1988). Liveryman, Merchant Taylors' Co., 1987. *Recreations:* Do-it-Yourself, classical sites, reading, ski-ing. *Address:* 27 High View, Pinner, Middlesex HA5 3NZ. *T:* (020) 8868 0657. *Club:* Oxford and Cambridge.

PASCALL, David Lewis, CBE 1993; Managing Director, Pascall Associates, European business and financial consultancy, since 2008; *b* 5 Feb. 1949; *s* of Robert Lewis Pascall and Dorothy Pascall (*née* Smith); *m* 1980, Carolyn Judith White; one *s* two *d*. *Educ:* Queen Mary's Grammar Sch., Basingstoke; Univ. of Birmingham (BSc 1st Cl. Hons Chem. Engrg 1970); INSEAD, Fontainebleau (MBA Dist. 1979). With British Petroleum Co. plc, 1967–93: posts in oil refining, trading, finance and business management in UK and, 1974–79, Germany and France; Divl Manager, BP Finance Internat., 1986–89; Manager: BP Share Sale, 1987; Project 1990 (cultural change prog.), 1989–93; Finance Dir, 1993–94, Chief Exec., Asia Pacific, 1994–95, MAI plc; Finance Dir to Hon. Sir Rocco Forte, 1996–98; Eur. Transaction Dir, Prin. Finance Gp, Nomura Internat., 2000–02; Man. Dir, Terra Firma Capital Partners Ltd, 2002–07. On secondment to: Central Policy Rev. Staff, Cabinet Office, 1982–83; No 10 Policy Unit, 1983–84. Non-exec. Dir, Colt Gp Ltd, 1999–2000. Advr, MoD Defence Costs Review, 1994. Mem., 1990–91, Chm., 1991–93, Nat. Curriculum Council; Mem. Exec. Cttee, Field Studies Council, 1993–99. Mem., Develt Adv. Council, Univ. of Birmingham, 2005–. Foundn Gov., Sir John Cass and Redcoat Comprehensive Sch., Stepney, 1995–2001. Mem., Nat Soc., 1994–2000. FRSA 1993. *Recreations:* my family, current affairs, golf. *Address:* 31 Lanchester Road, N6 4SX. *T:* (020) 8883 7708; *e-mail:* david@pascallassociates.co.uk. *Clubs:* Highgate Golf, Trevose Golf.

PASCO, Adam Gerhold; Editor, BBC Gardeners' World magazine, since 1991; Editorial Director, BBC Magazines' Gardening Group, since 2003; *b* 11 Jan. 1957; *s* of Cecil Filmer Pasco and Sheila Mary Pasco (*née* Gerhold); *m* 1992, Jayne Petra Fisher; one *s* one *d*. *Educ:* North East Surrey Coll. of Tech. (HND Applied Biology 1977); Univ. of Nottingham (BSc Horticulture 1982). Technical Editor, 1982–84, Editor, 1984–88, Garden Answers magazine; Editor, Garden News, 1988–90. Gardening Correspondent, Daily Telegraph, 1995–2000; Ed., then Editl Dir, BBC Easy Gardening magazine, 2002–06. *Publications:* Collins Complete Garden Manual, 1998; Greenfingers Book, 1999; Collins Gardeners' Calendar, 2000. *Recreations:* gardening, cookery, photography, writing, walking, travel, family life.

PASCO, Richard Edward, CBE 1977; actor; Hon. Associate Artist, Royal Shakespeare Company; *b* 18 July 1926; *s* of Cecil George Pasco and Phyllis Irene Pasco; *m* 1st, Greta (*née* Watson) (marr. diss.); one *s*; 2nd, 1967, Barbara Leigh-Hunt, *qv*. *Educ:* Colet Court; King's Coll. Sch., Wimbledon; Central Sch. of Speech and Drama (Gold Medallist). Served HM Forces, 1944–48. 1st stage appearance, She Stoops to Conquer, 1943; 1st London appearance, Zero Hour, Lyric, 1944; 1st New York appearance, The Entertainer, 1958. London appearances include: leading roles, English Stage Co., Royal Court, 1957; The Entertainer, Palace, 1957; The Lady from the Sea, Queen's, 1961; Teresa of Avila, Vaudeville, 1961; Look Homeward, Angel, Phoenix, 1962; The New Men, Strand, 1962; The Private Ear and the Public Eye, Globe, 1963; Bristol Old Vic: Henry V (title role), Berowne in Love's Labour's Lost, 1964; Peer Gynt (title role), Angelo in Measure for Measure, Hamlet (title role), 1966 (and world tour); Ivanov, Phoenix, 1965; The Italian Girl, Wyndham's, 1968. Joined RSC, 1969; leading roles include: Becket, Murder in the

Cathedral, Aldwych, 1972; (alternated with Ian Richardson) Richard and Bolingbroke in Richard II, Stratford-on-Avon, 1973, and Stratford and Aldwych, 1974; Jacques in As You Like It, 1973; tour of Amer. univs; Jack Tanner in Man and Superman, Malvern Festival, tour and Savoy, 1977; Timon in Timon of Athens, Clarence in Richard III, Arkady Schatslivtses in The Forest, Stratford, 1980–81; La Ronde, Aldwych, 1982; Soren in The Seagull, Stratford, tour and Barbican, 2000; National Theatre: The Father in Six Characters in Search of an Author, Pavel in Fathers and Sons, 1987; Rt Rev. Charlie Allen in Racing Demon, 1990, 1993; Sir Peter Edgecombe in Murmuring Judges, 1991, 1993; Birling in An Inspector Calls, 1992; Malcolm Pryce in Absence of War, 1993; Boss Findley in Sweet Bird of Youth, 1994. Many foreign tours; accompanied HSH Princess Grace of Monaco at Edinburgh, Stratford and Aldeburgh Festivals and on tour of USA, 1977–78. Frequent appearances at Aldeburgh, Brighton, Windsor and Harrogate festivals, Stratford-upon-Avon Poetry Festival etc. Recent films: A Watcher in the Woods; Wagner; Mrs Brown. Countless TV and radio appearances; recent television series: Sorrell & Son; Drummonds; Hannay; Inspector Morse; Absence of War; Kavanagh QC, Hetty Wainthropp Investigates, etc. Many recordings of poems, plays, recitals, etc. Life Trustee, Shakespeare Birthplace Trust, 1992. *Publications:* (contrib.) Shakespeare in Perspective, 1982; (contrib.) Time and Concord: Aldeburgh Festival recollections, 1997; (contrib.) Acting in Stratford, 1997. *Recreations:* music, gardening, reading. *Address:* c/o Michael Whitehall Ltd, 10 Lower Common South, SW15 1BP. *Club:* Garrick.

PASCO, Rowanne, (Mrs William FitzGerald); writer and broadcaster; *b* 7 Oct. 1938; *d* of John and Ann Pasco; *m* 1994, Rev. William FitzGerald (*d* 2004). *Educ:* Dominican Convent, Chingford; Ursuline Convent, Ilford; Open Univ. (BA Hons). Reporter, 1956–57, Editor, 1957–58, Chingford Express; Publicity Officer, NFU, 1958–59; Account Exec., Leslie Frewin PR, 1959–60; Travel Rep., Horizon Holidays, 1960–64; Publicity Asst, Paramount Pictures Corp., Hollywood, 1964–66; Publicity Officer, Religious Progs, Radio and TV, BBC, 1966–71; Reporter, BBC Radio London, 1971–72; TV Editor, Ariel, BBC Staff Newspaper, 1972–74; Radio 4 Reporter, 1974–76; Researcher, Religious Progs, BBC TV, 1976–77; Producer and Presenter, Religious Progs, BBC Radio, 1977–78; Dep. Editor, 1979–81, Editor, 1981–87, The Universe; Religious Editor, TV-am, 1987–92; religious correspondent, GMTV, 1993–94; Editl Advr, CCJ, 1994–2006; Presenter, Daily Service, BBC Radio 4, 2005–. *Publications:* (ed with Fr John Redford) Faith Alive, 1988, New Catechism edn, 1994; Answers to One Hundred & One Questions on the Catechism, 1995; Why I am a Catholic, 1995. *Recreations:* cats, gardening, Italy, creative cooking. *Address:* 12 The Dell, Blockley, Glos GL56 9DB.

PASCOE, Alan Peter, MBE 1975; Chairman, Fast Track, since 1998; *b* 11 Oct. 1947; *s* of late Ernest George Frank Pascoe and of Joan Rosina Pascoe; *m* 1970, Della Patricia (*née* James); one *s* one *d*. *Educ:* Portsmouth Southern Grammar Sch.; Borough Road Coll. (Cert. in Educn); London Univ. (BEd Hons). Master, Dulwich Coll., 1971–74; Lectr in Physical Educn, Borough Road Coll., Isleworth, 1974–80. Dir, 1976–83, Man. Dir, 1983, Chm., 1985–98, CEO, 1994–98, Alan Pascoe Associates Ltd, then API Gp of Cos; Chm., Carat Sponsorship, 1987–92; Dir, WCRS, then Aegis Gp, 1986–92. Vice Chm., London 2012 Olympic Bid, 2003–05. Member: Sports Council, 1974–80; Minister for Sport's Working Party on Centres of Sporting Excellence; BBC Adv. Council, 1975–79. European Indoor Champion, 50m Hurdles, 1969; Europ. Games Silver Medallist, 110m Hurdles, 1971; Silver Medal, Olympic Games, Munich, 4×400m Relay, 1972; Europa Gold Cup Medallist, 400m Hurdles, 1973; Commonwealth Games Gold Medal, 400m Hurdles, and Silver Medal, 4×400m Relay, 1974; Europ. Champion and Gold Medallist in both 400m Hurdles and 4×400m Relay, 1974; Europa Cup Gold Medallist, 400m Hurdles, 1975; Olympic Finalist (injured), Montreal, 1976; Europe's Rep., World Cup, 1977. DUniv Brunel, 1997. Hollis Sports Person of the Year, 2004. *Publication:* An Autobiography, 1979. *Recreations:* theatre, sport. *Address:* Fast Track, One Brewers Green, Buckingham Gate, SW1H 0RH.

PASCOE, Martin Michael; QC 2002; *b* 1953; *s* of late Michael Raymond Pascoe and Dorothy Agnes Pascoe. *Educ:* Christ Church, Oxford (BA Juris. 1976, BCL 1977). Called to the Bar, Lincoln's Inn, 1977; in practice, specialising in corporate and internat. insolvency law. *Address:* 3–4 South Square, Gray's Inn, WC1R 5HP. *T:* (020) 7696 9900, *Fax:* (020) 7696 9911; *e-mail:* martinpascoe@southsquare.com.

PASCOE, Dr Michael William; Head of Science, Camberwell College of Arts (formerly Camberwell School of Arts and Crafts), 1981–90; *b* 16 June 1930; *s* of Canon W. J. T. Pascoe and Mrs D. Pascoe; *m* 1st, 1956, Janet Clark (marr. diss. 1977); three *d*; 2nd, 1977, Brenda Hale Reed; one *d*. *Educ:* St John's, Leatherhead; Selwyn Coll., Cambridge (BA, PhD). MInstP. Res. Student (Tribology), Cambridge, 1951–55; Physicist: Mount Vernon Hosp., Northwood, 1956–57; British Nylon Spinners Ltd, 1957–60; Chemist/Physicist, ICI Paints Div., 1960–67; Lectr (Polymer Science), Brunel Univ., 1967–77; Principal Scientific Officer, 1976–79, Keeper of Conservation and Technical Services, 1979–81, British Museum. Tutor and Counsellor, Open Univ., 1971–76. Occasional Lectr: Winchester Coll., 1989–90; Univ. of Stirling, 1991–; Camberwell Coll. of Arts; Vis. Lectr in Materials, Univ. of Brunel, 1995 and 1999. Consultant to: Royal Acad. of Arts (Great Japan exhibn), 1982–; Mary Rose Trust, 1978–83; Council for the Care of Churches, 1980–91; Public Record Office (Domesday exhibn), 1986; Science Museum, 1988; Parliament of Guyana, 1991–; Govt and cultural instns of Guatemala on conservation matters, 1996–. FRSA. *Publications:* contrib. to books on polymer tribol. and technol.; articles in scientific, engrg and conservation jls on tribol., materials technol. and on conservation methods. *Recreations:* painting and drawing, active in University of the Third Age, *inter alia*.

PASCOE, Nigel Spencer Knight; QC 1988; a Recorder of the Crown Court, since 1979; *b* 18 Aug. 1940; *er s* of late Ernest Sydney Pascoe and of Cynthia Pascoe; *m* 1964, Elizabeth Anne Walter; two *s* four *d*. *Educ:* Epsom Coll. Called to the Bar, Inner Temple, 1966, Bencher, 1996; Leader, Western Circuit, 1995–98; a Pres., Mental Health Review Tribunal, 2002–. Chm., Bar Public Affairs Cttee, 1996–98. County Councillor for Lyndhurst, Hants, 1979–84. Founder and Editor, All England Qly Law Cassettes, 1976–85; Chm., Editl Bd, Counsel mag., 2000–07. *Publications:* The Trial of Penn and Mead, 1985; The Nearly Man, 1994; Pro Patria, 1996; Who Killed William Rufus?, 2000; Without Consent, 2004; To Encourage the Others, 2006; articles in legal jls. *Recreations:* theatre, devising and presenting with Elizabeth Pascoe legal anthologies, after-dinner speaking, cricket, play writing, broadcasting. *Address:* 3 Pump Court, Temple, EC4Y 7AJ. *T:* (020) 7353 0711. *Club:* Garrick.

PASCOE, Gen. Sir Robert (Alan), KCB 1985; MBE 1968; Adjutant General, 1988–90; Aide de Camp General to the Queen, 1989–91, retired; *b* 21 Feb. 1932; *er s* of late C. and Edith Mary Pascoe; *m* 1955, Pauline (*née* Myers); one *s* three *d*. *Educ:* Tavistock Grammar Sch.; RMA, Sandhurst. rcds, psc. Commissioned Oxford and Bucks LI, 1952; served with 1 Oxf. Bucks, 1 DLI and 4 Oxf. Bucks (TA), 1953–57; Middle East Centre for Arab Studies, Lebanon, 1958–59; 1st Cl. Interpretership (Arabic); GSO2 Land Forces Persian Gulf, 1960–62; sc Camberley, 1963; Co. Comd 2RGJ, UK and Malaysia, 1964–66

(despatches (Borneo) 1966); GSO2 HQ 2 Div. BAOR, 1967–68; Co. Comd 1RGJ, UK and UNFICYP, 1968–69; Second in Comd 2RGJ, BAOR, 1969; MA to QMG, 1970–71; Comd 1RGJ, 1971–74, BAOR and NI (despatches (NI) 1974); Col General Staff HQ UKLF, 1974–76; Comd 5 Field Force BAOR, 1976–79; rcds 1979; Asst Chief of Gen. Staff (Operational Requirements), MoD, 1980–83; Chief of Staff, HQ, UKLF, 1983–85; GOC Northern Ireland, 1985–88. Rep. Col Comdt, RGJ, 1988–90; Colonel Commandant: 1st Bn Royal Green Jackets, 1986–91; Army Legal Corps, 1988–90. Hon. Col, Oxfordshire ACF, 1991–2002; Vice Pres., Oxfordshire ACF League, 2002–. Mem. Adv. Bd, The Rifles, 2007–. Chm., Belautruche (UK) plc, 1997–2000; non-exec. Dir, Belautruche NV, 1997–2000. Chairman of Governors: Royal Sch., Bath, 1988–96 (Governor, 1981–96); Royal High Sch., Bath, 1996–. Gov., King Edward VII's Hosp., London, 2006– (Mem. of Council 1995–2006). President: Army LTA, 1986–91; Army Boxing Assoc., 1989–90; RGJ Golf Soc., 1999–2005; Reg. Forces Employment Assoc., 1997–99 (Chm., 1994–97); Potterne Br., RBL, 2006–; Chm., Ex-Services Resettlement Gp, 1994–98. Mem. and Vice Pres., Royal Patriotic Fund Corp., 1992–; Patron, Retired Officers Assoc., 1991–2001. Chairman: 43rd and 52nd Club, 1992–2002; Oxford and Bucks LI Mus. Trustees, 1992–2002. Hon. Associate, Girls' Day Sch. Trust, 2007. Freeman, City of London, 1992; Hon. Liveryman, Fruiterers' Co., 1992. *Recreations:* gardening, golf, fishing, tennis, ski-ing.

PASCOE-WATSON, George William; Political Editor, The Sun, since 2006; *b* Edinburgh, 21 Aug. 1966; *s* of John and Margaret Pascoe-Watson. *Educ:* George Heriot's Sch., Edinburgh; Royal High Sch., Edinburgh; Napier Coll., Edinburgh. The Sun: reporter, 1988–94; political corresp., 1994–96; Dep. Political Ed., 1996–2006. *Recreation:* golf. *Address:* Press Gallery, House of Commons, SW1A 0AA. *Clubs:* Soho House; Richmond Golf.

PASHA, Dr Syed Aziz, OBE 2005; Secretary General, Union of Muslim Organisations of the UK and Eire, since 1970; *b* 10 July 1930; *s* of Prof. Syed Rauf Pasha and Azmatunnisa Begum. *Educ:* Madras Univ. (BSc, BL); Wisconsin Univ. (LLM); New York Univ. Law Sch. (SJD). Advr to Indian Delegn to UN, 1961–62; Internat. Law Consultant to Matthew Bender, NY, 1963–64; Advocate, Madras High Court, 1964–65; post-doctoral res. on Islamic law, SOAS, Univ. of London, 1965–70. *Recreations:* debating, lecturing, sports. *Address:* Union of Muslim Organisations of UK and Eire, 109 Campden Hill Road, W8 7TL. *T:* (020) 7221 6608.

PASHLEY, Prof. Donald William, FRS 1968; Professor of Materials, Imperial College of Science, Technology and Medicine, 1979–92, now Professor Emeritus and Senior Research Fellow; *b* 21 April 1927; *s* of late Harold William Pashley and Louise Pashley (*née* Clarke); *m* 1954, Glenys Margaret Ball; one *s* one *d*. *Educ:* Henry Thornton Sch., London; Imperial Coll., London (BSc). 1st cl. hons Physics, 1947; PhD 1950. Research Fellow, Imp. Coll., 1950–55; TI Res. Labs, Hinxton Hall: Res. Scientist, 1956–61; Gp Leader and Div. Head, 1962–67; Asst Dir, 1967–68; Dir, 1968–79 (also Dir of Research, TI Ltd, 1976–79); Imperial College: Hd, Dept of Materials, 1979–90; Dean, Royal Sch. of Mines, 1986–89; Mem. Governing Body, 1986–89. Mem. Council, Royal Soc., 1981–83. Rosenhain Medal, Inst. of Metals, 1968. *Publications:* (jtly) Electron Microscopy of Thin Crystals, 1965; numerous papers on electron microscopy and diffraction, thin films and epitaxy in Phil. Mag., Proc. Roy. Soc., etc. *Address:* 11 Birch Court, The Gables, Oxshott, Leatherhead, Surrey KT22 0SD. *T:* (01372) 844518; Department of Materials, Imperial College, SW7 2AZ.

PASLEY, Sir Robert Killigrew Sabine, 6th Bt *cr* 1794, of Craig, Dumfriesshire; *b* 23 Oct. 1965; *s* of Sir Malcolm Pasley, 5th Bt, FBA and of Virginia Killigrew (*née* Wait); S father, 2004. *Heir:* *b* Humphrey Sabine Pasley, *b* 4 Dec. 1967.

PASQUA, Charles Victor; Senator (RPF) for Hauts-de-Seine, since 2004; *b* 18 April 1927; *s* of late André Pasqua and Françoise (*née* Rinaldi); *m* 1947; one *s*. *Educ:* Grasse High Sch.; Law Inst., Nice; Univ. of Aix-en-Provence (degree in Law). Sales Rep., then Sales Dir, 1962–63; Dir for sales in France and exports, 1963–68. Deputy (UDR) for Hauts-de-Seine, 1968–73; President: Centre National de la Libre Enterprise; Amicale Parlementaire Présence et Action du Gaullisme, 1972–73; Nat. Sec., then Dep. Gen. Sec., UDR, 1974–76; Senator (RPR) for Hauts-de-Seine, 1977–86, 1988–93 and 1995–99; Pres., RPR in Senate, 1981–86 and 1988–93; Minister of Interior, 1986–88; Minister of State and Minister for the Interior and Town and Country Planning, 1993–95. Pres., Gen. Council for Hauts-de-Seine, 1973–76 and 1988–2004. Mem. (RPF) for France, 1999–2004, and Pres., Union pour l'Europe des Nations Gp, 1999–2006, EP. Jt Founder and Pres., RPF, 1999–. Croix du Combattant volontaire de la Résistance; Médaille de la France Libre; Officier de la Légion d'Honneur. *Publications:* La Libre enterprise un état d'esprit, 1964; L'ardeur nouvelle, 1985; Que demande le peuple, 1992. *Recreation:* travel. *Address:* c/o RPF, 120 avenue Charles de Gaulle, 92200 Neuilly, France; Sénat, 15 rue de Vaugirard, 75006 Paris, France.

PASSLEY, Patrick Derek; Founder, and Managing Director, Paralegal Charity, since 1994; UK Delegate, Consultative Commission on Industrial Change, European and Economic Social Committee, Brussels, since 2004; *b* London, 10 Oct. 1965; *s* of Ivan Augustus Passley and Lurline Isamanda Passley; *m* 1991, Jean Francis; two *d*. *Educ:* Poly. of E London (LLB Hons); Middlesex Univ. (CertEd; Assessors Trainers Award Cert.). Law Lectr, Barnet Coll., 1991–2002. Commission for Racial Equality: Mem., 1999–2003; Chm., Nat. Sports Cttee, 2001; Official Observer on Disability Rights Commn, 2000–03; Special Advr to Trevor Philips, 2003–04; nominated CRE Comr for the Formal Investigation into CPS, 2000–01, and into Prison Service, 2000–03. Member Council: Prince's Trust, 2001–; King George's Jubilee Trust, 2001–. Member: Equity Sub-gp, Sport England, 2000–03; Mgt Cttee, Sporting Equals, CRE/Sport England, 2005–; Communications Cttee, FA, 2003–04; Adult Learning Cttee, Nat. LSC, 2001–; London E Local LSC, 2001–03. Sec., African and Caribbean Finance Forum, 2001–03. Jt Council for Anglo-Caribbean Churches, 2003–. *Recreations:* amateur boxing (former Nat. Amateur Boxing Champion and Commonwealth Rep. for England at Super Heavyweight, 1989–90), movies, current affairs, sport. *Address:* Paralegal Charity, 2 Fireman's Cottages, Tottenham Green Enterprise Centre, Town Hall Approach Road, N15 4RX. *T:* 0845 130 7095, *Fax:* 0845 130 7096; *e-mail:* ppassley@paralegalcharity.org.uk.

PASSMORE, George; artist; *b* Plymouth, Devon, 1942. *Educ:* Dartington Hall Coll. of Art; Oxford Sch. of Art; St Martin's Sch. of Art. Collaboration with Gilbert Proesch, as Gilbert and George. Gallery exhibitions include: Modern Fears, 1980, The Believing World, 1983, New Pictures, 1987, Worlds & Windows, 1990, New Democratic Pictures, 1992, Anthony d'Offay Gall.; The Rudimentary Pictures, Milton Keynes Gall., 2000; New Horny Pictures, White Cube[2], 2001; Perversive Pictures, NY, 2004; museum exhibitions include: The Paintings, 1971, Photo-Pieces 1971–80, 1981, Whitechapel Art Gall.; Pictures 1982 to 85, Hayward Gall., 1987; Enclosed and Enchanted, MOMA, Oxford, 2000; The Dirty Words Pictures (retrospective), Serpentine Gall., 2002; Gilbert & George: major exhibition (retrospective), Tate Modern, 2007; living sculpture includes: The Red Sculpture; Underneath the Arches; The Singing Sculpture; Our New Sculpture. Work in permanent collections incl. Nat. Portrait Gall., Tate Modern and San Francisco

Mus. of Modern Art. Represented GB, Venice Biennale, 2005. (Jtly) Turner Prize, 1986. *Publications:* (as George), with Gilbert Proesch: Lost Day; Oh, the Grand Old Duke of York; What Our Art Means. *Address:* c/o White Cube^2, 48 Hoxton Square, N1 6PB.

PASTINEN, Ilkka, Hon. KCMG 1976; Finnish Ambassador to the Court of St James's, 1983–91; *b* 17 March 1928; *s* of Martti and Ilmi Pastinen; *m* 1950, Eeva Marja Viitanen; two *d.* Entered Diplomatic Service, 1952; served Stockholm, 1955; Perm. Mission to UN, 1957–60; Peking, 1962–64; London, 1966–69; Ambassador and Dep. Representative of Finland to UN, 1969–71; Special Representative of Sec. Gen. of UN to Cttee of Disarmament, 1971–75; Ambassador and Perm. Representative of Finland at UN, NY, 1977–83. Kt Comdr of Order of White Rose of Finland, 1984. *Address:* Maneesikatu 1–3B, Helsinki, Finland. *Clubs:* Athenæum, Travellers; Swinley Forest Golf.

PASTON-BEDINGFELD, Sir Edmund George Felix, 9th Bt *cr* 1661; Major late Welsh Guards; Managing Director, Handley Walker (Europe) Ltd, 1969–80; *b* 2 June 1915; *s* of Sir Henry Edward Paston-Bedingfield, 8th Bt and Sybil (*d* 1985), *e d* of late H. Lyne Stephens of Grove House, Roehampton; *S* father, 1941; *m* 1st, 1942, Joan Lynette (*née* Rees) (*d* 1965); one *s* one *d*; 2nd, 1957, Agnes Kathleen (*d* 1974), *d* of late Miklos Gluck, Budapest; 3rd, 1975, Mrs Peggy Hannaford-Hill (*d* 1991), Fort Victoria, Rhodesia; 4th, 1992, Sheila Riddell (*née* Finlayson Douglas). *Educ:* Oratory School; New College, Oxford. Under-Sec., Head of Agricultural Div., RICS, 1966–69. Liveryman, Bowyers' Co., 1988–. *Heir:* *s* Henry Edgar Paston-Bedingfeld, *qv.* *Address:* 4 Finsbury Place, Bury St Edmunds, Suffolk IP33 1NU. *T:* (01284) 788160.

PASTON-BEDINGFELD, Henry Edgar; *see* Bedingfeld.

PATAKI, George Elmer; Governor, New York State, 1995–2006; Principal, Pataki-Cahill Group LLC; Of Counsel, Chadbourne and Parke; *b* 24 June 1945; *s* of Louis Pataki and Margaret Pataki; *m* Elizabeth (Libby) Rowland; two *s* two *d.* *Educ:* Peekskill High Sch.; Yale Univ. (BA 1967); Columbia Univ. Sch. of Law (JD 1970). Associate, Dewey, Ballantine, Bushby, Palmer and Wood, 1970–74; Partner, Plunkett & Jaffe, 1974–89. Mem., State Assembly 91st AD, 1985–92; Ranking Minority Member: Assembly Envmtl Conservation Cttee, 1987–90; Assembly Educn Cttee, 1991–92; Mem., State Senate 37th SD, 1993–95; Chm., State Ethics Cttee, 1993–95. Mayor, Peekskill, Westchester City, 1982–84. Co-proprietor, Pataki Farm, Peekskill, NY. *Recreations:* hiking in the woods, ski-ing, basketball, working on the family farm. *Address:* 21st Century Freedom PAC, 355 Lexington Avenue - 4th Floor, New York, NY 10017, USA.

PATE, Prof. John Stewart, FRS 1985; FAA 1980; FLS; Professor of Botany, University of Western Australia, 1974–2000, now Emeritus; *b* 15 Jan. 1932; *s* of Henry Stewart Pate and Muriel Margaret Pate; *m* 1959, Elizabeth Lyons Sloan, BSc; three *s.* *Educ:* Campbell College; Queen's Univ., Belfast (BSc, MSc, PhD, DSc). FLS 1990. Lectr, Sydney Univ., 1956–60; Lectr, Reader, Personal Chair in Plant Physiology, Queen's Univ. Belfast, 1960–73. Vis. Fellow, Univ. of Cape Town, 1973. Individual Excellence Award, AMEEF, 1998. *Publications:* (ed with J. F. Sutcliffe) Physiology of the Garden Pea, 1977; (ed with A. J. McComb) Biology of Australian Plants, 1981; (with K. W. Dixon) Tuberous, Cormous and Bulbous Plants, 1983; (ed with J. S. Beard) Kwongan: plant life of the sandplain, 1984; (ed with K. A. Meney) Australian Rushes: biology, identification and conservation of Restionaceae and allied families, 1999; (ed jtly and contrib.) Agriculture as a Mimic of Natural Ecosystems, 1999; reviews on carbon:nitrogen metabolism and biology of Australian flora; reviews and articles on understanding how plants can bioengineer soil profiles. *Recreations:* music, writing books on nature study, hobby farming, academic contact. *Address:* School of Plant Biology, University of Western Australia, 35 Stirling Highway, Crawley, WA 6009, Australia; 681 Mount Shadforth Road, Denmark, WA 6333, Australia.

PATEL, family name of **Barons Patel**, **Patel of Blackburn** and **Patel of Bradford**.

PATEL, Baron *cr* 1999 (Life Peer), of Dunkeld in Perth and Kinross; **Narendra Babubhai Patel,** Kt 1997; Consultant Obstetrician, Tayside Teaching Hospitals NHS Trust, Dundee, 1974–2003, now Hon. Consultant; Hon. Professor, University of Dundee, 1974–2003; *b* 11 May 1938; *m* 1970, Dr Helen Dally; twin *s* one *d.* *Educ:* Univ. of St Andrews (MB, ChB 1964). MRCOG 1969, FRCOG 1988; FRSE 1999. Chairman: Acad. of Med. Royal Colls, Scotland, 1994–95; Acad. of Med. Royal Colls, UK, 1996–98; Specialist Trng Authority, 1998–2001; Clinical Standards Bd for Scotland, 1999–2003; NHS Quality Improvement, Scotland, 2002–; Member: Council, GMC, 1998–2003; Armed Forces Pay Review Bd, 2000–. Chm., Stem Cell Steering Cttee, 2003–; Vice-Pres., All Party Parly Gp on Maternity Services, 2002–, on Infertility Services, 2003–; Mem., Sci. and Technol. Cttee, H of L, 2000, 2004, 2005–. Pres., RCOG, 1995–98 (Hon. Sec., 1987–92; Vice-Pres., 1992–95); Vice Pres., FIGO, 2000–03. Chancellor, Dundee Univ., 2006–. Founder FMedSci 1998. Hon. Fellowships: FACOG 1996; FSOGC 1997; FSACOG 1997; FICOG 1997; FRCPE 1997; FRCSE 1997; FRCPGlas 1998; FRCS 1998; FSLCOG 1998; FRANZCOG 1998; FRCA 1998; FRCPI 2000; FFPH 2003; FRCGP 2004; FRCPsych 2005; Eur. Soc. of Perinatal Medicine, 2002. Hon. Mem., German, Finnish, Argentinian, Chilean and Italian Socs of Obstetrics and Gynaecology. Hon. DSc: Napier, 1996; Aberdeen, 2001; St Andrews, 2001; Hon. MD: Stellenbosch, 2001; Athens, 2004; Hon. LLD Dundee, 2004. *Publications:* books and articles on pre-term labour, foetal monitoring, birth handicap, obstetrics, etc. *Recreations:* occasional golf, walking. *Address:* Department of Obstetrics, University of Dundee, Dundee DD1 4HN. *T:* (01382) 632959.

PATEL OF BLACKBURN, Baron *cr* 2000 (Life Peer), of Langho in the co. of Lancashire; **Adam Hafejee Patel;** *b* Gujarat, India, 7 June 1940; *m* 1964, Ayesha; four *s* four *d.* *Educ:* Maharaja Sayajirao Univ. of Baroda, India (BCom). Accountant with chartered accountants Ivan Jacques, Blackburn and S. & R. D. Thornton, Preston, 1967–74; Chief Internal Auditor, Zamtan, Lusaka, Zambia, 1975–76; Man. Dir, Comet Cash and Carry Co. Ltd, Blackburn, 1977–97. Mem., Labour Party, 1966–. Founder Mem., Blackburn Community Relns Council, later Blackburn with Darwen Racial Equality Council (Hon. Vice Pres.; former Treas., Vice-Chm. then Chm.); Chm., Blackburn and Dist Commonwealth Friendship Soc., 1966–67; founder Gen. Sec., Blackburn Indian Workers Assoc., 1967–74 (Pres., 1977–). Mem., Home Secretary's Race Relns Adv. Forum; Chm., British Hajj Delegn, FCO, 2001–. Founder Director: Lancs TEC; Blackburn Partnership. Jt Chm., Christian/Muslim Inter-Faith Forum; Member: Muslim Council of Britain; Lancs CC Standing Adv. Council on Religious Educn. Chm. and Trustee, W Brookhouse Community Centre, Blackburn. JP Blackburn, 1984–95. *Recreations:* community and social work, gardening, football, cricket. *Address:* Snodworth Hall, Snodworth Road, Langho, Lancs BB6 8DS.

PATEL OF BRADFORD, Baron *cr* 2006 (Life Peer), of Bradford, in the County of West Yorkshire; **Kamlesh Kumar Patel,** OBE 1999; a Lord in Waiting (Government Whip), since 2008; Professor, since 2000, and Head, International School of Communities, Rights and Inclusion, since 2008, University of Central Lancashire; Chairman, Mental Health Act Commission, since 2002 (Member, 1995–2001; Vice-Chairman, 2001–02); *b* 28 Sept. 1960; *s* of Sudhindra Kumar Patel and Savita Devi Patel; *m* 1998, Yasmin Saloojee; two *s*, and two step *d.* *Educ:* Univ. of Huddersfield (DipSW; CQSW). Ambulance man, 1981–83; social worker, 1983–87; Specialist Case Worker, Bradford Social Services, 1987–89; Manager, The Bridge Project (voluntary orgn for substance abuse/mental health), 1987–95; University of Central Lancashire: Sen. Lectr, 1995–98, Principal Lectr in Health and Social Care Policy, 1998–2000; Hd, Centre for Ethnicity and Health, 2000–08. Nat. Strategic Dir, Nat. Inst. for Mental Health in England, 2003–04 (on secondment); Nat. Dir, Black and Minority Ethnic Mental Health Prog., DoH, 2004–07; Expert Ministerial Advr to Sec. of State for DCLG, 2008. Hon. Lectr, Univs of Huddersfield, Lancaster, Salford and Northumbria, 1991–95. Member: Commn for Healthcare Audit and Inspection, 2003–06; (and Trustee) UK Drug Policy Commn, 2007–. Chm., Nat. Prison Drug Treatment Review Gp; Member: Adv. Council on Misuse of Drugs, 1990–96; Nat. Treatment Agency, 2001–; Global Task Force, UNICEF, 2006–. Patron: Men's Health Forum, 2006–; Sharing Voices Bradford, 2006–; Bridge Proj., Bradford, 2008. Hon. DLitt Manchester Metropolitan, 2007; Hon. Dr Civil Law Huddersfield, 2008. Plaque of Recognition (India), 1999. *Publications:* numerous contribs to books, jls, Home Office and DoH Reports on drugs, alcohol, mental health, community engagement, research, black and minority ethnic health and social care. *Recreations:* cricket, cricket coach. *Address:* Kipping Barn, Lower Kipping Lane, Thornton, Bradford BD13 3JT; House of Lords, SW1A OPW. *e-mail:* patelkk@parliament.uk, kkpatel@uclan.ac.uk.

PATEL, Bhikhu Chhotabhai; Co-founder and Managing Director, Waymade Healthcare plc and associated companies; *b* Kenya, 1 Aug. 1947; *s* of late Chhotabhai and of Shantaben Patel; *m* 1975, Shashikala Naranbhai Patel; one *s* two *d.* *Educ:* Univ. of Bristol (BA Arch.; DipArch.). RIBA 1978. (With V. C. K. Patel) co-founded: Waymade Healthcare plc, 1984; Amdipharm, 2002. CCMI 2002. Mem., Lions Clubs Internat. (Melvin Jones Fellow; Recognition of Distinguished Leadership Award, 2004). Hon. LLD Bristol, 2006. (Jtly) UK Entrepreneur of the Year, 2001. *Recreations:* swimming, walking, travelling, reading.
See also V. C. K. Patel.

PATEL, Chaitanya, CBE 1999; FRCP; Chairman, Court Cavendish Group, since 2007; *b* 14 Sept. 1954; *s* of Bhupendra and Ashru Patel; *m* (marr. diss.); two *d.* *Educ:* Southampton Univ. (BM 1979). MRCP 1982, FRCP 1999. MRC Res. Fellow, Pembroke Coll., Oxford, 1985; Investment Banker, Merrill Lynch and Lehman Brothers, 1985–89; founded Court Cavendish plc, 1989, subseq. Care First plc; Chief Exec., Westminster Health Care Ltd, 1999–2002; CEO, Priory Gp, 2002–07. Member: Better Regulation Task Force, 1997–2002; DoH Task Force for Older People, 1997–2002; Dir, Acute Bd, Independent Healthcare Assoc., 2003–05. Dir, Bridges Community Ventures, 2006–. Trustee: Help the Aged, 2000–02; IPPR, 2000– (Sec., 2000–07); Windsor Leadership Trust, 2001–. CCMI; FRSA. DUniv Open, 2002. *Recreations:* golf, music, theatre, travelling, films, photography. *Address:* *e-mail:* chai@courtcavendish.com. *Clubs:* Royal Automobile; Queenwood Golf.

PATEL, Praful Raojibhai Chaturbhai; company director; investment adviser in UK, since 1962; Chairman, Asia Fund Ltd, since 1984; *b* Jinja, Uganda, 7 March 1939; *s* of Raojibhai Chaturbhai Patel, Sojitra, Gujarat, India, and Maniben Jivabhai Lalaji Patel, Dharmaj, Gujarat; unmarried. *Educ:* Government Sec. Sch., Jinja, Uganda; London Inst. of World Affairs, attached to University Coll., London (Extra Mural Dept). Sec., Uganda Students Union, 1956–58; Deleg. to Internat. Youth Assembly, New Delhi, 1958; awarded two travel bursaries for visits to E, Central and S Africa, and Middle East, to study and lecture on politics and economics; arrived in Britain as student, then commenced commercial activities, 1962; increasingly involved in industrial, cultural and educational projects affecting immigrants in Britain. Spokesman for Asians in UK following restriction of immigration resulting from Commonwealth Immigrants Act 1968; Hon. Sec., All Party Parly Cttee on UK Citizenship, 1968–82; Founder and Council Mem., UK Immigration Advisory Service, 1970–82; Mem., Uganda Resettlement Bd, 1972–74; Hon. Sec., Uganda Evacuees Resettlement Advisory Trust, 1974–2000; Mem., Indian Govt Consultative Cttee on non-resident Indian investments, 1986–91; Pres., Nava Kala India Socio-Cultural Centre, London, 1962–75; Chm. Bd of Trustees, Swaminarayan Hindu Mission, UK, 1970–76; Jt Convener, Asian Action Cttee, 1976; Director: Shree Ganesh Foundn, 1999–; Indo-British Cultural Exchange, 2002– (Hon. Sec., 1980–82); Chm. and Trustee, Manava Trust, 1979–; Trustee: Charutar Arogya Mandal Trust, 1980–; India Overseas Trust, 2002–; Kailas Manasarovar Trust, 2002–. Gen. Sec., Internat. Ayurveda Foundn, 2003–. Contested (Lab) Brent North, 1987. Producer: ballet, Nritya Natika Ramayana, 1982; film, Kailas Manasarovar Yatra, 1997. Asian Times Award, 1986; Neasden Swaminarayan Mandir Award. *Publications:* articles in newspapers and journals regarding immigration and race relations, natural health issues, politics and business. *Recreations:* cricket, campaigning and lobbying, current affairs, promoting traditional Ayurveda medicines and inter-faith co-operation, collection of 2005 Ganesh Murtis and Hindu artefacts. *Address:* 60 Bedford Court Mansions, Bedford Avenue, WC1B 3AD. *T:* (020) 7580 0897, *Fax:* (020) 7436 2418; Puja Corporation Ltd, 3rd Floor, Readymoney Mansion, 43 Veer Nariman Road, Bombay 400023, India. *T:* (22) 2049248, *Fax:* (22) 2048938; *e-mail:* prcpatel@vsnl.com.

PATEL, Rashmita; *see* Shukla, R.

PATEL, Vijaykumar Chhotabhai Kalidas; principal Co-founder, 1984, and Chief Executive Officer, since 1989, Waymade Healthcare plc and associated companies; *b* Kenya, 10 Nov. 1949; *s* of late Chhotabhai and of Shantaben Patel; *m* 1975, Smita Kanaiyalal Patel; two *s.* *Educ:* Leicester Sch. of Pharmacy (BSc Pharm.). MRPS 1974. Opened first pharmacy, Leigh-on-Sea, Essex, 1975, subseq. expanded to chain of pharmacies, then supplier of pharmaceuticals; (with B. C. Patel) co-founded: Waymade Healthcare plc, 1984; Amdipharm, 2002. CCMI 2002; FRSA. Mem., Lions Clubs Internat. (Melvin Jones Fellow). (Jtly) UK Entrepreneur of the Year, 2001. *Recreations:* collector of watches and clocks, cars, keep fit, travelling, swimming, hill-walking.
See also B. C. Patel.

PATEMAN, Prof. John Arthur Joseph, FRS 1978; FRSE 1974; Emeritus Professor of Genetics, Australian National University; *b* 18 May 1926; *s* of John and Isobel May Pateman; *m* 1952, Mary Phelps; one *s* two *d.* *Educ:* Clacton County High Sch., Essex; University Coll., Leicester. BSc, PhD(Lond); MA(Cantab). Lectr, Univ. of Sheffield, 1954–58; Sen. Lectr, Univ. of Melbourne, Australia, 1958–60; Lectr, Univ. of Cambridge, 1960–67; Prof., Flinders Univ., S Australia, 1967–70; Prof. of Genetics, Univ. of Glasgow, 1970–79; Prof. of Genetics, ANU, 1979–88 (Exec. Dir, Centre for Recombinant DNA Res., 1982–88). Fellow, Churchill Coll., Cambridge, 1961–67. *Publications:* scientific papers in genetical, biochemical and microbiological jls. *Recreations:* reading, music, walking. *Address:* 1 Abberbury Road, Oxford OX4 4ET. *T:* (01865) 748275. *Club:* Oxford and Cambridge.

PATERSON, Alasdair Talbert; Librarian, 1994–2006, also Director of Information Services, 2006, University of Exeter; *b* 22 Oct. 1947; *s* of Talbert Robertson Paterson and

Alys Morton Paterson (*née* Campbell); *m* 1st, 1967, Corinne Brenda Norton (marr. diss. 1975); one *s*; 2nd, 1976, Ann Mary Cecilia Mulheirn; one *s* one *d*. *Educ:* Leith Acad.; Royal High Sch., Edinburgh; Univ. of Edinburgh (MA 1st cl. Hons 1970); Univ. of Sheffield (MA 1972). ALAI 1990. Asst Librarian, Univ. of Liverpool, 1972–86; Deputy Librarian: UC Cork, 1986–89; Univ. of Sheffield, 1989–94. Mem., Devon and Exeter Instn, 1994–. Eric Gregory Award, Soc. of Authors, 1975. *Publications:* Bibliography of Studies in Regional Industrial Development, 1978; The Floating World, 1984; Brief Lives, 1987; articles in prof. jls. *Recreations:* literature, the arts, travel, gardening, walking, watching sport, boules. *Address:* Taddyforde House North, New North Road, Exeter EX4 4AT. *T:* (01392) 430498. *Club:* Isca Pétanque (Exeter).

PATERSON, Alexander Craig, (Alastair), CBE 1987; FREng; Senior Partner, Bullen and Partners, Consulting Engineers, 1969–88, retired (Partner 1960–69); *b* 15 Jan. 1924; *s* of Duncan McKellar Paterson and Lavinia (*née* Craig); *m* 1947, Betty Hannah Burley (*d* 2008); two *s* two *d*. *Educ:* Glasgow High Sch.; Royal Coll. of Science and Technol. (ARCST); Glasgow Univ. (BSc). FICE 1963; FIMechE 1964; FIStructE 1970; FREng (FEng 1983); FCIArb 1968. Commd REME, 1944; served India and Burma, attached Indian Army, 1944–47. Engineer: with Merz and McLellan, 1947–58; with Taylor Woodrow, 1958–60. Mem., Overseas Projects Bd, 1984–87. Institution of Structural Engineers: Mem. Council, 1976–89; Vice Pres., 1981–84; Pres., 1984–85; Institution of Civil Engineers: Mem. Council, 1978–81 and 1982–91; Vice-Pres., 1985–88; Pres., 1988–89. Pres., British Section, Société des Ingénieurs et Scientifiques de France, 1980; Chm., British Consultants Bureau, 1978–80; Member: Council, British Bd of Agrément, 1982–95; Engrg Council, 1987–90. Mem. Court, Cranfield Inst. of Technol., 1970–80. Hon. DSc Strathclyde, 1989. *Publications:* professional and technical papers in engrg jls. *Recreations:* sailing, gardening. *Address:* Willows, The Byeway, West Wittering, Chichester, West Sussex PO20 8LJ. *T:* (01243) 514199. *Club:* Caledonian.

PATERSON, Bill; *see* Paterson, W. T.

PATERSON, Prof. Sir Dennis (Craig), Kt 1976; MB, BS 1953, MD 1983; FRCS, FRACS; Director and Chief Orthopaedic Surgeon, Adelaide Children's Hospital, 1966–95; Consultant Orthopaedic Surgeon, Queen Victoria Hospital, 1968–95; Clinical Associate Professor, University of Adelaide, since 1990; *b* 14 Oct. 1930; *s* of Gilbert Charles Paterson and Thelma Drysdale Paterson; *m* 1st, 1955, Mary (*d* 2004), *d* of Frederick Mansell Hardy; one *s* three *d*; *m* 2nd, 2006, Katalin Clara Maria Line. *Educ:* Collegiate Sch. of St Peter; Univ. of Adelaide (MB, BS 1953; MD 1983). FRCS 1958, FRACS 1961. Res. Med. Officer: Royal Adelaide Hosp., 1954; Adelaide Children's Hosp., 1955; Registrar, Robert Jones & Agnes Hunt Orthop. Hosp., Oswestry, Shropshire, 1958–60; Royal Adelaide Hospital: Sen. Registrar, 1960–62; Cons. Orthop. Surg., 1964–86; Cons. Orthop. Surg., Repatriation Gen. Hosp., Adelaide, 1962–70; Adelaide Children's Hospital: Asst Hon. Orthop. Surg., 1964–66; Sen. Hon. Orthop. Surg., 1966–70; Mem. Bd of Management, 1976–84; Chm., Med. Adv. Cttee, 1976–84; Chm., Med. Staff Cttee, 1976–84. Amer./British/Canadian Trav. Prof., 1966. Chairman: Trauma Systems Cttee for SA, 1994–2001; SA Road Safety Consultative Council, 1994–98; Southern Partnership, 1998–2002. Archbishop's Appeal Cttee, 1994–; Member: Nat. Road Trauma Adv. Council, 1990–95; Bd of Management, McLaren Vale and Fleurieu Visitors Centre, 1995–2002 (Chm., 1998–2002). Royal Australasian Coll. of Surgeons: Mem., Bd of Orthop. Surg., 1974–82, 1984–85 (Chm., 1977–82); Mem., Court of Examnrs, 1974–84; Mem., SA Cttee, 1974–78; Fellow: British Orthopaedic Assoc.; RSocMed; Member: Aust. Orthopaedic Assoc. (Censor-in-Chief, 1976–80; Dir, Continuing Educn, 1982–85); AMA; Internat. Scoliosis Res. Soc.; SICOT (Aust. Nat. Delegate, 1975–84, First Vice-Pres., 1984–87; Pres., 1987–90); Paediatric Orthopaedic Soc.; W Pacific Orthopaedic Soc.; Hon. Mem., American Acad. of Orthopaedic Surgeons, 1981. Pres., Crippled Children's Assoc. of South Australia Inc., 1970–84 (Mem. Council, 1966–70). Life Mem., S Aust. Cricket Assoc. Queen's Jubilee Medal, 1977. *Publications:* over 80 articles in Jl of Bone and Joint Surg., Clin. Orthopaedics and Related Res., Aust. and NZ Jl of Surg., Med. Jl of Aust., Western Pacific Jl of Orthop. Surg. *Recreations:* tennis, golf, gardening, vigneron. *Address:* 26 Queen Street, Glenunga, SA 5064, Australia. *T:* (8) 83792669, *Fax:* (8) 83796449. *Clubs:* Adelaide, Royal Adelaide Golf (Adelaide).

PATERSON, Douglas McCallum, CBE 2006; Chief Executive, Aberdeen City Council, 1995–2008; *b* 20 Nov. 1949; *s* of Douglas James Paterson and Violet Joan Paterson (*née* McCallum); *m* 1971, Isobel Stewart Beaton; two *d*. *Educ:* Aberdeen Univ. (MA Hons Econs 1971; DipEd 1976; MEd Hons 1981); Aberdeen Coll. of Educn (PGCE Dist. 1976); Robert Gordon Univ. (Dip Mgt 1990, DipM 1990). Manager, John Wood Gp, 1971–75; Grampian Regional Council: teacher, then head teacher, 1976–86; Advr in Educn, 1986–90; Depute Dir of Educn, 1990–92; Sen. Depute Dir of Educn, 1992–94; Dir of Educn, 1994–95. Hon. LLD Aberdeen, 2005. *Recreations:* walking, theatre, local history and culture, music, D-I-Y.

PATERSON, Francis, (Frank), FCILT; General Manager, Eastern Region, British Rail, York, 1978–85; Member, British Railways (Eastern) Board, 1978–85; Chairman, North Yorkshire Family Practitioner Committee, 1987–91; *b* 5 April 1930; *s* of Francis William Paterson and Cecilia Eliza Reid Brownie; *m* 1950, Grace Robertson (*d* 1996); two *s* two *d*. *Educ:* Robert Gordon's Coll., Aberdeen. Joined LNER as Junior Clerk, 1946; clerical and supervisory positions in NE Scotland; management training, Scotland, 1956–59; various man-management, operating and marketing posts, Scotland, Lincs and Yorks, 1960–66; Operating Supt, Glasgow North, 1967–68; Sales Manager, Edinburgh, 1968; Asst Divl Manager, S Wales, 1968–70; Dir, United Welsh Transport, 1968–70; Harbour Comr, Newport Harbour, 1968–70; Divl Manager, Central Div., Southern Region, 1970–75; Director: Southdown Motor Services Ltd, 1970–73; Brighton, Hove & District Omnibus Co., 1970–73; Dep. Gen. Man., Southern Region, 1975–77; Chief Freight Manager, British Railways Bd, 1977–78. Dir, N Yorks Moors Rly plc, 1993–2000. Vice-Chm., Nat. Railway Mus. Cttee, 1984– (Mem., 1978–); Member: CBI Southern Regional Council, 1975–77; CBI Transport Policy Cttee, 1977–78; BBC NE Adv. Council, 1987–91; Chm., BBC Local Radio Adv. Council, Radio York, 1987–91. Vice Chm., York and Selby CPRE, 2002–. President: St Andrews Soc. of York, 1989–90; Rotary Club of York, 2002–03. Trustee: Friends of Nat. Railway Museum, 1988– (Chm., 2002–); York Civic Trust, 2004–. Mem. Court, Univ. of York, 1981–92. FCILT (FCIT 1978 (Mem. Council, CIT, 1979–84); FILT 1999). OStJ 1980. *Publications:* papers to transport societies. *Recreations:* transport, travel, hill walking, country pursuits, Scottish culture, enjoying grandchildren. *Address:* Alligin, 97 Main Street, Askham Bryan, York YO23 3QS. *T:* (01904) 708478; *e-mail:* frankpaterson@talktalk.net.

PATERSON, His Honour Frank David; a Circuit Judge (formerly County Court Judge), 1968–93; *b* 10 July 1918; *yr s* of late David Paterson and Dora Paterson, Liverpool; *m* 1953, Barbara Mary, 2nd *d* of late Oswald Ward Gillow and Alice Gillow, Formby; one *s* two *d*. *Educ:* Calderstones Preparatory Sch. and Quarry Bank High Sch., Liverpool; Univ. of Liverpool (LLB). Called to Bar, Gray's Inn, 1941; Warden, Unity Boys' Club, Liverpool, 1941; Asst Warden, Florence Inst. for Boys, Liverpool, 1943. Practised on Northern Circuit. Chairman: Min. of Pensions and Nat. Insce Tribunal, Liverpool, 1957; Mental Health Review Tribunal for SW Lancashire and Cheshire, 1963. Asst Dep. Coroner, City of Liverpool, 1960. Pres., Merseyside Magistrates' Assoc., 1978–93; Jt Pres., Council of HM Circuit Judges, 1987. Hon. LLD Liverpool, 1993. *Address:* Vailima, 2 West Lane, Formby, Liverpool L37 7BA. *T:* (01704) 874345. *Club:* Athenæum (Liverpool).

PATERSON, Gil(bert); Member (SNP) Scotland West, Scottish Parliament, since 2007; Proprietor, Gils' Motor Factors, since 1973; *b* 11 Nov. 1942; *m* (marr. diss.); one *s*. *Educ:* Possilpark Secondary Sch. Company owner and director. Mem., Strathclyde Regl Council, 1975–78. Mem. (SNP) Central Scotland, Scottish Parlt, 1999–2003; Member: Equal Opportunities Cttee, 2001–03; Procedures Cttee, 2003; Convener, Cross-Party Gp on Men's Violence against Women and Children, 1999–2003. Contested (SNP): Glasgow Central, June 1980; Strathkelvin and Bearsden, 1987; Airdrie & Shotts, Scottish Parlt, 2003. Mem. Nat. Exec., 1995–98, Vice Convenor Fundraising, 2003–, SNP. Mem. Bd, Rape Crisis, 2003–. *Recreations:* reading, climbing, motorcycling, ski-ing, snowboarding, researching oriental ceramics. *Address:* (office) 280–290 Colston Road, Bishopbriggs, Strathkelvin G64 2BE.

PATERSON, Prof. Ian, PhD; FRS 2005; Professor of Organic Chemistry, University of Cambridge, since 2001; Professorial Fellow, Jesus College, Cambridge, since 2002; *b* 4 May 1954; *s* of Angus and Violet Paterson; *m* 1977, Nina Kuan. *Educ:* Kirkton High Sch., Dundee; Univ. of St Andrews (BSc 1976); Peterhouse, Cambridge (PhD 1979). Res. Fellow, Christ's Coll., Cambridge, 1978–79; NATO/SERC Postdoctoral Res. Fellow, Columbia Univ., NY, 1979–80; Lectr in Chemistry, UCL, 1980–83; University of Cambridge: Univ. Lectr in Chemistry, 1983–97; Reader in Organic Chemistry, 1997–2001; Teaching Fellow, Jesus Coll., 1983–2001. Various consultancies with pharmaceutical cos. MRSC 1980; MACS 1980. *Publications:* extensive articles in jls incl. Angewandte Chemie, Organic Letters, Jl of ACS, Tetrahedron Letters, Organic and Biomolecular Chemistry. *Recreation:* gardening. *Address:* Department of Chemistry, University of Cambridge, Lensfield Road, Cambridge CB2 1EW.

PATERSON, James Rupert; HM Diplomatic Service, retired; *b* 7 Aug. 1932; *s* of late Major Robert Paterson, MC, Seaforth Highlanders and Mrs Josephine Paterson; *m* 1956, Kay Dineen; two *s* two *d*. *Educ:* Nautical Coll., Pangbourne; RMA, Sandhurst. Commnd RA, 1953 (Tombs Meml Prize); Staff Coll., Camberley, 1963; retd from Army with rank of Major, 1970; joined FCO, 1970; First Sec., Pakistan, 1972; Dep. High Comr, Trinidad and Tobago, 1975; Ambassador to the Mongolian People's Republic, 1982; Consul-General, Istanbul, 1985, Geneva, 1989–92. *Recreations:* reading, travel, golf. *Address:* c/o Barclays Bank, Deal, Kent CT14 6EP.

PATERSON, James Veitch; Sheriff of the Lothian and Borders (formerly Roxburgh, Berwick and Selkirk) at Jedburgh, Selkirk and Duns, 1963–2000; *b* 16 April 1928; *s* of late John Robert Paterson, ophthalmic surgeon, and Jeanie Gouinlock; *m* 1st, 1956, Ailie (*d* 2003), *o d* of Lt-Comdr Sir (George) Ian Clark Hutchison, RN; one *s* one *d*; 2nd, 2004, Elspeth, widow of William Marshall Colledge. *Educ:* Peebles High School; Edinburgh Academy; Lincoln College, Oxford; Edinburgh University. Admitted to Faculty of Advocates, 1953. *Recreations:* fishing, shooting, gardening. *Address:* Sunnyside, Melrose, Roxburghshire TD6 9BE. *T:* (01896) 822502. *Club:* New (Edinburgh).

PATERSON, Rt Rev. John Campbell; *see* Auckland (NZ), Bishop of.

PATERSON, Very Rev. John Munn Kirk; Minister Emeritus of St Paul's Parish Church, Milngavie (Minister, 1970–87); Moderator of the General Assembly of the Church of Scotland, 1984–85; *b* 8 Oct. 1922; *s* of George Kirk Paterson and Sarah Ferguson Paterson (*née* Wilson); *m* 1946, Geraldine Lilian Parker; two *s* one *d*. *Educ:* Hillhead High School, Glasgow; Edinburgh Univ. MA, BD. RAF, 1942–46 (Defence and Victory medals, Italy Star, 1945). Insurance Official, 1940–58 (ACII 1951); Assistant Minister, 1958–64; Ordained Minister of Church of Scotland, 1964–. Hon. DD Aberdeen, 1986. *Recreations:* fishing, hill walking. *Club:* Royal Over-Seas League (Edinburgh).

PATERSON, Prof. Michael Stewart, PhD; FRS 2001; Professor of Computer Science, University of Warwick, since 1979; *b* 13 Sept. 1942. *Educ:* Trinity Coll., Cambridge (BA 1964; PhD 1968). Lectr, 1971–74, Reader, 1974–79, in Computer Sci., Univ. of Warwick. *Address:* Department of Computer Science, University of Warwick, Coventry CV4 7AL.

PATERSON, Owen William; MP (C) North Shropshire, since 1997; *b* 24 June 1956; *s* of late Alfred Paterson and of Cynthia Owen; *m* 1980, Rose Ridley; two *s* one *d*. *Educ:* Radley Coll.; Corpus Christi Coll., Cambridge (MA Hist.). British Leather Co.: Sales Dir, 1980; Man. Dir, 1993–97. Pres., European Tanners' Confedn, 1996–97. Contested (C) Wrexham, 1992. *Recreations:* travel, history, trees, riding, hunting, racing, poultry. *Address:* House of Commons, SW1A 0AA.

PATERSON, Rt Rev. Robert Mar Erskine; *see* Sodor and Man, Bishop of.

PATERSON, William Alexander; *see* Alexander, Bill.

PATERSON, Prof. William Edgar, OBE 1999; PhD; FRSE; Professor of German and European Politics, University of Birmingham, 1994–2008, now Emeritus; Director, Institute for German Studies, University of Birmingham, 1994–2005 and 2006–08, now Emeritus; *b* Blair Atholl, Perthshire, 26 Sept. 1941; *s* of late William Paterson, FRICS, FLAS, Land Agent, and of Winnie Paterson (*née* McIntyre); *m* 1st, 1964, Jacqueline Cramb (*d* 1974); two *s*; 2nd, 1979, Phyllis MacDowell; one *d*, and one step *s* one step *d*. *Educ:* Morrison's Acad.; Univ. of St Andrews (MA, Class Medallist); London Sch. of Econs (S. H. Bailey Schol.; MSc, PhD 1973). FRSE 1994. Lectr in Internat. Relns, Univ. of Aberdeen, 1967–70; University of Warwick: Volkswagen Lectr in German Politics, 1970–75; Sen. Lectr, 1975–82; Reader, 1982–89; Prof. and Chm. of Dept, 1989–90; Salvesen Prof. of Eur. Insts, and Dir, Europa Inst., Univ. of Edinburgh, 1990–94. Jt Ed., German Politics, 1991–2001; Member, Editorial Board: Jl Common Mkt Studies, 1991–2003 (Co-Ed., 2003–08); Internat. Affairs, 1993–; Co-Editor: Palgrave European Union Studies, 1992–; New Perspectives in German Studies, 1998–; Palgrave Studies in European Union Politics, 2005–. Mem., ESRC Res. Priorities Bd, 1995–99; Chm., One Europe or Several? prog. for ESRC, 2001–03. Mem., Königswinter Conf. Steering Cttee, 1994–. Chairman: Assoc. for Study of German Politics, 1974–76 (Hon. Vice Pres., 2000); Univ. Assoc. for Contemporary Eur. Studies, 1989–94; Chm., German-British Forum, 2005– (Vice-Chm., 1999–2005). Member: Adv. Bd, Centre for British Studies, Humboldt Univ., Berlin, 1997–2008; Kuratorium, Allianz Kulturstiftung, 2000–04. Associate Fellow, RIIA, 1994; AcSS 2000. FRSA 1998. Lifetime Achievement Award: Assoc. for Study of German Politics, 2004; Univ. Assoc. for Contemporary European Studies, 2007. Officer's Cross, Order of Merit (FRG), 1999. *Publications:* The SPD and European Integration, 1974; *jointly:* Social Democracy in Post-War Europe, 1974; The Federal Republic of Germany and the European Community, 1987; Government and the

Chemical Industry, 1988; Governing Germany, 1991; A History of Social Democracy in Post-War Europe, 1991; The Kohl Chancellorship, 1998; The Future of the German Economy, 2000; Germany's European Diplomacy, 2000; *edited jointly:* Social and Political Movements in Western Europe, 1976; Social Democratic Parties in Western Europe, 1977; Foreign Policy Making in Western Europe, 1978; Sozialdemokratische Parteien in Europa, 1978; The West German Model, 1981; The Future of Social Democracy, 1986; Developments in West German Politics, 1989; Politics in Western Europe Today, 1990; El Futuro de la Social Democracia, 1992; Developments in German Politics, 1992; Rethinking Social Democracy in Western Europe, 1993; Developments in German Politics 2, 1996; Developments in German Politics 3, 2003; Governance in Contemporary Germany, 2005; The German Crisis, 2008; The German Presidency of the European Union, 2009; contrib. over 100 articles to edited collections and learned jls. *Recreation:* walking. *Address:* Institute for German Studies, University of Birmingham, Pritchatts Road, Edgbaston, Birmingham B15 2TT. *T:* (0121) 414 7183; 220 Myton Road, Warwick CV34 6PS. *T:* (01926) 492492; 6 Port Road, Palnackie, Dumfriesshire DG7 1PQ. *T:* (01556) 600395; *e-mail:* w.e.paterson@bham.ac.uk. *Club:* Athenæum.

PATERSON, William Tulloch, (Bill), actor, since 1968; *b* 3 June 1945; *s* of late John Paris Paterson and of Ann Tulloch Paterson; *m* 1984, Hildegard Bechtler; one *s* one *d*. *Educ:* Whitehill Sen. Secondary Sch., Glasgow; RSAMD (FRSAMD 2005). First professional engagement, Glasgow Citizens' Theatre, 1968; Asst Dir, Citizens' Theatre for Youth, 1970–72; Founder Mem., 7:84 (Scotland) Theatre Co. *Stage:* The Cheviot, the Stag and the Black Black Oil, 1973; Writer's Cramp, 1977; Whose Life is it Anyway?, Savoy, 1978; Guys and Dolls, NT, 1982; Schweyk, NT, 1983; Death and the Maiden, Royal Court, 1992; Misery, Criterion, 1993; Mongrel's Heart, Edinburgh, 1994; Ivanov, Almeida, 1997; Marriage Play, RNT, 2001; *films:* Comfort and Joy, The Killing Fields, 1984; Defence of the Realm, 1985; A Private Function, 1986; The Adventures of Baron Munchausen, 1987; The Witches, 1989; Truly Madly Deeply, 1991; Chaplin, 1992; Richard III, 1996; Hilary and Jackie, 1998; Complicity, 2000; Crush, 2001; Bright Young Things, 2003; Rag Tale, 2005; Amazing Grace, 2006; Miss Potter, 2007; *television series and serials:* Smiley's People, 1981; Auf Wiedersehen Pet, 1986; The Singing Detective, 1987; Traffik, 1989; Tell Tale Hearts, 1992; Hard Times, 1993; The Writing on the Wall, 1995; The Crow Road, 1996; Wives and Daughters, 1999; The Whistleblower, 2001; Zhivago, 2002; Danielle Cable Eye Witness, 2003; Sea of Souls, 2005; Criminal Justice, 2008. *Publication:* Tales from the Backgreen, 2008. *Address:* c/o Gordon and French, 12–13 Poland Street, W1V 3DE.

PATERSON-BROWN, Dr June, CVO 2007; CBE 1991; JP; Lord-Lieutenant of Roxburgh, Ettrick and Lauderdale, 1998–2007; Chief Commissioner, Girl Guides Association, and Commonwealth Chief Commissioner, 1985–90; *b* 8 Feb. 1932; *d* of Thomas Clarke Garden and Jean Martha (*née* Mallace); *m* 1957, Dr Peter N. Paterson-Brown; three *s* one *d*. *Educ:* Esdaile Sch.; Edinburgh Univ. (MB, ChB). MO in Community Health, 1960–85. Scottish Chief Comr, Girl Guides Assoc., 1977–82; Vice-Pres., Guide Assoc., 1992–; Pres., Roxburghshire, Guide Assoc., 1993–. Non-exec. Dir, Border Television, 1980–2000; Chm., Borders Children's Panel Adv. Cttee, 1982–85; Trustee: Prince's Trust, 1982–94 (Vice-Chm., 1982–92); MacRobert Trusts, 1987–2002; Chm., Scottish Standing Conf. Voluntary Youth Organisations, 1982–85. Chm. Cttee, Duke of Edinburgh's Award Scheme, Roxburgh, 1970–85. DL 1990, JP 1999, Roxburgh, Ettrick and Lauderdale. Paul Harris Fellow, Rotary Internat., 1990. Silver Jubilee Medal, 1977; Golden Jubilee Medal, 2002. *Recreations:* golfing, fishing, tennis, music, reading. *Address:* Norwood, Hawick, Roxburghshire TD9 7HR. *T:* (01450) 372352. *Club:* Lansdowne.

PATEY, William Charters, CMG 2005; HM Diplomatic Service; Ambassador to Saudi Arabia, since 2007; *b* 11 July 1953; *s* of William Maurice Patey and Christina Kinnell Patey; *m* 1978, Vanessa Carol Morrell; two *s*. *Educ:* Trinity Acad., Edinburgh; Univ. of Dundee (MA Hons). Joined FCO, 1975; MECAS, 1977–78; Commercial Attaché, Abu Dhabi, 1978–81; Second Sec., Tripoli, 1981–84; FCO, 1984–88; First Sec. (Political), Canberra, 1988–92; Dep. Head, UN Dept, 1992–93, Inspector, 1994–95, FCO; Dep. Head of Mission and Consul-Gen., Riyadh, 1995–98; Hd, Middle East Dept, FCO, 1999–2002; Ambassador: to Sudan, 2002–05; to Iraq, 2005–06. Mem., Oxford Energy Policy Club, 2000–. Pres., Khartoum Cheshire Home, 2002–05. Hon. Pres: St Margaret's Film Soc., 1996. Trustee, Kids for Kids Charity, 2002–; Patron, Together for Sudan, 2003–. *Recreations:* tennis, theatre, golf. *Address:* c/o Foreign and Commonwealth Office, King Charles Street, SW1A 2AH.

PATHAK, Kirit Kumar, OBE 1997; Chairman, Patak's Foods Ltd, since 1990 (Chief Executive, 1990–2007); *b* 12 Sept. 1952; *s* of late Laxmishanker Gopalji and of Shanta Gaury Pathak; *m* 1976, Meena Desai (*see* M. Pathak); two *s* one *d*. *Educ:* Banbury Technical Coll.; Lancaster Poly. Joined Patak's (family Indian food business) at age 17. Member: NW Industrial Develt Bd, 1998–; UK Trade and Investment, 1999–. Mem. Council, Food From Britain, 1998–2003; Vice-Pres., FDF, 2003–. Corporate Hon. Fellow, Liverpool John Moores Univ., 2002. Hon. Dr Business Management UCE Birmingham, 1996. *Recreations:* meditation, football, tennis, ski–ing, trekking, horse riding, swimming, cooking, DIY. *Address:* Patak's Foods Ltd, Kiribati Way, Leigh, Lancs WN7 5RS. *T:* (01942) 267000, *Fax:* (01942) 267070; *e-mail:* info@pataksfoods.co.uk.

PATHAK, Meena, OBE 2001; Director, 1981–2007, and Deputy Chairperson, 2000–07, Patak's Foods Ltd; *b* 12 Aug. 1956; *d* of Col Naishad Desai and Dr Hansa Desai; *m* 1976, Kirit Kumar Pathak, *qv*; two *s* one *d*. *Educ:* Bombay Internat. Sch.; hotel mgt and food technol. Bd Mem., Univ. of Central Lancashire, 2000–. Hon. Fellow, Bolton Inst., 2002. Hon. Doctorate Central Lancashire, 1992. *Publications:* The Flavours of India, 2002; Indian Cooking for Family and Friends, 2003; Meena Pathak Celebrates Indian Cooking, 2007. *Recreations:* meditation, music, arts, reading, sports (cricket). *Address:* Patak's Foods Ltd, Kiribati Way, Leigh, Lancs WN7 5RS. *T:* (01942) 267000, *Fax:* (01942) 267070; *e-mail:* meena.pathak@pataksfoods.co.uk.

PATIENCE, Adèle; *see* Williams, J. A.

PATIENCE, Andrew; QC 1990; **His Honour Judge Patience;** a Circuit Judge, since 1999; *b* 28 April 1941; *s* of late William Edmund John Patience and Louise Mary Patience; *m* 1975, Jean Adèle Williams, *qv*; one *s* one *d*. *Educ:* Whitgift School, Croydon; St John's College, Oxford (MA). Called to the Bar, Gray's Inn, 1966; a Recorder, 1986–99; Resident Judge, Maidstone Crown Court, 2000–; Hon. Recorder of Dover, 2001–. *Recreations:* mimicry, complaining, horse racing. *Address:* The Law Courts, Barker Road, Maidstone, Kent ME16 8EQ. *Club:* Oxford and Cambridge.

PATMORE, Prof. (John) Allan, CBE 1993; Professor of Geography, University of Hull, 1973–91, Professor Emeritus, since 1991; Vice-Chairman, Sports Council, 1988–94 (Member, 1978–94); *b* 14 Nov. 1931; *s* of John Edwin Patmore and Marjorie Patmore; *m* 1956, Barbara Janet Fraser; one *s* two *d*. *Educ:* Harrogate Grammar Sch.; Pembroke Coll., Oxford (MA, BLitt). Served RAF, Educn Br., 1952–54. Department of Geography, University of Liverpool: Tutor, 1954–55; Asst Lectr, 1955–58; Lectr, 1958–69; Sen. Lectr,

1969–73; University of Hull: Dean of Social Science, 1979–81; Pro-Vice-Chancellor, 1982–85. Visiting Professor: Univ. of Southern Illinois, 1962–63; Univ. of Canterbury, NZ, 1978. Pres. 1979–80, Trustee 1979–88, Hon. Mem., 1991, Geographical Assoc.; Pres., Sect. E, BAAS, 1987–88. Pres., N Yorks Moors Assoc., 1993–2000; Member: N York Moors National Park Cttee, 1977–92; Nat. Parks Review Panel, 1990–91; Countryside Commn, 1992–98; Inland Waterways Amenity Adv. Council, 1993–94; Bd, Nat. Lottery New Opportunities Fund, 1998–2004. Friends of National Railway Museum: Chm., 1992–2002; Vice-Chm., 2002–; Chm., Executive, 2002–; Mem. Adv. Cttee, Nat. Railway Mus., 1988–2004. Methodist Local Preacher, 1959–. JP Hull, 1975–2001. Hon. DLitt Loughborough, 1993. *Publications:* Land and Leisure, 1970; People, Place and Pleasure, 1975; Recreation and Resources, 1983; Leisure and Mission, 2000. *Recreations:* pursuing railway history, enjoying the countryside.

PATNICK, Sir (Cyril) Irvine, Kt 1994; OBE 1980; Chairman, Watt Solutions Ltd, since 2004; *b* Oct. 1929; *m* 1960, Lynda Margaret (*née* Rosenfield); one *s* one *d*. *Educ:* Sheffield Poly. FCIOB. Member: Sheffield City Council, 1967–70; Sheffield MDC, 1971–88; S Yorks CC, until abolition in 1986 (Opposition Leader, 1973–86); Dep. Chm., S Yorks Residuary Body, 1985–87; Chm., Cons. Party Local Govt Adv. Cttee, 1989–90. Contested (C) Sheffield, Hillsborough, 1970, 1979. MP (C) Sheffield, Hallam, 1987–97; contested (C) same seat, 1997. An Asst Govt Whip, 1989–90; a Lord Comr of HM Treasury (Govt Whip), 1990–94. Member: Envmt Select Cttee, 1994–97; Cttee of Selection, 1997; Dep. Chm., Channel Tunnel Rail Link Bill Select Cttee, 1995–96. Vice-Chm., Cons. Party Back Bench Envmt Cttee, 1988–89. Member: Council of Europe, 1995–97; WEU, 1995–97. Mem., Cons. Party NEC, 1987–89. Chm., Yorks and Humberside Council for Sport and Recreation, 1979–85; Member: Sheffield Community Health Council, 1974–75; Yorks and Humberside Tourist Bd, 1977–79; Governor, Sports Aid Foundn, Yorks and Humberside, 1980–85. Chm., Keyturn Solutions Ltd, 1997–2004. Hon. Life Vice-Pres., ACC Ltd, 2003. Patron, Home Business Alliance, 1999–. Freeman, City of London, 1996.

PATNICK, Julietta, CBE 2005; Director, NHS Cancer Screening Programmes, since 1995; *b* 10 June 1957; *d* of Barry Freeman and Shirley (*née* Samuels); *m* 1978, Michael Patnick; one *s* one *d*. *Educ:* Univ. of Sheffield (BA Hons Ancient Hist. and Classical Civilisation 1978). FFPH 2002. Co-ordinator, Breast Screening, Trent Regl HA, 1987–90; Nat. Co-ordinator, NHS Breast Screening Prog., 1990–94. Member: Care Record Develt Bd, 2004–07; Medicines for Women's Health Expert Working Gp, 2006–. Hon. Fellow in Public Health, 2004, Vis. Prof. in Cancer Screening, 2008–, Oxford Univ. *Recreations:* spending time with family, reading classics and history, eating good food in good company. *Address:* NHS Cancer Screening Programmes, Fulwood House, Old Fulwood Road, Sheffield S10 3TH. *T:* (0114) 271 1063, *Fax:* (0114) 271 1089; *e-mail:* julietta.patnick@cancerscreening.nhs.uk.

PATON, Rt Hon. Lady; Ann Paton; PC 2007; a Senator of the College of Justice in Scotland, since 2000; *d* of James McCargow and Ann Dunlop or McCargow; *m* 1974, Dr James Y. Paton; no *c*. *Educ:* Laurel Bank Sch.; Univ. of Glasgow (MA 1972; LLB 1974). Admitted to the Scottish Bar, 1977. Standing Junior Counsel: to the Queen's and Lord Treasurer's Remembrancer (excluding *Ultimus Haeres*), 1979; in Scotland to Office of Fair Trading, 1981; QC (Scot.) 1990; Advocate Depute, 1992–94 Member: Criminal Injuries Compensation Bd, 1995–2000; Parole Bd, 2003–07. Dir, Scottish Council of Law Reporting, 1995–2000. Mem. Governing Body, Queen Margaret UC, 2001–04. *Publications:* Map of Sheriffdoms and Sheriff Court Districts in Scotland, 1977, 2nd edn 1980; (Jt Asst Editor) Gloag and Henderson, Law of Scotland, 8th edn 1980, to 10th edn 1995; (with R. G. McEwan) A Casebook on Damages in Scotland, 1983, 2nd edn as Damages in Scotland (sole author), 1989, re-titled Damages for Personal Injuries in Scotland, 1997; Faculty Digest Supplement 1971–1980, 1995; contrib. Scottish Current Law Statutes, Session Cases, Scots Law Times, and Green's Reparation Bulletin. *Recreations:* sailing, tennis, cycling, music, art.

PATON, Alasdair Chalmers, CEng, FICE, FCIWEM; Chief Executive, Scottish Environment Protection Agency, 1995–2000; *b* Paisley, 28 Nov. 1944; *o s* of David Paton and Margaret Elizabeth Paton (*née* Chalmers); *m* 1969, Zona Gertrude Gill; one *s* one *d*. *Educ:* John Neilson Instn, Paisley; Univ. of Glasgow (BSc). Assistant Engineer: Clyde Port Authy, 1967–71; Dept of Agric. and Fisheries for Scotland, 1971–72; Sen. Engineer, Scottish Develt Dept, 1972–77; Engineer, Public Works Dept, Hong Kong Govt, 1977–80; Scottish Development Department: Sen. Engineer, 1980–84; Principal Engineer, 1984–87; Dep. Chief Engineer, 1987–91; Dir and Chief Engineer, Water and Waste Directorate, Scottish Office Envmt Dept, 1991–95. *Recreations:* Rotary, sailing, golf. *Address:* Oriel House, Academy Square, Limekilns, Fife KY11 3HN. *Club:* Royal Scots (Edinburgh).

PATON, Ann; *see* Paton, Hon. Lady.

PATON, Douglas Shaw F.; *see* Forrester-Paton.

PATON, Maj.-Gen. Douglas Stuart, CBE 1983 (MBE 1961); FFPH; Commander Medical HQ BAOR, 1983–85; retired 1986; *b* 3 March 1926; *s* of Stuart Paton and Helen Kathleen Paton (*née* Hooke); *m* 1957, Jennifer Joan Land; two *d*. *Educ:* Sherborne; Bristol University. MB ChB 1951; FFPH (FFPHM 1989; FFCM 1982, MFCM 1973). Commissioned RAMC, 1952; served Middle East (Canal Zone), Malaya, Hong Kong and UK, 1952–61; 16 Para Bde, 1961–66; jssc 1966; CO Mil. Hosp., Terendak, Malaysia, 1967–70; MoD, 1970–73; CO Cambridge Mil. Hosp., Aldershot, 1973–76; rcds 1977; DDMS HQ 1 (BR) Corps, 1978–81; Dep. Dir-Gen., Army Med. Services, MoD, 1981–83. QHP 1981–86. Hon. Col 221 (Surrey) Field Amb. RAMC(V), TA, 1988–92. Chm., RAMC Assoc., 1988–98. Mem. Bd of Governors, Moorfields Eye Hosp., 1988–91. CStJ 1986. *Publications:* contribs to Jl RAMC. *Recreations:* golf, travel, opera, gardening. *Address:* Brampton, Springfield Road, Camberley, Surrey GU15 1AB.

PATON, Hon. (Frederick) Ranald N.; *see* Noel-Paton.

PATON, Ven. Michael John Macdonald; Archdeacon of Sheffield, 1978–87, Archdeacon Emeritus, since 1988; *b* 25 Nov. 1922; *s* of late Rev. William Paton, DD, and Grace Mackenzie Paton (*née* Macdonald); *m* 1952, Isobel Margaret Hogarth; one *s* four *d*. *Educ:* Repton School; Magdalen Coll., Oxford (MA). Indian Army, 1942–46; HM Foreign Service, 1948–52; Lincoln Theological Coll., 1952–54; Deacon 1954, priest 1955; Curate, All Saints', Gosforth, Newcastle upon Tyne, 1954–57; Vicar, St Chad's, Sheffield, 1957–67; Chaplain, United Sheffield Hosps, 1967–70; Vicar, St Mark's, Broomhill, Sheffield, and Chaplain, Weston Park Hosp., 1970–78. *Publications:* contrib. to: Essays in Anglican Self-criticism, 1958; More Sermons from Great St Mary's, 1971; Religion and Medicine, 1976; Mud and Stars, 1991. *Recreations:* hill walking, music, birdwatching. *Address:* 947 Abbeydale Road, Sheffield S7 2QD. *T:* (0114) 236 6148.

PATON, William; Director, TÜV Suddeutschland, since 2001; *b* 29 Nov. 1941; *s* of Matthew Paton and Elizabeth Paton (*née* Shearer); *m* 1964, Elizabeth Anne Marr; two *s*.

Educ: Douglas Ewart Sch., Newton Stewart; Univ. of Glasgow (BSc Hons Physics). Seismologist, SSL Ltd, 1964; Mgt Trainee, Colvilles Ltd, 1965; National Engineering Laboratory: scientific posts, 1965–80; Dir of Ops, 1990–95; Dir, 1995–97; Chief Exec., TÜV Product Service Ltd, 1997–2001. Dir and Sen. Exec., Nat. Engrg Assessment Gp, 1997–. Patents relating to improvements in carbon fibre processing technol., engrg designs and sports equipment. *Publications:* various articles in technical jls. *Recreations:* golf, travel. *Address:* 2 Wester Balrymonth, St Andrews, Fife KY16 8NN. *T:* (01334) 472131.

PATON WALSH, Jill, CBE 1996; self-employed author, since 1966; *b* 29 April 1937; *d* of John Llewelyn Bliss and Patricia Paula DuBern; *m* 1961, Antony Paton Walsh (separated; he *d* 2003); one *s* two *d*. *Educ:* St Michael's Convent, Finchley; St Anne's Coll., Oxford (BA English; MA; DipEd). Schoolteacher, Enfield Girls' Grammar Sch., 1959–62. Arts Council Creative Writing Fellowship, Brighton Poly., 1976–77, 1977–78; Gertrude Clark Whitall Meml Lectr, Library of Congress, 1978; vis. faculty mem., Center for Children's Lit., Simmons Coll., Boston, Mass, 1978–86. A Judge, Whitbread Lit. Award, 1984; Chm., Cambridge Book Assoc., 1987–89; former Mem., Management Cttee, Soc. of Authors; Member: Cttee, Children's Writers' and Illustrators' Gp; Adjunct British Bd, Children's Literature New England. FRSL 1996. *Publications: fiction:* Farewell, Great King, 1972; Lapsing, 1986; A School for Lovers, 1989; The Wyndham Case, 1993; Knowledge of Angels, 1994; A Piece of Justice, 1995; The Serpentine Cave, 1997; Thrones, Dominations (completion of novel by Dorothy L. Sayers), 1998; A Desert in Bohemia, 2000; Presumption of Death (with material by Dorothy L. Sayers), 2002; Debts of Dishonour, 2006; The Bad Quarto, 2007; *for children:* The Island Sunrise: pre-historic Britain, 1975; *fiction:* Hengest's Tale, 1966; The Dolphin Crossing, 1967; (with Kevin Crossley-Holland) Wordhoard, 1969; Fireweed (Book World Fest. Award), 1970; Goldengrove, 1972; Toolmaker, 1973; The Dawnstone, 1973; The Emperor's Winding Sheet (jtly, Whitbread Prize), 1974; The Butty Boy, 1975 (US edn as The Huffler); Unleaving (Boston Globe/Horn Book Award), 1976; Crossing to Salamis, The Walls of Athens, and Persian Gold, 1977–78 (US combined edn as Children of the Fox, 1978); A Chance Child, 1978; The Green Book, 1981 (re-issued as Shine, 1988); Babylon, 1982; Lost & Found, 1984; A Parcel of Patterns (Universe Prize), 1984; Gaffer Samson's Luck, 1985 (Smarties Prize Grand Prix, 1984); Five Tides, 1986; Torch, 1987; Birdy and the Ghosties, 1989; Grace, 1991; When Grandma Came, 1992; Matthew and the Sea-Singer, 1992; Pepi and the Secret Names, 1994; When I Was Little Like You, 1997. *Recreations:* photography, gardening, reading. *Address:* c/o David Higham Associates, 5–8 Lower John Street, Golden Square, W1R 4HA. *T:* (020) 7437 7888.

PATRIARCA, Stephen Richard; Principal (formerly Headmaster), William Hulme's Grammar School, Manchester, 2000–08 (city academy from 2007); *b* 3 May 1953; *s* of Ronald and late Maureen Patriarca. *Educ:* Sweyne Sch., Rayleigh; UC of Swansea (BA Hons 1995). Asst English Master, 1978–95, Dep. Headmaster, 1995–2000, Hulme GS, Oldham. Mem. Council, Royal Inst. of Philosophy. Trustee, Anglo Austrian Soc., 2002–. *Recreations:* travel, music, art, cooking, wine. *Address:* 297 Frederick Street, Oldham OL8 4HX. *Club:* East India.

PATRICK, Andrew; HM Diplomatic Service; Deputy Head of Mission, Afghanistan, since 2007; *b* 28 Feb. 1966; *s* of Henry Patrick and Carol Patrick (*née* Biddle). *Educ:* Poltair Sch., Cornwall; Univ. of Bristol (BSc Hons Maths 1987); City Univ., London (Dip. in Law 1988). Joined FCO, 1988; Third, later Second Sec., Nicosia, 1991–95; First Sec., NATO, Brussels, 1995–96; Asst Private Sec. to Sec. of State, FCO, 1997–2000; Dep. Hd, News Dept, FCO, 2001–04; Dep. High Comr, S Africa, 2004–07. *Address:* c/o Foreign and Commonwealth Office, King Charles Street, SW1A 2AH.

PATRICK, Gail; *see* Patrick, L. G.

PATRICK, Graham McIntosh, CMG 1968; CVO 1981; DSC 1943; Under Secretary, Department of the Environment, 1971–81, retired; *b* 17 Oct. 1921; *m* 1945, Barbara Worboys; two *s*. *Educ:* Dundee High Sch.; St Andrews Univ. RNVR (Air Branch), 1940–46. Entered Ministry of Works, 1946; Regional Director: Middle East Region, 1965–67; South West Region, DoE, 1971–75; Chm., South West Economic Planning Bd, 1971–75; Dir, Scottish Services, PSA, 1975–81. *Address:* 20 Woodlands, Budleigh Salterton, Devon EX9 6AT.

PATRICK, (Lilian) Gail; Sheriff of Tayside, Central and Fife at Kirkcaldy, 1991–2001; part-time Sheriff, since 2001; *b* 24 Dec. 1941; *d* of Alexander Findlay McFadzean, MA, LLB and Elizabeth Fullerton McFadzean (*née* Fenton); *m* 1967, Spencer Francis Rodger, LLB, WS, *s* of Francis and Isabel Patrick; one *s* three *d*. *Educ:* Radleigh Sch., Glasgow; Marr Coll., Troon; St Andrews Univ. (MA); Edinburgh Univ. (LLB). Enrolled as solicitor, 1966; pt-time practice, 1967–79; Lecturer and Tutor: Glasgow Univ., 1967–82; Edinburgh Univ., 1980–82, 1985–90; pt-time Procurator Fiscal Depute, 1979–80; admitted to Faculty of Advocates, 1981; Standing Jun. Counsel, Scottish Educn Dept, 1986–91; Chm., Social Security Appeal Tribunal, 1986–91; Reporter, Scottish Legal Aid Bd, 1986–91; Temp. Sheriff, 1988–91; called to the Bar, Lincoln's Inn, 1990. *Recreations:* golf, hill-walking, cycling, fishing, music. *Clubs:* Murrayfield Golf (Edinburgh), Bonar Bridge and Ardgay Golf, Dornoch Golf, Elie and Earlsferry Golf.

PATRICK, Simon John; Clerk of Delegated Legislation, House of Commons, since 2006; *b* 13 Oct. 1956; *s* of John Patrick and Mary Patrick (*née* Ansell). *Educ:* Merchant Taylors' Sch.; Pembroke Coll., Cambridge (BA Maths 1978, MA 1982). House of Commons: a clerk, 1978–: Clerk: Cttee of Public Accts, 1986–89; Employment Cttee, 1989–91; Table Office, 1991–95; Nat. Heritage Cttee, 1995–97; Treasury Cttee, 1998–2001; Jl Office, 2001–05; Europ. Scrutiny Cttee, 2005–06. *Publication:* (an Asst Ed) Erskine May's Parliamentary Practice, 23rd edn 2004. *Recreations:* classical music, typography, computing. *Address:* House of Commons, SW1A 0AA.

PATTEN, family name of **Barons Patten** and **Patten of Barnes**.

PATTEN, Baron *cr* 1997 (Life Peer), of Wincanton in the co. of Somerset; **John Haggitt Charles Patten;** PC 1990; Senior Advisor, Charterhouse Development Capital Ltd, since 2001; *b* 17 July 1945; *s* of late Jack Patten and Maria Olga (*née* Sikora); *m* 1978, Louise Alexandra Virginia Charlotte Rowe (*see* Lady Patten); one *d*. *Educ:* Wimbledon Coll.; Sidney Sussex Coll., Cambridge (PhD 1972). University Lectr, 1969–79, Fellow, Hertford Coll., 1972–94, Univ. of Oxford. Oxford City Councillor, 1973–76. MP (C) City of Oxford, 1979–83; Oxford W and Abingdon, 1983–97. PPS to the Ministers of State at the Home Office, 1980–81; Parliamentary Under-Secretary of State: NI Office, 1981–83; DHSS, 1983–85; Minister of State for Housing, Urban Affairs and Construction, DoE, 1985–87; Minister of State, Home Office, 1987–92; Sec. of State for Educn, 1992–94. Advr, 1996–2000, non-exec. Dep. Chm., 2000–01, Charterhouse plc; non-executive Director: Lockheed Martin UK Ltd, 1999–2003; Lockheed Martin UK Holdings Ltd, 2003–. UK Advr, Lockheed Martin Overseas Corp., 1997–; Advr, Thomas Goode & Co. Ltd, 1997–; Sen. Advr, Barros Technologies Ltd, 2008–. Jt Pres., Atlantic Council of the UK, 2005–. Hon. Fellow, Harris Manchester Coll., Oxford, 1996. *Publications:* The Conservative Opportunity (with Lord Blake), 1976; English Towns, 1500–1700, 1978; (ed) Pre-Industrial England, 1979; (ed) The Expanding City, 1983; (with Paul Coones) The Penguin Guide to the Landscape of England and Wales, 1986; Things to Come: the Tories in the 21st Century, 1995. *Recreation:* talking to my wife and daughter. *Address:* House of Lords, SW1A 0PW.

PATTEN OF BARNES, Baron *cr* 2005 (Life Peer), of Barnes in the London Borough of Richmond; **Christopher Francis Patten,** CH 1998; PC 1989; Chancellor: University of Newcastle, since 1999; University of Oxford, since 2003; Co-Chairman, International Crisis Group, since 2004; *b* 12 May 1944; *s* of late Francis Joseph Patten and Joan McCarthy; *m* 1971, Mary Lavender St Leger Thornton; three *d*. *Educ:* St Benedict's School, Ealing; Balliol College, Oxford (Hon. Fellow, 2000). Conservative Research Dept, 1966–70; Cabinet Office, 1970–72; Home Office, 1972; Personal Asst to Chairman of Conservative Party, 1972–74; Director, Conservative Research Dept, 1974–79. Governor and C-in-C, Hong Kong, 1992–97; Chm., Ind. Commn on Policing for NI, 1998–99. MP (C) Bath, 1979–92; contested (C) same seat, 1992. PPS to Chancellor of Duchy of Lancaster and Leader of House of Commons, 1979–81, to Secretary of State for Social Services, 1981; Parly Under-Sec. of State, NI Office, 1983–85; Minister of State, DES, 1985–86; Minister of State (Minister for Overseas Develt), FCO, 1986–89; Sec. of State for the Envmt, 1989–90; Chancellor of Duchy of Lancaster, 1990–92; Chm. of Cons. Party, 1990–92. Vice Chm., Cons. Parly Finance Cttee, 1981–83; Mem., Select Cttees on Defence and Procedure, 1982–83. Mem., Eur. Commn, 1999–2004. Dir, Independent Newspapers, 1998–99. Hon. FRCPE 1994. Hon. Fellow, St Antony's Coll., Oxford, 2003. Hon. DJur: Massachusetts, 1999; Birmingham, 2001; Bath, 2003; Hon. DCL: Newcastle, 1999; Oxford 2003; Hon. DLitt: Sydney, 2001; Exeter, 2002; Ulster, 2004; DUniv: Keele, 2002; Stettin, 2004; Hon. DBA Kingston, 2003. *Publications:* The Tory Case, 1983; East and West, 1998; Not Quite the Diplomat, 2005. *Recreations:* reading, tennis, gardening. *Address:* House of Lords, SW1A 0PW. *Clubs:* Athenæum, Beefsteak, Royal Automobile, Oxford and Cambridge; All England Lawn Tennis, Queen's.

PATTEN, Lady; Louise Alexandra Virginia Charlotte Patten; Senior Adviser, Bain & Co. Inc., since 1997; *b* 2 Feb. 1954; *m* 1978, John Haggitt Charles Patten (*see* Baron Patten); one *d*. *Educ:* St Paul's Girls' Sch., Hammersmith; St Hugh's Coll., Oxford (MA Hons). Manager, Citibank NA, 1977–81; Resident Vice Pres., Wells Fargo Bank NA, 1981–85; Partner: PA Consulting Gp, 1985–93; Bain & Co. Inc., 1994–97. Director: Hilton Gp plc, 1993–2003; Harveys Furnishings plc, 1993–2000; GUS (formerly Gt Universal Stores) plc, 1997–2006; Somerfield plc, 1998–2005 (Actg Chm., 1999–2000); Brixton plc, 2001– (Chm., 2003–); Bradford & Bingley plc, 2003–; Marks & Spencer plc, 2006–. *Recreations:* talking with my husband, our daughter and her ponies. *Address:* c/o Bain & Co. Inc., 40 Strand, WC2N 5HZ. *T:* (020) 7969 6000.

PATTEN, Brian; poet; *b* 7 Feb. 1946. Regents Lectr, Univ. of Calif (San Diego), 1985. FRSL 2003. Freedom, City of Liverpool, 2001. Hon. Fellow, Liverpool John Moores Univ., 2002. Cholmondeley Award for Poetry, 2002. *Publications: poetry:* Penguin Modern Poets, 1967; Little Johnny's Confession, 1967; Notes to the Hurrying Man, 1969; The Irrelevant Song, 1971; The Unreliable Nightingale, 1973; Vanishing Trick, 1976; The Shabby Angel, 1978; Grave Gossip, 1979; Love Poems, 1981; Clare's Countryside: a book on John Clare, 1982; New Volume, 1983; Storm Damage, 1988; Grinning Jack (Selected Poems), 1990; Armada, 1996; The Blue and Green Ark, 1999; New Selected Poems, 2007; Collected Love Poems, 2008; *novel:* Mr Moon's Last Case, 1975 (Mystery Writers of Amer. Special Award, 1976); *for younger readers:* The Elephant and the Flower, 1969; Jumping Mouse; 1971; Emma's Doll, 1976; The Sly Cormorant and the Fish: adaptations of The Aesop Fables, 1977; (ed) Gangsters, Ghosts and Dragonflies, 1981; Gargling with Jelly, 1985; Jimmy Tag-along, 1988; Thawing Frozen Frogs, 1990; (ed) The Puffin Book of Twentieth Century Children's Verse, 1991; Grizzelda Frizzle, 1992; The Magic Bicycle, 1993; Impossible Parents, 1994; The Utter Nutters, 1994; (ed) The Puffin Book of Utterly Brilliant Poetry, 1998; Beowulf and the Monster, 1999; Juggling with Gerbils, 2000; Little Hotchpotch, 2000; Impossible Parents Go Green, 2000; The Story Giant, 2001; Ben's Magic Telescope, 2003; (with Roger McGough) The Monsters' Guide to Choosing a Pet, 2004; Puffin Book of Modern Children's Verse, 2006; *plays:* The Pig And The Junkle, 1975; (with Roger McGough) The Mouth Trap, 1982; Blind Love, 1983; Gargling with Jelly, 1989; *recordings:* Brian Patten Reading His Own Poetry, 1969; British Poets Of Our Time, 1974; Vanishing Trick, 1976; The Sly Cormorant, 1977; Grizzelda Frizzle and other stories, 1995; The Mersey Sound, 1997. *Address:* c/o Rogers, Coleridge and White, 20 Powis Mews, W11 1JN. *Club:* Chelsea Arts.

PATTEN, Louise Alexandra Virginia Charlotte; *see* Lady Patten.

PATTEN, Hon. Sir Nicholas (John), Kt 2000; **Hon. Mr Justice Patten;** a Judge of the High Court of Justice, Chancery Division, since 2000; *b* 7 Aug. 1950; *s* of late Peter Grenville Patten and Dorothy Patten (*née* Davenport); *m* 1984, Veronica Mary Schoeneich (marr. diss. 1998); two *s* one *d*. *Educ:* Tulse Hill Sch.; Christ Church, Oxford (Open Schol.; MA; BCL (1st Cl. Hons Jurisprudence)). Called to the Bar, Lincoln's Inn, 1974, Bencher, 1997; QC 1988; a Dep. High Court Judge, 1998–2000. Vice-Chancellor, Co. Palatine of Lancaster, 2005–. Chm., Chancery Bar Assoc., 1997–99. *Recreation:* gardening. *Address:* Royal Courts of Justice, Strand, WC2A 2LL.

PATTENDEN, Prof. Gerald, FRS 1991; Research Professor of Organic Chemistry, Nottingham University, since 2005 (Pro-Vice-Chancellor, 1997–2003); *b* 4 March 1940; *s* of Albert James and Violet Eugene Pattenden; *m* 1969, Christine Frances Doherty; three *d*. *Educ:* Brunel Univ. (BSc); Queen Mary College London (PhD, DSc; Hon. Fellow, 2000). CChem, FRSC. Lectr, UC, Cardiff, 1966–72; Nottingham University: Lectr, 1972–75; Reader, 1975–80; Prof., 1980–88; Sir Jesse Boot Prof. of Organic Chem., 1988–2005; Hd of Dept of Chem., 1988–96. Chm., Org. Chem. Cttee, SERC, 1992–94. Mem. Council, Royal Soc., 2001–03. Royal Society of Chemistry: Pres., Perkin Div., 1995–97 (Scientific Ed., Perkin Trans); Corday-Morgan Medal and Prize, 1975; Simonsen Lect. and Medal, 1987; Tilden Lect. and Medal, 1991; Award for Synthetic Organic Chem., 1992; Pedler Lect. and Medal, 1993; Award for Heterocyclic Chem., 1994; Award for Natural Product Chemistry, 1997; Hugo Müller Lect. and Medal, 2001; Robert Robinson Lect., 2007. *Publications:* editor of several books; over 470 contribs to internat. jls of chemistry. *Recreations:* sport, DIY, gardening. *Address:* School of Chemistry, The University, Nottingham NG7 2RD. *T:* (0115) 951 3530, *Fax:* (0115) 951 3535; *e-mail:* gp@nottingham.ac.uk.

PATTERSON, Ben; *see* Patterson, G. B.

PATTERSON, (Constance) Marie, (Mrs Barrie Devney), CBE 1978 (OBE 1973); National Officer, Transport and General Workers' Union, 1976–84 (National Woman Officer, 1963–76); Member of General Council of TUC, 1963–84 (Chairman, 1974–75 and 1977); *b* 1 April 1934; *d* of Dr Richard Swanton Abraham; *m* 1st, 1960, Thomas Michael Valentine Patterson (marr. diss. 1976); 2nd, 1984, Barrie Devney. *Educ:* Pendleton High Sch.; Bedford Coll., Univ. of London (BA). Member: Exec., Confedn of Shipbuilding and Engrg Unions, 1966–84 (Pres., 1977–78); Hotel and Catering Trng Bd,

1966–87; Equal Opportunities Commn, 1975–84; Central Arbitration Commn, 1976–94; Legal Aid Adv. Cttee, 1988–90; Council, Office of Banking Ombudsman, 1992–2001. Dir of Remploy, 1966–87. Lay Mem., Press Council, 1964–70. Chm. Council, Queen's Coll., Harley St, 1994–2000; Mem. Court, LSE, 1984–2005 (Mem. Council, 2000–02). Chm., Galleon Trust, 1998–2005. FRSA 2000. Hon. DSc Salford, 1975. *Recreations:* sight-seeing, jig-saws.

PATTERSON, Eric, MBE 1970; HM Diplomatic Service, retired; Consul-General, 1982–88 and Counsellor (Commercial), 1986–88, Auckland; *b* 2 May 1930; *s* of Richard and Elizabeth Patterson; *m* 1st, 1953, Doris Mason (*d* 1999); two *s*; 2nd, 2001, Charlotte Pellizzaro (*née* Bathurst). *Educ:* Hookergate Grammar Sch., Co. Durham. Served Royal Signals, 1948–50. Local govt service, 1947–50; Lord Chancellor's Dept, 1950–52; BoT, 1952–62; Asst Trade Comr, Halifax, NS, 1962–67; Second Sec. (Commercial), Khartoum, 1967–70; First Sec. (Commercial), The Hague, 1970–74; FCO, 1974–76; First Sec. (Commercial), Warsaw, 1976–80; FCO, 1980–82. *Recreations:* golf, photography, fly-fishing. *Address:* 45A Bleakhouse Road, Howick, Auckland, New Zealand.

PATTERSON, Frances Silvia; QC 1998; a Recorder, since 2000; *m* 1980, Dr Graham Nicholson; three *s*. *Educ:* Queen's Sch., Chester; Leicester Univ. Called to the Bar, Middle Temple, 1977, Bencher, 2005; Asst Recorder, 1997–2000; Hd of Chambers, 2004–. *Address:* Kings Chambers, 36 Young Street, Manchester M3 3FT. *T:* (0161) 832 9082.

PATTERSON, George Benjamin, (Ben); Director, CJA Consultants Ltd, since 2004; *b* 21 April 1939; *s* of late Eric James Patterson and Ethel Patterson; *m* 1970, Felicity Barbara Anne Raybould; one *s* one *d*. *Educ:* Westminster Sch.; Trinity Coll., Cambridge (MA); London Sch. of Economics. Lecturer, Swinton Conservative Coll., 1961–65; Editor (at Conservative Political Centre), CPC Monthly Report, 1965–74; Dep. Head, London Office of European Parlt, 1974–79. MEP (C) Kent W, 1979–94; contested (C) Kent W, Eur. Parly elecns, 1994. Prin. Administrator, Internal Market, then Econ. and Monetary Affairs Div., DG for Res., EP, 1994–2004. Mem (C), Hammersmith LBC, 1968–71. Contested (C) Wrexham, 1970. MInstD. *Publications:* The Character of Conservatism, 1973; Direct Elections to the European Parliament, 1974; Europe and Employment, 1984; Vredeling and All That, 1984; VAT: the zero rate issue, 1988; A Guide to EMU, 1990; A European Currency, 1994; Options for a Definitive VAT System, 1995; The Co-ordination of National Fiscal Policies, 1996; The Consequences of Abolishing Duty Free Within the EU, 1997; Adjusting to Asymmetric Shocks, 1998; The Feasibility of a Tobin Tax, 1999; The Determination of Interest Rates, 1999; Exchange Rates and Monetary Policy, 2000; Tax Co-ordination in the European Union, 2002; Background to the Euro, 2002; Taxation in Europe: recent developments, 2003. *Recreations:* reading science fiction, walking. *Address:* Elm Hill House, High Street, Hawkhurst, Kent TN18 4XU. *T:* (01580) 752780; 38 Le Village, 09300 Montségur, France. *T:* (5) 61640119.

PATTERSON, Harry; novelist; *b* 27 July 1929; *s* of Henry Patterson and Rita Higgins Bell; *m* 1st, 1958, Amy Margaret Hewitt (marr. diss. 1984); one *s* three *d*; 2nd, 1985, Denise Lesley Anne Palmer. *Educ:* Roundhay Sch., Leeds; Beckett Park Coll. for Teachers; London Sch. of Economics as external student (BSc(Hons) Sociology). FRSA. NCO, The Blues, 1947–50. 1950–58: tried everything from being a clerk to a circus tent-hand; 1958–72: variously a schoolmaster, Lectr in Liberal Studies, Leeds Polytechnic, Sen. Lectr in Education, James Graham Coll. and Tutor in Sch. Practice, Leeds Univ.; since age of 41, engaged in full-time writing career. Dual citizenship, British/Irish. DUniv Leeds Metropolitan, 1995. *Publications include:* (as Jack Higgins): Prayer for the Dying, 1973 (filmed 1985); The Eagle has Landed, 1975 (filmed 1976); Storm Warning, 1976; Day of Judgement, 1978; Solo, 1980; Luciano's Luck, 1981; Touch the Devil, 1982; Exocet, 1983; Confessional, 1985 (filmed 1985); Night of the Fox, 1986 (filmed 1989); A Season in Hell, 1989; Cold Harbour, 1990; The Eagle Has Flown, 1990; Angel of Death, 1995; Drink with the Devil, 1996; Day of Reckoning, 2000; Edge of Danger, 2001; Bad Company, 2003; Dark Justice, 2004; (as Harry Patterson): The Valhalla Exchange, 1978; To Catch a King, 1979 (filmed 1983); Dillinger, 1983; Walking Wounded (stage play), 1987; and many others (including The Violent Enemy, filmed 1969, and The Wrath of God, filmed 1972) under pseudonyms (Martin Fallon, Hugh Marlowe, Henry Patterson); some books trans. into 42 languages. *Recreations:* tennis, old movies. *Address:* c/o Ed Victor Ltd, 6 Bayley Street, WC1B 3HB.

PATTERSON, Marie; *see* Patterson, C. M.

PATTERSON, Dr Mark Jonathan Lister; Hon. Consultant Haematologist, Manchester Royal Infirmary, since 1997; Consultant Haematologist, Mid Cheshire NHS Trust, since 1996; *b* 2 March 1934; *s* of Alfred Patterson and Frederica Georgina Mary Lister Nicholson; *m* 1958, Jane Teresa Scott Stokes; one *s* two *d*. *Educ:* privately; St Bartholomew's Hosp. Med. Coll., Univ. of London (MB 1959). MRCP. Jun. hosp. appts at St Bartholomew's Hosp., Royal Postgrad. Med. Sch., and MRC Exptl Haematol. Unit; Consultant Haematologist to Nat. Heart and Chest Hosps, 1967–84. Mem., GLC, 1970–73 and 1977–81; contested (C) Ealing N, Feb. 1974. *Recreations:* medicine, politics. *Address:* Wolverton Manor, Shorwell, Newport, Isle of Wight PO30 3JS. *T:* (01983) 740609.

PATTERSON, Paul Leslie; composer; Manson Professor of Composition, Royal Academy of Music, since 1997; Artistic Director, Park Lane Group Young Composer Forum, since 1998; formed: Manson Ensemble, 1968; The Patterson Quintet, 1982; *b* 15 June 1947; *s* of Leslie and Lilian Patterson; *m* 1981, Hazel Wilson; one *s* one *d*. *Educ:* Royal Academy of Music. FRAM 1980. Freelance composer, 1968–; Arts Council Composer in Association, English Sinfonia, 1969–70; Director, Contemporary Music, Warwick Univ., 1974–80; Prof. of Composition, and Hd of Composition and Twentieth Century Music, RAM, 1985–97; Composer in Residence: SE Arts Assoc., 1980–82; Bedford School, 1984–85; Southwark Fest., 1989–91; James Allen School, Dulwich, 1990–91; Three Spires Fest., Truro, 1992–94; NYO, 1997–; Guest Prof., Yale Univ., 1989–90; Vis. Prof. of Composition, Univ. of Canterbury, Christchurch, 2000–; Vis. Composition Tutor, RNCM, 2002–. Artistic Dir, Exeter Fest., 1991–97; Artistic Advr, N Devon Fest., 1999–. Chm., Mendelssohn Scholarship, Royal Schs of Music, 1997–. Member: Exec. Cttee, Composers Guild, 1972–75; Council, SPNM, 1975–81, 1985–; Adv. Council, BBC Radio London, 1986–; Adv. Cttee, Arts Council's Recordings Panel, 1986–94; Artistic Director of RAM Festivals: Lutosławski, 1984; Penderecki, 1986; Messiaen, 1987; Henze, 1988; Berio, 1989; Carter, 1990; Da Capo, 1993; Schnittke, 1994; Ligeti, 1995; film music, 1996; Birtwistle, 1997; Donatoni, 1998; Russian, 1999; Pärt, 2000; Kagel, 2001; Besio, 2004. Featured Composer at: Three Choirs Fest., Patterson at South Bank Fest., 1988; Cheltenham Fest., 1988, 1990; Peterborough Fest., 1989; Exeter Fest., 1991; Presteigne Fest., 2001. Performances world wide by leading orchestras and soloists and ensembles; also film and TV music. Numerous recordings. Pres., RAM Club, 1993–94. FRSA 1989. Hon. FLCM 1997. Lesley Boosey Award, Royal Philharmonic Soc., 1996. OM, Polish Ministry of Culture, 1987. *Publications:* Rebecca, 1968; Trumpet Concerto, 1969; Time Piece, 1972; Kyrie, 1972; Requiem, 1973; Comedy for Five Winds, 1973; Requiem, 1974; Fluorescences, 1974; Clarinet Concerto, 1976; Cracowian Counterpoints, 1977; Voices of Sleep, 1979; Concerto for Orchestra, 1981; Canterbury Psalms, 1981; Sinfonia, 1982; Mass of the Sea, 1983; Deception Pass, 1983; Duologue, 1984; Mean Time, 1984; Europhony, 1985; Missa Brevis, 1985; Stabat Mater, 1986; String Quartet, 1986; Magnificat and Nunc Dimittis, 1986; Propositions, 1987; Trombone Quartet, 1987; Suite for Cello, 1987; Sorriest Cow, 1987; Tides of Mananan, 1988; Te Deum, 1988; Tunnel of Time, 1989; White Shadows, 1989; Symphony, 1990; The End, 1990; Mighty Voice, 1991; Violin Concerto, 1992; Little Red Riding Hood, 1992; Magnificat, 1993; Music for Opening Channel Tunnel, 1994; Overture: Songs of the West, 1995; Soliloquy, 1996; Rustic Sketches, 1997; Hell Angels, 1998; Gloria, 1999; Western Winds, 1999; Millennium Mass, 2000; Deviations, 2001; Cello Concerto, 2002; Jubilee Dances, 2002; Three Little Pigs, 2003; Bug for Solo Harp, 2003; Harpo Maniac, 2004; Fifth Continent, 2005; Orchestra on Parade, 2005. *Recreations:* sailing, croquet, swimming, computing. *Address:* 31 Cromwell Avenue, Highgate, N6 5HN. *T:* (020) 8348 3711.

PATTERSON, Most Hon. Percival (Noel James), ON 2002; PC 1992; QC 1983; Prime Minister of Jamaica, 1992–2006; *b* 10 April 1935; *s* of Henry Patterson and Ina James; *m* (marr. diss.); one *s* one *d*. *Educ:* Somerton Primary, St James; Calabar High Sch., Kingston; Univ. of the West Indies (BA Hons English 1958); LSE (LLB 1963). Called to the Bar, Middle Temple, 1963; admitted to Jamaican Bar, 1963; private legal practice, Kingston. Senator, Leader of Opposition Business, 1969–70; MP (PNP) SE, then Eastern, Westmoreland, Jamaica, 1972–80 and 1989–2006; Minister of Industry, Trade and Tourism, 1972–77; Dep. Prime Minister, 1978–80, 1989–91; Minister: of Foreign Affairs and Foreign Trade, 1978–80; of Devel̀t Planning and Production, 1989–90; of Finance and Planning, 1990–91; of Defence, 1992–2006. People's National Party: Mem. Exec. Council, 1964; Vice-Pres., 1969; Chm., 1983–92; Pres. and Leader, 1992–2006. Agricola Medal, FAO, 2001; Golden Star Award, Caribbean and Latin Amer. Action Gp, 2002; Chancellor's Medal, Univ. of W Indies, 2006. Order of Francisco Morazán, Gran Cruz Placa de Oro (Honduras), 1990; Order of Águila Azteca (Mexico), 1990; Order of Liberator Simon Bolivar (Venezuela), 1st Class, 1992; Order of San Martin (Argentina), 1992; Order of Gran Cruz Gonzalo Jiménez de Quesada (Colombia), 1994; Order of Jose Marti (Cuba), 1997; Order of the Volta (Ghana), 1999; Gran Cruz Placa de Orode Juan Mora Fernández (Costa Rica), 2001; Grand Cross, Nat. Order of Civil Merit (Spain), 2006; Order of Belize, 2006; Grand Cross, Order of Southern Cross (Brazil), 2006; Order of Excellence (Guyana), 2006. *Recreations:* music (jazz/Jamaican), sports (cricket, boxing, track and field, tennis). *Address:* Heisconsults, Life of Jamaica Centre, 10th Floor, 28–48 Barbados Avenue, Kingston 5, Jamaica.

PATTIE, Rt Hon. Sir Geoffrey (Edwin), Kt 1987; PC 1987; Senior Partner, Terrington Management LLP, since 1999; Chairman, GEC-Marconi, 1996–99 (Joint Chairman, 1991–96); *b* 17 Jan. 1936; *s* of late Alfred Edwin Pattie, LDS, and Ada Olive (*née* Carr); *m* 1960, Tuëma Caroline (*née* Eyre-Maunsell); one *s* (one *d* decd). *Educ:* Durham Sch.; St Catharine's Coll., Cambridge (BA 1959, MA; Fellow Commoner, 2005; Hon. Fellow, 2007). Called to Bar, Gray's Inn, 1964. Served: Queen Victoria's Rifles (TA), 1959–61; (on amalgamation) Queen's Royal Rifles (TA), now 4th Royal Green Jackets, 1961–65; Captain, 1964, Hon. Col, 1996–99, Dep. Col Comdt (TA and Cadets), 1999–2007. Mem. GLC, Lambeth, 1967–70; Chm. ILEA Finance Cttee, 1968–70. Marketing Dir, 1997–98, Dir of Communications, 1998–99, GEC. Contested (C) Barking, 1966 and 1970. MP (C) Chertsey and Walton, Feb. 1974–1997. Parly Under Sec. of State for Defence for the RAF, 1979–81, for Defence Procurement, 1981–83; Minister of State: for Defence Procurement, 1983–84; DTI (Minister for IT), 1984–87; Vice-Chm., Cons. Party, 1990–97. Sec., Cons. Parly Aviation Cttee, 1974–75, 1975–76, Vice Chm., 1976–77, 1977–78; Jt Sec., Cons. Parly Defence Cttee, 1975–76, 1976–77, 1977–78, Vice Chm., 1978–79; Mem., Cttee of Public Accounts, 1976–79; Vice-Chm., All Party Cttee on Mental Health, 1977–79. Mem. General Synod of Church of England, 1970–75. Chm., Intellectual Property Inst., 1994–99. Chm. of Governors, London Coll. of Printing, 1968–69. Trustee, Excalibur Scholarship Scheme, 1992–. FRSA 1990. Hon. LLD Sheffield, 1996. *Publications:* Towards a New Defence Policy, 1976; (with James Bellini) A New World Role for the Medium Power: the British Opportunity, 1977; One of our Delegations is Missing, 2002. *Recreations:* opera, theatre, following Middlesbrough Football Club. *Address:* Terrington Management, 45 Great Peter Street, SW1P 3LT. *Clubs:* Reform, Royal Green Jackets.

PATTINSON, Kristina; *see* Harrison, K.

PATTISON, David Arnold, PhD; Best Value Inspector, Audit Commission, 2000–06; *b* 9 Feb. 1941; *s* of David Pattison and Christina Russell Bone; *m* 1967, Anne Ross Wilson; two *s* one *d*. *Educ:* Glasgow Univ. (BSc 1st Cl. Hons, PhD). Planning Assistant, Dunbarton County Council, 1966–67; Lecturer, Strathclyde Univ., 1967–70; Head of Tourism Division, Highlands and Islands Development Board, 1970–81; Chief Exec., Scottish Tourist Board, 1981–85; Dir of Leisure and Tourism Consulting, Arthur Young Group, 1985–90; Principal Associate: Cobham Resource Consultants, 1990–96; Scott Wilson Resource Consultants, 1996–98; Dir, David A. Pattison Associates, 1998–2000. Mem. Council, Inland Waterways Amenity Adv. Council, 2001–05. Hon. Prof., Queen Margaret Coll., Edinburgh, 1992. Hon. Pres., Scottish YHA, 1995–. *Publications:* Tourism Development Plans for: Argyll, Bute, Ayrshire, Burgh of Ayr, Ulster. *Recreations:* reading, watching soccer and Rugby, golf, gardening. *Address:* 7 Cramond Glebe Gardens, Cramond, Edinburgh EH4 6NZ.

PATTISON, Rev. Prof. George Linsley, DD; Lady Margaret Professor of Divinity, University of Oxford, since 2004; Canon of Christ Church, Oxford, since 2004; *b* 25 May 1950; *s* of George William Pattison and Jean Pattison; *m* 1971, Hilary Christine Cochrane; one *s* two *d*. *Educ:* Perse Sch., Cambridge; Edinburgh Univ. (MA, BD); Durham Univ. (PhD 1983, DD 2004). Ordained deacon, 1977, priest, 1978; Curate, St James' Church, Benwell, Newcastle upon Tyne, 1977–80; Priest-in-charge, St Philip and St James' Church, Kimblesworth, Co. Durham, 1980–83; Res. Student, Durham Univ., 1980–83; Rector, Badwell Ash, Great Ashfield, Hunston and Stowlangtoft with Langham, Suffolk, 1983–91; Dean of Chapel, King's Coll., Cambridge, 1991–2001; Associate Prof. of Theol., 2002–03, Vis. Prof. of Theol., 2005–, Univ. of Aarhus, Denmark. Vis. Res. Prof., Univ. of Copenhagen, 1997, 2000. Vice-Pres., Modern Churchpeople's Union, 1999–. Has broadcast on BBC Radio 3, Radio 4 and World Service on subjects of art and religion. Editor, Modern Believing, 1994–98. *Publications:* Art, Modernity and Faith, 1991, 2nd edn 1998; Kierkegaard: the aesthetic and the religious, 1992, 2nd edn 1999; (ed) Kierkegaard on Art and Communication, 1993; (with Sister Wendy Beckett) Pains of Glass, 1995; (with S. Platten) Spirit and Tradition, 1996; Agnosis: theology in the void, 1996; Kierkegaard and the Crisis of Faith, 1997; (ed with S. Shakespeare) Kierkegaard: the self in society, 1998; The End of Theology and the Task of Thinking About God, 1998; Poor Paris!, 1998; Anxious Angels, 1999; The Later Heidegger, 2000; A Short Course in the Philosophy of Religion, 2001; Kierkegaard's Upbuilding Discourses, 2002; Kierkegaard, Religion and the Nineteenth Century Crisis of Culture, 2002; A Short Course in Christian Doctrine, 2005; The Philosophy of Kierkegaard, 2005; Thinking About God in an Age of Technology, 2005; articles on theology, philosophy of religion and the arts in specialist and non-specialist jls. *Recreations:* family life, music, films, theatre, visiting cities. *Address:* Priory House, Christ Church, Oxford OX1 1DP.

PATTISON, Sir John (Ridley), Kt 1998; DM; FRCPath, FMedSci; Professor of Medical Microbiology, University College London, 1984–2004, now Emeritus; *b* 1 Aug. 1942; *s* of Tom Frederick and Elizabeth Pattison; *m* 1965, Pauline Evans; one *s* two *d*. *Educ:* Barnard Castle Sch.; University Coll., Oxford (BSc, MA; BM, BCh 1968; DM 1975); Middlesex Hosp. Med. Sch. FRCPath 1985. Asst Lectr in Pathology, then Lectr in Virology, Middx Hosp. Med. Sch., 1970–75; Lectr, then Sen. Lectr in Virology, St Bartholomew's and London Hosp. Med. Colls, 1976–77; Prof. of Medical Microbiol., KCH Med. Sch., 1977–84; Dean, UCL Med. Sch., 1990–98; Vice-Provost, UCL, 1994–99; Dir of R&D, DoH and NHS, 1999–2004 (on secondment). Hon. NHS Consultant, UCH, subseq. UCL Hosps NHS Trust, 1984–2004; Hon. Consultant, PHLS, 1980–2003 (Board Mem., 1989–95); Sen. Med. Advr, MRC, 1996–99. Mem., MRC, 1992–95, 1999–2004 (Mem., Grants Cttee, 1985–87, Systems Bd, 1988–92; Chm., Physiol Medicine and Infection Bd, 1992–95); Chm., Spongiform Encephalopathy Adv. Cttee, 1995–99 (Mem., 1994–95). Mem. Council, Soc. of Gen. Microbiol., 1981–87. Member of Board: LSHTM, 1989–92; Inst. of Child Health, 1992–96; Inst. of Neurology, 1995–97. Member: Mgt Cttee, King's Fund, 1993–99 (Dep. Chm., 1994–99); King's Fund London Commn, 1994–95. Editor-in-Chief, Epidemiology & Infection, 1980–94; Mem. Council, Internat. Jl Exptl Pathology, 1979–. Founder FMedSci 1998. *Publications:* (ed jtly) Principles & Practice of Clinical Virology, 1987, 5th edn 2004; (ed jtly) Practical Guide to Clinical Virology, 1989; (ed jtly) Practical Guide to Clinical Bacteriology, 1995; papers and reviews on aspects of medical virology, esp. rubella virus and parvovirus infections. *Recreations:* family, windsurfing, books. *Address:* 17 Broadwater Lane, Towcester, Northants NN12 6JF. *T:* (01327) 352116; *e-mail:* portsea200@btopenworld.com.

PATTISON, Michael Ambrose, CBE 1996; Director, Sainsbury Family Charitable Trusts, 1995–2006; *b* 14 July 1946; *s* of late Osmond John Pattison and Eileen Susanna Pattison (*née* Cullen); *m* 1975, Beverley Jean, *d* of Genevieve and Hugh Webber, Florida, USA; one *d*. *Educ:* Sedbergh School; University of Sussex (BA Hons 1968). Min. of Overseas Develt, 1968; Asst Private Sec. to Minister, 1970; seconded to HM Diplomatic Service as First Sec., Perm. Mission to UN, New York, 1974; ODA, 1977; Private Sec. to successive Prime Ministers, 1979–82; ODA, 1982, Establishment Officer, 1983–85; Chief Exec. and Sec. Gen., RICS, 1985–95; Dir, Surveyors Holdings Ltd, 1985–95. Mem. Council, British Consultants Bureau, 1985–95. Non-exec. Dir, Ordnance Survey, 1997–2001. Trustee, Battersea Arts Centre Trust, 1988–94. Member: Cambridge Univ. Careers Service Syndicate, 1989–93; HEFCE Appeals Panel, 1999–; Gov., Thames Poly., subseq. Greenwich Univ., 1989–97 (Pro-Chancellor, 1994–97). Vis. Fellow, City Univ., 1990–. FRSA 1990. *Recreations:* cricket, Real tennis, golf, local history, countryside. *Address:* 8 Bimport, Shaftesbury, Dorset SP7 8AX. *T:* (01747) 852017. *Clubs:* Athenæum; Warwickshire CC.

PATTISON, Rev. Prof. Stephen Bewley, DLitt; Professor of Religion, Ethics and Practice, University of Birmingham, since 2007; *b* 14 Sept. 1953; *s* of Theodore Pattison and Rosamund Audrey Pattison (*née* Greening); *m* 2003, Charmian Beer. *Educ:* Selwyn Coll., Cambridge (BA); Edinburgh Theol Coll. (Dip. in Pastoral Studies 1978); Univ. of Edinburgh (PhD 1982; DLitt 2001); Univ. of Birmingham (MSocSc 1991). Ordained deacon, 1978, priest, 1980; Asst Curate, All Saints' Ch, Gosforth, 1978–79; Chaplain, Edinburgh Theol Coll., 1982–83; Lectr, Dept of Theol., Univ. of Birmingham, 1983–88; Chief Officer, Central Birmingham CHC, 1988–90; Lectr, then Sen. Lectr, Sch. of Health and Social Welfare, Open Univ., 1990–98; Dist. Sen. Res. Fellow, 1998–2000, Prof. and Head, 2000–07, Sch. of Religious and Theol Studies, Cardiff Univ. Vis. Sen. Res. Fellow, Jesus Coll., Oxford, 2004–05. Gifford Lectr, Aberdeen Univ., 2007. *Publications:* A Critique of Pastoral Care, 1987, 3rd edn 2000; Alive and Kicking: towards a practical theology of healing and illness, 1988; Pastoral Care and Liberation Theology, 1994; The Faith of the Managers, 1997; Shame: theory, therapy, theology, 2000; (ed jtly) The Blackwell Reader in Pastoral and Practical Theology, 2000; (ed jtly) Values in Professional Practice, 2004; The Challenge of Practical Theology, 2006; Seeing Things: deepening relations with visual artefacts, 2007. *Recreation:* growing things. *Address:* Department of Religion and Theology, University of Birmingham, Edgbaston, Birmingham B15 2TT. *T:* (07951) 145989; *e-mail:* sbpattison@hotmail.com.

PATTISON, Stephen Dexter, CMG 2003; DPhil; HM Diplomatic Service, retired; Head, International Business Development, Dyson, since 2007; *b* 24 Dec. 1953; *s* of George Stanley and May Elizabeth Pattison; *m* 1987, Helen Chaoushis; one *d*. *Educ:* Sir George Monoux Sch.; Queens' Coll., Cambridge (BA 1976); Wadham Coll., Oxford (DPhil 1980). Joined FCO, 1981: Second Sec., Nicosia, 1983–86; FCO, 1986–89; First Sec., Washington, 1989–94; Dep. Hd, Non-Proliferation Dept, FCO, 1994–96; Dir of Trade Promotion and Consul-Gen., Warsaw, 1997–2000; Hd, UN Dept, FCO, 2000–03; Fellow, Harvard Univ., 2003–04; Dir, Internat. Security, FCO, 2004–07. *Recreations:* the arts, cricket. *Address:* c/o Dyson, Tetbury Hill, Wilts SN16 0RP.

PATTRICK, Prof. Richard Annandale Douglas, PhD; Professor of Earth Science, since 2001, and Associate Dean, Graduate Education, since 2007, University of Manchester; *b* 31 March 1953; *s* of Dr Francis Gilson Pattrick and Hope Annandale Pattrick; *m* 1979, Sheila Margaret Murdoch; two *s* one *d*. *Educ:* Univ. of St Andrews (BSc Hons Geol.); Univ. of Strathclyde (PhD Applied Geol. 1980). University of Manchester: Lectr in Geol., 1979–98; Reader in Mineralogy, 1998–2001; Hd, Grad. Sch., 2001–03; Hd, Sch. of Earth, Atmospheric and Envmtl Sci., 2003–07. Vice Pres., Mineralogical Soc., 1988–92. *Publications:* (with D. A. Polya) Mineralisation in the British Isles, 1993; (ed with D. J. Vaughan) Mineral Surfaces, 1995; contribs on metallogenesis, applied mineralogy and envmtl geosci. in peer reviewed jls. *Recreations:* sport: tennis (county level, student international), hockey (student international), supporter of Macclesfield Town FC. *Address:* University of Manchester, Manchester M13 9PL; *e-mail:* richard.pattrick@manchester.ac.uk. *Clubs:* Cavendish Golf (Buxton); Macclesfield Town Football (Vice-Pres.).

PATTULLO, Sir (David) Bruce, Kt 1995; CBE 1989; Governor, Bank of Scotland, 1991–98 (Group Chief Executive, 1988–96); *b* 2 Jan. 1938; *s* of late Colin Arthur Pattullo and Elizabeth Mary Bruce; *m* 1962, Fiona Jane Nicholson; three *s* one *d*. *Educ:* Rugby Sch.; Hertford Coll., Oxford (BA). FCIBS. Commnd Royal Scots and seconded to Queen's Own Nigeria Regt. Gen. Man., Bank of Scotland Finance Co. Ltd, 1973–77; Chief Exec., British Linen Bank Ltd, 1977–78 (Dir, 1977–98); Bank of Scotland: Dep. Treas., 1978; Treas. and Gen. Manager (Chief Exec.), 1979–88; Dir, 1980–98; Dep. Governor, 1988–91. Director: Melville Street Investments, 1973–90; Bank of Wales, 1986–98; NWS Bank plc, 1986–98; Standard Life Assurance Co., 1985–96. Chm., Cttee, Scottish Clearing Bankers, 1981–83, 1987–89; Pres., Inst. of Bankers in Scotland, 1990–92 (a Vice-Pres., 1977–90). First Prizeman (Bilsland Prize), Inst. of Bankers in Scotland, 1964. FRSE 1990. Hon. LLD Aberdeen, 1995; DUniv Stirling, 1996; Hon. DBA Strathclyde, 1998. *Recreations:* tennis, hill walking. *Address:* 6 Cammo Road, Edinburgh EH4 8EB. *Clubs:* Caledonian; New (Edinburgh).

PAUFFLEY, Hon. Dame Anna (Evelyn Hamilton), DBE 2003; **Hon. Mrs Justice Pauffley;** a Judge of the High Court of Justice, Family Division, since 2003; *b* 13 Jan. 1956; *d* of late Donald Eric Hamilton Pauffley and Josephine Sybil Pauffley; *m* 2001, Frank Harris. *Educ:* Godolphin Sch., Salisbury; London Univ. (BA Hons). Called to the Bar, Middle Temple, 1979, Bencher 2003; QC 1995; a Recorder, 1998–2003. Hon. LLD City, 2005. *Address:* Royal Courts of Justice, Strand, WC2A 2LL.

PAUK, György; Order of the Hungarian Republic, 1998; international concert violinist; Professor at Guildhall School of Music and Drama; Professor, Royal Academy of Music, since 1987; Professor Emeritus, Franz Liszt Academy, Budapest, since 2007; *b* 26 Oct. 1936; *s* of Imre and Magda Pauk; *m* 1959, Susanne Mautner; one *s* one *d*. *Educ:* Franz Liszt Acad. of Music, Budapest. Toured E Europe while still a student; won three internat. violin competitions, Genoa 1956, Munich 1957, Paris 1959; soon after leaving Hungary, settled in London, 1961, and became a British citizen. London début, 1961; seasonal appearances there and in the provinces, with orchestra, in recital and chamber music; also plays at Bath, Cheltenham and Edinburgh Fests and London Promenade Concerts; performs in major European music venues; US début, under Sir George Solti, with Chicago Symph. Orch., 1970, followed by further visits to USA and Canada to appear with major orchs; holds master classes in many US univs, major music schs in Japan and Internat. Mozart Acad., Prague; Vis. Prof., Winterthur Conservatorium, Switzerland, 1996; plays regularly in Hungary following return in 1973; overseas tours to Australia, NZ, S America, S Africa, Middle and Far East; many performances for BBC, incl. Berg and Bartók concertos, with Boulez. As conductor/soloist, has worked with the English, Scottish and Franz Liszt chamber orchs and London Mozart Players; guest dir, Acad. of St Martin-in-the-Fields; with Peter Frankl and Ralph Kirshbaum, formed chamber music trio, 1973; performances at major fests; public concerts in GB have incl. complete Brahms and Beethoven Cycles; the trio has also made many broadcasts for the BBC. First performances: Penderecki's Violin Concerto, Japan, 1979, UK, 1980; Tippett's Triple Concerto, London, 1980; Lutosawski's Chain 2, with composer conducting, Britain, The Netherlands and Hungary, 1986–87; Sir Peter Maxwell Davies' Violin Concerto, Switzerland, 1988; William Mathias' Violin Concerto, Manchester, 1991. Has made many recordings including: Bartok Sonatas (among top records in US, 1982), and Bartok's music for solo violin, with piano, for two violins and violin concertos; Tippett Concerto (Best Gramophone Record Award, 1983); Berg Concerto (Caecilia Prize, Belgium, 1983); complete sonatas for violin and harpsichord by Handel; all violin concertos and orch. works by Mozart; Brahms Sonatas. Hon. GSM 1980. Hon. RAM 1990. Bartók Pásztory Prize, Hungary, 2008.

PAUL, family name of **Baron Paul**.

PAUL, Baron *cr* 1996 (Life Peer), of Marylebone in the City of Westminster; **Swraj Paul;** Padma Bhushan; Chairman: Caparo Group Ltd, since 1978; Caparo Industries Plc, since 1981; Caparo Inc., USA, since 1988; *b* 18 Feb. 1931; *s* of Payare and Mongwati Paul; *m* 1956, Aruna Vij; three *s* one *d* (and one *d* decd). *Educ:* Punjab Univ. (BSc); Mass Inst. of Technol. (BSc, MSc (Mech. Engrg)). Began work as Partner in family-owned Apeejay Surrendra Gp, India, 1953; came to UK in 1966 and estabd first business, Natural Gas Tubes Ltd; Caparo Group Ltd formed in 1978 as holding co. for UK businesses involved in engrg, hotel and property develt, investment; Caparo Industries Plc (engrg, metals) formed in 1981. Founder Chm., Indo-British Assoc., 1975–2000. Chancellor: Univ. of Wolverhampton, 1999–; Univ. of Westminster, 2006–; Pro-Chancellor, Thames Valley Univ., 1998–2000. FRSA. Padma Bhushan (equivalent to British Peerage), 1983. Hon. PhD Amer. Coll. of Switzerland, Leysin, 1986; Hon. DSc: (Econ) Hull, 1992; Buckingham, 1999; DUniv: Bradford, 1997; Central England, 1999; Hon. DLitt Westminster, 1997. Corporate Leadership Award, MIT, 1987. Freeman, City of London, 1998. *Publications:* Indira Gandhi, 1984, 2nd edn 1985; Beyond Boundaries, 1998. *Address:* Caparo House, 103 Baker Street, W1U 6LN. *T:* (020) 7486 1417. *Clubs:* MCC, Royal Automobile; Royal Calcutta Turf, Royal Calcutta Golf (Calcutta); Cricket of India (Bombay).

PAUL, Alan Roderick, CMG 1997; Partner, Executive Access Ltd, Hong Kong, since 2004 (Director, 2001–04); *b* 13 May 1950; *s* of late Roderick Ernest Paul and of Hilda May Paul (*née* Choules); *m* 1979, Rosana Yuen-Ling Tam; one *s* one *d*. *Educ:* Wallington High Sch. for Boys; Christ Church, Oxford (Scholar; MA Modern Langs, 1st class Hons). HM Diplomatic Service, 1972–2001: FCO, 1972–73; language training, Univs of Cambridge and Hong Kong, 1973–75; FCO, 1975–77; Peking, 1977–80; FCO, 1980–84; Head of Chancery, The Hague, 1984–87; Asst Head, 1987–89, Head, 1989–91, Hong Kong Dept, FCO; Counsellor and Dep. Sen. Rep., 1991–97, Sen. Rep. (with personal rank of Ambassador), 1997–2000, Sino-British Jt Liaison Gp, Hong Kong; FCO, 2000–01. *Recreations:* gardening, genealogy, philately, music. *Address:* Executive Access, 13th/14th Floor, Prince's Building, 10 Chater Road, Hong Kong.

PAUL, Geoffrey David, OBE 1991; Consultant, Sternberg Foundation, since 1996; *b* 26 March 1929; *s* of Reuben Goldstein and Anne Goldstein; *m* 1st, 1952, Joy Stirling (marr. diss. 1972); one *d*; 2nd, 1974, Rachel Mann; one *s*. *Educ:* Liverpool, Kendal, Dublin. Weekly newspaper and news agency reporter, 1947–57; asst editor, Jewish Observer and Middle East Review, 1957–62; Jewish Chronicle, 1962–96: successively sub-editor, foreign editor, Israel corresp., deputy editor; Editor, 1977–90; US Affairs Editor, 1991–96. Dir, Anglo-Israel Assoc., 2001–03. FRSA 1998. *Publication:* Living in Jerusalem, 1981. *Address:* 1 Carlton Close, West Heath Road, NW3 7UA.

PAUL, George William; DL; Chairman, J. P. Morgan Fleming Overseas Investment Trust, since 2001; *b* 25 Feb. 1940; *s* of William Stuart Hamilton Paul and Diana Violet Anne Martin; *m* 1st, 1963, Mary Annette Mitchell (*d* 1989); two *s* one *d*; 2nd, Margaret J. Kilgour (*née* Hedges). *Educ:* Harrow; Wye Coll., Univ. of London (BSc Agric Hons). Pauls & Whites Foods: Marketing Dir, 1968; Managing Dir, 1972; Pauls & Whites: Dir, 1972; Group Managing Dir, 1982; Chm., Pauls, 1985; Harrisons & Crosfield: Dir, 1985; Jt Chief Exec., 1986; Chief Exec., 1987–94; Chm., 1994–97; Norwich Union: Dir, 1990–2000; Vice-Chm., 1992–94; Chm., 1994–2000; Dep. Chm., CGNU, then Aviva, 2000–05. Chairman: Agricola Holdings Ltd, 1998–2000; Agricola Gp Ltd, 2000–; Notcutts Ltd, 2006– (Dir, 1998–). Mem., Jockey Club; Chm., Jockey Club Estates Ltd, 1991–2005. High Sheriff, 1990, DL, 1991, Suffolk. *Recreations:* theatre, country sports, sailing. *Clubs:* Boodle's, Farmers'.

PAUL, Rev. Canon John Douglas; Dean of Moray, Ross and Caithness, 1991–92, retired; *b* 13 Sept. 1928; *s* of George Anson Moncreiff Paul and Vivian (*née* Ward); *m* 1969, Mary Susan Melody Woodhouse. *Educ:* Winchester Coll.; Edinburgh Univ. (MA); Ely Theol Coll. Asst Curate, Portsmouth, 1954–56; Missionary Priest, Mozambique, 1956–70; Archdeacon, Mozambique, 1965–70; Rector: Castle Douglas, 1970–75; Portobello, 1975–80; Holy Trinity, Elgin, with St Margaret's, Lossiemouth, 1980–92. Hon. Canon and Synod Clerk, Dio. of Moray, Ross and Caithness, 1989–91; Hon.

Canon, St Andrew's Cathedral, Inverness, 1992–. *Publication:* Mozambique: Memoirs of a Revolution, 1975. *Recreation:* travel. *Address:* 2 The Avenue, Gifford EH41 4QX. *T:* (01620) 810547. *Club:* Royal Scots (Edinburgh).

PAUL, Robert Cameron, CBE 1996; FREng; Chief Executive, Albright & Wilson plc, 1995–97; *b* 7 July 1935; *m* 1st, 1965, Diana Kathleen Bruce (*d* 2001); two *d*; 2nd, 2003, Catherine Frances Young. *Educ:* Rugby Sch.; Corpus Christi Coll., Cambridge (BA 1958; MEng 1992); UCL (Dip Astronomy 2006). Nat. Service, 2nd Lieut RE, 1953–55. Chemical Engineer, ICI, Runcorn, 1959; Dir, ICI Fibres, 1976; Dep. Chm., Mond Div., ICI, 1979; Dep. Chm. and Man. Dir, Albright & Wilson, 1986–95. Non-exec. Dir, Courtaulds plc, 1994–98. President: IChemE, 1990–91; Chemical Industries Assoc., 1995–97. FREng (FEng 1990); FRAS 2006. Hon. DEng Birmingham, 1990. *Recreations:* music (piano), astronomy. *Address:* 2 Devonshire Place, Kensington, W8 5UD.

PAUL, Air Marshal Sir Ronald Ian S.; *see* Stuart-Paul.

PAULET, family name of **Marquess of Winchester**.

PAULIN, Prof. Roger Cole, DrPhil, LittD; Schröder Professor of German, University of Cambridge, 1989–2005, now Emeritus; Fellow, Trinity College, Cambridge since 1989; *b* 18 Dec. 1937; *s* of Thomas Gerald Paulin and Paulina (*née* Duff); *m* 1966, Traute Fielitz; one *s* one *d*. *Educ:* Otago Boys' High Sch., Dunedin, NZ; Univ. of Otago (MA); Heidelberg Univ. (DrPhil); MA, LittD (Cantab). Asst Lectr, Univ. of Birmingham, 1963–64; Lectr, Univ. of Bristol, 1965–73; Fellow and Coll. Lectr in German, Trinity Coll., Cambridge, 1974–87; Univ. Lectr, Univ. of Cambridge, 1975–87; Henry Simon Prof. of German, Univ. of Manchester, 1987–89. Mem., Editl Bd, Literatur-Lexikon, 1988–93. *Publications:* Ludwig Tieck: a literary biography, 1985, 2nd edn 1986 (trans. German, 1988); The Brief Compass, 1985; Ludwig Tieck, 1987; Theodor Storm, 1991; Wilhelm Jerusalem, 1999; Shakespeare in Germany, 2003. *Recreation:* gardening. *Address:* 45 Fulbrooke Road, Cambridge CB3 9EE. *T:* (01223) 322564.

PAULIN, Thomas Neilson; poet and critic; G. M. Young Lecturer in English, University of Oxford, since 1994; Fellow, Hertford College, Oxford, since 1994; *b* 25 Jan. 1949; *s* of Douglas and Mary Paulin; *m* 1973, Munjiet Kaur Khosa; two *s*. *Educ:* Hull Univ. (BA); Lincoln Coll., Oxford (BLitt). English Department, University of Nottingham: Lectr, 1972–89; Reader in Poetry, 1989–94; Prof. of Poetry, 1994. NESTA Fellow, 2000–03. Hon. DLitt: Saskatchewan, 1987; Stafford, 1995; Hull, 2000. *Publications:* Thomas Hardy: the poetry of perception, 1975; A State of Justice, 1977 (Eric Gregory Award, 1976, Somerset Maugham Award, 1978); The Strange Museum, 1980 (Geoffrey Faber Meml Award, 1982); Liberty Tree, 1983; The Riot Act, 1985; Ireland and the English Crisis, 1985; (ed) The Faber Book of Political Verse, 1986; The Hillsborough Script, 1987; Fivemiletown, 1987; Seize the Fire, 1989; (ed) The Faber Book of Vernacular Verse, 1990; Minotaur: poetry and the nation state, 1992; Walking a Line, 1994; Writing to the Moment: selected critical essays, 1996; The Day-Star of Liberty: William Hazlitt's radical style, 1998; The Wind Dog, 1999; The Invasion Handbook, 2002; The Road to Inver, 2004; Crusoe's Secret: the aesthetics of dissent (essays), 2005; The Secret Life of Poems, 2008. *Address:* c/o Faber & Faber, 3 Queen Square, WC1N 3AU.

PAULUSZ, Jan Gilbert; a Recorder of the Crown Court, 1980–2001; *b* 18 Nov. 1929; *s* of Jan Hendrik Olivier Paulusz and Edith (*née* Gilbert); *m* 1973, Luigia Maria Attanasio. *Educ:* The Leys Sch., Cambridge. Called to the Bar, Lincoln's Inn, 1957; South Eastern Circuit, 1959–2001. *Recreations:* mountain walking, photography.

PAUNCEFORT, Bernard Edward, OBE 1983; HM Diplomatic Service, retired 1986; Administrator, Tristan da Cunha, South Atlantic, 1989–92; *b* 8 April 1926; *o s* of Frederick George Pauncefort and Eleanor May (*née* Jux); *m* 1956, Patricia Anne (*d* 2004), *yr d* of Charles Ernest Leah and Alice (*née* Kendal-Banks). *Educ:* Wandsworth School. RAFVR 1942–44; Royal Fusiliers, 1944–48. Metropolitan Police Civil Staff, 1948–53; HM Colonial Service, 1953; Malaya, 1953–56; Tanganyika, 1956–63; CRO, 1963–67; First Sec., Zambia, 1967–68; Consul, Cape Town, 1969–72; Lord Pearce's staff, Rhodesia, 1971–72; Head of Chancery, Madagascar, 1972–73; FCO, 1973–76; Sec. to Seychelles Electoral Review Commn, 1976; Head of Chancery, Burma, 1976–78; Dir, British Inf. Services, S Africa, 1978–80; Lord Soames' staff, Rhodesia-Zimbabwe, 1979–80; Administrator, Ascension Island, 1980–82; FCO, 1982–83; Counsellor and Chief Sec., Falkland Is, 1983–85; Counsellor, FCO, 1985–86; Under-Sec., Govt of the Turks & Caicos Is, W Indies, 1986–88. Zimbabwe Medal, 1980. *Recreations:* dogs, birds, waterways. *Address:* 10 New Church Road, Uphill, Weston-super-Mare BS23 4UY.

PAUNCEFORT-DUNCOMBE, Sir Philip; *see* Duncombe.

PAVEY, Martin Christopher; educational consultant; *b* 2 Dec. 1940; *s* of Archibald Lindsay Pavey and Margaret Alice Pavey (*née* Salsbury); *m* 1969, Louise Margaret (*née* Bird); two *s*. *Educ:* Magdalen College Sch., Oxford; University Coll., London (Hons English); Nottingham Univ. (MA English); Univ. of Cambridge (Dip. Educn). Wigglesworth & Co., London and E. Africa (Shipping and Finance), 1956–62; Assistant Master: King's Sch., Ely, 1962–64; Lancing Coll., 1968–71; Fairham Comprehensive School, Nottingham: Head of English, 1971–75; Dep. Headmaster, 1975–76; Headmaster, 1976–81; Headmaster: Cranbrook School, 1981–88; Latymer Upper School, Hammersmith, 1988–91. Chm., AgeCare, RSAS, 2002–. *Recreations:* art architecture, cinema. *Address:* 5 Vineyards, Bath BA1 5NA.

PAVORD, Anna, (Mrs T. D. O. Ware); Gardening Correspondent, The Independent, since 1986; *b* 20 Sept. 1940; *d* of Arthur Vincent Pavord and Christabel Frances (*née* Lewis); *m* 1966, Trevor David Oliver Ware; three *d*. *Educ:* Univ. of Leicester (BA Hons English). PA/Dir, Line Up, BBC2, 1963–70; contributor, Observer Mag., 1970–92; writer and presenter, Flowering Passions, Channel 4 TV, 1991–92. Associate Editor, Gardens Illustrated, 1993–2008. Member: NT Gardens Panel, 1996–2006 (Chm., 2002–06); English Heritage Parks and Gardens Panel, 2001–. Hon. DLitt Leicester, 2005. Veitch Meml Gold Medal, 2001. *Publications:* Foliage, 1990; The Flowering Year, 1991; Gardening Companion, 1992; Hidcote, 1993; The Border Book, 1994; The New Kitchen Garden, 1996; The Tulip, 1999; Plant Partners, 2001; The Naming of Names, 2005. *Recreations:* sailing, walking, gardening, visiting Guyana. *Address:* c/o The Independent, Independent House, 191 Marsh Wall, E14 9RS. *T:* (020) 7005 2000.

PAWLAK, Witold Expedyt; His Honour Judge Pawlak; a Circuit Judge, since 2004; *b* 1947; *s* of Felicjan and Jolanta Pawlak; *m* 1971, Susan Dimsdale; one *s* one *d*. *Educ:* Trinity Coll., Cambridge (BA 1969; MA). Called to the Bar, Inner Temple, 1970; in practice, 1970–2004; a Recorder, 1995–2004. *Address:* Woodhall House, Lordship Lane, Wood Green, N22 5LF.

PAWLEY, Prof. (Godfrey) Stuart, PhD; FRS 1992; FRSE; Professor of Computational Physics, University of Edinburgh, 1985–2002, now Emeritus; *b* 22 June 1937; *s* of George Charles Pawley and Winifred Mary (*née* Wardle); *m* 1961, Anthea Jean Miller; two *s* one *d*. *Educ:* Bolton Sch.; Corpus Christi Coll., Cambridge (MA, PhD 1962). FRSE 1975. Chem. Dept, Harvard Univ., 1962–64; University of Edinburgh: Lect, 1964–69; Reader, 1970–85. Guest Prof., Chem. Dept, Århus Univ., Denmark, 1969–70. *Publications:* (contrib.) An Introduction to OCCAM 2 programming, 2nd edn, 1989; numerous scientific papers. *Recreations:* choral singing, mountain walking, rock gardening (seed reception manager, Scottish Rock Gdn Club). *Address:* Acres of Keillour, Methven, Perth PH1 3RA. *T:* (01738) 840874.

PAWLEY, (Robert) John; Director of Professional Services, Valuation Office Agency, 1995–99; *b* 10 Sept. 1939; *s* of Frederick Clifford and Marjorie Pawley; *m* 1965, Simone Elizabeth Tayar; two *s*. *Educ:* Plymouth Coll.; Exeter Univ. (BA). Private practice, Plymouth, 1962–71; joined Valuation Office, 1972; Dist Valuer, Waltham Forest, 1977, Haringey, 1978–81; Suptg Valuer, Chief Valuer's Office, London, 1981–84, Cambridge, 1984–87; Asst Chief Valuer, 1987–88; Dep. Chief Valuer, Inland Revenue Valuation Office, later Dep. Chief Exec. (Technical), Valuation Office Agency, 1989–95. *Recreations:* 18th century English naval history and exploration, period model boats, antiques.

PAWLEY, Stuart; *see* Pawley, G. S.

PAWSEY, James Francis; Director: Shilton Consultants LLP, since 2006; Alavan Consulting Ltd 2003–05; *b* 21 Aug. 1933; *s* of William Pawsey and Mary Mumford; *m* 1956, Cynthia Margaret Francis; six *s* (including twins twice). *Educ:* Coventry Tech. School; Coventry Tech. Coll. Dir, Love Lane Investments, 1995–. MP (C) Rugby, 1979–83, Rugby and Kenilworth, 1983–97; contested (C) Rugby and Kenilworth, 1997. Parliamentary Private Secretary: DES, 1982–83; DHSS, 1983–84; to Minister of State for NI, 1984–86. Member: Parly Scientific Cttee, 1982–97; Select Cttee of Parly Comr for Admin, 1983–97 (Chm., 1993); Select Cttee on Standing Orders, 1987–97; Exec., 1922 Cttee, 1989–97; Liaison Cttee, 1993–97; Ct of Referees, 1993–97; Chm., Cons Parly Educn Cttee, 1985–97; Mem. Exec., IPU, 1984–97; Chm., W Midlands Gp of Cons. MPs, 1993–97. Member: Rugby RDC, 1965–73; Rugby Borough Council, 1973–75; Warwickshire CC, 1974–79; former Chm. and Pres., Warwickshire Assoc. of Parish Councils. Mem., Team 2000, 1999–. KLJ. *Publication:* The Tringo Phenomenon, 1983. *Address:* Shilton House, Shilton, near Coventry CV7 9HT.

PAWSON, Prof. Anthony James, CH 2006; OC 2000; PhD; FRS 1994; FRSC 1994; Senior Scientist, since 1985, and Director, 2002–05, Samuel Lunenfeld Research Institute, Mount Sinai Hospital, Toronto; Professor, Department of Molecular and Medical Genetics, University of Toronto, since 1985; *b* 18 Oct. 1952; *s* of Henry Anthony Pawson, OBE and Hilarie Anne Pawson (*née* Bassett); *m* 1975, Margaret Anne Luman; two *s* one *d*. *Educ:* Clare Coll., Cambridge (BA); London Univ. (PhD). Grad. Student, ICRF, London, 1973–76; Postdoctoral Fellow, Univ. of Calif, Berkeley, 1976–80; Asst Prof., Univ. of BC, 1981–85. Terry Fox Cancer Res. Scientist, Nat. Cancer Inst. of Canada, 1988–98; Internat. Res. Schol., Howard Hughes Med. Inst., 1991–2001; Apotex Prof. of Molecular Oncology, Mt Sinai Hosp., 1991–. Associate Mem., EMBO, 2003; Foreign Associate, US NAS, 2004; For. Mem., Amer. Acad. of Arts and Scis, 2004; Fellow, Amer. Acad. of Microbiol., 2004. Gairdner Foundn Internat. Award, 1994; Amer. Assoc. for Cancer Res. Inc./Pezcoller Internat. Award, 1998; Dr H. P. Heineken Prize for Biochem. and Physics, Royal Netherlands Acad. of Arts and Scis, 1998; Flavelle Medal, RSC, 1998; Dist. Scientist Award, MRC of Canada, 1998; Killam Prize for Health Scis, Canada Council for the Arts, 2000; J. Allyn Taylor Internat. Prize in Medicine, Univ. of Western Ont., 2000; Michael Smith Prize for Health Res., CIHR, 2002; Poulsson Medal, Norwegian Soc. of Pharmacol. and Toxicol., 2004; Wolf Prize in Medicine, Wolf Foundn, Israel, 2005. *Publications:* papers in Nature, Cell, Science, Molecular and Cell Biol., Proc. Nat. Acad. of Sci. (USA), Jl Virology, EMBO Jl, Jl Biol Chem., Oncogene and other learned jls. *Recreations:* reading, theatre, fly-fishing, ski-ing, baseball. *Address:* Samuel Lunenfeld Research Institute, Mount Sinai Hospital, 600 University Avenue, Toronto, ON M5G 1X5, Canada. *T:* (416) 5868262; 34 Glenwood Avenue, Toronto, ON M6P 3C6, Canada. *T:* (416) 7632266.

PAWSON, Anthony John Dalby; Head of Defence Export Services, Ministry of Defence, since 2007; *b* 14 Oct. 1946; *s* of Donald Pawson and Kathleen (*née* Goodwin); *m* 1969, Kathleen Chisholm (*d* 2004); one *s* one *d*. *Educ:* Kent Coll., Canterbury; City Univ. (BSc 1st Class Hons Computer Science). MoD 1967; Private Sec. to Chief of Air Staff, 1978–80; First Sec., UK Delgn to NATO, Brussels, 1981–83; Private Sec. to Sec. of State for NI, 1990–92; RCDS 1992; Asst Under-Sec. of State (Fleet Support), MoD, 1993–95; Under-Sec. (Overseas and Defence), Cabinet Office, 1995–97; Ministry of Defence: Dir Gen. Marketing, 1997–98; Dir Gen. Defence Export Services, 1998–2003; Dir Gen. of Corp. Communication, 2003–04; Dep. Chief of Defence Intelligence, 2004–07. *Recreations:* Rugby, cricket. *Address:* Ministry of Defence, Main Building, Whitehall, SW1A 2HB. *Clubs:* Civil Service; Tunbridge Wells Rugby Football; Borderers' Cricket.

PAWSON, John Ward, RDI 2005; architectural designer; *b* 6 May 1949; *s* of James Stoddart Pawson and Winifred Mary Pawson (*née* Ward); *m* 1989, Catherine Mary Clare Berning; one *s*; one *s* by Hester van Roijen. *Educ:* Eton; Architectural Assoc. Sch. Dir, W. L. Pawson and Son Ltd, Halifax, 1967–73; Lectr, Nagoya Univ. of Commerce, 1974–77. *Architectural projects* include: van Roijen Apt, London, 1981; Bruce Chatwin Apt, London, 1982; Waddington Galls, London, 1983; Neuendorf House, Mallorca, 1989; Calvin Klein Store, NY, 1995; Cathay Pacific Lounges, Hong Kong, 1998; Pawson House, London, 1999; Monastery of Our Lady of Novy Dvur, Bohemia, 2004; Sackler Crossing, Royal Botanic Gardens, Kew, 2006; 50 Gramercy Park North, NY, 2006. *Publications:* Minimum, 1996; Mini-Minimum, 1998; Barn (photography by Fi McGhee), 1999; (ed) Architecture of Truth, by Lucien Hervé, 2000; (with Annie Bell) Living and Eating, 2001; Themes and Projects, 2002; Leçons du Thoronet, 2006; *relevant publications:* John Pawson, 1992; Critic, 1995; John Pawson Works, by Deyan Sudjic, 2000, rev. edn 2005. *Address:* Unit B, 70–78 York Way, N1 9AG. *T:* (020) 7837 2929, *Fax:* (020) 7837 4949; *e-mail:* email@johnpawson.com.

PAXMAN, Jeremy Dickson; journalist, author and broadcaster; *b* 11 May 1950; *s* of Arthur Keith Paxman and Joan McKay Dickson; partner, Elizabeth Ann Clough; one *s* two *d* (of whom one *s* one *d* are twins). *Educ:* Malvern College; St Catharine's College, Cambridge (Exhibnr; Hon. Fellow, 2000). Reporter: N Ireland, 1974–77; BBC TV Tonight, 1977–79; Panorama, 1979–85; The Bear Next Door; presenter: Breakfast Time, 1986–89; Newsnight, 1989–; Did You See?, 1991–93; You Decide—with Paxman, 1995–96; Start The Week, R4, 1998–2002; Chairman: University Challenge, 1994–; Times Past, Times Present, R4, 1996. Hon. Fellow, St Edmund Hall, Oxford, 2000. Hon. LLD Leeds, 1999; Hon. DLitt Bradford, 1999; DUniv Open, 2006. Award for Internat. Current Affairs, RTS, 1985; Award for best personal contribution to television, Voice of Viewer and Listener, 1993, 1998, 2006; Richard Dimbleby Award, BAFTA, 1996, 2000; Interview of the Year, RTS, 1997 and 1998; BPG Award, 1998; Variety Club Media Personality of the Year, 1999; Presenter of the Year, RTS, 2001, 2007. *Publications:* (jtly) A Higher Form of Killing: the secret story of gas and germ warfare, 1982; Through the Volcanoes: a Central American journey, 1985; Friends in High Places: who runs Britain?, 1990; Fish, Fishing and the Meaning of Life, 1994; The Compleat Angler, 1996; The

English: a portrait of a people, 1998; The Political Animal, 2002; On Royalty, 2006. *Recreations:* food, books, fishing. *Address:* c/o Capel and Land, 29 Wardour Street, W1D 6PS. *Clubs:* Garrick, Chelsea Arts; Piscatorial Society.
See also T. G. Paxman.

PAXMAN, Timothy Giles, LVO 1989; HM Diplomatic Service; Ambassador to Mexico, since 2005; *b* 15 Nov. 1951; *s* of Arthur Keith Paxman and Joan McKay Paxman (*née* Dickson); *m* 1980, Segolene Claude Marie Cayol; three *d*. *Educ:* Malvern Coll.; New Coll., Oxford. DoE, 1974–76; Dept of Transport, 1976–78; Ecole Nat. d'Admin, Paris, 1978–79; joined FCO, 1980: 1st Secretary: UK Perm. Rep. to EC, 1980–84; FCO, 1984–88; Head of Chancery, Singapore, 1988–92; on secondment to Cabinet Office, 1992–94; Counsellor (Econ. and Commercial), Rome, 1994–98; Counsellor (Pol Affairs), UK Perm. Repn to EU, Brussels, 1999–2002; Minister and Dep. Hd of Mission, Paris, 2002–05. *Recreations:* sailing, ski-ing, jazz and blues music, cinema, golf. *Address:* c/o Foreign and Commonwealth Office, King Charles Street, SW1A 2AH.
See also J. D. Paxman.

PAXTON, John; author, also writing as Jack Cherrill; Editor, The Statesman's Year-Book, 1969–90; *b* 23 Aug. 1923; *m* 1950, Joan Thorne; one *s* one *d*. Head of Economics department, Millfield, 1952–63. Joined The Statesman's Year-Book, 1963, Dep. Ed., 1968; Consultant Editor, The New Illustrated Everyman's Encyclopaedia, 1981–84. Jt Treas., English Centre, Internat. PEN, 1973–78; Chm., West Country Writers' Assoc., 1993–95. *Publications:* (with A. E. Walsh) Trade in the Common Market Countries, 1965; (with A. E. Walsh) The Structure and Development of the Common Market, 1968; (with A. E. Walsh) Trade and Industrial Resources of the Common Market and Efta Countries, 1970; (with John Wroughton) Smuggling, 1971; (with A. E. Walsh) Into Europe, 1972; (ed) Everyman's Dictionary of Abbreviations, 1974, 2nd edn 1986, as Penguin Dictionary of Abbreviations, 1989; World Legislatures, 1974; (with C. Cook) European Political Facts 1789–1999, 3 vols, 1975–2000; The Statesman's Year-Book World Gazetteer, 1975, 4th edn, 1991; (with A. E. Walsh) Competition Policy: European and International Trends and Practices, 1975; The Developing Common Market, 1976; A Dictionary of the European Economic Community, 1977, 2nd edn, A Dictionary of the European Communities, 1982; (with C. Cook) Commonwealth Political Facts, 1979; (with S. Fairfield) Calendar of Creative Man, 1980; Companion to Russian History, 1984, 2nd edn as Encyclopedia of Russian History, 1993; Companion to the French Revolution, 1988; The Statesman's Year-Book Historical Companion, 1988; (with G. Payton) Penguin Dictionary of Proper Names, 1991; European Communities (a bibliography), 1992; Calendar of World History, 1999; (with W. G. Moore) Penguin Encyclopedia of Places, 1999; Imperial Russia: a reference handbook, 2000; Dictionary of Financial Abbreviations, 2002; Leaders of Russia and the Soviet Union: from the Romanov dynasty to Vladimir Putin, 2004; contrib. to Keesing's Contemporary Archives, Children's Britannica, TLS. *Recreation:* music (listening). *Address:* Moss Cottage, Hardway, Bruton, Somerset BA10 0LN. *T:* (01749) 813423.

PAXTON, (Peter) Robin; Director, Nimbus Communications Limited, since 2007; Associate Director, Criticaleye; *b* 14 April 1951; *s* of late Richard Gordon Paxton and of Marion Paxton; *m* 1987, Linda Jane French; two *s*. *Educ:* Leighton Park Sch.; Sussex Univ. (BA Hons); LSE (MScEcon); Nuffield Coll., Oxford. Joined London Weekend Television, 1977; Managing Director: LWT Broadcasting Ltd, 1993–94; Carlton Television (India), 1995–97; Walt Disney TV Internat. (Asia-Pacific), 1997–2001; Discovery Networks, EMEA, 2002–07.

PAYE, Jean-Claude; Chevalier de la Légion d'Honneur; Commandeur de l'Ordre National du Mérite; Chevalier de l'Ordre National du Mérite agricole; Croix de la Valeur militaire; Attorney at Law, Paris, since 2002; *b* 26 Aug. 1934; *s* of late Lucien Paye and of Suzanne Paye (*née* Guignard); *m* 1963, Laurence Hélène Marianne Jeanneney; two *s* two *d*. *Educ:* Lycée Bugeaud, Algiers; Lycée Carnot, Tunis; Faculté de droit, Tunis; Institut d'Etudes Politiques, Paris; Ecole Nationale d'Administration. Government service, 1961–64; Technical Adviser to Sec. of State for Scientific Research, 1965; Advisor to Minister of Social Affairs, 1966; Chief Adviser to Vice-Pres., EEC, 1967–73; Adviser, Embassy, Bonn, 1973; Asst Principal Private Sec. to Minister of Foreign Affairs, 1974–76; Diplomatic Advr to Prime Minister, 1976–79; Head of Economic and Financial Affairs, Ministry of Foreign Affairs, 1979–84; Sec.-Gen., OECD, 1984–96 (Pres., Exec. Cttee in special Session, 1980–84); Mem., Conseil d'Etat, France, 1996–2000. *Address:* 1 Place A. Deville, 75006 Paris, France.

PAYKEL, Prof. Eugene Stern, FRCP, FRCPE, FRCPsych; Professor of Psychiatry, University of Cambridge, 1985–2001, now Emeritus Professor (Head of Department, 1985–2000); Professorial Fellow, Gonville and Caius College, Cambridge, 1985–2001, now Emeritus Fellow; *b* 9 Sept. 1934; *s* of late Joshua Paykel and Eva Stern Paykel; *m* 1969, Margaret, *d* of late John Melrose and Joan Melrose; two *s*. *Educ:* Auckland Grammar Sch.; Univ. of Otago (MB ChB, MD; Stuart Prize, Joseph Pullar Schol., 1956); DPM London. Maudsley Hosp., 1962–65; Asst Prof. of Psychiatry and Co-Dir/Dir, Depression Res. Unit, Yale Univ., 1966–71; Consultant and Sen. Lectr, 1971–75, Reader, 1975–77, Prof. of Psychiatry, 1977–85, St George's Hosp. Med. Sch., Univ. of London. Chief Scientist's Adviser and Mem., Mental Illness Res. Liaison Gp, DHSS, 1984–88; Chm., Jt Cttee on Higher Psychiatric Trng, 1990–95. Previously examiner Univs of Edinburgh, Nottingham, Manchester, London, and RCPsych. Mem., Neurosciences Bd, MRC, 1981–85, 1995–99. Mem., Bethlem Royal and Maudsley Hosp. SHA, 1990–94. Vice Pres., RCPsych, 1994–96 (Chm., Social and Community Psych. Sect., 1984–88); Zonal Rep., World Psychiatric Assoc., 1993–99 (Chm., Pharmaco-psychiatry Sect., 1993–98); Hon. Mem., British Assoc. for Psychopharmacology, 1991 (Pres., 1982–84); President: Marcé Soc., 1992–94; Collegium Internat. Neuropsychopharmacologicum, 2000–02. Trustee, Mental Health Foundn, 1988–95. Founder FMedSci 1998; Hon. FRCPsych 2001 (MRCPsych 1971, FRCPsych 1977). Hon. Mem., Assoc. of Eur. Psychiatrists, 2007. Foundations Fund Prize for Res. in Psychiatry, 1978; BMA Film Competition Bronze Award, 1981; Anna Monika Stiftung 2nd Prize, 1985; Eur. Coll. of Neuropsychopharmacol.-Lilly Award for Clin. Neurosci., 2001. Jt Editor, Jl of Affective Disorders, 1979–93; Editor, Psychological Medicine, 1994–2006; Member, Editorial Board: Social Psychiatry; Jl of Affective Disorders; Acta Psychiatrica Belgica, etc. *Publications:* The Depressed Woman, 1974; Psychopharmacology of Affective Disorders, 1979; Monoamine Oxidase Inhibitors: the state of the art, 1981; Handbook of Affective Disorders, 1982, 2nd edn 1992; Community Psychiatric Nursing for Neurotic Patients, 1983; papers on depression, psychopharmacology, social psychiatry, life events, evaluation of treatment. *Recreations:* opera, music, theatre. *Address:* Department of Psychiatry, University of Cambridge, Douglas House, 18E Trumpington Road, Cambridge CB2 8AH. *T:* (01223) 741930.

PAYNE, Alan Jeffrey, CMG 1988; HM Diplomatic Service, retired; *b* 11 May 1933; *s* of Sydney Ellis Payne and Lydia Payne; *m* 1959, Letitia Freeman; three *s*. *Educ:* Enfield Grammar Sch.; Queens' Coll., Cambridge (Exhibnr). FIL 1962. RN, 1955–57. EMI, London, later Paris, 1957–62; Secretariat, NATO, Paris, 1962–64; joined Diplomatic Service, 1965; Commonwealth Relations Office (later FCO), 1965–67; British High Commn, Kuala Lumpur, 1967–70; FCO, 1970–72; British Embassy, Budapest, 1972–75; Counsellor, Mexico City, 1975–79; FCO, 1979–82; Consul-General, Lyons, 1982–87; High Comr, Jamaica, and Ambassador (non-resident) to Haiti, 1987–89. Sec. Gen., Internat. Primary Aluminium Inst., 1989–97. *Recreations:* music, theatre, growing trees, restoring old cars. *Club:* Royal Automobile.

PAYNE, (Andrew John) Sebastian, MW; Chief Buyer, International Exhibition Co-operative Wine Society, since 1985; *b* 3 April 1947; *s* of John Laurence Payne and Dorothy Gwendoline Payne (*née* Attenborough); *m* 1973, Frances Elizabeth Harrison; two *d*. *Educ:* Tonbridge Sch. (Schol.); Trinity Coll., Oxford (BA Lit. Hum. and Med. and Mod. Greek 1970; MA 1973). MW 1977. F. & E. May, wine shippers, 1970–73; IEC Wine Soc., 1973–. Mem., Govt Wine Adv. Cttee, 1993–. Chm., Inst. of Masters of Wine, 1995–96. Chevalier, Ordre Nat. du Mérite Agricole (France), 1999. *Address:* International Exhibition Co-operative Wine Society, Gunnelswood Road, Stevenage SG1 2BG. *T:* (01438) 761283. *Club:* Travellers.
See also G. J. N. Payne.

PAYNE, Anthony Edward; freelance composer and writer; *b* 2 Aug. 1936; *s* of Edward Alexander Payne and Muriel Margaret Elsie Payne (*née* Stroud); *m* 1966, Jane Marian Manning, *qv*. *Educ:* Dulwich Coll.; Durham Univ. (BA Hons Music 1961). Composition Tutor: London Coll. of Music, 1983–85; Sydney Conservatorium, 1986; Univ. of W Australia, 1996; Vis. Milhaud Prof., Mills Coll., Calif, 1983. Contributor: Daily Telegraph, 1964–; Times, 1964–; Independent, 1986–; Country Life, 1995–. FRCM 2005. Hon. DMus: Birmingham, 2001; Kingston, 2002; Durham, 2007. *Compositions:* principal works include: Paraphrases and Cadenzas, 1969; Paean, 1971; Phoenix Mass, 1972; Concerto for Orchestra, 1974; The World's Winter, 1976; String Quartet, 1978; The Stones and Lonely Places Sing, 1979; Song of the Clouds, 1980; Springs Shining Wake, 1981; A Day in the Life of a Mayfly, 1981; Evening Land, 1981; The Spirit's Harvest, 1985; The Song Streams in the Firmament, 1986; Half Heard in the Stillness, 1987; Sea Change, 1988; Time's Arrow, 1990; Symphonies of Wind and Rain, 1991; A Hidden Music, 1992; Orchestral Variations, 1994; Empty Landscape, 1995; completion of Elgar's Third Symphony, 1997; Piano Trio, 1998; Scenes from the Woodlanders, 1999; Of Knots and Skeins, 2000; Visions and Journeys, 2002; Poems of Edward Thomas, 2003; Storm Chorale for Solo Violin, 2004; Horn Trio, 2004; completion of Elgar's Sixth Pomp and Circumstance March, 2005; Windows on Eternity, 2006; Piano Quintet, 2007. *Publications:* Schoenberg, 1968; Frank Bridge—Radical and Conservative, 1976, 2nd edn 1984; Elgar's Third Symphony: the story of the reconstruction, 1998; articles in learned jls, incl. Musical Times, Tempo, Listener, etc, 1962–. *Recreations:* cinema, English countryside. *Address:* 2 Wilton Square, N1 3DL. *T:* (020) 7359 1593, *Fax:* (020) 7226 4369; *e-mail:* paynecomp@googlemail.com.

PAYNE, Christine Grace; General Secretary, Equity, since 2005; *b* 30 Dec. 1956; *d* of Jeffrey and Shirley Brass; *m* 1981, Terry Payne; one *d*. *Educ:* Loughborough Univ. (BSc Hons Psychol.); Middlesex Poly. (Dip. Industrial Relns and Trade Union Studies). Joined Equity, 1979: TV Commercials Orgnr, 1981–91; Asst Sec., recorded perfs, 1991–99; Asst Gen. Sec., live perfs, 1999–2005. *Address:* c/o Equity, Guild House, Upper St Martin's Lane, WC2H 9EG. *T:* (020) 7379 6000; *e-mail:* cpayne@equity.org.uk.

PAYNE, Prof. Christopher Charles, OBE 1997; DPhil; consultant on biological science, since 2003; *b* 15 May 1946; *s* of Rupert George Payne and Evelyn Violet (*née* Abbott); *m* 1969, Margaret Susan Street; one *s* one *d*. *Educ:* Wadham Coll., Oxford (MA, DPhil). CBiol, FIBiol 1995; FIHort 1991. Post-Doctoral Fellow, Univ. of Otago, NZ, 1972; SSO, NERC, Oxford, 1973–77; PSO, 1977–83, Head, Entomology Dept, 1983–86, Glasshouse Crops Res. Inst., Littlehampton; Head, Crop Protection Div., Inst. of Horticultural Res., E Malling, 1987–90; Chief Exec., Horticulture Research Internat., 1990–99; Prof. of Horticulture and Landscape, Univ. of Reading, 1999–2003. Vis. Prof. of Plant Scis, Univ. of Reading, 2003–. Hon. Professor: Univ. of Warwick, 1991–99; Univ. of Birmingham, 1995–99. Chm., Assured Produce Scheme, 2001–06; Dir, Assured Food Standards, 2003–06; Sen. Exec., Nat. Horticultural Forum, 2004–05. Trustee, Royal Botanic Gdns, Kew, 1997–2003. Editor in Chief, Biocontrol Science and Technology, 1991–2000. *Publications:* (with R. Hull and F. Brown) Virology: directory and dictionary of animal, bacterial and plant viruses, 1989; numerous contribs to books and learned jls. *Recreations:* gardening, walking, cycling, family and social history. *Address:* Old Thatch, 15 North Street, Marcham, Oxon OX13 6NG. *T:* (01865) 391185; *e-mail:* oldthatch@btinternet.com. *Club:* Farmers'.

PAYNE, Christopher Frederick, CBE 1987; QPM 1975; DL; Chief Constable of Cleveland Constabulary, 1976–90; *b* 15 Feb. 1930; *o s* of late Gerald Frederick Payne, OBE, BEM, QPM, and Amy Florence Elizabeth Payne (*née* Parker); *m* 1952, Barbara Janet Saxby; one *s* three *d*. *Educ:* Christ's Coll., Finchley; Hendon Technical Coll. CIMgt (CBIM 1987). Joined Metropolitan Police, 1950; Sen. Comd. course, 1965; Home Office R&D Br., 1968–70; Comdr 'X' Div., 1971–74; Comdr Airport Div., 1974–76. Dep. Chm., Metrop. Police Friendly Soc., 1971–76; Police Advr to ACCs' Social Services Cttee, 1979–90; Chm., Public Order Sub-Cttee, ACPO, 1981–88; Pres., Chief Constables' Club, 1989–90. Sen. Vis. Res. Fellow, Univ. of Bradford, 1991–2001. Adviser to: Chemical Hazards Unit, Qld Govt, 1989–90; UN Disaster Relief Org. External Services, 1990–96; Emergency Planning Advr, BRCS, Cleveland, 1990–94. County Dir, St John Ambulance, 1978–85, Comdr, SJAB, 1985–89, Chm., St John Council, 1986–89, Cleveland. Chm., Cleveland Mental Health Support Gp, 1981–86; Vice-Pres., Cleveland Youth Assoc., 1983–95; Vice Chm., Royal Jubilee and Prince's Trusts Cttee for Durham and Cleveland, 1984–90. Chm., Castlegate Quay Trust, 1991–2005. Chm. Mgt Develt Cttee and Mem. Exec. Bd, Inst. of Mgt, 1998–2001. Freeman, City of London, 1988. DL Cleveland, 1983, N Yorks, 1996. CStJ 1985 (OStJ 1980). *Publications:* various articles on contingency planning and management. *Recreations:* painting, philately, gardening. *Address:* c/o The Chief Constable's Office, PO Box 70, Ladgate Lane, Middlesbrough TS8 9EH.

PAYNE, Prof. David Neil, CBE 2004; FRS 1992; FREng; Director, Optoelectronics Research Centre, since 1995 (Deputy Director, 1989–95), and Professor of Photonics, since 1991, University of Southampton; *b* 13 Aug. 1944; *s* of Raymond and Maisie Payne. *Educ:* Univ. of Southampton (BSc, PhD). FREng 2005; FIET (FIEE 2005). Commissioning Engineer, English Electric Co., 1962; University of Southampton: Research Asst, 1969; Jun. Res. Fellow, 1971; Pirelli Res. Fellow, 1972, Sen. Res. Fellow, 1978, Principal Res. Fellow, 1981; Pirelli Reader, 1984. Chm., SPI Optics Inc., 2000–05 (Dir, 2005–). Fellow, Optical Soc. of America, 1995; Foreign Member: Norwegian Acad. of Scis, 2004; Russian Acad. of Scis, 2006. Awards include: Rank Prize for Optoelectronics, 1991; IEEE/OSA John Tyndall Award, 1991; Computers and Communications Prize, Foundn for Computer and Communications Promotion in Japan, 1993; Franklin Medal, Franklin Inst., 1998; Edward Rhein Foundn Basic Res. Award, Germany, 2000; Mountbatten Medal, IEE, 2001; Kelvin Medal (jt award of 8 engrg socs), 2004; Microptics Award, Optical Soc. of Japan, 2005. *Publications:* numerous contribs to learned jls. *Recreations:* cooking, motorcycling, gardening. *Address:* Optoelectronics Research Centre, The University, Southampton SO17 1BJ. *T:* (023) 8059 3583.

PAYNE, (Geoffrey John) Nicholas; Director, Opera Europa, since 2003; *b* 4 Jan. 1945; *s* of John Laurence Payne and Dorothy Gwendoline Payne (*née* Attenborough); *m* 1986, Linda Jane Adamson; two *s*. *Educ:* Eton Coll. (King's Schol.); Trinity Coll., Cambridge (BA Eng Lit). Finance Assistant, Royal Opera House, 1968–70; Subsidy Officer, Arts Council, 1970–76; Financial Controller, Welsh National Opera, 1976–82; Gen. Adminr, Opera North, 1982–93; Dir, Royal Opera, Covent Garden, 1993–98; Gen. Dir, ENO, 1998–2002. *Address: e-mail:* nicholas.payne@opera-europa.org.

See also A. J. S. Payne.

PAYNE, Henry Salusbury Legh D.; *see* Dalzell Payne.

PAYNE, Rev. James Richmond, MBE 1982; ThL; General Secretary, Bible Society in Australia, 1968–88; Chairman, United Bible Societies World Executive Committee, 1976–88; *b* 1 June 1921; *s* of late R. A. Payne, Sydney, New South Wales; *m* 1943, Joan, *d* of late C. S. Elliott; three *s*. *Educ:* Drummoyne High School; Metropolitan Business College, Moore Theological College, Sydney. Served War of 1939–45: AIF, 1941–44. Catechist, St Michael's, Surry Hills, NSW, 1944–47; Curate, St Andrew's, Lismore, NSW, 1947–50; Rector, St Mark's, Nimbin, NSW, 1950–52; Chaplain, RAAF, Malta and Amberley, Qld, 1952–57; Rector, St Stephen's, Coorparoo, Qld, 1957–62; Dean of Perth, Western Australia, 1962–68. Hon. Commissary in Australia for Anglican Bp of Central Tanganyika, E Africa, 1988–. JP, ACT, 1969. *Publications:* Around the World in Seventy Days, 1965; And Now for the Good News, 1982. *Recreations:* sport, walking, reading, family. *Address:* 10/42 Jinka Street, Hawker, ACT 2614, Australia. *T:* (2) 62546722.

PAYNE, Jane Marian, (Mrs A. E. Payne); *see* Manning, J. M.

PAYNE, Keith, VC 1969; OAM 2006; *b* 30 Aug. 1933; *s* of Henry Thomas Payne and Remilda Payne (*née* Hussey); *m* 1954, Florence Catherine Payne (*née* Plaw); five *s*. *Educ:* State School, Ingham, North Queensland. Soldier, Department of Army, Aug. 1951–75; 1 RAR, Korea, 1952–53; 3 RAR, Malaya, 1963–65; Aust. Army Trng Team, Vietnam, 1969 (Warrant Officer; awarded VC after deliberately exposing himself to enemy fire while trying to cover his outnumbered men); WO Instructor: RMC, Duntroon, ACT, 1970–72; 42 Bn, Royal Qld Regt, Mackay, 1973–75; Captain, Oman Army, 1975–76. Member: VC and GC Assoc.; Legion of Valour, USA; Aust. Army Training Team Vietnam Assoc.; Life Member: Totally and Permanently Disabled Soldiers' Assoc. (Mackay Centre); Korea & SE Asia Forces Assoc.; Special Operations Assoc., USA; RSL (also Sarina Sub Br.). Patron, TRY-Sponsored Aust. Cadet Corp Units (Victoria). Freeman City of Brisbane and of Shire of Hinchinbrook. Vietnamese Cross of Gallantry, with bronze star, 1969; US Meritorious Unit Citation; Vietnamese Unit Citation Cross of Gallantry with Palm; DSC (US); SSM (US). *Recreations:* football, fishing, hunting. *Address:* 1 Forest Court, Andergrove, Mackay, Qld 4740, Australia. *T:* (7) 49552794.

PAYNE, Leonard Sidney, CBE 1983; Director, J. Sainsbury Ltd, 1974–86; Adviser on Distribution and Retailing, Coopers & Lybrand, since 1986; *b* 16 Dec. 1925; *s* of Leonard Sydney Payne and Lillian May Leggatt; *m* 1944, Marjorie Vincent; two *s*. *Educ:* Woodhouse Grammar School. FCCA, FCILT. Asst Accountant, Peek Frean & Co. Ltd, 1949–52; Chief Accountant, Administrator of various factory units, head office appts, Philips Electrical Industries, 1952–62; Dep. Gp Comptroller, Morgan Crucible Co. Ltd, 1962–64; British Road Services Ltd: Finance Dir, 1964–67; Asst Man. Dir, 1967–69; Man. Dir, 1969–71; Dir of Techn. Services and Develt, Nat. Freight Corp., 1971–74, Vice-Chm. Executive 1974. President: Freight Transport Assoc., 1980–82; Chartered Inst. of Transport, 1983–84. Chm., CBI Transport Policy Cttee, 1980–86. CCMI. *Recreations:* gardening, swimming, squash, chess. *Address:* Apartment 5, Evenholme, Green Walk, Bowdon, Altrincham, Cheshire WA14 2SL.

PAYNE, Nicholas; *see* Payne, G. J. N.

PAYNE, Nicholas Milne; Chairman, National Gardens Scheme, 2002–08; *b* 14 May 1937; *s* of Robert Orlando Payne and Frances Elisabeth Payne; *m* 1985, Mona Helen de Ferranti (*née* Cunningham); one step *s* two step *d*. *Educ:* St Edward's Sch., Oxford; Trinity Hall, Cambridge (MA). Commercial Dir, Caradon Rolinx, 1964–87. Chm., NW Reg., NACF, 1993–2004; Chm., Friends of Manchester City Galls, 1984–; Trustee: Clonter Opera, 1984–2002; Tabley House Collection Trust, 1993–; Manchester City Galls Trust, 2001–. *Recreations:* gardening, music, the arts. *Address:* The Mount, Whirley, Macclesfield, Cheshire SK11 9PB. *T:* and *Fax:* (01625) 426730; *e-mail:* ngs@themount1.freeserve.co.uk.

PAYNE, Sir Norman (John), Kt 1985; CBE 1976 (OBE 1956; MBE (mil.) 1944); FREng; Chairman, BAA plc (formerly British Airports Authority), 1977–91 (Chief Executive, 1972–77); *b* 9 Oct. 1921; *s* of late F. Payne, Folkestone; *m* 1946, Pamela Vivien Wallis (separated; she *d* 2006); four *s* one *d*. *Educ:* John Lyon Sch., Harrow; City and Guilds Coll., London. BSc Eng Hons. FCGI, FICE, FCIT; FREng (FEng 1984). Royal Engrs (Captain), 1939–45 (despatches twice); Imperial Coll. of Science and Technology London (Civil), 1946–49; Sir Frederick Snow & Partners, 1949, Partner 1955; British Airports Authority: Dir of Engrg, 1965; Dir of Planning, 1969, and Mem. Bd 1971. Pres., West European Airports Assoc., 1975–77; Chairman: Airports Assoc. Co-ordinating Council, 1976; Aerodrome Owners' Assoc., 1983–84. Chm., British Sect., Centre for European Public Enterprise, 1979–82. Chm., NICG, 1982–83; Comr, Manpower Services Commn, 1983–85. Pres., CIT, 1984–85. CBIM (FBIM 1975); RAeS 1987. FIC 1989; FRSA 1990. Hon. FIStructE, 1988; Hon. FRIBA 1991. Hon. DTech Loughborough, 1985. *Publications:* various papers on airports and air transport. *Recreations:* travel, gardening. *Address:* L'Abri, La route des Merriennes, St Martin, Guernsey, CI GY4 6NS.

PAYNE, Peter Charles John, PhD; MSc(AgrEng); farmer, 1975–2000; *b* 8 Feb. 1928; *s* of late C. J. Payne, China Clay Merchant, and Mrs F. M. Payne; *m* 1961, Margaret Grover; two *s* one *d*. *Educ:* Plymouth Coll.; Teignmouth Grammar School; Reading University. BSc Reading 1948; Min. of Agriculture Scholar, Durham Univ., MSc(AgrEng) 1950; Scientific Officer, Nat. Institute of Agricultural Engineering, 1950–55; PhD Reading 1954; Lecturer in Farm Mechanisation, Wye College, London Univ., 1955–60; Lecturer in Agricultural Engineering, Durham Univ., 1960–61; Principal, Nat. Coll. of Agricultural Engineering, Silsoe, 1962–75 (Hon. Fellow, 1980); Visiting Professor: Univ. of Reading, 1969–75; Cranfield Inst. of Technology, 1975–80. Chm., Agricl Panel, Intermed. Technol. Develt Gp, 1979–86. Vice-Pres., Section III, Commn Internationale du Génie Rural, 1969. FIAgrE 1968; FRAgSs 1971; CEng 1980. *Publications:* various papers in agricultural and engineering journals. *Recreation:* sailing. *Address:* 5 Mulberry Quay, Market Strand, Falmouth TR11 3HD. *T:* (01326) 318880.

PAYNE, Sebastian; *see* Payne, A. J. S.

PAYNE, Most Rev. (Sidney) Stewart; Metropolitan of the Ecclesiastical Province of Canada and Archbishop of Western Newfoundland, 1990–97, retired; *b* 6 June 1932; *s* of Albert and Hilda Payne; *m* 1962, Selma Carlson Penney, St Anthony, Newfoundland; two *s* two *d*. *Educ:* Elementary and High School, Fogo, Newfoundland; Memorial Univ. of Newfoundland (BA); Queen's Coll., Newfoundland (LTh); BD(General Synod). Incumbent of Mission of Happy Valley, 1957–65; Rector, Parish of Bay Roberts, 1965–70; Rector, Parish of St Anthony, 1970–78; Bishop of Western Newfoundland, 1978–97. DD *hc*: Univ. of King's Coll., Halifax, NS, 1981; Queen's Coll., St John's, NL, 2006. *Address:* PO Box 2255, RR1 Stn Main, Corner Brook, NL A2H 2N2, Canada.

PAYNE, Stephen Michael, OBE 2004; RDI 2006; CEng; FRINA; Vice President and Chief Naval Architect, Carnival Corporate Shipbuilding, Southampton, since 2004; President, Royal Institution of Naval Architects, since 2007; *b* 28 Jan. 1960; *s* of Michael John Robert Payne and Pauline Patricia Payne. *Educ:* Univ. of Southampton (BSc Eng (Hons) Ship Sci. 1984). CEng 2002; FRINA 2002. Naval architect, Marconi Radar Systems, Chelmsford, 1984–85; Jun. Naval Architect, 1985–87, Naval Architect, 1987–92, Sen. Naval Architect, 1992–95, Technical Marine Planning Ltd, London; Carnival Corporation, 1995–: Sen. Naval Architect, 1995; Project Manager: MS Rotterdam (VI), 1995–97; MS Costa Atlantica, 1997–98; Chief Designer, then Proj. Manager, RMS Queen Mary 2, 1998; Dir, Proj. Mgt, Carnival Corporate Shipbuilding, 2000–04. Mem. Council, 2005–, Exec. Cttee, 2006–, RINA. Co-founder, Future Engineers 2008, in assoc. with RAEng. Freeman, City of London, 2004; Liveryman, Co. of Shipwrights, 2005– (Freeman, 2004). Hon. DSc Southampton, 2007. Bronze Medal, RINA, 1988; Special Achievement Award, RAEng, 2006; MN Medal, 2006. *Publications:* Grande Dame: Holland America Line and the SS Rotterdam, 1990; MS Statendam, 1993; contribs to Naval Architect, Ships Monthly, Steamboat Bill, Designs, Cruise Industry News. *Recreations:* public speaking, model-ship making, writing, cooking, airships, history of passenger ships. *Address:* c/o Royal Institution of Naval Architects, 10 Upper Belgrave Street, SW1X 8BQ.

PAYNTER, Alan Guy Hadley; Commissioner, 1997–2000, and Director, Corporate Services, 1999–2000, HM Customs and Excise; *b* 5 Nov. 1941; *s* of Leslie Alan Paynter and Dorothy Victoria Paynter (*née* Voak); *m* 1964, Mary Teresa Houghton; two *d*. *Educ:* East Ham Grammar Sch.; Central London Poly. (Post-grad. DMS 1972). EO, then HEO, MPBW, 1960–72 (Asst Private Sec. to Minister of Public Bldg and Works, 1968–71); HM Customs and Excise: Sen. Exec. Officer, 1972; Principal, 1978; on secondment to Overseas Containers Ltd, 1981–83; Sen. Principal, Computer Services, 1983–87; Asst Sec., 1987; Head, 1989–93, Dir, 1993–99, Information Systems; Mem. of Board, 1993–2000. Hon. Treas., Thorpe Bay Bowling Club, 2006–. Chm. of Trustees, Havens Hospices, 2007–. *Recreations:* golf, bowling, reading, theatre, gardening.

PAYNTER, Prof. John Frederick, OBE 1985; Professor of Music, 1982–97, and Head of Department of Music, 1983–94, University of York, now Professor Emeritus; *b* 17 July 1931; *s* of late Frederick Albert Paynter and late Rose Alice Paynter; *m* 1st, 1956, Elizabeth Hill (*d* 1998); one *d*; 2nd, 2003, Joan Minnetta Burrows (*née* Lee). *Educ:* Emanuel Sch., London; Trinity Coll. of Music, London (GTCL 1952). DPhil York, 1971. Teaching appts, primary and secondary schs, 1954–62; Lectr in Music, City of Liverpool C. F. Mott Coll. of Educn, 1962–65; Principal Lectr (Head of Dept of Music), Bishop Otter Coll., Chichester, 1965–69; Lectr, Dept of Music, Univ. of York, 1969, Sen. Lectr, 1974–82. Composer and writer on music-educn. Dir, Schs Council Proj., Music in the Secondary School Curriculum, 1973–82. Gen. Editor, series, Resources of Music, 1969–93; Jt Editor, British Jl of Music Educn, 1984–97. FRSA 1987. Hon. GSM 1985. Leslie Boosey Award, Royal Philharmonic Soc./PRS, 1998. *Publications:* (with Peter Aston) Sound and Silence, 1970; Hear and Now, 1972; (with Elizabeth Paynter) The Dance and the Drum, 1974; All Kinds of Music, vols 1–3, 1976, vol. 4, 1979; Sound Tracks, 1978; Music in the Secondary School Curriculum: trends and developments in class music teaching, 1982; Sound and Structure, 1992; Thinking and Making, 2008; editor and contributor to: A Companion to Contemporary Musical Thought, 1992; Between Old Worlds and New: occasional writings on music by Wilfrid Mellers, 1997; contributor to: How Music Works, 1981; Musik og Skola, 1981; Musikalische Erfahrung: Wahrnehmen, Erkennen, Aneignen, 1992; Zwischen Aufklärung & Kulturindustrie, 1993; Music Education: international viewpoints, 1994; Powers of Being: David Holbrook and his work, 1995; articles in Internat. Jl of Music Educn, British Jl of Music Educn, La Discussione, Popular Music, Música Arte y Proceso, beQuadro, Musica Domani, Psychol. of Music; scripts and commentaries for radio and TV; *musical compositions:* choral and instrumental works including: Landscapes, 1972; The Windhover, 1972; May Magnificat, 1973; God's Grandeur, 1975; Sacraments of Summer, 1975; Galaxies for Orchestra, 1977; The Voyage of St Brendan, 1978; The Visionary Hermit, 1979; The Inviolable Voice, 1980; String Quartet no 1, 1981; Cantata for the Waking of Lazarus, 1981; The Laughing Stone, 1982; Contrasts for Orchestra, 1982; Variations for Orchestra and Audience, 1983; Conclaves, 1984; Piano Sonata, 1987; Time After Time, 1991; String Quartet no 2, 1991; Four Sculptures of Austin Wright (for solo viola and orch.), 1991–94; Melting (for solo piano), 1997; Holding On (for viola and piano), 1998; Breakthrough (double piano duet), 2000; Memorials (unacc. choir), 2000; Ouverture d'Urgence (double piano duet), 2002; Binsey Poplars (voice and prepared piano), 2004; The Habit of Perfection (voice and piano), 2004; Of Time and Place (soprano, recorder and piano), 2004; Sequela (recorder and optional percussion), 2004; Inscape (unacc. choir), 2005; When the Time Comes (piano), 2007; The Oxen (choir and piano), 2007.

PEACE, Elizabeth Ann, CBE 2008; Chief Executive, British Property Federation, since 2002; *b* Birmingham, 5 Dec. 1952; *d* of Herbert Powers and Gwendoline Powers (*née* Burbridge); *m* 1978, Nigel David Peace; two *s*. *Educ:* King Edward VI Camp Hill Grammar Sch. for Girls, Birmingham; Royal Holloway Coll., Univ. of London (BA Hons Hist.). Admin trainee, then Grade 7, MoD, 1974–91; Dir, Corporate Affairs and Co. Sec., Qinetiq plc (formerly DERA), 1991–2002. Pres., Farnborough Aerospace Consortium, 1996–2002. Non-exec. Dir, Planning Inspectorate, 2005–08. Chm., Eur. Property Fedn, 2004–. Hon. Fellow, Coll. of Estate Mgt, 2008. Liveryman, Chartered Surveyors' Co., 2007. *Recreations:* opera, reading, gardening and conservation, keeping age at bay, hounding offspring - and shopping. *Address:* c/o British Property Federation, 1 Warwick Row, SW1E 5ER. *T:* (020) 7828 0111; *e-mail:* lpeace@bpf.org.uk. *Club:* Reform.

PEACE, John Wilfred; Chairman: Burberry, since 2002; Experian, since 2006; Deputy Chairman, Standard Chartered Bank, since 2007; *b* 2 March 1949; *m* 1971, Christine Blakemore; three *d*. *Educ:* Sandhurst. Experian (formerly CCN): Founding Dir, 1980; Man. Dir, 1991–96; Chief Exec., 1996–2000; Chief Exec., Great Universal Stores, later GUS, plc, 2000–06. *Recreations:* horse riding, golf. *Address:* Experian, Cardinal Place, 80 Victoria Street, SW1E 5JL.

PEACH, Prof. (Guthlac) Ceri (Klaus), DPhil; Professor of Social Geography, Oxford University, 1992–2007, now Emeritus; Fellow and Tutor, St Catherine's College, Oxford, 1969–2007, now Emeritus Fellow; Professor of Social Geography, Institute for Social Change, University of Manchester, since 2007; *b* 26 Oct. 1939; *s* of Wystan Adams Peach and Charlotte Marianne (*née* Klaus); *m* 1964, Susan Lesley Godfrey; two *s* one *d*. *Educ:* Howardian High Sch., Cardiff; Merton Coll., Oxford (MA, DPhil). Oxford University: Demonstrator, 1964–66; Faculty Lectr in Geography, 1966–92; Strakosch Fellow, 1969; Hd of Dept, Sch. of Geography, 1995–98; St Catherine's College: Dean, 1971–73; Sen. Tutor, 1973–77; Finance Bursar, 1981–84; Domestic Bursar, 1986–89; Vice-Master, 1990–92; Pro-Master, 1993–94. Mem., Hebdomadal Council, Oxford Univ., 1996–2001. Visiting Fellow: Dept of Demography, ANU, 1972; Dept of Sociology, Yale Univ., 1977; Visiting Professor: Dept of Geog., Univ. of BC, 1998; Dept of Sociology, Harvard Univ., 1998; Office of Population Res., Princeton Univ., 2006–07; Fulbright Vis. Prof., Dept of Geog., Univ. of Calif, Berkeley, 1985. Ethnic Geography Dist. Schol. Award, Assoc. of Amer. Geographers, 2008. *Publications:* West Indian Migration to Britain: a social geography, 1968; Urban Social Segregation, 1975; (ed jtly) Ethnic Segregation in Cities, 1981; (ed jtly) Geography and Ethnic Pluralism, 1984; (ed jtly) South Asians Overseas, 1990; The Caribbean in Europe, 1991; The Ethnic Minority Populations of Great Britain, 1996; (ed jtly) Islam in Europe, 1997; (ed jtly) Global Japan, 2003. *Recreations:* travelling, reading, computing. *Address:* St Catherine's College, Oxford OX1 3UJ. *Club:* Leander (Henley).

PEACH, Sir Leonard (Harry), Kt 1989; a Civil Service Commissioner, 1995–2000; *b* 17 Dec. 1932; *s* of late Harry and Beatrice Peach; *m* 1958, Doreen Lilian (*née* Barker); two *s*. *Educ:* Queen Mary's Grammar Sch., Walsall; Pembroke Coll., Oxford (MA; Hon. Fellow, 1996); LSE (Dip. Personnel Management). Research Asst to Randolph S. Churchill, 1956; personnel management posts, 1956–62; IBM UK Ltd: personnel management posts, 1962–71; Dir of Personnel, 1971–72; Gp Dir, Personnel, IBM Europe, Africa, Middle East (based Paris), 1972–75; Dir, Personnel and Corporate Affairs, 1975–85 and 1989–92; seconded to DHSS, 1985–89: Dir, Personnel, NHS Management Bd, 1985; Chief Exec., NHS Management Bd, 1986–89 (in rank of 2nd Perm. Sec.); Chairman: NHS Training Authy, 1986–91; Skillbase Ltd, 1990–94; Standards Develt Cttee, Management Charter Initiative, 1989–97; Development Partnership Consultancy, 1993–2006; Mgt Verification Consortium Bd, 1995–99; UKCC Commn on Educn and Trng of Nurses, Midwives and Health Visitors, 1998–99 (report Fitness for Practice, 1999); Dep. Chm., Regulatory Decisions Cttee, FSA, 2001–05; Member: Data Protection Tribunal, 1985–99; Civilian Trng Bd and Personnel Bd, MoD, 1992–2000; Forensic Science Service Remuneration Cttee, 1999–2005; non-exec. Dir, Appeals Service, 2004–06 (Chm., Audit Cttee, 2004–06); Mem., Audit Cttee, DWP, 2004–06. Chm., Police Complaints Authy, 1992–95; Comr for Public Appts, 1995–99; Comr for Public Appts in NI, 1995–99. Non-exec. Dir, Royal London Hosp., 1991–94. Chm., PSI, 1991–2001. Chm., Nationwide Pension Fund, 2002–03 (Dep. Chm., 1992–2002); Director: IBM UK Rentals, 1971–76; IBM UK Holdings, 1976–85, and 1989–92; IBM UK Pensions Trust, 1989–92; IBM UK Trust, 1989–92; PIA, 1993–97 (Dep. Chm., Memship and Discipline Cttee, 1996–2001); non-executive Director: Nationwide Anglia Bldg Soc., 1990–93; Coutts Consulting plc, 1993–99; Affinity Internet Hldgs plc, 2001–03. Pres., IPM, and Chm., IPM Services Ltd, 1983–85 and 1991–98 (President's Gold Medal, 1988); Chairman: Inst. of Continuing Professional Develt, 1998–2006; Selection Bd, RICS Disciplinary Panels and Bds, 2001–06; President: Manpower Soc., 1991–97; Assoc. of Business Schs, 1993–99. Vice-President: British Sports Assoc. for Disabled, 1988–; Industrial Participation Soc., 1989–2004. Chm., Remuneration and Succession Cttee, SCOPE, 1996–2003. Chairman: Quentin Hogg Trust, 1999–; Regent Street Poly. Trust, 1999–. Chm., Univ. of Westminster, 1993–99; Vice-Chm., Morley Coll., 1993–99; Gov., Portsmouth Grammar Sch., 1976–2001. CCIPD. Hon. FFOM, RCP, 1994. Hon. Fellow, Thames Polytechnic, 1990. Hon. DSc: Aston, 1991; UWE, 2000; Hon. DLitt Westminster, 1998; Hon. DCL Huddersfield, 2000. *Publications:* report on appt processes of judges and QCs in England and Wales, 1999; articles on personnel management and social responsibility. *Recreations:* opera, theatre, cricket, gardening. *Address:* Crossacres, Meadow Road, Wentworth, Virginia Water, Surrey GU25 4NH. *T:* (01344) 842258. *Clubs:* Oxford & Cambridge University; Wentworth Golf.

PEACOCK, Prof. Sir Alan (Turner), Kt 1987; DSC 1945; MA; FBA 1979; FRSE; Hon. Research Professor in Public Finance, Heriot-Watt University, since 1987; *b* 26 June 1922; *s* of late Professor A. D. Peacock, FRSE and of Clara Mary (*née* Turner); *m* 1944, Margaret Martha Astell Burt; two *s* one *d*. *Educ:* Grove Acad.; Dundee High School; University of St Andrews (1939–42, 1945–47). Royal Navy, 1942–45 (Lieut RNVR). Lecturer in Economics: Univ. of St Andrews, 1947–48; London Sch. of Economics, 1948–51 (Hon. Fellow, 1980); Reader in Public Finance, Univ. of London, 1951–56; Prof. of Economic Science, Univ. of Edinburgh, 1957–62; Prof. of Economics, Univ. of York, 1962–78; Prof. of Economics, and Principal-designate, University Coll. at Buckingham, 1978–80, Principal, 1980–83; Vice-Chancellor, Univ. of Buckingham, 1983–84, Professor Emeritus, 1985–; Exec. Dir, David Hume Inst., Edinburgh, 1985–90 (Hon. Pres., 2002–05). Seconded from Univ. of York as Chief Economic Adviser, Depts of Industry and Trade, 1973–76. Visiting Prof. of Economics, Johns Hopkins Univ., 1958. Keynes Lectr, British Acad., 1994. Mem., 1959–87, Chm., 1991–93, Adv. Council, IEA (Trustee, 1987–93; Hon. Fellow, 1994); Member: Commission of Enquiry into land and population problems of Fiji, 1959; Departmental Committee on Electricity in Scotland, 1961; Council, REconS, 1961–78; Cttee of Enquiry on impact of rates, 1964; Commn on the Constitution, 1970–73; SSRC, 1972–73; Cttee of Inquiry on Retirement Provision, 1984; Chm., Rowntree Inquiry into Corporate Takeovers, 1990–91. Chm., UN Adv. Mission to Russian Fedn on Social Protection, 1992. Pres., Internat. Inst. of Public Finance, 1966–69. Mem., Arts Council, 1986–92; Chairman: Arts Council Enquiry on Orchestral Resources, 1969–70; Cttee on Financing the BBC, 1985–86; Scottish Arts Council, 1986–92. Non-exec. Director: Economist Intelligence Unit Ltd, 1977–84; Caledonian Bank plc, 1991–96. FRSE 1989. Corr. Fellow, Accademia Nazionale dei Lincei, Rome, 1996. Hon. Mem., Royal Soc. of Musicians, 1996. DUniv: Stirling, 1974; Brunel, 1989; York, 1997; Hon. DEcon Zürich, 1984; Hon. DSc: Buckingham, 1986; Edinburgh, 1990; Hon. LLD: St Andrews, 1990; Dundee, 1990; Dr *hc:* Catania, 1991; Lisbon, 1999; Turin, 2001. *Publications:* Economics of National Insurance, 1952; (ed) Income Redistribution and Social Policy 1954; National Income and Social Accounting (with H. C. Edey), 1954, 3rd imp. 1967; The National Income of Tanganyika (1952–54) (with D. G. M. Dosser), 1958; The Growth of Public Expenditure in the UK, 1890–1955 (with J. Wiseman), 1961; Economic Theory of Fiscal Policy (with G. K. Shaw), 1971, 2nd edn, 1976; The Composer in the Market Place (with R. Weir), 1975; Welfare Economics: a liberal re-interpretation (with C. K. Rowley), 1975; Economic Analysis of Government, 1979; (ed and contrib.) Structural Economic Policies in West Germany and the UK, 1980; (ed jtly) Political Economy of Taxation, 1981; (ed and contrib.) The Regulation Game, 1984; (ed jtly) Public Expenditure and Government Growth, 1985; Waltz Contrasts (for piano solo), 1988; Public Choice Analysis in Historical Perspective, 1992; (with G. Bannock) Corporate Takeovers and the Public Interest, 1991; Paying the Piper, 1993; (ed jtly) Cultural Economics and Cultural Policies, 1994; Political Economy of Economic Freedom, 1997; (ed) The Political Economy of Heritage, 1998; (with B. Main) What Price Civil Justice?, 2000; Calling the Tune, 2001; The Enigmatic Sailor, 2003; Public Broadcasting Without the BBC?, 2004; (with I. Rizzo) The Heritage Game: economics, policy and practice, 2008; articles on applied economics in Economic Jl, Economica and other journals. *Recreations:* trying to write music, wine spotting. *Address:* 5/24 Oswald Road, Edinburgh EH9 2HE. *T:* (0131) 667 5677; *e-mail:* pavone@blueyonder.co.uk. *Clubs:* Reform; New (Edinburgh).

PEACOCK, Hon. Andrew (Sharp), AC 1997; Chairman, MFS Ltd, since 2007; *b* 13 Feb. 1939; *s* of late A. S. Peacock and Iris Peacock. *Educ:* Scotch Coll., Melbourne, Vic; Melbourne Univ. (LLB). Former Partner, Rigby & Fielding, Solicitors; Chm., Peacock and Smith Pty Ltd, 1962–69. Army Reserve (Captain), 1966–94. Pres., Victorian Liberal Party, 1965–66; MP (L) Kooyong, Australia, 1966–94; Minister for Army and Minister assisting Prime Minister, 1969–71; Minister for Army and Minister asstg Treasurer, 1971–72; Minister for External Territories, Feb.–Dec. 1972; Mem., Opposition Exec., 1973–75; Oppos. Shadow Minister for For. Affairs, 1973–75, 1985–87; Minister for: the Envmt, 1975; Foreign Affairs, 1975–80; Industrial Relns, 1980–81; Industry and Commerce, 1982–83; Leader of the Parly Liberal Party, and of the Opposition, 1983–85; Dep. Leader, Liberal Party and Dep. Leader, Opposition, 1987–89; Leader, Parly Liberal Party, and of the Opposition, 1989–90; Shadow Attorney-Gen. and Shadow Minister for Justice, 1990–92; Shadow Minister: for Trade, 1992–93; for Foreign Affairs, 1993–94; Australian Ambassador to the USA, 1997–2000. Pres., Boeing Australia, 2002–07. Chm., Internat. Democrat Union, 1989–92. Mem., Business Council of Australia, 2003–07. Mem., Internat. Adv. Panel, Graduate Sch. of Govt, Univ. of Sydney, 2003–. *Recreations:* horse racing, sailboarding, Australian Rules football. *Address:* MFS Ltd, Level 6, 56 Pitt Street, Sydney, NSW 2000, Australia. *Clubs:* Australian (Sydney); Melbourne, Melbourne Cricket, Victoria Racing, Melbourne Racing (Melbourne); Moonee Valley Racing.

PEACOCK, Elizabeth Joan; JP; DL; *b* 4 Sept. 1937; *d* of late John and Dorothy Gates; *m* 1963, Brian David Peacock; two *s*. *Educ:* St Monica's Convent, Skipton. Asst to Exec. Dir, York Community Council, 1979–83; Administrator, four charitable trusts, York, 1979–83. County Councillor, N Yorks, 1981–84. MP (C) Batley and Spen, 1983–97; contested (C) same seat, 1997, 2001. PPS to Minister of State, Home Office, 1991–92, to Minister for Social Security and disabled people, 1992. Mem., Select Cttee on Employment, 1983–87. Chairman: All Party Trans Pennine Gp, 1988–94; All Party Wool Textile Gp, 1989–97. Hon. Sec., Yorks Cons. MPs, 1983–88; Vice Chm., Cons. Back-bench Party Organisation Cttee, 1985–87; Mem. Exec. Cttee, 1922 Cttee, 1987–91; Mem. Exec., CPA, 1987–92. Mem., BBC Gen. Adv. Council, 1987–93; Chm., BBC Yorkshire Regl Audience Council (formerly Local Regl Cttee, Yorks), 2006–. Vice Pres., Yorks Area Young Conservatives, 1984–87; Pres., Yorks Area Cons. Trade Unionists, 1991–98 (Vice Pres., 1987–91). FRSA 1990 (Chm., Yorks Reg., 2003–06). JP Macclesfield, 1975–79, Bulmer East 1983; DL W Yorks, 1998. *Recreations:* reading, motoring. *Address:* Spen House, George Lane, Notton, Wakefield, W Yorks WF4 2NQ.
See also J. D. Peacock.

PEACOCK, Eric; *see* Peacock, W. E.

PEACOCK, Geraldine, CBE 2001; Chair, Charity Commission for England and Wales, 2004–06; *b* 26 Jan. 1948; *d* of late Peter Davies and of Joyce Davies (*née* Pullin); *m* 1971, Harry Peacock (marr. diss. 1988); three *s*. *Educ:* Redland High Sch., Bristol; Durham Univ. (BA Hons Sociology 1969); Univ. of California; Univ. of Newcastle upon Tyne (CQSW 1981; post-grad. dip. in Applied Social Work Studies 1981). Teaching Asst, Univ. of California, and Heroin Addiction Counsellor, San Bernadino State Prison, 1969–70; Med. Social Worker, Durham Hosp. Bd, 1970–72; Lectr in Criminology, Teesside Poly., 1972–75; Social Worker: Thalidomide Children's Trust, 1975–85; Lady Hoare Trust for Handicapped Children, 1975–79; Course Co-ordinator, Open Univ., 1975–82; Lectr in Social Work, Queen's Coll., Glasgow, 1982–86; Dep. Dir, London Boroughs Training Cttee, 1986–89; Chief Executive: Nat. Autistic Soc., 1989–97; Guide Dogs for the Blind Assoc., 1997–2003. Associate Fellow, Skoll Centre for Social Entrepreneurship, Saïd Business Sch., Oxford Univ., 2006–; Vis. Fellow, Centre for Charity Effectiveness, Cass Business Sch., London, 2007–. A Civil Service Comr, 2001–04; Comr and Bd Mem., Commn on Unclaimed Assets, 2006–. HM Treasury: Mem., Social Investment Taskforces, 2000–06; Chm., Futurebuilders Taskforce, 2003–04; Member: Strategy Unit Adv. Panel on Charity Law and Regulation, Cabinet Office, 2002–06; Action Community Unit Adv. Panel, Home Office, 2002–06. Columnist: Third Sector mag., 1999–, and other charity mags. Non-exec. Dir, Carbon Search. Member: Exec. Cttee, ACEVO (formerly ACENVO), 1994–2006 (Chm., 1996–2000); Council, Industrial Soc., 1996–2001; Exec. Cttee, NCVO, 2000–03 (Trustee, 1999–2006). Vice-Chm., Internat. Fedn of Guide Dog Schs for the Blind, 2001–03. Member: Social Enterprise Initiative Adv. Bd, Harvard Business Sch., 2003–; Business Adv. Forum, Saïd Business Sch., Oxford Univ., 2006–; Trustee, Movers and Shakers; Patron: Rainbow Trust; Autism Speaks; CDFA. Hon. LLD Teesside, 2005. *Publications:* (jtly) Social Work and Received Ideas, 1988; (ed jtly) The Haunt of Misery: essays in helping and caring, 1989; Appraising the Chief Executive, 1996; The Magic Roundabout: a guide to social investment for charities, 2004. *Recreations:* theatre, cinema, art, literature, family. *Address:* 3 Cathedral Green, Wells, Somerset BA5 2UD. *T:* 07939 664816; *e-mail:* office@geraldinepeacock.co.uk.

PEACOCK, Ian Douglas, OBE 1998; Chief Executive, Lawn Tennis Association, 1986–96; *b* 9 April 1934; *s* of Andrew Inglis Peacock and Minnie Maria (*née* King); *m* 1962, Joanna Hepburn MacGregor (marr. diss. 2007); one *s* one *d*. *Educ:* Sevenoaks Sch. Pilot Officer, RAF, 1953–54. Slazengers Ltd, 1955–83, Man. Dir 1976–83; Sports Marketing Surveys Ltd, 1984–85. President: British Sports & Allied Industry Fedn, 1984–85; UK Tennis Industry Assoc., 2008–. Director: Golf Foundn, 1982– (Chm., 1996–2003; Vice Pres., 2003–; Chm., Golf Ball Cttee, 1976–96); LTA Trust, 1988–96; Queen's Club Ltd, 1993–96; Wembley Nat. Stadium Ltd, 1998–2002; British Tennis Foundn, 1998–2007; Tennis Foundn, 2007–. Trustee: Torch Trophy Trust, 1993– (Chm., 1998–2006; Vice Pres., 2006–); English Nat. Stadium Trust, 1998–. *Recreations:* golf, ski-ing, painting. *Address:* 135 More Close, St Paul's Court, West Kensington, W14 9BW. *Clubs:* Royal Air Force, All England Lawn Tennis and Croquet, Queen's; Royal Ashdown Forest Golf (Forest Row).

PEACOCK, (Ian) Michael, OBE 2005; Chairman: UBC Media Group plc (formerly Unique Broadcasting Co. Ltd), 1989–95; The Michael Peacock Charitable Foundation, since 1990; *b* 14 Sept. 1929; *e s* of Norman Henry and Sara Barbara Peacock; *m* 1956, Daphne Lee; two *s* one *d*. *Educ:* Kimball Union Academy, USA; Welwyn Garden City Grammar School; London School of Economics (BSc Econ.; Hon. Fellow, 2004). BBC Television: Producer, 1952–56; Producer Panorama, 1956–58; Asst Head of Television Outside Broadcasts, 1958–59; Editor, Panorama, 1959–61; Editor, BBC Television News, 1961–63; Chief of Programmes, BBC 2, 1963–65; Controller, BBC 1, BBC Television Service, 1965–67; Managing Dir, London Weekend Television Ltd, 1967–69; Chm., Monitor Enterprises Ltd, 1970–89; Man. Dir, Warner Bros TV Ltd, 1972–74; Exec. Vice-Pres., Warner Bros Television Inc., 1974–76. Dir, Video Arts Ltd, 1972–89; Pres., Video Arts Inc., 1976–78; Man. Dir, Dumbarton Films Ltd (formerly Video Arts Television), 1978–87; Chairman: Video Answers, 1989–90; Publishing Projects plc, 1990–92. Dep. Chm., Piccadilly Radio, 1988–89; Man. Dir, Truly Classic Yachts Ltd, 1994–2002. IPPA:

First Chm., 1981–82; Mem. Council, 1983–88. Mem., Ct of Governors, LSE, 1982– (Chm., Campaign for the LSE, 2001–04). Hon. FTCL 2003. *Recreation:* sailing. *Address:* 21 Woodlands Road, Barnes, SW13 0JZ. *T:* (020) 8876 2025. *Club:* Savile.

PEACOCK, Ian Rex; Chairman: Mothercare plc, since 2002; MFI Furniture Group plc, 2000–06; *b* 5 July 1947; *s* of Mervyn (George) and Evelyn (Joyce) Peacock; *m* 1973, Alyanee Chya-Rochana; one *s. Educ:* Kingswood Grammar Sch.; Trinity Coll., Cambridge (MA). Economist: Unilever Plc, 1968–73; Cripps Warburg Ltd, 1973–75; Kleinwort Benson Gp, 1975–94 (Gp Dir, 1990–94); Co Head, Merchant Banking Div., USA, 1994–97, Chief Operating Officer, Investment Banking, 1997–98; BZW Ltd; Special Advr, Bank of England, 1998–2000. Non-exec. Dir, Norwich & Peterborough Bldg Soc., 1997–2005; Director: Lombard Risk Mgt, 2000– (Dep. Chm., 2004–); i-documentsystems, 2000–03. Chm., Family Mosaic Housing Assoc., 2007–. Trustee: WRVS, 2001–07; PHG Foundn, 2007–. *Recreations:* music, particularly opera, squash, gardening, travel. *Address:* Mothercare plc, Cherry Tree Road, Watford, Herts WD24 6SH. *Club:* Athenæum.

PEACOCK, James; *see* Peacock, W. J.

PEACOCK, Prof. John Andrew, PhD; FRS 2007; FRSE; Professor of Cosmology, University of Edinburgh, since 1998; *b* 27 March 1956; *s* of Arthur John Peacock and Isobel Watson Peacock (*née* Moir); *m* 1982, Catherine Heather Lewis; one *s* two *d. Educ:* Jesus Coll., Cambridge (BA 1977; PhD 1981). Res. astronomer, 1983–92, Hd of Res., 1992–98, Royal Observatory, Edinburgh. FRSE 2006. *Publication:* Cosmological Physics, 1999. *Recreations:* playing classical clarinet, hill walking. *Address:* Institute for Astronomy, University of Edinburgh, Royal Observatory, Blackford Hill, Edinburgh EH9 3HJ. *T:* (0131) 668 8100, *Fax:* (0131) 668 8416; *e-mail:* jap@roe.ac.uk.

PEACOCK, Jonathan David; QC 2001; *b* 21 April 1964; *s* of Brian David Peacock and Elizabeth Joan Peacock, *qv; m* 1997, Charlotte Ann Cole; one *s* one *d. Educ:* King's Sch., Macclesfield; Nunthorpe Grammar Sch., York; Corpus Christi Coll., Oxford (MA Juris 1st Cl.). Called to the Bar, Middle Temple, 1987 (Sen. Schol.). *Recreation:* cricket. *Address:* 11 New Square, Lincoln's Inn, WC2A 3QB. *T:* (020) 7242 4017. *Clubs:* United and Cecil; Brigands (Hants).

PEACOCK, Michael; *see* Peacock, I. M.

PEACOCK, Peter James, CBE 1998; Member (Lab) Highland and Islands, Scottish Parliament, since 1999; *b* 27 Feb. 1952; *s* of James and Doreen Peacock; *m* 1973, Shona Pearson; two *s. Educ:* Hawick High Sch.; Jordanhill Coll. of Educn (Dip. Youth Work and Community Studies 1973). Community Educn Officer, Orkney CC, 1973–75; Area Officer for Highland, Grampian, Tayside, Orkney, Shetland and Western Isles, and Central Policy Advr, Scottish Assoc. of CABx, 1975–87; Partner, The Apt Partnership, 1987–96. Member: Highland Regl Council (Dep. Leader; Chm. Finance Cttee), 1982–96; (Lab) Highland Council, 1995–99 (Leader/Convenor; Chm., Policy and Resources Cttee). Scottish Executive: Dep. Minister for Children and Educn, 1999–2000, for Finance and Local Govt, then for Finance and Public Services, 2000–03; Minister for Educn and Young People, 2003–06. Vice Pres., COSLA. Former Member: Bd, Scottish Natural Heritage; European Cttee of Regions; Scottish Economic Council; Bd, Scottish Post Office; Bd, Cairngorm Partnership. Chm., Scottish Library and Information Council, 1991–94; former Chairman: Moray Firth Community Radio; Community Work North; former Member: Scottish Valuation Adv. Council; Centres for Highlands and Islands Policy Studies. *Address:* (office) PO Box 5717, Inverness IV1 1YT.

PEACOCK, (William) Eric, CMG 2003; DBA; DL; non-executive Director, Exemplas Holdings Ltd (Chief Executive, 1996); Chief Executive, Business Link Hertfordshire, 1996–2006; *b* 22 Sept. 1944; *s* of Robert and Violet Peacock; *m* 1988, Carole Nicholls; one *s. Educ:* Bellahouston Acad.; Queen's Univ. Belfast (MBA 1974, DBA 1976). Barbour Ltd, 1960–79, Man. Dir, 1974–79; Managing Director: Hollis Gp plc, 1979–83; Hartsford Dales Ltd, 1983–93; Chm. and CEO, Babygro plc, 1983–88; Man. Dir, Missenden Abbey Management Develt Centre, 1993–96. Chairman: Cafe Slim Ltd, 2002–; What If, 2002–; Stevenage Packaging Ltd, 2003–; Eupak Ltd, 2003–; 4 Less Finance Plc, 2004–; Silent Edge Ltd, 2004–; Rialto Gp Ltd, 2004–. Non-executive Director: Hertfordshire Univ. Business Sch., 2002–; FCO, 2003–; DTI, later BERR. Gp Chm., Acad. for Chief Execs Ltd, 1997–. Chm., Peacock Foundn, 1987–. DL Herts 2003. *Recreations:* enthusiast and alchemist. *Address:* Green Fallow House, Bury Rise, Bovingdon, Herts HP3 0DN. *T:* (01442) 832154; *e-mail:* eric.peacock@chiefexecutive.com.

PEACOCK, Dr (William) James, AC 1994; BSc, PhD; FRS 1982; FAA; Chief, Division of Plant Industry, 1978–2003, Fellow, since 2004, Commonwealth Scientific and Industrial Research Organization; Chief Scientist, Australian Government, 2006–08; *b* 14 Dec. 1937; *m* 1961, Margaret Woodward; one *s* two *d. Educ:* Katoomba High Sch.; Univ. of Sydney (BSc, PhD). FAA 1976. CSIRO Postdoctoral Fellow, 1963 and Vis. Associate Prof. of Biology, 1964–65, Univ. of Oregon; Res. Consultant, Oak Ridge National Lab., USA, 1965; res. staff, Div. of Plant Industry, CSIRO, 1965–. Adjunct Prof. of Biology, Univ. of Calif, San Diego, 1969; Vis. Prof. of Biochem., Stanford Univ., 1970; Vis. Distinguished Prof. of Molecular Biol., Univ. of Calif, LA, 1977. Pres., Aust. Academy of Sci., 2002–06. For. Associate, US Nat. Acad. of Scis, 1990; For. Fellow, Indian Nat. Science Acad., 1990. FTSE (FTS 1988); FAIAST (FAIAS 1989). Hon. DSc Charles Sturt, 1996; Hon. DScAg NSW, 2002. Edgeworth David Medal, Royal Soc. of NSW, 1967; Lemberg Medal, Aust. Biochem. Soc., 1978; BHP Bicentennial Prize for Pursuit of Excellence in Science and Technol., 1988; CSIRO Medal for Leadership of Div. of Plant Industry, 1989; Burnet Medal, Aust. Acad. of Sci., 1989; (jtly) Prime Minister's Prize for Science (inaugural winner), 2000. *Publications:* editor of 5 books on genetics and molecular biology; approx. 330 papers. *Recreations:* cultivation of native plants, bush-walking. *Address:* 16 Brassey Street, Deakin, ACT 2600, Australia. *T:* (home) (2) 62814485.

PEACOCKE, Prof. Christopher Arthur Bruce, FBA 1990; Professor of Philosophy, Columbia University, since 2004; *b* 22 May 1950; *s* of late Rev. Dr Arthur Robert Peacocke, MBE; *m* 1980, Teresa Anne Rosen; one *s* one *d. Educ:* Magdalen College Sch., Oxford; Exeter Coll., Oxford (MA, BPhil, DPhil). Kennedy Schol., Harvard Univ., 1971; Sen. Schol., Merton Coll., Oxford, 1972; Jun. Res. Fellow, Queen's Coll., Oxford, 1973; Prize Fellow, All Souls Coll., Oxford, 1975; Fellow and Tutor, New Coll., Oxford, and CUF Lectr in Philosophy, 1979–85; Susan Stebbing Prof. of Philosophy, KCL, 1985–88; Waynflete Prof. of Metaphysical Philosophy, Univ. of Oxford and Fellow of Magdalen Coll., Oxford, 1989–2000; Prof. of Philosophy, New York Univ., 2000–04. Visiting Professor: Berkeley, 1975; Ann Arbor, 1978; UCLA, 1981; Maryland, 1987; NY Univ. 1996–99; Vis. Fellow, ANU, 1981; Fellow, Center for Advanced Study in the Behavioral Sciences, Stanford, 1983; Vis. Res. Associate, Center for Study of Language and Information, Stanford, 1984; Leverhulme Personal Res. Professorship, 1996–2000. Whitehead Lectr, Harvard, 2001; Immanuel Kant Lectr, Stanford, 2003. Pres., Mind Assoc., 1986; Mem., Steering Cttee, European Soc. for Philosophy and Psychology, 1991–95. Hon. DLitt Warwick, 2007. *Publications:* Holistic Explanation: action, space,

interpretation, 1979; Sense and Content, 1983; Thoughts: an essay on content, 1986; A Study of Concepts, 1992; Being Known, 1999; The Realm of Reason, 2004; Truly Understood, 2008; papers on philosophy of mind and language, and philosophical logic, in Jl of Philosophy, Philosophical Rev., etc. *Recreations:* music, visual arts. *Address:* Department of Philosophy, Columbia University, 1150 Amsterdam Avenue, 708 Philosophy Hall, MC 4971, New York, NY 10027, USA. *T:* (212) 8543384.

PEAKE, family name of **Viscount Ingleby.**

PEAKE, David Alphy Edward Raymond; Chairman, BNP Paribas (formerly Banque Nationale de Paris) UK Hldgs Ltd, 1997–2005 (Director, since 1974); Director, BNP Paribas (formerly Banque Nationale de Paris) SA, 1998–2004; *b* 27 Sept. 1934; *s* of Sir Harald Peake, AE and Mrs Resy Peake, OBE; *m* 1962, Susanna Kleinwort; one *s* one *d. Educ:* Ampleforth Coll.; Christ Church, Oxford (MA History, 1958). 2nd Lieut Royal Scots Greys, 1953–55. Banque Lambert, Brussels, 1958–59; J. Henry Schroder Wagg & Co. Ltd, 1959–63; Kleinwort Benson Ltd, 1963–93: Dir, 1971–93; Vice-Chm., 1985–87; Chm., 1988–89; Chm., Kleinwort Benson Group plc, 1989–93 (Dir, 1986–96); Hargreaves Group, 1964–86: Dir, 1964–86; Vice-Chm., 1967–74; Chm., 1974–86; Dir, M&G Gp, 1979–87. Pt-time Mem. of Bd, British Liby, 1990–96. Chairman: City and Inner London N TEC, 1990–93; 21st Century Learning Initiative (UK) (formerly Educn 2000 Trust), 1994–; Mem., BOTB, 1993–96. Chm., Chipping Norton Theatre Ltd, 1995–. Trustee, Harefield Hosp. Fund, 1994–95. Mem. Council, Goldsmiths Coll., Univ. of London, 1997–2004. Mem. Ct of Assts, Goldsmiths' Co., 1992– (Prime Warden, 2003–04). *Recreations:* reading, country sports. *Address:* Home Farm, Bourton-on-the-Hill, Moreton-in-Marsh GL56 9AF. *Clubs:* Brooks's, Pratt's, Cavalry and Guards.

PEAKE, John Fordyce; consultant; Associate Director (Scientific Development), Natural History Museum, 1989–92; *b* 4 June 1933; *s* of late William Joseph Peake and of Helena (*née* Fordyce); *m* 1963, Pamela Joyce Hollis; two *d. Educ:* City of Norwich Grammar Sch.; University Coll. London (BSc). National Trust, 1955–56; Norwich Technical Coll., 1956–58; Nature Conservancy Studentship, 1958–59; British Museum (Natural History): Research Fellow, 1959–61; Sen. Scientific Officer, 1961–69; PSO, 1969–71; Dep. Keeper, 1971–85; Keeper of Zoology, 1985–89. Hon. Research Associate, Bernice P. Bishop Mus., Honolulu, 1972–. Royal Society: Member: Aldabra Research Cttee, 1972–77; Southern Zones Cttee, 1982–86; Unitas Malacologica: Treas. 1962–63, Mem. Council, 1963–75; Vice Pres., Malacological Soc. of London, 1976–78; Council Mem., Zoological Soc. of London, 1985–88. *Publications:* (editor and contributor with Dr V. Fretter) Pulmonates, 3 vols, 1975–79; papers on taxonomy, biogeography and ecology of terrestrial molluscs in sci. jls. *Recreations:* gardening, local history. *Address:* Crows Nest, Back Lane, Blakeney, Holt, Norfolk NR25 7NP. *T:* (01263) 740388.

PEAKE, John Morris, CBE 1986; Chairman: Cambridgeshire Careers Guidance Ltd, 1995–98; Careers Services National Association, 1997–98; *b* 26 Aug. 1924; *s* of late Albert Edward Peake and Ruby Peake (*née* Morris); *m* 1953, Elizabeth Rought; one *s* one *d. Educ:* Repton School; Clare College, Cambridge (Mech. Scis Tripos; MA 1949); Royal Naval College, Greenwich (Dip. Naval Arch.). CEng, FIMechE; CMath, FIMA. Royal Corps of Naval Constructors, 1944–50; Personnel Administration Ltd, 1950–51; Baker Perkins (BP): joined 1951; Dir, parent co., 1956; Jt Man. Dir, BP Ltd, 1963–66; Man. Dir, BP Pty, 1969–74, in Australia; Pres., BP Inc., 1975–77, in USA; Dep. Man. Dir, BP Holdings, 1978–79, Man. Dir, 1980–85; Chm., Baker Perkins plc, 1984–87. Member: Council, CBI, 1980–89 (Chairman: Overseas Schols Bd, 1981–87; Educn and Trng Cttee, 1986–88); Council, BTEC, 1986–89 (Chm., Bd for Engineering, 1985–91); MSC, subseq. Trng Commn, 1986–88; RSA Examinations Bd, 1987–93 (Chm., 1989–93); RSA Council, 1989–93; Design Council, 1991–93 (Chm. Educn Cttee, 1990–94); Chm., Greater Peterborough Partnership, 1994–95; Vice Chm., Gtr Peterborough TEC, 1990–94. Chm., Nene Park Trust, 1988–93. Hockey Silver Medal, London Olympics, 1948. FRSA; CCMI. Hon. DTech CNAA, 1986. *Recreations:* sport, travel. *Address:* Old Castle Farmhouse, Stibbington, Peterborough PE8 6LP. *T:* (01780) 782683. *Clubs:* East India, MCC; Hawks (Cambridge).

PEAKER, Prof. Malcolm, DSc, PhD; FRS 1996; FZS, FIBiol, FRSE; Director, Hannah Research Institute, Ayr, 1981–2003; Hannah Professor, University of Glasgow, 1981–2003; *b* 21 Aug. 1943; *s* of Ronald Smith Peaker and Marian (*née* Tomasin); *m* 1965, Stephanie Jane Large; three *s. Educ:* Henry Mellish Grammar Sch., Nottingham; Univ. of Sheffield (BSc Zoology; DSc); Univ. of Hong Kong (SRC NATO Scholar; PhD). FZS 1969; FIBiol 1979; FRSE 1983. Inst. of Animal Physiology, ARC, 1968–78; Head, Dept of Physiol., Hannah Res. Inst., 1978–81. Chm. Bd, London Zoo, 1992–93; Vice-Pres., Council, Zoological Soc. of London, 1992–94; Mem. Council, RSE, 1999–2002. Mem., Rank Prize Funds Adv. Cttee on Nutrition, 1997–. Scientific Governor, British Nutrition Foundn, 1997– (Chm., 2002–04). Non-exec. Dir, Edinburgh Instruments Ltd, 2004–. Raine Distinguished Visitor, Univ. of WA, 1998. Munro Kerr Lecture, Munro Kerr Soc., 1997; Annual Lecture, Edinburgh Centre for Rural Res./RSE/Inst. of Biol., 2000; Dist. Lectr, Univ. of Hong Kong, 2000. Hon. DSc Hong Kong, 2000. Mem. Editorial Board: Jl of Dairy Science, 1975–78; Internat. Zoo Yearbook, 1978–82; Jl of Endocrinology, 1981–91; Procs of RSE, 1989–92; Mammary Gland Biology and Neoplasia, 1993–2000; Editor, British Jl of Herpetology, 1977–81. *Publications:* Salt Glands in Birds and Reptiles, 1975; (ed) Avian Physiology, 1975; (ed) Comparative Aspects of Lactation, 1977; (ed jtly) Physiological Strategies in Lactation, 1984; (ed jtly) Intercellular Signalling in the Mammary Gland, 1995; (ed jtly) Biological Signalling and the Mammary Gland, 1997; papers in physiol, endocrinol, zool, biochem., vet. and agricl science jls. *Recreations:* vertebrate zoology, natural history, golf, grumbling about bureaucrats. *Address:* Rushmere, 13 Upper Crofts, Alloway, Ayr KA7 4QX. *Club:* Royal Troon Golf.

PEARCE, Prof. Alastair Tom Parslow, PhD; Principal, Rose Bruford College, since 2001; *b* 9 Dec. 1953; *s* of Tom and Florence Pearce; *m* Dr Maureen Cleary. *Educ:* Royal Acad. of Music (LRAM); King's Coll., London (BMus, MMus; PhD). Nat. Advr for Computing in the Arts, Univ. of Oxford, 1972–82; University of Central England: Vice-Principal, Birmingham Conservatoire, 1994–98; Dean, Fac. of Educn, 1998–2001. *Publications:* contribs to music jls and articles on managing performing arts higher educn. *Recreations:* fine wine, cooking, writing. *Address:* Rose Bruford College, Lamorbey Park Campus, Burnt Oak Lane, Sidcup, Kent DA15 9DF. *T:* (020) 8308 2601, *Fax:* (020) 8308 2624; *e-mail:* alastair.pearce@bruford.ac.uk.

PEARCE, Andrew; Deputy Head of Distributive Trades Unit, European Commission, Brussels, 1994–2002; *b* 1 Dec. 1937; *s* of late Henry Pearce, Liverpool cotton broker, and Evelyn Pearce; *m* 1966, Myra Whelan (*d* 2006); three *s* one *d. Educ:* Rydal School, Colwyn Bay; University of Durham (BA). Formerly in construction industry; in Customs Dept, EEC, Brussels, 1974–79. Contested (C) Islington North, 1969 and 1970; Mem. (C) Cheshire W, Eur. Parlt, 1979–89; contested: (C) Cheshire W, EP elecn, 1989; (C) Ellesmere Port and Neston, 1992; (Pro Euro C) NW Reg., EP elecn, 1999. Founder and Vice-Pres., British Cons. Assoc. in Belgium; Vice-Pres., Consultative Assembly of Lomé Convention, 1980–89. Chm., Internat. Trade Cttee, British Retail Consortium, 1990–93; Vice Chm., European Business Develt Gp, 1991–93, Mem. Council, 2004–, Liverpool

Chamber of Commerce. Chairman: Friends of Nat. Museums Liverpool, 2004–; Liverpool Heritage Forum, 2005–; Mem. Council, Merseyside Civic Soc., 2004–. Governor: Archway Comprehensive School, 1967–70; Woodchurch High Sch., Birkenhead, 1985–90; Nugent Sch., Liverpool, 1992–94. FRSA 2004. *Address:* Laurel Cottage, 59 Stanley Lane, Eastham, Wirral CH62 0AQ. *Club:* Athenæum (Liverpool).

PEARCE, Andrew John; HM Diplomatic Service; Deputy Head of Mission, Bangkok, since 2004; *b* 7 Oct. 1960; *s* of Edward Peter Pearce and Renee Joyce Pearce; *m* 1986, Pornpun Pathumvivatana; one *s* one *d. Educ:* St Catherine's Coll., Oxford (MA 1st Cl. Hons Chemistry 1983). Joined FCO, 1983; Third Sec., Nr East and N Africa Dept, FCO, 1983–84; lang. trng, SOAS, London, 1984–85; Second Sec. (Pol), Bangkok, 1985–88; Head: Chemical Weapons Sect., Arms Control and Disarmament Dept, FCO, 1988–90; Iberian Sec., S European Dept, FCO, 1990–92; First Secretary: Pol and Public Affairs, Tel Aviv, 1992–96; Econ. Affairs, Pretoria, 1996–2000; Counsellor and Dep. Hd of Mission, Bucharest, 2001–03. *Recreations:* tennis, long-distance walking, exploring, cat rearing. *Address:* British Embassy, Wireless Road, Bangkok 10300, Thailand. *T:* (2) 714 3733; *e-mail:* andy.pearce@fco.gov.uk.

PEARCE, Brian; *see* Pearce, J. B.

PEARCE, Christopher Donovan James; Chief Executive Officer, Proteome Sciences (formerly Electrophoretics International) plc, since 1991; *b* 1 March 1953; *m* 1981, Sandra Lynette Jenkins; two *s* one *d* (and one *d* decd). *Educ:* St John's Coll., Hurstpierpoint. AIIMR 1977. Partner, Scott Goff Hancock & Co., 1971, acquired by Smith New Court Securities plc, 1986, Dir, 1986–90; Exec. Chm. and Jt Founder, Fitness First, 1992–2003; non-exec. Dir, Fitness First Hldgs Ltd, 2003–05. Mem., London Stock Exchange, 1978–90; MSI (Dip) 1990. *Recreations:* theatre, ballet, opera, Rugby, golf, tennis. *Address:* Proteome Sciences plc, Coveham House, Downside Bridge Road, Cobham, Surrey KT11 3EP. *Clubs:* Burhill Golf, Oxshott Sports; Old Johnian Rugby Football.

PEARCE, Sir (Daniel Norton) Idris, Kt 1990; CBE 1982; TD 1972; DL; Deputy Chairman, English Partnerships, 1993–2001; *b* 28 Nov. 1933; *s* of late Lemuel George Douglas Pearce and Evelyn Mary Pearce; *m* 1963, Ursula Helene Langley (marr. diss. 1997); two *d. Educ:* West Buckland Sch.; College of Estate Management. FRICS. Commnd RE, 1958; comd 135 Field Survey Sqdn, RE(TA), 1970–73. Joined Richard Ellis, 1959: Partner, 1961–92; Man. Partner, 1981–87; Consultant, 1992–2000. Chairman: English Estates, 1989–94; Flexit Cos, 1993–98; Varsity Funding, 1995–2000; Redburgh Ltd, 1996–2000; Director: The Phoenix Initiative, 1991; ITC, 1992–94; Nat. Mortgage Bank, 1992–97; Swan Hill (formerly Higgs & Hill), 1993–2002; Dusco UK Ltd, 1993–2002; Innisfree, 1996–2006; Millennium & Copthorne Hotels, 1996–2006; Regalian, 1998–2001; Resolution, 1998–2002. Royal Instn of Chartered Surveyors: Member: Gen. Council, 1980–94; Management Bd, 1984–91; Chm., Parly and Public Affairs Cttee, 1984–89; Vice Pres., 1986–90; Pres., 1990–91. Chm., Internat. Assets Valuation Standards Cttee, 1981–86. Member: Adv. Panel for Instnl Finance in New Towns, 1974–80; Sec. of State for Health and Social Security Inquiry into Surplus Land in the NHS, 1982; PSA Adv. Bd, 1981–86; FCO Adv. Panel on Diplomatic Estate, 1985–97; Financial Reporting Review Panel, 1991–93; Bd, London Forum, 1993–2001; Property Advr, NHS Management Bd, 1985–90; Dep. Chm., Urban Regeneration Agency, 1993–2001; Dir, London First Centre, 1995–2001. Chm., Higher Educn Funding Council for Wales, 1992–96; Member: UFC, 1991–93; HEFCE, 1992–96. Vice Chm., Greater London TA&VRA, 1991–94 (Mem. 1970–98; Chm., Works and Bldgs Sub-Cttee, 1983–90). Chm. Develt Bd, Nat. Art-Collections Fund, 1988–92. Dir, English Courtyard Assoc., 2007–. Member: Court, City Univ., 1987–2000; Council, Univ. of Surrey, 1993–2004 (Pro-Chancellor, 1994–2004, now Emeritus; Chm., 1998–2001); Council, Reading Univ., 1997–2000; Comr, Royal Hosp., 1995–2001. Chairman: Governors, Stanway Sch., Dorking, 1982–85; W Buckland Sch. Foundn, 2002–07. Trustee, Rochester Bridge Trust, 1991–94. Governor: Peabody Trust, 1992–2003; RCA, 1997–. Contested (C) Neath, 1959. DL Greater London, 1986. Hon. Fellow: Coll. of Estate Management, 1987; Univ. of Wales Cardiff, 1997; Centenary Fellow, Thames Poly., 1991; Companion, De Montfort Univ., 1992. Hon. Col, 135 Indep. Topographic Sqn, RE(V), TA, 1989–94. FRSA 1989. Hon. DSc: City, 1990; Oxford Poly., 1991; Salford Univ., 1991; Hon. DEng West of England, 1994; Hon. DTech E London, 1999; DUniv Surrey, 2004. *Publications:* A Call to Talent, 1993; various articles on valuation and property matters. *Recreations:* reading, opera, ballet, travel. *Club:* Brooks's.

PEARCE, Edward Robin; author and political commentator; *b* 28 March 1939; *s* of late Frank Pearce and Olive Pearce (*née* Johnson); *m* 1966, Deanna Maria Stanwell (*née* Singer); one *d. Educ:* Queen Elizabeth Grammar Sch., Darlington; St Peter's Coll., Oxford (MA); Univ. of Stockholm. Res. Asst, Labour Party, Transport Hse, 1964–66; Res. Officer, Police Fedn, 1966–68; with Douglas Mann & Co., solicitors, 1968–70; teacher, S Shields, 1970–75; contributor, Sunday Express, 1975–77; Leader-writer, Daily Express, 1977–79; Parliamentary sketch-writer: Daily Telegraph, 1979–87; freelance career, 1987–: columnist: Sunday Times, 1987–90; The Guardian, 1990–95; The Scotsman, 1998–2000; Commissioning Editor, Punch, 2000–02; contrib. Punch, Sunday Telegraph, Daily Mail, The Herald (Glasgow), Evening Standard, Wall St Jl, Sunday Tribune (Dublin), New Statesman, Spectator, History Today, Encounter, Tatler, New Republic (Washington), London Rev. of Books, Lit. Rev., TLS, Prospect, Yorkshire Post, Guardian Online, etc. Panel Member: The Moral Maze, Radio 4, 1991–95; Dateline, BBC World Service TV, 1997–2002; contrib. News Talk, LBC, 1989–92. Columnist of Year Award, What the Papers Say, 1987; Peter Wilson Award, League Against Cruel Sports, 1993. *Publications:* The Senate of Lilliput, 1983; Hummingbirds and Hyenas, 1985; Looking Down on Mrs Thatcher (collected Commons sketches), 1987; The Shooting Gallery, 1989; The Quiet Rise of John Major, 1990; Election Rides, 1992; Machiavelli's Children, 1993; The Lost Leaders, 1997; Lines of Most Resistance: the Lords, the Tories and Ireland 1886–1914, 1999; Denis Healey: a life in our times, 2002; Reform! the fight for the 1832 Reform Act, 2003; The Diaries of Charles Greville, 2005; The Great Man: a life of Sir Robert Walpole, 2007. *Recreations:* listening to classical music, esp. Schubert, watching cricket, esp. Lancashire, and football, esp. Oldham Athletic, reading history, esp. 18th Century, travel, esp. Italy, wandering around old towns, esp. ones with bookshops. *Address:* Ryedale House, Thormanby, York YO61 4NN. *Clubs:* Reform; Easingwold Cricket.

PEARCE, Gareth David, FCA; Chairman: Smith & Williamson, since 2000; Nexia International, since 2000; *b* 13 Aug. 1953; *s* of late Howard Spencer Pearce; *m* 1984, Virginia Louise Miller; four *d. Educ:* Abingdon Sch.; Balliol Coll., Oxford (MA). FCA 1997 (ACA 1979). Peat Marwick Mitchell & Co., 1975–81; Electra Investment Trust plc, 1982–86, Dir, Electra Mgt plc, 1984–86; Smith & Williamson, Chartered Accountants: Dir, 1986–; Hd, Corporate Finance Dept, 1986–95; Man. Dir, 1995–2000. *Recreations:* chess, fishing, reading, travelling. *Address:* Bewley Court, Lacock, Wilts SN15 2PG. *T:* (01249) 730573. *Club:* Hurlingham.

PEARCE, Most Rev. George Hamilton, SM; Archbishop Emeritus of Suva (R.C.); *b* 9 Jan. 1921; *s* of George H. Pearce and Marie Louise Duval. *Educ:* Marist Coll. and Seminary, Framingham Center, Mass, USA. Entered Seminary, 1940; Priest, 1947; taught in secondary sch. in New England, USA, 1948–49; assigned as missionary to Samoa, 1949; consecrated Vicar Apostolic of Samoa, 1956; first Bishop of Apia, 1966; Archbishop of Suva, 1967–76, retired 1976. *Address:* Cathedral Rectory, 30 Fenner Street, Providence, RI 02903, USA. *T:* (401) 3312434.

PEARCE, Howard John Stredder, CVO 1993; HM Diplomatic Service, retired; Governor of the Falkland Islands and Commissioner, South Georgia and the South Sandwich Islands, 2002–06; *b* 13 April 1949; *s* of late Ernest Victor Pearce and Ida (*née* Booth); *m* 2004, Caroline Thomée; one *d. Educ:* City of London Sch.; Pembroke Coll., Cambridge (MA, LLB). Joined HM Diplomatic Service, 1972; FCO, 1972–74; Third Sec., Buenos Aires, 1975–78; FCO, 1978–83; First Sec. and Hd of Chancery, Nairobi, 1983–87; FCO, 1987–90; Sen. Associate Mem., St Antony's Coll., Oxford, 1990–91; Dep. Hd of Mission, Budapest, 1991–94; Fellow, Center for Internat. Affairs, Harvard Univ., 1994–95; Hd, Central European Dept, FCO, 1996–99; High Comr, Malta, 1999–2002. Mem., Exec. Cttee, VSO, 1988–90. Chairman: S Georgia Heritage Trust, 2006–; Exhibiting Socs of Scottish Artists, 2008–. Officer's Cross (Republic of Hungary), 1999. *Recreations:* classical music, opera, reading, travel. *Club:* Oxford and Cambridge.

PEARCE, Sir Idris; *see* Pearce, Sir D. N. I.

PEARCE, Jessica Mary; *see* Hand, J. M.

PEARCE, (John) Brian, OBE 2000; Director, The Inter Faith Network for the United Kingdom, 1987–2007; *b* 25 Sept. 1935; *s* of late George Frederic Pearce and Constance Josephine Pearce; *m* 1960, Michelle Etcheverry; four *s. Educ:* Queen Elizabeth Grammar Sch., Wakefield; Brasenose Coll., Oxford (BA). Asst Principal: Min. of Power, 1959; Colonial Office, 1960; Private Sec. to Parly Under-Sec. of State, 1963; Principal: Colonial Office, 1964; Dept of Economic Affairs, 1967; Principal Private Sec. to Sec. of State for Economic Affairs, 1968–69; Asst Sec., Civil Service Dept, 1969, Under-Sec., 1976; Under-Sec., HM Treasury, 1981–86, retd. MLitt Lambeth, 1993. *Recreations:* comparative theology, music, architecture. *Address:* 124 Court Lane, SE21 7EA.

PEARCE, Prof. John Martindale, DPhil; FRS 2006; Professor of Psychology, Cardiff University, since 1992; *b* 6 Dec. 1947; *s* of Jack and Mavis Pearce; *m* 1976, Victoria Anne Bradley; one *s* two *d. Educ:* Univ. of Leeds (BSc Hons); Univ. of Sussex (DPhil). Lectr, Sch. of Psychol., Cardiff Univ., 1980–92. Vis. Prof., Dept of Psychol., Duke Univ., 1987–88; Vis. Fellow, Inst. of Advanced Study, Indiana Univ., Bloomington, 1999; Vis. Erskine Fellow, Univ. of Canterbury, Christchurch, 2001. Ed., Qly Jl of Experimental Psychology: Comparative and Physiological Psychology, 1997–2000. *Publications:* Introduction to Animal Cognition, 1987; Animal Learning and Cognition, 1997. *Recreations:* music, travelling in remote places. *Address:* School of Psychology, Cardiff University, Cardiff CF10 3YG. *T:* (029) 2087 4483, *Fax:* (029) 2087 4848; *e-mail:* pearcejm@cf.ac.uk.

PEARCE, Rev. Neville John Lewis; Priest-in-charge, Swainswick/Woolley, Diocese of Bath and Wells, 1993–98; Chief Executive, Avon County Council, 1982–89; *b* 27 Feb. 1933; *s* of John and Ethel Pearce; *m* 1958, Eileen Frances Potter; two *d. Educ:* Queen Elizabeth's Hosp., Bristol; Silcoates Sch., Wakefield; Univ. of Leeds (LLB Hons 1953, LLM 1954); Trinity Theol Coll., Bristol. Asst Solicitor: Wakefield CBC, 1957–59; Darlington CBC, 1959–61; Chief Asst Solicitor, Grimsby CBC, 1961–63, Dep. Town Clerk, 1963–65; Dep. Town Clerk, Blackpool CBC, 1965–66; Town Clerk, Bath CBC, 1967–73; Dir of Admin and County Solicitor, Avon CC, 1973–82. Ordained (C of E), 1991; Asst Curate, St Swithin, Walcot, Bath, 1991–93. *Recreations:* family support, a West Highland terrier, supporting leaderless churches. *Address:* Penshurst, Weston Lane, Bath BA1 4AB. *T:* (01225) 426925.

PEARCE, Nicholas Robin; Head of Strategic Policy, Prime Minister's Office, since 2007; *b* 24 May 1968; *s* of late Peter Bailes Pearce and of Lynda Margaret Pearce; *m* 2000, Rebecca Asher; one *s. Educ:* Univ. of Manchester (BA Hons); Balliol Coll., Oxford (MPhil Politics). Res. Asst to Bryan Davies, MP, 1993–97; Res. Fellow in Educn, IPPR, 1997; Special Advr to Leader of H of C, 1998; Sen. Res. Fellow in Educn, IPPR, 1998–99; Advr (pt-time), Social Exclusion Unit, 1998–99; Special Adviser: to Sec. of State for Educn and Employment, 1999–2001; to Home Sec., 2001–03; Dir, IPPR, 2004–07. *Publications:* (with J. Hillman) Wasted Youth, 1998; (ed with J. Hallgarten) Tomorrow's Citizens, 2000; (ed with W. Paxton) Social Justice: building a fairer Britain, 2005; (jtly) Freedom's Orphans, 2006; (ed with J. Margo) Politics for a New Generation, 2007. *Recreations:* twentieth century architecture, travel in South America. *Address: e-mail:* nicholasrpearce@googlemail.com.

PEARCE, Peter Huxley; Director, Landmark Trust, since 1995; *b* 16 May 1956; *s* of Dr Alan John Pearce and Marion Joyce (*née* Wright); *m* 1983, Christina Zalichi; two *s. Educ:* Reading Univ. (BSc Hons Rural Estate Mgt). FRICS 1981. National Trust: Man. Land Agent, E Midlands Reg., 1982–87, Southern Reg., 1988–95; Dir, Uppark Repair Project, 1989–95. Trustee, Edward James Foundn. *Recreations:* historic buildings, music, fishing, landscape and conservation, family life. *Address:* The Landmark Trust, Shottesbrooke, Maidenhead, Berks SL6 3SW. *T:* (01628) 825920.

PEARCE, Prof. Robert Alasdair; Vice-Chancellor, University of Wales, Lampeter, since 2003; *b* 28 Nov. 1951; *s* of Walter Charles Pearce and Dorothy Kate Pearce. *Educ:* George Dixon's Grammar Sch.; Cotham Grammar Sch.; Sir Thomas Rich's Sch.; Pembroke Coll., Oxford (BA Hons (Jurisprudence) 1973; BCL 1974; MA 1978). Lectr in Law: Univ. of Newcastle upon Tyne, 1974–79; Univ. of Lancaster, 1979–80; Lectr, then Statutory Lectr, UC, Cork, NUI, 1981–89; University of Buckingham: Sen. Lectr in Law, 1989–90; Prof. of Law of Property and Equity, 1990–2003; Dean, Acad. Affairs, 1993–94; Pro-Vice-Chancellor, 1994–2002; Actg Vice-Chancellor, 2000–01. Welsh Supernumerary Fellow, Jesus Coll., Oxford, 2007–08. Auditor, HEQC, then QAA, 1993–2003; Mem., Adv. Cttee on Degree Awarding Powers, QAA, 2003–; Chm., Postgrad. Internat. Assessment Bd, Irish Res. Council for Humanities and Social Scis, 2006–07 (Bd Mem., 2004–05). Chairman: Oxford Univ. Law Course Adv. Cttee, 1971–72; Univs Assoc. for Lifelong Learning Cymru, 2004–. Mem., Future Skills Wales, 2003–06. Parkside Housing Group, Windsor: Dir, 1998–2003; Vice-Chm., 2000–02; Chm., 2002–03. Mem., Cttee of Mgt, Rockboro Sch. Assoc., 1983–87; Governor: Pebble Brook Sch., Aylesbury, 1997–2000; Rycotewood Coll., Thame, 2000–03 (Vice-Chm., 2001–03). Hon. LLD Buckingham, 2007. *Publications:* A Commentary on the Succession Act 1965, 2nd revd edn 1986; (with I. J. Dawson) Licences Relating to the Occupation or Use of Land, 1979; Land Law (Irish Law Texts), 1985, 2nd edn with Dr John Mee, 2000; (with A. J. Stevens) The Law of Trusts and Equitable Obligations, 1995, 4th edn 2006; (with A. J. Stevens and N. Jackson) Land Law, 1997, 4th edn 2008. *Recreations:* smallholding, fishing. *Address:* University of Wales, Lampeter, Lampeter, Ceredigion SA48 7ED. *T:* (01570) 424704, *Fax:* (01570) 424988.

PEARCE, Robert Edgar; QC 2006; *b* 22 June 1953; *s* of Edgar Pearce and Stella Mary Louise Pearce (*née* Dimock); *m* 1984, Janice Linscott; two *d*. *Educ:* Whitgift Sch.; Christ Church, Oxford (BA 1st Cl. Jurisprudence 1975; BCL 1976). Called to the Bar, Middle Temple, 1977; in practice at Chancery bar, 1978–. Standing Counsel to the Charity Commn, 2001–06. *Publications:* (contrib. ed.) Butterworths Civil Court Practice, annually 1997–; various articles. *Recreation:* music. *Address:* Radcliffe Chambers, 11 New Square, Lincoln's Inn, WC2A 3QB. *T:* (020) 7831 0081, *Fax:* (020) 7405 2560; *e-mail:* rpearce@radcliffechambers.com.

PEARCE, Prof. Robert Penrose, FRMetS; FRSE; Professor of Meteorology and Head of Department of Meteorology, University of Reading, 1970–90, now Emeritus Professor; *b* 21 Nov. 1924; *s* of Arthur Penrose Pearce and Ada Pearce; *m* 1951, Patricia Frances Maureen Curling; one *s* two *d*. *Educ:* Bishop Wordsworth Sch., Salisbury; Imperial Coll., London (BSc, ARCS, DIC, PhD). Asst, Meteorological Office, 1941–43. Served RAF, 1943–47 (commnd 1945). Lectr, then Sen. Lectr in Mathematics, Univ. of St Andrews, 1952–66; Reader in Phys. Climatology, Imperial Coll., 1966–70. Pres., Royal Meteorological Soc., 1972–74 (Hon. Mem., 1998); Chm., World Meteorol Org. Working Gp in Trop. Meteorology, 1978–90. *Publications:* Observer's Book of Weather, 1980; (co-ed) Monsoon Dynamics, 1981; (ed) Meteorology at the Millennium, 2002; sci. papers in meteorol jls. *Recreations:* walking, gardening, bridge, music. *Address:* Schiehallion, 27 Copped Hall Way, Camberley, Surrey GU15 1PB. *T:* (01276) 501523.

PEARCE-HIGGINS, Daniel John; QC 1998; **His Honour Judge Pearce-Higgins;** a Circuit Judge, since 2004; *b* 26 Dec. 1949; *m*. *Educ:* St Paul's Sch., London; Univ. of Bristol (BSc Philosophy and Politics). Called to the Bar, Middle Temple, 1973; an Asst Recorder, 1995–99; a Recorder, 1999–2004. Mem., Mental Health Review Tribunal, 2000–. CEDR accredited mediator, 1999–2004. FCIArb 1999–2004. *Address:* c/o Midland Circuit Secretariat, The Priory Courts, 33 Bull Street, Birmingham B4 6DW.

PEARCEY, Oliver Henry James; historic environment consultant, since 2006; Special Projects Director, English Heritage, 2004–06; *b* 13 June 1951; *s* of Lawrence Henry Victor Pearcey and Gladys Winifred Pearcey (*née* Bond); *m* 1979, Elizabeth Platts; two *d*. *Educ:* Westminster Sch.; Univ. of Sussex (BSc Biochem). Department of the Environment: Admin trainee, 1972–78; Principal, 1978–85; on secondment to GLC, 1981–83; English Heritage: Team Leader, 1985–88, Head, 1988–91, Historic Bldgs Div.; Dir, Conservation, Midlands Reg., 1991–94; Dep. Dir, 1994–97, Dir, 1997–2002, Conservation; Designation Dir, 2002–04. Mem., IHBC, 1998. *Recreations:* industrial archaeology, English salt-glaze stoneware, reading voraciously. *Address:* 48 Westville Road, W12 9BD. *T:* (020) 8749 2793.

PEAREY, David Dacre; HM Diplomatic Service; Governor, British Virgin Islands, since 2006; *b* 15 July 1948; *s* of William Pearey and Dorothy Pearey; *m* 1996, Susan Anne (*née* Knowles); one *d*. *Educ:* Oundle Sch.; Bristol Univ. (BSc Hons Econs). Joined MoD as trainee, 1971; Pvte Sec. to Parly Under Sec. of State for Defence (RAF), 1974–76; joined FCO, 1979; First Secretary: Ankara, 1979–82; Energy and Policy Planning Depts, FCO, 1983–87; Dep. High Comr, Kampala, 1987–90; Southern European and Inspectorate Depts, FCO, 1990–95; Counsellor, Lagos, 1995–99; Dep. High Comr, Karachi, 2000–04; High Comr, Malaŵi, 2004–06. Mem., Glyndebourne Fest. Soc., 1998–. FRGS 1993. *Recreations:* travel, mountains, opera, walking, reading. *Address:* Government House, Tortola, British Virgin Islands; *e-mail:* dandspearey@aol.com. *Clubs:* Travellers, Hurlingham.

PEARL, David Stephen, PhD; **His Honour Judge Pearl;** a Circuit Judge, since 1994; President, Care Standards Tribunal, since 2002; *b* 11 Aug. 1944; *s* of late Chaim Pearl and Anita Pearl (*née* Newman); *m* 1st, 1967, Susan Roer (marr. diss.); three *s*; 2nd, 1985, Gillian Farr (*née* Maciejewska); one step *s* one step *d*. *Educ:* George Dixon Grammar Sch., Birmingham; Westminster City Sch.; Birmingham Univ. (LLB); Queens' Coll., Cambridge (Sen. Scholar; LLM, MA, PhD). Called to the Bar, Gray's Inn, 1968, Bencher, 2002; Cambridge University: Asst Lectr in Law, 1967–72; Lectr, 1972–89; Res. Fellow, Queens' Coll., 1967–69; Fellow and Dir of Studies in Law, Fitzwilliam Coll., Cambridge, 1969–89 (Life Fellow, 1989); Prof. of Law and Dean, Sch. of Law, UEA, 1989–94, Hon. Prof., 1995–; a Recorder, 1992–94. Immigration Appeals Adjudicator, 1980–92; Chm., 1992–97, Pres., 1998–99, Immigration Appeal Tribunal; Chief Immigration Adjudicator, 1994–98. Mem., Judicial Appts Commn, 2006–. Judicial Studies Board: Member: Civil and Family Cttee, 1994–96; Tribunals Cttee, 1996–99, 2004–; Dir of Studies, 1999–2001. Vice-Pres., Internat. Soc. for Family Law, 1991–97. Yorke Prize, Cambridge, 1972; Shaw Prize, Boston Coll. Law Sch., 1985; Van Heyden de Lancy Prize, Cambridge, 1991. *Publications:* A Textbook on Muslim Law, 1979, 3rd edn as Muslim Family Law (with W. Menski), 1998; Interpersonal Conflict of Laws in India, Pakistan and Bangladesh, 1980; (with K. Gray) Social Welfare Law, 1980; (jtly) Family Law and Society, 1983, 6th edn 2008; Family Law and Immigrant Communities, 1986; (with A. Grubb) Blood Testing AIDS and DNA Profiling, 1990; (jtly) Butterworth's Immigration Law Service, 1991–2007; (ed jtly) Clarke, Hall and Morrison on Children, 2004–. *Recreations:* helping my wife with the horses, goats and chickens, very amateur dramatics. *Address:* Care Standards Tribunal, 18 Pocock Street, SE1 0BW. *T:* (020) 7960 0673. *Club:* Reform.

PEARL, Prof. Laurence Harris, PhD; FRS 2008; Professor of Protein Crystallography and Section Chairman, Institute of Cancer Research, since 1999; *b* Manchester, 18 June 1956; *s* of Monty and Carole Pearl; *m* 1994, Frances M. G.; two *s* one *d*. Prof. of Structural Biol., UCL, 1996–99. Mem., EMBO, 2005. FMedSci 2007. *Publications:* contrib. scientific jls. *Recreations:* feeding my family, juggling, computer animation. *Address:* Institute of Cancer Research, Chester Beatty Laboratories, 237 Fulham Road, SW3 6JB. *T:* (020) 7153 5422; *e-mail:* Laurence.Pearl@icr.ac.uk.

PEARL, Patricia; Her Honour Judge Pearl; a Circuit Judge, since 2006; *b* Derby, 5 June 1953; *d* of Thomas Andrew Smallwood and Eva May Smallwood; *m* 1975; one *d*; partner, Ian S. Hilton. *Educ:* Parkfield Cedars Grammar Sch., Derby; Rugby High Sch. for Girls; Lady Margaret Hall, Oxford (BA Hons Geog. 1974). Admitted solicitor, 1977; a District Judge, 1998–2006. *Publications:* Small Claims Procedure: a practical guide, 4th edn 2008; (contrib. ed) Civil Procedure (The White Book). *Recreations:* photography, walking the long-distance footpaths of Britain. *Address:* Barnet County Court, Regents Park Road, Finchley, N3 1BQ. *T:* (020) 8343 4272.

PEARL, Valerie Louise, DPhil; FRHistS; President, New Hall, Cambridge, 1981–95; *b* 31 Dec. 1926; *d* of late Cyril Raymond Bence, sometime MP and Florence Bence; *m* 1949, Morris Leonard Pearl (*d* 2000); one *d*. *Educ:* King Edward VI High Sch., Birmingham; St Anne's Coll., Oxford (Exhibnr; Hon. Fellow, 1994); BA Hons Mod. History; MA, DPhil (Oxon). Allen Research Studentship, St Hugh's Coll., Oxford, 1951; Eileen Power Studentship, 1952; Sen. Research Studentship, Westfield Coll., London, 1962; Leverhulme Research Award, 1962; Graham Res. Fellow and Lectr in History, Somerville Coll., Oxford, 1965; Reader in History of London, 1968–76, Prof. of History of London, 1976–81, University College London. Convenor of confs to found The London Journal, Chm. of Editorial Bd, Editor-in-Chief, 1973–77; McBride Vis. Prof., Cities Program, Bryn Mawr Coll., Pennsylvania, 1974; Lectures: Woodward, Yale Univ., New Haven, 1974; Indian Council for Soc. Sci., Calcutta, New Delhi, 1977; John Stow Commem., City of London, 1979; James Ford Special, Oxford, 1980; Sir Lionel Denny, Barber Surgeons' Co., 1981. Literary Dir, Royal Historical Soc., 1975–77; Pres., London and Middx Archaeol. Soc., 1980–82; Governor, Museum of London, 1978; Comr, Royal Commn on Historical MSS, 1983; Syndic: Cambridge Univ. Library, 1982; Cambridge Univ. Press, 1984. Trustee, Henry and Procter Fellowships, 1985. FSA 1976. *Publications:* London and the Outbreak of the Puritan Revolution, 1625–43, 1961; Change and Stability in 17th Century London (inaugural lecture, Univ. of London), 1978; (ed jtly) History and Imagination: essays for Hugh Trevor-Roper, 1981; (ed) J. Stow, The Survey of London, 1987; Studies in Social Change in Puritan London, Parts 1, 2 (trans. Japanese, ed S. Sugawara), 1994; contributor to: Studies in London History (ed W. Kellaway, A. Hollaender), 1969; The Interregnum (ed G. Aylmer), 1972; Puritans and Revolutionaries (ed K. Thomas, D. Pennington), 1978; The Tudor and Stuart Town (ed J. Barry), 1990; also to learned jls and other works, including Trans Royal Hist. Soc., Eng. Historical Rev., History of English Speaking Peoples, Past and Present, Archives, Economic Hist. Rev., History, Jl of Eccles. History, Times Literary Supplement, The London Journal, London Rev. of Books, Albion, Listener, BBC, Rev. of English Studies, (jtly) Proc. Mass. Hist. Soc., DNB Missing Persons, Urban History, Encyclopedia Americana. *Recreations:* walking and swimming.

PEARLMAN, Her Honour Valerie Anne, CBE 2008; a Circuit Judge, 1985–2008; Designated Family Circuit Judge, 1991–2008 (a Senior Circuit Judge, 2003–08); *b* 6 Aug. 1936; *d* of late Sidney and Marjorie Pearlman; *m* 1972; one *s* one *d*. *Educ:* Wycombe Abbey Sch. Called to the Bar, Lincoln's Inn, 1958, Bencher, 2002; a Recorder, 1982–85. Member: Parole Bd, 1989–94; Civil and Family Cttee, Judicial Studies Bd, 1992–97; Chm., Home Sec's Adv. Bd on Restricted Patients, 1991–98; Mem., Cttee on Mentally Disordered Offenders, Mental Health Foundn, 1992–95. Mem., Council of Circuit Judges, 1998–2001; Vice-Pres., Inner London Magistrates' Assoc., 1999–. Patron, Children UK (formerly British Juvenile and Family Courts Soc.), 2000–. Member: Council, Marlborough Coll., 1989–97; Governing Body, Godolphin and and Latymer Sch., 1998–2003. Patron, Suzy Lamplugh Trust, 1987–. *Recreations:* gardening, reading.

PEARMAN, Hugh Geoffrey; architecture and design critic, Sunday Times, since 1986; Editor, RIBA Journal, since 2006; *b* 29 May 1955; *s* of late Douglas Pearman and of Tegwyn Pearman (*née* Jones); *m* 2005, Kate Hobson; two *s* two *d*. *Educ:* Skinners' Sch., Tunbridge Wells; St Chad's Coll., Durham Univ. (BA Hons Eng. Lang. and Lit.). Asst Editor, Building Design Magazine, 1978–82; Communications Editor, BDP, 1982–86. Member: Envmtl and Arts Panel, South Bank Employers' Gp, 1990–2000; Architectl Adv. Panel, Arts Council of GB, then of England, 1992–95; Council, RSA, 2004–06 (Chm., Art for Architecture Adv. Panel, 2000–04). Curator, British Council internat. touring exhibn, 12 for 2000: Building for the Millennium, 1998–2000. Vis. teacher in architecture, Univ. of Greenwich, 1999–2000. Founder and Juror, Stirling Prize for Architecture, 1996–98; judge, various architecture competitions. FRSA 1990. Hon. FRBS 1996; Hon. FRIBA 2001. Frequent contributor to television and radio. *Publications:* Excellent Accommodation, 1984; Rick Mather: urban approaches, 1992; The Ark, London, 1993; Contemporary World Architecture, 1998; Equilibrium: the work of Nicholas Grimshaw and Partners, 2000; (introd.) Ten Years, Ten Cities: Terry Farrell and Partners 1991–2001, 2002; (introd.) 30 Bridges, 2002; The Deep, 2002; The Architecture of Eden, 2003; Airports: a century of architecture, 2004; articles in newspapers, magazines and periodicals. *Recreation:* pottering. *Address:* 29 Nelson Road N8 9RX. *T:* (020) 8348 4838; *e-mail:* hughpearman@blueyonder.co.uk.

PEARS, David Francis, FBA 1970; Student of Christ Church, Oxford, 1960–88, now Emeritus; Professor of Philosophy, Oxford University, 1985–88; *b* 8 Aug. 1921; *s* of late Robert and Gladys Pears; *m* 1963, Anne Drew; one *s* one *d*. *Educ:* Westminster Sch.; Balliol Coll., Oxford. Research Lecturer, Christ Church, 1948–50; Univ. Lectr, Oxford, 1950–72, Reader, 1972–85; Fellow and Tutor, Corpus Christi Coll., 1950–60. Visiting Professor: Harvard, 1959; Univ. of Calif, Berkeley, 1964; Rockefeller Univ., 1967; UCLA, 1979; Hill Prof., Univ. of Minnesota, 1970; Humanities Council Res. Fellow, Princeton, 1966. Mem., l'Institut Internat. de Philosophie, 1978– (Prés., 1988–90); For. Corresp. Fellow, Amer. Acad. of Arts and Scis, 1998. *Publications:* (trans. with B. McGuinness), Wittgenstein, Tractatus Logico-Philosophicus, 1961, repr. 1975; Bertrand Russell and the British Tradition in Philosophy, 1967, 2nd edn 1972; Ludwig Wittgenstein, 1971; What is Knowledge?, 1971; (ed) Russell's Logical Atomism, 1973; Some Questions in the Philosophy of Mind, 1975; Motivated Irrationality, 1984; The False Prison: a study of the development of Wittgenstein's philosophy, vol. I, 1987, vol. II, 1988; Hume's System, 1990; Paradox and Platitude in Wittgenstein's Philosophy, 2006. *Address:* 7 Sandford Road, Littlemore, Oxford OX4 4PU. *T:* (01865) 778768.

PEARS, Dr Iain George; author; *b* 8 Aug. 1955; *s* of George Derrick Pears and Betty Mitchell Pears (*née* Proudfoot); *m* 1985, Ruth Harris; two *s*. *Educ:* Wadham Coll., Oxford (BA, MA); Wolfson Coll., Oxford (DPhil). Correspondent for Reuters: Italy, 1983–84; London, 1984–87; USA, 1987–89; France, 1989–90. *Publications:* The Discovery of Painting, 1988; The Raphael Affair, 1990; The Titian Committee, 1991; The Bernini Bust, 1992; The Last Judgement, 1993; Giotto's Hand, 1994; Death and Restoration, 1995; The Instance of the Fingerpost, 1997; The Immaculate Deception, 1999; The Dream of Scipio, 2002; The Portrait, 2005. *Recreation:* print collecting. *Address:* 52 St John Street, Oxford OX1 2LQ. *T:* (01865) 513009; *e-mail:* iainpears@hotmail.com.

PEARS, Mary Madeline; *see* Chapman, M. M.

PEARS, Tim(othy); novelist; *b* 15 Nov. 1956; *s* of William Steuart Pears and Jill (*née* Scurfield); *m* 1998, Hania Porucznik; one *s* one *d*. *Educ:* Exeter Sch.; National Film and Television Sch. (Directing course 1993). Various jobs, including building labourer, farm worker, night porter, teacher, museum gall. manager, etc. *Publications:* In the Place of Fallen Leaves, 1993 (Ruth Hadden Meml Award, 1993; Hawthornden Prize, 1994); In a Land of Plenty, 1997 (televised, 2001); A Revolution of the Sun, 2000; Wake Up, 2002; Blenheim Orchard, 2007. *Recreations:* football coaching, urban exploring, rural wandering. *Address:* 462 Banbury Road, Oxford OX2 7RG. *T:* (01865) 552605; *e-mail:* pearznik@yahoo.co.uk.

PEARS, Trevor Steven; Executive Chairman, Pears Foundation, since 2000; Director, William Pears Group, since 1986; *b* London, 18 June 1964; *s* of Clive and Clarice Pears; *m* 1993, Daniela; one *s* two *d*. *Educ:* City of London Sch.; City of London Poly. (BA Hons Business Law). *Recreations:* golf, swimming, salsa dancing.

PEARSE, Barbara Mary Frances, (Mrs M. S. Bretscher), PhD; FRS 1988; Staff Scientist, Medical Research Council Laboratory of Molecular Biology, Cambridge, 1981–2005; *b* 24 March 1948; *d* of Reginald William Blake Pearse and Enid Alice (*née* Mitchell); *m* 1978, Mark Steven Bretscher, *qv*; one *s* one *d*. *Educ:* The Lady Eleanor Holles Sch., Hampton, Middx; University Coll. London (BSc Biochemistry, PhD; Fellow, 1996). MRC Res. Fellowship, 1972–74; Beit Meml Fellowship, 1974–77; SRC Advanced

Fellowship, 1977–82; CRC Internat. Fellowship Vis. Prof., Stanford Med. Centre, USA, 1984–85. Mem., EMBO, 1982–. EMBO Medal, 1987. *Publications:* contribs to sci. jls. *Recreations:* wild flowers, planting trees, fresh landscapes. *Address:* Ram Cottage, 63 Commercial End, Swaffham Bulbeck, Cambridge CB5 0ND. *T:* (01223) 811276.

PEARSE, Sir Brian (Gerald), Kt 1994; FCIB; Deputy Chairman, Britannic Assurance Plc, 1997–2002; Chief Executive, Midland Bank, 1991–94; *b* 23 Aug. 1933; *s* of Francis and Eileen Pearse; *m* 1959, Patricia M. Callaghan; one *s* two *d*. *Educ:* St Edward's Coll., Liverpool. Martin's Bank Ltd, 1950; Barclays Bank, 1969–91: Local Dir, Birmingham, 1972; Gen. Man., 1977; Chief Exec. Officer, N America, 1983; Finance Dir, 1987–91; Dir, Midland Bank, 1994–95. Chm., Lucas Industries, later LucasVarity, PLC, 1994–98; non-executive Director: Smith & Nephew, 1993–2002; HSBC plc, 1992–94. Chm., Assoc. for Payments Clearing Services, 1987–91. Director: British American Chamber of Commerce, 1987–98; Private Finance Panel, 1993–95; BOTB, 1994–97; Charities Aid Foundn Bank, 1998–92. Chairman: Young Enterprise, 1992–95; British Invisibles, 1994–97; Housing Corp., 1994–97; Dep. Chm., Tor Homes, 1998–2003. Chm. Council, Centre for Study of Financial Innovation, 1998–. Member: Council for Industry of Higher Educn, 1994–98; City Promotion Panel, 1995–97; Bd of Banking Supervision, 1998–2001. Treas., KCL, 1992–99 (FKC 1996). Pres., CIB, 1993–94. Trustee, Charities Aid Foundn, 1995–99. Gov., Univ. of Plymouth, 1997–2006 (Chm. Govs, 2002–06). Chm., Finance Cttee, 2006–, Trustee, 2007–, Dio. of Plymouth. *Recreations:* Rugby football, opera. *Address:* Flat 7, 14 Gloucester Street, SW1V 2DN. *Club:* Royal Automobile.

PEARSE, Rear-Adm. John Roger Southey G.; *see* Gerard-Pearse.

PEARSON, family name of **Viscount Cowdray** and **Baron Pearson of Rannoch**.

PEARSON OF RANNOCH, Baron *cr* 1990 (Life Peer), of Bridge of Gaur in the district of Perth and Kinross; **Malcolm Everard MacLaren Pearson;** Chairman, PWS Holdings plc; *b* 20 July 1942; *s* of Col John MacLaren Pearson; *m* 1st, 1965, Francesca Frua De Angeli (marr. diss. 1970); one *d*; 2nd, 1977, Hon. Mary (marr. diss. 1995), *d* of Baron Charteris of Amisfield, GCB, GCVO, QSO, OBE, PC; two *d*; 3rd, 1998, Caroline, *d* of Major Hugh Launcelot St Vincent Rose. *Educ:* Eton. Founded Pearson Webb Springbett, now PWS group of reinsurance brokers, 1964, Chm., 1970–. Member: H of L Select Cttee on Eur. Communities, 1992–96; Sub-cttee C on Envmt and Social Affairs, 1992–95. Founded Rannoch Trust, 1984 (Exec. Trustee). Mem., CNAA, 1983–93 (Hon. Treas., 1986–93). Patron: Nat. Soc. for Mentally Handicapped People in Residential Care (Rescare), 1994–; British Register of Chinese Herbal Medicine, 1998–. *Recreations:* stalking, fishing, golf. *Address:* House of Lords, SW1A 0AA. *Clubs:* White's; Swinley Forest Golf.

PEARSON, Prof. Andrew David John, MD; FRCP, FRCPCH; Cancer Research UK Professor of Paediatric Oncology and Head, Paediatric Section, Institute of Cancer Research, University of London, since 2005; Head, Children's Unit, and Hon. Consultant Paediatric Oncologist, Royal Marsden Hospital Foundation NHS Trust, since 2005; *b* 2 March 1955; *s* of John and Jean Pearson; *m*; two *s* three *d*; *m* 2006, Gaby Charlton; one *d*. *Educ:* Univ. of Newcastle upon Tyne (MB BS 1st Cl. Hons 1977); DCH 1980; MD 1989. MRCP 1979, FRCP 1992; FRCPCH 1996. MRC Lilly Internat. Travelling Fellow, Dept. of Paediatrics, Univ. of Minnesota, 1983–84; Sen. Registrar in Paediatric Oncology, 1984, Hon. Sen. Registrar, 1985–89, Royal Victoria Inf., Newcastle upon Tyne; Hon. Consultant Paediatrician, Newcastle HA, 1989–94; Hd, Dept of Paediatric Oncology, Children's Services Directorate, 1992–2005, and Hon. Consultant Paediatric Oncologist, 1994–2005, Newcastle upon Tyne Hosps NHS Trust; University of Newcastle upon Tyne: Lectr, 1985–89, Sen. Lectr, 1989–94, in Paediatric Oncology, Dept of Child Health; Prof. of Paediatric Oncology, Sch. of Clinical Med. Scis, 1994–2005; Postgrad. Sub-Dean, 1998–2002, Dean of Postgrad. Studies, 2002–05, Fac. of Med. Scis. Trustees, Inst. of Cancer Res., 2005–. United Kingdom Cancer Study Group: Chm., Neuroblastoma Wkg Gp, 1991–95; Chm., Biol Studies Cttee, 1996–2002; Hd, Div. of Therapeutics, 1999–; Co-Chm., UKCCSG/Childhood Leukaemia Wkg Party Clin. Res. Governance Gp, 2003–06; Chm., 2003–06. Chairman: Europ. Neuroblastoma Study Gp, 1994–99; Europe Neuroblastoma (SIOPEN), Internat. Soc. of Paediatric Oncology, 1998–2001 (Founding Chm.), 2005–07; Co Chm., Internat. Neuroblastoma Risk Gp Strategy Cttee, 2004–. *Publications:* over 260 articles on children's cancer res., particularly neuroblastoma, drug develt and pharmacol. *Recreation:* walking. *Address:* Institute of Cancer Research, 15 Cotswold Road, Sutton, Surrey SM2 5NG. *T:* (020) 8661 3453, *Fax:* (020) 8661 3617; *e-mail:* andrew.pearson@icr.ac.uk.

PEARSON, Anthony James, CBE 2002; Director of Security, Prison Service, 1993–99; *b* 2 Nov. 1939; 2nd *s* of Leslie Pearson and Winifred Pearson (*née* Busby); *m* 1964, Sandra Lowe; two *d*. *Educ:* Saltley Grammar Sch., Birmingham; Exeter Univ. (BA Hons 1961); Oxford Univ. (Dip. Soc. and Public Admin 1962). Assistant Prison Governor: Maidstone, 1963–67; Albany, 1967–69; Parkhurst, 1970–72; Dep. Governor, Wandsworth Prison, 1972–73; Prison Service HQ, 1973–77; Prison Governor: Gartree, 1977–81; Brixton, 1981–85; HM Dep. Chief Inspector of Prisons, 1985–87; Prison Service Headquarters: Hd of Div., 1987–89; Hd, Directorate of Telecommunications, 1989–91; Area Manager, 1991–93. Trustee: Centre for Crime & Justice Studies, 1998– (Chm., 2002–); Butler Trust, 1999– (Dep. Chm., 2001–); Langley House Trust, 2001–. *Recreations:* Rugby, cricket (armchair expert).

PEARSON, Rev. Canon Brian William; Partner, Woodspring Psychological Services, since 2006; *b* 18 Aug. 1949; *s* of Victor William Charles Pearson and Florence Irene (*née* Webster); *m* 1974, Althea Mary Stride; two *s*. *Educ:* Roan Sch. for Boys, Blackheath; Brighton Polytechnic (BSc Hons); City Univ. (MSc); Ordination Training (Southwark Ordination Course); MTh Oxford 1994. Systems Engineer: IBM UK, 1967–71; Rohm and Haas UK, 1971–72; Lectr, Thames Polytechnic, 1972–81; College Head of Dept, Northbrook Coll., W Sussex, 1981–88; Bishop's Research Officer and Communications Officer, Bath and Wells, 1988–91; Archbishop's Officer for Mission and Evangelism and Tait Missioner, dio. of Canterbury, 1991–97; Hon. Canon, Canterbury Cathedral, 1992; Gen. Dir, CPAS, 1997–2000; Dir of Studies for Ordained Local Ministry, and Priest i/c, Leek Wootton, diocese of Coventry, 2000–06. Ministerial Trng Advr, Bath and Wells Dio., 2007–; Lectr (pt-time), Strode Coll., 2006–. Trustee, Christians in Sport, 1996–2001. Non-executive Director: Trinity Coll., Bristol, 1997–2000; Christian Research, 2000–03; 2K Plus Internat. Sports Media, 2004–. Regl Rep., Over The Wall Orgn, 2002–06. Hon. Chaplain: Warwicks Police HQ, 2000–06; Centrex Police Trng Centre, Ryton, 2002–06; Avon and Somerset Police, 2007–. Fellow, Coll. of Preachers, 1995. *Publications:* Yes Manager: Management in the local church, 1986; (with George Carey) My Journey, Your Journey, 1996; How to Guide: managing change, 1996; (contrib.) A Preacher's Companion, 2004. *Recreations:* cricket, theatre, cinema, music, learning more about life through the experiences of two energetic and creative sons, travel, enjoying the humour God has placed in His world. *Address:* London House, New Street, Somerton, Som TA11 7NU.

PEARSON, David Compton Froome; Deputy Chairman, Robert Fleming Holdings Ltd, 1986–90 (Director, 1974–90); *b* 28 July 1931; *s* of late Compton Edwin Pearson, OBE and of Marjorie (*née* Froome); *m* 1st, 1966, Venetia Jane Lynn (marr. diss. 1994); two *d*; 2nd, 1997, Mrs Bridget Thomson. *Educ:* Haileybury; Downing Coll., Cambridge (MA). Linklaters & Paines, Solicitors, 1957–69 (Partner, 1961–69); Dir, Robert Fleming & Co. Ltd, 1969–90; Chairman: The Fleming Property Unit Trust, 1971–90; Gill & Duffus Group Plc, 1982–85 (Dir, 1973–85); Robert Fleming Securities, 1985–90; River & Mercantile Investment Management Ltd, 1994–96; Dep. Chm., Austin Reed Group Plc, 1977–96 (Dir, 1971–96); Director: Blue Circle Industries Plc, 1972–87; Lane Fox and Partners Ltd, 1987–91; Fleming Income & Growth Investment Trust plc (formerly River & Mercantile Trust Plc), 1994–2001; Chesterton International Plc, 1994–98. Mem., Finance Act 1960 Tribunal, 1978–84. Mem., Wessex Regl Cttee, NT, 1995–2004. *Recreations:* gardening, walking. *Address:* The Manor, Berwick St John, Shaftesbury, Dorset SP7 0EX. *T:* (01747) 828363. *Clubs:* Brooks's, Army and Navy.

PEARSON, David Robert Stanley, FSA; FCLIP; Director, Research Library Services, University of London, since 2004; *b* 7 May 1955; *s* of Robert Edward Orlando Pearson and Gladys Pearson (*née* Goldsworthy); *m* 1987, Lynne Wallace; one *s*. *Educ:* St Bees Sch., Cumbria; Sidney Sussex Coll., Cambridge (BA 1977); Loughborough Univ. (DipLib). FCLIP 2001; FSA 2005. Curator, Eighteenth-century Short Title Catalogue, BL, 1986–92; Hd, Collection Develt, Nat. Art Liby, 1992–96; Librarian, Wellcome Trust, 1996–2004. Vice-Pres., Bibliographical Soc., 1995– (Hon. Sec., 1994–2002). *Publications:* Provenance Research in Book History, 1994; Oxford Bookbinding 1500–1640, 2000; (ed) For the Love of the Binding: studies in bookbinding history, 2000; English Bookbinding Styles 1450–1800, 2005; Books as History, 2008. *Recreations:* bibliography, walking by the sea. *Address:* The Old Vicarage, 10 Copperfields, Royston, Herts SG8 5BH. *T:* (01763) 241379; *e-mail:* drspearson@dsl.pipex.com.

PEARSON, Derek Leslie, CB 1978; Deputy Secretary, Overseas Development Administration (formerly Ministry of Overseas Development), 1977–81; *b* 19 Dec. 1921; *s* of late George Frederick Pearson and Edith Maud Pearson (*née* Dent); *m* 1956, Diana Mary (*d* 2005), *d* of late Sir Ralph Freeman; no *c*. *Educ:* William Ellis Sch.; London Sch. of Economics (BSc (Econ)). Served War of 1939–45; Lieut (A) (O) RNVR and subseq. Channel Air Div.; Lt-Comdr (A) RNVR, 1956. Colonial Office, 1947; seconded to Kenya, 1954–56; Principal Private Sec. to Sec. of State for Colonies, 1959–61; Dept of Technical Cooperation, 1961; Asst Sec., 1962; ODM, 1964; Under Secretary: CSD, 1970–72; Min. of Overseas Develt, 1972–75; Dep. Sec., Cabinet Office, 1975–77. *Address:* Langata, Little London Road, Horam, Heathfield, East Sussex TN21 0BG. *Clubs:* Naval, Civil Service.

PEARSON, (Edward) John (David); Hon. Director General, European Commission, since 2001; *b* 1 March 1938; *s* of Sydney Pearson and Hilda Beaumont; *m* 1963, Hilary Stuttard; three *s* two *d*. *Educ:* Huddersfield Coll.; Emmanuel Coll., Cambridge (MA). Admin. Trainee, London Transport Exec., 1959; Asst Principal, MoT, 1960, Principal 1965; Sen. Principal, DoE, 1971; European Commission: Head of Div., Transport Directorate-Gen., 1973–81; Dir, Fisheries Directorate-Gen., 1981–91; Dir, Regl Policy and Cohesion Directorate-Gen., 1991–98; Dep. Financial Controller, EC, 1999–2001 (Acting Financial Controller, July–Aug. 2000). *Recreations:* orienteering (Pres., Belgian Orienteering Assoc., 1982–87; Chm., Develt and Promotion Cttee, 1986–88, Mem. Council, 1988–94, Internat. Orienteering Fedn), hill-walking (Pyrenees High Level Route from Atlantic to Mediterranean in 43 days, 2006), writing (magazine articles published on ornithology, the Hungarian language, mountaineering, Arthur Ransome). *Address:* Mas d'en Clarimon, Route de Paloll à la Selva, 66400 Céret, France. *T:* (4) 68833458; *e-mail:* hilaryandjohnpearson@hotmail.com.

PEARSON, Sir (Francis) Nicholas (Fraser), 2nd Bt *cr* 1964, of Gressingham, Co. Palatine of Lancaster; *b* 28 Aug. 1943; *s* of Sir Francis Fenwick Pearson, 1st Bt, MBE and of Katharine Mary, *d* of Rev. D. Denholm Fraser; *S* father, 1991; *m* 1978, Henrietta Elizabeth, *d* of Comdr Henry Pasley-Tyler. *Educ:* Radley Coll. Commnd The Rifle Brigade, 1961; ADC to: Army Comdr, Far East, 1967; C-in-C, Far East, 1968. Dir, Hill & Delamain Ltd, 1970–75; Dep. Chm., Claughton Manor Brickworks, 1978; Chm., Turner Gp Ltd, 1979; Director: Intercontinental Hotel Group Ltd, 1989–92; Virgin Atlantic Airlines, 1989–92; Saison Hldgs BV, 1990–93. Trustee: Ruskin Foundn; Temenos Foundn. Prospective Parly Cand. (C), Oldham West, 1976–79. *Recreations:* shooting, fishing. *Heir:* none. *Address:* c/o National Westminster Bank, 55 Main Street, Kirkby Lonsdale, Cumbria. *Club:* Carlton.

PEARSON, Rt Rev. Geoffrey Seagrave; *see* Lancaster, Bishop Suffragan of.

PEARSON, Dr Graham Scott, CB 1990; CChem, FRSC; Hon. Visiting Professor of International Security, Department of Peace Studies, University of Bradford, since 1996; Assistant Chief Scientific Adviser (Non-Proliferation), Ministry of Defence, 1995–96; *b* 20 July 1935; *s* of Ernest Reginald Pearson and Alice (*née* Maclachlan); *m* 1960, Susan Elizabeth Meriton Benn; two *s*. *Educ:* Woodhouse Grove Sch., Bradford; St Salvator's Coll., Univ. of St Andrews (BSc 1st Cl. Hons Chemistry, 1957; PhD 1960). Postdoctoral Fellow, Univ. of Rochester, NY, USA, 1960–62; joined Scientific Civil Service, 1962; Rocket Propulsion Estab., 1962–69; Def. Res. and Develt Staff, Washington, DC, 1969–72; PSO to Dir Gen. Res. Weapons, 1972–73; Asst Dir, Naval Ordnance Services/ Scientific, 1973–76; Technical Adviser/Explosives, Materials and Safety (Polaris), 1976–79; Principal Supt, Propellants Explosives and Rocket Motor Estab., Westcott, 1979–80; Dep. Dir 1, 1980–82 and Dep. Dir 2, 1982–83, RARDE, Fort Halstead; Dir Gen., ROF (Res. and Develt), 1983–84; Dir, Chemical Defence Estabt, later Dir Gen., Chemical and Biol Defence Estabt, Porton Down, 1984–95. Fellow, IUPAC, 2004. *Publications:* (ed jtly) Strengthening the Biological Weapons Convention, 1996; The UNSCOM Saga: chemical and biological weapons non-proliferation, 1999; (ed jtly) Key Points for the Fifth Review Conference, 2001; (ed jtly) Scientific and Technical Means of Distinguishing Between Natural and Other Outbreaks of Disease, 2001; (ed jtly) Maximizing the Security and Development Benefits from the Biological and Toxin Weapons Convention, 2002; (ed jtly) The Implementation of Legally Binding Measures to Strengthen the Biological and Toxin Weapons Convention, 2004; The Search for Iraq's Weapons of Mass Destruction: inspection, verification and non-proliferation, 2005; (ed jtly) Key Points for the Sixth Review Conference, 2006; Hidcote: the garden and Lawrence Johnston, 2007; contributor to: Advances in Photochemistry, vol. 3, 1964; Advances in Inorganic and Radio Chemistry, vol. 8, 1966; Oxidation and Combustion Reviews, vol. 3, 1968 and vol. 4, 1969; Biological Weapons: Weapons of the Future?, 1993; Non-Conventional Weapons Proliferation in the Middle East, 1993; Verification after the Cold War, 1994; Weapons Proliferation in the 1990s, 1995; Verification 1997, 1997; Biological Weapons: limiting the threat, 1999; Biological Warfare: modern offense and defense, 2000; Deadly Cultures: biological weapons since 1945, 2006; Terrorism, War or Disease? Unraveling the Use of Biological Weapons, 2008; articles on combustion, and on chemical and biological defence and arms control, in scientific jls, and on Hidcote and Lawrence Johnston in horticultural jls; official reports. *Recreations:* walking, photography, reading, archival research, gardening. *Address:* Department of Peace Studies, University of Bradford, Bradford, W Yorks BD7 1DP. *T:* (01274) 234188.

PEARSON, Ian Howard; His Honour Judge Pearson; a Circuit Judge, since 2004; *b* 30 May 1949; *s* of Harry Seabourn and Elsie Margaret Pearson; *m* 1971, Sian Williams; two *d. Educ:* Farnham Grammar Sch.; Univ. of Leicester (LLB Hons); Coll. of Law, Guildford. Admitted as solicitor, 1973; Partner, Tanner & Taylor, Solicitors, Hants and Surrey, 1975–94; a Judge Advocate (pt time), 1992; Dep. Judge Advocate, 1994–95; Asst JAG, 1995–2004; Vice JAG, 2004; Asst Recorder, 1999–2000; a Recorder, 2000–04. Mem. (Lab), Rushmoor BC, 1986–94. Contested (Lab) Aldershot, 1987. *Recreations:* travel, literature, visual arts, food and wine, sport, avoiding watching opera. *Address:* Portsmouth Crown Court, Winston Churchill Way, Portsmouth, Hants PO1 2EB. *T:* (023) 9289 3000.

PEARSON, Ian Phares, PhD; MP (Lab) Dudley South, since 1997 (Dudley West, Dec. 1994–1997); Economic Secretary to HM Treasury and Department for Business, Enterprise and Regulatory Reform, since 2008; *b* 5 April 1959; *m* 1988, Annette Pearson; one *s* two *d. Educ:* Brierley Hill GS; Balliol Coll., Oxford (BA Hons PPE); Warwick Univ. (MA, PhD). Mem. (Lab) Dudley MBC, 1984–87. Local Govt Policy Res. Officer, Lab. Party, 1985–87; Dep. Dir, Urban Trust, 1987–88; business and economic develt consultant, 1988–91; Jt Chief Exec., W Midlands Enterprise Bd, 1991–94. An Asst Govt Whip, 2001–02; a Lord Comr of HM Treasury (Govt Whip), 2002–03; Parly Under-Sec. of State, NI Office, 2002–05; Minister of State (Minister for Trade), FCO and DTI, 2005–06; Minister of State, DEFRA, 2006–07; Minister of State (Minister for Sci. and Innovation), DIUS, 2007–08. *Address:* House of Commons, SW1A 0AA.

PEARSON, John; *see* Pearson, E. J. D.

PEARSON, Prof. John Richard Anthony, PhD, ScD; FRS 2005; Scientific Consultant, Schlumberger Cambridge Research, since 1996 (Scientific Adviser, 1982–95); Chairman, Pearson Publishing Group, since 1993; *b* Cairo, 18 Sept. 1930; *s* of Charles Robert Pearson and Olive Pearson (*née* Nock); *m* 1954, Emma Margaret Anderson; three *s* one *d. Educ:* English Sch., Cairo; Bedford Modern Sch.; Trinity Coll., Cambridge (BA 1953; PhD 1958; ScD 1975); Harvard Univ. (AM 1954). CEng 1970; FIMMM; MIChemE 1970. Nat. Service, 2nd Lieut, Royal Signals, 1948–50; Tech. Officer, ICI Ltd, 1957–59; Res. Scientist, Metal Box Co., 1959–60; Asst Dir Res., Dept of Chemical Engrg, Univ. of Cambridge, 1960–73; Dir of Studies in Maths and Fellow, Trinity Hall, Cambridge, 1961–73; Prof. of Chemical Engrg, Imperial Coll., London Univ., 1973–82. Visiting Professor: Princeton Univ., 1967; Univ. of Wisconsin, 1967; Rice Univ., 1969; MIT, 1973–76; Univ. of Sydney, 1982; Univ. of Louvain, 1994–95; D. A. Katz Lectr, Univ. of Michigan, 1975; Fairchild Schol., CIT, 1978–79, 1981; MTS Prof., Univ. of Minnesota, 2004. Hon. Professorial Fellow: Univ. of Wales, 1984–; Univ. of Birmingham, 1995–. Member and Chairman: UNIDO Tech. Assistance Cttee, Planta Piloto de Ingenieria Quimica, Argentina, 1973–79; Yucca Mountain Peer Rev. Cttee, US Dept of Energy, 2002–03; Mem., Internat. Geometrical Cttee, Govt of France, 1996–99. Pres., British Soc. of Rheology, 1980–82 (Gold Medal, 1986). Foreign Assoc., NAE, 1980. Hon. DSc Minnesota, 2002. *Publications:* Mechanical Principles of Polymer Melt Processing, 1966; Polymer Melt Processing, 1985; papers on engrg sci. in scientific jls. *Recreations:* Real tennis and other ball games (now mostly passive), travel, opera, wine. *Address:* Pearson Publishing Group, Chesterton Mill, French's Road, Cambridge CB4 3NP; *e-mail:* jrap@pearson.co.uk. *Clubs:* MCC; Cambridge University Real Tennis.

PEARSON, Captain John William, CBE 1981; Regional Administrator, Mersey Regional Health Authority, 1977–81; *b* 19 Sept. 1920; *s* of Walter and Margaret Jane Pearson; *m* 1945, Audrey Ethel Whitehead; two *s. Educ:* Holloway Sch. FCIS, FHA, FCCA, IPFA. Served War, RA (Field), 1939–46. Hospital Service, LCC, 1947–48; NW Metropolitan Regional Hosp. Bd, 1948–49; Northern Gp, HMC, Finance Officer, 1949–62; Treasurer: St Thomas' Bd of Governors, 1962–73; Mersey Regional Health Authority, 1973–77. Pres., Assoc. of Health Service Treasurers, 1970–71. *Recreations:* tennis, golf, gardening, snooker. *Address:* 20 Weare Gifford, Shoeburyness, Essex SS3 8AB. *T:* (01702) 585039.

PEARSON, Keith Philip, MA; FRSE; Headmaster, George Heriot's School, Edinburgh, 1983–97; *b* 5 Aug. 1941; *s* of Fred G. and Phyllis Pearson; *m* 1965, Dorothy (*née* Atkinson); two *d. Educ:* Madrid Univ. (Dip. de Estudios Hispanicos); Univ. of Cambridge (MA; Cert. of Educn). FRSE 1995. Teacher, Rossall Sch., 1964–72 (Head of Mod. Langs, 1968–72); George Watson's College: Head of Mod. Langs, 1972–79; Dep. Principal, 1979–83. *Recreations:* sport, mountains, music, DIY.

PEARSON, Very Rev. Kevin; Dean of the Diocese of Edinburgh, since 2004; Rector, St Michael and All Saints, Edinburgh, since 1995; Provincial Director of Ordinands, Scottish Episcopal Church, since 1991; *b* 27 Aug. 1954; s of Edward and Nancy Pearson; *m* 1992, Dr Elspeth Atkinson. *Educ:* Leeds Univ. (BA 1975); Edinburgh Univ. (BD 1979); Edinburgh Theol Coll. Ordained deacon, 1979, priest, 1980; Curate, St Mary, Horden, 1979–81; Chaplain, Leeds Univ., 1981–87; Rector, St Salvador, Edinburgh, 1987–93; Chaplain, Napier Poly., subseq. Napier Univ., 1988–94; Diocesan Dir of Ordinands, Dio. Edinburgh, 1990–95; Associate Rector, Old St Paul, Edinburgh, 1993–94; Priest-in-charge, Linlithgow, 1994–95. Hon. Canon, St Mary's Cathedral, Edinburgh, 2003–04. *Recreations:* Italy, the Victorian novel, food and drink. *Address:* The Rectory, 203 Gilmore Place, Edinburgh EH3 9PN; *e-mail:* PDO@scotland.anglican.org.

PEARSON, Prof. Margaret Anne, PhD; Deputy Vice-Chancellor, Keele University, 2004–07; *b* 13 Oct. 1952; *d* of late Charles Yorke and of Betty Yorke; one *s* one *d. Educ:* Newnham Coll., Cambridge (BA Hons Geog. 1975; MA 1977); RGN 1978; Liverpool Univ. (PhD Geog. 1985). Student Nurse, 1975–78, Staff Nurse, 1978–79, Sheffield AHA; Res. Officer, then Dir, Centre for Ethnic Minorities Health, Bradford Univ., 1982–84; Lectr in Health Policy, Nuffield Inst. for Health Services Studies, Leeds Univ., 1983–85; University of Liverpool: Lectr, then Sen. Lectr, in Med. Sociology, 1985–93; Prof. of Health and Community Care, 1993–96; Regl Dir of R&D, DoH/NHS Exec. NW, 1996–2001; Dep. Dir, NHS Human Resources, DoH, 2001–04. Member: UK Commn on Human Medicines, 2005–; Bd, UK Sector Skills Develt Agency, 2006–. Chm., Main Panel C (Nursing and Midwifery, Dentistry, Pharmacy and Allied Health Professions and Subjects), 2008 RAE. Hon. MFPH 1995. *Recreations:* family, music (flute player), reading, textile art.

PEARSON, Michael; *see* Pearson, T. M.

PEARSON, Prof. Michael George, FRCP; Professor of Clinical Evaluation, University of Liverpool, since 2007 (Professor of Medicine, 2003–07); Consultant Physician, University Hospital, Aintree, Liverpool, since 1984; *b* 11 Jan. 1950; *s* of Dr C. Andrew Pearson, OBE and Jean M. Pearson; *m* 1973, Diane Kay Park; three *d. Educ:* Culford Sch., Bury St Edmunds; Gonville and Caius Coll., Cambridge (MA; MB BChir 1975); Liverpool Univ. Med. Sch. FRCP 1991. Royal College of Physicians: Associate Dir, 1997–98, Dir, 1998–2006, Clinical Effectiveness and Evaluation Unit; Dir, Clinical Standards, 2005–07. Trustee Dir, Respiratory Educn Training (formerly Resource) Centres, 1998–; Dir, Nat. Collaborating Centre for Chronic Conditions, 2000–04. Hon. Prof., Dept of Biol Scis, Salford Univ., 1991–. Non-exec. Dir, Health and Social Care Inf. Centre, 2005–. Mem. Exec., British Thoracic Soc., 1995–99. *Publications:* Questions in Respiratory Medicine, 1994; Controversies in Chronic Obstructive Pulmonary Diseases, 2003; contrib. numerous papers to scientific jls. *Recreations:* gardening, music. *Address:* 12 Willow Hey, Maghull, Liverpool L31 3DL; *e-mail:* michael.pearson@liverpool.ac.uk.

PEARSON, Sir Nicholas; *see* Pearson, Sir F. N. F.

PEARSON, Maj.-Gen. Ronald Matthew, CB 1985; MBE 1959; Director Army Dental Service, 1982–85, retired; *b* 25 Feb. 1925; *s* of Dr John Pearson and Sheila Pearson (*née* Brown); *m* 1956, Florence Eileen Jack; two *d. Educ:* Clifton Hall Sch., Ratho, Midlothian; Glasgow Acad.; Glasgow Univ./Glasgow Dental Hosp. LDS RFPS(Glas) 1948; FBIM 1979. Civilian Dental Practice, 1948–49. Commnd RADC, 1949; served: RWAFF, 1950–53; UK, 1953–57; BAOR, 1957–60; UK, 1961–67; CO No 1 Dental Gp, BAOR, 1967–70; CO Army Dental Centres, Cyprus, 1970–73; CO No 8 Dental Gp, UK, 1973–75; CO No 4 Dental Gp, UK, 1975–76; Dep. Dir Dental Service, UKLF, 1976–78; Dep. Dir Dental Service, BAOR, 1978–82. QHDS, 1978–85. CStJ 1983. *Recreations:* trout fishing, photography, gardening, caravanning. *Address:* 27 Glenearn Court, Pittenze Street, Crieff, Perthshire PH7 3LE.

PEARSON, Siobhan Mary; *see* Kenny, S. M.

PEARSON, Sybil Angela Margaret, (Mrs Michael Pearson); *see* Jones, S. A. M.

PEARSON, Gen. Sir Thomas (Cecil Hook), KCB 1967 (CB 1964); CBE 1959 (OBE 1953); DSO 1940, and Bar, 1943; DL; retired 1974; *b* 1 July 1914; *s* of late Vice-Admiral J. L. Pearson, CMG; *m* 1947, Aud, *d* of late Alf Skjelkvale, Oslo; two *s. Educ:* Charterhouse; Sandhurst. 2nd Lieutenant Rifle Bde, 1934. Served War of 1939–45, M East and Europe; CO 2nd Bn The Rifle Bde, 1942; Dep. Comdr 2nd Independent Parachute Bde Gp 1944; Dep. Comdr 1st Air-landing Bde 1945; GSO1 1st Airborne Div. 1945; CO 1st Bn The Parachute Regt 1946; CO 7th Bn The Parachute Regt 1947; GSO1 (Land Air Warfare), WO, 1948; JSSC, GSO1, HQ Malaya, 1950; GSO1 (Plans), FARELF, 1951; Directing Staff, JSSC, 1953; Comdr 45 Parachute Bde TA 1955; Nat. Defence Coll., Canada, 1956; Comdr 16 Indep. Parachute Bde 1957; Chief of Staff to Dir of Ops Cyprus, 1960; Head of Brit. Mil. Mission to Soviet Zone of Germany, 1960; Major-General Commanding 1st Division, BAOR, 1961–63; Chief of Staff, Northern Army Group, 1963–67; Comdr, FARELF, 1967–68; Military Sec., MoD, 1968–72; C-in-C, Allied Forces, Northern Europe, 1972–74; psc 1942; jssc 1950; ndc Canada 1957. ADC Gen. to the Queen, 1974. Col Comdt, the Royal Green Jackets, 1973–77. Fisheries Mem., Welsh Water Auth., 1980–83. DL Hereford and Worcester, 1983. Haakon VII Liberty Cross, 1948; Medal of Honour, Norwegian Defence Assoc., 1973. *Recreations:* field sports, yachting. *Clubs:* Naval and Military; Kongelig Norsk Seilforenning.

PEARSON, (Thomas) Michael, MBE 2007; Trustee and Member Council, Cruse Bereavement Care, since 1986 (Hon. Officer, since 1987; Chair, 1992–2005); human resources adviser in private and charity/voluntary sectors, since 2001; *b* 23 Dec. 1941; *s* of Harold Hird Pearson and Mary Anderson Pearson (*née* Preston); *m* 1967, Margaret Green; one *s* one *d. Educ:* Lancaster Royal Grammar Sch.; Univ. of Liverpool (BA Hons Soc. Studies 1966); Univ. of Kent (BA Hons Archaeol Studies 2007). Chartered CCIPD (CIPM 1990). Career in personnel mgt/human resources: Glaxo Gp, 1966–85; Smiths Industries Group, 1985–2000: Dir of Personnel, Healthcare Gp, 1987–94, Personnel Dir, then Human Resources Dir, Portex Ltd, 1994–2000. Mem., Employment Tribunals, 1995–. Vice-Pres., IPM, 1990–92. Governor, Chichester Coll., W Sussex, 1992–2004 (Vice-Chm., Governing Body, 1992–2003). *Recreations:* archaeology, visiting historic places and gardens. *Address:* Rose Cottage, Belcaire Close, Lympne, Hythe, Kent CT21 4JR. *T:* and *Fax:* (01303) 269557; *e-mail:* mike.pearson@ukgateway.net.

PEART, Brian; Under-Secretary, Ministry of Agriculture, Fisheries and Food, 1976–85; *b* 17 Aug. 1925; *s* of late Joseph Garfield Peart and Frances Hannah Peart (*née* English); *m* 1952, Dorothy (*née* Thompson); one *s* one *d. Educ:* Wolsingham Grammar Sch.; Durham Univ. (BA). Served War, RAF, 1943–47. Agricultural Economist, Edinburgh Sch. of Agric., 1950–57; Sen. Agricultural Economist, 1957–64; Regional Farm Management Adviser, MAFF, West Midlands Region, 1964–67; Chief Farm Management Adviser, MAFF, 1967–71; Regional Manager, MAFF, Yorks/Lancs Region, 1971–74; Head of Intelligence and Trng Div., 1974–76; Chief Administrator, ADAS, 1976–80; Under Sec., Lands Gp, MAFF, 1980–85. Kellogg Fellow, USA, 1960. *Recreations:* golf, genealogy, bridge, The Times crossword. *Address:* 18 Derwent Close, Claygate, Surrey KT10 0RF. *Club:* Farmers'.

PEART, Icah Delano Everard; QC 2002; a Recorder, since 2000; *b* 19 Jan. 1956; *s* of Everard Leopold Peart and Doreen Mildred Peart; partner, Linda Torpey; two *s* one *d. Educ:* Ashmead Boys' Secondary Sch., Reading; London Sch. of Econs (LLB Hons); Coll. of Law. Called to the Bar, Middle Temple, 1978, Bencher, 2005; in practice specialising in criminal law; Asst Recorder, 1997–2000. *Recreations:* reading, cinema, watching Reading FC (Mem. Supporters' Club), my children. *Address:* Garden Court Chambers, 57–60 Lincoln's Inn Fields, WC2A 3LS. *T:* (020) 7993 7600, *Fax:* (020) 7993 7700; *e-mail:* icahp@gclaw.co.uk.

PEART, Michael John, CMG 1995; LVO 1983; HM Diplomatic Service, retired; *b* 15 Dec. 1943; *s* of Joseph Albert William Peart and Thelma Theresa Peart (*née* Rasmussen); *m* 1968, Helena Mary Stuttle; one *s* (one *d* decd). *Educ:* Gillingham County Grammar Sch., Kent. Prison Dept, Home Office, 1960–65; FCO 1966–69; served Blantyre, 1969–71; Warsaw, 1972–75; Mexico City, 1975–80; FCO, 1980–83; Dhaka, 1983–86; FCO, 1987–91; Ambassador, Lithuania, 1991–94; Ambassador, later High Comr, Fiji, and High Comr, Kiribati, Nauru and Tuvalu, 1995–97. Chm., British-Lithuanian Soc., 2000–. Chm., Tiltas Trust, 2007–. Pres. Elect, Rotary Club of Sherborne Castles. Grand Cross of Commander, Order for Merits (Lithuania), 2006. *Recreations:* music, reading, walking. *Address:* Amberleigh Cottage, 2 Dunstan Street, Sherborne, Dorset DT9 3SE.

PEART, Prof. Sir (William) Stanley, Kt 1985; MD; FRS 1969; Professor of Medicine, University of London, at St Mary's Hospital Medical School, 1956–87, now Emeritus; *b* 31 March 1922; *s* of J. G. and M. Peart; *m* 1947, Peggy Parkes (*d* 2002); one *s* one *d. Educ:* King's College School, Wimbledon; St Mary's Hospital Medical Sch. (MB, BS (Hons) 1945; MD 1949). FRCP 1959. Lecturer in Medicine, St Mary's Hospital, 1950–56. Master, Hunterian Inst., RCS, 1988–92. Wellcome Trust: Trustee, 1975–94; Dep. Chm., 1991–94; Consultant, 1994–98; Beit Trustee, 1986–2003. Goulstonian Lectr, 1959, Croonian Lectr, 1979, RCP. Founder FMedSci 1998. Hon. For. Mem., Académie Royale de Médicine de Belgique, 1984. Hon. FIC 1988; Hon. FRCA 1991; Hon. FRCS 1995; Hon. Fellow, UCL, 1997. Hon. DSc Edinburgh, 1993. Stouffer Prize, Amer. Heart Assoc., 1968; Nuffield Medal, RSM, 1990; Buchanan Medal, Royal Soc., 2000.

Publications: chapters in: Cecil-Loeb, Textbook of Medicine; Renal Disease; Biochemical Disorders in Human Disease; articles in Biochemical Journal, Journal of Physiology, Lancet. *Recreations:* ski-ing, reading, tennis. *Address:* 17 Highgate Close, N6 4SD.

PEASE, family name of **Barons Gainford** and **Wardington**.

PEASE, Sir (Alfred) Vincent, 4th Bt *cr* 1882; *b* 2 April 1926; *s* of Sir Alfred (Edward) Pease, 2nd Bt (*d* 1939), and his 3rd wife, Emily Elizabeth Pease (*d* 1979); *S* half-brother, 1963; unmarried. *Educ:* Bootham School, York; Durham Sch. of Agric., Houghall. *Heir: b* Joseph Gurney Pease [*b* 16 Nov. 1927; *m* 1953, Shelagh Munro, *d* of C. G. Bulman; one *s* one *d*]. *Address:* The Roseberry, Flatts Lane, Nunthorpe, Middlesbrough, Cleveland TS7 0PQ. *T:* (01287) 636453.

PEASE, Sir Richard Thorn, 3rd Bt *cr* 1920; DL; Chairman, Yorkshire Bank, 1986–90 (Director, 1977; Deputy Chairman, 1981–86); *b* 20 May 1922; *s* of Sir Richard Arthur Pease, 2nd Bt, and Jeannette Thorn (*d* 1957), *d* of late Gustav Edward Kissel, New York; *S* father, 1969; *m* 1956, Anne, *d* of late Lt-Col Reginald Francis Heyworth; one *s* two *d*. *Educ:* Eton. Served with 60th Rifles, Middle East, Italy and Greece, 1941–46 (Captain). Director: Owners of the Middlesbrough Estate Ltd, 1954–86; Barclays Bank, 1964–89; Bank of Scotland, 1977–85; Grainger Trust PLC, 1986–94; Vice-Chairman: Barclays Bank Ltd, 1970–82; Barclays Bank UK Management, 1971–82; Chm., Foreign and Colonial High Income Trust, 1990–92. DL Northumberland, 1990. *Heir: s* Richard Peter Pease, *b* 4 Sept. 1958.

PEASE, Robert John Claude; HM Diplomatic Service, retired; Counsellor (Administration) and Consul-General, British Embassy, Moscow, 1977–80; *b* 24 April 1922; *s* of Frederick Robert Hellier Pease and Eileen Violet Pease (*née* Beer); *m* 1945, Claire Margaretta Whall; one *s* two *d*. *Educ:* Cattedown Road Sch., Plymouth; Sutton High Sch., Plymouth. Served War of 1939–45; Telegraphist, RN, 1942; commnd Sub Lt RNVR, 1944. Clerk, Lord Chancellor's Dept, Plymouth County Court, 1939, Truro County Court, 1946; Foreign Office, 1948; Moscow, 1952; HM Consul, Sarajevo, 1954; 2nd Sec., Bangkok, 1958; HM Consul, Gdynia, 1959, Düsseldorf, 1961; 1st Sec., Pretoria, 1964, Bombay, 1966; FCO, 1969; Dep. High Commissioner, Mauritius, 1973. *Recreations:* golf, opera. *Address:* Palmetto, Kiln Close, Prestwood, Bucks, HP16 9DJ.

PEASE, Rosamund Dorothy Benson; Under Secretary, Department of Health, 1989–95; *b* 20 March 1935; *d* of Helen Bowen (*née* Wedgwood) and Michael Stewart Pease; one *s*. *Educ:* Chester Sch., Nova Scotia; Perse Sch., Cambridge; Mount Sch., York; Newnham Coll., Cambridge (BA Classical Tripos). Asst Principal, Min. of Health, 1958; Principal, 1965; Asst Sec., Pay Board, 1973; Office of Manpower Economics, 1974; Cabinet Office, 1975–76; DHSS, 1976; Office of Population Censuses and Surveys, 1983; Under Sec., NI Office, 1985. *Recreations:* music, gardening, family.

PEASE, Sir Vincent; *see* Pease, Sir A. V.

PEAT, Adam Erskine; Public Services Ombudsman for Wales, 2006–08; *b* 30 Nov. 1948; *s* of late Raymond Basil Peat and Cynthia Elisabeth Peat; *m* 1973, Christine Janet Champion; one *s* one *d*. *Educ:* Stowmarket Co. Grammar Sch.; Pembroke Coll., Oxford (MA). Joined Welsh Office, 1972: Principal, 1977; Private Sec. to Sec. of State for Wales, 1983–84; Asst Sec., 1984–89; Chief Exec., Tai Cymru, 1989–98; Gp Dir, Welsh Office, 1998–99; Dir, Local Govt Gp, subseq. Local Govt, Housing & Culture Dept, then Local Govt, Communities & Culture Dept, Nat. Assembly for Wales, 1999–2003; Local Govt Ombudsman and Health Service Ombudsman for Wales, 2003–06, and Welsh Admin Ombudsman, 2004–06. *Recreations:* music, walking, ski-ing.

PEAT, Sir Gerrard (Charles), KCVO 1988; FCA; Partner, Peat Marwick Mitchell & Co., Chartered Accountants, 1956–87; Auditor to the Queen's Privy Purse, 1980–88 (Assistant Auditor, 1969–80); *b* 14 June 1920; *s* of Charles Urie Peat, MC, FCA, sometime MP and Ruth (*née* Pulley); *m* 1949, Margaret Josephine Collingwood; one *s*. *Educ:* Sedbergh Sch. FCA 1961. Served War, RAF and ATA (pilot), 1940–45 (Service Medals; Badge of Honour for services in ATA in WWII, 2008); Pilot, 600 City of London Auxiliary Sqdn, 1948–51. Underwriting Mem. of Lloyd's, 1973–; Member: Cttee, Assoc. of Lloyd's Members, 1983–89; Council of Lloyd's, 1989–92. Member: Corp. of City of London, 1973–78; Worshipful Co. of Turners, 1970–. Hon. Treasurer, Assoc. of Conservative Clubs, 1971–78. Jubilee Medal, 1977. *Recreations:* travel, shooting, fishing, golf. *Address:* Flat 10, 35 Pont Street, SW1X 0BB. *T:* (020) 7245 9736. *Clubs:* Boodle's, MCC.

PEAT, Jeremy Alastair; a Trustee, BBC, since 2006 (a Governor, 2005–06); Director, David Hume Institute, since 2005; *b* 20 March 1945; *s* of John Scott Grainger Peat and Pamela Mary Peat (*née* Stephany); *m* 1972, Philippa Ann Jones; two *d*. *Educ:* Univ. of Bristol (BA Hons 1968); University College London (MSc 1977). FCIBS 1999. Govt Econ. Service, 1969–80; Hd, Employment Policy Unit, Govt of Botswana, 1980–84; HM Treasury, 1984–85; Sen. Econ. Advr, Scottish Office, 1985–93; Gp Chief Economist, Royal Bank of Scotland, 1993–2005. Bd Mem., Signet Accreditation Co. Ltd, 2007–. Vis. Prof., Univ. of Edinburgh, 1998; Hon. Prof., Heriot-Watt Univ., 1994. Vice Chm., SHEFC, 1999–2005. Mem., Competition Commn, 2005–. FRSE 2005; FRSA. Hon. LLD Aberdeen, 1997. *Publications:* (with Stephen Boyle) An Illustrated Guide to the Scottish Economy, 1999; (ed jtly) Scotland in a Global Economy: the 20:20 vision, 2002. *Recreations:* golf, tennis, reading, films, watching TV, walking dog. *Address:* Croft Dyke, Roslin Glen, Midlothian EH25 9PX. *T:* (0131) 440 2247; *e-mail:* jeremy.peat@bbc.co.uk.

PEAT, Ven. Lawrence Joseph; Archdeacon of Westmorland and Furness, 1989–95, now Emeritus; *b* 29 Aug. 1928; *s* of Joseph Edward and Lilian Edith Peat; *m* 1953, Sheila Shipway; three *s* three *d*. *Educ:* Lincoln Theological College. Curate of Bramley, Leeds, 1958–61; Rector of All Saints', Heaton Norris, Stockport, 1961–65; Vicar of Bramley, Leeds, 1965–73; Team Rector of Southend-on-Sea, 1973–79; Vicar of Skelsmergh, Selside and Longsleddale, Cumbria, 1979–86; RD of Kendal, 1984–88; Team Vicar of Kirkby Lonsdale, 1986–88. Canon of Carlisle Cathedral, 1988–95, now Emeritus. *Recreations:* walking, music. *Address:* 32 White Stiles, Kendal, Cumbria LA9 6DJ. *T:* (01539) 733829.

PEAT, Sir Michael (Charles Gerrard), KCVO 1998 (CVO 1994); FCA; Principal Private Secretary to the Prince of Wales and the Duchess of Cornwall, since 2005 (Private Secretary to the Prince of Wales, 2002–05); *b* 16 Nov. 1949; *m* 1976, Deborah Sage (*née* Wood); two *s* two *d* (and one *s* decd). *Educ:* Eton; Trinity Coll., Oxford (MA; Hon. Fellow, 2004); INSEAD, Fontainebleau (MBA). FCA 1975. KPMG Peat Marwick, 1972–93; Dir, Finance and Property Services, HM Household, 1990–96; Keeper of the Privy Purse, Treas. to the Queen, and Receiver-Gen., Duchy of Lancaster, 1996–2002.

PEATTIE, Catherine; Member (Lab) Falkirk East, Scottish Parliament, since 1999; *b* 24 Nov. 1951; *d* of late Ian Roxburgh and Catherine Cheape (*née* Menzies); *m* 1969, Ian Peattie; two *d*. *Educ:* Moray Secondary Sch., Grangemouth. Shop worker, 1966–68; factory worker, 1968–69; Trng Supervisor, 1970–75; Field Worker and Trng Officer, SPPA, 1980–86; Develt worker, Volunteer Network, Falkirk, 1986–90; Community Develt worker, Langlees Community Flat, Falkirk, 1990–91; Manager, Community Outreach, 1991–93; Dir, Falkirk Voluntary Action Resource Centre, 1993–99. Scottish Parliament: Convener, Equal Opportunities Cttee, 2003–07; Dep. Convener, Transport, Infrastructure and Climate Change Cttee, 2007–; Mem., Scottish Commn for Public Audit, 2003–07. *Address:* Scottish Parliament, Edinburgh EH99 1SP; *e-mail:* cathy.peattie.msp@scottish.parliament.uk; (constituency office) 5 Kerse Road, Grangemouth FK3 8HQ.

PEATTIE, Charles William Davidson, MBE 2003; freelance cartoonist, since 1985; *b* 3 April 1958; *s* of Richard Peattie and Frances Peattie; *m* 1st, 1988, Siobhan Clark (marr. diss.); two *d*; 2nd, 2005, Claudia Granados; two *s*. *Educ:* Charterhouse; St Martin's Sch. of Art (BA Fine Art). Portrait painter, 1980–85; artist: Alex cartoon (written with Russell Taylor) in: London Daily News, 1987; The Independent, 1987–91; Daily Telegraph, 1992–; Celeb cartoon (written with Mark Warren and Russell Taylor) in Private Eye, 1987–. *Television:* co-writer: Lenny Henry in Pieces (series), 1991; Passion Killers, 1999; Celeb (series), 2002. Writer, producer, animator, Alex (stage play), Arts Th., 2007. *Publications:* (with Mark Warren) Dick, 1987; Celeb, 1991; (co-designed with Phil Healey) Incredible Model Dinosaurs, 1994; The Original Celeb Gary Bloke, 2002; with Russell Taylor, Alex Year Books, 1987–: Alex, 1987; The Unabashed Alex, 1988; Alex II: Magnum Force, 1989; Alex III: Son of Alex, 1990; Alex IV: The Man with the Golden Handshake, 1991; Alex V: For the Love of Alex, 1992; Alex Calls the Shots, 1993; Alex Plays the Game, 1994; Alex Knows the Score, 1995; Alex Sweeps the Board, 1996; Alex Feels the Pinch, 1997; The Full Alex, 1998; The Alex Technique, 1999; The Best of Alex 1998–2001, 2001; The Best of Alex, annually 2002–07. *Address:* c/o Alex, PO Box 39447, N10 3PA. *T:* (020) 8374 1225. *Clubs:* Groucho, Soho House.

PÉBEREAU, Michel; Chairman, BNP Paribas, since 2000 (Chief Executive Officer, 2000–03); *b* 23 Jan. 1942; *m* 1962, Agnès Faure; two *s* two *d*. *Educ:* Ecole Polytechnique; Ecole Nationale d'Administration. Inspecteur Général des Finances honoraire. Inspecteur des Finances, 1967–70; Rep., later Tech. Advr, Cabinet of Minister of Econ. and Finance, 1970–74; Rep., Sub-Dir, Asst Dir and Hd of Service, Treasury Directorate, Ministry of Econ. and Finances, 1971–82; Dir, then Rep., Cabinet of Minister of Econ., 1978–81; Crédit Commercial de France: Man. Dir, 1982–87; Chm. and Chief Exec. Officer, 1987–93; Chm. and CEO, Banque Nationale de Paris, 1993–2000; Chm., Banque Paribas, 1999–2000. Chairman: French Banking Fedn, 2002–03 (Chm., Mkt and Investment Banking Commn, 2000–); French Banking Assoc., 2002–04; European Banking Fedn, 2004–; Bd, Institut de l'Entreprise, 2005–; Supervisory Bd, French Aspen Inst., 2005–; IIEB, 2006–. Director: BNP Paribas UK Ltd; Lafarge; Saint-Gobain; Total; Société Anonyme des Galeries Lafayette; Mem., Supervisory Bd, AXA. Institute of Political Studies, Paris: Sen. Lectr, 1967–78; Prof., 1980–2000; Mem., 1984–, Chm., 1988–, Mgt Cttee; Sen. Lectr, Nat. Sch. of Statistics and Econ. Admin, 1968–79. Mem., Acad. des Scis Morales et Politiques. Dep. Chm., Commn of Control for Film Industry, 1981–85; Chm., Commn for Selective Assistance for Film Distribn, 1987–89. Commandeur: Legion of Honour; Nat. Order of Merit (France). *Publications:* La Politique Economique de France, 3 Vols; science fiction book reviews for La Recherche, 1983–2002, for Le Journal du Dimanche, 2003–. *Address:* c/o BNP Paribas, 3 rue d'Antin, 75002 Paris, France.

PECK, David Arthur; Clerk to Merchant Taylors' Company, 1995–2006; *b* 3 May 1940; *s* of late Frank Archibald Peck and Molly Peck (*née* Eyels); *m* 1968, Jennifer Mary Still; one *s* two *d*. *Educ:* Wellingborough Sch.; St John's Coll., Cambridge (MA). Admitted Solicitor, 1966; Partner, Birkbeck Julius Coburn & Broad, 1967; Sen. Partner, Birkbeck Montagu's, 1985–91; Partner, Penningtons, 1991–95. Mem. Council, Radley Coll., 1993–. *Recreations:* golf, walking, cinema. *Address:* 26 Chepstow Place, W2 4TA. *Clubs:* MCC (Cttee, 1998–2001); Hawks (Cambridge).

See also Maj.-Gen. R. L. Peck.

PECK, Sir Edward (Heywood), GCMG 1974 (KCMG 1966; CMG 1957); HM Diplomatic Service, retired; *b* 5 Oct. 1915; *s* of Lt-Col Edward Surman Peck, IMS, and Doris Louise Heywood; *m* 1948, Alison Mary MacInnes; one *s* two *d* (and one *d* decd). *Educ:* Clifton College; The Queen's College, Oxford. 1st Cl. Hons (Mod. Langs), 1937; Laming Travelling Fellow, 1937–38. Entered Consular Service, 1938; served in Barcelona, 1938–39; Foreign Office, 1939–40; Sofia, 1940; Ankara, 1940–44; Adana, 1944; Iskenderun, 1945; Salonica, 1945–47; with UK Deleg. to UN Special Commn on the Balkans, 1947; Foreign Office, 1947–50; seconded to UK High Commissioner's Office, Delhi, 1950–52; Counsellor, Foreign Office, 1952–55; Dep. Comdt, Brit. Sector, Berlin, 1955–58; on staff of UK Commissioner-General for S-E Asia, 1959–60; Assistant Under-Secretary of State, Foreign Office, 1961–66; British High Commissioner in Kenya, 1966–68; Dep. Under-Secretary of State, FCO, 1968–70; British Perm. Rep. to N Atlantic Council, 1970–75. Dir, Outward Bound (Loch Eil), 1976–90; Mem. Council, Nat. Trust for Scotland, 1982–87. Hon. Vis. Fellow in Defence Studies, Aberdeen Univ., 1976–85. Hon. LLD Aberdeen, 1997. *Publications:* North-East Scotland (Bartholomew's Guides Series), 1981; Avonside Explored, 1983; The Battle of Glenlivet, 1994. *Recreations:* hill-walking, travel, reading history. *Address:* Easter Torrans, Tomintoul, Banffshire AB37 9HJ. *Club:* Alpine.

PECK, Maj.-Gen. Richard Leslie, CB 1991; FRGS; CEng, FICE; Director, The Churches Conservation Trust (formerly Redundant Churches Fund), 1992–97; *b* 27 May 1937; *s* of late Frank Archibald Peck and Molly Peck (*née* Eyels); *m* 1962, Elizabeth Ann, *d* of late Major Denis James Bradley and Barbara Edith Amy Bradley (*née* Metcalfe); two *s* one *d*. *Educ:* Wellingborough Sch.; Royal Mil. Acad., Sandhurst; Royal Mil. Coll. of Science, Shrivenham. BScEng. Commnd RE, 1957; served Cyprus, Libya, Germany, UK; psc 1969; Bde Major 5 Inf. Bde, 1969–71; Sqn Comd BAOR, 1972–73; Directing Staff, Staff Coll., 1973–77; CO 21 Engr Regt, 1977–79; Asst Mil. Sec., 1979–81; Comd 19 Inf. Bde, 1981–83; RCDS 1984; Dir Army Service Conditions, MoD, 1985; Dir Personnel, Staff of CDS, 1985–87; Engr-in-Chief (Army), 1988–91. Mem., Lord Kitchener Nat. Meml Fund, 1992– (Treas., 1999–). Col Comdt, RE, 1991–97; Col, Queen's Gurkha Engineers, 1991–96. Pres., London-West Br., SSAFA Forces Help, 2008–. Freeman, City of London, 1991; Mem., Engineers' Co., 1990–. *Recreations:* Association football, cricket, golf, shooting, ski-ing, Rugby football. *Clubs:* MCC; I Zingari, Free Foresters, Band of Brothers, Cryptics; Royal Mid-Surrey Golf.

See also D. A. Peck.

PECK, Stanley Edwards, CBE 1974; BEM 1954; QPM 1964; DL; HM Inspector of Constabulary, 1964–78; *b* 24 Jan. 1916; *er s* of late Harold Edwards Peck, Edgbaston and Shanghai; *m* 1st, 1939, Yvonne Sydney Edwards (*d* 1994), *er d* of late John Edwards Jessop, LDS; two *s* two *d*; 2nd, 1996, Elizabeth Beddows. *Educ:* Solihull School; Birmingham University. Served with RAF, 1941–45 (Flt-Lt). Joined Metropolitan Police, 1935; Chief Inspector and Supt, New Scotland Yard, 1950–54; Asst Chief Constable, Staffs, 1954–61; Chief Constable, Staffs, 1961–64. DL Staffs, 1962. Pres., Royal Life Saving Soc., UK, 1969–74 (Chm., East Midlands Region, RLSS, 1968–80). OStJ. *Recreations:* golf and dog walking. *Address:* April Cottage, Butchers Hill, Ickleton, Saffron Walden, Essex CB10 1SR. *Club:* Royal Air Force.

PECKFORD, Hon. (Alfred) Brian; PC (Can.) 1982; Premier of the Province of Newfoundland and Labrador, 1979–89; *b* Whitbourne, Newfoundland, 27 Aug. 1942; *s* of Ewart Peckford and Allison (*née* Young), St John's; *m* 1st, 1969, Marina Dicks; three *d*; 2nd, 1986, Carol Ellsworth; one *s*. *Educ:* Lewisporte High Sch.; Memorial Univ. of Newfoundland (BAEd). Schoolmaster, 1962–63 and 1966–72. MHA (Progressive C) Green Bay, 1972–89; Special Asst to Premier, 1973; Minister: of Dept of Municipal Affairs and Housing, 1974; of Mines and Energy, 1976, also of Rural Development, 1978. Leader of Progressive Cons. Party, Newfoundland and Labrador, 1979–89. President: Peckford Consulting Ltd (formerly Peckford Inc.), 1989–; Ming Financial Corp., Vancouver. Hon. LLD Meml Univ. of Newfoundland, 1986. *Recreations:* reading, sport, swimming, ski-ing. *Address:* 441 West Crescent Road, Qualicum Beach, BC V9K 1J5, Canada.

PECKHAM, Arthur John; UK Permanent Representative, Food and Agriculture Organisation, Rome, 1977–80; *b* 22 Sept. 1920; *s* of Richard William Peckham and Agnes Mercy (*née* Parker); *m* 1949, Margaret Enid Quirk; two *s* one *d*. *Educ:* The Judd Sch., Tonbridge. RAF (Pilot), 1942–46, 59 Sqdn Coastal Command. Cadet, Min. of Labour and Nat. Service, 1948; Colonial Office: Asst Principal, 1950; Private Sec. to Perm. Under-Sec., 1952; Principal, 1954; Counsellor (Technical Assistance), Lagos, 1964; Asst Sec., Min. of Overseas Develt, 1966; Minister, FAO, Rome, 1977. *Recreation:* gardening. *Address:* 147A Newmarket Road, Norwich NR4 6SY.

PECKHAM, Prof. Catherine Stevenson, CBE 1998; MD, FRCP, FRCOG, FRCPath, FFPH; Professor of Paediatric Epidemiology, since 1985, and former Head, Centre for Paediatric Epidemiology and Biostatistics, Institute of Child Health, University of London; Hon. Consultant, Hospital for Sick Children, Great Ormond Street, 1985–2002; *b* 7 March 1937; *d* of late Alexander King, CMG, CBE; *m* 1958, Sir Michael John Peckham, *qv*; three *s*. *Educ:* St Paul's Girls' Sch.; University Coll., London (MB BS, MD). FFPH (FFPM 1980); FRCP 1988; FRCPath 1991; FRCOG 1994. Reader in Community Medicine and Head of Dept, Charing Cross Hosp. Med. Sch., 1980–85. Member: Standing Med. Adv. Cttee, DoH, 1992–2001; Health Adv. Cttee, British Council, 1992–95; Bd, PHLS, 1989–92; Children Nationwide, Scientific Adv. Cttee, 1994–; Chairman: Steering Cttee on Epidemiol Res., Surveillance and Forecasting, WHO Global Prog. on AIDS, 1991–93; Exec. Cttee, British Paediatric Surveillance Unit, 1993–; Adv. Cttee on Dangerous Pathogens, DoH, 1999–2002; London Children's Taskforce, 2001–; Military Health Res. Adv. Gp, 2001–; Confidential Enquiries Adv. Cttee, NICE, 2002–; Medical Foundn for AIDS Res. & Sexual Health, 2002–. Member: Fulbright Commn, 1987–95; Bd of Govs, St Paul's Sch., 1992– (Dep. Chm., 2001–); Nuffield Council of Bioethics, 2000–06 (Vice-Chm., 2003–06); Council, Inst. of Educn, 2001–05; UK Women's Forum, 1990–; ASA, 1993–99. Founder FMedSci 1998; Founder FRCPCH. Harding Award, Action Research, 1993; James Spence Medal, RCPCH, 2003. *Publications:* The Peckham Report: national immunization study, 1989; chapters and papers on infections in pregnancy and early childhood, national cohort studies and epidemiology of common childhood conditions. *Recreation:* flute.

PECKHAM, Sir Michael (John), Kt 1995; FRCP, FRCS, FRCR, FRCPath; Founder, and Director, School of Public Policy, University College London, 1996–2000; *b* 2 Aug. 1935; *s* of William Stuart Peckham and Gladys Mary Peckham; *m* 1958, Catherine Stevenson King (*see* Prof. C. S. Peckham); three *s*. *Educ:* St Catharine's Coll., Cambridge (MA; Hon. Fellow, 1998); University College Hosp. Med. Sch., London (MD). MRC Clin. Res. Schol., Inst. Gustav Roussy, Paris, 1965–67; Institute of Cancer Research, London: Lectr, 1967–71; Sen. Lectr, 1971–74; Prof. of Radiotherapy, 1974–86; Dean, 1984–86; Dir, BPMF, 1986–90; Dir, R&D, DoH, 1991–95. Consultant: Royal Marsden Hosp., 1971–86; to Royal Navy, 1974–86. Mem., MRC, 1991–95; Mem., MRC Cell Biology and Disorders Bd, 1977–81. Member, Special Health Authority: Gt Ormond St Hosp., 1988–90; Brompton Nat. Heart and London Chest Hosps, 1986–90; Hammersmith and Queen Charlotte's Hosps, 1989–90. President: European Soc. of Therapeutic Radiology and Oncology, 1983–85; British Oncological Assoc., 1986–88; Fedn of European Cancer Socs, 1989–91; Mem., British Council Scientific Adv. Cttee, 1988–92. Vice-Chm., Council, ICRF, 1988–91. Chairman: BUPA Foundn, 1996–2004; Nat. Educn Res. Forum, 1999–2006; OST Foresight, Future of Healthcare, 1999–2000; Develt Forum, 2000–05; MS Soc. Sci. and Develt Bd, 2001–06; Macmillan Cancer Support Observatory, 2003–07. Founder: Bob Champion Cancer Trust, 1983; British Oncological Assoc., 1985; Co-founder, European Soc. of Therapeutic Radiology and Oncology, 1988. Mem., Inst. of Medicine, Nat. Acad. of Scis, Washington, 1995. Pres., Internat. Adv. Cttee, Canadian Inst. of Health Res., 2000–05. Trustee: Louise Buchanan Meml Trust, 1973–99; Guy's and St Thomas' Charitable Foundn, 1996–2000. Editor-in-Chief, European Jl of Cancer, 1989–95. Artist; RA summer exhibn, 2004; one-man exhibitions: Oxford, 1965; London, 1970, 1976, 1982, 1989, 1992, 1997, 2001, 2004; Edinburgh, 1989. Fellow: UCL, 1995; UCL Hosps, 1998; Inst. of Cancer Res., 1999. Founder FMedSci 1998. Dr *hc*: Univ. de Franche-Comté at Besançon, 1991; Catholic Univ. of Louvain, 1993; Hon. DSc: Loughborough, 1992; Exeter, 1996; London, 2007. *Publications:* Management of Testicular Tumours, 1981; (jtly) The Biological Basis of Radiotherapy, 1983; (jtly) Primary Management of Early Breast Cancer, 1985; (jt sen. editor) Oxford Textbook of Oncology, 1995; (with M. Marinker) Clinical Futures, 1998; A Model for Health: innovation and the future of health services, 1999. *Address:* 6 Crescent Place, SW3 2EA.

PEDDER, William Arthur; Director, Corporate Affairs, Hutchison Whampoa (Europe) Ltd, since 2006; *b* 20 Sept. 1950; *s* of Vice Adm. Sir Arthur Reid Pedder, KBE, CB, and Dulcie, *d* of O. L. Bickford; *m* 1983, Rosemarie Ghazaros; one *s* one *d*. *Educ:* Winchester Coll.; Merton Coll., Oxford (BA). Lieut, RN, 1972–79. Hogg Robinson Insce Gp, 1979–82; Manager, Lazard Bros, 1982–85; Dir, Dresdner Kleinwort Wasserstein, 1987–2001; Chief Exec., Invest·UK, subseq. Inward Investment, UK Trade & Investment, 2001–06. *Recreations:* sailing, theatre, ski-ing, tennis, shooting. *Address:* Hutchison Whampoa (Europe) Ltd, Hutchison House, 5 Hester Road, SW11 4AN. *T:* (020) 7350 5790; *e-mail:* williampedder@hwel.co.uk.

PEDDIE, Hon. Ian James Crofton; QC 1992; a Recorder, since 1997; *b* 17 Dec. 1945; *s* of Baron Peddie, MBE, JP, LLD and Hilda Mary Alice (*née* Bull), (Lady Peddie); *m* 1976, Susan Renée Howes; two *s* two *d*. *Educ:* Gordonstoun Sch.; University Coll. London (LLB Hons). Called to the Bar, Inner Temple, 1971; Asst Recorder, 1992–97. *Recreations:* family life, classic cars. *Address:* Garden Court Chambers, 57–60 Lincoln's Inn Fields, WC2A 3LS. *T:* (020) 7993 7600, *Fax:* (020) 7993 7700.

PEDDIE, Peter Charles, CBE 1983; Adviser to the Governor, and Head of Legal Unit, Bank of England, 1992–96; *b* 20 March 1932; *s* of Ronald Peddie and Vera Peddie (*née* Nicklin); *m* 1960, Charlotte Elizabeth Ryan; two *s* two *d*. *Educ:* Canford Sch., Wimborne; St John's Coll., Cambridge (BA 1954; MA 1977). Admitted Solicitor, 1957; Freshfields: articled, 1954–57; Asst Solicitor, 1957–60; Partner, 1960–92; Consultant, 1992. Mem., Standing Cttee on Company Law, Law Soc., 1972–92. Mem. Council, Middlesex Hosp. Med. Sch., 1977–88; Special Trustee, Middlesex Hosp., 1977–92. Gov., Canford Sch., 1981–94. Hon. QC 1997. *Recreations:* gardening, foreign travel. *Address:* Bannisters Farmhouse, Mattingley Green, Hook, Hants RG27 8LA. *T:* (0118) 932 6570. *Clubs:* Athenæum, City of London.

PEDELTY, Sir Mervyn (Kay), Kt 2005; FCA, FCIB; Chief Executive: Co-operative Bank, 1997–2004; Co-operative Insurance Society, 2002–04 (Director, 1998–2004); Co-operative Financial Services, 2002–04; *b* 16 Jan. 1949; *s* of late William Hopper Pedelty and of Muriel Pedelty; *m* 1st, 1983, Carol (decd); 2nd, 1998, Jill Wesson (*née* Hughes); one *s*, and one step *d*. *Educ:* Felixstowe GS; AMP, Harvard Business Sch. ACA 1971, FCA 1976. Scrutton, Goodchild & Sanderson, 1966–71; Whinney Murray & Co., 1971–73; British Leyland Ltd, 1973–76; Divl Finance Dir, 1976–80, Divl Man. Dir, 1980, Plantation Hldgs, then Phicom plc; Divl Man. Dir, Gould Inc., 1981–83; Finance Dir and Asst Man. Dir, Abacus Electronics Hldgs plc, 1983–87; Finance Dir, TSB Banking and Insurance, 1987–92; Chief Exec., Commercial Ops, TSB Gp plc, 1992–95; Partner, LEK Consulting LLP, 1995–97. Dir and Dep. Chm., Unity Trust Bank plc, 1997–2004; Exec. Cttee, Co-operative Gp (CWS) Ltd, 1997–2004. Non-executive Director: Hiscox plc, 2005–06; Hiscox Insurance Co. Ltd, 2005–; Hiscox Ltd (incorp. Bermuda), 2006–; Friends Provident plc, 2006–; Sen. Advr, Permira Advrs LLP, 2005–. Member: The Co-operative Commn, 2000–02; Employer Task Force on Pensions, DWP, 2003–05. Chairman: Sustainability NW, 1998–2003; Manchester Investment and Development Agency Service, 1999–2003; FTSE4Good Policy Cttee, 2001–; Manchester Enterprises Ltd, 2002–05 (Dir, 2000–); Dep. Chm., NW Business Leadership Team, 1997–2005. Vice-Pres., Community Foundn for Gtr Manchester, 2000–05. Mem., Chief Exec.'s Cttee, BBA, 1999–2005; Dir, ABI, 2003–05. Trustee: Triumph over Phobia, 1995–; Symphony Hall, Birmingham, subseq. Performances Birmingham, 1996–. FCIB 1992; FRSA 1997. Freeman, City of London, 1996; Liveryman, Tin Plate Workers' Alias Wire Workers' Co., 1997; Mem., Guild of Internat. Bankers, 2002. *Recreations:* charity and community work, the countryside and the environment, music, art, ski-ing. *Address:* PO Box 50416, London W8 7YU. *Club:* Royal Automobile.

PEDERSEN, Prof. (Knud) George, OC 1993; OOnt 1994; OBC 2002; PhD; FCCT; FRSA; Professor, The University of Western Ontario, 1985–96 (President and Vice-Chancellor, 1985–94); Chancellor, University of Northern British Columbia, 1998–2004; *b* 13 June 1931; *s* of Hjalmar Nielsen Pedersen and Anna (*née* Jensen); *m* 1st, 1953, Joan Elaine Vanderwarker (*d* 1988); one *s* one *d*; 2nd, 1988, Penny Ann Jones. *Educ:* Vancouver Normal Sch. (Dip. in Teaching 1952); Univ. of BC (BA History and Geography, 1959); Univ. of Washington (MA 1964); Univ. of Chicago (PhD 1969). FCCT 1977; FRSA 1983. Schools in North Vancouver: Teacher, Highlands Elem. Sch., 1952–56; Vice-Principal, North Star Elem. Sch., 1956–59; Principal, Carisbrooke Elem. Sch., 1959–61; Vice-Principal, Handsworth Sec. Sch., 1961–63; Principal, Balmoral Sec. Sch., 1963–65; Univ. of Chicago: Teaching Intern, 1966; Staff Associate, Midwest Admin Center, 1965–66, Res. Associate (Asst Prof.), 1966–68; Asst Prof., Ontario Inst. for Studies in Educn and Univ. of Toronto, 1968–70; Asst Prof. and Associate Dir, Midwest Admin Center, Div. of Social Sciences, Univ. of Chicago, 1970–72; Faculty of Educn, Univ. of Victoria: Associate Prof., 1972–75; Dean, 1972–75; Vice-Pres. (Academic), and Prof., Univ. of Victoria, 1975–79; President and Professor: Simon Fraser Univ., 1979–83; Univ. of British Columbia, 1983–85; Interim Pres., Univ. of Northern BC, 1995; Pres., Royal Roads Univ., 1995–96. Universities Council of British Columbia: Mem., Prog. Co-ordinating Cttee, 1975–78; Mem., Business Affairs Cttee, 1975–78; Mem., Long-range Planning Cttee, 1979–85; Mem. Council, Ontario Univ., 1985–94 (Chm.). Chm., Adv. Cttee on Educnl Planning, Min. of Educn (Prov. of BC), 1977–78; Member: Jt Bd of Teacher Educn, Prov. of BC, 1972–75; BC Council for Leadership in Educn, 1973–80; Interior Univ. Progs Bd, Min. of Educn, 1977–78. Member, Board of Directors: Assoc. of Univs and Colls of Canada, 1979–84 (Mem., Adv. Cttee, Office of Internat. Develt, 1979–83; Chm., 1989–91); Public Employers' Council of BC, 1979–84; Vancouver Bd of Trade, 1983–85; Pulp and Paper Res. Inst. of Canada, 1983–85; Corporate and Higher Educn Forum, 1988–94; President: N Vancouver Teachers' Assoc., 1962–63; N Vancouver Principals' and Vice-Principals' Assoc., 1963–64; Vice-Pres., Inter-American Orgn for Higher Educn, 1991–93 (Mem. Bd of Dirs, 1979–85); Sec.-Treasurer, Canadian Assoc. of Deans and Directors of Educn, 1972–73 and 1973–74; Mem., Exec. Bd, ACU, 1991–94. Member: BoT, Vancouver, 1983–85; Nat. Council, Canadian Human Rights Foundn, 1984–. Mem., Bd of Dirs, MacMillan Bloedel Ltd, 1984–86. Member, Board of Governors: Arts, Sciences and Technol. Centre, 1980–85; Leon and Thea Koerner Foundn, 1981–85; Member: Bd of Trustees, Discovery Foundn, 1980–85; Bd, Bill Reid Foundn, 2000–07 (Pres., 2000–02). Consultant, Salzburg Seminar, Austria, 1999–. Hon. LLD: McMaster, 1996; Simon Fraser 2003; Northern BC, 2005; Hon. DLitt: Emily Carr Inst. of Art and Design, 2003; Fraser Valley Univ. Coll., 2007. Confedn of Canada 125th Anniversary Medal 1992; Golden Jubilee Medal, 2003. *Publications:* The Itinerant Schoolmaster: a socio-economic analysis of teacher turnover, 1973; chapters in books on educn; articles in Administrator's Notebook (Univ. of Chicago), selected articles for Elem. Sch. Principals, Res. in Educn, Educn and Urban Soc., Educn Canada, Teacher Educn, Resources in Educn, Elem. Sch. Jl, Jl of Educnl Admin, and Canadian Jl of Univ. Continuing Educn; book reviews; proc. of confs and symposia; governmental and institutional studies and reports. *Address:* 2232 Spruce Street, Vancouver, BC V6H 2P3, Canada. *T:* (604) 7332400; *e-mail:* pgpedersen@telus.net. *Club:* Semiahmoo Golf and Country (Blaine, Washington).

PEDERSEN, Prof. Roger Arnold Lugo, PhD; Professor of Regenerative Medicine, Department of Surgery, School of Clinical Medicine, University of Cambridge, since 2002; *b* 1 Aug. 1944; *s* of Viggo Bernhardt Pedersen and Emily Anita Pedersen (*née* Lugo); *m* 2006, Elizabeth Jane Sowton; two *d*, and two step *d*. *Educ:* Stanford Univ. (AB with Dist. 1965); Yale Univ. (PhD 1970). Postdoctoral Fellow, Johns Hopkins Univ., 1970–71; University of California, San Francisco: Asst Prof., 1971–79; Associate Prof., 1980–84; Prof., 1985–2001; University of Cambridge, 2001–: Dir, Prog. in Stem Cell Medicine, Cambridge Stem Cell Initiative, 2004–. Member: Soc. for Develtl Biology; Internat. Soc. for Stem Cell Res. *Publications:* (ed jtly) Experimental Approaches to Mammalian Embryonic Development, 1986; (ed jtly) Animal Applications of Research in Mammalian Development, 1991; (ed jtly) Current Topics in Developmental Biology, Vols 30–48, 1995–2000; (ed jtly) Handbook of Stem Cells, Vol. 1, Embryonic Stem Cells, 2004; (ed jtly) Human Embryonic Stem Cells, 2005; (ed jtly) Essentials of Stem Cell Biology, 2006; over 100 peer-reviewed articles in scientific jls, 1971–. *Recreations:* violin playing and making, flying (single engine airplanes). *Address:* Cambridge Institute for Medical Research, Wellcome Trust/MRC Building, Hills Road, University of Cambridge, Cambridge CB2 0XY. *T:* (01223) 763366, *Fax:* (01223) 763350; *e-mail:* roger@stemcells.cam.ac.uk.

PEDLEY, Rt Rev. (Geoffrey) Stephen; Bishop Suffragan of Lancaster, 1998–2005; *b* 13 Sept. 1940; *s* of Geoffrey Heber Knight and Muriel Pedley; *m* 1970, Mary Frances Macdonald; two *s* one *d*. *Educ:* Marlborough College; Queens' College, Cambridge (MA); Cuddesdon Theological College. Curate: Liverpool Parish Church, 1966; Holy Trinity, Coventry, 1969; Rector of Kitwe, Zambia, 1971–77; Vicar of St Peter's, Stockton,

1977–88; Rector, Whickham, 1988–93; Residentiary Canon, Durham Cathedral, 1993–98. Chaplain to the Queen, 1984–98. Hon. Asst Bishop, Dio. of Newcastle, 2005–. *Recreations:* architecture, English literature, travel. *Address:* The Blue House, Newbrough, Northumberland NE47 5AN.

PEDLEY, Prof. Timothy John, PhD, ScD; FRS 1995; G. I. Taylor Professor of Fluid Mechanics, since 1996, and Head of Department of Applied Mathematics and Theoretical Physics, 2000–05, University of Cambridge; Fellow of Gonville and Caius College, Cambridge, 1973–89 and since 1996; *b* 23 March 1942; *s* of Richard Rodman Pedley and Jean Mary Mudie Pedley (*née* Evans); *m* 1965, Avril Jennifer Martin Uden; two *s*. *Educ:* Rugby Sch.; Trinity Coll., Cambridge (BA 1963; MA, PhD 1967; ScD 1982). Post-doctoral Fellow, Johns Hopkins Univ., 1966–68; Res. Associate, then Lectr, Physiol. Flow Studies Unit and Dept of Maths, Imperial Coll. London, 1968–73; Department of Applied Mathematics and Theoretical Physics, University of Cambridge: Asst Dir of Res., 1973–77; Lectr, 1977–89; Reader in Biolog. Fluid Dynamics, 1989; Prof. of Applied Maths, Univ. of Leeds, 1990–96. EPSRC Sen. Res. Fellow, 1995–2000. Chm., World Council for Biomechanics, 2002–06; President: IMA, 2004–05; Cambridge Philosophical Soc., 2006–07. Lectures: G. I. Taylor, Univ. of Cambridge, 1998; Clifford, Tulane Univ., 2003; Rutherford Meml, NZ, 2003; Talbot, Univ. of Illinois, 2004; Ludwig Prandtl Meml, Zurich, 2007. Foreign Associate, US NAE, 1999; Fellow: Amer. Inst. of Med. and Biol Engrg, 2001; Amer. Phys. Soc., 2005; Foreign Fellow, Nat. Acad. of Sci., India, 2007. Editor, Jl of Fluid Mechanics, 2000–06. *Publications:* (ed) Scale Effects in Animal Locomotion, 1977; (jtly) The Mechanics of the Circulation, 1978; The Fluid Mechanics of Large Blood Vessels, 1980; (ed with C. P. Ellington) Biological Fluid Dynamics, 1995; numerous articles in fluid mechanics and biomechanics jls. *Recreations:* bird-watching, running, reading. *Address:* Oakhurst Farm, 375 Shadwell Lane, Leeds LS17 8AH; Department of Applied Mathematics and Theoretical Physics, Centre for Mathematical Sciences, Wilberforce Road, Cambridge CB3 0WA. *T:* (01223) 339842.

PEEBLES, Prof. Phillip James Edwin, FRS 1982; Professor of Physics, 1965, and Albert Einstein Professor of Science, 1984, Princeton University, now Professor Emeritus; *b* Winnipeg, 25 April 1935; *s* of Andrew Charles Peebles and Ada Marian (*née* Green); *m* 1958, Jean Alison Peebles; three *d*. *Educ:* Univ. of Manitoba (BSc 1958); Princeton Univ. (MA 1959; PhD 1962). Member: Amer. Phys. Soc.; Amer. Astron. Soc.; AAAS; Internat. Astron. Union; Fellow: Amer. Physical Soc.; Amer. Acad. of Arts and Scis; Royal Soc. of Canada. Hon. DSc: Univ. of Toronto, 1986; Univ. of Chicago, 1986; McMaster Univ., 1989; Univ. of Manitoba, 1989. *Publications:* Physical Cosmology, 1971; The Large Scale Structure of the Universe, 1979; (ed jtly) Objects of High Redshift, 1980; Quantum Mechanics, 1992; Principles of Physical Cosmology, 1993. *Address:* 24 Markham Road, Princeton, NJ 08540, USA; Joseph Henry Laboratory, Princeton University, Princeton, NJ 08544, USA.

PEEK, Bruno Mark, OBE 2000; MVO 2002; Pageantmaster, organiser and co-ordinator, national and international events, since 1981; Chairman, Beacon Millennium Ltd; *b* 12 Sept. 1951; adopted *s* of George and Mildred Peek; one *d*; *m* 1st (marr. diss.); 2nd (marr. diss. 1999); one step *d*. *Educ:* Alderman Leach Secondary Sch., Gorleston, Great Yarmouth. Event organiser and consultant, English Tourist Bd (Mem., England Entertains Exec. Cttee, 1984); Develt Dir, Sparks Creative Services, 1989–92. Major nat. and internat. events include: Operation Sea Fire (chain of beacon fires), 1981; Great Armada Pageant, 1987–88; Fire over England (beacon signal fires), 1988; Beacon Europe (beacon signal fires), 1992; 50th Anniv. Celebrations, VE Day, 1995; Great British Poppy Chain for 75th Anniv. of RBL, 1996; Beacon Millennium, Millennium Flame, 1999–2000; Nelson Returns to England for Great Yarmouth Pageant, 2000; Golden Jubilee Summer Party, Golden Jubilee Summer Party Torch Relay, Golden Jubilee Dinner, 2002; Nelson's Farewell to Norfolk, Royal Norfolk Show, 2005; VC and GC Dinner for 60th Anniv. Celebrations, end of World War II, 2005; Trafalgar Weekend, 2005; Rededication of Nelson's Monument, Great Yarmouth, 2007; Grand Tour of 50 English cities of the Loving Cup of England, 2007; Nat. St George's Day Banquet, Banqueting House, Whitehall, 2007; Service of Commemoration of Falkland Islands conflict and Heroes' Dinner, Old Royal Naval Coll., Greenwich, 2007; Celebration Dinner and Ball, Diamond Wedding Anniversary of the Queen and Duke of Edinburgh, 2007; official visit of Loving Cup of England to Malta, 2008; St George's Day Reception, Westminster Hall, 2008. Coordinator, Enjoy England Celebrate St George's Day campaign, 2008. Trustee, 1998–, and Internat. Co-ordinator, 2000–, Covenant Home Ministries (Kisumu) Kenya. Freedom of the City of London, 1989. *Recreations:* walking, gardening. *Address:* 21 Coverdale, Carlton Colville, Lowestoft, Suffolk NR33 8TD. *T:* 07737 262913.

PEEK, Sir Richard Grenville, 6th Bt *cr* 1874, of Rousden, Devon; *b* 3 Feb. 1955; *s* of Sir William Grenville Peek, 5th Bt and of Lucy Jane Peek (*née* Dorrien-Smith); *S* father, 2004; *m* 1983, Melanie Jane Waterson; three *s*. *Educ:* Eton. *Heir:* *s* Timothy Grenville Peek, *b* 21 Nov. 1989.

PEEK, Vice-Adm. Sir Richard (Innes), KBE 1972 (OBE 1944); CB 1971; DSC 1945; *b* 30 July 1914; 2nd *s* of late James Norman and Kate Ethel Peek; *m* 1943, Margaret Seinor (*née* Kendall) (*d* 1946); one *s*; *m* 1952, Mary Catherine Tilley (*née* Stops) (*d* 2005); two *d*. *Educ:* Royal Australian Naval College. Joined RAN, 1928; served War of 1939–45 in HMS Revenge, HMAS Cerberus, Hobart, Australia, Navy Office; Korean War Service in HMAS Tobruk, 1951; Flag Officer Comdg HMA Fleet, 1967–68; Chief of Naval Staff, Australia, 1970–73. Legion of Merit (US), 1951. *Recreation:* gardening. *Address:* 10 Galway Place, Deakin, ACT 2600, Australia. *Clubs:* Royal Automobile (Sydney); Royal Commonwealth Society (Canberra).

PEEL, family name of **Earl Peel**.

PEEL, 3rd Earl *cr* 1929; **William James Robert Peel,** GCVO 2006; PC 2006; DL; Bt 1800; Viscount Peel, 1895; Viscount Clanfield, 1929; Lord Chamberlain of HM Household, since 2006; *b* 3 Oct. 1947; *s* of 2nd Earl Peel and Kathleen (*d* 1972), *d* of Michael McGrath; *S* father, 1969; *m* 1st, 1973, Veronica Naomi Livingston (marr. diss. 1987), *d* of Alastair Timpson; one *s* one *d*; 2nd, 1989, Hon. Mrs Charlotte Hambro, *yr d* of Baron Soames, PC, GCMG, GCVO, CH, CBE and of Lady Soames, *qv*; one *d*. *Educ:* Ampleforth; University of Tours; Cirencester Agric. Coll. Duchy of Cornwall: Mem., Prince's Council, 1993–96; Lord Warden of the Stannaries and Keeper of the Privy Seal, 1994–2006. Mem., Nature Conservancy Council for England, then English Nature, 1991–96; Chm., 1994–2000, Pres., 2000–08, Game and Wildlife Conservation Trust (formerly Game Conservancy Trust); former Mem. Cttee, Yorkshire Dales Nat. Park. President: Yorks Wildlife Trust, 1989–96; Gun Trade Assoc., 1993–99; Chm., Standing Conf. on Country Sports, 2001–06. Elected Mem., H of L, 1999–; Mem., Sub-Cttee D, H of L Select Cttee on EU (Envmt and Agric.), 2004–. DL N Yorks, 1998. *Heir:* *s* Viscount Clanfield, *qv*. *Address:* Eelmire, Masham, Ripon, N Yorks HG4 4PF.

PEEL, Catherine Anne; *see* Mackintosh, C. A.

PEEL, David Alexander Robert; Inquiry Manager (formerly Reference Secretary, then Inquiry Secretary), Competition (formerly Monopolies and Mergers) Commission, since 1996; *b* 12 Nov. 1940; *s* of late Maj. Robert Edmund Peel and Sheila Mary (*née* Slattery); *m* 1971, Patricia Muriel Essery; two *s*. *Educ:* St Edmund's Coll., Ware; University Coll., Oxford. Building labourer, New Scotland Yard devlt, 1963; joined MoT, 1964; Private Sec. to Minister of State, 1967; Principal, 1968; DoE, 1970; First Sec., UK Perm. Repn to EC, Brussels, 1972; Private Sec. to Minister for Transport, 1975; Asst Sec., Depts of Transport and the Environment, 1976–90: Nat. Roads Prog. and Highway Policy, 1982; Okehampton Bypass (Confirmation of Orders) Act, 1985; Interdeptl Review on Using Private Enterprise in Govt, 1986; Office Services, 1987–90; Under Sec., Dir of Admin Resources, DoE, 1990–96. *Recreations:* allotment gardening, ballet, baroque architecture.

PEEL, Prof. John David Yeadon, FBA 1991; Professor of Anthropology and Sociology, with reference to Africa, School of Oriental and African Studies, University of London, 1989–2007, now Professor Emeritus; *b* 13 Nov. 1941; *e s* of late Prof. Edwin Arthur Peel and Nora Kathleen Yeadon; *m* 1969, Jennifer Christine Ferial (marr. diss. 2000), *d* of K. N. Pare, Leicester; three *s*. *Educ:* King Edward's Sch., Birmingham; Balliol Coll., Oxford (Scholar; BA 1963, MA 1966); LSE (PhD 1966); DLit London 1985. Asst Lectr, then Lectr in Sociology, Nottingham Univ., 1965–70; Lectr in Sociology, LSE, 1970–73; Charles Booth Prof. of Sociology, 1975–89, Dean, Faculty of Social and Envmtl Studies, 1985–88, Univ. of Liverpool; Dean of Undergraduate Studies, SOAS, 1990–94. Vis. Reader in Sociology and Anthropology, Univ of Ife, Nigeria, 1973–75; Vis. Prof. in Anthropology and Sociology, Univ. of Chicago, 1982–83; Marett Lectr, 1993, Associate, Inst. of Develt Studies, 1973–94. Pres., African Studies Assoc. of UK, 1996–98; Vice-Pres., British Acad., 1999–2000. Chm. Trustees, Internat. African Inst., 2006– (Editor, Africa, and Officer, 1979–86); Gen. Editor, Internat. African Library, 1986–. Frazer Lectr, Univ. of Oxford, 2000; Galton Lectr, 2003; Roy H. Rappaport Lectr, 2003. Amaury Talbot Prize, RAI, 1983, 2000; Herskovits Award, African Studies Assoc., USA, 1984, 2001. *Publications:* Aladura: a religious movement among the Yoruba, 1968; Herbert Spencer: the evolution of a sociologist, 1971; (ed) Herbert Spencer on Social Evolution, 1972; Ijeshas and Nigerians, 1983; Religious Encounter and the Making of the Yoruba, 2000; articles in anthropological, sociological and Africanist jls; *festschrift:* Christianity and Social Change in Africa: essays in honour of J. D. Y. Peel, ed Toyin Falola, 2005. *Recreations:* gardening, fell-walking, old churches. *Address:* 80 Archway Road, N19 3TT. *T:* (020) 7272 9487.

PEEL, Rev. Jonathan Sidney, CBE 1994; MC 1957; Vice Lord-Lieutenant of Norfolk, 1981–2005; Ordained Local Minister, Horning Benefice, Diocese of Norwich, since 2001; *b* 21 June 1937; *s* of Major D. A. Peel, MC (killed in action 1944) and Hon. Mrs David Peel (*née* Vanneck); *m* 1965, Jean Fulton Barnett, *d* of Air Chief Marshal Sir Denis Barnett, GCB, CBE, DFC; one *s* four *d*. *Educ:* Norwich Sch.; Eton; St John's Coll., Cambridge (BA Land Economy; MA 1970); Norwich Dio. OLM Scheme. Commnd, Rifle Bde, Royal Green Jackets, 1956; served Malaya, 1956–57; UN forces, Congo (Zaire), 1960–61; Cyprus, 1962–63; resigned, 1966. Dir, Norwich Union Insce Gp, 1973–98; Chm., Pleasureworld plc, 1986–89. Vice Pres., Norfolk Naturalists Trust, 1984–2000; National Trust: Mem. Exec. Cttee, 1982–2002; Mem. Council, 1984–2002; Dep. Chm., 1992–2002; Chm., Cttee for East Anglia, 1981–90; Chm., Properties Cttee, 1990–2000. Norfolk Scouts Association: Dist Comr, 1971–75; Comr for Norwich, 1975–77; County Comr, 1977–81. Chairman: E Anglian Br., Royal Forestry Soc., 1979–81; Norfolk Police Authority, 1983–89; Norfolk Churches Trust, 1983–85; The Broads Authority, 1985–97; Norwich Sch., 1985–2003; How Hill Trust, 1987–2007; Pres., Norfolk Assoc. for the Advancement of Music, 1978–93. Mem., Norfolk CC, 1973–97 (Chm., Planning and Transportation Cttee, 1990–93). JP North Walsham, 1973–86. High Sheriff, Norfolk, 1984. Ordained deacon, 2000, priest, 2001, C of E. Hon. DCL UEA, 2005. *Publication:* (with M. J. Sayer) Towards a Rural Policy for Norfolk, 1973. *Recreations:* forestry, music. *Address:* Barton Hall, Barton Turf, Norwich NR12 8AU. *T:* (01692) 536250. *Clubs:* Boodle's; Norfolk (Norwich).

PEEL, Robert Edmund Guy, FIH; Chairman, Peel Hotels plc, since 1998; *b* 13 March 1947; *s* of John and Joanna Peel. *Educ:* Eton Coll. FIH (FHCIMA 1985). Various hotel appts, Europe, 1964–66; Queen Anne's Hotels & Properties, then Trust Houses Ltd, later Trust House Forte plc, 1966–76; Dir, 1976–98, Chief Exec., 1977–97, Mount Charlotte Investments, later Thistle Hotels plc. Director: Brierley Investments Ltd, 1992–96; Ivory & Sime Discovery Trust, 1994–2005. Dir, London Tourist Bd, 1994–98. *Recreations:* deep sea fishing, marine biology, tennis, gardening. *Address:* (office) 19 Warwick Avenue, Maida Vale, W9 2PS. *Club:* White's.

PEERS, Most Rev. Michael Geoffrey; Primate of the Anglican Church of Canada, 1986–2004; *b* 31 July 1934; *s* of Geoffrey Hugh Peers and Dorothy Enid Mantle; *m* 1963, Dorothy Elizabeth Bradley; two *s* one *d*. *Educ:* University of British Columbia (BA Hons); Universität Heidelberg (Zert. Dolm.-Interpreter's Certificate); Trinity Coll., Toronto (LTh). Deacon 1959, priest 1960; Curate: St Thomas', Ottawa, 1959–61; Trinity, Ottawa, 1961–65; University Chaplain, Diocese of Ottawa, 1961–66; Rector: St Bede's, Winnipeg, 1966–72; St Martin's, Winnipeg, with St Paul's Middlechurch, 1972–74; Archdeacon of Winnipeg, 1969–74; Rector, St Paul's Cathedral, Regina, 1974–77; Dean of Qu'Appelle, 1974–77; Bishop of Qu'Appelle, 1977–82; Archbishop of Qu'Appelle and Metropolitan of Rupert's Land, 1982–86. Ecumenist-in-Residence, Toronto Sch. of Theol., Univ. of Toronto, 2004–06. Hon. DD: Trinity Coll., Toronto, 1978; St John's Coll., Winnipeg, 1981; Wycliffe Coll., Toronto, 1987; Univ. of Kent, 1988; Montreal Dio. Coll., 1989; Coll. of Emmanuel and St Chad, Saskatoon, 1990; Thorneloe Univ., 1991; Univ. of Huron Coll., 1998; Lutheran Theol Seminary, Saskatoon, 2001; Vancouver Sch. of Theol., 2003; Episcopal Divinity Sch., Cambridge, Mass, 2004; Gen. Theol Seminary, NY, 2007; Hon. DCL Bishop's Univ., Lennoxville, 1993. *Publication:* Grace Notes: journeying with the Primate 1995–2004, 2005. *Address:* 195 Westminster Avenue, Toronto, ON M6R 1N9, Canada. *T:* (416) 5318958.

PEET, Ronald Hugh, CBE 1974; Chief Executive, Legal & General Group plc, 1972–84; *b* 12 July 1925; *s* of Henry Leonard and Stella Peet; *m* 1st, 1949, Winifred Joy Adamson (*d* 1979); two *s* two *d*; 2nd, 1981, Lynette Judy Burgess Kinsella. *Educ:* Doncaster Grammar Sch.; Queen's Coll., Oxford (MA). Served in HM Forces, Captain RA, 1944–47. Legal and General Assurance Society Limited: joined 1952; emigrated to Australia, 1955; Sec., Australian Branch, 1955–59; Asst Life Manager, 1959–65; Manager and Actuary for Australia, 1965–69; returned to UK as General Manager (Ops), 1969; Dir, 1969–84; Chm., 1980–84. Chairman: Aviation & General Insurance Co. Ltd, 1978–80; Stockley Plc, 1984–87; PWS Holdings plc, 1987–88; Director: AMEC Plc, 1984–96; Howard Gp plc, 1985–86; Independent Insurance Group plc, 1988–99. Director: City Arts Trust Ltd, 1976–90 (Chm., 1980–87); Royal Philharmonic Orchestra Ltd, 1977–88; English National Opera, 1978–84, 1985–95. Chm., British Insurance Assoc., 1978–79. FIA. *Recreations:* music, opera. *Address:* 9 Marlowe Court, Petyward, SW3 3PD. *Clubs:* Hurlingham, City of London.

PEGDEN, Jeffrey Vincent; QC 1996; **His Honour Judge Pegden;** a Circuit Judge, since 2007; *b* 24 June 1950; *s* of George Vincent Pegden and Stella Blanche Katherine

Pegden; *m* 1981, Delia Mary Coonan; one *s* one *d. Educ:* Univ. of Hull (LLB Hons 1972). Called to the Bar, Inner Temple, 1973, Bencher, 2002; a Recorder, 1996–2007. Mem., Crown Court Rules Cttee, 2001–07. FRSA. *Recreations:* reading, music, walking, sailing, clockmaker.

PEGGIE, Robert Galloway Emslie, CBE 1986; Commissioner for Local Administration (Ombudsman) in Scotland, 1986–94; Chairman, Scottish Local Government Staff Commission, 1994–97; *b* 5 Jan. 1929; *s* of John and Euphemia Peggie; *m* 1st, 1955, Christine Jeanette Simpson (*d* 2000); one *s* one *d*; 2nd, 2001, Janice Helen Renton. *Educ:* Lasswade High Sch. Certified accountant; Accountancy apprenticeship, 1946–52; Accountant in industry, 1952–57; Public Service, Edinburgh City, 1957–74; Chief Exec., Lothian Regl Council, 1974–86. Trustee, Lloyds TSB Foundn, 1995–98. Mem., Gen. Convocation and Court, Heriot-Watt Univ., 1988–97 (Convener, Finance Cttee, 1989–97); Governor, Edinburgh Coll. of Art, 1989–99 (Vice-Chm., 1995–97; Chm., 1998–99). DUniv Heriot-Watt, 1998. *Recreation:* golf. *Address:* 9A Napier Road, Edinburgh EH10 5AZ. *T:* (0131) 229 6775.

PEI, Ieoh Ming, FAIA, RIBA; architect; Founding Partner, Pei Cobb Freed & Partners (formerly I. M. Pei & Partners), Architects, New York, 1955–96; *b* Canton, China, 26 April 1917; naturalized citizen of USA, 1954; *m* 1942, Eileen Loo; three *s* one *d. Educ:* St John's Middle Sch., Shanghai; MIT (BArch 1940); Harvard Grad. Sch. of Design (MArch 1946). FAIA 1964. Nat. Defense Res. Cttee, 1943–45; Asst Prof., Harvard Grad. Sch. of Design, 1945–48; Dir Architecture, Webb & Knapp Inc., 1948–55; Wheelwright Travelling Fellow, Harvard, 1951. Designed Nat. Center for Atmospheric Res., Boulder, Colo, 1961–67; other projects include: John F. Kennedy Library, Boston, 1965–79; E Building, Nat. Gall. of Art, Washington, 1968–78; Morton H. Myerson Symphony Center, Dallas, 1982–89; Four Seasons Hotel, NY, 1989–93; Rock and Roll Hall of Fame and Mus., Cleveland, 1990–95; also church, hosp., municipal and corporate bldgs, schs, libraries and museums in US; numerous projects worldwide include: Fragrant Hill Hotel, Beijing, 1979–82; Bank of China, Hong Kong, 1982–89; expansion and renovation, The Louvre, Paris, 1983–93; Suzhou Mus., China, 2006. Member: Nat. Council on Humanities, 1966–70; Urban Design Council, NYC, 1967–72; AIA Nat. Urban Policy Task Force, 1970–74; Nat. Council on Arts, 1981–84. Member: Nat. Acad. Design, 1965; Amer. Acad. Arts and Scis, 1967; AAIL, 1975 (Chancellor, 1978–80); Institut de France, 1983. Hon. RA 1993. Hon. Degrees include: Pennsylvania, Columbia, NY, Brown, Colorado, Chinese Univ. of Hong Kong, Amer. Univ. of Paris. Numerous awards including: Arnold Brunner Award, Nat. Inst. Arts and Letters, 1961; Medal of Honour, NY Chapter, AIA, 1963; Thomas Jefferson Meml Medal for Architecture, 1976; Gold Medal, AAAL, 1979; Gold Medal, AIA, 1979; La Grande Médaille d'Or L'Académie d'Architecture, France, 1981; Architectural Firm Award, AIA, 1968; Praemium Imperiale, US, 1989; Ambassador for the Arts Award, 1994; Gold Medal, Architectural Soc. of China, Beijing, 1994; Jerusalem Prize for Arts and Letters, 1994; Jacqueline Kennedy Onassis Medal, Municipal Arts Soc., NY, 1996. Medal of Liberty, US, 1986; Officier de La Légion d'Honneur, 1993; US Medal of Freedom, 1993.

PEIRCE, Rev. Canon (John) Martin; Canon Residentiary of Christ Church, Oxford, 1987–2001, now Canon Emeritus, and Oxford Diocesan Director of Ordinands, 1985–2001; *b* 9 July 1936; *s* of Martin Westley and Winifred Mary Peirce; *m* 1968, Rosemary Susan Milne; two *s. Educ:* Brentwood Sch.; Jesus Coll., Cambridge (MA); Westcott House, Cambridge. Served Royal Air Force, 1954–56. Teacher, St Stephen's Coll., Hong Kong, 1960–64; Curate, St John Baptist, Croydon, 1966–70; Team Vicar, St Columba, Fareham, 1970–76; Team Rector, Langley, Slough, 1976–85. *Recreations:* walking, gardening. *Address:* 8 Burwell Meadow, Witney, Oxon OX28 5JQ. *T:* (01993) 200103.

PEIRCE, Robert Nigel; HM Diplomatic Service; Consul-General, Los Angeles, since 2005; *b* 18 March 1955; *s* of Kenneth Frank Peirce and Margaret Peirce. *Educ:* Taunton Sch.; St Catherine's Coll., Oxford (MA); Faculty of Oriental Studies, Univ. of Cambridge. Joined FCO, 1977; Hong Kong, 1979–80; Peking, 1980–83; FCO, 1983–85; Cabinet Office, 1985–86; Dep. Political Advr, Hong Kong, 1986–88; Private Sec. to Sec. of State for Foreign and Commonwealth Affairs, 1988–90; UK Mission to UN, 1990–93; Political Advr to Governor, Hong Kong, 1993–97; RCDS, 1998; Sec., Ind. Commn on Policing for NI, 1998–99; Counsellor, Washington, 1999–2004. *Recreations:* family, friends, speculation. *Address:* c/o Foreign and Commonwealth Office, King Charles Street, SW1A 2AH. *Club:* Hong Kong (Hong Kong).

PEIRIS, Prof. (Joseph Sriyal) Malik, DPhil; FRCPath; FRS 2006; Professor, Department of Microbiology, University of Hong Kong; Scientific Director, HKU-Pasteur Research Centre; *b* Sri Lanka. *Educ:* Univ. of Ceylon (MB BS 1972); Univ. of Oxford (DPhil 1981). Dept. of Microbiol., Univ. of Peradeniya, 1982–88; virologist, Royal Victoria Infirmary, Newcastle upon Tyne, 1988–95; Univ. of Hong Kong, 1995–. Knight, Légion d'Honneur (France), 2007. *Publications:* articles in jls and chapters in books. *Address:* Department of Microbiology, University of Hong Kong, University Pathology Building, Queen Mary Hospital Compound, Pokfulam Road, Hong Kong.

PEIRSE, Sir Henry Grant de la Poer B.; *see* Beresford-Peirse.

PEIRSE, Air Vice-Marshal Sir Richard (Charles Fairfax), KCVO 1988; CB 1984; Registrar and Secretary, Order of the Bath, 2002–06; *b* 16 March 1931; *s* of late Air Chief Marshal Sir Richard Peirse, KCB, DSO, AFC and late Lady Peirse; *m* 1st, 1955, Karalie Grace Cox (marr. diss. 1963); two *d*; 2nd, 1963, Deirdre Mary O'Donovan (*d* 1976); (one *s* decd); 3rd, 1977, Anna Jill Margaret Long (*née* Latey). *Educ:* Bradfield Coll.; RAF Coll., Cranwell. Commnd 1952; 2nd TAF No 266 Sqdn and HQ 2 Gp, 1952; Flying Instructor, Cranwell, 1956; Air Staff No 23 Gp, 1960; Staff Coll., 1962; Flt Comdr No 39 Sqdn and OC Ops Wg, Luqa, Malta, 1963; Air Sec.'s Dept, 1965; jssc 1968; OC No 51 Sqdn, 1968; Dep. Captain, The Queen's Flight, 1969; RCDS 1972; OC RAF Waddington, 1973; Dep. Dir, Op Requirements, 1976; Dir of Personnel (Air), 1977; Dir of Op Requirements, 1980; AOC and Comdt, RAF Coll. Cranwell, 1982; Defence Services Sec., 1985–88, retd. Gentleman Usher of the Scarlet Rod, Order of the Bath, 1990–2002. *Recreations:* theatre, archaeology. *Address:* Bemerton House, Lower Bemerton, Salisbury, Wilts SP2 9NH. *T:* (01722) 321921. *Club:* Royal Air Force.

PELHAM, family name of **Earls of Chichester** and **Yarborough**.

PELHAM, Clare Elizabeth; Chief Executive, Judicial Appointments Commission, since 2006; *b* 11 May 1959; *m* 1983, Prof. David Barr; one *s* one *d. Educ:* London Sch. of Econs (BSc Econ 1980). Home Office: Principal, 1987–93; Hd, Efficiency and Consultancy, 1993–95; Hd, Police Strategy, 1995–97; Customer Satisfaction Mgr, IBM, 1997–98; Dir of Corporate Affairs, HM Prison Service, 1998–2001; Dir, Cabinet Office, 2001–02; Dir, Coca-Cola Co., GB and Ire., 2002–03; Sen. Dir, Rev. of Immigration Enforcement, Home Office, 2004; Dir, DCA, 2004–06. *Recreation:* chauffeuring teenagers round London. *Address:* Judicial Appointments Commission, Steel House, 11 Tothill Street, SW1H 9LJ; *e-mail:* clare.pelham@jac.gsi.gov.uk.

PELHAM, Hugh Reginald Brentnall, PhD; FRS 1988; Director, Medical Research Council Laboratory of Molecular Biology, Cambridge, since 2006 (Deputy Director, 1996–2006); *b* 26 Aug. 1954; *s* of late Reginald A. and Pauline M. Pelham; *m* 1st, 1976, Alison Slowe (marr. diss. 1989); 2nd, 1996, Mariann Bienz, *qv*; one *s* one *d. Educ:* Marlborough Coll., Wiltshire; Christ's Coll., Cambridge (MA, PhD). Research Fellow, Christ's Coll., 1978–84; Dept of Embryology, Carnegie Instn of Washington Baltimore, Md, 1979–81; Mem., Scientific Staff, MRC Lab. of Molecular Biol., Cambridge, 1981–, Hd, Cell Biol. Div., 1992–2006. Visitor, Univ. of Zürich, 1987–88. Mem., EMBO, 1985. Founder FMedSci 1998. Colworth Medal, Biochemical Soc., 1988; EMBO medal, 1989; Louis Jeantet Prize for Medicine, 1991; King Faisal Internat. Prize for Sci., 1996; Croonian Lecture and Medal, Royal Soc., 1999. *Publications:* papers in sci. jls on molecular and cell biology. *Address:* MRC Laboratory of Molecular Biology, Hills Road, Cambridge CB2 0QH. *T:* (01223) 248011.

PELHAM BURN, Angus Maitland; DL; Vice Lord-Lieutenant for Kincardineshire, 1978–2000; Director, Bank of Scotland, 1977–2000 (Director, 1973–2001, Chairman, 1977–2001, North Local Board); *b* 13 Dec. 1931; *s* of late Brig. Gen. H. Pelham Burn, CMG, DSO, and late Mrs K. E. S. Pelham Burn; *m* 1959, Anne R. Pelham Burn (*née* Forbes-Leith); four *d. Educ:* Harrow; N of Scotland Coll. of Agriculture. Hudson's Bay Co., 1951–58. Director: Aberdeen and Northern Marts Ltd, 1970–86 (Chm., 1974–86); Jessfield Ltd, 1970–88; Aberdeen Meat Marketing Co. Ltd, 1973–86 (Chm., 1974–86); Prime Space Design (Scotland) Ltd, 1981–87; Status Timber Systems, 1986–90; Skeendale Ltd, 1987–88; Abtrust Scotland Investment Co., 1989–96; Dana Petroleum plc, 1999–2008; Chairman and Director: MacRobert Farms (Douneside) Ltd, 1970–87; Pelett Administration Ltd, 1973–94; Taw Meat Co., 1984–86; Oilcats Ltd, 2006–07; Chairman: Aberdeen Asset Mgt (formerly Aberdeen Trust) plc, 1993–2000; Scottish Provident Instn, 1995–98 (Dir, 1975–98; Dep. Chm., 1991–95). Chm., Aberdeen Airport Consultative Cttee, 1986–; Mem., Accounts Commn, 1980–94 (Dep. Chm., 1992–94). Chm., Global Philanthropic Internat. Ltd, 2002–; Dir, Global Philanthropic Ops Pty Ltd, 2004–. Mem. Council, Winston Churchill Meml Trust, 1984–93; Dir., Aberdeen Assoc. for Prevention of Cruelty to Animals, 1975–95 (Chm., 1984–89). Pres., Aberdeen Br., Inst. of Marketing, 1987–90. Member: Kincardine CC, 1967–75 (Vice Convener, 1973–75); Grampian Regional Council, 1974–94. Member, Queen's Body Guard for Scotland (Royal Co. of Archers), 1968–. Hon. FInstM. JP Kincardine and Deeside, 1984–2005; DL Kincardineshire 1978. LlD Robert Gordon Univ., 1996. CStJ 1995 (OStJ 1978). *Recreations:* photography esp. wildlife, hill walking, vegetable gardening. *Address:* Kennels Cottage, Dess, Aboyne, Aberdeenshire AB34 5AY. *T:* (013398) 84445, *Fax:* (013398) 84430; *e-mail:* snow.bunting@virgin.net. *Clubs:* Sloane; Royal Northern (Aberdeen).

PELIZA, Sir Robert (John), KBE 1998 (OBE 1989); ED 1955; company director, since 1962; Speaker, House of Assembly, Gibraltar, 1989–96; *b* 16 Nov. 1920; *s* of late Robert Peliza; *m* 1950, Irma Risso; three *s* four *d. Educ:* Christian Brothers' Coll., Gibraltar. Served in Gibraltar Defence Force (now Royal Gibraltar Regt), 1939–61. Founder Mem., Integration with Britain Party (first leader), 1967; Chief Minister, 1969–72, apptd following Gen. Elections, 1969; elected MHA, 1969–84; Leader of the Opposition, 1972–73. Pres., Gibraltar Br., CPA, 1989–. Hon. Col, Gibraltar Regt, 1993–98. *Recreations:* walking, painting, reading, jogging, cycling, rowing. *Address:* 125 Beverley Drive, Edgware, Middlesex HA8 5NH. *T:* and *Fax:* (020) 8952 1712; *e-mail:* rjpeliza@pelizar.freeserve.co.uk.

PELL, His Eminence Cardinal George; *see* Sydney, Archbishop of, (RC).

PELL, Gordon Francis; Chairman, Regional Markets (formerly Chief Executive Director and Chairman, Retail Banking and Wealth Management), Royal Bank of Scotland Group, since 2001; Chief Executive, Coutts Group, since 2002; *b* 23 Feb. 1950; *s* of Denis and Anne Pell; *m* 1971, Marian Leak; two *s* one *d. Educ:* Wellington Coll.; Southampton Univ. (BA). FCIB; FCIBS. With Lloyds Bank, then Lloyds TSB, 1971–2000: Dir, Distribution, 1996–98; Gp Dir, Retail Banking, 1998–2000; Exec. Dir and Chief Exec., Retail Banking, Royal Bank of Scotland Gp, 2000–01. Dir, Race for Opportunity, 1998–; Member: Nat. Employment Panel, 2005–; FSA Practitioners' Panel, 2006–. FRSA 1999. *Recreations:* riding, opera. *Address:* Regional Markets, Royal Bank of Scotland, 280 Bishopsgate, EC2M 4RB.

PELLEREAU, Maj.-Gen. Peter John Mitchell, MA, CEng, FIMechE, FIMgt; Secretary, Association of Consulting Engineers, 1977–87; *b* Quetta, British India, 24 April 1921; *s* of late Col J. C. E. Pellereau, OBE and Mrs A. N. V. Pellereau (*née* Betham); *m* 1949, Rosemary, *e d* of late S. R. Garnar; two *s. Educ:* Wellington Coll.; Trinity Coll., Cambridge (BA 1942, MA 1957). Commnd into Royal Engrs, 1942; War Service in NW Europe, 1944–45; OC 26 Armd Engr Sqdn, RE, 1946; ptsc, psc, 1950–51; Sec., Defence Research Policy Cttee, 1960; Asst Mil. Sec., WO, 1961; CO 131 Parachute Engr Regt RE TA, 1963; Mil. Dir of Studies, RMCS, 1965; Asst Dir RE Equipment Devel t, 1967; Sen. Mil. Officer, Royal Armament R&D Estabt, 1970; Vice-Pres., 1973–75, Pres., 1975–76, Ordnance Board; retired 1976. Hon. Col, RE (Vol.) (Explosive Ordnance Disposal), 1980–86. Liveryman: Worshipful Co. of Plumbers, 1977–92; Worshipful Co. of Engineers, 1984–92. Mem., Smeatonian Soc. of Civil Engineers, 1981– (Pres., 2002). Vice-Pres., Surrey Hockey Umpires' Assoc., 1979–85; Pres., Oxted Hockey Club, 1975–84. Mem., Wolfe Soc. Cttee, 1978– (Vice Pres., 2007); Chm., Westerham Motorway Action Gp, 1993–2001. *Recreation:* golf. *Address:* Woodmans Folly, Crockham Hill, Edenbridge, Kent TN8 6RJ. *T:* and *Fax:* (01732) 866309.

PELLEW, family name of **Viscount Exmouth**.

PELLEW, Dr Jill Hosford; Vice-President, GrenzebachGlier Europe, 2000–07; *b* 29 April 1942; *d* of late Prof. Frank Thistlethwaite, CBE and Jane (*née* Hosford); *m* 1965, Mark Edward Pellew, *qv*; two *s. Educ:* Cambs High Sch. for Girls; St Hilda's Coll., Oxford (BA 1964; MA 1968); Queen Mary Coll., London (MA 1970); PhD London 1976. MoD, 1964–66; part-time univ. teaching, Univ. of Saigon, Univ. of Sussex, Hollins Coll., Va, American Univ., Washington, 1967–89; Exec. Sec., Chatham Hse Foundn, Washington, 1984–89; Develt Officer, St Hilda's Coll., Oxford, 1989–90; Dir of Develt, Imperial Coll. of Science, Technology and Medicine, London, 1991–94; Dir, Develt Office, Univ. of Oxford, 1994–99; Fellow, Trinity Coll., Oxford, 1995–99. Mem., Council, British Sch. at Rome, 2003–; Mem. Adv. Council and Trustee, Inst. Historical Res., Univ. of London, 2005–; Trustee: Council for Advancement and Support of Educn (Europe), 1996–99; Estorick Foundn, 1999–; Schola Cantorum of Oxford, 2003–. *Publications:* The Home Office 1848–1914: from clerks to bureaucrats, 1982; (ed with S. Cassese) The Comparative History of Public Administration: the merit system, 1987; (ed with D. Cannadine) History and Philanthropy: past, present, future, 2008; various articles in learned jls on admin. hist. *Recreations:* reading, listening to music, entertaining family and friends. *Address:* 51 St George's Square, SW1V 3QN. *Club:* Reform.

PELLEW, Mark Edward, CVO 2000 (LVO 1980); HM Diplomatic Service, retired; Chief Executive to the Secretary General, Anglican Communion, 2002–05; *b* 28 Aug. 1942; *e s* of late Comdr Anthony Pownoll Pellew, RN retd, and of Margaret Julia

Critchley (*née* Cookson); *m* 1965, Jill Hosford Thistlethwaite (*see* J. H. Pellew); two *s*. *Educ:* Winchester; Trinity Coll., Oxford (BA). Entered HM Diplomatic Service, 1965; FO, 1965–67; Third Sec., Singapore, 1967–69; Second Sec., Saigon, 1969–70; FCO, 1970–76; First Sec., Rome, 1976–80; Asst Head of Personnel Ops Dept, FCO, 1981–83; Counsellor: Washington, 1983–89; on secondment to Hambros Bank, 1989–91; Head of N America Dept, FCO, 1991–96; Ambassador to the Holy See, 1998–2002. Chm., Hosting for Overseas Students, 2005–. *Recreations:* singing, playing the horn. *Address:* 51 St George's Square, SW1V 3QN. *Club:* Hurlingham.

See also R. A. Pellew.

PELLEW, Robin Anthony, OBE 2006; PhD; Chief Executive, National Trust for Scotland, 2001–06; *b* 27 Sept. 1945; *s* of late Comdr Anthony Pownoll Pellew, RN and Margaret Julia Critchley (*née* Cookson); *m* 1974, Pamela Daphne Gibson MacLellan; one *s* one *d*. *Educ:* Marlborough Coll.; Edinburgh Univ. (BSc 1968); University College London (MSc 1972; PhD 1981). Sen. Res. Scientist, Serengeti Res. Inst., Tanzania, 1973–78; BBC Natural History Unit, 1978–79; Res. Fellow, Physiology Lab., Cambridge, 1979–82; Cambridge University Press: Sen. Editor, 1982–86; Editorial Manager, 1986–87; Dir, Conservation Monitoring Centre, IUCN, 1987–88; Dir, World Conservation Monitoring Centre, Cambridge, 1988–93; Dir and Chief Exec., WWF-World Wide Fund for Nature, 1994–99; Chief Exec., Animal Health Trust, 1999–2001. Member: Envmt Cttee, RSA, 1993–98; UK Round Table on Sustainable Develt, 1995–99; Conservation and Science Cttee, 1997–2001, Inst. of Zool. Cttee, 1997–2001, Zool. Soc. of London. *Publications:* numerous scientific papers on wild life management and conservation in professional jls. *Recreations:* travel, watching wild life. *Address:* 32 Selwyn Gardens, Cambridge CB3 9AY.

See also M. E. Pellew.

PELLING, Andrew John; MP (C) Croydon Central, since 2005; *b* 20 Aug. 1959; *s* of Anthony Adair Pelling, *qv*; *m* Sanae (marr. diss.); one *s* two *d*; *m* 2006, Lucy Slaytor. *Educ:* New Coll., Oxford (MA PPE; Sec. and Librarian, Oxford Union Soc., 1979–80; Pres., Cons. Assoc., 1980). Croydon Borough Council: Mem. (C), 1982–2006; Chm., Educn, 1988–94; Dep. Leader, 1996–2002, Leader, 2002–05, Cons. Gp. Greater London Authority: Mem. (C) Croydon and Sutton, London Assembly, 2000–08; Cons. spokesman on London business, 2000–04; Chm., Audit Panel, 2001–04; Mem., Private Investment Commn, 2002–04; London Assembly: Chairman: Graffiti Investigative Cttee, 2001–02; Public Services Cttee, 2002–04; Budget Cttee, 2004–05. Member: Croydon Police Consultative Cttee, 2000–; LSC, London S, 2001–04. Mem., CATE, 1990–94. Mem., S Wandle Valley Partnership, 2001–05. *Recreations:* children, Jack Russells. *Address:* House of Commons, SW1A 0AA.

PELLING, Anthony Adair; President, Byrd Theatre Foundation, Richmond, since 2002; *b* 3 May 1934; *s* of Brian and Alice Pelling; *m* 1st, 1958, Margaret Lightfoot (*d* 1986); one *s* one *d*; 2nd, 1989, Virginia Glen-Calvert. *Educ:* Purley Grammar Sch.; London Sch. of Economics. BSc (Econ); MIPM. National Coal Board, 1957–67; entered MPBW as Principal, 1967; Asst Sec., 1970, Under Sec., 1981, DoE; seconded as Dep. Dir, Business in the Community, 1981–83; Dept of Transport, 1983–85; London Regional Dir, DoE, 1987–91; Dir, Construction Policy, DoE, 1991–93. Dir, GJW Government Relations Ltd, London and Washington, 1993–95. Pres., ESU, Richmond, 1998–2000; Chm., Region IV, and Mem. Nat. Bd, US ESU, 2000–02; Mem. Bd, Guardian Foundn, United Methodist Family Services, VA, 2007–. *Recreations:* music, theatre. *Address:* 70 West Square Drive, Richmond, VA 23238–6158, USA; *e-mail:* gjw1995pel@aol.com. *Clubs:* Reform; Kiwanis (Richmond, VA).

See also A. J. Pelling.

PELLING, Prof. Christopher Brendan Reginald, DPhil; Regius Professor of Greek, University of Oxford, and Student of Christ Church, Oxford, since 2003; *b* 14 Dec. 1947; *s* of Reginald Charles Pelling and (Frances Lilian) Brenda Pelling; *m* 1973, Margaret Ann Giddy; one *s* one *d* (and one *s* decd). *Educ:* Balliol Coll., Oxford (BA 1970); Christ Church, Oxford (DPhil 1975). Res. Fellow, Peterhouse, Cambridge, 1972–74; Lectr, 1974–75, McConnell Laing Fellow and Praelector in Classics, 1975–2003, University Coll., Oxford. Adjunct Prof. of Hist., Utah State Univ., 1998–; Visiting Professor: Washington and Lee Univ., Lexington, Va, 1986, 1989, 1997, 2000; Univ. of N Carolina, Chapel Hill, 2002. *Publications:* Plutarch: life of Antony, 1988; (ed) Characterization and Individuality in Greek Literature, 1990; (ed) Greek Tragedy and the Historian, 1997; Literary Texts and the Greek Historian, 2000; Plutarch and History, 2002; articles in learned jls. *Recreations:* cricket, golf, music, conviviality. *Address:* Christ Church, Oxford OX1 1DP. *T:* (01865) 276204, *Fax:* (01865) 276150; *e-mail:* chris.pelling@chch.ox.ac.uk. *Club:* MCC.

PELLING, (Philip) Mark; QC 2003; **His Honour Judge Pelling;** a Specialist Chancery Senior Circuit Judge, since 2006; *b* 27 June 1956; *s* of Philip Clive and Jean Rosemary Pelling; *m* 1986, Charlotte Jones; one *s* one *d*. *Educ:* Bancroft's Sch., Woodford Green; King's Coll., London (LLB; AKC). Called to the Bar, Middle Temple, 1979; Accredited Mediator, CEDR, 2000; a Recorder, 2004–06. Board of Governors, Ravensbourne College of Design and Communication, London: Mem., 1992–2000; Chm., Audit Cttee, 1994–95; Chm., Standing Cttee, 1995–97; Chm., 1997–2000. *Publication:* (with R. A. Purdie) Matrimonial and Domestic Injunctions, 1982, 2nd edn 1987. *Recreations:* sailing, flying, shooting. *Address:* Manchester Civil Justice Centre, 1 Bridge Street West, Manchester M60 9DJ. *Clubs:* Royal Western Yacht; Royal Plymouth Corinthian Yacht.

PELLING, Rowan Dorothy; Founding Editor, Erotic Review, 1996–2004; *b* 17 Jan. 1968; *d* of Ronald and Hazel Pelling; *m* 1995, Angus MacKinnon; one *s*. *Educ:* Walthamstow Hall, Sevenoaks; St Hugh's Coll., Oxford. Columnist, Independent on Sunday, 2000–. Dir, Dedalus Ltd. Judge, Man Booker Prize, 2004. *Publications:* The Erotic Review Bedside Companion, 2000; (ed) The Decadent Handbook, 2006. *Recreations:* cinema, gossip, rocking horses, buying vintage underwear, naked river swimming at Newnham swimming club. *Address:* *e-mail:* rowan@pelling.demon.co.uk. *Clubs:* Chelsea Arts, Academy, Blacks.

PELLY, Deborah Susan; *see* Mattinson, D. S.

PELLY, Derek Roland, (Derk); Deputy Chairman, Barclays Bank PLC, 1986–88 (Vice Chairman, 1984–85); *b* 12 June 1929; *s* of late Arthur Roland Pelly and Elsie Pelly; *m* 1953, Susan Roberts; one *s* two *d*. *Educ:* Marlborough; Trinity Coll., Cambridge. Served RA, 1947–49 (2nd Lieut). Entered Barclays Bank, 1952; Local Director: Chelmsford, 1959; Luton, 1969; Vice Chm., 1977–85, Chm., 1986–87, Barclays Internat. Ltd. Dir, The Private Bank & Trust Co., 1989–94. Member: Milton Keynes Develt Corp., 1976–85; Council, ODI, 1984–89. Mem. Cttee, Family Assce Soc., 1988–91. Dir, Chelmsford Dio. Bd of Finance, 1989–96. Governor: London House for Overseas Graduates, 1985–91; Chelmsford Coll., 1994–95. *Recreation:* painting. *Address:* Kenbank, St John's Town of Dalry, Kirkcudbrightshire DG7 3TX. *T:* (01644) 430424.

PELLY, Sir Richard (John), 7th Bt *cr* 1840, of Upton, Essex; farmer, since 1991; *b* 10 April 1951; *s* of Richard Heywood Pelly, 2nd *s* of Sir Alwyne Pelly, 5th Bt, MC and of Mary Elizabeth Pelly (*née* Luscombe); *S* uncle, 1993; *m* 1983, Clare Gemma Dove; three *s*. *Educ:* Wellington Coll., Berks; Wadham Coll., Oxford (BA Agriculture and Forestry Science). ACA 1978–82. Price Waterhouse, London, 1974–78; Birds Eye Foods Ltd, 1978–81; New Century Software Ltd, 1981–99. *Recreation:* hunting. *Heir:* *s* Anthony Alwyne Pelly, *b* 30 Oct. 1984. *Address:* The Manor House, Preshaw, Upham, Southampton SO32 1HP. *T:* (01962) 771757.

PEMBER, Susan Alison, OBE 2000; Director, Further Education and Learning and Skills Performance Group (formerly Adult Basic Skills Strategy Group, then Apprenticeships and Skills for Life), Department for Innovation, Universities and Skills (formerly Department for Education and Skills), since 2000; *b* 23 Dec. 1954; *d* of Bernard Pember and Muriel Pember; one *s*; *m* 1996, Brian Hudgell. *Educ:* Glamorgan Coll. of Educn (Cert Ed); Poly. of Wales, Pontypridd (BEd Univ. of Wales). Lectr, Redbridge Coll., 1977–83; Sen. Lectr, Southgate Coll., 1983–86; Educn Officer, 1986–87, Sen. Educn Officer, 1987–91, London Bor. of Enfield; Principal, Canterbury Coll., 1991–2000. *Recreations:* textiles, ski-ing, gardening. *Address:* Department for Innovation, Universities and Skills, Sanctuary Buildings, Great Smith Street, SW1P 3BT. *T:* (020) 7925 6978.

PEMBERTON; *see* Leigh-Pemberton, family name of Baron Kingsdown.

PEMBERTON, Col Alan Brooke, CVO 1988; MBE 1960; *b* 11 Sept. 1923; *s* of Eric Harry Pemberton (Canadian by birth) and Phyllis Edith Pemberton (*née* Brooke-Alder); *m* 1952, Pamela Kirkland Smith, of Winnipeg, Canada; two *s*. *Educ:* Uppingham School; Trinity College, Cambridge. Commissioned Coldstream Guards, 1942; war service in Italy and NW Europe; ADC to Earl Alexander of Tunis, Governor-General of Canada, 1951–52; ADC to Gen. Sir Gerald Templer, High Comr to Malaya, 1952–53; Commanded 1st Bn Coldstream Guards, 1963–66; Regtl Lt-Col, 1966–67; retired 1967 (Hon. Col). Queen's Body Guard, Yeomen of the Guard: Exon, 1967; Ensign; Clerk of the Cheque; Lieutenant, 1985–93. Chm. and Man. Dir, Diversified Corporate Services Ltd, 1970–85. Special Constable, A Div., Metropolitan Police, 1975–76. *Recreations:* reading, travel. *Address:* Searchers, Wildmoor, Sherfield-on-Loddon, Hook, Hants RG27 0HQ. *Club:* Boodle's.

PEMBERTON, Sir Francis (Wingate William), Kt 1976; CBE 1970; DL; FRICS; company director; *b* 1 Oct. 1916; *s* of late Dr William Warburton Wingate (assumed Arms of Pemberton, by Royal Licence, 1921) and Viola Patience Campbell Pemberton; *m* 1st, 1941, Diana Patricia (*d* 1999), *e d* of late Reginald Salisbury Woods, MD, and Irene Woods, CBE, TD; two *s*, 2nd, 2002, Mrs Mary Dadd. *Educ:* Eton; Trinity Coll., Cambridge (MA). Senior Consultant, Bidwells, Chartered Surveyors, 1980–89. Director: Agricultural Mortgage Corp. Ltd, 1969–91; Barclays Bank UK Ltd, 1977–81; Severn Trent Property Ltd, 1990–95. Chm. Adv. Cttee, Inst. of Animal Physiology and Genetics Res. (Cambridge and Edinburgh), 1983–90; Hon. Dir, Royal Show, 1963–68; Royal Agricultural Society of England: Mem. Council, 1951– (Pres., 1974–75, Dep. Pres., 1975–76); Chm. Exec. Bd, 1969–71; Trustee, 1969–; Gold Medal for distinguished services to agric., 1989. Trustee, Robinson Coll., Cambridge, 1973–85. Member: Water Resources Board, 1964–74; Winston Churchill Meml Trust, 1965–80; Economic Planning Council for East Anglia, 1965–74; National Water Council, 1974–81; Water Authorities Superannuation Pension Fund (Dep. Chm., Fund Management and Policy Cttee), 1983–89. High Sheriff, Cambridgeshire and Isle of Ely, 1965–66; DL Cambs, 1979. *Address:* The Flat, Trumpington Hall, Cambridge CB2 9LH. *T:* (01223) 841941. *Club:* Farmers'.

PEMBERTON, Gary Milton, AC 1999; Chairman, Racing NSW, since 2004; *s* of Eric Pemberton; *m* Margaret Whitford; four *c*. *Educ:* Fort Street High Sch. Australian Wool Bd, 1961–72; joined Brambles Industries Ltd, 1972: Chief Exec., 1982–93; Dep. Chm., 1994–96; Chairman: Qantas Airways Ltd, 1993–2000; TAB Ltd, 1997–2002; Billabong International, 2002–06; Director: Commonwealth Bank, 1989–93; John Fairfax Hldgs Ltd, 1992–93; CSR Ltd, 1993–94. Chief Exec. Officer, 1994–95, Pres., 1995–96, Sydney Organising Cttee of the Olympic Games.

PEMBERTON, Prof. John, MD London; FRCP, FFPH; DPH Leeds; Professor of Social and Preventive Medicine, The Queen's University, Belfast, 1958–76; *b* 18 Nov. 1912; British; *m* 1937, Winifred Ethel Gray; three *s*. *Educ:* Christ's Hospital; University College and UCH, London. House Physician and House Surgeon, University College Hospital, 1936–37; Rowett Research Institute under the late Lord Boyd Orr, 1937–39; Rockefeller Travelling Fellow in Medicine, Harvard, Mass., USA, 1954–55; Director of MRC Group for research on Respiratory Disease and Air Pollution, and Reader in Social Medicine, University of Sheffield, 1955–58. Mem., Health Educn Council, DHSS, 1973–76. Co-founder, Internat. Epidemiol Assoc., 1957. Milroy Lectr, RCP, 1976. *Publications:* (with W. Hobson) The Health of the Elderly at Home, 1954; (ed) Recent Studies in Epidemiology, 1958; (ed) Epidemiology: Reports on Research and Teaching, 1963; Will Pickles of Wensleydale, 1970; articles in Lancet, BMJ, etc. *Recreations:* reading, TV, walking, painting. *Address:* Iona, Cannon Fields, Hathersage, Hope Valley S32 1AG.

PEMBROKE, 18th Earl of, *cr* 1551, **AND MONTGOMERY,** 15th Earl of, *cr* 1605; **William Alexander Sidney Herbert;** Baron Herbert of Cardiff, 1551; Baron Herbert of Shurland, 1605; Baron Herbert of Lea (UK); *b* 18 May 1978; *s* of 17th Earl of Pembroke and Montgomery, and Claire Rose Herbert (*née* Pelly); S father, 2003. *Educ:* Bryanston Sch.; Sheffield Hallam Univ. (1st cl. Hons Industrial Design). Two years as product designer, Conran & Partners. Runs Wilton Estate. *Recreations:* scuba diving, ski-ing.

PEÑA, Paco; musician; flamenco guitar player, since 1954; Professor of Flamenco, Rotterdam Conservatory, since 1985; *b* 1 June 1942; *s* of Antonio Peña and Rosario Perez; *m* 1982, Karin Vaessen; two *d*. *Educ:* Córdoba, Spain. London début, 1968; New York début, 1983; founded: Paco Peña Flamenco Co., 1970; Centro Flamenco Paco Peña, Córdoba, 1981; composed Misa Flamenca, 1991, Requiem for the Earth, 2004; produced Musa Gitana, 1999, Voces y Ecos, 2002. Ramón Montoya Prize, 1983. Officer, Order of Merit (Spain), 1997. *Address:* c/o MPM London, 1 Prince of Wales Road, NW5 3LW. *T:* (020) 7681 7475, (020) 7681 7476; c/o Karin Vaessen, 4 Boscastle Road, NW5 1EG. *Fax:* (020) 7485 2320.

PENDER, 3rd Baron *cr* 1937; **John Willoughby Denison-Pender;** Joint Chairman, Bremar Trust Ltd, 1977–83; Chairman, J. J. L. D. Frost plc, 1983–84; *b* 6 May 1933; *s* of 2nd Baron Pender, CBE and Camilla Lethbridge (*d* 1988), *o d* of late Willoughby Arthur Pemberton; *S* father, 1965; *m* 1962, Julia, *yr d* of Richard Nevill Cannon; one *s* two *d*. *Educ:* Eton. Formerly Lieut, 10th Royal Hussars and Captain, City of London Yeomanry (TA). Dir, Globe Investment Trust Ltd. Vice Pres., Royal Sch. for Deaf Children, 1992– (Treas., 1999–2004). Steward: Folkestone Racecourse, 1985–2003; Lingfield Park, 1989–2003. *Heir:* *s* Hon. Henry John Richard Denison-Pender [*b* 19 March 1968; *m* 1994, Vanessa, *d* of John Eley, NSW, Australia; one *s* one *d*]. *Address:* North Court, Tilmanstone,

Kent CT14 0JP. *T:* (01304) 611726. *Clubs:* White's, Pratt's.
See also Viscount Esher.

PENDER, David James; Sheriff of North Strathclyde, since 1995; *b* 7 Sept. 1949; *s* of James and Isa Pender; *m* 1974, Elizabeth Jean McKillop; two *s* two *d. Educ:* Queen's Park Sen. Secondary Sch., Glasgow; Edinburgh Univ. (LLB Hons). Qualified as Solicitor, 1973; Partner, MacArthur Stewart, Solicitors, Oban, 1977–95. Sec., Oban Faculty of Solicitors, 1977–95. *Recreations:* travel, bridge, reading. *Address:* Sheriff's Chambers, Paisley Sheriff Court, St James Street, Paisley PA3 2HW. *T:* (0141) 887 5291.

PENDER, Simon Charles; Sheriff of North Strathclyde at Dumbarton, since 2004; *b* 23 June 1953; *s* of Robert R. E. Pender and Jean Elisabeth (*née* Haddow); *m* 1984, Linda Jeanne Miller; two *s* two *d. Educ:* Trinity Coll., Glenalmond; Univ. of Heidelberg; Univ. of Edinburgh (LLB). Solicitor, 1976–99: Partner: Breeze Paterson & Chapman, 1980–95; Dundas & Wilson, CS, 1995–99; Temp. Sheriff, 1995–99; Sheriff of S Strathclyde, Dumfries and Galloway at Hamilton, 1999–2004. Mem., Royal Scottish Pipers' Soc. *Recreations:* sailing, playing the great Highland bagpipe, ski-ing and various other sports, including golf, shooting and cycling. *Address:* Sheriff Court House, Church Street, Dumbarton G82 1QR. *T:* (01389) 763266; *e-mail:* sheriff.scpender@scotcourts.gov.uk. *Clubs:* Glasgow Highland; Royal Northern and Clyde Yacht, Mudhook Yacht.

PENDERECKI, Krzysztof; Rector, State Academy of Music, Kraków, 1972–87; Professor of Composition, School of Music, Yale University, New Haven, Conn, 1973–78; *b* Debica, Poland, 23 Nov. 1933; *s* of Tadeusz Penderecki and Zofia Penderecki; *m* 1965, Elzbieta Solecka; one *s* one *d. Educ:* State Acad. of Music, Kraków, Poland (Graduate 1958). Compositions include: Threnody to the Victims of Hiroshima, 1960 (52 strings); Passion According to St Luke, 1965–66 (oratorio); Dies irae, 1967; Utrenja, 1969–71 (oratorio); Devils of Loudon, 1969 (opera); Cello Concerto No 1, 1971–72; First Symphony, 1972; Magnificat, 1974 (oratorio); Awakening of Jacob, 1974 (orchestra); Paradise Lost, 1976–78 (rappresentazione for Chicago Lyric Opera; Milton libretto, Christopher Fry); Violin Concerto, 1977; Te Deum, 1979–80; (Christmas) Symphony No 2, 1980; Lacrimosa, 1980; Agnus Dei (for chorus a cappella), 1981; Cello Concerto No 2, 1982 (Grammy Award, Nat. Acad. of Recording Arts and Scis, 1988); Viola Concerto, 1983; Polish Requiem, 1983–84; Die schwarze Maske, 1986 (opera); Veni creator and Song of Cherubin (for chorus a cappella), 1987; Das unterbrochene Gedanke (for string quartet), 1988; Symphony No 3, 1988–95; Symphony No 4, 1989; Ubu Rex, 1991 (opera); Symphony No 5, 1991–92; Sinfonietta per archi, 1992; Flute Concerto, 1992–93; Quartet for clarinet and string trio, 1993; Violin Concerto No 2, 1995 (Grammy Award, 1999); Seven Gates of Jerusalem (oratorio), 1997; Credo (oratorio), 1998; Sextett, 2000; Concerto grosso per tre violocelli, 2000; Concerto per pianoforte e orch., 2001; Concerto grosse No 2 per 5 clarinetti, 2004; Largo per violoncello ed orchestra, 2003; Symphony No 8, Lieder der Vergänglichkeit, 2005–07. Hon. Professor: Moscow Tchaikovsky Conservatory, 1997; Beijing Conservatory. Hon. Dr: Univ. of Rochester, NY; St Olaf Coll., Northfield, Minn; Katholieke Univ., Leuven; Univ. of Bordeaux; Georgetown Univ., Washington; Univ. of Belgrade; Universidad Autónoma, Madrid; Adam Mickiewicz Univ.; Warsaw Univ.; Acad. of Music, Cracow and Warsaw; Univ. of Glasgow; Duquesne Univ., Pittsburgh. Member: RAM (Hon.); Akad. der Künste, Berlin (Extraordinary); Akad. der Künste der DDR, Berlin (Corresp.); Kungl. Musikaliska Akad., Stockholm; Accad. Nazionale di Santa Cecilia, Rome (Hon.); Acad. Nacional de Bellas Artes, Buenos Aires (Corresp.); Royal Acad. of Music, Dublin; Akad. der schönen Künste, Munich (Corresp.); Hon. Foreign Mem., Amer. Acad. Arts and Letters. Grosser Kunstpreis des Landes Nordrhein-Westfalen, 1966; Prix Italia, 1967/68; Gottfried von Herder Preis der Stiftung FvS zu Hamburg, 1977; Prix Arthur Honegger, 1977; Sibelius Prize, Wihouri Foundn, 1983; Premio Lorenzo Magnifico, 1985; Wolf Prize, 1987; Manuel de Falla Gold Medal, Accademia de Bellas Artes, Granada, 1989; Grawemeyer Award, Univ. of Louisville, 1992; Internat. Music Council/UNESCO Prize for Music, 1993; Prime Time Emmy Award, Acad. of Television Arts and Scis, 1995 and 1996; Crystall Award, Econ. Forum, Davos, 1997; Music Award, City of Duisburg, 1999; Cannes Classical Award, 2000; Prince of Asturios Award, 2001; Praemium Imperiale, 2004. Das Grosse Verdienstkreuz des Verdienstordens (Germany), 1990. *Publications:* all works published. *Recreations:* dendrology, gardening. *Address:* Schott Musik International, Concert Opera Media Division, Weihergarten 5, 55116 Mainz, Germany. *T:* (6131) 2460, *Fax:* (6131) 246250.

PENDERED, Richard Geoffrey; Chairman, Bunge & Co., 1987–90; *b* 26 Sept. 1921; *s* of Richard Dudley Pendered and Adèle Pendered (*née* Hall); *m* 1953, Jennifer Preston Mead; two *s* two *d. Educ:* Winchester College (Scholar); Magdalene College (Scholar). GCCS Bletchley, 1940–52 (renamed GCHQ); Bunge & Co., 1952–90, Dir, 1957, Man. Dir, 1963–86. *Recreations:* fishing, shooting, golf. *Address:* Wildcroft, The Hollow, West Chiltington, Pulborough, W Sussex RH20 2QA.

PENDLEBURY, Edward; Assistant Under Secretary of State (Sales Administration), Ministry of Defence, 1983–85, retired; *b* 5 March 1925; *s* of Thomas Cecil Pendlebury and Alice (*née* Sumner); *m* 1957, Joan Elizabeth Bell; one *s. Educ:* King George V Sch., Southport; Magdalen Coll., Oxford (MA). Served War, RNVR, 1943–46. Asst Principal, Min. of Food, 1949–53; Principal: MAFF, 1953–56; MoD (British Defence Staff, Washington), 1956–60; MAFF, 1960–66; Asst Secretary: DEA, 1966–70; MoD, 1970–80; Exec. Dir (Civilian Management), MoD, 1980–83. *Recreations:* gramophone, gazing. *Address:* 11 Newlands Court, Evesham Road, Stow-on-the-Wold, Glos GL54 1HN.

PENDLEBURY, Graham; Director, Environment and International, Department for Transport, since 2007; *b* 7 Oct. 1958; *s* of Alan Pendlebury and Margaret Elizabeth Pendlebury (*née* Moore); *m* 1991, Jill Amanda Thatcher; one *s. Educ:* Bolton Sch. (Boys' Div.); Sidney Sussex Coll., Cambridge (MA Hons Hist. 1981). Entered Civil Service, 1984; grad. trainee, 1986–90; Grade 7, Cabinet Office, then Dept of Transport, then DETR, 1990–99; Hd, Policy Strategy Integration Div., DETR, then DTLR, 1999–2001; Hd, Aviation Envmtl Div., DTLR, then DfT, 2001–04; Dir, Road and Vehicle Safety and Standards, DfT, 2004–07. *Publication:* Aspects of the English Civil War in Bolton and its Neighbourhood 1640–1660, 1983. *Recreations:* history, reading, walking, playing with my son, fretting about Bolton Wanderers FC. *Address:* Department for Transport, Great Minster House, 76 Marsham Street, SW1P 4DR. *T:* (020) 7944 6050; *e-mail:* graham.pendlebury@dft.gsi.gov.uk.

PENDOWER, John Edward Hicks, FRCS; Dean, Charing Cross and Westminster Medical School, 1989–93; *b* 6 Aug. 1927; *s* of Thomas Curtis Hicks Pendower and Muriel May Pendower (*née* Newbury); *m* 1st, 1960, Kate Tuohy (*d* 1987); one *s* two *d*; 2nd, 1989, Mrs Paulette Gleave. *Educ:* Dulwich College; King's College London; Charing Cross Hosp. Med. Sch. (MB BS (Hons Med.) 1950). FRCS 1955. Called to the Bar, Inner Temple, 1972. Served RAMC. Charing Cross Hosp. and St Mark's Hosp., 1950–62; Harvey Cushing Fellow, Harvard Med. Sch., 1959–60; Consultant Surgeon: Mayday Hosp., Croydon, 1964–89; Charing Cross Hosp., 1965–87 (Vice Dean, 1979–84; Sub Dean, Charing Cross and Westminster Med. Sch., 1984–87); former examr in surgery, London Univ. Mem., Hammersmith and Fulham, subseq. Riverside, HA, 1983–90. Special Trustee, Charing Cross Hosp.; Chm. Trustees, Sargent Cancer Care for Children (formerly Malcolm Sargent Cancer Fund for Children), 1992–2001 (Trustee, 1988–92). *Recreations:* formerly squash rackets, now walking; collecting campaign medals. *Address:* 2 Brockham Warren, Boxhill Road, Tadworth, Surrey KT20 7JX. *T:* 01737 843108.

PENDRED, Piers Loughnan; Director General, International Psychoanalytical Association, 2000–07; *b* 24 Aug. 1943; *s* of Loughnan Wildig Pendred and Dulcie Treen Hall; *m* 1973, Carol Ann Haslam; one *s* one *d. Educ:* Ardingly College; Trinity Hall, Cambridge (MA Fine Arts and Architecture). VSO teacher, S India, 1965–67; British Council, 1967–99: Television Officer, Sudan, 1967–69, Ethiopia, 1969–71; TV Training Officer, London, 1972–76; Head of Production, 1976–81; Dir, Design, Production and Publishing, 1981–84; Dir, Press and Inf., 1984–87; Controller, later Dir of Finance, 1987–94; Special Asst to Dir-Gen., 1994–95; Asst Dir-Gen., 1996–99. Sen. Exec. Programme, London Business Sch., 1987. Trustee, Centre for Internat. Briefing, 1996–99.

PENDRY, family name of **Baron Pendry.**

PENDRY, Baron *cr* 2001 (Life Peer), of Stalybridge in the County of Greater Manchester; **Thomas Pendry;** PC 2000; *b* 10 June 1934; *m* 1966, Moira Anne Smith (separated 1983); one *s* one *d. Educ:* St Augustine's, Ramsgate; Oxford Univ. RAF, 1955–57. Full time official, Nat. Union of Public Employees, 1960–70; Mem., Paddington Borough Council, 1962–65; Chm., Derby Labour Party, 1966. MP (Lab) Stalybridge and Hyde, 1970–2001. An Opposition Whip, 1971–74; a Lord Comr of the Treasury and Govt Whip, 1974, resigned 1977; Parly Under-Sec. of State, NI Office, 1978–79; Opposition spokesman on NI, 1979–81, on overseas development, 1981–82, on regional affairs and devolution, 1982–84, on sport and tourism, 1992–97. Member: Select Cttee on Envmt, 1987–92; Select Cttee on Members' Interests, 1987–92. Founder Mem., and Chm., 1980–92, All Party Football Gp; Chairman: All Party Tourism Gp; All Party Sports Cttee. Member: Speaker's Conf., 1973; UK delegn to WEU and Council of Europe, 1973–75. Pres., Football Foundn, 2003– (Chm., 1999–2003); Chm., Football Trust, 1997–99. Steward, British Boxing Bd of Control, 1987–. President: Stalybridge Public Band; Music Users Council, 1997–; Patron, Nat. Fedn of Football Supporters, 1998–. Freeman, Bor. of Tameside and Lordship of Mottram in Longendale, 1995. *Recreations:* sport; football, cricket, boxing (sometime Middleweight Champion, Hong Kong; boxed for Oxford Univ.). *Address:* House of Lords, SW1A 0PW. *Clubs:* Royal Air Force, MCC, Lord's Taverners; Vincent's (Oxford).

PENDRY, Sir John (Brian), Kt 2004; PhD; FRS 1984; Professor of Theoretical Solid State Physics, Department of Physics, Imperial College of Science, Technology and Medicine, University of London, since 1981 (Head, Department of Physics, 1998–2001); Dean, Royal College of Science, 1993–96; *b* 4 July 1943; *s* of Frank Johnson Pendry and Kathleen (*née* Shaw); *m* 1977, Patricia Gard. *Educ:* Downing Coll., Cambridge (MA; PhD 1969; Hon. Fellow, 2005). Res. Fellow in Physics, Downing Coll., Cambridge, 1969–72; Mem. of Technical Staff, Bell Labs, USA, 1972–73; Sen. Asst in Res., Cavendish Lab., Cambridge Univ., and Fellow in Physics and Praelector, Downing Coll., 1973–75; SPSO and Head of Theory Gp, Daresbury Lab., 1975–81. Mem., PPARC, 1998–2002. *Publications:* Low Energy Electron Diffraction, 1974; Surface Crystallographic Information Service, 1987; scientific papers. *Recreations:* music, gardening, photography. *Address:* The Blackett Laboratory, Imperial College of Science, Technology and Medicine, SW7 2AZ. *T:* (020) 7594 7606. *Club:* Athenæum.

PENFOLD, Peter Alfred, CMG 1995; OBE 1986; international consultant; formerly HM Diplomatic Service; *b* 27 Feb. 1944; *s* of Alfred Penfold and Florence (*née* Green); *m* 1st, 1972, Margaret Quigley (marr. diss. 1983); 2nd, 1992, Celia Dolores Koenig. *Educ:* Sutton Co. Grammar Sch. Joined Foreign Service, 1963; Bonn, 1965–68; Kaduna, 1968–70; Latin American Floater, 1970–72; Canberra, 1972; FCO, 1972–75; Second Secretary: Addis Ababa, 1975–78; Port of Spain, 1978–81; First Sec., FCO, 1981–84; Dep. High Comr, Kampala, 1984–87; First Sec., FCO, 1987–91; Gov., BVI, 1991–95; Special Advr on Drugs in the Caribbean, 1995–96; High Comr, Sierra Leone, 1997–2000; Sen. Conflict Advr, DFID, 2001. Chm., UK Assoc., Milton Margai Sch. for the Blind, Sierra Leone, 2004–. *Recreations:* travel, flying, mountaineering, reading. *Address:* Fisherman's Wharf, Abingdon, Oxfordshire OX14 5RX.

PENFOLD, Maj.-Gen. Robert Bernard, CB 1969; LVO 1957; *b* 19 Dec. 1916; *s* of late Bernard Hugh Penfold, Selsey, and late Ethel Ives Arnold; *m* 1940, Ursula, *d* of late Lt-Col E. H. Gray; two *d. Educ:* Wellington; RMC, Sandhurst. 2nd Lieut, Royal Leics Regt, 1936; commnd into 11th Sikh Regt, Indian Army, 1937; served in NWFP and during War of 1939–45 in Middle East, Central Mediterranean Forces; Instructor, Staff Coll., Quetta, 1946–47; transf. to British Army, RA, 1947; RN Staff Coll., 1953; Secretary, British Joint Services Mission, Washington, 1957–59; comdg 6 King's African Rifles, Tanganyika, 1959–61; Comdr 127 Inf. Bde (TA), 1962–64; Security Ops Adviser to High Commissioner, Aden, 1964–65; Imperial Defence Coll., 1966; Chief of Defence Staff, Kenya, 1966–69; GOC South East District, 1969–72. Gen. Manager and Chief Exec., Royal Hong Kong Jockey Club, 1972–80. Chm., Horseracing Adv. Council, 1980–86. *Recreations:* shooting, golf, gardening. *Address:* Park House, Amport, Andover, Hants SP11 8BW. *Club:* Army and Navy.

PENGELLY, Richard Anthony; Under Secretary, Welsh Office, 1977–85; *b* 18 Aug. 1925; *s* of Richard Francis Pengelly and Ivy Mildred Pengelly; *m* 1st, 1952, Phyllis Mary Rippon; one *s*; 2nd, 1972, Margaret Ruth Crossley; two *s* one *d. Educ:* Plymouth Coll.; School of Oriental and African Studies; London Sch. of Economics and Political Science (BScEcon). Served War: Monmouthshire Regt and Intell. Corps, 1943–47. Joined Min. of Supply as Asst Principal, 1950, Principal, 1954; NATO Defence Coll., 1960–61; Asst Sec., Min. of Aviation, 1964; RCDS 1971; Min. of Defence, 1972. *Recreations:* ski-ing, golf. *Address:* Byways, Wern Goch Road, Cyncoed, Cardiff, S Wales CF23 6SD. *T:* (029) 2076 4418.

PENHALIGON, Dame Annette, DBE 1993; Member (Lib Dem): Restormel Borough Council, Cornwall, since 2003; Cornwall County Council, since 2005; *b* 9 Feb. 1946; *d* of late Owen Bennett Lidgey and Mabel Lidgey; *m* 1968, David Charles Penhaligon, MP (*d* 1986); one *s* one *d*; *m* 1994, Robert William Egerton. *Educ:* Truro Girls' Grammar Sch. Subpostmistress, Chacewater PO, 1967–79; Sec. to husband, David Penhaligon, MP (L) Truro, 1974–86. Mem. (L, then Lib Dem), Carrick DC, Cornwall, 1987–94. Non-exec. Dir, Cornwall Independent Radio, 1992–2002. *Publication:* Penhaligon, 1989. *Recreation:* supporting charities helping people with learning disabilities. *Address:* Trevillick House, Fore Street, Grampound, Truro, Cornwall TR2 4RS. *T:* (01726) 884451.

PENLEY, William Henry, CB 1967; CBE 1961; PhD; FREng; engineering consultant, since 1985; *b* 22 March 1917; *s* of late William Edward Penley and late Clara (*née* Dodgson), Wallasey, Cheshire; *m* 1st, 1943, Raymonde Evelyn (*d* 1975), *d* of late Frederick Richard Gough, Swanage, Dorset; two *s* one *d*; 2nd, 1977, Marion Claytor (*d* 2004), *d* of late Joseph Enoch Airey, MBE, Swanage, Dorset; 3rd, 2006, Joanna Anderson-Doig, *d* of late Richard Barnett, Hedge End, Hants. *Educ:* Wallasey Grammar Sch.;

Liverpool Univ.; BEng, 1937; PhD, 1940. FIET (MIEE 1964); FRAeS 1967; FRSA 1975; FREng (FEng 1978). Head of Guided Weapons Department, Royal Radar Establishment, 1953–61; Director, Royal Radar Establishment, 1961–62; Director-General of Electronics Research and Development, Ministry of Aviation, 1962–64; Deputy Controller of Electronics, Ministry of Aviation, then Ministry of Technology, 1964–67; Dir, Royal Armament R&D Establishment, 1967–70; Chief Scientist (Army), 1970–75, Dep. Controller, Establishments and Res. B, 1971–75, MoD; Controller, R&D Establishments, and Research, MoD, and Professional Head of Science Gp of the Civil Service, 1976–77; Chm., Appleton Lab. Establishment Cttee, 1977–79; Dep. Dir, Under Water Weapons, Marconi Space and Defence Systems Ltd, Stanmore, 1979–82; Engrg Dir, Marconi Underwater Systems Ltd, 1982–85. Vis. Res. Fellow, Bournemouth Univ., 1996–2002. Sec., Swanage Choral and Operatic Soc., 1986–2000; Pres., Defence Electronics History Soc., 2003–. Vice-Chm., Purbeck Radar Mus. Trust, 1998–. Silver Jubilee Medal, 1977. *Address:* 28 Walrond Road, Swanage, Dorset BH19 1PD. *T:* (01929) 425042. *Club:* Royal Commonwealth Society.

PENMAN, Alistair, PhD; Chairman, Leatherhead Food International, since 2005; *b* 25 Oct. 1943; *s* of late Archibald Penman and Jean Penman; *m* 1968, Gina Hawthorn. *Educ:* Musselburgh Grammar Sch.; Univ. of Edinburgh (BSc Hons 1966; PhD 1969). Unilever: joined as Res. Scientist, 1969; Hd, Food Res., Rotterdam, 1989–95; Dir, Colworth House Lab., 1996–2003. Mem., BBSRC, 2002–08 (Chm., Audit Cttee, 2004–08; Chm., Diet and Health Res. Industry Club). Chm. Governing Body, Inst. of Food Res., 1998–2002. Trustee, E Malling Trust for Horticl Res., 2004–. Hon. Prof., Tea Res. Inst., Hangzhou, 1999. FIFST 1999. *Publications:* several scientific papers and patents. *Recreations:* golf, reading, walking. *Address:* Tregenna, Bubnell Lane, Baslow, Derbys DE45 1RL; *e-mail:* alistair@penman2510.freeserve.co.uk. *Clubs:* Sickleholme Golf, Chatsworth Golf.

PENMAN, Ian Dalgleish, CB 1987; Deputy Secretary, Central Services, Scottish Office, 1984–91; *b* 1 Aug. 1931; *s* of late John B. Penman and Dorothy Dalgleish; *m* 1963, Elisabeth Stewart Strachan; three *s*. *Educ:* Glasgow Univ. (MA Classics); Balliol Coll., Oxford (MA Lit. Hum.; Snell Exhibnr and Ferguson Scholar). National Service, RAF, 1955–57 (Educn Br.). Asst Principal, HM Treasury, 1957–58; Scottish Office, 1958–91; Private Sec. to Parly Under-Sec. of State, 1960–62; Principal, Scottish Develt Dept, 1962–69; Asst Sec., Estab. Div., 1970–72; Asst Sec., Scottish Home and Health Dept, 1972–78; Under-Sec., Scottish Develt Dept, 1978–84. Member: Chm.'s Panel, CSSB, 1991–95; Sec. of State's Panel of Inquiry Reporters, 1992–94; Council on Tribunals, 1994–2001 (Mem., Scottish Cttee, 1994–2001); Church of Scotland Cttee on Probationers, 1994–97; C of S Bd of Ministry, 1997–2003. Chm., Viewpoint Housing Assoc., 1991–95; Chief Exec., Scottish Homes, April–Oct. 1991. *Recreations:* walking, music, travel. *Address:* 1/3 Fettes Rise, Edinburgh EH4 1QH. *T:* (0131) 552 2180. *Club:* New (Edinburgh).

PENN, Charles Richard, TD 1990; PhD; Chief Development Officer, Syntaxin, since 2005; *b* 12 June 1957; *s* of Lt Col Charles Edward Penn and Mary Elizabeth Penn; *m* 1980, Elizabeth Jane Dawson; two *d*. *Educ:* Christ Church, Oxford (MA 1979); Wolfson Coll., Cambridge (PhD 1982). Res. Fellow, Wolfson Coll., Cambridge, 1982–84; SSO, Inst. for Animal Health, 1984–88; Sen. Res. Associate, Glaxo R&D, 1988–95; Sen. Med. Strategy Hd, Glaxo Wellcome, 1995–98; Dir for R&D, Centre for Applied Microbiol. and Res., subseq. HPA Porton Down, 1998–2005. Vis. Professorial Fellow, Univ. of Bath, 1999–2005. TAVR (RE), 1975–92. Co-inventor on patent, oxathiolane nucleoside analogues (treatment for AIDS/HIV). *Publications:* papers in professional jls, inc. Nature. *Recreations:* marine biology (inc. rearing cephalopods), fishing, DIY, family holidays. *Address:* Syntaxin, Unit 4-10, The Quadrant, Barton Lane, Abingdon, Oxon OX14 3YS. *T:* (01235) 552100, *Fax:* (01235) 552200; *e-mail:* charles.penn@syntaxin.com.

PENN, Jeremy John Harley; Chief Executive, Baltic Exchange, since 2004; *b* 11 March 1959; *s* of Comdr Geoffrey Briscoe Penn and Barbara Penn (*née* Beverley Robinson); marr. diss.; one *s* one *d*. *Educ:* Warwick Sch., Warwick; Corpus Christi Coll., Oxford (MA 1981); Harvard Business Sch. (AMP 1999). Reuters Gp plc, 1981–2001: Man. Dir, Reuters Asia, 1997–99; Dep. CEO, Reuterspace Div., 1999–2001; ind. consultant, 2002–03; Baltic Exchange, 2003–. *Recreations:* theatre, running, ski-ing, joinery. *Address:* The Baltic Exchange, 38 St Mary Axe, EC3A 8BH; *e-mail:* JPenn@Balticexchange.com. *Club:* Tanglin (Singapore).

PENN, Richard; Commissioner for Standards, National Assembly for Wales, since 2005; Chair, South Wales Probation Board, since 2001; *b* 4 Oct. 1945; *s* of George Stanley; *m* 1968, Jillian Mary Elias; three *s* one *d*. *Educ:* Canton High Sch., Cardiff; University Coll., Cardiff (BSc Econs Jt Hons); University Coll., Swansea (DipEd). MBPS. Lectr, University Coll., Cardiff, 1968–70; Glamorgan, then W Glamorgan, CC, 1970–76; Asst Chief Exec., Cleveland CC, 1976–78; Dep. Chief Exec., W Midlands CC, 1978–81; Chief Executive: Knowsley Metropolitan Council, 1981–89; City of Bradford Metropolitan Council, 1989–98. Member: EOC, 1997–2002; Legal Services Commn, 2000–03; Advr, Nat. Assembly for Wales, 2000–. FCMI; FRSA. *Recreations:* family, Rugby Union, theatre, good food. *Address:* c/o National Assembly for Wales, Crickhowell House, Cardiff Bay, Cardiff CF99 1NA. *Club:* Royal Over-Seas League.

PENN, Sean Justin; actor, director and writer; *b* Burbank, Calif, 17 Aug. 1960; *s* of Leo Penn and Eileen Penn (*née* Ryan); *m* 1st, 1985, Madonna Louise Veronica Ciccone, *qv* (marr. diss. 1989); 2nd, 1996, Robin Wright; one *s* one *d*. *Educ:* Santa Monica High Sch.; studied acting with Peggy Feury. Joined LA Gp Repertory Theater (backstage work; dir, Terrible Jim Fitch (one-act play)); moved to NYC, 1980; *theatre includes:* Earthworms, 1980; Heartland, 1981; Slab Boys, 1983; Hurlyburly, 1988; The Late Henry Moss, 2000. *Films include:* Taps, 1981; Fast Times at Ridgemont High, 1982; Summerspell, Bad Boys, 1983; Crackers, Racing with the Moon, 1984; The Falcon and the Snowman, 1985; At Close Range, Shanghai Surprise, 1986; Colors, Judgement in Berlin, Cool Blue, 1988; Casualties of War, We're No Angels, 1989; State of Grace, 1990; The Last Party, Carlito's Way, 1993; Dead Man Walking, 1996; U-Turn, She's So Lovely (also prod.), The Game, Hugo Pool, 1997; As I Lay Dying (also prod.), Loved (also prod.), The Thin Red Line, Hurlyburly, Sweet and Lowdown, Being John Malkovich, 1999; Up at the Villa, The Weight of Water, 2000; Before Night Falls, 2001; I Am Sam, 2002; Mystic River (Academy Award for best actor), 2003; It's All About Love, 21 Grams, 2004; The Interpreter, The Assassination of Richard Nixon, 2005; All the King's Men, 2006; *director:* The Pledge, 2001; *director and writer:* The Indian Runner, 1991; The Crossing Guard, 1995; Autumn of the Patriarch, 1999; Into the Wild, 2007. *Address:* Suite 2500, 2049 Century Park East, Los Angeles, CA 90067, USA.

PENNANT; *see* Douglas-Pennant.

PENNANT-REA, Rupert Lascelles; Chairman, Henderson Group, since 2005; *b* 23 Jan. 1948; *s* of late Peter Athelwold Pennant-Rea and Pauline Elizabeth Pennant-Rea; *m* 1986, Helen Jay; one *s*, and one *s* one *d* by previous marriage, and two step *d*. *Educ:* Peterhouse, Zimbabwe; Trinity Coll., Dublin (BA); Manchester Univ. (MA). Confedn of Irish Industry, 1970–71; Gen. and Municipal Workers Union, 1972–73; Bank of England, 1973–77; The Economist, 1977–93, Editor, 1986–93; Dep. Gov., Bank of England, 1993–95; Chairman: The Stationery Office, 1996–2005; PGI plc (formerly Plantation & Gen. Investments), 1997–; Security Printing and Systems, 1999–2006; Acuity VCT plc (formerly Electra Kingsway VCT), 2002–. Non-executive Director: British American Tobacco, 1995–2007; Sherritt Internat. Inc., 1995–2007; First Quantum Minerals, 2001–; Gold Fields, 2002–; Go Ahead Gp, 2002–; Times Newspapers, 2003–; The Economist, 2006–. Trustee: Action Med. Res., 2000–07; Wincott Foundn, 2000–. Chm., Shakespeare Schs Fest., 2001–. Gov., Peterhouse, Zimbabwe, 1994–. *Publications:* Gold Foil, 1979; (jtly) Who Runs the Economy?, 1980; (jtly) The Pocket Economist, 1983; (jtly) The Economist Economics, 1986. *Recreations:* music, tennis, golf, fishing, family. *Address:* Henderson Group, 4 Broadgate, EC2M 4DA. *Clubs:* MCC, Reform; Harare (Zimbabwe).

PENNECK, Stephen John, CStat, FSS; Executive Director, Methodology, Office for National Statistics, since 2008; *b* 25 June 1951; *s* of Norman James Penneck and Rose Esther Penneck; *m* 1979, Pauline Ann Tunnell; two *d*. *Educ:* Southampton Univ. (BSc Social Sc 1972); Birmingham Univ. (MSocSc 1973). Cadet statistician, CSO, 1972–73; Asst and Sen. Asst Statistician, 1973–78, Statistician, 1978–85, DTI; OFT, 1985–91; CSO, 1991–93; Chief Statistician, Hd of Profession, DTI, 1993–96; Office for National Statistics: Director: Nat. Accounts Div., 1997–2000; Nat. Stats and Policy Div., 2000–03; Statistical Outputs Gp, 2003–05; Exec. Dir, Surveys and Admin. Sources, 2005–08. Vice Pres., Internat. Assoc. for Official Statistics, 2007–. Mem. (LibDem), Sutton LBC, 1983–94 (Chm., Educn Cttee, 1986–91; Dep. Leader, 1988–94). Governor: Greenshaw High Sch., 1983–2004; All Saints (Benhilton) Primary Sch., 1986–2006. *Publications:* contrib. articles to Econ. Trends, Statistical News and conf. proceedings. *Recreations:* gardening, walking, travel, music. *Address:* Office for National Statistics, Cardiff Road, Newport, S Wales NP10 8XG. *T:* (01633) 812989, *Fax:* (01633) 652811; *e-mail:* stephen.penneck@ons.gov.uk.

PENNEFATHER, Maj.-Gen. David Anthony Somerset, CB 1996; OBE 1991; Commandant General, Royal Marines, 1996–98; *b* 17 May 1945; *s* of late Capt. R. R. S. Pennefather, RN and Rachael Ann Pennefather (*née* Fawcitt); *m* 1972, Sheila Elizabeth Blacklee (*d* 2002); one *s* one *d*. *Educ:* Wellington Coll. Entered RM, 1963; commando service incl. US Marine Corps exchange, 1965–76; Army Staff Coll., 1977 (psc(m)); commando service and MoD, 1978–85; DS, Army Staff Coll., 1986–88; CO, 42 Commando, 1988–90; rcds 1991; hcsc 1992; Comdr, 3rd Commando Bde, 1992–94; Dir of Operations for Bosnia, JHQ Wilton, 1994; COS to CGRM, 1995; Comdr, Rapid Reaction Force Ops Staff, Bosnia, 1995; Sen. DS (Navy), RCDS, 2000 and 2002. Chm. Trustees, Royal Marines Mus., 2007–. Sec., Royal Humane Soc., 2004–07. Liveryman, Co. of Clockmakers, 1973– (Mem., Ct of Assts, 1998–; Master, 2006–07). Comdr, Legion of Merit (USA), 1997. *Recreations:* fell-walking, forestry, fishing. *Club:* Army and Navy.

PENNEY, Most Rev. Alphonsus Liguori; Archbishop (RC) of St John's (Newfoundland), 1979–91, now Emeritus; *b* 17 Sept. 1924; *s* of Alphonsus Penney and Catherine Penney (*née* Mullaly). *Educ:* St Bonaventure's Coll., St John's, Newfoundland; University Seminary, Ottawa (LPh, LTh). Assistant Priest: St Joseph's Parish, St John's, 1950–56; St Patrick's Parish, St John's, 1956; Parish Priest: Marystown, Placentia Bay, Newfoundland, 1957; Basilica Parish, St John's, 1969. Prelate of Honour, 1971. Bishop of Grand Falls, Newfoundland, 1972. Hon. LLD, Memorial Univ. of Newfoundland, 1980. Confederation Medal, 1967. *Recreations:* walking, golf. *Address:* 23 Mayor Avenue, St John's, NL A1C 4N4, Canada.

PENNEY, Jennifer Beverly; Senior Principal, Royal Ballet, retired 1988; *b* 5 April 1946; *d* of Beverley Guy Penney and Gwen Penney. *Educ:* in Canada (grades 1–12). Entered Royal Ballet Sch., 1962; joined Royal Ballet, 1963; became soloist during 1967, principal dancer during 1970, and senior principal dancer during 1974. Evening Standard Award, 1980. *Recreation:* painting (water-colours). *Address:* 2.258 Lower Ganges Road, Saltspring Island, BC V8K 1S7, Canada.

PENNEY, John Anthony, CMG 2000; translator and lecturer, since 2000; *b* 30 Oct. 1940; *s* of late William Welch Penney and of Lily Penney; *m* 1st, 1968, Mary Hurley; 2nd, 1995, Miriam Franchini. *Educ:* Madrid Univ. (Dip. of Hispanic Studies 1960); St Catharine's Coll., Cambridge (BA (Hons) Mod. Langs, 1963; MA 1966); Nat. Autonomous Univ. of Mexico; Univ. of Paris IX, Ecole Supérieure d'Interpretation et de Traducteurs. HM Diplomatic Service, 1966–99: Jt Res. Dept, FCO, 1966–68; Lima, 1968–72; Hd, Americas Unit, FCO Res. & Analysis Dept, 1973–95; 1st Sec., Political Cttee, CSCE, UKMIS to UN, Geneva, 1974–75; Central Amer. and Caribbean Dept, FCO, 1977–78; Havana, 1978; Mexico and Central Amer. Dept, FCO, 1981–82; Paris, 1984–86; Santiago de Chile, 1988; Chief FCO Interpreter (Spanish), 1986–99; Antarctic Treaty UK Inspection Team, 1989; Minister-Counsellor, Consul-Gen., Dep. Hd of Mission and Commercial Manager, Brasilia, 1995–99. *Recreation:* music. *Address:* SMDB, Conj 4, Lote 3, Casa A, Lago Sul, Brasilia 71680–040, Brazil. *T:* (61) 33665344; *e-mail:* penneyjohn@gmail.com.

PENNEY, Penelope Anne; Headmistress, Haberdashers' Aske's School for Girls, Elstree, 1991–2005; *b* 30 Sept. 1942; *d* of late Richard Chamberlain, TD and (Lydia) Joan (*née* Kay); *m* 1963, Rev. William Affleck Penney; one *s* two *d*. *Educ:* Chatelard Sch., Switzerland; Bristol Univ. (BA Hons 1964). Head of Langs and Communications, Astor of Hever Sch., Maidstone, 1974–79; Headmistress: Prendergast Sch., Catford, 1980–86; Putney High Sch. (GPDST), 1987–91. Educn Advr, London Diocesan Bd for Schools, 2005–. Pres., GSA, 1994–95 (Chm., Inspections Cttee, 2001–03); Mem., Teacher Induction Panel, ISC, 1999–2003. Freeman, City of London, 1993; Liveryman, Haberdashers' Co., 2005. FCMI (FIMgt 1995); MInstD 1995. FRSA; FZS. *Publications:* Hearing the Squirrel's Heartbeat, 2006; Go and Open the Door, 2008. *Recreations:* education, fast cars, grandparental duties. *Address:* 6 Devonshire Court, 26A Devonshire Street, W1G 6PJ. *T:* (020) 7935 0649; *e-mail:* p.a.penney@btinternet.com.

PENNICOTT, Maj.-Gen. Brian Thomas, CVO 1994; Extra Gentleman Usher to the Queen, since 2008 (Gentleman Usher, 1995–2007); management consultant, 1998–2001; *b* 15 Feb. 1938; *s* of Thomas Edward Pennicott and Vera Ethel (*née* Gale); *m* 1962, Patricia Anne Chilcott; two *s* three *d*. *Educ:* Portsmouth Northern Grammar Sch.; RMA, Sandhurst. Commnd, RA, 1957; RMCS, Shrivenham, 1969–70; Staff Coll., Camberley, 1971; GSO2 (W), Project Management Team 155mm Systems, 1972–73; NDC, Latimer, 1976–77; CO 29 Commando Regt, RA, 1977–80; SO1 Mil. Sec.'s Br. 6, MoD, 1980–82; Comdr Artillery, Falkland Is, 1982; Asst Mil. Attaché, Washington, 1982–83; Comdr Artillery, 1 Armd Div., 1983–86; NDC, Canada, 1986–87; Dep. Mil. Sec. (A), 1987–89; Dir, RA, 1989–91; Defence Services Sec., 1991–94 and ACDS (Personnel and Reserves), 1992–94. Gp Security Advr, 1994–95, Gp Personnel Manager, later Gp Human Resources Manager, 1995–96, Sun Alliance Gp; Gp Human Resources Manager, Royal & Sun Alliance Insurance Gp, 1996–98. Chm., Inksane (formerly BrandGuardian) Ltd (Hong Kong), 1999–2002. Chm., Simplyhealth Gp Ltd (formerly Hospital Saving Assoc., subseq. HSA Gp Ltd), 1999–. Col Comdt, RA, 1991–96; Hon. Col, 289 Commando

Battery, RA(V), 1991–99. Chm., Army FA, 1991–94. *Recreations:* golf, bridge. *Address:* c/o Lloyds TSB, Cox's & King's Branch, PO Box 1190, 7 Pall Mall, SW1Y 5NA. *Club:* Army and Navy.

PENNICOTT, Ian; QC 2003; *b* 5 Sept. 1958; *s* of Roy Stephen Pennicott and Patricia Dorothy Pennicott; *m* 1991, Andrea Clare (*née* Whitlock); two *d. Educ:* Kingston Poly. (BA Hons); Corpus Christi Coll., Cambridge (LLM). Called to the Bar: Middle Temple, 1982; Hong Kong, 1984; in practice, specialising in building and engineering law, and construction related professional negligence. MCIArb. *Publications:* (contrib.) Keating on Building Contracts, 5th edn 1991 to 8th edn 2006; (contrib.) Halsbury's Laws of England, Vol. 4 (3), Building Contractors, Architects, Engineers, Valuers and Surveyors, reissue 2002; (consultant ed.) Halsbury's Laws of England, Vols 19 (1) and (2), Fuel and Energy, reissue 2007, Vol. 39 (14), Cross-Country Pipelines, reissue 2008. *Recreations:* golf, Southampton Football Club. *Address:* Keating Chambers, 15 Essex Street, WC2R 3AU. *T:* (020) 7544 2600, *Fax:* (020) 7240 7722; *e-mail:* ipennicott@keatingchambers.com. *Club:* Frilford Heath Golf (Oxon).

PENNING, Michael Allan; MP (C) Hemel Hempstead, since 2005; *b* 28 Sept. 1957; *s* of Brian and Freda Penning; *m* 1988, Angela Louden; two *d. Educ:* Appleton Comp. Sch., Benfleet; King Edmund Comp. Sch., Rochford. Served Grenadier Guards, 1974–79; RAMC, 1979–81; Essex Fire and Rescue Service, 1981–88; freelance media consultant, 1999–2000; Dep. Hd, News and Media, Conservative Party, 2000–04. Contested (C) Thurrock, 2001. GSM 1976. *Recreations:* keen angler, passionate Rugby Union supporter. *Address:* House of Commons, SW1A 0AA. *T:* (020) 7219 3000; *e-mail:* penningm@parliament.uk.

PENNING-ROWSELL, Prof. Edmund Charles, OBE 2006; FRGS; Head, Flood Hazard Research Centre, since 1970, Professor of Geography, since 1984, and Pro Vice-Chancellor (Research), since 1997, Middlesex University (formerly Middlesex Polytechnic); *b* 1 May 1946; *s* of late Edmund Lionel Penning-Rowsell and Margaret Penning-Rowsell; *m* 1968, Jacqueline Pritchett; two *d. Educ:* Chipping Norton Grammar Sch.; Sidcot Friends Sch.; University Coll. London (BSc 1967; PhD 1970; MA 1986). Lectr, Enfield Coll. of Technol., 1970–84; Dean of Social Sci., Middx Poly., then Middx Univ., 1984–97. FRGS 2000. *Publications:* (with J. Chatterton) The Benefits of Flood Alleviation: a manual of assessment techniques, 1977; (with D. J. Parker) Water Planning in Britain, 1980; (jtly) Floods and Drainage: British policies for hazard reduction, agricultural improvement and wetland conservation, 1986; (jtly) The Economics of Coastal Management: a manual of benefit assessment techniques, 1992; (jtly) The Benefits of Flood and Coastal Risk Management: a manual of assessment techniques, 2005. *Recreations:* wine, gardening. *Address:* Corner Cottage, Coln Rogers, Cheltenham, Glos GL54 3LB. *T:* (01285) 720470; *e-mail:* Edmund@Penningrowsell.com.

PENNINGTON, Hugh; *see* Pennington, T. H.

PENNINGTON, Michael Vivian Fyfe; freelance actor and writer; *b* 7 June 1943; *s* of late Vivian Maynard Cecil Pennington and Euphemia Willock (*née* Fyfe); *m* Katharine Ann Letitia Barker (marr. diss.); one *s. Educ:* Marlborough Coll.; Trinity Coll., Cambridge (BA English). RSC, 1964–65; BBC, ITV, Woodfall Films Ltd, West End Theatre, Royal Court Theatre, etc, 1966–74; RSC, 1974–81: roles included Berowne, Angelo and Hamlet; Crime and Punishment, Lyric Hammersmith, 1983; National Theatre: Strider, 1984; Venice Preserv'd, 1984; Anton Chekhov, 1984; The Real Thing, Strand, 1985; Jt Artistic Dir, English Shakespeare Co., 1986–93: three world tours playing Henry V, Richard II, Coriolanus, Leontes, Macbeth, and Dir, Twelfth Night; Playing with Trains, RSC, 1989; Vershinin, The Three Sisters, Gate, Dublin, 1990; The Gift of the Gorgon, Barbican, 1992, Wyndhams, 1993; Dir, Twelfth Night, Tokyo, 1993; Hamlet, Gielgud, 1994; Taking Sides, Chichester, transf. Criterion, 1995; Dir, Twelfth Night, Chicago, 1996; The Entertainer, Hampstead, 1996; Waste, The Seagull, The Provok'd Wife, Anton Chekhov, Old Vic, 1997; The Misanthrope, Filumena, Major Barbara, Piccadilly, 1998; Gross Indecency, Gielgud, 1999; Timon of Athens, RSC, 1999; The Guardsman, Albery, 2000; What the Butler Saw, nat. tour, 2001; The Shawl, Sheffield Crucible, 2001; The Front Page, Chichester, 2002; John Gabriel Borkman, English Touring Th., 2003; Dir, A Midsummer Night's Dream, Regent's Park, 2003; The Seagull, Edinburgh Fest., 2003; The Madness of George III, W Yorks Playhouse, 2003; When the Night Begins, Hampstead, 2004; Colder Than Here, Soho, 2005; The Cosmonaut's Last Message, Donmar, 2005; Nathan the Wise, Hampstead, 2005; The Best of Friends, Hampstead and nat. tour, 2006; The Bargain, nat. tour, 2007; Little Nell, Th. Royal, Bath, 2007; Sweet William (solo Shakespeare show), NT, internat. tour and W End, 2007; Taking Sides, Chichester, 2008; *television* includes: Oedipus the King, 1985; Return of Sherlock Holmes, 1986; Dr Terrible's House of Horrible, 2001; Trial and Retribution, 2007. *Publications:* Rossya—A Journey Through Siberia, 1977; The English Shakespeare Company, 1990; Hamlet: a user's guide, 1995; Twelfth Night: a user's guide, 1999; Are You There, Crocodile: inventing Anton Chekhov, 2002; A Midsummer Night's Dream: a user's guide, 2005; Sweet William—Twenty Thousand Hours with Shakespeare, 2008. *Recreations:* music, literature. *Address:* c/o Curtis Brown, Haymarket House, 28–29 Haymarket, SW1Y 4SP.

PENNINGTON, Prof. (Thomas) Hugh, PhD; FRCPath, FRCPE, FMedSci; FRSE; Professor of Bacteriology, University of Aberdeen, 1979–2003, now Emeritus (Dean, Faculty of Medicine, 1987–92); *b* 19 April 1938; *s* of Thomas Wearing Pennington and Dorothy Pennington; *m* 1965, Carolyn Ingram Beattie; two *d. Educ:* Lancaster Royal Grammar Sch.; St Thomas's Hosp. Med. Sch. (MB BS (Hons), Clutton Medal, Bristowe Medal, Beaney Scholarship; PhD). FRCPath 1990. House appts, St Thomas's Hosp., 1962–63; Asst Lectr, 1963–66, Lectr, 1966–67, Dept of Med. Microbiology, St Thomas's Hosp. Med. Sch.; Postdoctoral Fellow, Univ. of Wisconsin, 1967–69; Mem. Scientific Staff, 1969–70, Lectr, 1970–75, Sen. Lectr, 1975–79, MRC Virology Unit and Dept of Virology, Univ. of Glasgow. Chairman: Expert Gp on 1996 E.coli O157 outbreak in Central Scotland, 1996–97; Public Inquiry into 2005 Welsh E.coli outbreak, 2006–; Member: Scottish Food Adv. Cttee, Food Standards Agency, Scotland, 2000–05; Broadcasting Council for Scotland, 2000–05 (Vice Chair, 2003–05); BBC Rural Affairs Adv. Cttee, 2000–; World Food Prog. Tech. Adv. Gp, 2002–07. Gov., Rowett Res. Inst., 1980–88, 1995–2004; Mem., Bd of Dirs, Moredun Res. Inst., 2003–06. Pres., Soc. for Gen. Microbiology, 2003–07. Lectures: Pumphandle, John Snow Soc., 1997; Appleyard, BVA, 1997; Col Stock, APHA, 1999; Frank May, Leicester Univ., 2001; Victor Horsley, BMA, 2003; Sampson Gamgee, Birmingham Med. Inst., 2004; Al-Hammadi, RCPE, 2007. Founder FMedSci 1998; FRES 1957; FRSA 1997; FRSE 1997; FRCPE 1998. Hon. DSc: Lancaster, 1999; Strathclyde, 2001; Aberdeen, 2003; Hull, 2004. Caroline Walker Award, 1997; John Kershaw Meml Prize, RIPH&H, 1998; Silver Medal, Royal Scottish Soc. of Arts, 1999; Thomas Graham Medal, Royal Glasgow Philosophical Soc., 2001; 25th Anniv. Award for Achievement, Soc. of Food Hygiene Technol., 2004. *Publications:* (with D. A. Ritchie) Molecular Virology, 1975; When Food Kills, 2003; papers on molecular virology, molecular epidemiology and systematics of pathogenic bacteria; contrib. London Review of Books. *Recreations:* collecting books, dipterology. *Address:* University of Aberdeen, Medical School Buildings, Aberdeen AB25 2ZD. *T:* (01224) 645136.

PENNY, family name of **Viscount Marchwood**.

PENNY, Nicholas Beaver, MA, PhD; Director, National Gallery, since 2008; *b* 21 Dec. 1949; *s* of Joseph Noel Bailey Penny, QC; *m* 1st, 1971, Anne Philomel Udy (marr. diss.); two *d*; 2nd, 1994, Mary Agnes Wall. *Educ:* Shrewsbury Sch.; St Catharine's Coll., Cambridge (BA, MA); Courtauld Inst., Univ. of London (MA, PhD). Leverhulme Fellow in the History of Western Art, Clare Hall, Cambridge, 1973–75; Lectr, History of Art Dept, Univ. of Manchester, 1975–82; Sen. Res. Fellow, History of Western Art, King's Coll., Cambridge, 1982–84; Keeper of Western Art, Ashmolean Mus., Oxford, and Professorial Fellow, Balliol Coll., Oxford, 1984–89; Clore Curator of Renaissance Painting, 1990–2002, Keeper, 1998–2002, Nat. Gall.; Sen. Curator of Sculpture and Decorative Arts, Nat. Gall. of Art, Washington, 2002–08. Slade Prof. of Fine Art, Univ. of Oxford, 1980–81; Mellon Prof. at Center for Advanced Study in the Visual Arts, Nat. Gall. of Art, Washington, 2000–02. Mem., Amer. Acad. Arts and Scis., 2007. Cavaliere nell'Ordine al merito della Repubblica Italiana, 1990. *Publications:* Church Monuments in Romantic England, 1977; Piranesi, 1978; (with Francis Haskell) Taste and the Antique, 1981; Mourning, 1981; (ed jtly) The Arrogant Connoisseur, 1982; (with Roger Jones) Raphael, 1983; (ed) Reynolds, 1986; Alfred and Winifred Turner, 1988; (with Robert Flynn Johnson) Lucian Freud, Works on Paper, 1988; Ruskin's Drawings, 1988; (jtly) From Giotto to Dürer, 1991; Catalogue of European Sculpture in the Ashmolean Museum: 1540 to the present day, 3 vols, 1992; The Materials of Sculpture, 1993; Picture Frames, 1997; (jtly) From Dürer to Veronese, 1999; The Sixteenth Century Italian Paintings in the National Gallery, vol. 1, 2004, vol. 2, 2008; (with A. Radcliffe) Art of the Renaissance Bronze, 2004; reviews for London Review of Books; articles in Apollo, Burlington Magazine, Connoisseur, Jl of Warburg and Courtauld Insts, Past and Present, and elsewhere. *Address:* National Gallery, Trafalgar Square, WC2N 5DN.

PENNY, Patricia Joyce; *see* Longdon, P. J.

PENNYCUICK, Prof. Colin James, FRS 1990; Senior Research Fellow, University of Bristol, since 1997 (Research Professor in Zoology, 1993); *b* 11 June 1933; *s* of Brig. James Alexander Charles Pennycuick, DSO and Marjorie Pennycuick; *m* Sandy; one *s. Educ:* Wellington College; Merton College, Oxford (MA); Peterhouse, Cambridge (PhD). Lectr in Zoology, 1964–75, Reader, 1975–83, Bristol Univ.; seconded as Lectr in Zoology, Univ. of Nairobi, 1968–71, as Dep. Dir, Serengeti Res. Inst., 1971–73; Maytag Prof. of Ornithology, Univ. of Miami, 1983–92. *Publications:* Animal Flight, 1972; Bird Flight Performance, 1989; Newton Rules Biology, 1992; Modelling the Flying Bird, 2008. *Recreation:* gliding. *Address:* School of Biological Sciences, University of Bristol, Woodland Road, Bristol BS8 1UG.

PENRHYN, 7th Baron *cr* 1866; **Simon Douglas-Pennant;** *b* 28 June 1938; *s* of late Hon. Nigel Douglas-Pennant and Margaret Dorothy Douglas-Pennant (*née* Kirkham); *S* uncle, 2003; *m* 1963, Josephine Maxwell, *yr d* of Robert Upcott; two *s* two *d. Educ:* Eton Coll.; Clare Coll., Cambridge (BA Hons). Dir, Brintons Ltd, Kidderminster, 1990–98. *Recreations:* sport (golf, tennis), music, travelling. *Heir: s* Hon. Edward Sholto Douglas-Pennant, *b* 6 June 1966. *Address:* The Old Vicarage, Church Road, Castlemorton, Malvern, Worcs WR13 6BQ. *T:* (01684) 833513; *e-mail:* simon.dp@ukonline.co.uk. *Clubs:* MCC; County Cricketers Golf Society; Free Foresters, I Zingari, Greenjackets, Butterflies, Band of Brothers.

PENRITH, Bishop Suffragan of, since 2002; **Rt Rev. James William Scobie Newcome;** *b* 24 July 1953; *s* of John Newcome and Jane Newcome (*née* Scobie); *m* 1977, Alison Margaret (*née* Clarke); two *s* two *d. Educ:* Marlborough Coll.; Trinity Coll., Oxford (BA Mod. Hist. 1974, MA 1978); Selwyn Coll., Cambridge (BA Theol. 1977, MA 1981); Ridley Hall, Cambridge. Ordained deacon, 1978, priest, 1979; Asst Curate, All Saints, Leavesden, 1978–82; Minister, Bar Hill LEP, 1982–94; Tutor in Pastoral Studies, Ethics and Integrating Theology, Ridley Hall, Cambridge, 1983–88; RD, N Stowe, 1993–94; Residentiary Canon, Chester Cathedral, 1994–2002; Diocesan Dir of Ordinands, 1994–2000, of Ministry, 1996–2002, dio. Chester. Mem., Soc. for Study of Christian Ethics, 1985–. FRSA. *Publications:* (contrib.) Setting the Church of England Free, 2003; book reviews for Anvil. *Recreations:* film, contemporary novels, cross-country running, furniture restoration. *Address:* Holm Croft, 13 Castle Road, Kendal, Cumbria LA9 7AU. *T:* (01539) 727836, *Fax:* (01539) 734380; *e-mail:* bishop.penrith@carlislediocese.org.uk.

PENROSE, Rt Hon. Lord; George William Penrose; PC 2001; a Senator of the College of Justice in Scotland, 1990–2005; *b* 2 June 1938; *s* of late George W. Penrose and Janet L. Penrose; *m* 1964, Wendy Margaret Cooper; one *s* two *d. Educ:* Glasgow Univ. (MA, LLB). CA. Advocate, 1964; QC 1978; Advocate Depute, 1986; Home Advocate Depute, 1988. Procurator to Gen. Assembly of Ch of Scotland, 1984–90. Pres., Scottish procs of Aircraft and Shipbuilding Industries Arbitration Tribunal, 1977–83; Mem., panel of Chairmen, Financial Services Tribunal, 1988–90. Leader, Equitable Life Inquiry, 2001–04. Chm. Court, Heriot-Watt Univ., 2008–. Hon. LLD Glasgow, 2000; DUniv Stirling, 2001. *Recreation:* walking. *Address:* c/o Court of Session, Parliament House, Edinburgh EH1 1RQ.

PENROSE, Anne Josephine, (Mrs J. Penrose); *see* Robinson, A. J.

PENROSE, George William; *see* Penrose, Rt Hon. Lord.

PENROSE, John David; MP (C) Weston-super-Mare, since 2005; *b* 22 June 1964; *s* of late David Goronwe Penrose and of Anna Jill Penrose (who *m* 1995, Tom Lawrie); *m* 1995, Hon. Diana Mary Harding, *d* of Baron Harding of Petherton, *qv*; two *d. Educ:* Ipswich Sch.; Downing Coll., Cambridge (BA Hons 1986); Columbia Univ., NY (MBA 1991). J. P. Morgan, 1986–90; McKinsey & Co., 1992–94; Commercial Dir, Academic Books Div., Thomson Publishing, 1995–96; Man. Dir, Longman sch. textbooks for UK and Africa, Pearson plc, 1996–2000; Chm., Logotron, 2001–. Contested (C): Ealing Southall, 1997; Weston-super-Mare, 2001. PPS to Chm., Cons. Policy Rev., 2006–. Mem., Amnesty Internat. Mem., Blagdon and Dist Beekeeping Club. *Recreations:* fishing, beekeeping, listening to other people's opinions, worrying while my wife rides in steeplechases and celebrating when she wins. *Address:* House of Commons, SW1A 0AA. *Clubs:* Weston-super-Mare Conservative; Weston-super-Mare Constitutional.

PENROSE, Prof. Oliver, FRS 1987; FRSE; Professor of Mathematics, Heriot-Watt University, 1986–94, now Professor Emeritus; *b* 6 June 1929; *s* of Lionel S. Penrose, FRS, and Margaret Penrose (*née* Leathes); *m* 1953, Joan Lomas Dilley; two *s* one *d* (and one *s* decd). *Educ:* Central Collegiate Inst., London, Ont; University Coll. London (BSc); Cambridge Univ. (PhD). FRSE 1989. Mathematical Physicist, English Electric Co., Luton, 1952–55; Res. Asst, Yale Univ., 1955–56; Lectr, then Reader, in Mathematics, Imperial Coll., London 1956–69; Prof. of Mathematics, Open Univ., 1969–86. *Publications:* Foundations of Statistical Mechanics, 1970, repr. 2005; about 80 papers in physics and maths jls; a few book reviews and book chapters. *Recreations:* making music,

chess. *Address:* 29 Frederick Street, Edinburgh EH2 2ND. *T:* (0131) 225 5879.
See also Sir R. Penrose.

PENROSE, Sir Roger, OM 2000; Kt 1994; FRS 1972; Rouse Ball Professor of Mathematics, University of Oxford, 1973–98, now Emeritus; Fellow of Wadham College, Oxford, 1973–98, now Emeritus; *b* Colchester, Essex, 8 Aug. 1931; *s* of Lionel Sharples Penrose, FRS; *m* 1959, Joan Isabel Wedge (marr. diss. 1981); three *s*; *m* 1988, Vanessa Dee Thomas; one *s*. *Educ:* University Coll. Sch.; University Coll., Univ. of London (BSc spec. 1st cl. Mathematics), Fellow 1975; St John's Coll., Cambridge (PhD; Hon. Fellow, 1987). NRDC (temp. post, Feb.–Aug. 1956); Asst Lectr (Pure Mathematics), Bedford Coll., London, 1956–57; Research Fellow, St John's Coll., Cambridge, 1957–60; NATO Research Fellow, Princeton Univ. and Syracuse Univ., 1959–61; Research Associate King's Coll., London, 1961–63; Visiting Associate Prof., Univ. of Texas, Austin, Texas, 1963–64; Reader, 1964–66, Prof. of Applied Mathematics, 1966–73, Birkbeck Coll., London. Visiting Prof., Yeshiva, Princeton, Cornell, 1966–67 and 1969; Lovett Prof., Rice Univ., Houston, 1983–87; Distinguished Prof. of Physics and Maths, Syracuse Univ., NY, 1987–. Member: London Mathematical Soc.; Cambridge Philosophical Soc.; Inst. for Mathematics and its Applications; International Soc. for General Relativity and Gravitation. Adams Prize (Cambridge Univ.), 1966–67; Dannie Heineman Prize (Amer. Phys. Soc. and Amer. Inst. Physics), 1971; Eddington Medal (with S. W. Hawking), RAS, 1975; Royal Medal, Royal Soc., 1985; Wolf Foundn Prize for Physics (with S. W. Hawking), 1988; Dirac Medal and Prize, Inst. of Physics, 1989; Einstein Medal, 1990; Copley Medal, Royal Soc., 2008. *Publications:* Techniques of Differential Topology in Relativity, 1973; (with W. Rindler) Spinors and Space-time, Vol. 1, 1984, Vol. 2, 1986; The Emperor's New Mind, 1989 (Science Book Prize, 1990); Shadows of the Mind, 1994; (jtly) The Large, the Small and the Human Mind, 1997; The Road to Reality, 2004; many articles in scientific jls. *Recreations:* 3 dimensional puzzles, doodling at the piano. *Address:* Mathematical Institute, 24–29 St Giles, Oxford OX1 3LB. *T:* (01865) 273538.

PENRY-DAVEY, Hon. Sir David (Herbert), Kt 1997; **Hon. Mr Justice Penry-Davey;** a Judge of the High Court of Justice, Queen's Bench Division, since 1997; *b* 16 May 1942; *s* of late Watson and Lorna Penry-Davey; *m* 1970, Judy Walter; two *s* one *d*. *Educ:* Hastings Grammar Sch.; King's Coll., London (LLB Hons; FKC 1998). British Univs debating tour of Canada, 1964. Called to the Bar, Inner Temple, 1965, Bencher, 1993; a Recorder, 1986–97; QC 1988; Leader, S Eastern Circuit, 1992–95; a Dep. High Court Judge, 1994–97; Presiding Judge, Northern Circuit, 2000–03. Dep. Chm., Security Vetting Appeals Panel, 2004–. Chm., Gen. Council of the Bar, 1996 (Vice-Chm., 1995). *Recreations:* music, golf, cycling, hill-walking. *Address:* Royal Courts of Justice, Strand, WC2A 2LL.

PENTECOST, Prof. Brian Leonard, OBE 2000; MD; FRCP; Medical Director, British Heart Foundation, 1993–99; *b* 12 March 1934; *s* of Leonard Austin Pentecost and Florence Pentecost; *m* 1958, Janice Morgan Jones; one *s* two *d* (and one *d* decd). *Educ:* Erith Grammar Sch.; St Mary's Med. Sch., Univ. of London (MB BS 1957; MD 1965). FRCP 1972. Jun. appts, St Mary's, Brompton and Hammersmith Hosps; Jun. Med. Specialist, RAMC, 1959–61; Consultant Physician and Cardiologist, United Birmingham Hosps, 1965–93; Dean of Postgraduate Med. and Dental Educn, 1987–91, Hon. Prof. of Medicine, 1991–96, now Emeritus, Univ. of Birmingham. Consultant Advr in Cardiology to CMO, 1986–93. Member: Med. Subcttee, UGC, 1985–89; Cttee on Safety of Medicines, 1984–89, 1996–98. Royal College of Physicians: Examnr, 1977–92; Mem. Council, 1979–82; Censor, 1982–84; Linacre Fellow, 1991–94; Med. Co-ordinator, Jt Cttee on Higher Med. Educn, 1991–94. Mem. Council, 1973–77, Sec., 1976–80, British Cardiac Soc. Chm. Trustees, Royal Medical Benevolent Fund, 2001–07. Gov., The Health Foundation (formerly PPP Medical Healthcare Trust), 1998–2004. Hon. DSc Aston, 1998. *Publications:* contribs on cardiovascular medicine to books and scientific jls. *Recreations:* gardening, theatre, golf. *Address:* 37 Farquhar Road, Edgbaston, Birmingham B15 3RA. *Club:* Army and Navy.

PENTLAND, Ven. Raymond Jackson; QHC 2006; Archdeacon for the Royal Air Force, since 2006; *b* 14 July 1957; *s* of Adam Jackson Pentland and Edith Henderson Pentland; *m* 1979, Christine Ann Lyth; one *s* one *d*. *Educ:* Cowdenknowes High Sch.; William Booth Meml Coll.; St John's Coll., Nottingham (DPS 1988); Open Univ. (BA 1990); Westminster Coll., Oxford (MTh 2002; Farmington Fellow, 2004). Salvation Army Officer, 1979–86; ordained deacon, 1988, priest, 1989; Asst Curate, St Jude's, Nottingham, 1988–90; Chaplain, 1990–2005, Comd Chaplain, 2005–06, RAF. Mem., Gen. Synod, 2005–. Hon. Canon, Lincoln Cathedral, 2006–. *Publications:* contrib. Political Theol. *Recreations:* gourmet cuisine, travel, modern military history. *Address:* 9 Shelley Close, Medmenham, Marlow SL7 2SE. *T:* (01628) 477680; *e-mail:* r.pentland@btopenworld.com. *Club:* Royal Air Force.

PENTREATH, Prof. Richard John, (Jan), DSc, PhD; CBiol, FIBiol; CRadP; FSRP; Research Professor, Environmental Systems Science Centre, University of Reading, 2000–07, now Professor Emeritus; *b* 28 Dec. 1943; *s* of John Alistair Dudley Pentreath and Mary Lena (*née* Gendall); *m* 1965, Elisabeth Amanda Leach; two *d*. *Educ:* Humphry Davy Grammar Sch.; QMC, London (BSc (Special)); DSc London; Univ. of Auckland (PhD). FIBiol 1980; CBiol 1984; FSRP 1989. Commonwealth Schol., 1966–68; SRC Fellow, 1969; Fisheries Radiobiol Lab., MAFF, 1969–89: Hd, Aquatic Envmtl Protection Div. and Dep. Dir, Fisheries Res., 1988–89; Chief Scientist, and Dir Water Quality, NRA, 1989–95; Chief Scientist, and Dir, Envmtl Strategy, EA, 1995–2000. Member: NERC, 1992–98; Adv. Bd, Centre for Social and Econ. Res. on Global Envt, 1994–2005; Res. Assessment Panel, HEFC, 1995–96, 1999–2001; Council, Marine Biol Assoc. of UK, 1998–2000; Council, Assoc. for Schs Science Engrg and Technol., 1998–2000; Internat. Commn on Radiol Protection, 2003– (Chm., Cttee 5, Envmtl Protection, 2005–); Trustee, SAHFOS, 2001–; Indep. Mem., JNCC, 2000–06. Pres., Cornwall Sustainable Bldg Trust, 2005–. Hon. Prof., UEA, 1996–; Vis. Prof., ICSTM, 1997–2003. Pres., Cornwall Wildlife Trust, 2003–. Hon. DSc: Hertfordshire, 1998; UWE, 1999; Plymouth, 2002. *Publications:* Nuclear Power, Man and the Environment, 1980; contrib. numerous scientific papers. *Recreations:* Cornish history, crewing tall ships, visual arts. *Address:* Camelot House, Ropewalk, Penpol, Truro, Cornwall TR3 6NA. *T:* (01872) 862838.

PENZER, Dr Geoffrey Ronald, CChem, FRSC; Partner, Penzer Allen, since 1992; *b* 15 Nov. 1943; *s* of Ronald and Dora Penzer; *m* 1966, Sylvia Elaine (*née* Smith); one *s* one *d*. *Educ:* Merchant Taylors' Sch.; St John's Coll., Oxford (MA; DPhil 1969). CChem, FRSC 1979. Jun. Res. Fellow, Merton Coll., Oxford, 1967–69; Res. Chemist, Univ. of Calif, 1969–70; Lectr in Biol Chem., Univ. of York, 1970–75; British Council: Science Officer, Cairo, 1975–80; Science Officer, Mexico, 1980–84; Dir, Technical Co-operation Training Dept, 1984–87; Dir, Management Div., and Manager, HQ Location Project, 1987–91. Dir, Penzer Allen Ltd and Open Book Inspections, 1993–. Trustee: Outset, 1994–2002; BSS, 2001–. FCMI (FIMgt 1993). *Publications:* contrib. scientific books and jls. *Recreations:* music, landscapes, walking. *Address:* c/o Penzer Allen, Windward Lodge, West Kingsdown, Sevenoaks, Kent TN15 6AH.

PENZIAS, Dr Arno Allan; Venture Partner, New Enterprise Associates, since 1998; *b* 26 April 1933; *s* of Karl and Justine Penzias; *m*; one *s* two *d*; *m* 1996, Sherry Levit Penzias. *Educ:* City Coll. of New York (BS Physics, 1954); Columbia Univ. (MA Physics, 1958; PhD Physics, 1962). Bell Laboratories: Mem., Technical Staff, 1961–72; Head, Radio Physics Res., 1972–76; Dir, Radio Res. Lab., 1976–79; Exec. Dir, Research, Communications Sciences, 1979–81; Vice-Pres., Research, 1981–95; Vice-Pres. and Chief Scientist, AT&T Bell Laboratories, 1995–96; Lucent Technologies, Bell Labs Innovations: Vice-Pres. and Chief Scientist, 1996–98; Sen. Tech. Advr, 1998–2000. Lectr, Princeton Univ., 1967–72, Vis. Prof., Astrophysical Scis Dept, 1972–85; Res. Associate, Harvard Univ., 1968–80; Adjunct Prof., State Univ. of NY, Stony Brook, 1974–84; Lee Kuan Yew Dist. Vis., Nat. Univ. of Singapore, 1991. Lectures: Kompfner, Stanford Univ., 1979; Gamow, Colorado Univ., 1980; Jansky, NRAO, 1983; Michelson Meml, Dept US Navy, 1985; Tanner, Southern Utah State Coll., 1987; Klopsteg, Northwestern Univ., 1987; NSF Distinguished, 1987; Regent's, Univ. of Calif., Berkeley, 1990; Einstein, Princeton, 1996. Member: Sch. of Engrg and Applied Science (Bd Overseers), Univ. Pennsylvania, 1983–86; Union Councils for Soviet Jews Adv. Bd, 1983–95; NSF Industrial Panel on Science and Technology, 1982–92; CIT Vis. Cttee, 1977–79; NSF Astronomy Adv. Panel, 1978–79; MNAS, 1975–; Wissenschaftliche Fachbeirat, Max-Planck Inst., Bonn, 1978–85 (Chm., 1981–83); Technology Adv. Council, EarthLink Network Inc., 1996–98; Board of Directors: IMNET, 1986–92; A. D. Little, 1992–2001; Duracell, 1995–96; LCC, 1996–2001; Warpspeed, 1996–2001. Vice-Chm., Cttee of Concerned Scientists, 1976– (Mem., 1975–). Mem., National Acad. of Engrg, 1990. Hon. MIEEE, 1990. Trustee, Trenton State Coll., 1977–79. Hon. degrees: Paris Observatory, 1976; Wilkes Coll., City Coll. of NY, Yeshiva Univ., and Rutgers Univ., 1979; Bar Ilan Univ., 1983; Monmouth Coll., 1984; Technion-Israel Inst. of Technology, Pittsburgh Univ., Ball State Univ., Kean Coll., 1986; Ohio State Univ., Iona Coll., 1988; Drew Univ., 1989; Lafayette Coll., 1990; Columbia Univ., 1990; George Washington Univ., 1992; Rensselaer Polytechnic Inst., 1992; Pennsylvania Univ., 1992; Bloomfield Coll., 1994; Ranken Tech. Coll., 1997; Hebrew Union Coll., 1997; Oxford, 2002. Henry Draper Medal, National Acad. of Sciences, 1977; Herschel Medal, RAS, 1977; (jtly) Nobel Prize for Physics, 1978; Townsend Harris Medal, City Coll. NY, 1979; Newman Award, City Coll. NY, 1983; Joseph Handleman Prize in the Scis, 1983; Grad. Faculties Alumni Award, 1984; Big Brothers Inc. of NY, City Achievement in Science Award, 1985; Priestly Award, Dickinson Coll., 1989; Pake Prize, APS, 1990; NJ Literary Hall of Fame, 1991; Pender Award, Pennsylvania Univ., 1992; NJ Science/Technology Medal, R&D Council of NJ, 1996; Industrial Res. Inst. Medalist, 1998. Mem. Editorial Bd, Annual Revs of Astronomy and Astrophysics, 1974–78; Associate Editor, Astrophysical Jl Letters, 1978–82. *Publications:* Ideas and Information: managing in a high-tech world, 1989; Digital Harmony: business, technology & life after paperwork, 1995; 100 published articles, principally in Astrophysical Jl. *Address:* 2490 Sand Hill Road, Menlo Park, CA 94025, USA.

PEPINSTER, Catherine; Editor, The Tablet, since 2004; *b* 7 June 1959; *d* of late Michel Joseph Pepinster and of Winifred Pepinster (*née* Jones); *m* 2003, Kevin Charles Morley. *Educ:* Manchester Univ. (BA (Econ. and Soc. Sci.) 1980); City Univ., London (Postgrad. Dip. Journalism 1981); Heythrop Coll., Univ. of London (MA (Philos. and Religion) 2002). Local newspaper reporter, Manchester and London, 1981–85; Property Correspondent, Sheffield Morning Telegraph, 1985–86; Chief Reporter, Estates Times, 1986; News Ed., Building, 1987–89; reporter, The Observer, 1989–90; News Ed., Time Out, 1990–94; Asst News Ed., The Independent, 1994–95; Dep. News Ed., 1995–97, News Ed., 1997–98, Independent on Sunday; Features Ed., The Independent, 1998; Asst Ed., 1999–2002, Exec. Ed., 2002–04, Independent on Sunday. *Publication:* (ed) John Paul II: reflections from The Tablet, 2005. *Recreations:* walking, reading, architecture, Belgian culture. *Address:* The Tablet, 1 King Street Cloisters, Clifton Walk, W6 0QZ. *T:* (020) 8748 8484, *Fax:* (020) 8748 1550; *e-mail:* cpepinster@thetablet.co.uk. *Club:* Reform.

PEPPARD, Nadine Sheila, CBE 1970; race relations consultant, 1983–2003; *b* 16 Jan. 1922; *d* of late Joseph Anthony Peppard and May Peppard (*née* Barber). *Educ:* Macclesfield High Sch.; Manchester Univ. (BA, Teacher's Dip.). French teacher, Maldon Grammar Sch., 1943–46; Spanish Editor, George G. Harrap & Co. Ltd, 1946–55; Trg Dept, Marks and Spencer, 1955–57; Dep. Gen.-Sec., London Council of Social Service, 1957–64; Nat. Advisory Officer for Commonwealth Immigrants, 1964–65; Gen. Sec., Nat. Cttee for Commonwealth Immigrants, 1965–68; Chief Officer, Community Relations Commn, 1968–72; Adviser on Race Relations, Home Office, 1972–83, retd. *Publications:* (trans.) Primitive India, 1954; (trans.) Toledo, 1955; various professional articles. *Address:* 321 The Cedars, Abbey Foregate, Shrewsbury SY2 6BY. *T:* (01743) 235124.

PEPPÉ, Comdr William Lawrence Tosco, OBE 1987; Vice Lord-Lieutenant of Ross, Cromarty, Skye and Lochalsh, since 2005; *b* 25 Nov. 1937; *s* of Lt-Col William Tosco Hill Peppé, DSO, OBE, MC and Alison Mary (*née* Johnson); *m* 1966, Deirdre Eva Preston Wakefield; three *s*. *Educ:* Wellington Coll.; King's Coll., Cambridge. Joined RN, 1955; Commanding Officer: 892 Naval Air Sqn, 1974–76; HMS Diomede, 1980–81; retd 1991. Chm., Skye and Lochalsh Access Forum, 2007. JP Skye and Lochalsh, 1992–2007; DL Ross and Cromarty, Skye and Lochalsh, 1996. Hon. Sheriff, Portree and Lochmaddy, 2007. *Recreation:* country. *Address:* Glendrynoch Lodge, Carbost, Isle of Skye IV47 8SX.

PEPPER, Sir David (Edwin), KCMG 2005; DPhil; Director, Government Communications Headquarters, 2003–08; *b* 8 Feb. 1948; *s* of Samuel Edwin Pepper and Rose Pepper (*née* Pell); *m* 1970, Margaret Meehan; two *s*. *Educ:* Chigwell Sch.; St John's Coll., Oxford (MA, DPhil 1972). Joined Government Communications Headquarters, 1972: Principal, 1979; Grade 5, 1984; RCDS 1991; Dir of Admin, 1995–98; on loan to Home Office as Dir, Corporate Develt, 1998–2000; Dir, Policy and Resources, 2000–03. *Recreations:* walking, music, reading, cooking.

PEPPER, Prof. Gordon Terry, CBE 1990; Hon. Visiting Professor, Sir John Cass Business School, City of London (formerly City University Business School), 1987–90 and since 1998 (Director, Centre for Financial Markets, 1988–97 and Professor, 1991–97); Chairman, Lombard Street Research Ltd, since 2000 (Director, since 1998); *b* 2 June 1934; *s* of Harold Terry Pepper and Jean Margaret Gordon Pepper (*née* Furness); *m* 1958, Gillian Clare Huelin; three *s* one *d*. *Educ:* Repton; Trinity College, Cambridge (MA); FIA, FSIP. Equity & Law Life Assurance Soc., 1957–60; W. Greenwell & Co.: Partner, 1962; Joint Senior Partner, 1980–86; Chairman, Greenwell Montagu & Co., 1986–87; Dir and Sen. Advr, Midland Montagu, 1985–90; Chm., Payton Pepper & Sons Ltd, 1987–97. Member: Cttee on Industry and Finance, NEDC, 1988–90; ESRC, 1989–93; Adv. Cttee, Dept of Applied Econs, Cambridge Univ., 1992–97; Shadow Monetary Policy Cttee, 1997–; Council of Econ. Advrs to Opposition front bench, 1999–2006. *Publications:* Money, Credit and Inflation, 1990; Money, Credit and Asset Prices, 1994; Inside Thatcher's Monetarist Revolution, 1998; (with M. Oliver) Monetarism under Thatcher - Lessons for the Future, 2001; Liquidity Theory of Asset Prices, 2006; papers to Jl of Inst. of Actuaries. *Recreations:* sailing, family. *Address:* Staddleden, Sissinghurst, Cranbrook, Kent TN17 2AN. *T:* (01580) 712852, *Fax:* (01580) 714853; *e-mail:* gordonpepper@btopenworld.com. *Clubs:* Reform, Royal Ocean Racing.

PEPPER, Sir Michael, Kt 2006; FRS 1983; Pender Professor of Nanoelectronics, University College London, since 2009; Fellow of Trinity College, Cambridge, since 1982 (Senior Research Fellow, 1982–87; Professorial Fellow, 1987–2009); *b* 10 Aug. 1942; *s* of Morris and Ruby Pepper; *m* 1973, Jeannette Denise Josse, MB, BS, FRCPsych; two *d*. *Educ:* St Marylebone Grammar Sch.; Reading Univ. (BSc Physics, 1963; PhD Physics, 1967); MA 1987, ScD 1989, Cantab. FInstP 1991. Res. Physicist, Mullard Ltd, 1967–69; res. in solid state physics, The Plessey Co., Allen Clark Res. Centre, 1969–73; Cavendish Lab., 1973– (in association with The Plessey Co., 1973–82); Warren Res. Fellow of Royal Soc., Cavendish Lab., 1978–86; Principal Res. Fellow, GEC plc, Hirst Res. Centre, 1982–87; Prof. of Physics, Univ. of Cambridge, 1987–2009, now Emeritus. Jt Man. Dir, 1991–2007, Sen. Adviser, 2007–, Toshiba Res. Europe Ltd (formerly Toshiba Cambridge Res. Centre Ltd); Jt Founder and Dir, TeraView Ltd, 2001–. Mem., Univ. Council, 1993–97, 2000, Gen. Bd of Faculties, 1995–99, and various cttees of Council and Bd, 1993–99, Cambridge. Vis. Prof., Bar-Ilan Univ., Israel, 1984; Lectures: Inaugural Mott, Inst. of Physics, 1985; Royal Soc. Review, 1987; Rankin, Liverpool Univ., 1987; G. I. Taylor, Cambridge Philosophical Soc., 1988; Resnick, Bar-Ilan Univ., 1995; Mountbatten Meml, IEE, 2003; Bakerian, Royal Soc., 2004; Saha Meml, Kolkata, 2008. Past and present mem. of various cttees and panels of Inst. of Physics (Editl Bd, Jl of Physics, Condensed Matter, 1991–96), Royal Soc. (Associate Editor, 1983–89; Mem. Council, 1999–2001), Rutherford Meml Cttee, 1987–91, DTI and SERC (Cttees on Solid State Devices, Semiconductors, 1984–89); Mem., Council for Industry and Higher Educn, 2005–08. Fellow, Amer. Physical Soc., 1992. Hon. DSc: Bar-Ilan, 1993; Linköping, 1997. Guthrie Prize and Medal, Inst. of Physics, 1985; Hewlett-Packard Prize, European Physical Soc., 1985; Hughes Medal, 1987, Royal Medal, 2005, Royal Soc.; Mott Prize and Medal, Inst. of Physics, 2000. *Publications:* papers on semiconductors and solid state physics in jls. *Recreations:* whisky tasting, reading, travel. *Address:* London Centre for Nanotechnology, University College London, 17–19 Gordon Street, WC1H 0AH; *e-mail:* m.pepper@ee.ucl.ac.uk, mp10000@cam.ac.uk. *Clubs:* Athenæum; Arsenal Football.

PEPPER, Michael Peter Gregory, PhD; independent international statistical consultant, since 2004; *b* 2 June 1945; *s* of Arthur Pepper and Anne (*née* Panian); *m*; two *s* one *d*. *Educ:* Dr Challoner's Grammar Sch., Amersham; London Univ. (BSc Maths (Ext.)); Essex Univ. (MSc); PhD Bath. Res. Fellow, Univ. of Bath, 1970–74; Statistician, Dept of Energy, 1974–79; Sen. Statistician, Govt of Botswana, 1979–81; Statistician, Dept of Energy, 1981–86; Chief Statistician and Dir of Stats, Welsh Office, 1986–93; Hd of Price and Business Statistics Gp, CSO, subseq. ONS, 1993–2002; Exec. Dir, Business Transformation, ONS, 2002–04. *Recreations:* squash, travel, gardening, choral music. *Address:* The Rise, 145 Heol Isaf, Radyr, Cardiff CF15 8DX.

PEPPER, Terence, OBE 2002; Curator of Photographs and Exhibitions Organiser, National Portrait Gallery, since 1978; *b* 2 Jan. 1949; *s* of (Herbert Walter) Trevor Pepper and (Catherine) Rosemary (*née* Earle); partner, Rosalind Crowe. *Educ:* Epsom Coll.; Queen Mary Coll., Univ. of London (LLB); Council of Legal Educn; Sch. of Librarianship, Ealing Tech. Coll. ALA 1977. Asst Librarian, 1975, Librarian, 1976–78, NPG. Mem. Council, John Kobal Foundn, 1992–. Hon. FRPS 2002. *Publications:* exhibition catalogues: Monday's Children: fair and famous of the 1920s and 1930s, 1977; Camera Portraits by E. O. Hoppe, 1978; Photographs by Norman Parkinson: fifty years of portraits and fashion, 1981; Howard Coster's Celebrity Portraits, 1985; (contrib. with D. Mellor) Cecil Beaton, 1986; Portraits Helmut Newton, 1988; Lewis Morley: photographer of the sixties, 1989; (with J. Kobal) The Man Who Shot Garbo: the photographs of Clarence Sinclair Bull, 1989; Dorothy Wilding: the pursuit of perfection, 1991; The Lure of the Limelight: James Abbe, photographer of cinema and stage, 1995; High Society: photographs 1897–1914, 1998; (curated with P. Hoare) Icons of Pop, 1999; Horst Portraits, 2001; Cecil Beaton: Portraits, 2004 (German edn 2005); Angus McBean: Portraits, 2006. *Recreations:* swimming, cinema, reading Sunday newspapers, pop music. *Address:* c/o National Portrait Gallery, 2 St Martin's Place, WC2H 0HE. *T:* (020) 7306 0055, *Fax:* (020) 7306 0056; *e-mail:* tpepper@npg.org.uk.

PEPPIATT, Hugh Stephen Kenneth; Chairman, Moorfields Eye Hospital, 1991–98 (Special Trustee, 1991–2000); *b* 18 Aug. 1930; *s* of late Sir Leslie Peppiatt, MC and Lady (Cicely) Peppiatt; *m* 1960, Claire, *e d* of late Ian Douglas Davidson, CBE and Claire Davidson; three *s* two *d*. *Educ:* Winchester College; Trinity College, Oxford (schol.; MA); Univ. of Wisconsin. 2nd Lt, Coldstream Guards, 1948–50. Partner, Freshfields, Solicitors, 1960–90: Resident Partner, New York, 1977–81; Sen. Partner, 1982–90. Director: Greig Fester Gp, 1990–97; Hardy Oil & Gas, 1992–98; Benfield Greig Gp plc, 1997–99. Dir, St John Eye Hosp., Jerusalem, 1998–2005. Trustee, Help the Aged, 1991–97. CStJ 2003. *Recreations:* hillwalking, fly fishing, birdwatching. *Address:* 28 Bathgate Road, Wimbledon, SW19 5PN. *T:* (020) 8947 2709. *Clubs:* City of London; Royal Wimbledon Golf; Larchmont Yacht (New York).

PEPPITT, His Honour John Raymond; QC 1976; a Circuit Judge, 1991–2000; *b* 22 Sept. 1931; *s* of late Reginald Peppitt and Phyllis Claire Peppitt; *m* 1960, Judith Penelope James; three *s*. *Educ:* St Paul's Sch.; Jesus Coll., Cambridge (BA Classical Tripos). Called to the Bar, Gray's Inn, 1958, Bencher, 1982–2000; a Recorder, 1976–91. *Recreation:* collecting water-colours. *Address:* The Old Rectory, Snargate, Romney Marsh, Kent TN29 0EW. *Club:* Farmers'.

PEPYS, family name of **Earl of Cottenham**.

PEPYS, Prof. Mark Brian, MD, PhD; FRCP, FRCPath, FMedSci; FRS 1998; Professor of Medicine, Head of Department of Medicine, and Hon. Consultant Physician, Royal Free and University College Medical School, London, since 1999; Founder, and Head of National Health Service National Amyloidosis Centre, since 1999; *b* 18 Sept. 1944; *s* of Prof. Jack Pepys, MD, FRCP, FRCPE, FRCPath, and Rhoda Gertrude Pepys (*née* Kussel); *m* 1971, Dr Elizabeth Olga Winternitz; one *s* one *d*. *Educ:* Trinity Coll., Cambridge (BA, MA; MD 1982; PhD 1973); UCH Med. Sch., London. FRCP 1981; FRCPath 1991. Sen. Schol., 1964–65, Res. Schol., 1970–73, Fellow, 1973–79, Trinity Coll., Cambridge; MRC Trng Fellow, Dept of Pathology, Univ. of Cambridge, 1970–73; Registrar, then Sen. Registrar and Asst Lectr in Medicine, Hammersmith Hosp., 1973–75; Sen. Lectr, Hd of Immunology and Hon. Consultant Physician, Royal Free Hosp. Sch. of Medicine, 1975–77; Sen. Lectr in Medicine, 1977–80, Hon. Consultant Physician, 1977–99, Reader, 1980–84, Prof. of Immunol Medicine, 1984–99, RPMS, then ICSM, Hammersmith Hosp. Goulstonian Lectr, 1982, Lumleian Lectr, 1998, Harveian Orator, 2007, RCP; Sir Arthur Sims Travelling Prof., RCS, 1991; Kohn Lectr, RCPath, 1991; Chandos Lectr, Renal Assoc., 2000; Heberden Orator and Medallist, British Soc. for Rheumatology, 2002. Member Council: Royal Soc., 2003–05; Acad. of Med. Scis, 2003–06. Hon. Mem., Assoc. of Physicians of GB and Ireland, 1998. Founder FMedSci 1998. Fellow: UCL, 2003; Faculty of Medicine, Imperial Coll. London, 2004. Moxon Trust Medal, RCP, 1999; Glaxo Smith Kline Prize and Lect., Royal Soc., 2007; Ernst Chain Prize, 2008. *Publications:* contrib. articles on immunology, acute phase proteins and amyloidosis in learned jls. *Recreations:* ski-ing, tennis, surfing, wine. *Address:* 22 Wildwood Road, NW11 6TE. *T:* (020) 8455 9387. *Club:* Hurlingham.

PERAHIA, Murray, Hon. KBE 2004; FRCM; pianist and conductor; Principal Guest Conductor, Academy of St Martin-in-the-Fields, since 2001; *b* New York, 19 April 1947; *s* of David and Flora Perahia; *m* 1980, Naomi Shohet (Ninette); two *s*. *Educ:* High Sch. of Performing Arts; Mannes College (MS); studied piano with Jeanette Haien, M. Horszowski, Arthur Balsam. FRCM 1987; FRAM 1994. Co-Artistic Dir, Aldeburgh Fest., 1981–89; Hon. Dir, Britten-Pears Sch. for Advanced Musical Studies, 1981–. Won Kosciuszko Chopin Prize, 1965; début Carnegie Recital Hall, 1966; won Leeds Internat. Piano Festival, 1972; Avery Fisher Award, 1975; regular tours of Europe, Asia, USA; numerous recordings include complete Mozart Piano Concertos (as dir and soloist with English Chamber Orch.), complete Beethoven Piano Concertos (with Bernard Haitink and Royal Concertgebouw), Bartók Sonata for Two Pianos and Percussion (Grammy Award, 1989); Gramophone award for Handel and Scarlatti recording, 1997; Gramophone award for Bach English Suites recording, 1999; Chopin Études (Grammy Award, 2002). Hon. Fellow, Jesus Coll., Cambridge, 2007. *Address:* c/o IMG Artists-Europe, The Light Box, 111 Power Road, W4 5PY.

PERCEVAL, family name of **Earl of Egmont**.

PERCEVAL, Michael; HM Diplomatic Service, retired; Consul-General, Barcelona, 1992–96; *b* 27 April 1936; *o s* of late Hugh Perceval and Guida Brind; *m* 1968, Alessandra Grandis; one *s* one *d*. *Educ:* Downside Sch.; Christ Church, Oxford (Schol.; 2nd Cl. Hons English Lit.). Served Royal Air Force, Nicosia, 1956–60; film production asst, Athens, 1960; freelance correspondent, Madrid, 1961–69; joined FCO, 1970; First Sec. (Press), UK Rep. to EC, Brussels, 1972–74; First Sec. and subseq. Head of Chancery, British High Commission, Nicosia, 1974–78; Asst Head of Mexico and Caribbean Dept, FCO, 1978–79; Counsellor, Havana, 1980–82; Counsellor (Political and Economic) and Consul-Gen., Brasilia, 1982–85; Counsellor (Commercial), Rome, 1985–89; Consul-General, São Paulo, 1990–92. *Publication:* The Spaniards, 1969, 2nd edn 1972. *Recreations:* music, walking, the Mediterranean.

PERCHARD, Colin William, CVO 1997; OBE 1984; Chairman, Jersey Arts Trust, since 2001; Minister (Cultural Affairs), India, British Council, 1993–2000; *b* 19 Oct. 1940; *m* 1970, Elisabeth Penelope Glynis, *d* of Sir Glyn Jones, GCMG, MBE; three *s*. *Educ:* Victoria Coll., Jersey; Liverpool Univ. (BA Hons History); Internat. Inst. for Educnl Planning, UNESCO, Paris (DipEd Planning and Admin). British Council: Asst Rep., Blantyre, Malawi, 1964–68; Regional Officer, Africa S of the Sahara, 1968–71; Asst Rep., Calcutta, 1971–72; Officer i/c Dhaka, 1972; Rep., Seoul, 1973–76; Dir, Technical Co-operation Trng Dept, 1976–79; Internat. Inst. for Educnl Planning, Paris, 1979–80; Rep., Harare, 1980–86; Controller, Africa Div., 1986–90; Dir and Cultural Counsellor, Turkey, 1990–93. *Recreations:* theatre, music, cooking. *Address:* La Source, Rue de la Vignette, St Martin, Jersey JE3 6HY.

PERCHE, Neisha; *see* Crosland, N.

PERCIVAL, Allan Arthur, LVO 1996; consultant, UK Embassy, Kabul, Afghanistan, since 2007; *b* 28 Oct. 1950; *s* of Arthur Percival and Rita Margaret Percival. *Educ:* Grimsby Wintringham Grammar Sch. Press Officer, MoD, 1973–82; Chief Inf. Officer, HQ NI, 1982–86; DDPR (Army), 1986–89; NI Office, 1989–93; Press Sec. to Prince of Wales, 1993–96; Dep. Press Sec., Prime Minister's Office, 1996–98; Dir of Communications, LCD, subseq. DCA, 1998–2004; consultant: Kathmandu, Nepal, 2004–07; London, 2004–07. *Recreations:* friends, military history, reading. *Address:* 47 Kindersley Way, Abbots Langley, Herts WD5 0DG. *T:* (01923) 260882.

PERCIVAL, Prof. Ian Colin, PhD; FRS 1985; Professor of Theoretical Physics, 1991–96, Research Professor in Physics, since 2000, Queen Mary (formerly Queen Mary College, then Queen Mary and Westfield College), University of London; *b* 27 July 1931; *m* 1955, Jill Cuff (*née* Herbert) (*d* 1999); two *s* one *d*. *Educ:* Ealing County Grammar Sch.; UCL (BSc, PhD; Fellow, 1986). FRAS. Lectr in Physics, UCL, 1957–61; Reader in Applied Maths, QMC, 1961–67; Prof. of Theoret. Physics, Univ. of Stirling, 1967–74; Prof. of Applied Maths, QMC, 1974–91. Naylor Prize, London Mathematical Soc., 1985; Alexander von Humboldt Foundn Award, 1993; Dirac Medal and Prize, Inst. of Physics, 1999. *Publications:* (with Derek Richards) Introduction to Dynamics, 1983; (with Owen Greene and Irene Ridge) Nuclear Winter, 1985; Quantum State Diffusion, 1998; papers in learned jls on scattering theory, atomic and molecular theory, statistical mechanics, classical dynamics and theory of chaos and foundations of quantum theory. *Address:* Queen Mary, University of London, Mile End Road, E1 4NS. *T:* (020) 7882 5555; *e-mail:* i.c.percival@qmul.ac.uk.

PERCIVAL, John, MBE 2002; freelance dance critic, since 1950; Joint Dance Critic, The Independent, since 1996; *b* 16 March 1927; *s* of Cecil Ernest Percival and Mua Phoebe Margaret Mary Percival (*née* Milchard); *m* 1954, Freda Betty Margaret Thorne-Large (marr. diss. 1972); *m* 1972, Judith Alymer Cruickshank. *Educ:* Sir George Monoux Grammar Sch., Walthamstow; St Catherine's Coll., Oxford (MA). On admin. staff, LCC, then GLC and ILEA, 1951–90. Archivist, Ballet Annual, 1960–64; ballet critic, New Daily, 1960–65; Associate Editor, 1964–81, Editor, 1981–94, Dance & Dancers; Chief Dance Critic, The Times, 1965–94; London correspondent: Dance Mag. (NY), 1965–89; German annual, Ballett, 1966–87; London dance critic, NY Times; Chm. and Dir, Dance & Dancers Ltd, 1991–94; Eur. correspondent, Ballet Review (NY), 1996–. Advr, Nureyev Foundn, 1993–. Mem. Cttee, Gulbenkian Foundn. Has broadcast on radio and TV in Britain, Europe, America and Australia. *Publications:* Antony Tudor, 1963; Modern Ballet, 1970, rev. edn 1980; The World of Diaghilev, 1971, rev. edn 1979; Experimental Dance, 1971; Nureyev: aspects of the dancer, 1975, rev. edn 1979 (trans. Italian 1981, Japanese 1983); The Facts about a Ballet Company, 1979; Theatre in My Blood: a biography of John Cranko, 1983 (trans. German 1985); (with Alexander Bland) Men Dancing, 1984; contributed to: Enciclopedia dello Spettacolo, 1966; Marcia Haydee, Ballerina, 1975; Encyclopaedia of Dance and Ballet, 1977; Das Ballett und die Künste, 1981; John Neumeier und das Hamburger Ballett, 1983, 2nd edn 1993. *Recreations:* watching dance and writing and talking about it, reading thrillers, eating with friends. *Address:* 36 Great James Street, WC1N 3HB. *T:* (020) 7405 0267. *Club:* Critics' Circle (Past Pres.).

PERCIVAL SMITH, Ven. (Anthony) Michael; Archdeacon of Maidstone, 1979–89; *b* 5 Sept. 1924; *s* of Kenneth and Audrey Smith; *m* 1950, Mildred Elizabeth; two *d*. *Educ:* Shrewsbury; Gonville and Caius Coll., Cambridge (MA); Westcott House Theological Coll. Served Army, Rifle Brigade, 1942–46. Cambridge, 1946–48; Westcott House, 1948–50. Deacon 1950, priest 1951; Curate, Holy Trinity, Leamington, 1950–53; Domestic Chaplain to Archbishop of Canterbury, 1953–57; Vicar of All Saints, Upper Norwood, 1957–66; Vicar of Yeovil, 1966–72; Prebendary of Wells Cathedral, 1968–72; RD of Murston, 1968–72; Vicar of St Mildred's, Addiscombe, Croydon, 1972–80; Hon. Canon of Canterbury Cathedral, 1980–; Diocesan Dir of Ordinands, 1980–89; RD of

Rye, 1991–93. *Recreations:* reading, walking. *Address:* Birchwood House Rest Home, Stockland Green Road, Speldhurst, Tunbridge Wells TN3 0TU.

PERCY, family name of **Duke of Northumberland**.

PERCY, Earl; George Dominic Percy; *b* 4 May 1984; *e s* and *heir* of Duke of Northumberland, *qv. Educ:* Eton. A Page of Honour to the Queen, 1996–98. *Address:* Alnwick Castle, Alnwick, Northumberland NE66 1NG.

PERCY, Algernon Eustace Hugh H.; *see* Heber-Percy.

PERCY, John Pitkeathly, (Ian), CBE 1997; CA; Deputy Chairman: Weir Group plc, since 2005 (Director, since 1996); Ricardo plc, since 2005 (Director, since 2000); *b* 16 Jan. 1942; *s* of John Percy and Helen Glass Percy (*née* Pitkeathly); *m* 1965, Sheila Isobel Horn; two *d. Educ:* Edinburgh Acad. Qualified as a Chartered Accountant with Graham Smart & Annan, Edinburgh, 1967; Grant Thornton: Partner, Edinburgh, 1970–78; London, 1978–91; Managing Partner, 1981–88; Sen. Partner, 1988–93; Chairman: Accounts Commn for Scotland, 1992–2000; Audit Scotland, 1998–2000; Companies House, 2002–06. Director: William Wilson (Holdings), 1993–2005; Kiln plc, 1998–2005 (Chm., 2002–05); Cala Gp Ltd, 2000–. Dir, Scottish Legal Aid Bd, 2000–06; Mem., Internat. Auditing Practices Cttee, 1995–2000. Hon. Prof. of Accounting and Auditing, Aberdeen Univ., 1988–. Pres., Inst. of Chartered Accountants of Scotland, 1990–91 (Sen. Vice-Pres., 1989–91). Chm. Court, Queen Margaret Univ., Edinburgh, 2004–. Freeman, City of London, 1983; Liveryman, Painter Stainers' Co., 1983. FRSA 1989. Hon. LLD Aberdeen, 1999. *Recreations:* golf, fishing. *Address:* 4 Westbank, Easter Park Drive, Edinburgh EH4 6SL. *T:* (0131) 312 6446, *Fax:* (0131) 312 6775. *Clubs:* Royal Automobile, Institute of Directors; New (Edinburgh); Denham Golf; Royal & Ancient (St Andrews), Hon. Company of Edinburgh Golfers.

PERCY, Rev. Canon Prof. Martyn William, PhD; Principal, Ripon College Cuddesdon, since 2004, and Oxford Ministry Course, Oxford, since 2006; Professor of Theological Education, King's College London, since 2004; *b* 31 July 1962; *s* of Roy Percy and Sylvia Percy (*née* Owens); *m* 1989, Emma Bray; two *s. Educ:* Merchant Taylors' Sch., Northwood; Univ. of Bristol (BA Hons 1984); Univ. of Durham (Cert. Counselling 1990); KCL (PhD 1993); Univ. of Sheffield (MEd 2003); Univ. of Oxford (MA 2004). Publisher, 1984–88; ordained deacon, 1990, priest, 1991; Curate, St Andrew's, Bedford, 1990–94; Chaplain and Dir of Theol. and Religious Studies, Christ's Coll., Cambridge, 1994–97; Dir of Studies, Sidney Sussex Coll., Cambridge, 1995–97; Dir, Lincoln Theol Inst. for Study of Religion and Society, 1997–2004; Sen. Lectr, 1997–2000, Reader, 2000–03, Univ. of Sheffield; Reader, Univ. of Manchester, 2003–04. Prof. of Theol. and Ministry, Hartford Seminary, Conn, USA, 2002–08. Vis. Fellow, Regent's Park Coll., Oxford, 2006–. Hon. Canon, Sheffield Cathedral, 1997–2004, Canon Theologian, 2004–. Mem. Council and Dir, ASA, 2000–06; Member: Faith and Order Adv. Gp, 1998–2006; HEFCE RAE Panel (Humanities), 2005–08; Indep. Complaints Panel, Portman Gp, 2006–. Founder and Co-Chair, Soc. for Study of Anglicanism, 2003–. Chair, Cliff Coll. Council, 2002–06. Trustee, William Temple Foundn, 2002–. Patron, St Francis Children's Soc., 1998–. Ed., Modern Believing, 1997–2005. Freeman, City of London, 1989. FRSA 2000. *Publications:* Words, Wonders and Power: understanding contemporary Christian fundamentalism and revivalism, 1996; (ed) Intimate Affairs: spirituality and sexuality in perspective, 1997; Power and the Church: ecclesiology in an age of transition, 1998; Richard Hooker: an introduction, 1999; (ed) Previous Convictions: studies in religious conversion, 2000; (ed with G. R. Evans) Managing the Church?: order and organisation in a secular age, 2000; (ed) Calling Time: religion, society and change at the turn of the millennium, 2000; (ed with A. Walker) Restoring the Image: essays in honour of David Martin, 2001; (ed jtly) Darkness Yielding, 2001; Salt of the Earth: religious resilience in a secular age, 2002; (ed with I. Jones) Fundamentalism, Church and Society, 2002; (ed with S. Lowe) The Character of Wisdom: essays in honour of Wesley Carr, 2004; Engaging Theology: Christianity and contemporary culture, 2005; Clergy: the origin of species, 2006; (ed with I. Markham) Why Liberal Churches are Growing, 2006. *Recreations:* reading, cinema, listening to jazz. *Address:* Ripon College Cuddesdon, Oxford OX44 9EX. *T:* (01865) 874404, *Fax:* (01865) 875431; *e-mail:* mpercy@ripon-cuddesdon.ac.uk. *Club:* Athenæum.

PERCY, His Honour Rodney Algernon; a Circuit Judge, 1979–93; caravan site operator, 1993–99, general handyman on the site, since 2000; *b* 15 May 1924; 3rd *s* of late Hugh James Percy, Solicitor, Alnwick; *m* 1948, Mary Allen (*d* 2002), *d* of late J. E. Benbow, Aberystwyth; one *s* three *d. Educ:* Uppingham; Brasenose Coll., Oxford (MA). Lieut, Royal Corps of Signals, 1942–46, served in Burma, India, Malaya, Java. Called to Bar: Middle Temple, 1950; Lincoln's Inn, 1987 (*ad eund*). Dep. Coroner, N Northumberland, 1957; Asst Recorder, Sheffield QS, 1964; Dep. Chm., Co. Durham QS, 1966–71; a Recorder of the Crown Court, 1972–79. Pres., Tyneside Marriage Guidance Council, 1983–87; Founder Mem., Family Conciliation Service for Northumberland and Tyneside, 1982–93 (Pres., 1988–93). *Publications:* (ed) Charlesworth on Negligence, 4th edn 1962 to 6th edn 1977, 7th edn (Charlesworth & Percy on Negligence) 1983 to 9th edn 1997, consultant ed., 10th edn 2001 to 11th edn 2006; (contrib.) Atkin's Court Forms, 2nd edn, Vol. 20, 1982, rev. edn 1987, 1993 (title Health and Safety at Work), and Vol. 29, 1983, rev. edn 1991 (title Negligence). *Recreations:* golf, gardening, hill walking, King Charles Cavalier spaniels, beach-combing. *Address:* Brookside, Lesbury, Alnwick, Northumberland NE66 3AT. *T:* (01665) 830326/830000.

PEREIRA, Margaret, CBE 1985; BSc; FIBiol; Controller, Home Office Forensic Science Service, 1982–88; *b* 22 April 1928. *Educ:* La Sainte Union Convent, Bexley Heath; Dartford County Grammar School for Girls; Chelsea Coll. of Science and Technol. BSc 1953. Joined Metropolitan Police Forensic Science Lab., New Scotland Yard, 1947; Dep. Dir, Home Office Forensic Science Central Res. Estab., 1976; Director, Home Office Forensic Science Laboratory: Aldermaston, 1977; Chepstow, 1979.

PEREIRA, Most Rev. Simeon Anthony; Archbishop of Karachi, (RC), 1994–2002, now Archbishop Emeritus; *b* 19 Oct. 1927. Ordained priest, 1951; consecrated Bishop, 1971; Bishop of Islamabad-Rawalpindi, 1973–93; Co-adjutor Bishop of Karachi, 1993–94. *Address:* c/o Monastery of Angels, Plot No 213, Deh Landhi, Karachi 75120, Pakistan.

PEREIRA GRAY, Prof. Sir Denis (John), Kt 1999; OBE 1981; FRCP, FRCGP, FMedSci; General Medical Practitioner, 1962–2000; Professor of General Practice, University of Exeter, 1986–2001, now Emeritus (Director of Postgraduate Medical School, 1987–97); President, Royal College of General Practitioners, 1997–2000; *b* 2 Oct. 1935; *s* of late Dr Sydney Joseph Pereira Gray and Alice Evelyn Gray; forename Pereira changed to surname by deed poll; *m* 1962, Jill Margaret Hoyte; one *s* three *d. Educ:* Exeter Sch.; St John's Coll., Cambridge (MA); St Bartholomew's Hosp. Med. Sch. MB BChir. FRCGP 1973; FRCP 1999. Sen. Lectr in Charge, Univ. of Exeter, 1973–86. Regional Adviser in Gen. Practice, 1975–2000; Consultant Adviser in Gen. Practice to Chief MO, DHSS, 1984–87. Mem., GMC, 1994–2003; Chm., Jt Cttee on Postgrad. Trng for Gen. Practice, 1994–97. Trustee, The Nuffield Trust (formerly Nuffield Provincial Hosps Trust), 1994–2006 (Chm., 2003–06). Chm. Council, RCGP, 1987–90 (Hon. Editor, Journal, 1972–80, Publications, 1976–2000); Vice-Chm., 1998–2000, Chm., 2000–02, Acad. of Medical Royal Colls. Editor, Medical Annual, 1983–87. Pres., Watch?, 2007–08; Patron, Nat. Assoc. for Patient Participation. Lectures: James Mackenzie, RCGP, 1977; Pfizer, N England Faculty, RCGP, Gale Meml, SW England Faculty, RCGP, 1979; Eli Lilly, Haliburton Hume Meml, Newcastle upon Tyne and Northern Counties Med. Soc., Northcott Meml, Barnstaple, Harvard Davis, Denbigh, McConaghey Meml, Lifton, 1988; Murray Scott Meml, Aberdeen, 1990; Harben Meml, London, 1994; Sally Irvine, Ashridge Mgt Coll., 1995; Albert Wander, RSocMed, 1998; Andrew Smith, Durham, 1998; David Bruce, London, 1999; Frans Huygen, Nijmegen, Netherlands, 2001; Long Fox, Bristol, 2002. Founder FMedSci 1998. Hon. FRSH 1997; Hon. FFPH 1997; Hon. FIHM 2000 (FHSM 1997); Hon. FRCPI 2001; Hon. FFGDP 2003; Hon. Fellow, QMC, Univ. of London, 2000. Hon. DSc De Montfort, 1997; Hon. DM Nottingham, 2003. Gold Medal, Hunterian Soc., 1966, 1969; Sir Charles Hastings Prize, BMA, 1967, 1970; George Abercrombie Award, RCGP, 1978; Foundn Council Award, RCGP, 1980; Sir Harry Platt Prize, Modern Medicine Jl, 1981; Silver Medal, SIMG, 1989; Gold Medal, RIPH&H, 1999. *Publications:* Running a Practice (jtly), 1978, 3rd edn 1981; Training for General Practice, 1981; Forty Years On: the story of the first forty years of the RCGP, 1992; articles in Lancet, BMJ, Jl RCGP, British Jl Gen. Pract. *Recreation:* reading. *Address:* Alford House, 9 Marlborough Road, Exeter EX2 4TJ. *T:* (01392) 218080.

PERES, Shimon; President of Israel, since 2007; Member of Knesset, 1959–2007; *b* 1923; *s* of Yitzhak and Sarah Persky; *m* 1945, Sonia Gelman; two *s* one *d. Educ:* New York Univ.; Harvard Univ. Head of Naval Services, 1948–49; Head of Israel Defense Min. delegn to US, 1949–52; Dir-Gen., Defense Min., 1953–59; Dep. Defense Minister, 1959–65; Sec. Gen., Rafi Party, 1965–68; Minister: of Immigrant Absorption, 1969–70; of Transport and Communications, 1970–74; of Information, 1974; of Defense, 1974–77; Acting Prime Minister, 1977; Prime Minister, 1984–86 and 1995–96; Vice Premier, 1986–90; Minister of Foreign Affairs, 1986–88 and 1992–95; Minister of Finance, 1988–90. Chm., Israel Labour Party, 1977–92 and 1995–97; Vice-Pres., Socialist Internat., 1978. (Jtly) Nobel Peace Prize, 1994. *Publications:* The Next Phase, 1965; David's Sling, 1970; Tomorrow is Now, 1978; From These Men, 1980; Entebbe Diary, 1991; The New Middle East, 1993; Battling for Peace: memoirs, 1995. *Recreation:* reading. *Address:* Office of the President, 3 Hanassi Street, Jerusalem 92188, Israel.

PERETZ, David Lindsay Corbett, CB 1996; independent consultant to international organisations, since 1999; *b* 29 May 1943; *s* of Michael and April Peretz; *m* 1966, Jane Wildman; one *s* one *d. Educ:* The Leys Sch., Cambridge; Exeter Coll., Oxford (MA). Asst Principal, Min. of Technol., 1965–69; Head of Public Policy and Institutional Studies, IBRO, 1969–76; HM Treasury: Principal, 1976–80; Asst Sec., External Finance, 1980–84; Principal Pvte Sec. to Chancellor of Exchequer, 1984–85; Under-Secretary: Home Finance, 1985–86; Monetary Gp, Public Finance, 1986–90; UK Exec. Dir, IMF and World Bank, and Economic Minister, Washington, 1990–94; Dep. Dir, Internat. Finance, HM Treasury, 1994–99. Chair, Indep. Adv. Cttee on Develt Impact, DFID, 2007–. *Recreations:* walking, gardening, listening to music. *Address: e-mail:* dlcperetz@yahoo.co.uk.

PÉREZ DE CUÉLLAR, Javier, Hon. GCMG 1992; Ambassador of Peru to France, 2001–04; holds personal rank of Ambassador; *b* 19 Jan. 1920; *m* Marcela (*née* Temple); one *s* one *d. Educ:* Law Faculty, Catholic Univ., Lima, Perú. Joined Peruvian Foreign Ministry, 1940; Diplomatic Service, 1944; Sec., Peruvian Embassies in France, UK, Bolivia and Brazil and Counsellor, Embassy, Brazil, 1944–60; Mem., Peruvian Delegn to First Session of Gen. Assembly, UN, 1946; Dir, Legal, Personnel, Admin, Protocol and Political Affairs Depts, Min. of Foreign Affairs, Perú, 1961–63; Peruvian Ambassador to Switzerland, 1964–66; Perm. Under-Sec. and Sec.-Gen. of Foreign Office, 1966–69; Ambassador of Perú to USSR and to Poland, 1969–71; Perm. Rep. of Perú to UN, 1971–75 (Rep. to UN Security Council, 1973–74); Special Rep. of UN Sec.-Gen. in Cyprus, 1975–77; Ambassador of Perú to Venezuela, 1978; UN Under-Sec.-Gen. for Special Political Affairs, 1979–81; Sec.-Gen., UN, 1982–91. Prime Minister and Foreign Minister, Peru, 2000–01. Pres., World Commn on Culture and Develt, UN/UNESCO, 1992–; Chm. Emeritus, Inter-Amer. Dialogue, 1992–. Former Professor: of Diplomatic Law, Academia Diplomática del Perú; of Internat. Relations, Academia de Guerra Aérea del Perú. LLD *hc:* Univ. of Nice, France, 1983; Carleton Univ., Ottawa, 1985; Osnabruck Univ., 1986; Coimbra Univ., 1986; Oxford, 1993; other hon. degrees include: Jagiellonian Univ., Poland, 1984; Charles Univ. Czechoslovakia, 1984; Sofia Univ., Bulgaria, 1984; Universidad Nacional Mayor de San Marcos, Perú, 1984; Vrije Universiteit Brussel, Belgium, 1984; Sorbonne Univ., Paris, 1985; Cambridge Univ., 1989; Univ. of Salamanca, 1991; Oxford Univ., 1993. Various internat. awards including: Prince of Asturias Prize, 1987; Olof Palme Prize, 1989; Jawaharlal Nehru Award, 1989. Grand Cross, Order of El Sol (Perú); foreign decorations include: US Medal of Freedom; Grand Cross, Legion of Honour (France). *Publications:* Manual de Derecho Diplomático, 1964; Anarchy or Order, 1992; Pilgrimage for Peace, 1997. *Address:* Avenida Aurelio Miró Quesada 1071, Lima 27, Perú. *Clubs:* Travellers (Paris); Nacional, Ecuestre Huachipa, Jockey (Lima, Perú).

PÉREZ ESQUIVEL, Adolfo; sculptor; Hon. President: Servicio Paz y Justicia en América Latina, since 1986; Servicio Paz y Justicia Argentina, since 1973; President, International League for the Rights and Liberation of Peoples, since 1987; *b* 26 Nov. 1931; *m* 1956, Amanda Guerreño; three *s. Educ:* Nat. Sch. of Fine Arts, Buenos Aires. Prof. of Art, Manuel Belgrano Nat. Sch. of Fine Arts, Buenos Aires, 1956–76; Prof., Faculty of Architecture and Urban Studies, Univ. Nacional de la Plata, 1969–73; Gen. Co-ordinator, Servicio Paz y Justicia en América Latina, 1974–86. Work in permanent collections: Buenos Aires Mus. of Modern Art; Mus. of Fine Arts, Córdoba; Fine Arts Mus., Rosario. Joined group dedicated to principles of militant non-violence, and engaged in projects to promote self-sufficiency in urban areas, 1971; founded Paz y Justicia magazine, 1973. Co-founder, Ecumenical Movement for Human Rights, Argentina; Pres., Permanent Assembly for Human Rights. Premio la Nación de Escultura; Pope John XXIII prize, Pax Christi Orgn, 1977; Nobel Peace Prize, 1980. *Address:* Servicio Paz y Justicia, Piedras 730, CP 1070, Buenos Aires, Argentina.

PERFECT, Fiona Elizabeth; *see* Rae, F. E.

PERFECT, Henry George, FICE, FCIWEM; Chairman: Babtie Group Ltd, 1996–2002; British Water, 2000–02; *b* 31 March 1944; *s* of George Hunter Perfect and Constance Mary Perfect (*née* Holland); *m* 1971, Kathleen Margaret Lilian Bain; two *s* one *d. Educ:* West Bridgford Grammar Sch., Nottingham; Birmingham Univ. (BSc Civil Engrg); Glasgow Univ. (MEng Foundn Engrg). FICE 1987; FCIWEM (FIWEM 1992). Asst Engr, C. H. Dobbie & Partners, 1965–69; Babtie Shaw & Morton, subseq. Babtie Group: Engr (projects incl. Kielder Water Scheme, and numerous reservoir, water and sewerage projects), 1969–83; Associate, 1983–86; Partner, 1987–93; Man. Dir, Water Business,

1994–95. *Publications:* several papers on civil and water engrg. *Recreations:* hill walking, cycling. *Address:* 15 Thorn Road, Bearsden, Glasgow G61 4BS.

PERHAM, Linda; JP; Chair, East Living housing association, since 2006; *b* 29 June 1947; *d* of George Sidney Conroy and Edith Louisa Conroy (*née* Overton); *m* 1972, Raymond John Perham; two *d. Educ:* Mary Datchelor Girls' Sch.; Univ. of Leicester (BA Special Hons Classics); Ealing Tech. Coll. Postgrad. Dip. Liby Assoc.; MCLIP (ALA 1972). Library Asst, London Borough of Southwark, 1966; Inf. Officer, GLC Research Liby, 1970–72; City of London Polytechnic: Archives and Publications Librarian, 1972–76; Staff Develt Librarian, 1976–78; Cataloguer, Fawcett Liby, 1981–92; Bibliographical Librarian, Epping Forest Coll., 1992–97. MP (Lab) Ilford N, 1997–2005; contested (Lab) same seat, 2005. Mem., Select Cttee on Trade and Industry, 1998–2005; Chairman: All Party Gp on Libraries, 1998–2005; All Party Gp on Crossrail, 2003–05; Vice Chairman: All Party Gp on Male Cancers, 1998–2005; All Party Gp on Men's Health, 2001–05; Labour Friends of Israel, 2001–; Hon. Secretary: All Party Gp on Ageing and Older People, 1998–2005; British-Israel Parly Gp, 1998–2005; All Party Parly Gp on Corporate Social Responsibility, 2001–05; All Party Gp on Patient and Public Involvement in Health, 2004–05. London Borough of Redbridge: Councillor, 1989–97; Mayor, 1994–95; Chm., Highways Cttee, 1995–96, Leisure Cttee, 1996–97. Mem., Consumer Council for Water, London & SE (formerly Thames), 2005–; Consumer Dir, TrustMark, 2006–. Vice Chair, London Voluntary Service Council, 2005–; Board Member: East Thames Gp, 2006–; Housing and Community Assoc., 2006–. Trustee, Friends of the Women's Library, 2005–. FRSA 2005. Hon. FCLIP 2003. JP: Redbridge, 1990; Newham, 2006; Redbridge, 2007. *Publications:* Directory of GLC Library Resources, 1970, 2nd edn 1971; Greater London Council Publications 1965–71, 1972; Libraries of London, 1973; How to Find Out in French, 1977. *Recreations:* organising quizzes, arts, cinema, theatre, sudoku, watching tennis. *Address: e-mail:* lindaperham@hotmail.com.

PERHAM, Rt Rev. Michael Francis; *see* Gloucester, Bishop of.

PERHAM, Nancy Jane; *see* Lane, N. J.

PERHAM, Prof. Richard Nelson, ScD; FMedSci; FRS 1984; Master, St John's College, Cambridge, 2004–07 (Fellow, since 1964); *b* 27 April 1937; *s* of Cyril Richard William Perham and Helen Harrow Perham (*née* Thornton); *m* 1969, Nancy Jane Lane, *qv;* one *s* one *d. Educ:* Latymer Upper School; St John's College, Cambridge; BA 1961, MA 1965, PhD 1965, ScD 1976; Scholar; Slater Studentship, 1961–64; Henry Humphreys Prize, 1963. Nat. Service RN, 1956–58. Cambridge University: MRC Scholar, Lab. of Molecular Biol., 1961–64; Univ. Demonstrator in Biochem., 1964–69, Lectr, 1969–77; Reader in Biochemistry of Macromolecular Structures, 1977–89; Head, Dept of Biochem., 1985–96; Prof. of Structural Biochem., 1989–2004; Res. Fellow, St John's Coll., 1964–67, Tutor, 1967–77, Pres., 1983–87. Helen Hay Whitney Fellow, Dept of Molecular Biophysics, Yale Univ., 1966–67; EMBO Fellow, Max-Planck-Institut für Medizinische Forschung, Heidelberg, 1971; Drapers' Vis. Prof., Univ. of New South Wales, 1972; Biochem. Soc. Visitor, Aust. and NZ, 1979; Fogarty Internat. Scholar, NIH, USA, 1990–93. Member: EMBO, 1983; SRC Enzyme Chem. and Tech. Cttee, 1973–75; Enzyme Panel, Biol. Scis Cttee, 1975–76; SERC Science Bd, 1985–90; Biochem. Soc. Cttee, 1980–84; British Nat. Cttee for Biochem., 1982–87; Dir's Adv. Gp, AFRC Inst. of Animal Physiology, 1983–86; Exec. Council, Novartis (CIBA) Foundn, 1989–2002 (Trustee, 2002–08); Chm., Biol Scis Cttee, SERC, 1987–90 (Mem., 1983–85); Pres., Section D (Biological Scis), BAAS, 1987–88. Chm., Scientific Adv. Cttee, Lister Inst. of Preventive Medicine, 2000–06 (Mem., 1992–98). Mem., Marshall Aid Commemoration Commn, FCO, 1999–2005 (Vice-Chm., 2004–05). Mem., Academia Europaea, 1992. Syndic, CUP, 1988–2004. FRSA 1988; FMedSci 2005. Max Planck Res. Prize, 1993; Novartis Medal and Prize, 1998; Silver Medal, Italian Biochem. Soc., 2000; Edman Prize, Internat. Assoc. of Protein Structure Analysis and Proteomics, 2008. *Publications:* (ed) Instrumentation in Amino Acid Sequence Analysis, 1975; papers in sci. jls. *Recreations:* gardening, rowing (Lady Margaret BC), theatre, nosing around in antique shops. *Address:* St John's College, Cambridge CB2 1TP. *T:* (01223) 338600. *Clubs:* Oxford and Cambridge; Hawks (Cambridge).

PERKINS, Alice Elizabeth, CB 2002; Director General, Corporate Development Group (formerly Head of Civil Service Corporate Management), Cabinet Office, 2000–05; *b* 24 May 1949; *d* of Derrick Leslie John Perkins and Elsa Rose Perkins, CBE (*née* Rink); *m* 1978, John Whitaker Straw, *qv;* one *s* one *d. Educ:* North London Collegiate Sch. for Girls; St Anne's Coll., Oxford (BA Hons Modern Hist. 1971; Hon. Fellow 2006). Joined CS, DHSS, 1971; Principal, 1976–84; Asst Sec., DHSS, then DSS, 1984–90; Dir of Personnel, DSS, 1990–93; Under Sec., Defence Policy and Materiel Gp, HM Treasury, 1993–95; Dep. Dir, Public Spending, HM Treasury, 1995–98; Dir, Corporate Mgt, DoH, 1998–2000. Non-executive Director: Littlewoods Orgn, 1997–2000; Taylor Nelson Sofres, 2005–; BAA, 2006. Exec. Coach, JCA Gp, 2006–. Ext. Mem. Council, Oxford Univ., 2006–. *Recreations:* gardening, looking at paintings.

PERKINS, Brian Temple; newsreader, BBC Radio 4, 1965–69 and 1978–2003; freelance broadcaster, since 2003; *b* 11 Sept. 1943; *s* of Ray and Laurel Perkins; *m* 1964, Joan Russell; one *s* two *d. Educ:* Wanganui and Wellington, NZ. Broadcaster: NZ Broadcasting Co., 1962–64; BBC, 1965–69; double bass player, NZBC SO, 1970–75; broadcaster: Radio NZ, 1975–78; BBC, 1978–2003. *Recreations:* music, fell-walking, France. *T:* (01483) 233919.

PERKINS, Crispian G. S.; *see* Steele-Perkins.

PERKINS, Prof. Donald Hill, CBE 1991; FRS 1966; Professor of Elementary Particle Physics, 1965–93, and Fellow of St Catherine's College, since 1965, Oxford University; *b* 15 Oct. 1925; *s* of George W. and Gertrude Perkins; *m* 1955, Dorothy Mary (*née* Maloney); two *d. Educ:* Malet Lambert High School, Hull. BSc London 1945; PhD London 1948; 1851 Senior Scholar, 1948–51. G. A. Wills Research Associate in Physics, Univ. of Bristol, 1951–55; Lawrence Radiation Lab., Univ. of California, 1955–56; Lectr in Physics, 1956–60, Reader in Physics, 1960–65, Univ. of Bristol. Mem., SERC, 1985–89. Hon. DSc: Sheffield, 1982; Bristol, 1995. Guthrie Medal, Inst. of Physics, 1979; Holweck Medal and Prize, Société Française de Physique, 1992; Royal Medal, Royal Soc., 1997; High Energy Physics Prize, Eur. Physical Soc., 2001. *Publications:* The Study of Elementary Particles by the Photographic Method (with C. F. Powell and P. H. Fowler), 1959; Introduction to High Energy Physics, 1972, 4th edn 2000; Particle Astrophysics, 2003; about 50 papers and review articles in Nature, Physical Review, Philosophical Magazine, Physics Letters, Proc. Royal Soc., Nuovo Cimento, etc. *Recreations:* squash, tennis. *Address:* 25 Shingle Bank Drive, Milford-on-Sea, Lymington SO41 0WQ. *T:* (01590) 641930.

PERKINS, Douglas John David; Co-founder, Co-owner and Managing Director, Specsavers Optical Group Ltd, since 1984; *b* Llanelli, 2 April 1943; *s* of Philip Denzil Perkins and Muriel Ester Perkins (*née* Thomas); *m* 1967, Mary Lesley Bebbington (*see* Dame M. L. Perkins); one *s* two *d. Educ:* Advanced Technology Coll. of Wales, Cardiff; British Optical Assoc. (Dip. Contact Lens Practice). FCOptom. Co-owner and optometrist, Bebbington and Perkins Gp, 1966–80. Liveryman, Spectacle Makers' Co. Hon. Fellow: Cardiff Univ., 2005; Swansea Inst., 2006. Hon. Dr Anglia Ruskin, 2006. *Recreations:* walking, yoga, grandchildren, watching Rugby and cricket. *Address:* Hautes Falaises, Fort George, St Peter Port, Guernsey GY1 2SR. *T:* (01481) 725901, *Fax:* (01481) 725968; *e-mail:* dougp@gg.specsavers.com.

PERKINS, Prof. Edwin Arend, PhD; FRS 2007; FRSC; Professor of Mathematics, since 1989, and Canada Research Chair in Probability, since 2001, University of British Columbia; *b* 31 Aug. 1953; *s* of John Albert Perkins and Karin Brita (*née* Kunst); *m* 1974, Karen Marie Woitak; one *s* two *d. Educ:* Univ. of Toronto (BSc 1975); Univ. of Illinois (PhD 1979). University of British Columbia: Postdoctoral Fellow, 1979–80; NSERC Univ. Res. Fellow, 1980–81; Asst Prof. of Maths, 1982–85; Associate Prof. of Maths, 1985–89. Prof. Associé, Univ. of Strasbourg, 1984; SERC Res. Fellow, Cambridge Univ., 1986–87; Vis. Prof., Univ. of Wisconsin, 2000–01. FRSC 1988. *Publications:* Dawson-Watanabe Superprocesses and Measure-valued Diffusions, 1999; contribs to Memoirs Amer. Maths Soc. *Recreations:* hiking, cross-country ski-ing, canoeing. *Address:* Department of Mathematics, University of British Columbia, Vancouver, BC V6T 1Z2, Canada. *T:* (604) 8226670, *Fax:* (604) 8226074; *e-mail:* perkins@math.ubc.ca.

PERKINS, Prof. John Douglas, CBE 2007; PhD; FIChemE, FIMA; CEng, FREng; Vice President and Dean of Engineering and Physical Sciences, University of Manchester, since 2004; *b* 18 March 1950; *s* of late Douglas Herbert and of Isobel Mary Perkins; *m* 1975, Chantal Marie Lestavel (marr. diss. 1992); one *s. Educ:* Imperial Coll., London (BSc Eng; PhD 1976; DIC). ACGI 1971, FCGI 1996; FIChemE 1986; CEng 1986; CMath 1992; FIMA 1992; FREng 1993; CSci 2004. Demonstrator in Chem. Engrg, Univ. of Cambridge, 1973–77; Lectr in Chem. Engrg, 1977–83, Sen. Lectr, 1983–85, Imperial Coll., London; ICI Prof. of Process Systems Engrg, Univ. of Sydney, Aust., 1985–88; Imperial College, University of London: Prof. of Chem. Engrg, 1988–99; Dir, Centre for Process Systems Engrg, 1992–98; Hd, Dept of Chem. Engrg and Chem. Technol., 1996–2001; Courtaulds Prof. of Chem. Engrg, 2000–04; Principal, Faculty of Engrg, 2001–04. Pres., IChemE, 2000–01 (Dep. Pres., 1999–2000; Mem. Council, 1997–2002); Vice Pres., RAEng, 2007– (Mem. Council, 2004–). FRSA 2004. *Recreations:* orienteering, reading. *Address:* University of Manchester, PO Box 88, Sackville Street, Manchester M60 1QD. *T:* (0161) 306 9111, *Fax:* (0161) 306 9109.

PERKINS, John Vernon; District Judge (Magistrates' Courts) (formerly Metropolitan Stipendiary Magistrate), since 1999; *b* 13 June 1950; *s* of late Sidney and Lilian Florence Perkins; *m* 1975, Margaret Craig; one *s* one *d. Educ:* Tottenham Grammar Sch. Admitted Solicitor, 1975; Articled Clerk, 1970–75, Asst Solicitor, 1975–80, Partner, 1980–99 (Sen. Partner, 1988–99), J. B. Wheatley & Co. Mem., London Criminal Courts Solicitors' Assoc., 1975–99 (Hon. Mem. 1999). *Recreations:* walking, swimming, gardening. *Address:* c/o Principal Chief Clerk's Office, Secretariat Department, 65 Romney Street, SW1P 3RD.

PERKINS, Jonathan David; a Senior Immigration Judge, Asylum and Immigration Tribunal (formerly a Vice President, Immigration Appeal Tribunal), since 2003; *b* 15 Feb. 1958; *s* of Thomas Edward Perkins and Constance Perkins; *m* 1991, Margaret Anne Jackson; one *s* one *d. Educ:* Brierley Hill Grammar Sch.; University Coll. Cardiff (LLB Wales). Called to the Bar, Middle Temple, 1980; barrister, Midland and Oxford Circuit, 1981–99; Immigration Appeals Adjudicator, pt-time, 1993–99, full-time, 1999–2003. Methodist local preacher, 1988–. *Recreations:* church work, model making. *Address:* Asylum and Immigration Tribunal, Field House, Breams Building, Chancery Lane, EC4A 1DZ. *T:* (020) 7073 4200; *e-mail:* perkins.family@btinternet.com.

PERKINS, Maj.-Gen. Kenneth, CB 1977; MBE 1955; DFC 1953; Commander, Sultan's Armed Forces, Oman, 1975–77 (successfully concluded Dhofar War); *b* 15 Aug. 1926; *s* of George Samuel Perkins and Arabella Sarah Perkins (*née* Wise); *m* 1st, 1949, Anne Theresa Barry (marr. diss. 1984); three *d;* 2nd, 1985, Hon. Celia Sandys, *d* of Rt Hon. Lord Duncan-Sandys, CH, PC and Diana, *d* of Rt Hon. Sir Winston Churchill, KG, OM, CH, FRS; one *s* one *d. Educ:* Lewes County Sch. for Boys; New Coll., Oxford. Enlisted 1944; commnd RA 1946; various appts in Middle and Far East, BAOR and UK until 1965, incl. air OP pilot in Korean War, Malayan Emergency, and Staff Coll. Quetta 1958; Instructor, Staff Coll. Camberley, 1965–66; CO 1st Regt Royal Horse Artillery, 1967–69; GSO 1 Singapore, 1970; Comdr 24 Bde, 1971–72; RCDS 1973; Central Staff, MoD, 1974; Maj.-Gen., 1975; Asst Chief of Defence Staff (Ops), 1977–80; Dir, Military Assistance Office, MoD, 1980–82. Defence Advr, BAe, 1982–86. Col Comdt, RA, 1980–85. Vice Pres., Sultan of Oman's Armed Forces Assoc., 1994– (Chm., 1987–94). Mem. Council, Res. Inst. for Study of Conflict, 1992–2000. Mil. Advr, The Sun newspaper, 1991–2006. Chm., Politicians' Complaints Commn, 1992–93. Trustee, Battlefield Trust, 1998–2001. Selangor Distinguished Conduct Medal (Malaya), 1955; Hashemite Order of Independence, first class, 1975; Order of Oman, 1977. *Publications:* Weapons and Warfare, 1987; A Fortunate Soldier (autobiog.), 1988; Khalida (novel), 1991; articles in press and professional jls. *Recreations:* writing, painting (exhibited RA), cycling. *Address:* 88 Church Street, Great Bedwyn, Marlborough, Wilts SN8 3PF.

PERKINS, Dame Mary (Lesley), DBE 2007; Co-founder and Co-owner, Specsavers Optical Group Ltd, since 1984; *b* 14 Feb. 1944; *d* of late (George) Leslie Bebbington and of Eileen Hilda Constance Bebbington (*née* Mawditt); *m* 1967, Douglas John David Perkins, *qv;* one *s* two *d. Educ:* Fairfield Grammar Sch., Bristol; Advanced Technol. Coll. of Wales, Cardiff. FBOA 1965. Co-owner and optometrist, Bebbington and Perkins, 1966–80. Dir, Guernsey Trng Agency. Freeman, City of London; Liveryman, Spectacle Makers' Co. Dir, Womens' Refuge Guernsey; Pres., Age Concern Guernsey; Patron, Everywoman Ltd. Hon. Fellow, Cardiff Univ., 2005. *Address:* Specsavers Optical Group Ltd, La Villiaze, St Andrews, Guernsey GY6 8YP.

PERL, Alfredo; pianist; *b* Chile, 25 June 1965. *Educ:* German Sch., Santiago; Univ. de Chile, Santiago; Cologne Conservatoire; with Maria Curcio in London. First performance at age of 9; début in Internat. Piano Series, Queen Elizabeth Hall, 1992; first recital at Wigmore Hall, 1994, and performed complete Beethoven Sonata cycle, 1996–97; UK recital appearances include: BBC Manchester and Scotland; Bridgewater Hall; St John's Smith Sq. Concert Series; has performed worldwide, including: Vienna Musikverein; London Barbican; Rudolfinum, Prague; Munich Herkulessaal; Izumi Hall, Osaka; Teatro Colón, Buenos Aires; Sydney Town Hall; Nat. Arts Centre, Ottawa; Great Hall, Moscow Conservatoire; orchestral appearances include: LSO; BBC SO; RPO; Hague Residentie; Florida Philharmonic; Leipzig Radio; Adelaide SO; Melbourne SO; Mozarteum Orch.; Orch. de la Suisse Romande; MDR Leipzig; début at BBC Prom. Concerts, with BBC Philharmonic Orch., 1997. Has made numerous recordings, incl. complete Beethoven Sonatas. *Address:* c/o HarrisonParrott Ltd, 12 Penzance Place, W11 4PA.

PERL, Prof. Martin Lewis, PhD; FInstP; Professor of Physics, Stanford Linear Accelerator Center, Stanford University, California, 1963–2004, now Emeritus; *b* 24 June 1927; *s* of Oscar Perl and Fay Rosenthal Perl; *m;* three *s* one *d. Educ:* Polytechnic Univ.,

NY (BE Chem. 1948); Columbia Univ., NY (PhD Physics 1955). FInstP 1998. Chemical Engr, General Electric Co., 1948–50; Research Asst, Columbia Univ., 1950–55; Instructor, Asst Prof. and Associate Prof., Univ. of Michigan, 1955–63; Chm. of Faculty, Stanford Univ., 1991–. Mem., US Nat. Acad. of Scis, 1980–. Hon. DSc Chicago, 1990. Wolf Prize in Physics, Wolf Foundn, Israel, 1982; Nobel Prize in Physics, 1995. *Publications:* High Energy Hadron Physics, 1974; Physics Careers, Employment and Education, 1977; The Search for New Elementary Particles, 1992; The Tau-Charm Factory, 1994; Reflections on Experimental Science, 1996; numerous in physics and in science education. *Recreations:* collecting mechanical antiques, swimming, gardening. *Address:* Stanford Linear Accelerator Center, Stanford University, Stanford, CA 94309, USA. *T:* (650) 9262652.

PERLMAN, Itzhak; violinist and conductor; *b* Tel Aviv, 31 Aug. 1945; *s* of Chaim and Shoshana Perlman; *m* 1967, Toby Lynn Friedlander; two *s* three *d. Educ:* Studied at Tel Aviv Acad. of Music with Ryvka Goldgart, and at Juilliard Sch., NY, under Dorothy Delay and Ivan Galamian. First solo recital at age of 10 in Israel; New York début, 1958. Leventritt Meml Award, NY, 1964. Tours extensively in USA and plays with all major American symphony orchestras; has conducted major orchestras worldwide incl. NY, Chicago, LA, Boston and Berlin Philharmonic Orchestras, LPO, Amsterdam Concertgebouw; recital tours of Canada, South America, Europe, Israel, Far East and Australia; Principal Guest Conductor, Detroit SO, 2001–; Music Advr, St Louis SO, 2003–05. Has recorded numerous works for violin. Teacher, Juilliard Sch. and Perlman Music Prog. Has received many Grammy Awards. Hon. degrees: Harvard; Yale; Brandeis. *Recreation:* cooking. *Address:* c/o IMG Artists, Carnegie Hall Tower, 152 West 57th Street, 5th Floor, New York, NY 10019, USA.

PERMAN, Raymond John; Chairman: Social Investment Scotland, since 2002; Access to Finance Expert Group (formerly Small Business Investment Taskforce), Department of Business, Enterprise and Regulatory Reform (formerly Department of Trade and Industry), since 2005; Good Practice Ltd, since 2005; *b* 22 Aug. 1947; *s* of late Leonard Perman and Gladys Perman (*née* Rockingham); *m* 1974, Fay Young, writer and editor; three *s. Educ:* Univ. of St Andrews; BA Hons Open Univ.; Univ. of Edinburgh (MBA 1987). Journalist: Westminster Press, 1969–71; The Times, 1971–75; Financial Times, 1976–81; Dep. Editor, Sunday Standard, 1981–83; Man. Dir, Insider Publications Ltd, 1983–94; Director: Caledonian Publishing plc, 1994–96; GJWS, 1997–98; Chief Exec., Scottish Financial Enterprise, 1999–2003. Mem. Bd, Scottish Enterprise, 2004–. Chm., Scottish Adv. Council, WWF, 2000–04; Trustee, WWF UK, 2001–04. Mem. Court, Heriot-Watt Univ., 2003–. *Publications:* numerous newspaper and magazine articles. *Recreations:* forestry, painting, playing bass with the Blues Condition. *Address:* Social Investment Scotland, 1 St Andrew Square, Edinburgh EH2 2BD. *T:* (0131) 558 7706.

PERMANAND, Rabindranath; High Commissioner in London for Trinidad and Tobago, 1993–96; *b* 17 July 1935; *s* of late Ram Narais Permanand and of Kalawatee Permanand (*née* Capildeo); *m* 1969, Ursel Edda Schmid; one *s* one *d. Educ:* Queen's Royal Coll., Trinidad; Univ. of Calcutta (BA Hons); Univ. of Delhi (MA); Univ. of West Indies (Dip. Internat. Relations). History Teacher, Queen's Royal Coll., 1959–66; joined Min. of Foreign Affairs, 1966; Dep. High Comr, Georgetown, Guyana, 1966–69; First Sec., Ottawa, 1969–72; Chief of Protocol, 1973–77; Counsellor and Minister Counsellor, Brussels, 1977–81; Consul-Gen., Toronto, 1981–84; Head, Political Div., 1984–88; Ambassador and Perm. Rep. to UN, Geneva, 1988–93. *Recreations:* reading, music, walking, cricket. *Address:* 1607 Scott Crescent, Kelowna, BC V1Z 2Y2, Canada.

PEROWNE, Rear-Adm. (Benjamin) Brian, CB 2001; Chief Executive, Home Farm Trust, since 2001; *b* 24 July 1947; *s* of Rear-Adm. Benjamin Cubitt Perowne, CB and of Phyllis Marjorie Perowne (*née* Peel); *m* 1975, Honora Rose Mary Wykes-Sneyd; two *s. Educ:* Gresham's Sch., Holt; BRNC, Dartmouth. Joined RN, 1965; RN Staff Coll., 1977; HM Yacht Britannia, 1980–82; CO, HMS Alacrity, 1982–83; Staff, CBNS Washington, 1986–88; CO, HMS Brazen, 1988–89; Asst Dir (Strategic Systems), MoD, 1989–90; Chief Naval Signals Officer, MoD, 1990–92; rcds 1993; Commodore Clyde and Naval Base Comdr, 1994–96; Dir Gen., Fleet Support (Ops and Plans), 1996–99; Chief Exec., Naval Bases and Supply Agency, 1999–2001, and Chief of Fleet Support, 2000–01. ADC to the Queen, 1994–96. Trustee: Bletchley Park Trust, 2000–08; Assoc. for Real Change, 2001–. *Recreations:* family, people, country and maritime, most sports. *Address:* c/o Home Farm Trust, Merchants House, Wapping Road, Bristol BS1 4RW. *Club:* Army and Navy.

PEROWNE, Adm. Sir James (Francis), KBE 2000 (OBE 1983); Deputy Supreme Allied Commander Atlantic, 1998–2002; *b* 29 July 1947; *s* of late Lt Comdr John Herbert Francis Perowne and Mary Joy Perowne (*née* Dibb); *m* 1st, 1971, Susan Anne Holloway (marr. diss. 1990); four *s*; 2nd, 1992, Caroline Nicola Grimson. *Educ:* Sherborne Sch.; BRNC Dartmouth. CO, HMS Opportune, 1976–77; CO, HMS Superb, 1981–83; Staff of CBNS Washington, 1983–86; CO, HMS Boxer, 1986–88; Asst Dir, Naval Warfare, 1988–90; Captain, Second Submarine Sqdn, 1990–92; Captain, Sixth Frigate Sqdn and CO, HMS Norfolk, 1992–94; Sen. Naval Member, RCDS, 1995–96; Flag Officer Submarines, 1996–98; Comdr Submarines (NATO), Eastern Atlantic and Northwest Europe, 1996–98; COS (Ops) to C-in-C Fleet, 1996–98. Chm., Central and Eastern (formerly Central, subseq. Midland) Region Cttee, Consumer Council for Water (formerly Watervoice), 2002–. Member: MoJ (formerly DCA) Judiciary Review Bd, 2006–; GMC Fitness to Practice Panel, 2006–08; GMC Interim Orders Panel, 2008–. Pres., Submarines Assoc., 2002–; Chm., Submarine Officers' Life Members Assoc., 2002–. Pres., Assoc. of RN Officers and Royal Naval Benevolent Soc. for Officers, 2003–; Chairman: British Red Cross Queen Mother Meml Fund, 2003–06; The James Caird Soc., 2006–; Trustee, British Forces Foundn, 2002–. Patron, HMS Protector Assoc., 2007–. *Recreations:* golf, canal boating. *Address:* c/o ARNO, 70 Porchester Terrace, W2 3TP; *e-mail:* jamesperowne@aol.com. *Club:* Royal Navy of 1765 and 1785.

PERRETT, Prof. David I., DPhil; FBA 2005; FRSE; Professor of Psychology, University of St Andrews; *b* 11 April 1954. *Educ:* Univ. of St Andrews (BSc 1976); Univ. of Oxford (DPhil 1981). FRSE 1999. Lectr, then Reader in Psychol., Univ. of St Andrews. President's Award, BPsS, 2000. *Publications:* articles in learned jls. *Address:* School of Psychology, University of St Andrews, St Mary's College, South Street, St Andrews, Fife KY16 9JP.

PERRETT, His Honour Desmond Seymour; QC 1980; a Circuit Judge, 1992–2005; Resident Judge, Shrewsbury Crown Court, 2001–05; *b* 22 April 1937; *s* of His Honour John Perrett and Elizabeth Mary Perrett (*née* Seymour); *m* 1961, Pauline Merriel (*d* 2005), *yr d* of late Paul Robert Buchan May, ICS, and of Esme May; one *s* one *d. Educ:* Westminster Sch. National Service, RN, 1955–57: midshipman RNVR, 1955; Suez, 1956, and Cyprus, 1957. Called to the Bar, Gray's Inn, 1962, Bencher, 1989; Oxford Circuit, 1963–72; Midland and Oxford Circuit, 1972–; a Recorder, 1978–92; Mem., Senate of the Inns of Court and of the Bar, 1983–87. Chm. Disciplinary Appeals Cttee, Cricket Council, 1986–97. *Recreations:* cricket, fishing, shooting. *Address:* The Old Bakehouse, Cartway, Bridgnorth, Shropshire WV16 4BG. *Clubs:* MCC; BB, IZ, Arabs Cricket.

PERRIN, Charles John, CBE 2004; Deputy Chairman, Hambros Bank Ltd, 1986–98 (Chief Executive, 1995–98); *b* 1 May 1940; *s* of late Sir Michael Perrin, CBE, and Nancy May, *d* of late Rt Rev. C. E. Curzon; *m* 1966, Gillian Margaret, *d* of late Rev. M. Hughes-Thomas; two *d. Educ:* Winchester; New Coll., Oxford (Schol.; MA; Hon. Fellow, 1999). Called to the Bar, Inner Temple, 1965. Joined Hambros Bank, 1963, Dir, 1973–98; Chm., Hambro Pacific, Hong Kong, 1983–94; Dir, Hambros PLC, 1985–98. Non-exec. Dir, Harland and Wolff, 1984–89. Chairman: Retroscreen Virology, 1993–; MRC Pension Trust, 2004–. Mem., Royal Brompton Nat. Heart and Lung Hosps SHA, 1993–94; non-exec. Dir, Royal Brompton Hosp. NHS Trust, 1994–98; Vice Chm., Royal Brompton & Harefield NHS Trust, 1998–2007. Member Council: Univ. of London, 1994–; QMW, 1997– (Treas., 1999–); Central Sch. of Speech and Drama, 2006–. Hon. Treas., UK Assoc. for International Year of the Child, 1979; Vice-Chm., UK Cttee for UNICEF, 1972–91. Governor: Queen Anne's Sch., Caversham, 1981–2006; London Hosp. Med. Coll., 1991–95. Trustee: Med. Res. Foundn, 2006–; Nuffield Trust, 2006–; RCP, 2007–. Hon. MRCP 1999. *Publication:* Darwinism Today (Endeavour Prize Essay, 1958). *Recreation:* sailing. *Address:* 4 Holford Road, Hampstead, NW3 1AD. *T:* (020) 7435 8103. *Club:* Athenæum.

PERRIN, Air Vice-Marshal Norman Arthur; Secretary General, ECTEL (European Conference of Telecommunications Industry Associations), 1991–97; *b* 30 Sept. 1930; *s* of late Albert Arthur and Mona Victoria (*née* Stacey); *m* 1956, Marie (*née* Bannon), *d* of late Peter and Lucy Bannon; one *s. Educ:* Liverpool Collegiate School; Hertford College, Oxford; RAF Technical College. BA; CEng, FRAeS. Nat. Service commn, Airfield Construction Branch, RAF, Suez Canal Zone, 1951–53; perm. commn, Tech. Branch, 1953; Advanced GW course, 1956–57; Air Ministry, 1958–61; HQ 11 Group, 1961–62; Staff Coll., 1963; 390 Maintenance Units, FEAF, 1964–65; OC Eng Wing, RAF Seletar, 1966–67; JSSC 1967; Op. Requirements, SAGW, 1967–70; Chief Instructor, Systems Engineering, RAF Coll., 1970–72; Group Captain Plans, HQ Maintenance Comd, 1972–75; C. Mech. Eng., HQ Strike Comd, 1975–78; RCDS 1979; Dir Air GW MoD (PE), 1980–83; Vice-Pres. (Air), Ordnance Board, 1983: Pres., Ordnance Board, 1984–86. Dir, TEMA, 1987–91. *Recreations:* bridge, crosswords, Liverpool FC watching, choral singing. *Address:* c/o Barclays Bank, 10 High Street, Marlow, Bucks SL7 1AR. *Club:* Royal Air Force.

PERRING, Sir John (Raymond), 2nd Bt *cr* 1963, of Frensham Manor, Surrey; TD 1965; Chairman, Perrings Finance Ltd, since 1987; *b* 7 July 1931; *e s* of Sir Ralph Perring, 1st Bt and Ethel Mary (*d* 1991); *S* father, 1998; *m* 1961, Ella Christine, *e d* of late Tony and Ann Pelham; two *s* two *d. Educ:* Stowe School. Nat. Service, then TA, RA, 1949–60; Royal Fusiliers (City of London), 1960–65. Joined family business, Perring Furnishings, 1951, Dir 1957, Jt Man. Dir 1964, Vice-Chm., 1972, Chm., 1981–88. Nat. Pres., Nat. Assoc. of Retail Furnishers, 1971–73; Mem. Council, Retail Consortium, 1972–91 (Chm., non-food policy cttee, 1987–91); Mem. EDC (Distributive Trades), 1974–78. City of London: Sheriff, 1991–92; One of HM Lieutenants, 1963–; Assistant, Merchant Taylors' Co., 1980, Master, 1988, 1994; Master, Furniture Makers' Co., 1978. Trustee, Ranyard Meml Charitable Trust, 1983–2004 (Chm., 1990–2001); Chm., Wimbledon DFAS, 1998–2002. Gov., Bishopsgate Foundn, 1993–2002. President: Bishopsgate Ward Club, 1997–98; Old Stoic Soc., 2002–03. FRSA. OStJ 1986. *Recreations:* outdoor pursuits. *Heir: s* John Simon Pelham Perring, *b* 20 July 1962. *Clubs:* City Livery, Royal Automobile; Royal Wimbledon Golf; Bembridge Sailing.

PERRINGS, Prof. Charles Aubrey, PhD; Professor of Environmental Economics, Arizona State University, since 2005; *b* 7 July 1949; *s* of Aubrey and Noelle Perrings; *m* 2005, Ann Kinzig. *Educ:* SOAS, Univ. of London (BA Hons 1973, PhD 1976). Lectr in Econs, Nat. Univ. of Lesotho, 1976–78; Lectr, Sen. Lectr, then Associate Prof. of Econs, Univ. of Auckland, 1979–90; Prof. of Econs, Univ. of Calif, Riverside, 1991–92; Prof. of Envmtl Economics, Univ. of York, 1992–2005. Vis. Prof. of Econs, Univ. of Botswana, 1987–89. Ed., Envmt and Develt Econs, 1995–. Hon. Fellow, Beijer Inst., Royal Swedish Acad. of Scis, 1996–. *Publications:* Economy and Environment: a theoretical essay on the interdependence of economic and environmental systems, 1987 (trans. Italian 1992); (ed jtly) Biodiversity Conservation: problems and policies, 1994; (ed jtly) Biological Diversity: economic and ecological issues, 1995; Sustainable Development and Poverty Alleviation in Sub-Saharan Africa: the case of Botswana, 1996; (ed jtly) The Development of Ecological Economics, 1997; Economics of Ecological Resources: selected essays, 1997; (ed) The Economics of Biodiversity Conservation in Sub-Saharan Africa: mending the Ark, 2000; (ed jtly) The Economics of Biological Invasions, 2000; (ed jtly) Natural Resource Accounting and Economic Development, 2003; numerous papers in jls in natural and social scis, proceedings, and ed collections. *Recreations:* music, reading, walking. *Address:* School of Life Sciences, Arizona State University, Box 874501, Tempe, AZ 85287-4501, USA.

PERRINS, Prof. Christopher Miles, LVO 1987; DPhil; FRS 1997; Director, Edward Grey Institute of Field Ornithology, 1974–2002, Professor of Ornithology, 1992–2002, Leverhulme Emeritus Fellow, 2002–04, Oxford University; Fellow, Wolfson College, Oxford, 1970–2002, now Emeritus; *b* 11 May 1935; *s* of Leslie Howard Perrins and Violet Amy (*née* Moore); *m* 1963, Mary Ceresole Carslake; two *s. Educ:* Charterhouse; QMC (BSc Hons Zool.; Hon. Fellow, QMW, 1996); Oxford Univ. (DPhil). Edward Grey Institute of Field Ornithology, University of Oxford: Research Officer, 1963–66; Sen. Res. Officer, 1966–84; Reader, 1984–92. Mem., General Bd of Faculties, Oxford Univ., 1983–91, 1995–99 (Chm., Bldgs Cttee, 1995–99); Delegate, OUP, 1994–2002. The Queen's Swan Warden, 1993–. President: Internat. Ornithol Congress, 1990–94; European Ornithologists' Union, 1997–99; BOU, 2003–07; Hon. Corresp. Mem. 1976–83, Hon. Fellow 1983–, Amer. Ornithologists' Union; Hon. Corresp. Mem. 1991–2002, Hon. Fellow 2002, German Ornithologists' Union; Hon. Fellow: Netherlands Ornithologists' Union, 1992; Spanish Ornithologists' Union, 2004. Godman-Salvin Medal, British Ornithologists Union, 1988; Conservation Medal, RSPB, 1992. *Publications:* (ed with B. Stonehouse) Evolutionary Ecology, 1977; British Tits, 1979; (with T. R. Birkhead) Avian Ecology, 1983; (ed with A. L. A. Middleton) The Encyclopaedia of Birds, 1985; (with M. E. Birkhead) The Mute Swan, 1986; New Generation Guide: Birds, 1987; (ed with J. D. Lebreton and G. J. M. Hirons) Bird Population Studies, 1991; (Senior Ed.) Birds of the Western Palearctic, vol. VII, 1993, vols VIII and IX, 1994; (ed with D. W. Snow) The Birds of the Western Palearctic, concise edn, 2 vols, 1998; (ed) The New Encyclopedia of Birds, 2003. *Recreations:* photography, walking. *Address:* Edward Grey Institute of Field Ornithology, Department of Zoology, University of Oxford, South Parks Road, Oxford OX1 3PS. *T:* (01865) 271169.

PERRIS, Sir David (Arthur), Kt 1977; MBE 1970; JP; Secretary, Trades Union Congress West Midlands Regional Council, 1974–94; Vice President, Birmingham Hospital Saturday Fund, since 2000 (Vice-Chairman, 1975–85; Chairman, 1985–2000); *b* 25 May 1929; *s* of Arthur Perris; *m* 1955, Constance Parkes, BPharm, FRPharmS; one *s* one *d. Educ:* Sparkhill Commercial Sch., Birmingham. Film distribution industry, 1944–61; Reed Paper Group, 1961–65; Vice-Chm., ATV Midlands Ltd, 1980–81; Dir, Central Independent Television plc, 1982–83 (Vice Chm., W Midlands Bd). Sec.,

Birmingham Trades Council, 1966–83; a Chm., Greater Birmingham Supplementary Benefits Appeal Tribunal, 1982–89. Chairman: Birmingham Regional Hosp. Bd, 1970–74; West Midlands RHA, 1974–82; NHS National Trng Council, 1975–82; Mem. Bd of Governors, United Birmingham Hosps, 1965–74; Mem., Birmingham Children's Hosp. House Cttee, 1958–71 (Chm. 1967–71). Member: W Mids Econ. Planning Council, 1968–70; W Midlands Rent Assessment Panel, 1969–99; Midlands Postal Bd, 1974–81. Chairman: Central Telethon Trust, 1987–96; W Midlands Charitable Trust Gp, 1991–93; Pres., W Midlands Charity Trustees' Forum, 1999– (Chm., 1995–99). Life Governor, Univ. of Birmingham, 1972; Elective Gov. Birmingham & Midland Inst., 1989– (Vice Pres., 2008–). Mem. Council, Magistrates' Assoc., 1995–98 (Chm., 1975–86, Pres., 1986–98, Birmingham Br.); Pres., Public Service Announcements Assoc., subseq. Community Media Assoc., 1983–98; Pres., British Health Care Assoc., 1995–98 (Vice-Pres., 1994). Patron, Birmingham Rathbone Soc., 1998–. Life Fellow, British Fluoridation Soc., 1987. Hon. LLD Birmingham, 1981. JP Birmingham, 1961. *Recreation:* reading. *Address:* Broadway, 21 Highfield Road, Moseley, Birmingham B13 9HL. *T:* (0121) 449 3652.

PERRIS, John Douglas; HM Diplomatic Service, retired; *b* 28 March 1928; *s* of Frank William Perris and Alice Perris; *m* 1954, Kathleen Mary Lewington; one *s* two *d*. *Educ:* St Paul's, Knightsbridge; Westminster City Sch. Entered FO, 1945; Bahrain, 1951; Bucharest, 1953; Hamburg, 1955; FO, 1957; Tehran, 1960; Second Sec. (Admin), Caracas, 1963; Second Sec. (Econ.), Berlin, 1966; First Sec. (Admin), Baghdad, 1969; FCO (Inspectorate), 1972; First Sec./Head of Chancery/Consul, Tegucigalpa, 1974; First Sec. (Consular and Immigration), New Delhi, 1976; FCO, 1979; Counsellor (Admin), Bonn, 1982–86. *Recreations:* sport (non-active), reading (thrillers). *Address:* 128 Wakehurst Road, SW11 6BS. *T:* (020) 7228 0521.

PERROTT, John Gayford; HM Diplomatic Service, retired; British High Commissioner, The Gambia, 2000–02; *b* 5 July 1943; *s* of Dr Charles Hardy Perrott and Dr Phylis Perrott (*née* Dearns); *m* 1964, (Joan) Wendy Lewis; one *s* one *d*. *Educ:* Newport High Sch. Joined CRO, later FCO, 1962; Karachi, 1966–69; Ankara, 1970–72; Calcutta, 1973–76; Kathmandu, 1979–84; Istanbul, 1984–88; St Helena, 1993–97. *Recreations:* walking, golf.

PERROW, (Joseph) Howard; Chairman, Co-operative Union Ltd, 1975–83; Chief Executive Officer and Secretary, Greater Lancastria Co-operative Society Ltd, 1976–83; *b* 18 Nov. 1923; *s* of Joseph and Mary Elizabeth Perrow; *m* 1947, Lorraine Strick; two *s*. *Educ:* St Just, Penzance, Cornwall; Co-operative Coll., Stanford Hall, Leics (CSD). Joined Penzance Co-operative Soc., 1940. Served RAF, 1943–47. Various managerial positions in Co-operative Movement: in W Cornwall, with CRS N Devon, Carmarthen Soc., Silverdale (Staffs) and Burslem Socs; Mem., Co-operative Union Central Exec., 1966–83, Vice-Chm., 1973–75; Vice-Chm., NW Sectional Bd, 1970–75; Director: CWS, 1970–83; Nat. Co-operative Chemists, 1973–83; Greater Manchester Independent Radio, 1973–83; Mem., Central Cttee, Internat. Co-operative Alliance, 1975–83; Mem. Council (rep. Co-operative Union), Retail Consortium, 1976–83. President, Co-operative Congress, 1979. *Recreations:* football, cricket. *Address:* Blue Seas, Cliff Road, Mousehole, Penzance, Cornwall TR19 6QT. *T:* (01736) 731330. *Club:* Bolitho's (St Just).

PERRY, family name of **Baroness Perry of Southwark**.

PERRY OF SOUTHWARK, Baroness *cr* 1991 (Life Peer), of Charlbury in the County of Oxfordshire; **Pauline Perry;** President, Lucy Cavendish College, Cambridge University, 1994–2001; *b* 15 Oct. 1931; *d* of John George Embleton Welch and Elizabeth Welch; *m* 1952, George Walter Perry; three *s* one *d*. *Educ:* Girton Coll., Cambridge (MA; Hon. Fellow 1995). Teacher in English Secondary Sch., Canadian and American High Schs, 1953–54 and 1959–61; High School Evaluator, New England, USA, 1959–61; Research Fellow, Univ. of Manitoba, 1956–57; Lecturer in Philosophy: Univ. of Manitoba, 1957–59; Univ. of Massachusetts at Salem, 1960–62; Lectr in Education (part-time), Univ. of Exeter, 1962–66; Tutor for In-Service Trng, Berks, 1966–70; Part-time Lectr in Educn, Dept of Educational Studies, Oxford Univ., 1966–70; HM Inspector of Schools, 1970–86; Staff Inspector, 1975; Chief Inspector, 1981. Dir, S Bank Poly., 1987–92; Vice-Chancellor, S Bank Univ., 1992–93. Alexander Stone Lectr in Rhetoric, Glasgow, 1999. Member: Cttee on Internat. Co-operation in Higher Educn, British Council, 1987–97; ESRC, 1988–91; Governing Body, Institute of Develt Studies, Sussex Univ., 1987–94; Bd, South Bank Centre, 1992–94; NI Higher Educn Council, 1992–94; Nat. Adv. Council on Educn and Training Targets, 1992–95; Prime Minister's Adv. Panel on Citizen's Charter, 1993–97; Overseas Project Bd, 1993–98; Royal Soc. Project Sci. Bd of Patrons, 1995–2003; H of L Select Committee: on Science and Technol., 1992–95 (Chair, Inquiry into Energy Efficiency, 2004–05); on Scrutiny of Delegated Powers, 1994–98; on relationships between local and central govt, 1995–96; on Stem Cell Research, 2001–02; on Religious Offences, 2002–03; on Sci. and Technol., 2003–; Jt Select Cttee of Commons and Lords on Human Rights, 2000–03; Ecclesiastical Cttee, 2002–; Chairman: DTI Export Gp for Educn and Trng Sector, 1993–98; Judges Panel on Citizen's Charter, 1997–2004; Inquiry into Animals in Scientific Experiments, Nuffield Council on Bio-Ethics, 2003–05; Cttee on Quality and Standards, C&G, 2005–; Advr on Police Trng to Home Office, 1991–93. Co-Chm., Policy Gp on Public Services, Cons Party, 2006–07. President: London & City Br., Inst. of Mgt, 2000–; Higher Educn Foundn, 2002–06. Rector's Warden, Southwark Cath., 1990–94. MInstD; CCMI (CIMgt 1993). Mem. Court, Univ. of Bath, 1991–99; Trustee: Bacon's City Technol. Coll., 1991–; Cambridge Univ. Foundn, 1997–2006; Pro-Chancellor, Univ. of Surrey, 2001–06; Vice-Pres., C&G, 1994–99; Pres., CIFE, 2000–. Gov., Gresham's Sch., 2000–06. Patron, British Friends of Neve Shalom-Wahat al Salaam, 2005–. Freeman, City of London, 1992; Liveryman, Bakers' Co., 1992–; Hon. Freeman, Fishmongers' Co., 2006. Hon. FCollP 1987; Hon. FRSA 1988; Hon. FCGI 2000. Hon. Fellow: Sunderland Polytechnic, 1990; Lucy Cavendish Coll., 2001; Roehampton Univ., 2005 Hon. LLD: Bath, 1991; Aberdeen, 1994; Hon. DLitt: Sussex, 1992; South Bank, 1994; City, 2000; DUniv Surrey, 1995; Hon. DEd Wolverhampton, 1994. Mem., Pedagogical Acad., Swedish Acad. of Sci., 1992. *Publications:* Case Studies in Teaching, 1969; Case Studies in Adolescence, 1970; Your Guide to the Opposite Sex, 1970; The Womb in Which I Lay, 2003; *contributions to:* Advances in Teacher Education, 1989; Women in Education Management, 1992; Public Accountability and Quality Control in Higher Education, 1990; The Future of Higher Education, 1991; Technology: the challenge to education, 1992; What is Quality in Higher Education?, 1993; Education in the Age of Information, 1993; School Inspection, 1995; Women and Higher Education, 1996; Against the Tide: women leaders in American and British higher education, 1996; Higher Education Reform, 2000; Diversity and Excellence, 2001; Creative Church Leadership, 2004; articles in various educnl jls; freelance journalism for radio and TV. *Recreations:* music, walking, cooking. *Address:* House of Lords, SW1A 0PW.

PERRY, Alan Joseph; Director, Whitehall Strategic Management Consultants Ltd, 1992–95; *b* 17 Jan. 1930; *s* of late Joseph and Elsie Perry; *m* 1961, Vivien Anne Ball; two *s*. *Educ:* John Bright Grammar Sch., Llandudno; Dartford Grammar Sch. Served RE, 1948–50. HM Treasury, 1951–68 and 1970–78; CSD, 1968–70; Principal 1968, Asst Sec. 1976; Counsellor (Economic), Washington, 1978–80; Asst Sec., HM Treasury, 1980–86; Advr on Govt Affairs, Ernst & Whinney, 1986–88; Dir, Public Sector Services, Ernst & Young, 1989–92. Chm., Review of BBC External Services, 1984.

PERRY, David Gordon; Chairman: Anglian Group, 1996–2001; John Waddington, later Waddington, plc, 1993–97; *b* 26 Dec. 1937; *s* of late Elliott Gordon Perry and Lois Evelyn Perry; *m* 1961, Dorne Mary Busby; four *d*. *Educ:* Clifton Coll.; Christ's Coll., Cambridge. Management Trainee and Sales Exec., ES&A Robinson Ltd, 1960–66; Sales Dir 1966–69, Man. Dir 1969–78, Fell & Briant Ltd (subsid. of British Printing Corp.); British Printing Corporation: Chm. and Chief Exec., Packaging Div., 1978–80; Dir, 1980–81; John Waddington plc: Dep. Man. Dir, 1981–82; Man. Dir, 1982–88; Chief Exec., 1988–92. Non-executive Director: Whitecroft plc, 1991–95; Dewhirst Gp plc, 1992–2001; National & Provincial Building Soc., 1993–96; Kelda Gp plc (formerly Yorkshire Water plc), 1996–2000; Minorplanet Systems plc, 1997–2007 (Chm., 2004–07); Euler Hermes UK (formerly Euler Hldgs UK, then Euler Trade Indemnity) plc, 1998–2008; Bellway plc, 1999–. CCMI (CBIM 1985). FRSA 1990. *Recreation:* Rugby football (Cambridge Blue 1958, England XV 1963–66, Captain 1965). *Address:* Deighton House, Deighton, York YO19 6HQ. *Clubs:* Oxford and Cambridge, MCC.

PERRY, Sir David (Howard), KCB 1986; Chief of Defence Equipment Collaboration, Ministry of Defence, 1985–87, retired; *b* 13 April 1931; *s* of Howard Dace Perry and Annie Evelyn Perry; *m* 1961, Rosemary Grigg; one *s* two *d*. *Educ:* Berkhamsted Sch.; Pembroke Coll., Cambridge (MA). CEng, FRAeS. Joined Aero Dept, RAE, 1954; Aero Flt Div., 1954–66; Aero Projs Div., 1966–71; Head of Dynamics Div., 1971–73; RCDS, 1974; Head of Systems Assessment Dept, RAE, 1975–77; Ministry of Defence (Procurement Executive): Dir-Gen. Future Projects, 1978–80; Dir-Gen. Aircraft 1, 1980–81; Dep. Controller of Aircraft, 1981–82, Controller of Aircraft 1982; Chief of Defence Procurement, 1983–85. *Recreations:* gardening, painting. *Address:* 23 Rectory Road, Farnborough, Hants GU14 7BU.

PERRY, George Henry; *b* 24 Aug. 1920; *s* of Arthur and Elizabeth Perry; *m* 1944, Ida Garner; two *d*. *Educ:* elementary sch. and technical college. Engineering Apprentice, 1934–41. Naval Artificer, 1941–46 (Atlantic and Italy Stars; 1939–45 Star). Railway Fitter, 1946–66. Derby Town Councillor, 1955–66. Chairman: Derby Water Cttee, 1957–61; S Derbys Water Board, 1961–66; Derby Labour Party, 1961–62; Secretary, Derby Trades Council, 1961–66. Contested (Lab) Harborough, 1964; MP (Lab) Nottingham South, 1966–70. *Recreation:* walking.

PERRY, Grayson; artist in ceramics; occasional broadcaster and journalist; *b* 24 March 1960; *m* 1992, Philippa Fairclough; one *d*. *Educ:* King Edward VI Grammar Sch., Chelmsford; Braintree Coll. of Further Educn; Portsmouth Poly. (BA Fine Art). *Solo exhibitions* include: James Birch Gall., London, 1984, 1985; The Minories, Colchester, 1986; Birch & Conran, London, 1987, 1988, 1990; Garth Clark Gall., NY, 1991; David Gill Gall., London, 1991–92; Clara Scremini Gall., Paris, 1994; Anthony d'Offay Gall., London, 1994, 1996–97; Laurent Delaye Gall., London, 2000; fig-1, London, 2000; Guerilla Tactics, Stedelijk Mus., Amsterdam and Barbican Art Gall., 2002; Tate St Ives, 2004; Victoria Miro Gall., London, 2004, 2006; Gall. Il Capricorno, Venice, 2005; Andy Warhol Mus., Pittsburgh, 2006; The Collection, Lincoln, 2006; Mus. of 21st Century Contemp. Art, Kanazawa, Japan; *group exhibitions* include: ICA, 1981–82; Garth Clark Gall., NY, 1990, 1999; Whitechapel Gall., 1996, 2000; Crafts Council and Amer. Crafts Mus., NY, 1997–98; Richard Salmon Gall., London and Kettle's Yard, Cambridge, 1997–98; Stedelijk Mus., Amsterdam, Hydra Foundn, Greece, 1999; Laurent Delaye Gall., Saatchi Gall., 2001; Courtauld Inst., 2001–03; Blue Gall., London, Vancouver Art Gall., 2003; Tate Liverpool, 2004; Auckland Art Gall., NZ, 2005; MOMA, NY, 2006; *work in public collections* including British Council, Crafts Council, Saatchi Collection, Pottery Mus., Stoke-on-Trent, MOMA, Glasgow, Stedelijk Mus., Amsterdam and Hydra Foundn, Greece. Turner Prize, 2003. *Publications:* Cycle of Violence, 1992; (with W. Jones) Portrait of the Artist as a Young Girl, 2006. *Address:* c/o Victoria Miro Gallery, 16 Wharf Road, N1 7RW.

PERRY, Hugh; *see* Perry, V. H.

PERRY, Jacqueline Anne, (Mrs V. Levene); QC 2006; barrister; attorney at law; *b* 7 March 1952; *d* of late Clarence and Diana Perry; *m* 1980, Victor Levene; one *s*. *Educ:* Copthall Co. Grammar Sch. for Girls; Lady Margaret Hall, Oxford (BA 1973, MA 1977). Called to the Bar, Gray's Inn, 1975, Bencher, 2005; practising as barrister, 1975–, specialising in personal injury, and clinical and professional negligence; admitted to Bar, California, 2001; practising as attorney, California; Associate, Schuler & Brown, Van Nuys, Calif, 2006–. Mediator and Mem., ADR (UK) Ltd, 2000. Grade A Advocacy Teacher, Gray's Inn. Broadcaster, as Nicola Charles: Granada TV, 1989–94; BBC Radio, 1990–96. *Publications:* as Nicola Charles: (jtly) Rights of Woman, 1990; (jtly) Know Your Law, 1995. *Recreations:* cinema, theatre, motor cruising, cooking, reading (both high and low brow). *Address:* 2 Temple Gardens, Temple EC4Y 9AY. *T:* (020) 7822 1200, *Fax:* (020) 7822 1300; *e-mail:* jperry@2tg.co.uk.

PERRY, John; *see* Perry, R. J.

PERRY, Rt Rev. John Freeman; Bishop of Chelmsford, 1996–2003; *b* 15 June 1935; *s* of Richard and Elsie Perry; *m* 1959, Gay Valerie Brown; three *s* two *d*. *Educ:* Mill Hill School; London College of Divinity (ALCD); LTh St John's Coll., Nottingham, 1974; MPhil Westminster Coll., Oxford, 1986. Assistant Curate: Christ Church, Woking, 1959–62; Christ Church, Chorleywood, 1962–63; Vicar, St Andrew's, Chorleywood, 1963–77; RD of Rickmansworth, 1972–77; Warden, Lee Abbey, Lynton, Devon, 1977–89; RD of Shirwell, 1980–84; Suffragan Bishop of Southampton, 1989–96. Hon. Canon, Winchester Cathedral, 1989–96. Took seat in H of L, 2000. Member: Bd of Ministry, 1989–2002; Bd, Christian Solidarity Worldwide, 2004–; Chm., Cttee for Ministry of and among Deaf and Disabled, 1989–2001. Chairman: Burrswood, 1989–2003; Lee Abbey Movt, 2004–. Gov., Monkton Combe Sch., Bath, 2004–. Hon. Dr Anglia Poly. Univ., 2000. *Publication:* Effective Christian Leadership, 1983. *Recreations:* a large family, walking, sport, travel, classical music, films. *Address:* Foxbury, Gutch Common, Semley, Shaftesbury, Dorset SP7 9AZ.

PERRY, Rev. John Neville; *b* 29 March 1920; *s* of Robert and Enid Perry; *m* 1946, Rita Dyson Rooke; four *s* four *d*. *Educ:* The Crypt Gram. Sch., Gloucester; Univ. of Leeds (BA 1941), College of the Resurrection, Mirfield. Asst Curate, All Saints', Poplar, 1943–50; Vicar, St Peter De Beauvoir Town, Hackney, 1950–63; Vicar, St Dunstan with St Catherine, Feltham, Middx, 1963–75; Rural Dean of Hounslow, 1967–75; Archdeacon of Middlesex, 1975–82; Rector of Orlestone with Ruckinge and Warehorne, Kent, 1982–86. Mem. Latey Cttee on the Age of Majority, 1966–67. *Recreation:* relief wood carving. *Address:* 73 Elizabeth Crescent, East Grinstead, West Sussex RH19 3JG.

PERRY, John Scott, (Jack); Chief Executive, Scottish Enterprise, since 2004; *b* 23 Nov. 1954; *s* of George Michael Perry, CBE and Madalynn Heber; *m* 1977, Lydia; one *s* two *d*. *Educ:* Glasgow Univ. (BSc (Pure Sci.) 1975); Strathclyde Univ. (Postgrad. Dip. Accountancy 1976). CA (ICAS) 1979; Certified Public Accountant (USA) 1985. Ernst & Young, 1976–2003: Managing Partner, Glasgow, 1995–2003; Regl Industry Leader, Technol. Communications and Entertainment, Scotland and NI, 1999–2003. Chm., CBI Scotland, 2001–03 (Mem. Council, 1996–); Chm., Regl Chairmen, Mem., President's Cttee, CBI. Chm., TMRI Ltd, 2007–. Former Mem., Ministerial Task Force on Econ. Forums. Chm. Bd of Dirs, Craigholme Sch.; Vis. Tutor, Leadership Trust. *Recreations:* golf, ski-ing, reading, current affairs. *Address:* Scottish Enterprise, 150 Broomielaw, Atlantic Quay, Glasgow G2 8LU. *T:* (0141) 228 2421, *Fax:* (0141) 228 2040; *e-mail:* Jack.Perry@scotent.co.uk. *Clubs:* Glasgow Academical; Royal and Ancient Golf, Western Gailes Golf.

PERRY, John William; Chairman, Trace Computers, 1996–2001 (non-executive Director, 1994–96 and 2001–04); *b* 23 Sept. 1938; *s* of John and Cecilia Perry; *m* 1961, Gillian Margaret; two *d*. *Educ:* Wallington Grammar Sch.; Brasenose Coll., Oxford (MA). Burroughs: Dir of Marketing, UK, 1967–71, Europe Africa Div., 1977–78; Group Dir, Internat. Marketing, 1978–80; Vice-President: Strategic Planning, 1981; Financial Systems Gp., 1983; Central USA, 1985–86; Man. Dir, Burroughs UK, 1986; Chm. and Man. Dir, Unisys, 1987–94; Corporate Officer, 1990, Pres., Financial Services, 1993–94, Unisys Corp.; Director, 1987–94: Sperry; Burroughs Machines; BMX Information Systems; BMX Holdings; Unisys Holdings; Convergent Technologies (UK). Trustee, Information Age Project, 1989. Mem., Bd of Governors, Polytechnic of East London, 1989. *Recreations:* gardening, reading, music. *Address:* The Great Barn, Sandpit Lane, Bledlow, Bucks HP27 9QQ.

PERRY, Jonathan Peter Langman; Chairman, Paragon Group of Companies PLC (formerly National Home Loans Holdings), 1992– 2007; *b* 6 Sept. 1939; *s* of Thomas Charles Perry and Kathleen Mary Perry; *m* 1965, Sheila Johnson; two *s* one *d*. *Educ:* Peter Symonds Sch., Winchester. FCA. Butler Viney Childs, 1956–62; Cooper Brothers, 1962–66; Morgan Grenfell & Co., 1966–88 (Dir, 1973–88); Principal, Perry Associates, 1988–90; Chm. and Chief Exec., Ogilvie Adams & Rinehart, 1990–92; Vice-Chm., HSBC Investment Banking, 1997–99. *Recreations:* sailboat racing, golf, music. *Address:* c/o Paragon Group of Companies PLC, St Catherines Court, Herbert Road, Solihull, W Midlands B91 3QE. *Clubs:* Brooks's; Royal Yacht Squadron, Itchenor Sailing; West Sussex Golf.

PERRY, Prof. Malcolm John, PhD, ScD; Professor of Theoretical Physics, University of Cambridge, since 2005; Fellow and Lecturer in Mathematics, Trinity College, Cambridge, since 1986; *b* Birmingham, 13 Nov. 1951; *s* of John and Joan Perry; partner, Anna Nikola Żytkow. *Educ:* King Edward's Sch., Birmingham; St John's Coll., Oxford (BA Phys 1973); King's Coll., Cambridge (MA 1977; PhD 1978; ScD 1999). Res. Fellow, King's Coll., Cambridge, 1977–81; Mem., Inst. for Advanced Study, Princeton, 1978–79; Asst Prof., Princeton Univ., 1979–86; University of Cambridge: Royal Soc. Univ. Res. Fellow, Dept of Applied Maths and Theoretical Phys, 1986–93; Newton Lectr, 1994–98; Asst Dir of Res., 1999–2000; Reader in Theoretical Phys, 2000–05. *Publications:* articles in professional jls. *Recreations:* early and classical music, mountaineering. *Address:* Trinity College, Cambridge CB2 1TQ. *T:* (01223) 338400; *e-mail:* mjp1@cam.ac.uk.

PERRY, Rev. Canon Michael Charles, MA; Canon Residentiary, 1970–98, now Canon Emeritus, and Sub-Dean, 1985–98, Durham Cathedral; Senior Chaplain to the Bishop of Durham, 1993–98; *b* 5 June 1933; *o s* of late Charlie Perry; *m* 1963, Margaret, *o d* of late John Middleton Adshead; two *s* one *d*. *Educ:* Ashby-de-la-Zouch Boys' Grammar Sch.; Trinity Coll., Cambridge (Sen. Schol.); Westcott House, Cambridge. Asst Curate of Berkswich, Stafford, 1958–60; Chaplain, Ripon Hall, Oxford, 1961–63; Chief Asst for Home Publishing, SPCK, 1963–70; Archdeacon of Durham, 1970–93. Examining Chaplain to Bishop of Lichfield, 1965–74. Sec., Archbishops' Commn on Christian Doctrine, 1967–70. Diocesan Chm., 1970–81, Mem. Council, 1975–81, USPG; Mem., 1981–88, Vice-Chm., 1982–88, Hosp. Chaplaincies Council, Gen. Synod; Mem. Council for the Deaf, Gen. Synod, 1986–90. Mem., Durham HA, 1982–88. Trustee, 1970–96, Chm., 1982–96, Lord Crewe's Charity; Chm., Churches' Fellowship for Psychical and Spiritual Studies, 1986–95 (Pres., 1998–2008). Lectures: Selwyn, NZ, 1976; Marshall Meml, Melbourne, 1976; Beard Meml, London, 1977; Maurice Elliott Meml, London, 1986; Shepherd Meml, Worcester, 1988. DD Lambeth, 2003. Editor: Church Quarterly, 1968–71; Christian Parapsychologist, 1978–2008. *Publications:* The Easter Enigma, 1959; The Pattern of Matins and Evensong, 1961; (co-author) The Churchman's Companion, 1963; Meet the Prayer Book, 1963; (contrib.) The Miracles and the Resurrection, 1964; (ed) Crisis for Confirmation, 1967; (co-author) Declaring The Faith: The Printed Word, 1969; Sharing in One Bread, 1973; The Resurrection of Man, 1975; The Paradox of Worship, 1977; A Handbook of Parish Worship, 1977, 2nd edn 1989; (contrib.) Yes to Women Priests, 1978; (co-author) A Handbook of Parish Finance, 1981, 3rd edn 1992; Psychic Studies: a Christian's view, 1984; Miracles Then and Now, 1986; (ed) Deliverance, 1987, 2nd edn 1996; Gods Within: a critical guide to the New Age, 1992; Psychical and Spiritual, 2003. *Address:* 57 Ferens Park, The Sands, Durham DH1 1NU. *T:* (0191) 386 1891.

PERRY, Sir Michael (Sydney), GBE 2002 (CBE 1990; OBE 1978); Kt 1994; Chairman, Centrica plc, 1997–2004; *b* 26 Feb. 1934; *s* of Sydney Albert Perry and Jessie Kate (*née* Brooker); *m* 1958, Joan Mary Stallard; one *s* two *d*. *Educ:* King William's Coll., IoM; St John's Coll., Oxford (MA). Unilever, 1957–96: Chm., Lever Brothers (Thailand) Ltd, 1973–77; Pres., Lever y Asociados SACIF, Argentina, 1977–81; Chm., Nippon Lever KK, 1981–83; Jt Man. Dir, UAC Internat., 1983–85, Chm., 1985–87; Dir, Unilever plc and Unilever NV, 1985–96; Personal Products Co-ordinator, 1987–91; Vice-Chm., 1991–92, Chm., 1992–96, Unilever plc; Vice Chm., Unilever NV, 1992–96. Non-executive Director: Bass plc, 1991–2001 (Dep. Chm., 1996–2001); British Gas plc, 1994–97; Marks and Spencer plc, 1996–2001; Royal Ahold BV, 1997–2004; non-exec. Chm., Dunlop Slazenger Gp Ltd, 1996–2001; Chm., Chairmen's Counsel Ltd, 2006–. Mem., BOTB, 1986–92; Jt Chm., Netherlands British Chamber of Commerce, 1989–93; Chairman: Japan Trade Gp, 1991–99; Sen. Salaries Rev. Body, 1995–2002; Marketing Council, 1996–99. Pres., Advertising Assoc., 1993–96. Pres., Liverpool Sch. of Trop. Med., 1997–2002 (Vice-Pres., 1991–97); Trustee, IPPR, 2004–08; Member Council: Cheltenham Coll., 1995–2000; Alice Ottley Sch., Worcester, 2001–. Chm., Shakespeare Globe Trust, 1993–2006; Trustee: Leverhulme Trust, 1991–2008 (Chm., 2008–); Glyndebourne Arts Trust, 1996–2004; Dyson Perrins Mus. Trust, 2000–. CCMI (CBIM 1992). FRSA 1992. Hon. LLD South Bank, 1995; DUniv Brunel, 1995; Hon. DSc Cranfield, 1995. *Recreations:* music (choral), walking. *Clubs:* Oriental; Worcestershire Golf.

PERRY, Nicholas Proctor; Director General, Criminal Justice and Policing, Northern Ireland Office, since 2008; *b* 24 May 1958; *s* of Very Rev. Thomas Perry and Joyce Perry (*née* Proctor); *m* 1988, Belinda Jane Neill (marr. diss. 1998); one *s* one *d*. *Educ:* St Columba's Coll., Dublin; Trinity Coll., Dublin (BA Hons 1980). Joined HM Customs and Excise, 1981; MoD, 1984–91 (Private Sec. to Parly Under-Sec., Defence Procurement, 1987–89); Northern Ireland Office, 1991–: Asst Sec., 1994; Principal Private Sec. to Sec. of State for NI, 1998–2000; Associate Dir, 2003–04, Dir Gen., 2004–08, Policing and Security. *Publications:* (ed) Major General Oliver Nugent and the Ulster Division 1915–1918, 2007; (contrib.) Oxford DNB; contrib. books and jls on military history. *Recreations:* cricket, military history. *Address:* c/o Northern Ireland Office, Stormont, Belfast BT4 3TT.

PERRY, Norman Henry, PhD; Chairman, Public Services Group, HBJ Gateley Wareing LLP, since 2007; *b* 5 March 1944; *s* of late Charles and Josephine Perry; *m* 1970, Barbara Ann Marsden; two *s*. *Educ:* Quintin Sch., NW8; University Coll. London (BA 1965; PhD 1969). Lectr in Geography, UCL, 1965–69; Sen. Res. Officer, GLC, 1969–73; Sen. Res. Fellow, SSRC Survey Unit, 1973–75; joined DoE, 1975; Principal, London and Birmingham, 1975–80; Asst Sec., W Midlands Regl Office, 1980–86; Head of Inner Cities Unit (G4), Dept of Employment, then DTI, 1986–88; Under Sec., and Dir W Midlands, DTI, 1988–90; Chief Exec. and Policy Co-ordinator, Wolverhampton MBC, 1990–95; Chief Executive: Solihull MBC, 1995–2000; Housing Corpn, 2000–04. Non-executive Director: English Partnerships, 2002–04; THFC plc, 2003–04; Merlion Gp plc, 2004–07. Dir, Wolverhampton TEC, 1990–95; Gov., Univ. of Wolverhampton, 1993–95; Mem., Adv. Bd, Inst. of Public Mgt, Warwick Univ., 2005–. Company Sec., Solihull Business Partnership Ltd, 1996–2000; Dir, Central Careers Ltd, 1996–99. Sec., Soc. of Metropolitan Chief Execs, 1998–2000; Chm., Assoc. of Local Authority Chief Execs, 1995–96. Mem., Adv. Body, Almshouse Assoc., 2005–. FCMI (FIMgt 1983); FRSA 1996. *Publications:* (contrib.) European Glossary of Legal and Administrative Terminology, 1974, 1979, 1988; contribs to books and learned jls in fields of geography, planning, organisational sociology and urban policy. *Address:* The Beeches, Howe Road, Watlington, Oxon OX49 5EL.

PERRY, Roy James; Member (C) South East Region, England, European Parliament, 1999–2004 (Wight and Hampshire South, 1994–99); *b* 12 Feb. 1943; *s* of George and Dora Perry; *m* 1968, Veronica Haswell; two *d*. *Educ:* Tottenham County Grammar Sch.; Exeter Univ. Marks & Spencer, 1964–66; Lectr in Govt and Politics, 1966–75, Sen. Lectr, 1975–94, Southampton Tech. Coll. Leader, Test Valley Borough Council, 1985–94. Cons. spokesman on educn, culture and media, EP, 1994–2004; EPP co-ordinator, Petitions Cttee, 1999–2004 (Vice-Pres., 1999–2004). Mem., Hants CC, 2005– (Exec. Mem., Ext. Affairs). Chairman: Hants Strategic Partnership, 2005–; Test Valley Arts Foundn. Trustee, Hampshire Museums Trust, 1998–. *Recreations:* bridge, French travel and food. *Address:* c/o Tarrants Farmhouse, Maury Lane, West Wellow, Romsey, Hants SO51 6DA.

PERRY, (Rudolph) John; QC 1989; *b* 20 Feb. 1936; *s* of Rudolph Perry and late Beatrice (*née* Tingling, subseq. Robertson); *m* (marr. diss.); one *d*. *Educ:* Ruseas High Sch., Lucea, Jamaica; Southgate Technical Coll.; London Sch. of Economics (LLB (Hons), LLM); Univ. of Warwick (MA (Industrial Relations)). Lectr (part-time), LSE, 1970–78; Lectr, 1971, Sen. Lectr, 1974–78, City of London Poly. Called to the Bar, Middle Temple, 1975; in practice, 1976–; an Asst Recorder, 1988, Recorder, 1992–2002. Mem. Panel of Chairmen, Public Disciplinary Appeals Tribunals, 1997–. *Recreations:* watching cricket, travel, cinema. *Address:* 1 Mitre Court Buildings, Temple, EC4Y 7BS.

PERRY, Prof. Samuel Victor, BSc (Liverpool), PhD, ScD (Cantab); FRS 1974; Professor of Biochemistry, 1959–85, now Emeritus, and Head of Department of Biochemistry, 1968–85, University of Birmingham; *b* 16 July 1918; *s* of late Samuel and Margaret Perry; *m* 1948, Maureen Tregent Shaw; one *s* two *d*. *Educ:* King George V Sch., Southport; Liverpool Univ.; Trinity Coll., Cambridge. Served in War of 1939–45, home and N Africa; Royal Artillery, 1940–46, Captain; POW 1942–45. Research Fellow, Trinity Coll., Cambridge, 1947–51; Commonwealth Fund Fellow, University of Rochester, USA, 1948–49; University Lecturer, Dept of Biochemistry, Cambridge, 1950–59. Member: Standing Cttee for Research on Animals, ARC, 1965–72; Biol Scis and Enzyme Cttees, SRC, 1968–71; Medical Res. Cttee, Muscular Dystrophy Gp of GB, 1970–90; Systems Bd, MRC, 1974–77; Research Funds Cttee, British Heart Foundn, 1974–82; British Nat. Cttee for Biochemistry, 1978–87 (Chm., 1982–87); Council, Royal Soc., 1986–88; Chairman: Cttee of Biochemical Soc., 1980–83; Adv. Bd, Meat Res. Inst., 1980–85. Croonian Lectr, Royal Soc., 1984. FAAAS 1987. Hon. Mem., Amer. Soc. of Biol Chemists, 1978; Corresponding Mem., Société Royale des Sciences, Liège, 1978; Mem., Accad. Virgiliana, Mantova, 1979; Foreign Mem., Accademia Nazionale dei Lincei, 1989. CIBA Medal, Biochemical Soc., 1977. *Publications:* scientific papers in Biochemical Journal, Nature, Biochemica Biophysica Acta, etc. *Recreations:* gardening, building stone walls, Rugby football (Cambridge, 1946, 1947, England, 1947, 1948). *Address:* Cae Bach, Fishguard Road, Dinas Cross, Newport, Pembrokeshire SA42 0XB. *T:* (01348) 811447.

PERRY, Rev. Dr Simon; Joint Minister, Bloomsbury Central Baptist Church, since 2006; *b* 10 Sept. 1969; *s* of Bill and Joan Perry; *m* 1994, Rachel Olyott; three *s* one *d*. *Educ:* Oxford Univ. (BTh 1998); Bristol Univ. (PhD 2005). Data Analyst, Special Reaction Force, RAF, 1987–94; Minister, Fivehead Baptist Church, Somerset, 1998–2003; Chaplain, Fitzwilliam Coll., Cambridge, 2003–06. *Recreations:* rowing, running, guitar. *Address:* Bloomsbury Central Baptist Church, 235 Shaftesbury Avenue, WC2H 8EP. *T:* (020) 7240 0544, *Fax:* (020) 7836 6843; *e-mail:* revslammer@googlemail.com.

PERRY, Prof. (Victor) Hugh, DPhil; Professor of Experimental Neuropathology, University of Southampton, since 1998; *b* 18 April 1952; *s* of Eric and Marie Perry; *m* 1992, Jessica Duxbury; one *s* two *d*. *Educ:* Magdalen Coll., Oxford (BA Hons 1974; MA; DPhil 1977). University of Oxford: Royal Soc. Locke Res. Fellow, 1982–86; Wellcome Trust Sen. Res. Fellow, 1986–95; Prof. of Exptl Neuropathology, 1996–98; Dir, Southampton Neurosci. Gp, 2001–. Mem., Nuffield Council on Bioethics, 2006–. FMedSci 2005. *Publications:* Macrophages and the Nervous System, 1994; contrib. three book chapters; 239 papers and 51 reviews in scientific jls. *Recreations:* reading, walking, sailing, gardening. *Address:* School of Biological Sciences, University of Southampton, Southampton, Hants SO16 7PX. *T:* (023) 8059 5931, *Fax:* (023) 8059 2711; *e-mail:* vhp@soton.ac.uk.

PERRY, William Arthur; Command Secretary (Adjutant General, Personnel and Training Command), Ministry of Defence, 1994–97; *b* 5 Aug. 1937; *s* of Arthur Perry and Elizabeth Grace (*née* Geller); *m* 1962, Anne Rosemary Dight; two *d*. *Educ:* St Dunstan's Coll.; Kellogg Coll., Oxford (MSc 2004). Min. of Aviation, 1960–61; Second Sec. (Defence Supply), Bonn, 1964–66; Min. of Technology, then MoD, 1966–74; First Sec., UK Delegn to NATO, 1974–77; Head, Defence Secretariat 8, MoD, 1978–80; Counsellor (Defence Supply), Bonn, 1980–84; Regl Marketing Dir, Defence Exports Services Orgn, 1984–88; Asst Sec., MoD (PE), 1988–92; Dir (Finance and Secretariat), Air 1, MoD (PE), 1992–94. Mem., Royal Patriotic Fund Corp., 1994–97. Trustee, Wilts Archaeological and Natural History Soc. and Wilts Heritage Mus., 2001– (Chm., 2004–). *Recreations:* opera, gardening, genealogy.

PERRY, Dr William James, Hon. KBE 1998; Michael and Barbara Berberian Professor, Freeman Spogli Institute for International Studies and School of Engineering, Stanford University, since 1997; Secretary of Defense, United States of America, 1994–97; *b* Pa, 11 Oct. 1927; *m* Lee; three *s* two *d. Educ:* Butler High Sch., Butler, Pa; Carnegie Tech.; Stanford Univ. (BS Maths, MS); Penn State Univ. (PhD Maths). Served US Army: Fort Belvoir, Japan and Okinawa, 1946–47; Army Reserves, 1950–55. Dir, Electronic Defense Labs, Sylvania/General Telephone; Exec. Vice Pres., Hambrecht and Quist Inc.; Founder, ESL Inc., 1964, Pres., 1964–77; Under-Sec. of Defense for Res. and Engrg, 1977–81; Stanford University: Co-Dir, Center for Internat. Security and Arms Control, 1988–93; Chm., Technol. Strategies & Alliances, 1985–93; Dep. Sec. of Defense, 1993–94. Mem., Nat. Acad. Engrg; Fellow, Amer. Acad. Arts and Scis. Distinguished Public Service Medal, Dept of Defense, 1980 and 1981; Distinguished Service Medal, NASA, 1981; Medal of Achievement, Amer. Electronics Assoc., 1980; US Presidential Medal of Freedom, 1997. *Address:* Stanford University, CA 94305, USA.

PERSAUD, Dr Rajendra Dhwarka, FRCPsych; Consultant Psychiatrist, Maudsley Hospital, since 1994; *b* 13 May 1963; *s* of Prof. Bishnudat Persaud and Dr Lakshmi Seeteram; *m* 1994, Maria Francesca Cordeiro; one *s* one *d. Educ:* Haberdashers' Aske's Sch., Elstree; University Coll. London (BSc 1st Cl. Hons Psychol.; MB BS Medicine; MSc; Fellow 2002); Birkbeck Coll., London (Dip Phil); Inst. of Psychiatry, London (MPhil). MRCPsych 1991, FRCPsych 2005; DHMSA 1992. HO, UCH, 1986–87; SHO, Maudsley Hosp., 1987–90; Research Fellow: Johns Hopkins Med. Sch., Baltimore, 1990–91; Inst. of Neurol., 1991–93; Lectr, 1993–2000, Sen. Lectr, 2000, Inst. of Psychiatry. Vis. Gresham Prof. of Psychiatry, 2004–. Presenter, All in the Mind, BBC Radio 4; writer and presenter of TV series, incl. Psychology of Hostage Negotiation. Mem., Med. Soc. of London, 2003. *Publications:* Staying Sane: how to make your mind work for you, 1999; From the Edge of the Couch: bizarre psychiatric cases and what they teach us about ourselves, 2003; The Motivated Mind, 2005; Simply Irresistible, 2007; contrib. papers to BMJ, The Lancet, British Jl Psychiatry, New England Jl Medicine. *Recreations:* poker, tennis, golf, theatre. *Address:* Bethlem Royal and Maudsley Hospitals NHS Trust, Monks Orchard Road, Beckenham, Kent BR3 3BX. *T:* (020) 3228 4634; *e-mail:* sphardp@iop.kcl.ac.uk. *Clubs:* Athenæum, Savile, Reform, Queen's.

PERSEY, Lionel Edward; QC 1997; a Recorder, since 2002; *b* 19 Jan. 1958; *s* of Dr Paul Ronald Persey and Irene Persey; *m* 1984, Lynn Mear; one *s. Educ:* Haberdashers' Aske's Sch., Elstree; Birmingham Univ. (LLB Hons 1980). Called to the Bar, Gray's Inn, 1981; in practice as commercial and maritime barrister, 1982–; Mem., Supplementary Panel, Jun. Treasury Counsel, 1992–97. *Recreations:* classical music, opera, reading, gardening. *Address:* Quadrant Chambers, Quadrant House, 10 Fleet Street, EC4Y 1AU. *T:* (020) 7583 4444, *Fax:* (020) 7583 4455; *e-mail:* lionel.persey@quadrantchambers.com. *Club:* Reform.

PERSKE, Betty Joan; *see* Bacall, B. J.

PERSSON, Göran; Senior Advisor, JKL Group, Stockholm, since 2007; Prime Minister of Sweden, 1996–2006; *b* 20 Jan. 1949; *m* Annika Persson (marr. diss. 2002); *m* 2003, Anitra Steen; two *d* from a previous marriage. *Educ:* Orebro Univ. Organising Sec., 1971, Mem. of Bd, 1972–75, Swedish Social Democratic Youth League; mil. service, 1973–74; Sec., Workers' Educn Assoc., Sörmland, 1974–76; Chairman: Katrineholm Educn Authy, 1977–79; Bd of Educn, Södermanland Co., 1982–89. Mem., Riksdag (MP), 1979–84, 1991–94; Municipal Comr, Katrineholm, 1985–89; Minister for Schs and Educn, 1989–91; Minister of Finance, 1994–96. Chm., Swedish Social Democratic Party, 1996–2007. Vice-Chm., Oppunda Savings Bank, 1976–89; Chm., Södermanland Co-op. Soc., 1976–89; Nat. Auditor, Swedish Co-op. Wholesale Soc., 1988–89. Vice-Chm., Nordic Mus., 1983–89. *Address:* JKL Group, Box 1405, Sveavägen 24–26, 111 84 Stockholm, Sweden.

PERSSON, Rt Rev. William Michael Dermot; Suffragan Bishop of Doncaster, 1982–92; an Assistant Bishop, diocese of Bath and Wells, since 1994; *b* 27 Sept. 1927; *s* of Leslie Charles Grenville Alan and Elizabeth Mercer Persson; *m* 1957, Ann Davey; two *s* one *d. Educ:* Monkton Combe School; Oriel Coll., Oxford (MA); Wycliffe Hall Theological Coll. National service, Army, 1945–48; commissioned, Royal Signals. Deacon 1953, priest 1954; Curate: Emmanuel, South Croydon, 1953–55; St John, Tunbridge Wells, 1955–58; Vicar, Christ Church, Barnet, 1958–67; Rector, Bebington, Cheshire, 1967–79; Vicar, Knutsford with Toft, 1979–82. General Synod: Mem., House of Clergy, 1975–82, House of Bishops, 1985–92; Chm., Council for Christian Unity, 1991–92. *Recreations:* gardening, writing poetry. *Address:* Ryall's Cottage, Burton Street, Marnhull, Sturminster Newton, Dorset DT10 1PS.

PERT, Prof. Geoffrey James, PhD; FRS 1995; FInstP; Professor of Computational Physics, University of York, since 1987; *b* 15 Aug. 1941; *s* of Norman James Pert and Grace Winifred Pert (*née* Barnes); *m* 1967, Janice Ann Alexander; one *d. Educ:* Norwich Sch.; Imperial Coll., Univ. of London (BSc; PhD 1966). FInstP 1979. University of Alberta: Fellow, 1967–68; Asst Prof., 1968–70; University of Hull: Lectr, 1970–74; Sen. Lectr, 1974–78; Reader, 1978–82; Prof., 1982–87. *Publications:* papers in learned scientific jls. *Recreations:* hill-walking, gardening. *Address:* Department of Physics, University of York, Heslington, York YO1 5DD. *T:* (01904) 432250.

PERT, Michael; QC 1992; **His Honour Judge Pert;** a Circuit Judge, since 2004; *b* 17 May 1947; *s* of Lieut Henry McKay Pert (RN, retd) and Noreen (*née* Murphy); *m* 1971, Vivien Victoria Braithwaite (marr. diss. 1993); one *s* two *d. Educ:* St Boniface's Coll., Plymouth; Manchester Univ. (LLB Hons). Called to the Bar, Gray's Inn, 1970. A Recorder, 1988–2004. *Recreations:* beekeeping, sailing.

PERTH, 18th Earl of, *cr* 1605; **John Eric Drummond;** Baron Drummond of Cargill, 1488; Baron Maderty, 1609; Baron Drummond, 1686; Lord Drummond of Gilston, 1685; Lord Drummond of Rickertoun and Castlemaine, 1686; Viscount Strathallan, 1686; Hereditary Thane of Lennox and Hereditary Steward of Menteith and Strathearn; *b* 7 July 1935; *e s* of 17th Earl of Perth, PC and Nancy Seymour, *d* of Reginald Fincke, NYC; *S* father, 2002; *m* 1963, Margaret Ann (marr. diss. 1972), *o d* of Robin Gordon; two *s*; *m* 1988, Mrs Marion Elliot. *Educ:* Trinity Coll., Cambridge; Harvard Univ. (MBA). *Heir: s* Viscount Strathallan, *qv.*

PERTH (Australia), Archbishop of, since 2005; **Most Rev. Roger Adrian Herft;** Metropolitan of the Province of Western Australia, since 2005; *b* 11 July 1948; *s* of Richard Clarence and Esmie Marie Herft; *m* 1976, Cheryl Oranee Jayasekera; two *s. Educ:* Royal College, Colombo; Theological Coll. of Lanka. BTh, BD (Serampore). Employed at Carson Cumberbatch & Co. Ltd, 1966–69; theol coll., 1969–73; deacon 1972, priest 1973; Assistant Curate: Holy Emmanuel Church, Moratuwa, 1972; St Luke's Church, Borella, with chaplaincy to Colombo Prison, 1973; Vicar: Holy Emmanuel, Moratuwa, 1976; SS Mary and John Nugegoda, 1979; Parish Consultant, Diocese of Waikato, NZ, 1983; Bishop of Waikato, 1986–93; Bishop of Newcastle, NSW, 1993–2005. Chaplain, Lambeth Conf. of Bishops, 1998; Archbishop of Canterbury's rep. on L'Arche Internat.

Church Leaders' Commn, 1998–. Sub-Prelate, WA Commandery, Order of St John of Jerusalem. *Publications:* (co-ed) Encounter with Reality, 1971; Christ's Battlers, 1997. *Recreations:* reading, avid follower of cricket. *Address:* GPO Box W2067, Perth, WA 6486, Australia. *T:* (8) 93257455, *Fax:* (8) 93256741.

PERTH (Australia), Archbishop of, (RC), since 1991; **Most Rev. Barry James Hickey,** OAM 1982; *b* 16 April 1936; *s* of G. Hickey. *Educ:* Christian Brothers Coll., WA; St Charles Seminary, WA; Propaganda Fide Coll., Rome; Univ. of WA. Dir, Centacare, Perth (Catholic Family Welfare), 1972–82; Episcopal Vicar for Social Welfare, 1982–84; Parish Priest of Highgate, WA, 1983–84; Bishop of Geraldton, WA, 1984–91. Mem., Bd of Inst. of Family Studies, Melbourne, 1980–83; Chairman: Nat. Liturgical Commn, 1995–2000; Bishops' Cttee for the Media, 2000–06; Bishops' Cttee for Evangelisation and Mission, 2000–03; Bishops' Commn for Aborigines and Torres Strait Islanders, 2006–. Mem., Australian Citizenship Council, 1998–2000. Centenary Award (Federation Medal), Australia, 2003. *Recreations:* tennis, walking. *Address:* Archbishop's House, Victoria Square, Perth, WA 6000, Australia.

PERTH (Australia), Assistant Bishop of; *see* Burton, Rt Rev. Dr M. G.

PERTH, (St Ninian's Cathedral), Provost of; *see* Farquharson, Very Rev. H. B.

PERU, Bishop of, since 1998; **Rt Rev. (Harold) William Godfrey;** *b* 21 April 1948; *s* of Charles Robert Godfrey and Irene Eva Godfrey (*née* Kirk); *m* 1968, Judith Moya (*née* Fenton); one *s* two *d. Educ:* Chesterfield School; King's Coll., Univ. of London (AKC); St Augustine's Coll., Canterbury. VSO, Isfahan, Iran, 1966–67; Asst Curate, Warsop with Sookholme, Diocese of Southwell, 1972–75; Team Vicar of St Peter and St Paul, Hucknall Torkard, 1975–86; Bishop of Southwell's Ecumenical Officer, 1981–82; Rector of Montevideo, 1986–87, Archdeacon of Montevideo, 1986–87; Asst Bishop of Argentina and Uruguay, 1987–88; Bishop of Uruguay, 1988–98; Asst Presiding Bishop, Prov. of Southern Cone of America, 1989–95. Consultant for Confessional Affairs, Min. of Justice, Peru, 2004–; Pres., Interconfessional Cttee of Peru, 2004–. Founder Mem., Jesus Caritas Fraternity (Anglican Communion), 1974. *Recreations:* walking, music. *Address:* Apartado 18–1032, Miraflores, Lima 18, Peru. *T:* and *Fax:* (1) 4484855; *e-mail:* wgodfrey@amauta.rcp.net.pe.

PERVEZ, Sir (Mohammed) Anwar, Kt 1999; OBE 1992; Chairman, Bestway Group Ltd, since 2004 (Managing Director, 1975–2004); *b* 15 March 1935. *Educ:* Jhelum, Pakistan. Chm., Batleys Ltd, 2005–. Board Member: Fedn of Wholesale Distributors; Nat. Grocers Benevolent Fund. Founder, Bestway Foundn Charitable Trust. *Address:* Bestway Group Ltd, Abbey Road, Park Royal, NW10 7BW. *T:* (020) 8453 1234.

PERY, family name of **Earl of Limerick.**

PERY, Viscount; Felix Edmund Pery; *b* 16 Nov. 1991; *s* and *heir* of Earl of Limerick, *qv.*

PESARAN, Prof. (Mohammad) Hashem, FBA 1998; PhD; Professor of Economics, Cambridge University, and Fellow of Trinity College, Cambridge, since 1988; *b* 30 March 1946; *s* of Jamal and Effat Pesaran; *m* 1969, Marion Fay Swainston; three *s* two *d. Educ:* Salford Univ. (BSc 1968); Cambridge Univ. (PhD 1972). Jun. Res. Officer, Dept of Applied Econs, Cambridge Univ., and Lektor, Trinity Coll., Cambridge, 1971–73; Asst to Vice-Governor, 1973–74, and Head of Econ. Res. Dept, 1974–76, Central Bank of Iran; Under-Sec., Min. of Educn, Iran, 1977–78; Teaching Fellow, and Dir of Studies in Econs, Trinity Coll., Cambridge, 1979–88; Lectr in Econs, 1979–85, and Reader in Econs, 1985–88, Cambridge Univ. Prof. of Econs, and Dir, Program in Applied Econometrics, UCLA, 1989–93; Research Fellow: Inst. for Study of Labour, Bonn, 1999–; CESifo (Center for Economic Studies and Ifo Institute for Econ. Res.) Res. Network, Munich, 2000–. Visiting Lecturer: Harvard Univ., 1982; Dutch Network for Quantitative Econs, Groningen, 1985; Vis. Fellow, ANU, 1984 and 1988; Visiting Professor: Univ. of Rome, 1986; Univ. of Calif, LA, 1987–88; Univ. of Pennsylvania, 1993; Univ. of S Calif, 1995, 1997, 1999 and 2003. Director: Camfit Data Ltd, 1986–; Acorn Investment Trust, 1987–89 and 1991–93; Cambridge Econometrics, 1985, 1988–89 and 1992–96 (Hon. Pres., 1996–); (non-exec.), Chiltern Gp plc, 1999–2003; Vice Pres., Tudor Investment Corp., 2000–02. Member: HM Treasury Academic Panel, 1993–; Academic Econometric Panel, ONS, 1997–2002; Outside Mem., Meteorol Office, 1994–97. Member: Bd of Trustees, Econ. Res. Forum of Arab Countries, Iran and Turkey, 1996–2001 (Mem. Adv. Bd and Res. Fellow, 1993–96); World Bank Council for the Middle East and N Africa region, 1996–2000; Bd of Trustees, British Iranian Trust, 1997–; Charter Mem., Oliver Wyman Inst., 1997–2000. Mem. Council, Royal Econ. Soc., 2007–. Fellow, Econometric Soc., 1990. Founding Ed., Jl of Applied Econometrics, 1985–. Hon. DLitt Salford, 1993. *Publications:* World Economic Prospects and the Iranian Economy—a short term view, 1974 (also Persian) (with L. J. Slater) Dynamic Regression: theory and algorithms, 1980 (trans. Russian, 1984); (ed with T. Lawson) Keynes' Economics: methodological issues, 1985; The Limits to Rational Expectations, 1987; (with B. Pesaran) Data-FIT: an interactive software econometric package, 1987 (paperback edn, as Microfit, 1989); (ed with T. Barker) Disaggregation in Economic Modelling, 1990; (with B. Pesaran) Microfit 3.0, 1991, Microfit 4.0, 1997, Microfit 4.1, 2001; (ed with S. Potter) Non-Linear Dynamics, Chaos and Econometrics, 1993; Handbook of Applied Econometrics, Vol. I (ed with M. Wickens), 1995, Vol. II (ed with P. Schmidt), 1997; (jtly) Energy Demand in Asian Developing Economies, 1998; (ed jtly) Analysis of Panels and Limited Dependent Variables, 1999; (jtly) Global and National Macroeconometric Modelling: a long-run structural approach, 2006; (ed with J. Nugent) Explaining Growth in the Middle East, 2007; scientific papers in econ. and econometric jls (Best Paper award 2002–04, Econometric Reviews; Best Paper Award 2004–05, Internat. Jl of Forecasting; Multa Scripsit Award, Jl of Econometric Theory, 2008). *Recreations:* basketball (half-blue, Cambridge University), squash, swimming. *Address:* Trinity College, Cambridge CB2 1TQ. *T:* (01223) 335216; *e-mail:* hashem.pesaran@econ.cam.ac.uk.

PESCOD, Prof. Mainwaring Bainbridge, OBE 1977; CEng, FICE, FCIWEM, FCIWM; Corporate Fellow, SEC Ltd, since 2003; Tyne and Wear Professor of Environmental Control Engineering, 1976–98, now Emeritus, and Head of Department of Civil Engineering, 1983–98, University of Newcastle upon Tyne; *b* 6 Jan. 1933; *s* of Bainbridge and Elizabeth Pescod; *m* 1957, Mary Lorenza (*née* Coyle); two *s. Educ:* Stanley Grammar Sch., Co. Durham; King's Coll., Univ. of Durham (BSc); MIT (SM). CEng 1973, FICE 1980; FCIWEM (FIPHE 1971; FIWES 1983; FIWEM 1987; MIWPC 1967); FCIWM (FIWM 1997; MInstWM 1985). Lectr in Engrg, Fourah Bay Coll., Freetown, Sierra Leone, 1957–61; Asst Engr, Babtie, Shaw & Morton, CCE, Glasgow, 1961–64; Asst and Associate Prof. of Environmental Engrg, 1964–72, Prof. and Head of Div. of Environmental Engrg, 1972–76, Asian Inst. of Technol., Bangkok, Thailand. Chm. and Man. Dir, Envmtl Technology Consultants, 1988–2003. Mem., Northumbrian Water Authority, 1986–89; Director: Northumbrian Water Group, 1989–97; Motherwell Bridge Envirotec, 1991–95; Chm., MB Technology (Malaysia) Sdn Bhd, 1996–2002.

Publications: (ed with D. A. Okun) Water Supply and Wastewater Disposal in Developing Countries, 1971; (ed. with A. Arar) Treatment and Use of Sewage Effluent for Irrigation, 1988; (ed) Urban Solid Waste Management, 1991; pubns on water supply, wastewater treatment, environmental pollution control and management in learned jls and conf. proc. *Recreations:* golf, reading, advisory assignments in developing countries. *Address:* Tall Trees, High Horse Close Wood, Rowlands Gill, Tyne and Wear NE39 1AN. *T:* (01207) 542104. *Clubs:* British, Royal Bangkok Sports (Bangkok, Thailand).

PEŠEK, Libor, Hon. KBE 1996; Music Director, 1987–97, Conductor Laureate, since 1997, Royal Liverpool Philharmonic Society and Orchestra; *b* 22 June 1933. *Educ:* Academy of Musical Arts, Prague (studied conducting, piano, 'cello, trombone). Worked at Pilsen and Prague Opera Houses; Founder Director, Prague Chamber Harmony, 1958–64; Chief Conductor, Slovak Philharmonic, 1980–81; Conductor in residence, Czech Philharmonic, 1982– (tours and fests, Europe, Russia, Far East); guest conductor: Los Angeles Philharmonic, St Louis Symphony and other US orchestras; The Philharmonia, LSO, Orchestre Nat. de France, and other European orchestras; numerous recordings incl. much Czech repertoire. Pres., Prague Spring Fest. Hon. DMus Liverpool Polytechnic, 1989. *Recreations:* physics, Eastern philosophy and literature, particularly Kafka, Dostoyevsky and Tolstoy. *Address:* c/o IMG Artists (Europe), The Light Box, 111 Power Road, Chiswick, W4 5PY.

PESHAWAR, Bishop of; see Rumalshah, Rt Rev. M. K.

PESKETT, Stanley Victor, MA; Principal, Royal Belfast Academical Institution, 1959–78; *b* 9 May 1918; *o s* of Sydney Timber and Mary Havard Peskett; *m* 1948, Prudence Eileen, OBE 1974, *o d* of C. R. A. and M. A. Goatly; two *s* one *d* (and one *d* decd). *Educ:* Whitgift Sch.; St Edmund Hall, Oxford. Served War, 1939–46 (despatches) in Royal Marines, Norway, Shetland, Normandy, India and Java; Lt-Col, 1944; two Admiralty awards for inventions. Senior English Master, 1946–59, Housemaster 1954–59, The Leys School. Mem. Cttee, Headmasters' Conf., 1976; Mem. Council, Headmasters' Assoc., and Pres., Ulster Headmasters' Assoc., 1973–75; Chm., Northern Ireland Cttee, Voluntary Service Overseas, 1969–78; Founder Pres., Irish Schools Swimming Assoc., 1968–69 (Chm., Ulster Branch, 1968–78); Chm., NI Branch, School Library Assoc., 1964–73; Governor, Belfast Sch. of Music, 1974–77; Mem. Adv. Council, UDR, 1975–78. *Publications:* The Metfield Clock, 1980; (contrib.) People, Poverty and Protest in Hoxne Hundred 1780–1880, 1982; Only For a Day, 1984; Our Names, 1985; Wheelock 'Founder of Medfield', 1992; Monumental Inscriptions, Metfield, Suffolk, 1992; articles in educational jls. *Address:* Huntsman and Hounds Cottage, Metfield, Harleston, Norfolk IP20 0LB. *T:* (01379) 586425.

See also R. W. Seymour.

PESKIN, Richard Martin; Chairman, Great Portland Estates plc, 1986–March 2009; *b* 21 May 1944; *s* of Leslie and Hazel Peskin; *m* 1979, Penelope Howard Triebner; one *s* two *d. Educ:* Charterhouse; Queens' Coll., Cambridge (MA, LLM). Great Portland Estates, 1967–: Dir, 1968; Asst Man. Dir, 1972–78; Jt Man. Dir, 1978–84; Man. Dir, 1984–2000. FRSA 1989. CCMI (CBIM 1989). *Recreations:* crosswords, composing limericks, fine wine, racing, golf. *Address:* 41 Circus Road, NW8 9JH. *T:* (020) 7289 0492. *Clubs:* MCC, Royal Automobile; Wentworth Golf.

PESSINA, Stefano; Executive Chairman, Alliance Boots Ltd, since 2007 (Executive Deputy Chairman, 2006–07); *b* 4 June 1941; *s* of Oreste Pessina and Elena Fusco Pessina; separated; one *s* one *d.* Various academic posts; independent business consultant; work in pharmaceutical wholesaling, 1976–; Founder, Alliance Santé Gp, merged with UniChem plc, 1997, to form Alliance UniChem Gp; Chief Exec., 2001–04, Exec. Dep. Chm., 2004–06, Alliance UniChem plc; merged with Boots Gp, 2006, to form Alliance Boots Ltd. *Recreations:* yachting, art. *Address:* Alliance Boots Ltd, Sedley Place, 4th Floor, 361 Oxford Street, W1C 2JL; *e-mail:* stefano.pessina@allianceboots.com.

PESTELL, Catherine Eva; see Hughes, C. E.

PESTELL, John Edmund; Partnership Secretary, Linklaters & Paines, 1990–94; *b* 8 Dec. 1930; *s* of late Edmund Pestell and Isabella (*née* Sangster); *m* 1958, Muriel Ada (*née* Whitby); three *s. Educ:* Roundhay Sch.; New Coll., Oxford (State Scholar; MA). National Service, 1949–50. Jt Intell. Bureau, 1953–57; Asst Principal, WO, 1957–60; Private Sec. to Parly Under Sec. of State for War, 1958–60; Principal, WO and MoD, 1960–70; Admin. Staff Coll., Henley, 1963; Private Sec. to Minister of Defence (Equipment), 1969–70; Asst Sec., MoD, 1970–72; Press Sec. (Co-ordination), Prime Minister's Office, 1972–74; Asst Sec., CSD, 1974–76, Under Sec., 1976–81; Under Sec., HM Treasury, 1981–84; Asst Under-Sec. of State, MoD, 1984–88; Resident Chm., CSSB, 1988–90. Mem., CS Pay Res. Unit Bd, 1978–80. Governor, Cranleigh Sch., 1975–95. *Address:* New House, Bridge Road, Cranleigh, Surrey GU6 7HH. *T:* (01483) 273489. *Club:* Athenæum.

See also C. E. Hughes.

PESTON, family name of Baron Peston.

PESTON, Baron *cr* 1987 (Life Peer), of Mile End in Greater London; **Maurice Harry Peston;** Professor of Economics at Queen Mary College, University of London, 1965–88, now Emeritus; *b* 19 March 1931; *s* of Abraham and Yetta Peston; *m* 1958, Helen Conroy; two *s* one *d. Educ:* Belle Vue School, Bradford; Hackney Downs School; London School of Economics (BSc Econ; Hon. Fellow, 1995); Princeton Univ., NJ, USA. Scientific Officer, then Sen. Scientific Officer, Army Operational Research Group, 1954–57; Asst Lecturer, Lectr, Reader in Economics, LSE, 1957–65. Economic Adviser: HM Treasury, 1962–64; Min. of Defence, 1964–66; H of C Select Cttee on Nationalised Industries, 1966–70, 1972–73; Special Adviser to Sec. of State for Education, 1974–75, to Sec. of State for Prices, 1976–79. Chairman: H of L Cttee on Monetary Policy, 1998–2001; H of L Econ. Affairs Cttee, 2001–. Chairman: Pools Panel, 1991–95; NFER, 1991–97; Office of Health Econs, 1991–2000; Member: CNAA (and Chm. of Econs Bd), 1967–73; SSRC (Chm. of Econs Bd), 1976–79; Council of Royal Pharmaceutical Soc. of GB, 1986–96; Hon. Mem., RPSGB, 1996. Fellow: Portsmouth Poly., 1987; QMW, 1992; LSE 1995. Hon. FInstAM 1998. Hon. DEd E London, 1994; Hon. DPhil Guildhall, 1999. *Publications:* Elementary Matrices for Economics, 1969; Public Goods and the Public Sector, 1972; Theory of Macroeconomic Policy, 1974, 2nd edn 1982; Whatever Happened to Macroeconomics?, 1980; The British Economy, 1982, 2nd edn 1984; ed and contrib. to many other books; articles in economic jls. *Address:* House of Lords, SW1A 0PW. *T:* (020) 7219 3000.

See also R. J. K. Peston.

PESTON, Robert James Kenneth; Business Editor, BBC News, since 2006; *b* 25 April 1960; *s* of Baron Peston, *qv*; *m* 1998, Siân E. Busby; one *s*, and one step *s. Educ:* Highgate Wood Comp. Sch.; Balliol Coll., Oxford (BA PPE 1982). City Editor, Independent on Sunday, 1991–92; Financial Times: Banking Editor, 1992–93; Hd of Investigations, 1993–95; Political Editor, 1995–2000; Financial Editor and Asst Editor, 2000; Editl Dir,

CSQuest.com, 2000–02; Associate Editor, Spectator, 2000–01; City Ed. and Asst Ed., Sunday Telegraph, 2002–06. Columnist: New Statesman, 2001–02; Sunday Times, 2001–02. TV documentary, Super-Rich: the greed game, 2008. Member: Adv. Bd, SOAS; Bd, Media Standards Trust. Investigative Journalist of the Year, What the Papers Say awards, 1993; Sen. Financial Journalist of the Year, Harold Wincott awards, 2005; Scoop of the Year, London Press Club awards, 2005; Scoop of the Year, RTS TV Journalism Awards, 2007; Business News/Current Affairs Prog. of the Year, Wincott Foundn, 2007; Journalist of the Year, and Scoop of the Year, Business Journalist of Year Awards, 2007–08; Broadcast News Journalist of the Year and Documentary of the Year, Work Foundn Workworld Media Awards, 2007; Private Equity and Venture Capital Digital Journalist of the Year, 2007. *Publications:* Brown's Britain, 2005; Who Runs Britain?, 2008. *Recreations:* Arsenal, dance/ballet. *Address:* Room 4220, Television Centre, Wood Lane, W12 7RJ. *T:* (020) 8576 4433; 125 Dukes Avenue, N10 2QD; *e-mail:* robert@peston.com.

PETCH, Barry Irvine, FCA; General Manager, IBM Financing International Ltd, 1989–93; *b* 12 Oct. 1933; *s* of Charles Reginald Petch and Anne (*née* Fryer); *m* 1966, Anne Elisabeth (*née* Johannessen); two *s* one *d. Educ:* Doncaster Grammar Sch.; Kingston Univ. (MA 1998). FCA 1967. IBM United Kingdom Ltd, 1959–80; Controller, IBM Europe, 1981–83; Vice-Pres., Finance, IBM Europe, 1983–89. Part-time Mem., Price Commn, 1973–77. Director: Pathfinder NHS Trust, 1995–99; IBM UK Pensions Trust Ltd, 1997–2000. Hon. Treas., RNID, 1998–2001. *Recreations:* tennis, golf, sailing. *Club:* Reform.

PETERBOROUGH, Bishop of, since 1996; **Rt Rev. Ian Patrick Martyn Cundy;** Assistant Bishop, Diocese of Ely, since 2004; *b* 23 April 1945; *s* of late Henry Martyn Cundy and Kathleen Ethel Cundy; *m* 1969, Josephine Katherine Boyd; two *s* one *d. Educ:* Monkton Combe Sch.; Trinity Coll., Cambridge (BA 1967; MA 1971); Tyndale Hall, Bristol. Ordained: deacon, 1969; priest, 1970; Asst Curate, Christ Church, New Malden, 1969–73; Tutor and Lectr in Church History, Oak Hill Coll., London, 1973–77; Team Rector, Mortlake with East Sheen, 1978–83; Warden, Cranmer Hall, St John's Coll., Durham, 1983–92; Suffragan Bishop of Lewes, 1992–96. Church Comr, 2004–. Chm., Council for Christian Unity, 1998–2008. Pres., St John's Coll., Durham, 1999–2008. Trustee, Uppingham and Oakham Schs, 1996–. *Publication:* Ephesians—2 Thessalonians, 1981. *Recreations:* walking, music, photography, vintage cars. *Address:* Bishop's Lodging, The Palace, Peterborough, Cambs PE1 1YA. *T:* (01733) 562492, *Fax:* (01733) 890077.

PETERBOROUGH, Dean of; see Taylor, Very Rev. C. W.

PETERKEN, Laurence Edwin, CBE 1990; consultant, since 1996; Special Projects Director, NHS in Scotland, 1993–96; *b* 2 Oct. 1931; *s* of Edwin James Peterken and Constance Fanny (*née* Giffin); *m* 1st, 1955, Hanne Birgithe Von Der Recke (decd); one *s* one *d*; 2nd, 1970, Margaret Raynal Blair; one *s* one *d. Educ:* Harrow Sch. (Scholar); Peterhouse, Cambridge (Scholar); MA. Pilot Officer, RAF Regt, Adjt No 20 LAA Sqdn, 1950–52. Service Div. Manager, Hotpoint Ltd, 1961–63, Commercial Dir, 1963–66; Man. Dir, British Domestic Appliances Ltd, 1966–68; Dir, British Printing Corporation Ltd, 1969–73; Debenhams Ltd: Man. Dir, Fashion Multiple Div., 1974–76; Management Auditor, 1976–77; Controller, Operational Services, GLC, 1977–85; Acting Dir, Royal Festival Hall, 1983–85, to implement open foyer policy; Gen. Man., 1986–93, Dir, 1989–93, Gtr Glasgow Health Bd. Chairman: Working Party on Disposal of Clinical Waste in London, 1982–83; GLC Chief Officers' Guild, 1983–85; Member: Scottish Health Management Efficiency Gp, 1986–95; Scottish Health Clinical Resources and Audit Gp, 1989–93; Scottish Health Service Adv. Council, 1989–93; Criminal Injuries Compensation Appeal Panel, 1997–2006; Lay Member, Professional Conduct Committee: Nursing and Midwifery Council, 2004–; CIMA, 2005–. Vice Chm., RIPA, W of Scotland, 1991–93. Trustee: Rodolfus Choir, 1998–; Council for Music in Hosps, 2004–08 (Mem., Scottish Cttee, 1997–2008). Churchwarden, Haslemere Parish Church, 1985–86. *Recreations:* music, golf. *Address:* Carlston, Kilbarchan Road, Bridge of Weir, Renfrewshire PA11 3EG. *Club:* Athenæum.

PETERKIN, Maj. Gen. (Anthony) Peter G.; see Grant Peterkin.

PETERS, Prof. (Adrien) Michael, MD; FRCR, FRCP, FRCPath, FMedSci; Professor of Applied Physiology, Brighton and Sussex Medical School, and Hon. Consultant in Nuclear Medicine, Royal Sussex County Hospital, Brighton, since 2004; *b* 17 May 1945; *s* of Adrien John Peters and Barbara Muriel Peters; *m* 1st; one *s*; 2nd, 1980, Rosemary Cox; two *s* one *d. Educ:* St Mary's Hosp. Med. Sch., Univ. of London (BSc, MSc); Univ. of Liverpool (MB ChB, MD 1970). FRCR 1995; FRCPath 1996; FRCP 1997. GP, NSW, Australia, 1974–78, Liverpool, 1978–79; Res. Fellow, RPMS 1979–82; Res. Physician, Glaxo Gp Res. Ltd, 1982–84; Sen. Lectr in Diagnostic Radiol., 1984–89, Reader in Nuclear Medicine, 1989–95, RPMS; Prof. of Diagnostic Radiol., RPMS, then ICSM, 1995–99; Prof. of Nuclear Medicine, Univ. of Cambridge, 1999–2004. Consultant in Paediatric Radiol., 1984–88, Hon. Consultant, 1988–93 and 1996–2001, Hosp. for Sick Children, Gt Ormond St; Hon. Consultant: Hammersmith Hosp., 1984–99; Addenbrooke's Hosp., 1999–2004. FMedSci 2002. *Publications:* Physiological Measurement with Radionuclides in Clinical Practice, 1998; (ed) Nuclear Medicine in Radiological Diagnosis, 2003; numerous contribs to learned jls. *Recreations:* football, jazz. *Address:* Brighton and Sussex Medical School, G25 Audrey Emerton Building, Eastern Road, Brighton BN2 5BE. *T:* (01273) 523360.

PETERS, Alan George, OBE 1990; furniture maker, since 1962; *b* 17 Jan. 1933; *s* of George Peters, BEM and Evelyn Gladys Amy Peters (*née* Weeks); *m* 1962, Laura Robinson; one *s* one *d. Educ:* Petersfield and Cowplain schools; Shoreditch Teacher Trng Coll., Egham (Dip. with distinction); Central Sch. of Arts and Crafts, London. Apprenticed to Edward Barnsley, CBE, 1949–56. Crafts Council Bursary, Japan, 1975; Winston Churchill Fellow, S Korea and Taiwan, 1980; Guest Advr, NZ Crafts Council, 1984. Vice-Pres., Devon Guild of Craftsmen, 1987–2003 (Hon. Vice-Pres., 2003–). Founder Academician, SW Acad. of Fine and Applied Arts, 2000. Trustee, Crafts Study Centre, Bath, 1990–99. Exhibitions: Alan Peters Furniture, Cheltenham and touring, 1985–86; 30 Pieces for 30 Years, Bedales Gall., Petersfield, 1992; Crafts Council nat. and touring exhibns, 1973–; work exhibited in: museums, incl. V&A, Cheltenham, Bristol, Leicester, Plymouth, Portsmouth and Bath; Crafts Council Collection; seating for Earth Gall., Gall. of Modern Art, Glasgow, 1996. Fellow, Soc. of Designer-Craftsmen, 1968 (Centennial Medal, 1988; Hon. Fellow, 2005). Hon. Fellow, Somerset Guild of Craftsmen, 2006. Award of Distinction, Furniture Soc., USA, 2002; Gane Trust Award, 2005. *Publications:* Cabinetmaking: the professional approach, 1984; (ed) The Technique of Furniture Making, by Ernest Joyce, 1987, 4th edn 1997. *Recreations:* cycling, walking, real ale. *Address:* Aller Studio, 3 Mart Road, Minehead, Somerset TA24 5BJ.

PETERS, Most Rev. Arthur Gordon; Archbishop of Nova Scotia and Metropolitan of the Ecclesiastical Province of Canada, 1997–2002 (Bishop of Nova Scotia, 1984–2002); *b* 21 Dec. 1935; *s* of William Peters and Charlotte Peters (*née* Symes); *m* 1962, Elizabeth Baert; one *s* two *d. Educ:* High School, North Sydney, NS; Univ. of King's College,

Halifax, NS (BA 1960, BST 1963, BD 1973). Student, Parish of Waverley, 1961–63; deacon 1962, priest 1963, Nova Scotia; Morris Scholar, 1963, at Canterbury (Eng.), Geneva, Jerusalem, Norton (dio. Durham, Eng.); Rector: Weymouth, NS, 1964–68; Annapolis-Granville, NS, 1968–73; Christ Church, Sydney, NS, 1973–82; Bishop Coadjutor of Nova Scotia, 1982–84. Hon. DD Univ. of King's College, 1982. *Recreations:* swimming, ski-ing, reading, skating, photography. *Address:* 113–5 Ramsgate Lane, Halifax, NS B3P 2S6, Canada.

PETERS, (Boris) Kai (Georg); Chief Executive, Ashridge, since 2003; *b* 26 Sept. 1962; *s* of late Gerhard Peters and Hilla Westerhold Peters. *Educ:* Glendon Coll.; York Univ., Toronto; Univ. of Quebec at Chicoutimi; Erasmus Univ., Rotterdam. Man. Dir, Westerhold, 1989–; Rotterdam School of Management: Dir, MBA Progs, 1994–99; Dean, 2000–03. *Publications:* chapters and articles about mgt of educn. *Recreations:* food, travel, commuting against the flow from London. *Address:* Ashridge Business School, Berkhamsted, Herts HP4 1NS. *T:* (01442) 841041, *Fax:* (01442) 841002.

PETERS, Sir (David) Keith, Kt 1993; FRCP; FRS 1995; Interim Director, MRC National Institute for Medical Research, Mill Hill, since 2006; Regius Professor of Physic, University of Cambridge, 1987–2005, now Emeritus; Fellow, Christ's College, Cambridge, 1987–2005, now Hon. Fellow; *b* 26 July 1938; *s* of Herbert Lionel and Olive Peters; *m* 1st, 1961, Jean Mair Garfield (marr. diss. 1978); one *s* one *d*; 2nd, 1979, Pamela Wilson Ewan (CBE 2007); two *s* one *d*; one *d* by Dr Elizabeth Warburton. *Educ:* Welsh National Sch. of Medicine (MB BCh 1961). MRCP 1964, FRCP 1975; FRCPath 1991; FRCPE 1995. Junior posts in United Cardiff Hosps, 1961–65; Med. Research Council, Clinical Res. Fellowship, 1965–68; Lectr in Med., Welsh Nat. Sch. of Med., 1968–69; Royal Postgraduate Medical School: Lectr, 1969; Sen. Lectr, 1974; Reader in Med., 1975; Prof. of Medicine and Dir, Dept of Medicine, 1977–87; Consultant Physician, Hammersmith Hosp., 1969–87. Member: MRC, 1984–88 (Chm., MRC Physiological Systems Bd, 1986–88); ACOST, 1987–90; Council for Sci. and Technol. (Jt Chm., 2004–07); Chairman: NRPB, 1994–98; Council of Hds of Med. Schs and Deans of UK Faculties of Medicine, 1996–97. Chairman: Nat. Kidney Res. Fund, 1980–86 (Trustee, 2000–01); BHF, 1998–2002. Gov. and Mem., PPP Foundation, 1998–2002 (Chm., 2002). Member: Bd, Amersham Plc, 2000–04 (Mem., Sci. Adv. Bd, 1998– (Chm., 2001–04)); Chm., Sci. Adv. Bd, GE Healthcare Technologies, 2005–07; Sen. Advr in R & D, GlaxoSmithKline. Mem. Council, Royal Soc., 1999–2001. Chm. Council, Cardiff Univ., 2004–. Foreign Mem., Amer. Philos. Soc., 1999. Founder FMedSci 1998 (Pres., 2002–06). Hon. Fellow: Univ. of Wales Coll. of Medicine, 1997; ICSM, 1999; Cardiff Univ., 2001; Univ. of Wales, Swansea, 2001. Hon. MD: Wales, 1987; Nottingham, 1996; Paris, 1996; Birmingham, 1998; Bristol, 2005; St Andrews, 2006; Edinburgh, 2007; Hon. DSc: Aberdeen, 1994; Leicester, 1999; Glasgow, 2001; Sussex, 2004; Keele, 2006. *Publications:* (ed jtly) Clinical Aspects of Immunology, 4th edn 1982, 5th edn 1993; in various jls on immunology of renal and vascular disease. *Recreations:* tennis, chess. *Club:* Garrick.

PETERS, Kai; *see* Peters, B. K. G.

PETERS, Sir Keith; *see* Peters, Sir D. K.

PETERS, Martin Trevor, CB 1991; CEng, FRAeS; Technical Planning Director, British Aerospace plc, 1992–94; *b* 23 Dec. 1936; *s* of Reginald Thomas Peters and Catherine Mary Peters (*née* Ings); *m* 1958, Vera Joan Horton (*d* 2004); one *s*. *Educ:* Aylesbury Grammar Sch.; Watford Tech. Coll.; High Wycombe Coll. of Further Educn. MIMechE, CEng 1968; FRAeS 1988. Airtech, 1953–55; RAF, 1955–57; Airtech, 1957–59; RPE Westcott, 1959–64; NGTE Pyestock, 1964–71; MoD, 1971–77; Supt of Engineering, A&AEE Boscombe Down, 1977–79; NAMMA, Munich, 1979–81; Dir, Aircraft Post Design Services, MoD (PE), 1981–83; RCDS, 1984; Dir-Gen. Aircraft, 1984–87; Dep. Controller Aircraft, 1987–89; Dir, RAE, 1989–91; Tech. Dir, BAe Commercial Aircraft Ltd, 1991–92. *Recreations:* walking, music, 18th century ship modelling. *Address:* 96 East Avenue, Talbot Woods, Bournemouth BH3 7DD.

PETERS, Dame Mary (Elizabeth), DBE 2000 (CBE 1990; MBE 1973); Managing Director, Mary Peters Sports Ltd, 1977; *b* 6 July 1939; *d* of Arthur Henry Peters and Hilda Mary Peters. *Educ:* Portadown Coll., Co. Armagh; Belfast Coll. of Domestic Science (DipDomSc). Represented Great Britain: Olympic Games: 4th place, Pentathlon, 1964; 1st, Pentathlon (world record), 1972; Commonwealth Games: 2nd, Shot, 1966; 1st, Shot, 1st Pentathlon, 1970; 1st, Pentathlon, 1974. Member: Sports Council, 1974–80, 1987–94; NI Sports Council, 1974–93 (Vice-Chm., 1977–81); Ulster Games Foundn, 1984–93; NI BBC Broadcasting Council, 1981–84; NI Tourist Bd, 1993–2002. Dir, Churchill Foundn Fellowship Scholarship, Calif, 1972. Asst Sec., Multiple Sclerosis Soc., 1974–78. President: NI WAAA, 1985–87; British Athletic Fedn, 1996–98; Ulster Sports and Recreation Trust, 1996– (Trustee, 1972); Mem., Women's Cttee, IAAF, 1995–97. Hon. Senior Athletic Coach, 1975–; BAAB Pentathlon Coach, 1976; Team Manager: GB women's athletic team, European Cup, 1979; GB women's athletic team, Moscow, 1980 and Los Angeles, 1984. President: OAPs' Coal and Grocery Fund; Lady Taverners, NI; Vice-President: Assoc. of Youth Clubs; NI Assoc. of Youth Clubs; Riding for the Disabled; Driving for the Disabled; Action Cancer; Patron: NIAAA, 1981–; Friends of Royal Victoria Hosp., Belfast, 1988–96. Freeman of Lisburn, 1998. Awards: BBC Sports personality, 1972; Athletic Writers', 1972; Sports Writers', 1972; Elizabeth Arden Visible Difference, 1976; Athletics, Dublin (Texaco), 1970 and 1972; British Airways Tourist Endeavour, 1981; Living Action, 1985; Evian Health, 1985. Hon. DSc New Univ. of Ulster, 1974; DUniv QUB, 1998; Hon. DLitt Loughborough, 1999. *Publication:* Mary P., an autobiography, 1974. *Address:* Willowtree Cottage, River Road, Dunmurry, Belfast, N Ireland BT17 9DP.

PETERS, Michael; *see* Peters, A. M.

PETERS, Nigel Melvin; QC 1997; a Recorder of the Crown Court, since 1998; *b* 14 Nov. 1952; *s* of Sidney Peters and Maisie Peters (*née* Pepper). *Educ:* Hasmonean GS; Leicester Univ. (LLB 1975). Called to the Bar, Lincoln's Inn, 1976 (Mansfield Schol.; Bencher, 2006); Asst Recorder, 1994–98. *Recreations:* cricket, Real tennis, travel, food, wine. *Address:* 18 Red Lion Court, EC4A 3EB. *T:* (020) 7520 6000. *Club:* MCC (Mem. Cttee, 1999–).

PETERS, Prof. Richard Stanley, BA (Oxon), BA (London), PhD (London); Professor of the Philosophy of Education, University of London Institute of Education, 1962–82, now Emeritus Professor; Dean, Faculty of Education, London University, 1971–74; *b* 31 Oct. 1919; *s* of late Charles Robert and Mabel Georgina Peters; *m* 1943, Margaret Lee Duncan; one *s* two *d*. *Educ:* Clifton Coll., Bristol; Queen's Coll., Oxford; Birkbeck Coll., University of London. War service with Friends' Ambulance Unit and Friends' Relief Service in E London, 1940–44. Classics Master, Sidcot School, Somerset, 1944–46; Birkbeck Coll., University of London: Studentship and part-time Lecturer in Philos. and Psychol., 1946–49; full-time Lecturer in Philos. and Psychol., 1949–58; Reader in Philosophy, 1958–62. Visiting Prof. of Education: Grad. School of Education, Harvard Univ., 1961; Univ. of Auckland, 1975; Visiting Fellow, Australian National Univ., 1969. Part-time lectureships, Bedford Coll., LSE; Tutor for University of London Tutorial Classes Cttee and Extension Cttee. Member, American National Academy of Education, 1966. *Publications:* (revised) Brett's History of Psychology, 1953; Hobbes, 1956; The Concept of Motivation, 1958; (with S. I. Benn) Social Principles and the Democratic State, 1959; Authority, Responsibility and Education, 1960; Ethics and Education, 1966; (ed) The Concept of Education, 1967; (ed) Perspectives on Plowden, 1969; (with P. H. Hirst) The Logic of Education, 1970; (ed with M. Cranston) Hobbes and Rousseau, 1971; (ed with R. F. Dearden and P. H. Hirst) Education and the Development of Reason, 1972; Reason and Compassion (Lindsay Meml Lectures), 1973; (ed) The Philosophy of Education, 1973; Psychology and Ethical Development, 1974; (ed) Nature and Conduct, 1975; (ed) The Role of the Head, 1976; Education and the Education of Teachers, 1977; (ed) John Dewey Reconsidered, 1977; Essays on Educators, 1981; Moral Development and Moral Education, 1981. *Address:* e-mail: Bengtrans@aol.com.

PETERS, Air Vice-Marshal Robert Geoffrey, CB 1992; Clerk to the Guild of Air Pilots and Air Navigators, 1998–2000; *b* 22 Aug. 1940; *s* of Geoffrey Ridgway Peters and Henriette Catharine Peters; *m* 1966, Mary Elizabeth (*née* Fletcher); one *d* three *s*. *Educ:* St Paul's Sch., London; RAF Coll., Cranwell (Gen. Duties/Pilot). Beverley C Mk1 Pilot Nos 34 and 47 Sqdns, Singapore and UK, 1961–66; Flt Comdr, No 46 Sqdn (Andovers), RAF Abingdon, 1967–68; MoD Central Staffs (Asst MA to Chief Adviser Personnel and Logistics), 1968–69; OC Flying Trng Sqdn, Air Electronics and Air Engr Trng Sch., RAF Topcliffe, 1970–72; RAF Staff Coll., Bracknell, 1973; Air Sec.'s Dept, MoD, 1974–76; OC 10 Sqdn (VC10), RAF Brize Norton, 1977–78; Directorate of Forward Policy (RAF), MoD, 1979–81; PSO to Dep. SACEUR(UK), SHAPE, Belgium, 1981–83; OC RAF St Mawgan, 1984–85; RCDS 1986; Comdr, RAF Staff and Air Attaché, Washington, 1987–90; Comdt, RAF Staff Coll., Bracknell, 1990–93; Dir of Welfare, RAF Benevolent Fund, 1993–97. President: RAF Fencing Union, 1986–93; Combined Services Fencing Assoc., 1988–97. Freeman, City of London, 1977; Liveryman, Co. of Coachmakers and Coach Harness Makers, 1977; Upper Freeman, GAPAN, 1997–2000. QCVSA 1973. *Recreations:* golf, sailing. *Club:* Naunton Downs Golf.

PETERS, Roger; Regional Employment Judge (formerly Regional Chairman of Employment Tribunals), Southampton, since 2004; *b* 25 April 1945; *s* of Frederick James and Lilian Ivy Peters; *m* 1973, Isobel Susan Bell Briggs; three *s*. *Educ:* Reading Blue Coat Sch.; Coll. of Law. Admitted solicitor, 1968; Solicitor, Blandy & Blandy, Reading, 1968–71; Asst Chief Legal Officer, Redditch Develt Corp., 1971–76; Principal Legal Officer, S Yorks CC, 1976–81; Chief Solicitor, Leeds Perm. Bldg Soc., 1981–87; Partner, Staffurth & Bray, Bognor Regis, 1987–94; Chairman, Employment Tribunals: Manchester, 1995–96; London, 1997–2003. Legal corresp., Hospitality mag., 1987–95. *Publications:* Essential Law for Catering Students, 1992, 2nd edn 1995; (jt author and ed.) Health and Safety: liability and litigation, 1995; articles in Solicitors' Jl. *Recreations:* listening to classical music, dinghy sailing. *Address:* Regional Office of Employment Tribunals, Dukes Keep, Marsh Lane, Southampton SO14 3EX.

PETERS, Siobhan, CMG 2007; Team Leader, Energy, Environment and Agriculture, HM Treasury, since 2007; *b* Welwyn Garden City, 27 June 1970; *d* of Susan Peters; one *s* one *d*. *Educ:* Wadham Coll., Oxford (BA Hons Oriental Studies 1991); Open Univ. (MA Envmt Policy 2004). Auditor, Touche Ross, 1992–96; Desk Officer, FCO, London and Beijing, 1997–2004; Hd, G8 Climate Change Unit, DEFRA, 2004–05; Hd, Review Team, Stern Review of the Econs of Climate Change, HM Treasury, 2005–07. *Recreation:* family life. *Address:* HM Treasury, 1 Horse Guards Road, SW1A 2HQ.

PETERS, Prof. Timothy John, PhD, DSc; Professor of Clinical Biochemistry, King's College, London, 1988–2004; Hon. Consultant Physician and Chemical Pathologist, King's College Hospital, 1988–2004; Hon. Senior Research Fellow, Institute of Archaeology and Antiquity, University of Birmingham; *b* 10 May 1939; *s* of Stanley and Paula Peters; *m* 1965, Judith Mary Bacon; one *s* two *d*. *Educ:* King Edward VI Sch., Macclesfield; Univ. of St Andrews (MB ChB (Hons) 1964; MSc 1966; DSc 1986); RPMS, Univ. of London (PhD 1970); Univ. of Birmingham (MA 2006). MRCPE 1969, FRCPE 1986; MRCP 1970, FRCP 1976; MRCPath 1983, FRCPath 1988. MRC Trng Fellow, RPMS, 1967–70; MRC Travelling Fellow, Rockefeller Univ., NY, 1970–72; Lectr, Sen. Lectr, then Reader, RPMS, and Hon. Cons. Physician, Hammersmith Hosp., 1972–79; Head, Div. of Clin. Cell Biology, MRC Clin. Res. Centre, 1979–88; Head, Dept of Clin. Biochemistry, 1988–2004, Sub-Dean for Postgrads and Higher Degree, Sch. of Medicine, 1988–2000, KCL; Associate Dean, London and SE Region, London Univ., 2000–04. Foundation Ed., Addiction Biology, 1995–2003. FRSA 1998. *Publications:* (ed) Alcohol Misuse: a European perspective, 1996; (ed jtly) International Handbook of Alcohol Dependence and Problems, 2001; (ed jtly) Skeletal Muscle: pathology, diagnosis and management of disease, 2002; over 500 articles on subcellular fractionation, alcohol misuse and toxicology, porphyria and iron metabolism, absorption and toxicology. *Recreations:* industrial archaeology and history. *Address:* 24 Mount View, Mount Avenue, Ealing, W5 1PR.

PETERS, Prof. Wallace, MD, DSc; FRCP; Director, 1999–2003, Consultant, 2004, Centre for Tropical Antiprotozoal Chemotherapy (formerly Tropical Parasitic Diseases Unit), Northwick Park Institute for Medical Research; Professor of Medical Protozoology, London School of Hygiene and Tropical Medicine, University of London, 1979–89, now Emeritus; *b* 1 April 1924; *s* of Henry and Fanny Peters; *m* 1954, Ruth (*née* Scheidegger). *Educ:* Haberdashers' Aske's Sch.; St Bartholomew's Hosp., London. MB BS, 1947; MRCS, DTM&H. Served in RAMC, 1947–49; practised tropical medicine in West and East Africa, 1950–52; Staff Mem., WHO, Liberia and Nepal, 1952–55; Asst Dir (Malariology), Health Dept, Territory of Papua and New Guinea, 1956–61; Research Associate, CIBA, Basle, Switzerland, 1961–66; Walter Myers Prof. of Parasitology, Univ. of Liverpool, 1966–79; Dean, Liverpool Sch. of Tropical Medicine, 1975–78; Jt Dir, Malaria Reference Lab., PHLS, 1979–89; Hon. Res. Fellow, Internat. Inst. of Parasitology, then CABI Bioscience, 1992–99; Hon. Prof. Res. Fellow, Imperial Coll., 2000–. Vice-Pres. and Pres., Brit. Soc. Parasit., 1972–76; President: Brit. Sect., Soc. Protozool., 1972–75; Royal Soc. of Trop. Medicine and Hygiene, 1987–89 (Vice-Pres., 1982–83, 1985–87; Hon. Fellow, 1997). Chm., WHO Steering Cttee on Chemotherapy of Malaria, 1975–83; Member: Expert Adv. Panel, WHO, 1967–2005; WHO Steering Cttees on Leishmaniasis, 1979; Editorial Bd, Ann. Trop. Med. Parasit., 1966–79; Trop. Med. Research Bd, MRC, 1973–77; Scientific Council, Inst. of Cellular and Molecular Path., 1981–84; Parasitol. Bd, Institut Pasteur, 1979–87; Sec., European Fedn Parasit., 1979–84 (Vice-Pres., 1975–79). Hon. Consultant on malariology to the Army, 1986–89. Hon. Fellow, Amer. Soc. of Tropical Medicine and Hygiene, 1995. Dr *hc*, Univ. René Descartes, Paris, 1992. Rudolf Leuckart Medal, German Soc. of Parasitol., 1980; King Faisal Internat. Prize in Medicine, 1983; Le Prince Medal, Amer. Soc. of Tropical Medicine and Hygiene, 1994; Emile Brumpt Medal and Prize, Soc. de Pathologie Exotique, Paris, 1999; Manson Medal, RSTM&H, 2004. *Publications:* A Provisional Checklist of Butterflies of the Ethiopian Region, 1952; Chemotherapy and Drug Resistance in Malaria, 1970, 2nd edn 1987; (with H. M. Gilles) A Colour Atlas of Tropical

Medicine and Parasitology, 1977, 6th edn (with G. Pasvol), as Atlas of Tropical Medicine and Parasitology, 2007; (ed with R. Killick-Kendrick) Rodent Malaria, 1978; (ed with W. H. G. Richards) Antimalarial Drugs, 2 vols, 1984; (ed with R. Killick-Kendrick) The Leishmaniases in Biology and Medicine, 1987; A Colour Atlas of Arthropods in Clinical Medicine, 1992; numerous papers in jls, on trop. med. and parasitology. *Recreation:* photography. *Address:* Department of Infectious and Tropical Disease, London School of Hygiene and Tropical Medicine, Keppel Street, WC1E 7HT; *e-mail:* wallacepeters2@aol.com.

PETERS, William, CMG 1981; LVO 1961; MBE 1959; HM Diplomatic Service, retired; *b* 28 Sept. 1923; *o s* of John William Peters and Louise (*née* Woodhouse), Morpeth, Northumberland; *m* 1st, 1944, Catherine B. Bailey (*d* 1997); no *c*; 2nd, 2004, Gill Rosemary Casebourne. *Educ:* King Edward VI Grammar Sch., Morpeth; Balliol Coll., Oxford (MA Lit. Hum. 1948); LSE and SOAS. War Service, Queen's Royal Rifles, KOSB, and 9th Gurkha Rifles, 1942–46. Joined HMOCS as Asst District Comr, Gold Coast, 1950; served in Cape Coast, Bawku and Tamale; Dep. Sec., Regional Comr, Northern Region, 1958–59; apptd to CRO as Asst Prin., 1959; Prin., 1959; 1st Sec., Dacca, 1960–63; 1st Sec., Cyprus, 1963–67; Head of Zambia and Malaŵi Dept, CRO, 1967–68; Head of Central African Dept, FCO, 1968–69; Dir, Internat. Affairs Div., Commonwealth Secretariat, 1969–71; Counsellor and Head of Chancery, Canberra, 1971–73; Dep. High Comr, Bombay, 1974–77; Ambassador to Uruguay, 1977–80; High Comr in Malaŵi, 1980–83. Member: Royal African Soc., 1980–85 (Hon. Treas., 1983–85); RSAA, 1987– (Mem., Editl Bd, 1990–2003); Exec., S Atlantic Council, 1985– (Vice Chm., 1997–2002); Churches Refugee Network, 2002–05; Chairman: Exec. Cttee, Lepra, 1984–92; Ethnic Minorities Sub-Cttee, Abbeyfield Soc., 1991–95; Council and Exec. Cttee, USPG, 1991–94 (Vice-Pres., 1994–; Governor, 1996–2004); Tibet Soc. of UK, 1986–94; Co-Founder, Jubilee 2000, 1994; Vice-Pres., Jubilee 2000 Coalition, 1997–2000 (Bd Mem., 1998–2000); Bd Mem., Jubilee Debt Campaign, 2001–06; Trustee, Tibet Relief Fund of UK, 1985–93 (Vice-Pres., 1994–); President: Downs Br., Royal British Legion, 1986–2003; Rotary Club of Deal, 1989–90; Dover Dist Assoc., Neighbourhood Watch, 2000–. Chm. of Govs, Walmer Sch., later Walmer Science Coll., 1996–2006. FCMI (FBIM 1984); FRSA 2000. MLitt Lambeth, 2001. Alchemist Award, Common Purpose, 2000; Gandhi Internat. Peace Award, Gandhi Foundn, 2001. *Publications:* Diplomatic Service: Formation and Operation, 1971; (with M. Dent) Confronting a Global Crisis, 1998; (with M. Dent) The Crisis of Poverty and Debt in the Third World, 1999; contribs to Jls of Asian Affairs and of African Administration; Illustrated Weekly of India; Noticias (Uruguay); Army Qly and Defence Review; Bull. of Assoc. of Christian Economists, USA; Christian Aid; Oxford; Round Table. *Recreation:* music. *Address:* 12 Crown Court, Middle Street, Deal, Kent CT14 7AG. *T:* (01304) 365640; *e-mail:* peterslvo@aol.com. *Clubs:* Oxford and Cambridge, Royal Commonwealth Society.

PETERS, Rt Hon. Winston (Raymond); PC 1998; MP Tauranga, since 1984 (Nat., 1984–93, NZ First, since 1993); Minister of Foreign Affairs and Trade, since 2005; Leader, New Zealand First Party, since 1993; *b* 11 April 1946; *s* of Len Peters and Joan (*née* McInnes); *m* 1973; one *s* one *d*. *Educ:* Auckland Univ. (BA 1969; LLB 1973); DipEd. With Russell, McVeagh, lawyers, 1974–78; estabd own legal practice, Howick, 1982. MP (Nat.) Hunua, 1979–81; Minister of Maori Affairs and i/c of Iwi Transition Agency, 1990–93; Dep. Prime Minister and Treasurer, NZ, 1996–98. *Address:* Parliament Office, Parliament Buildings, PO Box 18–041, Wellington, New Zealand.

PETERSEN, Niels Helveg; MP (Social Liberal) Denmark, 1966–74, and since 1977; *b* 17 Jan. 1939; *s* of Lilly and Kresten Helveg Petersen; *m* 1984, Kirsten Lee, MD; two *s*. *Educ:* Univ. of Copenhagen (LLB 1965); Univ. of Stanford, Calif. Chief of Cabinet, Danish EU Comr, 1974–77; Chm., Parly Group, 1978–88; Minister for Economic Affairs, 1988–90; Minister for Foreign Affairs, 1993–2000. *Recreations:* chess, tennis, soccer football. *Address:* Folketinget, Christiansborg, 1240 Copenhagen, Denmark. *T:* (45) 33375500.

PETERSEN, Prof. Ole Holger, CBE 2008; MD; FRCP; FRS 2000; George Holt Professor of Physiology, since 1981, and MRC Research Professor, since 1998, University of Liverpool; *b* 3 March 1943; *s* of Rear Adm. Joergen Petersen, Royal Danish Navy, and Elisabeth Klein, pianist; *m* 1st, 1968, Nina Bratting Jensen (marr. diss. 1995); two *s*; 2nd, 1995, Nina Burdakova. *Educ:* Univ. of Copenhagen Med. Sch. (MB ChB 1969; MD 1972). FRCP 2001. Lectr, 1969–73, Sen. Lectr, 1973–75, Inst. of Med. Physiology, Univ. of Copenhagen; Wellcome-Carlsberg Travelling Res. Fellow, Dept of Pharmacology, Univ. of Cambridge, 1971–72; Symers Prof. of Physiology, Univ. of Dundee, 1975–81. Vis. Prof., Stellenbosch Univ., 2000. Morton Grossman Meml Lectr, UCLA, 1985; Halliburton Lectr, KCL, 1986; Jacobaeus Prize Lectr, Nordic Insulin Foundn, 1994; Keynote Lectr, Gordon Res. Conf. on Calcium Signaling, Mass, USA, 2003, on Salivary Glands and Exocrine Secretion, Calif, USA, 2005; IUPS Lectr, FEPS Congress, Bratislava, 2007. President: FEPS, 2001–03; Physiological Soc. (UK), 2006–08; Sec.-Gen., IUPS, 2001–; Member Council: Bioscis Fedn, 2004–08; Royal Soc., 2004–06 (Vice-Pres., 2005–06). Chm., Eur. Editl Bd, Physiological Reviews, 2003–. MAE 1988; Foreign Mem., Royal Danish Acad. of Scis and Letters, 1988; Hon. Member: Polish Physiological Soc., 1993 (Czubalski Medal, 1993); Hungarian Physiological Soc., 2002; Hungarian Acad. of Scis, 2004. FMedSci 1998. Jubilee Medal, Charles Univ., Prague, 1998; Purkyne Medal, Czech Acad. of Scis, 2003. *Publications:* The Electrophysiology of Gland Cells, 1980; (jtly) Landmarks in Intracellular Signalling, 1997; Measuring Calcium and Calmodulin Inside and Outside Cells, 2001; Human Physiology, 2007; more than 200 articles in scientific jls on intracellular signalling mechanisms. *Recreation:* classical music. *Address:* MRC Secretory Control Research Group, Physiological Laboratory, University of Liverpool, Crown Street, Liverpool L69 3BX. *T:* (0151) 794 5342, *Fax:* (0151) 794 5323, 794 5327; *e-mail:* o.h.petersen@liverpool.ac.uk; 5 Mount Park Court, Woolton Park, Liverpool L25 6JP. *T:* (0151) 428 8085.

PETERSHAM, Viscount; Charles Henry Leicester Stanhope; *b* 20 July 1945; *s* and *heir* of 11th Earl of Harrington, *qv*; *m* 1966, Virginia Alleyne Freeman Jackson, Mallow (marr. diss. 1983); one *s* one *d*; *m* 1984, Anita Countess of Suffolk and Berkshire. *Educ:* Eton. *Heir:* *s* Hon. William Henry Leicester Stanhope [*b* 14 Oct. 1967; *m* 2001, Candida, *e d* of Ian Bond; one *d*]. *Address:* 2 Astell House, Astell Street, SW3 3RX.

See also Viscount Linley.

PETERSON, Col Sir Christopher (Matthew), Kt 1994; CBE 1983; TD 1952; Chairman, Cardiff Health Foods Ltd, since 1988; *b* 22 Feb. 1918; *s* of Oscar Peterson and Minnie Dee; *m* 1945, Grace Winifred McNeil (*d* 2000); one *s* one *d* (and one *s* decd). *Educ:* St Illtyd's Coll., Cardiff; Cardiff Tech. Coll. Shipbroker Office, Cardiff Docks, 1936–39; served RASC, 1940–46 (Capt.). Joined S Wales India Rubber Co., subseq. SWIRCO-Newton Gp, 1952, Chm., 1968–79; Dir, Dorada Hlgs plc, 1979–83; Chairman: Wales Local Bd, Commercial Union Assce Co., 1972–77; J. McNeil (Cameras), 1983–92; Randall Cox (Photographic), 1984–92; Cox & Tarry Ltd, 1984–89; Stanton-King Orgn, 1985–89; Taff Ely Enterprise Partnership, 1989–91; SWIRCO-Hall, 1990–92. Member: Cardiff City Council, 1968–71; S Glam CC, 1973–85. JP City of Cardiff, 1973; DL 1977, High Sheriff 1981–82, S Glam. Served TA, 1946–65; CO, 1961–65 (Lt-Col), Hon. Col, 1972–77, 157 Regt RCT. Mem., Imperial Soc. of Knights Bachelors. CStJ 1997. *Recreation:* walking. *Address:* 6 Cranbourne Way, Pontprennau, Cardiff CF23 8SL. *T:* (029) 2073 3793. *Clubs:* Army and Navy; Cardiff and County.

PETERSON, Colin Vyvyan, CVO 1982; Lay Assistant to Bishop of Winchester, 1985–94; *b* 24 Oct. 1932; *s* of late Sir Maurice Drummond Peterson, GCMG; *m* 1966, Pamela Rosemary Barry; two *s* two *d*. *Educ:* Winchester Coll.; Magdalen Coll., Oxford. Joined HM Treasury, 1959; Sec. for Appointments to PM and Ecclesiastical Sec. to the Lord Chancellor, 1974–82; Under Sec., Cabinet Office (MPO), 1982–85. *Recreation:* fishing. *Address:* Easter Cottage, 62 Edgar Road, Winchester, Hants SO23 9TN. *T:* (01962) 890258.

PETERSON, Rev. David Gilbert, PhD; Research Fellow, Moore Theological College, Sydney, since 2007; Principal, Oak Hill Theological College, 1996–2007; *b* 29 Oct. 1944; *s* of Gilbert Samuel and Marie Jean Peterson; *m* 1970, Lesley Victoria (*née* Stock); three *s*. *Educ:* Univ. of Sydney (MA); Moore Theol Coll., Sydney (BD (Lond.)); Univ. of Manchester (PhD 1978). Ordained deacon, 1968, priest, 1969; St Matthew's, Manly, dio. of Sydney, 1968–71; Lectr, Moore Theol Coll., 1971–75, 1978–79, 1984–96; Post-grad. study, Univ. of Manchester and Sunday Asst, St Mary's, Cheadle, dio. of Chester, 1975–78; Rector and Sen. Canon, St Michael's, Provisional Cathedral, Wollongong, dio. of Sydney, 1980–83. Hon. Vis. Prof., Middlesex Univ., 2004–. *Publications:* Hebrews and Perfection, 1982; Engaging with God, 1992; Possessed by God, 1995; The Book of Acts and its Theology, 1996; Where Wrath and Mercy Meet: proclaiming the atonement today, 2001; The Word Made Flesh: evangelicals and the incarnation, 2003; Christ and His People in the Book of Isaiah, 2003; Holiness and Sexuality, 2004. *Recreations:* golf, swimming, music. *Address:* 1 Vista Street, Belrose, NSW 2085, Australia.

PETERSON, Hon. David Robert; PC (Can.) 1992; QC (Can.) 1980; Senior Partner, since 1991, and Chairman, since 1998, Cassels Brock & Blackwell LLP; *b* 28 Dec. 1943; *s* of Clarence Marwin Peterson and Laura Marie (*née* Scott); *m* 1974, Shelley Christine Matthews; two *s* one *d*. *Educ:* Univ. of Western Ontario (BA Phil./PolSci); Univ. of Toronto (LLB). Called to Bar, Ontario, 1969. Chm. and Pres., C. M. Peterson Co. Ltd, 1969–75; MLA for London Centre, Ontario, 1975–90; Leader, Liberal Party of Ontario, 1982–90; Leader of the Opposition, 1982–85; Premier of Ontario, 1985–90. Chm. and Dir of public cos. CStJ 1987. Chevalier, Légion d'Honneur (France), 1994. *Recreations:* theatre, riding, jogging, ski-ing, tennis, scuba diving, golf, reading, gardening. *Address:* Cassels Brock & Blackwell LLP, 40 King Street W, Suite 2100, Scotia Plaza, Toronto, ON M5H 3C2, Canada. *Club:* London (Ontario) Hunt.

PETERSON, Rev. Canon John Louis, ThD; Canon for Global Justice and Reconciliation, Diocese of Washington, since 2005; *b* 17 Dec. 1942; *s* of J. Harold Peterson and Edythe V. Peterson; *m* 1966, Kirsten Ruth Bratlie; two *d*. *Educ:* Concordia Coll. (BA 1965); Harvard Divinity Sch. (STB 1968); Chicago Inst. for Advanced Theol Studies (ThD 1976). Instr, OT and Syro-Palestinian Archaeol., Seabury-Western Theol Seminary, Evanston, 1968–76; Canon Theologian and Admin. Asst to Bishop, dio. of Western Michigan, 1976–82; Vicar, St Stephen's Plainwell, Mich, 1976–82; Dean of St George's Coll., and Canon Residentiary, St George's Cathedral, Jerusalem, 1982–94, Hon. Canon, 1995–; Sec. Gen., Anglican Consultative Council, 1995–2004. Hon. Canon: Cathedral Ch of Christ the King, Kalamazoo, Mich, 1982–; Cathedral Church of Christ, Canterbury, 1995; St Michael's Cathedral, Kaduna, Nigeria, 1999–; St Paul's Cathedral, 2000–05; All Saints Cathedral, Mpwapwa, Tanzania, 2002–; St Dunstan's Cathedral, Benoni, SA, 2004–; Cathedral of St Peter and St Paul, 2005–. Hon. DD: Virginia Theol Seminary, 1993; Univ. of South (Sewanee), 1996; Seabury-Western Theol Seminary, 1997. *Publications:* A Walk in Jerusalem, 1998; contrib. Anchor Bible Dictionary, 1992. *Address:* Washington National Cathedral, Mount St Alban, Washington, DC 20016–5094, USA.

PETERSON, Will; *see* Billingham, M. P. D.

PETHERBRIDGE, Edward; actor and director; *b* 3 Aug. 1936; *s* of late William and Hannah Petherbridge; *m* 1st, 1957, Louise Harris (marr. diss. 1980); one *s*; 2nd, 1981, Emily Richard, actress; one *s* one *d*. *Educ:* Grange Grammar Sch., Bradford; Northern Theatre Sch. Early experience in repertory and on tour; London début, Dumain in Love's Labours Lost and Demetrius in A Midsummer Night's Dream, Regent's Park Open Air Theatre, 1962; All in Good Time, Mermaid, and Phoenix, 1963; with Nat. Theatre Co. at Old Vic, 1964–70, chief appearances in: Trelawny of the Wells, Rosencrantz and Guildenstern are Dead, A Flea in her Ear, Love for Love, Volpone, The Advertisement, The Way of the World, The White Devil; Alceste in The Misanthrope, Nottingham, Lulu, Royal Court, and Apollo, 1970; John Bull's Other Island, Mermaid, Swansong, opening of Crucible, Sheffield, 1971; Founder Mem., Actors' Co., 1972; chief appearances at Edinburgh Fests, NY, and on tour, 1972–75: 'Tis Pity she's a Whore, Rooling the Roost, The Way of the World, Tartuffe, King Lear; also devised, dir. and appeared in Knots (from R. D. Laing's book), The Beanstalk, a wordless pantomime, and dir. The Bacchae; RSC tour of Australia and NZ, 1976; dir. Uncle Vanya, Cambridge Theatre Co., 1977; Chasuble in The Importance of Being Earnest, and dir., devised and appeared in Do You Love Me (from R. D. Laing's book), Actors' Co. tour and Round House, 1977; Crucifer of Blood, Haymarket, 1979; Royal Shakespeare Company: tour, 1978, Twelfth Night; Three Sisters, 1979; Suicide, Newman Noggs in Nicholas Nickleby (Best Supporting Actor, London Drama Critics' Award, 1981), No Limits to Love, 1980; Nicholas Nickleby, Broadway, 1981; Twelfth Night, British Council tour (Philippines, Singapore, Malaysia, China and Japan), followed by season at Warehouse, London, 1982; Peter Pan, Barbican, 1983; The Rivals, NT, 1983; Strange Interlude, Duke of York's, 1984, Broadway, 1985 (Olivier Award, 1984); Love's Labours Lost, Stratford, 1984; Co-Dir, McKellen Petherbridge Co. at NT, 1984–86, acting in Duchess of Malfi, The Cherry Orchard, The Real Inspector Hound, and The Critic, 1985, company appeared at Internat. Theatre Fests, Paris and Chicago, 1986; Busman's Honeymoon, Lyric, Hammersmith, 1988; The Eight O'Clock Muse, one-man show, Riverside Studios, 1989; Alceste in The Misanthrope, co-prodn with Bristol Old Vic, 1989; The Power and the Glory, Chichester, 1990; Cyrano de Bergerac (title rôle), Greenwich, 1990; Point Valaine, and Valentine's Day (musical, from Shaw's You Never Can Tell), Chichester, 1991; Noël & Gertie, Duke of York's, 1991; The Seagull, RNT, 1994; Twelfth Night, Barbican, 1996; The Merry Wives of Windsor, Stratford, 1996; Cymbeline, Hamlet, Krapp's Last Tape, Stratford, 1997, transf. Barbican, NY, Washington and Edinburgh, 1997–98, Arts Th., 1999; The Accused, Haymarket Theatre Royal, 2000; The Relapse, RNT, 2001; The Woman in White, Palace Th., 2004; Donkeys' Years, Comedy, 2006; Office Suite, Chichester, 2007. Numerous television appearances include: Vershinin in Three Sisters (from RSC prod.); Lytton Strachey in No Need to Lie; Newman Noggs in Nicholas Nickleby (from RSC prod.); Gower in Pericles; Lord Peter Wimsey; Marsden in Strange Interlude; Uncle in Journey's End; No Strings. Hon. DLitt Bradford, 1989. *Recreations:*

listening to music, photography, theatre history. *Address:* c/o United Agents, 12–26 Lexington Street, W1F 0LE.

PETHICA, Prof. John Bernard, PhD; FRS 1999; SFI Research Professor, since 2001, and Professor of Physics, Trinity College, Dublin; Chief Scientific Adviser, National Physical Laboratory, Teddington, since 2007; Fellow of St Cross College, Oxford, since 1986. *Educ:* Trinity Hall, Cambridge (BA 1974; PhD 1978); MA Oxon. Lectr, Dept of Materials, 1987, Prof. of Materials Sci., 1996–2001, Vis. Prof., 2001–, Univ. of Oxford; Sony Corp. R&D Prof. (on leave of absence), Japan, 1993–94; Founding Dir, Centre for Res. on Adaptive Nanostructures and Nanodevices, Trinity Coll., Dublin, 2002–05. Dir, Nano Instruments Inc., Knoxville, Tenn, 1985–98. Mem. Council, Royal Soc., 2004–06. Rosenhain Medal and Prize, Inst. of Materials, 1997; Hughes Medal, Royal Soc., 2001; Holweck Medal, Soc. Française de Physique, 2002. *Publications:* contribs to jls. *Address:* Department of Physics, Trinity College, Dublin 2, Ireland.

PETIT, Sir Dinshaw Manockjee, 5th Bt *cr* 1890, of Petit Hall, Bombay; *b* 21 Jan. 1965; *er s* of Sir Dinshaw Manockjee Petit, 4th Bt and of his 1st wife, Nirmala Nanavatty; *S* father, 1998; *m* 1994, Laila, *d* of Homi Commissariat; one *s* one *d*. President: N. M. Petit Charities, 1998–; Sir D. M. Petit Charities, 1998–; F. D. Petit Sanatorium, 1998–; Persian Zoroastrian Amelioration Fund, 1998–; Petit Girls' Orphanage, 1998–; D. M. Petit Gymnasium, 1998–; Native Gen. Dispensary, 1998–; J. N. Petit Inst., 2004–. Trustee: Soc. for Prevention of Cruelty to Animals, 1998–; Concern India, 2005–; Member: Exec. Cttee, B. D. Petit Parsi Gen. Hospital, 1998–; Mgt Cttee, Garib Zarthostiona Rehethan Fund, 2003–. *Heir: s* Rehan Jehangir Petit, *b* 4 May 1995. *Address:* Petit Hall, 66 Nepean Sea Road, Bombay 400006, India.

PETIT, Roland; Officier de la Légion d'honneur; Chevalier des Arts et des Lettres; Commandeur de l'Ordre National du Mérite, 2002; French choreographer and dancer; Artistic Director and Choreographer, Ballet National de Marseille, 1972–97; *b* Villemomble, 13 Jan. 1924; *m* 1954, Renée (Zizi) Jeanmaire; one *d*. *Educ:* Ecole de Ballet de l'Opéra de Paris. L'Opéra de Paris, 1940–44; founded Les Vendredis de la Danse, 1944, Les Ballets des Champs-Elysées, 1945, Les Ballets de Paris de Roland Petit, 1948; Artistic Dir and Choreographer, Ballets de Marseille. Choreographic works include: Les Forains, 1945; Le Jeune Homme et la Mort, 1946; Les Demoiselles de la nuit, 1948; Carmen, 1949; Deuil en 24 heures, 1953; Le Loup, 1953; Les Chants de Maldoror, 1962; Notre Dame de Paris, 1965; L'éloge de la Folie, 1966; Paradise Lost, 1967; Les Intermittences du coeur, 1974; L'Arlésienne, 1974; La Symphonie fantastique, 1975; La Dame de Pique, 1978 (new version, 2001); Die Fledermaus, Le Chat Botté, 1985; Coppelia, The Blue Angel, 1985; Pink Floyd Ballet; Ma Pavlova, 1986; Charlot Danse Avec Nous, 1991; Clavigo, 1999; Duke Ellington Ballet, 2001, etc; choreographer and dancer: La Belle au Bois Dormant; Cyrano de Bergerac. Appeared in films: Hans Christian Andersen; Un, Deux, Trois, Quatre (arr. ballets, for film, and danced in 3); 4 ballets, Black Tights. *Address:* c/o ATER, Via Giardini 466/G, 41100 Modena, Italy.

PETITGAS, Franck R.; Global Co-Head, Investment Banking, Morgan Stanley & Co.; *b* Nantes, 25 Feb. 1961; *s* of Victor and Denise Petitgas; *m* 1985, Catherine Gex; one *s*. Trustee: Tate, 2008–; Chichester Harbour Trust; Member Council: Serpentine Gall.; Artangel. Conseiller du Commerce Exterieur, UK. *Recreations:* yachting, ski-ing, arts, history. *Address: e-mail:* franck.petitgas@ms.com. *Clubs:* Royal Ocean Racing; Bosham Sailing.

PETO, Sir Henry (Christopher Morton Bampfylde), 5th Bt *cr* 1927, of Barnstaple, co. Devon; *b* 8 April 1967; *s* of Sir Michael Henry Basil Peto, 4th Bt and Sarah Susan, *y d* of Major Sir Dennis Stucley, 5th Bt; *S* father, 2008; *m* 1998, Louise Imogen, *y d* of Christopher Balck-Foote; one *s* two *d*. *Educ:* Eton; Oxford Brookes Univ. MRICS. *Heir: s* Jake Christopher Bampfylde Peto, *b* 11 Oct. 2004.

PETO, Sir Henry (George Morton), 4th Bt *cr* 1855; *b* 29 April 1920; *s* of Comdr Sir Henry Francis Morton Peto, 3rd Bt, RN, and Edith (*d* 1945), *d* of late George Berners Ruck Keene; *S* father, 1978; *m* 1947, Frances Jacqueline, JP, *d* of late Ralph Haldane Evers; two *s*. *Educ:* Sherborne; Corpus Christi College, Cambridge. Served War with Royal Artillery, 1939–46. Manufacturing industry, 1946–80. *Heir: s* Francis Michael Morton Peto [*b* 11 Jan. 1949; *m* 1974, Felicity Margaret, *d* of late Lt-Col John Alan Burns; two *s*].

PETO, Sir Richard, Kt 1999; FRS 1989; Professor of Medical Statistics and Epidemiology, University of Oxford, since 1992; Fellow of Green Templeton College (formerly Green College), Oxford, since 1979; *b* 14 May 1943; *s* of Leonard Huntley Peto and Carrie Clarinda Peto; *m* 1970, Sallie Messum (marr. diss.); two *s*, and two *s* by Gale Mead (*d* 2001). *Educ:* Trinity Coll., Cambridge (MA Natural Sci.); Imperial Coll., London (MSc Statistics). Research Officer: MRC, 1967–69; Univ. of Oxford, 1969–72; Lectr, Dept of Regius Prof. of Medicine, 1972–75, Reader in Cancer Studies, 1975–92, Univ. of Oxford. Founder FMedSci 1998. *Publications:* Natural History of Chronic Bronchitis and Emphysema, 1976; Quantification of Occupational Cancer, 1981; The Causes of Cancer, 1983; Diet, Lifestyle and Mortality in China, 1990, 2nd edn 2006; (jtly) Mortality from Smoking in Developed Countries 1950–2000, 1994, 2nd edn 2006. *Recreations:* science, children. *Address:* Richard Doll Building, Old Road Campus, Roosevelt Drive, Oxford OX3 7LF. *T:* (01865) 552830/743801.

PETRE, family name of **Baron Petre**.

PETRE, 18th Baron *cr* 1603; **John Patrick Lionel Petre;** Lord-Lieutenant of Essex, since 2002; *b* 4 Aug. 1942; *s* of 17th Baron Petre and Marguerite Eileen, *d* of late Ion Wentworth Hamilton; *S* father, 1989; *m* 1965, Marcia Gwendolyn, *d* of Alfred Plumpton; two *s* one *d*. *Educ:* Eton; Trinity College, Oxford (MA). DL Essex, 1991. KStJ 2003. *Heir: s* Hon. Dominic William Petre [*b* 9 Aug. 1966; *m* 1998, Marisa Verna, *o d* of Anthony J. Perry; one *s* one *d*]. *Address:* Writtle Park, Highwood, Chelmsford, Essex CM1 3QF.

PETRE, His Honour Francis Herbert Loraine; a Circuit Judge, 1972–97; Chairman, Police Complaints Authority, 1989–92; *b* 9 March 1927; *s* of late Maj.-Gen. R. L. Petre, CB, DSO, MC and Mrs Katherine Sophia Petre; *m* 1958, Mary Jane, *d* of late Everard C. X. White and Sydney Mary Carleton White (*née* Holmes); three *s* one *d*. *Educ:* Downside; Clare Coll., Cambridge. Called to Bar, Lincoln's Inn, 1952; Dep. Chm., E Suffolk QS, 1970; Dep. Chm., Agricultural Lands Tribunal (Eastern Area), 1972; a Recorder, 1972; Regular Judge, Central Criminal Court, 1982–93. Mem., Parole Bd, 1997–2000. *Address:* The Ferriers, Bures, Suffolk CO8 5DL.

PETRIE, David Dick; Member (C) Highlands and Islands, Scottish Parliament, April 2006–2007; *b* 10 Dec. 1946; *s* of David and Beatrice Petrie; *m* 1974, Grace Munro; one *d*. *Educ:* Trinity Acad., Edinburgh; Heriot-Watt Univ., Edinburgh (BSc Civil Engrg 1971); Moray House Sch. of Educn, Edinburgh (PGCE Maths 2004). CEng 1975–2003. Engr, Roads Dept, Argyll CC, 1971–75; Chartered Engr and Manager, Roads and Water Services, Strathclyde Regl Council, 1975–96; Manager, W of Scotland Water, 1996–2002; Community Relns Manager, Scottish Water, 2002–03; Maths Probationer, Oban and Lochaber High Sch., 2004–06. Mem., Highlands and Is Regl Cttee, Scottish Cons. and Unionist Party, 1999–2002; Chm. Oban Br., and Exec. Mem., Argyll and Bute Scottish Cons. and Unionist Assoc. 1999–2002. Contested (C): Argyll and Bute, Scottish Parlt, 1999, 2003; Argyll and Bute, 2001; Western Isles, Scottish Parlt, 2007. *Recreations:* family, politics, current affairs, travel, golf, swimming. *Address:* Ardbeg, Duncraggan Road, Oban, Argyll PA34 5DU. *T:* and *Fax:* (01631) 564145; *e-mail:* petriedave@hotmail.com. *Clubs:* Oban Lorne Rugby Football (Capt., 1974–75; Pres., 1997–99); Glencruitten Golf; Rotary (Oban) (Pres., 1994–95).

PETRIE, Sir Peter (Charles), 5th Bt *cr* 1918, of Carrowcarden; CMG 1980; Adviser on European and Parliamentary Affairs to Governor of Bank of England, 1989–2003; HM Diplomatic Service, retired; *b* 7 March 1932; *s* of Sir Charles Petrie, 3rd Bt, CBE, FRHistS and Jessie Cecilia (*d* 1987), *d* of Frederick James George Mason; *S* half-brother, 1988; *m* 1958, Countess Lydwine Maria Fortunata v. Oberndorff, *d* of Count v. Oberndorff, The Hague and Paris; two *s* one *d*. *Educ:* Westminster; Christ Church, Oxford. BA Lit. Hum., MA. 2nd Lieut Grenadier Guards, 1954–56. Entered HM Foreign Service, 1956; served in UK Delegn to NATO, Paris 1958–61; UK High Commn, New Delhi (seconded CRO), 1961–64; Chargé d'Affaires, Katmandu, 1963; Cabinet Office, 1965–67; UK Mission to UN, NY, 1969–73; Counsellor (Head of Chancery), Bonn, 1973–76; Head of European Integration Dept (Internal), FCO, 1976–79; Minister, Paris, 1979–85; Ambassador to Belgium, 1985–89. Member: Franco-British Council, 1994–2002 (Chm., British section, 1997–2002); Inst de l'Euro, Lyon, 1995–99; Acad. de Comptabilité, 1997–. Mem. Council, City Univ., 1997–2002. Chevalier, Légion d'Honneur (France), 2006. *Recreations:* country pursuits. *Heir: s* Charles James Petrie [*b* 16 Sept. 1959; *m* 1981, France de Hauteclocque; three *s* (one *d* decd)]. *Address:* 16A Cambridge Street, SW1V 4QH; 40 rue Lauriston, 75116 Paris, France; Le Hameau du Jardin, Lestre, 50310 Montebourg, France. *Clubs:* Brooks's, Beefsteak; Jockey (Paris).

PETROW, Judith Caroline; *see* Bingham, J. C.

PETT, Maj.-Gen. Raymond Austin, CB 1995; MBE 1976; DL; Chairman: Coventry and Rugby Hospital Co. plc, since 2002; Walsall Hospital Co. plc, since 2007; *b* 23 Sept. 1941; *s* of late Richard John Austin Pett and Jessie Lyle Pett (*née* Adamson); *m* 1965, (Joan) Marie McGrath Price, *d* of FO Bernard Christopher McGrath, RAF (killed in action 1943) and of Mrs Robert Henry Benbow Price; one *s* one *d*. *Educ:* Christ's Coll.; RMA Sandhurst; rcds, psc. Commnd Lancashire Regt (Prince of Wales's Vols), 1961; regtl service in GB, BAOR, Swaziland and Cyprus; seconded 2nd Bn 6th QEO Gurkha Rifles, Malaysia and Hong Kong, 1967–69; Instr, RMA Sandhurst, 1969–72; Staff Coll., 1972–73; DAA&QMG, HQ 48 Gurkha Inf. Bde, 1974–75; 1st Bn, Queen's Lancashire Regt, 1976–78; GSO2 ASD 3, MoD, 1978–80; CO, 1st Bn King's Own Royal Border Regt, 1980–82; Staff Coll. (HQ and Directing Staff), 1983–84; Col ASD 2, MoD, 1984; Col Army Plans, MoD, 1985; Comd Gurkha Field Force, 1985–86, and Comd 48 Gurkha Inf. Bde, 1986–87, Hong Kong; RCDS 1988; Dir, Army Staff Duties, MoD, 1989–91; DCS and Sen. British Officer, HQ AFNORTH, 1991–94; Dir of Infantry, 1994–96. Dir of Capital Projects, Royal Hosps NHS Trust, 1996–97; Chief Exec., Barts and the London NHS Trust, 1997–2000; Chairman: Derby Healthcare plc, 2005–07; Central Notts Hosps plc, 2006–07; Managing Director: HCP (Bidding) Ltd, 2004–06; HCP Defence Projects Ltd, 2001–04; Director: HCP (Holdings) Ltd, 2001–06; Healthcare Projects Ltd, 2001–06. Col, 6th QEO Gurkha Rifles, 1988–94; Col Comdt, King's Div., 1994–97. Trustee: Gurkha Welfare Trust, 1988–2007; Somerset ACF Trust, 2008–. Chm., Army Mountaineering Assoc., 1994–96. Vice-Pres., Mid-Somerset Agricl Soc., 1996–. FRSA 1997. Freeman, City of London, 2000; Liveryman, Painter Stainers' Co., 2000–. DL Somerset, 2007. *Recreations:* the arts, house restoration, cross-country ski-ing. *Clubs:* Army and Navy, Ronnie Scott's.

PETTEGREE, Prof. Andrew David Mark, DPhil; Professor of Modern History, University of St Andrews, since 1998; *b* 16 Sept. 1957; *s* of Kenneth William Pettegree and Jean Dorcas Pettegree; *m* 1995, Jane Karen Ryan; two *d*. *Educ:* Oundle Sch.; Merton Coll., Oxford (BA 1979; MA, DPhil 1983). Hanseatic Schol., Hamburg, 1982–84; Res. Fellow, Peterhouse, Cambridge, 1984–86; University of St Andrews: Lectr, 1986–94; Reader, 1994–98; Founding Dir, St Andrews Reformation Studies Inst., 1993–2004. FRHistS 1986 (Literary Dir, 1998–2003). *Publications:* Foreign Protestant Communities in Sixteenth Century London, 1986; Emden and the Dutch Revolt, 1992; The Early Reformation in Europe, 1992; Marian Protestantism, 1996; Reformation World, 2000; Europe in the Sixteenth Century, 2002; Reformation and the Culture of Persuasion, 2005. *Recreations:* golf, tennis. *Address:* School of History, University of St Andrews, St Andrews, Fife KY16 9AL; *e-mail:* admp@St-And.ac.uk. *Club:* MCC.

PETTIFER, Julian; freelance writer and broadcaster; *b* 21 July 1935; *s* of Stephen Henry Pettifer and Diana Mary (*née* Burton); unmarried. *Educ:* Marlborough; St John's Coll., Cambridge. Television reporter, writer and presenter: Southern TV, 1958–62; Tonight, BBC, 1962–64; 24 Hours, BBC, 1964–69; Panorama, BBC, 1969–75; Presenter, Cuba—25 years of revolution (series), ITV, 1984; Host, Busman's Holiday, ITV, 1985–86. Numerous television documentaries, including: Vietnam, War without End, 1970; The World About Us, 1976; The Spirit of '76, 1976; Diamonds in the Sky, 1979; Nature Watch, 1981–82, 1985–86, 1988, 1990, 1992; Automania, 1984; The Living Isles, 1986; Missionaries, 1990; See for Yourself, 1991; Assignment, 1991; Nature, 1992; The Culling Fields, 1999; Warnings from the Wild, 2000, 2001; radio broadcasts include: Asia File, 1995–, and Crossing Continents, 1999–, BBC Radio 4; The Sixties, BBC Radio 2, 2000. Trustee, Royal Botanic Gdns, Kew, 1993–96. President: Berks, Bucks and Oxfordshire Naturalists Trust, 1990–; RSPB, 1995–2001 and 2004–; Vice-Pres., RSNC, 1992–. Reporter of the Year Award, Guild of Television Directors and Producers, 1968; Cherry Kearton Award for Contribution to Wildlife Films, RGS, 1990; Mungo Park Medal, RSGS, 1998. *Publications:* (jtly) Diamonds in the Sky: a social history of air travel, 1979; (jtly) Nature Watch, 1981; (jtly) Automania, 1984; (jtly) Missionaries, 1990; (jtly) Nature Watch, 1994. *Recreations:* gardening, sport, cinema. *Address:* c/o Curtis Brown, 28–29 Haymarket, SW1Y 4SP. *T:* (020) 7396 6600. *Club:* Queen's.

PETTIFER, Richard Edward William, MBE 2008; PhD; General Secretary, PRIMET, since 2007; Executive Director, Royal Meterological Society, 1998–2006; *b* 19 Sept. 1941; *s* of Reginald Charles Edward Pettifer and Irene May Pettifer (*née* Bradley); *m* 1st, 1965, Colleen Rosemary Adams (*d* 1984); one *s* two *d*; 2nd, 1986, Maureen Eileen Macartney (*née* McCullough); one step *d*. *Educ:* Ealing County Grammar Sch. for Boys; London Polytechnic; Queen's Univ., Belfast (BSc 1st cl. Physics 1969; PhD Laser and Atmos. Physics 1975). FRMetS 1979; CMet 1994; CEnv 2005. Asst Dir, Meteorological Office, 1980–85; Managing Director: Vaisala (UK) Ltd, 1985–98; Scientific and Technical Mgt Ltd, 1998–2005. Chm., COST Project 43, 1978–84; Vice Pres., CIMO, 1980–84. *Publications:* approx. 100 papers, book contribs, public reports, etc on meteorological/oceanographic instrumentation and measurements. *Recreations:* gardening, golf, cricket, community support projects. *Address:* The Croft, 22 Vyne Road, Sherborne St John, Hants RG24 9HX. *T:* 07739 212227; *e-mail:* richard.pettifer@dsl.pipex.com. *Clubs:* Meteorological; Weybrook Park Golf; Eversley Cricket.

PETTIFOR, Prof. David Godfrey, CBE 2005; PhD; FRS 1994; Isaac Wolfson Professor of Metallurgy, Oxford University, since 1992; Fellow, St Edmund Hall, Oxford, since 1992; *b* 9 March 1945; *s* of late Percy Hayward Pettifor and Margaret Cotterill; *m* 1st, 1969, Lynda Ann Potgieter (marr. diss. 1989); two *s*; 2nd, 2004, Diane Gold. *Educ:* Univ. of Witwatersrand (BSc Hons 1967); PhD Cantab 1970. Lectr, Dept of Physics, Univ. of Dar es Salaam, 1971; Res. Asst, Cavendish Lab., Cambridge, 1974; Vis. Res. Scientist, Bell Labs, USA, 1978; Imperial College, London: Lectr and Reader, Dept of Mathematics, 1978–88; Prof. of Theoretical Solid State Physics, 1988–92. Lectures: Mott, Inst. of Physics, 1993; Maddin, Univ. of Pa, 1995. Hume-Rothery Award, Minerals, Metals and Materials Soc., USA, 1995; Armourers' and Brasiers' Award, Royal Soc., 1999. *Publications:* Bonding and Structure of Molecules and Solids, 1995; papers incl. Structures maps for pseudo-binary and ternary phases (Inst. of Metals Prize, 1989). *Recreation:* walking. *Address:* Department of Materials, University of Oxford, Parks Road, Oxford OX1 3PH. *T:* (01865) 273751.

PETTIGREW, Prof. Andrew Marshall, PhD; FBA 2003; AcSS; Dean of Management School, and Professor of Strategy and Organisation, University of Bath, since 2003; *b* 11 June 1944; *s* of late George Pettigrew and Martha (*née* Marshall); *m* 1967, Mary Ethna Veronica Moores; three *s* (one *d* decd). *Educ:* Corby Grammar Sch.; Liverpool Univ. (BA 1965; Dip. Ind. Admin 1967); Manchester Univ. (PhD Bus. Admin 1970). Res. Associate, Manchester Business Sch., 1966–69; Vis. Asst Prof., Yale Univ., 1969–71; Lectr, London Business Sch., 1971–76; Warwick Business School, University of Warwick: Prof. of Organisational Behaviour, 1976–85; Dir, Centre for Corporate Strategy and Change, 1985–95; Prof. of Strategy and Orgn, 1995–2003; Associate Dean of Res., 2002–03. Vis. Schol., 1981, Vis. Prof., 2001, Harvard Business Sch.; Vis. Schol., Stanford Univ., 1982. Member: Industry and Employment Cttee, ESRC, 1984–87; Jt Cttee, ESRC and SERC, 1988–91; Council, ESRC, 2005–; Bd, Eur. Foundn for Mgt Develt, 2006– (Vice Pres., 2008–); Dep. Chm., Mgt Studies Panel, RAE, UFC, 1992. Fellow: British Acad. of Mgt, 1996 (Chm., 1986–90; Pres., 1990–93); Acad. of Mgt, 1997; SMS, 2005; AcSS 1999. Hon. Dr Linköping, 1989. *Publications:* The Politics of Organisational Decision Making, 1973; (with E. Mumford) Implementing Strategic Decisions, 1975; The Awakening Giant: continuity and change in ICI, 1985; The Management of Strategic Change, 1987; (with R. Whipp) Managing Change for Competitive Success, 1991; (jtly) Shaping Strategic Change: making change in the NHS, 1992; (jtly) The New Public Management in Action, 1996; (with E. Fenton) The Innovating Organisation, 2000; (jtly) The Handbook of Strategy and Management, 2002; (jtly) Innovative Forms of Organising, 2003; articles in professional jls. *Recreations:* antiquarian horology, military history, Herefordshire. *Address:* School of Management, University of Bath, Claverton Down, Bath BA2 7AY. *T:* (01225) 383052; *e-mail:* a.m.pettigrew@bath.ac.uk.

PETTIGREW, Colin William; Floating Sheriff of North Strathclyde at Paisley, since 2002; *b* 19 June 1957; *s* of Thomas Whitelaw Pettigrew and Mary Macrae Pettigrew (*née* Muir); *m* 1981, Linda McGill; one *s* one *d*. *Educ:* High Sch. of Glasgow; Glasgow Univ. (LLB Hons). Admitted as solicitor and NP, 1980. Trainee solicitor, 1978–80, Asst Solicitor, 1980–82, McClure Naismith Brodie & Co., Glasgow; Asst Solicitor, 1982–83, Partner, 1983–2002, Borland Johnson & Orr, subseq. Borland Montgomerie Keyden, Glasgow. Elder, Church of Scotland. *Recreations:* Rugby, golf, gardening, travel. *Address:* Paisley Sheriff Court House, St James Street, Paisley PA3 2HW. *T:* (0141) 887 5291.

PETTIGREW, Prof. John Douglas, FRS 1987; FAA 1987; Professor of Physiology, 1983, now Emeritus, and Director, Vision, Touch and Hearing Research Centre, since 1988, University of Queensland; *b* 2 Oct. 1943; *s* of John James Pettigrew and Enid Dellmere Holt; *m* 1968, Rona Butler (marr. diss. 1996); one *s* two *d*. *Educ:* Katoomba High Sch.; Univ. of Sydney (BSc Med., MSc, MB BS). Jun. Resident MO, Royal Prince Alfred Hosp., 1969; Miller Fellow 1970–72, Res. Associate 1973, Univ. of California, Berkeley; Asst Prof. of Biology 1974, Associate Prof. of Biology 1978, CIT; Actg Dir, National Vision Res. Inst. of Aust., 1981. *Publications:* Visual Neuroscience, 1986; numerous pubns in Nature, Science, Jl of Physiol., Jl of Comp. Neurol., Exp. Brain Res., etc. *Recreations:* bird watching, mountaineering. *Address:* 207/180 Swann Road, Taringa, Qld 4068, Australia. *T:* (7) 38711062.

PETTIGREW, Hon. Pierre Stewart; PC (Canada) 1996; Executive Advisor, International, Deloitte & Touche, Toronto; Chairman, The Warwick Commission; *b* 18 April 1951. *Educ:* Univ. du Québec à Trois Rivières (BA Philos.); Balliol Coll., Oxford (MPhil Internat. Relns 1976). Dir, Pol Cttee, NATO Assembly, Brussels, 1976–78; Exec. Asst to Leader of Quebec Liberal Party, 1978–81; Foreign Policy Advr to Prime Minister, 1981–84; Vice Pres., Samson Bélair Deloitte & Touche Internat. (Montreal), 1985–95. MP (L) Papineau, Quebec, 1996–2006. Minister: for Internat. Co-operation, 1996; responsible for La Francophonie, 1996; of Human Resources Develt, 1996–99; for Internat. Trade, 1999–2003; of Health, of Intergovtl Affairs, and responsible for Official Langs, 2003–04; of Foreign Affairs, 2004–06. Hon. LLD Warwick, 2008. *Publication:* Pour une politique de la confiance, 1999. *Address: e-mail:* nstelfox@deloitte.ca.

PETTIGREW, Sir Russell (Hilton), Kt 1983; FInstD; FCILT; Chairman, Chep Handling Systems NZ Ltd, 1980–93; *b* 10 Sept. 1920; *s* of Albert and Bertha Pettigrew; *m* 1965, Glennis Olive Nicol; one *s* one *d*. *Educ:* Hangatiki Sch., King Country; Te Kuiti Dist High Sch. Served War, Naval Service, 1941–44 (Service Medals). Hawkes Bay Motor Co., 1935–40; Pettigrews Transport, 1946–63; formed Allied Freightways (now Freightways Holdings Ltd), 1964. Chairman: NZ Maritime Holdings Ltd, 1981–89; AGC NZ, 1984–88; Dep. Chm., NZ Forest Products, 1980–88 (Dir, 1975–90). FCILT (FCIT 1972) (Life Mem. 1995); Fellow, NZ Inst. of Dirs, 1972; Life Mem., NZ Road Transport Assoc., 1981. Paul Harris Fellow, Rotary Internat., 2003. Freedom, City of Napier, 2004. Knighthood for services to the Transport Industry. *Publication:* article in The Modern Freight Forwarder and the Road Carrier, 1971. *Recreations:* farming, Rugby, horse racing. *Club:* Hawkes Bay (New Zealand).

PETTIT, Sir Daniel (Eric Arthur), Kt 1974; Chairman, PosTel Investment Management (formerly Post Office Staff Superannuation Fund), 1979–83; *b* Liverpool, 19 Feb. 1915; *s* of Thomas Edgar Pettit and Pauline Elizabeth Pettit (*née* Kerr); *m* 1940, Winifred (*d* 2004), *d* of William and Sarah Bibby; two *s*. *Educ:* Quarry Bank High Sch., Liverpool; Fitzwilliam Coll., Cambridge (MA; Hon. Fellow, 1985). School Master, 1938–40 and 1946–47; War Service, Africa, India, Burma, 1940–46 (Major, RA); Unilever: Management, 1948–57; Associated Company Dir and Chm., 1958–70. Chm., Nat. Freight Corp., 1971–78 (part-time Mem. Bd, 1968–70); Member: Freight Integration Council, 1971–78; National Ports Council, 1971–80; Bd, Foundn of Management Educn, 1973–84; Waste Management Adv. Council, 1971–78; Chm., EDC for Distributive Trades, 1974–78. Chairman: Incpen, 1979–90; RDC Properties, 1987–2004; Director: Lloyds Bank Ltd, 1977–78 (Chm., Birmingham & W Midlands Bd, 1978–85); Lloyds Bank (UK) Ltd, 1979–85; Bransford Partnership, 1979–; Black Horse Life Assurance Co. Ltd, 1983–85; Lloyds Bank Unit Trust Managers Ltd, 1981–85. Mem. Council, British Road Fedn Ltd. Hon. Col, 162 Regt RCT (V). Freeman, City of London, 1971; Liveryman, Worshipful Co. of Carmen, 1971. CCMI; FCILT (Pres. 1971–72); FRSA; FIMMM; MIPD. *Publications:* various papers on transport and management matters. *Recreations:* cricket, Association football (Olympic Games, 1936; Corinthian FC, 1935–); fly-fishing. *Address:* Bransford Court Farm, Worcester WR6 5JL. *Clubs:* Farmers', MCC; Hawks (Cambridge).

PETTITT, Adam Sven, MA; Head Master, Highgate School, since 2006; *b* 5 Feb. 1966; *s* of Robin Garth Pettitt and Elizabeth Margaret Pettitt (*née* Jenkins); *m* 1997, Barbara Sauron; two *s* one *d*. *Educ:* Hailsham Sch.; Eastbourne Sixth Form Coll.; New Coll., Oxford (BA Mod and Medieval Langs 1988; MA 1995). Eton Coll., 1988–92; Hd of German, Oundle Sch., 1992–94; Hd of Mod. Langs, Abingdon Sch., 1994–98; Second Master, Norwich Sch., 1998–2006. *Recreations:* cross-country running, reading, old buildings. *Address:* Highgate School, North Road, N6 4AY. *T:* (020) 8340 1524, *Fax:* (020) 8340 7674. *Club:* Athenæum.

PETTITT, Sir Dennis, Kt 1998; Leader, Nottinghamshire County Council, 1981–2001; *b* 21 Aug. 1925; *m* 1949, Dorothy Mary. Served War of 1939–45. Electrician; trade unionist; Kenya, 1950–60; Vice Chm., Kenya League, 1952–53. Member (Lab): Birmingham CC, 1962–68; Broxtowe BC, 1974–99 (Leader, Lab Gp, 1974–77; Hon. Alderman, 2003); Notts CC, 1977–2001 (Leader, Lab Gp, 1979–2001; Hon. Alderman, 2001). Chm., ACC, 1988–89, 1991–92. Mem., Cttee of the Regions, EU, 1993–2001. Contested (Lab) Carlton, Oct. 1974. Hon. Citizen, Poznan, Poland, 2001. Commander's Cross, Order of Merit (Poland), 1993. *Address:* 32 Scalby Close, Eastwood, Notts NG16 3QQ.

PETTITT, Gordon Charles, OBE 1991; transport management consultant, 1993–2000; Managing Director, Regional Railways, British Rail, 1991–92; *b* 12 April 1934; *s* of Charles and Annie Pettitt; *m* 1956, Ursula Margareta Agnes Hokamp; three *d*. *Educ:* St Columba's Coll., St Albans; Pitman's Coll., London. FCILT. British Rail, 1950–92: Freight Sales Manager, Eastern Reg., 1976; Chief Passenger Manager, Western Reg., 1978; Divl Manager, Liverpool Street, Eastern Reg., 1979; Dep. Gen. Manager, 1983, Gen. Manager, 1985, Southern Reg.; Dir, Provincial, 1990–91. Director: Connex Rail Ltd, 1997–98; Heathrow Express Operating Co. Ltd, 1997–99; Network Rail Property Adv. Bd, 2003–06. Pres., Instn of Railway Operators, 2000–02. Governor, Middlesex Univ. (formerly Polytechnic), 1989–95. *Recreations:* walking, foreign travel, Victorian art. *Address:* Beeches Green, Woodham Lane, Woking, Surrey GU21 5SP.

PETTS, Prof. Geoffrey Eric, PhD; Vice Chancellor and Rector, University of Westminster, since 2007; *b* 28 March 1953; *s* of Horace and Eva Petts; *m* 1977, Judith Irene Armitt (*see* Prof. J. I. Petts). *Educ:* St Michael's Primary Sch., Tenterden; Ashford Grammar Sch.; Univ. of Liverpool (BSc Hons Geol and Phys. Geog. 1974); Univ. of Exeter; Univ. of Southampton (PhD 1978). Lectr, Dorset Inst. of Higher Educn, 1977–79; Loughborough University: Lectr, 1979–86; Sen. Lectr, 1986–89; Prof. of Phys. Geog., 1989–94; Hd, Dept of Geog., 1991–94; University of Birmingham: Prof. of Phys. Geog., 1994–2007; Dir, Centre for Envmtl Res. and Trng, 1997–2007; Hd, Sch. of Geog., 1998–2001; Pro Vice Chancellor, 2001–07. Visiting Professor: KCL, 2003–Aug. 2009, Univ. of Birmingham, 2007–. Founding Editor-in-Chief, Regulated Rivers: Research and Management, subseq. River Research and Applications, 1986–. Member Scientific Advisory Board: Prep. Gp for Internat. Lake Envmts Cttee, UNEP, 1985; Mgt of Land-Water Ecotones, UNESCO Man and Biosphere prog., 1989–97; Long-term Monitoring Upper Mississippi River, Fish and Wildlife Service, US Dept of Interior, 1989–1999; Water Res., ICSU, 1996–2003; Eco-Hydrology, UNESCO Internat. Hydrol. Prog., 1998–2000. Co-Chm., Eur. Network for Scientific and Tech. Co-operation, Large Alluvial Rivers, 1986–89; Dir, Internat. Water Resources Assoc., 1992–95. Member: British Soc. of Geomorphol. (formerly British Geomorphol Res. Gp) (Chm., Pubns Sub-cttee, 1986–89); British Hydrol Soc. (Sec., 1988–90); Freshwater Biol Assoc. (Mem. Council, 1999–2003). Mem. Bd, London Higher, 2007–. FRGS; FRSA 2003. Busk Medal, RGS, 2006. *Publications:* Rivers, 1983; Impounded Rivers: perspectives for ecological management, 1984; (with I. D. L. Foster) Rivers and Landscapes, 1985; (ed jtly) Alternatives in River Regulation, 1989; (ed jtly) Historical Analysis of Large Alluvial Rivers in Western Europe, 1989; (ed jtly) Water, Engineering and Landscape, 1990; (ed jtly) Lowland Floodplain Rivers: geomorphological perspectives, 1992; (ed jtly) River Conservation and Management, 1992; (ed jtly) Rivers Handbook, vol 1, 1992, vol 2, 1994; (ed jtly) Hydrosystemes Fluviaux, 1993 (Hydrosystems, 1996); (ed jtly) Changing River Channels, 1995; (ed) Man's Influence on Freshwater Ecosystems and Water Use, 1995; (ed jtly) River Restoration, 1996; (ed jtly) River Flows and Channel Forms, 1996; (ed jtly) River Biota, 1996; (ed jtly) Global Perspectives on River Conservation, 2000; (with J. Heathcote and D. Martin) Urban Rivers: our inheritance and future, 2002; (ed jtly) Braided Rivers, 2006. *Recreations:* walking, gardening, cricket, hockey, golf, the Arctic, painting and sketching. *Address:* University of Westminster, 309 Regent Street, W1B 2UW. *T:* (020) 7911 5115, *Fax:* (020) 7911 5103; *e-mail:* G.Petts@westminster.ac.uk. *Club:* East India.

PETTS, Prof. Judith Irene, PhD; Professor of Environmental Risk Management, since 1999, and Pro-Vice-Chancellor (Research and Knowledge Transfer), since 2007, University of Birmingham (Head, School of Geography, Earth and Environmental Sciences, 2001–07); *b* 7 Jan. 1954; *d* of Alexander and Rene Armitt; *m* 1977, Prof. Geoffrey Eric Petts, *qv*. *Educ:* Univ. of Exeter (BA Hons (Geog.) 1975); Loughborough Univ. (PhD 1996). MCIWM 2002. Loughborough University: Lectr, Centre for Extension Studies, 1987–95; Sen. Lectr, 1995–97, Dir, 1997–99, Centre for Hazard and Risk Mgt. Member: Council, NERC, 2000–06; Royal Commn on Envmtl Pollution, 2005–; EPSRC Societal Issues Panel, 2006–. FRSA 2003; AcSS 2007. *Publications:* (with G. Eduljee) Environmental Impact Assessment for Waste Treatment and Disposal Facilities, 1994; (jtly) Risk-based Contaminated Land Investigation and Assessment, 1997; (ed) Handbook of Environmental Impact Assessment, 1999. *Recreations:* travelling to remote places (particularly the Arctic), walking. *Address:* University of Birmingham, Edgbaston, Birmingham B15 2TT.

PETTY, Very Rev. John Fitzmaurice; Chaplain, Mount House Residential Home for the Elderly, Shrewsbury, 2001–07; *b* 9 March 1935; *m* 1963, Susan Shakerley; three *s* one *d*. *Educ:* RMA Sandhurst; Trinity Hall, Cambridge (BA 1959, MA 1965); Cuddesdon College. Commnd RE, 1955; seconded Gurkha Engineers, 1959–62; resigned commission as Captain, 1964. Deacon 1966, priest 1967; Curate: St Cuthbert, Sheffield, 1966–69; St Helier, Southwark Dio., 1969–75; Vicar of St John's, Hurst, Ashton-under-Lyne, 1975–87; Area Dean of Ashton-under-Lyne, 1983–87; Provost, then Dean, Coventry Cathedral, 1988–2000. Hon. Canon of Manchester Cathedral, 1986. Trustee, Simeon Trust, 2003–. Hon. DLitt Coventry, 1996. *Recreations:* cycling, ski-ing. *Address:* 4 Granville Street, Copthorne, Shrewsbury SY3 8NE. *T:* (01743) 231513.

PETTY, Prof. Michael Charles, PhD, DSc; Professor of Engineering, University of Durham, since 1994; Co-Director, Durham Centre for Molecular Electronics, since 1987; *b* 30 Dec. 1950; *s* of John Leonard Petty and Doreen Rosemary Petty (*née* Bellarby); *m* 1998, Anne Mathers Brawley; one step *d*. *Educ:* Sussex Univ. (BSc 1st Cl. Hons Electronics 1972; DSc 1994); Imperial Coll., London (PhD 1976). University of Durham:

Lectr in Applied Physics, 1976–88; Sen. Lectr, Sch. of Engrg, 1988–94; Chm., Sch. of Engrg, 1997–2000; Sir James Knott Res. Fellow, 2000–01; Chm. Council, St Mary's Coll., 2002–. Non-exec. Dir, Centre of Excellence for Nanotechnol., Micro and Photonic Systems, 2004–06. *Publications:* Langmuir-Blodgett Films, 1995; Introduction to Molecular Electronics, 1996; Molecular Electronics, 2007; numerous contribs on molecular electronics and nanoelectronics to scientific jls. *Recreations:* Yorkshire Dales, horse riding, supporter of Crystal Palace FC. *Address:* School of Engineering, University of Durham, South Road, Durham DH1 3LE. *T:* (0191) 334 2419. *Club:* Sedgefield Social.

PETTY, William Henry, CBE 1981; County Education Officer, Kent, 1973–84; *b* 7 Sept. 1921; *s* of Henry and Eveline Ann Petty, Bradford; *m* 1948, Margaret Elaine, *o d* of Edward and Lorna Bastow, Baildon, Yorks; one *s* two *d. Educ:* Bradford Grammar Sch.; Peterhouse, Cambridge; London Univ. MA 1950, BSc 1953. Served RA, India and Burma, 1941–45. Admin, teaching and lectrg in London, Doncaster and N R Yorks, 1946–57; Sen. Asst Educn Officer, W R Yorks CC, 1957–64; Dep. County Educn Officer, Kent CC, 1964–73. Member: Council and Court, Univ. of Kent at Canterbury, 1974–84, 1992–; Local Govt Trng Bd, Careers Service Trng Cttee, 1975–84; Careers Service Adv. Council, 1976–84; Trng and Further Educn Cons. Gp, 1977–83; Vital Skills Task Gp, 1977–78; Manpower Services Commn, SE Counties Area Bd, 1978–83; Bd of Dirs, Industrial Trng Service, 1978–97; Exec. Mem. and Sec. for SE Reg., Soc. of Educn Officers, 1978–82; Pres., Soc. of Educn Officers, 1980–81; Chm., Assoc. of Educn Officers, 1979–80 (Vice-Chm., 1978–79); Member: JNC for Chief Officers, Officers' side, 1974–84 (Chm., 1981–84); C of E Bd of Educn, Schs Cttee, 1981–86; County Educn Officers' Soc., 1974–84 (Chm., 1982–83); Youth Trng Task Gp, 1982; National Youth Trng Bd, 1983–84; Kent Area Manpower Bd, 1983–84; Canterbury Diocesan Bd of Educn, 1984–92 (Vice-Chm., 1989–92); Consultant, Further Educn Unit, 1984–90. Dir, Sennocke Services Ltd, 1989–97. Governor: Christ Church Coll., Canterbury, 1974–94 (Chm., 1992–94; Vice-Chm., 1988–92); Sevenoaks Sch., 1974–97; YMCA Nat. Coll., 1992–94. Hon. DLitt Kent, 1983. Prizewinner: Cheltenham Fest. of Lit., 1968; Camden Fest. of Music and Arts, 1969; Swanage Fest. of the Arts, 1995; Greenwood Prize, 1978; Lake Aske Meml Award, 1980; Kent Fedn of Writers Prize, 1995; White Cliffs Prize, Cruse Bereavement Care, 2000; Envoi Prize, Envoi mag., 2004; Essex Poetry Fest. Prize, 2006; Newark Poetry Soc. Prize, 2007. *Publications:* No Bold Comfort, 1957; Conquest, 1967; (jtly) Educational Administration, 1980; Executive Summaries (booklets), 1984–90; Springfield, 1994; (with Robert Roberts) Genius Loci, 1995; The Louvre Imperial, 1997; Interpretations of History, 2000; No-one Listening, 2002; Breaking Time, 2005; Hijacked over China with Jane Austen, 2006; But Someone Liked It, 2008; contrib. educnl and lit. jls and anthologies. *Recreations:* literature, travel. *Address:* Willow Bank, Moat Road, Headcorn, Kent TN27 9NT. *T:* (01622) 890087. *Club:* Oxford and Cambridge.

PETTY-FITZMAURICE, family name of **Marquess of Lansdowne**.

PEYTON, Kathleen Wendy; writer (as K. M. Peyton); *b* 2 Aug. 1929; *d* of William Joseph Herald and Ivy Kathleen Herald; *m* 1950, Michael Peyton; two *d. Educ:* Wimbledon High Sch.; Manchester Sch. of Art (ATD). Taught art at Northampton High Sch., 1953–55; started writing seriously after birth of first child, although had already had 4 books published. *Publications: as Kathleen Herald:* Sabre, the Horse from the Sea, 1947, USA 1963; The Mandrake, 1949; Crab the Roan, 1953; *as K. M. Peyton:* North to Adventure, 1959, USA 1965; Stormcock Meets Trouble, 1961; The Hard Way Home, 1962; Windfall, 1963, USA (as Sea Fever), 1963; Brownsea Silver, 1964; The Maplin Bird, 1964, USA 1965 (New York Herald Tribune Award, 1965); The Plan for Birdsmarsh, 1965, USA 1966; Thunder in the Sky, 1966, USA 1967; Flambards Trilogy (Guardian Award, 1970; televised, 1977): Flambards, 1967, USA 1968; The Edge of the Cloud, 1969, USA 1969 (Carnegie Medal, 1969); Flambards in Summer, 1969, USA 1970; Fly-by-Night, 1968, USA 1969; Pennington's Seventeenth Summer, 1970, USA (as Pennington's Last Term), 1971; The Beethoven Medal, 1971, USA 1972; The Pattern of Roses, 1972, USA 1973 (televised); Pennington's Heir, 1973, USA 1974; The Team, 1975; The Right-Hand Man, 1977; Prove Yourself a Hero, 1977, USA 1978; A Midsummer Night's Death, 1978, USA 1979; Marion's Angels, 1979, USA 1979; Flambards Divided, 1981; Dear Fred, 1981, USA 1981; Going Home, 1983, USA 1983; Who, Sir? Me, Sir?, 1983 (televised); The Last Ditch, 1984, USA (as Free Rein), 1983; Froggett's Revenge, 1985; The Sound of Distant Cheering, 1986; Downhill All the Way, 1988; Darkling, 1989, USA 1990; Skylark, 1989; No Roses Round the Door, 1990; Poor Badger, 1991, USA 1991; Late to Smile, 1992; The Boy Who Wasn't There, 1992, USA 1992; The Wild Boy, 1993; Snowfall, 1994, USA 1998; The Swallow Tale, 1995; Swallow Summer, 1996; Swallow the Star, 1997; Unquiet Spirits, 1997; Firehead, 1998; Blind Beauty, 1999; Small Gains, 2003; Greater Gains, 2005; Blue Skies and Gunfire, 2006; Minna's Quest, 2007; No Turning Back, 2008. *Recreations:* walking, gardening, sailing. *Address:* Rookery Cottage, North Fambridge, Chelmsford, Essex CM3 6LP.

PEYTON, Ven. Nigel; JP; Archdeacon of Newark, since 1999; *b* 5 Feb. 1951; *s* of Hubert Peyton and Irene Louise Peyton (*née* Ellis); *m* 1981, Anne Marie Thérèse (*née* McQuillan), *widow* of Colin Campbell; one *s* one *d* (and one *d* decd). *Educ:* Latymer Upper Sch.; Univ. of Edinburgh (MA 1973; BD 1976); Edinburgh Theol Coll.; Union Theol Seminary, NY (Scottish Fellow, 1976; STM 1977). Deacon 1976, priest 1977; Chaplain, St Paul's Cathedral, Dundee, 1976–82; Dio. Youth Chaplain, Brechin, 1976–85; Priest-in-charge, All Souls, Invergowrie, 1979–85; Vicar, All Saints, Nottingham, 1985–91; Priest-in-charge, Lambley, 1991–99; Dio. Ministry Develt Advr, Southwell, 1991–99. Chaplain: University Hosp., Dundee, 1982–85; Nottingham Bluecoat Sch., 1990–92. Bishops' Selector, 1992–2000, Sen. Selector, 2001–. Proctor in Convocation, 1995–. Dir, Ecclesiastical Insce Gp, 2005–. JP Nottingham, 1987. *Publication:* Dual Role Ministry, 1998. *Recreations:* music, reading, gardening, walking, real ale. *Address:* (office) Dunham House, Westgate, Southwell, Notts NG25 0JL. *T:* (01636) 817206; *e-mail:* archdeacon-newark@southwell.anglican.org; (home) 4 The Woodwards, Newark, Notts NG24 3GG. *T:* (01636) 612249, *Fax:* (01636) 611952; *e-mail:* nigel@peytons.fsnet.co.uk. *Club:* Nottingham Forest Football.

PEYTON, Oliver; Founder and Chairman, Peyton and Byrne (formerly Gruppo Ltd); *b* 26 Sept. 1961; *s* of Patrick Peyton; *m* 1999, Charlotte Polizzi; one *s. Educ:* Leicester Poly. (Textiles course 1979). Founder, The Can night club, Brighton, 1981; owner, import business, 1985–92; owner, Gruppo Ltd, 1993; proprietor of restaurants: Atlantic Bar and Grill, Regent Palace Hotel, London, 1994–2005; Coast, Mayfair, 1995–2000 (Best Restaurant, The Times; Restaurant of Year, Time Out, 1998); Mash, Oxford Circus, 1998–; Isola, subseq. Iso-bar, Knightsbridge, 1999–2004; The Admiralty, Somerset House, 2000–02 (Best New Restaurant, Time Out); Inn the Park, St James's Park, 2004–; National Dining Rooms and National Café, Nat. Gall., 2006–; Wallace Restaurant, Wallace Collection, 2006; Meals Café and Bakery, Heal's, Tottenham Ct Rd, 2006–. *Address:* Peyton Events, 19–21 Great Portland Street, W1W 8QB. *T:* (020) 7637 7300.

PEYTON-JONES, Julia, OBE 2003; Director, Serpentine Gallery, since 1991, and Co-Director, Exhibitions and Programmes; Professor, University of the Arts, London, since 2008; *b* 18 Feb. 1952; *d* of late Jeremy Norman Peyton-Jones and Rhona Gertrude Jean (*née* Wood); *m* 1975, Prosper Riley-Smith (marr. diss. 1985). *Educ:* Tudor Hall; Byam Shaw Sch. of Drawing and Painting (Dip BSD; LCAD); Royal Coll. of Art (MA; Sen. Fellow, 2008). LWT/Byam Shaw Bursary, 1973–74, 1974–75; John Minton Travelling Schol., 1978. Started 20th century Picture Dept, Phillips, auctioneers, 1974–75; Lectr, Painting and Humanities Depts, Edinburgh Sch. of Art, 1978–79; Organiser: Atlantis Gall., London, 1980–81; Wapping Artists' Open Studios Exhibn, 1981–82; Tolly Cobbold Eastern Arts 4th Nat. Exhibn, Cambridge and tour, 1982–84; Raoul Dufy 1877–1953 exhibn, Hayward Gall., 1983–84; Linbury Prize for Stage Design (selection and exhibn), 1986–87 (Mem., Exec. Cttee, 1988–96); Sponsorship Officer, Arts Council and S Bank Bd, 1984–87; Curator, Hayward Gall., 1988–91. Arts Council: Collection Purchaser, 1989–90; Mem., Visual Arts Projects Cttee, 1991–93; Mem., Visual Arts, Photography and Architecture Panel, 1994–96. Member: Westminster Public Art Adv. Panel, 1996–; Artists' Film and Video Adv. Panel, 1997–99. Jury Member: Citibank Private Banking Photography Prize, 1997; BP Portrait Award, NPG, 1997–99; Turner Prize, 2000. Trustee: Public Art Develt Trust, 1987–88; Chisenhale Trust, 1987–89; New Contemporaries Exhibn, 1988–90; The Place, 2002. Painter, 1974–87; exhibitions include: Riverside Studios (individual), 1978; ICA, 1973; John Moores, Liverpool, 1978; Royal Scottish Acad., 1979. Mem. Ct of Govs, London Inst., 1998–2002. Hon. FRIBA 2003; Hon. FRCA 1997. *Recreations:* contemporary arts in general, visual arts in particular. *Address:* Serpentine Gallery, Kensington Gardens, W2 3XA.

PFEIFFER, Michelle; actress; *b* Santa Ana, Calif, 29 April 1958; *d* of late Dick Pfeiffer and of Donna Pfeiffer; *m* 1st, 1981, Peter Horton (marr. diss.); 2nd, 1993, David E. Kelley; one *s*; one adopted *d. Educ:* Fountain High Valley Sch., Calif. Co-owner, Via Rosa (production co.), 1989–. *Theatre:* Playground in the Fall, LA, 1981; Twelfth Night, NY 1989. *Films include:* Falling in Love Again, 1980; Grease 2, 1982; Scarface, 1983; Into the Night, Ladyhawke, 1985; Sweet Liberty, 1986; Amazon Women on the Moon, The Witches of Eastwick, 1987; Married to the Mob, 1988; Tequila Sunrise, Dangerous Liaisons, The Fabulous Baker Boys (Best Actress, Golden Globe Awards, 1990), 1989; The Russia House, 1990; Frankie and Johnny, 1991; Batman Returns, 1992; Love Field, 1993; The Age of Innocence, Wolf, My Posse Don't Do Homework, 1994; Dangerous Minds, Up Close and Personal, To Gillian on her 37th Birthday, 1996; One Fine Day (also exec. prod.), Privacy, 1997; A Thousand Acres (also prod.), 1998; The Deep End of the Ocean, A Midsummer Night's Dream, 1999; The Story of Us, What Lies Beneath, 2000; I Am Sam, 2002; White Oleander, 2003; Hairspray, 2007; Stardust, 2007. *Television includes:* Delta House, The Solitary Man, 1979; B. A. D. Cats, 1980; Collie and Son, Splendour in the Grass, The Children Nobody Wanted, 1981; One Too Many, 1983; Power, Passion and Murder, Natica Jackson, 1987. *Address:* c/o CAA, 2000 Avenue of the Stars, Los Angeles, CA 90067, USA.

PFIRTER, Rogelio (Francisco Emilio); Director-General, Technical Secretariat, Organization for the Prohibition of Chemical Weapons, since 2002; *b* 25 Aug. 1948; *s* of Rogelio and Amanda Pfirter von Mayenfisch; *m* 1980, Isabel Serantes Braun. *Educ:* Colegio Inmaculada SJ, Argentina; Universidad de Litoral (grad as lawyer); Inst. of Foreign Service, Argentina. Third Sec., S America Dept, 1974; Second, then First Sec., Perm. Mission to UN, 1975–80; Counsellor: Undersecretariat of Foreign Affairs, 1980–81; London, 1982; Minister Counsellor, then Minister Plenipotentiary, Perm. Mission to UN, 1982–90; Alternate Perm. Rep. to UN, 1989; Dep. Hd, Foreign Minister's Cabinet, 1990–91; Dir, Internat. Security, Nuclear and Space Affairs, 1991; Under-Sec., Foreign Policy, 1992; Mem., Posting and Promotion Bd, 1993–95; Argentine Ambassador to UK, 1995–2000; Pres., Argentine Delegn, River Plate Commn, 2000–02; Under-Sec., Foreign Policy, 2002. Mem., Bd of Dirs, Argentine Nat. Commn for Space Activities, 1994–95. Pres., General Assembly, IMO, 1993–97; Member: UN Adv. Bd on Disarmament Matters, 1993–96; UN High-Level Meeting with Regl and Other Govtl Orgns, 2004–. Order of Merit, Cavaliere di Gran Croce (Italy), 1992; Order of Merit (Chile), 1992; Order of Isabel la Católica (Spain), 1994; Nat. Order of Merit in the Great Cross (Colombia), 2005. *Publications:* (jtly) Cuentos Originales, 1965; articles on policy. *Address:* (office) Johan de Wittlaan 32, 2517 JR The Hague, Netherlands. *Clubs:* White's; Haagsche (Hague); Circulo de Armas (Buenos Aires).

PHAROAH, Prof. Peter Oswald Derrick, MD; FRCP, FRCPCH, FFPHM; Professor of Public Health (formerly of Community Health), University of Liverpool, 1979–97, now Professor Emeritus; *b* 19 May 1934; *s* of Oswald Higgins Pharoah and Phyllis Christine Gahan; *m* 1960, Margaret Rose McMinn; three *s* one *d. Educ:* Lawrence Memorial Royal Military School, Lovedale, India; Palmers School, Grays, Essex; St Mary's Hospital Medical School. MD, MSc. Graduated, 1958; Med. House Officer and Med. Registrar appointments at various London Hosps, 1958–63; MO and Research MO, Dept of Public Health, Papua New Guinea, 1963–74; Sen. Lectr in Community Health, London School of Hygiene and Tropical Medicine, 1974–79. *Publication:* Endemic Cretinism, 1971. *Recreations:* walking, philately. *Address:* 11 Fawley Road, Liverpool L18 9TE. *T:* (0151) 724 4896.

PHELAN, His Honour Andrew James; a Circuit Judge, 1974–95; *b* 25 July 1923; *e s* of Cornelius Phelan, Kilganey House, Clonmel, Eire; *m* 1950, Joan Robertson McLagan; one *s* two *d. Educ:* Clongoweswood, Co. Kildare; National Univ. of Ireland (MA); Trinity Coll., Cambridge. Called to: Irish Bar, King's Inns, 1945; English Bar, Gray's Inn, 1949. Jun. Fellow, Univ. of Bristol, 1948–50; in practice at English Bar, 1950–74. *Publications:* The Law for Small Boats, 2nd edn, 1970; Ireland from the Sea, 1998; Turning Tides: a voyage through the Irish Sea, 2003. *Recreations:* sailing, mountain walking. *Clubs:* Royal Cruising, Bar Yacht.

PHELAN, Sean Patrick; Founder, Multimap.com, 1995; *b* 8 April 1958; *s* of Anthony Michael Phelan and Gwendoline Theresa Phelan (*née* Stock); partner, Audrey Mandela. *Educ:* St Ignatius Coll., Enfield; Univ. of Sussex (BSc Electronic Engrg); Institute Theseus, Sophia Antipolis, France (MBA). With Geac Computers, 1982–89; Principal Analyst, Yankee Gp Europe, 1991–95; Principal Consultant, Telecommunications and Media Convergence Practice, KPMG, 1995. *Recreations:* sailing, travel. *Address:* Multimap.com, 165 Fleet Street, EC4A 2DY. *T:* (020) 7632 7700, *Fax:* (020) 7681 2094; *e-mail:* sean@multimap.com.

PHELPS, Anthony John, CB 1976; Deputy Chairman, Board of Customs and Excise, 1973–82; *b* 14 Oct. 1922; *s* of John Francis and Dorothy Phelps, Oxford; *m* 1st, 1949, Sheila Nan Rait (*d* 1967), *d* of late Colin Benton Rait, Edinburgh; one *s* two *d*; 2nd, 1971, Janet M. T. Dawson (*d* 2008), *d* of late Charles R. Dawson, Edinburgh. *Educ:* City of Oxford High Sch.; University Coll., Oxford. HM Treasury, 1946; Jun. Private Sec. to Chancellor of the Exchequer, 1949–50; Principal, 1950; Treasury Rep. in Far East, 1953–55; Private Sec. to the Prime Minister, 1958–61; Asst Sec., 1961; Under-Sec., 1968. Freeman, City of Oxford, 1971. *Publication:* (with Sir Richard Hayward) A History of Civil Service Cricket, 1993. *Recreations:* music, watching sport. *Address:* 1 Woodsyre, Sydenham Hill, SE26 6SS. *T:* (020) 8670 0735. *Clubs:* City Livery, MCC.

PHELPS, Prof. Edmund Strother, PhD; McVickar Professor of Political Economy, Columbia University, New York, since 1982; *b* 26 July 1933; *s* of Edmund Strother Phelps and Florence Esther Phelps (*née* Stone); *m* 1974, Viviana Regina Montdor. *Educ:* Amherst Coll., (BA 1955); Yale Univ. (PhD 1959). Economist, RAND Corp., 1959–60; Asst Prof., 1960–62, Associate Prof., 1963–66, Yale Univ.; Professor of Economics: Univ. of Pennsylvania, 1966–71; Columbia Univ., 1971–78, 1979–82; New York Univ., 1978–79. Nobel Prize in Economics, 2006. *Publications:* Fiscal Neutrality Toward Economic Growth, 1965; Golden Rules of Economic Growth, 1966; (jtly) Microeconomic Foundations of Employment and Inflation Theory, 1970; Inflation Policy and Unemployment Theory, 1972; Studies in Macroeconomic Theory, vol. 1, 1979, vol. 2, 1980; Political Economy, 1985; (jtly) The Slump in Europe, 1988; Structural Slumps, 1994; Rewarding Work, 1997; Enterprise and Inclusion in the Italian Economy, 2002; articles in learned jls. *Address:* Department of Economics, Columbia University, 1004 International Affairs Building, 420 West 118th Street, New York, NY 10027, USA; (home) 45 East 89th Street, New York, NY 10128–1251, USA.

PHELPS, Howard Thomas Henry Middleton; President, Brewery Court Ltd, since 2005 (Chairman, 1990–94; Vice-President, 2004); *b* 20 Oct. 1926; *s* of Ernest Henry Phelps, Gloucester, and Harriet (*née* Middleton); *m* 1949, Audrey (*née* Ellis) (*d* 2005); one *d*; *m* 2008, Mrs Carolyn Sibbald. *Educ:* Crypt Grammar Sch., Gloucester; Hatfield Coll.; Durham Univ. (BA Hons Politics and Econs 1951). National Coal Board, Lancs, Durham and London, 1951–72, finally Dep. Dir-Gen. of Industrial Relations; Personnel Dir, BOAC, 1972; British Airways: Gp Personnel Dir, 1972; Bd Mem., 1973–83; Dir of Operations, 1979–86. Dir, P&OSN Co., 1986–89; Chairman: Sutcliffe Catering Gp, 1986–88; Sterling Guards Ltd, 1986–89; Earls Court and Olympia Ltd, 1986–89; Niccol Centre Ltd, 1989–90. Non-exec. Chm., QA Training Ltd, Cirencester, 1989–94; non-exec. Dir, Alden Press Ltd, Oxford, 1990–97. FRAeS; FCILT (FCIT 1975; FILT 1980). Chm., Alice Ruston Housing Assoc., 1973–84; President: Durham Univ. Soc., 1988–99 (Chm., 1975–88); Hatfield Assoc., 1983–90. Chm. Council, Durham Univ., 1992–97 (Mem., 1985–88); Dep. Chm., Governing Body, Middlesex Polytechnic, 1987–89 (Vis. Prof., 1987–); Chairman: Cirencester Tertiary Coll., 1990–99; Rendcomb Coll., Cirencester, 1986–91; Assoc. of Colleges, 1996–98. Pres., Brewery Arts, Cirencester. Hon. DCL Durham, 1995. *Recreations:* gardening, musical appreciation. *Address:* Tall Trees, Chedworth, near Cheltenham, Glos GL54 4AB. *T:* (01285) 720324. *Club:* Bull (Cirencester).

PHELPS, Maurice Arthur; human resource consultant, since 1989; Managing Director, Maurice Phelps Associates, since 1989; Managing Partner, Emslie Phelps Consultancy Group, since 1990; *b* 17 May 1935; *s* of H. T. Phelps; *m* 1960, Elizabeth Anne Hurley; two *s* one *d*. *Educ:* Wandsworth School; Corpus Christi College, Oxford Univ. BA Hons Modern History. Shell Chemical Co. Ltd, 1959–68; Group Personnel Planning Adviser, Pilkington Bros Ltd, 1968–70; Group Personnel Dir, Unicorn Industries Ltd, 1970–72; Dir of Labour and Staff Relations, W Midland Passenger Transport Exec., 1973–77; Dir of Personnel, Heavy Vehicle Div., Leyland Vehicles Ltd, 1977–80; Bd Mem. for Personnel and Industrial Relations, 1980–87, non-exec. Bd Mem., 1987–90, British Shipbuilders; Dir, British Ferries, and Dep. Chm. and HR Dir, Sealink UK Ltd, 1987–89. Jt Founding Partner, Emslie Phelps Associates, subseq. Emslie Phelps First, 1989–2003; Human Resource Consultant: Value Through People Ltd, 1991–; Saratoga (Europe), 1993–. Freeman: City of London, 1995; Co. of Watermen and Lightermen, 1995. *Publications:* The People Policy Audit, 1999; Human Resources Benchmarking, 2002; A Thameside Family, 2007; The Adventures of Mr Golly, 2007. *Address:* Abbotsfield, Goring Heath, S Oxon RG8 7SA.

PHILIP, Rt Hon. Lord; Alexander Morrison Philip; PC 2005; a Senator of the College of Justice in Scotland, 1996–2007; *b* 3 Aug. 1942; *s* of late Alexander Philip, OBE and Isobel Thomson Morrison; *m* 1971, Shona Mary Macrae; three *s*. *Educ:* High School of Glasgow; St Andrews University (MA 1963); Glasgow University (LLB 1965). Solicitor, 1967–72; Advocate 1973; Advocate-Depute, 1982–85; QC (Scotland), 1984; Chm., Scottish Land Court, 1993–96; Pres., Lands Tribunal for Scotland, 1993–96. Chm., Medical Appeal Tribunals, 1988–92. *Publication:* contrib. Oxford DNB. *Recreations:* golf, piping. *Address:* c/o Parliament House, Parliament Square, Edinburgh EH1 1RQ. *Clubs:* Western (Glasgow); Royal Scottish Pipers' Society (Edinburgh); Hon. Co. of Edinburgh Golfers, Prestwick Golf.

PHILIP, Alexander Morrison; *see* Philip, Rt Hon. Lord.

PHILIPPE, André J., Hon. GCVO 1972; Dr-en-Droit; Luxembourg Ambassador to the United States of America, 1987–91; *b* Luxembourg City, 28 June 1926. Barrister-at-Law, Luxembourg, 1951–52. Joined Luxembourg Diplomatic Service, 1952; Dep. to Dir of Polit. Affairs, Min. of Foreign Affairs, 1952–54; Dep. Perm. Rep. to NATO, 1954–61 and to OECD, 1959–61; Dir of Protocol and Legal Adviser, Min. of For. Affairs, 1961–68; Ambassador and Perm. Rep. to UN and Consul-Gen., New York, 1968–72 (Vice-Pres., 24th Session of Gen. Assembly of UN, 1969); Ambassador to UK, Perm. Rep. to Council of WEU, and concurrently Ambassador to Ireland and Iceland, 1972–78; Ambassador to France, 1978–84; Ambassador to UN, NY, 1984–87. Commander: Order of Adolphe Nassau (Luxembourg); Légion d'Honneur (France); Grand Officer: Order of Merit (Luxembourg), 1983; Order of Oaken Crown (Luxembourg), 1988. *Address:* 25 rue Adolphe, 1116 Luxembourg.

PHILIPPS, family name of **Viscount St Davids** and **Baron Milford**.

PHILIPPS, Charles Edward Laurence; Chief Executive, Amlin plc, since 1999; *b* 20 Jan. 1959; *s* of Peter Anthony Philipps and Suzannah Margaret Philipps; *m* 1984, Fiona Land; one *s* two *d*. *Educ:* Eton Coll. Chartered Accountant, 1983. Binder Hamlyn, 1979–83; County Bank, subseq. NatWest Markets Corporate Finance, 1983–97 (Dir, 1993–97); Finance Dir, Angerstein Underwriting Trust plc, 1997–99. *Recreations:* country pursuits, golf. *Address:* c/o Amlin plc, St Helen's, 1 Undershaft, EC3A 8ND. *T:* (020) 7746 1000, *Fax:* (020) 7746 1696. *Club:* Boodle's.

PHILIPS, Justin Robin Drew; District Judge (Magistrates' Courts) (formerly Metropolitan Stipendiary Magistrate), since 1989; Lead Judge, Dedicated Drug Court, London, since 2005; *b* 18 July 1948; *s* of late Albert Lewis Philips, Solicitor and of Henrietta Philips (*née* Woolfson). *Educ:* John Lyon School, Harrow; College of Law, London. Called to the Bar, Gray's Inn, 1969; practised criminal bar, 1970–89; Chm., Youth Court, 1993–; an Asst Recorder, 1994–99; a Recorder, 1999–2006. Mem., Adv. Council on Misuse of Drugs, 2008–. Hon. Sec., Hendon Reform Synagogue, 1990–94 (Mem. Council, 1979–90). Trustee, Tzedek Charity, 1993–; Patron, DrugFam. *Recreations:* music, Judaic studies, attempting to keep fit. *Address:* c/o West London Magistrates' Court, 181 Talgarth Road, W6 8DN. *T:* 0845 600 8889.

PHILIPSON, Garry, DFC 1944; Managing Director, Aycliffe and Peterlee Development Corporation, 1974–85; *b* 27 Nov. 1921; *s* of George and Marian Philipson; *m* 1949, June Mary Miller Somerville (*d* 1997); one *d*. *Educ:* Stockton Grammar Sch.; Durham Univ. (BA(Hons)). Jubilee Prize, 1947. Served War, RAFVR (2 Gp Bomber Comd), 1940–46. Colonial Service and Overseas Civil Service, 1949–60. Various Dist and Secretariat posts, incl. Clerk, Exec. Council and Cabinet Sec., Sierra Leone; Principal, Scottish Devlt Dept, 1961–66; Under Sec., RICS, 1966–67; Dir, Smith and Ritchie Ltd, 1967–70; Sec., New Towns Assoc., 1970–74; Vice-Chm. (NE), North Housing Assoc., 1985–92. Trustee, Dales-Care, 1988–91. *Publications:* Aycliffe and Peterlee New Towns 1946–88, 1988; press articles and contribs to various jls. *Recreations:* country pursuits, history. *Address:* Little Lodge Farm, Lane End Common, North Chailey, East Sussex BN8 4JH. *T:* (01825) 723027. *Club:* Royal Air Force.

PHILIPSON-STOW, Sir (Robert) Matthew, 6th Bt *cr* 1907, of Cape Town, Colony of Cape of Good Hope, and Blackdown House, Lodsworth, Co. Sussex; engineer with MacViro Consultants Inc., since 1989; *b* 29 Aug. 1953; *s* of Sir Christopher Philipson-Stow, 5th Bt, DFC and Elizabeth Nairn Philipson-Stow (*née* Trees); *S* father 2005, but his name does not appear on the Official Roll of the Baronetage; *m* 2001, Wendy Bracken (*née* Harrel); one step *d*. *Educ:* Univ. of Waterloo (BASc 1978). PEng. MacLaren Engineers Inc., 1978–89. *Recreations:* ice-hockey, golf, cabinetry, ski-ing, reading. *Heir:* *b* Rowland Frederick Philipson-Stow [*b* 2 Sept. 1954; *m* 1979, Mary Susan (*née* Stroud); one *s* one *d*]. *Address:* 32 John Street, Thornhill, ON L3T 1X8, Canada. *T:* (905) 8892219; *e-mail:* matthew.stow@sympatico.ca.

PHILLIMORE, family name of **Baron Phillimore**.

PHILLIMORE, 5th Baron *cr* 1918, of Shiplake, Oxfordshire; **Francis Stephen Phillimore;** Bt 1881; barrister; *b* 25 Nov. 1944; *o s* of 4th Baron Phillimore and Anne Elizabeth Phillimore (*d* 1995), *e d* of Major Arthur Algernon Dorrien-Smith, DSO; *S* father, 1994; *m* 1971, Nathalie Berthe Louisa Pequin; two *s* one *d*. *Educ:* Eton Coll.; Trinity Coll., Cambridge (BA). Called to the Bar, Middle Temple, 1972. Member: Shiplake Parish Council, 1995– (Chm., 1998–2002); Eye and Dunsden Parish Council, 2003–. Mem., Ct of Assistants, Fishmongers' Co., 2001–. Trustee, Venice in Peril Fund, 1996–. Steward, Hurlingham Polo Assoc., 1998–. *Recreations:* polo, sailing, the arts, shooting, Venetian rowing. *Heir:* *er s* Tristan Anthony Stephen Phillimore, *b* 18 Aug. 1977. *Address:* Coppid Hall, Binfield Heath, Henley-on-Thames, Oxon RG9 4JR. *T:* (01491) 573174. *Clubs:* Brooks's, Pratt's, City Barge; Royal Yacht Squadron.

PHILLIPS, family name of **Barons Phillips of Sudbury** and **Phillips of Worth Matravers**.

PHILLIPS OF SUDBURY, Baron *cr* 1998 (Life Peer), of Sudbury in the co. of Suffolk; **Andrew Wyndham Phillips,** OBE 1996; founding Partner, Bates, Wells & Braithwaite, solicitors, London, 1970; *b* 15 March 1939; *s* of late Alan Clifford Phillips and Dorothy Alice Phillips (*née* Wyndham); *m* 1968, Penelope Ann Bennett; one *s* two *d*. *Educ:* Uppingham; Trinity Hall, Cambridge (BA 1962). Qualified solicitor, 1964. Co-founder, 1971 and first Chm., Legal Action Gp; founder and first Chm., 1989–2000, first Pres., 2000–, Citizenship Foundn; Initiator and First Pres., Solicitors' Pro Bono Gp (Law Works), 1997–; Mem., Nat. Lottery Charities Bd, 1994–96. Trustee, Scott Trust (Guardian/Observer), 1992–2002. Dir, Faraday Underwriting Ltd, 1999–. Pres., British-Iranian Chamber of Commerce, 2002–. Mem. various Parly cttees and gps. Trustee and Patron of various charities incl. Trustee, Gainsborough's House. Presenter, London Programme, LWT, 1980–81; regular broadcaster, as Legal Eagle, Jimmy Young Show, BBC Radio Two, 1976–2001. Chancellor, Univ. of Essex, 2003–. Contested: (Lab) Harwich, 1970; (L) Saffron Walden, July 1977 and 1979; (L/Alliance) Gainsborough and Horncastle, 1983; (L) NE Essex, European Parlt, 1979. *Publications:* The Living Law; Charitable Status: a practical handbook, 1980, 5th edn 2003; (jtly) Charity Investment: law and practice. *Recreations:* the arts, local history, architecture, golf, cricket, walking. *Address:* River House, The Croft, Sudbury, Suffolk CO10 1HW. *T:* (01787) 882151.

PHILLIPS OF WORTH MATRAVERS, Baron *cr* 1999 (Life Peer), of Belsize Park in the London Borough of Camden; **Nicholas Addison Phillips,** Kt 1987; PC 1995; Senior Lord of Appeal in Ordinary, 2008–Oct. 2009; President of the Supreme Court of the United Kingdom, from Oct. 2009; *b* 21 Jan. 1938; *m* 1972, Christylle Marie-Thérèse Rouffiac (*née* Doreau); two *d*, and one step *s* one step *d*. *Educ:* Bryanston Sch.; King's Coll., Cambridge (MA; Hon. Fellow, 2004). Nat. Service with RN; commnd RNVR, 1956–58. Called to Bar, Middle Temple (Harmsworth Scholar), 1962, Bencher, 1984. In practice at Bar, 1962–87; Jun. Counsel to Minister of Defence and to Treasury in Admiralty matters, 1973–78; QC 1978; a Recorder, 1982–87; a Judge of High Court of Justice, QBD, 1987–95; a Lord Justice of Appeal, 1995–98; a Lord of Appeal in Ordinary, 1999–2000; Master of the Rolls, 2000–05; Hd of Civil Justice, 2000–05; Lord Chief Justice, 2005–08. Mem., Panel of Wreck Comrs, 1979–87. Chairman: Law Adv. Cttee, British Council, 1991–97; Council of Legal Educn, 1992–97; BSE Inquiry, 1998–2000; Lord Chancellor's Adv. Cttee on Public Records, 2000–05; Member: Adv. Council, Inst. of Eur. and Comparative Law, 1999–2007; Council of Mgt, British Inst. of Internat. and Comparative Law, 1999–; Adv. Council, Inst. of Global Law, 2000–; President: British Maritime Law Assoc., 2005– (Vice Pres., 1993–2005); Network of Presidents of Supreme Cts of EC, 2006–08. Trustee, Magna Carta Trust, 2000–05. Governor, Bryanston Sch., 1975–2008 (Chm. of Governors, 1981–2008); Visitor: Nuffield Coll., Oxford, 2000–05; UCL, 2000–05; Darwin Coll., Cambridge, 2005–. Liveryman: Drapers' Co.; Shipwrights' Co. Hon. Fellow: Soc. of Advanced Legal Studies, 1999–; UCL, 2006. Hon. LLD: Exeter, 1998; Birmingham, 2003; London, 2004; Hon. DCL City, 2003; Hon. LLD Internat. Inst. of Maritime Law, 2007. *Recreations:* sea, mountains, Mauzac. *Address:* House of Lords, SW1A 0PW. *Clubs:* Brooks's, Garrick.

PHILLIPS, Adam; psychoanalyst in private practice; writer; *b* 19 Sept. 1954; *s* of Eric and Jacqueline Phillips; partner, Judith Clark; two *d*. *Educ:* Clifton Coll., Bristol; St John's Coll., Oxford. Principal Child Psychotherapist, Charing Cross Hosp., 1990–97. Vis. Prof., English Dept, Univ. of York, 2006–. Gen. Ed., New Penguin Freud, 2003–. *Publications:* Winnicott, 1988; On Kissing, Tickling and Being Bored, 1992; On Flirtation, 1994; Terrors and Experts, 1995; Monogamy, 1996; The Beast in the Nursery, 1997; Darwin's Worms, 1999; Promises, Promises, 2000; Houdini's Box, 2001; Equals, 2002; Going Sane, 2005; Side-Effects, 2007; (with L. Bersani) Intimacies, 2008.

PHILLIPS, Adrian Alexander Christian, CBE 1998; freelance environmental consultant; *b* 11 Jan. 1940; *s* of Eric Lawrance Phillips, *qv*; *m* 1963, Cassandra Frances Elaïs Hubback, MA Oxon, *d* of D. F. Hubback, CB; two *s*. *Educ:* The Hall, Hampstead; Westminster Sch.; Christ Church, Oxford (1st Cl. Hons MA Geography). MRTPI 1966; FRGS 1984. Planning Services, Min. of Housing and Local Govt, 1962–68; Sen. Research Officer and Asst Director, Countryside Commission, 1968–74; Special Asst, Executive Director, United Nations Environment Programme (UNEP), Nairobi, Kenya, 1974–75; Head, Programme Coordination Unit, UNEP, Nairobi, 1975–78; Director of Programmes, IUCN, Switzerland, 1978–81; Dir, then Dir Gen., Countryside Commn, 1981–92; Prof. of Countryside and Envmtl Planning, City and Regl Planning Dept, UWCC, 1992–2001. Chairman: Commn on Nat. Parks and Protected Areas, IUCN, 1994–96 (Dep. Chm., 1988–94); World Commn on Protected Areas, IUCN, 1996–2000;

Sen. Advr on World Heritage, IUCN, 2000–04; Chm., Policy Cttee, CPRE, 2001–06. Chm., Cttee for Wales, RSPB, 1992–98. Trustee: WWF UK, 1997–2003; Woodland Trust, 2004–; Chm., Glos Envmtl Trust, 2001–; Mem., Bd of Trustees, NT, 2005–. FRSA 1983. Hon. FLI. *Publications:* (ed jtly) Countryside Planning, 2004; articles and chapters on envmtl and conservation topics. *Recreations:* walking, stroking the cats. *Address:* 2 The Old Rectory, Dumbleton, near Evesham, Worcs WR11 7TG. *T:* (01386) 882094; *e-mail:* adrianp@wcpa.demon.co.uk. *Club:* Royal Over-Seas League.

PHILLIPS, Alan; *see* Phillips, D. A.

PHILLIPS, Alan David John, CMG 1999; adviser on human and minority rights; Executive Director, Minority Rights Group, 1989–2000; *b* 4 April 1947; *s* of Reginald and Irene Phillips; *m* 1970, Hilary Siddell; one *s* two *d*. *Educ:* Brighton Coll.; Warwick Univ. (BSc Hons 1st class Physics; Pres., Students' Union, 1968–69). Systems Auditor, Rank Xerox, 1970–73; Gen. Sec., World Univ. Service (UK), 1973–81; Dep. Dir, British Refugee Council, 1982–89. NGO Expert to UK and EC delegns at intergovtl Human Rights fora, 1991–; UK nominated indep. expert, 1998–, Vice Pres., 1999, Pres., 2006–, Council of Europe Adv. Cttee, Framework Convention on Nat. Minorities. Advr to Prime Minister of Kosovo, 2004–. Mem., Cttee, Council for Assisting Refugee Academics, 1998–. Advr on Roma to EU and Council of Europe, 2003–. Chm., Brighton and Hove Organic Gardening, 2001–. Hon. LLD Warwick, 2005. *Publications:* British Aid for Overseas Students, 1980; UN Minority Rights Declaration, 1993; Universal Minority Rights, 1995; (contrib.) World Directory of Minorities, 1997; Ethnicity, Pluralism and Human Rights, 2003; (contrib.) Mechanisms for the Implementation of Minority Rights, 2004. *Recreations:* family, organic gardening, swimming, education. *Address: e-mail:* aphillips@gmx.net. *Club:* Brighton and Hove Allotment Soc.

PHILLIPS, Alice Mary; Headteacher, St Catherine's School, Bramley, since 2000; *b* 1 Aug. 1960; *d* of David and Lesley Alban; *m* 1986, Simon John Phillips; one *d*. *Educ:* Kendal High Sch.; Newnham Coll., Cambridge (BA 1982). Teacher of English, 1983–93, Hd, Dept of English, 1989–93, Royal Masonic Sch., Rickmansworth; Dep. Hd, Tormead Sch., 1993–99. FRSA. MInstD. *Recreations:* gardening, singing, cooking, music, ballet. *Address:* St Catherine's School, Bramley, Surrey GU5 0DF. *T:* (01483) 899605, *Fax:* (01483) 899606; *e-mail:* headmistress@stcatherines.info. *Club:* University Womens'.

PHILLIPS, Andrew Bassett; Head, Legal Deposit Review, British Library, 1996–99; *b* 26 Sept. 1945; *s* of William Phillips and Doreen (*née* Harris); *m* 1976, Valerie Cuthbert; two *s* one *d*. *Educ:* Newport High Sch.; Reading Univ. (BA). MCLIP. British Nat. Bibliography Ltd, 1969–70; Research Officer, Nat. Libraries ADP Study, 1970–71; Admin. Officer, Nat. Council for Educnl Technol., 1971–73; British Library: various posts in Bibliographic Servs and Ref. (subseq. Humanities and Social Scis) Divs, 1973–86; Dir, Public Services and Planning and Admin, 1987–90; Dir, Humanities and Social Scis, 1990–96. Part-time Lectr, West London Coll., 1972–75. Director: Cedar Audio Ltd, 1992–94; Saga Continuation Ltd, 1993–99. Advr, British Univs Film and Video Council, 2000–06. Member: Governing Body, City Lit. Inst., 1982–87; Archives Cttee, St Bartholomew's Hosp., 2000–; Sec., Friends of the British Liby, 2004–06 (Mem. Council, 1990–2002); Trustee: Black Country Mus. Develt Trust, 2004–; Harvard House Meml Trust, 2008–. Hon. Fellow, Shakespeare's Birthplace, 2003– (Trustee, 1991–2003). *Publications:* (ed) The People's Heritage, 2000; (contrib.) Inventing the 20th Century, 2000; various reviews, articles. *Address:* 23 Meynell Road, E9 7AP. *T:* (020) 8985 7413. *Club:* London Press.

PHILLIPS, Anne, (Mrs Basil Phillips); *see* Dickinson, V. A.

PHILLIPS, Prof. Anne, PhD; FBA 2003; Professor of Political and Gender Theory, London School of Economics, since 1999; *b* 2 June 1950; *d* of Frederick Phillips and Margaret Hill; *m* 1982, Ciaran Driver; two *s*. *Educ:* Univ. of Bristol (BSc Philos. and Pols 1971); Sch. of Oriental and African Studies, London (MSc W African Pols 1972); City Univ., London (PhD 1982). Lectr, 1975–88, Reader, 1988–90, in Politics, City of London Poly.; Prof. of Politics, London Guildhall Univ., 1990–99. Adjunct Prof., ANU, 2002–05. Hon. Dr phil Aalborg, 1999. *Publications:* Hidden Hands: women and economic policies, 1983; Divided Loyalties: dilemmas of sex and class, 1987; The Enigma of Colonialism, 1989; Engendering Democracy, 1991, 2nd edn 1997; Democracy and Difference, 1993; The Politics of Presence, 1995, 2nd edn 1998; Which Equalities Matter?, 1999; Multiculturalism without Culture, 2007. *Recreations:* swimming, reading novels, gardening. *Address:* Government Department, London School of Economics, Houghton Street, WC2A 2AE. *T:* (020) 7955 6979, *Fax:* (020) 7955 6408; *e-mail:* a.phillips@lse.ac.uk.

PHILLIPS, Anne Fyfe; *see* Pringle, A. F.

PHILLIPS, Rev. Canon Anthony Charles Julian; Headmaster, King's School, Canterbury, 1986–96; *b* 2 June 1936; *s* of Arthur Reginald Phillips and Esmée Mary Phillips; *m* 1970, Victoria Ann Stainton; two *s* one *d*. *Educ:* Kelly Coll., Tavistock (schol.); King's Coll., London (BD, 1st cl.; AKC, 1st cl.); Archibald Robertson Prize, 1962; Jun. McCaul Hebrew Prize, 1963); Gonville and Caius Coll., Cambridge (PhD 1967); College of the Resurrection, Mirfield. Solicitor, 1958; ordained priest, 1967; Curate, Good Shepherd, Cambridge, 1966–69; Dean, Chaplain and Fellow, Trinity Hall, Cambridge, 1969–74; Chaplain and Fellow, 1975–86, Domestic Bursar, 1982–84, St John's Coll., Oxford; Lecturer in Theology: Jesus Coll., Oxford, 1975–86; Hertford Coll., Oxford, 1984–86; S. A. Cook Bye Fellow, Gonville and Caius Coll., 1984; Canon Theologian, Dio. of Truro, 1986–2002; Chapter Canon, Truro Cath., 2001–02, now Canon Emeritus. Hon. Chaplain to Bishop of Norwich, 1970–71; Examining Chaplain to: Bp of Oxford, 1979–86; Bp of Manchester, 1980–86; Bp of Wakefield, 1984–86; Hon. Canon, Canterbury Cathedral, 1987–96. Archbps of Canterbury and York Interfaith Cons. for Judaism, 1984–86. Dir, Royal Cornwall Poly. Soc., 2003– (Chm., 2004–). Governor: Sherborne Sch., 1997–2001; Sherborne Sch. for Girls, 1997–2001; Cornwall Coll., 1997–2001, 2004–05; SPCK, 1998–2006 (Chair of Publishing, 2000–05). SBStJ 2003. *Publications:* Ancient Israel's Criminal Law, 1970; Deuteronomy (Cambridge Bible Commentary), 1973; God BC, 1977; (ed) Israel's Prophetic Tradition, 1982; Lower Than the Angels, 1983, 1996; Preaching from the Psalter, 1987; The Passion of God, 1995; Essays on Biblical Law, 2002; Entering into the Mind of God, 2002; Standing up to God, 2005; David: a story of passion and tragedy, 2008; contrib. to: Words and Meanings (ed P. R. Ackroyd and B. Lindars), 1968; Witness to the Spirit (ed W. Harrington), 1979; The Ministry of the Word (ed G. Cuming), 1979; Heaven and Earth (ed A. Linzey and P. Wexler), 1986; Tradition and Unity (ed Dan Cohn-Sherbok), 1991; Glimpses of God (ed Dan Cohn-Sherbok), 1993; Splashes of God Light (ed T. Copley and others), 1997; articles in theol jls, The Times, Expository Times, etc. *Recreations:* gardening, beachcombing. *Address:* The Old Vicarage, 10 St Peter's Road, Flushing, Falmouth, Cornwall TR11 5TP. *T:* (01326) 377217. *Club:* Sloane.

PHILLIPS, Prof. Calbert Inglis, FRCS, FRCSE; Professor of Ophthalmology, University of Edinburgh and Ophthalmic Surgeon, Royal Infirmary, Edinburgh,

1972–90, now Professor Emeritus; *b* 20 March 1925; *o s* of Rev. David Horner Phillips and Margaret Calbert Phillips; *m* 1962, Christina Anne Fulton, MB, FRCSE; one *s*. *Educ:* Glasgow High Sch.; Robert Gordon's Coll., Aberdeen; Aberdeen Univ. MB, ChB Aberdeen 1946; DPH Edinburgh 1950; FRCS 1955; MD Aberdeen 1957; PhD Bristol 1961; MSc Manchester 1969; FRCSE 1973. Lieut and Captain, RAMC, 1947–49. House Surgeon: Aberdeen Royal Infirmary, 1946–47 (House Phys., 1951); Aberdeen Maternity Hosp., 1949; Glasgow Eye Infirmary, 1950–51; Asst, Anatomy Dept, Glasgow Univ., 1951–52; Resident Registrar, Moorfields Eye Hosp., 1953–54; Sen. Registrar, St Thomas' Hosp. and Moorfields Eye Hosp., and Res. Asst, Inst. of Ophthalmology, 1954–58; Consultant Surg., Bristol Eye Hosp., 1958–63; Alexander Piggott Wernher Trav. Fellow, Dept of Ophthal., Harvard Univ., 1960–61; Consultant Ophthalmic Surg., St George's Hosp., 1963–65; Prof. of Ophthal., Manchester Univ., and Hon. Consultant Ophthalmic Surg. to United Manchester Hosps, 1965–72. Hon. FBOA 1975. *Publications:* (ed jtly) Clinical Practice and Economics, 1977; Basic Clinical Ophthalmology, 1984; Logic in Medicine, 1988, 2nd edn 1995; (jtly) Ophthalmology: a primer for medical students and practitioners, 1994; papers in Eur., Amer., and Japanese Jls of Ophthal., Nature, Brain, BMJ, etc, mainly on intra-ocular pressure and glaucoma, retinal detachments, ocular surgery and hereditary diseases. *Address:* 5 Braid Mount Crest, Edinburgh EH10 6JN.

PHILLIPS, Caryl, FRSL; writer; Professor of English, Yale University, since 2005; *b* 13 March 1958. *Educ:* Queen's Coll., Oxford (BA English 1979; Hon. Fellow, 2006). Writer in Residence: Literary Criterion Centre, Mysore, India, 1987; Univ. of Stockholm, Sweden, 1989; Nat. Inst. of Educn, Singapore, 1994; Amherst College, Massachusetts: Vis. Writer, 1990–92; Writer in Residence, 1992–94; Prof. of English and Writer in Residence, 1994–98; Barnard College, Columbia University: Prof. of English and Henry R. Luce Prof. of Migration and Social Order, 1998–2005; Dir, Initiatives in the Humanities, 2003–05. Visiting Professor: NY Univ., 1993; Univ. of WI, Barbados, 1999–2000. British Council Fiftieth Anniversary Fellow, 1984; Guggenheim Fellow, 1992; Rockefeller Foundn (Bellagio) Residency, 1993; Fellow, Centre for Scholars and Writers, NY Public Liby, 2002–03. Ed., Faber Caribbean series, 1998–2001. FRSL 2000. Humanities Schol. of the Year, Univ. of WI, 1999. Hon. AM Amherst, 1995; DUniv: Leeds Metropolitan, 1997; York, 2003; Hon. LittD Leeds, 2003; Hon. MA Yale, 2006. Giles Cooper Award, BBC, 1984; Bursary in Drama, Arts Council of GB, 1984; Martin Luther King Meml Prize, 1987; James Tait Black Meml Prize, 1994; Lannan Foundn Literary Award, 1994. *Publications:* plays: Strange Fruit, 1981; Where There is Darkness, 1982; The Shelter, 1984; novels: The Final Passage, 1985; A State of Independence, 1986; Higher Ground, 1989; Cambridge, 1991; Crossing the River, 1993; The Nature of Blood, 1997; A Distant Shore, 2003 (Commonwealth Writers Prize, 2004); Dancing in the Dark, 2005; screenplays: Playing Away, 1987; The Mystic Masseur (Silver Ombu award for best screenplay, Mar del Plata Film Fest.), 2002; non-fiction: The European Tribe, 1987; The Atlantic Sound, 2000; A New World Order, 2001; Foreigners, 2007; anthology: (ed) Extravagant Strangers, 1997; (ed) The Right Set: the Faber Book of Tennis, 1999. *Recreations:* running, golf. *Address:* c/o Georgia Garrett, A. P. Watt Ltd, 20 John Street, WC1N 2DR.

PHILLIPS, Sir David; *see* Phillips, Sir J. D.

PHILLIPS, Prof. David, OBE 1999; Professor of Physical Chemistry, 1989–2006, Hofmann Professor of Chemistry, 1999–2006, now Professor Emeritus, and Dean, Faculties of Life Sciences and Physical Sciences, 2002–06; Imperial College of Science, Technology and Medicine; *b* 3 Dec. 1939; *s* of Stanley and Daphne Ivy Phillips; *m* 1970, Caroline Lucy Scoble; one *d*. *Educ:* South Shields Grammar-Technical Sch.; Univ. of Birmingham (BSc, PhD). Post doctoral Fellow, Univ. of Texas, 1964–66; Vis. Scientist, Inst. of Chemical Physics, Acad. of Scis of USSR, Moscow, 1966–67; Lectr 1967–73, Sen. Lectr 1973–76, Reader 1976–80, in Phys. Chem., Univ. of Southampton; Royal Institution of Great Britain: Wolfson Prof. of Natural Philosophy, 1980–89; Actg Dir, Jan.–Oct. 1986; Dep. Dir, 1986–89; Head, Dept of Chemistry, Imperial Coll., London, 1992–2002. Vice-Pres. and Gen. Officer, BAAS, 1988–89. Mem., Faraday Council, RSC, 1990–93. Nyholm Lectr, RSC, 1994. Chm., London Gifted and Talented, 2003–. Michael Faraday Award, Royal Soc., 1997. *Publications:* (jtly) Time-Correlated Single-Photon Counting, 1984; Polymer Photophysics, 1985; (jtly) Jet Spectroscopy and Dynamics, 1995; over 585 res. papers and revs in sci. lit. on photochem., photophys. and lasers. *Recreations:* music, travel, tennis. *Address:* 195 Barnett Wood Lane, Ashtead, Surrey KT21 2LP. *T:* (01372) 274385. *Club:* Athenæum.

PHILLIPS, His Honour (David) Alan; a Circuit Judge, 1983–95; Chancellor, diocese of Bangor, 1988–95; *b* 21 July 1926; *s* of Stephen Thomas Phillips, MC and Elizabeth Mary Phillips; *m* 1960, Jean Louise (*née* Godsell); two *s*. *Educ:* Llanelli Grammar Sch.; University Coll., Oxford (MA). Left school, 1944. Served War, Army, 1944; commnd, 1946, RWF; Captain (GS), 1947; demobilised, 1948. Oxford, 1948–51. Lectr, 1952–59. Called to Bar, Gray's Inn, 1960. Stipendiary Magistrate for Mid-Glamorgan, 1975–83; a Recorder of the Crown Court, 1974–83. *Recreations:* music, chess, swimming.
See also S. E. Phillips.

PHILLIPS, Prof. David George, DPhil; FRHistS, AcSS; Professor of Comparative Education, University of Oxford, since 2000; Fellow of St Edmund Hall, Oxford, since 1984; *b* 15 Dec. 1944; *s* of late George and Doris Phillips; *m* 1968, Valerie Mary Bache; two *d*. *Educ:* Sir Walter St John's Sch., Battersea; BA London 1966; St Edmund Hall, Oxford (DipEd 1967; MA; DPhil 1984). Assistant teacher: Huntingdon Grammar Sch., 1967–69; Chipping Norton Sch., 1969–75; University of Oxford: Tutor, then Univ. Lectr, Dept of Educnl Studies, 1975–96; Reader in Comparative Educn, 1996–2000. Member: Teacher Educn Commn of Wissenschaftsrat, 1990–91; Council, 1992–94, Scientific Cttee, 1992–98, German Inst. for Internat. Educnl Res., Frankfurt-am-Main; Educnl Sci. Commn, Ministry of Sci., Res. and the Arts, Baden-Württemberg, 2003–04; Chm., British Assoc. for Internat. and Comparative Educn, 1998–2000. AcSS 2002; FRHistS 2002. FRSA 1987. Editor, Oxford Review of Education, 1984–2003; Series Editor, Oxford Studies in Comparative Educn, 1991–; Ed., Res. in Comparative and Internat. Educn, 2006–; Chm. Editl Bd, Comparative Educn, 2009–. *Publications include:* Zur Universitätsreform in der Britischen Besatzungszone 1945–48, 1983; (ed) German Universities After the Surrender, 1983; (with Veronica Stencel) The Second Foreign Language, 1983; (ed) Which Language?, 1989; (with Caroline Filmer-Sankey) Diversification in Modern Language Teaching, 1993; Pragmatismus und Idealismus: das Blaue Gutachten und die Britische Hochschulpolitik in Deutschland 1948, 1995; (ed) Education in Germany: tradition and reform in historical context, 1995; (ed jtly) Learning from Comparing, vol. 1, 1999, vol. 2, 2000; (ed) Education in Eastern Germany since Unification, 2000; Reflections on British Interest in Education in Germany in the Nineteenth Century, 2002; (jtly) Towards a Structural Typology of Cross-National Attraction in Education, 2002; (ed jtly) Can the Japanese Change Their Education System?, 2003; (ed jtly) Implementing European Union Education and Training Policy: a comparative study of issues in four member states, 2003; (ed jtly) Educational Policy Borrowing: historical perspectives, 2005; (jtly) Comparative and International Education: an introduction to theory, method and practice, 2006; festschrift: (ed Hubert Ertl) Cross-

National Attraction in Education: accounts from England and Germany, 2006; numerous articles in jls. *Recreations:* art history, antiquarian books. *Address:* Department of Education, 15 Norham Gardens, Oxford OX2 6PY; St Edmund Hall, Oxford OX1 4AR.

PHILLIPS, David John; QC 1997; a Recorder, since 1998; a Deputy High Court Judge, since 2001; *b* 4 May 1953; *s* of Hon. Sir (John) Raymond Phillips MC, and of Hazel Bradbury Phillips; *m* 1981, Ann Nicola Beckett, *d* of late Ronald Beckett; one *s* one *d*. *Educ:* Rugby Sch.; Aix-en-Provence Univ.; Balliol Coll., Oxford (BA (Jurisprudence) 1977; MA 1996). Called to the Bar, Gray's Inn, 1976 (Arden, Atkin, Mould & Reid Prize, 1977), Bencher, 2004; admitted Bar of Gibraltar, 2004; Mem., Bar of Eastern Caribbean, 2005; Mem., Wales and Chester Circuit, 1983; Asst Recorder, 1994–98; Hd of Chambers, 199 Strand, 2000–06. Chairman: FA Premier League Tribunal, 2003–; Sports Dispute Resolution Panel, 2003–; Judicial Chm., Nat. Greyhound Racing Club's Appeal Tribunal, 2006–. Dir, Disability Law Service, 1999–. Mem. Cttee, Barristers' Benevolent Assoc., 1993– (Jt Hon. Treas., 1999–). *Recreations:* hill walking, cinema. *Address:* Wilberforce Chambers, 8 New Square, Lincoln's Inn, WC2A 3QP. *T:* (020) 7306 0102; *e-mail:* dphillip@wilberforce.co.uk.

PHILLIPS, Diane Susan, CB 2000; Director, Transport Strategy, Department for Transport (formerly of the Environment, Transport and the Regions, then Department for Transport, Local Government and the Regions), 2000–02; *b* 29 Aug. 1942; *d* of Michael Keogh and Jessie (*née* Tite); *m* 1967, John Phillips; two *d*. *Educ:* Univ. of Wales. NEDO, 1967–72; Civil Service, 1972–: Principal, DoE, 1972–77, Cabinet Office, 1977–78; Asst Sec., Dept of Transport, 1978–80; Department of the Environment, then Department of the Environment, Transport and the Regions, now Department for Transport, Local Government and the Regions, 1981–: Grade 4, Local Govt Finance, 1988–90; Under Sec. (Grade 3) and Principal Finance Officer, Property Hldgs, 1990–94; Dir, Social Housing Policy and Resources, 1994–98; Dir, Roads and Traffic, 1998–2000; Dep. Hd, Integrated Transport Taskforce, 2000. Mem. Bd, London & Quadrant Housing Trust, 1998–. Gov., St George's Coll., Weybridge, 1995–2004. *Address:* 60 Portmore Park Road, Weybridge, Surrey KT13 8EU.

PHILLIPS, Rt Rev. Donald David; *see* Rupert's Land, Bishop of.

PHILLIPS, Eric Lawrance, CMG 1963; retired; *b* 23 July 1909; *s* of L. Stanley Phillips and Maudie Phillips (*née* Elkan), London, NW1; *m* 1938, Phyllis Bray (*d* 1991), artist; two *s*, and one step *d*; one *d* by Pauline Sharpe. *Educ:* Haileybury Coll.; Balliol Coll., Oxford (Scholar, BA). With Erlangers Ltd, 1932–39. Served War of 1939–45, Captain, RA. Principal, Bd of Trade, 1945, Monopolies Commn, 1949; Asst Secretary, Monopolies Commn, 1951, Bd of Trade, 1952; Under-Sec., Bd of Trade, 1964–69; Sec., Monopolies Commn, 1969–74; consultant to Monopolies and Mergers Commn, 1974–75. Hon. Chm., Abbeyfield West London Soc., 1980–86. *Recreation:* looking at pictures, places and buildings. *Address:* The Old Prebendal House, Station Road, Shipton-under-Wychwood, Chipping Norton OX7 6BQ.
See also A. A. C. Phillips.

PHILLIPS, Sir Fred (Albert), Kt 1967; CVO 1966; QC (Barbados) 1991; *b* 14 May 1918; *s* of Wilbert A. Phillips, Brighton, St Vincent. *Educ:* London Univ. (LLB); Toronto Univ.; McGill Univ. (MCL); Hague Acad. of International Law. Called to the Bar, Middle Temple. Legal Clerk to Attorney-General of St Vincent, 1942–45; Sen. Officer, Secretariat, 1945–47; Windward Island: Chief Clerk, Governor's Office, 1948–49; District Officer/Magistrate of District III, 1949–53; Magistrate, Grenada, and Comr of Carriacou, 1953–56; Asst Administrator and MEC, Grenada, 1957–58 (Officer Administrating the Govt, April 1958); Senior Asst Sec., Secretariat, Fedn of W Indies (dealing with constitutional development), 1958–60; Permanent Sec. (Sec. to Cabinet), 1960–62 (when Fedn dissolved); actg Administrator of Montserrat, 1961–62; Sen. Lectr, Univ. of W Indies and Sen. Resident Tutor, Dept of Extra-mural Studies, Barbados, 1962–63; Sen. Asst Registrar, Coll. of Arts and Science, Univ. of W Indies, 1963–64; Sen. Res. Fellow, Faculty of Law and Centre for Developing Area Studies, McGill Univ., 1964–65; Guggenheim Fellow, 1965; Administrator of St Kitts, 1966–67; Governor, St Kitts/Nevis/Anguilla, 1967–69; Chief Legal Advr for Cable & Wireless in the Caribbean, 1969–97. Chairman, Constitutional Review Commission: Grenada, 1984; St Kitts and Nevis, 1998; Antigua and Barbuda, 1999, 2000 and 2001. Has attended numerous conferences as a Legal or Constitutional Adviser. KStJ 1968. Hon. LLD West Indies, 1989. *Publications:* Freedom in the Caribbean: a study in constitutional change, 1977; The Evolving Legal Profession in the Commonwealth, 1978; West Indian Constitutions: post-Independence reforms, 1985; Caribbean Life and Culture: a citizen reflects, 1991; Commonwealth Caribbean Constitutional Law, 2002; Ethics of the Legal Profession, 2004; papers in various jls. *Recreations:* reading, legal writing. *Address:* Sandy Lane, Hodges Bay, PO Box 3298, St John's, Antigua.

PHILLIPS, Sir (Gerald) Hayden, GCB 2002 (KCB 1998; CB 1989); DL; Chairman: National Theatre, since 2004; HansonWesthouse Ltd, since 2007 (Senior Partner, Hanson Westhouse LLP, 2006); Deputy Chairman, Hanson Logistics, since 2007; Charities Consultant to HRH the Prince of Wales, since 2004 and HRH Duchess of Cornwall, since 2005; *b* 9 Feb. 1943; *s* of Gerald Phillips and Dorothy Phillips; *m* 1st, 1967, Dr Ann Watkins (marr. diss.); one *s* one *d*; 2nd, 1980, Hon. Laura Grenfell; one *s* two *d*. *Educ:* Cambridgeshire High Sch.; Clare Coll., Cambridge (MA); Yale Univ., USA (MA). Home Office: Asst Principal, 1967; Economic Adviser, 1970–72; Principal, 1972–74; Asst Sec., and Principal Private Sec. to Sec. of State for Home Dept, 1974–76; Dep. Chef de Cabinet to Pres., Commn of European Communities, 1977–79; Asst Sec., Home Office, 1979–81, Asst Under-Sec. of State, 1981–86; Dep. Sec., Cabinet Office (MPO, subseq. Office of the Minister for the Civil Service), 1986–88; Dep. Sec., HM Treasury, 1988–92; Permanent Secretary: DNH, later Dept for Culture, Media and Sport, 1992–98; LCD, 1998–2003; Dept for Constitutional Affairs, 2003–04; Clerk of the Crown in Chancery, 1998–2004. Reviewer: the Honours System, 2004; the Funding of Political Parties, 2006–07; Chm., Inter-Party Talks on Political Funding, 2007. Director: St Just Farms Ltd, 1997–; Global Solutions Ltd, 2005–. Adviser: Hanson Capital, 2004–06; Englefield Capital, 2004–. Member: Council, KCL, 1993–99; Ct of Govs, Henley Mgt Coll., 1993–2002; Council, Marlborough Coll., 1997– (Chm., 2006–); Bd, Inst. of Advanced Legal Studies, 1998–2004; Fitzwilliam Mus. Trust, 1999–2005; Salisbury Cathedral Council, 2002–; Chm., Salisbury Cathedral Fabric Adv. Cttee, 2006–. Lay Canon, Salisbury Cathedral, 2008–. Gov., Wilts Historic Buildings Trust, 2006–. Patron, Salisbury Spinal Injuries Trust, 2007–. Hon. Bencher, Inner Temple, 1998. DL Wilts, 2007. *Publications:* Review of the Honours System, 2004; Strengthening Democracy: fair and sustainable funding of political parties, 2007. *Recreations:* theatre, other arts, shooting and fishing, India. *Address:* Homington Farm, Homington, Salisbury, Wilts SP5 4NG. *Clubs:* Brooks's, Pratt's.

PHILLIPS, Dr Helen Mary; Chief Executive, Natural England, since 2006; *b* 29 May 1966; *d* of James Phillips and Anne Phillips (*née* Duggan); *m* 1991, Desmond Ryan; one *s* one *d*. *Educ:* University Coll., Dublin (BSc Hons 1987; PhD 1993). Environment Agency: Regl Tech. Planning Manager, 1996–97, Regl Planning Manager, 1997–98, Midlands Reg.; Area Manager, Thames Reg., 1998–2001; Head of Strategic Develt, 2001; Dir, Wales, 2002–06. *Recreation:* walking. *Address:* Natural England, 1 East Parade, Sheffield S1 2ET.

PHILLIPS, Ian, FCA; Director, M & G Equity Investment Trust, since 2000; *b* 16 July 1938; *s* of Wilfrid and Dorothy Phillips; *m* 1961, Fay Rosemary Stoner; two *s*. *Educ:* Whitgift Sch., South Croydon. Articled clerk, Hatfield Dixon Roberts Wright & Co., Accountants, 1955–61; Robert J. Ward & Co., Accountants, 1961–65; John Lewis' Partnership, 1965–69; London Transport Executive: Director of Corporate Planning, 1969–75; Chief Business Planning Officer, 1975–78; Group Planning Director, 1978–80; Mem. Board, LTE, later LRT, 1980–84; Dir, Finance and Planning, BRB, 1985–88; Finance Dir, BBC, 1988–93; Chief Exec., BBC Pension Services Ltd, 1990–96; Chm., BBC Enterprises Ltd, 1991–93. Chairman: OUP Pension Fund, 1995–2006; Severn Trent Pension Fund, 1998–2004; Chm., Investment Adv. Cttee, PanEuropean Property Unit Trust (Mem., 1996–). Bd Mem., Gloucestershire Hosps NHS Foundn Trust, 2002–. *Recreations:* sport, politics, reading, family. *Address:* 5 The Croft, Carpenters Lane, Cirencester, Glos GL7 1EE.

PHILLIPS, Prof. Ian, MD; FRCP, FRCPath, FFPH; Professor of Medical Microbiology, 1974–96 (at St Thomas' Hospital, 1974–82), and Clinical Dean, 1992–96, United Medical and Dental Schools of Guy's and St Thomas's Hospitals, now Emeritus Professor; *b* 10 April 1936; *s* of late Stanley Phillips and Emma (*née* Price). *Educ:* St John's Coll., Cambridge (MA, MD); St Thomas's Hosp. Med. Sch. (MB BChir). FRCPath 1981; FRCP 1983; FFPH (FFPHM 1996). House Officer, St Thomas' Hosp., 1961–62; Lecturer in Microbiology: St Thomas's Hosp. Med. Sch., 1962–66; Makerere UC, 1966–69; Sen. Lectr, 1969–72, Reader, 1972–74, St Thomas's Hosp. Med. Sch.; Chm., Dist Mgt Team, St Thomas' Hosp., 1978–79; Hon. Cons. Microbiologist, St Thomas' Hosp., subseq. Guy's and St Thomas's Hosp. NHS Trust, 1969–96, now Emeritus Consultant; Chm., Pathology, Guy's and St Thomas's Hosp. NHS Trust, 1990–96. Civil Consultant, RAF, 1979–2000. Mem., Veterinary Products Cttee, 1981–85. An editor, Clinical Microbiology and Infection, 1997–2005. Mem. Council, RCPath, 1974–76 and 1987–90; Chairman: Brit. Soc. for Antimicrobial Chemotherapy, 1979–82; Assoc. of Med. Microbiologists, 1989–93; Pres., European Soc. for Clinical Microbiol. and Infectious Diseases, 1995–96. Member: S London Botanical Inst.; BSBI. Hon. Mem., Croatian Acad. of Med. Sci., 1997. Freeman, City of London, 1975; Liveryman, Soc. of Apothecaries, 1975. *Publications:* (ed jtly) Laboratory Methods in Antimicrobial Chemotherapy, 1978; (jtly) Microbial Disease, 1979; contrib. chapters and papers. *Recreations:* botany, music. *Clubs:* Athenæum, Royal Society of Medicine.

PHILLIPS, (Ian) Peter, OBE 2004; JP; Director, Kroll Buchler Phillips Ltd, 1999–2005; Chairman, Kroll (formerly Buchler Phillips) Lindquist Avey, 1997–2005; *b* 13 Oct. 1944; *s* of Bernard Phillips and Constance Mary Clayton; *m* 1970, Wendy Berne; one *s* one *d*. *Educ:* Highgate Sch.; Sorbonne, Paris. FCA, FCCA, FIPA. Partner, Bernard Phillips & Co., 1968; UK Head of Corporate Recovery Services, Arthur Andersen & Co., 1982–88; Chm., Buchler Phillips Gp, 1988–99. Jt Administrator, British and Commonwealth Holdings, 1990; Court Receiver, Estate of Robert Maxwell, 1991. Dir, Jt Insolvency Monitoring Unit, 1997–98; Mem., Insolvency Tribunal, 1997–. Pres., Insolvency Practitioners Assoc., 1988–89. Member: Lord Chancellor's Adv. Cttee on JPs for City and Westminster; 2nd and 3rd Selection Panels, Gtr London Magistrates' Cts Authy, 2002–04. Mem., Global Adv. Bd, Centre for Internat. Business and Mgt, Judge Inst. of Mgt, Cambridge Univ., 1999–. Trustee: Israel-Palestine Centre for Res. and Inf., 1991–96; Papyrus (Prevention of Suicide) Co. Ltd, 2000–04; Restorative Justice Consortium, 2006–07. Treas., N Kensington Neighbourhood Law Centre, 1970–76. Chm., Hampstead Theatre, 1997–2001 (Dir, 1991–2004; Mem., Adv. Council, 2004–). Mem., British Acad. of Experts, 1991–. Accredited Relate Counsellor, 2006. JP Inner London, 1979 (Dep. Chm., Highbury Corner Bench). Mem., Magic Circle, 2003–. *Recreations:* theatre, baroque and modern jazz music, horse riding, coastal path walking, close-up magic. *Address:* The Fourth House, 5 Turner Drive, NW11 6TX. *T:* 07836 572277.

PHILLIPS, Jeremy Patrick Manfred; QC 1980; *b* 27 Feb. 1941; *s* of late Manfred Henry Phillips, CA, and late Irene Margaret (*née* Symondson); *m* 1962, Margaret Ann (*née* Adams) (marr. diss. 1968); *m* 1968, Virginia Gwendoline (*née* Dwyer) (marr. diss. 1974); one *s* (and one *s* decd); *m* 1976, Judith Gaskell (*née* Hetherington); two *s* two *d*. *Educ:* St Edmund's Sch., Hindhead, Surrey; Charterhouse. Apprentice Accountant, Thomson McLintock & Co., 1957–61. Called to Bar, Gray's Inn, 1964; in practice, accountancy and commercial law, 1964–2003; Head of Chambers: 2 Temple Gdns, 1990–98; New Ct Chambers, 2000–03; DTI Inspector, affairs of Queens Moat Houses plc, 1993. Owner and Dir of Ops, Kentwell Hall, Long Melford, Suffolk, 1971–; originator of domestic living history events in UK with Kentwell's Annual Historical Re-Creations of Tudor Domestic Life, 1978–. Founding Dir, CARE Britain. *Publications:* contrib. early edns of Cooper's Students' Manual of Auditing, Cooper's Manual of Auditing and various pamphlets, papers, guides, etc, on Kentwell Hall and Tudor period. *Recreations:* historic buildings, Tudor history, constitutional issues, cricket. *Address:* Kentwell Hall, Long Melford, Suffolk CO10 9BA.

PHILLIPS, John; *see* Phillips, M. J.

PHILLIPS, John Andrew, CBE 2006; **His Honour Judge Phillips;** a Circuit Judge, since 1998; Director of Studies, Judicial Studies Board of England and Wales, since 2007; *b* 26 May 1950; *s* of Jack and Mary Nolan Phillips; *m* 1993, Moira Margaret Kynnersley; two *d*. *Educ:* Fitzwilliam Coll., Cambridge (MA). Mem., Fitzwilliam String Quartet, Quartet in Residence, York Univ., 1971–74; called to the Bar, Gray's Inn, 1976, Bencher, 2008; in practice at the Bar, 1977–98. *Recreation:* playing the violin. *Address:* Judicial Studies Board, 9th Floor, Millbank Tower, Millbank, SW1P 4QU.

PHILLIPS, Sir (John) David, Kt 2000; QPM 1994; lecturer, writer, company director; *b* 22 April 1944; *s* of late Percy Phillips and of Alfreda Phillips; *m* 1970, Nancy Wynn Rothwell; one *s*. *Educ:* Leigh Grammar Sch.; Manchester Univ. (BA 1st Cl. Hons Econs). Served: Lancs Constabulary, 1963–84; Gtr Manchester Constabulary, 1984–89; Dep. Chief Constable, Devon and Cornwall, 1989–93; Chief Constable of Kent, 1993–2003; Dir, Nat. Centre of Policing Excellence, 2003–05. Chm., Nat. Crime Faculty; Pres., ACPO, 2001–03. CCMI 2002. *Recreations:* history, golf.

PHILLIPS, Hon. Prof. John Harber, AC 1998; QC (Vic.) 1975; Chief Justice of Victoria, 1991–2003; Provost, Sir Zelman Cowen Centre, Victoria University, Melbourne, since 2003; *b* 18 Oct. 1933; *s* of Anthony and I. Muriel Phillips; *m* 1962, Helen Isobel Rogers; two *s* one *d*. *Educ:* De La Salle Coll., Malvern; Univ. of Melbourne (LLB). Called to the Bar: Victoria, 1959; Middle Temple, 1979; practised at Victorian Bar, 1959–84; Justice: Supreme Court of Victoria, 1984–90; Federal Court of Australia, 1990–91. Mem., Victorian Bar Council, 1974–84; Chairman: Criminal Bar Assoc., 1982, 1983; Nat. Crime Authy, 1990–91; Chm., Nat. Inst. of Forensic Sci., 1991–. Pres., French Australian Lawyers Soc., 2000–. Vis. Prof. of Advocacy, Monash Univ., 1988–89. Hellenic Dist. for Service to Greek community of Victoria, 1992, 2000; Australian

Hellenic Council Award, 2003. *Publications:* (jtly) Forensic Science and the Expert Witness, 1985; Advocacy with Honour, 1986; The Trial of Ned Kelly, 1987; Poet of the Colours: the life of John Shaw Neilson, 1988; *plays:* By a Simple Majority: the trial of Socrates, 1990; Conference with Counsel, 1991; The Cab Rank Rule, 1995; Starry Night with Cypresses: the last hours of Vincent van Gogh, 2003; (for sch. children) Murder at Blue Hills, 2003; *poetry:* Wounds, 2001 (trans. Italian); Lament for an Advocate, 2005. *Address:* Sir Zelman Cowen Centre, Victoria University, Level 2, 295 Queen Street, Melbourne, Vic 3000, Australia.

PHILLIPS, John Randall; Member, 1995–99, Chairman, 1995–96, then Lord Mayor, 1996–97, Cardiff City and County Council; *b* 22 April 1940; *s* of James Phillips and Charlotte Phillips (*née* Phelps); *m* 1967, Margaret Ray Davies; one *s* one *d*. *Educ:* Cardiff High Sch.; University Coll., Cardiff (BA Econ. 1961). Dip. Soc. Studies 1967. Cardiff City Council, 1963–66; Glam CC, 1967–74; Mid Glam CC, 1974–96: Principal Trng Officer, 1974–82; Principal Asst (Child Abuse), 1982–89; Dist Social Services Officer, Cynon Valley, 1989–94; Principal Officer, 1994–96. Cardiff City Council: Member (Lab), 1972–96; Chm. of Personnel, 1974–76 and 1979–83; Dep. Leader, Labour Gp, 1986, Ldr, 1990–94; Vice Chm., 1987, Chm., 1990, Policy; Leader, 1990–94; Dep. Lord Mayor, 1994–95. Mem., Cardiff Bay Develt Corp., 1990–99. First Pres., UWIC, 1996–97. *Recreations:* politics, listening to music. *Address:* 15 Kyle Crescent, Whitchurch, Cardiff CF14 1ST. *T:* (029) 2062 4878.

PHILLIPS, Jonathan, PhD; Permanent Secretary, Northern Ireland Office, since 2005; *b* 21 May 1952; *s* of Gilbert Reginald Phillips and Ruby May Phillips (*née* Hughes); *m* 1974, Amanda Rosemary Broomhead; two *s*. *Educ:* Queen Mary's Grammar Sch., Walsall; St John's Coll., Cambridge (BA 1973; PhD 1978); London Univ. Inst. of Educn (PGCE 1974). Department of Trade, later Department of Trade and Industry, 1977–93: seconded: to CBI econs directorate, 1982–83; as Sec., Cttee of Inquiry into regulatory arrangements at Lloyd's, 1986–87; Asst Sec., 1987–93; Under-Sec., 1993; Dir, Exec. Agencies, Dept of Transport, 1993–96; Department of Trade and Industry: Dir, Investigations and Enforcement, 1996–98; Dir, Finance and Resource Mgt, 1998–2000; Dir Gen., Resources and Services, 2000–02; Operating Strategy Dir, Sea Systems, BAE Systems, 2002 (on secondment); Pol Dir, NI Office, 2002–05. Non-exec. Dir, Forward Trust Gp, 1995–96. Gov., St Saviour's and St Olave's Sch., Southwark, 1998–2005. *Address:* (office) 11 Millbank, SW1P 4PN. *T:* (020) 7210 6456; *e-mail:* jonathan.phillips@nio.x.gsi.gov.uk. *Club:* Athenæum.

PHILLIPS, Leslie Samuel, CBE 2008 (OBE 1998); actor, director, producer; *b* 20 April 1924; *s* of late Frederick and Cecelia Phillips; *m* 1st, 1948, Penelope Bartley (marr. diss. 1965; she *d* 1981); two *s* two *d*; 2nd, 1982, Angela Scoular; one step *s*. *Educ:* Chingford Sch.; Italia Conti Stage Sch. Army, 1942–45 (Lieut, DLI; invalided out). *Theatre* includes: début, Peter Pan, London Palladium, 1937; Zeal of Thy House, Garrick, 1938; Otello, and Turandot, Covent Garden, 1939; Dear Octopus, Queen's, 1939–40; Nutmeg Tree, Lyric, 1941–42; The Doctor's Dilemma, Haymarket, 1942; Daddy Long-Legs, Comedy, 1947–48; Charley's Aunt, Saville, 1948; On Monday Next, Comedy, 1949; For Better, For Worse, Comedy, 1952–54; Diary of a Nobody, Arts, 1954; Lost Generation, Garrick, 1955; The Whole Truth, Aldwych, 1955–56; The Big Killing, Shaftesbury, 1961–62; Boeing-Boeing, Apollo, 1963–65; The Deadly Game (also dir), Savoy, 1967; The Man Most Likely To… (also dir), Vaudeville, 1968–69, tour, S Africa, 1970–71, Duke of York's, 1972, tour of Australia, 1974; Sextet, Criterion, 1977–78; Canaries Sometimes Sing, tour, 1978; Not Now Darling, Savoy, 1979, world tour, 1980; Pygmalion, tour, 1980; The Cherry Orchard, Haymarket, 1983; Chapter 17, tour, 1983; Passion Play, Wyndham's, 1984–85; Pride and Prejudice, tour, 1988; Taking Steps, world tour, 1989; Painting Churches, Playhouse, 1992; August, tour of Wales, 1994; Love for Love, Chichester, 1996; Merry Wives of Windsor, RSC, 1997; Camino Real, 1998; On The Whole It's Been Jolly Good, Edin. Fest., 1999, Hampstead, 2000; Naked Justice, W Yorks Playhouse, 2001, 2002; The Play What I Wrote, Wyndhams, 2003; more than 100 *films*, including: A Lassie from Lancashire, 1938; The Citadel, 1938; Four Feathers, 1938; Mikado, 1938; Climbing High, 1939; Proud Valley, 1939; Thief of Baghdad, 1939; Train of Events, 1949; Sound Barrier, 1949; Pool of London, 1950; Gamma People, 1955; The Smallest Show on Earth, 1956; Brothers in Law, 1956; High Flight, 1957; Les Girls, 1957; Carry on Nurse, 1958; I Was Monty's Double, 1958; Carry on Constable, 1959; This Other Eden, 1959; Ferdinando, 1959; Doctor in Love, 1960; Very Important Person, 1961; In the Doghouse, 1961; Raising the Wind, 1961; Crooks Anonymous, 1962; Fast Lady, 1962; The Longest Day, 1963; Doctor in Clover, 1965; You Must Be Joking, 1965; Maroc 7 (also prod.), 1966; Some Will Some Won't, 1969; Doctor in Trouble, 1970; Magnificent Seven Deadly Sins, 1971; Don't Just Lie There, 1973; Spanish Fly, 1975; Out of Africa, 1986; Empire of the Sun, 1987; Scandal, 1988; Mountains of the Moon, 1989; King Ralph, 1990; August, 1995; Day of the Jackal, 1997; Cinderella, 1999; Saving Grace, 2000; Lara Croft: Tomb Raider, 2001; Thunderpants, 2001; Harry Potter and the Philosopher's Stone, 2001; Collusion, 2002; Harry Potter and the Chamber of Secrets, 2002; Carry On Columbus, 2002; Churchill: the Hollywood years, 2002; Colour Me Kubrick, 2004; Walking With Shadows, 2004; Millions, 2005; Venus, 2007; Is There Anybody There?, 2008; *television* includes: Morning Departure (first TV from Alexandra Palace), 1948; My Wife Jacqueline, 1952; Our Man at St Mark's, 1963; Impasse, 1963; The Reluctant Debutante, 1965; The Gong Game, 1965; Foreign Affairs, 1966; Blandings Castle, 1967; Very Fine Line, 1968; The Suit, 1969; Casanova, 1973; Redundant and the Wife's Revenge, 1983; You'll Never See Me Again, 1983; Mr Palfrey of Westminster, 1985; Monte Carlo, 1986; Rumpole, 1988; Summer's Lease, 1989; Comic Strip, 1989, 1990, 1991; Chancer, 1989–90; Who Bombed Birmingham, 1990; Life After Life, 1990; Thacker, 1991; The Trials of Oz, 1991; Boon, 1992; Lovejoy, 1992; Bermuda Grace, 1993; The Changeling, 1993; Vanity Dies Hard, 1993; Love on a Branch Line, 1993; House of Windsor, 1994; Two Golden Balls, 1994; Honey for Tea, 1994; The Canterville Ghost, 1995; L for Liverpool, 1998; Dalziel & Pasco, 1998; The Best of British, 2000; Sword of Honour, 2000; Take a Girl Like You, 2000; Into the Void, 2001; Legends, 2002; Monarch of the Glen, 2002; Holby City, 2002; Midsomer Murders, 2002; Unto the Wicked, 2002; Where The Heart Is, 2003; The Last Detective, 2007; Miss Marple, 2007; Harley Street, 2008; Edgar Wallace series: The Pale Horse, 1996; Tales from the Crypt, 1996; *radio* includes: The Navy Lark, 1959–76; Three Men in a Boat, 1962; Vera Lynn Story, 1973; Would the Last Businessman to Leave England Please Turn out the Light, 1977–78; Round the World in 80 Days, 1991–92; Red Riding Hood and the Wolf's Story, 1994; England Their England, 1994; Wind in the Willows, 1994; Tuth in Dark Places, 1994–95; Falling Heads, 1995; Philip and Rowena, 1995; Envious Casca, 1996; Half a Sixpence, 1996; Me and Little Boots, 2000; Maclean the Memorex Years, 2000; Cousin Bette, 2000; Tales from the Backbench, 2001; Democracy and Language, 2001; Les Miserables, 2002; Hitchhiker's Guide to the Galaxy, 2003; Cads, 2004; Dr Who, 2004. Vice Pres., Royal Theatrical Fund; Founder Mem., Theatre of Comedy; Vice Pres., Disabled Living Foundn, 2002–. Award for lifetime achievement in films, Evening Standard, 1997; Comic Icon Award, 2003, Greatest Living Englishman Award, 2006, Loaded mag.; Dilys Powell Award for Lifetime Achievement in Film, London Critics Circle, 2007; Best Supporting Actor, BIFA, 2007; Best Trouper Award, Oldie mag., 2007. *Publication:* Hello: the autobiography, 2006. *Recreations:* cats, restoration, racing, collecting, gardening, classical music, weaving, chess, all sport. *Address:* c/o Independent Talent Group Ltd, 76 Oxford Street, W1D 1BS. *T:* (020) 7636 6565.

PHILLIPS, Malcolm Edward, MD; FRCP; Consultant Physician and Nephrologist, Hammersmith Hospitals NHS Trust (formerly Charing Cross Hospital), 1981–2005, now Honorary Consulting Physician and Nephrologist (Director of Renal Services, 1994–2001); *b* 24 March 1940; *s* of Albert H. Phillips and Kathleen M. Phillips; *m* 1967, Rona Lendon; one *s* one *d*. *Educ:* Charing Cross Hosp. Med. Sch., London (MB BS 1964; MD 1979). MRCS 1964; FRCP 1986. Jun. hosp. med. posts, Fulham Hosp. and Charing Cross Hosp., 1964–81; Wellcome Trust Fellow, Univ. of Naples, 1970–72; Gen. Manager, 1989, Med. Dir, 1995–97, Charing Cross Hosp. Med. Advr, Parly and Health Service Ombudsman's Office, 2005–; Panellist, Fitness to Practice Panel, GMC, 2006–. Canterbury Trustbank Vis. Prof., Christchurch, NZ, 1997. Pres., W London Medico-Chirurgical Soc., 2005–06. *Publications:* articles in jls. *Recreations:* cricket, philately, keyboard. *Address:* The Ridings, 26 Pelhams Walk, Esher, Surrey KT10 8QD. *T:* (01372) 461098.

PHILLIPS, Margaret Corinna, (Mrs D. R. Hunt), FRCO; Professor of Organ, Royal College of Music, since 1996; concert organist; *b* 16 Nov. 1950; *d* of John George Phillips and Cora Frances (*née* Hurford); *m* 1983, Dr David Richard Hunt, MA, ARCO. *Educ:* Sittingbourne Grammar Sch. for Girls; Maidstone Grammar Sch. for Girls; Royal Coll. of Music (ARCM). GRSM 1971; FRCO 1971. Director of Music, St Lawrence Jewry next Guildhall, London, 1976–85; Prof. of Organ and Harpsichord, London Coll. of Music, 1985–91; Tutor in Organ Studies, RNCM, 1993–97 (Vis. Tutor, 1997–2005). Co-founder with Dr D. R. Hunt, and Chm., English Organ Sch. and Museum, Milborne Port, Som, 1996–. Pres., IAO, 1997–99; Mem. Council, RCO, 1982–2003. Recitals throughout Europe, USA, Mexico and Australia; radio broadcasts, UK, Scandinavia, Netherlands, Australia, USA; numerous recordings of solo organ music and with The Sixteen, BBC Singers, etc. *Publications:* articles on style and performance of organ music. *Recreations:* reading, tennis, playing the violin. *Address:* The Manse, Chapel Lane, Milborne Port, Sherborne DT9 5DL. *T:* (01963) 250899.

PHILLIPS, Marisa, DLitt; President, Mental Health Review Tribunal, since 1990; *b* 14 April 1932; *d* of Dr and Mrs J. Fargion; *m* 1956, Philip Harold Phillips; one *s* one *d*. *Educ:* Henrietta Barnet Sch., London; Univ. of Redlands, California (Fulbright Schol.; BA Hons); Rome Univ. (DLitt). Called to Bar, Lincoln's Inn, 1963. On return from Redlands Univ., worked for US Inf. Service, Rome, 1954–56; spent one year in Berlin, as husband then in Army; period of work with Penguin Books; read for the Bar, joining DPP as Legal Asst, 1964; Legal Adviser, Police Complaints Bd, 1977; returned to DPP, 1979; Asst Dir, DPP, 1981; Principal Asst DPP, 1985; Asst Hd of Legal Services, 1986–87, Dir of Legal Casework, 1987–90, Crown Prosecution Service. Sen. Legal Advr, Banking Ombudsman, 1990–. Comr, Mental Health Act Commn, 1991–96; Chm., Rent Assessment Panel, 1992–. Trustee, Camden Victim Support, 2006–. *Recreations:* music, theatre, foreign travel.

PHILLIPS, Captain Mark Anthony Peter, CVO 1974; ADC(P); Chef d'Equipe and Coach, US Three Day Event Team, since 1993; Consultant, Gleneagles Mark Phillips Equestrian Centre, 1992–97 (Director, 1988–92); *b* 22 Sept. 1948; *s* of late P. W. G. Phillips, MC, and Anne Patricia (*née* Tiarks); *m* 1st, 1973, HRH The Princess Anne (marr. diss. 1992); one *s* one *d*; 2nd, 1997, Sandy Pflueger; one *d*. *Educ:* Marlborough Coll.; RMA Sandhurst. Joined 1st The Queen's Dragoon Guards, July 1969; Regimental duty, 1969–74; Company Instructor, RMA Sandhurst, 1974–77; Army Trng Directorate, MoD, 1977–78, retired. Personal ADC to HM the Queen, 1974–. Student, RAC Cirencester, 1978. Chm., British Olympic Equestrian Fund, subseq. British Equestrian Fedn Fund, 1989–. In Three Day Equestrian Event, GB winning teams: Team Championships: World, 1970; European, 1971; Olympic Gold Medallists (Team), Olympic Games, Munich, 1972; Olympic Silver Medallists (Team), Olympic Games, Seoul, 1988; Mem., Equestrian Team (Reserve), Olympic Games, Mexico, 1968 and Montreal, 1976. Winner, Badminton Three Day Event, 1971, 1972, 1974, 1981. Dir, Glos TEC, 1991–98. Hon. FBHS 2005. Liveryman: Farriers' Co.; Farmers' Co.; Carmen's Co.; Loriners' Co.; Freeman: City of London; Yeoman, Saddlers' Co. *Recreations:* riding, Rugby football, athletics. *Address:* Aston Farm, Cherington, Tetbury, Glos GL8 8SW. *Club:* (Hon. Mem.) Buck's.

See also under Royal Family.

PHILLIPS, Mark Paul; QC 1999; a Recorder, 2000–07; *b* 28 Dec. 1959; *s* of Norman John Phillips and Wendy Sharron Phillips; *m* 1984, Deborah Elizabeth Fisher; one *s* two *d*. *Educ:* John Hampden Sch., High Wycombe; Univ. of Bristol (LLB 1982; LLM 1983). Called to the Bar, Inner Temple, 1984; in practice, 1986–; Asst Recorder, 1998–2000. Pres., Insolvency Lawyers' Assoc., 2002–03; Member: Council, Assoc. of Business Recovery Professionals, 2004– (Fellow, 2004); Internat. Insolvency Inst., 2007–. *Publications:* (ed jtly) Butterworth's Insolvency Law Handbook, 1987, 9th edn 2007; contrib. chapter on Insolvency in: Byles on Bills of Exchange, 26th edn 1983; Paget's Law of Banking, 10th edn 1989 to 13th edn 2007; chap. on insolvency procedures in Insolvency of Banks: managing the risks, 1996. *Recreations:* watching football, motor sport, ski-ing, theatre. *Address:* 3–4 South Square, Gray's Inn, WC1R 5HP. *T:* (020) 7696 9900, *Fax:* (020) 7696 9911; *e-mail:* markphillips@southsquare.com.

PHILLIPS, (Mark) Trevor, OBE 1999; broadcaster and journalist; Chair, Equality and Human Rights Commission, since 2006; *b* 31 Dec. 1953; *s* of George Milton Phillips and Marjorie Eileen Phillips (*née* Canzius); *m* 1981, Asha Bhownagary; two *d*. *Educ:* Queen's Coll., Georgetown, Guyana; Imperial Coll., London (BSc; ARCS). Pres., NUS, 1978–80; London Weekend Television: researcher, 1980–81; producer, Black on Black, The Making of Britain, 1981–86; reporter, This Week, Thames TV, 1986–87; London Weekend Television: Editor, London Prog., 1987–92; Hd, Current Affairs, 1992–94; Presenter: London Prog., 1987–2000; Crosstalk, 1994–2000; The Material World, 1998–2000. Man. Dir, Pepper Prodns, 1994–. Mem. (Lab), 2000–03, Chm., 2000–01 and 2002–03, Dep. Chm., 2001–02, London Assembly, GLA. Chairman: Runnymede Trust, 1993–98; Hampstead Theatre, 1993–97; London Arts Bd, 1997–2000; CRE, 2003–06. FRSA 1995. Hon. MA N London, 1995; Hon. DLitt: Westminster, 1999; South Bank, 2001; City, 2002. Journalism Award, RTS, 1988 and 1993; Best Documentary Series (for Windrush), RTS, 1998. Chevalier, Légion d'Honneur (France), 2007. *Publications:* Windrush: the irresistible rise of multi-racial Britain, 1998; Britain's Slave Trade, 1999. *Recreations:* music, running, crosswords. *Address:* (office) 3 More London, Riverside, Tooley Street, SE1 2RG. *Clubs:* Groucho, Home House.

PHILLIPS, Max; Assistant Under Secretary of State, Ministry of Defence, 1977–84; *b* 31 March 1924; *m* 1953, Patricia Moore; two *s* two *d*. *Educ:* Colston's Sch., Bristol; Christ's Hospital; Magdalene Coll., Cambridge (Schol.; 1st cl. Hist. Tripos, pts I and II; MA). Served War, RA, 1943–46. Appointed to Home Civil Service, 1949; Colonial Office, 1949–59; Sec., Nigeria Fiscal Commn, 1957–58; UKAEA, 1959–73; Procurement Exec., MoD, 1973–74; HM Treasury, 1974–77; retired 1984, re-employed as Asst Sec., MoD,

1984–87. Chm., Guildford Evening DFAS, 2003–06. Gov., Christ's Hospital, 1979– (Almoner, 1981–92). *Recreations:* modern myths, exploring the imagination and the countryside. *Address:* 2 Wilderness Farmhouse, Onslow Village, Guildford, Surrey GU2 7QP. *T:* (01483) 561308.

PHILLIPS, Melanie; columnist, Daily Mail, since 2001; *b* 4 June 1951; *d* of late Alfred and Mabel Phillips; *m* 1974, Joshua Rufus Rozenberg, *qv*; one *s* one *d*. *Educ:* Putney High Sch. for Girls; St Anne's Coll., Oxford (BA 1973). Grad. trainee, Evening Echo, Hemel Hempstead, 1974–76; staff writer, New Society, 1976–77; Guardian: reporter, 1977; social services corresp., 1978–80; leader writer, 1980–84; news ed., 1984–87; Asst Ed. and columnist, 1987–93; columnist: Observer, 1993–98; Sunday Times, 1998–2001. *Publications:* The Divided House, 1980; (with J. Dawson) Doctors' Dilemmas, 1984; All Must Have Prizes, 1996, 3rd edn 1998; The Sex-Change Society: feminised Britain and the neutered male, 1999; The Ascent of Woman, 2003, 2nd edn 2004; Londonistan, 2006. *Recreations:* family, friends, theatre, cinema, learning to swim. *Address:* c/o Daily Mail, Northcliffe House, 2 Derry Street, W8 5TT. *T:* (020) 7938 6000; *e-mail:* melanie@melaniephillips.com.

PHILLIPS, (Mervyn) John, AO 2004 (AM 1987); Chancellor, University of Western Sydney, since 2001; *b* 1 April 1930; *m* 1956, Moya, *d* of A. C. Bleazard; one *s* one *d*. *Educ:* De La Salle Coll., Ashfield; Univ. of Sydney (BEc). Commonwealth Bank of Australia, 1946–60; Reserve Bank of Australia, 1960–92: Manager for PNG, 1962–64; Chief Manager, Internat. Dept, 1976–79, Securities Markets Dept, 1980–82, Financial Markets Group, 1983–85; Adviser, 1982; Chief Admin. Officer, 1985–87; Dep. Gov. and Dep. Chm., 1987–92; Chm., I. B. J. Australia Bank Ltd, 1992–2002; Dir, CBOA Credit Union, 1964–73 (Chm., 1967–72); Chm., Note Printing Australia, 1990–93; Director: QBE Insurance Gp, 1992–2002; Alcoa of Australia, 1992–96; Aust. Gas Light Co., 1992–2003 (Chm., 1996–); O'Connell Street Associates Pty, 1992–; Woolworths Ltd, 1993–2001; GRW Property Ltd, 1994–98; WMC Ltd, 1996–2002. Chairman: For. Investment Review Bd, 1997–; Aust. Charities Fund, 2001–. Member: PNG Currency Conversion Commn, 1965–66; NSW Credit Union Adv. Cttee, 1968–72; Govt Cttees on PNG Banking, 1971–73; Off-shore Banking in Australia, 1984; Prime Minister's Task Force on Internat. Monetary Reform, 2000; Medical Indemnity Policy Reform Panel, 2003. Nat. Treas., Australian Catholic Relief, subseq. Caritas Australia, 1993–2001. Mem., Finance Cttee, Archdio. Sydney, 2002–. Member: Senate, Australian Catholic Univ., 1991–98; Adv. Council, Australian Grad. Sch. of Management, 1991–2001. Mem., Pontifical Council, Cor Unum, 1994–2000. FAICD; Sen. Fellow, Fin. Services Inst. of Australasia. GCSG 2004. *Address:* O'Connell Street Associates Pty Ltd, 6 O'Connell Street, Sydney, NSW 2000, Australia. *T:* (2) 92231822.

PHILLIPS, Prof. Nelson William, PhD; Professor of Strategy and Organizational Behaviour, Tanaka Business School, Imperial College London, since 2005; *b* 7 Nov. 1962; *s* of Murray and Lucille Phillips. *Educ:* Univ. of Calgary (BSc, MBA); Univ. of Alberta (PhD 1995). Asst Prof., 1993–98, Associate Prof., 1998–2002, Faculty of Mgt, McGill Univ.; Beckwith Prof. of Mgt Studies and MBA Dir, Judge Inst. of Mgt, and Fellow, Hughes Hall, Cambridge Univ., 2002–05. *Publications:* (with C. Hardy) Discourse Analysis, 2002; contribs to Acad. of Mgt Jl, Organization Science, Organization Studies, Jl Mgt Studies. *Address:* Tanaka Business School, Imperial College London, S Kensington Campus, SW7 2AZ. *T:* (020) 7589 5111, *Fax:* (020) 7823 7685; *e-mail:* n.phillips@imperial.ac.uk.

PHILLIPS, Prof. Owen Martin, FRS 1968; Decker Professor of Science and Engineering, Johns Hopkins University, 1975–98, now Emeritus; *b* 30 Dec. 1930; *s* of Richard Keith Phillips and Madeline Lofts; *m* 1953, Merle Winifred Simons; two *s* two *d*. *Educ:* University of Sydney; Trinity Coll., Cambridge (Hon. Fellow, 1997). ICI Fellow, Cambridge, 1955–57; Fellow, St John's Coll., Cambridge, 1957–60; Asst Prof., 1957–60, Assoc. Prof., 1960–63, Johns Hopkins Univ.; Asst Director of Research, Cambridge, 1961–64; Prof. of Geophysical Mechanics, Johns Hopkins Univ., 1963–68, of Geophysics, 1968–75. Mem. Council, Nat. Center of Atmospheric Research, Boulder, Colorado, 1964–68; Member: US Nat. Cttee Global Atmospheric Research Project, 1968; Res. Co-ord. Panel, Gas Research Inst., 1981–85; Principal Staff, Applied Phys. Lab., 1982–90. Associate Ed., Jl of Fluid Mechanics, 1964–95; Regl Ed., Proc. of Royal Soc. series A, 1992–98; Mem. Adv. Cttee, Annual Review of Fluid Dynamics, 1995–98. Mem.-at-large, Amer. Meteorol. Soc. Publications Commn, 1971–75; Pres., Maryland Acad. of Scis, 1979–85. Sec., Bd of Trustees, Chesapeake Res. Consortium, 1973–74 (Trustee, 1972–75); Vis. Cttees, Univ. of Michigan Res. Initiatives, 1990–93, 1994–97. Mem., US NAE, 1996. Adams Prize, Univ. of Cambridge, 1965; Sverdrup Gold Medal, Amer. Meteorol. Soc., 1975. *Publications:* The Dynamics of the Upper Ocean, 1966, 3rd edn 1976, Russian edn 1968, Chinese edn 1983; The Heart of the Earth, 1968, Italian edns 1970, 1975; The Last Chance Energy Book, 1979, Japanese edn 1983; (ed) Wave Dynamics and Radio Probing of the Ocean Surface, 1985; Flow and Reactions in Permeable Rocks, 1990; various scientific papers in Jl Fluid Mechanics, Proc. Cambridge Philos. Soc., Jl Marine Research, Proc. Royal Society, Deep Sea Research, Journal Geophys. Research. *Address:* 462 Heron Point, Chestertown, MD 21620–1681, USA. *T:* (410) 7787579. *Clubs:* Johns Hopkins (Baltimore); Quissett Yacht (Mass).

PHILLIPS, Prof. Paddy Andrew, FRACP, FACP; Chief Medical Officer, Department of Health, South Australia, since 2008; Professor of Medicine, Flinders University, Adelaide, since 1997; Consultant, Flinders Medical Centre and Repatriation Hospitals, Adelaide, since 1997 (Head of Medicine, 1997–2008); *b* 26 Oct. 1956; *s* of Walter Alfred Peter Phillips and Lilian Phillips (*née* Watt); *m* 1995, Lynda Jane Dandie; one *s* one *d*. *Educ:* Univ. of Adelaide (MB, BS); Univ. of Oxford (DPhil; MA 1997). Intern, Royal Adelaide Hosp., 1980; Hon. Sen. House Officer, John Radcliffe Hosp., Oxford, 1981–83; Resident MO and Registrar, Prince Henry's Hosp., Melbourne, 1984–86; Fellow in Clinical Pharmacology, 1987, Res. Fellow, 1988–90, Consultant, 1988–96, Austin Hosp., Melbourne; Sen. Lectr, 1990–94, Associate Prof., 1994–96, Dept of Medicine, Melbourne Univ.; May Reader in Medicine, Nuffield Dept of Clinical Medicine, Univ. of Oxford, and Professorial Fellow, New Coll., Oxford, 1996–97; Consultant, Oxford Radcliffe NHS Trust, 1996–97. *Publications:* scientific papers in physiol., pharmacol., cardiovascular disease, health services research. *Recreations:* gardening, fly fishing, ski-ing, music. *Address:* South Australia Department of Health, Citicentre Building, Hindmarsh Square, Adelaide, SA 5000, Australia. *T:* (8) 82266000.

PHILLIPS, Patricia Ruth; HM Diplomatic Service; Ambassador to Angola and concurrently to São Tomé and Príncipe, since 2007; *b* 11 March 1962; *d* of Alan and Diana Phillips. *Educ:* N London Collegiate Sch.; Newnham Coll., Cambridge (BA Hist. 1984). MAFF, 1984–91; Fulbright Fellow, Univ. of Minnesota, 1991–92; First Secretary: Washington, 1992–97; FCO, 1997–2002; Counsellor (Econ.), The Hague, 2002–04; Dep. Hd of Mission, Amman, 2004–07. *Recreations:* playing the trumpet, history, walking. *Address:* c/o Foreign and Commonwealth Office, King Charles Street, SW1A 2AH.

PHILLIPS, Peter; *see* Phillips, I. P.

PHILLIPS, Sir Peter (John), Kt 1990; OBE 1983; Chairman, Principality Building Society, 1991–2000 (Deputy Chairman, 1988–91); *b* 18 June 1930; *s* of Walter Alfred Phillips and Victoria Mary Phillips; *m* 1956, Jean Gwendoline Williams; one *s* one *d*. *Educ:* Radley College; Pembroke College, Oxford (MA). Joined Aberthaw and Bristol Channel Portland Cement Co., 1956, Jt Man. Dir, 1964–83; Western Area Dir, Blue Circle Industries, 1983–84; Dep. Chm., 1985, Chm., 1987–93, A. B. Electronic Products Gp. Dep. Chm. Bd of Governors, Univ. of Glam., 1996–98; Chm. Council, Univ. of Wales, Cardiff, 1998–2004 (Vice-Chm., 1997–98). *Recreations:* walking, fishing, reading. *Address:* Great House, Llanblethian, near Cowbridge, South Glam CF7 7JG. *T:* (01446) 775163. *Club:* Cardiff and County.

PHILLIPS, Peter Sayer; Founder and Musical Director, The Tallis Scholars, since 1973; Music Critic, The Spectator, since 1983; Director of Music, Merton College, Oxford, since 2008; *b* 15 Oct. 1953; *s* of Nigel Sayer Phillips and Patricia Ann Witchell (*née* Wyatt); *m* 1st, 1987, Clio (marr. diss. 1993), *d* of D. O. Lloyd-Jacob, *qv*; 2nd, 1997, Caroline Trevor; one *s*. *Educ:* Winchester Coll.; St John's Coll., Oxford (Organ Scholar). Teacher: Oxford Univ., 1976–81; Trinity Coll. of Music, 1980–84; RCM, 1981–88. Co-founder and Artistic Director: Gimell Records, 1981–; Tallis Scholars Summer Schs, Oakham, 2000–, Seattle, 2005–, Sydney, 2007–. Has conducted Dutch Chamber Choir, Collegium Vocale Gent, BBC Singers, Finnish Radio Choir, Woodley Ensemble, Tudor Choir of Seattle, Markell's Voices of Novosibirsk, Musix of Budapest, Taipei Chamber Singers. Mem., Early Music Cttee, Arts Council, 1987–88. Ed., Early Music Gazette, 1980–82; cricket correspondent, Spectator, 1989; Prop. and Adv. Ed., Musical Times, 1995–. Many awards for recordings made by Tallis Scholars, incl. Gramophone Record of the Year, 1987, and Early Music Record of the Year, 1987, 1991, 1994 and 2005, Gramophone magazine. Chevalier de l'Ordre des Arts et des Lettres (France), 2005. *Publications:* English Sacred Music 1549–1649, 1991; (contrib.) Companion to Medieval and Renaissance Music, 1992; What We Really Do, 2003; contrib. Spectator, Guardian, Musical Times, New Republic, Listener, Early Music, Music and Letters, Music and Musicians, 24 Hours, Royal Acad. magazine, Evening Standard, BBC Music Magazine. *Recreations:* black and white photography, cricket, cooking, Arabia. *Address:* 22 Gibson Square, N1 0RD. *T:* (020) 7354 0627, (020) 7226 8047; 48 rue des Francs Bourgeois, 75003 Paris, France. *T:* 42724461; Merton College, Merton Street, Oxford OX1 4JD. *Clubs:* Chelsea Arts, MCC.

PHILLIPS, (Rachel) Sarah, OBE 2005; DL; Chairman, Victim Support, since 2005; *b* 8 Feb. 1943; *d* of late Air Cdre John Lawrance Kirby, CB, CBE, JP, DL and Rachel Kirby; *m* 1966, Peter, *s* of Maj.-Gen. Sir Farndale Phillips, KBE, CB, DSO, and Lady (Lovering Catherine) Phillips; one *s* one *d*. *Educ:* Benenden Sch.; Heidelberg. Qualified as: LTA coach, 1978; remedial tutor, Kingsbury Centre, Washington, 1983; diagnosed with MS, 1981. Trustee, 1992–2005, Chm., 1998–2005, Multiple Sclerosis Society of GB and NI; Chm., Colchester Br., MS Soc., 1989–98; Chm., Homes Cttee, MS Soc., 1993–98; Trustee, Internat. Fedn of MS Socs, now MS Internat. Fedn, 1997– (Pres. and Chm., 2004–; Chm., Nominating Cttee, 2002–03, Hon. Sec., 2003–04). Chm., Disability Adv. Gp, NHS Appts Commn, 2003–07. Non-executive Director: Mid Essex Community and Mental Health Trust, 2000–01; N Essex Partnership NHS Foundn Trust (formerly N Essex Mental Health Partnership NHS Trust), 2001–Nov. 2009. Mem., Registration and Conduct Cttees, Gen. Social Care Council, 2003–. Comr, Royal Hosp. Chelsea, 2007–. Trustee, Leonard Cheshire, 1999–2002. DL Essex, 2005. *Recreations:* bridge, choral singing. *Address:* Wistaria House, Coggeshall, Essex CO6 1UF. *Club:* Royal Commonwealth Society.

PHILLIPS, Raymond Mark; Adviser to Central and East European Governments, since 1998; Director of Policy and Process Design, Employment Service, Department for Education and Employment, 1995–97; *b* 15 April 1944; *s* of Vernon Phillips and Claudia Phillips; *m* 1968, Janet Harris; four *s*. *Educ:* Cowbridge Grammar Sch.; UC Cardiff. Department of Employment: Operational Planning and Res., 1976–78; Pay Policy Advr, 1978–79; Asst Sec., Standing Commn on Pay Comparability, 1979–80; Regl Gen. Manager, Trng Services Agency, 1980–82; Exec. Dir, Employment Service, 1982–83; Regional Director: MSC, 1983–86; Employment and Enterprise Gp, 1986–87; Regl Dir, 1987–93, Dir of Inf. and Systems, 1993–95, Employment Service, Dept. of Employment. *Recreations:* gardening, cosmology, running, tennis. *Address:* Stockport, Cheshire.

PHILLIPS, Richard Charles Jonathan; QC 1990; *b* 8 Aug. 1947; *yr s* of Air Commodore M. N. Phillips, MD, ChB, DMRD and Dorothy E. Phillips; *m* 1978, Alison Jane Francis (OBE 1991); one *d*. *Educ:* King's School, Ely; Sidney Sussex College, Cambridge (Exhibnr). Called to the Bar, Inner Temple, 1970. Asst Parly Boundary Comr, 1992–. *Recreations:* travel, natural history, photography, walking. *Address:* Francis Taylor Building, Temple, EC4Y 7BY. *T:* (020) 7353 8415.

PHILLIPS, Dr Richard Peter, CMG 2006; Director, Customer Services and Innovation, British Council, since 2007; *b* 2 May 1950; *s* of William Leslie Phillips and Dorothy May Phillips; *m* 1st, 1976, Alice Detoya (*d* 2003); one *s* one *d*; 2nd, 2006, Adele Sinclair (*née* McNaughton). *Educ:* Univ. of Bristol (BSc Hons Chem. 1971; PhD Inorganic Chem. 1975); Huddersfield Poly. (PGCE 1981). Pt-time Tutor of Chem., Univ. of Bristol, 1971–74; Vis. Prof. of Chem., Mindanao State Univ., Philippines, 1974–76; Field Officer, Philippines, 1976–77, Field Dir, Indonesia, 1978–80, VSO; HM Diplomatic Service, 1981–82; joined British Council, 1982: Sci. Officer, Yugoslavia, 1983–85; Sen. Sci. Officer, London, 1985–89; Educn Officer/Dep. Dir, Indonesia, 1989–93; Hd, Mgt Services, London, 1993–95; Contract Ops Dir, Manchester, 1995–2000; Dir, Indonesia, 2000–03; Prog. Dir, Finance and Business Systems, 2003–06. *Publications:* contrib. various papers to Chemical Communications and Jl Inorganic Chemistry. *Recreations:* scuba-diving, tennis, sailing, reading. *Address:* c/o British Council, 10 Spring Gardens, SW1A 2BN; *e-mail:* richard.phillips@britishcouncil.org.

PHILLIPS, Rear Adm. Richard Thomas Ryder, CB 1998; FNI; Director, Ryder Phillips Associates, since 2004; Chief Executive Officer/Clerk, Worshipful Company of Haberdashers, since 2005; *b* 1 Feb. 1947; *s* of late Thomas Hall Phillips and Arabella Phillips; *m* 1st, 1969, Susan Elizabeth Groves (*d* 1996); one *d*; 2nd, 1999, Belinda Susan Kelway Round Turner; one step *s* one step *d*. *Educ:* Kingsland Grange, Shrewsbury; Wrekin Coll. BRNC Dartmouth, 1965; Commanding Officer: HMS Scimitar, 1974; HMS Hubberston, 1978; ndc Canberra, 1981; Directorate of Naval Plans, 1982; Commanding Officer: HMS Charybdis, 1985; HMS Scylla, 1986; Asst Dir, Defence Op. Requirements (Maritime), 1987; CO, HMS Cornwall, and Capt., 8 Frigate Sqn, 1988; Capt., RN Presentation Team, 1991; Cabinet Office Top Mgt Prog., 1992; COS, Flag Officer Surface Flotilla, 1992; CO, HMS Illustrious, 1993–96; ACDS Op. Requirements (Sea Systems), 1996–99. ADC to the Queen, 1993. Director: Marconi Naval Systems, 1999–2000; BAE SYSTEMS, 2000–04. Special Advr, Internat. Energy Adv. Council, 2004–. Younger Brother, Trinity Hse, 1984. FNI 1999; Associate Fellow, RUSI, 2004. *Recreations:* shooting, gardening, sailing. *Clubs:* Royal Yacht Squadron, Cargreen Sailing.

PHILLIPS, Robin, OC 2005; actor and director; *b* 28 Feb. 1940; *s* of James William Phillips and Ellen Anne (*née* Barfoot). *Educ:* Midhurst Grammar School, Sussex. Trained as director, actor and designer, Bristol Old Vic Co.; first appearance, Bristol, as Mr Puff in

The Critic, 1959; Associate Dir, Bristol Old Vic, 1960–61; played at Lyric, Hammersmith, 1961, Chichester Fest., 1962, and with Oxford Playhouse Co., 1964. Asst Dir, Timon of Athens and Hamlet, Royal Shakespeare Co., Stratford upon Avon, 1965; Dir or Associate Dir, Hampstead, Exeter, (Thorndike) Leatherhead, 1966–69; Artistic Dir, Stratford Festival, Canada, 1974–80; Artistic Dir, Grand Theatre Co., London, Ontario, 1982; Dir, Young Company, Stratford Festival Theatre, 1986; Dir Gen., The Citadel Theatre, Edmonton, Canada, 1990–95. Hon. Dr Univ. of Western Ontario, 1982. Guild Shield, Conestoga Coll., 1982. *London productions include:* Tiny Alice, RSC, Aldwych, 1970; Abelard and Heloise, Wyndhams and Broadway; The Two Gentlemen of Verona, Stratford and Aldwych, 1970; Miss Julie, for RSC (also directed film); Virginia, Haymarket, 1981; Long Day's Journey Into Night, Lyric, 2000; Ghosts, Comedy, 2001; *Chichester:* Caesar and Cleopatra and Dear Antoine, 1971; played Dubedat in The Doctor's Dilemma and directed The Lady's Not for Burning and The Beggar's Opera, 1972; The Jeweller's Shop, 1982; Antony and Cleopatra, 1985; *Greenwich:* formed Company Theatre and apptd Artistic Dir, 1973: plays directed include: The Three Sisters, Rosmerholm, Zorba; *Stratford Festival productions include:* 1975: The Two Gentlemen of Verona and The Comedy of Errors (both also Nat. tour), Measure for Measure, Trumpets and Drums and The Importance of Being Earnest; 1976–78: Hamlet, The Tempest, Antony and Cleopatra, A Midsummer Night's Dream, The Way of the World, Richard III, The Guardsman, As You Like It, Macbeth, The Winter's Tale, Uncle Vanya, The Devils, Private Lives, Hay Fever, Judgement; 1979: Love's Labours Lost, The Importance of Being Earnest, King Lear; 1980: Virginia, Long Day's Journey into Night; 1986: Cymbeline; 1987: The School for Scandal, As You Like It, Romeo and Juliet, Journey's End; 1988: Twelfth Night, King Lear, Oedipus, The Critic; 1993: King John; *Edmonton productions include:* A Midsummer Night's Dream, The Crucible, 1989; The Philadelphia Story, 1990; Never the Sinner, The Mousetrap, Romeo and Juliet, Democracy, 1991; Lend Me A Tenor, Fallen Angels, Oedipus, Man of La Mancha (also Toronto, 1993), Black Comedy, Invisible Friends, The Royal Hunt of the Sun, Hamlet, As You Like It, 1992; La Bête, The Two of Us, She Stoops to Conquer, Saint Joan, Oliver!, Aspects of Love (also Toronto, US tour), 1993; Cyrano de Bergerac, Macbeth, Hay Fever (also Winnipeg), Caesar and Cleopatra, A Man for All Seasons, The Music Man, 1994; Richard III, The Cherry Orchard, The Beggar's Opera, The Alberta Quilt, 1995; *other productions include:* The Marriage of Figaro, 1993, Beatrice and Benedict, 1996, Canadian Opera Co., Toronto; Owen Wingrave, Glyndebourne Touring Opera, 1995; Jekyll and Hyde, NY, 1997; Don Carlos, The Misanthrope, Soulpepper Th. Co., 1998. *Films:* as actor: Decline and Fall, David Copperfield (title part), Tales from the Crypt; as director: The Wars, Miss Julie, Waiting for the Parade. *Television:* Wilfred Desert in The Forsyte Saga; Constantin in The Seagull. *Address:* Wildwood House, RR3, Lakeside, ON N0M 2G0, Canada.

PHILLIPS, Sir Robin Francis, 3rd Bt *cr* 1912; Owner and Principal, Ravenscourt Theatre School, London, since 1989; *b* 29 July 1940; *s* of Sir Lionel Francis Phillips, 2nd Bt, and Camilla Mary, *er d* of late Hugh Parker, 22 Chapel Street, Belgrave Square, SW1; *S* father, 1944. *Educ:* Aiglon Coll., Switzerland. Chief Air Traffic Control Officer, Biggin Hill, 1970–78; Hazel Malaone Management, 1978–81; Devonair Radio, 1981–83; Radio Luxembourg, 1984; Hd of Casting, Corona Stage School, 1985–89. *Heir:* none. *Address:* 12 Manson Mews, Queens Gate, SW7 5AF; Ravenscourt Theatre School, 8–30 Galena Road, Hammersmith, W6 0LT.

PHILLIPS, Prof. Robin Kenneth Stewart, FRCS, FRCSE, FRCPSGlas; Consultant Surgeon, since 1987, and Clinical Director, since 2004, St Mark's Hospital, Harrow; *b* 18 Nov. 1952; *s* of John Fleetwood Stewart Phillips and Mary Gordon Phillips (*née* Shaw); *m* 1975, Janina Fairley Nowak; one *s* one *d*. *Educ:* Sherborne Sch. for Boys; Royal Free Hosp. Med. Sch. (MB BS 1975); MS London 1984. FRCS 1979; FRCSE 2002; FRCPSGlas *ad eundem*, 2004. Higher surgical trng with St Mary's Gp of Hosps, 1980–85; St Mark's Hospital: Resident Surgical Officer, 1986; Chm., Surgery, 1993–97; Dean, Acad. Inst., 1999–2002; Sen. Lectr in Surgery, St Bartholomew's Hosp., London, 1987–90; Consultant Surgeon, Homerton Hosp., London, 1990–93; Civilian Consultant in Colorectal Surgery to the RN, 2001–. Dir, CRUK (formerly ICRF) Polyposis Registry, 1993–. President: British Colostomy Assoc., 2001–05; Sect. of Coloproctology, RSocMed, 2006–07. Prof. of Colorectal Surgery, Imperial Coll., London, 2000–. *Publications:* edited: Familial adenomatous polyposis and other polyposis syndromes, 1994; Fistula-in-ano, 1996; A Companion to Specialist Surgical Practice: colorectal surgery, 1997, 3rd edn 2005; Frontiers in Coloproctology, 2005; contrib. numerous peer-reviewed res. articles, mainly in familial adenomatous polyposis (an inherited form of bowel cancer), anal fistula and other painful conditions. *Recreations:* fly-fishing, being walked by the dog. *Address:* St Mark's Hospital, Harrow, Middx HA1 3UJ. *T:* (020) 8235 4251, *Fax:* (020) 8235 4277; *e-mail:* m.gun@imperial.ac.uk. *Club:* Royal Society of Medicine.

PHILLIPS, (Ronald) William; fruit grower, 2002–06; Director: NB Selection Ltd, 1991–2002; Norman Broadbent International, 1998–2002; *b* 21 April 1949; *s* of late Ronald Phillips and Phoebe Nora Haynes; *m* 1979, Dorothy Parsons. *Educ:* Steyning Grammar Sch.; University College of Wales, Aberystwyth (BScEcon). Joined CS, 1971; served in Dept of Transport, PSA, DoE, Develt Commn (Private Sec. to Lord Northfield); Asst County Sec., Kent CC, 1979–80; UK Expert to EC Council of Ministers Wkg Party on Environmental Impact Assessment, 1980–83; Greater London Reg. Office, DoE (Local Govt Reorganisation), 1983–86; Head of Policy Unit, 1986–87, Man. Dir, 1987–91, Westminster CC. FRSA 1990; FCMI (FBIM 1990). JP Maidstone, 1992–96. *Recreation:* travel. *Address:* Livesey Cottage, Livesey Street, Teston, Kent ME18 5AY.

PHILLIPS, Rory Andrew Livingstone; QC 2002; *b* 30 May 1961; *s* of Peter and Jean Phillips; *m* 1987, Claire Imogen Haggard; two *s* one *d*. *Educ:* Eton; King's Coll., Cambridge (MA). Called to the Bar, Inner Temple, 1984; Jun. Counsel to the Crown (A Panel), 1999–2002. *Recreations:* music, conversation. *Address:* 3 Verulam Buildings, Gray's Inn, WC1R 5NT.

PHILLIPS, Sarah; *see* Phillips, R. S.

PHILLIPS, Siân, CBE 2000; actress; *d* of D. Phillips and Sally Phillips; *m* 1st, 1954, Dr D. H. Roy (marr. diss. 1960); 2nd, 1960, Peter O'Toole, *qv* (marr. diss. 1979); two *d*; 3rd, 1979, Robin Sachs (marr. diss. 1992). *Educ:* Pontardawe Grammar Sch.; Univ. of Wales (Cardiff Coll.) (BA Hons English; Fellow, 1982); RADA (Maggie Albanesi Scholarship, 1956; Bancroft Gold Medal, 1958). BBC Radio Wales, mid 1940s–, and BBC TV Wales, early 1950s–; Newsreader and Announcer, and Mem. Rep. Co., BBC, 1953–55; toured for Welsh Arts Council with National Theatre Co., 1953–55; Arts Council Bursary to study drama outside Wales, 1955. Mem., Arts Council Drama Cttee, 1970–75. Governor: St David's Trust, 1970–73; Welsh Coll. of Music and Drama, 1992–. *Theatre:* London: Hedda Gabler, 1959; Ondine, and the Duchess of Malfi, 1960–61 (1st RSC season at Aldwych); The Lizard on the Rock, 1961; Gentle Jack, Maxibules, and The Night of the Iguana, 1964; Ride a Cock Horse, 1965; Man and Superman, and Man of Destiny, 1966; The Burglar, 1967; Epitaph for George Dillon, 1972; A Nightingale in Bloomsbury Square, 1973; The Gay Lord Quex, 1975; Spinechiller, 1978; You Never Can Tell, Lyric, Hammersmith, 1979; Pal Joey, Half Moon, 1980 and Albery, 1981; Dear Liar, Mermaid, 1982; Major Barbara, NT, 1982; Peg, Phoenix, 1984; Gigi, Lyric, Shaftesbury Ave., 1985; Thursday's Ladies, Apollo, 1987; Brel, Donmar, 1987; Paris Match, Garrick, 1989; Vanilla, Lyric, 1990; The Manchurian Candidate, Lyric, Hammersmith, and nat. tour, 1991; Painting Churches, Playhouse, 1992; The Glass Menagerie, Cambridge Theatre Co. nat. tour, 1989; Ghosts, Welsh Arts Council tour, and Sherman Theatre, Wales, 1993; The Lion in Winter, UK nat. tour, 1994; An Inspector Calls, NY, 1995; A Little Night Music, RNT, 1995; Marlene, nat. tour, 1996, Lyric, 1997, S Africa, Paris, 1998, NY, 1999; Lettice and Lovage, tour, 2001; My Old Lady, LA, 2001, NY, 2002; The Old Ladies, UK tour, 2003; The Dark, Donmar Th., 2004; The Play What I Wrote, UK tour, The Unexpected Man, UK tour, 2005; Great Expectations, RSC, 2005–06; Rockaby, Barbican and Gate, Dublin, 2006; Quartet, USA, 2006; Regrets Only, NY, 2007; Les Liaisons Dangereuses, NY, 2008; Calendar Girls, UK tour, 2008; concert tours, UK and US, 2000, UK 2001; *cabaret:* NY, 2000, RNT and tour, 2001; Divas at the Donmar, Donmar Th., 2001; UK concert tour, 2003; Both Sides Now, 2007, 2008. *TV drama series include:* Shoulder to Shoulder, 1974; How Green was my Valley, 1975; I, Claudius, 1976; Boudicca, and Off to Philadelphia in the Morning, 1977; The Oresteia of Aeschylus, 1978; Crime and Punishment, 1979; Sean O'Casey (RTE), 1980; Winston Churchill, The Wilderness Years, 1981; Language and Landscape (6 bilingual films, Welsh and English), 1985; The Snow Spider, 1988; Shadow of the Noose, 1989; Emlyn's Moon, 1990; Perfect Scoundrels, 1990; Tonight at 8.30: Hands Across the Sea; The Astonished Heart; Ways and Means, 1991; The Borrowers, 1992, 1993; The Aristocrats, 1999; Nikita, The Magician's House, 2000; The Last Detective, 2002; Midsomer Murders, 2006; Canu Grwndi, 2006; *TV films* include: A Painful Case (RTE), 1985; While Reason Sleeps; Return to Endor, 1986 (USA); Siân (biographical), 1987, 2002; Heidi, 1993; Mind to Kill (also in Welsh), 1995; Summer Silence (musical, also in Welsh), 1995. *Films* include: Becket, 1963; Goodbye Mr Chips, and Laughter in the Dark, 1968; Murphy's War, 1970; Under Milk Wood, 1971; The Clash of the Titans, 1979; Dune, 1984; Ewocks Again, and The Doctor and the Devils, 1985; Valmont, 1989; Age of Innocence, 1994; House of America, 1996; Alice Through the Looking Glass, 1999; Coming and Going, 2000; The Gigolos, 2007. Has made recordings, incl. Peg, Gigi, I remember Mama, Pal Joey, Bewitched, Bothered and Bewildered, A Little Night Music, Marlene. RTS Annual Lecture (Eng. and Welsh transmissions), 1993. FWNCMD, 1991; Fellow, Cardiff Coll., Univ. of Wales, 1983; Hon. Fellow: Polytechnic of Wales, 1988; Trinity Coll., Carms, 1998; Univ. of Wales Swansea, 1998. Hon. DLitt Wales, 1984. Critics Circle Award, New York Critics Award, and Famous 7 Critics Award, for Goodbye Mr Chips, 1969; BAFTA Award for How Green was my Valley and I, Claudius, 1978; Royal Television Soc. Award for I, Claudius (Best Performer), 1978; Lifetime Achievement Award, BAFTA Wales, 2000. Mem., Gorsedd of Bards, 1960 (for services to drama in Wales). *Publications:* Siân Phillips' Needlepoint, 1987; autobiography: Private Faces, 1999; Public Places, 2001; gen. journalism (Vogue, Cosmopolitan, Daily Mail, 3 years for Radio Times, Country Living, Options). *Recreations:* gardening, needlepoint, drawing. *Address:* c/o Dalzell Beresford, 26 Astwood Mews, SW7 4DE.

PHILLIPS, Stephen Edmund; QC 2002; barrister; a Recorder, since 2000; *b* 10 Oct. 1961; *s* of His Honour (David) Alan Phillips, *qv*; *m* 1998, Sonia (*née* Tolaney). *Educ:* King's Sch., Chester; University Coll., Oxford (MA Oxon; Martin Wronker Prize, 1983). Called to the Bar, Gray's Inn, 1984 (Birkenhead Award, 1984; Reid Scholarship; David Karmel Prize, 1985; Bencher, 2006); an Asst Recorder, 1999–2000. General commercial practice, specialising in banking, commercial contracts, civil fraud and professional negligence. *Recreations:* hill walking, football, tennis. *Address:* 3 Verulam Buildings, Gray's Inn, WC1R 5NT. *T:* (020) 7831 8441, *Fax:* (020) 7831 8479; *e-mail:* sphillips@3vb.com.

PHILLIPS, Stephen James; freelance writer, producer and broadcaster; *b* 28 May 1947; *s* of James Ronald Phillips and Diana Betty Phillips (*née* Bradshaw); *m* 1988, Simone Lila Lopez; two *d*. *Educ:* Univ. of London (ext. BA Hons Ancient Hist.); St John's Coll., Cambridge (Dip. Classical Archaeol.). Reporter and critic, Yorks Evening Post, 1965–69; critic and feature writer, Daily Express, 1969–72; Manager, Holiday Village, Thasos, Greece, 1973; BBC reporter and presenter, 1973–76; Gen. Administrator, Prospect Theatre Co., Old Vic, 1976–78; presenter, Kaleidoscope and other BBC programmes, 1978–81; Arts Corresp., ITN and Channel Four, 1982–89; Series Ed., Signals, 1989–91; exec. producer, Antelope Films, 1992–2000; Hd of Arts, 1991–95, Arts consultant, 1996–2000, Meridian Broadcasting; Culture/communications consultant: Arts Sponsorship Panel, J. Sainsbury plc, 1990–2003; RIBA, 2000–. Lectr, Dramatic Writing MA, 1997–2007, Vis. Res. Fellow, 1999–2007, Sussex Univ. Member: Arts Council of England, 1994–98 (Chm., Touring Adv. Panel, 1994–98); SE Arts Bd, 1999–2002; SE England Regl Assembly and Exec. Cttee, 2000–02; Vice Chm., SE Regl Cultural Consortium, 2000–03. Chm., Isaac Newton Arts Trust, 2002–. Board Member: Tricycle Theatre, Kilburn, 1982–2002 (Chm., 1984–94); English Nat. Ballet, 1996–2005; Chichester Fest. Theatre, 1999–2003; Chm., Arts for Everyone Lottery Panel, 1996–98. Chm., Friends of Herstmonceux Castle, 1995–2002; Trustee: Brighton's West Pier, 1997–2007; RIBA Cultural Trust, 2003– (Vice Chair, 2007–); Patron, Brighton Dome Appeal. Hon. FRIBA 2003. *Recreations:* theatre, history, Mediterranean travel, family. *Address:* 2 James Court, James Avenue, Herstmonceux, East Sussex BN27 4PA.

PHILLIPS, Timothy Dewe, CBE 2007; Chairman: All England Lawn Tennis and Croquet Club, since 2000; Committee of Management, Wimbledon Championships, since 2000; *b* 22 April 1942; *s* of late Warren Phillips and Marjorie Phillips (*née* Thornton); *m* 1969, Elizabeth Wheeldon; two *s* one *d*. *Educ:* Mill Hill Sch.; Merton Coll., Oxford (MA; Hon. Fellow 2008); Harvard Business Sch. (AMP). British Airways, 1966–2001: worked overseas in various mgt posts based in Hong Kong, Zambia, Brunei, Lebanon, The Gulf, Australia and Italy, 1969–83; Head Office, London, 1983–2001: General Manager: Africa, 1983–84; UK, 1984–86; Hd, Logistics and Dep. Ops Dir, 1986–88; Dep. Mktg Dir, 1989–91; Regl Gen. Manager, Europe, 1992–94; Hd, Regs, 1994–96; Hd, Community Relns, 1996–2001. Played in 3 of the 4 Grand Slam tennis events incl. Wimbledon; semi-finalist, Men's Doubles, US Nationals, 1964. Mem., Internat. Tennis Clubs of GB, US and Australia. *Recreations:* tennis, squash, hockey (Triple Blue at Oxford). *Address:* All England Club, Church Road, Wimbledon, SW19 5AE. *T:* (020) 8971 2223. *Clubs:* All England Lawn Tennis, Queen's; Vincent's (Oxford).

PHILLIPS, Tom, CBE 2002; RA 1989 (ARA 1984); RE 1987; RP 1999; painter, writer and composer; *b* 25 May 1937; *s* of David John Phillips and Margaret Agnes (*née* Arnold); *m* 1961, Jill Purdy (marr. diss. 1988); one *s* one *d*; *m* 1995, Fiona Maddocks, *qv*. *Educ:* St Catherine's College, Oxford (MA; Hon. Fellow, 1992); Camberwell School of Art. NDD. One man shows: AIA Galleries, 1965; Angela Flowers Gall., 1970–71; Marlborough Fine Art, 1973–75; Dante Works, Waddington Galleries, 1983; retrospective exhibitions: Gemeente Museum, The Hague, 1975; Kunsthalle, Basel, 1975; Serpentine, 1975; 50 years of Tom Phillips, Angela Flowers Gall., 1987; Mappin Art Gall., Sheffield, 1987; Nat. Gall., Jamaica, 1987; Bass Mus., Miami, 1988; Nat. Gall., Australia, 1988; City Art Inst., Sydney, 1988; Nat. Portrait Gall., 1989; N Carolina Mus., 1990; Royal Acad., 1992; V&A, 1992; Ulster Mus., 1993; Yale Center, USA, 1993; S London Art Gall., 1998; Dulwich Picture Gall., 1998; Modern Art Mus., Fort Worth, 2001; Flowers Gall., London, 2004; Flowers Gall., NY, 2005; work in collections: British

Museum, Tate Gall., V&A, Nat. Portrait Gall., Imperial War Mus., Ashmolean Mus., Oxford, Mus. Fine Arts, Budapest, MOMA NY, Philadelphia Museum, Bibliothèque Nationale, Paris, Gemeente Museum, Boymans Museum, Rotterdam, Nat. Museum, Stockholm, Nat. Gall. of Australia; designed tapestries for St Catherine's, Oxford; music: first perf. opera Irma, 1973; York, 1974; ICA, 1983; recordings incl. Irma, 1980 (new version, 1988); Intervalles/Music of Tom Phillips 1982; Six of Hearts, 1997; television: co-dir, Dante series, 1984–89 (1st prize Montreal Fest., 1990; Prix Italia, 1991); film scripts: Tom Phillips (Grierson Award, BFI, 1976; Golden Palm Award, Chicago, 1976); The Artist's Eye (TV film), 1988; Twenty Sites (TV film), 1989; designer, The Winter's Tale, Globe Theatre, 1997; designer and translator, Otello, ENO, 1998; designer, The Entertainer, Derby Playhouse, 2003. Curator: Africa: the art of a continent, RA, 1995, Berlin and NY, 1996; We Are The People, NPG, 2004. Slade Prof. of Fine Art, Univ. of Oxford, 2005–06; Visitor, IAS, Princeton, 2005–. Chairman: RA Library, 1987–95; RA Exhibns Cttee, 1995; Vice-Chm., British Copyright Council, 1984–88. Chm., Aurea Foundn, NY, 1995–98; Trustee: Ruskin House, 1996–2002; Nat. Portrait Gall., 1998–2006; BM, 1999–2007. Pres., Heatherley's Sch. of Art, 2003–. Hon. Pres., S London Artists, 1987–. Hon. Fellow, London Inst., 1999. Francis Williams Prize, V&A 1983; First Prize, Hunting Gp of Cos, 1988. *Publications*: Trailer, 1971; A Humument, 1980, 4th rev. edn 2005; illustr. trans. Dante's Inferno, 1982; Works/Texts to 1974, 1975; Heart of a Humument, 1985; The Class of Forty-Seven, 1990; Works/Texts vol. II, 1992; Humument Supplement, 1992; Plato's Symposium, 1992; (with Salman Rushdie) Merely Connect, 1994; (ed) Africa: the art of a continent, 1995; Music in Art, 1997; Aspects of Art, 1997; (illustrator) Waiting for Godot, 2000; The Postcard Century, 2000; We Are The People, 2004; Merry Meetings, 2005. *Recreations*: ping pong, cricket, postcards. *Address*: 57 Talfourd Road, SE15 5NN. *T*: (020) 7701 3978, *Fax*: (020) 7703 2800; *e-mail*: tom@tomphillips.co.uk. *Clubs*: Chelsea Arts, Groucho; Surrey County Cricket.

PHILLIPS, Tom Richard Vaughan, CMG 1998; HM Diplomatic Service; Ambassador to Israel, since 2006; *b* 21 June 1950; *s* of late Comdr Tom Vaughan Gerald Phillips, DSC, OBE, RN and of Margaret Sproull (*née* Gameson); *m* 1986, Anne de la Motte; two *s*. *Educ*: Harlow Technical Coll.; Exeter Univ.; Jesus Coll., Oxford; Wolfson Coll., Oxford (MLitt). Journalist, West Herts and Watford Observer, 1969–72; DHSS, 1977–83; FCO, 1983–85; First Sec., Harare, 1985–88; FCO, 1988–90; Dep. Head of Mission and Consul-Gen., Tel Aviv, 1990–93; Counsellor, Washington, 1993–97; Hd, Eastern Adriatic Dept, FCO, 1997–99; High Comr to Uganda, 2000–02; UK Special Rep. for Afghanistan, 2002; Dir, S Asia and Afghanistan, FCO, 2003–06. *Publication*: (as Tom Vaughan) No Second Prize, 1993. *Address*: BFPO 5404, HA4 6EP.

PHILLIPS, Trevor; *see* Phillips, M. T.

PHILLIPS, Trevor Thomas; *see* Phillips, Tom.

PHILLIPS, Vernon Francis, CPFA; FCA; Chief Executive, Bedfordshire County Council, 1989–92, retired; *b* 7 July 1930; *s* of Charles and May Phillips; *m* 1955, Valerie P. Jones; two *s* one *d*. *Educ*: Wilson Sch., Reading. CIPFA (Hons) 1954; ASAA 1958; FCA 1970. Berkshire CC, 1946–53; Swindon BC, 1953–55; Bristol City Council, 1955–58; Coventry City Council, 1958–61; Dep. Borough Treas., Luton CB, 1962–73; County Treas., Bedfordshire CC, 1973–89. Adviser to ACC, 1985–92. Member: Soc. of County Treas., 1973–; Assoc. of County Chief Execs, 1989–95; SOLACE, 1989–95. Chm., Bedford Citizens Housing Assoc., 1999–2004. Mem., Bedford Rotary Club. *Recreations*: reading, music (listening), dancing, walking, paperweights, stained glass windows, photography. *Address*: 5 Troon Close, Bedford MK41 8AY. *T*: (01234) 345628.

PHILLIPS, William; *see* Phillips, R. W.

PHILLIPS, Dr William Daniel; physicist; National Institute of Standards and Technology Fellow, since 1995; Distinguished University Professor of Physics, University of Maryland, since 2001 (Adjunct Professor, 1992–2001); *b* 5 Nov. 1948; *s* of William Cornelius Phillips and Mary Catherine Savine Phillips; *m* 1970, Jane Van Wynen; two *d*. *Educ*: Juniata Coll. (BS Physics 1970); Massachusetts Inst. of Technol. (PhD Physics 1976). Chaim Weizmann Fellow, MIT, 1976–78; physicist, Nat. Bureau of Standards, later Nat. Inst. of Standards and Technol., 1978–95. Eastman Vis. Prof., Oxford Univ., 2002–03. Fellow: Amer. Physical Soc., 1986; Optical Soc. of America, 1994 (Hon. Mem., 2004); Amer. Acad. of Arts and Scis, 1995. Member: NAS, 1997; Pontifical Acad. of Scis, 2004. Gold Medal, Dept of Commerce, 1993; Michelson Medal, Franklin Inst., 1996; Nobel Prize in Physics, 1997; Schawlow Prize, Amer. Physical Soc., 1998. *Publications*: contrib. numerous articles in Physical Rev. Letters and other professional jls, and in proc. nat. and internat. confs. *Recreations*: photography, tennis, gospel music, Bible study. *Address*: 100 Bureau Drive, Stop 8424, National Institute of Standards and Technology, Gaithersburg, MD 20899–8424, USA.

PHILLIPS GRIFFITHS, Allen; *see* Griffiths.

PHILLIPSON, Prof. David Walter, LittD; FBA 2002; FSA; Director, Cambridge University Museum of Archaeology and Anthropology, 1981–2006 and Professor of African Archaeology, University of Cambridge, 2001–06; Fellow, Gonville and Caius College, Cambridge, 1988–2006, now Emeritus; *b* 17 Oct. 1942; *s* of late Herbert Phillipson and Mildred Phillipson (*née* Atkinson); *m* 1967, Laurel Lofgren; one *s* one *d*. *Educ*: Merchant Taylors' Sch., Northwood; Gonville and Caius Coll., Cambridge (BA 1964; MA 1968); PhD 1978, LittD 2003, Cantab. Sec. and Inspector, Nat. Monuments Commn, N Rhodesia, then Zambia, 1964–73; Asst Dir, British Inst. in Eastern Africa, 1973–78; Keeper of Archaeol., Ethnography and Hist., Glasgow Mus., 1979–81; Reader in African Prehistory, Univ. of Cambridge, 1991–2001. Ed., African Archaeol Rev., 1987–94. Reckitt Archaeol Lectr, British Acad., 2000; Dist. Lectr in African Archaeol., Univ. of Florida, 2006. Hon. Vis. Prof., Addis Ababa Univ., 2006. FSA 1979 (Frend Medal, 2005). *Publications*: (ed) Mosi-oa-Tunya: a handbook to the Victoria Falls Region, 1975; Prehistory of Eastern Zambia, 1976; Later Prehistory of Eastern and Southern Africa, 1977; African Archaeology, 1985, 3rd edn 2005; The Monuments of Aksum, 1997; Ancient Ethiopia, 1998; Archaeology at Aksum, Ethiopia, 1993–97, 2000; Archaeology in Africa and in Museums, 2003; Ancient Churches of Ethiopia, 2008; numerous contribs to ed vols and learned jls. *Recreation*: bibliomania. *Address*: 11 Brooklyn Terrace, Threshfield, Skipton, N Yorks BD23 5ER. *T*: (01756) 753965. *Club*: Oxford and Cambridge.

PHILLIS, Sir Robert (Weston), Kt 2004; Chief Executive, Guardian Media Group, 1997–2006; Chairman: Guardian Newspapers Ltd, 1997–2006; Greater Manchester Newspapers Ltd, 1997–2006; Trader Media Group Ltd, 2000–06; All3Media, since 2004; *b* 3 Dec. 1945; *s* of Francis William Phillis and Gertrude Grace Phillis; *m* 1966, Jean (*née* Derham); three *s*. *Educ*: John Ruskin Grammar Sch.; Nottingham Univ. (BA Industrial Econs 1968). Apprentice, printing industry, 1961–65; Thomson Regional Newspapers Ltd, 1968–69; British Printing Corp. Ltd, 1969–71; Lectr in Industrial Relations, Edinburgh Univ. and Scottish Business Sch., 1971–75; Vis. Fellow, Univ. of Nairobi, 1974; Personnel Dir, later Man. Dir, Sun Printers Ltd, 1976–79; Managing Director: Independent Television Publications Ltd, 1979–82 (Dir, 1979–87); Central Independent

Television plc, 1981–87 (non-exec. Dir, 1987–91); Gp Man. Dir, Carlton Communications, 1987–91; Chief Exec., ITN, 1991–93; Dep. Dir-Gen., BBC, 1993–97; Man. Dir, BBC World Service, 1993–94; Chm., BBC Enterprises Ltd, 1993–94; Chm., later Chief Exec., BBC Worldwide, 1994–97. Chairman: Zenith Productions Ltd, 1984–91; GMG Endemol Entertainment, 1997–2000; GMG Radio Hldgs, 1999–2003. Director: ITN Ltd, 1982–87 and 1991–93; Worldwide Television News Corp., 1991–93; Jazz FM, 1999–2006; Radio Investments, 1999–2004; Artsworld Channels, 2000–02; Elizabeth Phillips Hughes Hall Co., 2001–; ITV plc, 2005–07. Chm., Ind. Rev. of Govt Communications, 2003–04; Mem., Ind. Rev. of Crime Statistics, 2006. Director: Periodical Publishers Assoc., 1979–82; ITCA, 1982–87; Internat. Council, Nat. Acad. of Television Arts and Scis, 1985– (Vice Chm. (Internat.), 1994–97; Life Fellow, 1997); LTA, 2005–; Vice-Pres., EBU, 1996–97. Dir and Trustee, Television Trust for the Environment, 1985–2006; Dir, Teaching Awards Trust, 2001–. Hon. Prof., Stirling Univ., 1997; City Fellow, Hughes Hall, Univ. of Cambridge, 2002–06 (MA 2006). FRSA 1984; FRTS 1988 (Chm., 1989–92; Vice Pres., 1994–2004; Pres., 2004–). Hon. Fellow: Cardiff Univ., 2004; Univ. of the Arts, London, 2006. Hon. DLitt: Salford, 1999; City, 2000; Nottingham, 2003. *Recreations*: ski-ing, golf, military and political history. *Clubs*: Garrick, Reform, Groucho.

PHILO, Gordon Charles George, CMG 1970; MC 1944; HM Diplomatic Service, retired; *b* 8 Jan. 1920; *s* of Charles Gilbert Philo and Nellie Philo (*née* Pinnock); *m* 1952, Mavis (Vicky) Ella (*d* 1986), *d* of John Ford Galsworthy and Sybel Victoria Galsworthy (*née* Strachan). *Educ*: Haberdashers' Aske's Hampstead Sch.; Wadham Coll., Oxford (Methuen Schol. in Modern History, 1938). Served War, HM Forces, 1940–46: Royal West African Frontier Force, 1942–43; Airborne Forces, Normandy and Europe, 1944–45; India 1945–46. Alexander Korda Scholar, The Sorbonne, 1948–49; Lectr in Modern History, Wadham Coll., 1949–50; Foundn Mem., St Antony's Coll., Oxford, 1950–51. Foreign Office, 1951; Russian course, Christ's Coll., Cambridge, 1952–53; Istanbul, Third Sec., 1954–57; Ankara, Second Sec., 1957–58; FO, 1958–63; Kuala Lumpur, First Sec., 1963–67; FO, 1968; Consul-Gen., Hanoi, 1968–69; FCO, 1969–78. Extended Interview Assessor, Home Office Unit, CSSB, 1978–90. Chm. Council, Kipling Soc., 1986–88, 1997–99. Kesatria Mangku Negara (Hon.), Order of Malaysia, 1968. *Publications*: (jtly with wife, as Charles Forsyte): Diplomatic Death, 1960; Diving Death, 1962; Double Death, 1965; Murder with Minarets, 1968; The Decoding of Edwin Drood, 1980; articles in various jls. *Recreations*: travel, writing. *Address*: 10 Abercorn Close, NW8 9XS. *Club*: Athenæum.

PHILP, Prof. Ian, CBE 2008; MD; FRCP, FRCPE; Hon. Consultant and Professor in Health Care for Older People, University of Sheffield, since 1994; National Director for Older People (formerly Older People's Services, then Older People's Services and Neurological Conditions), Department of Health, 2000–08; *b* 14 Nov. 1958; *s* of Thomas Philp and Nancy Philp (*née* Yule); *m* 1984, Elizabeth Anne Boyd; one *s* two *d*. *Educ*: Univ. of Edinburgh (MB ChB, MD 1990). FRCPE 1993; FRCP 1994. Trained in geriatric medicine, general medicine, rehabilitation and public health in UK and USA, 1981–90; Hon. Consultant and Sen. Lectr in Geriatric Medicine, Univ. of Southampton, 1990–94. Founder, and Mem., Core Academic Gp, Sheffield Inst. for Studies on Ageing, 1999–. Developed EASY-Care and COPE Index, instruments for assessing needs of older people and family carers, used worldwide. Team Leader, UK Hosp. Doctor Team of the Year, 1999. Co-presenter, BBC TV series, How To Live Longer. Hon. FFPH. Queen's Anniv. Prize for Higher Educn, 2002. *Publications*: (ed) Assessing Elderly People, 1994; (ed) Outcomes Assessment, 1998; (ed) Carers of Older People in Europe, 2001; numerous contribs to acad. and med. press on care of older people. *Recreations*: cinema, travelling with family. *Address*: 2nd Floor, Samuel Fox House, Northern General Hospital, Herries Road, Sheffield S5 7AU.

PHILPOT, Nicholas Anthony John; His Honour Judge Philpot; a Circuit Judge, since 1992; *b* 19 Dec. 1944; *s* of late Oliver Lawrence Spurling Philpot, MC, DFC, and Margaret Nathalie Forsyth (*née* Owen); *m* 2008, Bahia Naïdji; two *s* and one step *d*. *Educ*: Winchester Coll.; New Coll., Oxford (BA PPE 1966). VSO, Bolivia, 1966–67. Called to the Bar, Lincoln's Inn, 1970; Asst Recorder, 1987–90; Recorder, 1990–92. *Address*: c/o Inner London Crown Court, Newington Causeway, SE1 6AZ.

PHILPOTT, Hugh Stanley; HM Diplomatic Service; Deputy Head, Overseas Territories Department, Foreign and Commonwealth Office, and Deputy Commissioner, British Indian Ocean Territory, since 2005; *b* 24 Jan. 1961; *s* of Gordon Cecil Haig Philpott and Janet Philpott (*née* Guy, now Downer); *m* 1984, Janine Frederica Rule; one *d*. *Educ*: Brockenhurst Coll. Barclays Bank Internat., 1979; FCO, 1980; Oslo, 1982–84; Third Secretary: Budapest, 1985–86; Arabic lang. trng, 1987–88; Baghdad, 1988–90; Second Secretary: FCO, 1990–93; Washington, 1993–97; First Secretary: DFID, 1997–99; FCO, 1999–2001; Counsellor and Dep. Hd of Mission, Muscat, 2001–04. *Recreations*: beach hut enthusiast, computers, growing walnuts. *Address*: c/o Foreign and Commonwealth Office, King Charles Street, SW1A 2AH; Crouttes, Orne, France.

PHIPPARD, Sonia Clare; Director, Food and Farming (EU, International and Analysis) (formerly Director, Analysis and Common Agricultural Policy Strategy), Department for Environment, Food and Rural Affairs, since 2006; *b* 8 Jan. 1960; *d* of Brig. Roy Phippard and Gillian Phippard (*née* Menzies); *m* 2001, Michael Hartley. *Educ*: Wadhurst Coll.; Somerville Coll., Oxford (BA Physics 1981). Joined Civil Service Department, later Cabinet Office (MPO), 1981: on secondment to DES, 1987–89; Private Sec. to Sec. of Cabinet, 1989–92; Asst Sec., Next Steps Project Dir, 1992–94; on secondment to Coopers and Lybrand, 1995–97; Dep. Dir, 1997–99, Head, 2000–01, Central Secretariat, Cabinet Office; Dir, Sustainable Agriculture and Livestock Products, DEFRA, 2001–06. *Recreations*: amateur dramatics, food, time with friends. *Address*: Department for Environment, Food and Rural Affairs, 9 Millbank, c/o 17 Smith Square, SW1P 3JR.

PHIPPEN, (Conway) Paul; Managing Partner, 1999–2008, Head of Litigation Department, since 2008, Macfarlanes, Solicitors; *b* 30 Jan. 1957; *s* of late Rev. Charles Dennis Phippen and of Margaret Helen Phippen; *m* 1981, Jennifer Caroline Nash; two *s* one *d*. *Educ*: Kingswood Sch., Bath; Exeter Univ. (LLB). Admitted solicitor, 1982; Partner, Macfarlanes, 1989–. *Address*: Macfarlanes, 20 Cursitor Street, EC4A 1LT. *T*: (020) 7831 9222, *Fax*: (020) 7831 9607; *e-mail*: paul.phippen@macfarlanes.com.

PHIPPS, family name of **Marquess of Normanby.**

PHIPPS, Belinda Clare; Chief Executive, National Childbirth Trust, since 1999; *b* 11 April 1958; *d* of Leonie May Kerslake; partner, Nigel John Simmons; three *d*. *Educ*: The Holt Grammar Sch., Wokingham; Bath Univ. (BSc Hons Microbiol. 1980); Ashridge Management Coll. (MBA 1992). Glaxo Pharmaceuticals, 1980–90; Man. Dir, NHS Blood Transfusion Service, 1991–94; co-ordinating Wells report on London Ambulance Service, 1995; CEO, East Berks Community Trust, 1996–99. *Recreation*: ballroom dancing. *Address*: National Childbirth Trust, Alexandra House, Oldham Terrace, W3 6NH. *T*: 0870 770 3236.

PHIPPS, Colin Barry, PhD; Chairman, Desire Petroleum plc, since 1996; *b* 23 July 1934; *s* of Edgar Reeves Phipps and Winifred Elsie Phipps (*née* Carroll); *m* 1956, Marion May Phipps (*née* Lawrey); two *s* two *d*. *Educ:* Townfield Elem. Sch., Hayes, Middx; Acton County; Swansea Grammar; University Coll. London (BSc 1st cl. Hons Geol. 1955); Birmingham Univ. (PhD Geol. 1957). Royal Dutch/Shell Geologist: Holland, Venezuela, USA, 1957–64; Consultant Petroleum Geologist, 1964–79; Dep. Chm. and Chief Exec., 1979–83, Chm., 1983–95, Clyde Petroleum. Chairman: Greenwich Resources plc, 1989–2002; Recycling Services Gp Ltd, 1996–2004. Chm., Brindex (Assoc. of British Independent Oil Exploration Cos), 1983–86. MP (Lab) Dudley W, Feb. 1974–1979. Mem., Council of Europe/WEU, 1976–79. Contested: (Lab) Walthamstow E, 1969; (SDP/L Alliance) Worcester, 1983; (SDP/L Alliance) Stafford, 1987. Founder mem., SDP; Mem. SDP Nat. Cttee, 1984–89; Chm., W Midland Regional council, SDP, 1986–89. FGS 1956; FInstPet 1972; CGeol 1991; CSci 2005; Mem. Instn of Geologists, 1978. Chairman: Twentieth Century British Art Fair, 1988–93; Falklands Conservation (formerly Falkland Islands Foundn), 1990–92 (Trustee, 1983–99); English String Orch., 1990–92 (Dir, 1985–92). *Publications:* (co-ed) Energy and the Environment: democratic decision-making, 1978; What Future for the Falklands?, 1977 (Fabian tract 450); contrib.: Qly Jl Geol Sci., Geol. Mag., Geol. Jl, etc. *Recreation:* playing with my grandchildren. *Address:* Mathon Court, Mathon, Malvern WR13 5NZ. *T:* (01684) 892267. *Clubs:* Reform, Chelsea Arts; Oporto Cricket and Tennis.

PHIPPS, Maj. Gen. Jeremy Julian Joseph, CB 1997; Director: Saladin Security Ltd, since 2007; Bibury Club, Salisbury Racecourse, since 2004; *b* 30 June 1942; *s* of Lt Alan Phipps, RN (killed in action, 1943), 2nd *s* of Rt Hon. Sir Eric Phipps, GCB, GCMG, GCVO, and Hon. Veronica Phipps, 2nd *d* of 16th Lord Lovat, KT, GCVO, KCMG, CB, DSO; *m* 1974, Susan Louise, *d* of late Comdr Wilfrid and Patricia Crawford; one *s* one *d*. *Educ:* Ampleforth Coll.; RMA, Sandhurst. Commnd Queen's Own Hussars, 1962; served in Germany, Middle East, Far East; student, US Armed Forces Staff Coll., Norfolk, Va, 1980; commanded Queen's Own Hussars, 1981–83; COS, RMA, Sandhurst, 1983–85; Comdr 11th Armoured Bde, 1985–89; Dir Special Forces, 1989–93; Sen. British Loan Service Officer, Sultanate of Oman, 1993–96; retd 1997. Man. Dir, Network Internat., 1997–2000; Dir of Special Accounts, Control Risks Gp, 2000–02; Dir of Security, Jockey Club, 2002–03; Dir, Derby House Stabling, 2003–05; Dir of Global Risks, Group 4 Security, 2005–07. Order of Achievement (1st cl.), (Sultanate of Oman), 1995. *Recreations:* shooting, trout fishing, sailing, ski-ing. *Address:* Drummonds Branch, Royal Bank of Scotland, 49 Charing Cross, SW1A 2DX. *Clubs:* White's, Special Forces; Houghton.

See also Sir C. E. Maclean of Dunconnel, Bt.

PHIPPS, John Christopher; His Honour Judge Phipps; a Circuit Judge, since 1996; *b* 29 Aug. 1946; *s* of Thomas Phipps and Jane Bridget Phipps; *m* 1969, Elizabeth Bower; one *s* three *d*. *Educ:* Liskeard GS, Cornwall; Univ. of Liverpool (LLB Hons 1967). Called to the Bar, Middle Temple, 1970; practised on Northern Circuit, 1971–96; Asst Recorder, 1989–93; Recorder, 1993–96. *Recreations:* theatre, opera. *Address:* Liverpool Crown Court, Queen Elizabeth II Law Courts, Derby Square, Liverpool L2 1XA.

PHIPPS, Air Vice-Marshal Leslie William, CB 1983; AFC 1959; *b* 17 April 1930; *s* of late Frank Walter Phipps and Beatrice Kate (*née* Bearman). *Educ:* SS Philip and James Sch., Oxford. Commnd RAF, 1950; served, 1951–69: Fighter Sqdns; Stn Comdr, RAF Aqaba, Jordan; OC No 19 (F) Sqdn; Central Fighter Estab.; RN Staff Coll.; HQ 1 (British) Corps; Stn Comdr, RAF Labuan, Borneo; OC No 29 (F) Sqdn; Jt Services Staff Coll.; Dir, RAF Staff Coll., 1970–72; Comdr, Sultan of Oman's Air Force, 1973–74; RCDS, 1975; Comdr, UK Team to Kingdom of Saudi Arabia, 1976–78; Dir of Air Def. and Overseas Ops, 1978–79; Air Sec., (RAF), 1980–82; Sen. Directing Staff, RCDS, 1983; retired. BAe (Mil. Aircraft Div.), 1984–91. Service with nat. and local charities, 1991–. *Recreations:* sailing, squash, music. *Address:* 33 Knole Wood, Devenish Road, Sunningdale, Berks SL5 9QR. *Clubs:* Royal Air Force; Royal Air Force Yacht.

PHIZACKERLEY, Ven. Gerald Robert; Archdeacon of Chesterfield, 1978–96, now Emeritus; *b* 3 Oct. 1929; *s* of John Dawson and Lilian Mabel Ruthven Phizackerley; *m* 1959, Annette Catherine, *d* of Cecil Frank and Inez Florence Margaret Baker; one *s* one *d*. *Educ:* Queen Elizabeth Grammar School, Penrith; University Coll., Oxford (Open Exhibnr; MA); Wells Theological Coll. Curate of St Barnabas Church, Carlisle, 1954–57; Chaplain of Abingdon School, 1957–64; Rector of Gaywood, Bawsey and Mintlyn, Norfolk, 1964–78; Rural Dean of Lynn, 1968–78; Hon. Canon of Norwich Cathedral, 1975, of Derby Cathedral, 1978; Priest-in-charge, Ashford-in-the-Water with Sheldon, 1978–90. Fellow, Woodard Corporation, 1981. JP Norfolk, 1972. *Publication:* (ed) The Diaries of Maria Gyte of Sheldon, Derbyshire, 1913–1920, 1999. *Recreations:* books, theatre, Border collies. *Address:* Archway Cottage, Hall Road, Leamington Spa, Warwickshire CV32 5RA. *T:* (01926) 332740.

PHYSICK, John Frederick, CBE 1984; DrRCA; FSA; Deputy Director, Victoria and Albert Museum, 1983; *b* 31 Dec. 1923; *s* of Nino William Physick and Gladys (*née* Elliott); *m* 1954, Eileen Mary Walsh; two *s* one *d*. *Educ:* Battersea Grammar Sch. Home Guard, 1940–42; Royal Navy, 1942–46 (Petty Officer Airman) (volunteer, 1941). Joined Victoria and Albert Museum, as Museum Asst, Dept of Engraving, Illustration and Design, 1948; Research Asst, 1949; Sen. Research Asst, 1965; Asst Keeper, Dept of Public Relations and Educn, 1967; Keeper, Dept of Museum Services, 1975–83; Sec. to Adv. Council, 1973–83; Asst to Dir, 1974–83. Leverhulme Trust Emeritus Fellow, 1984–86. Pres., Church Monument Soc., 1984–86, 1996–2001 (Hon. Vice-Pres., 2001–); Vice-Pres., Public Monuments and Sculpture Assoc., 1999– (Mem. Adv. Cttee, 1991–98); Chm., Monuments Sub-Cttee, 1984–2001 (Mem., 1978–2001), Conservation Cttees, 1993–2001 (Mem., 1984–93), Council for Care of Churches; Member: Rochester DAC for the Care of Churches, 1964–91 (Vice-Chm., 1987–91); RIBA Drawings Cttee, 1975; Cathedrals Adv. Cttee, 1977–81; Council, British Archaeol Assoc., 1985–88; Westminster Abbey Architectural Adv. Panel, 1985–98; Rochester Cathedral Fabric Cttee, 1987– (Vice-Chm., 1992–); Jt Diocesan Archaeol Survey Cttee, 1994–2005, Jt Diocesan Books and Documents Cttee, 1994–, Canterbury and Rochester; Guildford Cath. Fabric Adv. Cttee, 1999–2004. Mem. Council, Soc. of Antiquaries, 1991–93. Trustee, London Scottish Regt, 1977–87. Mem., Cttee of Mgt, Gunnis Dictionary of British Sculptors, 1999–2007. Freeman, City of London, 1997. DLitt Lambeth, 1996. Silver Jubilee Medal, 1977. *Publications:* Catalogue of the Engravings of Eric Gill, 1963; (ed) Handbook to the Departments Prints and Drawings and Paintings, 1964; The Duke of Wellington in caricature, 1965; Designs for English Sculpture 1680–1860, 1969; The Wellington Monument, 1970; (jtly) Victorian Church Art, 1971; Five Monuments from Eastwell, 1973; (with M. D. Darby) Marble Halls, 1973; Photography and the South Kensington Museum, 1975; (with Sir Roy Strong) V&A Souvenir Guide, 1977; The Victoria and Albert Museum—the history of its building, 1982; (ed) V&A Album II, 1983; (ed) Sculpture in Britain 1530–1830, 2nd edn 1988; (contrib.) Change and Decay, the Future of our Churches, 1977; (contrib.) Westminster Abbey, 1986; (contrib.) The Royal College of Art, 1987; (introd.) Westminster Abbey: the monuments, 1989; (contrib.) Design of the Times, 1996; (contrib.) The Dictionary of Art, 1996; (contrib.) The Albert Memorial, 2000; (contrib.) Kensal Green Cemetery, 2001; (contrib.) Westminster Abbey: the Lady Chapel of Henry VII, 2003; (contrib.) Biographical Dictionary of British Sculptors 1660–1851, 2009. *Recreations:* photography, genealogy, completing the inventory of monuments, Westminster Abbey. *Address:* 49 New Road, Meopham, Kent DA13 0LS. *T:* (01474) 812301; 14 Park Street, Deal, Kent CT14 6AG. *T:* (01304) 381621.

PIACHAUD, Prof. David François James; Professor of Social Policy (formerly Social Administration), London School of Economics, since 1987; *b* 2 Oct. 1945; *s* of late Rev. Preb. François A. Piachaud and Mary R. Piachaud; *m* 1988, Louise K. Carpenter, *d* of late Rev. Dr E. F. Carpenter, KCVO; one *s* one *d*. *Educ:* Westminster Sch.; Christ Church, Oxford (MA); Univ. of Michigan (MPA). Economic Asst, DHSS, 1968–70; Lectr, 1970–83, Reader, 1983–87, LSE. Policy Advr, Prime Minister's Policy Unit, 1974–79. Mem., Commn on Life Chances and Child Poverty, Fabian Soc., 2004–06. *Publications:* The Causes of Poverty (jtly), 1978; The Cost of a Child, 1979; (jtly) Child Support in the European Community, 1980; The Distribution and Redistribution of Incomes, 1982; (jtly) The Fields and Methods of Social Planning, 1984; (jtly) The Goals of Social Policy, 1989; (jtly) The Price of Food, 1997; (jtly) Understanding Social Exclusion, 2002; (jtly) Making Social Policy Work, 2007; contribs to learned jls and periodicals. *Recreations:* gardening, carpentry, travelling. *Address:* London School of Economics, Houghton Street, WC2A 2AE. *T:* (020) 7405 7686.

PIANO, Renzo; architect; *b* 14 Sept. 1937; *m* 1st, 1962, Magda Ardnino; two *s* one *d*; 2nd, Milly Rossato. *Educ:* Milan Poly. Sch. of Architecture. Works include: Pompidou Centre, Paris (with Sir Richard Rogers), and IRCAM, 1977; Schlumberger research labs, Paris, 1984; Menil Collection Mus., Houston, 1986; S Nicola Football Stadium, Bari, Italy, 1990; Kansai Internat. Airport, Osaka, 1994; Concert Hall, hotel and shopping mall, Lingotto, Turin, 1994–96; Contemp. Art Mus. and Congress Centre, Lyon, 1996; Mus. of Sci. and Technol., Amsterdam, and Beyeler Foundn Mus., Basle, 1997; Daimler Benz projects for redevelopment of Potsdamer Platz, Berlin, 1997–98; KPN Telecom office tower, Rotterdam, 2000; Aurora Place high rise office block, Sydney, 2000; numerous exhibitions worldwide. Hon. FAIA, 1981; Hon. FRIBA, 1985; Hon. Fellow: Amer. Acad. of Arts and Scis, 1993; Amer. Acad. of Arts and Letters, 1994. RIBA Gold Medal, 1989; Kyoto Prize, Inamori Foundn, 1990; Erasmus Prize, Amsterdam, 1995; Pritzker Architect Prize, USA, 1998. Cavaliere di Gran Croce (Italy), 1989; Officier, Ordre Nat. du Mérite (France), 1994; Officier, Légion d'Honneur (France), 2000. *Publications:* (jtly) Antico é bello, il recupero della città, 1980; Chantier ouvert au public, 1985; Progetti e Architetture 1984–1986, 1986; Renzo Piano, 1987; (with R. Rogers) Du Plateau Beaubourg au Centre G. Pompidou, 1987; (jtly) Le Isole del tesoro, 1989; Renzo Piano Building Workshop 1964–1988, 1989; Renzo Piano Building and Projects 1971–1989, 1989; Renzo Piano Building Workshop 1964–1991: in search of a balance, 1992; The Making of Kansai International Airport Terminal, 1994; Giornale di Bordo, 1997; Fondation Beyeler: une maison de l'art, 1998. *Address:* Via Rubens 29, 16158 Genoa, Italy; 34 rue des Archives, 75004 Paris, France.

PIATKUS, Judy; Managing Director and Publisher, Piatkus Books, 1979–2007; *b* 16 Oct. 1949; *d* of Ralph and Estelle Assersohn; *m* 1st, 1971, Brian Piatkus; one *s* two *d*; 2nd, 1990, Cyril Ashberg. *Educ:* S Hampstead High Sch. for Girls. Dip. Psychodynamic Psychotherapy 2001. *Publications:* (as Judy Ashberg): Little Book of Women's Wisdom, 2001; Lovers' Wisdom, 2004. *Recreations:* reading, cooking, travelling, working as a counsellor. *Web:* www.judypiatkus.com.

PICARDA, Hubert Alistair Paul; QC 1992; *b* 4 March 1936; *s* of late Pierre Adrien Picarda, Docteur en Droit (Paris), Avocat à la Cour d'Appel de Paris, Barrister, Middle Temple, and Winifred Laura (*née* Kemp); *m* 1976, Ann Hulse (marr. diss. 1995); one *s* one *d*; *m* 2000, Sarah Elizabeth, *d* of His Honour Judge William Alan Belcher Goss. *Educ:* Westminster Sch.; Magdalen Coll., Oxford (Open Exhibnr in Classics; BA Jurisprudence 1961; MA; BCL 1963); University Coll. London (Bunnell Lewis Prize for Latin Verse, 1962). Called to the Bar, Inner Temple, 1962, *ad eundem* Lincoln's Inn and Gray's Inn, 1965; in practice at Chancery Bar, 1964–; Night Lawyer, Daily Express, 1964–72; Lectr, Holborn Coll. Law, Langs and Commerce, 1965–68. Visiting Lecturer: Malaysian Bar Council, 1994, 1995, 1996; Law Soc. of Singapore, 1994, 1996; Hong Kong, 1994; Sarawak, 1995; Singapore Legal Acad., 1999; Cayman Islands Law Sch., 2003; WA Lee Equity Lectr, Brisbane, 2001; Max Planck Inst., Heidelberg Univ., 2006. Mem., Senate and Bar Council, 1978–81. Pres., Charity Law Assoc., 1992–2005; Mem., Trust Law Cttee, 1995–. Pres., Inst. Conveyancers, 2000. Pres., Hardwicke Soc., 1968–72; Member: Classical Assoc.; Horatian Soc.; London Roman Law Gp. Managing Editor: Charity Law and Practice Rev., 1992–2004; Receivers, Administrators and Liquidators Qly, 1994–99 (Consulting Editor, 1999–); Member, Editorial Board: Butterworths Jl of Internat. Banking and Financial Law, 1995–; Trust Law Internat., 1992–. *Publications:* Study Guide to Law of Evidence, 1965; Law and Practice Relating to Charities, 1977, 3rd edn 1999; Law Relating to Receivers, Managers and Administrators, 1984, 4th edn 2006; (ed) Receivers, in Halsbury's Laws of England, 4th edn, reissue, 1998; (ed) Charities, in Halsbury's Laws of England, 4th edn, reissue, 2001; (contrib.) Dictionary of British Classicists, 2004; contrib. legal periodicals and The Spectator. *Recreations:* Spain in World War II, Andalusian baroque churches, Latin, music, conversation. *Address:* Top Floor, 9 Old Square, Lincoln's Inn, WC2A 3SR. *T:* (020) 7242 3566; *e-mail:* hpicarda@aol.com. *Clubs:* White's, Turf, Pratt's, Beefsteak.

PICCARD, Dr Jacques; scientist; President, Foundation for the Study and Preservation of Seas and Lakes; *b* Belgium, 1922; Swiss Citizen; *s* of late Prof. Auguste Piccard (explorer of the stratosphere, in lighter-than-air craft, and of the ocean depths, in vehicles of his own design); *m* 1953, Marie Claude (*née* Maillard); two *s* one *d*. *Educ:* Brussels; Switzerland. Grad., Univ. of Geneva, 1946; Dip. from Grad. Inst. of Internat. Studies. Asst Prof., Univ. of Geneva, 1946–48. With his father, he participated in design and operation of the first deep diving vessels, which they named the bathyscaph (deep ship); this vessel, like its successor, operated independently of a mother ship; they first constructed the FNRS-2 (later turned over to the French Navy) then the Trieste (ultimately purchased by US Navy); Dr J. Piccard piloted the Trieste on 65 successive dives (the last, 23 Jan. 1960, was the record-breaking descent to 35,800 feet in the Marianas Trench, off Guam in the Pacific Ocean). He built in 1963, the mesoscaph Auguste Piccard, the first civilian submarine, which made, in 1964–65, over 1,100 dives carrying 33,000 people into the depths of Lake Geneva; built (with Grumman) 2nd mesoscaph, Ben Franklin, and in 1969 made 1.500 miles/30 days drift dive in Gulf Stream. Founded: Fondation pour l'Etude et la Protection de la Mer et des Lacs, 1966 (built research submersible, F. A.-FOREL, 1978); Institut International d'Ecologie, 1972. Hon. doctorate in Science, Amer. Internat. Coll., Springfield, Mass, 1962; Hon. DSc Hofstra Univ., 1970. Holds Distinguished Public Service Award, etc. *Publications:* The Sun beneath the Sea, 1971; technical papers and a popularized account (trans. many langs) of the Trieste, Seven Miles Down (with Robert S. Dietz). *Address:* (office) Fondation pour l'Etude et la Protection de la Mer et des Lacs, 1096 Cully, Switzerland. *T:* (21) 7992565.

PICK, Hella Henrietta, CBE 2000; writer and journalist; Consultant and Ameurus Conference Organiser, Weidenfeld Institute for Strategic Dialogue, since 1997; *b* 24 April 1929; *d* of Ernst Pick and Johanna Marie Pick (*née* Spitz). *Educ:* Fairfield PNEU Sch., Ambleside; London Sch. of Econs (BSc Econ). Commercial Ed., West Africa mag., 1958–60; The Guardian: UN Corresp., 1960–67; Europe Corresp., 1967–72; Washington Corresp., 1972–75; East-West Affairs Corresp., 1975–82; Diplomatic Ed., 1983–94; Associate Foreign Affairs Ed., 1994–96. Goldenes Ehrenzeichen (Austria), 1980; Grosses Verdienstkreuz (Germany), 2002. *Publications:* Simon Wiesenthal: a life in search of justice, 1996, 2nd edn 2000; Guilty Victim: Austria from the Holocaust to Haider, 2000. *Recreations:* walking, swimming, travel, opera. *Address:* Flat 11, 115 Haverstock Hill, NW3 4RY. *T:* (020) 7586 3072; *e-mail:* hpick@aol.com. *Clubs:* University Women's, PEN (also Austria).

PICK, Prof. Otto, CMG 2002; Ambassador at Large, Czech Ministry of Foreign Affairs, since 2000; *b* 4 March 1925; *m* 1948, Zdenka Hajek; one *s* two *d*. *Educ:* Prague English Grammar Sch.; Appleby Grammar Sch.; Faculty of Laws, Charles Univ., Prague (grad. 1948); Queen's Coll., Oxford (BA 1950). Military service, UK, 1943–45. BBC, 1950–58; Rockefeller Res. Student, LSE, 1958–61; Ext. Dir, Council of African-British Relns, 1963–66; Dir, Atlantic Inf. Centre for Teachers, 1966–76; University of Surrey: Prof. of Internat. Relns, 1973–83, now Prof. Emeritus; Dean, Human Studies, 1976–79; Pro-Vice-Chancellor, 1981–83; Dir, Czechoslovak Service Radio Free Europe, 1983–85; Prof., Munich Univ., and Professorial Lectr, Johns Hopkins Bologna, 1986–91; Prof. of Political Sci., Charles Univ., Prague, 1991–2000; Dir, Inst. of Internat. Relns, Prague, 1993–98; Dep. Minister of Foreign Affairs, Czech Republic, 1998–2000. Co-chair, Czech-German Co-ordination Council, 2000–04. Chm. Council, Diplomatic Acad., Prague, 2007–. DUniv Surrey, 2003. Grand Cross of Merit (Germany), 2002. *Publications:* (with J. Critchley) Collective Security, 1974; (ed with H. Maull) The Gulf War, 1989; (ed) The Cold War Legacy in Europe, 1991; numerous contribs to edited collections and articles in relevant jls in UK, US, Germany, Italy, etc. *Recreations:* gardening, walking, theatre, especially opera. *Address:* Laz 228, 26241 Bohutin, Czech Republic; 1 Whitegate Gardens, Harrow Weald, Middx HA3 6BW.

PICKARD, David Keith; General Director, Glyndebourne, since 2001; *b* 8 April 1960; *s* of Roger Willows Pickard and June Mary Pickard; *m* 1991, Annette Elizabeth Finney; two *s*. *Educ:* King's Sch., Ely (Choir Sch.); St Albans Sch.; Corpus Christi Coll., Cambridge (Choral Schol.; MA Music). Co. Manager, Royal Opera, 1984–87; Administrator, New Shakespeare Co., 1987–89; Man. Dir, Kent Opera, 1989–90; Asst Dir, Japan Fest. 1991, 1990–92; Artistic Administrator, Eur. Arts Fest., 1992–93; Chief Exec., Orch. of Age of Enlightenment, 1993–2001. Trustee, Shakespeare Globe Trust, 2005–. *Recreations:* playing piano duets, cooking. *Address:* c/o Glyndebourne, Lewes, E Sussex BN8 5UU. *T:* (01273) 812321, *Fax:* (01273) 812783; *e-mail:* david.pickard@glyndebourne.com.

PICKARD, John Anthony, (Tony); professional tennis coach; *b* 13 Sept. 1934; *s* of John William Pickard and Harriet Haywood Pickard; *m* 1958, Janet Sisson; one *s* twin *d*. *Educ:* Ripley Sch.; Diocesan Sch., Derby; Derby Tech. Coll. Worked under Harry Hopman, Australia (LTA), 1953–54; Sherwood Foresters, 1954–56; Mem., British Davis Cup team, 1958–63; Dir, Chellaston Brick Co., Derby, 1965; Dir, 1967, Man. Dir, 1971, F. Sisson & Sons and subsidiaries, Langley Mill; Captain, under-21 tennis team, winning Galea Cup, 1972; non-playing Captain, British Davis Cup team, 1973–76, 1991–94. Professional tennis coach to Stefan Edberg, 1985–94, to Greg Rusedski, 1997–98. GB Coach of the Year, 1988. *Recreations:* golf, walking, cars, spending time at home, football. *Clubs:* All England Lawn Tennis; International Tennis Clubs of GB, America, Germany, Sweden; Ripley Tennis; Lindrick Golf.

PICKARD, Prof. John Douglas, FRCS, FRCSE, FMedSci; Professor of Neurosurgery, University of Cambridge, since 1991; Consultant Neurosurgeon, Addenbrooke's Hospital, Cambridge, since 1991; Chairman, Wolfson Brain Imaging Centre, since 1995; Professorial Fellow, St Catharine's College, Cambridge, since 1991; *b* 21 March 1946; *s* of late Reginald James Pickard and Eileen Muriel Pickard (*née* Alexander); *m* 1971, Charlotte Mary, *d* of late Robert Stuart Townshend and Maureen Charlotte Townshend (*née* Moran); one *s* two *d* (and one *s* decd). *Educ:* King George V Grammar Sch., Southport; St Catharine's Coll., Cambridge (BA 1st Class 1967; MA); King's Coll. Hosp. Med. Sch., London (MB BChir 1970; MChir 1981 (distinction)). KCH, 1970–72; Inst. of Neurol Sci., Glasgow, 1972–73; Falkirk Hosp., 1973–74; Univ. of Pennsylvania Hosp., 1974–75; Registrar, Sen. Registrar, Lectr in Neurosurgery, Inst. of Neurol Sci., Glasgow, 1976–79; Consultant Neurosurgeon, Wessex Neurol Centre, Southampton, 1979–91; Sen. Lectr, 1979, Reader, 1984, Prof. of Clin. Neurol Scis, 1987–91, Univ. of Southampton. Pres., Soc. of British Neurological Surgeons, 2006–08. Founder Trustee, Brain and Spine Foundn. Founder FMedSci 1998. *Publications:* numerous articles in med. and sci. jls. *Recreation:* family life. *Address:* Academic Neurosurgical Unit, Addenbrooke's Hospital, Cambridge CB2 2QQ. *T:* (01223) 336946. *Club:* Athenæum.

PICKARD, Sir (John) Michael, Kt 1997; FCA; Chairman: National House-Building Council, 1998–2002; London Docklands Development Corporation, 1992–98 (Deputy Chairman, 1991–92); Deputy Chairman, Epsom Downs Racecourses Ltd, 2003–06; *b* 29 July 1932; *s* of John Stanley Pickard and Winifred Joan Pickard; *m* 1959, Penelope Jane (*née* Catterall); three *s* one *d*. *Educ:* Oundle School. Finance Dir, British Printing Corp., 1965–68; Man. Dir, Trust Houses Ltd/Trusthouse Forte Ltd, 1968–71; Founder Chm., Happy Eater Ltd, 1972–86; Dep. Chief Exec., 1986–88, Chief Exec., 1988–92, Sears plc; Chairman: Grattan plc, 1978–84; Courage Ltd and Imperial Brewing & Leisure Ltd, 1981–86; Dep. Chief Exec., Imperial Gp plc, 1985–86; Chm., Freemans, 1988–92. Director: Brown Shipley Hlgs, 1986–93; Electra Investment Trust plc, 1989–2002; Nationwide Building Soc., 1991–94; Pinnacle Leisure Gp Ltd (formerly Wates Leisure), 1992–99; London First, 1992–2002 (Dep. Chm., 1998–2002); Bentalls plc, 1993–2001; Racecourse Leisure Corp., 1993–96; United Racecourses (Holdings) Ltd, 1995–2003; Chairman: Bullough plc, 1996–2002; Servus (formerly Opus) Hldgs, 1997–2001; London First Centre, 1998–2001; The Housing Forum, 1999–2002; Freeport, 2001–03. Chairman: Council, Roedean Sch., 1980–91; Govs, Oundle Sch., 2004–07 (Gov., 1988–2000). Member: Bd, BTA, 1968–71; Cttee, AA, 1994–99. Mem., Court of Assistants, Co. of Grocers, 1990– (Master, 1996). Hon. LLD E London, 1997. *Recreations:* cricket, golf. *Clubs:* Boodle's, Pilgrims, MCC; Walton Heath Golf; Headley Cricket.

PICKARD, Nigel; Director of Family Entertainment (formerly Family & Children's Programming), RDF Television, since 2006; *m*; three *c*. Film ed., floor manager, trainee dir, then Asst Dir, Southern TV, 1972–82; TVS: Sen. Dir, 1982–85, Exec. Prod., 1985–86, Children's Dept; Controller, Children's and Family Programming, 1986–92; Controller of Entertainment and Drama Features, Scottish TV, 1992–93; Dir of Progs, 1993–96, Gen. Manager, 1996–97, Family Channel; Vice-Pres. of Prodn, and Gen. Manager, Challenge TV, Flextech TV, 1997–98; Controller: Children's and Youth Progs, ITV Network Ltd, 1998–2000; Children's Progs, BBC, 2000–02; Dir of Progs, ITV, 2003–06. Mem., Children's and Animation Cttee, Producers Alliance for Cinema and TV, 2006–. *Address:* RDF Media, Gloucester Building, Kensington Village, Avonmore Road, W14 8RF.

PICKARD, Tony; *see* Pickard, J. A.

PICKEN, Simon Derek; QC 2006; a Recorder, since 2005; *b* 23 April 1966; *s* of Keith and Ann Picken; *m* 1992, Sophie Victoria Seddon; one *s* three *d*. *Educ:* Cardiff High Sch.; University Coll., Cardiff (LLB Hons 1987); Magdalene Coll., Cambridge (LLM 1988). Called to the Bar, Middle Temple, 1989; in practice as a barrister, 1989–, specialising in commercial law. *Publication:* Good Faith and Insurance Contracts, 2nd edn 2004. *Recreations:* Rugby Union, Italy, fine wine. *Address:* 7 King's Bench Walk, EC4Y 7DS; 115 St James's Drive, SW17 7RP; Boccali, Pian de Marte, Umbria, Italy.

PICKERING, Prof. Alan Durward, PhD, DSc; CBiol, FIBiol; Director, CEH Windermere (formerly Institute of Freshwater Ecology), 1995–2001 (acting Director, 1993–95); *b* 7 Sept. 1944; *s* of Frank Hadfield Pickering and Olive Pickering (*née* Page); *m* 1969, Christine Mary Pott; two *s* one *d*. *Educ:* Ecclesfield Grammar Sch.; Univ. of Nottingham (BSc 1st cl. Zoology 1966; PhD 1970; DSc 1986). CBiol, FIBiol 1995. Res. Physiologist, Freshwater Biological Assoc., 1969–89; Head, Windermere Lab., 1989–93. Associate Prof., Dept of Biology and Biochemistry, Brunel Univ., 1991–2002. *Publications:* (ed) Stress and Fish, 1981; numerous articles in scientific jls. *Recreations:* gardening, woodwork, golf, sailing, travel.

PICKERING, Alan Michael, CBE 2004; Senior Consultant (formerly Partner), Watson Wyatt, since 1992; *b* 4 Dec. 1948; *s* of Frank and Betty Pickering; *m* 1982, Christine Tull. *Educ:* Exhall Grange Sch., Coventry; Univ. of Newcastle upon Tyne (BA Hons Politics and Social Admin). APMI 1981. With BR, 1967–69; Hd, Membership Services Dept, EETPU, 1972–92. Member: Occupational Pensions Bd, 1992–97; Bd, Pensions Regulator, 2005–; Chairman: Nat. Assoc. of Pension Funds, 1999–2001; Plumbing Ind. Pension Scheme, 2001–; Eur. Fedn of Retirement Provision, 2001–04. Trustee, Pre-Retirement Assoc., 2005–; Chm., Life Acad., 2006–. Pres., Blackheath Harriers, 1992. *Publication:* A Simpler Way to Better Pensions, 2002. *Recreations:* running, gardening, horse racing, travel. *Address:* c/o Watson Wyatt Ltd, 21 Tothill Street, SW1H 9LL. *T:* (020) 7227 2132, *Fax:* (020) 7222 9182. *Club:* Blackheath and Bromley Harriers Athletic.

PICKERING, Prof. Brian Thomas; Deputy Vice-Chancellor, University of Bristol, 1992–2001, now Emeritus Professor (Hon. Fellow, 2002); *b* 24 May 1936; *s* of Thomas Pickering and Dorothy May Pickering; *m* 1965, Joan Perry (*d* 2005); two *d*. *Educ:* Haberdashers' Aske's Hatcham Boys' Sch.; Univ. of Bristol (BSc 1958; PhD 1961; DSc 1974). Research Biochemist, Hormone Res. Lab., Univ. of California, 1961–62; Scientific Staff, NIMR, MRC, 1963–65; University of Bristol: Lectr in Biochem. and Pharmacol., 1965–70 (Mem., MRC Gp for Res. in Neurosecretion); Lectr in Anatomy and Biochem., 1970–72; Reader in Anatomy and Biochem., 1972–78; Prof. of Anatomy and Head of Dept, 1978–92; Dean, Faculty of Medicine, 1985–87. Vis. Prof., Univ. of Geneva, 1977; Anatomical Soc. Review Lectr, 1984. Mem., Bristol & Weston HA, 1988–90; non-exec. Dir, United Bristol Healthcare NHS Trust, 1990–98. Mem., Animal Grants Bd, AFRC, 1988–94 (Chm., 1991–94). Associate Editor, Jl of Endocrinology, 1972–77. European Society for Comparative Endocrinology: Sec. and Treasurer, 1971–77; Vice-Pres., 1986–90; Pres., 1990–94; Sec., British Neuroendocrine Gp, 1986–92; mem., other learned bodies. Hon. Fellow, Romanian Acad. of Med. Sci., 1991. Hon. MD Carol Davila, Bucharest, 1994; Hon. LLD Bristol, 2001. Medal, Soc. for Endocrinology, 1977. *Publications:* contribs to professional jls. *Address:* 51 Eastfield Road, Bristol BS9 4AE.

PICKERING, Errol Neil, PhD; Director General, International Hospital Federation, 1987–98; *b* 5 May 1938; *s* of Russell Gordon and Sylvia Mary Pickering. *Educ:* York Univ., Canada (BA Hons); Univ. of Toronto (DipHA); Univ. of New South Wales (PhD). Asst Administrator, St Michael's Hosp., Toronto, 1971–73; Executive Director: Aust. Council on Hosp. Standards, 1973–80; Aust. Hosp. Assoc., 1980–87. Dir, Health Care Risk Solutions Ltd, 1994–98. Pres., UNICEF Australia, 1984–86. Vice Pres., RSPCA, Gold Coast, 2006–. Chm., Internat. Assoc. Forum, 1990–92. Bd Mem., European Soc. of Assoc. Execs, 1995–98. *Publications:* many articles on hosp. and health policy issues. *Recreations:* classical music, bridge. *Address:* 13 Firestone Court, Robina Woods, Qld 4226, Australia.

PICKERING, Ven. Fred; Archdeacon of Hampstead, 1974–84, Archdeacon Emeritus, since 1984; *b* 18 Nov. 1919; *s* of Arthur and Elizabeth Pickering; *m* 1948, Mabel Constance Threlfall; one *s* one *d*. *Educ:* Preston Grammar Sch.; St Peter's Coll., Oxford; St Aidan's Theol Coll., Birkenhead. BA 1941 (PPE), MA 1945. Curate: St Andrew's, Leyland, 1943–46; St Mary's, Islington, 1946–48; Organising Sec. for Church Pastoral Aid Soc. in NE England, 1948–51; Vicar: All Saints, Burton-on-Trent, 1951–56; St John's, Carlisle, 1956–63; St Cuthbert's, Wood Green, 1963–74; Rural Dean of East Haringey, 1968–73; Exam. Chaplain to Bp of Edmonton, 1973–84. *Address:* Flat 8, Fosbrooke House, Clifton Drive, Lytham St Annes, Lancs FY8 5RQ. *T:* (01253) 667018.

PICKERING, Janet Dolton; Headmistress, Withington Girls' School, since 2000; *b* 21 June 1949; *d* of George Browning and Marjorie Dolton Haywood; *m* 1971, William Ronald Pickering; two *s*. *Educ:* Bridlington High Sch.; Malton Grammar Sch.; Univ. of Sheffield (BSc 1st Cl. Biochem.). SRC res. student, Univ. of Sheffield, 1970–73; Scientific Officer, Hallamshire Hosp. Med. Sch., 1973–75; Teaching Fellow, Univ. of Leeds, 1975–79; freelance proof-reader, editor, indexer (sch. sci. texts and scientific jls), 1980–88; part-time teacher and tutor, Gordonstoun Sch., 1983–85; King's School, Canterbury, 1986–97: teacher, tutor, housemistress, 1990–94; Dep. Hd, 1994–97; Hd, St Bees Sch., Cumbria, 1998–2000. HMC/ISI Inspector, 1994–. Chm., Sen. Mistresses Gp, 1995–96, Mem., Inspections Cttee, 2004–, GSA; Co-Chm., Sports Sub-Cttee, GSA/HMC, 2004–. Governor: Copthorne Prep. Sch., 1995–97; Windlesham House Sch., 1996–98; Branwood Prep. Sch., 2001–; Colfe's Sch., 2005–; Chetham's Sch. of Music, 2005–; Bury Grammar Schs, 2008–. *Publications:* (jtly) Nucleic Acid Biochemistry, 1982; (contrib.) Children's Britannica, 4th edn 1988; contrib. articles to Jl Gen. Micro., Inserm, Hum. Hered. *Recreations:* reading, theatre, cinema, natural history, travel, running. *Address:* 119 Dane Road, Sale, Cheshire M33 2BY. *T:* (0161) 962 0764. *Club:* University Women's.

PICKERING, Prof. John Frederick; business management and economic consultant; Professor of Business Strategy, Bath University, 1997–2000; *b* 26 Dec. 1939; *er s* of William Frederick and Jean Mary Pickering; *m* 1967, Jane Rosamund Day; two *d*. *Educ:* Slough Grammar Sch.; University Coll. London (BSc Econ; PhD; DSc Econ); MSc Manchester. In indust. market res., 1961–62; Lectr, Univ. of Durham, 1964–66, Univ. of Sussex, 1966–73; Sen. Directing Staff, Admin. Staff Coll., Henley, 1974–75; UMIST: Prof. of Industrial Economics, 1975–88; Vice-Principal, 1983–85; Dep. Principal, 1984–85; Dean, 1985–87; Vice-Pres. (Business and Finance), 1988–90, actg Pres., 1990–91, Dep. Pres., 1991–92, Portsmouth Poly.; Dep. Vice Chancellor, Portsmouth Univ., 1992–94. Visiting Professor: Durham Univ. Business Sch., 1995–98; Sch. of Mgt, Univ. of Southampton, 2001–04. Mem., UGC Business and Management Studies sub-cttee, 1985–88. Dir, Staniland Hall Ltd, 1988–94; Dir and Chm., Univ. of Portsmouth (formerly Portsmouth Polytechnic) Enterprise Ltd, 1989–94. Consultant, NIESR, 1994–97. Mem., Gen. Synod of Church of England, 1980–90; Church Comr for England, 1983–90; Mem., Archbishop's Commn on Urban Priority Areas, 1983–85; Pres., BCMS-Crosslink (formerly BCMS), 1986–92. Member: Council of Management, Consumers' Assoc., 1969–73, 1980–83; Retail Prices Index Adv. Cttee, 1974–95; Monopolies and Mergers Commn, 1990–99; Competition Appeal Tribunal (formerly Appeals Panel, Competition Commn), 2000–; Strategic Adv. Bd for Intellectual Property Policy, 2008–. Chm. Trustees, Vocational Training Charitable Trust, 2004–06 (Trustee, 2004–06). *Publications:* Resale Price Maintenance in Practice, 1966; (jtly) The Small Firm in the Hotel and Catering Industry, 1971; Industrial Structure and Market Conduct, 1974; The Acquisition of Consumer Durables, 1977; (jtly) The Economic Management of the Firm, 1984; papers and articles in learned jls in economics and management. *Recreations:* music, cricket, theatre. *Address:* 1 The Fairway, Rowlands Castle, Hants PO9 6AQ. *T:* (023) 9241 2007, *Fax:* (023) 9241 3385. *Club:* Royal Commonwealth Society.

PICKERING, His Honour Richard Edward Ingram; a Circuit Judge, 1981–98; *b* 16 Aug. 1929; *s* of late Richard and Dorothy Pickering; *m* 1962, Jean Margaret Eley; two *s*. *Educ:* Birkenhead Sch.; Magdalene Coll., Cambridge (MA). Called to the Bar, Lincoln's Inn, 1953; has practised on Northern Circuit, 1955–81 (Junior, 1960–61); a Recorder of the Crown Court, 1977–81. Admitted as advocate in Manx Courts (Summerland Fire Inquiry), 1973–74. Councillor, Hoylake UDC, 1961–64; Legal Chm., Min. of Pensions and Nat. Insurance Tribunal, Liverpool, 1967–77; pt-time Chm., Liverpool Industrial Tribunal, 1977–79; Nominated Judge, NW Reg. (formerly Judicial Mem., Merseyside), Mental Health Rev. Tribunal, 1984–2001 (Legal Mem., 1967–79; Regional Chm., 1979–81); Northern Circuit Rep., Cttee, Council of Circuit Judges, 1984–89. Pres., League of Friends, Clatterbridge Hosp., 2001–. *Recreations:* walking, bowls, gardening, study of military history. *Address:* Trelyon, Croft Drive, Caldy, Wirral CH48 2JN. *Clubs:* Athenæum (Liverpool); Union (Cambridge).

PICKERING, Robert Mark; Chief Executive, Cazenove Group Ltd and JPMorgan Cazenove, 2005–08; *b* 30 Nov. 1959; *s* of Richard Pickering and Lorna Pickering (*née* Browne); *m* 1st, 1983, Harriet Jump (marr. diss. 2005); two *s* one *d*; 2nd, 2006, Miho Umino. *Educ:* Westminster Sch.; Lincoln Coll., Oxford (MA Law). Admitted solicitor, 1982; Solicitor: Allen & Overy, 1982–85; Cazenove & Co., 1985–2001 (Partner, 1993); Cazenove Gp plc, 2001–05 (Chief Exec., 2002–05). *Recreations:* fishing, drinking wine, art. *Clubs:* Flyfishers'; Vincent's (Oxford); Links (New York).

PICKERING, Thomas Reeve; Vice Chairman, Hills & Company, since 2006; Co-Chairman, International Crisis Group, since 2006; *b* Orange, NJ, 5 Nov. 1931; *s* of Hamilton R. Pickering and Sarah C. (*née* Chasteney); *m* 1955, Alice J. Stover; one *s* one *d*. *Educ:* Bowdoin Coll. (AB); Fletcher Sch. of Law and Diplomacy (MA); Univ. of Melbourne (MA). Served to Lt-Comdr, USNR, 1956–59. Joined US For. Service, 1959; For. Affairs Officer, Arms Control and Disarmament Agency, 1961; Political Advr, US Delegn to 18 Nation Disarmament Conf., Geneva, 1962–64; Consul, Zanzibar, 1965–67; Counselor, Dep. Chief of Mission, Amer. Embassy, Dar-es-Salaam, 1967–69; Dep. Dir Bureau, Politico-Mil. Affairs, State Dept, 1969–73; Special Asst to Sec. of State and Exec. Sec., Dept of State, 1973–74; Amb. to Jordan, 1974–78; Asst Sec. for Bureau of Oceans, Internat. Environmental and Sci. Affairs, Washington, 1978–81; Ambassador: to Nigeria, 1981–83; to El Salvador, 1983–85; to Israel, 1986–88; Ambassador and US Perm. Rep. to UN, 1989–92; Ambassador: to India, 1992–93; to Russia, 1993–96; Under Sec. for Political Affairs, US Dept of State, 1997–2000. Sen. Vice Pres., Internat. Relations, Boeing Co., 2001–06. Mem. Council, For. Relns, IISS, 1973–. Phi Beta Kappa. Hon. LLD: Bowdoin Coll., 1984; Atlantic Union Coll., 1990; Tufts Univ., 1990; Hebrew Union Coll., 1991; Willamette Univ., 1991; Drew Univ., 1991; Franklin Pierce Coll., 1991; Hofstra, 1992; Lafayette Coll., 1992. *Address:* Hills & Co., 420 20th Street NW, Washington, DC 20036, USA. *Club:* Cosmos (Washington).

PICKETT, Prof. George Richard, DPhil; FRS 1997; Professor of Low Temperature Physics, University of Lancaster, since 1988. *Educ:* Magdalen Coll., Oxford (BA 1962; DPhil). Lectr, then Sen. Lectr, later Reader, Dept of Physics, Univ. of Lancaster. *Address:* Department of Physics, University of Lancaster, LA1 4YB; Thornber, Bentham, Lancaster LA2 7AQ. *T:* (01524) 261288.

PICKETT, Prof. John Anthony, CBE 2004; PhD, DSc; FRS 1996; Scientific Director, Rothamsted Centre for Sustainable Pest and Disease Management, since 2007; Head of Biological Chemistry Department (formerly Department of Insecticides and Fungicides, then Biological and Ecological Chemistry Department), Rothamsted Research (formerly IACR-Rothamsted), since 1984; *b* 21 April 1945; *s* of Samuel Victor Pickett and Lilian Frances Pickett (*née* Hoar); *m* 1970, Ulla Birgitta Skålèn; one *s* one *d*. *Educ:* King Edward VII Grammar Sch., Coalville; Univ. of Surrey (BSc Hons Chem 1967; PhD Organic Chem 1971); DSc Nottingham 1993. CChem 1975, FRSC 1982; CSci 2004. Postdoctoral Fellow, UMIST, 1970–72; Chem. Dept, Brewing Res. Foundn (flavour active components of hops and malt), 1972–76; Dept of Insecticides and Fungicides, Rothamsted Exptl Stn (semiochem. aspects of insect chem. ecology), 1976–83. Special Prof., Sch. of Biol., Univ. of Nottingham, 1991–. Lectures: Boyce Thompson Inst. for Plant Res., Cornell Univ., 1991; Alfred M. Boyce, Univ. of California, Riverside, 1993; Woolhouse, Soc. for Experimental Biology, York Univ., 1998; Barrington Meml, Univ. of Nottingham, 1999; Cameron-Gifford, Univ. of Newcastle, 2000; Andersonian Chem. Soc. Centenary, Univ. of Strathclyde, 2006; H. R. MacCarthy Pest Mgt, Univ. of BC, 2007; Croonian, Royal Soc., 2008. Mem. Council, Royal Soc., 2000–02. Rank Prize for Nutrition and Crop Husbandry, 1995; Silver Medal, Internat. Soc. of Chem. Ecology, 2002. *Publications:* numerous papers and patents. *Recreation:* jazz trumpet playing. *Address:* Biological Chemistry Department, Rothamsted Research, Harpenden, Herts AL5 2JQ. *T:* (01582) 763133.

PICKETT, Philip; Director, New London Consort, since 1978. *Educ:* Guildhall Sch. of Music and Drama (Maisie Lewis Foundn Award; Wedgewood Award; FGSM 1985). Prof. of Recorder and Historical Performance Practice, GSMD, 1972–97. Began career as trumpet player; subseq. took up recorder, crumhorn, shawm, rackett, etc; as soloist, has performed with many leading ensembles, incl. Acad. of St Martin-in-the-Fields, London Chamber Orch., Polish Chamber Orch., English Chamber Orch., London Mozart Players; with New London Consort, performs a wide repertoire of medieval, Renaissance and Baroque music; resident early music ensemble, S Bank Centre; nat. and internat. concerts and recitals, incl. BBC Proms, and regular performances at art fests. Dir of Early Music, Globe Theatre, 1993–; Artistic Director: Purcell Room Early Music Series, 1993–; Aldeburgh Early Music Fest., 1994–97 (also Founder); Early Music Fest., S Bank Centre, 1996–2003. Appearances on radio and television; film soundtracks. Solo recordings incl. Handel recorder concertos and trio concertos, and Vivaldi and Telemann concertos. *Publications:* articles in books and jls. *Address:* New London Consort, 8/9 Rust Square, SE5 7LG.

PICKETT-HEAPS, Prof. Jeremy David, PhD; FRS 1995; FAA; Professor, School of Botany, University of Melbourne, since 1988; *b* 5 June 1940; *s* of Harold Arthur Pickett-Heaps and Edna Azura (*née* May); *m* 1st, 1965, Daphne Charmian Scott (*d* 1970); one *s* one *d*; 2nd, 1977, Julianne Francis Jack; two *s*. *Educ:* Clare Coll., Cambridge (BA; PhD 1965). Fellow, Research Sch. of Biol Sci., ANU, 1965–70; Prof., Dept of Molecular, Cellular and Developmental Biol., Univ. of Colorado, 1970–88. FAA 1992. *Publications:* Green Algae, 1972; numerous scientific res. papers. *Recreations:* various. *Address:* PO Box 1113, Carlton, Vic 3053, Australia. *T:* (3) 96540300.

PICKFORD, David Michael, FRICS; Chairman, Committee of Management, Lionbrook (formerly Lilliput) Property Unit Trust, 1984–2002; *b* 25 Aug. 1926; *s* of Aston Charles Corpe Pickford and Gladys Ethel Pickford; *m* 1956, Elizabeth Gwendoline Hooson; one *s* two *d*. *Educ:* Emanuel Sch., London; Coll. of Estate Management. FRICS 1953. Hillier Parker May & Rowden, 1943–46; LCC, 1946–48; London Investment & Mortgage Co., 1948–57; Haslemere Estates plc, 1957–86: Man. Dir, 1968–83; Chm., 1983–86; Dir, City & Metropolitan Building Soc., 1986–90; Chairman: Exeter Park Estates, 1986–91; Luis Palau Europe Ltd, 1980–2001; Dabet Ltd, 1986–2004; Compco Hldgs PLC, 1987–2002; Louth Estates (No 2) Ltd, 1989–2000; Brushfield Properties Ltd, 1990–2000; Stonechange Ltd, 1990–97; Wigmore Property Investment Trust Plc, 1993–96; Chairman, Committee of Management: Gulliver Develts Property Unit Trust, 1987–2000; Swift Balanced Property Unit Trust, 1993–97. President: London Dist, The Boys' Bde, 1967–86 (Hon. Life Pres., 1986); Christians in Property, 1990– (Chm., 1978–90); Chm., Drug and Alcohol Foundn, 1987–90 (Vice-Pres., 1990–92); Director: Mission to London, 1980–2000; London and Nationwide Missions, 1982–; Billy Graham Evangelistic Assoc., 1986–; Youth with a Mission, 1986–95; CARE Campaigns Ltd (also Trustee), 1987–; Trustee: David Pickford Charitable Foundn, 1968–; Pickford Trust, 1972–; Prison Fellowship, 1989–2001 (Chm. Trustees, 1990–93); London Prison Creative and Counselling Trust, 1991–93; Genesis Arts Trust, 1994–96. *Recreations:* sheep farming, youth work, gardening. *Address:* Elm Tree Farm, Mersham, near Ashford, Kent TN25 7HS. *T:* (01233) 720200, *Fax:* (01233) 720522.

PICKFORD, Michael Alan, CB 1994; FIA; Directing Actuary, Supervision of Insurance Companies and Friendly Societies, Government Actuary's Department, 1989–95; *b* 22 Aug. 1937. *Educ:* City of Oxford Sch. Govt Actuary's Dept, 1958–95.

PICKFORD, Stephen John, CB 2004; Managing Director, International and Finance Directorate, HM Treasury, since 2007; *b* 26 Aug. 1950; *s* of Frank and May Pickford; *m* 1978, Carolyn M. Ruffle; two *s*. *Educ:* St John's Coll., Cambridge (BA Hons 1971; MA 1974); Univ. of British Columbia (MA 1984). Economist, Dept of Employment, 1971–79; HM Treasury: Economist, 1979–85; Dep. Press Sec., 1985–87; Sen. Economic Advr, 1987–89, 1993–98; Manager, Macroeconomics, New Zealand Treasury, 1989–93; UK Exec. Dir, IMF and World Bank, 1998–2001; Minister (Econ.), British Embassy, Washington, 1998–2001; Dir, Internat. Finance, 2001–06, Europe, 2006–07, HM Treasury. *Publication:* (contrib.) Government Economic Statistics, 1989. *Recreations:* running, ski-ing. *Address:* HM Treasury, 1 Horse Guards Road, SW1A 2HQ.

PICKING, Anne; *see* Moffat, A.

PICKLES, Eric Jack; MP (C) Brentwood and Ongar, since 1992; *b* 20 April 1952; *m* 1976, Irene. *Educ:* Greenhead Grammar Sch.; Leeds Polytechnic. Joined Conservative Party, 1968; Young Conservatives: Area Chm., 1976–78; Nat. Vice-Chm., 1978–80; Nat. Chm., 1980–81; Conservative Party: Member: Nat. Union Exec. Cttee, 1975–91; One Nation Forum, 1987–91; Nat. Local Govt Adv. Cttee, 1985– (Chm., 1992–93); Lectr, Cons. Agents Examination Courses, 1988–; Local Govt Editor, Newsline, 1990–92; a Vice-Chm., 1993–97; Dep. Chm., 2005–. Bradford Council: Councillor, 1979–91; Chm., Social Services, 1982–84; Chm., Educn, 1984–86; Leader, Cons. Gp, 1987–91; Leader of Council, 1988–90. Dep. Leader, Cons. Gp, AMA, 1989–91. PPS to Minister for Industry, 1993; Opposition frontbench spokesman on social security, 1998–2001; Shadow Transport Minister, 2001–02; Shadow Sec. of State for Local Govt and the Regions, 2002–07, for Communities and Local Govt, 2007–. Chm., All Party Film Gp, 1997–2004; Vice-Chm., Cons. Envmt, Transport and Regions Cttee, 1997–98. Mem., Council of Europe, 1997–. Mem., Yorks Area RHA, 1982–90. *Recreations:* film buff, opera, serious walking. *Address:* House of Commons, SW1A 0AA.

PICKLES, His Honour James; a Circuit Judge, 1976–91; *b* 18 March 1925. Practised at Bradford, 1949–76; a Recorder of the Crown Court, 1972–76. *Publications:* Straight from the Bench, 1987; Judge for Yourself, 1992; Off the Record (novel), 1993. *Address:* Hazelwood, Heath Road, Halifax, West Yorks HX3 0BA.

PICKTHALL, Colin; *b* 13 Sept. 1944; *s* of Frank Pickthall and Edith (*née* Bonser), Dalton-in-Furness; *m* 1973, Judith Ann Tranter; two *d*. *Educ:* Univ. of Wales (BA); Univ. of Lancaster (MA). Teacher, Ruffwood Comprehensive Sch., Kirkby, 1967–70; Edge Hill College of Higher Education: Sen. Lectr in English Lit., 1970–83; Head, European Studies, 1983–92. County Councillor, Ormskirk, Lancs CC, 1989–93. Contested (Lab) Lancashire West, 1987; MP (Lab) Lancs W, 1992–2005. *Recreations:* fell-walking, gardening, cricket, theatre. *Address:* 25 Fountain Street, Ulverston, Cumbria LA12 7EQ.

PICKTHORN, Sir James (Francis Mann), 3rd Bt *cr* 1959, of Orford, Suffolk; Partner, Pickthorn, estate agents and chartered surveyors, since 1994; *b* 18 Feb. 1955; *o s* of Sir Charles William Richards Pickthorn, 2nd Bt and of Helen Antonia, *o d* of Sir James Gow Mann, KCVO; *S* father, 1995; *m* 1998, Clare, *yr d* of Brian Craig-McFeely; two *s*. *Educ:* Eton; Reading Univ. (BSc Estate Management). With Healey & Baker, 1977–82; Debenham Tewson & Chinnocks, 1982–86; Kinney & Green, 1986–94 (Partner, 1991–94); founded Pickthorn, 1994. TA (HAC), 1978–98. *Recreation:* sailing. *Heir:* *s* William Edward Craig Pickthorn, *b* 2 Dec. 1998. *Address:* 45 Ringmer Avenue, SW6 5LP; (office) Pickthorn, 24 Lime Street, EC3M 7HS. *T:* (020) 7621 1380.

PICKUP, David Cunliffe; Chief Executive, Sports Council Trust Company, 1993–94; Director General, Sports Council, 1988–93; *b* 17 Sept. 1936; *s* of Robert and Florence Pickup; *m* 1960, Patricia Moira Aileen (*née* Neill); three *s*. *Educ:* Bacup and Rawtenstall Grammar Sch. Min. of Education, 1955–63; MPBW, 1964–71 (incl. periods as Pvte Sec. to four Ministers); Department of the Environment: Prin. Pvte Sec. to Minister for Housing and Construction, 1971–72; Asst Sec., 1972; Housing, 1972–75; Personnel, 1975–77; Under Sec., 1977; Regl Dir, Northern Reg., 1977–80; Housing, 1980–84; Local Govt, 1984–85; Dep. Sec., Assoc. of Dist Councils, 1986–88. Dir, Bromley Mytime, 2004–; Bd Mem., Proactive S London (formerly S London Sport and Physical Activity Partnership), 2006–. FRSA 1992. *Publications:* Not Another Messiah, 1996; Bracken Point, 2002; Legacy, 2005. *Recreations:* reading, music, sport, walking. *Address:* 15 Sandford Road, Bromley, Kent BR2 9AL. *T:* (020) 8402 2354.

PICKUP, David Francis William, CB 2002; Attorney General of the Falkland Islands, since 2007; *b* 28 May 1953; *s* of Joseph and Muriel Pickup; *m* 1975, Anne Elizabeth Round. *Educ:* Poole Grammar Sch.; Polytechnic of Central London (Univ. of London

External LLB Hons). Called to the Bar, Lincoln's Inn, 1976, Gibraltar, 1988. Joined Treasury Solicitor's Dept as Legal Asst, 1978, Sen. Legal Asst, 1981; Grade 5 1987; Estabt Finance and Security Officer, 1988–90; Grade 3, Chancery Litigation Div., 1990; Legal Advr, MoD, 1991–95; Solicitor (Grade 2), HM Customs and Excise, subseq. HM Revenue and Customs, 1995–2005; Dir Gen., HMRC, 2006–07. *Recreations:* playing and watching cricket, ski-ing, listening to music, food and wine, travel. *Address:* (office) Attorney General's Chambers, Cable Cottage, Stanley, Falkland Islands. *T:* 28460; *e-mail:* dpickup@sec.gov.fk. *Clubs:* Pyrford Cricket; Herefordshire Golf.

PICKUP, Ronald Alfred; actor; *b* 7 June 1940; *s* of Eric and Daisy Pickup; *m* 1964, Lans Traverse, USA; one *s* one *d*. *Educ:* King's Sch., Chester; Leeds Univ. (BA); Royal Academy of Dramatic Art. Repertory, Leicester, 1964; Royal Court, 1964 and 1965–66; National Theatre, 1965, 1966–73, 1977: appearances include: Rosalind, in all-male As You Like It, 1967; Richard II, 1972; Edmund, in Long Day's Journey into Night, 1971; Cassius, in Julius Caesar, 1977; Philip Madras, in The Madras House, 1977; Norman, in Norman Conquests, Globe, 1974; Play, Royal Court, 1976; Hobson's Choice, Lyric, Hammersmith, 1981; Astrov, in Uncle Vanya, Haymarket, 1982; Allmers in Little Eyolf, Lyric, Hammersmith, 1985; Gayev, in The Cherry Orchard, Aldwych, 1989; Amy's View, RNT, 1997, NY, 1999; Peer Gynt, Romeo and Juliet, RNT, 2000; Proof, Donmar Warehouse, 2002; Col Redfern in Look Back in Anger, Th. Royal, Bath, 2006; Uncle Vanya, Rose Th., Kingston, 2008; *films:* Three Sisters, 1969; Day of the Jackal, 1972; Joseph Andrews, 1976; 39 Steps, Zulu Dawn, 1978; Nijinsky, 1979; Never Say Never Again, John Paul II, 1983; Eleni, Camille (remake), 1984; The Mission, 1985; The Fourth Protocol, 1986; Bring Me the Head of Mavis Davis, 1996; Breathtaking, 1999; Evilenko, 2004; Greyfriars Bobby, 2006; *television:* series and serials: Dragon's Opponent, 1973; Jennie, Fight Against Slavery, 1974; Tropic, 1979; Life of Giuseppe Verdi, 1982; Wagner, 1982; Life of Einstein, 1983; Moving, 1984; The Fortunes of War, 1987; Behaving Badly, 1988; A Time to Dance, 1992; My Friend Walter, 1992; The Riff Raff Element, 1993, 1994; Ivanhoe, 1996; Hornblower, 1998; Dalziel and Pascoe, 1999; Holby City, 2005–07; The Worst Week of my Life, Feather Boy, 2004; other: The Philanthropist, Ghost Trio, The Discretion of Dominic Ayres, 1977; Memories, Henry VIII, 1978; England's Green and Pleasant Land, Christ Hero, 1979; The Letter, Ivanhoe, 1981; Orwell on Jura, 1983; The Rivals, 1986; The Attic, Chekhov in Yalta, 1988; A Murder of Quality, 1990; Absolute Hell, 1991; The War that Never Ends, 1991; The Golden Years, 1992; In the Cold Light of Day, 1994; Milner, 1994; A Case of Coincidence, 1994; A Very Open Prison, 1995; The Dying Day, Henry IV (title rôle), 1995; Cherished, 2003. *Recreations:* listening to music, walking, reading.

PICTET, François-Charles; Ambassador of Switzerland to Austria, 1990–94, and Ambassador on Special Mission to the Holy See, 1993–97; *b* Geneva, 21 July 1929; *e s* of Charles Pictet, Geneva, and Elisabeth (*née* Decazes), France; *m* 1st, 1954, Elisabeth Choisy (*d* 1980), Geneva; three *s*; 2nd, 1983, Countess Marie-Thérèse Althann, Austria. *Educ:* College Calvin, Geneva; Univ. of Geneva (Faculty of Law). Called to the Swiss Bar, 1954. Joined Swiss Federal Dept of Foreign Affairs, 1956; Attaché, Vienna, 1957; Sec., Moscow, 1958–60; 1st Sec., Ankara, 1961–66; Dep. Dir, Internat. Orgns, Dept of For. Affairs, Berne, 1966–75; Minister Plenipotentiary, 1975; Ambassador to Canada and (non-resident) to the Bahamas, 1975–79; Ambassador, Perm. Rep. to Internat. Orgns in Geneva, 1980–84; Ambassador to UK, 1984–89, to the Netherlands, 1989–90; Hd of Swiss Delgn to CSCE, Vienna, 1991–93. *Address:* 6 rue Robert-de-Traz, 1206 Geneva, Switzerland. *T:* (22) 7890086.

PICTON, Martin Thomas; His Honour Judge Picton; a Circuit Judge, since 2005; *b* 20 Jan. 1958; *s* of Gerald and Daphne Picton; *m* 1992, Dr Susan Wensley; three *s* one *d*. *Educ:* Haberdashers' Aske's Sch., New Cross; King's Coll. London (LLB). Called to the Bar, Middle Temple, 1981; tenant, Albion Chambers, Bristol, 1982–2005; a Recorder, 1998–2005. *Recreations:* running, ski-ing, bringing up four children. *Address:* Gloucester Crown Court, PO Box 9051, GLX 2XG. *T:* (01452) 420100, *Fax:* (01452) 833599.

PIDDINGTON, Philip Michael, CBE 1988; HM Diplomatic Service, retired; Counsellor, Foreign and Commonwealth Office, 1987–90; *b* 27 March 1931; *s* of Percy Howard Piddington and Florence Emma (*née* Pearson); *m* 1955, Sylvia Mary Price; one *s* one *d*. *Educ:* Waverley Grammar Sch., Birmingham. Served HM Forces, 1949–51. Entered Min. of Works, 1947; FO, 1952; Jedda, 1956; Tokyo, 1962–66; First Sec., Lagos, 1969–71; Consul: NY, 1971–73; Istanbul, 1973–77; First Sec., FCO, 1978–83; Counsellor and Consul-Gen., Brussels, 1983–87. *Recreations:* riding, walking, photography. *Address:* The Pump House, St Mary's Road, East Claydon, Bucks MK18 2NA. *T:* (01296) 712302.

PIDGEON, Caroline Valerie; Member (Lib Dem), London Assembly, Greater London Authority, since 2008; *b* Eastleigh, Hants, 29 Sept. 1972; *d* of Eric and Valerie Pidgeon; *m* 2006, Paul Miles. *Educ:* Univ. of Wales, Aberystwyth (BSc Econ Hons). Political Researcher: Cllr Rose Colley, Southwark BC, 1994–96; Brent Council, 1996–99; Communications Manager: Croydon HA, 1999–2002; Guy's and St Thomas' NHS Foundn Trust, 2002–06. Mem., Southwark BC, 1998– (Dep. Leader, 2002–04; Exec. Mem., for Educn, 2004–06, for Children's Services, 2006–08). *Recreations:* cinema, modern art. *Address:* Greater London Authority, City Hall, The Queen's Walk, SE1 2AA. *T:* (020) 7701 4648; *e-mail:* caroline.pidgeon@london.gov.uk.

PIDGEON, Sir John (Allan Stewart), Kt 1989; Chairman, since 1980, and Managing Director, since 1960, F. A. Pidgeon & Son and associated companies; *b* 15 July 1926; *s* of Frederick Allan Pidgeon and Margaret Ellen Pidgeon, MBE; *m* 1st, 1952, Sylvia Dawn (*d* 1991); one *s* four *d*; 2nd, 1993, Mrs Pamela Barbara Howell. *Educ:* Church of England Grammar Sch., Brisbane. Fellow, Aust. Inst. of Building; FIDA. Served 2nd AIF, 1944–45. Joined F. A. Pidgeon & Son Pty, 1946. Director: Suncorp Building Soc., 1976–91; Folkestone Ltd, 1985–95. Chm., Builders' Registration Bd of Qld, 1985–93. Pres., Qld Master Builders' Assoc., 1970–72 (Trustee, 1978–). Chm., Salvation Army Adv. Bd., 1988–93. FAICD. *Recreations:* ski-ing, tennis, swimming. *Address:* 14 Otway Street, Holland Park, Brisbane, Qld 4121, Australia. *T:* (7) 38971137; Great Brampton House, Madley, Hereford HR2 9NA. *Clubs:* Brisbane, Queensland, Tattersalls, Polo, Brisbane Amateur Turf (Brisbane); Brisbane Yacht.

PIEBALGS, Andris; Member, European Commission, since 2004; *b* 17 Sept. 1957; *m* Anda; one *s* two *d*. *Educ:* Univ. of Latvia (degree in physics). Teacher, then Headmaster, Secondary Sch. No 1, Valmiera, 1980–88; Desk Officer, then Hd of Dept, Min. of Educn, Latvia, 1988–90; Minister of Educn, 1990–93; MP, 1993–94; Minister of Finance, 1994–95; Ambassador to Estonia, 1995–97; Perm. Rep. of Latvia to EU, 1998–2003; Dep. Sec. of State, Min. of Foreign Affairs, 2003–04; Hd of Cabinet, Latvian Mem. of EC, 2004. *Address:* European Commission, 200 rue de la Loi, 1049 Brussels, Belgium.

PIËCH, Ferdinand; Chairman, Supervisory Board: Volkswagen AG, since 2002 (Member, 1992–2002, Chairman, 1993–2002, Board of Management); Man AG, since 2007; *b* Vienna, 17 April 1937; *s* of Dr jur Anton Piëch and Louise (*née* Porsche). *Educ:* in Switzerland; Tech. Univ. of Zurich. Mem., Management Bd i/c R and D, Audi NSU Auto Union AG/Audi AG, 1975–88; Chm., Bd of Management, Audi AG, 1988–92. Dr *hc* Vienna Technical Univ., 1984. *Address:* c/o Volkswagen AG, Brieffach 1880, 38436 Wolfsburg, Germany.

PIENAAR, John Adrian; Chief Political Correspondent, since 2002, and Presenter, The Weekend News, since 2006, BBC Radio Five-Live; *b* 2 Nov. 1956; *s* of Eric and Johanna Pienaar; *m* 1st, 1980, Denise Walsh (marr. diss.); one *s* one *d*; 2nd, Penny Davies; two *d*. *Educ:* Ravenswood Sch., Bromley. Political staff, Press Assoc., 1980–86; Political Correspondent: Independent, 1986–92; BBC News, 1992–. *Recreations:* reading, history, novels, almost anything, watching films, watching Crystal Palace FC. *Address:* BBC Westminster, 4 Millbank, SW1P 3JQ; *e-mail:* john.pienaar@bbc.co.uk.

PIEŃKOWSKI, Jan Michał; author and illustrator, since 1958; Founder Director, Gallery Five Ltd, 1961; *b* 8 Aug. 1936; *s* of late Jerzy Dominik Pieńkowski and Wanda Maria Pieńkowska. *Educ:* Cardinal Vaughan Sch., London; King's Coll., Cambridge (MA Classics and English). Art Dir, J. Walter Thompson, William Collins, and Time and Tide, London, 1958–61. Work includes graphics and murals, posters and greeting cards, children's TV, and book illustration. *Stage designs:* Meg and Mog Show, 1981–88; Beauty and the Beast, Royal Opera House, 1986; Théâtre de Complicité, 1988; Sleeping Beauty, Euro Disney, 1992. Kate Greenaway Medal, Library Assoc., 1972 and 1979. *Publications:* illustrator: A Necklace of Raindrops, 1968; The Kingdom under the Sea, 1971; Tale of a One Way Street, 1978; Past Eight O'Clock, 1986; A Foot in the Grave, 1989; M.O.L.E., 1993, etc; (co-author and illustrator) Meg and Mog series, 1973–90 (televised, 2004); illustrator/author: Nursery series, 1973–91; Haunted House, 1979; Robot, 1981; Dinner Time, 1981 (new large-format edn 2007); Christmas, 1984; Little Monsters, 1986 (new large-format edn 2007); Small Talk, 1988; Easter, 1989; Fancy That, 1990; Phone Book, 1991; Christmas Kingdom, 1991; Door Bell, 1992; Road Hog, 1993; ABC Dinosaurs, 1993; Toilet Book, 1994; 1001 Words, 1994; Furrytails series, 1994; Nursery Cloth Books series, 1994; Botticelli's Bed and Breakfast, 1996; Nursery Pop-Up series, 1996–97; Tickle-me Books, 1997; Good Night, 1998; Bel and Bub series, 2000; The Monster Pet, 2000; Pizza!, 2001; The Cat with Nine Lives, 2001; The Animals went in Two by Two, 2001; Meg, Mog and Og, 2003; Meg's Mummy, 2004; The First Noël, 2004; The Fairy Tales, 2005; Mog's Missing, 2005; Haunted House, 25th anniversary edn, 2005; The First Christmas, 2006; Meg & Mog Touch and Feel Counting Book, 2006; The Thousand Nights and One Night, 2007; Meg and Mog, 35th anniversary edn, 2007; Nut Cracker, 2008. *Recreations:* keeping bantams, Latin, drawing from life on computer. *Address:* Oakgates, Barnes. *Club:* Polish Hearth.

PIERCE, Rt Rev. Anthony Edward; Bishop of Swansea and Brecon, 1999–2008; *b* 16 Jan. 1941; *s* of Gwynfor Pierce and Martha Jane Pierce (*née* Owen). *Educ:* Dynevor Sch., Swansea; University Coll., Swansea (BA Hons Hist. 1963); Linacre Coll., Oxford (BA Hons Theol 1965; MA 1971); Ripon Hall, Oxford. Deacon 1965, priest 1966; Curate: St Peter, Swansea, 1965–67; St Mary and Holy Trinity, Swansea, 1967–74; Vicar of Llwynderw, 1974–92; Priest-in-charge, St Barnabas, Swansea, 1992–96; Canon Res., Brecon Cathedral, 1993; Archdeacon of Gower, 1995–99; Vicar, St Mary, Swansea, 1996–99. Sec., Dio. Conf. and Dio. Patronage Bd, 1991–95; Dio. Dir of Educn, 1992–96. Mem., Prov. Selection Panel, 1984–97; Chm., Social Action Sect., 1985–90, Chm. Div. Social Responsibility, 1990–92, Prov. Bd of Mission. Chm., Ecumenical Aids Monitoring Gp (Wales), 1988–95. University College, Swansea: Bp's Chaplain to Anglican Students, 1971–74; Mem. Ct of Govs, 1981–; Chaplain, 1984–88. Mem. Council, Univ. of Wales, Swansea, 1995–. Chaplain, Singleton Hosp., 1980–95; Co-ordinator, Hosp. Chaplains, 1982–95. Hon. Ed., Welsh Churchman, 1972–75. Sub-Prelate, Order of St John, Priory of Wales, 2002. *Recreations:* reading, theatre, music. *Address:* 2 Coed Ceirios, Swansea Vale, Swansea SA7 0NU.

PIERCE, Karen Elizabeth, (Mrs C. F. Roxburgh), CMG 2008; HM Diplomatic Service; Deputy Permanent Representative, UK Mission to United Nations, New York, with personal rank of Ambassador, and President, UN Trusteeship Council, since 2006; *b* 23 Sept. 1959; *d* of Derek Robert Pierce and Barbara Florence Pierce; *m* 1987, Charles Fergusson Roxburgh; two *s*. *Educ:* Penwortham Girls' High Sch.; Girton Coll., Cambridge (BA Hons English 1981; MA 1991). Joined FCO, 1981; Tokyo, 1984–87; Security Policy Dept, FCO, 1987–91; Washington, 1991–96; Eastern Dept, then Eastern Adriatic Dept, FCO, 1996–99; Head: Newsroom, FCO, 1999–2000; EU Dept (Bilateral), FCO, 2001–02; Eastern Adriatic Dept, FCO, 2002–06. *Recreations:* collecting fridge magnets, according to my children 'being with them'. *Address:* c/o Foreign and Commonwealth Office, King Charles Street, SW1A 2AH.

PIERCY, family name of **Baron Piercy**.

PIERCY, 3rd Baron *cr* 1945, of Burford; **James William Piercy;** *b* 19 Jan. 1946; *s* of 2nd Baron Piercy and Oonagh Lavinia (*d* 1990), *d* of late Major Edward John Lake Baylay, DSO; *S* father, 1981. *Educ:* Shrewsbury; Edinburgh Univ. (BSc 1968). AMIEE; FCCA. *Heir:* *b* Hon. Mark Edward Pelham Piercy [*b* 30 June 1953; *m* 1979, Vivien Angela, *d* of His Honour Judge Evelyn Faithfull Monier-Williams, *qv*; one *s* three *d*]. *Address:* 36 Richford Street, W6 7HP.

PIERI, Frank; Sheriff of South Strathclyde, Dumfries and Galloway at Hamilton, since 2005; *b* 10 Aug. 1954; *s* of Ralph Pieri and Teresa Pieri; *m* 1977, Dorothy Telfer; two *d*. *Educ:* St Aloysius Coll., Glasgow; Univ. of Glasgow (LLB 1974). Solicitor, 1976–93; called to the Scottish Bar, 1994; in practice as Advocate, 1994–2000; Immigration Adjudicator (full time), 2000–04. Member: Council, Scottish Law Agents Soc., 1981–93; Council of Immigration Judges, 2003. *Recreations:* ambling, crime fiction, opera, Partick Thistle FC. *Address:* Hamilton Sheriff Court, Beckford Street, Hamilton ML3 0BT. *T:* (01698) 282957; *e-mail:* sherifffpieri@scotcourts.gov.uk. *Club:* Glasgow Art.

PIERS, Sir James (Desmond), 11th Bt *cr* 1661, of Tristernagh Abbey, Westmeath; Partner, Fasken Martineau DuMoulin (formerly Russell & DuMoulin), lawyers, since 1982; *b* 24 July 1947; *s* of Sir Charles Robert Fitzmaurice Piers, 10th Bt and Ann Blanche Scott (*d* 1975); *S* father, 1996; *m* 1975, Sandra Mae Dixon; one *s* one *d*. *Educ:* Univ. of Victoria (BA 1969); Univ. of British Columbia (LLB 1973). Called to the Bar, British Columbia, 1974, Yukon Territory, 1975. *Heir:* *s* Stephen James Piers, *b* 14 Sept. 1979. *Address:* Fasken Martineau DuMoulin, 2100–1075 West Georgia Street, Vancouver, BC V6E 3G2, Canada.

PIETRONI, Prof. Patrick Claude, FRCP, FRCGP; Director, International Institute for the Study of Cuba, London Metropolitan University, since 2008; *b* 8 Nov. 1942; *s* of Michael and Jeannette Pietroni; *m* 1st, 1963, Theresa Wilkinson (marr. diss.); two *s* one *d*; 2nd, 1977, Marilyn Miller. *Educ:* Guy's Hosp. Med. Sch. (MB BS 1966). MRCP 1973, FRCP 2000; FRCGP 1985; MFPH (MFPHM 2000). MO, RAMC, 1967–69; Principal, Gen. Practice, 1971–; Associate Prof., Family Medicine, Univ. of Cincinatti, 1978–80; Sen. Lectr in Gen. Practice, St Mary's Hosp. Med. Sch., 1981–93; Prof. and Dir, Centre for Community Care and Primary Health, Univ. of Westminster, 1993–97; Dean, Postgrad. Gen. Practice, N Thames (West) Dept of Postgrad. Med. and Dental Educn,

London Univ., 1996–2001; Dir, Educnl Support Unit, London Region, NHS Exec., 2001–04. Dir, 4Ps Res. and Develt Unit, 2001–04. Hon. DSc Westminster, 2001. *Publications:* Holistic Living, 1986; The Greening of Medicine, 1990; Innovation in Community Care and Primary Health, 1995. *Recreations:* tennis, riding, bridge, opera.

PIGEON, Michel, PhD; Rector, Laval University, Canada, 2002–07; *b* 1945; *s* of Louis-Philippe Pigeon and Madeleine Gaudry; *m* 1968, Marie-José des Rivières; two *d*. *Educ:* Laval Univ. (BA 1963, BScA 1967); ICSTM (MPhil 1969); Univ. Pierre et Marie Curie, Paris (PhD 1984). Laval University: Department of Civil Engineering: Asst Prof., 1972–77; Associate Prof., 1977–87; Tenured Prof., 1987; Dir, 1999–2001; Dir, Interuniv. Res. Centre on Concrete, 1992–98, 2000–01; Vice Dean, Res., Sci. and Engrg Faculty, 2001; Dean, Sci. and Engrg Faculty, 2002. *Publications:* (with R. Pleau) Durability of Concrete in Cold Climates, 1995; book chapters and articles in learned jls. *Address:* c/o Office of the Rector, Laval University, Education Sciences Pavilion, Suite 1656, Québec City, QC G1K 7P4, Canada.

PIGGOTT, Ven. Andrew John; Archdeacon of Bath, since 2005; *b* 27 Sept. 1951; *s* of David Geoffrey John and Joyce Vera Piggott; *m* 1979, Ruth Elizabeth Morris; two *d*. *Educ:* Queen Mary Coll., London (BSc(Econ) 1972); Leeds Univ. (PGCE 1973); Nottingham Univ. (DipTh 1984). Various teaching posts, 1973–83; ordained deacon, 1986, priest, 1987; Curate, St Philip with St James, Dorridge, 1986–89; Team Vicar, St Chad's, Kidderminster, 1989–94; Incumbent, St Lawrence, Biddulph, 1994–99; Church Pastoral Aid Society: Ministry and Vocations Advr, 1999–2001; Acting Gen. Dir, 2000–01; Patronage Sec., 2001–05. *Address:* 56 Grange Road, Saltford, Bristol BS31 3AG. *T:* (01225) 873609, *Fax:* (01225) 874110; *e-mail:* adbath@bathwells.anglican.org.

PIGGOTT, Donald James; Director-General, British Red Cross Society, 1980–85; *b* 1 Sept. 1920; *s* of late James Piggott and Edith Piggott (*née* Tempest); *m* 1974, Kathryn Courtenay-Evans, *e d* of late William and Gwendoline Eckford. *Educ:* Bradford Grammar School; Christ's College, Cambridge (MA); London School of Economics. Served Army in NW Europe and India, 1941–46. PA to Finance and Supply Director, London Transport, 1947–50; Shell-Mex and BP Ltd, 1951–58; Manager Development Div., Marketing Dept, British Petroleum Co. Ltd, 1958–73; BRCS: Dir, Internat. Affairs, 1973; Head of Internat. Div., 1975; Asst Dir-Gen. International, 1980. Member: Central Appeals Adv. Cttee, BBC and IBA, 1980–83; Jt Cttee, St John and Red Cross, 1980–91; Dep. Pres., Suffolk Br., BRCS, 1987–93. Liveryman, Co. of Carmen, 1988–. FRSocMed 1993. OStJ 1983. *Recreations:* music, theatre. *Address:* Beech Tree House, The Green, Tostock, Bury St Edmunds, Suffolk IP30 9NY. *T:* (01359) 270589. *Clubs:* Hawks (Cambridge); Achilles.

PIGGOTT, Lester Keith; jockey, 1948–85 and 1990–95; trainer, 1985–87; *b* 5 Nov. 1935; *s* of late Keith Piggott and Iris Rickaby; *m* 1960, Susan Armstrong; two *d*. Selection of races won: the Derby (9 times): 1954 (on Never Say Die); 1957 (on Crepello); 1960 (on St Paddy); 1968 (on Sir Ivor); 1970 (on Nijinsky); 1972 (on Roberto); 1976 (on Empery); 1977 (on The Minstrel); 1983 (on Teenoso); St Leger (8 times); The Oaks (6 times); 2,000 guineas (5 times); 1,000 guineas (twice). In many seasons 1955–85 he rode well over 100 winners a year, in this country alone; rode 4,000th winner in Britain, 14 Aug. 1982; record 30th classic win, 1 May 1992; Champion Jockey 11 times, 1960, 1964–71, 1981, 1982; rode frequently in France; won Prix de l'Arc de Triomphe on Rheingold, 1973, on Alleged, 1977 and 1978; won Washington, DC, International on Sir Ivor, 1968 (first time since 1922 an English Derby winner raced in USA), on Karabas, 1969, on Argument, 1980. *Publication:* (with Sean Magee) Lester's Derbys, 2004; *relevant publication:* Lester, the Official Biography, by Dick Francis, 1986. *Recreations:* swimming, water ski-ing, golf. *Address:* Florizel, Newmarket, Suffolk CB8 0NY. *T:* (01638) 662584.

PIGNATELLI, Frank, CBE 2005; Chief Executive, University for Industry, Scotland, 1999–2006; *b* 22 Dec. 1946; *s* of Frank and Elizabeth Pignatelli; *m* 1969, Rosetta Anne McFadyen; one *s* one *d*. *Educ:* Univ. of Glasgow (MA; DipEd, MEd); Jordanhill Coll. of Educn (Secondary Teachers Cert.). Teacher, St Mungo's Acad., Glasgow, 1970; Hd of Dept, St Gregory's Secondary Sch., Glasgow, 1974; Asst Headteacher, St Margaret Mary's Secondary Sch., Glasgow, 1977; Strathclyde Region: Educn Officer, Renfrew Div., 1978; Asst Dir of Educn, 1983; Depute Dir of Educn, 1985; Dir of Educn, 1988–96; Gp Dir, Human Resources, Associated Newspapers, London, 1996–97; Chm. and Man. Dir, Exec. Support and Develt Consultancy, 1997–2000; Chief Exec., ScotBIC, 1998–99. Hon. Lectr in Educn, 1988–90, Vis. Prof., 1990–, Univ. of Glasgow Sch. of Educn; Vis. Prof. of Mgt Educn, Univ. of Glasgow Business Sch., 1997–. Chairman: RIPA (West of Scotland), 1990–93; Scottish Mgt and Enterprise Council, 1999–; Scottish Skills and Employability Network, 1999–; Member: Adv. Scottish Council for Educn and Trng Targets, 1993–96; Bd, SCOTVEC, 1993–96 (Fellow, 1996); UK Nuffield Langs Inquiry, 1998–2000; Ministerial Trade Union Wkg Pty on Lifelong Learning, 2000–. Chairman: Technol. Review Gp, 1993–; Nat. Cttee for Review of Post 16 educn and trng, 1993–; Assoc. for Mgt Educn and Trng in Scotland, 1998–; Scottish Parlt Futures Forum Project Bd, 2007. Pres., Glasgow and West of Scotland Inst. of Mgt, 2001–; Hon. Pres., Scottish Assoc. for Language Teaching, 1998–2000. CCMI (CIMgt 2000; FBIM 1989; Pres., Renfrewshire, 1991–93). FRSA 1992; FSQA 1997; FICPD 1999; FSC 2006. DUniv Paisley, 1993; Hon. DEd Abertay, 2003. *Publications:* Basic Knowledge 'O' French, 1974; Higher French Past Papers, 1975; Scottish Education Policy Review, 1994; contributor, World Year Book in Education, TES. *Recreations:* swimming, genealogy, do-it-yourself, reading. *Address:* 10 Whittingehame Drive, Glasgow G12 0XX. *T:* (0141) 334 3458; *e-mail:* frank@pignatelli.co.uk.

PIGOT, Sir George (Hugh), 8th Bt *cr* 1764, of Patshull, Staffs; Managing Director, Custom Metalcraft Ltd, since 1998; *b* 28 Nov. 1946; *s* of Maj.-Gen. Sir Robert Pigot, 7th Bt, CB, OBE, DL, and Honor (*d* 1966), *d* of Captain Wilfred St Martin Gibbon; *S* father, 1986; *m* 1st, 1967, Judith Sandeman-Allen (marr. diss. 1973); one *d*; 2nd, 1980, Lucinda Jane (marr. diss. 1993), *d* of D. C. Spandler; two *s*; 3rd, 2006, Odette, *yr d* of Walter Stanley, Port Elizabeth, SA. *Educ:* Stowe. Man. Dir, Padworth Fisheries Ltd, 1981–95; Dir, Southern Trout Ltd, 1993–95 (Man. Dir, 1994–95); business consultant, Positive Response, 1995–; Sec.-Gen., Residential Sprinkler Assoc., 1998–2003; Chief Exec., Fire Sprinkler Assoc., 2003–07. Member: Council, British Trout Assoc., 1986–93 (Hon. Treas., 1990–92); Fish Farming Exec. Cttee, NFU, 1987–90 (Chm. Health and Technical Sub-Cttee, 1989–90). *Recreations:* classic cars, golf. *Heir:* s George Douglas Hugh Pigot, *b* 17 Sept. 1982. *Address:* Mill House, Mill Lane, Padworth, near Reading, Berks RG7 4JX.

PIGOTT, Sir (Berkeley) Henry (Sebastian), 5th Bt *cr* 1808; farmer; *b* 24 June 1925; *s* of Sir Berkeley Pigott, 4th Bt, and Christabel (*d* 1974), *d* of late Rev. F. H. Bowden-Smith; *S* father, 1982; *m* 1954, (Olive) Jean, *d* of John William Balls; two *s* one *d*. *Educ:* Ampleforth College. Served War with Royal Marines, 1944–45. *Recreation:* sailing (blue water). *Heir: er s* David John Berkeley Pigott [*b* 16 Aug. 1955; *m* 1st, 1981 (marr. diss.); 2nd, 1986, Julie Wiffen (marr. diss.); one *d*]. *Address:* Brook Farm, Shobley, Ringwood, Hants BH24 3HT. *T:* (01425) 474423.

PIGOTT, Prof. Christopher Donald, PhD; Director, University Botanic Garden, Cambridge, 1984–95; *b* 7 April 1928; *s* of John Richards Pigott and Helen Constance Pigott (*née* Lee); *m* 1st, 1954, Margaret Elsie Beatson (*d* 1981); one *d*; 2nd, 1986, Sheila Lloyd (*née* Megaw). *Educ:* Mill Hill School; University of Cambridge. MA, PhD. Asst Lectr, and Lectr, Univ. of Sheffield, 1951–60; Univ. Lectr, Cambridge, 1960–64; Fellow of Emmanuel Coll., Cambridge, 1962–64; Prof. of Biology, Univ. of Lancaster, 1964–84, Prof. Emeritus, 1995–; Professorial Fellow, Emmanuel Coll., Cambridge, 1984–95; Member: Nature Conservancy, 1971–73; Nature Conservancy Council, 1979–82; Council, 1980–92, Properties Cttee, 1990–2002, Nat. Trust; Home Grown Timber Adv. Cttee, 1987–94, Res. Users Adv. Gp, 1993–96, Forestry Commn; Foreign Correspondent, Acad. d'Agriculture de France (Silviculture), 1982–. *Publications:* contribs to sci. jls (ecology and physiology of plants). *Recreations:* walking, gardening, drawing. *Address:* Greenbank, Cartmel, Grange-over-Sands LA11 7ST.

PIGOTT, Ronald Wellesley, FRCS, FRCSI; Consultant Plastic Surgeon, Frenchay Hospital, Bristol, 1969–93, Hon. Consultant, since 1993; *b* 16 Sept. 1932; *s* of Thomas Ian Wellesley Pigott and Kathleen Muriel (*née* Parsons); *m* 1958, Sheila King; four *s*. *Educ:* Oakham Sch., Rutland; Univ. of Dublin (BA, MB, BCh, BAO). FRCSI 1960; FRCS 1962. Short service commn, Parachute Field Ambulance, 1960–62. Sen. Registrar, Plastic Surgery, Stoke Mandeville Hosp., 1962–68; Robert Johnson Fellow, Univ. of Miami, 1967. Pioneered endoscopy of velopharyngeal isthmus in the condition of velopharyngeal incompetence; developed split screen recording of endoscopic and radiological examn of velopharyngeal isthmus with A. P. W. Makepeace; pioneered computer-based assessment of symmetry for application to cleft lip and nose deformity with B. Coghlan and D. Matthews. President: Eur. Assoc. of Plastic Surgeons, 1992–93; British Assoc. of Aesthetic Plastic Surgeons, 1993. James Halloran Bennet Medal in Surgery, 1956; James Berry Prize 1979, Jacksonian Prize 1979, RCS; Mowlem Award, Brit. Assoc. Plastic Surgeons, 1982. *Publications:* chapters regarding investigation and treatment of cleft lip and palate in: Advances in the Management of Cleft Lip and Palate, 1980; Clinics in Plastic Surgery, 1985; Scott Brown's Paediatric Otolaryngology, 5th edn 1987; Current Therapy in Plastic and Reconstructive Surgery, 1989; article on develt of endoscopy of palatopharyngeal isthmus, Proc. Royal Soc., 1977; articles in Lancet, Brit. Jl Plastic Surgery, Plastic Reconstructive Surgery, Annals Plastic Surgery, Scandinavian Jl Plastic Reconstructive Surgery. *Recreations:* formerly hockey (represented Ireland, University of Dublin and Army and Combined Services), tennis (represented Univ. of Dublin), painting, sculpture, gardening.

PIGOTT-BROWN, Sir William Brian, 3rd Bt *cr* 1902; *b* 20 Jan. 1941; *s* of Sir John Pigott-Brown, 2nd Bt (killed in action, 1942) and Helen (who *m* 1948, Capt. Charles Raymond Radclyffe), *o d* of Major Gilbert Egerton Cotton, Priestland, Tarporley, Cheshire; *S* father, 1942. *Heir:* none.

PIGOTT-SMITH, Timothy Peter; actor and director; *b* 13 May 1946; *s* of late Harry Thomas Pigott-Smith and of Margaret Muriel (*née* Goodman); *m* 1972, Pamela Miles; one *s*. *Educ:* Bristol Univ. (BA Hons 1967); Bristol Old Vic Theatre Sch. Appeared with: Bristol Old Vic, 1967–69; Prospect Th. Co., 1970–71; RSC, 1972–75; Birmingham, Cambridge, Nottingham and Royal Court Th., 1975–77; *stage appearances include:* Benefactors, Vaudeville, 1984; Bengal Lancer (one-man show), Leicester, transf. Lyric, Hammersmith, 1985; Coming in to Land, Antony and Cleopatra, Entertaining Strangers, Winter's Tale, Cymbeline, and Tempest, NT, 1986–88; dir, Samuel Beckett's Company, Donmar Warehouse (Edinburgh Fest. Fringe award), 1987; Artistic Dir, Compass Th., 1989–92; Brutus in Julius Caesar, 1990; Salieri in Amadeus, 1991; Saki—an anthology, 1991; Mr Rochester in Jane Eyre, Playhouse, 1993; The Picture of Dorian Gray, Lyric, 1994; Retreat, Orange Tree, Richmond, 1995; The Letter, Lyric, 1995; Mary Stuart, The Alchemist, RNT, 1996; Heritage, Hampstead, 1997; The Iceman Cometh, Almeida, 1998, transf. Old Vic, then NY, 1999; Five Kinds of Silence, Lyric, 2000; Cassius in Julius Caesar, RSC, 2001; Scrooge in A Christmas Carol, Lyric Hammersmith, 2002; Ezra Mannon in Mourning Becomes Electra, NT, 2003; Agamemnon in Hecuba, Donmar Warehouse, 2004; Women Beware Women, RSC, 2006; The Exonerated, Riverside, 2006; See How They Run, Duchess, 2006; Pygmalion, Th. Royal Bath and tour, 2007, transf. Old Vic, 2008; Little Nell, Th. Royal Bath and tour, 2007; director: Royal Hunt of the Sun, 1989; Playing the Wife, 1992; Hamlet, Regent's Park, 1994; The Real Thing, UK tour, 2005. *Films:* Aces High, 1975; Joseph Andrews, 1977; Sweet William, 1978; The Day Christ Died, 1979; Richard's Things, 1981; Clash of the Titans, 1981; Escape to Victory, 1981; Hunchback of Notre Dame, 1982; State of Emergency, 1985; Life Story (Best TV Film, BAFTA), 1987; The True Adventures of Christopher Columbus, 1992; The Remains of the Day, 1993; The Bullion Boys, 1993; The Shadowy Third, 1994; Four Feathers, Laissez Passer, Bloody Sunday, Gangs of New York, 2002; Johnny English, 2003; Alexander, 2004; Entente Cordiale, V for Vendetta, Flyboys, 2005; *television: series and serials:* Dr Who, 1970; Glittering Prizes, 1975; North and South, 1975; Wings, 1976; Eustace and Hilda, 1977; The Lost Boys, 1978; The Wilderness Years, 1978; Fame is the Spur, 1982; The Jewel in the Crown (Best TV Actor, BAFTA; TV Times Best Actor; BPG Best Actor), 1984; The Chief, 1989–91; The Vice, 2001; Kavanagh QC, 2001; Dr Terrible's House of Horrible, 2001; Inspector Lynley Mysteries, 2002; Spooks, 2002; North and South, 2004; Poirot: Taken at the Flood, 2006; Holby Blue, 2007; Midsomer Murders, 2008; *plays:* No Mama No, 1976; Measure for Measure, 1978; School Play, 1979; Henry IV part 1, 1980; Eroica, 2003; *documentaries:* Calcutta Chronicles (presenter and writer), 1996; Innocents, 2001; Pompeii: the last day, 2003; Peter Ackroyd's London, 2004. Hon. DLitt: Leicester, 2002; Bristol. *Publication:* Out of India, 1987. *Recreations:* music, sport.

PIKE, Prof. (Edward) Roy, PhD; FRS 1981; Clerk Maxwell Professor of Theoretical Physics, University of London at King's College, since 1986 (Head of School of Physical Sciences and Engineering, 1991–94); *b* 4 Dec. 1929; *s* of Anthony Pike and Rosalind Irene Pike (*née* Davies); *m* 1955, Pamela Sawtell; one *s* two *d*. *Educ:* Southfield Grammar Sch., Oxford; University Coll., Cardiff (BSc, PhD; Fellow, 1981). CPhys, FInstP, CMath, FIMA. Served Royal Corps of Signals, 1948–50. Fulbright Schol., Physics Dept, MIT, 1958–60; Royal Signals and Radar Estabt Physics Group, 1960: theoretical and experimental research condensed matter physics and optics; Individual Merit: SPSO 1967; DCSO 1973; CSO, 1984–90. Vis. Prof. of Maths, Imperial Coll., London, 1985–86. Chairman: Adam Hilger Ltd, 1981–85; Oval (114) Ltd, 1984–85; non-executive Director: Richard Clay plc, 1985–86; Stilo Technology Ltd, 2002–04 (Chm., 1995–2002); Stilo Internat. plc, 2002–04 (Chm., 2000–02); Phonologica Ltd, 2004–06. Govt assessor, SRC Physics Cttee, 1973–76. Mem. Council: Inst. of Physics, 1976–85 (Vice-Pres. for Publications, 1981–85); European Physical Soc., 1981–83; Director: NATO Advanced Study Insts, 1973, 1976; NATO Advanced Res. Workshops, 1987–88, 1991 and 1996. Hon. Editor: Journal of Physics A, 1973–78; Optica Acta, 1978–83; Quantum Optics, 1989–94. Nat. Science Foundn Vis. Lectr, USA, 1959; Lectures: Univ. of Rome, 1976; Univ. of Bordeaux, 1977; Simon Fraser Univ., 1978; Univ. of Genoa, 1980. FKC 1993. Charles Parsons medal and lecture, Royal Society, 1975; MacRobert award (jtly) and lecture, Council of Engrg Instns, 1977; Worshipful Co. of Scientific Instrument Makers Annual Achievement award (jtly), 1978; Committee on Awards to Inventors award, 1980;

Guthrie Medal and Prize, Inst. of Physics, 1996. Confrérie St-Etienne, 1980–. *Publications:* (jtly) The Quantum Theory of Radiation, 1995; (ed) High Power Gas Lasers, 1975; edited jointly: Photon Correlation and Light Beating Spectroscopy, 1974; Photon Correlation Spectroscopy and Velocimetry, 1977; Frontiers in Quantum Optics, 1986; Fractals, Noise and Chaos, 1987; Quantum Measurement and Chaos, 1987; Squeezed and Non-classical Light, 1988; Photons and Quantum Fluctuations, 1988; Inverse Problems in Scattering and Imaging, 1991; Photon Correlation and Light Scattering Spectroscopy, 1997; Scattering, 2002; numerous papers in scientific jls. *Recreations:* music, languages, woodwork. *Address:* 3a Golborne Mews, North Kensington, W10 5SB; 8 Bredon Grove, Malvern, WR14 3JR.

PIKE, Rt Rev. Eric; Bishop of Port Elizabeth, 1993–2001; *b* 11 Nov. 1936; *s* of Eric and Elizabeth Pike; *m* 1st, 1963, Wendy Anne Walker; one *s* one *d*; 2nd, 1977, Joyce Davidson; two step *s* three step *d*. *Educ:* Graaff Reinet Teachers' Training Coll. (Primary Teachers Cert. 1957); St Paul's Theol Coll., Grahamstown (DipTh 1968). Worked in Govt Service, Transkei, SA, 1955; taught at Queen's Coll. Boys' High Sch., 1958–65; ordained deacon, 1968, priest, 1969; Asst Priest, St John's, E London, 1969–71; Rector: St Paul's, Komga, 1971–72; St Mark's, E London, 1972–77; Archdeacon of E London and Operation Outreach, 1978–87; Rector, St Alban's, E London, 1987–89; Suffragan Bishop of Grahamstown, 1989–93. *Recreations:* walking, gardening. *Address:* Farne, 11 Barling Crescent, Fish Hoek 7975, South Africa.

PIKE, Lt-Gen. Sir Hew (William Royston), KCB 1997; DSO 1982; MBE 1977; Lieutenant, HM Tower of London, 2004–07; *b* 24 April 1943; *s* of Lt-Gen. Sir William Pike, KCB, CBE, DSO; *m* 1966, Jean, *d* of Col Donald Matheson, RAMC; one *s* two *d*. *Educ:* Winchester Coll.; RMA Sandhurst. Commissioned Parachute Regt, 1962; 3 Para, Middle East, Guyana, UK, 1963–66; ADC, UK and Norway, 1966–67; 1 Para, Middle East, UK, 1967–70; Sch. of Infantry, 44 Para Bde (V), 1970–74; Staff College, 1975; Brigade Major, 16 Para Bde, 1976–77; Co. Comdr, 3 Para Germany and UK, 1978–79; CO, 3 Para, UK and Falkland Is Campaign, 1980–83 (despatches 1981); Comd 22 Armd Bde, Bergen-Hohne, 1987–90; RCDS 1990; GOC 3rd (UK) Div., 1992–94; Comdt, RMA, Sandhurst, 1994–95; Dep. C-in-C, and Inspector Gen. TA, HQ Land Comd, 1995–97; Dep. Comdr, SFOR, Bosnia, 1997–98; GOC and Dir of Mil. Ops, NI, 1998–2000. Dir, GAP Activity Projects, 2001–06. Chm. Govs, Treloar Sch., 2001–08; Trustee, Treloar Trust, 2001–08. Freeman, City of London, 1982. Hon. Liveryman, Haberdashers' Co., 2004. *Publication:* From the Front Line—Family Letters and Diaries: 1914 to the Falklands and Afghanistan, 2008. *Recreation:* country pursuits. *Address:* c/o Lloyds TSB, Castle Street, Farnham, Surrey.

PIKE, Sir Michael (Edmund), KCVO 1989; CMG 1984; HM Diplomatic Service, retired; *b* 4 Oct. 1931; *s* of Henry Pike and Eleanor Pike; *m* 1962, Catherine (*née* Lim); one *s* two *d*. *Educ:* Wimbledon Coll.; London Sch. of Econs and Polit. Science; Brasenose Coll., Oxford (MA 1956). Service in HM Armed Forces, 1950–52. Editor, Cherwell, Oxford Univ., 1954; part-time News Reporter, Sunday Express, 1954–55; Feature Writer and Film Critic, Surrey Comet, 1955–56; joined HM Foreign (now Diplomatic) Service, 1956; Third Secretary: FO, 1956–57; Seoul, 1957–59; Second Secretary: Office of Comr Gen. for Singapore and SE Asia, 1960–62; Seoul, 1962–64; FO, 1964–68; First Sec., Warsaw, 1968–70; FCO, 1970–73; First Sec., Washington, 1973–75; Counsellor: Washington, 1975–78; Tel Aviv, 1978–82; RCDS, 1982; Ambassador to Vietnam, 1982–85; Minister and Dep. UK Perm. Rep. to NATO, Brussels, 1985–87; High Comr, Singapore, 1987–90. Political Affairs Advr, Sun Internat. Exploration and Production Co., 1991–93; Dir, AIB Govett Asian Smaller Cos Investment Trust, 1993–2001. Member: Bid Cttee, British Olympic Bid: Manchester 2000, 1991–93; Bid Cttee, English Commonwealth Games Bid, Manchester 2002, 1994–95; Sensitivity Review Unit, FCO, 1992–2001. Special Rep. of Sec. of State for Foreign and Commonwealth Affairs, 1992–99; HM Govt Co-ordinator, Conf., Britain in the World, 1995. Dir, Greenwich Millennium Trust, 1995–2000; Co-Chm., Greenwich Town Centre Management Agency, 1993–2001; Vice-Chm., Greenwich Develt Agency, 1998–2003 (Mem., 1997–2003); Member: Greenwich Tourism Partnership, 1998–2001; Cutty Sark Wkg Gp, Maritime Greenwich - World Heritage Site Partnership, 2002–04; Probity and Conduct Panel, Greenwich LBC, 2002–. Pres., Union of Catholic Students of GB, 1955–56; Director: Housing Justice (formerly Catholic Housing Aid Soc.), 1995–2004; Catholic Housing Aid Soc. (Central London), 2003–; Nat. New Infant and Parent Network, 1995–99. Chm., Editorial Bd, Asian Affairs, 2002–. *Recreations:* reading, running, contemplating London. *Address:* 5 Crooms Hill, SE10 8ER.

PIKE, Peter Leslie; *b* 26 June 1937; *s* of Leslie Henry Pike and Gladys (*née* Cunliffe); *m* 1962, Sheila Lillian Bull; two *d*. *Educ:* Hinchley Wood County Secondary Sch. (Commercial Dept); Kingston Technical Coll. Pt 1 Exam., Inst. of Bankers. National Service, RM, 1956–58. Midland Bank, 1954–62; Twinings Tea, 1962–63; Organiser/Agent, Labour Party, 1963–73; Mullard (Simonstone) Ltd, 1973–83. Mem., GMBATU (Shop Steward, 1976–83). Member (Lab): Merton and Morden UDC, 1962–63; Burnley BC, 1976–84 (Leader, Labour Gp, 1980–83; Gp Sec., 1976–80). MP (Lab) Burnley, 1983–2005. Opposition front bench spokesperson: on Rural Affairs, 1990–92; on Housing, 1992–94. Member: Envmt Select Cttee, 1984–90; Procedural Select Cttee, 1995–97; Regulatory Reform Cttee (formerly Deregulation Select Cttee), 1995–2005 (Chm., 1997–2005); Modernisation Select Cttee, 1997–2005; Liaison Cttee, 1997–2005; Speakers Panel of Chairmen, 2001–05; Chm., Rights of Way Rev. Cttee, 1997–2005. All-Party Groups: Chairman: Romania Gp, 1994–2005; Southern Africa Gp; Mongolia Gp; Joint Chairman: Road Passenger Transport Gp, 1995–2005; Kidney Gp, 2001–05; Associate Parly Transport Forum, 1997–2001; Vice Chairman: Paper Industry Gp; Homelessness Gp; (Jt), Manufacturing Gp; Kashmir Gp, 2005; Secretary: Pakistan Gp, 1997–2005; Building Socs Gp, 1997–2005; Jt Sec., Overseas Develt Gp; Treas., Road Transport Study Gp, 1997–2000. Chm., PLP Envmt Cttee, 1987–90. Chairman: Clarets Trust, 2005–; Burnley, Pendle and Rossendale Learning Difficulties Partnership, 2005–; Burnley Emmaus, 2005–; Burnley Area Community Credit Union, 2007–; Member Board: Burnley Youth Th.; Burnley Area Self Help Agency, 2005–; Pendle CAB, 2005–; SW Burnley Enterprise, 2005– (Chm., 2007–); Burnley Homestart, 2006–; Mem. Cttee, Burnley Civic Soc., 2005–; President: Burnley WEA, 2005–; Friends of Freshfields, 2005–; Treas., Friends of St Peters, 2006–. Member: Nat. Trust, 1974–; CND; Anti-Apartheid. *Recreation:* Burnley Football Club supporter. *Address:* 30 Deerpark Road, Burnley, Lancs BB10 4SD. *T:* (01282) 434719; *e-mail:* peterl.pike@btinternet.com. *Club:* Byerden House Socialist.

PIKE, Sir Philip Ernest Housden, Kt 1969; Chief Justice of Swaziland, 1970–72, retired; *b* 6 March 1914; *s* of Rev. Ernest Benjamin Pike and Dora Case Pike (*née* Lillie); *m* 1st, 1943, Phyllis Kelvin Calder; one *s* one *d*; 2nd, 1959, Millicent Locke Staples (*d* 1996); 3rd, 2004, Patricia Ethne Hodson. *Educ:* De Carteret School, and Munro Coll., Jamaica; Middle Temple, London. Barrister at Law, 1938. Crown Counsel, Jamaica, 1947–49; Legal Draftsman, Kenya, 1949–52; Solicitor General, Uganda, 1952–58; QC (Uganda) 1953; Attorney General, Sarawak, 1958–65; QC (Sarawak) 1958; Chief Justice, High Court in Borneo, 1965–68; Judge, High Court of Malawi, 1969–70, Actg Chief Justice, 1970. Coronation Medal, 1953. PNBS-Sarawak, 1965; Malaysia Commemorative Medal, 1967; PMN Malaysia 1968. *Recreations:* golf, gardening. *Address:* 3 Earlewood Court, 180/184 Ron Penhaligon Way, Robina, Qld 4226, Australia.

PIKE, Dr Richard Andrew, CEng, CSci; FRSC; FIMechE; FIChemE; FIET; FEI; Chief Executive, Royal Society of Chemistry, since 2006; *b* 2 April 1950; *s* of Tudor Morgan Pike and Eileen Mary (*née* Oxley); *m* 1986, Fiona Elizabeth Henry; one *s* two *d*. *Educ:* Gosport Co. Grammar Sch.; Downing Coll., Cambridge (BA 1st Cl. Engrg; MA; PhD 1977). CEng 1987; FIMechE 1988; FIChemE 1991; FEI 1992; FIET (FIEE 1996); CSci 2004; FRSC 2006. Joined British Petroleum as univ. apprentice, 1968; Maintenance Engr, BP Llandarcy, 1971–72; res. student, Cambridge, 1972–75; Develt Engr, BP Engrg, London, 1975–80; Area Commissioning Engr, Sullom Voe Terminal, Shetland, 1980–82; Business Develt Co-ordinator, Jt Ventures, London, 1982–83; Develt Supt, Pipelines and Facilities, Aberdeen, 1984–85; Offshore Prodn Engr, Forties, North Sea, 1985–86; Manager Technical, Sullom Voe Terminal, 1986–88; Manager, Jt Venture, Japan, 1988–89; Gen. Manager, Chems, BP Far East, Tokyo, 1989–93; Pres., BP Chems, Japan, 1991–93; Dir, Samsung-BP Chems, S Korea, 1989–91; Dir Gen., IMechE, 1993–98; Ops Manager, Cambridge Management Consulting, 1998–2000; Sen. Associate, Gaffney, Cline & Associates, 2000–06. *Publications:* articles in jls, magazines and newspapers on engrg, sci. and educn. *Recreations:* reading, swimming (first person to swim from Yell to Unst and mainland to Yell, Shetland Is, 1980), languages, travel. *Address:* Royal Society of Chemistry, Burlington House, Piccadilly, W1J 0BA. *T:* (020) 7437 8656.

PIKE, Roy; *see* Pike, E. R.

PIKE, Roy Ernest; Headmaster, Torquay Boys' Grammar School, since 1987; *b* Taunton, 1 May 1948; *s* of Ernest and Nora Pike; *m* 1971, Philippa Gordon; two *s* four *d*. *Educ:* Ilminster Grammar Sch.; St Luke's Coll., Exeter (BEd 1970); University Coll. London (BA Hons 1977 ext.). Torquay Boys' Grammar School: History Teacher, 1970; Hd of Dept, 1975–83; Pastoral Hd, 1977–83; Dep. Headmaster, 1983–87. Mem. Cttee, Foundn and Aided Schs Nat. Assoc. (formerly Grant Maintained Schs Adv. Cttee, then Foundn and Voluntary Aided Schs Assoc.), 1993–. Trustee, Torbay Coast and Countryside Trust, 2002–. FRSA. *Publications:* (contrib.) The Beacon School Experience: case studies in excellence, vol. 1, 2000, developing the curriculum, vol. 2, 2002. *Recreations:* family, tennis, country pursuits, conservation of natural and built environment. *Address:* Torquay Boys' Grammar School, Shiphay Manor Drive, Torquay TQ2 7EL. *T:* (01803) 615501, *Fax:* (01803) 614613; *e-mail:* rpike@tbgs.torbay.sch.uk.

PIKE, Air Vice-Marshal Warwick John; Director General, RAF Medical Services, 2002–04; *b* 31 Dec. 1944; *s* of Captain Thomas Pike and late Molly (*née* Buckley); *m* 1968, Susan Margaret Davies-Johns (*d* 2007); two *s* two *d*. *Educ:* Sir John Port Sch.; Guy's Hosp., London (MB BS 1968); London Sch. of Hygiene and Tropical Medicine (MSc 1988). MRCS, LRCP 1968; DObstRCOG 1975; MRCGP 1975; DAvMed 1979; MFOM 1993. Joined RAF, 1970; served in UK, Singapore, Hong Kong and Germany; CO, Princess Mary's Hosp., Akrotiri, Cyprus, 1990–92; Dir, Med. Personnel, 1992–94; Asst Dir of Med. Co-ordination, Surgeon Gen.'s Dept, MoD, 1994–96; Dir, Primary Health Services, 1996–99; QHP 1997–2004; COS, later Chief Exec., Defence Secondary Care Agency, 1999–2002. *Recreations:* walking, theatre, history. *Address:* 23 High Street, Alconbury, Huntingdon PE28 4DS; *e-mail:* warwick.pike@virgin.net. *Club:* Royal Air Force.

PILBROW, Richard Hugh; Founder and Chairman, Theatre Projects Consultants, 1957–2006, now Chairman Emeritus; *b* 28 April 1933; *s* of Arthur Gordon Pilbrow and Marjorie Pilbrow; *m* 1st, 1958, Viki Brinton; one *s* one *d*; 2nd, 1974, Molly Friedel; one *d*. *Educ:* Cranbrook Sch.; Central Sch. of Speech and Drama. Stage Manager, Teahouse of the August Moon, 1954; Lighting Designer for over 200 prodns in London, New York, Paris and Moscow, incl.: Brand, 1959; Blitz, 1962; Zorba, 1968; Annie, 1978; The Little Foxes, Windy City, 1982; Singin' In the Rain, 1983; Heliotrope Bouquet, 1991; Four Baboons Adoring the Sun, 1992; The Magic Flute, LA, 1993; Showboat, 1993; The Life, 1997; Our Town, 2003; The Boy Friend, 2005; The Sleeping Beauty, Amer. Ballet Th., 2007; A Tale of Two Cities, 2008; for Nat. Theatre Co., 1963–, incl. Hamlet, 1963, Rosencrantz and Guildenstern are Dead, 1966; Heartbreak House, 1975; Love for Love, 1985. Theatrical Producer in London of prodns incl.: A Funny Thing Happened on the Way to the Forum, 1963, 1986; Cabaret, 1968; Company, 1972; A Little Night Music, 1975; West Side Story, 1984; The Mysteries, Lyceum, 1985; I'm Not Rappaport, 1986. Film Prod., Swallows and Amazons, 1973; TV Productions: All You Need is Love—the story of popular music, 1975; Swallows and Amazons for Ever, 1984; Dir, Mister, 1971. Theatre Projects Consultants have been consultants on over 800 theatres and arts centres, incl. Disney Concert Hall, LA, Kimmel Performing Arts Centre, Philadelphia, New Amsterdam Theatre, NY, Nat. Theatre of GB, Barbican Theatre, and theatres and arts centres in Canada, Iran, Hong Kong, Saudi Arabia, Mexico, Iceland, Nigeria, Singapore, USA, etc. Co-founder, Soc. of British Theatre Designers, 1975; Fellow, Assoc. of British Theatre Technicians, 2003–; Jt Pres., Assoc. of Lighting Designers, 2003– (Chm., 1982–85); Member: Drama Panel, Arts Council of GB, 1968–70; Soc. of West End Theatre; Council, London Acad. of Music and Drama. Fellow, US Inst. of Theatre Tech., 2001. FRSA. *Publications:* Stage Lighting, 1970, 3rd edn 1991; Stage Lighting Design, 1997; (with Patricia Mackay) The Walt Disney Concert Hall—The Backstage Story, 2003. *Recreations:* The Hebrides, cooking, dogs. *Address:* 78 Barrack Hill Road, Ridgefield, CT 06877, USA. *Club:* Garrick.

PILCHER, Rosamunde, OBE 2002; writing and publishing short stories and novels, since 1944; *b* 22 Sept. 1924; *d* of Charles Montagu Lawrence Scott and Helen Scott; *m* 1946, Graham Pilcher; two *s* two *d*. *Educ:* St Clare's, Polwithen, Penzance; Howell's Sch., Llandaff, Cardiff. Author of Year, Bertelsmann Book Club, Germany, 1991; Berliner Zeitung Kulturpreis, 1993; Deutscher Videopreis, 1996; Bambi Award, Bunte magazine, 1997; Goldene Kamera Award, Hörzu, 1998. *Publications:* Sleeping Tiger; Another View; End of Summer; Snow in April; Empty House; Day of the Storm; Under Gemini; Wild Mountain Thyme; Carousel; Blue Bedroom; The Shell Seekers (Amer. Booksellers' Assoc. award, 1991; televised); September, 1990; Voices in Summer; Flowers in Rain; Coming Home, 1995 (Romantic Novelist of the Year, RNA, 1996; televised, 1998); The World of Rosamunde Pilcher; Winter Solstice, 2000. *Recreations:* walking, gardening, reading, travel. *Address:* Penrowan, Longforgan, Dundee DD2 5ET.

PILDITCH, Sir Richard (Edward), 4th Bt *cr* 1929; *b* 8 Sept. 1926; *s* of Sir Philip Harold Pilditch, 2nd Bt, and Frances Isabella, *d* of J. G. Weeks, JP, Bedlington, Northumberland; *S* brother, Sir Philip John Frederick Pilditch, 3rd Bt, 1954; *m* 1950, Pauline Elizabeth Smith; one *s* one *d*. *Educ:* Charterhouse. Served War of 1939–45, RNVR and RN, 1944–46, incl. service in India and Ceylon. *Recreation:* fishing. *Heir:* *s* John Richard Pilditch, *b* 24 Sept. 1955.

PILE, Colonel Sir Frederick (Devereux), 3rd Bt *cr* 1900; MC 1945; *b* 10 Dec. 1915; *s* of Gen. Sir Frederick Alfred Pile, 2nd Bt, GCB, DSO, MC; *S* father, 1976; *m* 1st, 1940, Pamela (*d* 1983), *d* of late Philip Henstock; two *d*; 2nd, 1984, Mrs Josephine Culverwell.

Educ: Weymouth; RMC, Sandhurst. Joined Royal Tank Regt, 1935; served War of 1939–45, Egypt and NW Europe; commanded Leeds Rifles, 1955–56; Colonel GS, BJSM, Washington, DC, 1957–60; Commander, RAC Driving and Maintenance School, 1960–62. Secretary, Royal Soldiers' Daughters' School, 1965–71. *Publication:* Better than Riches, 1993. *Recreations:* fishing, cricket, travelling. *Heir: nephew* Anthony John Devereux Pile [*b* 7 June 1947; *m* 1977, Jennifer Clare Youngman; two *s* one *d*]. *Club:* MCC.

PILGER, John Richard; journalist, author and film-maker; *s* of Claude Pilger and Elsie (*née* Marheine); one *s* one *d*. *Educ:* Sydney High Sch. Cadet journalist, Sydney Daily Telegraph, Australia, qualified, 1961; freelance journalist, Italy, 1962; Reuter, London, 1962; feature writer, chief foreign correspondent, Daily Mirror, London, 1962–86 (reporter, Vietnam War, 1966–75, Cambodia, 1979–91, etc); columnist, New Statesman, 1991–; contributor: The Guardian, The Independent, NY Times, Sydney Morning Herald, The Age, Melbourne, Aftonbladet, Sweden; Mail and Guardian, SA, Il Manifesto, Italy. Campaigns incl. Thalidomide 'X list' victims, and Australian Aboriginal land rights. Documentary film-maker, 1970–, films include: The Quiet Mutiny, 1970; A Faraway Country (Czechoslovakia), 1977; Year Zero: the silent death of Cambodia, 1979; Nicaragua, 1983; Japan Behind the Mask, 1986; The Last Dream, 1988; Death of a Nation: the Timor conspiracy, 1994; Vietnam: the last battle, 1995; Inside Burma: land of fear, 1996; Breaking the Mirror: the Murdoch Effect, 1997; Apartheid Did Not Die, 1998; Paying the Price: killing the children of Iraq, 2000; The New Rulers of the World, 2001; Palestine is Still the Issue, 2002; Breaking the Silence, 2003; Stealing a Nation, 2004; The War on Democracy, 2007. Edward Wilson Fellow, Deakin Univ., Aust., 1995; Vis. Prof., Cornell Univ., USA, 2004–. Hon. DLitt: Staffordshire, 1994; Kingston, 1999; Rhodes Univ., SA; DPhil *hc* Dublin City, 1995; Hon. DArts Oxford Brookes, 1997; Hon. LLD St Andrews, 1999; DUniv Open, 2001. Awards include: Descriptive Writer of the Year, 1966; Reporter of the Year, 1967; Journalist of the Year, 1967, 1979; Internat. Reporter of the Year, 1970; News Reporter of the Year, 1974; Campaigning Journalist of the Year, 1977; UN Media Peace Prize and Gold Medal, 1979–80; George Foster Peabody Award, USA, 1990; Reporters Sans Frontiers Award, France, 1990; Richard Dimbleby Award, 1991; US TV Academy Award (Emmy), 1991; Premis Actual Award, Spain, 1996; Sophie Prize for Human Rights, 2003; RTS Award, 2005. *Publications:* The Last Day, 1975; Aftermath: the struggle of Cambodia and Vietnam, 1981; The Outsiders, 1984; Heroes, 1986; A Secret Country, 1989; Distant Voices, 1992; Hidden Agendas, 1998; The New Rulers of the World, 2002; (ed) Tell Me No Lies: investigative journalism and its triumphs, 2004; Freedom Next Time, 2006. *Recreations:* swimming, sunning, mulling. *Address:* 57 Hambalt Road, SW4 9EQ. *T:* (020) 8673 2848; *e-mail:* jpmarheine@hotmail.com.

PILGRIM, Cecil Stanley, CCH 1986; High Commissioner for Guyana in London, 1986–92, and concurrently Ambassador (non-resident) to France, the Netherlands and Yugoslavia; *b* 1 Feb. 1932; *s* of Errol Pilgrim and Edith Pilgrim; *m* 1979, Cita I. Pilgrim; one *d*. *Educ:* Queen's Coll., Guyana; Univ. of Guyana (BSc; post graduate course in Internat. Relations). Diplomatic Cadet, Guyana, 1967; Second Sec., Jamaica, 1969; First Sec., China, 1974; Counsellor, USSR, 1978; Ambassador, Cuba, 1979. *Recreations:* reading, music, badminton, walking, cricket, enjoys sports of all types.

PILGRIM, Martin George; public policy consultant, since 2007; Chief Executive, Association of London Government, subseq. London Councils, 1997–2007; *b* 10 Feb. 1950; *s* of late George and Audrey Pilgrim; *m* 1974, Angela Muriel Staples; two *d*. *Educ:* Arden St Co. Primary Sch., Gillingham; Gillingham Grammar Sch.; Univ. of Kent at Canterbury (MA Mgt). CIPFA. Various posts, Kent CC, 1968–81; Association of Metropolitan Authorities: Under Sec. (Finance), 1981–96; Dep. Sec., 1996–97. Dir, Film London, 2005–; Associate Dir, CriticalEYE, 2007–. Chm., London Regl Council, Prince's Trust, 2007–; Chair, London Sustainability Exchange, 2007–. Trustee, Daycare Trust, 2007–. *Publications:* articles in acad. jls and local govt press. *Recreations:* keeping fit, hill-walking, moderate ski-ing, France and French. *Address:* 73 Hamelin Road, Gillingham, Kent ME7 3ER. *T:* (01634) 574852.

PILKINGTON, family name of **Baron Pilkington of Oxenford**.

PILKINGTON OF OXENFORD, Baron *cr* 1995 (Life Peer), of West Dowlish in the county of Somerset; **Rev. Canon Peter Pilkington;** Chairman, Broadcasting Complaints Commission, 1992–96; Hon. Canon of Canterbury Cathedral, 1975–90, now Canon Emeritus; *b* 5 Sept. 1933; *s* of Frank and Doris Pilkington; *m* 1966, Helen (*d* 1997), *d* of Charles and Maria Wilson; two *d*. *Educ:* Dame Allans Sch., Newcastle upon Tyne; Jesus Coll., Cambridge (BA 1955; MA 1958). Schoolmaster, St Joseph's Coll., Chidya, Tanganyika, 1955–57; ordained 1959; Curate in Bakewell, Derbys, 1959–62; Schoolmaster, Eton College, 1962–75, Master in College, 1965–75; Headmaster, King's Sch., Canterbury, 1975–86; High Master, St Paul's Sch., 1986–92. Mem., Parole Bd, 1990–95. *Address:* Oxenford House, near Ilminster, Somerset TA19 0PP. *T:* (01460) 52813. *Clubs:* Beefsteak, Garrick, Pratt's.

PILKINGTON, Air Vice-Marshal Michael John, CB 1991; CBE 1982; Air Officer Commanding Training Units, Royal Air Force Support Command, 1989–92, retired; *b* 9 Oct. 1937; *s* of David and Mary Pilkington; *m* 1960, Janet Rayner; one *d*. *Educ:* Bromley Grammar Sch. psc rcds. Commnd Royal Air Force, 1956; Bomber Sqdns, No 35, No 83, No 27, 1959–70; RAF sc 1971; HQ Near East Air Force, 1972–73; CO No 230 Vulcan OCU, 1974–75; Defence Policy Staff, 1977–78; CO RAF Waddington, 1979–81; RCDS 1982; Branch Chief Policy, SHAPE, 1982–85; DG of Trng, RAF, 1986–89. *Recreations:* golf, gardening, theatre, wine. *Clubs:* Royal Air Force; Gog Magog Golf.

PILKINGTON, Muriel Norma, MA; Headteacher, Wycombe High School, 1986–98; *b* 1 Jan. 1941; *d* of Norman Herbert Fosbury and Lilian Alice Fosbury; *m* 1st, 1962, Anthony Leonard Andrews; one *s*; 2nd, 1983, Derek Brogden Pilkington; one step *s* one step *d*. *Educ:* Woking County Grammar Sch.; Helene Lange Hochschule, Hamburg; Lady Margaret Hall, Oxford (BA 1962; MA 1970). Asst Teacher, Shephalbury Sch., Stevenage, 1962–64; 2nd in Dept, Hatfield Girls' Grammar Sch., 1964–66; Head of Dept/Faculty, Sir James Altham Sch., Watford, 1970–81; Dep. Head, Francis Bacon Sch., St Albans, 1981–86. Chm., Area 6 SHA, 1993–95. Consultant, Centre for Educnl Mgt, 1999–. Trustee: Whitmore Vale Housing Assoc., 1970–; London Arts Schs, 1994– (Mem. Council, 2000–08). Governor: Bucks Chilterns UC (formerly Bucks Coll., Brunel Univ.), 1993–2006 (consultant/guest lectr, 1999; Vice Chm., Council, 2001–06); Dr Challoner's High Sch., 2003–; Wimbledon High Sch., 2004–08. Contributor, Inf. for Sch. and Coll. Govs, 2003–07. FRSA 1990. Hon. PhD Bucks Chilterns UC, 2006. *Publication:* History of the Buckinghamshire New University, 2009. *Recreations:* music, jogging, gastronomy, travel. *Address:* 18 Woodside Drive, Bradwell Village, Burford, Oxon OX18 4XB.

PILKINGTON, Stephen Charles, CBE 2005; QPM 1998; PhD; DL; Chief Constable, Avon and Somerset Constabulary, 1998–2005; *b* 4 June 1948; *s* of Charles Leonard Pilkington and Joan Pilkington; *m* 1974, Anne Bernadette Brett; three *s*. *Educ:* Queen Elizabeth Coll., Univ. of London (BSc 1st cl. Hons Biology, 1969; PhD Plant Physiology, 1973). Joined Metropolitan Police, 1972; Constable, Battersea; seconded to American Police Force, 1984; Dep. Asst Comr, Central London, 1996–97. DL Somerset, 2005. *Recreations:* walking, ornithology, Rugby (spectator), cycling, kayaking and camping (holidays).

PILKINGTON, Sir Thomas Henry Milborne-Swinnerton-, 14th Bt *cr* 1635; *b* 10 March 1934; *s* of Sir Arthur W. Milborne-Swinnerton-Pilkington, 13th Bt and Elizabeth Mary (she *m* 1950, A. Burke), *d* of late Major J. F. Harrison, King's Walden Bury, Hitchin; *S* father, 1952; *m* 1961, Susan, *e d* of N. S. R. Adamson, Durban, South Africa; one *s* two *d*. *Educ:* Eton College. Sen. Steward, Jockey Club, 1994–98. *Recreations:* golf, racing. *Heir: s* Richard Arthur Milborne-Swinnerton-Pilkington [*b* 4 Sept. 1964; *m* 1994, Katya (marr. diss. 2000), *d* of T. J. Clemence; one *d*; *m* 2001, Henrietta Kirk; two *d*]. *Address:* King's Walden Bury, Hitchin, Herts SG4 8JU. *Club:* White's.

PILL, Rt Hon. Sir Malcolm (Thomas), Kt 1988; PC 1995; **Rt Hon. Lord Justice Pill;** a Lord Justice of Appeal, since 1995; *b* 11 March 1938; *s* of late Reginald Thomas Pill, MBE and Anne Pill (*née* Wright); *m* 1966, Roisin Pill (*née* Riordan), DL; two *s* one *d*. *Educ:* Whitchurch Grammar Sch.; Trinity Coll., Cambridge. MA, LLM, Dip. Hague Acad. of Internat. Law. Served RA, 1956–58; Capt., Glamorgan Yeomanry (TA), 1958–67. Called to Bar, Gray's Inn, 1962, Bencher, 1987; Wales and Chester Circuit, 1963 (Treas., 1985–87; Presiding Judge, 1989–93); a Recorder, 1976–87; QC 1978; a Judge of the High Court, QBD, 1988–95; a Judge, Employment Appeal Tribunal, 1992–95. 3rd Sec., Foreign Office, 1963–64 (delegns to UN Gen. Assembly, ECOSOC, Human Rights Commn). Dep. Chm., Parly Boundary Commn for Wales, 1993–95. Chairman: UNA (Welsh Centre) Trust, 1969–77, 1980–87; Welsh Centre for Internat. Affairs, 1973–76; Eur. Parly Boundary Cttee for Wales, 1993. Chm., UK Cttee, Freedom from Hunger Campaign, 1978–87. Trustee, Dominic Barker Trust, 1997–. Hon. Fellow, Univ. of Wales Cardiff, subseq. Cardiff Univ., 1998. Hon. LLD Glamorgan, 1998. *Publication:* A Cardiff Family in the Forties, 1999. *Address:* Royal Courts of Justice, Strand, WC2A 2LL. *Clubs:* Army and Navy; Cardiff and County.

PILLAR, Rt Rev. Kenneth Harold; Bishop Suffragan of Hertford, 1982–89; an Assistant Bishop, diocese of Sheffield, since 1990; *b* 10 Oct. 1924; *s* of Harold and Mary Pillar; *m* 1955, Margaret Elizabeth Davies; one *s* three *d*. *Educ:* Devonport High School; Queens' Coll., Cambridge (MA); Ridley Hall, Cambridge. Asst Curate, Childwall, Liverpool, 1950–53; Chaplain, Lee Abbey, Lynton, N Devon, 1953–57; Vicar: St Paul's, Beckenham, 1957–62; St Mary Bredin, Canterbury, 1962–65; Warden of Lee Abbey, Lynton, N Devon, 1965–70; Vicar of Waltham Abbey, Essex, 1970–82; RD of Epping Forest, 1976–82. *Recreations:* walking, music, reading. *Address:* 75 Dobcroft Road, Millhouses, Sheffield S7 2LS. *T:* (0114) 236 7902.

PILLAY, Prof. Gerald John, DTheol, PhD; Vice-Chancellor and Rector, Liverpool Hope University, since 2005 (Rector and Chief Executive, Liverpool Hope University College, 2003–05); *b* 21 Dec. 1953; *s* of Jimmy and Theena Pillay; *m* 1983, Nirmala Pillay; two *s*. *Educ:* Univ. of Durban-Westville (BA 1975; BD 1978; DTheol 1985); Rhodes Univ. (PhD 1984). Lectr, then Sen. Lectr in Church Hist., Univ. of Durban-Westville, 1979–87; Prof. of Church Hist., Univ. of SA, 1988–97; Foundn Prof. of Theology and Dean of Liberal Arts, Otago Univ., NZ, 1997–2003. *Publications:* Voices of Liberation, vol. 1, Albert Lutuli, 1993; Religion at the Limits?: Pentecostalism among Indian South Africans, 1994; (ed) A History of Christianity in South Africa, vol. 1, 1994; contribs to books and learned jls. *Recreations:* squash, gardening. *Address:* Liverpool Hope University, Hope Park, Liverpool L16 9JD. *T:* (0151) 291 3403, *Fax:* (0151) 291 3100; *e-mail:* pillayg@hope.ac.uk.

PILLING, Sir Joseph (Grant), KCB 2001 (CB 1995); Permanent Under-Secretary of State, Northern Ireland Office, 1997–2005; *b* 8 July 1945; *s* of late Fred and Eva Pilling; *m* 1968, Ann Cheetham; two *s*. *Educ:* Rochdale Grammar Sch.; King's Coll., London; Harvard. Asst Principal, 1966, Pvte Sec. to Minister of State, 1970, Home Office; Asst. Pvte Sec. to Home Sec., 1970–71; NI Office, 1972; Harkness Fellow, Harvard Univ. and Univ. of Calif at Berkeley, 1972–74; Home Office, 1974–78; Pvte Sec. to Sec. of State for NI, 1978–79; Home Office, 1979–84; Under Sec., DHSS, 1984–87; Dir of Personnel and Finance, HM Prison Service, Home Office, 1987–90; Dep. Under Sec. of State, NI Office, 1990–91; Dir-Gen., HM Prison Service, Home Office, 1991–92; Prin. Estabt and Finance Officer, DoH, 1993–97. Strategic Reviewer of CAA, 2007–08; Mem., Rev. of 30 Year Rule, 2007–08; Chairman: Rev. Gp on Sen. Appts in C of E, 2005–07; Koestler Trust, 2006–; Adv. Bd, Relationships Foundn, 2006–; Pres., New Bridge Foundn, 2006–; Member: Adv. Council, Mgt Sch., Imperial Coll., London, 1989–97; Bd of Trustees, Macmillan Cancer Support, 2005–; Council, Univ. of London, 2006–08; Dio. Bd of Finance, Oxford, 2006–. *Club:* Athenæum.

PILLING, Prof. Michael John, CBE 2008; PhD; CChem, FRSC; Research Professor, University of Leeds, since 2008; *b* 25 Sept. 1942; *s* of John and Joan Pilling; *m* 1966, Gwenda Madeline Harrison; one *s* one *d*. *Educ:* Bacup and Rawtenstall Grammar Sch.; Churchill Coll., Cambridge (MA, PhD). CChem, FRSC 1991. Cambridge University: SRC Fellow, 1967–68; Jun. Res. Fellow, Churchill Coll., 1967–70; ICI Fellow, 1969–70; Vis. Scientist, Nat. Bureau of Standards, USA, 1968–69; Lectr in Physical Chemistry, and Fellow and Tutor of Jesus Coll., Oxford Univ., 1970–89; Leeds University: Prof. of Physical Chem., 1989–2007; Pro-Vice-Chancellor, 1992–94; Hd of Sch. of Chem., 1995–98; Dean for Res., Faculty of Maths and Phys. Scis, 2000–02; Dir, NERC Distributed Inst. for Atmospheric Composition, 2002–07. Visiting Professor: Univ. of Oregon, 1975; Univ. of Maryland, 1980; Univ. of Rome, 1984; Stanford Univ., 1987; John Jeyes Lectr, RSC, 2001; Dist. Guest Lectr, Envmtl Chem. Gp, RSC, 2006. Pres., Faraday Div., RSC, 2003–06 (Vice Pres., 1991–98; Sec., 1992–98). Mem. Council, NERC, 1995–2000 (Chm., Atmospheric Science and Tech. Bd, 1995–2000); Chm., Air Quality Expert Gp, DEFRA, 2001–. Hon. Dr rer. nat. 2007 and Hon. Prof., 2007, Eötvös Loránd Univ., Budapest. Award in Reaction Kinetics, 1991, Michael Polanyi Medal, Gas Kinetics Gp, 1994, Award for Combustion and Hydrocarbon Oxidation Chem., 2001, RSC; Sugden Award, Combustion Inst., 1993. *Publications:* Reaction Kinetics, 1975; (ed jtly) Modern Gas Kinetics, 1985; (jtly) Reaction Kinetics, 1995; (jtly) Unimolecular Reactions, 1996; (ed) Low Temperature Combustion and Autoignition, 1997; res. papers in learned jls. *Recreation:* walking. *Address:* School of Chemistry, University of Leeds, Leeds LS2 9JT. *T:* (0113) 233 6451; *e-mail:* m.j.pilling@leeds.ac.uk.

PILLINGER, Prof. Colin Trevor, CBE 2003; PhD; FRS 1993; Professor of Planetary Science, Open University, since 1990; *b* 9 May 1943; *s* of Alfred Pillinger and Florence (*née* Honour); *m* 1975, Judith Mary Hay; one *s* one *d*. *Educ:* Kingswood Grammar Sch.; University Coll. Swansea, Univ. of Wales (BSc Hons Chem. 1965; PhD 1968; Hon. Fellow, 2003). Department of Chemistry, University of Bristol: Post Doctoral Fellow, 1968–72; BSC Fellow, 1972–74; Res. Associate, 1974–76; Res. Associate and Sen. Res. Associate, Dept of Earth Sci., Cambridge, 1976–84; Sen. Res. Fellow, Dept of Earth Sci., Open Univ., 1984–90. Gresham Prof. of Astronomy, 1996–2000. Lead Scientist, British-led Beagle 2 mission to land on Mars, 1997–. FRAS 1981 (Mem. Council, 1989–91); Fellow, Meteoritical Soc., 1986; FRGS 1993; Founder Mem., British Mass Spectrometry Soc. (Aston Medal, 2003). Fellow, UC Swansea, 2003. Hon. DSc Bristol, 1985. A. C.

Clarke Award, British Rocketry Oral Hist. Prog., 2005; Space Achievement Medal, BIS, 2005; Reginald Mitchell Medal, 2006. Asteroid 15614 named Pillinger. *Publications:* Beagle: from Darwin's epic voyage to the British mission to Mars, 2003; Space is a Funny Place, 2007; numerous papers in learned jls and contribs to radio and TV, UK and abroad. *Recreations:* farming, animals, soccer. *Address:* Planetary Sciences Research Institute, Open University, Milton Keynes MK7 6AA. *T:* (01908) 652119, *Fax:* (01908) 655910.

PIMENTA, His Eminence Simon Ignatius Cardinal; Archbishop of Bombay (RC), 1978–97, now Emeritus; *b* 1 March 1920; *s* of late Joseph Anthony Pimenta and Rosie E. Pimenta. *Educ:* St Xavier's Coll., Bombay (BA with Maths); Propaganda Univ., Rome (Degree in Canon Law). Secretary at Archbishop's House, and Vice-Chancellor and Defensor Vinculi, Bombay, 1954; Vice Rector of Cathedral, 1960; Visiting Prof. of Liturgy, Bombay Seminary, 1960; Episcopal Vicar for Liturgy and Pastoral Formation of Junior Clergy, 1968; Rector of the Cathedral, 1967, Rector of Seminary, 1971; Auxiliary Bishop, 1971; Coadjutor Archbishop with right of succession, 1977. President: Catholic Bishops' Conf. of India, 1982–88; (Latin Rite), Conf. of Catholic Bishops of India, 1994–96. Cardinal, 1988. *Publications:* (edited) The Catholic Directory of Bombay, 1960 and 1964 edns; Circulars and Officials of the Archdiocese of Bombay, vols I and II, 1964, vol. III, 1971; booklet on the Cathedral of the Holy Name, 1964; Priest for Ever (homilies), 1999; Memoirs and Milestones (autobiog.), 2000; Cardinal Valerian Gracias: his life and ministry, 2002. *Address:* Archbishop's House, 21 Nathalal Parekh Marg, Mumbai 400 001, India. *T:* 2021093, 2021193, 2021293, (personal) 22049696.

PINA-CABRAL, Rt Rev. Daniel (Pereira dos Santos) de; an Assistant Bishop, Diocese of Europe (formerly Auxiliary Bishop, Diocese of Gibraltar in Europe), since 1976; Archdeacon of Gibraltar, 1986–94; *b* 27 Jan. 1924; *m* 1951, Ana Avelina Pina-Cabral; two *s* two *d*. *Educ:* University of Lisbon (Licentiate in Law). Archdeacon of the North in the Lusitanian Church, 1965; Suffragan Bishop of Lebombo (Mozambique), Church of the Province of Southern Africa, 1967; Diocesan Bishop of Lebombo, 1968; Canon of Gibraltar, 1976–. *Address:* Rua Henrique Lopes de Mendonça 253–4° Dto-Hab. 42, 4150 Porto, Portugal. *T:* (22) 6177772.

PINCHAM, Roger James, CBE 1982; Chairman, Venture Consultants Ltd, since 1980; Consultant: Gerrard, 2000–06; Finn, since 2006; *b* 19 Oct. 1935; *y s* of late Sam and Bessie Pincham; *m* 1965, Gisela von Ulardt (*d* 1974); one *s* two *d*. *Educ:* Kingston Grammar School. National Service, RAF, 1954–56. With Phillips & Drew, 1956–88, Partner, 1967–76, consultant, 1976–88. Mem., London Stock Exchange, 1963–91; MSI, 1992–. Director: Market Access Internat., then Europ. Political Consultancy Gp., 1985–94; Gerrard Vivian Gray, subseq. Greig Middleton, 1988–2000; UKRD Ltd, 1991–2006; Cornwall Independent Radio Ltd, 1991–99; ICOR(LPG) Internat. Ltd, 1992–; County Sound Radio Network Ltd, 1998–2003. Contested (L) Leominster, 1970, Feb. and Oct. 1974, 1979, 1983. Liberal Party: Nat. Exec., 1974–75 and 1978–87; Assembly Cttee, 1974–87; Standing Cttee, 1975–83; Chm. of Liberal Party, 1979–82; Jt Negotiating Cttee with SDP, and signatory to A Fresh Start for Britain, 1981. Mem., Agenda Cttee, Congress for Democracy, 2001–. Pres., St John Ambulance, St Pancras Div., 1996–2000. Founder Chm., Gladstone Club, 1973–; First Chairman: Indep. Educnl Assoc., 1974–2007; St James and St Vedast Schools, 1974–2007; Mem. Council, City Appeal for Eng. Coll. in Prague, 1991–; Gov., Sidney Perry Foundn, 1993–; Founder Trustee, John Stuart Mill Inst., 1992–. Trustee: Princess Margarita of Romania Trust, 1994–2004; Nat. Benevolent Fund for the Aged, 2001–. Pres., Lloyd George Soc., 1996–. Pres., Kington Eisteddfod, 1978. FRSA 1994. Fellow, Churchill Meml, Fulton, Mo, 1997–. Freeman, City of London. Liveryman: Barbers' Co. (Master, 1993–94); Founders' Co.; Freeman, Co. of Watermen and Lightermen. *Publications:* (jtly) New Deal for Rural Britain, 1977; (ed) New Deal for British Farmers, 1978; (contrib.) Dictionary of Liberal Biography, 1998; (contrib.) Standing for Justice, 2001; (contrib.) Sheila Rosenberg: a Renaissance lady, 2004. *Recreations:* gardening, cricket, visiting Aldeburgh and Kullu. *Address:* Babbacombe, Snape Bridge, Saxmundham, Suffolk IP17 1ST. *T:* (01728) 688010. *Clubs:* Beefsteak, Reform, National Liberal, City of London, Royal Automobile; Surrey County Cricket, Norfolk County Cricket, Woolhope Naturalists' Field.

PINCHER, (Henry) Chapman; freelance journalist, novelist and business consultant; Assistant Editor, Daily Express, and Chief Defence Correspondent, Beaverbrook Newspapers, 1972–79; *b* Ambala, India, 29 March 1914; *s* of Major Richard Chapman Pincher, E Surrey Regt, and Helen (*née* Foster), Pontefract; *m* 1965, Constance, (Billee), Wolstenholme; one *s* one *d* (by previous *m*). *Educ:* Darlington Gram. Sch.; King's Coll., London (FKC 1979); Inst. Educn; Mil. Coll. of Science. Carter Medallist, London, 1934; BSc (hons Botany, Zoology), 1935. Staff Liverpool Inst., 1936–40. Joined Royal Armoured Corps, 1940; Techn SO, Rocket Div., Min. of Supply, 1943–46; Defence, Science and Medical Editor, Daily Express, 1946–73. Academician, Russian Acad. for Defence, Security and Internal Affairs, 2005. Hon. DLitt Newcastle upon Tyne, 1979. Granada Award, Journalist of the Year, 1964; Reporter of the Decade, 1966. Order of the Great Victory (Russia), 2006 (for war service). *Publications:* Breeding of Farm Animals, 1946; A Study of Fishes, 1947; Into the Atomic Age, 1947; Spotlight on Animals, 1950; Evolution, 1950; (with Bernard Wicksteed) It's Fun Finding Out, 1950; Sleep, and how to get more of it, 1954; Sex in Our Time, 1973; Inside Story, 1978; (jtly) Their Trade is Treachery, 1981; Too Secret Too Long, 1984; The Secret Offensive, 1985; Traitors—the Labyrinths of Treason, 1987; A Web of Deception, 1987; The Truth about Dirty Tricks, 1991; One Dog and Her Man, 1991; Pastoral Symphony (autobiog.), 1993; A Box of Chocolates, 1993; Life's a Bitch!, 1996; Tight Lines!, 1997; God's Dog, 1999; *novels:* Not with a Bang, 1965; The Giantkiller, 1967; The Penthouse Conspirators, 1970; The Skeleton at the Villa Wolkonsky, 1975; The Eye of the Tornado, 1976; The Four Horses, 1978; Dirty Tricks, 1980; The Private World of St John Terrapin, 1982; Contamination, 1989; original researches in genetics, numerous articles in scientific, agricultural and sporting jls. *Recreations:* fishing, natural history, country life; spy-hunting, ferreting in Whitehall and bolting politicians. *Address:* The Church House, 16 Church Street, Kintbury, near Hungerford, Berks RG17 9TR. *T:* (01488) 658397.

PINCHERA, Albert Anthony; Chief Operating Officer, HM Revenue and Customs (Prosecutions), since 2007; *b* 2 Sept. 1947; *s* of Albert Sestore Pinchera and Edith Pinchera (*née* DeLuca); *m* 1971, Linda Avril Garrad; one *d*. *Educ:* Upton House Sch.; University Coll. London (BSc Hons Geol.). Exploration Geologist, 1969–72; Boots Company plc: Buyer, 1972–74; Sen. Buyer, 1974–77; Asst Merchandise Controller, 1977–81; Mktg Controller, 1981–86; Business Gen. Manager, 1986–90; Man. Dir, Boots Opticians, 1990–95; Hd, Internat. Retail Develt, 1995–97; Chief Exec., Nat. Kidney Res. Fund, 1998–2003; Dir, Greater London Magistrates' Courts Authy, 2003–05; Dir, HM Courts Service, 2005–07. Non-exec. Dir, Queen's Univ. Hosp. Trust, 2001–06. *Recreations:* military history, art restoration, golf. *Address:* The Old School House, Elston, Notts NG23 5NP.

PINCHING, Prof. Anthony John, DPhil; FRCP; Associate Dean for Cornwall, Peninsula Medical School, since 2003; *b* 10 March 1947; *s* of John Pinching and Wilhelmina Hermina Pinching (*née* Jonkers); *m* 1971, Katherine Susan Sloper; two *s* two *d*. *Educ:* Sherborne Sch., Dorset; St John's Coll., Oxford (BA 1968); St Edmund Hall, Oxford; Oxford Univ. Med. Sch. (DPhil 1972; BM BCh, MA 1973). MRCP 1976; FRCP 1986. Royal Postgraduate Medical School, London: Registrar and Sen. Registrar, Medicine and Immunology, 1976–79; Res. Fellow (Immunology), 1979–82; St Mary's Hospital Medical School, London: Sen. Lectr in Clinical Immunology, 1982–89; Reader, 1989–92; Louis Freedman Prof. of Immunology, 1992–2003, and Hd, Div. of Molecular Pathology Infection and Immunity, 1998–2003, St Bartholomew's and the Royal London Sch. of Medicine and Dentistry, subseq. Bart's and The London Sch. of Medicine and Dentistry, QMW, London Univ.; Clinical Dir, Infection and Immunity, St Bartholomew's Hosp. and Royal Hosps NHS Trust, 1992–99. Vis. Prof., Univ. of Malta, 1986. Dep. Chm., CMO's Wkg Gp on CFS/ME, 2000–02; Principal Med. Advr, Action for ME, 2002–; Chm., CFS/ME Service Investment Steering Gp, DoH, 2003–06. Terrence Higgins Trust Award, 1986; Evian Health Award, 1990. *Publications:* (ed) AIDS and HIV Infection, 1986; (ed jtly) AIDS and HIV Infection: the wider perspective, 1988; (ed jtly) New Dictionary of Medical Ethics, 1997; res. papers on neuroanatomy, autoimmune disease, HIV and AIDS and other immuno-deficiency. *Recreations:* music, especially opera, playing clarinet, literature, especially 20th Century, writing poetry, hill-walking. *Address:* Peninsula Medical School Offices, Royal Cornwall Hospital, Truro TR1 3LJ.

PINCOTT, Leslie Rundell, CBE 1978; Managing Director, Esso Petroleum Co. Ltd, 1970–78; *b* 27 March 1923; *s* of Hubert George Pincott and Gertrude Elizabeth Rundell; *m* 1st, 1944, Mary Mae Tuffin (*d* 1996); two *s* one *d*; 2nd, 1997, Elaine Sunderland. *Educ:* Mercers' Sch. FCA. Served War, Royal Navy, 1942–46 (Lieut, RNVR). Broads Paterson & Co. (Chartered Accountants), 1946–50; joined Esso Petroleum Co. Ltd, 1950; Comptroller, 1958–61; Asst Gen. Manager (Marketing), 1961–65; Dir and Gen. Manager, Cleveland Petroleum Co. Ltd, 1966–68; Standard Oil Co. (NJ), 1968–70; Vice-Chm., Remploy Ltd, 1979–87 (Dir, 1975–87); Chairman: Canada Permanent Trust Co. (UK) Ltd, 1978–80; Stone-Platt Industries PLC, 1980–82; Edman Communications Gp PLC, 1982–87; BR Southern Bd, 1986–89 (Dir, 1977–86). Director: George Wimpey PLC, 1978–85; Highlands Fabricators Ltd, 1984–91. A Dep. Chm., 1978–79, Chm., 1979–80, Price Commn; Chairman: Hundred Gp of Chartered Accountants, 1978–79; Oxford Univ. Business Summer Sch., 1975–78; Printing Industries EDC, NEDO, 1982–88; Mem., Investment Cttee, London Develt Capital Fund (formerly part of Guinness Mahon), 1985–99. Chm., Wandle Housing Assoc., 1996–2000; Dir, Hurlingham Ct Ltd, 1999– (Chm., 2000–05, 2008–). Pres., District Heating Assoc., 1977–79. Vice-Pres., English Schs Athletics Assoc., 1977–; Mem. Council, ISCO, 1982–97. Mem., The Pilgrims, 1971–. *Recreations:* tennis, bowls, travel. *Address:* 53 Hurlingham Court, Ranelagh Gardens, SW6 3UP. *Club:* Hurlingham (Chm., 1988–92; Trustee, 1996–98).

PINDER, (John) Andrew, CBE 2004; Chairman, BECTA (formerly British Educational Communications and Technology Agency), since 2006; Managing Director, Andrew Pinder Consultancy Ltd, since 2004; *b* 5 May 1947; *s* of Norah Joan Pinder and William Gordon Pinder; *m* 1st, 1970, Patricia Munyard (marr. diss. 1980); one *d*; 2nd, 1981, Susan Ellen Tyrrell; one *d* and one step *s*. *Educ:* De La Salle Coll., Sheffield; Coleshill Grammar Sch., Warwicks; Univ. of Liverpool (BA Hons Social Studies). Inspector of Taxes, 1972–76; Board of Inland Revenue: Policy Div., 1976–79; Management Div., 1979–90, Under Sec., Dir of IT, 1989; Prudential Corporation: Dir of Systems, 1990–92; Dir, Gp Management Services, 1991–92; Dir, Systems and Business Ops, 1992–94; Citibank, 1995–99: Hd of Eur. Ops and Technol., 1995; Hd of Ops and Technol., Global Transaction Services, 1995–97; Hd of Eur. Br. Ops, Global Corp. Bank, 1998–99; indep. consultant on corporate and info. technol. strategy, 1999–2000; Prime Minister's e-envoy, Cabinet Office, 2000–04. Chairman: Dovetail Sabrina Ltd, 1998–2002; Dovetail of Shrewsbury Ltd, 1999–2002; Will Network Ltd, 2000–05; Indep. Nat. Will Register, 2000–04; non-executive Director: United Utilities plc, 2001–; Entrust Inc., 2004–06; Vertex Data Sciences, 2004–06; Spring Gp plc, 2005–. Mem., Intel Global Adv. Bd, 2005–. Chm., Shropshire Learning & Skills Council, 2000–01. FRSA 1995. Freeman, City of London, 1994; Liveryman, Co. of Information Technologists, 1995. *Recreations:* music, walking, gardening, reading, fly-fishing. *Address:* 6 Lambert Jones Mews, Barbican, EC2Y 8DP. *Clubs:* Institute of Directors, Century.

PINDER, John Humphrey Murray, OBE 1973; Professor, 1970–99, Hon. Professor, since 1999, College of Europe; *b* 20 June 1924; *s* of Harold Pinder and Lilian Pinder (*née* Murray); *m* 1964, Pauline Hawtayne Lewin. *Educ:* Marlborough Coll.; King's Coll., Cambridge (MA). Served RA, W African Artillery, 1943–47. Press Officer, Federal Union, 1950–52; EIU, 1952–64, Internat. Dir, 1957–64; Dir, PEP, then PSI, 1964–85. Member, Editorial Board: Government and Opposition, 1975–2001; Jl Common Mkt Studies, 1979–92. Pres., Union of Eur. Federalists, 1984–90 (Hon. Pres., 1990–); Vice-President: Eur. Movement (Internat.), 1990–2000; Eur. Movement (UK), 2001– (Vice Chm., 1975–90; Dep. Chm., 1990–98; Mem. Bd, 1998–2007); Member, Board: Inst. Eur. Envmtl Policy, 1990–2001; Trans Eur. Policy Studies Assoc., 1995–98; Member, Council: ODI, 1972–99; Hansard Soc., 1973–99; RIIA, 1985–91. Chairman: Federal Trust, 1985–2008; Pinder Centre Trustees, Pinder Trust, 1998–2006; James Madison Trust, 2001–; Trustee, One World Trust, 1993–2000. *Publications:* Britain and the Common Market, 1961; Europe against de Gaulle, 1963; (jtly) Europe after de Gaulle, 1969; (ed) The Economics of Europe, 1971; (ed) Fifty Years of PEP: looking forward 1931–1981, 1981; (jtly) Policies for a Constrained Economy, 1982; (ed) National Industrial Strategies and the World Economy, 1982; (ed jtly) One European Market?: a critical analysis of the Commission's internal market strategy, 1988; (ed jtly) Pacifism is not Enough: collected lectures and speeches of Lord Lothian, 1990; (jtly) Federal Union: the pioneers, 1990; The European Community and Eastern Europe, 1991; The Building of the European Union, 1991, 3rd edn 1998; (ed jtly) Maastricht and Beyond: building the European Union, 1994; (ed) Altiero Spinelli and the British Federalists, 1999; (ed) Foundations of Democracy in the European Union, 1999; (jtly) The European Union: a very short introduction, 2001, 2007; (jtly) The EU and Russia: the promise of partnership, 2002; (ed jtly) Multinational Federations, 2007. *Recreations:* music, walking, foreign languages and literature. *Address:* 26 Bloomfield Terrace, SW1W 8PQ. *Club:* Brooks's.

PINDLING, Dame Marguerite, DCMG 2007; Deputy to the Governor General of the Bahamas, since 2006; *b* 26 June 1932; *d* of Ruebin and Viola McKenzie; *m* 1956, Rt Hon. Sir Lynden Oscar Pindling, KCMG, OM, PC (*d* 2000); two *s* two *d*. *Educ:* South Andros All Age Sch., Andros Is., Bahamas. Businesswoman. *Publication:* The Life and Time of Dame Marguerite Pindling, 2007. *Recreations:* charitable work, Bahamas Red Cross Society. *Address:* Lynmar, Skyline Drive, Nassau, NP, Bahamas. *T:* 3271956; *e-mail:* thehomestore@coralwave.com.

PINE, Courtney, OBE 2000; jazz saxophonist; *b* 18 March 1964; *m* 1997, June Guishard; one *s* three *d*. *Albums* include: Journey to the Urge Within, 1987; Destiny's Song, 1988; The Vision's Tale, 1989; Closer to Home, 1990; Within the Realms of Our Dreams; To the Eyes of Creation; Modern Day Jazz Stories, 1995; Underground, 1997; Back in the Day, 2000; Devotion, 2003; Resistance, 2005; has also produced and arranged albums; contrib. to albums by other artists, incl. Mick Jagger, and to Larry Adler tribute album; has toured internationally. Presenter, Jazz Crusade, Radio 2. Jt producer, Jazzdaze (film), 2005. Hon. Prof., Thames Univ., 2005. Hon. DMus Westminster, 2005.

PINE, Prof. Cynthia Margaret, CBE 2006; PhD; Professor of Dental Public Health and Primary Dental Care, since 2002, Dean of Dental Studies, since 2003, University of Liverpool; *b* 2 Oct. 1953; *d* of Frederick and Nora Freeman; *m* 1992, Geoffrey Pine; two *d*, and one step *s*. *Educ:* Swanshurst Grammar Sch., Birmingham; Univ. of Manchester (BDS 1976; PhD 1982); Univ. of Dundee (MBA Dist. 2001). FDSRCSE 1977; FDSRCS 2004. Lectr, in Child Dental Health, 1982–85, in Dental Public Health, 1985–92, Univ. of Manchester; Dental Epidemiologist, NW RHA, 1985–92; University of Dundee: Sen. Lectr, 1992–99, Reader, 1999–2001, in Dental Public Health; Prof. of Dental Public Health, 2001–02. Hon. Consultant in Dental Public Health: Dundee Hosp., 1992–2001; Royal Liverpool Hosp., 2002–. Dir, WHO Collaborating Centre in Res. in Oral Health of Deprived Communities, 2003–. Non-exec. Dir, Aintree Univ. Hosp. NHS Foundn Trust, 2006; Mem., Health is Wealth Commn, 2007–. Gov., Birkenhead Sixth Form Coll., 2005–. FRSA 2007. *Publications:* Community Oral Health, 1997, 2nd edn 2007; over 100 articles in learned jls. *Recreations:* holidays with my family, reading, collecting porcelain, going to theatre and ballet. *Address:* Dental School, Pembroke Place, Liverpool L3 5PS. *T:* (0151) 706 5070; *e-mail:* cmpine@liv.ac.uk. *Club:* Royal Society of Medicine.

PINHEIRO, Prof. João de Deus, PhD, DSc; Professor of Engineering Sciences, University of Minho, since 1981; Member, European Parliament, since 2004; *b* Lisbon, 11 July 1945; *s* of Agostinho de Matos Salvador Pinheiro and Maria de Lurdes Rogado Pereira Salvador Pinheiro; *m* 1970, Maria Manuela Vieira Paisana; three *s* one *d*. *Educ:* Technol High Inst., Portugal (Licentiate in Chem. Engrg); Univ. of Birmingham (MSc Chem. Engrg, PhD Engrg Scis, DSc Engrg). University of Minho, Portugal: Dir, Dept of Planning, 1978–81; Dir, Sch. of Engrg, 1979–80; Associate Vice-Chancellor, 1981–82; Vice-Chancellor, 1984–85; Sec. of State for Educn and Schs Admin, 1982–83; Minister of Educn, then Minister of Educn and Culture, then Minister for Foreign Affairs, 1985–92; Mem., Nat. Parliament, for Viana do Castelo, 1985–87, for Porto, 1987–95; Mem., Nat. Council, Social Democratic Party, 1987; Pres., Cttee of Ministers, Council of Europe, 1991; Hon. Pres., Council of Ministers, NATO, 1990–91; Pres., Council of Ministers, EC, 1992; Mem., CEC, then EC, 1993–99. Pres., EPP, 2004–. Chm., Lusoturgolfes, 2001–; Vice-Chairman: Lusomundo Media, 2002–05; Sociedade Alentejana de Investimentos e Participaçoes, 2005–. Mem. 1979–83, Vice-Pres., 1983–84, Nat. Council for Scientific and Technol Res. Pres., Gen. Assembly, World Monument Fund Portugal, 2000–. Trustee, Ilídio Pinho Foundn, 2000–. For. Mem., Royal Acad. of Engrg, 1997. Grã-Cruz, Ordem Militar de Cristo (Portugal), 1993; numerous foreign decorations. *Recreations:* golf, tennis, reading, cinema, music, etc. *Address:* Rua José da Cunha Brochado No 7, 2750–397 Cascais, Portugal; *e-mail:* JPinheiro@europarl.eu.int. *Clubs:* Belas de Campo, Quinta da Marinha Golf and Tennis, Vilamoura Golfes (Portugal).

PINI, John Peter Julian; QC 2006; a Recorder, since 2000; *b* 27 Nov. 1954; *s* of Peter and Roberta Pini; *m* 1991, Yvonne Anne Coen, *qv*; one *s* one *d*, and one *d* from a previous marriage. *Educ:* Queen's Univ., Belfast (BA 1st Cl. Hons Philos. 1977); City Univ. (Dip. Law 1979). Called to the Bar, Gray's Inn, 1981 (Lord Justice Holker Exhibnr); criminal practitioner, SE Circuit, 1981–91, Midland Circuit, 1991–; Asst Recorder, 1999–2000. *Recreations:* jazz guitar, cookery, family. *Address:* 7 Bedford Row, WC1R 4BU. *T:* (020) 7242 3555; *e-mail:* jpini@7br.co.uk.

PINI, Yvonne Anne; *see* Coen, Y. A.

PININFARINA, Sergio; Cavaliere del Lavoro, 1976; engineer; Member, European Parliament (Liberal and Democratic Group), 1979–88; Chairman, Pininfarina SpA, 1966–2006, now Hon. Chairman; *b* 8 Sept. 1926; *s* of Battista Pininfarina and Rosa Copasso; *m* 1951, Giorgia Gianolio; one *s* one *d* (and one *s* decd). *Educ:* Polytechnic of Turin; graduated in Mech. Eng., 1950. Joined Pininfarina, 1950; Gen. Manager, 1960; Man. Dir, 1961–2003. President: Federpiemonte, 1983–88; OICA, 1987–89; Confindustria, 1988–92; Comitato Promotore Alta Velocità, 1991–; Vice-Pres., UNICE, 1990–94. Chm., Fidia; Board Member: Ferrari; Banca Passadore; Banca Brignone; Toro Assicurazioni; Edison; Indep. Internat. Univ. of Social Studies, Rome. Foreign Mem., Royal Swedish Acad. of Engrg Scis, 1988. Hon. Dr Econs, Indep. Internat. Univ. of Social Studies, Rome, 1993. Chevalier, Légion d'Honneur, 1979. Hon. RDI 1983. Compasso d'Oro, Assoc. for Industrial Design, 1995. *Recreation:* golf. *Address:* PO Box 295, 10100 Turin, Italy. *T:* (11) 70911; Pininfarina SpA, corso Stati Uniti 61, 10129 Turin, Italy. *Clubs:* Società Whist Accademia Filarmonica, Rotary, Subalpino, Artisti (Turin); Golf Torino, Golf Garlenda, Associazione Sportiva I Roveri.

PINKER, Prof. Robert Arthur, CBE 2005; international consultant, Press Complaints Commission, since 2004; Professor of Social Administration, London School of Economics and Political Science, 1993–96, now Emeritus; *b* 27 May 1931; *s* of Dora Elizabeth and Joseph Pinker; *m* 1955, Jennifer Farrington Boulton (*d* 1994); two *d*. *Educ:* Holloway County Sch.; LSE (Cert. in Social Sci. and Admin. 1959; BSc Sociology 1962; MSc Econ 1965). University of London: Head of Sociology Dept, Goldsmiths' Coll., 1964–72; Lewisham Prof. of Social Admin, Goldsmiths' Coll. and Bedford Coll., 1972–74; Prof. of Social Studies, Chelsea Coll., 1974–78; Prof. of Social Work Studies, LSE, 1978–93; Pro-Director, LSE, 1985–88; Pro-Vice-Chancellor for Social Scis, London Univ., 1989–90. Press Complaints Commission: Mem., 1991–2004; Privacy Comr, 1994–2004; Acting Chm., 2002–03; Chm., Bosnia-Hercegovina Press Council, 2003–05. Chm., British Library Project on Family and Social Research, 1983–86; Mem., Council, Advertising Standards Authority, 1988–95. Chm., Deptford Challenge Trust, 2005–. Chm. Governors, Centre for Policy on Ageing, 1988–94; Gov., BPMF, 1990–94; Mem. Council, Goldsmiths Coll., Univ. of London, 2001–07 (Hon. Fellow, 1999). Fellow, Soc. of Editors, 2004–. Chm., Editl Bd, Jl of Social Policy, 1981–86. *Publications:* English Hospital Statistics 1861–1938, 1964; Social Theory and Social Policy, 1971; The Idea of Welfare, 1979; Social Work in an Enterprise Society, 1990. *Recreations:* reading, writing, travel, unskilled gardening. *Address:* 76 Coleraine Road, Blackheath, SE3 7PE. *T:* (020) 8858 5320.

PINKER, Prof. Steven (Arthur), PhD; Johnstone Professor, Department of Psychology, Harvard University, since 2003; *b* Montreal, 18 Sept. 1954; *s* of Harry and Roslyn Pinker; US citizen; *m* 1st, 1980, Nancy Etcoff (marr. diss. 1992); 2nd, 1995, Ilavenil Subbiah. *Educ:* McGill Univ. (BA Psychol. 1976); Harvard Univ. (PhD Exptl Psychol. 1979). Postdoctoral Fellow, Center for Cognitive Sci., MIT, 1979–80; Assistant Professor, Department of Psychology: Harvard Univ., 1980–81; Stanford Univ., 1981–82; Massachusetts Institute of Technology: Asst Prof., Dept of Psychol., 1982–85; Associate Prof., 1985–89, Prof., 1989–2003, Dept of Brain and Cognitive Scis; Co-Dir, Center for Cognitive Scis, 1985–94; Dir, McDonnell-Pew Center for Cognitive Neurosci., 1994–99; Margaret MacVicar Faculty Fellow, 2000; Peter de Florez Prof., 2000–03. Hon. DSc McGill, 1999; Hon. PhD: Tel Aviv, 2003; Surrey, 2003. Dist. Scientific Award, 1984, Boyd R. McCandless Young Scientist Award, 1986, Amer. Psychol Assoc.; Troland Res. Award, NAS, 1993; Golden Plate Award, Amer. Acad. Achievement, 1999. *Publications:* Language Learnability and Language Development, 1984; (ed) Visual Cognition, 1985; (ed with J. Mehler) Connections and Symbols, 1988; Learnability and Cognition: the acquisition of argument structure, 1989; (ed with B. Levin) Lexical and Conceptual Semantics, 1992; The Language Instinct, 1994 (Wm James Bk Prize, Amer. Psychol Assoc., 1995); How the Mind Works, 1997 (LA Times Bk Prize, 1998; Wm James Bk Prize, Amer. Psychol Assoc., 1999); Words and Rules: the ingredients of language, 1999; The Blank Slate: the modern denial of human nature, 2002 (Eleanor Maccoby Book Prize, Amer. Psychol Assoc., 2003); The Stuff of Thought: language as a window into human nature, 2007; contrib. articles to Science, Cognition, Cognitive Sci. and other jls. *Recreations:* bicycling, photography. *Address:* Department of Psychology, Harvard University, William James Hall, 33 Kirkland Street, Cambridge, MA 02138, USA; *e-mail:* pinker@wjh.harvard.edu.

PINKERTON, Anthony James Moxon L.; *see* Lowther-Pinkerton.

PINKERTON, Prof. (Charles) Ross, MD; Director of Cancer Services, Mater Hospitals, Brisbane, since 2003; Professor of Oncology, University of Queensland, since 2003; Director of Paediatric Oncology, Royal Children's Hospital and Mater Children's Hospital, since 2007; *b* 6 Oct. 1950; *s* of Prof. John Henry McKnight Pinkerton, *qv*; *m* 1989, Janet Hardy; three *d*. *Educ:* Campbell Coll.; Queen's Univ., Belfast (MD 1981). Postgrad. trng in paediatrics, Dublin and London, 1976–80; trng in children's cancer, London and France, 1980–86. Consultant Paediatric Oncologist and Hd, Children's Unit, Royal Marsden Hosp., 1989–2003 (Sen. Res. Fellow, 1986–89); Prof. of Paediatric Oncology, Inst. of Cancer Res., London, 1995–2003. Chm., UK Children's Cancer Study Gp, 2000–. *Publications:* editor: Paediatric Oncology: clinical practice and controversies, 1991, 2nd edn 1997; Childhood Cancer Management, 1995; Clinical Challenges in Paediatric Oncology, 1998; over 200 papers on children's cancer management. *Recreation:* tennis. *Address:* 107 Ironbark Road, Chapel Hill, Qld 4069, Australia.

PINKERTON, Prof. John Henry McKnight, CBE 1983; Professor of Midwifery and Gynæcology, Queen's University, Belfast, 1963–85, now Emeritus; Gynæcologist: Royal Victoria and City Hospitals, Belfast, 1963–85; Ulster Hospital for Women and Children, 1963–85; Surgeon, Royal Maternity Hospital, Belfast, 1963–85; *b* 5 June 1920; *s* of late William Ross Pinkerton and Eva Pinkerton; *m* 1947, Florence McKinstry, MB, BCh, BAO; four *s*. *Educ:* Royal Belfast Academical Institution; Queen's Univ., Belfast. Hyndman Univ. Entrance Scholar, 1939; MB, BCh, BAO Hons; Magrath Scholar in Obstetrics and Gynæcology, 1943. Active service in HM Ships as Surg.-Lt, RNVR, 1945–47. MD 1948; MRCOG 1949; FRCOG 1960; FZS 1960; FRCPI 1977. Sen. Lectr in Obstetrics and Gynæcology, University Coll. of the West Indies, and Consultant Obstetrician and Gynæcologist to University Coll. Hosp. of the West Indies, 1953–59; Rockefeller Research Fellow at Harvard Medical Sch., 1956–57; Prof. of Obstetrics and Gynæcology, Univ. of London, at Queen Charlotte's and Chelsea Hosps and the Inst. of Obstetrics and Gynæcology, 1959–63; Obstetric Surgeon to Queen Charlotte's Hosp.; Surgeon to Chelsea Hosp. for Women. Vice-Pres., RCOG, 1977–80; Chm., Inst. of Obstetrics and Gynæcol., RCPI, 1984–87 (Hon. Fellow, 2007). Hon. DSc NUI, 1986. *Publications:* various papers on obstetrical and gynæcological subjects. *Address:* 41c Sans Souci Park, Belfast BT9 5QZ. *T:* (028) 9068 2956.

See also C. R. Pinkerton, W. R. Pinkerton.

PINKERTON, Ross; *see* Pinkerton, C. R.

PINKERTON, William Ross, CBE 1977; JP; HM Nominee for Northern Ireland on General Medical Council, 1979–83, retired; a director of companies; *b* 10 April 1913; *s* of William Ross Pinkerton and Eva Pinkerton; *m* 1943, Anna Isobel Lyness; two *d*. Managing Director, H. Stevenson & Co. Ltd, Londonderry, 1941–76. Mem., Baking Wages Council (NI), 1957–74. Mem. later Chm., Londonderry/Gransha Psychiatric HMC, 1951–69; Vice-Chm., then Chm., North West HMC, 1969–72; Chm., Western Health and Social Services Board, 1972–79; Member: Central Services Agency (NI), 1972–79; NI Health and Social Services Council, 1975–79; Lay Mem., Health and Personal Social Services Tribunal, NI, 1978–. Member, New Ulster Univ. Court, 1973–85, Council, 1979–85. Hon. Life Governor: Altnagelvin, Gransha, Waterside, St Columb's, Roe Valley, Strabane, Foyle and Stradreagh Hosps. JP Co. Londonderry, 1965–84, Div. of Ards, 1984–91, Div. of Craigavon, 1991. *Recreations:* yachting, fishing. *Address:* 9 Harwich Mews, Culcavey Road, Hillsborough, Co. Down, Northern Ireland BT26 6RH. *T:* (028) 9268 2421. *Club:* Royal Highland Yacht (Oban).

See also J. H. McK. Pinkerton.

PINNER, Ruth Margaret, (Mrs M. J. Pinner); *see* Kempson, R. M.

PINNINGTON, Roger Adrian, TD 1967; Chairman, SEA Group, since 2001; *b* 27 Aug. 1932; *s* of William Austin Pinnington and Elsie Amy Pinnington; *m* 1974, Marjorie Ann Pearson; one *s* three *d*. *Educ:* Rydal Sch., Colwyn Bay; Lincoln Coll., Oxford (MA). Marketing Dir, Jonas Woodhead & Sons, 1963–74; 1975–82: Vice Pres., TRW Europe Inc.; Man. Dir, CAM Gears Ltd; Pres., TRW Italia SpA; Dir Gen., Gemmer France; Pres., Torfinasa; Dep. Chm. and Chief Exec., UBM Group, 1982–85; Dir, Norcros, 1985–86; Dir and Chief Exec., Royal Ordnance PLC, 1986–87; Dir and Gp Chief Exec., RHP, subseq. Pilgrim House Gp, 1987–89. Chairman: Telfos Hldgs, subseq. Jenbacher Hldgs (UK), 1991–95; Lynx Holdings PLC, 1992–98; Cortworth PLC, 1994–97; British World Aviation Ltd, later BWA Gp plc, 1994–2000; Montanaro Hldgs Ltd, 1995–2001; Armour Gp plc, 1996–2001; Dep. Chm., Huntingdon Internat. Hldgs plc, 1998–99 (Chm., 1994–98). *Recreations:* gardening, arguing with Sally, collecting sauce bottle labels. *Address:* 2 Corrib House, 7 Clarence Terrace, Central Promenade, Douglas, Isle of Man IM2 4LS; *e-mail:* pinnington@hotmail.com. *Clubs:* Royal Automobile; Vincent's (Oxford).

PINNOCK, Comdr Harry James, RN retd; Director, Cement Makers' Federation, 1979–87; *b* 6 April 1927; *s* of Frederick Walter Pinnock and Kate Ada (*née* Shepherd); *m* 1st, 1962, Fru Inger Connie Åhgren (*d* 1978); one *d*; 2nd, 2002, Deborah Olivares, USA. *Educ:* Sutton Valence Sch. Joined RN, 1945; Midshipman, HMS Nelson, 1945–47; Sub-Lieut/Lieut, HMS Belfast, Far East, 1948–50; RN Rhine Flotilla, 1951–52; Staff of First Sea Lord, 1952–55; Lt-Comdr, Mediterranean Minesweepers, 1955–57; HMS Ceylon, E of Suez, 1957–59; Staff of C-in-C Plymouth, 1960–61; HQ Allied Naval Forces, Northern Europe, Oslo, 1961–63; Comdr, MoD, 1964–67, retd. Cement Makers' Fedn, 1970–87. Chm., Gala Day Services, 2007–. *Recreations:* walking, gardening, travel. *Address:* The Stables, Haining House, Selkirk TD7 5LR.

PINNOCK, Trevor, CBE 1992; ARCM; harpsichordist; conductor; Director, The English Concert, 1973–2003; *b* Canterbury, 16 Dec. 1946. *Educ:* Canterbury Cathedral Choir Sch.; Simon Langton Grammar Sch., Canterbury; Royal Coll. of Music, London (Foundn Scholar; Harpsichord and Organ Prizes). ARCM Hons (organ) 1965, FRCM 1996. London début with Galliard Harpsichord Trio (Jt Founder with Stephen Preston, flute and Anthony Pleeth, 'cello), 1966; solo début, Purcell Room, London, 1968. Formed The English Concert for purpose of performing music of baroque period on instruments in original condition or good modern copies, 1972, making its London début in English Bach Festival, Purcell Room, 1973. NY début at Metropolitan Opera, conducting Handel Giulio Cesare, 1988. Artistic Dir and Principal Conductor, 1991–96, Artistic Advr, 1996–98, Nat. Arts Centre Orch., Ottawa. Recordings of complete keyboard works of Rameau; Bach Toccatas, Partitas, Goldberg Variations, Concerti, Handel Messiah and Suites, Purcell Dido and Aeneas, orchestral and choral works of Bach, Handel, Vivaldi, complete symphonies of Mozart, etc. Hon. RAM 1988. Hon. DMus: Ottawa, 1993; Kent, 1995; Sheffield, 2005. Officier, Ordre des Arts et des Lettres (France), 1998. *Address:* c/o Ms Melanie Moult, Askonas Holt, Lincoln House, 300 High Holborn, WC1V 7JH. *T:* (020) 7400 1700.

PINSENT, Sir Christopher (Roy), 3rd Bt *cr* 1938; Lecturer and Tutor, Camberwell School of Art, 1962–86, retired; *b* 2 Aug. 1922; *s* of Sir Roy Pinsent, 2nd Bt, and Mary Tirzah Pinsent (*d* 1951), *d* of Dr Edward Geoffrey Walls, Spilsby, Lincs; *S* father, 1978; *m* 1951, Susan Mary, *d* of John Norton Scorer, Fotheringhay; one *s* two *d*. *Educ:* Winchester College. *Heir: s* Thomas Benjamin Roy Pinsent, *b* 21 July 1967. *Address:* Ramblers, The Cricket Green, Woodside Road, Chiddingfold, Surrey GU8 4UG.

PINSENT, Sir Matthew (Clive), Kt 2005; CBE 2001 (MBE 1992); oarsman; *b* 10 Oct. 1970; *s* of Rev. Ewen and Jean Pinsent; *m* 2002, Demetra Ekaterina Koutsoukos; twin *s* one *d*. *Educ:* Eton College; St Catherine's College, Oxford (BA Hons Geography 1993). Winner: coxless pairs: (with Tim Foster) Junior World Championship, 1988; (with Steven Redgrave): World Championship, 1991, 1993, 1994 and 1995; Olympic Gold Medal, 1992 and 1996; (with James Cracknell) coxed and coxless pairs, 2001, coxless pairs, 2002, World Championship; coxless fours: World Championship, 1997, 1998, 1999; Olympic Gold Medal, 2000 and 2004; Mem., Oxford Boat Race winning crew, 1990, 1991. Mem., IOC, 2002–04. *Publication:* A Lifetime in a Race, 2004. *Recreations:* golf, flying. *Club:* Leander (Henley-on-Thames).

PINSON, Barry; QC 1973; *b* 18 Dec. 1925; *s* of Thomas Alfred Pinson and Alice Cicily Pinson; *m* 1950, Miriam Mary; one *s* one *d*; *m* 1977, Anne Kathleen Golby. *Educ:* King Edward's Sch., Birmingham; Univ. of Birmingham. LLB Hons 1945. Fellow Inst. Taxation. Mil. Service, 1944–47. Called to Bar, Gray's Inn, 1949, Bencher 1981. Trustee, RAF Museum, 1980–98; Chm., Addington Soc., 1987–90. *Publications:* Revenue Law, 17 edns. *Recreations:* music, theatre, photography. *T:* (020) 7798 8450. *Club:* Sloane.

PINTER, Rabbi Abraham, (Avraham); Principal, Yesodey Hatorah Schools, since 1994; Dean, Beer Miriam Seminary, since 2008; *b* London, 21 Jan. 1949; *s* of Rabbi Samuel Pinter and Gertrude Pinter; *m* 1971, Rachel; two *s* five *d*. Mem. (Lab) Hackney BC, 1982–90. Chm., Chizuk, 1996–; Trustee, Union of Orthodox Hebrew Congregations, 1990– (Chm., Social Services, 1990–); Vice Chm., Ezer Lyoldos (Children and Families). *Address:* 6 Northdene Gardens, N15 6LX. *T:* (020) 8826 5500, *Fax:* (020) 8826 5505; *e-mail:* yeshatorah@aol.com.

PINTER, Lady Antonia; *see* Fraser, Antonia.

PINTER, Rabbi Avraham; *see* Pinter, Rabbi Abraham.

PINTER, Harold, CH 2002; CBE 1966; CLit 1998; FRSL; actor, playwright and director; Associate Director, National Theatre, 1973–83; *b* 10 Oct. 1930; *s* of Jack and Frances Pinter; *m* 1st, 1956, Vivien Merchant (marr. diss. 1980; she *d* 1982); one *s*; 2nd, 1980, Lady Antonia Fraser, *qv*. *Educ:* Hackney Downs Grammar Sch. Actor (mainly repertory), 1949–57. *Directed:* The Collection (co-dir with Peter Hall), Aldwych, 1962; The Birthday Party, Aldwych, 1964; The Lover, The Dwarfs, Arts, 1966; Exiles, Mermaid, 1970; Butley, Criterion, 1971; Butley (film), 1973; Next of Kin, Nat. Theatre, 1974; Otherwise Engaged, Queen's, 1975, NY 1977; Blithe Spirit, Nat. Theatre, 1977; The Rear Column, Globe, 1978; Close of Play, Nat. Theatre, 1979; The Hothouse, Hampstead, 1980 (for TV, 1982); Quartermaine's Terms, Queen's, 1981; Incident at Tulse Hill, Hampstead, 1982; The Trojan War Will Not Take Place, Nat. Theatre, 1983; The Common Pursuit, Lyric Hammersmith, 1984; Sweet Bird of Youth, Haymarket, 1985; Circe and Bravo, Wyndham's, 1986; Vanilla, Lyric, 1990; The New World Order, Royal Court, 1991; Party Time, Almeida, 1991 (for TV, 1992); Oleanna, Royal Court, 1993; Taking Sides, Criterion, 1995; Twelve Angry Men, Comedy, 1996; The Late Middle Classes, Watford, 1999; Celebration, and The Room, Almeida, 2000; No Man's Land, RNT, 2001; The Old Masters, Birmingham Rep., transf. Comedy, 2004. Fellow, BAFTA, 1997. Hon. DLitt: Reading, 1970; Birmingham, 1971; Glasgow, 1974; East Anglia, 1974; Stirling, 1979; Brown, 1982; Hull, 1986; Sussex, 1990; E London, 1994; Sofia, 1995; Bristol, 1998; London, 1999; Univ. of Aristotle, Thessaloniki, 2000; Florence, 2001; Turin, 2002; Nat. Univ. of Ireland, 2004; Leeds, 2007; Cambridge, 2008; Kragujevac, Serbia, 2008. Shakespeare Prize, Hamburg, 1970; Austrian State Prize for European Literature, 1973; Pirandello Prize, 1980; Donatello Prize, 1982; Elmer Holmes Bobst Award, 1984; David Cohen British Literary Prize, 1995; Laurence Olivier Special Award, 1996; Molière d'Honneur, Paris, 1997; Award for Literary Excellence, Sunday Times, 1997; Critics' Circle Award, 2000; Brianza Poetry Prize, 2000; South Bank Show Award, 2001; World Leaders Award, Canada, 2001; Hermann Kesten Medallion, 2001; Teatro Filodrammatici, 2004; 50th Anniversary Special Award, Evening Standard Theatre Awards, 2004; Wilfred Owen Poetry Prize, 2005; Kafka Prize, 2005; Nobel Prize for Literature, 2005; European Theatre Prize, 2006. Chevalier, Légion d'Honneur (France), 2007. *Plays:* The Room (stage 1957, television 1965); The Birthday Party, 1957 (stage 1958, television 1960 and 1987, film 1968); The Dumb Waiter, 1957 (stage 1960, television 1964 and 1987); The Hothouse, 1958 (stage 1980, television 1981); A Slight Ache, 1958 (radio 1959, stage 1961, television 1966); A Night Out, 1959 (radio and television, 1960); The Caretaker, 1959 (stage 1960 and 1991, film 1963, television 1966 and 1982); Night School, 1960 (television 1960 and 1982, radio 1966); The Dwarfs (radio 1960, stage 1963); The Collection (television 1961 and 1979, stage 1962); The Lover (television 1962 (Italia Prize) and 1977, stage 1963); Tea Party, 1964 (television 1965, stage 1970); The Homecoming, 1964 (stage 1965, film 1973); The Basement, 1966 (television 1967, stage 1970); Landscape, 1967 (radio 1968, stage 1969); Silence, 1968 (stage 1968); Night, 1969; Old Times, 1970 (stage 1971, television 1975); Monologue, 1972 (television 1973); No Man's Land, 1974 (stage 1975 and 1992, television 1978); Betrayal (stage 1978 (SWET Award, 1979) and 1991, film 1983); Family Voices, 1980 (radio 1981 (Giles Cooper Award, 1982), stage 1981); A Kind of Alaska, 1982 (stage and television 1984); Victoria Station (stage 1982); One for the Road (stage and television 1984); Mountain Language (stage 1988); The New World Order (stage 1991); Party Time (stage 1991, television 1992); Moonlight (stage 1993); Ashes to Ashes (stage 1996); Celebration (stage 2000); Sketches, 2002. *Screenplays:* The Caretaker, The Servant, 1962; The Pumpkin Eater, 1963; The Quiller Memorandum, 1966; Accident, 1967; The Birthday Party, The Homecoming, 1968; The Go-Between, 1969; Langrishe, Go Down, 1970 (adapted for television, 1978); A la Recherche du Temps Perdu, 1972; The Last Tycoon, 1974; The French Lieutenant's Woman, 1981; Betrayal, 1981; Victory, 1982; Turtle Diary, 1985; The Handmaid's Tale, 1987; The Heat of the Day, 1988; Reunion, 1989; The Trial, 1989; The Comfort of Strangers, 1990; Sleuth, 2007. *Publications:* The Caretaker, 1960; The Birthday Party, and other plays, 1960; A Slight Ache, 1961; The Collection, 1963; The Lover, 1963; The Homecoming, 1965; Tea Party, and, The Basement, 1967; (co-ed) PEN Anthology of New Poems, 1967; Mac, 1968; Landscape, and, Silence, 1969; Five Screenplays, 1971; Old Times, 1971; Poems, 1971; No Man's Land, 1975; The Proust Screenplay: A la Recherche du Temps Perdu, 1978; Betrayal, 1978; Poems and Prose 1949–1977, 1978; I Know the Place, 1979; Family Voices, 1981; Other Places, 1982; French Lieutenant's Woman and other screenplays, 1982; One For The Road, 1984; Collected Poems and Prose, 1986; (co-ed) 100 Poems by 100 Poets, 1986; Mountain Language, 1988; The Heat of the Day, 1989; The Dwarfs (novel), 1990; Party Time, 1991; Moonlight, 1993; (ed jtly) 99 Poems in Translation, 1994; Ashes to Ashes, 1996; Various Voices: prose, poetry, politics 1948–1998, 1998; Celebration, 2000. *Recreation:* cricket. *Address:* c/o Judy Daish Associates Ltd, 2 St Charles Place, W10 6EG.

PINTO, Amanda Eve; QC 2006; a Recorder, since 2004; *b* 28 July 1960; *d* of John and Marigold Pinto; *m* 1987, Charles Spencer Porter; one *s* two *d*. *Educ:* St Paul's Girls' Sch., London; Gonville and Caius Coll., Cambridge (BA Law 1982); Birkbeck Coll., London (Dip. Hist. of Art 1991). Called to the Bar, Middle Temple, 1983; in practice on S Eastern Circuit, specializing in criminal law, fraud and corporate crime. Mem., Cttee, Criminal Bar Assoc., 2007–. Contributor, amicus document to Iraqi High Tribunal, 2007. Contribs to Legal Network TV. *Publications:* (with M. Evans) Corporate Criminal Liability, 2003; contribs to Solicitors' Jl, Legal Week, Fraud Watch. *Recreations:* enjoying art, theatre and music, baking cakes, ski-ing, travelling, walking my dog. *Address:* (chambers) 5 Paper Buildings, Temple, EC4Y 7HB. *T:* (020) 7583 6117, *Fax:* (020) 7353 0075; *e-mail:* clerks@5pb.co.uk. *Club:* Hurlingham.

PIPE, Martin Charles, CBE 2000; racehorse trainer, National Hunt and flat racing, 1977–2006; *b* 29 May 1945; *m* 1971, Mary Caroline; one *s*. First trainer's licence, 1977; only British trainer to saddle 200 winners in a season, 1989; fifteen times champion trainer, National Hunt, to 2005; set new British record for Flat and jump winners with 2,989 winners, 2000. *Publication:* (with Richard Pitman) Martin Pipe: the champion trainer's story, 1992. *Address:* Pond House, Nicholashayne, near Wellington, Somerset TA21 9QY.

PIPER, Rt Rev. Dr Reginald John; Rector, St Paul's Anglican Church, Gymea, since 2007; Bishop of Wollongong, and an Assistant Bishop, Diocese of Sydney, 1993–2007; *b* 25 Feb. 1942; *s* of Leslie and Myra Elaine Piper; *m* 1967, Dorothy Patricia Lock; one *s* two *d* (and one *s* decd). *Educ:* Australian Nat. Univ. (BSc 1963); Moore Coll., Sydney (Theol. Schol. 1970); Melbourne Coll. of Divinity (BD 1975); Fuller Theol Seminary, LA (DMin 1992). Ordained deacon, 1966, priest, 1967; Curate: St Stephen's, Willougby, 1966–69; St Clement's, Lalor Park, 1970–71; Rector: St Aidan's, Hurstville Grove, 1972–75; Christ Church, Kiama, 1975–79; Holy Trinity, Adelaide, 1980–93. *Publications:* The Ephesus Plan, 1998; Forty Days with the Risen Lord, 2005; The Ephesus Code, 2006. *Address:* St Paul's Anglican Church, 131 Gymea Bay Road, Gymea, NSW 2227, Australia.

PIPPARD, Prof. Sir (Alfred) Brian, Kt 1975; FRS 1956; Cavendish Professor of Physics, University of Cambridge, 1971–82, now Emeritus; *b* 7 Sept. 1920; *s* of late Prof. A. J. S. Pippard; *m* 1955, Charlotte Frances Dyer; three *d*. *Educ:* Clifton Coll.; Clare Coll., Cambridge (BA 1941; MA 1945; PhD 1949; ScD 1966; Hon. Fellow 1973). Scientific Officer, Radar Research and Development Establishment, Great Malvern, 1941–45; Stokes Student, Pembroke Coll., Cambridge, 1945–46; Demonstrator in Physics, University of Cambridge, 1946; Lecturer in Physics, 1950; Reader in Physics, 1959–60; John Humphrey Plummer Prof. of Physics, 1960–71; Pres., Clare Hall, Cambridge, 1966–73 (Hon. Fellow, 1993). Visiting Prof., Institute for the Study of Metals, University of Chicago, 1955–56. Fellow of Clare Coll., Cambridge, 1947–66. Cherwell-Simon Memorial Lectr, Oxford, 1968–69; Eddington Meml Lectr, Cambridge, 1988. Pres., Inst. of Physics, 1974–76 (FInstP 1970, Hon. FInstP 1995). Hughes Medal of the Royal Soc., 1959; Holweck Medal, 1961; Dannie-Heineman Prize, 1969; Guthrie Prize, 1970; Lars Onsager Medal, Norwegian Univ. of Sci. and Technol., Trondheim, 2005. *Publications:* Elements of Classical Thermodynamics, 1957; Dynamics of Conduction Electrons, 1962; Forces and Particles, 1972; The Physics of Vibration, vol. 1, 1978, vol. 2, 1983; Response and Stability, 1985; Magnetoresistance, 1989; (ed and contrib.) 20th Century Physics, 1995; papers in Proc. Royal Soc., etc. *Recreation:* music. *Address:* 30 Porson Road, Cambridge CB2 8EU. *T:* (01223) 358713.

PIRIE, Madsen (Duncan), PhD; President, Adam Smith Institute, since 1978; *b* 24 Aug. 1940; *s* of Douglas Gordon Pirie and Eva (*née* Madsen). *Educ:* Univ. of Edinburgh (MA Hons 1970); Univ. of St Andrews (PhD 1974); MPhil Cantab 1997. Distinguished Vis. Prof. of Philosophy, Hillsdale Coll., Michigan, 1975–78. Mem., Adv. Panel on Citizen's Charter, 1991–95. *Publications:* Trial and Error and the Idea of Progress, 1978; The Book of the Fallacy, 1985; Privatization, 1988; Micropolitics, 1988; (with Eamonn Butler) The Sherlock Holmes IQ Book, 1995; How to Win Every Argument, 2006; Children of the Night, 2007; Dark Visitor, 2007; The Waters of Andros, 2007; Freedom 101, 2008. *Recreation:* calligraphy. *Address:* Adam Smith Institute, 23 Great Smith Street, SW1P 3BL.

PIRNIE, Graham John Campbell; HM Diplomatic Service, retired; Counsellor and Deputy Head of Mission, Abu Dhabi, 1998–2001; *b* 9 Aug. 1941; *s* of late Ian Campbell Pirnie and of Emily Elizabeth Pirnie; *m* 1st, 1967, Kathleen Gunstone (marr. diss. 2001); two *s* one *d*; 2nd, 2001, Dora Ines Guerrero Velez. *Educ:* Surbiton Grammar Sch.; Birmingham Univ. (BSocSc). Graduate VSO, 1963–64; joined Foreign and Commonwealth Office, 1965: Information Res. Dept, 1965; FCO, 1966–68; Third Sec. and Vice Consul, Phnom Penh, 1968–70; Commercial Officer, Paris, 1970–74; Second Sec. (Commercial), The Hague, 1974–77; FCO, 1977–82; First Sec. and Consul, Geneva, 1982–86; JSDC 1986; FCO, 1986–89; Dep. Head of Mission and Consul, Quito, 1989–93; FCO, 1993–95; Ambassador to Paraguay, 1995–98. *Recreations:* fell-walking, natural history, antiques restoration, reading (political autobiographies), cross country ski-ing. *Address: e-mail:* graham.pirnie@btinternet.com.

PIRNIE, Rear Adm. Ian Hugh, CB 1992; DL; FIET; Chairman, Morecambe Bay Health Authority, 1994–2002; *b* 17 June 1935; *s* of late Hugh and Linda Pirnie; *m* 1958, Sally Patricia (*née* Duckworth); three *d*. *Educ:* Christ's Hosp., Horsham; Pembroke Coll., Cambridge (MA). CEng 1986; FIET (FIEE 1986). Qualified in submarines, 1964; post-graduate educn, RMCS, Shrivenham, 1964–65; sea service in aircraft carriers, destroyers and submarines; commanded RNEC, Manadon, 1986–88; Chief, Strategic Systems Exec., MoD (in overall charge of Trident procurement prog.), 1988–92, RN retd, 1993. Chairman: Furness Enterprise Ltd, 1993–2000; Ashworth High Security Hosp., 1999; non-executive Director: Cumbria Ambulance Service, 1992–94; Cumbria and Lancs Strategic Health Authy, 2002–06. DL Cumbria, 2000. *Recreations:* fell walking, opera, classical music, topiary. *Club:* Army and Navy.

PIRRIE, David Blair, FCIB; Director of International and Private Banking, Lloyds Bank Plc, 1992–97; *b* 15 Dec. 1938; *s* of John and Sylvia Pirrie; *m* 1966, Angela Sellos; three *s* one *d*. *Educ:* Strathallen Sch., Perthshire; Harvard Univ. (Management Develt). FCIB 1987. Lloyds Bank: Gen. Man., Brazil, 1975–81; Dir, Lloyds Bank International, 1981–83; Gen. Man., Gp HQ, 1983–85; Sen. Dir, Internat. Banking, 1985–87; Sen. Gen. Man., UK Retail Banking, 1987–89; Dir, UK Retail Banking, 1989–92. *Recreations:* golf, theatre, music.

PIRZADA, Syed Sharif Uddin, SPk 1964; Hon. Senior Adviser to Chief Executive on Foreign Affairs, Law, Justice and Human Rights, Pakistan, 2000–08; Member, National Security Council, 1999–2008; Ambassador-at-Large, since 1999; Attorney-General of Pakistan, 1965–66, 1968–71 and 1977–89; *b* 12 June 1923; *s* of Syed Vilayat Ali Pirzada; *m* 1960; two *s* two *d*. *Educ:* University of Bombay. LLB 1945; barrister-at-law. Secretary, Provincial Muslim League, 1945–47; Managing Editor, Morning Herald, 1947; Prof., Sind Muslim Law Coll., 1947–55; Advocate: Bombay High Court, 1946; Sind Chief Court, 1947; West Pakistan High Court, 1955; Supreme Court of Pakistan, 1961; Senior Advocate Supreme Court of Pakistan; Foreign Minister of Pakistan, 1966–68; Minister for Law and Parly Affairs, 1979–85; Advr to Chief Martial Law Administrator and Federal Minister, 1978. Ambassador-at-Large with status of Federal Minister, 1989–93; Chm., Heritage Council, 1989–93. Sec.-Gen., Orgn of the Islamic Conf., 1984–88 (Chm. Cttee of Experts for drafting statute of Islamic Internat. Ct of Justice, 1980). Represented Pakistan: before International Tribunal on Rann of Kutch, 1965; before Internat. Ct of Justice regarding Namibia, SW Africa, 1971; Pakistan Chief Counsel before ICAO Montreal in complaint concerning overflights over Indian territory; Leader of Pakistan delegations to Commonwealth Conf. and General Assembly of UN, 1966; Mem., UN Sub-Commn on Prevention of Discrimination and Protection of Minorities, 1972–82 (Chm., 1968). Hon. Advisor, Constitutional Commn, 1961; Chm., Pakistan Company Law Commn, 1962; Mem., Internat. River Cttee, 1961–68; President: Pakistan Br., Internat. Law Assoc., 1964–67; Karachi Bar Assoc., 1964; Pakistan Bar Council, 1966; Inst. of Internat. Affairs. Led Pakistan Delegn to Law of the Sea Conferences, NY, 1978 and 1979, and Geneva, 1980. Member: Pakistan Nat. Gp, Panel of the Permanent Ct of Arbitration; Panel of Arbitrators and Umpires, Council of Internat. Civil Aviation Organisation; Panel of Arbitrators, Internat. Centre for Settlement of Investment Disputes, Washington; Internat. Law Commn, 1981–86. Chm., Nat. Cttee for Quaid-I-Azam Year, 2001–. *Publications:* Pakistan at a Glance, 1941; Jinnah on Pakistan, 1943; Leaders Correspondence with Jinnah, 1944, 3rd edn 1978; Evolution of Pakistan, 1962 (also published in Urdu and Arabic); Fundamental Rights and Constitutional Remedies in Pakistan, 1966; The Pakistan Resolution and the Historic Lahore Session, 1970; Foundations of Pakistan, vol. I, 1969, vol. II, 1970; Some Aspects of Quaid-i-Azam's Life, 1978; Collected Works of Quaid-i-Azam Mohammad Ali Jinnah, vol. I, 1985, vol. II, 1986. *Recreation:* bridge. *Clubs:* Sind (Karachi); Karachi Boat, Karachi Gymkhana.

PISANI, Edgard (Edouard Marie Victor); Chevalier de la Légion d'honneur; *b* Tunis, 9 Oct. 1918; *s* of François and Zoë Pisani. *Educ:* Lycée Carnot, Tunis; Lycée Louis-le-Grand, Paris. LèsL. War of 1939–45 (Croix de Guerre; Médaille de la Résistance). Chef du Cabinet, later Dir, Office of Prefect of Police, Paris, 1944; Dir, Office of Minister of Interior, 1946; Prefect: of Haute-Loire, 1946; of Haute-Marne, 1947; Senator (democratic left) from Haute-Marne, 1954; Minister of Agriculture, 1961; (first) Minister of Equipment, 1966; Deputy, Maine et Loire, 1967–68; Minister of Equipment and Housing, 1967; Conseiller Général, Maine et Loire, 1964–73; Mayor of Montreuil Bellay, 1965–75; Senator (socialist) from Haute-Marne, 1974–81; Mem., European Parlt, 1978–79 (Pres., Econ. and Monetary Affairs Cttee); Mem. for France, EEC, 1981–84; High Comr and Special Envoy to New Caledonia, 1984–85; Minister for New Caledonia, 1985–86. Member: Commn on Develt Issues (Brandt Commn), 1978–80; Economic and Social Cttee. Mem., Club of Rome, 1975. President: Inst. du Monde Arabe, 1988–95; Centre Internat. des Hautes Etudes Agronomiques Mediterraneenes, 1991–95. Dir, L'Evénement Européen, 1988–94. *Publications:* La région: pourquoi faire?, 1969; Le général indivis, 1974; Utopie foncière, 1977; Socialiste de raison, 1978; Défi du monde, campagne d'Europe, 1979; (contrib.) Pour la science, 1980; La main et l'outil, 1984; Pour l'Afrique, 1988; Persiste et Signe, 1992; Pour l'agriculture marchaude et ménagère, 1994; La passion de l'Etat, 1997; Une autre idée du Monde, 2001; Un vieil homme et le terre, 2004; Vive la Révolte, 2006; Le sens de l'Etat, 2008.

PISCHETSRIEDER, Bernd; Chairman, Board of Management, Volkswagen AG, 2002–06 (Member, 2000–06); *b* 15 Feb. 1948. *Educ:* Munich Technical Univ. (Diplom-Ingenieur). BMW, 1973–99: Production Planning Engineer, Munich, 1973–75; Head, Ops Control Dept, Munich factory, 1975–77; Head, Dingolfing factory, 1978–81; Dir of Production, Develt, Purchasing and Logistics, S Africa, 1982–85; Head, Quality Assurance, 1985–87; Head, Technical Planning, 1987–90; Dep. Mem., Process Engrg Bd, 1990 (Production); Mem., Bd of Mgt, 1991 (Production); Chm., Bd of Mgt, BMW AG, 1993–99.

PISSARIDES, Prof. Christopher Antoniou, PhD; FBA 2002; Norman Sosnow Professor of Economics, London School of Economics, since 2006 (Professor of Economics, since 1986); *b* 20 Feb. 1948; *s* of Antonios and Evdokia Pissarides; *m* 1986, Francesca Michela Cassano; one *s* one *d*. *Educ:* Essex Univ. (BA Econs 1970, MA Econs 1971); London Sch. of Econs (PhD 1974). Central Bank of Cyprus, 1974; Lectr, Univ. of Southampton, 1974–76; London School of Economics: Lectr, 1976–82; Reader, 1982–86; Prog. Dir, Centre for Econ. Performance, 1999–2007. Mem., Employment Taskforce, EC, 2003–04. Research Fellow: Centre for Economic Policy Res., London, 1994–; Inst. for Study of Labor (IZA), Bonn, 2001– (Prize in Labor Econs (jtly), 2005). Associate Ed., Economica, 1996– (Chm. Bd, 2007–); Mem., Editl Bd, AEJ Macroeconomics, 2007–. Specialist Advr, Treasury Cttee, H of C, 2001–05. Non-national Sen. Associate, Forum for Econ. Res. in Arab Countries, Iran and Turkey, 2002–. Mem., Monetary Policy Cttee, Central Bank of Cyprus, 2000–07. Member Council: REconS, 1996–2003; Econometric Soc., 2005–; Europ. Econ. Assoc., 2005–. Mem., Interim Governing Bd, Univ. of Cyprus, 1989–95. Fellow, Econometric Soc., 1997. *Publications:* Labour Market Adjustment, 1976; Equilibrium Unemployment Theory, 1990, 2nd edn 2000; contribs to professional jls, conf. proc. and ed books. *Recreations:* cooking, gardening, walking. *Address:* London School of Economics, Houghton Street, WC2A 2AE. *T:* (020) 7955 7513, *Fax:* (020) 7831 1840; *e-mail:* c.pissarides@lse.ac.uk.

PITAKAKA, Sir (Puibangara) Moses, GCMG 1995; Governor-General, Solomon Islands, 1994–99; *b* 24 Jan. 1945; *s* of Isaiah Puibangara and Lilian Tanaquana; *m* 1967, Lois Qilariava; three *s* four *d*. *Educ:* Goldie Coll., Western Prov., Solomon Is; Solomon Is Teachers' Coll.; Univ. of Birmingham; Univ. of S Pacific, Fiji; Univ. of Manchester; Queen Elizabeth House, Oxford Univ. School teacher, Solomon Is, 1964–66; Educn Officer, 1969–71; Dist Officer, Lands Officer and Magistrate, 1972–75; Honiara Town Clerk, Jan.–May 1976; Hd of Foreign Affairs, Prime Minister's Office, 1977–79; managed family business, 1980–81; Chm., N New Georgia Timber Co-op. Commn of Inquiry, 1982; Human Resources Develt Manager, Unilever Gp in Solomon Is, 1983–85; Leadership Code Commission: Comr, 1987–88; Chm., 1989–94. Chairman: Solomon Is Citizenship Commn, 1978–88; Nat. Educn Bd, 1980–86; Comr to Judicial and Legal Services Commn, 1981–83. Deacon, World Wide Church of God, 1993–. *Recreations:* reading, canoeing, swimming, jogging, table tennis. *Address:* c/o PO Box 52, Gizo, Western Province, Solomon Islands.

PITCHER, Sir Desmond (Henry), Kt 1992; CEng, FIET, FBCS; Chairman, United Utilities (formerly North West Water Group), 1993–98 (Director, 1990–98; Deputy Chairman, 1991–93); *b* 23 March 1935; *s* of George Charles and Alice Marion Pitcher; *m* 1st, 1961 (marr. diss.); twin *d*; 2nd, 1978 (marr. diss.); two *s*; 3rd, 1991, Norma Barbara Niven. *Educ:* Liverpool Coll. of Technology. MIEEE (USA). A. V. Roe & Co., Develt Engr, 1955; Automatic Telephone and Elec. Co. (now Plessey), Systems Engr, 1958; Univac Remington Rand (now Sperry Rand Ltd), Systems Engr, 1961; Sperry Univac: Dir, Systems, 1966; Managing Dir, 1971; Vice-Pres., 1974; Dir, Sperry Rand, 1971–76, Dep. Chm., 1974–76; Man. Dir, Leyland Vehicles Ltd, 1976–78; Dir, British Leyland, 1976–78; Man. Dir, Plessey Telecommunications and Office Systems, 1978–83; Dir, Plessey Co., 1979–83; Director: The Littlewoods Orgn, 1983–95 (Gp Chief Exec., 1983–93; Vice-Chm., 1993–95); National Westminster Bank, 1994–98; (Mem., Northern Adv. Bd, 1989–92). Chm. & Dir, Signbrick Ltd, 2001–; Dir, Steeltower Ltd, 2001–05. Chairman: Mersey Barrage Co., 1986–96; Merseyside Develt Corp., 1991–98. Pres., NW Chambers of Commerce, 1994–98. Vis. Prof. of Business Policy, Univ. of Manchester, 1993–98. Dir, CEI, 1979; Pres., TEMA, 1981–83. Dep. Chm., Everton Football Club, 1990–98 (Dir, 1987–98); Chm., Royal Liverpool Philharmonic Soc. Develt Trust, 1992–2005. Chm. and Trustee, Rocking Horse Appeal, Royal Liverpool Children's NHS Trust, 1996–2005; Trustee, Outward Bound, 2005–07. DL Merseyside, 1992–99. Freeman, City of London, 1987; Liveryman, Co. of Information Technologists, 1992–. CCMI; FRIAS; FRSA 1987; Hon. FIDE; Hon. Fellow, Liverpool John Moores Univ., 1993. Knight, Order of St Hubert (Austria), 1991. *Publications:* Institution of Electrical Engineers Faraday Lectures, 1974–75; Water Under the Bridge: 30 years in industrial management (autobiog.), 2003; various lectures on social implications of computers and micro-electronics. *Recreations:* golf, music. *Address:* Folly Farm, Sulhamstead, Berks RG7 4DF. *T:* (0118) 930 2326. *Clubs:* Brooks's, Royal Automobile; Royal Birkdale Golf; Royal Liverpool; Lancs CC.

PITCHERS, Hon. Sir Christopher (John), Kt 2002; a Judge of the High Court, Queen's Bench Division, 2002–08; *b* 2 Oct. 1942; *s* of late Thomas Pitchers and of Melissa Pitchers; *m* 1965, Judith Stevenson, MBE (*d* 2006); two *s*. *Educ:* Uppingham Sch.; Worcester Coll., Oxford. MA. Called to the Bar, Inner Temple, 1965, Bencher, 1996; a Recorder, 1981–86; a Circuit Judge, 1986–2002. Dir of Studies, Judicial Studies Bd, 1996–97 (Mem., Criminal Cttee, 1991–95; Jt Dir, 1995–96). Hon. Sec., Council of HM Circuit Judges, 1992–95 (Pres., 1999). Vice-Pres., NACRO, 1994–2002. Hon. LLD De Montfort, 2002.

PITCHFORD, Hon. Sir Christopher (John), Kt 2000; DL; **Hon. Mr Justice Pitchford;** a Judge of the High Court, Queen's Bench Division, since 2000; a Presiding Judge, Wales and Chester Circuit, 2002–05; *b* 28 March 1947; *s* of His Honour Charles Neville Pitchford; *m* 1st, 1970, Rosalind (*née* Eaton) (marr. diss. 1991); two *d*; 2nd, 1991, Denise (*née* James); two *s*. *Educ:* Duffryn Comprehensive Sch., Newport, Gwent; Queen's Coll., Taunton, Somerset; Queen Mary Coll., London (LLB). Called to the Bar, Middle Temple, 1969, Bencher, 1996; QC 1987; a Recorder, 1987–2000; a Dep. High Ct Judge, 1996–2000. Leader, Wales & Chester Circuit, 1999–2000. Arbitrator, Motor Insurers Bureau, 1994–2000. Chm., Criminal Cttee, Judicial Studies Bd, 2006–; Mem., Sentencing Guidelines Council, 2006–. Pres., Bedlinog RFC, 2002–. DL Mid Glamorgan, 2004. *Recreation:* fishing. *Address:* Royal Courts of Justice, Strand, WC2A 2LL.

PITFIELD, Hon. (Peter) Michael, CVO 1982; PC (Can.) 1984; QC (Can.) 1972; appointed Senator, Canada, Dec. 1982; *b* Montreal, 18 June 1937; *s* of Ward Chipman Pitfield and Grace Edith (*née* MacDougall); *m* 1971, Nancy Snow (decd); one *s* two *d*. *Educ:* Lower Canada Coll., Montreal; Sedbergh Sch., Montebello; St Lawrence Univ. (BASc; Hon. DLitt 1979); McGill Univ. (BCL); Univ. of Ottawa (DESD). Lieut, RCNR. Read Law with Mathewson Lafleur & Brown, Montreal (associated with firm, 1958–59); called to Quebec Bar, 1962; QC (Fed.) 1972; Admin. Asst to Minister of Justice and Attorney-Gen. of Canada, 1959–61; Sec. and Exec. Dir, Royal Commn on Pubns, Ottawa, 1961–62; Attaché to Gov.-Gen. of Canada, 1962–65; Sec. and Res. Supervisor of Royal Commn on Taxation, 1963–66; entered Privy Council Office and Cabinet Secretariat of Govt of Canada, 1965; Asst Sec. to Cabinet, 1966; Dep. Sec. to Cabinet (Plans), and Dep. Clerk to Council, 1969; Dep. Minister, Consumer and Corporate Affairs, 1973; Clerk of Privy Council and Sec. to Cabinet, 1975–79 and 1980–Nov. 1982; Sen. Adviser to Privy Council Office, Nov.–Dec. 1982. Rep., UN Gen. Assembly, 1983; Chm., Senate Cttee on Security and Intelligence, 1983. Director: Power Corp., Montreal; Trust Co., LaPresse; Great West Life Assurance Co.; Investor's Gp Ltd, Winnipeg; Fellow, Harvard Univ., 1974; Mackenzie King Vis. Prof., Kennedy Sch. of Govt, Harvard, 1979–80. Member: Canadian, Quebec and Montreal Bar Assocs; Can. Inst. of Public Admin; Can. Hist. Assoc.; Can. Polit. Sci. Assoc.; Amer. Soc. Polit. and Social Sci.; Internat. Commn of Jurists; Beta Theta Pi. Trustee, Twentieth Century Fund, NY; Member Council: Canadian Inst. for Advanced Res., Toronto; IISS. *Recreations:* squash, ski-ing, reading. *Address:* c/o The Senate, 111 Wellington Street, Ottawa, ON K1A 0A4, Canada. *Clubs:* University, Mount Royal, Racket (Montreal).

PITKEATHLEY, family name of **Baroness Pitkeathley**.

PITKEATHLEY, Baroness *cr* 1997 (Life Peer), of Caversham in the Royal co. of Berkshire; **Jill Elizabeth Pitkeathley,** OBE 1993; Chair: Children and Families Court Advisory and Support Service, since 2004; Advisory Panel on Futurebuilders, 2005–08; *b* 4 Jan. 1940; *d* of Roland Wilfred Bisson and Edith May Bisson (*née* Muston); *m* 1st, 1961, W. Pitkeathley (marr. diss. 1978); one *s* one *d*; 2nd, 2008, David Emerson. *Educ:* Ladies' Coll., Guernsey; Bristol Univ. (BA Econ). Social worker, 1961–64; Voluntary Service Co-ordinator, Manchester and Essex, 1970–83; Nat. Consumer Council, 1983–86; Dir, Nat. Council for Carers, 1986 until merger with Assoc. of Carers, 1988; Chief Exec., Carers Nat. Assoc., 1988–98; Chm., New Opportunities Fund, 1998–2004. Advr to Griffith's Rev. of Community Care, 1986–88; Mem., Health Adv. Service, 1993–97; Chm. Adv. Gp, 1999–2000, Interim Chair, 2001–02, Gen. Social Care Council. Chm., Adv. Body, OTS, Cabinet Office, 2008–. President: Community Council for Berks, 1998– (Vice-Pres., 1990–98); Volunteering England (formerly Nat. Centre for Volunteering), 2002–; Vice Pres., Carers UK, 2003–; Pres., Eurocarers, 2007–. Patron, Bracknell CVS. Mem. Bd of Governors, Nat. Inst. of Social Work, 1995–98. Hon. LLD: Bristol, 2002; London Metropolitan, 2002. *Publications:* When I Went Home, 1978; Mobilising Voluntary Resources, 1982; Volunteers in Hospitals, 1984; Supporting Volunteers, 1985; It's my duty, isn't it?, 1989; Only Child, 1994; (with David Emerson) Age Gap Relationships, 1996; Cassandra and Jane: a personal journey through the lives of the Austen sisters, 2004. *Recreations:* gardening, grand-children, writing. *T:* (office) (020) 7510 7066.

See also C. M. Wilson.

PITMAN, Sir Brian (Ivor), Kt 1994; Chief Executive, 1983–97, Chairman, 1997–2001, Lloyds TSB Group plc (formerly Lloyds Bank Plc); Senior Adviser, Morgan Stanley, since 2001; *b* 13 Dec. 1931; *s* of late Ronald Ivor Pitman and of Doris Ivy Pitman (*née* Short); *m* 1954, Barbara Mildred Ann (*née* Darby); two *s* one *d*. *Educ:* Cheltenham Grammar School. FCIB. Entered Lloyds Bank, 1952, Jt Gen. Manager, 1975; Exec. Dir, Lloyds Bank International, 1976, Dep. Chief Exec., 1978; Dep. Group Chief Exec., 1982, Dir, 1983–2001, Lloyds Bank Plc, subseq. Lloyds TSB Gp plc. Chm., Lloyds First Western

Corp., 1983–94; Director: Lloyds Bank California, 1982–86; Nat. Bank of New Zealand Ltd, 1982–97; Lloyds and Scottish Plc, 1983; Lloyds Bank International Ltd, 1985–87; Lloyds Merchant Bank Holdings Ltd, 1985–88; NBNZ Holdings Ltd, 1990–97; Carlton Communications Plc, 1998–2004; Tomkins PLC, 2000–07; Carphone Warehouse Gp, 2001–; Singapore Airlines Ltd, 2003–; ITV plc, 2003–08; Chm., Next plc, 1998–2002. Mem., Internat. Adv. Panel, Monetary Authy of Singapore, 1999–2001. President: BBA, 1996–97; CIB, 1997–98. Gov., Ashridge Mgt Coll., 1997–. Master, Guild of Internat. Bankers, 2002–03. Hon. DSc: City, 1996; UMIST, 2000. *Recreations:* golf, cricket, music. *Address:* Morgan Stanley, 20 Bank Street, Canary Wharf, E14 4AD. *Clubs:* MCC; Yorkshire CC; Gloucestershire CC; St George's Hill Golf.

PITMAN, Rt Rev. Cyrus Clement James; *see* Newfoundland, Eastern, and Labrador, Bishop of.

PITMAN, His Honour David Christian; a Circuit Judge, 1986–2006; a Deputy Circuit Judge, since 2006; *b* 1 Dec. 1936; 3rd *s* of Sir (Isaac) James Pitman, KBE, and Hon. Margaret Beaufort Pitman (*née* Lawson-Johnston); *m* 1971, Christina Mary Malone-Lee; one *s* two *d. Educ:* Eton Coll.; Christ Church, Oxford (BA (PPE) 1961, MA 1964). Editorial role in publishing books in Initial Teaching Alphabet, 1960–63; called to Bar, Middle Temple, 1963; commenced practice, 1964; a Recorder, 1986. National Service: 2nd Lieut, 60th Rifles, 1955–57; Territorial Army: Lieut Queen's Westminsters, KRRC, 1957–61; Captain, then Major, Queen's Royal Rifles (TA), 1961–67; Major, 5th (T) Bn RGJ, 1967–69. *Recreations:* music, the open air. *Address:* c/o The Crown Court, Snaresbrook, Hollybush Hill, E11 1QW.

PITMAN, Jennifer Susan, OBE 1998; professional racehorse trainer (National Hunt), 1975–99; Partner, DJS Racing, since 1996; author; *b* 11 June 1946; *d* of George and Mary Harvey; *m* 1st, 1965, Richard Pitman (marr. diss.); two *s*; 2nd, 1997, David Stait. *Educ:* Sarson Secondary Girls' School. Dir, Jenny Pitman Racing Ltd, 1975–99. Training of major race winners includes: Midlands National, 1977 (Watafella), 1990 (Willsford); Massey Ferguson Gold Cup, Cheltenham, 1980 (Bueche Giorod); Welsh National, 1982 (Corbiere), 1983 (Burrough Hill Lad), 1986 (Stearsby); Grand National, 1983 (Corbiere), 1995 (Royal Athlete); Mildmay/Cazalet Gold Cup, 1983 (Burrough Hill Lad), 1986 (Stearsby), 1993 (Superior Finish); Cheltenham Gold Cup, 1984 (Burrough Hill Lad), 1991 (Garrison Savannah); King George VI Gold Cup, 1984 (Burrough Hill Lad); Hennessy Gold Cup, Newbury, 1984 (Burrough Hill Lad); Whitbread Trophy, 1985 (Smith's Man); Ritz Club Chase, Cheltenham, 1987 (Gainsay); Philip Cornes Saddle of Gold Final, Newbury, 1988 (Crumpet Delite); Welsh Champion Hurdle, 1991 (Wonderman), 1992 (Don Valentino); Scottish National, 1995 (Willsford). Piper Heidsieck Trainer of the Year, 1983/84, 1989/90. *Publications:* Glorious Uncertainty (autobiog.), 1984; Jenny Pitman: the autobiography, 1998; *novels:* On the Edge, 2002; Double Deal, 2002; The Dilemma, 2003; The Vendetta, 2004; The Inheritance, 2005. *Address:* Owl's Barn, Kintbury, Hungerford, Berks RG17 9SX. *Club:* International Sporting.

PITOI, Sir Sere, Kt 1977; CBE 1975; MACE; Chairman, Public Services Commission of Papua New Guinea, 1971; *b* Kapa Kapa Village, SE of Port Moresby, 11 Nov. 1935; *s* of Pitoi Sere and Laka Orira; *m* 1957, Daga Leva; two *s* three *d. Educ:* Sogeri (Teachers' Cert.); Queensland Univ. (Cert. in Diagnostic Testing and Remedial Teaching); Univ. of Birmingham, UK (Cert. for Headmasters and Administrators). Held a number of posts as teacher, 1955–57, and headmaster, 1958–68, in Port Moresby, the Gulf district of Papua, Eastern Highlands, New Britain. Apptd a District Inspector of Schools, 1968. Chm., Public Service Bd, Papua New Guinea, 1969–76. Fellow, PNG Inst. of Management. *Recreation:* fishing. *Clubs:* Rotary (Port Moresby); Cheshire Home (PNG).

PITT, Sir Michael (Edward), Kt 2005; CEng, FICE; self-employed consultant; Chairman, South West Strategic Health Authority, since 2006; *b* 2 Feb. 1949; *s* of Albert and Doris Joan Pitt; *m* 1969, Anna Maria Di Claudio; two *d. Educ:* University College London (first class Hons BSc Engrg). CEng 1974; FICE 1989. Civil Servant, 1970–72; motorway design and construction, 1972–75; transportation planner in private sector and local govt, 1975–80; Asst County Surveyor, Northumberland CC, 1980–84; Dir of Property Services and Dir of Tech. Services, Humberside CC, 1984–90; Chief Executive: Cheshire CC, 1990–97; Kent CC, 1997–2005; Swindon BC, 2005–06. *Publications:* papers in technical jls. *Recreations:* family life, walking, the voluntary sector. *Address:* Garden Cottage, Foxley, Malmesbury, Wilts SN16 0JJ.

PITT, William F.; *see* Fox-Pitt.

PITT, William Henry; Managing Director, Perpetua Training Ltd, since 2004; *b* 17 July 1937; *m* 1961, Janet Pitt (*née* Wearn); one *d. Educ:* Heath Clark Sch., Croydon; London Nautical Sch.; Polytechnic of N London (BA Philos./Classics). Lighting Engineer, 1955–75; Housing Officer, Lambeth Borough Council, 1975–81. Gp Training Manager, Canary Wharf Gp plc, 1999–2004. Chm., Lambeth Br., NALGO, 1979–81. Joined Liberal Party, 1959; contested: (L) Croydon NW, Feb. and Oct. 1974, 1979, 1983; Thanet South (L/Alliance), 1987, (Lib Dem), 1992. MP (L) Croydon NW, Oct. 1981–1983; joined Labour Party, 1996. *Recreations:* photography, choral singing, listening to music, reading, walking, going to France. *Address:* 10 Inverness Terrace, Broadstairs, Kent CT10 1QZ.

PITT-BROOKE, John Stephen; Director General, Secretariat, Ministry of Defence, since 2006; *b* 9 Sept. 1950; *s* of late Reginald Pitt-Brooke and of Hilda (*née* Wright); *m* 1st, 1986, Rosalind (*d* 1996), *d* of Prof. William Mulligan, *qv*; two *s*; 2nd, 1999, Frances Way, *d* of B. T. McDade. *Educ:* Salford Grammar Sch.; Queens' Coll., Cambridge (MA). MoD, 1971–74; NI Office, 1974–77; Private Sec. to Minister of State for NI, 1975–77; MoD, 1978; NATO Defence Coll., 1980; Private Sec. to Permanent Under Sec., MoD, 1984–87; Cabinet Office, 1988–89; Ministry of Defence, 1989–: Head of Industrial Relns Div., 1989–92; Private Sec. to Sec. of State for Defence, 1992–94; Comd Sec., Land Comd, 1995–98; Fellow, Center for Internat. Affairs, Harvard Univ., 1998–99; Director General: Corporate Communications, 1999–2001; Civilian Personnel, 2001–04; Media and Communications, 2005–06. *Recreations:* family life, literature, cricket, baseball, Venice, supporting Manchester City Football Club. *Address:* c/o Ministry of Defence, Whitehall, SW1A 2HB.

PITT-RIVERS, Valerie; Lord-Lieutenant of Dorset, since 2006 (Vice Lord-Lieutenant, 1999–2006); *b* 23 Jan. 1939; *d* of Derek and Eva Scott; *m* 1964, George Anthony Lane-Fox Pitt-Rivers, OBE, DL. *Educ:* Prior's Field, Godalming. Advertising and public relns, 1957–63; worked for NHS, charities and the arts in Dorset, 1970–. Non-exec. Dir and Vice Chm., W Dorset Gen. Hosps NHS Trust, 1991–98. Founder, 1987, Chm., 1987–98, Arts in Hospital Project for NHS, Dorchester; Patron or Pres., numerous charitable orgns in Dorset. Trustee and Mem. Council, Royal Sch. of Needlework, 2000–06. DL Dorset, 1995. CStJ 2007. *Recreations:* gardens, opera. *Address:* Manor House, Hinton St Mary, Sturminster Newton, Dorset DT10 1NA.

PITTAM, Jonathan Charles; County Treasurer, Hampshire County Council, since 1997; *b* 9 June 1950; *s* of Brian and Sheila Pittam; *m* 1972, Mary Catherine Davey; two *s* one *d. Educ:* Tavistock Sch.; King's Coll., Univ. of London (BSc Hons). CPFA 1975. London Borough of Croydon: grad. trainee, 1971–73; Sen. Audit Asst, 1973; Accountant, 1973–75; Gp Accountant, 1975–76; Asst Prin. Accountant, 1976–78; Chief Accountant, 1979–80, Asst Dir, Finance and Admin, 1980–83, Cambs CC; Dep. Co. Treas., Hants CC, 1983–97. *Address:* Hampshire County Council, The Castle, Winchester, Hants SO23 8UB. *T:* (01962) 847400; *e-mail:* jon.pittam@hants.gov.uk.

PITTAWAY, David Michael; QC 2000; a Recorder, since 2000; *b* 29 June 1955; *s* of Michael Pittaway, JP, MRCVS, and Heather Yvette Pittaway (*née* Scott); *m* 1983, Jill Suzanne Newsam, *d* of Dr Ian Douglas Newsam, MRCVS; two *s. Educ:* Uppingham Sch.; Sidney Sussex Coll., Cambridge (Exhibnr; MA). Called to the Bar, Inner Temple, 1977 (Bencher, 1998); Asst Recorder, 1998; Midland and Oxford Circuit. Mem., Bar Council, 1999–2005. Chancellor, Peterborough Dio., 2006–. Legal Mem., Mental Health Review Tribunal, 2002–; Legal Assessor: GMC, 2002–04; RCVS, 2004–. Chm., Professional Negligence Bar Assoc., 2005–07. FCIArb 1992. *Publications:* (contrib.) Atkin's Court Forms, vol. 8, Carriers, 1990, rev. edn 2006, vol. 29(2), Personal Injury and Professional Negligence, 1996, rev. edn 2007, vol. 28, National Health Service, 2003; (Gen. Ed.) Pittaway & Hammerton, Professional Negligence Cases, 1998. *Recreations:* gardening, travel, music. *Address:* Hailsham Chambers, 4 Paper Buildings, Temple, EC4Y 7EX. *T:* (020) 7583 0816. *Clubs:* Garrick, Royal Automobile; Redclyffe Yacht (Wareham).

PITTILO, Prof. (Robert) Michael, PhD; FIBiol; Principal and Vice-Chancellor, Robert Gordon University, Aberdeen, since 2005; *b* 7 Oct. 1954; *s* of Robert Dawson Pittilo and Betsy Brown Pittilo (*née* Baird); *m* 1987, Dr Carol Margaret Blow. *Educ:* Kelvinside Acad., Glasgow; Univ. of Strathclyde (BSc Hons Biol.); NE London Poly. (PhD Biol. 1981). FIBiol 1994. Postdoctoral Res. Asst, Middx Hosp. Med. Sch., 1981–85; Hon. Res. Associate, University Coll. and Middx Sch. of Medicine, 1985–94; Kingston Polytechnic, subsequently Kingston University: Lectr, Sen. Lectr, then Reader, 1985–92; Prof. of Biomed. Scis and Hd, Dept of Life Scis, 1992–94; Dean: Faculty of Health and Social Care Scis, Kingston Univ. and St George's Hosp. Med. Sch., Univ. of London, 1995–2001; for Multiprofessional Educn, 1996–2001, and for Taught Postgrad. Courses, 1999–2001, St George's Hosp. Med. Sch., Univ. of London; Pro Vice-Chancellor, Univ. of Herts, 2001–05. Chm., Regulatory Wkg Gps for Herbal Medicine and Acupuncture, DoH, 2002–03 and 2006–; Mem., various nat. health cttees, 1997–. FLS 1980; FRSH 1993; FIBMS 1997; FRMS 2008. FRSA 2001. *Publications:* book chapters, articles, papers and reviews on the electron microscopy of parasitic protozoa, smoking, atherosclerosis and endothelial injury and health policy. *Recreations:* photography, mountain walking, motorcycling, cinema, music, clay shooting. *Address:* Office of the Principal and Vice-Chancellor, Robert Gordon University, Schoolhill, Aberdeen AB10 1FR. *T:* (01224) 262001, *Fax:* (01224) 262626; *e-mail:* R.M.Pittilo@rgu.ac.uk. *Clubs:* Royal Society of Medicine; Royal Northern and University (Aberdeen).

PITTS, Anthony Brian; His Honour Judge Pitts; a Circuit Judge, since 2002; *b* 18 May 1946; *s* of Sir Cyril Alfred Pitts, *qv*; *m* 1980, Sally-Jane Spencer; one *s* one *d. Educ:* Pembroke Coll., Oxford (BA Law). Called to the Bar, Gray's Inn, 1975; a Recorder, 1997–2002. *Recreations:* motor sport, guitar, France.

PITTS, Sir Cyril (Alfred), Kt 1968; Governor, University of Westminster (formerly Polytechnic of Central London), 1984–95 (Chairman of Governors, 1985–93); *b* 21 March 1916; *m* 1942, Barbara; two *s* one *d. Educ:* St Olave's; Jesus Coll., Cambridge. Chairman of ICI Companies in India, 1964–68; Chm., ICI (Export) Ltd and Gen. Manager, Internat. Coordination, ICI Ltd, 1968–78; Dir, ICI Americas Ltd, 1974–77; Dep. Chm., Ozalid Gp Holdings Ltd, 1975–77. Chairman: Process Plant EDC, 1979–83; Peter Brotherhood, 1980–83. President: Bengal Chamber of Commerce and Industry, and Associated Chambers of Commerce and Industry of India, 1967–68; British and S Asian Trade Assoc., 1978–83. Councillor, RIIA, 1968–77. Hon. DLitt Westminster, 1993. *Address:* 11 Middle Avenue, Farnham, Surrey GU9 8JL. *T:* (01252) 715864. *Clubs:* Oriental; Bengal (Calcutta).

See also A. B. Pitts.

PITTS, John Kennedy; Chairman, Legal Aid Board, 1988–95; *b* 6 Oct. 1925; *s* of Thomas Alwyn Pitts and Kathleen Margaret Pitts (*née* Kennedy); *m* 1st, 1957, Joan Iris Light (*d* 1986); 2nd, 1990, Julia Bentall. *Educ:* Bristol Univ. (BSc). Res. Officer, British Cotton Industry Res. Assoc., 1948–53; ICI, 1953–78; Dir, ICI Mond Div., 1969–71; Dep. Chm., ICI Agricl Div., 1972–77; Chairman: Richardsons Fertilizers, 1972–76; Hargreaves Fertilizers, 1975–77; Vice-Pres., Cie Neerlandaise de l'Azote, 1975–77. Chm. and Chief Exec., Tioxide Group, 1978–87. Mem., Tees and Hartlepool Port Authy, 1976–78; Chm., SASDA (formerly Shildon & Sedgefield Develt Agency), 1991–94. Pres., Chem. Industries Assoc., 1984–86. *Address:* Hall Garth House, Carthorpe, Bedale, N Yorks DL8 2LD. *Club:* Royal Automobile.

PITTS CRICK, Ronald; *see* Crick.

PITTSBURGH, Assistant Bishop of; *see* Scriven, Rt Rev. H. W.

PIX WESTON, John; *see* Weston.

PIZARRO, Artur; pianist; *b* Portugal. Performances with orchs incl. Philadelphia, LA Philharmonic, Baltimore Symphony, NHK Symphony (Tokyo), Montreal Symphony, Toronto Symphony, Hong Kong Philharmonic, Leipzig Chamber, Rotterdam Philharmonic, Vienna Symphony, Royal Philharmonic, BBC Symphony. Recitals worldwide. Numerous recordings. Winner, Leeds Internat. Piano Competition, 1990. *Address:* Tom Croxon Management Ltd, 22 Hurst Road, Buckhurst Hill, Essex IG9 6AB. *T:* (020) 8279 2516; *e-mail:* tom@tomcroxonmanagement.co.uk.

PIZZEY, Erin Patria Margaret; international founder of refuges for victims of domestic violence; *b* 19 Feb. 1939; *d* of late Cyril Edward Antony Carney, MBE and of Ruth Patricia Balfour-Last; *m* 1961, John Leo Pizzey (marr. diss. 1979); one *s* one *d. Educ:* St Antony's; Leweston Manor, Sherborne, Dorset. Somewhat chequered career as pioneering attracts frequent clashes with the law; appearances at such places as Acton Magistrates Court and the House of Lords could be considered milestones in the fulfilment of a career dedicated to defending women and children; Founder of first Shelter for Battered Wives (subseq. Women) and their children, 1971; helped fund and open Health Care Centre, Wandsworth Prison, 2001. Patron: Mankind Charity, 2002–; Derwentside Domestic Violence Forum, 2005–. Presenter, Domestic Violence is not a Gender Issue, Internat. Conf., Sacramento, 2008; held lectures about domestic violence and child advocacy for Slovenia Ombudsman, 2008. Member: Soc. of Authors; AFI; Smithsonian Instn; Royal Soc. of Literature. Patron, Care and Comfort Romania, 1998–. Attended Women of Achievement Lunch, Buckingham Palace, 2004. Diploma of Honour, Internat. order of volunteers for peace, 1981; Distinguished Leadership Award, World Congress of Victimology, 1987; San Valentino d'Oro prize for lit., 1994. *Publications:* (as

Erin Pizzey) Scream Quietly or the Neighbours Will Hear, 1974, 2nd edn 1978; Infernal Child (autobiog.), 1978; The Slut's Cookbook, 1981; Prone to Violence, 1982; Erin Pizzey Collects, 1983; Wild Child (autobiog.), 1996; (jtly) Grandmothers of the Revolution, 2000; (jtly) Women or Men - Who Are the Victims?, 2000; novels: The Watershed, 1983; In the Shadow of the Castle, 1984; The Pleasure Palace, 1986; First Lady, 1987; The Consul General's Daughter, 1988; The Snow Leopard of Shanghai, 1989; Other Lovers, 1991; Morning Star, 1991; Swimming with Dolphins, 1992; For the Love of a Stranger, 1993; Kisses, 1995; The Wicked World of Women, 1996; The Fame Game, 1999; poems and short stories. *Recreations:* wine, books, travel. *Address:* Flat 5, 29 Lebanon Park, Twickenham TW1 3DH. *T:* (020) 8241 6541; *e-mail:* erin.pizzey@blueyonder.co.uk.

PLAISTOWE, (William) Ian (David), FCA; Director of Audit and Business Advisory Practice for Europe, Arthur Andersen, 1993–2002; *b* 18 Nov. 1942; *s* of late David William Plaistowe and Julia (*née* Ross Smith); *m* 1968, Carolyn Anne Noble Wilson; two *s* one *d*. *Educ:* Marlborough Coll., Queens' Coll., Cambridge. Joined Arthur Andersen & Co., 1964; Partner, 1976; Head of Accounting and Audit practice, London, 1984–87; Dir of Acctg and Audit for UK and Ireland, 1987–93. Chm., Auditing Practices Bd of UK and Ireland, 1994–2002; Mem., Internat. Audit and Assurance Standards Bd, 2002–04. Institute of Chartered Accountants in England and Wales: Chairman: London Soc. of Chartered Accountants, 1981–82; Mem. Council, 1985–99; Vice-Pres., 1990–91; Dep. Pres., 1991–92; Pres., 1992–93. Mem. Council, Univ. of Buckingham, 2003–. Master, Co. of Chartered Accountants in England and Wales, 2002–03. *Publications:* articles in learned jls. *Recreations:* golf, tennis, squash, ski-ing, gardening. *Address:* Heybote, Ellesborough, Aylesbury, Bucks HP17 0XF. *T:* (01296) 622758. *Clubs:* Carlton; Moor Park Golf, Harewood Downs Golf.

PLANT, family name of **Baron Plant of Highfield**.

PLANT OF HIGHFIELD, Baron *cr* 1992 (Life Peer), of Weelsby in the County of Humberside; **Raymond Plant,** PhD; DLitt; Professor of Jurisprudence and Legal Philosophy, King's College London, since 2001; *b* 19 March 1945; *s* of Stanley and Marjorie Plant; *m* 1967, Katherine Sylvia Dixon; three *s*. *Educ:* Havelock Sch., Grimsby; King's Coll. London (BA); Hull Univ. (PhD 1971). Lectr, then Sen. Lectr in Philosophy, Univ. of Manchester, 1967–79; Prof. of Politics, 1979–94, Pro-Chancellor, 1996–99, Res. Prof., 1999–2001, Univ. of Southampton; Master, St Catherine's Coll., Oxford, 1994–99. Vis. Fellow, Corpus Christi Coll., Cambridge, 2006; Vincent Wright Prof., Inst. d'Etudes Politiques de Paris, Sciences Po, 2008. Lectures: Stevenson, Univ. of Glasgow, 1981; Agnes Cumming, UC Dublin, 1987; Stanton, 1989–90 and 1990–91, Boutwood, 2006, Univ. of Cambridge; Sarum, 1991; Bampton, 2007, Univ. of Oxford; Ferguson, Manchester Univ., 1994; Scott Holland, Manchester Cathedral, 1995; Charles Gore, Westminster Abbey, 1995; J. P. MacIntosh Meml, Edinburgh Univ., 1995; Eleanor Rathbone, Bristol Univ., 1997; G. Ganz, Southampton Univ., 2005; A. J. Milne, Durham, 2006. Chair: Labour Party Commn on Electoral Systems, 1991–93; Fabian Soc. Commn on Taxation and Citizenship, 1999–2000. President: Acad. of Learned Socs in Social Scis, 2000–01; NCVO, 1997–2002. Times columnist, 1988–92. Chm., Centrepoint, 2002–04. FKC 2008. Hon. Fellow: Cardiff Univ., 2000; St Catherine's Coll., Oxford, 2000; Harris Manchester Coll., Oxford, 2001. Hon. DLitt: London Guildhall Univ., 1993; Hull, 1994; DUniv York, 2007. *Publications:* Hegel, 1974, 2nd edn 1984; Community and Ideology, 1974; Political Philosophy and Social Welfare, 1981; Philosophy, Politics and Citizenship, 1984; Conservative Capitalism in Britain and the United States: a critical appraisal, 1988; Modern Political Thought, 1991; Politics, Theology and History, 2001. *Recreations:* music, opera, thinking about the garden, listening to my wife playing the piano, reading. *Address:* 6 Woodview Close, Bassett, Southampton SO16 3PZ. *T:* (01703) 769529.

PLANT, Dr Gordon Terence, FRCP, FRCOphth; Consultant Neurologist, National Hospital for Neurology and Neurosurgery, Moorfields Eye Hospital and St Thomas' Hospital, since 1991; *b* 4 July 1952; *s* of Thomas Edmund Plant and Sheila May Plant (*née* Atkinson); *m* 1978, Marilyn Jane Dirkin; three *d*. *Educ:* Downing Coll., Cambridge (BA 1974, MA 1977; MB BChir 1978; MD 1987). FRCP 1993; FRCOphth 2005. Hse Physician, St Thomas' Hosp., 1977; Hse Surgeon, Kingston Gen. Hosp., 1978; SHO, Westminster Hosp., 1978, Nat. Hosp., Queen Sq., 1979; Registrar in Neurol., Addenbrooke's Hosp., 1980–82. Wellcome Trust Res. Associate, Physiol Lab., Cambridge, 1982–85; Registrar, Nat. Hosp., Queen Sq., 1985–91; MRC Travelling Fellow, Smith-Kettlewell Res. Inst., San Francisco, 1989. Vis. Prof., City Univ. Member: British Is Neuro-ophthalmology Club, 1992–; Ophthalmic Club, 1996–. Editor-in-Chief, Neuro-ophthalmology, 2008–. *Publications:* Optic Neuritis, 1986; contribs to med., neurol, ophthalmol and visual sci. jls. *Recreations:* music, painting, book collecting. *Address:* 246 Sheen Lane, SW14 8RL. *T:* (020) 7829 8791, *Fax:* (020) 7833 8658; *e-mail:* gordon@plant.globalnet.co.uk.

PLANT, Prof. Jane Ann, (Mrs P. R. Simpson), CBE 1997; PhD; CEng, CGeol; FRSE, FIMM; Professor of Geochemistry, Imperial College London, since 2001; *b* 1 Feb. 1945; *d* of Ralph Lunn and Marjorie Lunn (*née* Langton); *m* 1st, 1967, Dr I. D. Plant (marr. diss. 1974); one *s*; 2nd, 1974, Prof. P. R. Simpson; one *s* one *d*. *Educ:* Liverpool Univ. (BSc 1966 with Dist.; BSc Hons 1967); Leicester Univ. (PhD 1977). CEng 1986; CGeol 1990; FRSE 2002. British Geological Survey: SO to Atomic Energy Div. (subseq. Geochem. Div.), 1967–71; SO, 1971; PSO, 1977; sabbatical year to work in N America, 1988; Hd, Applied Geochem. Gp, 1989–91; Asst Dir and Chief Geochemist, 1991–97; Chief Scientist and a Dir, 2000–05. Vis. Prof., Liverpool Univ., 1992; Special Prof., Nottingham Univ., 1996. Mem., Royal Commn on Envmtl Pollution, 1999–2006; Chair, Adv. Cttee on Hazardous Substances, 2001– (Chm., Stakeholders Forum). Freeman, City of London, 1999; Mem., Water Conservators' Co., 1999. FRGS 1998; FRSA 2000; FRSocMed 2005. DUniv Open, 1997; Hon. DSc: Exeter, 2001; Kingston, 2003; Keele, 2005; Åbo/Turku, 2005; Leicester, 2005. Lord Lloyd of Kilgerran Award, 1999. *Publications:* Your Life in Your Hands, 2000; (with G. Tidey) The Plant Programme, 2001; (with G. Tidey) Understanding, Preventing and Overcoming Osteoporosis, 2003; Prostate Cancer, 2004; (with G. Tidey) Eating for Better Health, 2005; numerous peer-reviewed papers and contrib. books on econ. and envmtl geochem. *Recreations:* gardening, theatre. *Address:* Earth Science and Engineering, Imperial College London, SW7 2AZ.

PLANT, Robert Anthony; singer and songwriter; solo singer, since 1980; *b* W Bromwich, Staffs, 20 Aug. 1948; *m* 1968, Maureen; one *s* one *d* (and one *s* decd). Lead singer, New Yardbirds, later Led Zeppelin, 1968–80; albums: Led Zeppelin, 1969; Led Zeppelin II, 1969; Led Zeppelin III, 1970; Untitled, 1971; Houses of the Holy, 1973; Physical Graffiti, 1975; Presence, 1976; In Through the Out Door, 1979; Coda, 1982; solo albums: Pictures at Eleven, 1982; The Principle of Moments, 1983; Shaken 'n' Stirred, 1985; Now and Zen, 1988; Manic Nirvana, 1989; Fate of Nations, 1993; Dreamland, 2002; Sixty Six to Timbuktu, 2003; with The Honeydrippers, The Honeydrippers Volume I, 1984; with Jimmy Page: No Quarter—Unledded, 1994; Walking into Clarksdale, 1998; with The Strange Sensation, Mighty ReArranger, 2005; with Alison Krauss, Raising Sand, 2007. *Address:* c/o Trinifold Management, 12 Oval Road, NW1 7DH.

PLANTIN, Marcus; Chief Executive, September Films, 2003–05; *b* 23 Oct. 1945. Producer/director, BBC TV, 1970–84; London Weekend Television: Head of Light Entertainment, 1985–87; Controller of Entertainment, 1987–90; Dir of Progs, 1990–92; ITV Network Dir, 1992–97; Dir of Progs, LWT, 1997–2001; Dir of Entertainment, Granada, 2001–02. FRTS. *Address:* The Lonsdale Healing Centre, 44A Lonsdale Road, SW13 9EB.

PLASKETT, Maj.-Gen. Frederick Joseph, CB 1980; MBE 1966; FCILT; Director General and Chief Executive, Road Haulage Association, 1981–88; *b* 23 Oct. 1926; *s* of Frederick Joseph Plaskett and Grace Mary Plaskett; *m* 1st, 1950, Heather (*née* Kington) (*d* 1982); four *d*; 2nd, 1984, Mrs Patricia Joan Healy. *Educ:* Wallasey Grammar Sch.; Chelsea Polytechnic. RN (trainee pilot, FAA), 1944–45; transf. to Army, 1945; commnd infantry (Green Howards), 1946; RASC, 1951; RCT, 1965; regimental and staff appts, India, Korea, Nigeria, Malaya, Germany and UK; Student, Staff Coll., Camberley, 1958; Jt Services Staff Coll., 1964; Instr, Staff Coll., Camberley, 1966–68; Management Coll., Henley, 1969; RCDS, 1975; Dir of Movements (Army), 1975–78; Dir Gen., Transport and Movements (Army), 1978–81, retired. Col Comdt, RCT, 1981–91 (Rep. Col Comdt, 1989). Chm., British Railways Bd, London Midland Region, 1989–92 (Mem., 1986–88). Director: Foden Trucks (Paccar UK) (formerly Sandbach Engrg Co.), 1981–97; RHA Insce Services Ltd, 1982–88; British Road Federation, 1982–88. Comr, Royal Hosp., Chelsea, 1985–88. Freeman, City of London, 1979; Liveryman, Co. of Carmen, 1979–. *Publications:* Shoot Like a Gentleman! (memoir), 2005; numerous articles in mil. and commercial jls on defence and transport related subjects. *Recreations:* fishing, sailing, gardening. *Address:* c/o National Westminster Bank, The Commons, Shaftesbury, Dorset SP7 8JY. *Club:* Army and Navy.

See also J. F. G. Logan.

PLASKITT, James Andrew; MP (Lab) Warwick and Leamington, since 1997; *b* 23 June 1954; *s* of late Ronald Plaskitt and of Phyllis Irene Plaskitt. *Educ:* Pilgrim Sch., Bedford; University Coll., Oxford (MPhil 1979; MA 1980). Lecturer in Politics: University Coll., Oxford, 1977–79; Christ Church, Oxford, 1984–86; Lectr in Govt, Brunel Univ., 1979–84; Oxford Analytica Ltd: Western European Editor, 1986–90; Dir of Consultancy, 1993–96. Mem. (Lab) Oxfordshire CC, 1985–97 (Leader, Labour Gp, 1990–96). Contested (Lab) Witney, 1992. Parly Under-Sec. of State, DWP, 2005–08. *Address:* House of Commons, SW1A 0AA.

PLASSNIK, Ursula, DIur; Minister for Foreign Affairs, Austria, since 2004; *b* 23 May 1956. *Educ:* elementary and grammar schs, Klagenfurt; High Sch., Foxcroft, Va; Vienna Univ. (DIur 1978); Coll. of Europe, Bruges (Postgrad. Dip.). Federal Ministry for Foreign Affairs, 1981–: COS of Vice Chancellor, 1997–2000, Federal Chancellor, 2000–04, Dr Wolfgang Schüssel, Federal Chancellery; Ambassador to Switzerland, 2004. *Address:* Ministry for Foreign Affairs, Minoritenplatz 8, 1014 Vienna, Austria. *T:* (5) 011500, *Fax:* (1) 5355091; *e-mail:* kabbm@bmaa.gv.at.

PLASTOW, Sir David (Arnold Stuart), Kt 1986; Chairman, Medical Research Council, 1990–98; *b* Grimsby, 9 May 1932; *s* of late James Stuart Plastow and Marie Plastow; *m* 1954, Barbara Ann May; one *s* one *d*. *Educ:* Culford Sch., Bury St Edmunds. Apprentice, Vauxhall Motors Ltd, 1950; joined Rolls-Royce Ltd, Motor Car Div., Crewe, Sept. 1958: apptd Marketing Dir, Motor Car Div., 1967; Managing Director: Motor Car Div., 1971; Rolls-Royce Motors Ltd, 1972; Vickers Plc: Dir, 1975–92; Man. Dir, 1980–86; Chief Exec., 1980–92; Chm., 1987–92. Dep. Chm., 1987–89, Jt Dep. Chm., 1989–94, Guinness PLC; Dep. Chm., TSB Gp, 1991–95; Chm., Inchcape plc, 1992–95; Regional Dir, Lloyds Bank, 1974–76; non-executive Director: GKN, 1978–84; Legal & General Gp Plc, 1985–87; Cable & Wireless, 1991–93; F. T. Everard & Sons, 1991–2001; Lloyds TSB, 1996–99. Trustee, Royal Opera House Trust, 1992–93 (Chm., 1992–93). Mem., European Adv. Council, Tenneco, 1984–86 and 1992–96; Bd Mem., Tenneco Inc., 1985–92, 1996–2004. Vice-Pres., Inst. of Motor Industry, 1974–82; Pres., SMMT, 1976–77, 1977–78 (Dep. Pres., 1978–79, 1979–80); Pres., Motor Industry Res. Assoc., 1978–81; Chm., Grand Council, Motor and Cycle Trades Benevolent Fund, 1976–82. Chm., Industrial Soc., 1983–87 (Mem., 1981); Dep. Chm., Listed Cos Adv. Cttee, 1987–90; Member: Council, CBI, 1983–92; BOTB, 1980–83; Engineering Council, 1980–83; Offshore Energy Technology Bd, 1985–86; Bd of Companions, BIM; Council, Regular Forces Employment Assoc. Patron, The Samaritans, 1987–99; Chm., 40th Anniversary Appeal Cttee, Mental Health Foundn, 1988–91; Gov., BUPA, 1990–95 (Dep. Chm., 1992–95). Chancellor, Univ. of Luton, 1993–2000 (Hon. Fellow, 1991). Chm. Governors, Culford Sch., 1979–2002. Pres., Crewe Alexandra FC, 1975–82. Liveryman, Worshipful Co. of Coachmakers & Coach Harness Makers. FRSA. Young Business Man of the Year Award, The Guardian, 1976. Hon. DSc Cranfield, 1978. *Recreations:* golf, music. *Clubs:* Boodle's; Royal and Ancient (St Andrews); Royal St George's (Sandwich); Senior Golfers' Society; Pine Valley Golf, Merion Golf.

PLATELL, Amanda Jane; writer and broadcaster; columnist, Daily Mail, since 2007; *b* 12 Nov. 1957; *d* of Francis Ernest Platell and Norma June Platell. *Educ:* Univ. of Western Australia (BA Hons Philosophy and Politics). Dep. Ed., Today newspaper, 1987–92; Man. Ed., Mirror Gp, 1993; Mktg Dir, 1993–95, Man. Dir, 1995–96, The Independent; Acting Ed., Sunday Mirror, 1996–97; Ed., Sunday Express, 1998–99; Hd of Media, Cons. Party, 1999–2001. *Publication:* Scandal, 1999. *Recreations:* travelling, cooking, cars, writing.

PLATER, Alan Frederick, CBE 2005; FRSL 1985; freelance writer, since 1960; *b* 15 April 1935; *s* of Herbert Richard Plater and Isabella Scott Plater; *m* 1st, 1958, Shirley Johnson (marr. diss. 1985); two *s* one *d*; 2nd, 1986, Shirley Rubinstein; three step *s*. *Educ:* Pickering Road Jun. Sch., Hull; Kingston High Sch., Hull; King's Coll., Newcastle upon Tyne. ARIBA (now lapsed). Trained as architect and worked for short time in the profession before becoming full-time writer in 1960; has written extensively for radio, television, films and theatre, also for The Guardian, Listener, New Statesman, etc. Vis. Prof., Univ. of Bournemouth, 2002–. Pres., Writers' Guild of GB, 1991–95 (Co-chair, 1986–87). Works include: *theatre:* A Smashing Day (also televised); Close the Coalhouse Door (Writers' Guild Radio Award, 1972); And a Little Love Besides; Swallows on the Water; Trinity Tales; The Fosdyke Saga; Fosdyke Two; On Your Way, Riley!; Skyhooks; A Foot on the Earth; Prez; Rent Party (musical); Sweet Sorrow; Going Home; I Thought I Heard a Rustling; Shooting the Legend; All Credit to the Lads; Peggy for You; Tales from the Backyard; Only a Matter of Time; Barriers; The Last Days of the Empire; Charlie's Trousers; Blonde Bombshells of 1943; Confessions of a City Supporter; Sweet William; Tales from the Golden Slipper; *films:* The Virgin and the Gypsy; It Shouldn't Happen to a Vet; Priest of Love; Keep the Aspidistra Flying; *television:* plays: So Long Charlie; See the Pretty Lights; To See How Far It Is (trilogy); Land of Green Ginger; Willow Cabins; The Party of the First Part; The Blacktoft Diaries; Thank You, Mrs Clinkscales; Doggin' Around; The Last of the Blonde Bombshells; Belonging; The Last Will and Testament of Billy Two Sheds; *biographies:* The Crystal Spirit; Pride of our Alley; Edward Lear—at the edge of the sand; Coming Through; series and serials: Z Cars;

Softly Softly; Shoulder to Shoulder; Trinity Tales; The Good Companions; The Consultant; Barchester Chronicles (adaptation of The Warden, and Barchester Towers, by Trollope); The Beiderbecke Affair; The Beiderbecke Tapes; The Fortunes of War (adaptation of Balkan and Levant trilogies by Olivia Manning); A Very British Coup (International Emmy; Golden Fleece of Georgia (USSR); Best Series BAFTA Award; Best Series RTS Award; Best Series Broadcasting Press Guild Award; Best Series and Grand Prix, Banff Internat. TV Fest., Canada); The Beiderbecke Connection; Campion (adapted from Margery Allingham); A Day in Summer (adaptation of J. L. Carr novel); Misterioso; A Few Selected Exits (adapted from Gwyn Thomas; Cymru Writing Award, BAFTA, Regl Programme Award, RTS, 1993); Oliver's Travels; Dalziel & Pascoe (from Reginald Hill); Lewis; *radio:* The Journal of Vasilije Bogdanovic (Sony Radio Award, 1983); All Things betray Thee (from Gwyn Thomas); The Lower Depths (from Gorky); Only a Matter of Time; Time Added On For Injuries; The Devil's Music; Abandoned Projects; Stories for Another Day. FRSA 1991. Hon. Fellow, Humberside Coll. of Higher Educn, 1983; Hon. DLitt: Hull, 1985; Newcastle, 2005; Hon. DCL Northumbria, 1997; DUniv Open, 2004. RTS Writer's Award, 1984/85; Broadcasting Press Guild Award, 1987; Writer's Award, BAFTA, 1988; Northern Personality Award, Variety Club of GB, 1989; Dennis Potter Award, BAFTA, 2005; Writer's Guild Lifetime Achievement Award, 2007. *Publications:* The Beiderbecke Affair, 1985; The Beiderbecke Tapes, 1986; Misterioso, 1987; The Beiderbecke Connection, 1992; Oliver's Travels, 1994; Doggin' Around, 2006; plays and shorter pieces in various anthologies. *Recreations:* reading, theatre, snooker, jazz, grandchildren, talking and listening. *Address:* c/o Alexandra Cann Representation, 2 St Thomas Square, Newport, Isle of Wight PO30 1SN. *T:* (020) 7938 4002. *Club:* Dramatists'.

PLATT, family name of **Baroness Platt of Writtle**.

PLATT OF WRITTLE, Baroness *cr* 1981 (Life Peer), of Writtle in the County of Essex; **Beryl Catherine Platt,** CBE 1978; FREng; DL; Chairman, Equal Opportunities Commission, 1983–88; *b* 18 April 1923; *d* of Ernest and Dorothy Myatt; *m* 1949, Stewart Sydney Platt (*d* 2003); one *s* one *d*. *Educ:* Westcliff High School; Girton Coll., Cambridge (MA; Fellow, 1988). CEng, FREng (FEng 1987); FRAeS (Hon. FRAeS 1994). Technical Assistant, Hawker Aircraft, 1943–46; BEA, 1946–49. Mem. Bd, British Gas, 1988–94. Member: Engineering Council, 1981–90; Engrg Training Authy, 1990–92; Meteorological Office Adv. Cttee (UK), 1992–99 (Chm., 1995–99). Member, Chelmsford RDC, 1958–74. Essex County Council: Mem., 1965–85; Alderman, 1969–74, Hon. Alderman, 2005; Vice-Chm., 1980–83; Chm., Education Cttee, 1971–80. Mem., H of L Select Cttee for Science and Technology, 1982–85, 1990–94, 1996–2001 and 2003–07, on Relationships between Central and Local Govt, 1995–96, on Stem Cell Res., 2001–02; Vice Pres., Parly Scientific Cttee, 1996–2000. Mem., Adv. Cttee on Women's Employment, 1984–88. Vice-Chairman: Technician Education Council, 1979–81; London Regional Adv. Council for Technology Education, 1975–81. President: Chelmsford Engrg Soc., 1979–80; Cambridge Univ. Engrs Assoc., 1987–2001; Assoc. for Sci. Educn, 1988; Pipeline Industries Guild, 1994–96; Vice-President: UMIST, 1985–92; Engrg Section, BAAS (Pres., 1988); ACC, 1992–97 (Mem. Educn Cttee, 1974–80); Member: CNAA, 1973–79; Council, CGLI, 1974–94; Cambridge Univ. Appointments Bd, 1975–79; Council, Careers Research and Adv. Centre, 1983–93; Council, RSA, 1983–88; COPUS, 1990–93; Council, Foundn for Sci. and Technology, 1991–97. Patron, Women into Sci. and Engrg, 1995–. Member of Court: Essex Univ., 1964–99; City Univ., 1969–78; Brunel Univ., 1985–92; Cranfield Inst. of Technology, 1989–2003; Chancellor, Middlesex Univ., 1993–2000. Trustee, Homerton Coll., 1970–81. Liveryman, Engineers' Co., 1988– (Mem., Ct of Assistants, 1995–2002, now Emeritus). DL Essex, 1983. Freeman, City of London, 1988. Fellow, 1987, Dir, 1989–94, Smallpeice Trust; Fellow, Manchester Polytechnic, 1989. FIGEM (FIGasE 1990); CInstE 1993; CIPD 1995; FRSA. Hon. FIMechE 1984; Hon. FITD 1994; Hon. FCP 1987; Hon. FIStructE 1991; Hon. FICE 1991; Hon. Fellow: Polytechnic of Wales, 1985; Women's Engrg Soc., 1988; UMIST, 1992. Hon. DSc: City, 1984; Salford, 1984; Cranfield, 1985; Nottingham Trent, 1993; Westminster, 1997; Sheffield, 2000; Anglia Ruskin, 2007; Southampton, 2008; DUniv: Open Univ., 1985; Essex, 1985; Middlesex, 1993; Sheffield Hallam, 2001; Hon. DEng Bradford, 1985; Hon. DTech: Brunel, 1986; Loughborough, 1993; Hon. LLD Cantab, 1988. European Engr, FEANI, 1987; Insignia Award *hc*, CGLI, 1988; RSC Parliamentary Award, 2007. *Recreations:* cooking, reading. *Address:* House of Lords, SW1A 0PW. *Club:* Oxford and Cambridge.

PLATT, Anthony Michael Westlake, CBE 1991; Chief Executive, London Chamber of Commerce and Industry, 1984–91; *b* 28 Sept. 1928; *s* of late James Westlake Platt, CBE and Veronica Norma Hope Platt (*née* Arnold); *m* 1st, 1952, Jennifer Susan Scott-Fox; three *s*; 2nd, 1984, Heather Mary Stubbs; one step *s* one step *d*; 3rd, 1987, Sarah Elizabeth Russell. *Educ:* Stowe School; Balliol College, Oxford (PPE 1951). Foreign Office, 1951, served Prague, 1953–54, NY, 1955–56; Shell Group of Cos: Switzerland, 1957; Guatemala, 1959; S Africa, 1961; Venezuela, 1963; London, 1969; The Hague, 1972; London, 1975–77 (Billiton UK); The Hague, 1977–78 (Billiton Internat.); Man. Dir, Consolidated Petroleum, London, 1979–84. Advr, Council of British Chambers in Europe, 1992–95. Freeman, City of London, 1991. *Publications:* (ed) Parallel 40 North to Eureka, 2000; Belovedest—A Marriage of Opposites, 2006. *Recreations:* walking, music, languages. *Address:* 17 Westgate Street, Bury St Edmunds, Suffolk IP33 1QG.
See also C. P. S. Platt.

PLATT, Prof. Colin Peter Sherard; Professor of History, Southampton University, 1983–99, now Emeritus; *b* 11 Nov. 1934; twin *s* of late James Westlake Platt and Veronica Norma Hope Arnold; *m* 1st, 1963, Valerie Ashforth (marr. diss. 1996); two *s* two *d*; 2nd, 1996, Claire Donovan. *Educ:* Collyers Grammar School, Horsham; Balliol College, Oxford (BA 1st cl., MA); Leeds University (PhD). Research Assistant in Medieval Archaeology, Leeds Univ., 1960–62, Lectr, 1962–64; Lectr, Sen. Lectr and Reader in History, Southampton Univ., 1964–83. *Publications:* The Monastic Grange in Medieval England, 1969; Medieval Southampton: the port and trading community AD 1000–1600, 1973; (with Richard Coleman-Smith) Excavations in Medieval Southampton 1953–1969, 2 vols, 1975; The English Medieval Town, 1976; Medieval England: a social history and archaeology from the Conquest to 1600 AD, 1978; The Atlas of Medieval Man, 1979; The Parish Churches of Medieval England, 1981; The Castle in Medieval England and Wales, 1982; The Abbeys and Priories of Medieval England, 1984; Medieval Britain from the Air, 1984; The Traveller's Guide to Medieval England, 1985; The National Trust Guide to late Medieval and Renaissance Britain, 1986; The Architecture of Medieval Britain: a social history (Wolfson Prize for History), 1990; The Great Rebuildings of Tudor and Stuart England: revolutions in architectural taste, 1994; King Death: the Black Death and its aftermath in late medieval England, 1996; Marks of Opulence: the why, when and where of western art 1000–1914, 2004; A Concise History of Jersey, 2009. *Recreations:* reading novels, visiting medieval antiquities. *Address:* The Old Rectory, Littlehempston, Totnes, Devon TQ9 6LY. *T:* (01803) 862598.
See also A. M. W. Platt.

PLATT, Dame Denise, DBE 2004 (CBE 1996); Chair, Commission for Social Care Inspection, since 2004; *b* 21 Feb. 1945; *d* of Victor Platt and May Platt (*née* Keeling). *Educ:* UCW, Cardiff (BSc Econ 1967); AIMSW 1968. Social Worker, then Sen. Social Worker, Middx Hosp., 1968–73; Sen. Social Worker, Guy's Hosp., 1973–76; Gp Leader, Southwark Social Services, 1976–78; Prin. Social Worker, Hammersmith Hosp., 1978–83; London Borough of Hammersmith and Fulham: Asst Dir, Social Services, 1983–86; Dir, 1986–95 (on leave of absence, 1994–95); Under Sec., Social Services, AMA, 1994–97; Hd of Social Services, LGA, 1997–98; Jt Hd, Social Care Gp, DoH, 1998–2001; Chief Inspector, Social Services Inspectorate, 1998–2004 and Dir of Children, Older People and Social Care Services, DoH, 2001–04. Pres., Assoc. Dirs of Social Services, 1993–94. Chm., Nat. AIDS Trust, 2006– (Trustee, 1987–98; Vice Chm., 1994–98); Trustee and Dir, FPA, 2005–; Trustee, NSPCC, 2007–. Member: Central Council Educn and Trng in Social Work, 1994–98; Youth Justice Task Force, 1997–98; Disability Rights Task Force, 1997–98; Ind. Reference Gp on Mental Health, 1997–98; Review Team, Strategic Review of London's Health Services, 1997–98; Ind. Review Bd, Cheshire CC Fire and Rescue Service, 2007–; Audit Commn, 2007–; Cttee on Standards in Public Life, 2008–. Governor: Nat. Inst. for Social Work, 1995–98 (Chm., 1997–99); Univ. of Bedfordshire, 2006–. Hon. DSocSc Brunel, 1998. *Publications:* various articles in social services press. *Recreations:* music, watercolours, walking, travel. *Address:* Commission for Social Care Inspection, 33 Greycoat Street, SW1P 2QF. *T:* (020) 7979 2000; *e-mail:* denise.platt@csci.gsi.gov.uk. *Club:* Reform.

PLATT, Eleanor Frances; QC 1982; a Recorder of the Crown Court, 1982–2004; a Deputy High Court Judge, Family Division, 1987–2004; *b* 6 May 1938; *er d* of late Dr Maurice Leon Platt and Sara Platt (*née* Stein), Hove, Sussex; *m* 1963; two *c*. *Educ:* Hove County School for Girls; University College London. LLB 1959. Called to the Bar, Gray's Inn, 1960; Jt Head of Specialist Family Law Chambers, 1990–2007. Mem., Matrimonial Causes Rule Cttee, 1986–90. Dep. Chm., NHS Tribunal, 1995–2001; Legal Assessor, GMC and GDC, 1995–2008; Mem., Gene Therapy Adv. Cttee, 1993–98. Treas., Family Law Bar Assoc., 1990–95 (Acting Chm., 1995); Pres., Jewish Family Mediation Register, 1998–. Chm., Law, Parly and Gen. Purposes Cttee, 1988–94, Dep. Chm. Defence Bd, 1997–2003, Vice Pres., 2003–06, Bd of Deputies of British Jews; Chm., New London Synagogue, 1994–99. Pres., Medico-Legal Soc., 2002–04 (Mem. Council, 1995–). *Recreations:* the arts, travel. *Address:* One Garden Court, Temple, EC4Y 9BJ. *T:* (020) 7797 7900; *e-mail:* platt@1gc.com.

PLATT, Sir Harold (Grant), Kt 1995; Chairman, Uganda Law Reform Commission, 1995–2000; *b* 11 March 1925; *s* of Rev. Harold George Platt and Frances Eaton Platt; *m* 1971, Eleonore Magdolna Gräfin Meran; one *d*. *Educ:* Ootacamund, S India; St Peter's Coll., Oxford. Called to the Bar, Middle Temple, 1952; joined Colonial Legal Service, 1954: Puisne Judge: Tanzania, 1965–73; Kenya, 1973–84; Judge of Court of Appeal, Kenya, 1984–89; Judge of Supreme Court, Uganda, 1989–95. *Recreations:* golf, tennis, gardening. *Address:* Johann Fuxgasse 8, 8010 Graz, Austria. *T:* (316) 323462. *Club:* Muthaiga Country (Kenya).

PLATT, Jane Christine; Chief Executive, National Savings and Investments, since 2006; *b* 8 Jan. 1957; *d* of George Platt and Miriam Platt (*née* Knowles); *m* 1980, David Bill. *Educ:* St Catherine's Coll., Oxford (MA). Sen. Pension Fund Manager, Mercury Asset Mgt, 1982–88; Dir, Business Develt, 1988–94, Man. Dir, 1994–95, BZW Investment Management; Chief Operating Officer, Barclays Asset Mgt, 1995–96; CEO, Barclays Stockbrokers and Barclays Bank Trust Co., 1996–2001; Chief Operating Officer, (Business Divs) Reuters, 2001–04. Non-executive Director: Edinburgh UK Investment Trust Plc, 2004–06; Witan Plc, 2005–06. Mem., Cornhill Club. *Recreations:* performing arts. *Address:* National Savings Investments, Charles House, 375 Kensington High Street, W14 8SD. *T:* (020) 7348 9469, *Fax:* (020) 7348 9353; *e-mail:* jane.platt@nsandi.com.

PLATT, John Richard; His Honour Judge Platt; a Circuit Judge, since 1992; *b* 21 Nov. 1942; *s* of Arthur James Platt and Joan Platt; *m* 1986, Jayne Mary Webb; two *d*. *Educ:* Sherborne Sch.; Trinity Hall, Cambridge. Partner, Lee Davies & Co., Solicitors, 1969–82; Registrar and District Judge, Bow County Court, 1982–92. *Publications:* A Guide to Judicial Pensions for Circuit Judges, 1995; A Guide to Judicial Pensions for District Judges, 1996; A Guide to Judicial Pensions for Stipendiary Magistrates, 1996; A Guide to the Judicial Pensions and Retirement Act, 1997; contribs to Jordans Civil Court Service, New Law Jl, Liverpool Law Review, Family Law. *Recreations:* wine and food, music, travel.

PLATT, Margaret; *see* Wright, M.

PLATT, Sir Martin Philip, 3rd Bt *cr* 1959, of Grindleford, co. Derby; *b* 9 March 1952; *o s* of Hon. Sir Peter Platt, 2nd Bt, AM and of Jean Halliday Platt (*née* Brentnall); *S* father, 2000; *m* 1971, Francis Corinne Moana, *d* of Trevor Samuel Conley; two *s* two *d*. *Heir: s* Philip Stephen Platt, *b* 17 Oct. 1972.

PLATT, Michael Edward Horsfall; Pensions Ombudsman, 1991–94; *b* 24 Aug. 1934; *s* of Fred Horsfall Platt and Alice Martha Taylor Platt (*née* Wilde). *Educ:* Taunton Sch.; The Queen's Coll., Oxford. Nat. Service, RAF, 1952–54. Min. of Labour, 1959; Min. of Pensions and Nat. Insurance, 1960; Min. of Social Security, 1966; Private Sec. to Minister of State, DHSS, 1968–70; Cabinet Office, 1970–71; DHSS, 1971–86; Chief Adjudication Officer, 1986–90. *Recreations:* theatre, music. *Address:* c/o Office of the Pensions Ombudsman, 11 Belgrave Road, SW1V 1RB. *T:* (020) 7834 9144.

PLATT, Stephen, (Steve); writer and journalist; *b* 29 Sept. 1954; *s* of Kenneth Norman Platt and Joyce (*née* Pritchard); one *d*. *Educ:* Longton High Sch., Stoke-on-Trent; Wade Deacon Sch., Widnes; LSE (BSc (Econ)). Teacher, Moss Brook Special Sch., Widnes, 1972–73; Dir, Self Help Housing Resource Library, Poly. of N London, 1977–80; Co-ordinator, Islington Community Housing, 1980–83; News Editor, subseq. Acting Editor, New Society, 1985–88; Editor: Roof, 1988; Midweek, 1988–89; columnist and writer, 1988–91; Editor, New Statesman and Society, 1991–96; freelance writer, 1996–. Editor, Enjoying the Countryside, 1988–; Editl Consultant, Channel 4, 1996–; Website and Contributing Ed., Time Team, 1999–; Dispatches Website Ed., 1999–. Hon. Chm., Medical Aid for Iraq, 1991–. *Publications:* various. *Recreations:* archaeology, amphibians, bears (real and fictional), countryside, football, growing things, mountains, music, poetry. *Address:* 46 Tufnell Park Road, N7 0DT. *T:* (020) 7263 4185; *e-mail:* mail@steveplatt.net. *Clubs:* Red Rose; Port Vale.

PLATT, Terence Charles, CB 1996; Deputy Under-Secretary of State and Principal Establishment Officer, Home Office, 1992–96; *b* 22 Sept. 1936; *yr s* of Bertram Reginald Platt, QPM and Nina Platt; *m* 1959, Margaret Anne Cotmore; two *s*. *Educ:* St Olave's and St Saviour's Grammar School; Joint Services School for Linguists; Russian Interpreter. HM Immigration Officer, 1957; Asst Principal, Home Office, 1962; Principal, 1966; Cabinet Office, 1970; Principal Private Sec. to Sec. of State for NI (Rt Hon. William Whitelaw), 1972–73; Asst Sec., Home Office, 1973–81; Asst Under-Sec. of State and Princ. Estabt and Finance Officer, NI Office, 1981–82; Asst Under-Sec. of State and Dir of Regimes and Services, Prison Dept, Home Office, 1982–86; Asst Under-Sec. of State

(Ops and Resources), Immigration and Nationality Dept, Home Office, 1986–92; Chief Inspector, Immigration Service, 1991–92. Mem., Civil Service Appeal Bd, 1997–2001. *Publication:* New Directions in Prison Design (Wkg Party Report), 1985. *Recreations:* photography, butterflies, water-colour painting.

PLATT, Prof. Trevor, PhD; FRS 1998; FRSC 1990; Head of Biological Oceanography, Bedford Institute of Oceanography, Nova Scotia, since 1972; *b* 12 Aug. 1942; *s* of John Platt and Lily Platt (*née* Hibbert); *m* 1988, Shuba Sathyendranath. *Educ:* Univ. of Nottingham (BSc); Univ. of Toronto (MA); Dalhousie Univ. (PhD 1970). Res. Scientist in Marine Ecology, Bedford Inst. of Oceanography, Nova Scotia, 1965–72.– Chairman: Jt Global Ocean Flux Study, 1991–93; Internat. Ocean-colour Co-ordinating Gp, 1996–; Pres., Amer. Soc. Limnology and Oceanography, 1990–92. *Publications:* numerous res. papers in scholarly jls. *Recreations:* cycling, fly-fishing, languages, music. *Address:* Bedford Institute of Oceanography, Dartmouth, NS B2Y 4A2, Canada. *T:* (902) 4263793.

PLATTEN, Rt Rev. Stephen George; *see* Wakefield, Bishop of.

PLATTS, (Charles) Graham (Gregory); His Honour Judge Platts; a Circuit Judge, since 2005; *b* 25 Aug. 1956; *s* of Arthur Platts and Georgina Platts; *m* 1985, Hazel Carty; one *s* one *d*. *Educ:* Fitzwilliam Coll., Cambridge (BA 1977). Called to the Bar, Gray's Inn, 1978; in practice specialising in clinical negligence and personal injury, 1978–2005; Asst Recorder, 1999–2000; a Recorder, 2000–05. Pt-time Legal Mem., 2002–05, Mem., Restricted Patient's Panel, 2007–, Mental Health Rev. Tribunal. *Recreations:* piano, walking, ski-ing, Manchester City FC.

PLATTS-MILLS, Mark Fortescue; QC 1995; *b* 17 Jan. 1951; *s* of John Faithful Fortescue Platts-Mills, QC; *m* 1982, Dr Juliet Anne Britton; one *s*. *Educ:* Bryanston Sch.; Balliol Coll., Oxford (BA Eng. Sci. and Econ.). Called to the Bar, Inner Temple, 1974; Bencher, Lincoln's Inn, 2006. *Recreations:* gardening, hockey, cricket. *Address:* 8 New Square, Lincoln's Inn, WC2A 3QP.

PLAYER, Dr David Arnott, FRCPE, FRCPsych, FFCM; District Medical Officer, South Birmingham Health Authority, 1987–91; *b* 2 April 1927; *s* of John Player and Agnes Gray; *m* 1955, Anne Darragh; two *s*. *Educ:* Calder Street Sch.; Bellahouston Acad., Glasgow; Glasgow Univ. (MB, ChB, DPH); DPM RCSI; St Andrews Univ. (MA Hons 1995). House Surgeon, Dumfries and Galloway Royal Infirmary, 1950; Consultant in Dermatology and VD, RAMC (Far East), 1950–52; House Surgeon, Western Infirmary, Glasgow, 1952; House Physician, Bridge of Earn Hosp., 1952–53; House Surgeon (Obst., Gyn. and Paed.), Halifax Royal Infirmary, 1953–54; GP, W Cumberland and Dumfriesshire, 1954–59; Registrar (Infectious Diseases), Paisley Infectious Diseases Hosp., 1959–60; Asst MOH, Dumfriesshire, 1960–62; Registrar (Psychiatry), Crichton Royal Hosp., Dumfries, 1962–64; MOH, Dumfries Burgh, 1964–70; MO (Mental Health Div.), SHHD and Med. and Psych. Adviser to Sec. of State for Scotland on Scottish Prison and Borstal Service, 1970–73; Dir, Scottish Health Educn Group, 1973–82; Dir Gen., Health Educn Council, 1982–87. Hon. Vis. Prof., Dept of Clinical Epidemiology and Gen. Practice, Royal Free Hosp. Sch. of Medicine, 1983–. *Publications:* articles in Health Bulletin, Internat. Jl of Health Educn, Scottish Trade Union Review. *Recreations:* golf, cycling. *Address:* 57 Learmonth Court, Edinburgh EH4 1PD.

PLAYER, Gary James; professional golfer, since 1953; *b* Johannesburg, 1 Nov. 1935; *s* of Francis Harry Audley Player and late Muriel Marie Ferguson; *m* 1957, Vivienne, *d* of Jacob Wynand Verwey; two *s* four *d*. *Educ:* King Edward Sch., Johannesburg. Won first, Dunlop tournament, 1956; major championship wins include: British Open, 1959, 1968, 1974; US Masters, 1961, 1974, 1978; US PGA, 1962, 1972; US Open, 1965; S African Open, thirteen times, 1956–81; S African PGA, 1959, 1960, 1969, 1979, 1982; Australian Open, seven times, 1958–74; Johnnie Walker Trophy, Spain, 1984; World Match Play Tournament, 1965, 1966, 1968, 1971, 1973. *Publications:* Golf Begins at 50 (with Desmond Tolhurst), 1988; To Be the Best, 1991; The Meaning of Life, 2000. *Address:* c/o Gary Player Group, 3930 RCA Boulevard, Suite 3001, Palm Beach Gardens, FL 33410–4214, USA.

PLAYFORD, His Honour Jonathan Richard; QC 1982; a Circuit Judge, 1998–2006; *b* 6 Aug. 1940; *s* of late Cecil R. B. Playford and Euphrasia J. Playford; *m* 1978, Jill Margaret Dunlop; one *s* one *d*. *Educ:* Eton Coll.; London Univ. (LLB). Called to the Bar, Inner Temple, 1962, Bencher, 1991; a Recorder, 1985–98. Mem., CICB, 1995–98. Freeman, Clockmakers' Co., 2004. *Recreations:* music, horology. *Address:* c/o Reading Crown Court, Old Shire Hall, Forbury, Reading RG1 3EH. *Clubs:* Garrick, Royal Automobile; Huntercombe Golf (Henley).

PLAYLE, Colin; Managing Director, Cicero, The Talking Company, since 1995; *b* 13 May 1933; *s* of James and Florence Playle; *m* 1st, 1957, Reena Mary Cuppleditch (marr. diss. 1975); two *d*; 2nd, 1976, Patricia Margaret Golds (*d* 1998); 3rd, 2007, Rosemary Margaret Henderson. *Educ:* University College London (BA Hons). CompIGasE. British Gas: Marketing and Customer Service, E Midlands Gas Bd, 1957–75; Regl Marketing Manager, E Midlands, 1975–78; Dir of Marketing, British Gas NE, 1978–86; Sen. Mem., British Gas Privatisation Team, 1986; HQ Dir, Industrial and Commercial Gas, London, 1988–91; Regl Chm., British Gas Scotland, 1991–94; Project Dir, Retail, 1994–95. Chm., Combined Heat and Power Assoc., 1991–93. Vis. Prof. in Business Studies, Liverpool Business Sch., 1997–. Co-ordinator, Azerbaijan, TAM programme, EBRD, 1999–2000. *Recreations:* ski-ing, ornithology, modern literature, theatrical productions. *Address:* Upton Barn, 83 Main Street, Upton, Newark, Notts NG23 5SY.

PLEDGER, Air Chief Marshal Sir Malcolm (David), KCB 2001; OBE 1988; AFC 1981; *b* 24 July 1948; *m* 1969, Betty Barker Kershaw; two *s*. *Educ:* Newcastle Univ. (BSc 1st Cl. Chemistry 1970). Commnd RAF, 1970; served RAF Stations at Akrotiri, Shawbury, Sek Kong, Upavon, RAF Staff Coll., and MoD, 1972–85; OC 240 Operational Conversion Unit, RAF Odiham, 1985–88, incl. tour as OC 78 Sqdn, RAF Mount Pleasant, Falkland Is; Air Sec.'s Dept, 1988–90; Station Comdr, RAF Shawbury, 1990–92; rcds 1993; Air Officer Plans, HQ RAF Strike Command, 1993–97; COS, Dep. C-in-C and AOC, Directly Administered Units, HQ RAF Logistics Comd, 1997–99; Air Mem. for Logistics and AOC-in-C, RAF Logistics Comd, 1999; DCDS (Personnel), 1999–2002; Chief of Defence Logistics, MoD, 2002–04. *Recreation:* golf. *Club:* Royal Air Force.

PLEMING, Nigel Peter; QC 1992; a Judge of the Courts of Appeal of Jersey and Guernsey, since 2007; *b* 13 March 1946; *s* of late Rev. Percy Francis Pleming and Cynthia Myra Pleming (later Mrs Leslie Tuxworth); *m* 1979, Evelyn Carol Joan Hoffmann; one *s* two *d*. *Educ:* King Edward VI Grammar Sch., Spilsby; Kingston Polytechnic (LLB); University Coll. London (LLM). Lectr, Kingston Poly., 1969–73; called to the Bar, Inner Temple, 1971, Bencher, 2001; in practice at the Bar, 1974–; Junior Counsel to the Crown (Common Law), 1987–92. Vice-Chm., Mental Health Act Commn, 1994–97; Mem., Govt working party on mental health reform, 1998–99. Hon. LLD Kingston, 1999.

Recreations: cricket, tennis, painting, blues guitar. *Address:* 39 Essex Street, WC2R 3AT. *T:* (020) 7832 1111. *Club:* Garrick.

PLENDER, John; *see* Plender, W. J. T.

PLENDER, Hon. Sir Richard (Owen), Kt 2008; **Hon. Mr Justice Plender**; a Judge of the High Court of Justice, Queen's Bench Division, since 2008; *b* 9 Oct. 1945; *s* of George Plender and Louise Mary (*née* Savage); *m* 1978, Patricia Clare (*née* Ward); two *d*. *Educ:* Dulwich Coll.; Queens' Coll., Cambridge (MA, LLB; Rebecca Squire Prize; LLD 1993); Univ. of Illinois (LLM; JSD 1972; College of Law Prize); Univ. of Sheffield (PhD 1973). Called to the Bar, Inner Temple, 1972 (Berridale-Keith Prize), Bencher, 1996; in practice at the Bar, 1974–2008; QC 1989; Recorder, 1998–2008. Consultant, UN Law and Population Programme, 1972–74; Legal Adviser, UN High Comr for Refugees, 1974–78; Legal Sec., Court of Justice of European Communities, 1980–83; Dir of Studies, 1987, Dir of Res., 1988, and Lectr, 1998, Hague Acad. of Internat. Law; Dir, Centre of European Law, KCL, 1988–91; Special Legal Advr to States of Jersey, 1988–. Leverhulme Fellow, Yale Law Sch., 1980; British Acad. Fellow, Soviet Acad. of Sciences, 1985; Sen. Mem., Robinson Coll., Cambridge, 1983–; Associate Prof., Univ. de Paris II (Univ. de Droit, d'Economie et des Sciences Sociales), 1989–90; Hon. Vis. Prof., City Univ., 1991–. *Publications:* International Migration Law, 1972, 2nd edn 1988; (ed and contrib.) Fundamental Rights, 1973; Cases and Materials on the Law of the European Communities, 1980 (with J. Usher), 3rd edn 1993; A Practical Introduction to European Community Law, 1980; (with J. Peres Santos) Introducción al Derecho Comunitario Europeo, 1984; Basic Documents on International Migration Law, 1988, 3rd edn 2006; (ed and contrib.) Legal History and Comparative Law: essays in honour of Albert Kiralfy, 1990; The European Contracts Convention: the Rome Convention on the Choice of Law for Contracts, 1991, 2nd edn 2001; (ed and contrib.) The European Courts Practice and Precedents, 1996, supplement 1997, as European Courts Procedure, 2000–; contribs in English, French, German and Spanish to jls and encyclopedias. *Recreations:* writing light verse, classical music (especially late nineteenth century orchestral). *Address:* Royal Courts of Justice, Strand, WC2A 2LL.

PLENDER, (William) John (Turner), FCA; contributor, leader writer and columnist, Financial Times, since 1981; Chairman, Quintain Estates and Development plc, since 2007 (non-executive Director, since 2004); *b* Cardiff, 9 May 1945; *s* of William Plender and Averil Maud Plender (*née* Turnbull); *m* 1st, 1972, Sophia Mary, *e d* of late Alistair and Nancy Crombie (marr. diss. 1989); one *s* two *d*; 2nd, 1997, Stephanie Julia Michell, *d* of late David and Joan Harris; two *s*. *Educ:* Downside Sch.; Oriel Coll., Oxford (BA). FCA 1970. Chartered Accountant, Deloitte, Plender, Griffiths & Co., 1967–70; Staff writer: Investors Chronicle, 1970–71; The Times, 1972–74; Financial Ed., Economist, 1974–79; Mem., Planning Staff, FCO, 1980–81; freelance journalist, publisher, author and broadcaster, 1982–. Chm., Pensions and Investment Res. Consultants, 1992–2002. Member: Co. Law Rev. Steering Gp, DTI, 1998–2001; Private Sector Adv. Gp on Corporate Governance, World Bank/OECD, 2002–. Mem., Quality of Mkts Adv. Cttee, London Stock Exchange, 1992–95; Chm., Adv. Council, Centre for Study of Financial Innovation, 1997–. Chm., Adv. Bd, Assoc. of Corporate Treasurers, 2002–. Sen. Wincott Award for Financial Journalism, 1994. *Publications:* That's The Way The Money Goes, 1981; (with P. Wallace) The Square Mile, 1985; A Stake in the Future, 1997; Going Off the Rails, 2003; (with A. Persaud) Ethics and Finance, 2007. *Recreation:* piano. *Address:* c/o The Financial Times, Number One, Southwark Bridge, SE1 9HL. *T:* (020) 7873 3000, *Fax:* (020) 7478 9438; *e-mail:* john.plender@ft.com, john.plender@quintain-estates.com. *Club:* Travellers.

PLENDERLEITH, Ian, CBE 2002; Deputy Governor and Member, Monetary Policy Committee, South African Reserve Bank, 2003–05; Executive Director, 1994–2002, Member, Monetary Policy Committee, 1997–2002, Bank of England; Chairman, BH Macro Ltd, since 2007; *b* 27 Sept. 1943; *s* of late Raymond William Plenderleith and Louise Helen Plenderleith (*née* Martin); *m* 1st, 1967, Kristina Mary Bentley (marr. diss. 2007); one *s* two *d*; 2nd, 2007, Elizabeth Ann Campbell Barrell. *Educ:* King Edward's Sch., Birmingham; Christ Church, Oxford (MA); Columbia Business Sch., NY (MBA; Beta Gamma Sigma Medal, 1971). Joined Bank of England, 1965; seconded to IMF, Washington DC, 1972–74; Private Sec. to Governor, 1976–79; Alternate Dir, EIB, 1980–86; Hd of Gilt-Edged Div., 1982–90; Asst Dir, 1986–90; Associate Dir, 1990–94. Dir, Bank of England Nominees Ltd, 1994–2002; Alternate Dir, BIS, 1994–2002; Sen. Broker to Comrs for Reduction of Nat. Debt, 1989–2002. Dir, London Stock Exchange (formerly Mem., Stock Exchange Council), 1989–2001 (Dep. Chm., 1996). Internat. Consultant, Invoice Clearing Bureau SA (Pty) Ltd, 2006–. Non-executive Director: Sanlam Ltd, 2006–; Medicapital Bank plc, 2006–; Bond Exchange of S Africa, 2007–; Mem., Adv. Panel, E-Clear plc, 2008–. Chairman: Stock Borrowing and Lending Cttee, 1990–95; G-10 Gold and Foreign Exchange Cttee, 1995–2001; Sterling Money Mkts Liaison Gp, 1999–2002; Corporation for Public Deposits, 2003–05; SA Money Mkts Liaison Gp, 2004–05; Co-Chm., Govt Borrowers Forum, 1991–94; Mem., G-10 Cttee on Global Financial System, 1994–2002. Member: Editl Cttee, OECD Study on Debt Management, 1990–93; Legal Risk Rev. Cttee, 1991–92; Financial Law Panel, 1992–94; Global Borrowers and Investors Forum Adv. Bd, 2003–05; Sen. Adv. Council, Internat. Capital Mkts Assoc., 2006–; Adv. Bd, Central Banking Pubns, 2006–. Member: Adv. Bd, Inst. of Archaeology Develt Trust, UCL, 1987–96; Bd of Overseers, Columbia Business Sch., 1991– (Mem., Adv. Bd, London Alumni Club, 2002, 2006–); London Old Edwardians Assoc. Cttee, 1996–2004 (Vice-Pres., 2004–); Ext. Adv. Panel, Oxford Math. Inst., 2000–03; Oxford Business Alumni Adv. Bd, 2002–03; Adv. Bd, Witwatersrand Business Sch., 2007–. Member: Fund-raising Planning Gp, St Bartholomew's Hosp., 1992–94; Fund-raising Planning Cttee, St Bartholomew's and The London Hosps, 1998–2003; Council, British Museum Soc., subseq. BM Friends, 1993–99, 2000–03 and 2005–; BM Townley Steering Gp, 2002–03; Adv. Bd, Actors Centre, 2002–; Council (formerly Develt Council), Shakespeare's Globe, 2002–; Bd, Christ Church Campaign, 2002– (Mem., Finance Cttee, 1998–2003); Chm., Reed's Sch. Foundn Appeal, 2006–07; Gov., Reed's Sch., 2007– (Chm., 2008–). Dir, City Arts Trust, 1997–2003. FSI 2006 (MSI 1991). Mem., Assoc. of Black Securities and Investment Professionals, 2005–. Fellow, ACT, 1989 (Mem. Adv. Bd, 2007–). Liveryman, Innholders' Co., 1977 (Mem., Investment Cttee, 2007–). *Recreations:* archaeology, theatre, cricket, long-distance walking. *Address:* Goldneys, River, Petworth, W Sussex GU28 9AU. *Clubs:* Athenæum (Mem., 2007–, Chm., 2008–, Investment Cttee), London Capital (Mem. Adv. Bd, 2002–), MCC; Tillington Cricket (Hon. Sec., 1983–2003).

PLETNEV, Mikhail Vasilievich; pianist, conductor and composer; *b* Archangel, Russia, 14 April 1957. *Educ:* Central Sch. of Music; Moscow State Conservatory (under Yakov Flier and Lev Vlasenko (piano), and Albert Leman (composition)). Founder and Principal Conductor, Russian Nat. Orch., 1990–99, now Conductor Laureate; Guest Conductor of orchs incl. Philharmonia, LSO, CBSO and Los Angeles Philharmonic. Piano recitals and tours with orchs worldwide; numerous recordings. Teacher, Moscow State Conservatory, 1981–. Works composed include: Classical Symphony; Triptych for Symphony Orch.; Fantasy on Kazakh Themes for Violin and Orch.; Capriccio for Piano and Orch.;

Concerto for Viola and Orch. Gold Medal, Tchaikovsky Internat. Piano Competition, 1978; State Prize of Russia, 1995, 2002. *Address:* c/o Salpeter Artists Management, 4 Denman Drive, NW11 6RG.

PLEWS, Derek Alexander; Partner, Media Outcomes, since 2006; *b* 14 Dec. 1960; *s* of Albert Alexander Plews and Doris Plews; *m* 1984, Sandra Elizabeth Joyce Ming; two *s*. *Educ:* Clondermott Sec. Sch., Londonderry. Reporter, Belfast Telegraph, 1979–82; Actg Ed., Londonderry Sentinel, 1982–85; Press Officer, MoD, 1985–91; Chief Press Officer, Employment Dept, 1991–94; Dep. Hd of Inf., Dept of Transport, 1994–97; Hd of News, DETR, 1997–98; Press Sec. to Dep. Prime Minister, 1998–2001; Dir of Communications, Assoc. of Train Operating Cos, 2001; Dir of News, MoD, 2001–02; Dir of Communication, ODPM, then DCLG, 2002–06. Major, London Regt (V) TA, attached to Media Ops Gp (V). *Recreations:* hill-walking, angling. *Address:* Media Outcomes, Satra Innovation Park, Rockingham Road, Kettering, Northants NN16 9JH.

PLEYDELL-BOUVERIE, family name of **Earl of Radnor**.

PLOMIN, Judith Frances; *see* Dunn, J. F.

PLOMIN, Prof. Robert, PhD; FBA 2005; Research Professor in Behavioural Genetics, and Deputy Director, MRC Research Centre on Social, Genetic, and Developmental Psychiatry, Institute of Psychiatry, King's College, London, since 1994; *b* 20 Feb. 1948; *m* 1987, Judith Frances Dunn, *qv*. *Educ:* DePaul Univ., Chicago (BA Psychology 1970); Univ. of Texas, Austin (PhD Psychology 1974). University of Colorado: Faculty Fellow, Inst. for Behavioral Genetics, 1974–86; Asst Prof., 1974–78; Associate Prof., 1978–82; Prof., 1982–86; Dist. Prof. and Dir, Center for Develtl and Health Genetics, Pennsylvania State Univ., 1986–94. Pres., Behavior Genetics Assoc., 1989–90. Ed., Sage Series on Individual Differences and Development, 1990–. *Publications:* (with A. H. Buss) Temperament: early developing personality traits, 1984; (with J. C. DeFries) Origins of Individual Differences in Infancy: the Colorado Adoption Project, 1985; Development, Genetics and Psychology, 1986; (ed with J. Dunn) The Study of Temperament: changes, continuities, and challenges, 1986; (jtly) Nature and Nurture in Infancy and Early Childhood, 1988; (with J. Dunn) Separate Lives: why siblings are so different, 1990; (jtly) Behavioral Genetics: a primer, 2nd edn 1990 to 4th edn 2001; (ed jtly) Nature and Nurture during Middle Childhood, 1994; (ed jtly) Separate Social Worlds of Siblings: impact of nonshared environment on development, 1994; Genetics and Experience: the interplay between nature and nurture, 1994; (jtly) The Relationship Code, 2000; numerous articles in learned jls. *Address:* MRC Centre for Social, Genetic and Developmental Psychiatry, Institute of Psychiatry, De Crespigny Park, Denmark Hill, SE5 8AF.

PLOTKIN, Prof. Gordon David, PhD; FRS 1992; FRSE; Professor of Computation Theory, Edinburgh University, since 1986; *b* 9 Sept. 1946; *s* of Manuel Plotkin and Mary (*née* Levin); *m* 1st, 1984, Lynda (*née* Stephenson) (marr. diss.); one *s*; 2nd, 1994, Hephzibah (*née* Kolban). *Educ:* Univ. of Glasgow (BSc 1967); Univ. of Edinburgh (PhD 1972). University of Edinburgh: Res. Associate and Res. Fellow, 1971–72; Lectr, 1975; Reader, 1982–86. BP Venture Res. Fellow, 1981–87; SERC Sen. Res. Fellow, 1992–97. MAE 1989. Royal Soc.-Wolfson Res. Merit Award, 2005–. *Publications:* (ed with G. Kahn) Semantics of Data Types, 1984; (ed with G. Huet) Logical Frameworks, 1991; (ed with J.-L. Lassez) Computational Logic: essays in honour of Alan Robinson, 1991; (ed jtly) Situation Theory and its Applications, 1991; (ed with G. Huet) Logical Environments, 1993; (ed with M. Dezani-Ciancaglini) Typed Lambda Calculi and Applications, 1995; (ed jtly) Proof, Language and Interaction: essays in honour of Robin Milner, 2000; contribs to jls of computer science and logic. *Recreations:* hill-walking, chess. *Address:* School of Informatics, University of Edinburgh, The King's Buildings, Edinburgh EH9 3JZ.

PLOTKIN, Prof. Henry Charles, PhD; Professor of Psychobiology, University College London, since 1993; *b* Johannesburg, 11 Dec. 1940; *s* of Bernard Solomon Plotkin and Edythe Plotkin (*née* Poplak); *m*, 1st, 1965, Patricia Ruehl (marr. diss. 1970); 2nd, 1975, Victoria Mary Welch; one *s* one *d*. *Educ:* Univ. of Witwatersrand (BSc 1st cl. Hons 1964); University College London (PhD 1968). Res. Asst, Univ. of Witwatersrand, 1964; Res. Scientist, MRC Unit on Neural Mechanisms of Behaviour, 1965–72; MRC Travelling Fellowship, Stanford Univ., Calif, 1970–71; Department of Psychology, University College London: Lectr, 1972–88; Reader, 1988–93; Head of Dept, 1993–98. *Publications:* Darwin Machines and the Nature of Knowledge, 1994; Evolution in Mind, 1997; The Imagined World Made Real, 2002; Evolutionary Thought in Psychology, 2004; Necessary Knowledge, 2007; *edited:* (with D. A. Oakley) Brain, Behaviour and Evolution, 1979; Essays in Evolutionary Epistemology, 1982; The Role of Behaviour in Evolution, 1988; articles in learned jls. *Recreations:* family, French house, growing old gracefully with music. *Address:* Department of Psychology, University College London, WC1E 6BT. *T:* (020) 7679 7573.

PLOURDE, Most Rev. Joseph Aurèle; Archbishop of Ottawa (RC), 1967–89, now Emeritus; *b* 12 Jan. 1915; *s* of Antoine Plourde and Suzanne Albert. *Educ:* Bathurst Coll.; Bourget Coll., Rigaud; Major Seminary of Halifax; Inst. Catholique, Paris; Gregorian Univ., Rome. Auxiliary Bishop of Alexandria, Ont., 1964. Hon. DEducn, Moncton Univ., 1969. *Address:* Jean-Paul II Residence, 1243 Kilborn Place, Ottawa, ON K1H 6K9, Canada.

PLOUVIEZ, Peter William; Chairman, Equity Trust Fund, 1992–2006; *b* 30 July 1931; *s* of C. A. W. and E. A. Plouviez; *m* 1978, Alison Dorothy Macrae; two *d* by previous marr. Gen. Sec., British Actors' Equity Assoc., 1974–91. FRSA 1992. *Address:* c/o Equity Trust Fund, 222 Africa House, 64 Kingsway, WC2B 6BD.

PLOWDEN, Hon. Francis John; Chairman, National Council for Palliative Care, since 2001; Member, Judicial Appointments Commission, since 2006; *b* 25 June 1945; *s* of Lord Plowden, GBE, KCB, and Lady Plowden, DBE; *m* 1984, Geraldine Wickman; one *s*. *Educ:* Eton; Trinity Coll., Cambridge (BA 1966). FCA 1969. Cooper Brothers, then Coopers & Lybrand, subseq. PricewaterhouseCoopers: consulting and acctg experience, UK, Ghana, the Gambia and Zaire, 1966–76; Partner, Nigeria, 1976–79; on secondment to HM Treasury/Cabinet Office Financial Mgt Unit, 1982–85; Partner, 1985; Hd, Govt Consulting, 1987–98; Man. Partner Internat. Affairs, and Mem. Internat. Exec. Cttee, 1995–98; Global Govt Leader, 1998–2001. Director: ITNET plc, 2001–05; Hedra plc, 2007–. Treas., Family Housing Assoc., 1979–84. Chm., Greenwich Foundn for the Old Royal Naval Coll., 2003–; Trustee: Royal Armouries, 1989–97; Royal Ballet Sch., 1989–2003; Anna Plowden Trust, 2000–. *Publication:* (with Sir Christopher Foster) The State Under Stress, 1996. *Recreations:* walking, ballet, theatre, built and natural environment. *Address:* 4 Highbury Road, SW19 7PR. *T:* (020) 8879 9841; *e-mail:* f.plowden@btopenworld.com. *Club:* Royal Automobile.
See also W. J. L. Plowden.

PLOWDEN, William Julius Lowthian, PhD; independent consultant; *b* 7 Feb. 1935; *s* of Lord Plowden, GBE, KCB, and Lady Plowden, DBE; *m* 1960, Veronica Gascoigne; two *s* two *d*. *Educ:* Eton; King's Coll., Cambridge (BA, PhD); Univ. of Calif, Berkeley (Commonwealth Fund Fellow). Staff Writer, Economist, 1959–60; BoT, 1960–65; Lectr in Govt, LSE, 1965–71; Central Policy Review Staff, Cabinet Office, 1971–77; Under Sec., Dept of Industry, 1977–78; Dir-Gen., RIPA, 1978–88; Exec. Dir, UK Harkness Fellowships, NY, 1988–91; Sen. Advr, Harkness Fellowships, London, 1991–98; UK Dir, Atlantic Fellowships, 1995–98. Hon. Prof., Dept of Politics, Univ. of Warwick, 1977–82; Vis. Prof. in Govt, LSE, 1982–88, 2002–; Vis. Prof., Univ. of Bath, 1992–95; Sen. Res. Associate, IPPR, 1992–94; Vis. Sen. Res. Fellow, London Business Sch., 1993–94; Vis. Res. Fellow, Constitution Unit, UCL, 1999–2002. Member: W Lambeth DHA, 1982–87; QCA, 1999–2002. Trustee: CSV, 1984–2004; Southern Africa Advanced Educn Project, 1986–95; Public Mgt Foundn, 1992–98. Mem. Ct of Govs, LSE, 1987–2006, Council, 2000–03. *Publications:* The Motor Car and Politics in Britain, 1971; (with Tessa Blackstone) Inside the Think Tank: advising the Cabinet 1971–1983, 1988; Mandarins and Ministers, 1994; (with Kate Jenkins) Governance and Nation-Building: the failure of international intervention, 2006. *Address:* 49 Stockwell Park Road, SW9 0DD. *T:* (020) 7274 4535.
See also F. J. Plowden.

PLOWDEN ROBERTS, Hugh Martin; Director, Argyll Group plc, 1983–95; *b* 6 Aug. 1932; *s* of Stanley and Joan Plowden Roberts; *m* 1st, 1956, Susan Jane Patrick (*d* 1996); two *d*; 2nd, 2000, Mrs Jane Hall (*d* 2007). *Educ:* St Edward's School, Oxford; St Edmund Hall, Oxford. BA 1954, MA 1956. FIGD 1980. Payne & Son Meat Group, 1954–60 (Dir, 1958); Asst Gen. Manager (Meat Group), Co-operative Wholesale Society, 1960–67; Allied Suppliers Ltd, 1967–82: Dir, 1971; Dep. Man. Dir, 1974; Man. Dir, 1978; Chm., 1980–82; Dir, Cavenham Ltd, 1979, Chm., 1981–82; Dep. Chm., Argyll Stores Ltd, 1983–85; Chm., Dairy Crest Foods, subseq. Dairy Crest Ltd, 1985–88; Dir, Lawson Mardon Group Ltd, 1987–91. Comr, Meat and Livestock Commn, 1975–79; Mem., MMB, 1983–89. *Recreations:* country pursuits. *Address:* Barn Cottage, Fulking, Henfield, W Sussex BN5 9NB. *T:* (01273) 857622. *Club:* Farmers'.

PLOWMAN, John Patrick; Director, John Plowman Associates Ltd (governance, strategy and policy analysis), since 2003; *b* 20 March 1944; *s* of late Robert and of Ruth Plowman, Lane End, Bucks; *m* 1973, Daphne Margaret Brock Kennett; two *s* one *d*. *Educ:* St Edward's Sch., Oxford; Grenoble Univ.; University Coll., Univ. of Durham (BA). MoD, 1967–75: Private Office, Minister of State for Defence, 1969–71; Resident Observer, CSSB, 1975; Cabinet Office, 1976–78; MoD and UK Delegn to UN Law of Sea Conf., 1979–81; Asst Sec., DoE, 1982–86; Counsellor, UK Repn to EC, 1986–90; Head, Envmtl Protection (Europe), 1990–93; Regl Dir for NW, DoE and Dept of Transport, 1993–94; Dir, Wildlife and Countryside, DoE, then DETR, 1994–98; Dir, Road Safety and Envmt, DETR, 1998–2001; Chm., Driver and Vehicle Operator Gp, DETR, subseq. DTLR, then DfT, 2001–02; Gp Modernisation Dir, Driver and Vehicle Operator Gp, DfT, 2003. Served Royal Marines Reserve, 1968–71. Dir and Trustee, Parly Adv. Council for Transport Safety, 2004–; Mem. Adv. Bd, 2004–06, Dir, 2006–, Roadsafe. Gov., Charlotte Sharman Sch., Southwark, 2002– (Chm., 2008). *Recreations:* music, fishing, gardening (English Gardening Sch., 2004), book collecting. *Club:* Royal Over-Seas League.

PLOWRIGHT, Dame Joan (Ann), (The Lady Olivier), DBE 2004 (CBE 1970); leading actress with the National Theatre, 1963–74; Member of the RADA Council; Vice-President, English Stage Company; *b* 28 Oct. 1929; *d* of late William Ernest Plowright and of Daisy Margaret (*née* Burton); *m* 1st, 1953, Roger Gage (marr. diss.); 2nd, 1961, (as Sir Laurence Olivier) Baron Olivier, OM (*d* 1989); one *s* two *d*. *Educ:* Scunthorpe Grammar School; Laban Art of Movement Studio; Old Vic Theatre School. First stage appearance in If Four Walls Told, Croydon Rep. Theatre, 1948; Bristol Old Vic and Mem. Old Vic Co., S Africa tour, 1952; first London appearance in The Duenna, Westminster, 1954; Moby Dick, Duke of York's, 1955; season of leading parts, Nottingham Playhouse, 1955–56; English Stage Co., Royal Court, 1956; The Crucible, Don Juan, The Death of Satan, Cards of Identity, The Good Woman of Setzuan, The Country Wife (transferred to Adelphi, 1957); The Chairs, The Making of Moo, Royal Court, 1957; The Entertainer, Palace, 1957; The Chairs, The Lesson, Phoenix, NY, 1958; The Entertainer, Royale, NY, 1958; The Chairs, The Lesson, Major Barbara, Royal Court, 1958; Hook, Line and Sinker, Piccadilly, 1958; Roots, Royal Court, Duke of York's, 1959; Rhinoceros, Royal Court, 1960; A Taste of Honey, Lyceum, NY, 1960 (Best Actress Tony Award); Rosmersholm, Greenwich, 1973; Saturday, Sunday, Monday, Queen's, 1974–75; The Sea Gull, Lyric, 1975; The Bed Before Yesterday, Lyric, 1975 (Variety Club of GB Award, 1977); Filumena, Lyric, 1977 (Soc. of West End Theatre Award, 1978); Enjoy, Vaudeville, 1980; The Cherry Orchard, Haymarket, 1983; The House of Bernada Alba, Globe, 1986; Time and the Conways, Old Vic, 1990; If We are Women, Greenwich, 1995; Absolutely! (perhaps), Wyndham's, 2003; Chichester Festival: Uncle Vanya, The Chances, 1962; St Joan (Best Actress Evening Standard Award), Uncle Vanya, 1963; The Doctor's Dilemma, The Taming of the Shrew, 1972; Cavell, 1982; The Way of the World, 1984; National Theatre: St Joan, Uncle Vanya, Hobson's Choice, opening season, 1963; The Master Builder, 1964; Much Ado About Nothing, 1967, 1968; Three Sisters, 1967, 1968; Tartuffe, 1967, 1968; The Advertisement, 1968; Love's Labour's Lost, 1968; The Merchant of Venice, 1970; A Woman Killed With Kindness, 1971; The Rules of the Game, 1971; Eden End, 1974; Mrs Warren's Profession, 1985. Produced The Travails of Sancho Panza, 1969; directed: Rites, 1969; A Prayer for Wings, 1985; Married Love, 1988. *Films include:* The Entertainer, 1960; Three Sisters, 1970; Equus; Britannia Hospital, 1982; Wagner, Revolution, 1985; Drowning by Numbers, The Dressmaker, 1988; I Love You to Death, Avalon, 1989; Stalin, 1992 (Golden Globe Award, 1993); Enchanted April, 1993 (Golden Globe Award, 1993); Denis the Menace, A Place for Annie, A Pin for the Butterfly, Widow's Peak, Last Action Hero, 1993; On Promised Land, Hotel Sorrento, A Pyromaniac's Love Story, The Scarlett Letter, 1994; Mr Wrong, 1995; Jane Eyre, 101 Dalmatians, Surviving Picasso, 1996; The Assistant, 1996; Dance with Me, 1998; America Betrayed, 1998; Tea with Mussolini, 1999; Return to the Secret Garden, Frankie and Hazel, Global Heresy, 2000; Callas Forever, 2001; George and the Dragon, I Am David, 2002; Bringing Down the House, 2003; Mrs Palfrey at the Claremont, 2006; The Spiderwick Chronicles, 2007; *films for TV:* The Merchant of Venice; Brimstone and Treacle, 1982; A Dedicated Man; Return of the Natives, 1994; Tom's Midnight Garden, 1998; This Could Be the Last Time, 1998; other *television* appearances include: Daphne Laureola, 1976; The Birthday Party, 1987; The Importance of Being Earnest, 1988; And a Nightingale Sang, 1989; House of Bernada Alba, 1991; Clothes in the Wardrobe, 1992. 18th annual Crystal Award, Women in Film, USA, 1994. Hon. DLitt Hull, 2001. *Publication:* And That's Not All (memoirs), 2001. *Recreations:* reading, music, entertaining. *Address:* c/o 41 Warbeck Road, W12 8NS.

PLOWRIGHT, Rosalind Anne, (Mrs J. A. Kaye), OBE 2007; mezzo-soprano; *b* 21 May 1949; *d* of Robert Arthur Plowright and Celia Adelaide Plowright; *m* 1984, J(ames) Anthony Kaye; one *s* one *d*. *Educ:* Notre Dame High Sch., Wigan; Royal Northern Coll. of Music, Manchester. LRAM. London Opera Centre, 1974–75; Glyndebourne Chorus and Touring Co., début as soprano, Agathe in Der Freischutz, 1975; WNO, ENO, Kent Opera, 1975–78; Miss Jessel in Turn of the Screw, ENO, 1979 (SWET award); début at Covent Garden as Ortlinde in Die Walküre, 1980; with Bern Opera, 1980–81, Frankfurt

Opera and Munich Opera, 1981; débuts: in USA (Philadelphia and San Diego), Paris, Madrid and Hamburg, 1982; at La Scala, Milan, Edinburgh Fest., San Francisco and New York (Carnegie Hall), 1983; at Deutsche Oper, Berlin, 1984; in Houston, Pittsburgh, Verona, Montpellier and Venice, 1985; in Rome, Florence and Holland, 1986; in Tulsa, Buenos Aires, Santiago di Chile, Israel and Bonn, 1987; with NY Phil. and Paris Opera, 1987; in Lausanne, Geneva, Oviedo and Bilbao, 1988; in Zurich, Copenhagen, Lisbon and Torre del Lago, 1989; with Vienna State Opera, 1990; in Nice, 1991; in Wiesbaden, 1992; in Leeds, 1993; in Athens and Bregenz, 1994; BBC Prom. Concerts; with Berlin Deutsche Staatsoper, 1996; with Scottish Opera, 1999; with Opera New Zealand, 2000; with Opera Holland Park, 2002; with NY Metropolitan Opera; Paris Châtelet, 2003; with Florence Maggio Musicale, 2004; Tokyo, Leipzig, 2006. Principal rôles as soprano include: Ariadne; Aida; Amelia in Un Ballo in Maschera; Leonora in Il Trovatore; Leonora in La Forza del Destino; Desdemona in Otello; Violetta in La Traviata; Medora in Il Corsaro; Elena in I Vespri Siciliani; Abigaille in Nabucco; Elisabetta in Don Carlos; Lady Macbeth; Manon Lescaut; Giorgetta in Il Tabarro; Suor Angelica; Norma; Alceste; Médée; Maddalena in Andrea Chénier; La Gioconda; Tatyana in Eugene Onegin; Tosca; principal rôles as mezzo-soprano include: Amneris in Aida; Kostelnicka in Jenufa; Fricka in Das Rheingold and Die Walküre; Ortrud in Lohengrin; Marfa in Khovanshchina. Has given recitals and concerts in UK, USA and Europe, made opera and concert recordings, and opera telecasts; acting début, House of Elliott, TV serial, 1993; The Man Who Made Husband Jealous, TV, 1997; Two's a Crowd, UK th. tour, 2002. Teacher of singing; masterclasses at Royal Acad. of Music, Guildhall Sch. of Music, RNCM and Trinity Coll. First prize, 7th Internat. Comp. for Opera Singers, Sofia, 1979; Prix Fondation Fanny Heldy, Acad. Nat. du Disque Lyrique, 1985. *Recreation:* fell walking. *Address:* c/o IMG Artists Management, The Light Box, 111 Power Road, Chiswick W4 5PY. *T:* (020) 7957 5822; *e-mail:* sgoldstone@imgartists.com.

PLOWRIGHT, Walter, CMG 1974; DVSc; FRS 1981; FRCVS; Head, Department of Microbiology, ARC Institute for Research on Animal Diseases, Compton, Berks, 1978–83; *b* 20 July 1923; 2nd *s* of Jonathan and Mahala Plowright, Holbeach, Lincs; *m* 1959, Dorothy Joy (*née* Bell). *Educ:* Moulton and Spalding Grammar Schs; Royal Veterinary Coll., London. DVSc (Pret.) 1964; MRCVS 1944; FRCVS 1977; FRVC 1987. Commissioned, RAVC, 1944–48; Colonial Service, 1950–64; Animal Virus Research Inst., Pirbright, 1964–71 (seconded E Africa, 1966–71); Prof. of Vet. Microbiology, RVC, 1971–78. Hon. Mem., Acad. Royale des Sciences d'Outre-Mer, Brussels, 1986. Hon. DSc: Univ. of Nairobi, 1984; Reading, 1986. J. T. Edwards Memorial Prize, 1964; R. B. Bennett Commonwealth Prize of RSA, 1972; Bledisloe Vet. Award, RASE, 1979; King Baudouin Internat. Devélt Prize, 1984; Dalrymple-Champneys Cup, BVA, 1984; Gold Award, Office Internat. des Epizooties, Paris, 1988; Outstanding Scientific Achievement Award, Animal Health Trust, 1991; Theiler Meml Trust Award, South Africa, 1994; World Food Prize, World Food Prize Foundn, Iowa, 1999. Moran, Order of the Burning Spear (Kenya), 2000. *Publications:* numerous contribs to scientific jls relating to virus diseases of animals. *Recreations:* gardening, reading on wine and investment, African history. *Address:* Whitehill Lodge, Goring-on-Thames, Reading RG8 0LL. *T:* (01491) 872891.

PLUMB, family name of **Baron Plumb**.

PLUMB, Baron *cr* 1987 (Life Peer), of Coleshill in the County of Warwickshire; **Charles Henry Plumb,** Kt 1973; DL; Member (C) The Cotswolds, European Parliament, 1979–99; *b* 27 March 1925; *s* of Charles and Louise Plumb; *m* 1947, Marjorie Dorothy Dunn; one *s* two *d*. *Educ:* King Edward VI School, Nuneaton. National Farmers Union: Member Council, 1959; Vice-President, 1964, 1965; Deputy-President, 1966, 1967, 1968, 1969; President, 1970–79. European Parliament: Chm., Agricl Cttee, 1979–82; Leader, EDG, 1982–87; Pres., 1987–89; Co-Chm., EU/ACP Jt Assembly, 1994; Vice-Pres., EPP, 1994–97; Leader, British Conservatives, 1994–97. Chm., British Agricl Council, 1975–79. Chm., Agricultural Mortgage Corp., 1994–95. Mem., Duke of Northumberland's Cttee of Enquiry on Foot and Mouth Disease, 1967–68; Member Council: CBI; Animal Health Trust. Chm., Internat. Agricl Trng Programme, 1987–. Pres., Royal Agric. Soc. of England, 1977, Dep. Pres. 1978; President: Internat. Fedn of Agricl Producers, 1979–82; Comité des Organisations Professionels Agricoles de la CEE (COPA), 1975–77. Pres., Nat. Fedn of Young Farmers' Clubs, 1976–; Patron, Warwicks Co. Fedn of YFC, 1974–; Hon. Pres., Ayrshire Cattle Soc. Pres., Nat. Sleep Assoc., 2000–. Chancellor, Coventry Univ., 1995–; Gov., RAC, Cirencester, 1995–. Liveryman, Farmers' Co. (Master, 2005–06). FRSA 1970; FRAgS 1974. DL Warwick 1977. Hon. Fellow, Wye Coll., London Univ., 1988. Hon. DSc: Cranfield, 1983; Silsoe Coll. of Technol., 1987; De Montfort, 1995; Hon. LLD Warwick, 1990; Hon. Dr Cheltenham & Gloucester Coll. of HE, 1999. Gold Medal, RASE, 1983; Robert Schuman Gold Medal, France, 1989. Ordén de Merito (Portugal), 1987; Order of Merit (Luxembourg), 1988; Grand Cross, Order of Civil Merit (Spain), 1989; Knight Comdr's Cross, Order of Merit (FRG), 1990 (Order of Merit, 1979); Grand Order of the Phoenix (Greece), 1997. *Recreations:* country pursuits, fishing. *Address:* The Dairy Farm, Maxstoke, Coleshill, Warwicks B46 2QJ. *T:* (01675) 463133, *Fax:* (01675) 464156; House of Lords, SW1A 0PW. *T:* (020) 7219 1233, *Fax:* (020) 7219 1649; *e-mail:* plumbh@parliament.uk. *Club:* Farmers'.

PLUMB, Alan; *see* Plumb, R. A.

PLUMB, Paula Maria H.; *see* Hay-Plumb.

PLUMB, Prof. (Raymond) Alan, PhD; FRS 1998; Professor of Meteorology, since 1988, and Director, Program in Atmospheres, Oceans and Climate, since 2003, Massachusetts Institute of Technology; *b* 30 March 1948; *s* of Tom and Dorothy Plumb; *m* 1981, Janet Gormly (marr. diss. 2007); one *s* one *d*. *Educ:* Manchester Univ. (BSc Physics 1969; PhD Astronomy 1972). SO, then SSO, Met. Office, Bracknell, 1972–76; Res. Scientist, then Principal Res. Scientist, CSIRO Div. of Atmospheric Res., Aspendale, Vic, 1976–88. *Publications:* (ed with R. A. Vincent) Middle Atmosphere, 1989; (with J. C. Marshall) Atmosphere, Ocean, and Climate Dynamics, 2007; numerous papers in refereed scientific jls, incl. Jl Atmospheric Scis, Jl Geophysical Res. *Recreations:* angling, hiking. *Address:* 76 Westford Street, Chelmsford, MA 01824, USA. *T:* (978) 2561402.

PLUMBLY, Sir Derek (John), KCMG 2001 (CMG 1991); HM Diplomatic Service; Chairman, Assessment and Evaluation Committee, Sudan, since 2008; *b* 15 May 1948; *s* of late John C. Plumbly and Jean Elizabeth (*née* Baker); *m* 1979, Nadia Gohar; two *s* one *d*. *Educ:* Brockenhurst Grammar Sch.; Magdalen Coll., Oxford (BA PPE). VSO, Pakistan, 1970; Third Sec., FCO, 1972; MECAS, 1973; Second Sec., Jedda, 1975; First Sec., Cairo, 1977; FCO, 1980; First Sec., Washington, 1984; Dep. Head of Mission, Riyadh, 1988; Head of Chancery, UK Mission to UN, NY, 1992–96; Internat. Drugs Co-ordinator, and Dir, Drugs and Internat. Crime, FCO, 1996–97; Dir, Middle East and N Africa, FCO, 1997–2000; Ambassador: to Saudi Arabia, 2000–03; to Egypt, 2003–07. Hon. Dr Loughborough, 2008. *Address:* c/o Foreign and Commonwealth Office, King Charles Street, SW1A 2AL. *Club:* Travellers.

PLUME, John Trevor; Regional Chairman, Industrial Tribunals (London North), 1984–87; *b* 5 Oct. 1914; *s* of William Thomas and Gertrude Plume; *m* 1948, Christine Mary Wells; one *d*. *Educ:* City of London School; Inns of Court School of Law. Called to the Bar, Gray's Inn, 1936, Bencher, 1969. Legal Associate Mem., Town Planning Inst., 1939; served Royal Artillery, 1940–46 (Captain). Practised at Bar, specialising in property law, 1936–76; Chm., Industrial Tribunals, 1976–87. Liveryman, Clockmakers' Co. *Recreations:* beekeeping, carpentry, gardening, fishing. *Address:* Mulberry Cottage, Forest Side, Epping, Essex CM16 4ED. *T:* (01992) 572389.

PLUMMER, family name of **Baron Plummer of St Marylebone**.

PLUMMER OF ST MARYLEBONE, Baron *cr* 1981 (Life Peer), of the City of Westminster; **(Arthur) Desmond (Herne) Plummer,** Kt 1971; TD 1950; JP; DL; President, Portman Building Society, 1990–2007 (Chairman, 1983–90); *b* 25 May 1914; *s* of late Arthur Herne Plummer and Janet (*née* McCormick); *m* 1941, Pat Holloway (Pres., Cons. Women's Adv. Cttee, Greater London Area, 1967–71) (*d* 1998); one *d*. *Educ:* Hurstpierpoint Coll.; Coll. of Estate Management. Served 1938–46, Royal Engineers, Field and Staff. Member: TA Sports Bd, 1953–79; London Electricity Consultative Council, 1955–66; St Marylebone Borough Council, 1952–65 (Mayor, 1958–59); LCC, for St Marylebone, 1960–65; Inner London Educn Authority, 1964–76. Greater London Council: Mem. for Cities of London and Westminster, 1964–73, for St Marylebone, 1973–76; Leader of Opposition, 1966–67 and 1973–74; Leader of Council, 1967–73. Member: South Bank Theatre Board, 1967–74; Standing Conf. on SE Planning, 1967–74; Transport Co-ordinating Council for London, 1967–69; Local Authorities Conditions of Service Adv. Bd, 1967–71; Exec. Cttee, British Section of Internat. Union of Local Authorities, 1967–74; St John Council for London, 1971–94; Exec. Cttee, Nat. Union Cons. and Unionist Assocs, 1967–76; Chm., St Marylebone Conservative Assoc., 1965–66. Chm., Horserace Betting Levy Bd, 1974–82. Chm., Nat. Employers' Life Assce, 1983–89; Pres., Met. Assoc. of Bldg Socs, 1983–89. Mem. Court, Univ. of London, 1967–77. Chairman: Epsom and Walton Downs Trng Grounds Man. Bd, 1974–82; National Stud, 1975–82; President: London Anglers' Assoc., 1976–; Thames Angling Preservation Soc., 1970–99. Liveryman, Worshipful Co. of Tin Plateworkers. FAI 1948; FRICS 1970; FRSA 1974; Hon. FASI (Hon. FFAS 1966). JP, Co. London, 1958; DL Greater London, 1970. KStJ 1986. *Publications:* Time for Change in Greater London, 1966; Report to London, 1970; Planning and Participation, 1973. *Recreations:* swimming (Capt. Otter Swimming Club, 1952–53); horse racing. *Address:* 4 The Lane, St Johns Wood, NW8 0PN. *Clubs:* Carlton (Chm., Political Cttee, 1979–84; Pres., 1984–98), Royal Automobile, MCC.

PLUMMER, (Arthur) Christopher (Orme), CC (Canada) 1968; actor; *b* Toronto, 13 Dec. 1929; *m* 1st, 1956, Tammy Lee Grimes; one *d*; 2nd, 1962, Patricia Audrey Lewis (marr. diss. 1966); 3rd, 1970, Elaine Regina Taylor. *Educ:* public and private schs, Montreal. French and English radio, Canada, 1949–52; Ottawa Rep. Theatre; Broadway: Starcross Story, 1951–52; Home is the Hero, 1953; The Dark is Light Enough, 1954 (Theatre World Award); The Lark, 1955; J. B., 1958 (Tony nomination); Arturo Ui, 1963; Royal Hunt of the Sun, 1965–66; Stratford, Conn, 1955: Mark Antony, Ferdinand; leading actor, Stratford Festival, Canada, 1956–67: Henry V, The Bastard, Hamlet, Leontes, Mercutio, Macbeth, Cyrano de Bergerac, Benedick, Aguecheek, Antony; Royal Shakespeare Co., Stratford-on-Avon, 1961–62: Benedick, Richard III; London debut as Henry II in Becket, Aldwych and Globe, 1961 (Evening Standard Best Actor Award, 1961); National Theatre, 1971–72: Amphytrion 38, Danton's Death; Broadway musical, Cyrano, 1973 (Outer Critics Circle Award and Tony Award for Best Actor in a Musical, NY Drama Desk Award); The Good Doctor, NY, 1974; Iago in Othello, NY, 1982 (Drama Desk Award); Macbeth, NY, 1988; No Man's Land, NY, 1994; Barrymore (one-man show), 1997 (Tony Award for Best Actor); King Lear, Stratford Fest., 2002, NY, 2004. *Films:* Stage-Struck, 1956; Across the Everglades, 1957; The Fall of the Roman Empire, 1963; The Sound of Music (Golden Badge of Honour, Austria), Daisy Clover, 1964; Triple Cross, 1966; Oedipus Rex, 1967; The Battle of Britain, 1968; Royal Hunt of the Sun, 1969; The Pyx, 1973; The Man Who Would Be King, 1975; Aces High, The Moneychangers (Emmy Award), 1976; International Velvet, The Silent Partner, 1978; Hanover Street, 1979; Murder by Decree, 1980 (Genie Award, Canada); The Disappearance, The Janitor, 1981; The Amateur, 1982; Dreamscape, 1984; Playing for Keeps, Lily in Love, 1985; Souvenir, 1989; Where The Heart Is, 1990; Twelve Monkeys, 1996; The Insider, 2000; Dracula 2001, Lucky Break, A Beautiful Mind, 2001; Ararat, Nicholas Nickleby, 2002; Blizzard, Gospel of John, 2003; National Treasure, 2004; Alexander, 2005; Inside Man, Syriana, 2006; Closing the Ring, 2007; Man in the Chair, 2008, and others. TV appearances, Britain, Denmark, and major N American networks, incl. Hamlet at Elsinore, BBC and Danish TV, 1964 (4 Emmy Award nominations). First entertainer to win Maple Leaf Award (Arts and Letters), 1982. *Recreations:* tennis, ski-ing, piano. *Clubs:* Players, River (New York).

PLUMMER, Maj.-Gen. Brian Peter, CBE 2002; Clerk to Worshipful Company of Skinners, since 2003; *b* 30 Aug. 1948. *Educ:* Univ. of Durham (BA). Commnd RWF, 1970; Regt and Staff Duty, 1974–85; jsdc, 1986; ASC, 1986–88; CO 1 RWF, 1989–91; HCSC, 1995; Comd, 1st Mechanised Bde, 1995–96; rcds, 1997; Comd, Combined Arms Trng Centre, 1998–99; Dir Gen. Trng Support, HQ Land Comd, 1999–2002. Col, RWF, 2001–05. *Address:* c/o RHQ RWF, Hightown Barracks, Wrexham, Clwyd LL13 8RD.

PLUMMER, Christopher; *see* Plummer, A. C. O.

PLUMMER, Peter Edward; Deputy Director, Department for National Savings, 1972–79; *b* 4 Nov. 1919; *s* of Arthur William John and Ethel May Plummer; *m* 1949, Pauline Wheelwright; one *s* one *d*. *Educ:* Watford Grammar Sch. Served War, REME, 1941–46. Customs and Excise, 1936–38; Dept for National Savings, 1938–79; Principal, 1956; Assistant Sec., 1964; seconded to Nat. Giro, 1970–71; Under-Sec., 1972. *Recreations:* gardening, photography. *Address:* Old Timbers, Farm Lane, Nutbourne, Chichester, W Sussex PO18 8SA. *T:* (01243) 377450.

PLUMPTON, Alan, CBE 1980; BSc; FREng, FIET; Chairman, Schlumberger plc, 1992–2001; Chairman, 1992–99, Director, 1999–2001, Beaufort Group PLC (formerly Beaufort Management Consultants); *b* 24 Nov. 1926; *s* of late John Plumpton and Doris Plumpton; *m* 1950, Audrey Smith; one *s* one *d*. *Educ:* Sunderland Technical Sch.; Durham Univ. (BSc Elec. Eng). FREng (FEng 1991). Pupil Engr, Sunderland Corp. Elec. Undertaking, 1942; various engrg and commercial appts, NEEB, 1948–61; Dist Manager, E Monmouthshire Dist, S Wales Electricity Bd, 1961–64. Admin. Staff Coll., Henley, 1963; Dep. Chief Commercial Engr, S Wales Elec. Bd, 1964–67; Chief Commercial Engr, S Wales Elec. Bd, 1967–72; Dep. Chm., London Elec. Bd, 1972–76, Chm., 1976–81; Dep. Chm., Electricity Council, 1981–86. Chairman: Ewbank Preece Group, 1986–92; Manx Electricity Authority, 1986–97; Schlumberger Measurement and Systems, 1988–92; Dir, Eleco Holdings, 1993–97. MInstD 1986; CCMI. Liveryman, Gardeners' Co. JP Mon, 1971–72. *Recreations:* golf, gardening. *Address:* Lockhill, Stubbs Wood, Amersham, Bucks HP6 6EX. *T:* (01494) 433791. *Club:* Harewood Downs Golf (Chm., 1996–98).

PLUMPTON, Denise Kathryn; Director of Information, Highways Agency, Department for Transport, since 2005; *b* 31 Oct. 1954; *d* of late Dennis Plumpton and Mabel Jenny Plumpton; partner, Peter John Finney. *Educ:* Univ. of Sheffield (BSc 1st Cl. Hons Maths 1976). Rover Gp, 1976–82; ISTEL, 1983–89; Powergen: Commercial Manager, 1989–96; IT Dir, 1996–99; Information Technology Director: TNT UK Ltd, 1999–2004; Sendo, 2004. MInstD. *Recreations:* Judge for British Racing and Sports Car Club, remembering to water hanging baskets in garden. *T:* (0121) 687 4130, *Fax:* (0121) 678 8406; *e-mail:* denise.plumpton@highways.gsi.gov.uk.

PLUMPTRE, family name of **Baron Fitzwalter.**

PLUMPTRE, Hon. (Wyndham) George; Director, Bonhams, since 2005; *b* 24 April 1956; 3rd *s* of 21st Baron Fitzwalter; *m* 1984, Alexandra Elizabeth Cantacuzene-Speransky; two *s* one *d. Educ:* Radley Coll.; Jesus Coll., Cambridge (BA Mod. Hist.). Author, journalist, lecturer and broadcaster, 1978–; Gardens Correspondent, 1993–95, columnist, 1995–97, The Times; Ed., Sotheby's Preview Mag., 1995–97; Dir, S Africa, Sotheby's, 1997–99; Founder and Editl Dir, greenfingers.com, 1999–2002. Trustee: Kent Gardens Trust, 1992–; Nat. Gardens Scheme, 2005–; Mem., SE Regl Cttee, Nat. Trust, 1993–96. *Publications:* Royal Gardens, 1981; Collins Book of British Gardens, 1985; The Fast Set, 1985; The Latest Country Gardens, 1988; Homes of Cricket, 1988; Garden Ornament, 1989; Cricket Cartoons and Caricatures, 1989; Back Page Racing, 1989; The Golden Age of Cricket, 1990; The Water Garden, 1993; The Garden Makers, 1993; Great Gardens, Great Designers, 1994; Edward VII, 1995; The Country House Guide, 1996; Classic Planting, 1998; Royal Gardens of Europe, 2005; Heritage Gardens, 2007. *Address:* The Old Laundry, Tudeley, Tonbridge, Kent TN11 0NW. *T:* (01732) 352314. *Clubs:* Pratt's, MCC (Mem., Arts and Liby Cttee, 1999–).

PLUMSTEAD, Isobel Mary, (Mrs N. J. Coleman); Her Honour Judge Plumstead; a Circuit Judge, since 2001; authorised to sit as Judge of High Court, Family Division, 2002; Designated Family Judge: Cambridge, 2003–Dec. 2009; Peterborough and Cambridge, 2007–Dec. 2009; *b* 19 July 1947; *d* of John Archibald Plumstead, DFM, MA and Nancy Plumstead (*née* Drummond); *m* 1971, Nicholas John Coleman, *qv*; one *s* two *d. Educ:* Norwich High Sch. for Girls (GPDST); St Hugh's College, Oxford (BA 1969; MA 1985); Inns of Court Sch. of Law. Blackstone Entrance Scholar, 1967, Colombos Prize for Internat. Law, 1970, Harmsworth Scholar, 1970–73, Middle Temple. Called to the Bar, Middle Temple, 1970, Bencher 2006; Registrar, Principal Registry, Family Div. of High Court, 1990; District Judge, Principal Registry, Family Div. of the High Ct, 1990–2001; Asst Recorder, 1994–98; a Recorder, 1998–2001. Member: Independent Schs Tribunal, 1992–2000; Family Cttee (formerly Civil and Family Cttee), 1993–99, Main Bd, 1997–99, Judicial Studies Bd; Hon. Sec., Council of HM Circuit Judges, 2009–. Trustee: New Parents' Infant Network (Newpin), 1989–96; Hackney and E London Family Mediation Service, 1993–96; Vice Pres., Family Mediators Assoc., 1999–. Gov., St Margaret's Sch., Hampstead, 1993–98. *Publications:* (contrib.) Emergency Remedies in the Family Courts, 1997; (contrib.) Rayden and Jackson on Divorce and Family Matters, 1997. *Recreation:* when time permits, spending the kids' inheritance. *Address:* Cambridge County Court, 197 East Road, Cambridge CB1 1BA. *Clubs:* Anmer Social; Hunstanton Golf.

See also J. C. Plumstead.

PLUMSTEAD, John Charles; His Honour Judge John Plumstead; a Circuit Judge, since 2006; *b* 7 Feb. 1953; *s* of John Archibald Plumstead, DFM, MA, and Nancy Plumstead (*née* Drummond); *m* 1984, Leonora Woollam (*d* 2004); one *d. Educ:* King Edward VI Norwich Sch.; Univ. of Liverpool (LLB 1974). Called to the Bar, Middle Temple, 1975 (Winston Churchill pupillage award); in practice as a barrister, 1975–2006; a Recorder, 2000–06. *Recreations:* life, liberty and the pursuit of happiness. *Address:* St Albans Crown Court, Bricket Road, St Albans, Herts AL1 3JW.

See also I. M. Plumstead.

PLUNKET, family name of **Baron Plunket.**

PLUNKET, 8th Baron *cr* 1827; **Robin Rathmore Plunket;** *b* 3 Dec. 1925; *s* of 6th Baron Plunket (*d* 1938) and Dorothé Mabel (*d* 1938), *d* of late Joseph Lewis and *widow* of Captain Jack Barnato, RAF; *S* brother, 1975; *m* 1951, Jennifer, *d* of late Bailey Southwell, Olivenhoutpoort, S Africa. *Educ:* Eton. Formerly Captain, Rifle Brigade. *Heir: b* Hon. Shaun Albert Frederick Sheridan Plunket, *b* 5 April 1931. *Address:* Rathmore, Chimanimani, Zimbabwe; 39 Lansdowne Gardens, SW8 2EL. *Club:* Boodle's.

PLUNKET GREENE, Mary, (Mrs Alexander Plunket Greene); see Quant, M.

PLUNKETT, family name of **Baron Dunsany,** and of **Baron Louth.**

PLUNKETT, (Andrew) Christopher; His Honour Judge Plunkett; a Circuit Judge, since 2005; *b* 31 March 1961; *s* of Anthony Penson Plunkett and Anne Malkin Plunkett; *m* 2001, Rachel Anne Stewart; two *s. Educ:* Warwick Univ. (LLB); Inns of Court Sch. of Law, London. Called to the Bar, Gray's Inn, 1983; a Recorder, 2002–05. *Recreations:* cycling, on and off road, reading. *Address:* The Crown Court at Leicester, Wellington Street, Leicester LE1 6HG. *T:* (0116) 222 5800, *Fax:* (0116) 222 5888. *Club:* Cyclists' Touring.

PLUNKETT, William Joseph; Valuer and Estates Surveyor, Greater London Council, 1977–81; *b* 8 Nov. 1921; *s* of John Joseph Archer and Marjorie Martin Plunkett; *m* 1949, Gwendoline Innes Barron; two *s* five *d. Educ:* Finchley Catholic Grammar Sch.; Coll. of Estate Management. BSc(Est. Man.). FRICS. RN, 1941–46; commnd, 1942; Lt RNVR. Dep. County Valuer, Middlesex CC, 1962–65; Asst Valuer, Valuation and Estates Dept, GLC, 1965–73; Dep. Valuer and Estates Surveyor, GLC, 1973–74; Dir of Valuation and Estates Dept, GLC, 1974–77. Mem., South Bank Polytechnic Adv. Cttee on Estate Management, 1973–76; Chm., Covent Garden Officers' Steering Gp, 1977–81. Mem. General Council, RICS, 1978–80 (Pres. Planning and Develt Div., 1978–79; Chm., S London Br. Cttee, 1976–77); Pres., Assoc. of Local Authority Valuers and Estate Surveyors, 1980–81. *Publications:* articles on Compensation, Valuation and Development. *Address:* 63 Radnor Cliff, Folkestone, Kent CT20 2JL. *T:* (01303) 248868.

PLUTHERO, John; Group Managing Director, Europe, Asia and US, since 2006, and Executive Chairman, International, since 2007, Cable & Wireless plc; *b* 10 Feb. 1964; *m*; one *d. Educ:* Colchester Royal Grammar Sch.; London Sch. of Econs (BSc 1st Cl. Hons Econs). Dir, Chelsea Harbour, P&O Develts, 1990–94; Strategy and Planning, Bass plc, 1994–95; Business Review Dir, Dixons Gp, 1995–98; Man. Dir, Mastercare DSG, 1998–99; Founder, Freeserve plc, subseq. Freeserve.com plc, CEO, 1998–2002; Chief Exec., Energis plc, 2002–05; Dir, UK Business, Cable & Wireless plc, 2005–06. MInstD. *Recreation:* modern art. *Address:* Cable & Wireless plc, 7th Floor, The Point, 37 North Wharf Road, Paddington Basin, W2 1LA.

PLYMOUTH, 3rd Earl of, *cr* 1905; **Other Robert Ivor Windsor-Clive;** DL; FRSA 1953; Viscount Windsor (UK 1905); 15th Baron Windsor (England, *cr* 1529); *b* 9 Oct.

1923; *e s* of 2nd Earl of Plymouth, PC and Lady Irene Charteris (*d* 1989), *d* of 11th Earl of Wemyss; *S* father, 1943; *m* 1950, Caroline Helen, *o d* of Edward Rice, Dane Court, Eastry, Kent; three *s* one *d. Educ:* Eton. Mem., Museums and Galls Commn (formerly Standing Commn on Museums and Galls), 1972–82; Chm., Reviewing Cttee on Export of Works of Art, 1982–85. DL County of Salop, 1961. *Heir: s* Viscount Windsor, *qv. Address:* The Stables, Oakly Park, Ludlow, Shropshire SY8 2JW.

PLYMOUTH, Bishop Suffragan of, since 2005; **Rt Rev. John Frank Ford;** *b* 14 Jan. 1952; *s* of Royston and Ivy Ford; *m* 1981, Bridget Barnard; three *s. Educ:* Charles Chute Sch., Basingstoke; Southampton Coll. of Technol.; Chichester Theol Coll.; University Coll., Chichester (MA 2004). Ordained deacon, 1979, priest, 1980; Curate, Christ Ch, Forest Hill, 1979–82; Vicar: St Augustine, Lee, 1982–91; Lower Beeding, and Domestic Chaplain to Bp of Horsham, 1991–94; Diocesan Missioner, Chichester, 1994–2000; Chichester Cathedral: Canon and Preb., 1997–2000; Precentor and Canon Residentiary, 2000–05. *Recreations:* cricket, theatre, food and wine, travel, Middle Eastern politics and culture. *Address:* 31 Riverside Walk, Tamerton Foliot, Plymouth PL5 4AQ. *T:* (01752) 769836, *Fax:* (01752) 769818; *e-mail:* bishop.of.plymouth@exeter.anglican.org.

PLYMOUTH, Bishop of, (RC), since 1986; **Rt Rev. Mgr Hugh Christopher Budd;** *b* 27 May 1937; *s* of John Alfred and Phyllis Mary Budd. *Educ:* St Mary's Primary School, Hornchurch, Essex; Salesian Coll., Chertsey, Surrey; Cotton Coll., North Staffs; English Coll., Rome. PhL; STD. Ordained Priest, 1962; post-ordination studies, 1963–65; Tutor, English Coll., Rome, 1965–71; Lectr at Newman Coll., Birmingham and part-time Asst Priest, Northfield, Birmingham, 1971–76; Head of Training, Catholic Marriage Advisory Council, National HQ, London, 1976–79; Rector, St John's Seminary, Wonersh, Surrey, 1979–85; Administrator, Brentwood Cathedral, Essex, Nov. 1985–Jan. 1986. *Recreations:* walking, cricket (watching), music (listening). *Address:* Bishop's House, 31 Wyndham Street West, Plymouth, Devon PL1 5RZ.

PLYMOUTH, Archdeacon of; see Wilds, Ven. A. R.

POCOCK, Dr Andrew John, CMG 2008; HM Diplomatic Service; Ambassador to Zimbabwe, since 2006; *b* 23 Aug. 1955; *s* of John Francis Pocock and Vida Erica Pocock (*née* Duruty); *m* 1995, Julie Mason. *Educ:* St Mary's Coll., Trinidad; Queen Mary Coll., London (BA, MA); Peterhouse, Cambridge (PhD 1987). Joined HM Diplomatic Service, 1981; Second, later First Sec., Lagos, 1983–86; First Secretary: Southern African Dept, FCO, 1986–87; Washington, 1988–92; Personnel Mgt Dept, FCO, 1992–94; Asst, S Asia Dept, FCO, 1994–95; Counsellor, on loan to RCDS, 1996; Dep. High Comr, Canberra, 1997–2001; Hd of African Dept (Southern), FCO, 2001–03; High Comr to Tanzania, 2003–06. Liveryman, Cutlers' Co., 1979–. *Recreations:* tennis, cricket, walking. *Address:* c/o Foreign and Commonwealth Office, King Charles Street, SW1A 2AH.

POCOCK, Gordon James; Director, Communications Educational Services Ltd, 1983–87; *b* 27 March 1933; *s* of late Leslie and Elizabeth Maud Pocock; *m* 1959, Audrey Singleton (*d* 1990). *Educ:* Royal Liberty Sch., Romford; Keble Coll., Oxford. Joined PO, 1954; Private Sec. to Dir Gen., 1958–59; Principal, 1960–68; Asst Sec., 1968–72; Dep. Dir, 1972–76; Dir, Ext. Telecommns, 1976–79; Dir, Telecommns Marketing, 1979, Sen. Dir, 1979–81; Chief Exec., Merlin Business Systems, BT, 1981–84. Fellow, Nolan Norton & Co., 1985–87. *Publications:* Corneille and Racine, 1973; Boileau and the Nature of Neo-Classicism, 1980; article on Nation, Community, Devolution and Sovereignty. *Recreations:* travel, theatre, local history. *Address:* 131 Lichfield Court, Sheen Road, Richmond, Surrey TW9 1AY. *T:* (020) 8940 7118.

POCOCK, Leslie Frederick, CBE 1985; Chairman, Liverpool Health Authority, 1982–86; *b* 22 June 1918; *s* of Frederick Pocock and Alice Helena Pocock; *m* 1946, Eileen Horton; two *s. Educ:* Emanuel School. FCCA. Chief Accountant: London & Lancashire Insurance Co. Ltd, 1959; Royal Insurance Co. Ltd, 1966; Chief Accountant and Taxation Manager, 1971, Dep. Gp Comptroller, 1974, Royal Insurance Gp; retired 1981. Gen. Comr of Income Tax, 1982–93. Dir, Federated Pension Services (Guarantee) Ltd, 1995–98. Pres., Assoc. of Certified Accountants, 1977–78. Mem., UK Central Council for Nursing, Midwifery and Health Visiting, 1983–87; Chm., Merseyside Residuary Body, 1985; Hon. Treas., 1986–96, Vice Chm., 1996–98, Merseyside Improved Houses, subseq. Riverside Housing Assoc. Chm. Governors, Sandown Coll., Liverpool, 1989–91. *Recreations:* gardening, bridge, crosswords. *Address:* Barn Lee, Tithebarn Close, Lower Heswall, Wirral, Merseyside CH60 0EY. *T:* (0151) 342 2917.

PODDAR, Prof. Ramendra Kumar, PhD; Professor of Biophysics, Calcutta University, 1973–95 (Vice-Chancellor, 1979–83); Member of Parliament (Rajya Sabha), 1985–93 (Vice-Chairman, 1987–89); *b* 9 Nov. 1930; *m* 1955, Srimati Jharna Poddar (*d* 1999); two *s* one *d. Educ:* Univ. of Calcutta (BSc Hons Physics, MSc Physics; PhD Biophysics); Associateship Dip., Saha Inst. of Nuclear Physics. Progressively, Research Asst, Lecturer, Reader, Associate Prof., Biophysics Div., Saha Inst. of Nuclear Physics, 1953–73. IAEA Advr to Govt of Mali, 1962. Study visits to Univ. of California, Berkeley, 1958–60, Cold Spring Harbor Biological Lab., 1960, Purdue Univ., 1960–61, California Inst. of Technology, 1970, CNRS, Paris, 1978. Advr, West Bengal Pollution Control Bd. Life Member: West Bengal Acad. of Science and Technol.; Indian Biophysical Soc.; Chm., Inst. of Wetland Management and Ecological Design, 1986–93. *Publications:* more than 50 research papers in the fields of biophysics, molecular biology and photobiology. *Address:* Department of Biophysics, Molecular Biology and Genetics, University College of Science, Calcutta 700009, India. *T:* (office) (33) 3508386; CF62 Salt Lake City, Calcutta 700064, India. *T:* (33) 3375646.

PODGER, Geoffrey John Freeman, CB 2003; Chief Executive, Health and Safety Executive, since 2005; *b* 3 Aug. 1952; *s* of late Leonard and Beryl Podger. *Educ:* Worthing High Sch. for Boys; Pembroke Coll., Oxford (Open Scholar; BA Medieval and Modern Langs 1974; MA 1977). MoD, 1974–82; Internat. Staff, NATO HQ, Brussels, 1977–79; Department of Health and Social Security, subseq. Department of Health, 1982–96; loaned to Falkland Islands Govt as Sec. to Port Stanley Hosp. Fire Inquiry, 1985; Private Sec. to Chm. (subseq. Chief Exec.), NHS Management Bd and Sec. to Bd, 1985–87; Principal Private Sec. to Sec. of State for Social Services, 1987–88; Head, Internat. Relations Unit, 1992–93; Under Sec. for Health Promotion, 1993–96; Hd of Food Safety and Sci. Gp, MAFF, 1996–97; Hd, Jt Food Safety and Standards Gp, MAFF and DoH, 1997–2000; Chief Exec., Food Standards Agency, 2000–03; Exec. Dir, European Food Safety Authy, 2003–05. Mem. Council, Inst. for Employment Studies, 2006– (Mem. Bd, 2007–). Hon. Vice Pres., IOSH, 2007. Hon. Fellow, IIRSM, 2007. *Address:* Health and Safety Executive, Redgrave Court, Merton Road, Bootle, Merseyside L20 7HS. *Club:* Athenæum.

PODMORE, Ian Laing; Chief Executive, Sheffield City Council, 1974–89; *b* 6 Oct. 1933; *s* of Harry Samuel Podmore and Annie Marion (*née* Laing); *m* 1961, Kathleen Margaret (*née* Langton); one *s* one *d. Educ:* Birkenhead School. Admitted Solicitor 1960. Asst Solicitor, Wallasey County Borough, 1960–63; Sen. Asst Solicitor, Southport Co.

Borough, 1963–66; Deputy Town Clerk: Southport, 1966–70; Sheffield, 1970–74. *Recreations:* golf, gardening, classics. *Club:* Abbeydale Golf.

POGGIO, Albert Andrew, OBE 2006 (MBE 1995); United Kingdom Representative of the Government of Gibraltar, since 1988; *b* 18 Aug. 1946; *s* of late Joseph Ernest and Sally Poggio; *m* 1966, Sally Sofaer (marr. diss. 1987); one *d*; partner, Doreen Isobel Mellor. *Educ:* Christian Brothers Coll., Gibraltar; Robert Montefiore Sch., London; City of London Coll. Chm., Vital Health Gp, 1990–2003; Dir, 1996–, Sen. Vice Pres., 2003–, Medcruise, Assoc. of Mediterranean Ports. Vice Pres., UK Overseas Territories Assoc. 1993– (Chm., 2004–05). Vice Chm., Calpe House Charitable Trust, 1989–; Dir, Friends of Gibraltar Heritage Trust, 1988–. *Recreations:* sports, military memorabilia, travelling. *Address:* (office) 150 Strand, WC2R 1JA. *T:* (020) 7836 0777, *Fax:* (020) 7240 6612; The Old House, Manor Place, Manor Park, Chislehurst, Kent BR7 5QJ; *e-mail:* a.poggio@gibraltar.gov.uk. *Clubs:* Reform, Royal Automobile; Casino Calpe (Gibraltar); Royal Gibraltar Yacht.

POGO, Most Rev. Ellison Leslie; *see* Melanesia, Archbishop of.

POGSON, Kevin Edward, CBE 2006; Regional Director for London, HM Courts Service, since 2006; *b* 5 Sept. 1950; *s* of Edward Pogson and Ivy (*née* Hubble); *m* 1977, Marilyn Elspeth Hyde; two *s*. *Educ:* state schools in London. Joined Lord Chancellor's Department, 1967; various positions at HQ, 1967–79; Knightsbridge Crown Court, 1979–86; Personnel Dept, 1987–92; Dir of Finance, 1992–99, of Change, 1999–2001, Court Service; Circuit Adminr, SE Circuit, LCD, 2001–02; Dir of Field Services, Court Service, 2003–04; SE Circuit Adminr, Court Service, subseq. Regl Dir for SE, HM Courts Service, 2004–06. *Recreations:* chess, music, cooking. *Address:* HM Courts Service, 2nd Floor, Rose Court, 2 Southwark Bridge, SE1 9HS. *Club:* UNATS Chess.

PÖHL, Karl Otto; Grosskreuz des Verdienstordens der Bundesrepublik Deutschland; Member, Shareholder Committee, Sal. Oppenheim Jr & Cie, since 1998 (Partner, 1992–98); Governor, Deutsche Bundesbank and German Governor, International Monetary Fund and Bank for International Settlements, 1980–91; *b* 1 Dec. 1929; *m* 1974; two *s* two *d*. *Educ:* Göttingen Univ. (Econs; Diplom.-Volkswirt). Div. Chief for Econ. Res., IFO-Institut, Munich, 1955–60; econ. journalist, Bonn, 1961–67; Mem. Exec., Fed. Assoc. of German Bank, Cologne, 1968–69; Div. Chief in Fed. Min. of Econs, Bonn, 1970–71; Dept Chief in Fed. Chancellery (Head, Dept for Econ. and Fiscal Policy), Bonn, 1971–72; Sec. of State in Fed. Min. of Finance, 1972–77; Dep. Governor, Deutsche Bundesbank, 1977–79; Chairman: EEC Monetary Cttee, 1976–77; Deputies of Gp of Ten, 1978–80; Gp of Ten, 1983–89; Cttee of Governors, Central Banks of EC Member States, 1990–91. Hon. DHL Georgetown Univ., 1983; Hon. DEconSc Ruhr Univ., 1985; Hon. DPhil Tel Aviv, 1986; Hon. Dr of Laws Univ. of Md, 1987; Hon. DSc: Buckingham, 1992; London, 1992; Hon. Dr Science Econ. Frankfurt, 2000. *Publications:* miscellaneous. *Address:* Sal. Oppenheim Jr & Cie, Untermainanlage 1, 60326 Frankfurt am Main, Germany.

POINTER, Martin John; QC 1996; barrister; *b* 17 July 1953; *s* of late Michael Edward Pointer and of Mary Isabel Pointer (*née* Simms); *m* 1st, 1985 (marr. diss. 1997); two *s* one *d*; 2nd, 2001, Janet Bridal. *Educ:* King's Sch., Grantham; Univ. of Leicester (LLB Hons). Called to the Bar, Gray's Inn, 1976 (Reid Schol., 1977). Fellow, Internat. Acad. of Matrimonial Lawyers, 1994. *Address:* 1 Hare Court, Temple, EC4Y 7BE. *T:* (020) 7797 7070. *Club:* Travellers.

POITIER, Sidney, KBE (Hon.) 1974; actor, film and stage; director; *b* Miami, Florida, 20 Feb. 1927; *s* of Reginald Poitier and Evelyn (*née* Outten); *m* 1950, Juanita Hardy (marr. diss.); four *d*; *m* 1975, Joanna Shimkus; two *d*. *Educ:* private tutors; Western Senior High Sch., Nassau; Governor's High Sch., Nassau. Served War of 1941–45 with 1267th Medical Detachment, United States Army. Started acting with American Negro Theatre, 1946. *Plays include:* Anna Lucasta, Broadway, 1948; A Raisin in the Sun, Broadway, 1959; *films include:* Cry, the Beloved Country, 1952; Red Ball Express, 1952; Go, Man, Go, 1954; Blackboard Jungle, 1955; Goodbye, My Lady, 1956; Edge of the City, 1957; Band of Angels, 1957; Something of Value, 1957; The Mark of the Hawk, 1958; The Defiant Ones, 1958 (Silver Bear Award, Berlin Film Festival, and New York Critics Award, 1958); Porgy and Bess, 1959; A Raisin in the Sun, 1960; Paris Blues, 1960; Lilies of the Field, 1963 (award for Best Actor of 1963, Motion Picture Academy of Arts and Sciences); The Bedford Incident, 1965; The Slender Thread, 1966; A Patch of Blue, 1966; Duel at Diablo, 1966; To Sir With Love, 1967; In the Heat of the Night, 1967; Guess Who's Coming to Dinner, 1968; For Love of Ivy, 1968; They Call Me Mister Tibbs, 1971; The Organization, 1971; The Wilby Conspiracy, 1975; Deadly Pursuit, 1988; Sneakers, 1991; Separate But Equal, 1990; Children of the Dust, 1995; To Sir With Love II, 1996; Mandela and De Klerk, One Man, One Vote, 1997; The Jackal, 1998; David and Lisa, 1998; Free of Eden, 1999; The Simple Life of Noah Dearborn, 1999; director and actor: Buck and the Preacher, 1972; A Warm December, 1973; Uptown Saturday Night, 1974; Let's Do It Again, 1975; A Piece of the Action, 1977; *director:* Stir Crazy, 1981; Hanky Panky, 1982. *Publications:* This Life (autobiography), 1980; The Measure of a Man: a spiritual autobiography, 2000. *Address:* c/o CAA, 2000 Avenue of the Stars, Los Angeles, CA 90067, USA.

POLAK, Dame Julia (Margaret), DBE 2003; FRCPath, FMedSci; Professor of Endocrine Pathology, London University, at Imperial College School of Medicine, 1984, now Emeritus; Head, Imperial College Interdisciplinary Group on Tissue Engineering, since 1997; Director, Centre for Tissue Engineering and Regenerative Medicine, Chelsea and Westminster Hospital, 1999; *b* 26 June 1939; *d* of Carlos and Rebeca Polak; *m* 1961, Daniel Catovsky, *qv*; two *s* one *d*. *Educ:* Univ. of Buenos Aires (MD 1964; Dip Histopath. 1966); DSc London, 1980. Hospital appts, Buenos Aires, 1961–67; Royal Postgraduate Medical School, London: Research Assistant in Histochemistry, 1968–69; Asst Lectr, Lectr, and Sen. Lectr, 1970–82; Reader, 1982–84; Dep. Dir, Dept of Histopathol., Hammersmith Hosp., 1988–99; Member: Exec. Cttee, Acad. Bd, RPMS, 1990–97; Med. Exec. Unit, Hammersmith Hosp., 1990–; Sub-Cttee in Biotech., London Univ., 1988–. Chm., British Endocrine Pathologists Gp, 1988–; Mem., Exec. Cttee of Council, Amer. Heart Assoc., 1989–. Mem., editl bds of med. jls. FMedSci 1999. Benito de Udaondo Cardiology Prize, 1967; Medal, Soc. of Endocrinology, 1984; Sir Eric Sharpe Prize for Oncology, Cable and Wireless, 1986–87. *Publications:* contribs to Nature and numerous professional jls. *Address:* Department of Chemical Engineering, Tissue Engineering and Regenerative Medicine, Imperial College, South Kensington Campus, SW7 2AZ. *T:* (020) 8237 2670, *Fax:* (020) 8746 5619; *e-mail:* julia.polak@ic.ac.uk.

POLAND, Rear-Adm. Edmund Nicholas, CB 1967; CBE 1962; *b* 19 Feb. 1917; 2nd *s* of late Major Raymond A. Poland, RMLI and Mrs F. O. Bayly Jones; *m* 1941, Pauline Ruth Margaret Pechell; three *s* one *d* (and one *d* decd). *Educ:* Royal Naval Coll., Dartmouth. Served at sea during Abyssinian and Palestine crises, Spanish Civil War; War of 1939–45: convoy duties, Norwegian waters; Motor Torpedo Boats, Channel and Mediterranean; Torpedo Specialist, 1943; Staff Officer Ops to Naval Force Comdr, Burma; Sqdn T. Officer, HMS Royalist; HMS Hornet, 1946; Flotilla Torpedo and Anti-Submarine Officer of Third Submarine Flotilla, HMS Montclare; Air Warfare Div., Admiralty, 1950; British Naval Staff, Washington, 1953; jssc 1955; Directorate of Tactics and Ship Requirements, Admiralty; comd RN Air Station, Abbotsinch, 1956; Nato Standing Gp, Washington; Director of Under Sea Warfare (Naval), Ministry of Defence, 1962; Chief of Staff to C-in-C Home Fleet, 1965–68; retired. Commander, 1950; Capt., 1956; Rear-Adm., 1965. Vice-Pres., Internat. Prisoners' Aid Assoc., 1978, Chm. (UK), 1979; Vice-Pres., Scottish Assoc. for Care and Resettlement of Offenders, 1979 (Dir, 1974–79). *Publications:* The Torpedomen, 1992; Majumba's Survival Trail, 1992. *Recreation:* gardening. *Address:* 39 Limmer Lane, Felpham, Bognor Regis, West Sussex PO22 7HD.

POLANYI, Prof. Hon. John Charles; PC (Can.) 1992; CC (Canada) 1979 (OC 1974); FRS 1971; FRSC 1966 (Hon. FRSC 1991); University Professor, since 1974 and Professor of Chemistry, since 1962, University of Toronto; *b* 23 Jan. 1929; *m* 1958, Anne Ferrar Davidson; one *s* one *d*; *m* 2004, Brenda Mary Bury. *Educ:* Manchester Grammar Sch.; Victoria Univ., Manchester (BSc, PhD, DSc). Research Fellow: Nat. Research Council, Ottawa, 1952–54; Princeton Univ., 1954–56; Univ. of Toronto: Lectr, 1956; Asst Prof., 1957–60; Assoc. Prof., 1960–62. Mem., Scientific Adv. Bd, Max Planck Inst. for Quantum Optics, Garching, Germany, 1982–92. Sloan Foundn Fellow, 1959–63; Guggenheim Meml Fellow, 1970–71, 1979–80; Sherman Fairchild Distinguished Scholar, CIT, 1982; Vis. Prof. of Chem., Texas A & M Univ., 1986; John W. Cowper Dist. Vis. Lectr, SUNY at Buffalo, 1986; Consolidated Bathurst Vis. Lectr, Concordia Univ., 1988; Beam Dist. Vis. Prof., Iowa Univ., 1992; Hitchcock Prof., Calif Univ., Berkeley, 1994; Lectures include: Centennial, Chem. Soc., 1965; Ohio State Univ., 1969 (and Mack Award); Reilly, Univ. of Notre Dame, 1970; Harkins Meml, Univ. of Chicago, 1971; Killam Meml Schol., 1974, 1975; F. J. Toole, Univ. of New Brunswick, 1974; Kistiakowsky, Harvard Univ., 1975; Camille and Henry Dreyfus, Kansas, 1975; Jacob Bronowski Meml, Toronto Univ., 1978; Hutchison, Rochester Univ., 1979; Priestley, Penn State Univ., 1980; Barré, Univ. of Montreal, 1982; Wiegand, Toronto Univ., 1984; Walker-Ames, Univ. of Washington, 1986; Morino, Japan, J. T. Wilson, Ont Sci. Centre, and Spiers Meml, Faraday Div., RSChem., 1987; Polanyi, IUPAC, W. B. Lewis, Atomic Energy of Canada Ltd, Killam, Univ. of Windsor, and Herzberg, Carleton Univ., 1988; C. R. Mueller, Purdue Univ., 1989; Phillips, Pittsburgh, 1991; Dove Meml, Toronto, 1992; Fritz London, Duke Univ., 1993; Linus Pauling, CIT, 1994; Hagey, Waterloo Univ., 1995. Hon. FRSE 1988; Hon. For. Mem., Amer. Acad. of Arts and Sciences, 1976; For. Associate, Nat. Acad. of Sciences, USA, 1978; Mem., Pontifical Acad. of Scis, 1986. Hon. DSc: Waterloo, 1970; Memorial, 1976; McMaster, 1977; Carleton, 1981; Harvard, 1982; Rensselaer, Brock, 1984; Lethbridge, Victoria, Ottawa, Sherbrooke, Laval, 1987; Manchester, York, 1988; Acadia, Univ. de Montréal, and Weizmann Inst. of Science, Israel, 1989; Univ. of Bari, Italy, Univ. of BC, and McGill Univ., 1990; Queen's, 1992; Free Univ., Berlin, 1993; Laurentian, Toronto, Liverpool, 1995; Hon. LLD: Trent, 1977; Dalhousie, 1983; St Francis Xavier, 1984; Concordia Univ., 1990; Calgary, 1994. Marlow Medal, Faraday Soc., 1963; Steacie Prize for Natural Scis, 1965; Chem. Inst. Canada Medal, 1976 (Noranda Award, 1967); Chem. Soc. Award, 1970; Henry Marshall Tory Medal, 1977, Michael Polanyi Medal, 1989, RSC; Remsen Award, Amer. Chem. Soc., 1978; (jtly) Wolf Prize in Chemistry, Wolf Foundn, Israel, 1982; (jtly) Nobel Prize for Chemistry, 1986; Killam Meml Prize, Canada Council, 1988; Royal Medal, 1989, Bakerian Prize, 1994, Royal Soc.; eponymous award, Canadian Soc. for Chem., 1992; Herzberg Canada Gold Medal, NSERC, 2008. KStJ 1987. *Film:* Concept in Reaction Dynamics, 1970. *Publications:* (with F. G. Griffiths) The Dangers of Nuclear War, 1979; papers in scientific jls, articles on science policy and on control of armaments. *Address:* Department of Chemistry, University of Toronto, 80 St George Street, Toronto, ON M5S 3H6, Canada; 1 Sullivan Street, Toronto, ON M5T 1B8, Canada.

POLDEN, Martin Alan, OBE 2006; Joint Founder, 1987, and Life President, Environmental Law Foundation (ELF) (Chairman, 1987–95); *b* 23 June 1928; *s* of Ralph Polden and Deborah Polden (*née* Tree); *m* 1956, Margaret Fry (*d* 1998); one *s* three *d*. *Educ:* Royal Grammar Sch., High Wycombe; LSE (LLB); Law Soc. Sch. of Law. Admitted solicitor, 1953; estabd Polden & Co., 1958, subseq. Polden Bishop & Gale, 1964; merged with Rubinstein Callingham, 1987, Sen. Partner, 1990–94; Consultant, Ross & Craig, 2001–. Member: All-Party Envmt Gp, 1993–; Planning and Envmtl Law Cttee, Law Soc., 1994–. Member: Green Alliance, 1990–; BAFTA, 1999–; Justice, 2000–. Founder, 1983, Trustee, 1983–2003, Gandhi Trust; Founding Trustee, Hugo Gryn Meml Trust, 1997–. Mem., Bd of Visitors, Wormwood Scrubs Prison, 1986–91. Fellow, Soc. for Advanced Legal Studies, 1998. FRSA 2000. *Publications:* The Law, the Environment and the Mosquito, 1990; The Environment and the Law: earth, air, fire and water, 1994; articles in legal and envmtl jls, and newspapers. *Recreations:* reading, writing, theatre, cinema, boating, walking, grandchildering and philosophying with them. *Address:* 29 Manor House Drive, NW6 7DE. *T:* (020) 8459 2584; 12 Southcliffe Road, Friars Cliff, Christchurch, Dorset BH23 4EN. *T:* (01425) 272548. *Club:* MCC.

POLDEN, Richard; His Honour Judge Polden; a Circuit Judge, since 2006; *b* 13 Nov. 1953; *s* of Stanley Richard Edward Polden and Gladys Mary Polden; *m* 1975, Susan James; one *s* one *d*. *Educ:* Knockhall Primary Sch.; Dartford Technical High Sch. for Boys; Coll. of Law, Guildford. Admitted Solicitor, 1978; joined Church Bruce Hawkes Brasington & Phillips Solicitors, Gravesend, 1978, Partner, 1980; a Dep. District Judge, 1993–95; District Judge, 1995; a Recorder, 2001–06. *Recreations:* football, dog walking, foreign travel, trying to play golf. *Address:* Bow County Court, 96 Romford Road, Stratford, E15 4EG. *T:* (020) 8536 5200; *e-mail:* polden@poldens.fsnet.co.uk. *Clubs:* Gravesend and Meopham Rotary; Gravesend 41; Mid Kent Golf.

POLE, Prof. Jack Richon, PhD; FBA 1985; FRHistS; Rhodes Professor of American History and Institutions, Oxford University, 1979–89; Fellow of St Catherine's College, since 1979; *b* 14 March 1922; *s* of Joseph Pole and Phœbe (*née* Rickards); *m* 1952, Marilyn Louise Mitchell (marr. diss. 1988); one *s* two *d*. *Educ:* King Alfred Sch.; Queen's Coll., Oxford Univ. (BA 1949); Princeton Univ. (PhD 1953). MA Cantab 1963. FRHistS 1970. Instr in History, Princeton Univ., 1952–53; Asst Lectr/Lectr in Amer. History, UCL, 1953–63; Cambridge University: Reader in Amer. History and Govt, 1963–79; Fellow, Churchill Coll., 1963–79 (Vice-Master, 1975–78); Mem., Council of Senate, 1970–74. Vis. Professor: Berkeley, 1960–61; Ghana, 1966; Chicago, 1969; Beijing, 1984. Commonwealth Fund Amer. Studies Fellowship, 1956; Fellow, Center for Advanced Study in Behavioral Sciences, 1969–70; Guest Schol., Wilson Internat. Center, Washington, 1978–79; Golieb Fellow, NY Univ. Law Sch., 1990; Sen. Res. Fellow, Coll. of William & Mary, Va, 1991; Leverhulme Trust Emeritus Fellow, 1991–93. Jefferson Meml Lectr, Berkeley, 1971; Richard B. Russell Lectr, Ga, 1981. Vice-Pres., Internat. Commn for History of Representative and Parly Instns, 1990–2000; Member: Council, Inst. for Early Amer. History and Culture, 1973–76; Acad. Européenne d'Histoire, 1981; Council, King Alfred Sch. Soc., 1981–84 (Hon. Fellow). Hon. Vice-Pres., British Amer. Nineteenth Century Historians, 2000–; Hon. Foreign Mem., Amer. Hist. Assoc., 2003. Hon. Fellow, Hist. Soc. of Ghana. *Publications:* Abraham Lincoln and the Working Classes of Britain, 1959; Abraham Lincoln, 1964; Political Representation in England and the Origins of the American Republic, 1966, 2nd edn 1971 (both edns also USA); (ed) The

Advance of Democracy, USA 1967; The Seventeenth Century: the origins of legislative power, USA 1969; (ed) The Revolution in America: documents of the internal development of America in the revolutionary era, 1971 (also USA); Foundations of American Independence 1763–1815, 1973 (USA 1972); The Decision for American Independence, USA 1975; The Idea of Union, USA 1977; The Pursuit of Equality in American History, USA 1978, 2nd edn 1993; Paths to the American Past, 1979 (also USA); The Gift of Government: political responsibility from the English Restoration to American Independence, USA 1983, 2008; (co-ed) Colonial British America: essays in the new history of the early modern era, USA 1983; (ed) The American Constitution: For and Against: the Federalist and Anti-Federalist papers, USA 1987; (co-ed) The Blackwell Encyclopedia of the American Revolution, 1991 (also USA), rev. edn as A Companion to the American Revolution, 2000; Freedom of Speech: right or privilege?, 1998; (ed) The Federalist, 2005; articles in Amer. Hist. Rev., William and Mary Qly, Jl of Southern Hist., etc., Enc. Brit., Enc. of Amer. Congress. *Recreations:* cricket, painting (exhibn Wolfson Coll., Oxford, 2001), writing. *Address:* 20 Divinity Road, Oxford OX4 1LJ; St Catherine's College, Oxford OX1 3UJ. *Clubs:* MCC; Trojan Wanderers Cricket (Co-founder, 1957).

POLE, Sir Peter Van Notten, 5th Bt *cr* 1791; FASA; ACIS; accountant, retired; *b* 6 Nov. 1921; *s* of late Arthur Chandos Pole and late Marjorie, *d* of late Charles Hargrave, Glen Forrest, W Australia; *S* kinsman, 1948; *m* 1949, Jean Emily, *d* of late Charles Douglas Stone, Borden, WA; one *s* one *d*. *Educ:* Guildford Grammar Sch. *Recreations:* reading, travel. *Heir: s* Peter John Chandos Pole [*b* 27 April 1952; *m* 1973, Suzanne Norah, BAppSc(MT), *d* of Harold Raymond Hughes; two *s* one *d*]. *Address:* 249 Dartnell Parade, Cambrai Village, 85 Hester Avenue, Merriwa, WA 6030, Australia.

POLIAKOFF, Prof. Martyn, CBE 2008; PhD; FRS 2002; Research Professor in Chemistry, University of Nottingham, since 1991; *b* 16 Dec. 1947; *s* of late Alexander Poliakoff, OBE and Ina Miriam Poliakoff (*née* Montagu); *m* 1969, Dr Janet Frances Keene; one *s* one *d*. *Educ:* Westminster Sch.; King's Coll., Cambridge (BA 1969, PhD 1973). CChem, FRSC 2002; CEng, FIChemE 2004. Sen. Res. Officer, Dept of Inorganic Chem., Univ. of Newcastle upon Tyne, 1972–79; Lectr in Inorganic Chem., 1979–85, Reader, 1985–91, Univ. of Nottingham. Hon. Prof. of Chem., Moscow State Univ., 1999–. Hon. ScD E Anglia, 2008. *Publications:* contrib. scientific papers to chem. jls. *Recreations:* hill-walking, second-hand books, architecture. *Address:* School of Chemistry, University of Nottingham, Nottingham NG7 2RD. *T:* (0115) 951 3386, *Fax:* (0115) 951 3058; *e-mail:* martyn.poliakoff@nottingham.ac.uk.
See also S. Poliakoff.

POLIAKOFF, Stephen, CBE 2007; playwright and film director; *b* 1 Dec. 1952; *s* of late Alexander Poliakoff, OBE and Ina Miriam Poliakoff (*née* Montagu); *m* 1983, Sandy Welch; one *s* one *d*. *Educ:* Westminster Sch.; King's Coll., Cambridge. *Plays:* Clever Soldiers, 1974; The Carnation Gang, 1974; Hitting Town, 1975; City Sugar (Evening Standard Most Promising Playwright Award), 1976; Strawberry Fields, NT, Shout Across the River, RSC, 1978; The Summer Party, 1980; Favourite Nights, 1981; Breaking the Silence, RSC, 1984; Coming in to Land, NT, 1987; Playing With Trains, RSC, 1989; Sienna Red, nat. tour, 1992; Sweet Panic, Hampstead, 1996, Duke of York's, 2003; Blinded by the Sun, RNT (Critics' Circle Best Play Award), 1996; Talk of the City, RSC, 1998; Remember This, RNT, 1999; *films:* Hidden City; Close My Eyes (Evening Standard Best British Film Award), 1992; Century, 1995; The Tribe, 1998; Food of Love, 1998; *TV plays include:* Caught on a Train (BAFTA Award), 1980; She's Been Away (Venice Film Festival Prize); Shooting the Past (serial) (PrixItalia), 1999; Perfect Strangers (serial), 2001 (Dennis Potter BAFTA Award, 2002); The Lost Prince (Emmy Award), 2003; Friends and Crocodiles, 2005; Gideon's Daughter, 2005; Joe's Palace, Capturing Mary, A Real Summer, 2007. *Publications:* all plays; Plays One, 1989; Plays Two, 1994; Plays Three, 1998. *Recreations:* watching cricket, going to the cinema. *Address:* 33 Devonia Road, N1 8JQ. *T:* (020) 7354 2695.
See also M. Poliakoff.

POLITZER, Prof. (Hugh) David, PhD; Richard Chace Tolman Professor of Theoretical Astrophysics, California Institute of Technology; *b* 31 Aug. 1949; *s* of Alan A. Politzer and Valerie T. Politzer (*née* Diamant). *Educ:* Michigan Univ. (BS 1969); Harvard Univ. (PhD 1974). Visiting Associate, 1975–76, Mem. of Faculty, 1976–, Prof. of Theoretical Physics, 1979–, Calif Inst. of Technol. (Jtly) Nobel Prize in Physics, 2004. *Address:* Particle Theory Group, California Institute of Technology, 1200 East California Boulevard, Pasadena, CA 91125, USA.

POLIZZI, Hon. Olga, (Hon. Mrs William Shawcross), CBE 1990; Director of Design, Rocco Forte Collection (formerly RF Hotels, later Rocco Forte Hotels), since 1996; Director: Tresanton Hotel Ltd, since 1996; Hotel Endsleigh Ltd, since 2004; Millers Bespoke Bakery Ltd, since 1996; Forte plc, 1983–96 (Managing Director, Building and Design Department, 1980–96); *d* of Baron Forte; *m* 1st, 1966, Alessandro Polizzi di Sorrentino (*d* 1980); two *d*; 2nd, 1993, Hon. William Hartley Hume Shawcross, *qv*. *Educ:* St Mary's Sch., Ascot. Westminster City Councillor, 1989–94. Trustee: Italian Hosp. Fund, 1992–; Trusthouse Charitable Foundn, 1997–; KCL, 1999– (Vice-Chm., Council); St Mary's Sch., Ascot, 1997– (Gov., 1988–97); Royal Opera House Endowment Fund, 2005–; King Edward VII's Hospital, 2007–. *Recreations:* walking, opera. *Address:* (office) 70 Jermyn Street, SW1Y 6NY.
See also Hon. Sir R. J. V. Forte.

POLKINGHORNE, Rev. Canon John Charlton, KBE 1997; PhD, ScD; FRS 1974; Fellow, Queens' College, Cambridge, since 1996 (President, 1989–96; Hon. Fellow, 1996); *b* 16 Oct. 1930; *s* of George Baulkwill Polkinghorne and Dorothy Evelyn Polkinghorne (*née* Charlton); *m* 1955, Ruth Isobel Martin (*d* 2006); two *s* one *d*. *Educ:* Elmhurst Grammar Sch.; Perse Sch.; Trinity Coll., Cambridge (MA 1956; PhD 1955; ScD 1974); Westcott House, Cambridge, 1979–81. Commonwealth Fund Fellow, California Institute of Technology, 1955–56; Lecturer in Mathematical Physics, Univ. of Edinburgh, 1956–58; Cambridge University: Fellow, Trinity Coll., 1954–86; Lecturer in Applied Mathematics, 1958–65; Reader in Theoretical Physics, 1965–68; Prof. of Mathematical Physics, 1968–79; Fellow, Dean and Chaplain of Trinity Hall, Cambridge, 1986–89 (Hon. Fellow, 1989). Hon. Prof. of Theoretical Physics, Univ. of Kent at Canterbury, 1985. Ordained deacon 1981, priest 1982; Curate: St Andrew's, Chesterton, 1981–82; St Michael's, Bedminster, 1982–84; Vicar of St Cosmus and St Damian in the Blean, 1984–86; Canon Theologian, Liverpool Cathedral, 1994–2005; Six Preacher, Canterbury Cathedral, 1996–. Member: SRC, 1975–79; Human Genetics Adv. Commn, 1996–99; Human Genetics Commn, 2000–02; Chairman: Nuclear Phys Bd, 1978–79; Cttee to Review the Research Use of Fetuses and Fetal Material, 1988–89; Task Force to Review Services for Drugs Misusers, 1994–96; Adv. Cttee on Genetic Testing, 1996–99. Member: C of E Doctrine Commn, 1989–95; Gen. Synod of C of E, 1990–2000. Chm. of Governors, Perse Sch., 1972–81; Governor, SPCK, 1984–2002. Licensed Reader, Diocese of Ely, 1975. Hon. DD: Kent, 1994; Durham, 1999; Hon. DSc: Exeter, 1994; Leicester, 1995; Marquette, 2003; Hon. DHum Hong Kong Baptist, 2006. Templeton Prize, 2002. *Publications:* (jtly) The Analytic S-Matrix, 1966; The Particle Play, 1979; Models of High Energy Processes, 1980; The Way the World Is, 1983; The Quantum World, 1984; One World, 1986; Science and Creation, 1988; Science and Providence, 1989; Rochester Roundabout, 1989; Reason and Reality, 1991; Science and Christian Belief, 1994; Quarks, Chaos and Christianity, 1994; Serious Talk, 1995; Scientists as Theologians, 1996; Beyond Science, 1996; Searching for Truth, 1996; Belief in God in an Age of Science, 1998; Science and Theology, 1998; Faith, Science and Understanding, 2000; (jtly) The End of the World and the Ends of Gods, 2000; (jtly) Faith in the Living God, 2001; (ed) The Work of Love, 2001; The God of Hope and the End of the World, 2002; Quantum Theory: a very short introduction, 2002; Living with Hope, 2003; Science and the Trinity, 2004; Exploring Reality, 2005; Quantum Physics and Theology, 2007; From Physicist to Priest: an autobiography, 2007; many articles on elementary particle physics in learned journals. *Recreation:* gardening. *Address:* Queens' College, Cambridge CB3 9ET.

POLL, Prof. (David) Ian (Alistair), OBE 2002; FREng, FRAeS, FAIAA, FCGI; Business Development and Technical Director, Cranfield Aerospace Ltd, since 2004 (Managing Director, 1995–99; Technical Director, 1999–2004); *b* 1 Oct. 1950; *s* of Ralph Angus Poll and Mary Poll (*née* Hall); *m* 1975, Elizabeth Mary Read; two *s* one *d*. *Educ:* Heckmondwike Grammar Sch.; Imperial Coll. London (BSc Hons); Cranfield Inst. of Tech. (PhD). FRAeS 1987; FREng (FEng 1996). Engineer, Future Projects, Hawker Siddeley Aviation, 1972–75; Res. Asst, 1975–78, Lectr, 1978–85, Sen. Lectr, 1985–87, Cranfield Inst. of Tech.; University of Manchester: Prof. of Aeronautical Engineering, and Dir of Goldstein Aeronaut. Engrg Lab., 1987–95; Man. Dir, Flow Science Ltd, 1990–95; Head, Dept. of Engineering, 1991–94; Prof. of Aerodynamics, subseq. Aerospace Engrg, and Hd, Coll. of Aeronautics, subseq. Dir, Cranfield Coll. of Aeronautics, Cranfield Univ., 1995–2004. Royal Aeronautical Society: Mem. Council, 1996–; Vice Pres., 1998–2000; Pres., 2001; Chairman: Learned Soc. Bd, 1996–2000; Strategic Review Bd, 2000–01; Uninhabited Air Vehicle Cttee, 2005–; Cranfield Univ. Br., 1997–. Member: Fluid Dynamics Panel, AGARD, 1990–97; Council, Air League, 1997–; Gen. Assembly, Internat. Council of the Aeronautical Scis, 1997– (Chm., Programme Cttee, 2006–; Pres., 2008–); Foresight Action Steering Cttee, SBAC, 1997–99; Aerospace Cttee, DTI, 1999–2004; Aerospace Technol. Steering Gp, DTI, 2004–; Council, Royal Acad. Engrg, 2004–07; Uninhabited Air Vehicle Steering Cttee, CAA, 2006–; Founder Mem., Greener-By-Design, 2000– (Mem., Steering Cttee, 2000–). Vice-Pres., Confedn of European Aerospace Socs, 2001–04. FAIAA 2000; ACGI 1972, FCGI 2004 (Vice Pres., City and Guilds Coll. Assoc., 2004–); Mem., RUSI, 2005. Liveryman, Co. of Coachmakers and Coach Harness Makers, 2001. Wilbur and Orville Wright Lectr, RAeS, 2002. Hodgson Prize, RAeS, 2001. *Publications:* more than 100 papers on fluid mechanics in learned jls and for tech. conferences. *Recreations:* golf, aviation, wine and conversation. *Address:* Cranfield Aerospace Ltd, Cranfield, Beds MK43 0AL. *T:* (01234) 754743; *e-mail:* d.i.a.poll@cranfield.ac.uk. *Clubs:* Athenæum, Royal Air Force.

POLLACK, Anita Jean; European consultant, since 2006; Head of European Policy (formerly European Liaison), English Heritage, 2000–06; *b* NSW, Australia, 3 June 1946; *d* of late John and Kathleen Pollack; *m* 1986, Philip Bradbury; one *d*. *Educ:* City of London Polytechnic (BA 1979); Birkbeck Coll., Univ. of London (MSc Polit. Sociology 1981). Advertising copy writer, Australia, 1963–69; book editor, 1970–75; student, 1976–79; Research Asst to Rt Hon. Barbara Castle, MEP, 1981–89. MEP (Lab) London SW, 1989–99; contested (Lab), EP elections: SE Region, 1999; London, 2004. *Recreation:* family. *Address:* 139 Windsor Road, E7 0RA.

POLLARD, Prof. Andrew John, PhD; Professor of Education, Institute of Education, University of London, since 2006; Director, ESRC Teaching and Learning Research Programme, since 2002; Fellow of Wolfson College, Cambridge, since 2000; *b* 13 Nov. 1949; *s* of Michael and Anne Pollard; *m* 1971, Rosalind Croft; one *s* one *d*. *Educ:* Univ. of Leeds (BA); Univ. of Lancaster (PGCE 1972); Univ. of Sheffield (MEd 1976; PhD 1981). Teaching in primary schools, 1972–81; Sen. Lectr, 1981–84, Principal Lectr, 1984–85, Oxford Poly.; Reader, 1985–90, Associate Dean, 1990–95, UWE; Prof. of Educn, Univ. of Bristol, 1996–2000; Prof. of Educn, Univ. of Cambridge, 2000–05. *Publications:* The Social World of the Primary School, 1985; Reflective Teaching, 1987, 5th edn 2005; (jtly) Changing English Primary Schools, 1994; The Social World of Children's Learning, 1996; (with A. Filer) The Social World of Pupil Career, 1999; (with P. Triggs) What Pupils Say: changing policy and practice in primary education, 2000; (with A. Filer) The Social World of Pupil Assessment, 2000. *Recreations:* sailing, gardening, bird watching. *Address:* Institute of Education, University of London, 20 Bedford Way, WC1H 0AL.

POLLARD, Maj.-Gen. Anthony John Griffin, CB 1992; CBE 1985; DL; General Officer Commanding, South West District, 1990–92, retired; *b* 8 April 1937; *s* of William Pollard and Anne Irene Griffin; *m* Marie-Luise; four *s*. *Educ:* Oakham Sch.; Jesus Coll., Cambridge. Commnd Royal Leics Regt, 1956; served Cyprus, Germany, Hong Kong, Borneo, Malta; Staff Coll., 1969; Staff 7 Armd Bde, 1970–72; Instr, Staff Coll., 1975–77; CO 1st Bn Royal Anglian Regt, 1977–79; (Norway, NI, Germany); QMG's Secretariat, 1980; Col, Tactical Doctrine, BAOR, 1981; Col, Ops and Tactical Doctrine, 1(BR) Corps, 1982; Comdr, British Forces, Belize, 1983–84; Comdt, Sch. of Infantry, 1984–87; Comdr, British Mil. Mission to Uganda, 1985–86; Dir Gen., Trng and Doctrine (Army), 1987–90. Dep. Col, Royal Anglian Regt, 1986–92; Colonel Commandant: Small Arms Sch. Corps, 1987–92; Queen's Div., 1990–92; Hon. Col Suffolk ACF, 1992–. Pres., Royal Tigers Assoc., 1996–. DL Suffolk, 1999. OStJ 2004 (Chm., St John Council, Suffolk, 2004–). *Recreations:* family, fishing, gardening, archaeology, ancient buildings. *Clubs:* Army and Navy, Victory Services (Vice Chm., 2003–).

POLLARD, Bernard, CB 1988; Deputy Secretary and Director General (Technical), Board of Inland Revenue, 1985–88; *b* 24 Oct. 1927; *m* 1961, Regina (*née* Stone); one *s* one *d*. *Educ:* Tottenham Grammar Sch.; London Univ. (BSc Econ; Gladstone Meml Prize (Econs), 1949). Called to the Bar, Middle Temple, 1968. Served RAF (Flying Officer), 1949–53. Entered Tax Inspectorate, Inland Revenue, 1953; Principal Inspector of Taxes, 1969; Asst Sec., 1973; Under Sec., 1979; Dir of Counter Avoidance and Evasion Div., 1981–85. *Recreations:* reading biographies, watching cricket and National Hunt racing. *Address:* 1 Albany House, 3 Balcombe Road, Poole, Dorset BH13 6DX. *T:* (01202) 763488.

POLLARD, Sir Charles, Kt 2001; QPM 1990; Chairman, Restorative Solutions Community Interest Company, since 2006; *b* 4 Feb. 1945; *s* of Humphrey Charles Pollard and Margaret Isobel Pollard (*née* Philpott); *m* 1972, Erica Jane Allison Jack; two *s* one *d*. *Educ:* Oundle Sch.; Bristol Univ. (LLB). Metropolitan Police, 1964; Sussex Police, 1980; Asst Chief Constable, Thames Valley Police, 1985–88; Dep. Asst Comr, i/c No 5 (SW) Area of London, Metropolitan Police, 1988–91; Chief Constable, Thames Valley Police, 1991–2002. Chm., Quality of Service Cttee, ACPO, 1993–94; Vice-Chm., Thames Valley Partnership (working for safer communities), 1992–2002; Mem., Youth Justice Bd for England and Wales, 1998–2006 (actg Chm., 2003–04). Chairman: Winchester

Restorative Justice Gp, 1999–2008; Justice Res. Consortium, 2002–05. Mem. Bd, Centre for Mgt and Policy Studies, 2000–02. Chm., Oxford Common Purpose, 1996–98. Vis. Fellow, Nuffield Coll., Oxford, 1993–2001. Hon. LLD: Buckingham, 2001; Bristol, 2003. *Publications:* contribs to nat. media and learned jls on policing, criminal justice and restorative justice. *Recreations:* tennis, walking, family pursuits. *Address:* Restorative Solutions Community Interest Company, 12 Nolan Close, St Andrews Ridge, Swindon, Wilts SN25 4GP. *Club:* Royal Over-Seas League.

POLLARD, Christopher Charles; Director, Out of the Blue Productions, since 2000; *b* 30 April 1957; s of Anthony Cecil and Margaret Noelle Pollard; *m* 1984, Margaret Ann Langlois; three *d. Educ:* Merchant Taylors' Sch., Northwood; Newland Park Coll. Gramophone, 1981–99: Editor, 1986–90; Man. Editor, 1990–93; Editl Dir, 1993–99. Director: Jethou, 1995–; John Griffiths Motorsport, 1999–; Newgate Motoring Solutions (formerly Newgate Finance), 2000–; Songlines Publications, 2002–; Kryotrans Internat., 2006–. *Recreations:* Rugby football, cricket, cars, music. *Address:* Beechcroft, Hotley Bottom, Great Missenden, Bucks HP16 9PL.

POLLARD, Eve, (Lady Lloyd), OBE 2008; *d* of late Ivor and Mimi Pollard; *m* 1st, 1968, Barry Winkleman (marr. diss. 1979); one *d*; 2nd, 1979, Sir Nicholas Lloyd, *qv*; one *s*. Fashion Editor: Honey, 1967–68; Daily Mirror Magazine, 1968–69; Women's Editor: Observer Magazine, 1970–71; Sunday Mirror, 1971–81; Asst Ed., Sunday People, 1981–83; Features Ed. and presenter, TV-am, 1983–85; Editor: Elle USA (launched magazine in NY), 1985–86; Sunday magazine, News of the World, 1986; You magazine, Mail on Sunday, 1986–88; Sunday Mirror and Sunday Mirror Magazine, 1988–91; Sunday Express and Sunday Express Magazine, 1991–94. Founder, Wedding Day magazine, 1999. Formerly contributor to Sunday Times. Member: English Tourism Council (formerly English Tourist Bd), 1993–2000; Competition Commn, 1999–2007; Mem., Newspaper Takeover Panel, Competition Commn, 1999–. Chair and Founder Mem., Women in Journalism, 1995–. Vis. Fellow, Bournemouth Univ., 2001–. *Publications:* Jackie: biography of Mrs J. K. Onassis, 1971; (jtly) Splash, 1995; (jtly) Best of Enemies, 1996; (jtly) Double Trouble, 1997; Unfinished Business, 1998; Jack's Widow, 2006. *Address:* c/o Noel Gay, 19 Denmark Street, WC2H 8NA.

POLLARD, (George) Nicholas; Head of News, British Sky Broadcasting, 1996–2006; *b* 15 Nov. 1950; *s* of Thomas Bewcastle Pollard and Helen Pollard; *m* 1981, Sally Jane Behenna; two *s. Educ:* Birkenhead Sch. Television journalist, BBC, 1977–80; ITN: television journalist, 1980–92; Exec. Producer, News at Ten, 1987–92; Producer, Election coverage, 1987, 1992; ind. producer, current affairs progs, 1992–94; Dir of Progs, Channel One TV, 1994–96. *Recreations:* family, walking, reading.

POLLARD, Kerry Patrick; JP; *b* 27 April 1944; *s* of late Patrick Joseph Pollard and of Iris Betty Pollard; *m* 1966, Maralyn Murphy; five *s* two *d. Educ:* St Joseph's Primary Sch., Heywood, Lancs; Thornleigh Coll., Bolton. Engr, British Gas, 1960–92; Co-ordinator, Homes for Homeless People, 1992; Dir and Co. Sec., Cherry Tree Housing Assoc., 1992–97. Member (Lab): St Albans DC, 1982–98; Herts CC, 1989–97. MP (Lab) St Albans, 1997–2005; contested (Lab) same seat, 1992, 2005. JP St Albans, 1984. *Recreations:* swimming, theatre, country walking.

POLLARD, L. Edwin, OBE 2003; High Commissioner for Barbados in the United Kingdom, 2003–08; *b* 21 May 1942; *m* 1968, Deanna Winifred Warner; one *s* one *d. Educ:* Combermere Sch., Barbados. CDipAF. Joined Barclays Bank plc, 1961: Staff and Industrial Relns Manager, Barclays, Caribbean; Asst Caribbean Dir (Mem., Barclays UK Exec. Cttee); Personal Sector and Offshore Dir; Product Develt and Mktg Dir, until 2000. Member Board: Barbados Inst. Banking and Finance; Securities Exchange of Barbados. FCIB. *Recreations:* golf, cricket, hockey, football. *Address:* c/o Barbados High Commission, 1 Great Russell Street, WC1B 3ND. *T:* (020) 7631 4975, *Fax:* (020) 7323 6872. *Club:* London Golf.

POLLARD, Nicholas; *see* Pollard, G. N.

POLLARD, His Honour Richard Frederick David; a Circuit Judge, 1990–2006; Senior Circuit Judge, Nottingham Crown Court, 2002–06; *b* 26 April 1941; *s* of William Pollard and Anne Irene Pollard (*née* Griffin), CBE; *m* 1964, Angela Susan Hardy; one *s* two *d. Educ:* Oakham School; Trinity College Dublin (BA); Univ. of Cambridge (Dip. Crim.). Called to the Bar, Gray's Inn, 1967, Bencher, 2001. *Recreations:* walking, art nouveau, looking out of the window. *Address: e-mail:* richardfdpollard@tiscali.co.uk.

POLLARD, Prof. Roger David, PhD; CEng, FREng, FIET, FIEEE; Professor of High Frequency Measurements, since 1995, and Dean, Faculty of Engineering, since 2003, University of Leeds; *b* 1 June 1946; *s* of late Mendel Pollard and Tilley Pollard (*née* Addess); *m* 1970, Anne Clara Price; two *d. Educ:* Hendon Co. Grammar Sch.; Univ. of Leeds (BSc 1972, PhD 1980). CEng 1979; FIEEE 1997; FIET (FIEE 2000); FREng 2005. University of Leeds: Lectr, 1974–85; Sen. Lectr, 1985–95; Hd, Sch. of Electronic and Electrical Engrg, 1999–2003. Consulting Engr, Agilent Technols (formerly Hewlett-Packard), 1981–. Pres., Microwave Theory and Techniques Soc., IEEE, 1998. Measurement Prize, IEE, 1999. *Publications:* papers, book chapters and patents on microwave active devices, circuits and measurements. *Recreations:* family, travel, reading. *Address:* School of Electronic and Electrical Engineering, University of Leeds, Leeds LS2 9JT; 1 Sandhill Crescent, Leeds LS17 8DY. *T:* (0113) 269 4861; *e-mail:* r.d.pollard@leeds.ac.uk.

POLLEN, Peregrine Michael Hungerford; Executive Deputy Chairman, 1975–77, Deputy Chairman, 1977–82, Sotheby Parke Bernet and Co.; *b* 24 Jan. 1931; *s* of late Sir Walter Michael Hungerford Pollen, MC, JP, and Lady Pollen; *m* 1958, Patricia Helen Barry; one *s* two *d. Educ:* Eton Coll.; Christ Church, Oxford. National Service, 1949–51. ADC to Sir Evelyn Baring, Governor of Kenya, 1955–57; Sotheby's, 1957–82: Dir, 1961; Pres., Sotheby Parke Bernet, New York, 1965–72. *Address:* The Farmhouse, Norton Hall, Mickleton, Glos GL55 6PU. *Clubs:* Brooks's, Beefsteak.

POLLEN, Sir Richard (John Hungerford), 8th Bt *cr* 1795, of Redenham, Hampshire; Director, Pollen Organics Ltd, since 2000; *b* 3 Nov. 1946; *o s* of Sir John Michael Hungerford Pollen, 7th Bt and Angela Pollen (*née* Russi, later Henderson); *S* father, 2003; *m* 1971, Christianne Mary, *d* of Sir Godfrey Agnew, KCVO, CB; four *s* three *d* (and one *s* decd). *Educ:* Worth Sch. Capel-Cure Myers, 1964–68; Financial Times, 1970–71; Charles Barker, 1971–79; Valin Pollen, 1979–91; Richard Pollen & Co., 1990–94; Ludgate Pollen, 1994–96; Communication Consultant, Pollen Associates, 1996–2000. Dir, Hampshire Fare, 2004–. FCIPR. *Publications:* (contrib.) The Management Audit, 1993; (contrib.) Maw on Corporate Governance, 1994. *Recreations:* riding, running, ski-ing, walking. *Heir: s* William Richard Hungerford Pollen, *b* 28 June 1976. *Club:* Royal Automobile.

POLLINGTON, Viscount; John Andrew Bruce Savile; *b* 30 Nov. 1959; *s* and *heir* of 8th Earl of Mexborough, *qv*.

POLLINI, Maurizio; pianist; *b* Milan, 5 Jan. 1942; *s* of Gino Pollini and Renata Melotti; *m* 1968, Maria Elisabetta Marzotto; one *s*. Has performed with all major orchestras, including: Chicago Symphony; Cleveland; Berlin Philharmonic; Boston Symphony; LPO; LSO; New York Philharmonic; Vienna Philharmonic; has played at Berlin, Prague, Salzburg and Vienna Fests. First Prize, Internat. Chopin Competition, Warsaw, 1960; Ernst von Siemens Music Prize, Munich, 1996. Has made numerous recordings. *Address:* c/o HarrisonParrott Ltd, 12 Penzance Place, W11 4PA.

POLLOCK, family name of **Viscount Hanworth**.

POLLOCK, Alexander; Sheriff of Grampian, Highland and Islands at Inverness, since 2005 (at Inverness and Portree, 2001–05); *b* 21 July 1944; *s* of late Robert Faulds Pollock, OBE, and Margaret Findlay Pollock; *m* 1975, Verena Francesca Gertraud Alice Ursula Critchley; one *s* one *d. Educ:* Rutherglen Academy; Glasgow Academy; Brasenose Coll., Oxford (Domus Exhibnr; MA); Edinburgh Univ. (LLB); Univ. for Foreigners, Perugia. Solicitor, Bonar Mackenzie & Kermack, WS, 1970–73; passed advocate, 1973; Advocate Depute, 1990–91; Sheriff (floating) of Tayside, Central and Fife at Stirling, 1991–93; Sheriff of Grampian, Highland and Is at Aberdeen and Stonehaven, 1993–2001. Contested (C) Moray, 1987. MP (C): Moray and Nairn, 1979–83; Moray, 1983–87. PPS to Sec. of State for Scotland, 1982–86, to Sec. of State for Defence, 1986–87. Mem., Commons Select Cttee on Scottish Affairs, 1979–82, 1986–87. Sec., British-Austrian Parly Gp, 1979–87. Mem., Queen's Body Guard for Scotland, Royal Co. of Archers, 1984–. *Publication:* (contrib.) Stair Memorial Encyclopaedia of Scots Law. *Recreations:* music, cycling, dogs. *Address:* Drumdarrach, Forres, Moray, Scotland IV36 1DW. *Clubs:* New (Edinburgh); Highland (Inverness).

POLLOCK, Prof. Allyson Mary; Professor of International Public Health Policy, University of Edinburgh, since 2005. *Educ:* Univ. of Dundee (BA Hons Physiol. 1979; MB ChB 1983); London Sch. of Hygiene and Tropical Medicine (MSc Community Medicine 1989). MFPH (MFPHM 1991). Prof. of Health Policy and Health Services Res., Sch. of Public Policy, UCL, 1998–2005, Hon. Prof., 2005–; Dir, R&D, UCL Hosps NHS Trust, 1998–2005. *Publications:* NHS plc: the privatisation of our health care, 2004; The New NHS Explained, 2006; contrib. BMJ, British Jl of Gen. Practice, Lancet, Jl of PHM, Public Law, Public Money and Mgt. *Address:* School of Health in Social Science, University of Edinburgh, Medical Quad, Teviot Place, Edinburgh EH8 9AG; *e-mail:* allyson.pollock@ed.ac.uk.

POLLOCK, Brian; *see* Pollock, P. B.

POLLOCK, Prof. Christopher John, CBE 2002; PhD, DSc; Hon. Professor, Institute of Rural Sciences, Aberystwyth University (formerly University of Wales, Aberystwyth), since 2007; Director, Institute of Grassland and Environmental Research, 1993–2007; *b* 28 March 1947; *s* of Neil Cunningham Pollock and Margaret Pollock (*née* Charlton); *m* 1970, Elizabeth Anne Bates; one *s* one *d. Educ:* Trinity Hall, Cambridge (BA 1968, MA 1972); Birmingham Univ. (PhD 1972; DSc 1993). Post-Doctoral Fellow, Botany Sch., Cambridge, 1971–74; joined Welsh Plant Breeding Station, now Inst. of Grassland and Envmtl Res., 1974; Head, Res. Gp, 1985; Head, Envmtl Biology Dept, 1989. Fulbright Fellow, Univ. of California, Davis, 1978–79; NATO Sen. Res. Fellow, Purdue Univ., 1987–92; Hon. Professor: Univ. of Wales, Aberystwyth, 1993; Nottingham Univ., 1994. Chairman: Scientific Steering Cttee for Farm-scale Trials of GM Crops, 1999–2005; Res. Priorities Gp for Sustainable Farming and Food, 2003–06; Adv. Cttee for Releases into the Envmt, 2003–; Mem., BBSRC, 2008–. FIBiol 1997; FRAgS 2000. *Publications:* (jtly) Carbon Partitioning Within and Between Organisms, 1992; (with J. F. Farrar) The Biology of Fructans, 1993; approx. 100 reviews; papers in sci. jls. *Recreations:* golf, walking, woodwork. *Address:* Institute of Rural Sciences, Aberystwyth University, Aberystwyth SY23 3AL. *T:* (01970) 624471. *Club:* St David's (Aberystwyth).

POLLOCK, David John Frederick; Director, The Continence Foundation, 1996–2001; *b* 3 Feb. 1942; *s* of late Leslie William Pollock and Dorothy Emily (*née* Holt); *m* 1976, Lois Jaques (marr. diss. 1991); one *s. Educ:* Beckenham and Penge Grammar Sch.; Keble Coll., Oxford (BA Lit. Hum. 1964; MA); London Business Sch. British Coal Corporation, 1964–90: Head of Central Secretariat, 1972–78; Head of Staff Planning and Orgn, 1980–90; Dir, ASH, 1991–94. Mem., Hackney BC, 1974–78. Sec., Charity Law Reform Cttee, 1972–77. Trustee (formerly Mem., Exec. Cttee), British Humanist Assoc., 1965–75 and 1997– (Chm., 1970–72); Mem. Bd, Rationalist Assoc. (formerly Rationalist Press Assoc.), 1979– (Chm., 1989–91); Pres., Eur. Humanist Fedn, 2006–. Treasurer, Hackney North Labour Party, 1989–92. *Publications:* Denial & Delay: the political history of smoking and health 1950–64, 1999; articles in humanist, health and other jls. *Recreations:* theatre, gardening. *Address:* 13 Dunsmure Road, N16 5PU. *T:* (020) 8800 3542, *Fax:* (020) 7502 0283; *e-mail:* david.pollock@virgin.net; *web:* www.david-pollock.me.uk.

POLLOCK, Sir George F(rederick), 5th Bt *cr* 1866; artist-photographer, since 1963; *b* 13 Aug. 1928; *s* of Sir (Frederick) John Pollock, 4th Bt and Alix l'Estom (*née* Soubiran); *S* father, 1963; *m* 1951, Doreen Mumford, *o d* of N. E. K. Nash, CMG; one *s* two *d. Educ:* Eton; Trinity Coll., Cambridge. BA 1953, MA 1957. 2nd Lieut, 17/21 Lancers, 1948–49. Admitted Solicitor, 1956, retd. Hon. FRPS (Past Pres.); Hon. MPAGB (J. S. Lancaster Medal for exceptional services to photography, 2003); EFIAP. FRSA. *Heir: s* David Frederick Pollock [*b* 13 April 1959; *m* 1985, Helena, *o d* of late L. J. Tompsett, OBE; one *d*]. *Address:* 83 Minster Way, Bath BA2 6RL. *T:* (01225) 464692. *Club:* Downhill Only (Wengen).

POLLOCK, Sir Giles (Hampden) Montagu-, 5th Bt *cr* 1872; management consultant, 1974–2002; *b* 19 Oct. 1928; *s* of Sir George Seymour Montagu-Pollock, 4th Bt, and Karen-Sofie (*d* 1991), *d* of Hans Ludwig Dedekam, Oslo; *S* father, 1985; *m* 1963, Caroline Veronica, *d* of Richard F. Russell; one *s* one *d. Educ:* Eton; de Havilland Aeronautical Technical School. With de Havilland Enterprise, 1949–56; Bristol Aeroplane Co. Ltd, 1956–59; Bristol Siddeley Engines Ltd, 1959–61; Associate Dir, J. Walter Thompson Co. Ltd, 1961–69; Director: C. Vernon & Sons Ltd, 1969–71; Acumen Marketing Group Ltd, 1971–74; 119 Pall Mall Ltd, 1972–78; Associate, John Stork & Partners, subseq. John Stork Internat., then Korn/Ferry Internat., 1980–2002. *Recreations:* bicycling, water ski-ing, walking. *Heir: s* Guy Maximilian Montagu-Pollock, *b* 27 Aug. 1966. *Address:* The White House, 7 Washington Road, SW13 9BG. *T:* (020) 8748 8491.

POLLOCK, Isobel Anne, (Mrs Graham Ramsden), CEng, FIMechE; Royal Academy of Engineering Visiting Professor in Engineering and Design, University of Leeds, since 2006; *b* Ballymoney, 10 Nov. 1954; *d* of Charles Wilson Pollock and late Elisabeth Margaret Pollock (*née* Watson); *m* 1980, Graham Ramsden (*d* 1997). *Educ:* Dalriada, Ballymoney; Imperial Coll., London (BScEng 1976). CEng 1981; FIMechE 1991. ICI, 1976–87; DuPont, 1987–96; Beatson Clark, 1997–99; Dir, Benbane Engrg Consultants, 1999–. Mem. Bd, Engrg Council UK, 2005–; Chm., DIUS (formerly DTI) Pathfinder Measurement Wkg Gp, 2006–. Vice Pres., IMechE, 2000–06. Trustee, Audi Design Foundn, 1999–. Liveryman, Engineers' Co., 2003–. Hon. DSc Huddersfield, 2004. *Recreations:* engineering heritage, family history research, bridge, golf. *Address:* Keyworth

Institute, University of Leeds, Woodhouse Lane, Leeds LS2 9JT. *Club:* Woodsome Hall Golf.

POLLOCK, His Honour (Peter) Brian; a Circuit Judge, 1987–2003; *b* 27 April 1936; *s* of late Brian Treherne Pollock and Helen Evelyn Pollock (*née* Holt-Wilson); *m* 1st, 1966, Joan Maryon Leggett (marr. diss. 1981); two *s* (and one *s* decd); 2nd, 1988, Jeannette Mary Nightingale; two step *s* one step *d*. *Educ:* St Lawrence College. Called to the Bar, Middle Temple, 1958. A Recorder of the Crown Court, 1986–87. *Recreations:* croquet, tennis, watching cricket, travel, walking, cooking, gardening. *Address:* 12 East Terrace, Budleigh Salterton, Devon EX9 6PG. *T:* (01395) 445535. *Clubs:* MCC; Budleigh Salterton Croquet.

POLTIMORE, 7th Baron *cr* 1831; **Mark Coplestone Bampfylde;** Bt 1641; Deputy Chairman, Sotheby's Europe, since 2006; *b* 8 June 1957; *s* of Captain the Hon. Anthony Gerard Hugh Bampfylde (*d* 1969) (*er s* of 6th Baron) and of Brita Yvonne (who *m* 2nd, 1975, Guy Elmes), *o d* of late Baron Rudolph Cederström; *S* grandfather, 1978; *m* 1982, Sally Anne, *d* of Dr Norman Miles; two *s* one *d*. Christie's: Associate Dir, 1984–87; Dir, 1987–2000; Dep. Chm., 1998–2000; Man. Dir, Eauctionroom.com, 2000–02; Sen. Dir, Sotheby's, 2002–06. *Publication:* (with Philip Hook) Popular Nineteenth Century Painting: a dictionary of European genre painters, 1986. *Heir: s* Hon. Henry Anthony Warwick Bampfylde, *b* 3 June 1985. *Address:* North Hidden Farm, Hungerford, Berks RG17 0PY. *Club:* White's.

POLWARTH, 11th Lord *cr* 1690 (Scot.); **Andrew Walter Hepburne-Scott;** *b* 30 Nov. 1947; *s* of 10th Lord Polwarth, TD and Caroline Margaret (*née* Hay); *S* father, 2005; *m* 1971, Anna, *e d* of late Maj. J. F. H. Surtees, OBE, MC; two *s* two *d*. *Educ:* Eton; Trinity Hall, Cambridge. JP Roxburgh Div., Scottish Borders, 1997–2005. *Heir: s* Master of Polwarth, *qv*. *Clubs:* New (Edinburgh); Knickerbocker (New York).

POLWARTH; Master of; Hon. William Henry Hepburne-Scott; *b* 21 March 1973; *s* and *heir* of Lord Polwarth, *qv*.

POLYNESIA, Bishop in, since 1975; **Most Rev. Jabez Leslie Bryce;** Archbishop and Co-Presiding Bishop, Anglican Church in Aotearoa, New Zealand and Polynesia, since 2006; *b* 25 Jan. 1935. *Educ:* St John's College, Auckland, NZ (LTh); St Andrew's Seminary, Manila, Phillipines (BTh). Deacon 1960, priest 1962, Polynesia; Curate of Suva, 1960–63; Priest-in-charge: Tonga, 1964; St Peter's Chinese Congregation, Manila, 1965–67; Archdeacon of Suva, 1967–69; Deputy Vicar-General, Holy Trinity Cathedral, Suva, 1967–72; Lectr, St John Baptist Theological Coll., Suva, 1967–69; Vicar of Viti Levu W, 1969–75; Archdeacon in Polynesia, 1969–75; Vicar-General of Polynesia, 1972–75. Chm., Pacific Conf. of Churches, 1976–86; Sec., S Pacific Anglican Council, 1970– (Chm., 1995–); Pres., WCC for Oceania, 1998–. *Recreations:* tennis, golf. *Address:* Bishop's House, PO Box 35, Suva, Fiji Islands. *T:* (office) 304716, (home) 302553, *Fax:* 302687.

POMEROY, family name of **Viscount Harberton**.

POMEROY, Brian Walter, CBE 2006; *b* 26 June 1944; *s* of Oscar Pomeroy and Eileen Pomeroy (*née* Rutter); *m* 1974, Hilary Susan Price; two *d*. *Educ:* King's Sch., Canterbury; Magdalene Coll., Cambridge (MA). FCA (ACA 1968). Partner, Touche Ross Mgt Consultants, subseq. Deloitte Consulting, 1975–99: on secondment as Under Sec., DTI, 1981–83; Man. Dir, 1987–95; Sen. Partner, 1995–99. Advr on public policy, esp. regulation and public-private partnerships. Deputy Chairman: Limit Underwriting Ltd, 2006–; QBE Insce Europe Ltd, 2006–; non-exec. Dir, Rover Gp plc, 1985–88. Member: Nat. Lottery Commn, 1999–2007 (Chm., 1999–2000, 2002–03); Audit Commn, 2003–; Gambling Commn, 2007– (Chm., 2008–). Mem., Cttee of Enquiry into Regulatory Arrangements at Lloyd's, 1986; Ind. Mem. Council, Lloyd's, 1996–2004; Dep. Chm., Lloyd's Regulatory Bd, 1996–2002. Chairman: Telecommunications Interconnection Cttee, 1988–91; Financial Inclusion Task Force, HM Treasury, 2005–; Payments Council, 2007–. Member: Disability Rights Task Force, 1997–99; Pensions Protection Investments Accreditation Bd, 2000–05; Bd, Social Market Foundn, 2000–; Ind. Inquiry into Drug Testing at Work, Joseph Rowntree Foundn, 2003–04; Financial Reporting Rev. Panel, 2004–. Mem., Commn on Taxation and Citizenship, Fabian Soc., 1998–2000. Mem. Council, Mgt Consultants Assoc., 1996–99. Chairman: AIDS Awareness Trust, 1993–96; Centrepoint, 1993–2001; Eur. Public Health Foundn, 1997–2002; Homeless Link, 2001–05; Raleigh Internat., 2005–07. Trustee: Money Advice Trust, 1999–; Children's Express, 2004–07; SPACE Studios, 2004–05; Lloyd's Charitable Trust, 2004–; Photographers' Gall., 2006– (Chm., 2008–); Chm. of Trustees, The King's Consort, 2000–05. Master, Mgt Consultants' Co., 2000–01. FRSA 1994. *Publications:* contrib. articles on public finance, regulation and public-private partnerships. *Recreations:* photography (ARPS 2004; MA 2006), listening to music, theatre, cycling. *Address:* 7 Ferncroft Avenue, NW3 7PG. *T:* (020) 7435 2584; *e-mail:* pomeroybw@aol.com.

PONCE-VIVANCO, (José) Eduardo; Permanent Representative of Peru to the United Nations Office in Geneva, since 2006; *b* 8 March 1943; *s* of José Eduardo Ponce-Mendoza and Laura Vivanco de Ponce-Mendoza; *m* 1969, Clemencia Hilbck; one *d*. *Educ:* Colegio Jesuita de San José de Arequipa, Peru; Univ. Nacional de San Agustín de Arequipa; Pontificia Univ. Católica del Perú; Peruvian Diplomatic Acad.; Univ. des Hautes Etudes Internat., Geneva. Third Secretary: to Internat. Orgns Under-Secretariat, 1967–68; Tokyo, 1968–70; Second Sec., Quito, 1971–75; Prof. of Peruvian Diplomatic Hist., Diplomatic Acad., Peru, 1976; Asst to Advr for Legal and Maritime Affairs of Minister's Office, 1976–77; Hd, Dept for Equador, Columbia and Venezuela, Under-Secretariat for Political Affairs, 1977; Asst Dir for Planning, Min. of Foreign Affairs, 1978–79; Perm. Rep. to UN and Internat. Orgns, Geneva, 1979–83; Minister, London, 1984; Perm. Rep. to Internat. Commodities Orgns, London, 1984; Ministry of Foreign Affairs: Dir, Territorial Sovereignty, 1985; Dir, America Dept, 1986; Asst Under-Sec., Bilateral Policy for American Affairs, 1987–88; Perm. Rep. to Latin American Integration Assoc. (ALADI), Montevideo, 1988–89; Ambassador to Ecuador, 1990–94; Vice-Minister, Internat. Policy and Sec. Gen. of Foreign Affairs, 1994–95; Ambassador: to UK, 1995–99; to Brazil, 1999; to Venezuela. Pres., Peruvian Delegn to UN World Water Conf., 1977; Mem., numerous Peruvian delegns to UN, Geneva and other internat. orgns. Grand Cross: Orden El Sol del Perú (Peru), 1995; Orden al Mérito Naval (Peru), 1996; Commander: Orden por Servicios Distinguidos (Peru), 1979; Defensor Calificado de la Patria (Peru), 1995; also decorations from Japan, Brazil and Bolivia. *Publications:* The Resolutions of the United Nations General Assembly, 1969; seminar documents; contrib. to Rev. Peruvian Diplomatic Acad. *Recreations:* tennis, music, ballet. *Clubs:* Queen's, Travellers, Naval and Military; Nacional, Terrazas (Lima); Arequipa (Arequipa).

PONCET, Jean André F.; *see* François-Poncet.

POND, Christopher; Director, Financial Capability, Financial Services Authority, since 2007; Chairman, Capacitybuilders UK Ltd, since 2005; *b* 25 Sept. 1952; *s* of Charles Richard Pond and Doris Violet Pond; *m* 1990, Carole Tongue, *qv* (marr. diss. 1999); one *d*; *m* 2003, Lorraine Melvin; one *s* one *d*. *Educ:* Univ. of Sussex (BA Hons Econs). Research Asst in Econs, Birkbeck Coll., Univ. of London, 1974–75; Res. Officer, Low Pay Unit, 1975–78; Lectr in Econs, CS Coll., 1978–79; Dir, Low Pay Unit, 1980–97. Contested (Lab) Welwyn Hatfield, 1987; MP (Lab) Gravesham, 1997–2005; contested (Lab) same seat, 2005; Parly Under-Sec. of State, DWP, 2003–05; Chief Exec., Nat. Council for One Parent Families, subseq. One Parent Families|Gingerbread, 2005–08. Vis. Lectr in Econs, Univ. of Kent, 1983–84; Hon. Vis. Prof. and Res. Fellow, Univ. of Surrey, 1984–86; Hon. Vis. Prof., Univ. of Middlesex, 1995–. Consultant, Open Univ., 1987–88 and 1991–92. Vice Chm., End Child Poverty, 2007–; Mem. Council, IFS, 2005–. FRSA 1992. *Publications:* (jtly) To Him Who Hath, 1977; (jtly) Taxation and Social Policy, 1981; (contrib.) Old and New Poverty, 1995; Out of Poverty: towards prosperity, 1996; (contrib.) Working for Full Employment, 1997; (contrib.) Beyond 2002, 1999. *Recreations:* running, reading, family. *Address:* Financial Services Authority, 25 North Colonnade, Canary Wharf, E14 5HS.

PONDER, Sir Bruce (Anthony John), Kt 2008; PhD; FRCP, FRCPath, FMedSci; FRS 2001; Li Ka Shing Professor of Oncology, University of Cambridge, since 2006; Director, Cancer Research UK Cambridge Research Institute, since 2005; Fellow, Jesus College, Cambridge, since 1993; *b* 25 April 1944; *s* of late Anthony West Ponder and Dorothy Mary Ponder (*née* Peachey); *m* 1969, Margaret Ann Hickinbotham; one *s* three *d*. *Educ:* Charterhouse Sch.; Jesus Coll., Cambridge (MA, MB BChir); St Thomas's Hosp. Med. Sch.; PhD London. FRCP 1987; FRCPath 2001. NHS hosp. appts, 1968–73; Clinical Research Fellow, ICRF, 1973–76; first Hamilton Fairley Fellow, CRC, at Harvard Med. Sch., 1977–78; Clinical Scientific Officer, ICRF, St Bartholomew's Hosp., 1978–80; Institute of Cancer Research: CRC Fellow and Sen. Lectr in Med., Royal Marsden Hosp., 1980–87; Reader in Human Cancer Genetics and Head, Section of Cancer Genetics, 1987–89; University of Cambridge: Dir, Cancer Res. UK (formerly CRC) Human Cancer Genetics Gp, 1989–; CRC Prof. of Human Cancer Genetics, 1992–96; CRUK (formerly CRC) Prof. of Clinical Oncology, 1996–2006. Hon. Consultant Physician: Royal Marsden Hosp., 1980–2003; Addenbrooke's Hosp., Cambridge, 1989–. Croonian Lectr, RCP, 1998. Gibb Fellow, CRC, 1990. Founder FMedSci 1998. Internat. Public Service Award, Nat. Neurofibromatosis Foundn, USA, 1992; Merck Prize, European Thyroid Assoc., 1996; Hamilton Fairley Award, European Soc. of Med. Oncology, 2004; Bertner Award, M. D. Anderson Hosp., 2007; Alfred Knudson Award for Cancer Genetics, Nat. Cancer Inst., USA, 2008; Ambuj Nath Bose Prize, RCP, 2008. *Publications:* papers on genetics, cancer, developmental biology. *Recreations:* gardening, travel, golf, wine. *Address:* Cancer Research UK Cambridge Research Institute, Robinson Way, Cambridge CB2 0RF. *T:* (01223) 404124; Sutton Fields, Bircham Road, Snettisham, Norfolk PE31 7NP. *Club:* Royal West Norfolk Golf (Brancaster).

PONSOLLE, Patrick Henry Jean; Managing Director and Vice Chairman, Morgan Stanley International Ltd, and President, Morgan Stanley SA, since 2001; *b* 20 July 1944; *s* of Jean Ponsolle and Marie-Rose Ponsolle (*née* Courthaliac); *m* 2nd, 1983, Nathalie Elie-Lefebvre; two *d*, and two step *s* two step *d*. *Educ:* Lycée Janson-de-Sailly, Paris; Lycée Henri IV, Paris; Ecole Normale Supérieure; Institut d'Etudes Politiques, Paris; Ecole Nationale d'Administration. Adminr, Min. of Econ. and Finance, 1973–77; Financial Attaché, French Embassy, Washington, 1977–79; Ministry of Economy and Finance: Chargé de Mission to Dir of Forecasting, 1980; Dep. Chief of Staff of Laurent Fabius, Minister responsible for the budget, 1981–83; Gen. Sec., Nat. Accounts and Budget Commn, France, 1980–81; Compagnie de Suez: Asst Dir Gen., 1983–87; Dir Gen., 1988–93; Adminr, 1991–93; Jt Chm., 1994–96, Exec. Chm., 1996–2001, Eurotunnel Gp; Chm., Eurotunnel SA, 1994–2001. *Address:* Morgan Stanley, 61 rue de Monceau, 75008 Paris, France.

PONSONBY, family name of **Earl of Bessborough** and of **Barons de Mauley**, **Ponsonby of Shulbrede** and **Sysonby**.

PONSONBY OF SHULBREDE, 4th Baron *cr* 1930, of Shulbrede; **Frederick Matthew Thomas Ponsonby;** Baron Ponsonby of Roehampton (Life Peer), 2000; JP; *b* 27 Oct. 1958; *o s* of 3rd Baron and of Ursula Mary, *yr d* of Comdr Thomas Stanley Lane Fox-Pitt, OBE, RN; *S* father, 1990. *Educ:* Holland Park Comprehensive Sch.; University Coll., Cardiff; Imperial Coll., London. FIMMM (FIMM 1996); CEng 1997. Councillor (Lab), London Borough of Wandsworth, 1990–94. Opposition frontbench spokesman on educn, H of L, 1992–97. Member: Sub-cttee C, European Select Cttee, H of L, 1997–98; Select Cttee on Sci. and Technol., H of L, 1998–99; Select Cttee on Constitution, 2001–02. Delegate: Council of Europe and WEU, 1997–2001; OSCE, 2001–. JP Westminster, 2006, Inner London Youth Panel, 2008. *Heir:* none. *Address:* House of Lords, SW1A 0PW.

PONSONBY, Sir Ashley (Charles Gibbs), 2nd Bt *cr* 1956; KCVO 1993; MC 1945; Director, J. Henry Schroder, Wagg & Co. Ltd, 1962–80; Lord-Lieutenant of Oxfordshire, 1980–96; *b* 21 Feb. 1921; *o s* of Col Sir Charles Edward Ponsonby, 1st Bt, TD, and Hon. Winifred (*d* 1984), *d* of 1st Baron Hunsdon; *S* father, 1976; *m* 1950, Lady Martha Butler, *yr d* of 6th Marquess of Ormonde, CVO, MC; four *s*. *Educ:* Eton; Balliol College, Oxford. 2nd Lieut Coldstream Guards, 1941; served war 1942–45 (North Africa and Italy, wounded); Captain 1943; on staff Bermuda Garrison, 1945–46. A Church Commissioner, 1963–80; Mem., Council of Duchy of Lancaster, 1977–92. DL Oxon, 1974–80. Hon. DArts Oxford Brookes, 1995; Hon. MA Oxon, 1996. *Heir: e s* Charles Ashley Ponsonby [*b* 10 June 1951; *m* 1983, Mary P., *yr d* of late A. R. Bromley Davenport and of Mrs A. R. Bromley Davenport, Over Peover, Knutsford, Cheshire; two *s* one *d*]. *Address:* Grim's Dyke Farm, Woodleys, Woodstock, Oxon OX20 1HJ. *T:* (01993) 811422. *Club:* Pratt's.

PONSONBY, Air Vice Marshal John Maurice Maynard, OBE 1999; Chief of Staff Operations, Headquarters Air Command, since 2007; *b* 8 Aug. 1955; *s* of Myles and Anne Ponsonby; *m* 1980, Marie-José Van Huizen; one *s* two *d*. *Educ:* Ampleforth Coll. Commn Royal Green Jackets, 1975–83; commnd RAF, 1983; qualified helicopter instructor, Hong Kong, Germany and UK, 1983–88; Flight Comdr, Germany, NI and Falkland Is, 1988–91; Staff HQ RAF Germany, 1991; Staff Coll., 1992; Staff, HQ No 1 Gp, MoD, 1993–95; Comd 27 Sqdn RAF, 1995–98; PSO to CDS, MoD, 1998–2000; HCSC, 2000; Station Comdr, RAF Aldergrove and Comdr Jt Helicopter Force, NI, 2000–02; AO Plans HQ Strike Comd, 2002–04; AOC Trng Gp and Chief Exec., Trng Gp Defence Agency, 2005–07. *Recreations:* flying, golf, tennis, military history. *Address:* c/o Lloyds TSB, 38 Blue Boar Road, Salisbury, Wilts SP1 1DB; *e-mail:* cepon@waitrose.com. *Club:* Royal Air Force.

PONSONBY, Robert Noel, CBE 1985; Controller of Music, BBC, 1972–85; *b* 19 Dec. 1926; *o s* of late Noel Ponsonby, BMus, Organist Christ Church Cathedral, Oxford, and Mary White-Thomson; *m* 1st, 1957, Una Mary (marr. diss.), *er d* of late W. J. Kenny; 2nd, 1977, Lesley Margaret Black (marr. diss.), *o d* of late G. T. Black. *Educ:* Eton; Trinity Coll., Oxford. MA Oxon, Eng. Litt. Commissioned Scots Guards, 1945–47. Organ Scholar, Trinity Coll., Oxford, 1948–50; staff of Glyndebourne Opera, 1951–55; Artistic Director of the Edinburgh International Festival, 1955–60; with Independent Television Authority,

1962–64; Gen. Administrator, Scottish Nat. Orchestra, 1964–72. Adminr, Friends of the Musicians Benevolent Fund, 1987–93. Director: Commonwealth Arts Festival, Glasgow, 1965; Henry Wood Promenade Concerts, 1974–86; Artistic Dir, Canterbury Fest., 1987–88. Artistic Adviser to Internat. Arts Guild of Bahamas, 1960–72. Chm., London Choral Soc., 1990–94; Programme Consultant, RPO, 1993–96. Mem., Music Adv. Panel, Arts Council of GB, 1986–89; Music Advr, Wingate Scholarships, 1988–2008. Trustee: Young Concert Artists Trust, 1984–89; Nash Concert Soc., 1988–2004; Michael Tippett Musical Foundn, 1989–. Governor, Purcell Sch., 1985–88. Hon. RAM 1975; Hon. Mem., ISM, 1992. FRSA 1979. *Publication:* Short History of Oxford University Opera Club, 1950. *Recreations:* fell-walking, bird-watching, English and Scottish painting, music. *Address:* 11 St Cuthbert's Road, NW2 3QJ.

PONTEFRACT, Bishop Suffragan of, since 2002; **Rt Rev. Anthony William Robinson;** *b* 25 April 1956; *m* 1981, Susan Boddy; two *s* one *d*. *Educ:* Bedford Modern Sch.; Salisbury and Wells Theol Coll. Ordained deacon, 1982, priest, 1983; Asst Curate, St Paul, Tottenham, 1982–85; Team Vicar, 1985–89, Team Rector, 1989–97, Resurrection, Leicester; Archdeacon of Pontefract, 1997–2003. Rural Dean, Christianity North, Leicester, 1992–97; Hon. Canon, Leicester Cathedral, 1994–97. *Address:* Pontefract House, 181a Manygates Lane, Wakefield WF2 7DR. *T:* (01924) 250781, *Fax:* (01924) 240490; *e-mail:* bishop.pontefract@wakefield.anglican.org.

PONTEFRACT, Archdeacon of; *see* Townley, Ven. P. K.

PONTI, Signora Carlo; *see* Loren, Sophia.

PONTIFEX, Brig. David More, CBE 1977 (OBE 1965; MBE 1956); General Secretary, Army Cadet Force Association and Secretary, Combined Cadet Force Association, 1977–87; *b* 16 Sept. 1922; *s* of Comdr John Weddall Pontifex, RN, and Monica Pontifex; *m* 1968, Kathleen Betsy (*née* Matheson); one *s* four *d*. *Educ:* Worth Preparatory Sch.; Downside Sch. Commnd The Rifle Brigade, 1942; served War, Italy (despatches); Staff Coll., Camberley, 1951; HQ Parachute Brigade, 1952–54; Kenya, 1954–56; War Office, 1956–58; Armed Forces Staff Coll., USA, 1958–59; Brigade Major, 63 Gurkha Brigade, 1961–62; CO 1st Bn Federal Regular Army, Aden, 1963–64; GSO1 2nd Div., BAOR, 1965–66; Col GS, Staff Coll., Camberley, 1967–69; Divisional Brig., The Light Div., 1969–73; Dep. Dir, Army Staff Duties, MoD, 1973–75; Dep. Comdr and COS, SE District, 1975–77, retired 1977. ADC to the Queen, 1975–77. *Address:* 68 Shortheath Road, Farnham, Surrey GU9 8SQ. *T:* (01252) 723284. *Club:* Naval and Military.

PONTIN, John Graham, OBE 2004; Chairman, JT Group Ltd, since 1961; Founder Trustee, Converging World, since 2007; *b* 2 June 1937; *s* of Charles Cyril Pontin and Phyllis (*née* Frieze); *m* 1st, 1966, Gillian Margaret Harris (marr. diss. 1971); one *s* one *d*; 2nd, 1977, Sylviane Marie-Louise Aubel (*d* 1998). *Educ:* Bristol Tech. Sch. (Building). Founder, JT Group, 1961. Chm., Dartington Hall Trust, 1984–97 (Trustee, 1980–97); Trustee, Quartet Community Foundn (formerly Gtr Bristol Community Trust, then Gtr Bristol Foundn), 1987–. FRSA. *Recreations:* gardening, walking. *Club:* Reform.

PONTIUS, Timothy Gordon; His Honour Judge Pontius; a Circuit Judge, since 1995; a Specialist Circuit Judge, Central Criminal Court, since 2008; *b* 5 Sept. 1948; *s* of Gordon Stuart Malzard Pontius and Elizabeth Mary (*née* Donaldson). *Educ:* Boroughmuir Sen. Secondary Sch., Edinburgh; London Univ. (external, LLB Hons). Called to the Bar, Middle Temple, 1972, Bencher, 2008; in practice at the Bar, 1972–88; Dep. Judge-Advocate, 1988–91; AJAG, 1991–95; a Recorder, 1993–95. *Recreations:* music, travel, swimming. *Address:* Central Criminal Court, Old Bailey, EC4M 7EH.

POOLE, family name of **Baron Poole**.

POOLE, 2nd Baron *cr* 1958, of Aldgate; **David Charles Poole;** *b* 6 Jan. 1945; *s* of 1st Baron Poole, PC, CBE, TD and Betty Margaret Gilkison (*d* 1988); *S* father, 1993; *m* 1967; one *s*; *m* 2004, Kate Watts. *Educ:* Dragon Sch., Oxford; Gordonstoun; Christ Church, Oxford (MA); INSEAD, Fontainebleau (MBA). Samuel Montagu & Co. Ltd, 1967–74; Bland Payne & Co. Ltd, 1974–78; Capel-Cure Myers, 1978–87; Bonomi Group, 1987–90; James Capel, 1992–94; Mem., Prime Minister's Policy Unit (on secondment), 1992–94, 1995–2002; Gp Chief Exec., Sturge, subseq. Ockham, Hldgs plc, 1994–2002. *Recreations:* sailing, ballet. *Heir:* *s* Hon. Oliver John Poole, *b* 30 May 1972. *Address:* *e-mail:* davidpoole300@hotmail.com. *Clubs:* Brooks's, City of London; Royal Yacht Squadron, Island Sailing.

POOLE, Dame Anne; *see* Poole, Dame Avril A. B.

POOLE, Anthony Cecil James; Head of Administration Department, House of Commons, 1985–88, retired; *b* 9 Oct. 1927; *s* of Walter James Poole and Daisy Poole (*née* Voyle); *m* 1951, Amelia Keziah (*née* Pracy); one *d*. *Educ:* Headlands Grammar School, Swindon. Served RN, 1945–47; Department of Employment, 1947–76; Principal Establishments Officer, Manpower Services Commn, 1976–80; House of Commons, 1980, Head of Establishments Office, 1981. *Recreations:* golf, gardening.

POOLE, Dame (Avril) Anne (Barker), DBE 1992; Chief Nursing Officer, Department of Health (formerly of Health and Social Security), 1982–92; *b* 11 April 1934; *d* of Arthur George and Norah Heritage; *m* 1959, John Percy Poole. *Educ:* High Sch., Southampton. SRN 1955, SCM 1957, Health Visitors Cert., 1958. Asst Chief Nursing Officer, City of Westminster, 1967–69; Chief Nursing Officer, London Borough of Merton, 1969–73; Area Nursing Officer, Surrey AHA, 1974–81; Dep. Chief Nursing Officer, DHSS, 1981–82. Non-exec. Dir, SW Surrey HA, 1993–96; Mem., Criminal Injuries Compensation Panel, 1996–2006. Trustee, Marie Curie Cancer Care (formerly Marie Curie Meml Foundn), 1992–2001. FRSocMed 1993; CCMI (CBIM 1984).

POOLE, David Arthur Ramsay; Managing Director, Blue Circle Industries, 1987–89; *b* 30 Sept. 1935; *s* of late Arthur Poole and Viola Isbol (*née* Ramsay); *m* 1961, Jean Mary Male; three *d*. *Educ:* King's Sch., Canterbury; St Edmund Hall, Oxford (MA Jurisprudence). Nat. service, 2nd Lieut, RA, 1955–57. Baring Bros & Co., 1960–65; APCM Ltd (now BCI), 1965–70; Wm Brandts & Co., 1970–73; British Caledonian Gp, 1973–75; Blue Circle Industries, 1976–89. *Recreations:* shooting, ski-ing, travel. *Address:* Dalwood Cottage, Long Reach, Ockham, Surrey GU23 6PF. *T:* and *Fax:* (01483) 284986. *Clubs:* East India, Royal Automobile.

POOLE, David James, PPRP (RP 1969); ARCA; artist; *b* 5 June 1931; *s* of Thomas Herbert Poole and Catherine Poole; *m* 1958, Iris Mary Toomer; three *s*. *Educ:* Stoneleigh Secondary Sch.; Wimbledon Sch. of Art; Royal Coll. of Art. National Service, RE, 1949–51. Sen. Lectr in Painting and Drawing, Wimbledon Sch. of Art, 1962–77. Pres., Royal Soc. of Portrait Painters, 1983–91. One-man exhibns, Zurich and London; exhibn of non-portrait work, Curwen and New Acad. Gall., London, 2008. Portraits include: the Queen, The Duke of Edinburgh, The Queen Mother, Prince Charles, Princess Anne, Princess Margaret, Earl Mountbatten of Burma and The Duke of Kent; Private Secretaries to the Queen: Sir Alan Lascelles, Sir Michael Adeane, Sir Martin Charteris, Sir Philip Moore, Sir William Heseltine, Sir Robert Fellowes, Sir Robin Janvrin; also distinguished members of govt, industry, commerce, medicine, the academic and legal professions. Work in private collections of the Queen and the Duke of Edinburgh, and in Australia, S Africa, Bermuda, France, W Germany, Switzerland, Saudi Arabia and USA. *Recreations:* French travel, food and drink. *Address:* Trinity Flint Barn, Weston Lane, Weston, Petersfield, Hants GU32 3NN. *T:* (01730) 265075.

POOLE, Isobel Anne; Sheriff of the Lothian and Borders, 1979–2007, at Edinburgh, 1986–2007; part-time Sheriff, all Scotland, since 2007; *b* 9 Dec. 1941; *d* of late John Cecil Findlay Poole, DM Oxon, and Constance Mary (*née* Gilkes), SRN. *Educ:* Oxford High Sch. for Girls; Edinburgh Univ. (LLB). Admitted to Faculty of Advocates, 1964. Formerly Standing Jun. Counsel to Registrar Gen. for Scotland. Ext. Examr in Comparative Criminal Procedure, Edinburgh Univ., 2001, 2002. Member: Sheriffs' Council, 1980–85; Scottish Lawyers European Gp, 1977–; Franco-British Lawyers Assoc. Chm., Edinburgh Sir Walter Scott Club, 2004–07. *Publication:* contrib. to Oxford DNB. *Recreations:* country, arts, houses, gardens, friends. *Address:* Sheriff's Chambers, Sheriff Court House, Chambers Street, Edinburgh EH1 1LB. *Clubs:* New, Scottish Arts (Edinburgh).

POOLE, Col Peter Michael, CBE 1992; TD 1964; Vice Lord-Lieutenant, County of Merseyside, 1994–2004; Consultant, Denton Clark & Co., 1995–2000; *b* 29 Sept. 1929; *s* of Reginald and Madeline Isobel Poole; *m* 1956, Diana Rosemary Hiam Wilson; three *s* one *d*. *Educ:* Sedbergh Sch.; Gonville and Caius Coll., Cambridge. FRICS (Ryde Meml Prizewinner, 1955); Fellow, CAAV. Univ. Officer, Cambridge, 1954–60; Chartered Surveyor and Land Agent; Principal, Poole & Partners, Liverpool, 1960–91; Partner, Denton Clark & Co., 1991–95. Mem., Lord Chancellor's Panel of Arbitrators, 1977–95; Chm., Merseyside Adv. Cttee on Gen. Comrs of Income Tax, 1993–2004. Dir, Merseyside Youth Assoc., 1973–2004. Liveryman and Mem., Chartered Surveyors' Co., 1980–. JP Liverpool 1976–96; DL Merseyside 1975. CO, 107 Corps Engr Regt, RE (TA), 1965–67; Brevet Col, 1967; Hon. Col, 75 Engr Regt, RE (V), 1972–80; Chm., North West TA&VRA, 1990–92; Hon. Mem., NW RFCA, 2003. *Publication:* The Valuation of Pipeline Easements and Wayleaves, 1962. *Recreations:* ornithology, golf, travel, photography. *Address:* Shelford, 3 Heron Court, Parkgate, Neston, Cheshire CH64 6TB. *T:* (0151) 336 2529. *Club:* Athenæum (Liverpool).

POOLE-WILSON, Prof. Philip Alexander, MD; FRCP, FMedSci; British Heart Foundation Simon Marks Professor of Cardiology, National Heart and Lung Institute (formerly Cardiothoracic Institute), Faculty of Medicine, Imperial College London (formerly Imperial College School of Medicine), since 1988; *b* 26 April 1943; *s* of late Denis Smith Poole-Wilson, CBE, MCh, FRCS and Monique Michelle Poole-Wilson; *m* 1969, Mary Elizabeth, *d* of late William Horrocks Tattersall, MA, MD and Joan Tattersall; two *s* one *d*. *Educ:* Marlborough Coll.; Trinity Coll., Cambridge (Major Scholar; MA, MD); St Thomas's Hosp. Med. Sch. FRCP 1983; FACC 1992. House appts, St Thomas' Hosp., Brompton Hosp., Hammersmith Hosp.; Lectr, St Thomas' Hosp.; British-American Travelling Fellowship from British Heart Foundn at UCLA, 1973–74; Cardiothoracic Institute, London University: Senior Lectr and Reader, 1976–83; Vice-Dean, 1981–84; apptd Prof. of Cardiology, 1983; Hon. Consultant Physician, Royal Brompton Hosp. (formerly at Nat. Heart Hosp.), 1976–. Chm., Cardiac Muscle Research Group, 1984–87; Mem. Council, British Heart Foundn, 1985–97; Founding Chm., British Soc. for Heart Failure, 1999–2001; World Heart Federation: Pres.-elect, 2001–03; Pres., 2003–04; European Society of Cardiology: Fellow, 1988; Mem. Bd, 1988–98; Sec., 1990–92; Pres.-elect, 1992–94; Pres., 1994–96. Strickland-Goodall Lectr, 1983, Bradshaw Lectr, 1993, Paul Wood Lectr, 1999, British Cardiac Soc. Founder FMedSci 1998. Le Prix Europe et Medicine, 2001. *Publications:* articles and contribs to books on physiology and biochemistry of normal and diseased heart. *Recreations:* sailing, gardening, opera. *Address:* Cardiac Medicine, National Heart and Lung Institute, Dovehouse Street, Imperial College London, SW3 6LY. *T:* (020) 7351 8179, *Fax:* (020) 7351 8113. *Clubs:* Athenæum; Parkstone Yacht.

POOLES, Michael Philip Holmes; QC 1999; a Recorder, since 2000; *b* 14 Dec. 1955; *s* of late Dennis John Pooles and of Joan Ellen Pooles; *m* 1982, Fiona Grant Chalmers; two *s*. *Educ:* Perse Sch., Cambridge; Queen Mary Coll., Univ. of London (LLB). Called to the Bar, Inner Temple, 1978; in practice at the Bar, 1980–; Asst Recorder, 2000. Hd, Hailsham Chambers, 2004–. Mem., Bar Standards Bd, 2006–. Gov., Perse Sch. *Publication:* (contrib.) Professional Negligence and Liability, 2001. *Recreations:* reading, gardening. *Address:* Hailsham Chambers, 4 Paper Buildings, Temple, EC4Y 7EX. *T:* (020) 7643 5000. *Club:* Royal Automobile.

POOLEY, Dr Derek, CBE 1995; consultant, Derek Pooley Associates, since 1998; Chairman, Waste Management Technology Ltd, since 2006; *b* 28 Oct. 1937; *s* of Richard Pike Pooley and Evelyn Pooley; *m* 1961, Jennifer Mary Davey; two *s* one *d*. *Educ:* Sir James Smith's Sch., Camelford, Cornwall; Birmingham Univ. (BSc 1958; PhD 1961). FInstP 1979. A. A. Noyes Res. Fellow, Calif Inst. of Technol., Pasadena, 1961–62; UKAEA, Harwell: Res. Scientist, 1962–68; Leader of Defects Gp, later of Physics Applications Gp, 1968–76; Head of Materials Develt Div., 1976–81; Dir of Non-nuclear Energy Res., 1981–83; Chief Scientist, Dept of Energy, 1983–86; Dep. Dir, 1986–89, Dir, 1989–90, Atomic Energy Estabt, Winfrith, later AEA Technol.; Dir, AEA Thermal Reactor Services, 1990–91; Man. Dir, Nuclear Business Gp, AEA Technol., 1991–94; Chief Executive: UKAEA Govt Div., 1994–96; UKAEA, 1996–97. Non-exec. Dir, UK Nirex Ltd, 1995–97; Dir, BNES Ltd, 1997–2000. Pres., British Nuclear Energy Soc., 1992–94; Chm., Scientific and Technical Cttee, Euratom, 1994–99. Mem., EU Adv. Gp on Energy, 2002–. *Publications:* Real Solids and Radiation, 1975; (contrib.) Radiation Damage Processes in Materials, 1975; (contrib.) Energy and Feedstocks in the Chemical Industry, 1983; A Radical Approach to Nuclear Decommissioning, 1995; (contrib.) Key Tasks for Future European Energy R&D, 2005. *Recreations:* history, astronomy, walking. *Address:* 11 Halls Close, Drayton, Abingdon, Oxon OX14 4LU. *T:* (01235) 537507.

POOLEY, Peter, CMG 1996; a Deputy Director General, European Commission, 1983–95, now an Hon. Director-General; Vice-President, Association Internationale des Anciens des Communautés Européennes, since 2005 (Chairman, UK Branch, since 2002); *b* 19 June 1936; *er* (twin) *s* of late W. M. Pooley, OBE, and Grace Lidbury, Truro; *m* 1966, Janet Mary, *er d* of Jack Pearson, Banbury; one *s* one *d*. *Educ:* Brentwood Sch.; Clare Coll., Cambridge (BA). Joined MAFF as Asst Principal, 1959; seconded to: Diplomatic Service, 1961–63 and 1979–82 (Minister (Agric.), Office of UK Perm. Rep. to EEC, Brussels); CSD, 1977–79; Under-Sec., 1979, Fisheries Sec., 1982, MAFF; Dep. Dir Gen., for Agric., 1983–89, for Develt, 1989–95 (Actg DG, 1992–95), EC. Interim Sec.-Gen., COPA/COGECA, 1995–96. Chm., British African Business Assoc., 1996–2001; with Business Council Europe-Africa, 1996–2002 (Pres., 1998). *Address:* The Lodge, 25 Rosebery Road, Alresford, Hampshire SO24 9HQ. *T:* (01962) 732779. *Club:* Oxford and Cambridge.

See also R. Pooley.

POOLEY, Robin, OBE 1997; Chairman, English Apples and Pears Ltd, 2000–07; *b* 19 June 1936; *yr* (twin) *s* of late W. Melville Pooley, OBE and of Grace M. Pooley (*née*

Lidbury); *m* 1972, Margaret Anne, *yr d* of Jack Pearson, Banbury; one *d*. *Educ:* Brentwood School. Various posts, Towers & Co. Ltd, 1954–71; Gen. Manager, CWS Gp, 1971–76; Man. Dir, Buxted Poultry Ltd, 1976–81; Chief Exec., Potato Marketing Bd, 1981–88; Managing Director: Anglian Produce Ltd, 1988–97; Anglian Potato Services Ltd, 1988–97; Chairman: Pseedco Ltd, 1995–98; Abbey Gp Ltd, 1997–2002; United Pig Marketing Ltd, 1999–2003. Director: North Country Primestock Ltd, 1996–2003; Smith and Holbourne, then Garden Isle, Ltd, 1997–2006. Chm., NFU Corporate, 1998–2003; Mem. Council, NFU, 1996–2003. Chm., MAFF Enquiry into meat hygiene, 1999; Mem., Scientific and Economic Co-ordinating Cttee, Min. of Agriculture for Italy, 1998–2007. Special Lectr in Mgt, Univ. of Nottingham, 1996–2008. Pres., CUPGRA, 1999, now Pres. Emeritus. Master, Co. of Butchers, 1987. *Recreations:* fly fishing, freemasonry. *Address:* Barn Hill House, Strumpshaw, Norfolk NR13 4NS. *T:* (01603) 715992. *Club:* Farmers'.

See also P. Pooley.

POORE, Duncan; *see* Poore, M. E. D.

POORE, Dr (Martin Edward) Duncan, MA, PhD; FIBiol, FRGS; consultant in conservation and land use, since 1983; *b* 25 May 1925; *s* of T. E. D. Poore and Elizabeth McMartin; *m* 1949, Judith Ursula, *d* of Lt-Gen. Sir Treffry Thompson, KCSI, CB, CBE, and late Mary Emily, *d* of Rev. Canon Medd; two *s*. *Educ:* Trinity Coll., Glenalmond; Edinburgh Univ.; Clare Coll., Cambridge. MA, PhD Cantab.; MA Oxon. MIEEM. GCCS, Bletchley Park and HMS Anderson, Colombo, 1943–45. Nature Conservancy, 1953–56; Consultant Ecologist, Hunting Technical Services, 1956–59; Prof. of Botany, Univ. of Malaya, Kuala Lumpur, 1959–65; Dean of Science, Univ. of Malaya, 1964–65; Lectr, Forestry Dept, Oxford, 1965–66; Dir, Nature Conservancy, 1966–73; Scientific Dir, Internat. Union for Conservation of Nature and Natural Resources, Switzerland, 1974–78; Prof. of Forest Science and Dir, Commonwealth Forestry Inst., Oxford Univ., 1980–83; Fellow of St John's Coll., Oxford, 1980–83; Dir, 1983–86, Sen. Consltnt, 1986–90, Forestry and Land Use Prog., Internat. Inst. for Envmt and Develt. Member: Thames Water Authority, 1981–83; Nature Conservancy Council, 1981–84. Pres., British Assoc. of Nature Conservationists, 1984–92 (Vice Pres., 1993–); Vice-Pres., Commonwealth Forestry Assoc., 1989–; Mem. Council, Scottish Wildlife Trust, 2001–04; Hon. Member: Botanical Soc. of Scotland, 1992; IUCN (World Conservation Union), 1978 (Hon. Mem., and Fred M. Packard Award, 1990, Commn for Nat. Parks and Protected Areas). FRSA. *Publications:* The Vanishing Forest, 1986; No Timber without Trees, 1990; (with Jeffrey Sayer) The Management of Tropical Moist Forest Lands, 1991; Guidelines for Mountain Protected Areas, 1992; (with Judy Poore) Protected Landscapes in the United Kingdom, 1992; Where Next?: reflections on the human future, 2000; Changing Landscapes: the development of the international tropical timber organisation and its influence on tropical forest management, 2003; (jtly) State of Tropical Forest Management, 2006; papers on ecology and land use in various jls and scientific periodicals. *Recreations:* hill walking, natural history, music, gardening, photography. *Address:* Balnacarn, Glenmoriston, Inverness-shire IV63 7YJ. *T:* (01320) 340261. *Club:* Royal Over-Seas League.

POORE, Sir Roger Ricardo, 7th Bt *cr* 1795, of Rushall, Wiltshire; *b* 21 Oct. 1930; *e s* of Nasionceno Poore, *b* of 5th Bt; *S* cousin, Sir Herbert Edward Poore, 6th Bt; *m* Norma Naso Poore (decd), *widow* of Roberto Poore. *Heir: nephew* Fernando Nasionceno Poore [*b* 1964; *m* Maria del Carmen; one *s*].

POOT, Anton, Hon. CBE 1989; Officer, Order of Oranje-Nassau (Netherlands), 1989; Managing Director, 1983–88, Chairman, 1983–89, Philips Electronics & Associated Industries Ltd; Chairman, Philips UK Ltd, 1985–89; *b* 23 Nov. 1929; *m* 1983, Jesmond Masters; one *s* one *d* by a former marriage. *Educ:* High School in Holland; electronics and economics, Holland and Johannesburg; Univ. of Surrey (BA 2002); Royal Holloway and Bedford New Coll., Univ. of London (MA 2004). NV Philips' Gloeilampenfabrieken, Hilversum, Utrecht, Eindhoven, 1946–51; Philips S Africa, Fedn of Rhodesia and Nyasaland, 1951–63; NV Philips' Gloeilampenfabrieken, Eindhoven, 1963–66; Chairman and Man. Dir, Philips East Africa, 1967–71; Man. Dir, Ada (Halifax) Ltd and Philips Electrical Ltd UK, 1971–76; Man. Dir, NV Philips' Gloeilampenfabrieken, Eindhoven, 1976–78; Chm. and Man. Dir, Philips Appliances Div., 1978–83. Hon. Freeman, Co. of Information Technologists, 1992. FRSA. *Recreations:* music, golf.

POOTS, Edwin; Member (DemU) Lagan Valley, Northern Ireland Assembly, since 1998; Minister for Culture, Arts and Leisure, since 2007; *b* 1965; *m*; four *c*. *Educ:* Wallace High Sch., Lisburn; Greenmount Agricl Coll. Farmer, Lagan Valley. Mem., NI Forum, 1996–98. Mem. (DemU) Lisburn CC. *Address:* Northern Ireland Assembly, Parliament Buildings, Belfast BT4 3XX; (office) Old Town Hall, 29 Castle Street, Lisburn, Co. Antrim BT27 4DH.

POPAT, Prashant; QC 2008; barrister, since 1992; *b* Saroti, Uganda, 24 Sept. 1968; *s* of Shantilal and late Saroj Popat; *m* 1991, Pritti Lakhani; one *s* one *d*. *Educ:* Mansfield Coll., Oxford (MA Jurisprudence 1990). Called to the Bar, Gray's Inn, 1992. Judicial Asst to Master of the Rolls, 1997. *Publications:* (jtly) Civil Advocacy: a practical guide, 1997, 2nd edn 2001; (contrib. ed.) Halsbury's Laws: practice and procedure, 2001. *Recreation:* chasing happiness. *Address:* Henderson Chambers, 2 Harcourt Buildings, Temple, EC4Y 9DB. *T:* (020) 7583 9020, *Fax:* (020) 7583 2686; *e-mail:* ppopat@hendersonchambers.co.uk.

POPAT, (Surendra) Andrew, CBE 1997; a Recorder, since 1998; *b* 31 Dec. 1943; *s* of late Dhirajlal Kurji Popat and Kashiben Popat (*née* Chitalia); *m* 1995, Suzanne Joy, *d* of Edward James Wayman and Beatrice Joyce Wayman; one *s*. *Educ:* Univ. of London (LLB); Univ. of Calif, Berkeley (LLM). Called to the Bar, Lincoln's Inn, 1969; Mem., Inner Temple, 1985; Associate Attorney, Willkie Farr & Gallaghar (NY), 1970–74; practising Barrister, specialising in criminal law, 1975–; Asst Recorder, 1992–98. Legal Mem., Criminal Injuries Compensation Appeals Panel, 2000–; Mem., Professional Conduct Cttee, 2000–, Professional Performance Cttee, 2002, GMC. Contested (C): Durham NE, 1983; Bradford S, 1992; London Reg., EP, 1999. Dir, John Patten's election campaign, 1987. Treas., Surbiton Cons. Assoc., 1985. Chm., Disraeli Club, 1993–. Trustee, Brooke Hosp. for Animals, 1998–2000. Freeman, City of London, 1987; Liveryman, Plaisterers' Co., 1987– (Mem. Ct of Assts, 2001–). *Recreations:* travel, theatre, cricket, tennis. *Address:* 9 King's Bench Walk, Temple, EC4Y 7DX. *T:* (020) 7353 3909. *Clubs:* Carlton, MCC.

POPE, His Holiness the; *see* Benedict XVI.

POPE, Cathryn Mary; soprano; *b* 6 July 1957; *m* 1st, 1982, Stuart Petersen (marr. diss. 1998); 2nd, 2003, Martin Barrell. *Educ:* Royal College of Music (ARCM); National Opera Studio. Début, ENO: Sophie, in Werther, 1983; Anna, in Moses, 1986; Susanna, in Marriage of Figaro, 1987; Gretel, in Hansel and Gretel, 1987; Oksana, in Christmas Eve, 1988; Despina, in Così fan tutte, 1988; Pamina, in Die Zauberflöte, 1989; Micaëla, in Carmen, 1993; Tatyana, in Eugene Onegin, 1994; Amsterdam: début, Gretel, 1990; Mélisande, in Pelléas et Mélisande, 1991; Elvira, in Don Giovanni, and Susanna, 1991; Opera Europa: Nedda, in Pagliacci, 1995; Giorgetta, in Il Tabarro; Nantes: Le Prostitué, in La Ronde. Numerous recordings.

POPE, Geoffrey Robert; Member (Lib Dem), London Assembly, Greater London Authority, 2005–08; *b* 9 April 1944; *s* of late George Pope and Stella Pope (*née* Edwards); *m* 1968, Margaret Victoria Thompson; one *s* one *d*. *Educ:* Kingsbury County Grammar Sch.; Hendon Coll. (HNC Applied Physics 1965). Mgt, SmithKline Beecham, 1969–98. Chm., Teddington Meml Hosp. and Community NHS Trust, 1998–2001; Dir, Kingston Hosp. NHS Trust, 2001–04. Mem. (Lib Dem) Richmond upon Thames LBC, 1982–98 (Mayor, 1989–90; Chm., Social Services, 1994–98). Chm., Transport Cttee, London Assembly, 2006–07. *Address: e-mail:* geoff.pope1@googlemail.com.

POPE, George Maurice, FRICS; independent surveyor, since 1999; *b* 12 Jan. 1943; *s* of Maj. John Pope; *m* 1968, Tessa Roselle Norman; one *s* two *d*. *Educ:* Eton. Capt., Coldstream Guards, 1962–69. With John D. Wood & Co., 1970–99, Chm., 1982–99. *Recreations:* racing, hunting, shooting, golf. *Address:* (office) 4 Pont Street, SW1X 9EL. *T:* (020) 7245 1277; Grounds Farm House, Fernham Road, Uffington, near Faringdon, Oxon SN7 7RD. *T:* (01367) 820234. *Clubs:* White's; Royal St George's Golf, Sunningdale Golf.

POPE, Gregory James; MP (Lab) Hyndburn, since 1992; *b* 29 Aug. 1960; *s* of Samuel J. Pope and Sheila M. (*née* Day); *m* 1985, Catherine M. Fallon; two *s* one *d*. *Educ:* St Mary's Coll., Blackburn; Univ. of Hull (BA Hons). Local govt officer, 1987–92. An Asst Govt Whip, 1997–99; a Lord Comr of HM Treasury (Govt Whip), 1999–2001. *Recreations:* walking, football, chess, music. *Address:* House of Commons, SW1A 0AA. *T:* (020) 7219 5842.

POPE, Jeremy James Richard, OBE 1985; DL; Chairman, English Farming and Food Partnership, 2003–08; *b* 15 July 1943; *s* of late Philip William Rolph Pope and of Joyce Winifred Harcourt Pope (*née* Slade); *m* 1969, Hon. Jacqueline Best; three *s*. *Educ:* Charterhouse; Trinity Coll., Cambridge. Law tripos, MA. Solicitor. Eldridge, Pope & Co., 1969–99: Finance and Planning Dir, 1972–82; Jt Man. Dir, 1982–88; Man. Dir, 1988–99; Chairman: Eldridge, Pope Fine Wines Ltd, 1999–2000; Milk Link Ltd, 2000–05; Chilworth Science Park Ltd, 2001–04; Exeter Investment Gp plc, 2003–04 (non-exec. Dir, 1999–2003). Chm., Smaller Firms Council, CBI, 1981–83; Member: NEDC, 1981–85; Top Salaries Review Body, 1986–93; Exec. Cttee, Food and Drinks Fedn, 1986–89 (Dep. Pres., 1987–89). Member: Royal Commn on Environmental Pollution, 1984–92; Wessex Regl Rivers Adv. Cttee, NRA, 1994–95; Bd, Bournemouth, Dorset and Poole LSC, 2001–04; Sustainable Farming and Food Strategy Implementation Gp, DEFRA, 2002–05. Chairman: Winterbourne Hosp. plc, 1981–89; Trustees, Wessex Medical Trust, 1993–97 (Trustee, 1991–97); Dorset Private Sector Forum, 1997–2000; Bournemouth, Dorset & Poole Economic Partnership, 1997–99; SW Chamber of Rural Enterprise, 2001–04; Dep. Chm., SW of England RDA, 1999–2004 (Bd Mem., 1998–2004). Mem., Wessex Regl Cttee, NT, 2007–. Dir, Weymouth and Portland Nat. Sailing Acad., 2004–. Gov., Forres Sch., Swanage, 1984–92; Mem. Council, Southampton Univ., 1999–2004. Trustee: Devonshire and Dorset Regtl Charity, 1994–2000; Tank Mus., 2000–; Jurassic Coast Trust (formerly World Heritage Coast Trust), 2004–; Chesil Trust, 2004–. Chm. Mgt Cttee, Mus. of Regts of Devon and Dorset, 1994–2000. DL Dorset, 2008. Liveryman: Gunmakers' Co., 1988; Innholders' Co., 1991 (Master, 2008–Oct. 2009). FRSA; ARAgS. Hon. DLitt Bournemouth, 1999. *Recreations:* shooting, fishing, gardening, cooking the resultant produce. *Address:* Field Cottage, West Compton, Dorchester, Dorset DT2 0EY. *T:* (01300) 320469.

POPE, Sir Joseph (Albert), Kt 1980; DSc, PhD (Belfast), WhSc; Director, since 1960, Consultant, since 1988, TQ International (formerly TecQuipment Group), Nottingham (Chairman, 1974–88); *b* 18 Oct. 1914; *s* of Albert Henry and Mary Pope; *m* 1940, Evelyn Alice Gallagher; one *s* two *d*. *Educ:* School of Arts and Crafts, Cambridge; King's College, London. Apprentice, Boulton & Pauls, Norwich, 1930–35. Whitworth Scholarship, 1935. Assistant Lecturer in Engineering, Queen's Univ., Belfast, 1938–44; Assistant Lecturer in Engineering, Univ. of Manchester, 1944–45; Lecturer, then Senior Lecturer, Univ. of Sheffield, 1945–49; Professor of Mechanical Engineering, Nottingham University, 1949–60; Research Dir, Mirrlees Nat. Research Div., Stockport, and Dir, Mirrlees National Ltd 1960–69; Vice-Chancellor, Univ. of Aston in Birmingham, 1969–79. Director: John Brown & Co. Ltd, 1970–82; Midlands Electricity Bd, 1975–80; Royal Worcester Ltd, 1979–83; Chm., W Midlands Econ. Planning Council, 1977–79. Gen. Treasurer, British Assoc., 1975–82; Pres., Whitworth Soc., 1978–79; Chm., Birmingham Civic Soc., 1978–79. Hon. LLD Birmingham, 1979; Hon. DUniv Heriot-Watt, 1979; Hon. DSc: Aston, 1979; Belfast, 1980; Salford, 1980; Nottingham, 1987. *Publications:* papers on the impact of metals and metal fatigue published in Proc. of Inst. of Mech. Engineers and Jl of Iron and Steel Inst. *Address:* 3 Mapperley Hall Drive, Nottingham NG3 5EP. *T:* (0115) 962 1146.

See also S. B. Pope.

POPE, Prof. Stephen Bailey, PhD, DSc (Eng); FRS 2007; Sibley College Professor of Mechanical Engineering, Cornell University, since 1998; *b* 26 Nov. 1949; *s* of Sir Joseph Albert Pope, *qv*; *m* 1979, Linda Ann Syatt; one *s* one *d*. *Educ:* Rydal Sch., Colwyn Bay; Imperial Coll., London (BSc (Eng.); MSc; PhD 1976; DIC); DSc (Eng) London 1986. ACGI. Mech. Engrg, Imperial Coll., London, 1972–77; Res. Fellow, Applied Maths, CIT, 1977–78; Asst Prof., then Associate Prof., of Mech. Engrg, MIT, 1978–81; Associate Prof., then Prof. of Mech. and Aerospace Engrg, Cornell Univ., 1982–. Dir, TQ Gp Ltd, 1995–. Fellow, Amer. Acad. Arts and Scis, 2007. *Publications:* Turbulent Flows, 2000; scientific articles in combustion and fluid dynamics. *Address:* Sibley School of Mechanical and Aerospace Engineering, Upson Hall, Cornell University, Ithaca, NY 14853, USA. *T:* (607) 2554314; *e-mail:* s.b.pope@cornell.edu.

POPHAM, Stuart Godfrey; Senior Partner, Clifford Chance, since 2003; *b* 20 July 1954; *s* of late George Godfrey Popham and Ena Majorie Popham; *m* 1978, Carolyn Dawe; one *s* two *d*. *Educ:* Southampton Univ. (LLB 1975). Admitted solicitor, 1978; joined Clifford-Turner, subseq. Clifford Chance, 1976: Partner, 1984; Hd of Finance, 2000–03. Chm., London Bd and Mem., Internat. Adv. Bd, CBI, 2005–. Member: Council, RIIA, 2005–; Adv. Forum, Saïd Business Sch., Oxford, 2005–. *Recreations:* sailing, theatre, ballet, water sports. *Address:* c/o Clifford Chance, 10 Upper Bank Street, E14 5JJ. *T:* (020) 7006 1000, *Fax:* (020) 7006 5555.

POPPLEWELL, Andrew John; QC 1997; a Recorder, since 2002; *b* 14 Jan. 1959; *s* of Sir Oliver Popplewell, *qv* and late (Catharine) Margaret Popplewell; *m* 1984, Debra Ellen Lomas; one *s* two *d*. *Educ:* Radley Coll.; Downing Coll., Cambridge (MA 1st cl. Law). Called to the Bar, Inner Temple, 1981. *Address:* Brick Court Chambers, 7–8 Essex Street, WC2R 3LD. *T:* (020) 7379 3550. *Club:* Hawks (Cambridge).

POPPLEWELL, Sir Oliver (Bury), Kt 1983; Judge of the High Court of Justice, Queen's Bench Division, 1983–99; *b* 15 Aug. 1927; *s* of late Frank and Nina Popplewell; *m* 1954, Catharine Margaret Storey (*d* 2001); four *s* (and one *s* decd); *m* 2008, Hon. Dame

Elizabeth Gloster, *qv*. *Educ:* Charterhouse (Schol.); Queens' Coll., Cambridge (Class. exhibnr; BA 1950; LLB 1951; MA); Harris Manchester Coll., Oxford (BA 2006; Hon. Fellow, 2006); London Sch. of Economics (MA 2008). FCIArb 1996. CUCC, 1949–51. Called to the Bar, Inner Temple, 1951, Bencher, 1978; QC 1969; Chartered Arbitrator; Accredited Mediator, 2000. Recorder, Burton-on-Trent, 1970–71; Dep. Chm., Oxon QS, 1970–71; a Recorder of the Crown Court, 1972–82. Indep. Mem., Wages Councils, 1962–82, Chm. 1973–82; Mem., Home Office Adv. Bd on Restricted Patients, 1981–82; Vice-Chm., Parole Bd, 1986–87 (Mem., 1985–87); Mem., Parole Review Cttee, 1987–88; Pres., Employment Appeal Tribunal, 1986–88 (Mem., 1984–85); Mem., London Court of Internat. Arbitration, 2000–. Chairman: Inquiry into Crowd Safety and Control at sports grounds, 1985–86; Sports Dispute Panel, 2000–; English Rep., ICC Commn into Corruption, 1999; Mem., Ct of Arbitration for Sport, 2000–. MCC: Mem. Cttee, 1971–74, 1976–79, 1980–97; Trustee, 1983–94; Pres., 1994–96. Gov., Sutton's Hosp. in Charterhouse, 1986–88. Trustee, Bletchley Park Trust, 1999–2008. *Publications:* Benchmark: life, laughter and the law, 2003; Hallmark: a judge at Oxford, 2008. *Recreations:* sailing, cricket, tennis. *Address:* Tuesday Cottage, Quainton, HP22 4AS. *Clubs:* Garrick, MCC; Hawks (Cambridge); Vincent's (Oxford); XL; Blakeney Sailing.
See also A. J. Popplewell.

PORCHESTER, Lord; George Kenneth Oliver Molyneux Herbert; *b* 13 Oct. 1992; *s and heir* of Earl of Carnarvon, *qv*.

PORRITT, Hon. Sir Jonathon (Espie), 2nd Bt *cr* 1963, of Hampstead, co. London; CBE 2000; freelance writer and broadcaster; Chairman, Sustainable Development Commission, since 2000; *b* 6 July 1950; *s* of Baron Porritt, GCMG, GCVO, CBE and Kathleen Mary (*d* 1998), 2nd *d* of A. S. Peck; *S* to Btcy of father, 1994; *m* 1986, Sarah Elizabeth Staniforth, *qv*; two *d*. *Educ:* Eton; Magdalen Coll., Oxford (BA (First Cl.) Modern Languages). ILEA Teacher, 1975–84: Head of English and Drama, Burlington Danes School, W12, 1980–84; Director: Friends of The Earth, 1984–90; Forum for the Future, 1996–. Co-Dir, Prince of Wales's Business and Envmtl Prog., 1994–. Presenter, Where on earth are we going?, BBC TV, 1990. Ecology Party: candidate: General Elections, 1979 and 1983; European Elections, 1979 and 1984; Local Elections, 1977, 1978, 1982; Party Council Member, 1978–80, 1982–84; Chairman, 1979–80, 1982–84. *Publications:* Seeing Green—the Politics of Ecology, 1984; Friends of the Earth Handbook, 1987; The Coming of the Greens, 1988; Where on Earth are We Going?, 1991; (ed) Save the Earth, 1991; Captain Eco (for children), 1991; Playing Safe: science and the environment, 2000; Capitalism as if the World Matters, 2005. *Recreation:* walking. *Heir: b* Hon. Jeremy Charles Porritt [*b* 19 Jan. 1953; *m* 1980, Penny, *d* of J. H. Moore; two *s*]. *Address:* 9 Lypiatt Terrace, Cheltenham, Glos GL50 2SX.

PORRITT, Sarah Elizabeth, (Hon. Lady Porritt); *see* Staniforth, S. E.

PORTAL, Sir Jonathan (Francis), 6th Bt *cr* 1901; FCA; freelance accountant, since 1993; *b* 13 Jan. 1953; *s* of Sir Francis Spencer Portal, 5th Bt, and of Jane Mary, *d* of late Albert Henry Williams, OBE; *S* father, 1984; *m* 1982, Louisa Caroline, *er d* of Sir John Hervey-Bathurst, Bt, *qv*; three *s*. *Educ:* Marlborough; Univ. of Edinburgh (BCom). FCA (ACA 1977). Gp Financial Controller, Henderson Admin, 1989–91; Finance Dir, Grosvenor Ventures Ltd, 1992–93. Treas., N Hants Br., CPRE. Gov., Old Malthouse Trust (formerly Old Malthouse Sch.). Mem., Clothworkers' Co. *Heir: s* William Jonathan Francis Portal, *b* 1 Jan. 1987. *Address:* Burley Wood, Ashe, Basingstoke, Hants RG25 3AG.

PORTARLINGTON, 7th Earl of, *cr* 1785; **George Lionel Yuill Seymour Dawson-Damer;** Baron Dawson 1770; Viscount Carlow 1776; *b* 10 Aug. 1938; *er s* of Air Commodore Viscount Carlow (killed on active service, 1944) and Peggy (who *m* 2nd, 1945, Peter Nugent; she *d* 1963), *yr d* of late Charles Cambie; *S* grandfather, 1959; *m* 1961, Davina, *e d* of Sir Edward Windley, KCMG, KCVO; three *s* one *d*. *Educ:* Eton. Page of Honour to the Queen, 1953–55. Director: G. S. Yuill & Co. Ltd, Sydney, 1964–; Australian Stock Breeders Co. Ltd, Brisbane, 1966–. *Recreations:* fishing, ski-ing, books. *Heir: s* Viscount Carlow, *qv*. *Address:* Gledswood, Melrose, Roxburghshire TD6 9DN. *T:* (01896) 822558, *Fax:* (01896) 823324; 118 Wolseley Road, Point Piper, NSW 2027, Australia. *T:* (2) 93639725, *Fax:* (2) 93274691. *Clubs:* Union, Australian (Sydney); Royal Sydney Golf.

PORTEN, Anthony Ralph; QC 1988; *b* 1 March 1947; *s* of late Ralph Charles Porten and of Joan Porten (*née* Edden); *m* 1970, Kathryn Mary (*née* Edwards); two *d*. *Educ:* Epsom Coll.; Emmanuel Coll., Cambridge (BA; Athletics Blue, 1967). Called to the Bar, Inner Temple, 1969, Bencher, 2002; joined Lincoln's Inn (*ad eund.*), 1973; Hd of Chambers, 2001–06; practising mainly in town and country planning and local government work. A Recorder, 1993–2001; Asst Boundary Comr, 2001–. Fellow, Soc. for Advanced Legal Studies, 1999. *Address:* Clive Cottage, Claremont Drive, Esher, Surrey KT10 9LU. *T:* (01372) 467513; 2–3 Gray's Inn Square, WC1R 5JH. *T:* (020) 7242 4986. *Clubs:* Royal Automobile; Hawks (Cambridge).

PORTEOUS, Christopher Selwyn, CBE 1993; Solicitor to Commissioner of Police for the Metropolis, 1987–95; *b* 8 Nov. 1935; *s* of Selwyn Berkeley Porteous (*né* Potous) and Marjorie Irene Porteous; *m* 1st, 1960, Brenda Jacqueline Wallis (marr. diss. 2005); four *d*; 2nd, 2007, Kathleen Patricia Horton. *Educ:* Dulwich Coll.; Law Society Sch. of Law. Articled to Clerk to Malling RDC, 1954–60; qual. as solicitor, 1960; LCC, 1960–62; Legal Asst with Scotland Yard, 1962–68; Sen. Legal Asst, 1968–76; Asst Solicitor, 1976–87. Pres., Assoc. of Police Lawyers, 1995–98; Mem., Solicitors European Gp, 1991–96. Anglican Reader, 1958–2002; Mem., Pastoral Cttee, Rochester Dio., 1984–88. Hon. Mem., ACPO, 1995. *Recreations:* reading, poetry, hymn writing, walking, local history. *Address:* c/o Boys and Maughan, 83 Station Road, Birchington, Kent CT7 9RB.

PORTEOUS, Prof. David John, PhD; FRCPE, FMedSci; FRSE; Professor of Human Molecular Genetics and Medicine, University of Edinburgh, since 1996; *b* 3 July 1954; *s* of John and Jean Porteous; *m* 1976, Rosemary Braid; three *d*. *Educ:* Aberdeen Grammar Sch.; Univ. of Edinburgh (BSc Biol Scis 1975; PhD Genetics 1978). FRCPE 2004. Res. Fellow, Univ. of Oxford, 1978–81; Jun. Res. Fellow, Wolfson Coll., Oxford, 1980–81; MRC Recombinant DNA Res. Fellow, MRC Mammalian Genome Unit, Edinburgh, 1981–84; MRC Human Genetics Unit, Edinburgh: Staff Scientist, 1984–86; scientific non-clinical career appt to MRC, Grade 1, 1986–93; Hd of Molecular Genetics, 1993–96. Scientific Advr, H of C Select Cttee on Sci. and Technol., 1994–96. Founder, Generation Scotland, 2007. Pioneered Cystic Fibrosis Gene Therapy, 1995; discovered DISC1, 2005. FMedSci 1999; FRSE 2001. *Recreations:* walking, cycling, windsurfing, ski-ing, reading, cinema, travelling, family, France. *Address:* Medical Genetics Section, Molecular Medicine Centre, University of Edinburgh, Crewe Road South, Edinburgh EH4 2XU. *T:* (0131) 651 1040, *Fax:* (0131) 651 1059; *e-mail:* david.porteous@ed.ac.uk.

PORTEOUS, James; DL; FREng, FIET; Chairman and Chief Executive, Yorkshire Electricity Group plc, 1990–92; *b* 29 Dec. 1926; *e s* of James and Isabella Porteous; *m* 1960, Sheila Beatrice (*née* Klotz); two *d*. *Educ:* Jarrow Grammar School; King's College, Durham University (BSc Hons). FREng (FEng 1986). NESCo Ltd, NE Electricity Bd, NE Div., BEA, 1945–62; Central Electricity Generating Board: Operations Dept, HQ, 1962–66; System Op. Eng., Midlands Region, 1966–70; Dir, Operational Planning, SE Region, 1970–72; NE Region, 1972–75; Dir-Gen., Midlands Region, 1975–84; Chm., Yorks Electricity Bd, 1984–90. Mem., Electricity Council, 1984–90; Director: Electricity Association Ltd, 1990–92; National Grid Company (Holdings) plc, 1990–92. Chm., BR (Eastern) Board, 1990–92 (Mem., 1986–90); Mem., E Midlands Economic Planning Council, 1976–79. Director: Peter Peregrinus Ltd, 1981–92, 1993–96; Merz and McLellan Ltd, 1992–96; Parsons Brinckerhoff Ltd, 1995–98; Nuclear Liabilities (formerly Nuclear Generation Decommissioning) Fund Ltd, 1996–2008; PB Power Ltd, 1998–2002. Vice-Pres., IEE, 1992–93 (Hon. FIET (Hon. FIEE 1997)). National Vice-President: Opportunities for People with Disabilities, 1990–92; Nat. Energy Action, 1992–2008. Hon. DSc Aston, 1990; Hon. DEng Bradford, 1991. DL N Yorks, 1991. *Recreations:* highland life, railways. *Club:* Caledonian.

PORTER, Alastair Robert Wilson, CBE 1985; Secretary and Registrar, Royal College of Veterinary Surgeons, 1966–91, retired; barrister; *b* 28 Sept. 1928; *s* of late James and Olivia Porter (*née* Duncan); *m* 1954, Jennifer Mary Priaulx Forman; two *s* one *d*. *Educ:* Irvine Royal Academy; Glasgow Academy; Merton Coll., Oxford (MA). Called to Bar, Gray's Inn, 1952. Resident Magistrate, N Rhodesia, 1954; Registrar of High Court of N Rhodesia, 1961; Permanent Secretary: Min. of Justice, N Rhodesia, 1964; Min. of Justice, Govt of Republic of Zambia, Oct. 1964. Mem., Fedn (formerly Liaison Cttee) of Veterinarians of the EEC, 1966–86, Sec.-Gen., 1973–79; Chm., EEC's Adv. Cttee on Veterinary Trng, 1986–87 (Vice-Chm., 1981–86). Lectures: Wooldridge Meml, BVA Congress, 1976; MacKellar Meml, Western Counties Veterinary Assoc., Tavistock, 1978; Weipers, Glasgow Univ., 1985; Keith Entwhistle Meml, Cambridge Univ., 1987. Vice-Chm., Haywards Heath Police Community Forum, 2000–02; Chm., Univ. of the Third Age, Haywards Heath, 2007–08. Hon. Member: BVA, 1978; British Small Animals Vet. Assoc., 1991; Australian Vet. Assoc., 1991; Latvian Vet. Assoc., 1997; Fedn of Veterinarians of Europe, 2002; Hon. Associate, RCVS, 1979. Vice-Pres., Blue Cross, 2006– (Gov., 1991–2000; Chm., Bd of Govs, 1995–98; Pres., 2000–05). Hon. DVMS Glasgow, 1994. Centenary Prize, 1981, and Victory Medal, 1991, Central Vet. Soc.; Akademische Ehrenbürger, Hannover Veterinary Sch., 1988. *Publication:* (jtly) An Anatomy of Veterinary Europe, 1972. *Address:* 4 Savill Road, Lindfield, West Sussex RH16 2NX. *T:* (01444) 482001.

PORTER, Amanda Eve; *see* Pinto, A. E.

PORTER, Andrew Brian; Music Critic, Times Literary Supplement, since 1997; *b* 26 Aug. 1928; *s* of Andrew Ferdinand Porter and Vera Sybil (*née* Bloxham). *Educ:* University Coll., Oxford (MA). Music Critic, Financial Times, 1952–72; Editor, Musical Times, 1960–67; Music Critic: New Yorker, 1972–92; The Observer, 1992–97. Vis. Fellow, All Souls Coll., Oxford, 1972–73; Bloch Prof., Univ. of Calif, Berkeley, 1980–81. Corresp. Mem., Amer. Musicol Soc., 1994. *Publications:* A Musical Season, 1974; The Ring of the Nibelung, 1976; Music of Three Seasons, 1978; Music of Three More Seasons, 1981; (ed with D. Rosen) Verdi's Macbeth: a sourcebook, 1984; The Tempest (opera libretto), 1985; Musical Events 1980–1983, 1987; Musical Events 1983–1986, 1989; The Song of Majnun (opera libretto), 1991; A Music Critic Remembers, 2000; *festschrift:* Words on Music (ed. C. Brook and D. Rosen), 2003; many opera translations; contrib. Music & Letters, Musical Qly, etc. *Address:* 9 Pembroke Walk, W8 6PQ.

PORTER, Andrew James; Political Editor, Daily Telegraph, since 2007; *b* Welwyn Garden City, 28 Sept. 1972; *s* of Arthur George Porter and Eileen Porter (*née* Nickolls). *Educ:* Dame Alice Owen's Sch.; Warwick Univ. (BA Hons Hist. and Pols); Cardiff Univ. (Postgrad. Dip. Journalism). Reporter, 1997–98, London Ed., 1998–2000, Western Morning News; Political Ed., Sunday Business, 2000–03; Business Corresp., 2003–04, Dep. Political Ed., 2004–06, Sunday Times; Dep. Political Ed., The Sun, 2006–07. *Recreations:* golf, football. *Address:* Press Gallery, House of Commons, SW1A 0AA. *T:* (020) 7219 5719; *e-mail:* andrew.porter@telegraph.co.uk. *Clubs:* Royal Automobile; Old Fold Manor Golf.

PORTER, Prof. Andrew Neil, PhD; Rhodes Professor of Imperial History, King's College, London, since 1993; *b* 12 Oct. 1945; *s* of Peter Tozer Porter and Muriel Betty Porter (*née* Luer); *m* 1972, Mary Faulkner; two *s*. *Educ:* Chester Cathedral Choir Sch.; Christ's Hosp., Horsham; St John's Coll., Cambridge (MA, PhD). LRAM. Lectr in History, Univ. of Manchester, 1970–71; King's College, London: Lectr in History, 1971–85; Reader, 1985–90; Head of History Dept, 1988–94 and 2000–01; Prof. of History, 1990–93; FKC 2005. Hon. Sec., RHistS, 1986–90 (FRHistS 1980); Convenor, History at Univs Defence Gp, 1992–96 (Mem., Steering Cttee, 1990–99); Chm., Adv. Council (formerly Bd of Mgt), Inst. of Commonwealth Studies, 1994–2001. Mem. Council, Friends of PRO, 1991–99. FRSA 1998. Editor, Jl of Imperial and Commonwealth History, 1979–90. *Publications:* The Origins of the South African War, 1980; Victorian Shipping, Business and Imperial Policy, 1986; (jtly) British Imperial Policy and Decolonization 1938–64, vol. 1, 1987, vol. 2, 1989; (ed jtly) Money, Finance and Empire 1790–1860, 1985; (ed jtly) Theory and Practice in the History of European Expansion Overseas, 1988; (ed) Atlas of British Overseas Expansion, 1991 (Japanese edn 1996); European Imperialism 1860–1914, 1994 (Korean edn 2001, Japanese edn 2006); (ed and contrib.) The Oxford History of the British Empire, Vol. III, The Nineteenth Century, 1999; (ed) Bibliography of Imperial, Colonial and Commonwealth History since 1600, 2002; (ed) The Imperial Horizons of British Protestant Missions, 1880–1914, 2003; Religion versus Empire? British Protestant Missionaries and Overseas Expansion 1700–1914 (Trevor Reese Meml Prize, Inst. of Commonwealth Studies), 2004. *Recreations:* playing chamber music, mountain walking, travel. *Address:* 5 Farm Close, Clun, Shropshire SY7 8LJ; Department of History, King's College London, Strand, WC2R 2LS. *T:* (020) 7848 1078.

PORTER, Rt Rev. Anthony; *see* Sherwood, Bishop Suffragan of.

PORTER, Prof. Arthur, OC 1983; MSc, PhD (Manchester); FIEE; FCAE; FRSC 1970; Professor of Industrial Engineering, and Chairman of Department, University of Toronto, Toronto, 1961–76, now Emeritus Professor; President, Arthur Porter Associates Ltd, since 1973; Associate, Institute for Environmental Studies, University of Toronto, since 1981; *b* 8 Dec. 1910; *s* of late John William Porter and Mary Anne Harris; *m* 1941, Phyllis Patricia Dixon; one *s*. *Educ:* The Grammar Sch., Ulverston; University of Manchester. Asst Lecturer, University of Manchester, 1936–37; Commonwealth Fund Fellow, Massachusetts Inst. of Technology, USA, 1937–39; Scientific Officer, Admiralty, 1939–45; Principal Scientific Officer, National Physical Laboratory, 1946; Prof. of Instrument Technology, Royal Military Coll. of Science, 1946–49; Head, Research Division, Ferranti Electric Ltd, Toronto, Canada, 1949–55; Professor of Light Electrical Engineering, Imperial College of Science and Technology, University of London, 1955–58; Dean of the College of Engineering, Saskatchewan Univ., Saskatoon, 1958; Acting Dir, Centre for Culture and Technology, Toronto Univ., 1967–68; Academic Comr, Univ. of W Ontario, 1969–71. Dir and Founding Chm., Scientists and Engineers for Energy and Environment Inc., 1981–84. Chairman: Canadian Environmental Adv. Council, 1972–75; Ontario Royal Commn on Electric Power Planning, 1975–80. Hon. DSc Manchester, 2004. *Publications:* An Introduction to Servomechanisms, 1950; Cybernetics Simplified, 1969; Towards a Community University, 1971; So Many Hills to Climb, 2004 (autobiog.); articles in Trans. Royal Society, Proc. Royal Society, Phil. Mag., Proc. Inst. Mech. Eng, Proc. IEE, Nature, etc. *Recreations:* travel, energy conservation. *Address:* 3314 Bermuda Village, Advance, NC 27006–9479, USA. *Club:* Bermuda Run Country (Advance, NC).

PORTER, Arthur Thomas, MRSL 1979; MA, PhD; Pro-Chancellor and Chairman of Court, University of Sierra Leone, Freetown, Sierra Leone, 1992–99 (Vice-Chancellor, 1974–84); *b* 26 Jan. 1924; *m* 1953, Rigmor Sondergaard (*née* Rasmussen) (*d* 2005); one *s* one *d*. *Educ:* Fourah Bay Coll. (BA Dunelm); Cambridge Univ. (BA (Hist Tripos), MA); Boston Univ. (PhD). Asst, Dept of Social Anthropology, Edinburgh Univ., UK, 1951–52. Prof. of History and Head of Dept of Hist., also Dir of Inst. of African Studies, Fourah Bay Coll., 1963–64; Principal, University Coll., Nairobi, Univ. of E Africa, 1964–70; UNESCO Field Staff Officer; Educl Planning Adviser, Min. of Educn, Kenya, 1970–74. Mem. Exec. Bd, UNESCO, 1976–80. Africanus Horton Meml Lectr, Edinburgh Univ., 1983; Fulbright Schol.-in-Residence, Bethany Coll., Kansas, 1986–87. Chm., Bd of Dirs, Sierra Leone Nat. Diamond Mining Co., 1976–85. Hon. LHD Boston 1969; Hon. LLD Royal Univ. of Malta, 1969; Hon. DLitt: Sierra Leone, 1988; Nairobi, 1994. Phi Beta Kappa 1972. Symonds Medal, ACU, 1985. *Publications:* Creoledom, a Study of the Development of Freetown Society, 1963; contribs to The Times, Africa, African Affairs. *Recreation:* photography. *Address:* 85 Marlborough Avenue, Ottawa, ON K1N 8E8, Canada; 81 Fitzjohn Avenue, Barnet, Herts EN5 2HN; 26b Spur Road, Wilberforce, PO Box 1363, Freetown, Sierra Leone, West Africa. *T:* (22) 231736.

PORTER, Sister Bernadette Mary, CBE 2005; PhD; Provincial Treasurer, Society of the Sacred Heart, since 2007; Vice-Chancellor, Roehampton University (formerly Rector and Chief Executive, Roehampton Institute, then University of Surrey Roehampton), 1999–2004 (Hon. Fellow, 2006); *b* 21 July 1952; *d* of Owen and Teresa Porter. *Educ:* Merrow Grange, Guildford; Digby Stuart Coll. (Cert Ed); King's Coll. London (BEd 1979; PhD 1989); Kingston Univ. (DMS). Mem., Soc. of the Sacred Heart, 1973–. Teacher: Woldington Sch., 1973–75; Sacred Heart, Newcastle, 1975–78; Our Lady's Convent, 1980–82; Kalunga Girls' Sch., Masaka, Uganda, 1982–83; Roehampton Institute, London: Lectr, 1983–89; Coll. Principal, 1989–99; Sen. Pro-Rector, 1995–99. Member: Council of Church Colls, 1989–2004; Council, Univ. of Surrey, 1999–2004; UUK, 1999–2004; Southwark Cathedral Council, 2001–; Cumberlege Commn, 2006–; Chm., Educn Cttee, RC dio. of Southwark, 2006–. Mem., Internat. Women's Forum, 2000–. Trustee: St Mary's Sch., Shaftesbury, 1999–; Higher Educn Foundn, 2002–05; Regent, Marymount Internat. Sch., 2002–05; Villiers Park Educnl Trust, 2004–. Chm. Trustees, Regenerate.com, 2005–; Mem., Neuro-disability Res. Trust, 2005–. Patron, Coll., of Teachers, 2005–. Governor: Wimbledon Sch. of Art, 2003–07; Heythrop Coll., 2007–. MInstD 1999. FRSA 1997. DUniv Middlesex, 2004. *Publications:* contrib. various articles. *Recreations:* gardening, walking, travel, music. *Address:* 10 Rodway Road, SW15 5DS; *e-mail:* bm.porter@btinternet.com. *Club:* Reform.

PORTER, David John; Head of Drama, since 1998 and Co-ordinator of Performance Studies, since 2002, Kirkley High School, Lowestoft; *b* 16 April 1948; *s* of late George Porter and of Margaret Porter; *m* 1978, Sarah Jane Shaw; two *s* two *d*. *Educ:* Lowestoft Grammar School; New College of Speech and Drama, London. Teacher, London, 1970–72; Dir and Co-Founder, Vivid Children's Theatre, 1972–78; Head of Drama, Benjamin Britten High School, Lowestoft, 1978–81; Conservative Party Agent: Eltham, 1982–83; Norwich North, 1983–84; Waveney, 1985–87. MP (C) Waveney, 1987–97; contested (C) same seat, 1997. Member, Select Committee: on Social Security, 1991–92; for Educn, 1992–96; for Educn and Employment, 1996–97. Dir, David Porter Freelance Communications, 1997–99. *Recreations:* family, Waveney area—past, present and future. *Address:* 11 Irex Road, Pakefield, Lowestoft, Suffolk NR33 7BU.

PORTER, Prof. Dorothy Elizabeth, (Mrs B. P. Dolan), PhD; FRHistS; Professor in History of the Health Sciences, since 2002 and Chair, since 2004, Department of Anthropology, History and Social Medicine, University of California, San Francisco; *b* 8 June 1953; *d* of John Dudley Mayne Watkins and Eileen Catherine Watkins (*née* Justice); *m* 1st, 1987, Roy Sydney Porter, FBA (marr. diss. 1997; he *d* 2002); 2nd, 2000, Brian Patrick Dolan. *Educ:* Univ. of Sussex (BA Sociol. 1976; MA Urban and Regl Studies 1977); University Coll. London (PhD 1984). FRHistS 1991. Fellow, Wellcome Inst. for Hist. of Medicine, 1985–88; Res. Associate, UCLA, 1988–89; Res. Fellow, Univ. of Calif., San Francisco, 1989–90; Vis. Asst Prof., Harvard Univ., 1990–91; Birkbeck College, University of London: Lectr, 1991–94, Sen. Lectr, 1994–97; Wellcome Reader in Hist. of Medicine, 1997–98; Prof. in the Hist. of Sci. and Medicine, 1998–2002; Pro-Vice Master for Internat. and Res. Students, 2001–02. Mem., Soc. for Social Hist. of Medicine, 1981. Founding Mem., Internat. Network for Hist. of Public Health, 1991; Member: Amer. Assoc. for Hist. of Medicine, 1990; Eur. Assoc. for Hist. of Medicine and Health, 1994. *Publications:* (with R. Porter) In Sickness and In Health: the British experience 1650–1850, 1988; (with R. Porter) Patient's Progress: doctors and doctoring in Eighteenth Century England, 1989; (ed jtly) The Codification of Medical Ethics, vol. 1, The Eighteenth Century, 1992; (ed with R. Porter) Doctors, Politics and Society: historical essays, 1993; (Introd.) John Ryle, Changing Disciplines, 1994; (ed) The History of Health and the Modern State, 1994, 2nd edn 2006; (ed) Social Medicine and Medical Sociology in the Twentieth Century, 1997; Health, Civilisation and the State: a history of public health from ancient to modern times, 1999, 2nd edn 2005. *Address:* Department of Anthropology, History and Social Medicine, School of Medicine, University of California, San Francisco, CA 94143–0850, USA. *T:* (415) 4768826, *Fax:* (415) 4766715; *e-mail:* dporter@itsa.ucsf.edu.

PORTER, Henry Christopher Mansel; writer and journalist; London Editor, Vanity Fair, since 1992; *b* 23 March 1953; *s* of Major H. R. M. Porter, MBE and Anne Victoria Porter (*née* Seymour); *m* 1990, Elizabeth Mary Elliot; two *d*. *Educ:* Wellington Coll.; Manchester Univ. (BA Hons). Columnist, Sunday Times, 1982–87; Editor: Illustrated London News, 1987–89; Correspondent Mag., 1989–90; Exec. Ed., Independent on Sunday, 1990–91; contributor, 1991–, to London Evening Standard, Guardian, Observer, Daily Telegraph, Independent on Sunday. *Publications:* Lies, Damned Lies, 1984; *novels:* Remembrance Day, 1999; A Spy's Life, 2001; Empire State, 2003; Brandenburg (CWA Ian Fleming Steel Dagger), 2005; The Master of the Fallen Chairs, 2008. *Recreations:* painting, walking, gardening, reading. *Address:* Lloyds Bank, Pershore, Worcs WR10 1BD.

PORTER, Ivor Forsyth, CMG 1963; OBE (mil.) 1944; HM Diplomatic Service, retired; *b* 12 Nov. 1913; *s* of Herbert and Evelyn Porter; *m* 1951, Ann, *o d* of late Dr John Speares (marr. diss., 1961); *m* 1961, Katerina, *o c* of A. T. Cholerton; one *s* one *d*. *Educ:* Barrow Grammar Sch.; Leeds Univ. (BA, PhD). Lecturer at Bucharest Univ., 1939–40; Temp. Secretary, at Bucharest Legation, 1940–41; Raiding Forces, 1941–45 (Major). Joined Foreign (subseq. Diplomatic) Service, May 1946, as 2nd Secretary in Sen. Branch; 1st Secretary 1948; transferred to Washington, 1951; Foreign Office, 1953; UK Delegation to NATO Paris as Counsellor and Head of Chancery, 1956; Nicosia, 1959 (Deputy Head UK Mission), Deputy High Commissioner, 1961–62, Cyprus; Permanent Rep. to Council of Europe, Strasbourg, 1962–65 (with personal rank of Minister); Dep. High Commissioner, Eastern India, 1965–66; Ambassador, UK Delegn to Geneva Disarmament Conf., 1968–71 (Minister, 1967–68); Ambassador to Senegal, Guinea, Mali and Mauritania, 1971–73; later Dir, Atlantic Region, Research Dept, FCO, retired. Comdr, Order of Cultural Merit (Romania), 2005. *Publications:* (as Ivor Crane) The Think Trap (novel), 1972; Operation Autonomous: with SOE in wartime Roumania, 1989; Michael of Romania: the King and the Country, 2005. *Recreations:* writing, walking. *Address:* 17 Redcliffe Road, SW10 9NP. *Clubs:* Travellers, PEN.

PORTER, James Forrest, CBE 1991; Director General (formerly Director) of the Commonwealth Institute, 1978–91; Leverhulme Research Fellow, 1991–99, Visiting Fellow, 1991–93, Head of International Development, 1993–95 and Acting Dean for New Initiatives, 1995–96, London University Institute of Education; *b* Frodsham, Cheshire, 2 Oct. 1928; *s* of Ernest Porter and Mary Violetta Porter; *m* 1952, Dymphna (*d* 2006), *d* of Leo Francis Powell, London; two *d*. *Educ:* Salford Grammar Sch.; LSE (BSc Sociol.); Univ. of London Inst. of Educn (MA). Asst Master, St George in the East Sec. Sch., Stepney, 1948–50; Leverhulme Scholar, Univ. of London, 1950–55; Lectr in Sociol. and Educn, Worcester Coll., 1955–60; Head of Educn Dept, Chorley Coll., 1960–62; Dep. Principal, Coventry Coll., 1962–67; Principal, Bulmershe Coll. of Higher Educn, Reading, 1967–78. Director: bi-annual internat. courses on teacher educn, Brit. Council, 1975, 1977, 1979, on Museum Educn, 1982; Adult Literacy Support Services Fund, 1977–81. Consultant: Finland, 1976; Unesco, Paris, 1979–; Commonwealth Fellow, Australia, 1977. Chm., Newsconcern Foundn, 1984–91; Member: Nat. Cttee of Inquiry into Teacher Educn and Trng (James Cttee), 1971; Educn Cttee, UGC, 1970–78; Educnl Adv. Council, IBA, 1970–80; Nat. Council for Dance Educn, 1978; Exec. Cttee, Internat. Council of Museums, 1981–87; Educn Council, BBC, 1987–92; President: British Comparative Educn Soc., 1983–84; World Educn Fellowship, 1989– (Chm., 1979–82). Member: UK Delegn to Unesco, Geneva, 1975 (Vice-Pres., Commn on Changing Role of Teacher); Unesco Missions to Morocco and Senegal, 1982, to Jordan, 1983. Mem., Educn Council, Royal Opera House, Covent Garden, 1985–91; Gov., Henley Coll. Corp., 2008–. Mem., Editorial Bd, Higher Education Review, 1974–; Chm., Editorial Bd, Commonwealth Today, 1985–89 (Mem., 1982). FRSA 1978; Hon. FCP 1978; FRGS 1984. *Publications:* (ed) Rural Development and the Changing Countries of the World, 1969; (with N. Goble) The Changing Role of the Teacher, Paris 1977; Reschooling and the Global Future: politics, economics and the English experience, 1999. *Recreations:* writing, river watching. *Address:* The Garden Flat, The Hermitage, 29 Vicarage Road, Henley-on-Thames RG9 1HT.

PORTER, Janet S.; *see* Street-Porter.

PORTER, Air Vice-Marshal John Alan, OBE 1973; CEng, FRAeS, FIET; Deputy Vice-Chancellor and Professor, University of Glamorgan, 1994–99, now Professor Emeritus; *b* 29 Sept. 1934; *s* of late Alan and Etta Porter; *m* 1961, Sandra Rose (marr. diss.); two *s*; *m* 2002, Veronica Kennedy. *Educ:* Lawrence Sheriff School, Rugby; Bristol Univ. (BSc); Southampton Univ. (Dip Soton). Commissioned in Engineer Branch, RAF, 1953; appts in UK, USA and Cyprus, 1953–79; Royal College of Defence Studies, 1980; Dep. Gen. Manager, NATO MRCA Develt and Production Agency (NAMMA), Munich, 1981–84; Dir-Gen. Aircraft 2, MoD(PE), 1984–88; Dir-Gen., Communications, Inf. Systems and Orgn (RAF), 1988–89; RAF retd, 1989. Dir, Communications-Electronics Security Gp, 1989–91; Dir, Sci. and Technol., GCHQ, 1991–94. Vis. Fellow, Cranfield Univ., 1994–97. Chm. Council, University Coll. Plymouth St Mark and St John, 2008–. Hon. DSc Glamorgan, 2005. *Recreations:* music, horology. *Address:* University of Glamorgan, Pontypridd, Mid Glam CF37 1DC. *Club:* Royal Air Force.

PORTER, Sir John Simon H.; *see* Horsbrugh-Porter.

PORTER, Leonard Keith; Chief Executive, Rail Safety and Standards Board, since 2003; *b* 17 March 1952; *s* of Leonard Oram Porter and Irene Anne Porter (*née* Whitfield); *m* 1983, Victoria Louise Wigham; one *s* two *d*. *Educ:* Grangefield Grammar Sch. for Boys, Stockton-on-Tees; Univ. of Leeds (BSc Hons Metallurgy). Commercial saturation diver, Subsea Offshore, 1977–81; Founder/Dir, MOM Gp, 1981–94; Dep. Chm. and Chief Exec., Marine Offshore Mgt, 1994–96; Dir, Global Transportation Business, Lloyds Register of Shipping, 1996–2003. *Publication:* A Handbook for Underwater Inspectors, 1992. *Recreations:* golf, Rugby (now spectating), scuba diving, interest in Sri Lanka, sustainable development, Boxer dogs. *Address:* 13 Silver Lane, Purley, Surrey CR8 3HJ. *T:* (office) (020) 7904 7700; *e-mail:* (home) dovecote13@aol.com, (office) len.porter@rssb.co.uk. *Clubs:* Woodcote Park Golf; Mars and Minerva Shooting (Bisley).

PORTER, Marguerite Ann, (Mrs Nicky Henson); Guest Artist, Royal Ballet Co., since 1986 (Senior Principal Dancer, 1976–85); *b* 30 Nov. 1948; *d* of William Albert and Mary Porter; *m* (marr. diss.); *m* 1986, Nicky Henson, *qv*; one *s*. *Educ:* Doncaster. Joined Royal Ballet School, 1964; graduated to Royal Ballet Co., 1966; soloist, 1972; Principal, 1976; favourite roles include: Juliet in Romeo and Juliet, Manon, Natalia in A Month in the Country; The Queen in Matthew Bourne's Swan Lake, NY, 1999. *Film:* Comrade Lady. Dir, Yorkshire Ballet Seminars, 2005–; Gov., Royal Ballet, 2006–. *Publication:* Ballerina: a dancer's life, 1989. *Recreations:* my family, friends. *Address:* c/o Richard Stone Partnership, 2 Henrietta Street, WC2E 8PS.

PORTER, Mark Edward; Creative Editor, The Guardian, since 2000; *b* 15 March 1960; *s* of Robert George Porter and Sybil Elizabeth Porter; *m* 2001, Elizabeth Hubbard; two *s*. *Educ:* Trinity Sch. of John Whitgift, Surrey; Trinity Coll., Oxford (BA Hons, MA 1985). Art Dir of several mags, 1986–93; freelance art dir and design consultant, 1993–95; Associate Art Dir, 1995–98, Art Dir, 1998–2000, The Guardian. Mem., AGI, 2004. *Publications:* contrib. to many books and jls on mag. and newspaper design. *Recreations:* family, food and cooking, Hispanophilia. *Address:* The Guardian, Kings Place, 90 York Way, N1 9AG; *e-mail:* info@markporter.com.

PORTER, Martin Hugh Ninnis; QC 2006; *b* 3 Nov. 1962; *s* of William Hugh Lancelot Porter and Elizabeth Hilary Porter (*née* Oddie); *m* 1989, Dr Kelly Jean Stanhope; two *d*. *Educ:* St John's Coll., Cambridge (BA 1984; LLM 1985). Called to the Bar, Inner Temple, 1986. *Recreations:* cycling, ski-ing, flying and drinking at moderate speed. *Address:* 2 Temple Gardens, EC4Y 9AY. *T:* (020) 7822 1200, *Fax:* (020) 7822 1300; *e-mail:* mporter@2tg.co.uk. *Club:* Thames Velo.

PORTER, Peter Neville Frederick, CLit 2006; FRSL; freelance writer, poet; *b* Brisbane, 16 Feb. 1929; *s* of William Ronald Porter and Marion Main; *m* 1st, 1961, Jannice Henry (*d* 1974); two *d*; 2nd, 1991, Christine Berg. *Educ:* Church of England Grammar Sch., Brisbane; Toowoomba Grammar Sch. Worked as journalist in Brisbane before coming to England in 1951; clerk, bookseller and advertising writer, before becoming full-time poet, journalist, reviewer and broadcaster in 1968. Chief work done in poetry and English literature. Hon. DLitt: Melbourne, 1985; Loughborough, 1987; Sydney, 1999; Queensland, 2001. Queen's Gold Medal for Poetry, 2002. *Publications:* Once Bitten, Twice Bitten, 1961; Penguin Modern Poets No 2, 1962; Poems, Ancient and Modern, 1964; A Porter Folio, 1969; The Last of England, 1970; Preaching to the Converted, 1972; (trans.) After Martial, 1972; (with Arthur Boyd) Jonah, 1973; (with Arthur Boyd) The Lady and the Unicorn, 1975; Living in a Calm Country, 1975; (jt ed) New Poetry 1, 1975; The Cost of Seriousness, 1978; English Subtitles, 1981; Collected Poems, 1983 (Duff Cooper Prize); Fast Forward, 1984; (with Arthur Boyd) Narcissus, 1985; The Automatic Oracle, 1987 (Whitbread Poetry Award, 1988); (with Arthur Boyd) Mars, 1988; A Porter Selected, 1989; Possible Worlds, 1989; The Chair of Babel, 1992; Millennial Fables, 1995; (ed) Oxford Book of Modern Australian Verse, 1996; (ed jtly) New Writing 5, 1996, 6, 1997; Dragons in their Pleasant Palaces, 1997; Collected Poems 1961–1999, 2 vols, 1999; Saving from the Wreck: essays on poetry, 2001; Max is Missing (poems), 2001 (Forward Prize, 2002); Afterburner, 2004. *Recreations:* buying records and listening to music; travelling in Italy. *Address:* 42 Cleveland Square, W2 6DA. *T:* (020) 7262 4289.

PORTER, Richard Bruce; Director of Operations, Vision 2020, since 2005; *b* 20 Jan. 1942; *s* of Maynard Eustace Prettyman Porter and Irene Marjorie Porter; *m* 1965, Susan Mary Early; two *d. Educ:* St Joseph's Coll., Ipswich; City of London Coll. (BSc Econ). Account Supervisor, A. C. Nielsen Co., 1965–70; Divl Manager, Brooke Bond Oxo Ltd, 1970–74; Market Develt Manager, Mackenzie Hill Hldgs, 1974–75; Management Consultant, 1975–79, Sen. Manager and Partner, 1984–94, KPMG Management Consulting; Project Economist, Engineering Science Inc., 1979–84; Exec. Dir, Sight Savers Internat., 1994–2005. *Publication:* (jtly) Science Parks and the Growth of High Technology, 1988. *Recreations:* tennis, hockey, reading, bridge, gardening. *Address:* 15 Park Road, Burgess Hill, W Sussex RH15 8EU. *T:* (01444) 232602. *Club:* Royal Over-Seas League.

PORTER, Prof. Robert, AC 2001; DM; FRACMA, FRACP, FAA; Director, Research Development, Faculty of Medicine, Health and Molecular Sciences, James Cook University, Queensland, since 1999 (Planning Dean (Medicine), 1998–99); *b* 10 Sept. 1932; *s* of late William John Porter and Amy Porter (*née* Tottman); *m* 1961, Anne Dorothy Steell; two *s* two *d. Educ:* Univ. of Adelaide (BMedSc, DSc); Univ. of Oxford (MA, BCh, DM). Rhodes Scholarship, South Australia, 1954; Radcliffe Travelling Fellowship in Med. Sci., University Coll., Oxford, 1962; Lectr, Univ. Lab. of Physiology, Oxford, 1960–67; Fellow, St Catherine's Coll., and Medical Tutor, Oxford, 1963–67; Prof. of Physiology and Chm., Dept of Physiology, Monash Univ., 1967–79; Howard Florey Prof. of Med. Res., and Dir, John Curtin Sch. of Med. Res., ANU, 1980–89; Dean, Faculty of Medicine, 1989–98, Dep. Vice Chancellor (Res.), 1992–93, Monash Univ. Sen. Fulbright Travelling Fellow and Vis. Prof., Washington Univ. Sch. of Medicine, St Louis, Mo, 1973; Fogarty Scholar-in-Residence, NIH, 1986–87. Member: Bd of Dirs, Alfred Gp of Hosps and Monash Med. Centre, 1989–99; Bd of Govs, Menzies Sch. of Health Res., Darwin, 1985–92; Bd of Management, Baker Med. Res. Inst., 1980–99. Hon. DSc Sydney, 2001. Centenary Medal, Australia, 2003. *Publications:* (with C. G. Phillips) Corticospinal Neurones: their role in movement, 1977; (with R. N. Lemon) Corticospinal function and voluntary movement, 1993; articles on neurophysiology and control of movement by the brain. *Recreations:* outdoor sports. *Address:* 2 Denison Court, Toomulla Beach, Qld 4816, Australia. *T:* (office) (7) 47815697.

PORTER, Rt Hon. Sir Robert (Wilson), Kt 1971; PC (NI) 1969; QC (NI) 1965; County Court Judge, Northern Ireland, 1978–95; *b* 23 Dec. 1923; *s* of late Joseph Wilson Porter and late Letitia Mary (*née* Wasson); *m* 1953, Margaret Adelaide, *y d* of late F. W. Lynas; one *s* one *d* (and one *d* decd). *Educ:* Model Sch. and Foyle Coll., Londonderry; Queen's Univ., Belfast. RAFVR, 1942–46; Royal Artillery (TA), 1950–56. Foundation Schol., Queen's Univ., 1947 and 1948; LLB 1949. Called to Bar: N Ireland, 1950; Ireland, 1975; Middle Temple, 1988. Lecturer in Contract and Sale of Goods, Queen's Univ., 1950–51; Jun. Crown Counsel, Co. Londonderry, 1960–63, Co. Down, 1964–65; Counsel to Attorney-General for N Ireland, 1963–64 and 1965; Recorder: of Londonderry, 1979–81; of Belfast, 1993–95. Vice-Chairman, 1959–61, Chairman, 1961–66, War Pensions Appeal Tribunal for N Ireland. MP (U) Queen's Univ. of Belfast, 1966–69, Lagan Valley, 1969–73, Parlt of N Ireland; Minister of Health and Social Services, N Ireland, 1969; Parly Sec., Min. of Home Affairs, 1969; Minister of Home Affairs, Govt of NI, 1969–70. Hon. Col, OTC, QUB, 1988–93. *Recreations:* gardening, golf. *Address:* Larch Hill, Church Close, Ballylesson, Belfast, N Ireland BT8 8JX. *Club:* Royal Air Force.

PORTER, Maj. Gen. Roderick John Murray, MBE 1994; Director, Force Strategic Engagement, Multinational Force Headquarters, Iraq, since 2008; *b* Tamerton Foliot, Devon, 29 June 1960; *s* of John William Porter and Jane Elisabeth Porter (*née* Langdon); *m* 1987, Martina Marianne Heslam; three *s. Educ:* Lipsom Vale Primary Sch., Plymouth; Mount House Sch., Tavistock; Sherborne Sch.; RMA Sandhurst; Univ. of Newcastle upon Tyne (BA Hons Combined Studies (German and Hist.)); US Army War Coll. (Combined/Jt Force Land Component Commander's Course). Platoon Comd, 1981–82, Regtl Signals Officer, 1985–87, Adjt, 1987–89, 1 RWF; SO3 G3 (Ops), HQ 4th Armd Bde (Germany and Gulf), 1989–91; Army Staff Course Div. II, 1991–92 (psc†); COS, HQ 4th Armd Bde (Germany and Bosnia), 1992–94; Co. Comd, 1 RWF (UK and Bosnia), 1994–96; SO1 Policy ACDS Operational Requirements (Land), 1997–99; CO, 1 RWF (NI), 1999–2001; Dep. Dir, Equipt Capability (Direct Battlefield Engagement), MoD, 2001–03; HCSC, Shrivenham, 2003; Bde Comd, 3 Inf. Bde (NI), 2003–04, 8 Inf. Bde (NI), 2004–05; Dir, Equipt Plans, MoD, 2006–08. Col, Royal Welsh, 2006–. Pres., Armed Forces Christian Union. *Recreations:* most sports, especially cricket, golf, dinghy sailing and Rugby (Rugby referee and Chm., Army and Combined Services Rugby Referees' Soc.); hill walking, reading, military and ancient history, music (especially classical, blues and rock; playing guitar, violin, saxophone). *Address:* c/o Regimental Headquarters, The Royal Welsh, Maindy Barracks, Cardiff CF14 3YE. *T:* (029) 2078 1202, *Fax:* (029) 2078 1357; *e-mail:* roddyporter@googlemail.com.

PORTER, Sally Curtis; *see* Keeble, S. C.

PORTER, Dame Shirley, (Lady Porter), DBE 1991; Councillor, Hyde Park Ward, 1974–93, Leader, 1983–91, Westminster City Council; Lord Mayor of Westminster, 1991–92; *b* 29 Nov. 1930; *d* of late Sir John (Edward) Cohen and Lady (Sarah) Cohen; *m* 1949, Sir Leslie Porter (*d* 2005); one *s* one *d. Educ:* Warren Sch., Worthing, Sussex; La Ramée, Lausanne, Switzerland. Founded Designers' Guild, 1970; Chairman: Neurotech Medical Systems, 1992–94; LBC, 1992–93; Dir, Capital Radio, 1982–88. Westminster City Council: Conservative Whip, 1974–77; Road Safety Cttee, 1974–82; Member: Co-ordinating Cttee, 1981–82; Chairman: Highways and Works Cttee, 1978–82 (Vice-Chm., 1977–78); Gen. Purposes Cttee, 1982–83; Policy Review Cttee, 1982–83; Policy and Resources Cttee, 1983–91. Chairman: (also Founder), WARS Campaign (Westminster Against Reckless Spending), 1981–84; Cleaner City Campaign, 1979–81; Pres., Eur. Conf. on Tourism and the Envmt, 1992–; Vice-Pres., Cleaner London Campaign, 1979–81; Mem. Exec., Keep Britain Tidy Gp, 1977–81. Pres., British Inst. of Cleaning Science, 1991–; Mem. Ct, Guild of Cleaners, 1976–2002. Former Dep. Chm., Bd, London Festival Ballet. Trustee, London Philharmonic Trust, 1991–93. Hon. Mem., London Community Cricket Assoc., 1989–. Governor, Tel Aviv Univ., 1982; Internat. Fellow, Porter Sch. of Envmtl Studies, Tel Aviv Univ., 2001–. JP Inner London, 1972–84; DL Greater London, 1988–94. FRSA 1989. Hon. PhD Tel Aviv, 1991. *Recreations:* golf, tennis, ballet. *Club:* Dyrham Park Golf.

PORTER, Stanley Leonard, CB 2005; Director, Winterbourne Consultancy Ltd, since 2006; *b* 16 March 1945; *s* of Leonard James and Lilian Elizabeth Porter; *m* 1966, Mary Roche; two *s* one *d. Educ:* King Edward VI Grammar Sch., Chelmsford. MCIPS 1994; FRAeS 1996. Ministry of Defence, 1963–2006: Asst Private Sec. to Minister of State for Defence Procurement, 1971–73; Principal, Tornado Finance, 1979–81; Asst Dir, Commercial, 1981–87; Director: Commercial Policy, 1987–89; Finance and Secretariat, 1989–92; Principal Dir, Commercial, 1992–98; Dir Gen., Commercial, 1998–2006 and Exec. Dir, Defence Procurement Agency, 1999–2006. *Recreations:* travel, gardening, my family. *Address:* 5 Orchard Close, Winterbourne, Bristol BS36 1BF. *T:* (01454) 775384; *e-mail:* stanporter@tiscali.co.uk.

PORTERFIELD, Dr James Stuart; retired; Reader in Bacteriology, Sir William Dunn School of Pathology, Oxford University, and Senior Research Fellow, Wadham College, Oxford, 1977–89; now Emeritus Fellow; *b* 17 Jan. 1924; *yr s* of late Dr Samuel Porterfield and Mrs Lilian Porterfield, Widnes, Lancs, and Portstewart, Co. Londonderry, NI; *m* 1950, Betty Mary Burch; one *d* (one *s* decd). *Educ:* Wade Deacon Grammar Sch., Widnes; King's Sch., Chester; Liverpool Univ. MB, ChB 1947, MD 1949. Asst Lectr in Bacteriology, Univ. of Liverpool, 1947–49; Bacteriologist and Virologist, Common Cold Res. Unit, Salisbury, Wilts, 1949–51; Pathologist, RAF Inst. of Pathology and Tropical Med., Halton, Aylesbury, Bucks, 1952–53; seconded to W African Council for Med. Res. Labs, Lagos, Nigeria, 1953–57; Mem. Scientific Staff, Nat. Inst. for Med. Res., Mill Hill, 1949–77; WHO Regional Ref. Centre for Arthropod-borne Viruses, 1961–65; WHO Collaborating Lab., 1965–89; Ref. Expert on Arboviruses, Public Health Lab. Service, 1967–76. Chm., Arbovirus Study Gp, Internat. Cttee for Nomenclature of Viruses, 1968–78; Meetings Sec., Soc. for General Microbiology, 1972–77; Vice-Pres., Royal Soc. for Tropical Med. and Hygiene, 1980–81 (Councillor, 1973–76); Secretary and Vice-Pres., Royal Institution, 1973–78. *Publications:* (ed) Andrewes' Viruses of Vertebrates, 5th edn, 1989; (ed) Exotic Viral Infections, 1995; contribs to Oxford DNB, medical and scientific jls. *Recreations:* fell-walking, gardening. *Address:* 8 Port Mill Court, Mills Way, Barnstaple, Devon EX31 1GW.

PORTES, Jonathan; Director, Children and Poverty, since 2006 and Chief Economist (Work), since 2002, Department for Work and Pensions (Director, Work, Welfare and Poverty, 2002–06); *b* 18 April 1966; *s* of Prof. Richard David Portes, *qv. Educ:* Balliol Coll., Oxford (BA Hons 1987); Princeton Univ. (MPA 1994). HM Treasury: various posts, 1987–91; Private Sec. and Speechwriter to the Chancellor of the Exchequer, 1991–92; Project Leader, Debt Mgt Review, 1994–95; Sen. Consultant, Nat. Economic Research Associates, 1995–98; Special Consultant, IMF, 1998–99; Project Leader, Performance and Innovation Unit, Cabinet Office, 1999–2000; Partner, Develt Strategies, 2000–02. Mem., ICA; FRSA. *Publications:* govt policy papers, econs jls and press articles. *Recreations:* walking, cooking. *Address:* Department for Work and Pensions, The Adelphi, 1–11 John Adam Street, WC2N 6HT; *e-mail:* jonathan.portes@dwp.gsi.gov.uk.

PORTES, Prof. Richard David, CBE 2003; DPhil; FBA 2004; Professor of Economics, London Business School, since 1995; President (formerly Director), Centre for Economic Policy Research, since 1983; *b* 10 Dec. 1941; *s* of Herbert Portes and Abra Halperin Portes; *m* 1st, 1963, Bobbi Frank (marr. diss. 2005); one *s* one *d*; 2nd, 2006, Hélène Rey; one *d. Educ:* Yale Univ. (BA 1962 *summa cum laude* maths and philosophy); Balliol and Nuffield Colls, Oxford (Rhodes Schol., Woodrow Wilson Fellow, Danforth Fellow; MA 1965; DPhil 1969). Official Fellow and Tutor in Econs, Balliol Coll., Oxford, 1965–69; Asst Prof. of Econs and Internat. Affairs, Princeton Univ., 1969–72; Prof. of Econs, Birkbeck Coll., Univ. of London, 1972–94 (Head, Dept of Econs, 1975–77 and 1980–83). Dir d'Etudes, Ecole des Hautes Etudes en Sciences Sociales, Paris, 1978–. Guggenheim Fellow, 1977–78; British Acad. Overseas Vis. Fellow, 1977–78; Res. Associate, Nat. Bureau of Econ. Res., Cambridge, Mass, 1980–; Vis. Prof., Harvard Univ., 1977–78; Dist. Global Vis. Prof., Haas Business Sch., Univ. of Calif at Berkeley, 1999–2000; Joel Stern Vis. Prof. of Internat. Finance, Columbia Business Sch., 2003–04. Vice-Chm., Econs Cttee, SSRC, 1981–84. Member: Bd of Dirs, Soc. for Econ. Analysis (Rev. of Econ. Studies), 1967–69, 1972–80 (Sec. 1974–77); Council on Foreign Relations, 1978–; Hon. Degrees Cttee, Univ. of London, 1984–89; Bellagio Gp on the Internat. Econ., 1990–; Franco-British Council, 1997–2002; Commn Economique de la Nation, France, 1999–2005; Conseil d'Admin, Fondation Banque de France, 1999–; ALSSS Commn on Social Scis, 2000–02; Gp of Econ. Policy Advrs, Presidency of EC, 2001–. Fellow, Econometric Soc., 1983–; Sec.-Gen., Royal Econ. Soc., 1992–2008 (Mem. Council, 1986–92; Exec. Cttee, 1987–2008); Council, European Econ. Assoc., 1992–96 (Fellow, 2004). Co-Chm., Bd of Governors, and Sen. Editor, Economic Policy, 1985–. Pres., Richard and Margaret Merrell Foundn, 1996–. Hon. DSc Univ. Libre de Bruxelles, 2000; Hon. PhD London Guildhall, 2000. *Publications:* (ed) Planning and Market Relations, 1971; The Polish Crisis, 1981; Deficits and Détente, 1983; (ed) Threats to International Financial Stability, 1987; (ed) Global Macroeconomics: policy conflict and cooperation, 1987; (ed) Blueprints for Exchange Rate Management, 1989; (ed) Macroeconomic Policies in an Interdependent World, 1989; (ed) Economic Transformation in Hungary and Poland, 1990; (ed) External Constraints on Macroeconomic Policy: the experience of Europe, 1991; (ed) The Path of Reform in Central and Eastern Europe, 1991; (ed) Economic Transformation in Central Europe, 1993; (ed) European Union Trade with Eastern Europe, 1995; Crisis? What Crisis? Orderly Workouts for Sovereign Debtors, 1995; Crises de la Dette, 2003; International Financial Stability, 2008; contribs to many learned jls. *Recreation:* living beyond my means. *Address:* London Business School, Regent's Park, NW1 4SA. *T:* (020) 7000 8424; *e-mail:* rportes@london.edu.
See also J. Portes.

PORTILLO, Rt Hon. Michael (Denzil Xavier); PC 1992; broadcaster and journalist; *b* 26 May 1953; *s* of late Luis Gabriel Portillo and of Cora Waldegrave Blyth; *m* 1982, Carolyn Claire Eadie. *Educ:* Harrow County Boys' School; Peterhouse, Cambridge (1st cl. Hons MA History). Ocean Transport & Trading Co., 1975–76; Conservative Res. Dept, 1976–79; Special Advr, Sec. of State for Energy, 1979–81; Kerr McGee Oil (UK) Ltd, 1981–83; Special Adviser: to Sec. of State for Trade and Industry, 1983; to Chancellor of the Exchequer, 1983–84. MP (C) Enfield, Southgate, Dec. 1984–1997; contested (C) same seat, 1997; MP (C) Kensington and Chelsea, Nov. 1999–2005. An Asst Govt Whip, 1986–87; Parly Under Sec. of State, DHSS, 1987–88; Minister of State, Dept of Transport, 1988–90; Minister of State for Local Govt, DoE, 1990–92; Chief Sec. to HM Treasury, 1992–94; Sec. of State for Employment, 1994–95, for Defence, 1995–97; Shadow Chancellor, 2000–01. Regular contributor to This Week, BBC1, 2003–; columnist, The

Sunday Times, 2004–. *Address:* c/o Suite 99, 34 Buckingham Palace Road, SW1W 0RH. *Club:* Chelsea Arts.

PORTLAND, 12th Earl of, *cr* 1689; **Timothy Charles Robert Noel Bentinck;** Viscount Woodstock, Baron Cirencester, 1689; Count of the Holy Roman Empire; actor (as Timothy Bentinck); *b* 1 June 1953; *s* of 11th Earl of Portland and Pauline (*d* 1967), *y d* of late Frederick William Mellowes; *S* father, 1997; *m* 1979, Judith Ann, *d* of John Robert Emerson; two *s. Educ:* Harrow; Univ. of East Anglia (BA Hons). Trained Bristol Old Vic Theatre Sch. Winner BBC Drama Schs Radio Competition, 1978. London theatre appearances include: Pirates of Penzance, Theatre Royal, Drury Lane, 1982; Reluctant Heroes, Theatre of Comedy, 1984; Hedda Gabler, King's Head Theatre, 1990; A Doll's House, Bridge Lane Theatre, London, 1992; Arcadia, Haymarket, 1994; Night Must Fall, Haymarket, 1996; *radio:* David Archer in The Archers; over 75 plays; *films:* North Sea Hijack, 1979; Pirates of Penzance, 1981; Winter Flight, 1985; Year of the Comet, 1992; Twelfth Night, 1995; Enigma, 2000; *television* includes: By the Sword Divided, 1983; Square Deal, 1989; Made in Heaven, 1990; Sharpe, 1993; Grange Hill, 1994; Strike Force, 1995; Prince Among Men, 1997; The Gathering Storm, 2002; Born and Bred, 2003; D-Day, Murder in Suburbia, 2004; Silent Witness, Frances Tuesday, The Thick of It, Broken News, Absolute Power, 2005; Doctors, Heartbeat, 2006; composer of theme music for Easy Money, BBC TV, 1984. Inventor of The Hippo (child-carrying device). HGV licence. *Recreations:* songwriting, ski-ing, swimming, house renovation, computer programming. *Heir:* s Viscount Woodstock, qv.

PORTMAN, family name of **Viscount Portman.**

PORTMAN, 10th Viscount *cr* 1873; **Christopher Edward Berkeley Portman;** Baron 1837; Chairman, Portman Settled Estates Ltd, since 1998; *b* 30 July 1958; *s* of 9th Viscount Portman and of Rosemary Joy Portman (*née* Farris); *S* father, 1999; *m* 1st, 1983, Caroline Steenson (marr. diss.); one *s*; 2nd, 1987, Patricia Martins Pim; two *s. Educ:* Marlborough Coll. *Recreations:* molecular nanotechnology, computer science, reading. *Heir:* e s Hon. Luke Oliver Berkeley Portman, *b* 31 Aug. 1984. *Address:* 38 Seymour Street, W1H 7BP. *T:* (020) 7563 1400. *Clubs:* Whites, Home House.

PORTSDOWN, Archdeacon of; *see* Reader, Ven. T. A. J.

PORTSMOUTH, 10th Earl of, *cr* 1743; **Quentin Gerard Carew Wallop;** DL; Viscount Lymington, Baron Wallop, 1720; Hereditary Bailiff of Burley, New Forest; *b* 25 July 1954; *s* of Oliver Kintzing Wallop (Viscount Lymington) (*d* 1984) and Ruth Violet (*d* 1978), *yr d* of Brig.-Gen. G. C. Sladen, CB, CMG, DSO, MC; *S* grandfather, 1984; *m* 1st, 1981, Candia (*née* McWilliam) (marr. diss. 1984); one *s* one *d*; 2nd, 1990, Annabel, *d* of Dr and Mrs Ian Fergusson; one *d. Educ:* Eton; Millfield. Non-exec. Dir, Grainger Trust plc, 1987–2002. Patron, Hants Br., BRCS, 1995–. Warden, St Andrew's Ch, Farleigh Wallop. Mem., Fishmongers' Co., 1997– (Mem., Court of Assts, 2006–). DL Hants, 2004. *Heir:* s Viscount Lymington, qv. *Address:* Farleigh House, Farleigh Wallop, Basingstoke, Hants RG25 2HT. *Clubs:* White's, Buck's, Pilgrims; International Association of Cape Horners; Hampshire Hunt.

PORTSMOUTH, Bishop of, since 1995; **Rt Rev. Kenneth William Stevenson,** PhD, DD, FRHistS; *b* 9 Nov. 1949; *s* of Frederik Robert and Margrete Stevenson; *m* 1970, Sarah Julia Mary (*née* Glover); one *s* three *d. Educ:* Edinburgh Acad.; Edinburgh Univ. (MA 1970); Southampton Univ. (PhD 1975); Manchester Univ. (DD 1987). FRHistS 1990. Ordained deacon, 1973, priest, 1974; Asst Curate, Grantham with Manthorpe, 1973–76; Lectr, Boston, 1976–80; part-time Lectr, Lincoln Theol Coll., 1975–80; Chaplain and Lectr, Manchester Univ., 1980–86; Team Vicar, 1980–82, Team Rector, 1982–86, Whitworth, Manchester; Rector, Holy Trinity and St Mary's, Guildford, 1986–95. Member: C of E Liturgical Commn, 1986–96; Faith and Order Advisory Gp, 1991–96; C of E Doctrine Commn, 1996–2003; Chm., C of E Bd of Educn and Nat. Soc. Council, 2003–. Chairman: Anglo-Nordic-Baltic Theol Conf., 1997– (Sec., 1985–97); Porvoo Panel, 2005– (Vice-Chm., 1999–2005). Vis. Prof., Univ. of Notre Dame, Indiana, 1983. Entered H of L, 1999. Comdr, Order of the Dannebrog (Denmark), 2006. *Publications:* Nuptial Blessing, 1982; Eucharist and Offering, 1986; Jerusalem Revisited, 1988; The First Rites, 1989; Covenant of Grace Renewed, 1994; (with H. R. McAdoo) The Mystery of the Eucharist in the Anglican Tradition, 1995; Handing On, 1996; The Mystery of Baptism in the Anglican Tradition, 1998; All the Company of Heaven, 1998; Abba Father: understanding and using the Lord's Prayer, 2000; (ed jtly) Love's Redeeming Work: The Anglican quest for holiness, 2001; Do This: the shape, style and meaning of the eucharist, 2002; The Lord's Prayer: a text in tradition, 2004; Rooted In Detachment: living the transfiguration, 2007; Watching and Waiting: a guide to the celebration of Advent, 2007; Take, Eat: reflections on the eucharist, 2008; (ed and contrib.) A Fallible Church: Lambeth essays, 2008; contribs to Scottish Jl of Theology, Ephemerides Liturgicae, Theology, etc. *Recreations:* historical biographies, Chinese cooking, walking, piano, Denmark. *Address:* Bishopsgrove, 26 Osborn Road, Fareham, Hants PO16 7DQ. *T:* (01329) 280247, *Fax:* (01329) 231538; *e-mail:* bishports@clara.co.uk. *Clubs:* Farmers, Nikaean, Nobody's Friends; Royal Yacht Squadron; Royal Naval and Royal Albert Yacht (Portsmouth).

PORTSMOUTH, Bishop of, (RC), since 1988; **Rt Rev. (Roger Francis) Crispian Hollis;** *b* 17 Nov. 1936; *s* of Christopher and Madeleine Hollis. *Educ:* Stonyhurst College; Balliol Coll., Oxford (MA); Venerable English College, Rome (STL). National Service as 2nd Lt, Somerset Light Infantry, 1954–56. Ordained priest, 1965; Assistant in Amesbury, 1966–67; RC Chaplain, Oxford Univ., 1967–77; RC Assistant to Head of Religious Broadcasting, BBC, 1977–81; Administrator, Clifton Cathedral, Bristol, 1981–87; Auxiliary Bishop of Birmingham (Bishop in Oxfordshire), 1987–88. Chm., Dept of Mission and Unity, 2001–05, Chm., Dept for Internat. Affairs, 2005–, Catholic Bishops' Conf. of England and Wales. *Recreations:* occasional golf, walking, cricket watching. *Address:* Bishop's House, Edinburgh Road, Portsmouth PO1 3HG.

PORTSMOUTH, Dean of; *see* Brindley, Very Rev. D. C.

POSKITT, Prof. Trevor John, DSc, PhD; consultant engineer, retired; Professor of Civil Engineering, Queen Mary and Westfield College (formerly Queen Mary College), University of London, 1972–94; *b* 26 May 1934; *s* of late William Albert Poskitt, Worthing, and Mrs D. M. Poskitt, Lincoln; *m* 1968, Gillian Mary, *d* of L. S. Martin, MBE, Romiley, Cheshire; one *s* one *d. Educ:* Corby Technical Sch.; Huddersfield Technical Coll.; Univ. of Leeds; Univ. of Cambridge. HND (Mech. Eng.); BSc Leeds, PhD Cambridge, DSc Manchester; CEng, FICE, FIStructE. Apprentice Engineer to Thos. Broadbent & Sons, Huddersfield, 1949–53; Graduate Assistant, English Electric Co. Ltd, 1958–60; Whitworth Fellow, 1960–63; Lectr, 1963–71, Senior Lectr, 1971–72, in Civil Engineering, Univ. of Manchester. *Publications:* numerous on civil engineering topics. *Recreations:* golf, music.

POSNANSKY, Jeremy Ross Leon; QC 1994; a Deputy High Court Judge, since 1997; *b* 8 March 1951; *s* of Anthony Posnansky and late Evelyn Davis (formerly Posnansky), JP;

m 1974, Julia Sadler, *d* of late Richard Sadler, MBE; two *d. Educ:* St Paul's Sch.; Coll. of Law. Called to the Bar, Gray's Inn, 1972 (Bencher, 2003), Antigua and Barbuda, 1995; in ind. practice at the Bar, 1972–2007; Asst Recorder, 1993–98; a Recorder, 1998–2002; admitted solicitor, 2007; Partner, Farrer & Co. LLP, 2007–. Mem., Family Courts Business and Service Cttees, Inner London, 1991–94. Fellow, Internat. Acad. of Matrimonial Lawyers, 1996. *Publications:* contrib. Internat. Family Law, Family Law. *Recreations:* scuba diving, travel, computers. *Address:* Farrer & Co., 66 Lincoln's Inn Fields, WC2A 3LH. *T:* (020) 7242 2022.

POSNER, Lindsay Steven; theatre director; *b* 6 June 1959; *s* of Dennis and Pauline Posner; *m* 2000, Megan Wheldon; one *s* two *d. Educ:* Exeter Univ. (BA Eng. Lit.); Royal Acad. Dramatic Art. Associate Dir, Royal Court Th., 1987–92; productions include: The Treatment; No One Sees the Video; Built on Sand; Blood; Downfall; Ambulance; Colquhoun and McBryde; Death and the Maiden, 1991 (Olivier Award for Best Play); Royal Shakespeare Co. productions include: Volpone, Taming of the Shrew, 1999; The Rivals, 2000; Twelfth Night, 2001; National Theatre: Tartuffe, 2002; Power, 2003; Almeida Theatre productions 2005–06 include: The Hypochondriac; Romance; Tom and Viv; Man and Boy; Dada; Love Counts; other productions include: American Buffalo, Young Vic, 1997; After Darwin, Hampstead Th., 1998; Sexual Perversity in Chicago, Comedy, 2003; A Life in the Theatre, Apollo, 2004; Oleanna, Garrick, 2004; Fool for Love, Apollo, 2005; The Birthday Party, Duchess, 2005; Fiddler on the Roof, Crucible, Sheffield, 2006, transf. Savoy, 2007; 3 Sisters on Hope Street, Everyman, Liverpool, 2008; *opera:* Giulio Cesare, Royal Opera Hse, 1997; *television* includes: The Maitlands, 1993; Two Oranges and a Mango, 1994. *Recreations:* Italian white wine, family, reading, a multiplicity of obsessions. *Address:* 58 Chaucer Road, W3 6DP. *T:* (020) 8993 5575; *e-mail:* l.posner@yahoo.com.

POSNER, Prof. Rebecca; Professor of the Romance Languages, University of Oxford, 1978–96, now Emeritus; Fellow, St Hugh's College, Oxford, 1978–96, Hon. Fellow, 1996; Research Associate, Oxford University Centre for Linguistics and Philology, since 1996; *b* 17 Aug. 1929; *d* of William and Rebecca Reynolds; *m* 1953, Michael Vivian Posner, CBE, one *s* one *d. Educ:* Somerville Coll., Oxford. MA, DPhil (Oxon); PhD (Cantab). Fellow, Girton Coll., Cambridge, 1960–63; Prof. of French Studies, Univ. of Ghana, 1963–65; Reader in Language, Univ. of York, 1965–78. Vis. Prof. of Romance Philology, Columbia Univ., NY, 1971–72; Vis. Senior Fellow, Princeton Univ., 1983; Emeritus Leverhulme Fellow, 1997. Vice-Pres., Philological Soc., 2000– (Pres., 1996–2000). *Publications:* Consonantal Dissimilation in the Romance Languages, 1961; The Romance Languages, 1966; (with J. Orr and I. Iordan) Introduction to Romance Linguistics, 1970; (ed with J. N. Green) Trends in Romance Linguistics and Philology: vol. 1, Romance Comparative and Historical Linguistics, 1980; vol. 2, Synchronic Romance Linguistics, 1981; vol. 3, Language and Philology in Romance, 1982; vol. 4, National and Regional Trends in Romance Linguistics and Philology, 1982; vol. 5, Bilingualism and Conflict in Romance, 1993; (contrib.) Legacy of Latin, ed R. Jenkyns, 1992; The Romance Languages, 1996 (trans. Spanish 1998); Linguistic Change in French, 1997; (contrib.) The History of the University of Oxford, vol. vii: Nineteenth Century Oxford, Part 2, 2000; (contrib.) Lexikon der Romanistischen Linguistik, vol. I, 1: Geschichte des Faches Romanistik, 2001; numerous articles. *Recreations:* walking, gardening, theatre, music. *Address:* St Hugh's College, Oxford OX2 6LE; Rushwood, Jack Straw's Lane, Oxford OX3 0DN. *T:* (01865) 763578.

POSNETT, Sir Richard (Neil), KBE 1980 (OBE 1963); CMG 1976; HM Diplomatic Service, retired; *b* 19 July 1919; *s* of Rev. Charles Walker Posnett, K-i-H, Medak, S India, and Phyllis (*née* Barker); *m* 1st; two *s* one *d*; 2nd, 1959, Shirley Margaret Hudson (*d* 2005); two *s* one *d. Educ:* Kingswood; St John's Coll., Cambridge (won 120 yards hurdles for Cambridge *v* Oxford, 1940). BA 1940, MA 1947. Called to the Bar, Gray's Inn, 1951. HM Colonial Administrative Service in Uganda, 1941; Chm., Uganda Olympic Cttee, 1956; Colonial Office, London, 1958; Judicial Adviser, Buganda, 1960; Perm. Sec. for External Affairs, Uganda, 1962; Perm. Sec. for Trade and Industry, 1963; joined Foreign (subseq. Diplomatic) Service, 1964; FO, 1964; served on UK Mission to UN, NY, 1966–70; briefly HM Comr in Anguilla, 1969; Head of W Indian Dept, FCO, 1970–71; Governor and C-in-C of Belize, 1972–76; Special Mission to Ocean Island, 1977; Dependent Territories Adviser, FCO, 1977–79; British High Comr, Kampala, 1979. UK Comr, British Phosphate Comrs, 1978–81. Governor and C-in-C, Bermuda, 1981–83. Mem., Lord Chancellor's Panel of Ind. Inspectors, 1983–89. First ascent of South Portal Peak on Ruwenzori, 1942. Member: RIIA; Royal Forestry Soc.; Royal African Soc. President: Kingswood Assoc., 1980; Godalming Joigny Friendship Assoc., 1987– (Chm., 1984–87); Eddystone Housing Assoc., 2003–. Gov., Kingswood Sch., 1985–93. KStJ 1972. *Publications:* (contrib.) Looking Back at the Uganda Protectorate, 1996; The Scent of Eucalyptus (autobiog.), 2001; articles in Uganda Journal, World Today, Empire & After. *Recreations:* ski-ing, golf, trees. *Address:* Bahati, Old Kiln Close, Churt, Surrey GU10 2JH. *Clubs:* Royal Commonwealth Society, Achilles; Hankley Common Golf; Privateers Hockey.

POST, Herschel, MBE 2006; International Managing Director, Business Development, 2000–05, and Director, 2003–05, Christie's International plc; *b* 9 Oct. 1939; *s* of Herschel E. and Marie C. Post; adopted British citizenship, 1992; *m* 1963, Peggy Mayne; one *s* three *d. Educ:* Yale Univ. (AB); Oxford Univ. (BA, MA); Harvard Law Sch. (LLB). Associate, Davis Polk & Wardwell, attorneys, 1966–69; Exec. Dir, Parks Council of NY, 1969–72; Dep. Adminr and Comr, Parks, Recreation and Cultural Affairs Admin, NYC, 1973; Vice-Pres., Morgan Guaranty Trust Co., 1974–83; Mem., Bd of Dirs, 1988–95, Dep. Chm., 1989–95, Internat. Stock Exchange, subseq. London Stock Exchange; Chief Operating Officer, Lehman Brothers Internat. (Europe) and Lehman Brothers Securities Ltd, 1990–94; Chief Operating Officer, 1994–95, Chief Exec. and Dep. Chm., 1995–2000, Coutts & Co. President: Shearson Lehman Global Asset Management, 1984–90; Posthorn Global Asset Management, 1984–90; Director: Euro-clear Clearance Systems plc, 1992–; Investors Capital Trust plc, 1999–; Ahli United Bank (UK) plc, 2001–; Ahli United Bank BSC, 2002–; CrestCo, 2002–; Threadneedle Asset Mgt, 2006–; Dep. Chm., EFG Private Bank Ltd, 2002–05. Pres., Woodcock Foundn (US), 2000–; Dir, Notting Hill Housing Gp, 2002–; Trustee: Earthwatch Inst. (Europe) (formerly Earthwatch Europe), 1988– (Chm., 1997–); You Can Do I.T., 2001–; Royal Opera House Benevolent Fund, 2002–. *Address:* 18 Kensington Park Gardens, W11 3HD. *T:* (020) 7229 5294, *Fax:* (020) 7912 0352. *Club:* Athenæum.

POST, Martin Richard, MA; Headmaster, Watford Grammar School for Boys, since 2000; *b* 3 Sept. 1958; *s* of Kenneth and Barbara Post; *m* 1999, Kate Watts; one *s. Educ:* Univ. of York (BA Eng. and Related Lit.); MA Educnl Mgt Open Univ. King's Sch., Rochester, 1982–84; Darwin Coll., Cambridge, 1984–85; Mill Hill Co. High Sch., 1985–89; Richard Hale Sch., 1989–95; Dep. Head (Pastoral and Finance), Watford GS for Boys, 1995–2000. FRSA 2004. *Recreations:* sports, reading, theatre. *Address:* Watford Grammar School for Boys, Rickmansworth Road, Watford, Herts WD18 7JF. *T:* (01923) 208900.

POSTE, Dr George (Henry), CBE 1999; FRCPath, FMedSci; FRS 1997; FRCVS; Chief Executive Officer, Health Technology Networks, since 2000; Director, Arizona Biodesign Institute, Arizona State University, since 2003; *b* 30 April 1944; *s* of late John H. Poste and of Kathleen B. Poste; *m* 1992, Linda Suhler; one *s* two *d*. *Educ:* Bristol Univ. (BVSc 1st. cl. hons 1966; DVM 1966; PhD Virology 1969). FRCVS 1987; FRCPath 1989; FIBiol 1998. Lectr, RPMS, Univ. of London, 1969–72; Prof. of Experimental Pathology, SUNY, 1972–80; SmithKline Beckman, then SmithKline Beecham: Vice Pres., R&D, 1980–88; Pres., R&D Technologies, 1989–90; Vice Chm. and Exec. Vice Pres., R&D, 1990–91; Dir, 1992–99; Pres., R&D, 1992–97; Chief Sci. and Technol. Officer, 1997–99. Partner, Care Capital, Princeton, 2000–; non-executive Chairman: diaDexus, 1997–; Structural Genomi X, 2000–; Illumina Maxygen and Orchid Bioscis. Pitt Fellow, Pembroke Coll., Cambridge, 1995–; Fellow, Hoover Inst., Stanford Univ., 2000–. Member: Human Genetics Adv. Cttee, 1996–99; US Defense Sci. Bd, 2000–. Governor, Center for Molecular Medicine and Genetics, Stanford Univ., 1992–. Founder FMedSci 1998. Hon. FRCP 1993; Hon. FRVC 2000. Hon. Fellow, UCL, 1999. Hon. DSc 1987, Hon. LLD 1995, Bristol; Hon. LLD Dundee, 1998; Hon. DSc Sussex, 1999. *Publications:* joint ed. of fifteen books; numerous reviews and papers in learned jls; column in FT. *Recreations:* automobile racing, military history, photography, helicopter piloting, exploring the deserts of American Southwest. *Address:* Health Technology Networks, 2338 Casmar Way, Gilbertsville, PA 19525, USA. *T:* (610) 7050828, *Fax:* (610) 7050810; *e-mail:* gposte@healthtechnetwork.com; Arizona Biodesign Institute, Arizona State University, Main Campus, PO Box 875001, Tempe, AZ 85287–5001, USA. *T:* (480) 7278662, *Fax:* (480) 9652765. *Club:* Athenæum.

POSTGATE, Prof. (John) Nicholas, FBA 1993; Professor of Assyriology, University of Cambridge, since 1994; Fellow, Trinity College, Cambridge, since 1982; *b* 5 Nov. 1945; *s* of Ormond Oliver Postgate and Patricia Mary Postgate (*née* Peet); *m* 1st, 1968, Carolyn June Prater (marr. diss. 1999); one *s* one *d*; 2nd, 1999, Sarah Helen Blakeney; one *s* one *d*. *Educ:* Winchester Coll.; Trinity Coll., Cambridge (BA Oriental Studies 1967; MA 1970). Lectr in Akkadian, SOAS, 1967–71; Fellow, Trinity Coll., Cambridge, 1970–74; Asst Dir, British Sch. of Archaeology, Iraq, 1971–75; Dir, British Archaeol. Expedn to Iraq, 1975–81; Lectr in Hist. and Archaeol. of Ancient Near East, 1981–85, Reader in Mesopotamian Studies, 1985–94, Univ. of Cambridge. Director of excavations: Abu Salabikh, S Iraq, 1975–89; Kilise Tepe, S Turkey, 1994–99, 2007–. *Publications:* Neo-Assyrian Royal Grants and Decrees, 1969; The Governor's Palace Archive, 1973; Taxation and Conscription in the Assyrian Empire, 1974; Fifty Neo-Assyrian Legal Documents, 1976; The First Empires, 1977; (ed) Abu Salabikh Excavations, vols 1–4, 1983–93; (with S. M. Dalley) Tablets from Fort Shalmaneser, 1984; The archive of Urad-Šerua and his family, 1988; Early Mesopotamia: society and economy at the dawn of history, 1992; (with F. M. Fales) Imperial administrative records, pt I 1992, pt II 1995; (with B. K. Ismail) Texts from Nineveh, 1993; (ed jtly) Concise Dictionary of Akkadian, 1999; (ed jtly) Excavations at Kilise Tepe 1994–98, 2007; The Land of Assur and the Yoke of Assur, 2007; (ed) Languages of Iraq, Ancient and Modern, 2007; articles in Iraq and other learned jls. *Address:* Trinity College, Cambridge CB2 1TQ. *T:* (01223) 338443.

POSTGATE, Prof. John Raymond, FRS 1977; FIBiol; Director, AFRC Unit of Nitrogen Fixation, 1980–87 (Assistant Director, 1963–80), and Professor of Microbiology, University of Sussex, 1965–87, now Emeritus; *b* 24 June 1922; *s* of Raymond William Postgate and Daisy Postgate (*née* Lansbury); *m* 1948, Mary Stewart (*d* 2008); three *d*. *Educ:* principally Woodstock Sch., Golders Green; Kingsbury County Sch., Middx; Balliol Coll., Oxford. BA, MA, DPhil, DSc. Research in chemical microbiology: with D. D. Woods on action of sulfonamide drugs, 1946–48, with K. R. Butlin on sulphate-reducing bacteria, 1948–59. Research on bacterial death, 1959–63, incl. Visiting Professor: Univ. of Illinois, 1962–63, working on sulphate-reducing bacteria; Oregon State Univ., 1977–78. President: Inst. of Biology, 1982–84; Soc. for Gen. Microbiology, 1984–87. Hon. DSc Bath, 1990; Hon. LLD Dundee, 1997. *Publications:* Microbes and Man, 1969, 4th edn 2000; Biological Nitrogen Fixation, 1972; A Plain Man's Guide to Jazz, 1973; Nitrogen Fixation, 1978, 3rd edn 1998; The Sulphate-Reducing Bacteria, 1979, 2nd edn 1984; The Fundamentals of Nitrogen Fixation, 1982; The Outer Reaches of Life, 1994; (with Mary Postgate) A Stomach for Dissent: the life of Raymond Postgate, 1994; Lethal Lozenges and Tainted Tea: a biography of John Postgate (1820–1881), 2001; ed, 4 scientific symposia; regular columnist in Jazz Monthly, 1952–72; numerous scientific papers in microbiol/biochem. jls; many jazz record reviews in specialist magazines; articles on jazz. *Recreations:* listening to jazz and attempting to play it. *Address:* 1 Houndean Rise, Lewes, Sussex BN7 1EG. *T:* (01273) 472675.

POSTGATE, Nicholas; *see* Postgate, J. N.

POSTINGS, David John; Chief Executive, Cattles plc, since 2007; *b* 22 Feb. 1960; *s* of Kenneth and Sheila Postings; *m* 1985, Joy Anne Young. *Educ:* Uplands Primary Sch., Wolverhampton; Smestow Sch., Wolverhampton. ACIB 1984; Dip. Financial Services 1989. Joined Barclays Bank, 1978: clerical and managerial roles, 1978–90; PA to Gp Chm., 1990–92; Br. Manager, Kensington, 1992–95; Chief Operating Officer, Large Corporate Banking, 1995–97; Managing Director: Barclays Sales Financing, 1997–99; IT and Ops Corporate Banking, 1999–2001; Barclays Enable, 2001–04; Lloyds TSB Business Banking, 2004–06; Lloyds TSB Commercial, 2006–07. *Recreations:* cycling, collecting wine in quantities I will never drink, supporting Wolverhampton Wanderers. *Address:* Cattles plc, Kingston House, Centre 27 Business Park, Wood Head Road, Birstall, Batley WF17 9TD.

POSTLETHWAITE, Peter William, OBE 2004; actor; *b* 16 Feb. 1945; partner, Jacqueline Morrish; one *s* one *d*. *Educ:* Bristol Old Vic Theatre Sch. *Stage* includes: Troilus and Cressida, Bristol Old Vic; Royal Shakespeare Company: Richard III; Cyrano de Bergerac; King Lear; Fair Maid of the West; a Midsummer Night's Dream; Macbeth, Bristol Old Vic and tour, 1997; The Homecoming, Royal Exchange Th., Manchester, 2002; *television* includes: The Muscle Market; Coast to Coast, 1987; The Bill; Martin Chuzzlewit, 1994; Between the Lines; Lost for Words, 1999; Alice in Wonderland, 2000; The Sins, 2000; *films* include: A Private Function, 1985; Distant Voices, Still Lives, 1988; The Dressmaker, 1989; The Last of the Mohicans, 1991; Alien 3, 1992; In the Name of the Father, 1993; Usual Suspects, 1995; Dragonheart, 1996; Brassed Off, 1996; Romeo and Juliet, 1997; The Lost World: Jurassic Park, 1997; Amistad, 1997; Serpent's Kiss, 1997; Among Giants, 1998; The Shipping News, 2002; Dark Water, The Constant Gardener, 2005; The Omen, 2006; Closing the Ring, 2007. *Address:* c/o Markham & Froggatt Ltd, 4 Windmill Street, W1P 1HF.

POTOČNIK, Janez, PhD; Member, European Commission, since 2004; *b* 22 March 1958; *m*; two *s*. *Educ:* Univ. of Ljubljana (BEc, MEc; PhD 1993). Econ. Analyst, SDK (APP) Agency, Kranj, 1983–84; Asst Dir, Inst. of Macroecon. Analysis and Develt, Ljubljana, 1984–87; Sen. Researcher, Inst. for Econ. Res., Ljubljana, 1988–93; Dir, Inst. of Macroecon. Analysis and Develt, Ljubljana, 1993–2001; Minister Councillor, Office of the Prime Minister, Slovenia, 2001–02; Minister for European Affairs, 2002–04. Asst Prof., Faculty of Law, Univ. of Ljubljana, 1991–2004. *Address:* European Commission, Rue de la Loi 200, 1049 Brussels, Belgium.

POTTER, Prof. Allen Meyers, PhD; James Bryce Professor of Politics, University of Glasgow, 1970–84, retired; *b* 7 March 1924; *s* of Maurice A. and Irene M. Potter; *m* 1949, Joan Elizabeth Yeo; two *d*. *Educ:* Wesleyan Univ., Conn (BA 1947, MA 1948); Columbia Univ., NY (PhD 1955). FSS 1967. Instructor, College of William and Mary, 1949–51; Lectr/Sen. Lectr, Univ. of Manchester, 1951–62; Vis. Professor, Univ. of Texas, 1960; Professor: Univ. of Strathclyde, 1963–65; Univ. of Essex, 1965–70; Pro-Vice-Chancellor, Univ. of Essex, 1969–70; Vice-Principal, Univ. of Glasgow, 1979–82. Dir, SSRC Data Bank, 1967–70. Member, US-UK Educational Commn, 1979–84. Governor, Glasgow Sch. of Art, 1979–82. *Publications:* American Government and Politics, 1955, 2nd edn 1978; Organised Groups in British National Politics, 1961; articles in American and British social science jls.

POTTER, Christopher Frank Rendall, OBE 2001; MA; Headmaster, Old Swinford Hospital, Stourbridge, 1978–2001; *b* 9 Sept. 1939; *s* of late Cedric Hardcastle Potter and Phyllis Potter (*née* Rendall); *m* 1971, Charlotte Ann Millis, San Francisco; two *s* three *d*. *Educ:* March Grammar Sch.; Trinity Coll., Cambridge (MA Classics). Ardingly College, Sussex: Asst Master, 1961–78; Head of Classics, 1964–78; Housemaster, 1966–78. Chief Examr in Archaeol., London Exam Bd, 1976–80. Chm., State Boarding Inf. Service, 1996–98. Schoolmaster Studentship, Christ Church, Oxford, 1989. Pres., Stourbridge Archaeol and Historical Soc., 1988; Chm., Ludlow Historical Res. Gp, 2005–. Chairman: Trustees, Knoll Sch., Kidderminster, 1989–; Govs, The Elms Sch., Colwall, 2004– (Vice Chm., 1985–2004). Churchwarden, St Laurence's, Ludlow, 2003–. *Publications:* (with T. W. Potter) Romano-British Village at Grandford, Cambridgeshire, 1980; (ed) Parish Register Transcripts: Romsley, Worcs, 1988; Stone, Worcs, 1989. *Recreations:* Italian opera, genealogy, red wine, the poetry of Horace. *Address:* St Leonard's House, Upper Linney, Ludlow SY8 1EF. *T:* (01584) 878770.

POTTER, Very Rev. Christopher Nicholas Lynden; Dean of St Asaph, since 2001; *b* 4 Oct. 1949; *s* of Sir (Joseph) Raymond (Lynden) Potter and of (Daphne) Marguerite Potter; *m* 1973, Jenny Lees; three *s* one *d*. *Educ:* Haileybury Coll.; Univ. of Leeds (BA (Hons) English/Fine Art 1971); St Asaph Diocesan Ordination Trng Course. Lectr, Tutor and Librarian, Bradford Art Coll., 1971–73; self-employed furniture designer and cabinet maker, 1975–90; ordained deacon, 1993, priest, 1994; Curate, Flint, 1993–96; Vicar of grouped parishes of Llanfair DC, Llanelidan, Efenechtyd and Derwen, 1996–2001. *Recreations:* hill walking, reading, mending things. *Address:* The Deanery, St Asaph, Denbighshire LL17 0RL. *T:* (01745) 583597.

POTTER, Dr David Edwin, CBE 1997; FREng; Founder, and Chairman, Psion plc, since 1980 (Chief Executive, 1980–99); a Director, Bank of England, since 2003; *b* 4 July 1943; *s* of Paul James Potter and Mary Agnes (*née* Snape); *m* 1969, Elaine Goldberg; three *s*. *Educ:* Trinity Coll., Cambridge (Exhibnr; MA); Imperial Coll., London (PhD 1970). Lectr, Blackett Lab., Imperial Coll., London, 1970–80. Commonwealth Schol., 1966–69; Asst Prof., UCLA, 1974. Director: Charterhouse Venture Fund Management Ltd, 1985–94; Press Assoc. Ltd, 1994–97 (Vice-Chm., 1995–97); London First Centre, 1994–2002; Finsbury Technology Trust, 1995–; Chairman: Symbian Ltd, 1998–2004; Knowledge=Power, 2000–02. Member: Nat. Cttee of Inquiry into Higher Educn (Dearing Cttee), 1996–97; HEFCE, 1997–2003; Council for Sci. and Technol., Cabinet Office, 1998–2004. Mem., London Regl Council, CBI, 1993–99. Vis. Fellow, Nuffield Coll., Oxford, 1998–. Gov., London Business Sch., 2000–. Lectures: Stockton, London Business Sch., 1998; Millennium, 10 Downing St, 1999; Tacitus, World Traders' Co., 2000. FRSA 1989; FREng 2001. Hon. Fellow: Imperial Coll., 1998; London Business Sch., 1998. Hon. DTech: Kingston, 1998; Oxford Brookes, 1999; Hon. DSc: Brunel, 1998; Westminster, 1998; Warwick, 1999; Sheffield, 1999; York, 2002; Edinburgh, 2002. Mountbatten Medal for Outstanding Services to Electronics Industry, Nat. Electronics Council, 1994. *Publications:* Computational Physics, 1972; contribs to various physics jls. *Recreations:* tennis, golf, flute, bridge, reading, ideas. *Address:* (office) 10 Park Crescent, W1B 1PQ. *Club:* Portland.

POTTER, David Roger William; Director, Noble Group, since 2000; Chairman, Camco International, since 2006; *b* 27 July 1944; *s* of late William Edward Potter and Joan Louise (*née* Frost); *m* 1966, Joanna Trollope, *qv* (marr. diss. 1983); two *d*; *m* 1991, Teresa Jill Benson; one *d*. *Educ:* Bryanston Sch.; University Coll., Oxford (MA). Nat. Discount Co., 1965–69; Managing Director: Credit Suisse First Boston and Credit Suisse White Weld, 1969–81; Samuel Montagu & Co. Ltd, 1981–89; Midland Montagu Corporate Banking, 1986–89; Gp Chief Exec., Guinness Mahon Holdings, 1990–98; Chm. and Chief Exec., Guinness Mahon & Co. Ltd, Merchant Bankers, 1990–98; Dep. Chm., Investec Bank (UK) Ltd, 1998–99. Chairman: EON Lifestyle, 2001–06; DictaScribe, 2001–03; Deltron Electronics, 2005–06; Director: Maybox plc, 1987–90; Thomas Cook, 1989–91; Tyndal plc, 1989–91; Rose Partnership, 2000; WMC Communications, 2001–03; New Media Spark, 2002–; Numerica Gp plc, 2003–05; Solar Integrated Technologies, 2004– (Chm., 2004–06); Quercus Publishing, 2006–; Vycon Inc., 2007–. Chm., London Film Commn, 1996–2000. Gov., Bryanston Sch., 1982–2007; Mem. Council, KCL, 1997–2007 (Treas., 1998–2007; FKC 2006); Mem. Adv. Council, Centre for the Study of Financial Innovation, 1990–. Chm., Nat. Film and Television Sch. Foundn, 2004– (Mem., 1997–2004); Trustee: Worldwide Volunteering for Young People (formerly Youth for Britain), 1994–; Nelson Mandela Children Foundn, 1998–. Mem., Adv. Bd, London Capital Club, 1995–. *Recreations:* shooting, gardening, golf. *Address:* (office) 6 Norland Square, W11 4PX; *e-mail:* david@davidpotter.org. *Club:* Vincent's (Oxford).

POTTER, Ernest Frank; Director, Finance, Cable & Wireless plc, 1979–87 (Director of Finance and Corporate Planning, 1977–79); *b* 29 April 1923; *s* of Frank William and Edith Mary Potter; *m* 1st, 1945, Madge (*née* Arrowsmith) (*d* 1990); one *s*; 2nd, 1992, Barbara (*née* Brewis-Levie). *Educ:* Dr Challoner's Grammar Sch., Amersham. FCMA, FCIS, MIMC. Commissioned Pilot and Navigator, RAF, 1941–49. Chief Accountant, Bulmer & Lumb Ltd, 1950–58; Director, Management Consulting, Coopers & Lybrand, 1959–71; British Steel Corporation, Cammell Laird Shipbuilders Ltd, 1972–77; Director (non-executive): Cable & Wireless (West Indies) Ltd, 1977–87; Bahrain Telecommunications Corp., 1982–89; Cable & Wireless North America Inc., 1980–87; Cable & Wireless Hongkong Ltd, 1982–87; Cable & Wireless (Leasing) Ltd, 1982–87; Bahrain Telecommunications Corp., 1982–89; Cable & Wireless Marine Ltd, 1984–87; Mercury Communications Ltd, 1985–87; Cable & Wireless (Bermuda) Ltd, 1986–87; General Hybrid Ltd, 1987–91; Cable Corp. Ltd, 1988–97; Windsor Cable Ltd, 1988–97; Telephone Corp. Ltd, 1988–92; Micrelec Gp, 1989–92; Chairman: Clebern Internat. Ltd, 1988–89; Holmes Protection Inc., 1990–91; Themes Internat., 1991–92. Mem., Accounting Standards Cttee, 1985–90. *Recreations:* golf, sailing. *Address:* 11 Ridgeway, St Ann's Park, Virginia Water, Surrey GU25 4TE. *T:* (01344) 842178. *Clubs:* Royal Air Force; Foxhills (Surrey); St Mawes Sailing.

POTTER, Jeremy Patrick L.; *see* Lee-Potter.

POTTER, John Herbert, MBE 1974; HM Diplomatic Service, retired; *b* 11 Jan. 1928; *s* of Herbert George and Winifred Eva Potter; *m* 1953, Winifred Susan Florence Hall (*d*

2000); one *d.* *Educ:* elementary education at various state schools. Electrical Engineering jobs, 1942–45; served HM Forces, 1945–48; GPO, 1948–53; Foreign Office, 1953–55; Commercial Attaché, Bangkok, 1955–57; FO, 1957–60; Istanbul, 1960; Ankara, 1960–64; Second Secretary, Information, 1962; Second Sec., Information, Addis Ababa, 1964; Vice-Consul, Information, Johannesburg, 1964–66; DSAO, later FCO, 1966–70; First Sec. (Administration): Brussels, 1970–74; Warsaw, 1974–76; FCO (Inspectorate), 1976–80; Counsellor (Admin) and Consul-Gen., Moscow, 1980–81; Counsellor (Admin), Bonn, 1981–82. *Recreations:* reading, languages, walking. *Address:* The Penthouse Flat, 37 Park Road, Bexhill-on-Sea, E Sussex TN39 3HX.

POTTER, Rt Hon. Sir Mark (Howard), Kt 1988; PC 1996; President of the Family Division and Head of Family Justice, since 2005; President, Court of Protection, since 2007; *b* 27 Aug. 1937; *s* of Prof. Harold Potter, LLD, PhD, and Beatrice Spencer Potter (*née* Crowder); *m* 1962, Undine Amanda Fay, *d* of Major James Miller, 5/6th Rajputana Rifles, and Bunty Miller, painter; two *s.* *Educ:* Perse Sch., Cambridge; Gonville and Caius Coll., Cambridge (Schol.; BA (Law Tripos) 1960; MA 1963; Hon. Fellow 1998). National Service, 15 Med. Regt RA, 1955–57 (commnd 1956); 289 Lt Parachute Regt RHA(TA), 1958–64. Asst Supervisor, Legal Studies, Girton, Gonville and Caius, Queens' and Sidney Sussex Colls, 1961–68; called to Bar, Gray's Inn, 1961, Bencher, 1987, Treasurer, 2004; in practice, 1962–88; QC 1980; a Recorder, 1986–88; a Judge of the High Court of Justice, QBD (Commercial Court), 1988–96; a Presiding Judge, Northern Circuit, 1991–94; a Lord Justice of Appeal, 1996–2005. Member: Supreme Ct Rule Cttee, 1980–84; Lord Chancellor's Civil Justice Review Cttee, 1985–88; Chm., Bar Public Affairs Cttee, 1987; Vice-Chm., Council of Legal Educn, 1989–91; Chairman: Lord Chancellor's Adv. Cttee on Legal Educn and Conduct, 1998–99; Legal Services Adv. Panel, subseq. Consultancy Panel, 2000–05. Mem. Council, Nottingham Univ., 1996–99. Trustee, Somerset House Trust, 1997–. Hon. FKC 2005. Hon. LLD London Guildhall, 2000. *Recreations:* family and sporting. *Address:* Royal Courts of Justice, Strand, WC2A 2LL. *Clubs:* Garrick, Saintsbury; St Enedoc Golf.

POTTER, Michael Nicholas; Executive Chairman, Seven Publishing, since 2003 (publishers of delicious, and Sainsbury's Magazine); *b* 17 Oct. 1949; *s* of Alan Edward and Evelyn Mabel Potter; *m* 1973, Janet Nyasa Griffiths; one *s* two *d.* *Educ:* Royal Grammar Sch., Guildford; London Univ. (BSc Econ. (ext.)). DipM, MCIM 1974. Joined Haymarket Publishing, 1971 (Publishing Dir, Campaign and Marketing, 1979–83); founded Redwood Publishing, 1983, Chm., 2001–03: launched over 50 mags, incl. BBC Top Gear, M & S Mag., Sky TV Guide. Dir, Prince's Trust Trading, 1999–2007; non-exec. Dir, 4 imprint plc, 2001–03. Mem. Council, Mktg Gp of GB, 1993– (Chm., 1995–97); Dir, PPA, 1995–2003; Mem., Assoc. of Publishing Agencies, 1993– (Chm., 1994–95). Member, Development Board: Nat. Portrait Gall., 1999–2007; Royal Court Th., 1999–2007. FRSA 1998. Marcus Morris Award for contrib. to magazine ind., PPA, 1998. *Recreations:* cars, motor-racing, theatre, opera, cinema, cricket. *Address:* Seven Publishing Ltd, 20 Upper Ground, SE1 9PD. *T:* (020) 7775 7775; *e-mail:* mpotter@7publishing.co.uk; (home) Hosey Rigge House, Westerham, Kent TN16 1TA. *Clubs:* Groucho, Fiorano.

POTTER, Rev. Philip Alford; General Secretary, World Council of Churches, 1972–84; *b* 19 Aug. 1921; *s* of Clement Potter and Violet Peters, Roseau, Dominica, Windward Is, WI; *m* 1st, 1956, Ethel Olive Doreen Cousins (*d* 1980), Jamaica, WI; 2nd, 1984, Rt Rev. Barbel von Wartenberg (now Bishop of Holstein-Lübeck). *Educ:* Dominica Grammar Sch.; United Theological Coll., Jamaica; London Univ. BD, MTh. Methodist Minister. Overseas Sec., British SCM, 1948–50; Superintendent, Cap Haitien Circuit, Methodist Church, Haiti, 1950–54; Sec., later Dir, Youth Dept, WCC, 1954–60; Sec. for WI and W Africa, Methodist Missionary Society, London, 1961–66; Dir, Commn on World Mission and Evangelism, and Associate Gen. Sec., WCC, 1967–72. Chaplain, Univ. of WI and Lectr, United Theol Coll. of WI, 1985–90. Mem., then Chm., Youth Dept Cttee, WCC, 1948–54; Chm., World Student Christian Fedn, 1960–68. Editor: Internat. Review of Mission, 1967–72; Ecumenical Rev., 1972–84. Hon. Doctor of Theology: Hamburg Univ., Germany, 1971; Geneva, 1976; Theol Inst. of Rumanian Orthodox Church, 1977; Humboldt Univ., Berlin, 1982; Uppsala, 1984; Hon. LLD W Indies, 1974; Hon. DD Birmingham, 1985; Hon. Dr Cape Town, 1998; Vienna, 2001. Niwano Peace Prize, Japan, 1986. *Publications:* (with Prof. Hendrik Berkhof) Key Words of the Gospel, 1964; The Love of Power or the Power of Love, 1974; Life in all its Fullness, 1981; (with Barbel von Wartenberg) Freedom is for Freeing, 1990; (jtly) Seeking and Serving the Truth: first hundred years of the World Student Christian Federation, 1997; chapter in Explosives Lateinamerika (ed by T. Tschuy), 1969; essays in various symposia; contrib. various jls, incl. Ecumenical Rev., Internat. Rev. of Mission, Student World. *Recreations:* swimming, hiking, music, geology. *Address:* Plönniesstrasse 6, 23560 Lübeck, Germany.

POTTER, Raymond, CB 1990; Deputy Secretary, 1986–93 (Courts and Legal Services, 1986–91), Head of the Court Service and Deputy Clerk of the Crown in Chancery, 1989–93, Lord Chancellor's Department; *b* 26 March 1933; *s* of William Thomas Potter and Elsie May Potter; *m* 1959, Jennifer Mary Quicke; one *s.* *Educ:* Henry Thornton Grammar School. Called to the Bar, Inner Temple, 1971, Bencher, 1989. Central Office, Royal Courts of Justice, 1950; Western Circuit, 1963; Chief Clerk, Bristol Crown Court, 1972; Dep. Circuit Administrator, Western Circuit, 1976; Circuit Administrator, Northern Circuit, 1982–86. Vice-Pres., Southern Rent Assessment Panel, 2001–03 (Pres., SW Panel, 1995–2001); Standing Chm., Strategic Health Authy Review Panel, 2003–. *Recreation:* painting. *Address:* 8 Robinson Way, Backwell, Bristol BS48 3BP. *Club:* Athenæum.

PÖTTERING, Hans-Gert; Member, since 1979 and President, 2007–June 2009, European Parliament; *b* Bersenbrück, 15 Sept. 1945; two *s.* *Educ:* Univ. of Bonn; Univ. of Geneva; Institut des Hautes Études Internationales, Geneva. Res. Asst, 1976–79; Lectr, Univ. of Osnabrück, 1989; Hon. Prof., 1995. European Parliament: Chm., Subcttee on Security and Disarmament, 1984–94; Vice-Chm., EPP Gp, 1994–99; Chm., EPP-ED Gp, 1999–2007; Head, EPP's and EPP-ED Gp's Working Party: on 1996 Intergovtl Conf., 1994–96; on EU Enlargement, 1996–99. Land Chm., Europa-Union in Lower Saxony, 1981–91; Chm., Europa-Union Deutschland, 1997–99. Chairman: Osnabrück Dist, Junge Union, CDU, 1974–76; Bersenbrück Br., CDU, 1974–80; Osnabrück Dist, CDU, 1990–; Mem. Exec. Cttee and Federal Exec., CDU; Mem., Bureau, EPP. Hon. Dr: Babeş-Bolyai; Opole. Walter Hallstein Prize, Frankfurt, 2007. Grand Order of Merit (Germany); Grand Decoration (Austria); Mérite Européen en or (Luxembourg); Grand Cross, Order of St Gregory the Great; Grand Order of Queen Jelena with Sash and Star (Croatia). *Publications:* Adenauers Sicherheitspolitik 1955–63, 1975; (with F. Wiehler) Die vergessenen Regionen, 1983; (with L. Kühnhardt) Europas vereinigte Staaten: annäherungen an werte und ziele, 1993; (with L. Kühnhardt) Kontinent Europa: kern, übergänge, grenzen, 1998; (with L. Kühnhardt) Weltpartner Europäische Union, 2001; Von der Vision zur Wirklichkeit: auf dem weg zur einigung Europas, 2004. *Address:* European Parliament, Rue Wiertz 60, 1047 Brussels, Belgium.

POTTERTON, Homan, FSA; art historian and writer; Editor, 1993–2002, and publisher, 2000–02, Irish Arts Review; Director, National Gallery of Ireland, 1980–88; *b* 9 May 1946; sixth *s* of late Thomas Edward Potterton and Eileen Potterton (*née* Tong). *Educ:* Kilkenny Coll.; Trinity Coll., Dublin (BA 1968, MA 1973); Edinburgh Univ. (Dip. Hist. Art 1971). FSA 1981. Cataloguer, National Gall. of Ireland, 1971–73; Asst Keeper, National Gall., London, 1974–80. Mem. Bd, GPA Dublin Internat. Piano Competition, 1987–92. HRHA 1982. *Publications:* Irish Church Monuments 1570–1880, 1975; A Guide to the National Gallery, 1976, rev. edn 1980 (German, French, Italian and Japanese edns 1977); The National Gallery, London, 1977; Reynolds and Gainsborough: themes and painters in the National Gallery, 1976; Pageant and Panorama: the elegant world of Canaletto, 1978; (jtly) Irish Art and Architecture, 1978; Venetian Seventeenth Century Painting (National Gallery Exhibn Catalogue), 1979; introd. to National Gallery of Ireland Illustrated Summary Catalogue of Paintings, 1981; (jtly) National Gallery of Ireland, 50 Pictures, 1981; Dutch 17th and 18th Century Paintings in the National Gallery of Ireland: a complete catalogue, 1986; Rathcormick: a childhood recalled, 2001; Potterton People and Places: three centuries of an Irish family, 2006; contrib. Burlington Mag., Apollo, Connoisseur, FT and Country Life. *Recreation:* genealogy. *Address:* Colombel Bas, 81140 Castelnau-de-Montmiral, France. *T:* and *Fax:* (5) 63405352; *e-mail:* hpotterton@free.fr; *web:* www.potterton.ie. *Clubs:* Royal Over-Seas League; St Stephen's Green (Dublin).

POTTINGER, Frank Vernon Hunter, RSA 1991; sculptor; *b* 1 Oct. 1932; *s* of William Pottinger and Veronica (*née* Irvine); *m* 1991, Evelyn Norah Smith; one step *s* two step *d.* *Educ:* Boroughmuir Secondary Sch.; Edinburgh Coll. of Art (DA 1963). Apprentice fitter engineer, 1948–53; nat. service, 1953–55; teacher: Portobello Secondary Sch., 1965–73; Aberdeen Coll. of Educn, 1973–85; vis. lectr, colls of art in Scotland, 1980–91; full-time artist, 1985–. *Address:* 30/5 Elbe Street, Edinburgh EH6 7HW. *T:* (0131) 553 5082.

POTTINGER, Graham Robert; Chief Executive, Scottish Mutual Assurance plc, 1997–2002 (Finance Director, 1992–96); Managing Director, Abbey National Financial Investment Services plc, 1997–2002; *b* 14 June 1949; *s* of Arthur and Mary Pottinger; *m* 1970, Dorothy McLean; one *s* one *d.* *Educ:* Jordanhill Coll. Sch., Glasgow; Glasgow Univ. (LLB). CA 1992; ACMA 1993. Peat Marwick Mitchell & Co., 1969–72; Partner, Deloitte Haskins & Sells, 1972–79; Controller, UK and Africa, Cargill Plc, 1980–92. Mem. Council, ICAS, 1995–2001.

POTTINGER, Piers Julian Dominic; Deputy Chairman (formerly Group Managing Director), Chime Communications plc, since 1993; *b* 3 March 1954; *s* of late W. G. Pottinger; *m* 1979, Carolyn Ann Rhodes; one *s* three *d.* *Educ:* Edinburgh Acad.; Winchester Coll. Trainee, J. Henry Schroder Wagg, 1972–74; Res. Analyst, Laurence Prust and Co., 1974–78; Exec., Charles Barker, 1978–80; Dir, Media Relations Manufacturers, Hanover, NY, 1980–82; Man. Dir, Sterling Financial Public Relations, 1982–85; Man. Dir, then Chm., Bell Pottinger (formerly Lowe Bell) Financial, 1985–. Director: Newmarket Investments plc (formerly British Bloodstock Agency plc), 2001–06 (Chm., 2001–06); Northern Racing Ltd, 2002–05; Chm., Sportech plc, 2006–. Former Member: Bd, Scottish Ballet; Gen. Council, Poetry Soc. Trustee, Foundn for Liver Res. (formerly Liver Res. Trust), 2001–; Vice-Pres., Nat. Soc. for Epilepsy, 2004–. *Recreations:* horse racing, golf, Real tennis. *Address:* The Old Rectory, Wixoe, Sudbury, Suffolk CO10 8UG. *T:* (01440) 785241. *Clubs:* Garrick, Turf; Jockey Club Rooms (Newmarket); Newmarket Real Tennis.

POTTS, Archibold; Director, Bewick Press, since 1989; *b* 27 Jan. 1932; *s* of late Ernest W. Potts and Ellen Potts; *m* 1957, Marguerite Elsie (*née* Elliott) (*d* 1983); one *s* one *d.* *Educ:* Monkwearmouth Central Sch., Sunderland; Ruskin and Oriel Colls, Oxford (Dip. Econ. and Pol. Sci., 1958; BA PPE 2nd cl. hons, 1960); ext. postgrad. student, London Univ. (Postgrad. CertEd 1964) and Durham Univ. (MEd 1969). Nat. Service, RAF, 1950–53. Railway Clerk, 1947–50 and 1953–56. Lecturer: N Oxfordshire Tech. Coll., 1961; York Tech. Coll., 1962–65; Rutherford Coll. of Technology and Newcastle upon Tyne Polytechnic, 1965–80; Head of Sch. of Business Admin, 1980–87, Associate Dean, Faculty of Business and Professional Studies, 1988, Newcastle upon Tyne Polytechnic. Moderator, history courses, Tyneside Open Coll. Network, 1992–2005. Tyne and Wear County Council: Councillor, 1979–86; Vice-Chm., Planning Cttee, 1981–86; Vice-Chm., Council, 1983–84; Chm., Council, 1984–85. Contested (Lab) Westmorland, 1979. Chm., NE Labour History Soc., 1990–96 (Vice Pres., 1997–); Mem., Exec. Cttee, Soc. for Study of Labour History, 1987–96. *Publications:* Stand True, 1976; Bibliography of Northern Labour History, 1982–; (ed) Shipbuilders and Engineers, 1987; Jack Casey, the Sunderland Assassin, 1991; The Wearside Champions, 1993; Jack London, the forgotten champion, 1997; Zilliacus, a life for peace and socialism, 2002; Headlocks and Handbags, 2005; contributions to: Dictionary of Labour Biography, vol. 2 1974, vol. 4 1977, vol. 5 1979, vol. 9 1993, vol. 11 2003, vol. 12 2005; Oxford DNB, 2004; articles on economics and history. *Recreations:* local history, watching old films. *Address:* 47 Graham Park Road, Gosforth, Newcastle upon Tyne NE3 4BJ. *T:* (0191) 284 5132. *Club:* Victory Service.

POTTS, Prof. David Malcolm, PhD, DSc; FREng, FICE; Professor of Analytical Soil Mechanics, since 1994, and Deputy Head, Department of Civil and Environmental Engineering, since 2001, Imperial College London; *b* 26 April 1952; *s* of Leonard Francis Potts and Doris Florence Potts; *m* 1974, Deborah Margot Peel; two *d.* *Educ:* King's Coll., London (BSc Eng); Churchill Coll., Cambridge (PhD 1976); Imperial Coll., London (DSc 1996). FICE 1997; FREng 2001. Res. Engr, Shell, Netherlands, 1976–79; Lectr, 1979–89, Reader, 1989–94, ICSTM. *Publications:* Finite Element Analysis in Geotechnical Engineering: theory, 1999; Finite Element Analysis in Geotechnical Engineering: application, 2001; numerous contribs to learned jls incl. Geotechnique, Internat. Jl Num. Anal. Meth. in Geomech., Internat. Jl Num. Meth. Engrg, Engrg Computations, Computers and Geotechnics, Canadian Geotechnical Jl, Computational Methods, Appl. Mech. Engrg, Geotechnical Engrg, Jl Geotechnical and Geoenvmtl Engrg. *Recreations:* fly fishing, swimming. *Address:* Department of Civil and Environmental Engineering, Imperial College London, Imperial College Road, SW7 2BU. *T:* (020) 7594 6084, *Fax:* (020) 7594 6150; *e-mail:* d.potts@imperial.ac.uk.

POTTS, Sir (Francis) Humphrey, Kt 1986; a Judge of the High Court of Justice, Queen's Bench Division, 1986–2001; *b* 18 Aug. 1931; *er s* of late Francis William Potts and Elizabeth Hannah (*née* Humphrey), Penshaw, Co. Durham; *m* 1971, Philippa Margaret Campbell, *d* of the late J. C. H. Le B. Croke and Mrs J. F. G. Downes; two *s* and two step *s.* *Educ:* Royal Grammar Sch., Newcastle upon Tyne; St Catherine's Society, Oxford (BCL 1954, MA 1957; Hon. Fellow, St Catherine's Coll., 2002). Barrister-at-Law, Lincoln's Inn, 1955 (Tancred Student, 1953; Cholmeley Scholar, 1954), Bencher, 1979; North Eastern Circuit, 1955; practised in Newcastle upon Tyne, 1955–71; QC 1971; a Recorder, 1972–86; admitted to Hong Kong Bar, 1984; Presiding Judge, NE Circuit, 1988–91. Member: Mental Health Review Tribunal, 1984–86; Criminal Injuries Compensation Bd, 1985–86; Parole Bd, 1992–96 (Vice-Chm., 1995–96); Chm., Special Immigration Appeals Commn, 1997–2001. Trustee, Mental Health Foundn, 1990–96. Pres., Norcare, 1997–99. *Address:* c/o Royal Courts of Justice, Strand, WC2A 2LL; Third Floor North, 4 Stone Buildings, Lincoln's Inn, WC2A 3XT.

POTTS, Paul John; Group Chief Executive, since 2000, and a Director, since 1995, PA Group; Editor-in-Chief, The Press Association, 1996–2006; *b* 21 Jan. 1950; *s* of late Michael Henry Potts and of Sylvia Brenda Potts; *m* 1st, 1976, Gabrielle Jane Fagan (marr. diss. 1994); one *s* two *d*; 2nd, 1994, Judith Anne Fielding. *Educ:* Worksop Coll. Gen. Reporter, Sheffield Star, 1968–74; Lobby Corresp., Yorkshire Post, 1974–78; General Reporter: Daily Telegraph, 1978–81; Mail on Sunday, 1981–82; Political Ed., News of the World, 1982–86; Political Ed., then Asst Ed., later Dep. Ed., Daily Express, 1986–95. Chm., CNW Gp (formerly Canada NewsWire), 2003– (Dir, 2000–); Mem., Nomination Cttee, Reuters Founders Share Co. Ltd, 2002–07. Mem., Code of Practice Cttee, 1996–2007. Patron, Sheffield Wednesday Supporters Trust, 2001. Hon. DLitt Sheffield, 2002. *Recreations:* military history, walking. *Address:* PA Group Ltd, 292 Vauxhall Bridge Road, SW1V 1AE. *T:* (020) 7963 7000. *Clubs:* Garrick, Royal Automobile.

POTTS, Robin; QC 1982; barrister; *b* 2 July 1944; *s* of William and Elaine Potts; *m*; one *s*; *m* Helen Elizabeth Sharp; two *s* one *d*. *Educ:* Wolstanton Grammar Sch.; Magdalen Coll., Oxford (BA, BCL). Called to the Bar, Gray's Inn, 1968, Bencher, 1993. Consulting Ed., Gore-Browne on Companies, 43rd and 44th edns. *Address:* 2 Harley House, Brunswick Place, NW1 4PR. *T:* (020) 7486 0897.

POTTS, Timothy Faulkner, DPhil; Director, Fitzwilliam Museum, Cambridge, since 2008; *b* 17 June 1958; *s* of Ian Faulkner Potts and Judy Potts; one *s* one *d*. *Educ:* Univ. of Sydney (BA Hons 1980); DPhil Oxon 1987. Res. Lectr, 1985–87, British Acad. Postdoctoral Res. Fellow, 1987–90, Christ Church, Oxford; Associate and Dir, Lehman Bros, NY and London, 1990–94; Director: Nat. Gall. of Victoria, Melbourne, 1994–98; Kimbell Art Mus., Texas, 1998–2007. *Publications:* Civilization: ancient treasures from the British Museum, 1990, 1997; Mesopotamia and the East: an archaeological and historical study of foreign relations *c* 3400–2000 BC, 1994; (ed jtly) Culture Through Objects: ancient Near Eastern studies in honour of P. R. S. Moorey, 2003; (ed) Kimbell Art Museum: handbook of the collection, 2003. *Address:* Fitzwilliam Museum, Trumpington Street, Cambridge CB2 1RB; *e-mail:* tp285@cam.ac.uk.

POULSEN, Ole Lønsmann, Hon. GCVO 2000; Ambassador of Denmark to India, since 2006; *b* 14 May 1945; *s* of Aage Lønsmann Poulsen, head teacher, and Tove Alice (*née* Gyldenstein); *m* 1973, Zareen Mehta; two *s*. *Educ:* Copenhagen Univ. (LLM 1971). Hd of Dept, Danchurchaid, 1969–73; joined Danish Diplomatic Service, 1973; Hd of Section, Min. of Foreign Affairs, Denmark, 1973–76; Advr, Asian Develt Bank, Manila, 1976–77; First Sec., New Delhi and Trade Comr, Bombay, 1977–80; Alternate Exec. Dir, World Bank, Washington, 1980–83; Dep. Head, 1983–85, Head, 1985–88, Dept of Internat. Develt Co-operation, then Under-Sec. for Multilateral Affairs (Ambassador), 1988–92, Min. of Foreign Affairs; Ambassador to Austria and Perm. Rep. to IAEA, UNIDO and UN, Vienna, also accredited to Slovenia and Bosnia Hercegovina, 1992–93; State Sec., Min. of Foreign Affairs, 1993–96; Ambassador: to UK, 1996–2001; to China, 2001–04; to Sweden, 2004–06. Chm., Industrial Develt Bd, UNIDO, 1990–91. Alternate Gov., World Bank and Gov. for Asian, African and Interamerican Develt Banks, 1989–92 and 1993–96. Chairman: Scandinavian Seminar Coll., 1975–76; Nordic Develt Fund, 1990–91. Comdr, 1999, Kt Comdr, 2005, Order of Dannebrog (Denmark); Grand Cross (Austria), 1993; Grand Cross (Sweden), 2006. *Recreations:* music, literature, sport. *Address:* Royal Danish Embassy, 11 Aurangzeb Road, New Delhi 110011, India.

POULTER, Brian Henry; Secretary, Northern Ireland Audit Office, 1989–2000; *b* 1 Sept. 1941; *s* of William Henry Poulter, PhC, MPS, and Marjorie Elizabeth Everett McBride; *m* 1968, Margaret Ann Dodds; one *s* twin *d*. *Educ:* Regent House Grammar Sch., Newtownards. Qual. as certified accountant, 1966. Hill, Vellacott and Bailey, Chartered Accountants, 1959–62; entered NICS, 1962; Min. of Health and Local Govt, 1962–65; Min. of Health and Social Services, 1965–71; Deputy Principal: Local Enterprise Develt Unit, 1971–74; Dept of Commerce, 1974–75; Chief Auditor 1975–81, Dep. Dir 1981–82, Dir 1982–87, Exchequer and Audit Dept; Dir, NI Audit Office, 1987–88. *Recreations:* reading, walking, cricket. *Address:* 20 Manse Road, Newtownards, Co. Down BT23 4TP.

POULTER, Jane Anne Marie; *see* Bonvin, J. A. M.

POULTER, John William; Chairman, Spectris plc, since 2001; *b* 22 Nov. 1942; *m* 1968, Margaret Winifred Thorn; one *s* one *d*. *Educ:* Berkhamsted Sch.; Queen's Coll., Oxford (MA). Joined Cambridge Instruments Gp, 1968, Marketing Dir, 1972–77; Dir and Gen. Manager, Robinsons Carton Packaging, 1977–81; Man. Dir, Vokes Ltd, and other BTR subsids, 1981–88; Spectris plc, 1988–: Gp Man. Dir, 1988–91; Chief Exec., 1991–2001. Chairman: Kymata Ltd, 1999–2001; Wyko Gp, 2001–04; Snell & Wilcox Ltd, 2002–; Filtronic plc, 2006–; non-executive Director: Lloyds Smaller Cos Investment Trust plc, 1992–2002; Crest Packaging plc, 1993–96; BTP plc, 1997–2000; Kidde plc, 2000–05; RAC plc, 2002–05; Smaller Cos Value Trust plc, 2002–; London Metal Exchange Ltd, 2003–05; MacQuarie European Infrastructure plc, 2003–05; Suffolk Life plc, 2006–. Gov., Ipswich Sch., 2000–. *Recreations:* sailing, walking, opera. *Address:* Spectris plc, Station Road, Egham, Surrey TW20 9NP. *T:* (01784) 470470, *Fax:* (01784) 439519; *e-mail:* john.poulter@spectris.com. *Club:* Oxford and Cambridge.

POULTON, Richard Christopher, MA; Director of Development, Round Square International Association of Schools, 2003–05; *b* 21 June 1938; *e s* of Rev. Christopher Poulton and Aileen (*née* Sparrow); *m* 1965, Zara, *o d* of late Prof. P. Crossley-Holland and Mrs J. Crossley-Holland; two *s* one *d*. *Educ:* King's Coll., Taunton; Wesleyan Univ., Middletown, Conn, USA; Pembroke Coll., Cambridge (BA 1961, CertEd 1962, MA 1965). Asst Master: Bedford Sch., 1962–63; Beckenham and Penge Grammar Sch., 1963–66; Bryanston School: Asst Master, 1966–80; Head of History Dept, 1971–76; Housemaster, 1972–80; Headmaster, Wycliffe Coll., 1980–86; Head Master, Christ's Hospital, Horsham, 1987–96; Founder Head Master, Internat. Sch. of the Regents, Pattaya, Thailand, 1996–97; Develt Officer, Inner Cities Young People's Project, 1998–2000; Clerk, All Saints Educnl Trust, 2001–04. Governor: Oxford and Cambridge Examinations Bd, 1987–90; Aiglon Coll., Switzerland, 1998–2000; Royal Bridewell Hosp., 1999–2004 and 2006–08; Beausoleil Internat. Coll., Switzerland, 2003–; Box Hill Sch., 2004–08; Presentation Gov., Christ's Hosp., 1999–. JP S Glos, 1985–86. Freeman, City of London, 1987; Liveryman, Ironmongers' Co., 1993– (Yeoman, 1990; Mem. Court, 1999–; Jun. Warden, 2006–07; Sen. Warden, 2007–08; Master, 2008–July 2009). FRSA 1994. *Publications:* Victoria, Queen of a Changing Land, 1975; Kings and Commoners, 1977; A History of the Modern World, 1980. *Recreations:* writing, choral music. *Address:* 2 Hill Cottages, Hoyle Lane, Heyshott GU29 0DU.

POUND, Sir John David, 5th Bt *cr* 1905; *b* 1 Nov. 1946; *s* of Sir Derek Allen Pound, 4th Bt; *S* father, 1980; *m* 1st, 1968 (marr. diss.); one *s*; 2nd, 1978, Penelope Ann, *er d* of late Grahame Arthur Rayden, Bramhall, Cheshire; two *s*. Liveryman, Leathersellers' Co. *Heir:* *s* Robert John Pound, *b* 12 Feb. 1973. *Address:* 106 Merrivale Lane, Turramurra, NSW 2074, Australia.

POUND, Rev. Canon Keith Salisbury; a Chaplain to the Queen, 1988–2003; *b* 3 April 1933; *s* of Percy Salisbury Pound and Annie Florence Pound. *Educ:* Roan School, Blackheath; St Catharine's Coll., Cambridge (BA 1954, MA 1958); Cuddesdon Coll., Oxford. Curate, St Peter, St Helier, Dio. Southwark, 1957–61; Training Officer, Hollowford Training and Conference Centre, Sheffield, 1961–64, Warden 1964–67; Rector of Holy Trinity, Southwark, with St Matthew, Newington, 1968–78; RD, Southwark and Newington, 1973–78; Rector of Thamesmead, 1978–86; Sub-Dean of Woolwich, 1984–86; Dean of Greenwich, 1985–86; Chaplain-Gen. and Archdeacon to Prison Service, 1986–93; Chaplain to HM Prison, Grendon and Spring Hill, 1993–98. Hon. Canon of Southwark Cathedral, 1985–. *Publication:* Creeds and Controversies, 1976. *Recreations:* theatre, music, books, crosswords. *Address:* Adeleine, Pett Road, Pett, East Sussex TN35 4HE. *T:* (01424) 813873. *Club:* Civil Service.

POUND, Stephen Pelham; MP (Lab) Ealing North, since 1997; *b* 3 July 1948; *s* of late Pelham Pound and Dominica James; *m* 1976, Marilyn Anne Griffiths; one *s* two *d*. *Educ:* London Sch. of Economics (BSc Econ., Dip. Indust. Relations). Seaman, 1967–69; Bus Conductor, 1969–70; Hosp. Porter, 1970–79; student, 1980–84; Housing Officer, Camden Council, 1984–88; Homeless Persons Officer, Hammersmith and Fulham Council, 1988–90; Housing Officer, Paddington Churches HA, 1990–97. Councillor, London Borough of Ealing, 1982–98. *Recreations:* Fulham FC, cricket, walking, collecting comics. *Address:* House of Commons, SW1A 0AA. *T:* (020) 7219 6238; 115 Milton Road, Hanwell, W7 1LG. *Clubs:* St Joseph's Catholic Social; Fulham Football Club Supporters'.

POUNDER, Prof. Robert Edward, (Roy), MD, DSc; FRCP; Professor of Medicine, Royal Free and University College Medical School, 1992–2005, now Professor Emeritus, University of London; Hon. Consultant Physician and Gastroenterologist, Royal Free Hospital, 1980–2005; *b* 31 May 1944; *s* of Edward Pounder and Annie Pounder (*née* Langdale); *m* 1972, Christine Lee; two *s*. *Educ:* Eltham Coll.; Peterhouse, Cambridge (BA 1st Cl. Hons Nat. Sci. 1966; BChir 1969; MB, MA 1970; MD 1977); Guy's Hosp. Med. Sch.; DSc (Med.) London 1992. MRCP 1971, FRCP 1984. Registrar, Central Middlesex Hosp., 1972–76; Sen. Registrar, St Thomas' Hosp., 1976–80; Royal Free Hospital School of Medicine: Sen. Lectr, 1980–85, Reader, 1985–92, in Medicine; Clin. Sub-Dean, 1986–88; Admissions Sub-Dean, 1992–95; Chm., Collegiate Cttee of Examrs, 1996–2003. Non-exec. Dir, Camden and Islington HA, 1996–2002 (Vice-Chm., 2001–02). Royal College of Physicians: Mem. Council, 1987–89 and 1997–2000; Vice-Pres., 2002–04; Associate Internat. Dir, Australasia and FE, 2004–. Member Council: British Digestive Foundn, 1987–98; British Soc. of Gastroenterology, 1996–2000 (Sec., 1982–86). Trustee, Alimentary Pharmacology and Therapeutics Trust, 1988–99. Chm., Friends of Peterhouse, 1999–2002 (Mem. Council, 1982–2002). Gov., St Paul's Sch., London, 2001– (Dep. Chm., 2007–). Founding Co-Editor, Alimentary Pharmacology and Therapeutics, 1987–; Ed.-in-Chief, GastroHep.com, 2000–. Hon. FRACP 2007. *Publications:* (ed) Long Cases in General Medicine, 1983, 2nd edn 1988; (ed) Doctor, There's Something Wrong with my Guts, 1983; (ed) Recent Advances in Gastroenterology, 6th edn 1986 to 10th edn 1994; (ed jtly) Diseases of the Gut and Pancreas, 1987, 2nd edn 1994 (trans. Italian and Greek); (ed jtly) Advanced Medicine, 1987; (ed jtly) A Colour Atlas of the Digestive System, 1989 (trans. Japanese); (ed) Landmark Papers: the histamine H_2-receptor antagonists, 1990; (ed jtly) Current Diagnosis and Treatment, 1996; (ed jtly) Inflammatory Bowel Disease, 1998; papers on pharmacological control of acid secretion, inflammatory bowel disease and med. workforce. *Recreations:* gardening, family life, travelling, encouraging skylarks. *Address:* High Tun Barn, Daglingworth, Cirencester, Glos GL7 7JA. *Fax:* (01285) 644126. *Club:* Garrick.

POUNDS, Prof. Kenneth Alwyne, CBE 1984; FRS 1981; Professor of Space Physics, 1973–2002, and Leverhulme Fellow, 2003–05, University of Leicester; *b* 17 Nov. 1934; *s* of Harry and Dorothy Pounds; *m* 1st, 1961, Margaret Mary (*née* Connell); two *s* one *d*; 2nd, 1982, Joan Mary (*née* Millit); one *s* one *d*. *Educ:* Salt Sch., Shipley, Yorkshire; University Coll. London (BSc, PhD; Fellow, 1993). Department of Physics, University of Leicester: Asst Lectr, 1960; Lectr, 1961; Sen. Lectr, 1969; Prof., 1973; Hd, Dept of Physics and Astronomy, 1986–2002; Chief Exec., PPARC (on leave of absence from Univ. of Leicester), 1994–98. Member: SERC, 1980–84 (Chm., Astronomy, Space and Radio Bd); Management Bd, British Nat. Space Centre, 1986–88; Pres., RAS, 1990–92. DUniv York, 1984; Hon. DSc: Loughborough, 1992; Sheffield Hallam, 1997; Warwick, 2001; Leicester, 2005. Gold Medal, RAS, 1989. *Publications:* many, in Monthly Notices, Nature, Astrophysical Jl, etc. *Recreations:* sport, music. *Address:* 12 Swale Close, Oadby, Leicester LE2 4GF. *T:* (0116) 271 9370.

POUNTNEY, David Willoughby, CBE 1994; freelance director; *b* 10 Sept. 1947; *s* of late Dorothy and Willoughby Pountney; *m* 1980, Jane Henderson; one *s* one *d*. *Educ:* St John's College Choir School, Cambridge; Radley College; St John's College, Cambridge (MA; Hon. Fellow, 2007). Joined Scottish Opera, 1970; 1st major production Katya Kabanova (Janacek), Wexford Fest., 1972; Dir of Productions, Scottish Opera, 1976–80; individual guest productions for all British Opera companies, also USA (Metropolitan Opera début, world première of The Voyage by Philip Glass, 1992), Aust., Italy, Germany, The Netherlands; Dir of Prodns, ENO, 1982–93; Intendant, Bregenzer Festspiele, 2004–. Productions for ENO include: Rusalka (Dvorak); Osud (Janacek); Dr Faust (Busoni); Lady Macbeth of Mtsensk (Shostakovich); Wozzeck (Berg); Pelléas and Mélisande (Debussy); Don Carlos (Verdi); Falstaff (Verdi); The Adventures of Mr Broucek (Janacek); The Fairy Queen (Purcell); Nabucco (Verdi), 2000; other major productions include: The Doctor of Myddfai (and libretto) (Peter Maxwell Davies), WNO, 1996; Julietta (Martinu), Opera North, 1997; Dalibor (Smetana), Scottish Opera, 1998; Guillaume Tell (Rossini), Vienna State Opera, 1998; Greek Passion, Bregenz, 1999, Royal Opera House, 2000; Faust (Gounod), Munich, 2000; Mr Emmet Takes a Walk (Peter Maxwell Davies), première, Orkney Fest., 2000; Jenufa, Vienna State Opera, 2002; Turandot, Salzburg Fest., 2002; Euryanthe, Netherlands Opera, 2003; Khovanshchina, WNO, 2007; La Juive, Zurich, 2007; Carmen, Bolshoi, Moscow, 2008; Die Soldaten, Lincoln Center Fest., NY, 2008. Martinu Medal, Prague, 2000. Chevalier de l'Ordre des Arts et des Lettres (France), 1993. *Publications:* (with Mark Elder and Peter Jonas) Power House, 1992; numerous trans. of opera, esp. Czech and Russian repertoire. *Recreations:* croquet, food and wine. *Address:* Château d'Azu, 71230 St Romain sous Gourdon, France. *Club:* Garrick.

POVER, Alan John, CMG 1990; HM Diplomatic Service, retired; High Commissioner to the Republic of Gambia, 1990–93; *b* 16 Dec. 1933; *s* of John Pover and Anne (*née* Hession); *m* 1964, Doreen Elizabeth Dawson; one *s* two *d*. *Educ:* Salesian College, Thornleigh, Bolton. Served HM Forces, 1953–55; Min. of Pensions and Nat. Insce, 1955–61; Commonwealth Relations Office, 1961; Second Secretary: Lagos, 1962–66; Tel Aviv, 1966–69; Second, later First, Sec., Karachi/Islamabad, 1969–73; First Sec., FCO, 1973–76; Consul, Cape Town, 1976–80; Counsellor, Diplomatic Service Inspector, 1983–86; Counsellor and Consul-Gen., Washington, 1986–90. *Recreations:* cricket, golf, gardening. *Club:* West Berkshire Golf.

POVEY, Sir Keith, Kt 2001; QPM 1991; HM Chief Inspector of Constabulary, 2002–05; *b* 30 April 1943; *s* of late Trevor Roberts Povey and Dorothy (*née* Parsonnage); *m* 1964, Carol Ann Harvey; two *d*. *Educ:* Abbeydale Grammar Sch., Sheffield; Sheffield Univ. (BA Law). Joined Sheffield City Police, 1962; Chief Superintendent, S Yorks, seconded as Staff Officer to Sir Lawrence Byford, HMCIC, 1984–86; Asst Chief Constable, Humberside, 1986–90; Dep. Chief Constable, Northants, 1990–93; Chief Constable, Leics, 1993–97; HM Inspector of Constabulary, 1997–2001. Hon. Secretary: ACPO General Purposes Cttee, 1994–96 (Chm., 1996–97); ACPO Crime Prevention Sub-cttee, 1994–96 (Chm., 1996–97). Hon. LLD Sheffield, 2004; Hon. DCL Northumbria, 2005. *Recreations:* jogging, flying (private pilot's licence).

POWELL; *see* Baden-Powell.

POWELL, family name of **Baron Powell of Bayswater**.

POWELL OF BAYSWATER, Baron *cr* 2000 (Life Peer), of Canterbury in the County of Kent; **Charles David Powell,** KCMG 1990; Chairman: LVMH (UK), since 2000; Capital Generation Partners, since 2006; *b* 6 July 1941; *s* of Air Vice-Marshal John Frederick Powell, *qv*; *m* 1964, Carla Bonardi; two *s*. *Educ:* King's Sch., Canterbury; New Coll., Oxford (BA). Diplomatic Service, 1963–83: served Helsinki, Washington, Bonn, Brussels (UK Perm. Repn to EU); Counsellor, 1979; Special Counsellor for Rhodesia negotiations, 1979–80; Private Sec. to the Prime Minister, 1984–91. Director: National Westminster Bank, 1991–2000; Jardine Matheson Hldgs, 1991–2000; Matheson & Co., 1991–; Mandarin Oriental Hotel Gp, 1992–; J. Rothschild Name Co., 1993–2003; Said Holdings, 1994–2000; LVMH Moet-Hennessy-Louis Vuitton, 1995–; British-Mediterranean Airways, 1998–2007 (Dep. Chm.); Caterpillar Inc., 2001–; Textron Inc., 2001–; Schindler Holdings, 2003–; Sen. Ind. Dir, Yell Gp, 2003–; Chairman: Phillips, 1999–2001; Sagitta Asset Mgt Ltd, 2000–05. Chm. Internat. Adv. Bd, Rolls Royce, 2000–; Member: Europ. Adv. Bd, Hicks Muse Tate & Furst, 2001–05; Internat. Adv. Council, Textron Corp., 1995–; International Advisory Board: Barrick Gold, 2000–; Magna Corp., 2002–; Alfa Gp, 2004–; ACE Insce, 2006–. Chairman: Singapore British Business Council, 1994–2001; Atlantic Partnership, 2004–; Pres., China-Britain Business Council, 1998–2007. Mem., EU Select Cttee, H of L, 2007–; Chm., All Party Parly Gp on Entrepreneurship, 2005–. Trustee: Aspen Inst., 1995–; British Mus., 2002–; Chm., Trustees, Oxford Business Sch. Foundn, 1998–. *Recreation:* walking. *Address:* House of Lords, SW1A 0PW.
See also Hon. H. E. Powell, J. C. Powell, J. N. Powell.

POWELL, Angela; *see* McNab, A.

POWELL, Christopher; *see* Powell, J. C.

POWELL, Gen. Colin Luther, Hon. KCB 1993; Legion of Merit, Bronze Star, Air Medal, Purple Heart; Secretary of State, USA, 2001–05; Strategic Limited Partner, Kleiner, Perkins, Caufield & Byers, since 2005; *b* 5 April 1937; *s* of late Luther Powell and Maud Ariel Powell (*née* McKoy); *m* 1962, Alma V. Johnson; one *s* two *d*. *Educ:* City Univ. of New York (BS Geology); George Washington Univ. (MBA). Commissioned 2nd Lieut, US Army, 1958; White House Fellow, 1972–73; Comdr, 2nd Brigade, 101st Airborne Div., 1976–77; exec. asst to Sec. of Energy, 1979; sen. mil. asst to Dep. Sec. of Defense, 1979–81; Asst Div. Comdr, 4th Inf. Div., Fort Carson, 1981–83; sen. mil. asst to Sec. of Defense, 1983–86; US V Corps, Europe, 1986–87; dep. asst to President 1987, asst 1987–89, for Nat. Security Affairs; General 1989; C-in-C, US Forces Command, Fort McPherson, April–Sept. 1989; Chm., Jt Chiefs of Staff, 1989–93. *Publication:* My American Journey (autobiog.), 1995 (UK title, A Soldier's Way). *Recreations:* racquetball, restoring old Volvos. *Address:* (office) Suite 700, 909 North Washington Street, Alexandria, VA 22314, USA; 1317 Ballantrae Farm Drive, McLean, VA 22101, USA.

POWELL, David Hebbert; HM Diplomatic Service; Ambassador to Norway, since 2006; *b* 29 April 1952; *s* of John Laycock Powell and Barbara Myrrha Powell (*née* Hebbert); *m* 1984, Gillian Mary Croft; one *d*. *Educ:* Fitzwilliam Coll., Cambridge (BA 1974). MoD, 1974–85; FCO, 1985–88; First Sec., Tokyo, 1988–92; FCO, 1992–95; Counsellor: Cabinet Office, 1995–97; UK Delegn to NATO, 1997–2001; Asst Dir, Human Resources, FCO, 2002–06. Mem., London Library. *Recreations:* reading, chess, Victorian crime. *Address:* British Embassy, Thomas Heftyes Gate 8, Oslo, Norway. *T:* 23132701, *Fax:* 23132789; *e-mail:* David.Powell@fco.gov.uk.

POWELL, His Honour (Dewi) Watkin; JP; a Circuit Judge, and Official Referee for Wales, 1972–92; *b* Aberdare, 29 July 1920; *o s* of W. H. Powell, AMICE and of M. A. Powell, Radyr, Glam; *m* 1951, Alice, *e d* of William and Mary Williams, Nantmor, Caerns; one *d*. *Educ:* Penarth Grammar Sch.; Jesus Coll., Oxford (MA). Called to Bar, Inner Temple, 1949. Dep. Chm., Merioneth and Cardigan QS, 1966–71; Dep. Recorder of Cardiff, Birkenhead, Merthyr Tydfil and Swansea, 1965–71; Junior, Wales and Chester Circuit, 1968; Liaison Judge for Dyfed, 1974–84, for Mid Glamorgan, 1984–91. Vice-Pres., South and Mid Glamorgan and Gwynedd branches of Magistrates' Assoc. Mem. Exec. Cttee, Plaid Cymru, 1943–55. Chairman: Constitutional Cttee, 1967–70; Govt of Wales Bill Drafting Gp, 1994–97; Constitutional Wkg Party, Parlt for Wales Campaign, 1994–; Member Council: Hon. Soc. of Cymmrodorion, 1965–93 (Chm., 1978–84; Vice Pres., 1984–); Cytun, 1993–98. Member, Court and Council: Univ. of Wales; Univ. of Wales Coll. of Cardiff (Vice Pres. and Vice Chm. of Council, 1987–98; Hon. Fellow). Hon. Mem., Gorsedd of Bards. President: Cymdeithas Theatr Cymru, 1984–89; Baptist Union of Wales, 1993–94; Pres., Free Church Council of Wales, 1994–98 (Vice-Pres., 1993–94). JP Mid Glamorgan. Hon. LLD Wales, 1997. *Publications:* Ymadroddion Llys Barn (Forensic Phraseology), 1974; (contrib.) Y Gair a'r Genedl, 1986; (contrib.) Lawyers and Laymen, 1986; (contrib.) Challenges to a Challenging Faith, 1995; (with John Osmond) Power to the People of Wales (Grym i Bobl Cymru), 1997; Cynulliad i Genedl, 1999. *Recreations:* gardening, reading theology, Welsh history and literature. *Address:* Nanmor, Morannedd, Cricieth, Gwynedd LL52 0PP.

POWELL, Earl Alexander, III, PhD; Director, National Gallery of Art, Washington, since 1992; *b* 24 Oct. 1943; *s* of Earl Alexander Powell and Elizabeth Powell; *m* 1971, Nancy Landry; three *d*. *Educ:* A. B. Williams Coll.; Harvard Univ. (PhD 1974). A. M. Fogg Art Mus. Teaching Fellow in Fine Arts, Harvard Univ., 1970–74 (Travelling Fellowship, 1973–74); Curator, Michener Collection and Asst Prof. of Art History, Univ. of Texas at Austin, 1974–76; National Gallery of Art, Washington: Mus. Curator, Sen. Staff Asst to Asst Director and Chief Curator, 1976–78; Exec. Curator, 1979–80; Dir, LA County Mus. of Art, 1980–92. Chm., US Commn of Fine Arts, 2005–; Member: Amer. Philos. Soc.; Assoc. of Art Museum Dirs; Cttee for Preservation of the White House; Fed. Council on Arts and Humanities; President's Cttee on Arts and Humanities. Trustee: American Fedn of the Arts; Morris and Gwendolyn Cafritz Foundn; Georgia O'Keeffe Foundn; Nat. Trust for Historic Preservation; White House Historical Assoc. Hon. DFA: Otis Parsons, 1987; Williams, 1993. King Olav Medal (Norway), 1978; Grand Official, Order of Infante D. Henrique (Portugal), 1995; Commendatore, Ordine al Merito (Italy), 1998; Chevalier, Légion d'Honneur (France), 2000; Officier, Ordre des Arts et des Lettres (France), 2004; Order of the Aztec Eagle (Mexico), 2007. *Publication:* Thomas Cole, 1990. *Address:* National Gallery of Art, 200B South Club Drive, Landover, MD 20785, USA. *T:* (202) 8426001. *Clubs:* Metropolitan (Washington); Knickerbocker (New York).

POWELL, Francis Turner, MBE 1945; Chairman, Laing & Cruickshank, Stockbrokers, 1978–80; *b* 15 April 1914; *s* of Francis Arthur and Dorothy May Powell; *m* 1940, Joan Audrey Bartlett (*d* 2003); one *s* one *d*. *Educ:* Lancing College. Served War, Queen's Royal Regt (TA), 1939–45 (Major). Joined L. Powell Sons & Co. (Stockbrokers), 1932, Partner, 1939; merged with Laing & Cruickshank, 1976. Mem. Council, Stock Exchange, 1963–78 (Dep. Chm., 1976–78). *Recreations:* golf, gardening. *Address:* 2 Horsley Court, East Horsley, Leatherhead, Surrey KT24 6QS.

POWELL, Geoffrey Colin, CBE 2005 (OBE 1995); Chairman, Jersey Financial Services Commission, since 1999; *b* 17 Sept. 1937; *s* of late Eric and Kate Powell; *m* 1962, Jennifer Mary Catt; three *d*. *Educ:* Wallington Co. Grammar Sch.; Jesus Coll., Cambridge (BA 1st Cl. Econs 1961). Econ. advr to NI Govt, 1963–68; States of Jersey: Econ. Advr, 1969–92; Chief Advr, 1992–98; Advr on Internat. Affairs, Chief Minister's Dept, 1999–. Chm., Offshore Gp of Banking Supervisors, 1981–. Chairman: Jersey Appeal, NSPCC Full Stop Campaign, 1999–; Jersey Child Care Trust, 2001–. Paul Harris Fellow, Rotary Club. *Publications:* Economic Survey of Jersey, 1971; Annual Reports on the Jersey Economy/Budget, 1969–1998; articles on Jersey econ., Jersey's role as an internat. finance centre, Jersey's relationship with the EU and role of offshore centres generally. *Recreations:* historical research, swimming, gardening, golf, grand-children. *Address:* (office) 14–18 Castle Street, St Helier, Jersey JE4 8TP. *T:* (01534) 822114, *Fax:* (01534) 822001; *e-mail:* c.powell@jerseyfsc.org. *Clubs:* United, Rotary (Jersey); Royal Jersey Golf.

POWELL, Hon. Hugh Eric; HM Diplomatic Service; UK Senior Representative in Helmand, since 2008; *b* 16 Feb. 1967; *s* of Baron Powell of Bayswater, *qv*; *m* 1993, Catherine Young; three *s*. *Educ:* Eton; Balliol Coll., Oxford (BA Hons 1988); Kennedy Sch. of Govt, Harvard (MPA 1990). Audit Commn, 1990–91; joined FCO, 1991; Second Sec., Paris, 1993–97; FCO, 1997–2000; First Sec., Berlin, 2000–03; Dir, Policy on Internat. Orgns, MoD, 2004; Hd, Security Policy Gp, FCO, 2005–08. *Recreation:* Left Back. *Address:* c/o Foreign and Commonwealth Office, King Charles Street, SW1A 2AH. *T:* (020) 7008 3000; *e-mail:* hugh.powell@fco.gov.uk.

POWELL, Prof. James Alfred, OBE 1996; DSc; CEng; Eur Ing; FIOA; Professor of Academic Enterprise, and Pro Vice Chancellor for Enterprise and Regional Affairs, Salford University, since 2001; *b* Sutton, 30 Oct. 1945; *s* of James Herbert Powell and Eileen Powell (*née* Newell); *m* 1969, Jennifer Elizabeth Morton; one *s*. *Educ:* De Burgh Sch., Tadworth; UMIST (BSc, MSc; AUMIST); Salford Univ. (PhD; DSc 2000). FIOA 1984; CEng 1996. ICI Schol., Salford Univ., 1970–71; Lectr, then Sen. Res. Associate, Sch. of Architecture, Dundee Univ., 1971–74; School of Architecture, Portsmouth Polytechnic: Reader in Building Utilisation, 1975–84; Prof. of Design Studies, 1984–91; Hd of Dept, 1990–91; Dep. Dean of Technol., Hd of Dept of Engrg and Mfg Systems and Lucas Prof. of Design Systems, Brunel Univ., 1991–94; Lucas Prof. of Informing Design Technol., 1994–2001, Dir of Acad. Enterprise, 1999–2001, Salford Univ. Science and Engineering Research Council: IT Applications Co-ordinator, 1988–93; Mem., Engrg Bd, 1988–93; Chm., Educn and Trng Cttee, 1988–93; IT Awareness in Engrg Co-ordinator, EPSRC, 1994. Mem., Learning Foresight Panel, OST, 1996–. Internat. Speaker, Nat. IT Council of Malaysia, 1998–. Designer, Menuhin Auditorium for Portsmouth String Quartet Fest., 1980. Award for Interactive Audio in Multi Media, European Multi Media Assoc., 1992. *Publications:* Design: Science: Methods, 1981; Changing Design, 1982; Designing for Building Utilisation, 1984; Noise at Work Regulations, 1990, 2nd edn 1994; Intelligent Command and Control Acquisition and Review using Simulation, 1992; The Powell Report: review of SERC engineering education and training, 1993; Informing Technologies for Construction, Civil Engineering and Transport, 1993; Neural Computing, 1994; Engineering Decision Support, 1995; Virtual Reality and Rapid Prototyping, 1995. *Recreations:* meditation, Tai Chi, cycling, squash, yoga, boating, painting. *Address:* Enterprise and Regional Affairs, University of Salford, Salford M5 4WT. *T:* (0161) 295 5464.

POWELL, Prof. Janet Tinka, PhD, MD; FRCPath; Professor of Vascular Medicine, University of Warwick, 2000–04; Medical Director, University Hospitals of Coventry and Warwickshire NHS Trust, 2000–04; *b* 1 Aug. 1945; *d* of Reginald Y. Powell and Mina Powell; partner, Douglas W. Ribbons (*d* 2002); one *s* one *d*. *Educ:* Lady Margaret Hall, Oxford (BA); King's Coll. London (PhD 1972); Univ. of Miami (MD 1981). FRCPath 2001. Asst Prof. of Medicine (Pulmonary), Univ. of Miami Sch. of Medicine, 1978–79; Hse Surgeon, Ysbyty Glan Clywd, 1982; Hse Physician, Bristol Royal Infirmary, 1982–83; SHO in Dermatol., Geriatrics and Medicine, St David's Hosp., Bangor, 1983; Charing Cross and Westminster Medical School: Lectr in Biochem. and Surgery, 1983–89; Sen. Lectr, 1989–91; Reader in Cardiovascular Biol., 1991–94; Prof. of Vascular Biol., 1994–97; Registrar in Chem. Pathol., Charing Cross Hosp., 1985–87; Imperial College School of Medicine: Chm., Vascular Scis and Diseases Gp, 1997–2000; Dean, 2000. Vis. Prof., ICSTM, subseq. Res. Prof., Imperial Coll. London, 2001–. Member: BMA, 1982; British Matrix Biol. Soc., 1984; Biochem. Soc., 1985; Vascular Surgical Soc., 1990; Surgical Res. Soc., 1990; British Atherosclerosis Soc., 1999. Member: Amer. Soc. Biochem. & Molecular Biol., 1975; Eur. Soc. for Vascular Surgery, 1992. Ed., Eur. Jl of Vascular and Endovascular Surgery, 2004–. *Publications:* numerous contribs to learned jls incl. New England Jl of Medicine, Lancet, BMJ and Nature. *Recreations:* hiking, cycling, theatre, film. *Address:* 8 The Square, Long Itchington, Warwickshire CV47 9PE; *e-mail:* Jtp700@aol.com.

POWELL, (John) Christopher; Chairman, National Endowment for Science, Technology and the Arts, since 2003; *b* 4 Oct. 1943; *s* of Air Vice-Marshal John Frederick Powell, *qv*; *m* 1973, Rosemary Jeanne Symmons; two *s* one *d*. *Educ:* St Peter's Sch., York; London Sch. of Econs (BSc Econ.). Worked in advertising agencies, in London, 1965–69; BMP, subseq. BMP DDB: Partner, 1969–82; Jt Man. Dir, 1975–85; Chief Exec., 1986–98; Chm., 1999–2003. Non-executive Director: Riverside Studios, 1989–; United Business Media (formerly United News & Media) plc, 1995–2006; Media Metrica, 2004–; Dr Foster LLP, 2006–; Mem. Corporate Finance Adv. Panel, PriceWaterhouseCoopers, 2005–. Dep. Chm., Riverside Community NHS Trust, 1994–2000; Chm., Ealing, Hammersmith & Hounslow HA, 2000–02. Chm., British Council Creative Industries Adv. Panel, 2002–; Dep. Chm., Public Diplomacy Bd, 2006–; Mem. Bd, Britain in Europe, 2005–. Pres., Inst. Practitioners in Advertising, 1993–95. Trustee, IPPR, 1999– (Chm., 2001–08). *Recreations:* riding, tennis, gardening, theatre. *Address:* DDBLondon Ltd, 12 Bishop's Bridge Road, W2 6AA. *T:* (020) 7258 3979.
See also Baron Powell of Bayswater, J. N. Powell.

POWELL, Air Vice-Marshal John Frederick, OBE 1956; Warden and Director of Studies, Moor Park College, 1972–77; *b* 12 June 1915; *y s* of Rev. Morgan Powell, Limpley Stoke, Bath; *m* 1939, Geraldine Ysolda (*d* 2003), *e d* of late Sir John Fitzgerald Moylan, CB, CBE; four *s*. *Educ:* Lancing; King's Coll., Cambridge (MA). Joined RAF Educnl Service, 1937; Lectr, RAF College, 1938–39; RAFVR (Admin. and Special

Duties) ops room duties, Coastal Comd, 1939–45 (despatches); RAF Educn Br., 1946; Sen. Instructor in History, RAF Coll., 1946–49; RAF Staff Coll., 1950; Air Min., 1951–53; Sen. Tutor, RAF Coll., 1953–59; Educn Staff, HQ FEAF, 1959–62; MoD, 1962–64; Comd Educn Officer, HQ Bomber Comd, 1964–66; OC, RAF Sch. of Educn, 1966–67; Dir of Educational Services, RAF, 1967–72; Air Commodore, 1967; Air Vice-Marshal, 1968. *Recreations:* choral music, gardening. *Address:* Barker's Hill Cottage, Donhead St Andrew, Shaftesbury, Dorset SP7 9EB. *T:* (01747) 828505. *Club:* Royal Air Force.

See also Baron Powell of Bayswater, J. C. Powell, J. N. Powell.

POWELL, John Lewis; QC 1990; a Recorder, since 2000; a Deputy High Court Judge; *b* 14 Sept. 1950; *s* of Gwyn Powell and Lilian Mary Powell (*née* Griffiths); *m* 1973, Eva Zofia Lomnicka; one *s* two *d*. *Educ:* Christ Coll., Brecon; Amman Valley Grammar Sch.; Trinity Hall, Cambridge (MA, LLB). Called to the Bar, Middle Temple, 1974 (Harmsworth Schol.), Bencher 1998. In practice, 1974–. Pres., Soc. of Construction Law, 1991–93; Member: Bar Council, 1997–2004 (Chm., Law Reform Cttee, 1997–98); Exec. Cttee, Commercial Bar Assoc. 2002–04. Contested (Lab) Cardigan, 1979. *Publications:* (with R. Jackson, QC) Professional Negligence, 1982, 5th edn; (with Eva Lomnicka) Encyclopedia of Financial Services Law, 1987; Palmer's Company Law, 24th edn 1987, 25th edn 1992; Issues and Offers of Company Securities: the new regimes, 1988; various articles. *Recreations:* travel, walking, sheep farming. *Address:* 4 New Square, Lincoln's Inn, WC2A 3RJ. *T:* (020) 7822 2000.

POWELL, John Mark Heywood; QC 2006; a Recorder, since 1997; *b* 18 July 1952; *s* of John Harford Powell, OBE, MC, and Lucinda Joan Eve Powell; *m* 1998, Carole Mary Symons-Jones; two *s* one *d*. *Educ:* Rugby Sch.; University Coll. London (BA Hons Hist. 1974). Solicitor, then Partner, Hugh James, solicitors, 1977–; barrister and solicitor, High Court of NZ, 1990–; HM Coroner, Monmouthshire, 1983–. Chm., Assoc. of Lawyers for Children, 1999–2001. Trustee: Triangle Trust, 2000–; Tros Gynnal, 2005–. Pres., Ebbw Vale RFC, 2002. *Recreations:* boating in Pembrokeshire, French history and French living, watching Ebbw Vale play Rugby. *Address:* Garden Cottage, Pantygelli, Abergavenny NP7 7HR. *T:* (01813) 850647; *e-mail:* jmhp@hotmail.co.uk. *Clubs:* MCC, Sloane; Cardiff and County (Cardiff); Dale Yacht; Club Athletic (Riberac).

POWELL, Jonathan Charles Boyd; JP; Chief Executive, Vitalise, since 2007; *b* 21 Jan. 1960; *s* of Jeremy Boyd Powell and Evangeline Anne Powell (*née* Simons); *m* 1993, Sarah Rhiannon Morgan; one *s* one *d*. *Educ:* Wellington Coll.; Southampton Univ. (BA Hons French and German). RN, 1983–89. RBL, 1990–2001 (Hd, Ops and Develt, 1997–2001); Chief Exec., IndependentAge, RUKBA, 2001–06. Director: Crossways Trust Ltd, 2002–06; IndependentAge Enterprises Ltd, 2003–06; Careways Ltd, 2007–. MInstD 2001; FRSA 2006. JP Ealing, 1995. *Address:* 22 Albany Road, W13 8PG; *e-mail:* jpowell@vitalise.org.uk.

POWELL, Jonathan Leslie; Director of Drama and Co-production, Carlton Television, 1993–2004; *b* 25 April 1947; *s* of James Dawson Powell and Phyllis Nora Sylvester (*née* Doubleday); *m* 1990, Sally Jane Brampton, *qv* (marr. diss.); one *d*. *Educ:* Sherborne; University of East Anglia. BA Hons (English and American Studies). Script editor and producer of drama, Granada TV, 1970–77; BBC TV: Producer, drama serials, 1977–83; Hd of Drama Series and Serials, 1983–87; Hd of Drama, 1987; Controller, BBC1, 1988–92. *TV serials include:* Testament of Youth, 1979 (BAFTA award); Tinker Tailor Soldier Spy, 1979; Pride and Prejudice, 1980; Thérèse Raquin, 1980; The Bell, 1982; Smiley's People, 1982 (Peabody Medal, USA); The Old Men at the Zoo, 1983; Bleak House, 1985; Tender is the Night, 1985; A Perfect Spy, 1987. Royal Television Soc. Silver Award for outstanding achievement, 1979–80. *Address:* Flat 1, 158 Lancaster Road, W11 1QU.

POWELL, Jonathan Nicholas; Managing Director, Investment Business Division, Morgan Stanley, since 2008; *b* 14 Aug. 1956; *s* of Air Vice-Marshal John Frederick Powell, *qv* and Geraldine Ysolda Powell (*née* Moylan); *m* 1st, 1980, Karen Elizabeth Drayne (marr. diss. 1997); two *s*; 2nd, 2007, Sarah Helm; two *d*. *Educ:* University Coll., Oxford (MA Hist.); Univ. of Pennsylvania (MA Hist.). With BBC, 1978; Granada TV, 1978–79; joined FCO, 1979; Lisbon, 1980–83; FCO, 1983–85; Member, British Delegation to: CDE, Stockholm, 1985; CSCE, Vienna, 1985–89; FCO, 1989–91; Washington, 1991–95; COS to Leader of the Opposition, 1995–97, to the Prime Minister, 1997–2007. *Publication:* Great Hatred, Little Room, 2008. *Recreations:* sailing, climbing, tennis. *Address:* Morgan Stanley, 20 Bank Street, Canary Wharf, E14 4AD; *e-mail:* Jonathan.Powell@morganstanley.com.

See also Baron Powell of Bayswater, J. C. Powell.

POWELL, Kenneth George; architectural critic and journalist; Consultant Director, Twentieth Century Society, 1995–2002; *b* 17 March 1947; *s* of Alan Powell and Winifred Alice Powell (*née* Hill); *m* 1969, Susan Harris-Smith. *Educ:* Canton High Sch. for Boys, Cardiff; London Sch. of Econs (BA 1968); Univ. of Manchester (MA Arch 1979). Research Assistant: Inst. of Historical Res., London, 1971–74; History of Univ. of Oxford, 1974–77; Temp. Lectr in Hist., UCL, 1977–78; worked in museums and as freelance researcher, 1978–84; Sec., SAVE Britain's Heritage, 1984–87; Architectural Corresp., Daily Telegraph, 1987–94; freelance writer. Member: Art and Architecture Cttee, Westminster Cathedral, 1994–2003; London DAC, 1996–; Historic Churches Cttee, Dio. of Leeds, 1996–; Fabric Cttee, Guildford Cathedral, 2006–; Hon. Sec., Architectural Assoc., 2006– (Mem. Council, 2002–). Hon. FRIBA 2000. *Publications:* Stansted: Norman Foster and the architecture of flight, 1991; Vauxhall Cross, 1992; (with R. Moore) Structures, Space and Skin, 1993; World Cities: London, 1993; Richard Rogers, 1994; Edward Cullinan Architects, 1995; Grand Central Terminal, 1996; Richard Rogers: complete works (I), 1999, (II), 2001, (III), 2006; Architecture Transformed, 1999; Jubilee Line Architecture, 2000; The City Transformed, 2000; (jtly) The National Portrait Gallery: an architectural history, 2000; New London Architecture, 2001, 2nd edn (with Cathy Strongman) as New London Architecture 2, 2007; The Modern House Today, 2001; Will Alsop: book 1, 2001, book 2, 2002; New Architecture in Britain, 2003; KPF: process and vision, 2003; Nottingham Transformed, 2006; contrib. many articles in Country Life, Architects Jl, etc. *Recreations:* architecture, food, wine and places, preferably Mediterranean or Celtic. *Address:* Flat 1, 78 Nightingale Lane, SW12 8NR. *T:* (020) 8673 3383.

POWELL, Prof. Kenneth Leslie, PhD; Head, Arrow Therapeutics, since 2007 (Chief Executive, 1998–2007); Hon. Professor, University College London, since 2000; *b* 23 July 1949; *s* of Alec and Ada Powell; *m* 1st, 1968, Anne (marr. diss. 1974); 2nd, 1975, Dorothy J. M. Purifoy; two *d*, and one step *s* one step *d*. *Educ:* Apsley Grammar Sch.; Univ. of Reading (BSc Microbiology 1970); Univ. of Birmingham (PhD 1973). Post-doctoral Fellow, 1973–75, Asst Prof., 1975–77, Baylor Coll. of Medicine, Houston; Lectr, 1978–85, Sen. Lectr, 1985–86, Univ. of Leeds; Wellcome Foundation: Head of: Biochemical Virology, 1986–88; Antiviral Res., 1988–90; Cell Biology, 1990–93; Biology, 1993–95; Dep. Dir, Cruciform Project, subseq. Wolfson Inst. for Biomed. Res., and Prof., UCL, 1995–2000. Vis. Prof., Univ. of Michigan, 1985. CEO, Inpharmatica Ltd, 1998–2000. *Publications:* more than 50 articles in learned jls. *Address:* Arrow Therapeutics Ltd, 7 Trinity Street, Borough, SE1 1DA. *T:* (020) 7015 1002.

POWELL, Prof. Lawrie William, AC 1990; MD, PhD; FRACP, FRCP; Professor of Medicine, University of Queensland, since 1975; Research Co-ordinator, Royal Brisbane and Women's Hospital, since 2000; *b* 4 Dec. 1934; *s* of Victor Alexander Powell and Ellen Evelyn (*née* Davidson); *m* 1958, Margaret Emily Ingram; two *s* three *d*. *Educ:* Univ. of Queensland (MB BS 1958; MD 1965; PhD 1973); Univ. of London; Harvard Medical Sch. FRACP 1975; FRCP 1991. Dir, Qld Inst. of Med. Res., 1990–2000. Hon. Lectr, Royal Free Hosp. and Univ. of London, 1963–65; Vis. Prof., Harvard Medical Sch., 1972–73. Mem. Bd, Australian Stem Cell Centre, 2007–. FTSE 1995. Hon. FRCP Thailand, 1997. DUniv Griffith, 1996. *Publications:* Metals and the Liver, 1978; Fundamentals of Gastroenterology, 1975, 6th edn 1995. *Recreations:* music, reading, chess, bushwalking. *Address:* Royal Brisbane and Women's Hospital, Brisbane, Qld 4029, Australia.

POWELL, Prof. Michael James David, FRS 1983; John Humphrey Plummer Professor of Applied Numerical Analysis, University of Cambridge, 1976–2001, now Emeritus; Fellow of Pembroke College, Cambridge, 1978–2001, now Emeritus; *b* 29 July 1936; *s* of William James David Powell and Beatrice Margaret (*née* Page); *m* 1959, Caroline Mary Henderson; two *d* (one *s* decd). *Educ:* Eastbourne Coll.; Peterhouse, Cambridge (Schol.; BA 1959; ScD 1979). Mathematician at Atomic Energy Research Estabt, Harwell, 1959–76; special merit research appt to banded level, 1969, and to senior level, 1975. For. Associate, NAS, US, 2001; Corresp. Mem., Australian Acad. of Sci., 2007. Hon. DSc UEA, 2001. George B. Dantzig Prize in Mathematical Programming, 1982; Naylor Prize, 1983, Sen. Whitehead Prize, 1999, London Math. Soc.; Gold Medal, IMA, 1996. *Publications:* Approximation Theory and Methods, 1981; papers on numerical mathematics, especially approximation and optimization calculations. *Recreations:* canals, golf, walking. *Address:* 134 Milton Road, Cambridge CB4 1LE.

POWELL, Sir Nicholas (Folliott Douglas), 4th Bt *cr* 1897; Company Director; *b* 17 July 1935; *s* of Sir Richard George Douglas Powell, 3rd Bt, MC, and Elizabeth Josephine (*d* 1979), *d* of late Lt-Col O. R. McMullen, CMG; *S* father, 1980; *m* 1st, 1960, Daphne Jean (marr. diss. 1987), 2nd *d* of G. H. Errington, MC; one *s* one *d*; 2nd, 1987, Davina Allsopp; two *s* one *d*. *Educ:* Gordonstoun. Lieut Welsh Guards, 1953–57. *Heir:* *s* James Richard Douglas Powell [*b* 17 Oct. 1962; *m* 1991, Susanna, *e d* of David Murray Threipland; two *s* one *d*]. *Address:* Lower Fresden House, Highworth, Wilts SN6 7PZ.

POWELL, Nikolas Mark; Director, National Film and Television School, since 2003; *b* 4 Nov. 1950; *s* of A. B. Powell and Jane Powell (*née* Weir); one *s* one *d*. *Educ:* Ampleforth Coll. Co-founder and Dir, Virgin Records, 1967–81; Co-Chm., Palace Gp of Cos Ltd, 1982–91; Chm., Scala Prodns Ltd, 1991–. Chm., 1995–2003, Vice Chm., 2004–, European Film Acad. Board Director: Film Consortium, 1996–2003; Northern Irish Film and TV Commn, 2001–. *Address:* National Film and Television School, Station Road, Beaconsfield, Bucks HP9 1LG. *Clubs:* Groucho, Soho House; European Producers.

POWELL, Prof. Percival Hugh, MA, DLitt, Dr Phil.; Professor of German, Indiana University, 1970–83, now Emeritus; *b* 4 Sept. 1912; 3rd *s* of late Thomas Powell and late Marie Sophia Roeser; *m* 1944, Dorothy Mavis Pattison (*née* Donald) (marr. diss. 1964); two *s* one adopted *d*; *m* 1966, Mary Kathleen (*née* Wilson); one *s*. *Educ:* University College, Cardiff (Fellow 1981); Univs of Rostock, Zürich, Bonn. 1st Class Hons German (Wales), 1933; Univ. Teachers' Diploma in Education, 1934; MA (Wales) Dist. 1936. Research Fellow of Univ. of Wales, 1936–38; Modern Languages Master, Towyn School, 1934–36; Dr Phil. (Rostock) 1938; Lektor in English, Univ. of Bonn, 1938–39; Asst Lectr, Univ. Coll., Cardiff, 1939–40; War Service, 1940–46 (Capt. Intelligence Corps); Lecturer in German, Univ. Coll., Leicester, 1946, Head of Department of German, 1954; Prof. of German, Univ. of Leicester, 1958–69. Barclay Acheson Prof. of Internat. Studies at Macalester Coll., Minn., USA, 1965–66. DLitt (Wales) 1962. British Academy Award, 1963; Fritz Thyssen Foundation Award, 1964; Leverhulme Trust Award, 1968. *Publications:* Pierre Corneilles Dramen in Deutschen Bearbeitungen, 1939; critical editions of dramas of Andreas Gryphius, 1955–72; critical edn of J. G. Schoch's Comœdia vom Studentenleben, 1976; Trammels of Tradition, 1988; Louise von Gall, 1993; Fervor and Fiction, 1996; Heinrich Burkart, 1997; (ed) Berliner Don Quixote, facsimile of 1832–33 edn, 2001; articles and reviews in English and foreign literary jls. *Recreation:* music. *Address:* c/o Department of Germanic Studies, Ballantine Hall, Indiana University, Bloomington, IN 47405, USA.

POWELL, Richard Stephen; HM Diplomatic Service; Deputy High Commissioner, Lagos, since 2007; *b* 19 Oct. 1959; *s* of late David Ronald Powell and of Audrey Grace Powell. *Educ:* Pwll Co. Primary Sch.; Llanelli Grammar Sch.; Emmanuel Coll., Cambridge (BA Natural Scis 1981); Imperial Coll., London (MBA 1997). Entered HM Diplomatic Service, 1981; FCO, 1981–82; Attaché, UK Mission to UN, NY, 1982; Third, later Second, Sec., Helsinki, 1983–88; FCO, 1988–92; First Secretary: Tokyo, 1992–96; FCO, 1997–2003; Dep. Hd of Mission, Helsinki, 2003–07; Dep. High Comr, Accra, 2007. *Recreations:* pottering, pubs. *Address:* c/o Foreign and Commonwealth Office, King Charles Street, SW1A 2AH; *e-mail:* Richard.Powell@fco.gov.uk.

POWELL, Dame Sally (Ann Vickers), DBE 2001; *b* 2 Oct. 1955; *d* of Alan Vickers Powell and Ena Esther Powell (*née* Crewe); *m* 1996, Iain Coleman, *qv*; one *s*. *Educ:* Royal Ballet Sch.; Univ. of Southampton (LLB 1984); Coll. of Law (Law Soc. Finals). Sadler's Wells Royal Ballet, 1974–80; joined Lewis Silkin, Solicitors, 1985; with Glazer Delmar, Solicitors, until 1997. Mem. (Lab) Hammersmith and Fulham London BC, 1986– (Cabinet Mem. for Regeneration). Dep. Leader, Assoc. of London Govt; Chm., Gtr London Enterprise; Dep. Chm., Business Link for London; Mem. Bd, London Develt Agency; Dep. Leader, Labour Gp, LGA. *Recreations:* theatre, football.

POWELL, Watkin; *see* Powell, D. W.

POWELL, William Rhys; barrister, arbitrator; *b* 3 Aug. 1948; *s* of late Rev. Canon Edward Powell and Anne Powell; *m* 1973, Elizabeth Vaudin; three *d*. *Educ:* Lancing College; Emmanuel College, Cambridge (BA 1970; MA 1973); DipArb Reading Univ. 2000. FCIArb 2001. Called to the Bar, Lincoln's Inn, 1971. MP (C) Corby, 1983–97; contested (C) same seat, 1997. PPS to Minister for Overseas Develt, 1985–86, to Sec. of State for the Envmt, 1990–92. Member, Select Committee: on Procedure, 1987–90; on Foreign Affairs, 1990–91; on Sci. and Technol., 1992–95; on Agriculture, 1995–97; Mem., Jt Parly Ecclesiastical Cttee, 1987–97; Joint Secretary: Cons. Back-bench For. Affairs Cttee, 1985 and 1987–90; Cons. Back-bench Defence Cttee, 1988–90; Chairman: All-Party Parly Gp for the Gulf, 1993–97; British-Italian Parly Gp, 1992–96; British-Taiwan Parly Gp, 1992–97; British-Mongolia Parly Gp, 1993–97; British-Tunisia Parly Gp, 1995–97. Jt Chm., CAABU, 1992–95; Mem. Council, British Atlantic Cttee, 1985–90. Fellow, Industry and Parlt Trust, 1991. As Private Mem. piloted Copyright (Computer Software) Amendment Act, 1985. Vis. Scholar, Academia Sinaca, Taiwan,

1999; Vis. Prof., Univ. of Kansai, Japan, 1999. *Address:* Regency Chambers, Market Square, Peterborough PE1 1XW. *Club:* Corby Conservative.

POWELL-JONES, John Ernest, CMG 1974; HM Diplomatic Service, retired; Ambassador to Switzerland, 1982–85; *b* 14 April 1925; *s* of late Walter James Powell-Jones and Gladys Margaret (*née* Taylor); *m* 1st, 1949, Ann Murray (marr. diss. 1967); one *s* one *d* (and one *s* decd); 2nd, 1968, Pamela Sale. *Educ:* Charterhouse; University Coll., Oxford (1st cl. Modern Hist.). Served with Rifle Bde, 1943–46. HM Foreign (now Diplomatic) Service, 1949; 3rd Sec. and Vice-Consul, Bogota, 1950–52; Eastern and later Levant Dept, FO, 1952–55; 2nd, later 1st Sec., Athens, 1955–59; News Dept, FO, 1959–60; 1st Sec., Leopoldville, 1961–62; UN Dept, FO, 1963–67; ndc Canada 1967–68; Counsellor, Political Adviser's Office, Singapore, 1968–69; Counsellor and Consul-General, Athens, 1970–73; Ambassador at Phnom Penh, 1973–75; RCDS 1975; Ambassador to Senegal, Guinea, Mali, Mauritania and Guinea-Bissau, 1976–79, to Cape Verde, 1977–79; Ambassador and Perm. Rep., UN Conf. on Law of the Sea, 1979–82. Chm., Inter Counsel UK Ltd, 1986–93. Member: Waverley BC, 1987–95; Wonersh Parish Council, 1987–99 (Vice-Chm., 1990–99). Chm., Wonersh United Charities, 1999–2005. Member: Bd, Surrey Historic Bldgs Trust, 1989–92; Council, SE England Agricl Soc., 1991–95. *Recreations:* gardening, walking. *Address:* Gascons, Gaston Gate, Cranleigh, Surrey GU6 8QY. *T:* (01483) 274313. *Club:* Travellers.
  See also M. E. P. Jones.

POWELL-SMITH, Christopher Brian, TD 1985; Chairman, Black & Decker Group Inc., since 1995 (Director, since 1980); *b* 3 Oct. 1936; *s* of Edgar and Theodora Powell-Smith; *m* 1964, Jennifer Goslett; two *s* two *d*. *Educ:* City of London Sch. Asst Solicitor, McKenna & Co., 1959; Nat. Service, 4th Regt, RHA, 1959–61; McKenna & Co.: Partner, 1964–97; Finance Partner, 1975–84; Managing Partner, 1984–87; Head, Corporate Dept, 1987–92; Sen. Partner, 1992–97; Partner, Cameron McKenna, 1997–99. Non-exec. Chm., KBC Advanced Technology plc, 2004– (Dir, 1997–); non-exec. Dir, MPG Gp Ltd, 1998–. Chm., Richmond Parish Lands Charity, 2000–05. CO and Regimental Col, HAC, 1975–79. *Recreations:* golf, choral singing. *Address:* 32 The Avenue, Kew, Richmond, Surrey TW9 2AJ. *T:* (020) 8395 0333; *e-mail:* cpowell_smith@compuserve.com. *Club:* Royal Mid-Surrey Golf.

POWER, Sir Alastair John Cecil, 4th Bt *cr* 1924, of Newlands Manor; *b* 15 Aug. 1958; *s* of Sir John Patrick McLannahan Power, 3rd Bt and of Melanie, *d* of Hon. Alastair Erskine; *S* father, 1984; *m* 1981, Virginia Newton; one *s* two *d*. *Heir: s* Mark Alastair John Power, *b* 15 Oct. 1989.

POWER, Prof. Anne Elizabeth, CBE 2000 (MBE 1983); PhD; Professor of Social Policy and Director, Postgraduate MSc/Diploma in Housing, London School of Economics, since 1997. *Educ:* Univ. of Manchester (BA Mod. Langs); London Sch. of Econs (Dip. Social Admin 1964); Univ. of Wisconsin (MA Sociol. 1966); PhD London 1985. Teacher, Tanzania, 1966; with Martin Luther King's End Slums Campaign, Chicago, 1966; Warden, Africa Centre, London, 1966–67; Co-ordinator: Friends Neighbourhood House, Islington, 1967–72; N Islington Housing Rights Project, 1972–79; Nat. Consultant, Priority Estates Project, DoE, 1979–89; Advr, Welsh Office and Rhondda BC, 1989–93. Co-ordinator and Res. Dir, prog. with Brookings Instn on Weak Mkt Cities, funded by Joseph Rowntree Foundn and DCLG, 2005–. Vis. Res. Associate, Dept of Social Policy, LSE, 1981–88. Founding Dir, Nat. Tenants' Resource Centre, 1991–; Dep. Dir, Centre for Analysis of Social Exclusion, 1997–. Adv. Mem., Panel of Experts to EC on urban problems; Member: Govt Sounding Bds, Housing, 1997–, Urban, 2000–; Urban Task Force, 1998–; Sustainable Develt Commn, 2000–. *Publications:* Property Before People: the management of Twentieth Century council housing, 1987; Housing Management: a guide to quality and creativity, 1991; Hovels to High-rise, 1993; (with R. Tunstall) Swimming Against the Tide, 1995; (with R. Tunstall) Dangerous Disorder, 1997; Estates on the Edge, 1997; (with K. Mumford) The Slow Death of Great Cities?, 1999; (with R. Rogers) Cities for a Small Country, 2000; (with K. Mumford) East Enders: family and community in East London, 2003; (with K. Mumford) Boom or Abandonment, 2003; Census Briefs: (with R. Lupton) Minority Ethnic Groups in Britain, 2004; (with R. Lupton) The Growth and Decline of Cities and Regions, 2005; (with J. Houghton) Jigsaw City, 2007; City Survivors, 2007; numerous governmental reports; contrib. articles in press on social policy and housing issues. *Address:* Department of Social Policy and Administration, London School of Economics, Houghton Street, WC2A 2AE; *e-mail:* anne.power@lse.ac.uk.

POWER, Mrs Brian St Quentin; *see* Stack, (Ann) Prunella.

POWER, Sir Noel (Plunkett), GBS 1999; Kt 1999; a Non-Permanent Judge: Hong Kong Court of Final Appeal, since 1997; Court of Appeal, Brunei Darussalam, since 2003 (President, since 2007); *b* 4 Dec. 1929; *s* of John Joseph Power and Hilda Power; *m* 1965, Irma Maroya; two *s* one *d*. *Educ:* Downlands Coll.; Univ. of Queensland (BA, LLB). Called to the Bar, Supreme Court of Queensland and High Court of Australia, 1955; Magistrate, Hong Kong, 1965–76; Pres., Lands Tribunal, Hong Kong, 1976–79; a Judge of the Supreme Court of Hong Kong, 1979–87; a Judge of Appeal, 1987–93; a Vice-Pres. of the Court of Appeal of the Supreme Court, then a Justice of Appeal, Appeal Court of the High Court, Hong Kong, 1993–99; Acting Chief Justice, Hong Kong, 1996–97. Chairman: Broadcasting Rev. Bd, HK, 1984–85; Univ. of HK Panel of Enquiry into allegations of political pressure, 2000. Chm., Hong Kong Island, 1984–99, Asia-Pacific Zone, 1994–99, Gold Coast, 1999–, Internat. Wine and Food Soc. Chm. Editl Bd, Hong Kong Law Reports, 1994–97. *Publications:* (ed) Lands Tribunal Law Reports, 1976–79. *Recreations:* travel, cooking, reading. *Address:* 44 Surfers Waters, 40 Cotlew Street, Southport, Qld 4215, Australia. *Clubs:* Hong Kong (Hong Kong); Queensland (Brisbane).

POWER, Prof. Philip Patrick, PhD; FRS 2005; Professor of Chemistry, University of California, Davis. *Educ:* Trinity Coll., Dublin (BA 1974); PhD Sussex 1977. Joined Univ. of Calif, Davis, 1981. Alexander von Humboldt Award, 1992; Mond Medal, RSC, 2004. *Publications:* articles in learned jls. *Address:* Department of Chemistry, University of California, Davis, CA 95616, USA.

POWER, Vince; Founder, Vince Power Music Group, 2005; *b* Co. Waterford, Ireland, 29 April 1947; *s* of late John Power and Brigid Power; *m* 1967 (marr. diss. 1979); three *c*; five *c* with former partners. *Educ:* Dungarvan Vocational Coll. Owner, chain of furniture shops, N London, 1964–82; Founder and Chm., Mean Fiddler Orgn, subseq. Mean Fiddler Music Gp plc, 1982–2005; opened club, Mean Fiddler, Harlesden, 1982; founder of clubs and bars: Powerhaus, Islington, 1988, moved to Finsbury Park, 1996; Subterania, 1988; The Grand, 1991; Jazz Cafe, 1992; The Forum, 1993; The Garage, 1993; Upstairs at the Garage, 1994; Crossbar, 1995; Mean Fiddler, Dublin, 1995; The Palace, Luton, 1995; The Complex, 1996; The Cube, 1996; Power's Bar, 1996; Zd, 1996; Bartok, 1998; Ion Bar and Restaurant, 1998; Point 101, 1998; The Rex, 1999; One Seven Nine, 2001; G-A-Y, 2002; Union-Undeb, Cardiff, 2003; Berkeley Square Cafe, 2003; acquired nightclubs: London Astoria, 2000; LA2, renamed Mean Fiddler, 2000; Media, 2002; Tunnel, 2002; Universe, 2002; promoter of events: Reading Fest., 1989–2005; Fleadh,

London, 1990–2005; Fleadh, Glasgow, 1992; Madstock, 1992, 1994, 1996, 1998; Fleadh Mor, Ireland, 1993; Neil Young, 1993; Phoenix Fest., 1993–97; Tribal Gathering, 1995–97; Paul Weller, 1996; The Sex Pistols, 1996; Big Love, 1996; Mount Universe, 1996; Jamiroquai, 1997; Fleadh New York, 1997–2005; Fleadh Chicago, 1998–2005; Fleadh San Francisco, 1998–2005; Creamfields, 1998; Pulp, 1998; Temptation, 1998; Fleadh Boston, 1999–2005; We Love...Homelands (formerly Homelands), 1999–2005; Homelands Scotland, 1999–2005; Homelands Ireland, 1999–2005; Leeds Fest., 1999–2005; Glasgow Green, 2000–05; Nat. Adventure Sports Weekender, 2001–; Dr Music Fest., Spain, 2003–; operational manager, Glastonbury Fest., 2002–05; co-owner, Tramore racecourse. *Address:* Vince Power Music Group, 54 Greek Street, W1D 3DS.

POWERS, Prof. Alan Adrian Robelou, PhD; Professor of Architecture and Cultural History, University of Greenwich, since 2007; *b* 5 Feb. 1955; *s* of Michael Powers and Frances Powers (*née* Wilson); *m* 1982, Susanna Curtis; one *s* one *d*. *Educ:* Bryanston Sch.; Clare Coll., Cambridge (BA 1977; PhD 1983). Dir, Judd Street Gall., 1985–91; Librarian and Tutor, Prince of Wales's Inst. of Architecture, 1992–2000; Sen. Lectr, 1999–2004, Reader in Architecture and Cultural Hist., 2004–07, Univ. of Greenwich. Curator: Modern Britain 1929–39, Design Mus., 1999; Serge Chermayeff, Kettle's Yard, Cambridge, 2001; Eric Ravilious, Imagined Realities, Imperial War Mus., 2003. Vice-Chm., Twentieth Century Soc., 1996–99; Chm., Pollock's Toy Mus. Trust, 1999–. Mem., Art Workers' Guild. Hon. FRIBA 2008. *Publications:* (jtly) The National Trust Book of the English House, 1985; Seaside Lithographs, 1986; The English Tivoli, 1988; Shop Fronts, 1989; Oliver Hill, 1989; Modern Block-Printed Textiles, 1992; Living with Books, 1999; Nature in Design, 1999; Francis Pollen, 1999; Living with Pictures, 2000; Serge Chermayeff, 2001; Front Cover, 2001; Children's Book Covers, 2003; The Twentieth Century House in Britain, 2004; Modern: the Modern movement in Britain, 2005; Modern Architectures in History: Britain, 2007. *Recreations:* painting, printmaking. *Address:* 99 Judd Street, WC1H 9NE. *T:* (020) 7387 3154; *e-mail:* a.powers@gre.ac.uk. *Club:* Double Crown.

POWERS, Dr Michael John; QC 1995; *b* 9 Feb. 1947; *o s* of late Reginald Frederick and of Kathleen Powers; *m* 1st, 1968, Meryl Hall (marr. diss. 2001); one *s* one *d*; 2nd, 2001, Pamela Barnes. *Educ:* Poole Grammar Sch.; Middlesex Hosp. Med. Sch., London Univ. (BSc, MB BS, DA). House Surgeon, Middlesex Hosp., 1972; House Physician, Royal S Hants Hosp., 1973; Sen. House Officer, Anaesthetics, Royal United Hosp., Bath, 1974; GP, Parson Drove, Cambs, 1975; Registrar in Anaesthetics, Northwick Park Hosp., Harrow, 1975–77; called to the Bar, Lincoln's Inn, 1979, Bencher, 1998; HM Asst Dep. Coroner, Westminster, 1981–87. Pres., S of England Coroners' Soc., 1987–88. FFFLM 2007. *Publications:* Thurston's Coronership: the law and practice on coroners, 1985; Medical Negligence, 1990, 4th edn (ed jtly), as Clinical Negligence, 2008; chapters in medical and legal texts on medico-legal subjects. *Recreations:* music, hill-walking, helicopter pilot. *Address:* Clerksroom, Equity House, Blackbrook Park Avenue, Taunton TA1 2PX. *T:* 0845 083 3000; *e-mail:* powersqc@medneg.co.uk. *Club:* Royal Society of Medicine.

POWERS-FREELING, Laurel Claire; Group Chief Executive, Dubai First International, since 2007; *b* 16 May 1957; *d* of Lloyd M. Powers and Catharine Berry Powers; *m* 1989, Dr Anthony Nigel Stanley Freeling; one *s* one *d*. *Educ:* Columbia Univ., NY (AB *cum laude*): Massachusetts Inst. of Technol. (Sloan Schol.). Sen. Consultant, Price Waterhouse, 1981–85; manager, McKinsey & Co., 1985–89; Corporate Finance, Morgan Stanley Internat., 1989–91; Dir, Corporate Strategy, Prudential Gp plc, 1991–94; Gp Finance Dir, Lloyds Abbey Life Gp plc, 1994–97; Lloyds TSB Group plc: Finance and Develt Dir, Retail, 1997–99; Man. Dir, Wealth Mgt, 1999–2001; Exec. Dir, Marks & Spencer Gp plc, 2001–04; CEO, Marks & Spencer Financial Services plc, 2001–04; Sen. Vice-Pres., UK Country Manager and Chm., American Express Insce Services Europe, 2005–07. Non-exec. Dir, Bank of England, 2002–05. Chm., Montisi Harpsichord Performance Centre, Siena, 2005–; Gov., RAM, 2007–; Dir, English Concert, 2008–. *Recreations:* interior design, sewing, music, restoring ancient buildings. *Address:* Dubai First International LLC, Monarch Tower, Level 25 (PO Box 114844), Dubai, UAE. *T:* 3050600, ext. 648, *Fax:* (4) 3050601; *e-mail:* laurel@powers-freeling.com.

POWERSCOURT, 10th Viscount *cr* 1743; **Mervyn Niall Wingfield;** Baron Wingfield, 1743; Baron Powerscourt (UK), 1885; *b* 3 Sept. 1935; *s* of 9th Viscount Powerscourt and Sheila Claude (*d* 1992), *d* of late Lt-Col Claude Beddington; *S* father, 1973; *m* 1st, 1962, Wendy Ann Pauline (marr. diss. 1974), *d* of R. C. G. Slazenger; one *s* one *d*; 2nd, 1979, Pauline (marr. diss. 1995), *d* of W. P. Van, San Francisco. *Educ:* Stowe; Trinity Coll., Cambridge. Formerly Irish Guards. *Heir: s* Hon. Mervyn Anthony Wingfield, *b* 21 Aug. 1963.
  See also Sir J. H. Langrishe, Bt.

POWIS, 8th Earl of, *cr* 1804; **John George Herbert;** Baron Clive (Ire.), 1762; Baron Clive (GB), 1794; Viscount Clive, Baron Herbert of Chirbury, Baron Powis, 1804; Assistant Professor, Redeemer College, Ontario, Canada, 1990–92; *b* 19 May 1952; *s* of 7th Earl of Powis and of Hon. Katharine Odeyne de Grey, *d* of 8th Baron Walsingham, DSO, OBE; *S* father, 1993; *m* 1977, Marijke Sophia, *d* of Maarten Nanne Guther, Ancaster, Canada; two *s* two *d*. *Educ:* Wellington; McMaster Univ., Ontario, Canada (MA; PhD 1994). Formerly Lectr, McMaster Univ. *Heir: s* Viscount Clive, *qv*. *Address:* Powis Castle Estate Office, Welshpool, Powys SY21 8RG.

POWLES, Prof. Raymond Leonard, CBE 2003; MD; FRCP; FRCPath; Professor of Haemato-Oncology, University of London, at Institute of Cancer Research, 1997–2004, now Emeritus; Head, Leukaemia and Myeloma Units, Parkside Cancer Clinic, Parkside Hospital, Wimbledon, since 2004; *b* 9 March 1938; *s* of late Leonard William David Powles and Florence Irene Powles (*née* Conolly); *m* 1980, Louise Jane Richmond; three *s* one *d*. *Educ:* Eltham Coll.; St Bartholomew's Hosp. Med. Coll. (BSc 1961; MB BS 1964; MD 1976). MRCP 1968; FRCP 1980; FRCPath 1993. House Physician and Surgeon, St Bartholomew's Hosp., 1965–66; RMO, Royal Marsden Hosp., 1967–68; Leukaemia Res. Fund Fellow, Ville Juif, Paris, 1968; Tata Meml Fund Fellow, Royal Marsden Hosp. and Inst. of Cancer Res., Sutton, 1969–72; SSO, ICRF, St Bartholomew's Hosp. and Royal Marsden Hosp., 1972–74; Physician in Charge, 1974–2003, and Gp Hd, Haemato-Oncology, 1993–2003, Leukaemia and Myeloma Units, Royal Marsden Hosp. Clin. Tutor, RCP, 1990; internat. lectures on leukaemia, myeloma and bone marrow transplantation. Member: MRC Wkg Party on Leukaemia, 1974–2003; Royal Marsden SHA, 1989–92; Standing Med. Adv. Sub-Cttee on Cancer, DoH, 1991–93; WHO Cttee on Internat. Programme Chernobyl Accident, 1990–92; Ind. Reconfiguration Panel, 2002–; Healthcare Inspections Adv. Panel, Cabinet Office Public Sector Team, 2002–. Chm., Nuclear Accidents Sub-Cttee, European Gp for Blood and Marrow Transplantation, 2001–. Bd Mem., European Soc. Med. Oncology, 1985–90; Scientific Advr, Internat. Myeloma Foundn, 1995–; American Society of Hematology: Mem., Scientific Cttee on hemopoetic growth factors, 2004– (Chm., 2006–08); Chm., Ad-Hoc Scientific Cttee on plasma cell biol., 2008–. Mem. Bd, BioPartners GmbH, 2000–07. Trustee, and Bd Mem., New Health Network, 2002–. Board Member: Bone Marrow

Transplantation, 1986–; Experimental Haematology, 1992–. Lifetime Achievement Award, Cancer Patients Aid Assoc., India, 1999. *Publications:* more than 1200 sci. papers, articles, and chapters in books on leukaemia, myeloma and bone marrow transplantation. *Recreations:* sport, travel, cinema. *Address:* Little Garratts, 19 Garratts Lane, Banstead, Surrey SM7 2EA. *T:* 07768 165882, *Fax:* (office) (020) 8605 9103; *e-mail:* myeloma@clara.co.uk.

See also T. J. Powles.

POWLES, Stephen Robert; QC 1995; **His Honour Judge Powles;** a Circuit Judge, since 2005; *b* 7 June 1948; *s* of late Andrew Frederick Arthur Powles and Nora (*née* Bristol); *m* 1975, Geraldine Patricia Hilda Adamson; one *s* one *d. Educ:* Westminster Sch.; University Coll., Oxford (MA). Called to the Bar: Middle Temple, 1972 (Harmsworth Maj. Exhibnr, 1971; Astbury Law Schol., 1972); Lincoln's Inn (*ad eundem*), 1977; a Recorder, 1994–2005. CEDR registered mediator, 2001–. Mem., Tribunal Panel, Accountancy Investigation and Discipline Bd, 2004–. Hon. CIMechE 2001. *Recreations:* hill-walking, sailing, my border terrier. *Address:* Judicial Communications Office, Thomas More Building, Royal Courts of Justice, Strand, WC2A 2LL.

POWLES, Prof. Trevor James, CBE 2003; PhD; FRCP; Consultant Breast Oncologist: St Anthony's Hospital, since 1978; Lister Hospital, since 2002; Parkside Oncology Clinic, since 2003; Consultant Physician in Breast Cancer, 1978–2003, Head of Breast Cancer Unit, 1993–2003, and Medical Director, Common Tumours Division, 2000–03, Royal Marsden Hospital; Professor of Breast Oncology, Institute of Cancer Research, London University, 1998–2003, now Emeritus; *b* 8 March 1938; *s* of late Leonard William David Powles and Florence Irene Powles (*née* Conolly); *m* 1968, Penelope Margaret Meyers; two *s* one *d. Educ:* Eltham Coll.; St Bartholomew's Hosp. Med. Coll. (PhD). FRCP 1983. House Physician and Registrar, Hammersmith Hosp., 1967–68; Med. Registrar, St Bartholomew's Hosp., 1965–70; MRC Clin. Res. Fellow, Inst. of Cancer Res., 1971–73; Sen. Registrar and Sen. Lectr, Royal Marsden Hosp., 1974–78. Visiting Professor: M. D. Anderson Cancer Center, Houston, 1993; Dana Farber Cancer Center, Harvard, Boston, 1996; Tom Baker Cancer Centre, Calgary, 1998. Director: Oncotech Inc., Calif, 1996–; Neothermia Inc., Ohio, 2000–. Vice Pres., Internat. Soc. for Prevention of Cancer, 1996–. Patron, Breast Cancer Care, 2003–. MInstD 2001. All Party Parly Gp Award for lifetime achievement in breast cancer, 2003; Brinker Award for Scientific Distinction, Komen Foundn, 2005. *Publications:* Breast Cancer Management, 1981; Prostaglandins and Cancer, 1982; Medical Management of Breast Cancer, 1991; scientific papers on diagnosis, prevention and treatment of breast cancer. *Recreations:* horse riding, ski-ing, reading. *Address:* Green Hedges, Coulsdon Lane, Chipstead, Surrey CR5 3QL; Parkside Oncology Clinic, 49 Parkside, Wimbledon, SW19 5NB. *T:* (020) 8247 3384, *Fax:* (020) 8247 3385. *Club:* Royal Automobile.

See also R. L. Powles.

POWLETT; *see* Orde-Powlett.

POWLEY, John Albert; Enquiry Officer, Post Office, 1991–96; *b* 3 Aug. 1936; *s* of Albert and Evelyn Powley; *m* 1957, Jill (*née* Palmer); two *s* one *d. Educ:* Cambridge Grammar Sch.; Cambridgeshire Coll. of Arts and Technology. Apprenticeship, Pye Ltd, 1952–57; RAF, 1957–59; retail shop selling and servicing radio, television and electrical goods, 1960–84. Member (C): Cambs CC, 1967–77, 1997– (Chm., Social Services Cttee, 1998–2005; Cabinet Mem. for finance and corp. services, 2005–); Cambridge City Council, 1967–79 (Leader, Cons. Group, 1973–79; Chm., Housing Cttee, 1972–74, 1976–79; Leader of Council, 1976–79). Contested (C): Harlow, 1979; Norwich S, 1987. MP (C) Norwich S, 1983–87. Chm., Soham Cons. Assoc., 1991–. Sec./Manager, Wensum Valley Golf Club, Taverham, Norfolk, 1989–90. *Recreations:* golf, cricket, football. *Address:* Kyte End, 70A Brook Street, Soham, Ely, Cambs CB7 5AE. *T:* (01353) 624552; *e-mail:* john.powley@cambridgeshire.gov.uk.

POWNALL, David; novelist and playwright, since 1970; *b* 19 May 1938; *s* of John Charles Pownall and Elsie Pownall (*née* Russell); *m* 1962, Glenys Elsie Jones (marr. diss. 1973; she *d* 1995); one *s*; partner 1972–89, Mary Ellen Ray; one *s*; *m* 1993, Jean Alexander Sutton; one *s. Educ:* Greasby Primary Sch., Wirral; Lord Wandsworth Coll., Long Sutton; Keele Univ. (BA Hons 1960). Grad. Trainee, then Personnel Officer, Ford Motor Co., 1960–63; Personnel Manager, Anglo-American Corp., Zambian Copperbelt, 1963–69. FRSL 1976. Hon. DLitt Keele, 2000. John Whiting Award, 1981; Giles Cooper Award, 1981, 1985; Sony Silver Award, 1993, 1994, Sony Gold Award, 1995. *Publications: novels:* The Raining Tree War, 1974; African Horse, 1975; God Perkins, 1977; Light on a Honeycomb, 1978; Beloved Latitudes, 1981; The White Cutter, 1987; The Gardener, 1988; Stagg and his Mother, 1990; The Sphinx and the Sybarites, 1993; The Catalogue of Men, 1999; The Ruling Passion, 2008; *plays:* The Dream of Chief Crazy Horse (for children), 1975; Music to Murder By, 1976; Motocar/Richard III Part Two, 1979; An Audience Called Edouard, 1979; Master Class, 1983; The Composer Plays, 1993; Death of a Faun, 1996; Radio Plays, 1998; Getting the Picture, 1998; Collected Plays, 2000; *short stories:* My Organic Uncle and other stories, 1976; The Bunch from Bananas (for children), 1980; *poetry:* Another Country, 1978; Poems, 2007; *non-fiction:* Between Ribble and Lune, 1980. *Recreations:* fishing, fell-walking, gardening, music. *Address:* c/o Johnson & Alcock Ltd, Clerkenwell House, 45/47 Clerkenwell Green, EC1R 0HT. *T:* (020) 7251 0125.

POWNALL, John Harvey; Director, DTI-North West, 1988–93; *b* 24 Oct. 1933; *s* of late Eric Pownall and Gladys M. Pownall; *m* 1958, Pauline M. Marsden, *o d* of William Denton Marsden; one *s* two *d. Educ:* Tonbridge School; Imperial College, London (BSc Eng Met). ARSM; MIMMM; CEng. Scientific Officer, Atomic Energy Research Estab., Harwell, 1955–59; Warren Spring Lab., DSIR, 1959–64; Dept of Economic Affairs, 1964–66; Board of Trade/Dept of Trade and Industry, 1966–83; Dir-Gen., Council of Mechanical and Metal Trade Assocs, 1983–85; Hd of Electricity Div., Dept of Energy, 1985–87; Under Sec., DTI, 1987, on secondment to CEGB, 1987–88. Mem. Council, 1989–2004, Pro-Chancellor, 2001–04, Salford Univ. (Chm., Estates Cttee, 1993–2003). *Publications:* papers in professional jls.

POWNALL, Brig. John Lionel, OBE 1972; Deputy Chairman, Police Complaints Authority, 1986–93 (Member, 1985–86); *b* 10 May 1929; *yr s* of late John Cecil Glossop Pownall, CB and Margaret Nina Pownall (*née* Jesson); *m* 1962, Sylvia Joan Cameron Conn, *d* of late J. Cameron Conn, WS and Florence Conn (*née* Lennox); two *s. Educ:* Rugby School; RMA Sandhurst. Commissioned 16th/5th Lancers, 1949; served Egypt, Cyrenaica, Tripolitania, BAOR, Hong Kong, Cyprus; psc, jssc; Comd 16th/5th The Queen's Royal Lancers, 1969–71; Adjutant-Gen.'s Secretariat, 1971–72; Officer i/c RAC Manning and Records, 1973–75; Col, GS Near East Land Forces/Land Forces Cyprus, 1975–78; Asst Dir, Defence Policy Staff, MoD, 1978–79; Brig. RAC, UKLF, 1979–82; Brig. GS, MoD, 1982–84; retired 1984. Col, 16th/5th The Queen's Royal Lancers, 1985–90. *Recreations:* country pursuits, arts. *Address:* Sweatmans, Milland, Liphook, Hampshire GU30 7JT. *Clubs:* Cavalry and Guards, Army and Navy.

POWNALL, Leslie Leigh, MA, PhD; Chairman, NSW Planning and Environment Commission, 1974–77, retired; *b* 1 Nov. 1921; *y s* of A. de S. Pownall, Wanganui, New Zealand; *m* 1943, Judith, *d* of late Harold Whittaker, Palmerston North. *Educ:* Palmerston North Boys' High Sch.; Victoria University College, University of Canterbury, University of Wisconsin. Asst Master, Christchurch Boys' High Sch., 1941–46; Lecturer in Geography: Christchurch Teachers' Coll., 1946–47; Ardmore Teachers' Coll., 1948–49; Auckland University College, 1949–51; Senior Lecturer in Geography, 1951–60, Prof. of Geography, 1960–61, Vice-Chancellor and Rector, 1961–66, University of Canterbury; Clerk of the University Senate, Univ. of London, 1966–74. Consultant, Inter-University Council for Higher Educn Overseas, London, 1963; Consultant to Chm. of Working Party on Higher Educn in E Africa, 1968–69. Member Meeting, Council on World Tensions on Social and Economic Development (S Asia and Pacific), Kuala Lumpur, Malaysia, 1964; Governor, Internat. Students Trust, London, 1967–74; Member: Central Governing Body, City Parochial Foundation, London, 1967–74 (Mem., Grants Sub-Cttee; Chm., Finance and Gen. Purposes Cttee); UK Commonwealth Scholarship Commn, 1979–80. *Publications:* New Zealand, 1951 (New York); geographic contrib. in academic journals of America, Netherlands and New Zealand. *Recreations:* music, literature. *Club:* University (Christchurch, NZ).

POWNALL, Michael Graham; Clerk of the Parliaments, House of Lords, since 2007; *b* 11 Oct. 1949; *s* of Raymond Pownall and Elisabeth Mary Pownall (*née* Robinson); *m* 1974, Deborah Ann, *e d* of T. H. McQueen; two *d. Educ:* Repton Sch.; Exeter Univ. Joined Parliament Office, House of Lords, 1971: seconded to CSD as Private Sec. to Leader of House and Govt Chief Whip, 1980–83; Estabt Officer and Sec. to Chm. of Cttees, 1983–88; Principal Clerk of Private Bills, 1988–90; Principal Clerk, Overseas Office, 1988–95; Clerk of Cttees, 1991–95; Clerk of the Journals, 1995–96; Reading Clerk and Principal Finance Officer, 1997–2003; Clerk Asst, 2003–07. *Recreations:* bird-watching, squash. *Address:* 13 Flanders Road, Chiswick, W4 1NQ. *T:* (020) 8994 0797.

POWNALL, (Stephen) Orlando (Fletcher); QC 2002; *b* 13 Nov. 1952; *s* of Alan Pownall and Carola Pownall (*née* Thielker); *m* 1978, Katherine Higgins; one *s* two *d. Educ:* Oundle Sch.; Faculté de Droit, Paris. Called to the Bar, Inner Temple, 1975, Bencher, 2007; Jun. Treasury Counsel, 1991–95; Sen. Treasury Counsel, CCC, 1995–2002. *Recreations:* Rugby, golf, painting, gardening. *Address:* 2 Hare Court, Temple, EC4Y 7BH.

POWRIE, Prof. William, PhD; CEng, FICE; Professor of Geotechnical Engineering, since 1995, and Head, School of Civil Engineering and the Environment (formerly Department of Civil and Environmental Engineering), 1999–2008, University of Southampton; *b* 25 Sept. 1959; *s* of William Powrie and Jean (*née* Darby); *m* 1988, Dr Christine Lorraine Solomon; three *s* one *d. Educ:* St Catharine's Coll., Cambridge (BA Engrg 1982; MA 1986; PhD Soil Mechanics 1986); King's Coll., London (MSc Construction Law and Arbitration 1991). CEng 1991; FICE 1997. Civil Engrg Trainee, British Rail (Eastern Reg.), 1978–82; Lectr in Civil Engrg, KCL, 1985–88; Queen Mary and Westfield College, London: Lectr in Civil Engrg, 1988–93; Reader in Civil Engrg, 1993–94. Chm., Southampton Univ. Res. into Sustainability and Envmt, 1998–. Geotechnical Cons. to W. J. Groundwater Ltd, Bushey, 1987–; Director: WJ Associates Ltd (geotechnical consultants), 1992–2003; Envmtl Services Assoc. Res. Trust, 1998–2002. Sponsor, Scientists for Global Responsibility (formerly Architects and Engrs for Social Responsibility), 2000–. Chm., DEFRA Technologies Adv. Cttee for Biodegradable Municipal Waste, 2005–. Hon. Editor and Chm. Editl Adv. Panel, ICE Procs (Geotech. Engrg), 1997–99, (Waste and Resource Mgt), 2005–. *Publications:* Soil Mechanics: concepts and applications, 1997, 2nd edn 2004; *c* 70 papers in acad. and professional jls incl. Geotechnique, ICE Procs, Procs ASCE, Canadian Geotech. Jl, Jl of Petroleum Sci. and Engrg, Waste Mgt and Res. and Internat. Jl of Rock Mechanics and Mining Scis. *Recreations:* music (playing and listening, mainly classical and jazz, piano, church organ and alto saxophone), cycling, walking, DIY. *Address:* School of Civil Engineering and the Environment, University of Southampton, Highfield, Southampton SO17 1BJ. *T:* (023) 8059 3214, *Fax:* (023) 8067 7519; *e-mail:* wp@soton.ac.uk.

POWYS, family name of **Baron Lilford**.

POYNTER, Kieran Charles, FCA; Chairman, 2000–08, and Senior Partner, since 2000, PricewaterhouseCoopers LLP; *b* 20 Aug. 1950; *s* of Kenneth and Betty Poynter; *m* 1977, Marylyn Melvin; three *s* one *d. Educ:* Salesian Coll.; Imperial Coll., London (BSc, ARCS). FCA 1977. Price Waterhouse, 1971–98, PricewaterhouseCoopers, 1998–: articled clerk, 1971; Partner, 1982; Dir, Insce Services, 1982–95; Member: Supervisory Bd, 1993–95; Mgt Bd, 1995–; Man. Partner, 1996–2000. Member: Insce Cttee, ICAEW, 1982–95; Life Accounting Cttee, ABI, 1992; Govt Task Force on Deregulation of Financial Services, 1993. Lloyd's Committees: Member: Accounting and Auditing Standards, 1988–90; Solvency and Reporting, 1994–95; Disputes Resolution Panel, 1996–97; Chm., Gooda Walker Loss Review, 1991–92. Member: Council for Industry and Higher Educn, 1997–; Council, NIESR, 2000–; President's Cttee, CBI, 2001–; Council, Prince of Wales' Internat. Business Leaders Forum, 2001–; Transatlantic Council, British American Business Inc., 2001–; Steering Cttee, Heart of the City, 2003–; Task Force on Ethnic Diversity, IPPR, 2005–06; President's Cttee, Employers Forum on Disability, 2006–; Council, British Olympic Appeal, 2008–. Trustee: Industry in Educn, 1999–; Royal Anniversary Trust, 2007–. Dir, Royal Automobile Club Ltd, 2007–. KHS 1999. *Publications:* contrib. various insurance articles to professional jls. *Recreations:* golf, watching sport, shooting. *Address:* (office) 1 Embankment Place, WC2N 6RH. *T:* (020) 7804 3188; 15 Montpelier Mews, SW7 1HB. *T:* (020) 7581 5812. *Club:* Royal Automobile.

POYNTZ, Rt Rev. Samuel Greenfield; Bishop of Connor, 1987–95; *b* 4 March 1926; *s* of James and Katharine Jane Poyntz; *m* 1952, Noreen Henrietta Armstrong; one *s* two *d. Educ:* Portora Royal School, Enniskillen; Univ. of Dublin. Mod., Mental and Moral Sci. and Oriental Langs, 1948; 1st cl. Div. Test., 1950; MA 1951; BD 1953; PhD 1960. Deacon 1950, priest 1951; Curate Assistant: St George's, Dublin, 1950–52; Bray, 1952–55; St Michan and St Paul, Dublin, 1955–59; Rector of St Stephen's, Dublin, 1959–67; Vicar of St Ann's, Dublin, 1967–78; Archdeacon of Dublin, 1974–78; Exam. Chaplain to Archbishop of Dublin, 1974–78; Bishop of Cork, Cloyne and Ross, 1978–87. Chairman: Youth Dept, British Council of Churches, 1965–69; Irish Council of Churches, 1986–88; Jt Chm., Irish Inter-Church Meeting, 1986–88; Vice-Pres., BCC, 1987–90. Member: Governing Body, UC Cork, 1978–87; Ct, Ulster Univ., 1987–2006. Hon. DLitt Ulster, 1995. *Publications:* The Exaltation of the Blessed Virgin Mary, 1953; St Stephen's—One Hundred and Fifty Years of Worship and Witness, 1974; Journey towards Unity, 1975; St Ann's—the Church in the heart of the City, 1976; (ed) Church the Way, the Truth, and Your Life, 1955; Our Church—Praying with our Church Family, 1983; (contrib.) Mary for Earth and Heaven: essays on Mary and ecumenism, 2002; (contrib.) Inter-Church Relations: developments and perspectives - a tribute to Bishop Anthony Farquhar, 2008. *Recreations:* interest in Rugby football, travel, stamp collecting. *Address:* 3 The Gables, Ballinteer Road, Dundrum, Dublin 16, Ireland. *T:* (1) 2966748.

POZNANSKY, Dulcie Vivien; *see* Coleman, D. V.

PRACY, Robert, FRCS; Dean of the Institute of Laryngology and Otology, University of London, 1981–85, retired; a Medical Chairman, Pensions Appeal Tribunals, since 1984 (Medical Member, since 1982); *b* 19 Sept. 1921; *s* of Douglas Sherrin Pracy and Gwendoline Blanche Power; *m* 1946, Elizabeth Patricia Spicer (*d* 2008); one *s* two *d* (and one *s* decd). *Educ:* Berkhamsted Sch.; St Bartholomew's Hosp. Med. Coll. (MB BS 1945); MPhil (Lond.) 1984. LRCP 1944; MRCS, FRCS 1953. Former Captain, RAMC. House Surgeon appts, St Bartholomew's Hosp.; formerly: Registrar, Royal Nat. Throat, Nose and Ear Hosp.; Consultant Surgeon: Liverpool Regional Board, 1954; United Liverpool Hosps, 1959; Alder Hey Childrens' Hosp., 1960; Royal Nat. Throat, Nose and Ear Hosp.; Hosp. for Sick Children, Gt Ormond St; Dir, Dept of Otolaryngology, Liverpool Univ. Mem. Ct of Examnrs, RCS and RCSI. Lectures: Yearsley, 1976; Joshi, 1978; Wilde, 1979; Semon, London Univ., 1980. Pres., British Assoc. of Otolaryngologists; FRSocMed (Pres., Sect. of Laryngology, 1982–83). Hon. FRCSI 1982; Hon. Fellow: Irish Otolaryngol Assoc.; Assoc. of Otolaryngologists of India; Polish Otolaryngological Assoc. *Publications:* (jtly) Short Textbook: Ear, Nose and Throat, 1970, 2nd edn 1974 (trans. Italian, Portuguese, Spanish); (jtly) Ear, Nose and Throat Surgery and Nursing, 1977; contribs to learned jls. *Recreations:* painting, engraving, theatre. *Address:* Ginkgo House, New Road, Moreton-in-Marsh, Glos GL56 0AS. *T:* (01608) 650740.

PRADA, Miuccia, PhD; Head of Prada SpA, since 1978; *b* 1949; *d* of late Luisa Prada; *m* 1987, Patrizio Bertelli; two *s*. Mime artist, Teatro Piccolo, Milan. Joined Prada, 1970; launched: women's clothing collection, 1988; Miu Miu, 1992; men's collection, 1994. Internat. Award, Council of Fashion Designers of America, 2004. *Address:* Prada SpA, Via Andrea Maffei 2, 20135 Milan, Italy.

PRAG, Prof. (Andrew) John (Nicholas Warburg), MA, DPhil; FSA; Keeper of Archaeology, Manchester Museum, 1969–2004, and Professor of Archaeological Studies, 2004–05, now Hon. Professor, University of Manchester; Hon. Research Fellow, School of Classics and History, since 2002, and Professor Emeritus of Classics, since 2005, University of Manchester; *b* 28 Aug. 1941; *s* of late Adolf Prag and Frede Charlotte (*née* Warburg); *m* 1969, Kay (*née* Wright); one *s* one *d*. *Educ:* Westminster Sch. (Queen's Scholar); Brasenose Coll., Oxford (Domus Exhibnr 1960; Hon. Scholar 1962; BA 1964; Dip. Classical Archaeol. 1966; Sen. Hulme Scholar, 1967; MA 1967; DPhil 1975). FSA 1977. Temp. Asst Keeper, Ashmolean Museum, Oxford, 1966–67; University of Manchester: Hon. Lectr, Dept of History, 1977–83, Dept of Archaeology, 1984–2005. Vis. Prof. of Classics, McMaster Univ., 1978; Vis. Fellow, British Sch. at Athens, 1994. Editor, Archaeological Reports, 1975–87. *Publications:* The Oresteia: iconographic and narrative tradition, 1985; (with Richard Neave) Making Faces Using the Forensic and Archaeological Evidence, 1997; (ed jtly) Periplous: papers on classical art and archaeology, 2000; (with J. Swaddling) Seianti Hanunia Tlesnasa: the story of an Etruscan noblewoman, 2002; (with Simon Timberlake) The Archaeology of Alderley Edge, 2005; Living with the Edge: Alderley's story, 2009; articles on Greek art and archaeology in learned jls. *Recreations:* travel, cooking, music. *Address:* Manchester Museum, The University, Manchester M13 9PL. *T:* (0161) 275 2665; *e-mail:* john.prag@manchester.ac.uk.
See also T. G. A. Prag.

PRAG, Derek; Member (C) Hertfordshire, European Parliament, 1979–94; *b* 6 Aug. 1923; *s* of late Abraham J. Prag and Edith Prag; *m* 1948, Dora Weiner; three *s*. *Educ:* Bolton Sch.; Emmanuel Coll., Univ. of Cambridge (Scholar; MA; Cert. of Competent Knowledge in Russian). Served War, Intelligence Corps, England, Egypt, Italy, Austria, 1942–47. Economic journalist with Reuters News Agency in London, Brussels and Madrid, 1950–55; Information Service of High Authority, European Coal and Steel Community, 1955–59; Head of Publications Div., Jt Information Service of European Communities, 1959–65; Dir, London Information Office of European Communities, 1965–73; ran own consultancy company on relations with EEC, 1973–79. Mem., 1982–94, Dep. Chm., 1989–94, Constitutional Cttee (EDG spokesman, 1982–84 and 1987–92; EPP dep. spokesman, and British Cons. spokesman, 1992–94; elected Chm., 1993, but stood down); Rapporteur, EU's internat. relns for European Parlt's draft treaty on European Union, adopted 1984; Prag report on seat of EC Institns and working place of European Parlt, adopted 1989. Political spokesman for European Democratic (Cons.) Group, 1984–87; Chm., European Parlt All-Party Disablement Gp, 1980–94; Vice-Pres., Eur. Parlt-Israel Intergroup, 1990–94; Founder Mem., Cons. Gp for Europe (Dep. Chm., 1974–77, 1991–93). Member: Anglo-Spanish Soc.; Luxembourg Soc. Hon. Dir, EEC Commn, 1974; Hon. Mem., EP, 1994. Hon. DLitt Hertfordshire, 1993. Silver Medal of European Merit, Fondation du Mérite Européen, 1974. Comdr, Order of Leopold II (Belgium), 1996. *Publications:* (with E. D. Nicholson) Businessman's Guide to the Common Market, 1973; various reports on Europe's internat. role, and booklets and articles on European integration. *Recreations:* reading, theatre, music, swimming, gardening; speaks seven languages. *Address:* 47 New Road, Digswell, Welwyn, Herts AL6 0AQ. *Clubs:* Royal Over-Seas League, Anglo-Belgian; Royal Automobile (Brussels).

PRAG, John; *see* Prag, A. J. N. W.

PRAG, Thomas Gregory Andrew; Chairman, Media Support Solutions, and Media Support Partnership, since 2001; *b* 2 Jan. 1947; *s* of late Adolf Prag and Frede Charlotte Prag (*née* Warburg); *m* 1970, Angela Hughes; three *s*. *Educ:* Westminster Sch.; Brasenose Coll., Oxford (MA PPE). Producer/presenter, BBC Radio Oxford, 1970–78; Prog. Organiser, BBC Highland, 1978–81; Man. Dir, 1981–2000, Chm., 2000–01, Moray Firth Radio; Mem. for Scotland, Radio Authority, 2001–03; Mem., Scottish Adv. Cttee, Ofcom, 2004– (Chm., 2006–). Pres., Inverness Chamber of Commerce, 1996–98; Mem. Bd, Inverness Harbour Trust, 2003–. Mem. Bd, Assoc. of Ind. Radio Contractors, subseq. Commercial Radio Cos Assoc., 1993–2000. Dir, 1993–2004, Chm., 2002–04, Highland Fest. Mem. Bd Governors, UHI Millennium Inst., 2002–; Chm., UHI Millennium Inst. Develt Trust, 2004–07. Mem. (Lib Dem), Highland Council, 2007–. FCMI (FBIM 1978); FRA 1998. *Recreations:* wife and family, acquiring old things – clocks, radios, etc, 1950 Convertible Daimler, casual gardener, sculler and cox, music, travel. *Address:* Windrush, Easter Muckovie, Inverness IV2 5BN. *T:* (01463) 791697; *e-mail:* thomas@prags.co.uk. *Clubs:* Inverness Rowing, Inverness Rotary (Pres., 2004–05).
See also A. J. N. W. Prag.

PRAIS, Prof. Sigbert Jon, FBA 1985; Senior Research Fellow, National Institute of Economic and Social Research, London, since 1970; *b* Frankfurt am Main, Germany, 19 Dec. 1928; *s* of Samuel and Bertha Prais; came to England as refugee, 1934; UK citizen, 1946; *m* 1971, Vivien Hennessy, LLM, solicitor; one *s* three *d*. *Educ:* King Edward's School, Birmingham; Univ. of Birmingham (MCom); Fitzwilliam Coll., Cambridge (PhD 1953; ScD 1974). Dept of Applied Economics, Cambridge, 1950–57; post-doctoral Fellow, Univ. of Chicago, 1953–54; research officer, NIESR, 1953–59; UN Tech. Assistance Orgn, 1959–60; IMF Washington, 1960–61; Finance Dir, Elbief Co., 1961–70. Vis. Prof. of Econs, City Univ., 1975–84. Mem. Council, Royal Economic Soc., 1979–83. Mem. Council, City Univ., 1990–94. Hon. DLitt City, 1989; Hon. DSc Birmingham, 2006. *Publications:* Analysis of Family Budgets (jtly), 1955, 2nd edn 1971; Evolution of Giant Firms in Britain, 1976, 2nd edn 1981; Productivity and Industrial Structure, 1981; Productivity, Education and Training, 1995; (jtly) From School to Productive Work in Britain and Switzerland, 1997; Social Disparities and the Teaching of Literacy, 2001; articles in economic and statistical jls, esp. on influence of educn on economic progress. *Address:* 83 West Heath Road, NW3 7TN. *T:* (020) 8458 4428; (office) (020) 7654 1939.

PRANCE, Sir Ghillean (Tolmie), Kt 1995; DPhil; FRS 1993; FLS, FIBiol; FRGS; Scientific Director, Eden Project, Cornwall, since 1999; *b* 13 July 1937; *s* of Basil Camden Prance, CIE, OBE and Margaret Hope Prance (*née* Tolmie); *m* 1961, Anne Elizabeth Hay; two *d*. *Educ:* Malvern Coll.; Keble Coll., Oxford (BA, MA, DPhil). FLS 1961; FIBiol 1988. New York Botanical Garden: Res. Asst, 1963–66; Associate Curator, 1966–68; B. A. Krukoff Curator of Amazonian Botany, 1968–75; Dir of Research, 1975–81; Vice-Pres., 1977–81; Senior Vice-Pres., 1981–88; Dir, Royal Botanic Gdns, Kew, 1988–99. Adjunct Prof., City Univ. of NY, 1968–99; Vis. Prof. in Tropical Studies, Yale, 1983–89; Vis. Prof., Reading Univ., 1988–; McBryde Prof., 2000–02, McBryde Sen. Res. Fellow, 2006–, Nat. Tropical Botanical Gdn, Kalaheo, Hawaii; Dir of Graduate Studies, Instituto Nacional de Pesquisas da Amazônia, Manaus, Brazil, 1973–75; 14 botanical expedns to Amazonia. President: Assoc. of Tropical Biol., 1979–80 (Hon. Fellow, 2007); Amer. Assoc. of Plant Taxonomists, 1984–85; Systematics Assoc., 1989–91; Econ. Botany Soc., 1996–97; Linnean Soc., 1997–2000; Internat. Assoc. for Plant Taxonomy, 1999–2005; Inst. of Biology, 2000–02; Internat. Tree Foundn, 2005–; Mem. Council, RHS, 1990–2000. FRGS 1989; Fellow: AAAS, 1990; Perak Acad., 2006; Corresponding Member: Brazilian Acad. of Scis, 1976; Botanical Soc. of America, 1994; Foreign Member: Royal Danish Acad. of Scis and Letters, 1988; Royal Swedish Acad. of Scis, 1989; Associate Mem., Third World Acad. of Scis, 1993; Hon. Mem., British Ecol Soc., 1996. Hon. Freeman, Gardeners' Co., 1997. Fil Dr *hc* Univ. Göteborgs, Sweden, 1983; Hon. DSc: Kent, Portsmouth, Kingston, 1994; St Andrews, 1995; Bergen Univ., Norway, 1996; Florida Internat. Univ., Herbert H. Lehman Coll., NY, and Sheffield Univ., 1997; Liverpool, 1998; Glasgow, Plymouth, 1999; Keele, Exeter, 2000. Henry Shaw Medal, Missouri Botanical Garden, St Louis, 1988; Linnean Medal, 1990; Internat. Cosmos Prize, Japan, 1993; Patron's Medal, RGS, 1994; Janaki Ammal Medal, Soc. of Ethnobotany, 1996; Internat. Award of Excellence, Botanical Res. Inst., Texas, 1998; Medalho do Mérito, Jardim Botânico, Rio de Janeiro, 1998; VMH 1999; Lifetime of Discovery Award, Discovery Channel and RGS, 1999; Fairchild Medal for Plant Exploration, Nat. Tropical Botanical Gdn, 2000; Dist. Econ. Botanist Award, Soc. of Econ. Botany, 2002; Graziela Maciel Barroso Prize, 2004; Allerton Award, Nat. Tropical Botanical Gdn, 2005. Ordem Nacional do Mérito Cientifico-Grã-Cruz (Brazil), 1995; Comendador da Ordem Nacional do Cruzeiro do Sul (Brazil), 2000. *Publications:* Arvores de Manaus, 1975; Algumas Flores da Amazonia, 1976; Extinction is Forever, 1977; Biological Diversification in the Tropics, 1981; Amazonia: key environments, 1985; Leaves, 1986; Manual de Botânica Econômica do Maranhão, 1988; Flowers for all Seasons, 1989; Out of the Amazon, 1992; Bark, 1993; The Earth Under Threat: a Christian perspective, 1996; Rainforests: water, fire, earth and air, 1997; Chrysobalanaceae of the World, 2003. *Recreations:* flower stamp collecting, bird watching. *Address:* The Old Vicarage, Silver Street, Lyme Regis, Dorset DT7 3HS. *T:* (01297) 444991, *Fax:* (01297) 444955; *e-mail:* gtolmiep@aol.com. *Club:* Explorers (New York) (Fellow).

PRANKERD, Thomas Arthur John, FRCP; Professor of Clinical Haematology, 1965–79 and Dean, 1972–77, University College Hospital Medical School; Hon. Consultant Physician: University College Hospital; Whittington Hospital; *b* 11 Sept. 1924; *s* of late H. A. Prankerd, Barrister-at-Law, and J. D. Shorthose; *m* 1950, Margaret Vera Harrison Cripps; two *s* (and one *s* one *d* decd). *Educ:* Charterhouse Sch.; St Bartholomew's Hospital Med. Sch. MD (London) Gold Medal 1949; FRCP 1962. Jr med. appts, St Bart's and University Coll. Hosp., 1947–60. Major, RAMC, 1948–50. Univ. Travelling Fellow, USA, 1953–54; Consultant Physician, University Coll. Hosp., 1960–65. Examr, RCP, and various univs. Goulstonian Lectr, RCP, 1963; Visiting Professor: Univ. of Perth, WA, 1972; Univ. of Cape Town, 1973. Mem., NE Thames RHA, 1976–79. Mem. Bd of Governors, UCH, 1972–74. Mem., Assoc. of Physicians, 1965. *Publications:* The Red Cell, 1961; Haematology in Medical Practice, 1968; articles in med. jls. *Recreations:* fishing, gardening, music. *Address:* 6 Stinsford House, Stinsford, Dorchester DT2 8PT. *T:* (01305) 751521.

PRASAD, Dr Sunand, RIBA; Senior Partner, Penoyre & Prasad Architects, since 1988; President, Royal Institute of British Architects, 2007–Aug. 2009; *b* 22 May 1950; *s* of Devi and Janaki Prasad; *m* 1982, Susan Francis; three *s*. *Educ:* Univ. of Cambridge Sch. of Architecture (MA); Architectural Assoc. (AA Dip.); PhD RCA 1988. RIBA 1987. Partner, Edward Cullinan Architects, 1978–84; Leverhulme Res. Fellow, RCA, 1985–88. Comr, Commn for Architecture and the Built Envmt, 1999–2006. Mem., Awards Gp, 1995–2000, Practice Cttee, 1999–2002, RIBA; Mem. Council, AA, 1997–2001. FRSA. *Publications:* contributor to: Le Corbusier: architect of the century, 1987; Paradigms of Indian Architecture, 1998; Macmillan Dictionary of Art, 1997; Design Quality, 2002; London: postcolonial city, 2002; Transformations: the architecture of Penoyre & Prasad, 2007; Changing Hospital Architecture, 2008. *Recreations:* music, sailboarding. *Address:* Penoyre & Prasad Architects, 28–42 Banner Street, EC1Y 8QE. *T:* (020) 7250 3477, *Fax:* (020) 7250 0844; *e-mail:* mail@penoyre-prasad.net.

PRASHAR, Baroness *cr* 1999 (Life Peer), of Runnymede in the county of Surrey; **Usha Kumari Prashar,** CBE 1995; Chairman, Judicial Appointments Commission, since 2006; *b* 29 June 1948; *d* of Nauhria Lal Prashar and Durga Devi Prashar; *m* 1973, Vijay Kumar Sharma. *Educ:* Duchess of Gloucester Sch., Nairobi; Wakefield Girls' High Sch. (Head Girl, 1966–67); Univ. of Leeds (BA Hons Pol. Studies); Univ. of Glasgow (postgrad. Dip. Social Admin). Race Relations Bd, 1971–76; Asst Dir, Runnymede Trust, 1976–77, Dir, 1976–84; Res. Fellow, PSI, 1984–86; Dir, NCVO, 1986–91; Dep. Chm., 1992–2000, Chm., 2000–05, Nat. Literacy Trust. CS Comr (part-time), 1990–96; Chm., Parole Bd, 1997–2000; First CS Comr, 2000–05. Non-executive Director: Channel 4, 1992–99; Unite plc, 2001–04; ITV, 2005–. Vice-Chm., British Refugee Council, 1987–89. Member: Arts Council of GB, 1979–81, Arts Council of England, 1994–97; Study Commn on the Family, 1980–83; Social Security Adv. Cttee, 1980–83; Exec. Cttee, Child Poverty Action Gp, 1984–85; GLAA, 1984–86; London Food Commn, 1984–90; BBC Educnl Broadcasting Council, 1987–89; Adv. Council, Open College, 1987–89; Solicitors' Complaints Bureau, 1989–90; Royal Commn on Criminal Justice, 1991–93; Lord Chancellor's Adv. Cttee on Legal Educn and Conduct, 1991–97; Council, PSI, 1992–97; Bd, Energy Saving Trust, 1992–98; King's Fund, 1998–2002. Hon. Vice-Pres., Council for Overseas Student Affairs, 1986–98. Trustee: Thames Help Trust, 1984–86; Charities Aid Foundn, 1986–91; Independent Broadcasting Telethon Trust, 1987–92; Acad. of Indian Dance, 1987–91; Camelot Foundn, 1996–2001; Ethnic Minority Foundn, 1997–2002; BBC World Service Trust, 2001–05; Miriam Rothschild and John Foster Trust, 2007–; Cumberland Lodge, 2007–; Chm., English Adv. Cttee, Nat. AIDS Trust, 1988–89; Patron: Sickle Cell Soc., 1986–; Elfrida Rathbone Soc., 1988–91. Chancellor, De Montfort Univ., 2000–06 (Gov., 1996–2006). FRSA. Hon. Fellow, Goldsmiths' Coll., Univ. of London, 1992. Hon. LLD: De Montfort, 1994; South Bank Univ., 1994; Greenwich, 1999; Leeds Metropolitan, 1999; Ulster, 2000; Oxford

Brookes, 2000. *Publications: contributed to:* Britain's Black Population, 1980; The System: a study of Lambeth Borough Council's race relations unit, 1981; Scarman and After, 1984; Sickle Cell Anaemia, Who Cares? a survey of screening, counselling, training and educational facilities in England, 1985; Routes or Road Blocks, a study of consultation arrangements between local authorities and local communities, 1985; Acheson and After: primary health care in the inner city, 1986. *Recreations:* reading, country walks, music, golf. *Address:* House of Lords, SW1A 0PW. *Club:* Royal Commonwealth Society (Trustee, 2001–; Chm., 2001–08).

PRATCHETT, Terence David John, OBE 1998; author; *b* 28 April 1948; *s* of David and Eileen Pratchett; *m* 1968, Lyn Purves; one *d*. *Educ:* High Wycombe Tech. High Sch.; Beaconsfield Public Library. Assorted journalism, 1965–80; Press Officer, CEGB, 1980–87. Chm., Soc. of Authors, 1994–95. Hon. DLitt Warwick, 1999. *Publications:* The Carpet People, 1971; The Dark Side of the Sun, 1976; Strata, 1981; The Colour of Magic, 1983; The Light Fantastic, 1986; Equal Rites, 1987; Mort, 1987; Sourcery, 1988; Wyrd Sisters, 1988; Pyramids, 1989; Truckers, 1989; Guards! Guards!, 1989; The Unadulterated Cat, 1989; Eric, 1989; (with N. Gaiman) Good Omens, 1990; Moving Pictures, 1990; Diggers, 1990; Wings, 1990; Reaper Man, 1991; Witches Abroad, 1991; Small Gods, 1992; Only You Can Save Mankind, 1992; Lords and Ladies, 1992; Johnny and the Dead, 1993; Men At Arms, 1993; Soul Music, 1994; Interesting Times, 1994; Maskerade, 1995; Johnny and the Bomb, 1996; Feet of Clay, 1996; Hogfather, 1996; Jingo, 1997; The Last Continent, 1998; Carpe Jugulum, 1998; The Fifth Elephant, 1999; (jtly) The Science of Discworld, 1999; (jtly) Nanny Ogg's Cookbook, 1999; The Truth, 2000; Thief of Time, 2001; The Amazing Maurice and his Educated Rodents, 2001 (Carnegie Medal, 2002); (jtly) The Science of Discworld II: The Globe, 2002; Night Watch, 2002; The Wee Free Men, 2003; Monstrous Regiment, 2003; A Hat Full of Sky, 2004; Going Postal, 2004; Thud!, 2005; Wintersmith, 2006; Making Money, 2007; Nation, 2008; (jtly) The Folklore of Discworld, 2008. *Recreation:* letting the mind wander. *Address:* c/o Colin Smythe, PO Box 6, Gerrards Cross, Bucks SL9 8XA. *T:* (01753) 886000.

PRATLEY, Alan Sawyer; Deputy Financial Controller, Commission of the European Communities, 1990–98 (Director, Financial Control, 1986–90); *b* 25 Nov. 1933; *s* of Frederick Pratley and Hannah Pratley (*née* Sawyer); *m* 1st, 1960, Dorothea Rohland (marr. diss. 1979); two *d*; 2nd, 1979, Josette Kairis (marr. diss. 1994); one *d*; 3rd, 1996, Marie-Hélène Ledivelec. *Educ:* Latymer Upper School; Sidney Sussex Coll., Cambridge (BA Modern Languages (German, Russian)). Head, German Dept, Stratford Grammar Sch., West Ham, 1958–60; Asst Dir, Examinations, Civil Service Commn, 1960–68; Home Office, 1968–73; Commission of the European Communities: Head, Individual Rights Div., 1973–79; Dep. Chef de cabinet to Christopher Tugendhat, 1979–80; Adviser to Michael O'Kennedy, 1980–81; Dir of Admin, 1981–86. *Recreations:* tennis, gardening. *Address:* 18 Avenue de l'Armée, 1040 Brussels, Belgium. *T:* and *Fax:* (2) 7352483; *e-mail:* alan.pratley@skynet.be.

PRATLEY, David Illingworth; Principal, David Pratley Associates, since 1996; *b* 24 Dec. 1948; *s* of Arthur George Pratley and Olive Constance Illingworth; *m* 1996, Caryn Faure Walker (*née* Becker) (*d* 2004). *Educ:* Westminster Abbey Choir Sch.; Westminster Sch.; Univ. of Bristol (LLB). PRO, Thorndike Theatre, Leatherhead, 1970–71; Gen. Asst, Queen's Univ. Festival, Belfast, 1971–73; Dep. Dir, Merseyside Arts Assoc., 1973–76; Dir, Greater London Arts Assoc., 1976–81; Regl Dir, Arts Council of GB, 1981–86; Chief Exec., Royal Liverpool Philharmonic Soc., 1987–88; Man. Dir, Trinity Coll. of Music, 1988–91; Dir of Leisure, Tourism and Econ. Develt, Bath CC, 1992–96. Chm., Alliance Arts Panel, 1987–88; Council Mem., Nat. Campaign for the Arts, 1986–92 (Chm., 1988–92); Dir, Dance Umbrella Ltd, 1986– (Chm., 1990–92). Lottery Policy Advr, Arts Council England (formerly Arts Council of England), 1996–. FRSA. *Recreations:* music, theatre, art, countryside, travel. *Address:* 54 Walnut Tree Walk, SE11 6DN. *Club:* Athenæum.

PRATT, family name of **Marquess Camden**.

PRATT, (Arthur) Geoffrey, CBE 1981; Hon. Secretary, Institution of Gas Engineers, 1982–87; *b* 19 Aug. 1922; *s* of William Pratt, Willington, Co. Durham; *m* 1st, 1946, Ethel, (Effie), Luck (*d* 1997); two *s* twin *d*; 2nd, 1998, Mrs Mavis Scargill (*d* 2002). *Educ:* King James I Grammar Sch., Bishop Auckland. CEng, FIGasE. Joined E Mids Gas Bd, 1951: Chief Engr, 1964; Dir of Engrg, 1967; Dep. Chm., S Eastern Gas Bd, 1970–72; Chm., SE Gas Region, 1972–81; part-time Mem., British Gas Corp., 1981–82. Chm., Metrogas Building Soc., 1977–85. Pres., IGasE, 1974–75; Hon. FIGEM (Hon. FIGasE 1987). *Recreations:* keep-fit, motoring. *Address:* 3 Hither Chantlers, Langton Green, Tunbridge Wells, Kent TN3 0BJ.

PRATT, Camden; *see* Pratt, R. C.

PRATT, Christopher Leslie; a District Judge (Magistrates' Courts) (formerly Metropolitan Stipendiary Magistrate), 1990–2007; *b* 15 Dec. 1947; *s* of late Leslie Arthur Cottrell Pratt and Phyllis Elizabeth Eleanor Pratt; *m* 1973, Jill Rosemary Hodges; two *s*. *Educ:* Highgate Sch. Admitted Solicitor, 1972. Court Clerk, Hendon, Harrow and Uxbridge Courts, 1967–72; Dep. Clerk to the Justices, Wimbledon and Uxbridge, 1972–76; Clerk to the Justices, Highgate, Barnet and S Mimms, 1976–90; Clerk to Barnet Magistrates' Courts Cttee and Trng Officer, Justices and staff, 1986–90. Mem. Council, Justices' Clerks' Soc., 1983–90 (Chm., Parly Cttee, Chm., Conf. and Social Cttee); Mem., Inner London Probation Cttee, 1996–2001. *Recreations:* conjuring (Vice Pres., The Magic Circle), cartophily. *Address:* c/o City of Westminster Magistrates' Court, 70 Horseferry Road, SW1P 2AX. *Club:* Magic Circle.

PRATT, Michael John; QC 1976; a Recorder of the Crown Court, 1974–94; *b* 23 May 1933; *o s* of W. Brownlow Pratt; *m* 1960, Elizabeth Jean Hendry; two *s* three *d*. *Educ:* West House Sch., Edgbaston; Malvern Coll. LLB (Birmingham). Army service, 2nd Lieut, 3rd Carabiniers (Prince of Wales's Dragoon Guards); Staff Captain. Called to the Bar, Middle Temple, 1954, Bencher, 1986; a Dep. High Court Judge, 1982–94. Chm. Govs, West House Sch., Edgbaston, 1975–2000; Gov., Malvern Coll., 1976–. *Recreations:* music, theatre, sport generally. *Address:* 9 Moorland Road, Edgbaston, Birmingham B16 9JP. *T:* (0121) 454 1071. *Clubs:* Cavalry and Guards; Edgbaston Golf.

PRATT, (Richard) Camden; QC 1992; a Recorder, since 1993; a Deputy High Court Judge (Family Division), since 1995; *b* 14 Dec. 1947; *s* of late Richard Sheldon Pratt, MA Oxon, and Irene Gladys Pratt; *m* 1973, (Dorothy Jane) Marchia Allsebrook. *Educ:* Boston Grammar Sch.; Westcliff High Sch.; Lincoln Coll., Oxford (MA Jurisp). Called to the Bar, Gray's Inn, 1970, Bencher, 2002. Chairman: Sussex Courts Liaison Cttee, 1993–; Sussex Sessions Bar Mess, 1994–2006; Mem., Area Criminal Justice Liaison Cttee, 1994–2002. *Recreations:* walking, sailing, travel, people. *Address:* 1 King's Bench Walk, Temple, EC4Y 7DB. *T:* (020) 7936 1500, *Fax:* (020) 7936 1590.

PRATT, Richard Charles; regulatory consultant; *b* 3 Nov. 1949; *s* of Charles Pratt and Rosemary Pratt (*née* Robson); *m* 1974, Christine Whiteman; one *s*. *Educ:* Eltham Coll.; Bristol Univ. (BSc Politics and Econs 1972); Sch. of Oriental and African Studies, London Univ. (MA 1973). Joined Civil Service, 1973; Press Officer, Prime Minister's Office, 1975–76; Asst Private Sec., Lord Privy Seal's Office, 1976; Head of Pay Negotiations Br., CSD, 1977–80; Head of Special Employment Measures Br., Dept of Employment, 1980–82; HM Treasury: Head of NI Public Expenditure Br., 1982–84; Mem., Central Unit for UK Budget, 1984–86; Head of Gen. Expenditure Div., 1986–87; Economic Counsellor, Washington, 1987–90 (on secondment); Head, EC Div. (EMU and Trade Policy), 1990–93; Advr to Sec. of State for Social Services on Expenditure Review, DSS, 1993; Head of Securities and Mkts Div., HM Treasury, 1993–95; Dir of External Affairs, LIFFE, 1995–98; Dir Gen., Jersey Financial Services Commn, 1999–2003. Ombudsman for KPMG, 2004–; Special Advr, RSM Robson Rhodes, 2004–06; Director: UK Financial Services Compensation Scheme, 2004–; Look Ahead Housing, 2008–. *Publications:* (ed) How to Combat Money Laundering and Terrorist Financing, 2005; (ed) Working Together: international cooperation between financial services regulators, 2007. *Recreations:* tennis, flying, travelling. *Address:* 40 Kestrel Avenue, SE24 0EB. *Club:* Jersey Aero.

PRATT, Richard James; QC 2006; a Recorder, since 2000; *b* 22 June 1956; *s* of Gordon Francis Pratt and Audrey Pratt (*née* Upton-Prowse); *m* 1987, Kim Lorraine Emmerson; two *d*. *Educ:* St Mary's Coll., Crosby, Liverpool; Lanchester Poly., Coventry (BA Hons 1978). Called to the Bar, Gray's Inn, 1980; in practice as barrister, 7 Harrington Street, Liverpool; Asst Recorder, 1997–2000. *Recreations:* watching Everton Football Club and old films, listening to music, practising ventriloquism. *Address:* 7 Harrington Street, Liverpool L2 9YH. *T:* (0151) 242 0707, *Fax:* (0151) 236 1120; *e-mail:* Rickpratt2@aol.com. *Club:* John Mc's (Liverpool).

PRATT, Prof. Robert John, CBE 2003; FRCN; Professor of Nursing and Director, Richard Wells Research Centre, Thames Valley University, since 1994; *b* 27 June 1941; *s* of Loren Delbert Pratt and Mary Jane Stubbs, and step *s* of Leonard William Paulson. *Educ:* Univ. of London (DN 1974); New Coll. of Calif, San Francisco (BA (Humanities) 1981); Chelsea Coll., London (MSc (Health Educn) 1984). Served US Navy, Hospital Corpsman, Fleet Marine Force, 1959–63. Various nursing appts, USA and UK, 1964–71; Charge Nurse, Charing Cross Hosp., 1971–76; Hd, Dept of Professional and Vocational Studies, Charing Cross Hosp. Sch. of Nursing, 1978–86; Vice Principal, Riverside Coll. of Health Studies, London, 1986–94. Pres., Infection Control Nurses Assoc. of British Isles, 2000–06; Patron, UK Nat. HIV Nurses Assoc., 1999–. FRCN 1999; FHEA 2007; FRSA 2006. *Publications:* HIV & AIDS: a foundation for nursing and healthcare practice, 1986, 6th edn 2009; (jtly) Tuberculosis: a foundation for nursing and healthcare practice, 2005; frequent articles in a variety of nursing and med. peer-reviewed jls. *Recreations:* theatre, cinema, travel, reading. *Address:* Richard Wells Research Centre, Thames Valley University, Paragon House, Boston Manor Road, Brentford, Middx TW8 9GA; *e-mail:* robert.pratt@tvu.ac.uk.

PRATT, Roger Allan, CBE 1996; Boundary Review Project Director, since 2000, Deputy Director of Campaigning, since 2005, Conservative Campaign Headquarters; Acting Secretary, National Conservative Convention, since 2006; *b* 28 Dec. 1950; *s* of late Allan Pratt and of Joyce Isobel Pratt (*née* Dodds); *m* 1st, 1975, Ann Heaton (marr. diss. 1993); one *s* one *d*; 2nd, 1993, Lynn Mary Tomlinson; one step *s* one step *d*. *Educ:* King Edward's Fiveways Sch., Birmingham. Organiser, E Midlands Area YC, 1971–72; NW Area Youth Develt Officer, 1972–74; Agent, Liverpool Wavertree Cons. Assoc., 1975–76; Nat. YC Organiser, 1976–79; Agent, Pendle, Burnley and Hyndburn Cons. Assocs, 1980–84; North West Area, then NW Region: Dep. Central Office Agent, 1984–89; Central Office Agent, 1989–93; Regl Dir, 1993; Dir, Cons. Pty in Scotland, 1993–97; Conservative Central Office: Dep. Dir, Campaigning Dept, 1997–98; Area Campaign Dir, London Western, and Regl Eur. Campaign Dir for London, 1998–2000; Dep. Dir of Ops, 2004. *Recreation:* cricket. *Address:* Conservative Central Office, 25 Victoria Street, Westminster, SW1H 0EX. *T:* (020) 7222 9000.

PRATT, Simon; His Honour Judge Pratt; a Circuit Judge, since 1995; *b* 23 June 1949; *s* of Harry James Roffey Pratt and Ann Loveday Pratt (*née* Peter); *m* 1974, Sheena Maynard; one *s* one *d*. Called to the Bar, Inner Temple, 1971; a Recorder, SE Circuit, 1989–95. Freeman, City of London, 1984. *Recreations:* music, walking, gardening, cookery, travel. *Address:* 3 Temple Gardens, Temple, EC4Y 9AU. *T:* (020) 7353 3102.

PRATT, Timothy Jean Geoffrey, CB 1993; Counsel to the Speaker (European Legislation), House of Commons, 1993–97; *b* 25 Nov. 1934; *s* of Geoffrey Cheeseborough Pratt and Elinor Jean (*née* Thomson); *m* 1963, Pamela Ann Blake; two *d*. *Educ:* Brighton College; Trinity Hall, Cambridge (MA). Called to the Bar, Middle Temple, 1959; in practice, 1959–61; joined Treasury Solicitor's Dept, 1961; Law Officers' Dept, 1972; DTI, 1974; Legal Advisor: Dir-Gen. of Fair Trading, 1979; Cabinet Office (European Secretariat), 1985; Dep. Treasury Solicitor, 1990–93. Vis. Fellow, 1998, Sen. Fellow, 1999–2001, Cambridge Univ. Centre for European Legal Studies. Advr on EU Law to BSE Inquiry, 1998–2000. *Address:* Game Keepers Cottage, Melton Park, Melton Constable, Norfolk NR24 2NG. *T:* (01263) 861577. *Club:* Oxford and Cambridge.

PRAWER, Prof. Siegbert Salomon, FBA 1981; Taylor Professor of German Language and Literature, University of Oxford, 1969–86, now Professor Emeritus; Professorial Fellow, 1969–86, Supernumerary Fellow, 1986–90, Hon. Fellow, 1990, The Queen's College, Oxford (Dean of Degrees, 1978–93); *b* 15 Feb. 1925; *s* of Marcus and Eleonora Prawer; *m* 1949, Helga Alice (*née* Schaefer); one *s* two *d* (and one *s* decd). *Educ:* King Henry VIII Sch., Coventry; Jesus Coll., Cambridge (Charles Oldham Shakespeare Scholar, 1945–46, MA 1950; Hon. Fellow, 1996); PhD Birmingham, 1953; LittD Cantab 1962; MA 1969, DLitt 1969, Oxon. Adelaide Stoll Res. Student, Christ's Coll., Cambridge, 1947–48; Asst Lecturer, Lecturer, Sen. Lecturer, University of Birmingham, 1948–63; Prof. of German, Westfield Coll., London Univ., 1964–69. Fulbright Exchange Schol., 1956; Visiting Professor: City Coll., NY, 1956–57; University of Chicago, 1963–64; Harvard Univ., 1968; Hamburg Univ., 1969; Univ. of Calif, Irvine, 1975; Otago Univ., 1976; Pittsburgh Univ., 1977; Visiting Fellow: Knox Coll., Dunedin, 1976; Humanities Research Centre, ANU, 1980; Tauber Inst., Brandeis Univ., 1981–82; Russell Sage Foundn, NY, 1988. Hon. Director, London Univ. Inst. of Germanic Studies, 1966–68. President: British Comp. Lit. Assoc., 1984–87 (Hon. Fellow, 1989); English Goethe Soc., 1990–94 (Vice-Pres., 1994–). Hon. Fellow, London Univ. Inst. Germanic Studies, 1987; Corresp. Fellow, Deutsche Akademie für Sprache und Dichtung, 1989. Hon. Mem., Modern Language Assoc. of America, 1986. Hon. Dr phil. Cologne, 1984; Hon. DLitt Birmingham, 1988. Goethe Medal, 1973; Friedrich Gundolf Prize, 1986; Gold Medal, German Goethe Soc., 1995. Co-editor: Oxford German Studies, 1971–75; Anglica Germanica, 1973–79. *Publications:* German Lyric Poetry, 1952; Mörike und seine Leser, 1960; Heine's Buch der Lieder: A Critical Study, 1960; Heine: The Tragic Satirist, 1962; The Penguin Book of Lieder, 1964; The Uncanny in Literature (inaug. lect.), 1965; (ed, with R. H. Thomas and L. W. Forster) Essays in German Language, Culture and Society, 1969; (ed) The Romantic Period in Germany, 1970; Heine's Shakespeare, a Study in Contexts (inaug. lect.), 1970; (ed) Seventeen Modern German Poets, 1971;

Comparative Literary Studies: an Introduction, 1973; Karl Marx and World Literature, 1976 (Isaac Deutscher Meml Prize, 1977); Caligari's Children: the film as tale of terror, 1980; Heine's Jewish Comedy: a study of his portraits of Jews and Judaism, 1983; A. N. Stencl: poet of Whitechapel (Stencl Meml Lect.), 1984; Coalsmoke and Englishmen (Bithell Meml Lecture), 1984; Frankenstein's Island: England and the English in the writings of Heinrich Heine, 1986; Israel at Vanity Fair: Jews and Judaism in the writings of W. M. Thackeray, 1992; (introd) Das Kabinett des Dr Caligari (first printing of original screenplay), 1996; Breeches and Metaphysics: Thackeray's German discourse, 1997; W. M. Thackeray's European Sketch Books: a study of literary and graphic portraiture, 2000; Sternberg's The Blue Angel, 2002; Werner Herzog's Nosferatu: Phantom of the Night, 2004; Between Two Worlds: the Jewish presence in German and Austrian film, 1910–1933, 2005; articles on German, English and comparative literature in many specialist periodicals and symposia. *Recreation:* portrait drawing. *Address:* 9 Hawkswell Gardens, Oxford OX2 7EX.

See also Mrs R. P. Jhabvala.

PRAWER JHABVALA, Ruth; *see* Jhabvala.

PREBBLE, David Lawrence; Master, Queen's Bench Division, Supreme Court of Justice, 1981–2001; *b* 21 Aug. 1932; *s* of late George Wilson Prebble and Margaret Jessie Prebble (*née* Cuthbertson); *m* 1959, Fiona W. Melville; three *d*. *Educ:* Cranleigh; Christ Church, Oxford. MA. National Service, 1950–52; commissioned in 3rd Carabiniers (Prince of Wales's Dragoon Guards); served TA, 1952–61, City of London Yeomanry (Rough Riders) TA (Captain). Called to the Bar, Middle Temple, 1957; practised at Bar, 1957–81. *Recreations:* reading; operetta; hounds and dogs; friends' horses; own wife and family; (not necessarily in foregoing order as to precedence). *Address:* Clunie Beag, Taybridge Road, Aberfeldy, Perthshire PH15 2BH. *T:* (01887) 820060.

PREBBLE, Stuart Colin; Managing Director, Liberty Bell Ltd, since 2002 (Joint Managing Director, 2002–05); *b* 15 April 1951; *s* of Dennis Stanley Prebble and Jean Margaret Prebble; *m* 1978, Marilyn Anne Charlton; one *d* (and one *d* decd). *Educ:* Univ. of Newcastle upon Tyne (BA Hons English Lang. and Lit.). Reporter, BBC TV News, 1975–80; Presenter, Granada TV, 1981; Producer, 1983–88, Editor, 1988–89, World in Action; Head of Regl Progs, Granada, 1989–90; Man. Dir, North East TV, 1990–91; Head of Factual Progs, Granada, 1992; Controller, ITV Network Factual Progs, 1993–96; Chief Exec., Granada Sky Broadcasting, 1996–98; Man. Dir, Channels and Interactive Media, Granada Media Gp, 1999; Chief Executive: ONdigital, subseq. ITV Digital, 1999–2002; ITV Network, 2001–02. *Publications:* A Power in the Land, 1988; The Lazarus File, 1989; The Official Grumpy Old Men Handbook, 2004; Grumpy Old Men: the secret diary, 2005; Grumpy Old Christmas, 2006; Grumpy Old Workers, 2007; Grumpy Old Drivers, 2008. *Recreations:* walking, cinema, music.

PREECE, Prof. Michael Andrew, MD; FRCP, FRCPCH; Professor of Child Health and Growth, Institute of Child Health, University College London, 1985–2007, now Emeritus; Medical Director, Great Ormond Street Hospital for Children, 2005–07; *b* 11 May 1944; *s* of Roy and Norah Preece; *m* 1977, Jan Baines; one *s*. *Educ:* Guy's Hosp. Med. Sch., Univ. of London (MB BS 1967; MD 1976; MSc 1977). FRCP 1982; FRCPCH 1997. Institute of Child Health, London University: Lectr In Growth and Develt, 1974–77; Sen. Lectr, 1977–83; Reader in Child Health and Growth, 1983–85. Visiting Professor: RPMS, later ICSM, 1994–2005; Hosp. for Sick Children, Univ. of Toronto, 2003; Lectures: Teale, RCP, 1990; Gaisford, Manchester Med. Soc., 1994. Guthrie Medal, British Paediatric Assoc., 1980. *Publications:* (with J. M. Tanner) The Physiology of Human Growth, 1989; (jtly) The Cambridge Encyclopaedia of Human Growth and Development, 1998; (jtly) Neoplasia: growth and growth hormone treatment, 2004. *Recreations:* nature photography, theatre, sport (mostly watching nowadays). *Address:* e-mail: mpreece@ich.ucl.ac.uk.

PREISS, Prof. David, FRS 2004; Professor of Mathematics, University of Warwick, since 2006; *b* 21 Jan. 1947; *s* of Alfred and Marta Preiss; *m* 1977, Irena; one *d*. *Educ:* Charles Univ., Prague (RNDr (Dr of Natural Sci.) 1970; Candidate of Sci. 1979). Various posts, Charles Univ., Prague, 1970–89; Astor Prof. of Maths, UCL, 1990–2006. Vis. posts at univs in Jerusalem, Palermo, Santa Barbara and Vancouver. *Publications:* res. papers, chiefly in mathematical analysis, in scientific jls. *Address:* Mathematics Institute, University of Warwick, Coventry CV4 7AL; *e-mail:* d.preiss@warwick.ac.uk.

PRENDERGAST, Prof. Christopher Alan Joseph, PhD; FBA 1996; Fellow, King's College, Cambridge, since 1970; Professor of Modern French Literature, Cambridge University, 1997–2003, now Professor Emeritus; *b* 27 Sept. 1942; *s* of James Prendergast and Celia (*née* Sevitt); *m* 1st, 1965, Shirley Busbridge (marr. diss. 1979); two *d*; 2nd, 1997, Inge Birgitte Siegumfeldt; one *d*. *Educ:* Keble Coll., Oxford (BA 1965; BPhil 1967); MA 1968, PhD 1989, Cantab. Lectr, Pembroke Coll., Oxford, 1967–68; Fellow, Downing Coll., Cambridge, 1968–70; Univ. Lectr, Cambridge Univ., 1968–89; Distinguished Prof. in French and Comparative Lit., Grad. Sch., CUNY, 1989–92; Reader in Modern French Lit., Cambridge Univ., 1992–97. Vis. Prof., 1998–2000, Hon. Prof., 2004, Univ. of Copenhagen, Denmark. *Publications:* Balzac: fiction and melodrama, 1978; The Order of Mimesis, 1986; (ed) Nineteenth-Century French Poetry, 1990; Paris and the Nineteenth Century, 1992; (ed jtly) Anthology of World Literature, 1994; (ed) Cultural Materialism, 1996; Napoleon and History Painting, 1997; The Triangle of Representation, 2000; (ed) Proust, In Search of Lost Time, 6 vols, 2002; (ed) Debating World Literature, 2004; The Classic: Sainte-Beuve and the nineteenth-century culture wars, 2007; The Fourteenth of July: and the taking of the Bastille, 2008. *Recreations:* gardening, cooking, opera. *Address:* 26 Bermuda Road, Cambridge CB4 3JX.

PRENDERGAST, Jonathan Barry, (John Barry), OBE 1999; composer; *b* York, 3 Nov. 1933; *s* of late Jack Prendergast; *m* 1978, Laurie; one *s*; three *d* from previous marriages. Founder, trumpeter and vocalist, John Barry Seven, 1957–62. Composer of stage musical, Billy, 1974; music for musical, Brighton Rock, 2004; film scores include: Beat Girl, 1960; Dr No, 1962; From Russia with Love, 1963; Zulu, 1964; Goldfinger, 1964; Thunderball, 1965; Born Free, 1966 (2 Acad. Awards); You Only Live Twice, 1967; The Lion in Winter, 1968 (Acad. Award); Midnight Cowboy, 1969; On Her Majesty's Secret Service, 1969; Mary, Queen of Scots, 1971; Diamonds Are Forever, 1971; A Doll's House, 1973; The Man with the Golden Gun, 1974; Moonraker, 1979; Body Heat, 1981; Octopussy, 1983; Out of Africa, 1985 (Acad. Award); A View to a Kill, 1985; Jagged Edge, 1985; Peggy Sue Got Married, 1986; The Living Daylights, 1987; Dances with Wolves, 1990 (Acad. Award); Chaplin, 1992; Indecent Proposal, 1993; The Specialist, 1994; The Scarlet Letter, 1995; Cry, the Beloved Country, 1995; Playing By Heart, 1998; Mercury Rising, 1998; Enigma, 2001. *Albums:* The Beyondness of Things, 1999; Eternal Echoes, 2001. *Address:* c/o Kraft-Engel Management, 15233 Ventura Boulevard, Sherman Oaks, CA 91403, USA.

PRENDERGAST, Sir Kieran; *see* Prendergast, Sir W. K.

PRENDERGAST, His Honour Robert James Christie Vereker; a Circuit Judge, 1989–2006; *b* 21 Oct. 1941; *s* of Richard Henry Prendergast and Jean (*née* Christie); *m* 1971, Berit, (Bibi), Thauland; one *d*. *Educ:* Downside; Trinity Coll., Cambridge (BA (Hons) Law; MA). Called to the Bar, Middle Temple, 1964; Harmsworth Law Schol.; S Eastern Circuit, 1964–89; an Asst Recorder, 1984–87; a Recorder, 1987–89. Chm., NE London Crown Court Liaison Cttee, 1984–89. Mem., S Eastern Circuit Wine Cttee, 1987–89. Pres., St Gregory's Soc., 1999–2002. *Recreations:* most gentle pursuits. *Address:* c/o 5 King's Bench Walk, Temple, EC4Y 7DN.

PRENDERGAST, Dame Simone (Ruth), DBE 1986 (OBE 1981); JP, DL; *b* 2 July 1930; *d* of late Mrs Neville Blond, OBE and late Norman Laski; *m* 1st, 1953, Albert Kaplan (marr. diss. 1957); 2nd, 1959, Christopher Anthony Prendergast, CBE (*d* 1998); one *s*. *Educ:* Queen's College; Cheltenham Ladies' College. Lady Mayoress of Westminster, 1968–69; Member: Lord Chancellor's Adv. Cttee for Inner London, 1981–91; Solicitors' Disciplinary Tribunal, 1986–2002; E London and Bethnal Green Housing Assoc., 1988–90; Exec. Cttee, Westminster Children's Soc., 1970–97 (Chm., 1980–90); Chairman: Jewish Refugees Cttee, 1980–96; Greater London Area Nat. Union of Conservative Assocs, 1984–87; E Grinstead Med. Res. Trust, 1984–; Blond McIndoe Centre for Med. Research, 1986–2004; Vice-Chm., Age Concern, Westminster, 1986–2002; Comr (part-time), CRE, 1996–98. Jt Treas., 1991–, Vice Pres., 1997–, Central British Fund for World Jewish Relief (Mem. Council, 1969–97); Life Patron, British Fedn of Women Zionists, 1994. Trustee, Kennedy Inst. of Rheumatology, 2003–. Comdt, Jewish Lads' and Girls' Bde, 1996–2000. Court of Patrons, RCS, 1987. FRSA 1988. JP Inner London 1971; DL Greater London 1982. Associate CStJ 1982. *Recreations:* reading, walking.

PRENDERGAST, Sir (Walter) Kieran, KCVO 1991; CMG 1990; HM Diplomatic Service, retired; Under-Secretary-General for Political Affairs, United Nations, New York, 1997–2005; independent consultant; *b* 2 July 1942; *s* of late Lt-Comdr J. H. Prendergast and Mai Hennessy; *m* 1967, Joan Reynolds; two *s* two *d*. *Educ:* St Patrick's College, Strathfield, Sydney, NSW; Salesian College, Chertsey; St Edmund Hall, Oxford. Turkish language student Istanbul, 1964; Ankara, 1965; FO (later FCO), 1967; 2nd Sec. Nicosia, 1969; Civil Service Coll., 1972; 1st Sec. FCO, 1972; The Hague, 1973; Asst Private Sec. to Foreign and Commonwealth Sec. (Rt Hon. Anthony Crosland, Rt Hon. Dr David Owen), 1976; UK Mission to UN, NY, 1979 (detached for duty Jan.–March 1980 at Govt House, Salisbury); Counsellor, Tel Aviv, 1982; Head of Southern African Dept, FCO, 1986–89; High Comr to Zimbabwe, 1989–92; High Comr to Kenya, 1992–95; Ambassador to Turkey, 1995–97. Sen. Advr, Centre for Humanitarian Dialogue, Geneva, 2006–; Chm., UN Follow-up Cttee on Bakassi Peninsula, 2006–. Non-executive Director: Blue Hackle, 2007–; Independent Diplomat, 2007–; Hakluyt & Co. Ltd, 2007–. Rhodesia Medal, 1980; Zimbabwe Independence Medal, 1980. *Recreations:* family, wine, walking, reading, rough shooting. *Address:* 26 Beckwith Road, SE24 9LG. *T:* (020) 7274 8445; Bonneval, Beaulieu-sur-Dordogne 19120, France. *T:* and *Fax:* (555) 912960; *e-mail:* prendergast.kieran@gmail.com. *Clubs:* Beefsteak, Garrick; Muthaiga (Nairobi).

PRENTER, Patrick Robert, CBE 1995; Chairman, Mactaggart Scott Holdings, Loanhead, Midlothian, since 2004; Lord-Lieutenant for Midlothian, since 2003; *b* 9 Sept. 1939; *s* of Robert Gibson Prenter, OBE and Katherine Emily Prenter (*née* Scott); *m* 1962, Susan, *d* of Francis Patrick, OBE and Isabel Patrick (*née* Spencer); two *s* two *d*. *Educ:* Loretto Sch., Musselburgh; Trinity Hall, Cambridge (BA Mech. Scis 1962). Man. Dir, 1967–99, Chm., 1991–2004, Mactaggart Scott & Co. Ltd. Tax Comr, 1985–2003. Dir, 1984–91, Vice Chm., 1990–91, Forth Ports Authy. Mem. Bd, Castle Rock Housing Assoc., 1975– (Chm., 1995–2000). Pres., Scottish Engrg Employers' Assoc., 1985–86. Dir, Scottish Chamber Orch., 1995–. JP Midlothian, 1980–2003. Gov., Loretto Sch., 1982–89. *Recreations:* music, opera, reading, golf, tennis, ski-ing. *Address:* Carlyle House, 5/2 East Suffolk Park, Edinburgh EH16 5PL. *T:* (0131) 667 4635; *e-mail:* patrick.prenter@btinternet.com; 9 Gondola Way, Gordons Bay, Western Cape, 7150, South Africa. *Clubs:* Royal Automobile; New (Edinburgh); Hon. Company of Edinburgh Golfers; Free Foresters.

PRENTICE, Dr Ann, OBE 2006; Director, MRC Collaborative (formerly Resource) Centre for Human Nutrition Research, since 1998; *b* 8 April 1952; *d* of Alexander Rubach and Beryl Ann Rubach; *m* 1976, Andrew Major Prentice; two *d*. *Educ:* Somerville Coll., Oxford (BA Hons Chemistry; MA 1977); Univ. of Surrey (MSc Med. Physics); Darwin Coll., Cambridge (PhD Natural Scis, 1978). Scientist, MRC Dunn Nutrition Gp, Keneba, Gambia, 1978–83; Scientist, 1984–91, Sen. Scientist, 1991–98, MRC Dunn Nutrition Unit, Cambridge. Hon. Prof., Shenyang Med. Coll., People's Republic of China, 1995–; Vis. Prof. KCL, 2003–. Pres., Nutrition Soc., 2004–07. *Publications:* book chapters and reviews; numerous contribs to peer-reviewed scientific jls. *Recreations:* music, theatre, literature, foreign travel. *Address:* MRC Collaborative Centre for Human Nutrition Research, Elsie Widdowson Laboratory, Fulbourn Road, Cambridge CB1 9NL. *T:* (01223) 426356.

PRENTICE, Bridget Theresa; JP; MP (Lab) Lewisham East, since 1992; Parliamentary Under-Secretary of State, Ministry of Justice (formerly Department for Constitutional Affairs), since 2005; *b* 28 Dec. 1952; *d* of James and Bridget Corr; *m* 1975, Gordon Prentice, *qv* (marr. diss. 2000). *Educ:* Glasgow Univ. (MA English Lit. and Mod. Hist.); London University: Avery Hill Coll. (PGCE); Southlands Coll. (Adv. Dip. in Careers Educn and Guidance); South Bank Univ. (LLB 1992). Teacher, ILEA, 1974–88. Councillor, Hammersmith and Fulham London BC, 1986–92. An Asst Govt Whip, 1997–98 and 2003–05. JP Inner London, 1985. *Recreations:* music, reading, crosswords, knitting, my three cats, football. *Address:* House of Commons, SW1A 0AA.

PRENTICE, Christopher Norman Russell; HM Diplomatic Service; Ambassador to Iraq, since 2007; *b* 5 Sept. 1954; *s* of Ronald Prentice and Sonia Prentice (*née* Bowring); *m* 1978, Marie-Josephine, (Nina), King; two *s* two *d*. *Educ:* Christ Church, Oxford (BA Lit.Hum., MA). Entered FCO, 1977; Arabic lang. student, MECAS, 1978; Third, later Second, Sec., Kuwait, 1980–83; First Secretary: on loan to Cabinet Office, 1983–85; Washington, 1985–89; FCO, 1989–94; Counsellor and Dep. Hd of Mission, Budapest, 1994–98; Counsellor, FCO, 1998–2002; Ambassador to Jordan, 2002–06; UK Special Rep., later FCO co-ordinator, Sudan Peace Process, 2006–07. *Recreations:* music, sport, reading, mountains. *Address:* c/o Foreign and Commonwealth Office, King Charles Street, SW1A 2AH. *Clubs:* Athenæum, Beefsteak, MCC.

PRENTICE, Prof. Daniel David; Allen & Overy Professor of Corporate Law, Oxford University, 1991–2008, now Emeritus; Fellow of Pembroke College, Oxford, since 1973; *b* 7 Aug. 1941; *s* of Thomas James Prentice and Agnes Prentice (*née* Fox); *m* 1965, Judith Mary Keane; one *s* one *d*. *Educ:* St Malachy's Coll., Belfast; Queen's Univ., Belfast (LLB); Univ. of Chicago (JD); MA Oxford (by special resolution). Called to the Bar, Lincoln's Inn, 1982; Mem., Erskine Chambers. Associate Prof., Univ. of Ontario, 1966–68; Lectr, UCL, 1968–73; Lectr, 1973–90, Reader, 1991, Univ. of Oxford. Vis. Prof., various univs incl. UCL, 2008–. Asst Editor, Law Qly Rev., 1988–. *Publication:* (ed) Chitty, Law of

Contracts, 25th edn 1983, 26th edn 1989, 29th edn 2004. *Address:* Pembroke College, Oxford OX1 1DW. *T:* (01865) 276438.

PRENTICE, Gordon; MP (Lab) Pendle, since 1992; *b* 28 Jan. 1951; *s* of Esther and William Prentice; *m* 1975, Bridget Theresa Corr (*see* B. T. Prentice) (marr. diss. 2000). *Educ:* Univ. of Glasgow (MA; Pres., Glasgow Univ. Union, 1972–73). Mercury House Publications, 1974–78; Local Govt Officer, 1978–81; Labour Party Policy Directorate, 1982–92. Mem. Council, London Borough of Hammersmith and Fulham, 1982–90 (Leader of Council, 1986–88). *Recreations:* cooking, hill walking, gardening. *Address:* House of Commons, SW1A 0AA. *T:* (020) 7219 3000.

PRENTICE, (Hubert Archibald) John, CEng; CPhys, FInstP; consultant on manufacturing and management strategies to several UK and USA companies; *b* 5 Feb. 1920; *s* of Charles Herbert Prentice and Rose Prentice; *m* 1947, Sylvia Doreen Elias; one *s*. *Educ:* Woolwich Polytechnic, London; Salford Univ. (BSc, MSc). MRAeS 1962, CEng 1970; FInstP 1967, CPhys 1985. Min. of Supply, 1939–56; R&D posts, res. estabts and prodn, MoD, 1956–60; Space Dept, RAE, Min. of Aviation, 1960–67; Head, Road User Characteristics Res., 1967–70, and Head, Driver Aids and Abilities Res., 1970–72, MoT; Head, Road User Dynamics Res., DoE, 1972–75; Counsellor (Sci. and Technol.), British Embassy, Tokyo, 1975–80. *Recreations:* walking, climbing. *Address:* 5 Foxhill Crescent, Camberley, Surrey GU15 1PR. *T:* (01276) 66373.

PRENTIS, David; General Secretary, UNISON, since 2001 (Deputy General Secretary, 1993–2000); President, Trades Union Congress, 2007–08; *b* Leeds. *Educ:* QMC, Univ. of London (BA Hist.); Univ. of Warwick (MA Industrial Relns). Member: TUC Gen. Council (Mem. Exec. Cttee); Trade Union Labour Party Liaison Cttee; Econ. Commn and Jt Policy Cttee, Labour Party; Bd, ACAS. Director: IPPR; Catalyst. Advr, Warwick Inst. of Governance and Public Mgt. Vis. Fellow, Nuffield Coll., Oxford. *Address:* UNISON, 1 Mabledon Place, WC1H 9AJ.

PRESCOTT, Prof. Edward C., PhD; W. P. Carey Professor of Economics, Arizona State University, since 2003; Senior Monetary Adviser, Federal Reserve Bank of Minneapolis, since 2003 (Senior Adviser, Research Department, 1981–2003); *b* 26 Dec. 1940; *s* of William Clyde Prescott and Mathilde Helwig Prescott; *m* 1965, Janet Dale Simpson; two *s* one *d*. *Educ:* Swarthmore Coll., Penn (BA 1962); Case Inst. of Technol. (MS 1963); Carnegie-Mellon Univ. (PhD 1967). Lectr, 1966–67, Asst Prof., 1967–71, Econs Dept, Univ. of Pennsylvania; Asst Prof., 1971–72, Associate Prof., 1972–75, Prof. of Econs, 1975–80, Carnegie-Mellon Univ.; Prof. of Econs, 1980–98, 1999–2003, Univ. of Minnesota; Prof. of Econs, Univ. of Chicago, 1998–99. Irwin Plein Nemmers Prize, 2002; (jtly) Nobel Prize in Economics, 2004. *Publications:* (with S. L. Parente) Barriers to Riches, 2000; contrib. learned jls. *Address:* Department of Economics, W. P. Carey School of Business, Arizona State University, Tempe, AZ 85287–3806, USA; Research Department, Federal Reserve Bank of Minneapolis, 90 Hennepin Avenue, Minneapolis, MN 55401–1804, USA.

PRESCOTT, John Barry, AC 1996; Chairman: ASC Pty Ltd (formerly Australian Submarine Corporation), since 2000; QR (formerly Queensland Rail), since 2006; *b* 22 Oct. 1940; *s* of late John Norman Prescott and Margaret Ellen (*née* Brownie); *m* 1985, Jennifer Cahill; one *s* two *d* (and one *d* decd). *Educ:* N Sydney Boys' High Sch.; Univ. of NSW (BComm Industrial Relns). Joined The Broken Hill Pty Co. Ltd as Industrial Relns Trainee, 1958: various industrial relns positions, 1958–69; Superintendent, Industrial Relns, Shipping and Stevedoring, Newcastle and Sydney, 1969–74; Asst Fleet Manager, Ops, Newcastle, 1974–79; Exec. Asst to Gen. Manager, Transport, 1979–80; Manager Ops, Transport, 1980–82; Gen. Manager, Transport, 1982–87; Exec. Gen. Manager and Chief Exec. Officer, BHP Steel, 1987–91; Dir, 1988–98; Man. Dir and CEO, 1991–98. Chm., Horizon Private Equity Pty Ltd, 1998–2005; Director: Tubemakers of Aust. Ltd, 1988–92; (non-exec.), Normandy Mining Ltd, 1999–2002; Member: Adv. Bd, Booz, Allen & Hamilton Inc., 1991–2003; Internat. Council, J. P. Morgan, 1994–2003; Asia Pacific Adv. Cttee, New York Stock Exchange Inc., 1995–2005. Chm., 2004–07, Patron, 2007–, Sunshine Coast Business Council; Member Board: Business Council of Aust., 1995–97; Walter and Eliza Hall Inst. of Med. Res., 1994–98; Bd of Trustees, Conf. Bd, 1995–2001. Mem. Internat. Council, Asia Soc., 1991–2003. Hon. LLD Monash, 1994; Hon. DSc NSW, 1995. *Recreations:* tennis, golf. *Address:* (office) Level 39, 140 William Street, Melbourne, Vic 3000, Australia. *Clubs:* Australian, Melbourne (Melbourne); Newcastle (Newcastle); Huntingdale Golf, National Golf (Vic).

PRESCOTT, Prof. John Herbert Dudley, PhD; FIBiol; FRAgS; Principal, Wye College, and Professor of Animal Production, University of London, 1988–2000, now Professor Emeritus; *b* 21 Feb. 1937; *s* of Herbert Prescott and Edith Vera Prescott; *m* 1960, Diana Margaret Mullock; two *s* two *d*. *Educ:* Haileybury; Univ. of Nottingham (BSc (Agric), PhD). FIBiol 1983; FRAgS 1986. Lectr in Animal Prodn, Univ. of Newcastle upon Tyne, 1963–72; Animal Prodn Officer in Argentina, FAO, UN, 1972–74; Head of Animal Prodn Advisory and Develt, E of Scotland Coll. of Agric., 1974–78; Prof. of Animal Prodn, Univ. of Edinburgh, 1978–84, and Head of Animal Div., Edinburgh Sch. of Agric., 1978–84; Dir, Grassland, later Animal and Grassland, Res. Inst., 1984–86; Dir, Grassland and Animal Prodn Res., AFRC, 1986–88. Visiting Professor: Univ. of Reading, 1985–88; UCW, Aberystwyth, 1988. Non-exec. Dir, Natural Resources Internat. Ltd, 1997–2000 (Actg Chm., 1996). Chm., Tech. Cttee on Response to Nutrients, AFRC, 1988–94. British Council: Member: Cttee for Internat. Co-operation in Higher Educn, 1989–2000; Agric. and Vet. Adv. Cttee, 1988–96; Vice-Chm., Sci., Engrg and Envmt Adv. Cttee, 1997–2001. Member: Adv. Bd, Centre for Tropical Vet. Medicine, 1978–84; Board of Directors: Hill Farming Res. Orgn, 1980–84; Hannah Res. Inst., 1981–84; Scientific Adv. Cttee, 1990–92, Governing Body, 1992–97, Macaulay Land Use Res. Inst.; various cttees on cattle and beef, MLC, 1969–90. President: British Soc. of Animal Prodn, 1988; Agricl and Forestry Sect., BAAS, 1994–95; Mem. Council, British Grassland Soc., 1984–87. Chairman: Stapledon Meml Trust, 1992–2004; Natural Resources Internat. Foundn, 1997–2004; Trustee, E Malling Trust for Horticl Res., 1998–. Member: Gov. Body and Corp., Hadlow Coll., 1988–98; Council: RVC, 1988–98, 2001–04; Univ. of Kent, 1988–2000. Liveryman, Farmers' Co., 2000–. FRSA 2000. Hon. Fellow: Inst. for Grassland and Envmtl Res., 1989; Wye Coll., 2000; ICSTM, 2001. *Publications:* scientific papers in Animal Prodn and Agricultural Science; technical articles. *Recreations:* farming, walking, wildlife, the countryside. *Club:* Farmers.

PRESCOTT, Rt Hon. John (Leslie); PC 1994; MP (Lab) Kingston upon Hull East, since 1997 (Kingston upon Hull (East), 1970–83; Hull East, 1983–97); Deputy Prime Minister, 1997–2007, and First Secretary of State, 2001–07; Deputy Leader of the Labour Party, 1994–2007; *b* 31 May 1938; *s* of late John Herbert Prescott, JP and Phyllis Prescott; *m* 1961, Pauline Tilston; two *s*. *Educ:* Ellesmere Port Secondary Modern Sch.; WEA; correspondence courses; Ruskin Coll., Oxford (DipEcon/Pol Oxon); Hull Univ. (BSc Econ). Trainee Chef, 1953–55; Steward, Passenger Lines, Merchant Navy, 1955–63; Ruskin Coll., Oxford, 1963–65; Recruitment Officer, General and Municipal Workers Union (temp.), 1965; Hull Univ., 1965–68. Full-time Official, National Union of Seamen, 1968–70. Contested (Lab) Southport, 1966. PPS to Sec. of State for Trade, 1974–76; opposition spokesman on Transport, 1979–81; opposition front bench spokesman on Regional Affairs and Devolution, 1981–83, on Transport, 1983–84 and 1988–93, on Employment, 1984–87 and 1993–94, on Energy, 1987–89; Mem., Shadow Cabinet, 1983–97; Sec. of State for the Envmt, Transport and the Regions, 1997–2001. Member: Select Cttee Nationalized Industries, 1973–79; Council of Europe, 1972–75; European Parlt, 1975–79 (Leader, Labour Party Delegn, 1976–79); British Delegn, Council of Europe and WEU, 2007–. Mem., NEC, Labour Party, 1989–. *Publications:* Not Wanted on Voyage, 1966; (jtly) Prezza: my story - pulling no punches, 2008. *Address:* House of Commons, SW1A 0AA.

PRESCOTT, Sir Mark, 3rd Bt *cr* 1938, of Godmanchester; racehorse trainer, in Newmarket; *b* 3 March 1948; *s* of late Major W. R. Stanley Prescott (MP for Darwen Div., 1943–51; 2nd *s* of Colonel Sir William Prescott, 1st Bt) and Gwendolen (who *m* 2nd, 1952, Daniel Orme (*d* 1972); she *d* 1992), *o c* of late Leonard Aldridge, CBE; *S* uncle, Sir Richard Stanley Prescott, 2nd Bt, 1965. *Educ:* Harrow. *Address:* Heath House, Moulton Road, Newmarket, Suffolk CB8 8DU. *T:* (01638) 662117.

PRESCOTT, Peter Richard Kyle; QC 1990; *b* 23 Jan. 1943; *s* of Richard Stanley Prescott and Sarah Aitchison Shand; *m* 1967, Frances Rosemary Bland; two *s* one *d*. *Educ:* St George's Coll., Argentina; Dulwich Coll.; University Coll. London (BSc); Queen Mary Coll., London (MSc). Called to the Bar, Lincoln's Inn, 1970, Bencher, 2001. *Publication:* The Modern Law of Copyright (with Hugh Laddie, QC, and Mary Vitoria), 1980, 3rd edn 2000. *Recreations:* music, reading, cooking. *Address:* 8 New Square, Lincoln's Inn, WC2A 3QP. *T:* (020) 7405 4321.

PRESCOTT, Dr Robert George Whitelock, FSAScot; Chairman, Department for Culture Media and Sport Advisory Committee on National Historic Ships, University of St Andrews, since 2006; *b* 9 Dec. 1938; *y s* of Edward Frank Whitelock Prescott and Ethel Prescott (*née* Shrubb); *m* 1st, 1964, Julia Margaret Palmer (marr. diss. 1982); two *d*; 2nd, 2005, Lloyd Carson. *Educ:* Latymer Upper Sch.; Peterhouse, Cambridge (BA 1961; PhD 1965). NATO Res. Fellow and Sen. Student, Royal Commn for Exhibn of 1851, Yale Univ., 1964–66; Sen. Asst in Res., Univ. of Cambridge, 1966–74; University of St Andrews: Lectr, then Sen. Lectr, 1974–2002; Co-founder, Scottish Inst. for Maritime Studies (Dir, 1984–2002); Caird Sen. Fellow, Nat. Maritime Mus., 2002–04. National Historic Ships Committee: Dir, Nat. Historic Ships Project, 1995–2001; Mem., 2003–06; Chm., 2005–06. Council Member: Royal Archaeol Inst., 1990–94; Soc. for Nautical Res., 1994–97 and 1999–2002; Scottish Executive/Scottish Museums Council: Scotland's Nat. Cultural Audit (Mem. Bd, 2000–02); Mem., RRS Discovery Conservation Cttee, 2004–06; Fife Mus Forum (Chm., 2004–07). Trustee: Nat. Mus. of Antiquities of Scotland, 1980–85; Scottish Fisheries Mus., 1977–2006 (Hon. Vice-Pres., 2007); frigate Unicorn, 1984–98; World Ship Trust, 1996–2001. Writer and presenter of radio and TV documentaries. FSAScot 1981. *Publications:* (with Ann V. Gunn) Lifting the Veil: research and scholarship in United Kingdom museums and galleries, 1999; articles and reviews in learned periodicals. *Recreations:* restoring and sailing historic ships, collecting books and things, watching birds, conversation, exploring the world of Samuel Pepys. *Address:* School of History, University of St Andrews, St Andrews, Fife KY16 9AL. *T:* (01334) 463017; *e-mail:* rgwp@st-andrews.ac.uk.

PRESCOTT-DECIE, Elizabeth Anne Scott, MA; Head Mistress, Godolphin School, Salisbury, 1980–89; *b* 28 Dec. 1942; *d* of Thomas Scott Hannay and Doreen Hewitt Hannay; *m* 2000, John Prescott-Decie. *Educ:* Heathfield Sch., Ascot; St Hugh's Coll., Oxford (MA). Assistant Mistress: St Mary's Sch., Calne, 1966–70; Moreton Hall Sch., Shropshire, 1970–72; St Michael's, Burton Park, Petworth, 1973–75; Dep. Headmistress, St George's Sch., Ascot, 1975–80. Governor: Norman Ct Sch., W Tytherley, 1982–; Prior's Field Sch., Godalming, 1991–; Stonar Sch., Melksham, 1999–.

PRESLAND, Frank George; Chief Executive: Twentyfirst Artists Ltd, since 2001; William A. Bong Ltd, and other companies in Elton John Group, since 1999; Sanctuary Group plc, since 2006; *b* 27 Feb. 1944; *s* of Reginald Charles Presland and Elsie Presland; *m*; one *s* one *d*. *Educ:* London Sch. of Economics (BSc Econ); University Coll. of Rhodesia and Nyasaland (Fairbridge Schol.). Admitted solicitor, 1973; Partner, Frere Cholmeley, 1976–92; Chm., Frere Cholmeley Bischoff, 1992–98, when co. merged with Eversheds; Jt Chm., Eversheds, 1998–99. Dir, Elton John AIDS Foundn, UK and USA, 1999–. *Recreation:* yachting. *Address:* (office) 1 Blythe Road, W14 0HG. *Club:* Little Ship.

PRESS, Dr Frank; Principal, Washington Advisory Group, since 1996; *b* 4 Dec. 1924; *m* 1946, Billie Kallick; one *s* one *d*. *Educ:* City Coll., NY (BS 1944); Columbia Univ. (MA 1946; PhD 1949). Columbia University: Res. Associate, 1946–49; Instr in Geology, 1949–51; Asst Prof. of Geology, 1951–52; Associate Prof., 1952–55; Prof. of Geophysics, 1955–65 and Dir, Seismol. Lab., 1957–65, CIT; Prof. of Geophysics and Chm., Dept of Earth and Planetary Scis, MIT, 1965–77; Sci. Advisor to Pres. and Dir, Office of Sci. and Tech. Policy, 1977–80; Prof., MIT, 1981; Pres., NAS, 1981–93; Cecil and Ida Green Sen. Fellow, Carnegie Instn of Washington, 1993–97. Member: President's Sci. Adv. Commn, 1961–64; Nat. Sci. Bd, 1970–; Lunar and Planetary Missions Bd, NASA; participant, bilateral scis agreement with People's Republic of China and USSR; US Deleg. to Nuclear Test Ban Negotiations, Geneva and Moscow. Mem., Acad. of Arts and Scis, and other US and internat. bodies. Life Mem., MIT Bd, 1985. Numerous awards, incl. Japan Prize, Sci. and Technol. Foundn of Japan, 1993, US Nat. Medal of Science, 1994, Lomonosov Gold Medal, Russian Acad. of Sci., 1998, and hon. degrees. Officer, Legion of Honour, 1989. *Publications:* (jtly) Propagation of Elastic Waves in Layered Media, 1957; (ed jtly) Physics and Chemistry of the Earth, 1957; (jtly) Earth, 1986; Understanding Earth, 1994, 4th edn 2005; numerous papers. *Address:* Suite 616 South, 2500 Virginia Avenue NW, Washington, DC 20037–1901, USA.

PRESS, Prof. Malcolm Colin, PhD; Professor of Ecology, and Head, College of Life and Environmental Sciences, University of Birmingham, since 2008; *b* 18 Sept. 1958; *s* of Kenneth and Sylvia Press. *Educ:* Kingsbury High Sch., London; Westfield Coll., Univ. of London (BSc (Envmtl Sci.) 1980); Univ. of Manchester (PhD (Botany) 1984). Res. Associate, UCL, 1985–89; Lectr, then Sen. Lectr, Univ. of Manchester, 1989–94; University of Sheffield: Reader, 1994–98; Prof. of Physiol Ecol., 1998–2008; Dir, Res. in the Envmt, 2001–08; Hd, Animal and Plant Scis, 2002–08. Pres., British Ecol Soc., 2007–Sept. 2009 (Mem. Council, 1992–2001). Ed., Jl Ecol., 2004–06. *Publications:* scientific papers and contribs to books on ecol., agric. and forestry. *Recreations:* Spanish language and culture, keeping fit. *Address:* College of Life and Environmental Sciences, University of Birmingham, Edgbaston, Birmingham B15 2TT. *T:* (0121) 414 8853; *e-mail:* m.c.press@bham.ac.uk.

PREST, Nicholas Martin, CBE 2001; Chairman: Aveva Group plc, since 2006; Cohort plc, since 2006; Shephard Group Ltd, since 2007; *b* 3 April 1953; *s* of Alan Richmond Prest and Pauline Chasey Prest (*née* Noble); *m* 1985, Anthea Joy Elisabeth Neal; one *s* two *d*. *Educ:* Manchester Grammar Sch.; Christ Church, Oxford (MA Hist. and Econs). Admin trainee, 1974, Principal, 1980–82, MoD; joined United Scientific Hldgs Plc, later Alvis Plc, 1982; Gp Mktg Dir, 1985–89; Chief Exec., 1989–2004; Chm., 1996–2004. Chm.,

Defence Manufrs Assoc., 2001–04; Mem., Nat. Defence Industries Council, 2001–04. *Recreations:* music, walking, shooting, watching cricket and Rugby. *Address:* 85 Elgin Crescent, W11 2JF. *T:* (020) 7792 4821. *Clubs:* Cavalry and Guards, MCC.

PRESTON, family name of **Viscount Gormanston**.

PRESTON, David Michael; Partner, Hosack & Sutherland, Solicitors, Oban, since 1978; President, Law Society of Scotland, 2002–03; *b* 26 Aug. 1952; *s* of Robert Matthew Preston and Lily Stewart Preston; *m* 1975, Sheila Elizabeth McMeekin; two *s*. *Educ:* Hillhead High Sch., Glasgow; Univ. of Dundee (LLB 1974). Depute Procurator Fiscal (pt-time), 1976–79; Clerk to Gen. Comrs of Income Tax, 1976–. Registrar, Episcopal Dio. Argyll and the Isles, 1977–. Mem. Council, Law Soc. of Scotland, 1990–. Chm., Oban Youth and Community Assoc., 1980–. Sec., Atlantis Leisure, Oban, 1991–2000. *Recreations:* sailing, ski-ing, golf, reading, family. *Address:* Hosack & Sutherland, Queen's Building, George Street, Oban PA34 5RZ. *Clubs:* Royal Highland Yacht, Oban Sailing (Cdre, 1992–93); Glencruitten Golf.

PRESTON, Dame Frances Olivia C.; *see* Campbell-Preston.

PRESTON, Geoffrey Averill; Assistant Counsel to Chairman of Committees, House of Lords, 1982–89; *b* 19 May 1924; *s* of George and Winifred Preston; *m* 1953, Catherine Wright. *Educ:* St Marylebone Grammar Sch. Barrister-at-Law. Served, RNVR, 1942–46. Called to Bar, Gray's Inn, 1950. Treasury Solicitor's Dept, 1952–71; Solicitor's Department: Dept of Environment, 1971–74; Dept of Trade, 1974–75; Under-Sec. (Legal), Dept of Trade, 1975–82. *Recreations:* gardening, carpentry, chess. *Address:* Ledsham, Glaziers Lane, Normandy, Surrey GU3 2DQ. *T:* (01483) 811250.

PRESTON, Helen Gillian; *see* Robinson, H. G.

PRESTON, Dr Ian Mathieson Hamilton, CBE 1993; FREng, FIET; Chairman, Motherwell Bridge Holdings, 1996–2001; *b* 18 July 1932; *s* of John Hamilton Preston and Edna Irene Paul; *m* 1958, Sheila Hope Pringle; two *s*. *Educ:* Univ. of Glasgow (BSc 1st cl. Hons; PhD). MInstP 1959; FIET (FIEE 1974); FREng (FEng 1982). Asst Lectr, Univ. of Glasgow, 1954–59; joined SSEB, 1959, Chief Engineer, Generation Design and Construction, 1972–77; Dir Gen., Generation Develt and Construction Div., CEGB, 1977–83; Dep. Chm., SSEB, 1983–90; Chief Exec., Scottish Power, 1990–95. Director: Deutsche (Scotland) (formerly Morgan Grenfell (Scotland)), 1994–2002; Clydeport plc, 1994–2000. Chairman: Mining Scotland, 1995–98; East of Scotland Water Authy, 1995–98. Pres., Scottish Council Develt and Industry, 1997–99 (Chm., 1992–97). Hon. FCIWEM 1995. *Recreations:* fishing, gardening. *Address:* 10 Cameron Crescent, Carmunnock, Glasgow G76 9DX.

PRESTON, Jeffrey William, CB 1989; Director General, Energy, Department of Trade and Industry, 1996–98; *b* 28 Jan. 1940; *s* of William and Sybil Grace Preston. *Educ:* Liverpool Collegiate Sch.; Hertford Coll., Oxford (MA Lit. Hum. 1966). Asst Principal, Min. of Aviation, 1963; Private Sec. to Permanent Sec., BoT, 1966; Principal: BoT, 1967; HM Treasury, 1970; DTI, 1973; Asst Sec., Dept of Trade, 1975–82; Under Sec. and Regional Dir, Yorks and Humberside Region, DTI, 1982–85; Dep. Sec., Industrial and Economic Affairs, Welsh Office, 1985–90; Dep. Dir Gen., OFT, 1990–96 (Acting Dir Gen., 1995). Vice-Pres., Hertford Soc., 2004– (Chm., 1987–95). FRSA. *Recreations:* travel, opera, wine. *T:* (020) 8940 7166. *Club:* Oxford and Cambridge (Chm., 1999–2001).

PRESTON, Kieran Thomas, OBE 2006; FCIT; Director General, West Yorkshire Passenger Transport Executive, since 1993; *b* 30 Nov. 1950; *s* of Charles Edward Preston and Mary Kate Preston; *m* 1974, Denise Marie Gregory; two *s*. *Educ:* Leeds Poly. (BA Hons Mgt and Admin). FCIT 1994. Local Govt Officer, various appts, 1972–89; Leeds City Council: Projects Dir, 1989–91; Actg Dir of Admin, 1991–92; Chief Services Officer, 1992–93. Chm., PTE Gp, 2001–05. FIPD (FIPM 1992). *Recreations:* keeping fit, horse riding, football, cricket, judo. *Address:* West Yorkshire Passenger Transport Executive, Wellington House, 40–50 Wellington Street, Leeds LS1 2DE; 15 Morritt Avenue, Leeds LS15 7EP. *T:* (0113) 260 9093.

PRESTON, Mark Robin; Group Chief Executive, Grosvenor, since 2008; *b* Westow, 20 Jan. 1968; *s* of Roger St Clair Preston and Polly Mary Preston (*née* Marriot); *m* 1997, Kate Whittaker; one *s* two *d*. *Educ:* Eton Coll.; Reading Univ. (BSc Land Mgt). MRICS 1992. Joined Grosvenor, 1989; seconded to Hong Kong, 1995–97; Gp Fund Mgt Dir, 1997–2002; Pres., Grosvenor USA, San Francisco, 2002–06; Chief Exec., Grosvenor Britain and Ireland, 2006–08. Non-exec. Dir, London Bd, Royal & Sun Alliance, 2006–08. Mem. Bd, Assoc. of Foreign Investors in Real Estate (Chm., 2007). *Recreations:* field sports. *Address:* Grosvenor, 70 Grosvenor Street, W1K 3JP. *T:* (020) 7408 0988. *Club:* Lansdowne.

PRESTON, Michael Richard, ATD; FCSD; consultant designer; *b* 15 Oct. 1927; *s* of Major Frederick Allan Preston, MC and Winifred Gertrude (*née* Archer); *m* 1st, 1955, Anne Gillespie Smith; 2nd, 1980, Judith Gaye James. *Educ:* Whitgift Sch.; Guildford Sch. of Art; Goldsmiths' Coll., London Univ. (NDD 1953; ATD 1954); Dip. in Humanities (London) 1964. FCSD (FSIAD 1972; MSIAD 1953). Served HM Forces, Queen's Royal Regt, 1944–48, Queen's Royal Regt, TA & HAC, 1948–61. Asst Art Master, Whitgift Sch., 1954–55; Drawing Master, Dulwich Coll., 1955–64; Science Mus., 1964–87; Head of Design, 1964–86; Keeper, Dept of Museum Services, 1987; designed exhibitions, including: Centenary of Charles Babbage, 1971; A Word to the Mermaids, 1973; Tower Bridge Observed, 1974; The Breath of Life, 1974; Nat. Rly Mus., York, 1975; Sci. and Technol. of Islam, 1976; Nat. Mus. of Photography, Bradford, 1977–83; Stanley Spencer in the Shipyard, 1979; Wellcome Mus. of Hist. of Medicine, 1980; Sci. and Technol. of India, 1982; The Great Cover-up Show, 1982; Beads of Glass, 1983; Louis Pasteur and Rabies, 1985. Advisory Assignments on Museum Projects: Iran, 1976–79; Spain, 1977–80; Germany, 1978–79; Canada, 1979–82, 1984–86; Trinidad, 1982–83; Turkey, 1984–94; Hong Kong, 1985; consultant to: Dean and Chapter of Canterbury, 1987–96; Wellcome Foundn, 1987–95; TAVRA Greater London, 1988–94; Mus. of East Asian Art, Bath, 1988–93; Design Expo '89, Nagoya; Bank of England Museum, 1989; Norwich Tourism Agency, 1989–91; Tricycle Theatre, 1989–90; Nat. Theatre, 1989–90; Scottish Office, 1990; English Heritage, 1990; Richmond Theatre, 1990; Accademia Italiana, 1990–94; Société Générale, 1992–95; Castrol Internat., 1994–95; Dean and Chapter of Westminster Abbey, 1997–98; Westminster CC, 1997–99. Mem., BTEC Validation Panel, 1986–92. Chm., Greenwich Soc., 1961–64. Society of Industrial Artists and Designers (now Chartered Society of Designers): Mem., 1953–; Vice-Pres., 1976, 1979–81; Chm., Membership Bd, 1976–79; Chm., Design Management Panel, 1976–80. Mem., ICOM, 1964–. Trustee, Vivat Trust, 1989–92. Hon. Keeper of Pictures, Arts Club, 1992–. Vis. Prof., NID, Ahmedabad, 1989–2000. Guild of Glass Engravers: Hon. FGGE 1980; Pres., 1986–92. FRSA 1955–68, 2001. *Recreations:* travel, food, conversation, jazz. *Clubs:* Arts; Australasian Pioneers', Union (Sydney).

PRESTON, Prof. Paul, CBE 2000; FRHistS; FBA 1994; Professor of International History, London School of Economics, since 1991; *b* 21 July 1946; *s* of Charles Ronald Preston and Alice Hoskisson; *m* 1983, Gabrielle Patricia Ashford-Hodges; two *s*. *Educ:* St Edward's Coll., Liverpool; Oriel Coll., Oxford. Lectr in Modern History, Univ. of Reading, 1974–75; Queen Mary College, University of London: Lectr and Reader in Modern History, 1975–85; Prof. of History, 1985–91. Marcel Proust Chair, Academia Europea de Yuste, 2006. Ramon Llull Internat. Prize, Catalonia, 2005. Comendador de la Orden de Mérito Civil (Spain), 1986; Gran Cruz, Orden de Isabel la Católica (Spain), 2007. *Publications:* (ed) Spain in Crisis, 1976; The Coming of the Spanish Civil War, 1978, 2nd edn 1994; (ed) Revolution and War in Spain 1931–1939, 1984; (with Denis Smyth) Spain, the EEC and NATO, 1984; The Triumph of Democracy in Spain, 1986; The Spanish Civil War 1936–1939, 1986; The Politics of Revenge, 1990; Franco, 1993 (Yorkshire Post Book of the Year, 1993); Las tres Españas del 36, 1998 (Así fue, 1998); Comrades! Portraits from the Spanish Civil War, 1999; Doves of War: four women of Spain, 2002; Juan Carlos: a people's king, 2004; We Saw Spain Die, 2008. *Recreations:* classical music, opera, modern fiction, wine, supporting Everton Football Club. *Address:* Department of International History, London School of Economics, Houghton Street, WC2A 2AE. *T:* (020) 7955 7107.

PRESTON, Peter John; journalist and writer; Co-Director, Guardian Foundation, since 1997; *b* 23 May 1938; *s* of John Whittle Preston and Kathlyn (*née* Chell); *m* 1962, Jean Mary Burrell; two *s* two *d*. *Educ:* Loughborough Grammar Sch.; St John's Coll., Oxford (MA EngLit; Hon. Fellow, 2003). Editorial trainee, Liverpool Daily Post, 1960–63; Guardian: Political Reporter, 1963–64; Education Correspondent, 1965–66; Diary Editor, 1966–68; Features Editor, 1968–72; Production Editor, 1972–75; Editor, 1975–95; Ed.-in-chief and Chm., Guardian and Observer, 1995–96; Editl Dir, Guardian Media Gp, 1996–98. Mem., Scott Trust, 1976–2004. British Exec. Chm., IPI, 1988– (World Chm., 1995–97); Chm., Assoc. of British Editors, 1996–99. Mem., UNESCO Adv. Gp on Press Freedom, 2000–03. Gov., British Assoc. for Central and Eastern Europe, 2000–. Hon. DLitt: Loughborough, 1982; City, 2000; Leicester, 2003; DU Essex, 1994. *Publications:* Dunblane: reflecting tragedy, 1996; The Fifty-First State (novel), 1998; Bess (novel), 1999. *Recreations:* football, films; four children. *Address:* The Guardian, Kings Place, 90 York Way, N1 9AG.

PRESTON, Sir Philip (Charles Henry Hulton), 8th Bt *cr* 1815, of Beeston St Lawrence, Norfolk; Partner, Bumphrey Preston Associates, architects; *b* 31 Aug. 1946; *s* of Lt-Col Philip Henry Herbert Hulton Preston, OBE, MC and Katherine Janet Preston (*née* Broomhall); *S* cousin, 1999, but his name does not appear on the Official Roll of the Baronetage; *m* 1980, Kirsi Sylvi Annikki, *d* of Eino Yrjö Pullinen; one *s* two *d*. *Educ:* Nautical Coll., Pangbourne. *Publication:* (ed jtly) The Battle of Crécy 1346, 2005. *Heir: s* Philip Thomas Henry Hulton Preston, *b* 1990. *Address:* 3 Place Gilbert Gaffet, Crécy-en-Ponthieu, 80150 Somme, Picardie, France.

PRESTON, Roberta Lynn; *see* Gilchrist, R. L.

PRESTON, Rosalind, OBE 1993; Co-Chairman, Inter Faith Network for UK, 2000–04 (Co-Vice-Chairman, 1994–2000); Vice President, Board of Deputies of British Jews, 1991–94; *b* 29 Dec. 1935; *d* of Benjamin and Marie Morris; *m* 1958, Ronald Preston; one *s* one *d*. *Educ:* Talbot Heath Sch., Bournemouth. Voluntary sector activity, 1960–; Nat. Pres., Nat. Council of Women, 1988–90; Hon. Vice Pres., British Section, Women's Internat. Zionist Orgn, 1999– (Vice Pres., 1993–99); Jt Hon. Sec., CCJ, 1996–2005. Dir (non-exec.), Harrow and Hillingdon Healthcare NHS Trust, 1994–96; Mental Health Manager, Central and NW London (formerly Brent, Kensington & Chelsea and Westminster) Mental Health NHS Trust, 2002–04. Chm., Nightingale Home, 2001–07. Trustee: Jewish Chronicle, 2000–08; Olive Tree Trust, 2004–. FRSA 1990. Paul Harris Fellow, Rotary Internat., 1992. *Recreations:* walking, reading newspapers, family and friends, international affairs. *Address:* 7 Woodside Close, Stanmore, Middx HA7 3AJ.

PRESTON, Simon John, OBE 2000; Organist and Master of the Choristers, Westminster Abbey, 1981–87; concert organist, since 1987; *b* 4 Aug. 1938. *Educ:* Canford Sch.; King's Coll., Cambridge (Dr Mann Organ Student; BA 1961; MusB 1962; MA 1964). ARCM, FRAM. Sub Organist, Westminster Abbey, 1962–67; Acting Organist, St Albans Abbey, 1968–69; Organist and Tutor in Music, Christ Church, Oxford, 1970–81. Conductor, Oxford Bach Choir, 1971–74. Artistic Dir, Calgary Internat. Organ Comp., 1990–2002. Has performed with major orchestras incl. Berlin Philharmonic, LA Philharmonic and Boston SO, as well as British orchestras; soloist, Last Night of the Proms, 2005. Tours to USA and performance in Far East, Australia and major Eur. countries, incl. Russia. FRSA. Hon. FRCO 1975; Hon. FRCCO 1986; Hon. FRCM 1986. Edison Award, 1971; Grand Prix du Disque, 1979; Performer of the Year Award, NY Chapter, Amer. Guild of Organists, 1987. *Recreations:* croquet, crosswords. *Address:* Little Hardwick, Langton Green, Tunbridge Wells, Kent TN3 0EY. *T:* (01892) 862042.

PRESTON, Susanna; *see* Gross, S.

PRESTON, Walter James, FRICS; Partner, Jones Lang Wootton, 1957–87, Consultant, 1987–99; *b* 20 March 1925; *s* of Walter Ronald and Agnes Ann McNeil Preston; *m* 1956, Joy Dorothea Ashton; two *s* one *d*. *Educ:* Dollar Academy, Perthshire. Served Royal Engineers, 1943–47. Jones Lang Wootton, 1948–99, Staff, 1948–57. Dir (non-exec.), Lynton Property and Reversionary plc, 1985–88. Liveryman: Chartered Surveyors' Co., 1977–; Vintners' Co., 1990–. *Recreation:* golf. *Clubs:* Carlton; Phyllis Court (Henley); Woking Golf; Trevose Golf and Country, St Enodoc Golf (North Cornwall).

PRESTWICH, Prof. Michael Charles, FRHistS; FSA; Professor of History, University of Durham, 1986–2008 (Pro-Vice-Chancellor, 1992–99 and Sub-Warden, 1997–99); *b* 30 Jan. 1943; *s* of late John Oswald Prestwich and Menna Prestwich; *m* 1973, Margaret Joan Daniel; two *s* one *d*. *Educ:* Charterhouse; Magdalen Coll., Oxford (MA, DPhil). FSA 1980. Res. Lectr, Christ Church, Oxford, 1965–69; Lectr in Mediaeval History, Univ. of St Andrews, 1969–79; Reader in Medieval History, Univ. of Durham, 1979–86. *Publications:* War, Politics and Finance under Edward I, 1972; The Three Edwards: war and state in England 1272–1377, 1980; Documents illustrating the Crisis of 1297–98 in England, 1980; Edward I, 1988; English Politics in the Thirteenth Century, 1990; Armies and Warfare in the Middle Ages, 1996; Plantagenet England, 1225–1360, 2005; articles in learned jls. *Recreation:* ski-ing. *Address:* 46 Albert Street, Western Hill, Durham DH1 4RJ. *T:* (0191) 386 2539.

PRETORIA, Bishop of, since 1998; **Rt Rev. Dr Johannes Thomas Seoka;** *b* 29 Aug. 1948; *s* of Isaac and Margaret Seoka; *m* 1980, Sybil Elizabeth Nomathonya; two *s*. *Educ:* school in Stanger; Eshowe Coll. of Educn, Zululand (grad. as teacher, 1971); St Bede's Coll., Umtata; Chicago Theol Seminary, Ill, USA (MTh); Univ. of Chicago (DMin); studies in industrial mgt, W Germany and USA. Deacon 1974, priest 1975, Natal; Curate, St Augustine, Umlazi, Natal, 1976–78; Rector, St Peter's, Greytown, 1978–80; Rector, St Hilda's, Senaoane, Soweto, 1980; seconded as Dir of Industrial Mission, 1981; Priest-in-Charge: Trinity Episcopal Church, Chicago, Ill, 1986; St James's, Diepkloof, Soweto,

1993–95; Church of the Good Shepherd, Tladi, Soweto, 1995–96; Dean of Pretoria and Rector, St Alban's Cathedral, 1996–98. Continuing urban and industrial work, including: Dir, Agency for Industrial Mission; Dir, Urban and Industrial Mission, 1994. CPSA Rep., Faith and Order Commn, WCC; Mem., WCC Adv. Gp on Urban and Rural Mission, 1983–. Hon. DD Gen. Theol Seminary, NY, 2006. *Publications:* contribs to books and magazines. *Address:* PO Box 1032, Pretoria 0001, S Africa. *T:* (12) 3222218; 237 Schoeman Street, Pretoria 0002, S Africa.

PRETTEJOHN, Nicholas Edward Tucker; Chief Executive, Prudential Assurance Company Ltd, since 2006; *b* 22 July 1960; *s* of Dr Edward Joseph Tucker Prettejohn and Diana Sally Prettejohn; *m* 1997, Claire Helen McKenna; two *d. Educ:* Balliol Coll., Oxford (BA 1st Cl. Hons PPE 1981; Pres., Oxford Union, 1980). Mgt Consultant, Bain & Co., 1982–91; Dir, Apax Partners, 1991–94; Dir of Corporate Strategy, NFC plc, 1994–95; Lloyd's of London: Head of Strategy, 1995–97; Man. Dir, Business Develt Unit, 1997–99, and N America Business Unit, 1998–99; Chief Exec., 1999–2005. Dep. Chm., Financial Services Practitioner Panel, 2007–. Chairman: English Pocket Opera, 2001–; Children's Music Workshop, 2006–; Trustee, Royal Opera House, 2005–. *Recreations:* opera, music, theatre, horse racing, golf, cricket, Rugby. *Address:* (office) Laurence Pountney Hill, EC4R 0HH. *Clubs:* Lloyd's Golf, Taunton and Pickeridge Golf, Huntercombe Golf, Walton Heath Golf, Minehead and West Somerset Golf.

PRETTY, Prof. Jules Nicholas, OBE 2006; Professor of Environment and Society, University of Essex, since 2000; *b* 5 Oct. 1958; *s* of John and Susan Pretty; partner, Gill Boardman; one *s* one *d. Educ:* Denes High Sch., Lowestoft; Univ. of York (BA Hons Biol. 1979); Imperial Coll., London (MSc Envmtl Technol. 1981). Res. Officer, Imperial Coll., London, 1985–86; Res. Associate and Associate Dir, 1986–91, Dir, 1991–97, Sustainable Agric. Prog., Internat. Inst. for Envmt and Develt; University of Essex: Vis. Prof., 1997; Dir, Centre for Envmt and Society, 1997–99, 2000–04; Hd, Dept of Biol Scis, 2004–08. A. D. White Prof.-at-Large, Cornell Univ., 2001–07. Dep. Chm., UK Adv. Cttee on Releases to the Envmt, 1999–. Trustee, Essex Wildlife Trust, 2005–. Presenter: Ploughing Eden (also writer), BBC Radio 4, 1999; The Magic Bean (also co-writer), BBC TV, 2001. FIBiol 2003; FRSA 2004. Chief Ed., Internat. Jl of Agricl Sustainability, 2002–. *Publications:* Unwelcome Harvest: agriculture and pollution (with G. R. Conway), 1991; Regenerating Agriculture: policies and practice for sustainability and self-reliance, 1995; (jtly) A Trainers' Guide to Participatory Learning and Action, 1995; The Living Land, 1998; (ed jtly) Fertile Ground: the impact of participatory watershed management, 1999; Agri-Culture: reconnecting people, land and nature, 2002; (ed) Guide to a Green Planet, 2002; (ed jtly) Waste Management, 2003; (ed) The Pesticide Detox: towards a more sustainable agriculture, 2005; (ed) The Earthscan Reader in Sustainable Agriculture, 2005; (ed) The Sage Major Work on the Environment, 2006; (jtly) Biological Approaches for Sustainable Soil Systems, 2006; (jtly) Guide to a Healthy Planet, 2006; (ed jtly) Sage Handbook on Environment and Society, 2007; The Earth Only Endures: on reconnecting with nature and our place in it, 2007; (ed) Sustainable Agriculture and Food, 4 vols, 2008; over 200 papers and articles. *Recreations:* walking, gardening, watching real football (Colchester United). *Address:* Department of Biological Sciences, University of Essex, Wivenhoe Park, Colchester, Essex CO4 3SQ. *T:* (01206) 873323, *Fax:* (01206) 872572; *e-mail:* jpretty@essex.ac.uk; *web:* www.julespretty.com.

PRETTY, Dr Katharine Bridget, FSA; Principal, Homerton College, Cambridge, since 1991; Pro-Vice-Chancellor, University of Cambridge, since 2004; *b* 18 Oct. 1945; *d* of M. W. and B. E. W. Hughes; *m* 1988, Prof. Tjeerd Hendrik van Andel. *Educ:* King Edward VI High Sch. for Girls, Birmingham; New Hall, Cambridge (MA, PhD). New Hall, Cambridge: College Lectr and Fellow in Archaeology, 1972–91; Admissions Tutor, 1979–85; Sen. Tutor, 1985–91; Emeritus Fellow, 1995–; University of Cambridge: Member: Council of Senate, 1981–89; Financial Bd, 1986–96; Gen. Bd, 1997–2004; Chm. Council, Sch. of Humanities and Social Scis, 1997–2004. Chairman: Rescue, 1978–83; OCR Examng Bd, 1998–. Governor: Bancroft's Sch., 1985–90; Felsted Sch., 1990–91; Leys Sch., 1993–98. Vice-Pres., RSA, 1998–2004. FSA 2000. *Recreations:* archaeology, botany, Arctic travel. *Address:* Homerton College, Cambridge CB2 8PH. *T:* (01223) 507131.

PREVEZER, Susan Rachel; QC 2000; a Recorder, since 2000; *b* 25 March 1959; *d* of late Prof. Sydney Prevezer and of Enid Margaret Prevezer (*née* Austin); *m* 1994, Benjamin Freedman; two *d. Educ:* St Paul's Girls' Sch.; Girton Coll., Cambridge (MA). Called to the Bar, Inner Temple, 1983. *Address:* Bingham McCutcheon (London) LLP, 41 Lothbury, EC2R 7HF.

PREVIN, André (George), Hon. KBE 1996; conductor, pianist and composer; Conductor Laureate, London Symphony Orchestra, since 1992; Music Director, Oslo Philharmonic, 2002–06; *b* Berlin, Germany, 6 April 1929; *s* of Jack Previn and Charlotte Epstein; *m* 1970; three *s* (inc. twin *s*), three *d; m* 1982, Heather (marr. diss.), *d* of Robert Sneddon; one *s; m* 2002, Anne-Sophie Mutter, *qv* (marr. diss. 2006). *Educ:* Berlin and Paris Conservatoires; private study with Pierre Monteux, Castelnuovo-Tedesco. Composer of film scores, 1950–62 (four Academy Awards). Music Dir, Houston Symphony Orchestra, 1967–69; Principal Conductor, London Symphony Orchestra, 1968–79, Conductor Emeritus, 1979; Music Director: Pittsburgh Symphony Orchestra, 1976–84; Los Angeles Phil. Orch., 1986–89; Music Dir, 1985–86, Prin. Conductor, 1987–91, RPO; Guest Conductor, most major orchestras, US and Europe, Covent Garden Opera, Salzburg Festival, Edinburgh Festival, Osaka Festival; Music Dir, London South Bank Summer Festival, 1972–74. Formed André Previn Jazz Trio, 1990. Member: Composers Guild of GB; Amer. Composers League; Dramatists League. Recording artist. Principal *compositions:* Cello Sonata; Violin Sonata, 1994; Bassoon Sonata; Guitar Concerto; Wind Quintet; Serenades for Violin; piano preludes; Piano Concerto, 1984; Trio for piano, oboe and bassoon, 1994; Principals, Reflections (for orchestra); Every Good Boy Deserves Favour (text by Tom Stoppard); Six Songs Mezzo-Soprano (text by Philip Larkin); Honey and Rue (text by Toni Morrison); Sally Chisum Remembers Billy the Kid (text by Michael Ondaatje); Four Songs for soprano, cello and piano (text by Toni Morrison), 1994; The Magic Number (for soprano and orch.), 1997; A Streetcar Named Desire (opera), 1998; Violin Concerto, 2002. Annual TV series: specials for BBC; PBS (USA). *Publications:* Music Face to Face, 1971; (ed) Orchestra, 1979; André Previn's Guide to Music, 1983; No Minor Chords (autobiog.), 1992; *relevant publications:* André Previn, by Edward Greenfield, 1973; Previn, by H. Ruttencutter, 1985.

PREVITE, His Honour John Edward; QC 1989; a Circuit Judge, 1992–2001; *b* 11 May 1934; *s* of late Lt Col K. E. Previte, OBE and Edith Frances (*née* Capper); *m* 1959, Hon. Phyllida Browne, *d* of 6th Baron Kilmaine, CBE; two *s. Educ:* Wellington Coll.; Christ Church, Oxford (MA). Called to the Bar, Inner Temple, 1959, Bencher, 1986; a Recorder, Western Circuit, 1987–92. *Recreations:* sailing, skiffing, Real tennis, gardening.

PREVOST, Sir Christopher (Gerald), 6th Bt *cr* 1805; *b* 25 July 1935; *s* of Sir George James Augustine Prevost, 5th Bt and Muriel Emily (*d* 1939), *d* of late Lewis William Oram; *S* father, 1985; *m* 1964, Dolores Nelly, *o d* of Dezo Hoffmann; one *s* one *d. Educ:* Cranleigh School. Served 60th Regt (formed by Prevost family) and Rifle Bde; Kenya

Service Medal, 1955. IBM, 1955–61; Pitney-Bowes, 1963–76; founder of Mailtronic Ltd, manufacturers and suppliers of mailroom equipment, 1977, Chm. and Man. Dir, 1977–91. Member: Huguenot Soc.; Soc. of Genealogists. *Heir: s* Nicholas Marc Prevost, *b* 13 March 1971.

PRIAULX, Andrew, MBE 2008; racing driver; *b* 10 Aug. 1973; *s* of Graham Ernold Priaulx and Judith Anne Priaulx; *m* 1997, Joanne Le Tocq; one *s* one *d. Educ:* Elizabeth Coll., Guernsey. Winner, British Hillclimb Championship, 1995; competed Formula Renault and British Formula 3, 1996; winner, British Renault Spider Cup Championship, 1999–2002; competed British Formula 3, 2000–02; joined BMW UK team, 2003; winner: European Touring Car Championship, 2004; World Touring Car Championship, 2005, 2006, 2007. Awards include: Lifetime Ambassador, States of Guernsey, 2005; BBC SW Sports Personality of Year, 2005. Gold Medal, British Racing Drivers Club, 2007; Gold Medal, BARC, 2006, 2007. *Recreations:* running, boating, family. *Address:* Andy Priaulx Racing, 2/37 York Place, Harrogate HG1 5RH. *Clubs:* British Racing Drivers, Midland Automobile, British Automobile Racing.

PRICE, Adam; MP (Plaid Cymru) Carmarthen East and Dinefwr, since 2001; *b* 23 Sept. 1968. *Educ:* Amman Valley Comprehensive Sch.; Saarland Univ.; Univ. of Wales Coll. of Cardiff (BA 1991). Res. Associate, Dept of City and Regl Planning, UWCC, 1991–93; Project Manager, 1993–95, Exec. Manager, 1995–96, Exec. Dir, 1996–98, Menter an Busnes; Man. Dir, Newidiem Econ. Develt Consultancy, 1998–2001. Contested (Plaid Cymru) Gower, 1992. *Publications:* The Collective Entrepreneur, (jtly) The Welsh Renaissance: innovation and inward investment in Wales, 1992; Rebuilding Our Communities: a new agenda for the valleys, 1993; Quiet Revolution? language, culture and economy in the nineties, 1994; The Diversity Dividend, 1996; (jtly) The Other Wales: the case for objective 1 funding post 1999, 1998. *Recreations:* contemporary culture, good friends, good food, travel. *Address:* (office) 37 Wind Street, Ammanford, Carmarthenshire SA18 3DN. *T:* (01269) 597677, *Fax:* (01269) 591334; House of Commons, SW1A 0AA. *T:* (020) 7219 8486.

PRICE, (Alan) Anthony; author and journalist; Editor, The Oxford Times, 1972–88; *b* 16 Aug. 1928; *s* of Walter Longsdon Price and Kathleen Price (*née* Lawrence); *m* 1953, Yvonne Ann Stone; two *s* one *d. Educ:* King's Sch., Canterbury; Merton Coll., Oxford (Exbnr; MA). Oxford & County Newspapers, 1952–88. *Publications:* The Labyrinth Makers, 1970 (CWA Silver Dagger); The Alamut Ambush, 1971; Colonel Butler's Wolf, 1972; October Men, 1973; Other Paths to Glory, 1974 (CWA Gold Dagger, 1974; Swedish Acad. of Detection Prize, 1978); Our Man in Camelot, 1975; War Game, 1976; The '44 Vintage, 1978; Tomorrow's Ghost, 1979; The Hour of the Donkey, 1980; Soldier No More, 1981; The Old Vengeful, 1982; Gunner Kelly, 1983; Sion Crossing, 1984; Here Be Monsters, 1985; For the Good of the State, 1986; A New Kind of War, 1987; A Prospect of Vengeance, 1988; The Memory Trap, 1989; Eyes of the Fleet, 1990. *Recreations:* military history, travelling, gardening, cooking. *Address:* Wayside Cottage, Horton-cum-Studley, Oxford OX33 1AW. *T:* (01865) 351326.

PRICE, (Arthur) Leolin, CBE 1996; QC 1968; *b* 11 May 1924; 3rd *s* of late Evan Price and Ceridwen Price (*née* Price), Hawkhurst, Kent; *m* 1963, Hon. Rosalind Helen Penrose Lewis, CBE (*d* 1999), *er d* of 1st Baron Brecon, PC, and Mabel, Baroness Brecon, CBE, JP; two *s* two *d. Educ:* Judd Sch., Tonbridge; Keble Coll., Oxford (Schol.; MA). War service, 1943–46 with Army: Capt., RA; Adjt, Indian Mountain Artillery Trng Centre and Depot, Ambala, Punjab, 1946. Treas., Oxford Union, 1948; Pres., Oxford Univ. Cons. Assoc., 1948. Tutor, Keble Coll., Oxford, 1951–59. Called to Bar, Middle Temple, 1949, Bencher, 1970–, Treas. 1990; Barrister of Lincoln's Inn, 1959. QC (Bahamas) 1969; QC (NSW) 1987; Barrister: BVI, 1994; Gibraltar, 1996. Member: Editorial Cttee, Modern Law Review, 1954–65; Bar Council Law Reform Cttee, 1969–75; Cttee, Soc. of Cons. Lawyers, 1971– (Vice-Chm., 1987–90). Director: SR (formerly Thornton) Pan-European Investment Trust (formerly Child Health Res. Investment Trust), 1980–99 (Chm., 1987–99; Pres., 1999–); Marine Adventure Sailing Trust plc, 1981–89; Thornton Asian Emerging Markets Investment Trust plc, 1989–95. Institute of Child Health: Chairman, 1976–2007; Fellow, 1996. Chm., Child Health Res. Appeal Trust, 1976–2007. Governor, Gt Ormond St Hosp. for Sick Children, 1972–92 (Trustee, 1992–2007); Mem., Falkland Islands Cttee, 1972–. Governor, Christ Coll., Brecon, 1977–. Chancellor, Diocese of Swansea and Brecon, 1982–99. Hon. Fellow UCL, 2001. *Publications:* articles and notes in legal jls. *Recreations:* conversation, politics, reading, sending letters to The Times. *Address:* 32 Hampstead Grove, NW3 6SR. *T:* (020) 7435 9843; 10 Old Square, Lincoln's Inn, WC2A 3SU. *T:* (020) 7405 0758, *Fax:* (020) 7831 8237; Moor Park, Llanbedr, near Crickhowell, Powys NP8 1SS. *T:* (01873) 810443, *Fax:* (01873) 810659; Selborne Chambers, 174 Phillip Street, Sydney, NSW 2000, Australia. *T:* (2) 92335188. *Clubs:* Carlton, Garrick.

See also V. W. C. Price.

PRICE, Barry David Keith, CBE 1991; QPM 1981; intelligence consultant, since 1993; Co-ordinator, National Drugs Intelligence Unit, 1987–92; *b* 28 June 1933; *s* of John Leslie Price and Lena Price; *m* 1953, Evelyne Jean Horlick; three *d. Educ:* Southall Grammar Sch. Metropolitan Police, 1954–75: Constable, uniform and CID, then through ranks to Det. Chief Supt; Asst Chief Constable, Northumbria Police, 1975–78; Dep. Chief Constable, Essex Police, 1978–80; Chief Constable, Cumbria Constabulary, 1980–87. Member: Adv. Council on the Misuse of Drugs, 1982–87; Drugs Intelligence Steering Gp, 1987–; Advr to ACPO Crime Cttee on drugs matters, 1985–88 (past Chm. and Sec.). President: English Police Golf Assoc., 1981–92; Northern Police Cricket League, 1983–87; Patron, NW Counties Schoolboys ABA, 1980–87. CCMI (FBIM 1975). SBStJ 1982 (County Dir, St John Amb. Assoc., 1981–87). Police Long Service and Good Conduct Medal, 1976. *Publications:* various articles in law enforcement and med. pubns. *Recreations:* golf, painting, gardening.

PRICE, (Benjamin) Terence; Secretary-General, Uranium Institute, 1974–86; *b* 7 Jan. 1921; *er s* of Benjamin and Nellie Price; *m* 1947, Jean Stella Vidal (*d* 2006); one *s* one *d. Educ:* Crypt School, Gloucester; Queens' College, Cambridge (Scholar). Naval electronics res., 1942–46; Lieut RNVR, 1945–46; Atomic Energy Research Establishment, Harwell (Nuclear Physics Division), 1947–59; Head of Reactor Development Division, Atomic Energy Estabt, Winfrith, 1959–60; Chief Scientific Officer, Ministry of Defence, 1960–63; Assistant Chief Scientific Adviser (Studies), Ministry of Defence, 1963–65; Director, Defence Operational Analysis Establishment, MoD, 1965–68; Chief Scientific Adviser, Min. of Transport, 1968–71; Dir of Planning and Development, Vickers Ltd, 1971–73. Chairman: OECD Transport Res. Gp, 1969–71; NEDO Mechanical Handling Sector Working Party, 1976–80. Mem., MRC Review Cttee on Industrial Psychology Res., 1964–66. Reviewer, CET, 1984–85. *Publications:* Radiation Shielding, 1957; Political Electricity, 1990; Political Physicist, 2004. *Recreations:* making music, writing. *Address:* Seers Bough, Wilton Lane, Jordans, Beaconsfield, Bucks HP9 2RG. *T:* (01494) 874589. *Club:* Athenæum.

PRICE, Bernard Albert, CBE 1997; DL; County Clerk and Chief Executive, Staffordshire County Council, and Clerk to the Lieutenancy, 1983–2003; Clerk to the

Staffordshire Police Authority, 1995–2003; *b* 6 Jan. 1944; *s* of Albert and Doris Price; *m* 1966, Christine Mary, *d* of Roy William Henry Combes; two *s* one *d*. *Educ:* Whitchurch Grammar Sch., Salop; King's Sch., Rochester, Kent; Merton Coll., Oxford (BA 1965, MA 1970). DMS, Wolverhampton Polytechnic, 1972. Articled, later Asst Solicitor, Worcs CC, 1966–70; Asst Solicitor, subseq. Dep. Dir of Admin, Staffs CC, 1970–80; Sen. Dep. Clerk, Staffs CC, 1980–83. Member: Council, Staffs Wildlife Trust, 2004–; W Mids Regl Cttee, NT, 2004–. Lay Mem., Chapter, Lichfield Cathedral, 2004–. DL Stafford, 2003. *Recreations:* sailing, walking. *Address:* The Cottage, Yeatsall Lane, Abbots Bromley, Rugeley, Staffs WS15 3DY. *T:* (01283) 840269.

PRICE, Hon. Charles H., II; Director, Mercantile Bancorporation, St Louis, 1991–96; *b* 1 April 1931; *s* of Charles Harry Price and Virginia (*née* Ogden); *m* 1969, Carol Ann Swanson; two *s* three *d*. *Educ:* University of Missouri. Chairman: Price Candy Co., 1969–81; American Bancorpn, 1973–81; American Bank & Trust Co., 1973–81; American Mortgage Co., 1973–81; Ambassador: to Belgium, 1981–83; to UK, 1983–89; Chm. Bd, Mercantile Bank, Kansas City, 1990–96. Non-executive Director: Hanson PLC, 1989–95; New York Times Co., 1989–95; Texaco Inc., 1989–2001; non-exec. Chm., Midwest Res. Inst., 1990–99 (Vice-Chm. and Mem. Exec. Cttee, 1978–81); Mem. Bd of Dirs, Civic Council, Greater Kansas City, 1979–80. Member: Young Presidents Orgn; IISS; World Business Council. Hon. Fellow, Regent's Coll., London, 1986. Hon. Dr Westminster Coll., Missouri, 1984; Hon. Dr of Laws Missouri, 1988. Salvation Army's William Booth Award, 1985; Kansas City Mayor's World Citizen of the Year, 1985, Trustee Citation Award, Midwest Res. Inst., 1987; Distinguished Service Award, Internat. Relations Council, 1989; Mankind Award, Cystic Fibrosis Foundn, 1990; Gold Good Citizen Award, Sons of the American Revolution, 1991; William F. Yates Medallion for Distinguished Service, 1996. *Recreations:* golf, shooting. *Address:* 1 West Armour Boulevard, Ste 300, Kansas City, MO 64111, USA. *Clubs:* White's, Mark's; Swinley Forest Golf; Eldorado Country (Palm Springs); Kansas City Country, River (Kansas City); Los Angeles Country (Los Angeles); Cypress Point (Monterey); Vintage (Palm Springs).

PRICE, Christopher; freelance journalist, consultant, and broadcaster; *b* 26 Jan. 1932; *s* of Stanley Price; *m* 1956, Annie Grierson Ross; two *s* one *d*. *Educ:* Leeds Grammar School; Queen's College, Oxford. Sec., Oxford Univ. Labour Club, 1953; Chm., Nat. Assoc. of Labour Student Organisations, 1955–56. Sheffield City Councillor, 1962–66; Dep. Chm., Sheffield Educn Cttee, 1963–66. Contested (Lab): Shipley, 1964; Birmingham, Perry Barr, 1970; Lewisham W, 1983. MP (Lab): Perry Barr Division of Birmingham, 1966–70; Lewisham W, Feb. 1974–1983; PPS to Secretary of State for Education and Science, 1966–67 and 1975–76; Chm., H of C Select Cttee on Educn, Science and the Arts, 1980–83. Mem., European Parlt, 1977–78. Dir, London Internat. Festival of Theatre Ltd, 1982–86; Pro-Asst Dir, The Polytechnic of the South Bank, 1983–86; Dir, Leeds Poly., 1986–92, Principal, Leeds Metropolitan Univ., 1992–94; Dir, 1991–95, Chm., 1994–95, Statesman & Nation Publishing Co. Ltd. Chm., Council, Nat. Youth Bureau, 1977–80; Member: Council, Inst. for Study of Drug Dependence, 1984–86; Bd, Phoenix House Ltd (Britain's largest gp of drug rehabilitation houses), 1986–87 (Chm., 1980–86); Council, Public Concern at Work, 1994–; Arts Council of England, 1997–98. Co-Chm., Campaign for Freedom of Information, 1990–94; Chair: Yorks and Humberside, then Yorks, Arts, 1997–2000 (Mem. Bd, 1994–2000; Chm., Audit Cttee, 1995–97); LGA Commn on Organisation of Sch. Year, 2000–03. Pres., BEMAS, 1992–94; Member: Delegacy, Univ. of London Goldsmiths' Coll., 1981–86; Court, Polytechnic of Central London, 1982–86; London Centre for Biotechnology Trust, 1984–86; Council, Open Univ., 1996–; Fellow, Internat. Inst. of Biotechnology, 1984. Vis. Sen. Fellow, Office of Public Management, 1994–96; Vis. Fellow, Centre for Policy Studies in Educn, Univ. of Leeds, 1994–97; Vis. Prof., UCE, 1996–. Vice Chm., Cttee for the Reunification of the Parthenon Marbles, 1997–. FRSA 1988. Editor, New Education, 1967–68; Founding Editor, The Stakeholder (Editor, 1997–2000); Educn corresp., New Statesman, 1969–74; Columnist: TES, 1983–85; THES, 1990–92. DUniv Leeds Metropolitan, 1994. *Publications:* (contrib.) A Radical Future, 1967; Crisis in the Classroom, 1968; (ed) Your Child and School, 1968; Which Way?, 1969; (contrib.) Life and Death of the Schools Council, 1985; (contrib.) Police, the Constitution and the Community, 1985. *Address:* 9 Pickwick Road, SE21 7JN.

See also H. M. Jackson.

PRICE, Prof. Christopher Philip, PhD; FRCPath; CChem, FRSC; President, Association for Clinical Biochemistry, 2003–06; *b* 28 Feb. 1945; *s* of Philip Bright Price and Frances Gwendoline Price; *m* 1968, Elizabeth Ann Dix; two *d*. *Educ:* Cirencester Grammar Sch.; Lanchester Poly. (BSc); Univ. of Birmingham (PhD 1973); MA Cantab 1983. CChem 1977; FRSC 1982; FRCPath 1989; Eur. Clinical Chemist 1999; CSci 2005. Basic Grade Clin. Biochemist, Coventry and Warwickshire Hosp., 1967–72; Principal Grade Clin. Biochemist, E Birmingham Hosp., 1972–76; Consultant Clinical Biochemist: Southampton Gen. Hosp., 1976–80; Addenbrooke's Hosp., Cambridge, 1980–88; Prof. of Clin. Biochem., London Hosp. Med. Coll., then QMW, 1988–2001; Dir of Pathol., The Royal Hosps, then Barts and the London, NHS Trust, 1995–2001; Vice-Pres., Outcomes Res., Diagnostics Div., Bayer HealthCare, Tarrytown, NY, 2002–05. Visiting Professor: in Clin. Biochem., Univ. of Oxford, 2002–; in Med. Diagnostics, Cranfield Univ., 2005–. Mem., Ind. Rev. of Pathology Services in England, 2006–08. Fellow, Acad. Clin. Biochem., 2000. Hon. DSc De Montfort, 1998. *Publications:* Centrifugal Analysers in Clinical Chemistry, 1980; Recent Advances in Clinical Biochemistry, Vol. 2, 1981, Vol. 3, 1985; Principles and Practice of Immunoassay, 1991, 2nd edn 1997; Point-of-Care Testing, 1999, 2nd edn 2004; Evidence-Based Laboratory Medicine, 2003, 2nd edn 2007; Point-of-Care Testing for Managers and Policymakers, 2006; Applying Evidence Based Laboratory Medicine: a step-by-step guide, 2008. *Recreations:* walking, concerts, dry stone walling.

PRICE, Sir Curtis (Alexander), KBE 2005; PhD; Principal, Royal Academy of Music, 1995–2008; *b* 7 Sept. 1945; *s* of Dalias Price and Lillian Price (*née* Alexander); adopted British nationality, 2006; *m* 1981, Rhian Samuel; one step *s*. *Educ:* Southern Illinois Univ. (BA 1967); Harvard Univ. (AM 1970; PhD 1974). Washington University, St Louis: Asst Prof., 1974–79; Associate Prof., 1979–82; King's College London: Lectr, 1982–85; Reader in Historical Musicology, 1985–88; King Edward Prof. and Head of Dept of Music, 1988–95; FKC 1994. Guggenheim Fellow, 1982–83. Pres., Royal Musical Assoc., 1999–2002. Hon. RAM 1993; Hon. FRNCM 2001; Hon. FRCM 2002. Einstein Award, Amer. Musicol. Soc., 1979; Dent Medal, Royal Musical Assoc., 1985. *Publications:* Music in the Restoration Theatre, 1979; Henry Purcell and the London Stage, 1984; Dido and Aeneas: a critical score, 1986; The Impresario's Ten Commandments, 1992. *Address:* e-mail: c.price@ram.ac.uk.

PRICE, David; *see* Price, G. D.

PRICE, David; His Honour Judge David Price; a Circuit Judge, since 2004; *b* 27 Sept. 1943; *s* of Bevan Glyn Price and Nora Price; *m* 1971, Jennifer Newton; two *s*. *Educ:* King Edward VI Sch., Stratford upon Avon; Univ. of Leeds (LLB). Called to the Bar, Inner Temple, 1968; in practice on Midland Circuit, 1968–93; a Recorder, 1992–2004. Asst Parly Boundary Comr, 1992; Chairman: Employment Tribunals, 1993–2004; Reinstatement Cttee, Reserve Forces, 1996–2004. *Recreations:* golf, music, theatre. *Address:* Derby Crown Court, The Morledge, Derby DE1 2XE. *T:* (01332) 622600, *Fax:* (01332) 622543; *e-mail:* HHJudgeDavid.Price@judiciary.gsi.gov.uk. *Club:* Market Harborough Golf.

PRICE, Sir David (Ernest Campbell), Kt 1980; DL; *b* 20 Nov. 1924; *o s* of Major Villiers Price; *m* 1960, Rosemary Eugénie Evelyn (*d* 2006), *o d* of late Cyril F. Johnston, OBE; one *d*. *Educ:* Eton; Trinity College, Cambridge; Yale University, USA; Rosebery Schol., Eton; Open History Schol., Trinity College, Cambridge. Served with 1st Battalion Scots Guards, CMF; subsequently Staff Captain (Intelligence) HQ, 56 London Div., Trieste, 1942–46. Trin. Coll., Cambridge, BA Hons, MA. Pres. Cambridge Union; Vice-Pres. Fedn of Univ. Conservative and Unionist Assocs, 1946–48; Henry Fellow of Yale Univ., USA, 1948–49. Industrial Consultant. Held various appts in Imperial Chemical Industries Ltd, 1949–62. MP (C) Eastleigh Div. of Hampshire, 1955–92; Parly Sec., Board of Trade, 1962–64; Opposition Front-Bench spokesman on Science and Technology, 1964–70; Parly Sec., Min. of Technology, June–Oct. 1970; Parly Sec., Min. of Aviation Supply, 1970–71; Parly Under-Sec. of State, Aerospace, DTI, 1971–72. Member: Public Accounts Cttee, 1974–75; Select Cttee on Transport, 1979–83; Select Cttee on Social Services, 1983–90; Select Cttee on Health, 1990–92; Vice-Pres., Parly and Scientific Cttee, 1975–79 and 1982–86 (Vice-Chm., 1965–70, Chm., 1973–75 and 1979–82). Vice-Chm., Cons. Arts and Heritage Cttee, 1979–81 and 1983–87; Chm., Cons. Shipping and Ship-Building Cttee, 1985–91; President: Wessex Area Cons. and Unionist Party, 1986–89 (Life Vice-Pres., 1991); Romsey and Waterside Cons. Assoc., 1993–99; Itchen Test and Avon Cons. Euro-Forum, 1994–99. British Representative to Consultative Assembly of the Council of Europe, 1958–61. Dir, Assoc. British Maltsters, 1966–70. Gen. Cons. to IIM (formerly IWM), 1973–90; Cons. to Union International Ltd, 1974–92; Non-exec. Dir, Southampton Univ. Hosps Trust, 1993–97. Vice-Pres., IIM, 1980–92. President: Wessex Glyndebourne Assoc., 1990–2001; Wessex Rehabilitation Assoc., 1990–2000; Chm., Hants CC Community Care Forum, 1993–96; Trustee: Wessex Medical Trust, 1988–96; Nuffield Theatre, 1990–; Mayflower Theatre, 1990–. Governor, Middlesex Hospital, 1956–60. FCMI. DL Hants, 1982. *Recreations:* swimming, arts and heritage, wine, cooking, gardening. *Address:* Forest Lodge, Moonhills Lane, Beaulieu, Hampshire SO42 7YW. *T:* (01590) 612537. *Clubs:* Beefsteak, Sloane.

PRICE, David William James; investment director and farmer; Chairman, F and C (formerly Foreign and Colonial) Management Ltd, 1999–2004; *b* 11 June 1947; *s* of Richard James Emlyn Price and Miriam Joan Dunsford; *m* 1971, Shervie Ann Lander Whitaker, *d* of Sir James Whitaker, 3rd Bt, OBE; one *s* one *d*. *Educ:* Ampleforth Coll.; Corpus Christi Coll., Oxford (MA). Director: Mercury Asset Management Gp, 1978–97 (Dep. Chm., 1985–97); S. G. Warburg and Co. Ltd, 1982–86; London Bd, Halifax Building Soc., 1993–96; Merrill Lynch European Investment (formerly Mercury Privatisation, then Mercury European Investment) Trust, 1994–2004; Scottish American Investment Co., 1997–; Booker plc, 1998–2000; Big Food Gp, 2000–04; Melchior Japan Investment Trust, 2006–; Chairman: Aberdeen All Asia Investment (formerly Govett Asian Recovery, later Gartmore Asia Pacific) Trust, 1998–; Gartmore Absolute Growth & Income Trust, 2000–04; Iceland Group, 2001–04. Dir, Heritage Trust of Lincs, 1997–; Trustee: Orders of St John Care Trust, 2001–; Schroder Foundn, 2004–. Councillor (C), London Borough of Lambeth, 1979–82. Mem. Council, KCL, 2001–. *Recreations:* history, gardening. *Address:* Harrington Hall, Spilsby, Lincs PE23 4NH. *T:* (01790) 753764. *Clubs:* Brooks's; Lincolnshire.

PRICE, Eric Hardiman Mockford; Proprietor, Energy Economics Consultancy, 1995–99; Director, Robinson Brothers (Ryders Green) Ltd, since 1985; *b* 14 Nov. 1931; *s* of Frederick H. Price and Florence N. H. Price (*née* Mockford); *m* 1963, Diana M. S. Robinson; one *s* three *d*. *Educ:* St Marylebone Grammar Sch.; Christ's Coll., Cambridge. Econs Tripos, 1955; MA 1958. FREconS, 1956; FSS 1958; MInstPet 1992. Army service, 1950–52; HAC, 1952–57. Supply Dept, Esso Petroleum Co. Ltd, 1955–56; Economist: Central Electricity Authority, 1956–57; Electricity Council, 1957–58; British Iron & Steel Fedn, 1958–62; Chief Economist, Port of London Authority, 1962–67; Sen. Econ. Adviser, Min. of Transport, 1966–69; Chief Econ. Adviser, Min. of Transport, 1969–71; Dir of Econs, 1971–75, Under Sec., 1972–76, Dir of Econs and Stats, 1975–76, DoE; Under Sec., Econs and Stats Div., Depts of Industry, Trade and Consumer Protection, 1977–80; Head of Econs and Stats Div., Dept of Energy, 1980–92; Chief Econ. Advr, Dept of Energy, later DTI, 1980–93. Special Consultant, Nat. Econ. Res. Associates, 1993–98. Member: Soc. of Business Economists, 1961; Expert Adv. Gp on Entry into Freight Transport Market, EEC, 1973–75; Northern Regional Strategy Steering Gp, 1976–77; Expert Gp on Venture Capital for Industrial Innovation, EEC, 1978–79; Soc. of Strategic and Long-range Planning, 1980–; Council, Internat. Assoc. of Energy Economists, 1981–85; Energy Panel, SSRC, 1980–83; Council, British Inst. of Energy Economics, 1986–2006 (Mem., 1980–2005; Hon. Fellow, 2006; Vice-Chm., 1981–82 and 1988–89; Chm., 1982–85); Steering Cttee, Jt Energy Programme, RIIA, 1981–89, Steering Cttee, Energy and Envmtl Prog., 1989–; Adv. Council, Energy Econs Centre, Univ. of Surrey, 1989–93. UK rep., Econ. Res. Cttee, European Council of Ministers of Transport, 1968–76; UK rep. on Six Nations' Prog. on Govt Policies towards Technological Innovation in Industry, 1977–80; Mem., World Bank's Groupe des Sages on Econs of Global Warming, 1990–93. Member, Advisory Board: Transport Studies Unit, Oxford Univ., 1973–75; Centre for Res. in Industrial, Business and Admin Studies, Univ. of Warwick, 1977–80. FInstD 1990. *Publications:* various articles in learned jls on transport and industrial economics, energy and energy efficiency, investment, public sector industries, technological innovation in industry, regional planning, environmental abatement policies, and East European energy issues. *Recreations:* tennis, squash, local history, horse racing. *Address:* Batchworth Heath Farm, London Road, Rickmansworth, Herts WD3 1QB. *Clubs:* Moor Park Golf (Hon. Mem.), Batchworth Park Golf; Riverside Health and Leisure (Northwood, Middx).

PRICE, Sir Francis (Caradoc Rose), 7th Bt *cr* 1815; QC (Can.) 1992; barrister and solicitor; *b* 9 Sept. 1950; *s* of Sir Rose Francis Price, 6th Bt and Kathleen June, *d* of late Norman W. Hutchinson, Melbourne; *S* father, 1979; *m* 1975, Marguerite Jean Trussler, retired Justice, Court of Queen's Bench, Alberta, *d* of late Roy S. Trussler, Victoria, BC; three *d*. *Educ:* Eton; Trinity College, Melbourne Univ. (Sen. Student 1971–72, LLB Hons 1973); Univ. of Alberta (LLM 1975); Canadian Petroleum Law Foundn Fellow, 1974–75. Admitted barrister and solicitor, Province of Alberta 1976, Northwest Territories 1978, Canada; Bencher, Law Soc. of Alberta, 1990–94. Lectr, 1979–89, and Course Head, 1983–89, Alberta Bar Admission Course. Chartered Arbitrator, Arbitration and Mediation Inst. of Canada, 1994. CLJ 2000. *Publications:* Pipelines in Western Canada, 1975; Mortgage Actions in Alberta, 1985; Conducting a Foreclosure Action, 1996; contribs to Alberta and Melbourne Univ. Law Revs, etc. *Recreations:* opera, cricket, theatre. *Heir: b* Norman William Rose Price [*b* 17 March 1953; *m* 1987, Charlotte Louise, *yr d* of late R. R. B. Baker]. *Address:* 9626 95th Avenue, Edmonton, AB T6C 2A4, Canada. *Club:* Faculty (Edmonton).

PRICE, Sir Frank (Leslie), Kt 1966; Chairman, Price-Brown Partnership (formerly Sir Frank Price Associates), 1985–2006; *b* 26 July 1922; *s* of G. F. Price; marr. diss.; one *s*; *m* Daphne Ling. *Educ:* St Matthias Church Sch., Birmingham; Vittoria Street Arts Sch. FRICS (FSVA 1960); FCIT 1969. Dir, 1958–68, Man. Dir, 1965–68, Murrayfield Real Estate Co.; Chairman: Birmingham Midland Investments, 1967–74; Alexander Stevens Real Estate, 1968–80; Wharf Holdings, 1968–72; Beagle Shipping, 1968–72; Butlers & Colonial Wharfs, 1971–76. Elected to Birmingham City Council, 1949; Alderman, 1958–74; Lord Mayor, 1964–65. Member: Council, Town and Country Planning Assoc., 1958–74; W Midlands Economic Planning Council, 1965–72; Nat. Water Council, 1975–79; Chm., British Waterways Bd, 1968–84. Founder/Chm., Midlands Art Centre for Young People, 1960–71; Chairman: W Midlands Sports Council, 1965–69; Telford Development Corporation, 1968–71; Comprehensive Develt Assoc., 1968–80; Dir, National Exhibn Centre, 1968–74. Member: Minister of Transport's Cttee of Inquiry into Major Ports, 1961; English Tourist Board, 1976–83; President: BAIE, 1979–83; Mojacar Assoc. of Commerce, 1994–. Mem., Fédn Internat. des Professions Immobilières. DL: Warwicks, 1970–77; West Midlands, 1974–77; Herefordshire and Worcestershire, 1977–84. Freeman, City of London; Liveryman, Basketmakers' Co., 1966–. Hon. Citizen, New Orleans, 1980. *Publications:* Being There (autobiog.), 2002; various pamphlets and articles on town planning, transport and public affairs. *Recreations:* painting, cruising. *Address:* Casa Noel, 42 Los Gallardos, Almeria 04630, Spain. *Club:* Reform.

PRICE, Gareth; broadcast management consultant, since 2005; *b* 30 Aug. 1939; *s* of Rowena and Morgan Price; *m* 1962, Mari Griffiths; two *s* one *d*. *Educ:* Aberaeron Grammar School and Ardwyn Grammar School, Aberystwyth; University College of Wales, Aberystwyth (BA Econ). Asst Lectr in Economics, Queen's Univ., Belfast, 1962–64; BBC Wales: Radio Producer, Current Affairs, 1964–66; Television Producer, Features and Documentaries, 1966–74; Dep. Head of Programmes, 1974–81; Head of Programmes, 1981–85; Controller, 1986–90; Thomson Foundation: Controller of Broadcasting, 1990–93; Dir, 1993–2005. Chm., Welsh Centre for Internat. Affairs, 2003–. Consultant, Asian Inst. for Broadcast Develt, 2005–. Vice-Chm., Communication and Inf. Cttee, UNESCO UK, 2006–. Hon. Sec., Elizabeth R. Fund, 2006–. Hon. Prof. of Communication, Univ. of Wales, Cardiff, 1994–99; Hon. Fellow, Univ. of Wales, Aberystwyth, 2000–. Elizabeth R Lifetime Achievement Award for Promoting Public Broadcasting, Commonwealth Broadcasting Assoc., 2006. *Publications:* David Lloyd George (with Emyr Price and Bryn Parry), 1981; Broadcast Management for Asians, 2006. *Address:* 98 Pencisely Road, Cardiff CF5 1DQ.

PRICE, Geoffrey Alan; DL; Chairman, Herefordshire Community Health Trust, 1997–2000. Local Govt finance posts in Glos CC, Cheshire CC, Southend-on-Sea and W Sussex CC, 1952–70; Dep. Co. Treas., 1970–76, Co. Treas., 1976–83, Hants CC; Chief Exec., 1983–93, Co. Treas., 1988–93, Hereford and Worcester CC; Clerk: to Lord Lieutenant, Hereford and Worcester, 1983–93; to West Mercia Police Authority, 1983–93; non-exec. Dir, Herefordshire HA, 1993–97. DL Hereford and Worcester, 1993.

PRICE, Prof. (Geoffrey) David, PhD; FGS; Professor of Mineral Physics, since 2006, and Vice Provost (Research), since 2007, University College London; *b* 12 Jan. 1956; *s* of Prof. Neville J. Price and Joan J. Price; *m* 1978, Prof. Sarah L. Price (*née* Millar); one *s* one *d*. *Educ:* Latymer Upper Sch.; Clare Coll., Cambridge (MA; PhD 1980). Royal Soc. Res. Fellow, 1983–88; Reader in Mineral Physics, 1988–91, Prof. of Mineral Physics, 1991–2006, UCL and Birkbeck Coll., London Univ.; Hd, Dept of Earth Scis, 1992–2002 and 2004–05, Vice Dean (Res.), 2003–06, Exec. Dean, 2006–07, Math. and Physical Scis, UCL. Ed., Earth and Planetary Sci. Letters, 2005–07. Pres., Mineralogical Soc. of GB, 2004–06 (Mem., 1977–; Schlumberger Medal, 1999); FGS 1992 (Murchison Medal, 2002); FMSA 1997; Fellow, Amer. Geophysical Union, 2005. MAE 2000. Louis Néel Medal, Eur. Geoscis Union, 2006. *Publications:* numerous papers in learned jls on mineralogy and geophysics. *Recreation:* philately. *Address:* Office of Vice Provost (Research), University College London, Gower Street, WC1E 6BT. *T:* (020) 7679 7083; *e-mail:* d.price@ucl.ac.uk.

PRICE, Rt Hon. George (Cadle), OCC 2001; PC 1982; Senior Minister, 1998–2003, and former Minister of Defence and National Emergency Management, Belize; *b* 15 Jan. 1919; *s* of William Cadle Price and Irene Cecilia Escalante de Price. *Educ:* Holy Redeemer Primary Sch., Belize City; St John's Coll., Belize City. Private Sec. to late Robert S. Turton; entered politics, 1944; City Councillor, 1947–65 (Mayor of Belize City several times); founding Mem., People's United Party, 1950; Party Sec., 1950–56; Leader, 1956–96; Mem., National Assembly, subseq. House of Reps, 1954–84, 1989–2003; under 1961 Ministerial System, led People's United Party to 100% victory at polls and became First Minister; under 1964 Self-Govt Constitution, title changed to Premier; Premier, 1964 until Independence, 1981; Prime Minister of Belize, 1981–84 and 1989–93; Leader of the Opposition, 1993, then Leader Emeritus, People's United Party. Has led delegns to Central American and Caribbean countries; spearheaded internationalization of Belize problem at internat. forums; addressed UN's Fourth Cttee, 1975, paving way for overwhelming victory at UN when majority of nations voted in favour of Belize's right to self-determination and territorial integrity. *Address:* c/o House of Representatives, Belmopan, Belize.

PRICE, Geraint; *see* Price, W. G.

PRICE, Gerald Alexander Lewin; QC 1992; His Honour Judge Gerald Price; a Circuit Judge, since 2000; *b* 13 Sept. 1948; *s* of Denis Lewin Price and Patricia Rosemary (*née* Metcalfe); *m* 1974, Theresa Elisabeth Iremonger-Watts; two *s*. *Educ:* Haileybury Coll.; College of Law; Inns of Court Law Sch. Called to the Bar, Middle Temple, 1969; in private practice, Cardiff, 1970–77; Bermuda: Resident Stipendiary Magistrate, 1977–81; Chief Stipendiary Magistrate and Sen. Coroner, 1981–84; in private practice, Cardiff, 1984–2000; a Recorder, 1990–2000. Chairman: Liquor Licence Authority, Land Valuation Appeals Tribunal, Price Control Commn and Jury Revising Tribunal, 1981–84. Mem., Commonwealth Magistrates and Judges Assoc., 1984–. Mem., RYA. *Recreations:* travel, classical music, sunshine, motorboating in Menorca. *Clubs:* Royal Commonwealth Society; Glamorgan Lawn Tennis and Croquet (Merthyr Mawr); Menorca Cricket.

PRICE, Isobel Clare M.; *see* McKenzie-Price.

PRICE, Sir James Keith Peter Rugge-, 10th Bt *cr* 1804, of Spring Grove, Richmond, Surrey; *b* 8 April 1967; *er s* of Sir Keith Rugge-Price, 9th Bt and of Jacqueline Mary Rugge-Price (*née* Loranger); *S* father, 2000. *Heir: b* Andrew Philip Richard Rugge-Price, *b* 6 Jan. 1970.

PRICE, James Richard Kenrick; QC 1995; *b* 14 Sept. 1948; *s* of Lt-Col Kenrick Jack Price, DSO, MC, 9th Lancers and Juliet Hermione, *d* of Marshal of the Royal Air Force Sir John Cotesworth Slessor, GCB, DSO, MC; *m* 1983, Hon. Virginia Yvonne, *d* of 5th Baron Mostyn, MC. *Educ:* Eton College; St Edmund Hall, Oxford. Called to the Bar, Inner Temple, 1974. Dir, Mostyn Estates Ltd, 1994–. *Recreations:* fine and decorative arts,

gardening, mountains, ski-ing, Corfu. *Address:* 5 Raymond Buildings, Gray's Inn, WC1R 5BP. *T:* (020) 7242 2902. *Clubs:* Brooks's, Beefsteak.

PRICE, John Alan; QC 1980; a Recorder of the Crown Court, since 1980; a Deputy Circuit Judge, since 1975; *b* 11 Sept. 1938; *s* of Frederick Leslie Price and Gertrude Davilda Alice Price; *m* 1964, Elizabeth Myra (*née* Priest) (marr. diss. 1982); one *s* one *d*; *m* 1984, Alison Elizabeth Curran (*née* Ward); two step *d*. *Educ:* Stretford Grammar Sch.; Manchester Univ. (LLB Hons 1959). Called to the Bar, Gray's Inn, 1961; in practice on Northern Circuit; Head of 60 King St Chambers, Manchester, 1978–80. *Recreations:* tennis, golf. *Club:* Wilmslow Golf.

PRICE, John Charles; His Honour Judge John Price; a Circuit Judge, since 2003; *b* 8 March 1945; *s* of Hubert and Betty Price. *Educ:* Wrekin Coll., Wellington, Shropshire; The Hill Sch., Pottstown, Pa, USA; Univ. of Birmingham (LLB Hons). Called to the Bar, Gray's Inn, 1969; in practice, 1969–2003; a Recorder of the Crown Court, 1990–2003. *Recreations:* tennis, sailing, ski-ing, maintaining friendships. *Address:* c/o Ministry of Justice, Selborne House, 54–60 Victoria Street, SW1E 6QW.

PRICE, Prof. John Frederick, MD; FRCP, FRCPCH; Consultant Paediatrician, King's College Hospital, since 1978; Professor of Paediatric Respiratory Medicine, University of London, since 1992; Clinical Director of Paediatrics, King's NHS Healthcare Trust, 1993–96 and since 1999; *b* 26 April 1944; *s* of Drs Cyril Frederick Price and Dora Elizabeth Price; *m* 1971, Dr Valerie Pickup; two *d*. *Educ:* Dulwich Coll.; St John's Coll., Cambridge (MB BCh; MA; MD 1986); Guy's Hosp., London. DCH 1973; FRCP 1985; FRCPCH 1997. MRC Trng Fellowship, Inst. of Child Health and Gt Ormond St Hosp., 1975–78; Hd, Acad. Dept of Child Health, 1995–98, and Chm., Div. of Child Health and Reproductive Medicine, 1995–98, GKT Med. and Dental Sch., KCL (formerly King's Coll. Sch. of Medicine and Dentistry), Univ. of London. Vis. Prof. and Ext. Examr, Hong Kong Univ. and Univ. of Malaya, 1997. Altounyan Address, Brit. Thoracic Soc., 1989; C. Elaine Field Lecture, Hong Kong Paediatric Soc., 1997, 2000. Sec., Paediatric Section, Royal Soc. Medicine, 1988–90; Chm., Brit. Paediatric Respiratory Soc., 1992–94; Council Member: Brit. Thoracic Soc., 1990–; European Respiratory Soc., 1990–95. Chm., Nat. Asthma Campaign, subseq. Asthma UK, 2003– (Trustee, 1990–); Trustee, Brit. Lung Foundn, 1990–95; Member: Med. Adv. Panel, Nat. Eczema Soc., 1987–91; Res. and Med. Adv. Cttee, Cystic Fibrosis Trust, 1993–. Associate Editor: Respiratory Medicine, 1987–93; European Respiratory Jl, 1990–93. *Publications:* (with J. Rees) ABC of Asthma, 1984, 3rd edn 1995; contrib. chapters in books; numerous articles in learned jls related to respiratory disease in childhood. *Recreations:* theatre, music, Austen, Trollope, conversations with family and friends. *Address:* Department of Child Health, Guy's, King's and St Thomas' School of Medicine, Bessemer Road, SE5 9PJ. *T:* (020) 3299 3215. *Club:* Hawks (Cambridge).

PRICE, Air Vice-Marshal John Walter, CBE 1979 (OBE 1973); UK Manager, Courage Energy Corporation (UK Manager, Altaquest Energy Corporation, 1997); *b* Birmingham, 26 Jan. 1930; *s* of late Henry Walter Price, MM, and Myrza Price (*née* Griffiths); *m* 1st, 1956, Margaret Sinclair McIntyre (*d* 1989), Sydney, Aust.; 2nd, 2004, Ilse Gertrud Burrows (*née* Koepke). *Educ:* Solihull Sch.; RAF Coll., Cranwell. Joined RAF, 1948; commnd 1950; Adjutant, No 11 (Vampire) Sqn, 1950–52; No 77 (Meteor) Sqn, RAAF, Korea, 1952–53 (mentioned in despatches, 1953); No 98 Sqn (Venoms and Vampires), 1953–54; No 2 (F) Op. Trng Unit (Vampires) and No 75 (F) Sqn (Meteors), RAAF, 1954–56; Cadet Wing Adjutant, RAF Tech. Coll., Henlow, 1956–60; RAF Staff Coll., 1960; Air Ministry (Ops Overseas), 1961–64; Comd No 110 Sqn (Sycamore and Whirlwind), 1964–66; Directing Staff, RAF Staff Coll., 1966–68; PSO to Chief of Air Staff, 1968–70; Comd No 72 (Wessex) Sqn, 1970–72; student, Coll. of Air Warfare, 1972; Dep. Dir Ops (Offensive Support and Jt Warfare), MoD (Air), 1973–75; sowc 1975–76; Comd RAF Laarbruch, 1976–78; Gp Capt. Ops, HQ Strike Comd, 1979; Dir of Ops (Strike), MoD (Air), 1980–82; ACAS (Ops), 1982–84, retd. Clyde Petroleum plc, 1984–95 (Manager, External Affairs and Exploration Admin, 1986–95). MRAeS 1971; CCMI (FBIM 1979, CIMgt 1997; Mem. Council, 1994–2000); MEI. Gov., Solihull Sch., 1979–2005 (Chm., 1983–2005). Freeman, City of London, 2001; Liveryman, Co. of Fuellers, 2001– (Mem. Court, 2003–; Jun. Warden, 2005). DL Hereford and Worcester, 1995–2005. *Recreations:* enjoying company of my wife and my friends, travel. *Address:* 2 Palace Yard, Hereford HR4 9BJ. *Clubs:* Army and Navy, Royal Air Force.

PRICE, Leolin; *see* Price, A. L.

PRICE, Leontyne; Opera Prima Donna (Soprano), United States; *b* 10 Feb. 1927. *Educ:* Public Schools, Laurel, Mississippi; Central State College, Wilberforce, Ohio (BA); Juilliard Sch. of Music, NY. Four Saints, 1952; Porgy and Bess, 1952–54. Operatic Debut on TV, 1955, as Tosca; Concerts in America, England, Australia, Europe. Operatic debut as Madame Lidouine in Dialogues of Carmelites, San Francisco, 1957; Covent Garden, Verona Arena, Vienna Staatsoper, 1958; five roles, inc. Leonora in Il Trovatore, Madame Butterfly, Donna Anna in Don Giovanni, Metropolitan, 1960–61; Salzburg debut singing soprano lead in Missa Solemnis, 1959; Aida in Aida, Liu in Turandot, La Scala, 1960; opened season at Metropolitan in 1961 as Minnie in Fanciulla del West; opened new Metropolitan Opera House, 1966, as Cleopatra in world premiere of Samuel Barber's Antony and Cleopatra; debut Teatre Dell'Opera, Rome, in Aida, 1967; debut Paris Opera, in Aida, 1968; debut Teatro Colon, Buenos Aires, as Leonora in Il Trovatore, 1969; opened season at Metropolitan Opera, in Aida, 1969. Numerous recordings. Vice-Chm., Nat. Inst. for Music Theatre. Member: Metropolitan Opera Assoc.; Bd of Dirs, Dance Theatre of Harlem; Bd of Trustees, NY Univ. Life Mem., NAACP. Fellow, Amer. Acad. of Arts and Sciences. Hon. Dr of Music: Howard Univ., Washington, DC, 1962; Central State Coll., Wilberforce, Ohio, 1968; Hon. DHL, Dartmouth Univ., 1962; Hon. Dr of Humanities, Rust Coll., Holly Springs, Miss, 1968; Hon. Dr of Humane Letters, Fordham Univ., New York, 1969. Hon. Mem. Bd of Dirs, Campfire Girls, 1966. Presidential Medal of Freedom, 1965; Spingarn Medal, NAACP, 1965; Nat. Medal of Arts, 1985; 18 Grammy Awards, Nat. Acad. Recording Arts and Scis. Order of Merit (Italy), 1966; Commandeur, Ordre des Arts et des Lettres (France), 1986. *Recreations:* cooking, dancing, shopping for clothes, etc, antiques for homes in Rome and New York.

PRICE, Dame Margaret (Berenice), DBE 1993 (CBE 1982); opera singer, retired 1999; formerly with Bayerische Staatsoper München; *b* Tredegar, Wales, 13 April 1941; *d* of late Thomas Glyn Price and of Lilian Myfanwy Richards. *Educ:* Pontllanfraith Secondary Sch.; Trinity Coll. of Music, London. Debut as Cherubino in Marriage of Figaro, Welsh Nat. Opera Co., 1962; debut, in same rôle, at Royal Opera House, Covent Garden, 1963; has subseq. sung many principal rôles at Glyndebourne, San Francisco Opera Co., Cologne Opera House, Munich State Opera, Hamburg State Opera, Vienna State Opera, Lyric Opera, Chicago, Paris Opera; La Scala, Milan; Metropolitan Opera House, NY. Major rôles include: Countess in Marriage of Figaro; Pamina in The Magic Flute; Fiordiligi in Così Fan Tutte; Donna Anna in Don Giovanni; Konstanze in Die Entführung; Amelia in Simone Boccanegra; Agathe in Freischütz; Desdemona in Otello; Elisabetta in Don Carlo; Amelia in Un Ballo In Maschera; title rôles in Aida, Norma and Ariadne auf Naxos. BBC recitals and concerts, also TV appearances. Has made recordings. Hon. FTCL; Hon. DMus

Wales, 1983. Elisabeth Schumann Prize for Lieder; Ricordi Prize for Opera; Silver Medal, Worshipful Co. of Musicians; Bayerische Kammersängerin. *Recreations:* cooking, driving, reading, walking, swimming. *Address:* c/o Stefan Hahn, Artist Management HRA, Tal 28, 80331 München, Germany.

PRICE, Mark Ian; Managing Director, Waitrose Ltd, since 2007; *b* 2 March 1961; *s* of Graham and Marjorie Price; *m* 1991, Judith Caroline Bolt; two *d. Educ:* Lanacster Univ. (BA Archaeol.). Managing Director: John Lewis, High Wycombe, 1992–95; John Lewis, Cheadle, 1995–98; Mktg Dir, 1998–2000, Dir of Selling and Mktg, 2000–05, Waitrose Ltd; Man. Dir, Partnership Develt, John Lewis, and Dir, John Lewis Partnership, 2005–07. Chm., On-Line Galls, 2007–. *Publication:* The Great British Picnic Guide, 2008. *Recreations:* picnics, gardening, shooting, fishing, golf. *Address:* Waitrose Ltd, Doncastle Road, Bracknell RG12 8YA. *T:* (01344) 824286, *Fax:* (01344) 824488; *e-mail:* Mark_Price@waitrose.co.uk.

PRICE, Michael Anthony, LVO 1991; HM Diplomatic Service, retired; High Commissioner, Fiji, 2000–02, also (non-resident) to Kiribati, Tuvalu and Nauru; *b* 13 Aug. 1944; *s* of Francis George and Lena Beatrice Price; *m* 1968, Elizabeth Anne Cook; one *s* one *d. Educ:* Forest Grammar Sch. Bd of Trade, 1964; Diplomatic Service, 1966–; served New Delhi, Freetown, Paris, Montreal; JSDC, 1983–84; Dep. Head of News Dept, FCO, 1984; First Sec. (Press and Public Affairs), Washington, 1988; Counsellor and HM Consul-Gen., Tokyo, 1992; on loan to No 10 Downing St, 1994–95; Counsellor, Paris, 1995–2000. *Recreations:* cricket, Gilbert and Sullivan, cooking. *Address:* Kasauli, Church Field, Monks Eleigh, Suffolk IP7 7JH.

PRICE, Nicholas Peter Lees; QC 1992; **His Honour Judge Nicholas Price;** a Circuit Judge, since 2006; *b* 29 Sept. 1944; *s* of Frank Henry Edmund Price, MBE (mil.) and Agnes Lees Price; *m* 1969, Wilma Ann Alison (*née* Steel); one *s* one *d. Educ:* Prince of Wales Sch., Nairobi; Edinburgh Univ. (LLB). Called to the Bar, Gray's Inn, 1968, Bencher, 2000; *ad eundem* Mem., Middle Temple; Asst Recorder, 1983–87; a Recorder, 1987–2006. Member: Gen. Council of the Bar, 1993–95 (Jt Vice Chm., Legal Services Cttee, 1994; Vice Chm., Public Affairs Cttee, 1995; Professional Standards Cttee, 2002–05; Vice Chm., Professional Conduct & Complaints Cttee, 2005–06); Gray's Inn Continuing Educn Cttee, 1998–2003 (Vice Chm., 1999–2000; Chm., 2001–03); Associate Mem., Criminal Bar Assoc., 1993–95. *Recreations:* watching Rugby, crosswords, destructive gardening, cinema. *Address:* Kingston-upon-Thames Crown Court, 6–8 Penrhyn Road, Kingston-upon-Thames, Surrey KT1 2BB.

PRICE, Nick; golfer; *b* Durban, 28 Jan. 1957; *m* Sue Price; one *s* two *d.* Wins include: US PGA, 1992, 1994; Open, Turnberry, 1994; Vardon Trophy, 1993; record for PGA Tournament lowest score (269), 1994. *Publication:* The Swing, 1997. *Address:* c/o Professional Golfers' Association Tour, 112 PGA Tour Boulevard, Ponte Vedra Beach, FL 32082, USA.

PRICE, Nigel Stewart; Master of the Supreme Court, Chancery Division, since 1999; *b* 18 May 1954; *s* of late Ernest Henry Price and Diana Price (*née* Lane). *Educ:* Billesley Infant and Jun. Schs; Moseley Grammar Sch., Birmingham; Christ's Coll., Cambridge (MA); Coll. of Law; City of Birmingham Poly. Admitted solicitor, 1978; articled clerk and Asst Solicitor, Clifford Turner, 1976–80; Asst Solicitor, Pinsent & Co., 1980–82; Lectr in Law, Univ. of Buckingham, 1983–86; Partner, Kimbell & Co., 1986–99; Dep. Master, Chancery Div., 1992–99; Immigration Adjudicator, 1996–98. *Publications:* contribs to legal jls. *Recreations:* languages, music, literature, ski-ing, dog walking. *Address:* Thomas More Building, Royal Courts of Justice, Strand, WC2A 2LL.

PRICE, Pamela Joan V.; *see* Vandyke Price.

PRICE, Rt Rev. Peter Bryan; *see* Bath and Wells, Bishop of.

PRICE, Peter Nicholas; European Strategy Counsel, since 1994; *b* 19 Feb. 1942; *s* of Rev. Dewi Emlyn Price and Kate Mary Price; *m* 1988, Joy Bhola; one *d. Educ:* Worcester Royal Grammar Sch.; Aberdare Boys' Grammar Sch.; Univ. of Southampton (BA (Law)); Coll. of Law, Guildford; KCL (Postgrad. Dip. in EC Law). Solicitor. Interviewer and current affairs freelance broadcaster, 1962–67; Asst Solicitor, Glamorgan CC, 1967–68; solicitor in private practice, 1966–67 and 1968–85; part-time EC consultant: Payne Hicks Beach, 1990–93; Howard Kennedy, 1993–2001; Standing Orders Comr, Nat. Assembly for Wales, 1998–99; pt-time Chm., Employment Tribunal, Cardiff, 2000–. Contested (C) Gen. Elecs: Aberdare 1964, 1966; Caerphilly 1970; Nat. Vice-Chm., Young Conservatives, 1971–72; Mem., Nat. Union Exec. Cttee, 1969–72 and 1978–79; Vice-Chm., Cons. Pol. Centre Nat. Cttee, 1978–79; Hon. Sec., For. Affairs Forum, 1977–79; Vice-Chm., Cons. Gp for Europe, 1979–81; Mem. Council, Europ. Movement, 1971–81. MEP (C): Lancashire W, 1979–84; London SE, 1984–94; Hon. MEP, 1994; European Parliament: Chm., Budgetary Control Cttee, 1989–92 (Vice-Chm., 1979–84, and its Rapporteur for series of 4 major reports on Community finances, 1985–86); spokesman for EDG, Legal Affairs Cttee, 1984–87, Budgets Cttee, 1986–89; Member: ACP/EEC Jt Assembly, 1981–94; Ext. Econ. Relns Cttee, 1992–94; delgns for relns with Japan, 1989–92, US Congress, 1992–94. Member: Lib Dem Federal Policy Cttee, 1998–; European Lib Dem. and Reformist (Party) Council, 1999–; Lib Dem Federal Finance Cttee, 2001–06. Contested (Lib Dem) Wales, EP elecn, 1999. Mem., Commn on Powers of Nat. Assembly for Wales, 2002–04. Non-executive Director: Bureau Veritas Quality Internat. Ltd, 1991–2001; Ravensbourne NHS Trust, 1998–99; Welsh Ambulance Services NHS Trust, 2005–. Mem., NEC, FPA, 1973–77 (Mem., then Chm., Long-term Planning Gp, 1973–76). Fellow, Industry and Parlt Trust, 1981–82; Vice-Pres., UK Cttee, Europ. Year of Small and Med.-sized Enterprises, 1983. Mem., RIIA. Vice-Pres., Llangollen Internat. Eisteddfod, 1981–. Governor, Thames Valley Univ., 1996–2005. *Publications:* misc. pol. pamplets and newspaper articles. *Recreations:* theatre, music, photography. *Address:* 37 Heol St Denys, Lisvane, Cardiff CF14 0RU. *T:* (029) 2076 1792; 60 Marlings Park Avenue, Chislehurst, Kent BR7 6RD. *T:* (01689) 820681; *e-mail:* peterprice@btinternet.com.

PRICE, Rev. Peter Owen, CBE 1983; BA; FPhS; RN retired; Minister of Blantyre Old Parish Church, Glasgow, 1985–96; *b* Swansea, 18 April 1930; *e s* of late Idwal Price and Florence Price; *m* 1957, Margaret Trevan (*d* 1977); three *d*; *m* 1996, Mary Hamill Robertson. *Educ:* Hutcheson's Grammar Sch., Glasgow; King Edward's Grammar Sch., Camp Hill, Birmingham; Wyggeston Sch., Leicester; Didsbury Theol Coll., Bristol. BA Open Univ. Ordained, 1960, Methodist Minister, Birmingham; commnd RN as Chaplain, 1960; served: HMS Collingwood, 1960; HQ 3 Cdo Bde, RM, 1962–64; Staff of C-in-C Med., 1964–68; RNAS Brawdy, 1968–69; HQ 3 Cdo Bde, 1969–70, HQ Cdo Forces, 1970–73, RM; HMS Raleigh, 1973; HMS Drake, 1974–78; BRNC Dartmouth, 1978–80; Principal Chaplain, Church of Scotland and Free Churches (Naval), MoD, 1981–84. Hon. Chaplain to the Queen, 1981–84. *Recreations:* freemasonry (Past Grand Chaplain, Grand Lodge of Scotland), warm water sailing, music, golf. *Address:* Duncraigan, 22 Old Bothwell Road, Bothwell, Glasgow G71 8AW.

PRICE, His Honour Philip John; QC 1989; a Circuit Judge, 1993–2008; *b* 16 May 1943; *s* of Ernest and Eunice Price; *m* 1967, Mari Josephine Davies; one *s* two *d. Educ:* Cardiff High Sch.; Pembroke Coll., Oxford (MA). Lectr in Law, Univ. of Leeds, 1966–70; called to the Bar, Gray's Inn, 1969; in practice on Wales and Chester Circuit and Temple, 1971–93; a Recorder, 1985–93. Chancellor, Dio. Monmouth, 1992–; Pres., Disciplinary Tribunal, Church in Wales, 2001–05. Member: Mental Health Rev. Tribunal, 1995–; Cttee, Council of Circuit Judges, 1998–2007 (Sen. Vice Pres., 2007). Mem., 1993–, Chm., Standing Cttee, 2005–, Governing Body, Church in Wales. Trustee, LATCH-Welsh Children's Cancer Charity, 1996– (Chm., 2006–). *Recreations:* architecture, books, cricket. *Address:* HMCS Wales, Churchill House, Churchill Way, Cardiff CF10 2HH. *Club:* Cardiff and County.

PRICE, Richard Alexander David; Chief Economist, since 2005, and Director of Corporate Performance, since 2008, Department for Environment, Food and Rural Affairs; *b* 18 Aug. 1967; *s* of Prof. Roger David Price and Heather Lynne Price; *m* 1999, Dr Luisa Affuso; one *s. Educ:* Hewett Sch., Norwich; Univ. of York (BA Econs 1987, MSc Econs 1989). Economist, HM Treasury, 1989–93; Nat. Econ. Res. Associates, 1993–97; Home and Legal Team, HM Treasury, 1997–99; Chief Economist, Home Office, 1999–2001; Performance and Innovation Unit, Cabinet Office, 2001; Strategy Advr to the Permanent Sec., Home Office, 2001–02; Hd of Enterprise Policy, HM Treasury, 2002–05. Non-exec. Dir, ETC Venues Ltd, 2005–06; alternate non-exec. Dir, Capital for Enterprise Bd, 2005. FRSA. *Publications:* various policy and res. papers and articles on econ. regulation, entrepreneurship, migration, crime reduction, envmtl econs and globalisation. *Recreations:* modern and contemporary art, exploring Italy, food. *Address:* Department for Environment, Food and Rural Affairs, 17 Smith Square, SW1P 3JR. *T:* (020) 7238 6900; *e-mail:* richard.price@defra.gsi.gov.uk.

PRICE, Richard Mervyn, OBE 1995; QC 1996; a Recorder, since 2004; *b* 15 May 1948; *s* of late William James Price and Josephine May Price; *m* 1971, Caroline Sarah (marr. diss. 2007), *d* of Geoffrey and Mary Ball; one *s* two *d. Educ:* King Edward VII Sch., Sheffield; King's Coll., London (LLB Hons). Called to the Bar, Gray's Inn, 1969, Bencher, 2002; Accredited Mediator, 1997. Standing Counsel on Election Law to Conservative Central Office, 1986–. Mem., Bar Council, 1998–2002 (Vice-Chm., 2002–04, Chm., 2005, Professional Conduct and Complaints Cttee); Mem., Bar Standards Bd, 2006–07 (Chm., Conduct Cttee, 2006–07). Legal Assessor to Disciplinary Cttee, RCVS, 2007–. *Publication:* (ed) Parker's Law and Conduct of Elections, 2003–; (cons. ed.) Halsbury's Laws of England, Elections and Referendums, 4th edn 2007 re-issue. *Recreations:* politics, theatre, films, music, walking, cycling. *Address:* Littleton Chambers, 3 King's Bench Walk North, Temple, EC4Y 7HR. *T:* (020) 7797 8600; Park Court Chambers, 16 Park Place, Leeds LS1 2SJ. *T:* (0113) 243 3277. *Clubs:* Garrick, Royal Automobile, St Stephen's.

PRICE, Richard Neville Meredith; His Honour Judge Richard Price; a Circuit Judge, since 1996; Resident Judge, Portsmouth and Newport Crown Courts, since 2004; *b* 30 May 1945; *s* of Christopher Llewelyn Price and Valerie Ruby Price (*née* Greenham); *m* 1971, Avril Judith Lancaster; three *s. Educ:* Marsh Court, Stockbridge, Hants; Sutton Valence, Kent. Admitted solicitor, 1970; Asst Recorder, 1985–90; called to the Bar, Middle Temple, 1990; Recorder, 1990–96; Hon. Recorder, City of Portsmouth, 2006–. *Recreations:* choral singing, sailing, reading, listening to music. *Address:* Portsmouth Combined Court Centre, Courts of Justice, Winston Churchill Avenue, Portsmouth, Hants PO1 2DL. *Clubs:* Royal London Yacht; Seaview Yacht (IoW).

PRICE, Air Vice-Marshal Robert George, CB 1983; *b* 18 July 1928; *s* of Charles and Agnes Price, Hale, Cheshire; *m* 1st, 1958, Celia Anne Mary Talamo (*d* 1987); one *s* four *d*; 2nd, 1989, Edith Barbara Dye. *Educ:* Oundle Sch.; RAF Coll., Cranwell. 74 Sqn, 1950; Central Flying Sch., 1952; 60 Sqn, 1956; Guided Weapons Trials Sqn, 1958; Staff Coll., 1960; Bomber Comd, 1961; JSSC 1964; CO 31 Sqn, 1965; PSO to Dep. SACEUR, 1968; CO RAF Linton-on-Ouse, 1970; RCDS 1973; Dep. Dir Operations, 1974; Group Captain Flying Trng, Support Comd, 1978; Dep. Chief of Staff, Support HQ, 2nd Allied Tactical Air Force, 1979; AOA, RAF Germany, 1980; AOA, HQ Strike Comd, 1981–83. *Recreations:* golf, ski-ing, bridge. *Club:* Royal Air Force.

PRICE, Sir Robert (John) G.; *see* Green-Price.

PRICE, Sarah Helena; HM Diplomatic Service; Head, Drugs and International Crime Department, Foreign and Commonwealth Office, since 2008; *b* 4 June 1966; *d* of John Michael Anthony Price and Mary Price; *m* 2006, Simon McGrath. *Educ:* Holy Child Sch., Edgbaston; Somerville Coll., Oxford (BA Hons Classics and Mod. Langs 1989). Joined FCO, 1990: Third Sec., FCO, 1990–92; Second Secretary: UK Delegn to CSCE, Helsinki, 1992; Prague, 1993–96; First Sec., FCO, 1996–99; on secondment to Finnish Foreign Ministry, 1999–2000; Dep. Hd of Mission, Belgrade, 2000–04; Dep. Hd, Counter-Proliferation Dept, FCO, 2004–07. *Address:* c/o Foreign and Commonwealth Office, King Charles Street, SW1A 2AH.

PRICE, Terence; *see* Price, B. T.

PRICE, Tristan Robert Julian; Group Finance Controller, M. P. Evans Group PLC, since 2006; *b* 24 Nov. 1966; *s* of Julian Price and Isolde (*née* Buchloh); *m* 1988, Judith Ann Torrance; three *s* one *d. Educ:* Tonbridge Sch.; Corpus Christi Coll., Cambridge (BA Hons Econs 1988); University Coll. London (MSc Econs 1993). FCA 2007 (ACA 1992). Coopers & Lybrand, 1988–91; Treuhandanstalt, Berlin, 1992; joined FCO, 1993, Econ. Advr, 1993–98; OECD, 1999–2002; rejoined FCO, 2003; Dep. Hd, Econ. Policy Dept, 2003; Hd, Financial Planning and Perf. Dept, 2003–06. *Publications:* (jtly) OECD Economic Surveys: Baltic States, 1999, Brazil, 2000, Yugoslavia, 2002. *Recreations:* my children, ski-ing, cycling, eating good cheese. *Address:* M. P. Evans Group PLC, 3 Clanricarde Gardens, Tunbridge Wells, Kent TN1 1HQ. *Club:* Commonwealth.

PRICE, Vivian William Cecil; QC 1972; *b* 14 April 1926; 4th *s* of late Evan Price, Hawkhurst, Kent; *m* 1961, Elizabeth Anne, *o c* of late Arthur Rawlins and Georgina (*née* Guinness); three *s* two *d. Educ:* Judd Sch., Tonbridge, Kent; Trinity Coll., Cambridge (BA); Balliol Coll., Oxford (BA). Royal Navy, 1946–49, Instructor Lieut. Called to the Bar: Middle Temple, 1954 (Bencher, 1979); Hong Kong, 1975; Singapore, 1979. Dep. High Court Judge (Chancery Div.), 1975–85; a Recorder of the Crown Court, 1984. Sec., Lord Denning's Cttee on Legal Educn for Students from Africa, 1960; Junior Counsel (Patents) to the Board of Trade, 1967–72; Mem., Patents Procedure Cttee, 1973. Mem., Incorporated Council of Law Reporting for England and Wales, 1980–85. *Address:* Redwall Farmhouse, Linton, Kent ME17 4AX. *T:* (01622) 743682. *Club:* Travellers.
See also A. L. Price.

PRICE, Prof. (William) Geraint, FRS 1988; FREng, FIMechE, FRINA; Professor of Ship Science, since 1990, and Head of School of Engineering Sciences, since 1998, University of Southampton; *b* 1 Aug. 1943; *s* of Thomas Price and Ursula Maude Price (*née* Roberts); *m* 1967, Jennifer Mary Whitten; two *d. Educ:* Merthyr Tydfil County Grammar Sch.; University Coll. Cardiff (Univ. of Wales) (G. H. Latham Open Sci.

Scholar; BSc, PhD); Univ. of London (DSc(Eng)). FRINA 1980; FREng (FEng 1986); FIMechE 1989. Res. Asst, later Lectr, UCL, 1969–81; Reader in Applied Mechanics, Univ. of London, 1981–82; Prof. of Applied Mechanics, Brunel Univ., 1982–90. Fellow: Japan Soc. for Promotion of Science, 1987; Y. S. Hui Foundn, 2004. Pres., RINA, 2001–04. Foreign Mem., Chinese Acad. of Engrg, 2000. *Publications:* Probabilistic Theory of Ship Dynamics, 1974; Hydroelasticity of Ships, 1979. *Recreations:* walking, Rugby, golf, barbecueing. *Address:* Tŷ Gwyn, 45 Palmerston Way, Alverstoke, Gosport, Hants PO12 2LY. *T:* (023) 9235 1719.

PRICE, William John R.; *see* Rea Price.

PRICE, Winford Hugh Protheroe, OBE 1983; FCA; City Treasurer, Cardiff City Council, 1975–83; *b* 5 Feb. 1926; *s* of Martin Price and Doris Blanche Price. *Educ:* Cardiff High Sch. IPFA 1952; FCA 1954. Served War, RAFVR, 1944–48. City Treasurer's and Controller's Dept, Cardiff, 1942; Dep. City Treasurer, Cardiff, 1973–75. Public Works Loan Comr, 1979–83. Treasurer and Financial Adviser, Council for the Principality, 1975–83; Financial Adviser, Assoc. of Dist Councils Cttee for Wales, 1975–83; Treasurer: The Queen's Silver Jubilee Trust (S Glam), 1976–83; Royal National Eisteddfod of Wales (Cardiff), 1978. Occasional lectr on local govt topics. *Publications:* contrib. to jls. *Recreation:* chess.

PRICE EVANS, David Alan; *see* Evans.

PRICHARD, David Colville Mostyn, MBE 2002; Headmaster, Wycliffe College, 1994–98; *b* 26 May 1934; *s* of Rev. George Mostyn Prichard and Joan Mary Mostyn Prichard; *m* 1992, Catherine Elizabeth Major (formerly Headmistress, Warwick Prep. Sch.). *Educ:* Radley Coll.; Pembroke Coll., Oxford (Captain of Boats; MA; Mem., Society Cttee, 1956–2005). FCollP. Asst Master, Monkton Combe Sch., 1955–68 (Dir, Centenary Appeal, 1962; Founder, GB 1st Vol. Police Cadets, 1964; CO, CCF, 1964–68); Headmaster, Port Regis, Motcombe Park, 1969–93. Founder, Nat. Conf. for Govs, Bursars and Heads, 1981–93; Chm., IAPS, 1989–90. Mem. Develt Cttee, SW Arts, 1998–2006. Trustee, Smallpeice Trust, 1980–2003; Chm., Smallpeice Enterprises, 1986–95; Co-Chm., Operation New World, 1992–99 (Trustee, 1992–); Vice President: Glos Pied Piper Appeal, 1995; Wycliffe Watermen, 1998–. Governor: Swanbourne House Sch., 1985–2000; Holmewood House Sch., 1987–98; Orwell Park Sch., 1995–98; St John's Sch., Chepstow, 1995–99; West Hill Park Sch., 1998–2002; Sherborne Prep. Sch., 1999–2006 (Chm., 2002–06); Mem., Govs' Adv. Body, Wycliffe Coll., 2006–. Trustee, Sherborne House Trust, 1998–2006. Mem. Cttee, Friends of Yeatman Hosp., 2000–03. Church Warden, Castleton Church, 1999–2005. Freeman, City of London, 1990; Liveryman, Lorimers' Co., 1990–. FRSA. *Publication:* Training for Service, 1967. *Recreations:* education, travel, gardening, rowing (OUBC Isis VIII). *Address:* Thornhill Lodge, North Road, Sherborne, Dorset DT9 3JW. *T:* (01935) 816539. *Clubs:* National, Carlton; Leander.

PRICHARD, Mathew Caradoc Thomas, CBE 1992; DL; Chairman, Agatha Christie Ltd, since 1976; *b* 21 Sept. 1943; *s* of late Major H. de B. Prichard and Rosalind Hicks; *m* 1st, 1967, Angela Caroline Maples (*d* 2004); one *s* two *d*; 2nd, 2007, Lucinda Mary Oliver. *Educ:* Eton College; New College, Oxford. BA (PPE). Penguin Books, 1965–69. Pres., Nat. Mus. of Wales, 1996–2002 (Mem. Court of Governors and Council, 1975–2007); Member: Welsh Arts Council, 1980–94 (Chm., 1988–94); Arts Council of GB, 1983–94. High Sheriff, Glamorgan, 1972–73; DL S Glam, 1994. *Recreations:* golf, cricket, bridge. *Address:* Pwllywrach, Colwinston, Cowbridge, Vale of Glamorgan CF71 7NJ. *T:* (01446) 772256. *Clubs:* Boodle's, MCC; Cardiff and County; Royal & Ancient Golf (St Andrews); Royal Porthcawl Golf, Loch Lomond Golf.

PRICHARD, Air Vice-Marshal Richard Augustin R.; *see* Riseley-Prichard.

PRICHARD-JONES, Sir David John Walter, 3rd Bt *cr* 1910, of Bron Menai, Anglesey; *b* 14 March 1943; *s* of Sir John Prichard-Jones, 2nd Bt and of Heather, *er d* of Sir Walter Nugent, 4th Bt; *S* father, 2007. *Educ:* Ampleforth; Christ Church, Oxford (BA). *Heir: cousin* Richard Stephen Prichard-Jones [*b* 23 Nov. 1952; *m* 2000, Jane Emma Lewsley; one *s* two *d* (of whom one *s* one *d* are twins)].

PRICKETT, Prof. (Alexander Thomas) Stephen, PhD; FEA; Margaret Root Brown Professor of English, and Director, Armstrong Browning Library, Baylor University, Texas, since 2003; *b* 4 June 1939; *s* of Rev. William Ewart Prickett and Barbara Browning (*née* Lyne); *m* 1st, 1967, Diana Joan Mabbutt; one *s* one *d*; 2nd, 1983, Maria Angelica Alvarez (marr. diss. 2001); 3rd, 2001, Patricia Erskine-Hill. *Educ:* Kent Coll., Canterbury; Trinity Hall, Cambridge (BA 1961; PhD 1968); University Coll., Oxford (DipEd). FAHA 1986. English teacher, Uzuakoli, E Nigeria, 1962–64; Asst Lectr, Lectr, and Reader, Univ. of Sussex, 1967–82; Prof. of English, ANU, Canberra, 1983–89; Regius Prof. of English Lang. and Lit., Univ. of Glasgow, 1990–2001. Vis. Lectr, Smith Coll., Mass, USA, 1970–71; Vis. Fulbright Prof., Univ. of Minnesota, 1979–80; Vis. Prof. of English, Duke Univ., USA, 2001–03. Trustee, Higher Educn Foundn, 1976–2004. President: Soc. for Study of Literature and Theology, 1991–2000; George MacDonald Soc., 1994–. Fellow, Soc. for Values in Higher Educn, USA, 1992; FRSA 1993; FEA 2004. *Publications:* Do It Yourself Doom, 1962; Coleridge and Wordsworth: the poetry of growth, 1970, 2nd edn 1980; Romanticism and Religion, 1976; Victorian Fantasy, 1979, 2nd edn 2005; Words and the Word: language poetics and biblical interpretation, 1986, 2nd edn 1988; England and the French Revolution, 1988; Reading the Text: biblical criticism and literary theory, 1991; (jtly) The Bible, 1991; Origins of Narrative: the romantic appropriation of the Bible, 1996; (ed) World's Classics Bible, 1997; The Bible and Literature: a reader, 1999; Narrative, Religion and Science, 2002; Education! Education! Education!: managerial ethics and the law of unintended consequences, 2002. *Recreations:* walking, ski-ing, drama. *Address:* Armstrong Browning Library, Baylor University, Waco, TX 76798–7152, USA.

PRICKETT, Air Chief Marshal Sir Thomas (Other), KCB 1965 (CB 1957); DSO 1943; DFC 1942; RAF retired; *b* 31 July 1913; *s* of late E. G. Prickett; *m* 1st, 1942, Elizabeth Gratian, (*d* 1984), *d* of late William Galbally, Laguna Beach, Calif, USA; one *s* one *d*; 2nd, 1985, Shirley Westerman. *Educ:* Stubbington House Sch.; Haileybury Coll. Assistant, later Manager, sugar estates, India with Begg Sutherland Ltd, 1932–37. Served Bihar Light Horse, Indian Army (Auxiliary). Joined RAF, 1937; Desert Air Force, Bomber Comd, 1939–44; RAF Delegn, Washington; Dep. Dir Trng, 1944–45; commanded RAF Tangmere, 1949–51; Group Captain operations, HQ Middle East Air Force, 1951–54; commanded RAF Jever, 1954–55; attended Imperial Defence Coll., 1956; Chief of Staff Air Task Force, 1956; Director of Policy, Air Ministry, 1957–58; SASO, HQ No 1 Group, 1958–60; ACAS (Ops) Air Ministry, 1960–63; ACAS (Policy and Planning) Air Ministry, 1963–64; AOC-in-C, NEAF, Comdr British Forces Near East, and Administrator, Sovereign Base Area, 1964–66; AOC-in-C, RAF Air Support Command, 1967–68; Air Mem. for Supply and Organisation, MoD, 1968–70; Dir, Goodwood Estate, 1970–78; Man. Dir, Goodwood Terrena, 1970–78. *Recreations:* polo, sailing, golf. *Address:* 46 Kingston Hill Place, Kingston upon Thames KT2 7QY. *Club:* Royal Air Force.

PRIDDIS, Rt Rev. Anthony Martin; *see* Hereford, Bishop of.

PRIDDLE, Robert John, CB 1994; Executive Director, International Energy Agency, 1994–2002; *b* 9 Sept. 1938; *s* of late Albert Leslie Priddle and Alberta Edith Priddle; *m* 1962, Janice Elizabeth Gorham; two *s*. *Educ:* King's Coll. Sch., Wimbledon; Peterhouse, Cambridge (MA). Asst Principal, Min. of Aviation, 1960, Principal 1965; Private Sec. to Minister for Aerospace, 1971–73; Asst Sec., DTI, 1973, and Dept of Energy, 1974; Under Sec., Dept of Energy, 1977–85; Under Sec., DTI, 1985–89; Dep. Sec. and Dir Gen. of Energy Resources, Dept of Energy, subseq. DTI, 1989–92; Dep. Sec., Corporate and Consumer Affairs, DTI, 1992–94. Pres., Conf. of European Posts and Telecommunications Administrations, 1987–89; Chm. Governing Bd, Internat. Energy Agency, 1991–92. Mem., Financial Reporting Council, 1992–94. Chevalier de la Légion d'Honneur (France), 2001. *Publication:* Victoriana, 1959, 2nd edn 1963. *Address:* 1 Stable Court, Stodham Lane, Liss, Hants GU33 7QX.

PRIDEAUX, Sir Humphrey (Povah Treverbian), Kt 1971; OBE 1945; DL; Chairman, Morland & Co., 1983–93 (Director, 1981–93; Vice Chairman, 1982); Chairman, Lord Wandsworth Foundation, 1966–92; *b* 13 Dec. 1915; 3rd *s* of Walter Treverbian Prideaux and Marion Fenn (*née* Arbuthnot); *m* 1939, Cynthia (*d* 2008), *er d* of late Lt-Col H. Birch Reynardson, CMG; four *s*. *Educ:* St Aubyns, Rottingdean; Eton; Trinity Coll., Oxford (MA). Commissioned 3rd Carabiniers (Prince of Wales's Dragoon Guards) 1936; DAQMG Guards Armd Div., 1941; Instructor, Staff Coll., 1942; AQMG 21 Army Gp, 1943; AA QMG Guards Armd Div., 1944; Joint Planning Staff, War Office, 1945; Naval Staff Coll., 1948; Commandant School of Administration, 1948; Chiefs of Staff Secretariat, 1950; retired, 1953. Director, NAAFI, 1956–73 (Man. Dir, 1961–65; Chm., 1963–73); Dir, London Life Association Ltd, 1964–88 (Vice-Pres., 1965–72; Pres., 1973–84); Chm., Brooke Bond Liebig Ltd, 1972–80 (Dir, 1968; Dep. Chm., 1969–71); Vice-Chm., W. H. Smith & Son Ltd, 1977–81 (Dir, 1969–77); Dir, Grindlays, 1982–85. DL Hants 1983. *Recreations:* country pursuits. *Address:* Kings Cottage, Buryfields, Odiham, Hants RG29 1NE. *T:* (01256) 703658. *Club:* Cavalry and Guards.

See also J. H. Prideaux.

PRIDEAUX, John Denys Charles Anstice, CBE 1994; PhD; Chairman: Superlink Ltd, since 2004; Festiniog Railway Co., since 2006; *b* 8 Aug. 1944; *s* of Denys Robert Anstice-Prideaux and Frances Hester Dorothy Anstice-Prideaux (*née* Glaze); *m* 1972, Philippa Mary (*née* Morgan); one *s* one *d*. *Educ:* St Paul's; Univ. of Nottingham (BSc, PhD). British Railways: Operational Research, 1965; Area Manager, Newton Abbot, 1972; Strategic Planning Officer, 1974; Divl Manager, Birmingham, 1980; Dir, Policy Unit, 1983–86; Dir, 1986–91, Man. Dir, 1991, InterCity; Man. Dir, New Ventures, 1992–94; Chm., Union Railways, 1992–93; Director: Green Arrow, 1994–95; Docklands Light Railway, 1994–98; Chairman: Prideaux and Associates, 1994–99; Angel Train Contracts, 1996–98 (Dir, 1998–2008); Image Scan Hldgs Plc, 1998–2000; Altram (Manchester) Ltd, 1999–2003. Member: Adv. Cttee on Trunk Road Assessment, 1977; Transport Cttee, SERC and ESRC, 1982; Planning and Envmt Cttee, ESRC, 1985. Chm., Festiniog Railway Trust, 1998–. Mem., Council, Manchester Business School, 1987. *Publications:* railway histories, papers on management and transport. *Recreations:* rural affairs, conservation, history, sailing, ski-ing, design. *Address:* Angel Trains, Portland House, Bressenden Place, SW1E 5BH.

PRIDEAUX, Julian Humphrey, OBE 1995; Deputy Director-General and Secretary, National Trust, 1997–2002; *b* 19 June 1942; 2nd *s* of Sir Humphrey Povah Treverbian Prideaux, *qv*; *m* 1967, Jill, 3rd *d* of R. P. Roney-Dougal; two *s*. *Educ:* St Aubyns, Rottingdean; Eton; Royal Agricultural Coll. (Dip. Estate Management). ARICS 1966, FRICS 1974. Land Agent with Burd & Evans, Shrewsbury, 1964–67; Agent to Col Hon. C. G. Cubitt and others, 1967–69; National Trust: Land Agent, Cornwall Region, 1969–77; Dir, Thames and Chilterns Region, 1978–86; Chief Agent, 1987–96. Mem. Council, 1987–, Trustee, 2003–05, Nat. Gardens Scheme; Trustee: Rural Housing Trust, 2001–; Chelsea Physic Gdn, 2003–; Goldsmiths Centre, 2007–. *Recreation:* walking. *Address:* Bellbrook, Donhead St Mary, Shaftesbury, Dorset SP7 9DL. *Club:* Farmers'.

PRIDHAM, Brian Robert; HM Diplomatic Service, retired; Hon. Research Fellow, Centre for Arab Gulf Studies, University of Exeter, 1995–2000 (Research Fellow, 1983–95; Director, 1985–86, 1987–95); *b* 22 Feb. 1934; *s* of Reginald Buller Pridham and Emily Pridham (*née* Winser); *m*, 1st, 1954, Fay Coles (marr. diss. 1996); three *s*; 2nd, Lorraine Patricia Waitt (*née* Moore). *Educ:* Hele's Sch., Exeter. MA Exon, 1984. RWAFF (Nigeria Regt), 1952–54; Foreign Office, 1954–57; MECAS, 1957–59; Bahrain, 1959; Vice-Consul, Muscat, 1959–62; Foreign Office, 1962–64; 2nd Sec., Algiers, 1964–66, 1st Sec., 1966–67; Foreign Office, 1967–70; Head of Chancery: La Paz, 1970–73; Abu Dhabi, 1973–75; Dir of MECAS, Shemlan, Lebanon, 1975–76; Counsellor, Khartoum, 1976–79; Head of Communications Ops Dept, FCO, 1979–81. University of Exeter: Lectr in Arabic, Dept of Arabic and Islamic Studies, 1984–87; Dep. Dir, Centre for Arab Gulf Studies, 1984–85. Dep. Hd, EU Observer Mission to Palestinian Elections, 1995–96; Hd, OSCE Observer Mission to Albanian Elections, 1997; Hd, EU Observer Mission to Tanzanian Elections, 2000. Jt Ed., New Arabian Studies series, 1994–2007. *Publications:* (ed) Contemporary Yemen: politics and historical background, 1984; (ed) Economy, Society and Culture in Contemporary Yemen, 1984; (ed) The Arab Gulf and the West, 1985; (ed) Oman: economic, social and strategic developments, 1986; The Arab Gulf and the Arab World, 1987; (trans.) Omani-French Relations 1715–1905, 1996. *Recreations:* shrubs, photography.

PRIDHAM, Kenneth Robert Comyn, CMG 1976; HM Diplomatic Service, retired; *b* 28 July 1922; *s* of late Colonel G. R. Pridham, CBE, DSO, and Mignonne, *d* of late Charles Cumming, ICS; *m* 1965, Ann Rosalind, *d* of late E. Gilbert Woodward, Metropolitan Magistrate, and of Mrs Woodward. *Educ:* Winchester; Oriel Coll., Oxford. Lieut, 60th Rifles, 1942–46; served North Africa, Italy, Middle East (despatches). Entered Foreign (subseq. Diplomatic) Service, 1946; served at Berlin, Washington, Belgrade and Khartoum, and at the Foreign Office; Counsellor: Copenhagen, 1968–72; FCO, 1972–74; Asst Under Sec. of State, FCO, 1974–78; Ambassador to Poland, 1978–81. Vis. Res. Fellow, RIIA, 1981–82. *Address:* c/o Lloyds TSB, 8/10 Waterloo Place, SW1Y 4BE. *Club:* Travellers.

PRIDHAM, Brig. Robert, OBE 1991; Clerk to the Grocers' Company, since 2006; *b* 9 Dec. 1949; *s* of late Kenneth Reginald Pridham, Grenadier Guards, and Theresia Pridham (*née* Berkemeier); *m* 1979, Jane Elizabeth Stibbon; four *d*. *Educ:* Hele's Sch., Exeter; RMCS Shrivenham (BSc Applied Sci. 1975); Univ. of Westminster (MA Internat. Liaison and Commns 2007). CEng 1998; FICE 1998. Enlisted Grenadier Guards, 1968; RMA Sandhurst, 1969–70; commnd RE, 1970; Troop Comd, Berlin and Cyprus, 1971; RMCS Shrivenham; Aide/Speechwriter, US Congress, Washington, 1972–75; Troop Comd, BAOR and NI, 1975–77; 3 Field Sqn, NI and Oman, 1977–79; Instructor, RMA Sandhurst, 1980; Army Comd and Staff Coll., Shrivenham and Camberley, 1981–82; Defence Operational Analysis Estabt, UK and Berlin, 1983–85; OC 39 Field Sqn BAOR, Canada and Australia, 1985–87; SO2 Mil Sec., MoD, 1987–88; SO1 Defence (Budget) Prog., MoD, 1988–90; CO 39 Engr Regt, UK, RAF Germany and Gulf, 1990–91; CRE

3rd UK Div., UK and France, 1991–94; Comdt RSME, 1995–97; RCDS, London and E Asia, 1998; Dir Staff Ops SHAPE, Mons, 1999–2000; lang. trng, Germany, 2001–02; Defence Attaché, Berlin, 2002–06. Member: British-German Assoc.; British-German Officers Assoc. FCIL 2006; FCMI 2006. *Recreations:* family, house-building, sports cars, opera, choral music, France, Germany, travel, biographies, rowing, langlauf. *Address:* Grocers' Hall, Princes Street, EC2R 8AD. *T:* (020) 7606 3113, *Fax:* (020) 7600 3082; *e-mail:* clerk@grocershall.co.uk.

PRIEST, Rear-Adm. Colin Herbert Dickinson C.; *see* Cooke-Priest.

PRIEST, Prof. Eric Ronald, PhD; FRS 2002; FRSE; James Gregory Professor of Mathematics, since 1997 and Wardlaw Professor, since 2002, University of St Andrews; *b* 7 Nov. 1943; *s* of Ronald Priest and Olive Vera Priest (*née* Dolan); *m* 1970, Clare Margaret Wilson; three *s* one *d*. *Educ:* Nottingham Univ. (BSc 1965); Leeds Univ. (MSc 1966; PhD 1969). FRSE 1985. St Andrews University: Lectr, 1968–77; Reader, 1977–83; Prof. of Theoretical Solar Physics, 1983–97. Marlar Lectr, Rice Univ., 1991; Lindsay Meml Lectr, Washington, 1998. Mem., Norwegian Acad. Scis and Letters, 1994. Hale Prize, AAS, 2002. *Publications:* Solar Magnetohydrodynamics, 1982 (trans Russian 1985); (jtly) Plasma Astrophysics, 1994; (jtly) Magnetic Reconnection: MHD Theory and Applications, 2000; *edited:* Solar Flare Magnetohydrodynamics, 1981; Solar System Magnetic Fields, 1985; Dynamics and Structure of Quiescent Solar Prominences, 1989; (jtly) Magnetic Flux Ropes, 1990; (jtly) Mechanisms of Chromospheric and Coronal Heating, 1991; (jtly) Advances in Solar System Magnetohydrodynamics, 1991 (trans. Russian 1995); (jtly) Reconnection in the Solar Corona and Magnetospheric Substorms, 1997; (jtly) A Crossroads for European Solar and Heliospheric Physics, 1998; over 400 res. papers and articles. *Recreations:* bridge, hill walking, aerobics, singing, having fun with my family. *Address:* Mathematical Institute, St Andrews University, St Andrews, Fife KY16 9SS. *T:* (01334) 463709.

PRIEST, Prof. Robert George, MD, FRCPsych; Professor of Psychiatry, University of London and Head of Department of Psychiatry at St Mary's Hospital Medical School, Imperial College of Science, Technology and Medicine, 1973–96, now Emeritus Professor; Hon. Consultant Psychiatrist, St Mary's Hospital, London, since 1973; *b* 28 Sept. 1933; *er s* of late James Priest and of Phoebe Priest; *m* 1955, Marilyn, *er d* of late Baden Roberts Baker and of Evelyn Baker; two *s*. *Educ:* University Coll., London and University Coll. Hosp. Med. Sch. MB, BS 1956; DPM 1963; MRCPE 1964; MD 1970; MRCPsych 1971 (Foundn Mem.); FRCPE 1974; FRCPsych 1974. Lectr in Psychiatry, Univ. of Edinburgh, 1964–67; Exchange Lectr, Univ. of Chicago, 1966; Consultant, Illinois State Psychiatric Inst., Chicago, 1966; Sen. Lectr, St George's Hosp. Med. Sch., London, 1967–73; Hon. Consultant: St George's Hosp., London, 1967–73; Springfield Hosp., London, 1967–73. University of London: Mem., Bd of Studies in Medicine, 1968–93 (Chm., 1987–89); Mem., Academic Adv. Bd in Medicine, 1987–90; Mem. Senate, 1989–93; Mem., Academic Council, 1989–93. Examiner in Psychiatry, NUI, 1975–78, 1980–83. Chm., Psychiatric Adv. Sub-Cttee, NW Thames RHA, 1976–79 (Vice-Chm., Reg. Manpower Cttee, 1980–83). Member: Council (Chm. Membership Cttee), British Assoc. for Psychopharmacology, 1977–81; World Psychiatric Assoc., 1980–93 (Mem. Cttee, 1985–93, Mem. Council, 1989–93); Central Cttee for Hosp. Med. Services, 1983–89 (Chm., Psych. Sub-Cttee, 1983–87); Pres., Soc. for Psychosomatic Res., 1980–81 (Vice-Pres., 1978–80); Chm., Mental Health Gp Cttee, BMA, 1982–85 (Mem. 1978–85, 1990–); Internat. Coll. of Psychosomatic Medicine: Fellow, 1977; Mem. Gov. Body and UK Delegate, 1978–81; Treasurer, 1981–83; Secretary, 1981–85; Vice-Pres., 1985–87; Royal College of Psychiatrists: Mem., Public Policy Cttee, 1972–80, 1983–89 (Chm., 1983–88); Mem. Council, 1982–88; Registrar, 1983–88; Chm., Gen. Psych. Cttee, 1985–89; Mem., Court of Electors, 1983–88 (Chm., Fellowship Sub-Cttee, 1984–88). A. E. Bennett Award, Soc. for Biol Psychiatry, USA (jtly), 1965; Doris Odlum Prize (BMA), 1968; Gutheil Von Domarus Award, Assoc. for Advancement of Psychotherapy and Amer. Jl of Psychotherapy, NY, 1970. *Publications:* Insanity: A Study of Major Psychiatric Disorders, 1977; (ed jtly) Sleep Research, 1979; (ed jtly) Benzodiazepines Today and Tomorrow, 1980; (ed) Psychiatry in Medical Practice, 1982; Anxiety and Depression, 1983, 3rd edn 1996; (ed) Sleep, 1984; (ed) Psychological Disorders in Obstetrics and Gynaecology, 1985 (Spanish edn 1987); (jtly) Minski's Handbook of Psychiatry, 7th edn, 1978, 8th edn as Handbook of Psychiatry, 1986; (jtly) Sleepless Nights, 1990; (jtly) Depression and Anxiety, 1992 (Spanish edn 1992); (jtly) Depression in General Practice, 1996; chapters in: Current Themes in Psychiatry, 1978; Mental Illness in Pregnancy and the Puerperium, 1978; Psychiatry in General Practice, 1981; Modern Emergency Department Practice, 1983; The Scientific Basis of Psychiatry, 1983, 2nd edn 1992; The Psychosomatic Approach: contemporary practice of wholeperson care, 1986; articles in BMJ, Brit. Jl of Psychiatry, Amer. Jl of Psychotherapy and other learned jls. *Recreations:* swimming, foreign languages, nature study. *Address:* Woodeaves, 29 Old Slade Lane, Richings Park, Iver, Bucks SL0 9DY. *T:* (01753) 653178.

PRIESTLEY, Clive, CB 1983; Chairman, St Bartholomew's Hospital Medical College Trust, since 1997 (Member, 1996–97); *b* 12 July 1935; *s* of late Albert Ernest and Annie May Priestley; *m* 1st, 1961, Barbara Anne Wells (marr. diss. 1984); two *d*; 2nd, 1985, Daphne June Challis Loasby, OBE, JP, DL, *o d* of late W. Challis and Dorothy Franks. *Educ:* Loughborough Grammar Sch.; Nottingham Univ. BA 1956; MA 1958. Nat. Service, RA, RAEC, 1958–60. Joined HM Home Civil Service, 1960; Min. of Educn, later DES, 1960–65; Schools Council, 1965–67; Harkness Commonwealth Fund Fellow, Harvard Univ., 1967–68; CSD, 1969–79; Prime Minister's Office, 1979–83 (Chief of Staff to Sir Derek Rayner); Under Sec., 1979–83; MPO, 1982–83; Div. Dir, British Telecom plc, 1983–88. Consultant: Corp. of London, 1988–90; Metropolitan Police Comr, 1989–91; LDDC, 1990–91; NEDC, 1992–93. Chm., Review of structure of arts funding in NI for govt, 1992, of responsibilities and gradings of chief officers of nat. museums, galleries and libraries, 1994; Assessor, Review of museums policy in NI, 1995. Member: Council, Univ. of Reading, 1984–86; Develt Trust, Univ. of Nottingham, 1994–97; Council, QMW, 1995–2002; Philharmonia Trust, 1985–87; Univ. of Cambridge Careers Service Syndicate, 1986–90; Adv. Council, Buxton Festival, 1987–97; Arts Council, of GB, 1991–94, of England, 1994–95 and 1996–97; British Soc. of Gastroenterology, 2000–05; Sec., Fundraising Cttee, Thiepval Proj., 2000–05; Chairman: London Arts Bd, 1991–97; Trafalgar Square 2000, 1996–98; Council for Dance Educn and Trng, 1997–2000. Vice-Pres., St Bartholomew's Hosp. Med. Coll., 1993–95 (Mem. Council, 1990–95). Governor: Royal Shakespeare Co., 1984–2004; City Lit. Inst., 1995–96; Trinity Coll. of Music, 1997–2005. Wandsman, St Paul's Cathedral, 1983–97; jt planner, Millennial Service for London, St Paul's Cathedral, 1998–2000. Hon. Perpetual Student, St Bartholomew's Hosp. Medical Coll., 1995; Hon. FTCL 1996; Hon. Fellow, QMUL, 2007. Freeman, City of London, 1989; Liveryman, Worshipful Co. of Glaziers and Painters of Glass, 1989–2002. *Publications:* financial scrutinies of the Royal Opera House, Covent Garden Ltd, and of the Royal Shakespeare Co., 1984. *Address:* Field House, Ham, Wilts SN8 3QR. *T:* and *Fax:* (01488) 669094; *e-mail:* ClivPrs@aol.com. *Club:* Army and Navy.

PRIESTLEY, Sir Julian (Gordon), KCMG 2007; Secretary-General, European Parliament, 1997–2007; *b* 26 May 1950; *s* of Arthur David Noel Priestley and Patricia (*née* Maynard). *Educ:* St Boniface's Coll., Plymouth; Balliol Coll., Oxford (BA Hons PPE). European Parliament, 1973–2007: Head of Div., Secretariat of Cttee on Energy, Res. and Technology, 1983–87; Dir, Parly Cttees, 1987–89; Sec.-Gen., Socialist Gp, 1989–94; Head, Private Office of the Pres., 1994–97. *Publication:* Six Battles that Shaped Europe's Parliament, 2008. *Recreations:* golf, cinema, reading. *Address:* 4 Clos du Quebec, 1410 Waterloo, Belgium.

PRIESTLEY, Kathleen, (Kate), (Mrs Alan Humphreys); Chairman, Local Government Leadership Centre, since 2004; *b* 25 Aug. 1949; *d* of late John Fletcher Taylor and Joan Taylor (*née* Hannon); *m* 1st, 1967 (marr. diss. 1983); one *s*; 2nd, 1985, Alan Humphreys. *Educ:* Notre Dame, Manchester; Manchester Univ. (CQSW); Edinburgh Univ. (MBA). Psychiatric social worker and Sen. Social Worker, Oldham, 1972–79; Manager, Mental Health Service, Salford, 1979–84; Chief Exec., Family Care, Edinburgh, 1984–89; Asst Dir, Social Services, Newcastle upon Tyne, 1989–92; Exec. Dir, Northern RHA, 1992–94; Department of Health: Dir, Purchase Performance Mgt, Northern and Yorkshire Reg., NHS Exec., 1994–97; Chief Exec., NHS Estates, 1998–2004; Chief Exec., Inventures, 2001–04. Non-exec. Dir, Scarborough Bldg Soc., 2001– (Vice-Chm., 2005–); Chm., Island Healthcare, 2003–. Non-executive Director: Nat. Property Bd, Dept of Constitutional Affairs, 2003–07; Living Independently, EU, 2006–07; Govt Office NE, 2008. Chm., Standing Cttee on Structural Safety, 2002–; Mem., Govt Skills Council, 2005–. Trustee, BRE Trust (formerly Foundn for the Built Envmt), 2003–08. FRSA 1999. Mem., Council, Univ. of Newcastle, 2005–. Hon. Fellow: Univ. of Manchester, 1993; Univ. of York, 1995; Inst. Healthcare Engrg and Estate Mgt, 2000. CompICE 2003; MInstD. *Recreations:* graphology, cooking and entertaining, opera. *Address:* Kitty Frisk House, Corbridge Road, Hexham, Northumberland NE46 1UN. *T:* (01434) 601533.

PRIESTLEY, Leslie William, TD 1974; FCIB; FCIM; Chairman, Tenax Capital Ltd, since 2005; *b* 22 Sept. 1933; *s* of Winifred and George Priestley; *m* 1960, Audrey Elizabeth (*née* Humber); one *s* one *d*. *Educ:* Shooters Hill Grammar School. Head of Marketing, Barclaycard, 1966–73; Asst Gen. Manager, Barclays Bank, 1974–77, Local Dir, 1978–79; Sec. Gen., Cttee of London Clearing Bankers, 1979–83; Dir, Bankers' Automated Clearing Services, 1979–83; Man. Dir, Barclays Insurance Services Co., 1983–84; Regional Gen. Manager, Barclays Bank, 1984–85; Dir and Chief Exec., TSB England & Wales plc (formerly TSB England and Wales and Central Trustee Savings Bank), 1985–89; Director: TSB Gp plc, 1986–89; Hill Samuel Bank, 1988–89; Pearce Signs Gp (formerly Pearce Gp Hldgs), 1989–2003. Chairman: CAA Pension Scheme Trustees, 1993–2003; Caviapen Investments Ltd, 1993–2003; Generali Pan Europe Ltd, 2006–; Vice-Chm., Guernsey Financial Services Commn, 2003–05 (Mem., 1999–2005); Director: London Electricity plc (formerly London Electricity Board), 1984–97; Pinnacle Insurance, 1990–2003; Omnia/ICL, 1991–94; London Chamber of Commerce and Industry, 1993–96; Expatriate Management Ltd, 1994–99; Prudential Banking plc, 1996–2006; Egg plc, 2000–06; Currencies Direct Ltd, 2006–. Banking Advr, Touche Ross & Co., 1990–96; Financial Services Advisor: ICL, 1991–97; Satyam Computer Services Ltd, 2005–08. Member: Monopolies and Mergers Commn, 1990–96; Bd, CAA, 1990–96. Member of Council: Chartered Inst. of Bankers, 1988–89; Assoc. for Payment Clearing Services, 1988–89. Vis. Fellow, UCNW, 1989–95. Consultant Editor, Bankers' Magazine, 1972–81. FCIM (FInstM 1987); CCMI; FRSA. *Publication:* (ed) Bank Lending with Management Accounts, 1981. *Recreations:* reading, gardening, swimming, golf. *Address:* Tenax Capital Ltd, Dominican House, 4 Priory Court, Pilgrim Street, EC4V 6DE. *Clubs:* Royal Automobile; Sundridge Park Golf, Chislehurst Golf.

PRIESTLEY, Prof. Maurice Bertram, MA, PhD; Professor of Statistics, University of Manchester Institute of Science and Technology, 1970–96 (Head of Department of Mathematics, 1973–75, 1977–78, 1980–85 and 1987–89), now Professor Emeritus, University of Manchester; *b* 15 March 1933; *s* of Jack and Rose Priestley; *m* 1959, Nancy, *d* of late Ralph and Hilda Nelson; one *s* one *d*. *Educ:* Manchester Grammar Sch.; Jesus Coll., Cambridge. BA (Wrangler, 1954), MA, DipMathStat (Cambridge); PhD (Manchester). Scientific Officer, RAE, 1955–56; Asst Lectr, Univ. of Manchester, 1957–60, Lectr, 1960–65; Vis. Professor, Princeton and Stanford Univs, USA, 1961–62; Sen. Lectr, UMIST, 1965–70; Dir, Manchester-Sheffield Sch. of Probability and Stats, and Hon. Prof. of Probability and Stats, Sheffield Univ., 1976–79, 1988–89, 1991–92. Mem. Court and Council, UMIST, 1971–74 and 1989–96. FIMS; FSS; Member Council: Royal Statistical Soc., 1971–75; Manchester Statistical Soc., 1986–96; Mem., ISI. Editor-in-chief, Jl of Time Series Analysis, 1980–. *Publications:* Spectral Analysis and Time Series, Vols I and II, 1981; Non-linear and non-stationary time series analysis, 1988; papers and articles in Jl RSS, Biometrika, Technom., Automatica, Jl of Sound and Vibration. *Recreations:* music, hi-fi and audio, golf. *Address:* School of Mathematics, University of Manchester, Oxford Road, Manchester M13 9PL. *T:* (0161) 306 3668.

PRIESTLEY, Philip John, CBE 1996; HM Diplomatic Service, retired; High Commissioner to Belize, 2001–04; *b* 29 Aug. 1946; *s* of late Frederick Priestley and Caroline (*née* Rolfe); *m* 1972, Christine Rainforth; one *s* one *d*. *Educ:* Boston Grammar Sch.; Univ. of East Anglia (BA Hons). FCO 1969; served Sofia and Kinshasa; First Sec., FCO, 1976; Wellington, 1979–83; FCO, 1984–87; Commercial Counsellor and Dep. Head of Mission, Manila, 1987–90; Ambassador to Gabon, 1990–91; Fellow, Center for Internat. Affairs, Harvard Univ., 1991–92; Consul-Gen., Geneva, 1992–95; Hd, N America Dept, FCO, 1996–2000. Vice-Pres. for Econ. Develt, Blue Diamond Ventures, 2006–. FRSA 1999. *Recreations:* golf, bridge, theatre.

PRIESTLEY, Dr Robert Henry; owner, Ro-Po Publishing, since 2007; *b* 19 March 1946; *s* of late Henry Benjamin Priestley, MA, BSc and Margaret Alice (*née* Lambert); *m* 1970, Penelope Ann Fox, BSc; two *d*. *Educ:* Brunts Grammar Sch., Mansfield; Univ. of Southampton (BSc 1967); Univ. of Exeter (PhD 1972); CS Coll. (Dip. in Consultancy Practice, 1999). FIBiol 1988. Plant Pathologist, Lord Rank Res. Centre, Rank Hovis McDougall, 1970–73; National Institute of Agricultural Botany: Cereal Pathologist, 1973–78; Head of Cereal Path. Section, 1978–82; Head of Plant Path. Dept, 1982–88; Gen. Sec., Inst. of Biol., 1989–97. Mgt consultant, HQ Strike Comd, RAF High Wycombe, 1998–2002; Principal Consultant and Lectr, Centre for Mgt and Policy Studies, Sunningdale Park, 2002–06. Sec., UK Cereal Pathogen Virulence Survey, 1974–82; Member: Council Fedn of British Plant Pathologists, 1980–81; Internat. Soc. for Plant Path., 1988–92; Treasurer, British Soc. for Plant Path., 1981–87; Member: British Nat. Cttee for Microbiology, 1982–89; Cttee of Management, Biol. Council, 1989–91; Bd, CSTI, 1989–97; Parly and Sci. Cttee, 1989–97; Chairman: European Communities Biol. Assoc., 1992–96; Eur. Biologist Registration Cttee, 1994–97. FCMI (FIMgt 1997). *Publications:* Football League Programmes of the late 1940s, 2007; consultancy reports; papers on diseases of crops; popular articles. *Recreations:* music, art, architecture, football. *Address:* 17 Wallingford Gardens, High Wycombe, Bucks HP11 1QS. *T:* (01494) 446660; *e-mail:* rhpriestley@hotmail.com.

PRIESTLY, Paul Graham; Permanent Secretary, Department for Regional Development, Northern Ireland, since 2007; *b* Belfast, 30 March 1958; *s* of Samuel Robert and Clara Priestly; *m* 1984, Pamela Ann Hawkins; one *s* two *d*. *Educ:* Grosvenor Grammar Sch., Belfast; Queen's Univ., Belfast (BA Hons 1st Cl. Geog.). Hd, Policing Reforms Div., NI Office, 1998–2000; Principal Private Sec. to Sec. of State for NI, 2000–02; Hd, Criminal Justice Reform Div., 2002–03, Dir of Resources, 2003–07, NI Office; Dir of Policy and Strategy, Office of the First Minister and Dep. First Minister, NI, 2007. *Recreations:* hill-walking, reading natural and military history, sailing, playing guitar (badly). *Address:* Department for Regional Development, Clarence Court, 10–18 Adelaide Street, Belfast BT2 8GB; *e-mail:* paul.priestly@drdni.gov.uk.

PRIESTMAN, Jane, OBE 1991; FCSD; design management consultant; *b* 7 April 1930; *d* of late Reuben Stanley Herbert and Mary Elizabeth Herbert (*née* Ramply); *m* 1954, Arthur Martin Priestman (marr. diss. 1986); two *s*. *Educ:* Northwood College; Liverpool Coll. of Art (NDD, ATD). Design practice, 1954–75; Design Manager, Gen. Manager, Architecture and Design, BAA, 1975–86; Dir, Architecture and Design, BRB, 1986–91. Member: LRT Design Panel, 1985–88; Jaguar Styling Panel, 1988–91; Percentage for Art Steering Gp, Arts Council, 1989–91; Council, Design Council, 1996–99; Design Panel, SE England Region, 2000–; Design Review Panel, Home Office, 2003–. Vis. Prof. of Internat. Design, De Montfort Univ., 1997–2001. Enabler, CABE, 2001–. Trustee, London Open House, 1995– (Chair of Trustees, 1998–). Governor: Commonwealth Inst., 1987–99; Kingston Univ. (formerly Kingston Polytechnic), 1988–96. Hon. FRIBA; FRSA. Hon. DDes: De Montfort, 1994; Sheffield Hallam, 1998. *Recreations:* textiles, city architecture, opera, travel. *Address:* 30 Duncan Terrace, N1 8BS. *T:* (020) 7837 4525. *Club:* Architecture.

PRIESTMAN, John David; Clerk of the Parliamentary Assembly of the Council of Europe, 1971–86; *b* 29 March 1926; *s* of Bernard Priestman and Hermine Bréal; *m* 1951, Nada Valić (*d* 1999); two *s* two *d*. *Educ:* private sch. in Paris; Westminster Sch.; Merton Coll. and Christ Church, Oxford (Hon. Mods, Lit. Hum.). Served Coldstream Guards, 1944–47, Temp. Captain. Third, subseq. Second, Sec., Belgrade, 1949–53; Asst Private Sec. to Rt Hon. Anthony Eden, 1953–55; joined Secretariat, Council of Europe, 1955; Head of Sec. Gen's Private Office, 1961; Sec., Cttee of Ministers, 1966; Dep. Clerk of Parly Assembly, 1968–71. Hon. Life Mem., Assoc. of Secretaries General of Parlt, 1986. Rep. in Alpes Maritimes, French Nat. Assoc. of Prison Visitors, 1987–99. *Recreations:* off-piste Alpine ski-ing, music, competition bridge, gastronomic research. *Address:* 6 rue Adolphe Wurtz, 67000 Strasbourg, France. *T:* 388354049.

PRIMAROLO, Rt Hon. Dawn; PC 2002; MP (Lab) Bristol South, since 1987; Minister of State, Department of Health, since 2007; *b* 2 May 1954; *m* 1972 (marr. diss.); one *s*; *m* 1990, Thomas Ian Ducat. *Educ:* Thomas Bennett Comprehensive Sch., Crawley; Bristol Poly.; Bristol Univ. Mem., Avon CC, 1985–87. Opposition front bench spokesman on health, 1992–94, on Treasury affairs, 1994–97; Financial Sec., HM Treasury, 1997–99; HM Paymaster Gen., 1999–2007. Mem., Select Cttee on Members' Interests, 1988–92. *Address:* House of Commons, SW1A 0AA; (office) PO Box 1002, Bristol BS99 1WH. *T:* (0117) 909 0063.

PRIMROSE, family name of **Earl of Rosebery**.

PRIMROSE, Sir John Ure, 5th Bt *cr* 1903, of Redholme, Dumbreck, Govan; *b* 28 May 1960; *s* of Sir Alasdair Neil Primrose, 4th Bt and of Elaine Noreen, *d* of Edmund Cecil Lowndes, Buenos Aires; *S* father, 1986; *m* 1st, 1983, Marion Cecilia (marr. diss. 1987), *d* of Hans Otto Altgelt; two *d*; 2nd, Claudia Ines Schwarz. *Heir: b* Andrew Richard Primrose [*b* 19 Jan. 1966. *Educ:* St Peter's School and Military Acad. BA].

PRIMUS, The; *see* Jones, Most Rev. Dr I., Bishop of Glasgow and Galloway.

PRINCE, David; Chief Executive, The Standards Board for England, 2004–08; *b* 31 May 1948; *s* of late Charles and Phyllis Grace Prince; *m* 1973, Davina Ann Pugh. *Educ:* Exeter Univ. (BA Hons English). CPFA. Hants CC Grad. Trainee, 1969–71; finance posts, Berks CC, 1971–76; Chief Accountant, Cambs CC, 1976–81, and Asst Co. Treasurer; Dep. Co. Treasurer, Herts CC, 1981–86; Dir, Finance and Admin, Cambs CC, 1986–91; Chief Exec., Leics CC, 1991–94; Audit Commission: Chief Exec., Dist Audit Service, then Dist Audit, 1994–2000; Dir of Ops, 2000–01; Dir of Strategy and Resources, 2001–03; Managing Dir, 2003–04. Lay Mem., Gen. Social Care Council. FRSA. *Recreations:* theatre, music, gardening.

PRINCE, Harold; theatrical director/producer; *b* NYC, 30 Jan. 1928; *s* of Milton A. Prince and Blanche (*née* Stern); *m* 1962, Judith Chaplin; two *d*. *Educ:* Univ. of Pennsylvania (AB 1948). Co-Producer: The Pajama Game, 1954–56 (co-prod film, 1957); Damn Yankees, 1955–57 (co-prod film, 1958); New Girl in Town, 1957–58; West Side Story, 1957–59; Fiorello!, 1959–61 (Pulitzer Prize); Tenderloin, 1960–61; A Call on Kuprin, 1961; They Might Be Giants, London 1961; Side By Side By Sondheim, 1977–78. Producer: Take Her She's Mine, 1961–62; A Funny Thing Happened on the Way to the Forum, 1962–64; Fiddler on the Roof, 1964–72; Poor Bitos, 1964; Flora the Red Menace, 1965. Director-Producer: She Loves Me, 1963–64, London 1964; Superman, 1966; Cabaret, 1966–69, London 1968, tour and NY, 1987; Zorba, 1968–69; Company, 1970–72, London 1972; A Little Night Music, 1973–74, London 1975 (dir. film, 1977); Pacific Overtures, 1976. Director: A Family Affair, 1962; Baker Street, 1965; Something For Everyone (film), 1970; New Phoenix Rep. prodns of Great God Brown, 1972–73, The Visit, 1973–74, and Love for Love, 1974–75; Some of my Best Friends, 1977; On the Twentieth Century, 1978; Evita, London 1978, USA 1979–83, Australia, Vienna, 1980, Mexico City, 1981; Sweeney Todd, 1979, London 1980; Girl of the Golden West, San Francisco Op., 1979; world première, Willie Stark, Houston Grand Opera, 1981; Merrily We Roll Along (musical) 1981; A Doll's Life (musical), 1982; Madama Butterfly, Chicago Lyric Op., 1982; Turandot, Vienna State Op., 1983; Play Memory, 1984; End of the World, 1984; Diamonds, 1985; The Phantom of the Opera, London, 1986, NY, 1988, Los Angeles, 1989, Canada, 1989; Roza, USA, 1987; Cabaret (20th anniversary revival), tour and Broadway, 1987; Kiss of the Spider Woman, 1990, Toronto, London, Broadway, 1993; (also adapted) Grandchild of Kings, 1992; Showboat, Toronto, 1993, NY, 1994; Parade (musical), NY, 1999; 3HREE, Philadelphia, 2000, LA, 2001; Hollywood Arms, Chicago, 2002. Directed for NY City Opera: Ashmedai, 1976; Kurt Weill's Silverlake, 1980; Candide, 1982, 1997; Don Giovanni, 1989; Faust, Metropolitan Opera, 1990; co-Director-Producer, Follies, 1971–72; co-Producer-Director: Candide, 1974–75; Merrily We Roll Along, 1981; A Doll's Life, 1982; Grind (musical), 1985. Antoinette Perry Awards for: The Pajama Game; Damn Yankees; Fiorello!; A Funny Thing Happened on the Way to the Forum; Fiddler on the Roof; Cabaret; Company; A Little Night Music; Candide; Sweeney Todd; Evita; The Phantom of the Opera; Show Boat, etc (total of 20); SWET award: Evita, 1977–78. Member: League of New York Theatres (Pres., 1964–65); Council for National Endowment for the Arts. Hon. DLit, Emerson College, 1971; Hon. Dr of Fine Arts, Univ. of Pennsylvania, 1971. Drama Critics' Circle Awards; Best Musical Award, London Evening Standard, 1955–58, 1972 and 1992; Tony Award for lifetime achievement, 2006. Kennedy Center Honoree, 1994. *Publication:* Contradictions: notes on twenty-six years in the theatre, 1974. *Recreation:* tennis. *Address:* Suite 1009, 10 Rockefeller Plaza, New York, NY 10020, USA. *T:* (212) 3990960.

PRINCE, Rose Amanda; food writer and columnist, Daily Telegraph, since 2002; *b* 4 Dec. 1963; *d* of 2nd Baron Jeffreys and of Sarah Clarke; *m* 1993, Dominic Prince; one *s* one *d*. *Educ:* Hatherop Castle Sch., Glos; St Mary's Wantage, Berks. Food columnist, Daily Express, 1998–2001; cook, Spectator mag., 1998–2005; columnist: The Tablet, 2004–; Resurgence, 2006–; contributor, 1998–: Spectator, New Statesman, Saveur (USA), Daily Mail, Sunday Telegraph, The Times. Reporter, Food Prog., BBC Radio 4. Prod., TV series, In the Foot Steps of Elizabeth David, 1999. Mem., H of L Cttee of Inquiry into misregulation of meat industry, 2000. Glenfiddich Food Writer of the Year, 2001. *Publications:* The New English Kitchen: changing the way you shop, cook and eat, 2005; The Savvy Shopper, 2006; The New English Table, 2008. *Recreations:* lunch, wine, sunbathing, children, reading, racing. *Address:* 177 Battersea Bridge Road, SW11 3AS. *T:* (020) 7223 9709, 07968 359376; *e-mail:* rose@roseprince.co.uk. *Clubs:* Bluebird; Sixpenny Handley Tennis.

PRINDL, Dr Andreas Robert, Hon. CBE 2001; Chairman, Nomura Bank International, 1990–97 (Managing Director, 1986–90); *b* 25 Nov. 1939; *s* of Frank Joseph Prindl and Vivian Prindl (*née* Mitchell); *m* 1963, Veronica Maria Koerber (marr. diss. 2004); one *s* one *d*. *Educ:* Princeton Univ. (BA); Univ. of Kentucky (MA, PhD). Morgan Guaranty Trust Company: NY and Frankfurt, 1964–70; Vice-Pres., IMM, London, 1970–76; Gen. Manager, Tokyo, 1976–80; CEO Saudi Internat. Bank, London, 1980–82; Vice-Pres., Mergers and Acquisitions, Morgan Guaranty, 1982–84; Man. Dir, Nomura Internat., 1984–86. Chm., Banking Industry Trng and Develt Council, 1994–96; Provost, Gresham Coll., 1996–99. President: Chartered Inst. of Bankers, 1994–95; Assoc. of Corporate Treasurers, 1996. Vis. Prof., People's Univ. of China, Beijing, 2000–. Mem. Council, Lloyd's, 2003–. Freeman, City of London, 1999; Liveryman: Musicians' Co., 1999– (Mem., Ct of Assts, 2001–; Master, 2006–07); World Traders' Co., 2000–. Hon. Treas., C&G, 1998–2000. Hon. Fellow, Acad. of Moral Sci., Beijing, 1998. Hon. DSc City, 1996. *Publications:* (jtly) International Money Management, 1972; Foreign Exchange Risk, 1976; Japanese Finance, 1981; Money in the Far East, 1986; (ed) Banking and Finance in Eastern Europe, 1992; (ed jtly) Ethical Conflicts in Finance, 1994; The First XV, 1995; A Companion to Lucca, 2000; A Companion to Angoulême, 2005 (trans. French as Du haut des remparts d'Angoulême, 2007); A Companion to Fauquier County, Virginia, 2008. *Recreations:* classical music, Asian art and history. *Address:* 48 Speed House, Barbican, EC2Y 8AT. *Club:* Reform.

PRING, Prof. Richard Anthony; Professor and Director of Department of Educational Studies, University of Oxford, 1989–2003; Fellow of Green College, Oxford, 1989–2003, now Emeritus; Lead Director, Nuffield Review of 14-19 Education and Training; *b* 20 April 1938; *s* of Joseph Edwin and Anne-Marie Pring; *m* 1970, Helen Faye Evans; three *d*. *Educ:* Gregorian Univ. and English College, Rome (PhL); University Coll. London (BA Hons Philosophy); Univ. of London Inst. of Education (PhD); College of St Mark and St John (PGCE). Asst Principal, Dept of Educn and Science, 1962–64; teacher in London comprehensive schools, 1965–67; Lectr in Education: Goldsmiths' Coll., 1967–70; Univ. of London Inst. of Educn, 1972–78; Prof. of Educn, Univ. of Exeter, 1978–89. Hon. DLitt Kent, 1995. Editor, British Jl of Educational Studies, 1986–2001. Bene Merenti Medal (Pius XII), 1958. Annual Award of Distinction, Aga Khan Univ., Karachi, 2007. *Publications:* Knowledge and Schooling, 1976; Personal and Social Education, 1984; The New Curriculum, 1989; Closing the Gap: liberal education and vocational preparation, 1995; (ed with Geoffrey Walford) Affirming the Comprehensive Ideal, 1997; Philosophy of Educational Research, 2000, 2nd edn 2004; Philosophy of Education: aims, theory, common sense and research, 2004; (ed with G. Thomas) Evidence Based Practice in Education, 2004; John Dewey: a philosopher of education for our time?, 2007. *Recreations:* running marathons, cycling, writing, campaigning for comprehensive schools. *Address:* Green Templeton College, Woodstock Road, Oxford OX2 6HG.

PRINGLE, Maj. Gen. Andrew Robert Douglas, CB 2000; CBE 1992 (MBE 1980); defence consultant, since 2002; Director, AP JOINTSOLUTIONS Ltd, since 2003; Chief of Staff, Permanent Joint Headquarters, 1998–2001; *b* 9 Oct. 1946; *s* of late Douglas Alexander Pringle and Wendy Pringle (*née* Gordon); *m* 1975, Jane Carolyn Mitchison; one *s* two *d*. *Educ:* Wellington Coll.; RMA, Sandhurst; RMCS, Shrivenham (BSc Hons). Commnd RGJ, 1967: served in UK, Cyprus, NI, Germany, 1967–77; Staff Coll., Camberley, 1977–78; Staff and Regtl appts, NI, 1979–82; Directing Staff, Staff Coll., Camberley, 1983–85; CO, 3rd Bn, RGJ, 1985–88; MoD, 1988–91; Higher Comd and Staff Course, 1990; rcds, 1991; Cabinet Office, 1992–94; Commander: 20 Armoured Bde, 1994–96; UN Sector SW, Bosnia, 1995; Dir, Land Warfare, 1996–97; Comdr, Multi-Nat. Div. (SW), Bosnia, 1997–98. Regtl (formerly Rep.) Col Comdt, Royal Green Jackets, 1999–2002; Col Comdt, 2nd Bn Royal Green Jackets, 1999–2001. Non-exec. Dir, Manpower Software plc, 2004–; Vice-Pres., Govt and Defence, Europe, Africa and Middle East, Kellogg Brown and Root Ltd, 2008–. QCVS 1996 and 1998. *Recreations:* reading, ski-ing, Cresta Run, a little light farming. *Clubs:* Army and Navy; St Moritz Tobogganing.

PRINGLE, Anne Fyfe, CMG 2004; HM Diplomatic Service; Ambassador to Russia, since 2008; *b* 13 Jan. 1955; *d* of George Grant Pringle and late Margaret Fyfe Pringle (*née* Cameron); *m* 1987, Bleddyn Glynne Leyshon Phillips. *Educ:* Glasgow High Sch. for Girls; St Andrews Univ. (MA Hons French and German). Joined FCO, 1977: Third Sec., Moscow, 1980–83; Vice Consul, San Francisco, 1983–85; Second Sec., UK Rep., Brussels, 1986–87; FCO, 1988–91; First Sec., Eur. Political Co-operation Secretariat, Brussels, 1991–93; Dep. Hd, Security Co-ordination Dept, then African Dept (Equatorial), FCO, 1994–96; Head, Common Foreign and Security Policy Dept, FCO, and European Correspondent, 1996–98; Head, Eastern Dept, FCO, 1998–2001; Ambassador to the Czech Republic, 2001–04; Dir, Strategy and Information, FCO, 2004–07. FRSA 2001. *Recreations:* sport, gardening, walking. *Address:* c/o Foreign and Commonwealth Office, King Charles Street, SW1A 2AH. *T:* (020) 7008 1500.

PRINGLE, Air Marshal Sir Charles (Norman Seton), KBE 1973 (CBE 1967); MA; FREng; *b* 6 June 1919; *s* of late Seton Pringle, OBE, FRCSI, Dublin; *m* 1946, Margaret, *d* of late B. Sharp, Baildon, Yorkshire; one *s*. *Educ:* Repton; St John's Coll., Cambridge. Commissioned, RAF, 1941; served India and Ceylon, 1942–46. Air Ministry, 1946–48; RAE, Farnborough, 1949–50; attached to USAF, 1950–52; appts in UK, 1952–60; STSO No 3 Group, Bomber Comd, 1960–62, and Air Forces Middle East, 1962–64; Comdt RAF St Athan and Air Officer Wales, 1964–66; MoD, 1967; IDC, 1968. Dir-Gen. of Engineering (RAF) MoD, 1969–70; Air Officer Engineering, Strike Command, 1970–73; Dir-Gen. Engineering (RAF), 1973; Controller, Engrg and Supply (RAF), 1973–76; Sen. Exec., Rolls Royce Ltd, 1976–78; Dir, Hunting Engineering Ltd, 1976–78; Dir and Chief Exec., SBAC, 1979–84. Director: FR Group plc, 1985–89; Aeronautical Trusts Ltd, 1987–97. President: RAeS, 1975–76; IMGTechE, 1979–82; Smeatonian Soc. of Civil Engrs, 2006; Vice-Chm., 1976–77, Chm., 1977–78, CEI. Mem., Defence Industries

Council, 1978–84. Member Council: Air League, 1976–92; CBI, 1979–84; RSA, 1978–83 and 1986–92. Chm. Governors, Repton Sch., 1985–92. Liveryman, Coachmakers' and Coach Harness Makers' Co., 1981–. FREng (FEng 1977). CCMI. Hon. FRAeS 1989. *Recreations:* photography, ornithology, motor sport. *Address:* Appleyards, Fordingbridge, Hants SP6 3BP; K9 Sloane Avenue Mansions, SW3 3JP. *T:* (020) 7584 3432. *Club:* Royal Air Force.

PRINGLE, Derek Raymond; Cricket Correspondent, The Daily Telegraph, since 2002; *b* Nairobi, 18 Sept. 1958; *s* of late Donald James Pringle and of Doris May Pringle (*née* Newton). *Educ:* St Mary's Sch., Nairobi; Felsted Sch., Essex; Fitzwilliam Coll., Cambridge (MA). Professional cricketer, Essex and England, 1978–93; Cricket Correspondent: Independent on Sunday, 1993–95; Independent, 1995–2002. *Publication:* England's Ashes, 2005. *Recreations:* photography, music, conchology. *Address:* c/o The Daily Telegraph, 111 Buckingham Palace Road, SW1W 0DT.

PRINGLE, Ian Derek; QC 2003; a Recorder, since 1998; *b* 19 Jan. 1957; *s* of late Dr Derek Hair Pringle and of Anne Collier Pringle (*née* Caw); *m* 1980, Mary Seeney; one *s* one *d*. *Educ:* Edinburgh Acad.; St Catharine's Coll., Cambridge (MA). Called to the Bar, Gray's Inn, 1979; in practice, specialising in criminal law; Mem., Guildhall Chambers, Bristol, 1981–. Mem. Council, Burden Neurol Inst., Bristol, 1996–. *Recreations:* history, sport, particularly football, Rugby, golf and athletics. *Address:* Guildhall Chambers, 23 Broad Street, Bristol BS1 2HG. *T:* (0117) 927 3366, *Fax:* (0117) 930 3829; *e-mail:* ian.pringle@guildhallchambers.co.uk. *Club:* Hibernian Football.

PRINGLE, Jack Brown, PPRIBA; Partner, Pringle Brandon, since 1986; President, Royal Institute of British Architects, 2005–07; *b* 13 March 1952; *s* of John and Grace Mason Pringle; divorced; two *d*. *Educ:* Bristol Univ. (BA Hons 1973; DipArch 1975). RIBA 1977. Architect: Powell and Moya, 1973–81; Jack Pringle Architects, 1981–86. Royal Institute of British Architects: Mem. Council, 1979–89 and 2003–; Vice-Pres. for Educn, 2003–; Chm., Professional Services Co., 2003–05. FRSA. Commandeur de l'Ordre des Arts et des Lettres (France), 2007. *Recreations:* flying (Private Pilot's Licence), racing offshore yachts, exhibitions, travelling with daughters. *Address:* Pringle Brandon, 10 Bonhill Street, EC2A 4QJ. *T:* (020) 7466 1000, *Fax:* (020) 7466 1050; *e-mail:* Jack-Pringle@Pringle-Brandon.co.uk.

PRINGLE, Sir John (Kenneth), Kt 1993; Justice of the High Court of Northern Ireland, 1993–99; *b* 23 June 1929; *s* of late Kenneth Pringle and Katie (*née* Batchen); *m* 1960, Ruth Henry; two *s* one *d*. *Educ:* Campbell Coll., Belfast; Queen's Univ., Belfast (BSc 1st Cl. Hons 1950; LLB 1st Cl. Hons 1953). Called to the Bar, NI, 1953, Bencher, 1973; QC (NI), 1970; Recorder of Belfast, 1984–93. Chm., Bar Council of NI, 1975–80. Member: Parades Commn for NI, 2000–05; Investigatory Powers Tribunal, 2001–06. *Recreations:* gardening, being outdoors.

PRINGLE, Jonathan Helier W.; *see* Watt-Pringle.

PRINGLE, Margaret Ann; Associate Director, Centre for the Study of Comprehensive Schools, since 1995; *b* 28 Sept. 1946. *Educ:* Holton Park Girls' Grammar Sch.; Somerville College, Oxford (MA, BLitt English Lang. and Lit.). English Teacher, Selhurst High School, Croydon, 1972–76; Head of English, Thomas Calton School, Peckham, 1976–81; Dep. Head, George Green's School, Isle of Dogs, 1981–86; Head, Holland Park Sch., 1986–95. *Recreations:* all food, all music, most dancing, and occasionally not thinking about education. *Address:* Flat 3, 64 Pembridge Villas, W11 3ET.

PRINGLE, Prof. Michael Alexander Leary, CBE 2001; FRCGP; Professor of General Practice, University of Nottingham, since 1993; *b* 14 May 1950; *s* of Alexander and Yvonne Pringle; *m* 1974, Nicola Mary Wood; three *d*. *Educ:* St Edward's Sch., Oxford; Guy's Hosp. Med. Sch. (MB BS 1973). FRCGP 1989. Vocational Trng Scheme for Gen. Practice, Reading, 1975–78. Principal in gen. practice, Collingham, Notts, 1979–2004; Lectr and Sen. Lectr, Dept of Gen. Practice, Univ. of Nottingham, 1983–93. GP Clinical Hd, NHS Connecting for Health, 2004–. Chm. Council, RCGP, 1998–2001. Co-Chm., Expert Ref. Gp for Diabetes Nat. Service Framework, 1999–2002. FMedSci 1999. Hon. FRCP 2000. *Publications:* (jtly) Managing Change in Primary Care, 1991; (ed) Change and Teamwork in Primary Care, 1993; (ed) Fellowship by Assessment, 1995; (jtly) A Guide for New Principals, 1996; (ed) Primary Care: core values, 1998; contrib. numerous chapters in books, res. articles and editorials in jls. *Recreations:* chess, reading, Italy, walking. *Address: e-mail:* mike.pringle@nottingham.ac.uk.

PRINGLE, Michael Stanley Robert; Member (Lib Dem) Edinburgh South, Scottish Parliament, since 2003; *b* 25 Dec. 1945; *s* of Robert Stanley Valdemar Pringle and Pauline Olga Pringle (*née* Brian); *m* 1971, Margaret Isobel Gilfillan Birkett; two *s*. *Educ:* Edinburgh Acad. Bank teller, Inst. of Bankers of Scotland, Royal Bank of Scotland, 1965–71; Trainee Hotel Manager, North British Trust Hotels, 1971–74; Man. Dir, TMM Ltd, 1974–92. Member: Edinburgh DC, 1992–96; Lothian Regl Council, 1994–96; Edinburgh CC, 1995–2003. *Recreations:* fishing, wine tasting, sport, cooking. *Address:* (constituency office) 4 Grange Road, Edinburgh EH9 1UH; Scottish Parliament, Edinburgh EH99 1SP. *T:* (0131) 348 5788; *e-mail:* mike.pringle.msp@scottish.parliament.uk.

PRINGLE, Lt Gen. Sir Steuart (Robert), 10th Bt *cr* 1683, of Stichill, Roxburghshire; KCB 1982; Commandant General Royal Marines, 1981–84; Chairman and Chief Executive, Chatham Historic Dockyard Trust, 1984–91; *b* 21 July 1928; *s* of Sir Norman H. Pringle, 9th Bt and Lady (Oonagh) Pringle (*née* Curran) (*d* 1975); *S* father, 1961; *m* 1953, Jacqueline Marie Gladwell; one *s* two *d* (and one *s* decd). *Educ:* Sherborne. Royal Marines: 2nd Lieut, 1946; 42 Commando, 1950–52; 40 Commando, 1957–59; Chief Instructor, Signal Trng Wing, RM, 1959–61; Bde Signal Officer, 3 Commando Bde, RM, 1961–63; Defence Planning Staff, 1964–67; Chief Signal Officer, RM, 1967–69; 40 Commando, Far East, 1969–71; CO 45 Commando Group, 1971–74; HQ Commando Forces, 1974–76; RCDS, 1977; Maj.-Gen. RM Commando Forces, 1978–79; Chief of Staff to Comdt Gen., RM, 1979–81. Col Comdt, RM, 1989–90, Representative Col Comdt, 1991–92. President: St Loye's Coll., 1984–2000; City of London Br., RM Assoc., 1984–2004; Vice-Pres., Officers Pensions Soc., 1984–99; Mem. Council, Union Jack Club, 1982–85; Vice-Patron, Royal Naval Benevolent Trust, 1984–. Liveryman, Plaisterers' Co., 1984. Hon. DSc City, 1982; Hon. LLD Exeter, 1994. Hon. Admiral, Texas Navy; Hon. Mem., Co. of Bear Tamers. *Publications:* (contrib) Peace and the Bomb, 1982; The Future of British Seapower, 1984; contribs to RUSI Jl, Navy International, etc. *Heir:* *s* Simon Robert Pringle [*b* 6 Jan. 1959; *m* 1992, Pamela Margaret, *d* of George Hunter; one *s* one *d*]. *Address:* 76 South Croxted Road, Dulwich, SE21 8BD. *Clubs:* Army and Navy, Royal Thames Yacht.

PRIOR, family name of **Baron Prior**.

PRIOR, Baron *cr* 1987 (Life Peer), of Brampton in the County of Suffolk; **James Michael Leathes Prior;** PC 1970; Chairman, The General Electric Company plc, 1984–98; *b* 11 Oct. 1927; 2nd *s* of late C. B. L. and A. S. M. Prior, Norwich; *m* 1954, Jane Primrose Gifford, 2nd *d* of late Air Vice-Marshal O. G. Lywood, CB, CBE; three *s* one *d*. *Educ:* Charterhouse; Pembroke College, Cambridge (1st class degree in Estate Management, 1950; Hon. Fellow, 1992). Commissioned in Royal Norfolk Regt, 1946; served in India and Germany; farmer and land agent in Norfolk and Suffolk. MP (C): Lowestoft, Suffolk, 1959–83; Waveney, 1983–87. PPS to Pres. of Bd of Trade, 1963, to Minister of Power, 1963–64, to Mr Edward Heath, Leader of the Opposition, 1965–70; Minister of Agriculture, Fisheries and Food, 1970–72; Lord Pres. of Council and Leader of House of Commons, 1972–74; Opposition front bench spokesman on Employment, 1974–79; Sec. of State for Employment, 1979–81; Sec. of State for NI, 1981–84. A Dep. Chm., Cons. Party, 1972–74 (Vice-Chm., 1965). Chairman: Allders, 1989–94; East Anglian Radio PLC, 1992–96; African Cargo Handling Ltd, 1998–2001; Ispat Energy Hldgs Ltd, 1998–2000; Ascot Underwriting Ltd, 2001–06; Dep. Chm., MSI Cellular Investments BV, 2000–04; Director: United Biscuits (Holdings), 1984–94; Barclays Bank, 1984–89; Barclays International, 1984–89; J. Sainsbury, 1984–92; Celtel, 2000–05; Member: Tenneco European Adv. Bd, 1986–97; Internat. Adv. Bd, Amer. Internat. Gp, 1988–2006. Chancellor, Anglia Poly. Univ., 1992–99 (Hon. PhD 1992). Chairman: Council for Industry and Higher Educn, 1986–91; Archbishops' Commn on Rural Areas, 1988–91; Great Ormond Street Wishing Well Appeal, 1985–89; Special Trustees, Great Ormond Street, 1989–94; Industry and Parliament Trust, 1990–94; Rural Housing Trust, 1990–99; Royal Veterinary Coll., 1990–99; Arab-British Chamber of Commerce, 1996–2004. *Publications:* (jtly) The Right Approach to the Economy, 1977; A Balance of Power, 1986. *Recreations:* cricket, tennis, golf, gardening. *Address:* House of Lords, SW1A 0PW. *Clubs:* MCC; Butterflies Cricket.

See also Hon. D. G. L. Prior.

PRIOR, (Alice) Mary, MBE 1999; Lord-Lieutenant of the County of Bristol, since 2007; *b* 22 April 1942; *d* of Harry Forty and Kathleen Louise Forty; *m* 1982, John Michael Prior; one *s* one *d*. *Educ:* Kingswood Grammar Sch. Bowater Paper Corp., 1959–65; Gen. Sales Manager, Sales Dir, then Sales and Mktg Dir, Alexandra plc, 1973–97. Trustee: St Monica Trust, 1999–; Quartet Community Foundn, 2004–; Patron, Bristol Cathedral Trust, 2005– (Trustee, 1988–2005). Patron or Pres., numerous charitable orgns in Bristol. DL County of Bristol, 1996. *Recreations:* reading, gardening, music. *Address:* Youngwood Farm, Youngwood Lane, Nailsea, Bristol BS48 4NR. *T:* (01275) 852374, *Fax:* (01275) 810031; *e-mail:* mary@youngwoodfarm.co.uk.

PRIOR, Anthony Basil, FRICS; Consultant Valuer: to Isle of Man Government, since 2001; to Institute of Revenues Rating & Valuation, since 2001; *b* 23 March 1941; *s* of Rev. Christopher Prior and May Prior (*née* Theobald); *m* 1967, Susan Margaret Parry; two *s*. *Educ:* Commonweal Grammar Sch., Swindon. FRICS 1977; IRRV 1988. Joined Valuation Office, 1967: Dist Valuer, Southampton, 1979–84; Superintending Valuer, Chief Valuer's Office, 1984–91; Regl Dir, Western Reg., later London Reg., 1991–98; Dir, Professional and Customer Services, and Mem., Mgt Bd, Valuation Office Agency, 1999–2001. Mem., Adv. Panel on Standards for the Planning Inspectorate, 2001–. Member: Rating Valuers' Assoc., 1984; Council, IRRV, 1988–. *Publication:* (jtly) Encyclopedia on Contractors Basis of Valuation, 1990. *Recreations:* bee-keeping, fly fishing, Greek and Roman history. *Address:* c/o Institute of Revenues Rating & Valuation, 41 Doughty Street, WC1N 2LF.

PRIOR, Clifford James, CBE 2002; Chief Executive, UnLtd, since 2006; *b* 14 Feb. 1957; *s* of Colin Prior and Beatrice (*née* Maber). *Educ:* Alleyn's Sch., Dulwich; St Catherine's Coll., Oxford (BA Biochem. 1978). Counsellor: Andover Crisis Support Centre, 1978–80; Social Services, Tower Hamlets LBC, 1980–82; Housing Asst, 1982–84, Area Manager, 1984–85, Special Projects Co-ordinator, 1985–88, New Islington and Hackney Housing Assoc.; Housing Services Manager, 1988–90, Asst Dir of Policy and Inf., 1990–92, Dir of Policy and Planning, 1992–94, Stonham Housing Assoc.; Progs Dir, Mental Health Foundn, 1994–98; Chief Exec., Nat. Schizophrenia Fellowship, subseq. Rethink, 1998–2006. Vice Chairman: Homeless Network, 1996–99; Long Term Med. Conditions Alliance, 2000–06; Member: NHS Mental Health Task Force, 2000–06; NHS Modernisation Bd, 2000–04; Nat. Leadership Gp, 2005–06; Medicines Commn, 2004–05; Third Sector Commissioning Task Force, 2005–06; Healthcare Commn, 2007–. Chm., Health and Social Care Gp, ACEVO, 2005–06; Comic Relief UK Grants Cttee, 2007–; FSE Trading Ltd, 2008–. Founder Member and Treasurer: Stonewall Housing Assoc., 1983–87; Strutton Housing Assoc., 1987–90; Chm. Supported Housing, Circle 33 Housing Trust, 1992–98. *Recreations:* scuba diving, travel, film, music, friends. *Address:* UnLtd, 123 Whitecross Street, EC1Y 8JJ. *T:* (020) 7566 1100, *Fax:* (020) 7566 1101; *e-mail:* cliffprior@unltd.org.uk.

PRIOR, Hon. David (Gifford Leathes); Chairman, Norfolk and Norwich University Hospital Trust, 2002–06 and since 2007; chairman and director of various private companies; *b* 3 Dec. 1954; *s* of Lord Prior, *qv*; *m* 1987, Caroline Henrietta Holmes; twin *s* and *d*. *Educ:* Charterhouse; Pembroke Coll., Cambridge (Exhibnr; MA Law 1976). Called to the Bar, Gray's Inn, 1977; Commercial Dir, British Steel, 1980–87. MP (C) N Norfolk, 1997–2001; contested (C) same seat, 2001. Vice Chm., 1998–99, Dep. Chm. and Chief Exec., 1999–2001, Conservative Party. *Recreations:* gardening, farming, most sports. *Address:* Swannington Manor, Swannington, Norwich NR9 5NR. *T:* (01603) 861560. *Club:* Royal Automobile.

PRIOR, Mary; *see* Prior, A. M.

PRIOR, Peter James, CBE 1980; DL; Chairman, H. P. Bulmer Holdings PLC, 1977–82 (Director, 1977–85; Managing Director, H. P. Bulmer Ltd, 1966–77); *b* 1 Sept. 1919; *s* of Percy Prior; *m* 1957, Prinia Mary (*d* 2001), *d* of late R. E. Moreau, Berrick Prior, Oxon; two *s*. *Educ:* Royal Grammar Sch., High Wycombe; London Univ. BSc(Econ). FCA, FIMC. Royal Berks Regt, 1939; Intell. Corps, 1944–46 (Captain) (Croix-de-Guerre 1944). Company Sec., Saunders-Roe (Anglesey) Ltd, 1948; Consultant, Urwick, Orr & Partners, 1951; Financial Dir, International Chemical Co., 1956; Financial Dir, British Aluminium Co., 1961; Dep. Chm., Holden Hydroman, 1984–88; Dir, Trebor, 1982–86. Member: English Tourist Bd, 1969–75; Midlands Electricity Bd, 1973–83; Chairman: Inquiry into Potato Processing Industry, 1971; Motorway Service Area Inquiry, 1977–78; Home Office Deptl Inquiry into Prison Discipline, 1984–85. Pres., Incorp. Soc. of British Advertisers' Council, 1980–83. FCMI (Mem. Council, BIM, 1974–82). Chm. Trustees, Leadership Trust, 1975–79; Member: Council, Regular Forces Employment Assoc., 1981–86; Council, Operation Raleigh, 1984–89. DL Hereford and Worcester, 1983. FRSA. Communicator of the Year Award, British Assoc. of Industrial Editors, 1982. *Publications:* Leadership is not a Bowler Hat, 1977; articles on management and leadership. *Recreations:* flying, motor-cycling, swimming, mountain walking, formerly parachuting (UK record for longest delayed drop (civilian), 1981). *Address:* Highland, Holbach Lane, Sutton St Nicholas, Hereford HR1 3DF. *T:* (01568) 797222. *Club:* Special Forces.

PRIOR, William Johnson, CBE 1979; CEng, FIET; Chairman, Manx Electricity Authority, 1984–85; retired; *b* 28 Jan. 1924; *s* of Ernest Stanley and Lilian Prior; *m* 1945, Mariel (*née* Irving); two *s* one *d*. *Educ:* Goole and Barnsley Grammar Schs. Barugh, Mexborough, Stuart Street (Manchester) and Stockport Power Stations, 1944–52; Keadby, 1952–56, Supt, 1954–56; Supt, Berkeley, 1957–58; Supt, Hinkley Point

Generating Station, 1959–66; CEGB and predecessors: Asst Reg. Dir (Generation), NW Region, 1967–70; Dir (Generation), SW Region, 1970–72; Dir-Gen., SE Region, 1972–76; Mem., Electricity Council, 1976–79; Chm., Yorks Electricity Bd, 1979–84. Member: NCB, 1977–83; Adv. Cttee on Safety of Nuclear Installations, 1980–87. *Recreation:* country walking. *Address:* Highfield House, Lime Kiln Lane, Kirk Deighton, Wetherby, W Yorks LS22 4EA. *T:* (01937) 584434.

PRISK, Mark Michael; MP (C) Hertford and Stortford, since 2001; *b* 12 June 1962; *s* of Michael Raymond Prisk and June Irene Prisk; *m* 1989, Lesley Titcomb. *Educ:* Truro Sch., Cornwall; Univ. of Reading (BSc (Hons) Land Mgt). Knight Frank & Rutley, 1983–85; Chartered Surveyor, 1985–; Dir, Derrick, Wade & Waters, 1989–91; Principal: Mark Prisk Connection, 1991–97; mp2, 1997–2001. Shadow Financial Sec., 2002–03; Shadow Paymaster Gen., 2003–04; Opposition Whip, 2004–05; Shadow Minister, Small Business and Enterprise, 2005–. Contested (C): Newham NW, 1992; Wansdyke, 1997. Nat. Vice Chm., FCS, 1981–82; Trustee, Industry and Parliament Trust, 2007–. Chm., Youth for Peace through NATO, 1983–85. Chm. Governors, Stratford GM Sch., 1992–93. *Recreations:* piano, choral music (Mem., Parlt Choir), Rugby and cricket supporter. *Address:* House of Commons, SW1A 0AA. *T:* (020) 7219 3000. *Club:* Saracens RF.

PRITCHARD, Arthur Alan, CB 1979; JP; formerly Deputy Under Secretary of State, Ministry of Defence; *b* 3 March 1922; *s* of Arthur Henry Standfast Pritchard and Sarah Bessie Myra Pritchard (*née* Mundy); *m* 1949, Betty Rona Nevard (*née* Little); two *s* one *d*. *Educ:* Wanstead High Sch., Essex. Board of Trade, 1939. RAFVR Pilot, 1941–52; CFS Instr, 1946. Joined Admiralty, 1952; Asst Sec., 1964; Royal College of Defence Studies, 1972; Asst Under-Sec. of State, Naval Personnel and Op. Requirements, MoD, 1972–76; seconded as Dep. Sec., NI Office, 1976–78; Secretary to the Admiralty Bd, 1978–81. Management consultant, 1984–89. Pres., Fordingbridge and Dist Community Assoc., 1996–2002 (Chm., 1990–95); Chm., Sandleheath Parish Council, 2001–03. JP Ringwood, 1986 (Totton and New Forest, 1981–86; Chm., Ringwood Bench, 1991–92). *Recreation:* walking. *Address:* Courtlands, Manor Farm Road, Fordingbridge, Hants SP6 1DY.

PRITCHARD, David Alan, CB 2006; Dean, Cardiff School of Management, University of Wales Institute, Cardiff, since 2006; *b* 23 March 1946; *s* of John Merfyn Pritchard and Anne Louise Pritchard; *m* 1970, Kathryn Henton; two *s*. *Educ:* UCNW, Bangor (BA Hons Econs). Welsh Office: Head: Industry Policy Div., 1989; Health Strategy and Rev. Div., 1990–97; Local Govt Policy and Finance Div., 1997–99; Welsh Assembly Government: Corporate Planning Unit, 1999–2000; Gp Dir, Econ. Devolt, then Econ. Devolt and Transport, Dept, 2000–06. Non-exec. Dir, Carbon Trust, 2001–. *Recreations:* walking, travelling, gardening. *Address:* Ty'r Ardd, Cardiff Road, Creigiau CF15 9NL. *T:* (029) 2089 0932.

PRITCHARD, David Peter; Deputy Chairman, Lloyds TSB Group plc, 2003–05; Chairman, Cheltenham & Gloucester, 2004–05; *b* 20 July 1944; *s* of Norman and Peggy Pritchard; *m* 1993, Elizabeth Cresswell; one *s* one *d*. *Educ:* Read Sch., Drax, Yorks; Southampton Univ. (BScEng 1966). Hawker Siddeley Aviation, 1966–71; Wm Brandt's Sons & Co., 1971–73; Edward Bates & Sons Ltd, 1973–78; Man. Dir, Citicorp Investment Bank, 1978–87; Vice Chm., Orion Royal Bank, 1987–88; Gen. Manager, Europe, Royal Bank of Canada, 1988–95; Treas., TSB Gp plc, 1995–96; on secondment to FSA, 1996–98; Gp Dir, Wholesale and Internat. Banking, Lloyds TSB Gp plc, 1998–2003. Chairman: Songbird Estates plc, 2005–; AIB Gp (UK) plc; non-executive Director: LCH.Clearnet Gp Ltd (formerly London Clearing House), 2001–07; Scottish Widows plc, 2003–07; Allied Irish Banks plc, 2007–. *Recreations:* cycling, Nordic ski-ing, photography. *Address:* 17 Thorney Crescent, SW11 3TT. *T:* (020) 7585 2253. *Club:* London Capital.

PRITCHARD, Frances Jean; *see* Judd, F. J.

PRITCHARD, Rear-Adm. Gwynedd Idris, CB 1981; *b* 18 June 1924; *s* of Cyril Idris Pritchard and Lily Pritchard; *m* 1975, Mary Thérèsa (*née* Curtin); three *s* (by previous marriage). *Educ:* Wyggeston Sch., Leicester. FCMI. Joined Royal Navy, 1942; Sub-Lieut 1944; Lieut 1946; Lt-Comdr 1954; Comdr 1959; Captain 1967; Rear-Adm. 1976; Flag Officer Sea Training, 1976–78; Flag Officer Gibraltar, 1979–81; retired list, 1981. Chm., SW Regl Planning Conf., 1990–93. Mem., Dorset CC, 1985–2001. *Recreations:* gardening, golf. *Address:* Hoofprints, Beach Road, Burton Bradstock, Dorset DT6 4RF.

PRITCHARD, Gwynn; *see* Pritchard, I. G.

PRITCHARD, (Iorwerth) Gwynn; independent television producer; Secretary General, International Public Television (INPUT) (formerly International Public Television Screening Conference), 2001–06; *b* 1 Feb. 1946; *s* of late Rev. Islwyn Pritchard and Megan Mair Pritchard; *m* 1st, 1970, Marilyn Bartholomew (*d* 1994); two *s* one *d*; 2nd, 1998, Althea Sharp. *Educ:* Bolton Sch.; King's Coll., Cambridge (MA). Producer and Director: BBC Television, London, 1969–78; BBC Wales, 1979–82; HTV Wales, 1982–85; Commissioning Editor, 1985–88, Sen. Commissioning Editor for Educn, 1989–92, Channel 4; Hd of Welsh Progs, then of Welsh Broadcasting, BBC Cymru/Wales, 1992–2001. Pres., INPUT Internat. Bd, 1988–93. Trustee: Welsh Writers Trust, 1990–; Broadcasting Support Services, 1990–92; Nat. Inst. for Adult and Contg Educn, 1990–92. Member Board: Sheffield Internat. Documentary Fest., 1993–96; Welsh (formerly Aberystwyth) Internat. Film Fest., 1993–98. Mem. Council, Coleg Harlech, 1992–2000; Gov., Ysgol Gynradd Pencae, 1992–2002. Winston Churchill Fellow, Winston Churchill Meml Trust, 1973; Huw Weldon Fellow, UCNW, Bangor, 1990–91. Chevalier de l'Ordre des Arts et des Lettres (France), 1990. *Recreations:* swimming, walking, cinema, reading. *Address:* 25 Westbourne Road, Penarth, Vale of Glamorgan CF64 3HA. *T:* (029) 2070 3608.

PRITCHARD, Rt Rev. John Lawrence; *see* Oxford, Bishop of.

PRITCHARD, John Michael; Founder and Chairman, Legalease Ltd, Publishers, since 1988; *b* 18 June 1949; *s* of Arthur Glyn Pritchard and Sybil Roderick Pritchard; *m* 1st, 1976, Mary Margaret Freeman (marr. diss. 1998); two *s* one *d*; 2nd, 1999, Hilary Baker. *Educ:* Penarth Grammar Sch.; Bristol Univ. Admitted solicitor, 1974; articled with Thompsons, solicitors, London; in practice with Powell Spencer, Kilburn, 1974–89. Chm., Internat. Centre for Commercial Law, 1997–. Editor-in-Chief of periodicals: Legal Business, 1990–; Practical Lawyer, 1991–; In House Lawyer, 1993–; European Legal Business, 1995–; Property Law Jl, 1997–. *Publications:* (ed) Penguin Guide to the Law, 1982, 5th edn, as New Penguin Guide to the Law: your rights and the law explained, 2001; (ed) Legal 500, annually 1988–; Young Solicitors' Handbook, 1990, rev. edn 1991; (ed) Who's Who in the Law: eminent practising lawyers in the UK, 1991; (ed) European Legal 500, annually 1991–; Which Firm of Solicitors?, 1993; Legal Experts, annually 1994–; (ed) Commercial Client Directory: guide to legal service buyers at the UK's top 15,000 companies, 1996; (ed) Asia Pacific Legal 500, annually 1996–; Kanzleien in Deutschland, annually 1997–; (ed) Cabinet's d'Avocats en France, annually, 1999–. *Recreation:* anything that does not involve lawyers. *Address:* c/o 12–14 Ansdell Street, W8 5BN. *T:* (020) 7396 9292, *Fax:* (020) 7396 9300.

PRITCHARD, Kenneth John, CB 1982; Director, Greenwich Hospital, 1987–92; *b* 18 March 1926; *s* of William Edward Pritchard and Ethel Mary Pritchard (*née* Cornfield); *m* 1st, 1949, Elizabeth Margaret Bradshaw (*d* 1978); two *d*; 2nd, 1979, Angela Madeleine Palmer; one *s* two *d*. *Educ:* Newport High Sch.; St Catherine's Coll., Oxford (MA 1951). Served Army, 1944–48; Indian Mil. Acad., Dehra Dun, 1945; served with 8th/12th Frontier Force Regt and 2nd Royal W Kent Regt. Asst Principal, Admiralty, 1951; Private Sec. to Sec. of State for Wales, 1964; Asst Sec., Min. of Aviation, 1966; RCDS, 1972; Principal Supply and Transport Officer (Naval), Portsmouth, 1978, Exec. Dir 1980; Dir Gen. of Supplies and Transport (Naval), MoD, 1981–86, retd. Vice Patron, Royal Naval Benevolent Trust, 1992–. Chm., Frome Tourist Information Ltd, 1996–. Freeman, City of London, 1988; Liveryman, Coopers' Co., 1988. Mem., Cousinerie de Bourgogne, 1997. FCIPS (FInstPS 1986). *Recreations:* tennis, music hall, good wine. *Address:* Pickford House, Beckington, Som BA11 6SJ. *T:* (01373) 830329.

PRITCHARD, Kenneth William, OBE 1992; WS; part-time Sheriff, 2000–03 (Temporary Sheriff, 1995–99); Secretary of the Law Society of Scotland, 1976–97; *b* 14 Nov. 1933; *s* of Dr Kenneth Pritchard, MB, BS, DPH, and Isobel Pritchard, LDS (*née* Broom); *m* 1962, Gretta (*née* Murray), BL, MBA, WS; two *s* one *d*. *Educ:* Dundee High Sch.; Fettes Coll.; St Andrews Univ. (BL). National Service, Argyll and Sutherland Highlanders, 1955–57; commnd 2nd Lieut, 1956; TA 1957–62 (Captain). Joined J. & J. Scrimgeour, Solicitors, Dundee, 1957, Sen. Partner, 1970–76; WS 1984. Hon. Sheriff, Dundee, 1978. Member: Sheriff Court Rules Council, 1973–76; Lord Dunpark's Cttee Considering Reparation upon Criminal Conviction, 1973–77; Secretary, Scottish Council of Law Reporting, 1976–97. Governor, Moray House Coll. of Educn, 1982–84; Mem. Ct, Univ. of Dundee, 1990–93. Mem., National Trust for Scotland Jubilee Appeal Cttee, 1980–82. Pres., Dundee High Sch. Old Boys Club, 1975–76; Captain of the Former Pupil RFC, Dundee High Sch., 1959–62. Hon. Prof. of Law, Strathclyde Univ., 1986–94. *Recreation:* golf. *Address:* 22/4 Kinellan Road, Edinburgh EH12 6ES. *T:* (0131) 337 4294. *Clubs:* New, Bruntsfield Links Golfing Society (Edinburgh); Hon. Company of Edinburgh Golfers (Muirfield).

PRITCHARD, Mark Andrew; MP (C) The Wrekin, since 2005; *b* 22 Nov. 1966; *s* of late Francis Pritchard and of Romona Pritchard; *m* 1997, Sondra Janae Spaeth. *Educ:* London Guildhall Univ. (MA Mktg Mgt); CIM Postgrad. Dip. Mktg; Elim Coll. (Cert. Theol. and Pastoral Studies). Parly researcher, 1994–95; founder and owner: Pritchard Communications Ltd, 1999–2007; Next Steps Mkt Res. Ltd, 2002–06. Member: Harrow BC, 1993–94; Woking BC, 2000–03. Contested (C) Warley, 2001. Member: Envmtl Audit Select Cttee, 2005–07; DWP Select Cttee, 2006–; Welsh Affairs Select Cttee, 2007–; Vice Chairman: All Party Parly Gp on Social Care, 2005–; All Party Parly Gp on Argentina, 2005–; All Party Parly Gp on Venezuela, 2006–; Chairman: All Party Parly Gp on the Philippines, 2006–; All Party Parly Gp Russia; Secretary: Cons. Parly Defence Cttee, 2006–; Cons. Parly Foreign Affairs Gp, 2006–; Mem., Cons. Homeland Security Team, 2006–; Comr, Cons. Human Rights Commn, 2006–. Member: Council, Bow Gp, 1993–94; Bd, Cons. Councillors Assoc., 2002–05. *Recreations:* walking miniature schnauzers (Mem., Miniature Schnauzer Club of GB), ski-ing, animal welfare. *Address:* c/o House of Commons, SW1A 0AA. *T:* (020) 7219 3000; *e-mail:* pritchardm@parliament.uk.

PRITCHARD, Mehmuda Nighat Mian; Trustee, BBC Trust, since 2006; Member, Independent Police Complaints Commission, since 2004; *b* 30 July 1962; *d* of Manzoor Alam and Naziran Mian; *m* 2003, Khalid Pritchard. *Educ:* Teesside High Sch. for Girls; Univ. of Birmingham (LLB Hons Law with French 1994); Coll. of Law, Chester. Admitted solicitor, 1989; articled clerk, then solicitor, Edge & Ellison, 1985–91; solicitor, Wansbroughs Willey Hargrave, 1991–94; Office for the Supervision of Solicitors, Law Soc., 1994–98. Mem., Police Complaints Authy, 1998–2004. *Recreations:* reading, trekking, travelling, charity fund raising, spending time with family and friends, trying to keep fit. *Address:* c/o Independent Police Complaints Commission, 90 High Holborn, WC1V 6BH. *T:* (020) 7166 3093; *e-mail:* mehmuda.mian.pritchard@ipcc.gsi.gov.uk.

PRITCHARD, Sir Neil, KCMG 1962 (CMG 1952); HM Diplomatic Service, retired; Ambassador in Bangkok, 1967–70; *b* 14 Jan. 1911; *s* of late Joseph and Lillian Pritchard; *m* 1943, Mary Burroughes (*d* 1988), Pretoria, S Africa; one *s*. *Educ:* Liverpool Coll.; Worcester Coll., Oxford. Dominions Office, 1933; Private Secretary to Permanent Under-Sec., 1936–38; Assistant Secretary, Rhodesia-Nyasaland Royal Commission, 1938; Secretary, Office of UK High Commissioner, Pretoria, 1941–45; Principal Secretary, Office of UK Representative, Dublin, 1948–49; Assistant Under-Secretary of State, Commonwealth Relations Office, 1951–54; Dep. UK High Commissioner: Canada, 1954–57; Australia, 1957–60; Actg Dep. Under-Sec. of State, CRO, 1961; British High Comr in Tanganyika, 1961–63; Deputy Under-Secretary of State, Commonwealth Office (formerly CRO), 1963–67. *Address:* Little Garth, Daglingworth, Cirencester, Glos GL7 7AQ.

PRITCHARD, Prof. Thomas Owen, OBE 2005; JP; Chairman, Cynefin Environmental Ltd, consultants in sustainable development, since 1991; Deputy Chairman, National Heritage Memorial Fund, 1999–2005; Professorial Fellow, University of Wales; *b* 13 May 1932; *s* of late Owen and Mary Pritchard; *m* 1957, Enyd Ashton; one *s* one *d*. *Educ:* Botwnnog Grammar Sch.; Univ. of Wales (BSc Hons Botany and Agric. Botany); Univ. of Leeds (PhD Genetics). Midlands Regl Officer and Head of Educn, Nature Conservancy, 1957–67; Dep. Dir for Wales, Nature Conservancy—NERC, 1967–73; Dir for Wales, NCC, 1973–91. Consultant, Council of Europe, 1968. Vis. Prof., Dept of Forestry and Resource Management, Univ. of California, Berkeley, 1981–. Dir, CTF Training Ltd, 1982–91; Chairman: Coed Cymru Ltd, 1983–92; Slate Ecology Co. Ltd, 1995–. Chairman: Bardsey Island Trust, 1987–93; Welsh Historic Gdns Trust, 1994–98 (Pres., 2001); Exec., POW Cttee, 1971–73; Country Cttee for Wales, Heritage Lottery Fund, 1999–2005; Envmt Protection Adv. Cttee for Wales, Envmt Agency, Wales, 2005–; Vice Chm. (Educn), IUCN, 1966–73; former Chm. and Mem., conservation and envmtl bodies, nat. and internat. Member: Genetical Soc.; British Ecological Soc. Member: Ct of Govs and Council: Univ. of Wales, Bangor (formerly UC, Bangor), 1981–; Nat. Museum of Wales, 1981–91. Member: Gorsedd of Bards, Royal Nat. Eisteddfod; Hon. Soc. of Cymmrodorion. FRSA. JP Bangor, 1978. *Publications:* Cynefin y Cymro, 1989; numerous contribs to sci. and educn jls. *Recreation:* sailing. *Address:* Graig Lwyd, 134 Ffordd Penrhos, Bangor, Gwynedd LL57 2BX. *T:* (01248) 370401.

PRITCHETT, Matthew, (Matt), MBE 2002; front page cartoonist for Daily Telegraph, since 1988; *b* 14 July 1964; *s* of Oliver Pritchett and Joan Pritchett (*née* Hill); *m* 1992, Pascale Charlotte Marie Smets; one *s* three *d*. *Educ:* Addey and Stanhope Sch.; St Martin's Sch. of Art. Freelance cartoonist for New Statesman, Punch and Spectator, 1986–88. Awards from: What the Papers Say, 1992, 2004, 2006; Cartoon Arts Trust, 1995, 1996, 1999, 2005, 2006; UK Press Gazette, 1996, 1998; British Press Awards, 2000, 2008.

Publications: Best of Matt, annually, 1991–; 10 Years of Matt, 2001. *Address:* c/o The Daily Telegraph, 111 Buckingham Palace Road, SW1W 0DT.

PRITTIE, family name of **Baron Dunalley**.

PROBERT, David Henry, CBE 1996; FCIS, FCMA, FCCA; Chief Executive, 1976–86, Executive Chairman, 1986–98, W. Canning plc (Director, 1976); *b* 11 April 1938; *s* of William David Thomas Probert and Doris Mabel Probert; *m* 1968, Sandra Mary Prince; one *s* one *d*. *Educ:* Bromsgrove High School. A Crown Agent for Oversea Govts and Admins, 1981–98 (Dep. Chm., 1985–90; Chm., 1990–98); Crown Agent for Holdings and Realisation Bd, 1981–98. Dir, Private Patients Plan Ltd, 1988–96; Chm., PPP Healthcare Group plc, 1996–98; Gov., PPP Medical Trust, 1998–99. Chairman: Leigh Interests plc, 1996–98 (Dir, 1995–98); Saville Gordon Estates plc, 1999–2001 (Dir, 1998–2001); Ash & Lacy plc, 1998–2000; Director: BSA Ltd, 1971–73; Mills and Allen International Ltd, 1974–76; HB Electronics plc, 1977–86; British Hallmarking Council, 1983–91; Linread Public Limited Company, 1983–90; ASD plc, 1985–90; Sandvik Ltd, 1985–90; Rockwool Ltd, 1988–90, 1992–94; Richard Burbridge Ltd, 1990–91; William Sinclair plc, 1994–2001; Hampson Industries plc, 1994–2002. Pres., Birmingham Chamber of Commerce and Industry, 1994–95 (Vice Pres., 1992–94). Gov., UCE, 1998–2001. Liveryman: Chartered Secretaries and Administrators' Co., 1984; Founders' Co., 1997. CCMI. *Recreations:* theatre, music, sport. *Address:* 4 Blakes Field Drive, Barnt Green, Worcs B45 8JT. *Club:* Lord's Taverners (Regl Chm., 1996–99).

PROBERT, (William) Ronald; Managing Director, Business Development, 1992–93, Member of the Board, 1985–93, Group Executive Member, 1989–93, British Gas plc (formerly British Gas Corporation), retired; *b* 11 Aug. 1934; *s* of William and Florence Probert; *m* 1957, Jean (*née* Howard); three *s*. *Educ:* Grammar Sch., Ashton-under-Lyne; Univ. of Leeds (BA). FIGEM. Entered gas industry, 1957; various marketing appts in E Midlands Gas Bd, 1957–67; Conversion Manager, 1967, Service Manager, 1971, Marketing Dir, 1973, E Midlands Gas Bd; Asst Dir of Marketing, 1975, Dir of Sales, 1977, British Gas Corp.; Man. Dir Marketing, British Gas, 1982–89; Man. Dir, Gas Supply and Strategy, 1989–92. Dir, E Berks NHS Trust, 1991–. CCMI. *Recreations:* narrowboats, music, winemaking. *Address:* 32 Austen Way, Gerrards Cross, Bucks SL9 8NW. *T:* (01753) 888527.

PROBINE, Dr Mervyn Charles, CB 1986; FRSNZ; FInstD; FNZIM; company director and consultant, since 1986; *b* 30 April 1924; *s* of Frederick Charles and Ann Kathleen Probine; *m* 1949, Marjorie Walker; one *s* one *d*. *Educ:* Univ. of Auckland (BSc); Victoria Univ. of Wellington (MSc); Univ. of Leeds (PhD). Physicist, DSIR, 1946–67; Dir, Physics and Engineering Lab., 1967–77; Asst Dir-Gen., DSIR, 1977–79; State Services Commission: Comr, 1979–80; Dep. Chm., 1980–81; Chm., 1981–86, retired. Chm., GEC (NZ), 1986–95; Dir, Fujitsu (NZ), 1986–2000. Chairman: Legislation Adv. Cttee, 1991–96; Insurance and Savings Ombudsman Commn, 1994–98. Trustee, Nat. Library of NZ, 1992–98. FRSNZ 1964; FNZIM 1985; FInstD 1993 (Dist. Fellow, 2004). *Publications:* numerous scientific research papers and papers on application of science in industry. *Recreations:* bridge, sailing, angling. *Address:* 10A Rodney Road, Northcote, Auckland, New Zealand. *T:* (9) 4198140. *Club:* Wellington (Wellington, NZ).

PROBY, Sir William Henry, 3rd Bt *cr* 1952, of Elton Hall, co. Huntingdon; DL; Chairman, MGM Assurance Ltd, since 2007; *b* 13 June 1949; *s* of Sir Peter Proby, 2nd Bt and Blanche Harrison (*née* Cripps); *S* father, 2002; *m* 1974, Meredyth Anne Brentnall; four *d*. *Educ:* Eton; Lincoln Coll., Oxford (MA); Brooksby Coll. of Agric. FCA. Price Waterhouse & Co., 1971–76; Morgan Grenfell & Co., 1976–80; Chief Exec., MWP Ltd, 1980–82; Elton Estates Co. Ltd, 1982–; Chm., Keygate Property Investments Ltd, 2003–. Pres., Historic Houses Assoc., 1994–99; Chm., Nat. Trust, 2003–08. Mem. Adv. Council, Tate Britain, 1999–. DL Cambs, 1995; High Sheriff, Cambs, 2001–02. *Address:* Elton Hall, Elton, Peterborough PE8 6SH. *T:* (01832) 280223, *Fax:* (01832) 280584; *e-mail:* whp@eltonhall.com. *Clubs:* Brooks's, Boodle's.

PROCHASKA, Dr Alice Marjorie Sheila, FRHistS; University Librarian, Yale University, since 2001; *b* 12 July 1947; *d* of John Harold Barwell and Hon. Sheila McNair; *m* 1971, Dr Franklyn Kimmel Prochaska; one *s* one *d*. *Educ:* Perse Sch. for Girls, Cambridge; Somerville Coll., Oxford (BA 1968; MA 1973; DPhil 1975). Assistant Keeper: London Museum, 1971–73; Public Record Office, 1975–84; Sec. and Librarian, Inst. of Historical Res., 1984–92; Dir of Special Collections, BL, 1992–2001. Chm., Nat. Council on Archives, 1991–95; Mem., Royal Commn on Historical MSS, 1998–2001. Member: History Working Gp on Nat. Curriculum, DES, 1989–90; Council, RHistS, 1991–95 (Vice Pres., 1995–99); Heritage Educn Trust, 1992–2001; Hereford Mappa Mundi Trust, 1992–95; Adv. Council, Inst. of Historical Res., 1992–2001; Library Panel, Wellcome Inst., 1993–97; Adv. Panel, Qualidata, Univ. of Essex, 1995–98; Sir Winston Churchill Archive Trust, 1995–2001; Steering Cttee, Digital Library Fedn, 2001–05 (Trustee, 2005–); Adv. Council, Yale Center for British Art, 2002–; Chairman: Section Panel, Rare Books and Manuscripts, IFLA, 1999–2003; Trustees of Lewis Walpole Library, 2001–; Chm., Collections and Access Cttee, 2003–05, Mem., Res., Trng and Learning Cttee, 2005–06, Chair, Special Collections Wkg Gp, 2007–, Assoc. of Res. Libraries; Bd Mem., Center for Res. Libraries, 2003–05 (Vice-Chair, 2005–07; Chair, 2007–). Gov., London Guildhall Univ., 1995–2001. Hon. Fellow: Inst. of Histl Res., London Univ., 2001; RHUL, 2002. *Publications:* London in the Thirties, 1973; History of the General Federation of Trade Unions 1899–1980, 1982; Irish History from 1700: a guide to sources in the Public Record Office, 1986; (ed jtly with F. K. Prochaska) Margaretta Acworth's Georgian Cookery Book, 1987; contribs to learned jls. *Recreations:* family life, collecting watercolours. *Address:* Sterling Memorial Library, Yale University, PO Box 208240, New Haven, CT 06520–8240, USA.

PROCTER, Jane Hilary; media consultant, since 2002; *m* 1985, Thomas Charles Goldstaub; one *s* one *d*. *Educ:* Queen's Coll., Harley St. Fashion Asst, Vogue, 1974–75; Asst Fashion Editor, Good Housekeeping, 1975–77; Actg Fashion Editor, Woman's Jl, 1977–78; Fashion Writer, Country Life, 1978–80; Freelance Fashion Editor, The Times, Sunday Times and Daily Express, 1980–87; Editor: British W, 1987–88; Tatler, 1990–99; Editl Dir, PeopleNews Network, 1999–2002. *Publication:* Dress Your Best, 1983. *Recreations:* sailing, ski-ing. *Address:* 32 Fernshaw Road, SW10 0TF.

PROCTER, (Mary) Norma; contralto; international concert singer; *b* Cleethorpes, Lincolnshire, 15 Feb. 1928. *Educ:* Wintringham Secondary Sch. Vocal studies with Roy Henderson, musicianship with Alec Redshaw, lieder with Hans Oppenheim and Paul Hamburger. London début, Southwark Cathedral, 1948; operatic début, Lucretia, in Britten's Rape of Lucretia, Aldeburgh Festival, 1959; Covent Garden début, Gluck's Orpheus, 1961. Specialist in concert works, oratorios and recitals; appeared with all major conductors and orchestras, and in all major festivals, UK and Europe; performed in Germany, France, Spain, Italy, Portugal, Holland, Belgium, Norway, Denmark, Sweden, Finland, Austria, Luxembourg, Israel, S America; BBC Last Night of the Proms, 1974. Many recordings. Hon. RAM 1974. *Address:* 194 Clee Road, Grimsby, NE Lincs DN32 8NG.

PROCTER, Robert John Dudley; Chief Executive, Lincolnshire County Council, 1983–95; *b* 19 Oct. 1935; *s* of Luther Donald Procter and Edith Muriel Procter; *m* 1962, Adrienne Allen; one *s* one *d*. *Educ:* Cheltenham Grammar School. Admitted Solicitor, 1961. Articled Clerk, Glos CC, 1956–61; Assistant Solicitor: Bath City, 1961–63; Cumberland CC, 1963–65; Lindsey County Council: Sen. Asst Solicitor, 1965–69; Asst Clerk, 1969–71; Dep. Clerk, Kesteven CC, 1971–73; Dir of Personnel, 1973–77, Dir of Admin, 1977–83, Lincolnshire CC. Chm., Assoc. of County Chief Execs, 1994–95. Mem., Warner Cttee of Inquiry into recruitment and selection of staff in children's homes, 1992. Vice Chm., Linkage Community Trust, 2001–04; Treas., Lincoln Cathedral Community Assoc., 2001–06. Chm. Govs, Lincoln Christ's Hosp. Sch. and Foundn, 2001–05. Chm., Eastgate Lincoln Bowls Club, 2007–08. *Recreations:* horse racing, swimming, family history, bowls. *Address:* Flat 3, The Lodge, 38B Nettleham Road, Lincoln LN2 1RE. *T:* (01522) 532105.

PROCTER, Sidney, CBE 1986; Commissioner, Building Societies Commission, 1986–93; company director; *b* 10 March 1925; *s* of Robert and Georgina Margaret Procter; *m* 1952, Isabel (*née* Simmons); one *d*. *Educ:* Ormskirk Grammar School. Served RAF, 1943–47. Entered former Williams Deacon's Bank, 1941; Asst General Manager, 1969; Dep. Dir, Williams & Glyn's Bank, 1970; Divl Dir, 1975; Exec. Dir, 1976–85; Asst Chief Executive, 1976; Dep. Chief Executive, 1977; Chief Exec., 1978–82; Dep. Gp Man. Dir, Royal Bank of Scotland Gp, 1979–82; Gp Chief Exec., 1982–85; Vice Chm., 1986; Director: Royal Bank of Scotland, 1978–86 (Vice Chm., 1986); Provincial Insurance Co., 1985–86; Dep. Chm., Provincial Group, 1991–94 (Dir, 1986–94); Chairman: Exeter Bank, 1991–97; Provincial Group Holdings, 1994–96. Adviser to Governor, Bank of England, 1985–87. Chm., Exeter Trust, 1986–97 (Dir, 1985–97).

PROCTOR, His Honour Anthony James; a Circuit Judge, 1988–2001; *b* 18 Sept. 1931; *s* of James Proctor and Savina Maud (*née* Horsfield); *m* 1964, Patricia Mary Bryan; one *d*. *Educ:* Mexborough Grammar Sch., Yorkshire; St Catharine's Coll., Cambridge (MA, LLM). Flying Officer, RAF, 1953–55. Articled to Sir Bernard Kenyon, County Hall, Wakefield, 1955–58; admitted Solicitor 1958. Sen. Prosecuting Solicitor, Sheffield Corp., 1959–64; Partner, Broomhead & Neals, Solicitors, Sheffield, 1964–74; Dist Registrar and County Court Registrar, Barrow in Furness, Lancaster, Preston, 1974–88; a Recorder, 1985–88; Hon. Recorder of Lancaster, 2000–05. Pres., Assoc. of Dist and Court Registrars, 1985–86. *Recreations:* fell walking, travel, genealogy.

PROCTOR, Harvey; *see* Proctor, K. H.

PROCTOR, (Keith) Harvey; Director, Proctor's Shirts and Ties, 1992; *b* 16 Jan. 1947; *s* of late Albert Proctor and Hilda Tegerdine. *Educ:* High School for Boys, Scarborough; Univ. of York (BA History Hons, 1969). Asst Director, Monday Club, 1969–71; Research Officer, Conservative 1970s Parliamentary Gp, 1971–72; Exec. Director, Parliamentary Digest Ltd, 1972–74; British Paper & Board Industry Federation: Asst Sec., 1974–78; Secretary, 1978–79; Consultant, 1979–87. MP (C): Basildon, 1979–83; Billericay, 1983–87. Mem., Exec. Council, Monday Club, 1983–87. Chief Exec., Richmond Bor. Chamber of Commerce, 1996–98 (Vice-Pres., 1990–92; Pres., 1992–94). Trustee, SW London Community Foundn, 1993–94; Chairman: Richmond Town Centre Cttee, 1995–97; Parkview Court Residents' Assoc., 1996–97 (Sec., 1994–96); Co-Chm., Richmond Victorian Evening Cttee, 1999–. Editor, News and Views, 1991–98. *Publication:* Billericay in Old Picture Postcards, 1985. *Recreations:* tennis, collecting British contemporary art.

PROCTOR, Prof. Michael Richard Edward, PhD, ScD; FRS 2006; FRAS, FIMA; Professor of Astrophysical Fluid Dynamics, University of Cambridge, since 2000; Teaching Fellow, since 1977, and Vice-Master, since 2006, Trinity College, Cambridge; *b* 19 Sept. 1950; *s* of Edward Francis Proctor and Stella Mary Major Proctor (*née* Jones); *m* 1st, 1973, Linda Irene Powell (marr. diss. 1998); two *s* one *d*; 2nd, 1999, Elizabeth Julia Colgate (*née* Nuttall); two step *s*. *Educ:* Stoke House Prep. Sch., Seaford; Shrewsbury Sch.; Trinity Coll., Cambridge (Entrance Scholar 1968; BA 1971, MA; PhD 1975; ScD 1994). FRAS 1977; FIMA 2007. University of Cambridge: Asst Lectr., 1977–81; Lectr, 1981–94; Reader, 1994–2000; Trinity College: Res. Fellow, 1974–77; Tutor, 1980–90, 1991–94; Dean, 1994–2006. Instructor and Asst Prof., MIT, 1975–77. *Publications:* over 130 articles in learned jls. *Recreations:* gardening, rowing, foreign travel, theatre, concerts. *Address:* 98 Long Road, Cambridge CB2 8HF. *T:* (01223) 841272, *Fax:* (01223) 338564; *e-mail:* mrep@cam.ac.uk. *Club:* Athenæum.

PROCTOR, Prof. Stephen John, FRCP, FRCPath; Professor of Haematological Oncology, University of Newcastle upon Tyne, since 1991; *b* 21 Nov. 1945; *s* of Jack and Betty Proctor; *m* 1971, Susan; one *s* two *d*. *Educ:* Morley Grammar Sch.; Univ. of Newcastle upon Tyne (MB BS 1970). FRCP 1985; FRCPath 1989. Sen. Lectr in Medicine and Haematology, Univ. of Newcastle upon Tyne, 1982–91. *Publications:* over 200 peer reviewed articles in scientific jls and med. jls. *Recreations:* gardening, horticulture, enjoying Northumberland, motoring, travel. *Address:* Academic Haematology Department, Medical School, Framlington Place, Newcastle upon Tyne NE2 4HH. *T:* (0191) 222 7791; *e-mail:* s.j.proctor@ncl.ac.uk.

PROCTOR, William Angus; Clerk of the Journals, House of Commons, 2003–04; *b* 1 May 1945; 3rd *s* of late George Longmate Proctor and Anne Ines Louis Proctor (*née* Angus); *m* 1969, Susan Irene Mottram; two *s* one *d*. *Educ:* Bristol Cathedral Sch. (chorister); Keele Univ. (BA Hons English and Political Instns). A Clerk, H of C, 1968–70 and 1972–2004; Res. Associate, Manchester Univ., 1970–72; Delegn Sec., H of C Overseas Office, 1972–74; Clerk, Select Committees on: Sci. and Technol., 1974–77; Procedure, 1977–79; Transport, 1979–82; Foreign Affairs, 1982–87; Sec., H of C Commn, 1987–92; Principal Clerk: of Financial Cttees and Clerk, Treasury and CS Cttee, 1992–95; of Standing Cttees, 1995–97; of Bills, 1997–99; of Delegated Legislation, 1999–2003. Procedural Advr to Pres., Council of Europe Assembly, 1989–92. *Publications:* (jtly) The European Parliament, 1973; (ed) The Parliamentary Assembly of the Council of Europe: procedure and practice, 9th edn (with J. Sweetman) 1990; contrib. articles and reviews to parly jls. *Recreations:* music, theatre, Landmarking. *Address:* *e-mail:* allproctors@btinternet.com.

PROCTOR-BEAUCHAMP, Sir Christopher Radstock; *see* Beauchamp.

PRODI, Romano; Prime Minister of Italy, 1996–98 and 2006–08; *b* Scandiano, Italy, 9 Aug. 1939; *m* Flavia Franzoni; two *s*. *Educ:* Catholic Univ. of Milan (degree in law); LSE (post-grad. studies; Hon. Fellow). Asst in Political Econs, 1963–71, Prof. of Industrial Organisation and Industrial Policy, 1971–99, Univ. of Bologna; Researcher: Lombard Inst. of Economic and Social Studies, 1963–64; Stanford Res. Inst., 1968. Prof. of Econs and Indust. Politics, Free Univ. of Trento, 1973–74; Vis. Prof., Harvard Univ., 1974. Minister of Industry, 1978–79; Chm., Inst. for Industrial Reconstruction, 1982–89, 1993–94. Chm., Ulivo (centre-left coalition gp), 1995. MP, Italy, 1996–99; Pres., Eur. Commn, 1999–2004; MP (Union), Italy, 2006–08. Hon. Mem., Real Academia de

Ciencias Morales y Politicas, Madrid. Hon. Dr: Madras; Sofia; Brown; Barcelona; Pisa; Ottawa; Seoul; Modena-Reggio; Hon. DCL Oxon, 2002. Premio Schumpeter, 1999.

PROESCH, Gilbert; artist; *b* Dolomites, Italy, 1943. *Educ:* Wolkenstein Sch. of Art; Hallein Sch. of Art; Munich Acad. of Art; St Martin's Sch. of Art. Collaboration with George Passmore, as Gilbert and George. Gallery exhibitions include: Modern Fears, 1980, The Believing World, 1983, New Pictures, 1987, Worlds & Windows, 1990, New Democratic Pictures, 1992, Anthony d'Offay Gall.; The Rudimentary Pictures, Milton Keynes Gall., 2000; New Horny Pictures, White Cube², 2001; Perversive Pictures, NY, 2004; museum exhibitions include: The Paintings, 1971, Photo-Pieces 1971–80, 1981, Whitechapel Art Gall.; Pictures 1982 to 85, Hayward Gall., 1987; Enclosed and Enchanted, MOMA, Oxford, 2000; The Dirty Words Pictures (retrospective), Serpentine Gall., 2002; Gilbert & George: major exhibition (retrospective), Tate Modern, 2007; living sculpture includes: The Red Sculpture; Underneath the Arches; The Singing Sculpture; Our New Sculpture. Work in permanent collections incl. Nat. Portrait Gall., Tate Modern and San Francisco Mus. of Modern Art. Represented GB, Venice Biennale, 2005. (Jtly) Turner Prize, 1986. *Publications:* (as Gilbert), with George Passmore: Lost Day; Oh, the Grand Old Duke of York; What Our Art Means. *Address:* c/o White Cube², 48 Hoxton Square, N1 6PB.

PROFIT, (George) Richard, CBE 2003 (OBE 1980); AFC 1974; FRAeS; Board Member, and Group Director, Safety Regulation, Civil Aviation Authority, 1997–2003; *b* 31 Oct. 1940; *s* of Richard George Profit and Lilian Cotterill Profit; *m* 1965, Pamela Shepherd; one *d. Educ:* Oldershaw Grammar Sch.; Army Staff Coll., Camberley; RCDS. FRAeS 1989; FSaRS 2004. Commissioned Royal Air Force, 1961: operational pilot, UK, Singapore, Germany, 1963–77; Officer Commanding: No 3 (F) Sqdn, 1977–80; RAF Coltishall, 1982–85; Inspector of Flight Safety, 1987–90; retd in rank of Air Cdre, 1990; Dir, Safety, Security and Quality Assurance, NATS Ltd, 1990–97; Hd, Aerodrome and Air Traffic Services, Safety Regulation Gp, CAA, 1997. Non-exec. Dir, Railway Safety Bd, 2001–03; Ind. non-exec. Dir, Rail and Safety Standards Bd, 2003–. *Publication:* Systematic Safety Management in the Air Traffic Services, 1995. *Recreations:* trout fishing, painting. *Club:* Royal Air Force.

PROKHOROVA, Violetta; *see* Elvin, V.

PROPHET, His Honour John; a Circuit Judge, 1997–2006; a Judge of the Employment Appeal Tribunal, 2002–06; *b* 19 Nov. 1931; *s* of Benjamin and Elsie Prophet; *m* 1961, Pauline Newby; three *d. Educ:* Trinity Coll., Cambridge (MA). Called to the Bar, Lincoln's Inn, 1956; Shell International, 1956–60; private practice at the Bar, 1960–63; Sen. Lectr, Law Faculty, Leeds Univ., 1968–76; full-time Chm. of Industrial Tribunals, 1976–88; Regl Chm. of Industrial Tribunals, Yorkshire and Humberside, 1988–97; Pres., Industrial, subseq. Employment, Tribunals for England and Wales, 1997–2002. Consultant, Nat. Assoc. of Local Councils, 1968–89. *Publications:* The Structure of Government, 1968; The Parish Councillor's Guide, 1974, 17th edn 2000; Fair Rents, 1976; The Councillor, 1979, 11th edn 1997. *Recreations:* tennis, chess, gardening, 8 grandchildren!

PROPHIT, Penny Pauline; Professor of Nursing Studies, University of Edinburgh, 1983–92 (Head of Department, 1983–88); *b* 7 Feb. 1939; *d* of C. Alston Prophit and Hortense Callahan. *Educ:* Marillac Coll., St Louis Univ., USA (BSN); Catholic Univ. of America (MSN, BNSc, PhD). Asst Prof., Catholic Univ. of America, 1975; Associate Professor: Univ. of Southern Mississippi, 1975; Louisiana State Univ. Med. Center, 1975; Cons., WHO, Europ. Office, Copenhagen, 1977; Prof., Katholieke Univ., Leuven, Belgium, 1977. Mental Welfare Comr for Scotland, 1985; Mem., UK Central Council for Nursing, Midwifery and Health Visiting, 1988. Delta Epsilon Sigma, Nat. Catholic Scholastic Honor Soc., 1966; Sigma Theta Tau, Internat. Nursing Scholastic Honor Soc., 1970; Sigma Epsilon Phi, Catholic Univ. of Amer. Honor Soc., 1975. *Publications:* (with Lynette Long) Understanding and Responding, 1982; res. articles on nursing care of the elderly, stress in nursing, interdisciplinary collaboration, etc. *Recreations:* jogging, reading and writing poetry and short stories, playing piano and listening to music of all kinds.

PROSSER, family name of **Baroness Prosser.**

PROSSER, Baroness *cr* 2004 (Life Peer), of Battersea in the London Borough of Wandsworth; **Margaret Theresa Prosser,** OBE 1997; Deputy Chair, Commission for Equality and Human Rights, since 2006; *b* 22 Aug. 1937; *d* of Frederick James and Lillian (*née* Barry); *m* (marr. diss.); one *s* two *d. Educ:* St Philomena's Convent, Carshalton; North East London Polytechnic (Post Grad. Dip. in Advice and Inf. Studies, 1977). Associate Mem., Inst. of Legal Execs, 1982. Advice Centre Organiser, Southwark Community Develt Project, 1974–76; Advr, Southwark Law Project, 1976–83; Transport and General Workers' Union: official, 1983–2002; Nat. Sec., 1984–92; Nat. Organiser, 1992–99; Dep. Gen. Sec., 1999–2002. Pres., TUC, 1995–96. Non-exec. Dir, Royal Mail, 2004–. Member: Equal Opportunities Commn, 1987–93; Employment Appeal Tribunal, 1995–2007; Central Arbitration Cttee, 2000–03; Low Pay Commn, 2000–05; Chair, Women's Nat. Commn, 2002–07. Treas., Labour Party, 1996–2001. *Recreations:* walking, gardening, reading. *Address:* Flat 34, 4 Grand Avenue, Hove, Sussex BN3 2LE.

PROSSER, Rt Hon. Lord; William David Prosser; PC 2000; a Senator of the College of Justice in Scotland and Lord of Session, 1986–2001; *b* 23 Nov. 1934; *yr s* of David G. Prosser, MC, WS, Edinburgh; *m* 1964, Vanessa, *er d* of Sir William O'Brien Lindsay, KBE, Nairobi; two *s* two *d. Educ:* Edinburgh Academy; Corpus Christi Coll., Oxford (MA); Edinburgh Univ. (LLB). Advocate, 1962; QC (Scotland) 1974; Standing Junior Counsel in Scotland, Board of Inland Revenue, 1969–74; Advocate-Depute, 1978–79; Vice-Dean, Faculty of Advocates, 1979–83; Dean of Faculty, 1983–86. Mem., Scottish Cttee, Council on Tribunals, 1977–84. Chm., Royal Fine Art Commn for Scotland, 1990–95. Chairman: Royal Lyceum Theatre Co., 1987–92; Scottish Historic Buildings Trust, 1988–98; Chamber Gp of Scotland, 1993–98; Edinburgh Sir Walter Scott Club, 1993–96; Scottish Architectural Educn Trust, 1994–2007; Mem., Franco-British Council, 1997–2007 (Trustee, 2002–07); Pres., Franco-British Lawyers' Soc., 1999–2002. Gov., UHI, 2001–. Hon. FRIAS 1995. Officier, Ordre des Arts et des Lettres (France), 2007. *Address:* 7 Randolph Crescent, Edinburgh EH3 7TH. *T:* (0131) 225 2709; 6 cité Pigalle, 75009 Paris, France. *T:* 40230433. *Clubs:* New, Scottish Arts (Edinburgh).

PROSSER, Charles; *see* Prosser, L. C.

PROSSER, Sir David (John), Kt 2005; FIA; Chief Executive, Legal & General Group, 1991–2006; *b* 26 March 1944; *s* of Ronald and Dorothy Prosser; *m* 1971, Rosemary Margaret Snuggs; two *d. Educ:* Univ. of Wales (BSc). Sun Alliance Group, 1965–69; Hoare Govett, 1969–73; CIN Management, 1973–88; Legal & General, 1988–2006. Director: SWALEC, 1991–96; InterContinental Hotels Gp, 2003–08; Investec plc, 2006–. Chm., Financial Services Skills Council, 2004–06. Mem. of Bd, ABI, 1994–97, 1999–2006. *Recreation:* family life. *Club:* Royal Automobile (Chm., 2007–).

PROSSER, His Honour (Elvet) John; QC 1978; a Circuit Judge, 1988–2001; Resident Judge, Newport (Gwent) Crown Court, 1993–2001; *b* 10 July 1932; *s* of David and Hannah Prosser; *m* 1957, Mary Louise Cowdry; two *d. Educ:* Pontypridd Grammar Sch.; King's Coll., London Univ. LLB. Flt Lt, RAF, 1957–59. Called to the Bar, Gray's Inn, 1956, Bencher, 1986; Mem., Senate of Inns of Court and the Bar, 1980–87; a Recorder, 1972–88; Leader, Wales and Chester Circuit, 1984–87. Part-time Chm. of Industrial Tribunals, 1975–81. An Asst Boundary Comr for Wales, 1977–2001. *Recreations:* watching cricket and television. *Address:* 15 Redwood Court, Llanishen, Cardiff CF14 5RD. *Clubs:* East India, Devonshire, Sports and Public Schools; Cardiff and County (Cardiff).

PROSSER, Gwynfor Mathews, (Gwyn) MP (Lab) Dover, since 1997; *b* 27 April 1943; *s* of late Glyndwr Jenkin Prosser and of Edith Doreen Prosser; *m* 1972, Rodina Beaton MacLeod; one *s* two *d. Educ:* Dunvant Sch., Swansea; Swansea Secondary Tech. Sch. Nat. Dip. Mech. Engrg; First Cl. Cert. Steam and Motor Engrg; CEng, MIMarEST. Merchant Navy Engr Cadet, 1960–65; sea-going Marine Engr, 1965–72; shore-based Marine Engr, Greenock and Saudi Arabia, 1972–79; Chief Engr, Sealink, 1979–92; OPCS, 1992–96. Mem., Select Cttee on Home Affairs, H of C, 2001–. Chm., Associated Parly Ports and Merchant Navy Gp, 2002–. Mem. (Lab), Kent CC, 1989–97 (Chm., Economic Develt Cttee, 1993–97). *Recreations:* hill walking, family outings, awaiting the revival of Welsh Rugby. *Address:* 26 Coombe Valley Road, Dover, Kent CT17 0EP. *Club:* Marine Officers' (Dover).

PROSSER, Sir Ian (Maurice Gray), Kt 1995; FCA; Chairman, InterContinental Hotels Group, 2003; Chairman and Chief Executive, 1987–2000, Executive Chairman, 2000–03, Six Continents (formerly Bass) PLC; *b* 5 July 1943; *s* of late Maurice and of Freda Prosser; *m* 1st, 1964, Elizabeth Herman (marr. diss. 2003); two *d*; 2nd, 2003, Hilary Prewer. *Educ:* King Edward's School, Bath; Watford Grammar School; Birmingham Univ. (BComm). Coopers & Lybrand, 1964–69; Bass Charrington Ltd, later Bass PLC, subseq. Six Continents PLC, 1969–2003: Financial Dir, 1978–84; Vice Chm., 1982–87; Gp Man. Dir, 1984–87. Director: Boots Co., 1984–96; Lloyds TSB Gp (formerly Lloyds Bank), 1988–99; BP, 1997– (Dep. Chm., 1999–); Glaxo Smithkline plc (formerly Smithkline Beecham PLC), 1999–; Sara Lee Corp., 2004–. Chm., Stock Exchange Listed Cos Adv. Cttee, 1992–98 (Mem., 1990–98). Chm., World Travel and Tourism Council, 2001–03. Chm., Brewers and Licensed Retailers Assoc. (formerly Brewers' Soc.), 1992–94 (Dir, 1983–2000). DUniv Birmingham, 2001. *Recreations:* bridge, theatre, music. *Clubs:* Home House; Leander.

PROSSER, Jeffrey; Chairman, Queen Elizabeth Hospital King's Lynn (formerly King's Lynn and Wisbech Hospitals) NHS Trust, 2000–05; *b* 13 June 1942; *s* of Trevor and Beryl Prosser; *m* 1st, 1968, Margaret Sumpter (marr. diss. 1988); three *s*; 2nd, 1989, Sandra Walmsley. *Educ:* University Coll., Cardiff (Dip. Social Services); Leicester Univ. (Dip. Social Work); UEA (BA 2004; MA 2006). Social worker, Herts CC, 1968–72; Principal Social Worker, Northwick Park Hosp., 1972–74; Divl Manager, Cambs CC, 1974–79; Asst Dir, Haringey LBC, 1979–82; Area Dir, Devon CC, 1982–84; Dep. Dir of Social Services, Enfield LBC, 1984–86; Gen. Manager, Tower Hamlets HA, 1986–89; Dir of Community Care, Court Cavendish plc, 1989–92; Controller of Community Services, 1993–95, Dir of Community Services, 1995–99, Dir of Social Affairs, 1999, London Bor. of Barnet. Chm., Flagship Hsg Gp, 1999–2006; Vice Chm., Peddars Way Housing Assoc., 1998–99. Chm., Red2Green, 2004–07; Dir, impressionsprints ltd, 2007–. Chm., Weeting Parish Council, 1999–2000. *Recreations:* gardening, cycling, photography. *Address:* The Old Rectory, Rectory Lane, Weeting, Brandon, Suffolk IP27 0PX. *T:* (01842) 812672.

PROSSER, Kevin John; QC 1996; tax barrister; a Recorder, since 2000; *b* 26 Aug. 1957; *s* of Sidney Ronald Prosser and Rita Lillian Prosser; *m* 1994, Mary Elizabeth Stokes; one *s* one *d. Educ:* Broxbourne Sch.; UCL (LLB); St Edmund Hall, Oxford (BCL). Called to the Bar, Lincoln's Inn, 1982, Bencher, 2005; Asst Recorder, 2000. Chm., Revenue Bar Assoc., 2008–. *Publication:* (with D. C. Potter) Tax Appeals, 1990. *Recreations:* opera, squash, reading. *Address:* 16 Bedford Row, WC1R 4EF. *T:* (020) 7414 8080. *Club:* Garrick.

PROSSER, (Leslie) Charles, DFA; consultant on quality of plans designing development, since 2005; *b* 27 Oct. 1939; *s* of Dr Leslie John Prosser and Eleanor Alice May (*née* Chapman); *m* 1960, Coral Williams; one *s* two *d. Educ:* Sedbergh Sch.; Bath Acad. of Art, Corsham; Slade Sch. of Fine Art (DFA); Kungl. Akademien Konsthögskolan, Stockholm; Inst. of Educn, Leeds Univ. (DAEd). Asst Lectr in Fine Art, Blackpool Sch. of Art, 1962–64; Leverhulme European Arts Research Award, Stockholm, 1964–65; Lectr in Fine Art, Leeds Coll. of Art, later Jacob Kramer Coll. of Art, 1965–76; Sec., Royal Fine Art Commn for Scotland, 1976–2005; research in art educn, 1974–75. Ed., Royal Fine Art Commn for Scotland pubns, 1976–2005. Mem. UK Cttee, Hong Kong Architecture Exhibn, Edinburgh, 1996–97. Mem., Scotch Malt Whisky Soc., Leith, 1991–. FRSA 1997; Hon. FRIAS 1997; Hon. MRTPI 2002. *Publications:* contrib. to environmental design jls. *Recreation:* pondering about structures. *Address:* 28 Mayfield Terrace, Edinburgh EH9 1RZ. *T:* (0131) 668 1141.

PROSSER, William David; *see* Prosser, Rt Hon. Lord.

PROTHEROE, Alan Hackford, CBE (mil.) 1991 (MBE (mil.) 1980); TD 1981; DL; journalist and media consultant; *b* 10 Jan. 1934; *s* of Rev. B. P. Protheroe and R. C. M. Protheroe; *m* 1st, 1956, Anne Miller (*d* 1999); two *s*; 2nd, 2004, Mrs Rosemary Margaret Louise Tucker. *Educ:* Maesteg Grammar Sch., Glamorgan. FCMI; MCIPR. Nat. Service, 2nd Lieut The Welch Regt, 1954–56; Lt-Col, Royal Regt of Wales (TA), 1979–84; Col, 1984–90. Reporter, Glamorgan Gazette, 1951–53; BBC Wales: Reporter, 1957–59; Industrial Correspondent, 1959–64; Editor, News and Current Affairs, 1964–70; BBC TV News: Asst Editor, 1970–72; Dep. Editor, 1972–77; Editor, 1977–80; Asst Dir, BBC News and Current Affairs, 1980–82; Asst Dir Gen., BBC, 1982–87. During BBC career wrote, produced, directed and presented films and radio programmes, reported wars, and travelled widely; seconded to Greek Govt to assist in reorganisation of Greek TV, 1973. Man. Dir, Services Sound and Vision Corp., 1988–94; Director: Visnews Ltd, 1982–87; Defence Public Affairs Consultants Ltd, 1987–93. Mem., Steering Cttee, EBU News Gp, 1977–87. Mem. Council, RUSI, 1984–87; Association of British Editors: Founder Mem., 1984–; Dep. Chm., 1984–87; Chm., 1987. Chm., Eastern Wessex Reserve Forces Assoc., 1991–99 (Dep. Chm., 1990–91). St James's Vice Pres., 1990–, and Mem. Bd of Mgt, 1992–, RBL; Dir, RBL Training, 1992–99. Hon. Col, TA Information Officers, 1991–96. DL Bucks, 1993. *Publications:* contribs to newspapers and specialist jls on industrial, media and defence affairs. *Recreations:* wine, travel, photography. *Address:* Amberleigh House, 60 Chapman Lane, Flackwell Heath, Bucks HP10 9BD. *T:* and *Fax:* (01628) 528492. *Club:* Army and Navy.

PROUD, Rt Rev. Andrew John; *see* Ethiopia and the Horn of Africa, Area Bishop of.

PROUDFOOT, Bruce; *see* Proudfoot, V. B.

PROUDFOOT, (George) Wilfred; owner, self-service stores; consultant in distribution; professional hypnotist and hypnotherapist, Master Practitioner of Neuro-Linguistic Programming; owner, Proudfoot School of Hypnosis and Hypnotherapy; *b* 19 Dec. 1921; *m* 1950, Margaret Mary, *d* of Percy Clifford Jackson, Pontefract, Yorks; two *s* one *d*. *Educ:* Crook Council Sch.; Scarborough Coll. Served War of 1939–45, NCO Fitter in RAF, 1940–46. Served Scarborough Town Council, 1950–58 (Chm. Health Cttee, 1952–58). MP (C) Cleveland Division of Yorkshire, Oct. 1959–Sept. 1964; PPS to Minister of State, Board of Trade, Apr.–July 1962, to Minister of Housing and Local Govt and Minister for Welsh Affairs (Rt Hon. Sir Keith Joseph, Bt, MP), 1962–64; MP (C) Brighouse and Spenborough, 1970–Feb. 1974; Minister of State, Dept of Employment, 1970; contested (C) Brighouse and Spenborough, Oct. 1974. Man. Dir, Radio 270, 1965–. Chm., Scarborough Cons. Assoc., 1978–80; Chm., Cleveland European Constituency Cons. Assoc., 1979–. Professional hypnotist; face lifted by Dr John Williams, USA, 1978. Chm., UK Guild of Hypnotist Examiners, 1983–; Mem., Virginia Satir Internat. Avanta Network, 1987–. *Publications:* The Two Factor Nation, or How to make the people rich, 1977; The Consumer Guide to Hypnosis, 1990. *Recreations:* reading, photography, caravanning, travel, walking, jogging. *Address:* 278 Scalby Road, Scarborough, North Yorkshire YO12 6EA. *T:* (01723) 367027.

PROUDFOOT, Prof. Nicholas Jarvis, PhD; FRS 2005; Brownlee-Abraham Professor of Molecular Biology, University of Oxford, since 2003; Fellow of Brasenose College, Oxford, since 1982; *b* Chicago, 6 June 1951; *s* of Malcolm Jarvis Proudfoot and Mary Proudfoot (*née* MacDonald); *m* 1975, Anne Semple; two *s*. *Educ:* Bedford Coll., London (BSc Biochem. 1972); King's Coll., Cambridge (PhD Molecular Biol. 1975). MRC Laboratory of Molecular Biology, Cambridge: MRC Res. Student, 1972–75; Jun. Beit Meml Res. Fellow, 1975–78; MRC Scientific Staff, 1978–79; Jun. Res. Fellow, St John's Coll., Cambridge, 1976–79; Sen. Res. Fellow, CIT, 1979–81; Res. Associate, Harvard Univ., 1981–82; University of Oxford: Lectr in Chemical Pathology, Sir William Dunn Sch. of Pathology, 1981–96; Prof. of Experimental Pathology, 1996–2003; Tutor in Biochem., Brasenose Coll., 1982–2003. Mem. EMBO, 1982. Royal Soc./Wolfson Res. Merit Award, 2002–. *Publications:* contrib. molecular biology/genetics jls. *Recreations:* amateur musician (horn player and baritone), walking, cycling. *Address:* 206 Divinity Road, Oxford OX4 1LS. *T:* (01865) 275566, *Fax:* (01865) 275556; *e-mail:* nicholas.proudfoot@path.ox.ac.uk.

PROUDFOOT, Prof. (Vincent) Bruce, OBE 1997; FSA 1963; FRSE 1979; FRSGS; Professor of Geography, University of St Andrews, 1974–93, Emeritus 1993; *b* 24 Sept. 1930; *s* of late Bruce Falconer Proudfoot; *m* 1961, Edwina Valmai Windram Field; two *s*. *Educ:* Royal Belfast Academical Instn; Queen's Univ., Belfast (BA, PhD). Research Officer, Nuffield Quaternary Research Unit, QUB, 1954–58; Lectr in Geography, QUB, 1958–59, Durham Univ., 1959–67; Tutor, 1960–63, Librarian, 1963–65, Hatfield Coll., Durham; Visiting Fellow, Univ. of Auckland, NZ, and Commonwealth Vis. Fellow, Australia, 1966; Associate Prof., 1967–70, Prof., 1970–74, Univ. of Alberta, Edmonton, Canada; Acting Chm., Dept of Geography, Univ. of Alberta, 1970–71; Co-ordinator, Socio-Economic Opportunity Studies, and Staff Consultant, Alberta Human Resources Research Council, 1971–72. Trustee, Nat. Mus. of Antiquities of Scotland, 1982–85. Chairman: Rural Geog. Study Gp, Inst. of British Geographers, 1980–84; Soc. for Landscape Studies, 1979–83. Royal Society of Edinburgh: Mem. Council, 1982–85 and 1990–91; Vice-Pres., 1985–88; Gen. Sec., 1991–96; Bicentenary Medal, 1997. Vice-Pres., Soc. of Antiquaries of Scotland, 1982–85; Pres., Section H (Anthrop. and Archaeol.), BAAS, 1985; Hon. Pres., Scottish Assoc. of Geography Teachers, 1982–84; Royal Scottish Geographical Society: Mem. Council, 1975–78, 1992–93; Chm. Council, 1993–99; Vice-Pres., 1993–; Hon. Editor, 1978–92; Fellow, 1991; Chm., Dundee Centre, 1993–99 (Mem., Cttee, 1976–93, 1999–2003). Lectures: Lister, BAAS, 1964; Annual, Soc. for Landscape Studies, 1983; Estyn Evans, QUB, 1985. *Publications:* The Downpatrick Gold Find, 1955; (with R. G. Ironside *et al*) Frontier Settlement Studies, 1974; (ed) Site, Environment and Economy, 1983; numerous papers in geographical, archaeological and soils jls. *Recreation:* gardening. *Address:* Westgate, Wardlaw Gardens, St Andrews, Scotland KY16 9DW. *T:* (01334) 473293. *Club:* Royal Scots (Edinburgh).

PROUDFOOT, Wilfred; *see* Proudfoot, G. W.

PROUDMAN, Hon. Dame Sonia Rosemary Susan, (Dame Sonia Cartwright), DBE 2008; **Hon. Mrs Justice Proudman;** a Judge of the High Court of Justice, Chancery Division, since 2008; *b* 30 July 1949; *d* of late Kenneth Oliphant Proudman and Sati Proudman (*née* Hekimian); *m* 1987, Crispian Cartwright; one *d*. *Educ:* St Paul's Girls' Sch. (Foundn Schol.); Lady Margaret Hall, Oxford (Open Schol.; BA 1st Cl. Hons Jurisprudence 1971; MA 1973). Called to the Bar, Lincoln's Inn, 1972 (Kennedy Schol., Buchanan Prize), Bencher, 1996; Oxford Univ. Eldon Law Schol., 1973; in practice at Chancery Bar, 1974–2008; QC 1994; Asst Recorder, 1996–2000; Recorder, 2000–08; Dep. High Court Judge, 2001–08. Mem., Panel of Chairmen, Competition Appeal Tribunal, 2008–. Member: Oxford Law Faculty Adv. Bd, 2000; QC Selection Panel, 2005. *Recreation:* taking enormous notice of hats and backchat. *Address:* Royal Courts of Justice, Strand, WC2A 2LL. *Clubs:* Hurlingham, CWIL.

PROUT, family name of **Baron Kingsland**.

PROUT, David Michael, PhD; Executive Director, Planning and Borough Development, Royal Borough of Kensington and Chelsea, since 2007; *b* 14 March 1963; *s* of late Prof. Charles Keith Prout and of Lesley Craven Prout; *m* 1992, Penelope Sarah Gibbs; two *d*. *Educ:* Magdalen Coll. Sch., Oxford; Wadham Coll., Oxford (BA Hons (Mod. Hist.) 1985); Courtauld Inst. of Art, London (PhD 1991). Joined Civil Service, 1993; various posts, DoE, 1993–95; UK Perm. Repn to EU, 1995–98; Private Sec., 1999–2001, Principal Private Sec., 2001–04, to Dep. Prime Minister; Dir of Local Govt Policy, ODPM, subseq. DCLG, 2004–07. *Recreations:* cycling, tennis, cinema, family, travel. *Address:* Royal Borough of Kensington and Chelsea, Town Hall, Hornton Street, W8 7NX. *T:* (020) 7361 2944; *e-mail:* david.prout@rbkc.gov.uk.

PROVAN, James Lyal Clark; politician, farmer, businessman; *b* 19 Dec. 1936; *s* of John Provan and Jean (*née* Clark); *m* 1960, Roweena Adele Lewis; twin *s* one *d*. *Educ:* Ardvreck Sch., Crieff; Oundle Sch., Northants; Royal Agricultural Coll., Cirencester. Member: Tayside Regional Council, 1978–82; Tay River Purification Bd, 1978–82. Chairman: McIntosh Donald Ltd, 1989–94; James McIntosh & Co., 1990–94. MEP (C): NE Scotland, 1979–89; S Downs W, 1994–99; SE Reg., England, 1999–2004; European Parliament: Quaestor, 1987–89; Cons. Chief Whip, 1994–96; Vice Pres. and Chief Whip, EPP, 1996–99; Vice Pres., 1999–2004; Member: Agriculture and Fisheries Cttee, 1979–89 (EDG spokesman on agricl and fisheries affairs, 1982–87); Environment, Consumer Affairs and Public Health Cttee, 1979–89; Chairman: Cross-Party Tourism Gp, 1996–2004; Conciliation Cttee to Council of Ministers, 1999–2002. Exec. Dir, Scottish Financial Enterprise, 1990–91; non-exec. Dir, CNH Global NV, 1999– (Director: New Holland Holdings NV, 1995–99; New Holland NV, 1996–99). Mem. Bd, Rowett Res. Inst., 1990–2004 (Chm., 1992–98); Mem., AFRC, 1990–94. Area President, Scottish NFU, 1965 and 1971; Treasurer, Perth and E Perthshire Conservative Assoc., 1975–77; Member, Lord Lieutenant's Queen's Jubilee Appeal Cttee, 1977. FRAgS 2000. FRSA 1987. *Publications:* The European Community: an ever closer union?, 1989; Europe's Freedom to Farm, 1996, 1998; Europe's Fishing Blues, 1997. *Recreations:* country pursuits, sailing, flying, musical appreciation, travel. *Address:* Summerfield, Glenfarg, Perth PH2 9QD. *Clubs:* Farmers', East India; Royal Perth Golfing Society.

PROVAN, Marie; *see* Staunton, M.

PROVERA, Marco T.; *see* Tronchetti Provera.

PROWSE, Philip (John); theatre director and designer; Professor of Theatre Design, Slade School of Fine Art, University College London, 1999–2003 (Head of Theatre Design Department, 1995–2003), now Professor Emeritus; *b* 29 Dec. 1937; *s* of late Alan William Auger Prowse and Violet Beatrice (*née* Williamson). *Educ:* King's Sch., Worcester; Malvern Coll. of Art; Slade Sch. of Fine Art. Professional début: Diversions for Royal Ballet, Royal Opera House, 1961; subsequent prodns and designs for opera, ballet and drama including: Glasgow Citizens' Theatre; rep. theatres; West End theatres; Royal Nat. Theatre; RSC, Barbican; Old Vic Theatre; Royal Opera; Royal Ballet; ENO; Sadler's Wells Royal Ballet; Birmingham Royal Ballet; WNO; Scottish Opera; Opera North; English Nat. Ballet (Festival Ballet); Scottish Ballet; prodns in Europe and US; festival appearances: Rome, Wiesbaden, Holland, Warsaw, Zurich, Belgrade, Edinburgh, Cologne, Hamburg, Venice, Parma, E Berlin, Halle, Caracas. Co-Dir, Glasgow Citizens' Theatre, 1970–2004. *Address:* c/o Cruickshank Cazenove, 97 Old South Lambeth Road, SW8 1XU.

PRUSINER, Prof. Stanley Ben, MD; Professor of Neurology, since 1984, and Professor of Biochemistry, since 1988, University of California at San Francisco; *b* 28 May 1942; *s* of Lawrence Albert Prusiner and Miriam Prusiner (*née* Spigel); *m* (marr. diss.); two *d*. *Educ:* Univ. of Pennsylvania (AB 1964; MD 1968). University of California at San Francisco: Med. Intern, 1968–69; Resident in Neurology, 1972–74; Asst Prof. of Neurology, 1974–80; Associate Prof., 1980–84; Prof., 1984–; Prof. of Virology, Univ. of Calif at Berkeley, 1984–. FAAAS 1998. Foreign Mem., Royal Soc., 1997. Max Planck Res. Award, Alexander von Humboldt Foundn and Max Planck Soc., 1992; Gairdner Foundn Award, 1994; Wolf Prize for Medicine, 1996; Nobel Prize in Physiology or Medicine, 1997. *Publications:* (ed) The Enzymes of Glutamine Metabolism, 1973; Slow Transmissible Diseases of the Nervous System, 2 vols, 1979; Prions, 1987; Prion Diseases of Humans and Animals, 1992; Molecular and Genetic Basis of Neurologic Disease, 1993, 3rd edn 2003; Prions, Prions, Prions, 1996, 2nd edn as Prion Biology and Diseases, 2004; more than 300 articles in learned jls. *Address:* University of California, 513 Parnassus Avenue, San Francisco, CA 94143, USA.

PRYCE, (George) Terry, CBE 1994; Chairman, G. T. Pryce (Farms) Ltd, since 1996; *b* 26 March 1934; *s* of Edwin Pryce and Hilda Florence (*née* Price); *m* 1957, Thurza Elizabeth Tatham, JP; two *s* one *d*. *Educ:* Welshpool Grammar Sch.; National Coll. of Food Technol. MFC, FIFST. Dir, various food cos in THF Gp, 1965–70; Asst Man. Dir, Dalgety (UK) Ltd, 1970–72; Man. Dir, Dalgety (UK) and Dir, DPLC, 1972–78; Man. Dir, 1978–81, Chief Exec., 1981–89, Dalgety PLC. Chairman: Solway Foods Ltd, 1990–94; York House Group Ltd, 1996–2003; Jas Bowman and Sons Ltd, 1999– (Dir, 1991–); Dir, H. P. Bulmer Holdings PLC, 1984–94. Chm., British Soc. for Horticultural Res., later Horticulture Res. Internat., 1990–97; Council Member: AFRC, 1986–94; UK Food and Drink Fedn, 1987–89; Mem. Adv. Bd, Inst. of Food Res., 1988–94. Chm., UK Food Assoc., 1986–88. CCMI. *Recreation:* sport. *Address:* 89 Brookmans Avenue, Brookmans Park, Hatfield, Herts AL9 7QG. *T:* (01707) 642039. *Clubs:* Athenæum, MCC.

See also S. C. C. Pryce.

PRYCE, Rt Rev. (James) Taylor; a Suffragan Bishop of Toronto (Area Bishop of York-Simcoe), 1985–2000; *b* 3 May 1936; *s* of James Pryce and Florence Jane (*née* Taylor); *m* 1962, Marie Louise Connor; two *s* one *d* (and one *s* decd). *Educ:* Bishop's Univ., Lennoxville, Quebec (BA, LST). Ordained deacon, 1962, priest, 1963; Asst Curate, Church of the Ascension, Don Mills, 1962–65; Incumbent: St Thomas' Church, Brooklin, Ont, 1965–70; St Paul's, Lorne Park, 1970–75; Christ Church, Scarborough, 1975–82; St Leonard's, North Toronto, 1982–85. Hon. DD Wycliffe Coll., 1986. *Address:* 12 Walnut Drive, RR#2, Shanty Bay, ON L0L 2L0, Canada.

PRYCE, Jonathan; actor; *b* 1 June 1947; lives with partner, Kate Fahy; two *s* one *d*. *Educ:* RADA. FRWCMD (FWCMD 1995). Patron: Friends United Network, 1992–; Facial Surgery Res. Foundn, Saving Faces, 2001–. *Theatre includes:* Comedians, Nottingham Playhouse, Old Vic, 1975, NY 1976 (Tony Award); title rôle, Hamlet, Royal Court, 1980 (Olivier Award); The Caretaker, Nat. Th., 1981; Accidental Death of an Anarchist, Broadway, 1984; The Seagull, Queen's, 1985; title rôle, Macbeth, RSC, 1986; Uncle Vanya, Vaudeville, 1988; Miss Saigon, Drury Lane, 1989 (Olivier Award and Variety Club Award), NY, 1991 (Tony Award for Best Actor in Musical, 1991); Oliver!, Palladium, 1994; My Fair Lady, RNT, transf. Theatre Royal, Drury Lane, 2001; The Reckoning, Soho Th., 2003; The Goat, or Who is Sylvia, Almeida, 2004, transf. Apollo, 2004; Dirty Rotten Scoundrels, NY, 2006; Glengarry Glen Ross, Apollo, 2007; *television includes:* Roger Doesn't Live Here Anymore (series), 1981; Timon of Athens, 1981; Martin Luther, 1983; Praying Mantis, 1983; Whose Line Is It Anyway?, 1988–; The Man from the Pru, 1990; Selling Hitler, 1991; Mr Wroe's Virgins, 1993; Thicker Than Water, 1993; David, 1997; HR, 2007; The Baker Street Irregulars, 2007; *films include:* Something wicked this way comes, 1982; The Ploughman's Lunch, 1983; Brazil, 1985; The Doctor and the Devils, 1986; Haunted Honeymoon, 1986; Jumpin' Jack Flash, 1987; Consuming Passions, 1988; The Adventures of Baron Munchausen, 1988; The Rachel Papers, 1989; Glengarry Glen Ross, 1992; The Age of Innocence, 1992; Barbarians at the Gate, 1992; Great Moments in Aviation, 1993; A Business Affair, 1993; Shopping, 1994; Carrington, 1995 (Best Actor Award: Cannes, 1995; Evening Standard, 1996); Evita, 1996; Regeneration, 1997; Tomorrow Never Dies, 1997; Ronin, 1998; Stigmata, 1999; Very Annie Mary, 2001; Bride of the Wind, 2001; The Affair of the Necklace, 2002; Unconditional Love, 2002; Pirates of the Caribbean: The Curse of the Black Pearl, 2003; What a Girl Wants, 2003; De-Lovely, 2004; The Brothers Grimm, 2005; Pirates of the Caribbean: Dead Man's Chest, 2006; Pirates of the Caribbean: At World's End, 2007; Leatherheads, 2007; *recordings include:* Miss Saigon; Nine—the Concert; Under Milk Wood; Cabaret; Oliver!; Evita; Hey Mr Producer; My Fair Lady. Hon. DLitt Liverpool, 2006. Special BAFTA Cymru, 2001. *Address:* c/o Julian Belfrage Associates, Adam House, 14 New Burlington Street, W1S 3BQ.

PRYCE, Prof. Roy; Director, 1983–90, Senior Research Fellow, 1990–99, Federal Trust for Education and Research; *b* 4 Oct. 1928; *s* of Thomas and Madeline Pryce; *m* 1954, Sheila Rose, *d* of Rt Hon. James Griffiths, CH; three *d*. *Educ:* Grammar Sch., Burton-on-Trent; Emmanuel Coll., Cambridge (MA, PhD). MA Oxon. Research Fellow: Emmanuel Coll., Cambridge, 1953–55; St Antony's Coll., Oxford, 1955–57; Head of London Information Office of High Authority of European Coal and Steel Community, 1957–60; Head of London Inf. Office, Jt Inf. Service of European Communities, 1960–64;

Rockefeller Foundn Res. Fellow, 1964–65; Dir, Centre for Contemp. European Studies, Univ. of Sussex, 1965–73; Directorate General for Information, Commission of the European Communities: Dir, 1973–78; Sen. Advr for Direct Elections, 1978–79; Chief Advr for Programming, 1979–81. Vis. Professorial Fellow, Centre for Contemporary European Studies, Univ. of Sussex, 1973–81; Visiting Professor: Coll. of Europe, Bruges, 1965–72; Eur. Univ. Inst., Florence, 1981–83; Eur. Inst. for Public Admin, Maastricht, 1983–88. *Publications:* The Italian Local Elections 1956, 1957; The Political Future of the European Community, 1962; (with John Pinder) Europe After de Gaulle, 1969, German and Ital. edns 1970; The Politics of the European Community, 1973; (ed) The Dynamics of European Union, 1987; (ed jtly) Maastricht and Beyond, 1994; Heathfield Park: a private estate and a Wealden town, 1996; Heathfield and Waldron: an illustrated history, 2000; Rotherfield Hall, 2002; Battle Abbey and the Websters, 2005. *Recreations:* gardening, local history.

PRYCE, Simon Charles Conrad; Chief Executive, BBA Aviation plc, since 2007; *b* 8 Dec. 1961; *s* of (George) Terry Pryce, *qv* and Thurza Elizabeth Pryce (*née* Tatham); *m* 1997, Katharine Mary Childs; two *s*. *Educ:* Haberdashers' Aske's Sch., Elstree; Reading Univ. (BSc Food Scis). Chartered Accountant. Dir, Lazard, 1987–96; Sen. Vice Pres., JPMorgan, 1996–97; GKN plc: Dir, Corporate Finance, 1997–2001; Chief Financial Officer, Automotive, 2001–04; Chief Exec., Diversified Businesses Gp, 2004–07. Dir, SMMT, 2005–07. MSI 1997. *Recreations:* sport, particularly ski-ing, Rugby, cricket, scuba and field sports, travel, opera, reading. *Address:* c/o BBA Aviation plc, 20 Balderton Street, W1K 6TL. *T:* (020) 7514 3999, *Fax:* (020) 7491 1853. *Club:* MCC; Brocket Hall Golf (Herts).

PRYCE, Rt Rev. Taylor; *see* Pryce, Rt Rev. J. T.

PRYCE, Terry; *see* Pryce, G. T.

PRYCE, Vicky, (Mrs C. M. P. Huhne); Chief Economic Adviser and Director General, Economics, Department for Business, Enterprise and Regulatory Reform (formerly Department of Trade and Industry), since 2002; Joint Head, Government Economic Service, since 2007 (Deputy Head, 2004–07); *b* Athens; *d* of late Nicolas Courmouzis and of Voula Courmouzis; *m* 1st, 1972, G. Pryce (marr. diss. 1981); two *d*; 2nd, 1984, Christopher Murray Paul Huhne, *qv*; two *s* one *d*. *Educ:* LSE (BSc Econs, MSc Monetary Econs). Economist, then Chief Economist, Williams & Glyn's Bank, 1973–83; Corporate Economist, Esso Europe, 1983–86; Chief Economist, then Partner, KPMG, 1986–2001; Partner, London Economics, 2001–02. Vis. Prof., Cass Business Sch., 2002–07. Chm., Good Corp., 2001–02. Member: Court, Co. of Mgt Consultants, 2001– (Third Warden, 2007–08); Council, REconS, 2002–07; Council, Univ. of Kent, 2005–; Bd of Trustees, RSA, 2006–. *Recreations:* theatre, cinema, Chelsea football supporter. *Address:* Department for Business, Enterprise and Regulatory Reform, 1 Victoria Street, SW1H 0ET; *e-mail:* vicky.pryce@berr.gsi.gov.uk. *Club:* Reform.

PRYDE, Roderick Stokes, OBE 1999; Regional Director, India and Sri Lanka, British Council, since 2005; *b* 26 Jan. 1953; *s* of William Gerard Pryde and Patricia Mary Pryde; *m* 1989, Susanne Mona Graham Hamilton; one *s* three *d*. *Educ:* George Watson's Coll., Edinburgh; Univ. of Sussex (BA Hons); UCNW, Bangor (PGCE, TESL). Lectr, Univ. of Dijon, 1975–76; English Teaching Co-ordinator, Cie Française des Pneumatiques, Michelin, 1979–81; British Council, 1981–: Asst Regl Lang. Officer, London, 1981–83; Dir of Studies, Milan, 1983–87; Regional Director: Andalucia, 1987–88; Bilbao, 1988–89; Director: Kyoto and Western Japan, 1990–94; English Lang. Centre, Hong Kong, 1994–98; Portugal, 1998–2000; Dir, Educnl Enterprises, 2000–02; Asst Dir-Gen., 2002–05. FRSA. *Recreations:* walking, family, reading. *Address:* c/o British Council, 10 Spring Gardens, SW1A 2BN. *T:* (020) 7930 8466. *Clubs:* Royal Commonwealth Society; Watsonian (Edinburgh).

PRYER, (Eric) John, CB 1986; Chief Land Registrar, 1983–90; Assistant Secretary, Council for Licensed Conveyancers, 1991–92; *b* 5 Sept. 1929; *s* of late Edward John and Edith Blanche Pryer; *m* 1962, Moyra Helena Cross; one *s* one *d*. *Educ:* Beckenham and Penge County Grammar Sch.; Birkbeck Coll., London Univ. (BA Hons). Called to the Bar, Gray's Inn, 1957. Exec. Officer, Treasury Solicitor's Dept, 1948; Legal Asst, HM Land Registry, 1959; Asst Land Registrar, 1965; Dist Land Registrar, Durham, 1976; Dep. Chief Land Registrar, 1981–83. Hon. Associate Mem., RICS, 1986. *Publications:* (ed) Ruoff and Roper, The Law and Practice of Registered Conveyancing, 5th edn 1986, 6th edn 1991; Land Registration Handbook, 1990; official pubns; articles in jls. *Recreation:* reading.

PRYKE, Sir Christopher Dudley, 4th Bt *cr* 1926, of Wanstead, co. Essex; *b* 17 April 1946; *s* of William Dudley Pryke and Lucy Irene Pryke (*née* Madgett); *S* uncle, 1998; *m* 1st, 1973, Angela Gay Meek (marr. diss. 1986); one *s*; 2nd, 1999, Marilyn Wright, *d* of late Gerald William Henry Williamson. *Educ:* Hurstpierpoint. MRICS. *Heir:* *s* James Dudley Pryke, *b* 29 Dec. 1977. *Address:* 23 Wavendon Avenue, Chiswick, W4 4NP.

PRYKE, Paula Shane, (Mrs P. Romaniuk); floral artist and author; *b* 29 April 1960; *d* of Ralph and Gladys Pryke; *m* 1987, Peter Romaniuk. *Educ:* Culford Sch.; Univ. of Leeds (BEd Hons Hist.). LRAM (Speech and Drama) 1985. Founder, Paula Pryke Flowers, London, 1998. Lectr and demonstrator on floral art around the world. Ambassador for Floral Industry Award, NFU, 2000. *Publications:* The New Floral Artist, 1993; Flower Innovations, 1995; Flower Celebrations, 1995; Simple Flowers, 1999; Candles, 1999; Wreaths and Garlands, 1999; Living Colour, 2001; Wedding Flowers, 2004; Classic Paula Pryke, 2004; The Flower School, 2006; Table Flowers, 2007; Seasonal Wreaths and Bouquets, 2008. *Recreations:* gardening, cooking, the arts. *Address:* The Flower House, Cynthia Street, N1 9JF. *T:* (020) 7837 7373; *e-mail:* paula@paula-pryke-flowers.com.

PRYKE, Roy Thomas; Director of the Virtual Staff College, University of Exeter, 2000–06; *b* 30 Nov. 1940; *s* of Thomas George and Nellie Matilda Pryke; *m* 1962, Susan Pauline Andrew; one *s* three *d*. *Educ:* Univ. of Wales (BA Hons); Univ. of Manchester (PGCE). Teacher, Manchester, 1963–71; Education Officer, Devon, 1971–79; Deputy Chief Education Officer: Somerset, 1980–82; Devon, 1983–87; Dep. Chief Educn Officer and Head of Operations, Cambridgeshire, 1987–89; Dir, Educn Services, Kent CC, 1989–98. Adviser to: Council of Local Educn Authorities, 1992–98; ACC, 1994–97; LGA, 1997–98; Chm., Assoc. of Chief Educn Officers, 1996–97. Chm., DFEE Adv. Gp, Schs Improvement Internat., 1999–2002; Mem., President of Zimbabwe's Commn on Educn and Trng, 1998–99. Vis. Prof. of Educn, 1998–2000, Hon. Fellow, 2006, Univ. of Exeter. Chm., Exmouth Community Assoc., 2007–. FRSA 1988; Hon. FCP 1991. Chevalier, Ordre des Palmes Académiques (France), 1994. *Publications:* contributor to: Open Plan Schools, 1978; The Head's Legal Guide, 1984; The Revolution in Education and Training, 1986; articles in Education Jl on curriculum and on education management. *Recreations:* foreign travel and languages, sailing, gardening, golf. *Address:* Marinhay, Douglas Avenue, Exmouth, Devon EX8 2EY. *T:* (01395) 277173.

PRYN, Maj.-Gen. William John, OBE 1973; MB, BS; FRCS, FRCSEd; Director of Army Surgery, and Consulting Surgeon to the Army, 1982–86, retired; *b* 25 Jan. 1928; *s* of late Col Richard Harold Cotter Pryn, FRCS, late RAMC and Una St George Ormsby (*née* Roe); *m* 1st, 1952, Alison Lynette (marr. diss.), 2nd *d* of Captain Norman Arthur Cyril Hardy, RN; two *s* one *d*; 2nd, 1982, June de Medina, *d* of Surg. Comdr Norman Bernard de Medina Greenstreet, RN; one step *s* one step *d*. *Educ:* Malvern Coll.; Guy's Hosp. Med. Sch., London Univ. (MB, BS 1951). MRCS, LRCP 1951; FRCS 1958; FRCSEd 1984. Trooper, 21st SAS Regt (Artists Rifles), TA, 1948–50. House appts, Gen. Hosp., Ramsgate and Royal Berks Hosp., Reading, 1951–52; commnd into RAMC, 1952; Regtl MO to No 9 Training Regt RE, 1952–53; surg. appts in mil. hosps in UK, Cyprus and N Africa, 1953–58; seconded as Surg. Registrar, Royal Postgrad. Med. Sch., Hammersmith Hosp., 1958–59; Officer i/c Surg. Div. and Consultant Surgeon to mil. hosps, Malaya, Singapore, N Borneo and UK, 1959–69; CO BMH Dhekelia, 1969–72; Sen. Consultant Surgeon in mil. hosps, UK and NI, 1972–77; Consulting Surgeon to BAOR, 1977–82; Consultant in Surgery to Royal Hosp., Chelsea, 1982–86; Hon. Consultant to S Dist, Kensington and Chelsea and Westminster AHA (T), 1981. Member: EUROMED Gp on Emergency Medicine, 1980–86; Specialty Bd in Surgery, and Reg. Trng Cttee in Gen. Surgery, Defence Medical Services, 1982–86; Med. Cttee, Defence Scientific Adv. Council, 1982–86; BMA, 1950–; Wessex Surgeons Club, 1976–. Member Council: RAMC, 1982–86; Mil. Surgical Soc., 1982–. Fellow, Assoc. of Surgeons of GB and Ireland, 1960 (Mem., Educn Adv. Cttee, 1982–86). QHS 1981–86. OStJ 1984. Mem., Editorial Bd, Injury, 1982–86. *Publications:* (contrib.) Field Surgery Pocket Book, 1981; original articles in the Lancet and British Jl of Surgery. *Recreations:* fishing, shooting and other country pursuits, golf, tennis, sailing, gardening, joinery, house maintenance.

PRYNNE, Andrew Geoffrey Lockyer; QC 1995; *b* 28 May 1953; *s* of late Maj.-Gen. Michael Whitworth Prynne, CB, CBE and Jean Violet Prynne; *m* 1977, Catriona Mary Brougham; three *d*. *Educ:* Marlborough Coll.; Univ. of Southampton (LLB Hons). Called to the Bar, Middle Temple, 1975. Mem., Lord Chancellor's Multi-Party Actions Wkg Gp, 1997–. Asst Boundary Comr, 2000–. CEDR Accredited Mediator, 2000. *Recreations:* sailing, shooting, ski-ing. *Address:* 2 Harcourt Buildings, Temple, EC4Y 9DB. *T:* (020) 7583 9020. *Clubs:* Royal Yacht Squadron, Royal Solent Yacht, Island Sailing (IoW); Bar Yacht.

PRYOR, Arthur John, CB 1997; PhD; competition consultant, since 1996; Head, Competition Policy Division, Department of Trade and Industry, 1993–96; *b* 7 March 1939; *s* of late Quinton Arthur Pryor, FRICS and Elsie Margaret (*née* Luscombe); *m* 1964, Marilyn Kay Petley; one *s* one *d*. *Educ:* Harrow County Grammar Sch.; Downing Coll., Cambridge (MA; PhD). Asst Lectr, then Lectr, in Spanish and Portuguese, UC Cardiff, 1963–66; Asst Principal, BoT and ECGD, 1966–69; Principal, DTI, 1970–73; First Sec., British Embassy, Washington, 1973–75; Principal, Dept of Trade, 1975–77; Assistant Secretary: Shipping Policy Div., Dept of Trade, 1977–80; Air Div., DoI, 1980–83; Department of Trade and Industry: Asst Sec., Internat. Trade Policy Div., 1984–85; Under Sec. and Regional Dir, W Midlands Region, 1985–88; Dir Gen., BNSC, 1988–93. Mem., Competition (formerly Monopolies and Mergers) Commn, 1998–2003; Competition Commn Appeal Panel, subseq. Competition Appeal Tribunal, 2000–. *Publications:* contribs to modern lang., space and competition jls. *Recreations:* tennis, golf, book collecting. *Address:* c/o Competition Appeal Tribunal, Victoria House, Bloomsbury Place, WC1A 2EB. *T:* (020) 7979 7979.

PRYOR, His Honour Brian Hugh; QC 1982; a Circuit Judge, 1986–2001; *b* 11 March 1931; *s* of Lt-Col Ronald Ernest Pryor, Royal Sussex Regt, and Violet Kathleen Pryor (*née* Steele); *m* 1955, Jane Mary Smith (*d* 2007); one *s* two *d*. *Educ:* Chichester High Sch.; University Coll., Oxford (Open Exhibnr Mod. History; BA Jurisprudence). Called to the Bar, Lincoln's Inn, 1956; Sir Thomas More Bursary, Lincoln's Inn, 1958. Member: SE Circuit Bar Mess, 1957; Kent County Bar Mess, 1957; Chm., Kent Bar Mess, 1979–82; Mem., SE Circuit Bar Mess Wine Cttee, 1979–82. A Recorder, 1981–86; Resident Judge, Woolwich Crown Court, 1993–99. Mem., Res. Ethics Cttee, Camberwell HA and King's Healthcare NHS Trust, 1990–95. *Recreation:* gardening.

PRYOR, Dr Francis Manning Marlborough, MBE 1999; Director of Archaeology, Flag Fen Bronze Age Centre, Peterborough, since 1987; *b* 13 Jan. 1945; *s* of late Robert Matthew Marlborough Pryor, MBE and Barbara Helen Pryor (*née* Robertson); *m* 1st, 1969, Sylvia Jean Page (marr. diss. 1977); one *d*; 2nd, 1988, Maisie Taylor. *Educ:* Eton; Trinity Coll., Cambridge (MA Archaeol. and Anthropol.; PhD 1985). Asst Curator, Royal Ontario Mus., Toronto, 1969–78; Welland Valley Field Officer, Cambs CC, 1978–82; Dir, Etton and Flag Fen Excavations, 1982–87. Vis. Prof. of Archaeol., Leicester Univ., 2007–. Pres., Council for British Archaeol., 1998–2005. Presenter, TV series: Britain BC, 2003; Britain AD, 2004. *Publications:* Excavations at Fengate, Peterborough, 4 vols, 1974–1984; Flag Fen, 1992; Prehistoric Farmers, 1998; Excavations at Etton, 1998; Sea Henge, 2001; The Flag Fen Basin, 2001; Britain BC, 2003; Britain AD, 2004; Britain in the Middle Ages, 2006. *Recreations:* gardening, playing the Anglo concertina, eating seafood, enjoying real ale. *Address:* Flag Fen Bronze Age Centre, The Droveway, Northey Road, Peterborough PE6 7QF. *T:* (01733) 313414, *Fax:* (01733) 349957; *e-mail:* office@flagfen.freeserve.co.uk.

PRYOR, John Pembro, MS; FRCS; consultant uroandrologist, retired; *b* 25 Aug. 1937; *s* of William Benjamin Pryor and Kathleen Pryor; *m* 1959, Marion Hopkins; four *s*. *Educ:* Reading Sch.; King's Coll. and King's Coll. Hosp. Med. Sch. (MB, BS). AKC 1961; FRCS 1967; MS London 1971. Training appointments: Doncaster Royal Infirm., 1965–66; Univ. of Calif, San Francisco, 1968–69; KCH and St Paul's Hosp., 1971–72; Consultant Urol Surgeon to KCH and St Peter's Hosp., 1975–94; Dean, Inst. of Urology, London Univ., 1978–85; Reader, Inst. of Urology, UCL and Hon. Cons. Urol Surgeon, St Peter's Hosp., 1994–99. Hunterian Prof., RCS, 1971 and 1995. Chairman: (first), British Andrology Soc., 1979–84; European Assoc. of Genital Microsurgeons, 1992–95; Impotence Assoc., 1999–2001; Eur. Sexual Alliance, 1999–2004; Trustees, Eur. Acad. for Sexual Medicine, 2004–; Pres., Eur. Soc. for Impotence Research, 1999–2001. Treas., British Jl of Urology, 1991–99. St Peter's Medal, British Assoc. of Urol Surgeons, 1995. *Publications:* (ed jtly) Andrology, 1987; (ed) Urological prostheses, appliances and catheters, 1992; (jtly) Impotence: an integrated approach to clinical practice, 1992; articles on urology and andrology in scientific jls. *Address:* The Beacon, Channel Way, Fairlight, E Sussex TN35 4BP. *T:* (01424) 814945.

PRYOR, His Honour Robert Charles; QC 1983; a Circuit Judge, 1991–2004; *b* 10 Dec. 1938; *s* of Charles Selwyn Pryor and Olive Woodall Pryor; *m* 1969, Virginia Sykes; one *s* one *d*. *Educ:* Eton; Trinity Coll., Cambridge (BA). National Service, KRRC, 2nd Lieut 1958. Called to the Bar, Inner Temple, 1963; a Recorder, 1989–91. Director, Sun Life Corp. (formerly Sun Life Assurance) plc, 1977–91.
See also Viscount Hampden.

PRYS-DAVIES, family name of **Baron Prys-Davies**.

PRYS-DAVIES, Baron *cr* 1982 (Life Peer), of Llanegryn in the County of Gwynedd; **Gwilym Prys Prys-Davies;** Partner, Morgan Bruce (formerly Morgan Bruce & Nicholas), Solicitors, Cardiff, Pontypridd, 1957–87, retired; *b* 8 Dec. 1923; *s* of William and Mary Matilda Davies; *m* 1951, Llinos Evans; three *d*. *Educ:* Towyn Sch., Towyn, Merioneth; University College of Wales, Aberystwyth. Served RN, 1942–46. Faculty of Law, UCW, Aberystwyth, 1946–52; President of Debates, Union UCW, 1949; President Students' Rep. Council, 1950; LLB 1949; LLM 1952. Admitted Solicitor, 1956. Contested (Lab) Carmarthen, 1966. Special Adviser to Sec. of State for Wales, 1974–78. Official opposition spokesman: on health, 1983–89; on N Ireland, 1982–93; on Welsh Office, 1987–95. Member, H of L Select Committee: on Parochial Charities Bill and Small Charities Bill, 1983–84; on murder and life imprisonment, 1988–89; on Central and Local Govt, 1995–96; Member: British-Irish Inter-Parly Body, 1990–96; Jt Cttee on Statutory Instruments, 1990–98; Delegated Powers and Deregulation Cttee, 1998–2002. Chm., Welsh Hosps Bd, 1968–74; Member: Welsh Council, 1967–69; Welsh Adv. Cttee, ITA, 1966–69; Working Party on 4th TV Service in Wales, Home Office and Welsh Office, 1975–76; Adv. Gp, Use of Fetuses and Fetal Material for Res., DHSS and Welsh Office, 1972; Econ. and Social Cttee, EEC, 1978–82. Chm., NPFA (Cymru), 1998–2001. Vice-Pres., Hon. Soc. of Cymmrodorion, 1993–. Pres., Univ. of Wales Swansea, 1997–2002; Vice-Pres., Coleg Harlech, 1989–95. Hon. Fellow: UCW, Aberystwyth, 1992; Trinity Coll., Carmarthen, 1995; Univ. of Wales Inst., Cardiff, 1995. Hon. LLD Wales, 1996. OStJ 1968. *Publications:* A Central Welsh Council, 1963; Y Ffermwr a'r Gyfraith, 1967; Llafur y Blynyddaedd, 1993. *Address:* Lluest, 78 Church Road, Tonteg, Pontypridd, Mid Glam CF38 1EN. *T:* (01443) 202462.

PRYS-ROBERTS, Prof. Cedric, DM; FRCA; Professor of Anaesthesia, University of Bristol, 1976–99, Emeritus since 2000; President, Royal College of Anaesthetists, 1994–97; *b* 8 Aug. 1935; *s* of late William Prys Roberts and Winifred Prys Roberts (*née* Osborne Jones); *m* 1961, Linda Joyce Bickerstaff; two *s* two *d*. *Educ:* Dulwich Coll.; St Bartholomew's Hosp. Med. Sch. (MB BS London); MA, DM Oxon; PhD Leeds. FANZCA; FCA; Hon. RCSI. Research Fellow, Univ. of Leeds, 1964–67; Clinical Reader in Anaesthetics, Oxford Univ., 1967–76; Fellow, Worcester Coll., Oxford, 1970–76; Hon. Cons. Anaesthetist, Radcliffe Infirmary, 1967–76; Prof. of Anaesthesia, Univ. of California, San Diego, 1974; Hon. Consultant Anaesthetist, Bristol Royal Infirmary and Bristol Royal Hosp. for Sick Children, 1976–99. Hunterian Prof., RCS, 1978. *Publications:* (ed) The Circulation in Anaesthesia, 1980; (ed) Pharmacokinetics of Anaesthesia, 1984; (ed) Monitoring in Anaesthesia and Intensive Care, 1994; (ed) International Practice of Anaesthesia, 2 vols, 1996; contribs to learned jls. *Recreations:* mountaineering, ski-ing, philately and postal history, music (playing trumpet). *Address:* Foxes Mead, Cleeve Hill Road, Cleeve, Bristol BS49 4PG.

PTASZYNSKI, André Jan; Chief Executive, Really Useful Group, since 2005; *b* 7 May 1953; *s* of Wladyslaw Ptaszynski and Joan Ptaszynski (*née* Holmes); *m* 1985, Judith Terry; two *s* two *d*. *Educ:* Ipswich Sch.; Jesus Coll., Oxford (BA 1975, MA 1978). Associate Dir, Crucible Th., Sheffield, 1978–80; ind. theatre and television producer, 1980–2000: produced over 50 West End and touring shows including: Return to the Forbidden Planet, West Side Story, Fosse, Chicago, Spend, Spend, Spend, Tommy, and Show Boat; produced sitcoms for BBC including Joking Apart (Bronze Rose, Montreux TV Fest., 1995); promoted live work of comedians including: Rowan Atkinson, Dave Allen, Victoria Wood, Eddie Izzard and League of Gentlemen; Chief Exec., Really Useful Th., 2000–05. Member, Board: Oxford Stage Co., 1990–97; RNT, 2001–. Pres., Soc. of London Th., 1996–99. *Recreations:* mountain trekking, fell-walking, cycling around London, reading, giving free advice to other motorists. *Address:* Hill Farm, Chiselhampton, Oxford OX44 7XH. *T:* (office) (020) 7240 0880; *e-mail:* andre@reallyuseful.co.uk.

PUAPUA, Rt Hon. Sir Tomasi, GCMG 2002; KBE 1998; PC 1982; Governor General of Tuvalu, 1998–2003; *b* 10 Sept. 1938; *s* of Fitilau and Olive Puapua; *m* 1971, Riana Tabokai; two *s* two *d*. *Educ:* King George V Secondary Sch.; Fiji Sch. of Medicine; Otago Med. Sch., NZ (DPH). Gilbert and Ellice Islands Colony Government: gen. med. practitioner, 1964–70; MO, Public Health, 1971–76; Tuvalu: MP Vaitupu, 1977–98; Prime Minister, 1981–89; Speaker of Parliament, 1993–98. *Recreations:* cricket, fishing, gardening, reading. *Address:* c/o Government House, Funafuti, Tuvalu.

PUBLICOVER, Ralph Martin; HM Diplomatic Service, retired; Ambassador to Angola, 2005–07; *b* 2 May 1952; *s* of John Publicover and Nora (*née* Bates); *m* 1973, Rosemary Sheward; one *s* two *d*. *Educ:* Haberdashers' Aske's Sch., Elstree; Univ. of Manchester (BA Econ 1973); Sch. of Oriental and African Studies, London. Joined HM Diplomatic Service, 1976; Second, then First Sec., Dubai, 1979–81; First Sec. (Econ.), Ottawa, 1981–85; Assessments Staff, Cabinet Office, 1985–87; First Sec., Washington, 1989–92; Dep. Hd, Central Europ. Dept, FCO, 1992–94; Deputy Head of Mission: Bucharest, 1994–97; Lisbon, 1998–2003; Hd, Consular Crisis Gp, FCO, 2003–04. *Recreations:* music, cricket, ancient monuments, ducks and geese. *Address:* c/o Foreign and Commonwealth Office, King Charles Street, SW1A 2AH.

PUDDEPHATT, Andrew Charles, OBE 2003; Director, Global Partners and Associates, since 2005; Visiting Fellow, London School of Economics and Political Science, since 2005; *b* 2 April 1950; *s* of Andrew Ross Puddephatt and Margaret McGuire; two *d*. *Educ:* Sidney Sussex College, Cambridge (BA 1971). Worked as teacher in 1970s; computer programmer, 1978–81. Councillor, Hackney Council, 1982–90 (Leader, 1986–89). Gen. Sec., NCCL, subseq. Liberty, 1989–95; Dir, Charter 88, 1995–99; Exec. Dir, Article 19, Internat. Centre Against Censorship, 1999–2005. *Recreations:* literature, music. *Address:* c/o Global Partners, 4th Floor, Holborn Gate, 26 Southampton Buildings, WC2A 1AH.

PUDDEPHATT, Prof. Richard John, OC 2007; PhD; FRS 1998; FRS (Can) 1991; Distinguished University Professor of Chemistry, University of Western Ontario (Professor of Chemistry, 1978); *b* 12 Oct. 1943; *s* of Harry and Ena Puddephatt; *m* 1979, Alice Ruth Poulton; one *s* one *d*. *Educ:* University Coll. London (BSc 1965; PhD 1968). Teaching Fellow, Univ. of Western Ont, 1968–70; Lectr, 1970–77, Sen. Lectr, 1977–78, Univ. of Liverpool. Canada Res. Chair, Univ. of Western Ont., 2001–. Sen. Editor, Canadian Jl Chem., 1998–. Royal Society of Chemistry: Noble Metals Award, 1991; Nyholm Award, 1997; Chemical Society of Canada: Alcan Award, 1985; Steacie Award, 1996; CIC Medal, 1998; Hellmuth Prize, 2000. *Publications:* The Periodic Table of the Elements, 1972, 2nd edn 1986; The Chemistry of Gold, 1978; contrib. numerous papers to learned jls, mostly on organometallic chemistry. *Recreations:* gardening, golf. *Address:* Department of Chemistry, University of Western Ontario, London, ON N6A 5B7, Canada. *T:* (519) 6792111.

PUENTE, Most Rev. Pablo; Apostolic Nuncio to the Court of St James's, 1997–2004; *b* 16 June 1931. Ordained priest, Dio. Santander, 1956; entered Diplomatic Service of Holy See, 1962: served in: Paraguay, Santo Domingo, Kenya, Secretariat of State, 1969–73; Lebanon, 1973–75; Yugoslavia, 1976–80; Pro-Nuncio: Indonesia, 1980–86; Senegal, Mali, Capo-Verde Is, Mauritania and Guinea Bissau, 1986–89; Nuncio: Lebanon, 1989–97; Kuwait (and delegate to Arabian Peninsula), 1993–97.

PUGH, Alastair Tarrant, CBE 1986; Chairman, Alistair Pugh and Associates, since 1988; *b* 16 Sept. 1928; *s* of Sqdn Leader Rev. Herbert Cecil Pugh, GC, MA, and Amy Lilian Pugh; *m* 1957, Sylvia Victoria Marlow (marr. diss. 2001); two *s* one *d*. *Educ:* Tettenhall Coll., Staffs; De Havilland Aeronautical Tech. Sch. FRAeS; FCILT. Design Dept, De Havilland Aircraft Co., 1949–52; Sen. Designer, H. M. Hobson, 1952–55; journalist, Flight, 1955–61; Channel Air Bridge, 1961–63; British United Airways, 1963–70: Planning Dir, 1968; British Caledonian Airways: Dir, R&D, 1970; Production Dir, 1973–74; Corporate Planning Dir, 1974–77; Dep. Chief Exec., 1977–78; Man. Dir, 1978–85; Exec. Vice-Chm./Dir of Strategy, British Caledonian Gp, 1985–88; Consultant, Goldman Sachs Internat. Ltd, 1988–2007. President: Inst. of Freight Forwarders, 1981–82; CIT, 1988–89. Trustee, Brooklands Mus. Trust, 1988–. *Recreation:* the chain-driven Frazer Nash. *Address:* England's Cottage, Sidlow Bridge, Reigate, Surrey RH2 8PN. *T:* (01737) 243456.

PUGH, Alun John; Chief Executive, Vestri Foundation, since 2008; Director, Snowdonia Society, since 2008; *b* 9 June 1955; *s* of Maurice Thomas Pugh, coal miner, and Violet Jane Pugh, nurse; *m* 1st, 1978, Janet Hughes (marr. diss. 2002); one *s* one *d*; 2nd, 2006, Mary Juliet Chaffé. *Educ:* Tonypandy Grammar Sch.; Poly. of Wales; UC, Cardiff. Lectr in Accounting, Bridgend Coll., 1983–87; Sen. Lectr, Newcastle Coll., 1987–92; Head of Sch., Llandrillo Coll., 1992–96; Asst Principal, W Cheshire Coll., 1996–99. Mem. (Lab) Clwyd W, Nat. Assembly for Wales, 1999–2007; Dep. Health and Social Services Sec., 2000–01; Dep. Educn Minister, 2001–03; Minister for Culture, the Welsh Lang. and Sports, 2003–07. Contested (Lab) Clwyd West, Nat. Assembly for Wales, 2007. *Recreation:* mountaineering. *Address: e-mail:* alunpugh@hotmail.com. *Club:* Oesterreichische Alpenverein (Innsbrück).

PUGH, Andrew Cartwright; QC 1988; *b* 6 June 1937; *s* of late Lewis Gordon Pugh and Erica Pugh; *m* 1984, Chantal Hélène Langevin; two *d*. *Educ:* Tonbridge; New Coll. Oxford (MA). Served Royal Sussex Regt, 1956–57. Bigelow Teaching Fellow, Law Sch., Univ. of Chicago, 1960–61. Called to the Bar, Inner Temple, 1961, Bencher, 1989. Recorder, 1990–2003. Legal Assessor, GMC and GDC, 1991–2007. Pres., Mental Health Review Tribunals, 2003–07. *Recreations:* gardening, reading, tennis. *Address:* Blackstone Chambers, Blackstone House, Temple, EC4Y 9BW. *T:* (020) 7583 1770. *Clubs:* Oxford and Cambridge; Waldron Cricket.

PUGH, Charles Edward, (Ted), CBE 1988; Managing Director, National Nuclear Corporation Ltd, 1984–87; *b* 17 Sept. 1922; *s* of Gwilym Arthur and Elsie Doris Pugh; *m* 1945, Edna Wilkinson; two *s* one *d*. *Educ:* Bolton and Salford Technical Colleges. CEng, MIMechE; FInstE 1987. Lancashire Electric Power Co., 1942–48; CEGB Project Manager responsible for design and construction of 6 power stations, 1951–71; Chief Electrical and Control and Instrumentation Engineer, CEGB, Barnwood, 1971–73; Special Services, CEGB, 1973–76; Dir of Projects, CEGB, 1976–82, with responsibility for completion of the AGR prog. of reactors; PWR Project Dir, NNC, 1982–84. Pres., Inst. of Energy, 1988–89. Hon. FINucE 1984. *Recreations:* power stations, sculpture, painting, music, gardening, walking, secure energy supplies for the UK.

PUGH, Edward Clevely; Director, British Council, Poland, 1994–97; *b* 14 Sept. 1937; *s* of late Edgar Pallister Pugh and Dora Lois Pugh (*née* Clevely); *m* 1962, Thirza Carolyn Browning; one *s* one *d*. *Educ:* Exeter Univ. (BA Econs and Govt 1962); SOAS, Univ. of London. Nat. Service, RN, 1955–57. Robinson Waxed Paper Co. Ltd, 1955 and 1962; British Council, 1963–97: Lectr, Tehran, 1963–67; Asst Rep., Tripoli, 1967–71; Regl Dir, Ndola, Zambia, 1971–74; Dep. Rep., 1974–75, Rep., 1975–77, Ethiopia; seconded to ODM, 1977–79; Dir, FE and Pacific Dept, London, 1979–80; Rep., Tanzania, 1980–83; Dep. Rep., Delhi, 1983–86; Rep., Thailand, 1986–90; Americas, Pacific and Asia Division: Asst Dir, 1990–91; Dep. Dir, 1991–92; Dir, 1992–93; Regl Dir, S Asia and Oceania, 1993–94. *Recreations:* reading, music, theatre, art, walking, swimming. *Address:* 43 Offham Road, W Malling, Maidstone, Kent ME19 6RB. *T:* (01732) 843317.

PUGH, Dame Gillian (Mary), DBE 2005 (OBE 1998); Chief Executive, Coram Family (formerly Thomas Coram Foundation for Children), 1997–2005; Chair, National Children's Bureau, since 2006; *b* 13 May 1944; *d* of Robert Quested Drayson, *qv*; *m* 1975, Gareth Nigel Pugh (*d* 1981); one *d*; *m* 1989, Martin Waldron; one step *s* two step *d*. *Educ:* Ashford Sch. for Girls; Univ. of Exeter (BA Hons). Editor: Careers Res. and Adv. Centre, Cambridge, 1966–67; Humanities Curriculum Project, Schs Council/Nuffield Foundn, 1967–70; Asst Dir of Information, Schs Council for Curriculum and Examinations, 1970–74; National Children's Bureau: Sen. Information Officer, 1974–77; Sen. Develt Officer, 1980–86; Dir, Early Childhood Unit, 1986–97; Develt Officer, Voluntary Council for Handicapped Children, 1978–80. Jt Editor, Children & Society, 1992–2003. Vis. Prof., London Univ. Inst. of Educn, 2000–. Member: Effective Preschool Educn Project Adv. Gp, DfEE, 1997–2006; Bd, Children's Workforce Develt Council, 2005–08; Bd, Trng and Develt Agency, 2006; Chair, Primary Educn Review, 2006–. Pres., Child Develt Soc., 1994–96; Chm., Parenting Educn and Support Forum, 1999–2006; Vice President: Preschool Learning Alliance, 1998–2003; British Assoc. of Early Childhood Educn, 1998–; Chair of Govs, Thomas Coram Early Childhood Centre, 1998–2005. Trustee: Nat. Family and Parenting Inst., 1999–2006; Friends Provident Charitable Foundn, 2005–. FRSA 1993. Hon. DEd: Manchester Metropolitan, 1994; West of England, 1998; DUniv Open, 1995. *Publications* include: (jtly) The Needs of Parents, 1984; Contemporary Issues in the Early Years, 1992, 4th edn 2006; Confident Parents, Confident Children, 1994; (jtly) Learning to Be a Parent, 1996; (jtly) Training to Work in the Early Years, 1998; London's Forgotten Children: Thomas Coram and the Foundling Hospital, 2007. *Recreations:* gardening, choral singing, walking, golf. *Address:* Weathervane, Old Shire Lane, Chorleywood, Herts WD3 5PW. *T:* (01923) 285505.

PUGH, Sir Idwal (Vaughan), KCB 1972 (CB 1967); Chairman, Chartered Trust Ltd, 1979–88; Director: Standard Chartered Bank, 1979–88; Halifax Building Society, 1979–88; *b* 10 Feb. 1918; *s* of late Rhys Pugh and Elizabeth Pugh; *m* 1946, Mair Lewis (*d* 1985); one *s* one *d*. *Educ:* Cowbridge Grammar Sch.; St John's Coll., Oxford (Hon. Fellow, 1979). Army Service, 1940–46. Entered Min. of Civil Aviation, 1946; Alternate UK Rep. at International Civil Aviation Organisation, Montreal, 1950–53; Asst Secretary, 1956; Civil Air Attaché, Washington, 1957–59; Under Secretary, Min. of Transport, 1959; Min. of Housing and Local Govt, 1961; Dep. Sec., Min. of Housing and Local Govt, 1966–69; Permanent Sec., Welsh Office, 1969–71; Second Permanent Sec., DoE, 1971–76. Parly Comr for Administration and Health Service Comr for England, Wales and Scotland, 1976–79. Chm., Develt Corp. of Wales, 1980–83. Chm., RNCM, 1988–92 (Hon. Mem., 1992); Vice-Pres., UC Swansea, 1988–94 (Hon. Fellow, 1995); President: Coleg Harlech, 1990–98; Cardiff Business Club, 1991–98. Hon. LLD Wales, 1988. *Address:* 5 Murray Court, 80 Banbury Road, Oxford OX2 6LQ. *Club:* Brooks's.

PUGH, John Arthur, OBE 1968; HM Diplomatic Service, retired; Chairman and Director, Numjai Restaurants, since 1998; *b* 17 July 1920; *er s* of late Thomas Pugh and

Dorothy Baker Pugh. *Educ:* Brecon Grammar Sch.; Bristol Univ. RN, 1941–45. Home CS, 1950–54; Gold Coast Admin. Service, 1955–58; Adviser to Ghana Govt, 1958–60; First Sec., British High Commn, Lagos, 1962–65; First Sec. (Economic), Bangkok, and British Perm. Rep. to Economic Commn for Asia and Far East, 1965–68; British Dep. High Comr, Ibadan, 1971–73; Diplomatic Service Inspector, 1973–76; High Comr to Seychelles, 1976–80. *Publications:* The Friday Man, 1992; editorial and other contributions to jls etc on political affairs, travel and history. *Recreations:* Oriental ceramics, travel. *Address:* Penybryn House, Hay on Wye, Hereford HR3 5RS. *T:* (01497) 820695. *Club:* Royal Commonwealth Society.

PUGH, Dr John David; MP (Lib Dem) Southport, since 2001; *b* 28 June 1948; *s* of James and Patricia Pugh; *m* 1971, Annette; one *s* three *d*. *Educ:* Maidstone Grammar Sch.; Durham Univ.; PhD Manchester; MPhil Nottingham; MA Liverpool. Head: Social Studies, Salesian High Sch., Bootle, 1972–83; Philosophy and Religious Studies, Merchant Taylors' Sch., Crosby, 1983–2001. Mem. (Lib Dem) Sefton MBC, 1987–2002 (Leader, Lib Dem Gp, 1992–2001; Leader of Council, 2000–01). *Publication:* The Christian Understanding of God, 1990. *Recreation:* cycling. *Address:* House of Commons, SW1A 0AA; 27 The Walk, Birkdale, Southport, Lancs PR8 4BG. *T:* (01704) 569025. *Club:* National Liberal.

PUGH, Peter David S.; *see* Storie-Pugh.

PUGH, Ted; *see* Pugh, C. E.

PUGSLEY, David Philip; His Honour Judge Pugsley; a Circuit Judge, since 1992; *b* 11 Dec. 1944; *s* of Rev. Clement Pugsley and Edith (*née* Schofield); *m* 1966, Judith Mary Mappin; two *d*. *Educ:* Shebbear College; St Catharine's College, Cambridge (MA); MPhil Birmingham, 1995. Called to the Bar, Middle Temple, 1968; practised Midland and Oxford Circuit until 1985; Chm. of Industrial Tribunals, Birmingham Reg., 1985–92; a Recorder, 1991–92. Pres., Council of Industrial Tribunal Chairmen, 1991–92; Mem., Parole Bd, 1999–2005. Mem., Editl Bd, Civil Court Procedure, 1999–. Freeman, City of London, 2006. *Publications:* (jtly) Industrial Tribunals Compensation for Loss of Pension Rights, 1990; (jtly) The Contract of Employment, 1997; (jtly) Butterworths Employment Compensation Calculator, 1999. *Recreations:* golf, fly fishing, theatre. *Address:* Derby Combined Court Centre, Morledge, Derby DE1 2XE.

PUIG de la BELLACASA, José Joaquín, Hon. GCVO 1986; Knight of Calatrava; Counsellor of State, Spain, since 1997 (Chairman, Council for Foreign Affairs, 1995–97); *b* 5 June 1931; *s* of José Maria Puig de la Bellacasa and Consuelo de Urdampilleta; *m* 1960, Paz de Aznar Ybarra; four *s* two *d*. *Educ:* Areneros Jesuit Coll., Madrid; Madrid Univ. Barrister-at-law. Entered Diplomatic Service, 1959; Dirección General Politica Exterior, 1961–62; Minister's Cabinet, 1962–69; Counsellor, Spanish Embassy, London, 1971–74; Private Sec. to Prince of Spain, 1974–75, to HM King Juan Carlos, 1975–76; Director-General: Co-op. Tecnica Internacional, 1976; Servicio Exterior, 1977–78; Under-Sec. of State for Foreign Affairs, 1978–80; Ambassador to Holy See, 1980–83; Ambassador to UK, 1983–90; Sec.-Gen., Spanish Royal Household, 1990–91; Ambassador to Portugal, 1991–95. Hon. Fellow, QMC, 1987. Grand Cross of Isabel la Católica; Grand Cross of Merito Naval; Encomienda de Numero de Carlos III; holds several foreign decorations. *Address:* Felipe IV 7, Madrid 28014, Spain. *Clubs:* Beefsteak, White's; Nuevo, Golf de Puerta de Hierro (Madrid).

PULFORD, Air Vice-Marshal Andrew Douglas, CBE 2004; Assistant Chief of the Defence Staff (Operations), since 2008; *b* 22 March 1958; *s* of Douglas and Jean Pulford; *m* 1982, Nicola Jane Pearse; one *s* one *d*. *Educ:* Magnus Grammar Sch., Newark. Support helicopter pilot, 1978–92; Fleet Air Arm Exchange, 1980–82; RAAF Exchange, 1985–87; OC 18 Sqn, 1996–99; PSO to CAS, 1999–2000; HCSC, 2001; OC RAF Odiham and Chinook Wing, 2002–03; Dir Air Resources and Plans, MoD, 2004–06; AOC No 2 Gp, 2007–08. *Recreations:* military history, motorcycling, old cars, sailing. *Address:* c/o Ministry of Defence, Main Building, Whitehall, SW1A 2HB. *Club:* Royal Air Force.

PULFORD, Richard Charles; Chief Executive, Society of London Theatre and Theatrical Management Association, since 2001; *b* 14 July 1944; *s* of late Charles Edgar Pulford and Grace Mary Pulford (*née* Vickors). *Educ:* Royal Grammar Sch., Newcastle upon Tyne; St Catherine's Coll., Oxford (BA Jurisprudence). Voluntary service in the Sudan, 1966–67; Home Civil Service, 1967–79: Department of Education and Science: Asst Principal, 1967–72, Principal, 1972–75; HM Treasury, 1975–77; Asst Secretary, DES, 1977–79. Arts Council of GB: Dep. Sec.-Gen., 1979–85; South Bank Planning Dir, 1985–86; Gen. Dir (Admin), South Bank Centre, 1986–92; consultant on cultural policy and admin, 1993–2001, including work with/for Min. of Culture, Bulgaria, Min. of Culture, Hungary, Arts Council of GB, Arts Council of England, British Council, Millennium Commn, London Arts Bd, Royal Opera House, Wales Millennium Centre, Birmingham Rep. Theatre. Bd Mem., Internat. Soc. of Performing Arts Administrators, 1988–92 (Pres., 1990–91); Member: South Bank Theatre Bd, 1985–92; Council, English Stage Co., 1989–2001; Dolphin Square Trust, 2000–; Bd, Nat. Campaign for the Arts, 2001–06 (Chm., 1992–96; Vice-Pres., 1996–2001); V&A Museum Cttee for Theatre Museum, 2002–. Pres., Performing Arts Employers League Europe, 2005–. Director: Stage One, 2002–; Stage One Club, 2004–05. Trustee, Crusaid and STAR Foundn, 1993–2001. *Publications:* articles in various newspapers and specialist magazines. *Recreations:* Brasiliana, trying to avoid respectability. *Address:* 905 Beatty House, Dolphin Square, SW1V 3PN. *T:* (020) 7798 8308, *Fax:* (020) 7387 6353.

PULHAM, Mary Helen; *see* Creagh, M. H.

PULLAN, Prof. Brian Sebastian, PhD; FBA 1985; Professor of Modern History, University of Manchester, 1973–98; *b* 10 Dec. 1935; *s* of late Horace William Virgo Pullan and Ella Lister Pullan; *m* 1962, Janet Elizabeth Maltby; two *s*. *Educ:* Epsom Coll.; Trinity Coll., Cambridge (MA, PhD); MA Manchester. Nat. Service, RA, 1954–56. Cambridge University: Res. Fellow, Trinity Coll., 1961–63; Official Fellow, Queens' Coll., 1963–72; Univ. Asst Lectr in History, 1964–67; Lectr, 1967–72; Dean, Faculty of Arts, Manchester Univ., 1982–84. Feoffee of Chetham's Hosp. and Library, Manchester, 1981–2004. Corresp. Fellow, Ateneo Veneto, 1986. Serena Medal, British Academy, 1991. *Publications:* (ed) Sources for the History of Medieval Europe, 1966; (ed) Crisis and Change in the Venetian Economy in the Sixteenth and Seventeenth Centuries, 1968; Rich and Poor in Renaissance Venice, 1971; A History of Early Renaissance Italy, 1973; The Jews of Europe and the Inquisition of Venice, 1983; (ed with Susan Reynolds) Towns and Townspeople in Medieval and Renaissance Europe: essays in memory of Kenneth Hyde, 1990; (ed with David Chambers) Venice: a documentary history 1450–1630, 1992; Poverty and Charity: Europe, Italy, Venice, 1400–1700, 1994; (with Michele Abendstern) A History of the University of Manchester 1951–73, 2000; (ed with Maureen Mulholland and Anne Pullan) Judicial Tribunals in England and Europe 1200–1700, 2003; (with Michele Abendstern) A History of the University of Manchester 1973–90, 2004; (ed) A Portrait of the University of Manchester, 2007; articles and reviews in learned jls and collections. *Recreations:* dogs, theatre. *Address:* 33 Green Pastures, Heaton Mersey, Stockport SK4 3RB.

PULLEIN-THOMPSON, Denis; *see* Cannan, D.

PULLEIN-THOMPSON, Josephine Mary Wedderburn, MBE 1984; writer; General Secretary, English Centre, International PEN, 1976–93; *b* 3 April 1924; *e d* of H. J. Pullein-Thompson, MC and Joanna Cannan, novelist. *Educ:* briefly at Wychwood Sch., Oxford. Horsewoman and writer; Vis. Comr, 1960–68, Dist Comr, 1970–76, Pony Club; Member: Cttee, Crime Writers' Assoc., 1971–73; Cttee, Children's Writers' Gp, Soc. of Authors, 1973–79 (Dep. Chm., 1978–79); English Centre of International PEN: Cttee, 1974–76; Pres., 1993–97; Vice Pres., 1997–. *Publications:* How Horses are Trained, 1961; (jtly) Ponies in Colour, 1962; Learn to Ride Well, 1966; Horses and Their Owners (anthology), 1970; Ride Better and Better, 1974; (with sisters) Fair Girls and Grey Horses: memories of a country childhood, 1996; *fiction:* It Began with Picotee (with sisters), 1946; Six Ponies, 1946; I had Two Ponies, 1947; Plenty of Ponies, 1949; Pony Club Team, 1950; The Radney Riding Club, 1951; Prince Among Ponies, 1952; One Day Event, 1954; Show Jumping Secret, 1955; Patrick's Pony, 1956; Pony Club Camp, 1957; The Trickjumpers, 1958; All Change, 1961, new edn as The Hidden Horse, 1982; Race Horse Holiday, 1971; Proud Riders (anthology), 1973; Black Ebony, 1975; Star Riders of the Moor, 1976; Fear Treks the Moor, 1978; Black Nightshade, 1978; Ride to the Rescue, 1979; Ghost Horse on the Moor, 1980; The No Good Pony, 1981; Treasure on the Moor, 1982; The Prize Pony, 1982; Black Raven, 1982; Pony Club Cup, 1982; Save the Ponies, 1984; Mystery on the Moor, 1984; Pony Club Challenge, 1984; Pony Club Trek, 1985; Suspicion Stalks the Moor, 1986; Black Swift, 1991; A Job with Horses, 1994; *crime:* Gin and Murder, 1959; They Died in the Spring, 1960; Murder Strikes Pink, 1963; (as J Mann) A Place with Two Faces, 1972; contrib. Oxford DNB. *Recreations:* travelling, gardening, reading, theatre going. *Address:* 16 Knivet Road, SW6 1JH.

See also D. Cannan.

PULLEN, Dr Roderick Allen; HM Diplomatic Service, retired; Fellow, Trinity College, Cambridge, since 2006; *b* 11 April 1949; *s* of late Derrick Brian Pullen and Celia Ada Pullen (*née* Wood); *m* 1971, Karen Lesley Sketchley; four *s* one *d*. *Educ:* Maidstone Grammar Sch.; Mansfield Coll., Oxford (MA); Sussex Univ. (DPhil). MoD, 1975–78; Second Sec., UK Delegn to NATO, 1978–80; MoD, 1980–81; First Sec., UK Delegn to CSCE, 1981–82; FCO, 1982–84; Dep. High Comr, Suva, 1984–88; FCO, 1988–90; Counsellor, Paris, 1990–94; Dep. High Comr, Nairobi, 1994–97; Dep. High Comr, Lagos, 1997–2000; High Comr, Ghana, 2000–04; Ambassador to Zimbabwe, 2004–06; UK Special Rep. to Sudan/Darfur Peace Process, 2006. *Address:* Trinity College, Cambridge CB2 1TQ.

PULLEYBLANK, Prof. Edwin George, PhD; FRSC; Professor of Chinese, University of British Columbia, 1966–87, now Emeritus; *b* Calgary, Alberta, 7 Aug. 1922; *s* of W. G. E. Pulleyblank, Calgary; *m* 1st, 1945, Winona Ruth Relyea (decd), Arnprior, Ont; one *s* two *d*; 2nd, 2002, Yihong Pan, Beijing. *Educ:* Central High School, Calgary; University of Alberta (BA Hons Classics 1942); University of London. Nat. Research Council of Canada, 1943–46. School of Oriental and African Studies, Univ. of London: Chinese Govt Schol., 1946; Lectr in Classical Chinese, 1948; PhD in Classical Chinese, 1951; Lectr in Far Eastern History, 1952; Professor of Chinese, University of Cambridge, 1953; Head, Dept of Asian Studies, Univ. of British Columbia, 1968–75. Fellow of Downing Coll., Cambridge, 1955–66. Corresp. Fellow, Italian Inst. for the Middle and Far East, 1993. *Publications:* The Background of the Rebellion of An Lu-Shan, 1955; Middle Chinese, 1984; Lexicon of Reconstructed Pronunciation in Early Middle Chinese, Late Middle Chinese and Early Mandarin, 1991; Outline of Classical Chinese Grammar, 1995; articles in Asia Major, Bulletin of School of Oriental and African Studies, etc. *Address:* c/o Department of Asian Studies, University of British Columbia, Vancouver, BC V6T 1Z2, Canada.

PULLINGER, John James; Librarian, House of Commons, since 2004; *b* 1 June 1959; *s* of Desmond and Kathleen Pullinger; *m* 1981, Alison Taylor; two *s* one *d*. *Educ:* Alleyn's Sch., Dulwich; Univ. of Exeter (BA 1st Cl. Hons Geog. and Stats 1980); Harvard Business Sch. (AMP 2003). Asst Statistician, then Sen. Asst Statistician, DTI, 1980–85; Section Hd, DoE, 1985–91; Hd of Pay Res., Office of Manpower Econs, 1991–92; Central Statistical Office, subseq. Office for National Statistics: Dir, Policy and Planning, 1992–96; Dir, Social and Regl Statistics, 1996–98; Exec. Dir, 1999–2004. *Recreations:* family, church, gardening, politics, current affairs. *Address:* House of Commons, SW1A 0AA; *e-mail:* pullingerj@parliament.uk.

PULLMAN, Philip Nicholas Outram, CBE 2004; FRSL; author and playwright; *b* 19 Oct. 1946; *s* of late Alfred and Audrey Pullman (*née* Merrifield); *m* 1970, Judith Speller; two *s*. *Educ:* Ysgol Ardudwy, Harlech; Exeter Coll., Oxford (BA English Lang. and Lit. 1968; Hon. Fellow, 2004). Teacher, Oxford Middle Schools, 1973–86; Lectr (part-time), Westminster Coll., Oxford, 1986–96. Patron, Centre for the Children's Book, 2000. Hon. Prof., Bangor Univ., 2008. Hon. Fellow: Westminster Inst. of Educn, 1999; Univ. of Wales, Bangor, 2003. Hon. DLitt: Oxford Brookes, 2002; UEA, 2003; DUniv: UCE, 2003; Surrey, 2003; Open, 2008; Hon. LLD Dundee, 2007. Hon. Freeman, City of Oxford, 2007. Booksellers Assoc. Author of the Year, 2000, 2001; Author of the Year, Br. Bk Awards, 2002; Eleanor Farjeon Award, 2003; Astrid Lindgren Memorial Award, 2005. *Plays:* Sherlock Holmes and the Adventure of the Limehouse Horror, 1984; The Three Musketeers, 1985; Frankenstein, 1986; Puss in Boots, 1997. *Publications: novels and stories:* Galatea, 1978; Count Karlstein, 1982, illustrated edn 1991; The Ruby in the Smoke, 1985 (Children's Book Award, Internat. Reading Assoc., 1988; televised 2006); The Shadow in the North, 1987; How To Be Cool, 1987; Spring-Heeled Jack, 1989; The Broken Bridge, 1990; The Tiger in the Well, 1991; The White Mercedes, 1992, re-issued as The Butterfly Tattoo, 1998; The Wonderful Story of Aladdin and the Enchanted Lamp, 1993; The Tin Princess, 1994; Thunderbolt's Waxwork, 1994; The Gas-Fitters' Ball, 1995; The Firework-Maker's Daughter, 1995 (Smarties Gold Award, 1996); His Dark Materials: Book One: Northern Lights, 1995 (US title: The Golden Compass) (Guardian Children's Fiction Award, 1996; Carnegie Medal, 1996; British Book Award: Children's Book of the Year, 1996; filmed, 2007); Book Two: The Subtle Knife, 1997; Book Three: The Amber Spyglass, 2000 (British Book Award: Children's Book of the Year, 2001; Whitbread Book of the Year, 2002; trilogy adapted for stage by Nicholas Wright, NT, 2003); Clockwork, or All Wound Up, 1996 (Smarties Silver Award, 1997); I Was a Rat!, 1999 (televised 2001); Mossycoat, 1999; Puss in Boots, 2000; Lyra's Oxford, 2003; The Scarecrow and His Servant, 2004; Aladdin, 2004; Once Upon a Time in the North, 2008; *plays:* Sherlock Holmes and the Adventure of the Limehouse Horror, 1993; Frankenstein, 1992. *Recreations:* drawing, music. *Address:* c/o A. P. Watt Ltd, 20 John Street, WC1N 2DR.

PULMAN, Prof. Stephen Guy, PhD; FBA 2001; Professor of Computational Linguistics, University of Oxford, since 2006; Fellow, Somerville College, Oxford, since 2000; *b* 1 Oct. 1949; *s* of Raymond Pulman and Celia Margaret Pulman; *m* 1989, Nicola Jane Verney; one *s* two *d*. *Educ:* Bedford Coll., London (BA Hons English 1972); Univ. of Essex (MA Theoretical Linguistics 1974; PhD Linguistics 1977). Lecturer: Dept of Lang.

and Linguistics, Univ. of Essex, 1977–78; Sch. of English and American Studies, UEA, 1978–84; University of Cambridge Computer Laboratory: Lectr, 1984–97; Reader in Computational Linguistics, 1997–2000; Dep. Hd, 1999–2000; Dir, 1988–97, Principal Scientist, 1998–2001, SRI Internat. (formerly Stanford Res. Inst.) Cambridge Computer Sci. Res. Centre; Prof. of Gen. Linguistics, Univ. of Oxford, 2000–06. *Publications:* Word Meaning and Belief, 1983; (jtly) Computational Morphology: practical mechanisms for the English lexicon, 1992; contrib. papers to Computational Linguistics, Artificial Intelligence, Linguistics and Philosophy, Philosophical Trans of Royal Soc., etc. *Recreations:* gardening, bird-watching, bell-ringing. *Address:* Somerville College, Oxford OX2 6HD.

PULVERTAFT, Rear-Adm. David Martin, CB 1990; Secretary, Defence, Press and Broadcasting Advisory Committee, 1992–99; *b* 26 March 1938; *s* of late Captain William Godfrey Pulvertaft, OBE, RN and Annie Joan Pulvertaft (*née* Martin); *m* 1961, Mary Rose Jeacock; one *s* two *d*. *Educ:* Canford Sch., Dorset; Britannia RN Coll., Dartmouth; RN Engineering Coll., Manadon. BSc (Eng) 1962. FIMechE 1989 (MIMechE 1974). HMS Ceylon, 1958–59; HMS Anchorite, Singapore, 1963–66; HMS Dreadnought, 1967–71; 10th Submarine Sqdn, 1971–72; HM Dockyard, Devonport, 1973–75; Nat. Defence Coll., Latimer, 1975–76; MoD 1976–78; HM Dockyard, Devonport, 1979–82; RCDS, 1983; MoD, 1984–87; Dir Gen. Aircraft (Navy), 1987–90; Dir Gen., Procurement and Support Orgn (Navy), 1990–92. Chm. of Trustees, Plymouth Naval Base Mus., 2001–05; Chm., SW Maritime Hist. Soc., 2000–03; Mem. Council, Soc. for Nautical Res., 2002–. *Recreations:* genealogy, printing, bookbinding, British warship figureheads. *Address:* Staffords, 3 Paternoster Row, Ottery St Mary, Devon EX11 1DP. *Club:* Army and Navy.

PULZER, Prof. Peter George Julius, PhD; FRHistS; Professorial Fellow, Institute for German Studies, University of Birmingham, 1996–99; Gladstone Professor of Government and Public Administration, University of Oxford, 1985–96, now Emeritus; Fellow of All Souls College, 1985–96, now Emeritus; *b* 20 May 1929; *s* of Felix and Margaret Pulzer; *m* 1962, Gillian Mary Marshall; two *s*. *Educ:* Surbiton County Grammar Sch.; King's Coll., Cambridge (1st Cl. Hons Historical Tripos 1950; PhD 1960); London Univ. (1st Cl. Hons BSc Econ 1954). FRHistS 1971. Lectr in Politics, Magdalen Coll. and Christ Church, Oxford, 1957–62; University Lectr in Politics, Oxford, 1960–84; Official Student and Tutor in Politics, Christ Church 1962–84. Visiting Professor: Univ. of Wisconsin, 1965; Sch. of Advanced Internat. Studies, Johns Hopkins Univ., 1972; Univ. of Calif, LA, 1972; Eric Voegelin, Munich Univ., 1988; Potsdam Univ., 1993; Technical Univ., Dresden, 1997; Humboldt Univ., Berlin, 2000; Leipzig Univ., 2003; Max Kade, Lafayette Coll., Easton, Pennsylvania, 2004. Chairman: Academic Adv. Cttee, Centre for German-Jewish Studies, Univ. of Sussex, 1997–; Leo Baeck Inst., London, 1998–; Mem. Governing Body, Historisches Kolleg, Munich, 1993–97. Hon. Vice-Pres., Internat. Assoc. for the Study of Germany Politics, 1997–. Hon. Dr rer. soc. oec. Innsbruck, 2007. Bundesverdienstkreuz (Germany), 2004; Grand Silver Medal of Honour for Meritorious Service to the Republic of Austria, 2008. *Publications:* The Rise of Political Anti-Semitism in Germany and Austria, 1964, 2nd edn 1988 (German edn 1966); Political Representation and Elections in Britain, 1967, 3rd edn 1975; Jews and the German State, 1992, 2nd edn 2003; German Politics 1945–1995, 1995; Germany 1870–1945: politics, state formation and war, 1997; (ed with K. R. Luther) Austria 1945–1995: fifty years of the Second Republic, 1998; (ed with Wolfgang Benz) Jews in the Weimer Republic, 1998; (contrib.) German-Jewish History in Modern Times, 1998; contrib. to jls, year books and symposia. *Recreations:* opera, walking. *Address:* All Souls College, Oxford OX1 4AL.

PUMPHREY, Sir (John) Laurence, KCMG 1973 (CMG 1963); HM Diplomatic Service, retired; Ambassador to Pakistan (formerly High Commissioner), 1971–76; *b* 22 July 1916; *s* of late Charles Ernest Pumphrey and Iris Mary (*née* Moberly-Bell); *m* 1945, Jean, *e d* of Sir Walter Buchanan Riddell, 12th Bt; four *s* one *d*. *Educ:* Winchester; New College, Oxford. Served War of 1939–45 in Army. Foreign Service from 1945. Head of Establishment and Organisation Department, Foreign Office, 1955–60; Counsellor, Staff of British Commissioner-General for SE Asia, Singapore, 1960–63; Counsellor, HM Embassy, Belgrade, 1963–65; Deputy High Commissioner, Nairobi, 1965–67; British High Comr, Zambia, 1967–71. Military Cross, 3rd Class (Greece), 1941. *Address:* Caistron, Thropton, Morpeth, Northumberland NE65 7LG.

PUNTER, Prof. David Godfrey, PhD; FSAScot; FEA; Professor of English, since 2000, and Research Dean, Faculty of Arts, since 2003, University of Bristol; *b* 19 Nov. 1949; *s* of Douglas Herbert and Hilda Mary Punter; *m* 1988, Caroline Mary Case; one *s* two *d*. *Educ:* Fitzwilliam Coll., Cambridge (BA 1970; PhD 1984); DLitt Stirling, 1999. FSAScot; FEA. Lectr, 1973–84, Sen. Lectr, 1984–86, in English, UEA; Prof. of English and Hd of Dept, Chinese Univ. of Hong Kong, 1986–88; Prof. of English, 1988–2000, and Hd of Dept, 1988–94 and 1996, Univ. of Stirling; Dean, Grad. Studies, Faculty of Arts, Univ. of Bristol, 2002–03. Vis. Prof. of Modern English, Fudan Univ., Shanghai, 1983. Dir, Develt of Univ. English Teaching Project, 1985–86. Fellow, Inst. Contemp. Scotland; FRSA; FHEA. *Publications:* The Literature of Terror: a history of Gothic fictions from 1765 to the present day, 1980, 2nd edn 1996; (jtly) Romanticism and Ideology: studies in English writing 1765–1830, 1981; Blake, Hegel and Dialectic, 1982; The Hidden Script: writing and the unconscious, 1985; (ed) Introduction to Contemporary Cultural Studies, 1986; William Blake: selected poetry and prose, 1988; The Romantic Unconscious: a study in narcissism and patriarchy, 1989; Selected Poems of Philip Larkin: notes, 1991; (ed) William Blake: new casebook, 1996; Romanticism, 1997; William Blake's Songs of Innocence and of Experience: notes, 1998; Gothic Pathologies: the text, the body and the law, 1998; (ed with G. Byron) Spectral Readings: towards a Gothic geography, 1999; (ed) A Companion to the Gothic, 2000; Writing the Passions, 2000; Postcolonial Imaginings: fictions of a new world order, 2000; Philip Larkin's The Whitsun Weddings and Selected Poems: advanced notes, 2003; William Blake's Songs of Innocence and of Experience: advanced notes, 2003; (with G. Byron) The Gothic, 2004; The Influence of Postmodernism on Contemporary Writing, 2005; (ed) Francis Latham, The Midnight Bell, 2007; Metaphor, 2007; Modernity, 2007; *poetry:* China and Glass, 1985; Lost in the Supermarket, 1987; Asleep at the Wheel, 1996; Selected Short Stories, 1999; contrib. numerous articles and book chapters. *Recreations:* gardening, walking, collecting maps. *Address:* Department of English, University of Bristol, Bristol BS8 1TB. *T:* (0117) 928 8082, *Fax:* (0117) 928 8860; *e-mail:* david.punter@bristol.ac.uk. *Clubs:* Oxford and Cambridge, Arts.

PURCELL, Philip James; President, Continental Investors LLC, since 2006; *b* 5 Sept. 1943; *m* 1964, Anne Marie McNamara; seven *s*. *Educ:* Univ. of Notre Dame (BBA 1964); LSE (MSc 1966); Univ. of Chicago (MBA 1967). Man. Dir, McKinsey & Co., 1967–78; Vice Pres. of Planning and Admin, Sears, Roebuck & Co., 1978–82; CEO, and Pres., subseq. Chm., Dean Witter Discover & Co., 1982–97; Chm. and CEO, Morgan Stanley Dean Witter & Co., subseq. Morgan Stanley, 1997–2005. Dir, NY Stock Exchange, 1991–96. *Address:* Continental Investors LLC, 227 West Monroe Street, Suite 5045, Chicago, IL 60606, USA.

PURCELL, (Robert) Michael, CMG 1983; HM Diplomatic Service, retired; Adviser and Secretary, East Africa Association, 1984–87; *b* 22 Oct. 1923; *s* of late Lt-Col Walter Purcell and Constance (*née* Fendick); *m* 1965, Julia Evelyn, *o d* of late Brig. Edward Marsh-Kellett; two *d*. *Educ:* Ampleforth Coll. Served 60th Rifles (Greenjackets), 1943–47 (Italian Campaign, 1944–45). Colonial Admin, Uganda, 1949–62, retd; 1st Sec., CRO, later FCO, 1964–68; 1st Sec. (Commercial/Economic), Colombo, 1968–69; FCO, 1969–71; 1st Sec. (Aid), Singapore, 1971–73; Head of Chancery, HM Legation to the Holy See, 1973–76; Counsellor and Dep. High Comr, Malta, 1977–80; Ambassador to Somali Democratic Republic, 1980–83. KCSG 1976. *Recreations:* country life, books, bridge. *Address:* French Mill Cottage, Shaftesbury, Dorset SP7 0LT. *T:* (01747) 853615.

PURCHAS, Christopher Patrick Brooks; QC 1990; a Recorder, since 1986; *b* 20 June 1943; *s* of Rt Hon. Sir Francis Purchas, PC and Patricia Mona Kathleen Purchas; *m* 1st, 1974, Bronwen Mary Vaughan (marr. diss. 1995); two *d*; 2nd, 1998, Diana, *widow* of Dr Ian Hatrick. *Educ:* Summerfield Sch.; Marlborough Coll.; Trinity Coll., Cambridge (MA). Called to the Bar, Inner Temple, 1966, Bencher, 1995. *Recreations:* golf, tennis, shooting, ski-ing. *Address:* Crown Office Chambers, Temple, EC4Y 7HJ. *T:* (020) 7797 8100.
See also R. M. Purchas.

PURCHAS, Robin Michael; QC 1987; a Recorder, since 1989; Deputy High Court Judge, since 1994; *b* 12 June 1946; *s* of Rt Hon. Sir Francis Brooks Purchas, PC and Patricia Mona Kathleen Purchas; *m* 1970, Denise Anne Kerr Finlay; one *s* one *d*. *Educ:* Summerfields; Marlborough College; Trinity College, Cambridge (MA). Called to the Bar, Inner Temple, 1968, Bencher, 1996. Mem., Bar Council, 1999–2002 (Chm., Educn and Trng Cttee, 2000–02). *Recreations:* opera, music, fishing, tennis, ski-ing, sailing, shooting, golf. *Address:* (chambers) Francis Taylor Building, Temple, EC4Y 7BY. *T:* (020) 7353 8415. *Clubs:* Boodle's, Lansdowne, Queen's; Royal West Norfolk Golf; Royal Worlington and Newmarket Golf; Brancaster Staithe Sailing.
See also C. P. B. Purchas.

PURCHASE, Kenneth; MP (Lab and Co-op) Wolverhampton North East, since 1992; *b* 8 Jan. 1939; *m* 1960, Brenda Sanders; two *d*. *Educ:* Springfield Secondary Modern Sch.; Wolverhampton Polytechnic (BA). Toolmaker: Lucas, 1960–68; Ever Ready, 1968–76; with Telford Development Corp., 1977–80; with Walsall MBC, 1981–82; Business Development Advr and Company Sec., Black Country CDA Ltd, 1982–92. Mem., Wolverhampton HA, 1972–87. Mem. (Lab) Wolverhampton CBC, subseq. MBC, 1970–90. Contested (Lab) Wolverhampton North East, 1987. PPS to Sec. of State for Foreign Affairs, 1997–2001, to Pres. of the Council and Ldr of the H of C, 2001–03. Mem., Select Cttee on Trade and Industry, 1993–97, on Foreign Affairs, 2005–; Jt Chm., All Party Exports Gp, 1993–; Chm., PLP Trade and Industry Cttee, 1992–97; Secretary: All Party Jazz Appreciation Soc., 1996–98; All-Party UK Bahrain Gp, 1997–; All-Party UK Egypt Gp, 1999–. *Address:* House of Commons, SW1A 0AA.

PURDEN, Roma Laurette, (Laurie), (Mrs J. K. Kotch), MBE 1973; journalist and writer; *b* 30 Sept. 1928; *d* of George Cecil Arnold Purden and Constance Mary Sheppard; *m* 1957, John Keith Kotch (*d* 1979); two *d*. *Educ:* Harecroft Sch., Tunbridge Wells. Fiction Editor, Home Notes, 1948–51; Asst Editor, Home Notes, 1951–52; Asst Editor, Woman's Own, 1952; Sen. Asst Editor, Girl, 1952–54; Editor of: Housewife, 1954–57; Home, 1957–62; House Beautiful, 1963–65; Good Housekeeping, 1965–73; Editor-in-Chief: Good Housekeeping, and Womancraft, 1973–77; Woman's Journal, 1978–88; Woman & Home, 1982–83. Dir, Brickfield Publications Ltd, 1978–80. Magazine Editor of the Year, 1979, British Soc. of Magazine Editors; Consumer Magazine of the Year awarded by Periodical Publishers Assoc. to Woman's Journal, 1985. *Address:* 174 Pavilion Road, SW1X 0AW. *T:* (020) 7730 4021.

PURDEW, Stephen James; Director, and Co-owner, Champneys Health Resorts; *b* 25 May 1959; *s* of late Robert and of Dorothy Purdew; one *s* one *d*. *Educ:* Midhurst Grammar Sch. Dir, Henlow Grange Health Farm, 1981– (Manager, 1981–90); acquisition of: Springs Health Hydro (Dir), 1990; Forest Mere Health Farm, 1997; Champneys, 2001, when all resorts rebranded under that name. *Address:* Champneys Health Resort, Henlow, Beds SG16 6DB. *T:* (01462) 811111, *Fax:* (01462) 815310.

PURDON, Maj.-Gen. Corran William Brooke, CBE 1970; MC 1945; CPM 1982; *b* 4 May 1921; *s* of Maj.-Gen. William Brooke Purdon, DSO, OBE, MC, KHS, and Dorothy Myrtle Coates; *m* 1945, Maureen Patricia (*d* 2008), *d* of Major J. F. Petrie, Guides Infantry, IA; one *s* one *d* (and one *s* decd). *Educ:* Rokeby, Wimbledon; Campbell Coll., Belfast; RMC Sandhurst. MBIM. Commnd into Royal Ulster Rifles, 1939; service with Army Commandos, France and Germany, 1940–45 (wounded; MC); 1st Bn RU Rifles, Palestine, 1945–46; GHQ MELF, 1949–51; psc 1955; Staff, Malayan Emergency, 1956–58; Co. Comdr, 1 RU Rifles, Cyprus Emergency, 1958; CO, 1st Bn RU Rifles, BAOR and Borneo Confrontation, 1962–64; GSO1 and Chief Instructor, Sch. of Infantry, Warminster, 1965–67; Comdr, Sultan's Armed Forces, Oman, and Dir of Ops, Dhofar War, 1967–70 (Sultan's Bravery Medal, 1968 and Distinguished Service Medal for Gallantry, 1969, Oman; CBE); Commandant: Sch. of Infantry, Warminster, 1970–72; Small Arms Sch. Corps, 1970–72; GOC, NW Dist, 1972–74; GOC Near East Land Forces, 1974–76, retired. Dep. Comr, Royal Hong Kong Police Force, 1978–81; St John Ambulance: Comdr, Wilts, 1981–84; Mem. Council, 1981–86; Pres., Devizes Div., 1993–2000. President: London Irish Rifles Assoc., 1993–; RUR Regtl Assoc., 1994–; Hon. Colonel: Queen's Univ. Belfast OTC, 1975–78; D (London Irish Rifles), 4th Bn Royal Irish Rangers, 1986–93. Pres. Army Gymnastic Union, 1973–76; Patron, Small Arms Sch. Corps Assoc., 1985–90. KStJ 1983 (Service Medal, 1999). Commendation Medal (Oman), 1970; Médaille d'Honneur de St Nazaire, 2000; Chevalier de la Légion d'Honneur (France), 2005; Pingat Jasa Malaysia, 2006. *Publications:* List the Bugle: reminiscences of an Irish soldier, 1993; articles in military jls. *Recreations:* physical training, dogs (English bull terriers, German shepherds). *Address:* Old Park House, Devizes, Wilts SN10 5JR. *Clubs:* Army and Navy; Hong Kong.

PURDUE, Marie Theresa; *see* Conte-Helm, M. T.

PURDY, Quentin Alexander; a District Judge (Magistrates' Courts), since 2003; *b* 23 Aug. 1960; *s* of late Gordon Purdy, OBE, FRCS and of Margaret Purdy; *m* 1988, Elizabeth Audrey Hazelwood; two *d*. *Educ:* Gresham's Sch., Holt; Leicester Poly. (BA Hons 1982); Inns of Court Sch. of Law, 1983; University Coll. London (LLM 1985). Called to the Bar, Gray's Inn, 1983; barrister, Common Law Chambers, London, 1983–2003; Actg Metropolitan Stipendiary Magistrate, 1998–2000; Dep. Dist Judge (Magistrates' Courts), 2000–03. Deacon, Dormansland Baptist Church, 2001–. Band Trust Award, 1983. *Recreations:* sailing, cycling, dog walking, foreign travel. *Address:* City of Westminster Magistrates' Court, 70 Horseferry Road, SW1P 2AX; Goldsmith Chambers, Goldsmith Building, Temple, EC4Y 7BL.

PURDY, (William) George, CBE 2002; Chief Scout, 1996–2004; *b* 16 April 1942; *s* of George Purdy and Amelia Jane Purdy (*née* McConnell); *m* 1969, Judith Sara Isabell Kerr; two *s*. *Educ:* Annadale Grammar Sch. NICS, 1960–91, 1993–96; Chief Exec., NI Software

Industry Fedn, 1991–93. Scout Leader, 1962–94, Chief Comr, NI, 1994–96, Vice Pres., 2007–, Scout Assoc. *Recreations:* golf, Rugby, tennis. *Address:* 16 Carshaulton Road, Donaghadee, Co. Down BT21 0QB.

PURKIS, Dr Andrew James, OBE 2002; Chief Executive, Tropical Health and Education Trust, since 2005; *b* 24 Jan. 1949; *s* of late Clifford Henry Purkis and Mildred Jeannie Purkis; *m* 1980, Jennifer Harwood Smith; one *s* one *d*. *Educ:* Highgate Sch.; Corpus Christi Coll., Oxford; St Antony's Coll., Oxford. 1st class Hons MA Mod. Hist. 1970; DPhil 1978. Home Civil Service, N Ireland Office, 1974; Private Sec. to Perm. Under-Sec. of State, NI Office, 1976–77; Head of Policy Unit, 1980, Asst Dir, 1986, NCVO; Dir, CPRE, 1987–91; Public Affairs Advr to the Archbishop of Canterbury, 1992–98; Chief Exec., Diana, Princess of Wales Meml Fund, 1998–2005. Member: Bd, Contact a Family (charity), 1986–93; Bd, Green Alliance, 1992–2004; Bd, Charity Commn, 2007–; Chair: Living Streets (formerly Pedestrians' Assoc.), 1999–2007; Empty Homes Agency, 2004–07. *Publications:* (with Paul Hodson) Housing and Community Care, 1982; (with Rosemary Allen) Health in the Round, 1983. *Recreations:* walking, surf-riding, bird-watching, music, theatre. *Address:* 38 Endlesham Road, Balham, SW12 8JL. *T:* (020) 8675 2439.

PURKISS, Robert Ivan, MBE 2000; independent consultant on diversity and change management; Managing Director, Different Realities Partnership, since 2004; *b* 11 Nov. 1945; *s* of Howard Flanagan and Betty Purkiss; *m* 1971, Monica Dell Richardson; two *d*. *Educ:* Toynbee Rd Boys' Sch.; Southampton Inst. of Higher Educn; Southampton Univ. (Dip. Industrial Relns). Chief Petty Officer, MN, 1961–72; Advr, Industrial Soc., 1972–74; Nat. Officer, Nat. Workers' Union of Jamaica, 1974–76; TGWU, 1976–2000 (Nat. Sec., 1989–2000); Chm., Eur. Monitoring Centre on Racism and Xenophobia, 2001–04. Mem., CRE, 1993–2001. Ind. Assessor for Public Appts, DTI, 2001–; Ind. Mem., Hampshire Police Authy, 2003–; Chair: Black & Ethnic Minorities Network, 2004–; Race and Diversity Policy, Assoc. of Police Authorities, 2005–. *Publications:* contrib. numerous articles on anti-racism, industrial relns and diversity. *Recreations:* football referee (Mem., Southampton Referees Soc.; Mem., Man. Cttee, Wessex League), athletics (Vice-Chm., Team Solent Athletics Club). *Address:* Penderyn, Norlands Drive, Otterbourne, Winchester SO21 2DT.

PURLE, Charles Lambert; QC 1989; **His Honour Judge Purle;** a Circuit Judge, since 2007; *b* 9 Feb. 1947; *s* of Robert Herbert Purle and Doreen Florence (*née* Button); *m* 1st, 1969, Lorna Barbara Brown (marr. diss. 1990); one *s* one *d*; 2nd, 1991, Virginia Dabney Hopkins Rylatt; two *s* two *d*. *Educ:* Nottingham Univ. (LLB 1969); Worcester Coll., Oxford (BCL 1971). Called to the Bar, Gray's Inn, 1970; in practice, 1972–2007. *Recreations:* opera, music, theatre, my children. *Address:* Priory Courts, 33 Bull Street, Birmingham B4 6DS.

PURNELL, Rt Hon. James; PC 2007; MP (Lab) Stalybridge and Hyde, since 2001; Secretary of State for Work and Pensions, since 2008; *b* 2 March 1970; *s* of John and Janet Purnell. *Educ:* Balliol Coll., Oxford (BA PPE). Researcher for Tony Blair, MP, 1990–92; Strategy Consultant, Hydra Associates, 1992–94; Res. Fellow, Media and Communications, IPPR, 1994–95; Hd, Corporate Planning, BBC, 1995–97; Special Advr to Prime Minister on culture, media, sport and the knowledge econ., 1997–2001. Mem. (Lab) Islington BC, 1994–95 (Chairman: Early Years Cttee; Housing Cttee). Parly Under-Sec. of State, DCMS, 2005–06; Minister of State, DWP, 2006–07; Sec. of State for Culture, Media and Sport, 2007–08. *Publications:* contrib. various publications for IPPR. *Recreations:* football, film, theatre, music. *Address:* House of Commons, SW1A 0AA. *Club:* Stalybridge Labour.

PURNELL, Nicholas Robert; QC 1985; a Recorder, since 1986; *b* 29 Jan. 1944; *s* of late Oliver Cuthbert Purnell and Pauline Purnell; *m* 1970, Melanie Stanway; four *s*. *Educ:* Oratory Sch.; King's Coll. Cambridge (Open Exhibnr; MA). Called to the Bar, Middle Temple, 1968 (Astbury Schol.), Bencher 1990; Junior of Central Criminal Court Bar Mess, 1972–75; Prosecuting Counsel to Inland Revenue, 1977–79; Jun. Treasury Counsel, 1979–85. Mem., Bar Council and Senate, 1973–77, 1982–85, 1989–91 (Chm., Legal Aid Fees Cttee, 1989–90); Member: Lord Chancellor's and Home Secretary's Working Party on the Training of the Judiciary, 1975–78; Crown Court Rules Cttee, 1982–88; Lord Chancellor's Adv. Cttee on Educn and Conduct, 1991–97; Criminal Cttee, Judicial Studies Bd, 1991–96. Chm., Criminal Bar Assoc., 1990–91. Governor, The Oratory Sch., 1994–. *Recreations:* living in France as much as possible, supporting Wimbledon AFC. *Address:* Cloth Fair Chambers, 39–40 Cloth Fair, EC1A 7NT.

See also P. O. Purnell.

PURNELL, Paul Oliver; QC 1982; a Recorder, since 1985; *s* of late Oliver Cuthbert and Pauline Purnell; *m* 1966, Celia Consuelo Ocampo; one *s* two *d*. *Educ:* The Oratory Sch.; Jesus Coll., Oxford (MA). Served 4th/7th Royal Dragoon Guards, 1958–62. Called to the Bar, Inner Temple, 1962, Bencher, 1991; Head of Chambers, 2007–. Jun. Treasury Counsel at Central Criminal Court, 1976–82. *Recreations:* tennis, windsurfing, motorcycling. *Address:* Farringdon Chambers, Gemini House, 180 Bermondsey Street, SE1 3TQ. *T:* (020) 7089 5700. *Clubs:* Cavalry and Guards, Hurlingham.

See also N. R. Purnell.

PURSE, Hugh Robert Leslie; barrister; part-time Chairman of Employment (formerly Industrial) Tribunals, 1996–2003; *b* 22 Oct. 1940; *s* of Robert Purse and Elsie Purse (*née* Kemp). *Educ:* St Peter's School, York; King's College London (LLB). Called to the Bar, Gray's Inn, 1964 (Atkin Scholar). Legal Asst, Dept of Employment, 1969; Legal Adviser to Price Commission, 1978–79; Govt legal service, 1979–96: Legal Advr, Dept of Employment, and Principal Asst Treasury Solicitor, 1988–96.

PURSEY, Nigel Thomas; Chief Executive, Staffordshire County Council, 2003–07; *b* 4 Aug. 1949. *Educ:* Manchester Univ. (MusB). CPFA 1975. Trainee Accountant, Cheshire CC, 1971–75; Accountant, Mid Glamorgan CC, 1975–78; Wiltshire County Council: Group Accountant, 1978–81; Chief Admin. Assistant (Finance), 1981–83; Chief Accountant, 1983–86; Asst County Treasurer, 1986–92; Shropshire County Council: County Treas., 1992–97; Chief Exec., 1997–2003. Clerk to: Shropshire Lieutenancy, 1997–2003; Staffs Lieutenancy, 2003–07; Staffs Police Authy, 2003–07. Dep. Chm., Shropshire Learning and Skills Council, 2001–03; Mem. Bd and Chair of Audit Cttee, Children's Workforce Develt Council, 2008–. Associate Master of the Music, Shrewsbury Abbey, 2001–. Treas., Pontesbury-Muheza Link Charity, 2008–. Gov., Staffs Univ., 2003–07. *Recreations:* music, walking, bridge, family activities.

PURSHOUSE, Michael, PhD; FIMechE, FIET, FREng; Senior Systems Engineer, Thales UK plc, since 2000; *b* Rotherham, 19 Sept. 1951; *s* of Edwin and Rita Purshouse; *m* 1981, Sabine Gabriele Rohrssen; two *d*. *Educ:* St John's C of E Sch., Mexborough; Mexborough Grammar Sch.; Sidney Sussex Coll., Cambridge (BA 1973; PhD 1978). FREng 2007. Undergrad. apprentice, BAC, Bristol, 1969–74; Acoustics Consultant, YARD Ltd, Glasgow, 1978–81; Res. Scientist, Fraunhofer-Gesellschaft, Stuttgart, Germany, 1981–83; Principal Consultant, YARD Ltd, 1984–92; Business Gp Manager, Naval Engrg, BAeSEMA Ltd, 1992–2000; Chief Engr, Thales CVF Team, 2000–03; Hd, Systems Engrg, Aircraft Carrier Alliance, 2003–06; Chief Engr, FRES-SOSI, 2007–. Hon. Prof., Dept of Physics and Astronomy, Univ. of Glasgow, 1997–; Fellow Commoner, Sidney Sussex Coll., Cambridge, 2004–. Mem., Exec. Cttee, Cambridge Univ. Engrs' Assoc., 2007–. Chm., Glasgow Panel, IMechE, 1992–95. Vice-Pres., Stephenson Soc., Sidney Sussex Coll., 1996–2006. Trustee Dir, Mt Pleasant Community Centre Ltd, 2007–. *Recreations:* Evelyn Waugh, Mozart, friends and family. *Address:* c/o Sidney Sussex College, Cambridge CB2 3HU; *e-mail:* mpurshouse@iee.org.

PURSSELL, Anthony John Richard; Governor, National Society for Epilepsy, since 1993 (Chairman, 1995–98); *b* 5 July 1926; *m* 1952, Ann Margaret Batchelor; two *s* one *d*. *Educ:* Oriel Coll., Oxford (MA Hons Chemistry). Managing Director: Arthur Guinness Son & Co. (Park Royal) Ltd, 1968; Arthur Guinness Son & Co. (Dublin) Ltd, 1973; Arthur Guinness & Sons plc, 1975–81; Jt Dep. Chm., 1981–83. Thames Valley and S Midlands Regl Bd, Lloyds Bank plc: Regl Dir, 1982–91; Chm., 1989–91. Member: IBA, 1976–81; Bd, CAA, 1984–90. Trustee and Hon. Treas., Oxfam, 1985–92. *Recreations:* travel, golf, books. *Address:* Allendale, 53 Bulstrode Way, Gerrards Cross, Bucks SL9 7QT. *Club:* Leander (Henley).

PURVES, Dame Daphne (Helen), DBE 1979; Senior Lecturer in French, Dunedin Teachers College, 1967–73, retired (Lecturer, 1963–66); *b* 8 Nov. 1908; *d* of Irvine Watson Cowie and Helen Jean Cowie; *m* 1939, Herbert Dudley Purves, CMG, FRSNZ (*d* 1993); one *s* two *d*. *Educ:* Otago Girls' High Sch., Dunedin, NZ; Univ. of Otago, Dunedin (MA 1st Cl. Hons English and French). Secondary sch. teacher, 1931–40 and 1957–63. Pres., NZ Fedn of University Women, 1962–64; Internat. Fedn of University Women: Mem., Cultural Relations Cttee, 1965–68, Convener, 1968–71; 3rd Vice-Pres., 1971–74; 1st Vice-Pres., 1974–77; Pres., 1977–80. Chm., National Theme Cttee, The Child in the World, NZ Nat. Commn for Internat. Year of the Child, 1978–80; Mem., Internat. Year of the Child Telethon Trust, 1978–81; Exec. Mem., NZ Cttee for Children (IYC) Inc., 1980–82. Mem., NZ Nat. Commn, Unesco, 1964–68. Pres., Friends of Olveston Inc., 1986–88. Mem., Theomin Gall. Management Cttee, 1986–91. *Relevant publication:* Nothing Like a Dame: a biography of Dame Daphne Purves, by Molly Anderson, 1998. *Recreations:* reading, croquet, bridge, travel, heraldry. *Clubs:* University (Dunedin); Punga Croquet (Pres., 1988–90); Dunedin Bridge, Otago Bridge.

PURVES, Elizabeth Mary, (Libby), (Mrs Paul Heiney), OBE 1999; writer and broadcaster; *b* 2 Feb. 1950; *d* of late James Grant Purves, CMG; *m* 1980, Paul Heiney, *qv*; one *d* (one *s* decd). *Educ:* Convent of the Sacred Heart, Tunbridge Wells; St Anne's Coll., Oxford (1st Cl. Hons Eng. Lang. and Lit.). BBC Local Radio (Oxford), 1972–76; Radio 4: Reporter, 1976–79, Presenter, 1979–81, Today; Presenter, Midweek, 1984–. Editor, Tatler, March–Oct. 1983, resigned; columnist, The Times, 1990–. Pres., Council for Nat. Parks, 2000–01. *Publications:* (ed) The Happy Unicorns, 1971; (ed) Adventures Under Sail, H. W. Tilman, 1982; Britain At Play, 1982; Sailing Weekend Book, 1985; How Not to be a Perfect Mother, 1986; Where Did You Leave the Admiral, 1987; (jtly) The English and their Horses, 1988; The Hurricane Tree, 1988; One Summer's Grace, 1989; How Not to Raise a Perfect Child, 1991; Getting the Story, 1993; Working Times, 1993; How Not to be a Perfect Family, 1994; (with Paul Heiney) Grumpers' Farm, 1996; Holy Smoke, 1998; Nature's Masterpiece: a family survival book, 2000; Radio - a True Love Story, 2002; *novels:* Casting Off, 1995; A Long Walk in Wintertime, 1996; Home Leave, 1997; More Lives Than One, 1998; Regatta, 1999; Passing Go, 2000; A Free Woman, 2001; Mother Country, 2002; Continental Drift, 2003; Acting Up, 2004; Love Songs and Lies, 2007. *Recreations:* sailing, walking, writing, radio. *Address:* c/o Rogers, Coleridge & White Ltd, 20 Powis Mews, W11 1JN. *Club:* Royal Cruising.

PURVES, Sir William, Kt 1993; CBE 1988; DSO 1951; Chairman, 1990–98, Chief Executive, 1990–92, HSBC Holdings plc; *b* 27 Dec. 1931; *s* of Andrew and Ida Purves; *m* 1st, 1958, Diana Troutbeck Richardson (marr. diss. 1988); two *s* two *d*; 2nd, 1989, Rebecca Jane Lewellen. *Educ:* Kelso High School. FIBScot; FCIB. National Service, with Commonwealth Div. in Korea (Subaltern; DSO). National Bank of Scotland, 1948–54; Hongkong and Shanghai Banking Corporation: Germany, Hong Kong, Malaysia, Singapore, Sri Lanka, Japan, 1954–70; Chief Accountant, Hong Kong, 1970; Manager, Tokyo, 1974; Sen. Manager Overseas Operations, 1976; Asst General Manager, Overseas Operations, 1978; General Manager, 1979; Executive Director, 1982–98; Dep. Chm., 1984–86; Chm. and Chief Exec., 1986–92; Chm., Midland Bank Plc, 1994–97 (Dir, 1987–98); Dir, Marine Midland Banks Inc., 1982–98. Chairman: British Bank of ME, 1979–98; Hakluyt & Co., Ltd, 2000–; non-executive Director: Shell Transport and Trading, 1993–2002; Reuters Founders Share Co. Ltd, 1995–; Trident Safeguards Ltd, 1999–2003; Aquarius Platinum, 2004–; Dep. Chm., Alstom, 1998–2003. Trustee and Dep. Chm., Imperial War Mus., 1996–2004. Hon. LLD: Sheffield, 1993; Hong Kong, 1994; Hon. DBA: Stirling, 1987; Hong Kong Poly., 1993; Napier, 1998; Hon. MBA Strathclyde, 1996; UMIST, 2001. GBM 1999. *Recreations:* golf, Rugby. *Address:* 100 Ebury Mews, SW1W 9NX. *Clubs:* Royal Automobile, Caledonian; Hong Kong Jockey.

PURVIS, Bryan John; Head Master, William Hulme's Grammar School, Manchester, 1997–99; *b* 6 Aug. 1947; *s* of Robert Hunt Purvis and Eleanor Liddel Purvis; *m* 1969, Irene Anne Griffiths; one *s* two *d*. *Educ:* Tynemouth High Sch.; Bedford Coll., London (BSc); Durham Univ. (MSc). Biology Master, St Joseph's Grammar Tech. Sch., Hebburn on Tyne, 1969–74; Dep. Headmaster and Head of Biology, King's Sch., Tynemouth, 1974–93; Head Master, Altrincham GS for Boys, 1993–97. *Recreations:* gardening, hill-walking, watching football (Manchester City) and Rugby. *Address:* Grange End, 219 Hale Road, Hale, Cheshire WA15 8DL. *T:* (0161) 980 4506; *e-mail:* BPrvs@aol.com. *Club:* East India, Devonshire, Sports and Public Schools.

PURVIS, Dawn; Member (PUP) Belfast East, Northern Ireland Assembly, since Jan. 2007; *b* 22 Oct. 1966; two *s*. *Educ:* Queen's Univ. Belfast (BA Hons 1st cl. Sociol. and Social Policy 2003). Researcher: Sch. of Envmtl Scis, Univ. of Ulster, Coleraine, 2004–06; Sch. of Sociology, Huddersfield Univ., 2006–07. Leader, PUP, 2007–. Mem., NI Policing Bd, 2006–07. *Address:* (office) 299 Newtownards Road, Belfast BT4 1AG. *T:* (028) 9022 5040, *Fax:* (028) 9022 5041; *e-mail:* movingforward@pup-ni.org.uk.

PURVIS, Air Vice-Marshal Henry R.; *see* Reed-Purvis.

PURVIS, Iain Younie; QC 2006; *b* 23 Aug. 1963; *s* of John Younie Purvis and Juliet Purvis (*née* Parker); *m* 1993, Beverley Jane Myers; two *s* one *d*. *Educ:* Royal Grammar Sch., High Wycombe; Clare Coll., Cambridge (BA Law 1984, MA); St Edmund Hall, Oxford (BCL). Called to the Bar, Gray's Inn, 1986. *Publication:* Working with Technology, 2001. *Recreations:* neolithic monuments, ski-ing, running. *Address:* 11 South Square, Gray's Inn, WC1R 5EY; *e-mail:* ipurvis@11southsquare.com.

PURVIS, Jeremy; Member (Lib Dem) Tweeddale, Ettrick and Lauderdale, Scottish Parliament, since 2003; *b* 15 Jan. 1974; *s* of George Purvis and Eileen Purvis. *Educ:* Brunel Univ. (BSc Hons Politics and Mod. Hist.). Personal Asst to Sir David Steel, later Lord Steel of Aikwood, 1995–98. Director: GJW Scotland, 1998–2001; McEwan Purvis, 2001–03.

Recreations: classic cars, painting, reading. *Address:* Scottish Parliament, Edinburgh EH99 1SP. *T:* (constituency office) (01896) 663656, *Fax:* (01896) 663655; *e-mail:* jeremy.purvis.msp@scottish.parliament.uk.

PURVIS, John Robert, CBE 1990; Member (C) Scotland, European Parliament, since 1999; Partner, Purvis & Co., since 1986; *b* 6 July 1938; *s* of Lt-Col R. W. B. Purvis, MC, JP, and Mrs R. W. B. Purvis, JP; *m* 1962, Louise S. Durham; one *s* two *d. Educ:* Cargilfield, Barnton, Edinburgh; Trinity Coll., Glenalmond, Perthshire; St Salvator's Coll., Univ. of St Andrews (MA Hons). National Service, Lieut Scots Guards, 1956–58. First National City Bank, New York, 1962–69: London, 1962–63; New York, 1963–65; Milan, 1965–69; Treasurer, Noble Grossart Ltd, Edinburgh, 1969–73; Man. Dir, Gilmerton Management Services Ltd, 1973–92. Mem. (C) Mid-Scotland and Fife, European Parlt, 1979–84, contested same seat, 1984; European Democratic Group, European Parliament: whip, 1980–82; spokesman on energy, research and technology, 1982–84; Vice-Pres., Economic and Monetary Affairs Cttee, 2001–. Vice Pres., Scottish Cons. and Unionist Assoc., 1987–89 (Chm., Industry Cttee, 1986–97); Mem., IBA, 1985–89 (Chm., Scottish Adv. Cttee, 1985–89); Mem., Scottish Adv. Cttee on Telecommunications, 1990–98. Director: James River Fine Papers Ltd, 1984–95; Edgar Astaire & Co. Ltd, 1993–94; Jamont NV, 1994–95; European Utilities Trust plc, 1994–2007; Curtis Fine Papers Ltd, 1995–2001; Crown Vantage Ltd, 1995–2001; Chairman: Kingdom FM Radio Ltd, 1998–2008 (Dir, 2008–); Belgrave Capital Management Ltd, 1999–. *Publication:* (section 'Money') in Power and Manoeuvrability, 1978. *Address:* European Parliament, Rue Wiertz 43, 1047 Brussels, Belgium. *T:* (2) 2845684; *e-mail:* john.purvis@europarl.europa.eu; PO Box 29222, St Andrews, Fife KY16 8WL. *T:* (01334) 475830; *e-mail:* purvisco@jpurvis.co.uk. *Clubs:* Cavalry and Guards, Farmers'; New (Edinburgh); Royal and Ancient (St Andrews).

PURVIS, Sir Neville, KCB 1992; Vice Admiral, retired; Chairman, Grays International of Cambridge, 2001–07; *b* 8 May 1936; *s* of Charles Geoffrey and Sylvia Rose Purvis; *m* 1970, Alice Margaret (*née* Hill) (marr. diss. 1998); two *s*; *m* 2008, Susan Legh Bancroft. *Educ:* Charterhouse; Selwyn College, Cambridge (MA). BRNC Dartmouth, 1953; reading engineering at Cambridge, 1954–57; joined submarine service, 1959; served in HM Ships Turpin, 1960, Dreadnought, 1963, Repulse, 1967; Naval Staff, 1970; Sqdn Engineer Officer, 3rd Submarine Sqdn, 1973; Staff of Flag Officer, Submarines, 1975; RCDS 1980; in Command, HMS Collingwood, 1985–87; Dir Gen., Future Material Projects (Naval), 1987–88; Dir Gen., Naval Manpower and Trng, 1988–90; Mem., Admiralty Bd, and Chief of Fleet Support, 1991–94; Chief Exec., BSI, 1994–96; Dir Gen., British Safety Council, 1997–2001; Chm., Reliance Secure Task Mgt, 2001–05. Chm., Council, Friends of Nat. Maritime Mus., 2002–05; Chm. and Trustee, Marine Soc. and Sea Cadets, 2005–07 (Trustee, Sea Cadets Assoc., 2003–05). President: Westminster Br., Royal Soc. of St George, 2007–; London Br., Submariners Assoc., 2007–. FInstD 1993; CCMI (CIMgt 1996); FRSA 1992. *Recreations:* wining and dining. *Address:* 11 Kingswood Terrace, Chiswick, W4 5BN.

PURVIS, Prof. Stewart Peter, CBE 2000; Partner, Content and Standards, Office of Communications, since 2007; *b* 28 Oct. 1947; *s* of late Peter and Lydia Purvis; *m* 1st, 1972 (marr. diss. 1993); one *d*; 2nd, 2004, Jacqui Marson; two *s. Educ:* Dulwich Coll.; Univ. of Exeter (BA). Presenter, Harlech TV, 1968–69; BBC News trainee, 1969; ITN journalist, 1972; Programme Editor, News At Ten, 1980; Editor, Channel Four News, 1983; Independent Television News: Dep. Editor, 1986; Editor, 1989; Editor-in-Chief, 1991–95; Chief Exec., 1995–2003. Dir, ITN Ltd, 1989–2003; Pres., Euronews, 1998–2002. News Internat. Prof. of TV Journalism, City Univ., 2003–; Vis. Prof. of Broadcast Media, Univ. of Oxford, 2004–05. Non-exec. Dir, Royal Marsden NHS Trust, 1999–2004. FRTS 1991. Hon. LLD Exeter, 2005. BAFTA Award for Best News or Outside Broadcast, 1986, 1987; BPG Award for Best News or Current Affairs Prog., 1988. *Address:* Office of Communications, Riverside House, 2a Southwark Bridge Road, SE1 9HA.

PUSACK, George Williams, MS; Chief Executive, Mobil Oil Australia Ltd, 1980–85, retired; *b* 26 Sept. 1920; *s* of George F. Pusack and Winifred (*née* Williams); *m* 1942, Marian Preston; two *s* one *d. Educ:* Univ. of Michigan; Univ. of Pennsylvania. BSE (AeroEng), BSE (Eng.Math), MS (MechEng). Aero Engr, US Navy, 1942–45; Corporal, US Air Force, 1945–46; Mobil Oil Corp.: Tech. Service and Research Manager, USA, 1946–53; Product Engrg Manager, USA, 1953–59; International Supply Manager, USA, 1959–69; Vice-Pres., N Amer. Div., USA, 1969–73; Regional Exec., Mobil Europe, London, 1973–76; Chm. and Chief Exec., Mobil Oil Co. Ltd, 1976–80. Pres., County Hospice, York, SC, 1989–91. Trustee, Victorian State Opera Foundn, 1983–85. Teacher, layreader, vestryman and warden of Episcopal Church (Trustee, York, SC, 1992–). *Recreations:* golf, travel. *Address:* 400 Avinger Lane #431, Davidson, NC 28036, USA. *T:* (704) 8961431. *Club:* River Hills Country (Pres., 1991) (Clover, USA).

PUSEY, Prof. Charles Dickson, DSc; FRCP, FRCPath, FMedSci; Professor of Medicine, since 2003, Head of Renal Section, Division of Medicine, since 1997, and Head of Postgraduate Medicine, since 2006, Imperial College, London; Hon. Consultant Physician, since 1984, and Lead Clinician, since 2001, Directorate of Renal Medicine and Transplantation, and Director of Education, since 2008, Imperial College Healthcare NHS Trust (formerly Hammersmith Hospitals NHS Trust). *Educ:* Corpus Christi Coll., Cambridge (BA 1969; MB BChir 1972; MA 1973); Guy's Hosp. Med. Sch., London Univ. (MSc 1983; DSc 2002). FRCP 1989; FRCPath 1997. House Officer and Jun. Med. Registrar, Guy's Hosp., 1972–74; Unit Med. Officer, Specialist then Sen. Specialist, in Medicine, RAF, 1974–79; Sen. Registrar, MRC Trng Fellow and Wellcome Trust Sen. Fellow in Clin. Sci., RPMS and Hammersmith Hosp., 1980–89; Sen. Lectr, Reader and then Prof. in Renal Medicine, RPMS and Imperial Coll., London, 1989–2002; Dir of Res. and Develt, Hammersmith Hosps NHS Trust, 2005–08. Acad. Registrar, RCP, 2001–05. Chm., Kidney Research UK, 2002–07. FMedSci 2002. *Publications:* Fast Facts: Renal Disorders, 2006; over 300 articles, reviews, and book chapters in field of renal medicine. *Recreations:* tennis, walking, music. *Address:* Renal Section, Division of Medicine, Imperial College London, Hammersmith Campus, Du Cane Road, W12 0NN. *T:* (020) 8383 3152, *Fax:* (020) 8383 2062; *e-mail:* c.pusey@imperial.ac.uk. *Club:* Athenæum.

PUSEY, Prof. Peter Nicholas, PhD; FRS 1996; FRSE; FInstP; Professor of Physics, University of Edinburgh, since 1991 (Head, Department of Physics and Astronomy, 1994–97 and 2000–03); *b* 30 Dec. 1942; *s* of late Harold Kenneth Pusey and Edith Joan Pusey (*née* Sparks); *m* 1966, Elizabeth Ann Nind; two *d. Educ:* St Edward's Sch., Oxford; Clare Coll., Cambridge (MA); Univ. of Pittsburgh (PhD 1969). FInstP 1981; FRSE 1996. Postdoctoral Fellow, IBM T. J. Watson Res. Center, Yorktown Heights, NY, 1969–72; SPSO, later Grade 6, RSRE, Malvern, 1972–91. *Publications:* numerous contribs in scientific literature. *Address:* School of Physics, University of Edinburgh, Mayfield Road, Edinburgh EH9 3JZ. *T:* (0131) 650 5255.

PUSINELLI, (Frederick) Nigel (Molière), CMG 1966; OBE 1963; MC 1940; HM Overseas Civil Service, retired; *b* 28 April 1919; second *s* of late S. Jacques and T. May Pusinelli, Frettenham, Norfolk and Fowey, Cornwall; *m* 1941, Joan Mary Chaloner (*d* 1999), *d* of late Cuthbert B. and Mildred H. Smith, Cromer, Norfolk and Bexhill-on-Sea, Sussex; one *d* (one *s* decd). *Educ:* Aldenham School; Pembroke College, Cambridge (BA Hons in law). Commissioned RA 1939; served BEF, 1940; India/Burma, 1942–45; Major, 1942; Staff College, Quetta, 1945. Administrative officer, Gilbert and Ellice Islands Colony, 1946–57. Transferred to Aden, 1958; Dep. Financial Sec. and frequently Actg Financial Sec. till 1962; Director of Establishments, 1962–68, and Assistant High Commissioner, 1963–68, Aden and Federation of South Arabia. Member E African Currency Board, 1960–62. Salaries Commissioner various territories in West Indies, 1968–70. Chm., Overseas Service Pensioners' Assoc., 1978–99 (Hon. Vice-Pres., 2004–). Chairman: Chichester Harbour Conservancy, 1987–90 (Vice-Chm., 1985–87; Mem., Adv. Cttee, 1971–2004); RYA Southern Region, 1979–96; Chichester Harbour Fedn of sailing clubs and yachting orgns, 1980–87. RYA Yachtsman's Award, 1996. *Publication:* Report on Census of Population of Gilbert and Ellice Islands Colony, 1947. *Recreation:* dinghy racing. *Address:* Mile End House, Westbourne, Emsworth, Hants PO10 8RP. *T:* (01243) 372915. *Clubs:* Royal Commonwealth Society; Royal Yachting Association, Cambridge University Cruising, Emsworth Sailing.

PUTIN, Vladimir Vladimirovich; Prime Minister of Russia, 1999 and since 2008; Chairman, United Russia Party, since 2008; *b* Leningrad, 7 Oct. 1952; *s* of late Vladimir Putin and Maria Putin; *m* 1983, Lyudmila; two *d. Educ:* Leningrad State Univ. (law degree, 1975). With KGB, in USSR and Germany, 1975–90; Adviser: to Rector, Leningrad State Univ., 1990; to Mayor of Leningrad, 1990–91; Chm., Cttee on Foreign Relations, Office of the Mayor, St Petersburg, 1991–94; first Dep. Mayor, and Chm. Cttee on Foreign Relations, St Petersburg, 1994–96; first Dep. Hd, Gen. Mgt Dept of Presidential Admin, 1996–97; Hd of Control Dept, 1997–98, first Dep. Hd of Admin, 1998, Kremlin; Dir, Fed. Security Service, Russia, 1998–99; Sec., Security Council, Russia, 1999; President of Russia, 2000–08. *Publication:* First Person (autobiog.), 2000. *Address:* White House, 2 Krasnopresnenskaya Naberezhnaya, Moscow 103274, Russia.

PUTNAM, Roger George, CBE 2007; Visiting Professor of Automotive Business, City University, since 2006; Chairman, Ford Motor Co. Ltd, 2002–05; *b* 17 Aug. 1945; *s* of George William Putnam and Peggy May Putnam (*née* Morgan); *m* 1969, Patricia Elizabeth Williams; one *s* one *d. Educ:* Haberdashers' Aske's Sch., Elstree. Public Relations Officer, 1966–68, Gen. Manager, Sales and Marketing, 1968–74, Lotus Cars Ltd; Director, Sales and Marketing: JCL Marine Ltd, 1974–76; Lotus Cars Ltd, 1976–82; Jaguar Cars Ltd, 1982–2002. Chairman: Jaguar Daimler Heritage Trust, 1985–; Retail Motor Strategy Gp, BERR, 2005–; The Learning Grid, 2007–. Non-exec. Director: Halcyon Days Ltd, 2002–; ITM Power plc, 2006–; Autologic Gp plc, 2007–. Dir, SMMT, 2002– (Pres., 2005–06). Pres., CIM (Midland), 2002. FIMI 1984. *Recreations:* collecting cameras, photography, theatre, reading. *Address:* c/o Society of Motor Manufacturers and Traders Ltd, Forbes House, Halkin Street, SW1X 7DS. *Club:* Royal Automobile.

PUTTNAM, family name of **Baron Puttnam.**

PUTTNAM, Baron *cr* 1997 (Life Peer), of Queensgate in the Royal Borough of Kensington and Chelsea; **David Terence Puttnam,** Kt 1995; CBE 1983; Chairman: Enigma Productions Ltd, since 1978; National Endowment for Science, Technology and the Arts, 1998–2003; Deputy Chairman, Channel Four, since 2006; *b* 25 Feb. 1941; *s* of Leonard Arthur Puttnam and Marie Beatrix Puttnam; *m* 1961, Patricia Mary (*née* Jones); one *s* one *d. Educ:* Minchenden Grammar Sch., London. Advertising, 1958–66; photography, 1966–68; film prodn, 1968–2000. Producer of feature films including: Bugsy Malone, 1976 (four BAFTA awards); The Duellists, 1977 (Jury Prize, Cannes); Midnight Express, 1978 (two Acad. Awards, three BAFTA Awards); Chariots of Fire, 1981 (four Acad. Awards, three BAFTA Awards, incl. awards for best film); Local Hero, 1982 (two BAFTA Awards); The Killing Fields, 1985 (three Acad. Awards, eight BAFTA Awards incl. Best Film); The Mission, 1986 (Palme d'Or, Cannes, 1986, one Acad. Award, three BAFTA awards, 1987). Chm. and Chief Exec. Officer, Columbia Pictures, 1986–88. Producer of films and series for television. Vis. Prof., Drama Dept, Bristol Univ., 1986–98. Director: National Film Finance Corp., 1980–85; Anglia Television Gp, 1982–99; Village Roadshow Corp., 1989–99; Chrysalis Group, 1993–96; Chairman: Internat. Television Enterprises Ltd, 1988–99; Spectrum Strategy Consultants, 1999–2006; Governor: National Film and Television Sch., 1974–2002 (Chm., 1988–96); LSE, 1997–2002 (Vis. Prof.); London Inst., 1998–2002; Member: Governing Council, Nat. Coll. for Sch. Leadership; Academic Adv. Bd, Inst. for Advanced Studies, Univ. of Bristol. Pres., UNICEF, 2002–; Vice President: BAFTA, 1993–2004; CPRE, 1995– (Pres., 1985–92). Member: British Screen Adv. Council, 1988–98; Arts Council Lottery Panel, 1995–98; Educn Standards Task Force, 1997–2002; British Educnl Communications and Technol. Agency; Arts and Humanities Res. Bd; Senate, Engrg Council. Chairman: Arts Adv. Cttee, British Council, 2001–03; Gen. Teaching Council, 1998–2001; Jt Scrutiny Cttee for Communications Bill, 2002; Media and Culture Sector Adv. Gp, QCA; Forum for the Future; Nat. Meml Arboretum; Nat. Mus. of Photography, Film and Television, 1994–2003. Trustee: Tate Gall., 1986–93; Science Museum, 1996–2004; Royal Acad. of Arts, 2000–03; Chm. Trustees, Nat. Teaching Awards, 1998–2008. Chancellor: Univ. of Sunderland, 1998–2007; Open Univ., 2007–. Lay Canon, Durham Cathedral, 2002–. FRGS; FRSA; FRPS; Fellow: BFI, 1997; BAFTA, 2006; FCGI 1999. Hon. Fellow: Manchester Polytechnic, 1990; Inst. of Educn, London Univ., 2007. Hon. FCSD 1990; Hon. FLI 1994. Hon. LLD Bristol, 1983; Hon. DLitt: Leicester, 1986; Sunderland, 1992; Bradford, 1993; Humberside, 1996; Westminster, 1997; Kent, 1998; London Guildhall, 1999; City, Nottingham, 2000; Heriot-Watt, 2001; Birmingham, 2002; Southampton, 2002; Keele, 2002; Hon. LittD Leeds, 1992; Hon. DLit QUB, 2001; Hon. Dr of Drama RSAMD, 1998; Hon. DPhil Cheltenham and Gloucester Coll. of Higher Educn, 1998; Hon. DSc (Med.) Imperial Coll., London, 1999; Hon. DFA American Univ. in London, 2000; Hon. Dr: Sheffield Hallam, 2000; Herzen Univ., St Petersburg, 2003; Nottingham Trent. Michael Balcon Award for outstanding contribn to British Film Industry, 1982, Fellowship, 2006, BAFTA; Benjamin Franklin Medal, RSA, 1996; Crystal Award, World Economic Forum, 1997; President's Medal, RPS, 2003. Commandeur de l'Ordre des Arts et des Lettres (France), 2006 (Officier, 1992). *Publications:* (with Brian Wenham) The Third Age of Broadcasting, 1982; (jtly) Rural England, 1988; What Needs to Change?, 1996; Undeclared War, 1997. *Recreations:* reading, going to the cinema. *Address:* House of Lords, SW1A 0PW. *Clubs:* Athenæum, Chelsea Arts, MCC.

PWAISIHO, Rt Rev. William Alaha, OBE 2004; Rector of Gawsworth, since 1999; Hon. Assistant Bishop of Chester, since 1997; *b* Solomon Is, 14 May 1948; *s* of Stephen Honiuhi and Esther Makatoro; *m* 1976, Sister Kate Kome Oikada; one *s* three *d* and one adopted *s. Educ:* C of E primary, sen. and secondary schs in Solomon Is; Bp Patterson Theol Coll., Kohimarama (Dip. in Theol. and Biblical Studies). Ordained deacon, 1974, priest, 1975; Chaplain to Archbp of Melanesia and to Central Police HQ, Honiara, 1976;

Curate, Mission Bay, Auckland, NZ (first missionary priest from Melanesia), 1977–78; Chaplain and Tutor, Bp Patterson Theol Coll., 1979–80; Dean, St Barnabas Provincial Cathedral, Honiara, 1980–81; Diocesan Bishop, Malaita, 1981–89; Tutor, Melanesian Brotherhood HQ, Tabalia, 1989–90; (first) Gen. Sec., Melanesian Bd of Mission, Honiara, 1990–95; Parish Priest, E of Honiara, 1995–97; Curate, St Anne and St Francis, Sale, UK, 1997–99. Chaplain to High Sheriff of Cheshire, 2002–03. Hon. Chaplain, Crimebeat in England and Wales, 2004–; Mem., Ethnic Minority Ind. Adv. Gp, Cheshire Constabulary. Member: Melanesian Mission UK; UK and NI Churches Together Pacific Forum. *Recreations:* football, Rugby, fishing, volleyball. *Address:* The Rectory, Church Lane, Gawsworth, Macclesfield, Cheshire SK11 9RJ. *T:* and *Fax:* (01260) 223201; *e-mail:* bishop.gawsworth@virgin.net. *Club:* Macclesfield Rotary.

PYANT, Paul; lighting designer, since 1988; *b* 22 July 1953; *s* of late Leonard Vincent Pyant and of Jean Phoebe Pyant (*née* Frampton); partner, Stephen Lawless. *Educ:* Royal Acad. of Dramatic Art (Hons Dip.). Lighting designs for: Glyndebourne Opera, 1974–, including: Death in Venice, Falstaff, 1990; Le Nozze di Figaro, 1991; Die Fledermaus, 2003; A Midsummer Night's Dream, 2006; English National Opera, 1985–, including: Xerxes, 1985; Lady Macbeth of Mtsensk, 1987; Street Scene (Scottish Opera/ENO), 1989; Royal National Theatre, 1988–, including: Wind in the Willows, 1990; The Madness of George III, 1991; Carousel, 1992 (NY, 1994, Japan, 1995); Candide, 1999; Streetcar Named Desire, 2003; Othello, 1997 (and Salzburg); 2000 Years, 2005; Houston Grand Opera, 1989–, incl. New Year, 1989; Royal Opera House, 1991–; Royal Shakespeare Co., 1991–, including: Richard III, 1992; The Tempest, 1993; Northern Ballet Theatre, 1991–, including: Romeo and Juliet, 1991; Cinderella, 1993; Dracula, 1996; Donmar Warehouse, 1992–, including: Assassins, 1992; Cabaret, 1993; Company, 1995; English National Ballet, 1993–, incl. Cinderella, 1996; LA Opera, 1995–, incl. The Elixir of Love, 1996; *theatre* includes: Orpheus Descending, Th. Royal, Haymarket, 1988 (NY, 1989); Hamlet, Old Vic, 2004; The Woman in White, Palace Th., 2004 (NY, 2005); Lord of the Rings, Toronto, 2006, Th. Royal, Drury Lane, 2007; opera work includes: productions in USA: for Metropolitan Opera, Seattle Opera, San Francisco Opera and Chicago Opera; in Australia and NZ; in Europe, incl. La Scala, Milan; ballet productions for: Royal NZ Ballet, Norwegian Nat. Ballet, Boston Ballet, Atlanta Ballet, Colorado Ballet and Asami Maki Ballet, Tokyo. *Recreations:* steam locomotives, gardening. *Address:* c/o Jeffrey Cambell Management, 11A Greystone Court, South Street, Eastbourne, E Sussex BN21 4LP. *T:* (01323) 411444; *e-mail:* cambell@theatricaldesigners.co.uk.

PYATT, David John; Principal Horn, London Symphony Orchestra, since 1998; *b* 26 Sept. 1973; *s* of John Douglas Pyatt and Frances Margaret Pyatt; *m* 1997, Catherine Anne Whiteside; one *s* one *d. Educ:* Watford Boys' Grammar Sch.; Selwyn Coll., Cambridge. Guest Principal Horn, Scottish Opera, 1994–96; Co-Principal Horn, BBC Nat. Orch. of Wales, 1996–98. Visiting Professor of Horn: GSM, 2000–; RAM, 2003–. Young Musician of the Year, BBC, 1988; Gramophone Young Artist of the Year, 1996. *Recreations:* cooking, eating and drinking enough to keep up with the Wine Society brochures. *Address:* c/o Clarion/Seven Muses, 47 Whitehall Park, N19 3TW. *T:* (020) 7272 4413, 5125, *Fax:* (020) 7281 9687; *e-mail:* caroline@c7m.co.uk.

PYE, Prof. (John) David, FLS; Professor of Zoology, Queen Mary and Westfield College (formerly Queen Mary College), University of London, 1973–91, now Emeritus Professor, Queen Mary, University of London; *b* 14 May 1932; *s* of Wilfred Frank Pye and Gwenllian Pye (*née* Davies); *m* 1958, Dr Ade Pye (*née* Kuku), Sen. Lectr, UCL, retd. *Educ:* Queen Elizabeth's Grammar School for Boys, Mansfield; University Coll. of Wales, Aberystwyth (BSc 1954, Hons 1955); Bedford Coll., London Univ. (PhD 1961). MInstP 2001, FInstP 2003. Research Asst, Inst. of Laryngology and Otology, London Univ., 1958–64; Lectr in Zoology, 1964–70, Reader, 1970–73, King's Coll. London; Head of Dept of Zoology and Comparative Physiology, Queen Mary Coll., 1977–82. A founder Dir, QMC Instruments Ltd, 1976–89. Linnean Society: Editor, Zoological Jl, 1981–85; Editl Sec. and Mem. Council, 1985–91; Vice-Pres., 1987–90; Mem., IEE Professional Gp Cttee E15, Radar, Sonar, Navigation and Avionics, 1983–86. Mem., RHS, 1988–. Member Editorial Boards: Zoolog. Soc., 1972–77, 1978–83, 1985–90; Jl of Exper. Biol., 1974–78; Jl of Comp. Physiol. A, 1978–96; Bioacoustics, 1987–. Royal Institution: Associate Mem., 1979–92; Mem., 1992–2002; delivered Friday discourses 1979, 1983, and televised Christmas Lects for Children, 1985–86; co-organizer, discussion evenings, 1994–2002; Mem. Council, 1999–2002; Vice Pres., 2001–02; Hon. Fellow, 2002. *Publications:* Bats, 1968; (with G. D. Sales) Ultrasonic Communication by Animals, 1974; (ed with R. J. Bench and A. Pye) Sound Reception in Mammals, 1975; Polarised Light in Science and Nature, 2001; articles and research papers. *Recreations:* baking and brewing, travel, arts. *Address:* Woodside, 24 St Mary's Avenue, Finchley, N3 1SN. *T:* (020) 8346 6869; (office) (020) 7882 3293.

PYE, Prof. Kenneth, ScD, PhD; CGeol, FGS; Managing Director, Kenneth Pye Associates Ltd, since 2004 (Founder Director, since 2002); *b* 24 Aug. 1956; *s* of Leonard Pye and Joyce Pye; *m* 1979, Diane Cadman (marr. diss. 2007); one *s* one *d. Educ:* Upholland Grammar Sch., Lancs; Hertford Coll., Oxford (Scholar; BA 1977; MA 1981); St John's Coll., Cambridge (PhD 1981; ScD 1992). CGeol 1995; FGS 1980. Cambridge University: NERC Postdoctoral Res. Fellow, 1980–82; Sarah Woodhead Res. Fellow, 1980–83, Non-stipendiary Fellow, 1983–89, Girton Coll.; Royal Society 1983 Univ. Res. Fellow, 1983–88; Reading University: Lectr in Quaternary Sedimentology, 1989–92; Reader in Sedimentology, 1992–94; Prof. of Envmtl Sedimentology, 1994–98; Royal Holloway, University of London: Prof. of Envmtl Geology, 1999–2004; Vis. Prof., 2004–07. Founder Director: Cambridge Envmtl Research Consultants Ltd, 1986–95; K. Pye Associates, 1998–. Expert Witness, forensic geology (criminal and civil investigations). Leverhulme Trust Fellowship, 1991; Leverhulme Trust Sen. Res. Fellowship, 1996. Sedgwick Prize, Univ. of Cambridge, 1984; British Geomorphological Research Group: Wiley Award, 1989; Gordon Warwick Award, 1991. *Publications:* Chemical Sediments and Geomorphology, 1983; Aeolian Dust and Dust Deposits, 1987; Aeolian Sand and Sand Dunes, 1990; Saltmarshes, 1992; The Dynamics and Environmental Context of Aeolian Sedimentary Systems, 1993; Aeolian Sediments Ancient and Modern, 1993; Sediment Transport and Depositional Processes, 1994; Environmental Change in Drylands, 1994; Backscattered Scanning Electron Microscopy and Image Analysis of Sediments and Sedimentary Rocks, 1998; Coastal and Estuarine Environments: sedimentology, geomorphology and geoarchaeology, 2000; Forensic Geoscience: principles, techniques and applications, 2004; Geological and Soil Evidence: forensic applications, 2007; contribs to learned jls. *Recreations:* world travel, visiting historic sites and houses, collecting rocks and minerals, reading. *Address:* Kenneth Pye Associates Ltd, Crowthorne Enterprise Centre, Crowthorne Business Estate, Old Wokingham Road, Crowthorne, Berks RG45 6AW. *T:* (01344) 751610.

PYE, William Burns, FRBS 1992; sculptor; *b* 16 July 1938; *m* 1963, Susan Marsh; one *s* two *d. Educ:* Charterhouse; Wimbledon Sch. of Art; Royal Coll. of Art (ARCA). Vis. Prof., Calif. State Univ., 1975–76. Pres., Hampshire Sculpture Trust, 2002–. Directed film, Reflections, 1971. *Solo exhibitions:* Winchester Great Hall, 1979; Hong Kong (retrospective), 1987; *public sculpture:* Zemran, South Bank, London, 1971; Curlicue, Greenland Dock, London, 1989; Cader Idris, Cardiff, 1998; *public water sculpture:* Slipstream and Jetstream, Gatwick Airport, 1988; Chalice, Fountain Sq., London, 1990; Water Wall and Portico, Expo '92, Seville, 1992; Orchid, the Peacocks, Woking, 1992; Cristos, St Christopher's Place, London, 1993; Confluence, Hertford, 1994; Downpour, British Embassy, Oman, 1995; Derby Cascade, Derby, 1995; Antony House, Cornwall, 1996; Archimedes Screw feature, West India Quay, London, 1997; Aquarena, Millennium Square, Bristol, 2000; Scaladaqua Tonda, Nat. Botanical Gardens, Wales, 2000; Tureen, St John's Coll., Cambridge, 2001; Monolith, Sunderland Winter Garden, 2001; Cornucopia, Millfield Sch., 2001; Scala Aquae Pembrochiana, Wilton House, 2001; Charybdis, Seaham Hall, Sunderland, 2001; Haberdashers' Co. new hall, 2002; Argosy, Lloyd's Register of Shipping, 2002; Divine Influx in Bath, Cross Bath, 2003; Jubilee Fountain, New Square, Lincoln's Inn, 2003; eight features for new gardens at Alnwick Castle, 2005; Sunken Garden, Aberglasney Gardens, Wales, 2005; *portrait bust of* Rt Hon. Douglas Hurd, Nat. Portrait Gall., 1996. Hon. FRIBA 1993. Prix de Sculpture, Vth Internat. Sculpture Exhibn, Budapest; Peace Sculpture Prize, W Midlands CC, 1984; ABSA Awards for Best Sculpture in UK (Gatwick Airport), 1988, and in Scotland (Glasgow), 1989; UENO Royal Museum Award, Japan, 1989. *Recreation:* playing the flute. *Address:* 43 Hambalt Road, Clapham, SW4 9EQ. *T:* (home) (020) 8673 2318, (studio) (020) 8682 2727.

PYLE, Derek Colin Wilson; Sheriff of Grampian, Highland and Islands at Inverness, since 2005; *b* 15 Oct. 1952; *s* of Colin Lawson Pyle and Mary Best Johnston Pyle; *m* 1980, Jean Blackwood Baillie May; five *s* one *d. Educ:* Royal High Sch., Edinburgh; Univ. of Edinburgh (LLB Hons). Law Apprentice, Lindsays, WS, Edinburgh, 1974–76; Partner, Dove Lockhart, WS, Solicitors, Edinburgh, 1977–80; Sole Partner, Wilson Pyle & Co., WS, Solicitors, Edinburgh, 1980–88; Partner, Henderson Boyd Jackson, WS, Solicitors, Edinburgh, 1989–99; Sheriff of Tayside, Central and Fife, 2000–05. *Recreations:* golf, writing unpublished best-sellers. *Address:* The Old Manor, Grange, Errol, Perthshire PH2 7SZ. *T:* (01821) 642198. *Club:* Craigielaw Golf.

PYLE, Prof. John Adrian, DPhil; FRS 2004; FRMetS; Director, Centre for Atmospheric Science, since 1992, and 1920 Professor of Physical Chemistry, since 2007, University of Cambridge; Fellow, St Catharine's College, Cambridge, since 1986; *b* 4 April 1951; *s* of Harold Pyle and Agnes Pyle (*née* Rimmer); *m* 1979, Elizabeth Caroline Lynnell Davies; one *s* two *d. Educ:* De La Salle Coll., Salford; Univ. of Durham (BSc Physics); Jesus Coll., Oxford (DPhil 1976). FRMetS 1976. Res. asst, Dept of Atmospheric Physics, Univ. of Oxford, 1976–82; Rutherford Appleton Lab., 1982–85; University of Cambridge: Lectr in Physical Chem., 1985–95; Reader in Atmospheric Chem., 1995–2000; Prof. of Atmospheric Sci., 2000–07; Head: Eur. Ozone Res. Co-ordinating Res. Unit, 1990–95; Atmospheric Chem. Modelling Support Unit, 1992–. Member: Stratospheric Ozone Rev. Gp, DoE, later DEFRA, 1986– (Chm., 1988–); EC DG Res. Panel on Stratospheric Ozone, 1990–; Subcttee on Envmtl Sci., ACOST, 1990–92; NERC Sci. and Technol. Bd, then Sci. and Implementation Strategy Bd, 2000–02. Mem. Council, Eur. Geophysical Soc., 1986–89. MAE 1993. Sec. II, RMetS, 1979–84. (Jtly) Eurotrac Award, Remote Sensing Soc., 1985; Interdisciplinary Award, RSC, 1991; (jtly) Körber Eur. Sci. Foundn Award, 1999; Adrian Gill Prize, RMetS, 2003. *Publications:* (ed jtly) Encyclopedia of Atmospheric Science, 2002; contrib. numerous papers to scientific jls. *Recreations:* hill walking, sport, supporting Bolton Wanderers. *Address:* Centre for Atmospheric Science, Department of Chemistry, Lensfield Road, Cambridge CB2 1EW. *T:* (01223) 336473, *Fax:* (01223) 763818; *e-mail:* john.pyle@atm.ch.cam.ac.uk.

PYM, Richard Alan, FCA; Chief Executive, Bradford & Bingley plc, since 2008; *b* 18 Sept. 1949. *Educ:* Exmouth Grammar Sch.; Univ. of Warwick (BSc 1971). FCA 1974. Thomson McLintock & Co., 1971–75; British Gas plc, 1975–77; BAT Industries plc, 1978–82; The Burton Gp plc, 1983–92; Alliance & Leicester plc: Gp Finance Dir, 1993–2001; Man. Dir, Retail Banking, 2001–02; Gp Chief Exec., 2002–07. Director: Selfridges plc, 1998–2003; Halfords plc, 2004– (Chm., 2006–); Old Mutual, 2007–. Vice-Pres., BBA, 2004–07.

PYMAN, Avril; *see* Sokolov, A.

PYMONT, Christopher Howard; QC 1996; a Recorder, since 2004; *b* 16 March 1956; *s* of John and Joan Pymont; *m* 1996, Meriel Rosalind, *d* of Roger and late Ann Lester; two *s* one *d. Educ:* Marlborough Coll.; Christ Church, Oxford (BA Hons 1977; MA 1979). Called to the Bar, Gray's Inn, 1979; in practice at the Bar, 1980–. *Address:* Maitland Chambers, 7 Stone Buildings, Lincoln's Inn, WC2A 3SZ. *T:* (020) 7406 1200.

PYNE, Kenneth John; cartoonist, since 1970; *b* London, 30 April 1951; *s* of John Ernest Pyne and Dorothy Maud Pyne. *Educ:* Holloway Co. Sch., London. First cartoon published in Punch, 1967; contributed to: The Times, TES, Daily Mirror, Mail on Sunday, Private Eye, Punch, Independent, Evening Standard, Daily Telegraph, The People, Observer, Guardian, Manchester Evening News, Hampstead & Highgate Express, Sunday Times, The Oldie, Reader's Digest, Which, Stern (Germany), Today, Sunday Express, Marketing Week, Spectator, New Statesman, The Listener, Radio Times, Esquire, House Beautiful, Fedn of Small Businesses, MoneyMarketing, FM World, etc. *Exhibitions:* Cartoonist Gall., London, 1991 and 1996; Barbican Centre, 1992; Burgh House, Hampstead, 2001; *work in collections*: V&A Mus.; Cartoon Art Trust Mus.; Salon Internat. du Pressin et d'Humour, Switzerland. Mem., British Cartoonist Assoc., 1979–. Cartoonist of Year, Cartoonist Club of GB, 1981; Strip Cartoonist of Year, 2001, Cartoonist of Year and Caricaturist of the Year, 2006, Cartoon Art Trust. *Publications:* The Relationship, 1981; Martin Minton, 1982; Silly Mid-off, 1985; This Sporting Life, 1986; In the Bleak Mid-winter, 1987; (with Craig Brown) 1966 and All That, 2005; work reproduced in numerous books. *Recreations:* walking, drawing, drinking, reading. *Address:* 15 Well Walk, Hampstead, NW3 1BY. *T:* (020) 7431 3480; *e-mail:* pyne9@hotmail.com.

PYOTT, David Edmund Ian, CBE 2006; Chairman and Chief Executive Officer, Allergan Inc., California, since 1998; *b* London, 13 Oct. 1953; *s* of Robert Macgregor Pyott and Margaret Pyott (*née* Martin); *m* 1990, Julianna Racz; three *s* one *d. Educ:* Glasgow Acad.; Univ. of Edinburgh (MA); Univ. of Amsterdam (Dip. Eur. and Internat. Law); London Business Sch. (MBA). Sandoz AG, Basel: Hd, Strategic Planning, Nutrition Div., 1980–83; Marketing Manager, Nutrition Div., Malaysia, Singapore, 1984–86; Gen. Manager, Nutrition Div., Austria, 1986–89; Gen. Manager, Nutrition Div., Spain, 1990–92; Chief Exec., Nutrition Div., USA, 1993–95; Mem., Exec. Bd, 1995–; Mem., Exec. Bd, Novartis Internat. AG, Basel, 1996–; Director: Avery Dennison Inc., Pasadena, Calif, 1999–; Edward Life Scis Corp., Irvine, Calif, 2000–. Director: California Healthcare Inst., 1998–; Biotechnol. Industry Orgn, 2005–. *Recreations:* ski-ing, mountaineering, cycling, travel, gardening, history. *Address:* Allergan Inc., 2525 Dupont Drive, Irvine, CA 92612, USA. *T:* (714) 2464500, *Fax:* (714) 2465918.

PYPER, Mark Christopher Spring-Rice; Principal (formerly Headmaster), Gordonstoun School, since 1990; *b* 13 Aug. 1947; *s* of late Arthur Spring-Rice Pyper and of Rosemary Isabel Pyper; *m* 1979, Jennifer Lindsay Gilderson; one *s* two *d*. *Educ:* Winchester College; Balliol College, Oxford; London Univ. (BA Mod. Hist. ext.). Asst Master, Stoke Brunswick Sch., East Grinstead, 1966–68; Asst Master, then Joint Headmaster, St Wilfrid's Sch., Seaford, 1969–79; Registrar, Housemaster, then Dep. Headmaster, Sevenoaks Sch., 1979–90. Dir, Sevenoaks Summer Festival, 1979–90. *Address:* Headmaster's House, Gordonstoun School, Elgin, Moray IV30 2RF. *T:* (01343) 837837. *Club:* MCC.

PYTCHES, Rt Rev. (George Edward) David; Vicar of St Andrew's, Chorleywood, Rickmansworth, 1977–96; *b* 9 Jan. 1931; 9th *c* and 6th *s* of late Rev. Thomas Arthur Pytches and late Eirene Mildred Pytches (*née* Welldon); *m* 1958, Mary Trevisick; four *d*. *Educ:* Old Buckenham Hall, Norfolk; Framlingham Coll., Suffolk; Univ. of Bristol (BA); Trinity Coll., Bristol; MPhil Nottingham, 1984. Deacon 1955, priest 1956; Asst Curate, St Ebbe's, Oxford, 1955–58; Asst Curate, Holy Trinity, Wallington, 1958–59; Missionary Priest in Chol Chol, Chile, 1959–62; in Valparaiso, Chile, 1962–68; Rural Dean, Valparaiso, 1966–70; Asst Bishop, 1970–72, Vicar General, 1971–72, Bishop, 1972–77, Dio. of Chile, Bolivia and Peru. Co-ordinator, Fellowship of Ind. Anglican Churches, 1992–; Founding Director, New Wine Family Conf., 1989–2000 (Trustee, 1999–); Founding Sponsor, and Trustee, Soul Survivor Youth Confs, 1993–2004; Co-ordinating Dir, Lakeside Family Conf., 1994–99. Dir, Kingdom Power Trust, 1987–2007. *Publications:* (contrib.) Bishop's Move, 1977; Come Holy Spirit, 1985; (contrib.) Riding the Third Wave, 1987; Does God Speak Today?, 1989; Some Said It Thundered, 1990; (jtly) New Wineskins, 1991; (contrib.) Planting New Churches, 1992; Prophecy in the Local Church, 1993; (contrib.) Recovering the Ground, 1995; (contrib.) Meeting John Wimber, 1996; (ed) John Wimber: his influence and legacy, 1998; Leadership for New Life, 1998; (ed) Burying the Bishop, 1999; (ed) Four Funerals and a Wedding, 1999; (ed) Out of the Mouths of Babes, 1999; Family Matters, 2002; Church Matters, 2002; Living at the Edge, 2002; (contrib.) Setting the Church of England Free, 2003; Can Anyone Be a Leader?, 2004; Upside Down Kingdom, 2007; If You Think My Preaching's Bad, Try My Jokes, 2008. *Recreations:* reading, travelling, enjoying twelve grandchildren. *Address:* Red Tiles, Homefield Road, Chorleywood, Rickmansworth, Herts WD3 5QJ. *T:* (01923) 283763, *Fax:* (01923) 283762; *e-mail:* pytches@btinternet.com.

Q

QADIR, Catherine Anne; *see* Stephens, C. A.

QESKU, Pavli; Ambassador of the Republic of Albania to the Court of St James's, 1993–97; *b* 16 June 1943; *s* of Mihal and Vasilika Qesku; *m* 1973, Lidia Daka; one *s* one *d*. *Educ:* Tirana State Univ. (English Language). Translator at State publishing house, 1968; English teaching, 1975; translator and editor at publishing house, 1978; Ministry of Foreign Affairs, 1993. *Recreations:* reading, writing, music.

QUADEN, Prof. Guy, PhD; Governor, National Bank of Belgium, since 1999 (Director, 1988–99); Member, Governing Council and General Council, European Central Bank, since 1999; *b* 5 Aug. 1945; *m* Brigitte Tilman; two *s*. *Educ:* Univ. of Liège (grad. Econ 1967; PhD Econ 1973); La Sorbonne (grad. Econ and Soc. Scis 1972). University of Liège: First Asst, 1974–76; Lectr, 1977; Prof. in Economic Policy, 1978–88; Special Prof., 1988–. Mem. Bd Dirs, BIS, 1994–; Alternate Governor: IDA, 1994–; IBRD, 1999–; IFC, 1999–; Governor, IMF, 1999–. Member: Conseil supérieur des Finances; Institut des Comptes nationaux. Officier: Ordre de Léopold (Belgium), 1987; Légion d'Honneur (France), 2001. *Publications:* Le budget de l'Etat belge, 1980; La crise de finances publiques, 1984; L'économie belge dans la crise, 1987; Politique économique, 1985, 2nd edn 1991. *Recreations:* football, music, literature. *Address:* National Bank of Belgium, Boulevard de Berlaimont 14, 1000 Brussels, Belgium. *T:* (2) 221 2096, *Fax:* (2) 221 3210.

QUAH, Prof. Danny, PhD; Professor of Economics, since 1996 and Head, Economics Department, since 2006, London School of Economics and Political Science; *b* Penang, Malaysia, 1958; *s* of Chong-eng Quah and Phaik-im Goh; two *s*. *Educ:* Princeton Univ. (AB 1980); Harvard Univ. (PhD Econs 1986). Asst Prof., Econs Dept, MIT, 1986–91; Lectr, then Reader in Econs, LSE, 1991–95. *Publications:* (ed) Oxford Handbook of Information and Communication Technologies, 2007; articles in Amer. Econ. Rev., Econometrica, Jl of Pol Economy, Econ. Jl, European Econ. Rev., Jl of Econ. Growth, Scandinavian Jl of Econs, Jl of Monetary Econs, etc. *Recreations:* Taekwon-do, running, videogaming. *Address:* Economics Department, London School of Economics and Political Science, Houghton Street, WC2A 2AE. *T:* (020) 7955 7535, *Fax:* (020) 7955 6592; *e-mail:* dq@econ.lse.ac.uk.

QUAN, Sir Henry (Francis), KBE 1997; JP; Managing Director, family business, since 1972; *b* 19 Dec. 1936; *s* of Augustine Quan Hong and Mary Woo; *m* 1961, Margaret Wong; three *s* one *d*. *Educ:* Canton, China; Sydney, Australia. Founder, Pres. and Vice-Pres., Solomon Is Chinese Youth Orgn; Founder, Chm. and Vice-Chm., Solomon Is Chinese Assoc. (now Hon. Life Pres.). JP Solomon Is. Independence Medal (Solomon Is), 1978; 10th Anniversary Medal (Solomon Is), 1988, 20th Anniversary Medal, 1998. *Recreation:* sport in general. *Address:* PO Box 209, Honiara, Solomon Islands. *T:* 22351. *Clubs:* Australian Jockey, Sydney Turf, South Sydney Junior Rugby League (Sydney).

QUANT, Mary, (Mrs A. Plunket Greene), OBE 1966; RDI 1969; Director, 1955–2000, Co-Chairman, 1991–2000, Mary Quant Group of companies; *b* 11 Feb. 1934; *d* of Jack and Mildred Quant; *m* 1957, Alexander Plunket Greene (*d* 1990); one *s*. *Educ:* Goldsmiths' College of Art (Hon. Fellow, 1993). Fashion designer. Founded Mary Quant Cosmetics, 1966. Mem., Design Council, 1971–74. Member: British/USA Bicentennial Liaison Cttee, 1973; Adv. Council, V&A Museum, 1976–78. Non-exec. Dir, House of Fraser, 1997–. Exhibition, Mary Quant's London, London Museum, 1973–74. FCSD (FSIA 1967); Sen. FRCA 1991; FRSA 1996. Hon. Dr Wales; hon. degree, Winchester Sch. of Art, 2000. Maison Blanche Rex Award (US), 1964; Sunday Times Internat. Award, 1964; Piavola d'Oro Award (Italy), 1966; Annual Design Medal, Inst. of Industrial Artists and Designers, 1966; Hall of Fame Award, British Fashion Council, 1990. *Publications:* Quant by Quant, 1966; Colour by Quant, 1984; Quant on Make-up, 1986; Classic Make-up and Beauty Book, 1996.

QUANTRILL, Prof. Malcolm, RIBA; architect, author and critic; Distinguished Professor of Architecture, Texas A&M University, 1986–2007, now Distinguished Professor Emeritus; Co-Founder, 1990, and Director, since 1996, Center for the Advancement of Studies in Architecture; *b* Norwich, Norfolk, 25 May 1931; *s* of Arthur William Quantrill and Alice May Newstead; *m* 1971, Esther Maeve, *d* of James Brignell Dand and Winifred Dand, Chester; two *s* two *d*. *Educ:* City of Norwich Sch.; Liverpool Univ. (BArch); Univ. of Pennsylvania (MArch); Univ. of Wroclaw (Doc. Ing Arch, now redesignated DScEng). RIBA 1961. Fulbright Scholar and Albert Kahn Meml Fellow, Univ. of Pennsylvania, 1954–55; Asst Prof., Louisiana State Univ., 1955–60; Lecturer: Univ. of Wales, Cardiff, 1962–65; UCL, 1965–66; Asst to Dir, Architectural Assoc., 1966–67, Dir, 1967–69; Lectr, Univ. of Liverpool, 1970–73; Dean, Sch. of Environmental Design, Polytechnic of N London, 1973–80; Prof. of Architecture and Urban Design, Univ. of Jordan, Amman-Jordan, 1980–83. Vis. Professor: Univ. of Illinois, Chicago, 1973–75; Carleton Univ., Ottawa, 1978; Gastprofessor, Technische Universität, Wien, 1975–77; Fellow, Graham Foundn for Advanced Studies in the Fine Arts, Chicago, 1984; Distinguished Prof., Assoc. of Coll. Schs of Architecture, 1990. Lectures: Sir William Dobell Meml in Modern Art, Sydney, NSW, 1978; Thomas Cubitt, London, 1993; Kivett Meml, Kansas City, 1994. Haecker Award, Assoc. of Architectl Res. Councils Consortium of N. America, 2002–03. Knight Commander, Order of Finnish Lion (Finland), 1988. *Plays performed:* Honeymoon, 1968; Life Class, 1968 (TV); Dust, 1990; radio plays include: The Fence, 1964; Let's Get This Straight, 1977; Immortal Bite, 1982. *Publications:* The Gotobed Trilogy (novels), 1962–64; Ritual and Response in Architecture, 1974; Monuments of Another Age, 1975; On the Home Front (novel), 1977; The Art of Government and the Government of Art, 1978; Alvar Aalto—a critical study, 1983; Reima Pietilä—architecture, context and modernism, 1985; The Environmental Memory, 1987; Reima Pietilä: one man's odyssey in search of Finnish architecture, 1988; (ed) Constancy and Change in Architecture, 1991; (ed) Urban Forms, Suburban Dreams, 1993; Finnish Architecture and the Modernist Tradition, 1995; The Culture of Silence, 1998; The Norman Foster Studio, 1999; (ed) Latin American Architecture: six voices, 2000; Julia Leiviska and the Continuity of Finnish Modern Architecture, 2001; (with Alfonso Corona-Martinez) The Architectural Project, 2003; The Unmade Bed of Architecture, 2004; Plain Modern: the architecture of Brian MacKay Lyons, 2005; (ed) Space and Place in the Mexican Landscape, 2007; articles in RIBA Jl, Arch. Assoc. Qly, Arch. Design, Jl of Arch. Educn, and Art Internat. *Club:* Garrick.

QUANTRILL, William Ernest; HM Diplomatic Service, retired; Ambassador to the Republic of Cameroon, and concurrently to the Central African Republic, Equatorial Guinea and the Republic of Chad, 1991–95; *b* 4 May 1939; *s* of late Ronald Frederick Quantrill and Norah Elsie Quantrill (*née* Matthews); *m* 1964, Rowena Mary Collins; three *s* one *d*. *Educ:* Colston's Sch., Bristol; Hatfield Coll., Univ. of Durham (BA Hons French). Entered FO, 1962; served Brussels, Havana, Manila, Lagos, 1964–80; Head of Training Dept, FCO, 1980–81; Dep. Head of Personnel Ops Dept, FCO, 1981–84; Counsellor and Hd of Chancery, Caracas, 1984–88; Dep. Gov., Gibraltar, 1988–90. *Recreations:* wild life, travel. *Address:* Tor House, 36 Newtown, Bradford-on-Avon, Wilts BA15 1NF. *T:* (01225) 866245.

QUARMBY, David Anthony, CBE 2003; MA, PhD; FCILT; consultant in transport, planning, tourism and economics, since 2006; Chairman, Strategic Rail Authority, 2004–06 (Deputy Chairman, 2002–04); *b* 22 July 1941; *s* of Frank Reginald and Dorothy Margaret Quarmby; *m* 1968, Hilmary Hunter; four *d*. *Educ:* Shrewsbury Sch.; King's Coll., Cambridge (MA); Leeds Univ. (PhD, Dip. Industrial Management). Asst Lectr, then Lectr, Dept of Management Studies, Leeds Univ., 1963; Economic Adviser, Economic Planning Directorate, Min. of Transport, 1966; London Transport Executive: Dir of Operational Research, 1970; Chief Commercial and Planning Officer, 1974; Mem., 1975–84; Man. Dir (Buses), 1978–84; Mem., London Regional Transport, 1984; Director: Homebase Ltd, 1987–89; Shaw's Supermarkets Inc., 1987–92; Jt Man. Dir, J. Sainsbury plc, 1988–96 (Dir, 1984–96). Chairman: English Tourist Bd, 1996–99; S London Business Leadership Ltd, 1996–99; BTA, 1996–2003; Docklands Light Railway Ltd, 1999–2001; SeaBritain 2005 Steering Gp, Nat. Maritime Mus., 2003–05; Dep. Chm., S London Econ. Develt Alliance, 1999–2003; Director: New Millennium Experience Co. Ltd, 1997–2001 (Chm., May–Sept. 2000; Dep. Chm., 2000–01); London First, 1998–2002; BRB (Shadow Strategic Rail Authy), 1999–2001; Ned Railways Ltd, 2007–; Colin Buchanan & Partners Ltd, 2007–; Member: Panel 2000, 1999–2002; London Sustainable Develt Commn, 2002–03; Ind. Transport Commn, 2007– (Chm., 2007–). Chm., Retail Action Gp for Crime Prevention, Home Office, 1995–96; Mem., Crime Prevention Agency Bd, Home Office, 1995–97; non-exec. Dir, Dept of Transport Central Mgt Bd, 1996–97, DETR Bd, 1997–98; Mem. Bd, Transport for London, 2000–04 (Ministerial Advr, 1999–2000). Mem. Bd, Elderhostel Inc., 2006–. Vice-President: Bus and Coach Council, 1981–84; CIT, 1987–91; Mem., Nat. Council, Freight Transport Assoc., 1985–88. Chm., Transport Res. Inst., Napier Univ., 2006–. Member: London Educn Business Partnership, 1988–92; Sch. Curriculum and Assessment Authy, 1993–95; Southwark Diocesan Synod, 1982–85; London Adv. Bd, Salvation Army, 1982–87; Mem., Friends' Council, 2004–07, Trustee, 2005–, Nat. Maritime Mus.; Trustee, St Paul's Cathedral Foundn, 2005–07. Dir, and Chm. Develt Cttee, Blackheath Concert Halls, 1990–94. Gov., 1987–98 (Chm., 1995–98), Chm., Finance Cttee, 1991–95, James Allen's Girls' Sch., London; Mem. Ct, Greenwich Univ., 2000–08. Pres., Inst. of Logistics, 1996–99. CompOR; CCMI; FTS 1997; FRSA 2006. Hon. DSc Huddersfield, 1999; Hon. DEng Napier. *Publications:* Factors Affecting Commuter Travel Behaviour (PhD Thesis, Leeds), 1967; contribs to Jl of Transport Economics and Policy, Regional Studies, Enterprise Management, and to books on transport, distribution, tourism, economics and operational research. *Recreations:* music, singing, walking, family life. *Address:* 13 Shooters Hill Road, Blackheath, SE3 7AR.

QUARME, Giles Thomas, RIBA; Principal, Giles Quarme & Associates, since 1989; *b* Chelsea, London, 19 June 1951; *s* of Philip Anthony Thomas and Wendy Kathlene Quarme; *m* 1987, Margaret Henrietta Augusta Casely-Hayford; one *d*. *Educ:* Marlborough Coll.; Univ. of East Anglia (BA Hons Art Hist. 1973); Univ. of Westminster (BA Hons Architecture 1976; DipArch 1979); Architectural Association (DipCons 1984). RIBA 1980. Sole practitioner in association with John Dickinson, RIBA, 1979–82; Co-Founder, Dickinson, Quarme & Associates, 1982–89. Surveyor of the Fabric, RNC, Greenwich, 1996–; Historic Bldg Advr to Foster & Partners on British Mus. Millennium proj., 1997. Projects include: restoration of Royal Victoria Patriotic Bldg Complex, Wandsworth, 1988 (Europa Nostra Award, 1988); restoration of High Comr of India's residence, London, 1995; restoration of 14 & 18 St Leonards Terrace, London, 1995; restoration of 49 Thames Street, Sunbury-on-Thames, 1996 (Spelthorne Design Award, 1996); Princess Diana Mus., Althorp Park, 1997; Queen Anne Court, RNC, Greenwich, 2000. Chm. Trustees, Ancient Monuments Soc., 2000– (Mem. Council, 1993–); Member: Adv. Cttee, 1991–92, Cttee, 1992, Save Britain's Heritage; British Acad. of Experts, 1993–; Exec. Council, ICOMOS UK, 1993–99; London Adv. Cttee, English Heritage, 1999–; Exec. Council, Georgian Gp, 1999–. FRSA 1986; Fellow, Royal Asiatic Soc., 1996. Freeman, Co. of Chartered Architects, 1994–. *Publications:* articles in ASCHB Transactions. *Recreations:* trying to understand historic events, analysing old buildings, walking on Exmoor. *Address:* 36 Smith Street, Chelsea, SW3 4EP. *T:* (020) 7582 0748; *e-mail:* mail@quarme.com. Giles Quarme & Associates, 7 Bishops Terrace, SE11 4UE.

QUARREN EVANS, His Honour (John) Kerry; a Circuit Judge, on South Eastern circuit, 1980–95; *b* 4 July 1926; *s* of Hubert Royston Quarren Evans, MC and Violet Soule Quarren Evans (*née* George); *m* 1958, Janet Shaw Lawson; one *s* one *d*. *Educ:* King Henry VIII Sch., Coventry; Cardiff High Sch.; Trinity Hall, Cambridge, 1948–51 (MA, LLM).

21st Glam. (Cardiff) Bn Home Guard, 1943–44; enlisted, Grenadier Gds, 1944; commnd Royal Welch Fusiliers, 1946, from OTS Bangalore; att. 2nd Bn The Welch Regt, Burma, 1946–47; Captain 1947. Admitted solicitor, 1953; Partner: Lyndon Moore & Co., Newport, 1954–71; T. S. Edwards & Son, Newport, 1971–80; Recorder, Wales and Chester Circuit, 1974–80. Clerk to Gen. Comrs of Income Tax, Dinas Powis Div., 1960–80; Chm., Newport Nat. Insurance Local Tribunal, 1968–71. *Recreations:* golf, Rugby football, oenology, staurologosophy, old things. *Address:* Coddleston, 8 Russett Hill, Gerrards Cross, Bucks SL9 8JY. *T:* (01753) 880819. *Clubs:* Arkaves (Cardiff); Woodpeckers, Denham Golf, Royal Porthcawl Golf, Crawshay's Welsh Rugby Football.

QUARTA, Roberto; Partner, Clayton, Dubilier & Rice, since 2001; non-executive Director, BAE Systems plc, since 2005; *b* 10 May 1949; *m*; one *s* one *d*. *Educ:* Italy and USA; Coll. of the Holy Cross, Mass, USA (BA 1971). Management Trainee, David Gessner, 1971–73; Worcester Controls Corp., 1973–78: Manager, Purchasing and Production Control; Vice-Pres., Internat. Procurement; BTR plc, 1979–85: Manufacturing Dir, Worcester Controls Corp.; Man. Dir, Worcester Controls UK; Group Man. Dir, Valves Group; Chief Exec., Hitchiner Manufacturing Corp., 1985–89; a Chief Divl Exec., BTR, 1989–93 (Dir, Main Bd, 1993); BBA Group plc: Dir, 1993–2007; Chief Exec., 1993–2000; Chm., 2000–07. Non-executive Director: PowerGen, 1996–2001; Equant NV, 2000–05; Azure Dynamics Corp., 2004–07. Trustee, Coll. of the Holy Cross. *Recreations:* aviation, music. *Address:* Clayton, Dubilier & Rice, Cleveland House, 33 King Street, SW1Y 6RJ.

QUARTANO, Ralph Nicholas, CBE 1987; Chairman, PosTel Investment Management Ltd, 1987–91 (Chief Executive, 1983–87); *b* 3 Aug. 1927; *s* of late Charles and Vivienne Mary Quartano; *m* 1st, 1954, Cornelia Johanna de Gunst (*d* 1996); two *d*; 2nd, 2006, Kathryn Margaret Brown. *Educ:* Sherborne Sch.; Pembroke Coll., Cambridge (MA). Bataafsche Petroleum Mij, 1952–58; The Lummus Co., 1958–59; Temple Press, 1959–65; Man. Director: Heywood Temple Industrial Publications, 1965–68; Engineering Chemical and Marine Press, 1968–70. The Post Office, 1971–74; Sen. Dir, Central Finance, 1973–74; Chief Exec., Post Office Staff Superannuation Fund, 1974–83. Dir, 1985–93, Dep. Chm., 1987–93, SIB. Director: London American Energy NV, 1981–88; Britoil plc, 1982–88; 3i Group plc (formerly Investors in Industry), 1986–97; John Lewis Partnership Pensions Trust, 1986–89; Clerical Medical Investment Group, 1987–98; Booker plc, 1988–98; British Maritime Technology Ltd, 1988–97 (Chm., 1995–97); Heitman Financial LLC, 1991–2000; Laird Group, 1991–98; Enterprise Oil, 1991–97; Lyonnaise Pension Trustees Ltd, 1994–2005; Chm., Murray Emerging Economies Trust plc, 1994–98. Member: Engrg Council, 1981–83; City Capital Markets Cttee, 1985–93; Investment Cttee, Pensioen Fonds PGGM, Netherlands, 1986–98; Investment Cttee, KPN (formerly PTT) Pensioen, Netherlands, 1988–98; Financial Reporting Council, 1990–93. City Advr to Dir-Gen., CBI, 1985–93. Sloan Fellow of London Business School. Gov., BUPA, 1987–98. Mem. Council, 1993–99, and Treas., 1994–99, RSA. Trustee, Monteverdi Trust, 1986–93. *Address:* 20 Oakcroft Road, SE13 7ED. *T:* (020) 8852 1607. *Club:* Athenæum.

QUAYLE, James Danforth, (Dan), JD; Chairman, Cerberus Global Investments, LLC, New York, since 2000; Vice-President of the United States of America, 1989–93; *b* 4 Feb. 1947; *m* 1972, Marilyn Tucker; two *s* one *d*. *Educ:* DePauw Univ. (BS 1969); Indiana Univ. (JD 1974). Admitted to Indiana Bar, 1974. Journalist, 1965–69, Associate Publisher and Gen. Manager, 1974–76, Huntington Herald Press; Investigator, Consumer Protection Div., Office of the Attorney General, Indiana, 1970–71; Admin. Assistant to Gov. of Indiana, 1971–73; Dir, Inheritance Tax Div., Indiana, 1973–74; Professor of Business Law, Huntington Coll., 1975. Mem. of Congress, 1976–80; Mem. for Indiana, US Senate, 1981–88. Chm., Circle Investors, Inc., 1993–. Vis. Prof., Thunderbird Internat. Business Sch., 1997–99. *Publications:* Standing Firm, 1994; The American Family, 1996; Worth Fighting For, 1999. *Address:* 7001 North Scottsdale Road, Suite 2010, Scottsdale, AZ 85253, USA.

QUAYLE, Quinton Mark; HM Diplomatic Service; Ambassador to Thailand, since 2007; *b* 5 June 1955; *s* of Eric Stanley Quayle and late Elizabeth Jean (*née* Thorne); *m* 1979, Alison Marshall; two *s*. *Educ:* Humphry Davy GS; Bristol Univ. (BA). Entered HM Diplomatic Service, 1977; Third, later Second Sec., Bangkok, 1979–82; FCO, 1983–86; Ecole Nat. d'Admin, Paris, 1986–87; First Sec., Paris, 1987–91; FCO, 1991–93; on secondment to Price Waterhouse Management Consultants, 1993–94; Dir, Jt Export Promotion Directorate, FCO, 1994–96; Counsellor, Consul-Gen. and Dep. Hd of Mission, Jakarta, 1996–99; Internat. Gp Dir, Trade Partners UK, British Trade Internat., 1999–2002; Ambassador to Romania, 2002–06. *Recreation:* book collecting. *Address:* c/o Foreign and Commonwealth Office, King Charles Street, SW1A 2AH.

QUAYLE, Maj.-Gen. Thomas David Graham, CB 1990; Vice Chairman, Salisbury NHS Foundation Trust, 2006–08; *b* 7 April 1936; *s* of Thomas Quayle and Phyllis Gwendolen Johnson; *m* 1962, Susan Jean Bradford; three *d*. *Educ:* Repton; Trinity College, Oxford. Commissioned RA 1958; Student, Indian Staff Coll., 1968; Comdr, The Chestnut Troop, 1971–72; Instructor, Staff Coll., Camberley, 1974–76; Comdr, 40 Field Regt (The Lowland Gunners), 1976–79; Comdr Artillery, 4th Armoured Div., 1981–83; Defence Attaché, Bonn, 1983–86; Comdr Artillery, 1st British Corps, 1987–90, retd. Ombudsman for Estate Agents (formerly for Corporate Estate Agents), 1990–99. Non-exec. Dir, Salisbury Health Care NHS Trust, 1999–2006. Mem., Mortgage Code Compliance Bd, 1999–2004. *Recreations:* fishing, bridge. *Address:* Oriole House, Figheldean, Salisbury, Wilts SP4 8JJ; *e-mail:* tdg.quayle@tiscali.co.uk.

QUEBEC, Archbishop of, since 2004; **Most Rev. Alexander Bruce Stavert;** Metropolitan of the Ecclesiastical Province of Canada, since 2004; *b* 1 April 1940; *s* of Ewart and Kathleen Stavert; *m* 1982, Diana Greig; one *s* two *d*. *Educ:* Lower Canada Coll., Montreal; Bishop's Univ., Lennoxville, PQ (BA 1961): Trinity Coll., Univ. of Toronto (STB 1964; MTh, 1976). Incumbent of Schefferville, Quebec, 1964–69; Fellow, 1969–70, Chaplain, 1970–76, Trinity Coll., Univ. of Toronto; Incumbent, St Clement's Mission East, St Paul's River, PQ, 1976–81; Chaplain, Bishop's Univ., Lennoxville, 1981–84; Dean and Rector, St Alban's Cathedral, Prince Albert, Sask., 1984–91; Bishop of Quebec, 1991–. Hon. DD Toronto, 1986. *Recreations:* swimming, ski-ing. *Address:* 31 rue des Jardins, Québec, QC G1R 4L6, Canada. *T:* (418) 6923858. *Club:* Garrison (Québec).

QUEBEC, Archbishop of, (RC), and Primate of Canada, since 2003; **His Eminence Cardinal Marc Ouellet,** PSS; *b* 8 June 1944. *Educ:* Amos Teacher Training Coll., Quebec; Grand Séminaire de Montréal (LTh Univ. of Montreal 1968); St Thomas Aquinas Pontifical Univ., Rome (LPh 1976); Gregorian Univ., Rome (Dr Dogmatic Theol. 1983). Ordained priest, 1968; Curate, St Sauveur, Val d'Or, 1968–70; teacher of philosophy, Major Seminary, Bogota; Faculty Member and Professor: Major Seminary, Manizales, Columbia, 1974; Grand Séminaire de Montréal; Major Seminary, Cali, Columbia, 1983 (Rector, 1984–89); Rector: Grand Séminaire de Montréal, 1990; St Joseph's Seminary, Edmonton, 1994; Titular Chair of Dogmatic Theol., John Paul II Inst., Lateran Pontifical Univ., 1996–2002; Sec., Pontifical Council for the Promotion of Christian Unity, 2001; Titular Bp, Agropoli, 2001; Cardinal, 2003. *Address:* (office) 1073 Boulevard René Levesque Ouest, Quebec, QC G1S 4R5, Canada.

QUEENSBERRY, 12th Marquess of, *cr* 1682; **David Harrington Angus Douglas;** Viscount Drumlanrig and Baron Douglas, 1628; Earl of Queensberry, 1633; Bt (Nova Scotia), 1668; late Royal Horse Guards; Professor of Ceramics, Royal College of Art, 1959–83; Partner, Queensberry Hunt design group; *b* 19 Dec. 1929; *s* of 11th Marquess of Queensberry and late Cathleen Mann; *S* father, 1954; *m* 1st, 1956, Mrs Ann Radford; two *d*; 2nd, 1969, Alexandra (marr. diss. 1986), *d* of Guy Wyndham Sich; three *s* one *d*; 3rd, 2000, Hsueh-Chun Liao; one *d*. *Educ:* Eton. Dir, Highland Stoneware. Mem. Council, Crafts Council; Pres., Design and Industries Assoc., 1976–78. Trustee: Laura Ashley Foundn; Paolozzi Foundn. Sen. FRCA, 1990. Hon. DDes Staffordshire, 1993. *Heir:* *s* Viscount Drumlanrig, *qv*.

QUEENSLAND, Metropolitan of; *see* Brisbane, Archbishop of.

QUEENSLAND, NORTH, Bishop of, since 2007; **Rt Rev. William James Ray;** *b* Yarram, Vic, 19 Oct. 1950; *s* of Vernon Henry Ray and Violet June Colbert; *m* 1978, Robin Adele, *d* of Rees William Llewellyn and Beryl Allison Koeteveld; one *s* one *d*. *Educ:* Yarram High Sch.; Frankston Teachers' Coll. (Teaching Dip.); Western Australian Coll. of Educn (BEd); Australian Coll. of Theology (ThL); Duke Univ., USA (MRE). Teacher, Stradbroke Primary Sch., 1973–75; Headteacher, Seaspray Primary Sch., 1976–77; Youth Officer, Dio. of Brisbane, 1978–81; Youth and Children's Officer, St Luke's, Toowoomba, 1981–83, 1986–87; Educn Officer, Dio. of Gippsland, 1987–91; Ministry Trng Officer, Dio. of Rockhampton, 1991–96; ordained deacon, 1992; Rector, St Luke's, Wandal, 1996–99; Dir Gen., Bd of Religious Educn, 2000–01 (Mem., 1974–97); Vicar: St George's, E Ivanhoe, 2001–03; St John the Divine, Croydon, 2003–07; Archdeacon of Maroondah, Melbourne, 2004–07. Chair, Diocesan Catechumenate Working Gp, 2002–; Mem., Archbishop in CI Exec., 2004–. CI Crescent Lagoon Sch., 1980–; Mem., Australian Coll. of Educn; Founding Mem., Academic Bd, Inst. of Theol. Educn, 1993–97; Trainer, Australian Educn for Ministry, 2005–07. Chaplain, Scouting Assoc., 1977–99. *Recreations:* walking, bushwalking, reading biographies and newspapers, cycling, movies, cooking. *Address:* PO Box 1244, Townsville, Qld 4810, Australia.

QUELCH, Prof. John Anthony, DBA; Senior Associate Dean and Lincoln Filene Professor of Business Administration, Harvard Business School, since 2001; *b* 8 Aug. 1951; *s* of late Norman Quelch and Laura Sally (*née* Jones); *m* 1978, Joyce Ann Huntley. *Educ:* Norwich Sch.; Exeter Coll., Oxford (BA 1972; Hon. Fellow, 2002); Wharton Sch., Univ. of Pennsylvania (MBA 1974); Harvard Univ. (DBA 1977; MS 1978). Asst Prof. of Business Admin, Univ. of Western Ontario, 1977–79; Harvard Business School: Asst Prof. of Business Admin, 1979–84, Associate Prof., 1984–88, Prof., 1988–93; Sebastian S. Kresge Prof. of Marketing, 1993–98; Dean and Prof. of Mktg, London Business Sch., 1998–2001. Chm., Massachusetts Port Authy, 2002–. Non-executive Director: Reebok Internat. Ltd, 1985–97; European Communication Mgt Ltd, 1988–97; WPP Gp plc, 1988–; US Office Products Co., 1995–97; Pentland Gp plc, 1997–99; Blue Circle Industries plc, 2000–01; easyJet plc, 2000–03; Inverness Medical Innovations Inc., 2003–; Loyalty Management UK Ltd, 2003–06; Pepsi Bottling Gp, 2005–; Gentiva Health Services, 2006–; Epiphany Biosciences, 2007–. Mem. Adv. Bd, PricewaterhouseCoopers Corporate Finance, 2002–03. Director: Council of Better Business Bureaux, 1995–97; Graduate Mgt Admissions Council, 1999–2001; Accion Internat., 2003–06. Mem., Internat. Adv. Bd, British Amer. Business Council (formerly British Amer. Business Inc.), 2001–; Mem., Adv. Bd, AT Kearney Internat. Policy Council, 2002–06; Dir, Americans For Oxford, 2006–. Hon. Consul Gen. of Morocco in New England, 2004–. CCMI (CIMgt 1998). FRSA 1998. *Publications:* (jtly) Advertising and Promotion Management, 1983; (jtly) Cases in Advertising and Promotion Management, 1983, 4th edn 1996; (jtly) Marketing Management, 1985, 2nd edn 1993; (jtly) Global Marketing Management, 1988, 5th edn 2005; How to Market to Consumers, 1989; Sales Promotion Management, 1989; (jtly) The Marketing Challenge of Europe 1992, 1990, 2nd edn 1991; (jtly) Ethics in Marketing, 1992; (jtly) Cases in Product Management, 1995; (jtly) Cases in Marketing Management and Strategy, 1996; (jtly) Cases in European Marketing Management, 1997; (jtly) Cases in Strategic Marketing Management: business strategies in Latin America, 2001; Business Strategies in Muslim Countries, 2001; (jtly) Marketing Management, 2004; (jtly) Problems and Cases in Health Care Marketing, 2004; (jtly) The Global Market, 2005; (jtly) The New Global Brands, 2006; (jtly) Business Solutions for the Global Poor, 2007; Readings in Modern Marketing, 2007; (jtly) Greater Good: how good marketing makes for better democracy, 2008; contribs to learned and professional jls. *Recreations:* squash, tennis. *Address:* Harvard Business School, Morgan Hall 185, Soldiers Field, Boston, MA 02163, USA. *T:* (617) 4956325, *Fax:* (617) 4965637; *e-mail:* jquelch@hbs.edu. *Clubs:* Brooks's, Harvard (Boston).

QUENTIN, Caroline; actress; *b* 11 July 1960; *d* of Frederick and Katie Emily Jones; adopted stage name of Quentin; *m* 1991, Paul James Martin, *qv* (marr. diss. 1999); *m* 2006, Sam Farmer; one *s* one *d*. *Educ:* Arts Educnl, Tring Park. *Theatre includes:* The Seagull, tour; Roots, RNT; Our Country's Good, Garrick; Low Level Panic, Sugar and Spice, Royal Court; Les Miserables, Barbican, transf. Palace; An Evening with Gary Lineker; A Game of Love and Chance, RNT; Les Enfants du Paradis, tour; Lysistrata; Mirandolina, Lyric, Hammersmith; The Live Bed Show, Garrick, 1994; The London Cuckolds, RNT, 1998; Life After Scandal, Hampstead, 2007; dir, Dead Funny, Palace, Watford, 1998. *Television includes:* series: Don't Tell Father, 1992; Men Behaving Badly, 1992–97; Jonathan Creek, 1997–2002; Kiss Me Kate, 1998–2002; The Innocent, 2001; Blue Murder, 2003–05; Life Begins, 2004–06; Von Trapped, 2004; *film:* An Evening with Gary Lineker, 1994. *Recreation:* bird-watching. *Address:* c/o Amanda Howard Associates, 21 Berwick Street, W1F 0PZ.

QUICK, Dorothy, (Mrs Charles Denis Scanlan); a District Judge (Magistrates' Courts) (formerly Metropolitan Stipendiary Magistrate), since 1986; *b* 10 Dec. 1944; *d* of Frederick and Doris Quick; *m* 1971, Charles Denis Scanlan; two *s*. *Educ:* Glanafan Grammar Sch., Port Talbot; University Coll. London (LLB). Called to the Bar, Inner Temple, 1969; barrister-at-law, 1969–86. Mem., British Acad. of Forensic Sciences, 1987–. *Recreations:* gardening, theatre, books. *Address:* c/o Highbury Corner Magistrates' Court, 51 Holloway Road, N7 8JA. *Club:* Reform.

QUICK, Robert Frederick, QPM 2003; Assistant Commissioner, Specialist Operations, Metropolitan Police Service, since 2008; *b* London, 25 April 1959; *s* of Robert Edward Quick and Patricia Quick; *m* 2001, Judith Jane Clark; one *s* four *d*. *Educ:* Exeter Univ. (MBA with Dist.); Civil Service Coll. Top Managers Prog.; Police Staff Coll., Bramshill (Police Strategic Comd Course 2001); Univ. of Cambridge (Dip. Applied Criminol. 2001). Metropolitan Police Service: Constable, Lambeth, 1978–82; Detective Constable, Brixton, Lambeth, 1982–84; Sergeant, 1984–87, Detective Sergeant, 1987–90, Catford, Lewisham; Detective Inspector, Lambeth, 1990–92, Greenwich, 1994–95; Detective Chief Inspector, SE London Crime Squad, 1995–96, Croydon, 1996–97; SO to Asst Comr, 1997–98; Superintendent, Southwark, 1998–99; Detective Chief Superintendent, Anti-Corruption Comd, New Scotland Yard, 1999–2001; Comdr, New Scotland Yard,

2001–03; Dep. Chief Constable, 2003–04, Chief Constable, 2004–08, Surrey Police. MInstD 2001. *Recreations:* ski-ing, walking, motorcycling, collector of classic motorcycles and motorcars. *Address:* Specialist Operations, New Scotland Yard, 10 Broadway, SW1H 0BG. *T:* (020) 7230 3515; *e-mail:* robert.quick@met.police.uk.

QUICKE, Sir John (Godolphin), Kt 1988; CBE 1978; DL; *b* 20 April 1922; *s* of Captain Noel Arthur Godolphin Quicke and Constance May Quicke; *m* 1953, Prudence Tinné Berthon, *d* of Rear-Adm. (E) C. P. E. Berthon; three *s* three *d*. *Educ:* Eton; New Coll., Oxford. Vice-Chm., North Devon Meat, 1982–86; Mem., SW Reg. Bd, National Westminster Bank, 1974–92. Chairman: Minister of Agriculture's SW Regional Panel, 1972–75; Agricl EDC, NEDO, 1983–88, Agricl Sector Gp, 1988–90; RURAL, 1983–96; Estates Panel, NT, 1984–92; Member: Consultative Bd for R&D in Food and Agric., 1981–84; Severn Barrage Cttee, 1978–80; Countryside Commn, 1981–88 (Chm., Countryside Policy Review Panel, 1986–87); Properties Cttee, NT, 1984–97. President: CLA, 1975–77; Royal Bath & West of England Soc., 1989–90. Mem. Bd of Governors, Univ. of Plymouth (formerly Polytechnic SW), 1989–93. DL Devon, 1985. Hon. FRASE, 1989. Hon. DSc: Exeter, 1989; Polytechnic South West, 1991. Bledisloe Gold Medal for Landowners, RASE, 1985. *Recreations:* reading, music, gardening. *Address:* Sherwood, Newton St Cyres, near Exeter, Devon EX5 5BT. *T:* (01392) 851216.

QUICKE, Rev. Michael John; C. W. Koller Professor of Preaching and Communication, Northern Baptist Theological Seminary, Chicago, since 2000; *b* 30 July 1945; *s* of George and Joan Quicke; *m* 1968, Carol Bentall; two *s*. *Educ:* Jesus Coll., Cambridge (MA); Regent's Park Coll., Oxford (MA). Nat. Sec. for Student Work, Baptist Union, 1967–69; Minister: Leamington Road Baptist Church, Blackburn, 1972–80; St Andrew's Street Baptist Church, Cambridge, 1980–93; Principal, Spurgeon's Coll., 1993–2000. Interim Preacher, First Baptist Ch, Wheaton, Ill., 2000–02. Religious Advr, ITV, 1987–88. Mem. Council, Baptist Union of GB, 1976–2000; Vice Chm., Doctrine Commn, 1990–95, Mem., Worship Commn, 1995–2005, Mem., Church Leadership Commn, 2006–, Baptist World Alliance. Member: Council of Mgt, Open Theol Coll., 1993–2000; Council, Evangelical Alliance, 1997–2000. Mem., Acad. of Homiletics, 1995–. Fellow, Coll. of Preachers, 1996 (Mem., Exec., 1996–2000). Hon. DD William Jewell Coll., Liberty, USA, 1994. *Publications:* Christian Apologetics, 1976; Something to Declare, 1996; On the Way of Trust, 1997; Doing Theology in a Baptist Way, 2000; 360 Degree Preaching, 2003; 360 Degree Leadership, 2006. *Recreations:* listening to sermons, music, travel. *Address:* Northern Baptist Theological Seminary, 660 East Butterfield Road, Lombard, IL 60148, USA.

QUIGLEY, Anthony Leslie Coupland, CEng, FIET; Tony Quigley Consulting, since 2001; *b* 14 July 1946; *s* of late Leslie Quigley and of Vera Barbara Rodaway (*née* Martin); *m* 1968, Monica Dean; one *s* two *d*. *Educ:* Apsley Grammar Sch.; Queen Mary Coll., Univ. of London (BSc Eng). Command Control and Computer Divs, ASWE, 1967–81 (Exchange Scientist, US Naval Surface Weapons Center, 1976–79); Supt, Command and Control Div., 1981–84, Hd, Command, Control and Assessment Gp, 1984–87, RARDE; Dep. Head, Science and Technology Assessment Office, Cabinet Office, 1987–90; Dir, SDI Participation Office, 1990–93, Asst Chief Scientific Advr (Nuclear), 1993–95, MoD; Under Sec., OST, 1995–99 (on secondment); Dir Gen., Scrutiny and Analysis, MoD, 1999–2001. Member, Council: Foundn for Sci. and Technol., 2001–; Kent Univ., 2003–. MInstD. *Publications:* technical papers on radar tracking and command and control. *Recreation:* golf. *Address:* 21 Yew Tree Road, Tunbridge Wells, Kent TN4 0BD. *Club:* Chartham Park Golf.

QUIGLEY, Conor; QC 2003; *b* 21 Feb. 1958; *s* of Edmond Gerard Quigley and Kathleen Theresa Quigley (*née* Murphy). *Educ:* King's Coll. London (LLB); MA Oxon. Called to the Bar, Gray's Inn, 1985; in practice as barrister specialising in EU law, 1985–. Fellow, LMH, Oxford Univ., 1991–96. Chm., Bar European Gp, 1992–94. *Publications:* European Community Contract Law, 1997; EC State Aid Law and Policy, 2002. *Recreations:* history, wine, Europe. *Address:* Brick Court Chambers, 7–8 Essex Street, WC2R 3LD. *T:* (020) 7379 3550, *Fax:* (020) 7379 3558; *e-mail:* conor.quigley@brickcourt.co.uk.

QUIGLEY, Sir George; *see* Quigley, Sir W. G. H.

QUIGLEY, Sir (William) George (Henry), Kt 1993; CB 1982; PhD; Chairman: Short Brothers, since 1999 (Director, since 1989); Ulster Bank Ltd, 1989–2001 (Deputy Chairman, 1988–89); *b* 26 Nov. 1929; *s* of William George Cunningham Quigley and Sarah Hanson Martin; *m* 1971, Moyra Alice Munn, LLB. *Educ:* Ballymena Academy; Queen's Univ., Belfast (BA (1st Cl. Hons), 1951; PhD, 1955). Apptd Asst Principal, Northern Ireland Civil Service, 1955; Permanent Secretary: Dept of Manpower Services, NI, 1974–76; Dept of Commerce, NI, 1976–79; Dept of Finance, NI, 1979–82; Dept of Finance and Personnel, NI, 1982–88. Director: Irish-American Partnership, 1989–; Nat. Westminster Bank, 1990–99; Independent News and Media (UK), 2001–; Chm., Natwest Pension Trustees Ltd, 1998–2002. Chairman: Co-operation North, 1994–96; NI Economic Council, 1994–98. Chm., Royal Group of Hospitals Trust, NI, 1992–95. Chm., NI Div., Inst. of Dirs, 1990–94; Member: Fair Employment Commn for NI, 1989–93; Council, NI Chamber of Commerce and Industry, 1989–92; Council, NI Div., CBI, 1990–95; Chm., Review of Parades Commn of NI, 2001–02. Chm., Scottish Fee Support Review, 1998–2000; Member: Nat. Cttee of Inquiry into Higher Educn, 1996–97; Qualifications and Curriculum Authority, 1997–99. Chm., Lothbury Property Trust, 2001–. President: Econ. and Social Res. Inst., 1999–2002; Inst. of Internat. Trade of Ireland, 1999–2001. Chm. Bd, Inst. of British-Irish Studies, UCD, 2006–. Professorial Fellow, QUB, 1989–93. Fellow, Inst. of Bankers in Ireland, 1989. MRIA 2007. CCMI. Hon. Fellow, IMgtI. Hon. LLD QUB, 1996; DUniv: Ulster, 1998; Open, 2005. Compaq Lifetime Achievement Award, 1997. *Publication:* (ed with E. F. D. Roberts) Registrum Iohannis Mey: The Register of John Mey, Archbishop of Armagh, 1443–1456, 1972. *Recreations:* historical research, reading, music, gardening. *Address:* Short Brothers Ltd, PO Box 241, Airport Road, Belfast BT3 9DZ.

QUILTER, Sir Anthony (Raymond Leopold Cuthbert), 4th Bt *cr* 1897; landowner since 1959; *b* 25 March 1937; *s* of Sir (John) Raymond (Cuthbert) Quilter, 3rd Bt and Margery Marianne (*née* Cooke); *S* father, 1959; *m* 1964, Mary Elise, *er d* of late Colonel Brian (Sherlock) Gooch, DSO, TD; one *s* one *d*. *Educ:* Harrow. Is engaged in farming. *Recreations:* shooting, golf. *Heir: s* Guy Raymond Cuthbert Quilter [*b* 13 April 1967; *m* 1992, Jenifer, *o d* of John Redvers-Cox; three *s*]. *Address:* Cliff Farm, Sutton, Woodbridge, Suffolk IP12 3JJ. *T:* (01394) 411246.

QUIN; *see* Wyndham-Quin, family name of Earl of Dunraven.

QUIN, Baroness *cr* 2006 (Life Peer), of Gateshead in the County of Tyne and Wear; **Joyce Gwendolen Quin;** PC 1998; *b* 26 Nov. 1944; *d* of late Basil Godfrey Quin, MC and Ida (*née* Ritson). *Educ:* Univ. of Newcastle upon Tyne (BA French, 1st Cl. Hons); Univ. of London (MSc Internat. Relns). Research Asst, Internat. Dept, Labour Party Headquarters, Transport House, 1969–72; Lecturer in French, Univ. of Bath, 1972–76; Resident Tutor, St Mary's Coll., and Lectr in French and Politics, Univ. of Durham, 1977–79. Mem. (Lab) European Parliament, S Tyne and Wear, 1979–84, Tyne and Wear, 1984–89. MP (Lab) Gateshead E, 1987–97, Gateshead E and Washington W, 1997–2005. Opposition front bench spokesman on trade and industry, 1989–92, on employment, 1992–93, on European affairs, 1993–97; Minister of State: Home Office, 1997–98; (Minister for Europe), FCO, 1998–99, MAFF, 1999–2001. Mem., Select Cttee on Treasury and Civil Service, 1987–89; Chairman: Franco-British Parly Relns Cttee, 2001–05; Regl Govt Gp, PLP, 2001–05; Mem., Franco-British Council, 2001– (Chm., 2007–). Vice-Chm., NE Constitl Convention, 2001–05. Vis. Prof., Centre for Urban and Regl Develt Studies, Newcastle upon Tyne Univ., 2001–; Vis. Parly Fellow, St Antony's Coll., Oxford, 2007–08. Hon. Fellow: Sunderland Polytechnic, subseq. Univ. of Sunderland, 1986; St Mary's Coll., Durham Univ., 1994. Hon. Freeman, Bor. of Gateshead, 2006. *Publications:* various articles in newspapers and journals. *Recreations:* North-East local history (Newcastle upon Tyne City Guide), music, theatre, walking, cycling. *Address:* House of Lords, SW1A 0PW.

QUINAN, Lloyd; Member (SNP) West Scotland, Scottish Parliament, 1999–2003; *b* 29 April 1957; *s* of Andrew and Ann Quinan. *Educ:* Queen Margaret Coll., Edinburgh. Actor, 1978–83; theatre dir, 1983–89; television presenter, producer and dir, 1989–99. Contested (SNP) Motherwell & Wishaw, Scottish Parlt, 2003. *Recreations:* reading, travel, music, football.

QUINCE, Peter; *see* Thompson, John W. McW.

QUINLAN, Rt Rev. (Alan) Geoffrey; a Bishop Suffragan, Diocese of Cape Town, 1988–98; *b* 20 Aug. 1933; *s* of late Robert Quinlan and Eileen Beatrice Quinlan; *m* 1963, Rosalind Arlen Sallie (*née* Reed); three *s* one *d*. *Educ:* Kelham Theological College. RAF, 1952–54. Deacon 1958, priest 1959; Asst Curate, St Thomas's, Leigh, Lancs, 1958–61; Rector: St Margaret's, Bloemfontein, 1962–68; St Michael and All Angels, Sasolburg, OFS, 1968–72; Warden, Community of Resurrection, Grahamstown and Chaplain, Grahamstown Training Coll., 1972–76; Priest-in-Charge of Training in Ministries and Discipleship, Cape Town Diocese, 1976–80; Rector, All Saints, Plumstead, Cape Town, 1980–88. Canon, St George's Cathedral, Cape Town, 1980–88. *Publications:* A Manual for Worship Leaders; Discipleship and the Alternative Society; Church-wardens' Handbook; My Personal Prayer Book, 2006. *Recreations:* chess, reading, bird-watching, computers, music, painting, philately. *Address:* 132 Woodley Road, Plumstead, Cape Town, 7800, South Africa.

QUINLAN, Sir Michael (Edward), GCB 1991 (KCB 1985; CB 1980); Director, Ditchley Foundation, 1992–99; *b* 11 Aug. 1930; *s* of late Gerald and Roseanne Quinlan; *m* 1965, (Margaret) Mary Finlay; two *s* two *d*. *Educ:* Wimbledon Coll.; Merton Coll., Oxford. (1st Cl. Hon. Mods, 1st Cl. LitHum; MA; Hon. Fellow, 1989). RAF, 1952–54. Asst Principal, Air Ministry, 1954; Private Sec. to Parly Under-Sec. of State for Air, 1956–58; Principal, Air Min., 1958; Private Sec. to Chief of Air Staff, 1962–65; Asst Sec., MoD, 1968; Defence Counsellor, UK Delegn to NATO, 1970–73; Under-Sec., Constitution Unit, Cabinet Office, 1974–77; Dep. Under-Sec. of State (Policy), MoD, 1977–81; Dep. Sec. (Industry), HM Treasury, 1981–82; Perm. Sec., Dept of Employment, 1983–88; Perm. Under-Sec. of State, MoD, 1988–92. Special Advr to Parly Cttees, 2002–06. Vis. Prof., KCL, 1992–95 and 2002–; Public Policy Scholar, Woodrow Wilson Center, Washington, 2000; Consulting Sen. Fellow, IISS, 2004–. Director: Lloyds Bank, 1992–95; Lloyds TSB Gp, 1996–98; Pilkington, 1992–99. Chm., Tablet Trust, 2001–. Trustee, Science Mus., 1992–2001. Governor, Henley Mgt Coll., 1983–88. Chm., CS Sports Council, 1985–89; Pres., CS Cricket Assoc., 1992–98. Pres., Merton Soc., 1992–95. CCMI (CBIM 1983). *Publications:* Thinking About Nuclear Weapons, 1997; European Defense Co-operation, 2001; (with Baron Guthrie of Craigiebank) Just War: the just war tradition: ethics in modern warfare, 2007; many articles on defence and public admin and ethics. *Recreations:* golf, watching cricket, listening to music. *Address:* 3 Adderbury Park, West Adderbury, Oxon OX17 3EN. *Clubs:* Royal Air Force, MCC, Lord's Taverners; Chipping Norton Golf.

QUINN, Aiden O'Brien; *see* Quinn, J. A. O'B.

QUINN, Andrea Helen, (Mrs R. Champ); conductor; Music Director and Chief Conductor, Symphony Orchestra of Norrlands Opera, Umeå, Sweden, since 2006; *b* 22 Dec. 1964; *d* of Desmond Bone and Theresa Bone (*née* MacLaren) (who *m* 1971, John Quinn); *m* 1991, Dr Roderick Champ; one *s* two *d*. *Educ:* Nottingham Univ. (BA Hons); Royal Acad. of Music (Adv. Cert. in Conducting; ARAM 1999). Music Director: London Philharmonic Youth Orch., 1993–96; Royal Ballet, 1998–2001; NY City Ballet, 2001–06. Hon. FTCL 2000. *Recreations:* horse riding, literature, Italian, art galleries. *Address:* Urishay Barn, Michaelchurch Escley, Herefordshire HR2 0LR. *T:* (01981) 510686; *e-mail:* quinnchamp@gmail.com.

QUINN, Andrew; Chief Executive, ITV, 1992–95; *b* 29 March 1937. Granada TV, 1964–92: Gen. Manager, 1977; Man. Dir, Granada Cable and Satellite, 1983; Man. Dir, 1987; Chief Exec., 1992. Dir, Border TV, 1996.

QUINN, Brian, CBE 1996; Managing Director, Brian Quinn Consulting (formerly Brian Quinn Consultancy plc), since 1996; *b* 18 Nov. 1936; *s* of Thomas Quinn and Margaret (*née* Cairns); *m* 1961, Mary Bradley; two *s* one *d*. *Educ:* Glasgow Univ. (MA Hons); Manchester Univ. (MA Econs); Cornell Univ. (PhD). FCIBS 1995. Economist, African Dept, IMF, 1964–70, Rep., Sierra Leone, 1966–68; joined Bank of England, 1970: Economic Div., 1970–74; Chief Cashier's Dept, 1974–77; Head of Information Div., 1977–82; Asst Dir, 1982–88; Head of Banking Supervision, 1986–88; Exec. Dir, 1988–96; Acting Dep. Gov., 1995. Chairman: Nomura Bank Internat., 1996–99; Celtic plc, 2000–07. Non-executive Director: GE Mortgage Insurance, 2004–; Qatar Finance Centre Regulatory Authy, 2006–. Chm., Financial Markets Gp, LSE, 1996–2000. Advisor: Singapore Govt, 1997–2002; Sumitomo-Mitsui Banking Corp., 2000–02; Consultant: World Bank, 1997–; IMF, 1997–; McKinsey and Co., 1998–; Mem. Bd of Dirs, Toronto Centre, 2008– (Mem. Adv. Bd 1998). Mem., City Disputes Panel, 2003–. Hon. Prof. of Econs and Finance, Glasgow Univ., 2006–. *Publications:* (contrib.) Surveys of African Economies, vol. 4, 1971; (contrib.) The New Inflation, 1976; articles in learned jls. *Recreations:* fishing, golf, cycling, football. *Address:* 14 Homewood Road, St Albans, Herts AL1 4BH. *Clubs:* Bankers', Reform; Tanfield Flyfishers'.

QUINN, Brian; *see* Quinn, J. S. B.

QUINN, Carolyn; Presenter: PM programme, BBC Radio 4, since 2000; Westminster Hour, BBC Radio 4, since 2007; *b* 22 July 1961; *d* of late Edward James Quinn and of Maureen Quinn; *m* 2003, Nigel Paul Morris. *Educ:* St Joseph's RC Primary Sch., Crayford; Dartford Grammar Sch. for Girls; Kent Univ. (BA Hons French 1983); Inst. of Educn, Univ. of London (PGCE). Clerical worker, Charing Cross Hosp., London, 1984–85; Irish Post newspaper, London, 1985–86; trainee, BBC Radio, Local Radio Reporter Scheme, 1986–87; reporter/producer, BBC Radio Solent, 1987–89; BBC Westminster, covering Parlt and politics, 1989–; political corresp., BBC, 1994–2006;

Presenter, Today prog., BBC Radio 4, 2004–08. *Recreations:* cycling, cinema, walking, jazz. *Address:* c/o BBC Radio 4, Television Centre, Wood Lane, W12 7RJ.

QUINN, (James) Aiden O'Brien; QC (Seychelles) 1973; Vice-President, Immigration Appeal Tribunal, 1996–2004 (Adjudicator, 1990–93; Special Adjudicator, 1993–96); Member, Special Immigration Appeals Commission, 1998–2002; *b* 3 Jan. 1932; *s* of late William Patrick Quinn (Comr, Gárda Siochána) and Helen Mary (*née* Walshe); *m* 1960, Christel Tyner; two *s* one *d. Educ:* Presentation Coll., Bray, Co. Wicklow, Ireland; University Coll., Dublin, NUI (BA, LLB Hons). Called to the Bar: Kings' Inns, Dublin, 1957; Inner Temple, 1967. National City Bank, Dublin, 1949–53; in practice at the Bar, under Colonial Office Scheme, 1958–60; Crown Counsel and Actg Sen. Crown Counsel, Nyasaland, 1960–64; Asst Attorney Gen. and Actg Attorney Gen., West Cameroon, 1964–66; Procureur Général, West Cameroon, and Avocat Général, Fed. Republic of Cameroon, 1966–68; Fed. Republic of Cameroon, 1968–72: Conseiller, Cour Fédérale de Justice; Judge, W Cameroon Supreme Court; Conseiller Technique (Harmonisation des Lois), Ministère de la Justice, Yaoundé; Président, Tribunal Administratif, Cameroun Occidental; Chargé de Cours, Ecole Nationale de l'Administration et de la Magistrature, Yaoundé; Republic of Seychelles: Attorney Gen., also of British Indian Ocean Territory, 1972–76; MLC, MEC and Mem. Parlt, 1972–76; Chief Justice, 1976–77; Actg Dep. Governor, 1974; Mem., Official Delegn on Self-Govt, 1975, and on Independence Constitutions, 1976; collab. with Prof. A. G. Chloros on translation and up-dating of Code Napoleon, 1975–76; Chm., Judicial Service Commn, 1976–77; Gilbert Islands (Kiribati): Chief Justice, 1977–81; Chm., Judicial Service Commn, 1977–81; set up new Courts' system, 1978; Mem., Council of State, 1979–81; Judge, High Court of Solomon Is, 1977–79; Special Prosecutor, Falkland Is, 1981; Botswana: Chief Justice, 1981–87; Chm., Judicial Service Commn, 1981–87; retired, 1987–89; Investment Advr, 1989–90. Mem., Panel of Experts of UN on Prevention of Crime and Treatment of Offenders, 1985–87. Chevalier, Ordre de la Valeur, Republic of Cameroon, 1967; Kiribati Independence Medal, 1979. *Publications:* Magistrates' Courts Handbook: West Cameroon, 1968; Kiribati, 1979; compiled and edited: West Cameroon Law Reports, 1961–68; Gilbert Islands Law Reports, 1977–79; Kiribati Law Reports, 1977–80; articles in Commonwealth Law Jl, The Magistrate, etc. *Recreations:* languages, travel, reading, swimming. *Address:* 24 Deer Park Drive, Newport, Shropshire TF10 7HB. *Club:* Lansdowne.

QUINN, (James Steven) Brian; Director General, International Institute of Communications, since 2003; *b* 16 June 1936; *s* of James and Elizabeth Quinn; *m* 1st, 1962, Blanche Cecilia James (marr. diss. 1987); two *s* one *d*; 2nd, 2004, Catherine Mann. *Educ:* St Mary's Coll., Crosby; Waterpark Coll., Ireland; University Coll., Dublin (BCL, LLB). Kings Inn, Dublin. Director: Johnson Radley, 1966–68; United Glass Containers, 1968–69; Head of Industrial Activities, Prices and Incomes Board, 1969–71; Dir, M. L. H. Consultants, 1971–79; Corporate Develt Advr, Midland Bank Internat., 1977–80; Chief Industrial Advr, Price Commn, 1977–78; Man. Dir, Visnews, 1980–86; Digital Computer Services: Dir, 1985–96; Chief Exec., 1989–92; Chm., 1992–96. Chairman: BrightStar Communications, 1983–85; BAJ Holdings, 1985–87; Harmer Holbrook, 1987–88; Signet Online, 1996–99; Loan Line Ltd, 1997–2000; Central Equipment Hldgs Ltd, 2003–04; Director: Telematique Services, 1985–90; QM Security Ltd. Legal res., TCD, 1995–97. Institute of Management (formerly British Institute of Management): CCMI (CBIM 1985; FBIM 1978); Mem. Council, 1981–87, 1990–98; Mem. Finance Cttee, 1981–84; Chm., City of London Branch, 1981–83; Vice Pres., 1983–90; Chm., Gtr London Regl Council, 1990–94. International Institute of Communications: Trustee, 1982–88, 1992–97; Chm., Exec. Cttee, 1984–88; Pres., 1988–91. Mem., Exec. Cttee, Inst. of European Trade and Technology, 1983–96. Trustee: Internat. Center of Communications, San Diego State Univ., 1990–. Chm., Finance Cttee, Great Japan Exhbn, 1979–82. Chm., Editl Bd, Professional Manager, 1993–98. *Recreations:* golf, reading, veteran vehicles. *Address:* 29 Bliss Mill, Chipping Norton, Oxon OX7 5JR. *Club:* Athenæum.

QUINN, Jane Elisabeth; Public Relations Consultant and Director, Bolton & Quinn Ltd, since 1981; *b* 2 March 1949; *d* of Dr Francis Prime and Barbara Prime; *m* 1st, 1971, Stephen Quinn (marr. diss. 1998); three *s*; 2nd, 2000, Martin Duignan. *Educ:* Convent of the Sacred Heart, Tunbridge Wells; Queen's Coll., London. Media buyer, Ogilvy & Mather, 1969–70; PR Exec., Prime Associates, 1970–72; Publicity Exec., Riverside Studios, 1978–81. Dir, Michael Clark Co., 2005–. Mem. Cttee, Human Rights Watch UK, 2005–. Dir, Art Baby, 2003–. *Address:* Bolton & Quinn Ltd, 10 Pottery Lane, W11 4LZ.

QUINN, Lawrence William; *b* 25 Dec. 1956; *s* of late Jimmy Quinn and Sheila Quinn; *m* 1983, Ann Eames. *Educ:* Pennine Way Schs, Carlisle; Harraby Sch., Carlisle; Hatfield Poly. (BSc). CEng; FICE. Formerly Planning Develt Engr, London NE, Railtrack. MP (Lab) Scarborough and Whitby, 1997–2005; contested (Lab) same seat, 2005. PPS to Minister of State, DTI, 2001–02, Cabinet Office, 2002–05. Chm., All Party Railways (formerly Rail Freight) Gp, 1997–2005; Secretary: Labour backbench Agriculture Cttee, 1997–2001; All Party Brazil Gp, 2000–05; Chairman: All Party Saudi Arabia Gp, 1998–2005; All Party Underground Space Gp, 2003–05. Sec., PLP Yorks and Humber Gp, 2001–05; PLP Rep., Nat. Policy Forum, 2001–05; Labour Party Policy Comr, 2001–. *Address:* Middle Offices, 29–31 Falsgrave Road, Scarborough YO12 5EA.

QUINN, Leo; Chief Executive Officer, De La Rue plc, since 2004; *b* 13 Dec. 1956; *s* of Kevin and Mary Quinn; *m* 1993, Elaine Fitzpatrick; two *s. Educ:* Portsmouth Poly. (BSc Hons Civil Engrg 1979); Imperial Coll., London (DIC Mgt Sci. 1982). Civil Engr, Balfour Beatty Construction, 1979–81; Planning Manager, Texas Instruments, UK and Portugal, 1982–84; Honeywell, 1984–2000: various posts in UK, Europe and USA; Pres., Honeywell H&BC Enterprise Solutions Worldwide, 2000; Pres. Europe, ME and Africa, Tridium Inc., 2000–01; Chief Operating Officer, Prodn Mgt Div., Invensys plc (USA), 2001–04. *Recreations:* ski-ing, theatre, water sports, shooting. *Address:* De La Rue plc, De La Rue House, Jays Close, Viables, Basingstoke, Hants RG22 4BS. *T:* (01256) 605326, *Fax:* (01256) 605347; *e-mail:* leo.quinn@uk.delarue.com.

QUINN, Niall Peter; QC 2006; a Recorder, since 1999; *b* 16 June 1950; *s* of late Michael Quinn and Sheelagh Quinn (*née* O'Hare); *m* 1st, 1970, Mary O'Flynn (*d* 1997); one *s* two *d*; 2nd, 2001, Linda Bamford (*née* Austin); two step *s. Educ:* Emanuel Sch.; Univ. of Manchester (LLB Hons 1971); Coll. of Law, London. Admitted solicitor, 1974; Foinette Quinn, then Woodfine Foinette Quinn, solicitors: Partner, 1975; Sen. Partner, 1984; Partner, 2000–. Asst Recorder, 1995–99. *Recreations:* Times crossword, karaoke. *Address:* Woodfines LLP, 125–131 Queensway, Bletchley MK2 2DH. *T:* (01908) 366333, *Fax:* (01908) 644096; *e-mail:* nquinn@woodfines.co.uk.

QUINN, Richard; *see* Quinn, T. R.

QUINN, Ruairi; TD (Lab) Dublin South-East, 1977–81 and since 1982; *b* 2 April 1946; *s* of Malachi Quinn and Julia Quinn; *m* 1st, 1969, Nicola Underwood; one *s* one *d*; 2nd, 1990, Liz Allman; one *s. Educ:* University Coll., Dublin (BArch, Higher Dip. in Ekistics). Dublin City Council: Mem., 1974–77; Leader, Lab Gp and Civic Alliance, 1991–93.

Mem., Seanad Eireann, 1976–77 and 1981–82; Minister of State, Envmt, 1982–83; Minister: for Labour, 1984–87, and for Public Service, 1986–87; for Enterprise and Employment, 1993–94; for Finance, 1995–97. Leader, Irish Labour Party, 1997–2002. *Publications:* Straight Left: a journey in politics, 2006; contrib. to Architects Jl, Irish Architect, Ekistics, Tilt. *Recreations:* reading, cooking, walking, music, gardening, cycling. *Address:* Dáil Eireann, Kildare Street, Dublin 2, Republic of Ireland.

QUINN, Dame Sheila (Margaret Imelda), DBE 1987 (CBE 1978); FRCN; President, Royal College of Nursing, 1982–86, now Life Vice President; *b* 16 Sept. 1920; *d* of late Wilfred Amos Quinn and Ada Mazella (*née* Bottomley). *Educ:* Convent of Holy Child, Blackpool; London Univ. (BScEcon Hons); Royal Lancaster Infirmary (SRN 1947); Birmingham (SCM); Royal Coll. of Nursing, London (RNT). FRCN 1978. Admin. Sister, then Principal Sister Tutor, Prince of Wales' Gen. Hosp., London, 1950–61; Internat. Council of Nurses, Geneva: Dir, Social and Econ. Welfare Div., 1961–66; Exec. Dir, 1967–70; Chief Nursing Officer, Southampton Univ. Hosps, 1970–74; Area Nursing Officer, Hampshire AHA (Teaching), 1974–78; Regional Nursing Officer, Wessex RHA, 1978–83. Member: E Dorset DHA, 1987–90; Dorset FHSA, 1990–96. Nursing Advr, BRCS, 1983–88. Pres., Standing Cttee of Nurses of EEC, 1983–91; Member: Council, Royal Coll. of Nursing, 1971–79 (Chm. Council, 1974–79; Dep. Pres., 1980–82); Bd of Dirs, Internat. Council of Nurses, 1977–85 (first Vice-Pres., 1981–85); Mem., EEC Adv. Cttee on Trng in Nursing, 1978–90. Consultant, Dreyfus Health Foundn, NY, 1999–. Hon. DSc (Social Sciences) Southampton, 1986. *Publications:* Nursing in The European Community, 1980; Caring for the Carers, 1981; ICN Past and Present, 1989; Nursing, the EC Dimension, 1993; A Dame Abroad (memoir), 2004; articles, mainly on internat. nursing and EEC, in national and internat. jls. *Recreations:* travel, gardening. *Clubs:* St John's House, Royal Society of Medicine.

QUINN, Stephen, CB 2008; Permanent Secretary, Department of Enterprise, Trade and Investment, Northern Ireland, since 2006; *b* 22 Aug. 1950; *s* of Thomas Charles Quinn and Jane Quinn (*née* Kirkpatrick); *m* 1983, Deirdre Mary Brady. *Educ:* Portora Royal Sch., Enniskillen; Trinity Coll., Dublin (BA Hons Hist. and Pol Sci.). Northern Ireland Civil Service: Dept of Finance, 1974–86 (Sec., Kincora Inquiry, 1984–85); Assistant Secretary: Dept of Health and Social Services, 1986–87; Dept of Finance and Personnel, 1987–90; Dept of Educn, 1990–92; Central Secretariat, 1992–94; Under Secretary: Dept of Finance and Personnel, 1994–98; DoE, 1998–99; Permanent Secretary: DoE, 1999–2002; Dept for Regl Develt, 2002–06. *Address:* c/o Department of Enterprise, Trade and Investment, Netherleigh, Massey Avenue, Belfast BT4 2JP.

QUINN, Terence James; Editor-in-Chief, APN Regional Newspapers, Australia and New Zealand, since 2004; *b* 17 Nov. 1951; *s* of Thomas Quinn and Shirley (*née* Anderson); *m* 1973, Patricia Anna-Maria Gillespie; one *s* one *d* (and one *s* decd). *Educ:* St Aloysius Coll., Glasgow. Editor: Telegraph & Argus, Bradford, 1984–89; Evening News, Edinburgh, 1989–92; Dep. Editl Dir, 1992–94, Editl Dir, 1994, Thomson Regl Newspapers; Editor, Daily Record, 1994–98; Sen. Vice Pres., Readership, Thomson Newspapers (US), 1998–2000; Pres., Reader Inc. (US), 2000–02; Publisher, Fairfax Sundays, NZ, 2002–04. *Recreations:* tennis, sailing, golf. *Address:* 300 Ann Street, Brisbane, Qld 4000, Australia; *e-mail:* tquinn@apnnewspapers.com.au.

QUINN, Dr Terence John, CBE 2004; FRS 2002; Emeritus Director, Bureau International des Poids et Mesures, Sèvres, France, since 2004 (Deputy Director, 1977–88; Director, 1988–2003); *b* 19 March 1938; *s* of John Henry and Olive Hilda Quinn; *m* 1962, Renée Marie Goujard; two *s. Educ:* Univ. of Southampton (BSc 1959); Univ. of Oxford (DPhil 1963). National Physical Laboratory, Teddington: Jun. Res. Fellow, 1962–64; Staff Mem., 1964–77. Vis. Scientist, Nat. Bureau of Standards, Washington, DC, 1967–68; Royal Soc. Vis. Fellow, Cavendish Lab., and Dist. Vis. Fellow, Christ's Coll., Cambridge, 1984–85. FInstP 1975; Fellow, APS, 1995; FAAAS 2001. Hon. Prof., Birmingham Univ., 2000. Hon. Dr Conservatoire Nat. des Arts et Métiers, Paris, 2000. Editor, Notes & Records of the Royal Soc., 2004–07. *Publications:* Temperature, 1983, 2nd edn 1990; papers in sci. press on thermometry, radiometry, mass standards, lab. gravitational experiments, fundamental phys. constants and gen. metrology. *Recreations:* photography, bee keeping. *Address:* 92 rue Brancas, 92310 Sèvres, France. *T:* (1) 46230656; *e-mail:* terry.quinn@physics.org. *Club:* Athenæum.

QUINN, (Thomas) Richard; jockey, 1978–2006; *b* 2 Dec. 1961; *s* of late Thomas Quinn and of Helen Quinn (*née* McDonald); *m* 1990, Fiona Christine Johnson (marr. diss. 1993); one *s* one *d. Educ:* Bannockburn High Sch. First winner, Kempton, 1981; Champion Apprentice, Europe, 1983, GB, 1984; 2nd in Jockey's Championship, 1996, 1999. Winning races include: Irish Oaks, 1986, 1990; French 1,000 Guineas, 1986; St Leger, 1990, 2001; Irish St Leger, 1990, 1995; Dewhurst Stakes, 1990; Prix Royal Oak, 1992; Italian Derby, 1994; Juddmonte Lockinge Stakes, 1996; Prix Vermeille, 1998; Oaks, 2000; has ridden winners in 25 countries worldwide. Vice-Pres., Jockey's Assoc., 1992–. *Address:* c/o Jockey Club, 42 Portman Square, W1H 0EN.

QUINTON, family name of **Baron Quinton.**

QUINTON, Baron *cr* 1982 (Life Peer), of Holywell in the City of Oxford and County of Oxfordshire; **Anthony Meredith Quinton,** FBA 1977; Chairman of the Board, British Library, 1985–90; *b* 25 March 1925; *s* of late Richard Frith Quinton, Surgeon Captain, RN, and late Gwenllyan Letitia Quinton; *m* 1952, Marcelle Wegier; one *s* one *d. Educ:* Stowe Sch.; Christ Church, Oxford (St Cyres Scholar; BA 1st Cl. Hons PPE 1949). Served War, RAF, 1943–46: flying officer and navigator. Fellow: All Souls Coll., Oxford, 1949–55; New Coll., Oxford, 1955–78 (Emeritus Fellow, 1980; Hon. Fellow, 1997); Pres., Trinity Coll., Oxford, 1978–87 (Hon. Fellow, 1987). Delegate, OUP, 1970–76. Mem., Arts Council, 1979–81; Vice Pres., British Acad., 1985–86. Visiting Professor: Swarthmore Coll., Pa, 1960; Stanford Univ., Calif, 1964; New Sch. for Social Res., New York, 1976–77; Brown Univ., 1994. Lecturer: Dawes Hicks, British Acad., 1971; Gregynog, Univ. of Wales, Aberystwyth, 1973; T. S. Eliot, Univ. of Kent, Canterbury, 1976; Robbins, Univ. of Stirling, 1987; Hobhouse, LSE, 1988; Tanner, Warsaw, 1988; R. M. Jones, QUB, 1988; Carter, Lancaster, 1989. President: Aristotelian Soc., 1975–76; Soc. for Applied Philosophy, 1988–91; Royal Inst. of Philosophy, 1990–2004; Assoc. of Indep. Libraries, 1991–97; Friends of Wellcome Inst., 1992–97. Chm., Kennedy Meml Trust, 1990–95. Governor, Stowe Sch., 1963–84 (Chm. Governors, 1969–75); Fellow, Winchester Coll., 1970–85. DHumLit NY Univ., 1987; DHum Ball State Univ., 1990. Order of Leopold II, Belgium, 1984. *Publications:* Political Philosophy (ed), 1967; The Nature of Things, 1973; Utilitarian Ethics, 1973; (trans.) K. Ajdukiewicz (with H. Skolimowski) Problems and Theories of Philosophy, 1973; The Politics of Imperfection, 1978; Francis Bacon, 1980; Thoughts and Thinkers, 1982; From Wodehouse to Wittgenstein, 1998. *Recreations:* sedentary pursuits. *Address:* A11 Albany, Piccadilly, W1J 0AL. *Clubs:* Garrick, Beefsteak.

QUINTON, Sir John (Grand), Kt 1990; Chairman, Barclays Bank PLC, 1987–92 (Deputy Chairman, 1985–87); *b* 21 Dec. 1929; *s* of William Grand Quinton and Norah May (*née* Nunn); *m* 1954, Jean Margaret Chastney; one *s* one *d. Educ:* Norwich Sch.; St

John's Coll., Cambridge (MA 1954); FCIB (FIB 1964). Joined Barclays Bank, 1953: Manager, King's Cross, 1965; seconded to Min. of Health as Principal, Internat. Div. and UK Deleg., World Health Assembly, 1966; Asst Gen. Manager, 1968; Local Dir, Nottingham, 1969; Reg. Gen. Manager, 1971; Gen. Manager, 1975; Dir and Sen. Gen. Man., 1982–84; Vice-Chm., 1985. Dep. Chm., Mercantile Credit Co. Ltd, 1975–79; Chairman: FA Premier League, 1992–99; George Wimpey PLC, 1993–95; non-exec. Dir, Norwich and Peterborough BS, 1993–99 (Dep. Chm., 1996–99). Chairman: Chief Exec. Officers, Cttee of London Clearing Bankers, 1982–83; Adv. Council, London Enterprise Agency, 1986–90; Office of the Banking Ombudsman, 1987–92; Cttee of London and Scottish Bankers, 1989–91; Metropolitan Police Cttee, 1995–2000. Member: City Capital Markets Cttee, 1981–86; NE Thames RHA, 1974–87; Accounting Standards Cttee, 1982–85; Econ. and Financial Policy Cttee, CBI, 1985–88 (Chm., 1987–88); Metropolitan Police Authy, 2000–06. Treasurer, Chartered Inst. of Bankers, 1980–86 (Pres., 1989–90); Hon. Treas. and Bd Mem., Business in the Community, 1986–91. Chairman: British Olympic Appeal, 1988; Royal Anniversary Trust Appeal, 1992. Trustee: Royal Acad. Trust, 1987–93; Westminster Abbey Trust, 1991–98; Thrombosis Res. Inst., 1993–2001; Chm. Bd of Trustees, Botanic Gdns Conservation Internat., 1991–99. Pres., East of England Show, 1992. Chm., Motability Finance Ltd, 1978–85; Gov., Motability, 1985– (Hon. Treas., 1998–2003); Vice-Chm., Motability Tenth Anniversary Trust Ltd, 1995–. Gov., Ditchley Foundn, 1987–92; Member: Court of Governors, Royal Shakespeare Theatre, 1986–2000; Court, Henley Coll., 1987–92. FRSA 1988. Chm., Chenies Parish Council, 2007–. Freeman: Norwich, 1952; City of London, 1989. *Recreations:* gardening, music, golf. *Address:* Chenies Place, Chenies, Bucks WD3 6EU. *Club:* Reform.

QUIRK, family name of **Baron Quirk**.

QUIRK, Baron *cr* 1994 (Life Peer), of Bloomsbury in the London Borough of Camden; **(Charles) Randolph Quirk,** Kt 1985; CBE 1976; FBA 1975; President, British Academy, 1985–89; Fellow of University College London; *b* 12 July 1920; *s* of late Thomas and Amy Randolph Quirk, Lambfell, Isle of Man; *m* 1st, 1946, Jean (marr. diss. 1979; she *d* 1995), *d* of Ellis Gauntlett Williams; two *s*; 2nd, 1984, Gabriele, *d* of Judge Helmut Stein. *Educ:* Cronk y Voddy Sch.; Douglas High Sch., IOM; University College London. MA, PhD, DLit London. Served RAF, 1940–45. Lecturer in English, University College London, 1947–54; Commonwealth Fund Fellow, Yale Univ. and University of Michigan, 1951–52; Reader in English Language and Literature, University of Durham, 1954–58; Professor of English Language in the University of Durham, 1958–60, in the University of London, 1960–68; Quain Prof. of English Language and Literature, University Coll. London, 1968–81; Vice-Chancellor, Univ. of London, 1981–85. Dir, Survey of English Usage, 1959–83. Member: Senate, Univ. of London, 1970–85 (Chm., Acad. Council, 1972–75); Ct, Univ. of London, 1972–85; Bd, British Council, 1983–91; BBC Archives Cttee, 1975–81; RADA Council, 1985–2004; Select Cttee on Sci., H of L, 1998–2003. President: Inst. of Linguists, 1975; Coll. of Speech Therapists, 1987–91; North of England Educn Conf., 1989; Vice-Pres., Foundn for Science and Technology, 1986–90; Governor: British Inst. of Recorded Sound, 1975–80; E-SU, 1980–85; Richmond Coll., London, 1981–2006; City Technology Colls, 1986–95. Chairman: Cttee of Enquiry into Speech Therapy Services, 1969–72; Hornby Educnl Trust, 1979–93; Anglo-Spanish Foundn, 1983–85; British Library Adv. Cttee, 1984–97; Vice-Chm., English Language Council, E-SU, 1985–. Trustee: Wolfson Foundn, 1987–; American Sch. in London, 1987–89; Royal Comr, 1851 Exhibn, 1987–95. Mem., Academia Europaea, 1988. Foreign Fellow: Royal Belgian Acad. of Scis, 1975; Royal Swedish Acad., 1987; Finnish Acad. of Scis, 1991; American Acad. of Arts and Scis, 1994. Hon. FCST; Hon. FCIL; Hon. Fellow: Imperial Coll., 1985; QMC, 1986; Goldsmiths' Coll., 1987; King's Coll., 1990; RHBNC, 1990. Hon. Bencher, Gray's Inn, 1992. Hon. Fil. Dr: Lund; Uppsala; Helsinki; Copenhagen; Hon. DU: Essex; Bar Ilan; Brunel; DUniv Open; Hon. DHC: Liège; Paris; Prague; Bucharest; Hon. DLitt: Reading; Newcastle upon Tyne; Durham; Bath; Salford; Queen Margaret; Southern California; Sheffield; Glasgow; Poznan; Nijmegen; Richmond Coll.; Hon. DCL Westminster; Hon. LLD: Leicester; London; Hon. DSc Aston. Jubilee Medal, Inst. of Linguists, 1973. *Publications:* The Concessive Relation in Old English Poetry, 1954; Studies in Communication (with A. J. Ayer and others), 1955; An Old English Grammar (with C. L. Wrenn), 1955, enlarged edn (with S. E. Deskis), 1994; Charles Dickens and Appropriate Language, 1959; The Teaching of English (with A. H. Smith), 1959, revised edn, 1964; The Study of the Mother-Tongue, 1961; The Use of English (with Supplements by A. C. Gimson and J. Warburg), 1962, enlarged edn, 1968; Prosodic and Paralinguistic Features in English (with D. Crystal), 1964; A Common Language (with A. H. Marckwardt), 1964; Investigating Linguistic Acceptability (with J. Svartvik), 1966; Essays on the English Language— Mediaeval and Modern, 1968; (with S. Greenbaum) Elicitation Experiments in English, 1970; (with S. Greenbaum, G. Leech, J. Svartvik) A Grammar of Contemporary English, 1972; The English Language and Images of Matter, 1972; (with S. Greenbaum) A University Grammar of English, 1973; The Linguist and the English Language, 1974; (with V. Adams, D. Davy) Old English Literature: a practical introduction, 1975; (with J. Svartvik) A Corpus of English Conversation, 1980; Style and Communication in the English Language, 1982; (with S. Greenbaum, G. Leech, J. Svartvik) A Comprehensive Grammar of the English Language, 1985; (with H. Widdowson) English in the World, 1985; Words at Work: lectures on textual structure, 1986; (with G. Stein) English in Use, 1990; (with S. Greenbaum) A Student's Grammar of the English Language, 1990; (with G. Stein) An Introduction to Standard English, 1993; Grammatical and Lexical Variance in English, 1995; (with K. Brown and others) Linguistics in Britain: personal histories, 2002; contrib. to: conf. proceedings and volumes of studies; papers in linguistic and literary journals. *Address:* University College London, Gower Street, WC1E 6BT. *T:* (020) 7219 2226. *Club:* Athenæum.

QUIRK, Barry John, CBE 2001; PhD; Chief Executive, London Borough of Lewisham, since 1994; *b* 20 Nov. 1953; *s* of John Quirk and Iris (*née* Cope; now Aldridge); three *s* one *d* by former *m*. *Educ:* London Univ. (ext. BSc Hons 1975); Portsmouth Poly. (PhD 1984). Head of Corporate Policy, London Borough of Newham, 1987–94; Asst Chief Exec., London Borough of Lewisham, 1987–94. Non-exec. Dir, HM Customs and Excise, subseq. Revenue and Customs, 2002–06. Pres., 2005–06, Chm., 2006–08, SOLACE. Vis. Fellow of Social Policy and Politics, Goldsmiths Coll., Univ. of London, 1998–.

QUIRK, John Stanton S.; *see* Shirley-Quirk.

QUIRKE, Pauline; actress; *b* 8 July 1959; *m* Steve; one *s* one *d*. *Educ:* Anna Scher Theatre Sch., London. Appeared in Dixon of Dock Green, BBC TV, 1968; A Tale of Two Cities, Royal Court Theatre, 1979; *television series include:* Angels, 1976; Shine on Harvey Moon, 1982; Rockliffe's Babies, 1987; Birds of a Feather (8 series), 1989–98; Jobs for the Girls, 1993; First Sign of Madness, 1996; Double Nougat, 1996; Real Women, 1997–99; Maisie Raine, 1998–99; Down to Earth, 2000–03; Office Gossip, 2001; Being April, 2002; North and South, 2004; *television drama includes:* The Sculptress, 1996; Our Boy, 1997; Deadly Summer, 1997; David Copperfield, 1999; The Flint Street Nativity, 1999. *Films include:* Little Dorrit, 1986; Getting it Right, 1988; The Return of the Soldiers, 1988; Still Lives— Distant Voices, 1989; The Canterville Ghost, 1997; Check-out Girl, 1998; Arthur's Dyke, 2000; Redemption Road, 2001. *Address:* c/o DB Management, Pinewood Studios, Iver, Bucks SL10 0NH.

QURESHI, Bashir Ahmed, FRCGP, FRCPCH, FFSRH; general practitioner, Hounslow, since 1969; Chairman, NHS Trusts Association, since 2006; *b* 25 Sept. 1935; one *s* four *d*. *Educ:* Nishtar Medical Coll., Multan, Pakistan (MB BS); DHMSA 1974; DCH 1976; DPMSA 1980. AFOM 1978; MRCGP 1976, FRCGP 1984; MICGP 1984; MFFP 1993; MRCPCH 1998, FRCPCH 2006; FFSRH (FFFP 2006). MO Paediatrics, Nishtar Hosp., Multan, Pakistan, 1961–64; med. doctor, UK hosps, 1964–69; MO (pt-time), British Army and HM Prisons, 1998–; Expert Witness in cultural, religious and ethnic issues in litigation, UK, 1992–. Chm. Council, 1997–98, Emeritus Vice Pres., 2005–, RSH; Dep. Chm. and Sec., Nat. Assoc. of Sessional GPs, 2007–. Dep. Chm., Local Med. Cttee, Hounslow, 2003–08; Med. Advr, London Area, British Red Cross, 2006–. Vice Pres., Hounslow Conservative Assoc., 2005–. Mem., Conservative Med. Soc., 1988–. Hon. FRSH 1998; Hon. Mem. APHA, 1998. Badge of Honour, British Red Cross, 1999; Plaque of Recognition, H of L, 2001. *Publications:* Transcultural Medicine, 1989, 2nd edn 1994; contrib. 12 chapters in med. books; over 170 articles in med. jls; handouts and 378 lects to med. meetings, mainly UK, USA, India and Tanzania. *Recreations:* music, dancing, travel, reading, theatre, dining out, holidays, public speaking. *T:* and *Fax:* (020) 8570 4008; *e-mail:* drbashirqureshi@hotmail.com; *web:* www.drbashirqureshi.com. *Clubs:* Royal Society of Medicine; Society of Authors.

QURESHI, Murad; Member (Lab) London Assembly, Greater London Authority, since 2004; *b* 27 May 1965. *Educ:* Univ. of E Anglia (BA 1987); University Coll. London (MSc 1993). Mem. (Lab) Westminster CC, 1998–2006. Member: Metropolitan Police Authy, 2004–06; London Fire and Emergency Planning Authy, 2004–. *Recreations:* football and cricket (playing and watching). *Address:* Greater London Authority, City Hall, Queen's Walk, SE1 2AA. *T:* (020) 7983 4400, *Fax:* (020) 7983 5679; *e-mail:* murad.qureshi@london.gov.uk.

QURESHI, Shamim Ahmed; a District Judge (Magistrates' Courts), since 2004; a Recorder, since 2005; *b* 28 Feb. 1960; *s* of Mohammed Aslam Qureshi and Sara Begum; *m* 1987, Shabina Akhtar Qureshi; three *s* one *d*. *Educ:* Bristol Poly. (BA Law). Called to the Bar, Gray's Inn, 1982; pupillage in London, 1982–83; Sen. Crown Prosecutor, CPS, 1984–89; in practice at the Bar, Bristol, 1989–2002; Immigration Adjudicator, 2002–04; Judge Advocate at Courts Martial (pt–time), 2001–. Served TA, 1986–2001 (Capt. 1998). TEM 1998. *Recreations:* golf, cricket, swimming, reading, travel. *Address:* The Law Courts, North Street, Wolverhampton WV1 1RA. *T:* (01902) 773151, *Fax:* (01902) 311738.

R

RA JONG-YIL, Dr; Ambassador of the Republic of Korea to Japan, since 2004; *b* 5 Dec. 1940; *s* of Ra Iong-Gwyn and Ra Gwi-Nye; *m* 1968, Ra Jae-Ja; one *s* three *d. Educ:* Seoul Nat. Univ. (BA Pol Sci, MA Pol Sci.); Trinity Coll., Cambridge (PhD Internat. Relns, 1972). Kyung Hee University, Korea: Prof. of Pol Sci., 1972–; Dean: Coll. of Econs and Pol Sci., 1980–81; Grad. Sch., 1988–92. Fellow Commoner, Churchill Coll., Cambridge, 1981; Fulbright Sen. Fellow, Univ. of Southern Calif, 1985. Vice-Chm., Forum of Democratic Leaders in Asia-Pacific, 1994; Mem., Exec. Cttee and Special Asst to Pres., Nat. Congress for New Politics, 1996–97; Hd, Admin. Office, Presidential Transition Cttee, 1997; 2nd and 1st Dir, Nat. Security Planning Bd, 1998; 1st Dir, Nat. Intelligence Service, 1998–99; Director-General: Res. Inst. of Peace Studies, 1999–2000; Circle Millennium Korea, 1999–2000; Special Assistant: to Pres., Foreign and Security Affairs, Millennium Democratic Party, 1999–2000; to Dir-Gen., Foreign Affairs, Nat. Intelligence Service, 2000–01; Ambassador of Republic of Korea to UK, 2001–03; Nat. Security Advr to Pres., 2003–04. *Publications:* Co-operation and Conflict, 1986; Points of Departure, 1992; Human Beings and Politics, 1995; Preparing for the New Millennium, 1998. *Recreations:* tennis, golf, Kendo, Aikido. *Address:* (office) 1–2–5 Minami Azabu, Minato-ku, Tokyo 106, Japan. *Clubs:* Seoul; Tokyo City, Ark Hills, Roppongi (Tokyo); Tokyo Lawn Tennis.

RABAN, Antony John; Conseiller, Relations Internationales, Association Bernard Gregory, 2003–07 (Committee Member, 1996–2002; Membre d'Honneur, since 2005); *b* 10 Dec. 1941; *s* of Rev. Harry Priaulx Raban and Freda Mary Raban (*née* Probert); *m* 1965, Sandra Gilham Brown. *Educ:* St John's Sch., Leatherhead; Corpus Christi Coll., Cambridge (MA Hist.). Asst Master, Doncaster GS, 1964–67; Careers Officer, 1967–69, Professional Asst, 1969–71, Cambs & Isle of Ely CC; Asst Sec. (Careers Advr), Oxford Univ. Careers Service, 1971–74; Careers Advr, 1974–92, Dir, 1992–2002, Cambridge Univ. Careers Service. Chm., Assoc. of Grad. Careers Adv. Services, 1979–81; Pres., Eur. Forum on Student Guidance, 1988–92; Mem. Council, CRAC, 1998–2002. *Publications:* Working in the European Union: a guide for graduate recruiters and job-seekers, 1985, 4th edn 1995; The Entry of New Graduates into the European Labour Market, 1991; From PhD to Employment, 2000, 2nd edn 2003; numerous reports and contribs to professional jls. *Recreations:* art history, France.

RABAN, Jonathan, FRSL; author; *b* 14 June 1942; *s* of late Rev. Canon J. Peter C. P. Raban and of Monica (*née* Sandison); *m* 1992, Jean Lenihan (marr. diss.); one *d. Educ:* Univ. of Hull (BA Hons English). Lecturer in English and American Literature: UCW, Aberystwyth, 1965–67; Univ. of E Anglia, 1967–69; professional writer, 1969–. FRSL 1975. Hon. DLitt Hull, 2005. *Publications:* The Technique of Modern Fiction, 1969; Mark Twain: Huckleberry Finn, 1969; The Society of the Poem, 1971; Soft City, 1973; Arabia Through the Looking Glass, 1979; Old Glory, 1981 (Heinemann Award, RSL, 1982; Thomas Cook Award, 1982); Foreign Land, 1985; Coasting, 1986; For Love and Money, 1987; God, Man & Mrs Thatcher, 1989; Hunting Mister Heartbreak, 1990 (Thomas Cook Award, 1991); (ed) The Oxford Book of the Sea, 1992; Bad Land, 1996 (National Book Critics Circle Award, 1997); Passage to Juneau, 1999; Waxwings, 2003; My Holy War, 2005; Surveillance, 2006. *Recreation:* sailing. *Address:* c/o Aitken Alexander Associates Ltd, 18–21 Cavaye Place, SW10 9PT. *Clubs:* Groucho; Rainier (Seattle).

RABBATTS, Heather Victoria, CBE 2000; Chief Executive, Millwall Holdings, since 2006; *b* 6 Dec. 1955; *d* of Thomas Rabbatts and Hyacinth Rabbatts; one *s* by Edmund Gerard O'Sullivan; *m* 2001, Michael Lee. *Educ:* London Sch. of Econs (BA Hons Hist.; MSc). Called to the Bar, Lincoln's Inn, 1981. Equalities Officer, then Parly Liaison Officer, Local Govt Inf. Unit, 1983–86; London Borough of Hammersmith and Fulham: Hd, Women's Dept, 1987–89; Dir of Personnel, 1989–91; Dep. Chief Exec. and Dir, Strategic Services, 1991–93; Chief Executive: Merton LBC, 1993–95; Lambeth LBC, 1995–2000; Man. Dir, 4Learning, Channel 4, 2002–06. A Gov., BBC, 1999–2002. Non-exec. Dir, Bank of England, 2003–07. Member: Bd, Qualifications and Curriculum Authority, 1997–99; Bd, British Council, 1998–2004; ESRC, 1998–2000. Trustee, Runnymede Trust, 1997–99. Gov., LSE, 1997–2004. *Recreations:* opera, literature, shopping, champagne. *Address:* c/o Millwall Holdings plc, The Den, Zampa Road, SE16 3LN.

RABBI, The Chief; *see* Sacks, The Chief Rabbi Sir J. H.

RABBITT, Prof. Patrick Michael Anthony, PhD; Research Professor in Gerontology and Cognitive Psychology, University of Manchester, 1983–2004, now Emeritus; *b* 23 Sept. 1934; *s* of Joseph Bernard Rabbitt and Edna Maude Smith; *m* 1st, 1955, Adriana Habers (marr. diss. 1976); one *s* two *d*; 2nd, 1976, Dorothy Vera Bishop, *qv. Educ:* Queens' Coll., Cambridge (MA, PhD); MA Oxon; Manchester Univ. (MSc). Scientific Staff, MRC Applied Psychology Unit, Cambridge, 1962–68; Univ. Lectr in Psychology, and Official Fellow, Queen's Coll., Univ. of Oxford, 1968–82; Prof. of Psychology, Univ. of Durham, 1982–83. University of Western Australia: Adjunct Prof. of Psychology, 1991–2003; Hon. Res. Fellow, then Sen. Res. Fellow, 2003–; Hon. Res. Fellow, then Sen. Res. Fellow, Dept of Exptl Psychol., Univ. of Oxford, 2004–. FRSA 1997. Hon. Mem., Experimental Psychol. Soc., 1999; Hon. FBPsS 1995. Hon. DSc Western Australia, 2001. *Publications:* (ed) Cognitive Gerontology, 1990; Methodology of Frontal and Executive Function, 1997; 342 papers in learned jls. *Recreations:* whisky, nostalgia. *Address:* Department of Experimental Psychology, University of Oxford, South Parks Road, Oxford OX1 3UD; 10 North Parade Avenue, Oxford OX2 6LX.

RABBITTS, Prof. Terence Howard, PhD; FMedSci; FRS 1987; Director, Leeds Institute of Molecular Medicine, University of Leeds, since 2006; *b* 17 June 1946; *s* of Joan and Frederick Rabbitts; *m* 1984, Pamela Gage; one *d*, and one step *s* one step *d. Educ:* John Ruskin Grammar School; Univ. of East Anglia (BSc); Nat. Inst. for Medical Research

(PhD). Research Fellow, Dept of Genetics, Univ. of Edinburgh, 1971–73; Mem., Scientific Staff, 1973–2006, Jt Hd of Protein and Nucleic Acid Div., 1988–2002, MRC Lab. of Molecular Biology, Cambridge. Chair, Scientific Advisory Board: Cambridge Antibody Tech., 1990–97; Quadrant Healthcare, 1992–2000; Oakes Lyman Consolidated Hldgs Ltd, 2002–07; Member: Sci. Adv. Bd, Domantis, 2001–08; Med. Adv. Bd, OLK Investments, 2007–. Mem., EMBO, 1981–. FMedSci 1998. Colworth Medal, 1981, Ciba Medal and Prize, 1993, Biochemical Soc. *Publications:* papers in scientific jls. *Address:* Leeds Institute of Molecular Medicine, Wellcome Trust Brenner Building, St James's University Hospital, Leeds LS9 7TF.

RABENIRINA, Rt Rev. Remi Joseph; Archbishop of the Indian Ocean, 1995–2005; Bishop of Antananarivo, since 1984; *b* 6 March 1938; *s* of Joseph Razafindrabe and Josephine Ramanantenasoa; *m* 1971, Elisabeth Razaizanany; two *s* four *d. Educ:* Protestant Church schs; St Paul's Theol Coll., Ambatoharanana, Madagascar; Univ. of Madagascar; St Chad's Theol Coll., Lichfield; Ecumenical Inst. of Bossey, Switzerland. School teacher, 1958–61; Parish Priest: St James', Toamasina, 1967–68; St Matthew's, Antsiranana, 1968–73; St John's, Ambohimangakely (Antananarivo), 1973–84; Diocesan Chancellor, Antananarivo, 1982–84. Chevalier, Officier et Commandeur de l'Ordre National (Malagasy). *Publications:* (in Malagasy) An Open Door: a short history of the beginning of the Anglican Church in Northern Madagascar, 1969; (trans.) J. C. Fenton, Preaching the Cross, 1990; Some of the Saints (biogs of Saints remembered in the Anglican Church Calendar, Madagascar), 1998. *Recreations:* reading, writing. *Address:* Evêché Anglican, Lot VK57 Ter, Ambohimanoro, 101 Antananarivo, Madagascar. *T:* (20) 2220827.

RABIN, Prof. Brian Robert; Professor of Biochemistry, 1988–93, now Emeritus, Fellow since 1984, University College, London; *b* 4 Nov. 1927; *s* of Emanuel and Sophia Rabin, both British; *m* 1954; one *s* one *d. Educ:* Latymer Sch., Edmonton; University Coll., London. BSc 1951, MSc 1952, PhD 1956. University College, London: Asst Lectr, 1954–57; Lectr, 1957–63; Reader, 1963–67; Prof. of Enzymology, 1967–70; Hd of Dept of Biochemistry, 1970–88. Rockefeller Fellow, Univ. of California, 1956–57. Founder Dir, London Biotechnology Ltd, 1985–. Invented prosthetogen-based diagnostic detection technol., and reverse polarity ADEPT for cancer treatment. *Publications:* numerous in Biochem. Jl, European Jl of Biochem., Nature, Proc. Nat. Acad. Sciences US, etc. *Recreations:* travel, listening to music, carpentry. *Address:* 22 Leaf House, Catherine Place, Harrow, Middx HA1 2JW. *T:* (020) 8861 5278. *Club:* Athenæum.

RABINOVITCH, Prof. Benton Seymour, FRS 1987; Professor of Chemistry, University of Washington, Seattle, 1957–86, now Emeritus; *b* 19 Feb. 1919; *s* of Samuel Rabinovitch and Rachel Schachter; *m* 1st, 1949, Marilyn Werby; two *s* two *d*; 2nd, 1980, Flora Reitman. *Educ:* McGill Univ. (BSc, PhD). Served Canadian Army overseas, Captain, 1942–46. Milton Fellow, Harvard Univ., 1946–48; University of Washington: Asst Prof., 1948–53; Associate Prof., 1953–57. Guggenheim Fellow, 1961–62. Fellow: Amer. Acad. of Arts and Scis, 1979; APS. Hon. Liveryman, Goldsmiths' Co., 2000. Hon. DSc Technion, Haifa, 1991. Sigma Xi Dist. Res. Award, 1981; Peter Debye Award, ACS, 1984; Michael Polanyi Medal, RSC, 1984. *Publications:* Physical Chemistry, 1964; Antique Silver Servers, 1990; Contemporary Silver, 2000; Contemporary Silver Pt II, 2005; (ed) annual reviews Phys. Chem., 1975–85; over 200 contribs to jls. *Recreation:* silversmithing. *Address:* Department of Chemistry Box 351700, University of Washington, Seattle, WA 98195, USA. *T:* (206) 5431636.

RABINOWITZ, Harry, MBE 1977; freelance conductor and composer; *b* 26 March 1916; *s* of Israel and Eva Rabinowitz; *m* 1st, 1944, Lorna Thurlow Anderson (marr. diss. 2000); one *s* two *d*; 2nd, 2001, Mitzi Scott. *Educ:* Athlone High Sch., S Africa; Witwatersrand Univ.; Guildhall Sch. of Music. Conductor, BBC Radio, 1953–60; Musical Dir, BBC TV Light Entertainment, 1960–68; Head of Music, LWT, 1968–77; freelance film, TV, radio and disc activities, 1977–. Conductor, world premieres of: Cats, New London Th., 1981; Song and Dance, Palace Th., 1982; Hollywood Bowl Concerts, 1983 and 1984; Boston "Pops" concerts, 1985, 1986, 1988–92; concerts with RPO, LSO and London Concert Orch.; *films:* conductor: La Dentellière, 1977; Mon Oncle d'Amérique, 1980; The Time Bandits, 1980; Chariots of Fire, 1981; Heat and Dust, 1982; The Missionary, 1983; Electric Dreams (actor/conductor), 1984; The Bostonians, 1984; Return to Oz, Lady Jane Grey, and Revolution—1776, 1985; F/X, and Manhattan Project, 1986; Masters of the Universe, Maurice, 1987; Simon Wiesenthal, Camille Claudet, 1988; Shirley Valentine (jt composer/conductor), Queen of Hearts, 1989; Music Box, Lord of the Flies, La Fille des Collines, 1990; Jalousie, La Tribu, Jesuit Joe, Iran Day of Crisis, Ballad of the Sad Café, J'embrasse pas, Pour Sascha, 1991; Howards End, The Ark and the Flood, 1992; The Remains of the Day, Taxi de Nuit, Moonfish, Petite Apocalypse, 1993; Grosse Fatigue, The Flemish Board, Mantegna & Sons, 1994; Jefferson in Paris, Jenny et Mr Arnaud, The Stupids, 1995; The Proprietor, Secret Agent, Star Command, Surviving Picasso, The English Patient, 1996; Tonka, Wings of the Dove, My Story So Far, 1997; City of Angels, Soldiers' Daughters Don't Cry, Place Vendôme, 1998; Message in a Bottle, Cotton Mary, The Talented Mr Ripley, 1999; The Golden Bowl, 2000; Obsession, 2001; Le Divorce, 2002; Bon Voyage, 2003; Cold Mountain, 2003; *television:* composer-conductor: Agatha Christie Hour, 1982; Reilly Ace of Spies, 1983; Glorious Day, 1985; Land of the Eagle, 1990; D. W. Griffiths Father of Film, Memento Mori, 1993; Project Ayrton Senna, 1995; Alien Empire, 1996; Battle of the Sexes, Impossible Journeys, 1998. Freeman, City of London, 1995. Gold Badge of Merit, British Acad. of Songwriters, Composers and Authors, 1985; award for lifetime contribution to Wavendon Allmusic, 1990. *Recreations:* listening to others making music, gathering edible fungi, wine tasting. *Address:* 7 East View Cottages, Pursers Lane, Peaslake, Surrey GU5 9RG. *T:* (01306) 730674; *e-mail:* mitziscott@aol.com.

RABINOWITZ, Laurence Anton; QC 2002; *b* 3 May 1960; *s* of Joseph and Mary Rabinowitz; *m* 1989, Suzanne Benster; two *s* one *d*. *Educ:* Univ. of Witwatersrand (BA, LLB); Merton Coll., Oxford (BA, BCL). Called to the Bar, Middle Temple, 1987, Bencher, 2008; in practice specialising in commercial law; Jun. Counsel to Crown, Chancery, 1995–2002. Gov., N London Collegiate Sch., 2008. *Publication:* (ed) Weinberg and Blank on Take-overs and Mergers, 5th edn, 1989. *Recreations:* sport, music, reading. *Address:* (chambers) One Essex Court, Temple, EC4Y 9AR. *T:* (020) 7583 2000, *Fax:* (020) 7583 0118; *e-mail:* lrabinowitz@oeclaw.co.uk.

RACE, (Denys Alan) Reg; management and policy consultant; Managing Director, Quality Health management consultants, since 1993; *b* 23 June 1947; *s* of Denys and Elsie Race. *Educ:* Sale Grammar School; Univ. of Kent (BA (Politics and Sociology), PhD (Politics)). Senior Research Officer, National Union of Public Employees, 1972. MP (Lab) Haringey, Wood Green, 1979–83. Contested (Lab) Chesterfield, 2001. Head of Programme Office, GLC, 1983–86; Special Res. Officer, ACTT, 1986; County Dir, Derbys County Council, 1988. Advr, Health Policy Adv. Unit, 1989–93. *Publications:* The Challenge Now (report on management and organisation of ACTT), 1986; numerous pamphlets and articles in Labour Movement press.

RACE, John William B.; *see* Burton-Race.

RACE, Steve, (Stephen Russell Race), OBE 1992; broadcaster, musician and author; *b* Lincoln, 1 April 1921; *s* of Russell Tinniswood Race and Robina Race (*née* Hurley); *m* 1st, Marjorie Clair Leng (*d* 1969); one *d*; 2nd, Léonie Rebecca Govier Mather. *Educ:* Lincoln Sch. (now Christ's Hospital Sch.); Royal Academy of Music. FRAM 1978. Served War, RAF, 1941–46; free-lance pianist, arranger and composer, 1946–55; Light Music Adviser to Associated-Rediffusion Ltd, 1955–60; presenter, Our World (first global TV Prog.) from Beatles' recording studio, 1967; conductor for many TV series incl. Tony Hancock and Peter Sellers Shows. Appearances in radio and TV shows include: My Music, A Good Read, Jazz in Perspective, Any Questions?, Kaleidoscope, Musician at Large With Great Pleasure, Desert Island Discs, Steve Race Presents the Radio Orchestra Show, The Two Worlds of Joseph Race; radio reviews in The Listener, 1975–80; long-playing records and commentary for Nat. Gall., London, Glasgow Art Gall. and Nat. Mus. of Wales, 1977–80. Dep. Chm., PRS, 1973–76. Member: Council, Royal Albert Hall of Arts and Scis, 1976–95; Exec. Council, Musicians' Benevolent Fund, 1985–95. FRSA 1975. Freeman, City of London, 1982. Governor of Tokyo Metropolis Prize for Radio, 1979; Wavendon Allmusic Media Personality of the Year, 1987; Radio Prog. of the Year, TV and Radio Industries Club Awards, 1988; Gold Badge of Merit for services to British music, BASCA, 1991. *Principal compositions:* Nicola (Ivor Novello Award); Faraway Music; The Pied Piper; incidental music for Richard The Third, Cyrano de Bergerac, Twelfth Night (BBC); Cantatas: Song of King David; The Day of the Donkey; Songs of Praise; My Music—My Songs; misc. works incl. ITV advertising sound-tracks (Venice Award, 1962; Cannes Award, 1963); film scores include: Calling Paul Temple, Three Roads to Rome, Against The Tide, Land of Three Rivers. *Publications:* Musician at Large: an autobiography, 1979; My Music, 1979; Dear Music Lover, 1981; Steve Race's Music Quiz, 1983; You Can't be Serious, 1985; The Penguin Masterquiz, 1985; (contrib.) With Great Pleasure, 1986; The Two Worlds of Joseph Race, 1988; (contrib.) The Illustrated Counties of England, 1984; contribs to DNB, Punch, Literary Review, Times, Daily Telegraph (crossword compiler, 1998–), Daily Mail, Independent, Listener, Country Living. *Recreations:* avoiding smokers, learning to lip-read. *Address:* Martins End Lane, Great Missenden, Bucks HP16 9HS.

RACEY, Prof. Paul Adrian, FRSE; FIBiol; Regius Professor of Natural History, University of Aberdeen, since 1993; *b* 7 May 1944; *s* of Albert and Esme Racey; *m* 1968, Anna Priscilla Notcutt; three *s*. *Educ:* Ratcliffe Coll.; Downing Coll., Cambridge (MA); London Univ. (PhD); Univ. of Aberdeen (DSc). FIBiol 1987; FRSE 1992. Rothamsted Experimental Station, 1965–66; Zoological Soc. of London, 1966–71; Res. Fellow, Univ. of Liverpool, 1971–73; University of Aberdeen: Lectr and Sen. Lectr in Zoology, 1973–85; Prof. of Zoology, 1985–93. Chairman: Chiroptera Specialist Gp, IUCN Species Survival Commn, 1986–; Bat Conservation Trust, 1990–96; Member: Scottish Exam. Bd, 1985–90; Management Cttee, Scottish Univs Res. and Reactor Centre, 1991–95 (Mem. Sci. Adv. Bd, 1986–90); Council, Fauna & Flora International (formerly Fauna & Flora Preservation Soc.), 1990– (Chm., Conservation Cttee, 1993–; Vice-Pres., 2006–); Bd of Govs, Macaulay Land Use Res. Inst., 1990–2001; NCC for Scotland, 1991–92; Terrestrial and Freshwater Sci. Cttee, NERC, 1991–94; Exec. Cttee, Mammal Soc., 1991–98; Res. Bd, 1992–94, Scientific Adv. Cttee, 1994–2001 (Chm., 1996–2001), SE Regl Bd, 1996–97, Scottish Natural Heritage; Council, Zool Soc. of London, 1999–2003 (Vice Pres., 2001–03; Member: Adv. Cttee for Sci. and Conservation, 1996–2000 (Chm., 1999–2000); Awards Cttee, 2003–07); Council for Scotland, WWF, 1997–2000. *Publications:* numerous res. papers in professional jls. *Recreations:* riding, sailing, walking, farming. *Address:* Chapelhouses, Oldmeldrum AB51 0AW. *T:* (01651) 872769.

RACKHAM, Dr Oliver, OBE 1998; FBA 2002; Fellow, since 1964, and Master 2007–08, Corpus Christi College, Cambridge; *b* 17 Oct. 1939; *s* of Geoffrey Herbert Rackham and Norah Kathleen Rackham (*née* Wilson). *Educ:* Norwich Sch.; Norwich City Coll.; Corpus Christi Coll., Cambridge (Natural Scis Tripos, BA 1961, MA 1964, PhD 1964). Jun. Proctor, 1996–97, Hon. Prof., 2006–, Cambridge Univ. DU Essex, 2000. *Publications:* Hayley Wood, its history and ecology, 1975; Trees and Woodland in the British Landscape, 1976, 2nd edn 1990; Ancient Woodland: its history, vegetation and uses in England, 1980, 2nd edn 2003; The History of the Countryside, 1986; Ancient Woodland of England: the woods of South-East Essex, 1986; The Last Forest: the story of Hatfield Forest, 1989; The Illustrated History of the Countryside, 1994; (with J. A. Moody) The Making of the Cretan Landscape, 1996; (with A. T. Grove) The Nature of Southern Europe: an ecological history, 2001; Treasures of Silver at Corpus Christi College, Cambridge, 2002; Woodlands, 2006. *Recreation:* archaeology, especially of carpentry. *Address:* Corpus Christi College, Cambridge CB2 1RH. *T:* (01223) 360144; *e-mail:* or10001@cam.ac.uk.

RADCLIFFE, Andrew Allen; QC 2000; a Recorder, since 2000; *b* 21 Jan. 1952; *s* of Reginald Allen Radcliffe and Sheila Radcliffe (*née* McNeil); *m* 1977 (marr. diss. 1990); two *s* one *d*; partner, Jane Alex Lewis. *Educ:* Birkenhead Sch.; St Edmund Hall, Oxford (BA Hons 1974). Called to the Bar, Middle Temple, 1975; Asst Recorder, 1998–2000. Mem. Cttee, Criminal Bar Assoc., 1998–2001. *Recreation:* sport. *Address:* 2 Hare Court, Temple, EC4Y 7BH. *T:* (020) 7353 5324. *Club:* Radlett Cricket.

RADCLIFFE, Anthony Frank, FSA; Hon. Keeper of Renaissance and Baroque Sculpture, Fitzwilliam Museum, since 1996; *b* Wivenhoe, Essex, 23 Feb. 1933; *s* of late Dr Walter Radcliffe and Muriel Laure Radcliffe (*née* Brée); *m* 1960, Enid Clair Cawkwell; two *s*. *Educ:* Oundle Sch.; Gonville and Caius Coll., Cambridge (MA). Victoria and Albert Museum: joined Dept of Circulation, 1958; transferred to Dept of Architecture and Sculpture, 1960; Res. Asst, Dept of Circulation, 1961–67; Asst to Dir, 1967–74; Asst Keeper, Dept of Architecture and Sculpture, 1974–79; Keeper of Sculpture, 1979–89; Head of Res., 1989–90; Keeper Emeritus, 1990–96. Mellon Sen. Vis. Curator, Nat. Gall. of Art, Washington, 1990; Guest Scholar, J. Paul Getty Mus., 1991, 1995; Samuel H. Kress Prof., CASVA, Nat. Gall. of Art, Washington, 1993–94. Member: Adv. Council, NACF, 1993–; Consultative Cttee, Burlington Magazine, 1990–. Medal, Accademia delle Arti del Disegno, Florence, 1986. Cavaliere Ufficiale al Merito della Repubblica Italiana, 2003. *Publications:* European Bronze Statuettes, 1966; Jean-Baptiste Carpeaux, 1968; (with J. Pope-Hennessy and T. Hodgkinson) The Frick Collection: an illustrated catalogue, III, IV, 1970; (with C. Avery) Giambologna, sculptor to the Medici, 1978; (with M. Baker and M. Maek Gérard) The Thyssen-Bornemisza Collection: Renaissance and later sculpture, 1992; The Robert H. Smith Collection: Bronzes 1500–1650, 1994; (jtly) The Robert H. Smith Collection: Art of the Renaissance Bronze 1500–1650, 2004; contribs to Burlington Mag., Apollo, Connoisseur, etc. *Address:* 203 Waller Road, SE14 5LX. *T:* (020) 7639 4605.

RADCLIFFE, Francis Charles Joseph; *b* 23 Oct. 1939; *s* of Charles Joseph Basil Nicholas Radcliffe and Norah Radcliffe (*née* Percy); *m* 1968, Nicolette, *e d* of Eugene Randag; one *s* two *d*. *Educ:* Ampleforth Coll.; Gonville and Caius Coll., Cambridge (MA). Called to the Bar, Gray's Inn, 1962; a Recorder of the Crown Court, 1979, until submitted 'Lawful marriage is good, just and indissoluble' (1540 Henry VIII c. 38). Contested (Christian: stop abortion candidate) York, 1979; founded York Christian Party, 1981. Chm., Life, York. *Recreations:* shooting, beagling, gardening, etc. *Address:* KBW, 3 Park Court, off Park Cross Street, Leeds LS1 2QH.

RADCLIFFE, Nora; Member (Lib Dem) Gordon, Scottish Parliament, 1999–2007; *b* 4 March 1946; *d* of late James Stuart MacPherson and Doreen MacPherson (*née* McRobb); *m* 1972, Michael Anthony Radcliffe; one *s* one *d*. *Educ:* Bowmore Primary Sch.; Peterculter Primary Sch.; High Sch. for Girls, Aberdeen; Aberdeen Univ. Hotel mgt, 1968–72; Grampian Health Board: Community Liaison Team, 1993–96; Primary Care Develt Team, 1996–99. Mem. (Lib Dem), Gordon DC, 1988–92. Contested (Lib Dem) Gordon, Scottish Parlt, 2007. *Recreations:* reading, walking, good food. *Address:* 3 King Street, Inverurie, Aberdeenshire AB51 4SY. *T:* (01467) 622575.

RADCLIFFE, Paula Jane, MBE 2002; professional athlete; Great Britain Women's Team Captain, since 1998; *b* 17 Dec. 1973; *d* of Peter Radcliffe and Patricia Radcliffe; *m* 2000, Gary Lough; one *d*. *Educ:* Loughborough Univ. (1st cl. Hons Mod. European Studies 1996). World Junior Champion, cross-country, 1992; European Champion: cross-country, 1998, 2003; 10,000m, 2002; Silver Medal for 10,000m, World Championships, 1999; World Champion: half marathon, 2000, 2001, 2003; cross-country, 2001, 2002; marathon, 2005; Commonwealth Champion, 5000m, 2002; winner of London Marathon, 2002, 2003 (World Record, 2 hours 15 mins 25 secs), 2005; winner of Chicago Marathon, 2002; winner of New York Marathon, 2004, 2007; European Record Holder: 10,000m (30 mins 1.09 secs, 2002), half marathon (1 hour 6 mins 47 secs, 2001), marathon; GB Record Holder: 3000m (8 mins 22.20 secs, 2002), 5000m (14 mins 29.11 secs, 2004), 10,000m (30 mins 1.10 secs, 2002), half marathon, marathon. DUniv: De Montfort, 2001; Loughborough, 2002. *Publication:* Paula: my story so far, 2004. *Recreations:* athletics!, travel, reading. *T:* (01509) 236431, *Fax:* 0870 1656171. *Club:* Bedford and County Athletic.

RADCLIFFE, Sir Sebastian Everard, 7th Bt *cr* 1813; *b* 8 June 1972; *s* of Sir Joseph Benedict Everard Henry Radcliffe, 6th Bt, MC and of Marcia Anne Helen (who *m* 1988, H. M. S. Tanner), *y d* of Major David Turville Constable Maxwell, Bosworth Hall, Husbands Bosworth, Rugby; *S* father, 1975; *m* 2005, Jacinta (*née* Lynch); one *d*. *Heir: cousin* Mark Hugh Joseph Radcliffe [*b* 22 April 1938; *m* 1963, Anne, twin *d* of Maj.-Gen. Arthur Evers Brocklehurst, CB, DSO; three *d*]. *Address:* Le Château de Cheseaux, 1033 Cheseaux, Vaud, Switzerland.

RADCLIFFE, Fr Timothy Peter Joseph, OP; Master of the Order of Preachers (Dominicans), 1992–2001; Sarum Canon of Salisbury Cathedral, since 2007; *b* 22 Aug. 1945; 3rd *s* of late Hugh John Reginald Joseph Radcliffe, MBE, and Marie-Therese, *d* of Maj.-Gen. Sir Cecil Pereira, KCB, CMG; *g s* of Sir Everard Radcliffe, 5th Bt. *Educ:* Downside; St John's College, Oxford (MA; Hon. Fellow, 1993). Entered Dominican Order, 1965; Chaplain to Imperial Coll., 1976–78; taught theology at Blackfriars, Oxford, 1978–88; Prior of Blackfriars, 1982–88; Faculty of Theology, Oxford Univ., 1985–88; Provincial of the English Province, OP, 1988–92. John Toohey Schol. in Residence, Sydney Univ., 1984. Grand Chancellor: Pontifical Univ. of St Thomas (Angelicum), Rome, 1992–2001; Univ. of Santo Tomas, Manila, 1992–2001; Theol. Faculty, Fribourg, 1992–2001; Ecole Biblique, Jerusalem, 1992–2001. Mem. Bd, CAFOD, 2002–. Pres., Conf. of Major Religious Superiors, 1991–92. Mem. Bd, New Blackfriars, 2003 (Chm., Editl Bd, 1983–88). Patron: Margaret Beaufort Inst., Cambridge, 1992–; Eckhart Soc., 1999–. Hon. STD Providence Coll., RI, 1993; Hon. LLD: Barry Univ., Florida, 1996; Molloy Coll., NY, 2005; Hon. DHumLit: Ohio Dominican Coll., 1996; Dominican Univ., Chicago, 2002; Aquinas Inst., St Louis Univ., 2007; Siena Heights Univ., 2007; Hon. DD Oxford, 2003; Hon. Dr Univ. Catholique de l'Ouest, 2006. Prix de littérature religieuse, Le syndicat des libraires de littérature religieuses de France, 2001; Spiritualités d'aujourd'hui, Le Centre Méditerranéen de Littérature, 2001. Hon. Citizen: Augusta (Italy); Sepahua (Peru). *Publications:* El Manantial de la Esperanza Salamanca, 1998; Sing a New Song: the Christian vocation, 2000; I Call You Friends, 2001; Seven Last Words, 2004; What is the Point of Being a Christian?, 2005 (trans. French; Prix des Lecteurs de la Procure, 2006; Michael Ramsey Prize, 2007); (ed) Just One Year, 2006; articles in books and periodicals. *Recreations:* walking and talking with friends, reading Dickens. *Address:* Blackfriars, St Giles, Oxford OX1 3LY. *T:* (01865) 278422.

RADCLYFFE, Sarah; Managing Director, Sarah Radclyffe Productions Ltd, since 1993; *b* 14 Nov. 1950; *d* of Charles Raymond Radclyffe, LVO and Helen Egerton Radclyffe; one *s* by Graham Bradstreet; *m* 1996, William Godfrey; one *s*. *Educ:* Heathfield Sch., Ascot. Jt Founder, 1984, Jt Man. Dir, 1984–93, Working Title; *films* produced include: My Beautiful Laundrette, 1984; Caravaggio, 1985; Wish You Were Here, 1985; Paperhouse, 1987; Sammy and Rosie Get Laid, 1988; A World Apart, 1988; Fools of Fortune, 1989; Robin Hood, 1990; Edward II, 1991; Sirens, 1993; Second Best, 1993; Bent, 1997; Cousin Bette, 1997; Les Misérables, 1997; The War Zone, 1998; There's Only One Jimmy Grimble, 1999; Love's Brother, 2003; Tara Road, 2004; Free Jimmy, 2006; How About You, 2007; The Edge of Love, 2008. Non-exec. Dir, Channel Four TV, 1995–99; Gov., BFI, 1996–99; Dir, Film Council, 2000–04. Simon Olswang Business Woman of the Year Award, 1993. *Recreations:* travel, ski-ing. *Address:* Sarah Radclyffe Productions Ltd, 10/11 St George's Mews, NW1 8XE; *e-mail:* sarah@srpltd.co.uk.

RADDA, Prof. Sir George (Karoly), Kt 2000; CBE 1993; MA, DPhil; FRS 1980; Professor and Head of Department of Physiology, Anatomy and Genetics, University of Oxford, since 2006; Professorial Fellow, Merton College, Oxford, 1984–2003 and since 2006; *b* 9 June 1936; *s* of Dr Gyula Radda and Dr Anna Bernolak; *m* 1st, 1961, Mary O'Brien (marr. diss. 1995); two *s* one *d*; 2nd, 1995, Sue Bailey. *Educ:* Pannonhalma, Hungary; Eötvös Univ., Budapest, Hungary; Merton Coll., Oxford (BA Cl. 1, Chem., 1960; DPhil 1962). Res. Associate, Univ. of California, 1962–63; University of Oxford: Lectr in Organic Chemistry, St John's Coll., 1963–64; Fellow and Tutor in Organic

Chem., Merton Coll., 1964–84; Lectr in Biochem., 1966–84, Hd of Dept of Biochem., 1991–96; British Heart Foundn Prof. of Molecular Cardiol., 1984–2003 (on leave of absence, 1996–2003); Chief Exec., MRC, 1996–2003. Vis. Prof., Cleveland Clinic, 1987. Medical Research Council: Mem. Council, 1988–92; Chm., Cell Biology and Disorders Bd, 1988–92; Chm., Human Genome Directed Programme Cttee, 1992–96; Hon. Dir, Unit of Biochemical and Clin. Magnetic Resonance, 1988–96. Member of Council: Royal Soc., 1990–92; ICRF, 1991–96 (Chm., Scientific Adv. Cttee, 1994–96). Chm., Singapore Bioimaging Consortium, 2005–; Res. Dir, Lab. of Metabolic Medicine, Singapore, 2005–. Non-exec. Dir, BTG plc, 1999–2005. Mem., various Editorial Bds of scientific jls including: Editor, Biochemical and Biophysical Research Communications, 1977–85; Man. Editor, Biochimica et Biophysica Acta, 1977–94 (Chm. Edtl Bd, 1989–94); Mem. Editorial Bd, Interface, 2004–. Founder Mem., Oxford Enzyme Gp, 1970–86; Pres., Soc. for Magnetic Resonance in Medicine, 1985–86. Mem., Fachbeirat, Max Planck Inst. für Systemphysiologie, Dortmund, 1987–93; Internat. Adv. Council Mem., Biomed. Res. Council, Singapore, 2003–06 (Bd Mem., 2005–). Trustee, Cancer Res. UK, 2003–06 (Dep. Chm., 2005–06). Mem., EMBO, 1997; MAE 1999; Fellow: Soc. of Magnetic Resonance, 1994; Internat. Acad. Cardiovascular Scis, 2001; Founding Fellow, Internat. Soc. Heart Res., 2000. Founder FMedSci 1998. Hon. Mem., Eur. Soc. of Magnetic Resonance and Biol., 2007. Hon. FRCR 1985; Hon. MRCP 1987, Hon. FRCP 1997; Hon. Fellow, Amer. Heart Assoc., 1988. Hon. DM Bern, 1985; Hon. DSc (Med) London, 1991; Hon. DSc: Stirling, 1998; Sheffield, 1999; Debrecen, Hungary, 2001; Birmingham, 2003; Univ. de la Méditerranée, 2003; Aberdeen, 2004; Düsseldorf, 2004; Semmelweis Univ., Budapest, 2004; Hull, 2005; Leicester, 2006. Colworth Medal, Biochem. Soc., 1969; Feldberg Prize, Feldberg Foundn, 1982; British Heart Foundn Prize and Gold Medal for cardiovascular research, 1982; CIBA Medal and Prize, Biochem. Soc., 1983; Gold Medal, Soc. for Magnetic Resonance in Medicine, 1984; Buchanan Medal, Royal Soc., 1987; Internat. Lectr and Citation, Amer. Heart Assoc., 1987; Skinner Lecture and Medal, RCR, 1989; Rank Prize in Nutrition, 1991; Medal of Merit, Internat. Acad. of Cardiovascular Res., 2006. *Publications:* articles in books and in jls of biochemistry and medicine. *Recreations:* opera, swimming, jazz. *Address:* Department of Physiology, Anatomy and Genetics, Sherrington Building, Parks Road, Oxford OX1 3PT.

RADEGONDE, Sylvestre Louis; Principal Secretary, Ministry of Foreign Affairs, The Seychelles, 2004–05; High Commissioner of The Seychelles to Malaysia, India, Australia and New Zealand, and Ambassador to Japan, Republic of Korea, China and Indonesia, 1998; *b* 16 March 1956. *Educ:* Seychelles Coll.; Polytechnic of Central London (MA Diplomatic Studies). Seychelles Police Force, 1974–85; Dir, Nat. Council for Children, 1985–86; Personnel Manager, Seychelles Hotels, 1986–87; Chief of Protocol and Desk Officer for Americas, Min. Planning and Ext. Relns, 1987–89; Counsellor and Actg High Comr, 1989–92, High Comr, 1992–93, London; Ambassador to EC and Belgium, 1993–97, concurrently to Germany, Netherlands and Luxembourg; Dir-Gen. of Internat. Relns, Min. of For. Affairs, 2004. *Recreations:* cooking, swimming. *Address:* c/o Ministry of Foreign Affairs, PO Box 656, Maison Quéau de Quinssy, Mont Fleuri, Mahé, Seychelles.

RADER, Gen. Paul Alexander; General of the Salvation Army, 1994–99; *b* 14 March 1934; *s* of Lt-Col Lyell Rader and Gladys (*née* Damon); *m* 1956, (Frances) Kay Fuller; one *s* two *d*. *Educ:* Asbury Coll. and Seminary, USA (BA, BD); Southern Baptist Seminary (MTh); Fuller Theol Seminary (DMiss). Salvation Army: trng work in Korea, 1962–73; Trng Principal, 1973; Educn Sec., 1974–76; Asst Chief Sec., 1976, Chief Sec., 1977–84, Korea; Trng Principal, USA Eastern Territory, 1984–87; Divl Comdr, 1987–89; Chief Sec., 1989; Territorial Comdr, USA Western, 1989–94. Pres., Asbury Coll., Wilmore, Ky, 2000–06. Hon. LLD Asbury Coll., USA, 1984; Hon. DD: Asbury Theol Seminary, USA, 1995; Roberts Wesleyan Coll., USA, 1998; Hon. LHD Greenville Coll., USA, 1997. *Recreations:* jogging, reading, music. *Address:* 3953 Rock Ledge Lane, Lexington, KY 40513, USA.

RADFORD, Dr David; Chairman, Devon Primary Care Trust, since 2006; *b* 22 April 1949; *s* of Ken and Dorothy Radford; *m* 1st, 1970, Josephine Mogridge; one *d*; 2nd, 1976, Madeleine Margaret Simms; two *d*. *Educ:* RN Sch., Malta; St John's Sch., Singapore; Manchester Univ. (BSc Hons Chem., MSc Organisation of Technology, PhD). Consumer Services Manager, CWS, 1974–75; Res. Dir, Welsh Consumer Council, 1975–77; Head of Res., Inst. of Housing, 1977–81; Asst Dir of Housing, Wolverhampton MBC, 1981–86; Asst Chief Exec., Wolverhampton MBC, 1986–90; Asst Chief Exec., Northants CC, 1990–97; Chief Exec., Somerset CC, 1997–2002; Lead Govt Official, Plymouth CC, 2003–06. Chm., SW Constitutional Convention, 2003–. *Recreations:* hill and coast walking, concert-going, sailing.

RADFORD, David Wyn; His Honour Judge Radford; Circuit Judge, since 1996, Senior Circuit Judge, since 2002; *b* 3 Jan. 1947; *s* of late Robert Edwin Radford, CB and of Eleanor Margaret Radford (*née* Jones); *m* 1972, Nadine Radford, *qv*; two *s* two *d*. *Educ:* Cranleigh Sch.; Selwyn Coll., Cambridge (MA, LLM). Called to the Bar, Gray's Inn, 1969; Asst Recorder, 1988; Recorder, 1993. *Recreations:* supporting Manchester City FC, theatre, walking, spending time with family. *Address:* Snaresbrook Crown Court, 75 Hollybush Hill, E11 1QW.

RADFORD, Georgina Margaret, (Gina), FRCP, FFPH; Director of Public Health, NHS Fife, since 2007; *b* 25 April 1955; *d* of Edward Arthur Radford and Elsie (*née* Burdon). *Educ:* Guildford Co. Grammar Sch. for Girls; Royal Free Hosp. Sch. of Medicine (MB BS 1979). DCH 1982; DRCOG 1983; MFPHM 1989, FFPH (FFPHM 1997); FRCP 2002. Consultant in Public Health Medicine, S and W Surrey DHA, 1988–94; Dir of Public Health, S and W Devon HA, 1994–97; Hd, Public Health Develt Unit, NHS Exec., DoH, 1997–99; Regl Dir of Public Health, E of England, DoH, 2000–06. *Recreations:* riding, singing/music, reading, travel, church warden and village duck warden! *Address:* Department of Public Health, NHS Fife, Cameron House, Cameron Bridge, Leven, Fife KY8 5RG. *T:* (01592) 226459.

RADFORD, Nadine Poggioli; QC 1995; a Recorder of the Crown Court, since 1995; *m* 1972, David Wyn Radford, *qv*; two *s* two *d*. Called to the Bar, Lincoln's Inn, 1974, Bencher, 1999; formerly an Assistant Recorder. *Address:* 15 New Bridge Street, EC4V 6AU.

RADFORD, Prof. Peter Frank, PhD; Professor, Department of Sport Sciences, Brunel University, 1997–2005 (Hon. Professor Associate, School of Sport and Education, 2007); *b* 20 Sept. 1939; *s* of Frank Radford and Lillian E. Radford (*née* Marks); *m* 1961, Margaret M. (*née* Beard); one *d*. *Educ:* Tettenhall Coll.; Cardiff Coll. of Educn (Dip. of Physical Educn); Purdue Univ., USA (MSc); Univ. of Glasgow (PhD 1978). Mem., GB Athletics Teams, 1958–64: held British 100m record, 1958–78; World Records: Jun. 100m and Jun. 200m, 1958; Indoor 50m, 1959; 200m and 220 yards, 1960; 4 × 110 yards Relay, 1963; Bronze Medals, 100m and 4 × 100m Relay, Olympic Games, Rome, 1960. Lectr and Asst Prof., Sch. of Physical Educn and Athletics, McMaster Univ., 1967–75; University of Glasgow: Professor and Head of Departments of: Physical Educn and Recreation, 1976–87; Physical Educn and Sports Sci., 1987–94; Head of Dept, 1997–2000, Dir of Res., 2000–05, Dept of Sport Scis, Brunel Univ. Vice-Chm., 1992–93, Chm., 1993–94, Exec. Chm., 1994–97, British Athletic Fedn. Scottish Sports Council: Mem., 1983–90; Mem., 1988–91, Chm., 1991–96, Drug Adv. Gp; Chm., Rev. of Coaching in Sport, 1991–93. Mem., Internat. Wkg Gp on Anti-Doping in Sport, 1991–93; Vice-Chm., 1992–94, Chm., 1994–98, Internat. Doping Convention, Council of Europe; Member: Saudi/British Memorandum of Understanding for Sport and Youth Welfare, 1990–2007; Compliance with Commitments Project, Council of Europe, 1998–99. Hon. DSc Wolverhampton, 2006. *Publications:* The Celebrated Captain Barclay, 2001; contrib. to various jls, conf. proc. and books on topics of sport, educn, sports science, sports history and doping control. *Recreations:* sports history 1650–1850, 18th and 19th century sporting art, gardening. *Address:* Bank House, 8 Sheep Street, Burford, Oxon OX18 4LT. *T:* (01993) 824836.

RADFORD, Timothy Robin; Science Editor, The Guardian, 1992–2005; *b* NZ, 9 Oct. 1940; *s* of Keith Ballantyne Radford and Agnes Radford; *m* 1964, Maureen Grace Coveney; one *s* one *d*. *Educ:* Sacred Heart Coll., Auckland. Reporter, NZ Herald, 1957–60; sub-ed., Fishing News, London, 1961–62; reporter, Hull Daily Mail, 1963–65; sub-ed., Dover Express, 1965–68; COI, 1968–73; joined The Guardian, 1973: Letters Ed., 1975–77; Arts Ed., 1977–80; Dep. Features Ed., 1980–88; Literary Ed., 1989–91. FRGS 1990. *Publications:* The Crisis of Life on Earth, 1990; (ed) Frontiers 01: science and technology 2001–02, 2002; (ed) Frontiers 03: new writing on cutting edge science by leading scientists, 2003. *Recreations:* reading, walking, travel. *Address:* 41 Downside Close, Eastbourne, E Sussex BN20 8EL.

RADICE, Baron *cr* 2001 (Life Peer), of Chester-le-Street in the County of Durham; **Giles Heneage Radice;** PC 1999; *b* 4 Oct. 1936. *Educ:* Winchester; Magdalen Coll., Oxford. Head of Research Dept, General and Municipal Workers' Union (GMWU), 1966–73. MP (Lab) Chester-le-Street, March 1973–1983, Durham North, 1983–2001. Front bench spokesman on foreign affairs, 1981, on employment, 1981–83, on education, 1983–87; Mem., Treasury and Civil Service Select Cttee, 1987–96; Chairman: Public Service Select Cttee, 1996–97; Treasury Select Cttee, 1997–2001. Chm., EU Economic and Financial Affairs Sub-cttee, H of L, 2002–06. Mem., Council, Policy Studies Inst., 1978–83. Chairman: European Movt, 1995–2001; British Assoc. for Central and Eastern Europe, 1997–2008 (Vice Chm., 1991–97); Franco British Council, 2002–07; Policy Network, 2007–. Parly Fellow, St Antony's Coll., Oxford, 1994–95. Order of Merit (Germany), 1996; Légion d'Honneur (France), 2004. *Publications:* Democratic Socialism, 1965; (ed jointly) More Power to People, 1968; (co-author) Will Thorne, 1974; The Industrial Democrats, 1978; (co-author) Socialists in Recession, 1986; Labour's Path to Power: the new revisionism, 1989; Offshore: Britain and the European idea, 1992; The New Germans, 1995; (ed) What Needs to Change, 1996; Friends & Rivals, 2002; Diaries 1980–2001: the political diaries of Giles Radice, 2004. *Recreations:* reading, tennis. *Address:* The Longhouse, 3 Gelston, near Grantham, Lincs NG32 2AE.

RADICE, Elizabeth Joy; Headmistress, Haberdashers' Aske's School for Girls, Elstree, since 2005; *b* 5 Feb. 1951; *d* of Donald and Joy Stephenson; *m* 1973, William Radice; two *d*. *Educ:* Wycombe Abbey Sch., High Wycombe; Somerville Coll., Oxford (BA Hons 1972). Hd of English, Sch. of St Helen and St Katharine, Abingdon, 1985–92; Dir of Studies, Royal Grammar Sch., Newcastle-upon-Tyne, 1996–98; Headmistress, Channing Sch., Highgate, London, 1999–2005. *Recreations:* books, theatre, film, cooking. *Address:* Haberdashers' Aske's School for Girls, Aldenham Road, Elstree, Herts WD6 3BT. *T:* (020) 8266 2300.

RADICE, Vittorio; Chief Executive, La Rinascente, since 2005; *b* Como, Italy, 2 April 1957; *m* Gemma; two *s*. *Educ:* Univ. of Milan. Head of Worldwide Sourcing, Home Furnishings Dept, Associated Merchandising Corp.; Buying Dir, Habitat Internat., 1990–92; Man. Dir, Habitat UK, 1992–96; Man. Dir, 1996–98, Chief Exec., 1998–2003, Selfridges plc; Exec. Dir, Home, Marks and Spencer plc, 2003–04. Non-executive Director: Abbey (formerly Abbey National) plc, 2001–04; Shoppers Stop India, 2001–; McArthurGlen, 2005–.

RADJI, Parviz Camran; diplomat; Ambassador of Iran to the Court of St James's, 1976–79; *b* 1936; *m* 1986, Golgoun Partovi. *Educ:* Trinity Hall, Cambridge (MA Econs). National Iranian Oil Co., 1959–62; Private Sec. to Minister of Foreign Affairs, 1962–65; Private Sec. to Prime Minister, subseq. Personal Asst, 1965–72; Special Adviser to Prime Minister, 1972–76. *Publication:* In the Service of the Peacock Throne: the diaries of the Shah's last Ambassador to London, 1983. *Address:* 20 Embankment Gardens, SW3 4LW.

RADNOR, 9th Earl of, *cr* 1765; **William Pleydell-Bouverie;** Bt 1713–14; Viscount Folkestone, Baron Longford, 1747; Baron Pleydell-Bouverie, 1765; *b* 5 Jan. 1955; *s* of 8th Earl of Radnor and Anne, *d* of Donald Seth-Smith, MC; *S* father, 2008; *m* 1996, Melissa, *d* of James Stanford, *qv*; four *s* two *d*. *Educ:* Harrow; Royal Agricultural Coll., Cirencester. *Heir:* *s* Viscount Folkestone, *qv*.

RADOMSKY, Rabbi David; educational consultant; *b* 4 Sept. 1956; *s* of Benjamin and Rachel Radomsky; *m* 1981, Naomi; three *s* one *d*. *Educ:* BA Hons, MA (Dist.); Teaching Dip. NPQH. Ordained rabbi; rabbi/teacher, Mid Rashiat Noam Yeshiva High Sch., Israel, 1982–85; Communal Rabbi, Dublin, 1985–88; Rabbi, Wembley Synagogue, 1988–93; pt-time Lectr, Jews' Coll., 1991–93; Dep. Headteacher, Immanuel Coll., 1993–2000; Headteacher, Hasmonean High Sch., 2000–06. *Address:* *e-mail:* Dradomsky@hotmail.com.

RAE, Barbara Davis, CBE 1999; RA 1996, RSA 1992 (ARSA 1980); RSW 1975; RGI; artist; *b* 10 Dec. 1943; *d* of James Rae and Mary (*née* Young); *m* twice; one *s*. *Educ:* Morrison's Acad., Crieff; Edinburgh Coll. of Art (Dip.; Postgrad. Travelling Schol.); Moray House Coll. of Education. Art Teacher: Ainsley Park Comprehensive, Edinburgh, 1968–69; Portobello Secondary Sch., Edinburgh, 1969–72; Lectr in Drawing, Painting and Printmaking, Aberdeen Coll. of Educn, 1972–75; Lectr in Drawing and Painting, Glasgow Sch. of Art, 1975–96; exchange teacher, Fine Art Dept, Univ. of Md, 1984. Resident artist: Ballinglen Arts Centre, Co. Mayo, 2002–; Cill Rialaig Project, Co. Kerry, 2003. Member: Art Panel, CNAA, 1986–93; Bd of Friends, Royal Scottish Acad.; Royal Fine Art Commn for Scotland, 1995–2005; Trustee, Arts Educnl Trust, 1986–90. Mem., SSA (Pres., 1983); Mem. Council, RSW, 1986–90, Vice-Pres. (E), 1991–. Member, Board of Trustees: British Sch. at Rome, 1997–2000; Hospitalfield House, Arbroath, 1997–99. Solo exhibitions include: New '57 Gall., Edinburgh, 1967, 1971; Univ. of York, 1969; Univ. of Aberdeen and Aberdeen Art Gall., 1974; Peterloo Gall., Manchester, 1975; Stirling Gall. and Greenock Arts Guild, 1976; Univ. of Edinburgh, 1978, 1979; Gilbert Parr Gall., London, 1977; Scottish Gall., Edinburgh, 1979, 1983, 1987, 1988, 1990, 1995, 1998, 2000, 2002, 2003, 2005, 2006; Festival Exhibn, Edinburgh, 2006; Wright Gall., Dallas, 1988; Leinster Fine Art, London, 1986; Glasgow Print Studio, 1987, 1992, 1997, 2003; Scottish Gall., London, 1989, 1990; Wm Jackson Gall., London, 1990, 1992; Perth Mus. and Art Gall., 1991; Clive Jennings Gall., London, 1992; Jorgensen Fine Art, Dublin, 1993, 1995, 2005; Waxlander Gall., Santa Fe, 1996; Bohun Gall., Henley on Thames, 1996; Art First, London, 1996, 1997, 1999, 2001, 2002; Graphic Studio Gall., Dublin,

1997, 2003, 2007; Printmakers Workshop, Edinburgh, 1997; Gall. Galtung, Oslo, 1998; Castlegate House Gall., Cumbria, 2003; North House Gall., Essex, 2004, New Prints, 2006; Tom Caldwell Gall., Belfast, 2004, 2006; Adam Gall., Bath, 2005; Sierra, Edinburgh Fest., 2006; Arizona, Richmond Hill Gall., Richmond, 2006; Adam Gall., London, 2008; Belfast Print Studio, 2008; touring exhibn, Scotland and Leeds, 1993–94; numerous gp exhibitions in Britain, Europe, USA, S America and Australia; works in public and private collections in Britain, Europe and America; commissions include: tapestry for Festival Theatre, Edinburgh, 1994; rug for Royal Mus. of Scotland, 1999; portraits. Hon. FRCA 2005 (FRCA 2003). Hon. DArts Napier, 1999; Hon. DLitt Aberdeen, 2003. Awards: Arts Council, 1968; Major Arts Council, 1975–81; Guthrie Medal, RSA, 1977; May Marshall Brown, RSW Centenary Exhibn, 1979; RSA Sir Wm Gillies Travel, 1983; Calouste Gulbenkian Printmaking, 1983; Alexander Graham Munro, RSW, 1989; Hunting Gp Prizewinner, 1990; Scottish PO Bd, RSA, 1990; Scottish Amicable, RGI, 1990; W. J. Burness, Royal Scottish Acad., 1990. *Relevant publication*: Barbara Rae, by B. Hare *et al*, 2008. *Recreation:* travelling. *Address:* c/o The Adam Gallery, 24 Cork Street, W1S 3NJ. *Club:* Glasgow Art.

RAE, Fiona Elizabeth, RA 2002; artist; *b* 10 Oct. 1963; *d* of Alexander Edward Ian Rae and Pamela Christine Rae; *m* 2002, Daniel Jonathan Perfect. *Educ:* Croydon Coll. of Art (Foundn Course Fine Art 1984); Goldsmiths Coll., London Univ. (BA 1st Cl. Hons Fine Art 1987). Artist Trustee, Tate, 2005–. Selected *solo exhibitions:* Kunsthalle Basel, 1992; ICA, London, 1993–94; Carré d'Art, Musée d'art contemporain de Nîmes, 2002–03; Timothy Taylor Gall., London, 2003, 2008; Signal, BBC commn, installation for Art Site, Broadcasting House Public Art Prog., London, 2003; PaceWildenstein, NY, 2006; selected *group exhibitions:* Freeze, Surrey Docks, London, 1988; Aperto, La Biennale di Venezia XLIV, 1990; Unbound: Possibilities in Painting, Hayward Gall., London, 1994; Sensation: Young British Artists from the Saatchi Collection, RA, London, Hamburger Bahnhof - Mus. für Gegenwart, Berlin and Brooklyn Mus. of Art, NY, 1997–2000; Painting Pictures: Painting and Media in the Digital Age, Kunstmus. Wolfsburg, 2003; Pictograms: the Loneliness of Signs, Kunstmus. Stuttgart, 2006–07. *Relevant publication:* Fiona Rae, by S. Wallis and J.-P. Criqui, 2002. *Address:* c/o Timothy Taylor Gallery, 15 Carlos Place, W1K 2EX. *T:* (020) 7409 3344, *Fax:* (020) 7409 1316; *e-mail:* mail@timothytaylorgallery.com.

RAE, Gordon Hamilton; Director General, Royal Horticultural Society, 1993–99; *b* 12 Sept. 1938; *s* of Peter and Gwendoline Elizabeth Rae; *m* 1965, Judith Elizabeth Pickup; one *s* two *d. Educ:* Bablake Sch., Coventry; Wye Coll., Univ. of London (BSc Agric. Hons); Clare Coll., Cambridge (Dip. Agric.); Imperial Coll. of Tropical Agric., Trinidad (DTA). Agricl and Dist Agricl Officer, HM Colonial Service, Kenya, 1962–65; ICI, 1965–93: Gen. Manager, Agricl Chemicals Div., ICI do Brasil, São Paulo, 1980–84; Gen. Manager, ICI Garden and Professional Products, 1989–92. Non-exec. Dir, D. J. Squire & Co. Ltd, 1999–2007. Jt Patron, Garden Media Guild, 2007–. FIHort 1996. VMH 1999. *Recreations:* gardening, family, travel, photography. *Address:* New House, Church Lane, Grayshott, Hindhead, Surrey GU26 6LY. *T:* (01428) 606025. *Club:* Farmers'.

RAE, Dr John; Vice-Chairman, AWE plc, 2001–02 (Chief Executive, 2000–01); *b* 29 Sept. 1942; *s* of late John Rae and of Marion Rae (*née* Dow); *m* 1968, Irene (*née* Cassells); one *s* one *d. Educ:* Rutherglen Academy; University of Glasgow (BSc 1964, PhD 1967). FInstE 1987; FInstP 1996. Lecturing and research in physics: Univ. of Glasgow, 1967–68; Univ. of Texas, 1968–70; Univ. Libre, Brussels, 1970–72; Queen Mary College London, 1972–74; Theoretical Physics Div., Harwell: Industrial Fellow, 1974–76; Leader, Theory of Fluids Group, 1976–85; Acting Div. Head, 1985; Chief Scientist, Dept of Energy, 1986–89; Chief Exec., AEA Envmt & Energy, 1990–93; Business Develt Dir, 1993–95, Dir, Nat. Envmtl Technology Centre, 1994–95, AEA Technology; Man. Dir, NPL Mgt Ltd, 1995–2000. Member: SERC, 1986–89; NERC, 1986–89. Pres., NPL Sports Club, 1996–2000. Freeman, City of London, 1997; Liveryman, Scientific Instrument Makers' Co., 1997–. *Publications:* scientific papers in professional jls. *Recreations:* music, especially singing; gardening, astronomy.

RAE, Rita Emilia Anna; QC (Scot.) 1992; Sheriff of Glasgow and Strathkelvin, since 1997; *b* 20 June 1950; *d* of Alexander Smith Cowie Rae and Bianca Bruno. *Educ:* Univ. of Edinburgh (LLB Hons). Apprentice, 1972–74, Asst Solicitor, 1974–76, Biggart Baillie & Gifford, Glasgow; Asst Solicitor and Partner, Ross Harper & Murphy, Glasgow, 1976–81; Advocate, 1982–; Temporary Sheriff, 1988–97; Temporary Judge of High Ct, 2004–. Tutor in Advocacy and Pleading, Strathclyde Univ., 1979–82. Vice-Chm., Parole Bd for Scotland, 2005–07 (Mem., 2001–07); Member: Sentencing Commn for Scotland, 2003–06; SACRO. Chm., Glasgow Br., Scottish Assoc. for Study of Delinquency, 2003– (Life Mem.). *Recreations:* classical music, opera, theatre, walking, gardening, learning piano. *Address:* Sheriff's Chambers, 1 Carlton Place, Glasgow G5 9DA. *T:* (0141) 429 8888.

RAE, Hon. Robert Keith; PC (Can.) 1998; OC 2000; OOnt 2004; QC (Can.) 1984; MP (Liberal) Toronto Centre, Canada, since 2008; Premier of Ontario, 1990–95; *b* 2 Aug. 1948; *s* of Saul Rae and Lois (*née* George); *m* 1980, Arlene Perly; three *d. Educ:* Ecole Internationale, Geneva; Univ. of Toronto (BA Hons 1969; LLB 1977); Balliol Coll., Oxford (BPhil 1971). MP for Broadview-Greenwood, Ontario, 1978–82; Finance Critic, New Democratic Party, 1979–82; MPP (NDP) York South, Ontario, 1982–95; Leader, Ontario New Democrats, 1982–96; Leader, Official Opposition, Ontario legislature, 1987–90. Partner, Goodmans LLP (formerly Goodmans Phillips & Vineberg), 1996–2007. Director: Tembec Ltd, 1997–; Trojan Technologies, 2001–. Adjunct Prof., Univ. of Toronto, 1997–; Sen. Fellow, Massey Coll., 1997–. Dir, Canadian Ditchley Foundn, 1997–. Chairman: Forum of Fedns, 1999–; Royal Conservatory of Music, 2000; Toronto SO, 2002; Canadian Unity Council, 2002–. Trustee, University Health Network, 1999–. Gov., Univ. of Toronto, 1999–; Nat. spokesperson, Leukemia Res. Fund of Canada, 1996–. Hon. LLD: Law Soc. of Upper Canada, 1998; Toronto, 1999; Assumption, 2001; Huntington, 2002. *Publications:* From Protest to Power, 1996; The Three Questions, 1998. *Recreations:* tennis, golf, ski-ing, fishing, reading. *Address:* House of Commons, 365 Confederation Building, Ottowa, ON K1A 0A6.

RAE, Air Vice-Marshal William McCulloch, CB 1993; Director, United Services Trustee, since 1996; *b* 22 June 1940; *s* of William Brewster Rae and Margaret Rae; *m* 1964, Helen, *d* of Thomas and Eileen Reading; two *d. Educ:* Aberdeen Grammar School; psc, ndc, rcds. RAF 1958; Nos 213, 10, 55 Sqns, 1960–64; CFS (helicopter element), 1965–67; Radar Res. Flying Unit, Pershore, 1968–70; Sqn Comdr, 6 FTS, 1970–72; Inspectorate of Recruiting, 1973; RAF Staff Coll., 1974; Air Sec's Dept, 1975–77; NDC, 1978; OC 360 Sqn, 1979–81; CDS Staff, 1981–82; Central Policy Staff, MoD, 1982–85; Station Comdr, RAF Finningley, 1985–87; RCDS, 1988; Branch Chief, Policy, SHAPE, 1989–91; Sen. DS (Air), RCDS, 1992–95; Sen. Assessor, Charter Mark, Cabinet Office, 1996–97. Dealer in early English barometers, 1997–2007. *Recreations:* antiques, fly-fishing, wine, golf. *Club:* Royal Air Force.

RAEBURN, David Antony; College Lecturer, New College, Oxford, since 2000; Grammatikos (tutor in Ancient Greek Language), Faculty of Literae Humaniores, 1991–96, Grocyn Lecturer, 1992–96, University of Oxford; *b* 22 May 1927; *e s* of late Walter Augustus Leopold Raeburn, QC; *m* 1961, Mary Faith, *d* of Arthur Hubbard, Salisbury, Rhodesia; two *s* one *d. Educ:* Charterhouse; Christ Church, Oxford (Schol., MA). 1st cl. hons Hon. Mods, 2nd in Greats. Nat. Service, 1949–51: Temp. Captain, RAEC. Asst Master: Bristol Grammar Sch., 1951–54; Bradfield Coll., 1955–58 (prod. Greek Play, 1955 and 1958); Senior Classics Master, Alleyn's Sch., Dulwich, 1958–62; Headmaster: Beckenham and Penge Grammar Sch., 1963–70 (school's name changed to Langley Park School for Boys, Beckenham in 1969); Whitgift Sch., Croydon, 1970–91. Schoolteacher Fellow-Commoner, Jesus Coll., Cambridge, 1980. Vis. Fellow, New Coll., Oxford, 1997. Chm. Classics Cttee, Schs Council, 1974–80; Pres., Jt Assoc. of Classical Teachers, 1983–85; Treas., HMC, 1984–89. FRSA 1969. *Publications:* trans. Ovid, Metamorphoses, 2004; trans. Sophocles, Electra and Other Plays, 2008; essays on education; articles on Greek tragedy and Greek play production. *Recreation:* play production (produced Cambridge Greek Play, 1980, 1983). *Address:* 41 Ritchie Road, 380 Banbury Road, Oxford OX2 7PW. *T:* (01865) 553075.

RAEBURN, Michael Edward Norman; (4th Bt, *cr* 1923, but does not use the title); *b* 12 Nov. 1954; *s* of Sir Edward Alfred Raeburn, 3rd Bt, and Joan, *d* of Frederick Hill; *S* father, 1977; *m* 1979, Penelope Henrietta Theodora (marr. diss. 1997), *d* of Alfred Louis Penn; two *s* three *d. Heir: s* Christopher Edward Alfred Raeburn, *b* 4 Dec. 1981.

RAEBURN, Susan Adiel Ogilvie; QC (Scot.) 1991; Sheriff of Glasgow and Strathkelvin, since 1993; *b* 23 April 1954; *d* of George Ferguson Raeburn and Rose Anne Bainbridge (*née* Morison). *Educ:* St Margaret's Sch. for Girls, Aberdeen; Edinburgh Univ. (LLB). Admitted to Faculty of Advocates, 1977; temp. Sheriff, 1988–93. Part-time Chairman: Social Security Appeal Tribunals, 1986–92; Med. Appeal Tribunals, 1992–93. *Recreations:* travel, the arts. *Address:* Sheriff's Chambers, Sheriff Court House, 1 Carlton Place, Glasgow G5 90A. *T:* (0141) 429 8888.

RAESIDE, Mark Andrew; QC 2002; *b* 27 Nov. 1955; *s* of Dr John Robertson Raeside and Anneli Raeside; *m* 1985, Alison, *d* of Major John Powell and Gertraud Powell; three *s* one *d. Educ:* Univ. of Kent; Wolfson Coll., Cambridge (BA; MPhil). FCIArb 2001. Called to the Bar, Middle Temple, 1982. Accredited Mediator, 2003; domestic and internat. commercial lawyer specialising in construction and engineering disputes. Military Cross (2nd class) (Estonia), 2004. *Recreations:* country pursuits and community life at West Sussex and Wester Ross estates, family life. *Address:* 1 Atkin Building, Gray's Inn, WC1R 5BQ. *T:* (020) 7404 0102, *Fax:* (020) 7405 7456.

RAFF, Prof. Martin Charles, FRS 1985; Professor of Biology, 1979–2002, now Emeritus, and Hon. Fellow, since 2004, University College London; Member, MRC Laboratory for Molecular Cell Biology and Cell Biology Unit, since 1995; *b* 15 Jan. 1938; *s* of David and Reba Raff; *m* 1979, Carol Winter; two *s* one *d* by a previous marriage. *Educ:* McGill Univ. (BSc; MD; CM). House Officer, Royal Victoria Hosp., Montreal, 1963–65; Resident in Neurology, Massachusetts General Hosp., 1965–68; Postdoctoral Fellow, Nat. Inst. for Med. Res., 1968–71; Sen. Res. Fellow, UCL, 1971–79; Dir, MRC Develtl Neurobiology Programme, 1971–2002. Chm., UK Life Scis Cttee, 1997–2001. Pres., British Soc. of Cell Biology, 1991–95. Founder FMedSci 1998. Foreign Hon. Mem., American Acad. of Arts and Scis, 1999; For. Associate Mem., NAS, US, 2003. Hon. DSc McGill, 2005; Vrije Univ. Brussel. *Publications:* (jtly) T and B Lymphocytes, 1973; (jtly) Molecular Biology of the Cell, 1983, 5th edn 2008; (jtly) Essential Cell Biology, 1997, 2nd edn 2004.

RAFFAN, Keith William Twort; Member (Lib Dem) Scotland Mid and Fife, Scottish Parliament, 1999–Jan. 2005; *b* 21 June 1949; *s* of A. W. Raffan, TD, MB, ChB, FFARCS and late Jean Crampton Raffan (*née* Twort), MB, ChB. *Educ:* Robert Gordon's Coll., Aberdeen; Trinity Coll., Glenalmond; Corpus Christi Coll., Cambridge (BA 1971; MA 1977). Parly Correspondent and sketch writer, Daily Express, 1981–83; internat. public relns consultant, NY, 1992–94; presenter, Welsh Agenda, HTV, 1994–98. Contested (C) Dulwich, Feb. 1974, and East Aberdeenshire, Oct. 1974; MP (C) Delyn, 1983–92. Mem., Select Cttee on Welsh Affairs, 1983–92. Introduced: Controlled Drugs (Penalties) Act (Private Member's Bill, 1985); Tourism (Overseas Promotion) (Wales) Act, 1991. Chief spokesman on home affairs, Scottish Lib Dem Party, 1998. Nat. Chm., PEST, 1970–74. *Clubs:* Chelsea Arts, Royal Automobile.

RAFFARIN, Jean-Pierre; Prime Minister of France, 2002–05; *b* 3 Aug. 1948; *s* of Jean Raffarin and Renée (*née* Michaud); *m* 1980, Anne-Marie Perrier; one *d. Educ:* Lycée Henri IV, Poitiers; Faculté de Droit, Paris-Assas; Ecole Supérieure de Commerce, Paris. Mktg Dept, Cafés Jacques Vabre, 1973–76; Advr, Office of Minister of Labour, 1976–81; Lectr, Inst. d'Etudes Politiques, Paris, 1979–88; Dir-Gen., Bernard Krief Communications, 1981–88; Gen. delegate, Inst. Euro-92, 1988–89. MEP (RPR-UDF), Poitou-Charentes, 1989–95; elected Mem. of Senate, for Vienne, 1995, 1997; Minister of Small and Medium Sized Businesses, Trade and Small Scale Industry, 1995–97. City Councillor, Poitiers, 1977–95; Regl Councillor, 1986–88, Chm., Regl Council, 1988–2002, Poitou-Charentes; Dep. Mayor, Chasseneuil-du-Poitou, 1995–2001. Nat. Delegate, Dep. Sec.-Gen. and Mem., Pol Bureau, 1977–, Nat. Sec., 1989–95, PR; Dep. Sec.-Gen. and Spokesman, 1993–95, Sec.-Gen, 1995–97, UDF; Vice-Chm., Democratie Libérale, 1997–. Pres., Assoc. of the Regions of France, 1998–2002. *Publications:* La vie en jaune, 1977; La publicité, nerf de la communication, 1983; L'avenir a ses racines, 1986; Nous sommes tous les régionaux, 1988; Pour une morale de l'action, 1992; Le livre de l'Atlantique, 1994; Pour une nouvelle gouvernance, 2002. *Recreations:* contemporary painting, regional literature.

RAFFERTY, Hon. Dame Anne (Judith), (Dame Anne Barker), DBE 2000; **Hon. Mrs Justice Rafferty;** a Judge of the High Court of Justice, Queen's Bench Division, since 2000; Presiding Judge, South Eastern Circuit, 2003–06; *m* 1977, Brian John Barker, *qv*; three *d* (and one *d* decd). *Educ:* Univ. of Sheffield (LLB; Hon. LLD 2005). Called to the Bar, Gray's Inn, 1973, Inner Temple *ad eundem*, 1996; Bencher, Gray's Inn, 1998; QC 1990; a Recorder, 1991–2000; Head of Chambers, 1994–2000; a Dep. High Court Judge, 1996–2000. Criminal Bar Association: Mem. Cttee, 1986–89; Sec., 1989–91; Vice-Chm., 1993–95; Chm., 1995–97; Chm., Bar Conf., 1992. Mem., Royal Commn on Criminal Justice, 1991–93. Member: SE Circuit Cttee, 1987–90; Pigot Cttee, 1988–89; Circuit Cttee, SE Circuit, 1991–94; Criminal Cttee, Judicial Studies Bd, 1998–2000. Gov., Expert Witness Inst., 1997–99. Mem., Appeal Ct, Oxford Univ., 2003–. Mem. Council, Eastbourne Coll., 1993–2006. *Address:* Royal Courts of Justice, Strand, WC2A 2LL.

RAFFERTY, Kevin Robert; Managing Editor, International Media Partners, New York, 1989; *b* 5 Nov. 1944; *s* of Leo and Thérèse Rafferty; *m* 1985, Michelle Misquitta. *Educ:* Marist Coll., Kingston upon Hull; Queen's Coll., Oxford (MA). Journalistic training, The Guardian, Sun, 1966–69; Financial Times, 1970–76; Founder Editor, Business Times Malaysia, 1976–77; Consultant Editor, Indian Express Gp, 1978–79; Foreign Correspondent, Financial Times, 1980; Asia Pacific Editor, Institutional Investor, 1981–87; Ed., The Universe, 1987–88. Founder Editor, then Associate Editor, Asia and Pacific Review, Saffron Walden, 1980–. *Publications:* City on the Rocks: Hong Kong's uncertain future, 1989; Inside Japan's Power Houses, 1995. *Recreations:* travelling, meeting ordinary people, reading. *Clubs:* Oxford and Cambridge; Foreign Correspondents (Hong Kong).

RAGGATT, Timothy Walter Harold; QC 1993; a Recorder, since 1994; *b* 13 April 1950; *s* of late Walter George and Norah Margaret Raggatt; *m* 1991, Carol Marion Allison; two *s* one *d*. *Educ:* Redditch County High Sch.; King's Coll. London (LLB 1971). Called to the Bar, Inner Temple, 1972, Bencher, 1999; Tutor, Inns of Court Sch. of Law, 1972–73; in practice on Midland and Oxford Circuit, 1974–; an Asst Recorder, 1991–94. Mem., Professional Assoc. of Diving Instructors, 1992–. *Recreations:* golf, scuba diving, bridge and snooker. *Address:* 4 King's Bench Walk, Temple, EC4Y 7DL; 3 Fountain Court, Steelhouse Lane, Birmingham B4 6DR. *Clubs:* Athenæum, Royal Automobile; Blackwell Golf (Birmingham).

RAGHUNATHAN, Prof. Madabusi Santanam, Padma Shri, 2001; PhD; FRS 2000; FIASc, FNA; Professor of Eminence, Tata Institute of Fundamental Research, Mumbai, since 1997; *b* 11 Aug. 1941; *s* of Madabusi Sudarsanam Iyengar Santanam and Ambuja Santanam; *m* 1968, Ramaa Rangarajan; one *s*. *Educ:* Vivekananda Coll., Univ. of Madras (BA Hons 1960); Bombay Univ. (PhD 1966). Tata Institute of Fundamental Research: Associate Prof., 1966–70; Prof., 1970–80; Sen. Prof., 1980–90; Distinguished Prof., 1990–97. FIASc 1974; FNA 1975; Fellow, Third World Acad. of Scis, 1994. Bhatnagar Award, Council of Scientific and Industrial Res., India, 1977; Third World Acad. Award, Trieste, 1991. *Publications:* Discrete Subgroups of Lie Groups, 1972; contrib. papers to Annals of Maths, Inventiones Mathematicae, etc. *Address:* Tata Institute of Fundamental Research, Homi Bhabha Road, Colaba, Mumbai 400 005, India. *T:* (office) (22) 22804654, (22) 22804545; (home) (22) 22804766.

RAGLAN, 5th Baron *cr* 1852; **FitzRoy John Somerset;** Chairman, Cwmbran New Town Development Corporation, 1970–83; *b* 8 Nov. 1927; *er s* of 4th Baron Raglan and Hon. Julia Hamilton, CStJ (*d* 1971), *d* of 11th Baron Belhaven and Stenton, CIE; *S* father, 1964; *m* 1973, Alice Baily (marr. diss. 1981), *yr d* of Peter Baily, Great Whittington, Northumberland. *Educ:* Westminster; Magdalen College, Oxford; Royal Agricultural College, Cirencester. Captain, Welsh Guards, RARO. Crown Estate Comr, 1970–74. Mem., Agriculture and Consumer Affairs sub-cttee, House of Lords Select Cttee on the European Community, 1974–83, 1985–90 (Chm., 1975–77). President: UK Housing Trust, 1983–89 (Chm., S Wales Region, 1976–89); United Welsh Housing Trust, 1989–. Pres., Pre Retirement Assoc., 1970–77, Vice-Pres. 1977–90. Chairman: Bath Preservation Trust, 1975–77; The Bath Soc., 1977–; Bugatti Owners' Club, 1988–97 (Patron, 1999–). President: Usk Civic Soc.; Bath Centre of Nat. Trust; Usk Rural Life Mus.; Monmouthshire Brecon and Abergavenny Canals Trust; Gwent Beekeepers Assoc.; S Wales Reg., RSMHCA, 1971–; Parity; Vice-Pres., Gwent Talking Newspaper for the Blind; Mem., Distinguished Members Panel, National Secular Soc.; Patron: Usk Farmers Club; The Raglan Baroque Players; Gwent County History Assoc.; Hospice of the Valleys; Mon Crossroads; Friends of Swanage Pier; Nat. Museums and Galleries of Wales; Trustee: Bugatti Trust; Cwmbran Arts Trust. JP 1958–97, DL 1971–97, Monmouthshire, then Gwent. *Recreation:* being mechanic to a Bugatti. *Heir: b* Hon. Geoffrey Somerset [*b* 29 Aug. 1932; *m* 1956, Caroline Rachel, *d* of late Col E. R. Hill, DSO; one *s* two *d*]. *Address:* Cefntilla, Usk, Monmouthshire NP15 1DG. *T:* (01291) 672050. *Clubs:* Beefsteak, Vintage Sports Car; Usk Farmers'.

RAHMAN, Prof. Atta-ur-, PhD, ScD; FRS 2006; Director, H. E. J. Research Institute of Chemistry, University of Karachi, since 1990; *b* Delhi, 20 Sept. 1942; *s* of Jameel-Ur-Rahman and Amtul Subhan Begum; *m* Nargis Jamal. *Educ:* Karachi Univ. (BSc 1963; MSc 1964); King's Coll., Cambridge (PhD 1968; ScD 1987; Hon. Life Fellow, 2007). Karachi University: Lectr, 1964–69; Asst Prof., 1969–74; Associate Prof., 1974–76; Prof. 1981–90; Co-Director, H. E. J. Research Inst. of Chem., 1977–80 and 1981–90. D. A. A. D. Fellow, Univ. of Tübingen, 1979, Co-ordinator Gen., Orgn of Islamic Conf. Standing Cttee on Scientific and Technol Co-operation, Islamabad, 1996–. Government of Pakistan: Minister: for Sci. and Technol., 2000–02; Min. of Educn, 2002; Min. of Sci. and Technol., 2003–04; Chm., Higher Educn Commn, 2002–; Advr to Prime Minister for Sci. and Technol., 2005–08. President: Chem. Soc. of Pakistan, 1992; Pakistan Acad. of Scis, 2003–06; Network Acad. of Scis of Islamic Countries, 2005–; Vice-Pres. (Central and S Asia), Acad. of Scis for the Developing World, 2007. FRSC 1981; Fellow: Pakistan Acad. of Scis, 1982; Islamic Acad. of Scis, 1988; Third World Acad. of Scis. Hon. DEd Coventry, 2007. Nishan-i-Imtiaz (Pakistan), 2002 (Tamgha-i-Imtiaz, 1983; Sitara-i-Imtiaz, 1991; Hilal-i-Imtiaz, 1998); Order of Golden Sash (Austria), 2007. *Publications:* contrib. books and jls. *Address:* H. E. J. Research Institute of Chemistry, International Centre for Chemical and Biological Sciences, University of Karachi, Karachi 75270, Pakistan.

RAHTZ, Prof. Philip Arthur; Professor of Archaeology, University of York, 1978–86, now Emeritus; *b* 11 March 1921; *s* of Frederick John Rahtz and Ethel May Rahtz; *m* 1st, 1940, Wendy Hewgill Smith (*d* 1977); three *s* two *d*; 2nd, 1978, Lorna Rosemary Jane Watts; one *s*. *Educ:* Bristol Grammar Sch. MA Bristol 1964. FSA. Served RAF, 1941–46. Articled to accountant, 1937–41; photographer (Studio Rahtz), 1946–49; schoolteacher, 1950–53; archaeological consultant, 1953–63; Univ. of Birmingham: Lectr, 1963–75; Sen. Lectr, later Reader, 1975–78. Pres., Council for British Archaeology, 1986–89. Hon. MIFA. Hon. DLitt Bristol, 2002. Frend Medal, Soc. of Antiquaries of London, 2003. *Publications:* Rescue Archaeology, 1973; Chew Valley Lake Excavations, 1978; Saxon and Medieval Palaces at Cheddar, 1979; Invitation to Archaeology, 1985, 2nd edn 1991; Tamworth Saxon Watermill, 1992; Glastonbury, 1993, 2nd edn 2003; Cannington Cemetery, 2000; Living Archaeology, 2001; contrib. nat. and regional jls in England, W Africa and Poland. *Recreations:* swimming, sunbathing, music. *Address:* The Old School, Harome, Helmsley, North Yorkshire YO62 5JE. *T:* (01439) 770862.

RAIKES, Vice-Adm. Sir Iwan (Geoffrey), KCB 1976; CBE 1967; DSC 1943; DL; Flag Officer Submarines, and Commander Submarines, Eastern Atlantic Area, 1974–76; retired 1977; *b* 21 April 1921; *s* of late Adm. Sir Robert Henry Taunton Raikes, KCB, CVO, DSO and bar, and Lady (Ida Guinevere) Raikes; *m* 1947, Cecilia Primrose Hunt; one *s* one *d*. *Educ:* RNC Dartmouth. Entered Royal Navy, 1935; HMS Sussex, 1939–40; HMS Repulse, 1940; HMS Beagle, 1941; specialised in Submarines, 1941; comd HM Submarines: Sealion, 1941–42; Saracen, 1942–43; H43, 1943; Varne, 1944; Virtue, 1946; Talent, 1948–49; Aeneas, 1952; Logistics Div., Allied Forces Mediterranean, 1953–55; Comdr SM Third Submarine Sqn, 1958–60; comd HM Ships: Loch Insh, 1961; Kent, 1968; Exec. Officer, HMS Newcastle, 1955–57; Dep. Dir, Undersurface Warfare, 1962–64; Dir, Plans & Operations, Staff of C-in-C Far East, 1965–66; JSSC, 1957; IDC, 1967. Rear-Adm., 1970; Naval Sec., 1970–72; Vice-Adm., 1973; Flag Officer, First Flotilla, 1973–74. Chm., United Usk Fisherman's Assoc., 1978–93. Mem., Governing Body, 1979–93, Rep. Body, 1982–93, Church in Wales. DL Powys, 1983. *Recreations:* shooting, fishing, gardening. *Address:* Aberyscir Court, Brecon, Powys LD3 9NW. *Club:* Naval and Military.

RAILTON, David; QC 1996; a Recorder, since 2000; *b* 5 June 1957; *s* of late Andrew Scott Railton, MC and of Margaret Elizabeth Railton (*née* Armit); *m* 1996, Sinéad Major; one *s* one *d*. *Educ:* Balliol Coll., Oxford (BA). Called to the Bar, Gray's Inn, 1979, Bencher, 2005. *Recreations:* cricket, golf. *Address:* Fountain Court, Temple, EC4Y 9DH.

RAILTON, Elizabeth Jane, CBE 2006; Programme Director, Together for Children, since 2007; *b* 21 Nov. 1952; *d* of John and Jill Nisbet; *m* 1974, James Lancelot Railton; two *s*. *Educ:* Somerville Coll., Oxford (MA, MSc). CQSW 1978. Social worker, 1974–86; Hertfordshire County Council: Social Services Manager, 1986–91; Asst Dir of Social Services, 1991–95; Dep. Dir, Social Services, 1995–96; Dir, Social Services, Cambs CC, 1998–2002; Essex County Council: Dep. Chief Exec., Learning and Social Care, 2003–05; Dir, Children's Services, 2005–06. Hon. Sec., Assoc. of Dirs of Social Services, 2002–06. Trustee, British Assoc. Adoption and Fostering, 2001–06. *Recreations:* shopping, travel. *Address:* Together for Children, Boundary House, 2 Wythall Green Way, Middle Lane, Birmingham B47 6LW; *e-mail:* liz.railton@togetherforchildren.co.uk.

RAINBOW, (James) Conrad (Douglas), CBE 1979; Chairman, Sovereign Country House Ltd, 1979–96; *b* 25 Sept. 1926; *s* of Jack Conrad Rainbow and Winifred Edna (*née* Mears); *m* 1974, Kathleen Margaret (*née* Holmes); one *s* one *d*. *Educ:* William Ellis Sch., Highgate; Selwyn Coll., Cambridge (MA). Asst Master, St Paul's Sch., London, 1951–60; HM Inspector of Schools, 1960–69; Dep. Chief Educn Officer, Lancashire, 1969–74, Chief Educn Officer, 1974–79. Vis. Prof., Univ. of Wisconsin, 1979. Education Consultant: ICI, 1980–85; Shell Petroleum Co. Ltd, 1980–; Advr to H of C Select Cttee on Educn, 1980–82. Mem., Exec. Cttee, Council of British Internat. Schs in EEC, 1975–91. Chairman of Governors: Northcliffe Sch., Hants, 1984–90; Elmslie Sch., Blackpool, 1994–98. *Publications:* various articles in educnl jls. *Recreations:* rowing (now as an observer), music, reading. *Address:* 7 Seville Court, Clifton Drive, Lytham St Annes, Lancs FY8 5RG. *T:* (01253) 737245. *Club:* Leander.

RAINBOW, Prof. Philip Stephen, DSc, PhD; CBiol, FIBiol; Keeper of Zoology, Natural History Museum, since 1997; *b* 21 Oct. 1950; *s* of Frank Evelyn Rainbow, OBE and Joyce May Victoria Rainbow (*née* Turner); *m* 1973, Mary Meaken; two *s*. *Educ:* Bedford Sch., Bedford; Clare Coll., Cambridge (MA); UCNW, Bangor (PhD 1975; DSc 1994). CBiol 1998, FIBiol 1998. Queen Mary College, later Queen Mary and Westfield College, University of London: Lectr, 1975–89; Reader in Marine Biology, 1989–94; Prof. of Marine Biology, 1994–97; Head, Sch. of Biol Scis, 1995–97; Vis. Prof., 1997. Mem., Darwin Initiative Adv. Cttee, DEFRA, 2003–. *Publications:* (ed jtly) Aspects of Decapod Crustacean Biology, 1988; (ed jtly) Heavy Metals in the Marine Environment, 1990; (ed jtly) Ecotoxicology of Metals in Invertebrates, 1993; (jtly) Biomonitoring of Trace Aquatic Contaminants, 1993, 2nd edn 1994; (ed jtly) Forecasting the Environmental Fate and Effects of Chemicals, 2001; numerous papers in scientific jls. *Recreations:* cricket, Rugby, natural history. *Address:* Department of Zoology, Natural History Museum, Cromwell Road, SW7 5BD. *T:* (020) 7942 5275. *Clubs:* Tetrapods, Zoological.

RAINE, Craig Anthony; poet; Fellow of New College, Oxford, since 1991; Editor, Areté, since 1999; *b* 3 Dec. 1944; *s* of Norman Edward Raine and Olive Marie Raine; *m* 1972, Ann Pasternak Slater; one *d* three *s*. *Educ:* Barnard Castle Sch.; Exeter Coll., Oxford (BA Hons in English; BPhil). College Lecturer, Oxford University: Exeter Coll., 1971–72; Lincoln Coll., 1974–75; Exeter Coll., 1975–76; Christ Church, 1976–79. Books Editor, New Review, 1977–78; Editor, Quarto, 1979–80; Poetry Editor: New Statesman, 1981; Faber & Faber, 1981–91. Cholmondeley Poetry Award, 1983; Sunday Times Writer of the Year, 1998. *Publications:* The Onion, Memory, 1978, 5th edn 1986; A Martian Sends a Postcard Home, 1979, 8th edn 1990; A Free Translation, 1981, 2nd edn 1981; Rich, 1984, 3rd edn 1985; The Electrification of the Soviet Union, 1986; (ed) A Choice of Kipling's Prose, 1987; The Prophetic Book, 1988; '1953', 1990; Haydn and the Valve Trumpet (essays), 1990; (ed) Rudyard Kipling: Selected Poetry, 1992; History: The Home Movie, 1994; Clay. Whereabouts Unknown, 1996; (ed jtly) New Writing 7, 1998; A la recherche du temps perdu, 2000; In Defence of T. S. Eliot (essays), 2000; Collected Poems 1978–1999, 2000; (ed) Rudyard Kipling: The Wish House and other stories, 2002; T. S. Eliot, 2006. *Recreations:* music, ski-ing. *Address:* c/o New College, Oxford OX1 3BN.

RAINE, John Stephen; County Director, then Chief Executive, Derbyshire County Council, 1989–97; *b* 13 April 1941; *s* of Alan and Ruby Raine; *m* 1961, Josephine Elizabeth Marlow; two *s*. *Educ:* Sir Joseph Williamson's Mathematical School, Rochester. MCIPR. Journalist; Kent Messenger, Sheffield Morning Telegraph, Sheffield Star, Raymond's News Agency, 1957–70; Derbyshire County Council: County Public Relations Officer, 1973–79; Asst to Clerk and Chief Exec., 1979–81; Asst Chief Exec., 1981–88; Dep. County Dir, 1988–89. Chairman: Derbys Probation Bd, 2001–07; Nat. Assoc. of Probation Bds for England and Wales, 2004–07. Chairman: Hearing Aid Council, 1997–2003; Derbys Assoc. for the Blind, 1997–2007. Non-exec. Dir, Chesterfield and N Derbys Royal Hosp. NHS Trust, 1998–2006; Chm., Derbys County NHS PCT, 2006–. *Recreations:* walking, travel, smallholding. *Address:* Prieston House, Melrose, Roxburghshire TD6 9HQ. *T:* (01835) 870219.

RAINE, June Munro, FRCP, FRCPE; Director, Vigilance and Risk of Medicines Management (formerly Post Licensing Division), Medicines and Healthcare products Regulatory Agency, since 2003 (Director, Post-Licensing Division, Medicines Control Agency, 1998–2003), Department of Health; *b* 20 June 1952; *d* of David Harris and Isobel Harris (*née* Munro); *m* 1975, Prof. Anthony Evan Gerald Raine (*d* 1995); one *s* one *d*. *Educ:* Herts & Essex High Sch.; Somerville Coll., Oxford (BA Hons 1st Cl. 1974; MSc 1976; BM BCh 1978). MRCP 1980, FRCP 2003; MRCGP 1982; FRCPE 1995. Department of Health: SMO, Medicines Div., 1985–89; Gp Manager, Medicines Control Agency, 1989–98; Principal Assessor to Medicines Commn, 1992–. Member: wkg gps on aspects of pharmaceutical regulation, EC; Foresight Healthcare Task Force (Public and Patients), DTI, 1999–2000. FRSocMed 2000. *Publications:* papers on pharmacology, adverse drug effects and regulation of medicines. *Recreations:* music, opera, travel, ski-ing. *Address:* Medicines and Healthcare products Regulatory Agency, Department of Health, Market Towers, 1 Nine Elms Lane, SW8 5NQ. *T:* (020) 7273 0400, *Fax:* (020) 7273 0675.

RAINE, Sandra Margaret; private consultant on company secretarial matters, since 2007; *b* 7 March 1958; *d* of Charles Kitchener Lovell and Mary Rosaline Lovell (*née* O'Hare); *m* 1980, Ian Henry Raine. *Educ:* Univ. of Newcastle upon Tyne (BA Hons Sociol. and Social Admin). ACIS 1986. Pensions Asst, Dunlop Ltd, 1980; Admin Officer, NE Council on Alcoholism, 1980–82; Sen. Admin Asst, Newcastle upon Tyne Poly., 1982–85; Asst Co-ordinator, Urban Programmes, Gateshead MBC, 1985–86; Asst Divl Dir, Berks Social Services, 1986–90; Asst Co. Sec., AA, 1990–91; Ben Fund Sec., Chartered Inst. Building, 1992–94; Sec. and Chief Exec., IGasE, 1994–99; Co. Sec., Paddington Churches Housing Assoc., subseq. Gp Co. Sec., Genesis Housing Gp Ltd, 1999–2003; Exec. Dir, Internat. Headache Soc., 2003–05. Trustee, Inst. of Plumbing and Heating Engrg, 2005–.

Liveryman, Plumbers' Co. *Recreations:* keep fit, cycling, reading. *Club:* Nirvana (Berkshire).

RAINER, Luise; actress and painter; *b* Vienna, 12 Jan.; *d* of Heinz Rainer; *m* 1937, Clifford Odets (from whom she obtained a divorce, 1940; he *d* 1963); *m* 1945, Robert (*d* 1989), *s* of late John Knittel; one *d*. *Educ:* Austria, France, Switzerland and Italy. Started stage career at age of sixteen under Max Reinhardt in Vienna; later was discovered by Metro-Goldwyn-Mayer talent scout in Vienna; came to Hollywood; starred in: Escapade, 1935; The Great Ziegfeld, 1936; The Good Earth, Emperor's Candlesticks, Big City, 1937; Toy Wife (Frou Frou), The Great Waltz, Dramatic School, 1938; Hostages, 1942; The Gambler, 1997; Poetry, 2001; received Motion Picture Academy of Arts and Sciences Award for the best feminine performance in 1936 and 1937. One-man exhibn of paintings at Patrick Seale Gallery, SW1, 1978. US tour in dramatised recitation of Tennyson's Enoch Arden with music by Richard Strauss, 1983–84. TV film (wrote and starred), By herself—a dancer, 1986. George Eastman Award, George Eastman Inst., Rochester, NY, 1982. Grand Cross 1st class, Order of Merit (Federal Republic of Germany), 1985. *Recreations:* formerly mountain climbing, now writing, painting.

RAINEY, Mary Teresa; Founder and Chairman, horsesmouth.co.uk, since 2005; *d* of Peter and Margaret Rainey. *Educ:* Glasgow Univ. (MA Hons); Aston Univ. Corporate Hd of Planning, Chiat/Day, US, 1983–89; CEO, Chiat/Day, London, 1989–93; Founding Partner, Rainey Kelly Campbell Roalfe, 1993–99; Jt CEO, 1999–2003, Chm., 2003–05, Rainey Kelly Campbell Roalfe/Y&R. Non-executive Director: WH Smith, 2003–08; SMG, 2005–07. Chm., Marketing Gp of GB. Member: Women's Advertising Club of London; Nat. Skills Commn. Founding Trustee, Timebank; Trustee, Demos. *Publications:* numerous contribs to jls of advertising and mkt res. industries incl. ADMAP and Market Leader. *Recreations:* reading, music, hill-walking. *Address: e-mail:* mt@mtrainey.com.

RAINEY, Simon Piers Nicholas; QC 2000; a Recorder, since 2001; *b* 14 Feb. 1958; *s* of Peter Michael Rainey and Theresa Cora Rainey (*née* Heffernan); *m* 1st, 1986, Pia Witlox (marr. diss. 1999); twin *s* one *d*; 2nd, 2000, Charlotte Rice. *Educ:* Cranbrook Sch.; Corpus Christi Coll., Cambridge (BA 1st Cl. Hons Law 1980; MA 1984); Univ. Libre de Bruxelles (Licence en Droit Européen (Dist) 1981). Called to the Bar, Lincoln's Inn, 1982; Western Circuit. *Publications:* Maritime Laws of West Africa, 1985; Ship Sale and Purchase, 1993; Law of Tug and Tow, 1996, 2nd edn 2002. *Recreations:* classical music, print-collecting, ski-ing. *Address:* Quadrant Chambers, 10 Fleet Street, EC4Y 1AU. *T:* (020) 7583 4444; *e-mail:* simon.rainey@quadrantchambers.co.uk.

RAINFORD, Rev. (Robert) Graham; Priest Administrator, Holy Trinity Church, Sloane Street, since 2005; *b* 23 April 1955; *s* of late Robert Rainford and Mary Madeline Victory Rainford (*née* Saunders); *m* 1979, Valerie Slater (marr. diss. 2006); two *s* one *d*; *m* 2006, Anne Barrett. *Educ:* Bootle Grammar Sch. for Boys; St Martin's Coll. of Educn, Lancaster (Cert Ed; BEd); St Stephen's House, Oxford. Schoolmaster, Seedfield Sch., Bury, 1977–81. Ordained deacon, 1983, priest, 1984; Curate, St Catherine with St Alban and St Paul, Burnley, 1983–86; Priest-in-charge, 1986–89, Vicar, 1989–2003, St Christopher, Hawes Side, Blackpool; Priest-in-charge, St Nicholas, Marton Moss, Blackpool, 2001–03; Area Dean of Blackpool, 2000–03; Sen. Chaplain to the Bishop of Dover and Canterbury Chaplain to the Archbishop of Canterbury, 2003–05. Industrial Chaplain, Blackpool Pleasure Beach, 1987–2003; Chaplain, Actors' Church Union, 1988–; Asst Theatre Chaplain, Marlowe Th., Canterbury, 2004–. Chm., House of Clergy, Blackburn Diocesan Synod, 2000–03; Hon. Canon, Blackburn Cathedral, 2001–03. Hon. Chaplain, Garden House Sch., Chelsea. Chairman of Governors: Marton Primary Sch., 1991–2003; Holy Trinity C of E Primary Sch., 2006–; Vice Chm. Govs, Hawes Side Primary Sch., Blackpool; Gov., St George's C of E High Sch., Blackpool, 2002–03. Non-magisterial Mem., Lord-Lieut of Lancs Adv. Cttee. *Recreations:* travel (pilgrimage), theatre, opera, music, art, architecture, reading, cooking, gardening. *Address:* Holy Trinity Church, Sloane Street, SW1X 9BZ. *T:* (020) 7730 7270; *e-mail:* priest@holytrinitysloanesquare.co.uk.

RAINGER, Peter, CBE 1978; FRS 1982; FREng; Deputy Director of Engineering, British Broadcasting Corporation, 1978–84, retired; *b* 17 May 1924; *s* of Cyril and Ethel Rainger; *m* 1st, 1953, Josephine Campbell (decd); two *s*; 2nd, 1972, Barbara Gibson. *Educ:* Northampton Engrg Coll.; London Univ. (BSc(Eng)). CEng, FIET; FREng (FEng 1979). British Broadcasting Corporation: Head of Designs Dept, 1968–71; Head of Research Dept, 1971–76; Asst Dir of Engrg, 1976–78. Chairman: Professional Gp E14, IEE, 1973–76; various working parties, EBU, 1971–84. Fellow, Royal Television Soc., 1969. Geoffrey Parr Award, Royal TV Soc., 1964; J. J. Thompson Premium, IEE, 1966; TV Acad. Award, Nat. Acad. of Arts and Scis, 1968; David Sarnoff Gold Medal, SMPTE, 1972. *Publications:* Satellite Broadcasting, 1985; technical papers in IEE, Royal TV Soc. and SMPTE jls. *Recreations:* sculpture, model engineering. *Address:* 22 Mill Meadow, Milford on Sea, Hants SO41 0UG.

RAINS, Prof. Anthony John Harding, CBE 1986; MS, FRCS; Professor of Surgery, Charing Cross Hospital Medical School, University of London, and Hon. Consultant Surgeon, Charing Cross Hospital, 1959–81; *b* 5 Nov. 1920; *s* of late Dr Robert Harding Rains and Mrs Florence Harding Rains; *m* 1943, Mary Adelaide Lillywhite; three *d*. *Educ:* Christ's Hospital School, Horsham; St Mary's Hospital, London. MB, BS London 1943; MS London 1952; MRCS; LRCP 1943; FRCS 1948. Ho. Surg. and Ho. Phys. St Mary's, 1943. RAF, 1944–47. Ex-Service Registrar to Mr Handfield-Jones and Lord Porritt, 1947–48; Res. Surgical Officer, Bedford County Hosp., 1948–50; Lectr in Surgery, Univ. of Birmingham, 1950–54, Sen. Lectr, 1955–59; Asst Dir, BPMF, Univ. of London, and Postgraduate Dean, SW Thames RHA, 1981–85. Hon. Consulting Surgeon, United Birmingham Hospitals, 1954–59; Hon. Consultant Surgeon to the Army, 1972–82. Royal College of Surgeons of England: Mem. Court of Examiners, 1968–74; Mem. Council, 1972–84; Dean, Inst. of Basic Med. Scis, 1976–82; Hunterian Trustee, 1982–95; Vice-President, 1983–84; Hon. Librarian, 1984–95. Chm., Med. Commn on Accident Prevention, 1974–83. Pres., Nat. Assoc. of Theatre Nurses, 1979–81. Trustee, Smith and Nephew Foundn, 1972–95. Sir Arthur Keith medal, RCS. Editor: Annals of RCS; Jl of RSocMed, 1985–94. *Publications:* (ed with Dr P. B. Kunkler) The Treatment of Cancer in Clinical Practice, 1959; Gallstones: Causes and Treatment, 1964; (ed) Bailey and Love's Short Practice of Surgery, 13th edn (ed with W. M. Capper), 1965, 20th edn (ed with C. V. Mann), 1988; Edward Jenner and Vaccination, 1975; Emergency and Acute Care, 1976; Lister and Antisepsis, 1977; 1,001 Multiple Choice Questions and Answers in Surgery, 1978, 4th edn 1996; (contrib.) A Millennium of Archdeacons, 2003; articles on the surgery of the gall bladder, on the formation of gall stones, inguinal hernia and arterial disease. *Recreations:* gardening, poetry. *Address:* 51 Peninsula Square, Winchester, Hants SO23 8GJ. *T:* (01962) 869419.

RAISER, Rev. Dr Konrad; General Secretary, World Council of Churches, 1993–2003; *b* Magdeburg, 25 Jan. 1938; *m* 1967, Elisabeth von Weizsäcker; four *s*. *Educ:* Univ. of Tübingen (DTheol 1970). Ordained into German Evangelical Ch., 1964; Asst Pastor, Württemberg, 1963–65; Lectr, Protestant Theol. Faculty, Tübingen, 1967–69; World Council of Churches: Study Sec., Commn on Faith and Order, 1969–73; Dep. Gen. Sec., 1973–83; Prof. of Systematic Theol. and Ecumenics, and Dir, Ecumenical Inst., Protestant Theol. Faculty, Univ. of Ruhr, 1983–93. *Publications:* Identität und Sozialität, 1971; Ökumene im Übergang, 1989 (Ecumenism in Transition, 1991); (contrib.) Dictionary of the Ecumenical Movement, 1991; Wir stehen noch am Anfang, 1994; To Be the Church, 1997; For a Culture of Life, 2002; Hoffen auf Gerechtigkeit und Versöhnung, 2002; Schritte auf dem Weg der Ökumene, 2005; many essays and articles. *Address:* Zikadenweg 14, 14055 Berlin, Germany.

RAISMAN, Prof. Geoffrey, DPhil, DM; FMedSci; FRS 2001; Director, Spinal Repair Unit, Institute of Neurology, and Professor of Neural Regeneration, University College London, since 2005; *b* 28 June 1939; *s* of Harry Raisman and Celia Raisman (*née* Newton); *m* 1958, Vivien Margolin; one *d*. *Educ:* Roundhay Sch., Leeds; Pembroke Coll., Oxford (Theodore Williams Open Schol. in Medicine; BA 1st Cl. Hons Animal Physiol. 1960); Christ Church, Oxford (MA, DPhil 1964; BM BCh 1965); DM Oxon 1974. Demonstrator, 1965–66, Schorstein Res. Fellow, 1965–67, Univ. Lectr, 1966–74, Dept of Human Anatomy, Oxford Univ. Med. Sch.; Res. Fellow, Dept of Anatomy, Harvard Univ., 1968–69; Fellow, 1970–74, Med. Tutor, 1973–74, Oriel Coll., Oxford; Head, Div. of Neurobiology, NIMR, 1974–2004. Scientific Director: Norman and Sadie Lee Res. Centre, Mill Hill, 1987–2004; Teijin Biomed. Centre, MRC Collaborative Centre, Mill Hill, 1992–97. Visiting Professor: in Neuroscis, KCL, 1977–82; of Anatomy and Develtl Biol., UCL, 1989–2004; Royal Soc. Exchange Prog. with China at Shanghai Physiol. Inst., Chinese Acad. of Scis, 1982; Norman and Sadie Lee Vis. Scientist, City of Hope Med. Center, Duarte, Calif, 1983. Member: MRC Co-ordinating Gp on Rehabilitation after Acute Brain Damage, 1977–85; MRC Neurobiol. and Mental Health Bd, 1980–83; Scientific Cttee, Internat. Spinal Res. Trust, 1986–. Trustee: British Neurol Res. Trust, 1987–95; American Friends of BNRT, 1995–. Mem., Editl Bds, incl. Brain Res., Anatomy and Embryol., Exptl Brain Res., Exptl Neurol. FMedSci 1999; FRSA 2002. Wakeman Award for Res. in Neuroscis, Duke Univ., N Carolina, 1980; Outstanding Contrib. to Neurosci. Award, British Neurosci. Assoc., 2004; Reeve-Irvine Res. Medal, UC Irvine, Calif, 2005. *Publications:* The Undark Sky: a story of four poor brothers, 2002; contrib. articles on brain structure and plasticity, sexual dimorphism in the brain and repair of spinal cord injury to scientific jls. *Recreations:* writing, travel, ancient civilisations, Chinese, Japanese. *Address:* Spinal Repair Unit, Institute of Neurology, University College London, Queen Square, WC1N 3BG. *T:* (020) 7676 2172, *Fax:* (020) 7676 2174; *e-mail:* G.Raisman@ion.ucl.ac.uk. *Club:* Royal Society of Medicine.

RAISMAN, Jeremy Philip; Senior Partner, Eversheds, London (formerly Jaques & Lewis), 1993–99; *b* 6 March 1935; *s* of Sir (Abraham) Jeremy Raisman, GCMG, GCIE, KCSI, and late Renee Mary (*née* Kelly); *m* 1963, Diana Rosamund Clifford, *d* of late Maj.-Gen. Cedric Rhys Price, CB, CBE; one *s* two *d*. *Educ:* Dragon Sch., Oxford; Rugby Sch. Articled, Norton Rose, 1953–59; admitted solicitor, 1959; Asst Solicitor, Clifford-Turner & Co., 1960–62; Asst Solicitor, then Partner, Nabarro Nathanson & Co., 1962–67; Partner, Jaques & Co., 1967, subseq. Jaques & Lewis, 1982, then Eversheds, London, 1995. *Recreations:* beagling (Jt Master, W Surrey & Horsell Beagles 1959–71), sailing, riding, trekking. *Address:* Winterdown, Holmbury St Mary, Dorking, Surrey RH5 6NL. *Clubs:* Bosham Sailing (Chichester); Rock Sailing (Wadebridge, Cornwall).

See also J. M. Raisman.

RAISMAN, John Michael, CBE 1983; Chairman, Shell UK Ltd, 1979–85; *b* 12 Feb. 1929; *er s* of Sir Jeremy Raisman, GCMG, GCIE, KCSI, and late Renee Mary Raisman; *m* 1953, Evelyn Anne, *d* of Brig. J. I. Muirhead, CIE, MC; one *s* two *d* (and one *d* decd). *Educ:* Dragon Sch., Oxford; Rugby Sch.; The Queen's Coll., Oxford (Jodrell Schol., MA Lit Hum). Joined Royal Dutch/Shell Group, 1953; served in Brazil, 1954–60; General Manager, Shell Panama, 1961–62; Asst to Exploration and Production Co-ordinator, The Hague, 1963–65; Gen. Man., Shell Co. of Turkey, 1966–69; President, Shell Sekiyu K. K. Japan, 1970–73; Head, European Supply and Marketing, 1974–77; Man. Dir, Shell UK Oil, 1977–78; Regional Co-ordinator, UK and Eire, Shell Internat. Pet. Co. Ltd, 1978–85; Shell UK Ltd: Dep. Chm., 1978–79; Chief Exec., 1978–85; Govt Dir, 1984–87, Dep. Chm., 1987–91, British Telecom. Chm., British Biotech plc, 1995–98 (Dir, 1993–98); Director: Vickers PLC, 1981–90; Glaxo Hldgs PLC, 1982–90; Lloyds Bank Plc, 1985–95; Lloyds Merchant Bank Hldgs Ltd, 1985–87; Candover Investments PLC, 1990–98; Tandem Computers Ltd, 1991–97; Lloyds TSB plc, 1996–98. Chairman: Adv. Council, London Enterprise Agency, 1979–85; UK Oil Industry Emergency Cttee, 1980–85; Council of Industry for Management Educn, 1981–85; Investment Bd, Electra-Candover Partners, 1985–95. Member: Council, CBI, 1979–90 (Chm., CBI Europe Cttee, 1980–88; Mem., President's Cttee, 1980–88); Council, Inst. of Petroleum, 1979–81; Council, Inst. for Fiscal Studies, 1982–; Governing Council, Business in the Community, 1982–85; Council, UK Centre for Econ. and Environmental Develt, 1985–89; Royal Commn on Environmental Pollution, 1986–87; Chm., Electronics Industry EDC, 1986–87. Chairman: Langs Lead Body, 1990–95; Council for Industry and Higher Educn, 1991–98 (Mem., 1988–98); Dep. Chm., Nat. Commn on Educn, 1991–2000; Pres., Council for Educn in World Citizenship, 1992–2003. Mem., Council for Charitable Support, 1986–91; Chairman: RA Trust, 1987–96 (Trustee, RA, 1983–); Trustees, British Empire and Commonwealth Mus., 2003–06. Governor, NIESR, 1983–; Pro-Chancellor, Aston Univ., 1987–93. CCMI (CBIM 1980). DUniv Stirling, 1983; Hon. LLD: Aberdeen, 1985; Manchester, 1986; UWE, 1998; Hon. DSc Aston, 1992. *Recreations:* golf, music, theatre, travel. *Address:* Netheravon House, Netheravon Road South, W4 2PY. *T:* (020) 8994 3731. *Clubs:* Brooks's; Royal Mid-Surrey; Sunningdale Golf.

See also J. P. Raisman.

RAISON, Dr John Charles Anthony, MA, MD; FFPH; Consultant in Public Health Medicine, Wessex Regional Health Authority, 1982–91, retired; *b* 13 May 1926; *s* of late Cyril A. Raison, FRCS, Edgbaston, Birmingham, and of Ceres Raison; *m* 1st, 1951 (marr. diss. 1982); one *s* two *d*; 2nd, 1983, Ann Alexander, *d* of Captain Faulkner, MM and Mrs J. H. R. Faulkner, Southampton; three step *d*. *Educ:* Malvern Coll.; Trinity Hall, Cambridge (MD); Birmingham Univ. Consultant Clinical Physiologist in Cardiac Surgery, Birmingham Reg. Hosp. Bd, 1962; Hon. Associate Consultant Clinical Physiologist, United Birmingham Hosps, 1963; Sen. Physiologist, Dir of Clinical Res. and Chief Planner, Heart Research Inst., Presbyterian-Pacific Medical Center, San Francisco, 1966; Chief Scientific Officer and Sen. Prin. Medical Officer, Scientific Services, DHSS, 1974–78; Dep. Dir, Nat. Radiological Protection Bd, 1978–81. Vis. Consultant, Civic Hosps, Lisbon (Gulbenkian Foundn), 1962; Arris and Gale Lectr, Royal College of Surgeons, 1965. Councillor, Southam RDC, 1955–59. *Publications:* chapters in books, and papers in medical jls on open-heart surgery, extracorporeal circulation, intensive care, scientific services in health care, and computers in medicine. *Recreations:* gardening, golf, singing. *Address:* 15 The Woodlands, Church Lane, Kings Worthy, near Winchester, Hants SO23 7QQ. *T:* (01962) 885722.

RAISON, Rt Hon. Sir Timothy (Hugh Francis), Kt 1991; PC 1982; Chairman: Advertising Standards Authority, 1991–94; Aylesbury Vale Community Healthcare NHS Trust, 1992–98; *b* 3 Nov. 1929; *s* of late Maxwell and Celia Raison; *m* 1956, Veldes Julia

Charrington; one *s* three *d*. *Educ:* Dragon Sch., Oxford; Eton (King's Schol.); Christ Church, Oxford (Open History Schol.). Editorial Staff: Picture Post, 1953–56; New Scientist, 1956–61; Editor: Crossbow, 1958–60; New Society, 1962–68. Member: Youth Service Develt Council, 1960–63; Central Adv. Council for Educn, 1963–66; Adv. Cttee on Drug Dependence, 1966–70; Home Office Adv., Council on Penal System, 1970–74; (co-opted) Inner London Educn Authority Educn Cttee, 1967–70; Richmond upon Thames Council, 1967–71. MP (C) Aylesbury, 1970–92; PPS to Sec. of State for N Ireland, 1972–73; Parly Under-Sec. of State, DES, 1973–74; Opposition spokesman on the Environment, 1975–76; Minister of State, Home Office, 1979–83; Minister of State, FCO, and Minister for Overseas Develt, 1983–86. Chm., Select Cttee on Educn, Science and the Arts, 1987–89. Sen. Fellow, Centre for Studies in Soc. Policy, 1974–77; Mem. Council, PSI, 1978–79; Vice-Chm. Bd, British Council, 1987–92. Trustee, BM, 1991–99. Mem. Council, Nat. Trust, 1997–2000. Nansen Medal (for share in originating World Refugee Year), 1960. *Publications:* Why Conservative?, 1964; (ed) Youth in New Society, 1966; (ed) Founding Fathers of Social Science, 1969; Power and Parliament, 1979; Tories and the Welfare State, 1990; various political pamphlets. *Recreations:* golf, gardening, history of art. *Club:* Beefsteak.

RAITZ, Vladimir Gavrilovich; airline and travel consultant; *b* 23 May 1922; *s* of Dr Gavril Raitz and Cecilia Raitz; *m* 1954, Helen Antonia (*née* Corkrey); three *d*. *Educ:* Mill Hill Sch.; LSE (BSc(Econ.), Econ History, 1942). British United Press, 1942–43; Reuters, 1943–48; Chm., Horizon Holidays, 1949–74 (pioneered holidays by air). Dir, Scantours Ltd, 1999–2005. Member: NEDC for Hotels and Catering Industry, 1968–74; Cinematograph Films Council, 1969–74; Ct of Governors, LSE, 1971–95. Cavaliere Ufficiale, Order of Merit (Italy), 1971. *Publication:* (with Roger Bray) Flight to the Sun: the story of the holiday revolution, 2001. *Recreation:* watching grandchildren grow up. *Address:* 32 Dudley Court, Upper Berkeley Street, W1H 7PH. *T:* (020) 7262 2592. *Club:* Reform.

RAJ, Prof. Kakkadan Nandanath; Hon. Emeritus Fellow, Centre for Development Studies, Trivandrum, Kerala State, since 1983 (Fellow, 1973–84); National Professor, since 1992; *b* 13 May 1924; *s* of K. N. Gopalan and Karthiayani Gopalan; *m* 1957, Dr Sarasamma Narayanan; two *s*. *Educ:* Madras Christian Coll., Tambaram (BA (Hons), MA, in Economics); London Sch. of Economics (PhD (Econ); Hon. Fellow, 1982). Asst Editor, Associated Newspapers of Ceylon, Nov. 1947–July 1948; Research Officer, Dept of Research, Reserve Bank of India, Aug. 1948–Feb. 1950; Asst Chief, Economic Div., Planning Commn, Govt of India, 1950–53; University of Delhi: Prof. of Economics, Delhi Sch. of Economics, 1953–73; Vice-Chancellor, 1969–70; Nat. Fellow in Economics, 1971–73; Jawaharlal Nehru Fellow, 1987–88. Mem., Economic Adv. Council to Prime Minister of India, 1983–91. Visiting Prof., Johns Hopkins Univ., Jan.-June, 1958; Vis. Fellow, Nuffield Coll., Oxford, Jan.–June, 1960. Corresp. Fellow, British Academy, 1972. Hon. Fellow, Amer. Economic Assoc. *Publications:* The Monetary Policy of the Reserve Bank of India, 1948; Employment Aspects of Planning in Underdeveloped Economies, 1956; Some Economic Aspects of the Bhakra-Nangal Project, 1960; Indian Economic Growth-Performance and Prospects, 1964; India, Pakistan and China-Economic Growth and Outlook, 1966; Investment in Livestock in Agrarian Economies, 1969; (ed jtly) Essays on the Commercialization of Indian Agriculture, 1985; Organizational Issues in Indian Agriculture, 1990; also articles in Economic Weekly, Economic and Political Weekly, Indian Economic Review, Oxford Economic Papers. *Address:* Nandavan, Kumarapuram, Trivandrum 695011, Kerala State, India. *T:* (home) (471) 443309, *T:* (office) (471) 448881, 448412.

RAKE, Sir Michael Derek Vaughan, Kt 2007; FCA; Chairman, British Telecommunications plc, since 2007; *b* 17 Jan. 1948; *s* of Derek Shannon Vaughan Rake and Rosamund Rake (*née* Barrett); *m* 1st, 1970, Julia (*née* Cook); three *s*; 2nd, 1986, Caroline (*née* Thomas); one *s*. *Educ:* Wellington Coll. FCA 1970. Turquands Barton Mayhew, London and Brussels, 1968–74; KPMG: Brussels, 1974; Partner, 1979–; Partner i/c of Audit, Belgium and Luxembourg, 1983–86; Sen. Resident Partner, ME, 1986–89; Partner, London office, 1989–; Mem., UK Bd, 1991– (Chm., 1998–); Regl Man. Partner, SE Reg., 1992–94; Chief Exec., London and SE Reg., 1994–96; Chief Operating Officer, UK, 1996–98; Sen. Partner, KPMG UK, 1998–2006; Chairman: KPMG Europe, 1999–2002; KPMG Internat., 2002–07. Mem., Task Force on US/UK Regulation, DTI, 2006–07; Chm., UK Commn for Employment and Skills, 2008–. Chm., BITC, 2004– (Dep. Chm., 1998–2004; Chm., Corporate Community Investment Leadership Team, 1998–2004); Member: Bd, Prince of Wales Internat. Business Leaders Forum, 1999–; Britain in Europe Business Leaders Gp, 2000–; President's Cttee, 2001–06, Internat. Adv. Cttee, 2005–, CBI; Internat. Financial Services London, 2001–06; Bd, Transatlantic Business Dialogue, 2004–; Bd, Business for New Europe, 2006–; London Financial High Level Stakeholder Gp, 2006–; Internat. Business Council, World Econ. Forum, 2006–. Mem., Adv. Bd, Cambridge Judge Inst., 2002–. MCMI 2006. Patron, Head Teachers Initiative, 2006–. Vice Pres., RNIB, 2003–. Reviseur d'Entreprise, Luxembourg. *Recreations:* polo, ski-ing. *Address:* BT Group plc, BT Centre, 81 Newgate Street, EC1A 7AJ. *Club:* Guards Polo Club (Mem. Bd, 2005–).

RALEIGH, Dr Jean Margaret Macdonald C.; *see* Curtis-Raleigh.

RALLI, Sir Godfrey (Victor), 3rd Bt *cr* 1912; TD; *b* 9 Sept. 1915; *s* of Sir Strati Ralli, 2nd Bt, MC; *S* father, 1964; *m* 1st, 1937, Nora Margaret Forman (marr. diss. 1947; she *d* 1990); one *s* two *d*; 2nd, 1949, Jean (*d* 1998), *er d* of late Keith Barlow. *Educ:* Eton. Joined Ralli Bros Ltd, 1936. Served War of 1939–45 (despatches), Captain, Berkshire Yeomanry RA. Dir and Vice-Pres., Ralli Bros Ltd, 1946–62; Chm., Greater London Fund for the Blind, 1962–82. *Recreations:* fishing, golf. *Heir: s* David Charles Ralli [*b* 5 April 1946; *m* 1975, Jacqueline Cecilia, *d* of late David Smith; one *s* one *d*]. *Address:* Panworth Hall, Ashill, Thetford, Norfolk IP25 7BB. *Club:* Naval and Military.

RALLING, (Antony) Christopher, OBE 1992; FRGS; freelance writer/director; *b* 12 April 1929; *s* of Harold St George Ralling and Dorothy Blanche Ralling; *m* 1963, Angela Norma (*née* Gardner); one *d*. *Educ:* Charterhouse; Wadham Coll., Oxford (BA 2nd Cl. Hons English). Joined BBC External Services, Scriptwriter, 1955; British Meml Foundn Fellowship to Australia, 1959; Dep. Editor, Panorama, BBC TV, 1964; joined BBC TV Documentaries, 1966; directed The Search for the Nile, 1972 (Amer. Acad. Award, 1972; Peabody Award, 1972); Mem., British Everest Expedn, 1975; produced The Voyage of Charles Darwin, 1978 (British Acad. Award, 1978; Desmond Davies British Acad. Award, 1978; RTS Silver Medal, 1979); Hd of Documentaries, BBC TV, 1980; left BBC to start Dolphin Productions, 1982; directed: The History of Africa, 1984; Chasing a Rainbow (Josephine Baker), 1986 (Amer. Acad. Award, 1986); Prince Charles at Forty, LWT, 1988; The Kon-Tiki Man, BBC, 1989; The Buried Mirror, BBC, 1992; A Diplomat in Japan, BBC, 1992; Return to Everest, Channel 4, 1993. FRGS 1978. *Publications:* Muggeridge Through the Microphone, 1967; The Voyage of Charles Darwin, 1978; Shackleton, 1983; The Kon-Tiki Man, 1990. *Recreations:* tennis, ski-ing. *Address:* Tankerville Cottage, Kingston Hill, Surrey KT2 7JH. *Club:* Alpine.

RALLS, Peter John Henry; QC 1997; **His Honour Judge Ralls;** a Circuit Judge, since 2008; *b* 18 July 1947; *s* of Ivan Jack Douglas Ralls and Sybil Gladys Child; *m* 1st, 1979, Anne Elizabeth Marriott (marr. diss. 1986); 2nd, 1997, Tonia Anne Clark; two *s* one *d*. *Educ:* Royal Russell Sch., Surrey; UCL (LLB Hons). Called to the Bar, Middle Temple, 1972; admitted Solicitor, 1981; returned to the Bar, 1982; an Asst Recorder, 1998–2000; a Recorder, 2000–08. Chm., Cowes Combined Clubs, 2001–. *Recreations:* yacht racing, cricket. *Address:* Southampton Crown Court, Courts of Justice, London Road, Southampton SO15 2XQ. *Clubs:* Brooks's, MCC; Royal London Yacht; Royal Yacht Squadron.

RALPH, Richard Peter, CMG 1997; CVO 1991; HM Diplomatic Service, retired; *b* 27 April 1946; *s* of Peter and Marion Ralph; *m* 1st, 1970 (marr. diss. 2001); one *s* one *d*; 2nd, 2002, Jemma Victoria Elizabeth Marlor. *Educ:* King's Sch., Canterbury; Edinburgh Univ. (MSc). Third Sec., FCO, 1969–70; Third, later Second, Sec., Vientiane, Laos, 1970–73; Second, later First, Sec., Lisbon, 1974–77; FCO, 1977–81; Head of Chancery, Harare, Zimbabwe, 1981–85; Counsellor, FCO, 1985–89; Head of Chancery and Congressional Counsellor, Washington, 1989–93; Ambassador to Latvia, 1993–95; Gov., Falkland Is, and Comr for S Georgia and S Sandwich Is, 1996–99; Ambassador: to Romania and to Moldova, 1999–2002; to Peru, 2003–06. Chairman: Anglo-Peruvian Soc.; S Georgia Soc. *Recreations:* motorcycles, tennis, reading, travelling. *Address:* 43 Albany Mansions, Albert Bridge Road, SW11 4PQ.

RALPHS, Enid Mary, (Lady Ralphs), CBE 1984; JP; DL; Chairman of the Council, 1981–84, Vice-President, since 1984, Magistrates' Association; *b* 20 Jan. 1915; *d* of Percy William Cowlin and Annie Louise Cowlin (*née* Willoughby); *m* 1938, Sir (Frederick) Lincoln Ralphs, Kt 1973 (*d* 1978); one *s* two *d*. *Educ:* Camborne Grammar Sch.; University Coll., Exeter (BA); DipEd Cambridge. Pres., Guild of Undergrads, Exeter, 1936–37; Vice-Pres., NUS, 1937–38. Teacher, Penzance Grammar Sch., 1937–38; Staff Tutor, Oxford Univ. Tutorial Classes Cttee, 1942–44; pt-time Sen. Lectr, Keswick Hall Coll. of Educn, 1948–80. Member: Working Party on Children and Young Persons Act 1969, 1977–78; Steering Cttee on Community Alternatives for Young Offenders, NACRO, 1979–82; Consultative Cttee on Educn in Norwich Prison, 1982–87; Home Office Adv. Bd on Restricted Patients, 1985–91; Chairman: Working Party on the Victim in Court, 1988; Working Party on Sentencing, a way ahead, 1989. Member: Religious Adv. Council, BBC Midland Reg., 1963–66; Guide Council for GB, 1965–68. President: Norwich and Dist Br., UNA, 1973–2002; Norfolk Guides (formerly Girl Guides), 1987–2002. Visitor, Wymondham Coll., 1991–. Trustee, Norfolk Children's Projects, 1982–2002. JP Norwich 1958; Chairman: Norwich Juvenile Panel, 1964–79; Norwich Bench, 1977–85; former Mem., Licensing Cttee; Mem., Domestic Panel, 1981–85; Vice-Pres., Norfolk Br., Magistrates' Assoc., 1986–; Dep. Chm., Norfolk Magistrates' Courts Cttee, 1978–85 (Chm., Trng Sub-Cttee); Mem., Central Council, Magistrates' Courts Cttees, 1974–81. DL Norfolk 1981. Hon. DCL East Anglia, 1989. *Publications:* (jtly) The Magistrate as Chairman, 1987; contribs to various jls. *Recreations:* gardening, travel. *Address:* Jesselton, 218 Unthank Road, Norwich NR2 2AH. *T:* (01603) 453382. *Clubs:* Royal Over-Seas League; Norfolk (Norwich).

RALSTON, Gen. Joseph W., DFC 1967; DSM 1990; Vice Chairman, The Cohen Group, since 2003; *b* 4 Nov. 1943; *m* 1989, Diana Dougherty; one *s* one *d*, and one step *s* one step *d*. *Educ:* Miami Univ. (BA Chemistry 1965); Central Michigan Univ. (MA Personnel Mgt 1976); John F. Kennedy Sch. of Govt, Harvard Univ. Commissioned USAF, Reserve Officer Trng Corps Program, 1965; F-105 Pilot, Laos and N Vietnam; US Army Comd and Gen. Staff Coll., 1976; Nat. War Coll., Washington, 1984; Asst Dep. COS (Ops), and Dep. COS (Requirements), HQ Tactical Air Comd, 1987–90; Dir, Tactical Progs, 1990–91, Opnl Requirements, 1991–92, HQ USAF; Comdr, Alaskan Comd, 11 Air Force, Alaskan N Amer. Aerospace Defense Comd Reg., and Jt Task Force Alaska, 1992–94; Dep. COS (Plans and Ops), HQ USAF, 1994–95; Comdr, Air Combat Comd, 1995–96; Vice Chm., Jt Chiefs of Staff, 1996–2000; SACEUR, NATO, and C-in-C, US European Comd, 2000–03. US Legion of Merit, DDSM, MSM, Air Medal, Air Force Commendation Medal. Highest degree, Mil. Order of Merit (Morocco), 1996; Officer, Legion of Honour (France), 1997; Kt Comdr's Cross, Order of Merit (Germany), 1999; Grand Cross, Royal Norwegian Order of Merit (Norway), 2000. *Recreations:* hunting, fishing, gardening. *Address:* The Cohen Group, 1200, 19th Street NW, Suite 400, Washington, DC 20036, USA.

RAMA RAU, Santha; free-lance writer, since 1945; English teacher at Sarah Lawrence College, Bronxville, NY, since 1971; *b* Madras, India, 24 Jan. 1923; *d* of late Sir Benegal Rama Rau, CIE and Lady Dhanvanthi Rama Rau; *m* 1st, 1951, Faubion Bowers (marr. diss. 1966); one *s*; 2nd, Gurdon W. Wattles. *Educ:* St Paul's Girls' School, London, England; Wellesley College, Mass, USA. Feature writer for the Office of War Information, New York, USA, during vacations from college, 1942–45. Hon. doctorate: Bates College, USA, 1961; Russell Sage College, 1965; Phi Beta Kappa, Wellesley College, 1960; Roosevelt Coll., 1962; Brandeis Univ., 1963; Bard Coll., NY, 1964. *Publications:* Home to India, 1945; East of Home, 1950; This is India, 1953; Remember the House, 1955; View to the South-East, 1957; My Russian Journey, 1959; A Passage to India (dramatization), 1962; Gifts of Passage, 1962; The Adventuress, 1971; Cooking of India, 1971 (2 vols); A Princess Remembers (with Rajmata Gayatri Devi of Jaipur), 1976; An Inheritance (with Dhanvanthi Rama Rau), 1977; many articles and short stories in New Yorker, Art News, Horizon, Saturday Evening Post, Reader's Digest, National Geographic, etc. *Address:* 508 Leedsville Road, Amenia, NY 12501, USA.

RAMADHANI, Rt Rev. John Acland; Bishop of Zanzibar and Tanga, 1980–2000, Bishop of Zanzibar, 2000–02; *b* 1 Aug. 1932. *Educ:* Univ. of Birmingham (DipTh 1975); Univ. of Dar-es-Salaam (BA 1967); Queen's Coll., Birmingham. Deacon 1975, Birmingham; priest 1976, Dar-es-Salaam; Asst Chaplain, Queen's Coll., Birmingham, 1975–76; Warden, St Mark's Theol Coll., Dar-es-Salaam, 1976–80; Archbishop of Tanzania, 1984–98. *Address:* PO Box 5, Zanzibar, Tanzania.

RAMAGE, (James) Granville (William), CMG 1975; HM Diplomatic Service, retired; *b* 19 Nov. 1919; *s* of late Rev. George Granville Ramage and Helen Marion (*née* Middlemass); *m* 1947, Eileen Mary Smith; one *s* two *d*. *Educ:* Glasgow Acad.; Glasgow University. Served in HM Forces, 1940–46 (despatches). Entered HM Foreign Service, 1947; seconded for service at Bombay, 1947–49; transf. to Foreign Office, 1950; First Sec. and Consul at Manila, 1952–56; South-East Asia Dept, FO, 1956–58; Consul at Atlanta, Ga, 1958–62; Gen. Dept, FO, 1962–63; Consul-General, Tangier, 1963–67; High Comr in The Gambia, 1968–71; Ambassador, People's Democratic Republic of Yemen, 1972–75; Consul General at Boston, Massachusetts, 1975–77. *Recreation:* music. *Address:* King's Head Court, London Road, Sawbridgeworth, Herts CM21 9JT. *T:* (01279) 860740.

RAMAGE, Prof. Robert, DSc; FRS 1992; CChem, FRSC; FRSE; Scientific Director, since 2002 and Vice President, since 2004, Almac Sciences (Scotland) Ltd (formerly Albachem Ltd, then CSS Albachem); Forbes Professor of Organic Chemistry, University of Edinburgh, 1984–2001; *b* 4 Oct. 1935; *s* of Robert Bain Ramage and Jessie Boag

Ramage; *m* 1961, Joan Fraser Paterson; three *d*. *Educ:* Whitehill Sen. Secondary Sch., Glasgow; Univ. of Glasgow (BSc Hons 1958; PhD 1961; DSc 1982). Fulbright Fellow and Fellow of Harvard Coll., 1961–63; Research at Woodward Res. Inst., 1963–64; Lectr then Sen. Lectr, Univ. of Liverpool, 1964–77; Prof., 1977–84, Head of Dept, 1979–84, UMIST; Head, Dept of Chem., Univ. of Edinburgh, 1987–90, 1997–2000; Dir, Edinburgh Centre for Protein Technology, 1996–2000. FRSE 1986; FRSA 1990. Dr (*hc*) Lille. *Recreations:* sport, gardening, current affairs. *Address:* Almac Sciences (Scotland) Ltd, Elvingston Science Centre, near Gladsmuir, E Lothian EH33 1EH. *T:* (01875) 408150.

RAMAKRISHNAN, Prof. Tiruppattur Venkatachalamurti, FRS 2000; Professor of Physics, 1981–84 and 1986–2003, and INSA Srinivasa Ramanujan Research Professor, 1997–2002, Indian Institute of Science, Bangalore; DAE Homi Bhabha Professor, Department of Physics, Banaras Hindu University, since 2003; *b* 14 Aug. 1941; *s* of Tiruppattur Ramaseshayyar Venkatachala-Murti and Jayalakshmi Murti; *m* 1970, Meera Rao; one *s* one *d*. *Educ:* Banaras Hindu Univ., Varanasi (BSc 1959; MSc 1961); Columbia Univ., NY (PhD 1966). Lectr, 1966, Asst Prof., 1967, Indian Inst. of Technol., Kanpur; Asst Res. Physicist, UCSD, 1968–70; Asst Prof., 1970–77, Prof. of Physics, 1977–80, Indian Inst. of Technol., Kanpur; Prof. of Physics, Banaras Hindu Univ., 1984–86. Vis. Res. Physicist, 1978–81, Vis. Prof., 1990–91, Princeton Univ. Consultant, Bell Labs, 1979–81. Pres., Indian Acad. of Scis, 2004–06. Fellow: INSA, 1984; APS, 1984; Third World Acad. of Scis, 1990. Padma Sri, 2001. *Publications:* (jtly) Physics, 1988, 2nd edn 1994; (with C. N. R. Rao) Superconductivity Today, 1990, 2nd edn 1997; about 100 research papers and 6 review articles. *Recreation:* trekking. *Address:* Department of Physics, Banaras Hindu University, Varanasi 221005, India; *e-mail:* tvrama@bhu.ac.in; Department of Physics, Indian Institute of Science, Bangalore 560012, India. *T:* (80) 3092579, 3600591.

RAMAKRISHNAN, Prof. Venkatraman, PhD; FRS 2003; Senior Scientist and Group Leader, Structural Studies Division, MRC Laboratory of Molecular Biology, Cambridge, since 1999. *Educ:* Baroda Univ., India (BSc 1971); Ohio Univ. (PhD 1976); Univ. of Calif, San Diego. Postdoctoral Fellow, Dept of Chem., Yale Univ., 1978–82; Res. Staff, Oak Ridge Nat. Lab., 1982–83; Brookhaven National Laboratory: Asst Biophysicist, 1983–85; Associate Biophysicist, 1985–88; Biophysicist, 1988–94; Sen. Biophysicist, 1994–95; Prof., Biochem. Dept, Univ. of Utah, 1995–99. *Address:* Structural Studies Division, MRC Laboratory of Molecular Biology, Hills Road, Cambridge CB2 0QH.

RAMAPHOSA, (Matamela) Cyril; Chairman, Shanduka Group, since 2000; *b* 17 Nov. 1952; *s* of late Samuel Ramaphosa and of Erdmuth Ramaphosa; *m* 1996, Tshepo Motsepe; two *s* two *d*. *Educ:* Sekano-Ntoane High Sch., Soweto; Univ. of North, Turfloop (BProc 1981). Detained under Terrorism Act for 11 months, 1974, and 6 months, 1976; active in Black People's Convention, 1975; articled clerk, Attorney Henry Dolovitz, 1977; Legal Advr, Council of Unions of SA, 1981–82; First Gen. Sec., NUM, SA, 1982–91; arrested and detained under Riotous Assemblies Act, 1984; organised first legal one day strike by black mineworkers, 1984; African National Congress: Mem., Nat. Exec. Cttee, 1991–; Sec.-Gen., 1991–96; Leader, ANC Delegn to Multi-Party Negotiations, 1992–94; Chm., Constitutional Assembly, Govt of Nat. Unity, 1994–96. Exec. Dep. Chm., New Africa Investments Ltd, 1996–99; Chm. and Chief Exec., Molope Gp, 1999–2000; Chairman: Rebhold Services (Pty), 2000–03; MCI Gp, 2003–. Dep. Chm., Commonwealth Business Council. Vis. Prof. of Law, Stanford Univ., USA, 1991. Hon. Dr: Massachusetts, 1992; Univ. of the North, 2002; Hon. PhD Port Elizabeth, 1995; Hon. LLD: Natal, 1997; Cape Town, 1997; Lesotho, 2002. *Recreation:* fly-fishing. *Address:* Suite 167, Private Bag X9924, Sandton, 2146, South Africa. *T:* (11) 3058900. *Club:* River (Johannesburg).

RAMBAHADUR LIMBU, Captain, VC 1966; MVO 1984; HM the Queen's Gurkha Orderly Officer, 1983–84; employed in Sultanate of Negara Brunei Darussalam, 1985–92; *b* Nov. 1939; *s* of late Tekbir Limbu; *m* 1st, 1960, Tikamaya Limbuni (*d* 1966); two *s*; 2nd, 1967, Punimaya Limbuni; three *s*. Army Cert. of Educn 1st cl. Enlisted 10th Princess Mary's Own Gurkha Rifles, 1957; served on ops in Borneo (VC); promoted Sergeant, 1971; WOII, 1976; commissioned, 1977. Hon. Captain (Gurkha Commnd Officer), 1985. *Publication:* My Life Story, 1978. *Recreations:* football, volley-ball, badminton, basketball. *Address:* Ward No 13 Damak, Nagar Palika, PO Box Damak, District Jhapa, Mechi Zone, East Nepal. *Clubs:* VC and GC Association, Royal Society of St George (England).

RAMGOOLAM, Dr the Hon. Navinchandra; MP Mauritius, since 1991; Prime Minister of Mauritius, 1995–2000 and since 2005; *b* 14 July 1947; *s* of Rt Hon. Sir Seewoosagur Ramgoolam, GCMG, PC (1st Prime Minister of Mauritius) and Lady Sushill Ramgoolam; *m* 1979, Veena Brizmohun. *Educ:* Royal Coll. of Surgeons, Dublin; London Sch. of Econs (LLB Hons; Hon. Fellow, 1998); Inns of Court Sch. of Law. LRCP, LRCSI 1975. Called to the Bar, Inner Temple, 1993. Mauritius Labour Party: Leader, 1991–; Pres., 1991–92. Leader of the Opposition, Mauritius, 1991–95. *Recreations:* reading, music, water ski-ing, chess. *Address:* Government House, Port-Louis, Mauritius. *Club:* Mauritius Turf.

RAMIN, Ileana, (Mme Manfred Ramin); *see* Cotrubas, I.

RAMMELL, William Ernest; MP (Lab) Harlow, since 1997; Minister of State, Foreign and Commonwealth Office, since 2008; *b* 10 Oct. 1959; *s* of William Ernest Rammell and Joan Elizabeth Rammell; *m* 1983, Beryl Jarhall; one *s* one *d*. *Educ:* University Coll., Cardiff (BA French). Pres., Cardiff Students' Union, 1982–83; mgt trainee, BR, 1983–84; NUS Regl Official, 1984–87; Hd of Youth Services, Basildon Council, 1987–89; General Manager: Students' Union, KCL, 1989–94; Univ. of London Union, 1994–97. PPS to Sec. of State for Culture, Media and Sport, 2001–02; Parly Under-Sec. of State, FCO, 2002–05; Minister of State: (Minister for Univs), DfES, 2005–07; DIUS, 2007–08. Chm., Lab Movt for Europe. *Recreations:* football, cricket, socialising. *Address:* House of Commons, SW1A 0AA. *T:* (020) 7219 3000; 9 Orchard Croft, Harlow, Essex CM20 3BA. *T:* (01279) 439706.

RAMOS, Gen. Fidel Valdez; President of the Philippines, 1992–98; *b* 18 March 1928; *s* of Narciso Ramos and Angela (*née* Valdez); *m* Amelita Martinez; five *d*. *Educ:* Nat. Univ. of Manila; USMA W Point; Univ. of Illinois. Active service in Korea and Vietnam; Dep. Chief of Staff, 1981, Chief of Staff, 1986, Philippines Armed Forces; Sec. of Nat. Defence, 1988. Leader, People's Power Party. Légion d'Honneur (France), 1987. *Address:* 26/F Urban Bank Plaza, Urban Avenue, Makati City, Philippines; 120 Maria Cristina Street, Ayala Alabang Village, Muntinlupa City, Philippines; *e-mail:* rpdeu@skyinet.net.

RAMOS-HORTA, José; President of East Timor, since 2007; *b* Dili, E Timor, 26 Dec. 1949; *s* of late Francisco Horta and of Natalina Ramos Filipe Horta; *m* 1978, Ana Pessoa (marr. diss.); one *s*. *Educ:* Hague Acad. of Internat. Law; Internat. Inst. of Human Rights, Strasbourg; Columbia Univ., NY; Antioch Univ. (MA 1984). Journalist, radio and TV correspondent, 1969–74; Minister for Ext. Affairs and Inf., E Timor, Dec. 1975; Perm. Rep. for Fretilin to UN, NY, 1976–89; Public Affairs and Media Dir, Embassy of Mozambique, Washington, 1987–88; Special Rep. of Nat. Council of Maubere Resistance, 1991; Foreign Minister, 2002–06, Prime Minister, 2006–07, E Timor. Founder Dir and Lectr, Diplomacy Trng Prog., 1990, and Vis. Prof., 1996, Law Faculty, Univ. of NSW. Member: Peace Action Council, Unrepresented Nations and Peoples Orgn, The Hague (UNPO Award, 1996); Exec. Council, Internat. Service for Human Rights, Geneva; Bd, E Timor Human Rights Centre, Melbourne. Sen. Associate Mem., St Antony's Coll., Oxford, 1987. Nobel Peace Prize (jtly), 1996. Order of Freedom (Portugal), 1996. *Publications:* Funu: the unfinished saga of East Timor, 1987; contrib. to newspapers and periodicals in Portugal, France, USA and Australia. *Recreation:* tennis. *Address:* Office of the President, Palácio das Cinzas, Cailcoli, Dili, East Timor. *T:* 3339999; *e-mail:* presidencia.republica.tl@gmail.com; (office) Rua São Lazaro 16, 1°, 1150 Lisbon, Portugal. *T:* (1) 8863727, *Fax:* (1) 8863791.

RAMPHAL, Sir Shridath Surendranath, OE 1983; GCMG 1990 (CMG 1966); OM (Jamaica) 1990; OCC 1991; Kt 1970; QC (Guyana) 1965, SC 1966; Secretary-General of the Commonwealth, 1975–90; Counsel, Guyana-Suriname UN Convention on the Law of the Sea Arbitration, since 2004; *b* 3 Oct. 1928; *s* of James and Grace Ramphal; *m* 1951, Lois Winifred King; two *s* two *d*. *Educ:* King's Coll., London (LLM 1952; FKC 1975). Called to the Bar, Gray's Inn, 1951 (Hon. Bencher 1981). Colonial Legal Probationer, 1951; Arden and Atkin Prize, 1952; John Simon Guggenheim Fellow, Harvard Law Sch., 1962. Crown Counsel, British Guiana, 1953–54; Asst to Attorney-Gen., 1954–56; Legal Draftsman, 1956–58; First Legal Draftsman, West Indies, 1958–59; Solicitor-Gen., British Guiana, 1959–61; Asst Attorney-Gen., West Indies, 1961–62, Attorney-Gen., Guyana, 1965–73; Minister of State for External Affairs, Guyana, 1967–72; Foreign Minister and Attorney General, Guyana, 1972–73; Minister, Foreign Affairs and Justice, 1973–75; Mem., Nat. Assembly, Guyana, 1965–75. Member: Ind. (Brandt) Commn on Internat. Develt Issues, 1977–83; Ind. (Palme) Commn on Disarmament and Security Issues, 1980–89; Ind. Commn on Internat. Humanitarian Issues, 1983–88; World (Brundtland) Commn on Environment and Develt, 1984–87; South Commn, 1987–90; Carnegie Commn on Preventing Deadly Conflict, 1994–98; Chm., W Indian Commn, 1990–92; Co-Chm., Commn on Global Governance, 1992–2000. Special Advr, Sec. Gen., UN Conf. on Envmt and Develt, 1992; Chm., UN Cttee on Develt Planning, 1984–87; Chief Negotiator on Ext. Economic Relations in Caribbean Reg., 1997–2001; Facilitator, Belize-Guatemala Dispute, 2002–02. Chairman: Internat. Adv. Cttee, Future Generations Alliance Foundn, Kyoto, 1994–97; Bd, Internat. Inst. for Democracy and Electoral Assistance, Stockholm, 1995–2001; Pres., Internat. Steering Cttee, Leadership in Envmt and Develt, 1991–98; Member: Bd, Internat. Develt Res. Centre, Ottawa, 1994–98; Council, Internat. Negotiating Network, Carter Centre, Atlanta, 1991–97. Mem., Internat. Commn of Jurists, 1970–. Chancellor: Univ. of Guyana, 1988–92; Univ. of Warwick, 1989–2002; Univ. of WI, 1989–. Visiting Professor: Exeter Univ., 1988; Faculty of Laws, KCL, 1988. Toronto Univ., 1995; Osgoode Hall Law Sch., Univ. of York, Toronto, 1995. FRSA 1981; CCMI (CBIM 1986). Fellow, LSE, 1979; Hon. Fellow, Magdalen Coll., Oxford, 1982; Companion, Leicester Poly., 1991. Hon. LLD: Panjab, 1975; Southampton, 1976; St Francis Xavier, NS, 1978; Univ. of WI, 1978; Aberdeen, 1979; Cape Coast, Ghana, 1980; London, 1981; Benin, Nigeria, 1982; Hull, 1983; Yale, 1985; Cambridge, 1985; Warwick, 1988; York, Ont, 1988; Malta, 1989; Otago, 1990; DUniv: Surrey, 1979; Essex, 1980; Hon. DHL: Simmons Coll., Boston, 1982; Duke Univ., 1985; Hon. DCL: Oxon, 1982; E Anglia, 1983; Durham, 1985; Hon. DLitt: Bradford, 1985; Indira Gandhi Nat. Open Univ., New Delhi, 1989; Hon. DSc Cranfield Inst. of Technology, 1987. Albert Medal, RSA, 1988; Internat. Educn Award, Richmond Coll., 1988; Rene Dubos Human Envmt Award, 1993. AC 1982; ONZ 1990; Comdr, Order of Golden Ark (Netherlands), 1994. *Publications:* One World to Share: selected speeches of the Commonwealth Secretary-General 1975–79, 1979; Nkrumah and the Eighties: Kwame Nkrumah Memorial Lectures, 1980; Sovereignty and Solidarity: Callander Memorial Lectures, 1981; Some in Light and Some in Darkness: the long shadow of slavery (Wilberforce Lecture), 1983; The Message not the Messenger (STC Communication Lecture), 1985; The Trampling of the Grass (Economic Commn for Africa Silver Jubilee Lecture), 1985; Inseparable Humanity: an anthology of reflections of Shridath Ramphal (ed Ron Sanders), 1988; An End to Otherness (eight speeches by the Commonwealth Secretary-General), 1990; Our Country, The Planet, 1992; contrib. various political, legal and other jls incl. International and Comparative Law Qly, Caribbean Qly, Public Law, Guyana Jl, Round Table, Foreign Policy, Third World Qly, RSA Jl Internat. Affairs. *Address:* The Garden House, Pleasant Hall Drive, Dayrells Road, Christchurch BB14030, Barbados, West Indies. *T:* 435 7531. *Clubs:* Athenæum, Royal Automobile, Travellers.

RAMPHUL, Sir Indurduth, Kt 1991; Governor, Bank of Mauritius, 1982–96; *b* 10 Oct. 1931; *m* 1962, Taramatee Seedoyal; one *s* one *d*. *Educ:* Univ. of Exeter (Dip. Public Admin). Asst Sec., Min. of Finance, 1966–67; Bank of Mauritius: Manager, 1967; Chief Manager, 1970; Man. Dir, 1973. Alternate Governor, IMF for Mauritius, 1982–96. *Recreations:* reading, swimming. *Address:* 9 Buswell Avenue, Quatre Bornes, Mauritius. *T:* 4541643, *Fax:* 4540559; *e-mail:* sirindur@internet.mu. *Clubs:* Mauritius Turf; Cadets.

RAMSAY, family name of **Earl of Dalhousie**.

RAMSAY OF CARTVALE, Baroness *cr* 1996 (Life Peer), of Langside in the City of Glasgow; **Meta Ramsay;** international affairs consultant; a Deputy Speaker, House of Lords2002–06; *b* 12 July 1936; *d* of Alexander Ramsay and Sheila Ramsay (*née* Jackson). *Educ:* Hutchesons' Girls' Grammar Sch.; Univ. of Glasgow (MA; MEd); Graduate Inst. of Internat. Studies, Geneva. President: Students' Rep. Council, Univ. of Glasgow, 1958–59; Scottish Union of Students, 1959–60; Associate Sec. for Europe, Co-ordinating Secretariat, Nat. Unions of Students, Leiden, Netherlands, 1960–63; Manager, Fund for Internat. Student Co-operation, 1963–67; HM Diplomatic Service, 1969–91: Stockholm, 1970–73; Helsinki, 1981–85; Counsellor, FCO, 1987–91. Foreign Policy Advr to Leader of Opposition, 1992–94; Special Advr to Shadow Sec. of State for Trade and Industry, 1994–95; a Baroness in Waiting (Govt Whip), 1997–2001. Mem., Intelligence and Security Cttee, 1997, 2005–07. Mem., Labour Finance and Industry Gp, 1997–. Mem., UK Parly delegn to NATO Parly Assembly, 2003–. Chm., Atlantic Council of the UK, 2001–. Co-Chair, Scottish Constitutional Convention, 1997–99; Chm., Scotland in Europe, 2004–. Hon. Vis. Res. Fellow in Peace Studies, Univ. of Bradford, 1996. Mem., Lewisham CHC, 1992–94. Chm., Bd of Governors, Fairlawn Primary Sch., Lewisham, 1991–97. Member: RIIA; Inst. of Jewish Policy Res.; Fabian Soc.; Labour Movement in Europe; Co-operative Party. FRSA 1995. Hon. DLitt Bradford, 1997; DUniv Glasgow, 2004. *Recreations:* theatre, opera, ballet. *Address:* House of Lords, SW1A 0PW. *T:* (020) 7219 5353. *Clubs:* Reform, University Women's.

RAMSAY, Lord; Simon David Ramsay; Lieutenant, 1st Battalion, Scots Guards; *b* 18 April 1981; *s* and *heir* of Earl of Dalhousie, *qv*. *Educ:* Harrow. *Recreations:* history of art, design and sculpture, country sports. *Address:* Brechin Castle, Brechin, Angus DD9 6SH.

RAMSAY, Sir Alexander William Burnett, 7th Bt *cr* 1806, of Balmain (also *heir-pres.* to Btcy of Burnett, *cr* 1626 (Nova Scotia), of Leys, Kincardineshire, which became dormant, 1959, on death of Sir Alexander Edwin Burnett of Leys, and was not claimed by Sir

Alexander Burnett Ramsay, 6th Bt, of Balmain); *b* 4 Aug. 1938; *s* of Sir Alexander Burnett Ramsay, 6th Bt and Isabel Ellice, *e d* of late William Whitney, Woodstock, New South Wales; *S* father, 1965; *m* 1963, Neryl Eileen, *d* of J. C. Smith Thornton, Trangie, NSW; three *s*. *Heir: s* Alexander David Ramsay [*b* 20 Aug. 1966; *m* 1990, Annette Yvonne, *d* of H. M. Plummer; three *d*]. *Address:* Bulbah, Warren, NSW 2824, Australia.

RAMSAY, Sir Allan (John Heppel Ramsay), KBE 1992; CMG 1989; HM Diplomatic Service, retired; Ambassador to the Kingdom of Morocco, 1992–96; *b* 19 Oct. 1937; *s* of Norman Ramsay Ramsay and Evelyn Faith Sorel-Cameron; *m* 1966, Pauline Therèse Lescher; two *s* one *d*. *Educ:* Bedford Sch.; RMA Sandhurst; Durham Univ. Served Army, 1957–70: Somerset Light Infantry, 1957–64; Trucial Oman Scouts, 1964–66; DLI, 1966–68. MECAS, 1968–69; entered FCO, 1970; First Sec. (Commercial), Cairo, 1973–76; First Sec. and Hd of Chancery, Kabul, 1976–78; Counsellor and Head of Chancery: Baghdad, 1980–83; Mexico City, 1983–85; Ambassador: to Lebanon, 1988–90; to Sudan, 1990–91. *Address:* Le Genest, 53190 Landivy, France.

RAMSAY, Andrew Charles Bruce, CB 2007; Director General, Partnerships and Programmes, Department for Culture, Media and Sport, since 2008; *b* 30 May 1951; *s* of Norman Bruce Ramsay and Marysha Octavia Ramsay; *m* 1983, Katharine Celia Marsh; two *d*. *Educ:* Winchester Coll.; Bedford Coll., London Univ. (BA). Joined DoE, 1974; Private Sec. to Parly Sec., Dept of Transport, 1978–80; Principal, DoE and Dept of Transport, 1980–85; Asst Sec., DoE, 1986–93; Under Sec. and Head of Arts, Sport and Lottery Gp, DNH, 1993–96; Under Sec. and Hd of Finance, Lottery and Personnel, then Corporate Services, Gp, DNH then DCMS, 1996–2000; Dir Gen., Creative Industries, Broadcasting, Gambling and Lottery Gp, 2000–04, Econ. Impact, 2004–06, Culture, Creativity and Economy, 2006–08, DCMS. *Recreations:* gardening, opera, birds. *Address:* Department for Culture, Media and Sport, 2–4 Cockspur Street, SW1Y 5DH; West Hall, Sedgeford, Hunstanton, Norfolk PE36 5LY.

RAMSAY, Andrew Vernon, CEng, FIET; Chief Executive Officer (formerly Executive Director), Engineering Council UK, since 2002 (Acting Director, 2001–02); *b* 7 July 1948; *s* of Douglas Charles Ramsay and Dorothy Isobel Ramsay (*née* Shankland); *m* 1971, Ruth Irene Mullen; one *s* one *d*. *Educ:* Churchill Coll., Cambridge (MA). CEng 1979; FIET (FIEE 2000). Student apprentice, AEI, 1966–70; Project Engr, GEC, 1970–72; various posts, CEGB, 1973–79; Dep. Sec., 1979–84, Sec. and CEO, 1985–97, CIBSE; Dir for Engrs Regulation, Engrg Council, 1997–2001; Construction Industry Council: Sec., 1988–90; Mem., 1990–97. FCIS 1982. *Recreations:* cycling, S London Swimming Club. *Address:* Engineering Council UK, 246 High Holborn, WC1V 7EX. *T:* (020) 3206 0500; *e-mail:* info@engc.org.uk. *Club:* Rumford.

RAMSAY, Maj.-Gen. Charles Alexander, CB 1989; OBE 1979; *b* 12 Oct. 1936; *s* of Adm. Sir Bertram Home Ramsay, KCB, KBE, MVO, Allied Naval C-in-C, Invasion of Europe, 1944 (killed on active service, 1945), and Helen Margaret Menzies; *m* 1967, Hon. Mary MacAndrew, *d* of 1st Baron MacAndrew, PC, TD; two *s* two *d*. *Educ:* Eton; Sandhurst. Commissioned Royal Scots Greys, 1956; attended Canadian Army Staff Coll., 1967–68; served abroad in Germany, Middle East and Far East; Mil. Asst to VCDS, 1974–77; commanded Royal Scots Dragoon Guards, 1977–79; Colonel General Staff, MoD, 1979–80; Comdr 12th Armoured Bde, BAOR and Osnabrück Garrison, 1980–82; Dep. Dir of Mil. Ops, MoD, 1983–84; GOC Eastern District, 1984–87; Dir Gen., Army Orgn and TA, 1987–89; resigned from Army. Col, Royal Scots Dragoon Guards, 1992–98. Director: John Menzies plc, 1990–2004; Morningside Mgt LLC USA, 1990–2004, and other cos; Chairman: Eagle Enterprises Ltd, Bermuda, 1991–95; Cockburns of Leith Ltd, 1992–2004. Member, Queen's Body Guard for Scotland, Royal Company of Archers. *Recreations:* field sports, horse racing, travel, country affairs. *Address:* Bughtrig, Coldstream, Berwickshire TD12 4JP. *Clubs:* Boodle's, Cavalry and Guards, Pratt's; New (Edinburgh).

RAMSAY, Douglas John; Parliamentary Counsel, since 2004; *b* 29 Nov. 1959; *s* of Douglas Ramsay and Susan McFadyen Ramsay; *m* 1999, Gillian Platt; one *s* one *d*. *Educ:* Northgate Grammar Sch., Ipswich; Univ. of Leeds (LLB 1981); Chester Coll. of Law. Articled clerk, then solicitor, Titmuss, Sainer & Webb, 1982–87; Office of the Parliamentary Counsel: Asst Parly Counsel, 1987–91; Sen. Asst Parly Counsel, 1991–94; Principal Asst Parly Counsel, 1994–98; Dep. Parly Counsel, 1998–2004, seconded to Law Commn, 1999–2002. *Recreations:* Rugby, football, my children. *Address:* Office of the Parliamentary Counsel, 36 Whitehall, SW1A 2AY.

RAMSAY, Gordon James, OBE 2006; Chef and Patron, Gordon Ramsay (Royal Hospital Road), since 1998; *b* 8 Nov. 1966; *s* of late Gordon Scott Ramsay and Helen Ramsay (*née* Mitchell); *m* 1996, Cayetana Elizabeth Hutcheson; one *s* three *d* (of whom one *s* one *d* are twins). *Educ:* Stratford-upon-Avon High Sch.; North Oxon Tech. Coll., Banbury (HND Hotel Mgt 1987). Professional footballer, Glasgow Rangers FC, 1982–85; worked: with Marco Pierre White at Harvey's, 1989–91; with Albert Roux at La Gavroche, 1992–93; in Paris kitchens of Guy Savoy and Joël Robuchon, 1993–94; chef/proprietor: Aubergine restaurant, 1994–98 (Michelin Star, 1995, 1997); Gordon Ramsay Restaurant, Chelsea, 1998– (Michelin Star, 2001); Pétrus, Mayfair, 1999–2003, at The Berkeley, 2003– (Michelin Star, 2000); Amaryllis, Glasgow, 2001–04 (Michelin Star, 2002); Gordon Ramsay at Claridge's, 2001– (Michelin Star, 2003); Gordon Ramsay at The Connaught, 2002–07 (Michelin Star, 2003); The Savoy Grill, 2003– (Michelin Star, 2004); Boxwood at The Berkeley, 2003–; Maze, Grosvenor Square, 2005–; Gordon Ramsay at The London, NY, 2006–; Gordon Ramsay at The Trianon Palace Hotel, Versailles, 2008–. Television includes series: Hell's Kitchen, 2004; Ramsay's Kitchen Nightmares (5 series), 2004– (BAFTA Award, 2005); The F Word (4 series), 2005–. *Publications:* Passion for Flavour, 1996; Passion for Seafood, 1999; A Chef for All Seasons, 2000; Just Desserts, 2001; Gordon Ramsay's Secrets, 2003; Gordon Ramsay's Kitchen Heaven, 2004; Gordon Ramsay makes it Easy, 2005; Gordon Ramsay's Sunday Dinners, 2006; The F Word, 2006; Humble Pie (autobiog.), 2006; Gordon Ramsay's Fast Food, 2007; Cooking for Friends, 2008. *Recreations:* salmon fishing, scuba diving, long distance running. *Address:* Gordon Ramsay Holdings Ltd, 1 Catherine Place, SW1E 6DX. *T:* (020) 7592 1370.

RAMSAY, Prof. John Graham, CBE 1992; FRS 1973; Professor of Geology, Eidgenössische Technische Hochschule and University of Zürich, 1977–92, now Professor Emeritus; *b* 17 June 1931; *s* of Robert William Ramsay and Kathleen May Ramsay; *m* 1st, 1952, Sylvia Hiorns (marr. diss. 1957); 2nd, 1960, Christine Marden (marr. diss. 1987); three *d* (and one *d* decd); 3rd, 1990, Dorothee Dietrich. *Educ:* Edmonton County Grammar Sch.; Imperial Coll., London. DSc, PhD, DIC, BSc, ARCS, FGS. Musician, Corps of Royal Engineers, 1955–57; academic staff Imperial Coll., London, 1957–73: Prof. of Geology, 1966–73; Prof. of Earth Sciences, Leeds Univ., 1973–76. Mem., NERC, 1989–92. Vice-Pres., Société Géologique de France, 1973. Hon. Prof. of Earth Sci., Univ. of Cardiff, 2002; Hon. Prof. of Geology, Ben-Gurion Univ., 2008. For. Associate, US Nat. Acad. of Scis, 1985. Dr *hc* Rennes, 1978. *Publications:* Folding and Fracturing of Rocks, 1967; The Techniques of Modern Structural Geology, vol. 1, 1983, vol. 2, 1987, vol. 3, 2000. *Recreations:* music composition, chamber music, ski-ing, writing poetry. *Address:* Cratoule, Issirac, 30760 St Julien de Peyrolas, France.

RAMSAY, Jonathan William Alexander, FRCS; Consultant Urologist: Charing Cross Hospital, since 1988; West Middlesex Hospital, since 1988; *b* 27 Oct. 1953; *s* of Raymond Ramsay, MBE, FRCS and Lillian Jane Ramsay, MBE (*née* Bateman); *m* 1983, Priscilla Jaqueline Russell Webster; two *s* one *d*. *Educ:* Bradfield Coll.; St Bartholomew's Hosp. Med. Coll. (MB BS, MS). FRCS 1981. Qualified, St Bartholomew's Hosp. (Brackenbury Schol.), 1977; Chief Asst (Urology), St Bartholomew's, 1985–88; Hon. Consultant Urologist, St Luke's Hosp. for Clergy, 1989–. Royal College of Surgeons: Regl Specialty Advr, 1995–; Mem., Court of Examrs, 1997–; Regl Advr, 1999–; Sec., Sect. Urology, RSocMed, 2006–. President: W London Medico-Chirurgical Soc., 1999; Eur. Intrarenal Surgery Soc., 1999–. Fellow, Eur. Bd of Urology, 1991. *Publications:* contribs on treatment of stones by minimally invasive techniques. *Recreations:* fishing, sailing. *Address:* Yew Trees House, Southlea Road, Datchet SL3 9BY; 149 Harley Street, W1N 1HG. *Clubs:* Athenæum, Royal Society of Medicine.

RAMSAY, Nicholas Harvey; Member (C) Monmouth, National Assembly for Wales, since 2007; *b* 10 June 1975; *s* of Graham George Ramsay and Carole Ann Mann, and step *s* of Andrew John Mann. *Educ:* Univ. of Durham (BA Jt Hons English and Philosophy); Cardiff Univ. (Postgrad. Dip. Applied Linguistics). Driving instructor, 2000–01; press officer/researcher, Nat. Assembly for Wales, 2001–07. Mem. (C) Monmouthshire CC, 2004–. Mem., Lions Club Internat. *Recreations:* tennis, reading, keen pub quizzer. *Address:* National Assembly for Wales, Cardiff Bay, Cardiff CF99 1NA. *T:* (029) 2089 8337; *e-mail:* Nicholas.Ramsay@wales.gov.uk.

RAMSAY, Patrick George Alexander; Controller, BBC Scotland, 1979–83; retired; *b* 14 April 1926; *yr s* of late Rt Rev. Ronald Erskine Ramsay, sometime Bishop of Malmesbury, and Winifred Constance Ramsay (*née* Partridge); *m* 1948, Hope Seymour Dorothy, *y d* of late Rt Rev. Algernon Markham, sometime Bishop of Grantham, and Winifred Edith Markham (*née* Barne); two *s*. *Educ:* Marlborough Coll.; Jesus Coll., Cambridge (MA). Served War, Royal Navy (Fleet Air Arm), 1944–46. Joined BBC as Report Writer, Eastern European Desk, Monitoring Service, 1949; Liaison Officer, US Foreign Broadcasts Information Service, Cyprus, 1951–52; Asst, Appts Dept, 1953–56; Sen. Admin. Asst, External Broadcasting, 1956–58; Admin. Officer News and Head of News Administration, 1958–64; Planning Manager, Television Programme Planning, 1964–66; Asst Controller: Programme Services, 1966–69; Programme Planning, 1969–72; Controller, Programme Services, 1972–79. General Managerial Advr, Oman Broadcasting Service, 1984–85. A Dir, Windsor Festival Soc., 1973–76. Councillor and Alderman, Royal Borough of New Windsor, 1962–67; Chm., Windsor and Eton Soc., 1971–76. FRSA. *Recreations:* fellwalking, gardening, foreign travel, history, looking in junk shops, thwarting bureaucrats. *Address:* Abcott Manor, Clungunford, Shropshire SY7 0PX.

RAMSAY, Richard Alexander McGregor; Director: Intelli Corporate Finance Ltd, since 2003 (Vice Chairman, 2003–05); The Shareholder Executive, since 2007; *b* 27 Dec. 1949; *s* of Alexander John McGregor Ramsay and Beatrice Kent La Nauze; *m* 1975, Elizabeth Catherine Margaret Blackwood; one *s* one *d*. *Educ:* Dalhousie Sch.; Trinity Coll., Glenalmond; Aberdeen Univ. (MA Hons in Politics and Sociology). ACA 1975; FCA. Price Waterhouse & Co., 1972–75; Grindlay Brandts, 1976–78; Hill Samuel & Co. Ltd, 1979–87 (Dir, 1984–87); on secondment as Dir, Industrial Develt Unit, DTI, 1984–86; Dir, 1988–91, Man. Dir, Corporate Finance Div., 1991–93, Barclays De Zoete Wedd; Director: Ivory & Sime, 1993–94; Ivory & Sime Investment Mgt, 1994–96; Finance Dir, Aberdeen FC, 1997–2000; Man. Dir for Regulation and Financial Affairs, Ofgem, 2001–03. Non-executive Director: Artemis AiM VCT plc, 2001– (Chm., 2001–03); Xploite plc, 2007–; Chm., Wolsey Group Ltd, 2008–. Consultant, Armstrong Bonham Carter, 2007–. *Recreations:* hill walking, ski-ing, classic cars, gardening. *Address:* The Little Priory, Sandy Lane, South Nutfield, Surrey RH1 4EJ. *T:* (01737) 822329.

RAMSAY, Robert, CMG 2000; DPhil; Director General for Research, European Parliament, 1989–99; *b* 11 Sept. 1940; *s* of Robert and Mabel Hamilton Ramsay; *m* 1963, Patricia Buckley; four *s* (and one *s* decd). *Educ:* Royal Belfast Academical Instn; Queen's Univ., Belfast (BA Hons); Univ. of Ulster (DPhil 1979). Commonwealth Fellow, Victoria Univ. of Wellington, 1963–65; entered NICS, 1965; Principal Private Sec. to Prime Minister, 1971–72; European Dir, Inward Investment, Brussels, 1972–74; Sec. to Economic Council, 1974–76; Principal Private Sec. to Sec. of State for NI, 1976–78; Under Sec., DoE, 1978–83; Sec. Gen., EDG, EP, 1983–87; Dir, President's Office, EP, 1987–89. Sen. Policy Advr on EU affairs, PRM European Lobbyists, Brussels, 1999–. Leverhulme Fellow, 1978. *Publication:* The Corsican Time Bomb, 1983. *Recreations:* sailing, European literature. *Address: e-mail:* ramsayrobert@hotmail.com. *Club:* Carlton.

RAMSAY-FAIRFAX-LUCY, Sir Edmund John William Hugh Cameron; *see* Fairfax-Lucy.

RAMSBOTHAM, family name of **Viscount Soulbury** and **Baron Ramsbotham**.

RAMSBOTHAM, Baron *cr* 2005 (Life Peer), of Kensington, in the Royal Borough of Kensington and Chelsea; **Gen. David John Ramsbotham,** GCB 1993 (KCB 1987); CBE 1980 (OBE 1974); HM Chief Inspector of Prisons for England and Wales, 1995–2001; *b* 6 Nov. 1934; *s* of Rt Rev. J. A. Ramsbotham; *m* 1958, Susan Caroline (*née* Dickinson); two *s*. *Educ:* Haileybury Coll.; Corpus Christi Coll., Cambridge (BA 1957, MA 1973; Hon. Fellow, 2001). Nat. Service, 1952–54; Rifle Bde, UK and BAOR, 1958–62; seconded to KAR, 1962–63; Staff Coll., 1964; Rifle Bde, Far East, 1965; Staff, 7 Armoured Bde, 1966–68; 3 and 2 Green Jackets (BAOR), 1968–71; MA to CGS (Lt-Col), 1971–73; CO, 2 RGJ, 1974–76; Staff, 4 Armd Div., BAOR, 1976–78; Comd, 39 Infantry Bde, 1978–80; RCDS, 1981; Dir of Public Relns (Army), 1982–84; Comdr, 3 Armd Div., 1984–87; Comdr, UK Field Army and Inspector Gen., TA, 1987–90; Adjt Gen., 1990–93; ADC Gen. to the Queen, 1990–93. Dir of Internat. Affairs, DSL Ltd, 1994–99. Chm., Hillingdon Hosp. NHS Trust, 1995. Mem. Council, IISS, 1996–2002. Col Comdt, 2nd Battalion, The Royal Green Jackets, 1987–92; Hon. Col, Cambridge Univ. OTC, 1987–93. FRSA 1999; FCGI 2000. Hon. DCL Huddersfield, 1999. *Publication:* Prisongate (memoirs), 2003. *Recreations:* sailing, shooting, gardening, art and art history. *Clubs:* Athenæum, MCC.

RAMSBOTHAM, Hon. Sir Peter (Edward), GCMG 1978 (KCMG 1972; CMG 1964); GCVO 1976; DL; HM Diplomatic Service, retired; *b* 8 Oct. 1919; *yr s* of 1st Viscount Soulbury, PC, GCMG, GCVO, OBE, MC; *S* brother, 2004 as 3rd Viscount Soulbury, but does not use the title; *m* 1st, 1941, Frances Blomfield (*d* 1982); two *s* (one *d* decd); 2nd, 1985, Dr Zaida Hall, *widow* of Ruthven Hall. *Educ:* Eton College; Magdalen College, Oxford (Hon. Fellow, 1991). Intelligence Corps, Europe, 1943–46 (Lt-Col; despatches; Croix de Guerre, 1945). Control Office for Germany and Austria from 1947; Regional Political Officer in Hamburg; entered Foreign Service, Oct. 1948; Political Division of Allied Control Commission, Berlin, Nov. 1948; transferred to Foreign Office, 1950; 1st Secretary, 1950; Head of Chancery, UK Delegation, New York, 1953; Foreign

Office, 1957; Counsellor, 1961, Head of Western Organisations and Planning Dept; Head of Chancery, British Embassy, Paris, 1963–67; Foreign Office, 1967–69 (Sabbatical year, Inst. of Strategic Studies, 1968); High Comr, Cyprus, 1969–71; Ambassador to Iran, 1971–74; Ambassador to the United States, 1974–77; Governor and C-in-C of Bermuda, 1977–80. Director: Lloyds Bank, 1981–90; Lloyds Bank Internat., 1981–83; Southern Regl Bd, Lloyds Bank, 1981–90 (Chm., 1983–90); Commercial Union Assurance Co., 1981–90. Trustee, Leonard Cheshire Foundn, 1981–94; Chairman: Ryder-Cheshire Foundn for the Relief of Suffering, 1982–99; World Meml Fund for Disaster Relief, 1992–96 (Trustee, 1989–); Gov., Ditchley Foundn, 1978–2007. Pres., British-American-Canadian Associates, 1994–97. Governor, King's Sch., Canterbury, 1981–90. DL Hants, 1992. Hon. LLD: Akron Univ., 1975; Coll. of William and Mary, 1975; Maryland Univ., 1976; Yale Univ., 1977. KStJ 1976. *Recreations:* gardening, fishing. *Address:* East Lane, Ovington, near Alresford, Hants SO24 0RA. *T:* (01962) 732515. *Club:* Garrick.

RAMSBOTTOM, Paul Benjamin; Executive Secretary, Wolfson Foundation, since 2007; Secretary, Wolfson Family Charitable Trust, since 2007; *b* 27 May 1976; *s* of Benjamin Ashworth Ramsbottom and Jean Margaret Ramsbottom (*née* Kelsall); *m* 2002, Karen Rachel Taylor; two *d. Educ:* St Albans Sch.; Corpus Christi Coll., Oxford (BA 1st Cl. Hons Modern Hist. 1997; MSt 1998). With Wolfson Foundation, 1998–: Grants Adminr, 1998–2000; Asst Exec. Sec., 2000–01; Dep. Exec. Sec., 2001–06. Chm., Savannah Educn Trust, 2004–. Trustee, Wolfson Res. Professorship of Royal Soc., 2007–. MRSocMed 2007. *Recreations:* exotic travel and food, theology, various sports. *Address:* The Wolfson Foundation, 8 Queen Anne Street, W1G 9LD. *T:* (020) 7323 5730, *Fax:* (020) 7323 3241.

RAMSBURY, Area Bishop of, since 2006; **Rt Rev. Stephen David Conway;** *b* 22 Dec. 1957; *s* of late David Conway and of Dorothy Isabella (*née* Jarman, now Lambert). *Educ:* Archbishop Tenison's Grammar Sch., London; Keble Coll., Oxford (BA Mod. Hist. 1980, MA 1984; PGCE 1981); Selwyn Coll., Cambridge (BA Theol. 1985; MA 2005); Westcott House, Cambridge. Asst Master, Glenalmond Coll., 1981–83; ordained deacon, 1986, priest, 1987; Curate: Heworth, 1986–89; Bishopwearmouth, 1989–90; St Margaret, Durham, 1990–94; Diocesan Dir of Ordinands, Durham, 1989–94; Priest i/c, subseq. Vicar, Cockerton, 1994–98; Sen. Chaplain to Bishop of Durham and Diocesan Communications Officer, 1998–2002; Archdeacon of Durham, and Canon Residentiary, Durham Cathedral, 2002–06. Mem., Gen. Synod of C of E, 1995–2000. Trustee, Affirming Catholicism, 2001– (Chm., Exec., 1997–2003). Chm., Bd of Trustees, Mental Health Matters, 2004–. *Publications:* (ed) Living the Eucharist, 2001; (contrib.) This is Our Calling, 2004; (contrib.) The Vicar's Guide, 2005. *Recreations:* walking, cinema, wine, cooking, travel, books. *Address:* Ramsbury Office, Southbroom House, London Road, Devizes, Wilts SN10 1LT. *T:* (01380) 729808, *Fax:* (01380) 738096; *e-mail:* ramsbury.office@salisbury.anglican.org. *Club:* Nobody's Friends.

RAMSDEN, David Edward John, CBE 2004; Managing Director, Macroeconomic and Fiscal Policy, and joint Head, Government Economic Service, HM Treasury, since 2007; *b* 9 Feb. 1964; *s* of late William Ramsden, OBE and of Elizabeth Ramsden (now Thompson); *m* 1993, Niccola Shearman; one *s* one *d. Educ:* Brasenose Coll., Oxford; London Sch. of Econs. Economist posts in DHSS and HM Treasury, 1986–98; HM Treasury: Head: EMU Policy Team, 1999–2003; O'Donnell Rev. Team, 2003; Dir, Tax and Budget, 2004–05; Dir, Macroeconomics and Fiscal Policy Gp, 2006–07. Mem., ESRC, 2008–. *Recreations:* cycling, rock climbing, mountain-walking, reading. *Address:* HM Treasury, 1 Horse Guards Road, SW1A 2HQ. *T:* (020) 7270 4318, *Fax:* (020) 7270 5735; *e-mail:* dave.ramsden@hm-treasury.gsi.gov.uk.

RAMSDEN, Prof. Herbert, MA, Dr en Filosofía y Letras; Professor of Spanish Language and Literature, University of Manchester, 1961–82, now Emeritus; *b* 20 April 1927; *s* of Herbert and Ann Ramsden; *m* 1953, Joyce Robina Hall, SRN, ONC, CMB; three *s* (incl. twin *s*) twin *d. Educ:* Sale Grammar Sch.; Univs of Manchester, Strasbourg, Madrid and Sorbonne. National Service, Inf. and Intell. Corps, 1949–51 (commnd). Travel, study and research abroad (Kemsley Travelling Fellow, etc), 1951–54; University of Manchester: Asst Lectr in Spanish, 1954–57; Lectr in Spanish, 1957–61; Pres., Philological Club, 1966–68. British Hispanists' rep., Nat. Council for Modern Languages, 1972–73; British rep., Asociación Europea de Profesores de Español, 1975–80. *Publications:* An Essential Course in Modern Spanish, 1959; Weak-Pronoun Position in the Early Romance Languages, 1963; (ed with critical study) Azorín, La ruta de Don Quijote, 1966; Angel Ganivet's Idearium español: A Critical Study, 1967; The Spanish Generation of 1898, 1974; The 1898 Movement in Spain, 1974; (ed with critical study) Lorca, Bodas de sangre, 1980; Pío Baroja: La busca, 1982; Pío Baroja: La busca 1903 to La busca 1904, 1982; (ed with critical study) Lorca, La casa de Bernarda Alba, 1983; Lorca's Romancero gitano, 1988; (ed, with critical study) Lorca, Romancero gitano: eighteen commentaries, 1988; articles in Bulletin of Hispanic Studies, Modern Language Review, Modern Languages, etc. *Recreations:* family, hill-walking, foreign travel. *Address:* 7 Burford Avenue, Bramhall, Stockport, Cheshire SK7 1BL. *T:* (0161) 439 4306.

RAMSDEN, Isobel Anne; *see* Pollock, I. A.

RAMSDEN, Rt Hon. James Edward; PC 1963; Chairman, The Hackfall Trust, since 1988; *b* 1 Nov. 1923; *s* of late Capt. Edward Ramsden, MC, and Geraldine Ramsden, OBE, Breckamore Hall, Ripon; *m* 1949, Juliet Barbara Anna, *y d* of late Col Sir Charles Ponsonby, 1st Bt, TD, and Hon. Lady Ponsonby, *d* of 1st Baron Hunsdon; three *s* two *d. Educ:* Eton; Trinity College, Oxford (MA). Commnd KRRC, 1942; served North-West Europe with Rifle Brigade, 1944–45. MP (C) Harrogate, WR Yorks, March 1954–Feb. 1974; PPS to Home Secretary, Nov. 1959–Oct. 1960; Under-Sec. and Financial Sec., War Office, Oct. 1960–Oct. 1963; Sec. of State for War, 1963–64; Minister of Defence for the Army, April–Oct. 1964. Director: UK Board, Colonial Mutual Life Assurance Society, 1966–72; Standard Telephones and Cables, 1971–81; Prudential Assurance Co. Ltd, 1972–91 (Dep. Chm., 1976–82); Prudential Corp. Ltd, 1979–91 (Dep. Chm., 1979–82). Dir, London Clinic, 1973–96 (Chm., 1984–96). Mem., Historic Buildings Council for England, 1971–72. Pres., Northern Horticultural Soc., 1996–2001. *Address:* 14 High Agnesgate, Ripon, North Yorks HG4 1QR. *T:* (01765) 692229, *Fax:* (01765) 605585; *e-mail:* james@oldslen.fsnet.co.uk. *Club:* Pratt's.

RAMSDEN, Sir John (Charles Josslyn), 9th Bt *cr* 1689, of Byram, Yorks; HM Diplomatic Service, retired; Ambassador to Croatia, 2004–08; *b* 19 Aug. 1950; *s* of Sir Caryl Oliver Imbert Ramsden, 8th Bt, CMG, CVO, and of Anne, *d* of Sir Charles Wickham, KCMG, KBE, DSO; *S* father, 1987; *m* 1985, (Jennifer) Jane Bevan; two *d. Educ:* Eton; Trinity Coll., Cambridge (MA). With merchant bank, Dawnay, Day & Co. Ltd, 1972–74. Entered FCO, 1975; 2nd Sec., Dakar, 1976; 1st Sec., MBFR, Vienna, 1978; 1st Sec., Head of Chancery and Consul, Hanoi, 1980; FCO, 1982–90; Counsellor, E Berlin, 1990; Counsellor and Dep. Hd of Mission, Berlin, 1991–93; Hd, Information Dept, FCO, 1993–96; UK Dep. Perm. Rep. to UN, Geneva, 1996–99; Hd, Central and NW Europe Dept, FCO, 1999–2003.

RAMSDEN, (John) Michael; Editor of Publications, Royal Aeronautical Society, 1989–93; *b* 2 Oct. 1928; *s* of John Leonard Ramsden and Edith Alexandra Ramsden; *m* 1953, Angela Mary Mortimer; one *s* one *d. Educ:* Bedford Sch.; de Havilland Aeronautical Tech. Sch. CEng, FRAeS. With de Havilland Aircraft Co. Ltd, 1946–55; Flight, 1955–89: Air Transport Editor, 1961–64; Editor, 1964–81; Editor-in-Chief, Flight International, 1981–89. Chm., Press and Broadcasting Side, Defence Press and Broadcasting Cttee, 1983–89. Dir, de Havilland Aircraft Mus., 1970–. Trustee, Geoffrey de Havilland Flying Foundn, 1992–. Pres., RAeS Hatfield Br., 2001–. Cumberbatch Trophy, GAPAN, 1981; Wakefield Gold Medal, RAeS, 1987; Douglas Weightman Award, Flight Safety Cttee, 1988. Silver Jubilee Medal, 1977. *Publications:* The Safe Airline, 1976, 2nd edn 1978 (Publications Award, Flight Safety Foundn, 1976); Caring for the Mature Jet, 1981; Chinook Justice, 2002. *Recreations:* light-aircraft flying, water-colour painting. *Club:* London School of Flying (Elstree).

RAMSDEN, Michael; *see* Ramsden, J. M.

RAMSDEN, Prof. Richard Thomas, FRCS; Consultant Otolaryngologist, Manchester Royal Infirmary, since 1977; Professor of Otolaryngology, University of Manchester, since 1994; *b* 30 Dec. 1944; *s* of late Thomas William Ramsden and Elaine Napier Ramsden (*née* Meikle); *m* 1st, 1968, Wendy Margaret Johnson (marr. diss. 1984); one *s* two *d*; 2nd, 1987, Eileen Gillian Richardson (*née* Whitehurst); two step *s. Educ:* Madras Coll., St Andrews; St Andrews Univ. (MB ChB 1968). FRCS 1972. Registrar in Otolaryngol., 1972–74, Sen. Registrar, 1974–75, RNTNEH; Sen. Registrar, Otolaryngol., London Hosp., 1975–77. TWJ Travelling Fellow to N America, 1978. Lectures: Subramaniam, Indian Soc. of Otolaryngol., McBride, Univ. of Edinburgh, 1987; Dalby, Otology Section, RSocMed, 1992; Younis, Pakistan Soc. of Otolaryngol., 1993; Wilde, Irish Otolaryngol Soc., Graham Fraser, Otology Section, RSocMed, 1994; Goldman, Groote Schoor Hosp., Univ. of Cape Town, 1998; Yearsley, RCS, 2001; Gordon Smyth, BAO-HNS, 2004; Susan Bellman, British Assoc. of Audiol Physicians, 2004; William F. House, American Neurol. Soc., 2005; Hunterian Oration, Hunterian Soc., 2008. Pres., British Assoc. of Otolaryngologists-Head and Neck Surgeons, 2006–Feb. 2009. FRCSE (*ad hominem*) 2000. Hon. Mem., German, Irish and Danish ENT socs; Corresp. Mem., Amer. Otological Soc., 2006. Dalby Prize, W. J. Harrison Prize, RSocMed; Jobson Horne Prize, BMA. *Publications:* chapters on aspects of otology and neuro-otology; contrib. learned jls of otology and neuro-otology. *Recreation:* none (sadly). *Address:* Elm House, 2 Mauldeth Road, Manchester M20 4ND. *T:* (0161) 434 9715. *Clubs:* Royal Society of Medicine; Wilmslow Golf; St Andrews New Golf; St Andrews Society of Manchester (Pres.).

RAMSEY, Basil Albert Rowland; Editor, Music & Vision, 1999; *b* 26 April 1929; *s* of Florence Lily Ramsey (*née* Childs) and Alfred John Rowland Ramsey; *m* 1953, Violet Mary Simpson; one *s* two *d. Educ:* State schools. ARCO. Novello & Co.: Music Editor, 1949; Head of Publishing, 1963; established own publishing Co., 1976; Serious Music Publishing Consultant, Filmtrax plc, 1987–90. Editor: Organists' Review, 1972–84; Music & Musicians, 1989–90; The Musical Times, 1990–92; Choir & Organ, 1993–98. *Publications:* The Music of Charles Camilleri, 1996; articles and reviews in Musical Times, 1955–93; regular contributor to weekly and daily press on musical matters. *Recreations:* reading, calligraphy. *Address:* 5 Victoria Avenue, Withernsea, East Yorks HU19 2LH.

RAMSEY, Brig. Gael Kathleen, CBE 1992 (MBE 1976); Chief Executive, British Executive Service Overseas, 1997–2004; *b* 8 June 1942; *d* of Lt Col William Hammond, MBE and Kathleen Hammond; *m* 1977 (marr. diss. 1996). *Educ:* Convent of Good Shepherd, Singapore; High Sch. for Girls, Worcester, Gloucester and Dover. Commissioned, WRAC, 1968; Dir, WRAC, 1989–92; ADC to the Queen, 1989–92; Dir Women (Army), 1992; Comdr, Aldershot Bde Area, 1992–95, retd. Dep. Col Comdt, AGC, 1998–2002. Freeman, City of London, 1991; Member: Guild of Freemen of City of London, 1992–; Council, WRAC Assoc., 1989– (Life Vice-Pres.). FInstD 1995. *Recreations:* golf, tennis, reading, needlework, travel, messing about with plants. *Clubs:* Army and Navy; Royal Cinque Ports Yacht.

RAMSEY, Prof. Norman Foster; Higgins Professor of Physics, Harvard University, since 1947; Senior Fellow, Harvard Society of Fellows, since 1971; *b* 27 Aug. 1915; *s* of Brig.-Gen. and Mrs Norman F. Ramsey; *m* 1940, Elinor Stedman Jameson (*d* 1983); four *d*; *m* 1985, Ellie A. Welch. *Educ:* Columbia Univ.; Cambridge Univ. (England). Carnegie Fellow, Carnegie Instn of Washington, 1939–40; Assoc., Univ. of Ill, 1940–42; Asst Prof., Columbia Univ., 1942–45; Research Assoc., MIT Radiation Laboratory, 1940–43; Cons. to Nat. Defense Research Cttee, 1940–45; Expert Consultant to Sec. of War, 1942–45; Gp Leader and Assoc. Div. Head, Los Alamos Lab. of Atomic Energy Project, 1943–45; Chief Scientist of Atomic Energy Lab. at Tinian, 1945; Assoc. Prof., Columbia Univ., 1945–47; Head of Physics Dept, Brookhaven Nat. Lab., 1946–47; Assoc. Prof., Harvard Univ., 1947–50; John Simon Guggenheim Fell., Oxford Univ., 1953–54; George Eastman Vis. Prof., Oxford Univ., 1973–74; Luce Prof. of Cosmology, Mt Holyoke, 1982–83; Prof., Univ. of Virginia, 1983–84. Dir Harvard Nuclear Lab., 1948–50, 1952; Chm., Harvard Nuclear Physics Cttee, 1948–60; Science Adviser, NATO, 1958–59; Fell. Amer. Phys. Soc. and Amer. Acad. of Arts and Sciences; Nat. Acad. of Sciences; Amer. Philos. Soc.; Foreign Associate, French Acad. of Science; Sigma Xi; Phi Beta Kappa; Amer. Assoc. for Advancement of Science, 1940– (Chm., Phys. Sect., 1976). Bd of Directors, Varian Associates, 1964–66; Bd of Trustees: Associated Univs; Brookhaven Nat. Lab., 1952–55; Carnegie Endowment for Internat. Peace; Univ. Research Assoc. (Pres., 1966–81, Pres. Emeritus 1981–); Rockefeller Univ., 1976–; Air Force Sci. Adv. Bd, 1948–54; Dept of Defense Panel on Atomic Energy, 1953–59; Bd of Editors of Review of Modern Physics, 1953–56; Chm. Exec. Cttee for Camb. Electron Accelerator, 1956–63; Coun. Amer. Phys. Soc., 1956–60 (Vice-Pres., 1977; Pres., 1978); Chm., Bd of Governors, Amer. Inst. of Physics, 1980–86. Gen. Adv. Cttee, Atomic Energy Commn, 1960–72. Chm., High Energy Accelerator Panel of President's Sci. Adv. Cttee and AEC, 1963. Chm. Bd, Physics and Astronomy Nat. Res. Council, 1986–89. Pres., Phi Beta Kappa, 1985 (Vice-Pres., 1982). Presidential Certificate of Merit, 1947; E. O. Lawrence Award, 1960; Davisson-Germer Prize, 1974; Award for Excellence, Columbia Univ. Graduate Alumni, 1980; Medal of Honor, IEEE, 1984; Rabi Prize, Frequency Control Symposium, IEEE, 1985; Monie Ferst Prize, Sigma Xi, 1985; Compton Award, Amer. Inst. of Physics, 1985; Rumford Premium, Amer. Acad. of Arts and Scis, 1985; Oersted Medal, Amer. Assoc. of Physics Teachers, 1988; Nat. Medal of Science, 1988; (jtly) Nobel Prize for Physics, 1989; Pupin Medal, Columbia Univ., 1992; Erice Science for Peace Prize, 1992; Einstein Medal, Optical and Quantum Electronics Soc., 1993; Vannevar Bush Award, US Nat. Sci. Bd, 1995; Alexander Hamilton Award, Columbia Univ., 1995. Hon. MA Harvard, 1947; Hon. ScD Cambridge, 1953; Hon. DSc: Case Western Reserve, 1968; Middlebury Coll., 1969; Oxford, 1973; Rockefeller Univ., 1986; Chicago, 1989; Houston, 1992; Michigan, 1993; Harvard, 2006; Hon. DCL Oxford, 1990. *Publications:* Experimental Nuclear Physics, 1952; Nuclear Moments, 1953; Molecular Beams, 1956; Quick Calculus, 1965; Spectroscopy with Coherent Radiation, 1999; and numerous articles in Physical Review and other scientific jls. *Recreations:* tennis, ski-ing, walking, sailing, etc. *Address:* 24 Monmouth Court, Brookline, MA 02446, USA. *T:* (617) 2772313.

RAMSEY, Hon. Sir Vivian (Arthur), Kt 2005; **Hon. Mr Justice Ramsey;** a Judge of the High Court, Queen's Bench Division, since 2005; Judge in charge, Technology and Construction Court, since 2007; *b* 24 May 1950; *s* of Rt Rev. Ian Thomas Ramsey and late Margretta Ramsey (*née* McKay); *m* 1974, Barbara Walker; two *s* two *d*. *Educ:* Harley Sch., Rochester, NY; Abingdon Sch., Oxon; Oriel Coll., Oxford (MA); City Univ. (Dip. Law). CEng, MICE 1977. Civil and Structural Engineer, Ove Arup & Partners, 1972–77, 1979–80; called to the Bar, Middle Temple, 1979, Bencher, 2002. Barrister and Arbitrator, 1981–2005; QC 1992; Head of Keating Chambers, 2002–05; Asst Recorder, 1998–2000; a Recorder, 2000–05. Special Prof., Dept of Civil Engineering, Nottingham Univ., 1990–; Vis. Prof., Centre of Construction Law, KCL, 2007–. Chm., Swanley Action Gp, 1989–2005. Editor, 1984–2005, Consultant Ed., 2005–, Construction Law Jl. *Publication:* (ed) Keating on Building Contracts, 7th edn, 2000, 8th edn, 2006. *Recreations:* building renovation, vineyards. *Address:* Royal Courts of Justice, Strand, WC2A 2LL.

RAMSEY, Waldo Emerson W.; *see* Waldron-Ramsey.

RAMSHAW, Wendy Anne Jopling, (Mrs D. J. Watkins), CBE 2003 (OBE 1993); RDI 2000; freelance artist and designer, since 1960; *b* 26 May 1939; *d* of Angus Ramshaw and Flora (*née* Hollingshead); *m* 1962, Prof. David John Watkins, *qv*; one *s* one *d*. *Educ:* Sunderland Girls' High Sch.; Saint Mary's Convent, Berwick-upon-Tweed; Coll. of Art and Industrial Design, Newcastle upon Tyne (NDD); Univ. of Reading (ATD); Central Sch. of Art and Design, London (postgrad. studies). Artist in Residence: Western Australian Inst. of Technol., 1978–79; Printmakers Workshop, Inverness, 1996; Pallant House, Chichester; Visiting Artist: in collaboration with Wedgwood, 1981–82; Glass Dept, RCA, 1985–86; Visiting Professor: San Diego State Univ., 1984; Bezalel Acad., Jerusalem, 1984; Dept of Goldsmithing, Silversmithing, Metalwork and Jewellery, RCA, 1998–2001. Patron, Contemporary Applied Arts, London. Lady Liveryman, Co. of Goldsmiths, 1986–. FCSD 1972; FRSA 1972. Hon. Fellow London Inst., 1999 (Governor, 2000–). *Exhibitions include:* Wendy Ramshaw - David Watkins: Goldsmiths Hall, London, 1973; Nat. Gall. of Victoria, 1978; Schmuckmuseum, Pforzheim, 1987; Wendy Ramshaw: V&A Mus., 1982; Retrospective, Bristol City Mus. & Art Gall., 1983; Jewellery Strategies/Jewellery Variations, Mikimoto, Tokyo, 1993; Picasso's Ladies: V&A Mus. and American Crafts Mus., NY, 1998; Institute Mathildenhohe, Darmstadt, 2001; Millennium Exhibn, Contemporary Applied Arts, London, 2000; Room of Dreams, Scottish Gall., Edinburgh, 2002; Blackwell, The Arts & Crafts House, Cumbria, 2004; Prospero's Table, SOFA, Chicago, 2004; Collect, V&A, 2005; *major commissions*: Bird of Paradise Gift from British Govt to Papua New Guinea, 1976; Garden Gate, St John's Coll., Oxford, 1993; Double Screen EH 9681, V&A Mus., 1996; semi-circular entrance gate, Mowbray Pk, Sunderland, 1998; Columbus screen, Canary Wharf, 1999; Queen's Millennium Medal, BM, 2000; glass door panels and brass handles, Southwark Cathedral, 2000; aluminium park gates, Sculpture at Goodwood, 2001; *work in public collections:* Australian Nat. Gall., Canberra; BM; Kunstindustrimuseet, Oslo; Musée des Art Décoratifs, Paris; Mus. of Mod. Art, Kyoto; Philadelphia Mus. of Art; Royal Mus. of Scotland, Edinburgh; Schmuckmuseum, Pforzheim; Science Mus., London; Smithsonian Inst., Cooper-Hewitt Nat. Design Mus., NY; Stedelijk Mus., Amsterdam; V&A Mus; Powerhouse, Sydney; Corning Mus. of Glass, Corning, USA; Nat. Mus. of Wales. Council of Industrial Design award, 1972; De Beers Diamond Internat. Award, 1975; Art in Architecture award, RSA, 1993. *Relevant publications:* Wendy Ramshaw (exhibn catalogue), 1982; From Paper to Gold (exhibn catalogue), 1990; Jewel Drawings and Projects: contemporary jewellery issues, 1998; Picasso's Ladies: jewellery by Wendy Ramshaw, 1998; Wendy Ramshaw: jewellery (Blackwell exhibn catalogue); The Big Works: Wendy Ramshaw, 2004. *Recreations:* visiting museums and art galleries, travelling. *Address:* c/o Faculty of Royal Designers for Industry, Royal Society of Arts, 8 John Adams Street, WC2N 6EZ.

RANA, Baron *cr* 2004 (Life Peer), of Malone in the County of Antrim; **Diljit Singh Rana,** MBE 1996; JP; Founder and Managing Director, Andras House Ltd, since 1981; *b* 20 Sept. 1938; *s* of Paras Ram Rana; *m* 1966, Uma Passi; two *s*. *Educ:* Punjab Univ. (BA (Econs) 1958). Founder and Chm., Indian Business Forum, 1985. Founder, Rana Charitable Trust, 1996; Chm., Thanksgiving Square, Belfast, 2002–. Vice Pres., UNICEF, 2004–. Hon. Indian Consul in NI, 2004–. President: S Belfast Safer Towns Assoc., 1991–93; Belfast Chamber of Trade, 1991–92; NI Chamber of Commerce and Industry, 2004–05. Gov., Lagan Coll., 1990–94. Hon. Dr: Ulster, 1999; QUB, 2003. JP Belfast, 1986. Pravasi Bharatiya Samman Award (India), 2007. *Address:* 13 Malone Park, Belfast BT9 6NH. *Clubs:* Ulster Reform, Dunmurry Golf (Belfast).

RANASINGHE, (Kulatilaka Arthanayake) Parinda; Chief Justice of Sri Lanka, 1988–91; *b* 20 Aug. 1926; *s* of Solomon Ranasinghe and Somawathie Ranasinghe; *m* 1956, Chitra (*née* Mapaguneratne); one *s* three *d*. *Educ:* Royal Coll., Colombo. Advocate of the Supreme Court; appointed Magistrate, 1958; District Judge, 1966–74; High Court Judge, 1974–78; Judge, Court of Appeal, 1978–82, Pres. 1982; Judge, Supreme Court, 1982–88. *Recreation:* walking. *Address:* 18/48 Muhandiram E. D. Dabare Mawatha, Colombo 5, Sri Lanka. *T:* (1) 508310.

RANATUNGA, Gen. Sugathapala Cyril; High Commissioner for Sri Lanka in London, 1993–95; *b* 19 Feb. 1930; *m* 1957, Myrtle Sumanasekera; two *s*. *Educ:* St Sylvester's Coll., Kandy; RMA Sandhurst. Joined Sri Lanka Army, as Officer Cadet, 1950; commnd Ceylon LI, 1952; Staff Coll., 1962–63; RCDS, 1974–75; COS, Sri Lanka Army, 1982–85; Sen. Exec. Dir, Airport and Aviation Services Ltd, 1983–85; Lt-Gen. 1985; GOC, Jt Ops Comd, 1985–88; Gen. 1986; Security Advr to Pres. and Sec. to Minister of State for Defence, 1989–90; Sec. to Min. of Defence, 1990–93. Chancellor, Sir John Kotelawela Defence Acad., 1990–. *Recreations:* reading, bridge, golf. *Address:* Erabubebela Estate, Mawanella, Sri Lanka. *Clubs:* Planters' Club (Kegalle); Nuwara Eliya Golf.

RANCHHODLAL, Sir Chinubhai Madhowlal, 3rd Bt *cr* 1913, of Shahpur, Ahmedabad, India; *b* 25 July 1929; *s* of 2nd Bt and Tanumati (*d* 1970), *d* of Javerilal Mehta; *S* father, 1990; grandfather, 1st Bt, was only member of Hindu Community to receive a baronetcy; *m* 1953, Muneera Khodad Fozdar; one *s* three *d*. Arjuna Award, 1972. *Heir: s* Prashant Ranchhodlal [*b* 15 Dec. 1955; *m* 1977, Swati Hrishikesh Mehta; three *d*]. *Clubs:* Willingdon, Cricket of India (Bombay).

RANDALL, family name of **Baron Randall of St Budeaux**.

RANDALL OF ST BUDEAUX, Baron *cr* 1997 (Life Peer), of St Budeaux in the co. of Devon; **Stuart Jeffrey Randall;** *b* 22 June 1938; *m* 1963, Gillian Michael; three *d*. *Educ:* University Coll., Cardiff (BSc Elect. Engrg). English Electric Computers and Radio Corp. of America, USA, 1963–66; Marconi Automation, 1966–68; Inter-Bank Res. Orgn, 1968–71; BSC, 1971–76; BL, 1976–80; Nexos Office Systems, 1980–81; Plessey Communications Systems, 1981–83. MP (Lab) Hull West, 1983–97. PPS to Shadow Chancellor of the Exchequer, 1984–85; Opposition front bench spokesman on Agricl, Food and Fisheries Affairs, 1985–87, on Home Affairs, 1987–92. *Recreations:* sailing, flying, jazz, opera. *Address:* House of Lords, SW1A 0PW.

RANDALL, (Alexander) John; MP (C) Uxbridge, since Aug. 1997; *b* 5 Aug. 1955; *s* of late Alec Albert Randall and of Joyce Margaret (*née* Gore); *m* 1986, Katherine Frances Gray; two *s* one *d*. *Educ:* Rutland House Sch., Hillingdon; Merchant Taylors' Sch., Herts; SSEES, Univ. of London (BA Hons Serbo-Croat Lang. and Lit. 1979). Dir, Randalls of Uxbridge Ltd, 1981– (Man. Dir, 1986–97). An Opposition Whip, 2000–March 2003, July 2003–05; Opposition Asst Chief Whip, 2005–. *Recreations:* ornithology, theatre, opera, travel, sport. *Address:* 36 Harefield Road, Uxbridge, Middx UB8 1PH. *T:* (01895) 239465. *Club:* Uxbridge Conservative.
See also P. A. Gore-Randall.

RANDALL, Jeff William; Editor-at-Large, The Daily Telegraph, since 2005; Presenter, Jeff Randall Live, Sky Television; *b* 3 Oct. 1954; *s* of Jeffrey Charles Randall and late Grace Annie (*née* Hawkridge); *m* 1986, Susan Diane Fidler; one *d*. *Educ:* Royal Liberty Grammar Sch., Romford; Univ. of Nottingham (BA Hons Econs); Univ. of Florida. Hawkins Publishers, 1982–85; Asst Editor, Financial Weekly, 1985–86; City Corresp., Sunday Telegraph, 1986–88; The Sunday Times: Dep. City Editor, 1988–89; City Editor, 1989–94; City and Business Editor, 1994–95; Asst Editor and Sports Editor, 1996–97; Editor, Sunday Business, 1997–2001; Business Ed., BBC, 2001–05. Dir, Times Newspapers, 1994–95; Dep. Chm., Financial Dynamics Ltd, 1995–96. Columnist, Sunday Telegraph, 2002–04. Hon. DLit: Anglia Poly. Univ., 2001; Univ. of Nottingham, 2006. Financial Journalist of the Year, FT-Analysis, 1991; Business Journalist of the Year, London Press Club, 2001; Sony Gold Award for best radio sports prog., The Bankrupt Game, BBC 5 Live, 2002; Broadcast Journalist of the Year and Decade of Excellence Award, Business Journalist of the Year Awards, 2003; Harold Wincott Award for Best Business Broadcaster, 2004; Communicator of the Year Award, PR Week, 2004; Best Broadcast Feature, Where's My Pension Gone?, Business Journalist of the Year Awards, 2007. *Recreations:* golf, horseracing, football. *Address:* Daily Telegraph, 111 Buckingham Palace Road, SW1W 0DT. *Clubs:* Brooks's; Wentworth; Langland Bay Golf.

RANDALL, John; *see* Randall, A. J.

RANDALL, John Norman; Registrar General for Scotland, 1999–2003; *b* 1 Aug. 1945; *s* of Frederick William Randall and Daphne Constance Randall (*née* Gawn); *m* 1st, 1967, Sandra Philpott (marr. diss. 1991); one *s* one *d*; 2nd, 1997, Eileen Wilson. *Educ:* Bromley Grammar Sch.; Bristol Univ. (BA Hons Geography); Glasgow Univ. (MPhil Town and Regl Planning 1968; MPhil Econs 1979). Economist: Dept of Economic Affairs, 1968–70; Scottish Office, 1970–85; Dep. Registrar Gen. for Scotland, 1985–89; Asst Sec., Scottish Office, 1989–99. Chm., Islands Book Trust, 2002–; Mem. Council, Butterfly Conservation, 2002–06. *Recreations:* hill walking, natural history. *Address:* 31 Lemreway, South Lochs, Isle of Lewis HS2 9RD.

RANDALL, John Paul; international consultant on higher education and professional training, since 2001; Chairman: Justice Sector Skills Council, since 2003; Police Negotiating Board and Police Advisory Board for England and Wales, since 2004; Police Advisory Board for Northern Ireland, since 2007; *b* 23 Nov. 1947; *s* of late E. T. (Ted) Randall and Mollie Randall (*née* Macrae); *m* (marr. diss.); one *s* one *d*; 2nd, 1993, Marie Catherine Hague. *Educ:* Wallington County Grammar Sch. for Boys; Univ. of York (BA Hons Biol and Educn 1971). National Union of Students: Dep. Pres., 1971–73; Pres., 1973–75; Civil Service Union: Asst Sec., 1975–77; Asst Gen. Sec., 1977–81; Dep. Gen. Sec., 1981–87; Dir, Professional Standards and Develt, Law Soc., 1987–97; Chief Exec., QAA, 1997–2001. Mem. Council, NCVQ, 1992–97 (Chm., Accreditation Cttee, 1993–96; Chm., NVQ Policy Cttee, 1996–97; Mem. Jt Cttee, NCVQ and Schools Curriculum and Assessment Authy, 1996–97); Mem. Bd, Internat. Network of QAAs, 1999–2001. Member: Information Tribunal, 2003–; Legal Services Consultative Panel, 2004–; Lay Assessor: Nat. Clin. Assessment Authy, 2003–; PMETB, 2006–. Quality Assurance Dir, Internat. Compliance Assoc., 2002–. Vis. Academic Advr, Univ. of HK, 2002; Tech. Sec., UGC (Hong Kong), 2003–04; Specialist Consultant, Asia Develt Bank Tech. Assistance Project, Commn on Higher Educn, Philippines, 2004; Consultant, Hong Kong Council on Academic Accreditation, 2005–. Mem. Council, C&G, 1999– (Mem. Exec. Cttee, 2004–). Mem. Bd of Mgt, Focus Housing Assoc., 1996–99. FRSA 1998. FCGI 2007. Hon. LLD Nottingham Trent, 1998. *Publications:* (contrib.) Higher Education Re-formed, 2000; articles in educnl and legal jls. *Recreations:* walking, music, wine, travel. *Address:* Orchard Cottage, The Rampings, Longdon, Worcs GL20 6AL; *e-mail:* john.randall23@btopenworld.com. *Clubs:* South London Harriers, Orion Harriers.

RANDALL, John Yeoman; QC 1995; a Recorder, since 1999; a Deputy High Court Judge, since 2000; *b* 26 April 1956; *s* of Richard and Jean Randall; *m* 1982, Christine Robinson; one *s* one *d*. *Educ:* Rugby Sch.; Loomis Inst., USA; Jesus Coll., Cambridge (MA). Called to the Bar: Lincoln's Inn, 1978, Bencher, 2003; NSW, 1979; WA, 2001; in practice at English Bar, 1980–; an Asst Recorder, 1995–99. Hd of Chambers, 2001–04. Mem., Legal Services Consultative Panel, 2000–. Vis. Fellow, Univ. of NSW, 2004–. *Recreations:* travel, sports, music. *Address:* St Philip's Chambers, 55 Temple Row, Birmingham B2 5LS. *T:* (0121) 246 7000, *Fax:* (0121) 246 7001; *e-mail:* clerks@st-philips.co.uk.

RANDALL, Philip Allan G.; *see* Gore-Randall.

RANDELL, Charles; Partner, Corporate Department, Slaughter and May, since 1989; *b* Rheindahlen, 6 June 1958; *s* of Keith and Annette Randell; *m* 1983, Celia Van Oss; three *s*. *Educ:* Streete Court Prep. Sch.; Bradfield Coll.; Trinity Coll., Oxford (BA Juris. 1979); College of Law, Guildford. Slaughter and May: Articled Clerk, 1980–82; Solicitor, 1982–89. Mem., Editl Bd, PLC Corporate Law, 1990–. *Publications:* (jtly) Public Company Takeovers in Germany, 2002; various articles relating to corporate law and corporate governance in PLC mag. *Recreations:* sailing, theatre, travel. *Address:* c/o Slaughter and May, One Bunhill Row, EC1Y 8YY.

RANDELL, Peter Neil; Head of Finance and Administration, Institute of Metals, 1984–89; *b* 18 Nov. 1933; *s* of Donald Randell and Dorothy (*née* Anthonisz); *m* 1962, Anne Loraine Mudie; one *s* one *d*. *Educ:* Bradfield Coll.; Wye Coll., Univ. of London (BSc (Agric) Hons). FCIS. Farming and other employments, Rhodesia, 1955–61; Asst to Sec., British Insulated Callenders Cables Ltd, 1962–65; Asst Sec., NRDC, 1965–73, Sec. 1973–83, Board Member 1980–81; Sec. Admin and Personnel, British Technology Gp (NRDC and NEB), 1981–83. *Recreations:* the outdoors, reading. *Address:* Wood Dene, Golf Club Road, Hook Heath, Woking, Surrey GU22 0LS. *T:* (01483) 763824.

RANDERSON, Jennifer Elizabeth; JP; Member (Lib Dem) Cardiff Central, National Assembly for Wales, since 1999; *b* 26 May 1948; *m* 1970, Dr Peter Frederick Randerson; one *s* one *d*. *Educ:* Bedford Coll., London Univ. (BA Hons History); Inst. of Educn, London Univ. (PGCE 1970). Teacher: Sydenham High Sch., 1970–72; Spalding High Sch., 1972–74; Llanishen High Sch., 1974–76; Lectr, Coleg Glan Hafren, Cardiff,

1976–99. Member (L, then Lib Dem): Cardiff City Council, 1983–96; Cardiff County Council, 1995–2000 (Leader of Opposition, 1995–99). National Assembly for Wales: Sec., then Minister, for Culture, Sports and the Welsh Lang., 2000–03; Lib Dem spokesperson on economic develt and finance, 2003–05, on health, finance and equal opportunities, 2005–07, on health, social services, local govt and finance, 2007–. Chair of Exec., Welsh Lib Dems, 1988–90. Contested: (L) Cardiff S and Penarth, 1987; (Lib Dem) Cardiff Central, 1992, 1997. JP Cardiff 1982. *Recreations:* travel, theatre and concert going, gardening. *Address:* National Assembly for Wales, Cardiff Bay, Cardiff CF99 1NA. *T:* (029) 2089 8355.

RANDLE, James Neville, FREng; RDI 1994; Chief Executive Officer, Lea Francis Ltd, since 2000 (Director, since 1997); *b* Birmingham, 24 April 1938; *s* of James Randle and Florence (*née* Wilkins); *m* 1963, Jean Violet Allen (*d* 2006); one *s* one *d*. *Educ:* Waverley Grammar Sch., Birmingham. MIMechE 1969, FIMechE 1980; FREng (FEng 1988). Rover Car Company: apprentice, 1954–59; design and develt engr, 1959–63; Project Manager, 1963–65; Jaguar: R&D Engr, 1965–72; Chief Res. Engr, 1972–78; Vehicle Engrg Dir, 1978–80; Product Engrg Dir, 1980–91. Hon. Prof., 1992–2006, Dir, Automative Engrg Centre, 1993–2006, Univ. of Birmingham. Chm., Randle Engrg and Design, 1994–; Dir, Volvo Aero Turbines, 1992–98. Institution of Mechanical Engineers: Mem. Bd, 1979–88, Chm., 1986–87, Automobile Div.; Mem. Council, 1986–93. Mem., Prince Philip Design Prize Cttee, 1992–95 and 1997–2002. Pres., Engrg Div., BAAS, 1995–96. Chm., Coventry Aeroplane Club, 2007–. FInstD 1986. FRSA 1989. Hon. FCSD 2000. James Clayton Prize, 1986, Crompton Lanchester Medal, 1986, IMechE. *Publications:* technical papers on automobile engrg design. *Recreations:* flying powered aircraft (private pilot's licence), sailing (yacht master's certificate), ski-ing, hill walking, designing automobiles. *Address:* Pear Tree House, High Street, Welford on Avon, Warwickshire CV37 8EF.

RANDLE, Prof. Valerie, PhD, DSc; Professor of Materials Engineering, since 1999, and Head of Materials Research, since 2007, Swansea University (formerly University of Wales Swansea); *b* 8 May 1953; *d* of Bertram and Edith Brushfield; *m* 1st, 1971, Michael Randle (decd); one *s* one *d*; 2nd, 2006, Victor Pinheiro. *Educ:* Univ. of Wales, Cardiff (BSc 1983; PhD 1986; DSc 1996). FIMMM 1993; CEng 1998. Royal Soc. Univ. Res. Fellow, Bristol Univ., 1987–92, UC of Swansea, 1992–95; Sen. Lectr, 1995–97, Reader, 1997–99, UC of Swansea, then Univ. of Wales Swansea. Volunteer, Cruse Bereavement Care. Welsh Woman of the Year, 1998. *Publications:* Microtexture Determination and its Applications, 1992, 2nd edn 2003; Grain Boundary Geometry in Polycrystals, 1993; (jtly) An Atlas of Backscatter Kikuchi Diffraction Patterns, 1994; The Role of the Coincidence Site Lattice in Grain Boundary Engineering, 1996; (with Olaf Engler) Introduction to Texture Analysis: macrotexture, microtexture and orientation mapping, 2000; 250 scientific papers in learned jls. *Recreations:* running, walking, swimming, yoga, meditation. *Address:* School of Engineering, Swansea University, Singleton Park, Swansea SA2 8PP. *T:* (01792) 295841, *Fax:* (01792) 295676; *e-mail:* v.randle@swansea.ac.uk.

RANDOLPH, Denys, BSc; CEng, MRAeS, FIProdE, FIET, FInstD; Director, Partnership Wines Ltd, 1995–2000; *b* 6 Feb. 1926; *s* of late Harry Beckham Randolph and Margaret Isabel Randolph; *m* 1951, Marjorie Hales; two *d*. *Educ:* St Paul's School: Queen's Univ., Belfast (BSc). Served Royal Engineers, 1944–48 (Captain). Queen's Univ., Belfast, 1948–52; post-grad. apprenticeship, Short Bros & Harland, 1952–55; Wilkinson Sword Ltd: Prod. Engr/Prod. Dir, Graviner Div., 1955–66; Man. Dir, Hand Tools Div., 1966–69; Chm., Graviner Div., 1969–79; Chm., 1972–79; Pres., 1980–85; Wilkinson Match Ltd: Dir, 1974–80; Chm., 1976–79. Chairman: Woodrush Investments Ltd, 1980–93; Poitires Eyots Ltd, 1972–93; Dir, Henley Distance Learning Ltd, 1985–94. Proprietor, Clapcot Vineyards, 1986–98. Institute of Directors: Chm., 1976–79; Vice-Pres., 1979–96. Past Master: Worshipful Co. of Scientific Instrument Makers, 1977; Cutlers' Co., 1986. Mem. Council, Brunel Univ., 1986–91; Governor, Henley Admin. Staff Coll., 1979–91. CIMgt; FRSA (Manufactures and Commerce). *Publication:* From Rapiers to Razor Blades—The Development of the Light Metals Industry (paper, RSA). *Recreation:* viticulture.

RANDS, Dr Michael Russell Wheldon; Director and Chief Executive, BirdLife International, since 1996; *b* 2 Aug. 1956; *s* of late Russell Fuller Rands and of Freda Millicent Rands; *m* 1984, Dr Gillian Frances Porter Goff; one *s* one *d*. *Educ:* Univ. of E Anglia (BSc Hons Envmtl Sci. 1978); Wolfson Coll., Oxford (DPhil 1982). Res. Biologist, Game Conservancy, 1982–86; Programme Dir, ICBP, 1986–94; Dir, Strategic Planning and Policy, BirdLife Internat., 1994–96. *Publications:* (with P. J. Hudson) Ecology and Management of Gamebirds, 1988; contrib. numerous papers to learned jls. *Recreations:* bird-watching, travelling with family, music. *Address:* BirdLife International, Wellbrook Court, Girton Road, Cambridge CB3 0NA.

RANELAGH, John O'B.; *see* O'Beirne Ranelagh.

RANFURLY, 7th Earl of, *cr* 1831 (Ire.); **Gerald François Needham Knox;** Baron Welles 1781; Viscount Northland 1791; Baron Ranfurly (UK) 1826; *b* 4 Jan. 1929; *s* of Captain John Needham Knox, RN (*d* 1967) (*g g g s* of 1st Earl) and Monica B. H. (*d* 1975), *d* of Maj.-Gen. Sir Gerald Kitson, KCVO, CB, CMG; *S* cousin, 1988; *m* 1955, Rosemary, *o d* of Air Vice-Marshal Felton Vesey Holt, CMG, DSO; two *s* two *d*. *Educ:* Wellington College. Served RN, 1947–60; retired as Lieut Comdr. Member of Stock Exchange, 1964; Partner in Brewin & Co., 1965; Senior Partner, 1982, Chm., 1987–95, Brewin Dolphin & Co. *Recreation:* foxhunting. *Heir:* *s* Edward John Knox [*b* 21 May 1957; *m* 1st, 1980, Rachel Sarah (marr. diss. 1984), *d* of F. H. Lee; 2nd, 1994, Johanna Humphrey, *d* of Sqdn Leader H. R. Walton, MBE; one *s* one *d*]. *Address:* Maltings Chase, Nayland, Colchester, Essex CO6 4LZ.

RANG, Prof. Humphrey Peter, DPhil; FRS 1980; Director, Sandoz, later Novartis, 1983–97, Institute for Medical Research, and Professor of Pharmacology, 1979–83 and 1995–2001, now Emeritus, University College London; *b* 13 June 1936; *s* of Charles Rang and Sybil Rang; *m* 1992, Isobel Heyman. *Educ:* University Coll. Sch.; University Coll. London (MSc 1960); UCH Med. Sch. (MB, BS 1961); Balliol Coll., Oxford (DPhil 1965). J. H. Burn Res. Fellow, Dept of Pharmacol., Oxford, 1961–65; Vis. Res. Associate, Albert Einstein Coll. of Medicine, NY, 1966–67; Univ. Lectr in Pharmacol., Oxford, 1966–72; Fellow and Tutor in Physiol., Lincoln Coll., Oxford, 1967–72; Prof. of Pharmacology: Univ. of Southampton, 1972–74; St George's Hosp. Med. Sch., London, 1974–79; Fellow, 1983, and Vis. Prof., 1983–95, UCL. Founder FMedSci 1998. *Publications:* Drug Receptors, 1973; Pharmacology, 1987; Drug Discovery and Development, 2006. *Recreations:* sailing, music, painting. *Address:* 1 Willow Road, NW3 1TH.

RANGER, Prof. Terence Osborn, DPhil; FBA 1988; Rhodes Professor of Race Relations, and Fellow of St Antony's College, University of Oxford, 1987–97, now Emeritus Professor and Fellow; *b* 29 Nov. 1929; *s* of Leslie and Anna Ranger; *m* 1953, Shelagh Campbell Clarke; three *d*. *Educ:* Highgate Sch.; Univ. of Oxford (BA, MA; DPhil 1960). Lecturer: RNC, Dartmouth, 1955–56; UC of Rhodesia and Nyasaland, 1957–63; Prof. of History, UC, of Dar es Salaam, 1963–69; Prof. of African History, Univ. of Calif, LA, 1969–74; Prof. of Modern History, Univ. of Manchester, 1974–87; Chm., Oxford Univ. Cttee on African Studies, 1987–94. Vis. Prof., Univ. of Zimbabwe, 1998–2001. Chm., Jl of Southern African Studies, 1976–92; Vice-Chm., Past and Present, 1987–. Hon. DLitt Zimbabwe, 1995. *Publications:* Revolt in Southern Rhodesia 1896–7, 1967; The African Voice in Southern Rhodesia 1898–1930, 1970; Dance and Society in Eastern Africa, 1975; Peasant Consciousness and Guerrilla War in Zimbabwe, 1985; Are We Not Also Men?, 1995; Voices From the Rocks: nature, culture and history in the Matopos mountains in Zimbabwe, 1999; (jtly) Violence and Memory: one hundred years in the dark forests of Matabeleland, 2000. *Recreations:* theatre, opera, walking. *Address:* 100 Woodstock Road, Oxford OX2 7NE; *e-mail:* terence.ranger@sant.ox.ac.uk. *Club:* Royal Commonwealth Society.

RANK-BROADLEY, Ian, FRBS; sculptor, since 1976; *b* 4 Sept. 1952; *s* of late John Kenneth Broadley and of Barbara Anne Broadley (*née* Barker); *m* 1980, Hazel G. Rank; one *s* one *d*. *Educ:* Epsom Sch. of Art; Slade Sch. of Fine Art; University Coll. London (Boise Travelling Schol., Italy). FRBS 1994. Effigy of: HM Queen Elizabeth II, for use on UK and Commonwealth coinage, 1998, and Golden Jubilee hallmark, 2002; HM Queen Elizabeth the Queen Mother, for Centenary Crown, 2000; the Queen for Golden Jubilee Crown and Medal, 2002; HRH Prince of Wales for 60th Birthday Crown, 2008; King George VI and Queen Elizabeth Diamond Stakes Trophy, 2005; Armed Forces Meml, 2007. *Works in public collections:* British Mus.; Nat. Portrait Gall.; Imperial War Mus.; Royal Mus. of Scotland; Fitzwilliam Mus.; Goldsmiths' Hall; London Library; Staatliche Mus., Berlin; Rijksmus., Leiden; Nat. Collection of Finland; Royal Swedish Coin Cabinet; All England Lawn Tennis & Croquet Club. Brother, Art Workers' Guild, 1995 (Mem. Cttee, 1999–2002; Trustee, 2002–05); Freeman: City of London, 1996; Goldsmiths' Co., 1996 (Mem., Modern Collection Cttee, 2004–). Prizewinner, XI Biennale Dantesca, Ravenna, Italy, 1996; first prize, Goldsmiths' Craft and Design Council Awards, 2000, 2002; Olin-Stones Prize, Soc. of Portrait Sculptors, 2002. *Recreations:* rowing, swimming. *Address:* Stanfields, Kingscourt Lane, Rodborough, Stroud, Glos GL5 3QR. *T:* (01453) 765985, *Fax:* (01453) 764064; *e-mail:* irb@ianrank-broadley.co.uk. *Club:* Gloucester Rowing.

RANKEILLOUR, 5th Baron *cr* 1932, of Buxted, co. Sussex; **Michael Richard Hope;** *b* 21 Oct. 1940; *s* of Hon. Richard Frederick Hope, OBE, *y s* of 1st Baron and Helen Hope (*née* Lambart); *S* cousin, 2005; *m* 1964, Elizabeth Rosemary, *e d* of Col F. H. Fuller; one *s* two *d*. *Educ:* Downside Sch.; Loughborough Coll. (Engrg Dip.). Prodn engr then mgt trainee, Pye Gp, Cambridge, 1961; IBM UK: tech. sales, 1965; Original Equipment Manufr Gp, 1969; marketing mgt, 1974; new business mgt, computer sales, 1979; retired 1997. Trustee: Norwich Open Christmas; All Saints Centre; Songbird Survival; St John's Catholic Cathedral. *Recreations:* fishing, wildlife. *Heir:* *s* Hon. James Francis Richard Hope [*b* 5 Aug. 1968; *m* 2000, Felicity Gallimore; one *s*]. *Address:* The Old Vicarage, Thurton, Norwich NR14 6AG. *T:* (01508) 480300; *e-mail:* michaelhope@vicaragethurton.fsnet.co.uk.

RANKIN, Andrew; QC 1968; a Recorder of the Crown Court, 1972–97; *b* 3 Aug. 1924; *s* of William Locke Rankin and Mary Ann McArdle, Edinburgh; *m* 1st, 1944, Winifred (marr. diss. 1963), *d* of Frank McAdam, Edinburgh; two *s* two *d* (and one *s* decd); 2nd, 1964, Veronica (*d* 1990), *d* of George Aloysius Martin, Liverpool; 3rd, 1991, Jenifer Margaret, *d* of Alfred George Hodges Bebington, Wirral. *Educ:* Royal High Sch., Edinburgh; Univ. of Edinburgh; Downing Coll., Cambridge. Served War of 1939–45: Sub-Lt, RNVR, 1943. BL (Edin.) 1946; BA, 1st cl. hons Law Tripos (Cantab), 1948. Royal Commonwealth Soc. Medal, 1942; Cecil Peace Prize, 1946; Lord Justice Holker Exhibn, Gray's Inn, 1947–50; Lord Justice Holker Schol., Gray's Inn, 1950–53; Univ. Blue, Edin., 1943 and 1946 and Camb., 1948. Lectr in Law, Univ. of Liverpool, 1948–52. Called to Bar, Gray's Inn, 1950. *Publications:* (ed, 4th edn) Levie's Law of Bankruptcy in Scotland, 1950; various articles in UK and foreign legal jls. *Recreations:* swimming, travel by sea, racing (both codes), watching soccer (especially Liverpool FC). *Address:* Chelwood, Pine Walks, Prenton, Birkenhead, Merseyside CH42 8LQ. *T:* (0151) 608 2987.

RANKIN, Ian James, OBE 2002; DL; novelist; *b* 28 April 1960; *s* of James Hill Rankin and Isobel Rankin (*née* Vickers); *m* 1986, Anna Miranda Harvey; two *s*. *Educ:* Beath Sen. High Sch.; Univ. of Edinburgh (MA Hons). Tax Collector, then punk musician, then alcohol researcher, then swineherd, then music journalist, 1986–90. Fulbright/Chandler Fellow, USA, 1991–92. Chm., Crime Writers Assoc., 1999–2000 (Short Story Dagger, 1994, 1996); Mem., Detection Club, 1998–. Book and culture reviewer, radio and newspapers. DL City of Edinburgh, 2007. Hon. DLitt: Abertay Dundee, 1999; St Andrews, 2000; Edinburgh, 2003; Open, 2005; Hull, 2006. Cartier Diamond Dagger Award for Lifetime Achievement, 2005. *Publications:* The Flood, 1986; Watchman, 1988; Westwind, 1989; Beggars Banquet, 2002; *Inspector Rebus series:* Knots and Crosses, 1987; Hide and Seek, 1990; Tooth and Nail, 1992; A Good Hanging and other stories, 1992; Strip Jack, 1992; The Black Book, 1993; Mortal Causes, 1994; Let it Bleed, 1995; Black and Blue (CWA Gold Dagger award), 1997; The Hanging Garden (Grand Prix du Roman Noir), 1998; Death is not the End (novella), 1998; Dead Souls, 1999; Set in Darkness, 2000; The Falls, 2001; Resurrection Men (MWA Edgar award), 2001; Question of Blood, 2003; Fleshmarket Close, 2004 (Best Crime Novel, British Book Awards, 2005); The Naming of the Dead, 2006 (Best Crime Novel, British Book Awards, 2007); Exit Music, 2007; *as Jack Harvey:* Witch Hunt, 1993; Bleeding Hearts, 1994; Blood Hunt, 1995. *Recreations:* couch potato, regular visitor to Edinburgh pubs, '70s rock music. *Address:* c/o Robinson Literary Agency, Block A511, The Jam Factory, 27 Green Walk, SE1 4TT. *Clubs:* Hallion, Oyster (Edinburgh).

RANKIN, Sir Ian (Niall), 4th Bt *cr* 1898, of Bryngwyn, Much Dewchurch, Co. Hereford; Chairman, I. N. Rankin Oil Ltd, since 1981; *b* 19 Dec. 1932; *s* of Lt-Col Arthur Niall Rankin (*d* 1965) (*yr s* of 2nd Bt) and Lady Jean Rankin, DCVO; *S* uncle, 1988; *m* 1st, 1959, Alexandra (marr. diss.), *d* of Adm. Sir Laurence Durlacher, KCB, OBE, DSC; one *s* one *d*; 2nd, 1980, Mrs June Norman (marr. diss. 1998), *d* of late Captain Thomas Marsham-Townshend; one *s*. *Educ:* Eton College; Christ Church, Oxford (MA). Lieut, Scots Guards. Chm., Slumberfleece Ltd, 1979–; Director: Lindsay and Williams Ltd, 1973; Bayfine Ltd and subsidiaries, 1974–85 (Jt Chm., 1974–81); Highgate Optical and Industrial Co. Ltd and subsidiary, 1976–84 (Jt Chm., 1976–81); New Arcadia Explorations Ltd, 1987–; Bristol Scotts, 1993–2001. Patron, Samaritans, 1991–; Mem. Council, Alexandra Rose Day, 1970–. Gov., Moorfields Eye Hosp., 2005–. *Publication:* Doomsday Just Ahead, 2004. *Recreations:* shooting, ski-ing, chess. *Heir:* *s* Gavin Niall Rankin, *b* 19 May 1962. *Address:* 97 Elgin Avenue, W9 2DA. *T:* (office) (020) 7286 0251, (home) (020) 7286 5117. *Clubs:* White's, Beefsteak, Pratt's; Royal Yacht Squadron.

RANKIN, James Deans, FREng, FIChemE; Senior Science and Technology Associate, ICI, 1995–2000; *b* 17 Feb. 1943; *s* of Dr James Deans Rankin and Florence Elizabeth (*née* Wight); *m* 1973, Susan Margaret Adams; one *s* one *d*. *Educ:* Merchiston Castle Sch., Edinburgh; Gonville and Caius Coll., Cambridge (MA). FREng (FEng 1987); FIChemE 1987. Joined ICI, 1965: Agricl Div., 1965–83; Process Technology Gp Manager, New Sci. Gp, 1983–88; Melinex R&D Manager, 1988–93; Technology, 1993–2000. Royal Acad. of Engrg Vis. Prof. of Engrg Design, Univ. of Oxford, 1997–2000; Vis. Prof., Univ.

of Manchester (formerly UMIST), 2000–. *Recreations:* steam boats, motoring. *Address:* Department of Chemical Engineering, University of Manchester, PO Box 88, Sackville Street, Manchester M60 1QD.

RANKIN, John James; HM Diplomatic Service; Director, Americas, Foreign and Commonwealth Office, since 2008; *b* 12 March 1957; *s* of late James Rankin, CBE, and Agnes Rankin (*née* Stobie); *m* 1987, Lesley Marshall; one *s* two *d. Educ:* Hutchesons' Boys' Grammar Sch.; Univ. of Glasgow (LLB 1st Cl. Hons); McGill Univ., Montreal (LLM with distinction). Solicitor and Mem., Law Soc. of Scotland. Lectr in Public Law, Univ. of Aberdeen, 1984–88; Asst, then Sen. Asst Legal Advr, FCO, 1988–90; Legal Advr, UKMIS and UKDIS, Geneva, 1991–94; Legal Counsellor, FCO, 1995; Dep. Head, OSCE Dept, 1996–98; Counsellor and Dep. Head of Mission, Dublin, 1999–2003; Consul Gen., Boston, 2003–08. *Publications:* articles on Scots law and international law. *Recreations:* tennis, golf, gardening, food. *Address:* c/o Foreign and Commonwealth Office, SW1A 2AH.

RANKIN, Maggie Mary; *see* Gee, M. M.

RANKIN, Rear-Adm. Neil Erskine, CB 1995; CBE 1988; Chairman, Scottish Environment LINK, since 2000; *b* 24 Dec. 1940; *s* of late James Hall Rankin and of Jean Laura Rankin (*née* Honeyman); *m* 1969, Jillian Mary Cobb; one *s* one *d. Educ:* HMS Conway; BRNC Dartmouth. Joined RN 1958; pilot's wings, 1963; CO HMS Achilles, 1977; CO HMS Bacchante, 1978; Comdr (Air), RNAS Yeovilton, 1979, HMS Invincible, 1981; Naval Air Warfare, MoD, 1982; COS, Flag Officer Third Flotilla, 1984; CO, Captain F8, HMS Andromeda, 1985; Sen. Naval Officer, Middle East, 1985; Dep. Dir, Naval Warfare, MoD, 1987; CO HMS Ark Royal, 1990; Comdr, British Forces Falkland Is, 1992–93; FO, Portsmouth, 1993–96. Chm., Caledonian Macbrayne Ltd, 1996–99. Director: Portsmouth Naval Base Property Trust, 1997–; Former Royal Yacht Britannia Trust, 1999–. Chm., Scottish Seabird Centre, 1997–; Mem., Central Council, King George's Fund for Sailors, 1997. Trustee, RZSScot, 2000. Mem., RNSA, 1995–. Comr, Queen Victoria Sch., Dunblane, 1999–. Liveryman, Shipwrights' Co., 1992–; Younger Brother, Trinity House, 1993–; Mem., Incorporation of Hammermen, Glasgow, 1998–. *Recreations:* Rugby (former Pres., Combined Services RFU, and RNRU, Pres., United Services Portsmouth RFC, 1994–96), sailing, golf. *Address:* c/o Lloyds TSB, Cox's & King's Branch, Pall Mall, SW1Y 5NA. *Clubs:* Royal Navy of 1765 and 1785, Naval; Royal Naval Golfing; North Berwick Golf; Gullane Golf; Royal Yacht Squadron; Royal Naval and Royal Albert Yacht; East Lothian Yacht.

RANKIN, Robert Craig McPherson, CompICE; Chairman, BKR Financial Ltd, 1988–2004; Director, British Shipbuilders, 1985–91; *b* 15 Aug. 1937; *s* of Robert Craig Rankin and Julia Rankin (*née* Duff); *m* 1963, Alison Barbara Black Douglas; one *s* one *d. Educ:* The Academy, Ayr; Royal College of Science and Technology, Glasgow. CompICE 1987. Dir, Balfour Beatty Construction (Scotland) Ltd, 1973–74; Dir 1974–83, Exec. Dir 1983–85, Balfour Beatty Construction Ltd; Balfour Beatty Ltd: Dir, 1983–88; Dep. Man. Dir, 1985–86; Man. Dir, 1986–87; Chief Exec., 1986–88; Dir, BICC PLC, 1987–88; Non-executive Director: London & Edinburgh Trust PLC, 1988–91; LDDC, 1989–93. CCMI (CBIM 1987). *Recreations:* opera, music.

RANKINE, Fiona Grace; *see* McLeod, F. G.

RANKINE, Jean Morag, (Mrs N. A. Hall); Deputy Director of the British Museum, 1983–97; *b* 5 Sept. 1941; *d* of late Alan Rankine and Margaret Mary Sloan Rankine (*née* Reid); *m* 1992, Norman Anthony Hall. *Educ:* Central Newcastle High Sch.; University College London (BA, MPhil; Fellow, 1990); Univ. of Copenhagen. Grad. Assistant, Durham Univ. Library, 1966–67; British Museum: Res. Assistant, Dept of Printed Books, 1967–73; Asst Keeper, Director's Office, 1973–78; Head of Public Services, 1978–83. *Recreations:* sculling, ski-ing, fell-walking, opera, motorcycling. *Address:* 49 Hartington Road, W4 3TS. *Clubs:* Thames Rowing; Clydesdale Amateur Rowing (Glasgow).

RANN, Hon. Michael David; MHA (ALP) Ramsay, South Australia, since 1993; Premier of South Australia, and Minister for the Arts and for Economic Development, since 2002, for Social Inclusion, since 2004 and for Sustainability and Climate Change, since 2006; *b* Sidcup, Kent, 5 Jan. 1953; *s* of Frederick George and Winifred Hetty Rann; *m* 1st, 1982, Jennifer Russell (marr. diss.); one *s* one *d*; 2nd, 2006, Sasha Carruozzo. *Educ:* Northcote Coll., NZ; Auckland Univ. (MA). Political Journalist, Radio NZ, 1976–77; Press Secretary: to Premier of SA, 1977–79, 1982–85; to Leader of the Opposition, 1979–82. MHA (ALP) Briggs, SA, 1985–93. South Australia Government: Minister: for Employment and Further Educn, of Youth Affairs, of Aboriginal Affairs, and Assisting Minister of Ethnic Affairs, 1989–92; for Business and Regl Develt, of Tourism and of State Services, 1992–93; Dep. Leader of the Opposition, and Shadow Minister for Regl Develt, Employment, Training and Further Educn, 1993–94; Leader of the Opposition, 1994–2002; Shadow Minister: for Industry, Manufacturing and Small Business, 1994–95; for Economic Develt, 1994–2002; for Jobs, 1998 and 2000–02; for Industry, 1999–2000; Minister for Volunteers, 2002–06. Mem., Parly Public Works Standing Cttee, 1986–89. Nat. Pres., ALP, 2008. Member: Australian Aboriginal Affairs Council, 1989–92; Australian Educn Council, 1990–92; SA Manuf. Council (Dep. Chm., 1992–93); Dep. Chm., Automotive Industry Task Force. Mem. Bd, Techsearch, 1986–89; Member Council: SA Inst. of Technol., 1986–89; Univ. of SA, 1994–97. Philip of Macedonia Award, Fed. Pan Macedonian Assoc., Australia, 1996; Nikki (Victory) Award, Aust. Hellenic Council, 1997. *Recreations:* reading, films, travel, soccer, arts, writing. *Address:* State Administration Centre, 15th Floor, 200 Victoria Square, Adelaide, SA 5000, Australia. *Clubs:* Northern (NZ); Salisbury United Soccer; South Adelaide Football, Adelaide United, Thunderbirds Netball, Port Adelaide Football.

RANNIE, Prof. Ian, FRCPath 1964; FIBiol 1964; Professor of Pathology (Dental School), University of Newcastle upon Tyne, 1960–81, Professor Emeritus 1981; *b* 29 Oct. 1915; *o s* of James Rannie, MA, and Nicholas Denniston McMeekan; *m* 1943, Flora Welch; two *s. Educ:* Ayr Academy; Glasgow University. BSc (Glas), 1935; MB, ChB (Glas), 1938; BSc Hons Pathology and Bacteriology (Glas), 1939; Hutcheson Research Schol. (Pathology), 1940. Assistant to Professor of Bacteriology, Glasgow, 1940–42; Lecturer in Pathology, 1942–60, King's College, Univ. of Durham. Consultant Pathologist, United Newcastle upon Tyne Hospitals, 1948–81, Hon. Consultant 1981–. Pres., International Soc. of Geographical Pathology, 1969–72; Vice-President: Assoc. of Clinical Pathologists, 1978–80; Internat. Union of Angiology. Hon. Mem., Hungarian Arteriosclerosis Res. Soc. *Publications:* papers on various subjects in medical journals. *Address:* Apartment G, 8 Osborne Villas, Newcastle upon Tyne NE2 1JU. *T:* (0191) 281 3163. *Club:* Royal Over-Seas League.

RANSFORD, John Anthony, CBE 1997; Deputy Chief Executive, Local Government Association, since 2005; *b* 19 Sept. 1948; *s* of Sydney George Ransford and Ethel Alice Ransford (*née* Peters); *m* 1971, Liz Hainsworth; one *s* one *d. Educ:* Letchworth Grammar Sch.; Univ. of Sussex (BA Hons Sociol.; MSocWork). CQSW 1972. Probation Officer, SE London Probation and After-Care Service, 1972–74; Kirklees Metropolitan Council: Trng Officer, Social Services Dept, 1974–77; Health Liaison Officer, 1977–79; Asst Dir, Social Services, 1979–82, Dir, 1982–87; Actg Chief Exec., 1987; Dir, Social Services, 1988–94, Chief Exec., 1994–99, N Yorks CC; Hd, Social Affairs, Health and Housing, subseq. Dir, Educn and Social Policy, LGA, 1999–2005. Hon. Sec., Assoc. of Dirs of Social Services, 1993–96. *Recreations:* theatre, foreign travel, current affairs. *Address:* Local Government Association, LGA House, Smith Square, SW1P 3HZ. *T:* (020) 7664 3236.

RANTZEN, Esther Louise, (Mrs Desmond Wilcox), CBE 2006 (OBE 1991); television producer/presenter, since 1968; *b* 22 June 1940; *d* of late Harry Rantzen and Katherine Rantzen; *m* 1977, Desmond John Wilcox (*d* 2000); one *s* two *d. Educ:* North London Collegiate Sch.; Somerville Coll., Oxford (MA). Studio manager making dramatic sound effects, BBC Radio, 1963; BBC TV: Researcher, 1965; Dir, 1967; Reporter, Braden's Week, 1968–72; Producer/Presenter, That's Life, 1973–94, scriptwriter, 1976–94; Producer, documentary series, The Big Time, 1976; Presenter: Esther Interviews …, 1988; Hearts of Gold, 1988; Esther, 1994–2002; That's Esther, 1999–; Producer/Presenter, Drugwatch, Childwatch, The Lost Babies, How to Have a Good Death and other progs on social issues; reporter/producer, various documentaries, religious and current affairs TV progs. Member: Nat. Consumer Council, 1981–90; Health Educn Authority, 1989–95; Task Force to review services for drug misusers, DoH, 1994. President: ChildLine, 2006– (Chair, 1986–2006); Meet-a-Mum Assoc.; Community Meeting Point, Harpenden; Assoc. of Young People with ME, 1996–; a Vice-President: ASBAH; Health Visitors' Assoc.; Nat. Deaf Children's Soc.; Iain Rennie Hospice at Home; Vice-Patron, Rose Road Appeal (people with disabilities in S Hants); Patron: Addenbrookes Kidney Patients Assoc.; Contact-a-Family (families of disabled children); DEMAND (furniture for the disabled); Downs Children's Assoc.; Children with Aids; Headway; Children Head Injuries Trust; Hesley Foundn; Komso Children's Hosp.; S Wessex Addiction Centre; ADFAM (Nat. Charity for Families and Friends of Drug Users); SIMR (Seriously Ill for Medical Research); John Grooms Assoc.; Hillingdon Manor Sch. for Autistic Children, 1999–; The New Sch. at West Heath (The Princess Diana Sch.), 2000–. Champion, Community Legal Service, 2000. Trustee: Ben Hardwick Meml Fund; NSPCC, 2006– (Hon. Mem., 1989). FRTVS 1995. Hon. DLitt: Southampton Inst. for FE, 1994; South Bank, 2000. Personality of 1974, RTS award; BBC TV Personality of 1975, Variety Club of GB; European Soc. for Organ Transplant Award, 1985; Special Judges' Award for Journalism, RTS, 1986; Richard Dimbleby Award, BAFTA, 1988; Snowdon Award for Services to Disabled People, 1996; RTS Hall of Fame Award, 1998; Lifetime Achievement Award, Women in Film and TV, 2005. SSStJ 1992. *Publications:* (with Desmond Wilcox) Kill the Chocolate Biscuit, 1981; Baby Love, 1985; (with Shaun Woodward) Ben: the story of Ben Hardwick, 1985; Esther (autobiog.), 2001; A Secret Life (novel), 2003; If Not Now, When?: living the baby boomer adventure, 2008. *Recreations:* family life, the countryside, appearing in pantomime. *Address:* c/o Billy Marsh Associates, 76a Grove End Road, St John's Wood, NW8 9ND.

RAO, Prof. Calyampudi Radhakrishna, Padma Vibhushan, 2001; FRS 1967; Eberly Professor of Statistics, 1988–2001, now Emeritus, and Director, Centre for Multivariate Analysis, since 1988, Pennsylvania State University; Adjunct Professor, University of Pittsburgh, since 1988 (University Professor, 1979–88); *b* 10 Sept. 1920; *s* of C. D. Naidu and A. Laksmikantamma; *m* 1948, C. Bhargavi Rao; one *s* one *d. Educ:* Andhra Univ. (MA, 1st Class Maths); Calcutta Univ. (MA, 1st Class Statistics; Gold Medal); PhD, ScD, Cambridge (Hon. Fellow, King's Coll., Cambridge, 1975). Indian Statistical Institute: Superintending Statistician, 1943–49; Professor and Head of Division of Theoretical Research and Training, 1949–64; Dir, Res. and Training Sch., 1964–76 (Sec., 1972–76); Jawaharlal Nehru Professor, 1976–84. Nat. Prof., India, 1987–92. Co-editor, Sankhya, Indian Jl of Statistics, 1964–72, Editor, 1972–96. Member, Internat. Statistical Inst., 1951 (Mem. Statistical Educn Cttee, 1958–; Treasurer, 1962–65; Pres.-elect, 1975–77, Pres., 1977–79, Hon. Mem. 1982); Chm., Indian Nat. Cttee for Statistics, 1962–70; President: Biometric Soc., 1973–75 (Hon. Life Mem., 1986); Indian Econometric Soc., 1971–76; Forum for Interdisciplinary Mathematics, 1982–84. Fellow: Indian Nat. Sci. Acad., 1953 (Vice-Pres., 1973, 1974); Inst. of Math. Statistics, USA, 1958 (Pres., 1976–77); Amer. Statistical Assoc., 1972; Econometric Soc., 1972; Indian Acad. of Scis, 1974; Founder Fellow: Third World Sci. Acad., 1983; Nat. Acad. of Scis, India, 1988; Nat. Acad. of Scis, USA, 1995; Foreign Mem., Lithuanian Acad. of Scis, 1997. Hon. Fellow: Royal Stat. Soc., 1969; Amer. Acad. of Arts and Scis, 1975; Calcutta Stat. Assoc., 1985; Biometric Soc., 1986; Finnish Statistical Soc., 1990; Inst. of Combinatorics and its Applications, 1995; Portuguese Statistical Soc., 2002. Shanti Swarup Bhatnagar Memorial Award, 1963; Guy Medal in Silver, Royal Stat. Soc., 1965; Padma Bhushan, 1968; Meghnad Saha Medal, 1969; J. C. Bose Gold Medal, 1979; S. S. Wilke's Meml Medal, 1989; Mahalandois Birth Centenary Gold Medal, 1996; Dist. Achievement Medal, Sect. on Stats and Envmt, Amer. Stat. Assoc., 1997; Carol and Emanuel Parzen Prize for statistical innovation, Texas A&M Univ., 2000; US Nat. Medal of Sci., 2001; Army Wilkes Medal, 2002; Srinivasa Ramanujan Medal, 2003; Mahalanobis Award, ISI, 2003. Hon. DSc: Andhra; Leningrad; Athens; Osmania; Ohio State; Philippines; Tampere; Neuchatel; Poznan; Indian Statistical Inst.; Colorado State; Hyderabad; Barcelona; Slovak Acad. of Scis; Guelph; Munich; Venkateswara; Waterloo; Brasilia; Athens; Kent; Cyprus; Wollongong; Oakland; Calcutta; Pretoria; Nova de Lisboa; Madras; Hon. DLitt: Delhi; Visva-Bharati. Hon. Prof., Univ. of San Marcos, Lima. *Publications:* (with Mahalanobis and Majumdar) Anthropometric Survey of the United Provinces, 1941, a statistical study, 1949; Advanced Statistical Methods in Biometric Research, 1952; (with Mukherjee and Trevor) The Ancient Inhabitants of Jebal Moya, 1955; (with Majumdar) Bengal Anthropometric Survey, 1945, a statistical study, 1959; Linear Statistical Inference and its Applications, 1965; (with A. Matthai and S. K. Mitra) Formulae and Tables for Statistical Work, 1966; Computers and the Future of Human Society, 1968; (with S. K. Mitra) The Generalised Inverse of Matrices and its Applications, 1971; (with A. M. Kagan and Yu. V. Linnik) Characterization Problems of Mathematical Statistics, 1973; (with J. Kleffe) Estimation of Variance Components and its Applications, 1988; Statistics and Truth, 1989; (with H. Toutenburg) Linear Models, 1995; (with D. N. Shanbhag) Choquet-Deny Type Functional Equations with Applications to Stochastic Models, 1994; (with M. B. Rao) Matrix Algebra and its Applications to Statistics and Econometrics, 1998. *Address:* Department of Statistics, 326 Thomas Building, Pennsylvania State University, University Park, PA 16802–2111, USA.

RAO, Prof. Chintamani Nagesa Ramachandra, Padma Shri, 1974; Padma Vibhushan, 1985; FRS 1982; CChem, FRSC; Hon. President and Linus Pauling Research Professor, Jawaharlal Nehru Centre for Advanced Scientific Research, Bangalore, India, since 2000 (President, 1989–99); *b* 30 June 1934; *s* of H. Nagesa Rao; *m* 1960, Indumati; one *s* one *d. Educ:* Univ. of Mysore (DSc); Univ. of Purdue, USA (PhD). Research Chemist, Univ. of California, Berkeley, 1958–59; Lectr, Indian Inst. of Science, 1959–63; Prof., Indian Inst. of Technology, Kanpur, 1963–76, Head of Chemistry Dept, 1964–68, Dean of Research, 1969–72; Jawaharlal Nehru Fellow, 1973–75; Indian Institute of Science, Bangalore: Chm., Solid State and Structural Chemistry Unit and Materials Res. Laboratory, 1977–84; Dir, 1984–94. Commonwealth Vis. Prof., Univ. of Oxford, and Fellow, St Catherine's Coll., 1974–75; Jawaharlal Nehru Vis. Prof., Univ. of Cambridge, and Professorial Fellow, Kings' Coll., Cambridge, 1983–84; Linnett Vis. Prof., Univ. of Cambridge, 1998; Gauss Prof., Acad. of Scis, Göttingen, 2003. Blackett Lectr, Royal Soc., 1991. US Nat. Acad. of Sci. Lect., 1993. President: INSA, 1985–86; IUPAC, 1985–87; Indian Sci. Congress, 1987–88; Indian Acad. of Scis, 1989–91; Materials Res. Soc. of India, 1989–91. Member: First Nat. Cttee of Science and Technology, Govt of India, 1971–74; Science Adv. Cttee to Union Cabinet of India, 1981–86 (Chm., 1997–98); Atomic Energy Commn of India, 1987–; Chm., Science Adv. Council to Prime Minister, 1985–89, 2005–. Member: Gen. Council, ICSU; Internat. Sci. Adv. Bd, UNESCO, 1996–99. Foreign Member: Slovenian Acad. of Scis, 1983; Serbian Acad. of Scis, 1986; Amer. Acad. of Arts and Scis, 1986; USSR Acad. of Scis, 1988; Czechoslovak Acad. of Scis, 1988; Polish Acad. of Scis, 1988; US Nat. Acad. of Scis, 1990; Pontifical Acad. of Scis, 1990; Amer. Philosophical Soc., 1995; Academia Europaea, 1997; Brazilian Acad. of Scis, 1997; European Acad. of Arts, Scis and Humanities, 1997; Japan Acad., 1998; Royal Spanish Acad. of Scis, 1999; French Acad of Scis, 2000; Founder Mem., Third World Acad. of Scis, 1983– (Pres., 2000–). Hon. Fellow: UWCC, 1997; St Catherine's Coll., Oxford, 2006; Hon. FInstP 2005. Hon. DSc: Purdue, 1982; Bordeaux, 1983; Sri Venkateswara, 1984; Roorkee, 1985; Banaras, Osmania, Mangalore and Manipur, 1987; Anna, Mysore, Burdwan, 1988; Wroclaw, 1989; Andhra, Karnatak, 1990; Bangalore, Hyderabad, Indian Inst. of Technology, Kharagpur, 1991; Oxford, 2007. Many awards and medals, incl.: Marlow Medal of Faraday Soc. (London), 1967; Royal Soc. of Chemistry (London) Medal, 1981; Centennial For. Fellowship of Amer. Chemical Soc., 1976; Hevrovsky Gold Medal, Czech. Acad. of Scis, 1989; Golden Jubilee Prize, CSIR, 1991; P. C. Ray Meml Award, 1994; Sahabdeen Award for Sci., Sri Lanka, 1994; Medal for Chemistry, Third World Acad. of Scis, 1995; Albert Einstein Gold Medal, UNESCO, 1996; Shatabdi Puraskar prize, Indian Sci. Congress Assoc., 1999; Centenary Medal, RSC, 2000; Hughes Medal, Royal Soc., 2000; Millennium Plaque of Honour, Indian Sci. Cong., 2001; Somiya Award, Internat. Union of Materials Res., 2004; India Sci. Prize, 2005; (jtly) Dan David Internat. Prize for Materials Sci., 2005; Chemical Pioneer, Amer. Inst. of Chemists, 2005. Comdr, Order of Rio Branco (Brazil), 2002; Chevalier, Légion d'Honneur (France), 2005. *Publications:* 41 books including: Ultraviolet and Visible Spectroscopy, 1960, 3rd edn 1975; Chemical Applications of Infrared Spectroscopy, 1963; Spectroscopy in Inorganic Chemistry, 1970; Modern Aspects of Solid State Chemistry, 1970; University General Chemistry, 1973; Solid State Chemistry, 1974; Phase Transitions in Solids, 1978; Preparation and Characterization of Materials, 1981; The Metallic and the Non-metallic States of Matter, 1985; New Directions in Solid State Chemistry, 1986; Chemistry of Oxide Superconductors, 1988; Chemical and Structural Aspects of High Temperature Oxide Superconductors, 1988; Bismuth and Thallium Superconductors, 1989; Advances in Catalyst Design, 1991; Chemistry of High Temperature Superconductors, 1991; Chemistry of Advanced Materials, 1992; Chemical Approaches to the Synthesis of Inorganic Materials, 1994; Transition Metal Oxides, 1995; Metal-Insulator Transition Revisited, 1995; Understanding Chemistry, 1999; Superconductivity Today, 1999; 1400 research papers. *Recreations:* gourmet cooking, gardening. *Address:* Jawaharlal Nehru Centre for Advanced Scientific Research, Jakkur Post, Bangalore 560064, India. *T:* (office) (80) 23653075, *T:* (home) (80) 23601410.

RAPER, (Alfred) Graham, CBE 1988; PhD; FREng; Chairman, Projecta, consulting engineers, 1987–99; Chief Executive and Deputy Chairman, Davy Corporation, 1985–87; *b* 15 May 1932; *s* of Hilda and Alfred William Raper; *m* 1st, Elizabeth Williams (marr. diss. 1975); two *s* one *d*; 2nd, Valerie Benson; one *s*. *Educ:* Lady Manners School, Bakewell; Univ. of Sheffield (BScTech Hons, PhD). FREng (FEng 1986); FIChemE. Asst Lectr, Univ. of Sheffield, 1955–57; Research Engineer, Head Wrightson Co., 1957–59; Technical Manager, Davy United Engineering, 1959–65; Steel Plant Manager, Highveld Steel & Vanadium, S Africa, 1965–69; joined Davy Corp., 1969; Vice-Chm., Kvaerner Davy, 1995–97. Non-exec. Dir, Vosper Thornycroft (UK) Ltd, 1995–2001. *Publications:* articles in jls of Iron & Steel Institute and British Association. *Recreations:* golf, gardening. *Address:* 54 Golf Links Road, Ferndown, Wimborne, Dorset BH22 8BZ. *T:* (01202) 873512.

RAPER, Maj.-Gen. Anthony John, CB 2006; CBE 1996 (MBE 1987); Quartermaster General, Ministry of Defence, 2002–06; *b* 14 April 1950. *Educ:* RMA Sandhurst; Selwyn Coll., Cambridge (BA 1974, MA 1976). Commnd Royal Signals, 1970; posts in UK, Germany, Cyprus, Bosnia and NATO; Commander: 4th Armoured Div. and Signal Regt, 1988–91; 1st Signal Bde, Allied Comd Europe, 1994–95; Defence Intelligence Staff; Directorate of Land Warfare; directing staff, RMA Sandhurst and Staff Coll.; Dir, Operational Requirements for Inf. and Communication Services; Chief Exec., Defence Communications Services Agency, 1998–2002; Dir Gen. Strategy and Logistics Develt, 2002–04; Defence Logistics Transformation Prog. Team Leader, 2004–05.

RAPHAEL, Adam Eliot Geoffrey; Editor, The Good Hotel Guide, since 2004; Associate Editor, Transport Times, since 2005; *b* 22 April 1938; *s* of Geoffrey George Raphael and Nancy Raphael (*née* Rose); *m* 1970, Caroline Rayner Ellis; one *s* one *d*. *Educ:* Arnold House, Charterhouse; Oriel Coll., Oxford (BA Hons History). 2nd Lieut Royal Artillery, 1956–58. Copy Boy, Washington Post, USA, 1961; Swindon Evening Advertiser, 1962–63; Film Critic, Bath Evening Chronicle, 1963–64; The Guardian: Reporter, 1965; Motoring Correspondent, 1967–68; Foreign Correspondent, Washington and S Africa, 1969–73; Consumer Affairs Columnist, 1974–76; Political Correspondent, The Observer, 1976–81, Political Editor, 1981–86; Presenter, Newsnight, BBC TV, 1987–88; an Asst Editor, 1988, Exec. Editor, 1988–93, The Observer; writer on Home Affairs, 1994, political correspondent, 1994–2004, The Economist. Awards include: Granada Investigative Journalist of the Year, 1973; British Press Awards, Journalist of the Year, 1973. *Publications:* My Learned Friends, 1989; Ultimate Risk: the inside story of the Lloyd's catastrophe, 1994. *Recreations:* tennis, golf, ski-ing. *Address:* 50 Addison Avenue, W11 4QP. *T:* (020) 7603 9133. *Clubs:* Garrick, Hurlingham, Royal Automobile.

RAPHAEL, Caroline Sarah; Commissioning Editor, BBC Radio Four, since 1997; *b* 15 Jan. 1958; *d* of Arnold Raphael and Lily Suzanne (*née* Shaffer); *m* 1982, Michael Eaves (marr. diss. 2001); one *s*. *Educ:* Putney High Sch.; Manchester Univ. (BA Hons Drama). Theatre director: Nuffield Theatre, 1980–81; Bristol Old Vic, 1981–83; Gate Theatre, London, 1983; Literary Agent and Publisher, Chappels Music, 1983; joined BBC Radio, 1984: Script Reader, Producer, Editor Drama, 1984–90; Editor Drama, Features, Youth Programmes, Radio 5, 1990–94; Hd of Drama, BBC Radio, 1994–97. Mem. Bd, Paines Plough Theatre Co., 1996–2000; Council Mem., NYT, 2005–. FRSA. *Recreations:* listening to radio, theatre, cinema, reading. *Address:* BBC, Broadcasting House, W1A 1AA. *T:* (020) 7580 4465.

RAPHAEL, Prof. David Daiches, DPhil, MA; Emeritus Professor of Philosophy, University of London, since 1983; *b* 25 Jan. 1916; 2nd *s* of late Jacob Raphael and Sarah Warshawsky, Liverpool; *m* 1942, Sylvia (*d* 1996), *er d* of late Rabbi Dr Salis Daiches and Flora Levin, Edinburgh; two *d*. *Educ:* Liverpool Collegiate School; University College, Oxford (scholar). 1st Class, Classical Moderations, 1936; Hall-Houghton Junior Septuagint Prizeman, 1937; 1st Class, Literae Humaniores, 1938; Robinson Senior Scholar of Oriel College, Oxford, 1938–40; Passmore Edwards Scholar, 1939. Served in Army, 1940–41. Temporary Assistant Principal, Ministry of Labour and National Service, 1941–44; temp. Principal, 1944–46. Professor of Philosophy, University of Otago, Dunedin, NZ, 1946–49; Lecturer in Moral Philosophy, Univ. of Glasgow, 1949–51; Senior Lecturer, 1951–60; Edward Caird Prof. of Political and Social Philosophy, Univ. of Glasgow, 1960–70; Prof. of Philosophy, Univ. of Reading, 1970–73; Prof. of Philosophy, Imperial Coll., Univ. of London, 1973–83 (Acad. Dir of Associated Studies, 1973–80; Head of Dept of Humanities, 1980–83; Hon. Fellow 1987). Visiting Professor of Philosophy, Hamilton Coll., Clinton, NY (under Chauncey S. Truax Foundation), and Univ. of Southern California, 1959; Mahlon Powell Lectr, Indiana Univ., 1959; Vis. Fellow, All Souls Coll., Oxford, 1967–68; John Hinkley Vis. Prof. of Political Sci., Johns Hopkins Univ., 1984. Independent Member: Cttee on Teaching Profession in Scotland (Wheatley Cttee), 1961–63; Scottish Agricultural Wages Board, 1962–84; Agricultural Wages Bd for England and Wales, 1972–78. Mem. Academic Adv. Cttee, Heriot-Watt Univ., Edinburgh, 1964–71; Mem. Cttee on Distribution of Teachers in Scotland (Roberts Cttee), 1965–66; Independent Member Police Advisory Board for Scotland, 1965–70; Member Social Sciences Adv. Cttee, UK Nat. Commission, UNESCO, 1966–74; Vice-Pres., Internat. Assoc. Philosophy of Law and Social Philosophy, 1971–87; Pres., Aristotelian Soc., 1974–75. Academic Mem., Bd of Governors, Hebrew Univ. of Jerusalem, 1969–81, Hon. Governor 1981–. Chm., Westminster Synagogue, 1987–89. *Publications:* The Moral Sense, 1947; Edition of Richard Price's Review of Morals, 1948; Moral Judgement, 1955; The Paradox of Tragedy, 1960; Political Theory and the Rights of Man, 1967; British Moralists 1650–1800, 1969; Problems of Political Philosophy, 1970, 2nd edn 1990; (ed jtly) Adam Smith's Theory of Moral Sentiments, 1976; Hobbes: Morals and Politics, 1977; (ed jtly) Adam Smith's Lectures on Jurisprudence, 1978; (ed jtly) Adam Smith's Essays on Philosophical Subjects, 1980; Justice and Liberty, 1980; Moral Philosophy, 1981, 2nd edn 1994; (trans. jtly with Sylvia Raphael) Richard Price as Moral Philosopher and Political Theorist, by Henri Laboucheix, 1982; Adam Smith, 1985; Concepts of Justice, 2001; The Impartial Spectator, 2007; articles in jls of philosophy and of political studies. *Address:* 54 Sandy Lane, Petersham, Richmond, Surrey TW10 7EL.

RAPHAEL, Frederic Michael; author; *b* 14 Aug. 1931; *s* of late Cedric Michael Raphael and of Irene Rose (*née* Mauser); *m* 1955, Sylvia Betty Glatt; two *s* (one *d* decd). *Educ:* Charterhouse; St John's Coll., Cambridge (MA (Hons)). FRSL 1964. *Publications: novels:* Obbligato, 1956; The Earlsdon Way, 1958; The Limits of Love, 1960; A Wild Surmise, 1961; The Graduate Wife, 1962; The Trouble with England, 1962; Lindmann, 1963; Darling, 1965; Orchestra and Beginners, 1967; Like Men Betrayed, 1970; Who Were You With Last Night?, 1971; April, June and November, 1972; Richard's Things, 1973; California Time, 1975; The Glittering Prizes, 1976; Heaven and Earth, 1985; After the War, 1988 (adapted for television, 1989); The Hidden I, 1990; A Double Life, 1993; Old Scores, 1995; Coast to Coast, 1998; Fame and Fortune, 2007; *short stories:* Sleeps Six, 1979; Oxbridge Blues, 1980 (also pubd as scripts of TV plays, 1984); Think of England, 1986; The Latin Lover, 1994; All His Sons, 1999; *biography:* Somerset Maugham and his World, 1977; Byron, 1982; *memoir:* Eyes Wide Open: a memoir of Stanley Kubrick and Eyes Wide Shut, 1999; A Spoilt Boy (autobiog.), 2003; Personal Terms series: Personal Terms (notebooks 1951–1969), 2001; Rough Copy (notebooks 1970–1973), 2004; Cuts and Bruises (notebooks 1974–1978), 2006; Ticks and Crosses (notebooks 1978–1981), 2008; *essays:* Bookmarks (ed), 1975; Cracks in the Ice, 1979; Of Gods and Men, 1992; France, the Four Seasons, 1994; The Necessity of Anti-Semitism, 1997; Karl Popper, 1998; (ed jtly and contrib.) The Great Philosophers from Socrates to Turing, 2000; The Benefits of Doubts, 2003; Some Talk of Alexander, 2006; *screenplays:* Nothing but the Best, 1964; Darling, 1965 (Academy Award); Two For The Road, 1967; Far From the Madding Crowd, 1967; A Severed Head, 1972; Daisy Miller, 1974; The Glittering Prizes, 1976 (sequence of TV plays) (Writer of the Year 1976, Royal TV Soc.); Rogue Male, 1976; (and directed) Something's Wrong (TV), 1978; School Play (TV), 1979; The Best of Friends (TV), 1979; Richard's Things, 1981; After the War (TV series), 1989; (and directed) The Man In The Brooks Brothers Shirt, 1991 (ACE Award); Eyes Wide Shut, 1999; For God's Sake (TV documentary series), 1998; Coast to Coast, 2004; *plays:* From The Greek, Arts, Cambridge, 1979; The Daedalus Dimension (radio), 1982; The Thought of Lydia (radio), 1988; The Empty Jew (radio), 1993; *translations:* Petronius: Satyrica, 2003; (with Kenneth McLeish): Poems of Catullus, 1976; The Oresteia, 1978 (televised as The Serpent Son, BBC, 1979); The Complete Plays of Aeschylus, 1991; Medea, 1994; Hippolytus, 1997; Aias, 1998; Bacchae, 1999. *Recreations:* tennis, having gardened. *Address:* c/o Steve Kenis & Co., Royalty House, 72–74 Dean Street, W1D 3SG. *Clubs:* Queen's, Savile.

RAPHAEL, Philip Montague, (Monty); Head of Fraud and Regulatory, Peters & Peters, solicitors, since 2005; *b* 8 Feb. 1937; *s* of Solomon and Sarah Raphael; *m* 1963, Leona Hartley; one *s* three *d* (and one *s* decd). *Educ:* Davenant Sch.; University Coll. London (LLB Hons). Admitted solicitor, 1962; Partner, Peters & Peters, 1965–2005. Vis. Prof., Kingston Univ., 2004–. Mem. Bd, Fraud Adv. Panel; Dir, Transparency Internat. (UK), 2006–. Trustee and Hon. Solicitor, Howard League for Penal Reform. *Publication:* The Proceeds of Crime Act: how it will work in practice, 2003. *Recreations:* obsessing about London, arts, travel, thinking very vigorously about exercise. *Address:* Peters & Peters, 15 Fetter Lane, EC4A 1BW. *T:* (020) 7822 7777, *Fax:* (020) 7822 7788; *e-mail:* montyr@petersandpeters.com. Capel & Land Ltd, 29 Wardour Street, W1D 6PS. *Clubs:* Royal Automobile, Savile.

RAPHAEL, Ven. Timothy John; Archdeacon of Middlesex, 1983–96; *b* 26 Sept. 1929; *s* of Hector and Alix Raphael; *m* 1957, Anne Elizabeth Shepherd; one *s* two *d*. *Educ:* Christ's College, Christchurch, NZ; Leeds Univ. (BA). Asst Curate, St Stephen, Westminster, 1955–60; Vicar of St Mary, Welling, Kent, 1960–63; Vicar of St Michael, Christchurch, NZ, 1963–65; Dean of Dunedin, 1965–73; Vicar, St John's Wood, London, 1973–83. *Recreations:* contemporary poetry, theatre, beach-combing. *Address:* 121 Hales Road, Cheltenham, Glos GL52 6ST. *T:* (01242) 256075.

RAPHOE, Bishop of, (RC), since 1995; **Most Rev. Philip Boyce,** DD; *b* 25 Jan. 1940; *s* of Joseph Boyce and Brigid Gallagher. *Educ:* Downings, Co. Donegal; Castlemartyr Coll., Co. Cork; Carmelite House of Studies, Dublin; Pontifical Theol Faculty (Teresianum), Rome (DD). Entered Discalced Carmelites, 1958; studied philosophy in Dublin and theology in Rome; ordained priest, 1966; on teaching staff of Pontifical Theol Faculty (Teresianum), Rome, 1972–95. Mem., Congregation for Divine Worship and Discipline of Sacraments, 1999–. *Publications:* The Challenge of Sanctity: a study of Christian perfection in the writings of John Henry Newman, 1974; Spiritual Exodus of John Henry Newman and Thérèse of Lisieux, 1979; (ed) Mary: the Virgin Mary in the life and writings of John Henry Newman, 2001; articles on themes of spiritual theology. *Address:* Ard Adhamhnáin, Letterkenny, Co. Donegal, Ireland. *T:* (74) 9121208.

RAPINET, Michael William; a Vice-President, 1997–2002, and Acting Vice-President, 2003–05, Immigration Appeal Tribunal; *b* 13 April 1935; *s* of Charles Herbert Rapinet and Eleanor Adelaide Rapinet (*née* Hunt); *m* 1962, Christina Mary, *d* of Captain William Eric Brockman, CBE, RN; one *s* one *d*. *Educ:* St Edward's Coll., Malta; St Joseph's Coll.,

London. Admitted Solicitor, 1957; Sen. Partner, Kidd Rapinet, 1958–85. Pt-time Chm., Industrial Tribunals, 1987–91; pt-time Chm., 1989–92, Chm., 1992–97, Immigration Tribunal. Pres., Council of Immigration Judges, 2000–01. Member (C): Wandsworth LBC, 1958–62; Berks CC, 1968–75 (Chm., Schs Cttee; Member: Finance Cttee; Personnel and Mgt Cttee). Liveryman, Tallow Chandlers' Co. Founder: Order of Malta Homes Trust, 1975; Orders of St John Care Trust (formerly Orders of St John Trust), 1975. CStJ 1988; Kt of Magistral Grace, 1973, Kt Grand Cross, 1996, SMO (Malta). *Recreations:* fishing, gardening, walking, reading, theatre, music. *Address:* Greenlands, Townsend Road, Streatley-on-Thames, Berks RG8 9LH. *T:* (01491) 871740. *Clubs:* Carlton; Leander.

RAPLEY, Prof. Christopher Graham, CBE 2003; PhD; Director, Science Museum, since 2007; Fellow: St Edmund's College, Cambridge, since 1999; University College London, since 2008; *b* 8 April 1947; *s* of Ronald Rapley and Barbara Helen Rapley (*née* Stubbs); *m* 1970, Norma Khan; twin *d. Educ:* Jesus Coll., Oxford (BA Hons Physics 1969; MA 1974; four shooting half blues); Manchester Univ. (MSc Radio Astronomy 1970); UCL (PhD X-ray Astronomy 1976); DSc Bristol 2008. FInstP 2008. Prof. of Remote Sensing Sci., UCL, 1991–97; Dir, British Antarctic Survey, 1998–2007. Exec. Dir, Internat. Geosphere-Biosphere Prog., Royal Swedish Acad. of Scis, 1994–97; Chm., ICSU Planning Gp, 2003–04, Mem., Jt Cttee, 2005–, for Internat. Polar Year 2007–08; Sen. Vis. Scientist, NASA Jet Propulsion Lab., 2006–. Pres., Internat. Scientific Cttee on Antarctic Res., 2006–08 (Vice Pres., 2000–04); Member: Earth Sci. Adv. Council, ESA, 2000–01; UK Deleg., Governing Council, ESF, 2000–03; Global Envmtl Res. Cttee, Royal Soc., 2007–. Sen. Associate, Cambridge Univ. Prog. for Industry, 2007–. Hon. Professor: UCL, 1998–; UEA, 1999–. Edinburgh Science Medal, Edinburgh Internat. Sci. Fest., 2008. *Publications:* more than 150 res. papers on space astronomy, remote sensing, global change, earth system sci. *Recreation:* digital photography. *Address:* 22 Artington Walk, Guildford, Surrey GU2 4EA. *T:* (01483) 851538.

RAPSON, Sydney Norman John, BEM 1984; *b* 17 April 1942; *s* of late Sidney Rapson and of Doris Rapson (*née* Fisher); *m* 1967, Phyllis Edna, *d* of Frank and Beatrice Williams; one *s* one *d. Educ:* Southsea and Paulsgrove Secondary Modern Sch.; Portsmouth Dockyard Coll. Apprentice aircraft fitter, 1958–63, Aircraft Engr, 1963–97, MoD. Member (Lab): Portsmouth CC, 1971–97 (Lord Mayor, 1990–91; Hon. Alderman, 1999); Hants CC, 1973–76. Non-exec. Dir, Portsmouth Healthcare NHS Trust, 1993–97. MP (Lab) Portsmouth N, 1997–2005; Team PPS, MoD, 2003–05. Freeman, City of London, 1990. Imperial Service Medal, 1998. *Address:* 79 Washbrook Road, Paulsgrove, Portsmouth, Hants PO6 3SB.

RASCH, Sir Simon (Anthony Carne), 4th Bt *cr* 1903, of Woodhill, Danbury, Essex; *b* 26 Feb. 1948; *s* of Sir Richard Guy Carne Rasch, 3rd Bt and Anne Mary (*d* 1989), *e d* of Maj. John Henry Dent-Brocklehurst, OBE; *S* father, 1996; *m* 1987, Julia, *er d* of Maj. Michael Godwin Plantagenet Stourton; one *s* one *d. Educ:* Eton; RAC Cirencester. MRICS (ARICS 1973). A Page of Honour to HM The Queen, 1962–64. *Heir: s* Toby Richard Carne Rasch, *b* 28 Sept. 1994. *Address:* The Manor House, Lower Woodford, Salisbury SP4 6NQ.

RASHBASS, Dr Barbara, FRCP; barrister-at-law; Director and Secretary: Wolfson Foundation, 1990–97; Wolfson Family Charitable Trust, 1989–97; *d* of late Leonard Cramer and Sarina (*née* Klinger); *m* 1956, Cyril Rashbass (*d* 1982); two *s* one *d. Educ:* Godolphin Sch., Salisbury; University Coll. London (MB, BS; Fellow 1999). DCH 1961; DPH 1968; FRCP 1995. Called to the Bar, Middle Temple, 1969. PMO, MRC, 1983–87. Dep. Chm., Harrow HA, 1982–84; non-exec. Dir, Harrow and Hillingdon Healthcare NHS Trust, 1998–2001. Mem., Med. Legal Soc., 1970–2002. FRSocMed 1989–2007. Trustee, Ronald Raven Cancer Res. Trust, 2000–02. *Recreations:* tennis, 'cello, gardening.

RASHLEIGH, Sir Richard (Harry), 6th Bt *cr* 1831; management accountant; self-employed, since 1990; *b* 8 July 1958; *s* of Sir Harry Evelyn Battie Rashleigh, 5th Bt and Honora Elizabeth (*d* 1987), *d* of George Stuart Sneyd; *S* father, 1984; *m* 1996, Emma, *o d* of John McGougan and Jennifer (*née* Dyke; she *m* 1987, Sir Antony Acland, *qv*); one *s* one *d. Educ:* Allhallows School, Dorset. Management Accountant with Arthur Guinness Son & Co., 1980–82; Dexion-Comino International Ltd, 1982–84; United Biscuits, 1985–88; Wessex Housing, 1988–90. *Recreations:* sailing, tennis, shooting. *Heir: s* David William Augustine Rashleigh, *b* 1 April 1997. *Address:* Menabilly, Par, Cornwall PL24 2TN. *T:* (01726) 815432. *Club:* Royal Fowey Yacht.

RASMUSSEN, Anders Fogh; MP (L) Greve, Denmark, since 1978; Prime Minister of Denmark, since 2001; *b* 26 Jan. 1953; *s* of Knud Rasmussen and Martha (*née* Fogh Andersen); *m* 1978, Anne-Mette; one *s* two *d. Educ:* Univ. of Aarhus (MSc Econs 1978). Consultant, Danish Fedn of Crafts and Small Industries, 1978–87. Folketing: Minister: for Taxation, 1987–92; for Econ. Affairs, 1990–92; spokesman for Liberal Party, 1992–98; Vice-Chairman: Housing Cttee, 1981–86; Econ. and Pol Affairs Cttee, 1993–98; Foreign Policy Bd, 1998–2001. Liberal Party: Mem., Mgt Cttee, 1984–87 and 1992–, Chm., 1998–2001, Parly Party; Vice-Chm., 1985–98, Chm., 1998–, nat. orgn. Nat. Chm., Liberal Youth of Denmark, 1974–76. Dr *hc* George Washington, 2002; Hon. LLD Hampden-Sydney Coll., Va, 2003. Awards: Adam Smith Award, 1993; Politician of the Year, Danish Mktg Assoc., 1998; Liberal of the Year, Jongeren Organisatie Vrijheid en Democratie, Holland, 2002; European Leader, Polish Leaders Forum, 2003; European of the Year, Danish Eur. Movt, 2003; Robert Schuman Medal, EP, 2003; Best Leader in Denmark, 2005; Årets Erhvervspolitiker, Dansk Erhvervssammenslutning, 2005. Medal of Merit in Gold (Denmark), 2002; Commander 1st Cl., Order of the Dannebrog (Denmark), 2002. Foreign decorations include: Grand Cross: Order of Merit (Portugal), 1992; Order of Merit (Germany), 2002; Order of Merit (Poland), 2003; Order of the Oak Crown (Luxembourg), 2003; Order of Nicaragua, 2003; Order of Star (Romania), 2004; Order of Polar Star (Sweden); Great Cross, Order Pedro Joaquín Chamorro (Nicaragua), 2003; Grand Duke Gediminas (Lithuania), 2004; Three Star Order (Latvia), 2005; Order of Stara Planina First Class (Bulgaria), 2006. *Publications:* Opgør med skattesystemet, 1979; Kampen om boligen, 1982; Fra socialstat til minimalstat, 1993. *Address:* Office of the Prime Minister, Christiansborg, Prins Jørgens Gård 11, 1218 Copenhagen K, Denmark. *T:* 33922201, *Fax:* 33114896; *e-mail:* stm@stm.dk.

RASMUSSEN, Poul Nyrup; Member (Social Democrats) for Denmark, European Parliament, since 2004; *b* 15 June 1943; *s* of Oluf Nyrup Rasmussen and Vera Nyrup Rasmussen; *m* 1st (marr. diss.); (one *c* decd); 2nd (marr. diss.); 3rd, 1994, Lone Dybkjær, MEP. *Educ:* Esbjerg Statsskole; Univ. of Copenhagen (MA Econs). With Danish Trade Union Council, 1980–86: in Brussels, 1980–81; Chief Economist, 1981–86; Man. Dir, Employees' Capital Pension Fund, 1986–88. Chm., SDP, 1992–2002 (Dep. Chm., 1987–92); MP (SDP) Herning-Kredsen, Denmark, 1988–2004; Prime Minister of Denmark, 1993–2001. Pres., PES, 2004–. *Address:* European Parliament, 60 Rue Wiertz, 1047 Brussels, Belgium.

RASSOOL, Bertrand Louis Maurice; Director, since 2005, Group Deputy Chief Executive Officer, since 2007 and Executive Chairman, Tourism and Leisure Division, since 2008, British American Investment Co. (Mauritius) Ltd; *b* 10 April 1957; *m* 1978, Estelle Guntier; one *s* two *d. Educ:* London Sch. of Econs (BSc Econs (Mathematical Econs and Econometrics)). Central Bank of Seychelles: economist, 1980; Asst Dir of Res., 1981–86; Dir of Res., 1986–88; Dir Gen., Planning and Econ. Co-operation Div., Min. of Planning and Ext. Relns, 1988–93; Principal Secretary: Min. of Foreign Affairs, Planning and Envmt, 1993–94; Min. of Industry, 1994–98; Min. of Tourism and Civil Aviation, 1998–99; High Comr of Seychelles to UK, 1999–2003. Non-exec. Dir, Trading Emissions plc (UK), 2007– (Advr, 2005–). *Recreations:* fishing, chess, horse-racing. *Address:* c/o British American Investment Co. (Mauritius) Ltd, 6th Floor, 25 Pope Hennessy Street, Port Louis, Mauritius.

RATCLIFF, Antony Robin Napier; Deputy Chairman and Chief Executive, Eagle Star Insurance, 1985–87; Visiting Professor, Sir John Cass Business School, City of London (formerly City University Business School), 1987–2005; *b* 26 Sept. 1925; *m* 1956, Helga Belohlawek, Vienna; one *s*. FIA 1953; Aktuar, DAV, 1994; ASA. Nat. Correspondent for England, Internat. Actuarial Assoc., 1965–70; Mem. Council, Assoc. of British Insurers (formerly British Insurance Assoc.), 1969–87. Pres., Inst. of Actuaries, 1980–82; Vice-President: London Insce Inst., 1964–; Chartered Insce Inst., 1983–84. Hon. Mem., Assoc. internat. pour l'Etude de l'Economie de l'Assurance, 1991– (Vice-Pres., 1986–90). Trustee, Soc. for the Protection of Life from Fire, 1989– (Chm., 1998–2000). Mem., Evangelische Forschungs-akad., Berlin. Corresponding Member: Deutsche Gesellschaft für Versicherungsmathematik; Verein zur Förderung der Versicherungswirtschaft. FRSA. Hon. Treasurer, German Christ Church, London; Trustee, St Paul's German Evangelical Reformed Ch Trust; Extraordinary Mem. of Synod, German-speaking Protestant Congregations in GB, 2003–. Messenger and Brown Prize-Winner, Inst. of Actuaries, 1963. Hon. DLitt City, 1986. Officer's Cross, Order of Merit (Germany), 2007. *Publications:* (jtly) Lessons from Central Forecasting, 1965; (jtly) Strategic Planning for Financial Institutions, 1974; (jtly) A House in Town, 1984; The Annals of the Deutsche Evangelische St Paulsgemeinde 1697–2007, 2008; contribs to Jl of Inst. of Actuaries, Trans of Internat. Congress of Actuaries, Jl London Insce Inst., Jl Chartered Insce Inst., Blätter der Deutschen Gesellschaft für Versicherungsmathematik. *Address:* 8 Evelyn Terrace, Richmond, Surrey TW9 2TQ. *Clubs:* Actuaries, Anglo-Austrian Society.

RATCLIFFE, Frederick William, CBE 1994; MA, PhD; JP; University Librarian, University of Cambridge, 1980–94, now Emeritus; Life Fellow, since 1994 (Fellow, 1980–94), and Parker Librarian, 1995–2000, Corpus Christi College, Cambridge; *b* 28 May 1927; *y s* of late Sydney and Dora Ratcliffe, Leek, Staffs; *m* 1952, Joyce Brierley; two *s* one *d. Educ:* Leek High Sch., Staffs; Manchester Univ. (MA, PhD); MA Cantab. Served in N Staffs Regt, 1945–48. Manchester University: Graduate Res. Scholarship, 1951; Res. Studentship in Arts, 1952; Asst Cataloguer and Cataloguer, 1954–62; Sub-Librarian, Glasgow Univ., 1962–63; Dep. Librarian, Univ. of Newcastle upon Tyne, 1963–65; University Librarian, 1965–80, Dir, John Rylands University Library, 1972–80, Manchester University. Trustee, St Deiniol's Library, Hawarden, 1975–98 (Hon. Fellow, 2000). Hon. Lectr in Historical Bibliography, Manchester Univ., 1970–80; External Prof., Dept of Library and Inf. Studies, Loughborough Univ., 1981–86; Hon. Res. Fellow, Dept of Library, Archive and Inf. Studies, UCL, 1987–; Sandars Reader in Bibliography, Cambridge Univ., 1988–89. Founder, later Pres., Consortium of Univ. Res. Libraries, 1984–94; Chm., Library Panel, The Wellcome Trust, 1988–94. Fellow, Chapter of Woodard Schools (Eastern Div.), 1981–97, now Emeritus (Vice-Provost, 1994–97). Chm., Adv. Cttee, Nat. Preservation Office, 1984–94. Trustee: Cambridge Foundn, 1989–94; Malaysian Commonwealth Studies Centre, 1994–98. Hon. FCLIP (Hon. FLA 1986). JP Stockport, 1972–80, Cambridge, 1981–97. Encomienda de la Orden del Merito Civil (Spain), 1988. *Publications:* Die Psalmenübersetzung Heinrichs von Mügeln, 1965; Preservation Policies and Conservation in British Libraries, 1984; many articles in learned journals. *Recreations:* book collecting, hand printing, cricket. *Address:* Ridge House, The Street, Rickinghall Superior, Diss, Norfolk IP22 1DY. *T:* (01379) 898232, (01379) 897199; *e-mail:* frederick@ratcliffe7375.freeserve.co.uk.

RATCLIFFE, James A.; Chairman, and Founder, Ineos plc, since 1998; *b* 18 Oct. 1952; *s* of Alan and Marie Ratcliffe; two *s. Educ:* Univ. of Birmingham (BSc); London Business Sch. (MBA). ACMA. CEO, Inspec, 1992–98 (Founder, 1992). *Recreations:* ski-ing, running, mountains, wine.

RATCLIFFE, (John) Michael; writer; *b* 15 June 1935; *s* of Donald Ratcliffe and Joyce Lilian Dilks; civil partnership 2006, Howard Lichterman. *Educ:* Cheadle Hulme Sch.; Christ's Coll., Cambridge (MA). Trainee journalist, Sheffield Telegraph, 1959–61; Asst Literary and Arts Editor, Sunday Times, 1962–67; Literary Editor, 1967–72, chief book reviewer, 1972–82, The Times; freelance writer, 1982–83; theatre critic, 1984–89, Literary Ed., 1990–95, Contributing Ed., 1995–96, Observer. Commended Critic of the Year, British Press Awards, 1989. Officer, Order of Merit (FRG), 2003. *Publications:* The Novel Today, 1968; The Bodley Head 1887–1987 (completed for J. W. Lambert), 1987. *Recreations:* music, travel, art, architecture, walking, gardening, cycling. *Address:* 4 Elia Street, N1 8DE. *T:* (020) 7837 1687; *e-mail:* elia@dircon.co.uk.

RATCLIFFE, Prof. Peter John, MD; FRCP, FMedSci; FRS 2002; Nuffield Professor of Clinical Medicine, University of Oxford, since 2004; Fellow, Magdalen College, Oxford, since 2004; *b* 14 May 1954; *s* of William and Alice Margaret Ratcliffe; *m* 1983, Fiona Mary MacDougall; two *s* two *d. Educ:* Lancaster Royal Grammar Sch.; Gonville and Caius Coll., Cambridge (MD 1987); St Bartholomew's Hosp., London (MB ChB). FRCP 1995. University of Oxford: Wellcome Sen. Fellow, 1990–92; Fellow, Jesus Coll., 1992–2004; Prof. of Renal Medicine, 1996–2004. Hon. Consultant Physician, Radcliffe Trust, Oxford, 1990–. FMedSci 2002; Member: EMBO, 2006; Amer. Acad. of Arts and Scis, 2007. *Publications:* contribs on aspects of renal and cell biology, particularly processes involved in cellular oxygen sensing. *Recreations:* fell-walking, gardening (when pressed). *Address:* Manor Farmhouse, 17 Church Street, Kidlington, Oxon OX5 2BA. *T:* (01865) 376570; *e-mail:* pjr@well.ox.ac.uk.

RATFORD, Sir David (John Edward), KCMG 1994 (CMG 1984); CVO 1979; HM Diplomatic Service, retired; Chairman, Tushinskaya Trust, since 1996; translator and language consultant, University of Lund, Sweden, since 1997; *b* 22 April 1934; *s* of George Ratford and Lilian (*née* Jones); *m* 1960, Ulla Monica, *d* of Oskar and Gurli Jerneck, Stockholm; two *d. Educ:* Whitgift Middle Sch.; Selwyn Coll., Cambridge (1st Cl. Hons Mod. and Med. Langs). National Service (Intell. Corps), 1953–55. Exchequer and Audit Dept, 1952; FO, 1955; 3rd Sec., Prague, 1959–61; 2nd Sec., Mogadishu, 1961–63; 2nd, later 1st Sec., FO, 1963–68; 1st Sec. (Commercial), Moscow, 1968–71; FCO, 1971–74; Counsellor (Agric. and Econ.), Paris, 1974–78; Counsellor, Copenhagen, 1978–82; Minister, Moscow, 1983–85; Asst Under-Sec., of State (Europe), 1986–90, and Dep. Political Dir, 1987–90, FCO; UK Rep., Permanent Council of WEU, 1986–90; Ambassador to Norway, 1990–94. Comdr, Order of the Dannebrog, Denmark, 1979.

Recreations: music, tennis, walking. *Address:* Wisborough Cottage, Wisborough Green, West Sussex RH14 0DZ; Käringön, Bohuslän, Sweden. *Club:* Travellers.

RATHBAND, Very Rev. Kenneth William; Rector, St Ninian's, Alyth, with St Catherine's, Blairgowrie, and St Anne's, Coupar Angus, since 1991; Dean of St Andrews, Dunkeld and Dunblane, since 2007; *b* 1960. *Educ:* Edinburgh Theol Coll.; Edinburgh Univ. (BD 1986). Ordained deacon, 1986, priest, 1987; Asst Curate, St Paul's Cathedral, Dundee, 1986–88; Team Vicar, St Martin's, Dundee, 1988–89; Asst Curate, St Philips and St James', Edinburgh, 1990–91. *Address:* 10 Rosemount Park, Blairgowrie PH10 6TZ. *T:* (01250) 872431; *e-mail:* krathband@btinternet.com.

RATHBONE, Prof. Dominic William, PhD; Professor of Ancient History, King's College London, since 2003; *b* 8 Feb. 1957; *s* of Norman and Christine Rathbone; *m* 1993, Yvette Erete. *Educ:* Christ's Hosp., Horsham; Jesus Coll., Cambridge (BA Classics; PhD 1986). Lectr in Classics, Univ. of Aberdeen, 1981–84; Lectr, 1985–93, Reader, 1993–2003, in Ancient Hist., KCL. *Publications:* Economic Rationalism and Rural Society in Third-Century AD Egypt, 1991; (ed jtly) Cambridge Ancient History, vol. xi, 2001; (ed jtly) Egypt from Alexander to the Copts: an archaeological and historical guide, 2004. *Recreations:* travel, DIY. *Address:* Department of Classics, King's College London, Strand, WC2R 2LS. *T:* (020) 7848 2343; *e-mail:* dominic.rathbone@kcl.ac.uk.

RATHBONE, William; Director and Chief Executive, Royal United Kingdom Beneficent Association and Universal Beneficent Association, 1988–2001; *b* 5 June 1936; *s* of William Rathbone and Margaret Hester (*née* Lubbock); *m* 1960, Sarah Kynaston Mainwaring (*d* 2006); one *s* one *d*. *Educ:* Radley Coll.; Christ Church, Oxford (MA 2nd Cl. Hons PPE 1959); IMEDE, Lausanne (Dip. Business Studies 1972). Nat. Service, RA, 1954–56. Ocean Group PLC, 1959–88: Elder Dempster Lines, 1959–69; tanker and bulk carrier div., 1969–71; Dir, Wm Cory & Sons Ltd, 1973–74; Gen. Manager, Ocean Inchcape Ltd, 1974–79; Exec. Dir, Gastransco Ltd, 1979–88. Dir, Rathbone Bros plc, 1994–2003. Trustee, Queen's Nursing Inst., 1974– (Vice-Chm., 1974–99); Pres., Community and Dist Nursing Assoc., 1984–99; Vice Pres., Christ Church (Oxford) United Clubs, 1991–. Trustee: Eleanor Rathbone Charitable Trust, 1958–; New England Co., 1974–; St Peter's Convent, Woking, 1992–2007; Hadfield Trust, 1997–; Southwark Cathedral Millennium Trust, 1998–; British Mus. Friends, 2003– (Vice-Chm., 2005–). Gov., Centre for Policy on Ageing, 2000–02. Liveryman, Skinners' Co., 1969–. *Recreations:* fishing, the arts, friends. *Address:* 7 Brynmaer Road, SW11 4EN. *T:* (020) 7975 1935. *Clubs:* Brooks's; Leander (Henley-on-Thames).

RATHCAVAN, 3rd Baron *cr* 1953, of The Braid, Co. Antrim; **Hugh Detmar Torrens O'Neill;** Bt 1929; *b* 14 June 1939; *o s* of 2nd Baron Rathcavan, PC (NI) and his 1st wife, Clare Désirée (*d* 1956), *d* of late Detmar Blow; *S* father, 1994; *m* 1983, Sylvie Marie-Thérèse Wichard du Perron; one *s*. *Educ:* Eton. Captain, Irish Guards. Financial journalism, Observer, Irish Times, FT; Dep. Chm., IPEC Europe, 1978–82; Chairman: Northern Ireland Airports, 1986–92; NI Tourist Board, 1988–96; Brasserie St Quentin 2002 Ltd, 2002–; Director: St Quentin, 1980–94; The Spectator, 1982–84; Old Bushmills Distillery Co., 1989–99; Savoy Management, 1989–94; Northern Bank Ltd, 1990–97; Berkeley Hotel Co. Ltd, 1995–97. Mem., BTA, 1988–96. Member: H of L European Select Cttee D, 1995–99; British-Irish Interparly Body, 1995–99. *Recreations:* food, travel. *Heir:* *s* Hon. François Hugh Nial O'Neill, *b* 26 June 1984. *Address:* Cleggan Lodge, Ballymena, Co. Antrim BT43 7JW. *T:* (028) 2568 4209, *Fax:* (028) 2568 4552; 14 Thurloe Place, SW7 2RZ. *T:* (020) 7584 5293, *Fax:* (020) 7823 8846; *e-mail:* lordrathcavan@btopenworld.com. *Clubs:* Beefsteak, Pratt's.

RATHCREEDAN, 3rd Baron *cr* 1916; **Christopher John Norton;** Director, Norton & Brooksbank Ltd, Pedigree Livestock Auctioneers, since 2003; *b* 3 June 1949; *er s* of 2nd Baron Rathcreedan, TD and Ann Pauline (*d* 2007), *d* of late Surg.-Capt. William Bastian, RN; *S* father, 1990; *m* 1978, Lavinia Anne Ross, *d* of late A. G. R. Ormiston; two *d*. *Educ:* Wellington Coll.; RAC Cirencester. Partner, Hobsons, Pedigree Livestock Auctioneers; founded Norton & Brooksbank, 1983, Partner, 1983–2003; Dir, KVN Stockdale Ltd, 1999–. *Recreations:* horse racing, gardening. *Heir:* *b* Hon. Adam Gregory Norton [*b* 2 April 1952; *m* 1980, Hilary Shelton, *d* of Edmond Ryan; two *d*]. *Address:* Stoke Common House, Purton Stoke, Swindon, Wilts SN5 4LL. *T:* (01793) 772492. *Club:* Turf.

RATHDONNELL, 5th Baron *cr* 1868; **Thomas Benjamin McClintock Bunbury;** *b* 17 Sept. 1938; *o s* of William, 4th Baron Rathdonnell and Pamela (*d* 1989), *e d* of late John Malcolm Drew; *S* father, 1959; *m* 1965, Jessica Harriet, *d* of George Gilbert Butler, Scatorish, Bennettsbridge, Co. Kilkenny; three *s* one *d*. *Educ:* Charterhouse; Royal Naval College, Dartmouth. Lieutenant RN. *Heir:* *s* Hon. William Leopold McClintock Bunbury [*b* 6 July 1966; *m* 2002, Emily Henrietta Dacres Dixon]. *Address:* Lisnavagh, Rathvilly, County Carlow, Ireland. *T:* (59) 9161104.

RATLEDGE, Prof. Colin, PhD; CChem, FRSC; CBiol, FIBiol; Professor of Microbial Biochemistry, University of Hull, 1983–2004, now Emeritus; *b* 9 Oct. 1936; *s* of Fred Ratledge and Freda Smith Ratledge (*née* Proudlock); *m* 1961, Janet Vivien Bottomley; one *s* two *d*. *Educ:* Bury High Sch.; Manchester Univ. (BSc Tech, PhD). AMCST; CChem, FRSC 1970; CBiol, FIBiol 1982. Res. Fellowship, MRC Ireland, 1960–64; Res. Scientist, Unilever plc, 1964–67; Hull University, 1967–: Lectr, 1967–73; Sen. Lectr, 1973–77; Reader, 1977–83; Head of Dept of Biochemistry, 1986–88. Visiting Lecturer: Australian Soc. of Microbiol., 1986; NZ Soc. of Microbiol., 1986; Kathleen Barton Wright Meml Lectr (Inst. of Biol./Soc. Gen. Microbiol.), 1995; Visiting Professor: Univ. of Malaya, 1993; Hong Kong Poly., 1994, 2001–02; Univ. of OFS, Bloemfontein, 1994; Ben-Gurion Univ. of the Negev, Israel, 2008. Mem., AFRC Food Res. Cttee, 1989–92; Chairman: AFRC Food Res. Grants Bd, 1989–92; AFRC Food-borne Pathogens Co-ord. Prog., 1992–95; Brit. Co-ordinating Cttee for Biotechnology, 1989–91; Inst. of Biol. Industrial Biol. Cttee, 1992–2001; Vice-Pres., SCI, 1993–96 (Chm. Biotechnol. Gp, 1990–91; Mem. Council, 1991–93); Sec., Internat. Cttee of Envmtl and Applied Microbiology, 1991–94; Mem., Biotechnology Cttee, Internat. Union of Biochemistry, 1984–97. Fellow, Internat. Inst. of Biotechnology, 1993. Editor: World Jl of Microbiol. and Biotechnol., 1987–; Biotechnology Techniques, 1988–99; Biotechnology Letters, 1996–. *Publications:* The Mycobacteria, 1977; Co-Editor: Microbial Technology: current state, future prospects, 1979; The Biology of the Mycobacteria, vol. 1 1982, vol. 2 1983, vol. 3 1989; Biotechnology for the Oils and Fats Industry, 1984; Microbial Technology in the Developing World, 1987; Microbial Lipids, vol. 1 1988, vol. 2 1989; Microbial Physiology and Manufacturing Industry, 1988; Biotechnology: Social and Economic Impact, 1992; Industrial Application of Single Cell Oils, 1992; Biochemistry of Microbial Degradation, 1993; Mycobacteria: molecular biology and virulence, 1999; Basic Biotechnology, 3rd edn 2006; Single Cell Oils, 2005; numerous scientific papers in biol science jls. *Recreations:* enjoying my grandchildren, hill walking, bonsai gardening. *Address:* Department of Biological Sciences, University of Hull, Hull HU6 7RX; *e-mail:* c.ratledge@hull.ac.uk; (home) 49 Church Drive, Leven, Beverley, E Yorks HU17 5LH. *T:* (01964) 542690.

RATNER, Gerald Irving; Chief Executive, geraldonline, since 2003; *b* 1 Nov. 1949; *s* of Leslie and Rachelle Ratner; *m* 1st (marr. diss. 1989); two *d*; 2nd, 1989, Moira Day; one *s* one *d*. *Educ:* Hendon Co. Grammar Sch. Chm. and Chief Exec., Ratners Gp, 1986–92. Director: Norweb, 1989–91; Workshop Health & Fitness Club, Henley, 1997–2003. *Publication:* The Rise and Fall… and Rise Again (autobiog.), 2007. *Recreation:* road cycling.

RATTEE, Sir Donald (Keith), Kt 1989; a Judge of the High Court of Justice, Chancery Division, 1993–2000 (Family Division, 1989–93); *b* 9 March 1937; *s* of Charles Ronald and Dorothy Rattee; *m* 1964, Diana Mary, *d* of John Leslie and Florence Elizabeth Howl; four *d*. *Educ:* Clacton County High School; Trinity Hall, Cambridge (Schol.; 1st cl. Pts I and II Law Tripos; MA, LLB). Called to Bar, Lincoln's Inn, 1962, Bencher, 1985, Treas., 2006; Second Junior Counsel to the Inland Revenue (Chancery), 1972–77; QC 1977; Attorney Gen. of the Duchy of Lancaster, 1986–89; a Recorder, 1989. Liaison Judge, Family Div. (NE Circuit), 1990–93; Mem., Gen. Council of the Bar, 1970–74. Chm., Inns of Court and Bar Educnl Trust, 1997–2004. *Recreations:* golf, walking, music, gardening. *Address:* 29 Shirley Avenue, Cheam, Surrey SM2 7QS. *Clubs:* Royal Automobile; Banstead Downs Golf (Banstead); Thurlestone Golf (Thurlestone, Devon).

RATTLE, Sir Simon, Kt 1994; CBE 1987; Chief Conductor and Artistic Director, Berlin Philharmonic Orchestra, since 2002; Principal Guest Conductor, Orchestra of the Age of Enlightenment, since 1992; *b* Liverpool, 19 Jan. 1955; *m* 1st, 1980, Elise Ross (marr. diss. 1995), American soprano; two *s*; 2nd, 1996, Candace Allen; one *s* by Magdalena Kozena. Won Bournemouth John Player Internat. Conducting Comp., when aged 19. Has conducted: Bournemouth Sinfonietta; Philharmonia; Northern Sinfonia; London Philharmonic; London Sinfonietta; Berliner Philharmoniker; Boston Symphony; Chicago Symphony; Cleveland; Concertgebouw; Stockholm Philharmonic; Toronto Symphony, etc. Débuts: Festival Hall, 1976; Glyndebourne, 1977; ENO, 1985; Royal Opera, 1990; Vienna Philharmonic, 1993; Philadelphia, 1993; Royal Albert Hall (Proms etc), 1976–; Asst Conductor, BBC Scottish Symphony Orch., 1977–80; Principal Conductor and Artistic Advr, 1980–90, Music Dir, 1990–98, CBSO. Associate Conductor, Royal Liverpool Philharmonic Soc., 1977–80; Principal Conductor, London Choral Soc., 1979–84; Artistic Dir, South Bank Summer Music, 1981–83; Principal Guest Conductor: Rotterdam Philharmonic, 1981–84; Los Angeles Philharmonic, 1981–92. Exclusive contract with EMI Records. Hon. Fellow, St Anne's Coll., Oxford, 1991. Hon. DMus: Birmingham, 1985; Birmingham Poly., 1985; Oxford, 1999. Shakespeare Prize, Toepfer Foundn, Hamburg, 1996; Albert Medal, RSA, 1997; Comenius Award, 2004; Hon. Schiller Award, 2005; Urania Medal, 2006; Goldena Kamera Award, 2006. Chevalier des Arts et des Lettres (France), 1995. *Address:* c/o Askonas Holt Ltd, Lincoln House, 300 High Holborn, WC1V 7JH. *T:* (020) 7400 1700.

RATTRAY, Hon. (Raphael) Carl, OJ 1994; President, Court of Appeal, Jamaica, 1993–99; *b* 18 Sept. 1929; *s* of late Benjamin Bruce Rattray and Agnes Agatha Rattray (*née* Wright); *m* 1951, Audrey Elaine Da Costa; two *s* two *d*. *Educ:* Beckford Smith's High Sch., Jamaica; Univ. of London (ext. LLB). Called to the Bar, Lincoln's Inn, 1956; Stipendiary Magistrate, Cayman Is, 1957–58; in private practice at Jamaican Bar, 1958–75; QC (Jamaica) 1969; Senator, Jamaican Parlt, 1975–83; Attorney Gen. and Minister of Justice, 1976–80; Leader: Govt Business in Senate, 1975–80; Opposition Business in Senate, 1980–83; Founding Mem., Rattray, Patterson, Rattray, 1981; in practice at Bar, 1981–89; MP (PNP), 1989–93; Attorney Gen. and Minister of Legal Affairs, 1989–92. Vice-Pres., Jamaican Bar Council, 1988–89. Hon. LLD Capital, Columbus, Ohio, 1990. *Publications:* Firstlings: a collection of poems, 1951; contrib. to Caribbean Law Rev., Jamaican Law Jl. *Recreations:* reading, writing, walking. *Address:* 4 Rockhampton Drive, Kingston 8, Jamaica. *T:* 9252723.

RAU, Santha Rama; *see* Rama Rau, S.

RAUSING, Dr Hans A., Hon. KBE 2006; *b* 25 March 1926; *s* of Ruben and Elisabeth Rausing; *m* 1958, Märit Norrby; one *s* two *d*. *Educ:* Univ. of Lund, Sweden. Tetra Pak: Man. Dir, 1954–83; Exec. Chm. and Chief Exec. Officer, 1983–91; Chm., Gp Bd, 1985–91; Chm. and Chief Exec. Officer, 1991–93, Hon. Chm., 1993–95, Tetra Laval Gp. Chm., Ecolean AB, Sweden, 2001–07 (Hon. Chm., 2008–); mem. of *c* 10 family-owned companies; Member, Board: Stockholms Enskilda Bank, Sweden, 1970–72; Skandinaviska Enskilda Banken, Sweden, 1973–82; South-Swedish Univs, Sweden, 1975–80; Business Internat., NY, 1975–79. Mem., Co-ordination Council for Foreign Investments, Russia, 1995. Hon. Prof., Univ. of Dubna, 1996; Vis. Prof., Mälardalens Högskola, Sweden, 2001. Mem., Russian Acad. of Inventors; Foreign Mem., Russian Acad. of Agriculture. Hon. Member: Royal Swedish Acad. of Engrg Scis, 1994; Acad. of Natural Scis, Russia, 1994; Hon. Fellow, Isaac Newton Inst., Cambridge, 2001; Fellow, Ashmolean Mus., Oxford, 2006. Hon. doctorates: Econs: Lund, 1979; Stockholm Sch. of Econs, 1987; Amer. Univ. in London; DTech: Royal Inst. of Technol., Stockholm, 1985; Mälardalen Univ., 2004; MD Lund, 2001; ScD Imperial Coll. London, 2005. *Address:* PO Box 216, Wadhurst, E Sussex TN5 6LW. *T:* (01892) 783693.

See also S. M. E. Rausing.

RAUSING, Dr Sigrid Maria Elisabet; philanthropist; publisher: Portobello Books, since 2005; Granta Publications, since 2005; *b* 29 Jan. 1962; *d* of Hans A. Rausing, *qv*; *m* 1st, 1996 (marr. diss. 2002); one *s*; 2nd, 2003, Eric Abraham. *Educ:* York Univ. (BA Hist.); University Coll. London (PhD Anthropol. 1997). Chm., Sigrid Rausing Trust, 1996–. Hon. Fellow, Dept of Anthropol., UCL, 1997–98. Mem. Bd, Atlantic Books, UK, 2006–. Mem. Bd, Human Rights Watch, NYC, 1997–. Trustee, Charleston Trust. Gov., Sevenoaks Sch. Human Rights Award, Internat. Service, 2004; Special Award for Philanthropy, Beacon Fellowship, 2005; Changing Face of Philanthropy Award, Women's Funding Network, 2006. *Publication:* History, Memory and Identity in Post-Soviet Estonia, 2004. *Recreations:* observing nature, human and otherwise, preferably in the company of dogs and horses. *Address:* 12–14 Addison Avenue, W11 4QR.

RAVEN, Amanda; *see* Game, A.

RAVEN, Prof. John Albert, FRS 1990; FRSE; CBiol, FIBiol; Boyd Baxter Professor of Biology, University of Dundee, since 1995; *b* 25 June 1941; *s* of John Harold Edward Raven and Evelyn Raven; *m* 1985, Linda Lea Handley. *Educ:* Wimbish County Primary Sch.; Friends' Sch., Saffron Walden; St John's College, Cambridge (MA, PhD). FRSE 1981; CBiol, FIBiol 1998. University of Cambridge: Research Fellow, and Official Fellow, St John's Coll., 1966–71; Univ. Demonstrator in Botany, 1968–71; Lectr, and Reader, 1971–80, Prof. (personal chair), 1980–95, Dept of Biol Scis, Univ. of Dundee. Hon. PhD Umeå, Sweden, 1995. *Publications:* Energetics and Transport in Aquatic Plants, 1984; (with Paul Falkowski) Aquatic Photosynthesis, 1997; numerous papers in learned jls and chapters in multi-author vols. *Recreations:* aviation, walking, literature. *Address:* Spital Beag, Waterside, Invergowrie, Dundee DD2 5DQ.

RAVEN, John Armstrong, CBE 1982; Director-General, International Express Carriers' Conference, 1991–93 and 1995–99 (Director (Facilitation), 1993–94); Adviser: World Bank, since 1983; International Air Cargo Association; *b* 23 April 1920; *s* of late John

Colbeck Raven; m 1st, 1945, Megan Humphreys (d 1963); one s one d; 2nd, 1965, Joy Nesbitt (d 1983); one step d. Educ: High Sch., Cardiff; Downing Coll., Cambridge (MA). Called to Bar, Gray's Inn, 1955. Dir, British Coal Exporters' Fedn, 1947–68; Section Head, Nat. Economic Develt Office, 1968–70. Dir-Gen., Assoc. of British Chambers of Commerce, 1972–74; Vice-Chm., SITPRO, 1974–82. Recreation: wondering. Address: 215 Avenue de Messidor, 1180 Brussels, Belgium. T: (2) 3457620. Club: Oxford and Cambridge.

RAVEN, Martin Clark; HM Diplomatic Service; Consul-General, São Paulo, and Director, Trade and Investment, Brazil, since 2006; b 10 March 1954; s of Basil Raven and Betty Raven (née Gilbert); m 1978, Philippa Michale Morrice Ruddick; two s. Educ: Bury Grammar Sch., Lancs; Univ. of Sussex (BA Intellectual Hist.). Joined HM Diplomatic Service, 1976: Korea/Mongolia Desk, then Yugoslavia/Albania Desk, FCO, 1976–78; Third Sec., Lagos, 1978; Hindi lang. trng, SOAS, 1979; Third, later Second Sec., Delhi, 1979–83; First Secretary: N America, then Non-Proliferation Depts, FCO, 1983–88; Human Rights and Social Issues, UK Mission to UN, NY and Alternate Rep. to Commn on Human Rights, 1988–92; Dep. Hd, S Atlantic and Antarctic Dept, FCO and Dep. Comr, British Antarctic Territory, 1993–96; Hd, Drugs and Internat. Crime Dept, FCO, 1996–98; Counsellor, Dep. Hd of Mission and Consul Gen., Stockholm, 1998–2001; on secondment as Dir, Services, Aid and Export Finance, Business Gp, Trade Partners UK, later UK Trade & Investment, 2001–06. Dir, BESO, 2001–05. Recreations: cycling, cinema, food, theatre, reading novels, listening to music, watching football and cricket, eating olives. Address: c/o Foreign and Commonwealth Office, King Charles Street, SW1A 2AH.

RAVENSCROFT, Ven. Raymond Lockwood; Archdeacon of Cornwall and Canon Librarian of Truro Cathedral, 1988–96; b 15 Sept. 1931; s of Cecil and Amy Ravenscroft; m 1957, Ann (née Stockwell); one s one d. Educ: Sea Point Boys' High School, Cape Town, SA; Leeds Univ. (BA Gen. 1953); College of the Resurrection, Mirfield. Assistant Curate: St Alban's, Goodwood, Cape, SA, 1955–58; St John's Pro-Cathedral, Bulawayo, S Rhodesia, 1958–59; Rector of Francistown, Bechuanaland, 1959–62; Asst Curate, St Ives, Cornwall, 1962–64; Vicar: All Saints, Falmouth, 1964–68; St Stephen by Launceston with St Thomas, 1968–74; Team Rector of Probus Team Ministry, 1974–88; RD of Powder, 1977–81; Hon. Canon of Truro Cathedral, 1982–88. Recreations: walking, reading, local history. Address: 19 Montpelier Court, St David's Hill, Exeter EX4 4DP. T: (01392) 430607.

RAVENSDALE, 3rd Baron cr 1911; **Nicholas Mosley,** MC 1944; Bt 1781; b 25 June 1923; e s of Sir Oswald Mosley, 6th Bt (d 1980) and Lady Cynthia (d 1933), d of 1st Marquess Curzon of Kedleston; S to barony of aunt, who was also Baroness Ravensdale of Kedleston (Life Peer), 1966, and to baronetcy of father, 1980; m 1st, 1947, Rosemary Laura Salmond (marr. diss. 1974; she d 1991); three s one d; 2nd, 1974, Mrs Verity Bailey; one s. Educ: Eton; Balliol College, Oxford. Served in the Rifle Brigade, Captain, 1942–46. Publications: (as Nicholas Mosley): Spaces of the Dark, 1951; The Rainbearers, 1955; Corruption, 1957; African Switchback, 1958; The Life of Raymond Raynes, 1961; Meeting Place, 1962; Accident, 1964; Experience and Religion, 1964; Assassins, 1966; Impossible Object, 1968; Natalie Natalia, 1971; The Assassination of Trotsky, 1972; Julian Grenfell: His Life and the Times of his Death, 1888–1915, 1976; The Rules of the Game: Sir Oswald and Lady Cynthia Mosley 1896–1933, 1982; Beyond the Pale: Sir Oswald Mosley 1933–1980, 1983; Efforts at Truth (autobiog.), 1995; Rules of the Game and Beyond the Pale, 1998; Time At War: a memoir, 2006; novels (series): Catastrophe Practice, 1979; Imago Bird, 1980; Serpent, 1981; Judith, 1986; Hopeful Monsters (Whitbread Prize), 1990; Children of Darkness and Light, 1996; The Hesperides Tree, 2001; Inventing God, 2003; Look at the Dark, 2005. Heir: s Hon. Shaun Nicholas Mosley [b 5 August 1949; m 1978, Theresa Clifford; five s one d]. Address: 2 Gloucester Crescent, NW1 7DS. T: (020) 7485 4514.

RAVENSWORTH, 9th Baron cr 1821; **Thomas Arthur Hamish Liddell;** Bt 1642; b 27 Oct. 1954; s of 8th Baron Ravensworth and Wendy, d of J. S. Bell; S father, 2004; m 1983, Linda, d of H. Thompson; one s one d. Educ: Gordonstoun; RAC Cirencester. Heir: s Hon. Henry Arthur Thomas Liddell, b 27 Nov. 1987.

RAVIV, Moshe; Ambassador of Israel to the Court of St James's, 1993–97; b Romania, 23 April 1935; s of David and Elka Raviv; m 1955, Hanna Kaspi; two s one d. Educ: Hebrew Univ., Jerusalem; Univ. of London (grad. Internat. Relations). Israel Ministry of Foreign Affairs: 2nd Sec., London, 1961–63; Office of Foreign Minister, Mrs Golda Meir, 1964–65; Political Sec. to Foreign Minister, Abba Eban, 1966–68; Counsellor, Washington, 1968–74; Dir, E European Div., 1974–76; Dir, N American Div., 1976–78; Ambassador to the Philippines, 1978–81; Dir, Economic Div., 1981–83; Minister, London, 1983–88; Dep. Dir Gen., i/c Information, 1988–93. Publication: Israel At Fifty: five decades of struggle for peace, 1998. Recreations: reading, chess, jogging.

RAWBONE, Rear-Adm. Alfred Raymond, CB 1976; AFC 1951; b 19 April 1923; s of A. Rawbone and Mrs E. D. Rawbone (née Wall); m 1943, Iris Alicia (née Willshaw); one s one d. Educ: Saltley Grammar Sch., Birmingham. Joined RN, 1942; 809 Sqdn War Service, 1943; CO 736 Sqdn, 1953; CO 897 Sqdn, 1955; CO Loch Killisport, 1959–60; Comdr (Air) Lossiemouth and HMS Ark Royal, 1961–63; Chief Staff Officer to Flag Officer Naval Air Comd, 1965–67; CO HMS Dido, 1968–69; CO RNAS Yeovilton, 1970–72; CO HMS Kent, 1972–73; Dep. ACOS (Operations), SHAPE, 1974–76. Comdr 1958; Captain 1964; Rear-Adm. 1974. Director: Vincents of Yeovil, 1983–86; Vindata, 1984–86; Vincents (Bridgewater) Ltd, 1984–86. Address: Blandings, Halstock Leigh, near Yeovil, Somerset BA22 9QU.

RAWCLIFFE, Prof. Carole, PhD; FSA, FRHistS; Professor of Medieval History, University of East Anglia, since 2002; b 18 Sept. 1946; d of Lewis and Betty Rawcliffe. Educ: Univ. of Sheffield (BA; PhD 1975). FRHistS 1978; FSA 2004. Asst Keeper, Commn on Historical MSS, 1972–74; Co-ed., medieval vols of The History of Parliament, 1974–92; University of East Anglia: Sen. Res. Fellow, Sch. of Hist., 1992–95; Sen. Lectr, 1995–98; Dir, Centre of E Anglian Studies, 1997–98 and 2005–08; Reader in Medical Hist., 1998–2002. Vis. Fellow, Huntington Liby, Calif, 1984. Mem. Council, Norfolk Record Soc., 1997–. Hon. Fellow, Norfolk Medico-Chirurgical Soc., 2003. Publications: The Staffords, Earls of Stafford and Dukes of Buckingham, 1978; (ed jtly) The History of Parliament: the House of Commons 1386–1421, 1993; Medicine and Society in Later Medieval England, 1995; Sources for the History of Medicine in Later Medieval England, 1995; The Hospitals of Medieval Norwich, 1995; Medicine for the Soul, 1999; (with R. G. Wilson) The History of Norwich, 2004; Leprosy in Medieval England, 2006; contribs to numerous collections of essays and learned jls on medieval medical, social and religious history. Recreations: art, music, swimming. Address: School of History, University of East Anglia, Norwich NR4 7TJ. T: (01603) 592872, Fax: (01603) 593519; e-mail: c.rawcliffe@uea.ac.uk.

RAWCLIFFE, Rt Rev. Derek Alec, OBE 1971; Bishop of Glasgow and Galloway, 1981–91; b 8 July 1921; s of James Alec and Gwendoline Rawcliffe; m 1977, Susan Speight

(d 1987). Educ: Sir Thomas Rich's School, Gloucester; Univ. of Leeds (BA, 1st cl. Hons English); College of the Resurrection, Mirfield. Deacon 1944, priest 1945, Worcester; Assistant Priest, Claines St George, Worcester, 1944–47; Asst master, All Hallows School, Pawa, Solomon Islands, 1947–53; Headmaster, 1953–56; Headmaster, S Mary's School, Maravovo, Solomon Is, 1956–58; Archdeacon of Southern Melanesia, New Hebrides, 1959–74; Assistant Bishop, Diocese of Melanesia, 1974–75; First Bishop of the New Hebrides, 1975–80; Asst Bishop, dio. of Ripon, 1991–96. New Hebrides Medal, 1980; Vanuatu Independence Medal, 1980. Publications: The Meaning of it All is Love (articles and essays), 2000; Pilgrimage to Melanesia, 2005; poems: The Stone and the Hazel Nut, 2000; Seasons of the Spirit, 2003; The White Blackbird, 2005. Recreations: music, poetry. Address: 7 Dorset Avenue, Leeds LS8 3RA. T: (0113) 249 2670.

RAWES, Francis Roderick, MBE 1944; MA; b 28 Jan. 1916; e s of late Prescott Rawes and Susanna May Dockery; m 1940, Dorothy Joyce (d 2004), d of E. M. Hundley, Oswestry; two s one d. Educ: Charterhouse; St Edmund Hall, Oxford. Served in Intelligence Corps, 1940–46; GSO3(I) 13 Corps; GSO1 (I) HQ 15 Army Group and MI14 WO. Asst Master at Westminster School, 1938–40 and 1946–64; Housemaster, 1947–64; Headmaster, St Edmund's School, Canterbury, 1964–78; Adminr, ISIS Assoc., 1979–83. C of E Lay Reader, 1979–96. Chm. Governing Body, Westonbirt Sch., 1983–91 (Governor, 1979–95). Address: Peyton House, Chipping Campden, Glos GL55 6AL.

RAWLEY, Alan David; QC 1977; a Recorder of the Crown Court, 1972–99; Fellow Commoner, Magdalene College, Cambridge, since 1991; b 28 Sept. 1934; er s of late Cecil David Rawley and of Theresa Rawley (née Pack); m 1964, Ione Jane Ellis; two s one d. Educ: Wimbledon Coll.; Brasenose Coll., Oxford. Nat. Service, 1956–58; commnd Royal Tank Regt. Called to the Bar, Middle Temple, 1958; Bencher, 1985. Dep. Chairman, Cornwall Quarter Sessions, 1971. Member: CICB, 1999–; CICAP, 2000–. Address: Outer Temple Chambers, 222 Strand, WC2R 1BA. T: (020) 7353 6381. Clubs: Garrick, Pilgrims, MCC.

RAWLINGS, Baroness cr 1994 (Life Peer), of Burnham Westgate in the County of Norfolk; **Patricia Elizabeth Rawlings;** b 27 Jan. 1939; d of Louis Rawlings and Mary (née Boas de Winter); m 1962, David Wolfson (see Baron Wolfson of Sunningdale) (marr. diss. 1967). Educ: Oak Hall, Haslemere, Surrey; Le Manoir, Lausanne; Florence Univ.; University Coll. London (BA Hons; Fellow 2005); London School of Economics (post grad. diploma course, Internat. Relns). Children's Care Cttee, LCC, 1959–61; WNHR Nursing, Westminster Hosp., until 1968. Contested (C): Sheffield Central, 1983; Doncaster Central, 1987. MEP (C) Essex SW, 1989–94; contested (C) Essex West and Hertfordshire East, Eur. parly elecns, 1994. European Parliament, 1989–94: EPP British Section Rep. on Conservative Nat. Union; Vice Pres., Albanian, Bulgarian and Romanian Delegn; EDG spokesman on Culture Cttee, substitute on Foreign Affairs Cttee; Dep. Whip, 1989–92. Opposition Whip, H of L, 1997–98; opposition spokesman on internat. develt and foreign affairs, H of L, 1998–. British Red Cross Society: Mem., 1964–; Chm., Appeals, London Br., until 1988; Nat. Badge of Honour, 1981, Hon. Vice Pres., 1988; Patron, London Br., 1997–. Member Council: British Bd of Video Classification, 1986–89; Peace through NATO; British Assoc. for Central and Eastern Europe, 1994–2008; Mem. Adv. Council, PYBT, 1998–; Special Advr to Ministry on Inner Cities, DoE, 1987–88. President: NCVO, 2002–07; British Antique Dealers Assoc., 2005–. Chm. Council, KCL, 1998–2007. Chm. of Govs, English Coll. Foundn, Prague, 2008–. Member: IISS; RIIA; EUW. Dir, English Chamber Orch. and Music Soc., 1980–2001. Trustee, Chevening Estate, 2002–. FKC 2003. Hon. LittD Buckingham, 1998. Hon. Plaquette, Nat. Assembly of Republic of Bulgaria, 2007. Order of the Rose, Silver Class (Bulgaria), 1991; Grand Official, Order of the Southern Cross (Brazil), 1997. Recreations: music, art, golf, ski-ing, travel. Address: House of Lords, SW1A 0PW. Clubs: Queen's, Grillions (Hon. Sec.), Pilgrims; Royal West Norfolk Golf.

RAWLINGS, Hugh Fenton, PhD; Director, Constitutional Affairs, Equality and Communications (formerly Strategic Policy, Legislation and Communications), Welsh Assembly Government, since 2007; b 24 Nov. 1950; s of William Rawlings and Marion Rawlings (née Hughes); m 1981, Felicity Gillian Douglas; one s one d. Educ: Worcester Coll., Oxford (BA Juris. 1973); London Sch. of Econs (PhD 1977). Lectr in Law, Univ. of Bristol, 1976–88; Welsh Office: Principal, Local Govt Finance Div., 1988–94; Hd, Culture and Recreation Div., 1994–97; Dep. Hd, Devolution Unit, 1997–99; National Assembly for Wales: Hd, European Affairs Div., 1999–2002; Sec., Commn on Local Govt Electoral Arrangements in Wales, 2002–03; Hd, Open Govt and Constitutional Affairs Div., 2003–04; Dir, Local Govt, Public Service and Culture, subseq. Local Govt and Culture, 2004–07. Publications: Law and the Electoral Process, 1988; articles in acad. legal jls. Recreations: reading, music, theatre, worrying about Welsh Rugby. Address: 9 Greenlawns, Penylan, Cardiff CF23 6AW; Welsh Assembly Government, Crown Buildings, Cathays Park, Cardiff CF10 3NQ. T: (029) 2080 1304; e-mail: hugh.rawlings@wales.gsi.gov.uk.

RAWLINGS, Flt Lieut Jerry John; President, Republic of Ghana, 1992–2001; b 22 June 1947; s of John Rawlings and Victoria Agbotui; m 1977, Nana Konadu Agyeman; one s three d. Educ: Achimota Sch., Accra; Ghana Military Acad. Enlisted in Ghana Air Force, 1967; commnd Pilot Officer, 1969; tried for mutiny, May 1979; forcibly released from cell, June 1979, by popular uprising; became Chm., Armed Forces Revolutionary Council; handed over to democratically elected Govt, Sept. 1979; overthrew Govt, Dec. 1981; Chm., Provisional Nat. Defence Council, 1982–92. Recreations: flying, swimming, riding, reading. Address: c/o PO Box 1627, Accra, Ghana.

RAWLINGS, Ven. John Edmund Frank; Archdeacon of Totnes, since 2005; b 15 April 1947; s of Edward and Ivy Rawlings; m 1969, Janette Mary Rawlings (née Alexander); one s one d. Educ: Godalming Grammar Sch.; King's Coll., London (AKC 1969); St Augustine's Coll., Canterbury. Ordained deacon, 1970, priest 1971; Curate: St Margaret's, Rainham, 1970–73; Tattenham Corner and Burgh Heath, 1973–76; Chaplain, RN, 1976–92; Vicar, Tavistock and Gulworthy, 1992–2005; RD Tavistock, 1997–2002; Preb., Exeter Cathedral, 1999–2005. Recreations: gardening, cooking, music (organ playing). Address: Blue Hills, Bradley Road, Bovey Tracey, Newton Abbot TQ13 9EU. T: (01626) 832064, Fax: (01626) 834947; e-mail: archdeacon.of.totnes@exeter.anglican.org.

RAWLINGS, Prof. Rees David, PhD; CEng; Professor of Materials Science, 1993–2007, now Emeritus, and Pro Rector (Educational Quality), 2000–08, Imperial College, London; b 30 Sept. 1942; s of Aubrey Rhys Islwyn Rawlings and Daphne Irene Rawlings (née Sangster); m 1964, Ann Margaret Halliday; two d. Educ: Sir Thomas Rich High Sch., Gloucester; Imperial Coll. (BSc Engrg 1st cl. Hons 1964; PhD Metallurgy 1967); ARSM 1964; DIC 1967; DSc London 1989. CEng 1980; FIMMM (FIM 1985); ILTM 2000. Imperial College: Lectr, 1966–81; Reader, 1981–93; acting Hd, Earth Resources Engrg, 1996–98; Dean, Royal Sch. of Mines, 1995–98; Mem. Governing Body, 1995–98; Mem. Court, 1998–2008; Partner, Matcon (Materials Consultants), 1974–90. Subject Specialist Assessor: HEFCE, 1996–98; HEFCW, 1997–98. Editor: Jl Materials Science, 2002–06 (Dep. Ed., 1993–2002); Jl Materials Science Letters, 2002–

(Dep. Ed., 1993–2002); Mem. Adv. Bd, Metal and Materials Internat., 2003–. Hon. FRCA, 2001. FCGI 2002. L. B. Pfeil Medal and Prize, Inst. of Materials, 1990. *Publications:* (jtly) Materials Science, 1974, 5th edn 2003; (jtly) Composite Materials: engineering and science, 1994; articles in learned jls, conf. proceedings and books on materials science. *Recreations:* sport (but no longer active), gardening, photography, theatre. *Address:* The Elms, 13 Wolverton Avenue, Kingston upon Thames, Surrey KT2 7QF. *Club:* Kingston Athletic and Polytechnic Harriers.

RAWLINS, Brig. Gordon John, OBE 1986; Partner, Hall Associates (Management Consultants), Trevone, since 2005; *b* 22 April 1944; *s* of Arthur and Joyce Rawlins; *m* 1st, 1965, Ann Beard (*d* 1986); one *s*; 2nd, 1986, Margaret Anne Ravenscroft; one step *s* one step *d*. *Educ:* Peter Symond's, Winchester; Welbeck College; RMA Sandhurst; RMCS Shrivenham (BSc Eng). CEng, FIET, psc. Commissioned REME, 1964; served Aden, Oman, Jordan, Hong Kong, BAOR, UK, 1964–77; Staff Coll., 1978; MoD 1978–80; 2 i/c 5 Armd Wksp, REME, BAOR, 1981–82; CO 7 Armd Wksp, REME, BAOR, 1982–84; MoD, 1984–87 (Sec. to COS Cttee, 1987); Comd Maint., 1 (BR) Corps, BAOR, 1988. Sec., Instn of Production, subseq. Manufacturing, Engrs, 1988–91; Dep. Sec., 1991–2000, Dir, Members Services, 2000–02, IEE. Liveryman, Turners' Co., 1991. *Recreations:* watching Rugby and cricket, messing about on the Helford. *Address:* The Smithy, Manaccan, Cornwall TR12 6HR. *Club:* Army and Navy.

RAWLINS, Prof. (John) Nicholas (Pepys), DPhil; FMedSci; Watts Professor of Psychology, University of Oxford, since 2005; Professorial Fellow, Wolfson College, Oxford, since 2008; *b* 31 May 1949; *s* of Surg. Vice-Adm. Sir John Stuart Pepys Rawlins, *qv*; *m* 1986, Prof. Susan Lynn Hurley (*d* 2007); two *s*. *Educ:* Winchester Coll.; University Coll., Oxford (BA 1971, MA 1976; DPhil 1977). Department of Experimental Psychology, University of Oxford: MRC Res. Asst, 1975–81; Royal Soc. Henry Head Fellow in Neurolog., 1981–83; Univ. Lectr in Psychol., 1983–98; Prof. of Behavioural Neurosci., 1998–2005; University College, Oxford: Weir Jun. Res. Fellow, 1978–81; Sen. Res. Fellow, 1981–87; Sir Jules Thorne Fellow and Praelector in Psychol., 1987–2005; Professorial Fellow, 2005–07; Emeritus Fellow, 2008–. Fogarty Foundn Res. Fellow, Johns Hopkins Univ., 1979–80. Neurosci. Grants Cttee, MRC, 1986–90; Wellcome Trust: Neurosci. Grants Cttee, 1995–2000; Mem., 2000–02, Chm., 2002–04, Basic Sci. Interest Gp; Co-Chm., Neurosci. Panel, 2004–07; Chm., Neurosci. Panel Cognitive and Higher Systems, 2004–07; Mem., Neurosci. Strategy Cttee, 2004–. Nuffield Council Panel on Bioethics, 2001–03. Trustee, Schizophrenia Res. Trust, 1995–. FMedSci 2006. *Publications:* (jtly) Brain Power: working out the human mind, 1999; over 190 articles in learned jls. *Recreations:* wine, cooking, gardens, walking, landscape, architecture, ski-ing, snorkelling. *Address:* Wolfson College, Oxford OX2 6UD; *e-mail:* nick.rawlins@psy.ox.ac.uk.

RAWLINS, Surg. Vice-Adm. Sir John (Stuart Pepys), KBE 1978 (OBE 1960; MBE 1956); *b* 12 May 1922; *s* of Col S. W. H. Rawlins, CB, CMG, DSO and Dorothy Pepys Cockerell; *m* 1944, Diana Margaret Freshney Colbeck (*d* 1992); one *s* three *d*. *Educ:* Wellington Coll.; University Coll., Oxford (Hon. Fellow, 1991); St Bartholomew's Hospital. BM, BCh 1945; MA, FRCP, FFPH, FRAeS. Surg. Lieut RNVR, HMS Triumph, 1947; Surg. Lieut RN, RAF Inst. Aviation Med., 1951; RN Physiol Lab., 1957; Surg. Comdr RAF Inst., Aviation Med., 1961; HMS Ark Royal, 1964; US Navy Medical Research Inst., 1967; Surg. Captain 1969; Surg. Cdre, Dir of Health and Research (Naval), 1973; Surg. Rear-Adm. 1975; Dean of Naval Medicine and MO i/c, Inst. of Naval Medicine, 1975–77; Actg Surg. Vice-Adm. 1977; Medical Dir-Gen. (Navy), 1977–80. QHP 1975. Chairman: Deep Ocean Engineering Inc., 1983–89; Medical Express Ltd, 1984–; Trident Underwater Engrg (Systems) Ltd, 1985–; General Offshore Corp. (UK) Ltd, 1988–91; Director: Diving Unlimited International Ltd, 1980–; Deep Ocean Technology Inc., 1989– (Chm., 1983–89); Deep Ocean Engrg, 1989–91. Pres., Soc. for Underwater Technology, 1980–84 (Hon. Fellow, 1986); Vice-Pres., Underseas Med. Soc.; Hon. Life Mem., British Sub-Aqua Club, 1983; Founder-Mem. European Underseas Biomed. Soc.; Fellow Aerospace Med. Soc. (Armstrong Lectr, 1980); FRAeS 1973; FRSocMed. Hon. Fellow, Lancaster Univ., 1986. Hon. DTech Robert Gordon's Inst. of Technology, 1991. Erroll-Eldridge Prize 1967; Sec. of US Navy's Commendation 1971; Gilbert Blane Medal 1971; Tuttle Meml Award 1973; Chadwick Medal and Prize 1975; Nobel Award, Inst. of Explosives Engrs, 1987; NOGI Award, US Acad. of Underwater Arts and Scis, 1998; Colin McLeod Award, British Sub-Aqua Club, 2000; Lowell Thomas Award, Explorers' Club, 2000; Man of the Year, British Council for Rehabilitation of the Disabled, 1964. *Publications:* papers in fields of aviation and diving medicine. *Recreations:* diving, fishing, stalking, riding. *Address:* Little Cross, Holne, Newton Abbot, S Devon TQ13 7RS. *T:* (01364) 631249, *Fax:* (01364) 631400. *Club:* Vincent's (Oxford).

See also J. N. P. Rawlins.

RAWLINS, Sir Michael (David), Kt 1999; DL; MD; FRCP, FRCPE, FFPM, FBPharmacolS, FMedSci; Ruth and Lionel Jacobson Professor of Clinical Pharmacology, University of Newcastle upon Tyne, 1973–2006, now Emeritus; Chairman, National Institute for Health and Clinical Excellence (formerly for Clinical Excellence), since 1999; *b* 28 March 1941; *s* of Rev. Jack and Evelyn Daphne Rawlins; *m* 1963, Elizabeth Cadbury Hambly; three *d*. *Educ:* St Thomas's Hosp. Med. Sch., London (BSc 1962; MB BS 1965); MD London 1973. FRCP 1977; FRCPE 1987; FFPM 1989. Lectr in Medicine, St Thomas's Hosp., London, 1967–71; Sen. Registrar, Hammersmith Hosp., London, 1971–72; Consultant Clinical Pharmacologist, Newcastle upon Tyne NHS Trust, 1973–2006. Vis. Res. Fellow, Karolinska Inst., Stockholm, Sweden, 1972–73; Public Orator, Univ. of Newcastle upon Tyne, 1990–93; Ruiting van Swieten Vis. Prof., Academic Med. Centre, Amsterdam, 1998; Hon. Prof., LSHTM, 2000–. Pres., NE Council on Addictions, 1991–; Chm., Adv. Council on Misuse of Drugs, 1998–2008; Vice-Chm., Northern RHA, 1990–94; Member: Nat. Cttee on Pharmacology, 1977–83; Cttee on the Safety of Medicines, 1980–98 (Chm., 1993–98); Cttee on Toxicity, 1989–92; Standing Gp on Health Technology Assessment, 1993–95. Chm., Newcastle SDP, 1981–84. Bradshaw Lectr, RCP, 1986; Welcome Lectr, Soc. of Apothecaries, 1996; Samuel Gee Lectr, 2005, Harveian Orator, 2008, RCP. DL Tyne and Wear, 1999. FRSocMed 1972; Founder FMedSci 1998; FBPharmacolS 2004. Hon. FRCA 2000. DUniv York. Univ. Medal, Helsinki, 1978; William Withering Medal, RCP, 1994; Dixon Medal, Ulster Med. Soc., 1995; Lilly Medal, British Pharmacol Soc., 1997; Paracelsus Medal, Univ. of Amsterdam, 1998; Bradlaw Oration and Medal, FDS RCS, 2002; Hutchinson Medal, RSocMed, 2003. *Publications:* Variability in Human Drug Response, 1973; (ed) Textbook of Pharmaceutical Medicine, 1994; articles on clinical pharmacology in med. and scientific jls. *Recreation:* music. *Address:* Shoreston House, Shoreston, near Seahouses, Northumberland NE68 7SX. *T:* (01665) 720203; Flat 3, 37 Lambs Conduit Street, WC1N 3NG. *Clubs:* Northern Counties (Newcastle); Bamburgh Castle Golf.

RAWLINS, Nicholas; *see* Rawlins, J. N. P.

RAWLINS, Brig. Peregrine Peter, MBE 1983; Clerk to the Grocers' Company, 1998–2006; *b* 3 March 1946; *s* of Lt-Col John Walter Rawlins, Northamptonshire Regt, and Elizabeth Joan Rawlins (*née* Delmé-Radcliffe); *m* 1976, Marlis Müller; one *s* one *d*. *Educ:* Malvern Coll.; RMA, Sandhurst; Lincoln Coll., Oxford (BA Hons Geography 1970). Royal Anglian Regiment: commnd 2nd Bn, 1966; Comd, 2nd Bn, 1985–87; Dep. Col, 1996–98. Staff Coll., 1978; Directing Staff, RMCS, 1988–90; COS, Directorate of Infantry, 1990–92; NATO Defence Coll., Rome, 1992; Defence Attaché, Bonn, 1992–96; Dep. Comdt, RMCS, 1996–98, retd. Gov., Dauntsey's Sch., 2007–. *Recreations:* bird watching, fishing, gardening, walking. *Address:* The Grey House, Low Road, Little Cheverell, Devizes, Wilts SN10 4JS.

RAWLINS, Peter Jonathan, FCA; business strategy consultant and executive coach, since 1994; *b* 30 April 1951; *e s* of late Kenneth Raymond Ivan Rawlins and of Constance Amande Rawlins (*née* Malzy); *m* 1st, 1973, Louise Langton (marr. diss. 1999); one *s* one *d*; 2nd, 2000, Christina Conway; three *s* one *d*. *Educ:* Arnold House Sch.; St Edward's Sch., Oxford; Keble Coll., Oxford (Hons English Lang. and Lit.; MA). Arthur Andersen & Co., 1972–85: Manager, 1977; Partner, 1983; UK Practice Develt Partner, 1984; full-time secondment to Lloyd's of London as PA to Chief Exec. and Dep. Chm., 1983–84; Dir, Sturge Holdings, and Man. Dir, R. W. Sturge & Co., 1985–89; Chief Exec., Internat., subseq. London, Stock Exchange, 1989–93; Director: Sturge Lloyd's Agencies, 1986–89; Wise Speke Holdings, 1987–89; non-exec. Dir, Lloyd-Roberts & Gilkes, 1989–94; Man. Dir (Europe, ME and Africa), Siegel & Gale Ltd, 1996–97; Director: Scala Business Solutions, NV, 1998–2000; Logistics Resources Ltd, 1999–2002; Oyster Partners Ltd, 2001–02; Cognito Ltd, 2007–; Chm., Higham Gp plc, 2004–05. Mem., Cttee, Lloyd's Underwriting Agents Assoc., 1986–89 (Treasurer, 1986–87; Dep. Chm., 1988); Mem., standing cttees, Council of Lloyd's, 1985–89. Non-exec. Dir, Royal Bournemouth and Christchurch Hosps NHS Foundn Trust, 2005–07. Director: London Sinfonietta Trust, 1985–88; Half Moon Theatre, 1986–88; Mem. Council and Dir, ABSA, 1982–96; Dir and Trustee, London City Ballet Trust, 1986–93; Mem., Develt Council, RNT, 1991–95; Vice-Chm., 2000, Chm., 2000–02, Spitalfields Fest. Chairman: London First Neighbourhood Approach, 1993–95; Assoc. for Res. into Stammering in Children, 1993–. FRSA 1990. *Recreations:* performing arts, tennis, shooting, travelling. *Address:* The White House, Hadlow Road, Tonbridge, Kent TN11 0AE. *T:* (01732) 852692, *Fax:* (01732) 852248; *e-mail:* peter@pjrawlins.co.uk. *Clubs:* City of London, MCC.

RAWLINSON, Sir Anthony Henry John, 5th Bt *cr* 1891; photographer and inventor; *b* 1 May 1936; *s* of Sir Alfred Frederick Rawlinson, 4th Bt and Bessie Ford Taylor (*d* 1996), *d* of Frank Raymond Emmatt, Harrogate; *S* father, 1969; *m* 1st, 1960, Penelope Byng Noel (marr. diss. 1967), 2nd *d* of Rear-Adm. G. J. B. Noel, RN; one *s* one *d*; 2nd, 1967, Pauline Strickland (marr. diss. 1976), *d* of J. H. Hardy, Sydney; one *s*; 3rd, 1977, Helen Leone (marr. diss. 1997), *d* of T. M. Kennedy, Scotland; one *s*. *Educ:* Millfield School. Coldstream Guards, 1954–56. *Recreations:* tennis, sailing. *Heir:* *s* Alexander Noel Rawlinson, *b* 15 July 1964.

RAWLINSON, Charles Frederick Melville; Deputy Chairman, Britten Sinfonia, since 1997 (Director, since 1988); *b* 18 March 1934; *s* of Rowland Henry Rawlinson and Olivia Melville Rawlinson; *m* 1962, Jill Rosalind Wesley; three *d*. *Educ:* Canford Sch.; Jesus Coll., Cambridge (MA). FCA, FCT. With A. E. Limehouse & Co., Chartered Accts, 1955–58; Peat Marwick Mitchell & Co., 1958–62; Morgan Grenfell & Co. Ltd, Bankers, 1962–94: Dir, 1970–87; Jt Chm., 1985–87; Morgan Grenfell Group PLC: Dir, 1985–88; Vice-Chm., 1987–88; Sen. Advr, 1988–94; Chm., Morgan Grenfell (Asia), Singapore, 1976–88, Hon. Pres., 1988–93; seconded as Man. Dir, Investment Bank of Ireland Ltd, Dublin, 1966–68; Director: Jefferson Smurfit Gp, 1969–83; Associated Paper Industries plc, 1972–91 (Chm., 1979–91); Willis Faber plc, 1981–89; Hedley Wright & Co. Ltd, 1994–99; Chm., Boxford Suffolk Gp, 1992–2000. Sen. Advr, West Merchant Bank, 1994–97. Chairman: The Hundred Gp of Finance Dirs, 1984–86; Industrial Mems Adv. Cttee on Ethics, ICAEW, 1991–99; Member: Chartered Accountants' Jt Ethics Cttee, 1994–2001; Council, ICAEW, 1995–97; Exec. Cttee, Jt Disciplinary Scheme, 1995–. Mem., Council, Order of St Etheldreda, Ely Cathedral, 1999–; Trustee, Ely Cathedral Trust, 2007–. Chm., Peache Trustees, 1980–2002; Hon. Vice Pres., NABC—Clubs for Young People, 1995– (Jt Hon. Treas., 1983–91; Dep. Chm., 1989–92; Chm., 1992–94). FRSA. *Recreations:* music, sailing, travel. *Address:* The Old Forge, Arkesden, Saffron Walden, Essex CB11 4EX. *Club:* Brooks's.

See also under Royal Family.

RAWLINSON, Dennis George Fielding, OBE 1978; JP; FCILT; company director; *b* 3 Sept. 1919; *s* of George and Mary Jane Rawlinson; *m* 1943, Lilian Mary; one *s* one *d*. *Educ:* Grocers' Co.'s Sch. Army, 1939–46. Various progressive positions in omnibus industry. Mem., Transport Tribunal, 1986–91. JP Darlington, 1971. *Recreations:* theatre, music, golf and various lesser sports. *Address:* 62 Cleveland Avenue, Darlington, Co. Durham DL3 7HG. *T:* (01325) 461254. *Club:* Army and Navy.

RAWLINSON, Ivor Jon, OBE 1988; HM Diplomatic Service, retired; career coach and career consultant, since 2007; *b* 24 Jan. 1942; *s* of Vivian Hugh Rawlinson and Hermione (*née* Curry); *m* 1976, Catherine Paule Caudal; one *s* two *d*. *Educ:* Christ Church, Oxford (MA). Joined FO, 1964; Polish lang. student, 1965–66; Warsaw, 1966–69; Bridgetown, 1969–71 (course at Univ. of W Indies); Second Sec., News Dept, FCO, 1971–73; Asst Private Sec. to Minister of State, FCO, 1973–74; Second Sec. (Econ.), Paris, 1974–78; First Secretary: FCO, 1978–80; (Commercial), Mexico City, 1980–84; Consul, Florence and Consul-Gen., San Marino, 1984–88; First Sec., later Counsellor (Inspectorate), FCO, 1988–93; RCDS, 1993; Consul-Gen., Montreal, 1993–98; Ambassador to Tunisia, 1999–2002; Hd, FCO Outplacement, 2002–07. Gov., Ryde Sch., IoW, 2005– (Vice-Chm., 2006–). Trustee, Pimpernel Trust, 2006–. *Recreations:* painting, tennis, collecting books, restoring farmhouse in France. *Address:* 29 Broxash Road, SW11 6AD. *T:* (020) 7228 5261.

RAWLINSON, Mark Stobart; Head, Corporate Department in London, Freshfields Bruckhaus Deringer LLP, since 2008; *b* Eccles, Manchester, 3 May 1957; *s* of Thomas Stobart Rawlinson and Barbara Rawlinson; *m* 1984, Julia Shepherd; three *s*. *Educ:* Haberdashers' Aske's Sch., Elstree; Sidney Sussex Coll., Cambridge (BA Hons 1979; MA Hons Law 1980); Guildford Law Sch. (Professional Exams Pt II). Freshfields Bruckhaus Deringer LLP (formerly Freshfields): articled clerk, 1982–84; Associate, 1984–90; Partner, 1990–; Hd, Trainee Recruitment, 2008–. *Recreations:* sport (4 Peaks Challenge, 1997, Engadin cross country ski marathon, 2005), Rugby, cricket, golf. *Address:* Freshfields Bruckhaus Deringer LLP, 65 Fleet Street, EC4Y 1HS. *T:* (020) 7832 7105, *Fax:* (020) 7108 7105. *Club:* Hawks'.

RAWLINSON, Richard Anthony; Vice President, Booz Allen Hamilton Inc., since 2004; *b* 11 Feb. 1957; *s* of Sir Anthony Rawlinson, KCB and Lady (Mary) Rawlinson; *m* 1991, Sharon Sofer; two *s*. *Educ:* Eton Coll. (King's Schol.); Christ Church, Oxford (BA Politics and Econs 1978; MA); Harvard Business Sch. (Baker Schol.; MBA 1983). J. Henry Schroder Wagg & Co. Ltd, 1978–81; Associates Fellow, Harvard Business Sch., 1983–84; Monitor Company: Cambridge, Mass, 1984–85; London, 1985–89; Tokyo, 1989–93;

Hong Kong, 1994–96; London, 1996–2001; Partner (formerly Dir), Monitor Co. Gp LP, 1993–2001. Chm. and Man. Dir, W. P. Stewart & Co. (Europe) Ltd, 2001–02; Dep. Man. Dir, W. P. Stewart & Co. Ltd, Bermuda, 2001–02. Mem., Competition (formerly Monopolies and Mergers) Commn, 1998–2005. FRGS 2002. *Publications:* (contrib.) Competition in Global Industries, 1986; articles in Harvard Business Review, Strategy & Business. *Recreations:* mountain walking, reading. *Address:* (office) 7 Savoy Court, Strand, WC2R 0JP. *Clubs:* Oxford and Cambridge, Hurlingham, Lansdowne.

RAWNSLEY, Andrew Nicholas James; author, broadcaster and journalist; Chief Political Columnist and Associate Editor, The Observer, since 1993; *b* 5 Jan. 1962; *s* of Eric Rawnsley and Barbara Rawnsley (*née* Butler); *m* 1990, Jane Leslie Hall; three *d*. *Educ:* Lawrence Sheriff Grammar Sch., Rugby; Rugby Sch.; Sidney Sussex Coll., Cambridge (schol.; 1st Cl. Hons Hist.; MA). BBC, 1983–85; The Guardian: reporter, 1985–87; sketchwriter, 1987–93. Ed.-in-Chief, PoliticsHome.com, 2008–. TV presenter: A Week in Politics, 1989–97; series: The Agenda, 1996; Bye Bye Blues, 1997; Blair's Year, 1998; What the Papers Say, incl. Rev. of the Year, 2002–07; The Sunday Edition, 2006–08; The Rise and Fall of Tony Blair, 2007; Gordon Brown: where did it all go wrong?, 2008; radio presenter, The Westminster Hour, 1998–2006; The Unauthorised Biography of the United Kingdom, 1999. FRSA 2001. Student Journalist of Year, Guardian/NUS Student Media Awards, 1982; Young Journalist of Year, British Press Awards, 1987; Columnist of Year, What the Papers Say Awards, 2000; Journalist of the Year, Channel Four Polit. Awards, 2003; Political Journalist of the Year, Public Affairs Awards, 2006; Commentator of Year, House Mag. Awards, 2008. *Publication:* Servants of the People: the inside story of New Labour, 2000, revd edn 2001 (Channel 4/Politico Book of the Year, 2001). *Recreations:* books, movies, mah-jong, scuba-diving, ski-ing. *Address:* The Observer, 119 Farringdon Road, EC1R 3ER. *T:* (020) 7713 4255; *e-mail:* Andrew.Rawnsley@Observer.co.uk; Press Gallery, House of Commons, SW1A 1AA.

RAWORTH, Sophie; Presenter, BBC One O'Clock News, since 2006; *b* Redhill, Surrey, 15 May 1968; *d* of Richard and Jenny Raworth; *m* 2003, Richard Winter; one *s* two *d*. *Educ:* Bute House Prep. Sch., Hammersmith; Putney High Sch.; St Paul's Girls' Sch.; Univ. of Manchester (BA Jt Hons French and German 1991); City Univ., London (Postgrad. Dip. Broadcast Journalism 1992). Joined BBC as trainee, 1992; reporter, BBC GMR Manchester, 1992–93; producer, Brussels office, 1993–95; Presenter: (and reporter) BBC Look North Leeds, 1995–97; BBC Breakfast, 1997–2002; (and reporter) Tomorrow's World, 1999–2002; BBC Six O'Clock News, 2003–06; Dream Lives, 2001; Judgemental, 2002. *Recreations:* my kids, running, photography, ski-ing, cinema, travelling, dreaming of travelling! *Address:* BBC Television Centre, Wood Lane, W12 7RJ.

RAWSON, Prof. Dame Jessica (Mary), DBE 2002 (CBE 1994); LittD; FBA 1990; Warden, Merton College, Oxford, since 1994; Professor of Chinese Art and Archaeology, since 2000, and Pro-Vice-Chancellor, since 2006, University of Oxford; *b* 20 Jan. 1943; *d* of Roger Nathaniel Quirk and Paula Quirk; *m* 1968, John Rawson; one *d*. *Educ:* New Hall, Cambridge (BA Hons History; LittD 1991; Hon. Fellow, 1997); London Univ. (BA Hons Chinese Lang. and Lit.). Asst Principal, Min. of Health, 1965–67; Department of Oriental Antiquities, British Museum: Asst Keeper II, 1967–71; Asst Keeper I, 1971–76; Dep. Keeper, 1976–87; Keeper, 1987–94. Visiting Professor: Kunsthistorisches Inst., Heidelberg, 1989; Dept of Art, Univ. of Chicago, 1994. Lectures: Barlow, Sussex Univ., 1979; Levintvitt Meml., Harvard, 1989; A. J. Pope, Smithsonian Instn, 1991; Harvey Buchanan, Cleveland Mus. of Art, 1993; Pratt Inst., 1998; Beatrice Blackwood, Oxford, 1999; Millennium, Oxford, 2000; Creighton, Univ. of London, 2000. Member: Nuffield Langs Inquiry, 1998–99; British Library Bd, 1999–2003; Scholars' Council, Library of Congress, Washington, 2005–. Chm., Oriental Ceramic Soc., 1993–96; Vice-Chm., Exec. Cttee, GB-China Centre, 1985–87. Governor: SOAS, Univ. of London, 1998–2003; Latymer and Godolphin Sch., 2004–08; St Paul's Girls' Sch., 2009–. Hon. DSc St Andrews, 1997; Hon. DLitt: London, 1998; Sussex, 1998; Newcastle, 1999. *Publications:* Chinese Jade Throughout the Ages (with John Ayers), 1975; Animals in Art, 1977; Ancient China, Art and Archaeology, 1980; Chinese Ornament: the lotus and the dragon, 1984; Chinese Bronzes: art and ritual, 1987; The Bella and P. P. Chiu Collection of Ancient Chinese Bronzes, 1988; Western Zhou Ritual Bronzes from the Arthur M. Sackler Collections, 1990; (with Emma Bunker) Ancient Chinese and Ordos Bronzes, 1990; (ed) The British Museum Book of Chinese Art, 1992; Chinese Jade from the Neolithic to the Qing, 1995; Mysteries of Ancient China, 1996; (with Evelyn Rawski) China, The Three Emperors 1662–1795, 2005; contrib. Proc. of British Acad. and learned jls. *Address:* Merton College, Oxford OX1 4JD. *T:* (01865) 276352, 276368, *Fax:* (01865) 276282.

RAWSON, Prof. Kenneth John, MSc; FREng; RCNC; consultant; Professor and Head of Department of Design and Technology, 1983–89, Dean of Education and Design, 1983–89, Brunel University; *b* 27 Oct. 1926; *s* of late Arthur William Rawson and Beatrice Anne Rawson; *m* 1950, Rhona Florence Gill; two *s* one *d*. *Educ:* Northern Grammar Sch., Portsmouth; HM Dockyard Technical Coll., Portsmouth; RN Colls, Keyham and Greenwich. RCNC; FREng (FEng 1984); FRINA. WhSch. At sea, 1950–51; Naval Construction Res. Estabt, Dunfermline, 1951–53; Ship Design, Admiralty, 1953–57; Lloyd's Register of Shipping, 1957–59; Ship and Weapons Design, MoD, Bath, 1959–69; Naval Staff, London, 1969–72; Prof. of Naval Architecture, University Coll., Univ. of London, 1972–77; Ministry of Defence, Bath: Head of Forward Design, Ship Dept, 1977–79; Dep. Dir, Ship Design and Chief Naval Architect (Under Sec.), 1979–83. Hon. DEng Portsmouth, 1995. *Publications:* Photoelasticity and the Engineer, 1953; (with E. C. Tupper) Basic Ship Theory, 1968, 5th edn 2001; Ever the Apprentice, 2006; contrib. numerous technical publications. *Recreations:* cabinet making, gardening, walking. *Address:* Moorlands, The Street, Chilcompton, Radstock BA3 4HB. *T:* (01761) 232793.

RAWSON, Air Vice-Marshal Paul David, CB 2007; Regional Director (Riyadh), Rolls-Royce International, since 2007; *b* 13 March 1953; *s* of Geoffry and Joyce Rawson; *m* 1975, Janet Elizabeth Fewster; one *s*. *Educ:* RAF Cranwell (HND Mech. Engrg); Open Univ. (BA). Joined RAF, 1972; completed Engr Officer trng, 1975; appts at Brize Norton, Waddington, Farnborough and Binbrook, 1975–83; Tech. Staff Officer, Ordnance Bd, then RAF Marham, subseq. Sen. Engr Officer, RAF Unit, Goose Bay, Canada, 1983–90; RAF St Athan, 1991–93; leader, VC10 Support Authy, Wyton, 1993–95; Sen. Engr Officer, St Athan, 1996–98; Logistics Support Services Agency, Wyton, 1998–2000; RCDS, 2000; ACOS Logistics, HQ Strike Comd, 2002–04; Team Comdr, MoD Saudi Arabian Armed Forces Project, 2004–06; Chief of Staff Support, HQ Strike Comd, 2006–07. *Recreations:* DIY, travel, golf, hill walking, ski-ing. *Address:* PO Box 88215, Riyadh 1162, Kingdom of Saudi Arabia. *T:* 07772 224820; *e-mail:* rawsonpd@hotmail.com.

RAWSTHORN, Judith Alison, (Alice); Design Critic, International Herald Tribune, since 2006; *b* 15 Nov. 1958; *d* of Peter Rawsthorn and Joan Rawsthorn (*née* Schofield). *Educ:* Clare Coll., Cambridge (MA). Grad. trainee journalist, Thomson Org., 1980–83; Journalist: Campaign Mag., 1983–85; Financial Times, 1985–2001; Dir, Design Mus., 2001–06. Chm., Design Adv. Gp, British Council, 2003–07; Mem., Arts Council England, 2007– (Lead Advr on Visual Arts, 2004–07; Chm., Turning Point Review of Contemporary Visual Arts). Trustee, Whitechapel Gall., 1998–. *Publications:* Yves Saint Laurent: a biography, 1996; Marc Newson, 2000. *Recreations:* art, architecture, film, reading, fashion. *Address:* International Herald Tribune, 40 Marsh Wall, E14 9TP; *web:* www.alicerawsthorn.com.

RAWSTHORNE, Anthony Robert; a Senior Clerk, House of Lords, 2001–05; *b* 25 Jan. 1943; *s* of Frederic Leslie and Nora Rawsthorne; *m* 1967, Beverley Jean Osborne; one *s* two *d*. *Educ:* Ampleforth College; Wadham College, Oxford. Home Office, 1966–97: Asst Sec., 1977; Crime Policy Planning Unit, 1977–79; Establishment Dept, 1979–82; Sec., Falkland Islands Review Cttee, 1982; Principal Private Sec., 1983; Immigration and Nationality Dept, 1983–86; Assistant Under-Secretary: Establishment Dept, 1986–91; Equal Opportunities and Gen. Dept, 1991; Asst Under-Sec., then Dep. Dir-Gen., Policy, Immigration and Nationality Directorate, 1991–97; Dir, Customs Policy, and a Comr, HM Customs and Excise, 1997–2000. Mem., Fitness to Practise Panel (formerly Professional Conduct Cttee), GMC, 2001–. *Recreations:* bridge, squash, holidays in France and Italy.

RAWSTHORNE, Rt Rev. John; *see* Hallam, Bishop of, (RC).

RAY, Hon. Ajit Nath; Chief Justice of India, Supreme Court of India, 1973–77; *b* Calcutta, 29 Jan. 1912; *s* of Sati Nath Ray and Kali Kumari Debi; *m* 1944, Himani Mukherjee; one *s*. *Educ:* Presidency Coll., Calcutta; Calcutta Univ. (Hindu Coll. Foundn Schol., MA); Oriel College, Oxford (MA; Hon. Fellow, 1975). Called to Bar, Gray's Inn, 1939; practised at Calcutta High Court, 1940–57; Judge, Calcutta High Court, 1957–69; Judge, Supreme Court of India, 1969–73. Pres., Governing Body, Presidency Coll., Calcutta, 1959–70; Vice-President: Asiatic Soc., 1963–65 (Hon. Treas. 1960–63); Internat. Law Assoc., 1977– (Pres., 1974–76; Pres., Indian Br., 1973–77); Indian Law Inst., New Delhi, 1973–77; Mem., Internat. Court of Arbitration, 1976–. Vice-Pres., Ramakrishna Mission Inst. of Culture, 1981–2006; Chm., Guru Saday Folk Art Soc., Calcutta, 1986–2004; Pres., Soc. for Welfare of Blind, Narendrapur, 1959–80. Mem., Karma Samiti (Exec. Council), 1963–67 and 1969–72, and Samsad (Court), 1967–71, Visva-Bharati Univ., Santiniketan. *Address:* 15 Panditia Place, Calcutta 700029, India. *T:* (33) 24541452. *Club:* Calcutta (Calcutta).

RAY, Christopher, PhD; High Master, Manchester Grammar School, since 2004; *b* 10 Dec. 1951; *m* 1976, Carol Elizabeth Morrison. *Educ:* Rochdale Grammar Sch.; UCL (BA; Pres. Students' Union, 1974–75); Churchill Coll., Cambridge (PhD 1982); Balliol Coll., Oxford. MInstP 1996; CPhys 1996. Admin and Overseas Depts, Bank of England, 1976–78; Asst Master Physics, Marlborough Coll., 1982–83; Sci. Educn Ed., OUP, 1984–88; Fellow, Nat. Univ. of Singapore, 1988–89; Asst Prof., Portland State Univ., Oregon, 1989–91; Teacher and Director of Studies: Framlingham Coll., 1991–96; King's Coll. Sch., Wimbledon, 1996–2001; Headmaster, John Lyon Sch., Harrow, 2001–04. Vis. Lectr in Philos. of Space and Time, Univ. of Oxford, 1987–88. Principal Sci. Scrutineer, QCA, 2000–02. Chairman: Ind. Schs ICT Cttee, 2003–05; N London Div., HMC, 2004; Educn and Acad. Policy Cttee, HMC/GSA, 2008– (Mem., 2002–04, 2007–). FRSA 2004. *Publications:* The Evolution of Relativity, 1987; Time, Space and Philosophy, 1991; (contrib.) A Companion to the Philosophy of Science, 2000; (contrib.) The Head Speaks Out, 2008. *Recreations:* fell-walking in the Lake District, opera, chess, crime fiction. *Address:* Manchester Grammar School, Old Hall Lane, Manchester M13 0XT. *T:* (0161) 244 7201, *Fax:* (0161) 257 2446. *Club:* East India.

RAY, Edward Ernest, CBE 1988; Chairman, C. T. Baker Ltd, since 1986; Senior Partner, Spicer and Pegler, Chartered Accountants, 1984–88 (Partner, 1957); *b* 6 Nov. 1924; *s* of Walter James Ray and Cecilia May Ray; *m* 1949, Margaret Elizabeth, *d* of George Bull; two *s*. *Educ:* Holloway Co. Sch.; London Univ. (External) (BCom). Served RN, 1943–46. Inst. of Chartered Accountants: Mem., 1950; FCA 1955; Council Mem., 1973; Vice Pres., 1980; Dep. Pres., 1981; Pres., 1982, 1983. Chm., London Chartered Accountants, 1972–73. Dir, SIB, 1985–90; Chm., Investors' Compensation Scheme Ltd, 1988–91; Member: City Capital Markets Cttee, 1984–88; Marketing of Investments Bd Organising Cttee, 1984–88. *Publications:* Partnership Taxation, 1972, 3rd edn 1987; (jtly) VAT for Accountants and Businessmen, 1972; contrib. accountancy magazines. *Recreations:* walking, birdwatching, golf.

RAY, Jane Rosemary; illustrator of children's books; *b* 11 June 1960; *d* of Donald Edwin Ray and Barbara May Ray (*née* Rowley); *m* 1988, David Temple; one *s* two *d*. *Educ:* Middlesex Univ. (BA Hons 3-D Design (Ceramics)). *Publications include:* author and illustrator: Noah's Ark, 1991; The Story of Creation, 1992; The Story of Christmas, 1992; Twelve Dancing Princesses, 1996; Hansel and Gretel, 1997; Can you catch a Mermaid, 2002; Adam and Eve and the Garden of Eden, 2004; The Apple Pip Princess, 2007; illustrator: A Balloon for Grandad, by Nigel Gray, 1989; The Happy Prince, by Oscar Wilde, 1994; Song of the Earth, by Mary Hoffman, 1995; Sun, Moon and Stars, by Mary Hoffman, 1998; Fairy Tales, by Berlie Doherty, 2000; Orchard Book of Love and Friendship, by Geraldine McCaughrean, 2000; The Bold Boy, by Malachy Doyle, 2001; The King of Capri, by Jeanette Winterson, 2003; Romeo and Juliet, re-written by Michael Rosen, 2004; Jinnie Ghost, by Berlie Doherty, 2005; Moonbird, by Joyce Dunbar, 2006; The Lost Happy Endings, by Carol Ann Duffy, 2006; various books illus. for Folio Soc., including: Myths and Legends of the Near and Middle East, 2003; Celtic Myths and Legends, 2006. *Recreations:* reading, gardening, listening to music, general domesticity. *Address:* c/o Rosemary Sandberg, 6 Bayley Street, WC1B 3HB. *T:* (home) (020) 8442 1748; *e-mail:* janeray41@aol.com; *web:* www.janeray.com.

RAY, Prof. John David, FBA 2004; FSA; Herbert Thompson Professor of Egyptology, University of Cambridge, since 2005 (Reader, 1977–2005); Fellow, Selwyn College, Cambridge, since 1979; *b* 22 Dec. 1945; *s* of late Albert Ray and of Edith Ray (*née* Millward); *m* 1997, Sonia Ofelia Falaschi. *Educ:* Latymer Upper Sch.; Trinity Hall, Cambridge (BA 1968, MA 1971; Thomas Young Medal). Res. Asst, Dept of Egyptian Antiquities, BM, 1970; Lectr in Egyptology, Univ. of Birmingham, 1970–77. Visiting Professor: Univ. of Chicago, 1984; Yale Univ., 1988. Reviewer: TLS, 1981–; The Times, 2001–. FSA 2000. *Publications:* The Archive of Hor, 1976; Reflections of Osiris: lives from Ancient Egypt, 2001; Demotic Papyri and Ostraca from Qasr Ibrim, 2005; The Rosetta Stone, 2007; articles in Jl of Egyptian Archaeology, Lingua Aegyptia, etc. *Recreations:* listening to Beethoven, reading Patrick O'Brian, being walked by a golden retriever. *Address:* Selwyn College, Cambridge CB3 9DQ; *e-mail:* jdr1000@cam.ac.uk.

RAY, Kenneth Richard, OBE 1996; FDSRCS, FRCS; Dean, Faculty of Dental Surgery, Royal College of Surgeons of England, 1992–95; Chairman, Joint Committee for Specialist Training in Dentistry, 1996–98; *b* 25 Jan. 1930; *s* of late John Thomas Ray and Edith Rose (*née* Hobbs); *m* 1958, Pamela Ann Thomas; one *s* two *d*. *Educ:* City of Oxford High Sch.; Univ. of Birmingham (LDS, BDS). FDSRCS 1959; FRCS 1995; FRACDS 1995. Hse Surgeon, Gen. Hosp., Birmingham, 1955; Sen. Hse Officer, Midlands Regl

Plastic and Jaw Surgery Centre, 1956; Registrar, then Sen. Registrar, Royal Dental Hosp. of London and St George's Hosp., 1957–60; Sen. Lectr and Hon. Cons. in Oral Surgery, Univ. of London at Royal Dental Hosp. Sch. of Dental Surgery, 1960–73; Cons. in Oral Surgery, Royal Berks Hosp., Reading and Oxford RHA, 1963–92. Mem., GDC, 1993–95. Chm., Central Cttee for Hosp. Dental Services, 1979–86; Mem., Jt Consultants Cttee, 1979–86 and 1992–95. Royal College of Surgeons: Mem. Bd, Fac. of Dental Surgery, 1981–95; Vice-Dean, 1989; Colyer Gold Medal, 1999; British Dental Association: Mem. Council, 1979–87; Pres., Berks, Bucks and Oxon Br., 1978; Pres., Hosp. Gp, 1979; Pres., BAOMS, 1985. UK Rep., EC Dental Liaison Cttee, 1981–89; UK Rep., EC Adv. Cttee on Trng of Dental Practitioners, 1981–92. Hon. Fellow, BDA, 1990; Hon. FDSRCSE 1997; Hon. FDSRCPSGlas 1998. *Publications:* articles in learned jls and contrib. to textbooks on oral and maxillofacial surgery, local analgesia and health service planning. *Recreations:* fell-walking, natural history, English inns. *Address:* Jacobs Spinney, Rag Hill, Aldermaston, Berks RG7 4NS. *T:* (0118) 971 2550. *Club:* Royal Society of Medicine.

RAY, Philip Bicknell, CMG 1969; Ministry of Defence 1947–76, retired; *b* 10 July 1917; *s* of late Basil Ray and Clare (*née* Everett); *m* 1946, Bridget Mary Robertson (decd); two *s* one *d. Educ:* Felsted Sch.; Selwyn Coll., Cambridge (MA). Indian Police, 1939–47 (Indian Police Medal, 1944). *Publication:* Jesus Through the Spyglass, 2005. *Address:* 3 South Green Road, Newnham, Cambridge CB3 9JP.

RAY, Hon. Robert (Francis); Senator for Victoria, 1981–2008; Minister for Defence, Australia, 1990–96, and Deputy Leader of Government in the Senate, 1993–96; *b* Melbourne, 8 April 1947; *m* (Victoria) Jane Petheram. *Educ:* Monash Univ.; Rusden State Coll. Former technical sch. teacher. Australian Labor Party: Mem., 1966–; Deleg., Vic. State Conf., 1970–96; Mem., Nat. Exec., 1983–98; Minister for Home Affairs and Dep. Manager of Govt Business in the Senate, 1987; Minister assisting the Minister for Transport and Communications, 1988; Minister for Immigration, Local Govt and Ethnic Affairs, 1988–90; Manager of Govt Business in the Senate, 1988–91. *Address:* Level 2, Suite 3, Illoura Plaza, 424 St Kilda Road, Melbourne, Vic 3004, Australia.

RAY, Rt Rev. William James; see Queensland, North, Bishop of.

RAYANANONDA, Vidhya, Hon. KCVO 1996; Ambassador for Thailand to the Court of St James's and concurrently to the Republic of Ireland, 1994–2002; *b* 2 March 1942; *s* of Adm. Thavil Rayananonda and M. L. Pensri Rayananonda; *m* 1971, Nantana; two *d. Educ:* Thammasat Univ., Thailand (BA Internat. Relns); USA (MA Pol Sci.); Nat. Defence Coll., Thailand. Joined Thai Diplomatic Service: Third Sec., Washington; Second Sec., SE Asian Div., Pol Affairs Dept; First Sec., Manila; Ministry of Foreign Affairs: Dir, FE Div., Pol Affairs Dept; Dep. Dir-Gen., Inf. Dept; Consul-Gen., LA, USA; Ambassador attached to Min. of Foreign Affairs; Dep. Sec.-Gen., then Sec.-Gen., to Prime Minister; Dir-Gen., Protocol Dept; Ambassador to Switzerland and Holy See. Kt Grand Cordon, Most Noble Order of Crown (Thailand), 1992; Kt Grand Cross (1st Cl.), Most Exalted Order of White Elephant (Thailand); Order of Sacred Treasure (Gold and Silver Star) (Japan). *Recreation:* playing golf. *Address:* c/o Royal Thai Embassy, 30 Queen's Gate, SW7 5JB.

RAYCHAUDHURI, Prof. Tapan Kumar, DPhil, DLitt; Professor of Indian History and Civilisation, University of Oxford, 1992–93; Fellow, St Antony's College, Oxford, 1973–93, now Emeritus; *b* 8 May 1926; *s* of Amiya Kumar and Prativa Raychaudhuri; *m* 1960, Pratima Sen-Roy; one *d. Educ:* Presidency Coll., Calcutta; Balliol Coll., Oxford. MA, DPhil Calcutta; MA, DPhil, DLitt Oxon. Lectr, Calcutta Univ., 1948–55; Dep. Dir, Nat. Archives of India, 1957–59 (Acting Dir, 1957–58); Delhi School of Economics: Reader in Econ. History, 1959–64; Prof., 1964–70; Dir, 1965–67; Prof. of History, Delhi Univ., 1971–72; Reader in Mod. S Asian History, Univ. of Oxford, 1973–92. Visiting Professor: Duke Univ., 1964; Univ. of Calif., Berkeley, 1964; Univ. of Penn., 1969; Harvard, 1969–70; El Colegio de Mexico, 1981; Univ. of Sydney, 1986. Fellow: Woodrow Wilson Center, 1993–94; Wissenschaftskolleg zu Berlin, 1997–98. Gen. Ed (with D. Kumar), Cambridge Economic History of India, 1982–83. Hon. DLitt: Burdwan, 1998; Calcutta, 2003; Vidyasagar, 2007. Padma Bhushan, 2007. *Publications:* Bengal under Akbar and Jahangir: an introductory study in social history, 1953, 2nd edn 1969; Jan Company in Coromandel 1605–1690: European trade and Asia's traditional economies, 1962; (ed with I. Habib) Cambridge Economic History of India, vol. I, 1982, vol. II, 1983; Europe Reconsidered: perceptions of the West in Nineteenth Century Bengal, 1986, 2nd edn 2003; Perceptions, Sensibilities, Emotions: essays on India's Colonial and post-Colonial experiences, 1999; (with G. Forbes) Memoirs of Dr Haimavati Sen: from child widow to lady doctor, 2000; (in Bengali): Romaathan, 1993; Bangalnama (memoirs), 2007; contrib. Desh mag. *Recreations:* travel, cinema, reading. *Address:* 1 Hawkswell Gardens, Oxford OX2 7EX. *T:* (01865) 559421; *e-mail:* tapanda@aol.com.

RAYFIELD, Rt Rev. Lee Stephen; see Swindon, Bishop Suffragan of.

RAYLEIGH, 6th Baron *cr* 1821; **John Gerald Strutt;** Company Chairman, since 1988; *b* 4 June 1960; *s* of Hon. Charles Richard Strutt (*d* 1981) (2nd *s* of 4th Baron) and of Hon. Jean Elizabeth, *d* of 1st Viscount Davidson, PC, GCVO, CH, CB; S uncle, 1988; *m* 1991, Annabel Kate, *d* of W. G. Patterson; four *s. Educ:* Eton College; Royal Agricultural College, Cirencester. Welsh Guards, 1980–84. Chairman: Lord Rayleigh's Farms Ltd, 1988–; Eastern Data Gp Ltd, 2005–. MRI. *Recreations:* cricket, gardening, shooting, silviculture. *Heir: s* Hon. John Frederick Strutt, *b* 29 March 1993. *Clubs:* Brooks's, White's, MCC.

See also Hon. B. C. Jenkin.

RAYMOND, Robert Jacques; director of banks and funds; *b* 30 June 1933; *s* of Henri Raymond and Andrée (*née* Aubrière); *m* 1970, Monique Brémond, MD. *Educ:* Sorbonne (Masters Econs 1955). With Bank of France, 1951–94: Audit Dept, 1958–66; Rep. in NY, 1966–67; Hd, Balance of Payments Div., 1969–73; Director: Internat. Affairs, 1973–75; Monetary Stats and Analysis, 1975–76; Dep. Sec. Gen., Conseil Nat. du Crédit, 1975–81; Dep. Hd, 1976–82, Dir Gen., 1982–90, Res. Dept; Dir Gen., Credit Dept, 1990–94; Dir Gen., European Monetary Inst., 1994–98; Perm. Rep. of European Central Bank to IMF, Washington, 1999; Chm. and CEO, Banque CPR–Paris, 1999–2001. Mem. Bd, various public financial instns in Paris, 1981–94. Chm., monetary experts, Cttee of Govs of EEC, 1981–91. Officier de la Légion d'Honneur (France), 1996 (Chevalier, 1984); Officier, Ordre national du Mérite (France), 1988. *Publications:* La Monnaie, 1976; (jtly) Les relations économiques et monétaires internationales, 1982, 3rd edn 1986; Les institutions monétaires en France, 1991, 2nd edn 1996; L'unification monétaire en Europe, 1993, 2nd edn 1996; L'Euro et l'unité de l'Europe, 2001. *Address:* 5 rue de Beaujolais, 75001 Paris, France.

RAYMOND, William Francis, CBE 1978; FRSC; agricultural science consultant; *b* 25 Feb. 1922; *m* 1949, Amy Elizabeth Kelk; three *s* one *d. Educ:* Bristol Grammar Sch.; The Queen's Coll., Oxford (MA). Research Officer, MRC, 1943–45; Head of Animal Science Div. and later Asst Dir, Grassland Research Inst., Hurley, 1945–72; Dep. Chief Scientist,

1972–81, Chief Scientist (Agriculture and Horticulture), 1981–82, MAFF. Mem., ARC, 1981–82. Sec., 8th Internat. Grassland Congress, 1960; President: Brit. Grassland Soc., 1974–75; Brit. Soc. Animal Production, 1981–82. Vis. Prof. in Agriculture, Wye Coll., 1978–83. Chm., Stapledon Meml Trust, 1983–93; Member: Policy Cttee, CPRE, 1993–96; Cttee, Family Farmers' Assoc., 1996– (Vice-Chm., 1998–); Hon. Treas., RURAL, 1984–; Chm., Internat. Agricl Res. Review, Council for Res. Policy, Denmark, 1992; Mem., Internat. Agricl Res. Review, Min. of Agric. and Forestry, Finland, 1996. Chm., Henley and Mapledurham Dist, CPRE, 2001–06. *Publications:* (with Shepperson and Waltham) Forage Conservation and Feeding, 1972, 5th edn 1996; EEC Agricultural Research Framework Programme, 1983; Research in Support of Agricultural Policies in Europe, FAO Regional Conf., Reykjavik, 1984; over 250 papers in scientific jls. *Recreation:* gardening. *Address:* Periwinkle Cottage, Christmas Common, Watlington OX49 5HR. *T:* (01491) 612942.

RAYNE, Hon. Robert (Anthony); Chief Executive Officer, LMS Capital plc, since 2007; Chairman, Derwent London plc, since 2007; *b* 30 Jan. 1949; *s* of Baron Rayne and late Margaret Marco; *m* 1974, Jane Blackburn (separated); one *s* one *d. Educ:* Malvern Coll.; New York Inst. of Finance. Dir, 1983–2001, CEO, 2001–07, London Merchant Securities plc; Director: First Leisure Corp. plc, 1983–2000; Westpool Investment Trust plc, 1984–; Weatherford Internat. Inc. (US), 1987–; First Call Gp plc, 1996–98; Crown Sports plc, 2001–03; Leo Capital plc, 2006–; Chairman: Golden Rose Communications plc, 1991–99; London Jazz Radio, 1991–99. Trustee: Rayne Foundn, 1977–; The Place To Be, 1993–. MInstD. *Recreations:* art, theatre, music. *Address:* 33 Robert Adam Street, W1U 3HR. *T:* (020) 7935 3555; *e-mail:* rrayne@lmscapital.com.

RAYNER, Claire Berenice, OBE 1996; writer and broadcaster; *b* 22 Jan. 1931; *m* 1957, Desmond Rayner; two *s* one *d. Educ:* City of London Sch. for Girls; Royal Northern Hosp. Sch. of Nursing, London (Gold Medal; SRN 1954); Guy's Hosp. (midwifery). Formerly: Nurse, Royal Free Hosp.; Sister, Paediatric Dept, Whittington Hosp. Woman's Own: Med. Correspondent, as Ruth Martin, 1966–75, as Claire Rayner, 1975–87; advice column: The Sun, 1973–80; The Sunday Mirror, 1980–88; Today, 1988–91; columnist, Woman, 1988–92. Radio and television broadcasts include: family advice, Pebble Mill at One, BBC, 1972–74; (co-presenter) Kitchen Garden, ITV, 1974–77; Contact, BBC Radio, Wales, 1974–77; Claire Rayner's Casebook (series), BBC, 1980, 1983, 1984; TV-am Advice Spot, 1985–92; A Problem Shared, Sky TV Series, 1989; Good Morning with Anne and Nick, BBC, 1992–93. Non-exec. Dir, Northwick Park Hosp., 1991–98; Associate non-exec. Dir, Royal Hosps NHS Trust, 1995–2000. Mem., Royal Commn on Long Term Care of the Elderly, 1997–98; Founder Mem., Forum on Children and Violence. FRSocMed; FRSA. President: Gingerbread; Patients' Assoc.; Nat. Assoc. of Bereavement Counsellors; British Humanist Assoc., 1999–2003 (Vice Pres., 2003–); Patron: Terrence Higgins Trust; Turning Point; Royal Philanthropic Soc., and others. Freeman, City of London, 1981. Hon. Fellow, Poly. of N London, 1988. Hon. doctorates: Oxford Brookes, 2000; Surrey, 2007; Middlesex. Med. Journalist of the Year, 1987; Best Specialist Consumer Columnist Award, 1988. *Publications:* Mothers and Midwives, 1962; What Happens in Hospital, 1963; The Calendar of Childhood, 1964; Your Baby, 1965; Careers with Children, 1966; Essentials of Out-Patient Nursing, 1967; For Children, 1967; Shall I be a Nurse, 1967; 101 Facts an Expectant Mother should know, 1967; 101 Key Facts of Practical Baby Care, 1967; Housework - The Easy Way, 1967; Home Nursing and Family Health, 1967; A Parent's Guide to Sex Education, 1968; People in Love, 1968 (subseq. publd as About Sex, 1972); Protecting Your Baby, 1971; Woman's Medical Dictionary, 1971; When to Call the Doctor - What to Do Whilst Waiting, 1972; The Shy Person's Book, 1973; Childcare Made Simple, 1973; Where Do I Come From?, 1975; (ed and contrib.) Atlas of the Body and Mind, 1976; (with Keith Fordyce) Kitchen Garden, 1976; (with Keith Fordyce) More Kitchen Garden, 1977; Family Feelings, 1977; Claire Rayner answers your 100 Questions on Pregnancy, 1977; (with Keith Fordyce) Claire and Keith's Kitchen Garden, 1978; The Body Book, 1978; Related to Sex, 1979; (with Keith Fordyce) Greenhouse Gardening, 1979; Everything your Doctor would Tell You if He Had the Time, 1980; Claire Rayner's Lifeguide, 1980; Baby and Young Child Care, 1981; Growing Pains, 1984; Claire Rayner's Marriage Guide, 1984; The Getting Better Book, 1985; Woman, 1986; When I Grow Up, 1986; Safe Sex, 1987; The Don't Spoil Your Body Book, 1989; Life and Love and Everything: children's questions, 1993; (autobiog.) How Did I Get Here From There, 2003; *fiction:* Shilling a Pound Pears, 1964; The House on the Fen, 1967; Starch of Aprons, 1967 (subseq. publd as The Hive, 1968); Lady Mislaid, 1968; Death on the Table, 1969; The Meddlers, 1970; A Time to Heal, 1972; The Burning Summer, 1972; Sisters, 1978; Reprise, 1980; The Running Years, 1981; Family Chorus, 1984; The Virus Man, 1985; Lunching at Laura's, 1986; Maddie, 1988; Clinical Judgements, 1989; Postscripts, 1991; Dangerous Things, 1993; First Blood, 1993; Second Opinion, 1994; Third Degree, 1995; Fourth Attempt, 1996; Fifth Member, 1997; The Performers: Book 1, Gower Street, 1973; Book 2, The Haymarket, 1974; Book 3, Paddington Green, 1975; Book 4, Soho Square, 1976; Book 5, Bedford Row, 1977; Book 6, Long Acre, 1978; Book 7, Charing Cross, 1979; Book 8, The Strand, 1980; Book 9, Chelsea Reach, 1982; Book 10, Shaftesbury Avenue, 1983; Book 11, Piccadilly, 1985; Book 12, Seven Dials, 1986; Poppy Chronicles: Book 1, Jubilee, 1987; Book 2, Flanders, 1988; Book 3, Flapper, 1989; Book 4, Blitz, 1990; Book 5, Festival, 1992; Book 6, Sixties, 1992; Quentin Quartet: Book 1, London Lodgings, 1994; Book 2, Paying Guests, 1995; *as Sheila Brandon: fiction:* The Final Year, 1962; Cottage Hospital, 1963; Children's Ward, 1964; The Lonely One, 1965; The Doctors of Downlands, 1968; The Private Wing, 1971; Nurse in the Sun, 1972; *as Ann Lynton:* Mothercraft, 1967; contrib. Lancet, Med. World, Nursing Times, Nursing Mirror, and national newspapers and magazines, incl. Design. *Recreations:* talking, party-giving, theatre-going. *Address:* PO Box 125, Harrow, Middx HA1 3XE.

See also J. Rayner.

RAYNER, David Edward, CBE 1992; FCILT; Director, South East Trains Ltd, 2003–06; *b* 26 Jan. 1940; *s* of Marjory and Gilbert Rayner; *m* 1966, Enid Cutty; two *d. Educ:* St Peter's School, York; Durham University (BSc Hons). Joined British Railways, 1963; Passenger Marketing Manager, BR Board, 1982; Dep. Gen. Manager, BR, London Midland Region, 1984–86; Gen. Manager, BR, Eastern Region, 1986–87; British Railways Board: Mem., 1987–94; Jt Man. Dir, 1987–89; Man. Dir, Engrg and Operations, 1989–92; Man. Dir, Safety and Operations, 1992–94; Bd Mem., Railtrack Gp, 1994–97; Dir Safety and Standards, Railtrack, 1994–97. Non-executive Chairman: Rail Investments Ltd, 1998–99; Oakburn Properties plc, 1998–2004; non-executive Director: Coll. of Railway Technol., subseq. Catalis Rail Trng, Ltd, 1998–2003 (Chm., 1998–2002); Connex Transport UK (formerly Connex Rail) Ltd, 1998–2003. Chm., Rail Industry Training Council, 1992–95. Vis. Prof., UCL, 1998–. Trustee: Science Mus., 1997–2006; York and N Yorks Community Foundn, 2000–07; York Museums (formerly York Museums and Gall.) Trust, 2002–07; York Glaziers Trust, 2004–; St Peter's Foundn, 2005–. Hon. Col, Railway Sqn, RLC (TA), 1992–99. *Recreation:* collector.

RAYNER, Jay; freelance writer, journalist and broadcaster; *b* 14 Sept. 1966; *s* of Desmond Rayner and Claire Berenice Rayner, *qv; m* 1992, Pat Gordon Smith; two *s. Educ:* Leeds Univ. (BA Hons Pol Studies 1987). Editor, Leeds Student newspaper, 1987–88; freelance journalist, The Observer, The Guardian, Independent on Sunday, Cosmopolitan and others, 1988–92; Feature Writer: The Guardian, 1992–93; Mail on Sunday, 1993–96; The Observer, 1996–, Restaurant Critic, 1999–. Presenter, BBC Radio: Stop Press, 1995–97; Papertalk, 1997–99 (Magazine Prog. of the Year, Sony Radio Awards, 1999); The Food Quiz, 2003–. Young Journalist of the Year, 1991, Critic of the Year, 2006, British Press Awards; Restaurant Critic of the Year, Glenfiddich Food and Drink Awards, 2001. *Publications:* Star Dust Falling, 2002; *novels:* The Marble Kiss, 1994; Day of Atonement, 1998; The Apologist, 2004; The Oyster House Siege, 2007; The Man Who Ate the World, 2008; contrib. to Arena, Esquire, Gourmet, Food and Wine. *Recreations:* lousy jazz pianist, cooking, my kids. *Address:* c/o Curtis Brown Group Ltd, Haymarket House, 28–29 Haymarket, SW1Y 4SP. *T:* (020) 7393 4400, *Fax:* (020) 7393 4401; *e-mail:* jay.rayner@observer.co.uk.

RAYNER, Rt Rev. Keith, AO 1987; Archbishop of Melbourne and Metropolitan of the Province of Victoria, 1990–99; Primate of Australia, 1991–99 (Acting Primate, 1989–91); *b* 22 Nov. 1929; *s* of Sidney and Gladys Rayner, Brisbane; *m* 1963, Audrey Fletcher; one *s* two *d. Educ:* C of E Grammar Sch., Brisbane; Univ. of Queensland (BA 1951; PhD 1964). Deacon, 1953; Priest, 1953. Chaplain, St Francis' Theol Coll., Brisbane, 1954; Mem., Brotherhood of St John, Dalby, 1955–58; Vice-Warden, St John's Coll., Brisbane, 1958; Rotary Foundn Fellow, Harvard Univ., 1958–59; Vicar, St Barnabas', Sunnybank, 1959–63; Rector, St Peter's, Wynnum, 1963–69; Bishop of Wangaratta, 1969–75; Archbishop of Adelaide and Metropolitan of South Australia, 1975–90. Pres., Christian Conference of Asia, 1977–81; Chm., International Anglican Theological and Doctrinal Commission, 1980–88. Hon. ThD Aust. Coll. of Theology, 1987; DUniv Griffith, 2001. *Address:* 36 Highfield Avenue, St Georges, SA 5064, Australia.

RAYNER, Miranda; *see* Hughes, M.

RAYNER, Prof. Peter John Wynn, PhD; Professor of Signal Processing, University of Cambridge, 1998–2002, now Emeritus; Fellow, Christ's College, Cambridge, 1969–2002, now Emeritus; *b* 22 July 1941; *s* of John Austin Rayner and Amelia Victoria Rayner; *m* 1960, Patricia Ann Gray; two *d. Educ:* Univ. of Aston (PhD 1968); MA Cantab 1969. Student apprentice, Pye TVT Ltd, 1957–62; Sen. Engr, Cambridge Consultants, 1962–65; Res. Student, Univ. of Aston, 1965–68; Cambridge University: Lectr, Dept of Engrg, 1968–90; Dir, Studies in Engrg, Christ's Coll., 1971–99; Reader in Inf. Engrg, 1990–98. Dir, Cedar Audio Ltd, 1989–; Advr to Bd, Autonomy Corp., 2000–. *Publications:* (with S. J. Godsill) Digital Audio Restoration, 1998; book chapters; numerous contribs to learned jls. *Recreations:* scuba-diving, flamenco and blues guitar, gardening, cycling. *Address:* 69 High Street, Oakington, Cambs CB4 5AG. *T:* (01223) 234203.

RAYNER, Samuel Alan Miles; Managing Director, Lakeland Ltd (formerly Lakeland Plastics Ltd), since 1974; *b* 31 May 1953; *s* of Alan and Dorothy Rayner; *m* 1978, Judy McIlvenny; two *s* one *d. Address:* Lakeland Ltd, Alexandria Buildings, Windermere LA23 1BQ.

RAYNER, Prof. Steve, PhD; James Martin Professor of Science and Civilization, University of Oxford, since 2003; Fellow, Keble College, Oxford, since 2003; *b* 22 May 1953; *s* of Harry Rayner and Esmé Rayner; *m* 1994, Heather Katz; one *d. Educ:* Univ. of Kent (BA Philos. and Theol. 1974); University Coll. London (PhD Anthropol. 1979). Res. Associate, Russell Sage Foundn, 1980–81; Vis. Schol., Boston Univ. Sch. of Public Health, 1982; Sen. Res. Staff, Oak Ridge Nat. Lab., 1983–91; Chief Scientist, Pacific Northwest Nat. Lab., 1991–99; Prof. of Envmt and Public Affairs, Columbia Univ., 1999–2003. Adjunct Asst Prof., Univ. of Tennessee, 1986; Vis. Associate Prof., Cornell Univ., 1990; Adjunct Associate Prof., Virginia Polytech., 1997–98. Dir, ESRC Sci. in Society Prog., 2002–08. Member: Intergovtl Panel on Climate Change, 1999–; Royal Commn on Envmtl Pollution, 2003–; Adv. Bd, UK Climate Impacts Prog., 2004–; Bd of Dirs, Foundn for Law, Justice and Soc., 2006–. *Publications:* (with Jonathan Gross) Measuring Culture, 1985; (with James Flanagan) Rules, Decisions and Inequality, 1988; (with Robin Cantor and Stuart Henry) Making Markets, 1992; (with Elizabeth Malone) Human Choice and Climate Change, 4 vols, 1998; articles in Climatic Change, Global Envmtl Change, Ecol Econs, Sci. and Public Policy, Science, Nature, Govt and Opposition, Social Studies of Sci., Risk Analysis, Evaluation Review, Econ. and Political Wkly, Industry and Higher Educn. *Recreations:* demolition, building, anything to do with boats. *Address:* James Martin Institute for Science and Civilization, Saïd Business School, Park End Street, Oxford OX1 1HP. *T:* (01865) 288938; *e-mail:* steve.rayner@sbs.ox.ac.uk. *Club:* Cosmos (Washington).

RAYNER JAMES, Jonathan Elwyn; *see* James.

RAYNES, Prof. (Edward) Peter, FRS 1987; Professor of Optoelectronic Engineering, University of Oxford, since 1998; Fellow of St Cross College, Oxford, since 1998; *b* 4 July 1945; *s* of Edward Gordon and Ethel Mary Raynes; *m* 1970, Madeline Ord; two *s. Educ:* St Peter's School, York; Gonville and Caius College, Cambridge (MA, PhD). CPhys, FInstP. Royal Signals and Radar Establishment, 1971–92: SPSO, 1981; DCSO, 1988–92; Chief Scientist, 1992–95, Dir of Res., 1995–98, Sharp Labs of Europe Ltd, Oxford. Rank Prize for Opto-electronics, 1980; Paterson Medal, Inst. of Physics, 1986; Special Recognition Award, Soc. for Information Display, 1987. *Publications:* (ed jtly) Liquid Crystals: their physics, chemistry and applications, 1983; numerous scientific papers and patents. *Recreation:* choral and solo singing. *Address:* Department of Engineering Science, University of Oxford, Parks Road, Oxford OX1 3PJ. *T:* (01865) 273024, *Fax:* (01865) 273905.

RAYNHAM, Viscount; Charles George Townshend; *b* 26 Sept. 1945; *s* and *heir* of 7th Marquess Townshend, *qv; m* 1st, 1975, Hermione (*d* 1985), *d* of Lt-Cdr R. M. D. Ponsonby and Mrs Dorothy Ponsonby; one *s* one *d*; 2nd, 1990, Mrs Alison Marshall, *yr d* of Sir Willis Combs, KCVO, CMG. *Educ:* Eton; Royal Agricultural College, Cirencester. Chm. and Dir, AIMS Ltd, 1977–87; Man. Dir, Raynham Workshops Ltd, 1986–94; Chm., Pera International, 1988–96. Gen. Comr, Income Tax, Norwich, 1989–97. Mem. Council, Design Gp Great Britain Ltd, 1984–90 (Chm., 1988); Mem. Council for Norfolk and Chief Steward, Royal Show, RASE, 1982–94. Pres., Fakenham Br., RBL, 2004–. Churchwarden, St Mary's, East Raynham, 1991–. *Heir: s* Hon. Thomas Charles Townshend, *b* 2 Nov. 1977. *Address:* Pattesley House, Fakenham, Norfolk NR21 7HT. *T:* (01328) 701818.

RAYNOR, Andrew Paul; Chief Executive, Tenon Group PLC, since 2003; *b* 24 May 1957; *s* of Laurence Edwin Raynor and Pamela Sylvia Raynor (*née* Skelton); *m* 1980, Karen Jane Robertson; three *d. Educ:* Leicester Polytech. (BA Hons Business Studies). FCA 1981. Partner, Stoy Hayward East Midlands, 1986; BDO Stoy Hayward East Midlands: Hd, Corporate Finance, 1994–97; Hd, Business Develt, 1997–2000; Managing Partner, 2000–01; Finance Dir, Tenon Group plc, 2002–03. *Publications:* various articles in financial related jls. *Recreations:* running, travel, searching for the children/children's dog, work! *Address:* Tenon Group PLC, 66 Chiltern Street, W1U 4GB. *T:* (020) 7535 5775; *e-mail:* andyraynor@aol.com.

RAYNOR, Philip Ronald; QC 1994; **His Honour Judge Raynor;** a Circuit Judge, since 2001; Specialist Circuit Judge, Technology and Construction Court, Salford, since 2006; *b* 20 Jan. 1950; *s* of Wilfred and Sheila Raynor; *m* 1974, Judith Braunsberg; one *s* one *d. Educ:* Roundhay Sch., Leeds; Christ's Coll., Cambridge (Schol., MA). Lectr in Law, Univ. of Manchester, 1971–74; called to the Bar, Inner Temple, 1973; in practice, 1973–2001; a Recorder, 1993–2001; Head of Chambers, 40 King Street, Manchester, 1996–2001. *Recreations:* travel, opera, dining out. *Address:* Manchester Civil Justice Centre, 1 Bridge Street West, Manchester M3 3FX.

RAYNSFORD, Rt Hon. Nick; *see* Raynsford, Rt Hon. W. R. N.

RAYNSFORD, Rt Hon. Wyvill Richard Nicolls, (Rt Hon. Nick); PC 2001; MP (Lab) Greenwich and Woolwich, since 1997 (Greenwich, 1992–97); *b* 28 Jan. 1945; *s* of Wyvill Raynsford and Patricia Raynsford (*née* Dunn); *m* 1968, Anne Raynsford (*née* Jelley); three *d. Educ:* Repton Sch.; Sidney Sussex Coll., Cambridge (MA); Chelsea Sch. of Art (DipAD). Market research, A. C. Nielsen Co. Ltd, 1966–68; Gen. Sec., Soc. for Co-operative Dwellings, 1972–73; SHAC: Emergency Officer, 1973–74; Research Officer, 1974–76; Dir, 1976–86; Partner, 1987–90, Dir, 1990–92, Raynsford and Morris, housing consultants; Dir, Raynsford Dallison Associates, housing consultants, 1992–93; Consultant, HACAS, 1993–97. Councillor (Lab) London Borough of Hammersmith & Fulham, 1971–75 (Chm., Leisure and Recreation Cttee, 1972–74). Contested (Lab) Fulham, 1987. MP (Lab) Fulham, April 1986–1987. Opposition front bench spokesman on London, 1993–97, on housing, 1994–97; Parly Under-Sec. of State, DoE and Dept of Transport, subseq. DETR, 1997–99; Minister of State: DETR, 1999–2001; DTLR, 2001–02; ODPM, 2002–05. Mem., Envmt Select Cttee, 1992–93. Chairman: NHBC Foundn, 2006–; Nat. Centre for Excellence in Housing, 2006–; Strategic Forum for Construction, 2008–; Dep. Chm., Construction Industry Council, 2005–06, 2008– (Chm., 2006–08). Pres., Nat. Home Improvement Council, 2008–. Hon. FRIBA 2007. *Publication:* A Guide to Housing Benefit, 1982, 7th edn 1986. *Recreation:* photography. *Address:* House of Commons, SW1A 0AA; 10 Charlton Road, Blackheath, SE3 7HG.

RAZ, Prof. Joseph, FBA 1987; Professor of the Philosophy of Law, 1985–2006, Research Professor in the Philosophy of Law, 2006–08, University of Oxford; Fellow of Balliol College, Oxford, 1985–2006, now Emeritus; Professor, Columbia Law School, New York, since 2002; *b* 21 March 1939. *Educ:* Hebrew University, Jerusalem (MJur 1963); University Coll., Oxford (DPhil 1967). Lectr, Hebrew Univ., Jerusalem, 1967–70; Research Fellow, Nuffield Coll., Oxford, 1970–72; Tutorial Fellow, Balliol Coll., Oxford, 1972–85. Vis. Prof., Columbia Law Sch., NY, 1995–2002. For. Hon. Mem., Amer. Acad. of Arts and Scis, 1992. Hon. Dr Catholic Univ., Brussels, 1993; Hon. PhD, KCL, 2008. *Publications:* The Concept of a Legal System, 1970, 2nd edn 1980; Practical Reason and Norms, 1975, 2nd edn 1990; The Authority of Law, 1979; The Morality of Freedom, 1986; Ethics in the Public Domain, 1994, rev. edn 1995; Engaging Reason, 2000; Value, Respect and Attachment, 2001; The Practice of Value, 2003. *Address:* Balliol College, Oxford OX1 3BJ. *T:* (01865) 277721.

RAZZALL, family name of **Baron Razzall**.

RAZZALL, Baron *cr* 1997 (Life Peer), of Mortlake in the London Borough of Richmond; **Edward Timothy Razzall,** CBE 1993; Partner, Argonaut Associates, since 1996; *b* 12 June 1943; *s* of late Leonard Humphrey and Muriel Razzall; *m* 1st, 1965, Elizabeth Christina Wilkinson (marr. diss. 1974); one *s* one *d*; 2nd, 1982, Deirdre Bourke Martineau (*née* Taylor Smith) (marr. diss. 2003). *Educ:* St Paul's Sch.; Worcester Coll., Oxford (Open Schol.; BA). Teaching Associate, Northwestern Univ., Chicago, 1965–66; with Frere Cholmeley Bischoff, solicitors, 1966–96 (Partner, 1973–96). Councillor (L), Mortlake Ward, London Borough of Richmond, 1974–98; Dep. Leader, Richmond Council, 1983–97. Treasurer: Liberal Party, 1986–87; Liberal Democrats, 1987–2000; Chm., Lib Dem Campaign Cttee, 2000–06. Pres., Assoc. of Lib Dem Councillors, 1990–95. European Lawyer of Year, Inst. of Lawyers in Europe, 1992. *Recreation:* all sports. *Address:* (office) Devonshire House, 146 Bishopsgate, EC2M 4JX. *Clubs:* National Liberal, Soho House, MCC.

REA, family name of **Baron Rea**.

REA, 3rd Baron *cr* 1937, of Eskdale; **John Nicolas Rea,** MD; Bt 1935; General Medical Practitioner, Kentish Town, NW5, 1957–62 and 1968–93; *b* 6 June 1928; *s* of Hon. James Russell Rea (*d* 1954) (2nd *s* of 1st Baron) and Betty Marion (*d* 1965), *d* of Arthur Bevan, MD; *S* uncle, 1981; *m* 1st, 1951, Elizabeth Anne (marr. diss. 1991), *d* of late William Hensman Robinson; four *s* two *d*; 2nd, 1991, Judith Mary, *d* of late Norman Powell. *Educ:* Dartington Hall School; Belmont Hill School, Mass, USA; Dauntsey's School; Christ's Coll., Cambridge Univ.; UCH Medical School. MA, MD (Cantab); FRCGP; DPH, DCH, DObstRCOG. Research Fellow in Paediatrics, Lagos, Nigeria, 1962–65; Lecturer in Social Medicine, St Thomas's Hosp. Medical School, 1966–68. Hon. Sec., Nat. Heart Forum, 2001– (Vice-Chm., Nat. Forum for Prevention of Coronary Heart Disease, 1985–95); Chairman: Healthlink Worldwide (formerly Appropriate Health Resources and Technology Action Gp), 1992–97; Parly Food & Health Forum, 1992–. Opposition spokesman on health, develt and co-operation, H of L, 1992–97; elected Mem., H of L, 1999. FRSocMed (Pres., Section of Gen. Practice, 1985–86). *Publications:* Interactions of Infection and Nutrition (MD Thesis, Cambridge Univ.), 1969; (jtly) Learning Teaching— an evaluation of a course for GP Teachers, 1980; articles on epidemiology and medical education in various journals. *Recreations:* music (bassoon), foreign travel, outdoor activities. *Heir: s* Hon. Matthew James Rea, *b* 28 March 1956. *Address:* 1 Littledene Cottages, Glynde, E Sussex BN8 6LA. *T:* (weekdays) (020) 7607 0546, *Fax:* (020) 7687 1219.

REA, Christopher William Wallace; Controller, Broadcast Productions (formerly Head of Communications), International Rugby Board, since 2000; *b* 22 Oct. 1943; *s* of Col William Wallace Rea and Helen Rea; *m* 1974, Daphne Theresa Manning; one *d. Educ:* High Sch. of Dundee; Univ. of St Andrews (MA). With BBC Radio Sports Dept, 1972–81; Rugby and Golf Corresp., Scotsman, 1981–84; Publisher and Ed., Rugby News Mag., 1984–88; Presenter, BBV TV Rugby Special, 1988–94; Asst Sec., then Head, Marketing and Public Affairs, MCC, 1995–2000. Rugby Corresp., Independent on Sunday, 1990–2000. Played Rugby Union for Scotland, 1968–71 (13 Caps); Mem., British Lions tour to NZ, 1971; played for Barbarians, 1971. *Publications:* Illustrated History of Rugby Union, 1977; Injured Pride, 1980; Scotland's Grand Slam, 1984. *Recreations:* golf, hill walking. *Address:* (office) Huguenot House, 35/38 St Stephen's Green, Dublin 2, Eire; 3 The Huntley, Carmelite Drive, Reading, Berks RG30 2SB. *Club:* Huntercombe Golf.

REA, Prof. Sir Desmond, Kt 2005; OBE 1996; PhD; Chairman: Northern Ireland Policing Board, since 2001; Ulster Orchestra, since 2008; *b* 4 March 1937; *s* of Samuel and Annie Rea; *m* 1969, Dr Irene Maeve Williamson; four *d. Educ:* Queen's Univ., Belfast (BSc Econ, MSc Econ; PhD); Univ. of Calif, Berkeley (MBA). Queen's University, Belfast: Lectr, then Sen. Lectr, in Business Admin, 1969–75; Asst Dean, Faculty of Econs and Social Scis, 1973–75; Hd of Dept and Prof. of Human Resource Mgt, Ulster Polytech., subseq. Univ. of Ulster, 1975–95, now Prof. Emeritus. Chairman (part-time): NI Schs Exams Council, 1987–90; NI Schs Exams and Assessment Council, 1990–94; NI Council for Curriculum, Exams and Assessment, 1994–98; NI Local Govt Staff Commn, 1989–96; NI Lab. Relns Agency, 1996–2002; Sec., Jt Ind. Gp for Study and Action, 1980–2004. Mem. Bd, Anglo-Irish Encounter, 1983–2004. Chm. Bd of Govs, Methodist Coll., Belfast, 2000–04. Ed., Quarterly Economic Outlook and Business Review, First Trust Bank, 1984–. *Publication:* (ed) Political Co-operation in Divided Societies: a series of papers relevant to the conflict in Northern Ireland, 1981. *Recreations:* reading, classical music, Rugby. *Address:* Northern Ireland Policing Board, Waterside Tower, 31 Clarendon Road, Clarendon Dock, Belfast BT1 3BG. *T:* (028) 9040 8500, *Fax:* (028) 9040 8525.

REA, Rev. Ernest; freelance broadcaster and writer; Head of Religious Broadcasting, BBC, 1989–2001; *b* 6 Sept. 1945; *s* of Ernest Rea and Mary Wylie (*née* Blue); *m* 1st, 1973, Kay (*née* Kilpatrick) (marr. diss 1994); two *s*; 2nd, 1995, Gaynor (*née* Vaughan Jones). *Educ:* Methodist Coll., Belfast; Queen's Univ., Belfast; Union Theological Coll., Belfast. Asst Minister, Woodvale Park Presb. Ch., Belfast, 1971–74; Minister, Bannside Presb. Ch., Banbridge, Co. Down, 1974–79; Religious Broadcasting Producer, BBC Belfast, 1979–84; Sen. Religious Broadcasting Producer, BBC S and W, 1984–88; Editor, Network Radio, BBC S and W, 1988–89; Hd of Religious Progs, BBC Radio, 1989–93. Presenter, Beyond Belief, BBC Radio 4, 2001–. *Recreations:* reading, watching cricket, playing tennis and golf, theatre, music. *Address:* The Coach House, Beechfield Road, Alderley Edge, Cheshire SK9 7AU.

REA, Dr John Rowland, FBA 1981; Lecturer in Documentary Papyrology, University of Oxford, 1965–96; Senior Research Fellow, Balliol College, Oxford, 1969–96, now Emeritus Fellow; *b* 28 Oct. 1933; *s* of Thomas Arthur Rea and Elsie Rea (*née* Ward); *m* 1959, Mary Ogden. *Educ:* Methodist Coll., Belfast; Queen's Univ., Belfast (BA); University Coll. London (PhD). Asst Keeper, Public Record Office, 1957–61; Res. Lectr, Christ Church, Oxford, 1961–65. *Publications:* The Oxyrhynchus Papyri, Vol. XL, 1972, Vol. XLVI, 1978, Vol. LI, 1984, Vol LV, 1988, Vol. LVIII, 1991, LXIII, 1996, also contribs to Vols XXVII, XXXI, XXXIII, XXXIV, XXXVI, XLI, XLIII, XLIX, L, LXII, LXIV; (with P. J. Sijpesteijn) Corpus Papyrorum Raineri V, 1976; articles in classical jls. *Address:* Aurolaine, 1 Shirley Drive, St Leonards-on-Sea, East Sussex TN37 7JW.

REA, Rupert Lascelles P.; *see* Pennant-Rea.

REA, Stephen James; actor and director; *b* Belfast, 31 Oct. 1949; *s* of James Rea and Jane Rea (*née* Logue); *m* 1983, Dolours Price; two *s*. *Educ:* Queen's Univ., Belfast. Trained at Abbey Theatre Sch., Dublin. Jt Founder, Field Day Theatre Co., 1980. *Theatre includes:* The Shadow of a Gunman; The Cherry Orchard; Miss Julie; High Society; Endgame; The Freedom of the City; Translations; The Communication Cord; Saint Oscar; Boesman and Lena; Hightime and Riot Act; Double Cross; Pentecost; Making History; Someone Who'll Watch Over Me; Uncle Vanya; Ashes to Ashes; Playboy of the Western World; Comedians; The Shaughraun; Cyrano de Bergerac, 2004; *director:* Three Sisters; The Cure at Troy; Northern Star. *Films include:* Angel, Loose Connections, 1983; Company of Wolves, 1984; The Doctor and the Devils, 1986; Life is Sweet, 1991; The Crying Game, 1992; Bad Behaviour, 1993; Princess Caraboo, Angie, Interview with the Vampire, 1994; Prêt-à-Porter, Between the Devil and the Deep Blue Sea, 1995; All Men are Mortal, Michael Collins, 1996; Trojan Eddie, A Further Gesture, 1997; The Butcher Boy, Still Crazy, 1998; In Dreams, The Life Before This, Guinevere, 1999; The End of the Affair, I Could Read the Sky, 2000; Evelyn, 2003; Bloom, Breakfast at Pluto, V for Vendetta, 2006; River Queen, 2008. *Television includes:* Four Days in July, 1984; The Kidnapper in Shergar, 1986; Hedda Gabler, 1993; The Shadow of a Gunman, 1995; Citizen X, 1995; Crime of the Century, 1996. *Address:* c/o Independent Talent Group Ltd, Oxford House, 76 Oxford Street, W1D 1BS.

REA PRICE, (William) John, OBE 1991; Director, National Children's Bureau, 1991–98; *b* 15 March 1937; *s* of late John Caxton Rea Price and of Mary Hilda Rea Price. *Educ:* University College Sch.; Corpus Christi Coll., Cambridge (MA); LSE (DSA; Cert. Applied Social Studies). London Probation Service, 1962–65; London Borough of Islington Children's Dept, 1965–68; Nat. Inst. for Social Work, 1968–69; Home Office, Community Develt Project, 1969–72; Dir of Social Services, London Borough of Islington, 1972–90. Pres., Assoc. of Dirs of Social Services, 1989–90. *Recreations:* cycling, archaeology, history of landscape. *Address:* 1 Old Store Gardens, Eastbridge, Leiston, Suffolk IP16 4SJ. *T:* (01728) 635083; *e-mail:* John.Reaprice@btinternet.com. *Club:* Reform.

READ, Miss; *see* Saint, D. J.

READ, Air Marshal Sir Charles (Frederick), KBE 1976 (CBE 1964); CB 1972; DFC 1942; AFC 1958; Chief of the Air Staff, RAAF, 1972–75, retired; *b* Sydney, NSW, 9 Oct. 1918; *s* of J. F. Read, Bristol, England; *m* 1946, Betty E., *d* of A. V. Bradshaw; three *s*. *Educ:* Sydney Grammar Sch. Former posts include: OC, RAAF Base, Point Cook, Vic., 1965–68; OC, RAAF, Richmond, NSW, 1968–70; Dep. Chief of Air Staff, 1969–72. *Recreation:* yachting. *Address:* 18 Ocean Drive, Safety Beach, Woolgoolga, NSW 2456, Australia. *T:* (2) 66540883.

READ, Sir David (John), Kt 2007; PhD; FRS 1990; Professor of Plant Sciences, Sheffield University, 1990–2004, now Emeritus; *b* 20 Jan. 1939; *s* of O. Read; *m* (marr. diss.); one *s*. *Educ:* Sexey's Sch., Bruton, Som; Hull Univ. (BSc 1960; PhD 1963). Sheffield University: Jun. Res. Fellow, 1963–66; Asst Lectr, 1966–69; Lectr, 1969–79; Sen. Lectr, 1979–81; Reader in Plant Sci., 1981–90. Chairman: Bd of Dirs, Rothamsted Research, 2003–; Res. Adv. Bd, Forestry Commn, 2004–. Vice-Pres. and Biol Sec., Royal Soc., 2003–. Mem. Bd Govs, Macaulay Res. Inst., 2003–. *Publications:* editor of numerous books and author of papers in learned jls mostly on subject of symbiosis, specifically the mycorrhizal symbiosis between plant roots and fungi. *Recreations:* walking, botany. *Address:* Minestone Cottage, Youlgrave, Bakewell, Derbys DE4 1WD. *T:* (01629) 636360.

READ, Prof. Frank Henry, FRS 1984; consultant engineer in charged particle optics, since 2002; Founder Director, CPO Ltd, since 2000; Professor Emeritus, University of Manchester (formerly Victoria University of Manchester), since 2002; *b* 6 Oct. 1934; *s* of late Frank Charles Read and Florence Louise (*née* Wright); *m* 1961, Anne Stuart (*née* Wallace); two *s* two *d*. *Educ:* Haberdashers' Aske's Hampstead Sch. (Foundn Scholar, 1946); Royal Coll. of Science, Univ. of London (Royal Scholar, 1952; ARCS 1955; BSc 1955). PhD 1959, DSc 1975, Victoria Univ. of Manchester. FInstP 1968; FIET (FIEE 1998); SMIEEE 2002; CEng; CPhys. University of Manchester: Lectr, 1959; Sen. Lectr, 1969; Reader, 1974; Prof. of Physics, 1975–98; Langworthy Prof. of Physics, 1998–2001; Res. Dean, Faculty of Sci., 1993–95; Res. Prof., 2001–02. Vis. Scientist: Univ. of Paris, 1974; Univ. of Colorado, 1974–75; Inst. for Atomic and Molecular Physics, Amsterdam, 1979–80. Consultant to industry, 1976–. Vice Pres., Inst. of Physics, 1985–89 (Chm., IOP Publishing Ltd, 1985–89); Member: Science Bd, SERC, 1987–90; Council, Royal Soc., 1987–89. Holweck Medal and Prize, Inst. of Physics and Soc. Française de Physique, 2000. Hon. Editor, Jl of Physics B, Atomic and Molecular Physics, 1980–84. *Publications:* (with E. Harting) Electrostatic Lenses, 1976; Electromagnetic Radiation, 1980; papers in physics and instrumentation jls. *Recreations:* stone-masonry, landscaping, riding. *Address:* Cumberland House, 9 Jordangate, Macclesfield SK10 1EG. *T:* (01625) 425759.

READ, Graham Stephen; QC 2003; *b* 17 Sept. 1957; *s* of Peter Denis Read and Dorothy Ruby Read; *m* 1983, Frances Margaret Catherine Daley; two *d*. *Educ:* Queen Mary's, Basingstoke; Trinity Hall, Cambridge (MA). Called to the Bar, Gray's Inn, 1981 (Arden Schol. 1980; Holker Schol. 1981). *Publications:* contrib. to various legal pubns. *Recreations:* walking, Roman and 20th century European history, concerts. *Address:* Devereux Chambers, Devereux Court, WC2R 3JH. *T:* (020) 7353 7534, *Fax:* (020) 7353 1724.
See also M. P. Read.

READ, Brig. Gregory, CBE 1984; Clerk to Vintners' Company, 1984–96; *b* 11 Oct. 1934; *s* of Edward Charles Read and Margaret Florence Maud Holdsworth; *m* 1957, Rosemary Patricia Frost; three *s*. *Educ:* Sherborne Sch.; RMA Sandhurst; RMCS Shrivenham (BSc Eng 1959); Open Univ. (BA Hons 2001). Commnd RTR, 1955; Comd 3 RTR, 1973–76; Comd RAC 1 (BR) Corps, 1979–81; Dir, Combat Develt, 1981; Dir, Battlefield Doctrine, 1982–84. Mem., Wine Standards Board, 1984–96; Trustee, Wine and Spirit Educn Trust, 1989–92. Vice-Chm., Riverpoint Charity, 1996–98 (Trustee, 1994–2001); Chm., S Wilts MENCAP, 2004– (Pres., 2000–04); Dir, Wessex Community Action, 2005–. *Recreations:* marathons, European history, travel. *Address:* The Girnel, Broad Chalke, Salisbury, Wilts SP5 5EN. *T:* (01722) 780276.

READ, Harry; British Commissioner, Salvation Army, 1987–90; Editor, Words of Life, 1990–2000; *b* 17 May 1924; *s* of Robert and Florence Read; *m* 1950, Winifred Humphries (*d* 2007); one *s* one *d*. *Educ:* Sir William Worsley Sch., Grange Town, Middlesbrough. Served RCS, 1942–47 (6th Airborne Div., 1943–45). Commnd Salvation Army Officer, 1948; pastoral work, 1948–54; Lectr, Internat. Training Coll., 1954–62; pastoral work, 1962–64; Divl Youth Sec., 1964–66; Lectr, Internat. Training Coll., 1966–72; Dir, Information Services, 1972–75; Divl Comdr, 1975–78; Principal, Internat. Training Coll., 1978–81; Chief Sec., Canada Territory, 1981–84; Territorial Comdr, Australia Eastern Territory, 1984–87. *Recreations:* writing, hymns, poetry. *Address:* 4 Kingswood, 29 West Cliff Road, Bournemouth, Dorset BH4 8AY. *T:* (01202) 766457.
See also J. L. Read.

READ, Imelda Mary, (Mel); Member (Lab) East Midlands Region, European Parliament, 1999–2004 (Leicester, 1989–94; Nottingham and Leicestershire North West, 1994–99); *b* Hillingdon, 8 Jan. 1939; *d* of Robert Alan Hocking and Teresa Mary Hocking; *m*; one *s* one *d*, and one step *s*. *Educ:* Bishopshalt Sch., Hillingdon, Middx; Nottingham Univ. (BA Hons 1977). Laboratory technician, Plessey, 1963–74; researcher, Trent Polytechnic, 1977–80; Lectr, Trent Polytechnic and other instns, 1980–84; Employment Officer, Nottingham Community Relations Council, 1984–89. European Parliament: Chair, British Labour Gp, 1990–92; Quaestor, 1992–94. Contested (Lab): Melton, 1979; Leicestershire NW, 1983. Member: Nat Exec. Council, ASTMS, 1975; NEC, MSF; TUC Women's Adv. Cttee; Chair, Regl TUC Women's Cttee. Hon. Pres., European Cervical Cancer Assoc., 2003–. *Publication:* (jtly) Against a Rising Tide, 1992. *Recreations:* beekeeping, gardening.

READ, Sir John (Emms), Kt 1976; FCA 1947; President, Charities Aid Foundation, 1994–98 (Trustee, 1985–98; Chairman of Trustees, 1990–94); *b* 29 March 1918; *s* of late William Emms Read and of Daysie Elizabeth (*née* Cooper); *m* 1942, Dorothy Millicent Berry (*d* 2004); two *s*. *Educ:* Brighton, Hove and Sussex Grammar Sch. Served Royal Navy, 1939–46 (rank of Comdr (S) RNVR); Admiral's Secretary: to Asst Chief of Naval Staff, Admty, 1942–45; to Brit. Admty Technical Mission, Ottawa, Canada, 1945–46. Ford Motor Co. Ltd, 1946–64 (Admin. Staff Coll., Henley, 1952), Dir of Sales, 1961–64; Dir, Electric and Musical Industries Ltd, 1965–87; EMI Group: Jt Man. Dir, 1967; Chief Exec., 1969–79; Dep. Chm., 1973–74; Chm., 1974–79; Thorn EMI: Dep. Chm., 1979–81, Dir, 1981–87. Director: Capitol Industries-EMI Inc., 1970–83; Dunlop Holdings Ltd, 1971–84; Thames Television, 1973–88 (Dep. Chm., 1981–88); Wonderworld plc, 1984–97; Hill Samuel Gp, 1987–88; Caflash (formerly Cafman) Ltd, 1990–98; Chairman: TSB Holdings Ltd, 1980–86; Trustee Savings Banks Central Bd, 1980–88; Central TSB Ltd, 1983–86; TSB England and Wales, 1983–86; TSB Gp plc, 1986–88; UDT, 1981–85; Target Gp plc, 1987–88; FI Group plc, 1989–93. Chm., EDC for Electronics Industry, 1977–80. Member: (part time), PO Bd, 1975–77; Engineering Industries Council, 1975–80; BOTB, 1976–79; Armed Forces Pay Review Body, 1976–83; Nat. Electronics Council, 1977–80; Groupe des Présidents des Grandes Enterprises Européennes, 1977–80. Vice-Pres., Inst. of Bankers, 1982–89. Gen. Partner, Midland Enterprise Bd for SE, 1991–98; Member: RN Film Corp., 1975–83; Brighton Festival Soc. Council of Management, 1977–82; CBI Council, 1977–90 (Mem., Presidents' Cttee, 1977–84; Chm., F&GP Cttee, 1978–84); White Ensign Assoc. Council of Management, 1979–95; Council, The Prince's Youth Business Trust, 1987–89; Nat. Theatre Develt Council, 1987–90; Court, Surrey Univ., 1986–96; Governing Body and F&GP Cttee, BPMF, London Univ., 1982–96 (Dep. Chm., 1987–96); Governing Council, Business in the Community, 1985–89; Council, British Heart Foundn, 1986–89; Chm., Inst. of Neurology Council of Management, 1980–97; Trustee: Westminster Abbey Trust, 1978–85; Brain Res. Trust, 1982–2002 (Chm., 1986–2002); Crimestoppers Trust (formerly Community Action Trust), 1987–2001; Eyeless Trust, 1991–2002; Dir and Trustee, Brighton Fest. Trust, 1977–92; Dir, NCVO Ltd, 1990–94. President: SABC Clubs for Young People (formerly Sussex Assoc. of Boys' Clubs), 1982–97; Cheshire Homes, Seven Rivers, Essex, 1979–85; Governor, Admin. Staff Coll., Henley, 1974–92 (Hon. Fellow 1993). CCMI (FBIM 1974); CompIERE 1974; FIB 1982. Hon. Fellow, UCL, 1999. DUniv. Surrey, 1989; Hon. DBA Internat. Management Centre, Buckingham, 1990. *Recreations:* music, arts, sports, various charities. *Address:* Flat 68, 15 Portman Square, W1H 9LL. *T:* (020) 7935 7888. *Club:* MCC.

READ, John Leslie, FCA; Chairman, Carvest Inc., since 1988; *b* 21 March 1935; *s* of Robert and Florence Read; *m* 1958, Eugenie Ida (*née* Knight); one *s* one *d*. *Educ:* Sir William Turner's School. Partner, Price Waterhouse & Co., 1966–75; Finance Dir, then Jt Chief Exec., Unigate plc, 1975–80; Chairman: Macarthy plc, 1989–92 (Dir, 1986–92); LEP Gp, 1982–91; Director: MB-Caradon Group (formerly Metal Box) plc, 1979–92; Equity Law Life Assurance Soc. plc, 1980–87; Border and Southern Stockholders Investment Trust, later Govett Strategic Investment Trust, 1985–92. Chm., Audit Commn for Local Authorities in England and Wales, 1983–86. *Recreations:* music, sport, reading, photography. *Address:* 2 Milbrook, Esher, Surrey KT10 9EJ. *Club:* Royal Automobile.
See also H. Read.

READ, Keith Frank, CBE 1997; CEng, FIMarEST; FIET; Chief Executive (formerly Director General), Institute of Marine Engineering, Science and Technology (formerly Institute of Marine Engineers), since 1999; *b* 25 April 1944; *s* of Alan George Read, OBE and Dorothy Maud Read (*née* Richardson); *m* 1966, Sheila Roberts; one *s* two *d*. *Educ:*

King's Sch., Bruton; Britannia Royal Naval Coll., Dartmouth; Royal Naval Engrg Coll., Manadon. CEng 1972; FIET (FIEE 1988); FIMarEST (FIMarE 1998). Joined Royal Navy, 1962: trng appts, 1963–67; HM Submarine Ocelot, 1968–69; Nuclear Reactor Course, RNC, Greenwich, 1969; HM Submarine Sovereign, 1970–73; Sen. Engr, HM Submarine Repulse, 1974–76; Staff of Capt. Submarine Sea Trng, 1976–79; Comdr 1980; Sch. Comdr, HMS Collingwood, 1980; Ops (E), MoD, 1981–84; jsdc 1984; Exec. Officer, Clyde Submarine Base, 1984–88; Capt. 1988; Dep. Dir, Naval Logistic Plans, 1989; rcds 1990; Capt. Surface Ship Acceptance, 1991–92; Naval Attaché, Rome and Albania, 1992–96; retd RN, 1996; Manager, Southern Europe, Ganley Gp, 1997–98. Dir, Engrg and Technol. Bd, 2001–02; Mem. Bd, Science Council, 2003–. Dir, Marine South East, 2008. Chm., Cttee of Chief Execs of Engrg Instns, 2004–. Member: Adv. Bd, Greenwich Maritime Inst., 1999–; Tech. Cttee, RNLI, 2002–. FRSA 2000. Freeman, City of London, 2000. *Recreations:* family, Italy, music, theatre, sailing. *Address:* Institute of Marine Engineering, Science and Technology, 80 Coleman Street, EC2R 5BJ. *T:* (020) 7382 2660.

READ, Leonard Ernest, (Nipper), QPM 1976; National Security Adviser to the Museums and Galleries Commission, 1978–86; *b* 31 March 1925; *m* 1st, 1951, Marion Alexandra Millar (marr. diss. 1979); one *d*; 2nd, 1980, Patricia Margaret Allen. *Educ:* elementary schools. Worked at Players Tobacco factory, Nottingham, 1939–43; Petty Officer, RN, 1943–46; joined Metropolitan Police, 1947; served in all ranks of CID; Det. Chief Supt on Murder Squad, 1967; Asst Chief Constable, Notts Combined Constabulary, 1970; National Co-ordinator of Regional Crime Squads for England and Wales, 1972–76. British Boxing Board of Control: Mem. Council, 1976–82; Admin. Steward, 1982–88; Vice Chm., 1988–96, Chm., 1996–2000; Vice Pres., 1991–97, Pres., 1997–2005; Vice Pres., 1989–, Sen. Vice Pres., 1997–2001, World Boxing Council; Vice-Pres., World Boxing Assoc., 1989–2001. Freeman, City of London, 1983. *Publications:* with James Morton: Nipper (autobiog.), 1991; Nipper Read: the man who nicked the Krays (autobiog.), 2001. *Recreations:* home computing, playing the keyboard. *Address:* 23 North Barn, Broxbourne, Herts EN10 6RR.

READ, Lionel Frank; QC 1973; a Recorder of the Crown Court, 1974–98; a Deputy High Court Judge, 1989–98; *b* 7 Sept. 1929; *s* of late F. W. C. Read and Lilian (*née* Chatwin); *m* 1956, Shirley Greenhalgh; two *s* one *d*. *Educ:* Oundle Sch.; St John's Coll., Cambridge (MA). Mons OCS Stick of Honour; commnd 4 RHA, 1949. Called to Bar, Gray's Inn, 1954 (Bencher, 1981; Treas., 2001); Mem., Senate of the Inns of Court and the Bar, 1974–77. A Gen. Comr of Income Tax, Gray's Inn Div., 1986–90. Chm., Local Government and Planning Bar Assoc., 1990–94 (Vice-Chm., 1986–90); Member: Bar Council, 1990–94; Council on Tribunals, 1990–96. *Recreations:* reading, travel. *Address:* Cedarwood, Church Road, Ham Common, Surrey TW10 5HG. *T:* (020) 8940 5247. *Clubs:* Garrick; Hawks (Cambridge).

READ, Malcolm James; District Judge (Magistrates' Courts) (formerly Metropolitan Stipendiary Magistrate), since 1993; *b* 4 May 1948; *s* of Frank James Cruickshank Read and Anne Elizabeth (*née* Oldershaw); *m*; one *s* by previous marriage. *Educ:* Wallington Independent Grammar Sch.; Council of Legal Educn. Called to the Bar, Gray's Inn, 1979; Clerk to Justices, Lewes Magistrates' Court, 1980–81; Clerk to: Hastings, Bexhill, Battle and Rye Justices, 1981–91; E Sussex Magistrates' Courts Cttee, 1981–91; in private practice, Brighton, 1991–93. *Recreations:* motor-cycling, golf (occasionally). *Address:* Thames Magistrates' Court, 58 Bow Road, E3 4DJ. *T:* (020) 8271 1201.

READ, Mark; Director of Strategy, WPP, since 2002; Chief Executive Officer, WPP Digital, since 2006; *b* London, 19 Nov. 1966; *s* of Ian and Linda Read. *Educ:* Trinity Coll., Cambridge (MA Econs 1988); Harvard Univ. (Henry Fellow 1999); INSEAD (MBA 2003). Corporate Develt, WPP, 1989–95; Principal, Booz Allen & Hamilton, 1995–99; CEO, Webrewards, 1999–2001. *Recreations:* ski-ing, sailing, wine, food. *Address:* WPP, 27 Farm Street, W1J 5RJ. *T:* (020) 7408 2204; *e-mail:* mread@wpp.com.

READ, Dr Martin Peter; non-executive Director, British Airways, since 2000; Senior Advisor: Candover Partners, since 2008; HCL, since 2008; *b* 16 Feb. 1950; *s* of late Peter Denis Read and of Dorothy Ruby Read; *m* 1974, Marian Eleanor Gilbart; one *s* one *d*. *Educ:* Queen Mary's Grammar Sch., Basingstoke; Peterhouse, Cambridge (BA Nat. Scis 1971); Merton Coll., Oxford (DPhil Physics 1974). CDipAF 1976; FIET (FIEE 2005). Posts in sales and marketing, finance, ops, and systems develt, UK and overseas, Overseas Containers Ltd, 1974–81; Corp. Commercial Dir, Marine Coatings, 1981–84, Gen. Manager, Europe, 1984–85, International Paint, part of Courtaulds; joined GEC Marconi, 1985; Gen. Manager, Marconi Secure Radio, 1986–87; Dir, Marconi Defence Systems Ltd, 1987–89; Man. Dir, Marconi Command and Control Systems Ltd, 1989–91; Gp Man. Dir, Marconi Radar and Control Systems Gp, 1991–93; Gp Chief Exec., LogicaCMG (formerly Logica) plc, 1993–2007. Non-executive Director: ASDA Gp plc, 1996–99; Southampton Innovations Ltd, 1999–2003; Boots Gp plc, 1999–2006. Member: President's Cttee, 2004–07, Internat. Adv. Bd, 2007–, CBI; Strategy Bd, DTI, 2005–06. Trustee: Hampshire Technology Centre, 1990–; Southern Focus (formerly Portsmouth Housing) Trust, 1992–2000; Shelter, 2004– (Mem. Finance Cttee, 2000–04); Dir, Portsmouth Housing Assoc., 1993–2007. Mem., Council for Industry and Higher Educn, 2000– (Trustee, 2007–). Gov., Highbury Coll., Portsmouth, 1989–99; Mem. Council, Southampton Univ., 1999– (Dep. Chm., 2008–). Hon. DTech Loughborough, 2000. *Publication:* article in Jl of Applied Physics. *Recreations:* French and German novels, drama, military history, travel, gardening. *Address:* c/o British Airways, Waterside, PO Box 365, Harmondsworth UB7 0GB.
See also G. S. Read.

READ, Mel; *see* Read, I. M.

READ, Piers Paul, FRSL; author; *b* 7 March 1941; 3rd *s* of Sir Herbert Read, DSO, MC and late Margaret Read, Stonegrave, York; *m* 1967, Emily Albertine, *o d* of Evelyn Basil Boothby, CMG and of Susan Asquith; two *s* two *d*. *Educ:* Ampleforth Coll.; St John's Coll., Cambridge (MA). Artist-in-residence, Ford Foundn, Berlin, 1963–64; Sub-Editor, Times Literary Supplement, 1965; Harkness Fellow, Commonwealth Fund, NY, 1967–68. Member: Council, Inst. of Contemporary Arts, 1971–75; Cttee of Management, Soc. of Authors, 1973–76; Literature Panel, Arts Council, 1975–77; Council, RSL, 2001–. Adjunct Prof. of Writing, Columbia Univ., NY, 1980. Bd Mem., Aid to the Church in Need, 1988–. Trustee, Catholic Nat. Liby, 1998–. Governor: Cardinal Manning Boys' Sch., 1985–91; More House Sch., 1996–2000. Chm., Catholic Writers' Guild (the Keys), 1992–97. TV plays: Coincidence, 1968; The House on Highbury Hill, 1972; The Childhood Friend, 1974; radio play: The Family Firm, 1970. *Publications:* novels: Game in Heaven with Tussy Marx, 1966; The Junkers, 1968 (Sir Geoffrey Faber Meml Prize); Monk Dawson, 1969 (Hawthornden Prize and Somerset Maugham Award; filmed 1997); The Professor's Daughter, 1971; The Upstart, 1973; Polonaise, 1976; A Married Man, 1979 (televised 1983); The Villa Golitsyn, 1981; The Free Frenchman, 1986 (televised 1989); A Season in the West, 1988 (James Tait Black Meml Prize); On the Third Day, 1990; A Patriot in Berlin, 1995; Knights of the Cross, 1997; Alice in Exile, 2001; *non-fiction:* Alive, 1974 (filmed 1992); The Train Robbers, 1978; Quo Vadis? the subversion

---

of the Catholic Church, 1991; Ablaze: the story of Chernobyl, 1993; The Templars, 1999; Alec Guinness, The Authorised Biography, 2003; Hell and Other Destinations, 2006. *Address:* 23 Ashchurch Park Villas, W12 9SP.

READ, Prof. Randy John, PhD; Professor of Protein Crystallography, University of Cambridge, since 1998; *b* 9 June 1957; *s* of John and Anne Read; *m* 1995, Penelope Effie Stein; one *s* one *d*. *Educ:* Univ. of Alberta, Edmonton (BSc 1979; PhD 1986). Asst Prof., 1988–93, Associate Prof., 1993–98, Univ. of Alberta. *Publications:* contrib. papers on methods in protein crystallography and applications to medically relevant proteins. *Address:* Cambridge Institute for Medical Research, Wellcome Trust/MRC Building, Hills Road, Cambridge CB2 0XY. *T:* (01223) 336500, *Fax:* (01223) 336827; *e-mail:* rjr27@cam.ac.uk.

READE, Brian Anthony; HM Diplomatic Service, retired; *b* 5 Feb. 1940; *s* of Stanley Robert Reade and Emily Doris (*née* Lee); *m* 1964, Averille van Eugen; one *s* one *d*. *Educ:* King Henry VIII Sch., Coventry; Univ. of Leeds (BA Hons 1963). Interlang Ltd, 1963–64; Lectr, City of Westminster Coll., 1964–65; 2nd Sec., FCO, 1965–69; 2nd Sec., Bangkok, 1970–71, 1st Sec., 1971–74; FCO, 1974–77; Consul (Econ.), Consulate-General, Düsseldorf, 1977–81; FCO, 1981–82; 1st Sec., Bangkok, 1982–84; Counsellor (ESCAP), Bangkok, 1984–86; Counsellor, FCO, 1986–93. *Recreations:* watching sport, conversation, reading. *Clubs:* Coventry Rugby Football; Royal Bangkok Sports (Thailand).

READE, David Jarrett; QC 2006; *b* 20 April 1961; *s* of John and Margaret Reade; *m* 1989, Linda Jane Whitfield; two *d*. *Educ:* Prince Henry's High Sch., Evesham; Univ. of Birmingham (LLB 1982). Called to the Bar, Middle Temple, 1983. Mem., Tufty Club, RoSPA, 1967–. *Publication:* (jtly) the Law of Industrial Action and Trade Union Recognition, 2004; (contrib.) Transfer of Undertakings, 2007. *Recreations:* tennis, football (W Bromwich Albion), Rugby, music. *Address:* Littleton Chambers, 3 King's Bench Walk North, Temple, EC4Y 7HR. *T:* (020) 7797 8600; *e-mail:* dr@djreade.com.

READE, Sir Kenneth Roy, 13th Bt *cr* 1661, of Barton, Berkshire; *b* 23 March 1926; *s* of Leverne Elton Reade (*d* 1943; 5th *s* of Sir George Compton Reade, 9th Bt), and Norma B. Ward; *S* cousin, 1982; *m* 1944, Doreen D. Vinsant; three *d*. *Heir:* none.

READE, Rt Rev. Nicholas Stewart; *see* Blackburn, Bishop of.

READER, David George; HM Diplomatic Service, retired; Ambassador to Cambodia, 2005–08; *b* 1 Oct. 1947; *s* of late Stanley Reader and of Annie Reader; *m* 1969, Elaine McKnight; one *s* one *d*. *Educ:* Barrow Grammar Sch. Entered FO, later FCO, 1964; Warsaw, 1969–72; Paris, 1972–74; Bucharest, 1974–76; FCO, 1976–79; Kinshasa, 1979–82; Kathmandu, 1982–84; FCO, 1984–87; Consul, Brisbane, 1987–92; First Sec. (Mgt) and Consul, Belgrade, 1992–96; FCO, 1996–98; Dir, Trade & Investment, Cairo, 1998–2001; High Comr, Kingdom of Swaziland, 2001–05. *Address:* c/o Foreign and Commonwealth Office, King Charles Street, SW1A 2AH. *Club:* Royal Over-Seas League.

READER, Martin Sheldon; Headmaster, Wellington School, Somerset, since 2006; *b* 28 May 1967; *s* of Phillip John Reader and Juliet Elaine Reader; *m* 1994, Amanda Elizabeth Dyton; one *s* one *d*. *Educ:* St Olave's Grammar Sch.; University Coll., Oxford (Exhibitioner; BA Hons Eng. Lang. and Lit. 1989; MPhil Eng. Studies 1991; MA 1993); Homerton Coll., Cambridge (QTS 2002); Univ. of Hull (MBA 2004). Assistant Master: St Edward's Sch., Oxford, 1991–97; Oundle Sch., 1997–2002; Dep. Head, Laxton Sch. (subseq. merged with Oundle), 2000–02; Dep. Head, 2002–04, Sen. Dep. Head, 2004–06, Reigate Grammar Sch. *Recreations:* birdwatching, ski-ing, gym, reading, spending time with family, local church involvement. *Address:* Wellington School, South Street, Wellington, Somerset TA21 8NT. *T:* (01823) 668800, *Fax:* (01823) 668844; *e-mail:* admin@wellington-school.org.uk.

READER, Ven. Trevor Alan John, PhD; Archdeacon of Portsdown, since 2006; *b* 3 Aug. 1946; *s* of Clement and Lucy Reader; *m* 1968, Lesley Suzanne Taubman (*d* 2005); six *d*. *Educ:* Portsmouth Poly. (BSc 1968, MSc 1970, Zoology (London Univ. external); PhD 1972); Southern Dios, MTS, Salisbury and Wells Theol Coll. Research Asst, 1968–72, Lectr/Sen. Lectr, 1972–86, Portsmouth Poly. Ordained deacon, 1986, priest, 1987; Asst Curate, St Mary, Alverstoke, 1986–89; Priest i/c, St Mary, Hook-with-Warsash, 1989–98; Priest i/c, Holy Trinity, Blendworth, with St Michael and all Angels, Chalton, with St Hubert, Idsworth, and Diocesan Dir of Non-Stipendiary Ministry, dio. Portsmouth, 1998–2003; Archdeacon of IoW, 2003–06. Bp of Portsmouth's Liaison Officer for Prisons, 2003–06; Bp of Portsmouth's Advr to Hospital Chaplaincy, 2006–. Dir, Portsmouth Educn Business Partnership, 2004–. *Publications:* (jtly) Teaching Christianity at Key Stage 2, 2001; 16 articles relating to work in parasitology in scientific jls. *Recreations:* walking, surfing, reading, vegetable gardening, relaxing with family. *Address:* 5 Brading Avenue, Southsea, Hants PO4 9QJ.

READHEAD, Simon John Howard; QC 2006; a Recorder of the Crown and County Court, since 2000; *b* 3 Feb. 1956; *s* of Frederick John Readhead and Kathleen Mary Readhead; *m* 1987, Siobhan Elizabeth Mary O'Mahony; two *s*. *Educ:* Tonbridge Sch.; Lincoln Coll., Oxford (MA, BCL). Called to the Bar, Middle Temple, 1979; Jun., Midland and Oxford Circuit, 1989–90. Asst Recorder, 1995–2000. Lectr in Law, Hammersmith and W London Coll., 1979–81. Mem., Costs Panel, Gen. Council of the Bar, 1995–. Mem. Mgt Cttee, Permanent Exhibn of Judicial and Legal Costume, Royal Courts of Justice, 1979–. Chm. Govs, King's House Sch., Richmond, 2007–. *Address:* 1 Chancery Lane, WC2A 1LF. *T:* 0845 634 6666, *Fax:* 0845 634 6667; *e-mail:* sreadhead@1chancerylane.com.

READING, 4th Marquess of, *cr* 1926; **Simon Charles Henry Rufus Isaacs;** Baron 1914; Viscount 1916; Earl 1917; Viscount Erleigh 1917; Sino-British business consultant; *b* 18 May 1942; *e s* of 3rd Marquess of Reading, MBE, MC, and of Margot Irene, *yr d* of late Percy Duke, OBE; *S* father, 1980; *m* 1979, Melinda Victoria, *yr d* of late Richard Dewar, Hay Hedge, Bisley, Glos; one *s* two *d*. *Educ:* Eton. Served 1st Queen's Dragoon Guards, 1961–64. Member of Stock Exchange, 1970–74. Director: Nelson Recovery Trust, 1998–; Cure Internat., 2004–; KICC, 2005–; Westminster Oil, 2005–. Trustee, Garden Tomb, Jerusalem, 2002–. Patron, Barnabas Fund, 1998–. *Heir:* *s* Viscount Erleigh, *qv*. *Address:* 7 Cecily Hill, Cirencester, Glos GL7 2EF. *Clubs:* Cavalry and Guards, White's, MCC, All England Lawn Tennis and Croquet; Stoke Park (Pres., 2005–07).

READING, Area Bishop of, since 2004; **Rt Rev. Stephen Geoffrey Cottrell;** *b* 31 Aug. 1958; *s* of John and Eileen Cottrell; *m* 1984, Rebecca Jane Stirling; three *s*. *Educ:* Belfairs High Sch. for Boys; Poly. of Central London (BA (Hons) Media Studies, 1979); St Stephen's House, Oxford. Ordained deacon, 1984, priest, 1985; Curate, Christ Ch, Forest Hill, 1984–88; Priest-in-charge, St Wilfrid's, Chichester, and Asst Dir of Pastoral Studies, Chichester Theol Coll., 1988–93; Diocesan Missioner, Wakefield, 1993–98; Springboard Missioner, 1998–2001; Canon Pastor, Peterborough Cathedral, 2001–04. *Publications:* (ed jtly) Follow Me: a programme of Christian nurture for all ages, 1991;

Sacrament, Wholeness and Evangelism: a Catholic approach, 1996; (jtly) Emmaus: the way of faith, 1996; Catholic Evangelism, 1998; Praying Through Life: at home, at work and in the family, 1998; Travelling Well: a companion guide to the Christian life, 2000; (jtly) Vital Statistics, 2002; (jtly) Youth Emmaus, 2003; On This Rock: Bible foundations for Christian living, 2003; I Thirst: the cross–the great triumph of love, 2003; From the Abundance of the Heart: Catholic evangelism for all Christians, 2006; Do Nothing to Change Your Life, 2007. *Recreations:* reading poetry, cooking, playing the guitar, trying to play the ukulele banjo, lino printing. *Address:* Bishop's House, Tidmarsh Lane, Tidmarsh, Reading RG8 8HA. *T:* (0118) 984 1216, *Fax:* (0118) 984 1218; *e-mail:* bishopreading@oxford.anglican.org.

READING, David Michael Ronald, OBE 2005; Director, Anaphylaxis Campaign, since 1996; *b* 17 Aug. 1947; *s* of Ronald George Frederick and Winifred Mabel Reading; *m* 1987, Sylvia Anne Cruickshank; two *d* (and one *d* decd). *Educ:* Godalming County Grammar Sch. Reporter, Surrey Advertiser, 1965–69; Sub-editor: Aldershot News, 1970–72, 1975–80, 1982–88, 1993–98; Reading Evening Post, 1972–73; Bedfordshire Times, 1973–74; Oxford Mail, 1974–75; Licensee Mag., 1980–82; Dep. Ed., Wokingham Times, 1988–93. Mem. Editl Bd, Food Allergy and Intolerance, 2001–. *Recreations:* guitar playing, films, ornithology, fitness. *Address:* Anaphylaxis Campaign, 1 Alexandra Road, Farnborough, Hants GU14 6BU. *T:* (01252) 373793; *e-mail:* david@anaphylaxis.org.uk.

READING, (Ian) Malcolm, RIBA; Founder, 1996, Malcolm Reading & Associates (now Malcolm Reading Consultants); *b* 11 June 1957; *s* of Harold William Reading and Margaret (*née* Fletcher); *m* 1988, Catherine Jane Ormell; one *s*. *Educ:* George Heriot's Sch., Edinburgh; Univ. of Bristol (BA Arch. 1979; DipArch 1983). RIBA 1986; FCSD 1992. Bernard Hartley, architects, 1983–86; Andrews Downie and Partners, architects, 1986–89; Moxley Frankl Architects, 1989–90; Dir, Architecture and Design, British Council, 1990–96. Trustee, Historic Royal Palaces, London, 2005–. FRSA 1993. Hon. FRGS 2005. *Publications:* Lubetkin and Tecton: architecture and social commitment, 1981; Lubetkin and Tecton, 1992. *Recreations:* cycling, walking, avoiding gardening. *Address:* (office) 45–46 Berners Street, W1T 3NE; *e-mail:* malcolm@malcolmreading.co.uk.

READING, Peter Gray, FRSL; writer, since 1970; *b* 27 July 1946; *s* of Wilfred Gray Reading and Ethel Mary Reading; *m* 1st, 1968, Diana Joy Gilbert (marr. diss. 1996); one *d*; 2nd, 1996, Deborah Joyce Jackson (marr. diss. 2002); 3rd, 2002, Penelope Anne Hamblen. *Educ:* Liverpool Coll. of Art (BA Fine Art and Painting). Art Teacher, Ruffwood Sch., 1967–68; Lectr, Liverpool Coll. of Art, 1968–70; animal feedmill worker, 1970–92. FRSL 1988. *Publications: poetry:* Water and Waste, 1970; For the Municipality's Elderly, 1974; The Prison Cell and Barrel Mystery, 1976; Nothing for Anyone, 1977; Fiction, 1979; Tom o'Bedlam's Beauties, 1981; Diplopic, 1983; 5x5x5x5x5, 1983; C, 1984; Ukulele Music, 1985; Going On, 1985; Stet, 1986; Final Demands, 1988; Perduta Gente, 1989; Shitheads, 1989; Evagatory, 1992; Last Poems, 1994; Eschatological, 1996; Collected Poems, vol. 1, 1995, vol. 2, 1996, vol. 3, 2003; Work in Regress, 1997; Chinoiserie, 1997; Ob, 1998; Apothegmatic, 1999; Marfan, 2000; untitled, 2001; Faunal, 2002; –273.15, 2005. *Recreations:* ornithology, natural sciences. *Address:* c/o Bloodaxe Books, Highgreen, Tarset, Northumberland NE48 1RP.

READING, Dr Peter Richard; Managing Director, PRSC Ltd; *b* 1 May 1956; *s* of Dr Harold Garnar Reading and Barbara Mary Reading (*née* Hancock); *m* 2001, Dr Catherine Austin (*née* Fountain); one *s* two *d*, and two step *d*. *Educ:* St Edward's Sch., Oxford; Gonville and Caius Coll., Cambridge (MA); Birmingham Univ. (PhD); Moscow State Univ. Health service mgt posts in London, 1984–94; Chief Executive: Lewisham and Guy's Mental Health NHS Trust, 1994–98; UCL Hosps NHS Trust, 1998–2000; Univ. Hosps of Leicester NHS Trust, 2000–07. CCMI. *Recreations:* children, animals, Oxford United, Russian history. *Address:* Cherry Trees, 26 Middle Lane, Nether Broughton, Melton Mowbray, Leics LE14 3HD. *T:* 07813 438932; *e-mail:* info@peterreading.co.uk.

REAMSBOTTOM, Barry Arthur; a Senior Secretary to the Speaker of the House of Commons, since 2002; *b* 4 April 1949; *s* of Agnes Reamsbottom. *Educ:* St Peter's RC Secondary Sch., Aberdeen; Aberdeen Academy. Scientific Asst, Isaac Spencer & Co., Aberdeen, 1966–69; Social Security Officer, DHSS, Aberdeen, 1969–76; Area Officer, NUPE, Edinburgh, 1976–79; Civil and Public Services Association: Head of Educn Dept, 1979–87; Editor, Press Officer, 1987–92; Gen. Sec., 1992–98; Gen. Sec., PCS, 1998–2002. Vice-Pres., Trade Union Cttee for European and Transatlantic Understanding, 1996–. Member: Amnesty Internat., 1978–; NUJ, 1987–. *Recreations:* reading, golf, art appreciation, politics, music, taking photographs, laughter and the love of friends. *Address:* 156 Bedford Hill, SW12 9HW.

REARDON, Rev. John Patrick, OBE 1999; General Secretary, Council of Churches for Britain and Ireland, 1990–99; Moderator, General Assembly of the United Reformed Church, 1995–96; *b* 15 June 1933; *s* of John Samuel Reardon and Ivy Hilda Reardon; *m* 1957, Molly Pamela Young; four *s* one *d*. *Educ:* Gravesend Grammar Sch. for Boys; University College London (BA Hons English); King's College London (postgraduate Cert. in Educn). Teacher, London and Gravesend, 1958–61; Minister, Horsham Congregational Church, 1961–68 (Chm., Sussex Congregational Union, 1967); Minister, Trinity Congregational Church, St Albans, 1968–72 (Chm., Herts Congregational Union, 1971–72); Sec., Church and Society Dept, 1972–90, and Dep. Gen. Sec., 1983–90, URC. *Publications:* More Everyday Prayers (contrib.), 1982; (ed) Leaves from the Tree of Peace, 1986; (ed) Threads of Creation, 1989; Together Met, Together Bound, 2007. *Recreations:* modern literature, photography, philately, travel. *Address:* 1 Newbolt Close, Newport Pagnell, Bucks MK16 8ND. *T:* (01908) 217559.

REARDON SMITH, Sir (William) Antony (John), 4th Bt *cr* 1920, of Appledore, Devon; Trustee and Chairman, Joseph Strong Frazer Trust, since 1980; Chairman, North Eastern Rubber Company Ltd, 1980–2004; *b* 20 June 1937; *e s* of Sir William Reardon Reardon-Smith, 3rd Bt and his 1st wife, Nesta Florence Phillips (*d* 1959); *S* father, 1995; *m* 1962, Susan Wight, *d* of Henry Wight Gibson; three *s* one *d*. *Educ:* Wycliffe Coll. Nat. Service, RN, Suez, 1956. Sir William Reardon Smith & Sons Ltd and Reardon Smith Line plc, 1957–85 (Dir, 1959–85); Director: London World Trade Centre, 1986–87; Milford Haven Port Authority, 1988–99; Marine and Port Services Ltd, Milford Docks, 1990–99. Member: Baltic Exchange, 1959–87 (Dir, 1982–87; Assoc. Mem., 1990–92); Chamber of Shipping Documentary Cttee, 1963–72 (Chm., 1968–72); Documentary Council, Baltic and Internat. Conf., 1964–82. Dir, UK Protection and Indemnity Club and Freight, Demurrage and Defence Assoc., 1968–80. Trustee: Royal Merchant Navy Sch. Foundn, 1966–2003 (Vice-Pres., 1992–); Bearwood Coll., 1966–2003; Member: Council, King George's Fund for Sailors, 1981–95; City of London Cttee, RNLI, 1976–2006. Liveryman: World Traders' Co., 1986–; Poulters' Co., 1991–; Shipwrights' Co., 1994–; Clerk to Fuellers' Co., 2002–. GCLJ 2002 (KLJ 1997; Bailiff, 2002). *Recreations:* golf, shooting. *Heir:* *s* William Nicolas Henry Reardon Smith [*b* 10 June 1963; *m* 2001, Julia, *er d* of D. Martin Slade]. *Address:* 26 Merrick Square, SE1 4JB. *T:* (020) 7403 5723. *Clubs:* Cardiff and County; Royal Porthcawl Golf.

REASON, Prof. James Tootle, CBE 2003; FBA 1999; FRAeS; FBPsS; Professor of Psychology, University of Manchester, 1977–2001, now Emeritus; *b* 1 May 1938; *s* of late George Stanley Tootle and Hilda Alice Reason; *m* 1964, Rea Jaari; two *d*. *Educ:* Royal Masonic Sch.; Univ. of Manchester (BSc 1962); Univ. of Leicester (PhD 1967). FBPsS 1988; FRAeS 1998. RAF Inst. of Aviation Medicine, 1962–64; Lectr and Reader, Dept of Psychology, Univ. of Leicester, 1964–76. Hon. DSc Aberdeen, 2002. Dist. Foreign Colleague Award, US Human Factors and Ergonomics Soc., 1995. Hon. FRCGP 2006. Dist. Service Award, RoSPA, 2006. *Publications:* Man in Motion, 1974; Motion Sickness, 1975; Human Error, 1990; Beyond Aviation Human Factors, 1995; Managing the Risks of Organizational Accidents, 1997; Managing Maintenance Error, 2003. *Recreations:* reading, gardening, walking, sailing. *Address:* Woodburn, Red Lane, Disley, Cheshire SK12 2NP. *T:* (01663) 762406; *e-mail:* reason@redlane.demon.co.uk.

REAY, 14th Lord *cr* 1628, of Reay, Caithness; **Hugh William Mackay;** Bt of Nova Scotia, 1627; Baron Mackay of Ophemert and Zennewijnen, Holland; Chief of Clan Mackay; *b* 19 July 1937; *s* of 13th Lord Reay and Charlotte Mary Younger; *S* father, 1963; *m* 1st, 1964, Hon. Annabel Thérèse Fraser (*see* A. T. Keswick) (marr. diss. 1978); two *s* one *d*; 2nd, 1980, Hon. Victoria Isabella Warrender, *d* of 1st Baron Bruntisfield, MC; two *d*. *Educ:* Eton; Christ Church. Mem., European Parlt, 1973–79 (Vice-Chm., Cons. Gp); Delegate, Council of Europe and WEU, 1979–86. Lord in Waiting (Govt Whip), 1989–91; Parly Under-Sec. of State, DTI, 1991–92; Mem., Select Cttee on European Communities, H of L, 1993–99 (Chm., Sub-Cttee on Food and Agric., 1996–99); elected Mem., H of L, 1999. *Heir:* *s* The Master of Reay, *qv*. *Address:* House of Lords, SW1A 0PW.

REAY, Master of; Aeneas Simon Mackay; *b* 20 March 1965; *s* and *heir* of 14th Lord Reay, *qv*. *Educ:* Westminster School; Brown Univ., USA. *Recreations:* most sports, especially football, cricket and shooting.

REAY, Lt-Gen. Sir Alan; *see* Reay, Lt-Gen. Sir H. A. J.

REAY, David William; Chairman, Northumberland Mental Health NHS Trust, 1992–2001; *b* 28 May 1940; *s* of late Stanley Reay and Madge Reay (*née* Hall); *m* 1964, Constance Susan Gibney; two *d*. *Educ:* Monkwearmouth Grammar School, Sunderland; Newcastle upon Tyne Polytechnic. Independent Television Authority, 1960–62; Alpha Television (ATV and ABC) Services Ltd, 1962–64; Tyne Tees Television Ltd, 1964–72; HTV Ltd: Engineering Manager, 1972–75; Chief Engineer, 1975–79; Dir of Engineering, 1979–84; Man. Dir, 1984–91, Chief Exec., 1991, Tyne Tees Television Hldgs. Chairman: Hadrian Television Ltd, 1988–91; Legend Television Ltd, 1989–91; Man. Dir, Tyne Tees Television Ltd, 1984–91; Director: Tyne Tees Music, 1984–91; Tyne Tees Enterprises, 1984–91; ITCA, now ITVA, 1984–91; Independent Television Publications, 1984–89; Tube Productions, 1986–91; ITN, 1990–91; Tyne and Wear Develt Corp., 1986–88; The Wearside Opportunity Ltd, 1988–91. Mem. Council, Univ. of Newcastle upon Tyne, 1989–94. CCMI (CBIM 1987); FRTS 1984; FRSA 1992. *Recreations:* walking, reading, music, watching soccer (particularly Sunderland AFC). *Address:* 11 The Links, Ascot, Berks SL5 7TN.

REAY, Prof. Diane, PhD; Professor of Education, University of Cambridge, since 2005; *b* 21 July 1949; *d* of Arthur James Sutton and Lilian Mary Sutton (*née* Smart); *m* 1971, Keith Reay (marr. diss. 1995); one *s* one *d*. *Educ:* Ashby Girls' Grammar Sch., Ashby-de-la-Zouch; Univ. of Newcastle upon Tyne (BA Hons Pols and Econs 1970; PGCE 1971); Inst. of Educn, London (MA 1987); South Bank Univ. (PhD 1995). Teacher, ILEA, 1971–90; Advr, Islington LEA, 1990–92; Res. Scholar, South Bank Univ., 1992–95; Res. Fellow, 1995–2001, Sen. Lectr, 2001–03, KCL; Prof., London Metropolitan Univ., 2003–05. Member: 2008 RAE Educn Panel; ESRC Res. Grants Bd, 2006–. AcSS 2007. *Publications:* Class Work: mothers' involvement in their children's schooling, 1998; (ed jtly) Activating Participation: parents and teachers working towards partnership, 2004; (jtly) Degrees of Choice: social class, race and gender in higher education, 2005. *Address:* Faculty of Education, University of Cambridge, Hills Road, Cambridge CB2 2PQ. *T:* (01223) 767600, *Fax:* (01223) 767602.

REAY, Lt-Gen. Sir (Hubert) Alan (John), KBE 1981; FRCP, FRCPE; Chairman, Lambeth Health Care (formerly West Lambeth Community Care) NHS Trust, 1992–97; Director General, Army Medical Services, 1981–85; *b* 19 March 1925; *s* of Rev. John Reay; *m* 1960, Ferelith Haslewood Deane, artist and printmaker; two *s* two *d* (and one *s* decd). *Educ:* Lancing College; Edinburgh Univ. MB, DTM&H, DCH. FRCPE 1968; FRCP 1972. Field Medical Services, Malaya, 1949–52 (despatches); Exchange Physician, Brooke Hosp., San Antonio, Texas, 1957; Command Paediatrician: Far East, 1962; BAOR, 1965; Adviser in Paediatrics, MoD (Army), 1968; Hon. Out-patient Consultant, Great Ormond Street Hosp., 1975–79, 1985–87; QHP 1976–85; Postgraduate Dean and Comdt, Royal Army Med. Coll., 1977–79; DMS, HQ BAOR, 1979–81. Hon. Col, 217 (London) General Hosp. RAMC (Volunteers) TA, 1986–90. Chm., Med. Cttee, Royal Star and Garter Home, 1986–92. Member Council: SSAFA, 1986–93; RSocMed, 1987–91 (Pres., Paediatric Section, 1984–85). Pres., Friends of St Thomas' Hosp., 1993–2003. Vice-Chm., Thames Reach Homelessness Project, 1992–94; Chm., Mosaic Clubhouse for people with mental illness, 1997–2001; Trustee: Children's Hospice for Eastern Reg., Cambridge, 1988–97; Buttle Trust, 1991–2002. Chief Hon. Steward, Westminster Abbey, 1985–97. Inaugural Lectr, Soc. of Armed Forces Med. Consultants, Univ. of Health Scis, Bethesda, 1984. FRCPCH 1997 (Hon. Mem., BPA, 1988); Hon. FRCGP 1985. CStJ 1981 (OStJ 1979). *Publications:* paediatric articles in med. jls. *Address:* 63 Madrid Road, Barnes, SW13 9PQ.

REAY, Dr John Sinclair Shewan; Director, Warren Spring Laboratory, Department of Trade and Industry, 1985–92; *b* Aberdeen, 8 June 1932; *s* of late George Reay, CBE and Tina (*née* Shewan); *m* 1958, Rhoda Donald Robertson; two *s* one *d*. *Educ:* Robert Gordon's College, Aberdeen; Univ. of Aberdeen; Imperial College, London (Beit Fellow). BSc, PhD, DIC. CChem, FRSC. Joined Scottish Agricultural Industries, 1958; Warren Spring Lab., Min of Technology, 1968; Head of Air Pollution Div., DoI, 1972–77; Head, Policy and Perspectives Unit, DTI, 1977–79; Head of Branch, Research Technology Div., DoI, 1979–81; Dep. Dir, Warren Spring Lab., 1981–85. *Publications:* papers on surface chemistry and air pollution. *Recreations:* playing violin, listening to music. *Address:* 13 Grange Hill, Welwyn, Herts AL6 9RH. *T:* (01438) 715587.

REAY-SMITH, Richard Philip Morley; DL; Vice-Chairman, Painshill Park Trust, since 1985 (first Chairman, 1980–85); *b* 24 Nov. 1941; *m* 1972, Susan Margaret Hill; two *s*. *Educ:* Stowe Sch.; Durham Univ. (LLB); Harvard Business Sch. (AMP). Barclays Bank 1963–98: Local Dir, Shrewsbury, 1984–87; Dep. Chief Exec., Central Retail Services Div., 1987–91; Chief Exec., Barclaycard, 1991–94; Man. Dir, Personal Banking, 1995–98; Chm., Barclays Life Assurance Co. Ltd, 1996–98; Chief Exec., UK Retail Banking, 1998. Director: Visa Internat. Services Assoc., 1991–98; Legal & General Bank Ltd, 2001–03. DL Surrey, 2004. FRSA. *Recreations:* sailing, music, travel, classic and vintage motorsport.

REBUCK, Gail Ruth, (Lady Gould of Brookwood), CBE 2000; Chairman and Chief Executive, Random House Group Ltd (formerly Random House UK), since 1991; *b* 10 Feb. 1952; *d* of Gordon and Mavis Rebuck; *m* 1985, Philip Gould (*see* Baron Gould of Brookwood); two *d*. *Educ:* Lycée Français de Londres; Univ. of Sussex (BA). Production Asst, Grisewood & Dempsey, 1975–76; Editor, then Publisher, Robert Nicholson Publications, 1976–78; Publisher, Hamlyn Paperbacks, 1978–82; Publishing Dir, Century Publishing, 1982–85; Publisher, Century Hutchinson, 1985–89; Chm., Random House Div., Random Century, 1989–91. Non-exec. Dir, BSkyB, 2002–. Mem., Creative Industries Taskforce, 1997–2000. Non-exec. Dir, Work Foundn, 2001–08. Trustee: IPPR, 1993–2003; Nat. Literacy Trust, 2007–. Member: Court, Univ. of Sussex, 1997–; Council, RCA, 1999–. FRSA 1989. *Recreations:* reading, travel. *Address:* Random House Group Ltd, 20 Vauxhall Bridge Road, SW1V 2SA. *T:* (020) 7840 8886.

RECKERT, Prof. (Frederick) Stephen, FBA 1994; Camoens Professor of Portuguese, University of London, 1967–82, now Emeritus; Co-Founder, Institute for Study of Symbology, New University of Lisbon, 1980; Hon. Senior Research Fellow, Institute of Romance Studies, University of London, since 1995; *b* 31 May 1923; *o c* of Frederick Carl Reckert and Aileen Templeton Adams Reckert; *m* 1st, 1946, Olwen Roberts (*d* 1963); two *s* one *d*; 2nd, 1965, Dídia Mateus Marques. *Educ:* Phillips Exeter Acad., USA; Saybrook Coll., Yale (BA *summa cum laude* 1945, ranked first in class); Trinity Coll., Cambridge (MLitt 1948); Berkeley Coll., Yale (PhD 1950). Japanese translator with RAF, Bletchley, 1943–45; Fellow, Berkeley Coll. and Asst Prof. of Spanish, Yale, 1948–58; Prof. and Head of Hispanic Studies, Univ. of Wales, 1958–66; Head, Portuguese and Brazilian Studies, Univ. of London, 1967–82. Visiting Professor: Univ. of Madrid, 1971; New Univ., Lisbon, 1974–78; Univ. of Rome, 1985; Kate Elder Lectr, London Univ., 1996; Guest Lectr, Univs of Lisbon, Coimbra, Oporto, Évora, Seville, Warsaw, Jagiellonian Univ. of Cracow. Corresp. Fellow: Hispanic Soc. of America; Portuguese Acad. of Scis.; Royal Spanish Acad. Hon. Fellow, Asociación Hispánica de Literatura Medieval. Mem., Phi Beta Kappa. Nobiling Medal for Medieval Studies, Brazil, 1978. Comendador, Order of Southern Cross (Brazil), 1979; Grand Cross, Order of Henry the Navigator (Portugal), 1990. *Publications:* (with Dámaso Alonso) Vida y Obra de Medrano, 1958; (with Helder Macedo) Do Cancioneiro de Amigo, 1976, 3rd edn 1996; Gil Vicente, 1977; (with Y. K. Centeno) Fernando Pessoa, 1978; Espírito e Letra de Gil Vicente, 1986; Um Ramalhete para Cesário, 1987; Beyond Chrysanthemums, 1993; Play it Again, Sam, 1997; From the Resende Songbook, 1998; Más allá de las neblinas de noviembre, 2001; The Presence of East Asia in Some Modern Portuguese Poets, 2001; Gil Terrón lletrudo está, 2001; The Sign of the City: visions of mythic space, 2003; Al alba venid, buen amigo, 2004; The Cantigas Mínimas of a Pan-Iberian Poet, 2005; Itinerario de un iberista, 2006; The Other Latin, 2008; as Frederick Carlson: A Perfeição, Musée de l'Homme, Contos da Palma da Mão, 1994; Brasil e Alguns Poemas, 1999; contribs to jls and collective vols. *Recreations:* poetry, music, travel, conviviality, ailurophilia. *Address:* Rua das Janelas Verdes 17–4°, 1200–690 Lisbon, Portugal. *T:* 213962292; Ayot Weir, Weybridge, Surrey KT13 8HR. *T:* (01932) 843589. *Clubs:* Oxford and Cambridge; PEN (Portuguese centre).

REDDAWAY, David Norman, CMG 1993; MBE 1980; HM Diplomatic Service; Ambassador to Ireland, since 2006; *b* 26 April 1953; *s* of late George Frank Norman Reddaway, CBE and of Jean Reddaway, OBE (*née* Brett); *m* 1981, Roshan Taliyeh Firouz; two *s* one *d*. *Educ:* Oundle Sch. (Schol.); Fitzwilliam Coll., Cambridge (Exhibnr; MA Hist.). Volunteer teacher, Ethiopia, 1972. Joined FCO, 1975; language student, SOAS, 1976 and Iran, 1977; Tehran: Third Sec. later Second Sec. (Commercial), 1977–78; Second Sec. later First Sec. (Chancery), 1978–80; First Secretary: (Chancery), Madrid, 1980–84; FCO, 1985–86; Private Sec. to Minister of State, 1986–88; (Chancery), New Delhi, 1988–90; Chargé d'Affaires, Tehran, 1990–93 (Counsellor, 1991); Minister, Buenos Aires, 1993–97; Hd, Southern European Dept, FCO, 1997–99; Dir, Public Services, FCO, 1999–2001; UK Special Rep. for Afghanistan, 2002; Vis. Fellow, Harvard Univ., 2002–03; High Comr, Canada, 2003–06. Hon. Vice-Pres., Raleigh Internat., 1998–. *Recreations:* ski-ing, tennis, Persian carpets and art. *Address:* c/o Foreign and Commonwealth Office, King Charles Street, SW1A 2AH. *Club:* Hawks (Cambridge).

REDDICLIFFE, Paul, OBE 1998; HM Diplomatic Service, retired; Research Analyst for Cambodia, Laos, Thailand, and Vietnam, Foreign and Commonwealth Office, 1997–2008; *b* March 1945; *m* 1974, Wee Siok Boi; two *s*. *Educ:* Bedford Mod. Sch.; Jesus Coll., Oxford (MA Lit. Hum. 1967); Sch. of Oriental and African Studies, Univ. of London (MA SE Asian Studies 1973); Univ. of Kent. VSO, Vientiane, Laos, 1968–70 and 1971–72; joined HM Diplomatic Service, 1977; Indochina Analyst, Res. Dept, FCO, 1977–85; First Sec., Canberra, 1985–89; Indochina Analyst, 1989–92, Hd, S and SE Asia Section, 1992–94, Res. later Res. and Analysis, Dept, FCO; Ambassador to Kingdom of Cambodia, 1994–97. *Recreations:* bird-watching, books, P. G. Wodehouse, history. *Address:* c/o Foreign and Commonwealth Office, King Charles Street, SW1A 2AH.

REDDIHOUGH, John Hargreaves; His Honour Judge Reddihough; a Circuit Judge, since 2000; Resident Judge, Grimsby Combined Court, since 2001; *b* 6 Dec. 1947; *s* of Frank Hargreaves Reddihough and Mabel Grace Reddihough (*née* Warner); *m* 1981, Sally Margaret Fryer; one *s* one *d*. *Educ:* Manchester Grammar Sch.; Univ. of Birmingham (LLB Hons). Called to the Bar, Gray's Inn, 1969; barrister, 1971–2000; Asst Recorder, 1991–94; Recorder, 1994–2000. *Recreations:* ski-ing, gardening, music, travel, reading, sport. *Address:* Grimsby Combined Court, Town Hall Square, Grimsby, S Humberside DN31 1HX. *T:* (01472) 265250.

REDDINGTON, (Clifford) Michael; Chief Executive, Liverpool City Council, 1986–88; *b* 14 Sept. 1932; *s* of Thomas Reddington and Gertrude (*née* Kenny); *m* 1968 Ursula Moor. *Educ:* St Michael's Coll., Leeds; St Edward's Coll., Liverpool; Liverpool Univ. BCom 1953; CPFA (IPFA 1958); MBCS 1964. Served RAF, 1958–60. City Treasury, Liverpool, 1953–58 and 1960–86; Dep. City Treasurer, 1974, City Treasurer, 1982–86. Mem., Indep. Inquiry into Capital Market Activities of London Borough of Hammersmith and Fulham, 1990. Chairman: Liverpool Welsh Choral Union, 1990–93; Convocation, Univ. of Liverpool, 1993–96; Trust Fund Manager, Hillsborough Disaster Appeal Fund, 1989–98; Chm., James Bulger Meml Trust, 1993–98. Mem. Governing Body, and Chm. Finance Cttee, Nugent Care Soc., 1992–2005. Mem., World Bank mission to govts of Macedonia, Latvia, Armenia and Yugoslavia, 1999–2005. *Recreations:* fell-walking, cooking. *Address:* Entwood, 18 Westwood Road, Noctorum, Prenton CH43 9RQ. *T:* (0151) 652 6081. *Club:* Athenæum (Liverpool).

REDDISH, Prof. Vincent Cartledge, OBE 1974; PhD, DSc; FRSE; Professor Emeritus, Edinburgh University, 1980; *b* 28 April 1926; *s* of William H. M. Reddish and Evelyn Reddish; *m* 1951, Elizabeth Waltho; two *s*. *Educ:* Wigan Techn. Coll.; London Univ. (BSc Hons, PhD, DSc). Lectr in Astronomy, Edinburgh Univ., 1954; Lectr in Radio Astronomy, Manchester Univ., 1959; Royal Observatory, Edinburgh: Principal Scientific Officer, 1962; Sen. Principal Sci. Off., 1966; Dep. Chief Sci. Off., 1974; Regius Prof. of Astronomy, Edinburgh Univ., Dir, Royal Observatory, Edinburgh, and Astronomer Royal for Scotland, 1975–80. FRSE 1965. Governor, Rannoch Sch., 1981–97. *Publications:* Evolution of the Galaxies, 1967; The Physics of Stellar Interiors, 1974; Stellar Formation, 1978; The D-Force, 1993; Publications on the Physics of Dowsing No. 4: interferometry and spin-torsion fields, 2003; numerous sci. papers in Monthly Notices RAS, Trans RSE, Nature and other jls. *Recreations:* gardening, sailing, ornithology, research into torsion fields. *Address:* 11 Rothes Drive, Murieston, Livingston, West Lothian EH54 9HR. *T:* and *Fax:* (01506) 414393.

REDDROP, Gemma; *see* Bodinetz, G.

REDESDALE, 6th Baron *cr* 1902; **Rupert Bertram Mitford;** Baron Mitford (Life Peer), 2000; *b* 18 July 1967; *s* of 5th Baron and of Sarah Georgina Cranstoun, *d* of Brig. Alston Cranstoun Todd, OBE; *S* father, 1991; *m* 1998, Helen, *e d* of David Shipsey; two *s* two *d*. *Educ:* Highgate Sch.; Newcastle Univ. (BA Hons Archaeology). Outdoor instructor, Fernwood Adventure Centre, South Africa, 1990–91. Lib Dem spokesman on overseas development, H of L, 1993–99, on defence, 2000–05, on energy, 2005; Member: H of L Select Cttee on Sci. and Technology, 1994–97; EU (D) Agric. Select Cttee, 1998–2000. Mem. Council, IAM, 1995–; Pres., Natural Gas Vehicle Assoc., 1997–2004; Chair, Red Squirrel Protection Partnership, 2006–. Hon. Vice Pres., Raleigh Internat., 2000–. *Recreations:* caving, climbing, ski-ing. *Heir:* *s* Hon. Bertram David Mitford, *b* 29 May 2000. *Address:* House of Lords, SW1 0PW. *Club:* Newcastle University Caving.

REDFERN, Rt Rev. Alastair Llewellyn John; *see* Derby, Bishop of.

REDFERN, Michael Howard; QC 1993; a Recorder, since 1999; *b* 30 Nov. 1943; *s* of Lionel William Redfern and Kathleen Roylance Redfern (*née* Brownston); *m* 1st, 1966, Sylvia Newlands (marr. diss. 1989); one *d*; 2nd, 1991, Diana Barbara Eaglestone, *qv*; one *d*, and two step *d*. *Educ:* Stretford Grammar Sch. for Boys; Leeds Univ. (LLB Hons). Teacher, 1967–68; Lectr in Law, 1968–69; called to the Bar, Inner Temple, 1970, Bencher, 2002. *Recreations:* music, sport (preferably participating), travel, history. *Address:* 24a–28 St John Street, Manchester M3 4DJ.

REDFERN, Philip, CB 1983; Deputy Director, Office of Population Censuses and Surveys, 1970–82; *b* 14 Dec. 1922; *m* 1951, Gwendoline Mary Phillips; three *d*. *Educ:* Bemrose Sch., Derby; St John's Coll., Cambridge. Wrangler, Mathematical Tripos, Cambridge, 1942. Asst Statistician, Central Statistical Office, 1947; Chief Statistician, Min. of Education, 1960; Dir of Statistics and Jt Head of Planning Branch, Dept of Educn and Science, 1967. *Recreation:* walking from Yorkshire to Wester Ross.

REDFORD, (Charles) Robert; American actor and director; *b* 18 Aug. 1937; *s* of Charles Redford and Martha (*née* Hart); *m* 1958, Lola Jean Van Wagenen (marr. diss. 1985); one *s* two *d*. *Educ:* Van Nuys High Sch.; Univ. of Colorado; Pratt Inst., Brooklyn; Amer. Acad. of Dramatic Arts. *Theatre:* appearances include: Tall Story, Broadway, 1959; Sunday in New York, Broadway, 1961–62; Barefoot in the Park, Biltmore, NY, 1963–64; *television:* appearances include, The Iceman Cometh, 1960; *films* include: as actor: War Hunt, 1962; Inside Daisy Clover, 1965; Barefoot in the Park, 1967; Butch Cassidy and the Sundance Kid, 1969; The Candidate, 1972; The Way We Were, 1973; The Sting, 1973; The Great Gatsby, 1974; All the President's Men, 1976; The Electric Horseman, 1979; The Natural, 1984; Out of Africa, 1985; Legal Eagles, 1986; Havana, 1990; Sneakers, 1992; Up Close and Personal, 1996; Spy Game, 2001; The Last Castle, 2002; The Clearing, 2004; An Unfinished Life, 2006; as director: Ordinary People, 1980 (Acad. Award for Best Dir, 1981); Milagro Beanfield War (also prod.), 1988; A River Runs Through It, 1992; Indecent Proposal (also actor), 1993; The River Wild, 1995; The Horse Whisperer (also actor), 1998; The Legend of Bagger Vance, 2001; Lions for Lambs (also actor), 2007. Hon. Academy Award, 2002. *Publication:* The Outlaw Trail, 1978. *Address:* c/o Sundance Institute, PO Box 684429, Park City, UT 84068, USA.

REDFORD, Robert; *see* Redford, C. R.

REDGRAVE, Adrian Robert Frank; QC 1992; a Recorder of the Crown Court, since 1985; *b* 1 Sept. 1944; *s* of Cecil Frank Redgrave and Doris Edith Redgrave; *m* 1967, Ann Cooper; two *s* one *d*. *Educ:* Abingdon Sch.; Univ. of Exeter (LLB 1966). Called to the Bar, Inner Temple, 1968. *Recreations:* tennis, wine, garden, France, Bangalore Phall. *Address:* 1 Chancery Lane, WC2A 1LF. *T:* 0845 634 6666.

REDGRAVE, Corin William; actor and director; *b* 16 July 1939; *s* of Sir Michael Redgrave, CBE and Rachel Kempson; *m* 1st, 1962, Deirdre Hamilton-Hill (marr. diss. 1975; she *d* 1997); one *s* one *d*; 2nd, 1985, Kika Markham; two *s*. *Educ:* Westminster Sch.; King's Coll., Cambridge (Classical Schol.; BA 1st cl. Hons (English)). Joined Royal Court Th. as Asst Dir, 1962; Founder, Moving Th. at Riverside Studios, 1994; Associate Artist, Alley Th., Houston, 1996; launched Lichfield Garrick Th., 2003. With Royal Shakespeare Co., 1972–73, 1996–97 and 2004: *plays* include: The Romans, 1973; The General from America, 1996; King Lear, 2004, transf. Albery, 2005; Royal National Theatre: *plays* include: Marat/Sade, 1997; Not About Nightingales, 1998; The Cherry Orchard, 2000; De Profundis, 2000; No Man's Land, 2001; Honour, 2003; Pericles, Shakespeare's Globe, 2005; *plays directed* include: Romeo and Juliet, Moscow; Lillian, Lyric Shaftesbury and Fortune, 1986; Real Writing, Moving Th., 1995; Ousama, USA, 1995; *films* include: A Man for All Seasons, 1966; The Charge of the Light Brigade, 1968; The Magus, 1968; Oh! What a Lovely War, 1969; When Eight Bells Toll, 1971; The Red Baron, 1971; Excalibur, 1981; In the Name of the Father, 1993; Four Weddings and a Funeral, 1994; Honest, 2000; Enigma, 2001; To Kill a King, 2003; Enduring Love, 2004; *television* includes: Canterbury Tales, 1969; David Copperfield, 1969; Wagner, 1983; The Ice House, 1997; Trial and Retribution, 1997; The Woman in White, 1997; Trial and Retribution IV, 2000, VI, 2002; The Forsyte Saga, 2002; Shameless, 2004. *Plays written* for BBC Radio 4: Roy and Daisy; Fool for the Rest of his Life; Blunt Speaking; Saint Lucy. Ed., The Marxist, 1988–. *Publications:* Michael Redgrave: my father, 1995; Julius Caesar (Actors on Shakespeare series), 2003. *Recreations:* tennis, piano. *Address:* c/o Sadie Feast Management, 10 Primrose Hill Studios, Fitzroy Road, NW1 8TR.

See also L. R. Redgrave, V. Redgrave.

REDGRAVE, Diane Catherine; Her Honour Judge Redgrave; a Circuit Judge, since 2008; *b* 28 May 1953; *d* of Norman Redgrave and Kathleen Redgrave; *m* 1981, Nicholas Harvey; one *s* one *d*. *Educ:* Notre Dame Collegiate Sch. for Girls, Leeds; Bristol Polytech. (BA Hons (Law) 1974). Lectr in Law, Leeds Polytech., 1974–78; Vis. Lectr in Law, Dept of Econs, Bradford Univ., 1976–77. Called to the Bar, Middle Temple, 1977; District Judge, Principal Registry, Family Div., 1998–2008; Recorder, 2002–08. *Recreations:* my family, walking, ski-ing, reading, gardening. *Address:* Bow County Court, 96 Romford Road, E15 4EG.

REDGRAVE, Lynn Rachel, OBE 2002; actress; *b* 8 March 1943; *d* of late Sir Michael Redgrave, CBE, and Rachel Kempson; *m* 1967, John Clark (marr. diss. 2000); one *s* two *d*. *Educ:* Queensgate Sch.; Central Sch. of Speech and Drama. Nat. Theatre of GB, 1963–66 (Tulip Tree, Mother Courage, Andorra, Hay Fever, etc); Black Comedy, Broadway 1966; The Two of Us, Slag, Zoo Zoo Widdershins Zoo, Born Yesterday, London 1968–71; A Better Place, Dublin 1972; My Fat Friend, Knock Knock, Mrs Warren's Profession, Broadway 1973–76; The Two of Us, California Suite, Hellzapoppin,

US tours 1976–77; Saint Joan, Chicago and NY 1977; Twelfth Night, Amer. Shakespeare Festival, Conn, 1978; Les Dames du Jeudi, LA, 1981; Sister Mary Ignatius Explains It All For You, LA, 1983; The King and I, N American Tour, 1983; Aren't We All, 1985, Sweet Sue, 1987, Love Letters, 1989, Broadway; Les Liaisons Dangereuses, Don Juan in Hell, LA, 1989–91; Three Sisters, Queen's, 1990; A Little Hotel on the Side, The Master Builder, Broadway, 1991–92; The Notebook of Trigorin, Ohio, 1996; The Mandrake Root, Conn, 2001; Noises Off, Piccadilly, 2001. One-woman show, Shakespeare for my Father, NY and US tour, 1993. *Films include:* Tom Jones, Girl with Green Eyes, Georgy Girl (NY Film Critics, Golden Globe and IFIDA awards, Academy nomination Best Actress), Deadly Affair, Smashing Time, Virgin Soldiers, Last of the Mobile Hotshots, Every Little Crook and Nanny, National Health, Happy Hooker, Everything You Always Wanted to Know about Sex, The Big Bus, Sunday Lovers, Morgan Stewart's Coming Home, Getting it Right, Midnight, Shine, Gods and Monsters (Best Supporting Actress, Golden Globe award, 1999), Strike, The Simian Line, Touched, The Annihilation of Fish, The Next Best Thing, How to Kill Your Neighbor's Dog, My Kingdom, Unconditional Love, Anita and Me. *Television includes:* USA: Co-host of nationally televised talk-show, Not For Women Only, appearances in documentaries, plays, The Muppets, Centennial, Beggarman Thief, The Seduction of Miss Leona, Rehearsal for Murder, The Old Reliable, Jury Duty, Whatever Happened to Baby Jane?, Calling the Shots, Toothless, Indefensible: the truth about Edward Brannigan, White Lies, Different, and series: Housecalls (CBS); Teachers Only (NBC); Chicken Soup (ABC); Rude Awakening; BBC: A Woman Alone, 1988; Death of a Son, 1989; Calling the Shots, 1994. *Publications:* Diet for Life (autobiog.) (US as This is Living), 1991; Journal: a mother and daughter's recovery from breast cancer, 2005. *Recreations:* cooking, gardening, horse riding.

REDGRAVE, Maj.-Gen. Sir Roy Michael Frederick, KBE 1979; MC 1945; FRGS; *b* 16 Sept. 1925; *s* of late Robin Roy Redgrave and Michelene Jean Capsa; *m* 1953, Caroline Margaret Valerie, *d* of Major Arthur Wellesley and Margaret Baker-Kirby; two *s*. *Educ:* Sherborne Sch. Served War of 1939–45: enlisted Trooper, Royal Horse Guards, 1943; Lieut, 1st Household Cavalry Regt, NW Europe, 1944–45. GSO III Intell., HQ Rhine Army, 1950; Canadian Army Staff Coll., 1955; GSO II Ops HQ, London Dist, 1956; Recce, Sqn Ldr, Cyprus, 1959 (despatches); Mil. Assistant to Dep. SACEUR, Paris, 1960–62; JSSC 1962; Comd Household Cavalry Regt (Mounted), 1963–64; Comd Royal Horse Guards (The Blues), 1965–67; AAG PS12, MoD, 1967–68; Chief of Staff, HQ 2nd Div., 1968–70; Comdr, Royal Armoured Corps, 3rd Div., 1970–72; Nat. Defence Coll., Canada, 1973; Comdt Royal Armoured Corps Centre, 1974–75; British Comdt, Berlin, 1975–78; Comdr, British Forces, Hong Kong, and Maj.-Gen. Brigade of Gurkhas, 1978–80. Hon. Col 31st Signal Regt (V), 1983–88. Dir Gen., Winston Churchill Meml Trust, 1980–82. Member: Council, Charing Cross and Westminster Med. Sch., 1981–85; Hammersmith SHA, 1981–85; Council, Victoria League for Commonwealth Friendship; Britain Nepal Soc., 1982–. Chairman: Hammersmith and Fulham HA, 1981–85; Lambrook Appeal, 1984–85; Charing Cross and West London Hosps, 1988–97 (Special Trustee, 1981–99); Trustee: Westminster and Roehampton Hosps, 1988–93; Governor General's Horse Guards, Canada, 1987–; Chelsea and Westminster Hosp., 1993–97; Governor, Commonwealth Trust, 1989–97. Guest Lectr, tours to N Cyprus, Mexico, NZ, Albania, High Arctic, N Africa, 1982–2002. Grand Master, OSMTH, Order of Knights Templar, 1998–2005. *Publications:* Balkan Blue, 2000; The Adventures of Colonel Daffodil, 2007. *Recreations:* native peoples, wildlife, archaeology, philately. *Address:* 44 Slaidburn Street, Chelsea, SW10 0JW. *Club:* Cavalry and Guards.

REDGRAVE, Sir Steven (Geoffrey), Kt 2001; CBE 1997 (MBE 1987); DL; oarsman; sports consultant; *b* 23 March 1962; *m* 1988, Elizabeth Ann Callaway; one *s* two *d*. *Educ:* Great Marlow Sch. Represented: Marlow Rowing Club, 1976–2000; Leander, 1987–2000. Rowed coxless pairs with Andrew Holmes, until 1989, then with Matthew Pinsent; subseq. rowed coxless fours with Matthew Pinsent, James Cracknell and Tim Foster; winner: Commonwealth Games, 1986 (single sculls, coxed fours, coxless pairs); World Championships, coxed pairs, 1986, coxless pairs, 1987, 1991, 1993, 1994 and 1995; Gold Medal, Olympic Games, 1984 (coxed fours), 1988, 1992 and 1996 (coxless pairs), 2000 (coxless fours); Gold Medal, World Championships, coxless fours, 1997, 1998 and 1999. Founded Sir Steve Redgrave Charitable Trust, 2001; Vice President: Diabetes UK; British Olympic Assoc. Hon. DCL. DL Bucks, 2001. *Publications:* Steven Redgrave's Complete Book of Rowing, 1992; (with Nick Townsend): A Golden Age (autobiog.), 2000; You Can Win at Life!, 2005. *Address:* PO Box 3400, Marlow, Bucks SL7 3WX. *T:* (01628) 483021. *Club:* Leander (Henley-on-Thames).

REDGRAVE, Vanessa, CBE 1967; actress, since 1957; *b* 30 Jan. 1937; *d* of late Sir Michael Redgrave, CBE, and Rachel Kempson; *m* 1962, Tony Richardson (marr. diss. 1967; he *d* 1991); two *d*; *m* Franco Nero; one *s*. *Educ:* Queensgate School; Central School of Speech and Drama. Frinton Summer Repertory, 1957; Touch of the Sun, Saville, 1958; Midsummer Night's Dream, Stratford, 1959; Look on Tempests, 1960; The Tiger and the Horse, 1960; Lady from the Sea, 1960; Royal Shakespeare Theatre Company: As You Like It, 1961, Taming of the Shrew, 1961, Cymbeline, 1962; The Seagull, 1964; The Prime of Miss Jean Brodie, Wyndham's, 1966; Daniel Deronda, 1969; Cato Street, 1971; The Threepenny Opera, Prince of Wales, 1972; Twelfth Night, Shaw Theatre, 1972; Antony and Cleopatra, Bankside Globe, 1973; Design for Living, Phoenix, 1973; Macbeth, LA, 1974; Lady from the Sea, NY, 1976, Roundhouse, 1979; The Aspern Papers, Haymarket, 1984; The Seagull, Queen's, 1985; Chekhov's Women, Lyric, 1985; The Taming of the Shrew and Antony and Cleopatra, Haymarket, 1986; Ghosts, Young Vic, transf. Wyndham's, 1986; Touch of the Poet, Young Vic, transf. Comedy, 1988; Orpheus Descending, Haymarket, 1988, NY, 1989; A Madhouse in Goa, Lyric, Hammersmith, 1989; Three Sisters, Queen's, 1990; When She Danced, Globe, 1991; Heartbreak House, Haymarket, 1992; The Liberation of Skopje, Antony and Cleopatra, Riverside, 1995; John Gabriel Borkman, NT, 1996; The Tempest, Globe, 2000; The Cherry Orchard, RNT, 2000; Lady Windermere's Fan, Haymarket, 2002; Long Day's Journey into Night, NY (Best Actress, Tony Award), 2003; Hecuba, Albery, 2005; The Year of Magical Thinking, NT, 2008. *Films:* Morgan—A Suitable Case for Treatment, 1966 (Cannes Fest. Award, Best Actress 1966); The Sailor from Gibraltar, 1967; Blow-Up, 1967; Camelot, 1967; Red White and Zero, 1967; Charge of the Light Brigade, 1968; Isadora, 1968; A Quiet Place in the Country, 1968; The Seagull, 1969; Drop-Out, 1970; La Vacanza, 1970; The Trojan Women, 1971; The Devils, 1971; Mary, Queen of Scots, 1972; Murder on the Orient Express, 1974; Out of Season, 1975; Seven Per Cent Solution, 1975; Julia, 1976 (Academy Award, 1977; Golden Globe Award); Agatha, 1978; Yanks, 1978; Bear Island, 1978; Playing for Time, 1980; My Body, My Child, 1981; Wagner, 1983; The Bostonians, 1984; Wetherby, 1985; Steaming, 1985; Comrades, 1987; Prick Up Your Ears, 1987; Consuming Passions, 1988; A Man For All Seasons, 1988; Orpheus Descending, 1990; Young Catherine, 1990; Whatever Happened to Baby Jane, 1990; The Ballad of the Sad Café, 1991; Howards End, 1992; The House of the Spirits, 1994; Mother's Boys, 1994; Little Odessa, 1995; A Month by the Lake, 1996; Mission: Impossible, 1996; Looking for Richard, 1997; Wilde, 1997; Smilla's Feeling for Snow, 1997; Mrs Dalloway, 1998; Deep Impact, 1998; Cradle Will Rock, 2000; Venus, 2007; Evening, 2007. Television incl. The Gathering Storm, 2002 (Best Actress, BPG awards, 2003). *Publications:* Pussies and Tigers (anthology of writings of school children), 1963; Vanessa Redgrave: an autobiography, 1991. *Address:* c/o Gavin Barker Associates, 2d Wimpole Street, W1G 0ED.

See also Joely Richardson, N. J. Richardson.

REDHEAD, Prof. Michael Logan Gonne, FBA 1991; Professor of History and Philosophy of Science, Cambridge University, 1987–97; Fellow, Wolfson College, Cambridge, 1988–97, now Emeritus Fellow (Vice-President, 1992–96); *b* 30 Dec. 1929; *s* of Robert Arthur Redhead and Christabel Lucy Gonne Browning; *m* 1964, Jennifer Anne Hill; three *s*. *Educ:* Westminster Sch.; University College London (BSc 1st Cl. Hons Physics 1950; PhD Mathematical Phys. 1970). FInstP 1982. Dir, Redhead Properties Ltd, 1962; Partner, Galveston Estates, 1970; Lectr, Sen. Lectr in Philosophy of Science, 1981–84, Prof., Philosophy of Physics, 1984–85, Chelsea Coll., Univ. of London; Prof. of Philosophy of Physics, King's College London, 1985–87; Hd, 1987–93, Chm., 1993–95, Dept of Hist. and Philosophy of Sci., Cambridge Univ. London School of Economics: Actg Dir, 1998–2001, Co-Dir, 2001–, Centre for Philosophy of Natural and Social Sci.; Centennial Prof. of Philosophy, 1999–2002. Tarner Lectr, Trinity Coll., Cambridge, 1991–94; Visiting Fellow: Pittsburgh Univ., 1985; Princeton Univ., 1991; LSE, 1994; All Souls Coll., Oxford, 1995; Vis. Prof., Essex Univ., 2004–07. Leverhulme Emeritus Fellow, 2008. Pres., British Soc. for Philos. of Sci., 1989–91. Mem., Acad. Internat. de Philosophie des Sciences, 1995. FKC 2000. Lakatos Award in Philosophy of Science, 1988. Editor, Studies in History and Philosophy of Modern Physics, 1993–2001. *Publications:* Incompleteness, Nonlocality and Realism, 1987; From Physics to Metaphysics, 1995; (with T. Debs) Objectivity, Invariance and Convention, 2007; (with T. Debs) God, Belief and Explanation, 2008; papers in learned jls. *Recreations:* tennis, poetry, music. *Address:* 119 Rivermead Court, Hurlingham, SW6 3SD. *T:* (020) 7736 6767. *Clubs:* Athenæum, Hurlingham.

REDIKER, Dennis L.; Chief Executive Officer, Standard Register, since 2000; *b* USA, 1 Jan. 1944; *m* 1st, 1965, Carolyn M. Hoehn; two *s*; 2nd, 1983, Sharon A.; one *d*. *Educ:* Del Mar High, Campbell, Calif; Univ. of Calif, Santa Barbara (BS Electrical Engrg 1966). MIEEE. Various rôles in Engrg, Sales, Product and Mkt Planning, IBM, 1966–83; Mead Corporation, 1983–93: Vice-Pres., Strategy and Mkt Develt, 1983–85 and Systems and Technol., 1985–86, Mead Data Central; Vice-Pres., Corporate Planning, Strategy and Planning, 1986–89; Pres., Mead Coated Board Div., 1989–93; English China Clays plc, subseq. ECC International Inc., 1993–99: Pres. and CEO, ECCI Ampac; Exec. Dir, 1995–99; Chief Executive: English China Clays plc, 1996–99; ECC Internat. Inc., 1999; CEO, Pigments and Additives Gp, Imerys, 1999–2000. *Address:* Standard Register, PO Box 1167, Dayton, OH 45401–1167, USA.

REDING, Dr Viviane; Member, European Commission, since 1999; *b* 27 April 1951; *m*; three *s*. *Educ:* Sorbonne, Paris (PhD). Journalist, Luxemburger Wort, 1978–99; Pres., Luxembourg Union of Journalists, 1986–98. MP (PCS) Luxembourg, 1979–89; MEP (EPP) Luxembourg, 1989–99. Nat. Pres., Christian-Social Women, 1988–93; Vice Pres., Parti Chrétien-Social, Luxembourg, 1995–99. *Address:* European Commission, 200 rue de la Loi, 1049 Brussels, Belgium.

REDMAN, Rev. Anthony James, FRICS; Partner, Whitworth Co. Partnership, Architects and Surveyors, since 1985 (Managing Partner, 1985–2002); *b* 1 May 1951; *s* of Alan Redman and Diana Redman (*née* Cooke); *m* 1974, Caroline Blackwood Ford; two *d*. *Educ:* Walton-on-Thames Secondary Modern Sch.; Surbiton Grammar Sch.; Univ. of Reading (BSc Hons Estate Mgt); East Anglian MTS; Anglia Ruskin Univ. (MA Pastoral Theol. 2005). FRICS 1998; IHBC 1998. Surveyor: Lister Drew and Associates, 1972–74; Suffolk CC, 1974–79; Asst Surveyor, Whitworth & Hall, 1979–85. Surveyor of Fabric, St Edmundsbury Cathedral, 1992–. Chm., RICS Bldg Conservation Gp, 1997–2000; Mem., RICS Conservation Bd, 2000–03. Ordained deacon, 2003, priest, 2004; NSM, N Bury Team, 2003–05; Asst priest NSM, Blackbourne Team, 2006–. Member: Gen. Synod of C of E, 1989–2003; Council for Care of Churches, 1990–2001 (Jt Vice Chm., 1996–2001); Westminster Abbey Fabric Adv. Commn, 1998–; St Albans DAC, 1998–2004; Cathedrals Fabric Commn for England, 1999–2003; Cathedrals Measure Revision Cttee, 2001–02. Mem., Baptist Union Listed Bldg Adv. Panel, 1997–. Mem., Romanian Hospice of Hope Appeal Cttee, 2003–. Liveryman, Masons' Co., 2008–. Freeman, City of London, 2008. *Publications:* (ed jtly) A Guide to Church Inspection and Repair, 1996; (ed with M. Carnell) A Taste of Transylvania, 2006. *Recreations:* gardening, painting, Romania, local history, avoiding household maintenance. *Address:* (office) 18 Hatter Street, Bury St Edmunds, Suffolk IP33 1NE. *T:* (01284) 760421; *e-mail:* TRedman@whitcp.co.uk.

REDMAN, Prof. Christopher Willard George, FRCP, FRCOG; Consultant and Clinical Professor of Obstetric Medicine, Nuffield Department of Obstetrics and Gynaecology, Oxford University, since 1992; Fellow of Lady Magaret Hall, Oxford, since 1988; *b* 30 Nov. 1941; *s* of late Roderick Oliver Redman and Annie Kathleen Redman (*née* Bancroft); *m* 1964, Corinna Susan Page; four *s* one *d*. *Educ:* St John's Coll., Cambridge (MA; MB, BChir). FRCP 1981; FRCOG (*ad eund*) 1993. Oxford University: Clinical Lectr, Dept of Regius Prof. of Medicine, 1970–76; Univ. Lectr and Consultant, Nuffield Dept of Obstetrics and Gynaecol., 1976–89; Clinical Reader and Cons., 1989–92. Pres., Internat. Soc. for Study of Hypertension in Pregnancy, 2006–08. *Publications:* scientific articles about pre-eclampsia in med. jls. *Recreation:* hill-walking. *Address:* Nuffield Department of Obstetrics and Gynaecology, John Radcliffe Maternity Hospital, Headington, Oxford OX3 9DU. *T:* (01865) 221009.

REDMAN, Maj.-Gen. Denis Arthur Kay, CB 1963; OBE 1942; retired; Colonel Commandant, REME, 1963–68; Director, Electrical and Mechanical Engineering, War Office, 1960–63; *b* 8 April 1910; *s* of late Brig. A. S. Redman, CB; *m* 1943, Penelope (*d* 2007), *d* of A. S. Kay; one *s* one *d*. *Educ:* Wellington Coll.; London Univ. (BSc (Eng) 1st class Hons). CEng. Commissioned in RAOC, 1934; served in Middle East, 1936–43; transferred to REME, 1942; Temp. Brig., 1944; DDME 1st Corps, 1951; Comdt REME Training Centre 1957–59. Graduate of Staff Coll., Joint Services Staff Coll. and Imperial Defence Coll. Pres., Ramsbury RBL, 1985–96. FCGI. *Recreations:* normal.

REDMAN, Maurice; Chairman, Scottish Region, British Gas Corporation, 1974–82 (Deputy Chairman, 1970–74); *b* 30 Aug. 1922; *s* of Herbert Redman and Olive (*née* Dyson); *m* 1960, Dorothy (*née* Appleton); two *d*. *Educ:* Hulme Grammar Sch., Oldham; Manchester Univ. BSc(Tech), 1st cl. Hons. Joined staff of Co. Borough of Oldham Gas Dept, 1943; Asst, later Dep. Production Engr, North Western Gas Bd, 1951; Chief Develt Engr, NW Gas Bd, 1957; Chief Engr, Southern Gas Bd, 1966; Dir of Engrg, Southern Gas Bd, 1970. Mem., Internat. Gas Union Cttee on Manufactured Gases, 1961–82. *Publications:* papers to Instn of Gas Engrs, Inst. of Fuel, various overseas conferences, etc. *Recreations:* gardening, music, photography. *Address:* Avington, 3 Cramond Regis, Edinburgh EH4 6LW. *T:* (0131) 312 6178. *Club:* New (Edinburgh).

REDMAYNE, Clive; retired aeronautical engineer; *b* 27 July 1927; *s* of late Procter Hubert Redmayne and Emma (*née* Torkington); *m* 1952, Vera Muriel, *d* of late Wilfred Toplis and Elsie Maud Toplis; one *s* one *d*. *Educ:* Stockport Sch. BSc (Hons Maths)

London External. CEng, MIMechE; FRAeS. Fairey Aviation Co.: apprentice, 1944–48; Stress Office, 1948–50; English Electric Co., Warton: Stress Office, 1950–51; A. V. Roe & Co., Chadderton: Stress Office, 1951–55; A. V. Roe & Co., Weapons Research Div., Woodford: Head of Structural Analysis, 1955–62; Structures Dept, RAE, 1962–67; Asst Director, Project Time and Cost Analysis, Min. of Technology, 1967–70; Sen. Officers' War Course, RNC, Greenwich, 1970; Asst Dir, MRCA, MoD(PE), 1970–74; Division Leader, Systems Engrg, NATO MRCA Management Agency (NAMMA), Munich, 1974–76; Chief Supt, A&AEE, Boscombe Down, 1976–78; Dir, Harrier Projects, MoD(PE), 1978–80; Director General, Future Projects, MoD(PE), 1980–81; Dir Gen. Aircraft 3, Procurement Exec., MoD, 1981–84. *Recreations:* reading, chess, bridge. *Address:* Bowstones, 5 Westbrook View, Stottingway Street, Upwey, Weymouth, Dorset DT3 5QA. *T:* (01305) 814691.

REDMAYNE, Hon. Sir Nicholas (John), 2nd Bt *cr* 1964; *b* 1 Feb. 1938; *s* of Baron Redmayne, DSO, PC (Life Peer) and Anne (*d* 1982), *d* of John Griffiths; *S* to baronetcy of father, 1983; *m* 1st, 1963, Ann Saunders (marr. diss. 1976; she *d* 1985); one *s* one *d*; 2nd, 1978, Christine Diane Wood Hewitt (*née* Fazakerley); two step *s*. *Educ:* Radley College; RMA Sandhurst. Grenadier Guards, 1957–62. Joined Grieveson, Grant, later Kleinwort Benson Securities, 1963; Dir, 1987, Chief Exec., 1994–96, Kleinwort Benson Ltd; Dir, 1989–96, Dep. Chm., 1996, Kleinwort Benson Gp; Chairman: Kleinwort Benson Securities, 1990–96; Kleinwort Benson Investment Mgt, 1995–96. *Recreations:* shooting, ski-ing. *Heir:* *s* Giles Martin Redmayne [*b* 1 Dec. 1968; *m* 1994, Claire Ann O'Halloran; two *s*]. *Address:* Walcote Lodge, Walcote, Lutterworth, Leics LE17 4JR.

REDMOND, Anthony Gerard, FCPA, CPFA; Chairman and Chief Executive, Commission for Local Administration, and Local Government Ombudsman, since 2001; *b* 18 May 1945; *s* of Alfonso and Florence Redmond; *m* 1973, Christine Mary Pinnington; two *s* two *d*. *Educ:* St Mary's Coll., Crosby. CPFA 1969; FCPA 2005. Liverpool City Council: various accountancy and audit posts, 1962–75; Chief Accountant, 1975–78; Dep. Treas., Wigan MBC, 1978–82; Treasurer: and Dep. Chief Exec., Knowsley MBC, 1982–87; Merseyside Police Authy, 1985–87; W London Waste Authy, 1987–2001; Chief Exec., London Borough of Harrow, 1987–2001. FRSA 1994. *Recreations:* sport, theatre, ballet, good food and fine wines. *Address:* Commission for Local Administration in England, Millbank Tower, Millbank, SW1P 4QP. *T:* (020) 7217 4620, *Fax:* (020) 7217 4621. *Clubs:* Wasps Rugby, Waterloo Rugby (Blundellsands), Lancashire Rugby; Cricketers; Guild of Freemen.

REDMOND, Ian Michael, OBE 2006; CBiol, FZS; independent wildlife biologist, since 1979; Head, Technical Support Team, since 2001, Chief Consultant, since 2005, UNEP/UNESCO Great Ape Survival Project, under contract to Born Free Foundation and United Nations Environment Programme; *b* 11 April 1954; *s* of Maj. Peter Redmond, RAMC (retd) and Margaret Redmond; *m* 1982, Caroline Ireland; two *s*. *Educ:* Beverley Grammar Sch., E Yorks; Kelvin Hall High Sch.; Univ. of Keele (BSc Hons Biol. with Geol. 1976). FZS 1979; MIBiol 1985, CBiol 1986. Res. Asst to Dr Dian Fossey, Karisoke Res. Centre, Rwanda, 1976–78; zoologist, Operation Drake, PNG, 1979; field conservationist, Fauna Preservation Soc., Mt Gorilla Project, Rwanda, 1980; zoologist/botanist, Operation Drake, Kenya, 1980; estabd Mt Elgon Elephant Caves Res. Project, Kenya, 1981–. Hon. Res. Associate, Dept of Psychol., Univ. of Hull, 1981–. Scientific Advr for, and sometimes featured in, numerous natural history documentaries, eg by BBC, Nat. Geographic, US and French TV, 1977–; freelance lecturer: UK and Africa, 1978–; N America, 1986–; public speaker, Foyles Lecture Agency, 1980–; freelance natural history photo-journalist, 1982–; reporter, BBC Wildlife Mag., 1983–84; Leader, Wildlife Special Interest Tours, 1983–2001. Consultant, 1986–, various conservation and animal welfare orgns, including: Dian Fossey Gorilla Fund (formerly Digit Fund); Born Free Foundn; Internat. Fund for Animal Welfare; Tusk Force; Internat. Primate Protection League; Bristol Zoo Gdns; WSPA, etc. Accredited observer, Convention on Internat. Trade in Endangered Species of Wild Fauna and Flora, Lausanne, 1989, Kyoto, 1992, Fort Lauderdale, 1994, Harare, 1997, Nairobi, 2000, Santiago, Chile, 2002; Bangkok, 2004. Founder: and Co-ordinator, African Ele-Fund, 1987– (Co-founder, Elefriends, subseq. part of Born Free Foundn, 1989); and Chm., UK Rhino Gp, 1993–; and Chm., Ape Alliance, 1996–. Mem., British Herpetological Soc., 1981–. Member: Yorks Wildlife Trust, 1970–; Jersey Wildlife Preservation Trust, 1973–; Fauna and Flora Internat., 1978–; E African Wildlife Soc., 1980–; Elephant Res. Foundn (formerly Elephant Interest Gp), 1982–; Primate Soc. of GB, 1982– (Mem. Conservation Wkg Party, 1988–; Mem. Council, 1996–99); Wildlife Conservation Soc. of Tanzania, 1992–; Elephant, Primates and Rhino/Tiger Wkg Gps, Species Survival Network, 1995–. Trustee: Orangutan Foundn-UK, 1993–; The Gorilla Organization (formerly Dian Fossey Gorilla Fund Europe), 2004–; Great Ape Film Initiative, 2006–. *Publications:* The Elephant in the Bush, 1990; (with V. Harrison) The World of Elephants, 1990; Monkeys and Apes, 1990; Wildlife at Risk: Gorillas, 1990; Wildlife at Risk: Elephants, 1990; The Elephant Book, 1990, 2nd edn 2001 (Friends of the Earth Earthworm Award, 1991); (jtly) Elephants - the Deciding Decade (Canada), 1991, 2nd edn 1997, UK edn as Elephants, Saving the Gentle Giants, 1993; Eyewitness Elephant, 1993; Eyewitness Gorilla and other primates, 1995; contrib. numerous scientific reports and papers, news reports and feature articles to wildlife mags worldwide, and newspapers incl. Guardian, Kuwait Times, Arab Post, Hong Kong Standard, Jakarta Post. *Recreations:* natural history, travel, outdoor activities, collecting antiquarian books and 78rpm records, minimum-intervention gardening and home maintenance. *Address:* PO Box 308, Bristol BS99 7LQ. *T:* and *Fax:* (0117) 924 6489; *e-mail:* ele@globalnet.co.uk.

REDMOND, Imelda; Chief Executive, Carers UK, since 2003; *b* 7 June 1959; *d* of Andy and Alice Redmond; *m* Jo Clare; one step *s*. *Educ:* Froebel Inst. (BA Hons (Social Admin) Univ. of London). Dir, Markfield Project, 1989–98; Dep. CEO, Carers UK, 1998–2003. *Address:* Carers UK, Longstone Court, 22 Great Dover Street, SE1 4LB.

REDMOND, Phil, CBE 2004; writer and television producer; Founder, The Mersey Television Co. Ltd (Chairman, 1981–2005); Chairman, Merseyfilm, since 2003; *m* Alexis Jane Redmond. *Educ:* Univ. of Liverpool (BA Hons). Writer, Grange Hill, 1978–81; Executive Producer: Brookside, 1982–2003; Hollyoaks, 1996–2005; Grange Hill, 2002–08. Creative Chair, 2008 Eur. Capital of Culture, Liverpool, 2007–. Chm. of Trustees, National Museums and Galleries of Liverpool, 2008–. Hon. Prof. of Media, 1989, Fellow, 1989, Liverpool John Moores Univ. FRSA 1996. *Recreations:* photography, boating, digital media. *Address:* (office) Merseyfilm, Tirley Garth, Willington, Tarporley, Cheshire CW6 0L2. *Club:* Groucho.

REDSHAW, Peter Robert Gransden; HM Diplomatic Service, retired; Group Security Adviser, Gallaher Ltd, 1996–2004; *b* 16 April 1942; *s* of late Robert Henry Gransden Redshaw and of Audrey Nita Redshaw (*née* Ward); *m* 1970, Margaret Shaun (*née* Mizon); one *s* two *d*. *Educ:* Boxgrove School; Charterhouse; Trinity College, Cambridge (MA). ACA. Price Waterhouse, 1964–67; FCO, 1968; Kampala, 1970–73; 1st Sec., 1971; FCO, 1973; Lagos, 1982–85; Counsellor, 1985; FCO, 1985–88; Kuala Lumpur, 1988–91; FCO, 1992–96. *Recreations:* books, sailing, travel. *Clubs:* Kampala; Woking Tennis & Croquet.

REDSHAW, Tina Susan; HM Diplomatic Service; Head of Environment, Energy and Infrastructure, UK Trade and Investment, Beijing, since 2008; *b* 25 Jan. 1961; *d* of Trevor Redshaw and Doreen Cooper; *m* 2001, Phong Phun Khoga Pun; one *d*. *Educ:* York Univ. (BA Hons Lang./Linguistics); Open Univ. (MSc Develt Mgt). Voluntary Service Overseas: Prog. Dir, China, 1990–94; Regl Prog. Manager, SE Asia, 1994–99; entered FCO, 1999; China Hong Kong Dept, 1999–2000; First Sec., Beijing, 2000–03; Ambassador, E Timor, 2003–06. *Recreations:* theatre, dance, jazz music, swimming. *Address:* c/o Foreign and Commonwealth Office, King Charles Street, SW1A 2AH; *e-mail:* tina.redshaw@fco.gov.uk.

REDWOOD, Rt Hon. John (Alan); PC 1993; DPhil; MP (C) Wokingham, since 1987; *b* 15 June 1951; *s* of William Charles Redwood and Amy Emma Redwood (*née* Champion); *m* 1974, Gail Felicity Chippington (marr. diss. 2004); one *s* one *d*. *Educ:* Kent Coll., Canterbury; Magdalen and St Antony's Colls, Oxford; MA, DPhil Oxon. Fellow, All Souls Coll., Oxford, 1972–87, 2003–05, 2007–. Investment Adviser, Robert Fleming & Co., 1973–77; Investment Manager and Dir, N. M. Rothschild & Sons, 1977–87; Norcros plc: Dir, 1985–89; Jt Dep. Chm., 1986–87; non-exec. Chm., 1987–89. Non-executive Chairman: Hare Hatch Hldgs Ltd (formerly Mabey Securities), 1999–2008; Concentric plc, 2003–; Pan Asset Capital Mgt, 2007–; non-exec. Dir, BNB, 2001–07. Adviser, Treasury and Civil Service Select Cttee, 1981; Head of PM's Policy Unit, 1983–85. Councillor, Oxfordshire CC, 1973–77. Parly Under Sec. of State, DTI, 1989–90; Minister of State: DTI, 1990–92; DoE, 1992–93; Sec. of State for Wales, 1993–95; Opposition front bench spokesman on trade and industry, 1997–99, on the envmt, 1999–2000; Shadow Sec. of State for De-regulation, 2004–05. Head, Cons. Parly Campaigns Unit, 2000–01; Chm., Cons. Party Policy Review on Econ. Competitiveness, 2005–. Vis. Prof., Middx Business Sch., 2000–. Governor of various schools, 1974–83. *Publications:* Reason, Ridicule and Religion, 1976; Public Enterprise in Crisis, 1980; (with John Hatch) Value for Money Audits, 1981; (with John Hatch) Controlling Public Industries, 1982; Going for Broke, 1984; Equity for Everyman, 1986; Popular Capitalism, 1988; The Global Marketplace, 1994; The Single Currency, 1995; Action Not Words, 1996; Our Currency, Our Country, 1997; The Death of Britain?, 1999; Stars and Strife, 2001; Just Say No, 2001; Singing the Blues, 2004; Superpower Struggles, 2005; I Want to Make a Difference, 2006; pamphlets on Cons. matters. *Recreations:* water sports, village cricket. *Address:* House of Commons, SW1A 0AA. *T:* (office) (020) 7219 4205, *T:* (home) (020) 7976 6603.

REDWOOD, Sir Peter (Boverton), 3rd Bt *cr* 1911; Colonel, late King's Own Scottish Borderers, retired 1987; *b* 1 Dec. 1937; *o s* of Sir Thomas Boverton Redwood, 2nd Bt, TD, and Ruth Mary Redwood (*née* Creighton, then Blair); *S* father, 1974; *m* 1964, Gilian, *o d* of John Lee Waddington Wood, Limuru, Kenya; three *d*. *Educ:* Gordonstoun. National Service, 1956–58, 2nd Lieut, Seaforth Highlanders; regular commn, KOSB, 1959; served in UK (despatches 1972), BAOR, Netherlands, ME, Africa and Far East; Staff Coll., Camberley, 1970; Nat. Defence Coll., Latimer, 1978–79. Dir, SERCO-IAL Ltd, 1992–95. Mem., Queen's Body Guard for Scotland (Royal Co. of Archers). Liveryman, Goldsmiths' Co. *Recreations:* shooting, silver and silversmithing. *Heir:* *half-b* Robert Boverton Redwood [*b* 24 June 1953; *m* 1978, Mary Elizabeth Wright; one *s* one *d*]. *Address:* c/o Royal Bank of Scotland, 8–9 Quiet Street, Bath BA1 2JN. *Club:* New (Edinburgh).

REECE, Sir Charles (Hugh), Kt 1988; Research and Technology Director, Imperial Chemical Industries, 1979–89; *b* 2 Jan. 1927; *s* of Charles Hugh Reece and Helen Youlle; *m* 1951, Betty Linford; two *d*. *Educ:* Pocklington Sch., E Riding; Huddersfield Coll.; Leeds Univ. (PhD, BSc Hons). FRSC 1981. ICI: joined Dyestuffs Div., 1949; Head of Medicinal Process Develt Dept, Dyestuffs Div., 1959; Manager, Works R&D Dept, 1965; Jt Research Manager, Mond Div., 1967; Dir, R&D, Mond Div., 1969; Dep. Chm., Mond Div., 1972; Chm., Plant Protection Div., 1975. Dir, Finnish Chemicals, 1971–75; Chm., Teijin Agricultural Chemicals, 1975–78; non-executive Director: APV plc (formerly APV Holdings), 1984–96; British Biotechnology Gp, 1989–95. Chm., Univ. of Surrey Robens Inst. of Indust. and Envtl Health and Safety Cttee, 1985–92; Member: ACARD, 1983–87, ACOST, 1987–89; Adv. Cttee on Industry, Cttee of Vice-Chancellors and Principals, 1983–; Council, RSC, 1985–86; SERC, 1985–89; ABRC, 1989–91; UFC, 1989–93; Royal Instn of GB, 1979–92 (Mem. Council, 1985–88); SCI; Parly and Sci. Cttee, 1979– (Vice-Chm., 1986). Hon. DSc: St Andrews, 1986; Queen's, 1988; Bristol, 1989; South West Poly., 1991; DUniv Surrey, 1989. *Publications:* reports and papers in learned jls. *Recreations:* sailing, gardening. *Address:* Heath Ridge, Graffham, Petworth, W Sussex GU28 0PT.

REECE, His Honour (Edward Vans) Paynter; a Circuit Judge, 1982–2003; *b* 17 May 1936; *s* of Clifford Mansel Reece and Catherine Barbara Reece (*née* Hathorn); *m* 1967, Rosamund Mary Reece (*née* Roberts); three *s* one *d*. *Educ:* Blundell's Sch.; Magdalene Coll., Cambridge (MA). Called to the Bar, Inner Temple, 1960; a Recorder of the Crown Court, 1980–82. *Recreations:* fishing, golf. *Clubs:* Garrick; New Zealand Golf.

REECE, Dr Henry Michael; Secretary to Delegates, and Chief Executive, Oxford University Press, since 1998; Fellow of Jesus College, Oxford, since 1998; *b* 10 Aug. 1953; *s* of David Reece and Persis Rebecca Reece; *m* 1993, Allison Jane King (marr. diss. 2005). *Educ:* Univ. of Bristol (BA 1st Cl. Hons); St John's Coll., Oxford (DPhil Modern Hist. 1981). Tutor in Hist., Univ. of Exeter, 1977–78; Prentice Hall International: Field Sales Editor, 1979–82; Academic Sales Manager, 1982–84; UK Sales Manager, 1984–85; Asst Vice-Pres., Simon & Schuster Internat., 1985–88; Exec. Ed., Allyn & Bacon (US), 1988–91; Man. Dir, Pitman Publishing, 1991–94; Executive Director: Longman Gp Ltd, 1994–95; Pearson Professional, 1995–97; Man. Dir, Financial Times Professional, 1997–98. Non-exec. Dir, Knowledge Pool Trng Ltd, 2000–01. Mem. Council, Publishers Assoc., 1999–2006 (Pres., 2004–05). *Recreations:* reading crime novels, watching Wales win at Rugby, running. *Address:* Oxford University Press, Great Clarendon Street, Oxford OX2 6DP. *T:* (01865) 353600.

REECE, Paynter; *see* Reece, E. V. P.

REECE, Richard Marsden, DPhil; FSA; Reader in Late Roman Archaeology and Numismatics, Institute of Archaeology, University College London, 1994–99; *b* 25 March 1939; *o s* of Richard Marsden Reece and Alice Reece (*née* Wedel). *Educ:* Cirencester Grammar Sch.; UCL (BSc Biochem. 1961); Wadham Coll., Oxford (DipEd 1962; DPhil 1972). FSA 1968. Asst Master, St John's Sch., Leatherhead, 1962–65; Head of Chem. Dept, St George's Sch., Harpenden, 1966–68; London Institute of Archaeology, subseq. Institute of Archaeology, University College London: Lectr, 1970–81; Sen. Lectr, 1981–93; Tutor to Arts students, 1988–91. Membre d'Honneur, Romanian Numismatic Soc.; Hon. FRNS 2003. *Publications:* Roman Coins, 1970; Excavations on Iona 1964–74, 1981; Coinage in Roman Britain, 1987, revd edn as Coinage of Roman Britain, 2002; My Roman Britain, 1988; Later Roman Empire, 1999; Roman Coins and Archaeology: collected papers, 2003; articles in learned jls. *Recreations:* reading novels, music. *Address:* The Apple Loft, The Waterloo, Cirencester, Glos GL7 2PU.

REED, Rt Hon. Lord; Robert John Reed; PC 2008; a Judge of the Inner House of the Court of Session, since 2008; *b* 7 Sept. 1956; *s* of George and Elizabeth Reed; *m* 1988, Jane Mylne; two *d. Educ:* George Watson's Coll.; Univ. of Edinburgh (LLB 1st Cl. Hons; Vans Dunlop Schol.); Balliol Coll., Oxford (DPhil). Admitted to Faculty of Advocates, 1983; called to the Bar, Inner Temple, 1991; Standing Junior Counsel: Scottish Educn Dept, 1988–89; Scottish Office Home and Health Dept, 1989–95; QC (Scot.) 1995; Advocate Depute, 1996–98; a Judge of the Outer House of the Court of Session, 1998–2008; Principal Commercial Judge, 2006–08; *ad hoc* Judge, European Court of Human Rights, 1999. Expert advr, EU/Council of Europe Jt Initiative with Turkey, 2002–04. Chm., Franco-British Judicial Co-operation Cttee, 2005–; Pres., EU Forum of Judges for the Envmt, 2006–08 (Vice Pres., 2008–); Member: Adv. Bd, British Inst. Internat. and Comparative Law, 2001–06; UN Task Force on Access to Justice, 2006–. Convener, Children in Scotland, 2006–. Chm., Centre for Commercial Law, Univ. of Edinburgh, 2008–. Hon. Professor: Glasgow Caledonian Univ., 2005–; Univ. of Glasgow, 2006–. *Publications:* Scottish Ed., European Law Reports, 1997–; (with J. M. Murdoch) A Guide to Human Rights Law in Scotland, 2001, 2nd edn 2008; contribs to various books and jls on public law. *Recreation:* music. *Address:* Parliament House, Parliament Square, Edinburgh EH1 1RQ.

REED, Adrian Harbottle, CMG 1981; HM Diplomatic Service, retired; Consul-General, Munich, 1973–80; *b* 5 Jan. 1921; *s* of Harbottle Reed, MBE, FRIBA, and Winifred Reed (*née* Rowland); *m* 1st, 1947, Doris Davidson Duthie (marr. diss. 1975); one *s* one *d*; 2nd, 1975, Maria-Louise, *d* of Dr and Mrs A. J. Boekelman, Zeist, Netherlands. *Educ:* Hele's Sch., Exeter; Emmanuel Coll., Cambridge. Royal Artillery, 1941–47. India Office, 1947; Commonwealth Relations Office, 1947; served in UK High Commission: Pakistan, 1948–50; Fedn of Rhodesia and Nyasaland, 1953–56; British Embassy, Dublin, 1960–62; Hd Econ. Relns, 1962–65, Far East and Pacific Depts, 1966–68, CO; Counsellor (Commercial), and Consul-Gen., Helsinki, 1968–70; Economic Counsellor, Pretoria, 1971–73. Chairman: Cold Harbour Working Wool Mus., 1983–86; Devon and Exeter Instn, 1989–2001; SW Maritime Hist. Soc., 1994–97; Devon Hist. Soc., 1994–2003. Bavarian Order of Merit, 1980. *Publications:* From Past to Present (autobiog.), 2006; articles and reviews on historical (mainly maritime) subjects. *Recreations:* maritime history, the English countryside. *Address:* Old Bridge House, Uffculme, Cullompton, Devon EX15 3AX. *T:* (01884) 840595.

REED, Alec Edward, CBE 1994; Founder, Reed Executive PLC, 1960; *b* 16 Feb. 1934; *s* of Leonard Reed and Anne Underwood; *m* 1961, Adrianne Mary Eyre; two *s* one *d. Educ:* Grammar School. FCMA, FCIM, FIPD. Founded: Reed Healthcare PLC; Medicare PLC; ICC PLC; Reed Business Sch.; Womankind Worldwide; Ethiopiaid; Women @ Risk; Acad. of Enterprise. President: Inst. of Employment Consultants, 1974–78; Internat. Confedn of Private Employment Agency Assocs, 1978–81. Hon. Prof., Enterprise and Innovation, Royal Holloway, Univ. of London, 1993–2003 (Fellow, RHBNC, 1988); Vis. Prof., London Metropolitan (formerly London Guildhall) Univ., 1999–2004; Hon. Prof., Warwick Univ., 2001–. Mem. Council, RHC, 1979–85. Hon. PhD London Guildhall, 1999. *Publications:* Innovation in Human Resource Management, 2002; Capitalism is Dead, Peoplism Rules, 2002. *Recreations:* family, cinema, tennis, riding, portrait painting. *Address:* Reed Executive PLC, 6 Sloane Street, SW1X 9LE.

REED, Andrew John; MP (Lab and Co-op) Loughborough, since 1997; *b* 17 Sept. 1964; *s* of James Donald Reed and Margaret Anne Reed; *m* 1992, Sarah Elizabeth Chester. *Educ:* Riverside Jun. Sch.; Stonehill High Sch.; Longslade Community Coll.; Leicester Poly. (BA Hons Public Admin 1987). Parly Asst to Keith Vaz, MP, 1987–88; Urban Regeneration Officer, Leicester CC, 1988–90; Sen. Economic Develt Officer, 1990–94, European Officer, 1994–97, Leics CC. Parliamentary Private Secretary: to Minister for Sport, 2000–01; to Sec. of State for Envmt, Food and Rural Affairs, 2001–03; to Paymaster General, 2005–07. *Recreations:* Rugby, volleyball, tennis, running. *Address:* House of Commons, SW1A 0AA. *Clubs:* Birstall Rugby Football, Leicester Rugby Football.

REED, Air Cdre April Anne, RRC 1981; Director of RAF Nursing Services, 1984–85, retired; *b* 25 Jan. 1930; *d* of Captain Basil Duck Reed, RN, and Nancy Mignon Ethel Reed. *Educ:* Channing Sch., Highgate. SRN, SCM. SRN training, Middlesex Hosp., 1948–52; midwifery training, Royal Maternity Hosp., Belfast, 1953; joined Royal Air Force, 1954; Dep. Matron, 1970; Sen. Matron, 1976; Principal Matron, 1981; Matron in Chief (Director), 1984. *Recreations:* sailing, ornithology, antiques, gardening, interest in oriental carpets. *Address:* 1 Garners Row, Burnham Thorpe, King's Lynn, Norfolk PE31 8HN. *Club:* Royal Air Force.

REED, Barry St George Austin, CBE 1988; MC 1951; Chairman, Austin Reed Group PLC, 1973–96; *b* 5 May 1931; *s* of late Douglas Austin Reed and Mary Ellen (*née* Philpott); *m* 1st 1956, Patricia (*née* Bristow) (*d* 2002); one *s* one *d*; 2nd 2005, Mary Rose (*née* Lee Warner), *widow* of N. S. Farquharson. *Educ:* Rugby Sch. Commnd Middlesex Regt (DCO), 1950; served Korea, 1950–51; TA, 1951–60. Joined Austin Reed Group, 1953; Dir, 1958–99; Man. Dir, 1966–85. National Westminster Bank: Dir, City and West End Regions, 1980–87; Dir, 1987–90; Chm., Eastern Regl Adv. Bd, 1987–92; Dir, UK Adv. Bd, 1990–92. Pres., Menswear Assoc. of Britain, 1966–67; Chairman: Retail Alliance, 1967–70; British Knitting and Clothing Export Council, 1985–89; Dir, British Apparel and Textile Confedn, 1992–99; Member: Bd, Retail Trading-Standards Assoc., 1964–78; Consumer Protection Adv. Cttee, 1973–79; European Trade Cttee, 1975–84; Cttee, Fleming American Exempt Fund, 1979–94; Council, Royal Warrant Holders Assoc., 1980– (Pres., 1990). Dir, Independent Broadcasting Telethon Trust Ltd, 1991–94. Pres., Vale of York Cons. Assoc., 1995–2000. Dir, Hambleton and Richmondshire Partnership Against Crime, 1997–99. Chm., Queen Elizabeth Scholarship Trust, 1990–95; Trustee, Third Age Challenge Trust, 1994–96. Member: Ripon and Leeds Dio. Synod, 1997–2006; Ripon and Leeds Dio. Bd of Finance, 1997–; Vice-Chm., 1997–2000, Chm., 2000–03, Ripon and Leeds Dio. Parsonages Bd; Chm., Ripon and Leeds Dio. Property and Estates Cttee, 2003–. Freeman, City of London, 1963; Liveryman, Glovers' Co., 1963– (Master 1980–81). DL Greater London, 1977–99; Rep. DL, London Borough of Hackney, 1980–86. FRSA. *Publications:* papers in clothing, textile and banking jls. *Recreations:* travel, gardens, reading. *Clubs:* Army and Navy, Pilgrims, MCC.
See also L. D. Reed.

REED, David; Director of Corporate Communications, Whitbread plc, 1990–2005; *b* 24 April 1945; *s* of Wilfred Reed and Elsie Swindon; *m* 1973, Susan Garrett, MA Oxon, MScEcon. *Educ:* West Hartlepool Grammar Sch. Former journalist and public relations adviser to Investors in Industry, Rank Xerox, Ernst & Whinney, Hewlett-Packard. Dir and Hd of Corporate and Financial PR, Ogilvy and Mather. MP (Lab) Sedgefield, Co. Durham, 1970–Feb. 1974. Trustee: Leonard Cheshire Foundn, 2005–; TB Alert, 2006–. *Publications:* many articles in national newspapers and other jls. *Recreations:* theatre, music, walking the dog. *Address:* St Luke's Cottage, Stonor, Oxon RG9 6HE.

REED, David; Regional Employment Judge (formerly Regional Chairman of Employment Tribunals), Newcastle upon Tyne, since 1998; *b* 11 Oct. 1946; *s* of Thomas and Olive Reed; *m* 1976, Sylvia Mary Thompson. *Educ:* London Univ. (LLB ext.). Admitted Solicitor (William Hutton Prize), 1972, in practice, 1972–91; full-time Chm., Industrial Tribunals, 1991–. *Address:* Quayside House, 110 Quayside, Newcastle upon Tyne NE1 3DX. *T:* (0191) 260 6900.

REED, Gavin Barras; *b* 13 Nov. 1934; *s* of late Lt-Col Edward Reed and Greta Milburn (*née* Pybus); *m* 1957, Muriel Joyce, *d* of late Humphrey Vaughan Rowlands; one *s* three *d. Educ:* Eton; Trinity Coll., Cambridge (BA). National Service, Fleet Air Arm Pilot, 1953–55. Joined Newcastle Breweries Ltd, 1958; Dir, Scottish & Newcastle Breweries Ltd, 1970–94; Gp Man. Dir, 1988–91, Gp Vice-Chm., 1991–94, Scottish & Newcastle plc; Chairman: John Menzies plc, 1997–2002 (Dir, 1992–2002); Hamilton & Inches Ltd, 1998–; Maclay Gp plc, 2001–; Dir, Burtonwood Brewery plc, 1996–2005. Chm., N Region, CBI, 1987–88. Liveryman, Brewers' Co., 1992–. *Recreation:* shooting. *Address:* Broadgate, West Woodburn, Northumberland NE48 2RN. *Club:* New (Edinburgh).

REED, Jamieson Ronald, (Jamie); MP (Lab) Copeland, since 2005; *b* 4 Aug. 1973; *s* of Ronald and Gloria Reed; *m*; three *s. Educ:* Whitehaven Sch.; Manchester Univ. (BA English 1994); Univ. of Leicester (MA Mass Communications 2000). Researcher: EP, 1995–97; and Advr, Labour Gp, Cumbria CC, 1997–2000; Manager, TU and Community Sellafield Campaign, 2000–01; Public Affairs, BNFL, 2001–05. *Recreations:* spending time with my family, American literature, modern history, music, football, fell walking, Rugby League. *Address:* House of Commons, SW1A 0AA. *T:* (office) (01946) 62024; *e-mail:* contact@copelandclp.fsnet.co.uk.

REED, Jane Barbara, CBE 2000; Director, Times Newspaper Holdings Ltd, since 2002; Director of Corporate Affairs, News International plc, 1989–2000; 2nd *d* of late William and Gwendoline Reed, Letchworth, Herts. *Educ:* Royal Masonic Sch.; sundry further educational establishments. Journalist on numerous magazines; returned to Woman's Own, 1965; Editor, 1970–79; Publisher, IPC Women's Monthly Group, 1979–81; Editor-in-Chief, Woman magazine, 1981–82; IPC Magazines: Asst Man. Dir, Specialist Educn and Leisure Gp, 1983; Man. Dir, Holborn Publishing Gp, 1983–85; Man. Editor (Features), Today, News (UK) Ltd, 1985–86; Man. Editor, Today, 1986–89. Pres., Media Soc., 1995. Director: Media Trust, 1994–; Nat. Acad. of Writing, 2001–. Member: Royal Soc. COPUS, 1986–96; Council, Nat. Literacy Trust, 1992–. Trustee, St Katharine and Shadwell Trust, 1992–. *Publications:* Girl About Town, 1964; (jtly) Kitchen Sink—or Swim?, 1982. *Address:* 1 Virginia Street, E98 1XY.

REED, Dr John Langdale, CB 1993; FRCP, FRCPsych; Medical Inspector, HM Inspectorate of Prisons, 1996–2002; *b* 16 Sept. 1931; *s* of John Thompson Reed and Elsie May Abbott; *m* 1959, Hilary Allin; one *s* one *d. Educ:* Oundle Sch.; Cambridge Univ.; Guy's Hosp. Med. Sch. FRCP 1974; FRCPsych 1974 (Hon. FRCPsych 1992). Maudsley Hosp., 1960–67; Consultant Psychiatrist and Sen. Lectr in Psychol Medicine, St Bartholomew's Hosp., 1967–96. SPMO, Health Care Div. (Medical), DHSS, subseq. DoH, 1986–93. Special Advr in Forensic Psychiatry, DoH, 1993–96. Chairman: DoH/Home Office Rev. of Services for Mentally Disordered Offenders, 1991–92; DoH Wkg Gp on High Security Psychiatric Care, 1992–93; DoH Wkg Gp on Psychopathic Disorder, 1992–93; Adv. Cttee on Mentally Disordered Offenders, 1993–96. Chm., Vanguard Housing Assoc., 1992–96. QHP 1990–93. *Publications:* (with G. Lomas) Psychiatric Services in the Community, 1984; papers on psychiatric services, on drug abuse, and on health care in prisons. *Recreations:* genealogy, opera, bridge, walking (preferably in the Lake District). *Address:* Willow Tree House, Westleigh Drive, Bromley BR1 2PN.

REED, Ven. John Peter Cyril; Archdeacon of Taunton, since 1999; *b* 21 May 1951; *s* of C. Gordon Reed and M. Joan Reed (*née* Stenning); *m* 1979, Gillian Mary Coles; one *s* one *d. Educ:* Monkton Combe Sch., Bath; King's Coll. London (BD, AKC 1978); Ripon Coll., Cuddesdon. With Imperial Group, 1969–73; Research and Marketing, Wales & the West Ltd, Cardiff, 1973–75. Deacon 1979, priest 1980; Curate, Croydon Parish Church, 1979–82; Precentor, St Albans Abbey, 1982–86; Rector, Timsbury and Priston and Chaplain for Rural Affairs, Archdeaconry of Bath, 1986–93; Team Rector, Ilminster and Dist Team Ministry, 1993–99. *Recreations:* family, cricket, tennis, fishing, countryside. *Address:* 4 Westerkirk Gate, Staplegrove, Taunton TA2 6BQ. *T:* (01823) 323838; *e-mail:* adtaunton@bathwells.anglican.org.

REED, John Shepard; Joint Chairman and Co-Chief Executive Officer, Citigroup, 1998–2000; *b* 7 Feb. 1939; *m* 1st, 1964, Sally Foreman (marr. diss.); four *c*; 2nd, 1994, Cindy McCarthy. *Educ:* Washington and Jefferson Coll. (BA Amer. Lit. 1961); MIT (BS Physical Metallurgy 1961; MS Mgt 1965). Served Corps of Engrs, US Army, Korea, 1962–64. Joined Citibank, later Citicorp, 1965; Planning Dept, Internat. Div., 1965–67; NY HQ, 1967; Asst Vice-Pres., 1968–69; Exec. Vice-Pres. and Hd of Operating Gp, 1970–74; Hd of Consumer Service Gp, 1974–79; Sen. Exec. Vice-Pres., 1979–82; Vice-Chm. i/c Individual Bank, 1982–84; Dir, 1982; Chm. and CEO, 1984–98; Citicorp merged with Travelers Gp to form Citigroup, 1998. Interim Chm., NY Stock Exchange, 2003–05 (Interim CEO, 2003–04). Dir, Altria Gp. *Address:* c/o Citigroup, 153 East 53rd Street, New York, NY 10022, USA.

REED, Dame Julie Thérèse; *see* Mellor, Dame J. T.

REED, Laurance Douglas; *b* 4 Dec. 1937; *s* of late Douglas Austin Reed and Mary Ellen Reed (*née* Philpott). *Educ:* Gresham's Sch., Holt; University Coll., Oxford (MA). Nat. Service, RN, 1956–58; worked and studied on Continent (Brussels, Bruges, Leyden, Luxembourg, Strasbourg, Paris, Rome, Bologna, Geneva), 1963–66; Public Sector Research Unit, 1967–69. MP (C) Bolton East, 1970–Feb. 1974; PPS to Chancellor of Duchy of Lancaster, 1973–74. Jt Sec., Parly and Scientific Cttee, 1971–74; Mem., Select Cttee on Science and Technology, 1971–74. *Publications:* Europe in a Shrinking World, 1967; An Ocean of Waste, 1972; Political Consequences of North Sea Oil, 1973; The Soay of Our Forefathers, 1986; Philpott of Fordingbridge, 1994. *Recreations:* gardening, historical research. *Address:* 1 Disraeli Park, Beaconsfield, Bucks HP9 2QE. *T:* (01494) 673153. *Club:* Carlton.
See also B. St G. A. Reed.

REED, Leslie Edwin, PhD; Chief Industrial Air Pollution Inspector, Health and Safety Executive, 1981–85; *b* 6 Feb. 1925; *s* of Edwin George and Maud Gladys Reed; *m* 1947, Ruby; two *s. Educ:* Sir George Monoux Grammar Sch., Walthamstow; University Coll. London (BScEng, MScEng, PhD). Engineering Officer, RNVR, 1945–47; Fuel Research Station, 1950–58; Warren Spring Laboratory, 1958–70; Central Unit on Environmental Pollution, DoE, 1970–79; Head, Air and Noise Div., DoE, 1979–81. *Address:* 20 Deards Wood, Knebworth, Herts SG3 6PG. *T:* (01438) 813272.

REED, Dr Malcolm Christopher, CBE 2004; FCILT, FIHT; Chief Executive, Transport Scotland, since 2005; *b* 24 Nov. 1944; *s* of James and Lilian Reed; marr. diss.; two *d. Educ:* Blue Coat Sch., Durham; Royal Grammar Sch., Newcastle upon Tyne; St Catherine's Coll., Oxford (MA); Nuffield Coll., Oxford; DPhil Oxon 1971. Asst Grade 1, Bodleian Liby, Oxford, 1968–69; Lectr, Dept of Econ. Hist., Univ. of Glasgow,

1969–74; Researcher, then Associate Dir, Planning Exchange, Glasgow, 1974–75; Planner, then Chief Public Transport Co-ordinator, Gtr Glasgow PTE, 1975–79; Strathclyde Regional Council: Chief Policy Planner, 1979–80; Sen. Exec. Officer, 1980–90; Asst Chief Exec., 1990–96; Dir Gen., Strathclyde PTE, 1997–2005. Interim Clerk, E Ayrshire Council, 1995. Railway Heritage Committee: Mem., 1994–99; Dep. Chm., 1996–99; Member: Adv. Cttee, Rail Safety & Standards Bd, 2003–05; Adv. Panel, Railway Heritage Trust, 2007–; Council, Instn of Engrs & Shipbuilders in Scotland, 2008–. FCILT (FCIT 1993); FIHT 2006; CIES 2007. FRSA. *Publications:* (ed) Railways in the Victorian Economy, 1969; Investment in Railways in Britain, 1975; A History of James Capel & Co., 1975; The London & North Western Railway: a history, 1996; contribs to Econ. Hist. Rev., Transport Hist., Scottish Jl Political Econ. *Recreations:* hill-walking, gardening, listening to music. *Address:* Transport Scotland, Buchanan House, 58 Port Dundas Road, Glasgow G4 0HF. *T:* (0141) 272 7110, *Fax:* (0141) 272 7111; *e-mail:* chiefexecutive@transportscotland.gsi.gov.uk. *Club:* Western (Glasgow).

REED, Philip Howard, OBE 2008; Director, Cabinet War Rooms, since 1993, and Churchill Museum, since 2005, Imperial War Museum; Executive Director, Churchill Centre, 2008; *b* 2 Nov. 1950; *s* of late William Reed and Mary Reed (*née* Fearon); *m* 1982, Sally Blaxland. *Educ:* Univ. of Leicester (BA Hons German 1973); Univ. of Bristol (MA 1974). Lexicographer, Harraps Ltd, 1973–74; Dep. Keeper, Dept of Documents, Imperial War Mus., 1974–93. *Publications:* various academic articles, papers and forewords. *Recreations:* opera, fine wines and haute cuisine. *Address:* c/o Churchill Museum and Cabinet War Rooms, Clive Steps, King Charles Street, SW1A 2AQ. *T:* (020) 7766 0120; *e-mail:* preed@iwm.org.uk.

REED, Robert John; *see* Reed, Rt Hon. Lord.

REED, Roger William Hampson, FCIS; DL; Chairman, South East Arts Board, 1995–2001; Member, Arts Council of England, 1996–98; Chairman, Pallant House Gallery Trust, 2002–07; *b* 23 Oct. 1938; *s* of late Thomas Henry Walter Reed and Lily Reed (*née* Hampson); *m* 1961, Jane Noelle Madeline Bowring Gabriel; one *s* one *d*. *Educ:* Trinity Sch. of John Whitgift; City of London Coll. FCIS 1968; FIET (FIEE 1990). Mgt trainee, Albright and Wilson Gp, 1957–61; Asst Co. Sec., Powell Duffryn Gp, 1961–62; Jt Chief Accountant, John Mowlem Gp, 1962–68; Ewbank Preece Group: Dir and Co. Sec., 1968–91; Chm., 1991–93; Chm., Old Ship Hotel (Brighton) Ltd, 1979–93; Dir, Regency Bldg Soc., 1984–88. Partner, Gratwicke Farm, 1982–. Founder Dir, Sussex Enterprise (formerly Sussex TEC), 1991–95. Chm., Sussex Br., Inst. Dirs, 1986–89. Trustee, Brighton Fest. Trust and Dir, Brighton Fest. Soc., 1980–95. Chm., Royal Alexandra Hosp. for Sick Children Centenary Fund and Rockinghorse Appeal, 1991–2004. Gov., Hurstpierpoint Coll., 1989–2001. Fellow, Woodard Foundn, 1993–2001. High Sheriff, 2004–05, DL 2005, W Sussex. FCIM 1982. *Recreations:* farming, the arts, cooking and entertaining, sport. *Address:* Gratwicke, Cowfold, W Sussex RH13 8EA. *T:* (01403) 864284. *Clubs:* Savile, MCC; Sussex; W Sussex Golf (Pulborough).

REED, Ruth Madeline, RIBA; Course Director, Birmingham School of Architecture, Birmingham City University (formerly University of Central England), since 2005; President elect, 2008–Sept. 2009, President, from Sept. 2009, Royal Institute of British Architects; *b* Winchester, 28 Sept. 1956; *d* of Roger and Pamela Green; *m* Donald Reed (separated); two *d*. *Educ:* Harlescott Grange Prim. Sch., Shrewsbury; Wakeman Sch., Shrewsbury; Sheffield Univ. (BA 1978; DipArch 1981; MA 1982). RIBA 1983. Architectural Asst, Welmar (Yorkshire) Ltd, 1981–83; Architect, Hadfield Cawkwell Davidson and Partners, 1983–87; Sen. Architect, S Yorks Housing Assoc., 1988–90; Sole Practitioner, 1992–2002, Partner, 2002–06, Reed Architects; Partner (pt-time), Green Planning Solutions LLP, 2007–. Pres., Royal Soc. of Architects in Wales, 2003–05; Vice Pres. Membership, RIBA, 2005–07. *Recreations:* gardening (especially buying plants), walking, photography, reading maps. *Address:* c/o Royal Institute of British Architects, 66 Portland Place, W1B 1AD; *e-mail:* ruth.reed@bcu.ac.uk.

REED, Prof. Terence James, (Jim), FBA 1987; Taylor Professor of the German Language and Literature, and Fellow, Queen's College, Oxford, 1989–2004, now Emeritus; *b* 16 April 1937; *s* of William Reed and Ellen (*née* Silcox); *m* 1960, Ann Macpherson; one *s* one *d*. *Educ:* Shooters' Hill Grammar Sch., Woolwich; Brasenose Coll., Oxford (MA). Sen. Scholar, Christ Church, Oxford, 1960–61; Jun. Res. Fellow, Brasenose Coll., Oxford, 1961–63; Fellow and Tutor in Mod. Langs, St John's Coll., Oxford, 1963–88 (Hon. Fellow, 1997). Schiller Prof., Univ. of Jena, 1999. Vis. Res. Scholar, Univ. of Göttingen, 2004–05. Pres., English Goethe Soc., 1995–; Member: Council, Goethe Soc., Weimar, 2003–; Academic Adv. Cttee, Weimar Classical Foundn, 2007–. Corresponding Member: Collegium Europaeum, Jena, 1991; Göttingen Acad. of Scis, 1997. Gold Medal, Goethe Soc., Weimar, 1999; Res. Prize, Humboldt Foundn, 2002. Co-founder and Editor, Oxford German Studies, 1965–; Editor, Oxford Magazine, 1985–2004. *Publications:* (ed) Death in Venice, 1972 (German edn 1983); Thomas Mann, The Uses of Tradition, 1974, 2nd edn 1997; The Classical Centre: Goethe and Weimar 1775–1832, 1980 (German edn 1982); Goethe, 1984 (German edn 1999; also Hebrew, Japanese, Korean, Persian and Spanish edns); (trans.) Heinrich Heine: Deutschland, a not so sentimental journey, 1986; Schiller, 1991; Death in Venice: making and unmaking a master, 1994; (trans. with D. Cram) Heinrich Heine, Poems, 1997; (trans.) Goethe: The Flight to Italy: diaries and letters 1786, 1999; (ed) Goethe: poems, 1999; (ed and trans. jtly) Goethe: poems, 2000; Humanpraxis Literatur (essays), 2001; (ed jtly) Thomas Mann: Erzählungen 1893–1912, 2 vols (text and commentary), 2004. *Recreation:* hill walking. *Address:* 91 Eynsham Road, Oxford OX2 9BY. *T:* (01865) 862946.

REED-PURVIS, Air Vice-Marshal Henry, CB 1982; OBE 1972; Sales Director, British Aerospace Dynamics Group, 1983–89; *b* 1 July 1928; *s* of late Henry Reed and of Nancy Reed-Purvis; *m* 1951, Isabel Price; three *d*. *Educ:* King James I School, Durham; Durham Univ. BSc Hons 1950. Entered RAF, 1950; various Op. Sqdns, 1951–58; Instr, Jt Nuclear Biological and Chemical Sch., 1958–60; RMCS Shrivenham (Nuclear Sci. and Tech.), 1961; MoD Staff, 1962–64; OC No 63 Sqdn, RAF Regt, Malaya, 1964–66; Exchange Duties, USAF, 1966–69; USAF War Coll., 1969–70; OC No 5 Wing RAF Regt, 1970–72; Gp Capt. Regt, HQ Strike Comd, 1972–74, HQ RAF Germany, 1974–76; ADC to the Queen, 1974–76; Dir, RAF Regt, 1976–79; Comdt Gen. RAF Regt and Dir Gen. of Security (RAF) 1979–83. Dir, Forces Help Soc. and Lord Roberts Workshops, 1986–97; Council Mem., Trustee and Dir, SSAFA/Forces Help, 1997–99. Vice Pres., Council for Cadet Rifle Shooting, 1985–. Pres., 2120 Sqdn ATC Welfare Cttee, 1995–2000. *Recreations:* golf, bridge and music. *Address:* Waterford House, Sherborne, Cheltenham, Glos GL54 3DR. *T:* (01451) 844199.

REEDER, John; QC 1989; *b* 18 Jan. 1949; *s* of Frederick and Barbara Reeder; *m* 1st, 1971, Barbara Kotlarz (marr. diss. 1994); 2nd, 1995, Pauline Madden. *Educ:* Catholic Coll., Preston; University Coll. London (LLM); PhD Birmingham 1976. Called to the Bar, Gray's Inn, 1971, NSW 1986. Lectr in Law, Univ. of Birmingham, 1971–76; commenced practice, 1976; Junior Counsel to the Treasury (Admiralty), 1981–89; a Recorder, 1991–97; Lloyd's salvage arbitrator, 1991–; CEDR Mediator, 2003–. Lawyer, PNG, 1984. Mem., Ferrari Owners' Club, 2003–. *Recreations:* motorsport, travel. *Address:* Stone Chambers, 4 Field Court, Gray's Inn, WC1R 5EA. *T:* (020) 7440 6900; 72 Bracondale Road, Norwich NR1 2BE.

REEDIE, Sir Craig (Collins), Kt 2006; CBE 1999; Chairman, British Olympic Association, 1992–2005; Member: International Olympic Committee, since 1994; Board, World Anti-Doping Agency, since 2000; *b* 6 May 1941; *s* of late Robert Lindsay Reedie and Anne Reedie; *m* 1967, Rosemary Jane Biggart; one *s* one *d*. *Educ:* High Sch., Stirling; Univ. of Glasgow (MA, LLB). Sec. and Pres., Scottish Badminton Union, 1966–81; Council Mem., Chm. and Pres., Internat. Badminton Fedn, 1970–84; Mem. Council and Treas., Gen. Assoc. of Internat. Sports Fedns, 1984–92. Board Member: Manchester 2002 Ltd, 2000–02; London 2012, 2003–05; London Organising Cttee for the Olympic Games, 2005–. Mem., NHS Resource Allocation Steering Gp, 1998–99. FRSA 1995. DUniv Glasgow, 2001; Hon. LLD St Andrews, 2005. *Recreations:* reading, golf, sport, sport and more sport. *Address:* Senara, Hazelwood Road, Bridge of Weir, PA11 3DB. *T:* (01505) 613434. *Clubs:* East India; Royal & Ancient Golf (St Andrews), Western Gailes Golf, Ranfurly Castle Golf.

REEDY, Norris John, (Jack); media consultant and lecturer, since 1994; Managing Director, The Speaking Business Ltd; *b* 1934; *s* of John Reedy; *m* 1964, Sheila Campbell McGregor; one *d*. *Educ:* Chorlton High Sch., Manchester; Univ. of Sheffield. Newspaper journalist, 1956–82, incl. Sunday Times and Guardian; Birmingham Post, 1964–82 (Editor, 1974–82); Regl Officer, Midlands, IBA, 1983–88; Sen. Nat. and Regl Officer, ITC, 1988–94; PRO, Inst. of Dirs (Midland Br.), 1994–99. Tutor in media skills and public speaking, RCN, 1985–. Mem., West Midlands Regl Bd and Coventry and Warwickshire Area Bd, The Prince's Trust; Chm., Warwickshire Badger Gp, 2005–; Vice Chm., Badger Trust, 2006–. Former Chm. W Midlands Region, and Nat. Vice-Pres., Guild of British Newspaper Editors; Sec., Midlands Centre, Royal Television Soc. Chm., House Cttee, Birmingham Press Club. *Recreations:* astronomy, riding, natural history, painting, photography. *Address:* The Old Manor, Rowington, near Warwick CV35 7DJ. *T:* (01564) 783129.

REEKIE, Jonathan Alistair James; Chief Executive, Aldeburgh Music, since 1997; *b* 2 Sept. 1964; *s* of Dr Andrew Reekie and Virginia Reekie; two *d*. *Educ:* Bristol Poly. (BA Business Studies). Co. Co-ordinator, Glyndebourne Fest., 1987–91; Gen. Manager, Almeida Th., 1991–97; Dir, Almeida Opera, 1991–2003. Mem., Bd of Dirs, Musica Nel Chiostro, Batignano, Italy, 1989–2005. Advr, Arts Prog. Cttee, Paul Hamlyn Foundn, 2007–. Trustee, Arts Foundn, 2000–. *Address:* Aldeburgh Music, Snape Maltings Concert Hall, Snape, Suffolk IP17 1SP. *T:* (01728) 687100, *Fax:* (01728) 687120; *e-mail:* enquiries@aldeburgh.co.uk.

REEKS, David Robin, TD 1974; Vice Lord-Lieutenant of Lanarkshire, since 2002; *b* 15 June 1935; *s* of Harry and Dorothy Reeks; *m* 1958, Kathleen Stephens; one *s* one *d*. *Educ:* Canford Sch.; London Univ. (BSc Eng ext.). Rig Design Engr, UKAEA, Dounreay, 1962–67; Reactor Thermal Engr, SSEB, 1967–89; Reactor Performance and Safety Engr, Scottish Nuclear, 1989–94. Mem. Cttee, and Volunteer Convoy Leader, Edinburgh Direct Aid to Bosnia and Kosovo, 1994–. TA, RE and RCT, 1962–90. DL Lanarks, 1989. *Recreations:* hill-walking, Scottish country dancing. *Address:* 3 Cedar Place, Strathaven, Lanarks ML10 6DW. *T:* and *Fax:* (01357) 521695; *e-mail:* d.reeks@talktalk.net.

REEMAN, Douglas Edward; writer (also as Alexander Kent); *b* 1924; *m* 1985, Kimberley Jordan. Served RN. *Publications: as Douglas Reeman:* A Prayer for the Ship, 1958; High Water, 1959; Send a Gunboat, 1960; Dive in the Sea, 1961; The Hostile Shore, 1962; The Last Raider, 1963; With Blood and Iron, 1964; HMS Saracen, 1965; Path of the Storm, 1966; The Deep Silence, 1967; The Pride and the Anguish, 1968; To Risks Unknown, 1969; The Greatest Enemy, 1970; Rendezvous - South Atlantic, 1972; Go in and Sink!, 1973; The Destroyers, 1974; Winged Escort, 1975; Surface with Daring, 1976; Strike from the Sea, 1978; A Ship Must Die, 1979; Torpedo Run, 1981; Badge of Glory, 1982; The First to Land, 1984; D-Day: a personal reminiscence (non-fiction), 1984; The Volunteers, 1985; The Iron Pirate, 1986; In Danger's Hour, 1988; The White Guns, 1989; Killing Ground, 1992; The Horizon, 1993; Sunset, 1994; A Dawn Like Thunder, 1996; Battlecruiser, 1997; Dust on the Sea, 1999; For Valour, 2000; Twelve Seconds to Live, 2002; Knife Edge, 2004; The Glory Boys, 2008; *as Alexander Kent:* To Glory We Steer, 1968; Form Line of Battle, 1969; Enemy in Sight!, 1970; The Flag Captain, 1971; Sloop of War, 1972; Command a King's Ship, 1973; Signal - Close Action!, 1974; Richard Bolitho, Midshipman, 1975; Passage to Mutiny, 1976; In Gallant Company, 1977; The Inshore Squadron, 1977; Midshipman Bolitho and the Avenger, 1978; Stand into Danger, 1980; A Tradition of Victory, 1981; Success to the Brave, 1983; Colours Aloft!, 1986; Honour this Day, 1987; With All Despatch, 1988; The Only Victor, 1990; Beyond the Reef, 1992; The Darkening Sea, 1993; For My Country's Freedom, 1995; Cross of St George, 1996; Sword of Honour, 1998; Second to None, 1999; Relentless Pursuit, 2001; Man of War, 2003; Band of Brothers, 2005; Heart of Oak, 2007. *Address:* c/o United Agents, 12–26 Lexington Street, W1F 0LE.

REES, family name of **Baron Rees**.

REES, Baron *cr* 1987 (Life Peer), of Goytre in the County of Gwent; **Peter Wynford Innes Rees;** PC 1983; QC 1969; chairman and director of companies; *b* 9 Dec. 1926; *s* of late Maj.-Gen. T. W. Rees, Indian Army, Goytre Hall, Abergavenny; *m* 1969, Mrs Anthea Wendell, *d* of late Major H. J. Maxwell Hyslop, Argyll and Sutherland Highlanders. *Educ:* Stowe; Christ Church, Oxford. Served Scots Guards, 1945–48. Called to the Bar, 1953, Bencher, Inner Temple, 1976; Oxford Circuit. Contested (C): Abertillery, 1964 and 1965; Liverpool, West Derby, 1966. MP (C): Dover, 1970–74 and 1983–87; Dover and Deal, 1974–83; PPS to Solicitor General, 1972; Minister of State, HM Treasury, 1979–81; Minister for Trade, 1981–83; Chief Sec. to HM Treasury, 1983–85. Dep. Chm., Leopold Joseph Holdings Plc, 1985–97; Dir, Fleming Mercantile Investment Trust, 1987–96; Chairman: LASMO, 1988–94; General Cable Ltd, 1990–95; CLM plc, 1994–99. Chm., Duty Free Confedn, 1987–99. Member: Council and Court of Governors, Museum of Wales, 1987–96; Museums and Galleries Commn, 1988–96. *Address:* 39 Headfort Place, SW1X 7DE; Goytre Hall, Abergavenny, Monmouthshire NP7 9DL. *Clubs:* Boodle's, Beefsteak, White's, Pratt's.

REES OF LUDLOW, Baron *cr* 2005 (Life Peer), of Ludlow in the county of Shropshire; **Martin John Rees,** OM 2007; Kt 1992; FRS 1979; Professor of Cosmology and Astrophysics, University of Cambridge, since 2002; Master of Trinity College, Cambridge, since 2004; President, Royal Society, since 2005; *b* 23 June 1942; *s* of late Reginald J. and Joan Rees; *m* 1986, Prof. Caroline Humphrey, *qv*. *Educ:* Shrewsbury Sch.; Trinity Coll., Cambridge (Hon. Fellow, 1995); MA, PhD (Cantab). Fellow, Jesus Coll., Cambridge, 1967–69 (Hon. Fellow, 1996); Research Associate, California Inst. of Technology, 1967–68 and 1971; Mem., Inst. for Advanced Study, Princeton, 1969–70; Prof., Univ. of Sussex, 1972–73; Cambridge University: Plumian Prof. of Astronomy and Experimental Philosophy, 1973–91; Dir, Inst. of Astronomy, 1977–82 and 1987–91; Royal Soc. Res. Prof., 1992–2003; Fellow of King's Coll., Cambridge, 1969–72 and 1973–2003. Astronomer Royal, 1995–2007. Visiting Professor: Harvard Univ., 1972,

1986–88; Inst. for Advanced Studies, Princeton, 1982, 1995; Imperial Coll., London, 2001–; Hitchcock Vis. Prof., UC Berkeley, 1994; Regents Fellow of Smithsonian Instn, Washington, 1984–88; Oort Prof., Leiden, 1999; Hon. Prof., Univ. of Leicester, 2001–. Lectures: H. P. Robertson Meml, US Nat. Acad. Sci., 1975; Bakerian, Royal Soc., 1982; Danz, Univ. of Washington, 1984; UK-Canada Rutherford, Royal Soc./RSC, 1998; Pauli, Zurich, 1999; Leverhulme, 1999; Scribner, Princeton, 2000; Russell, Amer. Astron. Soc., 2004; Messenger, Cornell Univ., 2005; Gifford, Scottish Univs, 2007. Trustee: BM, 1996–2002; NESTA, 1998–2001; Inst. for Adv. Study, Princeton, 1998–; Kennedy Meml Trust, 1999–2004; IPPR, 2001–; Nat. Mus. of Sci. and Industry, 2003–. President: RAS, 1992–94; BAAS, 1994–95; Chm., Science Adv. Cttee, ESA, 1976–78; Member: Council, Royal Soc., 1983–85 and 1993–95; PPARC, 1994–97. Member: Academia Europaea, 1989; Pontifical Acad. of Sci., 1990; For. Hon. Mem., Amer. Acad. of Arts and Sciences, 1975; Foreign Associate, Nat. Acad. of Sciences, USA, 1982; Foreign Member: Amer. Phil. Soc., 1993; Royal Swedish Acad. Sci., 1993; Russian Acad. of Sci., 1994; Norwegian Acad. of Arts and Letters, 1996; Accademia Lincei, Rome, 1996; Royal Netherlands Acad. of Arts and Sciences, 1998; Finnish Acad. of Sci. and Letters, 2004; Associate Mem., TWAS: the Acad. of Scis for the Developing World, 2008. Hon. FIASc 1990; Hon. FInstP 2001. Hon. Fellow: Cardiff Univ., 1998; Darwin Coll., Cambridge, 2004; John Moores Univ., 2008; King's Coll., Cambridge, 2007. Hon. DSc: Sussex, 1990; Leicester, 1993; Copenhagen, 1994; Keele, Newcastle and Uppsala, 1995; Toronto, 1997; Durham, 1999; Oxford, 2000; Ohio and Exeter, 2006; Hull, 2007; Liverpool, 2008; Yale, 2008; DUniv Open, 2008. Heinemann Prize, Amer. Inst. Physics, 1984; Gold Medal, RAS, 1987; Guthrie Medal and Prize, Inst. of Physics, 1989; Balzan Prize, Balzan Foundn, 1989; Schwarzschild Medal, Astron. ges., 1989; Bruce Gold Medal, Astron. Soc. of Pacific, 1993; Science writing award, Amer. Inst. of Physics, 1996; Bower Award for Science, Franklin Inst., 1998; Rossi Prize, American Astron. Soc., 2000; Cosmology Prize, Gruber Foundn, 2001; Einstein Award, World Cultural Council, 2003; Michael Faraday Award, Royal Soc., 2004; (jtly) Crafoord Prize, Royal Swedish Acad., 2005; Niels Bohr Medal, UNESCO, 2005. Officier, Ordre des Arts et des Lettres (France), 1991. *Publications:* Perspectives in Astrophysical Cosmology, 1995; (with M. Begelman) Gravity's Fatal Attraction: black holes in the universe, 1996; Before the Beginning: our universe and others, 1997; Just Six Numbers, 1999; Our Cosmic Habitat, 2001; Our Final Century?, 2003; What We Still Don't Know, 2009; mainly scientific papers; numerous general articles. *Address:* c/o Trinity College, Cambridge CB2 1TQ. *T:* (01223) 338412; (office) (01223) 337548.

REES, Allen Brynmor; Regional Chairman, Employment (formerly Industrial) Tribunals, Birmingham, 1995–2004; *b* 11 May 1936; *s* of late Allen Brynmor Rees and Elsie Louise Rees (*née* Hitchcock); *m* 1961, Nerys Eleanor Evans; two *d*. *Educ:* Monmouth Sch.; UCW, Aberystwyth (LLB 1958). Admitted Solicitor, 1961. Partner, Francis Ryan and Co., 1961–62; Solicitor, SW Div., NCB, 1962; Rexall Drug and Chemical Co., 1962–65; Rees Page (incorp. Page Son and Elias, Skidmore Hares and Co., and Darbey-Scott-Rees), 1965–93, Sen. Partner, 1974–93; Chm., Employment (formerly Industrial) Tribunals, 1993–2004. Prin. Solicitor, Birmingham Midshires Building Soc., 1976–93. Chairman: W Midlands Rent Assessment Panel, 1968–93; Social Security Tribunals, 1980–93; Mem. Cttee, Legal Aid Bd, 1975–93. Columnist (Solicitors' Notebook), Solicitors' Jl, 1968–92; Ed., Employment Tribunals Chairman's Handbook, 1999–2006. *Recreations:* canoeing, ski-ing, gardening, walking, watching Rugby. *Address:* Rossleigh, Shaw Lane, Albrighton, Wolverhampton WV7 3DS; Yr Hen Ystabl, Meifod, Powys SY22 6BP. *Club:* Old Monmothians (Monmouth).

REES, Prof. Andrew Jackson; Regius Professor of Medicine, University of Aberdeen, 1994; *b* 11 June 1946; *s* of late Gordon Jackson Rees and of Elisabeth Rees; *m* 1st, 1972, Ann Duncan (marr. diss. 1974); 2nd, 1979, Daphne Elizabeth Wood (marr. diss. 1985); two *d*; 3rd, 1999, Renate Kain; two *c*. *Educ:* King William's Coll., Isle of Man; Liverpool Univ. (MB ChB 1969); London Univ. (MSc). Trained in gen. medicine and nephrology, at Liverpool, Guy's, and Hammersmith Hosps, 1969–79; Consultant Physician, Hammersmith Hosp., 1979–90; Prof. of Nephrology, RPMS, 1990–94. Vis. Prof., Nat. Jewish Hosp., Denver, 1983–84; Goulstonian Lectr, RCP, 1984. Chair, UK Renal Genetics Gp, 2005–. Pres., Nephrology Section, RSocMed, 1994–95. Chm., 1995–2000, Vice-Pres., 2000–, Nat. Kidney Res. Fund; Pres., Renal Assoc. of GB and Ireland, 2001–04; Mem. Council, Internat. Soc. of Nephrology, 1998–2003. FMedSci 2000. *Publications:* (ed with C. D. Pusey) Rapidly Progressive Glomerulonephritis, 1998; papers on pathogenesis and treatment of glomerulonephritis. *Recreations:* contemporary theatre and music, ski-ing.

REES, (Anthony) John (David); educational consultant, since 2003; *b* 20 July 1943; *s* of Richard Frederick and Betty Rees; *m*; one *s* one *d* (and one *d* decd). *Educ:* Newcastle Royal Grammar Sch.; Clare Coll., Cambridge (Exhibr; BA 2nd Cl. Hons Geog.); PGCE 1966. Head of Economics, Harrow Sch., 1966–80; Head Master, Blundell's Sch., Tiverton, Devon, 1980–92; Rector, Edinburgh Acad., 1992–95; Director: Harrow Sch. Devlt Trust, 1995–97; The Bradfield Foundn, 1998–2000; school master, Cheltenham Coll., 2000–03. Established Notting Dale Urban Study Centre, 1972; Vis. Tutor, London Inst. of Education, 1973–2007. Member Executive Committee: Queen's Silver Jubilee Appeal, 1976–82; and Admin. Council, Royal Jubilee Trusts, 1978–82; Chairman: Prince's Trust for Devon, 1981–83; Youth Clubs UK, 1987–89; Founder Dir, Mid Devon Enterprise Agency, 1984–91; Chm., Crested, 1996–97. Member: CoSIRA Cttee for Devon, 1981–83; Council, Drake Fellowship, 1981–; Admiralty Interview Bd, 1981–2005; Cttee, HMC, 1986–91; Prince of Wales Community Venture, 1985–; Board: Devon and Cornwall Prince's Youth Business Trust, 1987–92; Fairbridge in Scotland, 1992–95; Trustee: SFIA Educl Trust, 1996–; Talley Community Woodland, 2007–. *Publications:* articles on economics and community service in many jls incl. Economics, Youth in Society, etc. *Recreations:* hill walking, family and friends.

REES, Barbara; *see* Wilding, B.

REES, Brian, MA Cantab; Headmaster, Rugby School, 1981–84; *b* 20 Aug. 1929; *s* of late Frederick T. Rees; *m* 1st, 1959, Julia (*d* 1978), *d* of Sir Robert Birley, KCMG; two *s* three *d*; 2nd, 1987, Juliet Akehurst (*née* Gowan). *Educ:* Bede Grammar Sch., Sunderland; Trinity Coll., Cambridge (Scholar). 1st cl. Historical Tripos, Part I, 1951; Part II, 1952. Eton College: Asst Master, 1952–65; Housemaster, 1963–65; Headmaster: Merchant Taylors' Sch., 1965–73; Charterhouse, 1973–81. Pres., Conference for Independent Further Education, 1973–82; Chm., ISIS, 1982–84. Res. Fellow, City Univ., 1989–90. Patron, UC of Buckingham, 1973–91. Liveryman, Merchant Taylors' Co., 1981. *Publications:* A Musical Peacemaker: biography of Sir Edward German, 1987; (ed) History and Idealism: essays, addresses and letters of Sir Robert Birley, 1990; Camille Saint-Saëns: a life, 1999; contrib. Oxford DNB. *Recreations:* music, gardening. *Address:* 52 Spring Lane, Flore, Northampton NN7 4LS. *T:* (01327) 340621.

REES, Caroline, (Lady Rees of Ludlow); *see* Humphrey, C.

REES, Christina Henking Muller; media and public relations consultant, since 1985; writer, since 1986; broadcaster, since 1990; executive coach, since 2003; *b* 6 July 1953; *d* of John Muller, Jr and Carol Benton Muller; *m* 1978, Christopher Rees, *s* of late Richard Rees and Margaret (*née* Head); two *d*. *Educ:* Pomona Coll., Calif (BA English 1975); King's Coll., London (MA Theology 1998). Asst PR Officer, Children's Soc., 1985–87. Member: Gen. Synod of C of E, 1990–; Archbishops' Council, 1999–2000, 2006–; Chair: Women and the Church, 1996–; Women on the Move, 1999–; spokesperson, Movt for Ordination of Women, 1992–94. Mem., Central Religious Adv. Cttee, 2003–. Trustee: Li Tim-Oi Foundn, 1997–; Christian Assoc. of Business Executives, 2007–; Dir, The Churchfield Trust, 2000–. Consultant: IBA, 1979; BBC Children in Need Appeal, 1997–2000. Gov., Ripon Coll. Cuddesdon, 2000–. Contribs to radio and TV progs, 1990–, incl. Thought for the Day, Radio 4, 1991–. FRSA 2005. *Publications:* Sea Urchin, 1990; The Divine Embrace, 2000; (ed) Voices of This Calling, 2002; contrib. to The Times, Guardian, Independent, Christian publications, etc. *Recreations:* rare breeds, beachcombing, improving Anglo-American relations. *Address:* Churchfield, Pudding Lane, Barley, Royston, Herts SG8 8JX. *T:* (01763) 848822, 848472.

See also Rev. Canon R. M. Rees.

REES, Sir Dai; *see* Rees, Sir David A.

REES, Prof. David, FRS 1968; Emeritus Professor of Pure Mathematics, University of Exeter (Professor, 1958–83); *b* 29 May 1918; *s* of David and Florence Gertrude Rees; *m* 1952, Joan Sybil Cushen; four *d*. *Educ:* King Henry VIII Grammar School, Abergavenny; Sidney Sussex College, Cambridge. Manchester University: Assistant Lecturer, 1945–46, Lecturer, 1946–49; Cambridge University: Lecturer, 1949–58; Fellow of Downing College, Cambridge, 1950–58, Hon. Fellow, 1970–. Mem. Council, Royal Soc., 1979–81. Hon. DSc Exeter, 1993. Polya Prize, London Mathematical Soc., 1993. *Publications:* papers on Algebraic topics in British and foreign mathematical journals. *Recreations:* reading and listening to music. *Address:* 6 Hillcrest Park, Exeter EX4 4SH. *T:* (01392) 259398.

See also S. M. Rees.

REES, Sir David Allan, (Sir Dai Rees), Kt 1993; BSc, PhD, DSc; FRCPE, FMedSci; FRS 1981; FRSC, FIBiol; Medical Research Council scientist, 1996–2001; *b* 28 April 1936; *s* of James Allan Rees and Elsie Bolam; *m* 1959, Myfanwy Margaret Parry Owen; two *s* one *d*. *Educ:* Hawarden Grammar Sch., Clwyd; University Coll. of N Wales, Bangor, Gwynedd (BSc 1956; PhD 1959; Hon. Fellow, 1988); DSc Edinburgh, 1970. FRCPE 1999. DSIR Res. Fellow, University Coll., Bangor, 1959, and Univ. of Edinburgh, 1960; Asst Lectr in Chem., 1961, Lectr, 1962–70, Univ. of Edinburgh; Section Manager, 1970–72, Principal Scientist, 1972–82, and Sci. Policy Exec., 1978–82, Unilever Res., Colworth Lab.; Chm., Science Policy Gp for Unilever Res., 1979–82. Associate Dir (pt-time), MRC Unit for Cell Biophysics, KCL, 1980–82; Dir, Nat. Inst. for Med. Res., Mill Hill, 1982–87; Sec., subseq. Chief Exec., MRC, 1987–96. Vis. Professorial Fellow, University Coll., Cardiff, 1972–77. Philips Lecture, Royal Soc., 1984. Member: MRC, 1984–96; Council, Royal Soc., 1985–87. Pres., ESF, 1994–99. FKC 1989. Founder FMedSci 1998. Hon. FRCP 1986. Hon. DSc: Edinburgh, 1989; Wales, 1991; Stirling, 1995; Leicester, 1997; DUniv York, 2007. Colworth Medal, Biochemical Soc., 1970; Carbohydrate Award, Chemical Soc., 1970. *Publications:* various, on carbohydrate chem. and biochem. and cell biology. *Recreations:* river boats, reading, listening to music. *Address:* Ford Cottage, 1 High Street, Denford, Kettering, Northants NN14 4EQ. *T:* (01832) 733502; *e-mail:* drees@nimr.mrc.ac.uk.

REES, David Wyn; His Honour Judge Wyn Rees; a Circuit Judge, since 2005; Diversity and Community Relations Judge (formerly Ethnic Minority Liaison Judge) for South Wales, since 2005; *b* 6 Jan. 1948; *s* of late David Daniel Rees and Mariann Rees; *m* 1972, Gillian Anne Davies; two *d*. *Educ:* Ysgol Gynradd Gymraeg Aberdâr; Mountain Ash Grammar Sch.; University Coll. of Wales, Aberystwyth (BSc Hons 1969). Admitted solicitor, 1973; Partner, Spicketts, Solicitors, Pontypridd, 1974–88; Dep. Dist Judge, 1984–88; Dist Judge, 1988–2005; Asst Recorder, 1994–98; Recorder, 1998–2005. Judicial Studies Board: Dir, Seminars for Dist Judges, 1996–2001; Mem., Civil and Family Cttees, 1996–2001; Mem., Main Bd, 1999–2001; Mem., Equal Treatment Adv. Cttee, 2007–. Mem., Lord Chancellor's Standing Cttee for Welsh Lang., 1999–2005. Pres., Pontypridd and Rhondda Law Soc., 1985–86. Hon. Mem., Gorsedd of Bards, 2003–. *Recreations:* walking Wales, foreign travel, golf, the company of family and friends. *Address:* Pontypridd County Court, The Courthouse, Courthouse Street, Pontypridd, Rhondda Cynon Taf CF37 1JR. *T:* (01443) 490800, *Fax:* (01443) 480305.

REES, Edward Parry; QC 1998; *b* 18 June 1949; *s* of Edward Howell Rees and Margaret Rees Parry; *m* 1983, Kathleen Wiltshire; one *s* one *d*. *Educ:* University Coll. of Wales, Aberystwyth (LLB Hons). Called to the Bar, Gray's Inn, 1973. Hon. Fellow in Criminal Process, Univ. of Kent, 1992. *Publication:* Blackstone's Guide to the Proceeds of Crime Act, 2003. *Recreations:* family, garden. *Address:* 11 Doughty Street, WC1N 2PG. *T:* (020) 7404 1313.

REES, Eleri Mair; Her Honour Judge Rees; a Circuit Judge, and Liaison Judge for the Welsh Language, since 2002; *b* 7 July 1953; *d* of late Ieuan Morgan and Sarah Alice Morgan (*née* James); *m* 1975, Alan Rees. *Educ:* Ardwyn Grammar Sch., Aberystwyth; Univ. of Liverpool (LLB Hons). Called to the Bar, Gray's Inn, 1975. Clerk to Justices, Bexley Magistrates' Court, 1983–94; Metropolitan Stipendiary Magistrate, subseq. Dist Judge (Magistrates' Courts), 1994–2002; a Recorder, 1997–2002. Editor, Family Court Reporter, 1992–94. Mem., Magisterial Cttee, Judicial Studies Bd, 1989–94. *Publications:* contrib. various jls on subject of family law. *Recreations:* travel, cookery, ski-ing. *Address:* c/o Circuit Office, 2nd Floor, Churchill House, Churchill Way, Cardiff CF1 4HH.

REES, Gareth David; QC 2003; *b* 2 July 1956; *s* of Baron Merlyn-Rees, PC and Colleen (*née* Cleveley); *m* 2000, Lucia Boddington; two *d*, and one *s* two *d* from former marriage. *Educ:* Harrow Co. Sch. for Boys; Reading Univ. (BA Hons). Called to the Bar, Gray's Inn, 1981; in practice as barrister, 1981–. *Recreations:* sport, music, family, cinema. *Address:* 7 Bedford Row, WC1R 4BS. *Clubs:* MCC, Two Brydges.

REES, Prof. Geraint Ellis, PhD; Wellcome Senior Clinical Fellow, Wellcome Trust Centre for Neuroimaging, since 2003, and Professor of Cognitive Neurology, since 2006, Institute of Neurology, University College London; *b* 27 Nov. 1967; *s* of Olav Anelyf Rees and Rosemary Ann Rees (*née* Dawson); *m* 2000, Rebecca Ruth Roylance; one *s* one *d*. *Educ:* Gonville and Caius Coll., Cambridge (BA Med. Sci. Tripos 1988); New Coll., Oxford (BM BCh 1991); University Coll. London (PhD 1999). MRCP 1994; FRCP 2008. Pre-registration surgery, Glasgow Royal Infirmary, and medicine, John Radcliffe Hosp., Oxford, 1991–92; post-registration SHO posts at Hammersmith Hosp., Royal Brompton Hosp., St Thomas' Hosp. and National Hosp., 1991–94; Registrar, Queen Mary's Hosp., Roehampton, 1994–95; Clin. Res. Fellow, Inst. of Neurol., UCL, 1995–99; Wellcome Advanced Fellow: CIT, 1999–2001; Inst. of Cognitive Neurosci., UCL, 2001–02. Hon. Consultant, National Hosp. for Neurol. and Neurosurgery, 2004–. *Publications:* (ed jtly) Neurobiology of Attention, 2005; contrib. numerous articles to acad. jls. *Recreation:* attempting to achieve a better work/life balance. *Address:* Wellcome Trust

Centre for Neuroimaging, 12 Queen Square, WC1N 3BG. *T:* (020) 7679 5496, *Fax:* (020) 7813 1420; *e-mail:* g.rees@fil.ion.ucl.ac.uk.

REES, Prof. Graham Charles, PhD; FBA 2005; Research Professor of English, Queen Mary, University of London, since 1998; *b* 31 Dec. 1944; *s* of Charles Rees and Margaret Fernie Rees; *m* 1995, Maria Eve Wakely; one *d. Educ:* Univ. of Birmingham (BA 1966; MA 1968; PhD 1970). Asst Lectr in English, Shenstone New Coll., 1969–72; Lectr in English, 1972–74, Sen. Lectr, 1974–98, Wolverhampton Poly., subseq. Univ.; British Acad./Leverhulme Trust Sen. Res. Fellow, 1995–96. Part-time tutor, Open Univ., 1971–81. *Publications:* (ed) The Oxford Francis Bacon, vol. VI: philosophical studies *c*1611–*c*1619, 1996, vol. XIII: Instauratio Magna: last writings, 2000, vol. XI: Novum Organum, 2004. *Recreations:* book collecting, cats, gardens (but not gardening), Wagner, wine. *Address:* 14 Latchett Road, South Woodford, E18 1DJ. *T:* (020) 8505 9375; *e-mail:* g.c.rees@qmul.ac.uk.

REES, Helen; *see* Young, H.

REES, Prof. Hubert, DFC 1945; PhD, DSc; FRS 1976; Professor of Agricultural Botany, University College of Wales, Aberystwyth, 1968–91, now Emeritus; *b* 2 Oct. 1923; *s* of Owen Rees and Tugela Rees, Llangennech, Carmarthenshire; *m* 1946, Mavis Hill; two *s* two *d. Educ:* Llandovery and Llanelli Grammar Schs; University Coll. of Wales, Aberystwyth (BSc); PhD, DSc Birmingham. Served RAF, 1942–46. Student, Aberystwyth, 1946–50; Lectr in Cytology, Univ. of Birmingham, 1950–58; Sen. Lectr in Agric. Botany, University Coll. of Wales, Aberystwyth, 1958, Reader 1966. *Publications:* Chromosome Genetics, 1977; B Chromosomes, 1982; articles on genetic control of chromosomes and on evolutionary changes in chromosome organisation. *Recreation:* fishing. *Address:* Irfon, Llanbadarn Road, Aberystwyth, Dyfed SY23 1EY. *T:* (01970) 623668.

REES, Hugh Francis E.; *see* Ellis-Rees.

REES, Rt Rev. Ivor; *see* Rees, Rt Rev. J. I.

REES, John; *see* Rees, A. J. D., and Rees, P. J.

REES, Rev. Canon John; *see* Rees, Rev. Canon V. J. H.

REES, John Charles; QC 1991; *b* 22 May 1949; *s* of Ronald Leslie Rees and Martha Therese Rees; *m* 1970, Dianne Elizabeth Kirby; three *s* one *d. Educ:* St Illtyd's College, Cardiff; Jesus College, Cambridge (double first class Hons; BA (Law), LLB (Internat. Law), MA, LLM; repr. Univ. in boxing and Association Football; boxing Blue). Called to the Bar, Lincoln's Inn, 1972. Trustee and Governor, St John's College, Cardiff, 1987–. Administrative Steward, and Chm., Welsh Area Council, BBB of C. *Recreations:* all sport, esp. boxing and Association Football; theatre. *Address:* Marleigh Lodge, Druidstone Road, Old St Mellons, Cardiff CF3 9XD. *T:* (029) 2079 4918; 33 Park Place, Cardiff CF1 3BA. *Club:* Hawks (Cambridge).

REES, Rt Rev. (John) Ivor; Bishop of St Davids, 1991–95; *b* 19 Feb. 1926; *o s* of David Morgan Rees and Cecilia Perrott Rees; *m* 1954, Beverley Richards; three *s. Educ:* Llanelli Gram. Sch.; University Coll. of Wales (BA 1950); Westcott House, Cambridge. Served RN, Coastal Forces and British Pacific Fleet, 1943–47. Deacon 1952, priest 1953, Dio. St David's; Curate: Fishguard, 1952–55; Llangathen, 1955–57; Priest-in-Charge, Uzmaston, 1957–59; Vicar: Slebech and Uzmaston, 1959–65; Llangollen, 1965–74; Rural Dean of Llangollen, 1970–74; Rector of Wrexham, 1974–76; Dean of Bangor, 1976–88; Vicar of Cathedral Parish of Bangor, 1979–88; Archdeacon of St Davids and Asst Bp, Dio. of St Davids, 1988–91. Canon of St Asaph, 1975–76; Chaplain, Order of St John for County of Clwyd, 1974–76, County of Gwynedd, 1976–88. Hon. Fellow, Trinity Coll., Carmarthen, 1996. KStJ 2006 (SBStJ 1975, OStJ 1981, Sub-Prelate, 1993–2002). *Publications:* Monograph—The Parish of Llangollen and its Churches, 1971; Keeping 40 Days—Sermons for Lent, 1989. *Recreations:* music and good light reading. *Address:* Llys Dewi, 45 Clover Park, Uzmaston Road, Haverfordwest, Pembs SA61 1UE. *T:* (01437) 764846; *e-mail:* jir.1926@amserve.net.

REES, John Samuel; Editor, Western Mail, 1981–87; *b* 23 Oct. 1931; *s* of John Richard Rees and Mary Jane Rees; *m* 1957, Ruth Jewell; one *s* one *d. Educ:* Cyfarthfa Castle Grammar Sch., Merthyr Tydfil. Nat. Service, Welch Regt and RAEC, 1950–52. Reporter, 1948–50, Sports Editor, 1952–54, Merthyr Express; The Star, Sheffield: Reporter, 1954–56; Sub Editor, 1956–58; Dep. Chief Sub Editor, 1958–59; Dep. Sports Editor, 1959–61; Asst Editor, 1961–66; Dep. Editor, Evening Echo, Hemel Hempstead, 1966–69; Editor: Evening Mail, Slough and Hounslow, 1969–72; The Journal, Newcastle upon Tyne, 1972–76; Evening Post-Echo, Hemel Hempstead, 1976–79, Asst Man. Dir, Evening Post-Echo Ltd, 1979–81. Lectr, Centre for Journalism Studies, Univ. of Wales Coll. of Cardiff, 1988–92. *Recreations:* marquetry, watching cricket and rugby, walking, gardening. *Address:* 2 Alton Close, Whirlowdale Park, Sheffield S11 9QQ. *T:* (0114) 235 1028.

REES, Prof. Jonathan Laurence, FRCP, FRCPE; Grant Professor of Dermatology, University of Edinburgh, since 2000; *b* 10 Oct. 1957; *s* of William Rees and Maura (*née* West); *m* 1983, Anne Bradbury (marr. diss. 2006); two *d*; *m* 2007, Lisa Naysmith. *Educ:* Newcastle Univ. (BMedSci 1st Cl. Hons 1981; MB BS Hons 1982). MRCP 1985, FRCP 1993; FRCPE 2001. Vis. Fellow, 1st Hautklinik, Allgemeines Krankenhaus der Stadt Wien, Vienna, 1986; MRC Trng Fellow, Univ. of Newcastle upon Tyne, 1987–89; MRC Clinician Scientist, CNRS/INSERM Lab. de Génétique Moléculaire des Eucaryotes, Strasbourg, 1989–91; Prof. of Dermatology, Univ. of Newcastle upon Tyne, 1992–99. FMedSci 1998. *Publications:* papers on genetics of skin disease, particularly genetics of skin and hair colour (red hair) and on pigment, skin cancer, nature of clinical discovery and stats in medicine. *Recreations:* not being timetabled, Rugby, arguing about why medicine and medical research should be done. *Address:* Department of Dermatology, University of Edinburgh, Level 1, The Lauriston Building, Lauriston Place, Edinburgh EH3 9HA. *T:* (0131) 536 2041, *Fax:* (0131) 229 8769; *e-mail:* jonathan.rees@ed.ac.uk.

REES, Jonathan Nigel; Deputy Chief Executive (Policy) (formerly Deputy Director General (Policy)), Health and Safety Executive, since 2004; *b* 29 Sept. 1955; *s* of late Arthur Ernest Rees and of Thelma Maureen Rees; *m* 1996, Kathryn Jayne Taylor; one *s* one *d. Educ:* Jesus Coll., Oxford (MA Hons Modern History). Joined DTI, 1977; Private Sec. to Minister for Trade, 1981–84; EC, 1984–86 (on secondment); DTI, 1986–89; Industry Counsellor, UK Rep. to EU, 1989–94; Prime Minister's Policy Unit, 1994–97; Dir, Citizen's Charter Unit, then Modernising Public Services Gp, Cabinet Office, 1997–2000; Dir, Consumer and Competition Policy, DTI, 2000–04. *Recreations:* sport, travel, theatre. *Address:* Health and Safety Executive, Rose Court, 2 Southwark Bridge, SE1 9HS. *T:* (020) 7717 6000. *Club:* MCC.

REES, Prof. Judith Anne, CBE 2005; PhD; Professor of Environmental and Resources Management, London School of Economics, since 1995; *b* 26 Aug. 1944; *d* of late Douglas S. Hart and Eva M. Hart (*née* Haynes); *m* 1st, 1968, Prof. Raymond Rees, *qv* (marr. diss. 1972); 2nd, 1981, Prof. David Keith Crozier Jones. *Educ:* Bilborough Grammar Sch., Nottingham; London Sch. of Economics (BSc Econ 1965; MPhil 1967; PhD 1978). Lectr, Agricl Econs, Wye Coll., London Univ., 1967–69; Lectr, 1969–85, Sen. Lectr, 1985–89, in Geography, LSE; University of Hull: Prof. of Geography, 1989–95; Dean of Sch. of Geography and Earth Resources, 1991–93; Pro-Vice Chancellor, 1993–95; Pro-Dir, then Dep. Dir, LSE, 1998–2004. Nat. Water and Sewerage Policy Advr, Australian Dept of Urban and Regl Develt, 1974–75. Economic and Social Research Council: Member: Trng Bd, 1994–98; Global Envmtl Change Cttee, 1995–98; Council, 2004–; Chm., Trng and Develt Bd, 2004–; Member: Exec. Panel on Pollution Res., SSRC, 1977–80; Adv. Cttee, Centre for Regulated Industries, 1990–; Technical Adv. Cttee, Global Water Partnership, 1996–; Competition (formerly Monopolies and Mergers) Commn, 1996–2002; Link/Teaching Co. Scheme Bd, OST, 1997–2002; UN Sec. Gen's Adv. Bd on Water and Sanitation, 2004–; Chm., Ofwat Southern Customer Service Cttee, 1990–96. Member: Council, RGS, 1979–82 (Vice Pres., 1995–97); Council, Inst. of British Geographers, 1981–83. *Publications:* Industrial Demands for Water, 1969; Natural Resources Allocation, Economics and Policy, 1985, 2nd edn 1990; (jtly) The International Oil Industry: an interdisciplinary perspective, 1987; (jtly) Troubled Water, 1987; Water for Life, 1993; articles on water resources and envmtl mgt in books and learned jls. *Address:* London School of Economics, Houghton Street, WC2A 2AE. *T:* (020) 7955 6228.

REES, Laurence Mark; Creative Director, BBC TV History Programmes, since 2000; *b* 19 Jan. 1957; *s* of late Alan Rees and Margaret Julia Rees (*née* Mark); *m* 1987, Helena Brewer; two *s* one *d. Educ:* Solihull Sch.; Worcester Coll., Oxford (BA). Joined BBC TV, 1978: prodn trainee, 1978–79; writer/producer/dir, 1982–; Ed., Timewatch, BBC2, 1992–2002; Hd, History Progs Unit, BBC TV, 1999–2000. *Productions* include: Crisis (drama documentary), 1987; A British Betrayal, 1991; We Have Ways of Making You Think (History of Propaganda series), 1992; Nazis: a warning from history (series; awards include: BAFTA, IDA, Peabody, BPG), 1997; War of the Century (series), 1999; Horror in the East (series), 2000; Auschwitz: the Nazis and the 'Final Solution' (series; Grierson Award, History Today Prize), 2005; World War Two: behind closed doors, 2008; as Executive Producer, awards include: Emmy Awards, 1994 (2) and 1996; Amnesty Press Award, 1994; Internat. Documentary Assoc. Award, 1997; Western Heritage Award, 2000. Hon. DLitt Sheffield, 2005. *Publications:* Electric Beach (novel), 1990; Selling Politics, 1992; Nazis: a warning from history, 1997; War of the Century, 1999; Horror in the East, 2001; Auschwitz: the Nazis and the 'Final Solution', 2005 (History Book of the Year, British Book Awards, 2006); Their Darkest Hour: people tested to the extreme in World War Two, 2007; World War Two: behind closed doors, 2008. *Recreation:* my three children. *Address:* c/o Andrew Nurnberg Associates, Clerkenwell House, Clerkenwell Green, EC1R 0QX. *T:* (020) 7417 8800.

REES, Dame Lesley Howard, DBE 2001; MD, DSc; FRCP; FRCPath; Professor of Chemical Endocrinology, Bart's and The London School of Medicine and Dentistry, Queen Mary (formerly St Bartholomew's Hospital Medical College), University of London, 1978; *b* 17 Nov. 1942; *d* of Howard Leslie Davis and Charlotte Patricia Siegrid Young; *m* 1969, Gareth Mervyn Rees. *Educ:* Pates Girls' Grammar Sch., Cheltenham; Malvern Girls' Coll.; London Univ. (MB BS 1965; MD 1972; MSc 1974; DSc 1989). MRCP 1967, FRCP 1979; MRCPath 1976, FRCPath 1988. Editor, Clinical Endocrinology, 1979–84; Subdean, 1983–88, Dean, 1989–95, St Bartholomew's Hosp. Med. Coll.; Public Orator, London Univ., 1984–86. Chm., Soc. for Endocrinology, 1984–87; Sec.-Gen., Internat. Soc. of Endocrinology, 1984–2005. Mem., Press Complaints Commn, 1991–94. Royal College of Physicians: Dir, Internat. Office, 1997–99; Dir, Educn Dept, 1997–2001. Founder FMedSci 1998. *Recreations:* music, poetry, reading, ski-ing, administrative gardening. *Address:* 23 Church Row, Hampstead, NW3 6UP. *T:* and *Fax:* (020) 7794 4936. *Club:* Reform.

REES, Rt Rev. Leslie Lloyd; Bishop Suffragan of Shrewsbury, 1980–86; *b* 14 April 1919; *s* of Rees Thomas and Elizabeth Rees; *m* 1944, Rosamond Smith (*d* 1989); one *s* (and one *s* decd). *Educ:* Pontardawe Grammar Sch.; Kelham Theological College. Asst Curate, St Saviour, Roath, 1942; Asst Chaplain, HM Prison, Cardiff, 1942; Chaplain, HM Prison; Durham, 1945; Dartmoor, 1948; Vicar of Princetown, 1948; Chaplain, HM Prison, Winchester, 1955; Chaplain General of Prisons, Home Office Prison Dept, 1962–80. Chaplain to the Queen, 1971–80. Mem., Parole Bd, 1987–90. Hon. Canon of Canterbury, 1966–80, of Lichfield, 1980–; Hon. Asst Bishop, dio. of Winchester, 1987–2004. Freeman, City of London. ChStJ 1985. *Recreation:* music. *Address:* Blackwater Mill Retirement Home, Blackwater, Newport, Isle of Wight PO30 3BJ.

REES, Mary; *see* Rees, S. M.

REES, Sir Meuric; *see* Rees, Sir R. E. M.

REES, Rev. Canon Michael; *see* Rees, Rev. Canon R. M.

REES, Owen, CB 1991; Deputy Chairman, Qualifications, Curriculum and Assessment Authority for Wales, 1997–2006; *b* 26 Dec. 1934; *s* of late John Trevor and Esther Rees, Trimsaran, Dyfed; *m* 1958, Elizabeth Gosby (*d* 1991); one *s* two *d. Educ:* Llanelli Grammar Sch.; Univ. of Manchester. BA(Econ). Bank of London and South America, 1957; regional development work in Cardiff, Birmingham and London, BoT, 1959–69; Cabinet Office, 1969–71; Welsh Office, 1971–94: Asst Sec. (European Div.), 1972; Under Sec., 1977–94; Sec. for Welsh Educn, 1977–78; Head, Educn Dept, 1978–80; Dir, Industry Dept, 1980–85; Head, Economic and Regl Policy Gp, 1985–90; Head, Agriculture Dept, 1990–94. *Address:* 4 Llandennis Green, Cyncoed, Cardiff CF23 6JX. *T:* (029) 2075 9712.

REES, Prof. (Peter) John, FRCP, FRCPE; Professor of Medical Education, since 2006, and Consultant Physician, King's College London School of Medicine; *b* 2 March 1949; *s* of Joseph Thomas Rees and Doris Mary Williams; *m* 1973, Helen Mary Heath; one *s* one *d. Educ:* Whitchurch Grammar Sch., Cardiff; Christ's Coll., Cambridge (MB BChir; MA; MD); Guy's Hosp., London. FRCP 1988; FRCPE 2002. Guy's Hospital, later UMDS of Guy's and St Thomas' Hospitals, then Guy's, King's and St Thomas' Hospitals Medical and Dental School of King's College London, subseq. King's College London School of Medicine: Lectr, 1979–83; Sen. Lectr in Medicine, 1983–2006; Consultant Physician, 1983–; Asst Clin. Dean, 1993–2000; Gp Clin. Dir for Acute Med. Services, 1995–2000; Dep. Chm., Academic Bd, 1996–98; Site Dean, Guy's Hosp., 2000–05; Dean, Undergrad. Educn, 2005–. Non-exec. Mem., Lewisham and N Southwark HA, 1990–92; non-executive Director: Mildmay Mission Hosp., 1992–2005; Lewisham Hosp. Trust Bd, 1995–2006; Mem. Exec. Cttee, British Lung Foundn, 1988–95. *Publications:* (jtly) ABC of Asthma, 1984, 5th edn 2006; (jtly) Practical Management of Asthma, 1985, 2nd edn 1996; A Medical Catechism, 1986; (jtly) A New Short Textbook of Medicine, 1988; Diagnostic Tests in Respiratory Medicine, 1988; Asthma: family doctor guide, 1988; (jtly) A Colour Atlas of Asthma, 1989; (jtly) Aids to Clinical Pharmacology and Therapeutics, 1993; (jtly) Principles of Clinical Medicine, 1995; (jtly) Asthma: current perspectives, 1996; (jtly) 100 Cases in Clinical Medicine, 2000, 2nd edn 2007. *Recreations:*

theatre, opera, cricket, squash, walking. *Address:* Guy's Hospital, London Bridge, SE1 9RT. *T:* (020) 7188 3739.

REES, Peter Wynne, RIBA; FRTPI; The City Planning Officer, City of London Corporation (formerly Corporation of London), since 1987; *b* 26 Sept. 1948; *s* of Gwynne Rees, MM, CEng, MIMechE, FMES, and late Elizabeth Rodda Rees (*née* Hynam). *Educ:* Pontardawe Grammar Sch.; Whitchurch Grammar Sch., Cardiff; Bartlett Sch. of Architecture, UCL (BSc Hons); Welsh Sch. of Architecture, Univ. of Wales (BArch); Polytechnic of the South Bank (BTP). Architectural Asst, Historic Bldgs Div., GLC, 1971–72; Asst to Gordon Cullen, CBE, RDI, FSIA, 1973–75; Architect, Historic Areas Conservation, DoE, 1975–79; UK Rep., Council of Europe Wkg Parties studying New Uses for Historic Buildings and The Economics of Building Conservation, 1977–78; Asst Chief Planning Officer, London Bor. of Lambeth, 1979–85; Controller of Planning, Corp. of London, 1985–87. Trustee, Building Conservation Trust, 1985–91. Founder Mem. and Dir, British Council for Offices, 1989–. London Rep., EC (formerly European) Working Party on Technological Impact on Future Urban Change, 1989–92; Member: Steering Gp, London World City Study, 1990–91; Officers' Gp, London Pride Partnership, 1994–98; London Office Review Panel, 1996–. FRSA 1988. President's Award, British Council for Offices, 2003; Barbara Miller Award, Faculty of Building, 2004. *Publications:* City of London Local Plan, 1989; City of London Unitary Development Plans, 1994 and 2002; contribs to professional studies and jls. *Recreations:* swimming, Nordic ski-ing, playing the viola, music, tidying. *Address:* City Planning Officer, Guildhall, EC2P 2EJ. *T:* (020) 7332 1700. *Club:* Guildhall.

REES, Philip; a Recorder of the Crown Court, 1983–2008; *b* 1 Dec. 1941; *s* of John Trevor Rees and Olwen Muriel Rees; *m* 1969, Catherine Good; one *s* one *d*. *Educ:* Monmouth Sch.; Bristol Univ. (LLB Hons). Called to the Bar, Middle Temple, 1965. Former Asst Boundary Comr. *Recreations:* music, sport. *Address:* 33 South Rise, Llanishen, Cardiff CF14 0RF. *T:* (029) 2075 4364. *Club:* Cardiff and County (Cardiff).

REES, Prof. Philip Howell, CBE 2004; PhD; FBA 1998; Professor of Population Geography, University of Leeds, 1990–Sept. 2009; *b* 17 Sept. 1944; *s* of Foster and Mona Rees; *m* 1968, Laura Campbell; one *s* one *d*. *Educ:* King Edward's Sch., Birmingham; St Catharine's Coll., Cambridge (BA Geog. 1966; MA 1970); Univ. of Chicago (MA Geog. 1968; PhD 1973). University of Leeds: Lectr, 1970–80; Reader, 1980–90. Hofstee Vis. Fellow, Netherlands Interdisciplinary Demographic Inst., The Hague, 1995; Dist. Vis. Fellow, Univ. of Adelaide, 1996. Gill Meml Award, RGS, 1996. *Publications:* Spatial Population Analysis, 1977; Residential Patterns in American Cities, 1979; (ed jtly) Population Structures and Models, 1985; (ed) Migration Processes and Patterns, Vol. 2, 1992; (ed jtly) Population Migration in the European Union, 1996; The Determinants of Migration Flows in England, 1998; (ed jtly) The Census Data System, 2002; The Development of a Migration Model, 2002; e-Learning for Geographers, 2009. *Recreation:* walking. *Address:* School of Geography, University of Leeds, Leeds LS2 9JT. *T:* (0113) 233 3341; (home) 8 Moseley Wood Gardens, Cookridge, Leeds LS16 7HR. *T:* (0113) 267 6968.

REES, Prof. Ray; Professor of Economics, University of Munich, 1993–2008 (Dean of Economics Faculty, 1999–2000); *b* 19 Sept. 1943; *s* of Gwyn Rees and Violet May (*née* Powell); *m* 1976, Denise Sylvia (*née* Stinson); two *s*. *Educ:* Dyffryn Grammar Sch., Port Talbot; London School of Economics and Political Science (MScEcon). Lectr 1966–76, Reader 1976–78, Queen Mary Coll., Univ. of London; Economic Advr, HM Treasury (on secondment), 1968–72; Prof. of Econs, UC, Cardiff, 1978–87; Prof. of Econs, Univ. of Guelph, Ont, 1987–93. Member (part-time), Monopolies and Mergers Commn, 1985–87. *Publications:* A Dictionary of Economics, 1968, 3rd edn 1984; Public Enterprise Economics, 1975, 3rd edn 1992; Microeconomics, 1981, 3rd edn 2004; Economics: a mathematical introduction, 1991; Introduction to Game Theory, 1992; The Theory of Principal and Agent, 1992; Mathematics for Economics, 1996, 2nd edn 2001; The Economics of Public Utilities, 2006; The Microeconomics of Insurance, 2007; Public Economics and the Household, 2008; articles in Economic Jl, Amer. Econ. Rev., Jl of Political Econ., Jl of Public Econs, Economica, and others. *Recreations:* playing the guitar, walking in the Alps. *Address:* Ungererstrasse 34, 80802 Munich, Germany. *T:* (89) 33036706.

REES, Sir (Richard Ellis) Meuric, Kt 2007; CBE 1982; JP; FRAgS; Lord-Lieutenant for Gwynedd, 1990–99; Vice Chairman, Hill Farming Advisory Committee (Chairman, Committee for Wales); *b* Pantydwr, Radnorshire, 1924; *m*; three *d*. President: YFC in Wales, 1961; Merioneth Agricl Soc., 1972; Royal Welsh Agricl Show, 1978; former Chm., Welsh Council of NFU; Mem., CLA. Member: Agricl Trng Bd, 1974 (Chm., Cttee for Wales); Countryside Commn, 1981 (Chm., Cttee for Wales). Governor: Welsh Agricl Coll., Aberystwyth; Coleg Meirionnydd, Dolgellau; Inst. of Grassland and Animal Production, 1987; Inst. of Grassland and Environmental Res., 1990. Mem., Tywyn UDC, 1967–73. Chm., N Wales Police Authority, 1982–84. JP Tywyn, 1957 (Chm. of Bench, 1974–94); High Sheriff of Gwynedd, 1982–83; DL Gwynedd, 1988. FRAgS 1973. Hon. MSc Wales, 1999. KStJ 1997. *Address:* Escuan Hall, Tywyn, Gwynedd LL36 9HR.

REES, Rev. Canon (Richard) Michael; Canon Emeritus, Chester Cathedral, since 2000; *b* 31 July 1935; *s* of late Richard and Margaret (*née* Head); *m* 1958, Yoma Patricia; one *s* one *d*. *Educ:* Brighton College; St Peter's College, Oxford (MA Theol); Tyndale Hall, Bristol. Curate: Crowborough, 1959–62; Christ Church, Clifton, Bristol, 1962–64; Vicar: Christ Church, Clevedon, 1964–72; Holy Trinity, Cambridge, 1972–84; Proctor, General Synod for Ely Diocese, 1975–85; Chief Sec., Church Army, 1984–90; Residentiary Canon, Chester Cathedral and Canon Missioner, Dio. of Chester, 1990–2000; Vice-Dean, Chester Cathedral, 1993–2000; Cheshire County Ecumenical Officer, 1991–99. C of E Rep., BCC, 1983–90 (Moderator, Evangelism Cttee, 1986–90). Editor, Missionary Mandate, 1955–68. *Publication:* Celebrating the Millennium in the Local Church, 1997. *Recreations:* photography, filling waste paper baskets. *Address:* 65 Tennyson Avenue, King's Lynn, Norfolk PE30 2QJ. *T:* (01553) 691982.

REES, Prof. (Susan) Mary, PhD; FRS 2002; Professor of Mathematics, University of Liverpool, since 2002; *b* 31 July 1953; *d* of Prof. David Rees, *qv* and Joan Rees. *Educ:* St Hugh's Coll., Oxford (BA 1974, MSc 1975); Univ. of Warwick (PhD Maths 1978). Asst, then Associate Prof. of Maths, Univ. of Minnesota, 1982–84; Lectr, 1984–90, Sen. Lectr, 1990–2002, Univ. of Liverpool. *Publications:* contribs to Acta Mathematicae, Annales de l'Ecole Normale Supérieure, Jls of London Mathematical Soc., Inventiones Mathematicae, Ergodic Theory and Dynamical Systems, Asterisque, etc. *Recreations:* walking, choir-singing, listening to music, reading, gardening. *Address:* Department of Mathematical Sciences, Mathematics and Oceanography Building, University of Liverpool, Peach Street, Liverpool L69 7ZL. *T:* (0151) 794 4063, *Fax:* (0151) 794 4061; *e-mail:* maryrees@liv.ac.uk.

REES, Prof. Teresa Lesley, CBE 2003; PhD; AcSS; Professor of Social Sciences, since 2000, and Pro Vice Chancellor, since 2004, Cardiff University; *b* 11 June 1949; *d* of Gordon Leslie Baggs and Vera Geddes-Ruffle; *m* 1974, Gareth Meredydd Rees (marr. diss. 2004); two *s*. *Educ:* Univ. of Exeter (BA Hons Sociology and Politics); PhD Wales 1993. Res. Officer, Univ. of Exeter, 1970–73; Res. Fellow, UWIST, 1973–76; Sen. Res. Asst, Mid Glamorgan CC, 1977–78; University College, Cardiff: Res. Fellow, 1976–77, 1978–88; Dir, Social Res. Unit, and Lectr in Sociology, 1988–92; Bristol University: Sen. Res. Fellow, 1993–94; Reader, 1994–95; Prof. of Labour Mkt Studies, 1995–2000. Fellow, Sunningdale Inst., Nat. Sch. of Govt, 2007–. Member: EOC, 1996–2002; BBC Audience Council Wales, 2007–. Hon. Pres., S Wales Br., WEA, 1996–. AcSS 2001. FRSA. Hon. Fellow, Univ. of Lampeter, 2006. *Publications:* (ed jtly) Youth Unemployment and State Intervention, 1982; (ed jtly) Our Sisters' Land: the changing identities of women in Wales, 1994; Women and the Labour Market, 1992; Mainstreaming Equality in the European Union, 1998; Women and Work, 1999; (jtly) Adult Guidance and the Learning Society, 2000. *Recreations:* campaigning for gender equality, watching Oscar ceremonies. *Address:* Cardiff University, Main Building, Park Place, Cardiff CF10 3AT. *T:* (029) 2087 0659.

REES, Victoria Kirstyn; *see* Williams, V. K.

REES, Rev. Canon (Vivian) John (Howard); Principal Registrar, Province of Canterbury, since 2000; *b* 21 April 1951; *s* of Herbert John Rees and Beryl Rees; *m* 1980, Dianne Elizabeth Hamilton; two *d*. *Educ:* Skinners' Sch., Tunbridge Wells; Southampton Univ. (LLB 1972); Wycliffe Hall, Oxford (MA); MPhil Leeds 1984. Admitted Solicitor, 1975; Ecclesiastical Notary; Asst Solicitor, Cooke Matheson & Co., 1975–76; Hosp. Administrator, Multan, Pakistan, 1976; ordained deacon 1979, priest 1980; Asst Curate, Moor Allerton Team Ministry, Leeds, 1979–82; Chaplain and Tutor, Sierra Leone Theol Hall, Freetown, 1982–85; with Winckworth Sherwood, 1986– (Partner, 1988–). Proctor in Convocation for Oxford, 1995–2000; Legal Advr, ACC, 1996–; Diocesan Registrar, Dio. Oxford, 1998–. Provincial Canon, Canterbury Cathedral, 2001–. Mem., Legal Adv. Commn, General Synod, 2000– (Vice-Chm., 2001–). Treas., Ecclesiastical Law Soc., 1995–. *Recreations:* photography, walking, cycling, second-hand bookshops. *Address:* (office) 16 Beaumont Street, Oxford OX1 2LZ. *T:* (01865) 297200, *Fax:* (01865) 726274; (home) 36 Cumnor Hill, Oxford OX2 9HB. *T:* and *Fax:* (01865) 865875; *e-mail:* jrees@winckworths.co.uk, vjhrees@btinternet.com.

REES, William Howard Guest, CB 1988; Chief Veterinary Officer, State Veterinary Service, 1980–88; *b* 21 May 1928; *s* of Walter Guest Rees and Margaret Elizabeth Rees; *m* 1952, Charlotte Mollie (*née* Collins); three *s* one *d*. *Educ:* Llanelli Grammar Sch.; Royal Veterinary Coll., London (BSc). MRCVS; DVSM. Private practice, Deal, Kent, 1952–53; joined MAFF as Veterinary Officer, 1953; stationed Stafford, 1953–66; Divl Vet. Officer, Vet. Service HQ, Tolworth, 1966–69; Divl Vet. Officer, Berks, 1969–71; Dep. Regional Vet. Officer, SE Reg., 1971–73; Regional Vet. Officer, Tolworth, 1973–76, Asst Chief Vet. Officer, 1976–80. Mem., AFRC, 1980–88. FRASE 1988. Hon. FRCVS 2000. Bledisloe Award, RASE, 1988; Gold Medal, Office Internat. des Epizooties, 1994. *Recreations:* Rugby and cricket follower, golf.

REES LEAHY, Dr Helen Blodwen; Lecturer in Art Gallery and Museum Studies, since 2000, and Director, Centre for Museology, since 2002, School of Art History and Archaeology, University of Manchester; *b* 23 Aug. 1960; *d* of late Edward Elgar Rees and of Dorothy Rees (*née* Banham); *m* 1997, Dr Michael Gordon Leahy. *Educ:* Gaisford High Sch. for Girls, Worthing; New Hall, Cambridge (MA); City Univ.; Univ. of Manchester (PhD 1999). Information Officer, Conran Foundn, 1984–86; Curator, 1986–89, Dir, 1989–92, Design Mus.; Communications Dir, Eureka!, The Mus. for Children, 1992; Asst Dir and Head of Public Affairs, NACF, 1992–95. Member: Adv. Panel, Arts Council of England, 1992–95; Design Adv. Cttee, RSA, 1990–94; Visual Arts Advr, NW Arts Bd, 1996–. Gov., Design Dimension Educnl Trust, 1990–. Trustee: Cardiff Old Library Trust, 1995–2000; Cornerhouse, Manchester, 1996–2003; Yorkshire Sculpture Park, 2002–. Editor (and contrib.) Design Museum Publications, 1989–92. *Publications:* 14:24 British Youth Culture, 1986; (contrib.) The Authority of the Consumer, ed Nigel Whiteley, 1993; (contrib.) The Culture of Craft, ed Peter Dormer, 1997; (contrib.) Art History and its Institutions, ed Elizabeth Mansfield, 2002. *Recreations:* friends, films, books. *Address:* 37 Merchants House, 66 North Street, Leeds LS2 7PN. *T:* (0113) 245 0873; Centre for Museology, School of Art History and Archaeology, University of Manchester, Oxford Road, Manchester M13 9PL; *e-mail:* helen.rees@man.ac.uk.

REES-MOGG, family name of **Baron Rees-Mogg**.

REES-MOGG, Baron *cr* 1988 (Life Peer), of Hinton Blewitt in the County of Avon; **William Rees-Mogg,** Kt 1981; Chairman: Pickering & Chatto (Publishers) Ltd, since 1981; Fleet Street Publications, since 1995; *b* 14 July 1928; *s* of late Edmund Fletcher Rees-Mogg and late Beatrice Rees-Mogg (*née* Warren), Temple Cloud, Somerset; *m* 1962, Gillian Shakespeare Morris, *d* of T. R. Morris; two *s* three *d*. *Educ:* Charterhouse; Balliol Coll., Oxford (Brackenbury Scholar). President, Oxford Union, 1951. Financial Times, 1952–60, Chief Leader Writer, 1955–60; Asst Editor, 1957–60; Sunday Times, City Editor, 1960–61; Political and Economic Editor, 1961–63; Deputy Editor, 1964–67; Editor, The Times, 1967–81; columnist, 1992–; Mem., Exec. Bd, Times Newspapers Ltd, 1968–81; Director: The Times Ltd, 1968–81; Times Newspapers Ltd, 1978–81. Columnist, Mail on Sunday, 2004–. Chairman: Sidgwick & Jackson, 1985–89; NewsMax Media Inc., 2000–06; Director: GEC, 1981–97; E. F. G. Private Bank, 1993–2005; Private Financial Holdings, 1995–2005. Vice-Chm., Bd of Governors, BBC, 1981–86; Chairman: Arts Council of GB, 1982–89; Broadcasting Standards Council, 1988–93; IBC plc, 1994–98. Contested (C) Chester-le-Street, Co. Durham, By-election 1956; General Election, 1959. Treasurer, Institute of Journalists, 1960–63, 1966–68, Pres., 1963–64; Vice-Chm. Cons. Party's Nat. Advisory Cttee on Political Education, 1961–63. Pres., English Assoc., 1983–84. Mem., Internat. Cttee, Pontifical Council for Culture, 1983–87. Vis. Fellow, Nuffield Coll., Oxford, 1968–72. High Sheriff, Somerset, 1978. Hon. LLD Bath, 1977. *Publications:* The Reigning Error: the crisis of world inflation, 1974; An Humbler Heaven, 1977; How to Buy Rare Books, 1985; Picnics on Vesuvius: steps toward the millennium, 1992; (with James Dale Davidson): Blood in the Streets, 1988; The Great Reckoning, 1991; The Sovereign Individual, 1997. *Recreation:* collecting. *Address:* 17 Pall Mall, SW1Y 5LU. *Club:* Garrick.

REES-WILLIAMS, family name of **Baron Ogmore**.

REES-WILLIAMS, Jonathan, FRCO; Organist and Master of the Choristers, St George's Chapel, Windsor Castle, 1991–2002; *b* 10 Feb. 1949; *s* of Ivor and Barbara Rees-Williams; *m* 1985, Helen Patricia Harling; one *s* two *d*. *Educ:* Kilburn Grammar Sch.; Royal Academy of Music; New Coll., Oxford (Organ Scholar; MA 1972). LRAM, DipRAM 1969; ARAM 1984; FRCO 1968. Organist: St Edmund, Yeading, 1967; Church of the Ascension, Wembley, 1968; Actg Organist, New Coll., Oxford, 1972; Assistant Organist: Hampstead Parish Church and St Clement Danes, 1972–74; Salisbury Cathedral, 1974–78; Dir of Music, Salisbury Cathedral Sch., 1974–78; Organist and Master of Choristers, Lichfield Cathedral, 1978–91; Conductor, Lichfield Cathedral Special Choir, 1978–91. Chorusmaster, Portsmouth Festival Choir, 1974–78;

Accompanist and Asst Dir, Salisbury Musical Soc., 1974–78. *Recreations:* cycling, wine, railways, vintage model railways.

REESE, Prof. Colin Bernard, PhD, ScD; FRS 1981; FRSC; Daniell Professor of Chemistry, King's College, University of London, 1973–98, now Emeritus; *b* 29 July 1930; *s* of Joseph and Emily Reese; *m* 1968, Susanne Bird; one *s* one *d*. *Educ:* Dartington Hall Sch.; Clare Coll., Cambridge (BA 1953, PhD 1956, MA 1957, ScD 1972). 1851 Sen. Student, 1956–58; Research Fellow: Clare Coll., Cambridge, 1956–59; Harvard Univ., 1957–58; Official Fellow and Dir of Studies in Chem., Clare Coll., 1959–73; Cambridge University: Univ. Demonstrator in Chem., 1959–63; Asst Dir of Res., 1963–64; Univ. Lectr in Chem., 1964–73. FKC 1989. *Publications:* scientific papers, mainly in chemical jls. *Address:* 21 Rozel Road, SW4 0EY. *T:* (020) 7498 0230.

REESE, Colin Edward; QC 1987; FCIArb; a Recorder, since 1994; Deputy Judge, Technology and Construction Court (formerly Deputy Official Referee), High Court, since 1994; *b* 28 March 1950; *s* of late Robert Edward Reese and Katharine Reese (*née* Moore); *m* 1978, Diana Janet Anderson; two *s* one *d*. *Educ:* Hawarden Grammar School; King Edward VI School, Southampton; Fitzwilliam College, Cambridge (BA 1972; MA 1976). Called to the Bar, Gray's Inn, 1973 (Mould Schol., 1974; Bencher, 1998); admitted, *ad eund.*, Lincoln's Inn, 1976; in practice, 1975–. An Asst Parly Boundary Comr, 1992–. Legal Mem., Mental Health Review Tribunals, 2000–. Vice-Chm., Qualifications Cttee, Bar Standards Bd, 2006–. Vice Chm., 1997–2000, Chm., 2000–03, Technol. and Construction (formerly Official Referees) Bar Assoc. Dir, Bar Mutual Indemnity Fund Ltd, 2001–. Pres., Cambridge Univ. Law Soc., 1971–72. Liveryman, Bakers' Co., 1991–. *Address:* 1 Atkin Building, Gray's Inn, WC1R 5AT. *T:* (020) 7404 0102.

REEVE, Sir Anthony, KCMG 1992 (CMG 1986); KCVO 1995; HM Diplomatic Service, retired; High Commissioner (formerly Ambassador) to South Africa, 1991–96; *b* 20 Oct. 1938; *s* of Sidney Reeve and Dorothy (*née* Mitchell); *m* 1st, 1964, Pamela Margaret Angus (marr. diss. 1988); one *s* two *d*; 2nd, 1997, Susan Doull (*née* Collins), Durban, S Africa. *Educ:* Queen Elizabeth Grammar Sch., Wakefield; Marling Sch., Stroud; Merton Coll., Oxford (MA). Lever Brothers & Associates, 1962–65; joined HM Diplomatic Service, 1965; Middle East Centre for Arab Studies, 1966–68; Asst Political Agent, Abu Dhabi, 1968–70; First Secretary, FCO, 1970–73; First Sec., later Counsellor, Washington, 1973–78; Head of Arms Control and Disarmament Dept, FCO, 1979–81; Counsellor, Cairo, 1981–84; Head of Southern Africa Dept, FCO, 1984–86; Asst Under Sec. of State (Africa), FCO, 1986–87; Ambassador to Jordan, 1988–91. Dir, Barclays Private Bank Ltd, 1997–2001; Chm., Curzon Corp. (formerly Union-Castle Travel), 1998–. *Recreations:* golf, music. *Address:* Box Tree Cottage, Horsley, Stroud, Glos GL6 0QB. *Clubs:* Oxford and Cambridge; Leander (Henley-on-Thames); Minchinhampton Golf.

REEVE, Derek Charles; financial consultant; Director of Finance and Information Systems, Deputy Town Clerk and Deputy Chief Executive, Royal Borough of Kensington and Chelsea, 1991–2002; *b* 7 Dec. 1946; *s* of Charles Reeve and Sylvia Reeve (*née* Prynne); *m* 1968, Janice Rosina Williamson; one *s* one *d*. *Educ:* Dame Alice Owen's Grammar Sch. for Boys, Islington; Tottenham and E Ham Tech. Colls. Various posts, Islington LBC, 1965–74; Asst Borough Treas., Greenwich LBC, 1974–79; Dep. Dir of Finance, RBK&C, 1979–91. Actg Clerk, Western Riverside Waste Authy, 2005–06. Pres., Soc. of London Treasurers, 2000–2001. Vice-Chm. Govs, Sweyne Co. Primary Sch., Swanscombe, Kent, 2002– (Chm., Finance Cttee, 2002–); Chm., Interim Governing Body, Manor Community Primary Sch., Swanscombe, Kent, 2008–. *Recreations:* golf, painting (watercolours), reading, gardening, music, following Arsenal FC, genealogy, fly-fishing. *Address:* 5 Red Lodge Crescent, Bexley, Kent DA5 2JR. *Clubs:* The Warren; Birchwood Park Golf (Wilmington).

REEVE, John; non-executive Chairman, Coverzones Ltd, since 2007; *b* 13 July 1944; *s* of Clifford Alfred Reeve and Irene Mary Turnidge Reeve; *m* 1974, Sally Diane Welton; one *d*. *Educ:* Westcliff High School (Grammar). FCA. Selbey Smith & Earle, 1962–67; Peat Marwick McLintock, 1967–68; Vickers, Roneo Vickers Group, 1968–76; Wilkinson Match, 1976–77; Amalgamated Metal Corp., 1977–80; Group Finance Director: British Aluminium Co., 1980–83; Mercantile House Holdings, 1983–87; Dep. Man. Dir, 1988, Man. Dir, 1989, Sun Life Assurance Society plc; Gp Man. Dir, 1990–95, non-exec. Dir, 1995–96, Sun Life Corp. plc; Exec. Chm., Willis Corroon, subseq. Willis, Gp Ltd, 1995–2000. Non-exec. Chm., Alea Gp Hldgs (Bermuda) Ltd, 2003–07. Director: The English Concert, 1987– (Chm., 1993–2006); HMC Group plc, 1988–94; Temple Bar Investment Trust PLC, 1992– (Chm., 2003–); London First, 1998–2002. Pres., Inst. of Business Ethics, 1997–2000 (Mem. Adv. Council, 1986–91; Dep. Pres., 1991–96). Chm., E London Business Alliance, 2000–02; Member: E London Partnership Bd, 1991–2000 (Chm., 1996–2000); Council, BITC, 1995–2000; Life Insce Council, 1991–94, Bd, 1993–95, ABI; Bd, 1993–2001, Exec. Cttee, 1996–2001, Internat. Insurance Soc. Inc. Governor: Res. into Ageing, 1991–96; NIESR, 1995–2000. CCMI. FRSA 1999. *Recreations:* yachting, music, theatre. *Address:* Cliff Dene, 24 Cliff Parade, Leigh-on-Sea, Essex SS9 1BB. *T:* (01702) 477563, *Fax:* (01702) 479092; *e-mail:* reevej@compuserve.com. *Clubs:* Athenæum, Royal Ocean Racing; Essex Yacht.

REEVE, Rear Adm. Jonathon, CB 2003; CEng; Deputy Chief Executive, Warship Support Agency, and Navy Board Member for Logistics, 2001–04; *b* 1 Oct. 1949; *e s* of late Lawrence Alick Reeve and of Joan Reeve; *m* 1980, Jennifer Anne, *d* of Guy and Betty Wickman; one *s* one *d*. *Educ:* Marlborough Coll.; St Catharine's Coll., Cambridge (MA 1972). CEng, MIEE 1978, FIET (FIEE 2000). Joined Royal Navy, 1967: qualified submarines, 1974; HMS Renown, 1974–76; HMS Dreadnought, 1979–82; RNSC, 1982; Naval Sec.'s Dept, MoD, 1982–84; Strategic Systems Exec., 1985–88; Naval Manpower Trng, 1989–91; Capt. 1991; Asst Dir, MoD Defence Systems, 1991–93; Head of Integrated Logistics Support (Navy), Ship Support Agency, MoD, 1994–96; rcds 1997; Cdre 1998; Naval Base Comdr, Devonport, 1998–2000; COS (Corporate Develt) to C-in-C Fleet, 2000. Dir, OMG, 2006–. *Recreations:* golf, tennis, gardening. *Address:* c/o Naval Secretary, Fleet Headquarters, Whale Island, Portsmouth, Hants PO1 3LS. *Club:* Army and Navy.

REEVE, Prof. Michael David, FBA 1984; Fellow, Pembroke College, Cambridge, since 1984; *b* 11 Jan. 1943; *s* of Arthur Reeve and Edith Mary Barrett; *m* 1970, Elizabeth Klingaman (marr. diss. 1999); two *s* one *d*. *Educ:* King Edward's Sch., Birmingham; Balliol Coll., Oxford (MA). Harmsworth Senior Scholar, Merton Coll., Oxford, 1964–65; Woodhouse Research Fellow, St John's Coll., Oxford, 1965–66; Tutorial Fellow, Exeter Coll., Oxford, 1966–84, now Emeritus Fellow; Kennedy Prof. of Latin, 1984–2006, Dir of Res., Faculty of Classics, 2006–07, Cambridge Univ. Visiting Professor: Univ. of Hamburg, 1976; McMaster Univ., 1979; Univ. of Toronto, 1982–83. Fellow, Società Internazionale per lo Studio del Medioevo Latino, 1996; Corresp. Mem., Akademie der Wissenschaften, Göttingen, 1990; For. Mem., Istituto Lombardo, Milan, 1993. Editor, Classical Quarterly, 1981–86. *Publications:* Longus, Daphnis and Chloe, 1982; contribs to Texts and Transmission, ed L. D. Reynolds, 1983; Cicero, Pro Quinctio, 1992; Vegetius, Epitoma rei militaris, 2004; Geoffrey of Monmouth, De gestis Britonum, 2007; articles in European and transatlantic jls. *Recreations:* chess, music, gardening, mountain walking. *Address:* Pembroke College, Cambridge CB2 1RF.

REEVE, Robin Martin, MA; Head Master, King's College School, Wimbledon, 1980–97; *b* 22 Nov. 1934; *s* of Percy Martin Reeve and Cicely Nora Parker; *m* 1959, Brianne Ruth Hall; one *s* two *d*. *Educ:* Hampton Sch.; Gonville and Caius Coll., Cambridge (Foundation Schol.; BA 1957; MA). Asst Master, King's Coll. Sch., Wimbledon, 1958–62; Head of History Dept, 1962–80, and Dir of Studies, 1975–80, Lancing Coll. Member: CATE, 1993–94; ISC (formerly ISJC), 1991–99; Council, Brighton Coll., 1997–99; Council, Lancing Coll., 1997– (Chm., 1999–2008). *Publication:* The Industrial Revolution 1750–1850, 1971. *Recreations:* English history and architecture, gardening. *Address:* The Old Rectory, Coombes, Lancing, W Sussex BN15 0RS. *Club:* Athenæum.

REEVE, Roy Stephen, CMG 1998; HM Diplomatic Service, retired; Head, EU Planning Team, Kosovo, since 2008; *b* 20 Aug. 1941; *s* of Ernest Arthur Reeve and Joan Elizabeth (*née* Thomas); *m* 1964, Gill Lee; two *d*. *Educ:* Dulwich Coll.; LSE (BSc Econs 1965; MSc 1966). Joined FCO, 1966; Moscow, 1968–71; First Secretary: FCO, 1973–78; (Commercial) Moscow, 1978–80; Counsellor on loan to Home Civil Service, 1983–85; Dep. Consul-General, Johannesburg, 1985–88; Hd, Commercial Management and Export Dept, FCO, 1988–91; Consul-Gen., Sydney, 1991–95; Ambassador to Ukraine, 1995–99; OSCE Ambassador: to Armenia, 1999–2003; to Georgia, 2003–07. Hon. Sen. Res. Fellow, Centre for Russian and E European Studies, Univ. of Birmingham, 1999–. *Recreations:* Rugby Union, scuba diving.

REEVES, Antony Robert; Chief Executive, City of Bradford Metropolitan District Council, since 2006; *b* 10 Feb. 1965; *s* of Bob and Jackie Reeves; *m* 2002, Kathryn; one *s*. *Educ:* Bristol Poly. (BA Hons); Huddersfield Univ. (MBA 1996). Housing Officer, 1989, Sen. Housing Officer, 1989–90, Stockport MBC; Estate Action Team Leader, 1990, District Housing Manager, 1990–92, Calderdale MBC; Barnsley Metropolitan Borough Council: Prin. Housing Officer, 1992–93; Hd of Housing Ops, 1993–95; Hd of Housing, 1995–99; Actg Prog. Dir of Health, Home Care Services, 1999–2000; Exec. Dir of Housing and Property Services, 2000–03; Dep. Chief Exec., Wakefield MDC, 2003–06. *Recreations:* scuba diving, walking, golf, Rugby, reading, travel. *Address:* Bradford City Council, City Hall, Bradford BD1 1HY. *T:* (01274) 432001; *e-mail:* Tony.reeves@bradford.gov.uk.

REEVES, Dr Colin Leslie, CBE 1999; self-employed healthcare consultant, since 2003; *b* 4 April 1949; *s* of Leslie and Isabelle Reeves; *m* 1978, Christine Lloyd; two *d*. *Educ:* Birkenhead Sch.; Clare Coll., Cambridge (BA 1970; MA); UCNW, Bangor (MSc 1971; PhD 1973); DBA Cornell Univ. 1990. CPFA (IPFA 1976). Lectr, UCNW, Bangor, 1971–73; Accountancy and Audit Assistant, Warrington County Borough, 1973–75; Asst Treas., Ellesmere Port and Neston BC, 1975–80; Deputy Director of Finance: Stratford-on-Avon DC, 1980–84; NW Thames RHA, 1984–85; Director of Finance: Paddington and N Kensington DHA, 1985–86; NW Thames RHA, 1986–94; Dir of Finance and Performance, NHS Exec., 1994–2001; Dir, Accountancy Foundn Rev. Bd, 2001–03. Non-exec. Dir, and Chm., Audit Cttee, Oxford Radcliffe Hosps NHS Trust, 2005–. Member: Adv. Cttee on Mentally Disordered Offenders, 1993–94; Culyer Cttee on R&D, 1993–94; NHS Steering Gps on Capitation and on Capital, 1993–94; Chancellor of Exchequer's Pvte Finance Panel, 1994–95; Butler Cttee on review of Audit Commn, 1995; CMO's Nat. Screening Cttee, 1996–2001; Review of ONS, reporting to HM Treasury, 1999; Bd, Accountancy NTO, 1999–2001; Co-ordinating Gp on Audit and Accounting Issues, DTI/HM Treasury, 2002; Consultative Cttee on Review of the Listing Regime, FSA, 2002. Hon. Treas., Headway (brain injury charity), 2002–. *Publications:* The Applicability of the Monetary Base Hypothesis to the UK, the USA, France and West Germany, 1974; contrib. professional jls. *Recreations:* sport, especially cricket and golf, history of Test Match cricket, hockey (former regl internat. and county player). *Address:* Hillcrest, 82 Wallingford Road, Goring-on-Thames, Oxon RG8 0HN. *T:* (01491) 872166. *Clubs:* Royal Automobile, MCC; Goring and Streatley Golf; Flying Ferrets Golf Soc.; Henley Hawks Rugby Football.

REEVES, Rev. Donald St John, MBE 2008; Rector, St James's Church, Piccadilly, 1980–98; *b* 18 May 1934; *s* of Henry and Barbara Reeves. *Educ:* Sherborne; Queens' Coll., Cambridge (BA Hons 1957); Cuddesdon Theol Coll. 2nd Lieut, Royal Sussex Regt, 1952–54. Lectr, British Council, Beirut, 1957–60; Tutor, Brasted Theol Coll., 1960–61; Cuddesdon Theol Coll., 1961–63; deacon, 1963, priest, 1964; Curate, All Saints, Maidstone, 1963–65; Chaplain to Bishop of Southwark, 1965–68; Vicar of St Peter's, Morden, 1969–80. Mem., Gen. Synod of C of E, 1990–94. Dir, The Soul of Europe Project, 1999–. MLitt Lambeth, 2003. *Publications:* (ed) Church and State, 1984; For God's Sake, 1988; Making Sense of Religion, 1989; Down to Earth: a new vision, 1995. *Recreations:* playing the organ, bee-keeping, watching TV soap operas. *Address:* The Coach House, Church Street, Crediton EX17 2AQ. *T:* (01363) 775100, *Fax:* (01363) 773911. *Club:* Athenæum.

REEVES, Gordon; *see* Reeves, W. G.

REEVES, Dame Helen May, DBE 1999 (OBE 1986); Chief Executive (formerly Director), National Association of Victim Support Schemes, 1980–2005; *b* 22 Aug. 1945; *d* of Leslie Percival William Reeves and Helen Edith Reeves (*née* Brown). *Educ:* Dartford Grammar School for Girls; Nottingham University (BA Hons Social Admin. 1966). Probation Officer, Inner London Probation Service, 1967–79 (Senior Probation Officer, 1975–79). Member: Nat. Bd for Crime Prevention, 1993–95; Govt Working Gp on Vulnerable and Intimidated Witnesses, 1998–99; Home Office Steering Gp on Review of Sexual Offences, 1999; EC Cttee of Experts on Victims of Crime, 1998–99; Indep. Review of Criminal Stats, 2006; Chm., Council of Europe Expert Cttee on Victims of Crime and Terrorism, 2005–06. Vice Pres., World Soc. of Victimology, 1994–2006; Chm., Eur. Forum for Victim Services, 2001–05. Member: RSA Risk Commn, 2006–; Howard League Commn on Future of English Prisons. Hon. MA Nottingham, 1998; Hon. LLD: Warwick, 2001; Southampton Solent, 2004. *Recreations:* social and local history and architecture, food, gardens.

REEVES, Marc Barnaby; Editor, Birmingham Post, since 2006; *b* 25 Nov. 1965; *s* of late Frederick Reeves and of Mai Reeves (now Barnes); *m* 1988, Tessa Perrin (separated); two *d*. *Educ:* St Teresa's Primary Sch., Birmingham; Handsworth Grammar Sch., Birmingham; Birmingham Poly.; Oxford Brookes Univ. (CMS 2002; DMS 2003). Dep. Ed., Walsall Advertiser, 1988–89; Sub-ed., Focus Newspapers. Birmingham, 1989–91; Revise Ed., Computer Newspaper Services, Howden, 1991–92; Prodn Ed., Northampton Chronicle & Echo, 1992–94; Dep. Ed., Cumberland News, 1994–97; Ed., Reading Chronicle, 1997–2000; Editl Dir, Trinity Mirror Southern, 2000–06. FRSA. Mem., Lunar Soc. *Recreations:* collecting music and music trivia, military and political history, lazing in the garden, anything relating to Land Rovers (restoring, driving, losing money). *Address:* Birmingham Post, PO Box 78, Weaman Street, Birmingham B4 6AY. *T:* (0121) 234 5617.

REEVES, Nicholas Philip, CEnv; Executive Director, Chartered Institution of Water and Environmental Management, since 1998; artist and writer; *b* 11 Sept. 1952; *s* of late Philip George Reeves and Rachel Reeves (*née* Rivers); *m* 2001, Janet Maureen Eade; two *d*, and one step *s* one step *d*. *Educ:* Birmingham Coll. of Art and Design (DipAD 1973); University Coll. London (BA 1974; DMS 1980). Chartered Water and Envmt Manager. Artist and freelance journalist, 1973–88; one-man exhibn of paintings and drawings, Compendium Galls and Warwick Gall., 1973; group exhibitions of paintings and drawings: Ikon Gall., 1975; Middlesbrough Mus. and Art Gall., 1981; Royal Birmingham Soc. of Artists, 1976, 1977, 1978; Man. Dir, Land Technology Ltd, 1989–92; Hd, Envmt and Recreation, Broxbourne BC, 1992–94; Dir of Policy and Dep. Dir, Inst. of Leisure and Amenity Mgt, 1994–98. Non-exec. Dir, Force 3 Leisure Ltd, 1989–92. Chm., Centre for Amenity and Leisure Contracting Study and Research, Writtle Coll., Univ. of Essex, 1996–98. Mem., Council for Travel and Tourism, 1996–98; Advr, Southern Arts Bd, 1997–99; Member Board: Science Council, 1999–; Soc. for the Envmt, 2000– (Chm., Ext. Affairs Cttee, 2004); Green Flag Adv. Bd, DCLG, 2005–; Sustainable Organic Resources Partnership, 2006–; Mem. Cttee, Thames Recreation, Fisheries, Ecology Adv. Cttee, Envmt Agency, 2005–. Trustee, Brumcan, 2005–. Co-Founder, Green Flag Parks Award Scheme, 1995; Founder, Arts and the Envmt Network, 2007. Chm., Green Flag Awards Steering Gp, 2002–05; Mem., Envmt Awards Cttee, RSA, 2004. Co-Founder, John Wilkes Soc. Dining Club, 2007. FIHort 1990; FILAM 1994; FInstD 1995; FRSA 2004; FIAM 2005; FISPAL 2007; FRGS 2008. Hon. FCIWEM 2000. Freeman, City of London, 2000; Court Asst, Co. of Water Conservators, 2006–. *Publications:* A Guide to Business Planning for Leisure and Environment Managers, 2002; various papers on envmt and cultural affairs in learned jls and pubns; articles in the press. *Recreations:* collecting art, painting and drawing, Richard III Society, pubs and real ale, thinking out loud. *Address:* Chartered Institution of Water and Environmental Management, 15 John Street, WC1N 2EB. *T:* (020) 7831 3110, *Fax:* (020) 7405 4967; *e-mail:* nick@ciwem.org; Sunnyside Cottage, Stanwell Road, Horton, Berks SL3 9PE. *T:* (01753) 682900; *e-mail:* nickreeves1@tiscali.co.uk. *Club:* Reform.

REEVES, Prof. Nigel Barrie Reginald, OBE 1987; DPhil; FCIL; Pro-Vice-Chancellor for External Relations, Aston University, 1996–2007, now Professor Emeritus; *b* 9 Nov. 1939; *s* of Reginald Arthur Reeves and Marjorie Joyce Reeves; *m* 1982, Minou (*née* Samimi); one *s* one *d*. *Educ:* Merchant Taylors' Sch.; Worcester Coll., Oxford (MA); St John's Coll., Oxford (DPhil 1970). FCIL (FIL 1981). Lectr in English, Univ. of Lund, Sweden, 1964–66; Lectr in German, Univ. of Reading, 1968–74; Alexander von Humboldt Fellow, Univ. of Tübingen, 1974–75; University of Surrey: Prof. of German, 1975–90; Hd of Dept of Linguistic and Internat. Studies, 1979–90; Dean, Faculty of Human Studies, 1986–90; Prof. of German and Head of Dept of Modern Langs, Aston Univ., 1990–96. Guest Prof. of German, Royal Holloway Coll., London Univ., 1976; Vis. Prof., European Business Sch., 1981–88; Sen. Alexander von Humboldt Fellow, Univ. of Hamburg, 1986; UK Short-term Visitor to Japan, Japan Foundn, 1997. Chm., Nat. Congress on Langs in Educn, 1986–90; President: Nat. Assoc. of Language Advisers, 1986–91; Assoc. of Teachers of German, 1988–89; Vice-President: Conf. of University Teachers of German, 1995–97 (Vice-Chm., 1988–91); Inst. of Linguists, 1990–2008 (Chm. Council, 1985–88); Convenor, British Inst. of Traffic Educn Res., 2001–02; Member: Academic Adv. Council, Linguaphone Inst., 1991–2005; Modern Langs Steering Cttee, Open Univ., 1991–96; Academic Adv. Council, Univ. of Buckingham, 1994–2002; Bd, British Trng Internat., 1998–2001; SCOTLANG (SHEFC), 2000–02; Exec. Cttee, Univ. Council for Modern Langs, 2003–07; Steering Gp for Benchmarking, QAA, 2003–07; Assessor, Irish Res. Council for Humanities and Social Scis, 2001–02. Consultant, QCA, 2001–03; Mem., Langs Ladder Wkg Gp, DfES, 2004–06. Governor: Germanic Inst., Univ. of London, 1989–94; Matthew Boulton Further and Higher Educn Corp., Birmingham, 2002–07 (Chm., 1999–2002). Mem., Adv. Council, Worcester Coll. Soc., Oxford, 2000–08. Trustee, London Chamber of Commerce and Industry Commercial Educn Trust, 2001–08. FRSA 1986; CIEx 1987. Hon. Fellow, Hong Kong Translation Soc., 2006. Goethe Medal, Goethe Inst., Munich, 1989; Medal, European Foundn for Quality Management, 1996. Officer's Cross, Order of Merit (Germany), 1999. *Publications:* Merkantil-Tekniska Stilar, 2 Vols, 1965–66; Heinrich Heine: poetry and politics, 1974; (with K. Dewhurst) Friedrich Schiller: medicine, psychology and literature, 1978; (with D. Lake) Heinrich von Kleist, The Marquise von O. and other stories, 1978; (with D. Liston) Business Studies, Languages and Overseas Trade, 1985; (jtly) Making Your Mark: effective business communication in Germany, 1988; (with D. Liston) The Invisible Economy: a profile of Britain's invisible exports, 1988; (jtly) Franc Exchange, effective business communication in France, 1991; (jtly) Spanish Venture, basic business communication in Spain, 1992; (with C. Wright) Linguistic Auditing, 1996; (ed with H. Kelly-Holmes) The European Business Environment: Germany, 1997; (with R. West and A. Simpson) Pathways to Proficiency: the alignment of language proficiency scales for assessing competence in English Language, 2003; over 100 articles in learned jls on language, language educn, literature and overseas trade. *Recreations:* gardening, walking. *Address:* c/o Aston University, Aston Triangle, Birmingham B4 7ET.

REEVES, Rt Rev. Sir Paul Alfred, ONZ 2007; GCMG 1985; GCVO 1986; QSO 1990; Kt 1985; Chancellor, Auckland University of Technology, since 2005; *b* 6 Dec. 1932; 2nd *s* of D'Arcy Lionel and Hilda Mary Reeves; *m* 1959, Beverley Gwendolen Watkins; three *d*. *Educ:* Wellington Coll., New Zealand; Victoria Univ. of Wellington (MA); St John's Theol. Coll., Auckland (LTh); St Peter's Coll., Univ. of Oxford (MA; Hon. Fellow, 1980). Deacon, 1958; Priest, 1960; Curate: Tokoroa, NZ, 1958–59; St Mary the Virgin, Oxford, 1959–61; Kirkley St Peter, Lowestoft, 1961–63; Vicar, St Paul, Okato, NZ, 1964–66; Lectr in Church History, St John's Coll., Auckland, NZ, 1966–69; Dir of Christian Educn, Dio. Auckland, 1969–71; Bishop of Waiapu, 1971–79; Bishop of Auckland, 1979–85; Primate and Archbishop of New Zealand, 1980–85; Governor-General, NZ, 1985–90; Anglican Observer at UN, and Assisting Bishop, Episcopal Dio. of NY, 1991–93; Dean, Te Rau Kahikatea Theol Coll., Auckland, 1994–95. Chairman: Environmental Council, 1974–76; Bioethics Council, 2002–04; Queen Elizabeth II Nat. Trust, 2000–03. Dep. Leader, Commonwealth Observers, S African elections, 1994; Leader, Commonwealth Observers, Ghanaian elections, 1996; Special Envoy of Commonwealth Sec. Gen. to Guyana, 2002–06; Special Rep. of Commonwealth Sec. Gen. to Fiji, 2007–. Chm., Fijian Constitutional Review Commn, 1995–96. Visiting Professor: Univ. of Auckland, 1997–2000; Auckland Univ. of Technol., 2000–05. KStJ 1986. Hon. DCL Oxford, 1985; Hon LLD Wellington, 1989; Hon. DD: Gen. Theol Seminary, NY, 1992; Church Divinity Sch. of Pacific, San Francisco, 1994; Hon. Dr Edinburgh, 1994. Hon. CF (Fiji), 1999. *Recreations:* jogging, sailing, swimming. *Address:* 14B Victoria Avenue, Remuera, Auckland, New Zealand.

REEVES, Philip Thomas Langford, RE 1964; RSA 1976 (ARSA 1971); PPRSW; artist in etching and other mediums; Senior Lecturer, Glasgow School of Art, 1973–91; President, Royal Scottish Society of Painters in Water Colours, 1998–2005; *b* 7 July 1931; *s* of Herbert Reeves and Lilian; *m* 1964, Christine MacLaren (*d* 1994); one *d*. *Educ:* Naunton Park Sch., Cheltenham. Student, Cheltenham Sch. of Art, 1947–49. Army service, 4th/7th Royal Dragoon Guards, Middle East, 1949–51. RCA, 1951–54 (ARCA 1st Cl.); Lectr, Glasgow Sch. of Art, 1954–73. Founder Member: Edinburgh Printmakers Workshop, 1967; Glasgow Print Studio, 1972. Associate, Royal Soc. of Painter Etchers, 1954; RSW 1962; RGI 1981. Works in permanent collections: Arts Council; V&A; Gall. of Modern Art, Edinburgh; Glasgow Art Gall.; Glasgow Univ. Print Collection; Hunterian Art Gall., Glasgow; Manchester City Art Gall.; Royal Scottish Acad.; Aberdeen Art Gall.; Paisley Art Gall.; Inverness Art Gall.; Milngavie Art Gall.; Dept of the Environment; Dundee Art Gall.; Scottish Develt Agency; Stirling and Strathclyde Univs; British Govt Art Collection; Contemporary Art Soc. *Recreation:* walking. *Address:* 13 Hamilton Drive, Glasgow G12 8DN.

REEVES, William Desmond, CB 1993; Secretary, UK Management Board, PricewaterhouseCoopers, 1998–2004; *b* 26 May 1937; *s* of late Thomas Norman and Anne Reeves; *m* 1967, Aase Birte Christensen; two *d*. *Educ:* Darwen Grammar Sch.; King's Coll., Cambridge (BA Hist.). National service, RAEC, 1959–61. Joined Admiralty as Asst Principal, 1961; MoD, 1964; Asst Sec., 1973; seconded to Pay Board, 1973–74; Asst Under Sec. of State, Air, MoD (PE), 1982–84, Resources and Progs, MoD, 1984, Systems, Office of Management and Budget, MoD, 1985–88; Under Sec., Cabinet Office, 1989–92; Asst Under Sec. of State (Commitments), MoD, 1992–94. Partnership Sec., Coopers & Lybrand, 1994–98. *Recreation:* supporting Blackburn Rovers. *Address:* 2 Downs Bridge Road, Beckenham, Kent BR3 5HX.

REEVES, Prof. (William) Gordon, FRCP, FRCPath; Professor and Head of Department of Microbiology and Immunology, College of Medicine, Sultan Qaboos University, Muscat, Oman, 1993–98; *b* 9 July 1938; *s* of Rev. W. H. and Mrs E. L. Reeves; *m* 1970, Elizabeth Susan, *d* of Surg.-Comdr L. A. and Mrs P. Moules; one *s* one *d*. *Educ:* Perse Sch., Cambridge; Guy's Hosp. Med. Sch. (BSc, MB BS). MRCS, LRCP 1964; MRCP 1966; FRCP 1978; FRCPath 1985. HO and Med. Registrar appts at Guy's, Central Middx, Brompton, National, Middx, and University Coll. Hosps, 1964–68; Lecturer: Clinical Pharmacology, Guy's Hosp. Med. Sch., 1968–71; Immunology and Medicine, Royal Postgrad. Med. Sch., 1971–73; Consultant Immunologist, Nottingham HA, 1973–88; Nottingham University: Sen. Lectr, 1975–85; Prof. of Immunology, 1985–88; Editor, The Lancet, 1989–90; Med. Editor and Consultant, Communicable Disease Surveillance Centre, PHLS, 1991–93. Vis. Prof. in Immunology of Infectious Disease, St Mary's Hosp. Med. Sch., 1992–97. FRSocMed. Member: Soc. of Authors; Friends of Cathedral Music; Prayer Book Soc.; Bury Soc.; Soc. des Etudes du Lot. *Publications:* contribs to med. and scientific books and jls on medicine, immunology and infectious diseases. *Recreations:* returning to the piano, the bustle of town life, East Anglian landscapes.

REFFELL, Adm. Sir Derek (Roy), KCB 1984; Governor and Commander-in-Chief, Gibraltar, 1989–93; *b* 6 Oct. 1928; *s* of late Edward (Roy) and Murielle Reffell; *m* 1956, Janne Gronow Davis; one *s* one *d*. *Educ:* Culford Sch., Suffolk; Royal Naval Coll., Dartmouth. Various ships at Home, Mediterranean, West Indies and Far East, 1946–63; qualified Navigating Officer, 1954; Comdr 1963; Comd HMS Sirius, 1966–67; Comdr BRNC Dartmouth, 1968–69; Captain 1970; Naval Staff, 1971–74; Comd HMS Hermes, 1974–76; Director Naval Warfare, 1976–78; Commodore Amphibious Warfare, 1978–79; Asst Chief of Naval Staff (Policy), 1979–82; Flag Officer Third Flotilla and Comdr Anti-Submarine Group Two, 1982–83; Flag Officer, Naval Air Comd, 1983–84; Controller of the Navy, 1984–89, retd. Governor, Royal Sch., Hindhead, 1995–98. Trustee, Special Olympics UK, 1998–2002. Chm., Friends of Gibraltar Heritage Soc., 1994–2004. Master, Coachmakers' Company, 1998–99. KStJ 1989. *Recreations:* golf, painting.

REFSHAUGE, Maj.-Gen. Sir William (Dudley), AC 1980; Kt 1966; CBE 1959 (OBE 1944); ED 1965; Secretary-General, World Medical Association, 1973–76; Hon. Consultant to Australian Foundation on Alcoholism and Drugs of Dependence, since 1979; *b* 3 April 1913; *s* of late F. C. Refshauge, Melbourne; *m* 1942, Helen Elizabeth (*d* 2002), *d* of late R. E. Allwright, Tasmania; four *s* one *d*. *Educ:* Hampton High Sch.; Scotch Coll., Melbourne; Melbourne University. MB, BS (Melbourne) 1938; FRCOG 1961; FRACS 1962; FRACP 1963; Hon. FRSH 1967; FACMA 1967; FRACOG 1978. Served with AIF, 1939–46; Lt-Col, RAAMC (despatches four times). Medical Supt, Royal Women's Hosp., Melbourne, 1948–51; Col, and Dep. DGAMS, Aust., 1951–55; Maj.-Gen., and DGAMS, Aust., 1955–60; QHP, 1955–64. Commonwealth Dir-Gen. of Health, Australia, 1960–73. Chairman: Council, Aust. Coll. of Nursing, 1958–60 (Chm. Educn Cttee, 1951–58); Nat. Health and MRC, 1960–73; Nat. Fitness Council, 1960–73; Nat. Tuberculosis Adv. Council, 1960–73; Prog. and Budget Cttee, 15th World Health Assembly, 1962; Admin., Fin. and Legal Cttee 19th World Health Assembly (Pres., 24th Assembly, 1971); Exec. Bd, WHO, 1969–70 (Mem., 1967–70). Member: Council, Aust. Red Cross Soc., 1954–60; Mem. Nat. Blood Transfusion Cttee, ARCS 1955–60; Nat. Trustee, Returned Services League Aust., 1961–73, 1976–; Mem. Bd of Management, Canberra Grammar Sch., 1963–68; Mem. Bd of Trustees, Walter and Eliza Hall Inst. of Med. Res., Melbourne, 1977–86 (Chm., Ethics Cttee, 1983–88); Chm., Governing Bd, Menzies Sch. of Health Research, Darwin, 1983–87. Chm., ACT Cttee, Mem., Nat. Cttee and Mem. Nat. Exec., Sir Robert Menzies Foundn, 1979–84; Chm., Australian-Hellenic Meml Cttee, 1986–88. Hon. Life Mem., Australian Dental Assoc., 1966. Patron: Australian Sports Medicine Assoc., 1971–; ACT Br., Aust. Sports Medicine Fedn, 1980–; Totally and Permanently Incapacitated Assoc., ACT, 1982–; 2/2 (2nd AIF) Field Regtl Assoc., 1984–; Medical Assoc. for Prevention of War (MAPW), 1989–; ACT Hospice Soc., 1991–; 15 Field Ambulance Assoc., 1991–. Leader, Commemorative Tour of Europe for 60th anniversary, RSL. Nat. Pres., 1st Pan Pacific Conf. on alcohol and drugs, 1980. Hon MD Sydney, 1988. Anzac Peace Prize, 1990, Meritorious Medal, 1992, RSL. *Publications:* contribs to Australian Med. Jl, NZ Med. Jl, etc. *Recreation:* reading. *Address:* 13/95 Groom Street, Hughes, Canberra, ACT 2605, Australia. *Clubs:* Royal Society of Medicine (London); Naval and Military, Cricket (Melbourne); Commonwealth (Canberra).

REGAN, Charles Maurice; Clerk to the Trustees, Hampstead Wells and Campden Trust, 1985–93; Under-Secretary, Department of Health and Social Security, 1972–79 and 1981–85; *b* 31 Oct. 1925; *m* 1961, Susan (*née* Littmann) (*d* 1972); one *s* one *d*. *Educ:* Taunton Sch.; London Sch. of Economics and Political Science (BSc(Econ)). Academic research, 1950–52. Asst Principal, Min. of National Insurance, 1952; Principal Private Sec. to Minister of Pensions and National Insurance, 1962–64; Asst Sec., 1964; Treasury/Civil Service Dept, 1967–70; Under-Sec., DES, 1979–81. *Recreations:* walking, travel. *Address:* 35 Crediton Hill, NW6 1HS. *T:* (020) 7794 6404. *Club:* Athenæum.

REGAN, Rt Rev. Edwin; *see* Wrexham, Bishop of, (RC).

REGAN, Hon. Gerald Augustine; PC (Can.) 1980; QC (Can.) 1970; President, Hawthorne Developments, since 1984; lawyer; *b* Windsor, NS, 13 Feb. 1929; *s* of Walter E. Regan and Rose M. Greene; *m* 1956, A. Carole, *d* of John H. Harrison; three *s* three *d*. *Educ:* Windsor Academy; St Mary's and Dalhousie Univs, Canada; Dalhousie Law Sch. (LLB). Called to Bar of Nova Scotia, 1954. Liberal candidate in Provincial gen. elecs, 1956 and 1960, and in Fed. gen. elec., 1962. MP for Halifax, NS, House of Commons of

Canada, 1963–65; Leader, Liberal Party of Nova Scotia, 1965–80; MLA for Halifax-Needham, Provincial gen. elec., 1967, re-elected, 1970–74 and 1978; Premier of Nova Scotia, 1970–78, Leader of the Opposition 1978–80; Minister of Labour, Govt of Canada, 1980–81, Minister responsible for Fitness and Amateur Sport, 1980–82; Secretary of State for Canada, 1981–82; Minister for International Trade, 1982–84; Minister of Energy, Mines and Resources, June–Sept. 1984. Counsel, Patterson Palmer Law, Halifax. Mem., NS Barristers Soc.; Chm. Exec. Cttee, Commonwealth Parly Assoc., 1973–76; Mem., Canadian Delegn, UN, 1965. Chm., Trenton Works Inc.; former Chm., Canadian Exporters Assoc.; Dir., Marsh Canada Ltd Adv. Bd. *Recreations:* tennis, ski-ing. *Address:* (home) 140 Shore Drive, Bedford, NS B4A 2E4, Canada. *Club:* Halifax (Halifax, NS).

REGAN, Prof. Lesley, (Mrs John Summerfield), MD; FRCOG; Professor and Head of Department of Obstetrics and Gynaecology, Imperial College at St Mary's Hospital, London, since 1996; Deputy Head, Division of Surgery, Oncology, Reproductive Biology and Anaesthetics, Imperial College London, since 2005; *b* 8 March 1956; *d* of Jack Regan and Dorothy Hull (*née* Thorne); *m* 1990, Prof. John Summerfield; twin *d*, and two step *s* two step *d*. *Educ:* Royal Free Hosp. Sch. of Medicine (MB BS 1980; MD 1989). MRCOG 1985, FRCOG 1998. Sen. Registrar in Obstetrics and Gynaecology, Addenbrooke's Hosp., Cambridge, 1986–90; Teaching Fellow (Medicine), 1986–90, Dir of Medical Studies, 1987–90, Girton Coll., Cambridge; Sen. Res. Associate, MRC Embryo and Gamete Res. Gp, Univ. of Cambridge, 1987–89; Sen. Lectr, ICSM, and Hon. Consultant in Obstetrics and Gynaecology, St Mary's Hosp., London, 1990–96; Director: Miscarriage Service, St Mary's Hosp., 1990–; Subspecialty Trng Prog. in Reproductive Medicine for ICSM at St Mary's and Hammersmith Hosps, 1995–; Clinical Dir, Maternity, 2000–03, Gynaecology, 2002–05, St Mary's Hosp. Rosenfelder Vis. Fellow, Boston, USA, 1999; Vis. Prof., Harvard Centre of Excellence for Women's Health, 2000–02; RCOG Vis. Lectr to S Africa, 2004; Lectures: Alexander Gordon, Aberdeen Univ., 2003; Lettsomian, Med. Soc. of London, 2004; Green-Armytage, RCOG, 2006. Non-exec. Dir, W Middx Univ. Hosp. NHS Trust, 2006–. Professional Advisor: Miscarriage Assoc., 1992–; CHANA, 1994–; Industrial Relns Soc., 1994–; Twins and Multiple Births Assoc., 1996–. Member: Expert Adv. Panels in Reproductive Medicine and Contraception, FIGO, 1997; Wellcome Trust Adv. Bd (Clinical Interest Gp), 2002–04; Gynaecol Vis. Soc.; Soc. for Gynaecol Investigation, USA; Council, 2006–, Academic Cttee, 2006–, RCOG. Sec., Assoc. of Professors and Gynaecologists, 2001–; Pres., Assoc. of Early Pregnancy Units in the UK, 2005–. Trustee: Inst. of Obstetrics and Gynaecology, 1996–; Save the Baby, 1998–. Woman of Achievement Award, 2005, for services to reproductive medicine. *Publications:* Miscarriage: what every woman needs to know, 1997, 2nd edn 2001; Your Pregnancy Week by Week, 2005; numerous chapters in reproductive medicine textbooks; scientific articles on sporadic and recurrent pregnancy loss and uterine fibroids in BMJ, Lancet, Human Reproduction, British Jl of Obstetrics and Gynaecol., Amer. Jls of Obstetrics and Gynaecol. *Recreations:* mother to my twin girls, opera, creating a garden in the South of France. *Address:* Department of Obstetrics and Gynaecology, Imperial College at St Mary's Hospital London, South Wharf Road, Paddington, W2 1NY. *T:* (020) 7886 1731; *e-mail:* l.regan@imperial.ac.uk.

REGAN, Maj.-Gen. Michael Dalrymple, CB 1996; OBE 1985; Controller, The Army Benevolent Fund, 1997–2003; *b* 6 Jan. 1942; *s* of late M. L. R. Regan and G. I. Regan (*née* Dalrymple); *m* 1974, Victoria, *o d* of late Comdr V. C. Grenfell, DSO; two *d*. *Educ:* St Boniface's Coll.; RMA, Sandhurst. Commnd 1st KSLI, 1962; Instructor, Sch. of Infantry, 1968–70; Adjutant, 3rd LI, 1971–73; Staff Coll., Camberley, 1973–74; BM, 12th Mech. Bde, 1975–76; Company Comdr, 1st LI, 1977–78; MA to C-in-C, UKLF, 1979–82; CO, 3rd LI, 1982–84; Col MS 2, MoD, 1985; Comdr, 20th Armd Bde, 1986–87; RCDS, 1988; DCOS, HQ UKLF, 1989–91; GOC Wales and Western Dist (5 Div.), 1991–94; Dir Gen., AGC, 1994–95; COS, HQ Adjt Gen., 1995–96. Col, LI, 1992–96; Asst Col Comdt, AGC, 1995–96. Chm. Trustees, Shropshire Regimental Mus., 1998–2003; Trustee: Army Dependants Assurance Trust, 2003–; Royal Commonwealth Ex-Services League, 2006– (Council Mem., 2003–). *Recreations:* golf, ski-ing, sailing. *Clubs:* MCC, Army and Navy; Royal Yacht Squadron (Cowes).

REGAN, Michael John; HM Diplomatic Service; Counsellor, Harare, since 2004; *b* 17 Aug. 1955; *s* of late Brig. John Joseph Regan, OBE and Edith Nancy Cunliffe; *m* 1986, Carolyn Gaye Black; two *s*. *Educ:* St George's Coll., Weybridge; Nottingham Univ. (BA Jt Hons Econs and Agricl Econs). SSC, 3rd RTR, 1977–82. Insurance Broker, Fenchurch Gp, 1982–83; joined Diplomatic Service, 1983; FCO, 1983–86; Kabul, 1986–88; FCO, 1988–89; First Sec. (Chancery/Economic), Dubai, 1989–91, FCO, 1991–95; Counsellor (ESCAP), Bangkok, 1995–98; FCO, 1998–2004. *Recreations:* hockey, tennis, golf, sailing, walking. *Address:* c/o Foreign and Commonwealth Office, King Charles Street, SW1A 2AH. *Club:* Hankley Common Golf.

REGO, (Maria) Paula (Figueiroa), (Mrs Victor Willing); artist; *b* 26 Jan. 1935; *d* of José Fernandes Figueiroa Rego and Maria de S José Pavva Figueiroa Rego; *m* 1959, Victor Willing (*d* 1988); one *s* two *d*. *Educ:* St Julian's Sch., Carcavelos, Portugal; Slade School of Fine Art, UCL. First Associate Artist, Nat. Gall., Jan.–Dec. 1990. Selected solo exhibitions: (1st at) Soc. Nat. de Belas Artes, Lisbon, 1965; Gal. S Mamede, Lisbon, 1971; Gal. Modulo, Porto, 1977; Gal. III, Lisbon, 1978; Air Gall., London, 1981; Edward Totah Gall., 1982, 1985, 1987; Arnolfini, 1983; Art Palace, NY, 1985; Gulbenkian Foundn, 1988, 1999; Serpentine Gall. (retrospective), 1988; Marlborough Graphics (nursery rhymes), 1989; Nat. Gall., 1991–92; Marlborough Gall., 1992, 1994; Tate Gall., Liverpool (retrospective), 1997; Dulwich Picture Gall., 1998; Gulbenkian Foundn, Lisbon, 1999; Abbot Hall, Kendal, 2001; Yale Centre for British Art, 2002; Marlborough Fine Art, 2003, 2006, 2008; Tate Britain, 2004; Serralves Museum, Oporto, 2004–05; prints (retrospective), Talbot Rice Gall., Edinburgh, then Brighton Mus. and tour, 2005–07; Mus. Nacional Centro de Arte Reina Sofia, Madrid (retrospective), 2007, then Nat. Mus. of Women in the Arts, Washington, DC. Many collective shows include: ICA, 1965; S Paulo Biennale, 1969, 1985; British Art Show, 1985, 2000; Hayward Gall., 1994 and 1996; Saatchi Gall., 1994–95; Encounters, Nat. Gall., 2000; also in Japan, Australia, all over Europe. Large painting, Crivelli's Garden, in restaurant of Sainsbury Wing, Nat. Gall., 1992. Sen. Fellow, RCA, 1989. Hon. DLitt: St Andrews, 1999; E Anglia, 1999; Oxford, 2005; Hon. DFA Rhode Island Sch. of Design, 2000; Hon. Dr: London Inst., 2002; UCL, 2004; DUniv Roehampton, 2005. *Relevant Publications:* Paula Rego, by John McEwen, 1992, 3rd edn 2006; Paula Rego, by Fiona Bradley, 2002; Paula Rego: the complete graphic work, by T. G. Rosenthal, 2003; Paula Rego's Map of Memory, by Dr Maria Lisboa, 2003; Behind the Scenes, by John McEwen, 2008. *Recreations:* going to the movies, plays. *Address:* c/o Marlborough Fine Art, 6 Albemarle Street, W1X 4BY. *T:* (020) 7629 5161.

REHN, Olli Ilmari, DPhil; Member, European Commission, since 2004; *b* Mikkeli, Finland, 31 March 1962; *s* of Tauno and Vuokko Rehn; *m* 1995, Merja Maria Hakkarainen; one *d*. *Educ:* Macalester Coll., St Paul, Minn; Univ. of Helsinki (Master Soc. Sci. Political Sci. 1989); St Antony's Coll., Oxford (DPhil Internat. Political Econ. 1996). Mem., City Council, Helsinki, 1988–94; MP (Centre Party), 1991–95; Special Advr to Prime Minister, 1992–93; MEP, 1995–96; Hd of Cabinet, EC, 1998–2002; Prof. and Dir of Res., Dept of Political Sci. and Centre for European Studies, Univ. of Helsinki, 2002–03; Econ. Policy Advr to Prime Minister, 2003–04. Chm., Centre Youth, Finland, 1987–89; Dep. Chm., Centre Party, 1988–94. Chm., Finnish Delegn to Council of Europe, 1991–95; Vice-President: Liberal Gp, EP, 1995; European Movement of Finland, 1996–98. Chm., Football League of Finland, 1996–97. Player, association football, 1968–: FC Mikkelin Palloilijat (youth teams, 1968–78; 1st team, 1979–82); FC Finnish Parliament, 1991–; CS Eurocommission II, 1998–2002. Columnist in several newspapers and mags, 1985–. *Publications:* Pieni valtio Euroopan Unionissa (A Small State in the European Union), 1996; European Challenges of the Finnish EU Presidency, 2nd edn 1998; (contrib.) Decision-Making in the European Union: a clear introduction to a complex game, 1998; (contrib.) The Yearbook of Finnish Foreign Policy 2002, 2002; (contrib.) Liberalism in the European Union: the way forward, 2004; Europe's Next Frontiers, 2006; Suomen eurooppalainen valinta ei ole suhdannepolitikkaa, 2006. *Recreations:* political economy, rock and jazz, reading. *Address:* European Commission, Berlaymont 10/299, Rue de la Loi 200, 1049 Brussels, Belgium. *T:* (2) 2957957, *Fax:* (2) 2958561; *e-mail:* Olli.Rehn@ec.europa.eu.

REICH, Peter Gordon; Assistant Chief Scientist (G), Royal Air Force, 1984–86; *b* 16 Sept. 1926; *s* of Douglas Gordon Reich and Josephine Grace Reich; *m* 1948, Kathleen, *d* of Alan and Florence Lessiter, Banstead; three *d*. *Educ:* Sutton Grammar Sch.; London Univ. (BSc). FRIN 1967 (Bronze Medal, 1967). Served RN, 1944–47. Entered Civil Service as Scientific Officer, 1952; Armament Res. Estab., 1952–54; Opl Res. Br., Min. of Transport and Civil Aviation, 1955–60; RAE, 1960–68; Asst Dir of Electronics Res. and Develt (2), Min. of Technol., 1968–70; Asst Dir of Res. (Avionics, Space and Air Traffic), Min. of Aviation Supply, 1971–73; Supt, Def. Opl Analysis Estab., MoD, 1973–76; Mem., Reliability and Costing Study Gp, MoD, 1976–79; Counsellor (Defence Res.), Canberra, and Head of British Defence Res. and Supply Staffs, Australia, 1979–83. *Publications:* papers in Jl of Inst. of Nav., and Jl of Opl Res. Soc. *Recreations:* racquet games, walking, aural pleasures.

REICH, Steve; composer; *b* 3 Oct. 1936; *s* of Leonard Reich and June Carroll (*née* Sillman); *m* 1976, Beryl Korot; one *s*, and one *s* from previous *m*. *Educ:* Cornell Univ. (BA Hons Philos. 1957); Juilliard Sch. of Music; Mills Coll. (MA Music 1963); Inst. for African Studies, Univ. of Ghana. Guggenheim Fellow, 1978; Montgomery Fellow, Dartmouth Coll., 2000. Mem., AAAL, 1994. Founded ensemble, Steve Reich and Musicians, 1966, toured the world, 1971–. Music performed by major orchestras, including: NY Philharmonic; San Francisco Symphony; St Louis Symphony; Brooklyn Philharmonic; LA Philharmonic; BBC Symphony; London Symphony Orch.; commissions received include: Fest. d'Automne, Paris for 200th Anniv. of French Revolution, 1989; BBC Proms in honour of centennial, 1995. Member: Amer. Acad. of Arts and Letters, 1994; Bavarian Acad. of Fine Arts, 1995. Schuman Prize, Columbia Univ., 2000. Commandeur, Ordre des Arts et des Lettres (France), 1999. *Compositions include:* Drumming, 1971; Music for 18 Musicians, 1976 (Grammy Award for Best Small Ensemble recording, 1996); Eight Lines, 1979–83; Tehillim, 1981; The Desert Music, 1984; Sextet, 1985; Different Trains, 1988 (Grammy Award for Best Contemporary Composition, 1990); The Cave, 1993; Nagoyd Marimba, 1994; City Life, 1995; Proverb, 1995; Triple Quartet, 1999; Three Tales, 2002; Cello Counterpoint, 2003; You Are (variations), 2004; Daniel Variations, 2006. *Publications:* Writings About Music, 1974; Writings on Music 1965–2000, 2002. *Address:* c/o Andrew Rosner, Allied Artists, 42 Montpelier Square, SW7 1JZ.

REICHMANN, Paul; Executive Director, Canary Wharf Group plc, until 2004 (Chairman, until 2003); Chief Executive, Reichmann Group of Companies; *b* Vienna, 1930; *s* of Samuel and Renee Reichmann. Moved to Toronto, 1954; with brothers, formed Olympia and York Develts Ltd; completed First Canadian Place, Toronto (offices), 1975; purchased 8 office buildings in Manhattan, NY, 1976; completed building of World Financial Centre, NY, 1986; responsible for concept and realisation of Canary Wharf project, 1987. Trustee: Retirement Residences Real Estate Investment Trust; CPL Long Term Care Real Estate Investment Trust; former Trustee, IPC US Income Commercial Real Estate Investment Trust. *Address:* c/o Canary Wharf Group, One Canada Square, Canary Wharf, E14 5AB.

REID, Sir Alan; *see* Reid, Sir P. A.

REID, Alan; MP (Lib Dem) Argyll and Bute, since 2001; *b* 7 Aug. 1954; *s* of James Smith Reid and Catherine Graham Reid (*née* Steele). *Educ:* Prestwick Acad.; Ayr Acad.; Strathclyde Univ. (BSc Hons Pure & Applied Maths). Strathclyde Regional Council: Maths Teacher, 1976–77; Computer Programmer, 1977–85; Computer Project Manager, Glasgow Univ., 1985–2001. *Recreations:* playing chess, walking, reading, watching TV. *Address:* House of Commons, SW1A 0AA; 95 Alexandra Parade, Dunoon, Argyll PA23 8AL. *T:* (01369) 704840, *Fax:* (01369) 701212.

REID, Dr Alexander Arthur Luttrell; Director-General, Royal Institute of British Architects, 1994–2000; *b* 11 Jan. 1941; *s* of late Capt. Philip Reid, RN and of Louisa (*née* Luttrell); *m* 1st, 1964, Sara Louise Coleridge (marr. diss. 1987); two *d*; 2nd, 1988, Sian Tudor Roberts; one *s* one *d*. *Educ:* Winchester Coll. (Schol.); Trinity Coll., Cambridge (MA); University Coll., London (MSc; PhD 1974). Served RN, Lieut (helicopter pilot), 1962–67. Post Office Telecommunications: Hd, Long Range Studies, 1972–77; Director: Prestel, 1977–80; Business Systems, 1980–83; Acorn Computer Gp PLC, 1984–85; Octagon Investment Mgt Ltd, 1984–; Chief Exec., DEGW Ltd, 1991–94. Mem. (Lib Dem), Cambs CC, 2003–. Royal College of Art: Council Mem., 1988–90; Chm., 1990–93. *Recreations:* carpentry, sailing. *Address:* 27 Millington Road, Cambridge CB3 9HW. *T:* (01223) 356100.

REID, Sir Alexander (James), 3rd Bt *cr* 1897; JP; DL; *b* 6 Dec. 1932; *s* of Sir Edward James Reid, 2nd Bt, KBE, and Tatiana (*d* 1992), *d* of Col Alexander Fenoult, formerly of Russian Imperial Guard; *S* father, 1972; *m* 1955, Michaela Ann, *d* of late Olaf Kier, CBE; one *s* three *d*. *Educ:* Eton; Magdalene Coll., Cambridge. Nat. Certificate Agriculture (NCA). 2nd Lieut, 1st Bn Gordon Highlanders, 1951; served Malaya; Captain, 3rd Bn Gordon Highlanders (TA), retired 1964. Director: Ellon Castle Estates Co. Ltd, 1965–96; Cristina Securities Ltd, 1970–. Chm., 1994–2003, Hon. Pres., 2004–, Clan Donnachaidh Soc. Governor, Heath Mount Prep. Sch., Hertford, 1970, Chm., 1976–92. JP Cambridgeshire and Isle of Ely, 1971, DL 1973; High Sheriff, Cambridgeshire, 1987–88. *Heir:* *s* Charles Edward James Reid, *b* 24 June 1956. *Address:* Lanton Tower, Jedburgh, Roxburghshire TD8 6SU. *T:* (01835) 863443. *Club:* Caledonian.

REID, Andrew Milton; Deputy Chairman, Imperial Group, 1986–89; *b* 21 July 1929; *s* of late Rev. A. R. R. Reid, DD and of Lilias Symington Tindal; *m* 1st, 1953, Norma Mackenzie Davidson (*d* 1993); two *s*; 2nd, 1995, Audrey Janet Wilson Bruell. *Educ:* Glasgow Academy; Jesus Coll., Oxford. Imperial Tobacco Management Pupil, 1952; Asst Managing Director, John Player & Sons, 1975; Dir, Imperial Group Ltd, 1978; Chm., Imperial Tobacco Ltd, 1979–86. Dep. Chm., Trade Indemnity plc, 1994–96 (Dir, 1982–96); Dir, Renold PLC, 1983–96. Member, Tobacco Adv. Council, 1977–86.

Member: Council, RSCM, 1987–89; Court and Council, Bristol Univ., 1986–99; Board, Bristol Develt Corp., 1989–96 (Dep. Chm., 1993–). Chm. Governors, Colston's Collegiate Sch., 1986–94. Master, Soc. of Merchant Venturers of Bristol, 1991–92. High Sheriff of Avon, 1991. *Recreations:* sailing, golf, fishing. *Address:* Parsonage Farm, Publow, Pensford, near Bristol BS39 4JD.

REID, Andrew Scott; HM Coroner, Inner North London District of Greater London, since 2002; *b* 2 March 1965; *m* 2007, Suzanne Ellen Greenaway; twin *s* two *d. Educ:* Univ. of Nottingham Med. Sch. (BMedSci 1986; BM BS 1988); Nottingham Trent Univ. Sch. of Law (Postgrad. Dip. Law 1992; Solicitors Final Exam 1993). Pre-registration, sen. house officer and registrar posts in gen. medicine, surgery and histopathol., 1988–92; temp. Lectr in Human Morphol., Univ. of Nottingham, 1989–90; admitted solicitor, specialising in med. law and clin. negligence, 1995; In-house Solicitor and/or Clinical Risk Manager: NHS Litigation Authy, 1998–99; NHS Exec. Regl Medicolegal Service, 1999–2001; NW London Hosps NHS Trust, 2001–02. Asst Dep. Coroner, Notts, 1995–98; Dep. Coroner, N London, 1998–2002. Hon. Sen. Lectr in Pathology, Inst. of Cell and Molecular Sci., Queen Mary's Sch. of Medicine and Dentistry, London Univ., 2005–. Legal Mem., Mental Health Rev. Tribunal, 2002–. Mem., Human Tissue Authy, 2005–. Member: BMA, 1987–; Coroners' Soc. of England and Wales, 1995–. FRSocMed 1997; FFFLM 2006. *Publications:* (contrib.) The Pathology of Trauma, ed Prof. J. K. Mason, 2nd edn 1993; contrib. papers on epithelial cell kinetics, breast cancer and industrial disease to med. jls. *Recreation:* trying to enjoy life between moderation and excess as appropriate. *Address:* St Pancras Coroner's Court, Camley Street, NW1 0PP. *T:* (020) 7387 4882/4, *Fax:* (020) 7383 2485.

REID, Andrew Stephen; Senior Partner, Reid Minty LLP, Solicitors, since 1980; Deputy High Court Costs Judge (formerly Deputy Supreme Court Taxing Master), since 1991; Deputy District Judge: Principal Registry of the Family Division, since 2001; South Eastern Circuit, since 2002; farmer; *b* 2 March 1954; *s* of Leon Ralph Reid and Fay Marion Reid; partner, Corrina Bithell; one *d. Educ:* University College Sch.; University Coll. London (LLB Hons). ACIArb 1979, MCIArb. Admitted solicitor, 1979; founded Reid Minty, Solicitors, 1980. Mem., Radio Authy, 1994–99. Racehorse trainer, London, 1999–2006. *Recreations:* polo, hunting, gardening, shooting, sailing. *Address:* (office) Moss House, 15/16 Brooks Mews, W1K 4DS. *Clubs:* Annabel's, MCC; Belmont Polo; Guards' Polo; Oakley Hunt.

REID, Caroline Jean Vernon; Head of Infrastructure and Project Finance, Banca OPI SpA, SanPaolo Imi Banking Group, since 2001; *b* 6 April 1948; *d* of late Colin Beever and of Dorothy Beever; *m* 1970, Michael Francis Reid; two *s. Educ:* Lycée Châteaubriand, Rome; Bedford High Sch. for Girls; Univ. of Bristol (BSc Hons Econs and Stats). Asst economist, British Gas Council, 1969–71; with NIESR, 1972–74; joined European Investment Bank, 1974: Energy Economist, 1974–85; loan officer, Energy/Envmt Div., Dept for Lending, Rome, 1985–88, Hd of Div., 1988–94; Dir, Italy Dept, 1994–99; Dir Gen., Projects Directorate, 1999–2001. *Address:* c/o Banca OPI SpA, Viale dell'Arte 21, 00144 Rome, Italy. *T:* (6) 59592244; *e-mail:* caroline.reid@bancaopi.it.

REID, Caroline Oldcorn, PhD; a District Judge, Principal Registry, Family Division, since 2006 (Deputy District Judge, 2003–06); *b* 6 April 1948; *d* of late John Patterson Reid and Olwen Reid; *m* 1983, Dr Frank Patrick Burton, *qv;* two *s* one *d. Educ:* Holt Grammar Sch., Wokingham; Univ. of Sheffield (BA Hons Hist. 1969; PhD 1976); City Univ. (Dip Law 1981). Tutor Organiser, WEA, Sheffield, 1974–80; called to the Bar, Middle Temple, 1982; in practice as a barrister, 1984–2006, 14 Gray's Inn Square, 1994–2006. *Publications:* (contrib.) Evidence in Family Proceedings, 1999; (contrib.) Child Abuse, 3rd edn 2003, 4th edn 2008; (contrib.) The Family Court Practice, 2008. *Recreations:* my family, Suffolk, old things, garden design, building. *Address:* Principal Registry of the Family Division, First Avenue House, 42–49 Holborn, WC1V 6NP.

REID, David James Glover; Member, Arts Council of England, 1995–98 (Acting Deputy Chairman, 1997–98; Chairman, Audit Committee, 1996–98); *b* 14 Aug. 1936; *s* of Alexander Robert Reid and Maisie Cullen Mowat; *m* 1963, Norma Scott Elder Chalmers; two *s. Educ:* Edinburgh Royal High Sch.; Univ. of Edinburgh (BSc Maths and Math. Physics). Joined IBM, 1962; USA, 1967–75; Manager, IBM Product 3250, 1977; Graphics Product Manager, 1979; lab. ops Manager, 1983; Resident Dir for Scotland, N England and NI, 1985, for England, Wales and NI, 1990; retired, 1993. Chairman: Scottish Cttee, ABSA, 1986; Scottish Enterprise Foundn, 1986; Southern Regl Arts Bd, 1991–98; Business in the Arts South, 1991–98; Member: Scottish Econ. Council, 1988; Exec., Scottish Business in the Community, 1988. Trustee, Arts Foundn, 1996–98. Gov., Univ. of Portsmouth, 1991–96. *Recreations:* bridge, computing, music, sailing, theatre, walking.

REID, Derek Donald; Board Member, Scottish Enterprise Tayside, 1996–2003; *b* 30 Nov. 1944; *s* of Robert Slorach Reid and Selina Mons Lewis Reid (*née* Donald); *m* 1977, Janice Anne Reid; one *s* one *d. Educ:* Inverurie Acad., Aberdeen; Aberdeen Univ. (MA); Robert Gordon Inst. of Technol. (Dip. Personnel Mgt). Cadbury Schweppes: mgt trainee, 1968; Divl Dir, 1982–86; Founder Mem., Premier Brands and Dir, Tea Business after mgt buy-out, 1986–89; Man. Dir, Tea Business, 1989–90; Chief Exec., Scottish Tourist Bd, 1994–96; Dep. Chm., Sea Fish Industry Authy, 1996–2000; Chm., Scotland's Hotels of Distinction, 1998–2001; dir, various small cos. Vis. Prof. of Tourism, Abertay Univ., 2000–. Hon. DBA Robert Gordon Univ., Aberdeen, 1995. *Recreations:* golf, cricket, fishing, art appreciation, classical music. *Address:* Broomhill, Kinclaven, Stanley, Perthshire PH14 4QL. *T:* (01250) 883209. *Clubs:* Royal Perth Golf, Blairgowrie Golf.

REID, Dominic; *see* Reid, J. D.

REID, Elizabeth Margaret; Chief Executive, Specialist Schools and Academies Trust (formerly Technology Colleges, then Specialist Schools, Trust), since 2001; *b* 16 April 1947; *d* of John A. McConachie, MB ChB, FRCPE and J. Margaret McConachie, MB ChB; *m* 1st, 1970, Robin Reid, MA (marr. diss. 1975); 2nd, 1982, Martin J. Monk, BA Hons Oxon (marr. diss. 2000). *Educ:* Aberdeen Univ. (MA Hons 1969); London Univ. (MA Educnl Admin 1980). Asst Principal, CS, 1969–70; Inner London Education Authority: schoolteacher, 1970–78; Advr for 16–19 educn, 1978–79; Professional Asst, London Borough of Ealing, 1979–80; Asst Educn Officer, London Borough of Haringey, 1980–83; Sen. Principal Officer (Educn), AMA, 1983–85; Inner London Education Authority: Admin. Head, Further and Higher Educn Br., 1985–88; Dep. Dir of Educn (Further and Higher Educn), 1988–89; Dep. Provost, London Guildhall Univ. (formerly City of London Poly.), 1989–93; Director of Education: Lothian Regional Council, 1993–96; City of Edinburgh Council, 1996–98; London Borough of Hackney, 1998–2000. Vice Chm., Scottish Qualifications Authy, 1996–98. Mem. Bd, Enterprise Educn Trust, 2000–. Member: Ct of Govs, Univ. of the Arts, London (formerly London Inst.), 2001–; Bd, City and Islington Coll.; Fashion Retail Acad. Fellow, Inst. of Educn, 2008. FRSA 1989; FSQA 1998; Fellow, 48 Gp Club, 2007. *Publications:* (contrib.) Central and Local Control of Education After the Education Reform Act 1988, ed R. Morris, 1990; (contrib.) The Future of Higher Education, ed T. Schuller, 1991; (with R. Morris

and J. Fowler) Education Act 93: a critical guide, 1993. *Recreations:* theatre, opera, music, reading, gardening. *Address:* Specialist Schools and Academies Trust, 16th Floor, Millbank Tower, 21–24 Millbank, SW1P 4QP.

REID, Rt Rev. Gavin Hunter, OBE 2000; Bishop Suffragan of Maidstone, 1992–2000; *b* 24 May 1934; *s* of Arthur William Reid and Jean Smith Reid (*née* Guthrie); *m* 1959, Mary Eleanor Smith; two *s* one *d. Educ:* Roan Sch., Greenwich; Queen Mary Coll. and King's Coll., London Univ. (BA 1956); Oak Hill Theol Coll. Ordained, Chelmsford Cathedral: deacon, 1960; priest, 1961; Assistant Curate: St Paul's, East Ham, 1960–63; Rainham Parish Church, 1963–66; Publications Sec., CPAS, 1966–71; Editorial Sec., United Soc. for Christian Lit., 1971–74; Sec. for Evangelism, 1974–90, Consultant Missioner, 1990–92, CPAS; Advr, Gen. Synod Bd of Mission, 1990–92. Seconded: Nat. Dir, Mission England, 1982–85; Project Dir, Mission 89, 1988–89. Chairman: Archbishops' Adv. Gp for the Millennium, 1995–2000; CPAS Council of Reference, 2005–08. Pres., British Youth for Christ, 2001–04. *Publications:* The Gagging of God, 1969; The Elaborate Funeral, 1972; A New Happiness, 1974; To Be Confirmed, 1977; Good News to Share, 1979; Starting Out Together, 1981; To Reach a Nation, 1987; Beyond Aids, 1987; Lights that Shine, 1991; Brushing up on Believing, 1991; Our Place in his Story, 1994; To Canterbury with Love, 2002; various symposia. *Recreations:* golf, sailing, walking, birdwatching. *Address:* 17 Richard Crampton Road, Beccles, Suffolk NR34 9HN.

REID, Rt Hon. George (Newlands); PC 2004; journalist; Member for Ochil, Scottish Parliament, 2003–07; Presiding Officer, Scottish Parliament, 2003–07; Lord High Commissioner, General Assembly, Church of Scotland, 2008; *b* 4 June 1939; *s* of late George Reid, company director, and of Margaret Forsyth; *m* 1968, Daphne Ann MacColl; one *d,* and one *d* from previous marriage. *Educ:* Tullibody Sch.; Dollar Academy; Univ. of St Andrews (MA Hons). Pres., Students' Representative Council. Features Writer, Scottish Daily Express, 1962; Reporter, Scottish Television, 1964; Producer, Granada Television, 1965; Head of News and Current Affairs (Scottish Television), 1968; presenter, BBC, 1979. Head of Inf., 1984–86, Dir of Public Affairs, 1986–90, Dir of Internat. Promotion, 1990–92, League of Red Cross and Red Crescent Socs, Geneva. MP (SNP) Stirlingshire E and Clackmannan, Feb. 1974–1979; Mem., British Parly Delegn to Council of Europe and WEU, 1977–79. Scottish Parliament: Mem. Mid Scotland & Fife, 1999–2003, Ochil, 2003–07 (SNP, 1999–2003, when elected Presiding Officer); Dep. Presiding Officer, 1999–2003; Convener: Scottish Parly Bureau, 2003–07; Scottish Parly Corporate Body, 2003–07. Vice-Convener, SNP, 1997–99. Contested (SNP) Ochil, 1997. Dir, Scottish Council Res. Inst., 1974–77. Vis. Prof., Glasgow Univ., 2006–. Vice Chm., Carnegie Commn on Civil Soc., 2006–; Mem., Caucasus-Caspian Commn, 2007–08. Trustee: Glasgow Culture and Sport, 2007–; Edinburgh Internat. Tattoo, 2007–. Chief Red Cross deleg. to Armenia, Dec. 1988–Jan. 1989. Hon LLD St Andrews, 2005; DUniv: Queen Margaret UC, 2006; Edinburgh, 2007. *Address:* Coneyhill House, Bridge of Allan, Stirling FK9 4DU.

REID, Gordon; *see* Reid, J. G.

REID, Rev. Canon Gordon; *see* Reid, Rev. Canon W. G.

REID, Graham Livingstone, CB 1991; Director General of Strategy, International and Analytical Services, Department for Education and Employment, 1995–97; *b* 30 June 1937; *s* of late William L. Reid and of Louise M. Reid; *m* 1st, 1973, Eileen M. Loudfoot (marr. diss. 1983); 2nd, 1985, Sheila Rothwell (*d* 1997). *Educ:* Univ. of St Andrews (MA); Queen's Univ., Kingston, Canada (MA). Dept of Social and Economic Res., Univ. of Glasgow: Asst Lectr in Applied Economics, 1960, Lectr 1963, Sen. Lectr 1968, Reader 1971; Sen. Econ. Adviser and Head of Econs and Statistics Unit, Scottish Office, 1973–75; Dir, Manpower Intelligence and Planning Div., MSC, 1975–84; Department of Employment: Chief Economic Adviser and Hd, Economic and Social Div., 1984–88 and Dir, Enterprise and Deregulation Unit, 1987; Dep. Sec., Manpower Policy, 1988–90, Resources and Strategy, 1991, Indust. Relns and Internat. Directorate, 1991–95. Vis. Associate Prof., Mich State Univ., 1967; Vis. Res. Fellow, Queen's Univ., Canada, 1969. FRSA 1996. *Publications:* Fringe Benefits, Labour Costs and Social Security (ed with D. J. Robertson), 1965; (with K. J. Allen) Nationalised Industries, 1970 (3rd edn 1975); (with L. C. Hunter and D. Boddy) Labour Problems of Technological Change, 1970; (with K. J. Allen and D. J. Harris) The Nationalised Fuel Industries, 1973; contrib. to Econ. Jl, Brit. Jl of Indust. Relations, Scot. Jl of Polit. Econ., Indust & Lab. Relns Rev. *Recreations:* golf, music. *Address:* 24 Barley Way, Marlow SL7 2DP. *T:* (01491) 577005. *Club:* Phyllis Court (Henley-on-Thames).

REID, Henry William, (Harry); writer; Commissioning Consultant, St Andrew Press, since 2002; *b* 23 Sept. 1947; *s* of late William Reid and of Catherine Robertson Craighead Reid (*née* Maclean); *m* 1980, Julie Wilson Davidson; one *d. Educ:* Aberdeen Grammar Sch.; Fettes Coll.; Worcester Coll., Oxford (BA). The Scotsman: reporter, sports writer, leader writer, 1970–73; educn correspondent, 1973–77; Features Ed., 1977–81; Sport and Leisure Ed., Sunday Standard, 1981–82; Exec. Ed., 1982–83, Dep. Ed., 1983–97, Ed., 1997–2000, The Herald, Glasgow. Vis. Fellow, Faculty of Divinity, Univ. of Edinburgh, 2001–02. Mem., Church and Soc. Council, Ch of Scotland, 2005–06. Gov., Fettes Coll., 2002–. DUniv Glasgow, 2001; Dr *hc* Edinburgh, 2001. *Publications:* Dear Country: a quest for England, 1992; Outside Verdict: an old kirk in a new Scotland, 2002; Deadline: the story of the Scottish press, 2006. *Recreations:* exploring Scotland and European cities, hill walking, supporting Aberdeen FC, reading novels, listening to Bob Dylan. *Address:* 12 Comely Bank, Edinburgh EH4 1AN. *T:* (0131) 332 6690.

REID, Sir Hugh, 3rd Bt *cr* 1922; farmer; *b* 27 Nov. 1933; *s* of Sir Douglas Neilson Reid, 2nd Bt, and Margaret Brighton Young (*d* 1992), *d* of Robert Young Maxtone, MBE, JP; *S* father, 1971. *Educ:* Loretto. Royal Air Force, 1952–56; RAFVR, 1956–78 (Flying Officer, Training Branch, 1965–78). *Recreations:* ski-ing, travel. *Heir:* none. *Address:* Caheronaun Park, Loughrea, Co. Galway, Ireland; 4772 Vouni Village, Limassol District, Cyprus.

REID, Iain; arts consultant; Dean, The Arts Educational Schools, London, 1998–2006; *b* 27 March 1942; *s* of Jean Reid (*née* Money) and George Aitken Reid; *m* 1st, 1968, Judith Coke; 2nd, 1982, Kay Barlow; one *s* one *d. Educ:* Uppingham; RADA; Lancaster Univ. (MA). Actor, 1963–73; theatre administrator, 1973–77; Drama Officer, Greater London Arts, 1977–82; Dir of Arts, Calouste Gulbenkian Foundn (UK), 1982–89; Dir, Arts Co-ordination, later Arts Develt, Arts Council of GB, 1989–94; Dir of Combined Arts, Arts Council of England, 1994–98. FRSA 1992. *Address:* e-mail: Kay.in@btinternet.com.

REID, (James) Gordon; QC (Scot.) 1993; a Temporary Judge of the Court of Session and High Court of Justiciary, since 2002; *b* 24 July 1952; *s* of James R. Reid and Constance M. Lawrie or Reid; *m* 1984, Hannah Hogg Hopkins; two *s* one *d* (and one *s* decd). *Educ:* Melville Coll., Edinburgh; Edinburgh Univ. (LLB Hons). Solicitor, 1976–80; Advocate, 1980–; called to the Bar, Inner Temple, 1991. Part-time Chm., VAT and Duties

Tribunals, 1997–; Dep. Special Comr for Income Tax Purposes, 1997–. FCIArb 1994. *Recreations:* guitar, tennis. *Address:* Blebo House, by St Andrews, Fife KY15 5TZ.

REID, James Robert; QC 1980; **His Honour Judge Reid;** a Circuit Judge, since 1999; *b* 23 Jan. 1943; *s* of late Judge J. A. Reid, MC and Jean Ethel Reid; *m* 1974, Anne Prudence Wakefield, *qv* (marr. diss. 2002); two *s* one *d. Educ:* Marlborough Coll.; New Coll., Oxford (MA). FCIArb 1992. Called to the Bar, Lincoln's Inn, 1965, Bencher, 1988; a Recorder, 1985–99. Mem., Senate of Inns of Court and the Bar, 1977–80; Mem., Gen. Council of the Bar, 1990–96 (Chm., Professional Conduct Cttee, 1995–96). Chm., Barristers Benevolent Assoc., 1995–99 (Hon. Jt Treas., 1986–91; Dep. Chm., 1991–95). Mem., Court of Arbitration for Sport, 1999–; Chm., Football League Appeal Cttee, 2000–.

REID, Prof. Janice Clare, AM 1998; FASSA; Vice-Chancellor and President, University of Western Sydney, since 1998; *b* 19 Sept. 1947; *d* of Keith M. Reid and Joan C. Reid; one *d. Educ:* Presbyterian Girls' Coll., Adelaide; Univ. of Adelaide (BSc); Univ. of Hawaii (MA); Stanford Univ., USA (MA, PhD). FASSA 1991. High sch. teacher, PNG, 1968–69; Res. Officer/Asst, Dept of Community Medicine, Univ. of NSW, 1974–75; Sen. Lectr, then Associate Prof., Sch. of Public Health and Tropical Medicine, 1979–90, and Dir, Centre for Crosscultural Studies in Health and Medicine, 1988–92, Univ. of Sydney; Foundn Hd, Sch. of Community Health, Cumberland Coll. of Health Scis, 1987–91; Prof. of Community Health, Univ. of Sydney, 1990–91; Pro Vice-Chancellor (Acad.), Qld Univ. of Technol., 1991–98. Chm. or mem., various Nat. Health and MRC standing cttees, 1992–96; Member: Higher Educn Council, 1996–98; Gtr Western Sydney Econ. Develt Bd, 1998–2000; Integral Energy Bd, 2000–06; Fed. Council on Australian/Latin American Relns, 2001–06 (Chm., Educn Action Gp, 2003–06); Higher Educn Cttee, Ministerial Ref. Gp, Nat. Higher Educn Rev., 2002; Governing Bd, OECD Instnl Mgt in Higher Educn Prog., 2005– (Vice-Chm., 2007–); NSW Health Clinical Excellence Commn, 2007–. Mem., Australian Inst. Aboriginal and Torres Is Studies, 1981–; Dep. Chm., Qld Inst. Med. Res., 1994–97. Chm., Founder and Convener, Australian Soc. of Med. Anthropol., 1981–82. Mem., Qld Mus. Bd, 1992–97. Mem. Council, Blue Mts GS, 1998–2002; Gov., Westmead Millennium Inst., 2001–. Mem. Bd, Unisuper, 2006–. Mem. Adv. Bd, Western Sydney Salvation Army, 2001–. Trustee, Kedumba Drawing Award, 2001–02; Mem. Trust, NSW Art Gall., 2004–. Wellcome Medal, RAI, 1984. Centenary Medal, Australia, 2003. *Publications:* (ed) Body Land and Spirit, 1982; Sorcerers and Healing Spirits, 1983; edited with P. Trompf: The Health of Immigrant Australia, 1990; The Health of Aboriginal Australia, 1991; contrib. numerous chapters, papers and reports to various jls, incl. Social Sci. and Medicine, particularly on Aborigines, migrants and refugees and health. *Address:* The Chancellery, University of Western Sydney, PO Box 1000, St Marys, NSW 1790, Australia. *T:* (2) 96787801, *Fax:* (2) 96787809; *e-mail:* vc@uws.edu.au.

REID, Rt Hon. John; PC 1998; PhD; MP (Lab) Airdrie and Shotts, since 2005 (Motherwell North, 1987–97; Hamilton North and Bellshill, 1997–2005); *b* 8 May 1947; *s* of late Thomas Reid and Mary Reid; *m* 1st, 1969, Catherine (*née* McGowan) (*d* 1998); two *s*; 2nd, 2002, Carine Adler. *Educ:* St Patrick's Senior Secondary Sch., Coatbridge; Stirling Univ. (BA History, PhD Economic History). Scottish Research Officer, Labour Party, 1979–83; Political Adviser to Rt Hon. Neil Kinnock, 1983–86; Scottish Organiser, Trades Unionists for Labour, 1986–87. Opposition spokesman on children, 1989–90, on defence, 1990–97; Minister of State, MoD, 1997–98; Minister of Transport, 1998–99; Secretary of State: for Scotland, 1999–2001; for Northern Ireland, 2001–02; Minister without Portfolio and Chair, Labour Party, 2002–03; Leader of the H of C and Pres. of the Council, 2003; Secretary of State: for Health, 2003–05; for Defence, 2005–06; for the Home Dept, 2006–07. Member: Public Accounts Cttee, 1988–89; Armed Forces Cttee and Reserved Forces Cttee, 1996–97. Fellow, Armed Forces Parly Scheme, 1990–. *Recreations:* football, reading, crossword puzzles. *Address:* Parliamentary Advice Office, 115 Graham Street, Airdrie ML6 6DE. *T:* (01236) 748777, *Fax:* (01236) 748666.

REID, John Boyd, AO 1980; LLB; FAIM, FAICD; CPEng, FIEAust; Chairman Emeritus, Australian Graduate School of Management, since 2000 (Board Member, 1991–2002); former Chairman, James Hardie Industries Ltd (Director, 1964–96); *b* 27 Dec. 1929; *s* of Sir John Thyne Reid, CMG. *Educ:* Scotch College; Melbourne Univ. Chm., Comsteel Vickers Ltd, 1983–86; Vice-Chm., Qantas Airways, 1981–86 (Dir, 1977–86); Director: Broken Hill Pty Co., 1972–97; Barclays Internat. Australia, 1982–85; Bell Resources Ltd, 1987–88; Peregrine Capital Australia Ltd, 1991–95; Focus Publishing, 1991–. Chm., Australian Bicentennial Authy, 1979–85; Dir, World Expo 88, 1986–89; Member: Admin. Review Cttee, 1975–76; Indep. Inquiry into Commonwealth Serum Labs, 1978; Patron, Australia Indonesia Business Co-operation Cttee, 1979–88 (Pres., 1973–79); Dir, Thailand-Australia Foundn Ltd, 1993–96; Mem., Internat. Adv. Bd, Swiss Banking Corp., 1986–97; Chm., Review of Commonwealth Admin, 1981–82. Trustee and Internat. Counsellor, Conference Bd USA; Internat. Council, Stanford Res. Inst., USA. Chairman: NSW Educn and Trng Foundn, 1989–93; Cttee, Aust. Scout Educn and Trng Foundn, 1991; Museum of Contemp. Art, 1994–98. Chm. Council, Pymble Ladies Coll., 1975–82 (Mem., 1965–75); Governor, Ian Clunies Ross Meml Foundn, 1975–2000; Chm., Sydney Adv. Cttee, 1995–97, and Red Shield Appeal, 1993–94, Salvation Army. Mem., Inst. of Company Dirs. Life Governor, AIM (Sydney Div.). Hon. Fellow, Univ. of Sydney, 2004. Hon. DBus Charles Sturt Univ., NSW; Hon. PhD Queensland. Melbourne Univ. Graduate Sch. of Business Admin Award, 1983; John Storey Medal, AIM, 1985. *Address:* Australian Graduate School of Management, University of New South Wales, Sydney, NSW 2052, Australia. *Clubs:* Australian (Sydney); Royal Sydney Yacht Squadron.

REID, (John) Dominic, OBE 2003; Pageantmaster, Lord Mayor's Show, since 1992; Principal, Reid and Reid, since 1992; Director, 2010 Anniversary Programme, Royal Society, since 2007; *b* 24 Sept. 1961; *s* of late John Reid, OBE, DL and of Sylvia Reid; *m* 1991, Suzanne Jessup (*née* Schultz); one *d. Educ:* Oundle Sch. (Music Scholar); Downing Coll., Cambridge; University College London. RIBA 1991. SSLC, 49 Field Regt, Royal Artillery, 1981. Architect: Doshi-Raje, Ahmedabad, India, 1984–85; Austin-Smith:Lord, 1986–89; Richard Horden Associates Ltd, 1989–90; John and Sylvia Reid, 1990–92; Dir, Designer's Collaborative, 1996–2000; Chief Exec., London Film Commission, 1999–2000; Exec. Dir, Oxford and Cambridge Boat Race, 2000–04. FRSA 1991. Liveryman, Grocers' Co., 1999–. OStJ 1999. *Recreations:* telemarking, sailing, cycling. *Address:* The Barge, Hindringham Road, Great Walsingham, Norfolk NR22 6DR. *T:* (01328) 824420, *Fax:* (01328) 824422; *e-mail:* dominic@reidandreid.com. *Clubs:* HAC; Leander.

REID, Prof. John Low, OBE 2001; DM; Regius Professor of Medicine and Therapeutics, University of Glasgow, since 1989; Medical Director, Scottish Advisory Committee on Distinction Awards, Scottish Government (formerly Executive) Health Department, since 2005; *b* 1 Oct. 1943; *s* of Dr James Reid and Irene M. Dale; *m* 1964, Randa Pharaon; one *s* one *d. Educ:* Fettes Coll., Edinburgh; Magdalen Coll., Oxford. MA; DM; FRCP 1986; FRCPGlas 1979; FRCPI 1997; FRSE 1995. House Officer, Radcliffe Infirmary, Oxford, and Brompton Hosp., 1967–70; Res. Fellow, RPMS, 1970–73; Vis. Fellow, Nat. Inst. of Mental Health, USA, 1973–74; Royal Postgraduate Medical School: Sen. Lectr in Clin. Pharmacol., and Consultant Physician, 1975–77; Reader in Clin. Pharmacol., 1977–78; Regius Prof. of Materia Medica, Univ. of Glasgow, 1978–89; Clinical Dir, Acute Medicine, 1993–2000, Chm., Div. of Medicine, 2000–06, N Glasgow Univ. Hosps NHS Trust. Founder FMedSci 1998. *Publications:* Central Action of Drugs in Regulation of Blood Pressure, 1975; Lecture Notes in Clinical Pharmacology, 1982; Handbook of Hypertension, 1983; papers on cardiovascular and neurological diseases in clinical and pharmacological journals. *Recreations:* books, gardening, the outdoors. *Address:* Division of Cardiovascular and Medical Sciences, Western Infirmary, Glasgow G11 6NT. *T:* (0141) 211 2886.

REID, Rt Rev. John Robert; United Mission to Nepal, 1995–97; Bishop of South Sydney, 1983–93 (Assistant Bishop, Diocese of Sydney, 1972–93); *b* 15 July 1928; *s* of John and Edna Reid; *m* 1955, Alison Gertrude Dunn; two *s* four *d. Educ:* Melbourne Univ. (BA); Moore Coll., Sydney (ThL). Deacon 1955, Priest 1955; Curate, Manly, 1955–56; Rector, Christ Church, Gladesville, NSW, 1956–69; Archdeacon of Cumberland, NSW, 1969–72. *Recreation:* walking. *Address:* 35 Arden Avenue, Avoca Beach, NSW 2251, Australia.

REID, Prof. Kenneth Bannerman Milne, PhD; FMedSci; FRS 1997; Professor of Immunochemistry, University of Oxford, 1993–2008; Fellow, Green College, Oxford, 1986–2008, now Emeritus; Director, MRC Immunochemistry Unit, Oxford University, 1985–2008; *b* 22 Sept. 1943; *s* of John McBean Reid and Maria Anderson (*née* Smith); *m* 1969, Margery Robertson Gilmour; one *s* two *d. Educ:* Univ. of Aberdeen (BSc 1965; PhD 1968). SO, Fisheries Res. Unit, Aberdeen Univ., 1968–69; ICI Res. Fellowship, Dept Biochem., Univ. of Oxford, 1969–70; Mem., Scientific Staff, 1970–84, Dep. Dir, 1984–85, MRC Immunochemistry Unit, Dept of Biochemistry, Univ of Oxford. Fellow, EMBO, 1991; Founder FMedSci 1998. Second Wellcome Trust Lecture Award, 1981. *Publications:* Complement, 1988, 2nd edn 1995; author or co-author of numerous papers in jls such as Nature, Biochem. Jl, Jl Immunology. *Recreations:* hill-walking, racket sports (squash, tennis). *Address:* 4 Peacock Road, Headington, Oxford OX3 0DQ; Green Templeton College, at the Radcliffe Observatory, Woodstock Road, Oxford OX2 6HG.

REID, Prof. Kenneth Gilbert Cameron, CBE 2005; WS; FRSE; FBA 2008; Professor of Property Law, University of Edinburgh, since 1994; *b* 25 March 1954; *s* of Gilbert Beith Reid and Mary Henry Reid (*née* Sinclair); *m* 1981, Elspeth Christie; two *s* one *d. Educ:* Loretto; St John's Coll., Cambridge (MA); Univ. of Edinburgh (LLB). Admitted solicitor, 1980; WS 1999. University of Edinburgh: Lectr in Law, 1980–91; Sen. Lectr, 1991–94; Mem., Scottish Law Commn, 1995–2005. Vis. Prof., Tulane Law Sch., New Orleans, 2003; Fellow, Business and Law Res. Centre, Radboud Univ., Nijmegen, 2005–. Ed., Edinburgh Law Review, 2006–. FRSE 2000. *Publications:* (jtly) The Laws of Scotland: Stair Memorial Encyclopaedia, Vol. 18, 1993, rev. edn as The Law of Property in Scotland, 1996; (with G. L. Gretton) Conveyancing, 1993, 3rd edn 2004; (ed jtly) A History of Private Law in Scotland, 2000; Abolition of Feudal Tenure in Scotland, 2003; (ed jtly) Mixed Legal Systems in Comparative Perspective: property and obligations in Scotland and South Africa, 2004; (ed jtly) Exploring the Law of Succession: studies national, historical and comparative, 2007; numerous papers in learned jls. *Recreation:* classical music, both listening and doing. *Address:* School of Law, University of Edinburgh, Old College, South Bridge, Edinburgh EH8 9YL. *T:* (0131) 650 2015.

REID, Lesley Munro; *see* Shand, L. M.

REID, Leslie, CBE 1978; HM Diplomatic Service, retired; Director General, The Association of British Mining Equipment Companies, 1980–83; *b* 24 May 1919; *s* of late Frederick Sharples and Mary Reid; *m* 1942, Norah Moorcroft; three *d. Educ:* King George V Sch., Southport, Lancs. Served War of 1939–45, W Europe and SEAC, Major, XX The Lancashire Fusiliers. Board of Trade, 1947–49; Asst Trade Commissioner: Salisbury, Rhodesia, 1949–55; Edmonton, Alberta, 1955–56; Trade Comr, Vancouver, 1956–60; Principal, BoT, 1960–62; Trade Comr and Economic Advisor, British High Commn, Cyprus, 1962–64; BoT, 1964–66; 1st Sec., FCO, 1966–68; Sen. Commercial Sec., British High Commn, Jamaica, and 1st Sec., British Embassy, Port-au-Prince, Haiti, 1968–70; Commercial and Economic Counsellor, Ghana, 1970–73; Consul Gen., Cleveland, Ohio, 1973–79. *Recreations:* golf, reading. *Address:* Kingsdowne, Albert Terrace, Norwich NR2 2JD.

REID, Prof. Lynne McArthur; Simeon Burt Wolbach Professor of Pathology, Harvard Medical School, since 1976; Pathologist-in-Chief, Children's Hospital, Boston, 1976–90, now Pathologist-in-Chief Emeritus; *b* Melbourne, 12 Nov. 1923; *er d* of Robert Muir Reid and Violet Annie Reid (*née* McArthur). *Educ:* Wimbledon Girls' Sch. (GPDST); Janet Clarke Hall, Trinity Coll., Melbourne Univ.; Royal Melbourne Hosp. MB, BS Melb. 1946; MRACP 1950; MRCP 1951; FRACP, MRCPath (Foundn Mem.) 1964; FRCPath 1966; FRCP 1969; MD Melb. 1969. House Staff, Royal Melb. Hosp., 1946–49; Res. Fellow, Nat. Health and MRC, Royal Melb. Hosp. and Eliza Hall, 1949–51; Res. Asst, Inst. Diseases of Chest, 1951–55; Sen. Lectr founding Res. Dept of Path., Inst. Diseases of Chest, 1955; Reader in Exper. Path., London Univ., 1964; Prof. of Exper. Path., Inst. of Diseases of Chest (later Cardiothoracic Inst.), 1967–76; Hon. Lectr, UC Med. Sch., 1971–76; Hon. Consultant in Exper. Path., Brompton Hosp., 1963–76; Dean, Cardiothoracic Inst. (British Postgrad. Med. Fedn), 1973–76. 1st Hastings Vis. Prof. in Path., Univ. of California, 1965; Holme Lectr, UC Med. Sch., 1969; Walker-Ames Prof., Univ. of Washington, 1971; Neuhauser Lectr, 1976; Fleischner Lectr, 1976; Waring Prof., Stanford and Denver, 1977; Amberson Lectr, Amer. Thoracic Soc., 1978. Mem. Fleischner Soc., 1971 (Pres., 1977); 1st Hon. Fellow, Canadian Thoracic Soc., 1973; Chm., Cystic Fibrosis Res. Trust, 1974 (Mem. Med. Adv. Cttee 1964); Royal Soc. Medicine (Sect. Pathology): Vice-Pres. 1974; Standing Liaison Cttee on Sci. Aspects of Smoking and Health, 1971; Commn of European Cttees (Industrial Safety and Medicine), 1972; Mem. Bd of Governors, Nat. Heart and Chest Hosps, 1974; Manager, Royal Instn of Gt Britain, 1973 (Vice-Pres. 1974); Mem. Gov. Body, British Postgrad. Med. Fedn, 1974. *Publications:* The Pathology of Emphysema, 1967; numerous papers in sci. jls. *Recreations:* music, travel, reading. *Address:* Department of Pathology, Children's Hospital, 300 Longwood Avenue, Boston, MA 02115–5724, USA. *T:* (617) 3557440, *Fax:* (617) 7310954; 50 Longwood Avenue, #216, Brookline, MA 02446, USA. *Clubs:* University Women's; Harvard (Boston).

REID, Malcolm Herbert Marcus; Chief Executive, Life Assurance and Unit Trust Regulatory Organisation, 1986–89; *b* 2 March 1927; *s* of late Marcus Reid and Winifred Stephens; *m* 1st, 1956, Eleanor (*d* 1974), *d* of late H. G. Evans, MC; four *s*; 2nd, 1975, Daphne (*d* 2000), *e d* of Sir John Griffin, QC; 3rd, 2004, Carol Stephens, *d* of late E. Deason. *Educ:* Merchant Taylors' Sch.; St John's Coll., Oxford. Served in Navy, 1945–48 and in RNVR, 1949–53. Entered Board of Trade, 1951; Private Secretary to Permanent Secretary, 1954–57; Trade Comr in Ottawa, 1957–60; Board of Trade, 1960–63; Private Secretary to successive Prime Ministers, 1963–66; Commercial Counsellor, Madrid, 1967–71; Asst Sec., DTI, 1972–74; Under Sec., Dept of Industry, 1974–78, of Trade,

1978–83, DTI, 1983–84; Registrar, Registry of Life Assurance Commn, 1984–86. Dir, Mercury Life Assurance Co. Ltd, 1989–97. Mem., Appeal Cttee, ICA, 1990–96. *Recreations:* National Hunt racing, inland waterways. *Address:* 3 Church Street, St Ives, Cambs PE27 6DG. *T:* (01480) 468367. *Club:* Oxford and Cambridge.

REID, Prof. Miles Anthony, PhD; FRS 2002; Professor, Mathematics Institute, University of Warwick, since 1992; *b* 30 Jan. 1948; *s* of John Rollo Reid and Edna Mary Reid (*née* Frost); *m* 1978, Nayo Hagino; three *d. Educ:* Petit Lycée Condorcet, Paris; Bournemouth Sch. for Boys; Trinity Coll., Cambridge (BA 1969, PhD 1972, MA 1973). Res. Fellow, Christ's Coll., Cambridge, 1973–78; Lectr, 1978–89, Reader, 1989–92, Maths Inst., Univ. of Warwick. Visiting Professor: Univ. of Tokyo, 1990; Nagoya Univ., 1996–97; British Hispanic Foundn Queen Victoria Eugenia Prof. of Doctoral Studies, Complutense Univ., Madrid, 2002–03. *Address:* Mathematics Institute, University of Warwick, Coventry CV4 7AL. *T:* (024) 7652 3523, *Fax:* (024) 7652 4182; *e-mail:* miles@maths.warwick.ac.uk.

REID, Paul Campbell; QC 2001; a Recorder of the Crown Court, since 1993; *b* 27 March 1949; *s* of Stuart Wemyss Reid and Elsie Reid; *m* 1978, Pauline Brown; two *s. Educ:* Merchant Taylors' Sch., Crosby; Christ's Coll., Cambridge (MA). Called to the Bar, Gray's Inn, 1973; an Assistant Recorder, 1989–93. *Recreations:* tennis, amateur dramatics, acoustic guitar. *Address:* Lincoln House Chambers, 1 Brazennose Street, Manchester M2 5EL. *T:* (0161) 832 5701. *Clubs:* Liverpool Ramblers Association Football; Alderley Edge Cricket.

REID, Maj.-Gen. Peter Daer, CB 1981; *b* 5 Aug. 1925; *s* of Col S. D. Reid and Dorothy Hungerford (*née* Jackson); *m* 1958, Catherine Fleetwood (*née* Boodle); two *s* two *d. Educ:* Cheltenham College; Wadham Coll., Oxford. Commissioned into Coldstream Guards, 1945; transferred Royal Dragoons, 1947; served: Germany, Egypt, Malaya, Gibraltar, Morocco; Staff Coll., 1959; Comdg Officer, The Royal Dragoons, 1965–68; student, Royal College of Defence Studies, 1973; Commander RAC, 3rd Div., 1974–76; Dir, RAC, 1976–78; Chief Exec., Main Battle Tank 80 Proj., 1979–80; Dir, Armoured Warfare Studies, 1981; Defence Advr, GKN, 1983–88; Mil. Advr, Howden Airdynamics, 1982–88; Associate Mem., Burdeshaw Associates Ltd (USA), 1982–94; Defence Consultant, Vickers Defence Systems Ltd, 1989–94. *Recreations:* sailing, ski-ing, fishing, bird watching. *Address:* The Border House, Cholderton, near Salisbury, Wilts SP4 0DU. *Clubs:* Army and Navy; Royal Western Yacht; Kandahar Ski.

REID, Philip; *see* under Ingrams, R. R.

REID, Sir (Philip) Alan, KCVO 2007; Keeper of the Privy Purse, Treasurer to the Queen, and Receiver-General of the Duchy of Lancaster, since 2002; *b* 18 Jan. 1947; *s* of Philip Reid and Margaret Reid (*née* McKerracher); *m* 1971, Maureen Petrie; one *s* one *d. Educ:* Fettes Coll.; St Andrews Univ. (LLB Hons). Internat. Chm., KMG Tax Advisors, 1982–87; Nat. Dir of Taxation, KMG Thomson McLintock, 1983–87; KPMG Management Consultancy: Eur. Exec. Chm., 1994–98; UK Head, 1994–98; Global Chm., 1996–98; KPMG: UK Chief Financial Officer, 1998–2001; Eur. Chief Financial Officer, 1999–2001; Global Chief Financial Officer, 1999–2001; UK Chief Operating Officer, 2001–02. Pres., Mgt Consultancies' Assoc., 1997. Mem. Council, King's Fund, 2002–. Trustee: Royal Collection Trust, 2002–; Historic Royal Palaces, 2002– (Dep. Chm., 2007–). Gov., King Edward VII's Hosp. Sister Agnes, 2004–. Mem., ICAS, 1973; Fellow, Inst. Taxation, 1979. *Recreations:* family, Arsenal, cinema, theatre, golf, ski-ing. *Address:* Buckingham Palace, SW1A 1AA. *Club:* MCC.

REID, Sir Robert Paul, (Sir Bob), Kt 1990; Chairman, ICE Futures Europe (formerly International Petroleum Exchange), since 1999; Deputy Governor, Bank of Scotland, 1997–2004 (Director, 1987–2004); non-executive Director, HBOS, 2001–04; *b* 1 May 1934; *m* 1958, Joan Mary; three *s. Educ:* St Andrews Univ. (MA Pol. Econ. and Mod. Hist.). Joined Shell, 1956; Sarawak Oilfields and Brunei, 1956–59; Nigeria 1959–67 (Head of Personnel); Africa and S Asia Regional Orgn, 1967–68; PA and Planning Adviser to Chairman, Shell & BP Services, Kenya, 1968–70; Man. Dir, Nigeria, 1970–74; Man. Dir, Thailand, 1974–78; Vice-Pres., Internat. Aviation and Products Trading, 1978–80; Exec. Dir, Downstream Oil, Shell Co. of Australia, 1980–83; Co-Ordinator for Supply and Marketing, London, 1983; Dir, Shell International Petroleum Co., 1984–90; Chm. and Chief Exec., Shell UK, 1985–90; Chairman: BRB, 1990–95; London Electricity plc, 1994–97; Sears plc, 1995–99; British-Borneo Oil & Gas plc, 1995–2000; Sondex Ltd, 1999–2002. Director: British Borneo Petroleum, 1993–2000; AVIS Europe, 1997–2004 (Chm., 2002–04); Sun Life Assurance Co. of Canada, subseq. Sun Life Financial, 1997–2004; Siemens plc, 1998–2006. Chairman: Foundn for Management Educn, 1986–2003; BIM, 1988–90; Council, Industrial Soc., 1993–98; Foundn for Young Musicians, 1994–; Learning Through Landscapes, 2000–; Conservatoire for Dance and Drama, 2001. Dir, Merchants Trust, 1995–2008. Chancellor, Robert Gordon Univ., 1993–2004. CCMI. Hon. LLD: St Andrews, 1987; Aberdeen, 1988; Sheffield Hallam, 1995; South Bank, 1995; Hon. DSc Salford, 1990. *Recreations:* golf, opera. *Address:* ICE Futures, 1 St Katharine's Way, E1W 1VY. *T:* (020) 7265 3636; *e-mail:* Kathleen.Murray@theice.com. *Clubs:* MCC; Royal and Ancient Golf; Royal Melbourne (Melbourne); Royal Mid-Surrey Golf, Frilford Heath Golf.

REID, Seona Elizabeth, CBE 2008; Director, Glasgow School of Art, since 1999; *b* 21 Jan. 1950; *d* of George Robert Hall and Isobel Margaret Reid. *Educ:* Park Sch., Glasgow; Strathclyde Univ. (BA Hons Sociology); Liverpool Univ. (DBA). Business Manager, Lincoln Theatre Royal, 1972–73; Press and Publicity Officer, Northern Dance Theatre, 1973–76; Press and PRO, Ballet Rambert, 1976–79; freelance Arts consultant, 1979–80; Dir, Shape, 1980–87; Asst Dir, Strategy and Regl Develt, Greater London Arts, 1987–90; Dir, Scottish Arts Council, 1990–99. Member: Exec. Cttee, Universities Scotland; Scottish Adv. Cttee, British Council. Bd Mem., Cove Park, 2004–. Mem., Knowledge and Evaluation Cttee, AHRC (formerly AHRB), 2006–. Hon. Prof., Univ. of Glasgow, 1999. FRSA 1991. Hon. DArts Robert Gordon Univ., Aberdeen, 1995; Hon. DLitt Glasgow, 2001; Hon. DLit Glasgow Caledonian, 2004. *Recreations:* walking, travel, food, arts. *Address:* Glasgow School of Art, 167 Renfrew Street, Glasgow G3 6RQ. *T:* (0141) 353 4500, *Fax:* (0141) 353 4528; *e-mail:* s.reid@gsa.ac.uk.

REID, Stephen Ashton; Director of Operations, Tanaka Business School, Imperial College London, since 2004; *b* 13 May 1949; *s* of Tom and Enid Reid; partner, Margaret Bradley. *Educ:* Brighton, Hove & Sussex Grammar Sch.; City of Westminster Coll.; UMIST; Pembroke Coll., Oxford; Harvard Business Sch. Personnel Mgt, BBC, 1975–79; Industrial Relns and Design Mgt, Granada TV, 1980–87; General Manager: Granada TV News Ops, 1987–90; BBC Wales, 1991–93; Controller: Resources Regs BBC, 1993–95; Services, BBC, 1995–97; Projects Dir, BBC Resources, 1998–99; Chief Exec., energywatch, 2000–03. *Recreations:* piano playing, sport, modern fiction. *Address:* Tanaka Business School, Imperial College London, South Kensington, SW7 2AZ.

REID, Whitelaw; President, Reid Enterprises; *b* 26 July 1913; *s* of late Ogden M. Reid and Mrs Ogden M. Reid; *m* 1st, 1948, Joan Brandon (marr. diss. 1959); two *s*; 2nd, 1959, Elizabeth Ann Brooks; one *s* one *d. Educ:* Lincoln Sch., NYC; St Paul's Sch., Concord, New Hampshire; Yale Univ. (BA). New York Herald Tribune: in various departments, 1938–40; foreign correspondent, England, 1940; Assistant to Editor, 1946; Editor, 1947–55; Pres., 1953–55; Chm. of Bd, 1955–58; Director, 1946–65; Dir, 1946–65, Pres., 1946–62, Herald Tribune Fresh Air Fund. Served War of 1939–45, 1st Lieut naval aviator, USNR. Formerly Director: Farfield Foundn; Freedom House; Golden's Bridge Hounds Inc., 1970–83; Dir, Yale Westchester Alumni Assoc. Chm., NY State Cttee on Public Employee Security Procedures, 1956–57. Ambassador to inauguration of President Ponce, Ecuador, 1956. Member: Nat. Commn for Unesco, 1955–60; President's Citizen Advisers on the Mutual Security Program, 1956–57; Yale Alumni Board (Vice-Chm., 1962–64), Yale Univ. Council (Chm., Publications Cttee, 1965–70; Sec., Class of Yale 1936, 1986–91, 2004–; Co-Chm., Class 65th Reunion); Nat. Inst. of Social Sciences, 1959–95; Mem., Council on Foreign Relations, 1941–94. District Comr, Purchase Pony Club, 1964–70; Pres., New York State Horse Council (formerly Empire State Horsemen's Assoc.), 1975–80. Fellow, Pierson Coll., Yale, 1949–. *Address:* (home and office) Reid Enterprises, Ophir Farm North, 73 West Patent Road, Bedford Hills, NY 10507, USA. *Clubs:* Century, Overseas Press, Silurians, Pilgrims, Yale, Amateur Ski (New York); Metropolitan (Washington); Bedford Golf and Tennis; St Regis Yacht.

REID, William, CBE 1987; FSA; Director, National Army Museum, 1970–87; Consultative Director, The Heralds' Museum, 1988–92; *b* Glasgow, 8 Nov. 1926; *o s* of Colin Colquhoun Reid and Mary Evelyn Bingham; *m* 1958, Nina Frances Brigden. *Educ:* Glasgow and Oxford. Commnd RAF Regt, 1946–48. Joined staff of Armouries, Tower of London, 1956. Organising Sec., 3rd Internat. Congress of Museums of Arms and Military History, London, Glasgow and Edinburgh, 1963; Sec.-Gen., Internat. Assoc. of Museums of Arms and Military History, 1969–81, Pres., 1981–87, Hon. Life Pres., 1987; Member: British Nat. Cttee, ICOM, 1973–88; Council, Chelsea Soc., 1979–85; Founding Council, Army Records Soc., 1983–88. FSA 1965 (Mem. Council, 1975–76); FMA 1974–88, resigned. Trustee: The Tank Museum, 1970–87; RAEC Museum, 1985–99; Museum of Richmond, 1987–2003 (Patron, 2003–); Florence Nightingale Museum Trust, 1987–2000; Royal Hants Regt Mus., 1990–97; Lord Brock Meml Trust, 1994–2000; AGC Mus., 1999–2003. Mem., Conservative Adv. Cttee on the Arts and Heritage, 1988–2005. Vice Pres., Arms and Armour Soc., 2000–. Hon. Life Mem., Friends of the Nat. Army Mus., 1987; Hon. Member: Amer. Soc. of Arms Collectors, 1975; Indian Army Assoc., 1981–2007. Freeman, Scriveners' Co., 1989–98 (Liveryman, 1990); Freeman, City of London, 1989. *Publications:* (with A. R. Dufty) European Armour in the Tower of London, 1968; The Lore of Arms, 1976 (Military Book Society choice) (also trans. Chinese, French, German, Danish, Italian, Spanish and Swedish); We're certainly not afraid of Zeiss: Barr & Stroud binoculars and the Royal Navy, 2002; contribs to British and foreign jls. *Recreations:* the study of armour and arms, military history, music, bird-watching. *Address:* 66 Ennerdale Road, Richmond, Surrey TW9 2DL. *T:* (020) 8940 0904. *Club:* Athenæum.

REID, Rev. Canon William Gordon; Rector of St Clement's, Philadelphia, USA, since 2004; *b* 28 Jan. 1943; *s* of William Albert Reid and Elizabeth Jean Inglis. *Educ:* Galashiels Academy; Edinburgh Univ. (MA); Keble Coll., Oxford (MA); Cuddesdon College. Deacon 1967, priest 1968; Curate, St Salvador's, Edinburgh, 1967–69; Chaplain and Tutor, Salisbury Theological Coll., 1969–72; Rector, St Michael and All Saints, Edinburgh, 1972–84; Provost of St Andrew's Cathedral, Inverness, 1984–88; Chaplain of St Nicolas, Ankara, 1988–89, of St Peter and St Sigfrid's Church, Stockholm, 1989–92; Canon, Gibraltar Cathedral, 1992–98; Vicar-Gen., Dio. of Gibraltar in Europe, 1992–2003; Archdeacon in Europe, 1996–98; Dean of Gibraltar, 1998–2000; Archdeacon of Italy and Malta, and Chaplain of All Saints, Milan, 2000–03. Canon Emeritus, Gibraltar Cathedral, 2004. Councillor, Lothian Regional Council, 1974–84; Chm., Lothian and Borders Police Bd, 1982–84. *Publications:* (ed) The Wind from the Stars, 1992; Every Comfort at Golgotha, 1999. *Recreations:* travel and languages, Church and politics. *Address:* St Clement's Church, 2013 Appletree Street, Philadelphia, PA 19103, USA. *T:* (215) 563 1876. *Clubs:* New (Edinburgh); Union League (Philadelphia).

REID, Sir William (Kennedy), KCB 1996 (CB 1981); Chairman: Advisory Committee on Distinction Awards, 1997–2000; Mental Welfare Commission for Scotland, 1997–2000; Parliamentary Commissioner for Administration, and Health Service Commissioner for England, Scotland and Wales, 1990–96; *b* 15 Feb. 1931; 3rd *s* of late James and Elspet Reid; *m* 1959, Ann, *d* of Rev. Donald Campbell; two *s* one *d. Educ:* Robert Gordon's Coll.; George Watson's Coll.; Univ. of Edinburgh; Trinity Coll., Cambridge. MA 1st cl. Classics Edinburgh and Cantab. Ferguson scholar 1952; Craven scholar 1956. Nat. service, 1952–54. Min. of Educn, 1956; Cabinet Office, 1964; Private Sec. to Sec. of Cabinet, 1965–67; Sec., Council for Scientific Policy, 1967–72; Under Sec., 1974–78, Accountant-General, 1976–78, DES; Dep. Sec. (Central Services), Scottish Office, 1978–84; Sec., SHHD, 1984–90. Chm. of Govs, Scottish Police Coll., 1984–90. Member: Council on Tribunals, 1990–96; Commns for Local Administration in England and in Wales, 1990–96. A Dir, Internat. Ombudsman Inst., 1992–96. Chm. Council, St George's Sch. for Girls, 1997–2003. Lectures: Crookshank, RCR, 1994; Sydenham, Soc. of Apothecaries, 1994; Hunt, RCGP, 1996. Chm., Edinburgh Fest. of Music, Speech and Drama, 2006–. Queen Mother Fellow, Nuffield Trust, 1998. FRCPE 1997; FRSE 1999; Hon. FRCSE 2002. Hon. LLD: Aberdeen, 1996; Reading, 1998; Hon. DLitt Napier, 1998. *Recreation:* hill walking. *Address:* Darroch House, 9/1 East Suffolk Park, Edinburgh EH16 5PL. *Clubs:* Oxford and Cambridge; New (Edinburgh).

REID, William Macpherson; Sheriff of Tayside, Central and Fife, 1983–2004; *b* 6 April 1938; *s* of William Andrew Reid and Mabel McLeod; *m* 1971, Vivien Anne Eddy; three *d. Educ:* Elgin Academy; Aberdeen Univ.; Edinburgh Univ. MA; LLB. Admitted Advocate, 1963; Sheriff of: Lothian and Borders, 1978; Glasgow and Strathkelvin, 1978–83. *Address:* 28 Chemin des Darbounelles, 30400 St Siffret, Gard, France.

REID BANKS, Lynne; *see* Banks.

REIDHAVEN, Viscount, (Master of Seafield); James Andrew Ogilvie-Grant; *b* 30 Nov. 1963; *s* and *heir* of Earl of Seafield, *qv. Educ:* Harrow.

REIF, Prof. Stefan Clive, PhD, LittD; Professor of Medieval Hebrew Studies, Faculty of Oriental Studies, University of Cambridge, 1998–2006, now Emeritus; Fellow of St John's College, Cambridge, since 1998; Founder Director, Genizah Research Unit, 1973–2006, and Head, Oriental Division, 1983–2006, Cambridge University Library; *b* 21 Jan. 1944; *s* of late Peter and Annie Reif (*née* Rapstoff); *m* 1967, Shulamit, *d* of late Edmund and Ella Stekel; one *s* one *d. Educ:* Jews' Coll., Univ. of London (BA 1964); PhD London 1969; MA Cantab 1976; LittD Cantab 2002. Lectr in Hebrew and Semitic Langs, Univ. of Glasgow, 1968–72; Asst Prof. of Hebrew Lang. and Lit., Dropsie Coll., Philadelphia, 1972–73. Visiting Professor: Hebrew Univ. of Jerusalem, 1989, 1996–97; Univ. of Pennsylvania, 2001. President: Jewish Historical Soc. of England, 1991–92; British Assoc. for Jewish Studies, 1992; Cambridge Theological Soc., 2002–04. *Publications:* Shabbethai Sofer and his Prayer-Book, 1979; (ed) Interpreting the Hebrew Bible, 1982; Published Material from the Cambridge Genizah Collections, 1988; (ed) Genizah Research After

Ninety Years, 1992; Judaism and Hebrew Prayer, 1993; Hebrew Manuscripts at Cambridge University Library, 1997; A Jewish Archive from Old Cairo, 2000; Why Medieval Hebrew Studies?, 2001; (ed) The Cambridge Genizah Collections: their contents and significance, 2002; Problems with Prayers, 2006; over 300 articles. *Recreations:* squash, football, cooking matza-brei for his grandchildren. *Address:* Genizah Research Unit, Cambridge University Library, West Road, Cambridge CB3 9DR. *T:* (01223) 766370.

REIGATE, Archdeacon of; see Kajumba, Ven. D. S. K.

REIHER, Sir Frederick (Bernard Carl), KBE 1992; CMG 1982; Investment and finance consultant, 1992; Director, Harrisons & Crosfield (PNG) Ltd, 1982–91; Chairman, Harcos Trading (PNG) Ltd, 1982–91; *b* 7 Feb. 1945; *s* of William and Ruth Reiher; *m* 1974, Helen Perpetua; two *s* two *d*. *Educ:* Chanel Coll., Rabaul; Holy Spirit National Seminary, Port Moresby; Univ. of Papua New Guinea (BD). Private Sec. to Minister for Finance, PNG, 1973–76. Joined Diplomatic Service, 1976; established Diplomatic Mission for PNG in London, 1977; High Comr for PNG in London, 1978–80, concurrently accredited Ambassador to FRG, Belgium, EEC and Israel; Sec. of Dept of Prime Minister, PNG, 1980–82; formerly High Comr for PNG in Canberra; COS to Prime Minister of PNG, 2001. Chairman: PNG Agriculture Bank, 1986–91; PNG Nat. Airline Commn, 1992. *Address:* PO Box 7500, Boroko, Papua New Guinea. *Clubs:* Aviat Social & Sporting, South Pacific Motor Sports, Royal Yacht, PNG Pistol.

REILLY, David, FRCP, FFHom; Lead Consultant Physician, Centre for Integrative Care, Glasgow Homoeopathic Hospital, since 1990 (Director, Adhom Academic Departments, since 1985); Founding Director, WEL: Wellness Enhancement Learning Programme, since 2005; Hon. Senior Lecturer in Medicine, Glasgow University, since 1991; *b* 4 May 1955. *Educ:* Glasgow Univ. (MB ChB with commendation). MRCP 1981, FRCP 1993; MRCGP 1982; MFHom 1983, FFHom 1989. Various trng posts in conventional medicine, homoeopathy and complementary medicine, mind body medicine and holism; Hon. Sen. Registrar in Gen. Medicine and RCCM/MRC Res. Fellow, Univ. Dept of Medicine, Glasgow Royal Infirmary, 1987–90. Vis. Faculty Mem., Harvard Med. Sch., 1994–; Vis. Prof., Univ. of Maryland Sch. of Med., 1999–. Co-founding Ed., Interprofessional Care, 1992–96; Internat. Ed., Alternative Therapies in Health and Medicine, 1995–96. Co-Founder and Dir, AdHominem charity, 1998–. RAMC Meml Prize, 1978; Merit Award, Gtr Glasgow Health Council, 1998; NHS Merit Award, 2001; Person of the Year, Dynamic Place Awards, 2004. *Publications:* contrib. to numerous scientific pubns and book chapters exploring human healing and integrative processes. *Recreations:* living, loving, lounging and laughing. *Address:* Centre for Integrative Care, Glasgow Homoeopathic Hospital, 1053 Great Western Road, Glasgow G12 0XQ. *T:* (0141) 211 1621.

REILLY, David Nicholas, (Nick), CBE 2000; Group Vice-President, General Motors Corporation, since 2006 (Vice-President, 1997–2006); President, General Motors Asia Pacific Operations, since 2006; Chairman, GM Daewoo Auto and Technology, since 2006; *b* 17 Dec. 1949; *s* of late John Reilly and of Mona Reilly; *m* 1976, Susan Haig; one *s* two *d*. *Educ:* Harrow Sch.; St Catharine's Coll., Cambridge (MA). Investment Analyst, 1971–74; joined Gen. Motors, 1974; Finance Dir, Moto Diesel Mexicana, 1980–83; Supply Dir, Vauxhall Motors, 1984–87; Vice Pres., IBC, 1987–90; Manufg Dir, Vauxhall Ellesmere Port, 1990–94; Vice Pres., Quality, Gen. Motors Europe, 1994–96; Man. Dir, 1996–2001, Chm., 1996–2001, Vauxhall Motors Ltd; Chm., IBC Vehicles, 1996–2001; Vice-Pres. of Sales, Mktg and Aftersales, Gen. Motors Europe, 2001–02; Pres. and CEO, GM Daewoo Auto and Technol., 2002–06. Mem. Bd, Saab GB, 1996–. Chairman: Chester, Ellesmere, Wirral TEC, 1990–94; Trng Standards Council, 1997–2001; Adult Learning Inspectorate, 2001. Mem., Commn for Integrated Transport, 1999–2001. Pres., SMMT, 2001–02 (Vice Pres., 1996–2001). Chm., Econ. Affairs Cttee, CBI, 1999–2001. Chm., Oundle Sch. Foundn, 1997–2001. FIMI 1990 (Vice Pres., 1995). *Address:* GM (China) Investment Co. Ltd, 11th Floor, Jinmao Tower, 88 Century Avenue, Pudong, Shanghai 200212, China.

REILLY, Lt-Gen. Sir Jeremy (Calcott), KCB 1987; DSO 1973; Commander Training and Arms Directors, 1986–89, retired; *b* 7 April 1934; *s* of late Lt-Col J. F. C. Reilly and E. N. Reilly (*née* Moreton); *m* 1960, Julia Elizabeth (*née* Forrester); two *d* (and one *d* decd). *Educ:* Uppingham; RMA Sandhurst. Commissioned Royal Warwickshire Regt, 1954; served Egypt, Cyprus (Despatches), Ireland, Hong Kong, Germany, Borneo, BJSM Washington DC; psc 1965; Brigade Major, BAOR, 1967–69; Chief Instructor, RMA, 1969–71; CO 2nd Bn Royal Regt of Fusiliers, 1971–73 (DSO); Instructor, Staff Coll., 1974–75; Col GS (Army Deployment), MoD, 1975–77; PSO to Field Marshal Lord Carver and attached FCO (Rhodesia), 1977–79; Comdr 6 Field Force and UK Mobile Force, 1979–81; Comdr 4th Armoured Div., BAOR, 1981–83; Dir Battle Develt, MoD, 1983–84; ACDS (Concepts), MoD, 1985–86. Dep. Col, RRF (Warwickshire), 1981–86; Col, RRF, 1986–96; Col Comdt, The Queen's Div., 1988–90. *Address:* RHQ RRF, HM Tower of London, EC3N 4AB.

REILLY, Mary Margaret; Chairman, London Development Agency, 2004–08; *b* 22 May 1953; *d* of John Reilly and Helena Reilly; *m* 1979, Mark Corby; one *s* one *d*. *Educ:* Notre Dame Collegiate Sch., Leeds; University Coll. London (BA Hist.); London Business Sch. ACA 1978, FCA 1988. Partner, Deloitte & Touche LLP, 1987–. Chm. London Reg., Council, CBI, 2004–06. *Recreations:* travel, theatre, music, cooking. *Club:* Reform.

REILLY, Michael David, PhD; HM Diplomatic Service; Director, British Trade and Cultural Office, Taipei, since 2005; *b* 1 March 1955; *s* of late Hugh Aidan Reilly and Mary Sheila Reilly; *m* 1981, Won-Kyong Kang; one *s* one *d*. *Educ:* Ulverston Grammar Sch.; Barnard Castle Sch.; Univ. of Liverpool (BA 1975; PhD 1986). Joined HM Diplomatic Service, 1978: Seoul, 1979–84; First Secretary: FCO, 1984–88; UK Delegn to OECD, Paris, 1988–91; Seoul, 1991–93; FCO, 1994–96; Dep. Hd of Mission, Manila, 1997–2000; Head: Cultural Relns, subseq. Culture, Scholarships and Sport, Dept, FCO, 2000–02; SE Asia Dept, FCO, 2003–05. Dir, Visiting Arts, 2000–03. Patron, Coral Cay Conservation, 2000–. *Publications:* articles in academic jls. *Recreations:* ski-ing, scuba diving, steam engines. *Address:* c/o Foreign and Commonwealth Office, King Charles Street, SW1A 2AH. *T:* (020) 7008 3000.

REILLY, Nick; see Reilly, D. N.

REIMAN, Dr Donald Henry; Editor, Shelley and his Circle, Carl H. Pforzheimer Collection, New York Public Library, since 1986; Adjunct Professor of English, University of Delaware, since 1992; *b* 17 May 1934; *s* of Mildred A. (Pearce) Reiman and Henry Ward Reiman; *m* 1st, 1958, Mary A. Warner (marr. diss. 1974); one *d*; 2nd, 1975, Hélène Dworzan. *Educ:* Coll. of Wooster, Ohio (BA 1956; Hon. LittD 1981); Univ. of Illinois (MA 1957; PhD 1960). Instructor, 1960–62, Asst Prof. 1962–64, Duke Univ.; Associate Prof., Univ. of Wisconsin, Milwaukee, 1964–65; Editor, Shelley and his Circle, Carl H. Pforzheimer Liby, 1965–86. James P. R. Lyell Reader in Bibliography, Oxford Univ., 1988–89. Gen. Editor, Manuscripts of the Younger Romantics, 1984–98 (29 vols);

Editor-in-Chief, Bodleian Shelley MSS, 1984–2000 (23 vols). *Publications:* Shelley's The Triumph of Life, 1965; Percy Bysshe Shelley, 1969, 2nd edn 1990; (ed) The Romantics Reviewed, 9 Vols, 1972; (ed) Shelley and his Circle, vols V–VI, 1973, Vols VII–VIII, 1986, (ed with D. D. Fischer) Vols IX–X, 2002; (ed with D. D. Fischer) Byron on the Continent, 1974; (ed with S. B. Powers) Shelley's Poetry and Prose, 1977, 2nd edn (with N. Fraistat), 2001; (ed) The Romantic Context: Poetry, 128 vols, 1976–79; (ed jtly) The Evidence of the Imagination, 1978; English Romantic Poetry 1800–1835, 1979; Romantic Texts and Contexts, 1987; Intervals of Inspiration, 1988; The Study of Modern Manuscripts, 1993; (ed with N. Fraistat) The Complete Poetry of Percy Bysshe Shelley, vol. I, 2000, vol. II, 2004; contribs to scholarly books, reviews and learned jls. *Address:* 907 Aster Avenue, Newark, DE 19711–2631, USA. *T:* (302) 3687199; *e-mail:* dhreiman@udel.edu.

REINERS, William Joseph; Director of Research Policy, Departments of the Environment and Transport, 1977–78, retired 1978; *b* 19 May 1923; *s* of late William and Hannah Reiners; *m* 1952, Catharine Anne Palmer; three *s* one *d*. *Educ:* Liverpool Collegiate Sch.; Liverpool Univ. RAE Farnborough, 1944–46; Min. of Works, 1946–50; Head, Building Operations and Economics Div., Building Research Station, 1950–63; Dir of Research and Information, MPBW, 1963–71; Dir of Research Requirements, DoE, 1971–77. Chm., Aldwyck Housing Assoc., 1993–95 (Mem. Bd, 1980–97). *Publications:* various on building operations and economics. *Address:* Valais, 10 Berks Hill, Chorleywood, Herts WD3 5AQ. *T:* (01923) 448604.

REINFELDT, Fredrik; Prime Minister of Sweden, since 2006; Chairman, Moderate Party of Sweden, since 2003; *b* 4 Aug. 1965; *s* of Bruno and Birgitta Reinfeldt; *m* 1992, Filippa; two *s* one *d*. *Educ:* Stockholm Univ. (BSc Business Admin and Econs 1990). Dep. Chm., Swedish Conscripts Council, Swedish Defence Staff, 1986; Skandinaviska Enskilda Banken, Täby, 1986, 1987. Young Moderates: Dep. Chm., 1988–90, Chm., 1990–92, Regl Section, Stockholm; Mem., 1990–92, Chm., 1992–95, Exec. Cttee. Dep. Sec., 1990–91, Sec., 1991–, to Stockholm City Comr. Mem., Riksdag, 1991–; Alternate, Riksdag Cttee, on Taxation, 1991–94, on EU Affairs, 2001–02; Mem., 1994–2001, Dep. Chm., 2002–03, Riksdag Cttee on Finance, 1994–2001; Chm., Riksdag Cttee on Justice, 2001–02; Alternate, 2002–03, Mem., 2003–06, Riksdag Adv. Council on For. Affairs. Moderate Party: Mem. Regl Section, Stockholm, 1992–2003; Mem., Bd, 2002–; Mem., 1999–2003, Leader and First Dep. Chm., 2002–03, Chm., 2003–, Exec. Cttee, Moderate Party Gp, Riksdag. *Publications:* Det sovande folket, 1993; Projekt Europa: sex unga européer om Europasamarbetet, 1993; Nostalgitrippen, 1995; Stenen i handen på den starke, 1995; Väljarkryss: personvalshandbok, 2001. *Address:* Office of the Prime Minister, Rosenbad 4, 103 33 Stockholm, Sweden; *e-mail:* heidi.kumlin@primeminister.ministry.se.

REINHARDT, Prof. Tobias, DPhil; Corpus Christi Professor of the Latin Language and Literature, University of Oxford, since 2008; Fellow, Corpus Christi College, Oxford, since 2008; *b* Gross-Gerau, Germany, 31 Aug. 1971; *s* of Mathias and Sabine Reinhardt; *m* 1997, Eva Maria Martin; one *s* one *d*. *Educ:* Kronberg-Gymnasium, Aschaffenburg, Germany; Univ. of Frankfurt (Staatsexamen); Corpus Christi Coll., Oxford (DPhil 2000). Jun. Res. Fellow in Ancient Philosophy, Merton Coll., Oxford, 2001–02; Lectr in Classical Langs and Lit., Univ. of Oxford, 2002–08; Fellow and Tutor in Latin and Greek, Somerville Coll., Oxford, 2002–08. *Publications:* Das Buch E der Aristotelischen Topik, 2000; Cicero's Topica, 2003; (with M. Winterbottom) Quintilian Book 2, 2006; contrib. learned jls. *Address:* Corpus Christi College, Oxford OX1 4JF.

REINTON, Sigurd Evang, Hon. CBE 2007; Chairman, London Ambulance Service NHS Trust, since 1999; *b* 9 Nov. 1941; *s* of Dr Lars Reinton and Ingrid Evang Reinton (*née* Evang); *m* 1966, Arlette Jeanne Gisele Dufresne; two *d*. *Educ:* Lund Univ. (MBA 1964). Sales Dir, Audio-Nike AB, 1964–66; Account Supervisor, Young & Rubicam, 1966–68; Associate, 1968–76, Principal, 1976–81, Dir, 1981–88, McKinsey & Co., Inc.; Chm., Express Aviation Services, 1988–91; Dir, Aubin Hldgs Ltd, 1988–98; Chm., Mayday Healthcare NHS Trust, 1997–99. Director: Freewheel Film Finance Ltd, 2000–03; NATS Hldgs Ltd, 2007–. Mem., Nat. Council, NHS Confedn, 1998–2007; Dir, Ambulance Services Network (formerly Ambulance Services Assoc.), 2005– (Mem. Nat. Council, 2001–05); Mem., Adv. Bd, The Foundation, 2005–. *Publications:* contrib. McKinsey Qly and Financial Times on corporate leadership. *Recreations:* flying (private pilot's licence/instrument rating), sailing, theatre. *Address:* c/o London Ambulance Service NHS Trust, 220 Waterloo Road, SE1 8SD. *T:* (020) 7921 5185. *Club:* Royal Automobile.

REIS e SOUSA, Caetano, DPhil; FMedSci; Head, Immunobiology Laboratory, since 1998, and Senior Group Leader, since 2003, Cancer Research UK, London Research Institute (formerly Imperial Cancer Research Fund); *b* 24 Feb. 1968; *s* of Artur and Margarida Reis e Sousa. *Educ:* United World Coll. of the Atlantic; Imperial Coll. of Sci., Technol. and Medicine, London (BSc Hons Biol. 1989); Hertford Coll., Oxford (DPhil Immunology 1992). Vis. Fellow, 1993–97, Vis. Associate, 1998, Nat. Inst. of Allergy and Infectious Diseases, NIH, Bethesda; Res. Scientist, 1998–2003, Sen. Scientist, 2003–05, CRUK, London Res. Inst. (formerly ICRF). Hon. Sen. Res. Fellow, 1998–2003, Hon. Reader, 2003–05, Hon. Prof., 2005–, Dept of Immunology and Molecular Pathology, UCL; Hon. Reader, 2004–05, Hon. Prof., 2005–, Centre for Molecular Oncology, Inst. of Cancer, Queen Mary, Univ. of London. FMedSci 2006. Mem., EMBO, 2006. *Publications:* numerous articles in scientific jls incl. Nature, Science, Nature Immunology, Immunity, Jl of Experimental Medicine, etc. *Recreations:* reading, music, diving. *Address:* Immunobiology Laboratory, Cancer Research UK, London Research Institute, Lincoln's Inn Fields Laboratories, 44 Lincoln's Inn Fields, WC2A 3PX. *T:* (020) 7269 2832, *Fax:* (020) 7269 2833; *e-mail:* caetano@cancer.org.uk.

REISS, Charles Alexander; Political Editor, Evening Standard, 1985–2004; *b* 23 March 1942; *s* of Dr Joseph Charles Reiss and Jenny Francisca Reiss; *m* 1978, Sue Rosemary Newson-Smith; three *d*. *Educ:* Bryanston Sch., Dorset. Reporter: Hampstead & Highgate Express, 1964–66; London office, Glasgow Citizen, and Scottish Daily Express, 1966–68; Press Officer, Labour Party, 1968–71; Lobby Correspondent: E Anglia Daily Times, etc, 1971–73; Birmingham Post, 1973–75; Political Correspondent: and leader writer, Evening News, 1975–80; and chief leader writer, Evening Standard, 1980–85. Chm., Parly Lobby Journalists, 1995–96. Mem., Govt Communications Review Gp, 2003. *Recreations:* opera, walking, reading. *Club:* Royal Automobile.

REISS, David Anthony; Managing Director and Chairman, Reiss (Holdings) Ltd, since 1992; *b* London, 15 May 1943; *s* of late Joshua Reiss and Rita Reiss; *m* 1966, Rosemary June; one *s* two *d*. *Educ:* Carmel Coll.; Kingsway Day Coll., Oxon. Manufacturers' agent, 1964–66; co-founder, Oliver Shirts, shirt manufg co., 1966–71; opened Reiss store, Bishopsgate, London, 1971; opened flagship store, King's Road, Chelsea, 1980; own label brand, 1992; launched Women's Wear Div., 2000; opened flagship store, NY, 2003. *Recreations:* sport, soccer (Mem., Diamond Club), Arsenal, plays tennis and golf, running. *Address:* Reiss Building, 12 Picton Place, W1U 1BA. *T:* (020) 3075 2000, *Fax:* (020) 3075 2001; *e-mail:* davidreiss@reiss.co.uk.

REISS, Rev. Prof. Michael Jonathan, PhD; FIBiol; Professor of Science Education, Institute of Education, University of London, since 2001 (Head, School of Science, Mathematics and Technology, 2001–07); *b* 11 Jan. 1958; *s* of Herbert and Ann Reiss (*née* Scott); *m* 1982, Jenny L. Chapman. *Educ:* Westminster Sch., London; Trinity Coll., Cambridge (BA 1st Cl. Hons Natural Scis 1978; MA 1982; PhD 1982; PGCE 1983); E Anglian Ministerial Trng Course; Cambs Consultancy in Counselling (Grad. Counsellor 1993); Open Univ. (MBA 2002). FIBiol 1990. Teacher, Hills Rd VIth Form Coll., Cambridge, 1983–88 (Hd, Social Biol., 1987); University of Cambridge: Lectr and Tutor, Dept of Educn, 1988–94; Sen. Lectr, 1994–98; Reader in Educn and Bioethics, 1998–2000; Tutor, Homerton Coll., 1994–2000. Vis. Prof., Kristianstad Univ., Sweden, 2002; Hon. Vis. Prof., Univ. of York, 2000–. Inaugural Ed., Sex Education, 1999–. Dir of Educn, Royal Soc., 2006–08. Chief Exec., Sci. Learning Centre, London, 2003–. Ordained deacon, 1990, priest, 1991; Priest-in-charge, Boxworth, Elsworth and Knapwell, 1996–99, Toft, 2003–05, Dio. Ely. Specialist Advr to H of L Select Cttee on Animals in Scientific Procedures, 2001–02. Chm., Biosci. for Society Strategy Panel, BBSRC, 2004–07. Member: Adv. Cttee on Novel Foods and Processes, 1998–2001; Farm Animal Welfare Council, 2004–. Vice-Pres., Inst. Biol., 1994–97. FRSA 2006. Freeman, Salters' Co., 2004. *Publications:* The Allometry of Growth and Reproduction, 1989; Science Education for a Pluralist Society, 1993; (with R. Straughan) Improving Nature?: the science and ethics of genetic engineering, 1996 (trans. Chinese, Croatian, Japanese, Polish and Portuguese); (with J. L. Chapman) Ecology: principles and applications, 1992, 2nd edn 1999 (trans Italian); Understanding Science Lessons: five years of science teaching, 2000; (with J. M. Halstead) Values in Sex Education: from principles to practice, 2003; contrib. numerous acad. papers, chapters, curriculum materials, reports and other books. *Recreations:* visiting art galleries and museums, trying to keep fit. *Address:* Institute of Education, University of London, WC1H 0AL. *T:* (020) 7612 6776, *Fax:* (020) 7612 6792; *e-mail:* m.reiss@ioe.ac.uk.

REISS, Rev. Canon Robert Paul; Canon Treasurer of Westminster Abbey, since 2005; *b* 20 Jan. 1943; *s* of Paul Michael Reiss and Beryl Aileen Reiss (*née* Bryant); *m* 1985, Dixie Nichols; one *d*. *Educ:* Haberdashers' Aske's Sch., Hampstead; Trinity Coll., Cambridge (MA); Westcott House, Cambridge; Theol Inst., Bucharest, Rumania. Ordained deacon, 1969, priest, 1970; Asst Curate, St John's Wood Parish Church, London, 1969–73; Asst Missioner, Rajshahi, dio. of Dacca, Bangladesh, 1973; Chaplain, Trinity Coll., Cambridge, 1973–78; Selection Sec., ACCM, 1978–85 (Sen. Selection Sec., 1983–85); Team Rector of Grantham, dio. of Lincoln, 1986–96; Archdeacon of Surrey, 1996–2005. Mem., General Synod of C of E, 1990–2005. Trustee, Churches Conservation Trust, 2002–08. *Publication:* (contrib.) Say One for Me, 1992. *Recreations:* cricket, golf. *Address:* 1 Little Cloister, Westminster Abbey, SW1P 3PL. *Clubs:* Oxford and Cambridge, MCC.

REITH; Barony of (*cr* 1940); title disclaimed by 2nd Baron.
See under Reith, Christopher John.

REITH, Christopher John; farmer; *b* 27 May 1928; *s* of 1st Baron Reith, KT, PC, GCVO, GBE, CB, TD, of Stonehaven, and Muriel Katharine, *y d* of late John Lynch Odhams; *S* father, 1971, as 2nd Baron Reith, but disclaimed his peerage for life, 1972; *m* 1969, Penelope Margaret Ann, *er d* of late H. R. Morris; one *s* one *d*. *Educ:* Eton; Worcester College, Oxford (MA Agriculture). Served in Royal Navy, 1946–48; farming thereafter. *Recreations:* fishing, gardening, forestry. *Heir:* (*to disclaimed peerage*): *s* Hon. James Harry John Reith, *b* 2 June 1971. *Address:* Glendene, 13 Polinard, Comrie, Perthshire PH6 2HJ.

REITH, Douglas, CBE 1994; TD 1994; QC (Scotland) 1957; a Social Security (formerly National Insurance) Commissioner, 1960–92; *b* 29 June 1919; *s* of William Reith and Jessie McAllan; *m* 1949, Elizabeth Archer Stewart; one *s* one *d*. *Educ:* Aberdeen Grammar School; Aberdeen University (MA, LLB). Became Member of Faculty of Advocates in Scotland, 1946. Served in Royal Signals, 1939–46. Standing Junior Counsel in Scotland to Customs and Excise, 1949–51; Advocate-Depute, Crown Office, Scotland, 1953–57; Pres., Pensions Appeal Tribunal (Scotland), 1958–64; Chm., Nat. Health Service Tribunal (Scotland), 1963–65. *Address:* 2 Ravelston Court, Ravelston Dykes, Edinburgh EH12 6HQ. *T:* (0131) 337 0332. *Club:* New (Edinburgh).

REITH, Fiona Lennox; QC (Scot.) 1996; Sheriff of Lothian and Borders at Edinburgh, since 2007; *b* 17 July 1955; *d* of late Patrick Donald Metcalfe Munro and Francesca Diana Munro (*née* Fendall, later Sutherland); *m* 1979, David Stewart Reith, WS (marr. diss. 1990). *Educ:* Perth Acad.; Aberdeen Univ. (LLB). Solicitor, Edinburgh, 1979–82; admitted WS 1981; admitted to Faculty of Advocates, 1983; Standing Jun. Counsel in Scotland to Home Office, 1989–92; Advocate-Depute, 1992–95; Standing Jun. Counsel to Scottish Office Envmt Dept, 1995–96; Sheriff: of Tayside Central and Fife at Perth, 1999–2000; of Glasgow and Strathkelvin, 2000–07. Member: Sheriff Courts Rules Council, 1989–93; Council, Sheriffs' Assoc., 2003–06; Criminal Courts Rules Council, 2004–; Parole Bd for Scotland, 2004–07 (Vice-Chm., 2008–); Civil Justice Adv. Gp, 2004–05. External Examr in Professional Conduct, Faculty of Advocates, 2000–06. FSAScot. Mem., Scotch Malt Whisky Soc., Edinburgh. *Recreations:* walking, theatre, good food and wine, travel, pilates. *Address:* Sheriffs' Chambers, Sheriff Court House, 25 Chambers Street, Edinburgh EH1 1LB. *T:* (0131) 225 2525. *Club:* New (Edinburgh).

REITH, Gen. Sir John (George), KCB 2003 (CB 2000); CBE 1991 (OBE 1989); Lead Senior Mentor, NATO, since 2008; Deputy Supreme Allied Commander Europe, 2004–07; *b* 17 Nov. 1948; *s* of John and Jean Reith; *m* 1st, 1971, Cherry Parker; one *s* one *d*; 2nd, 1987, June Nightingale; two *s*. *Educ:* Elliots Green; RMA Sandhurst. Commnd, 1969; CO 1st Bn Parachute Regt, 1986–88 (despatches 1986); COS 1 Armd Div., 1988–91; Comd, 4 Armd Bde, 1992–94; Comd, UN Sector SW Bosnia, 1994; Dir, Internat. Orgns, 1994, Dir, Mil. Ops, 1995–97, MoD; Comdr, ACE Mobile Force (Land), 1997–99; Comdr, Albania Force, 1999; ACDS (Policy), MoD, 2000–01; Chief of Jt Ops, Permt Jt HQ, 2001–04. Freeman, City of London, 2000. QCVS 1994. *Recreations:* hill walking, gardening, good food. *Club:* Army and Navy.

REITH, Lesley-Anne; *see* Alexander, L.-A.

REITH, Martin; HM Diplomatic Service, retired; *b* 6 Dec. 1935; *s* of late James Reith and Christian (*née* Innes); *m* 1964, Ann Purves; four *s*. *Educ:* Royal High Sch. of Edinburgh. Served: India (Calcutta), 1957–59; Uganda, 1962–66; Scottish Office, Edinburgh, 1966–68; Australia (Canberra), 1969–72; Asst Head of Central and Southern Africa Dept, FCO, 1974–77; Commercial Sec., Beirut, 1977–78; UN Dept, FCO, 1979; Counsellor, NATO Def. Coll., Rome, 1980; Dep. High Comr, Malta, 1980–83; High Comr, Swaziland, 1983–87; Ambassador, Republic of Cameroon, 1987–91. *Recreations:* bridge, bowling, family history, Scottish country dancing, travel. *Address:* Ardnagaul House, Strathtay, by Pitlochry, Perthshire PH9 0PG.

REITH, Hon. Peter Keaston; company director and consultant; a Director, European Bank for Reconstruction and Development, since 2003; *b* 15 July 1950; *s* of Dr A. C. Reith and E. V. Sambell; *m* (separated); four *s*. *Educ:* Brighton Grammar Sch., Vic; Monash Univ. (BEc, LLB). Solicitor, 1974–82. MP (L) Flinders, Victoria, 1984–2001; Shadow Attorney-Gen., 1987–88; Shadow Industrial Relns, 1988–89; Shadow Minister of Educn, 1989–90; Shadow Treas., 1990–93; Dep. Leader of Opposition, 1990–93; Shadow Special Minister of State, 1993; Shadow Minister for Defence, 1994; responsibility for Native Title legislation, 1994; Shadow Minister: for Foreign Affairs, 1994–95; of Industrial Relns and Manager, Opposition Business in the House, 1995–96; Leader, House of Representatives, 1996–2001; Minister assisting Prime Minister for Public Service, 1996–97; Minister: for Industrial Relns, 1996–97; for Employment, Workplace Relns and Small Business, 1998–2000; for Defence, 2000–01. Pres., Shire, Phillip Is. Council, 1980–81. Sec., Newhaven Coll., Phillip Is., 1977–82. *Recreations:* reading, sailing, golf. *Address:* c/o EBRD, 186 Bishopsgate, EC2A 2JN.

REITZLE, Dr Wolfgang; Chief Executive, Linde Group, since 2003; *b* 7 March 1949. *Educ:* Munich Tech. Univ. (Dipl.Ing; Dipl. Wirtschafts Ing; Dr.Ing); Harvard Business Sch. (AMP). Joined BMW AG, Munich, 1976; Head: Pilot Plant and New Manufg Technologies, 1980–82; Powertrain Manufg, 1982–83; Asst to CEO, to co-ordinate Product Develt, 1983–84; Dir, Technical Planning, 1984–85; Dir Gen., Product Develt, 1985–86; Mem. Bd of Mgt, R & D, subseq. also Global Purchasing, and Sales and Marketing, 1986–99; Pres., Premier Automotive Group, Ford Motor Co., 1999–2002. Bundesverdienstkreuz (Germany), 1997. *Publication:* Roboter-Technik, 1981. *Recreations:* golf, ski-ing. *Address:* Linde AG, Leopoldstrasse 252, 80807 Munich, Germany.

RELLIE, Alastair James Carl Euan, CMG 1987; HM Diplomatic Service, retired; business consultant; *b* 5 April 1935; *s* of William and Lucy Rellie; *m* 1961, Annalisa (*née* Modin); one *s* two *d*. *Educ:* Michaelhouse, SA; Harvard Univ., USA (BA). Rifle Bde, 1958–60. Second Sec., FCO, 1963–64; Vice-Consul, Geneva, 1964–67; First Secretary: FCO, 1967–68; (Commercial), Cairo, 1968–70; Kinshasa, 1970–72; FCO, 1972–74; (and later Counsellor), UK Mission to UN, New York, 1974–79; FCO, 1979–92. Dir, Market Relations, BAe, 1993–2000. Mem. Bd, Eur. Defence Industries Gp, 1994–2000, and NATO Industrial Adv. Gp, 1994–2000 (Head, UK delegn to both Gps, 1998–2000). Mem. Council, UK Defence Manufrs Assoc., 1994–2000. *Address:* 50 Smith Street, SW3 4EP. *T:* (020) 7352 5734. *Club:* Brooks's.

RELPH, Simon George Michael, CBE 2004; independent film producer; Director: Skreba Films, since 1980; Greenpoint Films, since 1980; *b* 13 April 1940; *s* of Michael Leighton George Relph; *m* 1963, Amanda, *d* of Anthony Grinling, MC; one *s* one *d*. *Educ:* Bryanston School; King's College, Cambridge (MA Mech. Scis). Asst Dir, Feature Films, 1961–73; Production Administrator, Nat. Theatre, 1974–78; Chief Exec., British Screen Finance Ltd, 1985–90. Chairman: Children's Film and TV Foundn, 1999–2005; BAFTA, 2000–02 (Vice Chm., 1994–98, Trustee, 2004–); Director: Bristol Old Vic, 2000–06; South West Screen, 2001–; Mem. Council, RCA, 1989–99 (Hon. Fellow, 1999). Non-exec. Dir, Arts Alliance Media, 2006–. Chm., Screenwriters Fest., 2006–. Governor: BFI, 1991–97; Nat. Film and Television Sch., 2002–. *Films include:* Production Supervisor, Yanks, 1978; Executive Producer: Reds, 1980; Laughterhouse, 1984; Enchanted April, 1991; Hideous Kinky, 1998; Bugs, 2002; Producer/Co-Producer: The Return of the Soldier, 1981; Privates on Parade, 1982; Ploughman's Lunch, 1983; Secret Places, 1984; Wetherby, 1985; Comrades, 1986; Damage, 1992; The Secret Rapture, 1992; Camilla, 1993; Look Me in the Eye, 1994; Blue Juice, 1995; The Slab Boys, 1996; Land Girls, 1997. Chevalier, Ordre des Arts et des Lettres (France), 1992. *Publication:* Relph Report, 2002. *Recreations:* gardening, photography, golf. *Address:* The Old Malthouse, Westwood, Bradford-on-Avon, Wilts BA15 2AG.

REMEDIOS, Alberto Telisforo, CBE 1981; opera and concert singer; *b* 27 Feb. 1935; *s* of Albert and Ida Remedios; *m* 1st, 1958, Shirley Swindells (marr. diss.); one *s*; 2nd, 1965, Judith Annette Hosken; one *s* one *d*. *Educ:* studied with Edwin Francis, Liverpool, and with Joseph Hislop. Début: Sadler's Wells Opera, 1956; Proms, 1960; Royal Opera, Covent Gdn, 1965; San Francisco, 1973; Los Angeles, 1974; WNO, 1975; NY Met., 1976; San Diego, 1978; Scottish Opera, 1977. Principal tenor, Frankfurt Opera, 1968–70; Member: Royal Opera Co., 1982–84; Australian Opera Co., 1984–86. Repertoire of over 80 principal roles; notable for Wagner interpretations, esp. Walther von Stolzing, Siegmund, Siegfried and Tristan, Sadler's Wells/ENO, under direction of Sir Reginald Goodall, 1968–81; first British tenor since 1935 to sing Siegfried at Covent Gdn, 1980–81 and 1981–82 seasons. Conductors worked with include: Richard Bonynge, Sir Colin Davis, Sir Edward Downes and Sir Charles Mackerras. Gives lectures, workshops, masterclasses. Recordings include Wagner's Ring; Tippett's A Midsummer Marriage; Stravinsky's Oedipus Rex. Mem., Wagner Soc. Queen's Prize, RCM, 1957; 1st prize for Tenor (Bulgarian Song), Union of Bulgarian Composers, and 1st prize, Bulgarian Internat. Opera Contest, 1963; Sir Reginald Goodall Award, Wagner Soc., 1995. *Recreations:* soccer (Hon. Mem., Liverpool FC), motoring, record collecting, old radios and record players.

REMNANT, family name of **Baron Remnant**.

REMNANT, 3rd Baron *cr* 1928, of Wenhaston; **James Wogan Remnant,** CVO 1979; FCA; Bt 1917; Director, Bank of Scotland, 1989–96 (Director 1973–96, and Chairman, 1979–92, London Board); Chairman, National Provident Institution, 1990–95 (Director, 1963–95); *b* 23 Oct. 1930; *s* of 2nd Baron Remnant, MBE and Dowager Lady Remnant (*d* 1990); *S* father, 1967; *m* 1953, Serena Jane Loehnis, *o d* of Sir Clive Loehnis, KCMG; three *s* one *d*. *Educ:* Eton. FCA 1955. Nat. Service, Coldstream Guards, 1948–50 (Lt). Partner, Touche Ross & Co., 1958–70; Man. Dir, 1970–80, Chm., 1981–89, Touche, Remnant & Co.; Chairman: TR City of London Trust, 1978–90 (Dir, 1973–90); TR Pacific Investment Trust, 1987–94. Dep. Chm., Ultramar, 1981–91 (Dir, 1970–91); Director: Australia and New Zealand Banking Group, 1968–81 (Mem., Internat. Bd of Advice, 1987–91); Union Discount Co. of London, 1968–92 (Dep. Chm., 1970–86); London Merchant Securities, 1994–2002; London Authorities Mutual, 2007–, and other cos. Chm., Assoc. of Investment Trust Cos, 1977–79. A Church Comr, 1976–84. Chm., Institutional Shareholders Cttee 1977–78. Trustee, Royal Jubilee Trusts, 1990–2000 (Hon. Treasurer, 1972–80; Chm., 1980–89); President: Wokingham Constituency Cons. Assoc., 1981–96; Nat. Council of YMCAs, 1983–96; Florence Nightingale Foundn, 1987–2004; Chm., Learning Through Landscapes Trust, 1989–2000. Master, Salters' Co., 1995–96. GCStJ (Bailiff of Egle, 1993–99). *Heir:* *s* Hon. Philip John Remnant, *qv*. *Address:* Bear Ash, Hare Hatch, Reading RG10 9XR.

REMNANT, Hon. Philip John; Senior Adviser, Credit Suisse, since 2006; Chairman, Shareholder Executive, since 2007; *b* 20 Dec. 1954; *s* and *heir* of Baron Remnant, *qv*; *m* 1977, Caroline Elizabeth Clare Cavendish; one *s* two *d*. *Educ:* Eton Coll.; New Coll., Oxford (MA Law). ACA 1979. Peat, Marwick, Mitchell & Co., 1976–82; Kleinwort Benson Ltd, 1982–90 (Dir, 1988–90); Barclays de Zoete Wedd, 1990–97: Man. Dir, 1992–97; Hd, UK Corporate Finance, 1993–94; Dep. Hd, Global Corporate Finance, 1995–96; Co-Hd, Global M&A, 1997; Man. Dir and Dep. Hd, UK Investment Banking, Credit Suisse First Boston, 1997–2001; Dir Gen., Takeover Panel (on secondment), 2001–03; Hd, UK Investment Banking, Credit Suisse First Boston, 2003–04; Vice-Chm., Credit Suisse First Boston Europe, 2003–06. *Address:* Ham Farm House, Baughurst, Basingstoke, Hants RG26 5SD.

REMNICK, David Jay; Editor, The New Yorker, since 1998; *b* 29 Oct. 1958; *m* 1987, Esther B. Fein; two *s* one *d. Educ:* Princeton Univ. (BA). Washington Post: staff writer, 1982–88; Moscow corresp., 1988–92; staff writer, The New Yorker, 1992–98. Vis. Fellow, Council on Foreign Relns. *Publications:* Lenin's Tomb, 1993 (Pulitzer Prize, George Polk Award, 1994); Resurrection, 1997; The Devil Problem (and Other True Stories), 1997; King of the World, 1998; Reporting: writings from The New Yorker, 2007. *Address:* The New Yorker, 4 Times Square, New York, NY 10036, USA.

RENALS, Sir Stanley, 4th Bt *cr* 1895; formerly in the Merchant Navy; *b* 20 May 1923; 2nd *s* of Sir James Herbert Renals, 2nd Bt; *S* brother, Sir Herbert Renals, 3rd Bt, 1961; *m* 1957, Maria Dolores Rodriguez Pinto, *d* of late José Rodriguez Ruiz; one *s. Educ:* City of London Freemen's School. *Heir: s* Stanley Michael Renals, BSc, CEng, MIMechE, MIProdE [*b* 14 Jan. 1958; *m* 1982, Jacqueline Riley; one *s* one *d*]. *Address:* 52 North Lane, Portslade, East Sussex BN4 2HG.

RENDEL, David Digby; Member, West Berkshire Council, since 2007; *b* 15 April 1949; *s* of late Alexander Rendel and Elizabeth (*née* Williams); *m* 1974, Dr Susan Taylor; three *s. Educ:* Eton (schol.); Magdalen Coll., Oxford (BA); St Cross Coll., Oxford. Shell Internat., 1974–77; British Gas, 1977–78; Esso Petroleum, 1978–90. Mem., Newbury DC, 1987–95. MP (Lib Dem) Newbury, May 1993–2005; contested (Lib Dem) same seat, 2005. Lib Dem spokesman: on Local Govt, 1993–97; on Higher Educn, 2001–05. Member: Public Accounts Cttee, 1999–2003; Procedures Cttee, 2001–02. Ldr, Lib Dem Parly Welfare Team, 1997–99. *Address:* Hilltop Cottage, Hopgoods Green, Bucklebury, Berks RG7 6TA. *T:* (01635) 862534.

RENDELL, family name of **Baroness Rendell of Babergh**.

RENDELL OF BABERGH, Baroness *cr* 1997 (Life Peer), of Aldeburgh in the co. of Suffolk; **Ruth Barbara Rendell,** CBE 1996; crime novelist, since 1964; *b* 17 Feb. 1930; *d* of Arthur Grasemann and Ebba Kruse; *m* 1950, Donald Rendell; marr. diss. 1975; remarried Donald Rendell, 1977 (he *d* 1999); one *s. Educ:* Loughton County High School. FRSL. Arts Council National Book Award for Genre Fiction, 1981; Sunday Times Award for Literary Excellence, 1990. *Publications:* From Doon with Death, 1964; To Fear a Painted Devil, 1965; Vanity Dies Hard, 1966; A New Lease of Death, 1967; Wolf to the Slaughter, 1967 (televised 1987); The Secret House of Death, 1968; The Best Man to Die, 1969; A Guilty Thing Surprised, 1970; One Across Two Down, 1971; No More Dying Then, 1971; Murder Being Once Done, 1972; Some Lie and Some Die, 1973; The Face of Trespass, 1974 (televised, as An Affair in Mind, 1988); Shake Hands for Ever, 1975; A Demon in my View, 1976 (film 1991); A Judgement in Stone, 1977; A Sleeping Life, 1978; Make Death Love Me, 1979; The Lake of Darkness, 1980 (televised, as Dead Lucky, 1988); Put on by Cunning, 1981; Master of the Moor, 1982 (televised 1994); The Speaker of Mandarin, 1983; The Killing Doll, 1984; The Tree of Hands, 1984 (film 1989); An Unkindness of Ravens, 1985; Live Flesh, 1986; Heartstones, 1987; Talking to Strange Men, 1987; (ed) A Warning to the Curious—The Ghost Stories of M. R. James, 1987; The Veiled One, 1988 (televised 1989); The Bridesmaid, 1989 (film 2005); Ruth Rendell's Suffolk, 1989; (with Colin Ward) Undermining the Central Line, 1989; Going Wrong, 1990; Kissing the Gunner's Daughter, 1992; The Crocodile Bird, 1993; Simisola, 1994; (ed) The Reason Why, 1995; The Keys to the Street, 1996; Road Rage, 1997; A Sight for Sore Eyes, 1998; Harm Done, 1999; Adam and Eve and Pinch Me, 2001; The Babes in the Wood, 2002; The Rottweiler, 2003; Thirteen Steps Down, 2004; End in Tears, 2005; The Water's Lovely, 2006; Not in the Flesh, 2007; *short stories:* The Fallen Curtain, 1976; Means of Evil, 1979; The Fever Tree, 1982; The New Girl Friend, 1985; Collected Short Stories, 1987; The Copper Peacock, 1991; Blood Linen, 1995; Piranha to Scurfy, 2000; Collected Stories, 2007; (as Barbara Vine): A Dark-Adapted Eye, 1986 (televised 1994); A Fatal Inversion, 1987 (televised 1992); The House of Stairs, 1988; Gallowglass, 1990; King Solomon's Carpet, 1991; Asta's Book, 1993; No Night Is Too Long, 1994; The Brimstone Wedding, 1996; The Chimney Sweeper's Boy, 1998. *Recreations:* reading, walking, opera. *Address:* House of Lords, SW1A 0PW. *Clubs:* Groucho, Detection.

RENDLE, Michael Russel; Managing Director, British Petroleum plc, 1981–86; Chairman: Forestry Investment Management, since 1992 (Director since 1989); Willis Pension Trustees, since 1998 (Director, since 1986); Director, Willis Ltd, since 2005; *b* 20 Feb. 1931; *s* of late H. C. R. Rendle and Valerie Patricia (*née* Gleeson); *m* 1957, Heather, *d* of J. W. J. Rinkel; two *s* two *d. Educ:* Marlborough; New College, Oxford. MA. Joined Anglo-Iranian Oil Co. (now BP), 1954; Man. Dir, BP Trinidad, 1967–70; Man. Dir, BP Australia, 1974–78; Dir, BP Trading Ltd, 1978–81; Chairman: BP Chemicals Int., 1981–83; BP Coal, 1983–86; BP Nutrition, 1981–86; Dep. Chm., British-Borneo Petroleum Syndicate plc, 1986–2000. Deputy Chairman: Imperial Continental Gas Assoc., 1986–87; Tace, 1991; Chairman: Markheath, later TBI, 1991–95; Campbell & Armstrong PLC, 1996–98 (Dir, 1992–); Director: London Adv. Bd, Westpac Banking Corp. (formerly Commercial Bank of Australia), 1978–89; Willis Faber, then Willis Corroon plc, 1985–98; Petrofina SA, 1986–87; OIS International Inspection plc, 1993–96 (Chm., 1995–96); Medical Defence Union, 1998–2001. Mem. BOTB, 1982–86; Chm., European Trade Cttee, 1982–86. Chm. Social Affairs Cttee, UNICE, 1984–87; Mem. Internat. Council and UK Adv. Bd, INSEAD, 1984–86. Mem. Council, Marlborough Coll., 1987–95. *Recreations:* golf, music, outdoor sports, gardening. *Address:* c/o Willis Group Ltd, 10 Trinity Square, EC3P 3AX. *T:* (020) 7481 7152. *Clubs:* Vincent's (Oxford); Australian (Melbourne).

RENDLE, Peter Critchfield; Under-Secretary (Principal Finance Officer), Scottish Office, 1978–80, retired; *b* Truro, 31 July 1919; *s* of late Martyn and Florence Rendle; *m* 1944, Helen Barbara Moyes; three *s. Educ:* Queen Elizabeth's Sch., Hartlebury. Clerical Officer, Min. of Transport, 1936–49. Served War, Royal Navy, 1940–46 (Lieut RNVR). Min. of Town and Country Planning, 1949; Dept of Health for Scotland, 1950–59 (Sec., Guest Cttee on Bldg Legislation in Scotland); Scottish Home and Health Dept, 1959–63 and 1972–73; Scottish Educn Dept, 1963–72; Under Sec., Housing, Scottish Development Dept, 1973–78. Member: Legal Aid Central Cttee for Scotland, 1980–87; Scottish Is Councils Cttee of Inquiry, 1982–84; Scottish Legal Aid Bd, 1987–89. *Publication:* Rayner Report, Scrutiny of HM Inspectors of Schools in Scotland, 1981. *Recreations:* theatre, taking photographs. *Address:* 3/6 Caithness Place, Clark Road, Edinburgh EH5 3AE. *T:* (0131) 552 8024. *Clubs:* Royal Over-Seas League; Royal Scots (Edinburgh).

RENDLESHAM, 9th Baron *cr* 1806 (Ire.); **Charles William Brooke Thellusson;** *b* 10 Jan. 1954; *o s* of 8th Baron Rendlesham and his 2nd wife, Clare, *d* of Lt-Col D. H. G. McCririck; *S* father, 1999; *m* 1988, Lucille Clare, *d* of Rev. Henry Ian Gordon Cumming; one *d. Educ:* Eton. *Heir: uncle* Hon. Peter Robert Thellusson [*b* 25 Jan. 1920; *m* 1st, 1947, Pamela Tufnell (*née* Parker) (marr. diss. 1950); 2nd, 1952, Celia Walsh; two *s*].

RENÉ, (France) Albert; barrister-at-law; President of the Republic of Seychelles, 1977–2004 (re-elected, 1979, 1984, 1989, 1993, 1998, 2001); *b* Mahé, Seychelles, 16 Nov. 1935; *s* of Price René and Louisa Morgan; *m* 1st, 1956, Karen Handlay; one *d*; 2nd, 1975, Geva Adam; one *s*; 3rd, 1993, Sarah Zarqani; three *d. Educ:* St Louis Coll., Seychelles; Collège du Sacré Cœur, St Maurice, Valais, Switzerland; St Mary's Coll., Southampton, England; King's Coll., Univ. of London; Council of Legal Educn, 1956; LSE, 1961. Called to Bar, 1957. Leader, Founder, Pres., 1964–78, Seychelles People's United Party (first effective political party and liberation movement in Seychelles); MP, 1965; Mem. in Governing Council, 1967; Mem., Legal Assembly, 1970 and 1974; Minister of Works and Land Development, 1975; Prime Minister, 1976–77; Minister: of Transport, 1984–86; of Admin, Finance and Industries, Planning and External Relns, 1984–89; of Defence, 1986–92. Founder, Leader and Sec.-Gen., Seychelles People's Progressive Front, 1978. Order of the Golden Ark (1st cl.), 1982. *Address:* c/o President's Office, State House, Republic of Seychelles.

RENFREW, family name of **Baron Renfrew of Kaimsthorn**.

RENFREW OF KAIMSTHORN, Baron *cr* 1991 (Life Peer), of Hurlet in the District of Renfrew; **Andrew Colin Renfrew,** FBA 1980; Disney Professor of Archaeology, University of Cambridge, 1981–2004; Director, 1991–2004, Fellow, since 2004, McDonald Institute for Archaeological Research, Cambridge; *b* 25 July 1937; *s* of late Archibald Renfrew and Helena Douglas Renfrew (*née* Savage); *m* 1965, Jane Margaret, *d* of Ven. Walter F. Ewbank, *qv*; two *s* one *d. Educ:* St Albans Sch.; St John's Coll., Cambridge (Exhibr; Hon. Fellow, 2004); British Sch. of Archaeology, Athens. Pt I Nat. Scis Tripos 1960; BA 1st cl. hons Archaeol. and Anthrop. Tripos 1962; MA 1964; PhD 1965; ScD 1976. Pres., Cambridge Union Soc., 1961; Sir Joseph Larmor Award 1961. Nat. Service, Flying Officer (Signals), RAF, 1956–58. Res. Fellow, St John's Coll., Cambridge, 1968; Bulgarian Govt Schol., 1966; University of Sheffield: Lectr in Prehistory and Archaeol., 1965–70; Sen. Lectr, 1970–72; Reader, 1972; Prof. of Archaeology, Southampton Univ., 1972–81; Professorial Fellow, St John's Coll., Cambridge, 1981–86; Jesus College, Cambridge: Master, 1986–97; Professorial Fellow, 1997–2004; Emeritus Fellow and Hon. Fellow, 2004–. Visiting Lecturer: Univ. of Calif at Los Angeles, 1967; Univ. of Minnesota, 1987. Contested (C) Sheffield Brightside, 1968; Chm., Sheffield Brightside Conserv. Assoc., 1968–72. Member: Ancient Monuments Bd for England, 1974–84; Royal Commn on Historical Monuments (England), 1977–87; Historic Buildings and Monuments Commn for England, 1984–86; Ancient Monuments Adv. Cttee, 1984–2001; UK Nat. Commn for UNESCO, 1984–86 (Mem. Culture Adv. Cttee, 1984–86); Exec. Cttee, NACF, 2001–; Trustee: Antiquity Trust, 1974–; British Mus., 1991–2001; Chm., Hants Archaeol Cttee, 1974–81; a Vice-Pres., RAI, 1982–85. Chm., Governors, The Leys, 1984–92; Chm. Council, British Sch. at Athens, 2004–. Lectures: Dalrymple in Archaeol., Univ. of Glasgow, 1975 and 2000; George Grant MacCurdy, Harvard, 1977; Patten, Indiana Univ., 1982; Harvey, New Mexico Univ., 1982; Hill, Univ. of Minnesota, 1987; Tanner, Stanford Univ., 1993; Neubergh, Univ. of Göteborg, 1997; Hitchcock, Univ. of Calif, Berkeley, 1997; Kroon, Amsterdam, 1999; McDonald, Cambridge Univ., 1999; Rhind, Edinburgh, 2001; Sackler, Nat. Acad. of Scis, Washington, DC, 2005. Excavations: Saliagos near Antiparos, 1964–65; Sitagroi, Macedonia, 1968–70; Phylakopi in Melos, 1974–76; Quanterness, Orkney, 1972–74; Maes Howe, 1973–74; Ring of Brodgar, 1974; Liddle Farm, 1973–74. FSA 1968 (Vice-Pres., 1987–92); FSAScot 1970 (Hon. FSAScot 2001); Hon. FRSE 2001; Hon. Fellow, Archaeol. Soc. of Athens, 1990. For. Associate, Nat. Acad. of Scis, USA, 1997; Corresponding Member: Österreichische Akad. der Wissenschaften, 2000; Deutsches Archaeologisches Institut, 2004; Russian Acad. of Scis, 2006; Amer. Philosophical Soc., 2006. Freeman, City of London, 1987. Hon. LittD: Sheffield, 1987; Southampton, 1995; Liverpool, 2005; Dr *hc* Athens, 1991; Hon. DLitt: Edinburgh, 2005; St Andrews, 2006. Rivers Meml Medal, 1979, Huxley Meml Medal, 1991, RAI; Fyssen Prize, Fyssen Foundn, Paris, 1996; Lucy Wharton Drexel Medal, Univ. of Pennsylvania Mus., 2003; Latsis Prize, Eur. Sci. Foundn, 2003; Balzan Foundn Prize, 2004. *Publications:* (with J. D. Evans) Excavations at Saliagos near Antiparos, 1968; The Emergence of Civilisation, 1972; (ed) The Explanation of Culture Change, 1973; Before Civilisation, 1973; (ed) British Prehistory, a New Outline, 1974; Investigations in Orkney, 1979; (ed) Transformations: Mathematical Approaches to Culture Change, 1979; Problems in European Prehistory, 1979; (with J. M. Wagstaff) An Island Polity, 1982; (ed) Theory and Explanation in Archaeology, 1982; Approaches to Social Archaeology, 1984; The Prehistory of Orkney, 1985; The Archaeology of Cult, 1985; Archaeology and Language, 1987; (with G. Daniel) The Idea of Prehistory, 1988; The Cycladic Spirit, 1991; (with P. Bahn) Archaeology, 1991; (ed) America Past, America Present, 2000; Loot, Legitimacy and Ownership, 2000; (ed) Archaeogenetics, 2000; Figuring It Out, 2003; (with P. Bahn) Archaeology, the Key Concepts, 2005; (ed with P. Forster) Phylogenetic Methods and the Prehistory of Languages, 2006; (ed jtly) Markiani, Amorgos: an early bronze age fortified settlement, 2006; articles in archaeol jls. *Recreations:* modern art, numismatics, travel. *Address:* McDonald Institute for Archaeological Research, Downing Street, Cambridge CB2 3ER. *T:* (01223) 333521. *Clubs:* Athenæum, Oxford and Cambridge.

RENFREY, Rt Rev. Lionel Edward William; Dean of Adelaide, 1966–97; Assistant Bishop of Adelaide, 1969–89; *b* Adelaide, SA, 26 March 1916; *s* of late Alfred Cyril Marinus Renfrey and Catherine Elizabeth Rose Frerichs (*née* Dickson); *m* 1948, Joan Anne, *d* of Donald Smith, Cooke's Plains, SA; one *s* five *d. Educ:* Unley High School; St Mark's Coll., Univ. of Adelaide; St Barnabas' Theological Coll., Adelaide. BA (First Cl. Hons English), ThL (ACT) (Second Cl. Hons). Deacon 1940, priest 1941, Dio. Adelaide; Curate, St Cuthbert's, Prospect, 1940–43; Mission Chaplain, Mid Yorke Peninsula, 1943–44; Warden, Brotherhood of St John Baptist, 1944–47; Priest-in-charge: Berri-Barmera, 1948–50; Kensington Gardens, 1950–57; Rector, St James', Mile End, 1957–63; Rural Dean, Western Suburbs, 1962–63; Organising Chaplain, Bishop's Home Mission Soc., 1963–66; Editor, Adelaide Church Guardian, 1961–66; Archdeacon of Adelaide, 1965–66; Examining Chaplain to Bishop of Adelaide, 1965–85; Administrator (*sede vacante*), Diocese of Adelaide, 1974–75; Rector, Mallala and Two Wells, 1981–88. Patron: Prayer Book Soc. in Australia, 1980–; Monarchist League, 1994–. OStJ 1981 (SBStJ 1969). *Publications:* Father Wise: a Memoir, 1951; Short History of St Barnabas' Theological College, 1965; What Mean Ye By This Service?, 1978; (ed) Catholic Prayers, 1980; (ed) SS Peter and Paul Prayer Book, 1982; Arthur Nutter Thomas, Bishop of Adelaide 1906–1940, 1988; Their Happy Brotherhood: a history of the Dean and Chapter of the Diocese of Adelaide, 2006. *Recreation:* reading. *Address:* 13 Northcote Terrace, Medindie, SA 5081, Australia. *Club:* Adelaide (Adelaide).

RENNARD, Baron *cr* 1999 (Life Peer), of Wavertree in the county of Merseyside; **Christopher John Rennard,** MBE 1989; Chief Executive, Liberal Democrats, since 2003 (Director of Campaigns and Elections, 1989–2003; Chair, Liberal Democrat General Election Campaign); *b* 8 July 1960; *s* of late Cecil Langton Rennard and Jean Winifred Rennard (*née* Watson); *m* 1989, Ann McTegart. *Educ:* Mosspits Lane County Primary Sch.; Liverpool Blue Coat Sch.; Univ. of Liverpool (BA Hons Politics and Economics). Liberal Party: Agent, Liverpool Mossley Hill constituency, 1982–84; Area Agent, East Midlands region, 1984–88; Election Co-ordinator, Social & Liberal Democrats, 1988–89. *Recreations:* cooking, wine, France. *Address:* (office) 4 Cowley Street, SW1P 3NB; 19 Stockwell Park Road, SW9 0AP.

RENNELL, 4th Baron *cr* 1933, of Rodd, co. Hereford; **James Roderick David Tremayne Rodd;** Communications and Accounts Manager and Entertainment Director, Sports Vision; *b* 9 March 1978; *o s* of 3rd Baron Rennell and Phyllis (*née* Neill); *S* father, 2006. *Educ:* Wellesley House; Bryanston; Latymer; De Montfort Univ. *Recreations:* wide range of sports, esp. surfing, golf, cricket. *Heir:* none. *Address:* *e-mail:* james@sportsvision.co.uk.

RENNET, Roderick James, CBE 2000; CEng; FICE; Chief Executive, East of Scotland Water, 1996–2000; *b* 25 March 1942; *s* of James Mowat Rennet and Rachel Rennet; *m* 1965, Lesley Margaret Irving Love; one *s* one *d.* *Educ:* Dundee Inst. of Technol. (BSc Hons). CEng 1969; FICE 1986; FCIWEM (FIWEM 1987); FIWO 1992. Civil engrg apprentice, Dundee Harbour Trust, 1960–62; asst engr, Chester CBC, 1966–68; asst engr, then sen. engr, Durham CC, 1969–70; sen. engr, then principal engr, Dundee Corp., 1970–75; Tayside Regional Council: Depute Dir of Water Services, 1975–87; Dir of Water Services, 1988–95. *Recreations:* hill-walking, photography, cycling. *Address:* 1A Polwarth Terrace, Edinburgh EH11 1NF.

RENNIE, Alexander Allan, CBE 1980; QPM 1971; Chief Constable, West Mercia Constabulary, 1975–81, retired; *b* 13 June 1917; *s* of late Charles Rennie and Susan Parsons Rennie; *m* 1941, Lucy Brunt; one *s* one *d.* *Educ:* Ellon Acad., Aberdeenshire. Armed Services, 1941–45: commnd 30 Corps Royal Northumberland Fusiliers; active service in Europe (mentioned in despatches, 1945). Joined Durham County Constab., 1937; Chief Supt, 1963; Dep. Chief Constable, Shropshire, 1963–67; Dir, Sen. Comd Course, Police Coll., Bramshill, 1967–69; Asst Chief Constable, West Mercia, 1969–72, Dep. Chief Constable, 1973–75. OStJ 1975. *Recreations:* golf, hill walking. *Address:* 1 Rowan Court, Droitwich Spa, Worcs WR9 8AH.

RENNIE, Archibald Louden, CB 1980; Secretary, Scottish Home and Health Department, 1977–84, retired; *b* 4 June 1924; *s* of John and Isabella Rennie; *m* 1950, Kathleen Harkess; four *s.* *Educ:* Madras Coll.; St Andrews University (BSc). Minesweeping Res. Div., Admty, 1944–47; Dept of Health for Scotland, 1947–62; Private Sec. to Sec. of State for Scotland, 1962–63; Asst Sec., SHHD, 1963–69; Registrar Gen. for Scotland, 1969–73; Under-Sec., Scottish Office, 1973–77. Member: Scottish Records Adv. Council, 1985–94; Council on Tribunals, 1987–88. Gen. Council Assessor, St Andrews Univ. Court, 1984–85; Chancellor's Assessor and Finance Convener, 1985–89; Vice-Chm., Adv. Cttee on Distinction Awards for Consultants, 1985–94; Chm., Disciplined Services Pay Review Cttee, Hong Kong, 1988. Trustee, Lockerbie Air Disaster Trust, 1988–91; Dir, Elie Harbour Trust, 1989– (Chm., 1994–98). Mem. Bd, Madras Coll., 1994–99. Chm., Elie and Royal Burgh of Earlsferry Community Council, 2001–03. Cdre, Elie and Earlsferry Sailing Club, 1991–93. Hon. FDSRCS 1995. Hon. LLD St Andrews, 1990. *Publications:* The Harbours of Elie Bay: a history, 2008; odd verses. *Recreations:* reading, pottering, firth-watching. *Address:* The Laigh House, South Street, Elie, Fife KY9 1DN. *T:* (01333) 330741.

RENNIE, David James; His Honour Judge Rennie; a Circuit Judge, since 2001; *b* 8 March 1953; *s* of Michael Rennie and Margaret Rennie (*nee* McGrath); partner, Catherine O'Shea; two *s.* *Educ:* Cranleigh Sch.; Kingston Poly. (BA Hons Law). Called to the Bar, Inner Temple, 1976; in practice, specialising in criminal law; a Recorder, 1998–2001. *Recreations:* spending time in France, cooking, cinema, painting. *Address:* Lewes Crown Court, High Street, Lewes, E Sussex BN7 1YB.

RENNIE, William Cowan; MP (Lib Dem) Dunfermline and West Fife, since Feb. 2006; *b* 27 Sept. 1967; *s* of Alexander and Peta Rennie; *m* 1992, Janet Macfarlane; two *s.* *Educ:* Paisley Coll. of Technol. (BSc 1989). Agent for Paul Tyler, MP, 1990–94; Campaign Officer, Liberal Democrats, 1994–97; Chief Exec., Scottish Liberal Democrats, 1997–2001; self-employed consultant, 2001–03; Account Dir, McEwan Purvis, 2003–06. *Recreation:* running. *Address:* House of Commons, SW1A 0AA. *T:* (020) 7219 5054; *e-mail:* renniew@parliament.uk. *Club:* Carnegie Harriers.

RENNISON, Air Vice-Marshal David Ralph Grey, CB 2005; Director, Future Capability and International Support, Military Air Solutions, BAE Systems, since 2007; *b* 28 June 1951; *s* of Brian and Elizabeth Rennison; *m* 1975, Anne Scarth; one *s* one *d.* *Educ:* Royal Sch., Armagh; UMIST (BSc Electrical Engrg and Electronics); Univ. of Cranfield (MSc Corporate Mgt); RAF Coll., Cranwell. Joined RAF, 1970; various jun. officer appts, 1975–82; 3 Sqn Ldr appts, 1982–89; student, RAF Staff Coll., 1989; OC Engrg Wing, RAF Wildenrath, 1990–92; Wing Comdr Appointer, RAF Personnel Agency, 1992–94; Gp Capt., RAF Signals Engrg Estabt, 1994–97; Station Comdr, RAF Sealand, 1997–98; ACOS Communications and Inf. Systems, HQ Strike Comd, 1999–2002; Dir, Defence Inf. Infrastructure Prog., MoD, 2002–03; COS (Support), HQ Strike Comd, 2003–05; Air Mem. for Logistics, and Dir Gen. Logistics (Strike Envmt), Defence Logistics Orgn, MoD, 2006–07. *Recreations:* social golf, walking, jogging. *Address:* c/o Military Air Solutions, BAE Systems, Warton Aerodrome, Preston PR4 1AX. *Club:* Royal Air Force.

RENO, Janet; Attorney General of the United States of America, 1993–2001; *b* 21 July 1938. *Educ:* Cornell Univ. (AB Chem. 1960); Harvard Law Sch. (LLB 1963). Started legal career in private practice; Staff Dir, Judiciary Cttee, Florida House of Reps, 1971–72; Asst State Attorney, Florida, 1973–76; Partner, Steel, Hector & Davis, Miami, 1976–78; State Attorney, Miami, 1978–93. Pres., Fla Prosecuting Attorneys Assoc., 1984–85; American Bar Association: Member: Special Cttee on Criminal Justice in a Free Soc., 1986–88; Task Force on Minorities and the Justice System, 1992. Herbert Harley Award, Amer. Judicature Soc., 1981; Medal of Honor, Fla Bar Assoc., 1990. *Address:* c/o Department of Justice, 10th & Constitution Avenue NW, Washington, DC 20530, USA.

RENSHAW, Sir (John) David, 4th Bt *cr* 1903, of Coldharbour, Wivelsfield, Sussex; *b* 9 Oct. 1945; *s* of Sir Maurice Renshaw, 3rd Bt and his 1st wife, Isabel Bassett (*née* Popkin); *S* father, 2002; *m* 1970, Jennifer Murray (marr. diss. 1988); one *s* two *d.* *Educ:* Ashmole Sch., Southgate. Army, 1960–69; NAAFI, 1970–74; Meat and Livestock Commn, 1974–88; self-employed furniture maker, 1990–2002. *Recreations:* ski-ing, narrowboating, travel. *Heir:* *s* Thomas Charles Bine Renshaw, *b* 3 March 1976. *Address:* c/o Flat 8, Graham House, Birdcage Walk, Newmarket, Suffolk CB8 0NE; Chalet Stephen, L'epervier 1, Le Nouy, Thollon les Memises, 74500, France; *e-mail:* david.renshaw@chalet-stephen.org.

RENTON, family name of **Baron Renton of Mount Harry**.

RENTON OF MOUNT HARRY, Baron *cr* 1997 (Life Peer), of Offham in the co. of Sussex; **Ronald Timothy Renton;** PC 1989; DL; *b* 28 May 1932; *yr s* of R. K. D. Renton, CBE, and Mrs Renton, MBE; *m* 1960, Alice Fergusson of Kilkerran, Ayrshire; two *s* three *d.* *Educ:* Eton Coll. (King's Schol.); Magdalen Coll., Oxford (Roberts Gawen Schol.). First cl. degree in History, MA Oxon. Joined C. Tennant Sons & Co. Ltd, London, 1954; with Tennants' subsidiaries in Canada, 1957–62; Dir, C. Tennant Sons & Co. Ltd and Managing Dir of Tennant Trading Ltd, 1964–73; Director: Silvermines Ltd, 1967–84; Australia & New Zealand Banking Group, 1967–76; Fleming Continental European Investment Trust, 1992–2003 (Chm., 1999–2003), and other cos. Mem., BBC Gen. Adv. Council, 1982–84; Vice Chm., British Council, 1992–97; Mem., British Council Bd, 1997–99. Contested (C) Sheffield Park Div., 1970. MP (C) Mid-Sussex, Feb. 1974–1997. PPS to Rt Hon. John Biffen, MP, 1979–81, to Rt Hon. Geoffrey Howe, MP, 1983–84; Parly Under Sec. of State, FCO, 1984–85; Minister of State: FCO, 1985–87; Home Office, 1987–89; Parly Sec. to HM Treasury and Govt Chief Whip, 1989–90; Minister of State, Privy Council Office (Minister for the Arts), 1990–92. Member: Select Cttee on Nationalised Industries, 1974–79; Select Cttee on Nat. Heritage, 1995–97; Vice-Chm., Cons. Parly Trade Cttee, 1974–79; Chairman: Parly British-Hong Kong All-Party Gp, 1992–97; Cons. Foreign and Commonwealth Council, 1982–84; Member: Sub-Cttee A, 1997–2001, Sub-Cttee D, 2002– (Chm., 2003–06), EC Cttee, H of L; Chm., Information Cttee, H of L, 2006–; Vice-Pres., 1978–80, Pres., 1980–84, Cons. Trade Unionists; Fellow, Industry and Parlt Trust, 1977–79. Member: Adv. Bd, Know-How Fund for Central and Eastern Europe, 1992–2000; Develt Council, Parnham Trust, 1992–2000; Criterion Theatre Trust, 1992–97; APEX. DL East Sussex, 2004. Pres. Council, Roedean Sch., 1998–2005 (Mem., 1982–97). Trustee: Mental Health Foundn, 1985–89; Brighton West Pier Trust, 1997–2005. Founding Pres. (with Mick Jagger), Nat. Music Day, 1992–97; Chairman: Outsider Art Archive, 1995–2001; Sussex Downs Conservation Bd, 1997–2005; South Downs Jt Cttee, 2005–. Mem. Council, Univ. of Sussex, 2000–07; Pres. Council, Brighton Coll., 2007–. *Publications:* The Dangerous Edge (novel), 1994; Hostage to Fortune (novel), 1997; Chief Whip: the role, history and black arts of parliamentary whipping, 2004. *Recreations:* writing, messing about in boats, listening to opera, cultivating a Sussex vineyard. *Address:* House of Lords, SW1A 0PW. *Club:* Garrick.

RENTON, Air Cdre Helen Ferguson, CB 1982; Director, Women's Royal Air Force, 1980–86; *b* 13 March 1931; *d* of late John Paul Renton and Sarah Graham Renton (*née* Cook). *Educ:* Stirling High Sch.; Glasgow Univ. (MA). Joined WRAF, 1954; commnd, 1955; served in UK, 1955–60; Cyprus, 1960–62; HQ Staff, Germany, 1967; MoD Staff, 1968–71; NEAF, 1971–73; Training Comd, 1973–76; MoD Staff, 1976–78. Hon. ADC to the Queen, 1980–86. Hon. LLD Glasgow, 1981. *Publication:* (jtly) Service Women, 1977. *Recreations:* needlework, gardening, reading.

RENWICK, family name of **Barons Renwick** and **Renwick of Clifton**.

RENWICK, 2nd Baron *cr* 1964, of Coombe; **Harry Andrew Renwick;** Bt 1927; *b* 10 Oct. 1935; *s* of 1st Baron Renwick, KBE, and Mrs John Ormiston, Miserden House, Stroud, *er d* of late Major Harold Parkes, Alveston, Stratford-on-Avon; *S* father, 1973; *m* 1st, 1965, Susan Jane (marr. diss. 1989), *d* of late Captain Kenneth S. B. Lucking and Mrs Moir P. Stormonth-Darling, Lednathie, Glen Prosen, Angus; two *s*; 2nd, 1989, Mrs Homayoun Mazandi, *d* of late Col Mahmoud Yazdanparst Pakzad. *Educ:* Eton. Grenadier Guards (National Service), 1955–56. Partner, W. Greenwell & Co., 1964–80; Dir, General Technology Systems Ltd, 1975–93; Chm., European Information Society Group, 1994–2000 (Pres., 2000–). Mem., H of L Select Cttee on the European Communities, 1988–92, on Science and Technology, 1992–95; Hon. Sec., Parly Information Technology Cttee, 1991–2000 (Vice-Pres., 2006–). Vice-Pres., British Dyslexia Assoc., 1982– (Chm., 1977–82); Chm., Dyslexia Educnl Trust, 1986–2002. *Heir:* *s* Hon. Robert James Renwick, *b* 19 Aug. 1966. *Address:* 38 Cadogan Square, SW1X 0JL. *Clubs:* White's, Turf, Carlton.

RENWICK OF CLIFTON, Baron *cr* 1997 (Life Peer), of Chelsea in the Royal Borough of Kensington and Chelsea; **Robin William Renwick,** KCMG 1989 (CMG 1980); Vice-Chairman: Investment Banking, JP Morgan Europe, since 2001; JP Morgan Cazenove, since 2005; Deputy Chairman, Fleming Family and Partners, since 2000; *b* 13 Dec. 1937; *s* of late Richard Renwick, Edinburgh, and Clarice (*née* Henderson); *m* 1965, Annie Colette Giudicelli; one *s* one *d.* *Educ:* St Paul's Sch.; Jesus Coll., Cambridge (Hon. Fellow, 1992); Univ. of Paris (Sorbonne). Army, 1956–58. Entered Foreign Service, 1963; Dakar, 1963–64; FO, 1964–66; New Delhi, 1966–69; Private Sec. to Minister of State, FCO, 1970–72; First Sec., Paris, 1972–76; Counsellor, Cabinet Office, 1976–78; Rhodesia Dept, FCO, 1978–80; Political Adviser to Governor of Rhodesia, 1980; Vis. Fellow, Center for Internat. Affairs, Harvard, 1980–81; Head of Chancery, Washington, 1981–84; Asst Under Sec. of State, FCO, 1984–87; Ambassador to S Africa, 1987–91; Ambassador to Washington, 1991–95. Dir, 1996–2000, Dep. Chm., 1999–2000, Robert Fleming Hldgs Ltd. Chairman: Save & Prosper Gp, 1996–98; Fluor Ltd, 1996–; Director: Compagnie Financière Richemont AG, 1995–; British Airways plc, 1996–2005; Liberty Internat., 1996–2000; Canal Plus, 1997–2000; BHP Billiton plc, 1997–2005; Fluor Corp., 1997–; SABMiller plc (formerly South African Breweries), 1999–2008; Harmony Gold, 1999–2004; Kazakhmys plc, 2005–; Gem Diamonds Ltd, 2007–. Trustee, The Economist, 1996–. FRSA. Hon. LLD: Wits Univ., 1990; Amer. Univ. in London, 1993; Hon. DLitt: Coll. of William and Mary, 1993; Oglethorpe Univ., 1995. *Publications:* Economic Sanctions, 1981; Fighting with Allies, 1996; Unconventional Diplomacy, 1997. *Recreations:* tennis, trout fishing. *Address:* JP Morgan plc, 10 Aldermanbury, EC2V 7RF. *Clubs:* Brooks's, Hurlingham, Travellers.

RENWICK, David Peter; scriptwriter and author, since 1974; *b* 4 Sept. 1951; *s* of James George Renwick and Winifred May Renwick (*née* Smith); *m* 1994, Eleanor Florence (*née* Hogarth). *Educ:* Luton Grammar Sch.; Luton Sixth Form Coll.; Harlow Tech. Coll. (Nat. Proficiency Cert. in Journalism). Reporter/Sub-Editor, Luton News, 1970–74. (With Andrew Marshall) creator and writer: The Burkiss Way, BBC Radio 4; television: End of Part One, 1979–80; Whoops Apocalypse, 1982; The Steam Video Company, 1984; Hot Metal, 1986–88; Alexei Sayle's Stuff, 1989–91; If You See God, Tell Him, 1993; solo creator and writer: One Foot in the Grave, 1989–2000; Jonathan Creek, 1997–2008; Love Soup, 2005–08; stage play, Angry Old Men, 1994. *Publication:* One Foot in the Grave, 1993. *Address:* c/o Roger Hancock Ltd, 4 Water Lane, NW1 8NZ. *T:* (020) 7267 4418, *Fax:* (020) 7267 0705.

RENWICK, Sir Richard Eustace, 4th Bt *cr* 1921; *b* 13 Jan. 1938; *er s* of Sir Eustace Deuchar Renwick, 3rd Bt, and Diana Mary, *e d* of Colonel Bernard Cruddas, DSO; *S* father, 1973; *m* 1966, Caroline Anne, *er d* of Major Rupert Milburn; three *s.* *Educ:* Eton. *Heir:* *s* Charles Richard Renwick [*b* 10 April 1967; *m* 1993, Jane Ann Lyles (*née* Bush) (marr. diss. 2003); two *s*]. *Address:* Whalton House, Whalton, Morpeth, Northumberland NE61 3UZ. *T:* (01670) 775383. *Club:* Northern Counties (Newcastle).

REPORTER, Sir Shapoor (Ardeshirji), KBE 1973 (OBE 1969); Consultant on Economic and Political Matters concerning Iran, since 1962; *b* 26 Feb. 1921; *s* of Ardeshirji Reporter and Shirin Reporter; *m* 1952, Assia Alexandra; one *s* one *d.* *Educ:* Zoroastrian Public Sch., Teheran; matriculated in Bombay (specially designed course in Political Science under Cambridge Univ. Tutors, UK). PRO, British Legation, Teheran, 1941–43; in charge of Persian Unit of All India Radio, New Delhi, 1943–45; Teaching English, Imperial Staff Coll., Teheran, 1945–48; Political Adviser, US Embassy, Teheran, 1948–54; Free-lance Correspondent, 1954–62; Economic Consultant to major British interests in Iran, 1962–73. *Publications:* English-Persian Phrases, 1945 (Delhi); Dictionary of English-Persian Idioms, 1956 (Teheran); Dictionary of Persian-English Idioms, 1972 (Teheran Univ.). *Recreations:* tennis, walking, travelling.

REPP, Richard Cooper, DPhil; Master, St Cross College, Oxford, 1987–2003; *b* 1 April 1936; *s* of Robert Mathias Repp, Jun., and Martha Repp (*née* Cooper); *m* 1972, Catherine Ross MacLennan; one *s* one *d*. *Educ:* Shady Side Acad., Pittsburgh; Williams Coll., Mass (BA); Worcester Coll., Oxford (1st Cl. Hons Oriental Studies, MA, DPhil; Hon. Fellow 1989). Instr in Humanities, Robert Coll., Istanbul, 1959–62; Oxford University: Univ. Lectr in Turkish History, 1963–2003; Sen. Proctor, 1979–80; Vice-Chm., Staff Cttee, 1982–84; Member: Gen. Bd of the Faculties, 1982–84, 1985–89; Hebdomadal Council, 1991–2000; Pro-Vice-Chancellor, 1994–2003; Linacre College: Fellow, 1964–87, Hon. Fellow, 1987; Sen. Tutor, 1985–87. Chm., Visitors of the Ashmolean Mus., 1995–2002. Hon. Fellow, St Cross Coll., Oxford, 2003. Bicentennial Medal, Williams Coll., Mass, 2004. *Publications:* The Müfti of Istanbul, 1986; various articles on Ottoman history. *Recreations:* gardening, music. *Address:* St Cross College, Oxford OX1 3LZ. *T:* (01865) 278490. *Club:* Williams (New York).

REPTON, Bishop Suffragan of, since 2007; **Rt Rev. Humphrey Ivo John Southern;** *b* 17 Sept. 1960; *s* of late Guy Hugo Southern and of Rosamund Antonia Southern (*née* McAndrew); *m* 1996, Emma Jane, *o d* of Robin and Brenda Lush; two *d*. *Educ:* Harrow Sch.; Westminster Tutors; Christ Church, Oxford (MA 1986); Ripon Coll., Cuddesdon. Ordained deacon, 1986, priest, 1987; Assistant Curate: St Margaret's, Rainham, Kent, 1986–89; Walton-on-the-Hill, Liverpool, 1989–92; Vicar and Team Rector, Hale with Badshot Lea, Farnham, Surrey, 1992–99; Ecumenical Officer, Dio. of Guildford, 1992–99; Team Rector, Tisbury and Nadder Valley, Wilts, 1999–2007. Chm., House of Clergy, Dio. of Salisbury, 2004–07; Non-res. Canon and Prebendary, Salisbury Cathedral, 2006–07. *Publications:* contrib. to Theology. *Recreations:* conversation, cooking, horse racing, English Bull Terriers, reading widely and walking gently. *Address:* Repton House, Lea, Matlock, Derbyshire DE4 5JP. *T:* (01629) 534644, *Fax:* (01629) 534003; *e-mail:* bishop@repton.free-online.co.uk. *Club:* Brooks's.

RESNAIS, Alain; French film director; *b* Vannes, 3 June 1922; *s* of Pierre Resnais and Jeanne (*née* Gachet); *m* 1969, Florence Malraux; *m* 1998, Sabine Azéma. *Educ:* Collège St François-Xavier, Vannes; Institut des hautes études cinématographiques. Assistant to Nicole Védrée for film Paris 1900, 1947–48; has directed his own films (many of which have won prizes), since 1948. Short films, 1948–59, include: Van Gogh, 1948; Guernica (jtly with Robert Hessens), 1950; Les statues meurent aussi (jtly with Chris Marker), 1952; Nuit et brouillard, 1955. Full length films include: Hiroshima mon amour, 1959; L'année dernière à Marienbad, 1961; Muriel, 1963; La guerre est finie, 1966; Je t'aime, je t'aime, 1968; Stavisky, 1974; Providence, 1977; Mon Oncle d'Amérique, 1980; La vie est un roman, 1983; L'amour à Mort, 1984; Mélo, 1986; Je veux rentrer à la maison, 1989; Smoking, 1993; No Smoking, 1993; On connait la chanson, 1998; Coeurs, 2006 (UK as Private Fears in Public Places, 2007).

RESTREPO-LONDOÑO, Andrés; Order of Boyacá, Colombia; private financial consultant, since 1993; President, Empresa Colombiana de Petróleos-ECOPETROL, 1988–92; *b* 20 Jan. 1942; *m* 1968, Ghislaine Ibiza; one *s* three *d*. *Educ:* Universidad de Antioquia; Université de Paris (postgraduate courses, 1966). Professor and Head of Economic Dept., Univ. de Antioquia, 1967–68; Gen. Man., La Primavera chain of stores, 1969–76; Finance Man., Empresas Públicas de Medellín, 1976–79; Gen. Man., Carbones de Colombia (Colombian Coal Bd), 1979–80; Minister for Economic Develt, 1980–81; Ambassador to UK, 1981–82. Chm., Proban SA (Banana Exporting Co.), 1983–84; Pres., Industrias e Inversiones Samper SA (Cement Co.), 1985–88. Order Sol of Perú; Order Cruzeiro do Sul, Brazil. *Publications:* Carbones Térmicos en Colombia, Bases para una Política Contractual, 1981; several articles in El Colombiano, daily newspaper of Medellín, Colombia. *Recreations:* fishing, tennis. *Address:* Calle 136A No 57B-17, Bogotá, DE, Colombia; (office) Calle 93B No 12–28 Of. 303, Santafé de Bogotá, DC, Colombia. *T:* (1) 6217905, 6217954. *Club:* Lagartos (Bogotá).

RETTIE, (James) Philip, CBE 1987; TD 1962; farmer, since 1964; Director, Rettie & Co., since 1992; *b* 7 Dec. 1926; *s* of James Rettie and Rachel Buist; *m* 1st, 1955, Helen Grant; two *s* one *d*; 2nd, 1980, Mrs Diana Harvey (*née* Ballantyne). *Educ:* Trinity College, Glenalmond. Royal Engineers, 1945–48; RE (TA), 1949–65. Wm Low & Co. plc, 1948–85 (Chm., 1980–85); Mem., TSB Scotland Area Bd, 1983–88; Partner, Crossley & Rettie, 1989–95. Dir, Edinburgh and Glasgow Investment Co., 1989–2003. Chm., Sea Fish Industry Authority, 1981–87. Director: Unicorn Preservation Soc., 1990–2001; Tayside Conservation Trust, 1992–. Chm., Scottish Soc. for Employment of ex-Regular Sailors, Soldiers and Airmen, 1995–. Trustee, Scottish Civic Trust, 1983–2002. Hon. Col, Northern Gp Field Sqns, RE (T), 1982–89. *Recreations:* shooting, gardening, hill-walking, fishing. *Address:* Hill House, Ballindean, Inchture, Perthshire PH14 9QS. *T:* (01828) 686337.

REUBEN, David; Joint Chief Executive Officer, Reuben Brothers Ltd, since 1988; Trustee, Reuben Brothers Foundation, since 2002; *b* 14 Sept. 1938; *s* of David Sassoon Reuben and Nancy Reuben; *m* 1976, Debra; two *s* one *d*. *Educ:* Sir Jacob Sassoon High Sch.; Sir John Cass Coll., London (non-degree course Metallurgy). Mount Star Metals, 1958–74, Dir, until 1972; Dir, Metal Traders Gp, 1974–77; Chm., Trans World Metals Gp, 1977–2000. *Recreations:* painting, writing, golf, other sports. *Clubs:* Hurlingham; Wentworth, Coombe Hill Golf.

REUBEN, Simon David; Joint Chief Executive Officer, Reuben Brothers Ltd, since 1988; Trustee, Reuben Brothers Foundation, since 2002; *s* of David Sassoon Reuben and Nancy Reuben; *m* 1973, Joyce Nounou; one *d*. *Educ:* Sir Jacob Sassoon High Sch.; Sir John Cass Coll., London (degree not completed). Self-employed importer of carpets to UK, 1962–65; Man. Dir, J. Holdsworth & Co. Ltd, 1966–77; Man. Dir, Devereux Gp of Cos, 1970–77; Dir and Jt Principal, Trans World Metals Gp, 1977–2000. *Recreations:* film, history, avoiding cocktail parties. *Address: e-mail:* rb@reubros.com. *Clubs:* Hurlingham; Yacht Club de Monaco; Monte-Carlo Tennis.

REUPKE, Michael; journalist, since 1962; *b* Potsdam, Germany, 20 Nov. 1936; *s* of Dr Willm Reupke and Dr Frances G. Reupke (*née* Kinnear); *m* 1963, (Helen) Elizabeth Restrick; one *s* two *d*. *Educ:* Latymer Upper Sch., London; Jesus Coll., Cambridge (MA Mod. Langs); Collège d'Europe, Bruges. Pilot Officer, RAF, 1957–58. Joined Reuters, 1962; reporter, France, Switzerland, Guinea and West Germany, 1962–69; Asst European Manager, Gen. News Div., 1970–72; Chief Rep., West Germany, 1973–74; Manager, Latin America and the Caribbean, 1975–77; Editor-in-Chief, 1978–89; Gen. Manager, 1989. Director: Visnews, 1985–89; Compex (formerly Company Information Exchange), 1992–. Mem. Bd, Radio Authy, 1994–99. Member: IPI, 1978–97; Internat. Inst. of Communications, 1987–2003. Trustee, Reuter Foundn, 1982–89. *Recreations:* travel, cooking, wine. *Address:* 27A Upper High Street, Thame, Oxon OX9 3EX; 60 rue St Georges, 75009 Paris, France. *Clubs:* Royal Automobile; Leander (Henley-on-Thames).

REUTER, Edzard; Chairman, Board of Management, Daimler-Benz, 1987–95. *Educ:* Univs of Berlin and Göttingen (maths and physics); Free Univ. of Berlin (law). Research Asst, Free Univ. of Berlin Law Faculty, 1954–56; Universum Film, 1957–62; Manager, TV prod. section, Bertelsmann Group, Munich, 1962–64; Daimler-Benz: exec., finance dept, 1964; responsible for management planning and organization, 1971; Dep. Mem., Bd, 1973; Full Mem., Exec. Bd, 1976. Chm., U-blox AG, Thalwilz, Switzerland, 2001–. Mem.,: Bd of Trustees, Ernst Reuter Foundn, Berlin, 1988–; Chm., Bd of Trustees, Helga and Edzard Foundn, Stuttgart, 1998–. Chm., OTA Hochschule, Berlin, 2004–. Hon. Citizen, Berlin, 1998. *Publications:* Vom Geist der Wirtschaft, 1986; Horizonte der Wirtschaft, 1993; Schein und Wirklichkeit, 1998; Der schmale Grat des Lebens, 2007. *Address:* Taldorfer Strasse 14A, 70599 Stuttgart, Germany.

REVELL, Surg. Vice-Adm. Anthony Leslie, CB 1997; FRCA; Surgeon General, Ministry of Defence, 1994–97; *b* 26 April 1935; *s* of Leslie Frederick Revell and Florence Mabel (*née* Styles). *Educ:* King's Coll. Sch., Wimbledon; Ashford and Eastbourne Grammar Schs; Univ. of Birmingham Med. Sch. (MB, ChB); DA 1968. FRCA (FFARCS 1969). Joined RN, 1960; HMS Troubridge, 1960–62; HMS Dampier, 1962; HMS Loch Fada and 5th Frigate Sqdn, 1963; Anæsthetist, RN Hosp., Plymouth, 1964–65; HMS Eagle, 1965–67; Clin. Assistant, Radcliffe Infirmary, Oxford, Alder Hey Children's Hosp., Liverpool, and various courses, 1967–69; Anæsthetist, RN Hosp., Plymouth, 1969–70; RAF Hosps Nocton Hall and Akrotiri, Cyprus, 1970–72; ANZUK Mil. Hosp., Singapore, 1972–74; Cons. Anæsthetist, RN Hosp., Haslar, 1974–79; *ndc*, Latimer, 1979–80; Recruiter, MoD, 1980; Dir of Studies, Inst. of Naval Medicine, 1980–82; on staff, Surg. Rear-Adm. (Naval Hosps), 1982–84; Dir, Med. Personnel, 1984–86; RCDS, 1986; MO i/c, RN Hosp., Plymouth, 1987–88; on staff, C-in-C Fleet, 1988–90; Dir, Clinical Services, Defence Med. Directorate, 1990–91; Surg. Rear-Adm., Operational Med. Services, 1991–92; CSO (Med. and Dental) to C-in-C Fleet, 1992–93; Med. Dir Gen. (Navy), 1993–94; QHS, 1989–97. Member Council: Epsom Coll., 1997–; Royal Med. Foundn, 1997– (Vice Chm., 1999–2006; Chm., 2006–); Pilgrims Sch., Winchester, 1997–. Trustee, John Ellerman Foundn, 1997–. Chm., Winchester Fest., 2007–. FRSocMed 1970. Hon. MD Birmingham, 1996. CStJ 1993. *Publications:* Haslar: the Royal Hospital, 1979; (ed jtly) Proc. World Assoc. Anæsthetists, 1970. *Recreation:* choral music. *Address:* Willow Cottage, Domum Road, Winchester, Hants SO23 9NN. *Club:* Army and Navy.

REVELSTOKE, 6th Baron *cr* 1885, of Membland, co. Devon; **James Cecil Baring;** *b* 16 Aug. 1938; *yr s* of 4th Baron Revelstoke and Hon. Florence Fermor-Hesketh, 2nd *d* of 1st Baron Hesketh; *S* brother, 2003; *m* 1st, 1968, Aneta (marr. diss.), *yr d* of Erskine A. H. Fisher; two *s*; 2nd, 1983, Sarah (marr. diss. 1990), *d* of William Edward Stubbs, MBE; two *d*. *Educ:* Eton. *Heir: s* Hon. Alexander Rupert Baring, *b* 9 April 1970.

REW, Paul Francis, FCA; Partner, PricewaterhouseCoopers (formerly Price Waterhouse), since 1987; *b* 1953; *s* of late Lt Col Peter Rew and of Diana Edith Rew; *m* 1982, Mary Ellen Pleasant; two *d*. *Educ:* Churcher's Coll., Petersfield; Exeter Univ. (BSc Engrg Sci.). ACA 1977; FCA 1983. Price Waterhouse: articled, London, 1974; Johannesburg office, 1982–84; Partner, 1987; UK Energy and Utilities leader, 2003–; on secondment to DTI as Under Sec. and Dir, Industrial Develt Unit, 1992–94. Mem., Steering Bd, Insolvency Service, 1992–94. Mem., Bd of Mgt, St Bartholomew's and Queen Alexandra's Coll. of Nursing and Midwifery, 1990–95. *Recreations:* golf, tennis, humanistic psychology. *Address:* PricewaterhouseCoopers, 1 Embankment Place, WC2N 6NN. *T:* (020) 7804 4071.

REX, Prof. John Arderne; Research Professor on Ethnic Relations, 1984–90, now Emeritus, and Associate Director, Centre for Research in Ethnic Relations, 1974–90, University of Warwick; *b* 5 March 1925; *s* of Frederick Edward George Rex and Winifred Natalie Rex; *m* 1st, 1949, Pamela Margaret Rutherford (marr. diss. 1963); two *d*; 2nd, 1965, Margaret Ellen Biggs; two *s*. *Educ:* Grey Institute High Sch. and Rhodes University Coll., S Africa. BA (S Africa), PhD (Leeds). Served War, Royal Navy (Able Seaman), 1943–45. Graduated, 1948; Lecturer: Univ. of Leeds, 1949–62; Birmingham, 1962–64; Prof. of Social Theory and Institutions, Durham, 1964–70; Prof. of Sociology, Univ. of Warwick, 1970–79; Dir, SSRC Research Unit on Ethnic Relations, Univ. of Aston in Birmingham, 1979–84. Visiting Professor: Univ. of Toronto, 1974–75; Univ. of Cape Town, 1991; NY Univ., 1996. *Publications:* Key Problems of Sociological Theory, 1961; (with Robert Moore) Race Community and Conflict, 1967, 2nd edn 1973; Race Relations in Sociological Theory, 1970; Discovering Sociology, 1973; Race, Colonialism and the City, 1974; (ed) Approaches to Sociology, 1974; Sociology and the Demystification of the Modern World, 1974; (with Sally Tomlinson) Colonial Immigrants in a British City, 1979; Social Conflict, 1980; (ed) Apartheid and Social Research, 1981; Race and Ethnicity, 1986; The Ghetto and the Underclass, 1988; Ethnic Identity and Ethnic Organisation in Britain, 1991; (with Beatrice Drury) Ethnic Mobilisation in a Multicultural Europe, 1994; Ethnic Minorities in the Modern Nation State, 1996; (with Montserrat Guibernau) The Ethnicity Reader, 1997; (ed with Gurharpal Singh) Governance in Multicultural Societies, 2004; Ethnicité et Citoyenneté: la sociologie des societés multiculturelles, 2006. *Recreations:* politics, race relations work. *Address:* 33 Arlington Avenue, Leamington Spa, Warwicks CV32 5UD.

REYNOLD, Frederic; QC 1982; *b* 7 Jan. 1936; *s* of late Henry and Regina Reynold. *Educ:* Battersea Grammar School; Magdalen College, Oxford. BA Hons Jurisprudence. Called to the Bar, Gray's Inn, 1960, Bencher, 1991; commenced practice, 1963. *Publication:* The Judge as Lawmaker, 1967. *Recreations:* music, the arts, association croquet, dining out among friends. *Address:* 5 Hillcrest, 51 Ladbroke Grove, W11 3AX. *T:* (020) 7229 3848. *Club:* Parsons Green Croquet.

REYNOLDS, Alan (Munro); painter, maker of reliefs, and printmaker; *b* 27 April 1926; *m* 1957, Vona Darby. *Educ:* Woolwich Polytechnic Art School; Royal College of Art (Scholarship and Medal). One man exhibitions: Redfern Gall., 1952, 1953, 1954, 1956, 1960, 1962, 1964, 1966, 1970, 1972, 1974; Durlacher Gall., New York, 1954, 1959; Leicester Galleries, 1958; Aldeburgh, Suffolk, 1965; Arnolfini Gall., Bristol, 1971 (graphics); Annely Juda Fine Art, 1978, 1991, 2006; Juda Rowan Gall., 1982, 1986; Thomas Agnew, Albemarle Street Gall., 1982; Gall. Wack, Kaiserslautern, 1986, 1990, 1995, 1999; Galerie Lahumière, Paris, 1990; Galerie Art, Nürnberg, 1992; Gal. Konstruktiv Tendens, Stockholm, 2002; retrospective exhibitions: Wilhelm-Hack Mus., Ludwigshafen am Rhein, 1996; Städtische Galerie, Wolfsburg, 1996; Kettle's Yard, Cambridge, 2003; work in exhibitions: Carnegie (Pittsburgh) Internat., USA, 1952, 1955, 1958, 1961; Internat. Exhibn, Rome, (awarded one of the three equal prizes), subsequently Musée d'Art Moderne, Paris, and Brussels; British Council Exhibn, Oslo and Copenhagen, 1956; Redfern Gall., 1971; Spectrum, Arts Council of GB, 1971; British Painting 1952–77, Royal Academy, 1977; Galerie Loyse Oppenheim, Nyon, Switzerland, 1977; Galerie Renée Ziegler, Zürich, 1981; group exhibitions: Scottish Nat. Gall. of Modern Art, Edinburgh, 1984; Annely Juda Fine Art and Juda Rowan Gall., London, 1985; Galeries Renée Ziegler, Zürich, 1985–86; Annely Juda Fine Art, 1986 and 1996; Wilhelm-Hack Mus., Ludwigshafen am Rhein, 1987; Stiftung für Konkrete Kunst,

Reutlingen, 1992–93. Works acquired by: Tate Gall.; V&A; National Galleries of: S Aust.; Felton Bequest, Vic., Aust.; NZ; Canada; City Art Galleries of: Birmingham; Bristol; Manchester; Wakefield; Mus. of Modern Art, NY; Contemporary Art Soc.; British Council; Arts Council of GB; Rothschild Foundn; The Graves Art Gall., Sheffield; Nottingham Castle Mus.; Fitzwilliam Mus., Cambridge; Mus. of Modern Art, São Paulo, Brazil; Leeds Art Gall.; Toledo Art Gall., Ohio, USA; Oriel Coll., Oxford; Warwick Univ.; Mus. and Art Galls, Brighton and Plymouth; Texas Univ., Austin, USA; Berlin Nat. Gall.; McCrory Corp., NY; Wilhelm-Hack Mus., Ludwigshafen am Rhein; Louisiana Mus., Denmark; Tel Aviv Mus., Israel; Musée des Beaux Arts de Grenoble; Mus. Pfalzgalerie, Kaiserslautern, W Germany; Inst. für Kultur, Kunstsammlung Nordrhein-Westfalen, Düsseldorf. CoID Award, 1965; Arts Council of GB Purchase Award, 1967. *Relevant publication:* The Painter, Alan Reynolds, by J. P. Hodin, 1962. *Address:* Briar Cottage, High Street, Cranbrook, Kent TN17 3EN.

REYNOLDS, Albert; Member of the Dáil (TD) (FF), 1977–2003; Taoiseach (Prime Minister of Ireland), 1992–94; President, Fianna Fáil, 1992–94 (Vice-President, 1983–92); *b* Rooskey, Co. Roscommon, 3 Nov. 1932; *m* Kathleen Coen; two *s* five *d*. *Educ:* Summerhill Coll., Sligo. Minister: for Posts and Telegraphs, and for Transport, 1979–81; for Industry and Energy, March–Dec. 1982; Opposition spokesperson: for Industry and Employment, 1983–85; for Energy, 1985–87; Minister for: Industry and Commerce, 1987–88; Finance, 1988–91. Mem., Oireachtas Jt Cttee on Commercial State-Sponsored Bodies, 1983–87. Mem., Longford CC, 1974–79. Pres., Longford Chamber of Commerce, 1974–78. *Address:* 18 Ailesbury Road, Dublin 4, Ireland.

REYNOLDS, (Arthur) Graham, CVO 2000; OBE 1984; FBA 1993; Keeper of the Department of Prints and Drawings, 1961–74 (of Engraving, Illustration and Design, 1959–61), and of Paintings, Victoria and Albert Museum, 1959–74; *b* Highgate, 10 Jan. 1914; *o s* of late Arthur T. Reynolds and Eva Mullins; *m* 1943, Daphne, painter and engraver (*d* 2002), *d* of late Thomas Dent and Florence Haskett, Huddersfield. *Educ:* Highgate School; Queens' College, Cambridge. Joined staff of Victoria and Albert Museum, 1937. Seconded to Ministry of Home Security, 1939–45. Hon. Keeper of Portrait Miniatures, Fitzwilliam Mus., Cambridge, 1994–. Member: Adv. Council, Paul Mellon Centre for Studies in British Art, 1977–84; Reviewing Cttee on the Export of Works of Art, 1984–90. Trustee, William Morris Gallery, Walthamstow, 1972–75; Chm., Gainsborough's House Soc., Sudbury, 1977–79. Leverhulme Emeritus Fellowship, 1980–81. *Publications:* Twentieth Century Drawings, 1946; Nicholas Hilliard and Isaac Oliver, 1947, 2nd edn 1971; Van Gogh, 1947; Nineteenth Century Drawings, 1949; Thomas Bewick, 1949; An Introduction to English Water-Colour Painting, 1950, rev. edn 1988; Gastronomic Pleasures, 1950; Elizabethan and Jacobean Costume, 1951; English Portrait Miniatures, 1952, rev. edn 1988; Painters of the Victorian Scene, 1953; Catalogue of the Constable Collection, Victoria and Albert Museum, 1960, rev. edn 1973; Constable, the Natural Painter, 1965; Victorian Painting, 1966, 2nd edn 1987; Turner, 1969; A Concise History of Water Colour Painting, 1972; Catalogue of Portrait Miniatures, Wallace Collection, 1980; Constable's England, 1983; The Later Paintings and Drawings of John Constable, 2 vols, 1984 (Mitchell Prize); The Earlier Paintings and Drawings of John Constable, 2 vols, 1996; Catalogue of Portrait Miniatures, Metropolitan Museum of Art, 1996; The Sixteenth and Seventeenth Century Miniatures in the Collection of Her Majesty the Queen, 1999; Daphne Reynolds: a memoir, 2007; Editor of series English Masters of Black and White; contribs to Burlington Magazine, Apollo, etc. *Address:* The Old Manse, Bradfield St George, Bury St Edmunds, Suffolk IP30 0AZ. *T:* (01284) 386610. *Club:* Athenæum.

REYNOLDS, Barbara, MA Cantab; BA (Hons), PhD London; author, lexicographer; Reader in Italian Studies, University of Nottingham, 1966–78; *b* 13 June 1914; *d* of late Alfred Charles Reynolds; *m* 1st, 1939, Prof. Lewis Thorpe (*d* 1977); one *s* one *d*; 2nd, 1982, Kenneth Imeson (*d* 1994). *Educ:* St Paul's Girls' Sch.; UCL. Asst Lectr in Italian, LSE 1937–40. Chief Exec. and Gen. Editor, The Cambridge Italian Dictionary, 1948–81; Man. Editor, Seven, an Anglo-American Literary Review, 1980–2004. Mem. Coun. Senate, Cambridge Univ., 1961–62. University Lecturer in Italian Literature and Language, Cambridge, 1945–62 (Faculty Assistant Lecturer, 1940–45); Warden of Willoughby Hall, Univ. of Nottingham, 1963–69. Vis. Professor: Univ. of Calif., Berkeley, 1974–75; Wheaton Coll., Illinois, 1977–78, 1982; Trinity Coll., Dublin, 1980, 1981; Hope Coll., Mich., 1982. Hon. Reader in Italian, Univ. of Warwick, 1975–80. Pres., Dorothy L. Sayers Soc., 1995– (Chm., 1986–94). Hon. DLitt: Wheaton Coll., Illinois, 1979; Hope Coll., Mich., 1982; Durham Univ., 1995. Silver Medal for Services to Italian culture (Italian Govt), 1964; Edmund Gardner Prize, 1964; Silver Medal for services to Anglo-Veneto cultural relations, Prov. Admin of Vicenza, 1971; Cavaliere Ufficiale al Merito della Repubblica Italiana, 1978. *Publications:* (with K. T. Butler) Tredici Novelle Moderne, 1947; The Linguistic Writings of Alessandro Manzoni: a Textual and Chronological Reconstruction, 1950; rev. edn with introd., Dante and the Early Astronomers, by M. A. Orr, 1956; The Cambridge Italian Dictionary, Vol. I, Italian-English, 1962, Vol. II, English-Italian, 1981; (with Dorothy L. Sayers) Paradise: a translation into English triple rhyme, from the Italian of Dante Alighieri, 1962, 3rd edn 2004; (with Lewis Thorpe) Guido Farina, Painter of Verona, 1967; La Vita Nuova (Poems of Youth); trans. of Dante's Vita Nuova, 1969, 2nd edn 2004; Concise Cambridge Italian Dictionary, 1975; Orlando Furioso, trans. into rhymed octaves of Ariosto's epic, Vol. I, 1975 (Internat. Literary Prize, Monselice, Italy, 1976) Vol. II, 1977; (ed) Cambridge-Signorelli Dizionario Italiano-Inglese, Inglese-Italiano, 1986; (ed jtly) The Translator's Art, 1987; The Passionate Intellect: Dorothy L. Sayers' encounter with Dante, 1989; Dorothy L. Sayers: her life and soul, 1993; (ed) The Letters of Dorothy L. Sayers, Vol. I, 1995, Vol. II, 1997, Vol. III, 1998, Vol. IV, 2000, Vol. V, 2002; Dante: the poet, the political thinker, the man, 2006; numerous articles on Italian literature in learned jls. *Address:* 220 Milton Road, Cambridge CB4 1LQ. *T:* (01223) 565380, *Fax:* (01223) 424894. *Clubs:* University Women's (Chm., 1988–90), Royal Air Force.

See also A. C. Thorpe.

REYNOLDS, Christopher Douglas; Chief Executive Officer, Games Marketing Ltd, since 2004; *b* 24 March 1957; *s* of Geoffrey Butler and Margaret Williams (*née* Reynolds); *m* 1993, Deborah Pegden; one *s* one *d*. *Educ:* Ellesmere Coll.; St John's Coll., Durham Univ. (BA 1978). Mktg trainee, Grants of St James's, 1978–80; Product Manager, Eden Vale, 1980–82; various mktg roles, incl. Mktg and Sales Dir, Europe, Dunlop Slazenger Internat. Ltd, 1982–90; Vice-Pres., Apparel, Internat. Div., Reebok Internat. Ltd, 1990–93; Brand Dir, Pringle of Scotland, 1994–95; Vice-Pres., Mktg, Sara Lee Champion Europe, Florence, 1995–97; Founder Partner, Pegden Reynolds Consultancy, 1997–2000; Man. Dir, British Horseracing Bd, 2000–02. Non-executive Chairman: iKnowledge Ltd, 2002–06; Sound Decisions Ltd, 2007– (non-exec. Dir, 2002–07). MInstD 2000. *Recreations:* golf, tennis, squash, lapsed Rugby/cricket - too slow/old, family, wines - passionate collector/imbiber. *T:* (01483) 417679. *Clubs:* MCC; Hankley Common Golf (Tilford, Surrey); Guildford and Godalming Rugby.

REYNOLDS, Prof. David, CBE 2002; Professor of Education, University of Plymouth, since 2005; *b* 3 May 1949; *s* of Colin Reynolds and Joyce Reynolds (*née* Jones); *m* 1994,

Meriel Jones; two step *s*. *Educ:* Norwich Sch.; Univ. of Essex. Mem., Scientific Staff, MRC, 1971–75; Lectr in Social Admin, UC Cardiff, 1976–82; Lectr, then Sen. Lectr in Educn, UC Cardiff, subseq. UWCC, 1983–93; Professor: of Educn, Univ. of Newcastle upon Tyne, 1993–99; of Sch. Effectiveness and Sch. Improvement, Loughborough Univ., 1999–2000; of Leadership and Sch. Effectiveness, Univ. of Exeter, 2000–05. Guest Prof., Univ. of Shenyang, China, 2005–; Vis. Prof., Univ. of Southampton, 2007–. Mem., Literacy Task Force, 1996–97; Chm., Numeracy Task Force, 1997–98; Department for Education and Employment, subseq. Department for Education and Skills: Member: Literacy and Numeracy Strategy Gp, 1998–2001; Value Added Adv. Gp, 2003–05; Adviser: Teachers' Gp, 1999–2000; Standards and Effectiveness Unit, 2001–01; City Acad. Support Service, 2002–03; Innovation Unit, 2003–06. Member Board: British Educnl Communications and Technol. Agency, 1999–2003; TDA (formerly TTA), 2000–06; Educnl Broadcasting Council for Wales, 2005–07. Consultant, Tribal Educn, 2003–. Non-exec. Dir, Goal plc, 2000–02. Gov., Clifton Coll., 2003–; Chm., The Innovation Trust (Monkseaton Community High Sch.), 2007–. FRSA 1996. Co-Ed., School Effectiveness and Improvement: an internat. jl of res., policy and practice, 1991–2005. *Publications:* jointly: (ed) Studying School Effectiveness, 1985; The Comprehensive Experiment, 1987; Education Policies: controversies and critiques, 1989; (ed) School Effectiveness and School Improvement, 1989; International School Effects Research, 1992; (ed) School Effectiveness, 1992; Advances in School Effectiveness Research, 1994; (ed) Merging Traditions, 1996; Making Good Schools, 1996; (ed) Dilemmas of Decentralisation, 1996; Worlds Apart?, 1996; Improving Schools: performance and potential, 1999; The International Handbook of School Effectiveness Research, 1999, 2nd edn 2005; World Class Schools, 2002; Effective Teaching, 2001, 2nd edn as Effective Teaching: research, policy and practice, 2005; contrib. articles to acad. jls, professional jls and popular media. *Recreations:* walking, wine, travelling, opera. *Address:* Tondrugwaer Farm, Cross Inn, Llantrisant CF72 8NZ. *T:* (01443) 223417; *e-mail:* dreynolds1@plymouth.ac.uk, david@davidreynoldsconsulting.com.

REYNOLDS, Sir David James, 3rd Bt *cr* 1923; *b* 26 Jan. 1924; *er s* of Sir John Francis Roskell Reynolds, 2nd Bt, MBE, JP and Milicent (*d* 1931), *d* of late Major James Orr-Ewing and late Lady Margaret Orr-Ewing, *d* of 7th Duke of Roxburghe; *S* father, 1956; *m* 1966, Charlotte Baumgartner; one *s* two *d*. *Educ:* Downside. Active service in Army, 1942–47, Italy, etc; on demobilisation, Captain 15/19 Hussars. *Recreation:* sport. *Heir: s* James Francis Reynolds, *b* 10 July 1971. *Address:* Jersey, CI.

REYNOLDS, Prof. David James, PhD; FBA 2005; Professor of International History, University of Cambridge, since 2002; Fellow of Christ's College, Cambridge, since 1983; *b* 17 Feb. 1952; *s* of late Leslie Reynolds and Marian Reynolds (*née* Kay); *m* 1977, Margaret Philpott Ray; one *s*. *Educ:* Dulwich Coll.; Gonville and Caius Coll., Cambridge (BA, MA, PhD 1980). Choate Fellow, 1973–74, Warren Fellow, 1980–81, Harvard Univ.; Res. Fellow, Gonville and Caius Coll., Cambridge, 1978–80, 1981–83; University of Cambridge: Asst Lectr in History, 1984–88; Lectr, 1988–97; Reader in Internat. History, 1997–2002. *Publications:* The Creation of the Anglo-American Alliance, 1937–41, 1981 (Bernath Prize, Soc. for Historians of Amer. For. Relns, 1982); (jtly) An Ocean Apart: the relationship between Britain and America in the 20th century, 1988; Britannia Overruled: British policy and world power in the 20th century, 1991; (ed jtly) Allies at War: the Soviet, American, and British experience 1939–45, 1994; (ed) The Origins of the Cold War in Europe, 1994; Rich Relations: the American occupation of Britain 1942–45, 1995 (Soc. for Mil. Hist. Distinguished Book Award, 1996); One World Divisible: a global history since 1945, 2000; From Munich to Pearl Harbor: Roosevelt's America and the origins of the Second World War, 2001; In Command of History: Churchill fighting and writing the Second World War, 2004 (Wolfson Hist. Prize, 2005); From World War to Cold War: Churchill, Roosevelt and the international history of the 1940s, 2006; Summits: six meetings that shaped the twentieth century, 2007. *Address:* Christ's College, Cambridge CB2 3BU. *T:* (01223) 334900.

REYNOLDS, Deborah, CB 2008; PhD; Chief Veterinary Officer and Director General, Animal Health and Welfare, Department for Environment, Food and Rural Affairs, 2004–07; Visiting Professor, Royal Veterinary College; *b* 29 May 1953; *m*; one *s*. *Educ:* Univ. of Bristol (BVSc 1975); Univ. of Reading (PhD 1983). MRCVS. Vet. Res. Officer, Inst. of Animal Health; Vet. Investigation Service, State Vet. Service, MAFF, 1984–91; MAFF, 1991–94; Hd, Bacteriol. Dept, Vet. Labs Agency, 1994–97; Hd of Endemic Animal Diseases and Zoonoses, MAFF, 1997–2001; Veterinary Dir, Food Standards Agency, 2001–04. Member, Board: HPA, 2008–; Berkshire West NHS PCT, 2008–. *Address:* Brimstone Cottage, Upper Bucklebury, near Reading, Berks RG7 6QX. *T:* (01635) 860254, 07976 297190.

REYNOLDS, Prof. (Edward) Osmund (Royle), CBE 1995; MD; FRCP, FRCOG, FMedSci; FRS 1993; Professor of Neonatal Paediatrics, University College London (formerly University College Hospital) Medical School, 1976–96, now Emeritus Professor, University of London; *b* 3 Feb. 1933; *s* of Edward Royle Reynolds and Edna Reynolds; *m* 1956, Margaret Lindsay Ballard; two *s*. *Educ:* St Paul's Sch.; St Thomas' Hosp. Med. Sch. (Henry Myers Exhbn, 1958). BSc, MD London; DCH; FRCP 1975; FRCOG (*ad eundem*) 1983. Posts at St Thomas' Hosp., 1959–63; Research Fellow in Pediatrics: Harvard Med. Sch., 1963–64; Yale Med. Sch., 1964; Res. Asst, then Lectr and Sen. Lectr, UCH Med. Sch., 1964–76; Hd, Dept of Paediatrics, UCMSM, 1987–93. Consultant Paediatrician, UCH, 1969–94. Hon. Prof. of Paediatrics, Inst. of Child Health, 1994; William Julius Mickle fellow, Univ. of London, 1976–77. Numerous visiting professorships, incl. RSocMed Foundn Vis. Prof. to Amer. Acad. of Pediatrics, 1989. Specialist Advr (perinatal medicine), H of C Social Services and Health Select Cttees, 1978–92; Member: Scientific Adv. Panel, Foundn for Study of Infant Deaths, 1994–98; Bd of Management, Inst. of Child Health, 1990–96 (Hon. Fellow, 1996). President: BLISS (Baby Life Support Systems), 1982–97; Neonatal Soc., 1991–94. Trustee, Action Medical Research (formerly Action Research), 2002–04 (Mem., Scientific Adv. Cttee, 1981–87). Founding Scientific Patron, Liggins Inst., Univ. of Auckland, 2001. Foundn Fellow, UCL Hosps, 1999. Founder FMedSci 1998. Hon. FRCPCH 1997; Hon. FRSocMed 2000. Hon. Member: Argentine Paediatric Assoc.; Italian Soc. for Perinatal Medicine; British Assoc. of Perinatal Medicine, 1992 (Founder's Lectr, 1992). Lectures: Charles West, RCP, 1989; George Frederic Still Meml, BPA, 1995; Perinatal, Belfast, 1997. Dawson Williams Meml Prize, BMA, 1992; James Spence Medal, BPA, 1994; Maternité Prize, Europ. Assoc. of Perinatal Medicine, 1994; Harding Award, Action Research, 1995. *Publications:* chapters and papers on neonatal physiology and medicine. *Recreations:* travel, music, photography, sport (particularly fencing; mem., British foil team, 3rd in World Championship, Rome, 1955). *Address:* 72 Barrowgate Road, Chiswick, W4 4QU. *T:* (020) 8994 3326; 4 Ginge, Oxon OX12 8QR. *T:* (01235) 861494.

REYNOLDS, Eva Mary Barbara; see Reynolds, Barbara.

REYNOLDS, Dame Fiona Claire, (Dame Fiona Merrill), DBE 2008 (CBE 1998); Director-General, National Trust, since 2001; *b* 29 March 1958; *d* of Jeffrey Alan Reynolds and Margaret Mary (*née* Watson); *m* 1981, Robert William Tinsley Merrill;

three *d*. *Educ:* Rugby High Sch. for Girls; Newnham Coll., Cambridge (MA, MPhil 1980). Sec., Council for Nat. Parks, 1980–87; Asst Dir, 1987–91, Dir, 1992–98, CPRE; Dir, Women's Unit, Cabinet Office, 1998–2000. Global 500 Award, UN Envmt Programme, 1990. *Recreations:* hillwalking, classical music and opera, reading. *Address:* National Trust, Heelis, Kemble Drive, Swindon SN2 2NA.

REYNOLDS, Prof. Francis Martin Baillie, DCL; FBA 1988; Professor of Law, University of Oxford, 1992–2000, now Emeritus; Fellow of Worcester College, Oxford, 1960–2000, now Emeritus; *b* 11 Nov. 1932; *s* of Eustace Baillie Reynolds and Emma Margaret Hanby Reynolds (*née* Holmes); *m* 1965, Susan Claire Shillito; two *s* one *d*. *Educ:* Winchester Coll.; Worcester Coll., Oxford (BA 1956; BCL 1957; MA 1960; DCL 1986). Bigelow Teaching Fellow, Univ. of Chicago, 1957–58. Called to the Bar, Inner Temple, 1961, Hon. Bencher 1979. Reader in Law, Oxford Univ., 1977–92. Visiting Professor, Nat. Univ. of Singapore, UCL, Univ. of Melbourne, Monash Univ., Otago Univ., Univ. of Sydney, Univ. of Auckland, Univ. of Hong Kong; Hon. Prof. of Internat. Maritime Law, Internat. Maritime Law Inst., Malta. Hon. QC 1993. Gen. Editor, Lloyd's Maritime and Commercial Law Qly, 1983–87; Editor, Law Qly Review, 1987–. *Publications:* (ed jtly) Chitty on Contracts, 24th edn 1977, to 30th edn 2008; (ed jtly) Benjamin's Sale of Goods, 1st edn 1974, to 7th edn 2006; Bowstead on Agency, (ed jtly) 13th edn 1968, to 18th edn, as Bowstead and Reynolds on Agency, 2006; (ed jtly) English Private Law, 2000, 2nd edn 2008; (with Sir Guenter Treitel) Carver on Bills of Lading, 2001, 2nd edn 2006; published lectures and contribs to legal jls. *Recreations:* music, walking. *Address:* 61 Charlbury Road, Oxford OX2 6UX. *T:* (01865) 559323, *Fax:* (01865) 511894.

REYNOLDS, Gillian, MBE 1999; Radio Critic, The Daily Telegraph, since 1975; *b* 15 Nov. 1935; *d* of Charles Morton and Ada (*née* Kelly); *m* 1958, Stanley Reynolds (marr. diss. 1982); three *s*. *Educ:* St Anne's Coll., Oxford (MA; Hon. Fellow, 1996); Mount Holyoke Coll., South Hadley, Mass, USA. TV journalist, 1964–; Radio Critic, The Guardian, 1967–74; Programme Controller, Radio City, Liverpool, 1974–75. Vis. Fellow, Bournemouth Univ. Media Sch., 2002. Trustee, Nat. Museums Liverpool (formerly Nat. Museums and Galls on Merseyside), 2001–. Chm., Charles Parker Archive Trust, 1986–. Fellow (first to be apptd), Radio Acad., 1990; FRTS 1996. Hon. Fellow, Liverpool John Moores Univ., 2004. Media Soc. Award for distinguished contrib. to journalism, 1999. *Recreation:* listening to the radio. *Address:* Flat 3, 1 Linden Gardens, W2 4HA. *T:* (020) 7229 1893.

REYNOLDS, Graham; *see* Reynolds, A. G.

REYNOLDS, Guy Edwin K.; *see* King-Reynolds.

REYNOLDS, James Edward; Beijing Correspondent, BBC, since 2006; *b* 20 May 1974; *s* of Paul and Louise Reynolds. *Educ:* Westminster Sch.; Christ's Coll., Cambridge (BA Hons Modern Langs 1996). Joined BBC, 1997; S America corresp., 1998–2001; Middle East corresp., 2001–06. *Recreations:* studying the effects of galactic trash, floating in the Dead Sea. *Address:* c/o BBC News, Television Centre, Wood Lane, W12 7RJ. *T:* (020) 8743 8000; *e-mail:* james.reynolds@bbc.co.uk. *Club:* Frontline.

REYNOLDS, (James) Kirk; QC 1993; *b* 24 March 1951; *s* of late James Reynolds, sometime Judge of the High Ct, Eastern Reg. of Nigeria, and of Alexandra Mary (*née* Strain). *Educ:* Campbell Coll., Belfast; Peterhouse, Cambridge (MA). Called to the Bar, Middle Temple, 1974; Bencher, 2000. Hon. Mem., RICS, 1997. *Publications:* The Handbook of Rent Review, 1981; The Renewal of Business Tenancies, 1985, 2nd edn 1997; Dilapidations: the modern law and practice, 1995, 2nd edn 2004; Essentials of Rent Review, 1995. *Address:* Falcon Chambers, Falcon Court, EC4Y 1AA. *T:* (020) 7353 2484.

REYNOLDS, John; Director, Capabilities Programme, Department of Trade and Industry, 2005; *b* 14 Nov. 1950; *s* of Albert Victor Reynolds and Nina Eileen Reynolds (*née* Wolfenden); *m* 1973, Brenda O'Doherty; one *s* one *d*. *Educ:* HMS Worcester; UWIST (BSc Maritime Studies 1975). Navigating Officer, P&OSNCo., 1966–75; Res Scientist, Nat. Maritime Inst., 1975–84; Department of Trade and Industry, 1984–89: Shipbuilding Policy Div., 1984–87; Eur. Mgt of Technol. Prog., 1985–86; Tech. Asst to Chief Engr and Scientist, 1987–89; Head of Mobile Radio Licensing, Radiocommunications Agency, 1989–90; Dir of Resources, Lab. of Govt Chemist, 1991–96; Director: Radiocommunications Agency, 1996–98; Future and Innovation Unit, DTI, 1998–2001; Gp Dir, Strategy and Communications Gp, British Trade Internat., subseq. UK Trade and Investment, 2001–04. *Recreations:* tennis, cycling, gardening.

REYNOLDS, John; Lord Provost and Lord-Lieutenant, City of Aberdeen, 2003–07; *b* 5 April 1949; *s* of William and Anne Reynolds; *m* 1970, Helen Will; one *s* two *d*. *Educ:* Blackpool Grammar Sch. Posts in: entertainment ind. throughout UK, 1966–70; electrical retail trade, with Electric Rentals Gp/Granada, and John Reynolds news agency, 1970–96; self employed in travel business, Scottish Choice Itineraries, and news agency, 1996–. Member (Lib Dem): Aberdeen DC, 1986–96; Grampian Regl Council, 1994–96; Aberdeen CC, 1995– (Mem., Licensing Cttee, 1996–). Member: Grampian Jt Fire Bd; Aberdeen Licensing Bd; Aberdeen and Grampian Tourist Bd. Comr, Northern Lighthouse Bd. President: Voluntary Service Aberdeen; Aberdeen Br., RNLI; Vice-Pres., Shipwrecked Fishermen and Mariners' Royal Benevolent Soc.; Mem., Local Adv. Cttee, Royal Nat. Mission to Deep Sea Fishermen. Pres., Aberdeen Scout Council. Trustee, Nat. Liby of Scotland. Patron: Mental Health Aberdeen, 2003–; Aberdeen Internat. Youth Fest., 2003–. JP Aberdeen (Chm., JPs Adv. Cttee). *Recreations:* music, theatre, DIY, socialising. *Address:* Aberdeen City Council, Town House, Aberdeen AB10 1LP. *T:* (01224) 522637, *Fax:* (01224) 523747; *e-mail:* bgraham@aberdeencity.gov.uk.

REYNOLDS, Joyce Maire, FBA 1982; Fellow of Newnham College, 1951–84, now Hon. Fellow, and Reader in Roman Historical Epigraphy, 1983–84, University of Cambridge; *b* 18 Dec. 1918; *d* of late William Howe Reynolds and Nellie Farmer Reynolds. *Educ:* Walthamstow County High Sch. for Girls; St Paul's Girls' Sch., Hammersmith; Somerville Coll., Oxford (Hon. Fellow, 1988). Temp. Civil Servant, BoT, 1941–46; Rome Scholar, British Sch. at Rome, 1946–48; Lectr in Ancient History, King's Coll., Newcastle upon Tyne, 1948–51; Cambridge University: Asst Lectr in Classics, 1952–57; Univ. Lectr 1957–83; Dir of Studies in Classics, 1951–79 and Lectr in Classics, 1951–84, Newnham Coll. Woolley Travelling Fellow, Somerville Coll., Oxford, 1961; Mem., Inst. for Advanced Study, Princeton, USA, 1984–85; Vis. Prof., Univ. of Calif at Berkeley, 1987. President: Soc. for Libyan Studies, 1981–86; Soc. for the Promotion of Roman Studies, 1986–89. Corresponding Member: German Archaeol Inst., 1971–; Austrian Archaeol Inst., 1991–. Hon. DLitt Newcastle upon Tyne, 1984. Gold Medal, Soc. of Antiquaries of London, 2004. *Publications:* (with J. B. Ward Perkins) The Inscriptions of Roman Tripolitania, 1952; Aphrodisias and Rome, 1982; (with R. Tannenbaum) Jews and Godfearers at Aphrodisias, 1987; (ed) Christian Monuments of Cyrenaica, 2003; articles on Roman history and epigraphy in jls, 1951–. *Recreation:* walking. *Address:* Newnham College, Cambridge CB3 9DF.

REYNOLDS, Kirk; *see* Reynolds, J. K.

REYNOLDS, His Honour Martin Paul; a Circuit Judge, 1995–2006; a Deputy Circuit Judge, 2006–08; *b* 25 Dec. 1936; *s* of Cedric Hinton Fleetwood Reynolds and Doris Margaret (*née* Bryan); *m* 1961, Gaynor Margaret Phillips; three *s*. *Educ:* University College Sch., Hampstead; St Edmund Hall, Oxford (MA). ACIArb 1982. Called to the Bar, Inner Temple, 1962. Mem., Parole Bd, 2006–; Pres., Mental Health Rev. Tribunal (Restricted Cases), 1997–. Councillor, London Borough of Islington, 1968–71 and 1972–82. Contested (Lab) Harrow West, Oct. 1994. *Recreations:* navigating European waterways in a Dutch barge, gastronomy, music. *Clubs:* Savage; Bar Yacht.

REYNOLDS, Dr Martin Richard Finch; Associate Director of Health Policy and Public Health, East Riding Health Authority, 1993–99; *b* 26 July 1943; 2nd *s* of Gerald Finch Reynolds and Frances Bertha (*née* Locke); *m* 1965, Shelagh (*née* Gray); two *d*. *Educ:* Newton Abbot Grammar Sch.; Univ. of Bristol. MB ChB, DPH; FFPHM; FRCP. House posts in medicine, surgery, infectious diseases and paediatrics, 1966–67; Dep. Med. Officer, Glos CC, 1967–70; Sen. Dep. Med. Officer, Bristol City and Asst Sen. Med. Officer, SW Regional Hosp. Bd, 1970–74; Dist Community Physician, Southmead Dist of Avon AHA (Teaching) and Med. Officer for Environmental Health, Northavon Dist Council, 1974–79; Area Med. Officer, Wilts AHA, 1979–80; Regional MO/Chief Med. Advr, South Western RHA, 1980–86; Specialist in Community Medicine, 1986–89, Consultant in Public Health Medicine, 1989–93, Hull HA. Registrar, FPHM, 1995–97. Voluntary work with Wycliffe Associates for Bible trans., 1999–. *Publications:* contrib. various articles in professional jls on subjects in community medicine.

REYNOLDS, Michael Emanuel, CBE 1977; Founder/Owner, Susan Reynolds Books Ltd, 1977–84; *b* 22 April 1931; *s* of Isaac Mark and Henrietta Rosenberg; *m* 1964, Susan Geraldine Yates; two *d*. *Educ:* Haberdashers' Aske's (HSC). Marks & Spencer Ltd, 1951–61; Food Controller, British Home Stores Ltd, 1961–64; Spar (UK) Ltd, 1964–77: Trading Controller, 1964–67; Chm. and Managing Dir, 1967–77; BV Intergroup Trading (IGT), 1974–77: Founder Mem., Bd of Admin.; Dir, 1974–75; Chm. and Dir, 1975–77. *Recreations:* tennis, squash, bridge.

REYNOLDS, Maj.-Gen. Michael Frank, CB 1983; author (military history); *b* 3 June 1930; *s* of Frank Reynolds and Gwendolen Reynolds (*née* Griffiths); *m* 1955, Anne Bernice (*née* Truman); three *d*. *Educ:* Cranleigh; RMA Sandhurst (Infantry Prize). Commnd Queen's Royal Regt, 1950 (last Adjt, 1959); served Germany, Korea (severely wounded), Cyprus (EOKA emergency), Canada (exchange officer), Persian Gulf, Netherlands, Belgium; psc 1960; GSO 1 Ops, HQ AFCENT, 1970–71; CO 2 Queen's, BAOR and Ulster, 1971–73; GSO 1 Ops, N Ireland, 1973–74; Comdr 12 (Mech.) Bde, BAOR, 1974–76; RCDS, 1977; Dep. Adjt Gen., BAOR, 1978–80; Comdr, Allied Command Europe Mobile Force (Land), 1980–83; Asst Dir, IMS (Plans and Policy), HQ NATO, 1983–86. Col Comdt, The Queen's Division, 1984–86; (Last) Col, The Queen's Regt, 1989–92. Pres., E Anglian Aviation Soc., 1996–98. Comdr First Cl., Order of the Dannebrog (Denmark), 1990; Grand Cross, Order of Orange-Nassau (Netherlands), 1992. *Publications:* The Devil's Adjutant, 1995; Steel Inferno, 1997; Men of Steel, 1999; Sons of the Reich, 2002; Eagles and Bulldogs in Normandy 1944, 2003; Monty and Patton - Two Paths to Victory, 2005. *Recreations:* military history (especially Normandy and Battle of the Ardennes, 1944), writing.

REYNOLDS, Osmund; *see* Reynolds, E. O. R.

REYNOLDS, Sir Peter (William John), Kt 1985; CBE 1975; Director, Cilva Holdings plc, since 1989; *b* 10 Sept. 1929; *s* of Harry and Gladys Victoria Reynolds; *m* 1955, Barbara Anne, *d* of Vincent Kenneth Johnson, OBE; two *s*. *Educ:* Haileybury Coll., Herts. National Service, 2nd Lieut, RA, 1948–50. Unilever Ltd, 1950–70: Trainee Dir, Managing Dir, then Chm., Walls (Meat & Handy Foods) Ltd. Ranks Hovis McDougall: Asst Gp Managing Dir, 1971; Gp Man. Dir, 1972–81; Chm., 1981–89; Dep. Chm., 1989–93. Director: Guardian Royal Exchange Assurance plc, 1986–99; Boots Co. plc, 1986–2000; Avis Europe Ltd, 1988–2001; Pioneer International, until 1999; Nationwide Anglia Building Soc., 1990–92; Chm., Pioneer Concrete (Hldgs), 1990–99. Chairman: EDC Employment and Trng Cttee, 1982–87; Resources Cttee, Food and Drink Fedn (formerly Food and Drink Industries Council), 1983–86; Member: EDC for Food and Drink Manufg Industry, 1976–87; Consultative Bd for Resources Develt in Agriculture, 1982–84; Covent Garden Market Authority, 1989–97; Dir, Industrial Develt Bd for NI, 1982–89; Mem., Peacock Cttee on Financing the BBC, 1985–86. Dir, Freemantle Trust (formerly Bucks Comm. Housing Trust), 1992–2001. Gov., Berkhamsted Sch., 1985–2001; Life Gov., Haileybury, 1985. High Sheriff, Bucks, 1990–91. *Address:* Rignall Farm, Rignall Road, Great Missenden, Bucks HP16 9PE. *T:* (01240) 64714.

REYNOLDS, Prof. Philip Alan, CBE 1986; DL; Vice-Chancellor, University of Lancaster, 1980–85; *b* 15 May 1920; *s* of Harry Reynolds and Ethel (*née* Scott); *m* 1946, Mollie Patricia (*née* Horton); two *s* one *d*. *Educ:* Worthing High Sch.; Queen's Coll., Oxford (BA 1940, 1st Cl. Mod. Hist.; MA 1950). Served War, 1940–46: HAA and Staff, UK, ME and Greece; Major 1945. Asst Lectr, then Lectr in Internat. History, LSE, 1946–50; Woodrow Wilson Prof. of Internat. Politics, UCW Aberystwyth, 1950–64 (Vice-Principal, 1961–63); Prof. of Politics and Pro-Vice-Chancellor, Univ. of Lancaster, 1964–80. Vis. Professor: in Internat. Relations, Toronto, 1953; in Commonwealth History and Instns, Indian Sch. of Internat. Studies, New Delhi, 1958; Anspach Fellow, Univ. of Pa, 1971; Vis. Res. Fellow, ANU Canberra, 1977. Vice-Chm., Cttee of Vice-Chancellors and Principals, 1984–85; Chm., Brit. Internat. Studies Assoc., 1976, Hon. Pres., 1981–84; Mem. Council, RIIA, 1975–80. DL Lancs, 1982. Hon. DLitt Lancaster, 1985; DUniv Open, 1994. *Publications:* War in the Twentieth Century, 1951; Die Britische Aussenpolitik zwischen den beiden Weltkriegen, 1952 (rev. edn, 1954, as British Foreign Policy in the Inter-War Years); An Introduction to International Relations, 1971, 3rd edn 1994 (Japanese edn 1977, Spanish edn 1978, Chinese edn 1997); (with E. J. Hughes) The Historian as Diplomat: Charles Kingsley Webster and the United Nations 1939–46, 1976; contrib. New Cambridge Mod. Hist., History, Slavonic Rev., Pol. Qly, Pol. Studies, Internat. Jl, Internat. Studies, Brit. Jl of Internat. Studies, Educn Policy Bulletin, Higher Educn, Univs Qly, Minerva. *Recreations:* music, bridge, eating and drinking. *Address:* Lattice Cottage, Borwick, Carnforth, Lancs LA6 1JR. *T:* (01524) 732518.

REYNOLDS, Dr Roy Gregory, CMG 2000; Chief Executive, Commonwealth Development Corporation, 1994–99; *b* 4 May 1939; *s* of Henry Herbert Reynolds and Alice Emily Reynolds; *m* 1963, Monica Cecelia; one *s* one *d*. *Educ:* George Dixon Grammar Sch., Birmingham; Birmingham Univ. (BSc Chem. Eng 1960); Imperial Coll., London (PhD 1964). Shell Internat. Petroleum Co., 1964–92. Dir, 1999–, Chm., 2003–, J P Morgan Emerging Markets Investment Trust (formerly Fleming Emerging Markets Trust). Non-exec. Dir, LASMO plc, 1997–2001. *Recreations:* keeping fit, golf. *Club:* Royal Automobile.

REYNOLDS, Susan Mary Grace, FRHistS; FBA 1993; Senior Research Fellow, Institute of Historical Research, since 1993; Hon. Research Fellow, History Department of University College London, since 1987, and of Birkbeck College, since 1995; *b* 27 Jan. 1929; *d* of Hugh Reynolds and Maisie Reynolds (*née* Morten). *Educ:* The Study, Montreal; Howell's Sch., Denbigh; Lady Margaret Hall, Oxford (History Cl. II, MA); Dip. Archive Admin, UCL. FRHistS 1968. Archive Asst, 1951–52; Victoria County Histories, 1952–59; school teacher, 1959–64; Fellow and Tutor in Modern History, LMH, Oxford, 1964–86, Emeritus Fellow, 1986; Lectr in Modern History, Oxford Univ., 1965–86. Visiting Professor: Dartmouth Coll., USA, 1986–87; Central European Univ., Budapest, 1994. *Publications:* (ed) Register of Roger Martival, Bishop of Salisbury, vol. 3, 1965; Introduction to the History of English Medieval Towns, 1977; Kingdoms and Communities in Western Europe 900–1300, 1984, 2nd edn 1997; Fiefs and Vassals, 1994; Ideas and Solidarities of the Medieval Laity, 1995; articles in historical jls. *Address:* 19 Ridgmount Gardens, WC1E 7AR. *T:* (020) 7636 9043.

REYNOLDS, Prof. Vernon, PhD; Professor of Biological Anthropology, University of Oxford, 1996–2001, now Professor Emeritus; Fellow, Magdalen College, Oxford, 1987–2001, now Fellow Emeritus; Emeritus Fellow, School of Anthropology, University of Oxford, since 2008; *b* 14 Dec. 1935; *s* of Heinz Emil Max Rheinhold and Eva Marianne Rheinhold (*née* Rudenberg); name changed to Reynolds, 1949; *m* 1960, Frances Glover; one *s* one *d*. *Educ:* Collyer's Sch.; University Coll. London (BA Hons; PhD 1962). Univ. of London Travelling Schol. to study wild chimpanzees in Uganda, 1962; Lecturer: in Anthropol., Bristol Univ., 1966–72; in Biol Anthropol., Oxford Univ., 1972–96. Hon. Sen. Res. Fellow, Univ. of Sussex, 2002–. Founder and Hd, Budongo Forest Project, Uganda, 1990–. President's Award, Amer. Soc. Primatologists, 2000; Chm.'s Award, Cttee for Res. and Exploration, Nat. Geographic Soc., 2000. *Publications:* Budongo: a forest and its chimpanzees, 1965; The Apes, 1967; The Biology of Human Action, 1976, 2nd edn 1980; (jtly) Primate Social Behaviour, 1993; (jtly) The Biology of Religion, 1983, 2nd edn 1994; The Chimpanzees of the Budongo Forest, 2005; edited jointly: Human Behaviour and Adaptation, 1978; The Meaning of Primate Signals, 1984; The Sociobiology of Ethnocentrism, 1987; Fertility and Resources, 1990; Mating and Marriage, 1991; The Aquatic Ape: fact or fiction?, 1991; Human Populations: diversity and adaptation, 1995; Survival and Religion, 1995; contributed chapters; contrib. scientific jls. *Recreations:* dinghy sailing, bee-keeping. *Address:* Orchard House, West Street, Alfriston, E Sussex BN26 5UX. *T:* (01323) 871136; *e-mail:* vreynolds@btopenworld.com.

REYNTIENS, Nicholas Patrick, OBE 1976; Head of Fine Art, Central School of Art and Design, London, 1976–86; *b* 11 Dec. 1925; *s* of Nicholas Serge Reyntiens, OBE, and Janet MacRae; *m* 1953, Anne Bruce (*d* 2006); two *s* two *d*. *Educ:* Ampleforth; Edinburgh Coll. of Art (DA). Served Scots Guards, 1943–47. St Marylebone Sch. of Art, 1947–50; Edinburgh Coll. of Art, 1950–51. Founder (with wife, Anne Bruce, the painter), Reyntiens Trust, which ran art sch., Burleighfield, where pupils from UK, Ireland, France, Germany, Japan, Canada, Australia, New Zealand, US and Iceland learned art of stained glass, and which had facilities for tapestry design and teaching, a printing house for editioning in lithography, etching and silkscreen, as well as workshops for stained glass, ceramics, drawing and painting. Has lectured in USA, Spain, Mexico, France and Switzerland; British Council lectr, India, 1995–96; occasional Vis. Prof., Pilchuck Sch. of Glass, Washington State, USA. Many commissions, including glass for Liverpool RC Metropolitan Cathedral; for 35 years interpreted painters' designs into stained glass, as well as own commissions for stained glass, 1953–, including baptistery window, Coventry Cathedral, Eton Coll. Chapel, Churchill Coll., Cambridge, Robinson Coll., Cambridge, St Margaret's Westminster (all with John Piper), Derby Cathedral and Liverpool Metropolitan Cathedral Blessed Sacrament Chapel (with Ceri Richards), All Saints Basingstoke (with Cecil Collins); completed glazing of Christ Church Hall, Oxford, 1980–84; designed and painted Great West Window, Southwell Minster, Notts, 1995; commnd with son, John, to design and paint Lady Chapel, and entire south transept, Ampleforth Abbey, 2002. Retrospective exhibn of autonomous panels, Ontario, 1990. Member: Court, RCA; Adv. Cttee in Decoration, Brompton Oratory; Adv. Cttee in Decoration, Westminster Cathedral; Adv. Cttee, Westminster Abbey, 1981–95. Art Critic, Catholic Herald; art correspondent, The Oldie. *Publications:* Technique of Stained Glass, 1967, 2nd edn 1977; The Beauty of Stained Glass, 1990; has written for architectural, art, literary and political magazines and on cooking for Harpers & Queen. *Address:* Winterbourne Lodge, Ilford Bridges Farm, close Stocklinch, Ilminster, Som TA19 9HZ. *T:* (01460) 52241, *Fax:* (01460) 52241.

RHIND, Prof. David William, CBE 2001; FRS 2002; FBA; Vice-Chancellor and Principal, City University, 1998–2007; Member of Court, Bank of England, 2006–May 2009; *b* 29 Nov. 1943; *s* of late William Rhind and Christina Rhind; *m* 1966, Christine Young; one *s* two *d*. *Educ:* Berwick Grammar School; Bristol Univ. (BSc); Edinburgh Univ. (PhD); London Univ. (DSc). FRGS; FRICS 1991; FSS 2004. Research Fellow, Royal College of Art, 1969–73; Lectr then Reader, Univ. of Durham, 1973–81; Birkbeck College, London University: Prof. of Geography, 1982–91; Dean, Faculty of Economics, 1984–86; Governor, 1986–90; Hon. Fellow, 2000; Dir Gen. and Chief Exec., Ordnance Survey, 1992–98. Visiting Fellow: Internat. Trng Centre, Netherlands, 1975; ANU, 1979. Vice-Pres., Internat. Cartographic Assoc., 1984–91; Mem., Govt Cttee on Enquiry into handling of geographic inf., 1985–87; Advisor, H of L Select Cttee on Sci. and Tech., 1983–84; Mem., ESRC, 1996–2000. Chairman: Bloomsbury Computing Consortium Mgt Cttee, 1988–91; Royal Soc. Ordnance Survey Scientific Cttee, 1989–91; Commn on Social Scis, Acad. of Learned Socs for Social Scis, 2000–03; Statistics Commn, 2003– (Mem., 2000–03); Higher Educn Staff Develt Agency, 2001–04; Islington Improvement Bd, 2003–04; Adv. Panel on Public Sector Inf., 2008–. Mem., UK Statistics Authy, 2008–. Pres., Remote Sensing and Photogrammetric Soc., 2003–. Trustee, Nuffield Foundn, 2008–. Governor: City of London Girls' Sch., 1999–2001; Ashridge Mgt Coll., 2000–04; NIESR, 2004–. Mem. Council, 2003–04, Mem. F and GP Cttee, 2003–08, Royal Soc.; Hon. Sec., RGS, 1988–91. CCMI (CIMgt 1998). Hon. FBA 2002; Hon. FCII 2004. Hon. DSc: Bristol, 1993; Loughborough, 1996; Southampton, 1998; Kingston, 1999; Durham, 2001; London Metropolitan, 2003; Royal Holloway, London, 2004; St Petersburg State Poly., 2007. Centenary Medal, RSGS, 1992; Patron's Medal, RGS, 1997; Decade Award for Achievement, Assoc. for Geographic Inf., 1997. *Publications:* (jtly) Land Use, 1980; The Census User's Handbook, 1983; (jtly) Atlas of EEC Affairs, 1984; (jtly) Geographical Information Systems, 1991, revised 1999; (jtly) Postcodes: the new geography, 1992; Framework for the World, 1997; (jtly) Geographical Information Systems and Science, 2001, 2nd edn 2005; numerous papers on map-making and geographical information systems. *Recreations:* travelling, mowing the lawn. *Address:* 1 Cold Harbour Close, Wickham, Hants PO17 5PT.

RHODES, Gary, OBE 2006; chef and restaurateur; *b* 22 April 1960; *s* of Jean Rhodes (*née* Ferris) and step *s* of John Smellie; *m* 1989, (Yolanda) Jennifer Adkins; two *s*. *Educ:* Thanet Technical Coll., Broadstairs (C&G qualifs; Student of the Year, Chef of the Year, 1979). Commis, then Chef de Partie, Amsterdam Hilton, 1979–81; Sous Chef: Reform Club, 1982–83; Capital Hotel, Knightsbridge, 1983–85; Head Chef: Whitehall, Broxted, 1985–86; Castle Hotel, Taunton, 1986–90 (Michelin Star, annually, 1986–90); The Greenhouse, London, 1990–96 (Michelin Star, 1996); Chef and Co-Proprietor: city rhodes, 1997–2003 (Michelin Star, annually 1997–2003); Rhodes in the Square, 1998–2003 (Michelin Star, 1998–2003); Rhodes & Co., Manchester, and Edinburgh, 1999–2002 (Bib Gourmand Award, 2001); Rhodes at the Calabash Hotel, Grenada, 2003–; Rhodes Twenty Four, 2003– (Michelin Star, 2004–); Arcadian Rhodes, P&O liner, 2005–; Oriana Rhodes, P&O liner, 2006; Rhodes D7, Dublin, 2006–; Rhodes W1 Restaurant, London, 2007 (Michelin Star, 2008–); Rhodes Mezzanine, Dubai, 2007. Jt owner, Rhokett Patisserie, 2002–. Hon. Prof., Thames Valley Univ., 2003. FCGI 2005. *Television series:* Hot Chefs, 1988; Rhodes Around Britain, 1994; More Rhodes Around Britain, 1995; Open Rhodes Around Britain, 1996; Gary Rhodes, 1997; Gary's Perfect Christmas, 1998; Gary Rhodes' New British Classics, 1999; Masterchef, 2001; At the Table, 2001; Spring into Summer, 2002; Autumn into Winter, 2002; Hell's Kitchen, 2005. Rhodes on the Road (tour), 1997; Rhodes Across India, 2007; Rhodes Across China, 2008; columnist, BBC Good Food magazine, 1996–. *Publications:* Rhodes Around Britain, 1994; More Rhodes Around Britain, 1995; Open Rhodes Around Britain, 1996; Short-cut Rhodes, 1997; Fabulous Food, 1997; Sweet Dreams, 1998; New British Classics, 1999; At the Table, 2000; Spring into Summer, 2002; Autumn into Winter, 2002; The Complete Cookery Year, 2003; Keeping it Simple, 2005; Time to Eat, 2007; Rhodes 365, 2008. *Recreations:* driving, art, fashion. *Address:* Restaurant Associates, 4th Floor, 24 Martin Lane, EC4R 0DR. *Clubs:* Les Ambassadeurs, St James's.

RHODES, George Harold Lancashire, TD 1946; Regional Chairman of Industrial Tribunals, Manchester, 1985–88; *b* 29 Feb. 1916; *er s* of Judge Harold and Ena Rhodes of Bowdon, Cheshire. *Educ:* Shrewsbury School; The Queen's College, Oxford (MA 1941). Commissioned 52nd Field Regt RA TA, 1938; war service, BEF, 1940, Middle East, 1942, Italy, 1943–46 (Major). Called to the Bar, Gray's Inn, 1947; practised on N Circuit; the Junior, 1948; Office of Judge Advocate General (Army and RAF), 1953; Asst Judge Advocate General, 1967; Chm., Industrial Tribunals (Manchester), 1974, Dep. Regional Chm., 1975. *Address:* 42 Custerson Court, Saffron Walden, Essex CB11 3HF.

RHODES, John Andrew, FCILT; independent public transport consultant, since 1999; *b* 22 May 1949; *s* of George and Elsie Rhodes; *m* 1985, Marie Catherine Carleton. *Educ:* Queen Elizabeth Sch., Barnet; Wadham Coll., Oxford (MA Mod. History). Civil Service: various posts in DoE, Cabinet Office, Dept of Transport, 1971–87; Dir Gen., W Yorks PTE, 1988–92; Strategy and Planning Advr, BRB, 1992–93; Dir, Passenger Services Gp, Office of Rail Regulator, 1993–99. Chm., railway industry Delay Attribution Bd, 2004–. Non-exec. Dir, E and N Herts NHS Trust, 2000–02. Chm., Bishop's Stortford Civic Soc., 2000–07; Vice Chm., Bishop's Stortford Civic Fedn, 2007–. Hon. Sen. Res. Fellow, Constitution Unit, UCL, 2001–. FRSA 1997. *Recreations:* music, history, gardening. *Address:* 26 Warwick Road, Bishop's Stortford, Herts CM23 5NW. *T:* (01279) 656482.
See also P. J. Rhodes.

RHODES, Sir John (Christopher Douglas), 4th Bt *cr* 1919; *b* 24 May 1946; *s* of Sir Christopher Rhodes, 3rd Bt, and Mary Florence, *d* of late Dr Douglas Wardleworth; *S* father, 1964. *Heir: b* Michael Philip James Rhodes [*b* 3 April 1948; *m* 1973, Susan, *d* of Patrick Roney-Dougal; one *d*].

RHODES, Prof. John David, CBE 2000 (OBE 1992); PhD, DSc; FRS 1993; FREng; Chairman, 1994, Group Chief Executive, 2006, Filtronic plc (formerly Filtronic Comtek plc); Industrial Professor, Leeds University, since 1981, now Emeritus; *b* 9 Oct. 1943; *s* of Jack and Florence Rhodes; *m* 1965, Barbara Margaret Pearce; one *s* one *d*. *Educ:* Univ. of Leeds (BSc, PhD, DSc). FIEEE 1980; FIET (FIEE 1984); FREng (FEng 1987). Leeds University: Res. Asst, 1964–66; Res. Fellow, 1966–67; Sen. Res. Engr, Microwave Develt Labs, USA, 1967–69; Leeds University: Lectr, 1969–72; Reader, 1972–75; Prof., 1975–81. Chm., and CEO Filtronic Ltd, 1977. Hon. DEng: Bradford, 1988; Leeds, 2004; Hon. DSc Napier, 1995. Prince Philip Medal, Royal Acad. of Engrg, 2003. *Publication:* Theory of Electrical Filters, 1976. *Recreation:* golf. *Address:* Dabarda, West Winds, Moor Lane, Menston, Ilkley LS29 6QD.

RHODES, John David McKinnon; Head of Financial Capability, Citizens Advice, since 2006; *b* 20 Aug. 1950; *s* of John Ivor McKinnon Rhodes, *qv*; *m* 1984, Sarah Elizabeth Rickard; two *s* one *d*. *Educ:* Dulwich Coll.; Sussex Univ. (BA Hons); London Business Sch. (Sloan Fellow 1983). With Lithotype Inc., 1971–72; joined Department of Trade and Industry, 1972: Principal Private Sec. to Sec. of State for Trade, 1981–83; Asst Sec., Internat. Projects, 1984–86; Director: British Trade and Investment Office (USA), NY, 1987–90; EC Single Market Policy, 1991–94; Electricity and Nuclear Fuels, 1994–96; Nuclear Sponsorship, 1996–97; Sec., Low Pay Commn, 1997–98; Director: Infrastructure and Energy Projects, 1998–2000; BNFL Partnership Team, 2000–02; Dir, Innovation Gp, 2002–04; voluntary and public sector consultancy, 2005. *Recreations:* family, cooking. *Address:* 17 Stradella Road, SE24 9HN.

RHODES, John Ivor McKinnon, CMG 1971; *b* 6 March 1914; *s* of late Joseph Thomas Rhodes and late Hilda (*née* McKinnon); *m* 1939, Eden Annetta Clark (*d* 1990); one *s* one *d*. *Educ:* Leeds Modern School. Exec. Officer, WO, 1933; Financial Adviser's Office, HQ British Forces in Palestine, 1938; Major 1940; Asst Comd Sec., Southern Comd, 1944; Financial Adviser, London District, 1946; Principal 1947, Asst Sec. 1959, HM Treasury; Minister, UK Mission to UN, 1966–74. Member: UN Pension Board, 1966–71; UN Cttee on Contributions, 1966–71, 1975–77; Chm., UN Adv. Cttee on Admin. and Budgetary Questions, 1971–74; Senior Adviser (Asst Sec.-Gen.) to Administrator, UNDP, 1979–80. *Recreations:* gardening, playing the electronic organ. *Address:* Quintins, Watersfield, Pulborough, W Sussex RH20 1NE. *T:* (01798) 831634.
See also J. D. McK. Rhodes.

RHODES, Prof. Jonathan Michael, MD; FRCP, FMedSci; Professor of Medicine, University of Liverpool, since 1995; Consultant Gastroenterologist, Royal Liverpool University Hospital, since 1991; *b* 21 April 1949; *s* of late Wilfred Harry Rhodes and of Ellen Linda Rhodes (*née* Wreford); *m* 1978, Elizabeth Geraldine Helen Morris (*d* 2007); three *d*. *Educ:* Kingston Grammar Sch.; St John's Coll., Cambridge (MA); St Thomas's Hosp. Med. Sch. (MD 1982). FRCP 1989. House surgeon, St Thomas' Hosp., 1973; house physician and SHO, Kingston Hosp., 1974–75; SHO, Hammersmith Hosp., 1976; Registrar and Res. Fellow, Royal Free Hosp., 1976–81; Sen. Registrar, Queen Elizabeth and Selly Oak Hosps, Birmingham, 1981–85; Sen. Lectr, 1985–91, Reader, 1991–95, Univ. of Liverpool. Pres.-elect, 2002–03, Pres., 2003–04, Liverpool Medical Inst. Chairman: Educn Cttee, British Soc. Gastroenterology, 1996–2000; Gastroenterology Speciality Cttee, RCP, 1997–2001; Member: Exec. Cttee, Assoc. Physicians, 1999–2001; Council, RCP, 2003–06. FMedSci 1999. Avery Jones Res. Medal, British Soc. Gastroenterology, 1989; Bengt Ihre Medal, Swedish Med. Assoc., 2005. *Publications:* (ed jtly) Inflammatory Bowel Disease, 3rd edn 1997; contrib. papers on inflammatory bowel disease, colon cancer, lectins and glycobiology. *Recreations:* fell-walking, classical guitar, rowing coaching. *Address:* Department of Medicine, University of Liverpool, Liverpool L69 3GA. *T:* (0151) 706 4073. *Clubs:* Hawks (Cambridge); Leander (Henley); Bristol Owners.

RHODES, Nicholas Piers; QC 2008; a Recorder, since 2002; *b* 26 April 1958; *s* of Colin and Charlotte Rhodes; *m* 1999, Sally Ann; two *s*. *Educ:* Dover Coll. Jun. Sch.; Dover Coll.; Univ. of E Anglia (LLB Hons); Inns of Court Sch. of Law. Called to the Bar, Lincoln's Inn, 1981. *Recreation:* military history. *Address:* Charter Chambers, 33 John Street, WC1N 2AT. *T:* (020) 7618 4400, *Fax:* (020) 7618 4401; *e-mail:* Nick.Rhodes@charterchambers.com.

RHODES, Prof. Peter John, FBA 1987; Professor of Ancient History, University of Durham, 1983–2005, Hon. Professor, since 2005; *b* 10 Aug. 1940; *s* of George Thomas Rhodes and Elsie Leonora Rhodes (*née* Pugh); *m* 1971, Jan Teresa Adamson (marr. diss. 2001). *Educ:* Queen Elizabeth's Boys' Grammar Sch., Barnet; Wadham Coll., Oxford (minor schol.; BA (1st cl. Mods, 1st cl. Greats); MA; DPhil). Harmsworth Schol., Merton Coll., Oxford, 1963–65; Craven Fellow, Oxford Univ., 1963–65; Lectr in Classics and Ancient History, 1965, Sen. Lectr, 1977, Durham Univ. Jun. Fellow, Center for Hellenic Studies, Washington, DC, 1978–79; Visiting Fellow: Wolfson Coll., Oxford, 1984; Univ. of New England, Aust., 1988; Corpus Christi Coll., Oxford, 1993; All Souls Coll., Oxford, 1998; Leverhulme Res. Fellow, 1994–95; Langford Family Eminent Scholar, Florida State Univ., 2002; Invitation Fellow, Japan Soc. for the Promotion of Sci., 2005. Mem., Inst. for Advanced Study, Princeton, USA, 1988–89. Foreign Mem., Royal Danish Acad., 2005. *Publications:* The Athenian Boule, 1972; Greek Historical Inscriptions 359–323 BC, 1972; Commentary on the Aristotelian Athenaion Politeia, 1981; (trans.) Aristotle: the Athenian Constitution, 1984; The Athenian Empire, 1985; The Greek City States: a source book, 1986, 2nd edn 2007; (ed) Thucydides Book II, 1988; (ed) Thucydides Book III, 1994; (with D. M. Lewis) The Decrees of the Greek States, 1997; (ed with L. G. Mitchell) The Development of the Polis in Archaic Greece, 1997; (ed) Thucydides Book IV.1–Book V.24, 1999; Ancient Democracy and Modern Ideology, 2003; (with R. Osborne) Greek Historical Inscriptions 404–323 BC, 2003; (ed) Athenian Democracy, 2004; A History of the Classical Greek World 478–323 BC, 2005; (ed with E. E. Bridges and E. M. Hall) Cultural Responses to the Persian Wars, 2007; (ed with J. L. Marr) The 'Old Oligarch', 2008; articles and reviews in jls. *Recreations:* music, typography, travel. *Address:* Department of Classics, University of Durham, 38 North Bailey, Durham DH1 3EU. *T:* (0191) 334 1670.

See also J. A. Rhodes.

RHODES, Richard David Walton; JP; Headmaster, Rossall School, 1987–2001; *b* 20 April 1942; *er s* of Harry Walton Rhodes and Dorothy Rhodes (*née* Fairhurst); *m* 1966, Stephanie Heyes, 2nd *d* of Frederic William Heyes and Catherine Heyes; two *d*. *Educ:* Rossall Sch.; St John's Coll., Durham (BA 1963). Asst Master, St John's Sch., Leatherhead, 1964–75 (Founder Housemaster, Montgomery House, 1973–75); Deputy Headmaster, Arnold Sch., Blackpool, 1975–79, Headmaster, 1979–87. Member: Lancs CC Social Services Adv. Cttee, 1992–2001; Lancs Magistrates' Courts Cttee, 1993–96. Chairman: NW Div., HMC, 1987; Northern ISIS, 1993–95. Lay Mem., Family Health Services Appeal Authy, 2002–. Member: Independent Remuneration Panel, South Lakeland DC, 2003–08; Cumbria Probation Bd, 2004–08; Chair, Cumbria Bd, Nat. Probation Service, 2008–. JP Member: Cumbria Courts Bd, 2004–07; Cumbrian Lancs Courts Bd, 2007–. Member Council: Univ. of Salford, 1987–93; Lawrence House Sch., Lytham St Annes, 1988–93; Trustee, Lawrence House Trust, 1994–97 (Chm., 2000–08); Gov., Terra Nova Sch., Jodrell Bank, 1989–2005 (Chm. Govs, 2000–05). JP Fylde, 1978, Wyre, 1999, Furness, 2002. *Recreations:* photography, sports, motoring, gardening in the Lake District. *Address:* Fairview, Staveley in Cartmel, Newby Bridge, Ulverston, Cumbria LA12 8NS. *T:* (01539) 531634.

RHODES, Robert Elliott; QC 1989; a Recorder, since 1987; *b* 2 Aug. 1945; *s* of late Gilbert G. Rhodes, FCA and of Elly, who *m* 2nd, Leopold Brook (he *d* 2007); *m* 1971, Georgina Caroline (marr. diss. 1996), *d* of J. G. Clarfelt, *qv*; two *s* one *d*. *Educ:* St Paul's School; Pembroke Coll., Oxford. MA. Called to the Bar, Inner Temple, 1968, Bencher, 2007. Accredited Mediator, 2007. Second Prosecuting Counsel to Inland Revenue at Central Criminal Court and Inner London Crown Courts, 1979, First Prosecuting Counsel, 1981–89. Hd of Chambers, 1998–2003. Deputy Chairman: IMRO Membership Tribunal Panel, 1992–2001; ICAEW Appeal Cttee, 1998–2004; an AIDB Chm. of Disciplinary Tribunals, 2004–. *Recreations:* opera, ballet, theatre, reading, art, cricket, real tennis. *Address:* Outer Temple, 222–225 Strand, WC2R 1BA. *T:* (020) 7353 6381. *Clubs:* Garrick, Annabel's, MCC; Epee.

RHODES, Zandra Lindsey, CBE 1997; RDI 1976; DesRCA, FCSD; Managing Director, Zandra Rhodes Enterprises; *b* 19 Sept. 1940; *d* of Albert James Rhodes and Beatrice Ellen (*née* Twigg). *Educ:* Medway Technical Sch. for Girls, Chatham; Medway Coll. of Art; Royal Coll. of Art (DesRCA 1964). FSIAD 1982. With Alexander MacIntyre, set up print factory and studio, 1965; sold designs (and converted them on to cloth) to Foale and Tuffin and Roger Nelson; formed partnership with Sylvia Ayton and began producing dresses using her own prints, 1966; opened Fulham Road Clothes Shop, designing dresses as well as prints, first in partnership, 1967–68, then (Fulham Road shop closed) alone, producing first clothes range in which she revolutionised use of prints in clothes by cutting round patterns to make shapes never before used; took collection to USA, 1969; sold to Fortnum and Mason, London, 1969, Piero de Monzi, 1971; began building up name and business in USA (known for her annual spectacular Fantasy Shows); also started designing in jersey and revolutionised its treatment with lettuce edges and seams on the outside; with Knight and Stirling founded Zandra Rhodes (UK) Ltd and Zandra Rhodes (Shops) Ltd, 1975–86; opened first shop in London, 1975; others opened in Bloomingdales NY, Marshall Field, Chicago, Seibu, Tokyo and Harrods, London, 1976; new factory premises opened in Hammersmith, London, 1984; closed Mayfair shop, 1991, to show on a more personal and individual scale in her Hammersmith showroom. Since 1976 Zandra Rhodes has tried to reach a wider public through licensing her name in UK, USA, Australia and Japan, making full use of the Zandra Rhodes textile design talent for: wallpapers and furnishing fabrics, bathmats, men's ties, sheets and bed linen, printed shawls and scarves, hosiery, teatowels, kitchen accessories and jewellery. Notable licences include: Eve Stillman Lingerie (USA), 1977, Wamsutta sheets and pillowcases (USA), 1976, CVP Designs interior fabrics and settings (UK), 1977, Philip Hockley Decorative Furs (UK), 1986 and Zandra Rhodes Saris (India), 1987 (which she launched with 'West meets East' shows of Saris and Shalwar Chamises in Bombay and Delhi—the first Western designer to do so), Littlewoods Catalogues (UK), 1988 for printed T-shirts and Intasia sweaters; Hilmet silk scarves and men's ties (UK), 1989; Bonnay perfume, Coats Patons needlepoint (UK), 1993; Pologeorgis Furs (USA), Zandra Rhodes II handpainted ready-to-wear collection (HK, China), 1995; Grattons Catalogue sheets and duvets (UK), 1996; range of printed tops for Topshop (UK), 2002; Jewellery Licence, 2002; China licence for Royal Doulton, 2004. Designed stand with furniture and carpet for Hanover Expo, 2000. Designed: costumes for Magic Flute, San Diego Opera, 2001; costumes and sets for: Pearl Fishers, San Diego and Michigan, 2004, San Francisco and NY, 2005; Aida, ENO, 2007. Solo exhibitions: Oriel, Cardiff (Welsh Arts Council), 1978; Texas Gall., Houston, 1981; Otis Parsons, Los Angeles, 1981; La Jolla Museum of Contemporary Art, San Diego, 1982; ADITI Creative Power, Barbican Centre, 1982; Sch. of Art Inst., Chicago, 1982; Parsons Sch. of Design, NY, 1982; Art Museum of Santa Cruz Co., Calif, 1983; retrospective exhibition of 'Works of Art' with textiles, Museum of Art, El Paso, Texas, 1984; retrospective of Garments & Textiles (also Lead Speaker for Art to Wear exhibn), Columbus, Ohio, 1987; retrospectives for Seibu Seed Hall, Seibu, Tokyo, 1987 and 1991; Mint Mus., N Carolina, 1992; Athenæum Liby, La Jolla, 1996; water colour exhibition: Dyansen Galls, NY, LA and New Orleans, 1989; major group exhibitions: Nat. Gall. of Australia, 1993; V&A, 1994; RCA 1996. Work represented in major costume collections: UK: V&A; City Mus. and Art Gall., Stoke-on-Trent; Bath Mus.; Royal Pavilion Brighton Mus.; Platt Fields Costume Mus., Manchester; City Art Gall., Leeds; overseas: Metropolitan Mus., NY; Chicago Historical Soc.; Smithsonian Instn; Royal Ontario Mus.; Mus. of Applied Arts and Scis, Sydney; Nat. Mus. of Victoria, Melbourne; La Jolla Mus. of Contemp. Art; LA County Mus. of Art. Opening speaker, Famous Women of Fashion, Smithsonian Instn, Washington, 1978. Founded Fashion & Textile Mus., Bermondsey, 1996, opened to public, 2003. Hon. DFA Internat. Fine Arts Coll., Miami, Florida, 1986; Hon. Dr RCA, 1986; Hon. DD CNAA, 1987; Hon. DLitt Westminster, 2000; Hon. Dr London Inst., 2000; Hon. DHL Acad. of Art Coll., San Francisco, 2001. Designer of the Year, English Fashion Trade UK, 1972; Emmy Award for Best Costume Designs in Romeo and Juliet on Ice, CBS TV, 1984; Woman of Distinction award, Northwood Inst., Dallas, 1986; Top UK Textile Designer, Observer, 1990; Hall of Fame Award, British Fashion Council, 1995; citations and commendations from USA estabs. *Publications:* The Art of Zandra Rhodes, 1984, US edn 1985; The Zandra Rhodes Collection by Brother, 1988. *Recreations:* travelling, drawing, gardening, cooking. *Address:* (office) 81 Bermondsey Street, SE1 3XF. *T:* (020) 7403 5333, *Fax:* (020) 7403 0555; *e-mail:* zrhodesent@aol.com, zandra@zandrarhodes.com.

RHYMES, Rupert John, OBE 2002; Trustee and Chairman, The Theatres Trust, since 2002; Director, 2002–07, and Chairman, 2003–07, Bristol Old Vic; *b* 24 June 1940; *s* of Elson John Rhymes and Phyllis Rhymes (*née* Rawlings); *m* 1970, Susan Mary Chennells; one *s* one *d*. *Educ:* King Edward's Sch., Bath; Magdalen Coll., Oxford (BA Mod. Hist. 1962; MA). Box Office Clerk, RSC, Aldwych Theatre, 1962; Asst Manager, Sadler's Wells Theatre, 1963; Theatre Manager, Nat. Theatre, Old Vic, 1963–69; Sadler's Wells Opera, then English National Opera, 1969–87: Asst to Admin. Dir, then Head of Press and Publicity, then Gen. Manager, 1969–72, Co. Sec., and Admin. Dir, 1972–87; Chief Executive: SOLT, 1987–2001; Theatrical Mgt Assoc., 1987–2001. Chm., Oxford Stage Co., 1987–97. Director: West End Theatre Managers, 1978–87 (Pres., 1979–82; Vice Pres., 1982–83); Theatre Investment Fund, 1982–; Nat. Campaign for the Arts, 1988–2001 (Vice Chm., 1999–2001); Nat. Council for Drama Trng, 1997–2001. Dir, JFMG Ltd, 1997–. Founding Mem., later Mem. Exec. Council, Performing Arts Employers Assocs League, Europe, 1991–2001 (Chm., 2000–01). Trustee: Raymond Mander and Joe Mitchenson Theatre Collection, 1977–2001 (Chm., 1986–2001); Motley Design Course, 1985–; Chichester Fest. Theatre, 1998–2000; Stephen Arlen Meml Fund, 1993–; Olivier Foundn, 2007–. Gov., Central Sch. of Speech and Drama, 1990–2002 (Vice Chm., 1991–92). *Recreations:* finding time for theatre, protesting against further destruction in the city of Bath. *Address:* Honeysuckle Farm, Perrymead, Bath BA2 5AU. *T:* (01225) 834188.

RHYS, family name of **Baron Dynevor**.

RHYS, Prof. (David) Garel, CBE 2007 (OBE 1989); FIMI; SMMT Professor Emeritus of Motor Industry Economics, and former Director, Centre for Automotive Industry Research, Cardiff Business School, Cardiff University; *b* 28 Feb. 1940; *s* of Emyr Lewys Rhys and Edith Phyllis Rhys (*née* Williams); *m* 1965, Charlotte Mavis Walters; one *s* two *d*. *Educ:* Ystalyfera Grammar Sch.; University Coll., Swansea (BA); Univ. of Birmingham (MCom). IOTA 1972. Asst Lectr, then Lectr in Econs, Univ. of Hull, 1965–70; University College, Cardiff, subseq. University of Wales College of Cardiff, now Cardiff University: Lectr in Econs, 1971–77; Sen. Lectr, 1977–84; Prof. of Motor Industry Econs, 1984–2005; seconded to Cardiff Business Sch., UWIST, 1987–88, until merger with UC Cardiff to form UWCC; Head of Economics, 1987–99; Dir, Centre for Automotive Industry Res., 1991–2005. Member: RPI Adv. Cttee, 1992–96; Bd, WDA, 1994–99 (Special Advr, 1999–); UK Round Table on Sustainable Develt, 1996–2000; Motor Racing Industry Competitiveness Panel, DTI, 2003–; HEFCW, 2003–; National Assembly for Wales: Mem., Enterprise, Innovation and Ministerial Adv. Gp, 2006–; Chm., Economic Res. Adv. Panel, 2002–. Chm., Welsh Automative Forum, 2000–. Key Consultant, UNIDO, 1995–96; Consultant, EC, 2005–06. Advr to H of C and H of L select cttees, 1975–96. Pres., Inst. of the Motor Industry, 2004– (Vice-Pres., 1990–2004). Chm. of Trustees, Wales Video Gall., 2001–. FRSA 1991. Freeman, City of London, 2000; Liveryman, Carmen's Co., 2000–. *Publications:* The Motor Industry: an economic survey, 1972; The Motor Industry in the European Community, 1989; (contrib.) Industries in Europe: competition, trends and policy issues, 2003; (contrib.) Deep Integration: how transatlantic markets are leading globalisation, 2005; (contrib.) Outsourcing and Human Resource Management: an international survey, 2008; contrib. Jl Industrial Econs, Jl Transport Hist., Jl Transport Econs and Policy, Bulletin of Econ. Res., Scottish Jl of Political Economy, Industrial Relns Jl, Accounting and Business Res., Jl Econ. Studies, World Econs, Long Range Planning. *Recreations:* walking, gardening, theatre and opera, sports' spectator, amusing my grandchildren. *Address:* 14 Maes Yr Awel, Radyr, Cardiff CF15 8AN. *T:* (029) 2084 2714. *Club:* Royal Automobile.

RHYS-JAMES, Shani, MBE 2006; artist; *b* 2 May 1953; *d* of Harold Marcus Rhys-James and Jean (*née* Barker); *m* 1977, Stephen Alexander West; two *s*. *Educ:* Parliament Hill Girls' Sch.; Loughborough Coll. of Art; St Martin's Sch. of Art (BA Hons). Major touring exhibitions: Blood Ties, Wrexham Arts Centre, 1993; Facing the Self, Oriel Mostyn, Llandudno, 1997; The Inner Room, Stephen Lacey Gall., London, 2000; The Black Cot, Aberystwyth Arts Centre, 2003; one person shows: Martin Tinney Gall., Cardiff, 2005, 2008; Connaught Brown Gall., London, 2009. Mem., RCA, 1994. Gold Medal, Nat. Eisteddfod, 1992; Hunting/Observer Prize 1993; Welsh BBC Artist of the Year Award, 1994; Jerwood Prize, 2003; Creative Wales Award, Welsh Arts Council, 2006. *Publications:* Facing the Self, 1997; The Inner Room, 2000; (with Eve Ropek) The Black Cot, 2003; Imaging the Imagination, 2005; exhibition catalogues. *Recreations:* writing, vegetable gardening, restoring, music. *Address:* Dolpebyll, Llangadfan, Powys SY21 0PU. *T:* (01938) 820469; *e-mail:* shanirhysjames@btinternet.com.

RHYS JONES, Griffith; actor, writer, director and producer; *b* 16 Nov. 1953; *s* of Elwyn Rhys Jones and Gwyneth Margaret Jones; *m* 1981, Joanna Frances Harris; one *s* one *d*. *Educ:* Brentwood Sch.; Emmanuel Coll., Cambridge. BBC Radio Producer, 1976–79; *television:* Not the Nine O'Clock News (also co-writer), 1979–81; Alas Smith and Jones (also co-writer), 1982–87; Porterhouse Blue (serial), 1987; The World according to Smith and Jones, 1987; Small Doses (series of short plays) (writer, Boat People), 1989; A View of Harry Clark, 1989; Smith and Jones (also co-writer), 1992, 1995, 1997, 1998; Demob (drama series), 1993; Bookworm (presenter), 1994–2000; Restoration (presenter), 2003, 2004; Mine All Mine (drama serial), 2004; Restoration Village (presenter), 2006; Three Men in a Boat, 2006; Mountain (writer and presenter), 2007; Three Men in Another Boat, 2008; *theatre:* Charley's Aunt, 1983; Trumpets and Raspberries, 1985; The Alchemist, 1985; Arturo Ui, 1987; Smith & Jones (also co-writer), 1989–; The Wind in the Willows,

RNT, 1990; dir, Twelfth Night, RSC, 1991; The Revengers' Comedies, Strand, 1991; An Absolute Turkey, Globe, 1994; Plunder, Savoy, 1996; The Front Page, Donmar, 1997; *films:* Morons from Outer Space, 1985; Wilt, 1989; As You Like It, 1992; Staggered, 1994; Up and Under, 1998; Taliesin Jones, 2000; Puckoon, 2003; *opera:* Die Fledermaus, Royal Opera Covent Garden, 1989; *radio* series: (also writer) Do Go On, 1997–; (also writer) Griff Rhys Jones show, 2000–03. Director: TalkBack, Advertising and Production; Playback, 1987–; Smith Jones Campbell (formerly Smith Jones Brown & Cassie), 1988–99. Chm., Hackney Empire Appeal Cttee, 1998–2004. FRWCMD (FWCMD 1997); FRSA 2002. *Publications:* Janet lives with Mel and Griff, 1988; The Lavishly Tooled Smith and Jones; Smith and Jones Head to Head, 1992; To the Baltic with Bob, 2003; Semi-Detached, 2006; Mountain: exploring Britain's high places, 2007. *Address:* c/o Troika, 3rd Floor, 74 Clerkenwell Road, EC1M 5QA.

RHYS WILLIAMS, Sir (Arthur) Gareth (Ludovic Emrys), 3rd Bt *cr* 1918, of Miskin, Parish of Llantrisant, Co. Glamorgan; Chief Executive, Vitec Group plc, since 2001; *b* 9 Nov. 1961; *s* of Sir Brandon Rhys Williams, 2nd Bt, MP and of Caroline Susan, *e d* of L. A. Foster; *S* father, 1988; *m* 1996, Harriet, *d* of Maj. Tom Codner; two *s* one *d. Educ:* Eton; Durham Univ. (BSc Hons Eng); Insead (MBA). CEng; MIET; MIMechE; CCMI. Materials Manager, Lucas CAV, 1987–88; Managing Director: NFI Electronics, 1990–93; Rexam Custom Europe, 1992–96; Reg. Man. Dir, Central Europe, BPB plc, 1996–2000. *Recreations:* shooting, travel, chess. *Heir: s* Ludo Dhaulagiri Rhys Williams, *b* 12 Oct. 2001. *Address:* 9 Matheson Road, W14 8SN. *Club:* Garrick.

RIBBANS, Prof. Geoffrey Wilfrid, MA; Kenan University Professor of Hispanic Studies, Brown University, USA, 1978–99, now Emeritus; *b* 15 April 1927; *o s* of late Wilfrid Henry Ribbans and Rose Matilda Burton; *m* 1956, Magdalena Cumming (*née* Willmann) (*d* 2004), Cologne; one *s* two *d. Educ:* Sir George Monoux Grammar Sch., Walthamstow; King's Coll., Univ. of London. BA Hons Spanish 1st cl., 1948; MA 1953. Asst Lectr, Queen's Univ., Belfast, 1951–52; Asst, St Salvator's Coll., Univ. of St Andrews, 1952–53; Univ. of Sheffield: Asst Lectr, 1953–55; Lectr, 1955–61; Sen. Lectr, 1961–63; Gilmour Prof. of Spanish, Univ. of Liverpool, 1963–78; First Director, Centre for Latin-American Studies, 1966–70; Dean, Faculty of Arts, 1977–78; Chm., Dept of Hispanic and Italian Studies, Brown Univ., USA, 1981–84. Andrew Mellon Vis. Prof., Univ. of Pittsburgh, 1970–71; Leverhulme Res. Fellow, 1975; NEH Univ. Fellowship, 1991; Hon. Prof., Univ. of Sheffield, 1994–; Vis. Prof., Univ. of Salamanca, 1995. Lectures: Fundación Juan March, Madrid, 1984; E. Allison Peers, Univ. of Liverpool, 1985, 1994; Norman Maccoll, Univ. of Cambridge, 1985; Fordham Cervantes, NY, 1988; Raimundo Lido Meml, Harvard, 1998. Vice-Pres., Internat. Assoc. of Hispanists, 1974–80 (Pres., Local Organising Cttee, 8th Congress, Brown Univ., 1983); Pres., Anglo-Catalan Soc., 1976–78. Dir, Liverpool Playhouse, 1974–78. Editor, Bulletin of Hispanic Studies, 1964–78. Hon. Fellow, Inst. of Linguists, 1972. Corresp. Member: Real Academia de Buenas Letras, Barcelona, 1978; Hispanic Soc. of Amer., 1981. Hon. Mem., N American Catalan Soc., 2001. MA *ad eund.* Brown Univ., 1979. Special Prize for excellence in Galdós Studies, Las Palmas, 1997. Encomienda de la Orden de Isabel la Católica (Spain), 1997; J. M. Batista i Roca Prize for contributions to Catalan studies, Barcelona, 2000. *Publications:* Catalunya i València vistes pels viatgers anglesos del segle XVIIIè, 1955, 2nd edn 1993; Niebla y Soledad: aspectos de Unamuno y Machado, 1971; ed, Soledades, Galerias, otros poemas, by Antonio Machado, 1975, 17th rev. edn 2008; Antonio Machado (1875–1939): poetry and integrity, 1975; B. Pérez Galdós: Fortunata y Jacinta, a critical guide, 1977 (trans. Spanish 1989); (ed) Campos de Castilla, by Antonio Machado, 1989, 14th rev. edn 2003; History and Fiction in Galdós's Narratives, 1993; Conflicts and Conciliations: the evolution of Galdós's Fortunata y Jacinta, 1997; numerous articles on Spanish and Catalan literature in specialised publications; *festschrift:* Hispanic Studies in Honour of Geoffrey Ribbans, 1992. *Recreations:* travel, fine art. *Address:* c/o Department of Hispanic Studies, Box 1961, Brown University, Providence, Rhode Island 02912, USA.

RIBBINS, Maureen Margaret; Headmistress, Woldingham School, 1997–2000; *b* 16 Aug. 1947; *d* of Guy and Eileen Shoebridge; *m* 1969, Peter Michael St John Ribbins, Prof. of Educn Mgt, Birmingham Univ. *Educ:* St Joseph's Convent GS, Abbey Wood; Lady Margaret Hall, Oxford (MA Hons Physics 1968; PGCE 1969); Thames Poly. (MSc Hons Solid State Physics, London, 1972); Birkbeck Coll., London Univ. (BSc Botany 1977); Birmingham Univ. (Cert. in Higher Educn in Botanical Illustration, 2003). Teacher of Mathematics and Physics, Farringtons Sch., Chislehurst, 1969–73; Head of Science, Dartford Girls' GS, 1973–80; Headmistress: Walton Girls' High Sch., 1980–83; Wolverhampton Girls' High Sch., 1983–97. Assessor, Nat. Educn Assessment Centre, 1991–2001; accredited OFSTED Inspector, 1995–2001. Mem., Birmingham Soc. of Botanical Painters. *Publications:* reviews and articles in Jl of Educnl Admin, and Pastoral Care in Educn. *Recreations:* reading modern literature, Chinese brush painting, botanical illustration, walking dog, music.

RIBEIRO, Bernard Franciso, CBE 2004; FRCS; FRCP; Consultant General Surgeon, Basildon University Hospital, 1979–2008; President, Royal College of Surgeons of England, 2005–08; *b* 20 Jan. 1944; *s* of Miguel Augustus Ribeiro and Matilda Ribeiro; *m* 1968, Elisabeth Jean Orr; one *s* three *d* (incl. twin *d*). *Educ:* Dean Close Sch., Cheltenham; Middlesex Hosp. Med. Sch., London (MB BS 1967). LRCP 1967; MRCS 1967, FRCS 1972; FRCSEd (*ad hominem*) 2000; FRCP 2006; FRCA. Registrar, then Sen. Registrar, Middlesex Hosp., 1972–78; Lectr in Urology, Ghana Med. Sch., Accra, 1974. Mem. Bd of Visitors, HM Prison Chelmsford, 1982–92; Surgical Advr to Expert Adv. Gp on Aids (EAGA) and UK Adv. Panel for health care workers infected with blood-borne viruses (UKAP), DoH, 1994–2003. Hon. Sec., 1991–96, Pres., 1999–2000, Assoc. of Surgeons of GB and Ire; Mem. Council, RCS, 1998– (Chm., Quality Assurance and Inspection, 2002–05; Sen. Vice–res., Res., 2004–05); Med. Vice Chm. E England, Adv. Cttee on Clinical Excellence Awards, 2002–05. Mem., Test and Itchen Assoc., 1989–. Liveryman, Co. of Barbers, 1997– (Mem., Ct of Assts, 2006–). Mem., Editl Internat. Adv. Bd, Archives of Surgery, 2000–. Mem. Council, Dean Close Sch., Cheltenham, 2006–. Hon. Fellow: Ghana Coll. of Physicians and Surgeons, 2006; Acad. of Medicine, Malaysia and Singapore; Hon. FRCSI; Hon. FACS; FRCPSGlas; Hon. Mem., Acad. Nationale de Médecine. Hon. Liveryman, Cutlers' Co., 2008. *Publications:* (contrib.) Concise Surgery, 1998; (contrib.) Emergency Surgery: principles and practice, 2006; contrib. Archives of Surgery, Bull. of RCS. *Recreations:* fishing, riparian activities, shooting, interest in the history of war. *Address:* Borough Farm, Itchen Stoke, Alresford, Hants SO24 0QS. *T:* (01962) 733523; *e-mail:* bernard.ribeiro@btinternet.com. *Clubs:* Flyfishers'; Surgical Sixty Travelling.

RIBEIRO, Roberto Alexandre Vieira; Hon. Mr Justice Ribeiro; Permanent Judge, Hong Kong Court of Final Appeal, since 2000; *b* 20 March 1949; *s* of late Gilberto and Eleanora Vieira Ribeiro; *m* 1974, Susan Elizabeth Swan. *Educ:* La Salle Coll., Hong Kong; London Sch. of Econs (LLB 1971, LLM 1972; Hon. Fellow, 2007). Called to the Bar, Inner Temple (Hon. Bencher, 2003) and Hong Kong, 1978; Lectr, Faculty of Law, Univ. of Hong Kong, 1972–79; in practice at Hong Kong Bar, 1979–99; QC (Hong Kong) 1990; Judge, Court of First Instance, 1999, Justice of Appeal, 2000, Hong Kong. Pres., Alliance Francaise, Hong Kong, 2000–. Bd Mem., Hong Kong Internat. Film Fest., 2004–. Chevalier de la Légion d'Honneur (France), 2002; Chevalier, l'Ordre des Arts et des Lettres (France), 2002; Comdr, Ordre des Palmes Académiques (France), 2007. *Recreations:* dogs, wine, books. *Address:* Court of Final Appeal, 1 Battery Path, Central, Hong Kong. *T:* 21230012, *Fax:* 21210303; *e-mail:* rribeiro@netvigator.com. *Clubs:* Hong Kong, Lusitano, Jockey (Hong Kong).

RICE; *see* Spring Rice, family name of Baron Monteagle of Brandon.

RICE, Alice Elspeth Middleton T.; *see* Talbot Rice.

RICE, Prof. C(harles) Duncan, PhD; FRSE; FRHistS; Principal and Vice-Chancellor, University of Aberdeen, since 1996; *b* 20 Oct. 1942; *s* of James Inglis Rice and Jane Meauras Findlay (*née* Scroggie); *m* 1967, Susan Wunsch (*see* S. I. Rice); two *s* one *d. Educ:* Univ. of Aberdeen (MA 1st Cl. Hons Hist. 1964); Univ. of Edinburgh (PhD 1969). FRHistS 1996; FRSE 1998. Lectr, Univ. of Aberdeen, 1966–69; Yale University: Asst Prof. of Hist., 1970–75; Associate Prof., 1975–79; Prof. of History, Hamilton Coll., Clinton, NY, 1979–85; New York University: Prof. of History, 1985–96; Dean, Faculty of Arts and Sci., 1985–94; Vice-Chancellor, 1994–96. Dir, BT Scotland, 1998–2002; Vice Chm., Grampian Enterprise Ltd, 1999–2006. Board Member: Univs and Colls Employers' Assoc., 1997–2007; Rowett Res. Inst., 1998–; Scottish Opera, 1998–2004; Scottish Ballet, 1998–2003; Member: Council, Nat. Trust for Scotland, 1998–2004; Heritage Lottery Fund Cttee for Scotland, 2005–. Trustee, CASE Europe, 2005– (Chm. Bd, 2007–). Chm., UK Socrates-Erasmus Council, 1999–. FRSA 1996. Hon. DHL New York, 2004; Hon. DEd Robert Gordon, 2005. *Publications:* The Rise and Fall of Black Slavery, 1975; The Scots Abolitionists 1831–1961, 1982. *Recreations:* hill-walking, contemporary Scottish literature, opera. *Address:* University of Aberdeen, Regent Walk, King's College, Aberdeen AB24 3FX. *T:* (01224) 272134, 272135.

RICE, Condoleezza, PhD; Secretary of State, USA, since 2005; *b* Birmingham, Ala, 14 Nov. 1954. *Educ:* Univ. of Denver (BA Internat. Relns 1974; PhD 1981); Univ. of Notre Dame, Indiana. Prof., Stanford Univ., Calif, 1981–88; Dir, Soviet and E Eur. Affairs, Nat. Security Council, Special Asst to Pres. for nat. security affairs and Sen. Dir for Soviet Affairs, 1988–91; Stanford University, California: Prof., 1991–93; Provost, 1993–99; on leave of absence as foreign policy advr to George W. Bush, 2000–01; Nat. Security Advr, and Asst to the Pres. for Nat. Security Affairs, 2001–05. Hon. Dr Notre Dame, 1995. *Publications:* Uncertain Allegiance: the Soviet Union and the Czechoslovak Army, 1984; (with A. Dallin) The Gorbachev Era, 1986; (with P. Zelikow) Germany Unified and Europe Transformed, 1995; contrib. numerous articles on Soviet and E European foreign and defense policy. *Address:* Department of State, 2201 C Street NW, Washington, DC 20520, USA.

RICE, Dennis George, PhD; Social Security (formerly National Insurance) Commissioner, 1979–98; a Child Support Commissioner, 1993–98; a Recorder, 1991–97; *b* 27 Nov. 1927; *s* of George Henry Rice and Ethel Emily Rice; *m* 1959, Jean Beryl Wakefield; one *s. Educ:* City of London Sch.; King's Coll., Cambridge (Scholar and Prizeman; BA 1950, LLB 1951, MA 1955); London Sch. of Econs (PhD 1956). Called to the Bar, Lincoln's Inn, 1952. Served RAF, 1946–48. Entered J. Thorn and Sons Ltd, 1952; Dir, 1955; Man. Dir, 1956; Chm. and Man. Dir, 1958–69; in practice at Chancery Bar, 1970–79. Member: Cttee of Timber Bldg Manufrs Assoc., 1967–69; Cttee of Joinery and Woodwork Employers Fedn, 1968–69. *Publications:* Rockingham Ornamental Porcelain, 1965; Illustrated Guide to Rockingham Pottery and Porcelain, 1971; Derby Porcelain: the golden years, 1750–1770, 1983; English Porcelain Animals of the Nineteenth Century, 1989; Cats in English Porcelain of the Nineteenth Century, 2002; Dogs in English Porcelain of the Nineteenth Century, 2002; articles on company law in legal jls and on Rockingham porcelain in art magazines. *Recreations:* history of English porcelain, gardening. *Address:* Mouse Cottage, 28 Springett Avenue, Ringmer, E Sussex BN8 5HE. *Club:* Reform.

RICE, Maj.-Gen. Sir Desmond (Hind Garrett), KCVO 1989 (CVO 1985); CBE 1976 (OBE 1970); Vice Adjutant General, 1978–79; *b* 1 Dec. 1924; *s* of Arthur Garrett Rice and Alice Constance (*née* Henman); *m* 1954, Denise Ann (*née* Ravenscroft); one *d. Educ:* Marlborough College. Commissioned into The Queen's Bays, 1944; psc 1954; 1st The Queen's Dragoon Guards, 1958; jssc 1963; First Comdg Officer, The Royal Yeomanry, 1967–69; Col GS 4 Div., 1970–73; BGS (MO) MoD, 1973–75; rcds 1976; Director of Manning (Army), 1977–78. Col, 1st The Queen's Dragoon Guards, 1980–86. Sec., Central Chancery of Orders of Knighthood, 1980–89. An Extra Gentleman Usher to HM Queen, 1989–. *Recreations:* field sports, gardening. *Address:* Fairway, Malacca Farm, West Clandon, Surrey GU4 7UQ. *T:* (01483) 222677. *Club:* Cavalry and Guards.

RICE, His Honour Gordon Kenneth; a Circuit Judge, 1980–2000; *b* 16 April 1927; *m* 1967. *Educ:* Brasenose Coll., Oxford (MA). Called to the Bar, Middle Temple, 1957. *Address:* 4 Kings Road, Westcliff-on-Sea, Essex SS0 8BH.

RICE, Maureen; *see* Rice-Knight, M.

RICE, Maurice; *see* Rice, T. M.

RICE, Michael Penarthur Merrick, CMG 2002; FCIPR; Chairman, The Michael Rice Group Ltd, 1957–2005; *b* 21 May 1928; *s* of late Arthur Vincent Rice, Penarth, Glam, and Dora Kathleen (*née* Blacklock). *Educ:* Challoner Sch. Dir, Eastern England Television Ltd, 1964–83; Consultant/Advr, Govts of Egypt, Jamaica, Bahrain, Saudi Arabia and Oman; planner and designer, museums in Bahrain, Qatar, Saudi Arabia and Oman. Co-Founder, Public Relations Consultants Assoc. (Chm., 1978–81; Hon. Fellow, 1985); Advr, Bahrain British Foundn, 1980–2005; Chm., Bahrain Soc., 1997–; Mem., Internat. Assoc. of Egyptologists, 1990. Trustee, Soc. for Arabian Studies, 1978–. FCIPR (FIPR 1975). Aga Khan Award for Architecture, 1980. Order of Bahrain, 1st Cl., 2003. *Publications:* The Temple Complex at Barbar, Bahrain, 1983; Dilmun Discovered: the first hundred years of the archaeology of Bahrain, 1984; (ed jtly) Bahrain Through the Ages, 1986; Egypt's Making, 1990; The Archaeology of the Arabian Gulf, 1993; False Inheritance: Israel in Palestine and the search for a solution, 1996; The Power of the Bull, 1998; Egypt's Legacy: the archetypes of Western Civilization, 1997; Who's Who in Ancient Egypt, 1999; (ed jtly) Traces of Paradise: the archaeology of Bahrain 2500 BC–300 AD (exhibition catalogue), 2000; (ed jtly) Consuming Ancient Egypt, 2003; Swifter than the Arrow: the golden hunting hounds of Ancient Egypt, 2006. *Recreations:* collecting paintings, listening to music, the Eighteenth Century. *Address:* The North Wing, The Mansion House, Burley on the Hill, Oakham, Rutland LE15 7FH. *T:* (01572) 770696, *Fax:* (01572) 770694; *e-mail:* michaelricecmg@mac.com. *Club:* Athenæum.

RICE, Noel Stephen Cracroft, MD; FRCS, FRCOphth; Consulting Surgeon, Moorfields Eye Hospital, since 1996 (Consultant Surgeon, 1967–96); Hospitaller, St John of Jerusalem, 1996–2002; *b* 26 Dec. 1931; *s* of late Raymond Arthur Cracroft Rice and Doris Ivy Rice (*née* Slater); *m* 1st, 1957, Karin Elsa Brita Linell (*d* 1992); two *s* one *d*; 2nd, 1997, Countess Ulla Mörner. *Educ:* Haileybury and ISC; Clare Coll., Cambridge (MA,

BChir, MD); St Bartholomew's Hosp. House appts, St Bartholomew's Hosp., 1956–57; Jun. Specialist, RAF, 1957–60 (Flt Lt); Registrar, Sen. Registrar, Moorfields Eye Hosp., 1962–65; Sen. Lectr, 1965–70, Clin. Teacher, 1970–91, Dean, 1991–96, Inst. of Ophthalmology. Vice-Pres., Ophthalmol Soc.; Member: Council, Coll. of Ophthalmologists; Internat. Council of Ophthalmol.; Acad. Ophth. Internat. Vis. Prof., Nat. Univ. of Singapore. St Eric's Medal, Karolinska Inst., Stockholm. KStJ 1996. Order of the Falcon (Iceland). *Publications:* contribs to sci. jls on subjects related to ophthalmology. *Recreation:* fly fishing. *Clubs:* Oriental; Piscatorial Society.

RICE, Olwen Mary; freelance journalist; Editor, Woman's Weekly, 1993–98; *b* 2 Aug. 1960; *d* of James Rice and Mary Rice (*née* Wood); *m* 1990, Andrew Tilley; one *d. Educ:* Hagley Park Comprehensive Sch.; London Coll. of Printing. News Reporter, Oxford Mail, 1980–84; News Editor, Fitness mag., 1984–85; Health and Beauty Editor, Chat mag., 1985–87; Asst Editor, then Dep. Editor, Best, 1987–88; Editor, Living, 1988–93. *Recreations:* swimming, reading, cycling, writing.

RICE, Peter Anthony Morrish; stage designer; *b* 13 Sept. 1928; *s* of Cecil Morrish Rice and Ethel (*née* Blacklaw); *m* 1954, Patricia Albeck; one *s. Educ:* St Dunstan's Coll., Surrey; Royal Coll. of Art (ARCA 1951). Designed first professional prodn, Sex and the Seraphim, Watergate Theatre, London, 1951, followed by The Seraglio, Sadler's Wells Opera, 1952, and Arlecchino, Glyndebourne, 1954; subsequently has designed over 100 plays, operas and ballets, including: *plays:* Time Remembered, 1954; The Winter's Tale, and Much Ado About Nothing, Old Vic, 1956; Living for Pleasure, 1956; A Day in the Life of…, 1958; The Lord Chamberlain Regrets, and Toad of Toad Hall, 1961; The Farmer's Wife, The Italian Straw Hat, and Heartbreak House, Chichester, 1966; Flint, and Arms and the Man, 1970; Happy Birthday, 1977; Private Lives, Greenwich and West End, 1980; Present Laughter, Greenwich and West End, 1981; Cavell, and Goodbye Mr Chips, Chichester, 1982; The Sleeping Prince, Chichester and West End, 1983; Forty Years On, Chichester and West End, 1984; Thursday's Ladies, Apollo, 1987; Hay Fever, Chichester, and Re: Joyce!, Fortune, 1988; Don't Dress for Dinner, Apollo, 1990; Night Must Fall, Haymarket, 1996; The Importance of Being Earnest, Chichester, transf. Haymarket, 1999; *operas:* Count Ory, Sadler's Wells, 1962; Arabella, Royal Opera, 1964, Paris Opera, 1981, Chicago, 1984, and Covent Garden, 1986; The Thieving Magpie, and The Violins of St Jacques, Sadler's Wells, 1967; La Bohème, Scottish Opera, 1970; The Magic Flute, Ottawa, 1974; Tosca, Scottish Opera, 1980; The Secret Marriage, Buxton Fest., 1981; The Count of Luxembourg, Sadler's Wells, 1982, 1987; Death in Venice, Antwerp, and Die Fledermaus, St Louis, USA, 1983; Manon, Covent Garden, 1987; Così Fan Tutte, Ottawa, 1990, Hong Kong, 1991; Carmen, Hong Kong, 1992; Ottone, Tokyo, 1992, QEH, 1993; Madama Butterfly, Holland, 1993; L'Infedelta Delusa, Garsington, 1993; L'Etoile, La Bohème, Carmen, 1995–97, Martha, 2000, Castleward Opera, NI; Un Ballo in Maschera, Iris, Eugene Onegin, 1996–97, Così fan tutte, The Yeomen of the Guard, 2000, The Merry Widow, 2006, Opera Holland Park; *ballets:* Romeo and Juliet, Royal Danish Ballet, 1955, new prodn 1995, and London Festival Ballet, 1985; Sinfonietta, Royal Ballet, 1966; The Four Seasons, Royal Ballet, 1974. Theatre interiors: Vaudeville Theatre, London; Grand Theatre, Blackpool; His Majesty's Theatre, Aberdeen; Minerva Studio Theatre, Chichester. *Publications:* The Clothes Children Wore, 1973; Farming, 1974; Narrow Boats, 1976. *Recreation:* ancient films. *Club:* Garrick.

RICE, Rowena C.; *see* Collins Rice.

RICE, Susan Ilene, CBE 2005; FCIBS; FRSE; Chief Executive, Lloyds TSB Scotland, since 2000; *b* 7 March 1946; *m* 1967, Prof. C(harles) Duncan Rice, *qv*; two *s* one *d. Educ:* Wellesley Coll., Mass (BA); Univ. of Aberdeen (MLitt). Chartered Banker; FCIBS 2000; FRSE 2001. Dean, Saybrook Coll., Yale Univ., 1973–79; Staff Aide to Pres., Hamilton Coll., 1980–81; Dean of Students, Colgate Univ., 1981–86; Sen. Vice Pres. and Div. Hd, Nat West Bancorp., 1986–96; Dir, Business Projects, Hd, Branch Banking, then Man. Dir, Personal Banking, Bank of Scotland, 1997–2000. Non-exec. Dir, Bank of England, 2007–. CCMI 2003; FRSA 2004. Hon. DBA Robert Gordon Univ., 2001; Dr *hc* Edinburgh, 2003; Hon. DLitt Heriot-Watt, 2004; DUniv: Paisley, 2005; Glasgow, 2007. *Recreations:* opera, modern art, hill-walking, cycling. *Address:* 120 George Street, Edinburgh EH2 4LH.

RICE, Prof. (Thomas) Maurice, PhD; FRS 2002; Professor of Physics, Eidgenössische Technische Hochschule Hönggerberg, Zürich, 1981–2004, now Emeritus; *b* 26 Jan. 1939; *s* of James P. Rice and Maureen K. Rice (*née* Quinn); *m* 1966, Helen D. Spreiter; one *s* two *d. Educ:* University Coll., Dublin (BSc 1959, MSc 1960); Churchill Coll., Cambridge (PhD 1964). Asst Lectr, Birmingham Univ., 1963–64; Res. Associate, Univ. of Calif., San Diego, 1964–66; Mem., tech. staff, Bell Labs, Murray Hill, NJ, 1966–81. *Address:* Theoretische Physik, ETH Hönggerberg, 8093 Zürich, Switzerland. *T:* (1) 6332581, *Fax:* (1) 6331115; *e-mail:* rice@itp.phys.ethz.ch.

RICE, Sir Timothy (Miles Bindon), Kt 1994; writer and broadcaster; *b* 10 Nov. 1944; *s* of late Hugh Gordon Rice and of Joan Odette Rice; *m* 1974, Jane Artereta McIntosh; one *s* one *d*; partner Nell Sully; one *d. Educ:* Lancing Coll. EMI Records, 1966–68; Norrie Paramor Org., 1968–69. Lyrics for stage musicals (with music by Andrew Lloyd Webber): The Likes of Us, 1965; Joseph and the Amazing Technicolor Dreamcoat, 1968 (rev. 1973); Jesus Christ Superstar, 1970; Evita, 1976 (rev. 1978); Cricket, 1986; (with music by Stephen Oliver) Blondel, 1983; (with music by Benny Andersson and Björn Ulvaeus) Chess, 1984 (rev. 1986); (with music by Michel Berger and book by Luc Plamondon) Tycoon, 1992; (with music by Alan Menken) Beauty and the Beast, 1994 (some songs only); (with music by John Farrar) Heathcliff, 1996; (with music by Alan Menken) King David, 1997; (with music by Elton John) Aida, 1998; lyrics for film musicals: (with music by Alan Menken) Aladdin, 1992; (with music by Elton John) The Lion King, 1994, expanded for theatre, 1997; (with music by Elton John) The Road to El Dorado, 2000. Producer, Anything Goes, Prince Edward Theatre, 1989. Lyrics for songs, 1975–, with other composers, incl. Marvin Hamlisch, Rick Wakeman, Vangelis, Paul McCartney, Mike Batt, Francis Lai, John Barry, Freddie Mercury, Richard Kerr, Burt Bacharach, Graham Gouldman, Michael Kamen and Lalo Schifrin. Awards include: Oscar and Golden Globe for Best Original Film Song, A Whole New World (music by Alan Menken), 1992, for Can You Feel the Love Tonight (music by Elton John), 1994 and for You Must Love Me (music by Andrew Lloyd Webber), 1996; gold and platinum records in over 20 countries, 12 Ivor Novello Awards, 3 Tony Awards and 6 Grammy Awards. Broadcasting appearances over the years include Just a Minute, Countdown and Grumpy Old Men. Film début as actor in insultingly small rôle, The Survivor, 1980; even smaller rôle in About A Boy, 2002. Cameron Mackintosh Vis. Prof. of Contemporary Theatre, Univ. of Oxford, 2003. Chairman: Stars Organization for Spastics, 1983–85; Shaftesbury Avenue Centenary Cttee, 1984–86; Foundn for Sport and the Arts, 1991–; Pres., Lord's Taverners, 1988–90 and 2000. Mem. Council, Radley Coll., 1999–. Pres., Richmond Pk Cons. Assoc., 1996–2003. *Publications:* Heartaches Cricketers' Almanack, yearly, 1975–; (ed) Lord's Taverners Sticky Wicket Book, 1979; Treasures of Lord's, 1989; Oh, What a Circus (autobiog.), 1999; (with Andrew Lloyd Webber): Evita, 1978; Joseph and the Amazing Technicolor Dreamcoat, 1982; (jtly) Guinness Books of British Hit Singles and Albums and associated pubns, 1977–96, 31 books in all; (jtly) The Complete Eurovision Song Contest Companion, 1998. *Recreations:* cricket, history of popular music, chickens. *Clubs:* Athenæum, Garrick, MCC (Pres., 2002–03), Groucho, Dramatists', Saints and Sinners (Chm., 1990); Cricket Writers.

RICE, Victor Albert; Chief Executive, LucasVarity plc, 1996–99; President, Ravelin LLC, since 1999; *b* 7 March 1941; *o s* of late Albert Edward Rice and of Rosina Emmeline (*née* Pallant); *m* 1984, Corinne Sutcliffe. Left sch. at 16 to join Finance Dept, Ford UK, 1957; various finance posts with Ford, Cummins and Chrysler, 1957–70; Comptroller, Northern European Ops, Perkins Engines Gp, 1970–75; Corporate Comptroller, Massey Ferguson (Perkins' parent co.), 1975–78; Varity Corporation: Pres. and Chief Operating Officer, 1978–80; Chm. and CEO, 1980–96. Liveryman, Glaziers' Co., 1978–. Mem. Council, Univ. of Buffalo, 1999–. *Recreations:* golf, gardening, opera, ballet, theatre. *Address:* Ravelin LLC, Suite 202, 374 Delaware Avenue, Buffalo, NY 14202–1611, USA.

RICE-KNIGHT, Maureen, (Maureen Rice); Editor, Psychologies magazine, since 2005; *b* 13 Dec. 1958; *d* of Patrick Rice and Anastasia Rice (*née* McGuire); *m* 1986, David Peter Knight; one *s* one *d. Educ:* Gumley House Convent Grammar Sch., Isleworth; Polytechnic of Central London (BA Hons Media Studies). Magazines: Features Editor, Mizz, 1985; Dep. Editor, No 1, 1985; Editor, Mizz, 1986; Editor, 19, 1988; Editor, Options, 1991–98. *Recreations:* reading, cinema.

RICH, Michael Anthony; Regional Chairman, Industrial Tribunals, Southampton, 1987–96; *b* 16 March 1931; *s* of Joseph and Kate Alexandra Rich; *m* 1959, Helen Kit Marston, MB, BS; one *s* one *d. Educ:* Kimbolton Sch., Hunts; Leicester Univ. (LLM). Admitted Solicitor, 1954. Army Legal Aid, 1954–56; Partner, Rich and Carr, Leicester, 1960–76; Part-time Chm., 1972 and 1996–99, Permanent Chm., 1976, Industrial Tribunals. President: Leicester Law Soc., 1976–77; Council of Industrial Tribunal Chairmen, 1993–94. Trustee: Ulverscroft Foundn, 1972–97; Millennium Meml Hall Trust, 2005–. *Publications:* (with I. A. Edwards) Mead's Unfair Dismissal, 5th edn, 1994; Industrial Tribunal Chairmen's Handbook, 1997. *Recreations:* railway modelling, France. *Address:* 4 Hickory Drive, Harestock, Winchester, Hants SO22 6NJ.

RICH, His Honour Michael Samuel; QC 1980; a Circuit Judge, 1991–2005; *b* 18 Aug. 1933; *s* of late Sidney Frank Rich, OBE and of Erna Babette; *m* 1963, Janice Sarita Benedictus; three *s* one *d. Educ:* Dulwich Coll.; Wadham Coll., Oxford (MA, 1st Class Hons PPE). Called to the Bar, Middle Temple, 1958 (Bencher, 1985; Reader, 2006); a Recorder, 1986–91; Deputy High Court Judge: Chancery Div., 1992–2005; QBD, 1993–2005. Mem., Lands Tribunal, 1993–2006. Hon. Pres., Dulwich Soc., 2001. Medal of Merit, Boy Scouts Assoc., 1970. *Publication:* (jtly) Hill's Law of Town and Country Planning, 5th edn, 1968. *Address:* 18 Dulwich Village, SE21 7AL. *T:* (020) 8693 1957. *Clubs:* Garrick, Dulwich; Maccabæans.

RICH, Nigel Mervyn Sutherland, CBE 1995; Chairman, SEGRO (formerly Slough Estates) plc, since 2006; *b* 30 Oct. 1945; *s* of Charles Albert Rich and Mina Mackintosh Rich; *m* 1970, Cynthia Elizabeth (*née* Davies); two *s* two *d. Educ:* Sedbergh Sch.; New Coll., Oxford (MA). FCA. Deloittes, London and New York, 1967–73; Jardine Matheson, Hong Kong, Johannesburg, Manila, 1974–94; Man. Dir, Jardine Matheson Holdings, 1989–94; Chief Exec., Trafalgar House, 1994–96. Chairman: Hamptons Gp, 1997–2005; Exel plc, 2002–05; CP Ships, 2005; Xchanging plc, 2008– (Dep. Chm., 2006–08); Director: Matheson & Co., 1994–; John Armit Wines, 1996–; Pacific Assets, 1997–; KGR Absolute Return, 2005–; Bank of Philippine Is (Europe), 2007–. Co-Chm., Philippine British Business Council, 2001–; Dep. Chm., Asia House, 2005–. Hon. Steward, HK Jockey Club, 1994–. Chm. Govs, Downe House Sch., 2004–. Freeman, City of London, 1970; Liveryman, Tobacco Pipemakers' and Tobacco Blenders' Co., 1975– (Master, 2008–June 2009). *Recreations:* tennis, golf, horseracing. *Address:* SEGRO plc, Red Wolf House, 5–10 Bolton Street, W1J 8BA. *Clubs:* Boodle's, Hurlingham, Turf, MCC; Denham Golf; Royal and Ancient Golf; Royal St George's Golf; New Zealand Golf.

RICHARD, family name of **Baron Richard.**

RICHARD, Baron *cr* 1990 (Life Peer), of Ammanford in the County of Dyfed; **Ivor Seward Richard;** PC 1993; QC 1971; *b* 30 May 1932; *s* of Seward Thomas Richard, mining and electrical engineer, and Isabella Irene Richard; *m* 1st, 1956, Geraldine Moore (marr. diss. 1962); one *s*; 2nd, 1962, Alison Imrie (marr. diss. 1983); one *s* one *d*; 3rd, 1989, Janet Jones; one *s. Educ:* St Michael's Sch., Bryn, Llanelly; Cheltenham Coll.; Pembroke Coll., Oxford (Wightwick Scholar; BA (Jurisprudence) 1953, MA 1970; Hon Fellow, 1981). Called to Bar, Inner Temple, 1955, Bencher, 1985. Practised in chambers, London, 1955–74. UK Perm. Representative to UN, 1974–79; Mem., Commn of EEC, 1981–84; Chm., Rhodesia Conf., Geneva, 1976. Chm., Commn on Powers and Electoral Arrangements of Nat. Assembly for Wales, 2002–04. Parly Candidate, S Kensington, 1959; MP (Lab) Barons Court, 1964–Feb. 1974. Delegate: Assembly, Council of Europe, 1965–68; Western European Union, 1965–68; Vice-Chm., Legal Cttee, Council of Europe, 1966–67; PPS, Sec. of State for Defence, 1966–69; Parly Under-Sec. (Army), Min. of Defence, 1969–70; Opposition Spokesman, Broadcasting, Posts and Telecommunications, 1970–71; Dep. Spokesman, Foreign Affairs, 1971–74; Leader of the Opposition, H of L, 1992–97; Lord Privy Seal and Leader, H of L, 1997–98; Chm., H of L Select Cttee on Constitutional Reform Bill, 2004. Chm., World Trade Centre Wales Ltd (Cardiff), 1985–97; Dir, World Trade Centre (Hldgs) Ltd, 2002–. Pres., UK-Korea Forum for the Future, 2000–07. Member: Fabian Society; Society of Labour Lawyers; Inst. of Strategic Studies; Royal Inst. of Internat. Affairs. *Publications:* (jtly) Europe or the Open Sea, 1971; We, the British, 1983 (USA); (jtly) Unfinished Business, 1999; articles in various political jls. *Recreations:* playing piano, watching football matches, talking. *Address:* House of Lords, SW1A 0PW.

RICHARD, Alain; Member, Conseil d'Etat, France, 1993–95 and since 2002; *b* 29 Aug. 1945; *m* 1988, Elisabeth Couffignal; one *s* one *d*, and one *s* by a previous marriage. *Educ:* Lycée Henri IV, Paris; Univ. of Paris; Institut d'Etudes Politiques; Ecole Nationale d'Administration. Auditor, 1971, Maître des requêtes, 1978, Council d'Etat; teaching posts, Univs of Reims, Paris I, and Institut d'Etudes Politiques; Mem., Nat. Office, Parti Socialiste Unifié, 1972–74; Mayor, Saint-Ouen-l'Aumône, 1977–97 and 2001–; Deputy, 1978–93, Senator, 1995–97, for Val-d'Oise (Vice-Pres., Commission des Lois, 1981–86; Vice-Pres., Nat. Assembly, 1987–88); Minister of Defence, France, 1997–2002. Mem. Cttee, 1979, Exec. Bd, 1988, Parti Socialiste. Vice-Pres., Party of Eur. Socialists, 2003–. *Address:* 3 rue Dante, 75005 Paris, France; 28 rue René Clair, 95310 Saint Ouen l'Aumône, France.

RICHARD, Prof. Alison Fettes, PhD; DL; Vice-Chancellor, Cambridge University, since 2003; Fellow of Newnham College, Cambridge, since 2003; *b* 1 March 1948; *d* of Gavin and Joyce Richard; *m* 1976, Robert E. Dewar; two *d* (one *s* decd). *Educ:* Queenswood; Newnham Coll., Cambridge (BA 1969, MA); Queen Elizabeth Coll., London (PhD 1973). Yale University: Asst Prof., 1972–80; Associate Prof., 1980–86; Prof.

of Anthropol., 1986–2003; Provost, 1994–2002; Franklin Muzzy Crosby Prof. of the Human Envmt, 1998–2003, Emerita, 2003–; Dir, Yale Peabody Mus. of Natural Hist., 1991–94; Co-dir, Prog. of Conservation and Develt in Southern Madagascar, 1977–2003. Consultant, Species Survival Commn, IUCN, 1982–90. Member, Editorial Board: Folia Primatologica, 1982–95; Amer. Jl of Primatology, 1988–97. Member: Sci. Adv. Council, L. S. B. Leakey Foundn, 1986–96; Physical Anthropol. Rev. Panel, NSF, 1988–91; Sci. Adv. Council, Wenner-Gren Foundn for Anthropol Res., 1991–94; Nat. Council, 1992–95, Bd, 1995–2004, WWF-US; Bd, Liz Claiborne/Art Ortenberg Foundn, 1998–. Trustee, WWF Internat., 2007–. DL Cambs, 2004. Hon. Dr: Peking, 2004; Antananarivo, Madagascar, 2005; York, Canada, 2006; Edinburgh, 2006. Officier, Ordre National (Madagascar), 2005. *Publications:* Behavioral Variation: case study of a Malagassy lemur, 1978; Primates in Nature, 1985; contrib. numerous scientific articles on primate evolution, ecology and social behaviour to acad. jls. *Recreations:* opera, gardening, cooking. *Address:* Office of the Vice-Chancellor, University of Cambridge, The Old Schools, Trinity Lane, Cambridge CB2 1TN. *Club:* Athenæum.

RICHARD, Sir Cliff, Kt 1995; OBE 1980; singer, actor; *b* 14 Oct. 1940; *s* of late Rodger Webb and Dorothy Webb; *né* Harry Rodger Webb; changed name to Cliff Richard, 1958. *Educ:* Riversmead Sch., Cheshunt. Awarded 14 Gold Discs for records: Living Doll, 1959; The Young Ones, 1962; Bachelor Boy, 1962; Lucky Lips, 1963; Congratulations, 1968; Power to all Our Friends, 1973; Devil Woman, 1976; We Don't Talk Anymore, 1979; Wired for Sound, 1981; Daddy's Home, 1981; Living Doll (with The Young Ones), 1986; All I Ask of You (with Sarah Brightman), 1986; Mistletoe and Wine, 1988; The Millennium Prayer, 1999; also 37 Silver Discs and 3 Platinum Discs (Daddy's Home, 1981; All I Ask of You, 1986; The Millennium Prayer, 1999). Films: Serious Charge, 1959; Expresso Bongo, 1960; The Young Ones, 1962; Summer Holiday, 1963; Wonderful Life, 1964; Finders Keepers, 1966; Two a Penny, 1968; His Land, 1970; Take Me High, 1973. Own TV series, ATV and BBC. Stage: rep. and variety seasons; Time, Dominion, 1986–87; Heathcliff, Apollo, 1997. Top Box Office Star of GB, 1962–63 and 1963–64; UK's best-selling singles artist of all time, 2004. *Publications:* Questions, 1970; The Way I See It, 1972; The Way I See It Now, 1975; Which One's Cliff, 1977; Happy Christmas from Cliff, 1980; You, Me and Jesus, 1983; Mine to Share, 1984; Jesus, Me and You, 1985; Single-minded, 1988; Mine Forever, 1989; Jesus Here and Now, 1996; My Story: a celebration of 40 years in show business, 1998; (with Penny Junor) My Life, My Way, 2008. *Recreation:* tennis. *Address:* c/o PO Box 46C, Esher, Surrey KT10 0RB. *T:* (01372) 467752. *Club:* All England Lawn Tennis and Croquet.

RICHARDS, family name of **Baron Milverton.**

RICHARDS, Prof. (Adrian) John, PhD; Professor of Botany, University of Newcastle upon Tyne, 2002–04, now Professor Emeritus; *b* 26 Jan. 1943; *s* of Dr Taliesin Richards and Roonie Eileen Richards; *m* 1966, Sheila Mackie; one *s* two *d*. *Educ:* Leighton Park Sch., Reading; University Coll., Durham (BSc 1964; PhD 1968). Demonstrator, Botany Sch., Univ. of Oxford, 1967–70; University of Newcastle upon Tyne: Lectr, 1970–85; Sen. Lectr, 1985–96; Reader in Botany, 1996–2002. Mem., Jt Rock Gdn Cttee, RHS, 1995–. Vice-Pres., Botanical Soc. of British Isles, 2002–; Pres., Alpine Gdn Soc., 2003–06. *Publications:* Plant Breeding Systems, 1986, 2nd edn 1997; Primula, 1993, 2nd edn 2003; (with A. A. Dudman) Dandelions of the British Isles, 1997; numerous botanical papers, esp. in New Phytologist and Heredity. *Recreations:* Alpine gardening, plant exploration, mountain walking (especially in Greece), birding, photographing butterflies. *Address:* School of Biology, Ridley Building, University of Newcastle upon Tyne NE1 7RU. *T:* (0191) 222 8839, *Fax:* (0191) 222 5229.

RICHARDS, Alun; *see* Richards, R. A.

RICHARDS, Anne Helen; Chief Investment Officer, Aberdeen Asset Management plc, since 2003; *b* 7 Aug. 1964; *d* of Michael and Helen Finnigan; *m* 1991, Matthew John Richards; two *s*. *Educ:* Univ. of Edinburgh (BSc Hons Electronics and Elec. Engrg 1985); INSEAD (MBA 1992); CDipAF 1991. CEng 1992; MIET 1992; FSI 2007. Res. Fellow, European Lab. for Particle Physics, CERN, 1985–88; Consultant, Cambridge Consultants Ltd, 1989–91; Analyst, Alliance Capital Ltd, 1992–94; Portfolio Manager, J P Morgan Investment Mgt, 1994–98; Team Leader, Merrill Lynch Investment Managers, 1999–2002; Jt Man. Dir, Edinburgh Fund Managers plc, 2002–03. Mem. Council, Duchy of Lancaster, 2005–; Dir, Scottish Financial Enterprise, 2006–. Dir and Trustee, EveryChild, 2005–; Gov., Caledonian Res. Foundn, 2007–; Trustee, Univ. of Edinburgh Develt Trust, 2007–. *Recreations:* music, mountains, family, gardening. *Address:* Aberdeen Asset Management, Donaldson House, 87 Haymarket Terrace, Edinburgh EH12 5HD.

RICHARDS, (Anthony) Charles, LVO 2006 (MVO 1997); Deputy Master of HM Household and Equerry to the Queen, since 1999; *b* 20 Feb. 1953; *s* of Dudley Raymond Richards and Eleonora Caroline Richards (*née* Otter); *m* 1978, Serena Anne Spencer; three *s*. *Educ:* Marlborough Coll.; RMA Sandhurst. Commissioned Welsh Guards, 1973; served with 1st Bn Welsh Guards, UK and BAOR, 1973–82; seconded 1st Bn 2nd Gurkha Rifles, Hong Kong, 1982–84; Staff Coll., 1985; BAOR, 1986–90; 2 i/c 1st Bn Welsh Guards, UK, 1990–92; Staff Officer, HQ London Dist, 1992–94; Equerry to the Duke of Edinburgh, 1994–97; Div. Lt Col, Foot Guards, 1997–99, retired 1999. *Recreations:* shooting, fishing, travel. *Address:* Rotherby Grange, Melton Mowbray, Leics LE14 2LP. *T:* (01664) 434206.

RICHARDS, Arthur Cyril, FIA; consultant; *b* 7 April 1921; *s* of Ernest Arthur Richards and Kate Richards; *m* 1st, 1944, Joyce Bertha Brooke (marr. diss. 1974); two *s* two *d*; 2nd, 1975, Els Stoyle; two step *s* one step *d*. *Educ:* Tollington Sch., London. FIA 1949; FSVA 1962. Insurance, 1937–41. Served RAF, 1941–46. Insurance, consulting actuary, steel manufacture, investment banking, internat. property develt, 1946–64; Advr, Samuel Montagu & Co. Ltd, 1965–67; Gp Finance Dir, Bovis Ltd, 1967–71; United Dominions Trust Ltd: Gp Finance Dir, 1971–76; Gp Man. Dir, 1976–80; Chief Exec., 1981–83; Dir, 1978–88, Chm., 1983–88, Blackwood Hodge plc. Chm., Federated Land, 1982; Director: MSL Gp Internat., 1970–81; TSB Trust Co., 1981–88; Combined Lease Finance PLC, 1985–89; Hermes Gp, 1990–2002. *Recreations:* sailing, antiques.

RICHARDS, Brian Henry, CEng, FIET; consultant, Society of British Aerospace Companies, since 2002; *b* 19 July 1938; *s* of Alfred Edward Richards and Lilian Maud Richards (*née* Bennett); *m* 1961, Jane Wilkins; one *s* one *d*. *Educ:* Buckhurst Hill County Grammar Sch.; St John's College, Cambridge (Mech. Sci. Tripos, 1st Class Hons 1959, BA 1960; MA 1965). GEC Electronics, later Marconi Defence Systems, 1960–87: Guided Weapons Division: various develt, systems, project and gen. management appts, 1960–84; Dir, Guided Weapons, 1985; RCDS, 1986; Asst Man. Dir, 1987; Technical Dir, Hunting Engineering, 1988–90; Chief Exec., Atomic Weapons Estabt, 1990–94; Weapon Systems Dir, 1995–2001, Special Projects Dir, 2001–02, Dynamics Div., GEC-Marconi Dynamics, later Missile Systems Div., Alenia-Marconi Systems; Projects Advr, MBDA UK, 2002–03. *Recreations:* golf, listening to music, reading history, travel, water colour painting.

RICHARDS, Sir Brian (Mansel), Kt 1997; CBE 1990; PhD; Chairman: Alizyme plc, since 1996; Lipoxen plc, since 2005; *b* 19 Sept. 1932; *s* of Cyril Mansel Richards and Gwendolyn Hyde Richards; *m* 1st, 1952, Joan Lambert Breese (marr. diss. 2003); one *s* one *d*; 2nd, 2003, June Clark-Richards. *Educ:* Lewis Sch., Pengam, Glam; University Coll. of Wales, Aberystwyth (BSc); King's College London (PhD). British Empire Cancer Fellowship, 1955–57; Nuffield Fellowship, 1957; MRC Biophysics Research Unit, 1957–64; Reader in Biology, Univ. of London, 1964–66; Research Div., G. D. Searle & Co., 1966–86; Vice-Pres., UK Preclinical R&D, 1980–86; Chairman: British Bio-technology Ltd, 1986–89; British Bio-technology Gp, 1989–94; Oxford BioMedica plc, 1996–98; CeNes Ltd, 1996–98; LGC (Holdings) Ltd, 1996–2001; Peptide Therapeutics Group plc, 1997 (Exec. Chm., 1995–97; Dir, 1998–2003); Cozart Biosciences Ltd, 2001–07; MAN Alternative Investments Ltd, 2001–07. Director: Prelude Trust plc, 1997–2003; Innogenetics SA, 1997–2005; Drug Royalty Corp., 1998–2002; Summit (formerly Vastox) plc, 2005–08; Aitua Ltd, 2006–. Hon. Prof. in Life Scis, UCW, Aberystwyth, 1991–. Chm., Biotechnology Working Party, CBI, 1988; Mem., Res. and Manufg Cttee, CBI, 1988; Mem., Sci. Bd, SERC, 1987; Chairman: Biotechnology Jt Adv. Bd, SERC/DTI, 1989; Science-based Cos Cttee, London Stock Exchange, 1994; Member: Adv. Cttee for Genetic Modification (previously Manipulation), HSE, 1984–96; Gene Therapy Adv. Cttee, DoH, 1994–98; BBSRC, 1994–97; Consultant on Biotechnology, OECD, 1987; Specialist Advr, H of L Select Cttee II on Biotechnol. Regulation, 1993. Chm., Roslin Inst., 1995–99. Hon. DSc Abertay Dundee, 1997. *Publications:* papers in sci. jls. *Recreation:* gastronomic travel. *Address:* c/o Lipoxen plc, London Bioscience Innovation Centre, 2 Royal College Street, NW1 0NH.

RICHARDS, Carol Anne Seymour-; *see* Seymour, C. A.

RICHARDS, Charles; *see* Richards, A. C.

RICHARDS, Clare Mary Joan; *see* Spottiswoode, C. M. J.

RICHARDS, Hon. Sir David (Anthony Stewart), Kt 2003; **Hon. Mr Justice David Richards;** a Judge of the High Court, Chancery Division, since 2003; Vice Chancellor, County Palatine of Lancaster, since 2008; *b* 9 June 1951; *s* of late Kenneth Richards, MBE and Winifred Richards; *m* 1979, Gillian, *er d* of Lt-Col W. A. Taylor; one *s* twin *d*. *Educ:* Oundle; Trinity Coll., Cambridge (BA 1973; MA 1980). Called to the Bar, Inner Temple, 1974; Bencher, Lincoln's Inn, 2000. Junior Counsel (Chancery), DTI, 1989–92; QC 1992. *Address:* Royal Courts of Justice, Strand, WC2A 2LL. *Club:* Garrick.

RICHARDS, Sir David (Gerald), Kt 2006; Chairman: Premier League (formerly Football Association Premier League), since 1999; Football Foundation, since 2003; *b* 3 Oct. 1943; *m* Janet; one *s* one *d*. *Educ:* Comprehensive sch. Mech. engr with own business, 1970–2000; Chm., Sheffield Wednesday FC, 1990–2000. *Address:* Premier League, 30 Gloucester Place, W1U 8PL.

RICHARDS, Gen. Sir David (Julian), KCB 2007; CBE 2000; DSO 2001; Commander-in-Chief, Land Forces, since 2008; Aide-de-Camp General to the Queen, since 2008; *b* 4 March 1952; *s* of John Downie Richards and Pamela Mary Richards (*née* Reeves); *m* 1978, Caroline Reyne (*née* Bond); two *d*. *Educ:* Eastbourne Coll. (Hd Boy, Capt. of Rugger); UWCC (BA Politics and Econs 1974). CO 3rd Regt RHA, 1991–94; Col Army Plans, 1994–96; Comdr 4th Armoured Bde, 1996–98; Comdr Jt Force HQ, 1998–2001; Commander British Joint Task Force: East Timor, 1999; Sierra Leone, 2000; COS ACE RRC, 2001–02; ACGS, 2002–05; Commander: ARRC, 2005–07; NATO Internat. Security and Assistance Force, Afghanistan, 2006–07. Mem., RUSI, 1992– (Mem. Council, 1995–96). Admiral, Army Sailing Assoc., 2008–. *Publications:* articles in RUSI Jl, SA Inst. of Internat. Affairs Jl, British Army Rev., RA Jl and other mil. pubns. *Recreations:* offshore sailing, military history, riding, gardening, shooting. *Address:* c/o Regimental Headquarters Royal Artillery, Royal Artillery Barracks, Larkhill, Salisbury, Wilts SP4 8QT. *T:* (01980) 845788. *Clubs:* Army and Navy; Royal Artillery Yacht, Royal Cruising, British Kiel Yacht (Cdre, 2001–02; Adm., 2005–).

RICHARDS, David Pender, CBE 2005; Chairman: Prodrive, since 1984; Aston Martin Lagonda Ltd; *b* 3 June 1952; *s* of Geoffrey and Eileen Richards; *m* 1976, Karen Danahur; two *s* one *d*. *Educ:* Brynhyffryd Sch., Ruthin. Chartered accountancy articles, Cooke & Co., Liverpool, 1970–75; professional rally driver, 1976–81; World Rally Champion, 1981; Team Principal, BAR F1, 2002–04. *Recreations:* flying helicopters, tennis, classic sports cars, time with the family. *Address:* Prodrive, Banbury, Oxon OX16 3ER. *Clubs:* Royal Automobile; British Racing Drivers' (Silverstone).

RICHARDS, David Thomas; Director, Governance in Wales Programme, Welsh Assembly Government, since 2006; *b* 30 Nov. 1954; *s* of Ralph Henry Richards and Brenda Mary Elizabeth Richards; *m* 1979, Veryan Cumming Black; one *s* two *d*. *Educ:* Whitchurch High Sch., Cardiff; New Univ. of Ulster, Coleraine (BA Philosophy). Exec. Officer, DTI, 1978–79; Welsh Office: fast stream trainee, 1979–83; Principal: Housing Div., 1983–86; Local Govt Finance Div., 1986–90; Assistant Secretary: Econ. Policy Div., 1990–92; Industrial Policy Div., 1992–94; Finance Programmes Div., 1994–97; Principal Finance Officer, 1997–99; Finance Dir, Welsh Assembly Govt, 1999–2006. Chm., Steering Bd, UK Intellectual Property Office (formerly Patent Office), 2001–. *Recreations:* wine, books, playing the harp. *Address:* Welsh Assembly Government, Cathays Park, Cardiff CF10 3NQ. *T:* (029) 2082 5177.

RICHARDS, His Honour (David) Wyn; a Circuit Judge, 1998–2008; *b* 22 Sept. 1943; *s* of late Evan Gwylfa Richards and Florence Margretta Richards (*née* Evans); *m* 1972, Thelma Frances Hall; five *s*. *Educ:* Gwendraeth GS; Llanelli GS; Trinity Hall, Cambridge. Called to the Bar, 1968; a Recorder, 1985–98. Asst Comr, Boundary Commn for Wales, 1982–86, 1992–96.

RICHARDS, Edward Charles; Chief Executive, Ofcom, since 2006; *b* 29 Aug. 1965; *s* of Donald and Pat Richards; partner, Delyth Evans, *qv*; one *s* one *d*. *Educ:* London Sch. of Econs (BSc 1987; MSc 1989); Harvard Business Sch. (AMP 2005). Researcher, Diverse Prodns, 1988–89; Policy Advr, Nat. Communications Union, 1989–90; Advr to Gordon Brown, MP, 1990–92; Sen. Consultant, London Econs, 1992–95; Controller, Corporate Strategy, BBC, 1995–99; Sen. Advr, Prime Minister's Office, 1999–2003; Sen. Partner, 2003–05, Chief Operating Officer, 2005–06, Ofcom. *Recreations:* music, reading, film, theatre, sport, walking. *Address:* Ofcom, Riverside House, 2A Southwark Bridge Road, SE1 9HA. *T:* (020) 7981 3800, *Fax:* (020) 7981 3504.

RICHARDS, Sir Francis Neville, KCMG 2002 (CMG 1994); CVO 1991; DL; Director, Centre for Studies in Security and Diplomacy, University of Birmingham, since 2007; Chairman, National Security Inspectorate, since 2007; Governor and Commander-in-Chief, Gibraltar, 2003–06; *b* 18 Nov. 1945; *s* of Sir (Francis) Brooks Richards, KCMG, DSC and Hazel Myfanwy, *d* of Lt-Col Stanley Price Williams, CIE; *m* 1971, Gillian Bruce Nevill, *d* of late I. S. Nevill, MC and of Dr L. M. B. Dawson; one *s* one *d*. *Educ:* Eton; King's Coll., Cambridge (MA). Royal Green Jackets, 1967 (invalided, 1969). FCO, 1969; Moscow, 1971; UK Delegn to MBFR negotiations, Vienna, 1973; FCO, 1976–85 (Asst

Private Sec. to Sec. of State, 1981–82); Economic and Commercial Counsellor, New Delhi, 1985–88; FCO, 1988–90 (Head, S Asian Dept); High Comr, Windhoek, 1990–92; Minister, Moscow, 1992–95; Dir (Europe), FCO, 1995–97; Dep. Under-Sec. of State, FCO, 1997–98; Dir, GCHQ, 1998–2003. Chm., Internat. Adv. Bd, Altimo, 2008–. Chm., Bletchley Park Trust, 2007–; Trustee, Imperial War Mus., 2007–. DL Glos, 2007. KStJ 2003. *Recreations:* walking, travelling, riding. *Address:* King's Mill House, Painswick, Glos GL6 6RT. *Clubs:* Special Forces, Brooks's.

RICHARDS, Prof. George Maxwell, (Max), TC 2003; PhD; President, Trinidad and Tobago, since 2003; *b* 1 Dec.1931; *m* Jean Ramjohn; one *s* one *d.* *Educ:* Queen's Royal Coll., Port of Spain; Univ. of Manchester (BSc Tech 1955, MSc Tech 1957; Outstanding Alumnus Award, UMIST, 2003); Pembroke Coll., Cambridge (PhD 1963; Hon. Fellow, 2004). Trainee, United British Oilfields of Trinidad Ltd, 1950–51; Shell Trinidad Ltd: Asst Chemist, 1957–58, Chief Chemist, 1958–59; Auxiliary Plants Supervisor, 1959–60; Section Head: Distillation Processes, 1963–64; Catalytic Conversion Processes, 1964–65; Hd, Refinery Ops, 1965; University of the West Indies: Sen Lectr, 1965–70; Hd, Dept of Chem. Engrg, 1969–74; Prof. of Chem. Engrg, 1970–85, now Emeritus; Asst Dean, 1970–74, Dean, 1974–79, Faculty of Engrg; Dep. Principal, St Augustine Campus, and Pro-Vice-Chancellor, 1980–85; Principal, St Augustine, and Pro-Vice-Chancellor, 1985–96. Chm., Salaries Review Commn, 1977–2003. Hon. FIChemE, 2003. Hon. DLitt Sheffield, 2005. CMT (1st Class), 1977. *Address:* President's House, Queen's Park, Port of Spain, Trinidad and Tobago.

RICHARDS, Graham; *see* Richards, W. G.

RICHARDS, Sir (Isaac) Vivian (Alexander), KGN 1999; OBE 1994; cricketer; Chairman, West Indies Selection Committee, 2002–04; *b* St Johns, Antigua, 7 March 1952; *s* of Malcolm Richards; *m* Miriam Lewis; one *s* one *d.* *Educ:* Antigua Grammar School. First class débuts, Leeward Islands, 1971, India (for WI), 1974; played for: Somerset, 1974–86; Queensland, 1976–77; Rishton, Lancs League, 1987; Glamorgan, 1990–93; Capt., WI Cricket Team, 1985–91; played in 100th Test Match, 1988; scored 100th first class century, 1988; 100th Test Match catch, 1988; highest Test score, 291, *v* England, Oval, 1976; highest first class score, 322, *v* Warwicks, Taunton, 1985; fastest Test century *v* England, Antigua, 1986; highest number of Test runs by a West Indian batsman, 1991. WI team coach, tour of NZ, 1999. An ICC Ambassador. Hon. DLitt Exeter, 1986. *Publications:* (with David Foot) Viv Richards (autobiog.), 1982; (with Patrick Murphy) Cricket Masterclass, 1988; (with Michael Middles) Hitting across the Line (autobiog.), 1991; (with Bob Harris) Sir Vivian (autobiog.), 2000. *Recreations:* golf, tennis, music, football. *Address:* 36 Novello Street, SW6 4JB. *T:* (020) 7736 7420.

RICHARDS, Jeremy Simon; His Honour Judge Jeremy Richards; a Circuit Judge, since 2004; Designated Family Judge for Norfolk, since 2007; *b* 18 Sept. 1959; *s* of Richard Elwyn Richards and Rosemary Isobel Richards; *m* 1990, Lesley Isobel Seaton (*née* Buist); one *s* one *d.* *Educ:* Tywyn Sch.; UCW, Aberystwyth (LLB Hons). Called to the Bar, Gray's Inn, 1981; in practice as barrister, 1981–2004, specialising in children and family work for Official Solicitor, guardians and local authorities. Chm. (pt-time), Employment Tribunals, 1996–2004; Asst Recorder, 1998–2000, Recorder, 2000–04. *Recreations:* sailing, cooking. *Address:* Norwich County Court, The Law Courts, Bishopgate, Norwich NR3 1UR. *T:* (01603) 728200. *Clubs:* Norfolk (Norwich); Norfolk Punt.

RICHARDS, John; *see* Richards, A. J. and Richards, R. J. G.

RICHARDS, Dr John Arthur, OBE 1997; Leader, Climate Change Programme, British Council, since 2007; *b* 28 Nov. 1946; *s* of Clifford Alban Richards and Helen Mary Richards (*née* Shaw); *m* 1980, Asha Kasbekar; two *s.* *Educ:* Faringdon Sch.; The Coll., Swindon; Univ. of Surrey (BSc Hons (Chem.) 1969); Univ. of Nottingham (PhD (Organometallic Chem.) 1975). Plessey Co. Ltd: res., Allen Clarke Res. Centre, 1967–68; Manager, Components Gp, 1969–72; res., Centre de la recherche scientifique, Bordeaux, 1975–76; British Council: London, 1976–77; Bombay, 1977–80; Sci. Officer and Dep. Dir, Japan, 1981–87; on secondment to Cabinet Office, 1987–89; Dir, Sci. and Technol. Dept, London, 1989–92; Hd, Educn and Sci. Dept, 1992–94; Director: Thailand, 1995–2000; Hungary, 2000–03; Nigeria, 2003–06. *Recreations:* reading, canoeing and other water sports, travelling. *Address:* British Council, 10 Spring Gardens, SW1A 2BN.

RICHARDS, Prof. Keith Sheldon, PhD; Professor of Geography, University of Cambridge, since 1995; Fellow of Emmanuel College, Cambridge, since 1984 (Professorial Fellow, since 1995); *b* 25 May 1949; *s* of Maurice and Jean Richards; *m* 1973, Susan Mary Brooks. *Educ:* Falmouth Grammar Sch.; Jesus Coll., Cambridge (MA 1974; PhD 1975). Lectr, then Sen. Lectr, Lanchester Poly., 1973–78; Lectr, then Sen. Lectr, Univ. of Hull, 1978–84; University of Cambridge: Lectr, 1984–95; Reader in Physical Geog., 1995; Head of Geography Dept, 1994–99; Dir, Scott Polar Res. Inst., 1997–2002. Chm., Brit. Geomorph. Res. Gp, 1994–95; Mem., various NERC Cttees, 1990–93, 1995–97, Peer Review Coll., 2004–07. Vice-Pres. (Research), RGS, 2004–07; Pres., BAAS Geography Section, 2005–06. Mem./Chm., 2001 and 2008 RAE Panels. Cuthbert Peek Award, RGS, 1983. *Publications:* Stochastic Processes in One-dimensional Series: an introduction, 1979; (ed jtly) Geomorphological Techniques, 1982; Rivers: form and process in alluvial channels, 1982; (ed jtly) Geomorphology and Soils, 1985; (ed) River Channels: environment and process, 1987; (ed jtly) Slope Stability: geotechnical engineering and geomorphology, 1987; (ed jtly) Landform Monitoring, Modelling and Analysis, 1998; (ed jtly) Glacier Hydrology and Hydrochemistry, 1998; numerous papers on geomorphol., hydrology, river and slope processes in various jls. *Recreations:* reading, travel, opera. *Address:* Department of Geography, University of Cambridge, Cambridge CB2 3EN. *T:* (01223) 333393.

RICHARDS, Louise; Chief Executive, Computer Aid International, since 2007; *b* 11 July 1951; *d* of William and Evelyn Greene; *m* 1977, Anthony Richards. *Educ:* Univ. of Leicester (BA Hons). Head of International Department: NALGO, 1983–93; UNISON, 1993–2003; Chief Exec., War on Want, 2003–07. Board Member: Solidar, 2003–; Community HEART, 2003–; Justice for Colombia, 2003–. *Recreations:* music, theatre, film. *Address:* Computer Aid International, Unit 10, Brunswick Industrial Park, Brunswick Way, N11 1JL. *T:* (020) 8361 5540; *e-mail:* louise@computeraid.org.

RICHARDS, Prof. Martin Paul Meredith; Professor of Family Research, 1997–2005, now Emeritus, and Director of the Centre for Family Research, 1969–2005, Cambridge University; *b* 26 Jan. 1940; *s* of Paul Westmacott Richards and Sarah Anne Richards (*née* Hotham); *m* 1st, 1961, Evelyn Cowdy (marr. diss. 1966); 2nd, 1999, Sarah Smalley. *Educ:* Westminster Sch.; Trinity Coll., Cambridge (BA 1962; MA 1965; PhD 1965; ScD 1999). SRC Post-Doctoral Fellow, 1965–67; University of Cambridge: Res. Fellow, Trinity Coll., 1965–69; Mental Health Res. Fund Fellowship, 1970; Lectr in Social Psychology, 1970–89; Reader in Human Develt, 1989–97; Chm., Faculty of Soc. and Pol Scis, 1997, Head of Dept, 1996–99. Member: Biomedical Ethics (formerly Medicine and Society) Panel, Wellcome Trust, 1998–2006; Human Genetics Commn, 2000–05; Ethics and Governance Council, UK Biobank, 2006–. Vis. Fellow, Princeton Univ., 1966–67; Visitor, Centre for Cognitive Studies, Harvard Univ., 1967 and 1968; Winegard Vis. Prof., Univ. of Guelph, 1987; Hon. Vis. Prof., City Univ., 1992–94; de Lissa Fellow, Univ. of SA, 1993; William Evans Vis. Fellow, Univ. of Otago, 1997. Chm., Bardsey Is Trust, 1993–2000. *Publications:* (ed jtly) Race, Culture and Intelligence, 1972; (ed) The Integration of a Child into a Social World, 1974; (ed jtly) Benefits and Hazards of the New Obstetrics, 1977; (ed jtly) Separation and Special Care Baby Units, 1978; Infancy: the world of the newborn, 1980; (ed jtly) Parent-Baby Attachment in Premature Infants, 1983; Children in Social Worlds, 1986; (with J. Burgoyne and R. Ormrod) Divorce Matters, 1987; (ed jtly) The Politics of Maternity Care, 1990; (ed jtly) Obstetrics in the 1990s, 1992; (with J. Reibstein) Sexual Arrangements, 1992; (ed jtly) The Troubled Helix, 1996; (ed jtly) What is a Parent?, 1999; (ed jtly) Body Lore and Laws, 2002; (ed jtly) The Blackwell Companion to the Sociology of Families, 2003; (ed jtly) Children and their Families: contact, rights and welfare, 2003; (jtly) Supporting Children Through Family Change, 2003; (ed jtly) Kinship Matters, 2006; (ed jtly) Death Rites and Rights, 2007. *Recreations:* bird-watching, listening to blue grass music, alpine gardening. *Address:* c/o Centre for Family Research, University of Cambridge, Free School Lane, Cambridge CB2 3RF.

RICHARDS, Max; *see* Richards, G. M.

RICHARDS, Menna; Controller, BBC Wales, since 2000; *b* 27 Feb. 1953; *d* of late Penri T. Richards and of Dilys M. Richards; *m* 1985, Patrick Hannan. *Educ:* Maesteg Grammar Sch.; UCW, Aberystwyth (BA). Journalist, BBC Wales, 1975–83; HTV Wales: journalist, 1983–91; Controller, Factual and Gen. Programmes, 1991–93; Dir of Programmes, 1993–97; Man. Dir, 1997–99. Hon. Fellow: Univ. of Wales, Aberystwyth, 1999; NE Wales Inst., 2004; Cardiff Univ., 2007. FRTS 2001. *Recreations:* music, family, friends. *Address:* c/o BBC, Broadcasting House, Llandaff, Cardiff CF5 2YQ. *T:* (029) 2032 2001. *Clubs:* Royal Over-Seas League; Newport Boat.

RICHARDS, Prof. Michael Adrian, CBE 2001; MD; FRCP; Sainsbury Professor of Palliative Medicine, King's College London School of Medicine (formerly Guy's, King's and St Thomas' School of Medicine, King's College London), 1995–99; Chairman, National Cancer Research Institute, 2006–08; *b* 14 July 1951; *s* of Donald Hibbert Richards and Peronelle Imogen (*née* Armitage-Smith). *Educ:* Dragon Sch., Oxford; Radley Coll.; Trinity Coll., Cambridge (MA); St Bartholomew's Hosp., London (MB BChir, MD 1988). FRCP 1993. ICRF Res. Fellow, St Bartholomew's Hosp., 1982–86; ICRF Sen. Lectr, 1986–91, Reader in Med. Oncology, 1991–95, Guy's Hosp., London; Clinical Dir of Cancer Services, Guy's and St Thomas' Hosps, 1993–99. *Publications:* papers on breast cancer, cancer service delivery, palliative care, quality of life. *Recreations:* hill-walking, classical music. *Address:* Department of Palliative Medicine, St Thomas' Hospital, SE1 7EH. *T:* (020) 7188 4732; 42 Liberia Road, N5 1JR.

RICHARDS, Maj.-Gen. Nigel William Fairbairn, CB 1998; OBE 1987; Chairman, Confederation of British Service and Ex-Service Organisations, 1999–2002; *b* 15 Aug. 1945; *s* of late Lt-Col William Fairbairn Richards RA and of Marjorie May Richards; *m* 1968, Christine Anne Helen Woods; two *s* one *d.* *Educ:* Eastbourne Coll.; RMA Sandhurst; Peterhouse, Cambridge (MA). Commissioned, RA, 1965; regtl duty, 1966–76, UK, Germany, NI, Cyprus, Malaya; RN Staff Coll., 1976–77; MoD, 1978–80; Comd J Anti-Tank Battery, RHA, 1980–81; Directing Staff, RMCS, 1982–83; CO 7 Para Regt, RHA, 1983–86; MoD, 1986–88; Higher Comd and Staff Course, 1988; Comdr 5 Airborne Brigade, 1989–90; RCDS 1991; Dir Army Staff Duties, MoD, 1991–93; Chief of Combat Support, HQ Allied Command Europe Rapid Reaction Corps, 1994–96; GOC 4th Div., 1996–98. President: British Scouts Western Europe, 1994–96; Army Boxing and Hockey, 1996–98. Hon. Col, 7 Para Regt RHA, 1999–2005; Col Comdt, RA, 2001–06. Chm., Peterhouse Soc., 2001–04. *Recreations:* cricket, fishing, ski-ing, golf. *Address:* 14 Berkeley Place, Wimbledon, SW19 4NN. *Club:* Army and Navy.

RICHARDS, Prof. Peter, FMedSci; President, Hughes Hall, Cambridge, 1998–2006; *b* 25 May 1936; *s* of William and Barbara Richards; *m* 1st, 1959, Anne Marie Larsen (marr. diss. 1986); one *s* three *d*; 2nd, 1987, Dr Carol Anne Seymour, *qv.* *Educ:* Monkton Combe Sch.; Emmanuel Coll., Cambridge (BA 1957; MB BChir 1960; MA 1961; MD 1971; Hon. Fellow, 2002); St George's Hosp. Medical Sch.; Royal Postgraduate Medical Sch. (PhD 1966); FRCP 1976. Consultant Physician, St Peter's Hosp., Chertsey and Hon. Sen. Lectr in Medicine, St Mary's Hosp. Med. Sch., 1970–73; Sen. Lectr in Medicine, St George's Hosp. Med. Sch., 1973–79; Dean and Prof. of Medicine, 1979–95, Emeritus Prof., 1995, St Mary's Hosp. Med. Sch. (part of ICSTM, from 1988), Univ. of London; Pro-Rector (Medicine), Imperial Coll., 1988–95; Med. Dir, Northwick Park and St Mark's NHS Trust, 1995–98. Non-exec. Dir, W Suffolk Hosps NHS Trust, 2001–06. Chm., Council of Deans of UK Med. Schs and Faculties, 1994–95. Mem., Septemviri, Univ. of Cambridge, 2000–05. Med. Advr to Health Service Ombudsman, 1999–2001. Member: GMC, 1994–2003 (Dep. Chm., 1999–2002, Chm., 2002, Professional Conduct Cttee); Council, RCP, 1994–97. Mem. Council, Anglo-Finnish Soc., 1984–. Freeman, City of London, 1985; Liveryman, Soc. of Apothecaries, 1984–. Hon. Fellow, Hughes Hall, Cambridge, 2006. Founder FMedSci 1998. Kt, Order of White Rose (Finland), 2001. *Publications:* The Medieval Leper, 1977; (ed jtly) Clinical Medicine and Therapeutics, Vol. I, 1977, Vol. II, 1979; Understanding Water, Electrolyte and Acid/Base Metabolism, 1983; Learning Medicine, 1983, 17th edn 2006; Living Medicine, 1990; UCAS Guide to Entry to Medicine, 1996, 2nd edn 1997; (with S. Stockhill) The New Learning Medicine, 1997 (Soc. of Authors Prize for best gen. med. book, 1998); scientific papers esp. concerning kidney disease and criteria for selection of medical students in Lancet, BMJ, etc. *Recreations:* walking, listening to music, Finland, social history, cycling. *Address:* Barefords, 78 Commercial End, Swaffham Bulbeck, Cambs CB5 0NE. *T:* (01223) 812007; *e-mail:* pr229@cam.ac.uk. *Clubs:* Garrick; Hawks (Cambridge).

RICHARDS, Peter Graham Gordon; a District Judge (Magistrates' Courts) (formerly Stipendiary Magistrate), Staffordshire, 1991–2008; *b* 16 July 1939; *s* of David Gordon and Irene Florence Richards; *m* 1965, Jeanette Uncles (*d* 1997); two *d.* *Educ:* Univ. of London (LLM 1966). Schoolmaster, 1962–65; Lectr, 1965–68; called to the Bar, Middle Temple, 1968; Midland and Oxford Circuit, 1968–91. *Recreations:* sports broadcasting, travel, theatre, astronomy. *Address:* c/o Law Courts, Baker Street, Fenton, Stoke on Trent ST4 3BX.

RICHARDS, Philip Brian; His Honour Judge Philip Richards; a Circuit Judge, since 2001; *b* 3 Aug. 1946; *s* of late Glyn Bevan Richards and Nancy Gwenhwyfar Richards (*née* Evans); *m* 1st, 1971, Dorothy Louise George (marr. diss.); two *d*; 2nd, 1994, Julia Jones; one *d*, and one step *s.* *Educ:* Univ. of Bristol (LLB Hons). Called to the Bar, Inner Temple, 1969; Asst Recorder, 1995–2000; Recorder, 2000–01. *Publications:* (jtly) Government of Wales Bill, 1996; Report on Judicial training in the Welsh language, 2003. *Recreations:* music, sport, theatre, literature, the history, culture, languages and constitution of Wales. *Address:* Cardiff Crown Court, Cathays Park, Cardiff CF10 3PG. *T:* (029) 2041 4400. *Clubs:* Cardiff and County; Mountain Ash Rugby Football.

RICHARDS, Sir Rex (Edward), Kt 1977; DSc Oxon 1970; FRS 1959; FRSC; Chancellor, Exeter University, 1982–98; *b* 28 Oct. 1922; *s* of H. W. and E. N. Richards; *m* 1948, Eva Edith Vago; two *d. Educ:* Colyton Grammar School, Devon; St John's College, Oxford. Senior Demy, Magdalen College, Oxford, 1946; MA; DPhil; Fellow, Lincoln College, Oxford, 1947–64, Hon. Fellow, 1968; Research Fellow, Harvard University, 1955; Dr Lee's Prof. of Chemistry, Oxford, 1964–70; Fellow, Exeter College, 1964–69; Warden, Merton Coll., Oxford, 1969–84, Hon. Fellow, 1984; Vice-Chancellor, Oxford Univ., 1977–81; Hon. Fellow, St John's Coll., Oxford, 1968; Associate Fellow, Morse Coll., Yale, 1974–79. Director: IBM-UK Ltd, 1978–83; Oxford Instruments Group, 1982–91. Chm., BPMF, 1986–93; Dir, Leverhulme Trust, 1984–93; Chm., Task Force on Clinical Academic Careers, 1996–97. Member: Chemical Society Council, 1957, 1987–93; Faraday Society Council, 1963; Royal Soc. Council, 1973–75; Scientific Adv. Cttee, Nat. Gall., 1978–2007; ABRC, 1980–83; ACARD, 1984–87; Comr, Royal Commn for the Exhibition of 1851, 1984–97; Pres., Royal Soc. of Chemistry, 1990–92; Trustee: CIBA Foundn, 1978–97; Nat. Heritage Memorial Fund, 1980–84; Tate Gall., 1982–88, 1991–93; Nat. Gall., 1982–88, 1989–93; Henry Moore Foundn, 1989–2003 (Vice-Chm., 1993–94; Chm., 1994–2001); Chm., Nat. Gall. Trust, 1995–99 (Trustee, 1995–2007). Tilden Lectr, 1962. FRIC 1970. Hon. FRCP 1987; Hon. FBA 1990; Hon. FRAM 1991. Hon. DSc: East Anglia, 1971; Exeter, 1975; Leicester, 1978; Salford, 1979; Edinburgh, 1981; Leeds, 1984; Kent, 1987; Birmingham, 1993; London, 1994; Oxford Brookes, 1998; Warwick, 1999; Hon. LLD Dundee, 1977; Hon. ScD Cambridge, 1987. Centenary Fellow, Thames Polytechnic (subseq. Univ. of Greenwich), 1990. For. Associate, Académie des Sciences, France, 1995. Corday-Morgan Medal of Chemical Soc., 1954; Davy Medal, Royal Soc., 1976; Award in Theoretical Chemistry and Spectroscopy, Chem. Soc., 1977; Educn in Partnership with Industry or Commerce Award, DTI, 1982; Medal of Honour, Rheinische Friedrich-Wilhelms Univ., Bonn, 1983; Royal Medal, Royal Soc., 1986; President's Medal, Soc. of Chemical Ind., 1991. *Publications:* various contributions to scientific journals. *Recreation:* enjoying painting and sculpture. *Address:* Unit 4, West Heanton, Buckland Filleigh, Beaworthy, Devon EX21 5PJ. *T:* (01409) 281985.

RICHARDS, (Richard) Alun; Welsh Secretary in charge of Welsh Office Agriculture Department, 1978–81, retired; *b* 2 Jan. 1920; *s* of Sylvanus and Gwladys Richards, Llanbrynmair, Powys; *m* 1944, Ann Elonwy Mary, (Nansi), Price (decd), Morriston, Swansea; two *s. Educ:* Machynlleth County Sch.; Liverpool Univ. (BVSc, MRCVS, 1942). Veterinary Officer with State Vet. Service, Caernarfon and Glamorgan, 1943–57; Divl Vet. Officer, HQ Tolworth and in Warwick, 1957–65; Dep. Reg. Vet. Officer (Wales), 1965–67; seconded to NZ Govt to advise on control of Foot and Mouth disease, 1967–68; Reg. Vet. Officer, HQ Tolworth, 1968–71; Asst Chief Vet. Officer, 1971–77; Asst Sec., Welsh Dept, MAFF, 1977–78; Under-Sec., 1978. *Publications:* contrib. to vet. jls. *Recreations:* beekeeping, fishing, playing bridge. *Address:* Penrhiw, Cefnllan, Waunfawr, Aberystwyth SY23 3QB. *T:* (01970) 617107.
See also Rt Hon. Sir S. P. Richards.

RICHARDS, (Robert) John (Godwin); Chief Executive, Hammerson plc, since 1999; *b* 11 Jan. 1956; *m* 1987, Amanda Joseph; two *s. Educ:* Poly. of Wales (BSc). FRICS. Joined Hammerson plc, 1981; Dir, 1990–; UK Develt Dir, 1990–93; UK Man. Dir, 1993–97; Internat. Man. Dir, 1997–99. Pres., British Council of Shopping Centres, 2003–04. *Address:* Hammerson plc, 10 Grosvenor Street, W1K 4BJ. *T:* (020) 7887 1000.

RICHARDS, Roderick; Member (C) Wales North, National Assembly for Wales, 1999–2002; *b* 12 March 1947; *s* of Ivor George Richards and Lizzie Jane Richards (*née* Evans); *m* 1975, Elizabeth Knight; two *s* one *d. Educ:* Llandovery College; Univ. of Wales (BSc Econ). Short service commn, RM, 1969–71. Ministry of Defence, 1977–83; broadcaster and journalist, 1983–89; Special Adviser to Sec. of State for Wales, 1990. Contested (C): Carmarthen, 1987; Vale of Glamorgan, May 1989. MP (C) Clwyd North West, 1992–97; contested (C) Clwyd West, 1997. PPS to Minister of State, FCO, 1993–94; Parly Under-Sec. of State, Welsh Office, 1994–96. Mem. Welsh Affairs Select Cttee, 1992–93. Welsh Cons. Leader, 1998–99. *Recreations:* Rugby, cricket, walking, games. *Clubs:* Special Forces; Llanelli Rugby; Colwyn Bay Cricket.

RICHARDS, Rt Hon. Sir Stephen (Price), Kt 1997; PC 2005; **Rt Hon. Lord Justice Richards;** a Lord Justice of Appeal, since 2005; *b* 8 Dec. 1950; *s* of Richard Alun Richards, *qv*; *m* 1976, Lucy Elizabeth Stubbings, MA; two *s* one *d. Educ:* King's Coll. Sch., Wimbledon; St John's Coll., Oxford (open schol.; BA Lit.Hum. 1972; BA Jurisprudence 1974; MA 1977). Called to the Bar, Gray's Inn, 1975 (Arden Schol. and Bacon Schol.; Bencher, 1992); Second Jun. Counsel, 1987–89, Standing Counsel, 1989–91, to Dir Gen. of Fair Trading; a Jun. Counsel to the Crown, 1990–91, First Jun. Treasury Counsel, Common Law, 1992–97; an Asst Recorder, 1992–96; a Recorder, 1996–97; a Judge of High Court of Justice, QBD, 1997–2005; a Presiding Judge, Wales and Chester Circuit, 2000–03. Dep. Chm., Boundary Commn for Wales, 2001–05. Governor, King's Coll. Sch., Wimbledon, 1998–2007 (Chm., 2004–07). Hon. LLD Glamorgan, 2004. *Publication:* (ed jtly) Chitty on Contracts, 25th edn 1983, 26th edn 1989. *Recreations:* walking, relaxing in the Welsh hills. *Address:* Royal Courts of Justice, Strand, WC2A 2LL.

RICHARDS, Sir Vivian; *see* Richards, Sir I. V. A.

RICHARDS, Prof. (William) Graham, CBE 2001; DPhil, DSc; Professor of Chemistry, 1996–2007, and Chairman of Chemistry, 1997–2006, Oxford University; Fellow of Brasenose College, Oxford, since 1966; *b* 1 Oct. 1939; *o s* of Percy Richards and Julia Richards (*née* Evans); *m* 1st, 1970, Jessamy Kershaw (*d* 1988); two *s*; 2nd, 1996, Mary Elizabeth Phillips. *Educ:* Birkenhead Sch.; Brasenose Coll., Oxford (MA; DPhil 1964; DSc 1985). ICI Res. Fellow, Balliol Coll., Oxford, 1964 (Hon. Fellow, 2006); Res. Fellow, CNRS, Paris, 1965; Lectr, 1966–94, Reader in Computational Chemistry, 1994–96, Dept of Physical Chemistry, Oxford Univ. Director: Oxford Molecular Gp plc, 1989–99 (Founding Scientist, 1989, Chm., 1990–93); Isis Innovation Ltd, 1994–2007; Catalyst Biomedica Ltd, 1998–2003; IP Gp Plc (formerly IP2IPO Gp), 2000– (Chm., 2004–06); Oxeco Plc, 2006–; Chm. and Founding Scientist, Inhibox Ltd, 2002–. Res. Schol., Stanford Univ., 1975–76; Visiting Professor: Univ. of Calif at Berkeley, 1975–76; Stanford Univ., 1978–82. Mem., Bd of Dirs, Assoc. for Internat. Cancer Res., 1995–99. Editor, Jl of Molecular Graphics, 1984–96. Marlow Medal, 1972, Award for Theoretical Chem., 1989, RSC; Lloyd of Kilgerran Prize, Foundn for Sci. and Technol., 1996; Mullard Award, Royal Soc., 1998; Italgas Prize, 2001; Award for Computers in Chemical and Pharmaceutical Res., American Chemical Soc., 2004. *Publications:* Ab Initio Molecular Orbital Calculations for Chemists, 1970, 2nd edn 1983; Bibliography of Ab Initio Wave Functions, 1971, supplements, 1974, 1978, 1981; Entropy and Energy Levels, 1974; Structure and Spectra of Atoms, 1976; Quantum Pharmacology, 1977, 2nd edn 1983; Spin-Orbit Coupling in Molecules, 1981; Structure and Spectra of Molecules, 1985; The Problems of Chemistry, 1986; Computer-Aided Molecular Design, 1989; Energy Levels of Atoms and Molecules, 1994; Computational Chemistry, 1995; An Introduction to Statistical Thermodynamics, 1995. *Recreations:* sport, running, swimming. *Address:* Brasenose College, Oxford OX1 4AJ. *T:* (01865) 277830. *Club:* Vincent's (Oxford).

RICHARDS, Wyn; *see* Richards, D. W.

RICHARDSON, family name of **Baron Richardson of Duntisbourne** and **Baroness Richardson of Calow**.

RICHARDSON OF CALOW, Baroness *cr* 1998 (Life Peer), of Calow in the co. of Derbyshire; **Rev. Kathleen Margaret Richardson,** OBE 1996; Moderator, Churches' Commission for Inter-Faith Relations, 1999–2006; *b* 24 Feb. 1938; *d* of Francis and Margaret Fountain; *m* 1964, Ian David Godfrey Richardson; three *d. Educ:* St Helena Sch., Chesterfield; Stockwell Coll. (Cert Ed); Deaconess Coll., Ilkley; Wesley House, Cambridge. School teacher, 1958–61. Wesley Deaconess, Champness Hall, Rochdale, 1961–64; Lay Worker, Team Ministry, Stevenage, 1973–77; Minister, Denby Dale and Clayton West Circuit, 1979–87; ordained presbyter, 1980; Chm., West Yorks Dist, 1987–95. Pres., Methodist Conf., 1992–93; Moderator, Free Church Federal Council, subseq. Free Churches' Council, 1995–99; a President, Churches Together in England, 1995–99; Chm., Commn on Urban Life and Faith, 2004–06. Hon. DLitt Bradford, 1994; Hon. LLD Liverpool, 1999; Hon. DD Birmingham, 2000. *Recreations:* reading, needlework.

RICHARDSON OF DUNTISBOURNE, Baron *cr* 1983 (Life Peer), of Duntisbourne in the County of Gloucestershire; **Gordon William Humphreys Richardson,** KG 1983; MBE (mil.) 1944; TD 1979; PC 1976; DL; Governor, Bank of England, 1973–83, Member, Court of the Bank of England, 1967–83; Senior International Adviser, Morgan Stanley & Co. Inc., since 1997; *b* 25 Nov. 1915; *er s* of John Robert and Nellie Richardson; *m* 1941, Margaret Alison (*d* 2005), *er d* of Canon H. R. L. Sheppard; one *s* one *d. Educ:* Nottingham High School; Gonville and Caius College, Cambridge (MA, LLB). Commnd S Notts Hussars Yeomanry, 1939; Staff Coll., Camberley, 1941; served until 1946. Called to Bar, Gray's Inn, 1946 (Hon. Bencher, 1973); Mem. Bar Council, 1951–55; ceased practice at Bar, Aug. 1955. Industrial and Commercial Finance Corp. Ltd, 1955–57; Director: J. Henry Schroder & Co., 1957; Lloyds Bank Ltd, 1960–67 (Vice-Chm., 1962–66); Legal and General Assurance Soc., Ltd, 1956–70 (Vice-Chm. 1959–70); Rolls Royce (1971) Ltd, 1971–73; ICI Ltd, 1972–73; Chairman: J. Henry Schroder Wagg & Co. Ltd, 1962–72; Schroders Ltd, 1966–73; Schroder Banking Corp. Inc. (NY), 1968–73; Morgan Stanley Internat. Inc., 1986–95. Mem., Adv. Bd, Morgan Stanley Dean Witter; Chm. and Vice-Chm., Internat. Adv. Bd, Chase Manhattan. Chm., Industrial Develt Adv. Bd, 1972–73. Mem. Company Law Amendment Committee (Jenkins Committee), 1959–62; Chm. Cttee on Turnover Taxation, 1963. Member: Court of London University, 1962–65; NEDC, 1971–73, 1980–83; Trustee, National Gallery, 1971–73, Chm., Pilgrim Trust, 1984–88. One of HM Lieutenants, City of London, 1974–83; High Steward of Westminster, 1985–89; DL Glos, 1983. Deputy High Steward, Univ. of Cambridge, 1982–; Hon. Fellow: Gonville and Caius Coll., 1977; Wolfson Coll., Cambridge, 1977. Hon. LLD Cambridge, 1979; Hon. DSc: City Univ., 1976; Aston, 1979; Hon. DCL East Anglia, 1984. Benjamin Franklin Medal, RSA, 1984. *Address:* 25 St Anselm's Place, W1K 5AF. *T:* (020) 7629 4448. *Clubs:* Brooks's, Pratt's.
See also Sir John Riddell, Bt.

RICHARDSON, Anthony; *see* Richardson, H. A.

RICHARDSON, Sir Anthony (Lewis), 3rd Bt *cr* 1924; *b* 5 Aug. 1950; *s* of Sir Leslie Lewis Richardson, 2nd Bt, and of Joy Patricia, Lady Richardson, *d* of P. J. Rillstone, Johannesburg; *S* father, 1985; *m* 1985, Honor Gillian Dauney; one *s* one *d. Educ:* Diocesan College, Cape Town, S Africa. Stockbroker with L. Messel & Co., London, 1973–75; Insurance Broker with C. T. Bowring, London and Johannesburg, 1975–76; Stockbroker with Fergusson Bros, Hall, Stewart & Co., Johannesburg and Cape Town, 1976–78; Stockbroker with W. Greenwell & Co., London, 1979–81; with Rowe & Pitman, subseq. S. G. Warburg Securities, then SBC Warburg, London, 1981–99 (Dir, 1986–99), seconded to Potter Partners, Melbourne and Sydney, 1986–89, seconded to SBC Warburg, Johannesburg, 1996–99; Dir, Barclays Private Bank, London, 1999–. *Recreations:* various sports, photography. *Heir: s* William Lewis Richardson, *b* 15 Oct. 1992. *Address:* Triggs, Crondall Road, Crondall, Hampshire GU10 5RU. *Clubs:* Boodle's, Hurlingham.

RICHARDSON, Beverley Anne; Parliamentary Counsel, since 2005; *b* 17 May 1964. *Educ:* Girton Coll., Cambridge (BA 1986, MA 1990). Admitted as solicitor, 1990. Asst Parly Counsel, 1991–97; Sen. Asst Parly Counsel, 1997–2001; Dep. Parly Counsel, 2001–05. *Address:* Office of the Parliamentary Counsel, 36 Whitehall, SW1A 2AY. *T:* (020) 7210 6607.

RICHARDSON, Prof. Brian Frederick, FBA 2003; Professor of Italian Language, University of Leeds, since 1996; *b* 6 Dec. 1946; *s* of late Ronald Frederick Richardson, CBE and Anne Elizabeth Richardson (*née* McArdle); *m* 1973, Catherine Normand; three *d. Educ:* Lincoln Coll., Oxford (MA); Bedford Coll., London (MPhil). Lecturer in Italian: Univ. of Strathclyde, 1970–72; Univ. of Aberdeen, 1972–76; Lectr, 1977–89, Sen. Lectr, 1989–96, Univ. of Leeds. Gen. Editor, Modern Language Review, 2004–. *Publications:* (ed) N. Machiavelli, Il principe, 1979; (ed) Trattati sull'ortografia del volgare, 1984; Print Culture in Renaissance Italy, 1994; Printing, Writers and Readers in Renaissance Italy, 1999; (ed) G. F. Fortunio, Regole grammaticali della volgar lingua, 2001. *Recreations:* music, walking, gardening. *Address:* Department of Italian, School of Modern Languages and Cultures, University of Leeds, Leeds LS2 9JT.

RICHARDSON, David; Director, London Office, International Labour Organisation, 1982–91; *b* 24 April 1928; *s* of Harold George Richardson and Madeleine Raphaële Richardson (*née* Lebret); *m* 1951, Frances Joan Pring; three *s* one *d. Educ:* Wimbledon Coll.; King's Coll., London (BA Hons). FIPM 1986. RAF, 1949. Unilever, 1951. Inland Revenue, 1953; Min. of Labour, 1956; Sec., Construction Industry Training Bd, 1964; Chm., Central Youth Employment Exec., 1969; Royal Coll. of Defence Studies, 1971; Under Sec., Dept of Employment, 1972; Dir, Safety and Gen. Gp, Health and Safety Exec., 1975; Dir and Sec., ACAS, 1977. Director: The Tablet, 1985–98; Industrial Training Service Ltd, 1987–93. *Recreations:* music, walking, landscape gardening, ceramics. *Address:* 183 Banstead Road, Carshalton, Surrey SM5 4DP. *T:* (020) 8241 4614.

RICHARDSON, Rev. David John; His Honour Judge Richardson; a Circuit Judge, since 2000; an Additional Judge of the Employment Appeal Tribunal, since 2003; *b* 23 June 1950; *s* of Abraham Eric Richardson and Gwendoline Richardson (*née* Ballard); *m* 1980, Jennifer Margaret Richardson (*née* Cooke); one *s* one *d. Educ:* John Ruskin Grammar Sch., Croydon; Trinity Hall, Cambridge (BA 1971, MA; LLB 1972); Southwark Ordination Trng Course. Called to the Bar, Middle Temple, 1973; in practice, 1973–2000; an Asst Recorder, 1992–97; a Recorder, 1997–2000. Ordained deacon, 1985, priest, 1986; Hon. Curate, Emmanuel Church, S Croydon, 1985–. *Recreations:* walking, reading, supporter of Crystal Palace FC.

RICHARDSON, Prof. Genevra Mercy, CBE 2007; FBA 2007; Professor of Law, King's College London, since 2005; *b* 1 Sept. 1948; *d* of John Lawrence Richardson and Josephine Juliet Richardson; *m* 1977, Oliver Thorold (*see* Sir A. O. Thorold); one *s* one *d. Educ:* King's Coll., London (LLB, LLM). Res. Officer, Centre for Socio-Legal Studies, Oxford, 1974–78; Lectr, UEA, 1979–87; Lectr, 1987–89, Reader, 1989–94, Prof. of Public Law, 1994–2005, Dean, Faculty of Law, 1996–99, QMW, subseq. Queen Mary, Univ. of London. Chm., Expert Cttee Advising Ministers on Reform of Mental Health Legislation, 1998–99. Mem., Administrative Justice & Tribunals Council (formerly Council on Tribunals), 2001–. Member: Mental Health Act Commn, 1987–92; Animal Procedures Cttee, 1998–2006; Chm., Prisoner's Advice Service, 1994–2002. Mem. Council, MRC, 2001–08. Trustee, Nuffield Foundn, 2002–. Hon. FRCPsych 2004. *Recreations:* walking, travel. *Address:* School of Law, King's College, Strand, WC2R 2LS; *e-mail:* genevra.richardson@kcl.ac.uk.

RICHARDSON, George Barclay, CBE 1978; Warden, Keble College, Oxford, 1989–94 (Hon. Fellow, 1994); Pro-Vice-Chancellor, Oxford University, 1988–94; *b* 19 Sept. 1924; *s* of George and Christina Richardson; *m* 1957, Isabel Alison Chalk (marr. diss. 1998); two *s*. *Educ:* Aberdeen Central Secondary Sch. and other schs in Scotland; Aberdeen Univ. (BSc Physics and Maths, 1944); Corpus Christi Coll., Oxford (MA PPE 1949; Hon. Fellow, 1987). Admty Scientific Res. Dept, 1944; Lieut, RNVR, 1945. Intell. Officer, HQ Intell. Div. BAOR, 1946–47; Third Sec., HM Foreign Service, 1949; Student, Nuffield Coll., Oxford, 1950; Fellow, St John's Coll., Oxford, 1951–89, Hon. Fellow, 1989; University Reader in Economics, Oxford, 1969–73; Sec. to Delegates and Chief Exec., OUP, 1974–88 (Deleg., 1971–74). Economic Advr, UKAEA, 1968–74. Member: Economic Develt Cttee for Electrical Engineering Industry, 1964–73; Monopolies Commn, 1969–74; Royal Commn on Environmental Pollution, 1973–74; Council, Publishers Assoc., 1981–87. Mem., UK Delegation, CSCE Cultural Forum, 1985. Visitor, Ashmolean Mus., 1992–96. Hon. DCL Oxon, 1988; Hon. LLD Aberdeen, 1996. *Publications:* Information and Investment, 1960, 2nd edn 1991; Economic Theory, 1964; The Economics of Imperfect Knowledge, 1998; articles in academic jls. *Address:* 33 Belsyre Court, Woodstock Road, Oxford OX2 6HU. *Club:* Oxford and Cambridge.

RICHARDSON, George Taylor, CM 2002; OM 2000; Hon. Chairman: James Richardson & Sons, Limited, Winnipeg, Canada, since 2000 (Chairman, 1993–2000; President 1966–93; Vice-President 1954); RBC Dominion Securities Inc., since 1996; *b* 22 Sept. 1924; *s* of late James Armstrong Richardson and Muriel (*née* Sprague); *m* 1948, Tannis Maree Thorlakson; two *s* one *d*. *Educ:* Grosvenor Sch. and Ravenscourt Sch., Winnipeg; Univ. of Manitoba (BComm). Joined family firm of James Richardson & Sons Ltd, 1946. Hon. Dir, Canada's Aviation Hall of Fame. Hon. LLD: Manitoba; Winnipeg. *Recreations:* hunting, helicopter flying. *Clubs:* MB, St Charles (Winnipeg); Vancouver (Vancouver); Toronto (Toronto); Mill Reef (Antigua); Bear's Paw (Naples, Fla).

RICHARDSON, (Henry) Anthony; a Recorder of the Crown Court, 1978–96; a Deputy Traffic Commissioner and a Deputy Licensing Authority, North Eastern Traffic Area, 1989–93; barrister, retired; *b* 28 Dec. 1925; *er s* of late Thomas Ewan Richardson and Jessie (*née* Preston), Batley, W Yorks; *m* 1954, Georgina (*née* Lawford) (*d* 2004), *d* of late Rosamond Bedford and step *d* of late Gp Captain G. R. Bedford, MB, ChB, RAF retd. *Educ:* Giggleswick Sch.; Leeds Univ. (LLB 1950, LLM 1956). Called to the Bar, Lincoln's Inn, 1951; North-Eastern Circuit; Dep. Circuit Judge, 1972–78. Chm., a Police Disciplinary Appeal Tribunal, 1983. *Publications:* articles in legal periodicals. *Recreations:* walking, gardening, listening to music, British history.

RICHARDSON, Hugh; Head, Delegation of European Commission to Tokyo, since 2006; *b* 12 May 1947; *s* of Robert Richardson and Pauline (*née* Broadhurst); *m* (marr. diss.); two *s* two *d*; *m* 2000, Lisbeth Van Impe; one *d*. *Educ:* Pembroke Coll., Oxford (BA 1969; BCL 1970; MA 2002). Commission of the European Communities: with Secretariat Gen., 1974–79; Directorate-Gen. for External Relns, 1979–84; Counsellor and Dep. Head, Tokyo Delegn, 1984–88; Asst to DG for External Relns, 1988–91; Dir, Rights and Obligations, Directorate-Gen. for Personnel and Admin, 1991–96; Dep. Dir Gen., Jt Res. Centre, 1996–2002; Dep. Dir Gen., DG Res., 2002–04; Dep. Dir Gen., DG EuropeAid Co-operation Office, 2004–06. *Publication:* EC-Japan Relations: after adolescence, 1989. *Recreations:* sailing, ski-ing, running. *Address:* Delegation of European Commission to Japan, Europa House, 9–15 Sanban-cho, Chiyoda-ku, Tokyo 102–0075, Japan.

RICHARDSON, Rt Hon. Sir Ivor (Lloyd Morgan), Kt 1986; PCNZM 2002; PC 1978; SJD; President, Court of Appeal of New Zealand, 1996–2002 (Judge, 1977–96); Non-Permanent Judge, Hong Kong Court of Final Appeal, since 2003; *b* 24 May 1930; *s* of W. T. Richardson; *m* 1955, Jane, *d* of I. J. Krchma; three *d*. *Educ:* Canterbury Univ. (LLB); Univ. of Mich (LLM, SJD). Partner, Macalister Bros, Invercargill, 1957–63; Crown Counsel, Crown Law Office, Wellington, 1963–66; Victoria University of Wellington: Prof. of Law, 1967–73; Dean of Law Faculty, 1968–71; Pro-Chancellor, 1979–84; Chancellor, 1984–86; Dist. Vis. Fellow, 2002–; Partner, Watts & Patterson, Wellington, 1973–77. Chm., Cttees of Inquiry into Inflation Accounting, 1975–76, into Solicitors Nominee Cos, 1983. Chairman: Council of Legal Educn, 1983–92; Royal Commn on Social Policy, 1986–88; Orgnl Rev. of Inland Revenue Dept, 1993–94. Hon. LLD: Canterbury, 1987; Victoria, 1989. *Publications:* books and articles on legal subjects. *Address:* 16/127 Molesworth Street, Wellington 6011, New Zealand. *T:* (4) 4728826. *Club:* Wellington (Wellington, NZ).

RICHARDSON, Rev. Canon James John, OBE 2007; Hon. Canon Pastor, Sherborne Abbey, since 2009; *b* 28 March 1941; *s* of late James John Richardson and of Gladys May (*née* Evans); *m* 1966, Janet Rosemary Welstand; two *s* one *d*. *Educ:* Catford Central Sch.; Hull Univ. (BA); Sheffield Univ. (DipEd); Cuddesdon Coll., Oxford; MPhil Leicester 2008. Assistant Master, Westfield Comp. Sch., Sheffield, 1964–66; Curate, St Peter's Collegiate Church, Wolverhampton, 1969–72; Priest i/c, All Saints, Hanley, Stoke-on-Trent, 1972–75; Rector of Nantwich, 1975–82; Vicar of Leeds, 1982–88; Exec. Dir, CCJ, 1988–92; Priest-in-Charge: Gt Brington, Whilton and Norton (Northampton), dio. of Peterborough, 1993–96; E Haddon and Holdenby, Church and Chapel Brampton and Harlestone, 1994–96; St Augustine, Bournemouth, 2001–08; Team Rector, Bournemouth Town Centre Parish, 1996–2008. Hon. Canon, 1982–88, Canon Emeritus, 1988–, Ripon Cathedral. Chaplain: to Earl Spencer, 1993–96; to High Sheriff of Northants, 1995–96; to Mayor of Bournemouth, 2002–03 and 2006–07; to High Sheriff of Dorset, 2007–08. Chm., Racial Harassment Commn, Leeds, 1986–87; N of England Vice-Pres., UN Year of Peace, 1986–87. Chairman: Bournemouth Town Centre Detached Youth Project, 1997–2008; Churches Together in Bournemouth, 1998–2002; Director: Bournemouth Millennium Co., 1998–99; Hope FM Radio, 1998–2001. Member: Council, Centre for the Study of Judaism and Jewish/Christian Relations, Selly Oak Coll., 1989–94; Internat. Council of Christians and Jews Adv. Cttee, 1992–96. Member: Partnership Steering Cttee, Bournemouth BC, 2001–03; Bournemouth BC Standards Bd, 2003– (Vice-Chm., 2003–07; Chm., 2007–08); Bournemouth BC Schs Orgn Cttee, 2003–06; Bournemouth Town Centre Mgt Bd, 2003–08. Mem. Court, Leeds Univ., 1986–88; Chairman of Governors: Abbey Grange High Sch., Leeds, 1982–86; Leeds Grammar Sch., 1983–88; Governor: Leeds Girls' High Sch., 1982–88; Leeds Music Fest., 1982–88; Chm. Steering Gp, New Church Secondary Sch. for Bournemouth, 2001–03. FRSA 1991. Hon. Freeman, Bor. of Bournemouth, 2008. *Publications:* (contrib.) Four Score Years, 1989; contrib. Yorkshire Post, 1982–90. *Recreations:* leading pilgrimages to Israel, biography—especially life and times of Rupert Brooke, deciphering Elizabethan churchwardens' accounts. *Address:* 67 Acreman Street, Sherborne, Dorset DT9 3PH.

RICHARDSON, Prof. Jeremy John, PhD; Fellow, 1998–2003, and Senior Tutor, 2001–03, Nuffield College, Oxford, now Emeritus Fellow; *b* 15 June 1942; *s* of Samuel Radcliffe Richardson and Sarah Doris Richardson; *m* 1966, Anne Philippsen (marr. diss. 1993); one *s* one *d*; *m* 1994, Sonia Pauline Mazey; two *d*. *Educ:* Univ. of Keele (BA Hons Politics and Econs); Univ. of Manchester (MA Econ; PhD 1970). Asst Lectr, Lectr, then Reader, Univ. of Keele, 1966–82; Professor: Dept of Politics, Univ. of Strathclyde, 1982–92; Univ. of Warwick, 1992–95; Univ. of Essex, 1995–98; Nuffield Prof. of Comparative European Politics and Dir, Centre for European Politics, Economics and Society, Oxford Univ., 1998–2001. Ed., Jl of European Public Policy, 1993–. Hon. Dr Pol Sci., Umeå, 1995. *Publications:* The Policy-Making Process, 1969; (ed with R. Kimber) Campaigning for the Environment, 1974; (ed with R. Kimber) Pressure Groups in Britain: a reader, 1974; (with A. Grant Jordan) Governing Under Pressure: the policy process in a post-parliamentary democracy, 1979; (ed with R. Henning) Policy Responses to Unemployment in Western Democracies, 1984; (with J. Moon) Unemployment in the UK: politics and policies, 1985; (with A Grant Jordan) Government & Pressure Groups in Britain, 1987; (ed jtly) The Politics of Economic Crisis: lessons from Western Europe, 1989; (jtly) Local Partnership and the Unemployment Crisis in Britain, 1989; (with G. Dudley) Politics and Steel in Britain 1967–1988, 1990; (ed) Privatisation and Deregulation in Canada and Britain, 1990; (with S. Mazey) Lobbying in the European Community, 1993; (ed) Pressure Groups, 1993; (jtly) True Blues: the politics of Conservative Party membership, 1994; (jtly) Networks for Water Policy: a comparative perspective, 1994; (with W. Maloney) Managing Policy Change in Britain: the politics of water policy, 1995; (ed) European Union: power and policy-making, 1996, 3rd edn 2005; (with G. Dudley) Why Does Policy Change?: lessons from British transport policy 1945–1999, 2000. *Recreations:* gardening, DIY, walking, playing with the children. *Address:* 30 Queen's Avenue, Fendalton, Christchurch 8014, New Zealand. *T:* (3) 3559161.

RICHARDSON, Jeremy William; QC 2000; a Recorder, since 2000; a Deputy High Court Judge, Family Division, since 2004; *b* 3 April 1958; *s* of late Thomas William Sydney Raymond Richardson and of Jean Mary Richardson (*née* Revill); civil partnership 2006, David Carruthers. *Educ:* Forest Sch.; Queen Mary Coll., Univ. of London (LLB Hons 1979). Called to the Bar, Inner Temple, 1980, Bencher, 2007; in practice at the Bar, NE Circuit, 1982–; Asst Recorder, 1998–2000. Mem., Gen. Council of the Bar, 1992–94. Sec., NE Circuit, 1991–96. *Address:* KBW, The Engine House, 1 Foundry Square, Leeds LS11 5DL. *T:* (0113) 297 1200. *Club:* Athenæum.

RICHARDSON, Joely; actress; *b* 9 Jan. 1965; *d* of late Tony Richardson and of Vanessa Redgrave, *qv*; *m* 1992, Tim Bevan, *qv* (marr. diss. 2001); one *d*. *Educ:* Lycée Française de Londres; St Paul's Girls' Sch.; Pinellas Park High Sch., Florida; Thacher Sch., Calif; RADA. West End début, Steel Magnolias, Lyric, 1989; Lady Windermere's Fan, Haymarket, 2002. *Films include:* Wetherby, 1985; Drowning by Numbers, 1988; Shining Through, Rebecca's Daughters, 1992; Sister, My Sister, 1995; Loch Ness, Believe Me, 101 Dalmatians, Hollow Reed, 1996; Event Horizon, 1997; Wrestling with Alligators, Under Heaven, 1998; Maybe Baby, Return to Me, The Patriot, 2000; The Affair of the Necklace, 2002; *television includes:* Body Contact, 1987; Behaving Badly, 1989; Heading Home, 1991; The Storyteller, Lady Chatterley's Lover, 1993; The Tribe, Echo, 1998; Nip/Tuck, 2004–; Wallis and Edward, 2005. *Address:* c/o Finch and Partners, 4–8 Heddon Street, W1B 4BS.

See also N. J. Richardson.

RICHARDSON, John Burke; Head, Maritime Policy Task Force, European Commission, since 2005; *b* 22 Dec. 1944; *s* of Alan and Mary Richardson; *m* 1969, Irmtraud Hübner; three *d*. *Educ:* Downing Coll., Cambridge (BA Chemistry; MA 1970); University Coll. London (MSc Econs 1969). Economist, Unilever, 1969–73; joined European Commn, 1973: Negotiator for Internat. Trade in Services, 1982–88; Head of Unit: for USA, 1988–92; for Japan, 1992–96; Dep. Hd of Delegn to USA, 1996–2001; Ambassador and Hd, EC Delegn to UN, NY, 2001–05. Mem. Bd, Salzburg Global Seminar, 1998–. *Publications:* contrib. on trade in services and internat. relations to learned jls. *Recreations:* gardening, bird watching, Mediterranean life. *Address:* European Commission, 200 rue de la Loi, 1049 Brussels, Belgium. *Club:* International Château St Anne (Brussels).

RICHARDSON, John Charles; Managing Director, Historical Publications Ltd, since 1975; *b* 7 June 1935; *s* of Joseph and Vera Richardson; *m* 1st, 1957, Laura Caroline Bourne Webb (marr. diss. 1962); two *s*; 2nd, 1967, Elizabeth Noel Ballard (marr. diss. 1981); two *s*; 3rd, 1981, Helen Warnock English. *Educ:* Barking Abbey GS. J. Walter Thompson, 1965–72; KMP, 1974–84. Member: St Pancras BC, 1959–66; Camden BC, 1966–71. Joint Founder: GLAA, 1966; Camden Arts Centre, 1966; Chm., Bubble Theatre Co., 1968–74. Chm., Camden Hist. Soc., 1970–. *Publications:* The Local Historian's Encyclopedia, 1974; Covent Garden, 1979; Highgate: its history since the fifteenth century, 1983; Hampstead One Thousand, 1985; Islington Past, 1986; Highgate Past, 1989; Camden Town and Primrose Hill Past, 1991; London and its People, 1995; Covent Garden Past, 1995; Kentish Town Past, 1997; A History of Camden, 1999; The Annals of London, 2000; The Camden Town Book, 2007. *Recreations:* visiting the London Library, architecture. *Address:* 32 Ellington Street, N7 8PL. *T:* (020) 7607 1628.

RICHARDSON, John Francis; Director and Chief Executive, National & Provincial Building Society, 1985–86; *b* 16 June 1934; *s* of Francis and Stella Richardson; *m* 1960, Jacqueline Mary Crosby; two *d*. *Educ:* Wadham College, Oxford (PPE). FCBSI. Burnley Building Society, 1959–82; Chief General Manager, 1980–82; Dep. Chief Executive, National & Provincial Building Society, 1983–85. Pres., CBSI, 1985. *Recreations:* gardening, military history. *Address:* Low Gables, Spofforth Hill, Wetherby, West Yorks LS22 6SF.

RICHARDSON, Rt Rev. John Henry; Suffragan Bishop of Bedford, 1994–2002; Hon. Assistant Bishop, dioceses of Carlisle and Newcastle, since 2003; *b* 11 July 1937; *s* of John Farquhar Richardson and Elizabeth Mary Richardson; *m* 1963, Felicity-Anne Lowes; three *d*. *Educ:* Winchester; Trinity Hall, Cambridge (BA 1961; MA 1965); Cuddesdon Coll., Oxford. Nat. Service, 1956–58 (despatches, Malaya, 1958). Ordained deacon, 1963, priest, 1964; Asst Curate, St George's, Stevenage, 1963–66; Curate, St Mary's, Eastbourne, 1966–68; Vicar: St Paul's, Chipperfield, 1968–75; St Mary's, Rickmansworth, 1975–86; RD, Rickmansworth, 1977–86; Vicar, St Michael's, Bishops Stortford, 1986–93; Hon. Canon, St Albans Cathedral, 1986–2002. Hon. Fellow, Luton Univ., 2003. *Recreations:* walking, bird-watching, windsurfing, fishing, energetic gardening. *Address:* The Old Rectory, Bewcastle, Carlisle, Cumbria CA6 6PS. *T:* (016977) 48389. *Clubs:* Royal Automobile; Leander.

RICHARDSON, John Patrick; writer; *b* 6 Feb. 1924; *s* of Sir Wodehouse Richardson, KCB, DSO and Clara Pattie (*née* Crocker). *Educ:* Stowe; Slade Sch. of Art. US Rep., Christie's, 1964–72; Vice-Pres., M. Knoedler & Co., NYC, 1972–76; Man. Dir, Artemis Gp, London and New York, 1976–78; Editor-at-large, House and Garden (US), 1981–91; Contributing Ed., Vanity Fair, 1990–2006. Slade Prof. of Art History, Oxford, 1995–96. Corresp. FBA 1993. Whitbread Book of Year Award, 1991; La Vanguardia Book of Year Award, Barcelona, 1997. *Publications:* Picasso: watercolors and gouaches, 1956; Manet, 1958; Braque, 1959; A Life of Picasso, Vol. I, 1991, Vol. II, 1996; The Sorcerer's Apprentice: Picasso, Provence, and Douglas Cooper, 1999; Sacred Monsters, Sacred Masters: Beaton, Capote, Dali, Picasso, Freud, Warhol, and more, 2001; contrib. to TLS, Burlington Mag., New York Rev. of Books, New Yorker, etc. *Address:* 73 Fifth Avenue, New York City, NY 10003, USA; 263 West Meeting House Road, New Milford, CT 06776, USA.

RICHARDSON, Very Rev. John Stephen; Vicar of Wye and Brook with Hastingleigh, and Chaplain, Imperial College London (Wye College) (formerly Wye Agricultural College), since 2001; Priest-in-charge of Boughton Aluph and Eastwell, since 2004, and of Hinxhill, since 2007; *b* 2 April 1950; *s* of James Geoffrey and Myra Richardson; *m* 1972, Elizabeth Susan Wiltshire; one *s* two *d* (and one *s* decd). *Educ:* Haslingden Grammar Sch.; Univ. of Southampton (BA Hons Theology); St John's Theological Coll., Nottingham. Deacon 1974, priest 1975; Asst Curate, St Michael's, Bramcote, 1974–77; Priest-in-Charge, Emmanuel Church, Radipole and Melcombe Regis, 1977–80; Asst Diocesan Missioner and Lay Trainer Adviser, dio. of Salisbury and Priest-in-Charge of Stinsford, Winterborne Monkton and Winterborne Came with Witcombe, 1980–83; Vicar of Christ Church, Nailsea, 1983–90; Adviser in Evangelism, dio. of Bath and Wells, 1985–90; Provost, subseq. Dean, of Bradford, 1990–2001; Area Dean of West Bridge, 2003–. Dir, Spring Harvest, 1998–2003 and 2007–; Chm., Spring Harvest Charitable Trust, 1998–. Chaplain, W Yorks Police, 1995–2001. Bishop's Selector, ABM, 1993–97. Mem., General Synod, 1993–2001. Member: Exec. Bd, Common Purpose, 1992–2000; BBC North Adv. Panel, 1990–94; Bradford Breakthrough, 1992–2001; Council, Evangelical Alliance Management Gp, 1994–2000; Council, Scripture Union, 2000–07. Mem. Council, Bradford Chamber of Commerce, 1992–2001. Director: Mildmay Hosp., 2004– (Chm., 2007–); Kent Community Housing Trust, 2005–. Trustee: Acorn Healing Trust, 1990–2007; Spennithorne Hall, 1990–98; Northumbria Community, 2006–. Council Mem., St John's Theological Coll., Nottingham, 1988–94; Governor: Bradford Grammar Sch., 1990–2001; Giggleswick Sch., 1993–2001; Bradford Cathedral Community Coll. (formerly Fairfax Sch., then Bowling Community Coll.), 1994–2001. Chaplain to: High Sheriff, W Yorks, 1994–95, 2000–2001; High Sheriff, Kent, 2004–05. MInstD 1994. *Publication:* Ten Rural Churches, 1988. *Recreations:* football, cricket, North Western Municipal Bus Operators, walking, writing, broadcasting. *Address:* The Vicarage, Cherry Garden Crescent, Wye, Ashford, Kent TN25 5AS. *T:* (01233) 812450; *e-mail:* john.richardson@wyechurch.co.uk. *Clubs:* Farmers; Kent and Canterbury.

RICHARDSON, John Stephen; Headmaster, Cheltenham College, since 2004; *b* 2 Dec. 1953; *s* of Rev. James H. Richardson and Rachel Richardson (*née* Varley); *m* 1989, Ruth W. Vardy; two *s* one *d*. *Educ:* Rossall Sch.; Selwyn Coll., Cambridge (BA 1976; PGCE 1977). Dean Close School, Cheltenham, 1977–84: Teacher of Maths, Housemaster and Curriculum Dir; OC CCF/RAF Section; Eton College, 1984–92: Teacher of Maths, House List, Chapel Steward; Master i/c U16 Rowing; OC CCF/RAF Section; Treas., Eton Action; Headmaster, Culford Sch., Bury St Edmunds, 1992–2004. ISI Inspector, 1993–2004; Chm., East Div., HMC, 2000–02; Mem., NAHT. Vice Chm., Curriculum Evaluation and Mgt Centre, Durham Univ., 2000–04. Mem. Council of Reference, Cheltenham Youth for Christ, 2007–. Trustee, Ind. Schs Christian Alliance, 1994–2002. FRSA 2007. Foundn Fellow, Univ. of Gloucester, 2006. *Recreations:* reading, sailing, mountaineering. *Address:* College House, Thirlestaine Road, Cheltenham, Glos GL53 7AA. *T:* (01242) 705597; *e-mail:* jr@richardson1578.freeserve.co.uk. *Club:* East India.

RICHARDSON, Kenneth Augustus, CVO 1994; CBE 1989; JP; Secretary to the Cabinet, Bermuda, 1984–93; *b* 13 Feb. 1939; *s* of Augustus J. Richardson; *m* 1966, Brenda Joyce (*née* Smith); one *s* one *d*. *Educ:* Howard Univ., Washington (BSc); Manchester Polytechnic (Dip. Personnel Admin and Labour Relations). Teacher, Sandys Secondary School, Bermuda, 1964; Admin. Cadet, Colonial Sec.'s Office, 1967; Training and Recruitment Officer, Bermuda Govt, 1969; Perm. Sec., Labour and Home Affairs, 1974. Chm., Employment Tribunal, 1990–. Hon. Life Vice Pres., Bermuda Football Assoc., 1994. MIPM 1973; MInstD 1988. JP 1984. *Recreations:* sport (soccer, tennis). *Address:* Mahogany, 19 Trimingham Hill, Paget, Bermuda; PO Box HM 1703, Hamilton HM GX, Bermuda. *T:* 236 1788.

RICHARDSON, Margaret Ann, OBE 2005; FSA; Curator, Sir John Soane's Museum, 1995–2005 (Assistant Curator, 1985–95); *b* 11 Sept. 1937; *d* of late James Ballard and Edna (*née* Johnstone); *m* 1963, Anthony George Richardson; two *d*. *Educ:* Harrogate Coll.; University Coll. London (BA Hons; Fellow, 2001); Courtauld Inst. of Art (Acad. Dip.). FSA 1996. Asst Curator, 1963–68, Jt Dep. Curator, 1972–85, Drawings Collection, British Architectural Liby. Pres., Twentieth Century Soc., 1995–2003 (Mem. Cttee, 1984–2003); Trustee: Save Britain's Heritage, 1975–; Lutyens Trust, 1984– (Chm., 1994–2001); Greenwich Foundn for RNC, 1997–2004; Mem. Council, Nat. Trust, 2002–. Hon. Curator of Architecture, RA, 2005–. Hon. FRIBA 1994. *Publications:* (ed) RIBA Catalogue series, vols A, B, C–F, and S, 1969–76; Edwin Lutyens, 1973; Lutyens and the Sea Captain, 1981; (jtly) Great Drawings from the RIBA, 1983; Architects of the Arts and Crafts Movement, 1983; 66 Portland Place: the London headquarters of the RIBA, 1984; (jtly) The Art of the Architect, 1984; Sketches by Lutyens, 1994; (ed jtly) John Soane Architect: master of space and light, 1999. *Address:* 64 Albert Street, NW1 7NR. *T:* (020) 7387 7940.

See also J. G. Ballard.

RICHARDSON, Dame Mary, DBE 2001; Chief Executive, HSBC Global Education Trust, 2000–08; *b* 26 Feb. 1936; *d* of Lt George Arthur Habgood, RN, and Anna Jane Habgood; *m* 1960, Dr Donald Arthur Richardson; one *s* one *d*. *Educ:* Notre Dame High Sch., Wigan; Liverpool Univ. (BA, PGCE). Officer, WRAC, 1954–60. Pt-time teacher, St Adrian's Jun. Sch., 1963–72; Hd of Sixth Form, then Hd of English, Marlborough Sch., St Albans, 1977–85; Dep. Hd, Convent of Jesus and Mary, Willesden, 1985–86; Principal, Convent of Jesus and Mary Lang. Coll., 1986–2000. Member: Adv. Cttee on Indep./State Schs Partnerships, 1999–2002; Bd of Visitors, HM Prison Wormwood Scrubs, 1995–2002. Director: Technol. Colls, subseq. Specialist Schs and Academies, Trust, 2000– (Fellow 2005); Nat. Coll. Sch. Leadership, 2008–; Trustee, CfBT, 2001–06. President: London Youth Trust, 2003–05; SOS Children's Villages, UK, 2008–. Governor: Thornton Coll., Bucks, 1994–; City of London Schs (Boys), 2000–; ESU; Mem. Council, Royal Alexandra and Albert Sch., Reigate, 2007–; Trustee: Waterford Coll., Swaziland, 2002–04 and 2008–; Dulverton Trust; Marine Soc. and Sea Cadets; Future Hope, Calcutta, 2008–. FRSA 1996. Member: Newman Assoc., 1964; Baconian Soc., 2002; NADFAS, 2000. Freeman, City of London, 2000. Hon. Dr: Brunel, 2005; Richmond, 2007; City, 2008. *Publications:* Free to Play, Free to Pretend, Free to Imagine, drama textbooks for use in primary schs, 1972; contrib. professional periodicals. *Address:* 13 Abbey Avenue, St Albans, Herts AL3 4BJ. *T:* (01727) 859039; *e-mail:* MRicha3539@aol.com.

RICHARDSON, Michael Elliot; Director of Continuing Education and Lifelong Learning and Director, Institute of Continuing Education (formerly Director of Continuing Education and Secretary, Board of Continuing Education), University of Cambridge, 1990–2003; Fellow of Wolfson College, Cambridge, 1990–2003, now Emeritus; *b* 29 Sept. 1938; *s* of late Rev. Emery Lonsdale Richardson and Margaret Ann Richardson (*née* Elliot); *m* 1968, Gillian Miles Jones; two *d*. *Educ:* Pocklington Sch., York; St John's Coll., Cambridge (MA 1967); Lincoln Theol Coll.; Univ. of Nottingham (DipAdEd 1970). FCIPD. Schoolmaster, Middlesbrough Boys' High Sch., 1964–65; Adult Educn Tutor, Ibstock Community Coll., 1965–67; Principal, Alfreton Hall Adult Educn Centre, 1967–69; Open University, 1969–90: Dep. Regl Dir, Northern, 1969–76; Regl Dir, NW, 1976–79; Dir, Educnl Services for Cont. Educn, 1979–81; Pro-Dir, 1981–84, Dir, 1984–86, Centre for Cont. Educn; Pro-Vice Chancellor, Cont. Educn, 1985–90. Chm., Council for Educn and Training of Youth and Community Workers, 1985–90; Sec., UACE, 1998–2002 (Mem. Council, 1990–2003, now Life Mem.); Mem. Council, CRAC, 1990–98; Mem., numerous cttees and boards, 1980–. Trustee, Nat. Extension Coll., 1988–2003. DUniv Open 1994. FRSA. *Publications:* Preparing to Study, 1979; Continuing Education for the Post Industrial Society, 1982; contribs to educn jls. *Recreations:* gardening, angling, walking. *Address:* Holmlea, Station Road, Corbridge, Northumberland NE45 5AY.

RICHARDSON, Michael John, CB 2005; Chairman, Lewisham Primary Care Trust, since 2007; *b* 17 March 1946; *s* of Philip George Richardson, MBE and Susan Rowena (*née* Pearce); *m* 1967, Celia, *d* of Rev. Canon Peter and Daphne Bradshaw; one *s* one *d*. *Educ:* Eton Coll.; St Edmund Hall, Oxford (BA Lit.Hum. 1968). Joined HM Diplomatic Service, 1968; Hong Kong, 1969–71; 3rd, later 2nd Sec., Peking, 1972–74; 1st Secretary: FCO, 1974–75; EEC, 1976; Western European Dept, FCO, 1977–78; Private Secretary to: Minister of State, 1978–79; Lord Privy Seal, 1979–80; 1st Sec., Rome, 1980–85; Asst Head, EC Dept, 1985; Head, EC Presidency Unit, FCO, 1986–87; Department for Education, later DFEE, 1987–2001: Under Sec., 1992; Dir for Qualifications, 1995–98; Dir for Employment Policy, 1998–2001; Department for Work and Pensions: Director: for Work, Welfare and Fraud, 2001–02; for Work and Welfare Strategy, 2002–03; for Work, Welfare and Poverty, 2003–06. Dep. Chm., London & Quadrant Housing Assoc., 1998–. *Recreations:* family, reading, gardening, theatre-going. *Address:* 12 Northumberland Place, W2 5BS.

RICHARDSON, Miranda; actress; *b* 3 March 1958; *d* of William Alan Richardson and Marian Georgina Townsend. *Educ:* St Wyburn, Southport, Merseyside; Southport High Sch. for Girls; Bristol Old Vic Theatre Sch. Repertory: Manchester Library Theatre, 1979–80; Derby Playhouse, Duke's Playhouse, Lancaster, Bristol Old Vic and Leicester Haymarket, 1982–83; West End début, Moving, Queen's, 1980–81; Royal Court: Edmund, 1985; A Lie of the Mind, 1987; Etta Jenks, 1990; National Theatre: The Changeling, and Mountain Language, 1988; The Designated Mourner, 1996; Orlando, Edinburgh Fest., 1996; Aunt Dan and Lemon, Almeida, 1999. *Television:* series include: Agony; Sorrell and Son; Blackadder II and III; Die Kinder, 1990; The True Adventures of Christopher Columbus, 1992; A Dance to the Music of Time, 1998; The Life and Times of Vivienne Vyle, 2007; plays include: The Master Builder; The Demon Lover; After Pilkington; Sweet as You Are (RTS Award, 1987–88); Ball-trap on the Côte Sauvage, 1989; Old Times, 1991; Merlin, 1998; Alice in Wonderland, 2000; The Lost Prince, 2003; Gideon's Daughter, 2006; *films:* Dance with a Stranger (role, Ruth Ellis) (City Limits Best Film Actress, 1985; Evening Standard Best Actress, 1985; Variety Club Most Promising Artiste, 1985); Underworld; Death of the Heart; Empire of the Sun; The Mad Monkey; Eat the Rich; Redemption, 1991; Enchanted April, 1992 (Golden Globe Award, Best Comedy Actress, 1993); Mr Wakefield's Crusade, The Bachelor, 1992; Damage (BAFTA Award, Best Supporting Actress, 1993; NY Critics Circle Award; Film Critics Circle, Best Actress 1994; Royal Variety Club of GB, Best Film Actress of 1994); The Crying Game, 1992; Century, 1993; Tom and Viv (Best Actress, Nat. Bd of Review of Motion Pictures), La Nuit et Le Moment, 1994; Kansas City, Evening Star, 1996; Swann, 1997; Designated Mourner, Apostle, All For Love, Jacob Two Two and the Hooded Fang, The Big Brass Ring, 1998; Sleepy Hollow, Chicken Run (voice), Snow White, 2000; The Hours, Spider, 2001; The Actors, 2002; Rage on Placid Lake, Falling Angels, The Prince and Me, Phantom of the Opera, 2003; Harry Potter and the Goblet of Fire, 2005; Wah Wah, Spinning into Butter, Puffball, Southland Tales, 2006; Fred Claus, Provoked: a True Story, Young Victoria, 2007. *Recreations:* reading, walking, softball, gardening, music, junkshops, occasional art, animals. *Address:* c/o Independent Talent Group Ltd, Oxford House, 76 Oxford Street, W1D 1BS.

RICHARDSON, Natasha Jane; actress; *b* 11 May 1963; *d* of late Tony Richardson and of Vanessa Redgrave, *qv*; *m* 1st, 1990, Robert Michael John Fox, *qv* (marr. diss. 1994); 2nd, 1994, Liam Neeson (*see* W. J. Neeson); two *s*. *Educ:* Lycée Française de Londres; St Paul's Girls' Sch.; Central Sch. of Speech and Drama. Season at Leeds Playhouse; A Midsummer Night's Dream, New Shakespeare Co.; Ophelia in Hamlet, Young Vic; The Seagull, Lyric Hammersmith, tour and Queen's, 1985 (Most Promising Newcomer, London Drama Critics, 1986); China, Bush Th., 1986; High Society, Leicester Haymarket and Victoria Palace, 1987; Anna Christie, Young Vic, 1990 (Best Actress, London Drama Critics, 1992), NY, 1993 (Outer Critics Circle Award, 1993); Cabaret, NY (Tony, Outer Critics' Circle and Drama Desk Awards), 1998; Closer, NY, 1999; The Lady from the Sea, Almeida, 2003; A Streetcar Named Desire, NY, 2005. *Films:* Every Picture Tells a Story, 1985; Gothic; A Month in the Country, 1987; Patty Hearst, 1988; Fat Man and Little Boy, 1989; The Handmaid's Tale, The Comfort of Strangers, 1990 (Best Actress, London Evening Standard Awards, 1990); The Favour, the Watch and the Very Big Fish, 1992; Past Midnight; Widows Peak (Best Actress, Prague Film Fest., 1994), Nell, 1994; The Parent Trap, 1998; Blow Dry, 2001; Chelsea Walls, Wakin' up in Reno, 2002; Maid in Manhattan, 2003; Asylum, The White Countess, 2006; Evening, 2007. *Television:* In a Secret State, 1985; Ghosts, 1986; Hostages, 1992; Suddenly Last Summer, 1993; Zelda, 1993; Tales from the Crypt, 1996; Haven (series), 2000. Most Promising Newcomer Award, Plays and Players, 1986; Best Actress: Evening Standard Film Awards, 1990; London Theatre Critics, 1990; Plays and Players, 1990. *Address:* c/o Independent Talent Group Ltd, Oxford House, 76 Oxford Street, W1D 1BS.

See also Joely Richardson.

RICHARDSON, Rev. Neil Graham, PhD; Senior Research Scholar, The Queen's Foundation, since 2007; President, Methodist Conference, 2003–04; *b* 2 Dec. 1943; *s* of John and Ethel Richardson; *m* 1972, Rhiannon Bradshaw; three *s*. *Educ:* Queen's Coll., Oxford (BA Classics, Modern Hist.; MA 1970); Wesley House, Cambridge (BA Theol. 1971); Bristol Univ. (MLitt 1977, PhD 1992). Asst Tutor, Wesley Coll., Bristol, 1971–73; Minister, Oxford Circuit, 1973–77; Ecumenical Lectr, Bishop's Hostel, Lincoln, 1977–81; Minister, Manchester Mission Circuit, and Chaplain to Manchester Univ., 1981–84; Wesley College, Bristol: Tutor in New Testament Studies, 1984–95; Principal,

1995–2001; Superintendent Minister, Leeds NE Circuit, 2001–07. Res. Fellow, Queen's Coll., Birmingham, 2007–08. *Publications:* Was Jesus Divine?, 1979; The Panorama of Luke, 1982; Preaching from Scripture, 1983; Paul's Language About God, 1994; God in the New Testament, 1999; Paul for Today, 2008. *Recreation:* marathon running (London Marathon, 1995, 1999, 2000, 2004–07; first UK national Church leader to run the London Marathon whilst in office). *Address:* 14 Mortimer Drive, Orleton SY8 4JW.

RICHARDSON, Dr Nigel Peter Vincent; Headmaster, The Perse School, Cambridge, 1994–2008; *b* 29 June 1948; *s* of Vincent Boys Richardson and Jean Frances (*née* Wrangles); *m* 1979, (Averon) Joy James; two *s*. *Educ:* Highgate Sch.; Trinity Hall, Cambridge (MA Hist.); Bristol Univ. (PGCE); University Coll. London (PhD 2007). Uppingham School: Hist. Dept, 1971–89; Sixth Form Tutor, 1977–83; Second Master, 1983–89; Headmaster, Dragon Sch., Oxford, 1989–92; Dep. Headmaster and Dir of Studies, King's Sch., Macclesfield, 1992–94. Course Dir, Bell Sch., Cambridge, 1976–82. Chm., HMC, 2007 (Vice-Chm., 2007–08). Question compiler, Top of the Form, BBC Radio 4, 1982–87. Governor: Greycotes Sch., Oxford, 1989–92; King's Coll. Sch., Cambridge, 1998–2004; King's Sch., Ely, 2008–; Norwich Sch., 2008–; Magdalen Coll. Sch., Oxford, 2008–. Walter Hines Page Scholar, ESU, 2003. Ed., Conference and Common Room, 1999–2002. *Publications:* The Effective Use of Time, 1984, 2nd edn 1989; First Steps in Leadership, 1987; Typhoid in Uppingham: analysis of a Victorian town and school in crisis 1875–77, 2008 (British Assoc. for Local Hist. Award, 2008); various histories and biographies for school use; contrib. TES, The Times, Daily Telegraph, Daily Mail, etc. *Recreations:* history, music, writing, sport, gardening, travel. *Address:* 6 High Meadow, Harston, Cambridge CB22 7TR. *T:* (01223) 872469; *e-mail:* NPVRichardson@btinternet.com.

RICHARDSON, Rt Rev. Paul; Assistant Bishop of Newcastle, since 1998; *b* 16 Jan. 1947; *s* of late William and Ilene Richardson. *Educ:* Keswick Sch.; The Queen's Coll., Oxford (BA (Mod. History) 1968, (Theol.) 1970; MA 1975); Harvard Divinity Sch.; Cuddesdon Theol Coll. Ordained deacon, 1972, priest, 1973; Asst Curate, St John's, Earlsfield, 1972–75; Asst Chaplain, Oslo, Norway, 1975–77; Mission Priest, Nambaiyufa, PNG, 1977–79; Lectr, 1979–81, Principal, 1981–85, Newton Theol Coll.; Dean, St John's Cathedral, Port Moresby, 1985–86; Bishop of Aipo Rongo, PNG, 1987–95; Bishop of Wangaratta, 1995–97. *Recreations:* reading, walking, travel. *Address:* Close House, St George's Close, Jesmond, Newcastle upon Tyne NE2 2TF. *T:* (0191) 281 2556. *Club:* Melbourne.

RICHARDSON, Paul Brayshaw; a District Judge (Magistrates' Courts), since 2002; *b* 21 June 1948; *s* of Ronald and Enid Richardson; *m* 1973, Valerie Madeleine Hine; one *s* one *d*. *Educ:* Berkhamsted Sch.; Trinity Coll., Oxford (MA). Called to the Bar, Middle Temple, 1972; in practice as barrister, Northern Circuit, with chambers in Manchester, 1973–2002; Actg Stipendiary Magistrate, 1995–2002. *Recreations:* fly fishing, cricket, jugband music. *Address:* Manchester Magistrates' Court, Crown Square, Manchester M60 1PR.

RICHARDSON, Prof. Peter Damian, FRS 1986; Professor of Engineering and Physiology, Brown University, USA, since 1984; *b* West Wickham, Kent, 22 Aug. 1935; *s* of late Reginald William Merrells Richardson and Marie Stuart Naomi (*née* Ouseley). *Educ:* Imperial College, Univ. of London (BSc (Eng) 1955; PhD 1958; DSc (Eng) 1974; ACGI 1955; DIC 1958; DSc 1983); MA Brown Univ. 1965. Demonstrator, Imperial Coll., 1955–58; Brown University: Vis. Lectr, 1958–59; Research Associate, 1959–60; Asst Prof. of Engrg, 1960–65; Associate Prof. of Engrg, 1965–68; Prof. of Engrg, 1968–84; Chair, University Faculty, 1987– (Vice-Chair, 1986–87). Sen. Vis. Fellow, Univ. of London, 1967; Prof. d'échange, Univ. of Paris, 1968; leave at Orta Doğu Teknik Univ., Ankara, 1969. FASME 1983; Founding Fellow, AIMBE, 1991; FCGI 2003. Humboldt-Preis, A. von Humboldt Sen. Scientist Award, 1976; Laureate in Medicine, Ernst Jung Foundn, 1987. *Publications:* (with M. Steiner) Principles of Cell Adhesion, 1995; numerous articles in learned jls. *Recreations:* photography, travel, country life. *Address:* Box D, Brown University, Providence, Rhode Island 02912–9104, USA. *T:* (401) 8632687.

RICHARDSON, Prof. Robert Coleman, PhD; Floyd Newman Professor of Physics, since 1987, and Vice Provost for Research, since 1998, Cornell University; *b* 26 June 1937; *s* of Robert Franklin Richardson and Lois Richardson (*née* Price); *m* 1962, Betty Marilyn McCarthy; two *d*. *Educ:* Virginia Poly. Inst. and State Univ.; Duke Univ. Served US Army, 1959–60. Cornell University: Res. Associate, 1966–67; Asst Prof., 1968–71; Associate Prof., 1972–74; Prof. of Physics, 1975–86. Chm., C-5 Cttee, IUPAP, 1981–84; Mem., Bd of Assessment, Nat. Bureau of Standards, 1983–. FAAAS. (Jtly) Nobel Prize for Physics, 1996. *Publications:* (jtly) Discovering Complexity: decomposition and localization as strategies in scientific research, 1993; (jtly) Experimental Techniques in Condensed Matter Physics at Low Temperatures, 1998; articles in learned jls. *Address:* Department of Physics, Cornell University, 517 Clark Hall, Ithaca, NY 14853, USA.

RICHARDSON, Lt-Gen. Sir Robert (Francis), KCB 1982; CVO 1978; CBE 1975 (OBE 1971; MBE 1965); Lieutenant of the Tower of London, 1992–95; Administrator, MacRobert Trusts, 1985–95; *b* 2 March 1929; *s* of late Robert Buchan Richardson and Anne (*née* Smith); *m* 1st, 1956, Maureen Anne Robinson (*d* 1986); three *s* one *d*; 2nd, 1988, Alexandra Inglis (*née* Bomford); two step *s*. *Educ:* George Heriot's Sch., Edinburgh; RMA Sandhurst. Commnd into The Royal Scots, 1949; served in BAOR, Korea, and Middle East with 1st Bn The Royal Scots until 1960; Defence Services Staff Coll., India, 1960–61; psc 1961; GSO II MO4, MoD, 1961–64; jssc 1964; Brigade Major Aden Bde, 1967 (Despatches); GSO II ACDS (Ops), MoD, 1968–69; CO 1st Bn The Royal Scots, 1969–71; Col Gen. Staff, Staff Coll. Camberley, 1971–74; Comdr 39 Infantry Bde, Northern Ireland, 1974–75; Deputy Adjutant General, HQ BAOR, 1975–78; GOC Berlin (British Sector), 1978–80; Vice Adjutant Gen. and Dir of Army Manning, 1980–82; GOC NI, 1982–85. Col, The Royal Scots (The Royal Regt), 1980–90. Chairman: Greencastle Farming plc, 1995–2004; RSC Mgt Ltd, 1999–. Man. Trustee, BLESMA, 1995–2002 (Mem., National Adv. Cttee, 2000–04); Trustee, Scottish Civic Trust, 1997–2003. OStJ 1988. *Recreations:* golf, shooting, gardening. *Address:* c/o Bank of Scotland, PO Box 23688, The Mound, Edinburgh EH1 1WG. *Clubs:* Royal Scots (Trustee, 1995–) (Edinburgh); Hon. Co. of Edinburgh Golfers (Muirfield).

RICHARDSON, Hon. Ruth Margaret; consultant and company director; Ruth Richardson (NZ) Ltd, strategic and economic policy advice, since 1994; *b* 13 Dec. 1950; *d* of Ross Pearce Richardson and Rita Joan Richardson; *m* 1975, Andrew Evan Wright; one *s* one *d*. *Educ:* Canterbury Univ., NZ (LLB Hons 1971). Admitted to the Bar, 1973; Legal Adviser: Law Reform Div., Dept of Justice, 1972–75; Federated Farmers of NZ, 1975–80. MP (Nat. Party) Selwyn, NZ, 1981–94; Opposition spokesman: on Education and on Youth Issues, 1984–87; on Finance, 1987–90; Minister of Finance, 1990–93. Dir, Reserve Bank of NZ, 1999–2004. *Recreations:* running, swimming, gardening. *Address:* RD5, Christchurch, New Zealand. *T:* (3) 3479146.

RICHARDSON, Sir Simon Alaisdair S.; *see* Stewart-Richardson.

RICHARDSON, Stephen John; Chief Executive, Banking, Robert Fleming & Co., 1999; *b* 18 Jan. 1953; *m* 1978, Heather Mary Boor; one *s* one *d*. *Educ:* Imperial Coll., London (BSc Mech. Engrg). FCIB 1990. Barclays Bank plc, 1974–96: Dir, UK Personal Sector, 1989–93; Man. Dir, Barclaycall, 1993–95; Man. Dir, Save & Prosper Gp, 1996–98. Non-executive Director: FOCUS Central London Ltd, 1998; Proshare (UK) Ltd, 1999. *Recreations:* sport, music.

RICHARDSON, Maj.-Gen. Thomas Anthony, (Tony), CB 1976; MBE 1960; Secretary, Christmas Tree Growers Association of Western Europe, 1989–2003; *b* 9 Aug. 1922; *s* of late Maj.-Gen. T. W. Richardson, Eaton Cottage, Unthank Road, Norwich, and late Mrs J. H. Boothby, Camberley; *m* 1st, 1945, Katharine Joanna Ruxton Roberts (*d* 1988), Woodland Place, Bath; one *s* one *d*; 2nd, 1991, Anthea Rachel Fry, Wimbledon. *Educ:* Wellington Coll., Berks. Technical Staff Course, psc, Fixed Wing Pilot, Rotary Wing Pilot, Parachutist. War of 1939–45: enlisted, Feb. 1941; commissioned, RA, March 1942; Essex Yeomanry (France and Germany), 1942–45; Air Observation Post, 1945–46. Tech. Staff/G Staff, 1949–52, 1954–55, 1959–60, 1963–64; Regt duty, 1942–45, 1952–54, 1957–58, 1961–62. Instr, Mil. Coll. Science, 1955–56; CO, 7th Para, RHA, 1965–67; CRA, 2 Div., 1967–69; Dir, Operational Requirements (Army), 1969–71; Dir, Army Aviation, 1971–74; Defence and Military Advr, India, 1974–77. Col Comdt, RA, 1978–83. Asst Sec., 1978–80, Sec. 1980–84, Timber Growers England and Wales Ltd; Sec., British Christmas Tree Growers Assoc., 1980–98; Dep. Chm., 1984–86, Chm., 1986–88, Tree Council. Chm., Queen Mary's Roehampton Trust, 2001–02. President: Essex Yeomanry Assoc., 1982–2006 (Vice-Pres., 2006–); Surrey Normandy Veterans Assoc., 1993–; Normandy Veterans Assoc., 2007–; Pres./Chm., Air Observation Post Officers' Assoc., 2002–. *Recreations:* sailing, fishing. *Address:* The Lodge, 7 Woodhayes Road, Wimbledon, SW19 4RJ. *Club:* Army and Navy.

RICHARDSON, Sir Thomas (Legh), KCMG 2000 (CMG 1991); HM Diplomatic Service; Ambassador to Italy, 1996–2000; *b* 6 Feb. 1941; *s* of Arthur Legh Turnour Richardson and Penelope Margaret Richardson; *m* 1979, Alexandra Frazier Wasiqullah (*née* Ratcliff). *Educ:* Westminster Sch.; Christ Church, Oxford. MA (Hist.). Joined Foreign Office, 1962; seconded to Univ. of Ghana, 1962–63; FO, 1963–65; Third Sec., Dar-Es-Salaam, 1965–66; Vice-Consul (Commercial), Milan, 1967–70; seconded to N. M. Rothschild & Sons, 1970; FCO, 1971–74; First Sec., UK Mission to UN, 1974–78; FCO, 1978–80; seconded to Central Policy Review Staff, Cabinet Office, 1980–81; Head of Chancery, Rome, 1982–86; Head of Economic Relns Dept, FCO, 1986–89; UK Dep. Perm. Rep. to UN, with personal rank of Ambassador, 1989–94; Asst Under-Sec. of State (Western Europe), FCO, 1994–96. Gov., British Inst. of Florence, 2001–08 (Chm., 2003–08); Mem. Council, British Sch. at Rome, 2002–06. Hon. Pres., British-Italian Soc., 2007–. *Recreations:* reading, walking, travel, music.

RICHARDSON, Maj.-Gen. Tony; *see* Richardson, Maj.-Gen. Thomas A.

RICHARDSON-BUNBURY, Sir (Richard David) Michael; *see* Bunbury.

RICHBOROUGH, Bishop Suffragan of, since 2002; **Rt Rev. Keith Newton;** Provincial Episcopal Visitor, Canterbury, since 2002; *b* 10 April 1952; *s* of James Henry and Eva Newton; *m* 1973, Gillian Irene Newton (*née* Donnison); two *s* one *d*. *Educ:* Alsop High Sch., Liverpool; KCL (BD, AKC 1973); Christchurch Coll., Canterbury (PGCE 1974); St Augustine's Coll., Canterbury. Ordained deacon, 1975, priest, 1976; Curate, St Mary's, Gt Ilford, 1975–78; Vicar, i/c St Matthews, Wimbledon Team Ministry, 1978–85; Rector, St Paul's, Blantyre, Dio. Southern Malaŵi, 1985–86; Dean of Blantyre, 1986–91; Priest i/c, 1991–93, Vicar, 1993–2002, Holy Nativity, Knowle; Priest i/c, All Hallows, Easton, 1997–2002. RD, Brislington, 1995–99; Area Dean, Bristol S, 1999–2001. Hon. Canon: Southern Malaŵi, 1986–; Bristol Cathedral, 2000–02. *Recreation:* travel. *Address:* Richborough House, 6 Mellish Gardens, Woodford Green, Essex IG8 0BH.

RICHER, Julian, LVO 2007; Founder and Chairman, Richer Sounds plc, since 1978; *b* 9 March 1959; *s* of Percy Isaac Richer and Ursula Marion (*née* Haller); *m* 1982, Rosemary Louise Hamlet. *Educ:* Clifton Coll., Bristol. Salesman, Hi-Fi Markets Ltd, 1977; Founder and Chairman: JR Properties, 1989–; Audio Partnership plc, 1994–; Richer Consulting Ltd, 1996–2002; The Richer Partnership, 1997–; JR Publishing, 1998–; Lomo Ltd, 1998–2007; Definitely Mktg Ltd, 2000–05; Chairman: Home Ltd, 1999–2003; Grey Frog plc, 2000–04. Non-executive Director: Duchy Originals Ltd, 1998–2006; Urban Spaces Ltd, 1999–2003; Knutsford plc, 1999–2002; Poptones plc, 2000–05; WILink.com plc, 2000–03. Chm., Business Develt Gp, Henry Doubleday Res. Assoc., 1998–2002. Founder and Chm., Persula Foundn, 1994–; Mem., Leadership Gp, Amnesty Internat., 2004–07; Ambassador for Youth, 1998–; Patron: Gold Service Panel, Irwell Valley Housing Assoc., 1998– (Chm., Gold Service Evaluation Panel, 1998–2005); Big Issue, 1999; Youth Clubs UK 90th Anniv., 2000; Ambassador, Centrepoint, 2000–01; Vice-Pres., RSPCA, 2002–; Dep. Chm. and Mem., New Horizons Develt Bd, 1997–2002, Mem., Adv. Bd, 2002–04, RNIB. Dir, Whizz-Kids 10th Birthday Bd, 1999–2007. Hon. DBA: Kingston, 2001; Bournemouth, 2002. *Publications:* The Richer Way, 1995, 4th edn 2001; Richer on Leadership, 1999. *Recreations:* radio controlled models, drumming, reading, walking, travel. *Address:* c/o Richer Sounds plc, Richer House, Hankey Place, SE1 4BB. *T:* (020) 7403 1310.

RICHER, Rosalind Miriam; *see* Altmann, R. M.

RICHES, Anne Clare, (Mrs T. C. Coltman), OBE 1999; FSA; DL; free-lance architectural historian, since 1989; *b* 12 April 1943; *d* of late Rt Rev. Kenneth Riches and of Kathleen Mary Riches (*née* Dixon); *m* 1989, Timothy Charles Coltman. *Educ:* Headington Sch., Oxford; Edinburgh Univ. (MA 1965; Dip. Hist of Art 1966). FSA 1985. Historian, Historic Bldgs Div., GLC, 1966–78; Inspector, then Principal Inspector, Historic Bldgs and Monuments Directorate, Scottish Develt Dept, 1978–89. Society of Architectural Historians of Great Britain: Sec., 1978–83; Conf. Sec., 1978–85; Chm., 1985–88. Member: Adv. Panel, Railway Heritage Trust, 1985–2006; Nat. Cttee, Assoc. of Preservation Trusts, 1989–95; RCHME, 1991–99; Royal Commn on Ancient and Historical Monuments of Scotland, 1995–2004; Council for Care of Churches, 2001–. Trustee: Scottish Historic Bldgs Trust, 1989–; Theatres Trust, 1996–2005; Heritage Trust for Lincolnshire: Dir, 1990–; Chm., 2002–; Chm., Archaeol. Adv. Cttee, 1991–94; Chm., Bldgs Adv. Cttee, 1992–. Mem., Lincoln Cathedral Fabric Council, 1998–. DL Lincs, 2006. *Publications:* (with R. Barber) A Dictionary of Fabulous Beasts, 1972; Victorian Church Building and Restoration in Suffolk, 1982; (jtly) Building of Scotland: Glasgow, 1990; contrib. Architectl Hist. *Recreations:* gardening, hill-farming, visiting buildings. *Address:* Skellingthorpe Hall, Lincoln LN6 5UU. *T:* (01522) 694609.

RICHINGS, Lewis David George; *b* 22 April 1920; *s* of Lewis Vincent Richings and Jessie Helen (*née* Clements); *m* 1944, Margaret Alice Hume (*d* 2005); three *d*. *Educ:* Battersea Grammar Sch.; Devonport High Sch.; Darlington Grammar Sch.; London Sch. of Econs and Polit. Science (part-time). Served War, Army, 1939–46: commnd 2 Lieut Inf., 1940; attached 8 DLI, 1940–41; seconded 11 KAR, 1941–45; Actg Major, 1945; various postings, UK, 1945–46. MAFF, 1937–58; attached MoD, 1958; Gen.

Administrator, AWRE, 1958–65; Health and Safety Br., UKAEA, 1965–70; Sec., Nat. Radiol Protection Bd, 1970–79, Dep. Dir, 1978–80. Mem., Radiol Protection and Public Health Cttee, Nuclear Energy Agency, OECD, 1966–80 (Chm., 1972–74). FRSA. *Publications:* articles in press and jls on admin and technical matters relating to common land, rural electrification, earthquakes, and radiol protection. *Recreation:* boats. *Address:* 31 Kennedy Street, Blairgowrie, Vic 3942, Australia.

RICHMOND, 10th Duke of, *cr* 1675, **LENNOX**, 10th Duke of, *cr* 1675 (Scot.), **AND GORDON**, 5th Duke of, *cr* 1876; **Charles Henry Gordon-Lennox;** Baron Settrington, Earl of March, 1675; Lord of Torboulton, Earl of Darnley (Scot.), 1675; Earl of Kinrara, 1876; Duc d'Aubigny (France), 1684; Hereditary Constable of Inverness Castle; Lord-Lieutenant of West Sussex, 1990–94; *b* 19 Sept. 1929; *s* of 9th Duke of Richmond and Gordon, and Elizabeth Grace (*d* 1992), *y d* of late Rev. T. W. Hudson; *S* father, 1989; *m* 1951, Susan Monica, *o d* of late Colonel C. E. Grenville-Grey, CBE, Hall Barn, Blewbury, Berks; one *s* four *d*. *Educ:* Eton; William Temple Coll. 2nd Lieut, 60th Rifles, 1949–50. Chartered Accountant, 1956. Dir of Industrial Studies, William Temple Coll., 1964–68; Chancellor, Univ. of Sussex, 1985–98 (Treasurer, 1979–82). Church Commissioner, 1963–76; Mem. Gen. Synod of Church of England, formerly Church Assembly, 1960–80 (Chm., Bd for Mission and Unity, 1967–77); Mem., Central and Exec. Cttees, World Council of Churches, 1968–75; Chairman: Christian Orgn Res. and Adv. Trust, 1965–87; House of Laity, Chichester Diocesan Synod, 1976–79; Vice-Chm., Archbishop's Commn on Church and State, 1966–70; Member: W Midlands Regional Economic Planning Council, 1965–68; Steering Gp, W Sussex Economic Forum, 1997–; Bognor Regis Jt Regeneration Steering Gp, 2001–07; Chm., W Sussex Coastal Strip Enterprise Gateway Hub, 2000–06. Chairman: Goodwood Group of Cos, 1969–; Dexam International Holdings Ltd, 1969–; Ajax Insurance (Holdings) Ltd, 1987–89; John Wiley and Sons Ltd, 1992–99 (Dir, 1984–92); Dir, Radio Victory Ltd, 1982–87. Historic Houses Association: Hon. Treas., 1975–82; Chm., SE Region, 1975–78; Dep. Pres., 1982–86; President: Action in Rural Sussex (formerly Sussex Rural Community Council), 1973–2006 (Chm., Rural Housing Adv. Cttee, 1996–2006); British Horse Soc., 1976–78; South of England Agricultural Soc., 1981–82; SE England Tourist Bd, 1990–2003 (Vice-Pres., 1974–90); Chm., Assoc. of Internat. Dressage Event Organisers, 1987–94; Chairman: Rugby Council of Social Service, 1961–68; Dunford Coll., (YMCA), 1969–82; Dir, Country Gentlemen's Assoc. Ltd, 1975–89. Pres. (UK), African Med. and Res. Foundn, 1996–. Chairman: of Trustees, Sussex Heritage Trust, 1978–2001; Planning for Economic Prosperity in Chichester and Arun, 1984–89 (Pres., 1989–); Chichester Cathedral Develt Trust, 1985–91 (Pres., 1991–); Sussex Community Foundn, 2005–; Patron, Sussex Enterprise, 1987–. President: Chichester Festivities, 1975–; Sussex CCC, 1991–2001 (Patron, 2001–). DL W Sussex, 1975–90. CCMI (CBIM 1982). Freeman, City of Chichester, 2008. Hon LLD Sussex, 1986. Medal of Honour, British Equestrian Fedn, 1983. *Heir: s* Earl of March and Kinrara, *qv*. *Address:* Molecomb, Goodwood, Chichester, W Sussex PO18 0PZ. *T:* (office) (01243) 755000, (home) (01243) 527861, *Fax:* (office) (01243) 755005; *e-mail:* richmond@goodwood.co.uk.

RICHMOND, Archdeacon of; *see* Henderson, Ven. J.

RICHMOND, Bernard Grant; QC 2006; a Recorder, since 2002; *b* 25 May 1965; *s* of James Richmond and Carol Richmond (*née* Linstead); *m* 1995, Christa Elfriede, *d* of Rudolf and Ruth Veile. *Educ:* Stratford Comp. Sch.; City of London Poly. (LLB Hons 1986). Called to the Bar, Middle Temple, 1988, Bencher, 2005; in practice as a barrister, 1988–; apptd to Faculty, Middle Temple Advocacy, 1995, Dir of Studies, 2006–. *Recreations:* judo, Real tennis, battling with German grammar, conversing with my cats. *Address:* Lamb Building, Temple, EC4Y 7AS. *T:* (020) 7797 7788; *e-mail:* clerks@lambbuilding.co.uk. *Clubs:* Queen's, Kuwa no Kai Judo; Hyde Real Tennis.

RICHMOND, Sir David (Frank), KBE 2008; CMG 2004; HM Diplomatic Service, retired; Director General, Defence and Intelligence, Foreign and Commonwealth Office, 2004–07; Consultant, Bell Pottinger, since 2007; *b* 9 July 1954; *s* of Frank George Richmond and Constance Lillian Richmond (*née* Hilling); *m* 1990, Caroline Matagne; one *s* one *d*. *Educ:* Merchant Taylors' Sch.; Trinity Hall, Cambridge (BA). FCO, 1976; MECAS, 1977–78; Baghdad, 1979–82; Second, later First Sec., FCO, 1982–87; UK Rep., Brussels, 1987–91; Dep. Head, Near East and N Africa Dept, FCO, 1991–94; Head, Economic Relations Dept, FCO, 1994–96; Head of Chancery, UK Mission to UN, NY, 1996–2000; UK Rep. to Pol and Security Cttee, EU and UK Perm. Rep. to WEU, Brussels, with rank of Ambassador, 2000–03; UK Special Rep. for Iraq, 2004. Gov., Ditchley Foundn, 2004–. *Address:* c/o Bell Pottinger, 14 Curzon Street, W1J 5HN.

RICHMOND, Rt Rev. (Francis) Henry (Arthur); Hon. Assistant Bishop, diocese of Oxford, since 1999; Hon. Assistant Chaplain of Christ Church Cathedral, Oxford, since 2006; *b* 6 Jan. 1936; *s* of Frank and Lena Richmond; *m* 1966, Caroline Mary Berent; two *s* one *d*. *Educ:* Portora Royal School, Enniskillen; Trinity Coll., Dublin (MA); Univ. of Strasbourg (BTh); Linacre Coll., Oxford (MLitt); Wycliffe Hall, Oxford. Deacon, 1963, priest, 1964; Asst Curate, Woodlands, Doncaster, 1963–66; Sir Henry Stephenson Research Fellow, Sheffield Univ. and Chaplain, Sheffield Cathedral, 1966–69; Vicar, St George's, Sheffield, 1969–77; Anglican Chaplain to Sheffield Univ. and Mem. Sheffield Chaplaincy for Higher Education, 1974–77; Warden, Lincoln Theol Coll., and Canon and Prebendary of Lincoln Cathedral, 1977–85; Bishop Suffragan of Repton, 1986–98. Examng Chaplain to Bishop of Lincoln; Proctor in Convocation for Lincoln, 1980. Archbishop's ecumenical bishop for Old Catholic Churches, 1991–98. *Recreations:* listening to classical music, reading, theatre, walking, gardening. *Address:* 39 Hodges Court, Oxford OX1 4NZ. *T:* (01865) 790466.

RICHMOND, Sir Mark (Henry), Kt 1986; PhD, ScD; FRS 1980; Member, School of Public Policy, University College London, 1996–2005; *b* 1 Feb. 1931; *s* of Harold Sylvester Richmond and Dorothy Plaistowe Richmond; *m* 1st, 1958, Shirley Jean Townrow (marr. diss. 1999); one *s* one *d* (and one *d* decd); 2nd, 2000, Sheila Travers. *Educ:* Epsom College; Clare Coll., Cambridge. BA, PhD, ScD. Scientific Staff, MRC, 1958–65; Reader in Molecular Biology, Univ. of Edinburgh, 1965–68; Prof. of Bacteriology, Univ. of Bristol, 1968–81; Vice-Chancellor, and Prof. of Molecular Microbiol., Victoria Univ. of Manchester, 1981–90; Chm., SERC, 1990–94 (Mem., 1981–85); Gp Hd of Res., Glaxo Hldgs, 1993–95. Director: Whittington Hosp. NHS Trust, 1996–98; Core Gp plc, 1997–99; Ark Therapeutics plc, 1997–; Genentech Inc., 1999–2005; OSI Pharmaceuticals Inc., 1999–2006; Cytos AG, 1999–. Member: Bd, PHLS, 1976–85; Fulbright Cttee, 1980–84; Chairman: British Nat. Cttee for Microbiol., 1980–85; CVCP, 1987–89; Cttee on Microbiological Food Safety, 1989–91; Member: Genetic Manipulation Adv. Gp, 1976–84; Adv. Cttee on Genetic Manipulation, 1984–85; Internat. Scientific Adv. Bd, UNESCO, 1996–2001; Council, Cancer Res. UK (formerly CRC), 1997–2002 (Chm., CRC Technology, 1997–2002; Chm., Cancer Res. Ventures, 1999–2002). Pres., Epsom Coll., 1992–2001. Member: IBM Academic Adv. Bd, 1984–90; Knox Fellowship Cttee, 1984–87; CIBA-Geigy Fellowship Trust, 1984–91; Jarrett Cttee for University Efficiency, 1985; Governing Body, Lister Inst., 1987–90; Council, ACU, 1988–90; Council, Royal Northern Coll. of Music, 1990–92; Educn Cttee, Royal Anniversary Trust, 1994–97; Trustee: Nat. Gall., 1994–2000; Tate Gall., 1995–99; Dyson Perrins Mus., Worcester, 1993–2001. *Publications:* several in microbiology and biochemistry jls. *Recreation:* hill-walking. *Address:* School of Public Policy, University College London, 29–30 Tavistock Square, WC1H 9QU. *Club:* Athenæum.

RICHMOND, Prof. Peter, PhD, DSc; FInstP; Director, EPM Associates Ltd, since 1998; *b* 4 March 1943; *s* of John Eric Richmond and Nellie (*née* Scholey); *m* 1967, Christine M. Jackson (*d* 1995); one *s* one *d*. *Educ:* Whitcliffe Mount Grammar Sch., Cleckheaton; Queen Mary Coll., London (BSc, PhD); London Univ. (DSc). ICI Res. Fellow, Univ. of Kent, 1967–69; Univ. of NSW, 1969–71; Queen Elizabeth II Res. Fellow, Inst. of Advanced Studies, ANU, 1971–73; Unilever Res., 1973–82; Hd, Process Physics, AFRC Food Res. Inst., Norwich, 1982–86; Prof., Univ. of Loughborough, 1985–88; Dir, AFRC Inst. of Food Res., Norwich Lab., 1986–92; Gen. Man., CWS, 1992–96. Hon. Prof., UEA, 1986–; EU Marie Curie Fellow, 1998, Vis. Prof., Dept of Physics, 1998–, TCD. Mem., MAFF/DoH Adv. Cttee on novel foods and processes, 1988–94; Chm., Eur. Co-operation in Scientific and Tech. Res. P10, Physics of Risk, 2004–07. *Publications:* (with R. D. Bee and J. Mingins) Food Colloids, 1989; (with P. J. Frazier and A. Donald) Starch Structure and Functionality, 1997; contribs to learned jls. *Recreations:* music, walking, talking and eating with friends. *Club:* Athenæum.

RICHMOND, Timothy Stewart, MBE 1985; TD 1982; FCA; Vice Lord-Lieutenant of Nottinghamshire, since 2008; chartered accountant and adviser in business direction; *b* Edingley, 17 Nov. 1947; *s* of Stewart McKenzie Sylvester Richmond and Nancie Richmond (*née* Barber); *m* 1974, Susan Carol Spencer; two *s* two *d*. *Educ:* Birkdale Sch., Sheffield; Nottingham High Sch. ACA 1970; FCA 1979. Pannell Kerr Forster (PKF), Chartered Accountants: articles, 1966–70; qualified Asst, Manager, 1970–74; Partner, 1974–98; Man. Partner, Nottingham firm, 1980–85; Nat. Man. Partner, UK firm, 1985–94; Chm., internat. firm, 1994–98; Partner, GTN and predecessor firms, 1998–2008. Chairman: Huthwaite Internat. Ltd, 1998–; Clegg Gp Ltd, 2008– (non-exec. Dir, 2000–); Dir, Legal Practice Consortium Ltd, 2006–. Mem., Monopolies and Mergers Commn, 1997–2003. Dir, Nottingham HA, 1989–91. Chm., Connexions Notts Ltd, 2001–. Dir, Notts Community Foundn, 2003–05. Chm., English Churches Housing Gp, 1994–98. Pres., Nottingham, Derby and Lincoln Dist Soc. of Chartered Accountants, 2006–07 (Vice and Dep. Pres., 2004–06); Mem., Members Services Bd, ICAEW, 2007–. Mem. Council, Chartered Mgt Inst., 1998–2002 (CCMI). Dep. Chm., Nottingham Trent Univ. (formerly Nottingham Poly.), 1989–97 (Gov., 1984–98); Gov., New Coll., Nottingham, 2008–. Member: Southwell Cath. Council, 2000–07; Council of Friends of Southwell Cath., 2006–. Trustee, Notts Community Safety Trust, 2002–. Vice Chm. (Army), Nat. Council, Reserve Forces and Cadets Assoc. and Chm., E Midlands Assoc., 2003–. Commnd Royal Regt of Artillery TA, 1971 (2nd Lieut); OC (Maj.) 307 (S Notts Hussars Yeo. RHA) Observation Post Battery (V), 1982–85 (Hon. Col, 2002–); CO (Lt Col), E Midlands Univs OTC, 1988–91 (Hon. Col, 2005–); Dep. Bde Comdr (Col), 49 and 54 Bdes and TA Col for E Midlands, 1991–95; ADC (TA) to the Queen, 1992–95; Comdt, Notts ACF, 1997–2001. DL 1990, High Sheriff, 2002–03, Notts. Hon. DBA Nottingham Trent, 1998. *Recreations:* sailing, gardening. *Address:* Kirklington, Notts. *Clubs:* Army and Navy; Nottingham.

RICHMOND-WATSON, Julian Howard; Senior Steward, Jockey Club, since 2003; *b* 6 Dec. 1947; *s* of Sonny and Jean Richmond-Watson; *m* 1972, Sarah Gee; four *s*. *Educ:* Hawtrey Sch.; Radley Coll. Man. Dir and Chm. of private cos in the property, quarrying and packing fields. Mem., various racecourse boards. *Recreations:* horse-racing, shooting. *Address:* Wakefield Lodge, Potterspury, Northants NN12 7QX; *e-mail:* Julianrw@farming.co.uk. *Clubs:* Boodle's, Jockey.

RICHTER, Prof. Burton; Paul Pigott Professor in the Physical Sciences, Stanford University, USA, 1980 (Professor of Physics, 1967–2005, now Emeritus); Director, Stanford Linear Accelerator Center, 1984–99, now Emeritus (Technical Director, 1982–84); *b* 22 March 1931; *s* of Abraham Richter and Fannie Pollack; *m* 1960, Laurose Becker; one *s* one *d*. *Educ:* Massachusetts Inst. of Technology. BS 1952, PhD (Physics) 1956. Stanford University: Research Associate, Physics, High Energy Physics Lab., 1956–60; Asst Prof., 1960–63; Associate Prof., 1963–67; full Prof., 1967. Loeb Lectr, Harvard, 1974; De Shalit Lectr, Weizmann Inst., 1975; Astor Vis. Lectr, Oxford Univ., 2000. Member, Board of Directors: Varian Corp., then Varian Associates, 1989–99; Litel Instruments, 1990–; Varian Med. Systems, 1999–2002; AREVA Enterprises, 2003–. Chm., Bd on Physics and Astronomy, Nat. Res. Council/Nat. Acads of Sci., USA, 2003–06. Pres., IUPAP, 1999–2002 (Pres. Designate, 1997–99). FAPS 1984 (Pres., 1994); Fellow, Amer. Acad. of Arts and Scis, 1990 (Mem., 1989); Mem., Nat. Acad. of Scis, 1977. Laurea *hc* in Physics, Univ. of Pisa, 2001. E. O. Lawrence Award, 1975; Nobel Prize for Physics (jointly), 1976. *Publications:* over 300 articles in various scientific journals. *Address:* Stanford Linear Accelerator Center, PO Box 20450, Stanford University, Stanford, CA 94309–0450, USA.

RICKARD, Rear Adm. Hugh Wilson, CBE 1996; Chief Executive, Royal Anniversary Trust, 2004–06; *b* 1 Sept. 1948; *s* of Charles Thomas Rickard and Isobel Rickard; *m* 1982, Patricia Ann Seager; two *s* one *d*. *Educ:* Surbiton Co. Grammar Sch.; Northern Poly. (BSc London Hons). MCIL (MIL 1994). Joined RN, 1972; qualified as Meteorological and Oceanographic Officer, 1974; Naval Staff Course, 1982; UK Defence and Naval Attaché, The Hague, 1992–95; CO, HMS Raleigh, 1995–98; Sen. Naval DS, RCDS, 1998–2000. Chief Exec., Lib. Dems, 2000–03. Bursar, Claremont Fan Court Sch., 2006–. *Recreations:* sailing, bridge, hill-walking. *Address:* High Burrows, The Drive, Sutton, Surrey SM2 7DP. *T:* (020) 8661 6258.

RICKARD, Dr John Hellyar; independent consultant economist; *b* 27 Jan. 1940; *s* of Peter John Rickard and Irene Eleanor (*née* Hales); *m* 1963, Christine Dorothy Hudson; one *s* two *d*. *Educ:* Ilford County High Sch.; St John's Coll., Oxford (MA 1966; DPhil 1976); Univ. of Aston in Birmingham (MSc 1969). Lectr, Univ. of Aston, 1967–70; Economist, Programmes Analysis Unit, AEA, Harwell, 1970–72; Res. Associate, and Dep. Head, Health Services Evaluation Gp, Dept of Regius Prof. of Medicine, Univ. of Oxford, 1972–74; Econ. Adviser, Dept of Health, 1974–76; Sen. Econ. Adviser: Dept of Prices and Consumer Protection, 1976–78; Central Policy Review Staff, Cabinet Office, 1978–82; HM Treasury, 1982–84; Econ. Adviser, State of Bahrain, 1984–87; Chief Economic Advr, Dept of Transport, 1987–91; Under Sec. (Econs), HM Treasury, 1991–94; Chief Econ. Advr, Dept of Transport, 1994–95; IMF Fiscal Advr, Min. of Finance, Republic of Moldova, 1995. Trustee, Earl Mountbatten Hospice, IoW, 2003–. *Publications:* (with D. Aston) Macro-Economics: a critical introduction, 1970; Longer Term Issues in Transport, 1991; articles in books and learned jls. *Recreations:* sailing, music. *Address:* Bay House, Lanes End, Totland Bay, Isle of Wight PO39 0BE. *T:* (01983) 754669. *Club:* Island Sailing.

RICKARD, Prof. Peter, DPhil, PhD, LittD; Drapers Professor of French, University of Cambridge, 1980–82, Emeritus since 1983; Fellow of Emmanuel College, Cambridge, 1953, Professorial Fellow, 1980, Life Fellow, since 1983; *b* 20 Sept. 1922; *yr s* of Norman

Ernest Rickard and Elizabeth Jane (*née* Hosking); unmarried. *Educ:* Redruth County Grammar Sch., Cornwall; Exeter Coll., Oxford (Final Hons Mod. Langs (French and German), Cl. I, 1948; MA 1948); DPhil Oxon 1952; PhD Cantab 1952; LittD Cambridge 1982. Served War, 1st Bn Seaforth Highlanders and Intell. Corps, India, 1942–46. Heath Harrison Travelling Scholar (French), 1948; Amelia Jackson Sen. Scholar, Exeter Coll., Oxford, 1948–49; Lectr in Mod. Langs, Trinity Coll., Oxford, 1949–52; Univ. of Cambridge: Asst Lectr in French, 1952–57, Lectr, 1957–74; Reader in French Lang., 1974–80; Mem., St John's Coll., 1952–; Tutor, Emmanuel Coll., 1954–65. *Publications:* Britain in Medieval French Literature, 1956; La langue française au XVIe siècle, 1968; (ed with T. G. S. Combe) The French Language: studies presented to Lewis Charles Harmer, 1970; (ed and trans.) Fernando Pessoa, Selected Poems, 1971; A History of the French Language, 1974; Chrestomathie de la langue française au XVe siècle, 1976; (ed with T. G. S. Combe) L. C. Harmer, Uncertainties in French Grammar, 1979; The Embarrassments of Irregularity, 1981; The French Language in the 17th Century: contemporary opinion in France, 1992; The Transferred Epithet in Modern English Prose, 1996; articles in Romania, Trans Phil Soc., Neuphilologische Mitteilungen, Cahiers de Lexicologie, and Zeitschrift für Romanische Philologie. *Recreations:* travel, music. *Address:* Upper Rosevine, Portscatho, Cornwall TR2 5EW. *T:* (01872) 580582.

RICKARDS, Prof. (Richard) Barrie, CGeol, FGS; Professor of Palaeontology and Biostratigraphy, University of Cambridge, 2000–05, now Emeritus Professor; Curator, Sedgwick Museum of Geology, 1969–2005, now Hon. Curator; Fellow, Emmanuel College, Cambridge, 1977–2004, now Life Fellow; Hon. Curator, Emmanuel College Museum, 1994–99; *b* 12 June 1938; *s* of Robert Rickards and Eva (*née* Sudborough); *m* 1960, Christine Townsley (marr. diss. 1991); one *s*. *Educ:* Goole Grammar Sch.; Univ. of Hull (BSc; PhD 1963; DSc 1990); MA Cantab, 1969; ScD Cantab, 1976. FGS 1960; Founder MIFM 1969; CGeol 1990. Reckitt Scholar, Univ. of Hull, 1960–63; Curator, Garwood Library, UCL, 1963; Asst in Research, Univ. of Cambridge, 1964–66; SSO, BM (Natural History), 1967; Lectr, TCD, 1967–69; University of Cambridge: Lectr, 1969–90; Reader, 1990–2000; Official Lectr, Emmanuel Coll., 1977–2000. Founder and first Sec., Pike Anglers' Club; Founding Mem., Nat. Anglers' Council; Deleg., E Reg., 1987–2000, Mem., Gen. Purposes Cttee, 1989–2000, Nat. Fedn of Anglers; Mem. Council, Waterbeach Angling Club, 1980–84; first Fishery Manager, Leland Water, 1982–83. Consultant, Shakespeare Co. (UK) Ltd, 1988–. President: Lure Fishing Soc. of GB, 1992–; Nat. Assoc. of Specialist Anglers, 1993–2000; Specialist Anglers Alliance, 2001–; Trustee, Specialist Anglers' Conservation Gp, 1995–2000. Gov., Caldecote Co. Primary Sch., Cambs, 1994–95. Murchison Fund, 1982, Lyell Medal, 1997, Geol Soc.; John Phillips Medal, Yorks Geol Soc., 1988. *Publications:* Fishers on the Green Roads (novel), 2002; *angling:* (with R. Webb) Fishing for Big Pike, 1971, (sole author) 3rd edn, as Big Pike, 1986; Perch, 1974; (with R. Webb) Fishing for Big Tench, 1976, 2nd edn 1986; Pike, 1976; (with K. Whitehead) Plugs and Plug Fishing, 1976, and Spinners, Spoons and Wobbled Baits, 1977, rev. edn of both titles as A Textbook of Spinning, 1987; (with N. Fickling) Zander, 1979, 2nd edn 1990; (with K. Whitehead) Fishing Tackle, 1981; (with K. Whitehead) A Fishery of Your Own, 1984; Angling: fundamental principles, 1986; (with M. Gay) A Technical Manual of Pike Fishing, 1986; (ed) River Piking, 1987; (ed) Best of Pikelines, 1988; (with M. Gay) Pike, 1989; (with M. Bannister) The Ten Greatest Pike Anglers, 1991; (jtly) Encyclopaedia of Fishing, 1991; Success with Pike, 1992; Success with the Lure, 1993; (with M. Bannister) The Great Modern Pike Anglers, 2006; Richard Walker: biography of an angling legend, 2007; (with T. Baily) Nile Perch, 2008; over 700 articles on angling in newspapers and magazines; *geology:* Graptolites: writing in the rocks, 1991; (ed with D. C. Palmer) H. B. Whittington, Trilobites, 1992; (ed with S. Rigby) Graptolites in Colour: a teaching aid, 1998; upwards of 200 scientific articles and monographs in internat. jls, mostly on fossils (graptolites) and evolution. *Recreations:* angling, marathon running, angling administration (from local to national). *Address:* Emmanuel College, Cambridge CB2 3AP. *T:* (01223) 334282.

RICKERD, Martin John Kilburn, OBE 2004; MVO 1985; HM Diplomatic Service; Consul General, Atlanta, USA, since 2005; *b* 17 Aug. 1954; *s* of John Rickerd and Anne Rickerd (*née* Kilburn, later Greener); *m* 1976, Charmain Gwendoline Napier; two *s*. *Educ:* Lord Weymouth Sch. HM Diplomatic Service, 1972–: FCO, 1972–75; UK Delegn to NATO, Brussels, 1975–77; Wellington, 1977–80; Asst Private Sec. to Parly Under Sec. of State, FCO, 1980–82; Third Sec., Bridgetown, 1982–86; Consul, Milan, 1986–91; First Sec., FCO, 1991–95; Hd of Chancery, Singapore, 1995–98; on secondment to Standard Chartered Bank, London, 1998–2000; Dep. Hd of Mission, Abidjan, 2000–03; Hd, N America Team, FCO, 2003–05. *Address:* c/o Foreign and Commonwealth Office, King Charles Street, SW1A 2AH. *T:* (USA) (404) 9547700; *e-mail:* martin.rickerd@fco.gov.uk.

RICKETS, Brig. Reginald Anthony Scott, (Tony); Chairman, Irvine Housing Association, since 2002; *b* 13 Dec. 1929; *s* of Captain R. H. Rickets and Mrs V. C. Rickets (*née* Morgan); *m* 1952, Elizabeth Ann Serjeant; one *s* one *d*. *Educ:* St George's Coll., Weybridge; RMA Sandhurst. 2nd Lieut, RE, 1949; served with airborne, armoured and field engrs in UK, Cyrenaica, Egypt, Malaya, Borneo, Hong Kong and BAOR; special employment military forces Malaya, 1955–59; Staff Coll., Camberley, 1962; BM Engr Gp, BAOR, 1963–66; OC 67 Gurkha Indep. Field Sqn, 1966–68; DS Staff Coll., 1968–70; Comdt Gurkha Engrs/CRE Hong Kong, 1970–73; COS British Sector, Berlin, 1973–77; Col GS RSME, 1977–78; Chief Engr UKLF, 1978–81. Man. Dir, Irvine Develt Corp., 1981–95. Director: Enterprise Ayrshire, 1990–97; Kelvin Travel, 1995–98; Nobel Exhibn Trust, (The Big Idea), 1997–2002. President: Ayrshire Chamber of Industries, 1983–86; Ayrshire Chamber of Commerce and Industry, 1989–91; German-British Chamber of Industry and Commerce in Scotland, 1998–; Mem. Exec. Bd, Scottish Council (Develt and Industry), 1990–92. Chm., ASSET Enterprise Trust, 1996–97. Mem. Exec. Bd, Scottish Maritime Mus., 1986–. *Recreation:* sailing. *Address:* Burnbrae Cottage, Montgreenan, Ayrshire KA13 7QZ. *Club:* Royal Engineer Yacht (Commodore, 1979–81).

RICKETT, William Francis Sebastian; Director General, Energy, Department of Energy and Climate Change (formerly Department of Trade and Industry, then Department for Business, Enterprise and Regulatory Reform), since 2006; *b* 23 Feb. 1953; *s* of Sir Denis Rickett, KCMG, CB; *m* 1979, Lucy Caroline Clark; one *s* one *d*. *Educ:* Trinity Coll., Cambridge (BA 1974). Joined Department of Energy, 1975; Private Sec. to Perm. Under Sec. of State, 1977; Principal, 1978; Private Sec. to Prime Minister, 1981–83; seconded to Kleinwort Benson Ltd, 1983–85; Asst Sec., Oil Div., Dept of Energy, 1985; Asst Sec., Electricity Privatisation, 1987; Grade 4, Electricity Div., 1989; Under Sec., 1990; Dir Gen., Energy Efficiency Office, Dept of Energy, 1990–92, DoE, 1992–93; Dir of Finance (Central) and Principal Finance Officer, DoE, 1993–97; Dir of Town and Country Planning, DoE, then DETR, 1997–98; Dep. Sec. and Hd, Economic and Domestic Secretariat, Cabinet Office, 1998–2000; Hd, Integrated Transport Taskforce, subseq. Dir-Gen., Transport Strategy and Planning, DETR, 2000–01; Dir-Gen., Transport Strategy, Roads, Local and Maritime Transport, then Transport Strategy, Roads and Local Transport, then Strategy, Finance and Delivery, DTLR, subseq. DfT, 2001–04; on secondment to Ernst & Young from DfT, 2004–06. Chm., Governing Bd, Internat. Engrg Agency, 2007–. *Recreations:* children, painting, sports. *Address:* Department of Energy and Climate Change, 1 Victoria Street, SW1H 0ET.

RICKETTS, Prof. Martin John, DPhil; Professor of Economic Organisation, University of Buckingham, since 1987; *b* 10 May 1948; *s* of Leonard Alfred Ricketts and Gertrude Dorothy (*née* Elgar); *m* 1975, Diana Barbara Greenwood; one *s* one *d*. *Educ:* City of Bath Boys' Sch.; Univ. of Newcastle upon Tyne (BA Hons Econ.); Univ. of York (DPhil). Econ. Asst, Industrial Policy Gp, 1970–72; Res. Fellow, Inst. Econ. and Social Res., Univ. of York, 1975–77; University College at Buckingham, later University of Buckingham: Lectr in Econs, 1977–82; Sen. Lectr, 1982–85; Reader, 1985–87; Dean, Sch. of Business (formerly Sch. of Accountancy, Business and Econs), 1993–97; Pro-Vice-Chancellor, 1993. Economic Dir, NEDO, 1991–92. Vis. Prof., Virginia Poly. Inst. and State Univ., 1984. Hon. Prof., Heriot-Watt Univ., 1996. Trustee, Inst. of Econ. Affairs, 1992–. Chm., Buckingham Summer Fest., 2004–. *Publications:* (with M. G. Webb) The Economics of Energy, 1980; The Economics of Business Enterprise: new approaches to the firm, 1987, 3rd edn 2002; The Many Ways of Governance: perspectives on the control of the firm, 1999; papers on public finance, public choice, housing econs and econ. orgn. *Recreation:* music, student of piano and oboe. *Address:* 22 Bradfield Avenue, Buckingham MK18 1PR; School of Economics, University of Buckingham, Hunter Street, Buckingham MK18 1EG.

RICKETTS, Sir Peter (Forbes), KCMG 2003 (CMG 1999); HM Diplomatic Service; Permanent Under-Secretary of State, Foreign and Commonwealth Office, and Head of the Diplomatic Service, since 2006; *b* 30 Sept. 1952; *s* of Maurice and Dilys Ricketts; *m* 1980, Suzanne Julia Horlington; one *s* one *d*. *Educ:* Bishop Vesey's Grammar Sch.; Pembroke Coll., Oxford (MA; Hon. Fellow, 2007). Joined FCO, 1974; Singapore, 1975–78; UK Delegn to NATO, 1978–81; FCO, 1981–86, Private Sec. to Sec. of State for Foreign and Commonwealth Affairs, 1983–86; Washington, 1986–89; FCO, 1989–94, Head, Hong Kong Dept, 1991–94; Economic and Financial Counsellor, Paris, 1994–97; Dep. Pol Dir, FCO, 1997–99; Dir, Internat. Security, FCO, 1999–2000; Chm., Jt Intelligence Cttee, Cabinet Office (on secondment), 2000–01; Pol Dir, FCO, 2001–03; UK Perm. Rep., UK Delegn to NATO, 2003–06. *Recreations:* restoring Normandy farmhouse, Victorian art and literature. *Address:* c/o Foreign and Commonwealth Office, King Charles Street, SW1A 2AH. *T:* (020) 7270 3000.

RICKETTS, Simon Henry Martin, CB 2000; Ministry of Defence, 1975–2000; *b* 23 July 1941; *s* of late Ralph Robert Ricketts and Margaret Adeliza Mary (*née* Royds); *m* 1973, Annabel Ophelia Clare Lea (*d* 2003); one *s* one *d*. *Educ:* Ampleforth; Magdalen Coll., Oxford (BA Hons History). Senior Systems Analyst, George Wimpey & Co., 1963–71; Lectr in Liberal Studies, Hammersmith Coll. of Art and Building, 1967–68; Kulu Trekking Agency, 1971; Teacher, British Inst. of Florence, 1971–73; Royalties Clerk, Cape & Chatto Services, 1973–75. Mem., Friends of Georgian Soc. of Jamaica, 2001– (Trustee, 2004–07). *Publication:* (ed) The English Country House Chapel: building a Protestant tradition, by Annabel Ricketts, 2007. *Address:* c/o Lloyds TSB, 8 Fore Street, Budleigh Salterton, Devon EX9 6NQ. *Club:* Athenæum.

RICKETTS, Sir Stephen Tristram, 9th Bt *cr* 1828, of The Elms, Gloucestershire, and Beaumont Leys, Leicestershire; *b* 24 Dec. 1974; *s* of Sir (Robert) Tristram Ricketts, 8th Bt and of Ann Ricketts (*née* Lewis); *S* father, 2007. *Heir: uncle* John Stafford Ricketts [*b* 13 Feb. 1956; *m* 1986, Jacqueline Zifteh; one *s*].

RICKFORD, Jonathan Braithwaite Keevil, CBE 2001; solicitor, regulatory consultant; Professorial Fellow, British Institute of International and Comparative Law, since 2006 (Director, Company Law Centre, 2003–06); *b* 7 Dec. 1944; *s* of R. B. K. Rickford, MD, FRCS, FRCOG and of Dorothy Rickford (*née* Lathan); *m* 1968, Dora R. Sargant; one *s* two *d*. *Educ:* Sherborne School; Magdalen College, Oxford (MA (Jurisp.); BCL). Barrister, 1970–85; Solicitor, 1985–. Teaching Associate, Univ. of California Sch. of Law, 1968–69; Lectr in Law, LSE, 1969–72; Legal Asst, Dept of Trade, 1972–73; Senior Legal Assistant: Dept of Prices and Consumer Protection, 1974–76; Law Officers' Dept, Attorney General's Chambers, 1976–79; Dept of Trade and Industry (formerly Dept of Trade): Asst Solicitor (Company Law), 1979–82; Under Sec. (Legal), 1982–85; Solicitor, 1985–87; British Telecom: Solicitor and Chief Legal Advr, 1987–89; Dir of Govt Relns, 1989–93; Dir of Corporate Strategy, 1993–96; Project Dir, DTI's Review of Company Law, 1998–2001; Unilever Prof. in Eur. Corporate Law, Univ. of Leiden, Netherlands, 2002. Vis. Prof. of Law, LSE, 2003–. Mem., Competition (formerly Monopolies and Mergers) Commn, 1997–2004. Member: Europe Cttee, CBI, 1993–98; Council, European Policy Forum, 1993–. FRSA 1992. *Publications:* articles in learned jls. *Recreation:* sailing. *Clubs:* Reform; Bosham Sailing.

RICKINSON, Prof. Alan Bernard, PhD; FRS 1997; Professor of Cancer Studies, University of Birmingham, since 1983; *b* 12 Nov. 1943; *s* of Lawrence and Annie Rickinson; *m* 1968, Barbara; one *s* two *d*. *Educ:* Corpus Christi Coll., Cambridge (MA, PhD 1969). FRCP 1996. *Recreations:* walking, poetry. *Address:* Cancer Research UK Institute for Cancer Studies, University of Birmingham, Edgbaston, Birmingham B15 2TT. *T:* (0121) 414 4492.

RICKLETON, James David John; Assistant Auditor General, National Audit Office, since 2003; *b* 26 Aug. 1959; *s* of Jack and Jennifer Mary Rickleton; *m* 1998, Carol Anne Lyons; one *s* one *d*. *Educ:* Newcastle upon Tyne Poly. (BA Hons (Econs) 1980); City of London Poly. IPFA 1985. National Audit Office, 1981–: Audit trainee, 1981–86; Sen. Auditor, Financial Audit Tech. Support Team, 1986–88; Audit Manager, DES, 1988–92; Private Sec. to Comptroller and Auditor Gen., 1992–95; Dir of Audit, 1995–2003. *Recreations:* golf, reading, Newcastle United FC. *Address:* c/o National Audit Office, 157–197 Buckingham Palace Road, Victoria, SW1W 9SP. *T:* (020) 7798 7177, *Fax:* (020) 7798 7978; *e-mail:* jim.rickleton@nao.gsi.gov.uk.

RICKMAN, Alan; actor. *Educ:* Latymer Upper Sch.; Chelsea Sch. of Art (DipAD); Royal Coll. of Art; RADA. *Theatre* includes: The Devil is an Ass, Measure for Measure, Birmingham, Edinburgh Fest., Nat. Theatre, European tour, 1976–77; The Tempest, Captain Swing, Love's Labour's Lost, Antony and Cleopatra, RSC, 1978–79; The Summer Party, Crucible, 1980; Commitments, Bush, 1980; The Devil Himself, Lyric Studio, 1980; Philadelphia Story, Oxford Playhouse, 1981; The Seagull, Royal Court, 1981; Brothers Karamazov, Edinburgh Fest. and USSR, 1981; The Last Elephant, Bush, 1981; Bad Language, Hampstead, 1983; The Grass Widow, 1983, The Lucky Chance, 1984, Royal Court; As You Like It, Troilus and Cressida, Les Liaisons Dangereuses, Mephisto, RSC, 1985–86; Les Liaisons Dangereuses, West End and Broadway, 1986–87; Tango at the End of Winter, Edinburgh and West End, 1991; Hamlet, Riverside Studios and Brit. Tour, 1992; Antony and Cleopatra, RNT, 1998; Private Lives, Albery, 2001, NY, 2002; *director:* Desperately Yours, NY, 1980; (asst dir) Other Worlds, Royal Ct, 1983; Live Wax, Edin. Fest., 1986; Wax Acts, West End and tour, 1992; The Winter Guest, Almeida, 1995; My Name is Rachel Corrie, Royal Court, 2005, West End, Edin. Fest. and NY, 2006; Creditors, Donmar Warehouse, 2008; *films:* Die Hard, 1988; The January Man, 1989; Quigley Down Under, 1990; Truly, Madly, Deeply, Closetland, Close My

Eyes, Robin Hood, Prince of Thieves, 1991; Bob Roberts, 1992; Fallen Angels (TV, USA), Mesmer, 1993; An Awfully Big Adventure, 1995; Sense and Sensibility, Michael Collins, Rasputin, 1996; (dir) The Winter Guest (Best Film, Chicago Film Fest.; Premio Cinema Avvenire, OCIC Award, Venice Film Fest.), 1997; Dark Harbor, Judas Kiss, Dogma, 1999; Galaxy Quest, The Search for John Gissing, 2000; Blow Dry, Play, Harry Potter and the Philosopher's Stone, 2001; Harry Potter and the Chamber of Secrets, 2002; Love, Actually, 2003; Harry Potter and the Prisoner of Azkaban, Something the Lord Made, 2004; The Hitchhiker's Guide to the Galaxy, Harry Potter and the Goblet of Fire, 2005; Snow Cake, Perfume, Nobel Son, 2006; Harry Potter and the Order of the Phoenix, 2007; Sweeney Todd: The Demon Barber of Fleet Street, Bottle Shock, 2008; *television* includes: Thérèse Raquin, 1979; Barchester Chronicles, 1982; Pity in History, 1984; Revolutionary Witness, Spirit of Man, 1989; also radio performances. Bancroft Gold Medal, RADA, 1974; Seattle Film Fest. Best Actor, 1991; Time Out Award for Tango at the End of Winter, 1992; BAFTA Film Award for Best Supporting Actor, 1992; Evening Standard Film Award for Best Actor, 1992; Best Actor, Montreal Film Fest., 1994; Emmy Award for Best Actor, 1996; Golden Globe Award for Best Actor, 1997; Screen Actors Guild Award for Best Actor, 1997; Variety Club Award for Best Actor, 2002. *Publication*: (contrib.) Players of Shakespeare, Vol. 2, 1989. *Address*: c/o Independent Talent Group Ltd, Oxford House, 76 Oxford Street, W1D 1BS.

RICKMAN, Prof. Geoffrey Edwin, FBA 1989; Professor of Roman History, University of St Andrews, 1981–97, now Emeritus; *b* 9 Oct. 1932; *s* of Charles Edwin Rickman and Ethel Ruth Mary (*née* Hill); *m* 1959, Ann Rosemary Wilson; one *s* one *d. Educ*: Peter Symonds' Sch., Winchester; Brasenose Coll., Oxford (MA, DipClassArchaeol, DPhil). FSA 1966; FRSE 2001. Henry Francis Pelham Student, British Sch. at Rome, 1958–59; Jun. Res. Fellow, The Queen's Coll., Oxford, 1959–62; University of St Andrews: Lectr in Ancient History, 1962–68; Sen. Lectr, 1968–81; Master of the United Coll. of St Salvator and St Leonard, 1992–96; Pro-Vice-Chancellor, 1996–97. Vis. Fellow, Brasenose Coll., Oxford, 1981; Mem., IAS, Princeton, 1997–98. Mem., Faculty of Archaeol., History and Letters, 1979–87 (Chm., 1983–87), Chm. Council, 1997–2002, Hon. Fellow, 2002, British Sch. at Rome; Mem., Humanities Res. Bd, British Acad., 1995–98. *Publications*: Roman Granaries and Storebuildings, 1971; The Corn Supply of Ancient Rome, 1980. *Recreations*: opera, swimming, walking beside the sea. *Address*: 56 Hepburn Gardens, St Andrews, Fife KY16 9DG. *T*: (01334) 472063.

RICKS, Catherine Louise; Head, Sevenoaks School, since 2002; *b* 16 March 1961; *d* of Paul George Koralek, *qv*; *m* 1983, David Bruce Ricks. *Educ*: Camden Sch. for Girls, London; Balliol Coll., Oxford (MA Eng. Lit. 1982). Assistant Teacher: St Paul's Girls' Sch., 1985–87; King Edward's Sch., Birmingham, 1987–90; Latymer Upper Sch., 1990–92; Hd of Eng., St Edward's Sch., Oxford, 1992–97; Dep. Hd (Academic), Highgate Sch., 1997–2002. *Address*: Sevenoaks School, Sevenoaks, Kent TN13 1HU. *T*: (01732) 455133, *Fax*: (01732) 456143.

RICKS, Prof. Christopher Bruce, FBA 1975; Warren Professor of the Humanities, since 1998, and Co-Director, Editorial Institute, since 1999, Boston University (Professor of English, 1986–97); Professor of Poetry, University of Oxford, 2004–Oct. 2009; *b* 18 Sept. 1933; *s* of James Bruce Ricks and Gabrielle Roszak; *m* 1st, 1956, Kirsten Jensen (marr. diss.); two *s* two *d*; 2nd, 1977, Judith Aronson; one *s* two *d. Educ*: King Alfred's Sch., Wantage; Balliol Coll., Oxford (BA 1956; BLitt 1958; MA 1960; Hon. Fellow, 1989). 2nd Lieut, Green Howards, 1952. Andrew Bradley Jun. Res. Fellow, Balliol Coll., Oxford, 1957; Fellow of Worcester Coll., Oxford, 1958–68 (Hon. Fellow, 1990); Prof. of English, Bristol Univ., 1968–75; University of Cambridge: Prof. of English, 1975–82; King Edward VII Prof. of English Lit., 1982–86; Fellow, Christ's Coll., 1975–86 (Hon. Fellow, 1993). Visiting Professor: Berkeley and Stanford, 1965; Smith Coll., 1967; Harvard, 1971; Wesleyan, 1974; Brandeis, 1977, 1981, 1984. Lectures: Lord Northcliffe, UCL, 1972; Alexander, Univ. of Toronto, 1987; T. S. Eliot, Univ. of Kent, 1988; Clarendon, Univ. of Oxford, 1990; Clark, Trinity Coll., Cambridge, 1991. Pres., Assoc. of Literary Scholars and Critics, 2007–08. A Vice-Pres., Tennyson Soc.; Pres., Houseman Soc. Co-editor, Essays in Criticism. Fellow, American Acad. of Arts and Scis, 1991. Hon. DLitt: Oxon, 1998; Bristol, 2003. George Orwell Meml Prize, 1979; Beefeater Club Prize for Literature, 1980; Andrew W. Mellon Dist. Achievement Award, 2004. *Publications*: Milton's Grand Style, 1963; (ed) The Poems of Tennyson, 1969, rev. edn 1987; Tennyson, 1972, rev. edn 1989; Keats and Embarrassment, 1974; (ed with Leonard Michaels) The State of the Language, 1980, new edn 1990; The Force of Poetry, 1984; (ed) The New Oxford Book of Victorian Verse, 1987; (ed) A. E. Housman: Collected Poems and Selected Prose, 1988; T. S. Eliot and Prejudice, 1988; (ed with William Vance) The Faber Book of America, 1992; Beckett's Dying Words, 1993; Essays in Appreciation, 1996; (ed) Inventions of the March Hare: poems 1909–1917 by T. S. Eliot, 1996; (ed) The Oxford Book of English Verse, 1999; (ed) Selected Poems of James Henry, 2002; Reviewery, 2002; Allusion to the Poets, 2002; Dylan's Visions of Sin, 2003; Decisions and Revisions in T. S. Eliot, 2003; (ed) New and Selected Poems of Samuel Menashe, 2005; Tennyson: selected poems, 2007. *Address*: 39 Martin Street, Cambridge, MA 02138, USA. *T*: (617) 3547887; Lasborough Cottage, Lasborough Park, near Tetbury, Glos GL8 8UF. *T*: (01666) 890252.

RICKS, David Trulock, CMG 1997; OBE 1981; British Council Director, France, and Cultural Counsellor, British Embassy, Paris, 1990–96; *b* 28 June 1936; *s* of Percival Trulock Ricks and Annetta Helen (*née* Hood); *m* 1960, Nicole Estelle Aimée Chupeau; two *s. Educ*: Kilburn Grammar Sch.; Royal Acad. of Music; Merton Coll., Oxford (MA); Univ. of London Inst. of Educn; Univ. of Lille (LèsL). Teaching in Britain, 1960–67; joined British Council, 1967: Rabat, 1967–70; Univ. of Essex, 1970–71; Jaipur, 1971–74, New Delhi, 1974; Dar Es Salaam, 1974–76; Tehran, 1976–80; London, 1980–85; Rep., Italy, and Cultural Counsellor, British Embassy, Rome, 1985–90. Mem., Rome Cttee, Keats-Shelley Meml House, Rome, 1985–90; Founder Mem., Assoc. Bourses Entente Cordiale, 1996. Gov., British Inst., Florence, 1985–90. Mem., Municipal Council, Forcalquier, France, 2001–08. *Publications*: (jtly) Penguin French Reader, 1967; (jtly) New Penguin French Reader, 1992. *Recreations*: music, playing the piano, ski-ing. *Address*: Saint Jean, Boulevard Raoul Dufy, 04300 Forcalquier, France. *T*: 492752063. *Club*: Oxford and Cambridge.

RICKS, Robert Neville; Deputy Legal Adviser, Treasury Advisory Division, Treasury Solicitor's Department, 1998–2002; *b* 29 June 1942; *s* of Sir John Plowman Ricks. *Educ*: Highgate Sch.; Worcester Coll., Oxford (MA). Admitted Solicitor, 1967. Entered Treasury Solicitor's Dept as Legal Asst, 1969; Sen. Legal Asst, 1973; Asst Solicitor, 1981; Prin. Asst Solicitor, 1986; Legal Advr, DES, then DfEE, 1990–97; Special Projects Dir, Treasury Solicitor's Dept, 1997–98. *Recreations*: collecting original cartoons, wine. *Address*: 2 Eaton Terrace, Aberavon Road, E3 5AJ. *T*: (020) 8981 3722.

RICKSON, Ian; Artistic Director, Royal Court Theatre, 1998–2007; *b* 8 Nov. 1963; *s* of Richard and Eileen Rickson; one *s* by Kate Gould; *m* 2006, Polly Teale; one *d. Educ*: Essex Univ. (BA Eng and Eur. Lit. Hons); Goldsmiths' Coll., London Univ. (PGTC; Hon. Fellow, 2005). Freelance Dir, King's Head, The Gate, Chichester Fest. Theatre; Special

Projects Dir, Young Peoples' Th., 1991–92, Associate Dir, 1993–98, Royal Court Theatre. Plays directed include: Me and My Friend, Chichester, 1992; The House of Yes, Gate Th., 1993; La Serva Padrona (opera), Broomhill, 1993; The Day I Stood Still, RNT, 1997; The Hothouse, NT, 2007; *Royal Court Theatre:* Wildfire, Sab, Killers, 1992; Some Voices, Ashes and Sand, 1994; Mojo, Pale Horse, 1995; Chicago, The Lights, 1996; The Weir, 1997, transf. Duke of York's, then NY, 1998; Dublin Carol, 2000; Mouth to Mouth, transf. Albery, 2001; The Night Heron, 2002; Fallout, 2003; The Sweetest Swing in Baseball, 2004; Alice Trilogy, 2005; The Winterling, Krapp's Last Tape, 2006; The Seagull, 2007. Films directed: Krapp's Last Tape (BBC), 2007; Fallout, 2008.

RICKUS, Gwenneth Margaret, CBE 1981; Director of Education, London Borough of Brent, 1971–84; *b* 1925; *d* of Leonard William Ernest and Florence Rickus. *Educ*: Latymer Sch., Edmonton; King's Coll., Univ. of London. BA, PGCE. Teaching, 1948–53; Asst Sec., AAM, 1953–61; Education Administration: Middx CC, 1961–65; London Borough of Brent, 1965–84. Cllr (Lib Dem), New Forest DC, 1991–99. Co-opted Mem. Educn Cttee, Hampshire CC, 1985–97. Comr for Racial Equality, 1977–80. *Recreations*: reading, crafts, music.

RIDDELL, Alan Gordon; Associate Director, IRIS Consulting, since 2007; *b* 8 Sept. 1948; *s* of George Riddell and Elizabeth (*née* Mellin); *m* 1976, Barbara Kelly; two *d. Educ*: Greenock Acad.; Glasgow Univ. (MA Hons Mod. Hist. and Pol Econ.). History teacher, Greenock Acad., 1971–74; Hd of History, Eyemouth High Sch., 1974–75; Department of the Environment, 1975–97: Asst Private Sec. to Minister of Housing, 1981–83; Inner Cities Div., 1983–86; Private Rented Sector Div., 1986–87; Private Sec. to Minister for Local Govt, 1987–90; Hd, Private Rented Sector Div., 1990–92; Principal Private Sec. to Sec. of State, 1992–94; Sec., Cttee on Standards in Public Life (Nolan Cttee), 1994–97; Hd, Regeneration Policy Div., DETR, 1997–98; Regl Dir, Govt Office for E of England, 1998–2002; Dir of Ops, Neighbourhood Renewal Unit, subseq. Dir of Local Develt and Renewal, ODPM, then DCLG, 2002–07. Chm., Standards Cttee, Sevenoaks DC, 2001–. *Recreations*: walking, boats.

RIDDELL, Alistair; *see* Riddell, J. A.

RIDDELL, Christopher Barry; political cartoonist and illustrator; Political Cartoonist, The Observer, since 1995; *b* 13 April 1962; *s* of Morris and Pamela Riddell; *m* 1987, Joanna Burroughes; two *s* one *d. Educ*: Archbishop Tennison's Grammar Sch., London; Epsom Sch. of Art and Design (Foundn); Brighton Polytech. Art Sch. (BA 1st cl. Hons (Illustration)). Cartoonist: The Economist, 1988–96; The New Statesman, 1998–2006; Political Cartoonist, Independent and Independent on Sunday, 1990–95; Cover Artist, Literary Review, 1996–. *Publications*: Ben and the Bear, 1986; Humphrey Goes to the Ball, 1986; Humphrey of the Rovers, 1986; Humphrey the Hippo, 1986; Humphrey's New Trousers, 1986; Mr Underbed, 1986, 2nd edn 1997; Bird's New Shoes, 1987; The Fibbs, 1987; The Trouble with Elephants, 1988; When the Walrus Comes, 1989; The Wish Factory, 1990; The Bear Dance, 1990; The Emperor of Absurdia, 2006; The Da Vinci Cod: and other illustrations to unwritten books, 2006; Ottoline and the Yellow Cat, 2007; with Richard Platt: The Castle Diary: the journal of Tobias Burgess, 1999; The Pirate Diary: the journal of Jake Carpenter, 2001 (Kate Greenaway Medal, 2002); Platypus, 2001; Platypus and the Lucky Day, 2002; (with Martin Jenkins) Jonathan Swift's Gulliver (Kate Greenaway Medal), 2004; with Paul Stewart: The Edge Chronicles series, 1998–; The Rabbit and Hedgehog series, 1998–2001; The Blobheads series, 2000; The Muddle Earth series, 2003; Fergus Crane (Smarties Book Prize), 2004; Corby Flood (Nestlé Book Prize), 2005; Hugo Pepper (Nestlé Book Prize), 2006; Barnaby Grimes: curse of the nightwolf, 2007; illus. for many other authors. *Recreations*: writing, drawing, talking. *Address*: The Observer, 3–7 Herbal Hill, EC1R 5EJ. *T*: (020) 7837 4530. *Club*: Academy.

RIDDELL, (John) Alistair, OBE 1988; Treasurer, British Medical Association, 1987–96; *b* 11 Feb. 1930; *s* of Alexander Riddell and Mamie McFarlane MacKintosh; *m* 1st, 1956, Elizabeth Park McDonald Davidson (*d* 1999); one *s* three *d*; 2nd, 1999, Susan Anne Fraser, MD, FRCPGlas. *Educ*: Glasgow Acad.; Glasgow Univ. (MB ChB). FRCGP 1983; FRCPGlas 1996. GP E Glasgow, 1956–95; Clinical Asst, Geriatrics, Lightburn Hosp., 1968–78. Member: Glasgow Local Med. Cttee, 1964–95 (Med. Sec., 1978–91); Scottish GDC, 1975–82; Gen. Med. Services Cttee, 1972–96 (Negotiator, 1982–87; Vice-Chm., 1985–87); Chairman: Scottish Gen. Med. Services Cttee, 1983–86; Glasgow Area Med. Cttee, 1974–90. Mem. Council, BMA, 1983– (Chm., Community Care Cttee, 1991–94; Mem., 1982–2003, Chm., 2001–03, Scottish Council; Mem., 1982–2005, Chm., 2001–05, Charities Cttee); Mem., GMC, 1994–99 (Chm., Assessment Referral Cttee, 1997–99); Treas., Commonwealth Med. Assoc., 1989–2001. Dir, GP Finance Corp., 1975–90 (Vice-Chm., 1989–90); Dir, BMA Services, 1987–97; Chm., BMA Prof. Services, 1994–96. Dir, Silver Birch (Scotland) Ltd, 1996– (Chm., 1997–2002). Assessor, Scottish Community Foundn, 1997–2003. Mem., CAB Easter House, 1974–77. Mem., Bonnetmakers' Craft and Grand Antiquity Soc., Glasgow. *Publications*: contrib. BMJ and Scottish Med. Jl. *Recreations*: golf, ski-ing, sailing. *Address*: 27 Upper Glenburn Road, Bearsden, Glasgow G61 4BN. *T*: (0141) 942 0235.

RIDDELL, Sir John (Charles Buchanan), 13th Bt *cr* 1628; CVO 1990; CA; Extra Equerry to HRH the Prince of Wales, since 1990; Lord-Lieutenant of Northumberland, since 2000; Chairman, Northern Rock plc, 2000–04 (Director, 1981–1985, and 1990–2004; Deputy Chairman, 1992–99); *b* 3 Jan. 1934; *o s* of Sir Walter Buchanan Riddell, 12th Bt, and Hon. Rachel Beatrice Lyttelton (*d* 1965), *y d* of 8th Viscount Cobham; *S* father, 1934; *m* 1969, Hon. Sarah (LVO 1993), *o d* of Baron Richardson of Duntisbourne, *qv*; three *s. Educ*: Eton; Christ Church, Oxford. 2nd Lieut Rifle Bde, 1952–54. With IBRD, Washington DC, 1969–71; Associate, First Boston Corp., 1972–75; Director: First Boston (Europe) Ltd, 1975–78; UK Provident Instn, 1975–85; Northumbrian Water Gp, 1992–97; Alpha Bank London Ltd, 1995–2004; Chm., Govett Strategic Investment Trust, 1995–2004; Dep. Chm., Credit Suisse First Boston Ltd, 1990–95 (Dir, 1978–85). Dep. Chm., IBA, 1981–85; Private Sec., 1985–90, and Treasurer, 1986–90, to TRH the Prince and Princess of Wales; Member, Prince's Council, 1985–90. Contested (C): Durham NW, Feb. 1974; Sunderland S, Oct. 1974. Mem., Bloomsbury DHA, 1982–85; Dir, Poplar Housing and Regeneration Community Assoc., 1998–2000. Trustee, Guinness Trust, 1998–2001; Mem., Winston Churchill Meml Trust, 2000–07. Chm., Northumbria Regl Cttee, NT, 1995–2003. FRSA 1990. DL Northumberland, 1990. Heir: *s* Walter John Buchanan Riddell [*b* 10 June 1974; *m* 2003, Lucy, *d* of Selwyn Awdry; one *s* two *d* (of whom one *s* one *d* are twins)]. *Address*: Hepple, Morpeth, Northumberland NE65 7LN; 11 Farm Place, W8 7SX. *Clubs*: Garrick; Northern Counties (Newcastle upon Tyne).

See also Sir J. L. Pumphrey.

RIDDELL, His Honour Nicholas Peter; a Circuit Judge, 1995–2008; *b* 24 April 1941; *s* of late Peter John Archibald Riddell and Cynthia Mary Riddell (later Douglas); *m* 1976, Barbara Helen Glucksmann; three *d. Educ*: Harrow; Magdalene Coll., Cambridge (BA Cantab). Called to the Bar, Inner Temple, 1964; practised at the Bar, 1964–95. Mem. Bd, Circle 33 Housing Trust Ltd, 1998–. *Address*: 18 Myddelton Square, EC1R 1YE. *T*: (020) 7837 4034.

RIDDELL, Norman Malcolm Marshall; Chairman: Norman Riddell and Associates Ltd, since 1997; Novitas Partners LLP, since 2008; *b* 30 June 1947; *s* of Malcolm Riddell and Euphemia Richardson Riddell (*née* Wight); *m* 1969, Leila Jean White; three *s*. *Educ:* George Heriot's Sch., Edinburgh. MCIBS, AIIMR. National Commercial Bank and Royal Bank of Scotland, 1965–78; Man. Dir, Britannia Investment Services, 1978–86; Chief Executive: Capital House Investment Management, 1986–93; INVESCO plc, 1993–96; Chairman: United Overseas Gp plc, 1997–99; Savoy Asset Mgt plc, 1997–2000. Director: Charterhouse Gp, 1986–89; Life Assce Hldg Corp., 1995–2004; Asset Management Investment Co., 1997–2002; Clubhaus, 1999–2004; Improvement Pathway, 1999–2002; Progressive Value Mgt, 2000–; Progressive Income Products Ltd, 2000–; Pathway One VCT plc, 2001–; Family Assce Friendly Soc., 2006–. *Recreations:* plate collecting, gardening, most sports (spectator), travel, music, wine. *Address:* Norman Riddell and Associates Ltd, 68 King William Street, EC4N 7DZ. *Club:* Capital.

RIDDELL, Peter John Robert; Political Columnist, since 1991, and Assistant Editor (Politics), since 1993, The Times; *b* 14 Oct. 1948; *s* of late Kenneth Robert Riddell and Freda Riddell (*née* Young); *m* 1994, Avril Walker; one *d*. *Educ:* Dulwich Coll.; Sidney Sussex Coll., Cambridge (BA Hist. and Econs 1970, MA; Hon. Fellow, 2005). Joined Financial Times, 1970: Property Corresp., 1972–74; Lex Column, 1975–76; Economics Corresp., 1976–81; Political Editor, 1981–88; US Editor and Washington Bureau Chief, 1989–91; joined The Times, 1991, Political Editor, 1992–93. Regular broadcaster, Week in Westminster, Talking Politics, Radio 4, and on TV. Vis. Prof. of Political History, QMW, 2000–03. Chairman: Parly Press Gall., 1997; Council, Hansard Soc., 2007– (Mem., 1995–). Mem. Cttee, Centre for (formerly Inst. of) Contemp. British Hist., 1996–. FRHistS 1998. Hon. Fellow, Pol Studies Assoc., 2007. Hon. DLitt: Greenwich, 2001; Edinburgh, 2007. Wincott Award for Economic and Financial Journalism, 1981; House Magazine Political Journalist of the Year, 1986; Political Columnist of the Year, Political Studies Assoc., 2004. *Publications:* The Thatcher Government, 1983, rev. edn 1985; The Thatcher Decade, 1989, rev. edn as The Thatcher Era, 1991; Honest Opportunism, the rise of the career politician, 1993, rev. edn 1996; Parliament under Pressure, 1998, rev. edn as Parliament under Blair, 2000; Hug Them Close, 2003 (Pol Book of Year, Channel 4 Pol Awards, 2004); The Unfulfilled Prime Minister, 2005; contrib. chaps in books, including: A Conservative Revolution?, 1994; The Major Effect, 1994; The Blair Effect, 2001; British Politics since 1945, 2001; Reinventing Britain: Constitutional change under New Labour, 2007; contrib. to Spectator, New Statesman, Political Qly, British Journalism Rev., TLS, Jl of Legislative Studies. *Recreations:* watching cricket, opera, theatre. *Address:* 22 Falkland Road, NW5 2PX. *Clubs:* Garrick, MCC.

RIDDELL, Richard Rodford; freelance writer and researcher; Joint Head of Education, Amnesty International UK, since 2005; *b* 28 Jan. 1953; *m* 1975, Millie Mitchell; one *s* one *d*. *Educ:* Manchester Grammar Sch.; Magdalen Coll., Oxford (MA); Madeley Coll. of Educn (PGCE); Bulmershe Coll. of Higher Educn (MPhil). Teacher: John Mason Sch., Abingdon, 1975–77; Waingel's Copse Sch., Reading, 1977–81; Asst Educn Officer, Wilts CC, 1981–86; Educn Officer, Notts CC, 1986–90; Asst Dir of Educn, Avon CC, 1990–95; Dir of Educn, Bristol CC, 1995–2002. Vis. Fellow, UWE, 2002–. FRSA 1999. *Publication:* Schools For Our Cities, 2003. *Address: e-mail:* richardriddell@blueyonder.co.uk.

RIDDICK, Graham Edward Galloway; Director, Norman Broadbent, since 2007; *b* 26 Aug. 1955; *s* of late John Julian Riddick and Cecilia Margaret Riddick (*née* Ruggles-Brise); *m* 1988, Sarah Northcroft; one *s* two *d*. *Educ:* Stowe Sch., Buckingham; Univ. of Warwick (Chm., Warwick Univ. Cons. Assoc.). Sales management with Procter & Gamble, 1977–82; Coca-Cola, 1982–87. Gp Mktg Dir, subseq. Gp Mktg and Communications Dir, Onyx Environmental Gp plc, 1997–2000; Business Develt Dir, DeHavilland Information Services plc, 2000–05; Commercial Dir, Adfero Ltd, 2005–07. MP (C) Colne Valley, 1987–97 (first Cons. MP in Colne Valley for 102 years); contested (C) same seat, 1997. PPS to Financial Sec. to HM Treasury, 1990–92, to Sec. of State for Transport, 1992–94. Mem., Educn Select Cttee, 1994–96; Vice Chm., Cons. Trade and Industry Cttee, 1990; Secretary: Cons. Employment Cttee, 1988–90; All Party Textiles Gp, 1988–97. Pres., Yorks CPC, 1993–97. *Recreations:* fishing, shooting, sports, photography, bridge.

RIDDLE, Howard Charles Fraser; a District Judge (Magistrates' Courts) (formerly Metropolitan Stipendiary Magistrate), since 1995; *b* 13 Aug. 1947; *s* of Cecil Riddle and Eithne Riddle (*née* McKenna); *m* 1974, Susan Hilary Hurst; two *d*. *Educ:* Judd Sch., Tonbridge; London School of Economics (LLB); Coll. of Law. Admitted Solicitor, 1978. Sub-Editor, Penguin Books, 1969–70; Editor, McGill-Queens University Press, 1970–71; Publications Officer, Humanities and Social Science Res. Council, Canada, 1971–76; Solicitor, Edward Fail, Bradshaw and Waterson, 1976–95 (Sen. Partner, 1985–95). Vice-Chm., London Area Cttee, Legal Aid Bd, 1993–95; Mem., Sentencing Adv. Panel, 2004–; Chm., Legal Cttee, Council of Dist Judges (Magistrates' Courts), 2008–. *Publication:* (Contrib. Ed.) Wilkinson's Road Traffic Offences, 2008. *Recreations:* village activities, Rugby football, tennis, visiting France. *Address:* c/o Greenwich Magistrates' Court, 9 Blackheath Road, SE10 8PF. *T:* (020) 8276 1302. *Clubs:* Druidstone (Pembrokeshire); Tonbridge Juddians Rugby Football.

RIDDLE, Hugh Joseph, (Huseph), RP 1960; artist; portrait painter; *b* 24 May 1912; *s* of late Hugh Howard Riddle and late Christine Simons Brown; *m* 1936, Joan Claudia Johnson (*d* 1994); one *s* two *d*. *Educ:* Harrow; Magdalen Coll., Oxford; Slade School of Art; Byam Shaw School of Art and others. Specialises in portraits of children and adults; work includes HRH Prince Edward, aged 9, and HM the Queen. *Recreations:* sailing, swimming, gardening. *Address:* 18 Boulevard Verdi, Domaine du château de Tournon, Montauroux 83440, France.

RIDDLE, Philip Keitch, OBE 2008; Chief Executive, VisitScotland, since 2001; *b* 6 May 1952; *s* of Clifford Stanley Frederick Riddle and Anne Munro Riddle (*née* Black); *m* 1977, Catherine Mary Riddle (*née* Adams); three *s*. *Educ:* Dunfermline High Sch.; Trinity Hall, Cambridge (BA 1973, MA 1977); Univ. of Edinburgh (MBA 1977). Shell Group: various posts, marketing and trading, 1977–82; Hd, Oil and Gas Trading, Brunei Shell, 1982–85; Business Develt Manager, Shell Internat. Gas, 1985–88; Area Co-ordination, S America, Shell Internat., 1988–91; Man. Dir, Shell Namibia, 1991–94; Regl Develt Dir, Shell S Africa, 1994–95; Vice-Pres., Shell LPG Europe, 1995–99; Chm., Maximedia, 2000–01. Hon. Consul (Namibia), Govt of the Netherlands, 1991–94. Counsellor, Prince's Scotland Youth Business Trust, 2000–. *Recreations:* ski-ing, walking, reading, travel, making sense of Scotland. *Address:* VisitScotland, Ocean Point One, 94 Ocean Drive, Edinburgh EH6 6JH. *T:* (0131) 472 2201, *Fax:* (0131) 472 2207; *e-mail:* philip.riddle@visitscotland.com.

RIDEOUT, Prof. Roger William; Professor of Labour Law, University College, London, 1973–2000; *b* 9 Jan. 1935; *s* of Sidney and Hilda Rideout; *m* 1st, 1959, Marjorie Roberts (marr. diss. 1976); one *d*; 2nd, 1977, Gillian Margaret Lynch (*d* 2005). *Educ:* Bedford School; University Coll., London (LLB, PhD). Called to the Bar, Gray's Inn, 1964. National Service, 1958–60; 2nd Lt RAEC, Educn Officer, 1st Bn Coldstream Guards. Lecturer: Univ. of Sheffield, 1960–63; Univ. of Bristol, 1963–64. University Coll., London: Sen. Lectr, 1964–65; Reader, 1965–73; Dean of Faculty of Laws, 1975–77; Fellow, 1997. ILO missions to The Gambia, 1982–83, Somalia, 1989–90, Egypt, 1992–94. Part-time Chm., Industrial Tribunal, subseq. Employment Tribunals, 1984–2007, salaried 2003–07. ACAS panel arbitrator, 1981–; Vice-Pres., Industrial Law Society. FZS. Jt Editor, Current Legal Problems, 1975–92; Gen. Editor, Federation News, 1989–2001. *Publications:* The Right to Membership of a Trade Union, 1962; The Practice and Procedure of the NIRC, 1973; Trade Unions and the Law, 1973; Principles of Labour Law, 1972, 5th edn 1989; Bromham in Bedfordshire – a history, 2003. *Address:* 255 Chipstead Way, Woodmansterne, Surrey SM7 3JW. *T:* (01737) 213489.

RIDER, Prof. Barry Alexander Kenneth, PhD; Director, Institute of Advanced Legal Studies, University of London, 1995–2004, Hon. Senior Research Fellow, since 2004; Fellow Commoner, Jesus College, Cambridge, since 2001; Professorial Fellow, Development Studies Committee, University of Cambridge, since 2008; *b* 30 May 1952; *s* of Kenneth Leopold Rider and Alexina Elsie Rider (*née* Bremner); *m* 1976, Normalita Antonina Furto Rosales; one *d*. *Educ:* Bexleyheath Boys' Secondary Modern Sch.; Poly. of N London (Intermediate Ext. LLB 1970); Queen Mary Coll., London (LLB Hons 1973; PhD 1976); Jesus Coll., Cambridge (MA 1976; PhD 1978). Called to the Bar, Inner Temple, 1977. Univ. teaching officer, Univ. of Cambridge, 1980–95; Fellow, 1976–2001, Dean, 1989–96, Jesus Coll., Cambridge. Master of Witan Hall, incorp. Gyosei Internat. Coll., 2002–03. Vis. Sen. Fellow, Centre for Commercial Law Studies, QMC, 1979–90; University of London: Chm., Acad. Policy and Standards Cttee, Sch. of Advanced Study, 1997–2004; Mem., Bd of Mgt, Inst. of US Studies, 1997–2004. Various visiting academic appts, inc. Florida Univ., 1990–; Paul Hastings Prof. of Commercial Law, Univ. of Hong Kong, 2003. Honorary Professor: Dept of Mercantile Law, Univ. of the Free State (formerly Univ. of OFS), RSA, 1998–; Beijing Normal Univ., 2006–; Supreme People's Procuratorate Univ., PRC, 2006–; Remin Univ., 2006–. General Editor: Company Lawyer, 1980–; European Business Law Rev., 1996–; Jl Financial Crime, 1994–; Jl Money Laundering Control, 1996–; Amicus Curiae, 1997–; Internat. and Comparative Corporate Law Jl, 1998–; Internat. Jl of Disclosure and Governance, 2003–; Editor: CUP series on Corporate Law, 1996–; Kluwer series on Company and Financial Law, 1997–; Butterworth's series on Compliance, 2002–. Hd, Commonwealth Commercial Crime Unit, 1981–89; Exec. Dir, Centre for Internat. Documentation on Organised and Econ. Crime, 1989–. Special Advr to H of C Select Cttee on Trade and Industry, 1989–93. Internation Gen. Counsel, Internat. Compliance Assoc., 2007–. Chairman: Exec. Cttee, Soc. for Advanced Legal Studies, 1997–2004 (Mem., 2006–); Hamlyn Trust for Legal Educn, 2001–05. Former Consultant to various govtl agencies and to internat. bodies, incl. UNDP, IMF, Commonwealth Fund for Tech. Co-operation, and Commonwealth Secretariat. Consultant: Beachcroft LLP (formerly Beachcroft Wansbroughs), 2004–06; Islamic Financial Services Bd, 2005–. Mem., Bd of Advrs, Internat. Council for Capital Formation, 2003–. International Advisor: New England Sch. of Law, 2002–; Faculty of Law, Univ. of Cyprus, 2003–; Centre for Criminology, Univ. of Hong Kong, 2004–; Inst. of Criminal Justice, Beijing, 2006–. Mem. Court, City Univ., 2001–. Freeman, City of London, 1984; Mem., Court of Assts, 1998–, Master, 2007–08, Co. of Pattenmakers; Freeman, Guild of Educators, 2008–. Fellow, Inst. of Professional Investigators, 1980; FRSA 1997. Hon. Fellow, Soc. for Advanced Legal Studies, 2004. Hon. LLD: Dickinson Law Sch., USA, 1996; Free State, RSA, 2001. *Publications:* (jtly) The Regulation of Insider Trading, 1979; Insider Trading, 1983; (jtly) Guide to the Financial Services Act, 1987, 2nd edn 1989; (jtly) Insider Crime, 1993; (jtly) Guide to Financial Services Regulation, 1997; (jtly) Anti-Money Laundering Guide, 1999; (jtly) Market Abuse and Insider Dealing, 2002; *edited:* The Regulation of the British Securities Industry, 1979, CCH Financial Services Reporter, 3 vols, 1987; The Fiduciary, the Insider and the Conflict, 1995; Money Laundering Control, 1996; Corruption: the enemy within, 1997; Developments in European Company Law, vol. I 1997, vol. II 1998; International Tracing of Assets, 2 vols, 1997; Commercial Law in a Global Context, 1998; The Corporate Dimension, 1998; The Realm of Company Law, 1998; contrib. to numerous books and legal periodicals on company law, financial law and control of economic crime. *Recreations:* riding, historic houses. *Address:* Institute of Advanced Legal Studies, Charles Clore House, 17 Russell Square, WC1B 5DR. *T:* (020) 7862 5800; Jesus College, Cambridge CB5 8BL. *T:* (01223) 339483; *e-mail:* b.rider@jesus.cam.ac.uk. *Clubs:* Athenæum, Oxford and Cambridge, Civil Service.

RIDER, Gill; Director General, Civil Service Capability Group, Cabinet Office, since 2006; *b* London, 24 Oct. 1954; *d* of William and Ethel Rider; *m* 1986, David Paul Burke. *Educ:* Univ. of Southampton (BSc Hons Biol.; PhD Botany). FCIPD 2008. Accenture, 1979–2006: Man. Partner, Utilities Practice, Europe and S Africa, 1998–99; Mem., Global Exec. Cttee, 1999–2006; Man. Partner, Resources Operating Unit, EMEA, India and S America, 1999–2002; Chief Leadership Officer, 2002–06. Non-exec. Dir, De La Rue plc, 2006–. *Recreations:* entertaining, gardening, motor-racing, travel. *Address:* Cabinet Office, Room 3.14, Admiralty Arch, The Mall, SW1A 2WH. *T:* (020) 7276 1566, 2003; *e-mail:* gill.rider@cabinet-office.x.gsi.gov.uk.

RIDER, Stephen Henry; Presenter, F1 Grand Prix, 2006–08, and Champions League matches, since 2006, ITV Sport; *b* 28 April 1950; *s* of Alfred Charles Rider and Shirley Jeanette (*née* Walls); *m* 1985, Jane Eydmann; one *s* one *d*. *Educ:* Roan Grammar Sch., Blackheath. Local sports journalist, S London and sports presenter for London Broadcasting, 1969–76; Sports Presenter: Anglia TV, 1976–80; ITV Network, incl., World of Sport, 1980 Olympics, Midweek Sports Special, Network Golf, 1980–85; Network Presenter for BBC Sport: Main Presenter, Sportsnight, 1985–92; network golf coverage; Olympic Games, Seoul, 1988, Barcelona, 1992, Atlanta, 1996, Athens, 2004; Commonwealth Games, 1986, 1990, 1994 and 1998; main network golf presenter, 1991–2005; motor sport specialist; Presenter, Grandstand, 1985–2005 (Main Presenter, 1992–2005). Sports Presenter of Year, TRIC, 1994, RTS, 1995. *Recreations:* golf, family. *Address:* c/o Blackburn Sachs Associates, 2–4 Noel Street, W1F 8GB.

RIDGE, Anthony Hubert; Director-General, International Bureau, Universal Postal Union, Bern, 1973–74 (Deputy Director-General, 1964–73); *b* 5 Oct. 1913; *s* of Timothy Leopold Ridge and Magdalen (*née* Hernig); *m* 1938, Marjory Joan Sage (*d* 2007); three *s* one *d*. *Educ:* Christ's Hospital; Jesus College, Cambridge. Entered GPO, 1937; seconded to Min. Home Security, 1940; GPO Personnel Dept, 1944; PPS to Postmaster General, 1947; Dep. Dir, London Postal Region, 1949; Asst Sec., Overseas Mails, 1951, Personnel, 1954, Overseas Mails, 1956; Director of Clerical Mechanization and Buildings, and Member of Post Office Board, GPO, 1960–63. Mem., Postling Parish Council, 1979–87. Governor, Christ's Hosp. *Recreations:* music, languages, transport, gardening. *Address:* 36 Pegasus Court, St Stephen's Road, Cheltenham, Glos GL51 3GB. *T:* (01242) 519804. *Clubs:* Christ's Hospital, Oxford and Cambridge, Cambridge Society.

RIDGE, Rupert Leander Pattle; Adviser, Motivation Charitable Trust, since 2004; *b* 18 May 1947; *y s* of late Major Robert Vaughan Ridge and Marian Ivy Edith Ridge (*née* Pattle); *m* 1971, Mary Blanche Gibbs; two *s* two *d*. *Educ:* King's Coll., Taunton. Officer, LI, 1969–73. BAC, then British Aerospace Defence Ltd, 1973–94; Internat. Dir, Leonard Cheshire Foundn, then Dir, Leonard Cheshire Internat., 1994–2004. Trustee: Action around Bethlehem Children with Disability, 1994–2005 (Chm., 1998–2005); Wellspring Counselling, 2004– (Chm., 2006–). *Recreations:* gardening, being in the country. *Address:* (office) Motivation Charitable Trust, Brockley Academy, Brockley Lane, Backwell, Bristol BS48 4AQ.

RIDGWAY, Lt-Gen. Andrew Peter, CB 2001; CBE 1995; Lieutenant-Governor and Commander-in-Chief, Jersey, since 2006; *b* 20 March 1950; *s* of late Robert Hamilton Ridgway and of Betty Patricia Ridgway (*née* Crane); *m* 1974, Valerie Elizabeth Shawe; three *s* one *d*. *Educ:* Hele's Sch., Exeter; RMA, Sandhurst; St John's Coll., Cambridge (MPhil). Commnd RTR, 1970: served Germany, NI, Belize, Bosnia, Kuwait, Macedonia, Kosovo and UK; CO, 3 RTR, 1991–92; Col, Army Prog., MoD, 1992–93; Comdr, 7 Armd Bde, 1993–95 (Comdr, UN Sector SW Bosnia Herzegovina, Feb.–Nov. 1994); Dir, Operational Capability, MoD, 1995–97; Chief, Jt Rapid Deployment Force, 1997–98; COS, ACE RRC, 1998–2001 (COS, Kosovo Force, 1999); Hd, Defence Trng Review Implementation Team, 2001–02; Dir Gen. Trng and Educn, MoD, 2002; Chief of Defence Intelligence, MoD, 2003–06. Col Comdt, RTR, 1999–2006; Hon. Colonel: Cambridge Univ. OTC, 2003–; Westminster Dragoons, 2008–. Dir, Army Ice Sports, 1999–2006. CStJ 2007. *Recreations:* golf, fishing, walking, bobsleigh, beekeeping. *Address:* Government House, Jersey JE2 7GH. *T:* (01534) 441700. *Club:* Army and Navy.

RIDGWAY, David Frederick Charles, CMG 2000; OBE 1988; HM Diplomatic Service, retired; Assessor, Foreign and Commonwealth Office, 2001–07; Partner, CONSULAT Business Consultancy, since 2002; *b* 9 June 1941; *m* 1966, Dora Beatriz Siles; one *s* one *d*. Entered FO, 1960; served La Paz, Colombo and Durban, 1963–77; First Sec. (Commercial), Buenos Aires, 1980–82; FCO, 1982–84; Chargé d'Affaires *ai*, San Salvador, 1984–87; FCO, 1988–91; Dir of Trade Promotion, Madrid, 1991–95; Ambassador to: Bolivia, 1995–98; Cuba, 1998–2001. Chairman: Anglo-Central American Soc., 2005–07; Cuba Studies Trust, 2007–. *Address:* 84 Chesilton Road, SW6 5AB.

RIDLER, Vivian Hughes, CBE 1971; Printer to the University of Oxford, 1958–78; *b* 2 Oct. 1913; *s* of Bertram Hughes Ridler and Elizabeth Emmeline (*née* Best); *m* 1938, Anne Barbara Bradby, OBE, FRSL, poet (*d* 2001); two *s* two *d*. *Educ:* Bristol Gram. Sch.; MA Oxon 1958 (by decree; Corpus Christi College). Appren. E. S. & A. Robinson, Ltd, 1931–36. Works Manager University Press, Oxford, 1948; Assistant Printer, 1949–58. Pres., British Federation of Master Printers, 1968–69. Professorial Fellow, St Edmund Hall, 1966, Emeritus Fellow, 1978. *Recreations:* printing, theatre, cinema, cinematography. *Address:* 14 Stanley Road, Oxford OX4 1QZ. *T:* (01865) 247595.

RIDLEY, family name of **Viscount Ridley**.

RIDLEY, 4th Viscount *cr* 1900; **Matthew White Ridley,** KG 1992; GCVO 1994; TD 1960; JP; DL; Baron Wensleydale, 1900; Bt 1756; Lord-Lieutenant and Custos Rotulorum of Northumberland, 1984–2000; Lord Steward of HM Household, 1989–2001; *b* 29 July 1925; *e s* of 3rd Viscount Ridley; *S* father, 1964; *m* 1953, Lady Anne Lumley (*d* 2006), 3rd *d* of 11th Earl of Scarbrough, KG, GCSI, GCIE, GCVO, PC; one *s* three *d*. *Educ:* Eton; Balliol College, Oxford. MRICS (ARICS 1951). Coldstream Guards (NW Europe), 1943–46, Captain, 1946; Northumberland Hussars, 1947–64 (Lt-Col 1961, Bt Col 1964); ADC to Sir Evelyn Baring, Gov. of Kenya, 1952–53; Hon. Colonel: Northumberland Hussars Sqdn, Queen's Own Yeomanry, 1979–86; Queen's Own Yeomanry RAC TA, 1984–86; Northumbrian Univs OTC, 1986–90; Col Comdt, Yeomanry RAC TA, 1982–86. Director: Northern Rock Building Soc., 1962– (Chm., 1987–92); Tyne Tees Television, 1964–90; Barclays Bank (NE) Ltd, 1964–90; Municipal Mutual Insurance, 1982–93. Chm., NE Housing Assoc., 1970–74; Member: Layfield Cttee of Enquiry into Local Govt Finance, 1974–; Commonwealth War Graves Commn, 1991–99. Chm., Internat. Dendrology Soc., 1988–93; President: British Deer Soc., 1970–73; Natural Hist. Soc. of Northumbria, 1997–2005. Chm., N of England TA Assoc., 1980–84; Pres., TA & VRA Council, 1984–95 (Patron, 1995–); Vice-Pres., SSAFA. Chm., Newcastle Univ. Develt. Trust, 1981–84; Chancellor, 1978–80, Hon. Fellow, 1980, Newcastle upon Tyne Polytechnic; Chancellor, Newcastle Univ., 1989–99. Hon. FRHS 1986; Hon. FRICS 1986. JP 1957, CC 1958, CA 1963, DL 1968, Northumberland; Chm., Northumberland CC, 1967–74, Chm., new Northumberland CC, 1974–79; Pres., ACC, 1979–84. Pres., Blyth Spartans FC, 2000. KStJ 1984; Hon. DCL Newcastle, 1989. Order of Merit, West Germany, 1974. *Heir: s* Hon. Matthew White Ridley, *qv*. *Address:* Boston House, Blagdon, Seaton Burn, Newcastle upon Tyne NE13 6DB. *T:* (01670) 789236, *Fax:* (01670) 789560. *Clubs:* Boodle's, Pratt's; Northern Counties (Newcastle upon Tyne).

RIDLEY, Sir Adam (Nicholas), Kt 1985; Director General, London Investment Banking Association, 2000–05, Senior Adviser, 2005–06; Chairman of Trustees, Equitas Group of Companies, since 1996; *b* 14 May 1942; *s* of late Jasper Maurice Alexander Ridley and Helen Cressida Ridley (*née* Bonham Carter); *m* 1981, Margaret Anne Passmore; three *s* (inc. twin *s*). *Educ:* Eton Coll.; Balliol Coll., Oxford (1st cl. hons PPE 1965); Univ. of California, Berkeley. Foreign Office, 1965, seconded to DEA, 1965–68; Harkness Fellow, Univ. of California, Berkeley, 1968–69; HM Treasury, 1970–71, seconded to CPRS, 1971–74; Economic Advr to shadow cabinet and Asst Dir, 1974–79, Dir, 1979, Cons. Res. Dept; Special Advr to Chancellor of the Exchequer, 1979–84, to Chancellor of the Duchy of Lancaster, 1985. Director: Hambros Bank, 1985–97; Hambros PLC, 1985–97; Sunday Newspaper Publishing PLC, 1988–90 (Chm., 1990); non-executive Director: Leopold Joseph Holdings, 1997–2004; Morgan Stanley Bank Internat., 2006–; Hampden Agencies Ltd, 2007–. Chm., Names Adv. Cttee, 1995–96, Mem. Council, 1997–99, Mem., Regulatory Bd, 1997–99, Lloyds of London. Mem., National Lottery Charities Bd, 1994–2000 (Dep. Chm., 1995–2000). *Publications:* articles on regional policy, public spending, international and Eastern European economics, charities, and financial regulation. *Recreations:* music, pictures, travel. *Club:* Garrick.

RIDLEY, Prof. Brian Kidd, FRS 1994; Research Professor of Physics, University of Essex, 1991–2008, now Professor Emeritus; *b* 2 March 1931; *s* of Oliver Archbold Ridley and Lillian Beatrice Ridley; *m* 1959, Sylvia Jean Nicholls; one *s* one *d*. *Educ:* Univ. of Durham (BSc 1st Cl. Hons Physics, PhD). CPhys, FInstP. Research Physicist, Mullard Research Lab., Redhill, 1956–64; Essex University: Lectr in Physics, 1964–67; Sen. Lectr, 1967–71; Reader, 1971–84; Prof., 1984–91. Dist. Vis. Prof., Cornell Univ., 1967; Vis. Prof. at univs in USA, Denmark, Sweden and Holland. Paul Dirac Medal and Prize, Inst. of Physics, 2001. *Publications:* Time, Space and Things, 1976, 3rd edn 1995; The Physical Environment, 1979; Quantum Processors in Semiconductors, 1982, 4th edn 1999; Electrons and Phonons in Semiconductor Multilayers, 1997, 2nd edn 2008; On Science, 2001. *Recreations:* tennis, piano.

RIDLEY, Prof. Frederick Fernand, OBE 1978; PhD; Senior Fellow, School of Management (formerly Institute of Public Administration and Management), and Professor Emeritus, University of Liverpool, since 1995 (Professor of Political Theory and Institutions, 1965–95); *b* 11 Aug. 1928; *s* of late J. and G. A. Ridley; *m* 1967, Paula Frances Cooper Ridley, *qv*; two *s* one *d*. *Educ:* The Hall, Hampstead; Highgate Sch.; LSE (BScEcon, PhD); Univs of Paris and Berlin. Lectr, Univ. of Liverpool, 1958–65. Vis. Professor: Graduate Sch. of Public Affairs, Univ. of Pittsburgh, 1968; Coll. of Europe, Bruges, 1975–83. Manpower Services Commission, Merseyside: Chm., Job Creation Prog., 1975–77; Vice-Chm., 1978–87, Chm., 1987–88, Area Manpower Bd. Member: Jt Univ. Council for Social and Public Admin, 1964–95 (Chm., 1972–74); Exec., Polit. Studies Assoc., 1967–75 (Hon. Vice-Pres., 1995–); Council, Hansard Soc., 1970–94; Polit. Science Cttee, SSRC, 1972–76; Cttee, European Gp on Public Admin, 1973–92; Public and Social Admin Bd, CNAA, 1975–82; Social Studies Res. Cttee, CNAA, 1980–83 (Chm.); Academic Cttee, Assoc. Internat. de la Fonction Publique, 1988–93; Vice-Pres., Rencontres Européennes des Fonctions Publiques/Entretiens Universitaires pour l'Admin en Europe, 1990–2001. Member: Exec., Merseyside Arts (RAA), 1979–84; Adv. Council, Granada Foundn, 1984–98; Council, Hochschule für Verwaltungswissenschaft, Speyer, 1993–2005; Trustee, Friends of Merseyside Museums and Galleries, 1977–85. Pres., Politics Assoc., 1976–81 (Hon. Fellow, 1995). Editor: Political Studies, 1969–75; Parliamentary Affairs, 1975–2004. *Publications:* Public Administration in France, 1964; Revolutionary Syndicalism in France, 1970; The Study of Government, 1975; numerous articles and edited vols on political sci. and public admin. *Address:* Riversdale House, Grassendale Park, Liverpool L19 0LR. *T:* (0151) 427 1630.

RIDLEY, Hon. Matthew White, DL; DPhil; FRSL; FMedSci; Chairman, Northern Rock plc, 2004–07 (Director, 1994–2007); *b* 7 Feb. 1958; *s* and *heir* of 4th Viscount Ridley, *qv*; *m* 1989, Anya Hurlbert, *d* of Dr Robert Hurlbert, Houston, Texas; one *s* one *d*. *Educ:* Eton Coll.; Magdalen Coll., Oxford (BA Zoology 1979; DPhil Zoology 1983). Science Editor, 1983–87, Washington corresp., 1987–90, American Editor, 1990–92, The Economist; columnist, Sunday and Daily Telegraph, 1993–2000. Chm., Northern 2 VCT, 1999–; Director: Northern Investors, 1994–2007; PA Holdings Ltd, 1999–. Chm., Internat. Centre for Life, 1996–2003. DL Northumberland, 2007. FRSL 1999; FMedSci 2004. *Publications:* Warts and All, 1989; The Red Queen, 1993; The Origins of Virtue, 1996; Genome, 1999; Nature Via Nurture, 2003; Francis Crick, 2006. *Recreations:* fly fishing, natural history. *Address:* Blagdon Hall, Seaton Burn, Newcastle upon Tyne NE13 6DD.

RIDLEY, Michael; *see* Ridley, R. M.

RIDLEY, Sir Michael (Kershaw), KCVO 2000 (CVO 1992); Clerk of the Council, Duchy of Lancaster, 1981–2000; *b* 7 Dec. 1937; *s* of late George K. and Mary Ridley; *m* 1968, Diana Loraine McLernon; two *s*. *Educ:* Stowe; Magdalene College, Cambridge. MA. FRICS. Grosvenor Estate, Canada and USA, 1965–69, London, 1969–72; Property Manager, British & Commonwealth Shipping Co., 1972–81. A Gen. Comr of Income Tax, 1984–98. Chm., Standards Cttee, RBK&C, 2001–06. Mem., Adv. Panel, Greenwich Hosp., 1978–2002. Mem. Court, Lancaster Univ., 1981–2000. Trustee: St Martin's-in-the-Fields Almshouse Assoc., 1991–2005; Anne Duchess of Westminster Charity, 2004–. Dir, Feathers Clubs Assoc.; Pres., Assoc. of Lancastrians in London, 2000. Hon. Treas., Chartered Surveyors' Co., 1999–2002. *Recreation:* golf. *Address:* 37 Chester Row, SW1W 9JE. *Clubs:* Brooks's, Garrick; Royal Mid-Surrey Golf.

RIDLEY, Paula Frances Cooper, CBE 2008 (OBE 1996); JP; DL; MA; Chairman, Board of Trustees, Victoria and Albert Museum, 1998–2007; Director, Gulbenkian Foundation (UK), 1999–2007; *b* 27 Sept. 1944; *d* of Ondrej Clyne and Ellen (*née* Cooper); *m* 1967, Frederick Fernand Ridley, *qv*; two *s* one *d*. *Educ:* Kendal High Sch., Westmorland; Univ. of Liverpool (BA, MA). Lectr in Politics and Public Admin., Liverpool Polytechnic, 1966–71; Proj. Co-ordinator, Regeneration Projects Ltd, 1981–84; Dir, Community Initiatives Res. Trust, 1983–90; Consultant, BAT Industries Small Businesses Ltd, 1983–95; Bd Mem., Brunswick Small Business Centre Ltd, 1984–95; Associate, CEI Consultants, 1984–88. Chairman: Liverpool Housing Action Trust, 1992–2005; Public Interest Gen. Council, Office for Public Mgt, 2003–07; Dir, Merseyside Develt Corp., 1991–98. Mem., Royal Commn on Long Term Care for the Elderly, 1997–99. Presenter and Assoc. Editor, Granada Action, 1989–92; Mem., IBA, 1982–88. Chm., Stocktonwood County Primary Sch., 1976–79; Member: Liverpool Heritage Bureau, 1971–88; Management Cttee, Liverpool Victoria Settlement, 1971–86 (Vice-Chm., 1977–86); Granada Telethon Trust, 1988–94. Trustee: Tate Gall., 1988–98; Nat. Gall., 1995–98; Chm., Tate Gall., Liverpool, 1988–98. Liverpool University: Lady Pres., Guild of Undergraduates, Clerk of Convocation, 1972–74; Member: Court, 1972–; Council, 1998–2007; Life Governor, Liverpool and Huyton Colls, 1979–94. Merseyside Civic Society: Hon. Sec., 1971–82; Vice-Chm., 1982–86; Chm., 1986–91. Chm., Liverpool Biennial of Contemporary Art, 2008–. JP Liverpool, 1977. DL Merseyside, 1989. FRSA. Hon. FRIBA 2005. Hon. Fellow, Liverpool John Moores Univ., 2002. Hon. LLD Liverpool, 2003. *Address:* Riversdale House, Grassendale Park, Liverpool L19 0LR. *T:* (0151) 427 1630; 69 Thomas More House, Barbican, EC2Y 8BT. *T:* (020) 7628 8573.

RIDLEY, (Robert) Michael; Principal, Royal Belfast Academical Institution, 1990–2006; *b* 8 Jan. 1947; *s* of Maurice Roy Ridley and Jean Evelyn Lawther (*née* Carlisle); *m* 1985, Jennifer Mary Pearson; two *d*. *Educ:* Clifton Coll.; St Edmund Hall, Oxford (MA, Cert Ed). Wellington Coll., Berks, 1970–82 (Housemaster, 1975–82); Hd of English, Merchiston Castle Sch., Edinburgh, 1982–86; Headmaster, Denstone Coll., 1986–90. Mem., Rotary Club, Belfast, 1990–. *Recreations:* cricket (Oxford Blue, 1968–70; Ireland 1968), golf, reading, travel. *Clubs:* East India; Vincent's (Oxford); Royal County Down Golf (Newcastle, Co. Down); Boat of Garten Golf (Inverness-shire).

RIDLEY, Prof. Tony Melville, CBE 1986; FREng, FICE, FCILT; Professor of Transport Engineering (formerly Rees Jeffreys Professor), 1991–99, and Head of Department of Civil and Environmental Engineering (formerly Department of Civil Engineering), 1997–99, Imperial College of Science, Technology and Medicine, University of London, now Professor Emeritus, Imperial College London; *b* 10 Nov. 1933; *s* of late John Edward and Olive Ridley; *m* 1959, Jane (*née* Dickinson); two *s* one *d*. *Educ:* Durham Sch.; King's Coll. Newcastle, Univ. of Durham (BSc); Northwestern Univ., Ill (MS); Univ. of California, Berkeley (PhD); Stanford Univ., Calif (Sen. Exec. Prog.). Nuclear Power Group, 1957–62; Univ. of California, 1962–65; Chief Research Officer, Highways and Transportation, GLC, 1965–69; Director General, Tyne and Wear Passenger Transport Exec., 1969–75; Man. Dir, Hong Kong Mass Transit Rly Corp., 1975–80; Bd Mem., 1980–88, Man. Dir (Rlys), 1980–85, LTE, then LRT; Chm., 1985–88, Man. Dir, 1985–88, Chief Exec., 1988, London Underground Ltd; Man. Dir-Project, Eurotunnel, 1989–90 (Dir, 1987–90). Chm., Docklands Light Railway Ltd, 1987–88; Dir, London Transport Internat., 1982–88. Sen. Transport Advr, London 2012 Olympic Bid, 2004–05; Mem., Indep. Dispute Avoidance Panel for London 2012, 2008–. Chm., Building Schs for the Future Investments LLP, 2007–. President: Light Rail Transit Assoc., 1974–92; Assoc. for Project Mgt, 1999–2003; Commonwealth Engineers Council, 2000–; Internat. Pres., CILT (formerly CIT), 1999–2001 (Vice-Pres., 1987–90); Member: Council, ICE, 1990–97 (Chm., Transport Bd, 1990–93; Vice Pres., 1992–95; Pres., 1995–96); Senate, Engrg Council, 1997–2000 (Chm., Bd for the Engrg Profession, 1997–99); Exec. Council, WFEO, 2000–; Task Force 10 (Sci., Technol. and Innovation), UN Millennium Project, 2002–05. Trustee, RAC Foundn for Motoring, 1999– (Mem.,

Public Policy Cttee, 1997–). Freeman, City of London, 1982; Hon. Fellow, Paviors' Co., 2006–. FREng (FEng 1992); FHKIE, FITE, FIHT 1992 (Highways Award, 1988). FCGI 1996. Hon. FAPM 1996; Hon. FIA 1999. Hon. DTech Napier, 1996; Hon. DEng Newcastle upon Tyne, 1997. Herbert Crow Award (1st recipient), Carmen's Co., 2001; President's Award, Engrg Council, 2002. *Publications:* articles in transport, engrg and other jls. *Recreations:* theatre, music, international affairs. *Address:* Orchard Lodge, Stichens Green, Streatley, Berks RG8 9SU. *T:* (01491) 871075. *Clubs:* Royal Automobile; Hong Kong, Jockey (Hong Kong).

RIDLEY-THOMAS, Roger; Managing Director, Thomson Regional Newspapers Ltd, 1989–94; *b* 14 July 1939; *s* of late John Montague Ridley-Thomas, MB, ChB, FRCSE, Norwich, and Christina Anne (*née* Seex); *m* 1962, Sandra Grace McBeth Young; two *s* two *d*. *Educ:* Gresham's Sch. Served Royal Norfolk Regt, 1958–60. Newspaper Publisher: Eastern Counties Newspapers, 1960–65; Thomson Regional Newspapers, 1965–94 (Dir, 1985–94); Managing Director: Aberdeen Journals, 1980–84; Scotsman Publications, 1984–89; Director: Caledonian Offset, 1979–94; Radio Forth, 1978–81; TRN Viewdata, 1978–89; Thomson Scottish Organisation, 1984–89; Northfield Newspapers, 1984–89; The Scotsman Communications, 1984–94; The Scotsman Publications, 1984–94; Central Publications, 1984–94; Aberdeen Journals, 1980–84, 1990–94; Belfast Telegraph Newspapers, 1990–94; Chester Chronicle, 1990–94; Newcastle Chronicle & Journal, 1990–94; Western Mail & Echo, 1990–94; Cardrona Ltd, 1995–; Milex Ltd, 1996–2005; Adscene Gp plc, 1996–99; Roys (Wroxham) Ltd, 1997– (Chm., 2004–); Norfolk Christmas Trees Ltd, 2000–08; Chairman: Anglia FM, 1996–98; NorCor Hldgs plc, 1996–2000. Director: Aberdeen Chamber of Commerce, 1981–84; Scottish Business in the Community, 1984–89; Scottish Business Achievement Award Trust, 1985–2003; Edinburgh Ch. of Commerce and Manufrs, 1985–88. Pres., Scottish Daily Newspaper Soc., 1983–85; Mem. Council, CBI, 1983–86; Mem., Scottish Wildlife Appeal Cttee, 1985–88. *Recreations:* shooting, golf, tennis, travel. *Club:* New (Edinburgh).

RIDPATH, Ian William; author and broadcaster on astronomy and space; *b* 1 May 1947; *s* of late Alfred William Joseph Ridpath and Irene Florence Ridpath (*née* Walton). *Educ:* Beal Grammar Sch., Woodford. FRAS 1988 (Council Mem., 2004–07); Mem., Soc. of Authors; Assoc. of British Sci. Writers. Ed., Popular Astronomy (qly mag.), 1986–89. *Publications:* Worlds Beyond, 1975; (ed) Encyclopedia of Astronomy and Space, 1976; Messages from the Stars, 1978; The Young Astronomer's Handbook, 1981; Hamlyn Encyclopedia of Space, 1981; Life off Earth, 1983; Collins Pocket Guide to Stars and Planets, 1984, 4th edn as Collins Stars and Planets Guide, 2007; The Night Sky, 1985; (jtly) A Comet Called Halley, 1985; Concise Handbook of Astronomy, 1986; Dictionary of Astronomy and Astronautics, 1987; The Monthly Sky Guide, 1987, 7th edn 2006; Go Skywatching, 1987; Star Tales, 1988; (ed) Norton's Star Atlas, 18th edn 1989, 20th edn 2003; Giant Book of Space, 1989; Pocket Guide to Astronomy, 1990; Space, 1991; Book of the Universe, 1991; Philips Atlas of Stars and Planets, 1992, 4th edn 2004; (ed) Oxford Dictionary of Astronomy, 1997, 2nd edn 2007; Handbook of Stars and Planets, 1998, 2nd edn 2002; Gem Stars, 1999; (ed) Collins Encyclopedia of the Universe, 2001; The Times Space, 2002; The Times Universe, 2004; Eyewitness Companion to Astronomy, 2006; *for children:* Discovering Space, 1972; (ed) Man and Materials (series): Oil, Coal, Gas, Stone, Plastics, Minerals, 1975; Signs of Life, 1977; Space, 1979; Secrets of Space, 1980; Spacecraft, 1981; Stars and Planets, 1981; Secrets of the Sky, 1985; The Sun, 1987; The Stars, 1987; Outer Space, 1987; *contributions to:* Reader's Digest Library of Modern Knowledge, 1978; Hutchinson 20th Century Encyclopedia, 1987; Microsoft Encarta Encyclopedia, 1997–; Universe, 2005. *Recreations:* collecting antique star atlases and astronomically related stamps, distance running (Race Dir, Polytechnic Marathon, 1993–95), horse racing and riding. *Address:* 48 Otho Court, Brentford, Middlesex TW8 8PY. *T:* (020) 8568 6100; *e-mail:* ian@ianridpath.com.

RIDSDALE, Victoire Evelyn Patricia, (Paddy), (Lady Ridsdale), DBE 1991; *b* 11 Oct. 1921; *d* of Col J. and Edith Marion Bennett; *m* 1942, Julian Errington Ridsdale (later Sir Julian Ridsdale, CBE; *d* 2004); one *d*. *Educ:* Sorbonne. Sec., DNI, 1939–42; Sec. to her husband, 1953–2004. Chm., Conservative MPs' Wives, 1978–91. British Gold Hero Award, ARP/050, 1998. *Address:* 12 The Boltons, SW10 9TD. *T:* (020) 7373 6159.
See also Sir P. H. Newall.

RIESCO ZAÑARTU, Germán; commercial entrepreneur; Chilean Ambassador to the Court of St James's, 1990–93, and non-resident Ambassador to Ireland, 1992–93; *b* 17 Aug. 1941; *s* of Ignacio Riesco and Eliana Zañartu de Riesco; *m* 1974, Jacqueline Cassel; four *s* two *d*. *Educ:* Colegio San Ignacio, Santiago; Univ. of California, Davis (agric. degree; Special Award); Univ. of California, Berkeley (Economics). MP Nuble (National Party), 1969–73; Pres., Cttee on Economy, Chamber of Deputies; Dir, Agric. Planning Office, 1976–78. Vice-Pres., Nat. Party, 1983–88; Pres., Nat. Party for No Vote, 1988; Pres., PAC-Centre Alliance Party, 1988–90. Board Mem., Fundación Chile, 1983–90. Pres., Nat. Agric. Soc., Chile, 1979–81, 1981–83. Negotiator at FAO, World Bank and other internat. orgns. *Publications:* papers on Chilean agric. and econs. *Recreations:* music, theatre, tennis, ski-ing. *Address:* 5308 Agustín Denegri, Vitacura, Santiago, Chile. *T:* (562) 2182799, 2184049. *Clubs:* Chile, De La Union, Los Leones Country (Santiago, Chile).

RIFKIN, Joshua; Founder, and Director, The Bach Ensemble, since 1978; *b* 22 April 1944; *s* of Harry H. Rifkin and Dorothy (*née* Helsh); *m* 1st, 1970, Louise Litterick (marr. diss. 1984); 2nd, 1995, Helen Palmer; one *d*. *Educ:* Juilliard Sch. of Music (BS 1964); Princeton Univ. (MFA 1969). Musical Consultant, later Musical Dir, Nonesuch Records, NY, 1963–75; Brandeis University: Instructor, 1970–71; Asst Prof., 1971–77; Associate Prof., 1977–82. Visiting Professor, 1973–2002: NY Univ.; Harvard Univ.; Yale Univ.; Rutgers Univ.; Bard Coll.; Princeton Univ.; Stanford Univ.; King's Coll. London; Basel Univ.; Ohio State Univ.; Dortmund Univ. (Gambrinus Prof.); Munich Univ.; Univ. of N Carolina at Chapel Hill. Numerous concerts with Bach Ensemble in UK, Europe, US and Canada; Guest Conductor: English Chamber Orch., 1983, 1984; Scottish Chamber Orch., 1984, 1994; St Louis SO, 1985; Schola Cantorum Basiliensis, 1986, 1990, 1993, 1997, 2000; Victoria State SO, 1989; San Francisco SO, 1989; St Paul Chamber Orch., 1989; LA Chamber Orch., 1990; City of Glasgow SO, 1992; Cappella Coloniensis, Germany, 1993, 1994; Orch. Haydn/Bolzano, 1995; Solistas de México, BBC Concert Orch., and City of London Sinfonia, 1996; Jerusalem SO, Prague Chamber Orch., 1997; Nat. Arts Centre Orch., Houston SO, Camerata de las Américas, 1999; Bayerische Staatsoper, Munich, 2001; Israel Camerata, Jerusalem, 2002. Numerous recordings. Fellow, Wissenschaftskolleg, Berlin, 1984–86. Hon. PhD Dortmund, 1999. *Publications:* contrib. New Grove Dictionary of Music and Musicians, 1980; numerous articles in scholarly jls. *Recreations:* food, wine, cinema, theatre, computers, fiction. *Address:* *e-mail:* jrifkin@compuserve.com.

RIFKIND, Rt Hon. Sir Malcolm (Leslie), KCMG 1997; PC 1986; QC (Scot.) 1985; MP (C) Kensington and Chelsea, since 2005; *b* 21 June 1946; *yr s* of late E. Rifkind, Edinburgh; *m* 1970, Edith Amalia Rifkind (*née* Steinberg); one *s* one *d*. *Educ:* George Watson's Coll.; Edinburgh Univ. LLB, MSc. Lectured at Univ. of Rhodesia, 1967–68. Vis. Prof., Inst. for Advanced Studies in the Humanities, Edinburgh Univ., 1998. Called to Scottish Bar, 1970. Contested (C) Edinburgh, Central, 1970; MP (C) Edinburgh, Pentlands, Feb. 1974–1997; contested (C) same seat, 1997, 2001. Opposition front bench spokesman on Scottish Affairs, 1975–76; Parly Under Sec. of State, Scottish Office, 1979–82, FCO, 1982–83; Minister of State, FCO, 1983–86; Secretary of State: for Scotland, 1986–90; for Transport, 1990–92; for Defence, 1992–95; for Foreign and Commonwealth Affairs, 1995–97; Opposition front bench spokesman on work and pensions, 2005. Jt Sec., Cons. Foreign and Commonwealth Affairs Cttee, 1978; Member: Select Cttee on Europ. Secondary Legislation, 1975–76; Select Cttee on Overseas Develt, 1978–79. Hon. Pres., Scottish Young Conservatives, 1975–76; Pres., Scottish Cons.-Unionist Party, 1998–2002. Mem., Royal Co. of Archers, Queen's Body Guard for Scotland, 1992; Hon. Col, 162 Movt Control Regt (V), RLC, 1997–2005; Hon. Col, City of Edinburgh Univs OTC, 2004– (Hon. Dep. Col, 1999–2004). Pres., Edinburgh Univ. Develt Trust. Hon. LLD Napier, 1998; Dr *hc* Edinburgh, 2003. Commander: Order of Merit (Poland), 1998; Order of Grand Duke Gediminas (Lithuania), 2002. *Recreations:* walking, reading, field sports. *Address:* House of Commons, SW1A 0AA. *Clubs:* Pratt's, White's; New (Edinburgh).

RIGBY, Sir Anthony (John), 3rd Bt *cr* 1929, of Long Durford, Rogate. co. Sussex; *b* 3 Oct. 1946; *e s* of Lt-Col Sir (Hugh) John (Macbeth) Rigby, 2nd Bt and Mary Patricia Erskine Rigby (*née* Leacock); *S* father, 1999; *m* 1978, Mary Oliver; three *s* one *d*. *Educ:* Rugby. *Heir: e s* Oliver Hugh Rigby, *b* 20 Aug. 1979.

RIGBY, Brian, CBE 2003; Chairman, Walnut Tree Enterprises Ltd, since 2003; *b* 30 Aug. 1944; *s* of Donald Rigby and Margaret Rigby (*née* Dorrity); *m* 1966, Ann Passmore; one *s*. *Educ:* Birkenhead Sch.; Hertford Coll., Oxford (MA 1970); LSE (MSc 1972). Principal, DoE, 1971–77; British Telecommunications: joined, 1977; Dir, London, 1984–88; Dep. Man. Dir, Enterprises, 1988–92; Dir, Supply Mgt, 1992–97; Dir, Procurement Gp, HM Treasury, 1997–2000; Dep. Chief Exec., Office of Govt Commerce, 2000–03. Vis. Fellow, Warwick Business Sch., 2003–. Director: Oxford Radcliffe Hosp. NHS Trust, 2004–; Partnership for Schools, 2005–. Gov., Millfield Sch., Somerset, 2005–. *Recreations:* people, places.

RIGBY, Bryan; Chairman, Anglo German Foundation, since 1998 (Trustee, since 1992); *b* 9 Jan. 1933; *s* of William George Rigby and Lily Rigby; *m* 1978, Marian Rosamund; one *s* one *d* of a former marriage, and one step *s* one step *d*. *Educ:* Wigan Grammar Sch.; King's Coll., London (BSc Special Chemistry, Dip. Chem. Engrg). UKAEA Industrial Gp, Capenhurst, 1955–60; Beecham Gp, London and Amsterdam, 1960–64; Laporte Industries (Holdings) Ltd, 1964–78; Dep. Dir-Gen., CBI, 1978–83; Man. Dir, UK Ops, 1984–87, UK, Ireland and Scandinavia, 1987–93, BASF Group; Chairman: Streamline Hldgs, 1994–98; Elliott Ross Associates, 1998–2003. Dir, MEDEVA plc, 1993–99. Mem., Social Security Adv. Cttee, 1994–99; Chm., Nurses' Pay Review Body, 1995–98. Vice-Pres., BAAS, 1992–96; Gov., Henley Management Coll., 1993–2002. Chm., Scannappeal, 1999–. *Recreations:* music, golf, gardening. *Address:* Cluny, 61 Penn Road, Beaconsfield, Bucks HP9 2LW. *T:* (01494) 673206. *Club:* Reform.

RIGBY, Jean Prescott, (Mrs Jamie Hayes); mezzo-soprano; Principal, English National Opera, 1982–90; *d* of late Thomas Boulton Rigby and of Margaret Annie Rigby; *m* 1987, Jamie Hayes; three *s*. *Educ:* Birmingham Sch. of Music (ABSM 1976); Royal Acad. of Music (Dip.RAM; Hon. ARAM 1984; Hon. FRAM 1989). ARCM 1979; ABC 1996. Début: Royal Opera House, Covent Garden, 1983; Glyndebourne Festival Opera, 1984; rôles, 1990–, include: Nicklaus, in The Tales of Hoffmann, Olga in Eugene Onegin, Royal Opera; Isabella, in The Italian Girl in Algiers, Buxton; title rôle, La Cenerentola, and Idamante in Idomeneo, Garsington; Charlotte, in Werther, San Diego and Seattle; Irene, in Theodora, Geneviève, in Pelléas and Mélisande, Eduige, in Rodelinda, Hippolyta, in A Midsummer Night's Dream, and Emilia, in Otello, Glyndebourne; *English National Opera:* Penelope, in The Return of Ulysses; title rôle, in The Rape of Lucretia; Amastris, in Xerxes; Rosina, in The Barber of Seville; Helen, in King Priam; Maddalena, in Rigoletto; Ruth, in The Pirates of Penzance; Suzuki, in Madam Butterfly; Mrs Ford, in Sir John in Love. Several TV performances, videos and over fifty recordings. Hon. Fellow, Birmingham Conservatoire, 2007. *Recreations:* British heritage, sport, cooking. *Address:* c/o Askonas Holt Ltd, Lincoln House, 300 High Holborn, WC1V 7JH.

RIGBY, Sir Peter, Kt 2002; Chairman and Chief Executive, Specialist Computer Holdings Plc, since 1975; President, Specialist Computers International Ltd, since 2000; Chairman, Patriot Aviation Ltd, since 2002; *b* 29 Sept. 1943; *s* of late John and Phyllis Rigby; two *s*. Founder, Rigby Foundn Charitable Trust, 1995; Chm., Millennium Point Trust, 1996–2003. Chm., Mallory Court Hotel, 1997–. Trustee, RAF Mus., 2005–. DL W Midlands, 2000. DUniv UCE, 1998; Hon. DSc Aston, 2003. *Recreations:* flying, sailing, classical music. *Address:* Specialist Computer Holdings Plc, James House, Warwick Road, Birmingham B11 2LE. *T:* (0121) 766 7000, *Fax:* (0121) 766 2601; *e-mail:* peter.rigby@scc.com.

RIGBY, Peter William Jack, PhD; FMedSci; Chief Executive, Institute of Cancer Research, since 1999, and Professor of Developmental Biology, University of London; *b* 7 July 1947; *s* of Jack and Lorna Rigby; *m* 1st, 1971, Paula Webb (marr. diss. 1983); 2nd, 1985, Julia Maidment; one *s*. *Educ:* Lower Sch., John Lyon, Harrow; Jesus Coll., Cambridge (BA, PhD). MRC Lab. of Molecular Biol., Cambridge, 1971–73; Helen Hay Whitney Foundn Fellow, Stanford Univ. Med. Sch., 1973–76; Imperial College London: Lectr, then Sen. Lectr in Biochem., 1976–83; Reader in Tumour Virology, 1983–86; Vis. Prof., 1986–94 and 2000–; Head, Div. of Eukaryotic Molecular Genetics, NIMR, MRC, 1986–2000 (Head, Genes and Cellular Controls Gp, 1986–96). Chm., MRC Gene Therapy Co-ordinating Cttee, 1992–96; Member: MRC Cell Bd, 1988–92; EMBO, 1979; Science Council, Celltech, 1982–2003; Scientific Adv. Bd, Somatix Therapy Corp., 1989–97; Scientific Cttee, Cancer Res. Campaign, 1983–88, 1996–99; Strategy Bd, BBSRC, 2004–06; Bd, Genome Res. Ltd, The Wellcome Trust Sanger Inst., 2006–. Chairman, Scientific Advisory Board: Topotarget (formerly Prolifix Ltd), 1996–; Hexagen Technology Ltd, 1996–98; Member, Scientific Advisory Board: deVGen NV, 1998–2000; KuDOS Pharmaceuticals, 1999–2006. Non-executive Director: Royal Marsden NHS Foundn Trust, 2001–; Proacta Therapeutics, 2001–03. Member: Council, Acad. of Med. Scis, 2002–04; Bd of Govs, Beatson Inst. for Cancer Res., Glasgow, 2003–06 (Dep. Chm., 2006–07); Council, St George's, Univ. of London (formerly St George's Hosp. Med. Sch.), 2003–09; Bd of Govs, Wellcome Trust, 2008–; Bd of Trustees, Univ. of London, 2008–. Chm. Medical Res. Cttee, and Mem. Nat. Council, Muscular Dystrophy Campaign, 2003–07; Chm., Wellcome Trust Principal Res. Fellowship Interview Cttee, 2004–07. FMedSci 1999. European Editor, Cell, 1984–97. *Publications:* papers on molecular biology in sci. jls. *Recreations:* narrow boats, listening to music, sport. *Address:* Chester Beatty Laboratories: Institute of Cancer Research, 237 Fulham Road, SW3 6JB. *T:* (020) 7878 3824. *Club:* Athenæum.

RIGG, Dame Diana, DBE 1994 (CBE 1988); actress; *b* Doncaster, Yorks, 20 July 1938; *d* of Louis Rigg and Beryl Helliwell; *m* 1982, Archibald Stirling; one *d*. *Educ:* Fulneck Girls' Sch., Pudsey. Trained for the stage at Royal Academy of Dramatic Art. First appearance on stage in RADA prod. in York Festival, at Theatre Royal, York, summer,

1957 (Natella Abashwili in The Caucasian Chalk Circle); after appearing in repertory in Chesterfield and in York she joined the Royal Shakespeare Company, Stratford-upon-Avon, 1959; first appearance in London, Aldwych Theatre, 1961 (2nd Ondine, Violanta and Princess Berthe in Ondine); at same theatre, in repertory (The Devils, Becket, The Taming of the Shrew), 1961; (Madame de Tourvel, The Art of Seduction), 1962; Royal Shakespeare, Stratford-upon-Avon, Apr. 1962 (Helena in A Midsummer Night's Dream, Bianca in The Taming of the Shrew, Lady Macduff in Macbeth, Adriana in The Comedy of Errors, Cordelia in King Lear); subseq. appeared in the last production at the Aldwych, Dec. 1962, followed by Adriana in The Comedy of Errors and Monica Stettler in The Physicists, 1963. Toured the provinces, spring, 1963, in A Midsummer Night's Dream; subseq. appeared at the Royal Shakespeare, Stratford, and at the Aldwych, in Comedy of Errors, Dec. 1963; again played Cordelia in King Lear, 1964, prior to touring with both plays for the British Council, in Europe, the USSR, and the US; during this tour she first appeared in New York (State Theatre), 1964, in same plays; Viola in Twelfth Night, Stratford, June 1966; Heloise in Abelard and Heloise, Wyndham's, 1970, also at the Atkinson, New York, 1971; joined The National Theatre, 1972: in Jumpers, 'Tis Pity She's a Whore and Lady Macbeth in Macbeth, 1972; The Misanthrope, 1973, Washington and NY, 1975; Phaedra Britannica, 1975 (Plays and Players Award for Best Actress); The Guardsman, 1978; Pygmalion, Albery, 1974; Night and Day, Phoenix, 1978 (Plays and Players award, 1979); Colette, USA, 1982; Heartbreak House, Haymarket, 1983; Little Eyolf, Lyric, Hammersmith, 1985; Antony and Cleopatra, Chichester, 1985; Wildfire, Phoenix, 1986; Follies, Shaftesbury, 1987; Love Letters, San Francisco, 1990; All for Love, Almeida, 1991; Berlin Bertie, Royal Court, 1992; Medea, Almeida, 1992, transf. Wyndhams, 1993–94 (Evening Standard Drama Award), then NY, 1994 (Tony Award); Mother Courage, RNT, 1995; Who's Afraid of Virginia Woolf?, Almeida, 1996; Phèdre, and Britannicus, Albery, 1998; Humble Boy, RNT, 2001; Suddenly Last Summer, Albery, 2004; Honour, Wyndham's, 2006; All About my Mother, Old Vic, 2007; The Cherry Orchard, Chichester, 2008; *films include:* A Midsummer Night's Dream, Assassination Bureau, On Her Majesty's Secret Service, Julius Caesar, The Hospital, Theatre of Blood, A Little Night Music, The Great Muppet Caper, Evil Under the Sun (Film Actress of the Year Award, Variety Club, 1983), A Good Man in Africa; Heidi; *television appearances include:* Sentimental Agent, The Comedy of Errors, The Avengers (Special Award, BAFTA, 2000), Married Alive, Diana (US series), In This House of Brede (US), Three Piece Suite, The Serpent Son, Hedda Gabler, The Marquise, Little Eyolf, King Lear, Witness of the Prosecution, Bleak House, Mother Love (BAFTA award), Unexplained Laughter, Moll Flanders (serial), Rebecca (Emmy Award for Best Supporting Actress, 1997), The Mrs Bradley Mysteries, Victoria and Albert, Charles II: The Power and the Passion, and others. Chair, MacRoberts Arts Centre; Mem., BM Develt Fund. A Vice-Pres., Baby Life Support Systems (BLISS), 1984–. Cameron Mackintosh Vis. Prof. of Contemporary Theatre, Oxford Univ., 1999; Emeritus Fellow, St Catherine's Coll., Oxford. Chancellor, Stirling Univ., 1997–2008. Foreign Hon. Mem., American Acad. of Arts and Scis. *Publications:* No Turn Unstoned, 1982; So to the Land, 1994. *Recreations:* reading and trying to get organized. *Address:* c/o ARG, 4 Great Portland Street, W1W 8PA.

RIGG, (Ian) Malcolm; Director, Policy Studies Institute, since 2004; *b* 31 Jan. 1947; *s* of Donald Appleby Rigg and Marjorie Isobel Connell Rigg (*née* Smiley); *m* 1982, Lesley Saunders, DPhil; one *s*, and one step *s* one step *d*. *Educ:* Magdalen College Sch., Oxford; Enfield Coll. of Technol. (BA Business Studies). Director: IFF Res., 1978–82; Sample Surveys, 1982–83; Sen. Res. Fellow, PSI, 1984–90; Head of Inf., Consumers' Assoc., 1990–94; Dir of Res., COI Communications, 1994–97; Managing Director: BMRB Social Res., 1997–2000; BMRB Internat., 2001–04. Market Research Society: Mem. Council, 1995–97; Vice-Chm., 1996–97; Chairman: Professional Standards Cttee, 1995–97; Professional Develt Adv. Bd, 1997–2004. Mem. Cttee, Assoc. of Res. Centres in Soc. Scis, 2005–. AcSS. FRSA. *Publications:* Training in Britain: individuals' perspectives, 1989; Continuing Training in Firms and Trainer Development in Britain, 1991; (jtly) Electronic Government: the view from the queue, 1999; (jtly) HEFCE Strategic Review of Sustainable Development in Higher Education in England, 2008. *Recreations:* tandem triathlon, cycling up hills, social justice, music festivals, avant-garde jazz, poetry, Tottenham Hotspur season ticket holder (an annual entitlement to hope with minimal chance of fulfilment). *Address:* Policy Studies Institute, 50 Hanson Street, W1W 6UP. *T:* (020) 7911 7522, *Fax:* (020) 7911 7501; *e-mail:* m.rigg@psi.org.uk.

RIGGE, Marianne, (Mrs Trevor Goodchild), OBE 2000; Director, College of Health, 1983–2003; *b* 10 May 1948; *d* of late Dr Patrick Noel O'Mahony and of Elizabeth Nora O'Mahony (*née* Daly); *m* 1st, 1968, John Simon Rigge; two *d* (one *s* decd); 2nd, 1990, Trevor Goodchild. *Educ:* St Angela's Ursuline Convent, London; University College London (BA Hons French). PA, Consumers' Assoc., 1971–76; Res. Asst to Chm., Nat. Consumer Council, 1976–77; founder Dir, Mutual Aid Centre, 1977–83. Member: Clinical Outcomes Gp, 1993–97; Clinical Systems Gp, 1997–2000; NICE Partners Council, 1999–2002; Nat. Access Taskforce, 2000–02. Non-exec. Dir, Whipps Cross Univ. Hosp. NHS Trust, 2001–08. Editor, Self Health, 1985–87; columnist, Health Service Jl, 1999–2003. *Publications:* (with Michael Young) Mutual Aid in a Selfish Society, 1979; Building Societies and the Consumer, 1981; Hello, Can I Help You, 1981; Prospects for Worker Co-operatives in Europe, 1981; (with Michael Young) Revolution from Within, 1983; Annual Guide to Hospital Waiting Lists, 1984–92. *Recreations:* gardening, cooking, music. *Address:* 157 Whipps Cross Road, E11 1NP. *T:* (020) 8530 4420.

RIGGS, David George; Chief Financial Officer, Australian Government Solicitor, since 1998; *b* 6 May 1942. *Educ:* Bury GS; Manchester Univ. (BA Econ.). CPFA (IPFA 1963). With Bury CBC, 1958–68; Greater London Council, 1968–82: Finance Officer, 1968–74; Hd of Public Services Finance, 1974–76; Asst Comptroller of Finance, 1976–82; Dir of Finance, ILEA, 1982–90; Dir of Finance, Benefits Agency, 1991–98. *Address:* 48 Jacka Crescent, Campbell, ACT 2612, Australia.

RIGNEY, Howard Ernest; HM Diplomatic Service, retired; Consul-General, Lyons, 1977–82; *b* 22 June 1922; *o s* of late Wilbert Ernest and Minnie Rigney; *m* 1950, Margaret Grayling Benn (*d* 2002); one *s*. *Educ:* Univs of Western Ontario, Toronto and Paris. BA Western Ont. 1945, MA Toronto 1947. Lectr, Univ. of British Columbia, 1946–48; grad. studies, Paris Univ., 1948–50; COI, 1953–56; CRO, 1956; Regional Information Officer, Dacca, 1957–60, Montreal, 1960–63; CRO, 1963–65; FO/CO, 1965–67; Consul (Information), Chicago, 1967–69; Dep. Consul-Gen., Chicago, 1969–71; Head of Chancery and Consul, Rangoon, 1971–73; Head of Migration and Visa Dept, FCO, 1973–77. Hon. DLitt, Winston Churchill Coll., Ill, 1971. *Recreations:* opera, book-collecting, gardening. *Address:* The Old Forge, Frinstead, Sittingbourne, Kent ME9 0TF.

RIIS-JØRGENSEN, Birger; Ambassador of Denmark to the Court of St James's, since 2006; *b* 13 Jan. 1949; *s* of Jens and Thyra Jørgensen; *m* 1978, Karin Rasmussen, MEP; two *s*. *Educ:* Univ. of Copenhagen (MA Hist. 1974); studies in Sweden and USA. Res. Librarian, Royal Liby, Copenhagen, 1975; joined Danish Foreign Service, 1976; First Sec., Danish Delegn to NATO, Brussels, 1979–83; Hd of Section, Min. of For. Affairs, and Sec. to For. Affairs Cttee of Parlt, 1983–86; Counsellor, Secretariat for Europ. Political Co-operation, Brussels, 1987–88; Hd of Section and Dep. Hd of Dept, Danish Internat. Develt Agency, 1989–91; Ministry of Foreign Affairs: Hd, Africa Dept, 1991–94; Hd, Middle East and Latin America Dept, 1994–96; Under-Sec. for Bilateral Affairs, 1996–2000; State Sec. and Hd of Trade Council of Denmark, 2000–06. Member Board of Directors: Industrialisation Fund for Developing Countries, 1996–2000; Fund for Industrialisation of Eastern Europe, 1996–2000; Danish Co-Chm., US/Denmark/ Greenland Cttee for Econ., Technical, Scientific and Cultural Co-operation, 2004–06. Comdr of the Dannebrog (Denmark), 2004. *Recreations:* tennis, bicycling, sea-kayaking, swimming, modern history, classical music. *Address:* Royal Danish Embassy, 55 Sloane Street, SW1X 9SR. *T:* (020) 7333 0200, *Fax:* (020) 7333 0270; *e-mail:* lonamb@um.dk. *Clubs:* Athenæum, Travellers.

RILEY, Bridget Louise, CH 1999; CBE 1972; artist; *b* 24 April 1931; *d* of late John Riley and Louise (*née* Gladstone). *Educ:* Cheltenham Ladies' College; Goldsmiths' School of Art; Royal College of Art. ARCA 1955. Mem., RSA. Exhibitions: Gall. One, London, 1962–63; Drawings, Mus. of Modern Art, NY, 1966–67; (with Philip King) XXXIV Biennale Venice, 1968; (retrospective) British Council touring exhibn, Hanover, Berne, Dusseldorf, Turin, Prague, 1970–72; (retrospective) touring exhibn, US, Aust., Japan, 1978–80; Working with Colour, Arts Council of GB touring exhibn, 1984–85; According to Sensation: Paintings 82–92, Arts Council of GB touring exhibn, Germany and Hayward Gall., London, 1992; Paintings from the 60s and 70s, Serpentine Gall., London, 1999; Paintings 1982–2000 and Early Works on Paper, PaceWildenstein, NY, 2000; Reconnaissance, DIA Center for Arts, NY, 2001; (retrospective) Tate Britain, 2003; New Work, Krefeld, Germany, 2004; Mus. of Contemp. Art, Sydney, Aust., 2004–05. Public collections include: Tate Gallery; Victoria and Albert Museum; Arts Council; British Council; Museum of Modern Art, New York; Australian Nat. Gallery, Canberra; Museum of Modern Art, Pasadena; Ferens Art Gallery, Hull; Allbright Knox, Buffalo, USA; Museum of Contemporary Art, Chicago; Ulster Museum, Ireland; Stedelijk Museum, Amsterdam; Berne Kunsthalle; Mus. of Modern Art, Tokyo. Designed Colour Moves, for Ballet Rambert, 1983. Trustee, Nat. Gallery, 1981–88. Hon. DLitt: Manchester, 1976; Ulster, 1986; Oxford, 1993; Cambridge, 1995; De Montfort, 1996; Exeter, 1997; London, 2005. AICA critics Prize, 1963; Stuyvesant Bursary, 1964; Ohara Mus. Prize, Tokyo, 1972; Gold Medal, Grafik Biennale, Norway, 1980; Praemium Imperiale for Painting, 2003. *Address:* c/o Karsten Schubert, 5–8 Lower John Street, Golden Square, W1F 9DR.

RILEY, Christopher John; Associate, Oxera Consulting Ltd, since 2005; *b* 20 Jan. 1947; *s* of Bernard Francis Riley and Phyllis (*née* Wigley); *m* 1982, Helen Marion Mynett; two *s*. *Educ:* Ratcliffe Coll., Leicester; Wadham Coll., Oxford (MA Maths); Univ. of East Anglia (MA Econs). Economist, HM Treasury, 1969–77; Res. Fellow, Nuffield Coll., Oxford, 1977–78; Sen. Economic Advr, 1978–88, Under Sec., 1988–95, HM Treasury; Chief Economist, DoE, subseq. DETR, then DTLR, later DfT, 1995–2005. *Publications:* various articles in books and learned jls. *Recreation:* music, especially choral singing. *Address:* 10 Briarwood Road, SW4 9PX. *T:* (020) 7720 6263; *e-mail:* chris@h-riley.gotadsl.co.uk.

RILEY, Lt-Gen. Jonathon Peter, CB 2008; DSO 1996; Deputy Commander International Security Assistance Force, Afghanistan, 2007–08; *b* 16 Jan. 1955; *s* of John Sisson Riley and Joyce Riley (*née* Outen); *m* 1980, Kathryn Mary Beard (marr. diss. 2000); one *s* one *d*. *Educ:* St Mary's, Beverley; Kingston Sch.; UCL (BA Geog.); Leeds Univ. (MA Hist.); Cranfield Univ. (PhD 2006). Commnd Queen's Royal Regt, 1974; Staff Coll., 1987; Bde Major, 6th Armd Bde, 1989; transferred to RWF, 1990; mil. observer, Balkan war, 1992–93; DS, Staff Coll., 1993–94; CO, 1 RWF, 1994–96; COS, 1st Armd Div., 1996–98; Dep. Comdt, Multinat. Div. (SW), Bosnia, 1998–99; Commander: 1st Mechanized Bde, 1999–2001; Jt Task Force, and Mil. Advr to Govt of Sierra Leone, 2000–01; Dep. Comdt, Staff Coll., 2001–03; Dep. Comdg Gen., New Iraqi Army, 2003; rcds 2004; GOC British Troops, Iraq, and Comdg Gen., Multinat. Div. (SE), Iraq, 2004–05; Sen. British Mil. Advr, US Central Comd, 2005–07. Col, Royal Welch Fusiliers, 2005–06. Council Member: Army Records Soc., 2004–; RUSI, 2006–; CDISS, 2006–; Mem., Catholic Records Soc., 2005– Officer, Legion of Merit (US), 2005. *Publications:* History of the Queen's, 1988; From Pole to Pole, 1989, 2nd edn 2001; Soldiers of the Queen, 1992; White Dragon, 1995; Napoleon and the World War 1813, 2000; The Royal Welch Fusiliers 1945–2000, 2001; The Life and Campaigns of General Hughie Stockwell, 2006; Napoleon as a General, 2007; (ed) That Astonishing Infantry, 2007. *Recreations:* field sports, white water rafting, rowing, historical research, poetry and English literature. *Address:* Manor Afon, Aber-Giâr, Llanllwni, Carmarthenshire SA40 9SQ; *e-mail:* baggydad@hotmail.com. *Club:* Naval and Military.

RILEY, Very Rev. Kenneth Joseph, OBE 2003; Dean of Manchester, 1993–2005, now Emeritus; *b* 25 June 1940; *s* of Arthur and Mary Josephine Riley; *m* 1968, Margaret; two *d*. *Educ:* Holywell GS; UCW, Aberystwyth (BA 1961); Linacre Coll., Oxford (BA 1964; MA); Wycliffe Hall, Oxford. Ordained deacon, 1964, priest, 1965; Asst Curate, Emmanuel Ch., Fazakerley, Liverpool, 1964–66; Chaplain: Brasted Place Coll., 1966–69; Oundle Sch., 1969–74; Liverpool Univ., 1974–83; Vicar, Mossley Hill, Liverpool, 1975–83; RD, Childwall, 1982–83; Canon Treas., 1983–87, Canon Precentor, 1987–93, Liverpool Cathedral. *Publication:* Liverpool Cathedral, 1987. *Recreations:* music, drama, films. *Address:* 145 Turning Lane, Southport, PR8 5HZ.

RILEY, Philip Stephen; Chief Executive, Chrysalis Radio, 1999–2007; *b* 4 June 1959; *s* of James and Marie Riley; *m* 1992, Jean Fiveash; one *s* two *d*. *Educ:* Loughborough Univ. (BSc Hons 1980); Columbia Business Sch. (MBA Beta Gamma Sigma 1988). Prog. Dir, BRMB Radio, 1989–90; Managing Director: Radio Aire, 1990–94; 100.7 Heart FM, 1994–96; Chrysalis Radio, 1996–99. Member, Board: Commercial Radio Companies' Assoc., 1994–; Radio Advertising Bureau, 1996–; RAJAR, 2004–.

RILEY, Stephen Michael; Director, Maritime Heritage, National Maritime Museum, Greenwich, 2002–07; *b* 4 April 1950; *s* of Jack and Constance Riley; partner, Jane Avard Weeks; one *s* one *d*. *Educ:* Liverpool Univ. (BA Hons 1972); Univ. of Leicester (Post-grad. Cert. in Mus. Studies 1974). Curatorial trainee, Maritime Hist., Merseyside Co. Mus, Liverpool, 1972–76; National Maritime Museum, Greenwich: Dep. Hd, Dept of Ships and Antiquities, 1986–92; Director: Property and Tech. Services, 1993–95; Display Div., 1995–98; Neptune Court Re-develt Project, 1998–99; Nat. Maritime Mus. Galls, 1999–2001. *Recreations:* riding, classic boats and classic cars, photography, travel.

RILEY-SMITH, Prof. Jonathan Simon Christopher, FRHistS; Dixie Professor of Ecclesiastical History, Cambridge University, 1994–2005, now Emeritus; Fellow, Emmanuel College, Cambridge, 1994–2005; Librarian, Order of St John, since 2005; *b* 27 June 1938; *s* of late William Henry Douglas Riley-Smith and Elspeth Agnes Mary Riley-Smith (*née* Craik Henderson); *m* 1968, Marie-Louise Jeannetta, *d* of Wilfred John Sutcliffe Field; one *s* two *d*. *Educ:* Eton College; Trinity College, Cambridge (MA, PhD, LittD). Dept of Mediaeval History, University of St Andrews: Asst Lectr, 1964–65; Lectr, 1966–72; Faculty of History, Cambridge: Asst Lectr, 1972–75; Lectr, 1975–78; Chm., Bd,

1997–99; Queens' College, Cambridge: Fellow and Dir of Studies in History, 1972–78; Praelector, 1973–75; Librarian, 1973, 1977–78; Prof. of History, Univ. of London, 1978–94 (at RHC, 1978–85, at RHBNC, 1985–94); Head of Dept of History, RHC, then RHBNC, 1984–90. Stewart Short-Term Vis. Fellow, Princeton Univ., 2001. Lectures: Bampton, Columbia Univ., 2007; Robert M. Conway, Univ. of Notre Dame, 2008. Chairman: Bd of Management, Inst. of Historical Res., 1988–94 (Hon. Fellow, 1997); Victoria County Hist. Cttee, 1989–97; Pres., Soc. for the Study of the Crusades and the Latin East, 1990–95. Corres. Fellow, Medieval Acad. of America, 2006. KStJ 1969 (Librarian: Priory of Scotland, 1966–78; Grand Priory, subseq. Priory of England and the Islands, 1982–2007); KM 1971 (Officer of Merit, 1985). Prix Schlumberger, Acad. des Inscriptions et Belles-Lettres, Paris, 1988. *Publications:* The Knights of St John in Jerusalem and Cyprus, 1967; (with U. and M. C. Lyons) Ayyubids, Mamlukes and Crusaders, 1971; The Feudal Nobility and the Kingdom of Jerusalem, 1973; What were the Crusades?, 1977, 2nd edn 1992; (with L. Riley-Smith) The Crusades: idea and reality, 1981; The First Crusade and the Idea of Crusading, 1986; The Crusades: a short history, 1987, 2nd edn 2005 (trans. French, 1990, Italian, 1994); (ed) The Atlas of the Crusades, 1991 (trans. German 1992, French 1996); The Oxford Illustrated History of the Crusades, 1995; (with N. Coureas) Cyprus and the Crusades, 1995; (jtly) Montjoie, 1997; The First Crusaders, 1997; Hospitallers: the history of the Order of St John, 1999; Al seguito delle Crociate, 2000; (jtly) Dei gesta per Francos, 2001; (jtly) In Laudem Hierosolymitani, 2007; The Crusades, Christianity and Islam, 2008; articles in learned jls. *Recreation:* the past and present of own family. *Address:* Emmanuel College, Cambridge CB2 3AP. *T:* (01223) 334200.

RIMER, Rt Hon. Sir Colin (Percy Farquharson), Kt 1994; PC 2007; **Rt Hon. Lord Justice Rimer;** a Lord Justice of Appeal, since 2007; *b* 30 Jan. 1944; *s* of late Kenneth Rowland Rimer and Maria Eugenia Rimer (*née* Farquharson); *m* 1970, Penelope Ann Gibbs; two *s* one *d*. *Educ:* Dulwich Coll.; Trinity Hall, Cambridge (MA, LLB). Legal Assistant, Inst. of Comparative Law, Paris, 1967–68; called to the Bar, Lincoln's Inn, 1968, Bencher, 1994; QC 1988; in practice, 1969–94; a Judge of the High Court of Justice, Chancery Div., 1994–2007. *Recreations:* music, novels, walking. *Address:* Royal Courts of Justice, Strand, WC2A 2LL.

RIMER, Jennifer; Head Teacher, St Mary's Music School, Edinburgh, since 1996; *b* Kirkcaldy; *d* of James and Margaret Whitelaw; *m* 1971, David Rimer; three *d*. *Educ:* Buckhaven High Sch., Fife; Univ. of Edinburgh (BMus Hons 1969; DipEd 1970). LRAM 1968. Teacher, Church High Sch., Newcastle, 1970–72; Principal Teacher, Music, St David's High Sch., Dalkeith, 1972–77; Music and Piano Teacher, 1982–93, Hd, Acad. Music, Careers and Guidance, 1993–96, St Mary's Music Sch., Edinburgh. Examiner, setter and marker, SQA, 1978–2008. Founder Fellow, Inst. of Contemp. Scotland, 2000; Member: Sch. Leaders Scotland (formerly Headteachers' Assoc. of Scotland); Eur. Piano Teachers' Assoc., 1975–. Gov., George Heriots' Sch., 1990–2000; Dir, Edinburgh Youth Orch., 1990–93. *Publication:* contrib. Jl of Scottish Educn. *Recreations:* family, theatre, opera, concerts, art galleries, piano, viola, books, youth orchestras, walking, yoga. *Address:* St Mary's Music School, Coates Hall, 25 Grosvenor Crescent, Edinburgh EH12 5EL. *T:* (0131) 538 7766; *e-mail:* jrimer@st-marys-music-school.co.uk.

RIMINGTON, John David, CB 1987; Director-General, Health and Safety Executive, 1984–95; *b* 27 June 1935; *s* of late John William Rimington, MBE, and of Mabel Dorrington; *m* 1963, Dame Stella Rimington, *qv*; two *d*. *Educ:* Nottingham High Sch.; Jesus Coll., Cambridge (Cl. I Hons History, MA). Nat. Service Commn, RA, 1954–56. Joined BoT, 1959; seconded HM Treasury (work on decimal currency), 1961; Principal, Tariff Div., BoT, 1963; 1st Sec. (Economic), New Delhi, 1965; Mergers Div., DTI, 1969; Dept of Employment, 1970; Asst Sec. 1972 (Employment Policy and Manpower); Counsellor, Social and Regional Policy, UK perm. representation to EEC, Brussels, 1974; MSC, 1977–81; Under Sec. 1978; Dir, Safety Policy Div., HSE, 1981–83; Dep. Sec., 1984; Permanent Sec., 1992. Non-executive Director: Magnox Electric, 1996–98; BNFL, 1998–2000; Angel Trains Gp (formerly Angel Train Contracts) Ltd, 1999–2006. Mem. Nat. Council, 1995–2008, Vice Chm., 2001–07, Consumers' Assoc. Visiting Professor: Univ. of Strathclyde, 1997–99; Salford Univ., 1999–. CCMI (CIMgt 1993). Hon. DSc Sheffield, 1995. *Publications:* articles on risk; contrib. to RIPA Jl, New Asia Review, Trans IChemE, etc. *Recreations:* playing the piano, gardening, watching cricket. *Address:* 9 Highbury Hill, N5 1SU.

RIMINGTON, Dame Stella, DCB 1996; Director General, Security Service, 1992–96; *b* 1935; *m* 1963, John David Rimington, *qv*; two *d*. *Educ:* Nottingham High Sch. for Girls; Edinburgh Univ. (MA). Security Service, 1969. Non-executive Director: Marks & Spencer plc, 1997–2004; Whitehead Mann GKR (formerly GKR), 1997–2001; BG plc, 1997–2000; BG Gp, 2000–05; Royal Marsden NHS Trust, 1998–2001. Chm., Inst. of Cancer Res., 1997–2001. Trustee, RAF Mus., 1998–2001. Hon. Air Cdre, No 7006 (VR) Intelligence Sqn, RAuxAF, 1997–2001. Hon. LLD: Nottingham, 1995; Exeter, 1996; London Metropolitan, 2004; Liverpool, 2005. *Publications:* Open Secret (autobiog.), 2001; novels: At Risk, 2004; Secret Asset, 2006; Illegal Action, 2007; Dead Line, 2008. *Address:* PO Box 1604, SW1P 1XB.

RIMMER, Henry, (Harry), CBE 1994; DL; Member (Lab) Liverpool City Council, 1952–53 and 1987–96; Leader, Liverpool City Council, 1990–96; *b* 19 May 1928; *s* of Thomas and Sarah Ellen Rimmer; *m* 1st, 1951, Doreen Taylor (marr. diss. 1978); three *s* one *d*; 2nd, 1978, Joan Conder. *Educ:* Oulton High Sch.; Liverpool Collegiate Sch. Mem., Merseyside CC, 1981–86 (Dep. Leader, 1982–86). Member: Merseyside Police Authy, 1987–96 (Vice-Chm., 1990–92); Bd, Merseyside Develt Corp., 1991–98. Director: Wavertree Technology Park Co., 1987–96; Liverpool Airport PLC, 1989–96. DL Merseyside, 1997. *Recreations:* country walking, supporting Liverpool Football Club. *Address:* Flat 103 Ash Grange, Brookside Avenue, Knotty Ash, Liverpool L14 7NQ. *T:* (0151) 220 6022.

RIMMER, Air Vice-Marshal Thomas William, CB 2001; OBE 1987; FRAeS; Commander, British Forces Cyprus, 2000–03; *b* 16 Dec. 1948; *s* of William Thompson Rimmer and Elizabeth Comrie Rimmer (*née* Baird); *m* 1976, Sarah Caroline Hale; one *s* one *d*. *Educ:* Morrison's Academy, Crieff; Edinburgh Univ. (MA Hons 1970). FRAeS 1997. Graduated RAF Cranwell, 1972; served Central Flying Sch., RAF Linton-on-Ouse, RAF Bruggen, RAF Coltishall, to 1983; French Air Force Staff Coll., 1983–84; Chief Instructor, RAF Cottesmore, 1984–87; HQ RAF Germany, 1987–89; Head, RAF Presentation Team, 1989–90; Station Comdr, RAF Cottesmore, 1990–92; Senior UK Mil. Officer, WEU, 1992–94; rcds 1995; MoD, 1996–98; AOC and Comdt, RAF Coll., Cranwell, 1999–2000. Liveryman, Tallow Chandlers' Co., 1992–. QCVSA 1983. *Recreations:* offshore sailing, golf, gardening. *Club:* Royal Air Force.

RIMMINGTON, Rosemary Jean Neil; *see* Conley, R. J. N.

RINGEN, Mary Christina; *see* Chamberlain, M. C.

RINGEN, Prof. Stein; Professor of Sociology and Social Policy, and Fellow of Green Templeton College (formerly Green College), University of Oxford, since 1990; *b* 5 July 1945; *s* of John Ringen and Anna Ringen (*née* Simengard); *m* 2002, Prof. Mary Christina Chamberlain, *qv*. *Educ:* Univ. of Oslo (MA, dr. philos.). Broadcasting reporter, Norwegian Broadcasting Corp., 1970–71; Fellow, Internat. Peace Res. Inst., Oslo, 1971–72; Head of Secretariat, Norwegian Level of Living Study, 1972–76; Fellow, Inst. for Social Res., Oslo, 1976–78; Head of Res., Min. of Consumer Affairs and Govt Admin, Oslo, 1978–83; Prof. of Welfare Studies, Univ. of Stockholm, 1983–86; Sen. Res. Scientist, Central Bureau of Statistics, Oslo, 1986–88; Asst Dir Gen., Min. of Justice, Oslo, 1988–90. Mem., Royal Commn on Human Values, Norway, 1998–2001. FRSA. *Publications:* The Possibility of Politics, 1987, 3rd edn 2006; Citizens, Families and Reform, 1997, 2nd edn 2005; Reformdemokratiet, 1997; The Family in Question, 1998; Veien til det gode liv, 2000; What Democracy Is For, 2007; The Liberal Vision and Other Essays on Democracy and Progress, 2007. *Address:* University of Oxford, St Cross Building, Manor Road, Oxford OX1 3UQ. *T:* (01865) 281168; *e-mail:* stein.ringen@green.ox.ac.uk.

RINGROSE, Adrian Michael; Chief Executive, Interserve plc, since 2003; *b* 9 April 1967; *s* of Prof. John Robert Ringrose, *qv*; *m* 1995, Frances Jacombs; one *s* two *d*. *Educ:* Univ. of Liverpool (BA Hons Pol Theory and Instns 1988). MCIM 1991. London Electricity plc: Business Analyst, 1990–92; Commercial Manager, 1992–97; Hd, Business Develt, Building & Property Gp, 1997–2001; Man. Dir, Interserve FM Ltd, 2001–03. Pres., Business Services Assoc., 2007–. *Recreations:* family, sport, music, film, travel. *Address:* Interserve plc, Ruscombe Park, Twyford, Berks RG10 9JU.

RINGROSE, Ven. Hedley Sidney; Archdeacon of Cheltenham, since 1998; *b* 29 June 1942; *s* of Sidney and Clara Ringrose; *m* 1969, Rosemary Anne Palmer; one *s* two *d*. *Educ:* West Oxfordshire Coll.; Salisbury Theol Coll.; BA Open Univ. 1979. Deacon 1968, priest 1969; Curate: Bishopston, Bristol, 1968–71; Easthampstead, Berks, 1971–75; Vicar, St George, Gloucester with Whaddon, 1975–88; RD Gloucester City, 1983–88; Vicar of Cirencester, 1988–98; RD Cirencester, 1989–97; Hon. Canon, 1986–98, Reserved Canonry, 1998–, Gloucester Cathedral. Chairman: Dio. Bd of Patronage, 1990–98; Dio. House of Clergy, 1994–98; Dio. Bd of Education, 1998–. Mem., Gen. Synod of C of E, 1990–2005. Gov., Rendcomb Coll., 2000–. Trustee: Glenfall House, 1998–; Foundation of St Matthias, 1998– (Chm., 2005–); Sylvanus Lysons Trust, 2000–. *Recreations:* travel, family and friends, grandchildren, cycling, driving. *Address:* The Sanderlings, Thorncliffe Drive, Cheltenham, Glos GL51 6PY. *T:* (01242) 522923, *Fax:* (01242) 235925; *e-mail:* archdchelt@star.co.uk.

RINGROSE, Prof. John Robert, FRS 1977; FRSE; Professor of Pure Mathematics, 1964–93, now Emeritus, and a Pro-Vice-Chancellor, 1983–88, University of Newcastle upon Tyne; *b* 21 Dec. 1932; *s* of Albert Frederick Ringrose and Elsie Lilian Ringrose (*née* Roberts); *m* 1956, Jean Margaret Bates; three *s*. *Educ:* Buckhurst Hill County High School, Chigwell, Essex; St John's Coll., Cambridge (MA, PhD). Lecturer in Mathematics: King's Coll., Newcastle upon Tyne, 1957–61; Univ. of Cambridge (also Fellow of St John's Coll.), 1961–63; Sen. Lectr in Mathematics, Univ. of Newcastle upon Tyne, 1963–64. Pres., London Mathematical Soc., 1992–94. *Publications:* Compact Non-self-adjoint Operators, 1971; (with R. V. Kadison) Fundamentals of the Theory of Operator Algebras, 1983; mathematical papers in various research jls. *Address:* 6 Polwarth Road, Brunton Park, Newcastle upon Tyne NE3 5ND. *T:* (0191) 236 3035.

See also A. M. Ringrose.

RINGROSE, Peter Stuart, PhD; Chairman, Biotechnology and Biological Sciences Research Council, 2003–April 2009; *b* 9 Oct. 1945; *s* of Arthur Ringrose and Roma Margaret Ringrose (*née* Roberts); *m* 1966, Nancy Elaine Palmer; two *s* one *d*. *Educ:* Alderman Newton's Grammar Sch., Leicester; Corpus Christi Coll., Cambridge (BA 1967; PhD 1971). Hd Biochemistry, Hoffmann La Roche, UK, 1970–79; Div. Dir, Sandoz Forschungs-Institut, Vienna, 1979–82; Sen. Vice Pres., Global Drug Discovery, Pfizer Inc., UK, 1982–96; CSO, Bristol-Myers Squibb Co., NY, and Pres., Pharmaceutical Res. Inst., Princeton, 1997–2002. Chm. Pharmaceutical R&D Heads, Hever Gp, 1999–2002; non-exec. Director: Cambridge Antibody Technology, 2003–06 (Chm., Scientific Adv. Bd, 2003–06); Astex Therapeutics, 2005–; Rigel Pharmaceuticals, 2005–; Biotica Technol., 2007–; Technol. Strategy Bd, 2007–; Member Scientific Advisory Board: Accenture Life Sciences, 2003–; Merlin Biosciences, 2003–05; Cempra Pharmaceuticals, 2006–; Schering-Plough Inc., 2007–. Council Mem., Foundn for Sci. and Technol., UK, 2003–. Member: Policy Adv. Bd, Centre for Medicines Res. Internat., 1994–2001; Sci. and Regulatory Exec., Pharmaceutical Res. and Manufacturers of America, 1997–2002; US Council on Competitiveness, 1998–2002. Member: Chancellor's Ct of Benefactors, Oxford Univ., 1998–2003; Chemistry Adv. Bd, Cambridge Univ., 2001–; Bd of Governors, NY Acad. of Sciences, 2001–05. William Pitt Fellow, Pembroke Coll., Cambridge, 1998–2006 (Life Hon. Fellow, 2006). *Recreations:* sketching and painting, scuba diving, renovating old houses, Italian cooking. *Address:* Biotechnology and Biological Sciences Research Council, Polaris House, North Star Avenue, Swindon SN2 1UH; *e-mail:* peter.ringrose@bbsrc.ac.uk. *Club:* Athenæum.

RINK, John Stuart; Managing Partner, Allen & Overy, 1994–2003; *b* 25 Oct. 1946; *s* of Paul Lothar Max Rink and Mary Ida McCall Rink (*née* Moore); *m* 1971, Elizabeth Mary Pitkethly; one *s* one *d*. *Educ:* Sedbergh Sch.; London Univ. (LLB ext.). Allen & Overy: Trainee Solicitor, 1970–72; Asst Solicitor, 1972–77; Partner, 1977–2003; Man. Partner, Litigation Dept, 1989–94; Legal Dir, British Aerospace, 1994–95 (on secondment). Director: Brixton plc, 2003–06; Eversheds, 2004–; RSM Robson Rhodes, 2004–06. *Recreations:* golf, Rugby, walking, opera. *Address:* 2 Camp View, Wimbledon, SW19 4UL. *T:* (020) 8947 4800. *Clubs:* MCC, City Law; Royal Wimbledon Golf, Royal West Norfolk Golf; Windermere Motor Boat Racing.

RINTOUL, Dr Gordon Charles; Director, National Museums Scotland, since 2002; *b* 29 May 1955; *s* of Henry Rintoul and Janet Rintoul (*née* Brown); *m* 1997, Stephanie Jane Budden; one *s*. *Educ:* Allen Glen's Sch., Glasgow; Univ. of Edinburgh (BSc Hons Physics); Univ. of Manchester (MSc Sci., Technol. and Society; PhD Hist. of Sci. and Technol. 1982). Dip. Museums Assoc. Res. Supervisor, Chem. Mus. Develt Project, 1982–84; Consultant and Tutor, Open Univ., Milton Keynes, 1984; Curator, Colour Mus., Bradford, 1984–87; Dir, Catalyst: Mus. of the Chem. Industry, 1987–98; Chief Exec., Sheffield Galls and Museums Trust, 1998–2002. Member: Registration Cttee, Resource: Council for Museums, Archives and Libraries, 1995–2002; Bd, Scottish Cultural Resources Access Network (SCRAN), 2002–06. Member Council: Assoc. of Indep. Museums, 1989–2002 (Treas., 1991–97); Museums Assoc., 1998–2004. Hon. Prof., Univ. of Edinburgh. *Recreations:* travel, reading, cooking. *Address:* National Museums Scotland, Chambers Street, Edinburgh EH1 1JF. *T:* (0131) 247 4260, *Fax:* (0131) 247 4308; *e-mail:* g.rintoul@nms.ac.uk.

RIORDAN, Linda; MP (Lab and Co-op) Halifax, since 2005; *b* 31 May 1953; *d* of John Foulds Haigh and Mary Alice Haigh (*née* Helliwell); *m* Alan Riordan. *Educ:* Univ. of Bradford (BSc Hons). Formerly in banking. Pvte Sec. to Alice Mahon, MP, 2001–05.

Mem. (Lab), Calderdale MBC, 1995–. *Address:* (office) 2–4 Shaw Lodge House, Halifax HX3 9ET; House of Commons, SW1A 0AA.

RIORDAN, Stephen Vaughan; QC 1992; a Recorder, since 1990; *b* 18 Feb. 1950; *s* of Charles Maurice Riordan and Betty Morfydd Riordan; *m* 1983, Jane Elizabeth Thomas; two *d*. *Educ:* Wimbledon Coll.; Univ. of Liverpool (LLB Hons). Called to the Bar, Inner Temple, 1972; Asst Recorder, 1986–90. *Recreation:* singing. *Address:* 25–27 Castle Street, Liverpool L2 4TA. *T:* (0151) 236 5072.

RIORDAN, Thomas Messenger; Chief Executive, Yorkshire Forward, since 2006; *b* 9 April 1968; *s* of late Michael Riordan and of Juliet Riordan; *m* Louise; one *s* one *d*. *Educ:* Trinity Coll., Oxford (BA Hons Mod. Hist. 1989); Imperial Coll., London (MBA 1st Cl. 1997). Joined Civil Service, 1990, fast stream incl. rep. UK on internat. envmtl policy negotiations (climate change and biodiversity), 1990–96; Operational Hd, RDA Proj. Team, Govt Office for Yorkshire and Humber, 1997–99; Yorkshire Forward: Hd, Strategy, 1999–2000; Exec. Dir, Strategy and Policy, 2000–05; Dep. Chief Exec., 2005–06. *Publications:* articles on regl develt for Smith Inst. and New Local Govt Network. *Recreations:* football, Middlesbrough Football Club, horse racing, competitive dominoes, music. *Address:* Yorkshire Forward, Victoria House, 2 Victoria Place, Leeds LS11 5AE. *T:* (0113) 394 9700, *Fax:* (0113) 394 9780; *e-mail:* tom.riordan@yorkshire-forward.com. *Club:* Northallerton Working Mens'.

RIPA di MEANA, Carlo; Member for Italy, European Parliament, 1979–84 and 1994–99; *b* 15 Aug. 1929; *m* 1982, Marina Punturieri. Editor, Il Lavoro (Ital. Gen. Conf. of Labour weekly newspaper), and Editor, foreign dept, Unita (Ital. Communist Party daily paper), 1950–53; rep. of Italy on UIE, Prague, 1953–56; founded jointly Nuova Generazione, 1956; left Ital. Communist Party, 1957; founded jointly Passato e Presente, 1957 (chief editor); joined Italian Socialist Party (PSI), 1958; worked in publishing, Feltrinelli, Rizzoli, until 1966; Councillor for Lombardy (PSI), 1970–74 (Chm., Constitutional Cttee); leader, PSI Group, regional council; head, international relations PSI, 1979–80; left PSI 1993; Leader, Green Party, Italy, 1993–95. Comr, EEC Exec. Cttee, 1985–92; Minister for Environment, Italy, 1992–93. Councillor for Umbria, 2000–05. Pres., Inst. for Internat. Economic Cooperation and Develt Problems, 1983. Nat. Pres., Italia Nostra, 2005–07, Pres., Italia Nostra Roma, 2007. Sec.-Gen., Club Turati, Milan, 1967–76; Mem. Board, Scala Theatre, Milan, 1970–74; Mem. Council, Venice Biennale 1974–82 (Pres., 1974–79); founder Mem., Crocodile Club; Pres., Fernando Santi Inst.; Pres., Unitary Fedn, Italian Press abroad; Vice-Chm., Internat. Cttee for Solidarity with Afghan People, 1980–85. *Publications:* Un viaggio in Viet-Nam (A Voyage to Vietnam), 1956; A tribute to Raymond Roussel and his Impressions of Africa, 1965; Il governo audiovisivo (Audiovisual Government), 1973; Adieu La Terre, 1993; Salvare Il Pianeta, 1995; Sorci Verdi, 1997; Cane Sciolto, 2000; L'Ordine di Mosca: fernate la biennale del dissenso, 2007. *Recreations:* horse riding, sailing. *Address:* Via Ovidio 26, Int.2–00193 Rome, Italy.

RIPLEY, Prof. Brian David, PhD; FRSE; Professor of Applied Statistics, and Fellow of St Peter's College, University of Oxford, since 1990; *b* 29 April 1952; *s* of Eric Lewis Ripley and Sylvia May (*née* Gould); *m* 1973, Ruth Mary Appleton. *Educ:* Farnborough Grammar Sch.; Churchill Coll., Cambridge (MA, PhD). FIMS 1987; FRSE 1990. Lectr in Statistics, Imperial Coll., London, 1976–80; Reader, Univ. of London, 1980–83; Prof. of Statistics, Univ. of Strathclyde, 1983–90. Mem., Internat. Statistical Inst., 1982. Adams Prize, Univ. of Cambridge, 1987. *Publications:* Spatial Statistics, 1981; Stochastic Simulation, 1987; Statistical Inference for Spatial Processes, 1988; Modern Applied Statistics with S-Plus, 1994, 3rd edn 1999; Pattern Recognition and Neural Networks, 1996; S Programming, 2000; numerous papers on statistics and applications in astronomy, biology, chemistry and earth sciences. *Recreation:* natural history. *Address:* Department of Statistics, University of Oxford, 1 South Parks Road, Oxford OX1 3TG. *T:* (01865) 272861.

RIPLEY, Sir William (Huw), 5th Bt *cr* 1880, of Rawdon, Yorkshire and Bedstone, Salop; *b* 13 April 1950; *s* of Major Sir Hugh Ripley, 4th Bt, American Silver Star, and Dorothy Mary Dunlop Ripley (*née* Bruce-Jones); *S* father, 2003. *Educ:* Eton; McGill Univ., Montreal (BA Pol. Sci. and Eng. Lit.). Poet; local journalist; bookseller; printer; smallholder; factory worker (nightshift). Patron, St Edward's Church, Hopton Castle. Mem., Leintwardine History Soc. Friend, Gwasg Gregynog. *Publication:* (jtly) Bedstone Court: the story of a calendar house, 2007. *Recreations:* rare books, writing, the Welsh borderland, Herefordshire cider, border people, the Clun Valley, gardening, a private life. *Heir:* none. *Address:* The Old Post Office and Forge, Bedstone, Bucknell, Salop SY7 0BE; The Carpenter's Cottage, Bedstone, Bucknell, Salop.

RIPON, Dean of; *see* Jukes, Very Rev. K. M.

RIPON AND LEEDS, Bishop of, since 2000; **Rt Rev. John Richard Packer;** *b* 10 Oct. 1946; *s* of John and Muriel Packer; *m* 1971, Barbara Jack; two *s* one *d*. *Educ:* Manchester Grammar Sch.; Keble Coll., Oxford (MA); Ripon Hall, Oxford; York Univ. (DSA). Ordained deacon, 1970, priest, 1971; Curate, St Peter, St Helier, 1970–73; Director of Pastoral Studies: Ripon Hall, 1973–75; Ripon Coll., Cuddesdon, 1975–77; Chaplain, St Nicolas, Abingdon, 1973–77; Vicar, Wath Upon Dearne with Adwick Upon Dearne, 1977–86; Rural Dean of Wath, 1983–86; Rector, Sheffield Manor, 1986–91; Rural Dean of Attercliffe, 1990–91; Archdeacon of W Cumberland, 1991–96; Priest i/c of Bridekirk, 1995–96; Bp Suffragan of Warrington, 1996–2000. Mem., Gen. Synod of C of E, 1985–91, 1992–96 and 2000–. *Recreations:* history, walking. *Address:* Hollin House, Weetwood Avenue, Leeds LS16 5NG.

RIPPENGAL, Derek, CB 1982; QC 1980; Counsel to Chairman of Committees, House of Lords, 1977–99; *b* 8 Sept. 1928; *s* of William Thomas Rippengal and Margaret Mary Rippengal (*née* Parry); *m* 1963, Elizabeth Melrose (*d* 1973); one *d* (one *s* decd). *Educ:* Hampton Grammar Sch.; St Catharine's Coll., Cambridge (Scholar; MA). Called to Bar, Middle Temple, 1953 (Harmsworth schol.). Entered Treasury Solicitor's Office, 1958, after Chancery Bar and univ. posts; Sen. Legal Asst, 1961; Asst Treasury Solicitor, 1967; Principal Asst Treasury Solicitor, 1971; Solicitor to DTI, 1972–73; Dep. Parly Counsel, 1973–74, Parly Counsel, 1974–76, Law Commn. *Publication:* (contrib.) Halsbury's Laws of England, vol. 34 (Parliament), 4th edn, 1997. *Recreations:* music, fishing. *Address:* 62 Gwydir Street, Cambridge CB1 2LL. *Club:* Athenæum.

RIPPON, Angela, OBE 2004; broadcaster; presenter, Live with Angela Rippon, ITV News Channel, since 2004; *b* 12 Oct. 1944; *d* of John and Edna Rippon; *m* 1967, Christopher Dare (marr. diss.). *Educ:* Plymouth Grammar Sch. Journalist, The Independent, Plymouth; presenter and reporter, BBC TV, Plymouth, 1966–69; editor, producer and presenter, Westward TV, 1967–73; reporter, nat. news, 1973–75, newsreader, 1975–81, BBC TV; co-founder, and presenter, TV-am, 1983; arts and entertainment correspondent, WNEV-TV, Boston, USA, 1984–85; presenter, LBC, 1990–94. *Television series include:* presenter: Angela Rippon Reporting, 1980–81; Antiques Roadshow, 1980–83; In the Country, 1980–83; Masterteam, 1985–87; Come Dancing, 1988–91; What's My Line, 1988–90; compère, Eurovision Song Contest, 1976; also presenter, radio progs. Vice-President: British Red Cross, 1999–; English Nat. Ballet, 2004– (Chm., 2000–04). TRIC Newsreader of the Year, 1975, 1976, 1977. Hon. DHum Amer. Coll. in London, 1994. European Woman of Achievement, Women's EU, 2002. *Publications:* Riding, 1980; In the Country, 1980; Victoria Plum (children's stories), 1981; Mark Phillips: the man and his horses, 1982; Angela Rippon's West Country, 1983; Badminton: a celebration, 1987; Fabulous at 50 and Forever, 2003. *Address:* c/o Knight Ayton Management, 114 St Martin's Lane, WC2N 4BE.

RISCHARD, Jean-François; Vice-President for Europe, World Bank, 1998–2005; *b* 2 Oct. 1948; *s* of Dr Charles-Edouard Rischard and Huguette (*née* Navereau); *m* 1979, Jacqueline Salvo; three *s*. *Educ:* Univ. of Aix-en-Provence (LèsScEcons 1971; DèsScEcon 1973); Univ. of Luxembourg (Dr Law 1971); Harvard Business Sch. (MBA 1975). World Bank: Project Officer, Industrial Projects, 1975–82; Chief, Financial Mgt Div., 1982–86; Sen. Vice Pres., Internat. Fixed Income Mkts, Drexel Burnham Lambert, NY, 1986–90; World Bank: Dir, Investment Dept, 1990–93; Vice Pres., Finance and Private Sector Develt, 1993–98. Founding Comr, Global Inf. Infrastructure Commn, 1995–. Pres., Professional Bankers' Assoc., Washington, 1993–98. Mem., Governing Bd, Inst. of Develt Studies, Sussex, 2000. Officier, Couronne de Chêne (Luxembourg), 1995. *Publications:* High Noon: 20 global problems, 20 years to solve them, 2002; contrib. numerous articles on internat. finance, global issues and global governance problems. *Recreations:* ski-ing, golf, history, music.

RISELEY-PRICHARD, Air Vice-Marshal Richard Augustin; Principal Medical Officer, Royal Air Force Support Command, 1980–85, retired; Member, Swindon District Health Authority, 1988–90 (Associate Member, 1990–93); *b* 19 Feb. 1925; *s* of late Dr J. A. Prichard and Elizabeth (*née* Riseley); *m* 1953, Alannah *d* of late Air Cdre C. W. Busk, CB, MC, AFC; four *d*. *Educ:* Beaudesert Park; Radley Coll.; Trinity Coll., Oxford (MA, BM, BCh); St Bartholomew's Hosp., London. FFCM. Commnd RAF Med. Br., 1951; pilot trng, 1951–52; served at RAF Coll., Cranwell, 1953–56; Dep. Principal Med. Officer (Flying), HQ Transport Comd and HQ RAF Germany, 1956–63; RAF Staff Coll., 1964; SMO, British Forces, Aden, 1967; Dep. Principal Med. Officer, HQ Strike Comd, 1970–73; Commanding Officer: RAF Hosp. Wegberg, Germany, 1973–76; Princess Alexandra Hosp., Wroughton, 1977–80. QHS 1980–85. Hon. Air Cdre, No 4626, RAuxAF Sqn, 1986–2002. Gen. Comr of Income Tax, 1987–. Dir (non-exec.) and Vice Chm., Wiltshire Ambulance Service NHS Trust, 1993–. Mem., Armed Forces Cttee, BMA, 1989–. Governor: Dauntsey's Sch., 1982– (Vice-Chm., 1985–86, Chm., 1986); BUPA Medical Foundn, 1990–96. CStJ. *Recreations:* tennis, squash, bridge, gardening. *Address:* The Little House, Allington, Devizes, Wilts SN10 3NN. *T:* (01380) 860662. *Clubs:* Royal Air Force; All England Lawn Tennis.

RISIUS, Maj. Gen. Gordon, CB 2000; **His Honour Judge Risius;** a Circuit Judge, since 2003; *b* 10 July 1945; *s* of late Rudolf Risius and Irene Risius (*née* Spier); *m* 1980, Lucinda Mary, *d* of Marshal of the Royal Air Force Sir Michael Beetham, *qv*; one *s* two *d*. *Educ:* University College Sch.; Coll. of Law. Admitted Solicitor, 1972; commnd as Capt., Army Legal Services, 1973; served HQ Land Forces Hong Kong, HQ BAOR, HQ NI, MoD, HQ 4th Armd Div., HQ Land Forces Cyprus; Col, Army Legal Services 2, MoD, 1992–94; Brig. Legal, HQ BAOR/UKSC (Germany), 1994–95; Brig. Legal, HQ Land Command, 1995–96; Brig. Prosecutions, 1997; Dir, Army Legal Services and Army Prosecuting Authy, 1997–2003. Asst Recorder, 1991–95; a Recorder, 1995–2003; a Vice-Pres., Immigration Appeal Tribunal, 2003–05; a Sen. Judge, Sovereign Base Areas Court, Cyprus, 2007–. Dep. Col Comdt, AGC, 2004–. Vice-Pres., 1997–2003, Hon. Pres., 2003–, Internat. Soc. for Military Law and the Law of War; Mem., Internat. Inst. of Humanitarian Law, 1994–2003. *Publications:* articles on the law of war. *Recreations:* music, reading, computers, travel. *Address:* Reading Crown Court, Old Shire Hall, The Forbury, Reading RG1 3EH.

RISK, Douglas James; QC (Scot.) 1992; Sheriff Principal of Grampian, Highland and Islands, 1993–2001; *b* 23 Jan. 1941; *s* of James Risk and Isobel Katherine Taylor Risk (*née* Dow); *m* 1967, Jennifer Hood Davidson; three *s* one *d*. *Educ:* Glasgow Academy; Gonville and Caius Coll., Cambridge (BA 1963, MA 1967); Glasgow Univ. (LLB 1965). Admitted to Faculty of Advocates, 1966; Standing Junior Counsel, Scottish Education Dept, 1975; Sheriff of Lothian and Borders at Edinburgh, 1977–79; Sheriff of Grampian, Highland and Islands at Aberdeen and Stonehaven, 1979–93. Hon. Prof., Faculty of Law, Univ. of Aberdeen, 1994–2007 (Hon. Lectr, 1981–94). Burgess of Guild, City of Aberdeen, 2008–. *Club:* Royal Northern and University (Aberdeen).

RISK, Sir Thomas (Neilson), Kt 1984; FRSE; Governor of the Bank of Scotland, 1981–91 (Director, 1971; Deputy Governor, 1977–81); *b* 13 Sept. 1922; *s* of late Ralph Risk, CBE, MC, and Margaret Nelson Robertson; *m* 1949, Suzanne Eiloart; three *s* (and one *s* decd). *Educ:* Kelvinside Academy; Glasgow Univ. (BL). Flight Lieut, RAF, 1941–46; RAFVR, 1946–53. Partner, Maclay Murray & Spens, Solicitors, 1950–81; Director: Standard Life Assurance Co., 1965–88 (Chm., 1969–77); British Linen Bank, 1968–91 (Governor, 1977–86); Howden Group, 1971–87; Merchants Trust, 1973–94; MSA (Britain) Ltd, 1958–98; Shell UK Ltd, 1982–92; Barclays Bank, 1983–85; Bank of Wales, 1986–91; Chm., Scottish Financial Enterprise, 1986–89. Member: Scottish Industrial Develt Bd, 1972–75; Scottish Econ. Council, 1983–91; NEDC, 1987–91. Chm., Edinburgh Internat. Festival Endowment Fund, 1987–96. Chm., Univ. of Glasgow Trust, 1992–2004. Hon. Pres., Citizens Th., Glasgow, 1995–2002. FRSE 1988. Hon. LLD Glasgow, 1985; Dr *hc* Edinburgh, 1990. *Address:* 29/31 Inverleith Place, Edinburgh EH3 5QD. *T:* (0131) 552 0571. *Clubs:* Royal Air Force; New (Edinburgh).

RIST, Prof. John Michael, FRSC; Professor of Classics and Philosophy, University of Toronto, 1983–96, Emeritus Professor, since 1997; *b* 6 July 1936; *s* of Robert Ward Rist and Phoebe May (*née* Mansfield); *m* 1960, Anna Thérèse (*née* Vogler); two *s* two *d*. *Educ:* Trinity Coll., Cambridge (BA 1959, MA 1963). FRSC 1976. Univ. of Toronto: firstly Lectr, finally Prof. of Classics, 1959–80; Chm., Grad. Dept of Classics, 1971–75; Regius Prof. of Classics, Aberdeen Univ., 1980–83. Vis. Prof., Augustinianum, Rome, 1998–. Hon. PhilDr Santa Croce, Rome, 2002. *Publications:* Eros and Psyche, Canada 1964; Plotinus: the road to reality, 1967; Stoic Philosophy, 1969; Epicurus: an introduction, 1972; (ed) The Stoics, USA 1978; On the Independence of Matthew and Mark, 1978; Human Value, 1982; Platonism and its Christian Heritage, 1985; The Mind of Aristotle, 1989; Augustine, 1994; Man, Soul and Body, 1996; On Inoculating Moral Philosophy Against God, 2000; Real Ethics, 2001; What is the Truth?, 2008; contrib. classical and phil jls. *Recreations:* travel, swimming, hill-walking. *Address:* 14 St Luke's Street, Cambridge CB4 3DA.

RITBLAT, Sir John (Henry), Kt 2006; FRICS; Chairman, The British Land Company PLC, 1970–2006 (Managing Director, 1970–2004; Hon. President, 2007); *b* 3 Oct. 1935; *m* 1st, 1960, Isabel Paja (*d* 1979); two *s* one *d*; 2nd, 1986, Jill Zilkha (*née* Slotover). *Educ:* Dulwich Coll.; London Univ. College of Estate Management. FRICS 2000. Articles with West End firm of Surveyors and Valuers, 1952–58. Founder Partner, Conrad Ritblat & Co., Consultant Surveyors and Valuers, 1958; Chairman: Conrad Ritblat Gp plc,

1993–97; Colliers Conrad Ritblat Erdman, 2000–. Comr, Crown Estate Paving Commn, 1969–. Hon. Surveyor, King George's Fund for Sailors, 1979–. Member: Council, Business in the Community, 1987–; Prince of Wales' Royal Parks Tree Appeal Cttee, 1987–; British Olympic Assoc., 1979; Olympic Appeal Cttee, 1984, 1988, 1996 and 2000. Chm., Trustees, Wallace Collection, 2005–; Trustee, Tate Gall., 2006–; Member: Patrons of British Art, Tate Gall.; English Heritage; Royal Horticultural Soc.; Architecture Club; SPAB; NACF; British Library Bd, 1995–2003; Council, Royal Instn, 2002 (Life Fellow, 2001); Life Member: Nat. Trust; Zool Soc. of London; Georgian Gp; RGS; Trollope Soc. Patron, Investment Property Forum, 1999–. Trustee, Zool Soc. of London Develt Trust, 1986–89. Trustee, Internat. Students' Trust; Mem., Council of Govs, Internat. Students' House (Vice-Chm., 2007). Patron, London Fedn of Boys' Clubs Centenary Appeal; Founder Sponsor, Young Explorers' Trust; Sponsor, RGS, 1982–85; (sole), British Nat. Ski Championships, 1978–; Pres., British Ski and Snowboard Fedn (formerly British Ski Fedn), 1994– (Vice-Pres., 1984–89). Member, Board of Governors: London Business Sch., 1990– (Hon. Fellow, 2000; Chm. Govs, 2006–); The Weizmann Inst., 1991–; Dir and Gov., RAM, 1998– (Dep. Chm., 1999–; Hon. Fellow, 2000); Gov., Dulwich Coll., 2003–. FRGS 1982; CCMI; Life FRSA; Hon. FRIBA 2006. Hon. DLitt London Metropolitan, 2005. *Recreations:* antiquarian books and libraries, bees, Real tennis, golf, ski-ing. *Address:* Lansdowne House, Berkeley Square, W1J 6ER. *Clubs:* Carlton, Royal Automobile, MCC, The Pilgrims, Queen's; Cresta (St Moritz).

RITCHESON, Prof. Charles Ray; University Professor of History and University Librarian Emeritus, University of Southern California, since 1991; *b* 26 Feb. 1925; *s* of Charles Frederick and Jewell Vaughn Ritcheson; *m* 1st, 1953, Shirley Spackman (marr. diss. 1964); two *s*; 2nd, 1965, Alice Luethi; four *s*. *Educ:* Univs of Harvard, Zürich, Oklahoma and Oxford. DPhil (Oxon). FRHistS. Prof. and Chm. of History, Kenyon Coll., 1953–65; Chm. and Dir, Graduate Studies, Southern Methodist Univ., 1966–70; Lovell Prof. of History, Univ. of Southern Calif., 1971–74; Cultural Attaché, US Embassy, 1974–77; University of Southern California: Lovell Distinguished Prof. of History, 1977–84; Univ. Prof., Univ. Librarian, Dean and Special Asst. to Pres., 1984–91; Dist. Emeritus Prof., 2000. Vis. Prof., Univs of Edinburgh and Cambridge, 1965–66. Chm., British Inst. of the US, 1979–81; Exec. Sec., American Conf. on British Studies, 1971–74. Vice-Pres., Board of Dirs, Amer. Friends of Covent Garden, 1978–84; Exec. Vice Pres., Fund for Arts and Culture in Central and Eastern Europe, 1992–96; Member: National Council for the Humanities, 1983–87 and 1988–91; US Bd of Foreign Scholarships, 1987–88; Adv. Council, Amer. Ditchley Foundn, 1977–2001; Adv. Council, Univ. of Buckingham (formerly UC Buckingham), 1977–90; Examination Jury, Ecole Nat. de l'Admin, 1998–2000; Bd of Dirs, Trust for Mus. Exhibitions, 2003–05; Sen. Advr, Libya Project, 2005–. Member: Assoc. pour le Rayonnement d'Opéra à Paris, 1993–; French Archaeol Soc., 1998–; French Heritage Soc., 2002–. Hon. DLitt Leicester, 1976. *Publications:* British Politics and the American Revolution, 1954; Aftermath of Revolution: British policy toward the United States 1783–1795, 1969 (paperback, 1971); The American Revolution: the Anglo-American relation, 1969; (with E. Wright) A Tug of Loyalties, 1971. *Recreations:* horseback riding, swimming, opera. *Address:* 85 Boulevard Haussmann, 75008 Paris, France. *T:* 47424484. *Clubs:* Beefsteak, Brooks's; Cosmos (Washington).

RITCHIE, family name of **Baron Ritchie of Dundee.**

RITCHIE OF DUNDEE, 6th Baron *cr* 1905; **Charles Rupert Rendall Ritchie;** *b* 15 March 1958; *s* of 5th Baron Ritchie of Dundee and of Anne (*née* Johnstone); *S* father, 2008; *m* 1st, 1984, Tara Van Tuyl Koch (marr. diss. 1992); 2nd, 2003, Celina Lucie Traill (marr. diss.); one *s* one *d* (twins); one *s, b* 1994. *Educ:* Brickwall Sch., Northiam. *Heir: s* Hon. Sebastian Ritchie, *b* 31 July 2004. *Address:* Orchard Cottage, High Street, Hartfield, East Sussex TN7 4AA.

RITCHIE, Maj.-Gen. Andrew Stephenson, CBE 1999; Director, Goodenough College, since 2006; *b* 30 July 1953; *er s* of Rev. Canon David Caldwell Ritchie and Dilys (*née* Stephenson); *m* 1981, Camilla Trollope; one *s* two *d*. *Educ:* Harrow County Boys' Sch.; RMA Sandhurst; Durham Univ. (BA Hons). Commnd RA 1973; regtl service, UK, Belize, Rhodesia, Germany, 1974–84; sc 1985; SO 2 Dir of Mil. Ops, MoD, 1986–87; 3 RHA, Germany, Cyprus, UK, 1988–90; SO 1 Dir of Army Plans, MoD, 1990–92; CO 1 RHA, UK, 1992–95; COS 3 (UK) Div./Multinational Div. SW, Bosnia, 1995–96; hcsc, 1997; Comdr RA 3 (UK) Div., 1997–98; Dir Personal Services (Army), 1998–2000; rcds, 2001; Dir Corporate Communications (Army), MoD, 2001–02; GOC 4th Div., 2002–03; Comdt, RMA Sandhurst, 2003–06. Pres., RA Hunt, 2006–. Hon. Col 100 (Yeo.) Regt RA (V), 2000–. Mem. Council, Marlborough Coll., 2006–; Gov., Princess Helena Coll., 2006–. *Recreations:* hunting, opera, tennis, golf. *Address:* Goodenough College, Mecklenburgh Square, WC1N 2AB. *Club:* Boodle's.

RITCHIE, Anna, OBE 1997; PhD; FSA; consultant archaeologist; *b* 28 Sept. 1943; *d* of George and Margaret Bachelier; *m* 1968, Graham Ritchie; one *s* one *d*. *Educ:* UC, Cardiff (BA Hons); Univ. of Edinburgh (PhD 1970; Hon. Fellow, 2000). FSA 1977. Member, Ancient Monuments Bd for Scotland, 1990–99. Trustee: Nat. Museums of Scotland, 1993–2003; BM, 1999–2004. Vice-Pres., Soc. of Antiquaries of London, 1988–92; Pres., Soc. of Antiquaries of Scotland, 1990–93. Hon. FSAScot. *Publications:* Orkney and Shetland, 1985; Picts, 1989; Viking Scotland, 1993; Prehistoric Orkney, 1995; Orkney, 1996; Shetland, 1997; Iona, 1997; with G. Ritchie: Scotland: archaeology and early history, 1981; Scotland: an Oxford archaeological guide, 1998. *Address:* 11 Powderhall Rigg, Edinburgh EH7 4GG. *T:* (0131) 556 1128; *e-mail:* ritchie@anagram.abel.co.uk.

RITCHIE, Prof. David Alastair, DPhil; FInstP; Professor of Experimental Physics, University of Cambridge, since 2002; Fellow, Robinson College, Cambridge, since 1991; *b* Watford, 11 March 1959; *s* of Charles and Elizabeth Ritchie; *m* 1989, Linda Elizabeth Miller; two *d*. *Educ:* Watford Grammar Sch. for Boys; Hertford Coll., Oxford (BA Physics 1980); Univ. of Sussex (DPhil Physics 1986). FInstP 2005. Res. Asst, Univ. of Sussex, 1984–85; University of Cambridge: Res. Associate, 1985–91; Asst Dir of Res., 1991–99; Reader of Exptl Physics, 1999–2002. Gov., Watford GS for Boys, 2005–. Tabor Medal and Prize, Inst. of Physics, 2008. *Publications:* contrib. jl papers on physics and technol. of III–V semiconductors. *Recreations:* running, cycling, exploring the Gower peninsula. *Address:* Cavendish Laboratory, J. J. Thomson Avenue, Cambridge CB3 0HE. *T:* (01223) 337331, *Fax:* (01223) 337271; *e-mail:* dar11@cam.ac.uk.

RITCHIE, David Robert, CB 2001; Hon. Senior Research Fellow, University of Birmingham, since 2001; *b* 10 March 1948; *s* of late James Ritchie and of Edith Ritchie (*née* Watts); *m* 1989, Joan Gibbons. *Educ:* Manchester Grammar School; St John's College, Cambridge (BA, MA). Min. of Transport, 1970; DoE, 1970; Regl Dir, W Midlands Regl Office, Depts of the Envmt and Transport, 1989–94; Regl Dir, Govt Office for W Midlands, 1994–2001. Mem., Adjudication Panel for England, 2002–; Chm., Nat. Urban Forestry Unit, 2003–06. Mem., Bishop's Council, Dio. Birmingham, 1992–2004. Dir, Univ. Hosp. Birmingham NHS Foundn Trust, 2006–. Pres. Govs, The Queen's Foundn, 2007– (Vice-Pres., 2002–07). *Recreations:* fell-walking, cooking. *Address:* 14 Ashfield Road, Birmingham B14 7AS.

RITCHIE, Prof. Donald Andrew, CBE 2005; DL; FRSE; Professor of Genetics, University of Liverpool, 1978–2003, now Emeritus; Deputy Chairman, Environment Agency, 2000–05; *b* 9 July 1938; *s* of Andrew Ritchie and Winifred Laura (*née* Parkinson); *m* 1962, Margaret Jeanne (*née* Collister); one *s* one *d*. *Educ:* Latymer's Sch., London; Univ. of Leicester (BSc 1959); RPMS, London (PhD 1964). FIBiol 1978, CBiol 1985; FRSE 1979. MRC Microbial Genetics Res. Unit, London, 1959–64; Res. Associate, Biophysics Dept, Johns Hopkins Univ., 1964–66; Lectr, 1966–72, Sen. Lectr, 1972–78, Virology Dept, Univ. of Glasgow; Pro-Vice-Chancellor, Liverpool Univ., 1992–95. Royal Soc. Leverhulme Trust Sen. Res. Fellow, 1991–92; Royal Acad. of Engrg Vis. Prof., Univ. of Liverpool, 2004–06. Member: Science Bd, SERC, 1989–92; Biotechnol. Jt Adv. Bd, DTI, 1990–95; NERC, 1990–95; Bd, Envmt Agency, 1998–2005 (Dep. Chm., 2001–05). Mem. Council, Marine Biol Assoc., 1991–94; Professional Affairs Officer, Soc. for Gen. Microbiol., 1998–2001; Mem., Environment Cttee, 1996–99 and Finance Cttee, 1996–2002, Inst. of Biol. Chairman: Mil. Educn Cttee, Liverpool Univ., 1995–2006; Council of Mil. Educn Cttees of UK Univs, 2004–; King's Regt Mus. Trust, 2006–. Member: Council, Liverpool Sch. of Tropical Medicine, 1993–99; RFCA (formerly TAVRA), NW England & IOM, 1995–. Chairman: Merseyside Reg., NACF, 1996–2000; Liverpool Scottish Mus. Trust, 1999–. Governor: IOM Internat. Business Sch., 2000–; Shrewsbury Sch., 2003– (Dep. Chm., 2007–). Hon. Col Liverpool Univ. OTC, 2001–07. DL Merseyside, 2002. *Publications:* (with T. H. Pennington) Molecular Virology, 1971; (with K. M. Smith) Introduction to Virology, 1980; pubns on microbial molecular genetics and environmental microbiology in learned jls. *Recreations:* painting, gardening, walking, photography. *Address:* Glenfinnan, 19 Bertram Drive, Meols, Wirral CH47 0LG. *T:* (0151) 632 1985; *e-mail:* d.a.ritchie@liverpool.ac.uk. *Clubs:* Army and Navy; Athenæum (Liverpool).

RITCHIE, Sister Frances Dorothy Lyon, (Sister Frances Dominica), OBE 2006; FRCN; DL; Sister of All Saints Community, since 1966; Founder: Helen House Children's Hospice, 1982; Douglas House, Respice for Young People, 2003; *b* 21 Dec. 1942; *d* of Thomas Norman Ritchie and Margaret Armstrong Ritchie (*née* Paterson). *Educ:* Cheltenham Ladies' Coll.; Hosp. for Sick Children, Gt Ormond St (RSCN); Middlesex Hosp. (RGN). FRCN 1983. Entered Soc. of All Saints, Sisters of the Poor, 1966; professed, 1969; Mother Superior, 1977–89. Trustee, Helen & Douglas House, 2002–. Hon. FRCPCH 1998. MUniv Open, 2003; Hon. Dr: Oxford Brookes, 2003; London Metropolitan, 2004. DL Oxon, 2001. *Publication:* Just My Reflection: helping families to do things their way when their child dies, 1997, 2nd edn 2007. *Recreations:* dog walking at dawn, being alone in a country cottage with no television, telephone or alarm clock for a week at a time, friends. *Address:* All Saints Convent, St Mary's Road, Oxford OX4 1RU. *T:* (01865) 793841.

RITCHIE, Rear-Adm. George Stephen, CB 1967; DSC 1942; writer; retired hydrographer; *b* 30 Oct. 1914; *s* of Sir (John) Douglas Ritchie, MC and late Margaret Stephen, OBE 1946, JP, Officer of the Order of Orange-Nassau, *d* of James Allan, Methlick, Aberdeenshire; *m* 1942, Mrs Disa Elizabeth Smith (*née* Beveridge) (*d* 2000); three *s* one *d*. *Educ:* RNC, Dartmouth. Joined RN Surveying Service, 1936; attached Eighth Army, 1942–43; served in HM Survey Ship Scott for invasion of Europe, 1944; comd HMS Challenger on scientific voyage round world, 1950–51; comd HM New Zealand Survey Ship Lachlan and NZ Surveying Service, 1953–56; comd HM Surveying Ship Dalrymple, Persian Gulf, 1959; comd HM Surveying Ship Vidal, West Indies and Western Europe, 1963–65; ADC to the Queen, 1965; Hydrographer of the Navy, 1966–71; Vis. Research Fellow, Southampton Univ., 1971–72; Pres., Directing Cttee, Internat. Hydrographic Bureau, Monaco, 1972–82; Founder Pres., 1972–73, Emeritus Mem., 1988–, Hydrographic Soc. Hon. Member: Canadian Hydrographic Assoc., 1981; Hydrographic Soc. of SA, 1985; Challenger Soc., 1992 (Hon. Life Mem., 1993). Chm., Collieston Harbour Trustees, 1991–96. Columnist, Hydro Internat. jl, 1997–2007. Founder's Medal, RGS, 1972; Prix Manley-Bendall, Académie de Marine, Paris, 1977; Gold Medal, Royal Inst. of Navigation, 1978; Dalrymple Trophy, Internat. Hydrographic Orgn, 2006. *Publications:* Challenger, 1957; The Admiralty Chart, 1967, new edn 1995; No Day Too Long, 1992; As It Was - Highlights of Hydrographic History, 2003; papers on navigation and oceanography in various jls, including Developments in British Hydrography since days of Captain Cook (RSA Silver Medal, 1970). *Recreations:* conserving Collieston, boules, sea-fishing. *Address:* Sea View, Collieston, Ellon, Aberdeenshire AB41 8RS. *Clubs:* Reform; Royal Northern and University (Aberdeen) (Hon. Mem.); Collieston Boules; Monte Carlo (Emeritus Mem.).

RITCHIE, Hamish Martin Johnston; Chairman, Marsh & McLennan Companies UK Ltd, 2000–05; *b* 22 Feb. 1942; *s* of late James Martin Ritchie and Noreen Mary Louise Ritchie; *m* 1967, Judith Carol Young; one *s* one *d*. *Educ:* Loretto Sch.; Christ Church, Oxford (MA). Man. Dir, Hogg Robinson UK Ltd, 1980–81 (Dir, 1974–80); Chairman: Bowring London Ltd, 1981–93; Marsh Mercer Holdings Ltd (formerly Bowring Gp), 1983–; and Chief Exec., Bowring Marsh & McLennan Ltd, 1985–96; Marsh Europe SA, 1992–2001; Dir, Marsh Ltd, 1997–2005. Director: RAC, 1990–99; Halma plc, 1997–2002. Chm., BIBA, 2002–04 (Dep. Chm., 1987–91); Pres., Insurance Inst. of London, 1995–96. CCMI (CIMgt 1985). Trustee: Princess Royal Trust for Carers, 2000–05; Tower Hill Improvement Trust, 2005–; Chm., Oldhurst Trust, 2003–. Member: Barbican Centre Cttee, 2005–06; Develt Council, Historic Royal Palaces, 2005–06. Gov., English Nat. Ballet, 2001–05. *Recreations:* music, golf. *Address:* Oldhurst, Bulstrode Way, Gerrards Cross, Bucks SL9 7QT. *T:* (01753) 883262. *Clubs:* MCC, Royal Automobile; Royal & Ancient Golf (St Andrews) (Capt. 2008–Sept. 2009), Denham Golf, Rye Golf.

RITCHIE, Ian Carl, CBE 2000; RA 1998; RIBA; Principal, Ian Ritchie Architects, since 1981; Consultant, Rice Francis Ritchie, since 1987; *b* 24 June 1947; *s* of Christopher Charles Ritchie and Mabel Berenice (*née* Long); *m* 1972, Jocelyne van den Bossche; one *s*. *Educ:* Varndean, Brighton; Liverpool Sch. of Architecture; Polytechnic of Central London Sch. of Architecture (Dip. Arch. distinction). With Foster Associates, 1972–76; in private practice in France, 1976–78; Partner, Chrysalis Architects, 1979–81; Co-founder and Dir, RFR (Rice Francis Ritchie), 1981–87. Major works include: Ecology Gall., Nat. Hist. Mus.; B8, Stockley Park, London; Roy Square housing, Limehouse, London; Eagle Rock House, E Sussex; Culture Centre, Albert, France; roofs, Louvre Sculpture Courts, Paris; roof and glass facades, Mus. Nat. de Science, Techniques et de l'Industrie, La Villette, Paris; pharmacy, Boves, France; Fluy House, Picardy, France; Terrasson Cultural Greenhouse, France; HV Pylons for EDF, France (Millennium Product award, Design Council, 1999); glass towers, Centro de Arte Reina Sofia, Madrid; Leipzig Glashalle; Bermondsey Underground Stn, and Crystal Palace Concert Platform (Millennium Product award, Design Council, 1999), London; Scotland's Home of the Future, Glasgow; White City, London; Spire Monument, Dublin; Internat. Rowing Centre, Royal Albert Dock, London; Light Monument, Milan; Plymouth Th. Royal Production Centre; RSC Courtyard Th. Mem., Royal Fine Art Commn, now CABE, 1995–2001, now Emeritus Comr. Architectural Adviser: Natural Hist. Mus., 1991–95; to the Lord Chancellor, 1999–2004; BM, 2004–06; Advr, Ove Arup Foundn, 2002–. External examiner, RIBA, 1986–. Vis. Prof., Vienna Technical Univ., 1994–95; Special Prof., Sch.

of Civil Engrg, Leeds Univ., 2001–04; Prof. of Architecture, RA, 2005–. Mem., Technology Foresight Construction Panel, 1996–98. Chairman: Europan UK, 1997–2003; Collections and Library Cttee, RA, 2000– (Mem. Council, 2000–). Council Mem., Steel Construction Inst., 1994–97; Architects' Council of Europe rep. on European Construction Technology Platform, 2005–07. FRSA. Gov., 2001–, Mem., Internat. Council, 2005–, RSC. Hon. DLitt Westminster, 2000. Tableau de l'Ordre des Architectes Français, 1982; Architectural Design Silver Medal, 1982; IRITECNA (Italian state construction industry) European Prize, 1992; Eric Lyons Meml Award, for European housing, 1992; Robert Matthew Award, Commonwealth Assoc. of Architects, 1994; AIA Awards, 1997, 2003; Civic Trust Awards, 1998, 2002; Arts Bldg of the Year Award, Royal Fine Art Commn, 1998; Stephen Lawrence Prize, 1998; RIBA Awards, 1998, 2000, 2003, 2004, 2007; Acad. d'Architecture VII Silver Medal, 2000; Sports Bldg of the Year Award, Royal Fine Art Commn, 2000; Internat. Outstanding Structure Award, IABSE, 2000; Bldg of the Year Award, Royal Fine Art Commn, 2003; Innovation in Copper Award, Copper Develt Assoc. (UK), 2000, 2003. *Publications:* (Well) Connected Architecture, 1994; The Biggest Glass Palace in the World, 1997; Ian Ritchie Technoecology, 1999; Plymouth Theatre Royal TR2, 2003; The Spire, 2004; The Leipzig Glass Hall, 2006; The RSC Courtyard Theatre, 2006. *Recreations:* art, swimming, reading, writing, film making. *Address:* (office) 110 Three Colt Street, E14 8AZ. *T:* (020) 7338 1100; *e-mail:* iritchie@ianritchiearchitects.co.uk.

RITCHIE, Ian Charles Stewart; Director, City of London Festival, since 2005; *b* 19 June 1953; *s* of Kenneth John Stewart Ritchie and Wanda Margaret Angela Ritchie; *m* 1st, 1977, Angela Mary (marr. diss. 1993); two *d*; 2nd, 1997, Kathryn Alexandra McDowell, *qv. Educ:* Stowe Sch.; Royal Coll. of Music; Trinity Coll., Cambridge (MA); Guildhall Sch. of Music and Drama. General Manager, City of London Sinfonia, 1979–84; Artistic Dir, City of London Fest., 1983–84; Man. Dir, Scottish Chamber Orchestra, 1984–93; Gen. Dir, Opera North, 1993–94; arts mgt consultant, 1994–2005. Artistic Co-Dir, 1988–93, Dir, 2004–05, St Magnus Fest., Orkney; Dir, Highland Fest., 1994–96. Hon. Dir, Accord Internat., 2001–. *Recreations:* wine, walking, song. *Address:* 91 Lauderdale Tower, EC2Y 8BY. *T:* (020) 7638 4778; *e-mail:* ian@accordinternational.org. *Club:* MCC.

RITCHIE, Ian Cleland, CBE 2003; FRSE; CEng, FREng, FBCS; Chairman: Interactive University Ltd, since 2003; Computer Application Services Ltd, since 2005; Scapa Ltd, since 2006; *b* 29 June 1950; *s* of late Alexander Ritchie and Jean Russell Ritchie (*née* Fowler); *m* 1974, Barbara Allan Cowie (*d* 2001); one *s* one *d. Educ:* Heriot-Watt Univ. (BSc Hons Computer Sci. 1973). CEng 1991; FBCS 1992. Develt Engr/Manager, ICL, 1974–83; CEO and Man. Dir, Office Workstations Ltd (OWL), Edinburgh and Seattle, 1984–92 (OWL pioneered develt of hypertext (web-browsing) technol.; sold to Panasonic, 1989); special project, Heriot-Watt Univ., 1992–94. Chairman: Voxar Ltd, 1994–2002 (non-exec. Dir, 1994–2004); Orbital Software Gp Ltd, 1995–2001; Active Navigation (formerly Multicosm) Ltd, 1997–2004; Digital Bridges Ltd, 2000–03 (Dir, 2003–); Sonaptic Ltd, 2003–06; Dep. Chm., Vis Interactive, 1995–2004. Director: Northern Venture Trust PLC, 1996–2001; Scran, 1996–2004; Indigo Active Vision Systems Ltd, 1997–2000; Epic Gp PLC, 1998–2004; Scottish Enterprise, 1999–2005; Channel 4 TV, 2000–06; Bletchley Park Trust, 2000–; Scottish Science Trust, 2001–03; Mindwarp Pavilion Ltd, 2001–02; Dynamic Earth, 2004–. Chairman: Generation Science, 2005–; Connect Scotland, 2006–. Dir, Nat. Museums Scotland (formerly Nat. Museums of Scotland), 2003–. Member: PPARC, 1999–2002; SHEFC, 2002–05; SFC, 2005–. Dir, Scottish Inst. for Enterprise, 2001–06. Pres., BCS, 1998–99. Hon. Prof., Heriot-Watt Univ., 1993–. FREng 2001; FRSE 2002. DUniv Heriot-Watt, 2000; Hon. DSc Robert Gordon, 2001; Hon. DBA Abertay Dundee, 2002; Dr *hc* Edinburgh, 2003. *Publications:* New Media Publishing: opportunities from the digital revolution, 1996; contrib. various technol. papers and articles. *Recreations:* travel, theatre and arts, web-browsing. *Address:* Coppertop, Green Lane, Lasswade EH18 1HE. *T:* (0131) 663 9486. *Club:* Royal Over-Seas League.

RITCHIE, Ian Russell; Chief Executive, All England Lawn Tennis and Croquet Club, since 2005; *b* 27 Nov. 1953; *s* of Hugh Russell Ritchie and Sheelah Ritchie; *m* 1982, Jill Evelyn Middleton-Walker; two *s. Educ:* Leeds Grammar Sch.; Trinity Coll., Oxford (MA Jurisprudence). Called to the Bar, Middle Temple, 1976. Practised at the Bar, 1976–78; Industrial Relations Advr, EEF, 1978–80; Granada TV, 1980–88 (Head of Prodn Services, 1987–88); Dir of Resources, 1988–91, Man. Dir, 1991–93, Tyne Tees TV; Gp Dep. Chief Exec., Yorkshire Tyne Tees TV, 1992–93; Managing Director: Nottingham Studios, Central Television, 1993–94; London News Network, 1994–96; Chief Exec., 1996, Chief Operating Officer, 1996–97, Channel 5 Broadcasting; Partner and Man. Dir, Russell Reynolds Associates, 1997–98; CEO, Middle East Broadcasting, 1998–2000; CEO, Associated Press Television News, 2000–03; Vice-Pres., Global Business, and Man. Dir, Associated Press Internat., 2003–05. Dir, West Ham United plc, 1999–2002; Ind. Dir, Football League Ltd, 2004–. FRSA. *Recreations:* golf, tennis, theatre, music. *Address:* Virginia Water, Surrey. *Club:* Vincent's (Oxford).

RITCHIE, Jean Harris, (Mrs G. T. K. Boney); QC 1992; a Recorder, since 1993; *b* 6 April 1947; *d* of late Walter Weir Ritchie and of Lily (*née* Goodwin); *m* 1976, Guy Thomas Knowles Boney, *qv*; two *s. Educ:* King's Coll., London (LLB); McGill Univ., Montreal (LLM). Called to the Bar, Gray's Inn, 1970 (Churchill Sch., 1968; Bencher, 2000); on Western Circuit; Head of Chambers, 2000–04. Chairman: Clunis Inquiry (care in the community for patients suffering from schizophrenia), 1993–94; Inquiry into Clinical Governance (arising from actions of Rodney Ledward), 1999–2000. Member: Supreme Ct Rule Cttee, 1993–97; Judicial Studies Bd, 1998–2001 (Mem., Civil Cttee, 1997–2001); QC Selection Panel, 2006–. Member: Med. Ethics Cttee, King Edward VII Hosp., 2003–; City Panel, Treloar Trust, 2005–08. Chm. Govs, Norman Court Prep. Sch., W Tytherley, 1996–2000. *Publication:* (contrib.) Safe Practice in Obstetrics and Gynaecology, ed R. V. Clements, 1994. *Recreation:* family. *Address:* King's Head House, Stockbridge, Hants SO20 6EU.

RITCHIE, Dr John Hindle, MBE 1985; architect; development management consultant; *b* 4 June 1937; *s* of Charles A. Ritchie; *m* 1963, Anne B. M. Leyland; two *d. Educ:* Royal Grammar School, Newcastle upon Tyne; Univ. of Liverpool (BArch Hons); Univ. of Sheffield (PhD Building Science). Served RN, 1956–58. Science Research Council, 1963–66; Town Planner, Liverpool City Council, 1966–69; Rowntree Housing Trust, Univ. of Liverpool, 1969–72; R&D Architect, Cheshire County Council, 1972–74; Asst County Planner (Envmt), Merseyside CC, 1974–80; Merseyside Development Corporation: Dir of Develt, 1980–85; Chief Exec. and Mem., 1985–91. Chm., Merseyside Educn Training Enterprise Ltd, 1986–91; Member: Merseyside Tourism Bd, 1986–88; Internat. Organising Cttee, Grand Regatta Columbus '92, 1986–92; Board: Gardners Row Business Centre, 1987–90; Merseyside Enterprise Trust, 1988–91; Instant Muscle Ltd, 1993–95; Merseyside Sculptors Guild, 1993–97; Wirral Community Healthcare Trust, 1993–95; Landscape Trust, 1996–2001. Mem., Lord Chancellor's Panel of Ind. Inspectors, 1994–2003; consultant inspector, Planning Inspectorate, 2003–05. Gov., Liverpool Community Coll., 1995–. Major projects include: natural resource management, pollution control, land reclamation and urban conservation progs and projects, Merseyside Strategic Plan; Liverpool South Docks and Riverside reclamation and develt, Liverpool Internat. Garden Fest., 1984 (Civic Trust Award; Landscape Inst. 75th Anniv. Award, 2004); Albert Dock Conservation (European Gold Medal, 1986; Civic Trust Jubilee Award, 1987). CCMI. *Publications:* scientific and planning papers on urban environment obsolescence and regeneration. *Address:* Cartref, 46 The Mount, Heswall, Wirral CH60 4RD; *e-mail:* jhritchie@btinternet.com.

RITCHIE, Kathryn Alexandra; *see* McDowell, K. A.

RITCHIE, Dr Kenneth George Hutchison; Chief Executive, Electoral Reform Society, since 1997; *b* 8 Dec. 1946; *s* of William Ritchie and late Margaret Morton Ritchie (*née* Hutchison); *m* 1985, Elizabeth Anne Black; one *s* one *d. Educ:* George Heriot's Sch., Edinburgh; Edinburgh Univ. (BSc); Aston Univ. (PhD 1981). Maths teacher, VSO, Tanzania, 1968–69; systems analyst, ICI, 1970–73; Hd, Internat. Service, UNA, 1976–83; Exec. Dir, Appropriate Health Resources and Technologies Action Gp, 1983–88; Dep. Dir, British Refugee Council, 1988–94; UK Dir, Intermediate Technol., 1994–96. Hon. Treas., War on Want, 1980–85; Treas., Western Sahara Campaign, 1984–. Mem., Council for Advancement of Arab-British Understanding, 1989–94. Dir, Make Votes Count, 1998–; Bd Mem., FairVote/Center for Voting and Democracy, Washington, 2004–. Contested (Lab): Beckenham, 1987 and 1992; Daventry, 1997. FRSA. *Recreations:* golf, music, walking the dog. *Address:* 37 Ware Road, Barby, Rugby CV23 8UE. *T:* (01788) 890942.

RITCHIE, Margaret; Member (SDLP) South Down, Northern Ireland Assembly, since 2003; Minister for Social Development, since 2007; *b* 25 March 1958; *d* of late John Ritchie and Rose Ritchie (*née* Drumm). *Educ:* Queen's Univ., Belfast (BA). Mem. (SDLP) Down DC, 1985–. Mem., NI Forum, 1996. Parly Asst to Edward McGrady, MP, 1987–2003. *Address:* (office) 5 Irish Street, Downpatrick, Co. Down BT30 6BN; Northern Ireland Assembly, Parliament Buildings, Belfast BT4 3XX.

RITCHIE, Margaret Claire; Headmistress of Queen Mary School, Lytham, 1981–98; *b* 18 Sept. 1937; *d* of Roderick M. Ritchie, Edinburgh. *Educ:* Leeds Girls' High Sch.; Univ. of Leeds (BSc); London Univ. (PGCE). Asst Mistress, St Leonards Sch., St Andrews, 1960–64; Head of Science Dept, Wycombe Abbey Sch., High Wycombe, 1964–71; Headmistress, Queenswood Sch., 1972–81. JP Fylde, 1991–99, Preston PSD, 1999–2007. *Address:* 29 Walmer Road, Lytham St Annes, Lancs FY8 3HL.

RITCHIE, Peter, FCCA; Head of Finance, Fife Council, 1995–2001; *b* 16 March 1951. *Educ:* Kirkland High Sch.; Buckhaven High Sch. FCCA 1975. Fife CC, 1969–75; Fife Regional Council, 1975–: Chief Accountant, 1980–84; Sen. Asst Dir of Finance, 1984–88; Dep. Dir of Finance, 1988–95. *Recreations:* hill-walking, gardening, theatre, cinema, photography.

RITCHIE, Robert Blackwood, (Robin); grazier running family sheep and cattle property, Western Victoria, 1958–2001; *b* 6 April 1937; *s* of Alan Blackwood Ritchie and Margaret Louise (*née* Whitcomb); *m* 1965, Eda Natalie Sandford Beggs; two *s* one *d. Educ:* Geelong Grammar Sch.; Corpus Christi Coll., Cambridge (MA; Rowing Blue, 1958). Dir, Agricl Investments Australia, 1968–89 (Chm., 1968–85). Exec. Mem., Graziers Assoc. of Vic, 1968–72; Mem., National Rural Adv. Council, 1974–75; Chairman: Exotic Animal Disease Preparedness Consultative Council, 1990–95; Renewable Energy Authority, Vic, 1993–98. Dir-Gen., Min. for Economic Develt, Vic, 1981–83. Geelong Grammar School: Mem. Council, 1966–78 (Chm., 1973–78); Chief Exec., 1979–80 (during period between Head Masters). *Recreation:* sailing. *Address:* 42 Griffith Street, Port Fairy, Vic 3284, Australia. *T:* (55) 681447. *Club:* Melbourne (Melbourne).

RITCHIE, Shirley Anne; *see* Anwyl, S. A.

RITCHIE, Susan Rosemary; *see* Foister, S. R.

RITCHIE, Prof. William, OBE 1994; PhD; FRSGS; FRICS; FRSE; Director, Aberdeen Institute of Coastal Science and Management, King's College, University of Aberdeen, since 2002; *b* 22 March 1940; *s* of Alexander Ritchie and Rebecca Smith Ritchie; *m* 1965, Elizabeth A. Bell; two *s* one *d. Educ:* Glasgow Univ. (BSc, PhD 1966). FRSGS 1980; FRSE 1982; FRICS 1989. Research Asst, Glasgow Univ., 1963; Aberdeen University: Lectr, 1964–72; Sen. Lectr, 1972–79; Prof., 1979–95; Dean, 1988–89; Vice Principal, 1989–95; Vice-Chancellor, Lancaster Univ., 1995–2002; Interim Dir, Macaulay Inst., Aberdeen, 2006. Post-doctoral Vis. Prof. and Hon. Prof. appts in geog. and coastal geog., Louisiana State Univ., USA, at various times, 1971–95; Adjunct Prof., World Maritime Univ., Malmo, 2003–. DUniv Stirling, 2003; Hon. DSc Lancaster, 2003. *Publications:* Mapping for Field Scientists, 1977; Surveying and Mapping for Field Scientists, 1988, 4th edn 1996; The Environmental Impact of the Wreck of the Braer, 1994; numerous papers mainly in jls of physical and coastal geog. and envmtl mgt. *Address:* Aberdeen Institute of Coastal Science and Management, School of Geosciences, King's College, University of Aberdeen, Aberdeen AB24 3UE.

RITTER, Prof. Mary Alice, DPhil; FRCPath; Professor of Immunology, since 1991, and Pro-Rector for Postgraduate Affairs, since 2004 and for International Affairs, since 2005, Imperial College London; *b* 19 Dec. 1943; *d* of Douglas and Iris Buchanan Smith; *m* 1st, 1967, James Ritter (marr. diss. 1973); 2nd, 1976, Roger Morris; three *s. Educ:* Berkhamsted Sch. for Girls; St Hilda's Coll., Oxford (BA Hons Zool. 1966; Dip. Physical Anthropol. 1967; MA 1971); Wolfson Coll., Oxford (DPhil 1971). FRCPath 2006. Res. Associate, Univ. of Conn, 1976–78; Res. Fellow, ICRF, 1978–84; Royal Postgraduate Medical School, London, later Imperial College, London: Lectr in Immunol., 1982–86; Sen. Lectr, 1986–88; Reader, 1988–91; Vice Dean (Educn), 1992–97; Asst Vice Principal (Postgrad. Medicine), 1998–2000; Dir, Grad. Sch. of Life Scis and Medicine, 1999–2006; Hd, Dept of Immunol., 2004–06. Mem. Council, and Chm. Scientific Adv. Panel, Action Res., 1997–2000. FRSA 2004; FCGI 2006. *Publications:* (with I. N. Crispe) The Thymus, 1992 (trans. Japanese 1993); contrib. numerous articles to peer-reviewed scientific learned jls. *Recreations:* travelling, gardening, cycling, biography, baroque music, ballet, opera. *Address:* Imperial College London, Level 4, Faculty Building, South Kensington Campus, Exhibition Road, SW7 2AZ. *T:* (020) 7594 1412, *Fax:* (020) 7594 8802; *e-mail:* m.ritter@imperial.ac.uk.

RITTERMAN, Dame Janet (Elizabeth), DBE 2002; PhD; Vice-President, Royal College of Music, since 2005 (Director, 1993–2005); *b* 1 Dec. 1941; *d* of Charles Eric Palmer and Laurie Helen Palmer; *m* 1970, Gerrard Peter Ritterman. *Educ:* North Sydney Girls' High Sch.; NSW State Conservatorium of Music; Univ. of Durham (BMus 1971); King's Coll. London (MMus 1977; PhD 1985). Pianist, accompanist, chamber music player; Senior Lecturer in Music: Middlesex Poly., 1975–79; Goldsmiths' Coll., Univ. of London, 1980–87; Dartington College of Arts: Head of Music, 1987–90; Dean, Academic Affairs, 1988–90; Acting Principal, 1990–91; Principal, 1991–93; Hon. Vis. Prof. of Music Educn, Univ. of Plymouth, 1993–2005. Chm., Assoc. Bd of Royal Schs of Music (Publishing) Ltd, 1993–2005. Former Mem., music educn and arts orgns; Member: Arts

Council, 2000–02 (Mem., Music Panel, 1992–98); DfES Adv. Cttee, Music and Dance Scheme, 2001–05; Chm., Postgrad. Cttee, AHRB, 2002–04 (Mem. Postgrad. Panel, 1999–2002); Mem., Nominating Cttee, AHRC, 2005–. Member: Council, Royal Musical Assoc., 1994–2004 (Vice-Pres., 1998–2004); Bd, ENO, 1996–2004; Bd, NYO, 1999–2008; Bd of Dirs, The Voices Foundn, 2005–; Adv. Council, Inst. of Germanic Romance Studies, 2005–, Inst. of Musical Res., 2006–, Univ. of London; Vice-Pres., Nat. Assoc. of Youth Orchestras, 1993–. Chairman: Adv. Council, Arts Res. Ltd, 1997–2005; Fedn of British Conservatoires, 1998–2003; Member: Wissenschaftsrat, Bundesministerium für Bildung, Wissenschaft und Kultur, Austria, 2003–; Bd of Dirs, Anglo-Austrian Soc., 2005–. Member: Governing Body: Heythrop Coll., 1996–2006; Dartington Coll. of Arts, 2005–08; Middlesex Univ., 2006–; UC Falmouth, 2008–; Council, Goldsmiths Coll., 2002–07; Governor: Assoc. Bd, Royal Schs of Music, 1993–2005; Purcell Sch., 1996–2000. Mem., Nuffield Foundn Educn Adv. Cttee, 2007–. Trustee: Countess of Munster Musical Trust, 1993–; Plymouth Chamber Music Trust, 2006–. Mem. Ct, Musicians' Co., 2005–. FRNCM 1996; Fellow: Nene Coll., 1997; Dartington Coll. of Arts, 1997; Heythrop Coll., Univ. of London, 2007; High Educn Acad., 2007. Hon. RAM 1995; Hon. GSMD 2000; Hon. Sen. Fellow, RCA 2004. DUniv: Central England, 1996; Middx, 2005; Hon. DLitt Ulster, 2004. *Publications:* articles in learned jls, France and UK. *Recreations:* reading, theatre-going, country walking. *Address: e-mail:* jritterman@blueyonder.co.uk. *Club:* Athenæum.

RITTNER, Luke Philip Hardwick; Chief Executive, Royal Academy of Dance (formerly of Dancing), since 1999; *b* 24 May 1947; *s* of late George Stephen Hardwick Rittner and Joane (*née* Thunder); *m* 1974, Corinna Frances Edholm; one *d*. *Educ:* Blackfriars School, Laxton; City of Bath Technical Coll.; Dartington Coll. of Arts; London Acad. of Music and Dramatic Art. Asst Administrator, Bath Festival, 1968–71, Jt Administrator, 1971–74, Administrative Director, 1974–76; Founder, and Dir, Assoc. for Business Sponsorship of the Arts, 1976–83; Sec. Gen., Arts Council of GB, 1983–90; Dir, Marketing and Communications, then Corporate Affairs, Sotheby's Europe, 1992–99. Chm., English Shakespeare Co., 1990–94. UK Cultural Dir, Expo '92, Seville; Corporate Advr on cultural sponsorship to: Eurotunnel; J. Sainsbury plc. Non-exec. Bd Mem., Carlton Television, 1991–93. Member: Adv. Council, V&A Museum, 1980–83; Music Panel, British Council, 1979–83; Drama Panel, 1992–94 and 2007–, Dance Panel, 2003–04, Olivier Awards; Council, and Chm., Exec. Bd, LAMDA, 1994–. Chm., London Choral Soc., subseq. London Chorus, 1994–2005. Trustee: Bath Preservation Trust, 1968–73; Theatre Royal, Bath, 1979–82; City Ballet of London, 1997–2000; Foundn Trustee, Holburne Museum, Bath, 1981–83; Governor, Urchfont Manor, Wiltshire Adult Educn Centre, 1982–83. Patron, Dartington Coll. of Arts, 2002–. Hon. DA Bath, 2004; Hon. DCL Durham, 2005. *Recreations:* the arts, people, travel. *Address:* Royal Academy of Dance, 36 Battersea Square, SW11 3RA. *Club:* Garrick.

RIVA, Hilary; Chief Executive, British Fashion Council, since 2005; *b* Mansfield, 3 April 1957; three *s*. *Educ:* Poly. of Central London (BA Hons Soc. Sci. 1984). Arcadia Group: Buying and Merchandising Controller, Topshop, 1980–90; Buying and Merchandising Dir, Burton Gp, 1990–96; Man. Dir, Evans, 1996–98; Man. Dir, Dorothy Perkins, Topshop, Evans, Principles, 1998–2000; Man. Dir, Evans, Wallis, Warehouse, Principles, 2000–01; Man. Dir, Rubicon Retail Ltd, 2001–05. *Address:* Abbey House, Abbey Road, Faversham ME13 7BE. *T:* (01795) 834744; *e-mail:* hilary.riva@britishfashioncouncil.com.

RIVERDALE, 3rd Baron *cr* 1935, of Sheffield, co. York; **Anthony Robert Balfour;** Bt 1929; *b* 23 Feb. 1960; *s* of Hon. Mark Robin Balfour (*d* 1995) and Susan Ann Phillips (*d* 1996); *S* grandfather, 1998. *Educ:* Wellington. *Heir: cousin* Arthur Michael Balfour [*b* 24 Nov. 1938; *m* 1962, Rita Ann Fance; two *s* one *d*].

RIVERINA, Bishop of, since 2005; **Rt Rev. Douglas Stevens;** *b* 19 May 1952; *s* of Robert Henry Stevens and Dorothy Phyllis Cooper; *m* 1979, Denise Karen; two *d*. *Educ:* Newcastle Univ., NSW (BA); Aust. Coll. of Theol. (BTh Hons); Univ. of Dublin (MPhil); Melbourne Coll. of Divinity (Dr of Ministry Studies). Rector: Merriwa, 1981–84; Botton Point, 1986–90; Wingham, 1990–94; Nambucca Heads, 1994–99; Tweed Heads, 1999–2005. *Address:* PO Box 10, Narrandera, NSW 2700, Australia. *T:* (2) 69591648.

RIVERS, Valerie Lane-Fox P.; *see* Pitt-Rivers.

RIVETT, Dr Geoffrey Christopher; Senior Principal Medical Officer, Department of Health (formerly of Health and Social Security), 1985–92; *b* 11 Aug. 1932; *s* of Frank Andrew James Rivett and Catherine Mary Rivett; *m* 1976, Elizabeth Barbara Hartman; two *s* by previous marr. *Educ:* Manchester Grammar Sch.; Brasenose Coll., Oxford (MA 1st Cl. Hons Animal Physiol.); University Coll. Hosp. (BM, BCh); FRCGP, DObst RCOG. House Officer, Radcliffe Inf., Oxford, 1957; House Phys., London Chest Hosp., 1958; RAMC, 1958–60; GP, Milton Keynes, 1960–72; DHSS, subseq. DoH, 1972–92. Vice Chm., Council of Govs, Homerton NHS Foundn Trust. Liveryman: Soc. of Apothecaries, 1981–; Co. of Barbers, 1993–. ARPS 1971. *Publications:* The Development of the London Hospital System 1823–1982, 1986; From Cradle to Grave: fifty years of the NHS, 1998. *Recreations:* photography, house conversion. *Address:* 173 Shakespeare Tower, Barbican, EC2Y 8DR. *T:* (020) 7786 9617; *e-mail:* geoffrey@rivett.net; *web:* www.nhshistory.net. *Club:* Royal Society of Medicine.

RIVETT-CARNAC, Sir Miles (James), 9th Bt *cr* 1836, of Derby; DL; Vice Lord-Lieutenant of Hampshire, 2000–07; *b* 7 Feb. 1933; *s* of Vice-Adm. James William Rivett-Carnac, CB, CBE, DSC (2nd *s* of 6th Bt) (*d* 1970), and Isla Nesta Rivett-Carnac (*d* 1974), *d* of Harry Officer Blackwood; *S* brother, 2004; *m* 1958, April Sally Villar; two *s* one *d*. *Educ:* Royal Naval College, Dartmouth, RN, 1950–70 (despatches 1965); Commander, 1965; US Staff Coll., 1966; Commanded HMS Dainty, 1967–68; MoD, 1968–70. Joined Barings, 1971; Dir, Baring Bros & Co., 1976; Pres., Baring Bros Inc., 1978; Managing Dir, Baring Bros & Co., 1981; Dep. Chm., Barings plc, 1988–93; Chairman: Baring Asset Management, 1989–93; Baring Securities, 1993–94. Chm., Tribune Investment Trust, 1985–99. Director: London Stock Exchange, 1991–94; Allied Domecq (formerly Allied Lyons) plc, 1992–97. Chm., Hampshire Boys' Clubs, 1982–90. Mem. Council, King George V Fund for Sailors, 1989. Elder Brother, Trinity House, 1992–. High Sheriff, Hants, 1995, DL Hants, 1996. *Recreations:* tennis, golf, shooting, philately (FRPS). *Heir: s* Jonathan James Rivett-Carnac, *b* 14 June 1962. *Address:* 47 Broad Street, Alresford, Hants SO24 9AS. *T:* (01962) 779311. *Clubs:* White's, Naval and Military; Links, Racquet (NY).

RIVIERE, Rev. Jonathan Byam Valentine; Rector, Sandringham Group of Parishes, and Domestic Chaplain to the Queen, since 2003; Chaplain to the Queen, since 2007; *b* 4 Feb. 1954; *s* of late Anthony and of Ann Riviere; *m* 1987, Clare Hudson; two *s* one *d*. *Educ:* Westminster; RAC Cirencester; Cuddesdon Coll. Ordained deacon, 1983, priest, 1984; Curate, Wymondham, 1983–88; Team Vicar, Quidenham, 1988–94; Priest i/c, 1994, Rector, 1995–2003, Somerleyton Gp of Parishes. *Recreation:* sailing. *Address:* The Rectory, Sandringham, Norfolk PE35 6EH. *T:* (01485) 540587.

RIVLIN, Geoffrey; QC 1979; **His Honour Judge Rivlin;** a Circuit Judge, since 1989; a Senior Circuit Judge, since 2004; *b* 28 Nov. 1940; *s* of late M. Allenby Rivlin and late May Rivlin; *m* 1974, Maureen Smith, Hon. ARAM, Prof. of violin, RCM; two *d*. *Educ:* Bootham Sch.; Leeds Univ. (LLB). Called to the Bar, Middle Temple, 1963 (Colombos Prize, Internat. Law); Bencher, 1987. NE Circuit Junior 1967; a Recorder, 1978–89. Mem., Senate of Inns of Court and the Bar, 1976–79. Chm. Adv. Bd, Computer Crime Centre, QMW, 1996–2002. Hon. Recorder, City of Westminster, 2008. Governor: St Christopher's Sch., Hampstead, 1990–99; NLCS, Edgware, 1993–2003. *Publications:* First Steps in the Law, 1999, 4th edn, as Understanding the Law, 2006; Judges and Schools, 2002. *Address:* The Crown Court, Southwark, 1 English Grounds, SE1 2HU.

RIX, family name of **Baron Rix**.

RIX, Baron *cr* 1992 (Life Peer), of Whitehall in the City of Westminster and of Hornsea in Yorkshire; **Brian Norman Roger Rix,** Kt 1986; CBE 1977; DL; actor-manager, 1948–77; President, Mencap (The Royal Mencap Society, formerly Royal Society for Mentally Handicapped Children and Adults), since 1998 (Secretary-General, 1980–87; Chairman, 1988–98); Chairman, The Rix-Thompson-Rothenberg (formerly Mencap City) Foundation, since 1988 (Founder and Governor, since 1984); *b* 27 Jan. 1924; *s* of late Herbert and Fanny Rix; *m* 1949, Elspet Jeans Macgregor-Gray; two *s* one *d* (and one *d* decd). *Educ:* Bootham Sch., York. Stage career: joined Donald Wolfit, 1942; first West End appearance, Sebastian in Twelfth Night, St James's, 1943; White Rose Players, Harrogate, 1943–44. Served War of 1939–45, RAF and Bevin Boy. Became actor-manager, 1948; ran repertory cos at Ilkley, Bridlington and Margate, 1950; toured Reluctant Heroes and brought to Whitehall Theatre, 1950–54; Dry Rot, 1954–58; Simple Spymen, 1958–61; One For the Pot, 1961–64; Chase Me Comrade, 1964–66; went to Garrick Theatre, 1967, with repertoire of farce: Stand By Your Bedouin; Uproar in the House; Let Sleeping Wives Lie; after 6 months went over to latter, only, which ran till 1969; then followed: She's Done It Again, 1969–70; Don't Just Lie There, Say Something!, 1971–73 (filmed 1973); New Theatre, Cardiff, Robinson Crusoe, 1973; Cambridge Theatre, A Bit Between The Teeth, 1974; Fringe Benefits, Whitehall Theatre, 1976; returned to a theatre season with Dry Rot, Lyric Theatre, 1989; dir., You'll Do For Me!, tour, 1989. Entered films, 1951: subsequently made eleven, including Reluctant Heroes, 1951, Dry Rot, 1956. BBC TV contract to present farces on TV, 1956–72; first ITV series Men of Affairs, 1973; A Roof Over My Head, BBC TV series, 1977. Presenter, Let's Go …, BBC TV series (first ever for people with a learning disability), 1978–83; BBC Radio 2 series, 1978–80; occasional appearances in A Peer Round Whitehall, 2008–. Dir and Theatre Controller, Cooney-Marsh Group, 1977–80; Trustee, Theatre of Comedy, 1983–93; Arts Council: Mem., 1986–93; Chairman: Drama Panel, 1986–93; Monitoring Cttee, Arts and Disabled People, 1988–93; Indep. Develt Council for People with Mental Handicap, 1981–86; Friends of Normansfield, 1975–2003 (Pres., 2003–); Libertas, 1987–2006. Chancellor, Univ. of E London, 1997–. DL Greater London, 1987; Vice Lord-Lieut of Greater London, 1988–97. Hon. Fellow: Humberside Coll. of Higher Educn, 1984; Myerscough Coll., 2002; Hon. FRSocMed 1998; Hon. FRCPsych 1999. Hon. MA: Hull, 1981; Open, 1983; DUniv: Essex, 1984; Bradford, 2000; Hon. LLD: Manchester, 1986; Dundee, 1994; Exeter, 1997; Hon. DSc Nottingham, 1987. Evian Health Award, 1988; Communicator of the Year, RNID, 1990; Campaigner of the Year, Spectator, 1999; Yorks Lifetime Achievement Award, Yorkshire Awards, 1999; Lifetime Achievement Award, UK Charity Awards, 2001; Public Service Award, British Neurosci. Assoc., 2001; Lifetime Achievement Award, ePolitix Charity Champions Awards, 2004. *Publications:* My Farce from My Elbow: an autobiography, 1975; Farce about Face (autobiog.), 1989; Tour de Farce, 1992; Life in the Farce Lane, 1995; (ed and contrib.) Gullible's Travails, 1996; All About Us!: the story of people with a learning disability and Mencap, 2006. *Recreations:* cricket, amateur radio (G2DQU; Hon. Vice-Pres., Radio Soc. of GB, 1979), gardening. *Address:* House of Lords, SW1A 0PW. *Clubs:* Garrick, MCC, Lord's Taverners (Pres., 1970).

RIX, Rear Adm. Anthony John; Chief of Staff to Commander Allied Naval Forces Southern Europe, since 2007; *b* 12 Aug. 1956; *s* of Sir John Rix, MBE, and of Sylvia Gene Rix (*née* Howe). *Educ:* Sherborne Sch.; Britannia RNC. Joined RN, 1975; Commanding Officer: HMS Glasgow, 1995–96; HMS Marlborough, 1999–2000; Flag Officer Sea Trng, 2006–07. QCVS 2006. *Recreations:* tennis, shooting, fishing, sailing. *Address:* 30 Parkville Road, Fulham, SW6 7BX; *e-mail:* Anthony.Rix@btinternet.com. *Clubs:* Royal Yacht Squadron; Trinity House.

RIX, Rt Hon. Sir Bernard (Anthony), Kt 1993; PC 2000; **Rt Hon. Lord Justice Rix;** a Lord Justice of Appeal, since 2000; *b* 8 Dec. 1944; *s* of late Otto Rix and Sadie Silverberg; *m* 1983, Hon. Karen Debra, *er d* of Baron Young of Graffham, *qv*; three *s* two *d* (incl. twin *s*). *Educ:* St Paul's School, London; New College, Oxford (BA: Lit.Hum. 1966, Jur. 1968; MA; Hon. Fellow 2007); Harvard Law School (Kennedy Scholar 1968; LLM 1969). FCIArb 1999. Called to Bar, Inner Temple, 1970 (Bencher, 1990; Reader, 2004, Treasurer, 2005); QC 1981; a Recorder, 1990–93; a Judge of the High Court, QBD, 1993–2000; Judge in charge of Commercial List, 1998–99. Member: Senate, Inns of Court and Bar, 1981–83; Bar Council, 1981–83. Chm., Commercial Bar Assoc., 1992–93. Pres., Harvard Law Sch. Assoc. of UK, 2002–; Vice-Pres., British Insurance Law Assoc., 2006–. Dir, London Philharmonic Orchestra, 1986–. Vice-Chm., Central Council for Jewish Community Services, 1994–96 (author, report on youth services and orgns, 1994). Dir, Spiro Inst., 1995–99. Chm., British Friends of Bar-Ilan Univ., 1987–99 (Hon. Vice-Pres., 1999–); Mem. Bd of Trustees, Bar-Ilan Univ., 1988–99; Chm., Adv. Council, Centre of Commercial Law Studies, QMUL, 2003–; Trustee and Dir, British Inst. of Internat. and Comparative Law, 2003–. Patron, Wiener Library, 2006–. Hon. Fellow, QMUL, 2008. *Recreations:* music, opera, Italy, formerly fencing. *Address:* Royal Courts of Justice, Strand, WC2A 2LL.

RIX, Dr (Edward) Martyn; freelance writer and botanist, since 1978; Editor, Curtis's Botanical Magazine, since 2003; *b* 15 Aug. 1943; *s* of Edward Lionel Reussner Rix and Elizabeth Joyce Rix; *m* 1983, Alison Jane Goatcher; two *d*. *Educ:* Sherborne Sch., Dorset; Trinity Coll., Dublin (MA); Corpus Christi Coll., Cambridge (PhD). Res. Fellow, Univ. of Zürich, 1971–73; botanist, RHS, Wisley, 1974–78. FLS 2006. Gold Veitch Meml Medal, RHS, 1999; Tercentenary Bronze Medal, Linnean Soc. of London, 2008. *Publications:* The Art of the Botanist, 1981; Growing Bulbs, 1983; The Redouté Album, 1990; Subtropical and Dry Climate Plants, 2006; with R. Phillips: Bulbs, 1981; Freshwater Fish, 1985; Roses, 1988; Shrubs, 1989; Perennials, 2 vols, 1991; Vegetables, 1993; The Quest for the Rose, 1993; Conservatory and Indoor Plants, 1997; Annuals, 1999; The Botanical Garden, 2002; (with S. Sherwood) Treasures of Botanical Art, 2008. *Recreations:* fishing, sailing, travel. *Address:* c/o Macmillan Publishers Ltd, 20 New Wharf Road, N1 9RR.

RIX, Martyn; *see* Rix, E. M.

RIX, Michael David; National Executive Officer, GMB, since 2005; *b* 11 April 1963; *s* of Roy Rix; *m* 1984; one *s* one *d*. *Educ:* Primrose Hill High Sch., Leeds; Bradford and Ilkley TUC Coll.; various TUC/ASLEF educn projects. Left sch. at 16 with no formal qualifications; work experience, Yorks copper works, 1979; trainee driver, BR, Leeds, 1979–86; qualified BR driver, 1986. Leeds ASLEF: Mem., Br. Cttee, 1980–84; Asst Br. Sec., 1984–98; Br. Sec., 1988–98; Negotiating Chair, 1992; Dist Council Chm., 1995; Dist Sec., No 3 Reg., 1998; Gen. Sec., ASLEF, 1998–2003. Mem., TUC General Council, 2001–03. Mem., Labour Party, 1980–97, 2000–. Mem., Co-op Soc., Wortley Hall, PPPS. *Recreations:* football, especially Leeds United, watching Rugby league, watching Yorkshire CCC, swimming, reading, very little time though to pursue. *Address:* c/o GMB National Office, 22/24 Worple Road, SW19 4DD.

RIX, Timothy John, CBE 1997; Chairman, Longman Group Ltd, 1984–90 (Chief Executive, 1976–89); *b* 4 Jan. 1934; *s* of late Howard Terrell Rix and Marguerite Selman Rix; *m* 1st, 1960, Wendy Elizabeth Wright (marr. diss. 1967); one *d*; 2nd, 1967, Gillian Diana Mary Greenwood; one *s* one *d*. *Educ:* Radley Coll.; Clare Coll., Cambridge (BA); Yale Univ., USA. Sub-Lieut, RNVR, 1952–54. Mellon Fellow, Yale, 1957–58; joined Longmans, Green & Co. Ltd, subseq. Longman Gp, 1958; Overseas Educnl Publisher, 1958–61; Publishing Manager, Far East and SE Asia, 1961–63; Head of English Language Teaching Publishing, 1964–68; Divl Man. Dir, 1968–72; Jt Man. Dir, 1972–76. Director: Pearson Longman Ltd, 1979–83; Goldcrest Television, 1981–83; Yale Univ. Press, London, 1984–; ECIC (Management) Ltd, 1990–92; Blackie and Son Ltd, 1990–93; B. H. Blackwell Ltd, 1990–95; Blackwell Ltd, 1993–95; HEA Publishing Adv. Bd, 1993–95; Geddes and Grosset Ltd, 1996–98; Jessica Kingsley Publishers Ltd, 1997–2008; Frances Lincoln Ltd, 1997–; Meditech Media Ltd, 1997–2003; Scottish Book Source, 1999–2008. Chairman: Book Marketing Ltd, 1990–2003; Edinburgh University Press, 2001–07; Senior Consultant: Pofcher Co., 1990–95; van Tulleken Co., 1996–2007. Chm., Pitman Examns Inst., 1987–90. Publishers Association: Chm., Trng Cttee, 1974–78; Chm., Book Develt Council, 1979–81; Vice-Pres., 1980–81 and 1983–84; Pres., 1981–83. Chairman: Book Trust, 1986–88; Book House Training Centre, 1986–89; British Library Centre for the Book, 1990–96; Society of Bookmen, 1990–92; British Library Publishing, 1992–2003; Book Aid International, 1994–2006; Nat. Book Cttee, 1997–2003. Member: Exec. Cttee, NBL, 1979–86 (Dep. Chm., 1984–86); Publishers Adv. Panel, British Council, 1978–98 (Chm., 1994–98); Arts Council Literature Panel, 1983–86; British Library Adv. Council, 1982–86; British Library Bd, 1986–96; British Council Bd, 1988–97; Finance Cttee, Delegacy of OUP, 1992–2002; Bd, HEA, 1996–99; Adv. Council, Inst. of English Studies, London Univ., 1999–. Hon. Pres., Independent Publishers' Guild, 1993–2008. Governor: Bell Educnl Trust, 1990–2004 (Chm. Govs, 1995–2001); ESU, 1999–2005. CCMI (CBIM 1981); FRSA 1986. Hon. MA Oxford, 1992; DUniv Stirling, 2006. *Publications:* articles on publishing in trade jls. *Recreations:* reading, landscape, wine. *Address:* Flat 1, 29 Barrington Road, N8 8QT. *T:* (020) 8341 4160. *Club:* Garrick.

RIZA, Alper Ali; QC 1991; a Recorder of the Crown Court, since 2000; *b* 16 March 1948; *s* of Ali Riza and Elli Liasides; *m* 1981, Vanessa Frances Hall-Smith, *qv*; two *d*. *Educ:* American Academy, Larnaca, Cyprus; English Sch., Nicosia. Called to the Bar, Gray's Inn, 1973. Pupillage, 1974–75; Turnpike Lane Law and Advice, 1975–77; Appeals Lawyer, Jt Council for Welfare of Immigrants, 1977–82; private practice, 1982–. Founder Mem., Assoc. of Greek, Turkish and Cypriot Affairs, 1990–. Fellow, Inst. of Advanced Legal Studies; Mem., RIIA. Jt Editor, Butterworths's Immigration Law Service, 1991–95. *Recreations:* music, philosophy, drinking and smoking, sport, walking around London W2 and W11 esp. Hyde Park, Kensington Gardens and Holland Park. *Address:* Goldsmith Chambers, Goldsmith Building, Temple, EC4Y 7BL.

RIZA, Vanessa Frances; *see* Hall-Smith, V. F.

RIZK, Waheeb, CBE 1984 (OBE 1977); MA, PhD; FREng, FIMechE; Engineering Consultant, W R Associates, since 1986; *b* 11 Nov. 1921; *s* of Dr and Mrs I. Rizk; *m* 1952, Vivien Moyle, MA (Cantab); one *s* one *d* (and one *d* decd). *Educ:* Emmanuel College, Cambridge. MA, PhD. Joined English Electric Co., 1954, Chief Engineer, Gas Turbine Div., 1957, Gen. Manager, new div., combining gas turbines and industrial steam turbines, 1967; after merger with GEC became Man. Dir, GEC Gas Turbines Ltd, 1971; Chairman: GEC-Ruston Gas Turbines Ltd, 1983–86; GEC Diesels Ltd, 1983–86. Chm. of Bd, BSI, 1982–85. Pres., IMechE, 1984–85 (Mem. Council, 1978–89); Mem. Council, Fellowship of Engrg, 1982–85. Pres., Internat Council on Combustion Engines (CIMAC), 1973–77. Chm., Smallpeice Trust, 1991–98. Mem. Council, Cranfield Inst. of Technology, 1985–95; Member Court: Brunel Univ., 1986–99; Cranfield Univ., 1986–. Liveryman, Worshipful Co. of Engineers. Gold Medal, CIMAC, 1983. *Publications:* technical papers to IMechE, Amer. Soc. of Mech. Engineers and CIMAC. *Recreations:* intelligent tinkering with any mechanism, photography, old motor cycles. *Address:* 231 Hillmorton Road, Rugby CV22 5BD. *T:* (01788) 565093.

RIZZI, Carlo; conductor; Musical Director, Welsh National Opera, 1992–2002 and 2004–07; *b* 19 July 1960. *Educ:* Milan Conservatoire; Accademia Musicale Chigiana, Siena. Débuts: Australian Opera Co., 1989; Netherlands Opera, 1989; Royal Opera, 1990; WNO, 1991; Deutsche Oper, Berlin, 1992; Cologne Opera, 1992; Israel Philharmonic, 1993; Metropolitan Opera, NY, 1993; has made numerous recordings. *Address:* c/o Allied Artists Agency, 42 Montpelier Square, SW7 1JZ. *T:* (020) 7589 6243, *Fax:* (020) 7581 5269.

ROACH, Prof. Gary Francis, FRSE; Professor of Mathematics, University of Strathclyde, 1979–96, now Emeritus; *b* 8 Oct. 1933; *s* of John Francis Roach and Bertha Mary Ann Roach (*née* Walters); *m* 1960, Isabella Grace Willins Nicol. *Educ:* University Coll. of S Wales and Monmouthshire (BSc); Univ. of London (MSc); Univ. of Manchester (PhD, DSc). FRAS, FIMA, CMath. RAF (Educn Branch), Flying Officer, 1955–58; Research Mathematician, BP, 1958–61; Lectr, UMIST, 1961–66; Vis. Prof., Univ. of British Columbia, 1966–67; University of Strathclyde: Lectr, 1967; Sen Lectr, 1970; Reader, 1971; Prof., 1979; Dean, Faculty of Science, 1982–87. Mem., Edinburgh Mathematical Soc. (Past Pres.). Deacon, Incorp. of Bonnetmakers and Dyers of Glasgow, 1997–98. FRSA 1991. Hon. Fellow, Solvay Inst., 1998. Hon. ScD Lodz, 1993. OStJ 1992. *Publications:* Green's Functions, 1970, 2nd edn 1982; articles in learned jls. *Recreations:* mountaineering, photography, philately, gardening, music. *Address:* 11 Menzies Avenue, Fintry, Glasgow G63 0YE. *T:* (01360) 860335.

ROADS, Dr Christopher Herbert; Acting Chairman and (Founding) Managing Director, Historic Arms Exhibitions and Forts LLC, Oman, since 2001; consultant in museums and audio visual archives; *b* 3 Jan. 1934; *s* of late Herbert Clifford Roads and Vera Iris Roads; *m* 1976, Charlotte Alicia Dorothy Mary Lothian (marr. diss.); one *d*. *Educ:* Cambridge and County Sch.; Trinity Hall, Cambridge (MA; PhD 1961). Nat. Service, 2nd Lieut, RA, Egypt, 1952–54. Adviser to WO on Disposal of Amnesty Arms, 1961–62; Imperial War Museum: Keeper of Dept of Records, 1962–70; Dep. Dir-Gen. at Main Building, Southwark, 1964–79, at Duxford, Cambridge, 1976–79, HMS Belfast, Pool of London, 1978–79; Dir, Museums & Archives Develt Associates Ltd, 1977–85; Dir, Nat. Sound Archive, 1983–92; Associate Dir (Consultancy), R&D Dept, BL, 1992–94. UNESCO consultant designing major audio visual archives or museums in Philippines, Panama, Bolivia, Kuwait, Jordan, Saudi Arabia, etc, 1976–. Founder and Dir, Cambridge Coral/Starfish Res. Gp, 1968–; Director: Nat. Discography Ltd, 1986–92; Historic Cable Ship John W. Mackay, 1986–; AVT Communications Ltd, 1988–92; Cedar Audio Ltd, 1989–92. Chm., Coral Conservation Trust, 1972–; President: Historical Breechloading Small Arms Assoc., 1973–, Pres. for Life, 2003; Internat. Film and TV Council (UNESCO Category A), 1990–92 (Pres., Archives Commn, 1970–); Hon. Pres., World Expeditionary Assoc. (Vice Pres., 1971); Vice President: Duxford Aviation Soc., 1974–; English Eight Club, 1980–; Cambridge Univ. Rifle Assoc., 1987– (Mem. Council, 1955–87); Mem. Council, Scientific Exploration Soc., 1971–82; Sec., Nat. Archives Cttee, Internat. Assoc. of Sound Archives, 1988–92; Hon. Sec., Cambridge Univ. Long Range Rifle Club, 1979–; Mem., Home Office Reference Panel for Historic Firearms, 1997–2003; Chm., Heritage Arms Rescue, 1996–. Trustee: HMS Belfast Trust, 1970–78; Nat. Life Stories Collection, 1986–92; NSA Wild Life Sound Trust, 1986–92. Adjt, English VIII, 1964–88. Churchill Fellowship, 1970; Vis. Fellow, Centre of Internat. Studies, Univ. of Cambridge, 1983–84. FRGS. Liveryman, Gunmakers' Co., 1996; Freeman, City of London, 1996. Silver Jubilee Medal, 1977. Order of Independence, 2nd cl. (Jordan), 1977. *Publications:* The British Soldier's Firearm, 1850–1864, 1964; (jtly) New Studies on the Crown of Thorns Starfish, 1970; The Story of the Gun, 1978. *Recreations:* rifle shooting, marine and submarine exploration, wind surfing, motorcycling, videography. *Address:* The White House, 90 High Street, Melbourn, near Royston, Herts SG8 6AL. *T:* (01763) 260866, *Fax:* (01763) 262521; DX 12 Urbanización Bahia Dorada, 29693 Estepona, Málaga, Spain. *T:* and *Fax:* (95) 2796407; Historic Arms Exhibitions and Forts LLC, PO Box 3726, P. Code 112, Ruwi, Muscat, Sultanate of Oman. *T:* (office) 24501218, (residence) 99797326, *Fax:* (residence) 24596603. *Clubs:* Oxford and Cambridge; Hawks (Cambridge).

ROADS, Peter George, MD; FFPH; Regional Medical Officer, South West Thames Regional Health Authority, 1973–82, retired; *b* 14 Nov. 1917; *s* of Frank George Roads and Mary Dee Hill Roads (*née* Bury); *m* 1949, Evelyn Clara (*née* Daniel); one *s* one *d*. *Educ:* Bedford Sch.; St Mary's Hosp. Med Sch., London Univ. (MD); Hon. Society of Inner Temple. FFPH (FFCM 1974; FFPHM 1989). Served War, in China, 1944–46. MRC, Pneumoconiosis Unit, 1949–50; Dep. MOH, etc, City and Co. of Bristol, 1956–59; MOH, Principal Sch. Med. Officer and Port Med. Officer for City and Port of Portsmouth, 1959–73; Med. Referee to Portchester Crematorium, 1959–73, to Chilterns Crematorium, 1980–2005. Mem., Central Midwives Bd, 1964–76; Adviser on Health Services, Assoc. of Municipal Corporations, 1966–74. FRSocMed; Fellow, Soc. of Public Health (formerly of Community Medicine) (Pres., 1988–89). Chairman: Bucks Br., Historical Assoc., 1987–93; Bucks Family History Soc., 1990–93; Bucks Management Cttee, Oxford Diocesan Council for the Deaf, 1991–93. Mem. Deanery Synod, and Church Warden, Stone Dinton and Hartwell, 1988–91. *Publications:* Care of Elderly in Portsmouth, 1970; Medical Importance of Open Air Recreation (Proc. 1st Internat. Congress on Leisure and Touring), 1966. *Recreations:* open air, walking, forestry, history, touring. *Address:* Pasture Cottage, School Lane, Dinton, near Aylesbury, Bucks HP17 8UZ. *T:* (01296) 748504.

ROBARDS, Prof. Anthony William, OBE 2002; PhD, DSc; HSBC Professor of Innovation, University of York, since 2001; *b* 9 April 1940; *s* of Albert Charles Robards, Lamberhurst, Kent, and Kathleen Emily Robards; *m* 1st, 1962, Ruth Bulpett (marr. diss. 1985); one *s* one *d*; 2nd, 1987, Eva Christina, *d* of Bo Knutson-Ek, Lidingo, Sweden. *Educ:* Skinners' Sch.; UCL (BSc 1962; PhD 1966; DSc 1977); Inst. of Educn, Univ. of London (PGCE 1963); Dip RMS 1976. FIBiol 1978. Department of Biology, University of York: Lectr, 1966–70; Sen. Lectr, 1970–79; Reader, 1979–88; Prof. of Biol., 1988–2003; Pro-Vice-Chancellor for Ext. Relns, 1996–2004; Director: Inst. for Applied Biol., 1986–95; Industrial Develt, 1988–96. Visiting Research Fellow: ANU, 1975; Univ. of Stockholm, 1986. Dir, York Science Park (Innovation Centre) Ltd (Chm., 1995–2006); Chm., York Science Park Ltd, 1999–; non-exec. Chm., YorkTest Gp Ltd, 1999–. Mem., Co. of Merchant Adventurers, City of York, 1991–. *Publications:* (with U. B. Sleytr) Low Temperature Methods in Biological Electron Microscopy, 1985; 120 scientific articles. *Recreations:* horology, sailing, opera. *Address:* Shrubbery Cottage, Nun Monkton, Yorks YO26 8EW. *T:* (01423) 331023; The Innovation Centre, York Science Park, York YO10 5DG. *T:* (01904) 435105; *e-mail:* awr1@york.ac.uk.

ROBARTS, (Anthony) Julian; Director and Chief Executive, Iveagh Trustees Ltd, 1993–98; Managing Director, Coutts & Co., 1986–91; *b* 6 May 1937; *s* of late Lt-Col Anthony V. C. Robarts, DL and Grizel Mary Robarts (Grant); *m* 1961, Edwina Beryl Hobson; two *s* one *d*. *Educ:* Eton College. National Service, 11th Hussars (PAO), 1955–57; joined Coutts & Co., 1958, Dir, 1963, Dep. Man. Dir, 1976–86; Director: Coutts Finance Co., 1967–91; F. Bolton Group, 1970–; International Fund for Institutions Inc., USA, 1983–93; Chm., Hill Martin, 1993–2004; Regional Dir, Nat. Westminster Bank, 1971–92. Hon. Treasurer, 1969–2001, Vice-Pres., 2001–, Union Jack Club. Trustee: Beit Med. Meml Fellowships, 1993–2001; Sargent Cancer Care for Children, 1997–2000. *Recreations:* shooting, gardening, opera. *Address:* Bromley Hall, Standon, Ware, Herts SG11 1NY. *Clubs:* Brooks's, Pratt's, MCC.

ROBATHAN, Andrew Robert George; MP (C) Blaby, since 1992; *b* 17 July 1951; *s* of late Robert Douglas Brice Robathan and of Sheena Mary Martin (*née* Gimson); *m* 1991, Rachael Maunder; one *s* one *d*. *Educ:* Merchant Taylors' Sch., Northwood; Oriel Coll., Oxford (MA). Served Coldstream Guards, 1974–89 (on secondment to SAS, 1981–83, HQ, 1984–87), resigned as Major; rejoined Army for Gulf War, Jan.–April 1991 (COS, POW Guard Force). Councillor, London Borough of Hammersmith and Fulham, 1990–92. PPS to Minister of State for Nat. Heritage, 1995–97; opposition spokesman on: trade and industry, 2002–03; internat. develt, 2003; defence, 2004–05; Dep. Opposition Chief Whip, 2005–. Mem., Internat. Develt Select Cttee, 1997–2002, 2003–04; Chm., 1994–97, Vice-Chm., 1997–, All-Party Cycling Gp; Vice Chairman: Parly Renewable and Sustainable Energy Gp, 1992–94, 1997–; Cons. back bench Defence Cttee, 1993–94, 1997–2001 (Chm., 1994–95); Cons. NI Cttee, 1994–95, 1997–2001; Cons. Defence and Internat. Affairs Policy Gp, 2001–02. Captain, Tug of War Team, 1995–2000, Clay Pigeon Team., 1997–2007, H of C. Mem. Bd, Indict, 1998–2001; Trustee, Halo Trust, 2000–06 (Chm., 2003–06). *Recreations:* hill-walking, ski-ing, shooting, architecture, history, conservation. *Address:* House of Commons, SW1A 0AA. *T:* (020) 7219 3000.

ROBB, (David) Campbell; Director General, Office of the Third Sector, Cabinet Office, since 2006; *b* Glasgow, 14 May 1969; *m* 2007, Donna Murray; two *d*. *Educ:* Univ. of Edinburgh (MA Hons Pols and Mod. Hist.). Researcher for David Blunkett, MP, 1993–94; Press Officer for Chris Smith, MP, 1996–97; Hd of Campaigns, 1998–2001, Dir, Public Policy, 2001–05, NCVO; Advr to HM Treasury, 2005. *Recreations:* music, cooking, escaping to our allotment, reading. *Address:* Office of the Third Sector, 35 Great Smith Street, SW1P 3BQ. *T:* (020) 7276 6026; *e-mail:* DirectorGeneralOTS@cabinet-office.x.gsi.gov.uk.

ROBB, Sir John (Weddell), Kt 1999; Chairman, British Energy, 1995–2001; *b* 27 April 1936; *s* of John and Isabella Robb; *m* 1965, Janet Teanby; two *s* one *d*. *Educ:* Daniel Stewart's College, Edinburgh. Beecham Group: Marketing Exec., Toiletry Div., Beecham

Products, 1966; Man. Dir, Beecham (Far East), Kuala Lumpur, 1971; Vice-Pres., W. Hemisphere Div., Beecham Products, USA, 1974; Man. Dir, Food and Drink Div., Beecham Products, 1976; Group Board, 1980; Chm., Food and Drink Div., 1980; Chm., Beecham Products, 1984–85; Gp Man. Dir, 1985–88; Wellcome Plc: Dep. Chief Exec., 1989–90; Chief Exec., 1990–95; Chm., 1994–95. Non-exec. Dir, Uniq plc (formerly Unigate), 1996–2002. Dep. Chm., Horserace Betting Levy Bd, 1993–2006; Trustee, Royal Botanic Gdn, Edinburgh, 1997–2002. *Recreations:* golf, gardening, racing. *Clubs:* Turf; Sunningdale.

ROBB, Prof. Michael Alfred, PhD, DSc; FRS 2000; Professor of Chemistry, Imperial College, London, since 2004; *b* 19 Feb. 1944; *s* of Robert Fredrick Robb and Dorothy Estelle Robb; *m* 1st, 1967, Brenda Elizabeth Donald (*d* 2000); one *s*; 2nd, 2001, Elaine Murphy (*see* Baroness Murphy). *Educ:* Toronto Univ. (PhD 1970); DSc London 1987. King's College, London: Lectr, 1971–88; Reader, 1988–92; Prof. of Chemistry, 1992–2003; Hd, Dept of Chemistry, 2000–03. *Publications:* contrib. to chemistry jls. *Address:* Department of Chemistry, Imperial College London, SW7 2AZ. *T:* (020) 7594 5757.

ROBBIE, David Andrew; Finance Director, Rexam plc, since 2005; *b* Greenmount, Lancs; *s* of Frank Robbie and Dorothy Robbie (*née* Holt). *Educ:* St Andrews Univ. (MA). ACA 1990. Finance Director: CMG plc, 2000–03; Royal P&O Nedlloyd NV, 2004–05. Non-exec. Dir, BBC, 2007–. Trustee, Almeida Th. *Recreations:* theatre, opera, travelling. *Address:* Rexam plc, 4 Millbank, SW1P 3XR. *T:* (020) 7227 4155; *e-mail:* david.robbie@rexam.com. *Clubs:* Royal Automobile, Century.

ROBBINS, Christopher William; HM Diplomatic Service; Minister-Counsellor (formerly Consul General) and Deputy Head of Mission, Seoul, 2001; *b* 16 June 1946; *s* of William Henry Meech Robbins and Marion Elizabeth Millington Robbins (*née* Rees); *m* 1st, 1978 (marr. diss.); 2nd, 2000, Brigitte Anna Petronella van Dijk. *Educ:* Skinners' Sch., Tunbridge Wells; Univ. of Sussex (BA); Warburg Inst., Univ. of London (MPhil). Lectr in Philosophy, Univ. of York, 1969–75; Principal, Welsh Office, 1975–77; Adminr, Directorate of Economic and Social Affairs, Council of Europe, 1977–84; joined HM Diplomatic Service, 1984; EC Dept, FCO, 1984–87; First Sec., New Delhi, 1987–90; Asst Head, Central and Southern Africa Dept, 1990–91; Head, Projects and Export Policy Branch I, DTI (on secondment), 1991–94; Commercial Counsellor, The Hague, 1994–98, and Consul-Gen., Amsterdam, 1996–98; Ambassador to Lithuania, 1998–2001. *Publications:* (contrib.) La Santé Rationnée?, 1981; (contrib.) The End of an Illusion, 1984; articles in philosophical and social policy jls. *Recreation:* the enjoyment of beauty. *Address:* c/o Foreign and Commonwealth Office, SW1A 2AH.

ROBBINS, James; Diplomatic Correspondent, BBC, since 1998; *b* 19 Jan. 1954; *s* of late (Richard) Michael Robbins, CBE and (Rose Margaret) Elspeth Robbins (*née* Bannatyne); *m* 1981, Gillian Gee; one *d*. *Educ:* Westminster Sch.; Christ Church, Oxford (BA Hons PPE). BBC: News Trainee, 1977; Reporter: Belfast, 1979–83; BBC News, 1983–87; Southern Africa Corresp., 1987–92; Europe Corresp., 1993–97. *Recreations:* opera, music, tennis, cooking, walking, looking out of train windows. *Address:* BBC, Room 2505, Television Centre, Wood Lane, W12 7RJ. *T:* (020) 8624 8550.

ROBBINS, Prof. Keith Gilbert; Vice-Chancellor (formerly Principal), University of Wales (formerly St David's University College), Lampeter, 1992–2003; Senior Vice-Chancellor, University of Wales, 1995–2001; *b* 9 April 1940; *s* of Gilbert Henry John and Edith Mary Robbins; *m* 1963, Janet Carey Thomson; three *s* one *d*. *Educ:* Bristol Grammar Sch.; Magdalen and St Antony's Colls, Oxford (MA, DPhil); DLitt Glasgow. FRSE 1991. University of York: Asst Lectr in History, 1963; Lectr in Hist., 1964; Prof. of History, 1971–79, Dean of Faculty of Arts, 1977–79, UCNW, Bangor; Prof. of Modern Hist., Glasgow Univ., 1980–91. Visiting Professor: British Columbia Univ., 1983; Univ. of Western Australia, 1995. Lectures: Enid Muir, Newcastle Univ., 1981; A. H. Dodd, UCNW, Bangor, 1984; Raleigh, British Acad., 1984; Ford, Oxford Univ., 1986–87. Winston Churchill Travelling Fellow, 1990. Pres., Historical Assoc., 1988–91; Chm. Cttee, Hds of Higher Educn, Wales, 1996–98. Mem., and Chm. Res. Cttee, Humanities Res. Bd, British Acad., 1994–97; Mem., Arts and Humanities Res. Bd, 1998–2003. Pres., Old Bristolians' Soc., 1995–96. Editor, History, 1977–86; Member: Editorial Bd, Jl of Ecclesiastical History, 1978–93. Hon. DLitt: UWE, 1999; Wales, 2005. *Publications:* Munich 1938, 1968; Sir Edward Grey, 1971; The Abolition of War: The British Peace Movement 1914–1919, 1976; John Bright, 1979; The Eclipse of a Great Power: Modern Britain 1870–1975, 1983; The First World War, 1984; Nineteenth-Century Britain: integration and diversity, 1988; Appeasement, 1988; (ed) Blackwell Biographical Dictionary of British Political Life in the Twentieth Century, 1990; (ed) Protestant Evangelicalism, 1991; Churchill, 1992; History, Religion and Identity in Modern British History, 1993; Politicians, Diplomacy and War in Modern British History, 1994; A Bibliography of British History 1914–1989, 1996; Great Britain: identities, institutions and the idea of Britishness, 1997; The World since 1945: a concise history, 1998; The British Isles 1901–1951, 2002; Britain and Europe 1789–2005, 2005; England, Ireland, Scotland, Wales: the Christian Church 1900–2000, 2008; articles in Historical Jl, Internat. Affairs, Jl of Contemporary Hist., Jl of Ecclesiastical Hist., Jl of Commonwealth and Imperial Hist., etc. *Recreations:* music, gardening, walking. *Address:* Rhydyfran, Cribyn, Lampeter, Ceredigion SA48 7NH. *T:* (01570) 470349; *e-mail:* profkgr@clara.co.uk.

ROBBINS, Michael; *see* Robbins, R. F. M.

ROBBINS, Oliver; Director, Prime Minister's Private Office, since 2007; *b* 20 April 1975; *s* of Derek and Diana Robbins; *m* 2005, Sherry Birkbeck. *Educ:* Hertford Coll., Oxford (BA Hons PPE 1996). HM Treasury, 1996–2006: Hd, Corporate and Private Finance, 2003–06; Hd, Defence, Diplomacy and Intelligence, 2006; Principal Private Sec. to the Prime Minister, 2006–07. *Recreations:* walking, cooking. *Address:* c/o Prime Minister's Private Office, 10 Downing Street, SW1A 2AA. *T:* (020) 7930 4433. *Club:* National Liberal.

ROBBINS, Dr (Raymond Frank) Michael, CBE 1987; Director, Polytechnic South West (formerly Plymouth Polytechnic), 1974–89, Hon. Fellow, 1989; *b* 15 Feb. 1928; *s* of Harold and Elsie Robbins; *m* 1955, Eirian Meredith Edwards; two *d*. *Educ:* Grove Park Grammar Sch., Wrexham; UCW Aberystwyth. PhD 1954; FRIC 1962. Research Chemist, Monsanto Chemicals Ltd, 1954–55; Research Fellow, Univ. of Exeter, 1955–56; Lectr, Nottingham Coll. of Technology, 1956–59; Sen. Lectr, Hatfield Coll. of Technology, 1960–61; Head of Dept of Chem. Sciences, Hatfield Polytechnic, 1961–70; Dep. Dir, Plymouth Polytechnic, 1970–74. Chm., Sci. Prog. Adv. Gp, PCFC, 1989–92; Mem., British Accreditation Council, 1984–93. *Publications:* papers on organic chemistry in chem. jls, various reviews and articles in sci. and educnl press. *Recreations:* hill walking, creative gardening.

ROBBINS, Ven. Stephen; QHC 2005; Archdeacon for the Army, since 2004; Chaplain General, Ministry of Defence Chaplains (Army), since 2008; Honorary Canon, Salisbury Cathedral, since 2007; *b* 11 Aug. 1953; *s* of Joseph and Jane Robbins; *m* 1976, Susan Florence McCann; one *s* one *d*. *Educ:* Jarrow Grammar Sch.; King's Coll., London (BD AKC 1974). Ordained deacon, 1976, priest, 1977; Curate, Tudhoe Grange, Spennymoor, 1976–80; Priest-in-charge, then Vicar, Harlow Green, Gateshead, 1980–87; joined RAChD, 1987; Regtl Chaplain in Germany, 1987–94; Chaplain, Army Trng Regt, Bassingbourn, 1994–97; Sen. Chaplain, 8 Infantry Bde, Londonderry, 1997–99; Armed Forces Chaplaincy Centre, 1999–2001; Chaplain, RMA Sandhurst, 2001–02; Assistant Chaplain General: Germany, 2002–03; HQ Land Comd, 2003–06; Dir of Training, 2006–07, Dep. Chaplain Gen., 2007–08, MoD Chaplains (Army). *Recreations:* exploring Neolithic and Bronze Age earthworks, Newcastle United, trying to find a beer I don't like. *Address:* Ministry of Defence Chaplains (Army), Trenchard Lines, Upavon, Pewsey, Wilts SN9 6BQ. *T:* (01980) 615803, *Fax:* (01980) 615800; *e-mail:* armychaplains@armymail.co.uk.

ROBBINS, Stephen Dennis; His Honour Judge Robbins; a Circuit Judge, since 1994; *b* 11 Jan. 1948; *s* of late Lt-Col Dennis Robbins, OBE, TD and Joan Robbins (*née* Mason); *m* 1974, Amanda Smith, JP; three *d*. *Educ:* Orwell Park; Marlborough; Coll. d'Europe, Bruges (Churchill Award). Infantry, HAC, 1966–69. Called to the Bar, Gray's Inn, 1969; practised SE Circuit, 1972–94; Asst Recorder, 1983–87; Recorder, 1987–94. Former Mem., Overseas Cttee, Bar Council; Hon. Sec., London Common Law Bar Cttee; Hon. Legal Advr, Katharine Lowe Centre, Battersea, 1974–79. Pres., Mental Health Rev. Tribunals, 1994–. Mem., Parole Bd, 2001–. *Recreations:* collecting ephemera, shooting, swimming, walking, music. *Address:* Hillcrest Farm, Sevington, near Ashford, Kent TN24 0LJ. *T:* (01233) 502732; 1/2 The Studios, 17/19 Edge Street, Kensington Church Street, W8 7PN. *T:* (020) 7727 7216.

ROBBINS, Prof. Trevor William, PhD; FBPsS, FMedSci; FRS 2005; Professor of Experimental Psychology and Head of Department of Experimental Psychology, University of Cambridge, since 2002 (Professor of Cognitive Neuroscience, 1997–2002); Fellow, Downing College, Cambridge, since 1990; *b* 26 Nov. 1949; *s* of William Walter Robbins and Eileen Hilda Robbins; *m* 1979, Barbara Jacquelyn Sahakian; two *d*. *Educ:* Battersea GS; Jesus Coll., Cambridge (Schol.; BA 1st cl. Hons; MA; PhD). FBPsS 1990. Univ. Demonstrator, 1973–78, Univ. Lectr, 1978–92, Reader in Cognitive Neuroscience, 1992–97, Dept. of Exptl Psychology, Univ. of Cambridge. Chm. and Council Mem., Neuroscience Bd, MRC, 1995–99 (Mem., 1989–93); Council Mem., European Neuroscience Assoc., 1996–98; President: European Behavioural Pharmacology Soc., 1992–94; British Assoc. for Psychopharmacology, 1996–98. Ed., Psychopharmacology, 1980–. Fred Kavli Dist. Internat. Scientist Lectr, Soc. for Neurosci., 2005. Foreign Mem., American Coll. of Neuropsychopharmacology, 1994–. FMedSci 1999. Spearman Medal, BPsS, 1982; D. G. Marquis Award, Amer. Psychol Assoc., 1997; Dist. Scientist Award, European Behavioural Pharmacol. Soc., 2001; Medal, Coll. de France, 2004; Prize for Neuronal Plasticity, Fondn Ipsen, 2005. *Publications:* (ed jtly) Psychology for Medicine, 1988; (ed) Seminars in the Neurosciences: milestones in dopamine research, 1992; (ed jtly) The Prefrontal Cortex, 1998; Disorders of Brain and Mind 2, 2003; (ed jtly) Drugs and the Future, 2007; more than 500 articles in learned books and jls. *Recreations:* chess, cricket, cinema. *Address:* Department of Experimental Psychology, University of Cambridge, Downing Street, Cambridge CB2 3EB. *T:* (01223) 333551, *Fax:* (01223) 333564; *e-mail:* twr2@cam.ac.uk.

ROBBS, John Edward; Director, Wildlife and Countryside, Department for Environment, Food and Rural Affairs, since 2006; *b* 26 June 1955; *s* of Eric and Christine Robbs; *m* 1989, Jacqueline Tozer; two *s*. *Educ:* King Edward VII Sch., King's Lynn; Queens' Coll., Cambridge (MA); London Sch. of Econs (MSc Econ). Joined Ministry of Agriculture, Fisheries and Food, 1977: Private Sec. to Perm. Sec., 1981–82; Private Sec. to Minister, 1982–83; on secondment to UK Perm. Repn to EU, Brussels, 1985–89; Head: of Envmt Task Force Div., 1991–94; of Conservation Policy Div., 1994–95; of Fisheries (Common Fisheries Policy) Div., 1995–99; of EU Internat. Div., 1999–2000; of Food Industry, Competitiveness and Flood Defence Gp, 2000–01; Dir, Food Industry and Crops, DEFRA, 2001–06. *Recreations:* family, friends, gardening. *Address:* Department for Environment, Food and Rural Affairs, Nobel House, Smith Square, SW1P 3JR.

ROBERG, Rabbi Meir; Inspector of schools, UK, since 1997; Dean, Midrasha Institute, Lauder Foundation, Berlin (formerly at Frankfurt), since 2005; *b* 25 June 1937; *s* of late Julius and Hannchen Roberg; *m* 1961, Mirjam Nager; three *s* two *d*. *Educ:* Manchester Grammar Sch. (Gratrix Scholar); Talmudical Coll., Israel (Rabbinical Diploma); Univ. of London (BA 1st Cl. Hons 1960; DipEd 1970; MPhil 1972). Asst Teacher, 1960–62, Dep. Head, 1962–65, Yavneh Grammar Sch., London; Hasmonean High School: Asst Teacher and Head of Classics, 1965–71; Dep. Head, 1971–80; Headmaster, 1980–93; Principal of Jewish Day Schs and Dean of Talmudical Coll., Kiev, 1993–95; Hon. Consultant for Jewish schs and colls estbd in Ukraine following independence, 1995–2005. Lectr, Colls of Further Educn, 1962–93; Headmaster, Middx Regl Centre, 1965–73. Delegate, Internat. Religious Conf., Jerusalem, 1963 and 1980. Member: Keren Hatorah; Hendon Adass; Massoret Inst. (Chm., 1980–95); Assoc. of Headteachers of Jewish Day Schs (Pres., 1991–93; Life Pres., 1993–). *Publications:* (contrib.) Responsa Literature, 1996, 1998, 2000; reviews for Comparative Education, Jewish Tribune, and Parent-Teacher Monthly (NY). *Recreations:* Talmudic research, hiking. *Address:* 19 Sorotzkin Street, Jerusalem, Israel.

ROBERTS, family name of **Barons Clwyd**, **Roberts of Conwy** and **Roberts of Llandudno**.

ROBERTS OF CONWY, Baron *cr* 1997 (Life Peer), of Talyfan in the co. of Gwynedd; **Ieuan Wyn Pritchard Roberts,** Kt 1990; PC 1991; *b* 10 July 1930; *s* of late Rev. E. P. Roberts and Margaret Ann Roberts; *m* 1956, Enid Grace Williams; two *s* (and one *s* decd). *Educ:* Harrow; University Coll., Oxford. Sub-editor, Liverpool Daily Post, 1952–54; News Asst, BBC, 1954–57; TWW Ltd: News, Special Events and Welsh Language Programmes Producer, 1957–59; Production Controller, 1959–60; Exec. Producer, 1960–68; Welsh Controller, 1964–68; Programme Exec., Harlech TV, 1969. MP (C) Conway, 1970–83, Conwy, 1983–97. PPS to Sec. of State for Wales, 1970–74; opposition front bench spokesman on Welsh Affairs, 1974–79; Parly Under-Sec. of State, 1979–87, Minister of State, 1987–94, Welsh Office. Opposition front bench spokesman on Welsh Affairs, H of L, 1997–2007. Vice-Pres., Assoc. of District Councils, 1975–79. Mem. of Gorsedd, Royal National Eisteddfod of Wales, 1966. Member, Court of Governors: Nat. Library of Wales, 1970–91; Nat. Museum of Wales, 1970–91; University Coll. of Wales, Aberystwyth, 1970–91. Pres., Univ. of Wales Coll. of Medicine, 1997–2004; Vice Pres., Univ. of Cardiff, 2005–07. Hon. Fellow: Univ. of Wales, Bangor, 1995, Aberystwyth, 1997. Hon. LLD Wales, 2005. *Recreation:* gardening. *Address:* Tan y Gwalia, Conwy, Gwynedd LL32 8TY. *T:* (01492) 650371.

ROBERTS OF LLANDUDNO, Baron *cr* 2004 (Life Peer), of Llandudno in the County of Gwynedd; **Rev. John Roger Roberts;** Superintendent Methodist Minister, since 1965; *b* 23 Oct. 1935; s of Thomas Charles and Alice Ellen Roberts; *m* 1962, Eirlys Ann (*d* 1995); one *s* two *d*. *Educ:* John Bright Grammar Sch., Llandudno; Univ. of Wales, Bangor (BA Hons); Handsworth Methodist Coll., Birmingham. Methodist Minister,

1958–. President: Welsh Liberal Party, 1981–84; Welsh Lib Dems, 1990–96. Contested Conwy: (L) 1979; (L/Alliance) 1983, 1987; (Lib Dem) 1992, 1997. *Recreations:* travel, walking, music. *Address:* 22 Garth Court, Abbey Road, Llandudno, Conwy LL30 2HF. *T:* (01492) 876690; House of Lords, SW1A 0PW; *e-mail:* jrogerroberts@aol.com.

ROBERTS, Sir Adam; *see* Roberts, Sir E. A.

ROBERTS, Prof. Alan Clive, OBE 2001 (MBE 1982); TD 1969; PhD; JP; DL; Professor of Biomaterials in Surgery, University of Hull, since 1994; Consultant, Nuffield Hospital, Leeds, since 2002; *b* 28 April 1934; *s* of Major William Roberts, MBE and Kathleen Roberts; *m* 1956, Margaret Mary Shaw; two *s*. *Educ:* Gregg Sch., Newcastle upon Tyne; MPhil CNAA 1975; PhD Bradford Univ. 1988. CBiol 1971; FIBiol 1987; CIMechE 1995. Nat. Service, 1950–54. Scientific Officer, Royal Victoria Infirmary, Newcastle, 1954–56; Sen. Scientific Officer, Leeds Hosps, 1956–60; Prin. Clin. Scientist, Dept of Plastic Surgery, 1960–67, Consultant Clin. Scientist, 1990–, St Luke's Hosp., Bradford; Vis. Sen. Res. Fellow, Biomedical Scis, 1961–, Dir, Biomaterials Res. Unit, 1990–, Jt Dir, Inst. of Health Res., 1993–2003, Hon. Prof., 2000, Univ. of Bradford; Dir of R&D, Bradford Hosps NHS Trust, 1992–2003. Council of Europe Res. Fellow, Sweden, 1968. ADC to the Queen, 1980–83. Mem. Council, RSocMed, 2000– (Hon. Sub Dean, N Yorks, 2001–04; Treas., 2004–07; Vice Pres., 2007–); President: British Inst. of Surgical Tech., 1998– (Vice-Pres., 1996–98); Bradford Medico-Chirurgical Soc., 1995; Chm., Bradford Res. Ethics Cttee, 2003–; Partner, Health Professions Council, 2004–; Clin. Dir, Prosthetic Solutions, Univ. of Bradford, 2005. Mem., NY Acad. of Scis, 1987. Chm., COMEC, 1990–96; Chm., Court and Council, 1986–, Pro-Chancellor, 1986–2000, Dir, Westwood Hall, 1987–, Chm., Mil. Educn Cttee, 1996–, Univ. of Leeds; Dir, Univ. of Leeds Foundn, 1986–2000; Examiner, Sch. of Clin. Dentistry, Univ. of Sheffield, 1995–; Mem., Adv. Bd, Inst. of Cancer Therapeutics, Univ. of Bradford. Trustee: Edward Boyle Trust, 1986–97; Yorks Sculpture Park, 1995–; Isherwood Trust, 2004–. Mem. Council, BRCS, 1995 (Pres., W Yorks, 1983–2004; Badge of Honour, 1992); President: Leeds RBL; W Yorks SSAFA, 2000– (Chm., 1985–99); Leeds NSPCC, 2002–; Chm., W Riding Artillery Trust, 1983–; Trustee, ARNI Trust, 2007–. Col and Dep. Comdr, NE Dist TA, 1980–83; Hon. Col, 269 Batt., RA, 1983–; Col Comdt, RA, 1996–; Regtl Col, Leeds Univ. OTC, 2000–; Mem., HAC, 2000–. Patron, Age Concern, 1994–. Governor: Pocklington Sch., 1990–2001; Gateways Sch., Leeds, 2000–06. Hon. Freeman and Liveryman, Clothworkers' Co., 2000–. JP Leeds, 1977; DL W Yorks, 1982. CGIA, 1969, 1976, FCGI 1990 (Pres., City and Guilds Assoc., 1998–2003); FRSocMed 1993; FLS 1998. Hon. LLD Leeds, 2000; Hon. DSc: London, 2005; Bradford, 2007; Hon. DTech Brunel, 2007. Prince Philip Medal for Science, C&G, 1970. Lead researcher and inventor of: Indermil Tissue Adhesive, 1993; Zeflosil Prosthetic Adhesive, 2007. CStJ 2002 (Chm. Council, S & W Yorks, 2004–). Companion, Order of the League of Mercy, 2002. *Publications:* Obturators and Prosthesis for Cleft Palate, 1968; Facial Restoration by Prosthetic Means, 1975; Maxillo-Facial Prosthetics: a multi-disciplinary practice, 1975; numerous articles in med. and dental jls. *Recreations:* sculpture, silversmithing, avoiding holidays. *Address:* The Grange, Rein Road, Morley, Leeds, W Yorks LS27 0HZ. *T:* (0113) 253 4632. *Club:* Army and Navy.

ROBERTS, Alfred, PhD; Chief Executive, Institution of Engineering and Technology (formerly Institution of Electrical Engineers), 1999–2007; *b* 24 June 1945; *s* of Oswald and Ellen Roberts; *m* 1978, Elizabeth Ann King; one *s* one *d*. *Educ:* University Coll. London (BSc 1st cl. Hons 1967); Univ. of Manchester (PhD 1970). Central Electricity Generating Board: Res. Officer, 1971–73; Section Manager, Applied Physics, 1973–75; Div. Head, Engrg Sci., 1975–81; Regl Financial Controller, 1981–85; Gp Financial Controller, 1985–88; Dir, Engrg Services, 1988–89; Commercial Dir, PowerGen plc, 1989–98. *Publications:* articles in Nuclear Physics; conf. proceedings on nucleon transfer reactions; conf. papers on privatisation and deregulation of the electricity industry. *Recreations:* science, technology, history, music, literature, football.

ROBERTS, Allan Deverell; Counsel to the Chairman of Committees, House of Lords, since 2002; *b* 14 July 1950; *s* of Irfon Roberts and Patricia Mary (*née* Allan); *m* 1991, Irene Anne Graham Reilly; two *s* (and one *s* decd). *Educ:* Eton Coll. (King's Schol.); Magdalen Coll., Oxford (MA). Solicitor in private practice, 1974–76; Solicitor's Office, DHSS, 1976–96, Under-Sec. (Legal), 1989–96; Dir, Legal (Envmt, Planning and Countryside), DoE, 1996–97; Dir, Legal (Envmt, Housing and Local Govt), DETR, 1997–99; Dir, Legal (Legislation Unit), DETR, subseq. DTLR, 1999–2002. *Recreations:* tegestology, football, gardening. *Address:* House of Lords, SW1A 0PW.

ROBERTS, Alwyn; Pro Vice Chancellor, University of Wales, Bangor, 1994–97; *b* 26 Aug. 1933; *s* of late Rev. Howell Roberts and Buddug Roberts; *m* 1960, Mair Rowlands Williams; one *s*. *Educ:* Penygroes Grammar Sch.; Univ. of Wales, Aberystwyth and Bangor (BA, LLB); Univ. of Cambridge (MA). Tutor, Westminster Coll., Cambridge, 1959; Principal, Pachhunga Meml Govt Coll., Aijal, Assam, India, 1960–67; Lectr in Social Admin, University Coll., Swansea, 1967–70; University College of North Wales, later University of Wales, Bangor: Lectr, subseq. Sen. Lectr, Dept of Social Theory and Instns, 1970–79; Dir of Extra Mural Studies, 1979–95; Vice Principal, 1985–94. BBC National Governor for Wales, 1979–86; Chm., Broadcasting Council for Wales, 1979–86 (Mem., 1974–78); Member: Welsh Fourth TV Channel Auth., 1981–86; Gwynedd CC, 1973–81 (Chm., Social Services Cttee, 1977–81); Gwynedd AHA, 1973–80; Royal Commn on Legal Services, 1976–79; Parole Bd, 1987–90. Pres., Royal National Eisteddfod of Wales, 1994–96 (Vice-Chm., 1987–89; Chm., 1989–92; Mem. Council, 1979–); Chm., Acen (Cyf.), 1989–; Vice Chm., Arts Council of Wales, 1994–2000; Mem. Bd, Cwmni Theatr Cymru, 1982–86. Fellow, Nat. Eisteddfod of Wales, 2005. Hon. Fellow, Univ. of Wales, Aberystwyth, 1999. Hon. LLD Wales, 2000. *Address:* Brithdir, 43 Talycae, Tregarth, Bangor, Gwynedd LL57 4AE. *T:* (01248) 600007.

ROBERTS, Andrew, FRSL; writer; *b* 13 Jan. 1963; *s* of Simon and Katie Roberts; *m* 1st, 1995, Camilla Henderson (marr. diss. 2001); one *s* one *d*; 2nd, 2007, Susan Gilchrist. *Educ:* Cranleigh Sch.; Gonville and Caius Coll., Cambridge (exhibnr, Hon. Sen. Schol.; BA 1st Cl. Hons Hist.; MA; Chm., CU Cons. Assoc., 1984; Mem., Ct of Benefactors, 2002–06). Corporate broker, Robert Fleming Securities Ltd, 1985–88; freelance journalist, broadcaster and book reviewer, 1988–. Trustee: Roberts Foundn, 1989–; Margaret Thatcher Archive Trust, 2005–; Mem. Exec. Cttee, Friends of Lambeth Palace Library, 2003–. Member, Council: Bruges Gp, 2003–; Freedom Assoc., 2003–; British Weights and Measures Assoc., 2003–; Centre for Policy Studies, 2003–; Centre for Social Cohesion, 2007–; Global Vision, 2008–. Chm., Cons. Party Adv. Panel on Sch. History Teaching, 2005. Judge, Elizabeth Longford Historical Biography Prize, 2003, 2005–. Hon. Member: Guild of Battlefield Guides, 2006; Internat. Churchill Soc. (UK), 2007. FRSL 2001; FRSA 2004. Hon. DHL Westminster Coll., Fulton, Mo, 2000. *Publications:* The Holy Fox: a life of Lord Halifax, 1991; Eminent Churchillians, 1994; The Aachen Memorandum, 1995; Salisbury: Victorian Titan, 1999 (James Stern Silver Pen Award, Wolfson Award for Hist., 2000); The House of Windsor, 2000; Napoleon and Wellington, 2001; Hitler and Churchill: secrets of leadership, 2003; (ed) What Might Have Been, 2004; Waterloo: Napoleon's Last Gamble, 2005; (ed) The Correspondence Between Mr Disraeli and Mrs Brydges Willyams, 2006; A History of the English-Speaking Peoples since 1900, 2006 (Intercollegiate Studies Inst. Book Award, 2007); (ed) A Genius for War, 2008; Masters and Commanders, 2008. *Address:* 22 South Eaton Place, SW1W 9JA. *T:* (020) 7730 3091; *e-mail:* andrew@roberts-london.com. *Clubs:* Beefsteak, Brooks's, Garrick, Pilgrims, Walbrook (Hon. Mem.); University Pitt (Cambridge); Other Other (Wisconsin); St Louis Racquet (Hon. Mem.) (Missouri); Chaos (Hon. Mem.) (New York).

ROBERTS, Air Vice-Marshal Andrew Lyle, CB 1992; CBE 1983; AFC 1969; FRAeS; defence consultant; Chairman of Public Inquiries, Lord Chancellor's Panel of Independent Inspectors, since 1994; *b* 19 May 1938; *s* of Ronald and Norah Roberts; *m* 1962; three *d*. *Educ:* Cranbrook Sch.; RAF Coll., Cranwell. Commnd RAF, 1958; ADC to AOC No 18 Gp, 1965–66; Flight Comdr, 201 Sqdn, 1967–68 (AFC); RNSC, 1969; Personal Air Sec. to Parly Under-Sec. of State (RAF), MoD, 1970–71; i/c 236 Operational Conversion Unit, 1972–74; US Armed Forces Staff Coll., 1974; staff, SACLANT, 1975–77; i/c RAF Kinloss, 1977–79; Gp Capt. Ops, HQ Strike Command, 1980–82 (CBE); RCDS, 1983; Dir, Air Plans, MoD, 1984–86; C of S, HQ No 18 Gp, 1987–89; ACDS (Concepts), 1987–92; Hd of RAF Manpower Structure Study Team, 1992–94. Vice-Pres., Coastal Comd and Maritime Air Assoc., 2002– (founding Chm., 1995–2002). Trustee, Gwennili Trust (sailing for the disabled), 1995–. Organist, St Paul's Cathedral, Valletta, 1961. *Recreations:* cross-country and hill walking, natural history, classical music, church organ, choral singing, off-shore sailing. *Address:* c/o HSBC, 61 High Street, Staines, Middx TW18 4QW. *Club:* Royal Air Force.

ROBERTS, Angus Thomas; Director of Litigation and Prosecution, Post Office Solicitor's Office (formerly Principal Assistant Solicitor to General Post Office), 1965–74; *b* 28 March 1913; *s* of late Edward Roberts and late Margaret (*née* Murray); *m* 1940, Frances Monica, *d* of late Frederick and late Agnes Bertha Cane; two *s*. *Educ:* Felsted School. Admitted Solicitor, 1936. Entered Post Office Solicitor's Dept, 1939. Served in Royal Navy, 1941–46 (Lieut, RNVR). Asst Solicitor to GPO, 1951. *Recreations:* golf, fishing, gardening. *Address:* 8 Watermill Court, Bath Road, Woolhampton, Berks RG7 5RD. *T:* (0118) 971 3075.

ROBERTS, Ann; *see* Clwyd, Ann.

ROBERTS, (Anthony) John, CBE 1991; Board Member, since 2004, and Deputy Chairman, since 2005, British Educational Communications and Technology Agency; Board Member, 1985–2002, and Chief Executive, 1995–2002, Royal Mail Group (formerly The Post Office, then Consignia plc); Chairman, Post Office Ltd (formerly Post Office Counters Ltd), 1993–2002; *b* 26 Aug. 1944; *s* of Douglas and Margaret Roberts; *m* 1970, Diana June (*née* Lamdin); two *s*. *Educ:* Hampton Sch.; Exeter Univ. (BA Hons). Open Entrant, Administrative Class Civil Service, The Post Office, 1967; PA to Dep. Chairman and Chief Executive, 1969–71; Principal, Long Range Planning, 1971–74; Controller Personnel and Finance, North Western Postal Board, 1974–76; Principal Private Sec. to Chairman, 1976–77; Director, Chairman's Office, 1977–80; Secretary Designate, 1980–81, Sec., 1981–82; Dir, 1981–85, Man. Dir, 1985–93, Counter Services, subseq. Post Office Counters Ltd; Man. Dir, Gp Services, 1993–95; Chm., Subscription Services, 1993–95. Advr, Deloitte Consulting, 2003–05. Chm., South Thames TEC, 1989–92; Director: Internat. Posts Corp., 1996–2003; OFSTED, 2007–; Member: Govt New Deal Task Force, 1997–2003; CBI Educn and Trng Affairs Cttee, 1998–2003; Home Office Strategic Delivery Bd, 2003–05. Royal Mail Stamp Adv. Cttee, 2003–. Mem. Council, Inst. of Employment Studies, 1995–2003 (Pres., 1998–2003); Governor: Henley Mgt Coll., 1996–2006; Europ. Foundn for Quality Management, 1996–2001 (Pres., 1998–2001). FRSA 1992. Freeman, City of London, 1983. *Recreations:* golf, gardening, music. *Club:* Betchworth Park Golf.

ROBERTS, Barbara Haig; *see* MacGibbon, B. H.

ROBERTS, Prof. Benjamin Charles; Professor of Industrial Relations, London School of Economics, University of London, 1962–84, now Emeritus; *b* 1 Aug. 1917; *s* of Walter Whitfield Roberts and Mabel Frances Roberts; *m* 1945, Veronica Lilian (*d* 2001), *d* of George Frederick and Vera Lilian Vine-Lott; two *s*. *Educ:* London Sch. of Economics (Hon. Fellow, 1988); New Coll., Oxford (MA). Research Student, Nuffield Coll., Oxford, 1948–49; Part-time Lectr, Ruskin Coll., Oxford, 1948–49; London Sch. of Economics: Lectr in Trade Union Studies, 1949–56; Reader in Industrial Relations, 1956–62; Mem. Ct of Govs, 1964–69, 1979–83. Vis. Prof: Princeton Univ., 1958; MIT 1959; Univ. of Calif., Berkeley, 1965. Assoc., Internat. Inst. of Labour Studies, Geneva, 1966; Member: Council, Inst. Manpower Studies; British-N American Cttee; Nat. Reference Tribunal of Coal Mining Industry, 1970–93; Council, ACAS, 1979–86; Bruges Gp, 1990–. Editor, British Jl of Industrial Relations, 1963–89, Hon. Editor, 1990–. Pres., British Univs Industrial Relations Assoc., 1965–68; Pres., Internat. Industrial Relations Assoc., 1967–73. Consultant to EEC, 1976–79. Chm., Economists' Bookshop, 1979–87. Wincott Lecture, IEA, 1987. *Publications:* Trade Unions in the New Era, 1947; Trade Union Government and Administration in Great Britain, 1956; National Wages Policy in War and Peace, 1958; The Trades Union Congress, 1868–1921, 1958; Trade Unions in a Free Society, 1959; (ed) Industrial Relations: Contemporary Problems and Perspectives, 1962; Labour in the Tropical Territories of the Commonwealth, 1964; (ed) Manpower Planning and Employment Trends 1966; (with L. Greyfié de Bellecombe) Collective Bargaining in African Countries, 1967; (ed) Industrial Relations: Contemporary Issues, 1968; (with John Lovell) A Short History of the TUC, 1968; (with R. O. Clarke and D. J. Fatchet) Workers' Participation in Management in Britain, 1972; (with R. Loveridge and J. Gennard) Reluctant Militants: a study of industrial technicians, 1972; (with H. Okomoto and G. Lodge) Collective Bargaining and Employee Participation in Western Europe, North America and Japan, 1979; also Evidence to Royal Commn on Trade Unions, 1966, and Report to ILO on Labour and Automation: Manpower Adjustment Programmes in the United Kingdom, 1967; Industrial Relations in Europe: the imperatives of change, 1985; (with T. Kochan and N. Meltz) New Departures in Industrial Relations: developments in USA, the UK and Canada, 1988; Europe—Uniformity or Freedom?: the real EC questions, 1991. *Address:* 28 Temple Fortune Lane, NW11 7UD. *T:* (020) 8458 1421. *Clubs:* Reform, Political Economy.

ROBERTS, Bernard, FRCM; concert pianist; Piano Professor, Royal College of Music, 1962–99; *b* 23 July 1933; *s* of William Wright Roberts and Elsie Alberta Roberts (*née* Ingham); *m* 1st, 1955, Patricia May Russell (marr. diss. 1988); two *s*; 2nd, 1992, Caroline Ireland. *Educ:* William Hulme's Grammar Sch., Manchester; Royal Coll. of Music (ARCM 1951; FRCM 1982). Début as concert pianist, Wigmore Hall, 1957; recital, concerto and chamber music pianist, 1957–; has appeared with major British orchestras as soloist, incl. Promenade Concerts, 1979; recitals in UK and abroad, incl. master classes in major centres; has broadcast on BBC Radio 3. Member: Parikian-Fleming-Roberts Trio, 1975–84; Piano Trio with sons, 1991–2004. Piano Tutor, Chetham's Sch. of Music, Manchester, 2000–. FRWCMD 2004. DUniv Brunel, 1989. *Recreations:* philosophy, religion, model railways. *Address:* Uwchlaw'r Coed, Llanbedr, Gwynedd LL45 2NA. *T:* (01341) 241532; *e-mail:* caroline.ireland@virgin.net.

ROBERTS, Brian Stanley; HM Diplomatic Service, retired; educational consultant; *b* 1 Feb. 1936; *s* of Stanley Victor Roberts and Flora May (*née* McInnes); *m* 1st, 1961, Phyllis Hazel Barber (marr. diss. 1976); two *s*; 2nd, 1985, Jane Catharine Chisholm; one *d. Educ:* Liverpool Collegiate Sch., Christ's Coll., Cambridge (MA); Courtauld Institute, London (MA). Served Royal Navy, 1955–57. Staff, Edinburgh Univ., 1960–62; Lecturer in Art History, Goldsmiths' Coll., London, 1962–69; entered FCO, 1970: First Secretary, Capetown/Pretoria, 1972; FCO, 1974; attached to Hong Kong Govt, 1977; FCO, 1980; Counsellor, Stockholm, 1983–87; Cabinet Office, 1987. Teacher, Art Hist., Cheltenham Ladies' Coll., 1988–89; Head of Art Hist., Putney High Sch., 1989–97. *Recreations:* walking, looking at pictures. *Clubs:* Oxford and Cambridge, Lansdowne.

ROBERTS, Dr Brynley Francis, CBE 1993; Librarian, National Library of Wales, 1985–94; Moderator, General Assembly of the Presbyterian Church of Wales, 2001–02; *b* 3 Feb. 1931; *s* of Robert F. Roberts and Laura Jane Roberts (*née* Williams); *m* 1957, Rhiannon Campbell; twin *s. Educ:* Grammar School, Aberdare; University College of Wales, Aberystwyth (BA Hons Welsh, MA, PhD). Fellow, Univ. of Wales, 1956–57; Lectr, Sen. Lectr, Reader, Dept of Welsh, University Coll. of Wales, Aberystwyth, 1957–78; Prof. of Welsh Language and Literature, University Coll. Swansea, 1978–85. Sir John Rhys Fellow, Jesus Coll., Oxford, 1973–74; Leverhulme Emeritus Fellow, 1997; Res. Associate, Dublin Inst. for Advanced Studies, 2000–. Chairman: United Theological Coll., Aberystwyth, 1977–98; Gwasg Pantycelyn, Caernarfon, 1977–98. Pres., Welsh Library Assoc., 1985–94; Chm., Welsh Books Council, 1989–94 (Vice-Chm., 1986–89); Mem., 1994–2008); Mem., HEFCW, 1993–2000. Editor: Dictionary of Welsh Biography, 1987–; Y Traethodydd, 1999–. Hon. Fellow, Univ. of Wales, Swansea, 1996, Aberystwyth, 2000; Hon. Prof., Cardiff, 2001. Hon. FCLIP (Hon. FLA 1994). Hon. DLitt Wales, 1996. Sir Ellis Griffith Prize, 1962, Vernam Hull Prize, 2005, Univ. of Wales; Medal, Hon. Soc. of Cymmrodorion, 2007. *Publications:* Gwassanaeth Meir, 1961; Brut y Brenhinedd, 1971, 2nd edn 1984; Cyfranc Lludd a Llefelys, 1975; Brut Tysilio, 1980; Edward Lhuyd: the making of a scientist, 1980; Gerald of Wales, 1982; Itinerary through Wales, 1989; Studies on Middle Welsh Literature, 1992; (ed) Y Bywgraffiadur Cymreig 1951–1970, 1997; (ed) Dictionary of Welsh Biography 1941–1970, 2001; Breudwyt Maxen Wledic, 2005; (with Dewi W. Evans) Edward Lhwyd, Archaeologia Britannica: texts and translations, 2008; articles in learned jls. *Recreations:* gardening, music. *Address:* Hengwrt, Llanbadarn Road, Aberystwyth SY23 1HB. *T:* (01970) 623577.

ROBERTS, Carl Bertrand Westerby; High Commissioner of Antigua and Barbuda to the Court of St James's, and concurrently Ambassador to France, Germany, Spain and Italy, since 2004; *b* St John's, Antigua and Barbuda, 13 Oct. 1948; *s* of late Arthur E. S. Roberts and of Audrey E. Roberts; *m* 1974, Pauline Margaret A.; two *s* one *d. Educ:* Antigua Grammar Sch.; Northeastern Univ., Boston (BSEE Hons *magna cum laude* 1982); Univ. of WI, Barbados (MBA 1995); Univ. of Bradford (DBA 2004). Joined Cable & Wireless (WI) Ltd, 1967; Gen. Manager, Montserrat, 1995–97; Chief Executive: Cable & Wireless Dominica, 1997–2002; Cable & Wireless St Kitts & Nevis, 2002–04. Perm. Rep., UNESCO, Paris, 2004–; Dep. Perm. Rep., WTO, Geneva, 2004–. *Recreations:* cricket, tennis, golf, reading, singing. *Address:* High Commission for Antigua and Barbuda, 2nd Floor, 45 Crawford Place, W1H 4LP; *e-mail:* carl.roberts@antigua-barbuda.com. *Club:* Rotary (London).

ROBERTS, Rear-Adm. Cedric Kenelm, CB 1970; DSO 1952; *b* 19 April 1918; *s* of F. A. Roberts; *m* 1940, Audrey, *d* of T. M. Elias; four *s. Educ:* King Edward's Sch., Birmingham. Joined RN as Naval Airman 2nd Cl., 1940; commnd Temp. Sub-Lt (A), RNVR, 1940; sunk in HMS Manchester, 1942, Malta Convoy; interned in Sahara; released, Nov. 1942; Personal Pilot to Vice-Adm. Sir Lumley Lyster, 1943; HMS Trumpeter, Russian Convoys, 1944; perm. commn as Lt RN, HMS Vindex, Pacific, 1945; CO 813 Sqdn, 1948; Naval Staff Coll., 1949; CO 767 Sqdn, 1950–51; CO 825 Sqdn, 1951–52: served Korean War; shot down, rescued by US Forces; lent to RAN as Dep. Dir, Air Warfare, 1953–55; CO, RNAS Eglinton, 1958–59; Chief Staff Officer: FONFT, 1959–61; FOAC, 1961–62; Capt., HMS Osprey, 1962–64; Capt., RNAS Culdrose, 1964–65; Chief Staff Officer (Ops), Far East Fleet, 1966–67; Flag Officer, Naval Flying Training, 1968–71; retired 1971; farmed in Somerset, 1971–79; emigrated to Australia, 1979. Comdr 1952; Capt. 1958; Rear-Adm. 1968. Arctic Emblem, 2006. *Recreations:* sitting in the sun, drinking plonk, and watching the sheilas go by. *Address:* 11 Collins Street, Merimbula, NSW 2548, Australia. *T:* (2) 64951754.

ROBERTS, Cedric P.; see Prys-Roberts.

ROBERTS, Christopher William, CB 1986; Deputy Secretary, 1983–97, and Director-General of Trade Policy, 1987–97, Department of Trade and Industry; Senior Trade Adviser, Covington and Burling, since 1998; *b* 4 Nov. 1937; *s* of Frank Roberts and Evelyn Dorothy Roberts. *Educ:* Rugby Sch.; Magdalen Coll., Oxford (MA). Lectr in Classics, Pembroke Coll., Oxford, 1959–60; Asst Principal, BoT, 1960; Second Sec. (Commercial), British High Commn, New Delhi, 1962–64; Asst Private Sec. to Pres. of BoT, 1964–65; Principal, 1965; Cabinet Office, 1966–68; Private Sec. to Prime Minister, 1970–73; Asst Sec., 1972; Dept of Trade, 1973–77; Under Secretary: Dept of Prices and Consumer Protection, 1977–79; Dept of Trade, 1979–82; Chief Exec., BOTB, 1983–87. Non-exec. Dir, NHBC, 1998–2004. Chairman: Wine Standards Bd, 1999–2006; Liberalisation of Trade in Services Cttee, Internat. Financial Services London, 2000–05; Policy Cttee, European Services Forum, 2002–08. *Recreations:* travel, cricket, opera. *Address:* Tall Timbers, High Drive, Woldingham, Surrey CR3 7ED. *Clubs:* Oxford and Cambridge, MCC.

ROBERTS, Colin, CVO 2006; HM Diplomatic Service; Director, Overseas Territories, Foreign and Commonwealth Office, since 2008; Commissioner of the British Indian Ocean Territory and of the British Antarctic Territory, since 2008; *b* 31 July 1959; *s* of John Jeffrey Roberts and Avril Joyce Roberts (*née* Dowding); *m* 2000, Camilla Frances Mary Blair; two *s. Educ:* Winchester Coll.; King's Coll., Cambridge (BA Eng. Lit., MA); Courtauld Inst. of Art (MPhil 1982). Lectr, Ritsumeikan Univ., Kyoto, 1983–84; called to the Bar, Inner Temple, 1986; in private legal practice, 1986–89; entered HM Diplomatic Service, 1989; Second Sec. (Econ.), later First Sec. (Pol), Tokyo, 1990–94; First Secretary: EU Dept (Internal), FCO, 1995–96; (Pol/Mil.), Paris, 1997–98; Hd, Common Foreign and Security Policy Dept, FCO, 1998–2000; Pol Counsellor, Tokyo, 2001–04; Ambassador to Lithuania, 2004–08. *Publications:* contrib. occasional articles on art history. *Recreations:* mountain sports, natural history, tennis, reading. *Address:* c/o Foreign and Commonwealth Office, King Charles Street, SW1A 2AH. *Club:* Travellers.

ROBERTS, Colin, MD; FRCP, FRCPath; Consultant Medical Microbiologist, and Medical and Scientific Postgraduate Dean, Public Health Laboratory Service, 1993–99; Hon. Consultant Microbiologist, Oxford Radcliffe Hospitals NHS Trust, since 2007 (locum consultant microbiologist, 2000–07); *b* 25 Jan. 1937; *s* of Theophilus and Daisy Roberts; *m* 1961, Marjorie Frances Conway; two *s. Educ:* Univ. of Liverpool (BSc 1960; MB ChB 1963; MD 1968); Univ. of Manchester (Dip. Bact. (Dist.) 1972). MRCPath 1973, FRCPath 1986; MRCP 1996, FRCP 1999; FRIPH (FRIPHH 1992); FFPH (FFPHM 1997); FFPath, RCPI 2000. House physician/surgeon, 1963–64; Registrar in

Pathology, 1964–66, Sefton Gen. Hosp., Liverpool; Hon. Sen. Registrar, United Liverpool Hosps, 1966–70, and Lectr in Pathology, 1966–69, in Med. Microbiol., 1969–70, Univ. of Liverpool; Asst Microbiologist (Sen. Registrar), Regl Public Health Lab., Fazakerley Hosp., Liverpool, 1970–73; Liverpool Public Health Laboratory: Sen. Microbiologist, 1973–75; Consultant Med. Microbiologist, 1975–87; Dep. Dir, 1977–87; Dep. Dir, PHLS, London, 1987–93. Vis. Prof., Envmtl Health Div., Univ. of Strathclyde, 1993–2002; Hon. Prof., LSHTM, 1997–2008 (Study Unit Tutor in Hosp. Infection, Distance Learning, 2004–08). Chm., Dip. HIC Examiners' Cttee, 2007–08). Sec., Assoc. of Acad. Clin. Bacteriologists and Virologists, 2000–07; Hon. Treas., 2003–06, Pres. elect, 2007–09, Pres., Sept. 2009–, Pathology Sect., RSocMed. Chm., Central Sterilising Club, 1992–96. Mem. Editl Bd, Jl Clin. Pathol., 1992–97; Asst Ed., Jl of Hosp. Infection, 2004–. Founder FMedSci 1998; Founder Mem., Acad. of Med. Educators, 2007. Hon. FRCPCH 1996; Hon. Fellow, Liverpool John Moores Univ., 2001. Hon. Dip. HIC 1999. *Publications:* contrib. chapters, papers and proceedings, including: (contrib.) Infectious and Communicable Diseases in England and Wales, 1990; (ed jtly) Quality Control: principles and practice in the microbiology laboratory, 1991, 2nd edn 1999; (jtly) A Supervisor's Handbook of Food Hygiene and Safety, 1995; contribs to academic jls. *Recreations:* theatre, music, art, literature, sport (represented Wales at schoolboy and youth level in soccer). *Address:* Microbiology Department, Level 6, John Radcliffe Hospital, Headington, Oxford OX3 9DU. *T:* (01865) 220886. *Club:* Royal Society of Medicine.

ROBERTS, David Francis, CMG 2003; consultant and commentator on agricultural trade policy; Deputy Director General responsible for agricultural trade issues, European Commission, 1996–2002; *b* 28 Aug. 1941; *s* of Arthur Roberts and Mary Roberts; *m* 1974, Astrid Suhr Henriksen; two *s* one *d. Educ:* Priory Grammar School, Shrewsbury; Worcester College, Oxford (MA). Joined MAFF, 1964; seconded to FCO as First Sec. (Agric.), Copenhagen, 1971–74; Principal Private Sec. to Minister of Agriculture, 1975–76; seconded to HM Treasury as Head of Agric. Div., 1979–80; Under Sec., 1985, seconded to FCO as Minister (Agric.), UK Repn to the European Communities, Brussels, 1985–90; Dep. Dir Gen., resp. for agricl support, DG VI, EC, 1990–96. *Recreations:* sailing, squash, rowing. *Address:* 68 Beaulieu Avenue, SE26 6PW.

ROBERTS, David George; HM Diplomatic Service; on secondment to 3i Group plc, since 2008; *b* 11 April 1955; *s* of David Ceredig Roberts and Margaret (*née* Burns), Dolgellau, Wales; *m* 1985, Rosmarie Rita Kunz, Winterthur, Switzerland; one *s* one *d. Educ:* Bishop Vesey's Grammar Sch., Sutton Coldfield; Pembroke Coll., Oxford (MA Hons Mod. Hist. 1976). Joined FCO, 1976: Desk Officer, E Germany and WEU, 1976–77; Third, later Second, Sec. (Chancery), Jakarta, 1977–81; Second Sec. (Chancery), Havana, 1981–83; Desk Officer for nuclear deterrence, strategic defence and test ban matters, Defence and Arms Control and Disarmament Depts, FCO, 1983–86; Section Head for N Africa, Near East and N Africa Dept, FCO, 1986–88; First Secretary: (Eur. and Econ. Affairs), Madrid, 1988–90; (EU and Financial Affairs), Paris, 1990–94; Deputy Head: Hong Kong Dept, FCO, 1994–96; of Mission, and Consul Gen., Santiago, 1996–2000; of Mission, Dir of Trade and Investment and Consul Gen., Switzerland and Liechtenstein, 2000–05; Hd, Global Business, subseq. Sustainable Develt and Business, Gp, FCO, 2005–08. *Recreations:* enjoying languages (Spanish, French, German, Indonesian), attempting to keep fit, reading, gardening, listening to classical music, eating and drinking. *Address:* c/o Foreign and Commonwealth Office, King Charles Street, SW1A 2AH.

ROBERTS, (David) Gwilym (Morris), CBE 1987; FREng; Chairman: Acer Group Ltd, 1987–92; Acer-ICF Ltd, 1990–92; *b* 24 July 1925; *er s* of late Edward and Edith Roberts of Crosby; *m* 1st, 1960, Rosemary Elizabeth Emily (*d* 1973), *d* of late J. E. Giles of Tavistock; one *s* one *d*; 2nd, 1978, Wendy Ann, *d* of late Dr J. K. Moore of Beckenham and Alfriston. *Educ:* Merchant Taylors' School, Crosby; Sidney Sussex College, Cambridge (Minor Scholar, MA; Hon. Fellow, 1993). FICE, FIMechE; FREng (FEng 1986). Engineering Officer, RNVR, 1945–47; Lieut Comdr RNR, retired 1961. Asst Engineer, 1947–55, Partner, 1956–90 (Sen. Partner, 1981–90), John Taylor & Sons; principally development of water and wastewater projects, UK towns and regions, and Abu Dhabi, Bahrain, Egypt, Iraq, Kuwait, Mauritius, Qatar, Saudi Arabia and Thailand. Director: Acer Gp Ltd, 1987–92; various transportation projects in UK and abroad. Vis. Prof., Loughborough Univ., 1991–95. Chairman: BGS Programme Bd, 1989–93; Football Stadia Adv. Design Council, 1990–93; 2nd Severn Crossing Technical Adjudication Panel, 1991–97; Member: UK Cttee, IAWPRC, 1967–83; Bd of Control, AMBRIC (American British Consultants), 1978–92; (Construction Industry) Group of Eight, 1983–85, 1987–88; President: IPHE, 1968–69 (IPHE Silver Medal 1974; Gold Medal 1987); ICE, 1986–87 (Vice-Pres., 1983–86; Overseas Premium, 1978; Halcrow Premium, 1985; George Stephenson Medal, 1986). Council Member: Brighton Polytechnic, 1983–86; NERC, 1987–93; CIRIA, 1988–92. Member: Exec. Cttee, British Egyptian Soc., 1991–93; Nat. Cttee, British-Arab Univ. Assoc., 1991–93. Governor: Chailey Sch., 1988–92; Roedean Sch., 1989–93. Freeman, City of London, 1977; Liveryman: Engineers' Co., 1985; Constructors' Co., 1990; Water Conservators' Co., 2000. Hon. FCIWEM. *Publications:* (co-author) Civil Engineering Procedure, 3rd edn 1979; Built By Oil, 1995; From Kendal's Coffee House to Great George Street, 1995; Chelsea to Cairo, 2006; papers to Royal Soc., Arab League, ICE, IPHE. *Recreations:* tennis, golf, family history. *Address:* Flitteridge, Fletching, Uckfield TN22 3TL. *T:* (01825) 713684. *Clubs:* St Stephen's, Oxford and Cambridge; Piltdown Golf.

ROBERTS, (David) Paul; Director (Strategy and Development), Improvement and Development Agency, since 2005 (Strategic Adviser (Education and Children's Services), 2004–05); *b* 6 Sept. 1947; *s* of Percival and Nancy Roberts; *m* 1969, Helen Margaret Shone; two *d. Educ:* Univ. of Bristol (BSc Hons 1969; CertEd 1970); Cambridge Inst. Educn (AdvDip 1982). Maths Teacher, then Dir of Studies, Ipswich Sch., 1970–74; Dep. Hd Teacher, Harlington Upper Sch., Beds, 1974–83; Chief Inspector, then Dep. Dir of Educn, Notts CC, 1983–97; Dir of Educn, Nottingham CC, 1997–2001. Dir, Guideline Careers Co. Ltd, 1997–2001; Dir, Capita Strategic Educn Services, and Dir of Educn, Haringey Council, 2001–04. Advr to DCMS and DCSF (formerly DfES) Ministers on Creativity in Schs, 2005–; Chm., Creative and Cultural Educn Bd, DCSF and DCMS, 2007–. Mem. Cttee, Fellowship Prog., 2004–06, Mem., Innovation Cttee, 2006–, NESTA. FRSA. *Publications:* articles in educnl and maths jls. *Recreations:* arts, hill-walking. *Address:* 55 Dunster Road, West Bridgford, Nottingham NG2 6JE. *T:* (0115) 923 1775.

ROBERTS, Denis Edwin, CBE 1974 (MBE (mil.) 1945); Managing Director, Posts, The Post Office, 1977–80; *b* 6 Jan. 1917; *s* of late Edwin and Alice G. Roberts; *m* 1940, Edith (*née* Whitehead) (*d* 2002); two *s. Educ:* Holgate Grammar Sch., Barnsley. Served War of 1939–45, Royal Signals, France, N Africa, Italy and Austria. Entered Post Office, Barnsley, 1933; various appts, 1933–71; Dir Postal Ops, 1971–75; Sen. Dir, Postal Services, 1975–77. Mem., Industrial Tribunal, 1982–86. Chm., British Philatelic Trust, 1981–85. Freeman, Gardeners' Co. *Address:* 302 Gilbert House, Barbican, EC2Y 8BD. *T:* (020) 7638 0881. *Club:* City of London.

ROBERTS, Dennis Laurie Harold; Director for Surveys and Administrative Services, Office for National Statistics, since 2008; *b* 24 Jan. 1949; *s* of William Roberts and Vera Roberts; *m* 1980, Anne Mary Hillhouse; one *s*. *Educ:* Sheffield Univ. (BA, MSc). CSO, 1971–76; DoE, 1976–83; MoD, 1983–85; Department of the Environment: Head: Local Govt Finance Div., 1985–89; Water Envmt Div., 1989–92; Finance Div., 1992–94; OPCS, 1994–96; Dir, Socio-Economic Stats and Analysis Gp, 1996–98, Dir, Corp. Services Gp, 1998–99, ONS; Dir, Roads and Traffic Directorate, DETR, 2000–01; Dir, Road Transport Directorate, DTLR, then DfT, 2001–03; Dir, Registration Services and Dep. Registrar General for England and Wales, ONS, 2004–08. *Recreations:* walking, reading, watching football. *Address:* Office for National Statistics, Government Buildings, Cardiff Road, Newport NP10 8XG. *T:* (01633) 455517.

ROBERTS, Sir Denys (Tudor Emil), KBE 1975 (CBE 1970; OBE 1960); *b* 19 Jan. 1923; *s* of William David and Dorothy Elizabeth Roberts; *m* 1st, 1949, Brenda Marsh (marr. diss. 1973); one *s* one *d*; 2nd, 1985, Anna Fiona Dollar Alexander; one *s*. *Educ:* Aldenham; Wadham Coll., Oxford, 1942 and 1946–49 (MA 1948, BCL 1949; Hon. Fellow, 1984). Served with Royal Artillery, 1943–46, France, Belgium, Holland, Germany, India (Captain). English Bar, 1950–53; Crown Counsel, Nyasaland, 1953–59; QC Gibraltar 1960; QC Hong Kong 1964; Attorney-General, Gibraltar, 1960–62; Solicitor-General, Hong Kong, 1962–66; Attorney-General, Hong Kong, 1966–73; Chief Secretary, Hong Kong, 1973–78; Chief Justice, Hong Kong, 1979–88; Pres., Court of Appeal, Bermuda, 1988–94; Chief Justice, 1979–2001, Pres., Ct of Appeal, 2002–03, Negara Brunei Darussalam. Hon. Bencher, Lincoln's Inn, 1978. SPMB (Negara Brunei Darussalam), 1984. *Publications:* Smuggler's Circuit, 1954; Beds and Roses, 1956; The Elwood Wager, 1958; The Bones of the Wajingas, 1960; How to Dispense with Lawyers, 1964; Doing them Justice, 1986; I'll Do Better Next Time, 1995; Yes Sir But, 2000; Another Disaster, 2006. *Recreations:* cricket, walking, writing. *Address:* The Grange, North Green Road, Pulham St Mary, Norfolk IP21 4QZ. *Clubs:* MCC (Pres., 1989–90), Royal Commonwealth Society.

ROBERTS, Derek Franklyn, FCII, FCIB; Chairman, Yorkshire Building Society, 1997–2001; *b* 16 Oct. 1942; *s* of Frank Roberts, MBE, and May Evelyn Roberts; *m* 1969, Jacqueline (*née* Velho); two *s* one *d*. *Educ:* Park High Grammar Sch., Birkenhead; Liverpool Coll. of Commerce; Harvard Business Sch. (AMP (Grad.)). Royal Insurance Co. Ltd, 1961–72; Huddersfield Building Society: Insce Services Man., 1972; apptd to Executive, as Business Develt Man., 1975; Develt Man., 1979; on formation of Yorkshire Building Soc., 1982, apptd Asst Gen. Man. (Marketing); Dir and Chief Exec., 1987–96. Director: BWD Securities plc, 1988–92; Yorkshire Water Services (formerly Yorkshire Water), 1996–2005; Kelda Gp plc, 1999–2005. Dir, Bradford City Challenge Ltd, 1993–97; Mem., W Yorks Rural Develt Cttee, 1992–96. CCMI. *Recreations:* golf, gardening, ski-ing, keeping friendships in constant repair. *Address:* The Ark, 20 Arkenley Lane, Almondbury, Huddersfield HD4 6SQ. *T:* (01484) 426414. *Clubs:* Huddersfield Golf, Royal Liverpool Golf, Woodsome Hall Golf; Huddersfield Rugby Union FC.

ROBERTS, Sir Derek (Harry), Kt 1995; CBE 1983; FRS 1980; FREng, FInstP; Provost of University College London, 1989–99 and 2002–03; *b* 28 March 1932; *s* of Harry and Alice Roberts; *m* 1958, Winifred (*née* Short); one *s* one *d*. *Educ:* Manchester Central High Sch.; Manchester Univ. (BSc). Joined Plessey Co.'s Caswell Res. Lab., 1953; Gen. Man., Plessey Semiconductors, 1967; Dir, Allen Clark Res. Centre, 1969; Man. Dir, Plessey Microelectronics Div., 1973; Technical Dir, 1983–85, Jt Dep. Man. Dir (Technical), 1985–88, GEC. Pres., BAAS, 1996–97. Hon. DSc: Bath, 1982; Loughborough, 1984; City, 1985; Lancaster, 1986; Manchester, 1987; Salford, Essex, London, 1988; DUniv Open, 1984. *Publications:* about 20 pubns in scientific and technical jls. *Recreations:* reading, gardening. *Address:* University College London, Gower Street, WC1E 6BT. *T:* (020) 7679 7234.

ROBERTS, Sir (Edward) Adam, KCMG 2002; FBA 1990; Montague Burton Professor of International Relations, 1986–2007, Senior Research Fellow, Department of Politics and International Relations, since 2008, Oxford University; Fellow of Balliol College, Oxford, 1986–2007, now Emeritus; President, British Academy, from July 2009; *b* 29 Aug. 1940; *s* of late Michael Roberts, poet and Janet Roberts, OBE, writer (as Janet Adam Smith); *m* 1966, Frances P. Dunn; one *s* one *d*. *Educ:* Westminster School; Magdalen College, Oxford (BA 1962, MA 1981). Asst Editor, Peace News Ltd, 1962–65; Noel Buxton Student in Internat. Relations, LSE, 1965–68; Lectr in Internat. Relations, LSE, 1968–81; Alastair Buchan Reader in Internat. Relations, Oxford Univ., and Professorial Fellow, St Antony's Coll., Oxford, 1981–86; Leverhulme Res. Fellow, 2000–03. Member, Council: RIIA, 1985–91; IISS, 2002–08; Mem. Adv. Bd, UK Defence Acad., 2003–. Gov., Ditchley Foundn, 2001–. Hon. Fellow: LSE, 1997; St Antony's Coll., Oxford, 2006. *Publications:* (ed) The Strategy of Civilian Defence, 1967; (jtly) Czechoslovakia 1968, 1969; Nations in Arms, 1976, 2nd edn, 1986; (ed jtly) Documents on the Laws of War, 1982, 3rd edn 2000; (ed jtly) United Nations, Divided World, 1988, 2nd edn 1993; (ed jtly) Hugo Grotius and International Relations, 1990; Humanitarian Action in War, 1996; (ed jtly) The United Nations Security Council and War, 2008. *Recreations:* rock climbing, mountaineering. *Address:* Balliol College, Oxford OX1 3BJ. *T:* (01865) 277777. *Club:* Alpine.

ROBERTS, Eifion; *see* Roberts, H. E. P.

ROBERTS, Emyr Gordon, PhD; Director, Department for Social Justice and Local Government (formerly Department for Social Justice and Regeneration), Welsh Assembly Government, since 2005; *b* 6 Sept. 1958; *s* of Gordon and Awena Wyn Roberts; *m* 1999, Karen Turner; one *s* one *d*. *Educ:* Univ. of Reading (BA Hons 1979); Univ. of Wales, Aberystwyth (PhD 1989). NFU, 1982–91; Welsh Office: Principal, 1991–97; Hd, Financial Planning Div., 1997–2000; Hd, Econ. Planning Div., Nat. Assembly for Wales, 2001–03; Chief Exec., Welsh European Funding Office, 2003–05. *Address:* Welsh Assembly Government, Merthyr Tydfil Office, Rhydycar, Merthyr Tydfil CF48 1UZ. *T:* (01685) 729175, *Fax:* (01685) 729549; *e-mail:* emyr.roberts@wales.gsi.gov.uk.

ROBERTS, Prof. Geoffrey Frank Ingleson, CBE 1978; FREng; Chairman, British Pipe Coaters Ltd, 1978–88; Professor of Gas Engineering, University of Salford, 1983–89, Professorial Fellow, 1989–91; *b* 9 May 1926; *s* of late Arthur and Laura Roberts; *m* 1st, 1949, Veronica (*d* 1993), *d* of late Captain J. Busby, Hartlepool; two *d*; 2nd, 1995, Patricia, *widow* of Neville H. H. Johnson, Ilkley. *Educ:* Cathedral Sch., and High Sch. for Boys, Hereford; Leeds Univ. (BSc Hons). FIChemE; FInstE; FREng (FEng 1978). Pupil engr, Gas Light & Coke Co., and North Thames Gas Bd, 1947–50; North Thames Gas Board: Asst Engr, 1950–59; Stn Engr, Slough, 1959–61; Dept. Stn Engr, Southall Stn, 1961–66; Group Engr, Slough Group, 1966–68; Dep. Dir (Ops) Gas Council, 1968–71; Mem. for Production and Supply, Gas Council, later British Gas Corp., 1972–78; Mem. for External Affairs, British Gas Corp., 1979–81, retired. President: IGasE, 1980–81 (Hon. FIGEM 1983); Inst. of Energy, 1983–84. *Recreations:* woodwork, travel. *Address:* 2 Birchwood Court, South Parade, Ilkley, West Yorks LS29 9AW. *T:* (01943) 601671.

ROBERTS, George Arnott; Head of Administration Department, House of Commons, 1988–91; *b* 16 April 1930; *s* of David Roberts and Doris (*née* Sykes); *m* 1956, Georgina (*née* Gower); two *s* one *d*. *Educ:* Rastrick Grammar Sch.; London Univ. (extra-mural). Min. of Labour, then Dept of Employment, 1947–74; Advisory, Conciliation and Arbitration Service, 1974–85: Sec., Central Arbitration Cttee, 1978–80; Dir of Administration, 1980–83; Dir, London Region, 1983–85; House of Commons, 1985–91: Hd of Establishment Office, 1985–88. *Recreations:* golf, gardening. *Club:* Sonning Golf.

ROBERTS, Sir Gilbert (Howland Rookehurst), 7th Bt *cr* 1809; *b* 31 May 1934; *s* of Sir Thomas Langdon Howland Roberts, 6th Bt, CBE, and of Evelyn Margaret, *o d* of late H. Fielding-Hall; *S* father, 1979; *m* 1958, Ines, *o d* of late A. Labunski; one *s* one *d*. *Educ:* Rugby; Gonville and Caius Coll., Cambridge (BA 1957). CEng, MIMechE. *Heir: s* Howland Langdon Roberts, *b* 19 Aug. 1961. *Address:* 3340 Cliff Drive, Santa Barbara, CA 93109–1079, USA.

ROBERTS, Gillian Frances; Academic Registrar, University of London, 1983–2006; *b* 3 Nov. 1944; *d* of late Frank and Mabel Murray; *m* 1969, Andrew Clive Roberts. *Educ:* Sydenham High Sch.; Southampton Univ. (BA Hist., 1966). Academic Dept, London Univ., 1967–83. Trustee: City Parochial Foundn, 1993–2007; Resource Centre (London) Ltd (formerly London Vol. Sector Resource Centre), 1997–. *Address:* Flat 601, 7 High Holborn, WC1V 6DR. *T:* (020) 7430 2369.

ROBERTS, Prof. Gordon Carl Kenmure, PhD; Professor of Biochemistry, since 1986, Director, Henry Wellcome Laboratories for Structural Biology (formerly Leicester Biological NMR Centre), since 1986, and Head of School of Biological Sciences, since 2004, University of Leicester; *b* 28 May 1943; *s* of Rev. Douglas M. A. K. Roberts and Hilda (*née* Engelmann); *m* 1963, Hilary Margaret Lepper; two *s* one *d*. *Educ:* University Coll., London (BSc Hons Biochem. 1964); PhD Biochem. London 1967. Res. Chemist, Merck Sharp & Dohme Res. Labs, Rahway, NJ, 1967–69; Member scientific staff: MRC Molecular Pharmacol. Res. Unit, Dept of Pharmacol., Univ. of Cambridge, 1969–72; NIMR, 1972–86; Dir, Centre for Mechanisms of Human Toxicity, 1991–2000, Hd, Dept of Biochemistry, 2000–04, Leicester Univ. *Publications:* NMR in Molecular Biology (with O. Jardetzky), 1981; (ed) NMR of Biological Macromolecules, 1993; numerous papers in scientific jls. *Recreation:* gardening. *Address:* Henry Wellcome Laboratories for Structural Biology, Henry Wellcome Building, University of Leicester, PO Box 138, Lancaster Road, Leicester LE1 9HN. *T:* (0116) 229 7100.

ROBERTS, Gwilym; *see* Roberts, D. G. M.

ROBERTS, Gwilym Edffrwd, PhD; Member (Lab), Staffordshire County Council, since 2005; *b* 7 Aug. 1928; *s* of William and Jane Ann Roberts; *m* 1954, Mair Griffiths; no *c*. *Educ:* Brynrefail Gram. Sch.; UCW (Bangor); City Univ. BSc. Industrial Management, 1952–57; Lecturer (Polytechnic and University), 1957–66, 1970–74. Mem., Cannock Chase DC, 1983–2002 (Leader, 1992–99). MP (Lab): South Bedfordshire, 1966–70; Cannock, Feb. 1974–1983; PPS, DoI, 1976–79. Contested (Lab): Ormskirk, 1959; Conway, 1964; S Beds, 1970; Cannock and Burntwood, 1983, 1987. Chm., First Community NHS Trust, 1998–2001. Business Analyst, Economic Forecasting, Market and Operational Research, 1957. Institute of Statisticians: Vice-Pres., 1978; Hon. Officer, 1983–84; Editor, Newsletter, 1967–78. FCMI. Hon. FSS 1993. *Publications:* many articles on technical, political, parliamentary and European matters. *Recreations:* cricket, table tennis. *Address:* 18 Church Street, Rugeley, Staffs WS15 2AB. *T:* (01889) 583601.

ROBERTS, Sir Hugh (Ashley), KCVO 2001 (CVO 1998; LVO 1995); FSA; Director of the Royal Collection and Surveyor of the Queen's Works of Art, since 1996; *b* 20 April 1948; *s* of late Rt Rev. Edward James Keymer Roberts and Dorothy Frances, *d* of Rev. Canon Edwin David Bowser; *m* 1975, Hon. Priscilla Jane Stephanie Low (*see* Hon. P. J. S. Roberts); two *d*. *Educ:* Winchester Coll.; Corpus Christi Coll., Cambridge (MA). FSA 1994. With Christie Manson and Woods, 1970–87 (Dir, 1978–87); Dep. Surveyor of the Queen's Works of Art, 1988–96. Mem., Sec. of State's Adv. Gp, Historic Royal Palaces Agency, 1990–98. Member: Exec. Cttee, NACF, 1988–2000; Arts Panel, NT, 1988– (Chm., 1997–); Council, Attingham Trust, 1988–; Trustee: Harewood House Trust, 1986–; Historic Royal Palaces Trust, 1998–; Great Steward of Scotland's Dumfries House Trust, 2007–. Mem., Soc. of Dilettanti, 1991–. *Publications:* For the King's Pleasure: the furnishing and decoration of George IV's apartments at Windsor Castle, 2001; contrib. to Furniture History, Burlington Mag., Apollo, etc. *Recreation:* gardening. *Address:* Adelaide Cottage, Home Park, Windsor, Berks SL4 2JQ. *T:* (01753) 855581.

ROBERTS, His Honour (Hugh) Eifion (Pritchard); QC 1971; DL; a Circuit Judge, 1977–98; *b* 22 Nov. 1927; *er s* of late Rev. and Mrs E. P. Roberts, Anglesey; *m* 1958, Buddug Williams; one *s* two *d*. *Educ:* Beaumaris Grammar Sch.; University Coll. of Wales, Aberystwyth (LLB); Exeter Coll., Oxford (BCL). Called to Bar, Gray's Inn, 1953; practised as a Junior Counsel on Wales and Chester Circuit, Sept. 1953–April 1971. Dep. Chairman: Anglesey QS, 1966–71; Denbighshire QS, 1970–71; a Recorder of the Crown Court, 1972–77. Formerly Asst Parly Boundary Comr for Wales; Mem. for Wales of the Crawford Cttee on Broadcasting Coverage. Chm. Council, Univ. of Wales, Bangor. DL Clwyd, 1988. *Recreation:* gardening. *Address:* Maes-y-Rhedyn, Gresford Road, Llay, Wrexham, Clwyd LL12 0NN. *T:* (01978) 852292.

ROBERTS, Hugh Martin P.; *see* Plowden Roberts.

ROBERTS, Prof. Ian Gareth, PhD, LittD; FBA 2007; Professor of Linguistics and Fellow of Downing College, University of Cambridge, since 2000 (Head of Department of Linguistics, 2001–05); *b* 23 Oct. 1957; *s* of Idris Michael Roberts and Dorothy Sybil Roberts (*née* Moody); *m* 1993, Lucia Cavalli; one *s* one *d*. *Educ:* Stamford Sch.; Eirias High Sch., Colwyn Bay; UCNW (Bangor) (BA Hons Linguistics 1979); Univ. of Southern Calif (PhD 1985); LittD Cantab 2006. Translator, Motor Ind. Res. Assoc., Nuneaton, 1980–81; University of Geneva: Asst de linguistique anglaise, 1985–86; Maître-asst de linguistique générale, 1986–91; Professor: of Linguistics, UCNW (Bangor), then Univ. of Wales, Bangor, 1991–96; of English Linguistics, Univ. of Stuttgart, 1996–2000. Ed., Jl Linguistics, 1994–2000. *Publications:* The Representation of Implicit and Dethematised Subjects, 1987; Verbs and Diachronic Syntax, 1993; Comparative Syntax, 1996; Syntactic Change, 2003; Principles and Parameters in a VSO Language, 2005; Diachronic Syntax, 2007; contrib. numerous articles to learned jls. *Recreations:* reading, walking, music. *Address:* Downing College, Cambridge CB2 1DQ. *T:* (01223) 331733.

ROBERTS, Ian White; HM Diplomatic Service, retired; Hon. Visiting Fellow, 1985–99, Official Historian, since 1999, School of Slavonic and East European Studies, University College London; *b* 29 March 1927; *s* of George Dodd Roberts and Jessie Dickson Roberts (*née* White); *m* 1956, Pamela Johnston; one *d*. *Educ:* Royal Masonic Sch., Bushey, Herts; Gonville and Caius Coll., Cambridge (MA 1st Cl. Hons Mod. Langs). Served Royal Air Force (Pilot Officer), 1948–50; postgrad. student, Cambridge (Scarbrough Award), 1950. Joined Foreign Office, 1951–: Klagenfurt, 1952; Munich, 1954; Berlin, 1955; FCO, 1957–61; Second (later First) Secretary, Budapest, 1961–63; FCO, 1963; Bujumbura,

1965; FCO, 1965–66; Buenos Aires, 1966; FCO, 1969–74; Oslo, 1974–76; FCO, 1976–84; Counsellor, 1976. *Publications:* Nicholas I and the Russian Intervention in Hungary, 1991; History of School of Slavonic and East European Studies, University of London, 1991; articles in philatelic jls. *Recreations:* music, reading, philately. *Address:* c/o Lloyds TSB, 1 Butler Place, SW1H 0PR. *Club:* Travellers.

ROBERTS, Sir Ivor (Anthony), KCMG 2000 (CMG 1995); HM Diplomatic Service, retired; President, Trinity College, Oxford, since 2006; *b* 24 Sept. 1946; *s* of late Leonard Moore Roberts and Rosa Maria Roberts (*née* Fusco); *m* 1974, Elizabeth Bray Bernard Smith; two *s* one *d*. *Educ:* St Mary's Coll., Crosby; Keble Coll., Oxford (Gomm schol.; MA; Hon. Fellow 2001); FCIL (FIL 1991). Entered HM Diplomatic Service, 1968; MECAS, 1969; Third, later Second Sec., Paris, 1970–73; Second, later First Sec., FCO, 1973–78; First Sec., Canberra, 1978–82; First Sec., later Counsellor, FCO, 1982–88; Minister and Dep. Head of Mission, Madrid, 1989–93; Chargé d'Affaires, Belgrade, 1994–96; Ambassador to Yugoslavia, 1996–97; Sen. Associate Mem., St Antony's Coll., Oxford, 1997–98; Ambassador: to Ireland, 1999–2003; to Italy and to San Marino, 2003–06. Chm. Council, British Sch. of Archaeol. and Fine Arts, Rome, 2008–. Patron, Venice in Peril Fund. *Recreations:* opera, ski-ing, golf, photography. *Address:* President's Lodgings, Trinity College, Oxford OX1 3BH. *Clubs:* Oxford and Cambridge, Beefsteak; Downhill Only (Wengen).

ROBERTS, Hon. Jane; *see* Roberts, Hon. P. J. S.

ROBERTS, Dame Jane (Elisabeth), DBE 2004; FRCPsych; Consultant Child and Adolescent Psychiatrist, since 1993, Medical Director, 2002–2006, and Director, Quality and Performance, since 2006, Islington Primary Care Trust; *b* 23 Aug. 1955; *d* of Rev. Dr Fred Roberts and Nia Lora Roberts; *m* 2005, Prof. David Dunger; one *s* and one step *d*. *Educ:* Bristol Univ. (MB ChB 1980); Brunel Univ. (MSc 1991). MRCP 1983; MRCPsych 1986, FRCPsych 2004. Jun. posts in paediatrics, 1980–84; Registrar, Psychiatry, Maudsley Hosp., 1984–87; Sen. Registrar, Child and Adolescent Psychiatry, Tavistock Clinic, 1987–92; Locum Consultant, Child and Adolescent Psychiatry, Camden and Islington Community Health Services, NHS Trust, 1992–93. London Borough of Camden Council: Mem., 1990–2006; Dep. Leader, 1994–98, Leader, 2000–05; Chair, Educn Cttee, 1998–2000. Chair, Councillors' Commn, 2007. Mem. Bd, OFSTED, 2007–. Trustee: IPPR, 2005–; Parenting UK, 2006– (Chair, 2006–); Dir, New Local Govt Network, 2006–. Sen. Associate Fellow, Warwick Business Sch., 2006–. Hon. Fellow, UCL, 2005. Hon. DLaws Bristol, 2007. *Publications:* (ed with Dr S. Kraemer) The Politics of Attachment, 1996; academic articles in paediatrics and psychiatry. *Address:* 1 Countess Road, NW5 2NS.

ROBERTS, Jeremy Michael Graham; QC 1982; **His Honour Judge Jeremy Roberts;** a Circuit Judge, at the Central Criminal Court, since 2000; *b* 26 April 1941; *s* of late Lt-Col J. M. H. Roberts and E. D. Roberts; *m* 1964, Sally Priscilla Johnson, *d* of late Col F. P. Johnson, OBE. *Educ:* Winchester; Brasenose Coll., Oxford. BA. Called to the Bar, Inner Temple, 1965, Bencher, 1992. A Recorder, 1981–2000. Head of Chambers, 1997–2000. *Recreations:* racing, reading, theatre, opera, canals. *Address:* Central Criminal Court, Old Bailey, EC4M 7EH.

ROBERTS, John; *see* Roberts, A. J.

ROBERTS, John Anthony; QC 1988; FCIArb; a Recorder of the Crown Court, 1987–98; *b* Sierra Leone, 17 May 1928; *s* of late John Anthony Roberts of Brazil and Regina Roberts of Sierra Leone; *m* 1961, Eulette Valerie; one *s*. *Educ:* St Edward's RC Secondary Sch., Sierra Leone; Inns of Court Sch. of Law. Costs Clerk, Taylor Woodrow W Africa Ltd; Civil Servant, Sierra Leone; RAF 1952–62 (GSM Malaya), served UK, Europe, Near East, Far East, S Pacific; qualified Air Traffic Control Officer, 1962–64; qualified pilot; Civil Service, UK, 1964–69, incl. Inland Revenue; part time law student; called to the Bar, Gray's Inn, 1969, Bencher, 1996; Mem., Lincoln's Inn, 1972; Head of Chambers, 1975; Asst Recorder, 1983–87. First person of African ancestry to be appointed QC at the English Bar; called to the Bar in: Jamaica, 1973; Sierra Leone, 1975; Trinidad and Tobago, 1978; Bahamas, 1984; St Kitts and Nevis, 1988; Antigua, 2002; Barbados, 2002; Bermuda, 2003; Anguilla, 2006; Grenada, 2007. Judge, Supreme Cts of BVI and Anguilla, BWI, 1992–93. Bencher, Council of Legal Educn, Sierra Leone, 1990. Tutor, Inns of Ct Sch. of Law, London, 1990–92. Pres., UK Br., W Indian Ex-Servicemen's and Ex-Servicewomen's Assoc., 2000–03; Jt Pres., British Caribbean Assoc., UK, 2002–06. Hon. Citizen, Atlanta, Ga, USA, 1991. Freeman, City of London, 1996; Mem. Guild of Freemen, 1997. Hon. Citizen, BVI, 2000. Hon. DCL City, 1996. *Recreations:* music, singing in a choir (Latin Mass and Gregorian Chant), flying light aircraft, playing piano, organ and guitar, reading, dancing, athletics, boxing (former sprinter and boxer, RAF).

ROBERTS, John Arthur, CEng, FIET; Under-Secretary, Department of Energy, 1974–77; *b* 21 Dec. 1917; *s* of late John Richard and Emily Roberts; *m* 1st, 1944, Winifred Wilks Scott (*d* 1976); two *s* one *d*; 2nd, 1977, Rosetta Mabel Price. *Educ:* Liverpool Institute; Liverpool Univ. (BEng). Apprentice, Metropolitan-Vickers Electrical Co. Ltd, 1939. Served War, Royal Signals, 1940–46, Major. Sen. Lectr, Applied Science, RMA, Sandhurst, 1947–49; SSO and PSO, RAE, Farnborough, 1949–59; Head, Control and Computers Section, Applications Br., Central Electricity Generating Bd, 1959–62; Project Ldr, Automatic Control, CEGB, 1962–67; DCSO, Min. of Tech. and DTI, 1967–72; Under-Sec., DTI, 1972–74. *Address:* Damery, High Street, Wookey, Wells, Somerset BA5 1JZ. *T:* (01749) 678025.

ROBERTS, John Charles Quentin; Hon. Chairman, International Advisory Board of All-Russia State Library for Foreign Literature, Moscow, since 2004 (Member, 1991–93; Co-Chairman, 1994–2004); Director, Britain-Russia Centre (formerly Great Britain-USSR Association), 1974–93; *b* 4 April 1933; *s* of Hubert and Emilie Roberts; *m* 1st, 1959, Dinah Webster-Williams (marr. diss.); one *s* one *d*; 2nd, 1982, Elizabeth Roberts (*née* Gough-Cooper) (marr. diss.). *Educ:* Quainton Hall; King's Coll., Taunton (open scholar); Merton Coll., Oxford (MA). Royal Air Force CSC Interpreter, 1953; Russian Language Tutor, SSEES, Univ. of London, 1953; Shell International Petroleum Co. Ltd, 1956; Shell Co. of E Africa Ltd: Representative, Zanzibar and S Tanganyika, 1957, Kenya Highlands, 1958; PA to Man. Dir, Shell Austria AG Vienna, 1960; Pressed Steel Co. Ltd, Oxford, 1961; Asst Master, Marlborough Coll., 1963–74. Chairman: Organising Cttee for British Week in Siberia, 1978; Steering Cttee, British Month in USSR (Kiev), 1990. Mem. Council, Amer. Friends of the Russian Country Estate Inc., Washington, 1998–2003. Member Council: SSEES, Univ. of London, 1981–93; Academia Rossica, 2000–06; Vice Pres., Assoc. of Teachers of Russian, 1984–89. Governor, Cobham Hall, 1984–88. Trustee: Serge Rachmaninoff Foundn, 2002–06; Keston Inst., Oxford, 2003–07. Hon. Life Mem., GB-Russia Soc., 2002. Mem., Editl Adv. Bd, Herald of Europe, Moscow, 2001–. Tyutchev Gold Medal, Internat. Pushkin Foundn, 2004. *Publications:* Speak Clearly into the Chandelier: cultural politics between Britain and Russia 1973–2000, 2000 (Russian lang. edn 2001, Znamya Award); translations from Russian and French literature; contribs to specialist jls; occasional journalism. *Recreations:* family, reading, France. *Address:* 147 Beaufort Street, SW3 6BS. *T:* (020) 7376 3452. *Club:* Athenæum.

ROBERTS, John Edward, CBE 2004; FREng, FIET, FCCA; DL; Chief Executive, United Utilities, 1999–2006; *b* 2 March 1946; *s* of Arthur and Dora Roberts; *m* 1970, Pamela Baxter; one *s* one *d*. *Educ:* Liverpool Univ. (BEng). FCCA 1983; CEng, FIET (FIEE 1988); FREng 2002; DMS. Merseyside and North Wales Electricity Board, subseq. Manweb: Chief Accountant, 1984–90; Finance Dir, 1990–91; Man. Dir, 1991–92; Chief Exec., 1992–95; Chief Exec., S Wales Electricity, then Hyder Utilities, 1996–99. Dir, Hyder Gp, 1996–99. Mem., Royal Commn on Envmtl Pollution, 1998–2002. CCMI. Hon. Fellow, Liverpool John Moores Univ., 2004. DL Merseyside, 2006. Hon. DEng Liverpool, 2004. *Recreations:* scuba diving, walking, gardening.

ROBERTS, Dr John Esmond; Head, Chemicals and Nanotechnologies, since 2006, and Head, Noise and Local Environmental Quality, since 2008, Department for Environment, Food and Rural Affairs; *b* Bristol, 29 June 1951; *s* of Bill and Marian Roberts; *m* 1989, Lucy-Anne Collier; one *s* one *d*. *Educ:* Bishop Wordsworth Sch., Salisbury; Keble Coll., Oxford (MA, DPhil Chem. 1975). DoE, later DEFRA, 1975–; on secondment to Cabinet Secretariat, 1985–87; Local Govt Finance – Grants, 1987–91; Housing Gp Secretariat, 1991–92; Housing, Private Rented Sector, 1992–96; on secondment to LGA, 1996–97; Urban Policy, 1997–2001; Marine Envmt, 2001–06. Mem., Mgt Bd, Eur. Chemicals Agency, 2007–. Vice Pres., Stockholm Convention on Persistant Organic Pollutants, 2007–. *Recreations:* St Luke's Church, Wimbledon Park, Fulham Football Club. *Address:* Department for Environment, Food and Rural Affairs, Nobel House, 17 Smith Square, SW1P 3JR. *T:* (020) 7238 1569; *e-mail:* John.Roberts@defra.gsi.gov.uk.

ROBERTS, John Herbert; former tax administrator; *b* 18 Aug. 1933; *s* of late John Emanuel Roberts and Hilda Mary Roberts; *m* 1965, Patricia Iris; one *s* three *d*. *Educ:* Canton High Sch.; London School of Economics (BScEcon Hons). Entered Civil Service by Open Competition as Inspector of Taxes, 1954; National Service, commnd RASC, 1955–57; returned to Inland Revenue, 1957; Principal Inspector, 1974; Sen. Principal Inspector, 1979; Under Secretary, 1981; Director of Operations, 1981–85; Dir, Technical Div. 2, 1985–88; Dir, Compliance and Collection Div., 1988–92; Dir of Ops (DO2), 1992–93; consultant, overseas tax admin, 1994–99. *Recreations:* music, walking.

ROBERTS, John Houghton; His Honour Judge John H. Roberts; a Circuit Judge, since 1993; *b* 14 Dec. 1947; *s* of John Noel Roberts and Ida Roberts, Irby, Wirral; *m* 1st, 1972, Anna Elizabeth (marr. diss. 1990), *e d* of Peter and Elizabeth Sheppard; three *s*; 2nd, 1991, Mary, *er d* of Frederic and Patricia Wilkinson, Blundellsands. *Educ:* Calday Grange Grammar Sch., West Kirby; Trinity Hall, Cambridge (Schol.; BA 1st Cl. Hons Law Tripos; MA). Lectr in Law, Liverpool Univ., 1969–71; called to the Bar, Middle Temple, 1970 (Harmsworth Major Entrance Exhibn 1968; Astbury Law Schol. 1970). Practised Northern Circuit, 1970–93. Asst Recorder, 1983; Recorder, 1988–93; Resident Judge, Bolton Crown Court, 1997–2001. *Recreations:* Rugby football, golf, cricket, music. *Address:* Liverpool Crown Court, Queen Elizabeth II Law Courts, Derby Square, Liverpool L2 1XA. *T:* (0151) 473 7373. *Clubs:* Athenæum (Liverpool); Heswall Golf, Nefyn and District Golf; Oxton Cricket; Waterloo Football.

ROBERTS, Dr John Laing; independent consultant in health and economic policy, since 1997; Adviser: to the Indian Ocean Commission, since 2004; to the Commonwealth Secretariat, since 2004; Associate Professor, Department of Economics and Statistics, University of Mauritius, since 2006; *b* 26 Dec. 1939; *s* of Charles F. Roberts and May Roberts; *m* 1st, 1963, Meriel F. Dawes (marr. diss. 1980); three *d*; 2nd, 1981, Judith Mary Hare (marr. diss. 2002); 3rd, 2002, Bibi Bilkis Sheik Janny. *Educ:* Latymer Upper School; Univ. of Birmingham. PhD, BSocSc. FHA. NHS Nat. Administrative Trainee, 1962–63; Senior Administrative Asst, United Birmingham Hosps, 1964–66; Sen. Res. Associate, Dept of Social Medicine, Univ. of Birmingham, 1966–69; Dep. Dir, Res. Div., Health Education Council, 1969–74; Operational Services Gen. Administrator, S Glamorgan AHA (T), 1974–77; Regional Gen. Administrator, W Midlands RHA, 1977–82; Regional Administrator, 1983–85, Regl Prevention Manager, 1985–89, N Western RHA; Regl Advr in Health Services, WHO Office for Europe, Copenhagen, 1990–92; Consultant, WHO Office for Europe, 1992–94; Health Economist/Planner, Min. of Econ. Planning and Develt, Mauritius, 1994–98. Adviser to Government: of Malaŵi, 1999–2001; of Mauritius, 2000–04; consultant to UNEP on Africa envmt outlook, 2001–02; advr to UNEP, 2002–. Dir, Adhealth, 1989–96. Hon. Sen. Res. Fellow, Manchester Univ., 1990–2000. Mem. Editl Bd, Internat. Jl of Health Promotion, 1996–. *Publications:* papers on health education, health service administration, health and economics, the environment and sustainable development; PhD thesis, Studies of Information Systems for Health Service Resource Planning and Control. *Recreations:* swimming, hill walking, tennis. *Address:* 5 Ranmore Court, 101 Worple Road, SW19 8HB; Habasha, Morcellement Mont Choisy, Mont Choisy, Mauritius. *T:* 2655187; *e-mail:* jlrobertsy@aol.com.

ROBERTS, John Mervyn; His Honour Judge Mervyn Roberts; a Circuit Judge, since 1999; *b* 19 Feb. 1941; *s* of late Mervyn and Catherine Roberts; *m* 1972, Phillippa Ann Critien; one *d*. *Educ:* Hereford Cathedral Sch.; King's Coll., London (LLB Hons 1962). Called to the Bar, Inner Temple, 1963, Bencher, 2007; in practice at the Bar, 1963–99; a Recorder, 1994–99. Member: Criminal Injuries Compensation Bd, 1998–99; Parole Bd, 2002–. *Recreations:* music, golf, travel. *Address:* Inner London Crown Court, Sessions House, Newington Causeway, SE1 6AZ.

ROBERTS, Rear-Adm. John Oliver, CB 1976; MNI; Managing Director, Demak Ltd, International Consultants, since 1983; *b* 4 April 1924; *er s* of J. V. and M. C. Roberts; *m* 1st, 1950, Lady Hermione Mary Morton Stuart (marr. diss. 1960; she *d* 1969); one *d*; 2nd, 1963, Honor Marigold Gordon Gray (marr. diss. 1987); one *s* one *d*; 3rd, 1987, Sheila Violet Mary Traub (*née* Barker). *Educ:* RN Coll., Dartmouth. Served War: Midshipman, HMS Renown and Tartar, 1941–43; Sub-Lt, HMS Serapis, 1943–44; Lieut, 1945; Pilot Trg, 1944–46. HMS Triumph, 1947–49; RNAS, Lossiemouth, 1949–51; Flag-Lt to FOGT, 1952; Lt-Comdr, 1953; HMAS Vengeance and Sydney, 1953–54; RNVR, Southern Air Div., 1954–56; CO, No 803 Sqdn, HMS Eagle, 1957–58; Comdr, 1958; RNAS, Brawdy, 1958–60; CO, HMS St Bride's Bay, 1960–61; Naval Staff, 1962–64; Captain, 1964; CSO, Flag Officer Aircraft Carriers, 1964–66; CO, HMS Galatea, 1966–68; Naval Staff, 1968–70; CO, HMS Ark Royal, 1971–72; Rear-Adm., 1972; Flag Officer Sea Training, 1972–74; COS to C-in-C Fleet, 1974–76; Flag Officer, Naval Air Command, 1976–78. Non-exec. Dir, Aeronautical & General Instruments Ltd, 1981–82 (Head of Marketing and Sales, Defence Systems Div., 1980–81); Dir Gen., British Printing Industries Fedn, 1981–82. FRSA. *Recreations:* Rugby football, cricket, athletics, sailing, ski-ing. *Address:* Priory House, Blakesley, Northants. *Club:* East India, Devonshire, Sports and Public Schools.

ROBERTS, Julia Fiona; actress; *b* Smyrna, Georgia, 28 Oct. 1967; *d* of late Walter Roberts and of Betty Roberts; *m* 1st, 1993, Lyle Lovett (marr. diss. 1995); 2nd, 2002, Danny Moder; two *s* one *d* (of whom one *s* one *d* are twins). *Educ:* Campbell High Sch., Georgia. *Stage:* Three Days of Rain, NY, 2006; *films include:* Satisfaction, Mystic Pizza, 1988; Steel Magnolias, 1989 (Best Supporting Actress, Golden Globe Awards, 1990); Blood Red, Pretty Woman (Best Actress, Golden Globe Awards, 1991), Flatliners, 1990;

Sleeping with the Enemy, Hook, Dying Young, 1991; The Pelican Brief, I Love Trouble, Prêt-à-Porter, 1994; Something to Talk About, 1995; Mary Reilly, Everybody Says I Love You, Michael Collins, 1996; My Best Friend's Wedding, Conspiracy Theory, 1997; Stepmom, 1998; Notting Hill, Runaway Bride, 1999; Erin Brockovich, 2000 (Academy Award for Best Actress, 2000; Best Actress, BAFTA Awards, Golden Globe Awards, Screen Actors' Guild Awards, 2001); The Mexican, America's Sweethearts, 2001; Ocean's Eleven, 2002; Confessions of a Dangerous Mind, Full Frontal, 2003; Mona Lisa Smile, 2004; Closer, Ocean's Twelve, 2005; Ocean's Thirteen, Charlie Wilson's War, 2007; *television includes:* Crime Story, 1988; Baja Oklahoma, 1988; In the Wild, 1988.

ROBERTS, Julian; *see* Roberts, R. J.

ROBERTS, Prof. Kevin William Stuart, DPhil; FBA 2007; Sir John Hicks Professor of Economics, University of Oxford, since 1999; Fellow, Nuffield College, Oxford, since 1999; *b* 29 Feb. 1952; *s* of Basil Roberts and Dorothy Roberts (*née* Heaven); *m* 1981, Julia Clarke (marr. diss. 1996); two *d. Educ:* Cheltenham Grammar Sch.; Univ. of Essex (BA Math. Econ. 1973); Nuffield Coll., Oxford (BPhil Econ. 1975; DPhil Econ. 1977). Jun. Res. Fellow, St John's Coll., Oxford, 1975–77; Asst Prof., MIT, 1977–78; Univ. Lectr and Official Fellow, St Catherine's Coll., Oxford, 1978–82; Professor: of Econ. Theory, Univ. of Warwick, 1982–87; of Economics, LSE, 1987–99. Fellow, Econometric Soc., 1984. *Publications:* articles in internat. learned jls incl. Econometrica and Rev. Econ. Studies. *Recreations:* country walks, old buildings and their preservation. *Address:* 94 Southmoor Road, Oxford OX2 6RB. *T:* (01865) 558468.

ROBERTS, Prof. Lewis Edward John, CBE 1978; FRS 1982; Wolfson Professor of Environmental Risk Assessment, University of East Anglia, 1986–90, Emeritus Professor, since 1990; *b* 31 Jan. 1922; *s* of William Edward Roberts and Lilian Lewis Roberts; *m* 1948, Eleanor Mary Luscombe; one *s. Educ:* Swansea Grammar Sch.; Jesus Coll., Oxford (MA, DPhil). Clarendon Laboratory, Oxford, 1944; Scientific Officer, Chalk River Res. Estabt, Ont, Canada, 1946–47; AERE, Harwell, 1947, Principal Scientific Officer, 1952; Commonwealth Fund Fellow, Univ. of Calif, Berkeley, 1954–55; Dep. Head, Chemistry Div., 1966, Asst Dir, 1967, Dir, 1975–86, AERE. Mem., UKAEA, 1979–86. Pres., British Nuclear Energy Soc., 1985–87; Mem. Council and Vice Pres., Royal Instn, 1991–94. R. M. Jones Lectr, QUB, 1981; Rutherford Meml Lectr, Royal Soc., 1992. Governor, Abingdon Sch., 1978–86. *Publications:* Nuclear Power and Public Responsibility, 1984; Power Generation and the Environment, 1990; papers in qly revs and in scientific journals and IAEA pubns. *Recreations:* reading, gardening. *Address:* Penfold Wick, Chilton, Didcot OX11 0SH. *T:* (01235) 834309.

ROBERTS, Lynn Deborah; a District Judge, Principal Registry, Family Division, since 2001; *b* 25 Oct. 1956; *d* of Henry and Eva Roberts; *m* 1994, John Watson; one *s* one *d*, and one step *s* one step *d. Educ:* South Hampstead High Sch.; Brasenose Coll., Oxford (BA Hons (Mod. Hist.) 1979); Coll. of Law. Solicitor, 1986–88, Partner, 1988–2001, Hodge Jones and Allen; Deputy District Judge: County Courts, 1999–2001; Principal Registry, Family Div., 1999–2001. *Publication:* (contrib.) Raydon and Jackson, Divorce and Family Matters, 18th edn 2004. *Recreations:* cooking, crosswords, country walks. *Address:* Principal Registry of the Family Division, First Avenue House, 42–49 High Holborn, WC1V 6NP.

ROBERTS, Martin Geoffrey; Senior Consultant, Beachcroft Regulatory (formerly Beachcroft Wansbroughs) Consulting, since 2003; Director, PensionsRisk LLP, since 2007; *b* 3 July 1946; *s* of Arthur and Mary Roberts; *m* 1969, Christine Muriel George; two *s. Educ:* Priory Grammar Sch., Shrewsbury; Worcester Coll., Oxford (MA). Min. of Technology, 1970; Private Sec. to Minister without Portfolio, 1973–74; seconded: to FCO, 1979–82; to DoE as Controller, Yorks and Humberside Regl Office, 1984–85; Sec., BOTB, 1985–89; Hd of Investigations Div., 1992–96, Dir, Finance and Resource Mgt, 1996–98, DTI; Dir, Insurance, HM Treasury, 1998; Dir, Insce and Friendly Socs, 1999–2002, Sen. Insce Advr, 2002–03, FSA. Chm., Friendly Socs Commn, 1998–2002; Mem., Exports Guarantee Adv. Council, 2003–. Mem., Exec. Cttee, 1998–2003, Chm., Tech. Cttee, 2000–03, Internat. Assoc. of Insce Supervisors. *Recreation:* sailing. *Address:* Beachcroft Regulatory Consulting, 100 Fetter Lane, EC4A 1BN. *T:* (020) 7894 6203.

ROBERTS, Michael; *see* Roberts, T. M.

ROBERTS, Surgeon Rear Adm. Michael Atholl F.; *see* Farquharson-Roberts.

ROBERTS, Rev. Canon Michael Graham Vernon; Principal, Westcott House, Cambridge, 1993–2006; *b* 4 Aug. 1943; *s* of Walter Graham Southall Roberts and Pamela Middleton Roberts (*née* Abel, now Murray); *m* 1970, Susan Elizabeth (*née* Merry); one *s* two *d. Educ:* Eton Coll.; Keble Coll., Oxford (BA 1965; MA); Cuddesdon Coll.; Church Divinity Sch. of Pacific, Berkeley, Calif. (MDiv 1967). Curate, Exmouth, 1967–70; Chaplain, Clare Coll., Cambridge, 1970–74; Vicar, St Mark, Bromley, 1974–79; Tutor, Queen's Coll., Birmingham, 1979–85; Team Rector, High Wycombe, 1985–90; Vice-Principal, Westcott House, Cambridge, 1990–93. Hon. Canon, Ely Cathedral, 2004–. *Recreations:* gardening, walking, Brittany, reading. *Address:* La Herviais, 22100 Trévron, France. *T:* (2) 96835299.

ROBERTS, Michael John Wyn; HM Diplomatic Service; Ambassador to Slovakia, since 2007; *b* 4 July 1960; *s* of late Denys Murray Wyn Roberts and of Diana Roberts (*née* Marshall); *m* 1985, Margaret Anne Ozanne; one *s* two *d. Educ:* Bryanston Sch.; Brasenose Coll., Oxford (BA). Joined HM Diplomatic Service, 1984; Second, then First Sec., Athens, 1987–91; FCO, 1991–95; First Sec., UK Perm. Repn to EU, Brussels, 1995–99; Hd of Div., European Secretariat, Cabinet Office, 1999–2003; Dep. Hd of Mission, Ankara, 2004–07. *Recreations:* music, Chelsea FC, walking. *Address:* c/o Foreign and Commonwealth Office, King Charles Street, SW1A 2AH.

ROBERTS, Michèle Brigitte; novelist and poet; Professor of Creative Writing, University of East Anglia, 2002–07, now Emeritus; *b* 20 May 1949; *d* of Reginald George Roberts and Monique Pauline Joseph (*née* Caulle); *m* 1991, Laurence James Latter (marr. diss. 2005). *Educ:* Somerville Coll., Oxford (MA); University Coll. London. MCLIP (ALA 1972); FRSL 1999. British Council Librarian, Bangkok, 1973–74; writer, 1974–; Poetry Editor: Spare Rib, 1974; City Limits, 1981–83. Vis. Fellow in Creative Writing, UEA, 1992; Research Fellow in Writing, 1995–96, Vis. Prof., 1996–2001, Nottingham Trent Univ.; Writer-in-Residence, York Univ., 2008. Chm., Lit. Cttee, British Council, 1998–2001. Mem., Soc. of Authors. Chevalier, Ordre des Arts et des Lettres (France), 2001. *Publications: novels:* A Piece of the Night, 1978; The Visitation, 1983; The Wild Girl, 1984; The Book of Mrs Noah, 1987; In the Red Kitchen, 1990; Daughters of the House, 1992 (W. H. Smith Literary Award, 1993); Flesh and Blood, 1994; Impossible Saints, 1997; Fair Exchange, 1999; The Looking-Glass, 2000; The Mistressclass, 2003; Reader, I Married Him, 2005; *stories:* During Mother's Absence, 1993; Playing Sardines, 2001; *memoir:* Paper Houses, 2007; *poetry:* The Mirror of the Mother, 1986; Psyche and the Hurricane, 1991; All the Selves I Was, 1995; *plays:* The Journeywoman, 1988; Child-Lover, 1995; *film:* The Heavenly Twins, 1993; *essays:* Food, Sex and God: on inspiration and writing, 1998; *anthology:* (ed jtly) Mind Readings, 1996. *Recreations:* cooking, gardening. *Address:* c/o Gillon Aitken, Aitken Alexander Associates, 18–21 Cavaye Place, SW10 9PT. *T:* (020) 7373 8672.

ROBERTS, Patrick John; Director, Cognis Public Relations, since 2006; *b* 21 Oct. 1942; *s* of Frank and Hilda Mary Roberts; *m* 1978, Alison Mary Taylor; one *s* one *d. Educ:* Rotherham Grammar Sch.; Lincoln Coll., Oxford (BA Hons Modern Langs). Foreign Office, 1965; Bangkok, 1966; FCO, 1970; First Sec., Lagos, 1971; FCO, 1974; UK Repn to EEC, Brussels, 1977; FCO, 1980; Counsellor (Inf.), Paris, 1984. Edelman Public Relations Worldwide: Dir of Eur. Affairs, 1989–90; Dir of Public, then Business and Corporate, Affairs, 1991–95; Dep. Man. Dir, 1995–99. Consultant, Abel Hadden and Co. Ltd, 1999–2002; Principal Consultant, Kaizo, 2002–06. *Recreations:* cooking, photography. *Address:* 81 Fawnbrake Avenue, SE24 0BG. *T:* (020) 7274 3530. *Club:* Oxford and Cambridge.

ROBERTS, Paul; *see* Roberts, D. P.

ROBERTS, Prof. Paul Harry, PhD, ScD; FRS 1979; FRAS; Professor of Mathematics, since 1986, and Professor of Geophysical Sciences, Institute of Geophysics and Planetary Physics, University of California at Los Angeles; *b* 13 Sept. 1929; *s* of Percy Harry Roberts and Ethel Frances (*née* Mann); *m* 1989, Mary Frances (*née* Tabrett). *Educ:* Ardwyn Grammar Sch., Aberystwyth; University Coll. of Wales, Aberystwyth; Gonville and Caius Coll., Cambridge (George Green Student; BA, MA, PhD, ScD). FRAS 1955. Res. Associate, Univ. of Chicago, 1954–55; Scientific Officer, AWRE, 1955–56; ICI Fellow in Physics, 1956–59, Lectr in Phys, 1959–61, Univ. of Durham; Associate Prof. of Astronomy, Univ. of Chicago, 1961–63; Prof. of Applied Maths, Univ. of Newcastle upon Tyne, 1963–85. Fellow: Amer. Geophysical Union; Amer. Acad. of Arts and Scis. Editor, Geophysical and Astrophysical Fluid Dynamics, 1976–91. John Adam Fleming Medal, Amer. Geophysical Union, 1999. *Publications:* An Introduction to Magnetohydrodynamics, 1967; contrib. to Geophys. and Astrophys. Fluid Dyn., Jl Low Temp. Phys., Astrophys. Jl, Jl Fluid Mech., Jl Phys. Soc. and Proc. and Trans Royal Soc. *Recreations:* playing bassoon, chess. *Address:* Department of Mathematics, UCLA, Los Angeles, CA 90095–1555, USA. *T:* (310) 8257764, (310) 2062707.

ROBERTS, Peter John Martin; Headmaster, Bradfield College, since 2003; *b* 31 May 1963; *s* of Alfred John Victor and Pamela Roberts; *m* 1990, Marie Toudic; three *d. Educ:* Tiffin Boys' Sch., Kingston upon Thames; Merton Coll., Oxford (MA 1st cl. Hons (Mod. Hist.) 1985); Inst. of Educn, London (PGCE 1986). Winchester College: Asst Master, 1986–90; Hd of History, 1990–97; Master in Coll. (Housemaster to the Scholars), 1991–2003. *Recreations:* cricket, book binding, fell walking. *Address:* Crossways, Bradfield, Bradfield College, Reading, Berks RG7 6AR.

ROBERTS, Philip Bedlington; a Recorder of the Crown Court, 1982–93; Consultant, Scholfield Roberts & Hill, 1990–97; *b* 15 Dec. 1921; *s* of late R. J. S. Roberts, solicitor and A. M. Roberts; *m* 1944, Olive Margaret, *d* of E. R. Payne, Mugswell, Chipstead, Surrey; one *s* one *d. Educ:* Dawson Court, Kensington; St Matthew's Sch., Bayswater. RAFVR, 1940–46. Admitted solicitor, 1949; in private practice with Scholfield Roberts & Hill, 1950–75; part-time Chm. of Industrial Tribunals, 1966–75, 1990–94, Chm., 1975–84, Regional Chm. (Bristol), 1984–90, retd. Chairman: Nat. Insce Tribunals, 1959–75; Compensation Appeals Tribunal, 1962. Solicitor, Somerset British Legion, 1960–75. *Publications:* contribs to professional jls. *Recreations:* illiterate computing, fair weather gardening. *Club:* Royal Air Force.

ROBERTS, Phyllida Katharine S.; *see* Stewart-Roberts.

ROBERTS, Hon. (Priscilla) Jane (Stephanie), (Hon. Lady Roberts), CVO 2004 (LVO 1995; MVO 1985); Curator of the Print Room, Royal Library, since 1975 and Librarian, since 2002, Windsor Castle; *b* 4 Sept. 1949; *d* of 1st Baron Aldington, KCMG, CBE, DSO, TD, PC; *m* 1975, Hugh Ashley Roberts (*see* Sir H. A. Roberts); two *d. Educ:* Cranborne Chase School; Westfield College, Univ. of London (BA Hons); Courtauld Inst., Univ. of London (MA). *Publications:* Holbein, 1979; Leonardo: Codex Hammer, 1981; Master Drawings in the Royal Collection, 1985; Royal Artists, 1987; A Dictionary of Michelangelo's Watermarks, 1988; (jtly) Leonardo da Vinci, 1989; A Souvenir Album of Sandby Views of Windsor, 1990; A King's Purchase: King George III and the Collection of Consul Smith, 1993; Holbein and the Court of Henry VIII, 1993; Views of Windsor: watercolours by Thomas and Paul Sandby, 1995; Royal Landscape: the gardens and parks of Windsor, 1997; Ten Religious Masterpieces: a Millennium Celebration, 2000; (ed) Royal Treasures: a Golden Jubilee celebration, 2002; (ed and contrib.) George III and Queen Charlotte: patronage, collecting and Court taste, 2004; (jtly) Unfolding Pictures: fans in the Royal Collection, 2005; Queen Elizabeth II: a birthday souvenir album, 2006; Five Gold Rings: a royal wedding souvenir album, 2007; Charles, Prince of Wales: a birthday souvenir album, 2008; articles in Burlington Magazine, Apollo, Report of Soc. of Friends of St George's. *Recreations:* singing, sewing. *Address:* Adelaide Cottage, Home Park, Windsor, Berks SL4 2JQ. *T:* (01753) 855581.

ROBERTS, Ven. Raymond Harcourt, CB 1984; Chairman, Customer Service Committee for Wales, Office of Water Services, 1990–2001; licensed to officiate, diocese of Llandaff, since 1995; *b* 14 April 1931; *s* of Thomas Roberts and Carrie Maud Roberts. *Educ:* Pontywaun Grammar Sch., Risca, Mon; St Edmund Hall, Oxford (MA English); St Michael's Theol Coll., Llandaff. Nat. Service, RN, 1949–51. Deacon 1956, priest 1957, dio. of Monmouth (Curate of Bassaleg); Chaplain RNVR, 1958, RN, 1959; Destroyers and Frigates, Far East, 1959; HMS Pembroke, 1962; Dartmouth Trng Sqdn, 1963; RM Commando Course, 1965; 45 Commando, S. Arabia, 1965; RN Engrg Coll., 1967; HMS Bulwark, 1968; BRNC Dartmouth, 1970; HMS Ark Royal, 1974; Commando Trng Centre, RM, 1975; HMS Drake and HM Naval Base, Plymouth, 1979; Chaplain of the Fleet and Archdeacon for RN, 1980–84, Archdeacon Emeritus, 1985–; QHC, 1980–84; Hon. Canon, Cathedral of Holy Trinity, Gibraltar, 1980–84; Gen. Sec., Jerusalem and ME Church Assoc., 1985–89; licensed, dio. of Guildford, 1986–91; Hon. Chaplain, Llandaff Cathedral, 1991–95. Mem., Nat. Customer Council, Ofwat, 1993–2001. Chaplain: Welsh Livery Guild, 1993–2007; to the High Sheriff of S Glam, 1993–94; Drapers' Co., 1996–97; Submariners Assoc., 2000–06. Governor, Rougemont Sch., Gwent, 1993–2004. *Recreations:* cooking and listening to Mozart, not necessarily simultaneously. *Address:* 8 Baynton Close, Llandaff, Cardiff CF5 2NZ. *T:* (029) 2057 8044.

ROBERTS, Richard (David Hallam); occasional academic and writer, yachtmaster, bookbinder's mate, competent househusband, gardener, woodman, antiquarian cyclist; *b* 27 July 1931; *s* of Arthur Hallam Roberts, Barrister-at-law, sometime Attorney-General, Zanzibar, and Ruvé Constance Jessie Roberts; *m* 1960, Wendy Ewen Mount; three *s. Educ:* King's Sch., Canterbury; Jesus Coll., Cambridge. Commissioned into RA 6th Field Regt, 1952. Asst Master, King's Sch., Canterbury, 1956; Housemaster, 1957; Head of Modern Language Dept, 1961; Senior Housemaster, 1965; Headmaster: Wycliffe Coll., Stonehouse, 1967–80; King Edward's Sch., Witley, 1980–85. Chairman: Alde and Ore Assoc., 1991–94; Orford Town Trust, 1995–99. *Club:* Orford Sailing.

ROBERTS, Sir Richard John, Kt 2008; PhD; FRS 1995; Chief Scientific Officer, New England Biolabs, since 2005 (Director of Research, 1992–2005); *b* Derby, 6 Sept. 1943; *s* of John Walter Roberts and Edna Wilhelmina Roberts; *m* 1st, 1965, Elizabeth Dyson; one *s* one *d*; 2nd, 1986, Jean (*née* Tagliabue); one *s* one *d*. *Educ:* Bath Boys' Sch.; Sheffield Univ. (BSc Chem. 1965; PhD 1968). Harvard University: Res. Fellow, 1969–70; Res. Associate in Biochem., 1971–72; Cold Spring Harbor Laboratory: Sen. Staff Investigator, 1972–86; Asst Dir for Research, 1986–92. Miller Prof., UC Berkeley, 1991. Dist. Scientist and Res. Schol., Boston Univ., 2003–. Chm., Scientific Adv. Bd, Celera, 1998–2002; Advr to Dir, NASA Astrobiol. Prog., 2000–. Exec. Editor, Nucleic Acids Res., 1987– (Mem. Editl Bd, 1977–87); Panel Mem., NLM Study Section, Comp. Biol., 1993–95. Hon. MD: Uppsala, 1992; Bath, 1994; Hon. DSc Sheffield, 1994. (Jtly) Nobel Prize in Physiology or Medicine, 1993. *Publications:* numerous papers on restriction endonucleases, DNA methylases, computational molecular biology. *Recreations:* collecting games, croquet. *Address:* New England Biolabs, 240 County Road, Ipswich, MA 01938, USA. *T:* (978) 3807405.

ROBERTS, (Richard) Julian, FSA; Deputy Librarian, 1986–97, and Keeper of Printed Books, 1974–97, Bodleian Library, Oxford; Fellow of Wolfson College, Oxford, 1975–97, now Emeritus; *b* 18 May 1930; *s* of A. R. and K. M. Roberts; *m* 1957, Anne Ducé; one *s* one *d*. *Educ:* King Edward's Sch., Birmingham; Magdalen Coll., Oxford. MCLIP (ALA 1956); FSA 1983. Asst Keeper, BM, 1958–74. Vicegerent, Wolfson Coll., Oxford, 1983–85. Regents' Prof., UCLA, 1991. Pres., Bibliographical Soc., 1986–88. *Publications:* (ed) Beawty in Raggs: poems by Cardell Goodman, 1958; John Dee's Library Catalogue, 1990; (contrib.) Cambridge History of the Book in Britain, vol. 4, 2002; (contrib.) Cambridge History of Libraries in Britain and Ireland, vols 1 and 2, 2006; contrib. to Library, Book Collector, Bodleian Liby Record, Oxford DNB, etc. *Recreation:* antiquarianism. *Address:* St John's Farm House, Tackley, Oxford OX5 3AT. *T:* (01869) 331249.

ROBERTS, Prof. Ronald John, PhD; FRCPath, FIBiol, FRCVS; FRSE; Professor of Aquatic Pathobiology and Director, Institute of Aquaculture, University of Stirling, 1971–96, now Professor Emeritus; *b* 28 March 1941; *s* of Ronald George Roberts and Marjorie Kneale; *m* 1964, Helen, *d* of Gordon Gregor Macgregor; two *s*. *Educ:* Campbeltown Grammar Sch., Argyll; Univ. of Glasgow Vet. Sch. (PhD, BVMS). FIBiol 1984; FRCPath 1988; FRCVS 1992; FRSE 1978. Univ. of Glasgow: Asst in Microbiology, 1964–66; Lectr in Vet. Pathology, 1966–71. Hagerman Dist. Vis. Prof., Univ. of Idaho, 1997–. Consultant in Fish Diseases: Dept Agric. and Fisheries for Scotland, 1968–71; ODA, subseq. DFID, 1974–2001; FAO, Rome, 1978–83; World Bank, 1989. Dir, Machrihanish Marine Envmtl Res. Lab., 1991–96. Member: Cabinet Office Science Panel, 1993–94; Res. Grants Panel, SFHEFC (formerly SHEFC), 2001–; Vice-Chm., 2003–06, Mem., 2006–June 2009, Animal Health and Welfare Panel, European Food Safety Authy. Editor: Jl Fish Diseases, 1978–; Aquaculture Research (formerly Aquaculture and Fisheries Management), 1988–2000. Chairman: Stirling Aquaculture, 1987–95; Heronpisces Ltd, 2003–; Bradan Ltd, 2003–; Director: Stirling Salmon, 1987–94; Tarbert Fyne Foods, 1987–90; Stirling Aquatic Technology, 1987–90; Campbeltown and Kintyre Enterprise, 1992–2005 (Chm., 1996–2005); Landcatch Ltd, 1996–. Scientific Advr, Lithgow Gp, 1996–. Chm., Argyll and Bute Countryside Trust, 1994–2004; Sec., Lady Linda McCartney Meml Trust, 2000–. Buckland Prof. and Medallist, 1985–86; C-Vet Award, BVA, 1989; Dalrymple-Champneys Cup and Medal, BVA, 1990. Commander, Most Noble Order of the Crown (Thailand), 1992. *Publications:* (with C. J. Shepherd) Handbook of Salmon and Trout Diseases, 1974, 3rd edn 1996; Fish Pathology, 1978, 3rd edn 2000; various scientific publications on histopathology of fishes. *Recreations:* arboriculture, rhododendron culture, golf, squash, admiring and conserving the Scottish natural environment. *Address:* 9 Alexander Drive, Bridge of Allan, Stirling FK9 4QB. *T:* (01786) 833078; Carrick Point Farm, Ardnacross Shorelands, by Campbeltown, Argyll PA28 5QR. *T:* (01586) 554417. *Club:* Machrihanish Golf (Kintyre).

ROBERTS, Sir Samuel, 4th Bt *cr* 1919, of Ecclesall and Queen's Tower, City of Sheffield; barrister; *b* 16 April 1948; *s* of Sir Peter Geoffrey Roberts, 3rd Bt, and Judith Randell (*d* 1998), *d* of late Randell G. Hempson; *S* father, 1985; *m* 1977, Georgina Ann, *yr d* of David Cory; one *s* three *d*. *Educ:* Harrow School; Sheffield Univ. (LLB); Manchester Business School. Called to the Bar, Inner Temple, 1972. Chairman: Cleyfield Properties Ltd, 1984–; Wiltshire and Co. Ltd, 1988–; Angermann, Goddard and Loyd Ltd, 1994. *Heir:* *s* Samuel Roberts, *b* 12 Aug. 1989.

ROBERTS, Maj. Gen. Sir Sebastian (John Lechmere), KCVO 2007; OBE 1993; Chief of Staff, Royal College of Defence Studies, since 2007; *b* 7 Jan. 1954; *s* of Brig. John Mark Herbert Roberts, OBE and Nicola Helen Lechmere Roberts (*née* Macaskie); *m* 1979, Elizabeth Anne Muir; two *s* two *d*. *Educ:* Ampleforth; Balliol Coll., Oxford (BA, MA); RMA, Sandhurst; Army Staff Coll., Camberley. Commnd Irish Guards, 1977; Captain, Rendezvous Point Comdr, Op AGILA, Southern Rhodesia, 1979–86; Major, COS, 4th Armd Bde, Münster, 1987–89; CO, 1st Bn, Irish Guards, Belize and Berlin, 1989–91; Lt Col, MA to CGS, MoD, 1991–93; CO, 1st Bn, Irish Guards, London and E Tyrone, 1993–96; Col, Land Warfare 2 (Doctrine), Upavon, 1996–99; Brig., Dir Public Relns (Army), MoD, 1999–2002; rcds 2003; GOC London Dist and OC Household Div., 2003–07. Regtl Lt Col, 1999–2008, Col., 2008–, Irish Guards; Col Comdt, Media Ops Gp (Volunteers), 2006–. Hon. Col, 256 (City of London) Field Hosp. (Volunteers), 2007–. Liveryman, Girdlers' Co., 2005. *Publications:* The Bullingdon War Mag, 1976; Bertie Meets the Queen, 1978; Soldiering: the military covenant, 1998. *Recreations:* painting and drawing, conversation, rebus letters, public speaking, prayer, eating, drinking, travelling, reading, writing, 9 brothers and sisters, shooting and a Springer Spaniel. *Address:* Royal College of Defence Studies, Seaford House, Belgrave Square, SW1X 8NS. *Clubs:* Beefsteak, Pitt, Aspinalls.

ROBERTS, Prof. Simon Arthur, PhD; Professor of Law, London School of Economics and Political Science, since 1986; *b* 13 April 1941; *s* of Arthur and Margaret Roberts; *m* 1965, Marian Bernadt; one *s* one *d*. *Educ:* Tonbridge Sch.; London Sch. of Econs (LLB 1962; PhD 1968). Lectr, Inst. of Public Admin, Blantyre, Malaŵi, 1963–64; London School of Economics: Asst Lectr, 1965–68; Lectr, 1968–77; Sen. Lectr, 1977–81; Reader, 1981–86. Prof. Invité, Aix-en-Provence, 1990. Gen. Ed., Modern Law Rev., 1988–95. Advr on Customary Law, Govt of Botswana, 1968–73. Member: Lord Chancellor's Adv. Bd on Family Law, 1997–2002; Adv. Cttee on Civil Costs, 2007–. *Publications:* Order and Dispute, 1979; (with J. L. Comaroff) Rules and Processes, 1981; (with W. T. Murphy and T. Flessas) Understanding Property Law, 1987, 4th edn 2004; (with M. Palmer) Dispute Processes, 1998, 2nd edn 2005. *Recreations:* art, architecture, countryside. *Address:* London School of Economics, Houghton Street, WC2A 2AE. *T:* (020) 7955 7253; *e-mail:* simon.roberts@lse.ac.uk. *Club:* Surrey.

ROBERTS, Stephen Cheveley; Principal, Stamford Endowed Schools, since 2008; *b* 23 Aug. 1956; *s* of David Roberts and Elizabeth Roberts (*née* Thornborough); *m* 1985, Joanna Meryl Cunnison; two *s*. *Educ:* Mill Hill Sch.; University Coll., Oxford (BA 1978; PGCE 1979; MA 1982). Credit Analyst, Orion Bank, 1979–80; Asst Master, Christ's Hosp., Horsham, 1980–86; Oundle School: Hd of Physics, 1986–90; Housemaster, 1990–93; Headmaster, Felsted Sch., 1993–2008. *Recreations:* golf, hockey, music, reading. *Address:* Stamford Endowed Schools, St Paul's Street, Stamford, Lincs PE9 2BS. *T:* (01780) 750310. *Clubs:* East India; Vincent's (Oxford).

ROBERTS, Ven. Stephen John; Archdeacon of Wandsworth, since 2005; *b* 6 Dec. 1958; *s* of Percy Stanley Roberts and Brenda May Roberts. *Educ:* Newcastle-under-Lyme High Sch.; King's Coll. London (BD Hons 1981); Westcott House, Cambridge; Heythrop Coll. London (MTh 1999). Ordained deacon, 1983, priest, 1984; Asst Curate, St Mary, Riverhead, with St John, Dunton Green, 1983–86; Curate, St Martin-in-the-Fields, 1986–89; Vicar, St George, Camberwell, and Warden, Trinity Coll. Centre, Peckham, 1989–2000; Canon Treas., Southwark Cathedral, and Sen. Dir of Ordinands, Southwark Dio., 2000–05. *Recreations:* cycling, walking, music, travel. *Address:* 2 Alma Road, Wandsworth, SW18 1AB. *T:* (020) 8874 8567.

ROBERTS, Stephen Pritchard; baritone; professional singer, since 1972; *b* 8 Feb. 1949; *s* of Edward Henry Roberts and Violet Pritchard. *Educ:* Royal College of Music (schol.). ARCM 1969; GRSM 1971. Professional Lay-Cleric, Westminster Cathedral Choir, 1972–76; now sings regularly in London, UK and Europe, with all major orchs and choral socs; has also sung in USA, Canada, Israel, Hong Kong, Singapore and S America. Mem., Vocal Faculty, RCM, 1993–. *Opera* rôles include: Count, in Marriage of Figaro; Falke, in Die Fledermaus; Ubalde, in Armide; Ramiro, in Ravel's L'Heure Espagnole; Aeneas, in Dido and Aeneas; Don Quixote, in Master Peter's Puppet Show; Mittenhofer, in Elegy for Young Lovers; *television* appearances include: Britten's War Requiem; Weill's Seven Deadly Sins; Delius' Sea Drift; Handel's Jeptha; Handel's Judas Maccabaeus; Penderecki's St Luke Passion, 1983 Proms; Walton's Belshazzar's Feast, 1984 Proms; *recordings* include: Tippett's King Priam; Birtwistle's Punch and Judy; Gluck's Armide; Orff's Carmina Burana; Vaughan Williams' Five Mystical Songs, Epithalamion, Sea Symphony, Fantasia on Christmas Carols, Hodie, and Serenade; Elgar's Apostles, and Caractacus; Penderecki's St Luke Passion; Fauré's Requiem; Dyson's Canterbury Pilgrims; Stravinsky songs; works by J. S. Bach, C. P. E. Bach and Duruflé. *Address:* 144 Gleneagle Road, SW16 6BA. *T:* (020) 8516 8830.

ROBERTS, Stewart Brian, MA; Headmaster, Dauntsey's School, since 1997; *b* 21 March 1952; *s* of late Evan John and Joyce Roberts; *m* 1985, Anna Susan Norman; one *s* one *d*. *Educ:* Birkenhead Sch.; St Peter's Coll., Oxford (BA 1974; PGCE 1975; MA 1978). Asst Master, Birkenhead Sch., 1975–78; Asst Master, 1978–93, (Housemaster, 1984–93), Shrewsbury Sch.; Headmaster-des., Chand Bagh Sch., Lahore, 1994; Second Master, Dauntsey's Sch., 1995–97. Mem., P&O Scholarship Bd, 2001–05. Governor: St Francis Sch., Pewsey, 1997–2002; Shiplake Coll., 2003–. Freeman, City of London, 2000. *Address:* Headmaster's House, Dauntsey's School, West Lavington, near Devizes, Wilts SN10 4HE. *T:* (01380) 814500.

ROBERTS, Susan Holt, FRCP; National Clinical Director for Diabetes, 2003–08; *b* 28 Aug. 1945; *d* of David Holt Roberts and Joyce Eastoe Roberts (*née* How); *m* 1971, Christopher Kenneth Drinkwater; two *d*. *Educ:* Middlesex Hospital Medical Sch., London (BSc 1966; MB BS 1969); Univ. of Newcastle upon Tyne (MSc Clin. Biochem. 1975). FRCP 1986. Lectr in Medicine, Meml Univ. of Newfoundland, 1974–76; Consultant Physician, Northumbria Healthcare Trust, 1978–2008. *Publications:* articles and book chapters on med. topics incl. women in medicine, diabetes, healthcare delivery and patient educn. *Recreations:* walking, gardening, knitting, cats. *Address:* 30 Battle Hill, Hexham, Northumberland NE46 2EB. *T:* (01434) 600352; *e-mail:* sue.roberts@gofo.co.uk.

ROBERTS, Prof. (Thomas) Michael, PhD; CBiol, FIBiol; Chief Executive, Central Science Laboratory, Department for Environment, Food and Rural Affairs, 2001–08, now Consultant; *b* 12 May 1948; *e s* of Robert Stanley Roberts and Mary Roberts (*née* Cliffe); *m* 1968, Ann Vaughan-Williams; one *s* two *d*. *Educ:* St Asaph Grammar Sch.; Univ. of Wales, Swansea (BSc 1969; PhD 1972). CBiol 1991; FIBiol 1991; MIEEM 1995. Asst Prof., Dept of Botany, Univ. of Toronto, 1972–74; Lectr, Dept of Botany, Univ. of Liverpool, 1974–78; Section Head, Terrestrial Ecology, Biology Section, CEGB, 1978–89; Dir, Inst. of Terrestrial Ecology, 1989–99, Dir, Centre for Ecology and Hydrology, 1999–2001, NERC. Hon. Prof., York Univ., 1993–. Ed., Jl of Applied Ecology, 1981–86. Member: DoE Adv. Cttee on Hazardous Substances, 1992–2000; HSE Adv. Cttee on Genetic Modification, 1994–99; MAFF Adv. Cttee on Pesticides, 1996–2001; Adv. Bd, Jt Inst. for Food and Nutrition, Food and Drug Admin/Univ. of Maryland, USA, 2002–08; Chm., UK Man and Biosphere Cttee, 1993–2001; Trustee, Nat. Biodiversity Network, 2000–01. Mem. Bd, Yorks and Humber Sci. and Innovation Council, 2006–08. Mem., Yorks Philosophical Soc., 2003–. Vice-Pres., Reigate Priory CC and Little Shelford CC, 2000–. *Publications:* Planning and Ecology, 1984; Ecological Aspects of Radionuclide Releases, 1985; numerous articles on applied ecology in learned jls. *Recreations:* village cricket, real ale, golf. *Address:* Central Science Laboratory, Department for Environment, Food and Rural Affairs, Sand Hutton, York YO41 1LZ.

ROBERTS, Timothy David; QC 2003; a Recorder, since 1993; *b* 4 Oct. 1955; *s* of Norman and Heather Roberts; *m* 1986, Angela Shakespeare; two *d*. *Educ:* Guisborough Grammar Sch.; Southampton Univ. (LLB Hons). Called to the Bar, Gray's Inn, 1978, Bencher, 2007; Public Solicitor, Solomon Islands, 1979–81; joined Fountain Chambers, 1982, Hd of Chambers, 2000–; in practice, specialising in criminal law. *Recreations:* music, sailing. *Address:* Fountain Chambers, Cleveland Business Centre, 1 Watson Street, Middlesbrough, Cleveland TS1 2RQ. *T:* (01642) 804040, *Fax:* (01642) 804060. *Club:* Runswick Bay Sailing.

ROBERTS, Sir William (James Denby), 3rd Bt *cr* 1909; *b* 10 Aug. 1936; *s* of Sir James Denby Roberts, 2nd Bt, OBE, and of Irene Charlotte D'Orsey, *yr d* of late William Dunn, MB, CM; *S* father, 1973. *Educ:* Rugby; Royal Agricultural Coll., Cirencester. MRAC, FRICS. Farms at Strathallan Castle. *Recreation:* swimming. *Heir:* *nephew* James Elton Denby Roberts-Buchanan, *b* 12 July 1966. *Address:* Strathallan Castle, Auchterarder, Perthshire PH3 1JZ. *T:* (01764) 662131.

ROBERTS CAIRNS, Patricia Rose Marie, (Mrs D. A. O. Cairns), OBE 2000; freelance editorial consultant; Consultant, National Magazine Co., since 1999; *b* 27 Nov. 1947; *d* of late Maj. William Roberts, MBE, RA and Catherine (*née* Slawson); *m* 1993, Dr David A. O. Cairns. *Educ:* St Barnabas Sch., Woodford Green; Open Univ. (BA). Reporter, Independent Newspapers, Essex, 1965–68; features writer, IPC mags, 1968–72; Founder Editor, Girl About Town (London's first free mag.), 1972–80; feature writer, Femail, Daily Mail, 1980–82; Associate Editor, Family Circle, 1982–84; Editor, Over 21, 1984–89; Founder Editor, House Beautiful, 1989–95; Editor-in-Chief, Good Housekeeping, 1995–99. Member: Editl Cttee, Periodical Trng Council, 1992–; Women of Year Cttee, 1993–; BSME Cttee, 1993–99; Editl Public Affairs Cttee, PPA, 1993–99; Press Complaints Commn, 1998–99. FRSA. Launch Editor of Year, BSME, 1990; Editor of Year, PPA, 1992. *Publications:* Living Images: styling yourself to success, 1990; House

Beautiful Home Handbook, 1992. *Address:* Roseburn, Haywood Road, Moffat, Dumfriesshire DG10 9BU.

ROBERTS-WEST, Lt-Col George Arthur Alston-; *see* West.

ROBERTSHAW, Patrick Edward; His Honour Judge Robertshaw; a Circuit Judge, since 1994; *b* 7 July 1945; *s* of late George Edward Robertshaw and May (*née* Tallis); *m* 1972, Sally Christine Greenburgh (*née* Searle); two *s* two *d. Educ:* Hipperholme Grammar Sch.; Southampton Univ. (LLB). Called to the Bar, Inner Temple, 1968; a Recorder, 1989–94. *Publications:* The Inglorious Twelfth: the study of a 1950s murder trial, 2005; contrib. to legal periodicals. *Recreations:* reading, listening to music, travel, photography. *Address:* Sheffield Combined Court Centre, 50 West Bar, Sheffield S3 8PH. *T:* (0114) 281 2400.

ROBERTSON, family name of **Barons Robertson of Oakridge, Robertson of Port Ellen** and **Wharton**.

ROBERTSON OF OAKRIDGE, 2nd Baron *cr* 1961; **William Ronald Robertson;** Bt 1919; Member of the London Stock Exchange, 1973–95; *b* 8 Dec. 1930; *s* of General Lord Robertson of Oakridge, GCB, GBE, KCMG, KCVO, DSO, MC, and Edith (*d* 1982), *d* of late J. B. Macindoe; *S* father, 1974; *m* 1972, Celia Jane, *d* of William R. Elworthy; one *s. Educ:* Hilton Coll., Natal; Charterhouse; Staff Coll., Camberley (psc). Served The Royal Scots Greys, 1949–69. Mem. Salters' Co. (Master, 1985–86). *Heir: s* Hon. William Brian Elworthy Robertson, *b* 15 Nov. 1975.

ROBERTSON OF PORT ELLEN, Baron *cr* 1999 (Life Peer) of Islay in Argyll and Bute; **George Islay MacNeill Robertson,** KT 2004; GCMG 2004; PC 1997; Deputy Chairman, TNK-BP, since 2006; *b* 12 April 1946; *s* of George Philip Robertson and Marion I. Robertson; *m* 1970, Sandra Wallace; two *s* one *d. Educ:* Dunoon Grammar Sch.; Univ. of Dundee (MA Hons 1968). Res. Asst, Tayside Study, 1968–69; Scottish Organiser, G&MWU, 1970–78. MP (Lab) Hamilton, 1978–97, Hamilton South, 1997–99. PPS to Sec. of State for Social Services, 1979; opposition spokesman on Scottish Affairs, 1979–80, on Defence, 1980–81, on Foreign and Commonwealth Affairs, 1981–93; principal spokesman on European Affairs, 1984–93; principal opposition front bench spokesman on Scotland, 1993–97; Sec. of State for Defence, 1997–99. Sec.-Gen., NATO, 1999–2003. Chm., Scottish Labour Party, 1977–78; Mem., Scottish Exec. of Lab. Party, 1973–79, 1993–97. Dep. Chm., 2004–06, Sen. Internat. Advr, 2007–, Cable & Wireless plc; Chm., Cable & Wireless Internat., 2006–; non-executive Director: Smiths Gp plc, 2004–06; Weir Gp plc, 2004–; Adviser: Cohen Gp, USA, 2004–; Engelfield Capital, 2004–; Royal Bank of Canada, 2004–. Vice Chm. Bd, British Council, 1985–94; Mem. Council, RIIA, 1984–91 (Jt Pres., 2001–). Chm., John Smith Meml Trust, 2004–08. Gov. and Dep. Chm., Council, Ditchley Foundn, 1989–. Hon. Regtl Col, London Scottish (Volunteers), 2000–. Elder Brother, Trinity Hse, 2002–. Pres., Hamilton Burns Club, 2002. Hon. Guild Brother, Guildry of Stirling, 2004. FRSA 1999. Hon. FRSE 2003; Hon. Sen. Fellow, Foreign Policy Assoc., USA, 2000. Hon. LLD: Dundee, Bradford, 2000; Baku State Univ., Azerbaijan, 2001; Romanian Nat. Sch. of Pol and Admin Studies, 2003; French Univ., Yerevan, Armenia, 2003; Azerbaijan Acad. of Scis, 2003; St Andrews, 2003; Glasgow Caledonian, 2004; Hon. DSc RMCS Cranfield, 2000; DUniv: Paisley, 2006; Stirling, 2008. Knight Grand Cross: Order of Merit (Italy), 2003; Order of Oranje-Nassau (Netherlands), 2003; Comdr Grand Cross, Order of Three Stars (Latvia), 2004; Grand Cross: Order of the Star (Romania), 2000; Order of Merit (Germany), 2003; Order of Merit (Poland), 2003; Order of Merit (Hungary), 2003; Order of Merit (Luxembourg), 2003; Order of Isabel the Catholic (Spain), 2003; Order of Jesus (Portugal), 2003; Order of Grand Duke Gedeminos (Lithuania), 2003; Order of Stara Planina (Bulgaria), 2003; Order of King Petar Kresimir IV (Croatia), 2003; Order of Yaroslav the Wise (Ukraine), 2005; Grand Cordon, Order of Leopold (Belgium), 2003; Presidential Medal of Freedom (USA), 2003; First Class: Order of the Tarra Mariana (Estonia), 2004; Order of the White Two-Arm Cross (Slovakia), 2004; Order for Exceptional Services (Slovenia), 2006. *Publication:* Islay and Jura: photographs, 2006. *Recreations:* reading, family, photography, golf. *Address:* House of Lords, SW1A 0PW; 1 St James's Square, SW1Y 4PD. *Clubs:* Army and Navy, Royal Commonwealth Society; Islay Golf.

ROBERTSON, Alastair, PhD; Executive Director, CSIRO Science Strategy and Investment, since 2007; *b* 18 July 1949; *s* of Robert Russell Robertson and Brenda Scott Robertson; *m* 1975, Wendy Kathleen Purchase; one *s* one *d. Educ:* Univ. of Bath (BSc Hons Applied Biology 1973; PhD Plant Biochemistry 1976). FRSC 1983; FIFST 1983. Postdoctoral Fellow, Univ. of Cambridge, 1976–79; Process Biochemist, Sigma Chemical Co., 1979–81; Head of Chemistry and Biochemistry, 1981–86, Dir of Food Science, 1986–92, Campden and Chorley Wood Food Res. Assoc.; Head of Res. and Develt, 1992–95, Technical Dir, 1995–2000, Safeway Stores plc; Dir, Inst. of Food Res., BBSRC, 2000–03; Chief Exec., Food Sci. Australia, 2003–05; Gp Exec., CSIRO Agribusiness, 2005–07. Hon. Prof., UEA, 2000–03; Res. Prof., Univ. of Tasmania, 2004–. *Publications:* 50 articles in jls on biochemistry and food sci. areas. *Recreations:* gardening, music, angling, sports. *Address:* CSIRO Science Strategy and Investment, 5 Julius Avenue, Riverside Corporate Park, Delhi Road, North Ryde, NSW 2113, Australia.

ROBERTSON, Andrew James; QC 1996; *b* 14 May 1953; *s* of Pearson Robertson and Zillah Robertson (*née* Robinson); *m* 1981, Gillian Amanda Frankel; two *s* one *d. Educ:* Bradford GS; Christ's Coll., Cambridge (MA). Called to the Bar, Middle Temple, 1975; North Eastern Circuit; a Recorder, 1994–2002. *Recreations:* hockey, winter climbing, history. *Address:* 11 King's Bench Walk, Temple, EC4Y 7EQ.

ROBERTSON, Andrew Ogilvie, OBE 1994; Senior Partner, T. C. Young, 1994–2006; *b* 30 June 1943; *s* of Alexander McArthur Ogilvie Robertson and Charlotte Rachel Robertson (*née* Cuthbert); *m* 1974, Sheila Sturton; two *s. Educ:* Sedbergh Sch.; Edinburgh Univ. (LLB 1964). Apprentice Solicitor, Maclay Murray & Spens, 1964–67; Asst Solicitor, 1967–68, Partner, 1968, T. C. Young. Secretary: Erskine Hosp., 1976–2002 (Vice-Chm., 2006–); Fedn of Community Clydeside-based Housing Assocs, 1978–93 (also Treas.); Briggait Co. Ltd, 1983–88; Princess Royal Trust for Carers, 1990–2006 (Legal Advr, 1990–2006; Trustee, 2006–); Chairman: Post Office Users' Council for Scotland, 1988–99; Gtr Glasgow Community and Mental Health Services NHS Trust, 1994–97; Glasgow Royal Infirmary Univ. NHS Trust, 1997–99; Gtr Glasgow Primary Care NHS Trust, 1998–2004; Member: POUNC, 1988–99; Gtr Glasgow Health Bd, 1999– (Vice-Chm., 2004–07; Chm., 2007–). Chm., Lintel Trust (formerly Scottish Housing Assocs Charitable Trust), 1990–2007; Trustee, Housing Assocs Charitable Trust (UK), 1990–97. Non exec. Dir, Scottish Building Soc., 1994– (Chm., 2003–06). Gov., Sedbergh Sch., 2000–08. *Recreations:* climbing, sailing, swimming, reading, fishing. *Address:* 11 Kirklee Road, Glasgow G12 0RQ. *T:* (0141) 357 1555. *Club:* Western (Glasgow).

ROBERTSON, Angus; MP (SNP) Moray, since 2001; *b* 28 Sept. 1969. *Educ:* Broughton High Sch., Edinburgh; Univ. of Aberdeen (MA 1991). News Editor, Austrian Broadcasting Corp., 1991; reporter, BBC, Austria, etc, 1991–99; communications consultant and journalist, 1999–. SNP spokesman on foreign affairs, 2001–, on defence, 2003. Contested (SNP) Midlothian, Scottish Parlt, 1999. *Address:* (constituency office) 9 Wards Road, Elgin, Moray IV30 1NL; c/o House of Commons, SW1A 0AA.

ROBERTSON, Rev. Charles, LVO 2005; JP; Parish Minister, Canongate (The Kirk of Holyroodhouse), 1978–2005, now Minister Emeritus; Chaplain: to the Queen in Scotland, since 1991; to the High Constables and Guard of Honour of Holyroodhouse, since 1993; *b* 22 Oct. 1940; *s* of late Thomas Robertson and Elizabeth Halley; *m* 1965, Alison Margaret Malloch; one *s* two *d. Educ:* Camphill School, Paisley; Edinburgh Univ. (MA); New College, Edinburgh. Asst Minister, North Morningside, Edinburgh, 1964–65; Parish Minister, Kiltearn, Ross-shire, 1965–78. Chaplain to Lord High Comr, 1990, 1991, 1996 (the Princess Royal). Convener, Gen. Assembly's Panel on Worship, 1995–99 (Sec., 1982–95); C of S rep. on Joint Liturgical Group, 1984–99 (Chm., 1994–99). Mem., Broadcasting Standards Council, 1988–91, 1992–93. Chaplain: Clan Donnachaidh Soc., 1981–96; New Club, Edinburgh, 1986–; Moray House Coll. of Educn, then Edinburgh Univ. at Moray House, 1986–2002; No 2 (City of Edinburgh) Maritime HQ Unit, 1987–99, No 603 (City of Edinburgh) Sqn, 1999–, RAAF; Incorp. of Goldsmiths of City of Edinburgh, 2000–; Edinburgh Merchants' Co., 2002–; Edinburgh and Lothians Scots Guards Association, 2004–; Convenery of Trades of Edinburgh, 2005–. Lectr, St Colm's Coll., 1980–94. Mem., Historic Buildings Council for Scotland, 1990–99. Chairman: Bd of Queensberry House Hosp., 1989–96 (Mem., 1978–); Queensberry Trust, 1996–; Gov., St Columba's Hospice, 1986–2006; Trustee: Edinburgh Old Town Trust, 1987–94; Edinburgh Old Town Charitable Trust, 1994–; Edinburgh World Heritage Trust, 1999–2000; Church Hymnary Trust, 1987–; Carnegie Trust for the Univs of Scotland, 2005–; Pres., Church Service Soc., 1988–91. JP Edinburgh, 1980–2006. Sec. of cttees which compiled Hymns for a Day, 1983, Songs of God's People, 1988, Worshipping Together, 1991, Clann ag Urnaigh, 1991, Common Order, 1994, Common Ground, 1998; Sec., Cttee to Revise Church Hymnary, 1995–2004. *Publications:* (ed) Singing the Faith, 1990; (ed) St Margaret Queen of Scotland and her Chapel, 1994; (jtly) By Lamplight, 2000. *Recreations:* Scottish and Edinburgh history and literature, hymnody, collecting Canongate miscellanea. *Address:* 3 Ross Gardens, Edinburgh EH9 3BS. *T:* (0131) 662 9025. *Clubs:* Athenæum; Puffins, New (Hon. Mem.), Royal Scots (Hon. Mem.) (Edinburgh).

ROBERTSON, Christine Joyce; *see* Howe, C. J.

ROBERTSON, Daphne Jean Black, WS; Sheriff of Lothian and Borders at Edinburgh, 1996–2000; *b* 31 March 1937; *d* of Rev. Robert Black Kincaid and Ann Parker Collins; *m* 1965, Donald Buchanan Robertson, *qv. Educ:* Hillhead High Sch.; Greenock Acad.; Edinburgh Univ. (MA); Glasgow Univ. (LLB). Admitted solicitor, 1961; WS 1977; Sheriff of Glasgow and Strathkelvin, 1979–96.

ROBERTSON, Donald Buchanan; QC (Scot.) 1973; Temporary Judge, Court of Session, Scotland, 1991–2002; *b* 29 March 1932; *s* of Donald Robertson, yachtbuilder, Sandbank, Argyll, and Jean Dunsmore Buchanan; *m* 1st, 1955, Louise Charlotte, *d* of Dr J. Linthorst-Homan; one *s* one *d*; 2nd, 1965, Daphne Jean Black Kincaid (*see* D. J. B. Robertson). *Educ:* Dunoon Grammar Sch.; Glasgow Univ. (LLB). Admitted Solicitor, 1954; Royal Air Force (National Service), 1954–56. Passed Advocate, 1960; Standing Junior to Registrar of Restrictive Practices, 1970–73. Member: Sheriff Court Rules Council, 1972–76; Royal Commn on Legal Services in Scotland, 1976–80; Legal Aid Central Cttee, 1982–85; Criminal Injuries Compensation Bd, 1986–2002; Chm., VAT Tribunal, 1978–85. Hon. Sheriff, Lothian and Peebles, 1982–. FSA (Scot.) 1982. *Recreations:* shooting, numismatics, genealogy. *Address:* 11 Grosvenor Crescent, Edinburgh EH12 5EL. *T:* (0131) 337 5544; Cranshaws Castle, By Duns, Berwickshire TD11 3SJ. *T:* (01361) 890268. *Club:* New (Edinburgh).

ROBERTSON, Geoffrey Ronald; QC 1988; a Recorder, since 1999; barrister; author; *b* 30 Sept. 1946; *s* of Francis Albert Robertson and Bernice Joy (*née* Beattie); *m* 1990, Kathryn Marie Lette, *qv*; one *s* one *d. Educ:* Epping Boys' High Sch.; Univ. of Sydney (BA 1966; LLB Hons 1970); University Coll., Oxford (BCL 1972; Rhodes Schol.). Called to the Bar, Middle Temple, 1973, Bencher, 1997; Supreme Court of NSW, 1977, of Antigua, 1990, of Trinidad, 1992, of Malaysia, 1998, of Hong Kong, 2001, of Fiji, 2002, of Anguilla, 2007. An Asst Recorder, 1993–99. Head, Doughty Street Chambers, 1990–. Visiting Fellow: Univ. of NSW, 1977; Warwick Univ., 1980–81; Vis. Prof., Birkbeck Coll., and Queen Mary, London Univ., 1997–. Consultant on Human Rights to Attorney Gen. of Australia, 1983; Consultant (Commonwealth Secretariat) to Constitutional Convention, Seychelles, 1993. Chm., Inquiry into Press Council, 1982–83; Counsel: Royal Commn on Arms Trafficking, Antigua, 1990–91; Commn on Admin of Justice, Trinidad, 2000. Appeal Judge, UN Special Ct for Sierra Leone, 2002–07 (and Pres., 2002–04). Chm., Commn on UN Internal Justice Reform, 2006–07; Mem., UN Internal Justice Council, 2008–. Member: BFI Wkg Party on New Technologies, 1984; Exec. Council, ICA, 1987–97; Freedom of Inf. Campaign, 1987–; Charter 88, 1988–96; Justice, 1991–. Chm., BMA Cttee on Medical Inf. and Patient Privacy, 1994. Chm., Common Sense, 1998–. *Television:* Moderator, Hypotheticals, 1981–; writer and presenter, Tree of Liberty, 1982; Chm., The World This Week, 1987; writer and narrator, 44 Days (documentary), 1992. Editor, legal column, The Guardian, 1980–85. Freedom of Information Award, 1993. *Publications:* The Trials of Oz (play), 1973 (televised 1991); Whose Conspiracy?, 1974; Reluctant Judas, 1976; Obscenity, 1979; People Against the Press, 1983; (with A. Nicol) Media Law, 1984, 5th edn 2007; Hypotheticals, 1986; Does Dracula have Aids?, 1987; Freedom, the Individual and the Law, 6th edn 1989, 7th edn 1993; Geoffrey Robertson's Hypotheticals, 1991; The Justice Game, 1998; Crimes Against Humanity, 1999, 3rd edn 2006; The Tyrannicide Brief, 2005; The Levellers: the Putney debates, 2007; contribs to anthologies and learned jls. *Recreations:* tennis, opera, fishing. *Address:* Doughty Street Chambers, 11 Doughty Street, WC1N 2PL. *T:* (020) 7404 1313, *Fax:* (020) 7404 2283.

ROBERTSON, Air Marshal Graeme Alan, CBE 1988 (OBE 1985); Co-ordinator, British-American Community Relations, Ministry of Defence, since 2004; *b* 22 Feb. 1945; *s* of Ronald James Harold Robertson, DFC and Constance Rosemary (*née* Freeman); *m* 1972, Barbara Ellen (*née* Mardon); one *d. Educ:* Bancroft's Sch.; RAF Coll., Cranwell; BA Open Univ. Pilot: 8 Sqn, 1968–69; 6 Sqn, 1970–72; 228 OCU, 1972–73; Flight Commander: 550 TFTS, USAF, 1973–76; 56 Sqn, 1976–77; RAF Staff Coll., 1977–78; OR/Air Plans Staff, MoD, 1978–82; Commanding Officer: 92 Sqn, 1982–84; 23 Sqn, 1984–85; RAF Wattisham, 1985–87; Hon. ADC to the Queen, 1985–87; Dir of Air Staff Briefing and Co-ordination, MoD, 1987–88; RCDS, 1989; Dir of Defence Programmes, MoD, 1990–91; Dep. C-in-C, RAF Germany, 1991–93; AOC No 2 Gp, 1993–94; ACDS (Programmes), MoD, 1994–96; C of S and Dep. C-in-C, Strike Comd, 1996–98; Hon. Col, 77 Engr Regt (Vols), 1996–99. Defence and Air Advr, BAe, subseq. Sen. Mil. Advr, BAE Systems, 1999–2003. Man. Dir, Blackbourne Wells Ltd, 2003–. FRSA 1995; FRAeS 1997. Freeman, City of London, 1997. QCVSA 1973. *Recreations:* shooting, sailing, golf, winter sports. *Address:* c/o National Westminster Bank, Sleaford, Lincs NG34 7BJ. *Clubs:* Royal Air Force, MCC.

ROBERTSON, Hamish, CB 1992; MBE 1966; Under Secretary, Scottish Office Education Department (formerly Scottish Education Department), 1987–92; *b* 6 April 1931; *s* of James and Elizabeth Robertson, Huntly; *m* 1955, Barbara Suzanne Taylor, *d* of late Dr G. C. and I. H. McL. Taylor, Peterhead; two *s* two *d*. *Educ:* The Gordon Schs, Huntly; Aberdeen Univ. (MA). RA, 1952–54. Joined Colonial Admin. Service; Nyasaland, 1954–64; HMOCS, Malawi, 1964–67; Scottish Office: Principal, 1967; Asst Sec., 1973. *Recreations:* country pursuits. *Address:* 14 Harviestoun Road, Dollar FK14 7HG. *T:* (01259) 742374.

ROBERTSON, Hugh Michael, FRGS; MP (C) Faversham and Mid Kent, since 2001; *b* 9 Oct. 1962; *s* of George and June Robertson; *m* 2002, Anna Copson; one *s*. *Educ:* King's Sch., Canterbury; RMA Sandhurst; Reading Univ. (BSc Hons Land Mgt (Property Investment)). Served Life Guards, 1985–95 (Armourers' and Brasiers' Prize, 1986): active service: NI, 1988; UN Cyprus, 1988; Gulf War, 1991; Bosnia, 1994; i/c Household Cavalry on Queen's Birthday Parade and State Opening of Parlt as Field Officer of the Escort, 1993; Silver Stick Adjutant, 1994–95; retd in rank of Major; Schroder Investment Mgt, 1995–2001 (Asst Dir, 1999–2001). An Opposition Whip, 2002–04; Shadow Sports Minister, 2004–05; Shadow Minister for Sport and the Olympics, 2005–. Sec., Parly Fruit Gp., 2001–; Chm., All Party UN Gp, 2005–. Gov., Westminster Foundn for Democracy, 2005–. FRGS 1995. Sultan of Brunei's Personal Order of Merit, 1993. *Recreations:* cricket, hockey. *Address:* House of Commons, SW1A 0AA. *T:* (020) 7219 2643. *Clubs:* Cavalry and Guards, MCC (Playing Mem.).

ROBERTSON, Iain Samuel, CBE 2002; CA; Chairman, Corporate Banking and Financial Markets, Royal Bank of Scotland, 2001–05 (Chief Executive, 2000–01); *b* 27 Dec. 1945; *s* of Alfred and Kathleen Robertson; *m* 1972, Morag; two *s* two *d*. *Educ:* Jordanhill College Sch.; Glasgow Univ. (LLB). Industry and professional practice, 1966–72; Civil Servant, 1972–83; Dir, Locate in Scotland, 1983–86; Chief Exec., SDA, 1987–90; Gp Finance Dir, County Natwest, 1990–92; Royal Bank of Scotland: Man. Dir, Corporate and Instnl Banking Div., 1992–98; Chief Exec., UK Bank, 1998–2000. Non-executive Director: Scottish Development Finance, 1983–90; Selective Assets Trust plc, 1989–96; British Empire Securities & Gen. Trust plc, 1995–2007; BT (Scotland), 2004–08; Cairn Capital Ltd, 2004–08; John Menzies plc, 2004–. *Recreations:* golf, reading.

ROBERTSON, Ian, CA; Partner, Robertson Consultancy, since 2007; President, Institute of Chartered Accountants of Scotland, 2004–05; *b* 10 Aug. 1947; *s* of James Love Robertson and Mary Hughes Robertson (*née* Reid); *m* 1st, 1968, Susan Moira Scott (marr. diss.); two *s* one *d*; 2nd, 2001, Fiona Ann Hervey. *Educ:* Queen's Park Sch., Glasgow. CA 1969. Chief Accountant, Whitbread Scotland Ltd, 1973–76; Dir, J. & A. Ferguson Ltd, 1976–82; Chief Accountant, United Biscuits, Glasgow, 1982–84; Financial Controller, Terry's of York, 1984–87; Finance Dir, Dairy Div., 1987–90, Gp Finance Controller, 1991–94, Northern Foods plc; Finance Dir, 1994–2003, Gp Chief Exec., 2003–07, Wilson Bowden plc. Member: Financial Reporting Council, 2004–; Audit Adv. Bd, Scottish Parlt Corporate Body, 2007–. Mem. (C), 1973–84, Chm., 1980–84, Eastwood DC. Mem. Council, 1996–2003, Sen. Vice-Pres., 2003–04, ICAS. CCMI 2004 (FCMI 1976). *Recreations:* reading, music, travel, walking. *Address:* e-mail: ianochaye@aol.com.

ROBERTSON of Brackla, Maj.-Gen. Ian Argyll, CB 1968; MBE 1947; MA; DL; Vice-Lord-Lieutenant, Highland Region (Nairn), 1980–88; Representative in Scotland of Messrs Spink & Son, 1969–76; Chairman, Royal British Legion, Scotland, 1974–77 (Vice-Chairman, 1971–74); *b* 17 July 1913; 2nd *s* of John Argyll Robertson and Sarah Lilian Pitt Healing; *m* 1939, Marjorie Violet Isobel Duncan; two *d*. *Educ:* Winchester Coll.; Trinity Coll., Oxford. Brigade Major: 152 Highland Bde, 1943; 231 Infantry Bde, 1944; GSO2, Staff College, Camberley, 1944–45; AAG, 15 Indian Corps, 1945–46; GSO1, 51 Highland Div., 1952–54; commnd Seaforth Highlanders, 1954; Comdg 1st Bn Seaforth Highlanders, 1954–57; Comdg Support Weapons Wing, 1957–59; Comdg 127 (East Lancs) Inf. Bde, TA, 1959–61; Nat. Defence College, Delhi, 1962–63; Comdg School of Infantry, 1963–64; Commanding 51st Highland Division, 1964–66; Director of Army Equipment Policy, Ministry of Defence, 1966–68; retd. Mem. Council, Nat. Trust for Scotland, 1972–75. DL Nairn 1973. *Recreations:* various in a minor way. *Address:* Gardeners Cottage, Brackla, Cawdor, Nairn IV12 5QY. *T:* (01667) 404220. *Clubs:* Army and Navy, MCC; Vincent's (Oxford).

ROBERTSON, Rear-Adm. Ian George William, CB 1974; DSC 1944; *b* 21 Oct. 1922; *s* of late W. H. Robertson, MC, and Mrs A. M. Robertson; *m* 1947, Barbara Irène Holdsworth; one *s* one *d*. *Educ:* Radley College. Joined RNVR, 1941; qual. Pilot; Sub-Lt 1943; air strike ops against enemy shipping and attacks against German battleship Tirpitz, 1944 (DSC); Lieut, RN, 1945; flying and instructional appts, 1944–53; Comdr (Air): RNAS Culdrose, 1956; HMS Albion, 1958; in command: HMS Keppel, 1960; HMS Mohawk, 1963; RNAS Culdrose, 1965; idc 1968; in comd, HMS Eagle, 1970; Admiral Comdg Reserves, 1972–74; retd 1974. Comdr 1954; Captain 1963; Rear-Adm. 1972. Dir-Gen., Navy League, 1975–76; Scoutreach Resources Organiser, Scout Assoc., 1976–79. Pres., Craft Club, 1992–99. *Recreations:* golf, sailing, fishing. *Address:* The Studio, Bedford Place, Uckfield, E Sussex TN22 3LW. *T:* (01825) 764682. *Clubs:* Naval; Piltdown Golf.

ROBERTSON, James Andrew Stainton, PhD; Director, Private Finance Value for Money Studies, since 1995, and Chief Economist, since 2007, National Audit Office; *b* 23 April 1949; *s* of James Robertson and Margaret Elodie Robertson (*née* Stainton); *m* 1979, Ann Leatherbarrow; one *s* one *d*. *Educ:* Highgate Sch.; Univ. of Essex (BA Econs); LSE (MSc Econs, PhD). Sen. Econ. Asst and Econ. Advr, Dept of Employment, 1975–82; Econ. Advr, Dept of Energy, 1982–86; Senior Economic Adviser: DTI, 1986–89; Dept of Transport, 1989–90; Hd of Industrial and Regl Econs, DTI, 1990–93; Chief Econ. Advr, Dept of Employment, subseq. DFEE, 1993–95. *Publications:* contrib. various learned jls. *Recreations:* family, do-it-yourself, gardening. *Address:* National Audit Office, 151 Buckingham Palace Road, SW1W 9SP.

ROBERTSON, James Downie, RSA 1989 (ARSA 1974); RSW 1962; RGI 1980; Senior Lecturer in Fine Art (Drawing and Painting), 1975–96, Painter in Residence, 1996–98, Glasgow School of Art; *b* 2 Nov. 1931; *s* of Thomas Robertson and Mary Welsh; *m* 1970, Ursula Orr Crawford; two step *s* one step *d*. *Educ:* Hillhead High Sch., Glasgow; Glasgow Sch. of Art. DA Glasgow. Taught at Keith Grammar Sch., 1957–58; Glasgow School of Art: part time Lectr, 1959; Lectr in Drawing and Painting, 1967. Vis. Lectr, Art Schools and Univs, Scotland, England and overseas; one-man exhibitions, 1961–, UK, Ireland, Spain, USA, including: Christopher Hull Gall., London, 1984, 1987, 1989; Jorgensen Fine Art Gall., Dublin, 1995, 2005; Roger Billcliffe Gall., Glasgow, 2000, 2006; retrospective, Glasgow Sch. of Art, 2000; Scottish Gall., Edinburgh, 2008; numerous group exhibns; annual exhibns at RSA, RSW, RGI, RA; works in public collections of arts socs, art galleries (incl. RSA), corporations, banks, univs and in many private collections. Lectr, Sorbonne Univ., 2007. Hon. DLitt Glasgow, 2001. Awards: RGI, 1971, 1982, 1990; RSW, 1976, 1981, 1987, 1999; RSA, 1993 (Scottish Post Office Award); Shell Exploration and Production Award, 1985; Dunfermline Building Soc. Prize, RSA, 2001. *Recreations:* drawing, painting. *Address:* Carruthmuir, by Kilbarchan, Renfrewshire PA10 2QA. *T:* (01505) 613592. *Club:* Glasgow Art (Pres., 2001–03, 2004–06).

ROBERTSON, John; MP (Lab) Glasgow North West, since 2005 (Glasgow Anniesland, Nov. 2000–2005); *b* 17 April 1952; *s* of Charles Robertson and Agnes Millen Robertson (*née* Webster); *m* 1973, Eleanor Munro; three *d*. *Educ:* Shawlands Acad.; Langside Coll.; Stow Coll. (HNC Electrical Engrg). GPO, subseq. PO, then British Telecom, 1969–2000 (Customer Service Field Manager, BT, 1991–2000). PPS to Minister of State, FCO, 2005–. Chairman, All Party Parliamentary Groups: on telecommunications, subseq. communications, 2002–; on music, 2005– (Sec., 2003–05); on nuclear energy, 2005–; on Nigeria, 2005–. *Recreations:* football, cricket, reading, music. *Address:* House of Commons, SW1A 0AA; (constituency office) 131 Dalsetter Avenue, Glasgow G15 8TE. *T:* (0141) 944 7298. *Clubs:* Garrowhill Cricket, Cambus Athletic Football, Old Kilpatrick Bowling (Glasgow).

ROBERTSON, John David H.; *see* Home Robertson.

ROBERTSON, John Davie Manson, CBE 1993 (OBE 1978); DL; FRSE; Chairman, S. & J. D. Robertson Group, since 1979; *b* 6 Nov. 1929; *s* of late John Robertson and Margaret Gibson (*née* Wright); *m* 1959, Elizabeth Amelia Macpherson; two *s* two *d*. *Educ:* Kirkwall Grammar Sch.; Univ. of Edinburgh (BL). Anglo Iranian Oil Co., later BP, UK and ME, 1953–58; S. & J. D. Robertson Gp, 1958–. Dir, Stanley Services, Falkland Is, 1987–; Founder Chm., Orkney Today, 2003–; Chm., Orkney Media Gp, 2007–. Chairman: Kirkwall Ba' Cttee, 1977–; Orkney Health Bd, 1983–91 (Mem., 1974–79, Vice-Chm., 1979–83); Highland Health Bd, 1991–97; N of Scotland Water Authy, 1995–98. Member: Bd of Mgt, Orkney Hosps, 1970–74; Highlands and Is Consultative Council, 1988–91; Highlands and Is Enterprise, 1990–95; NHS Tribunal, 1990–; Chairman: Children's Panel, Orkney, 1971–76 (Chm., Adv. Cttee, 1977–82); Highlands and Is Savings Cttee, 1975–78; Scottish Health Mgt Efficiency Gp, 1985–95; Chm. and Vice-Chm., Scottish Health Bds Chairmen's Gp, 1995–97. Chm., Lloyds TSB Foundn for Scotland, 1997–99 (Trustee, 1989–99). Hon. Sheriff, Grampian Highland and Islands, 1977–. Hon. Vice Consul for Denmark, 1972–2004; Hon. Consul for Germany, 1976–2007. DL Sutherland, 1999. FRSE 2000; FRSA 1993. Hon. FCIWEM 1996. Knight, Order of Dannebrog (Denmark), 1982; Officer's Cross, Order of Merit (Germany), 1999 (Cavalier's Cross, 1986). *Publications:* Uppies and Doonies, 1967; (ed) An Orkney Anthology, 1991; Spinningdale and its Mill 1791-2000, 2000; The Kirkwall Ba', 2004; The Island of Fara 1739–2007. *Recreations:* shooting, fishing, history, art. *Address:* S. & J. D. Robertson Gp, Dunkirk, Shore Street, Kirkwall, Orkney KW15 1LG; Spinningdale House, Spinningdale, Sutherland IV24 3AD. *T:* (01862) 881240. *Club:* New (Edinburgh).

ROBERTSON, Rear Adm. John Keith, CB 1983; FIET; *b* 16 July 1926; *s* of G. M. and J. L. Robertson; *m* 1951, Kathleen (*née* Bayntun); one *s* three *d*. *Educ:* RNC Dartmouth; Clare Coll., Cambridge (BA 1949). FIET (FIEE 1981). RNC Dartmouth, 1940–43; served, 1943–83 (Clare Coll., Cambridge, 1946–49): HM Ships Queen Elizabeth, Zest, Gabbard, Aisne and Decoy; Staff, RNC Dartmouth; Grad. Recruiting; Weapon Engr Officer, HMS Centaur; Comdr, RNEC Manadon; RCDS; Captain Technical Intell. (Navy), 1974–76; Captain Fleet Maintenance, Portsmouth, 1976–78; Dir, Naval Recruiting, 1978–79; Dir, Management and Support of Intelligence, MoD, 1980–82; ACDS (Intelligence), 1982–83. *Recreations:* hockey, tennis, golf, wood carving. *Address:* Alpina, Kingsdown, Corsham, Wilts SN13 8BJ. *Clubs:* Corkscrew (Bath); Kingsdown Golf.

ROBERTSON, John Shaw; Rector, Dollar Academy, since 1994; *b* Glasgow, 7 April 1950; *s* of David and Margaret Robertson; *m* 1973, Mary Roy; one *s* one *d*. *Educ:* Univ. of Glasgow (MA English Lang. and Lit.; DipEd). English master, Housemaster, then Asst Headmaster, Daniel Stewart's & Melville Coll., 1973–87; Dep. Rector, Dollar Acad., 1987–93. Principal Examr, English (H), Scottish Exam. Bd, 1990–94. Headmasters' and Headmistresses' Conference: Member: Academic Policy Cttee, 1997–2003; Membership Cttee, 2003– (Chm., 2007–); Chm., Scottish Div., 2000. Mem., Dollar Burns Club. *Publications:* Stewart's Melville: the first ten years, 1984; contrib. articles on educn, curriculum, assessment and on Robertson Davies, Canadian novelist. *Recreations:* cricket (Scottish), music (English), literature (international). *Address:* Dollar Academy, Dollar FK14 7DU. *T:* (01259) 742511, *Fax:* (01259) 742867; *e-mail:* rector@dollaracademy.org.uk. *Clubs:* East India; Scottish Cricket Union (Life Member).

ROBERTSON, John William; Director, John Robertson Architects, since 2005; *b* 27 Aug. 1956; *s* of Ian Middleton Strachan Robertson and Agnes Ramsey Seaton Robertson; *m* 1984, Judy Peacock; one *s* two *d*. *Educ:* Univ. of Dundee (BSc 1976); Univ. of Liverpool (BArch Hons 1979). RIBA 1981. Partner, Fitzroy Robinson Partnership, 1986–93; Dir, Hurley Robertson and Associates, 1993–2005. Projects include: One Great St Helens, London (British Council for Offices Award, 2000); restoration and refurbishment of Daily Express Bldg, Fleet Street (Royal Fine Art Commn Award, 2001; City Heritage Award, 2002); 10 Queen St Place, EC4 (British Council for Offices Award, 2007); Park House, Finsbury Circus, 2008. Mem., City Architectural Forum, 1994–. *Publication:* contrib. Architecture Today. *Recreations:* bagpiping, golf, ski-ing, Norfolk terriers. *Address:* John Robertson Architects, 111 Southwark Street, SE1 0JF. *T:* (020) 7633 5100, *Fax:* (020) 7620 0091; *e-mail:* john.robertson@jra.co.uk. *Clubs:* Royal Automobile; Berkshire Golf.

ROBERTSON, John Windeler; Senior Partner, Wedd Durlacher Mordaunt, 1979–86; *b* 9 May 1934; *s* of late John Bruce Robertson and Evelyn Windeler Robertson; *m* 1st, 1959, Jennifer-Ann Gourdou (marr. diss.); one *s* one *d*; 2nd, 1987, Rosemary Helen Jane Banks. *Educ:* Winchester Coll. National Service, RNVR, 1953–55. Joined Wedd Jefferson & Co. (Members of Stock Exchange), 1955; Partner, 1961. Dep. Chm., Barclays de Zoete Wedd Securities Ltd (BZW), 1986–88. Dep. Chm., Stock Exchange, 1976–79 (Mem. Council, 1966–86); Dir, Securities Assoc., 1986–88. Mem., City Capital Markets' Cttee, 1981–88. Trustee, Lloyds TSB (formerly TSB) Foundn, 1991–98. Mem. Council, GDBA, 1989–2000 (Chm., 1993–2000). *Recreations:* marine art, bell ringing, walking. *Address:* Eckensfield Barn, Compton, near Chichester, West Sussex PO18 9NT. *T:* (023) 9263 1239. *Club:* City of London.

ROBERTSON, Kathryn Marie; *see* Lette, K. M.

ROBERTSON, Laurence Anthony; MP (C) Tewkesbury, since 1997; *b* 29 March 1958; *s* of James Robertson and Jean (*née* Larkin); *m* 1989, Susan (*née* Lees); two step *d*. *Educ:* St James C of E Sch., Farnworth; Farnworth Grammar Sch.; Bolton Inst. Higher Educn. Work study engr, 1976–82; industrial consultant, 1982–92; charity fundraising, 1992–97 (raised about £2 million for various charities). Contested (C): Makerfield, 1987; Ashfield, 1992. An Opposition Whip, 2001–03; Opposition front bench spokesman on economic affairs, 2003–05; Shadow Minister for NI, 2005–. Member: Envmt Audit Select Cttee, 1997–99; Social Security Select Cttee, 1999–2001; European Scrutiny Select Cttee, 1999–2002; Educn and Skills Select Cttee, 2001; Jt Cttee on Consolidation of Bills,

1997–2001; Secretary: Cons. Back Bench Constitutional Cttee, 1997–2001; 92 Gp, 2001–02. *Recreations:* sport (ran 6 marathons), particularly horseracing and golf, reading, writing, history. *Address:* House of Commons, SW1A 0AA. *T:* (020) 7219 4196; 22 High Street, Tewkesbury GL20 6DL. *T:* (01684) 291640.

ROBERTSON, Sir Lewis, Kt 1991; CBE 1969; FRSE; industrialist, administrator, and corporate recovery specialist; Trustee, Carnegie Trust for Universities of Scotland, since 1963 (Member, Executive Committee, 1963–2003; Chairman, 1990–2003); *b* 28 Nov. 1922; *s* of John Farquharson Robertson and Margaret Arthur; *m* 1950, Elspeth Badenoch (*d* 2001); two *s* one *d* (and one *s* decd). *Educ:* Trinity Coll., Glenalmond. Accountancy training; RAF Intelligence, Bletchley Park. Chm., 1968–70, and Man. Dir, 1965–70, Scott & Robertson Ltd; Chief Executive, 1971–76, and Dep. Chm., 1973–76, Grampian Holdings plc; Director: Scottish and Newcastle Breweries plc, 1975–87; Whitman (International) SA (formerly IC Industries (International) SA), Geneva, 1987–90; Bank of Edinburgh Group (formerly Aristuein), 1990–94; EFM Income Trust plc, 1991–99; Scottish Financial Enterprise, 1991–93; Berkeley Hotel Co., 1995–97; Chairman: Girobank Scotland, 1984–90; Borthwicks (formerly Thomas Borthwick & Sons plc), 1985–89; F. J. C. Lilley, subseq. Lilley, 1986–93; Triplex Lloyd, 1987–90 (F. H. Lloyd Hldgs, 1982–87; Triplex, 1983–87); Havelock Europa plc, 1989–92; Stakis plc, 1991–95; Postern Exec. Gp Ltd, 1991–96. Mem., 1975–76, Dep. Chm. and Chief Exec., Scottish Develt Agency, 1976–81. Chm., Eastern Regional Hosp. Bd (Scotland), 1960–70; Member: Provincial Synod, Episcopal Church of Scotland, 1963–83 (Chm. Policy Cttee, 1974–76); (Sainsbury) Cttee of Enquiry, Pharmaceutical Industry, 1965–67; Court (Finance Convener), Univ. of Dundee, 1967–70; Monopolies and Mergers Commn, 1969–76; Arts Council of GB (and Chm., Scottish Arts Council), 1970–71; Scottish Economic Council, 1977–83; Scottish Post Office Bd, 1984–90; British Council (Chm., Scottish Adv. Cttee), 1978–87; Council, BESO, 1995–98 (Chm., Scotland, 1995–98); Council, Scottish Business School, 1978–82; Restrictive Practices Court, 1983–96; Edinburgh Univ. Press Cttee, 1985–88; Bd, Friends of Royal Scottish Acad., 1986–95; Chairman: Bd for Scotland, BIM, 1981–83; Scotland, Imperial Soc. of Kts Bachelor, 1994–99. Mem., Adv. Bd, Edinburgh edn of Waverley novels, 1984–. Trustee: Foundn for Study of Christianity and Society, 1980–88; RSE Scotland Foundn, 1996–2000 (Chm., 1999–2000); Foundn for Skin Res., 2000–04; Scottish Cancer Foundn, 2000–06; Trustee and Mem. Bd, Advanced Mgt Prog., Scotland, 1996–2003. FRSE 1978 (Mem. Council, 1992–99; Treasurer, 1994–99; Bicentenary Medal, 2001); CCMI (CBIM 1976). Hon. FRCSE 1999. Hon. LLD: Dundee, 1971; Aberdeen, 1999; Hon. DBA Napier, 1992; DUniv: Stirling, 1993; Glasgow, 2003. Lifetime achievement award, Soc. of Turnaround Practitioners, 2004. *Recreations:* foreign travel, computer use, music, reading, listmaking, things Italian. *Address:* Flat 5, 29 Inverleith Place, Edinburgh EH3 5QD. *T:* (0131) 552 3045; *e-mail:* lr32scp@talk21.com. *Clubs:* Athenæum; New (Edinburgh).

ROBERTSON, Nelson; *see* Robertson, W. N.

ROBERTSON, Nicholas John; Chief Executive Officer, ASOS.com, since 1999; *b* Woking, Nov. 1967; *s* of John Spencer Robertson and Cynthia Mary Robertson; *m* 2004, Janine Coulson; one *d. Educ:* Canford Sch., Wimborne. Young and Rubicam, 1987–92; Carat UK, 1992–96; Entertainment Marketing UK Ltd, 1996–99. *Recreations:* ski-ing, Chelsea FC, cycling. *Address:* ASOS.com, Greater London House, Hampstead Road, NW1 7FB. *T:* (020) 7756 1000, *Fax:* (020) 7756 1001.

ROBERTSON, Prof. Norman Robert Ean, CBE 1991; FDSRCPSGlas; Professor of Orthodontics, 1970–92, Dean of the Dental School, 1985–92, University of Wales College of Medicine; Hon. Consulting Orthodontist, South Glamorgan Health Authority, since 1992 (Hon. Consultant in Orthodontics, 1970–92); *b* 13 March 1931; *s* of late Robert Robertson and Jean Robertson (*née* Dunbar); *m* 1954, Morag Wyllie, *d* of George McNicol, MA; three *s* two *d. Educ:* Hamilton Acad.; Glasgow Univ. (BDS); Manchester Univ. (MDS 1962; DDS 1969). FDSRCPSGlas 1967. Registrar, then Sen. Registrar in Orthodontics, Glasgow Dental Hosp., 1957–59; Lectr in Orthodontics, 1960–62, Sen. Lectr in Orthodontics, 1962–70, Manchester Univ. Member: GDC, 1985–94; Standing Dental Adv. Cttee, 1989–92; S Glamorgan HA, 1976–92. *Publications:* Oral Orthopaedics and Orthodontics for Cleft Lip and Palate, 1983; articles in dental and med. jls. *Recreation:* painting. *Address:* 26 Heol Tyn y Cae, Rhiwbina, Cardiff CF14 6DJ. *T:* (029) 2061 3439.

ROBERTSON, Patricia; QC 2006; *b* 1 Aug. 1964; *d* of George and Sheila Robertson; *m* 1991, Tom Henry; two *s* one *d. Educ:* St George's Sch., Edinburgh; Balliol Coll., Oxford (BA Mod. Hist.); City Univ. (Dip. Law). Called to the Bar, Inner Temple, 1988; in practice as a barrister, 1989–, specialising in commercial law, banking and financial services, professional negligence and regulatory law. CEDR accredited mediator, 2004–. Mem., Mediterranean Gardening Soc. *Publications:* (contrib.) Law of Bank Payment, ed by Brindle and Cox, 1996, 2004; (contrib.) Professional Negligence and Liability, ed by M. Simpson, 2006. *Recreations:* gardening on a grand scale, faking Renaissance masterpieces (for pleasure, not profit). *Address:* Fountain Court, Temple, EC4Y 9DH. *T:* (020) 7583 3335, *Fax:* (020) 7353 0329; *e-mail:* probertson@fountaincourt.co.uk.

ROBERTSON, Patrick Allan Pearson, CMG 1956; *b* 11 Aug. 1913; *s* of A. N. McI. Robertson; *m* 1st, 1939, Penelope Margaret Gaskell (*d* 1966); one *s* two *d*; 2nd, 1975, Lady Stewart-Richardson. *Educ:* Sedbergh School; King's College, Cambridge. Cadet, Tanganyika, 1936; Asst Dist Officer, 1938; Clerk of Exec. and Legislative Councils, 1945–46; Dist Officer, 1948; Principal Asst Sec., 1949; Financial Sec., Aden, 1951; Asst Sec., Colonial Office, 1956–57; Chief Sec., Zanzibar, 1958; Civil Sec., Zanzibar, 1961–64; Deputy British Resident, Zanzibar, 1963–64; retired, 1964. Associate Member, Commonwealth Parliamentary Association. *Recreations:* gardening, fishing. *Address:* Lynedale, Longcross, Chertsey, Surrey KT16 0DP. *T:* (01932) 872329.

See also Sir Simon Stewart-Richardson, Bt.

ROBERTSON, Raymond Scott; Director of Public Affairs (formerly Development Director), Halogen Communications, since 2002; *b* 11 Dec. 1959; *s* of late James Robertson and Marion Robertson. *Educ:* Glasgow Univ. (MA Hist. and Politics); Jordanhill Coll. Teacher, Hist. and Mod. Studies, Smithycroft Secondary Sch., Glasgow, 1982–83, Dumbarton Acad., 1983–89; NE Political Dir, 1989–92, Vice-Chm., 1993–95, Chm., 1997–2001, Scottish Cons Party. MP (C) Aberdeen South, 1992–97; contested (C): same seat, 1997; Eastwood, 2001. PPS to Min. of State, NI Office, 1994–95; Parly Under-Sec. of State, Scottish Office, 1995–97.

ROBERTSON, Prof. Ritchie Neil Ninian, DPhil; FBA 2004; Official Fellow of St John's College, Oxford, since 1989; Lecturer in German, since 1989, titular Professor, since 1999, University of Oxford; *b* 25 Dec. 1952; *s* of Alexander Ritchie Robertson and Elizabeth Robertson (*née* Ninian); *m* 1999, Katharine Mary Nicholas; one step *s* one step *d. Educ:* Nairn Acad.; Univ. of Edinburgh (MA 1st class Honours: English 1974; German 1976); Lincoln Coll., Oxford (DPhil 1981). Montgomery Tutorial Fellow, Lincoln Coll., Oxford, 1979–84; Fellow and Dir of Studies in Modern Langs, Downing Coll., Cambridge, 1984–89. Ed., Austrian Studies, 1990–99; Germanic Ed., MLR, 2000–. *Publications:* Kafka: Judaism, politics and literature, 1985 (trans. German 1988); Heine, 1988 (trans. German 1997); The 'Jewish Question' in German Literature 1749–1939, 1999; (ed) The Cambridge Companion to Thomas Mann, 2002; Kafka: a very short introduction, 2004 (trans. Japanese 2007); (ed with Katrin Kohl) A History of Austrian Literature 1918–2000, 2006. *Address:* 31 Frenchay Road, Oxford OX2 6TG; St John's College, Oxford OX1 3JP. *T:* (01865) 277437, *Fax:* (01865) 277435; *e-mail:* ritchie.robertson@sjc.ox.ac.uk.

ROBERTSON, Robert Henry; Australian diplomat, retired; *b* 23 Dec. 1929; *s* of James Rowland Robertson and Hester Mary (*née* Kay); *m* 2nd, 1958, Jill Bryant Uther (marr. diss. 1982); two *s* one *d*; 3rd, 1986, Isabelle Costa de Beauregard, *d* of Comte and Comtesse René Costa de Beauregard. *Educ:* Geelong Church of England Grammar Sch.; Trinity Coll., Univ. of Melbourne (LLB). Third Secretary, Australian High Commn, Karachi, 1954–56; Second Sec., Mission to UN, New York, 1958–61; First Sec., later Counsellor, Washington, 1964–67; Ambassador to Jugoslavia, Romania and Bulgaria, 1971–73; Asst Sec., Personnel Br., Dept of Foreign Affairs, Canberra, 1974–75; First Asst Sec., Western Div., 1975–76, Management and Foreign Service Div., 1976–77; Ambassador to Italy, 1977–81; Dep. High Comr in London, 1981–84; Perm. Rep. to UN in Geneva, 1984–88; Ambassador to Argentina, Uruguay and Paraguay, 1989–92. Chm., Exec. Cttee, UN High Comr for Refugees, 1987–88. *Address:* 53 Williams Road, Mount Eliza, Vic 3930, Australia. *T:* and *Fax:* (3) 97752078. *Club:* Melbourne.

ROBERTSON, Shirley Ann, (Mrs J. Boag), OBE 2005 (MBE 2001); sailor; *b* 15 July 1968; *d* of Iain Robertson and Elizabeth Ann Robertson (*née* Burnett); *m* 2001, Jamie Boag; one *s* one *d* (twins). *Educ:* Moray House, Edinburgh (BA Hons Recreation Mgt). Competitive Laser Cl. sailing, 1983–88, Europe Cl., 1988–2000. Member GB sailing team, Olympic Games: Barcelona, 1992; Atlanta, 1996; Gold Medal: Women's Singlehanded Europe Cl., Olympic Games, Sydney, 2000; three-person Women's Yngling Keelboat Cl., Olympic Games, Athens, 2004. World Sailor of the Year, ISAF, 2000. *Address:* 2 Langtry Place, Cowes PO31 7QQ. *Club:* Royal Corinthian Yacht.

ROBERTSON, Sholto David Maurice; *see* Robertson, Toby.

ROBERTSON, Brig. Sidney Park, MBE 1962; TD 1967; JP; Vice Lord-Lieutenant of Orkney, 1987–90; Director, S. & J. D. Robertson Group Ltd (Chairman, 1965–79); *b* 12 March 1914; *s* of John Davie Manson Robertson and Elizabeth Park Sinclair; *m* 1940, Elsa Miller Croy (*d* 1997); one *s* one *d. Educ:* Kirkwall Grammar Sch.; Edinburgh Univ. (BCom 1939; Hon. Fellow 1996). MIBS 1936. Served War; commnd RA, 1940 (despatches, NW Europe, 1945). Managerial posts, Anglo-Iranian Oil Co., ME, 1946–51; Manager, Operation/Sales, Southern Div., Shell Mex and BP, 1951–54; founded Robertson firm, 1954. Chm., Orkney Hosps Bd of Management/Orkney Health Bd, 1965–79. Maj. comdg 861 (Ind.) LAA Batt., RA (Orkney and Zetland) TA, 1956–61; Lt-Col comdg Lovat Scouts, TA, 1962–65; CRA 51st Highland Div., TA, 1966–67 (Brig.); Hon. Col, 102 (Ulster and Scottish) Light Air Defence Regt, RA (TA), 1975–80; Hon. Col Comdt, RA, 1977–80; Chm., RA Council of Scotland, 1980–84; Vice Pres., Nat. Artillery Assoc., 1977–; Pres., RBL Scotland, Kirkwall Br., 1957–97; Hon. Vice Pres., RBL Scotland, Highlands and Is Area, 1975–; Hon. President: Orkney Bn, Boys' Bde, 1972–; Friends of St Magnus Cathedral, 1994; Orkney Family History Soc., 1996–2005; Orkney Norway Friendship Assoc., 1999–2005; Vice-Pres., 1985, Life Vice Pres., 1989, RNLI (Chm., 1972–97, Pres., 1997–, Kirkwall Stn Cttee); Hon. Life Vice Pres., Longhope Lifeboat Mus. Trust, 2002; Patron, N Ronaldsay Heritage Trust, 1995–. Pres., Villars Curling Club, 1978–80, 1986–88. DL Orkney, 1968; Hon. Sheriff, Grampian, Highlands and Islands, 1969–. Freedom of Orkney, 1990. Hon. DLitt Napier, 2002. *Recreations:* travel, hill walking, angling. *Address:* Daisybank, Kirkwall, Orkney KW15 1LX. *T:* (01856) 872085. *Clubs:* Army and Navy, Caledonian; New (Edinburgh).

ROBERTSON, Simon Manwaring; Managing Partner, Simon Robertson Associates, since 2005; Chairman, Rolls-Royce plc, since 2005 (Director, since 2004); *b* 4 March 1941; *s* of David Lars Manwaring Robertson, CVO; *m* 1965, Virginia Stewart Norman; one *s* two *d. Educ:* Eton. Joined Kleinwort Benson, 1963; Dir, 1977–97; Dep. Chm., 1992–96; Chm., 1996–97; Man. Dir, Goldman Sachs Internat. and Pres., Goldman Sachs Europe Ltd, 1997–2005. Director: Inchcape, 1996–2005; London Stock Exchange, 1998–2001; Berry Bros & Rudd, 1998–; Invensys, 1999–2005; Royal Opera House Covent Garden Ltd, 2002–; HSBC Hldgs PLC, 2006–. Trustee: Eden Project, 2000–; St Paul's Foundn, 2000–; Royal Acad. Trust, 2001–; Royal Opera Hse Endowment Fund 2000, 2001–. *Recreations:* ski-ing, walking in the Alps. *Clubs:* Boodle's, White's; Racquet (New York).

ROBERTSON, Stanley Stewart John, CBE 1998; CEng, FIET, FCILT; safety engineering consultant; Managing Director, Robertson Safety Engineering Services Ltd, since 1998; Director, Metro Solutions Ltd, since 2005; *b* 14 July 1938; *s* of Jock Stanley Robertson and Florence Kathleen Robertson (*née* Carpenter); *m* 1961, Valerie Housley; two *s* two *d. Educ:* Liverpool Poly. (Dip. EE 1961). FIET (FIEE 1987); FCILT (FCIT 1998). Student engrg apprentice, UKAEA, 1956–62; Asst Electrical Engr, CEGB, 1961–67; Elec. Engrg Manager, Shell Chemicals UK, 1967–74; Health and Safety Executive: Sen. Electrical Inspector, 1974–77; Dep. Superintending Inspector, 1977–80; Superintending Inspector, 1980–91; Dep. Chief Inspector and Regl Dir, 1991–93; HM Chief Inspector of Railways, 1993–98. Chairman: HSE Tech. Cttee investigating radio frequency ignition hazards, St Fergus, Scotland, 1979; Rly Industry Adv. Cttee, HSC, 1993–98; HSE Cttee investigating safety of Forth Rail Bridge, 1995–96; Mem., HSE Tech. Cttee investigating collapse of railway tunnels at Heathrow Airport and New Austrian Tunnelling Method, 1994. Health and Safety Advr, Taiwan High Speed Rail Corp., 1999–2006. Chm., Nat. Inspection Council for Elec. Installation Contracting, 1993–95. Non-exec. Dir, NQA Ltd, 1993–95. *Publications:* several tech. papers on electrical and railway safety matters. *Recreations:* music, gardening. *Address: e-mail:* ssjrcbe@hotmail.com.

ROBERTSON, Stephen Peter; Director General, British Retail Consortium, since 2008; *b* Essex, 17 Nov. 1954; *m* Susan; three *s* two *d. Educ:* Univ. of Nottingham (BSc Hons Chem.). Eur. Mktg Manager, Mars Inc., 1986–92; Marketing Director: Mattel Toys, 1992–93; B&Q plc, 1993–2000; Chm., Screwfix Direct, 2000–02; Dir, Gp Communications, Kingfisher plc, 2002–04 (incl. Man. Dir, Ellen MacArthur sponsorship); Marketing Director: (interim) WH Smith plc, 2004; Woolworths Gp plc, 2004–07. Non-exec. Dir, Fresca Gp Ltd, 2005–. Fellow and former Chm., Marketing Soc. *Address:* British Retail Consortium, 21 Dartmouth Street, SW1H 9BP. *T:* (020) 7854 8900; *e-mail:* Stephen.Robertson@brc.org.uk.

ROBERTSON, Tina; *see* Tietjen, T.

ROBERTSON, Toby, (Sholto David Maurice Robertson), OBE 1978; director and actor, theatre, opera and television; *s* of David Lambert Robertson and Felicity Douglas (*née* Tomlin); *m* 1963, Teresa Jane McCulloch (marr. diss. 1981); two *s* two *d. Educ:* Stowe; Trinity Coll., Cambridge (BA 1952, MA 1981). Formerly an actor. Dir. first prof. prodn, The Iceman Cometh, New Shakespeare, Liverpool, 1958. Dir. plays, London,

Pitlochry and Richmond, Yorks, and for RSC, 1959–63. Member: Bd, Prospect Productions Ltd, 1964– (Artistic Dir, Prospect Theatre Co., 1964–79); Bd, Cambridge Theatre Co., 1970–74; Director: Old Vic Theatre, 1977–80, Old Vic Co., 1979–80; Acting Co., Kennedy Centre, Washington, 1983; Associate Dir, Circle Rep., New York, 1983–84; Dir, Theatr Clwyd, Mold, 1985–92. Drama Advr, Argo Records, 1979–; Prof. of Theatre, Brooklyn Coll., City Univ. NY, 1981–82; Hon. Prof. of Drama, 1987–90, Hon. Prof. of English, 1990–92, Fellow, 1996, UCNW. Lectures: Wilson Meml, Cambridge Univ., 1974; Hamlet, Athens Univ., 1978; Rikstheatre, Stockholm, 1980; Hamlet, Gulbenkian Foundn, Lisbon, 1987. Director of over 40 prodns for *Prospect Theatre Co.*, many staged in London and Edinburgh, 1964–79, including: The Soldier's Fortune; You Never Can Tell; The Confederacy; The Importance of Being Earnest; The Square; Howard's End; The Man of Mode; Macbeth; The Tempest; The Gamecock; A Murder of No Importance; A Room with a View; No Man's Land; The Beggar's Opera; The Servant of Two Masters; Edward II; Much Ado About Nothing; Boswell's Life of Johnson; Venice Preserved; King Lear and Love's Labour's Lost (Australian tour); Alice in Wonderland; Richard III; Ivanov; The Grand Tour; Twelfth Night, Pericles and The Royal Hunt of the Sun (internat. fests, Moscow, Leningrad and Hong Kong); The Pilgrim's Progress; A Month in the Country (Chichester Fest.); directed for *Old Vic Co.*: War Music; Antony and Cleopatra; Smith of Smiths; Buster; The Lunatic, The Lover and The Poet; Romeo and Juliet; The Government Inspector; The Padlock; Ivanov; Hamlet (Elsinore, and first visit by a British co., China, 1980); directed for *Theatr Clwyd*: Medea (also Young Vic), 1986; Barnaby and the Old Boys, 1987 (also Vaudeville, 1989); Edward III (jtly adapted, attrib. William Shakespeare) (also Cambridge and Taormina Fests), 1987; Captain Carvallo, 1988, transf. Greenwich; Revenger's Tragedy, 1988; The Old Devils, 1989; Othello, 1989; The Importance of Being Earnest, 1990; Enemy of the People, 1991, transf. Lyric Hammersmith; The Cherry Orchard, 1991 (also Brighton Festival); Marching Song, 1992; Hamlet (also Nat. Tour), 1991–92; The Seagull, 1992; Loot, 1995; directed *other productions*, including: Next Time I'll Sing to You, Greenwich, 1980; Beggar's Opera, Lyric, Hammersmith, 1980; Measure for Measure, People's Arts Theatre, Peking, 1981; Pericles, NY, 1981 (Obie award, 1982); Night and Day (opening prodn), 1982 and The Taming of the Shrew, 1983, Huntingdon Theatre Co., Boston; The Tempest (opening prodn), New Cleveland Playhouse, 1983; Love's Labour's Lost, Shakespeare Workshop, 1983, Circle Rep., 1984, NYC; York Cycle of Mystery Plays, York Fest., 1984; Midsummer Night's Dream, Open Air Theatre, Regent's Park, 1985; (jt dir) Antony and Cleopatra, The Taming of the Shrew, Haymarket, 1986; Coriolanus, festivals in Spain, 1986; You Never Can Tell, Haymarket, 1988; Richard II, Folger Theatre, Washington; Trelawny of the 'Wells', Comedy, 1992; The Old Devils, Philadelphia, 1993; The Taming of the Shrew, Regent's Park, 1993; Macbeth, Tel Aviv, 1994; Hamlet, Oberlin Coll., Ohio, 1997. *Opera:* for Scottish Opera, incl.: A Midsummer Night's Dream, 1972; Hermiston, 1975; Marriage of Figaro, 1977; for Opera Co. of Philadelphia: Elisir d'Amore (with Pavarotti and winners of Pavarotti competition), Dido and Aeneas, Oedipus Rex, 1982; Faust, 1984; Wiesbaden: A Midsummer Night's Dream, 1984; NY City Opera: Barber of Seville, 1984; Wexford Opera: The Kiss, 1984. Asst Dir, Lord of the Flies (film), 1961. Dir of more than 25 television prodns, incl.: The Beggar's Opera; Richard II; Edward II. *Recreation:* painting. *Address:* 32 Stamford Brook Road, W6 0XL. *Club:* Garrick.

ROBERTSON, Vernon Colin, OBE 1977; self employed consultant, specialising in environmental issues in developing countries; *b* 19 July 1922; *s* of Colin John Trevelyan Robertson and Agnes Muriel Robertson (*née* Dolphin). *Educ:* Imperial Service College, Windsor; Univ. of Edinburgh (BSc Agr subs. Forestry); Univ. of Cambridge (Dip Agr 1950; MA). Joined Home Guard, 1940; enlisted RA, 1941, commissioned 1942; served 12th HAC Regt RHA, N Africa, Italy, Austria, 1942–45 (despatches 1945); with 1st Regt RHA, Italy, 1945–46 (Adjutant). Staff, Sch. of Agric., Cambridge, 1950; joined Hunting Aerosurveys Ltd, 1953, as ecologist heading new natural resources survey dept; developed this into overseas land and water resource consultancy, renamed Hunting Technical Services Ltd (Managing Director, 1959–77; after retirement continuing as Director and Consultant until 1987), development planning in Africa, Asia and Latin America. Director: Hunting Surveys and Consultants Ltd, 1962–77; Groundwater Development Consultants (International) Ltd, 1975–85; Vice-Chm. and acting Chm., Environmental Planning Commn, Internat. Union for Conservation of Nature, 1972–78; Chm., Trop. Agric. Assoc. (UK), 1981–85; Mem. Bd, Commonwealth Develt Corp., 1982–90. *Publications:* articles in learned jls. *Recreations:* natural history, esp. plants and birds, gardening, painting, photography, music, sailing. *Address:* Brickfields, Quay Lane, Kirby-le-Soken, Essex CO13 0DP. *T:* (01255) 674585. *Club:* Honourable Artillery Company.

ROBERTSON, Air Cdre William Duncan, CBE 1968; Royal Air Force, retired; Senior Air Staff Officer, HQ 38 Group, Royal Air Force, 1975–77; *b* 24 June 1922; *s* of William and Helen Robertson, Aberdeen; *m* 1st, 1952, Doreen Mary (*d* 1963), *d* of late Comdr G. A. C. Sharp, DSC, RN (retd); one *s* one *d*; 2nd, 1968, Ute, *d* of late Dr R. Koenig, Wesel, West Germany; one *d*. *Educ:* Robert Gordon's Coll., Aberdeen. Sqdn Comdr, No 101 Sqdn, 1953–55, No 207 Sqdn, 1959–61. Gp Dir, RAF Staff Coll., 1962–65; Station Comdr, RAF Wildenrath, 1965–67; Dep. Dir, Administrative Plans, 1967; Dir of Ops (Plans), 1968; Dir of Ops Air Defence and Overseas, 1969–71; RCDS, 1971–72; SASO RAF Germany, 1972–74; SASO 46 Group, 1975. *Recreations:* golf, tennis. *Address:* Parkhouse Farm, Leigh, Surrey RH2 8QE. *Clubs:* Royal Air Force; Walton Heath Golf.

ROBERTSON, (William) Nelson, CBE 1996; FCII; Director, Alliance Trust, 1996–2002; *b* 14 Dec. 1933; *s* of James Bogue and Eleanor Robertson; *m* 1964, Sheila Catherine Spence; two *d*. *Educ:* Berwick Grammar Sch.; Edinburgh Univ. (MA). FCII 1963. Served RA, 1955–57. General Accident Fire & Life Assurance Corporation Ltd, later General Accident plc, 1958–95: Asst Gen. Man. (Overseas), 1972; Gen. Man., 1980; Dir, 1984; Dep. Chief Gen. Man., 1989; Gp Chief Exec., 1990–95. Director: Morrison Construction Gp, 1995–2001; Second Alliance Trust, 1996–2002; Edinburgh New Tiger Trust, 1996–2001; Scottish Community (formerly Caledonian) Foundn, 1996–99; Supervisory Bd, Scottish Amicable, 1997–2004; Edinburgh Leveraged Income Trust plc, 2001–02; Edinburgh Zeros 2008 plc, 2001–02. Bd Mem., ABI, 1991–95. Mem. Court, Univ. of Abertay, Dundee, 1996–99. *Recreations:* hill-walking, gardening. *Club:* Caledonian.

ROBERTSON-MACLEOD, (Roderick) James (Andrew); Consultant, Group 4 Securicor, since 2006; *b* 5 March 1951; *s* of Col Roderick Robertson-Macleod and Daphne Robertson-Macleod; *m* 1992, Karen Barclay; one *s* two *d*. *Educ:* Milton Abbey. Commnd Royal Green Jackets, 1970–80; Private Sec. to HSH Princess Grace of Monaco, 1980–82; Dir, Markham Sports Sponsorship, 1982–91; Chief Exec., Raleigh International, 1991–2003; Dir, Project Support, AEGIS Defence Services, 2004–06. *Recreations:* tennis, ski-ing, walking. *Address:* Hill House, Coneyhurst, W Sussex RH14 9DL. *T:* (01403) 786877; *e-mail:* jrobmac@btinternet.com.

ROBINS, David Anthony; Chairman: Henderson TR Pacific Investment Trust plc, since 2004 (Director, since 2003); New Philanthropy Capital, since 2001; Hackney Empire Ltd, since 2003 (Director, since 2001); Oriel Securities Ltd, since 2007; *b* 2 Sept. 1949; *s* of John Anthony Robins and Ruth Wenefrede Robins (*née* Thomas); *m* 1981, Joanna Christina Botting; two *s* one *d*. *Educ:* University Coll. London (BSc Econ). Economic Analyst, Investment and Res. Dept, Commonwealth Bank, Sydney, Australia, 1973–74; Economist, Overseas Dept, Bank of England, 1976–78; Exec., Japanese Dept, James Capel, 1978–80; Chief Internat. Economist, Phillips & Drew, 1980–86; Hd of Res., UBS Phillips & Drew Ltd, Tokyo, 1986–88; Hd, Internat. Securities Dept, UBS Securities Inc., NY, 1988–90; Functional Advr, Securities and Res., Union Bank of Switzerland, Zurich, 1990–93; Chief Exec. Officer, UBS UK Ltd, 1994–98; Exec. Vice Pres. and Hd, Region Europe, Union Bank of Switzerland, 1997–98; Chm. and Chief Exec. Officer, ING Barings, 1998–2000; Mem., Exec. Bd, ING Gp, 2000. Non-executive Director: MPC Investors Ltd, 2001–07; Bending Light Ltd, 2001–; LCH Clearnet Ltd, 2001– (Chm., 2003–07); Meggitt plc, 2002–; EMG Gp Ltd, 2004–. Dep. Chm., E London Business Alliance, 2000–06. Mem., Investment Adv. Cttee, Univs Superannuation Scheme, 2004–. Gov., Eltham Coll., 2001– (Chm., 2004–). *Recreations:* tennis, swimming, walking. *Address:* Oriel Securities Ltd, 125 Wood Street, EC2V 7AN.

ROBINS, John Vernon Harry; Chairman, Xchanging plc, since 2000; *b* 21 Feb. 1939; *s* of Col William Vernon Harry Robins, DSO and Charlotte Mary (*née* Grier); *m* 1962, Elizabeth Mary Banister; two *s* one *d*. *Educ:* Winchester Coll. Nat. Service, 2nd Lieut 2/10 Princess Mary's Own Gurkha Rifles, 1959–61. Man. Dir, SNS Communications Ltd, 1966–74; Chief Exec., Bally Gp (UK) Ltd, 1974–79; Group Financial Director: Fitch Lovell plc, 1979–84; Willis Faber, subseq. Willis Corroon Gp plc, 1984–94; Chief Exec., Guardian Royal Exchange plc, 1994–99; Chairman: Hyder plc, 1998–2000; Lane, Clark and Peacock (Actuaries), 2000–03; Austin Reed Gp plc, 2000–06. Director: Wellington Underwriting plc, 1999–2001; Axa Asia Pacific Hldgs Ltd, Melbourne, 1999–2002; Alexander Forbes Ltd (SA), 2002– (Dep. Chm., 2004–07). Chm., Policyholders Protection Bd, 1998–2000. Mem., Barbican Centre Cttee, 2003–. *Recreations:* clocks, Baroque music, grand-children. *Club:* Brooks's.

ROBINS, Group Captain Leonard Edward, CBE (mil.) 1979; AE 1958 (and 2 clasps); Inspector, Royal Auxiliary Air Force, 1973–83; *b* 2 Nov. 1921; *yr s* of late Joseph Robins, Bandmaster RM, and late Louisa Josephine (*née* Kent); *m* 1949, Jean Ethelwynne (Headteacher) (*d* 1985), *d* of late Roy and Bessie Searle, Ryde, IoW. *Educ:* Singlegate, Mitcham, Surrey; City Day Continuation School, EC. Entered Civil Service, GPO, 1936; War service, Radar Br., RAF, UK, SEAC, Ceylon, India, 1941–46; resumed with GPO, 1946; Min. of Health, 1948; Min. of Housing and Local Govt, 1962; DoE, 1970–80, retired. Airman, No 3700 (Co. of London) Radar Reporting Unit RAuxAF, 1950; Commissioned 1953, radar branch; transf. to No 1 (Co. of Hertford) Maritime HQ Unit RAuxAF, intelligence duties, 1960; OC No 1 Maritime Headquarters Unit, RAuxAF, 1969–73; Gp Capt., Inspector RAuxAF, 1973–83. ADC to the Queen, 1974–83. Selected Air Force Mem., Greater London TAVRA, 1973–83 and City of London TAVRA, 1980–84; Mem., HAC, 1997–. Patron, World War II Air Forces Radar Reunion, 2001, presided at Reunions, annually, 2003–. Lord Mayor of London's personal staff, as researcher and speech writer, 1977–78, 1980–81, 1982–83 and 1986–94. Pres., Wandsworth Victim Support Scheme, 1980–87. Trustee, Royal Foundn of Greycoat Hosp., 1983–88. Freeman, City of London, 1976. Coronation Medal, 1953; Silver Jubilee Medal, 1977. Officer of Merit with Swords, SMO Malta, 1986. DL Greater London, 1978–97, Rep. DL, Bor. of Wandsworth, 1979–97. FCMI. *Recreations:* naval, military and aviation history, book hunting, kipping, speech writing. *Address:* 5 Varley Terrace, Dean Street, Liskeard, Cornwall PL14 4AN. *T:* (01579) 348740. *Club:* Royal Air Force.

ROBINS, Sir Ralph (Harry), Kt 1988; DL; FREng; FRAeS; Chairman, Rolls-Royce plc, 1992–2003; *b* 16 June 1932; *s* of Leonard Haddon and Maud Lillian Robins; *m* 1962, Patricia Maureen Grimes; two *d*. *Educ:* Imperial Coll., Univ. of London (BSc; ACGI; FIC 1993). MIMechE; FREng (FEng 1988); FRAeS 1990. Development Engr, Rolls-Royce, Derby, 1955–66; Exec. Vice-Pres., Rolls-Royce Inc., 1971; Man. Dir, RR Industrial & Marine Div., 1973; Commercial Dir, RR Ltd, 1978; Chm., International Aero Engines AG, 1983–84; Rolls-Royce plc: Man. Dir, 1984–89; Dep. Chm., 1989–92; Chief Exec., 1990–92. Non-executive Director: Standard Chartered plc, 1988–2004; Schroders plc, 1990–2002; Marks & Spencer plc, 1992–2001; Cable and Wireless plc, 1994–2003 (non-exec. Chm., 1998–2003); Marshall Hldgs Ltd, 2004–. Chm., Defence Industries Council, 1986–2003; Pres., SBAC, 1986–87. Mem., Council for Sci. and Technology, 1993–98. DL Derbys, 2000. FCGI 1990. Hon. FRAeS; Hon. FIMechE 1996. Hon. DSc: Cranfield, 1990; Nottingham, 2002; DUniv Derby, 1992; Hon. DBA Strathclyde, 1996; Hon. DEng Sheffield, 2001. Commander's Cross, Order of Merit (Germany), 1996. *Recreations:* golf, music, classic cars. *Club:* Athenæum.

ROBINS, William Edward Charles; Metropolitan Stipendiary Magistrate, 1971–89; solicitor; *b* 13 March 1924; *s* of late E. T. and late L. R. Robins; *m* 1946, Jean Elizabeth, *yr d* of Bruce and Flora Forsyth, Carlyle, Saskatchewan, Canada; one *s* one *d*. *Educ:* St Alban's Sch. Served War: commissioned as Navigator, RAF, 1943–47. Admitted as a Solicitor, 1948; joined Metropolitan Magistrates' Courts' service, 1950; Dep. Chief Clerk, 1951–60; Chief Clerk, 1960–67; Sen. Chief Clerk, Thames Petty Sessional Div., 1968–71. Sec., London Magistrates' Clerks' Assoc., 1953–60 (Chm. 1965–71). Member, Home Office working parties, on: Magistrates' Courts' Rules; Legal Aid; Motor Vehicle Licences; Fines and Maintenance Orders Enforcement, 1968–71; Member: Lord Chancellor's Sub-Cttee on Magistrates' Courts' Rules, 1969–70; Adv. Council on Misuse of Drugs, 1973–86. Fellow Commoner, Corpus Christi Coll., Cambridge, Michaelmas 1975. *Recreations:* touring off the beaten track, music, theatre.

ROBINS, Maj.-Gen. William John Pherrick, CB 1998; OBE 1984 (MBE 1979); CEng, FIET; FBCS; Director, Bill Robins Ltd, since 2003; *b* 28 July 1941; *s* of John Robins and Helen Hamilton (*née* Urry); *m* 1st, 1967, Anne Marie Cornu (marr. diss. 1985); one *s* one *d*; 2nd, 1993, Kathy Walsh. *Educ:* Henry Mellish Grammar Sch., Nottingham; Welbeck Coll.; RMA Sandhurst; RMCS Shrivenham (BSc (Eng) London, 1966); Staff Coll., Camberley; Cranfield Inst. of Technology (MPhil (Information Systems) 1993). CEng 1991, FIET (FIEE 1992); FBCS 1995. 16 Parachute Bde, 1966–70; Special Communications, 1970–72; Germany and UK, 1972–79; CO 14 Signal Regt (Electronic Warfare), 1979–82; Mil. Asst to MGO, 1982–84; Army ADP Co-ordinator, 1984–87; Project Dir, 1987–89; Dir, CIS (Army), 1989–92; ACDS (Command, Control, Communications and Information Systems), 1992–94; Dir Gen., Information and Communication Services, MoD, 1995–98. Director: Marconi Radar and Defence Systems, 1998–99; Alenia Marconi Systems, 1999–2000; BAE SYSTEMS: Future Systems Dir, 2000–01; Dir, C4ISTAR Develt Avionics Gp, 2001–02; Dir, Advanced Concepts C4ISR Gp, 2002–03. Vis. Prof., Cranfield Univ., 2003–. Freeman, Information Technologists' Co., 2004. Hon. Fellow, Sch. of Defence Management, Cranfield Univ., 1994; Associate FRUSI 2002. *Recreations:* cartoons, looking at pictures, making high quality compost, running, hill walking. *Address:* c/o RHQ Royal Signals, Blandford Camp, Dorset DT11 8RH. *Clubs:* Special Forces, Army and Navy.

ROBINSON, family name of **Baron Martonmere**.

ROBINSON, Alastair; see Robinson, F. A. L.

ROBINSON, Sir Albert (Edward Phineas), Kt 1962; Director, E. Oppenheimer and Son (Pty) Ltd, 1963–2000; b 30 Dec. 1915; s of late Charles Phineas Robinson (formerly MP Durban, S Africa) and of late Mabel V. Robinson; m 1st, 1944, Mary Judith Bertram (née Bertish) (d 1973); four d; 2nd, 1975, Mrs Madeleine L'Estrange Royston-Piggot (née Barrett) (d 2005). Educ: Durban High School; Universities of Stellenbosch, London (LSE), Cambridge (Trinity Coll.) and Leiden; MA (Cantab). Pres., Footlights Club, Cambridge, 1936–37. Barrister, Lincoln's Inn. Served War of 1939–45, in Imperial Light Horse, Western Desert, N Africa, 1940–43. Member Johannesburg City Council, 1945–48 (Leader United Party in Council, 1946–47); MP (United Party), S African Parlt, 1947–53; became permanent resident in Rhodesia, 1953. Dep. Chm., General Mining and Finance Corp. Ltd, 1963–71; Chairman: Johannesburg Consolidated Investment Co., 1971–80; Rustenburg Platinum Mines, 1971–80; Australian Anglo American Ltd, 1980–85; Director: Anglo American Corp., Zimbabwe Ltd, 1964–86; Founders Bldg Soc., 1954–86; Rand Mines Ltd, 1965–71; Anglo American Corp. of SA Ltd, 1965–88; Johannesburg Consolidated Investment Co., 1965–85; Standard Bank Investment Corp., 1972–86; Director, in Zimbabwe and South Africa, of various Mining, Financial and Industrial Companies. Chm. Central African Airways Corp., 1957–61. Member, Monckton Commission, 1960; High Commissioner in the UK for the Federation of Rhodesia and Nyasaland, 1961–63. Chancellor, Univ. of Bophuthatswana, 1980–91. Hon. DComm Univ. of Bophuthatswana, 1990. Recreations: people, music and conversation. Address: 43 St Mary Abbots Court, Warwick Gardens, W14 8RB. Clubs: Carlton; Country (Johannesburg); Country (Durban).

ROBINSON, Alice; Her Honour Judge Alice Robinson; a Circuit Judge, since 2007; b Brentwood, Essex, 13 June 1959; d of Anthony Robinson and Anne Mary Robinson; m 1988, Antony John Cronk; one s one d. Educ: Haverstock Comp. Sch., London; University Coll., Cardiff (LLB 1st Cl. Hons 1982). Called to the Bar, Gray's Inn, 1983; in practice as barrister specialising in planning, property and public law; Supplementary Panel of Jun. Counsel to the Crown, Common Law, 1992–99; Recorder, 2003–07. Legal Mem., 2007–, Mem., Restricted Patients Panel, 2007–, Mental Health Rev. Tribunal. Asst Ed., Encyclopaedia of Planning Law and Practice, 2004–07. Publications: various articles in Jl of Planning Law and Judicial Rev. on Planning and Public Law. Recreations: hill walking, films, cooking. Address: Basildon Combined Court, The Gore, Basildon, Essex SS14 2BU.

ROBINSON, Alwyn Arnold; Managing Director, Daily Mail, 1975–89; b 15 Nov. 1929. Mem., Press Council, 1977–87 (Jt Vice-Chm., 1982–83).

ROBINSON, Ann; see Robinson, M. A.

ROBINSON, Dr Ann; Director General, National Association of Pension Funds Ltd, 1995–2000; b 28 Jan. 1937; d of Edwin Samuel James and Dora (née Thorne); m 1961, Michael Finlay Robinson; two s. Educ: St Anne's Coll., Oxford (MA); McGill Univ. (MA, PhD). Financial journalist, Beaverbrook Newspapers, 1959–61; University Lecturer: Durham, 1962–65; Bristol, 1970–72; Bath, 1972–75; Cardiff, 1972–89 (Sen. Lectr, 1987–89); Head of Policy Unit, Inst. of Dirs, 1989–95. Director: Great Western Hldgs, 1996–98; Almeida Capital, 2001–. ICSA Vis. Prof. of Corporate Governance, Bournemouth Univ., 2000–03. Member: Equal Opportunities Commn, 1980–85; Econ. and Social Cttee, EEC, 1986–93 (Chm., Industry Section, 1990–92); Welsh Arts Council, 1991–93; HEFCW, 1993–97; Competition (formerly Monopolies and Mergers) Commn, 1993–99; Bd, Harwich Haven Authy, 1999–2006; Pensions Protection and Investments Accreditation Bd, 2001–06; London Pensions Fund Authy, 2001–05. Dir, WNO, 1992–94. Member: Council, RIIA, 1991–97; Bd of Academic Govs, Richmond Coll., London, 1992–; Bd of Govs, Commonwealth Inst., 1992–97; Council, Clifton Coll. (Vice-Chm. Council, 1998–2003); Council, City Univ., 1998–2002. Trustee: Foundn for Business Responsibilities, 1997–2003; Dixons Retirement and Employee Security Scheme, 2000–06. Contested (C) S E Wales, EP election, 1979. Publications: Parliament and Public Spending, 1978; (jtly) Tax Policy Making in the United Kingdom, 1984; articles in acad. jls and chapters on public expenditure control by Parliament. Recreations: Alpine sports (summer and winter), gardening. Address: Northridge House, Usk Road, Shirenewton, Monmouthshire NP16 6RZ. Club: Reform.

ROBINSON, Anne Josephine; journalist and broadcaster; b 26 Sept. 1944; d of late Bernard James Robinson and Anne Josephine Robinson (née Wilson); m 1st, 1968, Charles Martin Wilson, qv (marr. diss. 1973); one d; 2nd, 1980, John Penrose (marr. diss. 2008). Educ: Farnborough Hill Convent; Les Ambassadrices, Paris. Reporter: Daily Mail, 1967–68; Sunday Times, 1968–77; Daily Mirror: Women's Editor, 1979–80; Asst Editor, 1980–93; columnist, 1983–93; columnist: Today, 1993–95; The Times, 1993–95; The Sun, 1995–97; The Express, 1997–98; The Times, 1998–2001; The Daily Telegraph, 2003–05. Presenter: Anne Robinson Show, Radio 2, 1988–93; Watchdog, 1993–2001; Guess Who Is Coming to Dinner, 2003; for BBC Television: Points of View, 1987–98 (also writer); Weekend Watchdog, 1997–2001; Going for a Song, 2000; The Weakest Link, 2000– (also USA, 2001–02); Test the Nation, 2002–07; Outtake TV, 2003–; Travels with an Unfit Mother, 2004; What's the Problem?, 2005. Hon. Fellow, Liverpool John Moores Univ., 1996. Publication: Memoirs of an Unfit Mother, 2001. Recreations: dogs, houses, gossip, decently cooked food, having opinions. Address: c/o Tracey Chapman, PO Box 50445, London W8 9BE. T: (020) 8870 6303; e-mail: Tracechapman@btinternet.com.

ROBINSON, Anthony John de G.; see de Garr Robinson.

ROBINSON, Rt Rev. Anthony William; see Pontefract, Bishop Suffragan of.

ROBINSON, Ariadne Elizabeth S.; see Singares Robinson.

ROBINSON, Arthur Alexander; Director of Computing Centre, University of Wales College of Cardiff (formerly at University of Wales Institute of Science and Technology), 1976–91; b 5 Aug. 1924; o s of Arthur Robinson and Elizabeth (née Thompson); m 1956, Sylvia Joyce Wagstaff; two s one d. Educ: Epsom Coll.; Clare Coll., Cambridge (MA); Univ. of Manchester (PhD). English Electric Co. Ltd, 1944; Ferranti Ltd, 1950; Dir and Gen. Man., Univ. of London Atlas Computing Service, 1962; Dir, Univ. of London Computer Centre, 1968; Dir, National Computing Centre Ltd, 1969–74. Publications: papers in Proc. IEE. Recreations: travel, gardening. Address: 6 Portland Close, Penarth, Vale of Glamorgan CF64 3DY.

ROBINSON, (Arthur) Geoffrey, CBE 1978; Chairman, Medway Ports Authority, 1978–87; b 22 Aug. 1917; s of Arthur Robinson and Frances M. Robinson; m 1st, 1943, Patricia MacAllister (d 1971); three s one d; 2nd, 1973, Hon. Mrs Treves, d of Rt Hon. Lord Salmon; three step s one step d. Educ: Lincoln Sch.; Jesus Coll., Cambridge (MA). Sch. of Oriental and African Studies, London Univ. Served War, RA, 1939–46. Solicitor, 1948; Treasury Solicitor's Dept, 1954–62; PLA, 1962–66; Man. Dir, Tees and Hartlepool Port Authority, 1966–77; Chm., English Indust. Estates Corp., 1977–83. Member:

National Dock Labour Bd, 1972–77; National Ports Council, 1980–81; Chm., British Ports Assoc., 1983–85. Publications: Hedingham Harvest, 1977; various articles. Recreation: music. Address: 96 Bluecoat Pond, Christ's Hospital, Horsham, W Sussex RH13 0TN.
See also P. H. Robinson.

ROBINSON, Hon. (Arthur Napoleon) Raymond, SC; President, Trinidad and Tobago, 1997–2003; b 16 Dec. 1926; s of late James Alexander Andrew Robinson, Headmaster, and Emily Isabella Robinson; m 1961, Patricia Rawlins; one s one d. Educ: Bishop's High Sch., Tobago; St John's Coll., Oxford (Hon. Fellow 1988). LLB (London); MA (PPE) Oxon. Called to Bar, Inner Temple; in practice, 1957–61. Treas., People's Nat. Movt (governing Party) 1956; Mem. Federal Parlt, 1958; MHR for Tobago East, 1961–71 and 1976–80; Minister of Finance, 1961–66; Dep. Political Leader of Party, 1966; Actg Prime Minister (during his absence), April and Aug. 1967; Minister of External Affairs, Trinidad and Tobago, 1967–70; Chm., Democratic Action Congress, 1971–86; Chm., Tobago House of Assembly, 1980–86; Leader, Nat. Alliance for Reconstruction, 1986–92; Prime Minister of Trinidad and Tobago, 1986–91. Member: Legal Commn on US Leased Areas under 1941 Agreement, 1959; Industrial Develt Corp., 1960; Council, Univ. of West Indies, 1960–62. Dir, Foundn for establishment of an Internat. Criminal Court, 1972–87. Member: UN Expert Gp on Crime and the Abuse of Power, 1979; Adv. Council, Nuclear Age Peace Foundn, 1994–; Pres. and Exec. Mem., Parliamentarians for Global Action, 1993–95. Hon. DCL Obafemi Awolowo Univ., Nigeria, 1991. Dist. Internat. Criminal Law Award, Internat. Criminal Court Foundn, 1977; Dist. Human Develt Award, Internat. Conf. on Human Rights and Humanitarian Law, UN Affiliate, 1983; Commendation Award, and Freeman, City of a Thousand Oaks, Calif, 1987; Dist. Service Award, Calif Lutheran Univ., 1987; Individual of the Year Award, Friends of Tobago Liby Cttee, 1995. Freeman: LA, 1988; Caracas, 1990. KStJ 1992. Gran Cordon, Orden de El Libertador (Venezuela), 1990; Chief of Ile Ife (Nigeria), 1991. Publications: The New Frontier and the New Africa, 1961; Fiscal Reform in Trinidad and Tobago, 1966; The Path of Progress, 1967; The Teacher and Nationalism, 1967; The Mechanics of Independence, 1971; Caribbean Man, 1986; articles and addresses. Address: 21 Ellerslie Park, Maraval, Trinidad and Tobago.

ROBINSON, Bill; see Robinson, P. W.

ROBINSON, Boz; see Robinson, B. L.

ROBINSON, Brian Gordon, CBE 1996; QFSM 1992; FIFireE; Commissioner for Fire and Emergency Planning (formerly Chief Officer, then Chief Fire Officer and Chief Executive), London Fire Brigade, 1991–2003; b 21 April 1947; s of Gordon and Theodora Robinson, Colchester, Essex; m 1996, Charmian Lesley Houslander-Green. FIFireE 1992. Joined London Fire Brigade, 1968; Accelerated Promotion Course, 1974, Sen. Course Dir, 1982, Fire Service Coll.; Divl Comdr, London, 1983; Asst Chief Officer, 1985; Dep. Chief Officer, 1990. OStJ 1992. Recreation: golf. Address: c/o London Fire Brigade Headquarters, 8 Albert Embankment, SE1 7SD. T: (020) 7587 4000.

ROBINSON, Air Vice-Marshal Brian Lewis, (Boz); Managing Director, Boz! Ltd, since 2002; Joint Managing Director, Boz Asia Co. Ltd, since 2007; b 2 July 1936; s of Frederick Lewis Robinson and Ida (née Croft); m 1962, Ann Faithfull; one s one d. Educ: Bradford Grammar Sch. Served, 1956–76: 74 Sqn; Oxford Univ. Air Sqn; 73 Sqn; Canberra Trials and Tactical Evaluation Unit; Directorate of Flight Safety, MoD; RAF Staff Coll.; RAF Valley; 2 ATAF Germany; Canadian Forces Comd and Staff Coll., and 411 Air Reserve Sqn, Toronto; Chief Instr, 4 Flying Trg Sch., 1976–78, OC, RAF Valley, 1978–80; Internat. Mil. Staff HQ, NATO, Brussels, 1980–82; Defence and Air Attaché, Moscow, 1983–86; Dir of Orgn and Quartering, RAF, MoD, 1986–88; RAF Long-term Deployment Study, 1988; AOC Directly Administered Units, and AO Admin, HQ Strike Command, 1989–91. Sen. Partner, Belmont Consultants, then Sole Exec., Belmont Aviation, 1991–2001. Display pilot: (Gnat), Kennet Aviation, 1997–2001; (Hunter): Classic Jets, 2001–02; Thunder City, Cape Town, 2001–02; Hunter Flying Club, 2002; (Gnat and Hunter), Delta Jets, 2002; Flying Instr, Bristol Flying Centre, 1997–2001; Mem., British Precision Flying Team, Krakow, 1998. Editor, Flight Safety section, Air Clues, 1967–69. Mem., RAF and British Bobsleigh teams, 1967–74. President: 74 Tiger Sqdn Assoc., 1992–2008; British Aviation Archaeol. Council, 2000–; Patron, Sky's the Limit, Cape Town Airport, 2002–. Gov., Edgehill Coll., Bideford, 1997–2001. FRAeS 2000. King Hussein Meml Sword, Royal Internat. Air Tattoo Cottesmore, 2001. Recreations: travel, writing. Address: 17 Cleevemont, Evesham Road, Cheltenham, Glos GL52 3JT. T: (01242) 237465; e-mail: boz74@tesco.net.
See also Sir J. C. N. Wakeley, Bt.

ROBINSON, Prof. Carol Vivien, PhD; FRS 2004; Royal Society Research Professor of Biological Chemistry, University of Cambridge, since 2006; b 10 April 1956; m 1982, Martin Robinson; two s one d. Educ: Canterbury Coll. of Technol. (ONC; HNC); Medway and Maidstone Coll.; RSC (grad.); Univ. of Swansea (MSc); Churchill Coll., Cambridge (PhD 1982). Res. Technician, Pfizer, 1972–79; MRC Trng Fellow, Univ. of Bristol, 1982–83; Post Doctoral Fellow, 1993–95, Royal Soc. Univ. Res. Fellow, 1995–2001, Univ. of Oxford; Prof. of Mass Spectrometry, Univ. of Cambridge, 2001–06. Biemann Medal, Amer. Soc. for Mass Spectrometry, 2003; Rosalind Franklin Award, Royal Soc., 2004. Publications: 120 pubns inc. book chapters, etc. Recreations: gardening, sport. Address: Department of Chemistry, University of Cambridge, Lensfield Road, Cambridge CB2 1EW. T: (01223) 763846, Fax: (01223) 763418; e-mail: cvr24@cam.ac.uk.

ROBINSON, Christopher John, CVO 1992 (LVO 1986); CBE 2004; Fellow, since 1991, and Organist and Director of Music, 1991–2003, St John's College, Cambridge; b 20 April 1936; s of late Prebendary John Robinson, Malvern, Worcs; m 1962, Shirley Ann, d of H. F. Churchman, Sawston, Cambs; one s one d. Educ: St Michael's Coll., Tenbury; Rugby; Christ Church, Oxford (BMus); MA (Oxon and Cantab). FRCO; Hon. RAM. Assistant Organist of Christ Church, Oxford, 1955–58; Assistant Organist of New College, Oxford, 1957–58; Music Master at Oundle School, 1959–62; Assistant Organist of Worcester Cathedral, 1962–63; Organist and Master of Choristers: Worcester Cathedral, 1963–74; St George's Chapel, Windsor Castle, 1975–91; Acting Dir of Music, Clare Coll., Cambridge, 2005–06. Conductor: City of Birmingham Choir, 1963–2002; Oxford Bach Choir, 1977–97; Leith Hill Musical Festival, 1977–80. President: RCO, 1982–84; Friends of Cathedral Music, 2004–. Chm., Ouseley Trust, 2002–07. Hon. Fellow, Birmingham City Univ. (formerly Birmingham Poly., later Univ. of Central England), 1990. Hon. FGCM 2002. Hon. MMus Birmingham, 1987; MusD Lambeth, 2002. Recreations: watching cricket, travel. Address: St John's College, Cambridge CB2 1TP.

ROBINSON, Sir Christopher Philipse, 8th Bt cr 1854, of Toronto; b 10 Nov. 1938; s of Christopher Robinson, QC (d 1974) (g s of 1st Bt) and Neville Taylor (d 1991), d of Rear-Adm. Walter Rockwell Gherardi, USN; S kinsman, Sir John Beverley Robinson, 7th Bt, 1988, but his name does not appear on the Official Roll of the Baronetage; m 1962,

Barbara Judith, *d* of late Richard Duncan (marr. diss.); two *s* (and one *s* decd). *Heir:* *s* Peter Duncan Robinson [*b* 31 July 1967; *m* Jennifer Ann Martin; two *s* one *d*].

ROBINSON, Prof. Colin, FSS, FEI; Professor of Economics, University of Surrey, 1968–2000, now Emeritus; Editorial Director, Institute of Economic Affairs, 1992–2002; *b* 7 Sept. 1932; *s* of late James Robinson and Elsie (*née* Brownhill); *m* 1st, 1957, Olga West; two *s*; 2nd, 1983, Eileen Marshall; two *s* two *d*. *Educ:* Univ. of Manchester (BA Econ). FSS 1970; FEI (FInstPet 1985). Economist, Procter and Gamble, 1957–60; Economist, subseq. Head of Economics Dept, Esso Petroleum Co., 1960–66; Econ. Advr, Natural Gas, Esso Europe, 1966–68. Mem., Monopolies and Mergers Commn, 1992–98. Fellow, Soc. of Business Economists, 2000. Outstanding Contribution to the Profession Award, Internat. Assoc. for Energy Economics, 1998. *Publications:* Business Forecasting, 1970; (with Jon Morgan) North Sea Oil in the Future, 1978; (with Eileen Marshall) Can Coal Be Saved?, 1985; Energy Policy, 1993; papers on energy economics and regulation in learned jls. *Recreations:* walking, music, home improvements.

ROBINSON, Cynthia Ann; Chief Executive, Queen Elizabeth's Foundation for Disabled People, since 2001; *b* 28 June 1951; *d* of Andrew Ian Robinson and Alys Congreve Sandys Robinson. *Educ:* Univ. of Nottingham (BSc Hons Biochem. 1972). Registered nutritionist, 1991; CDipAF 1993. Res. Biochemist, Roche Products, 1972–75; Res. Nutritionist, Slimming Magazine, 1975–80; Mkt Res. Exec., AGB Ltd, 1980–82; consultant nutritionist, 1982–; Hd of Communications, Cow & Gate, 1991–93; Dir of Communications, Marie Curie Cancer Care, 1993–98; Chief Exec., Fitness Industry Assoc., 1998–99. Dir, RYA, 1999–2002, 2004–07. Mem. Council, Royal Inst. of Navigation, 2004– (Chm., Small Craft Gp, 2007–). FRIN 2004. *Publication:* (contrib.) Good Health Fact Book, 1995. *Recreations:* sailing (RYA Yachtmaster Offshore instructor, 1983–, examiner, 1994–), gliding (British Gliding Assoc. instructor, 1984–90), flying. *Address:* Queen Elizabeth's Foundation for Disabled People, Leatherhead Court, Leatherhead, Surrey KT22 0BN. *Club:* Royal Thames Yacht (Hon. Mem.).

ROBINSON, Prof. David Antony, PhD; Director, International Corporate Coaching Pty Ltd, since 2003; Vice Chancellor and President, Monash University, 1997–2002; *b* 24 July 1941; *s* of Harry Robinson and Marjorie Newcombe Robinson (*née* Patchett); *m* 1st, 1965, Marjorie Rose Collins (marr. diss. 1970); 2nd, 1976, Yvonne Ann Salter (marr. diss. 2003); 3rd, 2006, Gael Edith Hayes. *Educ:* Royal Masonic Schs; University Coll., Swansea (BA, PhD 1967). University College, Swansea: Res. Asst, Dept of Sociol., 1964–67; Res. Fellow, DHSS Med. Sociol. Res. Centre, 1967–71; Lectr, then Sen. Lectr, DHSS-MRC Addiction Res. Unit, Inst. of Psychiatry, Univ. of London, 1974–80; University of Hull: Sen. Lectr and Actg Dir, 1980–82, Dir, 1982–91, Inst. for Health Studies; Prof. of Health Studies, 1984–91; Hd of Dept, Social Policy and Professional Studies, 1985–86; Dean, Sch. of Social and Pol Scis, 1986–89; Pro Vice-Chancellor, 1989–91; Co-Dir, ESRC Addiction Res. Centre, Univs of Hull and York, 1983–88; Dir, WHO Collaborating Centre for Res. and Trng in Psycho-social and Econ. Aspects of Health, 1986–91; Vice-Chancellor and Pres., Univ. of S Australia, 1992–96. Member: Editl Bd, Brit. Jl of Addiction, 1978–89; Editl Adv. Bd, Sociol. of Health and Illness, 1987–90. Member: Exec. Council of Soc. for Study of Addictions, 1979–82; Exec. Cttee, Nat. Council on Alcoholism, 1979–82; Exec. Cttee, Nat. Council on Gambling, 1980–87; Health Services Res. Cttee, MRC, 1981–84; Social Affairs Cttee, ESRC, 1982–85. Member: Australian Vice Chancellors Cttee, 1992–2002, Dir, 1995–96; Business/Higher Educn Round Table, 1992–97 (Dir, 1995–98); Australian Higher Educn Industrial Assoc., 1992–97 (Mem., Exec. Cttee, 1993–97; Vice Pres., 1995–97); Univ. Grants Cttee, HK, 2002; Aust. Govt Rep., Univ. Grants Cttee, Univ. of S Pacific, 2001–02. Chm., VERNet Pty Ltd, 2005–07. Director: Open Learning Agency of Australia Pty Ltd, 1994–2002; Foundn for Family and Private Business, 1997–2000; Monash Univ. Sunway Campus Malaysia Sdn Bhd, 1998–2002; Monash Univ. S Africa Ltd, 2000–02; Monash Southern Africa (Pty) Ltd, 2000–02; Olympic Games Knowledge Services Inc., 2002. Chm. Council, Victorian Inst. of Forensic Mental Health, 1998–2000. FAIM 1993; FAICD 2005. FRSA 1990. *Publications:* (jtly) Hospitals, Children and their Families, 1970; The Process of Becoming Ill, 1971; Patients, Practitioners and Medical Care: aspects of medical sociology, 1973, 2nd edn 1978; From Drinking to Alcoholism: a sociological commentary, 1976; (ed jtly) Studies in Everyday Medical Life, 1976; (with S. Henry) Self-help and Health: mutual aid for modern problems, 1977; Talking Out of Alcoholism: the self-help process of Alcoholics Anonymous, 1979; (with Y. Robinson) From Self-help to Health: a guide to self-help groups, 1979; (ed) Alcohol Problems: reviews, research and recommendations, 1979; (with P. Tether) Preventing Alcohol Problems: a guide to local action, 1986; (ed jtly) Local Action on Alcohol Problems, 1989; (ed jtly) Controlling Legal Addictions, 1989; (ed jtly) Manipulating Consumption: information, law and voluntary controls, 1990; (with A. Maynard et al) Social Care and HIV-AIDS, 1993; contrib. numerous pamphlets, book chapters and papers in learned and professional jls. *Recreations:* walking, bridge, painting, cinema. *Address:* 55/1 Sandilands Street, South Melbourne, Vic 3205, Australia. *T:* (3) 96825004.

ROBINSON, (David) Duncan, CBE 2008; DL; Director and Marlay Curator, Fitzwilliam Museum, Cambridge, 1995–2007; Master, Magdalene College, Cambridge, since 2002; Deputy Vice-Chancellor, University of Cambridge, since 2005; *b* 27 June 1943; *s* of Tom and Ann Robinson; *m* 1967, Elizabeth Anne Sutton; one *s* two *d*. *Educ:* King Edward VI Sch., Macclesfield; Clare Coll., Cambridge (MA); Yale Univ. (Mellon Fellow, 1965–67; MA). Asst Keeper of Paintings and Drawings, 1970–76, Keeper, 1976–81, Fitzwilliam Museum, Cambridge; Fellow and Coll. Lectr, Clare Coll., Cambridge, 1975–81; Dir, Yale Center for British Art, New Haven, Conn, and Chief Exec., Paul Mellon Centre for Studies in British Art, London, 1981–95; Adjunct Prof. of History of Art, and Fellow of Berkeley Coll., Yale Univ., 1981–95; Professorial Fellow, Clare Coll., Cambridge, 1995–2002, Fellow Emeritus, 2002. Mem. Cttee of Management, Kettle's Yard, Cambridge Univ., 1970–81, 1995– (Chm., Exhibns Cttee, 1970–81). Member: Art Panel, Eastern Arts Assoc., 1973–81 (Chm., 1979–81); Arts Council of GB, 1981 (Mem., 1978–81, Vice-Chm., 1981, Art Panel); Museums and Collections Cttee, English Heritage, 1996–2002; Assoc. of Art Mus. Dirs (USA), 1982–88; Bd of Managers, Lewis Walpole Library, Farmington Ct, USA, 1982–95; Council of Management, The William Blake Trust, 1983–; Vis. Cttee, Dept of Paintings Conservation, Metropolitan Museum of Art, NY, 1984–94; Walpole Soc., 1983– (Mem. Council, 1985–87, 1995–2000); Connecticut Acad. of Arts and Scis, 1991–95; Univ. Museums Gp, 1995– (Sec., 1997–99); Adv. Council, Paul Mellon Centre for Studies in British Art, 1997–2002; Arts and Humanities Res. Bd, 1998–2003; Chm., Art and Artifacts Indemnity Adv. Panel (USA), 1992–94 (Mem., 1991). Member, Board of Directors: New Haven Colony Historical Soc., 1991–94; Amer. Friends of Georgian Gp, 1992–95; E of England Museums, Libraries and Archives Council (formerly Mus Service East of England), 2001–03; The Burlington Magazine Publications Ltd, 2003–. Gov., Yale Univ. Press, 1987–95. Trustee: Yale Univ. Press, London, 1990–; Charleston Trust (USA), 1990–92; Fitzwilliam Mus. Trust, 1995–2007; Wingfield Arts Trust, 2001–03; Burlington Magazine Foundn, 2003–; Crafts Study Centre, Surrey Inst. of Art and Design, 2004–08; Henry Moore Foundn, 2006– (Chm., 2008–); Royal Collection, 2006–; Chm of Trustees, Prince's Drawing Sch., 2007–; Hon. Treas., NW Essex Collection Trust,

2003–07 (Chm., 2002–03). Governor: SE Museums Service, 1997–99; Gainsborough's House Soc., 1998–2002. Pres., Friends of Stanley Spencer Gall., Cookham, 1998–; Vice-Pres., NADFAS, 2000–06. FRSA 1990; FSA 2006. DL Cambs, 2004. Organised Arts Council exhibitions: Stanley Spencer, 1975; William Nicholson, 1980. *Publications:* Companion Volume to the Kelmscott Chaucer, 1975, re-issued as Morris, Burne-Jones and the Kelmscott Chaucer, 1982; Stanley Spencer, 1979, rev. edn 1990; (with Stephen Wildman) Morris & Company in Cambridge, 1980; Town, Country, Shore & Sea: English Watercolours from van Dyck to Paul Nash, 1982; Man and Measure: the paintings of Tom Wood, 1996; The Yale Center for British Art: a tribute to the genius of Louis I. Kahn, 1997; catalogues; articles and reviews in Apollo, Burlington Magazine, etc. *Address:* The Master's Lodge, Magdalene College, Cambridge CB3 0AG. *T:* (01223) 332144. *Clubs:* Garrick, Oxford and Cambridge.

ROBINSON, David Julien; film critic and festival director; *b* 6 Aug. 1930; *s* of Edward Robinson and Dorothy Evelyn (*née* Overton). *Educ:* Lincoln Sch.; King's Coll., Cambridge (BA Hons). Associate Editor, Sight and Sound, and Editor, Monthly Film Bulletin, 1956–58; Programme Dir, NFT, 1959; Film Critic: Financial Times, 1959–74; The Times, 1973–92; Editor, Contrast, 1962–63. Vis. Prof. of Film, Westfield Coll., Univ. of London. Director: Garrett Robinson Co., 1987–88; The Davids Film Co., 1988–. Guest Dir, Edinburgh Film Fest., 1989–91; Director: Channel 4 Young Film Maker of the Year Comp., Edinburgh Film Fest., 1992–95; Pordenone Silent Film Fest., Italy, 1997–. Has curated exhibns, incl. Musique et Cinéma muet, Musée d'Orsay, Paris, 1995. Films produced and directed: Hetty King—Performer, 1969; (Co-dir) Keeping Love Alive, 1987; (Co-dir) Sophisticated Lady, 1989. *Publications:* Hollywood in the Twenties, 1969; Buster Keaton, 1969; The Great Funnies, 1972; World Cinema, 1973, 2nd edn 1980 (US edn The History of World Cinema, 1974, 1980); Chaplin: the mirror of opinion, 1983; Chaplin: his life and art, 1985, 2001; (ed and trans.) Luis Buñuel (J. F. Aranda); (ed and trans.) Cinema in Revolution (anthology); (ed jtly) The Illustrated History of the Cinema, 1986; Music of the Shadows, 1990; Masterpieces of Animation 1833–1908, 1991; Richard Attenborough, 1992; Georges Méliès, 1993; Lantern Images: iconography of the magic lantern 1440–1880, 1993; Sight and Sound Chronology of the Cinema, 1994–95; Musique et cinéma muet, 1995; Charlot—entre rires et larmes, 1995; Peepshow to Palace, 1995; (jtly) Light and Image: incunabula of the motion picture, 1996. *Recreations:* collecting optical toys, model theatres. *Address:* 1 Winifred's Dale, Cavendish Road, Bath BA1 2UD. *T:* (01225) 420305.

ROBINSON, Derek, CBE 1979; Fellow of Magdalen College, Oxford, 1969–99, now Emeritus; Senior Research Officer, Oxford Institute of Economics and Statistics, 1961–99; *b* 9 Feb. 1932; *s* of Benjamin and Mary Robinson; *m* 1956, Jean Evelyn (*née* Lynch); one *s* one *d*. *Educ:* Barnsley Holgate Grammar Sch.; Ruskin Coll., Oxford; Lincoln Coll., Oxford. MA (Oxon), DipEcPolSci (Oxon). Civil Service, 1948–55. Sheffield Univ., 1959–60; Senior Research Officer, Oxford Inst. of Economics and Statistics, 1961–99. Economic Adviser, Nat. Bd for Prices and Incomes, 1965–67; Sen. Economic Adviser, Dept of Employment and Productivity, 1968–70; Dep. Chm., Pay Bd, 1973–74; Chm., SSRC, 1975–78. Mem., British Library Bd, 1979–82. Visiting Professor: Cornell Univ., 1983; Univ. of Hawaii, 1983. Chairman: Oxfordshire Dist Manpower Cttee, 1980–83 (Oxf. and S Bucks, 1975–79); Cttee of Inquiry into the remuneration of members of local authorities, 1977; Chilterns Area Bd, Manpower Services Commn Special Programmes, 1978–79. Inter-regional Adviser on Wage Policy, ILO, 1986–88. Mem., Internat. Reference Panel to Presidential Comprehensive Labour Market Commn, S Africa, 1995–96. *Publications:* Non-Wage Incomes and Prices Policy, 1966; Wage Drift, Fringe Benefits and Manpower Distribution, 1968; Workers' Negotiated Savings Plans for Capital Formation, 1970; (ed) Local Labour Markets and Wage Structures, 1970; Prices and Incomes Policy: the Austrian Experience (with H. Suppanz), 1972; Incomes Policy and Capital Sharing in Europe, 1973; (with J. Vincens) Research into Labour Market Behaviour, 1974; (with K. Mayhew et al) Pay Policies for the Future, 1983; Introduction to Economics, 1986; Monetarism and the Labour Market, 1986; Civil Service Pay in Africa, 1990; contributor to Bulletin of Oxford Univ. Inst. of Economics and Statistics, Industrial Relations Jl, etc. *Address:* 56 Lonsdale Road, Oxford OX2 7EP. *T:* (01865) 552276.

ROBINSON, Derek Anthony, DPhil; Keeper, Science Museum, London, 1978–99, retired; *b* 21 April 1942; *e* *s* of late Charles Frederick Robinson and Mary Margaret Robinson; *m* 1965, Susan Gibson (*d* 1991); two *s*. *Educ:* Hymers Coll., Hull; The Queen's Coll., Oxford (Hastings Scholar; BA 1963; MA, DPhil 1967). MRSC 2001. Post-doctoral Res. Fellow, Dept of Chemistry, Univ. of Reading, 1967–69; Mem. scientific staff, Molecular Pharmacology Unit of MRC, Cambridge, 1969–72; Sen. Asst in Res., Dept of Haematol Medicine, Cambridge Univ. Med. Sch., 1972–74; Science Museum: Asst Keeper I, Dept of Chem., 1974–77; Dep. Keeper (formerly Asst Keeper I), Wellcome Mus. of History of Medicine, and Sec. of Adv. Council, 1977–78; Keeper, Dept of Museum Services, 1978–87; Keeper, Dept of Physical Scis, later Head of Sci. Gp, then Head of Phys. Scis and Engrg Gp, 1987–98; Asst Dir (actg) and Hd of Collections, 1998–99. Mem., British Nat. Cttee for History of Sci., Medicine and Technology, 1987–88; Mem., CGLI, 1984–; Dir, Bd, Mus. Documentation Assoc., 1989–92. Trustee, Nat. Gas Mus., 1999–. Hon. Sec., Artefacts annual internat. confs, 2000–. *Publications:* contributions to: 2nd edn Acridines, ed R. M. Acheson, 1973; Vol. VI, The History of Technology, ed T. I. Williams, 1978; Cambridge General Encyclopaedia, ed D. Crystal, 1990; Making of the Modern World: milestones of science and technology, ed N. Cossons, 1992; Instruments of Science: an historical encyclopaedia, ed R. F. Bud and D. J. Warner, 1998; Musei, saperi e culture, Atti del Convegno, ed M. Gregorio, 2002; (ed jtly) Chymica Acta: an autobiographical memoir, by Frank Greenaway, 2007; papers on heterocyclic chemistry, molecular pharmacol., and leukaemia chemotherapy, in Jl Chem. Soc., Brit. Jl Pharmacol., and Biochem. Trans. *Recreations:* living and gardening in France, travel, walking. *Address:* 3 Broadwater Avenue, Letchworth Garden City, Herts SG6 3HE. *T:* (01462) 686961; *e-mail:* derekarobinson@aol.com. *Club:* Athenæum.

ROBINSON, Dickon Hugh Wheelwright, CBE 2003; RIBA; Member, Commission for Architecture and the Built Environment, since 2000; *b* 28 Dec. 1945; *s* of Hugh and Nancy Robinson (*née* Bartlett); *m* 1969, Charlotte Louise Clifton (*née* Gilmore); three *s* one *d*. *Educ:* St George's Sch., Hong Kong; King's Sch., Bruton; Portsmouth Coll. of Art (Dip Arch). RIBA 1971. Dept of Architecture, GLC, 1966–67; Scientific Control Systems (SCION), 1969–74; Sir John Burnet Tait Architects (hosp. design partnership), 1972–74; Westwood, Piet Poole and Smart, Architects, 1974–75; Housing Dept, Camden LBC, 1976–88; Dir, Develt and Tech. Services, Peabody Trust, 1988–2004; Man. Dir, Peabody Enterprises, 2004–05. Vis. Prof., Mackintosh Sch. of Architecture, 2002–. Retained Advisor: Grainger Trust plc, 2004–; Pocket Homes, Bath & NE Som DC, 2004–. Chairman: Cabespace, 2003; Building Futures, 2005; Mem., Urban Panel, English Heritage, 2000. Founder Member: Save Piccadilly Campaign, 1972–74; and First Chm., Soho Housing Assoc., 1973–80. Mem., Policy Cttee, British Property Fedn, 2000–03. Member: Mgt Cttee, Vision for London, 1994–98; Mgt Cttee, Centrepoint, 1995–99; Council, Urban Villages Forum, 1996–99; Mgt Cttee, St Mungo's, 1999–2000. Mem., Foyer Fedn for Youth, 1992 (Chm., 1994–2001). FRSA 1995. *Recreations:* twentieth century fine and applied art, architecture and books, apples, cider-making, orchards and trees, challenging received wisdom. *Address:* 4 Morgan House, 127 Long Acre, Covent Garden, WC2E 9AA; *e-mail:* dickon@ambooco.co.uk. *Club:* Architecture.

ROBINSON, Sir Dominick Christopher L.; *see* Lynch-Robinson.

ROBINSON, Rt Rev. Donald William Bradley, AO 1984; Archbishop of Sydney and Metropolitan of New South Wales, 1982–93; *b* 9 Nov. 1922; *s* of Rev. Richard Bradley Robinson and Gertrude Marston Robinson (*née* Ross); *m* 1949, Marie Elizabeth Taubman; three *s* one *d*. *Educ:* Sydney Church of England Grammar Sch.; Univ. of Sydney (BA); Queens' Coll., Cambridge (MA). Australian Army, 1941–45, Lieut Intell. Corps, 1944. Deacon 1950, Sydney; priest 1951; Curate, Manly, NSW, 1950–52; St Philip's, Sydney, 1952–53; Lecturer: Moore Coll., 1952–81 (Vice-Principal, 1959–72); Sydney Univ., 1964–81; Asst Bishop, Diocese of Sydney (Bishop in Parramatta), 1973–82. Hon. ThD Aust. Coll. of Theology, 1979. *Address:* 1 Jubilee Avenue, Pymble, NSW 2073, Australia. *T:* (2) 94493033.

ROBINSON, Duncan; *see* Robinson, David D.

ROBINSON, Emma-Jane; heritage consultant and researcher; University Librarian, University of London Library, 1994–2003; *b* 19 Aug. 1953; *d* of late Harold Frederick Wensley Cory and of Yvonne Margaret Cory (*née* Hales); *m* 1974, David John Robinson. *Educ:* Westonbirt Sch.; University Coll. of Wales, Aberystwyth (BSc); Inst. of Educn, London Univ. (PhD 2008). MCLIP (ALA 1981). Asst Librarian, then Sub-Librarian, Univ. of London Liby, 1989–94. Member: Consortium of Univ. Res. Libraries, 1994–2003; Consortium of European Res. Libraries, 1994–2003; Res. Libraries Gp, 1994–2003; BL Arts, Humanities and Social Scis Adv. Bd, 1997–2003. FRSA 1995. *Publications:* articles on cultural landscapes in academic and professional jls. *Recreations:* riding, walking, botanising, archaeologising. *Address:* 101 Colindeep Lane, Colindale, NW9 6DD.

ROBINSON, Eric; Corporate Director, Social Care and Health, Staffordshire County Council, since 2005; *b* 28 May 1960; *s* of Eric Robinson and Margaret Robinson; partner, Jacqueline Pratt; one *s* two *d*. *Educ:* University Coll. Cardiff (BSc; DMS). Qualified as social worker, 1982; Assistant Director of Social Services: Knowsley MBC, 1995–97; Lincs CC, 1997–2001; Director of Social Services: Enfield LBC, 2001–03; Cambridgeshire CC, 2003–05. *Recreations:* being a father, family life, Liverpool Football Club. *Address:* Staffordshire County Council, Martin Street, Stafford ST16 2LH. *T:* (07815) 999014; *e-mail:* eric.robinson@staffordshire.gov.uk.

ROBINSON, Eric Embleton; Director, Lancashire Polytechnic (formerly Preston Polytechnic), 1982–90; *b* 12 March 1927; *s* of Cyril Robinson and Florence Mary Embleton. *Educ:* local authority schools, Nelson and Colne, Lancs; London Univ. (MSc). Teaching, Prescot Grammar Sch., 1948, Acton Tech. Coll., 1949–56, Brunel Coll., 1956–62, Enfield Coll., 1962–70; Dep. Dir, NE London Polytechnic, 1970–73; Principal, Bradford Coll., 1973–82. Pres., Assoc. of Teachers in Tech. Instns, 1962; Exec. Mem., Nat. Union of Teachers, 1961–67; Member: Burnham Cttees, 1961–67; Nat. Council for Training and Supply of Teachers, 1964–66; Minister's Working Party on Polytechnics, 1965–66; Equal Opportunities Commn, 1976–81; CNAA, 1976–82; UNESCO Nat. Commn, 1975–78. Vice Pres., Socialist Educn Assoc., 1966–. Hon. Advr, Beijing Inst. of Business, 1987–; Hon. Vis. Prof., Wolverhampton University (formerly Wolverhampton Polytechnic), 1990–. Hon. Fellow, Sheffield Hallam Univ. (Sheffield City Polytechnic), 1990). Hon. DEd CNAA (E London), 1990; DUniv Central Lancs, 2006. *Publications:* The New Polytechnics, 1968; numerous articles and papers. *Address:* 8 Roundwood Avenue, Reedley, Burnley BB10 2LH. *T:* (01282) 447320. *Club:* Savile.

ROBINSON, (Francis) Alastair (Lavie); Group Vice-Chairman, Barclays Bank, 1992–96; *b* 19 Sept. 1937; *s* of late Stephen and Patricia Robinson; *m* 1961, Lavinia Elizabeth Napier; two *d*. *Educ:* Eton. Nat Service, 4th/7th Royal Dragoon Guards, 1956–58 (2nd Lieut). Mercantile Credit: management trainee, 1959; Gen. Manager, 1971; Mem. Board, 1978; Chief Exec. Officer and Pres., Barclays American, USA, 1981; Regional Gen. Manager, Asia-Barclays International, 1984; Barclays Bank: Dir Personnel, 1987; Exec. Dir, UK Ops, 1990–92; Exec. Dir, Banking Div., 1992–96. Non-executive Director: RMC Gp plc, 1996–2005; Marshall of Cambridge (Hldgs) Ltd, 1996–2006; Portman Bldg Soc., 1998–2004. *Recreations:* music, country pursuits.

ROBINSON, Prof. Francis Christopher Rowland, CBE 2006; PhD; Professor of History of South Asia, University of London, since 1990; *b* Southgate, 23 Nov. 1944; *s* of late Leonard Robinson and Joyce Robinson (*née* King); *m* 1971, Patricia Courtenay Hughes; one *s* one *d*. *Educ:* County Grammar Sch. for Boys, Bexhill-on-Sea; Trinity Coll., Cambridge (MA, PhD). Prize Fellow, Trinity Coll., Cambridge, 1969–73; Royal Holloway College, then Royal Holloway and Bedford New College, subseq. Royal Holloway, University of London: Lectr in History, 1973–85; Reader, 1985–90; Hd of Dept, 1990–96; Mem., Council, 1991–; Vice-Principal (Res. and Enterprise), 1997–2003; Sen. Vice-Principal, 2003–04; Mem., Academic Cttee, 1994–, Council, 1995–98, London Univ. Vis. Prof., S Asia Program, 1982 and 1986, Near East Program, 1985, Jackson Sch. of Internat. Studies, Univ. of Washington; Directeur d'Etudes Associé, Ecole des Hautes Etudes en Sciences Sociales, Paris, 1985, 2006–; Vis. Fellow, 2005–08, Fellow, 2008–, Oxford Centre for Islamic Studies; Vis. Prof., Faculty of History, Oxford Univ., 2008–. Member, Board of Management: Inst. of Histl Research, 1994–99; Inst. of Commonwealth Studies, 1994–99. Mem., SE England - India Adv. Bd, 2007–. Pres., RAS, 1997–2000, 2003–06 (Vice-Pres., 2000–03); Mem. Council, Soc. for S Asian Studies, 1998–2002. Trustee: Charles Wallace (Pakistan) Trust, 1999– (Chm. of Trustees, 2001–06); Surrey History Trust, 2001–; Sir Ernest Cassel Educnl Trust, 2005–. Governor: King Edward's Sch., Witley, 2002–; Jubilee High Sch., Addlestone, 2002–04. Ed.-in-Chief, Past in the Present Books, 2006–. FRSA 1997. Iqbal Centenary Medal (Pakistan), 1978. *Publications:* Separatism among Indian Muslims: the politics of the United Provinces' Muslims 1860–1923, 1974, 2nd edn 1993; (with F. Harcourt) Twentieth Century World History: a select bibliography, 1979; Atlas of the Islamic World since 1500, 1982; (with P. R. Brass) Indian National Congress and Indian Society 1885–1985, 1987; Varieties of South Asia Islam, 1988; (ed) Cambridge Encyclopedia of India, Pakistan, Bangladesh, Sri Lanka, 1989; (ed) Cambridge Illustrated History of the Islamic World, 1996; Islam and Muslim History in South Asia, 2000; The 'Ulama of Farangi Mahall and Islamic Culture in South Asia, 2001; Islam, South Asia and the West, 2007; The Mughal Emperors and the Islamic Dynasties of India, Iran and Central Asia 1206–1925, 2007; (ed) New Cambridge History of Islam, vol. 5: Islam in the Age of Western Domination, 2009; contrib. Modern Asian Studies, Asian Affairs, S Asia, Jl of Islamic Studies, Encyclopedia of Islam, Indian Sociology, etc. *Recreations:* ball games, gardening, people, books, travel, food and wine. *Address:* Department of History, Royal Holloway, University of London, Egham, Surrey TW20 0EX. *T:* (01784) 443995. *Clubs:* Athenæum; Hawks.

ROBINSON, Geoffrey; *see* Robinson, A. G.

ROBINSON, Geoffrey; MP (Lab) Coventry North West, since March 1976; *b* 25 May 1938; *s* of Robert Norman Robinson and Dorothy Jane Robinson (*née* Skelly); *m* 1967, Marie Elena Giorgio; one *s* one *d*. *Educ:* Emanuel School; Cambridge and Yale Univs. Labour Party Research Assistant, 1965–68; Senior Executive, Industrial Reorganisation Corporation, 1968–70; Financial Controller, British Leyland, 1971–72; Managing Director, Leyland Innocenti, Milan, 1972–73; Chief Exec., Jaguar Cars, Coventry, 1973–75; Chief Exec. (unpaid), Meriden Motor Cycle Workers' Co-op., 1978–80 (Dir, 1980–82). Chm., TransTec PLC, 1986–97. Dir, W Midlands Enterprise Bd, 1980–84. Opposition spokesman on science, 1982–83, on regional affairs and industry, 1983–86; HM Paymaster General, 1997–98. *Publication:* The Unconventional Minister: my life inside New Labour, 2000. *Recreations:* reading, architecture, gardens, football. *Address:* House of Commons, SW1A 0AA. *T:* (020) 7219 3000.

ROBINSON, Dr Geoffrey Walter, CBE 1998; FREng, FIET, FBCS; Director General and Chief Executive, Ordnance Survey, 1998–99; *b* 9 Nov. 1945; *s* of late George Robinson and Edith Margaret (*née* Wilson); *m* 1967, Edwina Jones; one *s* one *d*. *Educ:* Aireborough Grammar Sch.; Nottingham Univ. (BSc 1st Cl. Maths; PhD). IBM UK: Lab. posts, 1969–82; Manager of Scientific Centre, 1982–84; Technical Progs Advr, 1984–85; Technical Dir, 1986–88; Dir, Laboratories, 1988–92, 1994–96; Vice Pres., Networking Software Div., 1994–96; Dir of Technol., 1996–97; Chm., Transarc Corp., 1994–96; Dir, Pirelli UK, 2002–05. Chief Advr on Sci. and Technol., DTI, 1992–94. Dep. Chm., Foundn for Sci. and Technol., 1998–2000. Member: SERC, 1992–94; NERC, 1992–94; PPARC, 1994–98; CCLRC, 1995–98; Bd, QAA, 1997–2000; Bd, British Geol Survey, 2001– (Chm., 2002–04). Liveryman: Co. of Inf. Technologists, 1992; Scientific Instrument Makers' Co., 1996. Gov., King Alfred's Coll., Winchester, 1993–99 (Hon. DTech 1992). FBCS 1994 (Pres., 1995–96); FIET (FIEE 1994) (Vice Pres., IEE, 1998–2000); FREng (FEng 1994). FRSA 1992. DUniv Leeds Metropolitan, 1997. *Publications:* articles on science, technol. and society. *Recreation:* music. *Address:* Fardale, Hookwood Lane, Ampfield, Romsey, Hants SO51 9BZ. *T:* (023) 8025 1112; *e-mail:* gwr@fardale.org.

ROBINSON, George; Member (DemU) East Londonderry, Northern Ireland Assembly, since 2003; *b* Limavady, 30 May 1941; *m*; one *s* one *d*. *Educ:* Limavady Tech. Coll. Civil servant, retired. Mem. (DemU), Limavady BC, 1985– (Mayor, 2002). Northern Ireland Assembly: Mem., Regl Develt Cttee; Mem., Exec. Review Cttee. *Address:* (office) 6–8 Catherine Street, Limavady, Co. Londonderry BT49 9DB.

ROBINSON, Sir Gerrard Jude, (Sir Gerry), Kt 2004; Chairman: Arts Council England (formerly Arts Council of England), 1998–2004; Allied Domecq, 2002–05; *b* 23 Oct. 1948; *s* of Anthony and Elizabeth Ann Robinson; *m* 1st, 1970, Maria Ann Borg (marr. diss. 1990); one *s* one *d*; 2nd, 1990, Heather Peta Leaman; one *s* one *d*. *Educ:* St Mary's Coll., Castlehead. FCMA 1991. Works Accountant, Lesney Products, 1970–1974; Financial Controller, Lex Industrial Distribution and Hire, 1974–80; Coca Cola: Finance Dir, 1980–81; Sales and Mkting Dir, 1981–83; Man. Dir, 1983–84; Man. Dir, Grand Metropolitan Contract Services, 1984–87; Chief Exec., Compass Gp plc, 1987–91; Granada Group plc: Chief Exec., 1991–96; Chm., 1996–2000; Dir, 2001–03; Chairman: LWT, 1994–96; ITN, 1995–97; BSkyB, 1995–98; Granada Compass plc, 2000–01. Presenter television documentaries: I'll Show Them Who's Boss, 2003; Can Gerry Robinson Fix the NHS? (series), 2007. *Publication:* I'll Show Them Who's Boss: the six secrets of successful management, 2004. *Recreations:* golf, opera, chess, ski-ing, reading, music. *Club:* Wisley Golf.

ROBINSON, Helen Gillian, (Mrs Helen Preston), OBE 1992; Chief Executive, The New West End Co., 2000–05; *b* 4 Jan. 1940; *d* of Dr John Christopher Wharton and Gertrude Margaret (*née* Dingwall); *m* 1st, 1959, Philip Henry Robinson, *qv* (marr. diss. 1979); one *d* (one *s* decd); 2nd, 1980, Desmond Preston (*d* 1995). *Educ:* Roedean. Fashion Ed., UK and USA, Vogue Mag., 1960–70; Exec. Ed., Vogue Mag., 1970–75; Dir, Debenhams plc, 1975–86; Gp Mktg Dir, Conde Nast Pubns, 1986–88; Gp Man. Dir, Thomas Goode & Co. Ltd, 1988–93; general marketing and design mgt consultancies, 1993–96; Dir of Mktg, Asprey Gp, 1996–98; Mgt Consultant, MIA Pty Australia, 1999. Non-executive Director: BAA, 1978–95; LRT, 1984–95; London Electricity Plc, 1989–94; Churchill China Plc, 1996–98. Royal College of Art: Mem. Council, 1982–2000 (Vice Chm., 1992–2000); Chm., Staff Cttee, 1985–2000; Trustee, 2000–; Sen. Fellow, 2001. Gov. and Trustee (formerly Gov. and Mem., Exec. Cttee), Commonwealth Inst., 1994–2007; Trustee, Commonwealth Educn Trust, 2007–. Mem., Design Mgt Adv. Gp, London Business Sch., 1985–95. World Wide Fund for Nature: Trustee and Chm., WWF (UK) Ltd, 1989–95; Mem., Council of Ambassadors, 1999–2006 (Fellow, 2006–). Mem. Council, Cottage Homes (Retail Trade Charity), 1995–96. FRSA 1990; Hon. FCSD 1994. *Recreations:* theatre, cinema, music, art, cooking, wildlife, family. *Address:* 18 Doria Road, SW6 4UG. *T:* (020) 7736 8814, *Fax:* (020) 7731 2165.

ROBINSON, Sir Ian, Kt 2000; FREng, FIChemE; Chairman, Ladbrokes plc (formerly Hilton Group), since 2001; *b* 3 May 1942; *s* of Thomas Mottram Robinson and Eva Iris Robinson (*née* Bird); *m* 1967, Kathleen Crawford Leay; one *s* one *d*. *Educ:* Leeds Univ. (BSc); Harvard Univ. FIChemE 1982; FREng (FEng 1994). With Kellogg International Co. Ltd, 1964–72; Managing Director: Ralph M. Parsons Co. Ltd, 1972–86; John Brown Engrs & Constructors, 1986–92; Dir and Chm., Engrg Div., Trafalgar House plc, 1992–95; Chief Exec., Scottish Power plc, 1995–2001; Chm., Amey plc, 2001–03. Non-executive Director: Siemens plc, 2002–; Scottish & Newcastle plc, 2004–; Compass Gp plc, 2006–. Member: Takeover Panel, 2003–; Adv. Bd, CVC Capital Partners, 2004–06. Chm., Scottish Enterprise, 2001–03. *Recreations:* golf, gardening. *Address:* Ladbrokes plc, Imperial House, Imperial Drive, Rayners Lane, Harrow HA2 7JW. *Club:* Royal Automobile.

ROBINSON, Iris; MP (DemU) Strangford, since 2001; Member (DemU) Strangford, Northern Ireland Assembly, since 1999; *b* 6 Sept. 1949; *d* of Joseph and Mary Collins; *m* 1970, Peter David Robinson, *qv;* two *s* one *d*. *Educ:* Knockbreda Intermediate Sch.; Cregagh Tech. Coll. Mem. (DemU) Castlereagh BC, 1989– (Mayor 1992, 1995, 2000). *Recreation:* interior design. *Address:* House of Commons, SW1A 0AA; (constituency office) 12 North Street, Newtownards, Northern Ireland BT23 4DE. *T:* (028) 9182 7701.

ROBINSON, Jancis Mary, (Mrs N. L. Lander), OBE 2003; MW; wine writer and broadcaster; *b* 22 April 1950; *d* of late Thomas Edward Robinson and of Ann Sheelagh Margaret Robinson (*née* Conacher); *m* 1981, Nicholas Laurence Lander, *qv;* one *s* two *d*. *Educ:* Carlisle and County High Sch. for Girls; St Anne's Coll., Oxford (MA). Editor, Wine & Spirit, 1976–80; Founder and Editor, Drinker's Digest (subseq. Which? Wine Monthly), 1977–82; Editor, Which? Wine Guide, 1980–82; Sunday Times Wine Corresp., 1980–86; Evening Standard Wine Corresp., 1987–88; Financial Times Wine Corresp., 1989–; freelance journalism, particularly on wine, food and people, 1980–; freelance television and radio broadcasting, on various subjects, 1983–; Writer/Presenter: The Wine Programme, 1983 (Glenfiddich Trophy), 1985, 1987; Jancis Robinson Meets..., 1987; Matters of Taste, 1989, 1991; Vintners' Tales, 1992, 1998; Jancis Robinson's Wine Course, 1995 (Glenfiddich Trophy); The Food Chain, 1996; Taste,

1999; wine judging and lecturing, 1983–; Wine Consultant, British Airways, 1995–. Director: Eden Productions Ltd, 1989–2003; JancisRobinson.com Ltd, 2003–. Proprietor and principal contrib., jancisrobinson.com, 2000–. DUniv Open, 1997. *Publications*: The Wine Book, 1979, rev. edn 1983; The Great Wine Book, 1982 (Glenfiddich Award); Masterglass, 1983, rev. edn 1987; How to Choose and Enjoy Wine, 1984; Vines, Grapes and Wines, 1986 (André Simon Meml Prize, Wine Guild Award, Clicquot Book of the Year); Jancis Robinson's Adventures with Food and Wine, 1987; Jancis Robinson on the Demon Drink, 1988; Vintage Timecharts, 1989; (ed) The Oxford Companion to Wine, 1994 (6 internat. awards), 3rd edn 2006; Jancis Robinson's Wine Course, 1995, revd edn 2003; Jancis Robinson's Guide to Wine Grapes, 1996; Confessions of a Wine Lover (autobiog.), 1997; Jancis Robinson's Wine Tasting Workbook, 2000; Jancis Robinson's Concise Wine Companion, 2001; (with Hugh Johnson) The World Atlas of Wine, 5th edn 2001 and 6th edn 2007. *Recreations:* wine, food and words. *Address:* e-mail: jancis@jancisrobinson.com; *web:* www.janisrobinson.com.

ROBINSON, Jane; *see* Morrice, J.

ROBINSON, Joanna Lesley; *see* Simons, J. L.

ROBINSON, John Harris, FREng, FIChemE; Chairman: Consort Medical (formerly Bespak) plc, since 2004; Affinity Healthcare Ltd, since 2005; Oasis Healthcare Ltd, since 2007; Operating Partner, Duke Street Capital, since 2001; *b* 22 Dec. 1940; *s* of Thomas and Florence Robinson; *m* 1963, Doreen Alice Gardner; one *s* one *d*. *Educ*: Woodhouse Grove Sch.; Birmingham Univ. (BSc). CEng 1968, FREng (FEng 1998); FIChemE 1983. ICI plc, 1962–65; Fisons plc, 1965–70; PA Consulting Gp, 1970–75; Woodhouse and Rixson, 1975–79; Smith & Nephew plc: Man. Dir, Healthcare Div., 1979–82; Dir, 1982–89; Dep. Chief Exec., 1989–90; Chief Exec., 1990–97; Chm., 1997–99; Chairman: Low & Bonar PLC, 1997–2001; UK Coal (formerly RJB Mining) plc, 1997–2003; George Wimpey plc, 1999–2007 (non-exec. Dir, 1998); Railtrack, 2001–02; Paragon Healthcare Gp, 2002–06; non-executive Director: Delta plc, 1993–2001; Esporta Gp Ltd, 2006–07; Abbeyfield Soc., 2007–. Chm., Healthcare Sector Gp, DTI, 1996–2001; Mem., Industrial Develt Adv. Bd, DTI, 1998–2001. Mem., President's Cttee, CBI, 2001– (Chm., Technol. and Innovation Cttee, 1998–2001). Governor: Hymers Coll., Hull, 1983–; Woodhouse Grove Sch., 2003–; Chm. Council and Pro-Chancellor, Hull Univ. 1998–2006; Mem., Cttee of Univ. Chairmen, 1998–2006. President: IChemE, 1999; Inst. of Mgt, 2002. Liveryman, Engineers' Co. (Mem., Ct of Assts, 2005–; Middle Warden, 2008–April 2009). CCMI (CIMgt 1991); FRSA 1992. Hon. DEng Birmingham, 2000; DUniv Bradford, 2000; Hon. DBA Lincoln, 2002; Hon. DSc Hull, 2006. *Recreations:* golf, cricket, theatre. *Address:* 146 Artillery Mansions, Victoria Street, SW1H 0HX. *T:* (020) 7222 7303. *Clubs:* Athenæum; Brough Golf (E Yorks).

ROBINSON, Sir John (James Michael Laud), 11th Bt *cr* 1660; DL; Vice Lord-Lieutenant of Northamptonshire, since 2008; *b* 19 Jan. 1943; *s* of Michael Frederick Laud Robinson (*d* 1971) and Elizabeth (*née* Bridge); *S* grandfather, 1975; *m* 1968, Gayle Elizabeth (*née* Keyes) (High Sheriff, Northants, 2001–02); two *s* one *d*. *Educ*: Eton; Trinity Coll., Dublin (MA, Economics and Political Science). Chartered Financial Analyst. Chairman: St Andrews Hosp., Northampton, 1984–94; Northampton Gen. Hosp. NHS Trust, 1994–99. Pres., British Red Cross, Northants Br., 1982–90. DL Northants, 1984. *Heir: s* Mark Christopher Michael Villiers Robinson [*b* 23 April 1972; *m* 2002, Paula, *d* of late Donald Hendrick; one *d*]. *Address:* Cranford Hall, Cranford, Kettering, Northants NN14 4AL.

ROBINSON, Very Rev. (John) Kenneth; Dean of Gibraltar, 2000–03, now Emeritus; *b* 17 Dec. 1936; *s* of John Robinson and Elizabeth Ellen Robinson (*née* Blackburn); *m* 1965, Merrylyn Kay (*née* Young); one *s* one *d*. *Educ:* Balshaw's Grammar Sch., Leyland, Lancs; KCL (BD 1961). Ordained deacon, 1962, priest 1963; Assistant Curate: St Chad, Poulton-le-Fylde, 1962–65; Lancaster Priory, 1965–66; Chaplain, St John's Army Children's Sch., Singapore, 1966–68; Vicar, Holy Trinity, Colne, Lancs, 1968–70; Dir of Educn, dio. Windward Is, WI, 1971–74; Vicar, St Luke, Skerton, Lancaster, 1974–81; Area Sec., USPG, 1981–91; Minor Canon, St Edmundsbury Cathedral, 1982–91; Chaplain, Greater Lisbon, Portugal, 1991–2000; Archdeacon of Gibraltar, 1994–2002. *Recreations:* swimming, crossword puzzles, cooking. *Address:* 9 Poplar Drive, Coppull, Chorley, Lancs PR7 4LS.

ROBINSON, John Martin Cotton, DPhil, DLitt; FSA; antiquary; Partner, Historic Buildings Consultants, since 1988; *b* 10 Sept. 1948; *s* of John Cotton Robinson and Ellen Anne Cecilia Robinson, *e d* of George Adams, Cape Town, S Africa. *Educ*: Fort Augustus Abbey; St Andrews Univ. (MA 1st Cl. Hons 1970; DLitt 2002); Oriel Coll., Oxford (DPhil 1974). FSA 1979. Historic Buildings Div., GLC, 1974–86; Librarian to Duke of Norfolk, 1978–. Fitzalan Pursuivant Extraordinary, 1982–88; Maltravers Herald Extraordinary, 1988–. Heraldic Advr, NT, 1996–. Vice-Chm., Georgian Gp, 1990–; Chm., Art and Architecture Cttee, Westminster Cathedral, 1996–; Member: Prince of Wales Restoration Cttee, Windsor Castle, 1993–94; NW Cttee, NT, 1994–2005; Trustee, Abbot Hall Art Gall., 1990–. KM 1980. Architectural Editor, Survey of London, 1978–80. *Publications:* The Wyatts, 1979; Georgian Model Farms, 1980; Dukes of Norfolk, 1982; Latest Country Houses, 1983; Cardinal Consalvi, 1987; (with Thomas Woodcock) Oxford Guide to Heraldry, 1988; Temples of Delight, 1990; Guide to Country Houses of the North West, 1991; Treasures of English Churches, 1995; (with David Neave) Francis Johnson, Architect, 2001; The Staffords, 2002; The Regency Country House, 2005; Grass Seed in June, 2006. *Address:* Beckside House, Barbon, Carnforth, Lancs LA6 2LT. *T:* (office) (020) 7831 4398, *Fax:* (office) (020) 7831 8831; *e-mail:* mentmore@historical-buildings.co.uk. *Clubs:* Travellers, Beefsteak, Pratt's, Pitt, XV, Roxburghe (Sec., 1990–).

ROBINSON, Dr Keith; Chief Executive, Wiltshire County Council, since 1996; *b* 12 July 1951; *s* of Wes and Eileen Robinson; *m* 1976, Anne Elizabeth Wilkinson; one *s* one *d*. *Educ:* Sidney Sussex Coll., Cambridge (MA); Durham Univ. (MA); Manchester Univ. (PhD). Dept of Educn and Science, 1975–85; Leics CC, 1985–88; Bucks CC, 1988–93; Wilts CC, 1993–. *Recreations:* jazz, running. *Address:* County Hall, Trowbridge, Wilts BA14 8JF. *T:* (01225) 713100.

ROBINSON, Very Rev. Kenneth; *see* Robinson, Very Rev. J. K.

ROBINSON, Sir Kenneth, Kt 2003; PhD; author and consultant; *b* 4 March 1950; *s* of James Robinson and Ethel Robinson; *m* 1982, Marie Therese Watts; one *s* one *d*. *Educ*: Univ. of Leeds (BEd 1972); Inst. of Educn, Univ. of London (PhD 1982). Dir, Nat. Curriculum Council for Arts in Schs, 1985–89; Prof. of Educn, Univ. of Warwick, 1989–2001, now Emeritus; Sen. Advr, J. Paul Getty Trust, Los Angeles, 2001–06. Dir of Culture, Creativity and the Young, Council of Europe, 1996–98; Chm., Nat. Adv. Cttee on Creative and Cultural Educn, 1998–99. FRSA 1988. European Business Speaker of the Year, Speakers for Business, 2000. *Publications:* Learning Through Drama, 1977; Exploring Theatre and Education, 1980; (jtly) The Arts in Schools, 1982; The Arts and Higher Education, 1983; The Arts 5–16, 1990; Arts Education in Europe, 1997; All Our Futures:

creativity, culture and education, 1999; Out of Our Minds: learning to be creative, 2001. *Recreations:* theatre, music, cinema. *Address:* 2803 Colorado Avenue, Santa Monica, CA 90404, USA.

ROBINSON, Kenneth William; Member (UU) Antrim East, Northern Ireland Assembly, since 1998; *b* Belfast, 2 June 1942; *s* of Joseph Robinson and Anne Elizabeth (*née* Semple); *m* 1964, Louisa Morrison; three *s*. *Educ:* Whitehouse Primary Sch.; Ballyclare High Sch.; Stranmillis Coll. (Teacher's Cert. 1963); Queen's Univ., Belfast (BEd 1979). Principal Teacher: Lisfearty Primary Sch., 1975–77; Argyle Primary Sch., 1977–80; Cavehill Primary Sch., 1980–96. Mem., and Vice-Chm. Educn Cttee, N Eastern Educn and Liby Bd, 1985–93. Mem. (UU), Newtownabbey BC, 1985– (Mayor, 1991–92; Vice Chm., Econ. Develt Cttee, 1995–); Mem., Newtownabbey Dist Partnership Bd, 1996–. Chm., S Antrim Unionist Assoc., 1985–87. Governor: E Antrim Inst. Higher and Further Educn, 1985–93; Whiteabbey Primary Sch., 1985–; Hollybank Primary Sch., 1985–. Vice-Chm., Newtownabbey-Dorsten Twinning Assoc., 2001–. *Recreations:* foreign travel, caravanning, historical research, Association Football, swimming. *Address:* 5 Sycamore Close, Jordanstown, Newtownabbey, Co. Antrim BT37 0PL. *T:* (028) 9086 6056.

ROBINSON, Lee Fisher, CEng; Chairman: HMC Technology plc, since 1983; Demetal Ltd, since 2004; Metals Recovery Ltd, since 2005; Director, HMC Technology (Asiatic) Ltd, since 1997; *b* 17 July 1923; *m* 1st, 1944; three *d*; 2nd, 1976, June Edna Hopkins. *Educ:* Howard Sch.; Cardiff Tech. College. CEng, MICE; MCIArb. Royal Engrs, Sappers and Miners, IE, 1942–45. Turriff Const. Corp. Ltd, HBM (BCC), 1963; Man. Dir, Power Gas Corp. Ltd, 1964; Chief Exec. and Dep. Chm., Turriff Construction Corp., 1970–73. Director: Davy-Ashmore Ltd, 1970; Combustion Systems (NRDC), 1972–96 (Chm., 1978); Redwood Internat. (UK) Ltd, 1972; Altech SA, 1976–96; Protech SA, 1976–96; BCS Ltd, 1976–96; Charterhouse Strategic Development Ltd, 1976–80 (Gp Indust. Adviser, Charterhouse Gp); Ingeco Laing SA, 1977–96; RTR (Oil Sands) Alberta, 1977–96; RTR Canada Ltd, 1977–96; RTR SA (also Chief Exec.), 1977–96; RTL SA (also Vice-Pres.), 1977–96; Thalassa (North Sea) Ltd, 1980–96; Marcent Natural Resources Ltd (Man. Dir), 1980–96; Hydromet Mineral Co., 1983–96; Solvex Corp., 1988–96; Chairman: Graesser (Contractors) Ltd, 1979–96; Biotechna Ltd, 1982–96; ABG Ltd, 1993–96; Bio-Electrical Ltd, 1993–96; Chm. and Chief Exec. Officer, Biotechna Environmental Ltd, 1994–96. Consultant, Internat. Management Consultants, 1972–96. Chm., Warren Spring Adv. Bd, 1969–72; Mem. Adv. Council for Technology, 1968–69. Mem., Academy of Experts, 1996. *Publications:* Cost and Financing of Fertiliser Projects in India, 1967; various articles. *Address:* Flat 3, Athenaeum Hall, Vale-of-Health, NW3 1AP.

ROBINSON, Mark; *see* Robinson, S. M. P.

ROBINSON, Mark Noel Foster; Executive Director, Commonwealth Press Union, 1997–2002; *b* 26 Dec. 1946; *s* of late John Foster Robinson, CBE, TD and Margaret Eve Hannah Paterson; *m* 1982, Vivien Radclyffe (*née* Pilkington) (*d* 2004); one *s* one *d*. *Educ:* Harrow School; Christ Church, Oxford. MA Hons Modern History. Called to the Bar, Middle Temple, 1975. Research Assistant to Patrick Cormack, MP, 1970–71; Special Asst to US Congressman Hon. F. Bradford Morse, 1971–72; Special Asst to Chief of UN Emergency Operation in Bangladesh, 1972–73; Second Officer, Exec. Office, UN Secretary-General, 1974–77; Asst Dir, Commonwealth Secretariat, 1977–83. Consultant, 1987, Dir, 1988–91, non-exec. Dir, 1991–94, Leopold Joseph & Sons Ltd; non-exec. Dir, Leopold Joseph Hldgs, 1994–95. MP (C): Newport West, 1983–87; Somerton and Frome, 1992–97; contested (C): Newport West, 1987; Somerton and Frome, 1997. PPS to Sec. of State for Wales, 1984–85; Parly Under Sec. of State, Welsh Office, 1985–87; PPS to Minister for Overseas Develt and to Parly Under-Sec. of State, FCO, 1992–94, to Sec. of State for Foreign and Commonwealth Affairs, 1994–95, to Chief Sec. to Treasury, 1995–97. Member: Foreign Affairs Select Cttee, 1983–84; Welsh Affairs Cttee, 1992–97. Chm., UN Parly Gp, 1992–98 (Hon. Sec., 1983–85; Vice Chm., 1996–97); Mem. Cttee, British American Parly Gp, 1996–97. Mem., Commonwealth Develt Corp., 1988–92; Chm., Council for Educn in the Commonwealth, 1999–. Mem. Council, Winston Churchill Meml Trust, 1993–. Fellow, Industry and Parlt Trust, 1985. Member: RUSI; 1984; RIIA, 1984. FCMI (FBIM 1983); FRSA 1990. *Recreations:* include the countryside and fishing. *Clubs:* Brooks's, Pratt's, Travellers.

ROBINSON, Mary; President, Realizing Rights, Ethical Globalization Initiative, since 2002; *b* 21 May 1944; *d* of Aubrey and Tessa Bourke; *m* 1970, Nicholas Robinson; two *s* one *d*. *Educ:* Trinity Coll. Dublin (MA, LLB 1967; Hon. Fellow 1991); Harvard Law Sch. (LLM 1968). Called to the Bar, King's Inns, Dublin, 1967 (Hon. Bencher, 1991); Middle Temple, 1973 (Hon. Bencher, 1991); SC 1980. Reid Prof. of Constitutional and Criminal Law, 1969–75, Lectr in EC Law, 1975–90, TCD. Mem., Irish Senate, 1969–89; Pres. of Ireland, 1990–97; UN High Comr for Human Rights, 1997–2002. Member: Adv. Bd, Common Market Law Review, 1976–90; Internat. Commn of Jurists, 1987–90; Adv. Cttee, Inter-Rights, 1984–90; Vaccine Fund Bd, 2001–; Global Commn on Internat. Migration, 2003–. Chair, Council of Women World Leaders, 2003–. Hon. Pres., Oxfam Ltd, 2002–. Chancellor, Dublin Univ., 1998–. Extraordinary Prof., Univ. of Pretoria, 2003–; Prof. of Practice, Columbia Univ., 2004–. Chair, Irish Chamber Orch., 2003–. Mem., Haut Conseil de la Francophonie, 2003–. Mem., Club of Madrid, 2002– (Vice Pres., 2004–). MRIA 1992; Mem., Amer. Phil Soc., 1998. Hon. Fellow: Hertford Coll., Oxford, 1999; LSE, 1999. Hon. FRCOG 1995; Hon. FRCPsych; Hon. FRCPI; Hon. FRCSI; Hon. FIEI. DCL Oxford (by diploma), 1993; hon. doctorates: Austin; Basle; Brown; Buenos Aires; Caledonian; Cambridge; Columbia; Costa Rica; Coventry; Dublin; Dublin City; Dublin Inst. of Technol.; Duke; Edinburgh; Emory; Essex; Florence; Fordham; Harvard; Leuven; Liverpool; London; McGill; Melbourne; Mongolia; Montpellier; Northeastern; Nottingham; Nova, Lisbon; NUI; Open; Poznan; QUB; Rennes; St Andrews; St Mary's, Halifax; Schweitzer Internat., Geneva; Seoul; S Africa; Toronto; Uppsala; Victoria; Wales; Wheaton; Winnipeg; Yale. Grand Cross: Order of Merit, Chile, 2002; Order of the Southern Cross (Brazil), 2002; Military Order of Christ (Portugal), 2003; Grand Officier, Légion d'Honneur (France), 2003; Condecoración, Aquila Azteca (Mexico), 2002. *Address:* 271 Madison Avenue, Suite 1007, New York, NY 10016, USA; Massbrook House, Ballina, Co. Mayo, Ireland.

ROBINSON, (Maurice) Richard; President, since 1974, Chief Executive Officer, since 1975 and Chairman, since 1982, Scholastic Corporation; *b* 15 May 1937; *s* of Maurice Richard Robinson and Florence Liddell; *m* 1986, Helen Benham (marr. diss.); two *s*. *Educ:* Harvard Univ. (BA magna cum laude); Teachers Coll., Columbia Univ.; St Catharine's Coll., Cambridge. Teacher, Evanston High Sch., Ill, 1960–62; Scholastic: Asst Editor, 1962–64; Editorial Dir, 1964–70; Publisher, 1971–74. *Recreations:* tennis, swimming, jogging, books. *Address:* c/o Scholastic Corporation, 557 Broadway, New York, NY 10012, USA. *T:* (212) 3436700, *Fax:* (212) 3436701; *e-mail:* drobinson@scholastic.com. *Clubs:* University, Century (New York).

ROBINSON, Michael John, CMG 1993; HM Diplomatic Service, retired; Adviser, Government of Albania, Tirana, since 2003 (on secondment from FCO, 2003–04); *b* 19 Dec. 1946; *s* of George Robinson and Beryl Florence Naldrett Robinson; *m* 1971, Anne Jamieson Scott; two *s* two *d*. *Educ:* Cheadle Hulme Sch.; Worcester Coll., Oxford (BA

Hons Mod. Langs). Third Sec., FCO, 1969; Russian lang. student, 1969; Third, subseq. Second, Sec., Moscow, 1970; Second, subseq. First, Sec., Madrid, 1972; FCO, 1977; UK Delegn to CSCE, Madrid, 1980; First Sec. and Head of Chancery, Madrid, 1981; Chef de Cabinet to Sec. Gen., OECD, Paris (on secondment), 1982; Dep. Head, UK Delegn to UNESCO, Paris, 1985; First Sec., subseq. Counsellor, FCO, 1986; Dep. Head of Mission and Consul-Gen., subseq. Chargé d'Affaires, Belgrade, 1990; Dep. Gov., Gibraltar, 1995–98; on secondment as: Pol Advr, OSCE Presence in Albania, Tirana, 1999–2001; Sen. Pol Advr, OSCE Mission to Yugoslavia, 2001–02; Head of OSCE Office, Montenegro, 2002–03. Vis. Fellow, RIIA, 1994. *Publication:* Managing Milosevic's Serbia, 1995. *Recreations:* reading, music, travel. *Address:* c/o Foreign and Commonwealth Office, SW1A 2AH. *Clubs:* Royal Over-Seas League; Royal Gibraltar Yacht.

ROBINSON, Air Vice-Marshal Michael Maurice Jeffries, CB 1982; *b* 11 Feb. 1927; *s* of Dr Maurice Robinson and Muriel (*née* Jeffries); *m* 1952, Drusilla Dallas Bush; one *s* two *d.* *Educ:* King's Sch., Bruton; Queen's Coll., Oxford; RAF Coll., Cranwell. psa 1961, jssc 1965. MA History, Univ. of West of England, 1994. Commnd, 1948; 45 Sqdn, Malaya, 1948–51; CFS, 1953–55; OC 100 Sqdn, 1962–64; Comd, RAF Lossiemouth, 1972–74; Asst Comdt, RAF Coll., Cranwell, 1974–77; SASO No 1 Gp, 1977–79; Dir Gen. of Organisation (RAF), 1979–82, retd. Wing Comdr 1961, Gp Captain 1970, Air Cdre 1976, Air Vice-Marshal 1980. *Recreations:* golf, gardening, going to the opera. *Address:* 70 Southover, Wells, Somerset BA5 1UH. *Club:* Royal Air Force.

ROBINSON, Michael R.; *see* Rowan-Robinson, G. M.

ROBINSON, Michael Stuart; Chief Executive, United Kingdom Hydrographic Office, since 2006; *b* 17 May 1964; *s* of Albert Edward Robinson and Mary Robinson; *m* 1994, Lucie Kate; one *s* one *d.* *Educ:* Portsmouth Poly. (BSc Hons Computer Sci.). ACA 1989. Audit Manager, Price Waterhouse, 1986–92; Chief Internal Auditor, Black Horse Financial Services, 1992–97; Chief Executive: Clerical Med. Internat., 1997–2005; HBOS Europe Financial Services, 2005–06. *Recreations:* music, tennis, ski-ing, sailing. *Address:* c/o United Kingdom Hydrographic Office, Admiralty Way, Taunton, Som TA1 2DN; *e-mail:* mike.robinson@ukho.gov.uk.

ROBINSON, (Moureen) Ann, (Mrs Peter Robinson); Partner, Rush Communication Strategic Consultancy, since 2003; Director of Consumer Policy, uSwitch, since 2005; *d* of William and Winifred Flatley; *m* 1961, Peter Crawford Robinson. DHSS, 1969–74; Central Policy Review Staff, 1974–77; nurses and midwives pay, educn and professional matters, 1981–85; liaison with Health Authorities, NHS planning and review, 1985–86; social security operations, 1986–93; Dir of Policy and Planning, Benefits Agency, DSS, 1990–93; Chief Exec., The Spastics Soc., then Scope, 1993–95; Head, Govt Consultancy Computer Sciences Corp., 1995–96; Dir-Gen., British Retail Consortium, 1997–99; Chairman: Gas Consumers Council, 2000; London Electricity Consumer Cttee, 2000; energywatch (formerly Gas and Electricity Consumers Council), 2000–03. Member: GMC, 2003–; Prison Service Pay Review Body, 2004–08. Chm., Victim Support London, 1999–2001; Trustee, Foundn for Credit Counselling, 2000–08. *Recreations:* walking, fine wine, bridge. *Address: e-mail:* annrob@ntlworld.com.

ROBINSON, Prof. Muriel Anita, PhD; Principal, Bishop Grosseteste University College (formerly Bishop Grosseteste College), Lincoln, since 2003; *b* 21 Feb. 1954; *d* of Albert and Anita Robinson; *m* 1981, Richard Mosiewicz. *Educ:* Furzedown Coll., London (BEd English and Educn Studies 1976); Univ. of London Inst. of Educn (MA Lang. and Lit. 1985; PhD 1995). Teaching in primary schs, ILEA, 1976–85; Brighton Polytechnic, subseq. University of Brighton School of Education: Lectr, 1985, Sen. Lectr, 1987, English in Educn; Course Leader, 1990–97; Principal Lectr, 1993; Co-ordinator, Professional Develt Award Scheme, 1994–98; Dep. Hd of Sch., 1998–2000; Vice Principal, Newman Coll. of Higher Educn, Birmingham, 2000–03. Fellow, Higher Educn Acad. FRSA. *Publications:* Children Reading Print and Television, 1997; extensive range of chapters in learned books and articles in jls, mainly in field of children and media educn. *Recreations:* music, reading, film, cycling, walking, travel. *Address:* Bishop Grosseteste University College, Lincoln LN1 3DY. *T:* (01522) 527347, *Fax:* (01522) 530243; *e-mail:* m.robinson@bishopg.ac.uk.

ROBINSON, Ven. Neil; Archdeacon of Suffolk, 1987–94; *b* 28 Feb. 1929; *s* of James and Alice Robinson; *m* 1956, Kathlyn Williams; two *s* two *d.* *Educ:* Penistone Grammar School; Univ. of Durham (BA, DipTh). Curate of Holy Trinity Church, Hull, 1954–58; Vicar of St Thomas, South Wigston, Leicester, 1958–69; Rector and RD of Market Bosworth, Leicester, 1969–83; Residentiary Canon of Worcester Cathedral, 1983–87. *Recreation:* hill walking. *Address:* 16 Mallorie Court, Ripon, N Yorks HG4 2QG. *T:* (01765) 603075.

ROBINSON, Neil; Communications Consultant, London 2012 Olympic Games, since 2006; Director of Business Development, Ten Alps Digital, since 2007; *b* 25 April 1958; *s* of Arthur and Margery Robinson; *m* 1988, Susie Elizabeth Campbell; one *s.* *Educ:* Anfield Comprehensive Sch. Journalist: S Yorks Times, 1977–79; Evening Chronicle, Newcastle, 1979–86; Border Television: News Ed., 1986–87; Producer (various programmes), 1987–88; Head of News and Current Affairs, 1988–90; Controller of Programmes, 1990–2000; Dir of Programmes, 2000–04; Interim Dir of Communications, Liverpool Culture Co., European Capital of Culture, 2005. Dir, Cumbria Inward Investment Agency Ltd, 1997–2003; Partner, Newsmarket.com, NY, 2007–. European Bd Mem., Co-op. Internat. de la Recherche et d'Actions en Matière de Communication, 1998–. Dir, NW Media Charitable Trust Ltd, 1998–99. Member: Northern Production Fund Panel, Northern Arts, 1993–2000; Cttee, BAFTA Scotland, 1998–2003. Mem., RTS, 1988; FRSA 1995. *Address:* Fayrefield, High Bank Hill, Kirkoswald, Cumbria CA10 1EZ. *Club:* Groucho.

ROBINSON, Nicholas Anthony; Political Editor, BBC, since 2005; *b* 5 Oct. 1963; *s* of E. D. (Robbie) Robinson and Evelyn Robinson; *m* 1991, Pippa Markus; two *s* one *d.* *Educ:* University Coll., Oxford (BA Hons PPE). BBC, 1986–2002: Producer, then Dep. Ed., On The Record, 1988–92; Ed., The Vote Race, 1992; Dep. Ed., Panorama, 1992–95; Political Corresp., BBC News, 1995–97; Presenter, Radio Five Live, 1997–98; Chief Political Corresp., News 24, 1999–2002; Presenter, Westminster Live, 2001–02; Political Ed., ITV News, 2003–05. Columnist, The Times, 2003–. *Recreations:* Alice, Will and Harry, aspirant sailor, Hope Cove. *Address:* c/o BBC News, House of Commons, SW1A 1AA; *e-mail:* nick.robinson@bbc.co.uk.

ROBINSON, Oswald Horsley, CMG 1983; OBE 1977; HM Diplomatic Service, retired; *b* 24 Aug. 1926; *s* of Sir Edward Stanley Gotch Robinson, CBE, FSA, FBA, and Pamela, *d* of Sir Victor Horsley, CB, FRS; *m* 1954, Helena Faith, *d* of Dr F. R. Seymour; two *s* one *d.* *Educ:* Bedales Sch.; King's Coll., Cambridge. Served RE, 1943–48. Joined FO, 1951; served: Rangoon and Maymyo, 1954; FO, 1958; Mexico and Guatemala, 1961; Quito and Bogotá, 1963; FO (later FCO), 1965; Georgetown, Guyana, 1973; Bangkok, 1976; FCO, 1979–84. Dir, RCC Pilotage Foundn, 1985–95. *Publications:* (compiled) Atlantic Spain and Portugal, 1988; *edited:* Ports and Anchorages of the Antilles, 1991; North Africa, 1991; A Baltic Guide, 1992; Faeroes, Iceland and Greenland, 1994; Cruising Notes on the South Atlantic Coast of South America, 1996; Chile: Atacama Desert to Tierra del Fuego, 1998; Mediterranean Spain: part 1, 1998, part 2, 1999. *Recreation:* sailing. *Address:* Dunn House, The Green, Long Melford, Suffolk CO10 9DU. *Clubs:* Royal Cruising, Special Forces.

ROBINSON, Dr Patrick William, (Bill); Head of Economics, KPMG Forensic, since 2007; *b* 6 Jan. 1943; *s* of Harold Desmond Robinson and Joyce Grover; *m* 1st, 1966, Heather Jackson (*d* 1995); two *s* one *d*; 2nd, 1997, Priscilla Stille. *Educ:* Bryanston Sch.; St Edmund Hall, Oxford; DPhil Sussex 1969; MSc LSE 1971. Economic Asst, 10 Downing Street, 1969–70; Cabinet Office, 1970–71; Economic Adviser, HM Treasury, 1971–74; Head of Div., European Commn, 1974–78; Sen. Res. Fellow, London Business Sch., 1979–86; Adviser, Treasury and Civil Service Cttee, 1981–86; Dir, Inst. for Fiscal Studies, 1986–91; econ. columnist, The Independent, 1989–91; Special Advr to Chancellor of Exchequer, 1991–93; Dir, London Economics, 1993–99; Hd UK Business Economist, Corporate Finance and Recovery (formerly Financial Adv. Services), PricewaterhouseCoopers, 1999–2007. Mem., Retail Prices Index Adv. Cttee, 1988–91. Editor: Exchange Rate Outlook, LBS, 1979–86; Economic Outlook, LBS, 1980–86; IFS Green Budget, 1987–91. *Publications:* Medium Term Exchange Rate Guidelines for Business Planning, 1983; Britain's Borrowing Problem, 1993; numerous articles. *Recreations:* bassoon playing, opera, bridge, ski-ing, windsurfing. *Address:* KPMG, 20 Farringdon Street, EC4A 4PP. *T:* (020) 7311 3515. *Club:* Reform.

ROBINSON, Paul Anthony; Director of Children's Services, Wandsworth Borough Council, since 2007; *b* Birmingham, 9 Sept. 1953; *s* of Frank and Marie Robinson; *m* 1986, Alison Margaret Cheadle; one *s* one *d.* *Educ:* Leeds Univ. (BA Hons Hist. 1975); Christ's Coll., Liverpool (PGCE 1977). Auditor, Price Waterhouse, 1975–76; teacher, Doncaster GS, 1977–83; Professional Asst, Leics CC, 1983–85; Asst Educn Officer, Cambs CC, 1986–89; Asst Co. Educn Officer, Essex CC, 1989–92; Dep. Dir of Educn, 1992–94, Dir of Educn, 1994–2007, Wandsworth BC. Chm., London Aggregation Body, 2002–. Chm., Assoc. of London Chief Educn Officers, 1997–2004. Chm., London Grid for Learning Trust Co., 1995–. Gov., S Thames Further Educn Coll., 2001–. Chevalier, Ordre des Palmes Académiques (France), 2003. *Publication:* (contrib.) School Development Planning, 1989. *Recreations:* golf, gym, Rugby coaching, tennis, scuba-diving, theatre, cinema, eating and food, anything to do with castles. *Address:* Wandsworth Borough Council, Town Hall, Wandsworth High Street, SW18 2PU. *T:* (020) 8871 7890; *e-mail:* paul.robinson93@ntlworld.com. *Clubs:* Esher Rugby Union Football; Richmond Golf; Claygate Tennis.

ROBINSON, Air Vice-Marshal Paul Anthony, OBE 1994; FRAeS; defence and security consultant; *b* 8 Aug. 1949; *s* of Anthony and Eira Robinson; *m* 1971, Sarah Wood; one *s* one *d.* *Educ:* Peter Symonds' Sch., Winchester; RAF Coll., Cranwell; RAF Staff Coll., Bracknell. FRAeS 2001. Joined RAF, 1967; Harrier pilot, 1972–77, 1983–85 and 1989–91; qualified flying instructor, 1978; instructed on Gnat, Hawk, Harrier, Jetstream, Tutor and Vigilant aircraft; MoD (OR), 1987–89; OC 233 Operational Conversion Unit (Harrier), 1989–91; HQ 1 Gp, 1991–93; HQ 2 Gp, 1994–96; Stn Comdr, RAF Coll., Cranwell, 1996–98; COS, British Forces, Cyprus, 1998–2000; Comdt, CFS, 2000–01; Dep. Chief of Jt Ops, 2001–04. Liveryman, GAPAN, 2007. *Recreations:* sailing, fishing, shooting, golf. *Club:* Royal Air Force.

ROBINSON, Paul Nicholas; Managing Director, KidsCo Ltd, since 2007; *b* 31 Dec. 1956; *s* of Harold George Robert Robinson and Sonja Diana Robinson; *m* 1983, Gill; two *s.* *Educ:* Camberley Grammar Sch.; Manchester Univ. (BSc Hons Metallurgy 1978); Univ. of Bradford Sch. of Mgt (MBA Dist. 1996). Prog. Dir, Chiltern Radio Network, 1987–90; Head: of Programmes, BBC Radio 1, 1990–94; of Strategy and Develt, BBC, 1994–96; Man. Dir, Talk Radio UK, 1996–98; Vice-Pres., Walt Disney TV Internat., 1998–2000; Sen. Vice Pres., and Hd, Worldwide Prog. Strategy, Disney/ABC Cable Networks, 2000–03. Judge: BAFTA Awards; Sony Radio Awards. Member: Radio Acad., 1985; RTS 1998. *Recreations:* golf, gardening, popular music, taxi service for my children! *Address:* 234a Kings Road, SW3 5UA.

ROBINSON, Peter Damian, CB 1983; Deputy Secretary, Lord Chancellor's Department, 1980–86; *b* 11 July 1926; *s* of late John Robinson and Jill Clegg (*née* Easten); *m* 1st, 1956, Mary Katinka Bonner (*d* 1978), Peterborough; one *d* (and one *d* decd); 2nd, 1985, Mrs Sheila Suzanne Gibbins (*née* Guille). *Educ:* Corby Sch., Sunderland; Lincoln Coll., Oxford. MA. Royal Marine Commandos, 1944–46. Called to Bar, Middle Temple, 1951; practised common law, 1952–59; Clerk of Assize, NE Circuit, 1959–70; Administrator, NE Circuit, 1970–74; Circuit Administrator, SE Circuit, 1974–80; Dep. Clerk of the Crown in Chancery, Lord Chancellor's Dept, 1982–86. Advr on Hong Kong Judiciary, 1986. Member, Home Office Departmental Cttee on Legal Aid in Criminal Proceedings (the Widgery Cttee), 1964–66; Chm., Interdeptl Cttee on Conciliation, 1982–83. *Recreations:* reading, the countryside, antiques. *Address:* 15 Birklands Park, St Albans AL1 1TS.

ROBINSON, Rt Hon. Peter (David); PC 2007; MP (DemU) Belfast East, since 1979 (resigned seat Dec. 1985 in protest against Anglo-Irish Agreement; re-elected Jan. 1986); Member (DemU) Belfast East, since 1998, and First Minister, since 2008, Northern Ireland Assembly; *b* 29 Dec. 1948; *s* of David McCrea Robinson and Sheliah Robinson; *m* 1970, Iris Collins (*see* I. Robinson); two *s* one *d.* *Educ:* Annadale Grammar School; Castlereagh Further Education College. Gen. Secretary, Ulster Democratic Unionist Party, 1975–79, Dep. Leader, 1980–87. Member: (DemU) Belfast E, NI Assembly, 1982–86; NI Forum, 1996–98. Minister for Regl Develt, 1999–2000 and 2001–02, of Finance and Personnel, 2007–08, NI. Member, Castlereagh Borough Council, 1977–2007; Deputy Mayor, 1978; Mayor of Castlereagh, 1986. Member: Select Cttee on NI, 1994–2005; All-Party Cttee on Shipbuilding, 1992–. Mem., NI Sports Council, 1986. *Publications:* (jtly) Ulster—the facts, 1982; booklets include: The North Answers Back, 1970; Capital Punishment for Capital Crime, 1978; Ulster in Peril, 1981; Their Cry Was "No Surrender", 1989; The Union Under Fire, 1995. *Recreations:* golf, bowling. *Address:* 51 Gransha Road, Dundonald, Northern Ireland BT16 0HB; Strandtown Hall, 96 Belmont Avenue, Belfast BT4 3DE; *e-mail:* probin1690@aol.com, peter.robinson.mp@btconnect.com.

ROBINSON, Peter James, FCIS, FCIB; Chairman, Cobra Holdings Ltd, since 2006; Group Chief Executive, Forester Holdings (Europe) Ltd (formerly Forester UK, then Foresters UK Group), 1998–2006 (non-executive Director, since 2006); *b* 28 April 1941; *s* of Percival Albert Robinson and Lillian Caroline (*née* Pantling); *m* 1st, 1963 (marr. diss.); twin *s* one *d*; 2nd, 1984, Janice Helen Jones; two *d.* *Educ:* Erith Co. Grammar Sch.; City of London Poly. FCIS 1967; FCIB 1967. Woolwich Building Society: mgt trainee, 1963–68; PA to Gen. Managers, 1968–70; Ops and Mkting Manager, 1970–72; Co. Sec., 1972–75; Asst Gen. Manager (Develt), 1975–81; Gen. Manager (Ops), 1981–86; Dep. Chief Exec. and Dir, 1986–91; Man. Dir, 1991–95; Gp Chief Exec., Woolwich Building Soc., 1995; management consultant, 1997–98. Chm., Metropolitan Assoc. of Building Socs, 1992. Freeman, City of London, 1982. MInstD 1988; CCMI (CIMgt 1991).

Publications: contrib. articles to Finance Gazette, Economist, Mgt Today, various newspapers. *Recreations:* cricket, golf, gardening, dogs. *Address:* Quakers, Brasted Chart, Kent TN16 1LY. *Clubs:* Royal Automobile, MCC.

ROBINSON, Ven. Peter John Alan; Archdeacon of Lindisfarne, since 2008; *b* Carshalton, Surrey, 8 Dec. 1961; *s* of Alan and Sylvia Robinson; *m* 1986, Sarah Frances Walker; two *s*. *Educ:* Tiffin Boys Grammar Sch., Kingston-upon-Thames; St John's Coll., Cambridge (BA Hons 1983); St John's Coll., Univ. of Durham (BA Hons 1992; PhD 1997). Exec., Burmah Castrol, 1983–90; ordained deacon, 1995, priest, 1996; Asst Curate, North Shields, 1995–99; Priest-in-charge: St Martin's, Byker, 1999–2008; St Michael's, Byker, 2001–08. Dir, Urban Ministry and Theology Project, Newcastle E Deanery, 1999–2008. *Recreations:* fell-walking (especially in Northumberland), cricket, music (especially opera), reading (contemporary novels), travel (especially in Europe), family occasions, teaching theology. *Address:* 4 Acomb Close, Morpeth, Northumberland NE61 2YH. *T:* (01670) 503810, *Fax:* (01670) 503469; *e-mail:* pjarobinson@btinternet.com.

ROBINSON, Prof. Peter Michael, FBA 2000; Tooke Professor of Economic Science and Statistics, London School of Economics and Political Science, since 1995 (Professor of Econometrics, 1984–95); Leverhulme Trust Personal Research Professor, 1998–2003; *b* 20 April 1947; *s* of Maurice Allan Robinson and Brenda Margaret (*née* Ponsford); *m* 1981, Wendy Rhea Brandmark; one *d*. *Educ:* Brockenhurst Grammar Sch.; University Coll. London (BSc); London School of Economics (MSc); Australian National Univ. (PhD). Lectr, LSE, 1969–70; Asst Prof. 1973–77, Associate Prof. 1977–79, Harvard Univ.; Associate Prof., Univ. of British Columbia, 1979–80; Prof., Univ. of Surrey, 1980–84. Fellow, Econometric Soc., 1989; FIMS 2000. Mem., ISI, 2005–. Dr *hc* Universidad Carlos III, Madrid, 2000. Co-Editor: Econometric Theory, 1989–91; Econometrica, 1991–96; Jl of Econometrics, 1997–. *Publications:* (ed with M. Rosenblatt) Time Series Analysis, 1996; (ed) Time Series with Long Memory, 2003; articles in books, and in learned jls, incl. Econometrica, Annals of Statistics. *Recreation:* walking. *Address:* Department of Economics, London School of Economics and Political Science, Houghton Street, WC2A 2AE. *T:* (020) 7955 7516.

ROBINSON, Philip; Chief Executive, City of Bradford Metropolitan District Council, 2003–05; *b* 2 March 1949; *s* of late Clifford and Vera Robinson; *m* 1974, Irene Langdale. *Educ:* Grange Grammar Sch., Bradford. IPFA, IRRV. City of Bradford Metropolitan District Council: Principal Accountant, 1982–85; Asst Dir of Finance, 1985–87; Dir of Finance, 1987–95; Strategic Dir (Corporate Services), 1995–2000; Asst Chief Exec. (Policy and Corporate Support), 2000–03. *Recreations:* walking, music, theatre.

ROBINSON, Philip Edward Donald; Vice Chancellor, University of Chichester (formerly Principal, University College Chichester), 1996–2007; *b* 13 April 1943; *s* of late James Edward Robinson and Phyllis Robinson (*née* Colclough); *m* 1st, 1967, Pamela Joan Bolton (*d* 1972); one *d*; 2nd, 1975, Linda Jane Whitelaw; one *s* two *d*. *Educ:* Haslingden Grammar Sch.; St Paul's Coll., Cheltenham (CertEd 1964); Goldsmiths' Coll., London (BScSoc 1969); Inst. of Educn, London (MSc Econ. 1971). Lectr, then Sen. Lectr, Univ. of Keele, 1974–83; Hd of Educn, Westminster Coll., Oxford, 1983–87; Dean of Educn, then Sen. Pro Rector and Principal of Froebel Coll., Roehampton Inst., London, 1987–96. Inter-Univ. Council Vis. Fellow, Univ. Sains Malaysia, 1977–78. Chm., Council of Ch Univs and Colls, 2001–03; Vice Chm., GuildHE (formerly Standing Conf. of Principals), 2003–06; Bd Mem., QAA, 2000–04. Mem. Bd, Chichester Fest. Th., 2005–. Vice Chm., Bd of Govs, Central Sch. of Speech and Drama, 2003–; Gov., Chichester High Sch. for Girls, 1997–2003; Mem., Bd of Govs, South Downs Coll., 2005–. *Publications:* Education and Poverty, 1976; Perspectives on the Sociology of Education, 1981 (trans. Korean 1991); (with F. J. Coffield and J. Sarsby) A Cycle of Deprivation?, 1981; articles relating to educnl policy. *Recreations:* theatre, 18th century maritime history, Rugby Union football, long-distance walking, 18th and 19th century music. *Address:* The Drift, 11 Park Crescent, Emsworth, Hants PO10 7NT. *T:* (01243) 816050, *Fax:* (01243) 816063.

ROBINSON, Philip Henry; Member, Estates Committee, Canterbury Cathedral, 1993–99; *b* 4 Jan. 1926; *s* of Arthur Robinson and Frances M. Robinson; *m* 1st, 1959, Helen Gillian Wharton (*see* H. G. Robinson) (marr. diss. 1979); one *d* (one *s* decd); 2nd, 1985, Aneta Baring (*née* Fisher); two step *s*. *Educ:* Lincoln Sch.; Jesus Coll., Cambridge (Exhibr, MA); Sch. of Oriental and African Studies, London Univ.; NY Univ. Graduate Sch. of Business Admin. Member, Gray's Inn. Royal Navy, 1944–47; N. M. Rothschild & Sons, 1950–54; Actg Sec., British Newfoundland Corp., Montreal, 1954–56; Asst Vice-Pres., J. Henry Schroder Banking Corp., New York, 1956–61; J. Henry Schroder Wagg & Co. Ltd, 1961; Director: J. Henry Schroder Wagg & Co. Ltd, 1966–85; Siemens Ltd, 1967–86; Schroders & Chartered Ltd Hong Kong, 1971–85; Schroder International Ltd, 1973–85 (Exec. Vice-Pres., 1977–85); Standard Chartered PLC, 1986–91 (Chm., Audit Cttee, 1989–91); Chairman: Schroder Leasing Ltd, 1979–85; Sunbury Investment Co. Ltd, 1985–94; Berkertex Hldgs Ltd, 1987–88; Man. Trustee, Municipal Mutual Insurance Ltd, 1977–92 (Dep. Chm., 1992). Dir and Chm., Audit Cttee, CLF Municipal Bank, 1993–96; Dir, Capital Re Corp., NY, 1993–99 (Chm., Audit Cttee, 1994–98). Mem., Nat. Coal Board, 1973–77. Hon. Treasurer, Nat. Council for One Parent Families, 1977–79. *Recreations:* music, tennis. *Address:* Stone Hall, Great Mongeham, Deal, Kent CT14 0HB. *Club:* Sloane.

See also A. G. Robinson, Baron Revelstoke.

ROBINSON, Hon. Raymond; *see* Robinson, Hon. A. N. R.

ROBINSON, Richard; *see* Robinson, M. R.

ROBINSON, Richard John; a District Judge, Principal Registry, Family Division, since 2002; *b* 4 Aug. 1952; *s* of Peter Norton and Patricia Helen Robinson; *m* 1987, Joanna Lesley Simons, *qv*. *Educ:* Trinity Hall, Cambridge (BA 1974); SOAS, London (LLM 1976). Called to the Bar, Middle Temple, 1977, also Gray's Inn *ad eundem*; in practice as barrister, 1977–2002. *Recreations:* nature conservation (London Wildlife Trust, Galapagos Conservation Trust), birdwatching (partic. in hot climates). *Address:* Principal Registry of the Family Division, First Avenue House, 42–49 High Holborn, WC1V 6NP. *T:* (020) 7947 6000. *Clubs:* Norwich City Football; Charlton Athletic Football.

ROBINSON, Robert Henry; writer and broadcaster; *b* 17 Dec. 1927; *o s* of Ernest Redfern Robinson and Johanna Hogan; *m* 1958, Josephine Mary Richard; one *s* two *d*. *Educ:* Raynes Park Grammar Sch.; Exeter Coll., Oxford (MA). Editor of Isis, 1950. TV columnist, Sunday Chronicle, 1952; film and theatre columnist, Sunday Graphic, and radio critic, Sunday Times, 1956; editor Atticus, Sunday Times, 1960; weekly column, Private View, Sunday Times, 1962; film critic, Sunday Telegraph, 1965. Writer and presenter of TV programmes: Picture Parade, 1959; Points of View, 1961; Divided We Stand, 1964; The Look of the Week, 1966; Reason to Believe?, The Fifties, 1969; Chm., Call My Bluff, Ask The Family, 1967; The Book Programme, Vital Statistics, 1974; Word for Word, 1978; The Book Game, 1983 and 1985; Behind The Headlines, 1989–; films for TV: Robinson's Travels - the Pioneer Trail West, 1977; B. Traven: a mystery solved, 1978; From Shepherd's Bush to Simla, 1979; Robinson Cruising, 1981; The Auden Landscape, 1982; Robinson Country, 1983, 1987, 1993; In Trust—Houses and Heritage, 1986; The Magic Rectangle, 1986; presenter of: BBC radio current affairs programme Today, 1971–74; Chm., Brain of Britain, 1973–; Chm., Stop the Week, 1974–92; Ad Lib, 1989–; devised and presented: Conversations with Strangers, 1997; Divided We Stand, 1998; Odd Obits, 1999. Mem., Kingman Cttee on the teaching of the English Language, 1987–88. Pres., Johnson Soc. of Lichfield, 1982. Radio Personality of the Year: Radio Industries Club, 1973; Variety Club of GB, 1980. *Publications:* (ed) Poetry from Oxford, 1951; Landscape with Dead Dons, 1956; Inside Robert Robinson (essays), 1965; (contrib.) To Nevill Coghill from Friends, 1966; The Conspiracy, 1968; The Dog Chairman, 1982; (ed) The Everyman Book of Light Verse, 1984; Bad Dreams, 1989; Prescriptions of a Pox Doctor's Clerk, 1990; Skip All That, 1996; The Club, 2000. *Address:* 16 Cheyne Row, SW3 5HL. *Club:* Garrick.

ROBINSON, (Simon) Mark (Peter); Member (DemU) South Belfast, Northern Ireland Assembly, 1998–2007; *b* 12 May 1959; *s* of Desmond and Evelyne Robinson. *Educ:* Knockbreda High Sch.; Castlereagh Coll. of Further Educn (HNC); Belfast Coll. of Technol. Mechanical engr, 1977–89; Gen. Manager, 1989–95; Man. Dir, DCR Engrg, 1995–99. Mem. (DemU) Castlereagh BC, 1997. Governor: Knockbreda High Sch.; Belvoir Park Primary Sch. *Recreations:* musical theatre, golf. *Address:* c/o Parliament Buildings, Stormont, Belfast BT4 3XX.

ROBINSON, Stella; *see* Robson, S.

ROBINSON, Stephen Joseph, OBE 1971; FRS 1976; FREng, FIET; FInstP; Director, Royal Signals and Radar Establishment, Ministry of Defence, 1989–91, retired (Deputy Director, 1985–89); *b* 6 Aug. 1931; *s* of Joseph Allan Robinson and Ethel (*née* Bunting); *m* 1957, Monica Mabs Scott; one *s* one *d*. *Educ:* Sebright Sch., Wolverley; Jesus Coll., Cambridge (MA Natural Sciences). RAF, 1950–51. Mullard Res. Labs, 1954–72; MEL Div., Philips Industries (formerly MEL Equipment Co. Ltd), 1972–79; Product Dir, 1973–79; Man. Dir, Pye TVT Ltd, 1980–84. Vis. Prof., Birmingham Univ., 1990–91. Mem. Council, Royal Soc., 1982–. *Recreations:* sailing, ski-ing.

ROBINSON, Timothy James; tenor; *b* 10 May 1964; *s* of John Robinson and Sheila Robinson; *m* 1990, Elizabeth Marcus; two *s*. *Educ:* Uppingham Sch.; New Coll., Oxford (BA 1985); Guildhall Sch. of Music and Drama. Operatic début, Kudrjas in Katya Kabanova, Glyndebourne Fest. Opera, 1992; other Glyndebourne rôles incl. Jacquino in Fidelio, Janek in Makropulos Case, Shepherd/Sailor in Tristan, Grimoaldo in Rodelinda, Lysander in Midsummer Night's Dream; rôles with ENO incl. Fenton in Falstaff, Simpleton in Boris Godunov, Male Chorus in Rape of Lucretia, Captain Vere in Billy Budd; Principal, Royal Opera House, Covent Garden, 1995–2001, rôles incl. Ferrando in Così fan tutte, Froh in Das Rheingold, Jupiter in Semele; has also sung with Aix Opera, Opéra National de Paris, Salzburg Opera, Hamburg Opera, Lyon Opera, Welsh Nat. Opera. Has appeared in concert with leading orchestras incl. Royal Philharmonic, Berlin Philharmonic, Leipzig Gewandhaus and Vienna Philharmonic. Numerous recordings. *Recreations:* good food and wine, anything to do with sport, family holidays. *Address:* c/o Askonas Holt, Lincoln House, 300 High Holborn, WC1V 7JH.

ROBINSON, Tony; actor and writer; Vice-President, British Actors' Equity, 1996–2000; *b* 15 Aug. 1946; *s* of Leslie Kenneth Robinson and Phyllis Joan Robinson; one *s* one *d*. *Educ:* Wanstead Co. High Sch.; Central Sch. of Speech and Drama. Numerous appearances as child actor, incl. original stage version of Oliver!; theatre dir, 1968–78; work with Chichester Festival Th., RSC and NT; nationwide tour of 40 Years On, 1997; Tony Robinson's Cunning Night Out (on tour), 2005–07; *television* includes: Joey (documentary); Baldrick in Blackadder (4 series), 1983–89; Sheriff of Nottingham in Maid Marian and Her Merry Men (4 series) (also writer); My Wonderful Life (3 series), 1997–99; presenter of TV programmes, incl. Blood and Honey (OT series) (also writer); Time Team (15 series); The Good Book Guide (series); The Worst Jobs in History (2 series); The Real Da Vinci Code, 2005; Me & My Mum, 2006; documentaries in Africa for Comic Relief; writer for TV: Fat Tulip's Garden; Odysseus: the greatest hero of them all (13 episodes); *film:* The Never Ending Story III. Mem., Labour Party NEC, 2000–04. Hon. MA: Bristol, 1999; East London, 2003; Hon. PhD: Open, 2005; Exeter, 2005; Oxford Brookes, 2006. RTS and BAFTA awards; Internat. Prix Jeunesse. *Publications:* for children: Boodicaa and the Romans, 1989; Robert the Incredible Chicken, 1989; Keeping Mum/Driving Ambition, 1992; Hit Plays, 1992; Blood and Honey: story of Saul and David, 1993; Tony Robinson's Kings and Queens, 2000; Maid Marian and Her Merry Men series: How the Band Got Together, 1989; Beast of Bolsover, 1990; Whitish Knight, 1990; Rabies in Love, 1991; Worksop Egg Fairy, 1991; It Came From Outer Space, 1992; with Richard Curtis: Odysseus Goes Through Hell, 1996; Odysseus, Superhero!, 1996; Theseus, Monster-killer!, 1996; The Worst Children's Jobs in History, 2005; for adults: (with Mick Aston) Archaeology is Rubbish: a beginners guide to excavation, 2002; In Search of British Heroes, 2003; The Worst Jobs in History, 2004. *Recreations:* politics, Bristol City Football Club. *Address:* c/o Jeremy Hicks Associates, 114–115 Tottenham Court Road, W1T 5AH.

ROBINSON, Vivian; QC 1986; a Recorder, since 1986; *b* 29 July 1944; *s* of late William and Ann Robinson; *m* 1975, Louise Marriner; one *s* two *d*. *Educ:* Queen Elizabeth Grammar School, Wakefield; The Leys School, Cambridge; Sidney Sussex College, Cambridge (BA). Called to the Bar, Inner Temple, 1967 (Bencher, 1991). Liveryman, Gardeners' Co., 1976– (Mem., Court of Assistants, 1989–; Master, 2000–01). *Address:* Queen Elizabeth Building, Temple, EC4Y 9BS. *Clubs:* Garrick, Royal Automobile, MCC, Pilgrims.

ROBINSON, Sir Wilfred (Henry Frederick), 3rd Bt *cr* 1908; Staff, Diocesan College School, Rondebosch, South Africa, 1950–77, Vice-Principal, 1969–77; *b* 24 Dec. 1917; *s* of Wilfred Henry Robinson (*d* 1922) (3rd *s* of 1st Bt), and Eileen (*d* 1963), *d* of Frederick St Leger, Claremont, SA; *S* uncle, Sir Joseph Benjamin Robinson, 2nd Bt, 1954; *m* 1946, Margaret Alison Kathleen, *d* of late Frank Mellish, MC, Cape Town, SA; one *s* two *d*. *Educ:* Diocesan Coll., Rondebosch; St John's Coll., Cambridge (MA 1944). Served War of 1939–45, Devonshire Regt and Parachute Regt, Major. Finance Officer, Soc. of Genealogists, 1980–92. *Heir:* *s* Peter Frank Robinson [*b* 23 June 1949; *m* 1988, Alison Jane, *e d* of D. Bradley, Rochester, Kent; three *d*]. *Address:* 102 Riverview Gardens, Barnes, SW13 8RA.

ROBINSON, William Good; Deputy Secretary, Department of the Civil Service, Northern Ireland, 1978–80, retired; *b* 20 May 1919; *s* of William Robinson and Elizabeth Ann (*née* Good); *m* 1947, Wilhelmina Vaughan; two *d*. *Educ:* Clones High Sch.; Queen's Univ. of Belfast (BScEcon, BA). Served War, RAF, 1941–46 (Flt Lieut, Navigator). Entered NI Civil Service, 1938; Min. of Labour and National Insurance, NI, 1946–63; Principal, Min. of Home Affairs, NI, 1963; Asst Sec., 1967; Sen. Asst Sec., NI Office, 1973. *Recreations:* do-it-yourself, reading history. *Address:* Stormochree, 47 Castlehill Road, Belfast BT4 3GN. *T:* (028) 9020 7386.

ROBINSON, William Rhys Brunel; Under Secretary, Overseas Division, Department of Employment, 1980–89; *b* 12 July 1930; *s* of late William Robinson and Elizabeth Myfanwy Robinson (*née* Owen); *m* 1988, Pamela Mary Hall (*d* 2006). *Educ:* Chepstow Secondary Grammar Sch.; St Catherine's Soc., Oxford (MA, BLitt). Entered Min. of Labour, 1954; Asst Private Sec. to Minister, 1958–59; Principal, Min. of Labour, 1959; Asst Sec., 1966; London Sch. of Economics, 1972–73 (MSc Industrial Relations, 1973); Asst Sec., Trng Services Agency, 1973–75; Dep. Chief Exec., Employment Service Agency, 1975–77; Under-Sec. and Dir of Establishments, Dept of Employment, 1977–80. Chm., Governing Body, ILO, 1986–87. FSA 1978; FRHistS 1991. *Publications:* Early Tudor Gwent 1485–1547, 2002; articles in historical jls. *Recreation:* historical research. *Address:* 7 Shere Avenue, Cheam, Surrey SM2 7JU. *T:* (020) 8393 3019.

ROBISON, Maj. Gen. Garry Stuart; Commandant General Royal Marines, since 2006; Chief of Staff (Capability) to Commander-in-Chief Fleet, since 2008; *b* 10 June 1958; *s* of late George Desmond Robison and of Carole Margaret Robison (*née* Pugh); *m* 1982, Bridget Anne Clark; one *s* two *d*. *Educ:* Bemrose Grammar Sch., Derby; Christ's Coll., Cambridge (MPhil Internat. Relns 1999). Royal Marines: Officer trng, 1976–77; Company Comdr, 40 Commando, 1988–89; CO, 45 Commando, 1999–2000; Dep. Comdr, Iraq Survey Gp, 2003; Comdt, Commando Trng Centre, 2004–06; Comdr UK Amphibious Forces, 2006–08; Dep. Comdr (Stability), HQ ISAF, Afghanistan, 2007. President: RN Cricket; RM Cricket; RM Football; Vice Pres., RN Football. *Recreations:* cricket, football, music. *Address:* Chief of Staff (Capability), Fleet Headquarters, MP2–1, Leach Building, Whale Island, Portsmouth PO2 8BY. *T:* (023) 9262 5289, *Fax:* (023) 9262 5265; *e-mail:* robisong145@mod.uk. *Club:* Free Foresters Cricket.

ROBISON, Shona; Member (SNP) Dundee East, Scottish Parliament, since 2003 (North East Scotland, 1999–2003); Minister for Public Health, since 2007; *b* 26 May 1966; *d* of Robin and Dorothy Robison; *m* 1997, Stewart Hosie, *qv*; one *d*. *Educ:* Alva Acad.; Glasgow Univ.; Jordanhill Coll. Sen. Community Worker, City of Glasgow Council, 1993–99. Shadow Minister, Health (formerly Health and Community Care) Cttee, Scottish Parlt, 2003–07. Contested (SNP) Dundee E, 1997. *Address:* Scottish Parliament, Edinburgh EH99 1SP.

ROBLES, Marisa, FRCM; harpist; Professor of Harp, Royal College of Music, since 1971; *b* 4 May 1937; *d* of Cristobal Robles and Maria Bonilla; *m* 1985, David Bean; two *s* one *d* by previous marriage. *Educ:* Madrid National Sch.; Royal Madrid Conservatoire. Prof. of Harp, Royal Madrid Conservatoire, 1958–60. Recitals and solo appearances with major orchestras in UK, Europe, Africa, Canada, USA, South America, Japan, China and Australia. Mem., UK Harp Assoc. Recordings include concerti by Handel, Dittersdorf, Boildieu, Debussy, Rodrigo, Moreno-Buendia, solo repertoire by Beethoven, Mozart, Fauré, Hasselmans, Tournier, Guridi and others, and chamber music by Alwyn, Roussel, Britten, Ravel, Debussy and others. Hon. Royal Madrid Conservatoire 1958; Hon. RCM 1973; FRCM 1983. *Recreations:* theatre, gardening, indoor plants, family life in general. *Address:* 38 Luttrell Avenue, Putney, SW15 6PE. *T:* (020) 8785 2204. *Club:* Royal Over-Seas League.

ROBOROUGH, 3rd Baron *cr* 1938, of Maristow; **Henry Massey Lopes;** Bt 1805; *b* 2 Feb. 1940; *s* of 2nd Baron Roborough and Helen (decd), *o d* of Lt-Col E. A. F. Dawson; *S* father, 1992; *m* 1st, 1968, Robyn Zenda Carol (marr. diss. 1986), *e d* of John Bromwich; two *s* two *d*; 2nd, 1986, Sarah Anne Pipon, 2nd *d* of Colin Baker; two *d*. *Educ:* Eton. MRICS. Late Lt Coldstream Guards. Farmer, managing Maristow Estate, Plymouth. Racehorse owner and breeder. *Heir: s* Hon. Massey John Henry Lopes [*b* 22 Dec. 1969; *m* 1996, Jean, *d* of Peter George Underwood, Supreme Court of Tasmania; two *s* one *d*]. *Club:* Turf.

ROBOTTOM, Dame Marlene (Anne), DBE 2000; education consultant; Headteacher, Mulberry School for Girls, Tower Hamlets, London, 1991–2006; *b* 10 July 1950; *d* of Alan Joseph Robottom and Patricia Anne Robottom (*née* Gilkes). *Educ:* Coll. of All Saints, London (CertEd 1971); NE London Poly. (BEd 1981); Poly. of E London (MSc 1989). Tower Hamlets, subseq. Mulberry School: Teacher, 1971–72; Dep. Head of Dept, 1972–77; Hd of Dept, 1977–78; Hd of House, 1979–80; Hd of House and Second Dep. Headteacher, 1980–87; First Dep. Headteacher (Curriculum), 1987–90. *Recreations:* theatre, music, the arts. *Club:* Institute of Directors.

ROBSON, Agnes; Head of Corporate Services, Scottish Executive, 2000–04; *b* 6 Oct. 1946; *d* of John Wight and Agnes Margaret Wight (*née* Stark); *m* 1969, Godfrey Robson (marr. diss.); one *s*. *Educ:* Holy Cross Acad., Edinburgh; Edinburgh Univ. (MA Hons Politics and Mod. Hist.). Civil Servant, Dept of Employment, 1968–79; joined Scottish Office, 1985: Industry Department: Head: Energy Div., 1988–89; Nuclear Energy Div., 1989–90; Urban Policy Div., 1990–92; Dir, Primary Care, NHS Mgt Exec., Health Dept, 1992–2000. Mem., Scottish Health Council, 2005–. Non-exec. Dir, Royal Scottish Nat. Orch., 2006–. *Recreations:* opera, contemporary Scottish painting.

ROBSON, Alan; General Secretary, Confederation of Shipbuilding and Engineering Unions, 1993–2005; *b* 24 Dec. 1941; *s* of John William Robson and Bridgit Robson; *m* 1964, Joyce Lydia. *Educ:* Ellison C of E Sch. Fitter-turner, 1958–90; Asst Gen. Sec., AEU, 1990–93. *Recreations:* reading, supporting the arts, football. *Address:* 20 York Avenue, Jarrow, Tyne and Wear NE32 5LT. *T:* (0191) 421 6883. *Clubs:* Labour, Elmfield, Ex-Service Men's (Jarrow).

ROBSON, Prof. Alan David, AM 2003; PhD; FTSE, FAIAST; FACE; Vice Chancellor, University of Western Australia, since 2004; *b* 1 Feb. 1945; *s* of Thomas Robson and Anne Robson (*née* Cummings); *m* 1966, Gwenda Clarice Ferris; one *s* two *d*. *Educ:* Univ. of Melbourne (BAgrSc); Univ. of Western Australia (PhD 1970). FACE 2004. Res. agronomist, 1972–73; University of Western Australia: Lectr, 1974–80; Sen. Lectr, 1980–82; Associate Prof., 1982–83; Prof., 1984–, Hackett Prof. of Agric., 1996–; Dir, Centre for Legumes in Mediterranean Agric., 1992–93; Dep. Vice Chancellor, 1993–2004. FTSE 1989; FAIAST (FAIAS 1989). *Publications:* (ed) Copper in Soils and Plants, 1981; (ed) Soil Acidity and Plant Growth, 1989; (ed) Zinc in Soil and Plants, 1993; (ed) Management of Mycorrhizas in Agriculture, Horticulture and Forestry, 1994; numerous scientific contribs on mineral nutrition of plants. *Recreations:* sport, reading. *Address:* Vice Chancellery, M464, University of Western Australia, 35 Stirling Highway, Crawley, WA 6009, Australia; *e-mail:* Alan.Robson@uwa.edu.au.

ROBSON, Bryan, OBE 1990; Manager, Sheffield United Football Club, 2007–08; *b* 11 Jan. 1957; *s* of Brian and Maureen Robson; *m* 1978, Denise Brindley; one *s* two *d*. *Educ:* Lord Lawson Comprehensive Sch., Birtley. Player: West Bromwich Albion FC, 1974–81; Manchester United FC, 1981–94 (captain, winning team: FA Cup, 1983, 1985, 1990; European Cup Winners' Cup, 1991; Premier League, 1993, 1994); Manager: Middlesbrough FC, 1994–2001 (player-manager, 1994–97); Bradford City FC, 2003–04; W Bromwich Albion FC, 2004–06. Player, England Football Team, 1980–91 (90 appearances, 65 as captain, 26 goals). Hon. BA: Manchester, 1992; Salford, 1992. *Publication:* United I Stand (autobiog.), 1983. *Recreations:* horse racing, golf. *Address:* Malthouse Business Centre, 48 Southport Road, Ormskirk, Lancs L39 1QP. *T:* (01695) 586040, *Fax:* (01695) 586045. *Clubs:* West Bromwich Albion Football, Manchester United, Middlesbrough.

ROBSON, Carol; *see* Robson, E. C.

ROBSON, David Ernest Henry; QC 1980; a Recorder of the Crown Court (NE Circuit), 1979–2005; *b* 1 March 1940; *s* of late Joseph Robson and Caroline Robson; civil partnership 2006, Leslie Colwell. *Educ:* Robert Richardson Grammar Sch., Ryhope; Christ Church, Oxford (MA). Called to the Bar, Inner Temple, 1965 (Profumo Prize, 1963), Bencher, 1988. NE Circuit, 1965–. Artistic Dir, Royalty Studio Theatre, Sunderland, 1986–88. Pres., Herrington Burn YMCA, Sunderland 1987–2001. *Recreations:* acting, Italy. *Address:* 1 Tollgate Road, Hamsterley Mill, Rowlands Gill, Tyne and Wear NE39 1HF. *T:* (01207) 549989. *Club:* County (Durham).

ROBSON, Elizabeth; *see* Howlett, E.

ROBSON, Prof. Elizabeth Browel; Galton Professor of Human Genetics, University College London, 1978–93; *b* 10 Nov. 1928; *d* of Thomas Robson and Isabella (*née* Stoker); *m* 1955, George MacBeth, writer (marr. diss. 1975, he *d* 1992). *Educ:* Bishop Auckland Girls' Grammar Sch.; King's Coll., Newcastle upon Tyne; BSc Dunelm; PhD London, 1954; Dip. History of Art, Univ. of London, 2000. Rockefeller Fellowship, Columbia Univ., New York City, 1954–55; external scientific staff of MRC (London Hosp. Med. Coll. and King's Coll. London), 1955–62; Member and later Asst Director, MRC Human Biochemical Genetics Unit, University Coll. London, 1962–78; Hd, Dept of Genetics and Biometry, UCL, 1978–90. Jt Editor, Annals of Human Genetics, 1978–93. *Publications:* papers on biochemical human genetics and gene mapping in scientific jls. *Address:* 44 Sheen Road, Richmond, Surrey TW9 1AW.

ROBSON, (Elizabeth) Carol; HM Diplomatic Service, retired; Head, United Nations and Commonwealth Department, Department for International Development, 2004–05 (on secondment); *b* 14 Jan. 1955; *d* of James Henry Robson and Laura Robson (*née* Jacobson). *Educ:* Carlisle and County High Sch.; York Univ. (BA Physics 1977). Entered Diplomatic Service, 1977; Latin America floater, 1980–81; Russian lang. trng, 1981–82; Ulaanbaatar, 1983; Moscow, 1983–84; FCO, 1984; UKMIS, Geneva, 1987–92; Asst Head, SE Asia Dept, 1992–95; Head, Transcaucasus and Central Asia Unit, 1995–96; Counsellor, Consul-Gen. and Dep. Head of Mission, Stockholm, 1996–98; Dep. Dir, Ditchley Foundn, 1998–2001 (on special leave); Counsellor and Dep. Hd of Mission, Copenhagen, 2002–04. *Recreations:* diverse, including cooking, antiques, art, gardening, travel, visiting historic sites and houses, reading.

ROBSON, Eric; DL; freelance writer and broadcaster, since 1979; farmer, since 1987; *b* 31 Dec. 1946; *s* of James Walter Robson and Agnes Gourlay Robson; *m* 1st, 1976, Mary Armstrong (marr. diss. 1984); one *s* one *d*; 2nd, 1988, Annette Steinhilber; one *s* two *d*. *Educ:* Carlisle Grammar Sch. Border TV, 1966–; BBC TV and Radio, 1976–; BBC outside broadcast commentator, Trooping the Colour, the Cenotaph, handover of Hong Kong; Chm., Gardeners' Question Time, BBC Radio, 1995–; documentary producer and presenter. Chairman: Striding Edge Ltd, 1994–; Cumbria Tourist Bd, 2002–; Wainwright Soc., 2002–; Dir, Hadrian's Wall Heritage, 2006–. DL Cumbria, 2004. *Publications:* Great Railway Journeys of the World, 1981; Northumbria, 1998; Out of Town, 2002; After Wainwright, 2004; The Border Line, 2006; Outside Broadcaster, 2007. *Recreations:* painting, fell walking, cooking, avoiding housework. *Address:* Crag House Farm, Wasdale, Cumbria CA19 1UT. *T:* (01946) 726301. *Clubs:* Farmers'; St Augustine's Working Men's (Carlisle).

ROBSON, Euan Macfarlane; Chief Executive, Scottish Sustainable Energy Foundation, since 2007; *b* 17 Feb. 1954; *m* 1984, Valerie Young; two *d*. *Educ:* Univ. of Newcastle upon Tyne (BA Hons History 1976); Univ. of Strathclyde (MSc Political Sci. 1984). Teacher, King Edward VI Sch., Morpeth, 1977–79; Dep. Sec., Gas Consumers' Northern Council, Newcastle upon Tyne, 1981–86; Scottish Manager, Gas Consumers' Council, 1986–99. Mem. (L/All), Northumberland CC, 1981–89 (Chm., Highways Cttee, 1988–89; Hon. Alderman, 1989); L/All Gp Sec., 1981–87. Contested (L/All) Hexham, 1983, 1987. Scottish Parliament: Mem. (Lib Dem) Roxburgh and Berwickshire, 1999–2007; Lib Dem Rural Affairs spokesman, 1998–99, Justice and Home Affairs spokesman, 1999–2001, Health and Communities spokesman, 2005–07; Dep. Minister for Parlt, subseq. for Parly Business, 2001–03, for Educn and Young People, 2003–05; Convener, Lib Dem Parly party, 2005–07. Contested (Lib Dem) Roxburgh and Berwicks, Scottish Parlt, 2007. River Tweed Comr, 1994–2001. Founding Mem., Consumer Safety Internat.; Life Mem., Nat. Trust for Scotland. *Publications:* The Consumers' View of the 1990 EU Gas Appliances' Directive, 1991; George Houston: nature's limner, 1997; (contrib.) Kirkcudbright: 100 years of an artists' colony, 2000; Scotland, Poland and the European Union, 2002. *Recreation:* angling. *Address:* Elmbank, Tweedsyde Park, Kelso, Roxburghshire TD5 7RF. *T:* (01573) 225279.

ROBSON, Frank Elms, OBE 1991; Consultant, Winckworth Sherwood (formerly Winckworth & Pemberton), Solicitors, Oxford and Westminster, 1998–2002 (Partner, 1962–98; Senior Partner, 1990–94); *b* 14 Dec. 1931; *s* of Joseph A. Robson and Barbara Robson; *m* 1958, Helen (*née* Jackson); four *s* one *d*. *Educ:* King Edward VI Grammar Sch., Morpeth; Selwyn Coll., Cambridge (MA). Admitted solicitor, 1954. Registrar, Dio. Oxford, 1970–2000; Joint Registrar, Province of Canterbury, 1982–2000. Chm., Ecclesiastical Law Soc., 1996–2002; Vice-Chm., Legal Adv. Commn, Gen. Synod of C of E, 1990–2002. DCL Lambeth, 1991. *Recreations:* walking, clocks, following Oxford United. *Address:* 2 Simms Close, Middle Road, Stanton St John, Oxford OX33 1HB. *T:* (01865) 351393.

ROBSON, Godfrey, CB 2002; Director, Lloyds TSB Scotland, since 2001; Chairman, Frontline Consultants, since 2003 (Director, since 2003); *b* 5 Nov. 1946; *s* of late William James Robson and of Mary Finn; *m* (marr. diss.); one *s*. *Educ:* St Joseph's Coll., Dumfries; Edinburgh Univ. (MA). Joined Scottish Office, 1970; Pvte Sec. to Parly Under-Sec. of State, 1973–74, to Minister of State, 1974; Prin. Pvte Sec. to Sec. of State for Scotland, 1979–81; Assistant Secretary: Roads and Transport, 1981–86; Local Govt Finance, 1986–89; Under Sec., 1989; Scottish Fisheries Sec., 1989–93; Scottish Executive (formerly Scottish Office): Under Sec., Industrial Expansion, subseq. Economic and Industrial Affairs, 1993–2000; Dir of Health Policy, 2000–02. Sen. Policy Advr, ICAP, Washington DC, 2004–. Founding Chm., Nat. Jubilee Hosp., Clydebank, 2002–03; Dir and Trustee, Caledonia Youth, 2003–. *Recreations:* walking, travel by other means, reading history. *Address:* 50 East Trinity Road, Edinburgh EH5 3EN. *T:* (0131) 552 9519; Chemin Sous Baye, 84110 Vaison la Romaine, France. *T:* (4) 90371832.

ROBSON, Prof. James Scott, MD; FRCP, FRCPE; Professor of Medicine, University of Edinburgh, 1977–86, now Emeritus; Consultant Physician, and Physician in charge, Medical Renal Unit, Royal Infirmary, Edinburgh, 1959–86; *b* 19 May 1921; *s* of William Scott Robson, FSA and Elizabeth Hannah Watt; *m* 1948, Mary Kynoch MacDonald, MB

ChB, FRCPE, *d* of late Alexander MacDonald, Perth; two *s*. *Educ:* Edinburgh Univ. (Mouat Schol.). MB ChB (Hons) 1945, MD 1946; FRCPE 1960, FRCP 1977. Captain, RAMC, India, Palestine and Egypt, 1945–48. Rockefeller Student, NY Univ., 1942–44; Rockefeller Res. Fellow, Harvard Univ., 1949–50. Edinburgh University: Sen. Lectr in Therapeutics, 1959; Reader, 1961; Reader in Medicine, 1968. Hon. Associate Prof., Harvard Univ., 1962; Merck Sharp & Dohme Vis. Prof., Australia, 1968. External examnr in medicine to several univs in UK and overseas. Mem., Biomed. Res. Cttee, SHHD, 1979–84; Chm., Sub-cttee in Medicine, Nat. Med. Consultative Cttee, 1983–85. Pres., Renal Assoc., London, 1977–80. Hon. Mem., Australasian Soc. of Nephrology. Sometime Mem. Editl Bd, and Dep. Chm., Clinical Science, 1969–73, and other med. jls. *Publications:* (ed with R. Passmore) Companion to Medical Studies, vol. 1, 1968, 3rd edn 1985; vol. 2, 1970, 2nd edn 1980; vol. 3, 1974; contribs on renal physiology and disease to med. books, symposia and jls. *Recreations:* gardening, theatre, reading, writing, contemporary art of Scotland. *Address:* 1 Grant Avenue, Edinburgh EH13 0DS. *T:* (0131) 441 3508.

ROBSON, Sir John (Adam), KCMG 1990 (CMG 1983); HM Diplomatic Service, retired; Ambassador to Norway, 1987–90; *b* 16 April 1930; *yr s* of Air Vice-Marshal Adam Henry Robson, CB, OBE, MC; *m* 1958, Maureen Molly, *er d* of E. H. S. Bullen; three *d*. *Educ:* Charterhouse; Gonville and Caius Coll., Cambridge (Major Scholar; BA 1952, MA 1955, PhD 1958). Fellow, Gonville and Caius Coll., 1954–58; Asst Lectr, University Coll. London, 1958–60. HM Foreign Service (later Diplomatic Service), 1961; Second Sec., British Embassy, Bonn, 1962–64; Second, later First, Secretary, Lima, 1964–66; First Sec., British High Commn, Madras, 1966–69; Asst Head, Latin American Dept, FCO, 1969–73; Head of Chancery, Lusaka, 1973–74; RCDS, 1975; Counsellor, Oslo, 1976–78; Head of E African Dept, FCO, and Comr for British Indian Ocean Territory, 1979–82; Ambassador to Colombia, 1982–87. Leader, UK Delegn, Conf. on Human Dimension, CSCE, 1990–91. Panel Mem., Home Office Assessment Consultancy Unit, 1992–2000. Chm. Mgt Cttee, Seven Springs Cheshire Home, 1992–96; Mem. Internat. Cttee, Cheshire Foundn, 1996–2000. Mem. Ct, Kent Univ., 1990–99. Chm., Anglo-Norse Soc., 1998–2003. Royal Order of Merit (Norway), 1988. *Publications:* Wyclif and the Oxford Schools, 1961; articles in historical jls. *Recreation:* gardening. *Address:* Biggenden Oast, Paddock Wood, Tonbridge, Kent TN12 6ND. *Club:* Oxford and Cambridge.

ROBSON, John Gair, PhD, ScD; FRS 2003; Senior Research Professor in Vision Science, University of Houston, since 1997; Fellow of Gonville and Caius College, Cambridge, since 1965 (Life Fellow, 1995); *b* 27 June 1936; *s* of Thomas Robson and Kathleen (*née* Elwell); *m* 1958, Jane Macdonald; two *s* two *d*. *Educ:* Shrewsbury Sch.; St John's Coll., Cambridge (BA; PhD 1962; ScD 2004). Vis. Scientist, Bell Labs, Murray Hill, 1964; Vis. Prof. Northwestern Univ., 1964; Demonstrator in Physiol., 1962–65, Lectr in Physiol., 1966–83, Reader in Neurophysiol., 1983–96, Univ. of Cambridge. Champness Lectr, Spectacle Makers' Co., 1990. (Jtly) Friedenwald Award, Assoc. for Res. in Vision and Ophthalmol., 1983; Edgar J. Tillyer Award, Optical Soc. of America, 1996. *Publications:* numerous contribs on vision and visual neurophysiology to learned jls. *Address:* Herring's House, Wilbraham Road, Fulbourn, Cambridge CB21 5EU. *T:* (01223) 880277.

ROBSON, Rev. John Phillips, LVO 1999; Chaplain to the Queen, 1993–2002; an Extra Chaplain to the Queen, since 2002; Chaplain of the Queen's Chapel of the Savoy and Chaplain of the Royal Victorian Order, 1989–2002; *b* 22 July 1932; *s* of Thomas Herbert and Nellie Julia Robson. *Educ:* Hele's School, Exeter; Brentwood School; St Edmund Hall, Oxford (Liddon Exhibnr 1954); King's College London (AKC 1958). Deacon 1959, priest 1960; Curate, Huddersfield Parish Church, 1959–62; Asst Chaplain 1962–65, Senior Chaplain 1965–80, Christ's Hospital, Horsham; Senior Chaplain of Wellington College, Berks, 1980–89. *Recreations:* golf, cinema, theatre. *Address:* A2 Odhams Walk, Long Acre, WC2H 9SA. *T:* (020) 7240 7662. *Club:* Garrick.

ROBSON, Prof. Peter Neville, OBE 1983; FRS 1987; FREng; Professor of Electronic and Electrical Engineering, University of Sheffield, 1968–96, now Emeritus; *b* 23 Nov. 1930; *s* of Thomas Murton and Edith Robson; *m* 1957, Anne Ross Miller Semple; one *d*. *Educ:* Cambridge Univ. (BA); PhD Sheffield. FIET, FIEEE. Res. Engr, Metropolitan Vickers Electrical Co., Manchester, 1954–57; Lectr 1957–63, Sen. Lectr 1963–66, Sheffield Univ.; Res. Fellow, Stanford Univ., USA, 1966–67; Reader, University Coll. London, 1967–68. FREng (FEng 1983). *Publications:* Vacuum and Solid State Electronics, 1963; numerous papers on semiconductor devices and electromagnetic theory. *Address:* Department of Electronic and Electrical Engineering, Sheffield University, Mappin Street, Sheffield S1 3JD. *T:* (0114) 222 5131.

ROBSON, Air Vice-Marshal Robert Michael, OBE 1971; freelance journalist; sheep farmer, 1987–96; *b* 22 April 1935; *s* of Dr John Alexander and Edith Robson; *m* 1959, Brenda Margaret (*née* Croysdill); one *s* two *d*. *Educ:* Sherborne; RMA Sandhurst. Commissioned 1955; RAF Regt, 1958; Navigator Training, 1959; Strike Squadrons, 1965; Sqdn Comdr, RAF Coll., 1968; Defence Adviser to British High Comr, Sri Lanka, 1972; Nat. Defence Coll., 1973; CO 27 Sqdn, 1974–75; MoD staff duties, 1978; CO RAF Gatow, 1978–80; ADC to the Queen, 1979–80; RCDS 1981; Dir of Initial Officer Training, RAF Coll., 1982–84; Dir of Public Relations, RAF, 1984–87; Hd, RAF Study of Officers' Terms of Service, 1987; retired. Chairman: Turbo (UK) Ltd, 1995–98; Fuel Mechanics Ltd, 1995–97; Dir, Advanced Technology Industries Ltd, 1993–97; Chm., Prince's Trust, Lincs, 1993–96; Dir and Chm., Witham Hall Trust, 1995–2003; Gov., Witham Hall Sch., 1988–2006 (Chm. Govs, 1995–2003; Vice-Pres., 2003–06). Vice-Pres., SSAFA Forces Help, Lincs. FCMI (FBIM 1980). *Recreations:* fly fishing, golf. *Club:* Royal Air Force.

ROBSON, Sir Robert William, Kt 2002; CBE 1991; Founder, The Sir Bobby Robson Foundation, 2008; International Football Consultant, Republic of Ireland Football Team, 2006–07; *b* 18 Feb. 1933; *s* of Philip and Lilian Robson; *m* 1955, Elsie Mary Gray; three *s*. *Educ:* Langley Park Primary Sch.; Waterhouses Secondary Mod. Sch., Co. Durham. Professional footballer: Fulham FC, 1950–56 and 1962–67; West Bromwich Albion FC, 1956–62; twenty appearances for England; Manager: Vancouver FC, 1967–68; Fulham FC, 1968–69; Ipswich Town FC, 1969–82 (FA Cup Winners, 1978; UEFA Cup Winners, 1981); England Assoc. Football Team, and Nat. Coach, 1982–90; Manager, PSV Eindhoven, Netherlands, 1990–92 (Dutch Champions, 1990–91, 1991–92); Head Coach: Sporting Lisbon, Portugal, 1992–93; Futebol Clube Do Porto, Portugal, 1994–96 (Portuguese Champions, 1994–95, 1995–96; Portuguese Cup Winners, 1995; Super Cup Winners, 1994, 1995); Coach, Barcelona FC, 1996–98 (Spanish Super Cup, 1996; Eur. Cup Winners Cup, 1997; Spanish Cup, 1997); Head Coach, PSV Eindhoven, Netherlands, 1998–99 (Super Cup Winners, 1999); Manager, Newcastle Utd FC, 1999–2004. Hon. MA UEA, 1997; Hon. DCL Newcastle, 2003. Hon. Freeman, Newcastle upon Tyne, 2005. *Publications:* Time on the Grass (autobiog.), 1982; Farewell But Not Goodbye; my autobiography, 2005; with Bob Harris: So Near and Yet So Far: Bobby Robson's World Cup diary, 1986; Against The Odds, 1990; An Englishman Abroad, 1998. *Recreations:* golf, squash, reading, gardening. *Address:* The Sir Bobby Robson Foundation, Metropolitan House, Longrigg, Swalwell, Newcastle upon Tyne NE16 3AS.

ROBSON, Stella; Chair, Northern Sinfonia Board, 1998–2002; *b* 18 Feb. 1935; *d* of Charles Moreton Marchinton and Margaret Maude Backhouse; *m* 1998, Frank Robson; one *s* one *d* by a previous marriage. *Educ:* Aireborough Grammar Sch.; Princess Mary High Sch., Halifax; Univ. of Leeds (BA Hons English 1956). Housing Officer: Joseph Rowntree Village Trust, York, 1956–57; Rotherham BC, 1957–59; Students Accommodation Officer, King's Coll., Newcastle, 1959–63; Chair, Northern Arts, 1990–98. Mem., Arts Council of England, 1993–98. Trustee, North Music Trust, 2000–07. Mem. Bd, Darlington Housing Assoc., 2001–05. Member (Lab): Darlington BC, 1972–79, 1995– (Mayor of Darlington, 2005–06); Durham CC, 1981–97 (Hon. Alderman, 1997). *Recreations:* walking, the arts. *Address:* 40 Parkland Drive, Darlington DL3 9DU.

ROBSON, Sir Stephen Arthur, (Sir Steve), Kt 2000; CB 1997; PhD; Second Permanent Secretary, Finance, Regulation and Industry, HM Treasury, 1997–2001; *b* 30 Sept. 1943; *s* of Arthur Cyril Robson and Lilian Marianne (*née* Peabody); *m* 1974, Meredith Hilary Lancashire; two *s*. *Educ:* Pocklington Sch.; St John's Coll., Cambridge (MA, PhD); Stanford Univ., USA (MA). Joined Civil Service (HM Treasury), 1969; Private Sec. to Chancellor of the Exchequer, 1974–76; seconded to Investors in Industry plc, 1976–78; Under Sec., Defence Policy and Material Gp, 1987–89, Public Enterprises and Privatisation Gp, 1990–93; Dep. Sec., Industry and Financial Instns, later Finance, Regulation and Industry, 1993–97. Non-executive Director: Royal Bank of Scotland, 2001–; J P Morgan Cazenove (formerly Cazenove), 2001–; Partnerships UK, 2001–; Xstrata, 2002–; Financial Reporting Council, 2007–. *Recreation:* sailing. *Club:* Bosham Sailing.

ROCARD, Michel Louis Léon; Member (Party of European Socialists), European Parliament, since 1994; Prime Minister of France, 1988–91; *b* 23 Aug. 1930; *s* of late Yves Rocard and of Renée (*née* Favre); *m* 1st; one *s* one *d*; 2nd, 1972, Michèle Legendre (marr. diss.); two *s*. *Educ:* Lycée Louis-le-Grand, Paris; Univ. of Paris (Nat. Sec., Association des étudiants socialistes, 1953–55); Ecole Nationale d'Administration, 1956–58. Inspecteur des Finances, 1958; Econ. and Financial Studies Service, 1962; Head of Econ. Budget Div., Forecasting Office, 1965; Sec.-Gen., Nat. Accounts Commn, 1965. Nat. Sec., Parti Socialiste Unifié, 1967–73; candidate for Presidency of France, 1969; Deputy for Yvelines, 1969–73, 1978–81, 1986–93; Minister of Planning and Regl Develt, 1981–83; Minister of Agriculture, 1983–85; Mem., Senate, 1995–97. European Parliament: Chairman: Develt Cttee, 1997–99; Employment and Social Affairs Cttee, 1999–2001; Culture Cttee, 2002, 2004; Mem., Foreign Affairs Cttee, 2004–. Joined Parti Socialiste, 1974: Mem., Exec. Bureau, 1975–81 and 1986–88; Nat. Sec. in charge of public sector, 1975–79; First Sec., 1993–94. Mayor, Conflans-Sainte-Honorine, 1977–94. *Publications:* Le PSU et l'avenir socialiste de la France, 1969; Des militants du PSU présentés par Michel Rocard, 1971; Questions à l'Etat socialiste, 1972; Un député, pour quoi faire?, 1973; (jtly) Le Marché commun contre l'Europe, 1973; (jtly) L'Inflation au cœur, 1975; Parler vrai, 1979; A l'épreuve des faits: textes politiques 1979–85, 1986; Le coeur à l'ouvrage, 1987; Un pays comme le nôtre, 1989; L'art de la Paix, 1997; Les moyens d'en sortir, 1997; Le français langue des Droits de l'Homme?, 1998; Mes idées pour demain, 2000; Entretiens, 2001; Si la gauche savait, 2005. *Address:* 266 boulevard St Germain, 75007 Paris, France.

ROCH, Rt Hon. Sir John (Ormond), Kt 1985; PC 1993; a Lord Justice of Appeal, 1993–2000; *b* 19 April 1934; *s* of Frederick Ormond Roch and Vera Elizabeth (*née* Chamberlain); *m* 1st, 1967, Anne Elizabeth Greany (*d* 1994); three *d*; 2nd, 1996, Mrs Susan Angela Parry. *Educ:* Wrekin Coll.; Clare Coll., Cambridge (BA, LLB). Called to Bar, Gray's Inn, 1961, Bencher, 1985; QC 1976; a Recorder, 1975–85; a Judge of the High Court of Justice, QBD, 1985–93; Presiding Judge, Wales and Chester Circuit, 1986–90. Vice-Pres., RNLI, 2006– (Gov. and Mem. Mgt Cttee, 1996–2006). President: Haverfordwest Civic Soc., 2006–; Old Wrekinian Assoc., 2007–. *Recreations:* sailing, music. *Clubs:* Dale Yacht, Bar Yacht.

ROCHA, John, CBE 2002; fashion designer, since 1980; *b* 23 Aug. 1953; *s* of Henry and Cecilia Rocha; *m* 1990, Odette; one *s* two *d*. *Educ:* Croydon Coll. of Art and Design (Dip. Fashion). Hon. DLitt Ulster, 1994. British Designer of the Year, British Fashion Awards, 1994. *Publication:* Texture, Form, Purity, Detail, 2002. *Recreation:* fly fishing. *Address:* 10 Ely Place, Dublin 2, Ireland. *T:* (1) 6629225, *Fax:* (1) 6629226; *e-mail:* info@johnrocha.ie. *Clubs:* Hospital, Groucho.

ROCHAT, Dr Philippe Henri Pierre; Executive Director, Air Transport Action Group, Geneva; *b* 19 Oct. 1942; *m* 1967, Catherine Dupuy; two *s* one *d*. *Educ:* Gymnase de Lausanne; Lausanne Univ. (LLB 1966; LLD 1974). Journalist and reporter, Swiss Radio-TV, 1967–74; Asst to Dep. Dir, Federal Office for Civil Aviation, Bern, 1975–77; Admin. and Commercial Dir, Geneva Airport, 1977–85; International Civil Aviation Organisation Council: Alternate Rep. of Belgium, 1985–86; Rep. of Switzerland, 1986–89; Dir, Mkting and Envmt, Geneva Airport, 1989–91; Sec. Gen., ICAO, 1991–97. Air Law Professor: Geneva Univ.; Lausanne Univ. *Publications:* articles, reports and lectures on civil aviation and envmt, airports' structure and mgt, challenges in civil aviation, etc. *Recreations:* ski-ing, tennis, hiking, various cultural activities. *Address:* c/o Air Transport Action Group, PO Box 49, 1215 Geneva 15, Switzerland. *T:* (22) 7702670, *Fax:* (22) 7702686; *e-mail:* rochatp@atag.org.

ROCHDALE, 2nd Viscount *cr* 1960; **St John Durival Kemp;** Baron 1913; *b* 15 Jan. 1938; *s* of 1st Viscount Rochdale, OBE and Elinor Dorothea Pease, CBE, JP (*d* 1997); *S* father, 1993; *m* 1st, 1960, Serena Jane Clark-Hall (marr. diss. 1974); two *s* two *d*; 2nd, 1976, Elizabeth Anderton. *Educ:* Eton. *Heir:* *s* Hon. Jonathan Hugo Durival Kemp [*b* 10 June 1961; *m* 1994, Mingxian Zhu].

ROCHDALE, Archdeacon of; *see* Vann, Ven. C. E.

ROCHE, family name of **Baron Fermoy**.

ROCHE, Rt Rev. Arthur; *see* Leeds, Bishop of, (RC).

ROCHE, Barbara Maureen; Chairman, Metropolitan Support Trust, since 2007; Deputy Chairman, Metropolitan Housing Partnership (Board Member, since 2006); *b* 13 April 1954; *d* of late Barnett Margolis and Hannah (*née* Lopes Dias); *m* 1977, Patrick Roche; one *d*. *Educ:* JFS Comprehensive Sch., Camden; Lady Margaret Hall, Oxford (BA). Called to the Bar, Middle Temple, 1977. MP (Lab) Hornsey and Wood Green, 1992–2005; contested (Lab) same seat, 2005. Parly Under-Sec. of State, DTI, 1997–98; Financial Sec., HM Treasury, 1999; Minister of State: Home Office, 1999–2001; Cabinet Office, 2001–02; ODPM, 2002–03. Vis. Fellow, Univ. of Teesside; Vis. Prof., Univ. of Sunderland, 2008–. *Recreations:* theatre, detective fiction.

ROCHE, David; Chief Executive, Borders UK and Ireland Ltd, 2006–08; *b* 8 May 1961; *s* of Lawrence and Jocelyn Roche; *m* 1987, Johanna Kari; three *s*. *Educ:* Worth Sch.; Durham Univ. (BA Hons Psychol. 1983). Prodn Planner, Burlington Klopman, 1984–86;

Stock Control Manager, Hornes Ltd, 1986–89; Ops Manager, HMV UK Ltd, 1989–95; Product Director: HMV Europe Ltd, 1995–2002; Waterstone's Ltd, 2002–05. *Recreations:* golf, Rugby, scuba diving, flying, cooking, travel, reading. *Address:* Broadway House, 156 Hare Lane, Claygate, Surrey KT10 0RD. *T:* (01372) 469672, 07962 667982. *Clubs:* Soho House, MCC; Royal Wimbledon Golf.

ROCHE, Sir David (O'Grady), 5th Bt *cr* 1838 of Carass, Limerick; FCA; *b* 21 Sept. 1947; *s* of Sir Standish O'Grady Roche, 4th Bt, DSO, and of Evelyn Laura, *d* of Major William Andon; *S* father, 1977; *m* 1971, Hon. (Helen) Alexandra Briscoe Frewen, *d* of 3rd Viscount Selby; one *s* one *d* (and one *s* decd). *Educ:* Wellington Coll., Berks; Trinity Coll., Dublin. Chartered Accountant. Chairman: Baroc Energy Ltd, 2002–; Plaza Hldgs Ltd, 2003–; Strategic East European Fund; British-Serbian Chamber of Commerce. *Heir: s* David Alexander O'Grady Roche, *b* 28 Jan. 1976. *Address:* Bridge House, Starbotton, Skipton, N Yorks BD23 5HY. *T:* (01756) 760863; 20 Lancaster Mews, W2 3QE. *e-mail:* davidroche20@yahoo.co.uk. *Clubs:* Buck's; Kildare Street and University (Dublin); Royal Yacht Squadron.

ROCHE, Sir Henry John, (Sir Harry), Kt 1999; Chairman, Press Association, 1995–2008 (non-executive Director, 1988–2008); *b* 13 Jan. 1934; *s* of Henry Joseph Roche and Mary Ann Roche; *m* 1st, 1956, Shirley May Foreman (marr. diss. 1986); three *s*; 2nd, 1986, Heather Worthington. *Educ:* George Mitchell Sch., Leyton; Watford Coll. of Technol. (HND Printing Technol.). Apprentice engraver, until 1959; worked on shopfloor of Daily Mirror, 1959–69; Dep. Prodn Controller, Daily Mirror, 1969–70; Northern Prodn Controller, Mirror Gp Newspapers, Manchester, 1970–73; Prodn Dir, 1973–77, Man. Dir, 1977–85, Manchester Evening News; Man. Dir, The Guardian, 1985–88; Chm. and Chief Exec., Guardian Media Gp Plc, 1988–96; Chm., GMTV, 1989–92. Director: Johnston Press plc, 1993–2004 (Dep. Chm., 1995–2004); Jazz FM (formerly Golden Rose Communications) plc, 1995–2002 (Chm., 1999–2002). Chairman: Press Standards Bd of Finance Ltd, 1991–2003; Orgn for Promoting Understanding in Society, 1998–2002; Dep. Chm., Printers Charitable Corp., 1996–2000 (Dir, 1985–2000; Pres., 1993). Mem. Council, CPU, 1988–. FIP3 (FIOP 1993 (Pres., 1996–98)). Freeman, City of London, 1993. *Recreations:* golf, ski-ing, music (particularly jazz). *Clubs:* Royal Automobile; Dunham Forest Golf and Country (Cheshire).

ROCHE, Nicola; Director of Strategy, Government Olympic Executive, Department for Culture, Media and Sport, since 2007; *b* 27 Dec. 1956; *d* of Ronald and Shirley Roche. *Educ:* Harrogate Grammar Sch.; Univ. of York (BA Hons Hist. 1979); Birkbeck Coll., London (MA Hist. 1986). EDG, 1979–82; Prime Minister's Office, 1982–86; EDG, 1987–91; City and Inner London N TEC, 1991–93; Labour Attaché, Brussels, The Hague and Luxembourg, 1993–98; Private Office, DfEE, 1998–2001; Hd of Strategy, then Dir for Identity Cards, Children and Coroners, Home Office, 2001–04; Dir of Sport, DCMS, 2004–07. *Recreations:* athletics, walking, history, art. *Address:* Department for Culture, Media and Sport, 2–4 Cockspur Street, SW1Y 5DH. *T:* (020) 7211 6193, *Fax:* (020) 7211 6539; *e-mail:* Nicola.Roche@culture.gsi.gov.uk.

ROCHE, Patrick John; Member (NIU), Lagan Valley, Northern Ireland Assembly, 1999–2003 (UKU, 1998–99); *b* 4 March 1940; *m. Educ:* Trinity Coll., Dublin (BA Hons Econs and Politics); Durham Univ. (MA Politics). Posts in banking, 1957–66; Lecturer: in Economics, Ulster Univ., 1974–95; in Philosophy of Religion, Irish Baptist Coll., 1978–. *Publications:* (ed jtly) The Northern Ireland Question: myth and reality, 1991, perspectives and policies, 1994, Unionism, nationalism and partition, 1999; (jtly) An Economics Lesson for Irish Nationalists, 1996; The Appeasement of Terrorism and the Belfast Agreement, 2000; publications on political and econ. issues. *Recreation:* squash.

ROCHESTER, 2nd Baron, of the 4th creation, *cr* 1931, of Rochester in the County of Kent; **Foster Charles Lowry Lamb;** DL; *b* 7 June 1916; *s* of 1st Baron Rochester, CMG, and Rosa Dorothea (*née* Hurst); *S* father, 1955; *m* 1942, Mary Carlisle (*d* 2000), *yr d* of T. B. Wheeler, CBE; two *s* one *d* (and one *d* decd). *Educ:* Mill Hill; Jesus College, Cambridge. MA. Served War of 1939–45: Captain 23rd Hussars; France, 1944. Joined ICI Ltd, 1946: Labour Manager, Alkali Div., 1955–63; Personnel Manager, Mond Div., 1964–72. Pro-Chancellor, Univ. of Keele, 1976–86. Chairman: Cheshire Scout Assoc., 1974–81; Governors of Chester Coll., 1974–83. DL Cheshire, 1979. DUniv Keele, 1986. *Heir: s* Hon. David Charles Lamb [*b* 8 Sept. 1944; *m* 1969, Jacqueline Stamp; two *s*. *Educ:* Shrewsbury Sch.; Univ. of Sussex]. *Address:* 337 Chester Road, Hartford, Northwich, Cheshire CW8 1QR. *T:* (01606) 74733. *Clubs:* Reform, National Liberal, MCC; Hawks (Cambridge).

See also Hon. T. M. Lamb.

ROCHESTER, Bishop of, since 1994; **Rt Rev. Dr Michael James Nazir-Ali;** *b* 19 Aug. 1949; *s* of James and Patience Nazir-Ali; *m* 1972, Valerie Cree; two *s*. *Educ:* St Paul's School and St Patrick's Coll., Karachi; Univ. of Karachi (BA 1970, Econs Sociology and Islamic History); Fitzwilliam Coll. (PGCTh 1972; MLitt 1977; Hon. Fellow, 2006) and Ridley Hall, Cambridge; St Edmund Hall, Oxford (BLitt 1974; MLitt 1981; Hon. Fellow, 1999); ThD Aust. Coll. of Theol., NSW 1985; DHLitt Westminster Coll., Penn 2004. Assistant: Christ Church, Cambridge, 1970–72; St Ebbe's, Oxford, 1972–74; Burney Lectr in Islam, Cambridge, 1973–74; Tutorial Supervisor in Theology, Univ. of Cambridge, 1974–76; Assistant Curate, Holy Sepulchre, Cambridge, 1974–76; Tutor, then Sen. Tutor, Karachi Theol Coll., 1976–81; Assoc. Priest, Holy Trinity Cathedral, Karachi, 1976–79; Priest-in-charge, St Andrew's, Akhtar Colony, Karachi, 1979–81; Provost of Lahore Cathedral, 1981–84; Bishop of Raiwind, Pakistan 1984–86; Asst to Archbp of Canterbury, Co-ordinator of Studies and Editor for Lambeth Conf., 1986–89; Director-in-Residence, Oxford Centre for Mission Studies, 1986–89; Gen. Sec., CMS, 1989–94; Canon Theologian, Leicester Cathedral, 1992–94. Took seat in H of L, 1999. Mem., HFEA, 1998–2003 (Chm., Ethics and Law Cttee, 1998–2003). Sec., Archbp's Commn on Communion and Women in the Episcopate (Eames Commn), 1988–98; Chm., Wkg Party on Women in Episcopate, 2001–04; Archbishops' nominee, CCBI, 1990–94; Chairman: C of E Mission Theol Adv. Gp, 1992–2001; House of Bishops' Theol. Gp, 2004–; Member: ARCIC II, 1991–; C of E Bd of Mission, 1991–94, 1996–2001; Archbps' Council, 2000–05; House of Bishops' Standing Cttee, 2000–05; Internat. Anglican-Roman Catholic Commn for Unity and Mission, 2001–. Mem. Bd, Christian Aid, 1987–97. Vis. Prof., Univ. of Greenwich, 1996–. Paul Harris Rotary Fellow, 2005. DD Lambeth, 2005; Hon. DLitt: Bath, 2003; Greenwich, 2003; Hon. DD Kent, 2004. *Publications:* Islam: a Christian perspective, 1983; Frontiers in Muslim-Christian Encounter, 1987; Martyrs and Magistrates: toleration and trial in Islam, 1989; From Everywhere to Everywhere, 1990; Mission and Dialogue, 1995; The Mystery of Faith, 1995; Citizens and Exiles: Christian faith in a plural world, 1998; Shapes of the Church to Come, 2001; Understanding My Muslim Neighbour, 2002; Conviction and Conflict, 2006; The Unique and Universal Christ, 2008; *edited:* Working Papers for the Lambeth Conference, 1988; The Truth shall Make you Free: report of the Lambeth Conference, 1988; Trustworthy and True: Pastoral letters from the Lambeth Conference, 1988; articles and contribs to jls. *Recreations:* cricket, hockey, table tennis, reading fiction, humour and poetry, writing poetry. *Address:* Bishopscourt, St Margaret's Street, Rochester, Kent ME1 1TS. *T:* (01634) 842721.

ROCHESTER, Dean of; *see* Newman, Very Rev. A.

ROCHESTER, Archdeacon of; *see* Lock, Ven. P. H. D'A.

ROCHESTER, Terence Anthony, CB 1997; *b* 30 May 1937; *s* of Arthur Alfred Rochester and Winifred Mabel Rochester (*née* Smith); *m* 1966, Margaret Alexandra Fleming; one *s* one *d*. *Educ:* Southwest Essex Sch. FIHT. British Rail, 1953–59, 1961–65; Nat. Service, 2nd Lieut, RE, 1959–61; joined Dept of Transport, 1965; various posts, 1965–87; Director: Transport Eastern Region, 1987–89; Transport W Midlands Region, 1989–90; Construction Programme, W Midlands, 1990–91; Chief Highway Engineer, 1991–94; Civil Engrg and Envmtl Policy Dir, 1994–96, Quality Services Dir, 1996–97, Highways Agency. Chairman: Tech. Cttee B/525 Bldg and Civil Engrg Structures, BSI, 1997–2000; Construction Clients' Forum, 1997–2000; Mem., Govt Cttee on Thaumasite, 1998–99. Res. Fellow, Transport Res. Foundn. Pres., CIRIA, 1998–2001; Hon. Mem., British PIARC. *Recreations:* music, walking, DIY.

ROCK, David Annison, PPRIBA; FCSD; President, Royal Institute of British Architects, 1997–99; Partner, Camp 5, since 1992; *b* 27 May 1929; *s* of Thomas Henry Rock and Muriel Rock (*née* Barton); *m* 1st, 1954, Daphne Elizabeth Richards (marr. diss. 1986); three *s* two *d*; 2nd, 1989, Lesley Patricia Murray. *Educ:* Bede Grammar Sch., Sunderland; King's Coll., Durham (BArch 1952; CertTP 1953). ARIBA 1953, FRIBA 1967; MSIAD 1963, FCSD 1978. 2nd Lieut, RE, 1953–55. With Basil Spence and Partners, 1952–53 and 1955–58; David Rock Architect, 1958–59; Associate Partner, 1959–64, Equity Partner, 1964–71, Grenfell Baines & Hargreaves, later Building Design Partnership; Chm. and Man. Dir, Rock Townsend, 1971–92. Inventor, Workspace concept (sharing by several firms of central support services in a building), 1971; first RIBA/ARCUK approved Archt Developer, 1973. Major projects include: Bumpus Bookshop, W1, 1958; Univ. of Surrey Develt Plan, 1965; UN HQ and Austrian Nat. Conf. Centre, Vienna, 1970; Middlesex Poly., Bounds Green, 1975–88; (with Ralph Erskine) The London Ark, Hammersmith, 1993. Graham Willis Vis. Prof., Univ. of Sheffield, 1990–92. Founder Chairman and Director: 5 Dryden Street Collective, 1971–82; Barley Mow Workspace Ltd, 1973–92; Joint Founder: Construction Industry Council, 1986; Urban Design Alliance, 1997. Royal Institute of British Architects: Mem./Chm., Architecture Award Bds for 14 UK Regs, 1960–77; Mem., Vis. Bds, 20 univs and polys, 1973–81; Mem. Council, 1970–76, 1986–88, 1995–2001; Vice-Pres., 1987–88, 1995–97. Member: Architecture Bd, CNAA, 1975–81; Housing the Arts Cttee, Arts Council of GB, 1981–84; Lottery Awards Panel, Sports Council, 1995–97; Specialist Assessor, HEFCE, 1994–95; Hd, Lottery Architecture Unit, Arts Council of England, 1995–99. Finance Dir, HCL Ltd, 2003–05 and 2006–. Chm., Soc. of Architect Artists, 1986–92; Pres., Architects Benevolent Soc., 2003–07 (Vice Pres., 2000–03, 2007–); Trustee: Montgomery Sculpture Trust, 2000–05; S Norfolk Buildings Preservation Trust, 2003–05. *Solo painting exhibitions:* Durham, and Covent Garden, 1977; Ditchling, 1994, Harleston, 2007. Hon. FAIA 2002 (Hon. AIA 1998). Glover Medal, Northern Architectl Assoc., 1949; Henry Bell Saint Bequest, Univ. of Durham, 1950; Crown Prize, Walpamur Co., 1951; Soane Medallion, 1954, Owen Jones Studentship prize, 1960, RIBA; President's Medal, AIA, 1998. *Publications:* Vivat Ware!: strategies to enhance a historic town, 1974; The Grassroot Developers: a handbook for town development trusts, 1979; *illustrated:* B. Allsopp, Decoration and Furniture, 1950; D. Senior, Your Architect, 1964; articles and reviews in prof. and technical pubns, 1961–. *Recreations:* work, painting, watching TV sport. *Address:* Camp 5, The Beeches, 13 London Road, Harleston, Norfolk IP20 9BH. *T:* and *Fax:* (01379) 854897; *e-mail:* david.rock1@btinternet.com.

ROCK, Prof. Paul Elliot, FBA 2000; Professor of Social Institutions, London School of Economics and Political Science, 1995–2008, now Emeritus; *b* 4 Aug. 1943; *s* of Ashley Rock and Charlotte (*née* Dickson); *m* 1965, Barbara Ravid (*d* 1998); two *s*. *Educ:* London School of Economics (BScSoc); Nuffield Coll., Oxford (DPhil). London School of Economics: Asst Lectr, 1967; Lectr, 1970; Sen. Lectr, 1976; Reader in Sociology, 1980; Reader in Social Institutions, 1981; Prof. of Sociology, 1986–95; Dir, Mannheim Centre for Study of Criminology and Criminal Justice, 1992–95. Visiting Professor: Princeton Univ., 1974–75; Univ. of Pennsylvania, 2006–; Vis. Schol., Ministry of Solicitor Gen. of Canada, 1981–82; Fellow, Center for Advanced Study of Behavioral Scis, Stanford, Calif, 1996; Resident, Rockefeller Foundn Study Center, Bellagio, 2003. FRSA 1997. *Publications:* Making People Pay, 1973; Deviant Behaviour, 1973; The Making of Symbolic Interactionism, 1979; (with D. Downes) Understanding Deviance, 1982, 2nd edn 1988, rev. 1998; A View from the Shadows, 1986; Helping Victims of Crime, 1990; The Social World of an English Crown Court, 1993; Reconstructing a Women's Prison, 1996; After Homicide, 1998; Constructing Victims' Rights, 2004. *Address:* London School of Economics and Political Science, Houghton Street, Aldwych, WC2A 2AE. *T:* (020) 7955 7296.

ROCKEFELLER, David; banker; *b* New York City, 12 June 1915; *s* of John Davison Rockefeller, Jr and Abby Greene (Aldrich) Rockefeller; *m* 1940, Margaret (*d* 1996), *d* of Francis Sims McGrath, Mount Kisco, NY; two *s* four *d*. *Educ:* Lincoln School of Columbia University's Teachers College; Harvard Coll. (BS); London School of Economics; Univ. of Chicago (PhD). Sec. to Mayor Fiorello H. LaGuardia, 1940–41; Asst Regional Dir, US Office of Defense Health and Welfare Services, 1941. Served in US Army, N Africa and France, 1942–45 (Captain). Joined Chase National Bank, NYC, 1946; Asst Manager, Foreign Dept, 1946–47; Asst Cashier, 1947–48; Second Vice-Pres., 1948–49; Vice-Pres., 1949–51; Senior Vice-Pres., 1951–55; Chase Manhattan Bank (merger of Chase Nat. Bank and Bank of Manhattan Co.): Exec. Vice Pres., 1955–57; Dir, 1955–81; Vice-Chm., 1957–61; Pres. and Chm., Exec. Cttee, 1961–69; Chm. of Bd and Chief Exec. Officer, 1969–81; Chairman: Chase Internat. Investment Corp., 1961–75; Chase Internat. Adv. Cttee, 1980–2000; Rockefeller Brothers Fund Inc., 1981–87; The Rockefeller Group Inc., 1983–95; Rockefeller Center Properties Inc., 1985–92. Director: Internat. Exec. Service Corps (Chm., 1964–68); NY Clearing House, 1971–78; Center for Inter-American Relations (Chm. 1966–70); Overseas Develt Council; US-USSR Trade and Econ. Council, Inc.; Chairman: Rockefeller Univ., 1950–75; NYC Partnership, 1979–88; Hon. Chm., Americas Soc.; Hon. N America Chm., Trilateral Commn; Member: Council on Foreign Relations; Exec. Cttee, Museum of Modern Art (Chm., 1962–72, 1987–93); Harvard Coll. Bd of Overseers, 1954–60, 1962–68; Urban Develt Corp., NY State, Business Adv. Council, 1968–72; US Adv. Cttee on Reform of Internat. Monetary System, 1973–; Sen. Adv. Gp, Bilderberg Meetings; US Exec. Cttee, Dartmouth Conf.; Bd, Inst. of Internat. Economics. Director: Downtown-Lower Manhattan Assoc., Inc. (Chm., 1958–65); Internat. House, NY, 1940–63; Morningside Heights Inc., 1947–70 (Pres., 1947–57, Chm., 1957–65); B. F. Goodrich Co., 1956–64; Equitable Life Assce Soc. of US, 1960–65. Trustee: Univ. of Chicago, 1947–62 (Life Trustee, 1966); Carnegie Endowment for Internat. Peace, 1947–60; Council of the Americas (Chm., 1965–70, 1983–92); Historic Hudson Valley (formerly Sleepy Hollow Restorations), 1981–. Member: American Friends of LSE; US Hon. Fellows, LSE; Founding Mem., Business

Cttee for the Arts; Hon. Mem., Commn on White House Fellows, 1964–65; Hon. Chm., Japan Soc. World Brotherhood Award, Jewish Theol Seminary, 1953; Gold Medal, Nat. Inst. Social Sciences, 1967; Medal of Honor for city planning, Amer. Inst. Architects, 1968; C. Walter Nichols Award, NY Univ., 1970; Reg. Planning Assoc. Award, 1971. Hon. LLD: Columbia Univ., 1954; Bowdoin Coll., 1958; Jewish Theol Seminary, 1958; Williams Coll., 1966; Wagner Coll., 1967; Harvard, 1969; Pace Coll., 1970; St John's Univ., 1971; Middlebury, 1974; Univ. of Liberia, 1979; Rockefeller Univ., 1980; Hon. DEng: Colorado Sch. of Mines, 1974; Univ. of Notre Dame, 1987. Holds civic awards. Grand Croix, Legion of Honour, France, 2000 (Grand Officer, 1955); Order of Merit of the Republic, Italy; Order of the Southern Cross, Brazil; Order of the White Elephant and Order of the Crown, Thailand; Order of the Cedar, Lebanon; Order of the Sun, Peru; Order of Humane African Redemption, Liberia; Order of the Crown, Belgium; National Order of Ivory Coast; Grand Cordon, Order of Sacred Treasure, Japan, 1991. *Publications:* Unused Resources and Economic Waste, 1940; Creative Management in Banking, 1964; Memoirs, 2002. *Recreation:* sailing. *Address:* 30 Rockefeller Plaza, New York, NY 10112, USA. *Clubs:* Century, Harvard, River, Knickerbocker, Links, University, Recess (New York); New York Yacht.

ROCKEY, Patricia Mary, (Mrs D. C. Rockey); *see* Broadfoot, P. M.

ROCKHAMPTON, Bishop of, since 2003; **Rt Rev. Godfrey Charles Fryar;** *b* 5 Feb. 1950; *s* of Neville Gordon Fryar and Norma Emma Fryar (*née* Kloske); *m* 1977, Bronwyn Anne Horrocks; two *s* one *d*. *Educ:* All Souls' Sch., Charters Towers, Qld; St Francis Coll. (ThL 1972). Ordained deacon, 1973, priest, 1974; Bush Brother, Longreach, Cunnamulla and Quilpie, 1973–76; Parish Priest, Dawson Valley, N Rockhampton, N Mackay, Stafford, 1977–93; Dean, St Saviour's Cathedral, Goulburn, 1993–98; Asst Bishop, Wagga Wagga, and Vicar Gen., Dio. Canberra and Goulburn, 1998–2003. *Recreation:* bush walking. *Address:* PO Box 6158, Central Queensland Mail Centre, Rockhampton, Qld 4702, Australia. *T:* (7) 49273188, *Fax:* (7) 49229325; *e-mail:* bishop@anglicanrock.org.au.

ROCKLEY, 3rd Baron *cr* 1934; **James Hugh Cecil;** Director, Kleinwort Benson Group, 1986–98 (Chairman, 1993–96); *b* 5 April 1934; *s* of 2nd Baron Rockley, and Anne Margaret (*d* 1980), *d* of late Adm. Hon. Sir Herbert Meade-Featherstonhaugh, GCVO, CB, DSO; *S* father, 1976; *m* 1958, Lady Sarah Primrose Beatrix, *e d* of 7th Earl Cadogan, MC; one *s* two *d*. *Educ:* Eton; New Coll., Oxford. Wood Gundy & Co. Ltd, 1957–62; Kleinwort Benson Ltd, 1962–96. Chairman: Dartford River Crossing, 1988–93; Kleinwort Develt Fund, 1990–93; Midland Expressway, 1992–93; Hall & Woodhouse Ltd, 2000–; Director: Equity and Law, 1980–91; Christies Internat., 1989–98; Cobham (formerly FR Gp), 1990–2002; Abbey National, 1990–99; Foreign and Colonial Investment Trust, 1992–2003; Cadogan Gp Ltd, 1996–; Dusco (UK) Ltd, 1996–2000; Hypo Foreign & Colonial Mgt (Hldgs) Ltd, 1996–99. Mem., Design Council, 1987–93; Trustee, Nat. Portrait Gall., 1981–88. Chm. of Govs, Milton Abbey Sch., 2000–04. *Heir: s* Hon. Anthony Robert Cecil [*b* 29 July 1961; *m* 1988, Katherine Jane, *d* of G. A. Whalley; one *s* two *d*]. *Address:* The Bell House, Ellisfield, Basingstoke, Hants RG25 2QD. *T:* (01256) 381212.

ROCKLIFFE, Victor Paul L.; *see* Lunn-Rockliffe.

ROCKLIN, David Samuel; Chairman, Norton Opax, 1973–89; *b* 15 Aug. 1931; *s* of Alfred Rocklin and Ada Rebecca Rocklin; *m* 1955, Dorothy Ann; two *s* two *d*. *Educ:* Heles School, Exeter. Managing Director, Norton Opax, 1969–73. *Recreations:* books, travel, music, painting, good food and conversation.

RODAN, Hon. Stephen Charles; MHK, Garff, since 1995; Speaker, House of Keys, Isle of Man, since 2006; *b* 19 April 1954; *s* of Robert W. Rodan and Betty Rodan (*née* Turner); *m* 1977, Ana Maria Valentina Ballesteros Torres, Mexico City; two *d*. *Educ:* High Sch., Glasgow; Univ. of Edinburgh; Heriot-Watt Univ. (BSc Hons Pharmacy 1977). MRPharmS 1978. Pharmacist, Elgin, Inverness, 1978–80; Pharmacy Manager, Bermuda, 1980–87; Pharmacy Proprietor, I of M, 1987–. Mem., Laxey Village Commn, 1991–95 (Chm., 1993–95). Isle of Man Government: Chm., Planning Cttee, 1997–99; Minister: for Educn, 1999–2004; for Health and Soc. Security, 2004–06. Chairman: Liberal Club, Univ. of Edinburgh, 1974–76; Scottish Young Liberals, 1974–76; Mem. Nat. Exec., Scottish Liberal Party, 1975–77. Contested (Scots L) Moray and Nairn, 1979. Pres., Caledonian Soc. of Bermuda, 1983–85. Pipe Major, Cair Vie Manx Pipe Band, 1992–95. Chm., Laxey and Lonan Heritage Trust, 1995–. Pres., Laxey and Lonan Br., RBL, 1998–. *Recreations:* playing the bagpipes, speaking at Burns' dinners, visiting art galleries, books, travel, Isle of Man heritage. *Address:* Orry's Mount, Ballaragh Road, Laxey, Isle of Man IM4 7PE. *T:* and *Fax:* (01624) 861514; *e-mail:* steve.rodan@gov.im.

RODD, family name of **Baron Rennell**.

RODDA, James, (Jim), FCA; Hon. Treasurer, National Council for the Conservation of Plants and Gardens, since 2003; *b* 16 Aug. 1945; *s* of George Rodda and Ruby (*née* Thompson); *m* 1967, Angela Hopkinson; one *s* two *d*. *Educ:* Maldon Grammar Sch.; Reading Univ. (BA Hons); Leicester Univ. FCA 1971. Spicer and Pegler, 1967–71; Coopers and Lybrand, 1971–77; Thomas Cook Group, 1977–84; Lonconex Group, 1984–85; Mercantile Credit, 1985–86; London Commodity Exchange, 1986–91; Dir of Finance and Admin, House of Commons, 1991–96; Financial Dir, Nat. Film and Television Sch., 1996–2005. *Recreations:* railway rambling, music.

RODDA, Dr John Carrol, FRMetS; FRGS; President, International Association of Hydrological Sciences, 1995–2001; *b* 15 Aug. 1934; *s* of late J. Allen Rodda and Eleanor M. Rodda; *m* 1961, Annabel Brailsford Edwards; two *s*. *Educ:* UCW, Aberystwyth (BSc 1956; DipEd 1957; PhD 1960; DSc 1979). FRMetS 1961; MCIWEM 1976. DSIR Res. Fellow, 1960–62, Hydrologist, 1962–65, Hydraulics Res. Station, Wallingford; Hd, Catchment Res., Inst. Hydrology, Wallingford, 1965–69 and 1970–72; Consultant, WMO, Geneva, 1969–70 (on secondment); Head: Envmtl Pollution and Resources Unit, Directorate Gen. of Res., DoE, 1972–74; Data Acquisition Br., Water Data Unit, Reading, DoE, 1974–82; Asst Dir, Inst. Hydrology, Wallingford, 1982–88; Dir, Hydrology and Water Resources Dept, WMO, Geneva, 1988–95. Visiting Professor: Dept of Geog., Univ. of Strathclyde, 1976–79; Internat. Inst. for Infrastructure, Hydraulics & Envmt, Delft, 1976–97; Univ. of Perugia, 1983; Hon. Prof., Inst. Geog. and Earth Scis, Univ. of Wales, Aberystwyth, 1995–. Ed., 1972–79, Sec.-Gen., 1979–87, Internat. Assoc. Hydrological Scis; Sec./Treas., ICSU/Union Internat. des Assocs et Organismes Techniques Cttee on Water Res., 1982–87; Mem., Scientific Cttee on Water Res., ICSU, 1991–95; Mem. Exec. Cttee, IUGG, 1995–2001. UN International Decade for Natural Disaster Reduction: Member: Prep. Cttee, 1988–90; Scientific and Tech. Cttee, 1990–95; Chm., UN Admin. Co-ordinating Cttee, Sub-cttee on Water Resources, 1990–92; Chairman: Prog. Rev. Gp IV, Centre for Ecol. and Hydrol., NERC, 1996–2000; Commn on Water, World Humanities Action Trust, 1998–2000; Member: Bd of Govs, World Water Council, 1999–2001; Regl Envmt Protection Adv. Cttee, Envmt Agency, 2007–. Associate. Dir, Hydro-GIS Ltd, 2006–. Mem., Amer. Geophysical Union, 1960; Hon. Member: British Hydrological Soc., 1983; Amer. Water Resources Assoc., 1992; Hungarian Hydrological Soc., 1992. Chm., Oxon Agenda 21 Planning Gp, 1997–2001; Vice-Chm., Trust for Oxon's Envmt, 2001–03 (Mem. Bd, 1998–2000). Fellow, NERC Centre for Ecol. and Hydrol., 2004. FRGS 2003. Hugh Robert Mill Prize, RMetS, 1980; Internat. Hydrology Prize, Internat. Assoc. of Hydrol Scis/UNESCO/WMO, 2004. *Publications:* (jtly) Systematic Hydrology, 1976; (ed) Facets of Hydrology, 1976, Facets of Hydrology II, 1985 (trans. Russian); (jtly) Global Water Resource Issues, 1994; (ed jtly) Land Surface Processes in Hydrology: trials and tribulations of modeling and measurement, 1997; (ed jtly) World Water Resources at the Beginning of the Twenty-First Century, 2003; (ed jtly) The Basis of Civilisation - Water Science?, 2004. *Recreations:* walking, music, golf, environment. *Address:* Ynyslas, Brightwell cum Sotwell, Wallingford, Oxon OX10 0RG; *e-mail:* jandarodda@waitrose.com. *Club:* Goring and Streatley Golf.

RODDAM; *see* Holderness-Roddam.

RODDICK, (George) Winston, CB 2004; QC 1986; a Recorder, since 1987; Counsel General to National Assembly for Wales, 1998–2003; *b* Caernarfon, 2 Oct. 1940; *s* of William and Aelwen Roddick; *m* 1966, Cennin Parry; one *s* one *d*. *Educ:* Sir Huw Owen GS, Caernarfon; Tal Handak, Malta; University Coll. London (LLB, LLM). Called to the Bar, Gray's Inn, 1968, Bencher, 1997; Leader, Wales and Chester Circuit, 2007–. Member: Gen. Council of the Bar, 1992–95; Professional Conduct Cttee of the Bar, 1994–96; Employed Barristers Cttee, Bar Council, 2000–03; Chm., Bristol and Cardiff Chancery Bar Assoc., 1996–98. Hon. Recorder, Caernarfon, 2001–. Member: ITC, 1998; S4C Authy, 2005–. Member: Welsh Language Bd, 1988–93; Lord Chancellor's Adv. Cttee on Statute Law, 1999–2003; Standing Cttee on use of Welsh lang. in legal proceedings, 1999–. Mem. Editl Bd, Cambridge Jl of Financial Crime, 1995–98; Mem. Editl Bd, Wales Law Jl, 2001–06. Vice Pres., Univ. of Wales, Aberystwyth, 2000 (Hon. Fellow, 1999). Gov., Ysgol y Wern Sch., Cardiff, 1991–99. Pres., Cantorian Creigiau, 2000–. Vice Pres., Caernarfon Male Voice Choir, 1994–. Patron, Caernarfon RFC, 1994–. *Recreations:* walking the countryside, fishing. *Address:* Ely Place Chambers, 30 Ely Place, EC1N 6TD; 9 Park Place, Cardiff CF10 3DP. *T:* (home) (029) 2075 9376. *Club:* Caernarfon Sailing.

RODDIE, Prof. Ian Campbell, CBE 1988; TD 1967; FRCPI; Dunville Professor of Physiology, Queen's University, Belfast, 1964–87, now Emeritus; *b* 1 Dec. 1928; *s* of Rev. J. R. Wesley Roddie and Mary Hill Wilson; *m* 1st, 1958, Elizabeth Ann Gillon Honeyman (decd); one *s* three *d*; 2nd, 1974, Katherine Ann O'Hara (marr. diss.); one *s* one *d*; 3rd, 1987, Janet Doreen Saville (*née* Lennon). *Educ:* Methodist Coll., Belfast; Queen's Univ., Belfast. Malcolm Exhibnr, 1951, McQuitty Schol., 1953; BSc (1st cl. Hons Physiol.), MB BCh, BAO, MD (with gold medal), DSc; MRCPI; MRIA. Major RAMC (T&AVR); OC Med. Sub-unit, QUB OTC, retd 1968. Resident MO, Royal Victoria Hosp., Belfast, 1953–54; Queen's University, Belfast: Lectr in Physiology, 1954–60; Sen. Lectr, 1961–62; Reader, 1962–64; Dep. Dean, 1975–76, Dean, 1976–81, Faculty of Medicine; Pro-Vice-Chancellor, 1983–87; Head of Med. Educn, 1990–94, and Dep. Med. Dir, 1991–94, King Khalid Nat. Guard Hosp., Jeddah. Consultant Physiologist: NI Hosps Authority, 1962–72; Eastern Health Bd, NI, 1972–88. Staff Consultant, Asian Develt Bank, Manila, 1987–88; part-time consultant, IFC/African Project Develt Facility/World Bank, Washington, 1989–2004. Harkness Commonwealth Fund Fellow, Univ. of Washington, Seattle, 1960–61; Visiting Professor: Univ. of NSW, 1983–84; Chinese Univ. of Hong Kong, 1988–90; Res. Fellow, Japan Soc. for Promotion of Science, Matsumoto, Japan, 1984. External Examiner: Univs of Aberdeen, Baghdad, Benghazi, Birmingham, Bristol, Glasgow, Ireland, Jeddah, Jos, Lagos, Leeds, London, Sheffield, Southampton, Zimbabwe; RCS, RCSE, RCPGlas, RCSI. Chief Reg. Sci. Advr for Home Defence, NI, 1977–88; Member: Home Defence Sci. Adv. Conf., 1977–88; Eastern Area Health and Social Services Bd, NI, 1976–81; Physiol Systems Bd, MRC, 1974–76; Med. Adv. Cttee, Cttee of Vice-Chancellors and Principals, 1976–81; GMC, 1979–81; GDC, 1979–81. President: Royal Acad. of Medicine in Ireland, 1985–88; Biol Scis Sect., Royal Acad. of Medicine in Ireland, 1964–66; Ulster Biomed. Engrg Soc., 1979–83; Chm. Cttee, Physiol Soc., 1985–88 (Mem. Cttee, 1966–69; Hon. Mem., 1989). Arris and Gale Lectr, RCS, 1962. Conway Bronze Medal, Royal Acad. of Medicine in Ireland, 1977. *Publications:* Physiology for Practitioners, 1971, 2nd edn 1975; Multiple Choice Questions in Human Physiology, 1971, 6th edn 2004; The Physiology of Disease, 1975; papers on physiology and pharmacology of vascular, sudorific and lymphatic systems. *Address:* 32a Hazlewell Road, Putney, SW15 6LR. *T:* (020) 8789 1848; *e-mail:* ian.roddie@gmail.com. *Club:* Reform.

RODECK, Prof. Charles Henry, DSc; FRCOG, FRCPath, FMedSci; Professor of Obstetrics and Gynaecology, University College London, 1990–2007, now Emeritus; *b* 23 Aug. 1944; *s* of Heinz and Charlotte Rodeck; *m* 1971, Elisabeth (*née* Rampton); one *s* one *d*. *Educ:* University College London (BSc Anatomy 1966; Fellow 2003); UCH Med. Sch. (MB BS 1969); DSc (Med) London 1991. MRCOG 1975; FRCOG 1987; FRCPath 1994. House appts to 1975; King's College Hospital Medical School: Registrar, 1975; Lectr, 1976; Sen. Lectr/Consultant, 1978; Dir, Harris Birthright Res. Centre for Fetal Medicine, 1983–86; Prof., Inst. of Obstetrics and Gynaecol., RPMS, Queen Charlotte's and Chelsea Hosp., 1986–90. Member, Council: Obst. and Gyn. Sect., RSocMed; British Assoc. of Perinatal Med.; RCOG, 1991–92, 1996–2001 (Chm., Subspeciality Bd, 1989–92); Mem., Working Party on Antenatal Diagnosis, RCP, 1986–89; Chm., Steering Gp for Fetal Tissue Bank, MRC, 1989–92; Mem., EEC Working Party on Chorion Villus Sampling, 1983–85; Mem., Antenatal Screening Subgroup, DoH, 2001–05. Examr, RCOG and Univs of Aberdeen, Brussels, Dublin, Leiden, London, Nottingham, Oxford, Reading, Singapore, Stockholm; Visiting Professor: USA Univs; Hong Kong Univ. Pres., Internat. Fetal Medicine and Surgery Soc., 1986; Chm., Assoc. of Profs of Obst. and Gyn., 1995–2000; Chm., Fedn of Assocs of Clinical Profs, 2000–; Pres., Internat. Soc. for Prenatal Diagnosis, 2002–06; Mem. or Hon. Mem., med. socs Europe and USA; Founder FMedSci 1998. Mem., editl bds of professional jls, UK and overseas; Editor for Europe, Prenatal Diagnosis, 1985–. *Publications:* (ed) Prenatal Diagnosis, 1984; (ed) Fetal Diagnosis of Genetic Defects, 1987; (ed) Fetal Medicine, 1989; (co-ed) Prenatal Diagnosis and Screening, 1992; (co-ed) Fetus and Neonate, 1993; (co-ed) Fetal Medicine: basic science and clinical practice, 1999; articles on prenatal diagnosis and fetal medicine. *Recreations:* stroking the cats, looking out of aeroplanes, the Wigmore Hall, Spurs. *Address:* Department of Obstetrics and Gynaecology, University College London, 86–96 Chenies Mews, WC1E 6HX. *T:* (020) 7679 6060. *Club:* Athenæum.

RODEN, 10th Earl of, *cr* 1771 (Ire.); **Robert John Jocelyn;** Baron Newport 1743; Viscount Jocelyn 1755; Bt 1665; *b* 25 Aug. 1938; *s* of 9th Earl of Roden and Clodagh Rose (*d* 1989), *d* of Edward Robert Kennedy; *S* father, 1993; *m* 1st, 1970, Sara Cecilia (marr. diss. 1982), *d* of Brig. Andrew Dunlop; one *d*; 2nd, 1986, Ann Margareta Maria, *d* of Dr Gunnar Henning; one *s*. *Educ:* Stowe. *Heir: s* Viscount Jocelyn, *qv*.

RODENBURG, Patricia Anne, (Patsy), OBE 2005; Head of Voice: Guildhall School of Speech and Drama, since 1981; Royal National Theatre, 1990–2006; *b* 2 Sept. 1953; *d* of Marius Rodenburg and late Margaret Edna Rodenburg (*née* Moody). *Educ:* St Christopher's Sch., Beckenham; Central Sch. of Speech and Drama. Voice Tutor, Royal

Shakespeare Co., 1981–90; Head of Voice, Stratford Fest. Theatre, Canada, 1984–85; Associate: Michael Howard Studios, NY, 1994–; Royal Court Theatre, 1999–; Founding Dir, Voice and Speech Centre, London, 1989–; works regularly with Almeida Theatre, Shared Experience, Cheek-by-Jowl, Théâtre de Complicité, Donmar Warehouse; works extensively in theatre, TV and radio throughout Europe, N America, Australia, Africa and Asia with major theatre and opera cos. Distinguished Vis. Prof., Southern Methodist Univ., Dallas, 1987–. *Publications:* The Right to Speak, 1992; The Need for Words, 1993; The Actor Speaks, 1997; Speaking Shakespeare, 2002; Presence, 2007. *Recreations:* travelling, reading. *Address:* c/o Royal National Theatre, South Bank, SE1 9PX.

RODERICK, Caerwyn Eifion; Councillor, South Glamorgan County Council, 1980–96; *b* 15 July 1927; *m* 1952, Eirlys Mary Lewis; one *s* two *d*. *Educ:* Maes-y-Dderwen County Sch., Ystradgynlais; University Coll. of North Wales, Bangor. Asst Master, Caterham Sch., Surrey, 1949–52; Sen. Master, Chartesey Sch., LCC, 1952–54; Sen. Maths Master, Boys' Grammar Sch., Brecon, 1954–57; Method Study Engineer, NCB, 1957–60; Sen. Maths Master, Hartridge High Sch., Newport, Mon, 1960–69; Lecturer, Coll. of Educn, Cardiff, 1969–70. MP (Lab) Brecon and Radnor, 1970–79; PPS to Rt Hon. Michael Foot. Dist Officer, NUT, 1980–91. Mem. Council: UC, Cardiff; formerly Mem. Council, RCVS. *Address:* 29 Charlotte Square, Rhiwbina, Cardiff CF14 6NE. *T:* (029) 2062 8269.

RODERICK, Edward Joseph; Chairman, Truck Project Ltd, since 2005; Co-Chairman, Envestors (MENA) Ltd, since 2008; Group Chief Executive, Christian Salvesen PLC, 1997–2004; *b* 23 Oct. 1952; *s* of late Edward Deakin Roderick and Joan Roderick; *m* 1974, Denise Ann Rowan; two *s*. *Educ:* De La Salle Grammar Sch., Liverpool. National/International CPC. FCIL (FILog 1992). B&I Line, 1972–87 (Head, UK Freight Ops, 1984–87); Man. Dir, Alexandra Molyneux Transport, 1987–88; BET plc, 1988–90: Man. Dir, IFF, 1988–90; Gp Dir, UTCH Ltd, 1988–90; Director: UTL Ltd, 1988–90; Seawheel, 1988–90; Gen. Manager, UK and Iberia, Bell Lines, 1990–92; Divl Man. Dir, Hays Network Distbn and other directorships in Hays plc, 1992–95; Man. Dir, Industrial Div., 1996–97, Man. Dir, Logistics UK and Europe, 1997, Christian Salvesen PLC. Dir, Heywood Williams Gp plc, 2002–07. Chm., Passim Internat. Ltd, 2005–07. Director: Road Haulage Assoc., 1998–2000; Freight Transport Assoc., 2000–07. Sen. Vice-Pres., Global Logistics Agility Inc., 2007–08. Dir, Northern Ballet Theatre, 1997–2000. MInstD 1987; CCMI (CIMgt 2000). Hon. LLD De Montfort, 2001. *Recreations:* golf, opera, ballet, swimming, wife and family. *Address:* Campbell House, Northampton Road, Higham Ferrers, Rushden, Northants NN10 6AL. *T:* (01933) 419148.

RODGER OF EARLSFERRY, Baron *cr* 1992 (Life Peer), of Earlsferry in the District of North East Fife; **Alan Ferguson Rodger;** PC 1992; FBA 1991; a Lord of Appeal in Ordinary, since 2001; *b* 18 Sept. 1944; *er s* of Prof. Thomas Ferguson Rodger and Jean Margaret Smith Chalmers. *Educ:* Kelvinside Acad., Glasgow; Glasgow Univ. (MA, LLB); New Coll., Oxford (MA (by decree), DPhil; DCL; Hon. Fellow, 2005). Dyke Jun. Res. Fellow, Balliol Coll., Oxford, 1969–70 (Hon. Fellow, 1999); Fellow, New Coll., Oxford, 1970–72; Mem., Faculty of Advocates, 1974; Clerk of Faculty, 1976–79; QC (Scot.) 1985; Advocate Depute, 1985–88, Home Advocate Depute, 1986–88; Solicitor-Gen. for Scotland, 1989–92; Lord Advocate, 1992–95; a Senator of the Coll. of Justice in Scotland, 1995–96; Lord Justice Gen. of Scotland and Lord President of the Court of Session, 1996–2001. Member: Mental Welfare Commn for Scotland, 1981–84; UK Delegn to CCBE, 1984–89; Acad. of European Private Lawyers, 1994–. Maccabaean Lectr, British Acad., 1991. Visitor, St Hugh's Coll., Oxford, 2003–. FRSE 1992. Hon. Bencher: Lincoln's Inn, 1992; Inn of Court of NI, 1998. Hon. Mem., SPTL, subseq. SLS, 1992; Corresp. Mem., Bayerische Akad. der Wissenschaften, 2001. Pres., Holdsworth Club, 1998–99. Hon. Fellow, American Coll. of Trial Lawyers, 2008. Hon. LLD: Glasgow, 1995; Aberdeen, 1999; Edinburgh, 2001. *Publications:* Owners and Neighbours in Roman Law, 1972 (asst editor) Gloag and Henderson's Introduction to the Law of Scotland, 10th edn, 1995; (ed jtly) Mapping the Law, 2006; The Courts, the Church and the Constitution, 2008; articles mainly on Roman Law. *Recreation:* walking. *Address:* House of Lords, SW1A 0PW. *Club:* Athenæum.

RODGER, Martin Owen; QC 2006; a Recorder, since 2003; *b* 11 Feb. 1962; *s* of William Rodger and Elizabeth Rodger (*née* Tunney); *m* 1991, Catherine Murphy; two *s* one *d*. *Educ:* St Aloysius Coll., Glasgow; University Coll., Oxford (BA 1983). Called to the Bar, Middle Temple, 1986. *Address:* Falcon Chambers, Falcon Court, EC4Y 1AA. *T:* (020) 7353 2484; *e-mail:* rodger@falcon-chambers.com.

RODGER, Mary Elizabeth; *see* Francis, M. E.

RODGER, Prof. Nicholas Andrew Martin, DPhil; FBA 2003; FSA, FRHistS; Senior Research Fellow, All Souls College, Oxford, since 2008; *b* 12 Nov. 1949; *s* of Lt Comdr Ian Rodger and Sara Rodger; *m* 1982, Susan Eleanor Farwell; three *s* one *d*. *Educ:* Ampleforth Coll., York; University Coll., Oxford (BA 1971, MA; DPhil 1974). FRHistS 1980; FSA 1985. Asst Keeper, PRO, 1974–91; Anderson Sen. Res. Fellow, Nat. Maritime Mus., 1992–99; Sen. Lectr in Hist., 1999–2000, Prof. of Naval Hist., 2000–08, Exeter Univ. *Publications:* The Admiralty, 1979; (ed with G. A. Osbon) The Black Battlefleet, by G. A. Ballard, 1980; Exchequer Ancient Deeds DD Series, 1101–1645 (E211), 1983; Naval Records for Genealogists, 1985, 3rd edn 1998; (ed) The Naval Miscellany, Vol. V, 1985; The Wooden World: an anatomy of the Georgian Navy, 1986, 2nd edn 1988; (ed with G. J. A. Raven) The Anglo-Dutch Relationship in War and Peace 1688–1988, 1990; The Insatiable Earl: a life of John Montagu, Fourth Earl of Sandwich, 1718–1792, 1993; (ed jtly) British Naval Documents 1204–1960, 1993; (ed) Naval Power in the Twentieth Century, 1996; The Safeguard of the Sea: a naval history of Britain, Vol. I, 660–1649, 1997; (ed) Memoirs of a Seafaring Life: the narrative of William Spavens, 2000; The Command of the Ocean: a naval history of Britain, Vol. II, 1649–1815, 2004; (ed with R. Cock) A Guide to the Naval Records in the National Archives, 2006. *Address:* All Souls College, Oxford OX1 4AL. *T:* (01865) 279379, *Fax:* (01865) 279299.

RODGERS, family name of **Baron Rodgers of Quarry Bank**.

RODGERS OF QUARRY BANK, Baron *cr* 1992 (Life Peer), of Kentish Town in the London Borough of Camden; **William Thomas Rodgers;** PC 1975; Chairman, Advertising Standards Authority, 1995–2001; Leader, Liberal Democrats, House of Lords, 1998–2001; *b* 28 Oct. 1928; *s* of William Arthur and Gertrude Helen Rodgers; *m* 1955, Silvia (*d* 2006), *d* of Hirsch Szulman; three *d*. *Educ:* Sudley Road Council Sch.; Quarry Bank High School, Liverpool; Magdalen College, Oxford. General Secretary, Fabian Society, 1953–60; publisher's editor, 1961–64, 1970–72; management recruiter, 1972–74. Contested: (Lab) Bristol West, March 1957; (SDP) Stockton N, 1983; (SDP/Alliance) Milton Keynes, 1987. MP (Lab 1962–81, SDP 1981–83) Stockton-on-Tees, 1962–74, Teesside, Stockton, 1974–83; Parly Under-Sec. of State: Dept of Econ. Affairs, 1964–67, Foreign Office, 1967–68; Leader, UK delegn to Council of Europe and Assembly of WEU, 1967–68; Minister of State: BoT, 1968–69; Treasury, 1969–70; MoD, 1974–76; Sec. of State for Transport, 1976–79. Chm., Expenditure Cttee on Trade and Industry, 1971–74. Vice-Pres., SDP, 1982–87. Dir-Gen., RIBA, 1987–94. Borough Councillor, St Marylebone, 1958–62. Hon. FRIBA 1994; Hon. FIStructE 1993. *Publications:* Hugh Gaitskell, 1906–1963 (ed), 1964; (jt) The People into Parliament, 1966; The Politics of Change, 1982; (ed) Government and Industry, 1986; Fourth Among Equals, 2000; pamphlets, etc. *Address:* 43 North Road, N6 4BE.

RODGERS, Sir (Andrew) Piers (Wingate), 3rd Bt *cr* 1964, of Groombridge, Kent; Secretary, Royal Academy of Arts, London, 1982–96; *b* 24 Oct. 1944; second *s* of Sir John Rodgers, 1st Bt and Betsy (*d* 1998), *y d* of Francis W. Aikin-Sneath; *S* brother, 1997; *m* 1st, 1979, Marie Agathe Houette (marr. diss. 2000); two *s*; 2nd, 2004, Ilona Medvedeva; two *d*. *Educ:* Eton Coll.; Merton Coll., Oxford (BA 1st Cl. Honour Mods, Prox. acc. Hertford and De Paravicini Prizes). J. Henry Schroder Wagg & Co. Ltd, London, 1967–73: Personal Asst to Chairman, 1971–73; Director, International Council on Monuments and Sites (ICOMOS), Paris, 1973–79; Consultant, UNESCO, Paris, 1979–80; Member, Technical Review Team, Aga Khan Award for Architecture, 1980, 1983; Secretary, UK Committee of ICOMOS, 1981. Trustee, The Type Mus., London, 1991–2004 (Dir, 2001–04). Mem. Bd, Warburg Inst., Univ. of London, 1993–98. FRSA 1973. Mem., Court of Assts, Masons' Co., 1982–. Chevalier de l'Ordre des Arts et des Lettres (France), 1987; Chevalier de l'Ordre National du Mérite (France), 1991; Cavaliere dell'Ordine al Merito della Repubblica Italiana, 1992. *Publications:* articles on protection of cultural heritage. *Recreations:* books, music, Real tennis, Islamic art. *Heir:* *s* Thomas Rodgers, *b* 18 Dec. 1979. *Address:* Peverell, Bradford Peverell, Dorset DT2 9SE. *Clubs:* Brooks's, Pratt's.

RODGERS, Bríd; Director, Bord Bia, since 2004; *b* 20 Feb. 1935; *d* of Tom Stratford and Josephine (*née* Coll); *m* 1960, Antoin Rodgers; three *s* three *d*. *Educ:* St Louis Convent, Monaghan; University Coll., Dublin (BA Hons Mod. Langs; Higher DipEd). Exec. Mem., NI Civil Rights Assoc., 1970–71. Mem., Irish Senate, 1983–87. Mem. (SDLP), Craigavon BC, 1985–93. Social Democratic and Labour Party: Vice Chair, 1976–78; Chair, 1978–80; Gen. Sec., 1981–83; Delegate to Brooke/Mayhew Talks, 1991–92; elected in Upper Bann to Negotiations, 1996, Chair, Negotiating Team, 1996–98; Dep. Leader, 2001–04. Mem. (SDLP) Upper Bann, NI Assembly, 1998–2003. Minister of Agriculture & Rural Develt, NI, 1999–2002. Contested (SDLP) Tyrone West, 2001. *Recreations:* reading, music, golf. *Address:* 34 Kilmore Road, Lurgan, Co. Armagh BT67 9BP.

RODGERS, Derek; *see* Rodgers, R. F.

RODGERS, Joan, CBE 2001; soprano; *b* 4 Nov. 1956; *d* of Thomas and Julia Rodgers; *m* 1988, Paul Daniel, *qv*; two *d*. *Educ:* Univ. of Liverpool (BA Hons Russian); RNCM. FRNCM. Kathleen Ferrier Meml Scholarship, 1981. Début, Aix-en-Provence, 1982; Covent Garden début, 1984; NY Met. début, 1995; has appeared with all major British opera cos; has worked with many conductors, incl. Barenboim, Solti, Abbado, Rattle, Gardiner, Colin Davis, Andrew Davis, Salonen, Mehta, Harnoncourt; Mozart rôles incl. Susanna, Zerlina, Ilia, Fiordiligi, Elvira, Sandrina, Countess; other rôles incl. Cleopatra in Giulio Cesare, Ginevra in Ariodante, Tatyana in Eugene Onegin, Mélisande, Theodora, Governess in The Turn of the Screw, Marschallin in Der Rosenkavalier, Blanche in The Carmelites; regular recitals and concert performances in London, Australia, Vienna, Madrid, Los Angeles, New York, Chicago, Paris and Brussels; many recordings. *Recreations:* walking, spending time with my family. *Address:* c/o Ingpen & Williams Ltd, 7 St George's Court, 131 Putney Bridge Road, SW15 2PA.

RODGERS, Dr Patricia Elaine Joan; Permanent Secretary, Ministry of Foreign Affairs, Commonwealth of the Bahamas, since 2003; *b* 13 July 1948; *d* of late Dr Kenneth V. A. Rodgers, OBE and Anatol C. Rodgers, MBE. *Educ:* Univ. of Aberdeen (MA Hons English, 1970); Inst. of Internat. Relations, St Augustine, Trinidad (Dip. in Internat. Relns (Hons) 1972); Inst. Univ. des Hautes Etudes Internationales, Geneva (PhD 1977). Joined Ministry of Foreign Affairs, Nassau, Bahamas, 1970; Minister-Counsellor, Washington, 1978–83; Actg High Comr to Canada, 1983–86, High Comr, 1986–88; High Comr to UK, 1988–92, also Ambassador (non-resident) to: FRG and Belgium, 1988–92, to EC and France, 1989–92; Perm. Rep. to IMO, 1991–92; Chief of Protocol, Min. of For. Affairs, 1993–94; Perm. Sec., Min. of Tourism, 1995–2003. *Publication:* Mid-Ocean Archipelagos and International Law: a study of the progressive development of international law, 1981. *Recreations:* folk painting, gourmet cooking, theatre. *Address:* Ministry of Foreign Affairs, East Hill Street, PO Box N3746, Nassau, Bahamas.

RODGERS, Sir Piers; *see* Rodgers, Sir A. P. W.

RODGERS, Robert Frederick, (Derek); His Honour Judge Rodgers; a County Court Judge, Northern Ireland, since 1997; *b* 10 June 1947; *s* of Fred and Peggy Rodgers; *m* 1973, Kathleen Mary Colling; one *s* one *d*. *Educ:* Royal Belfast Academical Instn; Queen's Univ., Belfast (LLB 1970). J. C. Taylor & Co., solicitors, 1970–90; a District Judge, 1989–97. Life Sentence Review Comr, 2002–. Mem., Legal Adv. Cttee, C of I, 2002–. Chancellor, Diocese of Connor, 2008–. *Recreations:* reading, music, Rugby, sailing. *Address:* c/o Laganside Courts, PO Box 413, 45 Oxford Street, Belfast BT1 3LL. *T:* (028) 9032 8594, *Fax:* (028) 9031 5219; *e-mail:* drodgers.rcj@courtsni.gov.uk. *Clubs:* Ulster Reform; Carrickfergus Sailing; Ballymena Rugby Football.

RODLEY, Sir Nigel (Simon), KBE 1998; PhD; Professor of Law, University of Essex, since 1994; *b* 1 Dec. 1941; *s* of John Peter Rodley (*né* Hans Israel Rosenfeld) and Rachel Rodley (*née* Kantorowitz); *m* 1967, Lyn Bates. *Educ:* Clifton Coll.; Univ. of Leeds (LLB 1963); Columbia Univ. (LLM 1965); New York Univ. (LLM 1970); Univ. of Essex (PhD 1993). Asst Prof. of Law, Dalhousie Univ., 1965–68; Associate Economic Affairs Officer, UN HQ, NY, 1968–69; Vis. Lectr in Pol Sci., New Sch. for Social Res., NY, 1969–72; Res. Fellow, NY Univ. Center for Internat. Studies, 1970–72; Founder and Hd, Legal Office, Amnesty Internat., 1973–90; Vis. Lectr in Law, 1973–90, Res. Fellow, 1983, LSE; Reader in Law, Univ. of Essex, 1990–94. Dist. Vis. Scholar, Grad. Sch. of Internat. Studies, Univ. of Denver, 2002. Special Rapporteur on Torture, UN Commn on Human Rights, 1993–2001; Member: UN Human Rights Cttee, 2001– (Vice-Chm., 2003–04); Internat. Indep. Gp of Observers, Sri Lankan Commn of Inquiry, 2007–08. Comr, Internat. Commn of Jurists, 2003– (Exec. Cttee, 2004–06). Hon. FFFLM 2008. Hon. LLD Dalhousie, 2000. Goler T. Butcher Human Rights Medal, Amer. Soc. of Internat. Law, 2005. *Publications:* (ed jtly) International Law in the Western Hemisphere, 1974; (jtly) Enhancing Global Human Rights, 1979; The Treatment of Prisoners under International Law, 1987, 2nd edn 1999; (ed) To Loose the Bands of Wickedness: international intervention in defence of human rights, 1992; (ed jtly) International Responses to Traumatic Stress, 1996; numerous articles in learned jls and contribs to books. *Recreations:* music, theatre, cinema, crosswords, walking. *Address:* Department of Law, University of Essex, Wivenhoe Park, Colchester CO4 3SQ. *T:* (01206) 872562; (home) 1 Meyrick Crescent, Colchester CO2 7QX. *T:* (01206) 570732.

RODNEY, family name of **Baron Rodney**.

RODNEY, 10th Baron *cr* 1782; **George Brydges Rodney;** Bt 1764; *b* 3 Jan. 1953; *o s* of 9th Baron Rodney and Régine (*d* 2003), *d* of Chevalier Pangaert d'Opdorp, Belgium; *S* father, 1992; *m* 1996, Jane, *d* of Hamilton Rowan Blakeney; one *s*. *Educ:* Eton. *Heir: s* Hon. John George Brydges Rodney, *b* 5 July 1999. *Address:* 38 Pembroke Road, W8 6NU.

RODRIGUES, Sir Alberto, Kt 1966; CBE 1964 (OBE 1960; MBE (mil.) 1948); ED; Senior Unofficial Member Executive Council, Hong Kong, 1964–74; former Pro-Chancellor and Chairman of Executive Council, University of Hong Kong; *b* 5 Nov. 1911; *s* of late Luiz Gonzaga Rodrigues and Giovanina Remedios; *m* 1940, Cynthia Maria da Silva; one *s* two *d*. *Educ:* St Joseph's College and University of Hong Kong. MB BS Univ. of Hong Kong, 1934; FRCPE 1988. Post graduate work, London and Lisbon, 1935–36; Medical Practitioner, 1937–40; also Medical Officer in Hong Kong Defence Force. POW, 1940–45. Medical Practitioner, 1945–50; Post graduate work, New York, 1951–52; Resident, Winnipeg Maternity Hosp. (Canada), 1952–53; General Medical Practitioner, Hong Kong, 1953. Member: Urban Council (Hong Kong), 1940–41; 1947–50; Legislative Council, 1953–60; Executive Council, 1960–74. Med. Superintendent, St Paul's Hospital, 1953. Director: Jardine Strategic Hldgs (formerly Jardine Securities), 1969; Lap Heng Co. Ltd, 1970; HK & Shanghai Hotels Ltd, 1969; Peak Tramways Co. Ltd, 1971; Li & Fung Ltd, 1973; HK Commercial Broadcasting Co. Ltd, 1974; Hong Kong and Shanghai Banking Corporation, 1974–76. Officer, Ordem de Cristo (Portugal), 1949; Chevalier, Légion d'Honneur (France), 1962; Knight Grand Cross, Order of St Sylvester (Vatican), 1966. *Recreations:* cricket, hockey, tennis, swimming, badminton. *Address:* c/o University of Hong Kong, Pokfulam Road, Hong Kong. *Clubs:* Hong Kong Jockey, Hong Kong Country, Lusitano, Recreio (all Hong Kong).

RODRIGUES, Christopher John, CBE 2007; Chairman: VisitBritain, since 2007; International Personal Finance, since 2007; *b* 24 Oct. 1949; *s* of late Alfred John Rodrigues and of Joyce Margaret Rodrigues (*née* Farron-Smith); *m* 1976, Priscilla Purcell Young; one *s* one *d*. *Educ:* University College Sch.; Jesus Coll., Cambridge (BA Econs and Hist.; Pres., Cambridge Univ. Boat Club, 1971; rowing Blue, 1970 and 1971); Harvard Business Sch. (Baker Scholar; MBA 1976). With Spillers Foods, London, 1971–72; Foster Turner & Benson, London, 1972–74; McKinsey & Co., London, 1976–79; American Express, NY and London, 1979–88; Thos Cook Gp, 1988–95 (Chief Exec., 1992–95); Gp Chief Exec., Bradford & Bingley Bldg Soc., subseq. plc, 1996–2004; Chief Exec., Visa Internat., San Francisco, 2004–06. Non-executive Director: Energis PLC, 1997–2002; Hilton Gp, 2003–06; Ladbrokes plc, 2006–. Non-exec. Dir, FSA, 1997–2003. Mem. Exec. Cttee, NT, 1994–2004. Chm., Windsor Leadership Trust, 2007–. FRSA 1994. Steward, Henley Royal Regatta, 1998–. *Recreations:* cooking, ski-ing, rowing, shooting, opera, ballet. *Address:* VisitBritain, Thames Tower, Black's Road, W6 9EL. *T:* (020) 8563 3018. *Clubs:* Arts; Leander Rowing (former Chm.) (Henley); Hawks (Cambridge); Century (Harvard); Brook (NY).

RODRÍGUEZ-POSE, Prof. Andrés, PhD; Professor of Economic Geography, London School of Economics and Political Science, since 2004; *b* Madrid, 9 June 1966; *s* of José Luis and Josefina; *m* 1997, Leticia Verdú; one *s* one *d*. *Educ:* Complutense Univ. of Madrid (BA Geog. and Hist. 1989; PhD *summa cum laude* Geog. 1993); Universidad Nacional de Educación a Distancia (LLB Law 1991); Inst. of European Studies, Brussels (MSc dist. Eur. Studies 1991); European University Inst., Florence (PhD with dist. Soc. and Pol Scis 1996). Res. Dir, Cabinet for Planning and Spatial Develt, Galician Regl Govt, 1994–95; Lectr, 1995–2000, Sen. Lectr, 2000–02, Reader, 2002–04, in Econ. Geog., LSE. Vis. Prof. on Growth and Cohesion, College of Europe, Bruges, 2004–. Sec., Eur. Regl Sci. Assoc., 2001–06. Member, Board of Trustees: Internat. Centre for Advanced Econ. and Soc. Studies, Madrid, 2005–; Madrid Inst. for Advanced Studies, 2006–; Enterprise LSE Ltd, 2006–. Man. Ed., Envmt and Planning C: Govt and Policy, 2008–. Gill Meml Award, RGS, 2001. *Publications:* Reestructuración socioeconómica y desequilibrios regionales en la Unión Europea, 1995; The Dynamics of Regional Growth in Europe: social and political factors, 1998; The European Union: economy, society, and polity, 2002 (L'Unione Europea: economia, politica e società, 2003); (jtly) Local and Regional Development, 2006; more than 60 articles in learned jls. *Recreations:* reading, spending time with family and friends, swimming, listening to music (especially classical, R&B, rock, disco, funk). *Address:* Department of Geography and Environment, London School of Economics, Houghton Street, WC2A 2AE. *T:* (020) 7955 7971, *Fax:* (020) 7955 7412; *e-mail:* a.rodriguez-pose@lse.ac.uk.

RODRÍGUEZ IGLESIAS, Gil Carlos; Professor of International Public Law, Madrid Complutense University, since 2003; Director, Real Instituto Elcano, Madrid, since 2005; *b* 26 May 1946; *m* 1972, Teresa Díez Gutiérrez; two *d*. *Educ:* Oviedo Univ. (LLL 1968); Madrid Autonomous Univ. (doctorate 1975). Internat. law asst, then Lectr, Oviedo, Freiburg, Madrid Autonomous and Madrid Complutense Univs, 1969–82; Professor: Madrid Complutense Univ., 1982–83; Granada Univ., 1983–2003 (on leave 1986–2003); Judge, EC Court of Justice, 1986–2003; Pres., Court of Justice of Eur. Communities, 1994–2003. Hon. Bencher: Gray's Inn, 1995; King's Inns, Dublin, 1997. Hon. Dr: Univ. of Turin, 1996; Univ. of Babes-Bolyai' Cluj-Napoca, Romania, 1996; Univ. of Saarbrücken, Germany, 1997; Univ. of Oviedo, 2001; St Clement of Ohrid Univ. of Sofia, 2002; Hon. Dip. Romanian Acad., 2002. Walter-Hallstein Prize, City of Frankfurt, Johann-Wolfgang-Goethe Univ. of Frankfurt, and Dresdner Bank, 2003. Encomienda de la Orden de Isabel la Católica (Spain), 1976; Cruz de Honor de la Orden de San Raimundo de Peñafort (Spain), 1986; Gran Cruz, Orden del Mérito Civil (Spain), 1999; Grand Cross: Order of the Phoenix (Greece), 2001; Nat. Order of Star (Romania), 2002; Order of Merit (Luxembourg), 2004; Order of Isabel la Católica (Spain), 2005; Grande Ufficiale, Ordine al Merito (Italy), 2002. *Publications:* El régimen juridico de los monopolios de Estado en la Comunidad Económica Europea, 1976; various articles and studies on EC law and internat. law. *Address:* Faculty of Law, Madrid Complutense University, 28040 Madrid, Spain.

RODRÍGUEZ ZAPATERO, José Luis; Prime Minister of Spain, since 2004; *b* 4 Aug. 1960; *m*; two *d*. *Educ:* Univ. of León (Law Degree). Mem. (PSOE) for León, Congress of Deputies, 1986–. Sec. Gen., Socialist Fedn of León, 1988–2000; Pres., Socialist Parly Gp, Congress of Deputies, 2000–04; Vice-Pres., Socialist Internat., 2003. Mem., PSOE, 1979–, Sec. Gen., 2000–. *Address:* Presidencia del Gobierno, Complejo de la Moncloa, 28071 Madrid, Spain. *T:* (91) 3353535, *Fax:* (91) 3900217; *e-mail:* jlrzapatero@presidencia.gob.es.

RODWAY, Susan Caroline; QC 2002; *m* Dr Vanya Gant; two *s* two *d*. *Educ:* Cheltenham Ladies' Coll.; King's Coll., London (BA Hons); City Univ. (Dip. in Law). Accredited Mediator, 2000. Called to the Bar, Middle and Inner Temple, 1981. Mem., Clinical Standards Cttee, Guy's and St Thomas's NHS Trust, 1998–2001. Dep. Chm., NHS Tribunals, 2000–04. Mem., Professional Negligence Cttee, 2001–, and Personal Injuries Cttee, Bar Assoc. *Publications include:* (contrib.) Application of Neural Networks in Clinical Practice, 2000. *Recreations:* motorcycling, riding. *Address:* 39 Essex Street, WC2R 3AT; *e-mail:* susan.rodway@39essex.com.

RODWELL, His Honour Daniel Alfred Hunter, QC 1982; a Circuit Judge, 1986–2002; *b* 3 Jan. 1936; *s* of late Brig. R. M. Rodwell, AFC, and Nellie Barbara Rodwell (*née* D'Costa); *m* 1967, Veronica Ann Cecil; two *s* one *d*. *Educ:* Munro Coll., Jamaica; Worcester Coll., Oxford, 1956–59 (BA Law). National service, 1954–56; 2/Lieut 1st West Yorks, PWO, 1955; TA, 1956–67: Captain and Adjt 3 PWO, 1964–67. Called to Bar, Inner Temple, 1960. A Deputy Circuit Judge, 1977 and 2002–05; a Recorder, 1980–86. *Recreations:* gardening, sailing. *Address:* Roddimore House, Winslow Road, Great Horwood, Milton Keynes MK17 0NY.

RODWELL, Dr Warwick James, FSA, FSAScot, FRHistS; consultant archaeologist and architectural historian; *b* 24 Oct. 1946; *s* of late George and Olive Rodwell; *m* 1st, 1972, Kirsty Gomer (marr. diss. 1983); 2nd, 1984, Christine Bensted (marr. diss. 1999); 3rd, 2004, Diane Marie Gibbs. *Educ:* Southend High Sch. for Boys; Univ. of Nottingham (teaching cert. and dip. 1968); Univ. of London (BA Hons 1972; DLit 1998); Worcester Coll., Oxford (DPhil 1976; DLitt 1992); Univ. of Birmingham (MA 1979). FSAScot 1965; FSA 1977; FRHistS 1992. Res. Asst, MPBW, 1968–69; Dir, Cttee for Rescue Archaeol. in Avon, Glos and Somerset, 1975–81. Vis. Prof. in Archaeol., Univ. of Reading, 2002–. Consultant Archaeologist: Glastonbury Abbey, 1976–2005; Bristol Cath., 1976–; Wells Cath., 1977–; Lichfield Cath., 1982–; Westminster Abbey, 2004–. Directed major res. projs and/or excavations at Westminster Abbey, Dorchester Abbey, Lichfield Cath., Wells Cath. and parish churches at Barton-upon-Humber, Hadstock, Kellington and Rivenhall; directed res. and excavation campaigns in Jersey at Mont Orgueil Castle, Elizabeth Castle, Les Ecréhous Priory, St Lawrence Ch, St Helier Ch, Fishermen's Chapel and Hamptonne Farm. Member: Council for the Care of Churches, 1976–86; Cathedrals Adv. Commn, 1981–90; Cathedrals Fabric Commn for England, 1991–96; Member, Fabric Advisory Committee: Salisbury Cath., 1987–2006; Exeter Cath., 1999–2006. Mem., Coll. of Westminster Abbey, 2008–. Pres., Bristol and Gloucester Archaeol. Soc., 1999–2000. Trustee, Bath Archaeol. Trust, 1976–2005. Hon. Mem., La Société Jersiaise, 1998. Frend Medal, Soc. of Antiquaries, 1988. *Publications:* Small Towns of Roman Britain (with T. Rowley), 1975; Historic Churches: a wasting asset, 1977; Temples, Churches and Religion in Roman Britain, 1980; Archaeology of the English Church, 1981, 3rd edn 2005; (with J. Bentley) Our Christian Heritage, 1984; (with K. Rodwell) Rivenhall: investigations of a villa, church and village, vol. 1 1985, vol. 2 1993; The Fishermen's Chapel, Jersey, 1996; Origins and Early Development of Witham, Essex, 1993; Les Ecréhous, Jersey, 1996; (with M. Paton and O. Finch) La Hougue Bie, Jersey, 1999; Archaeology of Wells Cathedral, 2001; Westminster Abbey Chapter House and Pyx Chamber, 2002; Church Archaeology, 2005; Mont Orgueil Castle, Jersey, 2006; (with G. Leighton) Architectural Records of Wells by John Carter 1784–1808, 2006; numerous contribs to learned jls and multi-author vols. *Recreations:* visiting historic buildings, horology, bibliophilia. *Address:* 2c Little Cloister, Westminster Abbey, SW1P 3PA.

RODWELL, Sheila Anne; *see* Bingham, S. A.

ROE, Anthony Maitland, DPhil; CChem, FRSC; Executive Secretary, Council of Science and Technology Institutes, 1987–94; *b* 13 Dec. 1929; *s* of late Percy Alex Roe and Flora Sara Roe (*née* Kisch); *m* 1958, Maureen, *d* of late William James Curtayne and of Kathleen (*née* Wigfull); two *s* one *d*. *Educ:* Harrow Sch.; Oriel Coll., Oxford (BA, MA, DPhil). ARIC 1955; FRSC, CChem 1976. Commnd Intell. Corps, 1955–57. Univ. of Rochester, NY, 1957–59; Sen. Chemist, Smith Kline & French Res. Inst., 1959–65; Hd of Chemistry Gp, Smith Kline & French Labs Ltd, 1965–78; Dir of Chemistry, Smith Kline & French Res. Ltd, 1978–86. Royal Society of Chemistry: Mem. Council, 1982–85, 1987–91; Vice-Pres., Perkin Div., 1986–88; Chm., Heterocyclic Gp, 1986–88; Chm., 'Chemistry in Britain' Management Cttee, 1987–91. Founder Cttee Mem., Soc. for Drug Res., 1966–77; Member: Bd for Science, BTEC, 1985–88; Parly and Scientific Cttee, 1987–94. Chm., Welwyn Hatfield CAB, 1996–2000. *Publications:* research papers, patents and reviews in field of organic and medicinal chem. *Recreations:* travel, walking, good food and wine. *Address:* 10 Lodge Drive, Hatfield, Herts AL9 5HN. *T:* (01707) 265075.

ROE, Chang Hee; Senior Advisor, Federation of Korean Industries, 1998–2003; *b* 25 Feb. 1938; *m* 1963, Chung Ja Lee; one *s* one *d*. *Educ:* Seoul Nat. Univ., Korea (BA Econ 1960). Joined Min. of Foreign Affairs, 1960: Instructor ROK Air Force Acad., 1962–66; Dir of Legal Affairs, 1968–69; First Sec., Korean Embassy, Canada, 1969–72; Private Sec. to Minister of Foreign Affairs, 1972–73; Dir, Treaties Div., 1973–75; Counsellor, Sweden, 1975–78; Dep. Dir-Gen., American Affairs Bureau, 1978–80; Dir-Gen., Treaties Bureau, 1980–82; Minister and Dep. Chief of Mission, USA, 1982–85; Ambassador to Nigeria, 1985–88; Sen. Protocol Sec. to Pres., 1988–91; Ambassador and Perm. Rep. to UN, 1991–92; Vice Minister of Foreign Affairs, 1992–93; Ambassador to UK, 1993–96; Ambassador at Large, 1996–98. Guest Prof., Hanseo Univ., Korea, 1998–2001. Gov., Asia Europe Foundn, 2001–. *Recreations:* golf, ski-ing. *Address:* Hanyang Apt 62–606, Apkujong-dong, Kangnam-gu, Seoul 135–110, Korea.

ROE, David John, CBE 2001; Director, Change, Department for Culture, Media and Sport, since 2007; *b* 26 Nov. 1958; *s* of Malcolm Roe and Pauline Roe (*née* Baker); partner, Alison Mary Sharpe; one *s*. *Educ:* Selwyn Coll., Cambridge (BA 1981); Queen Mary Coll., London (MA 1983). Export Credits Guarantee Dept, 1983–85; DTI, 1985–92; HM Treasury, 1992–2000: Hd, Internat. Financial Instns, 1994–97; Hd, Financial Regulatory Reform, 1997–2000; on secondment to Charities Aid Foundn, 2001–02; Prime Minister's Strategy Unit, 2002–03; Hd, Strategy, Policy and Delivery, 2003–05, Dir, Strategy, 2005–07, DCMS. UK Alternate Dir (pt-time), EBRD, 1995–97. Parent Gov., Fielding Primary Sch., 2005–. Mem., ICA. *Recreations:* playing the saxophone, watching Brentford Football Club, seaside holidays, books. *Address:* Department for Culture, Media and Sport, 2–4 Cockspur Street, SW1Y 5DH. *T:* (020) 7211 6026, *Fax:* (020) 7211 6508; *e-mail:* david.roe@culture.gsi.gov.uk.

ROE, Geoffrey Eric; Director, Air Tanker Ltd, 2000–03 (Chairman, 2002–03); *b* 20 July 1944; *s* of Herbert William Roe and Florence Roe (*née* Gordon); *m* 1968, Elizabeth Anne Ponton; one *s* one *d*. *Educ:* Tottenham Grammar School. Min. of Aviation, 1963; Finance (R&D) Br., 1963–67; Asst Private Sec. to Sir Ronald Melville, 1967–69; Exports and Internat. Relations Div., Min. of Technology, 1969–74; Guided Weapons Contracts Branch, 1974–76; seconded British Aerospace, 1976–78; Rocket Motor Exec., 1978–81; Asst Dir Contracts (Air), 1981–86; Dir of Contracts (Underwater Weapons), 1986–89; Head, Material Co-ord. (Naval), 1989–90; Principal Dir, Navy and Nuclear Contracts, 1990–91; Director-General: Defence Contracts, MoD, 1991–95; Commercial, MoD, 1995; Aircraft Systems 2, 1995–96. Man. Dir, FR Aviation Gp (formerly FR Aviation Ltd), 1997–2002; Director: Cobham plc, 1997–2002; FR Aviation Services Ltd, 2000–02; FBS Ltd, 2000–02; FBH Ltd, 2000–02. Chm., Nat. Jet Systems, Australia, and Nat. Air Support, Australia, 2000–02. Dir, SBAC, 1998–2000. *Recreations:* ski-ing, fell-walking, sailing, private flying. *Address:* Pond Barton, Norton St Philip, Bath BA2 7NE. *Club:* Lymington Town Sailing.

ROE, Prof. Howard Stanley James, DSc; Director, Southampton Oceanography Centre, NERC and the University of Southampton, 1999–2005; Professor, University of Southampton, since 2000; *b* 23 May 1943; *s* of Eric James Roe and Freda Mary Roe (*née* Perkins); *m* 1970, Heather Anne Snelling; one *s* two *d. Educ:* Bedford Sch.; University Coll. London (BSc 1st Cl. Hons Zool. 1965; DSc Biol Oceanography 1998). Natural Environment Research Council: Scientific Officer, Whale Res. Unit, 1965–68; transferred to Biol. Dept, Nat. Inst. Oceanography, 1968; Project Co-ordinator for develt of Southampton Oceanography Centre, 1989–95; Hd, George Deacon Div., Inst. Oceanographic Scis, later Southampton Oceanography Centre, 1993–99 (Dep. Dir, 1997–99). Chairman: NERC Project Bd, RRS James Cook, 2002–07; Partnership for Observing the Global Ocean, 2003–05; DEFRA Science Audit of CEFAS, 2005–06. Member: Council for Ocean Policy Studies, Ship and Ocean Foundn, Japan, 2003–; Natural Scis Adv. Gp, English Nature, 2003–05. Chm., Ext. Rev. Cttee, Seoul Nat. Univ., 2002–. Mem., Challenger Soc. for Marine Sci. FIMarEST, 2003. *Publications:* contrib. numerous papers and reports to jls, etc, dealing with whale biology, biological oceanography and develt of sampling technol. *Recreations:* fishing, gardening, travel, amateur dramatics. *Address:* National Oceanography Centre Southampton, Empress Dock, Southampton SO14 3ZH; Barton Mere, Barton Court Avenue, New Milton, Hants BH25 7HD. *T:* (01425) 622092. *Club:* Christchurch Angling.

ROE, James Kenneth; Chairman, New Star Investment Trust, since 2005; Director, Jupiter International (formerly Jupiter Tyndall) Group, 1993–2000; Member, Monopolies and Mergers Commission, 1993–99; *b* 28 Feb. 1935; *s* of late Kenneth Alfred Roe and Zirphie Norah Roe (*née* Luke); *m* 1958, Marion Audrey Keyte (*see* Dame M. A. Roe); one *s* two *d. Educ:* King's Sch., Bruton. National Service commn, RN, 1953–55. Joined N. M. Rothschild & Sons, 1955; Director, 1970–92. Chm., China Investment Trust, 1993–98; Dep. Chm., Innovations Gp (formerly Kleeneze Holdings), 1985–96; Director: Rothschild Trust Corp., 1970–95; Jupiter European Investment Trust, 1990–2000; GAM Selection Inc., 1992–2005; Ronson (formerly Halkin Holdings), 1993–98 (Chm., 1993–97); Microvitec, 1993–97; JP Morgan Fleming (formerly Fleming) Income and Capital Investment Trust, 1995–2006; Whitehall Fund Managers Ltd, 1998–2000; Principle Capital Investment Trust, 2005–. FRSA 1991; FInstD 1993. *Recreations:* walking, reading, theatre, opera. *Clubs:* Brooks's, MCC.

ROE, Dame Marion (Audrey), DBE 2004; *b* 15 July 1936; *d* of William Keyte and Grace Mary (*née* Bocking); *m* 1958, James Kenneth Roe, *qv*; one *s* two *d. Educ:* Bromley High Sch. (GPDST); Croydon High Sch. (GPDST); English Sch. of Languages, Vevey, Switzerland. Member: London Adv. Cttee, IBA, 1978–81; Gatwick Airport Consultative Cttee, 1979–81; SE Thames RHA, 1980–83. Member (C): Bromley Borough Council, 1975–78; for Ilford N, GLC, 1977–86 (Cons. Dep. Chief Whip, 1978–82). Contested (C) Barking, 1979; MP (C) Broxbourne, 1983–2005. Parly Private Secretary to: Parly Under-Secs of State for Transport, 1985; Minister of State for Transport, 1986; Sec. of State for Transport, 1987; Parly Under Sec. of State, DoE, 1987–88. Member, Select Committee: on Agriculture, 1983–85; on Social Services, 1988–89; on Procedure, 1990–92; on Sittings of the House, 1991–92; Chairman: Select Cttee on Health, 1992–97 (Mem., 1988–89, 2000–01); H of C Admin. Cttee, 1997–2005 (Mem., 1991–97); Mem., Speaker's Panel of Chairmen, 1997–2005. Vice Chairman: All-Party Fairs and Showgrounds Gp, 1992–2005 (Jt Chm., 1989–92); All-Party Parly Garden Club, 1995–2005; All-Party Gp on Alcohol Misuse, 1997–2005; All-Party Gp on Domestic Violence, 1999–2005; Chairman: All-Party Hospice Gp, 1992–2005 (Sec., 1990–92); Jt Chm., All-Party Gp on Breast Cancer, 1997–2005; Mem., UNICEF Parly Adv. Cttee, 2002–05; Chairman: Cons. Back bench Horticulture and Markets Sub-Cttee, 1989–97 (Sec., 1983–85); Cons. Back bench Social Security Cttee, 1990–97 (Vice-Chm., 1988–90); Vice-Chairman: Cons. Back bench Environment Cttee, 1990–97; Cons. Parly Health Cttee, 1997–99; 1922 Cttee, 2001–05 (Mem. Exec., 1992–94; Sec., 1997–2001); Sec., Cons. Back bench Horticulture Cttee, 1983–85; Jt Sec., Cons. Back bench Party Orgn Cttee, 1985; Vice-Chm., British-Canadian Parly Gp, 1997–2005 (Sec., 1991–97); Mem., Adv. Cttee on Women's Employment, Dept of Employment, 1989–92; Substitute Mem., UK Delegn to Parly Assemblies of Council of Europe and WEU, 1989–92; Mem., Exec. Cttee, UK Br., CPA, 1997–2005 (Vice Chm., 2002–03); Inter-Parliamentary Union: Mem. Exec. Cttee, British Gp, 1997–98, 2001–05 (Vice-Chm., 1998–2001); Mem., Internat. Panel on Prohibition of Female Genital Mutilation, 2002–05. Chm., Nat. Council for Child Health and Well-being (formerly Child Health Gp), 2001–; Vice-Pres., Women's Nationwide Cancer Control Campaign, 1985–87, 1988–2001; Patron: UK Nat. Cttee for UN Develt Fund for Women, 2004– (Mem., 1985–87); Hospice of Hope, Romania, Serbia and Moldova, 2005–; Gov., Research into Ageing Trust, 1988–97; Managing Trustee, Parly Contributory Pension Fund, 1990–97; Mem., Internat. Women's Forum, 1992–2005; Trustee, Nat. Benevolent Fund for the Aged, 1999–. Vice-President: Capel Manor Horticultural and Envmtl Centre, 1994– (Chm., Trust Fund, 1989–94). Hoddesdon Soc., 2005–. Patron, Broxbourne Parly Cons Assoc., 2006– (Pres., Women's Section, 1983–). Mem. Council, Wine Guild of the UK, 2007–. Fellow, Industry and Parlt Trust, 1990. Freeman: City of London, 1981; Borough of Broxbourne, 2005; Liveryman, Gardeners' Co., 1993–. Hon. MIHort 1993. *Recreations:* family, theatre, ballet, opera, travel.

ROE, Dame Raigh (Edith), DBE 1980 (CBE 1975); JP; Director, Airlines of Western Australia, 1981–90; World President, Associated Country Women of the World, 1977–80; *b* 12 Dec. 1922; *d* of Alwyn and Laura Kurts; *m* 1941, James Arthur Roe; three *s. Educ:* Perth Girls' Sch., Australia. Country Women's Association: State Pres., 1967–70; National Pres., 1969–71. World Ambassador, WA Council, 1978–; Hon. Ambassador, State of Louisiana, USA, 1979–. Comr, ABC, 1978–83; Nat. Dir (Aust.), Queen Elizabeth II Silver Jubilee Trust for Young Australians, 1978–94. JP Western Australia, 1966. Australian of the Year, 1977; Brooch of Merit, Deutscher Landfrauenverband, Fed. Republic of Germany, 1980.

ROE, William Deas; Chairman: Highlands and Islands Enterprise, since 2004; Skills Development Scotland, since 2008; *b* Perth, Scotland, 9 July 1947. *Educ:* Edinburgh Univ. (BSc). Chm., Rocket Sci. UK Ltd, 2004–. Scotland Comr, UK Commn for Employment and Skills, 2008–. Vice Chm., Pension, Disability and Carers Service, DWP, 2008–. FRSA. *Recreations:* sailing, ski-ing, hill-walking, visual arts, music, travel. *Address:* 3A Northumberland Street, Edinburgh EH3 6LL. *T:* 07771 930880.

ROEBUCK, Roy Delville; barrister-at-law; *b* Manchester, 25 Sept. 1929; *m* 1957, Dr Mary Ogilvy Adams (*d* 1995); one *s. Educ:* various newspapers; Inns of Court Sch. of Law; Univ. of Leicester (LLM 1997; MA 2000). Called to the Bar, Gray's Inn, 1974. Served RAF (National Service), 1948–50 (wireless operator, FEAF). Journalist, Stockport Advertiser, Northern Daily Telegraph, Yorkshire Evening News, Manchester Evening Chronicle, News Chronicle, Daily Express, Daily Mirror and Daily Herald, and Asst Ed., Forward, 1950–66; freelance journalist, 1966–; columnist, London Evening News, 1968–70. Contested (Lab): Altrincham and Sale, 1964 and Feb. 1965; Leek, Feb. 1974. MP (Lab) Harrow East, 1966–70; Member, Select Committee: on Estimates, 1968–70; on Parly Comr, 1968–70; PA to Rt Hon. George Wigg, Paymaster-Gen., 1966–67; Advr to Lord Wigg, Pres. of Betting Office Licensees Assoc., 1975–83. Founder Mem., Labour Common Market Safeguards Cttee, 1967. Member: Islington CHC, 1988–92; Bd of Governors, Moorfields Eye Hospital, 1984–88. Fellow, Atlantic Council, 1993–. Governor, Thornhill Sch., Islington, 1986–88. *Recreations:* tennis, ski-ing, music, reading Hansard and the public prints. *Address:* 12 Brooksby Street, N1 1HA. *T:* (020) 7607 7057; Bell Yard Chambers, 116–118 Chancery Lane, WC2A 1PP. *T:* (020) 7306 9292. *Clubs:* Royal Automobile, Victory Services.

ROEG, Nicolas Jack, CBE 1996; film director; *b* 15 Aug. 1928; *s* of Jack Roeg and Gertrude Silk; *m* 1st, 1957, Susan (marr. diss.), *d* of Major F. W. Stephen, MC; four *s*; 2nd, Theresa Russell; two *s. Educ:* Mercers' Sch. Fellow, BFI, 1994–. Original story of Prize of Arms; Cinematographer: The Caretaker, 1963; Masque of the Red Death, 1964; Nothing But the Best, 1964; A Funny Thing Happened on the Way to the Forum, 1966; Fahrenheit 451, 1966; Far From the Madding Crowd, 1967; Petulia, 1968, etc; 2nd Unit Director and Cinematographer: Lawrence of Arabia, 1962; Judith, 1965; Co-Dir, Performance, 1968; Director: Walkabout, 1970; Don't Look Now, 1972; The Man who Fell to Earth, 1975; Bad Timing, 1979; Eureka, 1983; Insignificance, 1985; Castaway, 1986; Track 29, 1987; Aria, 1987; Sweet Bird of Youth, 1989; Witches, 1990; Cold Heaven, 1991; Heart of Darkness, 1993; Two Deaths, Hotel Paradise, Full Body Massage, 1995; Samson and Delilah, 1996; (also writer) The Sound of Claudia Schiffer, 2000; Puffball, 2007; Exec. Producer, Without You I'm Nothing, 1989; writer of screenplays: Ivanhoe, Kiss of Life, 1999; Night Train, 2001; (with Andrew Hislop) History Play, 2004–05. Hon. Prof. of Film Studies, Univ. of Exeter. Hon. DLitt Hull, 1995; Hon. DFA Brooklyn Coll., City Univ. of NY, 2003. *Address:* c/o Independent, 32 Tavistock Street, WC2E 7PB.

ROFF, Derek Michael, OBE 1972; HM Diplomatic Service, retired; *b* 1 Aug. 1932; *m* 1957, Diana Susette Barrow; three *s. Educ:* Royal Grammar Sch., Guildford; St Edmund Hall, Oxford (BA). National Service with The Cameronians (Scottish Rifles) and King's African Rifles, 1952–54. ICI Ltd, 1958–67; entered Foreign Office, 1967; Consul (Economic), Frankfurt, 1968; First Sec., UK Delegn to the European Communities, Brussels, 1970; Consul (Economic), Düsseldorf, 1973; First Sec., FCO, 1977; Counsellor, FCO, 1981–92. Regl Dir, BESO, 1993–97. Mem., Internat. Cttee, Leonard Cheshire, 1997–2005.

ROGAN, family name of **Baron Rogan**.

ROGAN, Baron *cr* 1999 (Life Peer), of Lower Iveagh in the county of Down; **Dennis Robert David Rogan;** Leader, Ulster Unionist Party in House of Lords, since 2001; President, Ulster Unionist Party, since 2004 (Chairman, 1996–2001; Hon. Secretary, 2001–04); *b* 30 June 1942; *s* of Robert Henderson Rogan and Florence Rogan; *m* 1968, Lorna Elizabeth Colgan; two *s. Educ:* Wallace High Sch., Lisburn; Belfast Inst. of Technol.; Open Univ. (BA). Moygashel Ltd, 1960–69; Wm Ewart & Co., 1969–72; Lamont Holdings plc, 1972–78; Chairman: (exec.) Associated Processors Ltd, 1985–; Stakeholder Communications Ltd, 2005–; Stakeholder Events Ltd, 2005–; Dep. Chm., Independent News & Media (Northern Ireland) Ltd, 2000–. Mem. Internat. Adv. Bd, Independent Newspapers, 2001–. Chm., Lisburn Unit of Mgt, Eastern Health Bd, 1984–85. Chairman: Ulster Young Unionist Council, 1968–69; S Belfast UU Constituency Assoc., 1992–96. Member: UK Br., CPA, 1999–; IPU, 2002–. Mem., Council, RFCA (NI), 2002–. Gov., Westminster Foundn for Democracy, 2005–. Patron, Somme Assoc., 2000–. *Recreations:* Rugby football, oriental carpets, shooting, gardening. *Address:* 31 Notting Hill, Belfast BT9 5NS. *T:* (028) 9066 2468. *Clubs:* Army and Navy; Ulster Reform (Belfast).

ROGAN, Rev. Canon John; Chaplain of St Mark's, Lord Mayor's Chapel, Bristol, 1999–2008; Canon Residentiary, 1983–93, and Chancellor, 1989–93, Bristol Cathedral (Precentor, 1983–89), Canon Emeritus since 1993; *b* 20 May 1928; *s* of William and Jane Rogan; *m* 1953, Dorothy Margaret Williams; one *s* one *d. Educ:* Manchester Central High School; St John's Coll., Univ. of Durham. BA 1949, MA 1951; DipTheol with distinction, 1954; BPhil 1981. Education Officer, RAF, 1949–52. Asst Curate, St Michael and All Angels, Ashton-under-Lyne, 1954–57; Chaplain, Sheffield Industrial Mission, 1957–61; Secretary, Church of England Industrial Cttee, 1961–66; Asst Secretary, Board for Social Responsibility, 1962–66; Vicar of Leigh, Lancs, 1966–78; Sec., Diocesan Bd for Social Responsibility, 1967–74, Chm. 1974–78; Rural Dean of Leigh, 1971–78; Hon. Canon of Manchester, 1975–78; Provost, St Paul's Cathedral, Dundee, 1978–83; Bishop's Adviser in Social Responsibility, dio. Bristol, 1983–93. *Publications:* (ed jtly) Principles of Church Reform: Thomas Arnold, 1962; (ed) Bristol Cathedral: history and architecture, 2000; Reading Roman Inscriptions, 2006. *Recreations:* medieval life, walking, music. *Address:* 84 Concorde Drive, Bristol BS10 6PX.

ROGÉ, Pascal; pianist; *b* Paris, 6 April 1951; two *s. Educ:* Paris Conservatoire. Débuts in Paris and London, 1969. Soloist with leading orchestras worldwide. Specialist in music of Ravel, Poulenc, Debussy and Satie. Numerous recordings. *Address:* c/o Balmer & Dixon Management AG, Kreuzstrasse 82, 8032 Zürich, Switzerland; c/o Clarion/Seven Muses, 47 Whitehall Park, N19 3TW.

ROGERS, family name of **Baron Rogers of Riverside**.

ROGERS OF RIVERSIDE, Baron *cr* 1996 (Life Peer), of Chelsea in the Royal Borough of Kensington and Chelsea; **Richard George Rogers,** CH 2008; Kt 1991; RA 1984 (ARA 1978); RIBA; architect; Chairman, Rogers Stirk Harbour + Partners (formerly Richard Rogers Architects Ltd), London and Tokyo; Director, River Cafe Restaurant, London; *b* 23 July 1933; *s* of Dada Geiringer and Nino Rogers; *m* 1st, 1961, Su Rogers; three *s*; 2nd, 1973, Ruth Elias (*see* Lady Rogers of Riverside); two *s. Educ:* Architectural Assoc. (AA Dipl.); Yale Univ. (MArch; Fulbright and Yale Scholar). Reith Lectr, 1995. Winner of numerous internat. competitions incl. for Centre Pompidou, Paris, 1971–77; Lloyd's HQ, City of London, 1978. Major internat. work includes: *masterplanning:* Royal Docks, London, 1984–86; Potsdamer Platz, Berlin, 1991; Shanghai Pu Dong District, 1994; Parc BIT, Mallorca, 1994; Dunkirk, 1998; E Manchester, 1999; Greenwich Peninsula, 2000; Singapore, 2001; Almada, Portugal, 2002; *airports and HQ buildings:* PA Technology, Cambridge, 1975–83; PA Technology, Princeton, NJ, 1984; Marseille Airport, 1992; Channel 4 HQ, London, 1994; European Court of Human Rights, Strasbourg, 1995; VR Techno offices and lab., Gifu, Japan, 1998; Daimler Chrysler, Berlin, 1999; Law Courts, Bordeaux, 1999; Millennium Experience, Greenwich, 1999; Montevetro Housing, Battersea, 2000; 88 Wood Street, London, 2000; Ashford Retail Designer Outlet, 2000; Lloyd's Register of Shipping, London, 2000; Broadwick Street, London, 2002; Nat. Assembly for Wales, Cardiff, 2005; New Area Terminal, Barajas Airport, Madrid, 2005 (Stirling Prize, 2006); Paddington Basin, London, 2005; Mossbourne Community Acad., Hackney, 2005; Law Courts, Antwerp, 2005; Terminal 5, Heathrow Airport, 2008. *Current projects include:* 122 Leadenhall Street, London;

Chelmsford Univ.; Bullring, Barcelona; L'Hospitalet Business Park, Barcelona; Silvercup Studios, NY; One Hyde Park, Knightsbridge, London; The Berkeley Hotel, London; Capodichino Tube Station, Naples; Jacob K. Javits Convention Centre, NY; Tower 3 on World Trade Centre site, NY. *Exhibitions worldwide include:* Royal Acad.; Mus. of Modern Art, NY; Louisiana Mus., Copenhagen. Teaching posts include: AA, London; Cambridge Univ.; Yale; UCLA. Chairman: Nat. Housing Tenants Resource Centre; Architecture Foundn, 1991–2001; Tate Gall. Trust, 1984–88; Govt Urban Task Force, 1998–2001; Vice-Chm., Arts Council of England, 1994–97; Mem., UN Architects' Cttee; Mem., Urban Strategies Adv. Council, Barcelona; Trustee: London First; UK Bd, Médecins du Monde. Hon. Mem., Royal Inst. of Architects, Scotland, 1999; Hon. FAIA 1986. Hon. Dr RCA. Royal Gold Medal for Arch., 1985; Thomas Jefferson Meml Foundn Medal in Architecture, 1999; Praemium Imperiale, 2000; Pritzker Prize, 2007. Chevalier de la Légion d'Honneur, France, 1986. Subject of several television documentaries and jl articles on architecture. *Publications:* Richard Rogers + Architects, 1985; A+U: Richard Rogers 1978–1988, 1988; Architecture: a modern view, 1990; (jtly) A New London, 1992; Cities for a Small Planet (Reith Lectures), 1997; Richard Rogers: the complete works, vol. 1, 1999, vol. 2, 2001, vol. 3, 2006; (with Anne Power) Cities for a Small Country, 2000; *relevant publications:* Richard Rogers, a biography, by Bryan Appleyard, 1986; Richard Rogers, by Kenneth Powell, 1994; The Architecture of Richard Rogers, by Deyan Sudjic, 1994; Richard Rogers Partnership, by Richard Burdett, 1995; Richard Rogers: architect of the future, by Kenneth Powell, 2006. *Recreations:* friends, art, architecture, travel, food. *Address:* (office) Thames Wharf, Rainville Road, W6 9HA. *T:* (020) 7385 1235.

See also P. W. Rogers.

ROGERS OF RIVERSIDE, Lady; Ruth Rogers; Chef and owner, River Cafe Restaurant, since 1987; *b* 2 July 1948; *d* of Frederick and Sylvia Elias; *m* 1973, Richard George Rogers (*see* Baron Rogers of Riverside); two *s*, and three step *s*. *Educ:* London Coll. of Printing (BA Hons Design). Penguin Books, 1970–73; Richard Rogers & Partners, 1973–87. *Publications:* with Rose Gray: River Cafe Cook Book, 1995; River Cafe Cook Book Two, 1997; Italian Kitchen, 1998; River Cafe Cook Book Green, 2000; River Cafe Cook Book Easy, 2003; River Cafe Two Easy, 2005. *Recreation:* ski-ing. *Address:* River Cafe Restaurant, Thames Wharf, Rainville Road, W6 9HA. *T:* (020) 7386 4200; *e-mail:* ruthrogers@rivercafe.co.uk.

ROGERS, Alan James, MA; Headmaster, Lodge International School, Kuching, Sarawak, Malaysia, since 2007; *b* 30 March 1946; *s* of William James Albert Rogers and Beatrice Gwendolyn Rogers (*née* Evans); *m* 1968, Sheila Follett; one *s* two *d*. *Educ:* Humphry Davy Grammar Sch., Penzance; Jesus Coll., Oxford (MA). Asst Master, Pangbourne Coll., 1969–73; Head of Geography and Geology, Arnold Sch., Blackpool, 1973–78; Head of Geography, Wellington Coll., 1978–82; Second Master and Dep. Headmaster, 1982–90, Headmaster, 1990–2006, Wellington Sch. *Publications:* articles on geographical educn in UK and Commonwealth jls. *Recreations:* alpine and rainforest environments, hockey, house restoration.

ROGERS, Alice; *see* Rogers, F. A.

ROGERS, Allan Ralph, FGS; *b* 24 Oct. 1932; *s* of John Henry Rogers and Madeleine Rogers (*née* Smith); *m* 1955, Ceridwen James; one *s* three *d*. *Educ:* University College of Swansea (BSc Hons Geology). Geologist, UK, Canada, USA, Australia, 1956–63; Teacher, 1963–65; Tutor-organiser, WEA, 1965–70, District Sec., 1970–79. Vis. Prof., Univ. of Glamorgan, 1997–. MP (Lab) Rhondda, 1983–2001. Opposition spokesman: on defence, 1987–92; on foreign affairs, 1992–94. Mem., Intelligence and Security Cttee, 1994–2001. European Parliament: Mem. (Lab) SE Wales, 1979–84; Vice-Pres., 1979–82. Non-exec. Dir, Buy As You View, 2001–. Bd Mem., British Geol Survey, 2001–05. Chm., Earth Sci. Educn Forum, 2002–. *Recreation:* all sports. *Address:* 8 Ingram Close, Juxon Street, SE11 6NN. *Club:* Workmen's (Treorchy).

ROGERS, Anthony Gordon; JP; **Hon. Mr Justice Rogers;** Vice-President of the Court of Appeal, Hong Kong, since 2000; *b* 16 Feb. 1946; *s* of late Gordon Victor Rogers and Olga Elena Rogers; *m* 1970, Barbara Ann Zimmern; one *s* two *d*. *Educ:* Beaumont Coll. Called to the Bar, Gray's Inn, 1969; practised at the Bar: London, 1970–76; Hong Kong, 1976–93; QC (Hong Kong) 1984; Judge of the High Court, 1993–97, Judge of the Court of Appeal, 1997–2000, Hong Kong. Chm., Hong Kong Bar Assoc., 1990, 1991. Mem., Basic Law Consultative Cttee, 1985–90; Chm., Standing Cttee on Company Law Reform, 1994–2004. JP Hong Kong 1988. Dir, 1992–, Sec., 1995–, Hong Kong China Rowing Assoc. *Recreations:* rowing, golf, music, keeping the family happy. *Address:* The Court of Appeal, The High Court, 38 Queensway, Hong Kong. *T:* 28254306, *Fax:* 25523327. *Clubs:* Thames Rowing, Sloane; Hong Kong, Hong Kong Country, Shek-O, Lion Rock Rowing (Hong Kong); Sydney Rowing.

ROGERS, Maj.-Gen. Anthony Peter Vernon, OBE 1985; law of war specialist; *b* 10 July 1942; *s* of Kenneth David Rogers and Eileen (*née* Emmott); *m* 1965, Anne-Katrin Margarethe, *d* of Dr Ewald Lembke; two *d*. *Educ:* Highgate Sch.; Coll. of Law; Liverpool Univ. (LLM 1994). Admitted Solicitor, 1965. Commnd as Capt., Army Legal Services, 1968; served HQ BAOR, Command Legal Aid Section, BAOR, MoD, SHAPE, HQ UKLF, 3 and 1 Armoured Divs; Col Army Legal Services 2, MoD, 1989–92; Brig. Legal, HQ BAOR, 1992–94; Dir, Army Legal Services, 1994–97, retd. Vice Pres., Internat. Soc. for Mil. Law and Law of War, 1994–97; Member: Internat. Inst. of Humanitarian Law, 1992–99 (Chm., Cttee for Mil. Instruction, 1993–97); Internat. Humanitarian Fact-Finding Commn, 2001–06 (Vice-Pres., 2004–06). Fellow: Lauterpacht Res. Centre for Internat. Law, Univ. of Cambridge, 1999– (Sen. Fellow, 2006–); Human Rights Centre, Univ. of Essex, 1999–2004 (Vis. Fellow, 2005–08); Yorke Dist. Vis. Fellow, Faculty of Law, Univ. of Cambridge, 2004. FRSA 1995. *Publications:* Law on the Battlefield, 1996, 2nd edn 2004; (jtly) ICRC Model Manual on The Law of Armed Conflict, 1999; (co-ed) UK MoD Manual of The Law of Armed Conflict, 2004; articles on law of war. *Recreations:* music, the arts, playing the piano (especially as accompanist) and bassoon, walking (preferably in mountains), cricket. *Address:* c/o Directorate of Army Legal Services, Trenchard Lines, Upavon, Wilts SN9 6BE. *T:* (01980) 615966.

ROGERS, General Bernard William; General, United States Army, retired; Supreme Allied Commander, Europe, 1979–87; *b* 16 July 1921; *s* of late Mr and Mrs W. H. Rogers; *m* 1944, Ann Ellen Jones; one *s* two *d*. *Educ:* Kansas State Coll.; US Mil. Acad. (BS); Oxford Univ. (Rhodes Scholar; BA, MA); US Army Comd Staff Coll., Fort Leavenworth, Kansas; US Army War Coll., Carlisle Barracks, Pa. CO 3rd Bn, 9th Inf. Regt, 2nd Inf. Div., Korea, 1952–53; Bn Comdr 1st Bn, 23rd Inf., 2nd Inf. Div., Fort Lewis, Washington, 1955–56; Comdr, 1st Battle Gp, 19th Inf., Div. COS, 24th Inf. Div., Augsburg, Germany, 1960–61; Exec. Officer to Chm., Jt Chiefs of Staff, Washington, DC, 1962–66; Asst Div. Comdr, 1st Inf. Div., Republic of Vietnam, 1966–67; Comdt of Cadets, US Mil. Acad., 1967–69; Comdg Gen., 5th Inf. Div., Fort Carson, Colo, 1969–70; Chief of Legislative Liaison, Office of Sec. to the Army, Washington, DC, 1971–72; Dep. Chief of Staff for Personnel, Dept of the Army, Washington, DC, 1972–74; Comdg Gen., US Army Forces Comd, Fort McPherson, Ga, 1974–76; Chief of Staff, US Army, Washington, DC, 1976–79. Hon. Fellow, University Coll., Oxford, 1979. Hon. LLD: Akron, 1978; Boston, 1981; Hon. DCL Oxon, 1983. Dist. Graduate Award, US Mil. Acad., 1995; George C. Marshall Medal, Assoc. of US Army, 1999. *Publications:* Cedar Falls-Junction City: a Turning Point, 1974; contribs to: Foreign Affairs, RUSI, 1982; Strategic Review, NATO's Sixteen Nations, 1983; Europa Archiv, Defense, NATO Review, 1984; Europäische Wehrkunde, Rivista Militaire, 1985; The Adelphi Papers, 1986; Soldat und Technik, 1987. *Recreations:* golf, reading. *Address:* 1467 Hampton Ridge Drive, McLean, VA 22101–6023, USA.

ROGERS, Brett; Director, Photographers' Gallery, London, since 2005; *b* 22 Dec. 1954; *d* of Bob and Jerry Rogers; *m* 1982, Alan Lowery (marr. diss. 2007); one *s* one *d*. *Educ:* Univ. of Sydney (BA Hons 1976); Courtauld Inst. of Art, Univ. of London (MA 1981). Exhibns Officer, 1976–78, Hd of Exhibns, 1978–80, Australian Gall. Dirs Council; Exhibns Officer, 1982–95, Hd of Exhibns and Dep. Dir, 1996–2005, Fine Arts Dept, British Council. *Publications:* Madame Yevonde: Be Original or Die, 1998; Reality Check: recent developments in British photography, 2003; To be continued......aspects of recent British and Finnish photography, 2005. *Recreations:* visual arts, theatre, swimming. *Address:* Photographers' Gallery, 5 Great Newport Street, WC2H 7HY. *T:* (020) 7841 5040; *e-mail:* Brett.Rogers@photonet.org.uk. *Club:* Adam Street.

ROGERS, Surgeon Rear-Adm. (D) Brian Frederick, CB 1980; Director of Naval Dental Services, 1977–80; *b* 27 Feb. 1923; *s* of Frederick Reginald Rogers, MIMechE, MIMarE, and Rosa Jane Rogers; *m* 1946, Mavis Elizabeth (*née* Scott); one *s* two *d*. *Educ:* Rock Ferry High Sch.; Liverpool Univ. (LDS 1945). House Surgeon, Liverpool Dental Hosp., 1945; joined RNVR, 1946; transf. to RN, 1954; served HMS Ocean, 1954–56 and HMS Eagle, 1964–66; Fleet Dental Surg. on staff of C-in-C Fleet, 1974–77; Comd Dental Surg. to C-in-C Naval Home Comd, 1977. QHDS 1977. *Recreations:* European touring, photography, DIY. *Address:* 22 Trerieve, Downderry, Torpoint, Cornwall PL11 3LY. *T:* (01503) 250526; Montana roja, Lanzarote, Canary Islands. *T:* (28) 517150.

ROGERS, Catherine W.; *see* Wyn-Rogers.

ROGERS, Christopher; *see* Rogers, L. C. G.

ROGERS, Ven. David Arthur; Archdeacon of Craven, 1977–86; *b* 12 March 1921; *s* of Rev. Canon Thomas Godfrey Rogers and Doris Mary Cleaver Rogers (*née* Steele); *m* 1951, Joan Malkin; one *s* three *d*. *Educ:* Saint Edward's School, Oxford (scholar); Christ's College, Cambridge (exhibitioner). BA 1947, MA 1952. War service with Green Howards and RAC, 1940–45; Christ's Coll. and Ridley Hall, Cambridge, 1945–49; Asst Curate, St George's, Stockport, 1949–53; Rector, St Peter's, Levenshulme, Manchester, 1953–59; Vicar of Sedbergh, Cautley and Garsdale, 1959–79; Rural Dean of Sedbergh and then of Ewecross, 1959–77; Hon. Canon of Bradford Cathedral, 1967. *Address:* 24 Towns End Road, Sharnbrook, Bedford MK44 1HY. *T:* (01234) 782650.

ROGERS, Dr David P., FRMetS; President and Chair of the Board, Health and Climate Foundation, since 2007; *b* 20 March 1957. *Educ:* UEA (BSc Hons); Univ. of Southampton (PhD). Navigating Officer, British MN; res. appts, Desert Res. Inst., Univ. of Nevada; Scripps Institution of Oceanography, University of California, San Diego: res. scientist; Associate Dir, Calif Space Inst.; Dir, Physical Oceanography Res. Div. and Dir, Jt Inst. for Marine Observations, 1989–2000; Dir, Office of Weather and Air Quality Res. and Associate Dir of Res., Nat. Oceanographic and Atmospheric Admin, USA, 2000–03; Vice Pres., Meteorol and Oceanographic Services, Sci. Applications Internat. Corp., Virginia, 2003–04; Chief Executive, Met Office, 2004–05. *Address:* *e-mail:* drogers@hc-foundation.org.

ROGERS, Prof. (Frances) Alice, PhD; Professor of Mathematics, King's College London, since 2007; *b* 13 Sept. 1947; *d* of John George Monroe and Jane Monroe (*née* Reynolds); *m* 1970, Richard Ian Rogers, *qv*; one *s* one *d*. *Educ:* New Hall, Cambridge (BA Maths 1968); Hughes Hall, Cambridge (PGCE); Imperial Coll., London (PhD). Secondary sch. teacher, 1969–76; SERC Res. Fellow, Imperial Coll., London, 1981–83; Department of Mathematics, King's College London: Res. Associate, 1983–84; SERC Adv. Res. Fellow, 1984–89; Royal Soc. Univ. Res. Fellow, 1989–94; Lectr, 1994–96; Reader, 1996–2007. Mem., Adv. Cttee on Maths Educn, 2007–. *Publications:* Supermanifolds: theory and applications, 2007; articles on mathematical physics in scientific jls. *Recreations:* gardening, history, hills, most things Italian. *Address:* 21 Keyes Road, NW2 3XB; *e-mail:* alice.rogers@kcl.ac.uk.

ROGERS, (George) Stuart L.; *see* Lawson-Rogers.

ROGERS, Hayley; Parliamentary Counsel, since 2007; *b* 16 July 1967; *d* of Peter Jordan and Ann Catherine Jordan (*née* Newman); *m* 1990, Steven Alexander Rogers. *Educ:* Univ. of Reading (LLB 1988); Coll. of Law, Guildford. Articled clerk, then solicitor, Boys and Maughan Solicitors, Margate, 1989–93; Asst Parly Counsel, 1993–98; Sen. Asst Parly Counsel, 1998–2002; Dep. Parly Counsel, 2002–07; Head Drafter, Tax Law Rewrite Project, HM Revenue and Customs, 2005–07. *Recreations:* walking, painting, gardening. *Address:* Parliamentary Counsel Office, 36 Whitehall, SW1A 2AY. *T:* (020) 7210 6847; *e-mail:* hayley.rogers@cabinet-office.x.gsi.gov.uk.

ROGERS, Very Rev. John; Dean of Llandaff, 1993–99, now Emeritus; *b* 27 Nov. 1934; *s* of William Harold and Annie Mary Rogers; *m* 1972, Pamela Mary Goddard; one *s* one *d*. *Educ:* Jones' W Monmouth Sch., Pontypool; St David's Coll., Lampeter (BA 1955); Oriel Coll., Oxford (BA 1957; MA 1960); St Stephen's House, Oxford, 1957–59. Ordained deacon, 1959, priest, 1960; Assistant Curate: St Martin's, Roath (dio. of Llandaff), 1959–63; St Sidwell's, Lodge, with Holy Redeemer, Ruimveldt, Guyana, 1963–67; Vicar: Holy Redeemer, Ruimveldt, Guyana, 1967–69; Wismar and Lower Demerara River Missions, 1969–71; Caldicot, 1971–77; Monmouth, 1977–84; Rector, Ebbw Vale, 1984–93. Rural Dean: Monmouth, 1981–84; Blaenau Gwent, 1986–93; Canon of St Woolos Cathedral, 1988–93. *Recreations:* gardening, fencing, reading. *Address:* Fron Lodge, Llandovery SA20 0LJ. *T:* (01550) 720089.

ROGERS, Prof. (John) Michael, DPhil; FSA; FBA 1988; Khalili Professor of Islamic Art, School of Oriental and African Studies, University of London, 1991–2000, now Emeritus; Hon. Curator, Nasser D. Khalili Collection of Islamic Art, Nour Foundation, since 1991; *b* 25 Jan. 1935. *Educ:* Ulverston Grammar Sch.; Corpus Christi Coll., Oxford (MA, DPhil). FSA 1974. Robinson Sen. Student, Oriel Coll., Oxford, 1958–61; Tutor in Philosophy, Pembroke and Wadham Colls, Oxford, 1961–65; Asst, then Associate, Prof. of Islamic Art and Archaeol., Center for Arabic Studies, Amer. Univ. in Cairo, 1965–77; Dep. Keeper, Dept of Oriental Antiquities, BM, 1977–91. Vis. Sen. Res. Fellow, Merton Coll., Oxford, 1971–72; Vis. Res. Fellow, New Coll., Oxford, 1998; Slade Prof. of Fine Art, Oxford Univ., 1991–92. Pres., British Inst. of Persian Studies, 1993–96. Corresp. Mem., Deutsches Archäologisches Inst., Berlin, 1988. Order of the Egyptian Republic, 2nd cl., 1969. *Publications:* The Spread of Islam, 1976; Islamic Art and Design 1500–1700, 1983; (with R. M. Ward) Süleyman the Magnificent, 1988; Mughal Painting, 1993, 2nd edn 2006; Empire of the Sultans: Ottoman art in the Khalili collection, 1995; (with M. B. Piotrovsky) Heaven on Earth: art from Islamic lands, 2004; Sinan, 2006; numerous articles on hist. and archaeol. of Islamic Turkey, Egypt, Syria, Iran and Central Asia. *Recreations:* walking, music, botany. *Address:* The Nour Foundation, 27 Liddell Road, Maygrove Road, NW6 2EW. *Club:* Beefsteak.

ROGERS, John Michael Thomas; QC 1979; **His Honour Judge John Rogers;** a Circuit Judge, since 1998; *m* 2006, Mrs Angela Victoria Galaud (*née* Ginders); one step *s* one step *d*, and one *d* from a former marriage. *Educ:* Rydal Sch.; Birkenhead Sch.; Fitzwilliam House, Cambridge (MA, LLB). Called to Bar, Gray's Inn, 1963, Bencher 1991. A Recorder, 1976–98. Leader, Wales and Chester Circuit, 1990–92. *Recreations:* farming, gardening. *Address:* Mold Crown Court, Mold CH7 1AE. *Clubs:* Reform; Pragmatist's (Wirral); Barbarians Rugby Football.

ROGERS, Air Chief Marshal Sir John (Robson), KCB 1982; CBE 1971; FRAeS; Executive Chairman, RAC Motor Sports Association, 1989–98; *b* 11 Jan. 1928; *s* of B. R. Rogers; *m* 1955, Gytha Elspeth Campbell; two *s* two *d*. *Educ:* Brentwood Sch.; No 1 Radio Sch., Cranwell; Royal Air Force Coll., Cranwell. OC 56(F) Sqdn, 1960–61; Gp Captain, 1967; OC RAF Coningsby, 1967–69; Air Commodore, 1971; Dir of Operational Requirements (RAF), 1971–73; Dep. Comdt, RAF Coll., 1973–75; RCDS, 1976; Air Vice-Marshal, 1977; Dir-Gen. of Organisation, RAF, 1977–79; AOC Training Units, RAF Support Comd, 1979–81; Air Mem. for Supply and Organisation, MoD, 1981–83; Controller Aircraft, MoD PE, 1983–86, retired. Director: British Car Auctions, 1986–90; First Technology Gp, 1986–93. Pres., Internat. Historic Commn, Fedn Internat. de l'Automobile, 1995–2004. Chm., Children's Fire and Burn Trust, 2000–04. FRAeS 1983. *Recreation:* motor racing. *Address:* c/o Lloyds TSB, 27 High Street, Colchester, Essex. *Clubs:* Royal Automobile (Vice-Chm., 1990–98; Life Vice Pres., 1999), Royal Air Force.

ROGERS, Prof. (Leonard) Christopher (Gordon), PhD; Professor of Statistical Science, University of Cambridge, since 2002. *Educ:* St John's Coll., Cambridge (BA 1975; PhD 1980). Lecturer: Univ. of Warwick, 1980–83; Univ. Coll. of Swansea, 1983–85; Univ. of Cambridge, 1985–91; Fellow of St John's Coll., Cambridge, 1985–91; Prof. of Math. Statistics, QMW, 1991–94; Prof. of Probability, Univ. of Bath, 1994–2002. *Publications:* (with David Williams) Diffusions, Markov Processes, and Martingales, vol. 1, Foundations, 1979, vol. 2, Itô calculus, 1987; articles in learned jls. *Address:* Department of Pure Mathematics and Mathematical Statistics, Centre for Mathematical Sciences, Wilberforce Road, Cambridge CB3 0WB.

ROGERS, Malcolm Austin, CBE 2004; DPhil; FSA; Ann and Graham Gund Director, Museum of Fine Arts, Boston, Mass, since 1994; *b* 3 Oct. 1948; *s* of late James Eric Rogers and Frances Anne (*née* Elsey). *Educ:* Oakham School; Magdalen College, Oxford (Open Exhibnr); Christ Church, Oxford (Senior Scholar). Violet Vaughan Morgan Prize, 1967; BA (Eng. Lang. and Lit. 1st cl.), 1969; MA 1973; DPhil 1976. National Portrait Gallery: Asst. Keeper, 1974–83; Dep. Keeper, 1983–85; Keeper, 1985–94; Dep. Dir, 1983–94. Freeman, City of London, 1992; Liveryman, Girdlers' Co., 1992. Chevalier de l'Ordre des Arts et des Lettres (France), 2007. *Publications:* Dictionary of British Portraiture, 4 vols (ed jtly), 1979–81; Museums and Galleries of London, 1983, 3rd edn 1991; William Dobson, 1983; John and John Baptist Closterman: a catalogue of their works, 1983; Elizabeth II: portraits of sixty years, 1986; Camera Portraits, 1989; Montacute House, 1991; (with Sir David Piper) Companion Guide to London, 1992; (ed) The English Face, by Sir David Piper, 1992; Master Drawings from the National Portrait Gallery, 1993; articles and reviews in Burlington Magazine, Apollo, TLS. *Recreations:* food and wine, opera, travel. *Address:* 540 Chestnut Hill Avenue, Brookline, MA 02445, USA. T: (617) 2320214; La Bastille, 10 The Common, Royalston, MA 01368, USA. *Clubs:* Beefsteak; Algonquin (Hon. Mem.), Wednesday Evening Club of 1777, Thursday Evening, Commercial, Odd Volumes (Boston).

ROGERS, Martin Hartley Guy; HM Diplomatic Service, retired; *b* 11 June 1925; *s* of late Rev. Canon T. Guy Rogers and Marguerite Inez Rogers; *m* 1959, Jean Beresford Chinn; one *s* three *d*. *Educ:* Marlborough Coll.; Jesus Coll., Cambridge. CRO, 1949; 2nd Sec., Karachi, 1951–53; CRO, 1953–56 and 1958–60; seconded to Govt of Fedn of Nigeria, 1956–57; ndc 1960–61; 1st Sec., Ottawa, 1961–62; Adviser to Jamaican Min. of External Affairs, 1963; CRO, later Commonwealth Office, 1963–68; Dep. High Comr, Bombay, 1968–71; Kaduna, 1972–75; High Comr, The Gambia, 1975–79; on loan to CSSB as Asst Dir, 1979–85. *Recreation:* bridge. *Address:* Rydal, Tower Road, St Helier, Jersey JE2 3HR. T: (01534) 731429.

ROGERS, Martin John Wyndham, OBE 2000; Director, Fellowships in Religious Education for Europe, since 2001; Co-director, Science and Religion in Schools Project, since 2002; *b* 9 April 1931; *s* of late John Frederick Rogers and Grace Mary Rogers; *m* 1957, Jane Cook; two *s* one *d*. *Educ:* Oundle Sch.; Heidelberg Univ.; Trinity Hall, Cambridge (MA); MA Oxon 1995. Henry Wiggin & Co., 1953–55; Westminster School: Asst Master, 1955–60; Sen. Chemistry Master, 1960–64; Housemaster, 1964–66; Under Master and Master of the Queen's Scholars, 1967–71; Headmaster of Malvern Coll., 1971–82; Chief Master, King Edward's Sch., Birmingham, Headmaster of the Schs of King Edward VIth in Birmingham, 1982–91; Dir, Farmington Inst. for Christian Studies, 1991–2001. Seconded as Nuffield Research Fellow (O-level Chemistry Project), 1962–64; Salter's Company Fellow, Dept of Chemical Engrg and Chemical Technology, Imperial Coll., London, 1969; Associate Fellow, Manchester, subseq. Harris Manchester, Coll., Oxford, 1991–2001. Chairman: Curriculum Cttee of HMC, GSA and IAPS, 1979–86; HMC, 1987; Mem. Council, GPDST, 1991–93. Chm., European Council, Nat. Assocs of Indep. Schs, 1994–97. Mem. Council, Birmingham Univ., 1985–92. Governor: Oundle Sch., 1988–2001; Westonbirt Sch., 1991–97; Elmhurst Ballet Sch., 1991–95; English Coll., Prague, 1991–2005. Chm., Millwood Educn Trust, 2001–04; Trustee: Sandford St Martin Trust, 1994–2003; Smallpeice Trust, 2000–02. *Publications:* John Dalton and the Atomic Theory, 1965; Chemistry and Energy, 1968; Gas Syringe Experiments, 1970; (co-author) Chemistry: facts, patterns and principles, 1972; Editor: Foreground Chemistry Series, 1968; Farmington Papers, 1993–2001. *Address:* Eastwards, 24 Millwood End, Long Hanborough, Oxon OX29 8BX. *Club:* East India, Devonshire, Sports and Public Schools.

ROGERS, Michael; see Rogers, J. M.

ROGERS, Nigel David; free-lance singer, conductor and teacher; Professor of Singing, Royal College of Music, 1978–2000; *b* 21 March 1935; *m* 1961, Frederica Bement Lord (*d* 1992); one *d*; *m* 1999, Lina Zilinskyte; one *d*. *Educ:* Wellington Grammar Sch.; King's Coll., Cambridge (MA). Studied in Italy and Germany. Professional singer, 1961–; began singing career in Munich with group Studio der frühen Musik. Is a leading specialist in field of Baroque music, and has made over 70 recordings from Monteverdi to Schubert; gives concerts, recitals, lectures and master classes in many parts of world; most acclaimed role in opera as Monteverdi's Orfeo. Formed vocal ensemble Chiaroscuro, to perform vast repertory of Italian Baroque music, 1979, later extended to include Chiaroscuro Chamber Ensemble and Chiaroscuro Baroque Orch. Has lectured and taught at Schola Cantorum Basiliensis, Basle, Switzerland. Hon. RCM 1981. *Publications:* chapter on Voice,

Companion to Baroque Music (ed J. A. Sadie), 1991; articles on early Baroque performance practice in various periodicals in different countries. *Address:* Wellington House, 13 Victoria Road, Deal, Kent CT14 7AS. T: and *Fax:* (01304) 379249.

ROGERS, Maj.-Gen. Norman Charles, FRCS 1949; consultant surgeon, retired; *b* 14 Oct. 1916; *s* of Wing Comdr Charles William Rogers, RAF, and Edith Minnie Rogers (*née* Weaver); *m* 1954, Pamela Marion (*née* Rose); two *s* one *d*. *Educ:* Imperial Service Coll.; St Bartholomew's Hosp. MB, BS London; MRCS, LRCP 1939. Emergency Commn, Lieut RAMC, Oct. 1939; 131 Field Amb. RAMC, Dunkirk (despatches, 1940); RMO, 4th Royal Tank Regt, N Africa, 1941–42; Italy, 1942–43 (POW); RMO 1st Black Watch, NW Europe, 1944–45 (wounded, despatches twice). Ho. Surg., St Bartholomew's Hosp., 1946–47; Registrar (Surgical) Appts, Norwich, 1948–52; Sen. Registrar Appts, Birmingham, 1952–56; granted permanent commn, RAMC, 1956; surgical appts in mil. hospitals: Chester, Dhekelia (Cyprus), Catterick, Iserlohn (BAOR), 1956–67; Command Consultant Surgeon, BAOR, 1967–69; Dir, Army Surgery, 1969–73; QHS, 1969–73. Clin. Supt, 1975–80, and Consultant, 1973–81, Accident and Emergency Dept, Guy's Hosp.; Civilian Consultant Surgeon: BMH Iserlohn, 1983–86; BMH Munster, 1986. *Publications:* contribs on surgical subjects. *Address:* 110 Mill Street, Kidlington OX5 2EF.

ROGERS, Parry; see Rogers, T. G. P.

ROGERS, Patricia Maureen S.; see Shepheard Rogers.

ROGERS, Paul; actor; *b* Plympton, Devon, 22 March 1917; *s* of Edwin and Dulcie Myrtle Rogers; *m* 1st, 1939, Jocelyn Wynne (marr. diss. 1955); two *s*; 2nd, 1955, Rosalind Boxall; two *d*. *Educ:* Newton Abbot Grammar School, Devon. Michael Chekhov Theatre Studio, 1936–38. First appearance on stage as Charles Dickens in Bird's Eye of Valour, Scala, 1938; Stratford-upon-Avon Shakespeare Memorial Theatre, 1939; Concert Party and Colchester Rep. Co. until 1940. Served Royal Navy, 1940–46. Colchester Rep. Co. and Arts Council Tour and London Season, Tess of the D'Urbervilles, 1946–47; Bristol Old Vic, 1947–49; London Old Vic (incl. tour S Africa and Southern Rhodesia), 1949–53; also at Edinburgh, London and in USA, 1954–57; London, 1958; tour to Moscow, Leningrad and Warsaw, 1960. Roles with Old Vic include numerous Shakespearean leads; Gloucester, in King Lear, 1989. Other parts include: Sir Claude Mulhammer in The Confidential Clerk, Edinburgh Festival and Lyric, London, 1953; Lord Claverton in The Elder Statesman, Edinburgh Fest. and Cambridge Theatre, London, 1958; Mr Fox in Mr Fox of Venice, Piccadilly, 1959; Johnny Condell in One More River, Duke of York's and Westminster, 1959; Nickles in JB, Phœnix, 1961; Reginald Kinsale in Photo Finish, Saville, 1962; The Seagull, Queen's, 1964; Season of Goodwill, Queen's, 1964; The Homecoming, Aldwych, 1965; Timon of Athens, Stratford-upon-Avon, 1965; The Government Inspector, Aldwych, 1966; Henry IV, Stratford-upon-Avon, 1966; Max in The Homecoming, New York, 1967 (Tony Award and Whitbread Anglo-American Award); Plaza Suite, Lyric, 1969; The Happy Apple, Apollo, 1970; Sleuth, St Martin's, 1970, NY, 1971; Othello, Bristol Old Vic, 1974; Heartbreak House, Nat. Theatre, 1975; The Marrying of Ann Leete, Aldwych, 1975; The Return of A. J. Raffles, Aldwych, 1975; The Zykovs, Aldwych, 1976; Volpone, The Madras House, Nat. Theatre, 1977; Eclipse, Royal Court, 1978; You Never Can Tell, Lyric, Hammersmith, 1979; The Dresser, New York, 1981, 1982; The Importance of Being Earnest, A Kind of Alaska, Nat. Theatre, 1982; The Apple Cart, Theatre Royal, Haymarket, 1986; Danger: Memory!, Hampstead, 1988; Other People's Money, Lyric, 1990. Appears in films and television. *Publication:* a Preface to Folio Soc. edition of Shakespeare's Love's Labour's Lost, 1959. *Recreations:* gardening, carpentry, books. *Address:* 9 Hillside Gardens, Highgate, N6 5SU. T: (020) 8340 2656.

ROGERS, Peter Brian, CBE 2001; Chief Executive, Independent Television Commission, 1996–2000; *b* 8 April 1941; *s* of late William Patrick Rogers and Margaret Elizabeth Rogers; *m* 1966, Jean Mary Bailey; one *s* two *d*. *Educ:* De La Salle Grammar Sch., Liverpool; Manchester Univ. (1st Cl. Hons BAEcon; Cobden Prize); London Sch. of Econs and Pol. Science, London Univ. (MSc Econs). Tax Officer, Inland Revenue, 1959–67; Res. Associate, Manchester Univ., 1967–68; Econ. Adviser, HM Treasury, 1968–73; Sen. Econ. Adviser, Central Policy Review Staff, Cabinet Office, 1973–74; Dir of Econ. Planning, Tyne and Wear CC (on secondment from Central Govt), 1974–76; Sen. Econ. Adviser, DoE, 1976–79; Dep. Chief Exec., Housing Corp., 1979–82; Dir of Finance, IBA, 1982–90; Dep. Chief Exec. and Dir of Finance, ITC, 1991–96. Dir, Channel Four Television Co., 1982–92. *Recreations:* woodwork, cycling. *Address:* Thorphinsty House, Cartmel Fell, Grange over Sands, Cumbria LA11 6NF. T: (01539) 552515; *e-mail:* pbrogers@btinternet.com.

ROGERS, Peter Richard; Master of Costs Office (Costs Judge), Supreme Court; *b* 2 April 1939; *s* of Denis Roynan Rogers and Lucy Gwynneth (*née* Hopwood); *m* 1966, Adrienne Winifred Haylock. *Educ:* Bristol Univ. (LLB Hons). Solicitor of the Supreme Court. Articled Clerk, then solicitor, Turner Kenneth Brown (formerly Kenneth Brown Baker Baker) (solicitors), 1961–92; Partner, 1968–92; Dep. Supreme Court Taxing Master, 1991–92; Taxing Master, now Costs Judge, Supreme Court, 1992–. Mem., London No 13 Legal Aid Cttee, 1980–92. General Editor, Greenslade on Costs, 1999– (Consulting Editor, 1995–99); Jt Editor, Costs Law Reports, 1997–. *Recreations:* weather, steam and other railways, environmental concerns. *Address:* Supreme Court Costs Office, Cliffords Inn, Fetter Lane, EC4A 1DQ. T: (020) 7936 6224.

ROGERS, Peter Standing; JP; Member (C) North Wales, National Assembly for Wales, 1999–2003; *b* 2 Jan. 1940; *s* of late Harold Rogers and of Joan Thomas; *m* 1973, Margaret Roberts; two *s*. *Educ:* Prenton Secondary Sch., Birkenhead; Cheshire Sch. of Agriculture. Farm Manager, 1962–65; Sales Manager, Ciba Geigy UK, 1965; self-employed farmer, 1965–. Contested: (C) Ynys Môn, Nat. Assembly for Wales, 2003; (Ind) Ynys Môn, 2005. JP Ynys Môn, 1990; High Sheriff, Gwynedd, 2008. *Recreations:* sports, all rural activities. *Address:* Bodrida, Brynsiencyn, Anglesey LL61 6NZ. *Clubs:* Old Birkonians (Birkenhead); Welsh Crawshays Rugby.

ROGERS, Peter William, CBE 2007; Eur Ing, FREng; Director, Stanhope Plc, since 1995; *b* 25 Oct. 1946; *s* of Dr Nino Rogers and Dada (*née* Geiringer); *m* 1971, Hélène Tombazis (marr. diss.); one *s* one *d*; *m* 1988, Barbara Peters; two *s*. *Educ:* Portsmouth Poly. (BSc). CEng 1975, FREng 2005; MICE 1975; Eur Ing 1989. Various construction industry appts, UK, USA, France, Holland and ME, 1970–84; Dir, Stanhope Properties Plc, 1985–95, resp. for construction of Broadgate, 1985–91. Advr on arts projects, incl., Nat. Gall., Glyndebourne Opera House, Royal Opera House, Tate Modern, Roundhouse, Serpentine Gall. and RSC, 1986–. Non-executive Director: Thomas Telford Ltd, 1989–92; Asite, 2000–; Firstbase, 2006– (Exec. Dir. 2004–06). Mem., Construction Industry Sector Gp, NEDO, 1988–92. Mem., Foresight Panel, DTI, 1994–95 and 2000–01. Advr, Heritage Lottery Fund, 1995–2000. Dir, Reading Construction Forum, 1994–99; Chairman: Strategic Forum for Construction, 2002–06 (Chm., 2012 Task Gp, 2005–); Constructing Excellence, 2003–08; DCLG (formerly ODPM) Steering Cttee for Sustainable Buildings, 2005–07; UK Green Bldg Council, 2006–. Trustee and Chm., Buildings Strategy Cttee, V&A Mus., 1999–2008. Visitor,

Ashmolean Mus., 2007–. FRSA 2001. Hon. FRIBA 2003. *Recreations:* theatre, ballet, art, music, travel, sailing, ski-ing. *Address:* Norfolk House, 31 St James's Square, SW1Y 4JJ. *T:* (020) 7170 1700, *Fax:* (020) 7170 1701; *e-mail:* peter.rogers@stanhopeplc.com. *Club:* Royal Yachting Association.

See also Baron Rogers of Riverside.

ROGERS, Philip John, MBE 1990; FREng, FInstP; Optical Design Consultant, VNF Ltd, since 2006; *b* 4 Oct. 1942; *s* of late John William Rogers and Lilian (*née* Fleet); *m* 1979, Wendy Joan Cross; one *s* two *d. Educ:* Burnley Grammar Sch.; North London Poly. (HNC Applied Physics 1965). CPhys 1990; CEng 1993. Optical Designer, Hilger & Watts, London, 1960–66; Pilkington PE, subseq. Pilkington Optronics, then Thales Optics Ltd: Optical Designer, 1966–69; Chief Optical Designer, 1969–2005; Chief Optics Engr, 3 sites, Pilkington Optronics Gp, 1994–2000. Vis. Prof., Cranfield Univ., 2007–; lecturing activities incl. OU TV broadcast, 1977. Mem., Thomson Coll., Paris, 1992–98. FInstP 1992; FREng 1998; Fellow: Internat. Soc. for Optical Engrg, 1991 (Dir, Bd, 1995–97); Optical Soc. of America, 1998. *Publications:* (contrib.) Electro Optical Displays, 1992; (contrib.) Optical Society of America Handbook of Optics, Vol. 1, 1995; conf. procs papers; contrib. 6 articles in jls; 27 patents covering infrared, night vision, avionic, visual and miscellaneous optics. *Recreations:* listening to music, armchair astronomy (some lecturing to astronomical societies), reading (history and science particularly), messing about on computers. *Address:* 24 Cilgant Eglwys Wen, Bodelwyddan, Denbighshire LL18 5US. *T:* (01745) 582498; *e-mail:* PhilJRog@aol.com.

ROGERS, Raymond Thomas, CPhys, FInstP; Managing Director, Dragon Health International (formerly Ray Rogers Associates), 1997–2006; *b* 19 Oct. 1940; *s* of late Thomas Kenneth Rogers and of Mary Esther Rogers (*née* Walsh); *m* 1964, Carmel Anne Saunders; two *s* one *d. Educ:* Gunnersbury Grammar Sch.; Birmingham Univ. (BSc). CPhys, FInstP 1962. Basic Med. Physicist, London Hosp., 1962–66; Sen. Med. Physicist, Westminster Hosp., 1966–70; Department of Health and Social Security, later Department of Health: PSO, Scientific and Tech. Br., 1970; Supt Engr, then Dir 1984; Asst Sec., Health Inf. Br., 1984–91; Under Sec., and Exec. Dir Information Mgt Gp, 1991–97. FRSA 1997. *Publications:* contribs to scientific jls and books. *Recreations:* trekking, opera, science, peace. *Address:* One Bannisters Road, Onslow Village, Guildford, Surrey GU2 5RA. *T:* (01483) 573078.

ROGERS, Col Richard Annesley C.; *see* Coxwell-Rogers.

ROGERS, Richard Ian; Director, Company Law and Investigations, Department of Trade and Industry, 1997–2003; *b* 10 June 1947; *s* of Charles Murray Rogers and Aileen Mary Seton Rogers (*née* Hole); *m* 1970, (Frances) Alice Monroe (*see* Prof. F. A. Rogers); one *s* one *d. Educ:* Monkton Combe Sch.; Queens' Coll., Cambridge (BA). Prison Asst Gov., 1969–72; Brent Family Service Unit, 1972–77; Civil Service, 1977–2003: Depts of Prices and Consumer Protection, of Trade, and of Industry; Department of Trade and Industry: British Steel Privatisation, 1986–88; Projects and Export Policy, 1989–92; Telecoms Policy, 1992–93; Sen. Staff Mgt, 1993–97; Chm., Company Law Review Steering Gp, 1998–2001. *Recreations:* mountains, music and opera, books, heavy gardening, motorcycling. *Address:* 21 Keyes Road, NW2 3XB.

ROGERS, Robert James; Clerk of Legislation, House of Commons, since 2006; *b* 5 Feb. 1950; *o s* of late Francis Barry Day Rogers and Jeanne Turner Prichard Rogers (*née* Prichard-Williams); *m* 1st, 1973, Sarah Elizabeth Anne Howard (marr. diss. 1976); 2nd, 1981, Constance Jane Perkins; two *d. Educ:* Tonbridge Sch. (Scholar); Lincoln Coll., Oxford (Scholar and Judd Exhibitioner; BA Hons 1971; Rhodes Res. Scholar 1971; MA 1978). MoD, 1971–72; House of Commons: an Asst Clerk, 1972; a Sen. Clerk, 1977; a Dep. Principal Clerk, 1985; Clerk: of Select Cttee on Defence, 1983–89; of Private Members' Bills, 1989–92; of Select Cttee on European Legislation, 1993–98; Parly Counsellor to the Pres., Parly Assembly of Council of Europe, 1992–95; Principal Clerk: of Delegated Legislation, 1998–99; of Select Cttees, 1999–2001; of Domestic Cttees, and Sec., H of C Commn, 2001–04; Clerk of the Journals, 2004–05; Principal Clerk of the Table Office, 2005–06. Ind. Chm., Standards Cttee, Herefords CC, 2002; Ind. Chm., 2002–06, Mem., 2006–, Standards Cttee, Herefords and Worcs Fire Authy; Ind. Mem., 2002–04, Chm., 2004–08, Selection Panel, Ind. Mem., Standards Cttee, 2007–, W Mercia Police Authy. Gov., Skinners' Co. Sch. for Girls, 2005. Chm., Hereford Cathedral Perpetual Trust, 2007–. Fellow, Industry and Parliament Trust, 1981. Associate, Nat. Sch. of Govt, 2007–. Liveryman, Skinners' Co., 2004 (Mem. Court, 2005–07). *Publications:* (with Rhodri Walters) How Parliament Works, 5th edn 2004, 6th edn 2006; contribs to various books and jls on European and Parly affairs. *Recreations:* music (church organist), cricket, sailing, shooting, the natural world. *Address:* Public Bill Office, House of Commons, SW1A 0AA. *T:* (020) 7219 3255; *e-mail:* rogersr@parliament.uk. *Club:* Travellers.

ROGERS, Ruth; *see* Rogers of Riverside, Lady.

ROGERS, Sheila; consultant, since 2005; *b* 29 March 1947; *d* of Charles Rogers and Peggy Baird; *m* Kenneth Hunter (marr. diss.); one *d. Educ:* Univ. of Winnipeg (BA 1976); Univ. of Manitoba (LLB 1979); CIPFA (AdvDip 1999). Legal Aid Manitoba, 1980–86, Dep. Dir, 1986; Equal Opportunities Commn for NI, 1989–98, Dir of Finance and Admin, 1993–98; Chief Exec., Commn for Racial Equality for NI, 1998–99; Dir of Race Unit, 1999–2002, and Asst Chief Exec., 2000–01, Equality Commn for NI; Commission for Racial Equality (on secondment): Hd, Community Policy and Progs, 2002–04; Dir, Strategy and Delivery, 2004; Chief Exec., 2004–05. *Publications:* (contrib.) Equal Opportunities: women's working lives, 1993; (contrib.) Workplace Equality: an international perspective on legislation, policy and practice, 2002. *Address: e-mail:* rogers.sheila@gmail.com. *Club:* Institute of Directors.

ROGERS, (Thomas Gordon) Parry, CBE 1991; Director, The Plessey Co. plc, 1976–86; *b* 7 Aug. 1924; *s* of late Victor Francis Rogers and Ella (*née* May); *m* 1st, 1947, Pamela Mary (*née* Greene) (marr. diss. 1973); one *s* seven *d*; 2nd, 1973, Patricia Juliet (*née* Curtis); one *s* one *d. Educ:* West Hartlepool Grammar Sch.; St Edmund Hall, Oxford (MA). Served RAC and RAEC, 1944–47. Procter & Gamble Ltd, 1948–54; Mars Ltd, 1954–56; Hardy Spicer Ltd, 1956–61 (Dir, 1957–61); IBM United Kingdom Ltd, 1961–74 (Dir, 1964–74); The Plessey Co. plc, 1974–86; Chairman: Percom Ltd, 1984–94; ECCTIS 2000 Ltd, 1989–97; Director: MSL Gp Internat. Ltd, 1970–78; ICL plc, 1977–79; Hobsons Publishing plc, 1985–90; Butler Cox plc, 1985–91; Norman Broadbent Internat. Ltd, 1985–90; Ocean Group plc, 1988–94; Future Perfect (Counselling) Ltd, 1986–92; PRIMA Europe Ltd, 1987–93; BNB Resources plc, 1990–94. Chm., Plessey Pension Trust, 1978–86; Trustee, BNB Resources Pension Trust, 1991–94. Chairman: BTEC, 1986–94; SW London Coll. HEC, 1989–91; IT Skills Agency, 1984–96; Salisbury HA, 1986–90; Commn on Charitable Fundraising, NCSS, 1970–76; Member: Employment Appeal Tribunal, 1978–87; Standing Cttee on Pay Comparability, 1980–81; Nat. Steering Gp, Trng and Vocational Educn Initiative, MSC, 1983–86; CBI/BIM Panel on Mgt Educn, 1968–78; CBI Employment Policy Cttee, 1980–86; Rev. Team, Children and Young Persons Benefits, DHSS, 1984–85; Oxford Univ. Appts Cttee, 1972–87; Member Council: CRAC, 1965–94; ISCO, 1988–95; Inst. of Manpower Studies, 1970–86; Indust. Participation Assoc., 1972–86; Inst. of Dirs, 1980–95 (Chm., 1985–88; Vice Pres., 1988–95); Inst. of Personnel Management, 1954– (Pres., 1975–77); EEF, 1980–86; Econ. League, 1982–86; E Europe Trade Council, 1982–85. Governor: Ashridge Management Coll., 1985–94; Warminster Sch., 1989–99; St Mary's Sch., Shaftesbury, 1991–94. Patron, Dorset Chamber Orch. Freeman, City of London, 1987; Mem., Information Technologists' Co., 1987–. CCIPD; CCMI; FRSA; FInstD. *Publications:* The Recruitment and Training of Graduates, 1970; contribs on management subjects to newspapers and jls. *Recreations:* birdwatching, golf, tennis, photography, listening to music. *Address:* St Edward's Chantry, Bimport, Shaftesbury, Dorset SP7 8BA. *T:* (01747) 852789.

ROGERSON, Rt Rev. Barry; Bishop of Bristol, 1985–2002; an Assistant Bishop, diocese of Bath and Wells, since 2003; *b* 25 July 1936; *s* of Eric and Olive Rogerson; *m* 1961, Olga May Gibson; two *d. Educ:* Magnus Grammar School; Leeds Univ. (BA Theology); Wells Theol Coll. Midland Bank Ltd, 1952–57; Curate: St Hilda's, South Shields, 1962–65; St Nicholas', Bishopwearmouth, Sunderland, 1965–67; Lecturer, Lichfield Theological Coll., 1967–71, Vice-Principal, 1971–72; Lectr, Salisbury and Wells Theol Coll., 1972–75; Vicar, St Thomas', Wednesfield, 1975–79; Team Rector, Wednesfield Team Ministry, 1979; Bishop Suffragan of Wolverhampton, 1979–85. Chm., ABM (formerly ACCM), 1987–93; Mem. Central Cttee, WCC, 1991–2002 (Mem., Faith and Order Commn, 1987–98); Pres., CTBI, 1999–2002. Chm., Melanesian Mission, 1979–2002. Hon. Freeman, City and County of Bristol, 2003. Hon. LLD Bristol, 1993; Hon. DLitt UWE, 2003. *Recreations:* cinema, stained glass windows. *Address:* Flat 2, 30 Albert Road, Clevedon, N Somerset BS21 7RR.

ROGERSON, Daniel John; MP (Lib Dem) Cornwall North, since 2005; *b* 23 July 1975; *s* of Stephen John Rogerson and Patricia Anne Rogerson (*née* Jones); *m* 1999, Heidi Lee Purser; two *s. Educ:* St Mary's Sch., Bodmin; Bodmin Coll.; Univ. of Wales, Aberystwyth (BSc Econ Pols 1996). Local govt officer, Bedford BC, 1996–98; admin. officer, De Montfort Univ., 1998–2002. Mem., Bedford BC, 1999–2002. *Recreations:* listening to blues music, reading, travel. *Address:* House of Commons, SW1A 0AA. *T:* (020) 7219 4707, *Fax:* (020) 7219 1018; *e-mail:* rogersond@parliament.uk. *Clubs:* Camelford Liberal, St Columb Liberal; St Lawrence's Social.

ROGERSON, Nicolas; Chairman, AIGIS Blast Protection Ltd; *b* 21 May 1943; *s* of late Hugh and Olivia Rogerson; *m* 1998, Hon. Caroline Elizabeth Tamara Le Bas (*d* 2001), *er d* of Baron Gilbert, *qv. Educ:* Cheam Sch.; Winchester Coll.; Magdalene Coll., Cambridge. Investors Chronicle, 1964–65; Executive, Angel Court Consultants, 1966–68; formed Dewe Rogerson, 1969: Chief Exec., Dewe Rogerson Gp, 1969–99; Chm., Dewe Rogerson Internat., 1985–99. Appeals Chm., King George's Fund for Sailors. *Recreations:* sailing, ski-ing, Real tennis, field sports, languages and European history. *Clubs:* Turf, Beefsteak; Royal Yacht Squadron.

ROGERSON, Paul, CBE 2007; Chief Executive, Leeds City Council, since 1999; *b* 10 June 1948; *s* of late John Rogerson and of Hilda Rogerson (*née* Hepworth); *m* 1971, Eileen Kane; four *s* two *d. Educ:* De La Salle Coll., Sheffield; Manchester Univ. (LLB, MA Econ). Called to the Bar, Gray's Inn, 1971; Lectr, Univ. of Leeds, 1969–75; Principal Legal Officer: Barnsley MBC, 1975–78; Kirklees MDC, 1978–89; Asst Dir/Chief Legal Officer, 1989–95, Exec. Dir, 1995–99, Leeds CC. Vis. Prof., Univ. of Louisville, USA, 1972–73. Jt Gen. Ed., Local Govt Law Reports, 1999–2001. *Recreation:* family and friends. *Address:* Civic Hall, Leeds LS1 1UR. *T:* (0113) 247 4554.

ROGERSON, Philip Graham; Chairman, Carillion, since 2005 (Deputy Chairman, 2004–05); *b* 1 Jan. 1945; *s* of Henry and Florence Rogerson; *m* 1968, Susan Janet Kershaw; one *s* two *d. Educ:* William Hulme's Grammar Sch., Manchester. FCA 1968. Dearden, Harper, Miller & Co., Chartered Accountants, 1962–67; Hill Samuel & Co. Ltd, 1967–69; Thomas Tilling Ltd, 1969–71; Steetley Ltd, 1971–72; J. W. Chafer Ltd, 1972–78; with ICI plc, 1978–92 (General Manager, Finance, 1989–92); British Gas, later BG plc: Man. Dir, Finance, 1992–94; Exec. Dir, 1994–98; Dep. Chm., 1996–98. Non-executive Chairman: Pipeline Integrity Internat., 1998–2002; Bertram Gp Ltd, 1999–2001; United Engineering Forgings Ltd, 1999–2001; KBC Advanced Technologies plc, 1999–2004; Project Telecom plc, 2000–03; Aggreko, 2002– (Dep. Chm., 1997–2002); Thus Gp plc, 2004–; Viridian Gp plc, 1999–2005 (Dep. Chm., 1998); Northgate plc, 2007– (non-exec. Dir, 2003–07); non-executive Director: Leeds Permanent Bldg Soc., then Halifax Bldg Soc., now Halifax plc, 1994–98; Limit plc, 1997–2000; Internat. Public Relations, 1997–98; Wates City of London Properties, 1998–2001; British Biotech, 1999–2003; Octopus Capital plc, 2000–01; CopperEye Ltd, 2001–03; Celltech Gp plc, 2003–04; Davis Service Gp, 2004–. Trustee, Changing Faces, 1997–. *Recreations:* golf, tennis, theatre.

ROGG, Lionel; organist and composer; Professor of Organ and Improvisation, Geneva Conservatoire de Musique, since 1961; *b* 1936; *m* Claudine Effront; three *s. Educ:* Conservatoire de Musique, Geneva (1st prize for piano and organ). Concerts or organ recitals on the five continents. Records include works by Alain, Buxtehude (complete organ works; Deutscher Schallplatten Preis, 1980), Couperin and Martin; also complete works of J. S. Bach (Grand Prix du Disque, 1970, for The Art of the Fugue). *Compositions:* Acclamations, 1964; Chorale Preludes, 1971; Partita, 1975; Variations on Psalm 91, 1983; Cantata "Geburt der Venus", 1984; Introduction, Ricerare and Toccata, 1985; Two Etudes, 1986; Monodies, 1986; Psalm 92, 1986; Piece for Clarinette, 1986; Face-à-face for two pianos, 1987; Organ Concerto, 1991. DèsL Univ. de Genève, 1989. *Publication:* Eléments de Contrepoint, 1969. *Address:* Conservatoire de Musique, Place Neuve, Geneva, Switzerland; 38A route de Troinex, 1234 Vessy-Genève, Switzerland.

ROH, Tae Woo, Hon. GCMG 1989; President of Republic of Korea, 1988–93; *b* 4 Dec. 1932; *m* 1959, Kim-Ok-Sook; one *s* one *d. Educ:* Korean Military Academy; Republic of Korea War College. Commander, Capital Security, 1978, Defence Security, 1980; retd as Army General; Minister of State for Nat. Security and Foreign Affairs, 1981; Minister of Sports, and of Home Affairs, 1982; President: Seoul Olympic Organizing Cttee, 1983; Asian Games Organizing Cttee, 1983; Korean Olympic Cttee, 1984. Mem., Nat. Assembly and Pres., Ruling Democratic Justice Party, 1985. Hon. Dr George Washington Univ., 1989. Order of Nat. Security Merit (Sam Il Medal) (Korea), 1967; Grand Order of Mugunghwa (Korea), 1988; foreign decorations, incl. France, Germany, Kenya, Paraguay. *Publications:* Widaehan pot'ongsaram ui shidae (A great era of the ordinary people), 1987, trans. Japanese, 1988; Korea: a nation transformed, 1990. *Recreations:* tennis, swimming, golf, music, reading.

ROHMER, Eric, (Maurice Henri Joseph Schérer); French film director and writer; *b* 21 March 1920; *s* of Désiré Schérer and Jeanne Monzat; *m* 1957, Thérèse Barbet. *Educ:* Paris. Teacher, 1942–55; journalist, 1951–55. Film critic, Revue du cinéma, Arts, Temps Modernes, La Parisienne, 1949–63; Jt Founder, La Gazette du cinéma (also former Jt Editor). Dir of educnl films for French television, 1964–70. Co-Dir, Société des Films du Losange, 1964–. Films include (director and writer): Charlotte et son steak (short film),

1951; Le signe du lion, 1959; La boulangère de Monceau (short film), 1962; La collectionneuse, 1966; Ma nuit chez Maud, 1969 (prix Max Ophüls, 1970); Le genou de Claire, 1970 (prix Louis-Delluc, prix Méliès, 1971); L'amour l'après-midi, 1972; La Marquise d'O, 1976; Perceval le Gallois, 1978; Le beau mariage, 1982; Pauline à la plage, 1982; Les nuits de la pleine lune, 1984; Le rayon vert (Lion d'or, Venice Film Fest., prix de la critique internationale), 1986; L'ami de mon amie, 1988; Conte de Printemps, 1989; Conte d'Hiver, 1992; L'Arbre, le maire et la médiathèque, 1993; Rendezvous in Paris, 1996; Conte d'Eté, 1996; Conte d'Automne, 1999; L'Anglaise et le Duc, 2001; Triple Agent, 2004; Les Amours d'Astrée et de Céladon, 2007. Best Dir Award, Berlin Film Fest., 1983; Lifetime Achievement Award, Venice Film Fest., 2001. *Publications:* Alfred Hitchcock, 1973; Charlie Chaplin, 1973; Six contes moraux, 1974; L'organisation de l'espace dans le "Faust" de Murnau, 1977; The Taste for Beauty (essays), 1992; De Mozart en Beethoven, 1996. *Address:* Les Films du Losange, 22 avenue Pierre 1er de Serbie, 75116 Paris, France.

ROHRER, Dr Heinrich; IBM Research Division, Zurich Research Laboratory, 1963–97, and IBM Fellow, 1986–97; *b* 6 June 1933; *s* of Henrich and Katharina Rohrer; *m* 1961, Rose-Marie Egger; two *d. Educ:* Federal Inst. of Technology, ETH, Zürich (Dr. sc. nat); PhD 1960. Post-doctoral Fellow, Rutgers Univ., 1961–63; joined IBM Res. Div. as Res. Staff Mem., 1963; then various managerial posts. Vis. Scientist, Univ. of Calif. at Santa Barbara, 1974–75. Mem. Bd, Swiss Fed. Insts of Technol., 1993–2003. Mem., Swiss Acad. of Technical Scis, 1988; For. Associate, US Acad. of Sci., 1988; Hon. Member: Swiss Physical Soc., 1990; Swiss Assoc. of Engrs and Architects, 1991; Zurich Physical Soc., 1992. Hon. Fellow, RMS, 1988. Hon. Dr: Rutgers, 1987; Marseille, 1988; Madrid, 1988; Tsukuba, Japan, 1994; Wolfgang Goethe Univ., Frankfurt, 1996; Tohoku, Japan, 2000. (Jtly) King Faisal Internat. Prize for Science, 1984; (jtly) Hewlett Packard Europhysics Prize, 1984; (jtly) Nobel Prize in Physics, 1986; (jtly) Cresson Medal, Franklin Inst., Philadelphia, 1987. *Recreations:* ski-ing, hiking, gardening.

ROITH, Oscar, CB 1987; FREng, FIMechE; Deputy Chairman, British Maritime Technology, 1997–2002 (Director, 1987–2002); Chief Engineer and Scientist, Department of Trade and Industry, 1982–87; *b* London, 14 May 1927; *s* of late Leon Roith and Leah Roith; *m* 1950, Irene Bullock; one *d. Educ:* Gonville and Caius Coll., Cambridge (minor schol.; Mech. Scis Tripos; MA). FIMechE 1967; FREng (FEng 1983); Eur Ing 1988. Research Dept, Courtaulds, 1948; Distillers Co. Ltd: Central Engrg Dept, 1952; Engrg Manager, Hull Works, 1962; Works Manager, 1968, Works Gen. Manager, 1969, BP Chemicals, Hull; General Manager: Engrg and Technical, BP Chemicals, 1974; Engrg Dept, BP Trading, 1977; Chief Exec. (Engrg), BP Internat., 1981. Dir, Trueland Ltd, 1987–2004. Mem., Yorks and Humberside Economic Planning Council, 1972–74. Comr, Royal Commn for Exhibition of 1851, 1988–98. Chm., Mech. and Electrical Engrg Requirements Bd, 1981–82; Member: Mech. Engrg and Machine Tools Requirements Bd, 1977–81; (non-exec.) Res. Cttee. British Gas, 1987–96; ACORD, 1982–87; ACARD, 1982–87; Process Plant EDC, NEDO, 1979–82; SERC, 1982–87; NERC, 1982–87; Bd (part-time), LRT, 1988–95; Chm., Res. Adv. Gp, PCFC, 1989–92. Pres., IMechE, 1987–88 (Dep. Pres., 1985–87; Mem. Council, 1981–92; Mem., Process Engrg Gp Cttee, 1962–68); Dep. Chm. Council, Foundn for Science and Technol., 1988–95; Hon. Sec., Mech. Engrg, Council of Fellowship of Engrg, 1988–91. Hon. Prof., Dept of Mgt Sci., Univ. of Stirling, 1992–95; Hon. Fellow, Univ. of Brighton, 1992. Governor: Brighton Polytechnic, 1988–91; ICSTM, 1990–98. CCMI; FRSA. Hon. DSc West of England, 1993. *Recreations:* cricket, gardening, walking. *Address:* 20 Wraymill House, Wraymill Park, Batts Hill, Reigate, Surrey RH2 0LJ. *T:* (01737) 779633. *Club:* Athenæum.

ROITT, Prof. Ivan Maurice, FRS 1983; Emeritus Professor of Immunology, University College London, since 1992; Professor, 1968–92, and Head of Department of Immunology, 1968–92, and of Rheumatology Research, 1984–92, University College and Middlesex School of Medicine (formerly Middlesex Hospital Medical School); Chief Scientist, NALIA Systems Ltd, since 2005; *b* 30 Sept. 1927; *e s* of Harry Roitt; *m* 1953, Margaret Auralie Louise, *d* of F. Haigh; three *d. Educ:* King Edward's Sch., Birmingham; Balliol Coll., Oxford (exhibnr; BSc 1950; MA 1953; DPhil 1953; DSc 1968; Hon. Fellow 2004). FRCPath 1973. Res. Fellow, 1953, Reader in Immunopathol., 1965–68, Middlesex Hosp. Med. Sch. Chm., WHO Cttee on Immunolog. Control of Fertility, 1976–79; Mem., Biol. Sub-Cttee, UGC. Mem., Harrow Borough Council, 1963–65; Chm., Harrow Central Lib. Assoc., 1965–67. Vis. Prof., Middx Univ., 2006. Florey Meml Lectr, Adelaide Univ., 1982. Hon. FRCP 1995. Hon. Dr Middx, 2007. (Jtly) Van Meter Prize, Amer. Thyroid Assoc., 1957; Gairdner Foundn Award, Toronto, 1964. *Publications:* Essential Immunology, 1971, 11th edn 2006; (jtly) Immunology of Oral Diseases, 1979; (jtly) Immunology, 1985, 7th edn 2006; (jtly) Current Opinion in Immunology (series), 1989–93; (jtly) Clinical Immunology, 1991; Slide Atlas of Essential Immunology, 1992; (with Peter J. Delves) Encyclopedia of Immunology, 1992, 2nd edn 2000; (ed jtly) Medical Microbiology, 1993, 4th edn 2007; 283 contribs to learned scientific jls. *Recreations:* tennis, golf, clarinet (modest), piano (very modest), banjo (subliminal), the contemporary novel, models of public debate. *Address:* Royal Free and University College London, Department of Immunology, Windeyer Institute of Medical Sciences, Cleveland Street, W1T 4JF.

ROJO, Tamara; Principal Dancer, Royal Ballet, since 2000; *d* of Pablo Rojo and Sara Diez. *Educ:* Centro de Danza de Victor Ullate. Compañía de Danza Victor Ullate, 1991–96; Guest Dancer, Scottish Ballet, 1996–97; Principal, English Nat. Ballet, 1997–2000. Guest Dancer: Ballet Nat. de Cuba; Deutsche Oper Ballet Berlin; Ballet de La Opera de Niza; Ente Publico Arena di Verona; Scottish Ballet; Ballet Victor Ullate, Madrid. Grand Prix Femme, Concours Internat. de Danse de Paris, 1994; Best Dancer of Year, Italian Critics, 1996; Award for Outstanding Achievements in Dance, Barclay's Th. Awards, 2000; Best Female Dancer of Year 2001, Critic's Circle Dance Awards, 2002. Medalla de Oro al Mérito en las Bellas Artes (Spain), 2002. *Address:* c/o Royal Ballet, Royal Opera House, Covent Garden, WC2E 9DD.

ROKISON, Kenneth Stuart; QC 1976; a Judge of the Courts of Appeal of Jersey and Guernsey, 2000–07; a former Deputy High Court Judge; *b* 13 April 1937; *s* of late Frank Edward and late Kitty Winifred Rokison; *m* 1973, Rosalind Julia (*née* Mitchell); one *s* two *d. Educ:* Whitgift School, Croydon; Magdalene College, Cambridge (BA 1960). Called to the Bar, Gray's Inn, 1961, Bencher, 1985–2003. A Recorder, 1989–94. *Recreations:* theatre, tennis, charity bicycle rides. *Address:* Ashcroft Farm, Gadbrook, Betchworth, Surrey RH3 7AH. *T:* (01306) 611244.

ROLAND, Prof. Martin Oliver, CBE 2003; DM; FRCP, FRCGP; FMedSci; Professor of General Practice, Manchester University, since 1992; Director: National Primary Care Research and Development Centre, since 1999; National School for Primary Care Research, since 2006; *b* 7 Aug. 1951; *s* of Peter Ernest Roland and Margaret Eileen Roland; *m* 1st, 1971, Gillian Chapman; one *s*; 2nd, 1979, Rosalind Thorburn; two *s* one *d. Educ:* Rugby Sch.; Merton Coll., Oxford (BA 1972; BM BCh 1975; DM 1989). MRCP 1978, FRCP 2001; FRCGP 1994. Lectr in Gen. Practice, St Thomas's Hosp. Med. Sch., 1979–83; Dir of Studies in Gen. Practice, Cambridge Univ. Sch. of Clinical Medicine, 1987–92. Mem., MRC Health Services Research Bd, 1992–96 (Chm. and Mem. MRC Council, 1994–96). FMedSci 2000. *Publications:* contribs on gen. practice, hosp. referrals, back pain, quality of care and out of hours care. *Recreations:* walking, opera. *Address:* National Primary Care Research and Development Centre, University of Manchester, Williamson Building, Oxford Road, Manchester M13 9PL. *T:* (0161) 275 7663.

ROLFE; *see* Neville-Rolfe.

ROLFE, Mervyn James, CBE 2000; JP, DL; FSAScot; Convener, Scottish Police Services Authority, since 2007; *b* 31 July 1947; *s* of Raymond Rolfe and late Margaret Rolfe; *m* 1977, Christine Margaret Tyrell; one *s. Educ:* Buckhaven High Sch., Fife; Dundee Univ. (MEd Hons); Abertay Dundee Univ. (MSc). FSAScot 1993. Civil servant, MSC, 1977–83; Co-ordinator, Dundee Resources Centre for Unemployed, 1983–87. Tayside Regional Council: Councillor, 1986–96; Convener of Educn, 1986–94; Depute Leader, 1990–94; Opposition Leader, 1994–96; Dundee City Council: Mem., 1995–2003; Convener of Econ. Develt and Depute Leader, 1999–2003; Lord Provost and Lord-Lieut of Dundee, 1996–99. Chief Exec., Dundee and Tayside Chamber of Commerce and Industry, 2002–06; Dir, Scottish Enterprise Tayside, 1992–96, 1999–2003. Chm., ESEP Ltd, 1999–. Member: General Teaching Council Scotland, 1986–96; Exec., COSLA, 1990–96. Mem. Court, Dundee Univ., 1986–2000. Vice Chm. of Govs, HM Frigate Unicorn Preservation Soc., 1998–; Hon. Col, 2 (City of Dundee) Signals Sqn, TA, 2003–. Hon. Fellow, Univ. of Abertay Dundee, 1999. FRSA 1992. JP 1988, DL 1999, Dundee. OStJ 1997. *Recreations:* reading, music, local history. *Address:* 17 Mains Terrace, Dundee DD4 7BX. *T:* (01382) 450073.

ROLFE, William David Ian, PhD; FRSE, FGS, FMA; Keeper of Geology, National Museums of Scotland, 1986–96; *b* 24 Jan. 1936; *s* of late William Ambrose Rolfe and Greta Olwen Jones; *m* 1960, Julia Mary Margaret, *d* of late Capt. G. H. G. S. Rayer, OBE; two *d. Educ:* Royal Liberty Grammar Sch., Romford; Birmingham Univ. (BSc 1957; PhD 1960). FGS 1960; FMA 1972; FRSE 1983. Demonstrator in Geol., UC of N Staffs, 1960; Fulbright Schol., and Asst Curator, Mus. of Comparative Zool., Harvard Coll., Cambridge, Mass, 1961–62; Geol. Curator, Univ. Lectr, then Sen. Lectr in Geol., Hunterian Mus., Univ. of Glasgow, 1962–81; Dep. Dir, 1981–86. Vis. Scientist, Field Mus. of Natural Hist., Chicago, 1981. Mem., Trng Awards Cttee, NERC, 1980–83. President: Palaeontol Assoc., 1992–94 (Vice-Pres., 1974–76); Soc. Hist. Natural Hist., 1996–99 (Vice-Pres., 1987). Geological Society of Glasgow: Ed., Scottish Jl of Geol., 1967–72; Pres., 1973–76; Geological Society: Editl Chm., Journal, 1973–76; Chm., Conservation Cttee, 1980–85; Murchison Fund, 1978; Tyrrell Res. Fund, 1982; Coke Medal, 1984; Edinburgh Geological Society: Pres., 1989–91; Clough Medal, 1997. FRSA 1985. *Publications:* (ed) Phylogeny and Evolution of Crustacea, 1963; Treatise on Invertebrate Paleontology, part R, 1969; Geological Howlers, 1980; papers on fossil phyllocarid crustaceans and palaeontol., esp. other arthropods, and hist. of 18th century natural sci. illustration. *Recreations:* visual arts, walking, music. *Address:* 4A Randolph Crescent, Edinburgh EH3 7TH. *T:* (0131) 226 2094.

ROLFE JOHNSON, Anthony, CBE 1992; tenor; *b* 5 Nov. 1940; *m* (marr. diss.); two *s*; *m* Elisabeth Jones Evans; one *s* two *d*. Has performed at Glyndebourne, Covent Garden, Hamburg State Opera, La Scala Milan, Royal Albert Hall, Coliseum, Queen Elizabeth Hall, Aldeburgh Festival, Royal Festival Hall, Barbican Centre, Wigmore Hall, Salzburg Festival, Metropolitan NY. Has appeared with all major British orchestras and with Chicago Symphony Orchestra, Boston Symphony Orchestra, New York Philharmonic Orchestra and others. *Current rôles include:* Ulisse, Orfeo (Monteverdi), Idomeneo, Aschenbach, Peter Grimes, Lucio Silla, Tamino. *Address:* c/o Askonas Holt, Lincoln House, 300 High Holborn, WC1V 7JH.

ROLLAND, Lawrence Anderson Lyon, PPRIBA; PPRIAS; FRSE; Senior Partner, Hurd Rolland Partnership (formerly L. A. Rolland & Partners, later Robert Hurd and Partners), 1959–97; President of Royal Institute of British Architects, 1985–87; *b* 6 Nov. 1937; *s* of Lawrence Anderson Rolland and Winifred Anne Lyon; *m* 1960, Mairi Melville; two *s* two *d. Educ:* George Watson Boys' College, Edinburgh; Duncan of Jordanstone College of Art. Diploma of Art (Architecture) 1959. ARIBA 1960; FRIAS 1965 (Pres., RIAS, 1979–81); FRSE 1989. Founder Mem., Scottish Construction Industry Group, 1979–81; Mem., Bldg EDC, NEDC, 1982–88. Mem. Bd, Architects' Registration Bd, 1996–2004 (Chm., Qualifications Adv. Gp, 2000–04). Architect for: The Queen's Hall, concert hall, Edinburgh; restoration and redesign of Bank of Scotland Head Office (original Architect, Sibbald, Reid & Crighton, 1805 and later, Bryce, 1870); much housing in Fife's royal burghs; British Golf Museum, St Andrews; General Accident Life Assurance, York; redesign, Council Chamber, GMC. Chairman: RIBA Educn Trust Fund, 1996–2003; RIBA Educn Funds Cttee, 1996–2003; Gen. Trustee, Church of Scotland, 1979– (Chm., Adv. Cttee on Artistic Matters, 1975–81); Mem. of Council and Bd, Nat. Trust for Scotland, 2005–. Chm. Bd. of Govs, Duncan of Jordanstone Coll. of Art, 1993–94; Chm. Court, Univ. of Dundee, 1997–2004 (Mem., 1993–; Chancellor's Assessor, 2002–). FRSA 1988. Hon. LLD Dundee, 2004. Winner of more than 20 awards and commendations from Saltire Soc., Stone Fedn, Concrete Soc., Civic Trust, Europa Nostra, RIBA, and Times Conservation Award. *Recreations:* music, fishing, food, wine, cars. *Address:* Blink Bonny Cottage, Newburn, nr Upper Largo, Leven, Fife KY8 6JF. *T:* (01333) 360383. *Club:* Reform.

ROLLINSON, Timothy John Denis; Director-General and Deputy Chairman, Forestry Commission, since 2004; *b* 6 Nov. 1953; *s* of William Edward Denis Rollinson and Ida Frances Rollinson (*née* Marshall); *m* 1975, Dominique Christine Favardin; one *s* two *d. Educ:* Chigwell Sch.; Edinburgh Univ. (BSc Hons). MICFor 1978, FICFor 1995; FIAgrE 2004; CEnv 2005. Forestry Commission: District Officer: Kent, 1976–78; New Forest, 1978–81; Head of: Growth and Yield Studies, 1981–88; Land Use Planning, 1988–90; Parly and Policy Div., 1990–93; Sec., 1994–97; Chief Conservator, England, 1997–2000; Head of Policy and Practice Div., 2000–03; Dir, Forestry Gp, 2003–04. Chairman: Forest Res. Co-ordination Cttee, 2000–04; Global Partnership on Forest Landscape Restoration, 2002–; Pres., Inst. of Chartered Foresters, 2000–02. Patron, Tree Aid, 2008. CCMI 2006. *Publications:* Thinning Control in British Woodlands, 1985; articles in forestry jls. *Recreations:* golf, swimming, food. *Address:* Forestry Commission, 231 Corstorphine Road, Edinburgh EH12 7AT. *T:* (0131) 314 6424. *Club:* Craigmillar Park Golf (Edinburgh).

ROLLO, family name of **Lord Rollo**.

ROLLO, 14th Lord *cr* 1651; **David Eric Howard Rollo;** Baron Dunning 1869; *b* 31 March 1943; *s* of 13th Lord Rollo and of Suzanne Hatton; *S* father, 1997; *m* 1971, Felicity Anne Christian, *o d* of Lt-Comdr J. B. Lamb; three *s. Educ:* Eton. Late Captain Grenadier Guards. *Heir: s* Master of Rollo, *qv. Address:* Pitcairns House, Dunning, Perthshire PH2 9BX. *Clubs:* Cavalry and Guards, Turf.

ROLLO, Master of; Hon. James David William Rollo; *b* 8 Jan. 1972; *s* and *heir* of Lord Rollo, *qv*; *m* 2001, Sophie Sara, *d* of Hubert de Castella; one *s* two *d*. *Educ:* Eton; Edinburgh Univ.

ROLLO, Prof. James Maxwell Cree, CMG 1998; Professor of European Economic Integration, University of Sussex, and Co-Director, Sussex European Institute, since 1999; *b* 20 Jan. 1946; *s* of late James Maxwell Cree Rollo and Alice Mary (*née* Killen); *m* 1970, Sonia Ann Halliwell; one *s* one *d*. *Educ:* Gourock High Sch.; Greenock High Sch.; Glasgow Univ. (BSc); London School of Economics (MSc Econ). Asst Economist, 1968–75, Economic Advr, 1975–79, MAFF; Economic Advr, FCO, 1979–81; Sen. Economic Advr, ODA, 1981–84; Dep. Head, Economic Advrs, FCO, 1984–89; Dir, Internat. Econs Programme, RIIA, 1989–93; Chief Economic Advr, FCO, 1993–98. Dir, ESRC Res. Prog., One Europe or Several?, 2001–03. Special Prof., Univ. of Nottingham, 1996–99. Trustee, Mus. of Migration and Diversity, Spitalfields, 2001–. Ed., Jl of Common Market Studies, 2003–. *Publications:* The New Eastern Europe: Western responses, 1990; (with John Flemming) Trade, Payments and Adjustment in Central and Eastern Europe, 1992; articles in learned jls. *Recreation:* having fun. *Address:* Sussex European Institute, University of Sussex, Falmer, Brighton BN1 9RG. *T:* (01273) 877265, *Fax:* (01273) 678571; *e-mail:* j.rollo@sussex.ac.uk.

ROLLS, Prof. Edmund Thomson, DPhil, DSc; Professor of Experimental Psychology, University of Oxford, 1996; Fellow and Tutor in Psychology, Corpus Christi College, Oxford, 1973; *b* 4 June 1945; *s* of Eric Fergus Rolls and May Martin Rolls (*née* Thomson); *m* 1969, Barbara Jean Simons (marr. diss. 1983); two *d*. *Educ:* Hardye's Sch., Dorchester; Jesus Coll., Cambridge (BA Preclinical Medicine 1967; MA); Queen's Coll., Oxford (Thomas Hardy Schol.); Magdalen Coll., Oxford (DPhil 1971); DSc Oxon 1986. Oxford University: Fellow by Exam., Magdalen Coll., 1969–73; Lectr in Exptl Psychol., 1973–96. Associate Dir, MRC Oxford IRC for Cognitive Neurosci., 1990–2003. Member: Soc. for Neurosci.; Physiological Soc.; Exptl Psychol. Soc. Secretary: Eur. Brain and Behaviour Soc., 1973–76; Council, Eur. Neurosci. Assoc., 1985–88; Membre d'Honneur, Société Française de Neurologie, 1994; Mem., Academia Europea. Canadian Commonwealth Fellow, 1980–81. Hon. DSc Toyama, 2005. Spearman Medal, BPsS, 1977. *Publications:* The Brain and Reward, 1975; (with B. J. Rolls) Thirst, 1982; (with A. Treves) Neural Networks and Brain Function, 1998; (jtly) Introduction to Connectionist Modelling of Cognitive Processes, 1998; The Brain and Emotion, 1999; (with G. Deco) Computational Neuroscience of Vision, 2002; Emotion Explained, 2005; Memory, Attention and Decision-Making, 2007. *Recreations:* yachting, windsurfing, music, including opera.

ROMAIN, Rabbi Dr Jonathan Anidjar, MBE 2004; Minister, Maidenhead Synagogue, since 1980; Chairman, Assembly of Rabbis, since 2007; *b* 24 Aug. 1954; *s* of Daniel and Gabrielle Romain; *m* 1981, Sybil Sheridan; four *s*. *Educ:* University Coll. London (BA Hons); Univ. of Leicester (PhD 1990). Semicha/Rabbinic Ordination, Leo Baeck Coll., London. Chaplain, Jewish Police Assoc., 2003–. Bd Mem., CCJ, 1989–. *Publications:* Signs and Wonders, 1985; The Jews of England, 1988; Faith and Practice, 1991; Tradition and Change, 1995; Till Faith us to Part, 1996; Renewing the Vision, 1996; Your God Shall Be My God, 2000; (ed) Reform Judaism and Modernity, 2004; God, Doubt and Dawkins, 2008. *Recreations:* tennis, completing a never-ending family tree, preaching what I think I ought to practise. *Address:* Grenfell Lodge, Ray Park Road, Maidenhead, Berks SL6 8QX. *T:* (01628) 673012.

ROMAIN, Roderick Jessel Anidjar; Metropolitan Stipendiary Magistrate, 1972–83; *b* 2 Dec. 1916; *s* of late Artom A. Romain and Winifred (*née* Rodrigues); *m* 1947, Miriam (*d* 1991), *d* of late Semtob Sequerra; one *s* one *d*. *Educ:* Malvern Coll.; Sidney Sussex Coll., Cambridge. Called to the Bar, Middle Temple, 1939. Commissioned from HAC to 27th Field Regt, RA, 1940. Served War of 1939–45; France and Belgium, also N Africa and Italy, JAG Staff, 1943–45; JA at Neuengamme War Crimes Trial. Admitted a Solicitor, 1949, in practice as Partner, in Freke Palmer, Romain & Gassman, until 1972; recalled to Bar, 1973; a Dep. Circuit Judge, 1975–78.

ROMAINE, Prof. Suzanne, PhD; Merton Professor of English Language, and Fellow of Merton College, Oxford University, since 1984. *Educ:* Bryn Mawr Coll., Penn (AB); Edinburgh Univ. (MLitt); PhD Birmingham Univ. Lectr in Linguistics, Birmingham Univ., 1979–84. *Publications:* Socio-historical Linguistics: its status and methodology, 1982; Sociolinguistic Variation in Speech Communities, 1982; Language of Children and Adolescents, 1984; Pidgin and Creole Languages, 1988; Bilingualism, 1989; (ed) Language in Australia, 1991; Language Education and Development, 1992; Language in Society: introduction to sociolinguistics, 1994; (ed) Cambridge History of the English Language, vol. IV, 1998; Communicating Gender, 1999; (with D. Nettle) Vanishing Voices, 2000. *Address:* Merton College, Oxford OX1 4JD.

ROMAN, Stephan; Regional Director, West Europe and North America, British Council, since 2005; *b* 29 March 1953; *s* of Victor and Muriel Roman; *m* 1986, Dorcas Pearmaine; one *s* two *d*. *Educ:* St Peter's Coll., Oxford (BA Hons Mod. Hist. 1974, MA); Univ. of Sheffield (MA Librarianship and Inf. Studies 1976). Libraries, Arts and Mus Dept, Coventry CC, 1974–78; British Council: Sudan and Yemen, 1979–82; Saudi Arabia and Gulf, 1983–86; Indonesia, 1986–91; Dir, Information Services, 1992–2001; Regl Dir, SE Europe, 2001–05. Order of Merit (Romania), 2004. *Publication:* The Development of Islamic Library Collections in Western Europe and North America, 1990. *Recreations:* walking, history, opera. *Address:* British Council, Rue de Trône/Troonstraat 108, 1050 Brussels, Belgium. *T:* (2) 5540464, *Fax:* (2) 2270849; *e-mail:* stephan.roman@britishcouncil.be.

ROMANES, Professor George John, CBE 1971; PhD; Professor of Anatomy, 1954–84, and Dean of Faculty of Medicine, 1979–83, Edinburgh University; Professor of Anatomy, Royal Scottish Academy, since 1983; *b* 2 Dec. 1916; *s* of George Romanes, BSc, AMICE, and Isabella Elizabeth Burn Smith; *m* 1945, Muriel Grace Adam (*d* 1992), Edinburgh; four *d*. *Educ:* Edinburgh Academy; Christ's College, Cambridge (BA, PhD); Edinburgh University (MB, ChB). Marmaduke Sheild Scholar in Human Anatomy, 1938–40; Demonstrator in Anatomy, Cambridge, 1939; Beit Memorial Fellow for Medical Research, Cambridge, 1944–46; Lectr in Neuroanatomy, Edinburgh Univ., 1946–54. Commonwealth Fund Fell., Columbia Univ., NY, 1949–50. Chm., Bd of Management, Edinburgh Royal Infirmary, 1959–74. Mem. Anatomical Soc. of Gt Brit. and Ireland; Mem. Amer. Assoc. of Anatomists; Assoc. Mem. Amer. Neurological Assoc. FRSE 1955; FRCSE 1958. Hon. DSc Glasgow, 1983. *Publications:* (ed) Cunningham's Textbook and Manuals of Anatomy; various papers on the anatomy and development of the nervous system in Jl of Anatomy and Jl of Comparative Neurology. *Recreations:* angling and curling. *Address:* Camus na Feannag, Kishorn, Strathcarron, Ross-shire IV54 8XA. *T:* (01520) 733273.

ROMANIUK, Paula Shane; *see* Pryke, P. S.

ROMANOW, Rt Hon. Roy John, OC 2003; PC (Can.) 2003; QC (Sask.); Senior Fellow in Public Policy, Department of Political Studies, University of Saskatchewan, Canada, since 2001; Senior Policy Fellow, Saskatchewan Institute of Public Policy, University of Regina, since 2001; *b* 1939; *s* of Mike and Tekla Romanow; *m* 1967, Eleanore Boykowich. *Educ:* Univ. of Saskatchewan (Arts and Law degrees). First elected to Saskatchewan Legislative Assembly, 1967; MLA (NDP) Saskatoon-Riversdale, 1967–82, 1986–2001; Dep. Premier, 1971–82; Attorney General, 1971–82; Minister of Intergovtl Affairs, 1979–82; Opposition House Leader for NDP Caucus, 1986; Leader, Saskatchewan NDP, 1987–2001; Premier, Saskatchewan, 1991–2001. Hd, Commn on Future of Health Care in Canada, 2001–02; Mem., Security Intelligence Rev. Cttee, 2003–08. Vis. Fellow, Sch. of Policy Studies, Queen's Univ., 2001–. *Publication:* (jtly) Canada Notwithstanding, 1984. *Address:* c/o Department of Political Studies, University of Saskatchewan, 9 Campus Drive, 919 Arts Building, Saskatoon, SK S7N 5A5, Canada.

ROME, Alan Mackenzie, OBE 1997; FSA; architect in private practice, 1960–2002; *b* 24 Oct. 1930; *s* of John and Evelyn Rome; *m* 1956, Mary Lilyan Barnard; one *s* one *d*. *Educ:* King's Sch., Bruton; Royal West of England Academy Sch. of Architecture (DipArch 1955). FRIBA 1971; FSA 1979. Pupil in office of Sir George Oatley, 1947–49; Nat. Service, RE, 1949–50; Asst to Stephen Dykes Bower at Westminster Abbey, 1955–60; Associate Architect with Michael Torrens and Alan Crozier Cole, 1960–64. Architect to: Glastonbury Abbey, 1972–96; Bath Abbey, 1976–97; Lancing Coll. Chapel, 1984–98 (now Architect Emeritus); St Mary Redcliffe, Bristol, 1986–2001, and other churches in Somerset, Devon and Wilts; Deans, Chapters and Cathedrals of: Leicester, 1971–97 (Consultant); Salisbury, 1974–92; Peterborough, 1976–89; Wells, 1979–94; Bristol, 1986–2001; St Edmundsbury, 1991–98; Truro, 1992–2001 (now Architect Emeritus). Member: Council for the Care of Churches, 1972–96 (Mem., Organs Adv. Cttee, 1991–96); Churches Conservation Trust (formerly Redundant Churches Fund), 1980–99; Cttee of Hon. Consulting Architects, Historic Churches Preservation Trust, 1990–95; Bath and Wells DAC, 1978–. Occasional Lectr, Bath and Bristol Univs. *Publications:* (jtly) Bristol Cathedral – History and Architecture, 2000; papers and addresses on architectural subjects. *Recreations:* walking, sketching, music. *Address:* 11 Mayfair Avenue, Nailsea, N Somerset BS48 2LR. *T:* (01275) 853215.

ROMINGER, Rev. Roberta Carol Sears; General Secretary, United Reformed Church, since 2008; *b* USA, 30 Aug. 1955; *d* of Robert Alden Sears and Janet Carol Sears (*née* Graef); *m* 1990, Rev. Dale Rominger. *Educ:* Univ. of California, Berkeley (BA 1977); Pacific Sch. of Religion, Berkeley (MDiv 1982). Ordained Minister, 1982; Minister: Tombstone Community Church, United Church of Christ, Arizona, 1982–85; York Rd URC, Woking, 1985–90; Worplesdon URC, Guildford, 1987–90; Wideopen URC, Newcastle-upon-Tyne, 1991–98; Kingston Park Ecumenical Church, Newcastle-upon-Tyne, 1993–98; Moderator, Thames North Synod, URC, 1998–2008. *Recreation:* playing the cello. *Address:* United Reformed Church, 86 Tavistock Place, WC1H 9RT. *T:* (020) 7916 2020, *Fax:* (020) 7916 2021.

ROMNEY, 8th Earl of, *cr* 1801; **Julian Charles Marsham;** Bt 1663; Baron of Romney, 1716; Viscount Marsham, 1801; *b* 28 March 1948; *s* of late Col Peter William Marsham, MBE and of Hersey (*née* Coke); *S* cousin, 2004; *m* 1975, Catriona Ann, *d* of Lt-Col Sir Robert Christie Stewart, *qv*; two *s* one *d*. *Educ:* Eton. High Sheriff, Norfolk, 2007. *Heir:* *s* Viscount Marsham, *qv*.

RONALD, Edith, (Mrs Edmund Ronald); *see* Templeton, Mrs Edith.

RONALDSHAY, Earl of; Robin Lawrence Dundas; Director: Fine Art Commissions Ltd, since 1997; Zetland Estates Ltd (formerly Dundas Estates Ltd), since 1999; Zetland Estates (Shetland) Ltd, since 2004; Stronghill Developments Ltd, since 2004; *b* 5 March 1965; *s* and *heir* of Marquess of Zetland, *qv*; *m* 1997, Heather, *d* of Robert Hoffman, Maryland, USA and Mrs Richard Cazenove, Cottesbrooke, Northants; four *d* (incl. twins). *Educ:* Harrow; Royal Agricl Coll., Cirencester. Director: Catterick Racecourse Co., 1988–2006; Redcar Racecourse Ltd (formerly Redcar Race Co.), 1989–2006; Man. Dir, Musks Ltd, 1993–99. Member: Richmond Burgage Pastures Cttee, 2000– (Chm., 2005–); Yorks Cttee, CLA, 2001–05. Treas., Yorks HHA, 2000–05 (Dep. Chm., 2005–). Trustee, Trebetherick Estate Club, 1995–. Chm., Aske Parish Meeting, 1998–. *Recreations:* tennis, golf, keeping up with my children. *Address:* The Estate Office, Aske, Richmond, N Yorks DL10 5HJ. *Club:* Slainte Mhah.

RONAY, Egon; Founder of the Egon Ronay hotel and restaurant guides (taken over by the Automobile Association, 1985, purchased by Leading Guides Ltd, 1992, all publishing rights reverted to Egon Ronay, 1997); *m* 1967, Barbara Greenslade; one *s*, and two *d* of previous marr. *Educ:* School of Piarist Order, Budapest; Univ. of Budapest (LLD); Academy of Commerce, Budapest. Dip. Restaurateurs' Guild, Budapest; FIH. After univ. degree, trained in kitchens of family's five restaurants; continued training abroad, finishing at Dorchester Hotel, London; progressed to management within family concern of 5 restaurants, of which eventually he took charge; emigrated from Hungary, 1946; Gen. Manager, Princes Restaurant, Piccadilly, then Society Restaurant, Jermyn Street, followed by 96 Restaurant, Piccadilly; opened own restaurant, The Marquee, SW1, 1952–55; started eating-out and general food, wine and tourism weekly column in Daily Telegraph and later Sunday Telegraph, 1954–60, also eating-out guide, 1957; weekly dining out column in Evening News, 1968–74; fortnightly gastronomic column, Sunday Times, 1986–92; Ed.-in-Chief, Egon Ronay Recommends (BAA Airports magazine), 1992–94. Constant team surveyance of catering and rating, BAA's 7 airports, 1992–2002. Founder and Pres., British Acad. of Gastronomes, 1983–; Mem. l'Académie des Gastronomes, France, 1979; Founder, Internat. Acad. of Gastronomy, 1985. Lifetime Achievement Award, Carlton London Restaurant Awards, 1999; Lifetime Achievement Award, Caterer and Hotelkeeper Award, 2001. Médaille de la Ville de Paris, 1983; Chevalier de l'Ordre du Mérite Agricole, 1987. *Publications:* Egon Ronay's Guide to Hotels and Restaurants, annually, 1956–85; Egon Ronay's Just A Bite, annually, 1979–85; Egon Ronay's Pub Guide, annually, 1980–85; Egon Ronay's Guide to 500 Good Restaurants in Europe's main cities, annually, 1983–85; The Unforgettable Dishes of My Life, 1989; Egon Ronay's Guide 2005 to the Top 200 Restaurants in the UK, 2005; Egon Ronay's 2006 Guide to the Best Restaurants and Gastropubs in the UK, 2005; various other guides to Britain and overseas, to ski resorts in Europe, to Scandinavian hotels and restaurants and to eating places in Greece.

RONAYNE, Prof. Jarlath, AM 2002; PhD; FRSC, FTSE; Vice-Chancellor, Sunway University College, Malaysia, since 2006 (Academic Director, 2004–06); Senior Associate, Ronayne Francis International, Melbourne, since 2005; Vice-Chancellor and President, Victoria University of Technology, Melbourne, 1991–2003, Distinguished Professorial Fellow, since 2004; *b* 3 Sept. 1938; *s* of late Michael Ronayne and Anne Ronayne (*née* Kenny); *m* 1st, 1965, Rosalind Hickman; two *s*; 2nd, 1995, Margaret Francis. *Educ:* Trinity Coll., Dublin (BA 1965; MA 1968; Hon. Fellow 1997); St John's Coll., Cambridge (PhD 1968). FRSC 1988; FTSE 1995. Lecturer: Dept of Applied Sci., Wolverhampton Poly., 1968–70; Dept of Sci. and Technol. Policy, Manchester Univ., 1970–74; Sen. Lectr, then Dir, Sci. Policy Res. Centre, Sch. of Sci., Griffith Univ., Brisbane, 1974–77; University of New South Wales: Prof. of Hist. and Philosophy of Sci., 1977–91; Hd of Dept of Hist. and Philosophy of Sci., 1977–83; Dean, Faculty of Arts, 1983–84; Pro-Vice-Chancellor,

1984–88; Dep. Vice-Chancellor, 1988–91; Prof. Emeritus, 1991. Hon. Prof., Shanghai Inst. Tourism, 1993; Visiting Fellow: Oriel Coll., Oxford, 1999; Wolfson Coll., Cambridge, 2004–. Member: Internat. Council on Sci. Policy Studies, 1984–; Exec. Cttee, Australian Higher Educn Industrial Assoc., 1996–99; Bd, Communications Law Centre, Sydney, 1996–2003; Standing Cttee on Internat. Matters, AVCC, 1998– (Leader, AVCC Delegn to India, 1998); Bd Dirs, Sunway Coll. Sdn Bhd, 2004–. Consultant to Commonwealth Dept of Employment, Educn and Youth Affairs, 1998. Mem., Victorian Educn Ministry Delegns to SE Asia and S America, 1998. Member Board: Melba Conservatorium of Music, Melbourne, 1995–; Playbox Theatre Co., Melb., 2000–03; Member: Academic Adv. Bd, Hong Kong Inst. of Technol., 2003–. Admissions Advr, RCSI, 2004–. Hon. Consul for Ireland in Victoria, 2002–. Manoel de Vilhena Award, Malta, 1999. *Publications:* Guide to World Science: Australia and New Zealand, 1975; (jtly) Science, Technology and Public Policy, 1979; Science in Government: a review of the principles and practice of science policy, 1983; Science and Technology in Australasia, Antarctica and Pacific Islands, 1989; First Fleet to Federation: Irish supremacy in colonial Australia, 2001, republd as The Irish in Australia: rogues and reformers, First Fleet to federation, 2003; contrib. numerous jl articles in chemistry and sci. policy, and book chapters in chemistry, hist. of sci. and sci. policy. *Recreations:* reading, especially Irish history. *Address:* PO Box 656, Williamstown, Vic 3016, Australia. *Clubs:* Union, University and Schools (Sydney); Naval and Military (Melbourne).

RONE, Ven. James; Archdeacon of Wisbech, 1995–2002; *b* 28 Aug. 1935; *s* of James and Bessie Rone; *m* 1st, 1956, Ivy Mylchreest (*née* Whitby) (*d* 1970); one *s* one *d*; 2nd, 1976, Mary Elizabeth (*née* Angove). *Educ:* Skerry's Coll., Liverpool; St Stephen's House, Oxford. FSCA 1971. RAMC, 1953–56. Accountant, ICI Ltd, 1957–64; Hawker Siddeley Dynamics, 1964–65; Subsidiary co. dir and Sec., Reed International, 1965–71; Gp Chief Accountant, Leigh & Sillavan, 1971–73; Finance Officer, Oxford Diocesan Bd of Finance, 1973–79. Ordained deacon 1980, priest 1981; Curate, Stony Stratford, dio. of Oxford, 1980–82; Vicar, SS Peter and Mary Magdalene, Fordham and Rector of Kennett, 1982–89; Canon Residentiary, Ely Cathedral, 1989–95. Mem., Gen. Synod of C of E, 1995–2002. MInstD. *Recreations:* walking, Rugby (now non-playing), classical music, theatre, good food and wine. *Address:* Little Housing, 32 Lumley Close, Ely, Cambs CB7 4FG. *T:* (01353) 667088. *Club:* Royal Over-Seas League.

RONEY, Joanne Lucille, FCIH; Chief Executive, Wakefield Council, since 2008; *b* 13 Sept. 1961; *d* of John William Roney and Grace (*née* Darnley). *Educ:* Univ. of Birmingham (MBA Public Admin 1996). Housing, Birmingham CC, 1977–89; Regl Dir, Sanctuary Housing Assoc., 1989–91; Dir of Housing, Kirklees MBC, 1991–99; Exec. Dir for Housing and Direct Services Orgn, 1999–2005, Exec. Dir for Neighbourhoods and Community Care, 2005–08, Sheffield CC. FCIH 2000 (Chm. Policy Bd, 2000–06). *Recreations:* travel, reading, music. *Address:* Wakefield Council, Town Hall, Wakefield WF1 2HQ.

RONEY, Peter John; Managing Director, Cambridge Associates Asia, Singapore, since 2008; *b* 12 Oct. 1949. *Educ:* Durham Univ. (BA Hons Pol. and Econs). Investment Manager, Derbys CC; Chief Investment Officer, S Yorks CC; CEO, Combined Actuarial Performance Services Ltd; Man. Dir, Halifax Financial Services Ltd; Chief Exec., Save & Prosper Gp Ltd, 1996–98; Man. Dir, Consumer Financial Services, Great Universal Stores PLC, 1998–2000; with Cambridge Associates, 2001–.

RONSON, Dame Gail, DBE 2004; Board Member, since 1992, and Deputy Chairman, since 2002, Jewish Care; Director, Royal Opera House, since 2001; *b* 3 July 1946; *d* of Joseph and Marie Cohen; *m* 1967, Gerald Maurice Ronson, *qv*; four *d*. *Educ:* Clarke's Coll. Co-Chm., St Mary's Hosp. Save the Baby Fund, 1985–96; Vice-Pres., Assoc. for Res. into Stammering in Childhood, 1991–. Jt Chm., Council for a Beautiful Israel, 1987–94. Trustee: Ronson Foundns, 1980–95; Royal Opera House Trust, 1985–; Home Farm Develt Trust, 1991–94; Gerald Ronson Foundn, 2005–. *Recreations:* opera and ballet lover. *Address:* Heron House, 19 Marylebone Road, NW1 5JL. *T:* (020) 7486 4477, *Fax:* (020) 8455 3756; *e-mail:* gailronson@heron.co.uk.

RONSON, Gerald Maurice; Chief Executive: Heron Corporation PLC; Heron International PLC; Chairman and Chief Executive, Snax 24 Corporation Ltd; *b* 27 May 1939; *s* of Henry and Sarah Ronson; *m* 1967, Gail (*see* Dame G. Ronson); four *d*. Chief Executive: Heron Corp. PLC, 1976– (Chm., 1978–93); Heron International PLC, 1983– (Chm., 1983–93). Chm. Trustees, Gerald Ronson Foundn, 2005–. Ambassador of Druse community on Mount Carmel. *Recreation:* work. *Address:* Heron House, 19 Marylebone Road, NW1 5JL. *T:* (020) 7486 4477.

ROOCROFT, Amanda Jane; soprano; *b* 9 Feb. 1966; *d* of Roger Roocroft and Valerie Roocroft (*née* Metcalfe); *m* 1999, David Gowland; three *s*. *Educ:* Southlands High Sch.; Runshaw Tertiary Coll.; Royal Northern Coll. of Music. Début as Sophie in Der Rosenkavalier, WNO, 1990; has sung at Glyndebourne, Royal Opera House, English Nat. Opera, Bayerische Staatsoper, BBC Promenade Concerts, Edinburgh Internat. Fest.; rôles include: Fiordiligi in Così fan Tutte; Donna Elvira in Don Giovanni; Pamina in Die Zauberflöte; Giulietta in I Capuleti e I Montecchi; Mimi in La Bohème; Amelia in Simon Boccanegra; Jenifer in The Midsummer Marriage; Eva in Die Meistersinger; Desdemona in Otello; Tatyana in Eugene Onegin; title rôles: in Katya Kabanova; in Jenufa; in The Merry Widow. *Address:* c/o Ingpen & Williams Ltd, 7 St George's Court, 131 Putney Bridge Road, SW15 2PA. *T:* (020) 8874 3222, *Fax:* (020) 8877 3113.

ROOK, Peter Francis Grosvenor; QC 1991; **His Honour Judge Rook;** a Circuit Judge, Central Criminal Court, since 2005; *b* 19 Sept. 1949; *s* of Dr Arthur James Rook and Frances Jane Elizabeth Rook (*née* Knott); *m* 1978, Susanna Marian Tewson; one *s* two *d*. *Educ:* Charterhouse; Trinity College, Cambridge (Open Exhibnr; MA Hist.); Bristol Univ. (Dip. Soc. Studies). Called to the Bar, Gray's Inn, 1973, Bencher, 2000; 2nd Standing Counsel to Inland Revenue at Central Criminal Court and Inner London Courts, 1981, 1st Standing Counsel, 1989; Asst Recorder, 1990–95; a Recorder, 1995–2005; Hd of Chambers, 18 Red Lion Court, 2002–05. Chm., Criminal Bar Assoc. of England and Wales, 2002–03 (Dir of Educn, 2003–05). Course Dir, Serious Sexual Offences Seminar, Judicial Studies Bd, 2006–. *Publication:* Rook and Ward on Sexual Offences, 1990, 3rd edn 2004. *Recreations:* tennis, squash, cricket, theatre, growing tropical plants. *Address:* Central Criminal Court, Old Bailey, EC4M 7EH. *Clubs:* MCC; Coolhurst Lawn Tennis and Squash.

ROOKE, Daphne Marie; author; *b* 6 March 1914; *d* of Robert Pizzey and Marie Knevitt; *m* 1937, Irvin Rooke; one *d*. *Educ:* Durban, S Africa. Hon. DLit Univ. of Natal, 1997. *Publications:* A Grove of Fever Trees, 1950, repr. 2008; Mittee, 1951, repr. 2008; Ratoons, 1953, repr. 2008; The South African Twins, 1953; The Australian Twins, 1954; Wizards' Country, 1957, repr. 2008; The New Zealand Twins, 1957; Beti, 1959; A Lover for Estelle, 1961; The Greyling, 1962, repr. 2008; Diamond Jo, 1965; Boy on the Mountain, 1969; Double Ex!, 1970; Margaretha de la Porte, 1974; A Horse of his Own, 1976; Three Rivers: a memoir, 2003. *Recreation:* walking. *Address:* 4 Brookfield Road, Coton, Cambridge CB23 7PT. *T:* (01954) 210585.

ROOKE, His Honour Giles Hugh, TD 1963; QC 1979; DL; a Circuit Judge, 1981–2001; Resident Judge, Canterbury, 1995–2001; *b* 28 Oct. 1930; *s* of late Charles Eustace Rooke, CMG, and Irene Phyllis Rooke; *m* 1968, Anne Bernadette Seymour, *d* of His Honour John Perrett; three *s* one *d* (and one *s* decd). *Educ:* Stowe; Exeter Coll., Oxford (MA). Kent Yeomanry, 1951–61, Kent and County of London Yeomanry, 1961–65 (TA), Major. Called to Bar, Lincoln's Inn, 1957; practised SE Circuit, 1957–81; a Recorder of the Crown Court, 1975–81. Hon. Recorder of Margate, 1980–2001. Mem. Council, Univ. of Kent at Canterbury, 1997–2003; Hon. Sen. Fellow, Univ. of Kent at Canterbury Law Sch., 1999–2002. Hon. Burgess, Margate, 2001. DL Kent, 2001. *Address:* St Stephen's Cottage, Bridge, Canterbury CT4 5AH. *T:* (01227) 830298. *Club:* Army and Navy.

ROOKE, James Smith, CMG 1961; OBE 1949; Grand Decoration of Honour in Gold, of the Austrian Republic, 1981; Chief Executive, British Overseas Trade Board, 1972–75; HM Diplomatic Service, retired; Lecturer, Diplomatic Academy, Vienna, 1980–97; *b* 6 July 1916; *s* of Joseph Nelson Rooke and Adeline Mounser (*née* Woodgate); *m* 1938, Maria Theresa Rebrec, Vienna; one *s* two *d*. *Educ:* Workington Grammar Sch.; University College, London; Vienna Univ. Apptd to Dept of Overseas Trade, 1938. Military service, 1940–45, KRRC and AEC. Second Secretary (Commercial), British Embassy, Bogotá, 1946; UK Delegation to ITO Conf., Havana, 1947; Dep. UK Commercial Rep., Frankfurt, 1948; First Secretary (Commercial), British Embassy, Rome, 1951; Consul (Commercial), Milan, 1954; Deputy Consul-General (Commercial), New York, 1955–59; HM Counsellor (Commercial) British Embassy, Berne, 1959–63, Rome, 1963–66; Minister (Commercial), British High Commn, Canberra, 1966–68; Minister (Economic), British Embassy, Paris, 1968–72. *Publication:* Trade and the Diplomat, 2006. *Recreations:* walking, swimming. *Address:* Flotowgasse 26/3/1, 1190 Vienna, Austria. *Club:* East India, Devonshire, Sports and Public Schools.

ROOKE, Very Rev. Patrick William; Dean of Armagh, and Keeper of the Robinson Public Library, since 2006; *b* 12 April 1955; *s* of late Rev. William Warburton Lloyd Rooke and of Lucy Gwendoline Rosemary Rooke; *m* 1979, Alison Isobel Forsythe; one *s* two *d*. *Educ:* Sandford Park Sch., Dublin; Gurteen Agricl Coll., Roscrea; Salisbury and Wells Theol Coll.; Open Univ. (BA); Irish Sch. of Ecumenics, Trinity Coll. Dublin (MPhil). Ordained deacon 1978, priest 1979; Curate, Mossley, 1978–81; Ballwillan, Portrush, 1981–83; Rector: Craigs, Dunaghy and Killagan, 1983–88; Ballymore, Tandragee, 1988–94; Agherton, Portstewart, 1994–2006; Canon Preb., Lisburn Cathedral, 2001–05; Archdeacon of Dalriada, 2005–06. Chm., Hard Gospel Cttee, C of I, 2005–. *Recreations:* gardening, swimming, supporting Rugby. *Address:* The Deanery, 43 Abbey Street, Armagh BT61 7DY. *T:* (028) 3752 3142, *Fax:* (028) 3752 4177; *e-mail:* dean@armagh.anglican.org.

ROOKE, Brig. Vera Margaret, CB 1984; CBE 1980; RRC 1973; Matron-in-Chief (Army) and Director of Army Nursing Services, 1981–84; *b* 21 Dec. 1924; *d* of late William James Rooke and Lily Amelia Rooke (*née* Cole). *Educ:* Girls' County Sch., Hove, Sussex. Addenbrooke's Hosp., Cambridge (SRN); Royal Alexandra Children's Hosp., Brighton (RSCN); St Helier Hosp., Carshalton (Midwifery). Joined Queen Alexandra's Royal Army Nursing Corps, 1951; appointments include: service in military hospitals, UK, Egypt, Malta, Singapore; Staff Officer in Work Study; Liaison Officer, QARANC, MoD, 1973–74; Assistant Director of Army Nursing Services and Matron: Military Hosp., Hong Kong, 1975; Royal Herbert Hosp. and Queen Elizabeth Military Hosp., Woolwich, 1976–78; Dep. Dir, Army Nursing Services, HQ UKLF, 1979–80. QHNS, 1981–84. Lt-Col 1972, Col 1975, Brig. 1981. *Recreations:* gardening, walking, cookery, opera. *Address:* c/o Lloyds TSB, 74 Church Road, Hove, Sussex BN3 2EE.

ROOKER, Baron *cr* 2001 (Life Peer), of Perry Barr in the County of West Midlands; **Jeffrey William Rooker;** PC 1999; CEng; *b* 5 June 1941; *m* 1972, Angela Edwards (*d* 2003). *Educ:* Handsworth Tech. Sch.; Handsworth Tech. Coll.; Warwick Univ. (MA); Aston Univ. (BScEng). CEng, FIET; MCMI. Apprentice toolmaker, King's Heath Engrg Co. Ltd, Birmingham, 1957–63; student apprentice, BLMC, 1963–64; Asst to Works Manager, Geo. Salter & Co., West Bromwich, 1964–65, Assembly Manager, 1965–67; Prodn Manager, Rola Celestion Ltd, Thames Ditton and Ipswich, 1967–70; Industrial Relations and Safety Officer, Metro-Cammell, Birmingham, 1971; Lectr, Lanchester Polytechnic, Coventry, 1972–74. MP (Lab) Birmingham, Perry Barr, Feb. 1974–2001. Opposition spokesman on social services, 1979–80, on social security, 1980–83, on treasury and economic affairs, 1983–84, on housing, 1984–87, on local government, 1987–88, on health and social services, 1990–92, on higher educn, 1992–93; Dep. Shadow Leader of H of C, 1994–97; Minister of State: MAFF, 1997–99; DSS, 1999–2001; Home Office, 2001–02; for Housing, Planning and Regeneration, ODPM, 2002–05; NI Office, 2005–06; DEFRA, 2006–08. Mem., Public Accounts Cttee, 1989–91. Chair, Labour Campaign for Electoral Reform, 1989–95. Mem. Council, Instn of Prodn Engrs, 1975–81. Lay Gov., Aston Univ., 2008–. Hon. DSc Aston, 2001; DUniv UCE, 2002. *Address:* House of Lords, SW1A 0PW. *T:* (020) 7219 6469, (home) (01242) 604507.

ROOKES, Caroline Mary; Director, Private Pensions, Retirement Planning and Older People, Department for Work and Pensions, since 2005; *b* 28 Oct. 1954; *d* of late James Harold Hartley and Mary Irene Hartley; *m* 1975, John William Rookes (marr. diss. 1985); partner, Michael Pearce. *Educ:* Fleetwood Grammar Sch.; Downer Grammar Sch.; Univ. of Lancaster (BA Hons English 1975). Civil Service, 1975–: various postings in DHSS, subseq. DSS; Inland Revenue, then HM Revenue and Customs: Head, Review of Analytical Services, 1999; Dir of Charities, 2000; Head, Share Scheme, 2000–02; Director: Savings, Pensions, Share Schemes, 2002–05; Individuals, 2005. *Recreations:* opera, fell walking, friends, family, good food and wine, all things Italian. *Address:* (office) 1–11 John Adam Street, WC2N 6HT. *T:* (020) 7962 8300; *e-mail:* caroline.rookes@dwp.gsi.gov.uk.

ROOKS, Robert John; Director General, Security and Safety, Ministry of Defence, since 2004; *b* 20 Nov. 1948; *s* of Ronald Sidney Rooks and Daisy Rooks; *m* 1970, Elizabeth Lewis; one *s* one *d*. *Educ:* Hardye's Sch., Dorchester; Liverpool Univ. (BEng Hons). Spacecraft Design Engr, BAC, 1970–72; Ministry of Defence, 1972–: Admin Trainee, Chief Exec. Dockyards, 1972–73; Adjutant Gen. Secretariat, 1973–74; Size, Shape and Cost of RAF Prog., Defence Secretariat, 1974–75; Private Sec. to Chief of Defence Procurement, 1975–78; Fighting Vehicles and Engrg, Equipment Secretariat, 1978–80; RAF Ops, Defence Secretariat, 1980–83; Mgt Services Orgn, 1983–85; Finance Mgt and Planning, 1985–88, Head, 1988–90, Controller Aircraft Secretariat; Head of: Adjutant Gen. Secretariat 2, 1990–93; Civilian Mgt (Personnel) 1, 1993–97; Dir of Orgn and Mgt, 1998–99; Comd Sec., RAF PTC, 1999–2003; Fellow, Weatherhead Center for Internat. Affairs, Harvard Univ., 2003–04. *Recreations:* sailing, travel, IT. *Address:* Ministry of Defence, Main Building, Whitehall, SW1A 2HB. *Club:* Royal Air Force.

ROOLEY, Anthony; lutenist; Artistic Director, The Consort of Musicke, since 1969; *b* 10 June 1944; *s* of Madge and Henry Rooley; *m* 1967, Carla Morris; three *d*; one *s* by Emma Kirkby (*see* Dame Emma Kirkby). *Educ:* Royal Acad. of Music. LRAM (Performers). Recitals in Europe, USA, Middle East, Japan, S America, New Zealand, Australia; radio and TV in UK, Europe and USA; numerous recordings, British and

German. Visiting Professor: York Univ., 1998–; Schola Cantorum Basiliensis, Basle, Switzerland, 1999–; Vis. Orpheus Scholar, Florida State Univ., Tallahassee, 2003–. Hon. FRAM 1990. *Publications:* Penguin Book of Early Music. 1982; Performance—revealing the Orpheus within, 1990. *Recreations:* food, wine, gardening, philosophy. *Address:* Stable Cottage, Church Road, Rotherfield, E Sussex TN6 3LG.

ROOME, Maj. Gen. Oliver McCrea, CBE 1973; Vice Lord-Lieutenant, Isle of Wight, 1987–95; *b* 9 March 1921; *s* of late Maj. Gen. Sir Horace Roome, KCIE, CB, CBE, MC, DL, late Royal Engineers; *m* 1947, Isobel Anstis (*d* 2003), *d* of Rev. A. B. Jordan; two *s* one *d. Educ:* Wellington Coll. Commissioned in Royal Engineers, 1940. Served War: UK, Western Desert, Sicily, Italy, 1939–45. Various appts, UK, Far and Middle East, Berlin, 1946–68; IDC, 1969; Director of Army Recruiting, 1970–73; Chief, Jt Services Liaison Organisation, Bonn, 1973–76; retired. Col Comdt, RE, 1979–84. County Comr, Scouts, Isle of Wight, 1977–85. DL Isle of Wight, 1981–96; High Sheriff of the Isle of Wight, 1983–84. *Recreations:* sailing, youth activities. *Address:* The White Cottage, Hill Lane, Freshwater, Isle of Wight PO40 9TQ. *Clubs:* Royal Ocean Racing, Royal Cruising; Royal Yacht Squadron; Royal Solent Yacht.

ROONEY, Michael John, RA 1991 (ARA 1990); Head of Painting, Royal Academy Schools, 1991–95; *b* 5 March 1944; *s* of Elisabeth and John Rooney; *m* 1st, 1967, Patricia Anne Lavender (marr. diss. 1984); one *s* one *d*; 2nd, 1988, Alexandra Grascher, Vienna; one *s. Educ:* primary and secondary schools; Sutton Sch. of Art; Wimbledon Sch. of Art (NDD); Royal Coll. of Art (MA RCA, ARCA); British Sch. at Rome (Austin Abbey Major Award). Part-time lectr, various art colls; artist-in-residence, Towner Art Gall., Eastbourne, 1983; one man exhibns in Holland, Austria, London, Edinburgh and other UK locations; jt exhibns in Chicago, NY, Portland (Oregon), and throughout Europe and UK; commissions include: painting for FT Centenary, 1988; London Transport Poster, 1990; tapestry for TSB Ltd, Birmingham, 1991; work in public collections: Sussex; Cumbria; Birmingham; Punta del Este, Uruguay; London; Govt Art Collection. Chm., Soc. of Painters in Tempera. Prizes include: Calouste Gulbenkian Printmakers' Award, 1984; John Player Portrait Award, Nat. Portrait Gallery, 1985; RA Summer Exhibn Awards, 1986, 1988, 1989; Chichester Arts Prize, 1995. *Recreations:* cooking, travel. *Address:* 106 Sandycombe Road, Kew, Richmond, Surrey TW9 2ER. *Club:* Chelsea Arts.

ROONEY, Terence Henry; MP (Lab) Bradford North, since Nov. 1990; *b* 11 Nov. 1950; *s* of Eric and Frances Rooney; *m* 1969, Susanne Chapman; one *s* two *d. Educ:* Buttershaw Comprehensive Sch.; Bradford Coll. Formerly: commercial insurance broker; Welfare Rights Advice Worker, Bierley Community Centre. Councillor, Bradford City, 1983–91 (Dep. Leader, 1990). *Address:* c/o House of Commons, SW1A 0AA.

ROOSE-EVANS, James Humphrey; freelance theatre director and author; non-stipendiary Anglican priest; *b* 11 Nov. 1927; *s* of Jack Roose-Evans and Catharina Primrose Morgan. *Educ:* St Benet's Hall, Oxford (MA). Started career in repertory, as an actor; Artistic Dir, Maddermarket Theatre, Norwich, 1954–55 (dir. English première of The Language of Flowers, 1955); Faculty of Juilliard Sch. of Music, NY, 1955–56; on staff of RADA, 1956–; founded Hampstead Theatre, 1959; Resident Dir, Belgrade Theatre, Coventry, 1961. Regularly tours USA, lecturing and leading workshops. Productions directed include: *Hampstead Theatre*: The Square, 1963; The Little Clay Cart (also adapted), 1964; Adventures in the Skin Trade, world première, The Two Character Play, world première, Letters from an Eastern Front (also adapted), 1966; An Evening with Malcolm Muggeridge (also devised), 1966; *West End*: Cider with Rosie (also adapted), 1963; Private Lives, 1963; An Ideal Husband, 1966; The Happy Apple, 1967; 84 Charing Cross Road (also adapted), 1981, NY 1982 (awards for Best Play and Best Dir, 2001), tour 2004; Seven Year Itch, 1986; The Best of Friends, 1988 (also prod Comédie des Champs-Elysées, Paris, 1989), Hampstead and tour, 2006; Temptation, 1990; Irving (also jt author with Barry Turner), 1995; Legend of Pericles, 1996; *other productions:* Venus Observed, Chichester, 1992; Pericles, 2000, Macbeth, 2001, Ludlow Fest. Author, Re: Joyce!, West End, 1991; The Bargain, Th. Royal, Bath and tour, 2007. Consultant, Theatre Mus. Founder and Chm., Bleddfa Trust-Centre for Caring and the Arts, subseq. Bleddfa Centre for Creative Spirit, Powys, 1974–; Bleddfa Lect., 2007. Columnist (Something Extra), Woman, 1986–88. Trng at Glasshampton Monastery, Worcs; ordained priest, 1981. *Publications:* adaptation of The Little Clay Cart, by King Sudraka, 1965; Directing a Play, 1968; Experimental Theatre, 1970, 4th rev. edn, 1988; London Theatre, 1977; play version of 84 Charing Cross Road, by Helene Hanff, 1983; Inner Journey, Outer Journey, 1987, rev. edn 1998 (US as The Inner Stage, 1990); (introd. and ed) Darling Ma: the letters of Joyce Grenfell, 1988; The Tale of Beatrix Potter, 1988; (with Maureen Lipman) Re:Joyce!, 1988; (introd and ed) The Time of My Life: wartime journals of Joyce Grenfell, 1989; (trans.) Obey, On the Edge of Midnight, 1989; Passages of the Soul: ritual today, 1994; Cider with Rosie (stage adaptation), 1994; One Foot on the Stage (biog. of Richard Wilson), 1996; Eminently Victorian: the story of Augustus Hare (play), 1996; Loving without Tears (stage adaptation of Molly Keane novel), 1996; The Christ Mouse, 2004; (devised and ed) The Cook-a-Story Book, 2005; What is Spirituality?, 2005; Holy Theatre, 2005; *for children:* The Adventures of Odd and Elsewhere, 1971; The Secret of the Seven Bright Shiners, 1972; Odd and the Great Bear, 1973; Elsewhere and the Gathering of the Clowns, 1974; The Return of the Great Bear, 1975; The Secret of Tippity-Witchit, 1975; The Lost Treasure of Wales, 1977. *Recreations:* gardening, writing. *Address:* c/o Sheil Land Associates, 43 Doughty Street, WC1N 2LF. *Club:* Garrick.

ROOT, Jane; President, 2006–07 and General Manager, 2004–07, Discovery Channel (Executive Vice-President, 2004–06); *b* 18 May 1957; *e d* of James William Root and Kathleen Root; *m* 2003, Ray Hill; one *d. Educ:* Sussex Univ.; London Coll. of Printing. Manager, Cinema of Women (Film Distribn Co.), 1981–83; freelance journalist and film critic, 1981–83; Lectr in Film Studies, UEA, 1981–84; Researcher, Open the Box, Beat Productions, 1983; Co-Creator, The Media Show, 1986; Jt Founder and Jt Man. Dir, Wall to Wall Television, 1987–96; Head of Independent Commng Gp, BBC, 1997–98; Controller, BBC2, 1999–2004. Theme Leader, Connecting With Audiences, BBC, 2001. Mem., Exec. Cttee, Edinburgh TV Fest. (Chair, 1995). *Publications:* Pictures of Women: sexuality, 1981; Open the Box: about television, 1983. *Address:* 4209 Thornapple Street, Chevy Chase, MD 20815, USA.

ROOTES, family name of **Baron Rootes**.

ROOTES, 3rd Baron *cr* 1959; **Nicholas Geoffrey Rootes;** author and freelance copywriter; Managing Director, Nick Rootes Associates Ltd, since 1997; *b* 12 July 1951; *s* of 2nd Baron Rootes and of Marian, *d* of Lt-Col H. R. Hayter, DSO and *widow* of Wing Comdr J. H. Slater, AFC; *S* father, 1992; *m* 1976, Dorothy Anne Burn-Forti (*née* Wood); one step *s* one step *d. Educ:* Harrow Sch. Trustee, Rootes Charitable Trust, 1992–; Patron, Assoc. of Rootes Car Clubs, 1993–. *Publications:* The Drinker's Companion, 1987; Doing a Dyson, 1996. *Recreations:* ski-ing, fly-fishing. *Heir: cousin* William Brian Rootes [*b* 8 Nov. 1944; *m* 1969, Alicia, *y d* of Frederick Graham Roberts, OBE; two *d*]. *Address:* 2 Cedars Road, Barnes, SW13 0HP. *T:* (020) 8255 7229. *Club:* Ski of Great Britain.

ROOTS, Guy Robert Godfrey; QC 1989; *b* 26 Aug. 1946; *s* of late William Lloyd Roots, QC and Elizabeth Colquhoun Gow (*née* Gray); *m* 1975, Caroline (*née* Clarkson); three *s. Educ:* Winchester College; Brasenose College, Oxford (MA). Called to the Bar, Middle Temple, 1969, Harmsworth Scholar, 1970, Bencher, 2000. Chm., Planning and Envmt, Bar Assoc., 2000–04. Fellow, Soc. of Advanced Legal Studies, 1998–. Liveryman, Drapers' Co., 1972. *Publications:* (ed) Ryde on Rating, 1986; (ed) Tottel's Compulsory Purchase and Compensation Service, 1999. *Recreations:* sailing, fishing, ski-ing, photography, woodworking. *Address:* Francis Taylor Building, Temple, EC4Y 7BY. *T:* (020) 7353 8415; *e-mail:* clerks@ftb.eu.com. *Club:* Itchenor Sailing.

ROOTS, Paul John; Director of Industrial Relations, Ford Motor Co. Ltd, 1981–86, retired; *b* 16 Oct. 1929; *s* of John Earl and Helen Roots; *m* 1950, Anna Theresa Pateman; two *s* two *d. Educ:* Dormers Wells Sch.; London Sch. of Economics; Open Univ. BA Hons 1993; Cert. in Personnel Admin. CCIPD; CCMI. RN, 1947–54: service in Korean War. Personnel Officer, Brush Gp, 1955; Labour Officer, UKAEA, 1956, Labour Manager, 1959; Ford Motor Co. Ltd: Personnel Manager, Halewood, 1962; Forward Planning Manager, 1966; Labour Relations Manager, 1969; Dir of Employee Relations, 1974. Vice-Pres., IPM, 1981–83. Chairman: CBI Health and Safety Policy Cttee, 1984–; CBI Health and Safety Consultative Cttee, 1984–; Member: Council of Management, CBI Educn Foundn, 1981–; CBI Working Party on the Employment of Disabled People, 1981–; CBI Employment Policy Cttee, 1983–; CBI Council, 1984–; Engrg Industry Training Bd, 1985–. *Publications:* (jtly) Communication in Practice, 1981; (jtly) Corporate Personnel Management, 1986; Financial Incentives for Employees, 1988; articles in personnel management jls. *Recreations:* riding, theatre, music.

ROOTS, William; Chief Executive and Director of Finance, City of Westminster, 1994–2000; *b* 12 April 1946; *s* of William Roots and Violet (*née* Frost); *m* 1st, 1963, Norma Jane Smith (marr. diss.); one *s* one *d*; 2nd, 1980, Susan Grace Sharratt; two *s. Educ:* Wandsworth Sch. Sun Life Assce Soc., 1962–64; joined GLC as trainee, 1964; Hd of Budget, 1980; London Borough of Southwark: Head of: Exchequer, 1980–81; Finance, 1982–82; Director of Finance: London Borough of Bexley, 1982–90; City of Westminster, 1990–94. Mem., CIPFA 1970. *Recreations:* sport (esp. Rugby), relaxing with friends, films. *Address: e-mail:* bill@roots88.fsnet.co.uk.

ROP, Anton; Member, National Assembly, Slovenia (Liberal Democrats, until 2007; Social Democrats, since 2007); Prime Minister of Slovenia, 2002–04; *b* 27 Dec. 1960. *Educ:* Univ. of Ljubljana (MA). Asst Dir, Slovene Inst. for Macroecon. Analysis and Develt, 1985–92. State Sec., Min. of Econ. Relations and Develt, 1993; Minister of Labour, Family and Social Affairs, 1996–2000, of Finance, 2000–02. Former Leader, Parly Gp, Liberal Democratic Party, until 2005. *Address:* National Assembly, Šubičeva 4, 1102 Ljubljana, Slovenia.

ROPER, family name of **Baron Roper**.

ROPER, Baron *cr* 2000 (Life Peer), of Thorney Island in the City of Westminster; **John Francis Hodgess Roper;** PC 2005; Liberal Democratic Chief Whip, House of Lords, 2001–05; Hon. Professor, Institute for German Studies, University of Birmingham, since 1999; *b* 10 Sept. 1935; *e s* of late Rev. Frederick Mabor Hodgess Roper and Ellen Frances (*née* Brockway); *m* 1959, (Valerie) Hope (*d* 2003), *er d* of late Rt Hon. L. John Edwards, PC, OBE, MP, and late Mrs D. M. Edwards; one *d. Educ:* William Hulme's Grammar Sch., Manchester; Reading Sch.; Magdalen Coll., Oxford; Univ. of Chicago. Nat. Service, commnd RNVR, 1954–56; studied PPE, Oxford, 1956–59 (Pres. UN Student Assoc., 1957; organised Univ. referendum on Nuclear Disarmament); Harkness Fellow, Commonwealth Fund, 1959–61; Research Fellow in Economic Statistics, Univ. of Manchester, 1961; Asst Lectr in Econs, 1962–64, Lectr 1964–70, Faculty Tutor 1968–70; RIIA: Editor of International Affairs, 1983–88; Head of Internat. Security Programme, 1985–88, and 1989–90; Dir of Studies, 1988–89; Associate Fellow, 1996–99; Hd, WEU Inst. for Security Studies, Paris, 1990–95. Vis. Prof., Coll. of Europe, Bruges, 1997–2000. Contested: (Lab) High Peak (Derbys), 1964; (SDP) Worsley, 1983. MP (Lab and Co-op 1970–81, SDP 1981–83) Farnworth, 1970–83; PPS to Minister of State, DoI, 1978–79; opposition front bench spokesman on defence, 1979–81; Social Democrat Chief Whip, 1981–83. Vice-Chairman: Anglo-German Parly Gp, 1974–83; Anglo-Benelux Parly Gp, 1979–83; Chm., British-Atlantic Gp of Young Politicians, 1974–75. Council of Europe: Consultant, 1965–66; Mem., Consultative Assembly, 1973–80; Chm., Cttee on Culture and Educn, 1979–80; Mem., WEU Assembly, 1973–80; Chm., Cttee on Defence Questions and Armaments, WEU, 1977–80. Hon. Treasurer, Fabian Soc., 1976–81; Chairman: Labour Cttee for Europe, 1976–80; GB/East Europe Centre, 1987–90; Council on Christian Approaches to Defence and Disarmament, 1983–89; Mem., Internat. Commn on the Balkans, 1995–96. Research Adviser (part-time), DEA in NW, 1967–69. Director: Co-op. Wholesale Soc., 1969–74; Co-op Insurance Soc., 1973–74. Pres., Gen. Council, UNA, 1972–78; Mem. Council, Inst. for Fiscal Studies, 1975–90; Mem. Gen. Adv. Council, IBA, 1974–79. Vice-Pres., Manchester Statistical Soc., 1971–. Trustee, Hist. of Parlt Trust, 1974–84. *Publications:* Towards Regional Co-operatives, 1967; The Teaching of Economics at University Level, 1970; The Future of British Defence Policy, 1985; (ed with Karl Kaiser) British-German Defence Co-operation, 1988; (ed with Yves Boyer) Franco-British Defence Co-operation, 1988; (ed with Nicole Gnesotto) Western Europe and the Gulf, 1992; (ed with Nanette Gantz) Towards a New Partnership, 1993; (ed with Laurence Martin) Towards a Common Defence Policy, 1995. *Recreations:* reading, travel. *Address:* House of Lords, SW1A 0PW. *T:* (020) 7219 3114. *Club:* Oxford and Cambridge.

See also Sir J. C. Jenkins, Rev. G. E. H. Roper.

ROPER, Brian Anthony; Chief Executive, since 2002, and Vice Chancellor, since 2004, London Metropolitan University; *b* 15 Dec. 1949; *s* of Harold Herbert Albert Roper and Elizabeth Roper (*née* Rooney); *m* 1971, Margaret Patricia Jones; one *s* one *d. Educ:* UWIST (BSc Hons Econs 1971); Univ. of Manchester (MA Econs 1973). Tutor in Econs, UWIST, 1971–72; Lectr in Econs, Teesside Poly., 1973–75; Sen. Lectr, then Principal Lectr, Leicester Poly., 1975–80; Hd, Sch. of Econs, Dean, Faculty of Social Scis and Asst Dir, Resources, Newcastle upon Tyne Poly., 1980–90; Dep. Vice Chancellor Acad. Affairs and Dep. Chief Exec., Oxford Poly., subseq. Oxford Brookes Univ., 1991–94; Vice-Chancellor and Chief Exec., Univ. of N London, 1994–2002. DUniv Chelyabinsk State, Russia, 2001; Hon. DLitt Pennsylvania, 2004; Hon. DTech Nizhni Novgorod, Russia, 2007. *Publications:* contrib. Econ. Theory and Policy, Higher Educn Policy and Mgt. *Recreations:* Rugby Union, Italian opera, Impressionist painting, hill-walking. *Address:* London Metropolitan University, 166–220 Holloway Road, N7 8DB. *T:* (020) 7753 5181. *Club:* Tynedale Rugby Football.

ROPER, Rev. Geoffrey Edward Hodgess; Associate General Secretary (Free Churches), and Secretary, Free Churches Group, Churches Together in England, 2001–05; *b* 24 April 1940; *y s* of late Rev. Frederick Mabor Hodgess Roper and Ellen Frances (*née* Brockway); *m* 1967, Janice Wakeham; one *s* one *d. Educ:* Christ's Hosp.; Magdalen Coll., Oxford (PPE); Mansfield Coll., Oxford (Theol.); MA Oxon. Ordained 1965; Minister: Trinity Congregational Church, Ifield, Crawley, 1965–71; Streatham

Congregational Church, 1971–78 (URC from 1972); Seaford URC, 1978–85; Christ Church, Chelmsford, 1985–95; Gen. Sec., Free Church Fed. Council, later Free Churches' Council, 1996–2001; Legacy & Restricted Funds officer, Council for World Mission, 2005–06; Cataloguing Asst (LMS archives), SOAS, 2006–07. Sec., URC Deployment Cttee, 1978–84; Convenor, URC Maintenance of Ministry Sub-Cttee, 2005–; URC Ecumenical Officer: Sussex East, 1979–85; Essex, 1986–95; Dir, URC Ministers Pension Fund, 2005–. Vice-Chm., Churches Main Cttee, 2004–05. Sec., Gen. Body of Dissenting Ministers and Deputies of the Three Denominations, 1998–2005. Chm., Churches Cttee for Hospital Chaplaincy, 2001–04; Mem., Eastbourne CHC, 1980–85 (Vice-Chm., 1983–84). British Isles Mem., Exec. Cttee, Leuenberg Doctrinal Conversations of Reformed and Lutheran Churches in Europe, 1987–94. Chair, King's Cross Develt Forum, 2006–. Director: Highway Trust, 1977–94; Farthing Trust, 1985–95; British and Internat. Sailors' Soc., 1999–2006. Sec., Friends of Dr Williams's Library, 2005– (Chm. of Cttee, 1991–2005). Trustee, St George's Chapel, Heathrow Airport, 1999–2005. Pres., Mansfield Coll. Assoc., 2005–. *Recreations:* family history, cycling, listening. *Address:* 25 Witley Court, Coram Street, WC1N 1HD.

See also Baron Roper.

ROPER, Michael, CB 1992; FRHistS; Keeper of Public Records, 1988–92; *b* 19 Aug. 1932; *s* of Jack Roper and Mona Roper (*née* Nettleton); *m* 1957, Joan Barbara Earnshaw; one *s* one *d*. *Educ:* Heath Grammar Sch., Halifax; Univ. of Manchester (BA, MA; Langton Fellow). Registered Mem., Soc. of Archivists, 1987. Public Record Office: Asst Keeper, 1959–70; Principal Asst Keeper, 1970–82; Records Admin Officer, 1982–85; Dep. Keeper of Public Records, 1985–88. Lectr (part time) in Archive Studies, UCL, 1972–87, Hon. Res. Fellow, 1988–; Dist. Visitor, Univ. of BC, 1994; Vis. Prof., Surugadai Univ., Japan, 1999. Sec., Adv. Council on Public Records, 1963–68; Vice-President: Soc. of Archivists, 1992– (Vice-Chm., 1983–84; Chm., 1985–86; Pres., 1989–92); British Records Soc., 1988–; RHistS, 1989–93 (Hon. Treas., 1974–80); Sec.-Gen., Internat. Council on Archives, 1988–92 (Sec. for Standardization, 1984–88; Hon. Mem., 1992); Hon. Sec., Assoc. of Commonwealth Archivists and Records Managers, 1996–2000. Chairman: Voices from the Past, 1992–95; English Record Collections, 1994–. Ext. Examr, Nat. Univ. of Ireland, 1982–86, Univ. of Liverpool, 1986–89, Univ. of London, 1988–93. Chm., Judy Segal Trust, 1990–98; Hon. Treasurer, Bethlem Art & Hist. Collections Trust, 1995–2007. Hon. DLitt Bradford, 1991. *Publications:* Yorkshire Fines 1300–1314, 1965; Records of the Foreign Office 1782–1939, 1969; (with J. A. Keene) Planning, Equipping and Staffing a Document Reprographic Service, 1984; Guidelines for the Preservation of Microforms, 1986; Directory of National Standards Relating to Archives Administration and Records Management, 1986; Planning, Equipping and Staffing an Archival Preservation and Conservation Service, 1989; Geresye to Jersey: the record endures, 1991; Records of the War Office and Related Departments 1660–1964, 1998; Records of the Foreign Office 1782–1968, 2002; (with C. Kitching) Yorkshire Fines 1314–1326, 2006; contribs to learned jls. *Recreations:* listening to music, gardening, walking the dog. *Address:* Sherwood House, Vicarage Road, Roxwell, Chelmsford, Essex CM1 4NY. *T:* (01245) 249033; *e-mail:* MRoper3784@aol.com.

ROPER, Prof. Warren Richard, FRS 1989; FRSNZ 1984; Professor of Chemistry, University of Auckland, New Zealand, 1984–2007, now Emeritus; *b* 27 Nov. 1938; *m* 1961, Judith Delcie Catherine Miller; two *s* one *d*. *Educ:* Nelson Coll., Nelson, NZ; Univ. of Canterbury, Christchurch, NZ (MSc, PhD). FNZIC. Postdoctoral Res. Associate, Univ. of N Carolina, 1963–65; Lectr in Chemistry, Univ. of Auckland, 1966. Vis. Lectr, Univ. of Bristol, 1972; Pacific W Coast Inorganic Lectr, 1982; Brotherton Vis. Res. Prof., Univ. of Leeds, 1983; Visiting Professor: Univ. de Rennes, 1984, 1985; Stanford Univ., 1988; Sydney Univ., 2001. Mellor Lectr, NZ Inst. of Chemistry, 1985; Centenary Lectr and Medallist, RSC, 1988; Glenn T. Seaborg Lectr, Univ. of Calif., Berkeley, 1995; Gordon Stone Lectr, Univ. of Bristol, 2003; Arthur D. Little Lectr, MIT, 2005. Fellow, Japan Soc. for Promotion of Science, 1992. Hon. DSc Canterbury, 1999. RSC Award in Organometallic Chemistry, 1983; ICI Medal, NZ Inst. of Chemistry, 1984; Hector Medal, Royal Soc. of NZ, 1991; 12th Inorganic Award, Royal Australian Inst. of Chemistry, 1992; Dwyer Medallist, Univ. of NSW, 2000. *Publications:* 200 sci. papers in internat. jls. *Recreations:* music, espec. opera, walking. *Address:* 26 Beulah Avenue, Rothesay Bay, Auckland 1311, New Zealand. *T:* (9) 4786940.

ROPER-CURZON, family name of **Baron Teynham**.

ROPNER, David; *see* Ropner, W. G. D.

ROPNER, Sir John (Bruce Woollacott), 2nd Bt *cr* 1952; *b* 16 April 1937; *s* of Sir Leonard Ropner, 1st Bt, MC, TD, and Esmé (*d* 1996), *y d* of late Bruce Robertson; *S* father, 1977; *m* 1st, 1961, Anne Melicent (marr. diss. 1970), *d* of late Sir Ralph Delmé-Radcliffe; two *d* (and one *d* decd); 2nd, 1970, Auriol (marr. diss. 1993; she *m* 1997, Marquess of Linlithgow, *qv*), *d* of late Captain Graham Lawrie Mackeson-Sandbach, Caerllo, Llangernyw; one *s* two *d*; 3rd, 1996, Diana Nicola, *d* of Peter Agnew. *Educ:* Eton; St Paul's School, USA. High Sheriff, N Yorks, 1991. *Recreation:* field sports. *Heir: s* Henry John William Ropner, *b* 24 Oct. 1981. *Address:* Thorp Perrow, Bedale, Yorks DL8 2PR.

See also Viscount Knutsford.

ROPNER, Sir Robert (Clinton), 5th Bt *cr* 1904; Director and Chairman, HR & F Management Services, since 2004; *b* 6 Feb. 1949; *s* of Sir Robert Douglas Ropner, 4th Bt and Patricia Kathleen (*née* Scofield); *S* father, 2004; *m* 1978, Diana Felicia Abbott; one *s* one *d* (twins). *Educ:* Harrow. FCA 1977. Global Funds Reporting Manager, Invesco Europe Ltd, 1999–2002. *Recreations:* motoring, ski-ing, gardening. *Heir: s* Christopher Guy Ropner, *b* 18 Jan. 1979. *Address:* 152 Bishops Road, SW6 7JG. *T:* (020) 7736 7482; *e-mail:* robert.ropner@btopenworld.com.

ROPNER, (William Guy) David; Director, Ropner PLC, 1953–94 (Chairman, 1973–85); *b* 3 April 1924; *s* of late Sir William Guy Ropner and Lady (Margarita) Ropner; *m* 1st, 1955, Mildred Malise Hare Armitage (marr. diss. 1978); one *d* three *s*; 2nd, 1985, Hon. Mrs Charlotte M. Taddei; one *s*. *Educ:* Harrow. FICS 1953. Served War, 1942–47: 2nd Lieut RA, Essex Yeomanry; Captain 3rd Regt, RHA. Joined Sir R. Ropner and Co. Ltd, 1947; dir of various Ropner PLC gp cos, 1953–94. Member: Lloyd's, 1952–91; Gen. Cttee, Lloyd's Register of Shipping, 1961–94; Pres., Gen. Council of British Shipping, 1979–80; Chairman: Deep Sea Tramp Section, Chamber of Shipping, 1970–72; Lights Adv. Cttee, GCBS, 1978–87; Merchant Navy Welfare Bd, 1980–94; Cleveland & Durham Industrial Council, 1980–94; Dir, British Shipowners Assoc., 1954–89. *Recreations:* country and garden pursuits. *Address:* Dolphin House, 99 Windsor Road, Chobham, Surrey GU24 8LE. *Club:* St Moritz Tobogganing.

ROQUES, (David) John (Seymour); Chairman, Portman Building Society, 1999–2006 (Director, 1995–2006); *b* 14 Oct. 1938; *s* of late Frank Davy Seymour Roques and of Marjorie Mabel Hudson; *m* 1963, Elizabeth Anne Mallender; two *s* one *d*. *Educ:* St Albans Sch. Mem., Inst. of Chartered Accountants of Scotland, 1962. Touche Ross & Co., later Deloitte & Touche: Partner, 1967; Partner in charge, Midlands region, 1973; Partner in charge, Scottish region, 1978; Partner in charge, London office, 1984; Man. Partner, 1990; Sen. Partner and Chief Exec., 1990–99. Non-executive Director: British Nuclear Fuels, 1990–2000; BBA Aviation plc, 1999–; Premier Farnell plc, 1999–; Chubb plc, 2003; Henderson Gp plc (formerly HHG plc), 2004–. Member: Financial Reporting Review Panel, 1991–94; Financial Reporting Council, 1996–2001. Gov., Health Foundn, 2001–05. FRSA. *Recreations:* Rugby football, racing, opera, gardening. *Address:* High Down, Cokes Lane, Chalfont St Giles, Bucks HP8 4TQ. *Clubs:* Brooks's, MCC; Lambourne Golf, Harewood Downs Golf.

RORKE, Prof. John, CBE 1979; PhD; FRSE; FIMechE; Professor of Mechanical Engineering, 1980–88, and Vice-Principal, 1984–88, Heriot-Watt University, now Professor Emeritus; *b* 2 Sept. 1923; *s* of John and Janet Rorke; *m* 1948, Jane Craig Buchanan; two *d*. *Educ:* Dumbarton Acad.; Univ. of Strathclyde (BSc, PhD). Lectr, Strathclyde Univ., 1946–51; Asst to Engrg Dir, Alexander Stephen & Sons Ltd, 1951–56; Technical Manager, subseq. Gen. Man., and Engrg Dir, Wm Denny & Bros Ltd, 1956–63; Tech. Dir, subseq. Sales Dir, Man. Dir, and Chm., Brown Bros & Co. Ltd (subsid. of Vickers Ltd), 1963–78; Man. Dir, Vickers Offshore Engrg Gp, 1978; Dir of Planning, Vickers Ltd, 1979–80. Chairman: Orkney Water Test Centre Ltd, 1987–94; Environment and Resource Technology Ltd, 1991–94. Pres., Instn of Engineers and Shipbuilders in Scotland, 1985–87. Hon. DEng Heriot-Watt, 1994. *Recreations:* golf, bridge. *Address:* 3 Barnton Park Grove, Edinburgh EH4 6HG. *T:* (0131) 336 3044. *Club:* Bruntsfield Links Golfing Society (Edinburgh).

ROSCOE, Alexis Fayrer; *see* Brett-Holt, A. F.

ROSCOE, Gareth; *see* Roscoe, J. G.

ROSCOE, Dr Ingrid Mary, FSA; Lord-Lieutenant, West Yorkshire, since 2004 (Vice Lord-Lieutenant, 2001–04); *b* 27 May 1944; *d* of late Dr Arthur Allen and Else (*née* Markenstam) and adopted *d* of late Brig. Kenneth Hargreaves; *m* 1963, John Richard Marshall Roscoe; one *s* two *d*. *Educ:* St Helen's, Northwood; Univ. of Leeds (BA; PhD 1990). FSA 1998. Res. Fellow, Huntington Library, 1988; Lectr in Sculpture Hist., Univ. of Leeds, 1990–96. Co. Rep., NACF, 1972–93; Ed., Ch Monuments Jl, 1993–2000; Ed. in Chief, A Biographical Dictionary of British Sculptors, 2000–09. Mem., Exec. Cttee, Walpole Soc., 2000–05. Chm. Trustees, 1996–03, High Steward, 2000–08, Selby Abbey; Trustee: Martin House Childrens' Hospice, 1989–98; York Minster, 2005–; Yorkshire Sculpture Park, 2006–; Founding Trustee, Hepworth Wakefield Charitable Trust, 2006–; President: Calderdale Community Foundn, 2004–; Safe Anchor Trust, 2006–; ABF W Yorks; RBL W Yorks; Patron: Nat. Mining Mus., 2004–; Yorks Volunteers Regtl Assoc., 2004–; Yorks Historic Churches, 2004–; W Yorks, Prince's Trust, 2005–; Yorks Archaeol Soc. Hon. Col, Leeds Univ. OTC, 2007–. Hon. DCL Huddersfield, 2007. OStJ 2006. *Publications:* (contrib.) The Royal Exchange, 1997; contrib. articles to Apollo, Gazette des Beaux-Arts, Grove Dictionary of Art, Walpole Soc. Jl, Oxford DNB, etc. *Recreations:* English cultural history, walking, grandchildren. *Address:* Church House, Nun Monkton, York YO26 8EW. *T:* (01423) 339145.

ROSCOE, (John) Gareth; barrister; Legal Adviser, Competition Commission, 2002–04 and 2005–07; Lawyer, Department for Work and Pensions, 2004–05; *b* 28 Jan. 1948; *s* of late John Roscoe and Ann (*née* Jones); *m* 1st, 1970, Helen Jane Taylor (marr. diss. 1979); one *d*; 2nd, 1980, Alexis Fayrer Brett-Holt, *qv*; one *s* one *d*. *Educ:* Manchester Warehousemen and Clerks' Orphan Schools (now Cheadle Hulme Sch.); Stretford Tech. Coll.; London Sch. of Economics and Political Science (LLB); Univ. of Leicester (LLM 2003). Called to the Bar, Gray's Inn, 1972; in practice, 1972–75; Legal Asst 1975–79, Sen. Legal Asst 1979, DoE; Law Officers' Dept, Attorney-General's Chambers, 1979–83; Asst Solicitor, 1983–87, Dep. Solicitor, 1987–89, DoE; Dir, BBC Enterprises Ltd, 1989–96; Legal Advr to the BBC, 1989–98; Company Sec., BBC Worldwide Ltd, 1996–98; Consultant Advr, DTI, 1999–2001. Non-executive Director: Optimum NHS Trust, 1995–97; King's Coll. Hosp. NHS Trust, 2001–04. Mem., Gen. Council of the Bar, 1987–90. Member: Adv. Cttee, Centre for Communications and Information Law, UCL, 1991–; Legal Cttee, EBU, 1989–98. Mem., Range Officers' Assoc., 2002–. *Recreations:* music, gardening and the company of friends. *Club:* Athenæum.

ROSE, Alan Douglas, AO 1994; Consultant, Phillips Fox Lawyers, since 2005 (General Counsel, 1999–2005); *b* 3 May 1944; *s* of late Willfred Allen Rose and Hazel Agnes Rose (*née* Heinemann-Mirre); *m* 1966, Helen Elizabeth Haigh; two *d*. *Educ:* Univ. of Queensland (BA 1966; LLB Hons 1969); LSE, Univ. of London (LLM 1979). Barrister, Supreme Court of Queensland, 1973; Dep. Sec., Dept of Prime Minister and Cabinet, 1982–86; Sec. to Aust. Dept of Community Services, 1986–87; Associate Sec. and Sec. to Aust. Attorney-Gen. Dept, 1987–94; Pres., Aust. Law Reform Commn, 1994–99. *Publications:* articles in legal jls and works on public admin. *Recreations:* surfing, ski-ing, reading, travelling. *Address:* PO Box 3296, Manuka, ACT 2603, Australia.

ROSE, Alison Mary; a District Judge (Magistrates' Courts), since 2002; *b* 31 May 1958; *d* of late Brian Henry Rose and of José Gwendoline Rose (*née* Rixon). *Educ:* Univ. of Exeter (LLB Hons 1979). Articled clerk, John H. Rosen & Co., 1980–82; admitted solicitor, 1983; Asst Solicitor, Rosen Hudson & Co., 1983–88; Partner, Hudson Freeman Berg, 1988–2000; Asst Solicitor, Farrell Matthews & Weir, 2000–02; Dep. Dist Judge (Magistrates' Courts), W Midlands, 1999–2002. *Address:* Thames Magistrates' Court, 58 Bow Road, E3 4DJ. *T:* (020) 8271 1219.

ROSE, Anthea Lorrainne, (Mrs H. D. Rose); Managing Director, Everywhere Associates Ltd, since 2004; *b* 2 Dec. 1946; *d* of Philip Brown and Muriel (*née* Seftor); *m* 1971, Hannan David Rose. *Educ:* St Hugh's Coll., Oxford (MA Mod. Hist.). Administrator, Open Univ., 1968–69; Personnel Officer, Beecham Pharmaceuticals, 1969–71; Administrator, Univ. of Kent, 1971–77; Chartered Association of Certified Accountants, later Association of Chartered Certified Accountants, 1977–2003: Under Sec., 1982–88; Dep. Chief Exec., 1988–93; Chief Exec., 1993–2003. Vis. Prof., Oxford Brookes Univ., 2002–07. Lay Mem., Nursing & Midwifery Council, 2006–07. Hon. DBA Kingston, 2002. *Recreations:* travel, food, wine. *Address:* (office) 11 Campden Hill Court, W8 7HX.

ROSE, Sir (Arthur) James, Kt 2007; CBE 1996; education consultant; Director of Inspection, Office for Standards in Education, 1994–99; *m* 1960, Pauline; one *d*. *Educ:* Kesteven College; Leicester University. HM Chief Inspector for Primary Educn, DES, subseq. DFE, 1986–92; Dep. Dir of Inspection, OFSTED, 1992–94. Leader: review of teaching of reading, DFES, 2006–; review of Primary Curriculum, DFES.

ROSE, Aubrey, CBE 1997 (OBE 1986); Deputy Chairman, Commission for Racial Equality, 1995 (Commissioner, 1991–95); *b* 1 Nov. 1926; *s* of Solomon Rosenberg and Esther Rosenberg (*née* Kurtz); *m* 1954, Sheila Ray Glassman (*d* 2007); one *s* one *d* (and one *s* decd). *Educ:* at various grammar schs incl. Central Foundn Sch., London. Admitted as solicitor, 1952; Sen. Partner, 1971–95. Chm., Legal Cttee, CRE, 1993–95. Founder Mem. and Treas., Commonwealth Human Rights Initiative, 1990–2003. Dep. Chm., British Caribbean Assoc., 1990–; Jt Chm., Indian-Jewish Assoc., 1996–2003 (Pres.). Sen.

Vice-Pres., Bd of Deputies of British Jews, 1991–97; Chm., Jewish Wkg Gp on Envmt, 1991–; Jt Patron, New Assembly of Churches, 1993–. Trustee, Project Fullemploy, 1994–. FRSA 1993. Freeman, City of London, 1965. DUniv N London, 2000. *Publications:* Judaism and Ecology, 1992; Jewish Communities of the Commonwealth, 1993; Journey into Immortality, 1997; Brief Encounters of a Legal Kind, 1997; The Rainbow Never Ends, 2005; Letters to My Wife: a tribute to Sheila Rose, 2007. *Recreations:* gardening, walking, various sports, writing, reading, lecturing, listening to music, being a grandfather. *Address:* 14 Pagitts Grove, Hadley Wood, Herts EN4 0NT. *T:* (020) 8449 2166.

ROSE, Barry Michael, OBE 1998; FRSCM; FRAM; Master of the Music, St Albans Abbey, 1988–97; *b* 24 May 1934; *s* of late Stanley George Rose and Gladys Mildred Rose; *m* 1965, Elizabeth Mary Ware; one *s* two *d*. *Educ:* Sir George Monoux Grammar Sch., Walthamstow; Royal Acad. of Music (ARAM). FRSCM 1973; FRAM 1989. First Organist and Master of the Choristers, new Guildford Cathedral, 1960–74; Sub-Organist, St Paul's Cath., 1974–77; Master of the Choir, 1977–84; Master of the Choirs, The King's School, Canterbury, 1985–88. Music Adviser to Head of Religious Broadcasting, BBC, 1970–90. Hon. FRCO 2003; Hon. FGCM 2004. Hon. DMus City, 1991; MUniv Surrey, 1992. *Recreation:* collecting and restoring vintage fountain-pens. *Address:* Level Crossing, Milking Lane, Draycott, Somerset BS27 3TL. *T:* and *Fax:* (01934) 744838; *e-mail:* brose80648@aol.com.

ROSE, Brian; HM Diplomatic Service, retired; *b* 26 Jan. 1930; *s* of Edwin and Emily Rose; *m* 1952, Audrey Barnes; one *d*. *Educ:* Canford Sch., Dorset. Intelligence Corps, 1948–50. Min. of Food, 1950–54; CRO, 1954; Peshawar, 1955–56; Ottawa, 1958–61; Kingston, Jamaica, 1962–65; Rome, 1966; Zagreb, 1966–68; Zomba, Malawi, 1968–71; FCO, 1971–74; Düsseldorf, 1974–77; E Berlin, 1977–78; Zürich, 1978–82; Consul-Gen., Stuttgart, 1982–85; Commercial and Econ. Counsellor, Helsinki, 1985–88. *Recreations:* tennis, music. *Club:* Travellers.

ROSE, Major Charles Frederick, CBE 1988 (MBE 1968); CEng, FICE; independent consultant in railway engineering and safety, 1989–98; *b* 9 July 1926; *s* of Charles James Rose and Ida Marguerite Chollet; *m* 1956, Huguette Primerose Lecoultre; one *s* one *d*. *Educ:* Xaverian Coll., Brighton; Royal School of Military Engineering, 1951–52 and 1957–59. Student engineer, Southern Railway Co., 1942–46; commnd RE, 1947; service with mil. railways, Palestine and Egypt, 1947–51; with a Field Sqdn in Germany, 1952–53; Engr SO, Korea, 1953–54; Instructor: Mons Officer Cadet Sch., 1954–57; Transportation Centre, Longmoor, 1959–62; OC a Field Sqdn, Germany, 1962–64; Instr, Royal Sch. of Mil. Engrg, 1964–66; Engr, RE road construction project, Thailand, 1966–68; Inspecting Officer of Railways, MoT, 1968–82; Chief Inspecting Officer of Railways, Dept of Transport, 1982–88. Chm., Anglo-French Channel Tunnel Safety Authy, 1987–89. *Recreations:* hill walking, foreign travel, music. *Address:* 13 Home Farm Road, Busbridge, Godalming, Surrey GU7 1TX. *T:* (01483) 416429.

ROSE, Christine B.; *see* Brooke-Rose.

ROSE, Rt Hon. Sir Christopher (Dudley Roger), Kt 1985; PC 1992; Chief Surveillance Commissioner, since 2006; a Lord Justice of Appeal, 1992–2006; *b* 10 Feb. 1937; *s* of late Roger and Hilda Rose, Morecambe; *m* 1964, Judith, *d* of late George and Charlotte Brand, Didsbury; one *s* one *d*. *Educ:* Morecambe Grammar Sch.; Repton; Leeds Univ. (LLB and Hughes Prize, 1957); Wadham Coll., Oxford (1st cl. hons BCL 1959, Eldon Scholar 1959; Hon. Fellow, 1993). Lectr in Law, Wadham Coll., Oxford, 1959–60; called to Bar, Middle Temple, 1960 (Bencher, 1983; Treas., 2002); Bigelow Teaching Fellow, Law Sch., Univ. of Chicago, 1960–61; Harmsworth Scholar, 1961; joined Northern Circuit, 1961; QC 1974; a Recorder, 1978–85; a Judge of the High Court, QBD, 1985–92; Presiding Judge, Northern Circuit, 1987–90. Vice-Pres., Court of Appeal (Criminal Div.), 1997–2006. Chm., Criminal Justice Consultative Council, 1994–2000. Mem., Senate of Inns of Court and Bar, 1983–85. UK Trustee, Harold G. Fox Foundn, 1995–2005. Hon. LLD Leeds, 2008. *Recreations:* playing the piano, listening to music, travel. *Address:* Office of Surveillance Commissioners, PO Box 29105, SW1V 1ZU. *Club:* Garrick.

ROSE, Clifford; *see* Rose, F.C.

ROSE, Sir Clive (Martin), GCMG 1981 (KCMG 1976; CMG 1967); HM Diplomatic Service, retired; *b* 15 Sept. 1921; *s* of late Rt Rev. Alfred Carey Wollaston Rose and Lois Juliet (*née* Garton); *m* 1946, Elisabeth Mackenzie (*d* 2006), *d* of late Rev. Cyril Lewis, Gilston; two *s* three *d*. *Educ:* Marlborough College; Christ Church, Oxford (MA). Rifle Bde, 1941–46 (Maj.; despatches): served in Europe, 1944–45; India, 1945; Iraq, 1945–46. CRO, 1948; Office of Deputy High Comr, Madras, 1948–49; Foreign Office, 1950–53; UK High Commn, Germany, 1953–54; British Embassy, Bonn, 1955; FO, 1956–59; 1st Sec. and HM Consul, Montevideo, 1959–62; FO, 1962–65; Commercial Counsellor, Paris, 1965–67; Imp. Defence Coll., 1968; Counsellor, British Embassy, Washington, 1969–71; Asst Under-Sec. of State, FCO, 1971–73; Ambassador and Head, British Delegn to Negotiations on Mutual Reduction of Forces and Armaments and Associated Measures in Central Europe (MBFR), Vienna, 1973–76; Dep. Secretary, Cabinet Office, 1976–79; Ambassador and UK Permanent Rep. on North Atlantic Council, 1979–82. Lectr to RCDS, 1979–87 (Mem., Adv. Bd, 1985–91). Consultant, Control Risks Gp, 1983–95; Dir, Control Risks Information Services Ltd, 1986–93 (Chm., 1991–93). Pres., Emergency Planning Assoc. (formerly Assoc. of Civil Defence and Emergency Planning Officers), 1987–93; Vice-Patron, RUSI, 1993–2001 (Chm. Council, 1983–86; Vice-Pres., 1986–93). Vice-Patron, Suffolk Preservation Soc., 2007– (Chm., 1985–88; Vice-Pres., 1988–2007). FRSA 1982; Hon. FICD 1989. *Publications:* Campaigns Against Western Defence: NATO's adversaries and critics, 1985, 2nd edn 1986; The Soviet Propaganda Network, 1988; The Unending Quest: a search for ancestors, 1996; Alice Owen: the life, marriages and times of a Tudor lady, 2006; (ed) Lavenham Remembers, 2006; Fanfare for Lavenham (epic poem), 2007; contrib. to FCO Occasional Papers. *Recreations:* gardening, reading Trollope, family history. *Address:* Chimney House, Lavenham, Sudbury, Suffolk CO10 9QT.

ROSE, David Edward; independent film and television producer; *b* 22 Nov. 1924; *s* of Alvan Edward Rose and Gladys Frances Rose; *m* 1st, 1952, Valerie Edwards (*d* 1966); three *s* three *d*; 2nd, 1966, Sarah Reid (marr. diss. 1988); one *d*, and one step *s* one step *d* adopted; 3rd, 2001, Karin Bamborough. *Educ:* Kingswood Sch., Bath; Guildhall Sch. of Music and Drama. Repertory Theatre, 1952; Ballets Jooss, and Sadler's Wells Theatre Ballet, 1954; BBC Television, 1954–81 (in production and direction; Head of Television Training, 1969; Head of Regional Television Drama, 1971–81); Sen. Commng Editor (Fiction), 1981–88, Hd of Drama, 1988–90, Channel Four TV. Member: BAFTA; Eur. Film Acad. Prix Italia TV Award (for film Medico), 1959; BAFTA Producer and Director's Award, (for Z Cars (prod original series)), 1963; BFI Award (for Film on Four and work of new writers and directors), 1985; Desmond Davies Award, BAFTA, 1987; Prix Roberto Rossellini (for Channel Four Television), Cannes Film Fest., 1987; Critics Circle Special Film Award, 1987; Gold Medal, RTS, 1988; BAFTA Fellowship, 1999.

ROSE, Dinah Gwen Lison; QC 2006; barrister; *b* 16 July 1965; *d* of Michael and Susan Rose; *m* 1991, Peter Kessler; two *d*. *Educ:* City of London Sch. for Girls; Magdalen Coll., Oxford (BA Hons Mod. Hist. 1987); City Univ. (Dip. Law 1988). Called to the Bar, Gray's Inn, 1989; in practice as barrister, 1989–, specialising in public and employment law and human rights. *Address:* Blackstone Chambers, Blackstone House, Temple, EC4Y 9BW. *T:* (020) 7583 1770, *Fax:* (020) 7822 7350; *e-mail:* dinahrose@blackstonechambers.com.

ROSE, Donald Henry Gair, LVO 1982; HM Diplomatic Service, retired; Consul-General, Jedda, 1983–86; *b* 24 Sept. 1926; *m* 1950, Sheila Munro; three *s*. HM Forces, 1944–48; Scottish Office, 1948–66; Commonwealth Office, 1966; Nairobi, 1967; Tripoli, 1971; First Sec., Cairo, 1974–77; FCO, 1977–79; High Comr, Kiribati, 1979–83. *Address:* 11 Buckstone Gardens, Edinburgh EH10 6QD.

ROSE, Prof. Francis Dennis, LLD, DCL; Professor of Commercial Law, University of Bristol, since 2000; *b* 11 Jan. 1950; *s* of Francis Joseph Rose and late Catherine Mary Rose (*née* Conlon); *m* 1974, Lynda Kathryn Banks; one *s* two *d*. *Educ:* Farnborough Grammar Sch.; Magdalen Coll., Oxford (BA 1972, BCL 1973, MA 1975; DCL 2007); UCL (PhD 1986); MA 1992, LLD 2006, Cantab. Called to the Bar, Gray's Inn, 1983; barrister; Associate Mem., Quadrant Chambers (formerly 2, then 4, Essex Court Chambers). Lecturer in Law: Liverpool Univ., 1973–75; Cardiff Law Sch., UWIST, 1975–77; UCL, 1977–85; Sen. Lectr, UCL, 1985–89; Lectr in Law, Univ. of Cambridge and Fellow, St John's Coll., Cambridge, 1989–92; Prof. of Commercial and Common Law, Univ. of Buckingham, 1993–99. Visiting Professor: UCL, 1992–94; Univ. of Natal, 1996; Internat. Maritime Law Inst., Malta, 2001–; Univ. of Auckland, 2002; Tulane Univ., 2005; Univ. of Queensland, 2007. Convener, Restitution Section, SLS (formerly SPTL), 1983– (Mem. Council, 1986–99; Sections Sec., 1990–96). Associate Ed., Current Legal Problems, 1983–85; Ed., 1983–87, Gen. Ed., 1987–, Lloyd's Maritime and Commercial Law Qly; Gen. Ed., Restitution Law Review, 1993–; Ed.-in-Chief, Company, Financial and Insolvency Law Review, 1997–99. Editl Dir, Mansfield Press, 1993–2000; Ed., Internat. Maritime and Commercial Yearbook, 2002–. *Publications:* The Modern Law of Pilotage, 1984; Kennedy and Rose, The Law of Salvage, 5th edn 1985 (jtly) and 6th edn 2001; (ed) New Foundations for Insurance Law, 1987; (ed) International Commercial and Maritime Arbitration, 1987; (ed) Restitution and the Conflict of Laws, 1995; (ed) Consensus Ad Idem, 1996; (ed) Failure of Contracts: contractual, restitutionary and proprietary consequences, 1997; General Average: law and practice, 1997, 2nd edn 2005; (ed) Restitution and Banking Law, 1998; (ed jtly) Lessons of the Swaps Litigation, 2000; (ed jtly) Restitution and Equity, vol. I, Resulting Trusts and Equitable Compensation, 2000; (ed) Lex Mercatoria, 2000; (ed) Restitution and Insolvency, 2000; Marine Insurance: law and practice, 2004; contribs to legal jls and books. *Recreations:* family, music, photography, collecting. *Address:* Faculty of Law, University of Bristol, Wills Memorial Building, Queen's Road, Bristol BS8 1RJ. *T:* (0117) 954 5318; *e-mail:* Francis.Rose@bristol.ac.uk.

ROSE, Dr F(rank) Clifford, FRCP; Hon. Consulting Neurologist, Charing Cross Hospital, since 1991; *b* 29 Aug. 1926; *s* of James and Clare Rose; *m* 1963, Angela Juliet Halsted; three *s*. *Educ:* King's Coll., London; Westminster Hosp. Med. Sch.; Univ. of California, San Francisco; Hôpital de la Salpêtrière, Paris. MB BS London; DCH; MRCS; FRCP 1971 (LRCP 1949, MRCP 1954). Medical Registrar, Westminster Hosp., 1955; Resident MO, National Hosp., Queen Square, 1957; Sen. Registrar, Dept of Neurology, St George's Hosp., 1960; Consultant Neurologist: Medical Ophthalmology Unit, St Thomas' Hosp., 1963–85; Moor House Sch. for Speech Disorders, 1965–70; Physician i/c, Dept. of Neurology, Regl Neuroscis Centre, Charing Cross Hosp., 1965–91; Dir, Academic Unit of Neuroscis, Charing Cross and Westminster Med. Sch., 1985–91; Dir, London Neurological Centre, 1991–2005; Prof. Associate, Dept of Health Scis, Brunel Univ., 1991–97. PMO, Allied Dunbar (formerly Hambro Life) Assurance Co., 1970–96. Mem., Wkg Pty on Stroke, RCP, 1988; Chairman: European Stroke Prevention Study, 1981–88; Res. Adv. Cttee, Assoc. for Res. in Multiple Sclerosis, 1987–91; Internat. Amyotrophic Lateral Sclerosis/Motor Neurone Disease Res. Foundn, 1987–90; Motor Neurone Disease Assoc., 1988–90 (Med. Patron, 1978–90; Scientific Advr, 1990–91); Ind. Doctors Forum, 1994–96 (Chm., Specialists' Cttee, 2003–05); Ciba Epilepsy Res. Award, 1997. Sen. Editor, Neuroepidemiology, 1991–96 (Dep. Editor, 1982–83; Editor, 1984–90); Editor: World Neurology, 1990–98; Jl of Hist. of Neuroscis, 1992–96; Co-editor, Headache Qly, 1991–95. President: Med. Soc. London, 1983–84 (Lettsomian Lectr, 1979; Treas., 1984–89; Internat. Sec., 1995–2007); Assurance Med. Soc., 1983–85; Section of Neurology, RSM, 1990–91; Sec.-Treas. Gen., World Fedn of Neurology, 1989–98. Trustee: Migraine Trust (Chm., 1988–96); The Way Ahead Appeal, 1986–91. Examr in Clinical Pharmacology and Therapeutics, Univ. of London. Guest Lectr, Scandinavian Migraine Soc., 1983. Hon. Member: Neurol Soc. of Thailand, 1992; Austrian Soc. of Neurol., 1992; Hon. Life Mem., Internat. Headache Soc., 1997. Harold Wolff Award, 1981 and 1984, and Distinguished Clinician Award, 1986, Amer. Assoc. for the Study of Headache; Louis Boshes Award, Northwestern Univ., Chicago, 1994; Lifetime Award, Internat. Soc. for the History of Neuroscis, 2003. *Publications:* (jtly) Hypoglycaemia, 1965, 2nd edn, 1981 (Japanese trans., 1988); (jtly) Basic Neurology of Speech, 1970, 3rd edn 1983; (ed) Physiological Aspects of Clinical Neurology, 1976; (ed) Medical Ophthalmology, 1976; (ed) Motor Neurone Disease, 1977; (ed) Clinical Neuroimmunology, 1978; (ed) Paediatric Neurology, 1979; (jtly) Optic Neuritis and its Differential Diagnosis, 1979; (ed jtly) Progress in Stroke Research 1, 1979; (ed jtly) Progress in Neurological Research, 1979; (jtly) Migraine: the facts, 1979 (Spanish trans., 1981); (ed) Clinical Neuroepidemiology, 1980; (ed) Animal Models of Neurological Disorders, 1980; (ed jtly) Research Progress in Parkinson's Disease, 1981; (ed) Metabolic Disorders of the Nervous System, 1981; (ed jtly) Progress in Migraine Research 1, 1981; (jtly) Stroke: The Facts, 1981 (Dutch trans., 1982); (ed jtly) Historical Aspects of the Neurosciences, 1982; (ed jtly) Cerebral Hypoxia in the Pathogenesis of Migraine, 1982; (ed) Advances in Stroke Therapy, 1982; (ed) Advances in Migraine Research and Therapy, 1982; (ed) Research Progress in Epilepsy, 1982; (ed jtly) Immunology of Nervous System Infections, 1983; (ed) The Eye in General Disease, 1983; (ed jtly) Progress in Stroke Research 2, 1983; (ed) Research Progress in Motor Neurone Disease, 1984; (ed) Progress in Migraine Research 2, 1984; (ed) Progress in Aphasiology, 1985; (ed) Modern Approaches to the Dementias (2 vols), 1985; (ed jtly) Neuro-oncology, 1985; (ed) Migraine: clinical and research advances, 1985; Handbook of Clinical Neurology: headache, 1986; (ed) Stroke: epidemiological, therapeutic and socio-economic aspects, 1986; (jtly) Atlas of Clinical Neurology, 1986 (Japanese trans., 1989); (ed jtly) Multiple Sclerosis: diagnostic, immunological and therapeutic aspects, 1987; (ed) Advances in Headache Research, 1987; (ed) Parkinson's Disease: clinical and research advances, 1987; (ed jtly) Physiological Aspects of Clinical Neuro-ophthalmology, 1987; (jtly) Answers to Migraine, 1987; (ed jtly) Aphasia, 1988; (ed) The Management of Headache, 1988; (ed jtly) Neuromuscular Stimulation, 1989; (ed) James Parkinson, his life and times, 1989; (ed) Control of the Hypothalamic-Pituitary-Adrenal Axis, 1989; (ed) New Advances in Headache Research, 1989; (ed) Neuroscience across the Centuries, 1989; (ed jtly) Clinical Trial Methodology in Stroke, 1989; (ed jtly) Amyotrophic Lateral Sclerosis: new advances in toxicology and epidemiology, 1990; (ed) Progress in Clinical Neurologic Trials:

amyotrophic lateral sclerosis, 1990; (ed) New Advances in Headache Research 2, 1991; (ed) Parkinson's Disease and the Problems of Clinical Trials, 1992; (ed) Molecular Genetics and Neurology, 1992; (ed) Advances in Clinical Neuropharmacology, 1993; (ed) ALS: from Charcot to the present and into the future, 1994; (ed) New Advances in Headache Research 3, 1994; (ed) Tropical Neurology, 1996; Towards Migraine 2000, 1996; A Short History of Neurology: the British contribution 1660–1910, 1999; Multiple Sclerosis at Your Fingertips, 2000; Twentieth Century Neurology: the British contribution, 2001; (jtly) Motor Neurone Disease at your fingertips, 2003; (ed) Neurology of the Arts, 2004; (jtly) Migraine, 2004; (jtly) Managing Your Multiple Sclerosis, 2004; The Neurobiology of Painting, 2006; Neurology of Music, 2009; History of British Neurology, 2009; papers in neurological and gen. med. jls. *Recreations:* reading, wine, bridge. *Address:* 7–8 Church Street, Little Bedwyn, Marlborough, Wilts SN8 3JQ. *T:* (01672) 870303. *Clubs:* Royal Society of Medicine, Savile.

ROSE, Gerald Gershon, PhD; CChem, FRSC; Director, Thornton Research Centre, Shell Research Ltd, 1975–80; *b* 4 May 1921; *m* 1945, Olive Sylvia; one *s* two *d*. *Educ:* Hendon County Grammar Sch.; Imperial Coll. of Science and Technology (BSc, ARCS, DIC, PhD). Joined Shell Group, 1944; served in refineries, Stanlow, Trinidad, Singapore and South Africa; General Manager, Shell/BP South Africa Petroleum Refineries, 1963; Manufacturing and Supply Director, Shell/BP Service Co., 1968; Manager, Teesport Refinery, 1971. *Recreations:* golf, tennis, gardening. *Address:* The Tithe Barn, Great Barrow, Chester, Cheshire CH3 7HW. *T:* (01829) 40623.

ROSE, Graham Hunt; a Master of the Supreme Court (Queen's Bench Division), since 1992; *b* 15 July 1937; *er s* of late William Edward Hunt Rose and Mary Musgrave Rose (*née* Kent); *m* 1962, Malvinia Ann Saunders (marr. diss. 1988); three *s*. *Educ:* Canford Sch.; University Coll., Oxford (MA). Nat. Service, RA, 1955–57: commnd 1956; active service, 1957. Called to the Bar, Inner Temple, 1961; practised at the Bar, 1961–92, Western Circuit. Jt Editor, Civil Procedure (formerly Supreme Court Practice), 1992–. *Recreations:* most ball games, mountaineering, gardening, birdwatching. *Address:* Royal Courts of Justice, Strand, WC2A 2LL. *Clubs:* Travellers; Parkstone Golf; Farnham Golf.

ROSE, Prof. Harold Bertram; Emeritus Professor of Finance, London Business School (formerly London Graduate School of Business Studies), since 1996 (Esmée Fairbairn Chair, 1965–75; Visiting Professor of Finance, since 1975); *b* 9 Aug. 1923; *s* of late Isaac Rose and Rose Rose (*née* Barnett); *m* 1st, 1949, Valerie Frances Anne Chubb (marr. diss. 1974); three *s* one *d*; 2nd, 1974, Diana Mary Campbell Scarlett; one *s* one *d*. *Educ:* Davenant Foundn Sch.; LSE (BCom). Served with RA in Britain, India and Burma, 1942–46 (Captain). Head of Econ. Intell. Dept, Prudential Assce Co., Ltd, 1948–58; Sen. Lectr, then Reader, in Economics, LSE, 1958–65; Member: Council, Consumers' Assoc., 1958–63; Central Adv. Council on Primary Educn (Plowden Cttee), 1963–65; Business Studies Cttee, SSRC, 1967–68, and Univ. Grants Cttee, 1968–69; Reserve Pension Bd, 1973–75; HM Treasury Inquiry into Value of Pensions, 1980; Special Adviser to: H of C Treasury and Civil Service Cttee, 1980–81; DoI, 1980–81. Gp Economic Advr, Barclays Bank, 1975–88. Director: Economist Newspaper, 1969–71; Abbey National Building Soc., 1975–83. Mem., Retail Prices Adv. Cttee, 1985–89. Trustee, IEA, 1975–98 (Chm., 1995–98); Trustee, Inst. for Study of Civil Soc., 2000–06 (Treas., 2000–04). Gov., The Hall Sch., 1987–95. *Publications:* The Economic Background to Investment, 1960; Disclosure in Company Accounts, 1963; Management Education in the 1970's, 1970; various papers in econ. and financial jls. *Address:* 33 Dartmouth Park Avenue, NW5 1JL. *T:* (020) 7485 7315; *e-mail:* harold@hbrose.co.uk. *Club:* Reform.

ROSE, Gen. Sir (Hugh) Michael, KCB 1994; CBE 1986; DSO 1995; QGM 1981; DL; Adjutant General, 1995–97; Aide de Camp General to the Queen, 1995–97; *b* 5 Jan. 1940; *s* of late Lt-Col Hugh Vincent Rose, IA and Mrs Barbara Phoebe Masters (*née* Allcard); *m* 1968, Angela Raye Shaw; two *s*. *Educ:* Cheltenham College; St Edmund Hall, Oxford (2nd Cl. Hons PPE; Hon. Fellow, 1995); Staff College; RCDS. Commissioned Gloucestershire Regt, TAVR, 1959; RAFVR, 1962; Coldstream Guards, 1964; served Germany, Aden, Malaysia, Gulf States, Dhofar, N Ireland (despatches), Falkland Is (despatches); BM 16 Para. Bde, 1973–75; CO 22 SAS Regt, 1979–82; Comd 39 Inf. Bde, 1983–85; Comdt, Sch. of Infantry, 1987–88; DSF, 1988–89; GOC NE Dist and Comdr 2nd Inf. Div., 1989–91; Comdt, Staff Coll., 1991–93; Comdr, UK Field Army and Insp. Gen. of TA, 1993–94; Comdr, UN Protection Force, Bosnia-Herzegovina, 1994–95; Dep. C-in-C, Land Comd, 1995. Col, Coldstream Guards, 1999–. Hon. Col, Oxford Univ. OTC, 1995–2000. DL Somerset, 2003. Hon. DLitt Nottingham, 1999. Comdr, Legion of Honour (France), 1995. *Publications:* Fighting for Peace, 1998; Washington's War, 2007. *Recreations:* sailing, ski-ing. *Address:* c/o Regimental HQ Coldstream Guards, Wellington Barracks, Birdcage Walk, SW1E 6HQ. *Club:* Pratt's.

ROSE, Irwin A., (Ernie), PhD; Researcher, Department of Physiology and Biophysics, University of California, Irvine, since 1997; *b* 16 July 1926; *s* of Harry Royze and Ella Greenwald; *m* 1955, Dr Zelda Budenstein; three *s* one *d* (incl. twin *s*). *Educ:* Univ. of Chicago (BS 1948; PhD 1952). Instructor in Biochem., Yale Univ. Med. Sch., 1954–63; Scientist, Fox Chase Cancer Center, Philadelphia, 1963–95. (Jtly) Nobel Prize in Chemistry, 2004. *Publications:* articles in learned jls. *Address:* Department of Physiology and Biophysics, University of California, Irvine, CA 92697–4560, USA.

ROSE, Jack, CMG 1963; MBE 1954; DFC 1942; *b* 18 Jan. 1917; *s* of late Charles Thomas Rose; *m* 1st, 1940, Margaret Valerie (*d* 1966), 2nd *d* of late Alec Stuart Budd; two *s*; 2nd, 1967, Beryl Elizabeth, 4th *d* of late A. S. Budd. *Educ:* Shooters Hill School; London University. Served RAF, 1938–46 (Wing Commander); served in fighter, fighter/bomber and rocket firing sqdns; France, 1940 and 1944; Battle of Britain; Burma, 1944–45. Joined Colonial Administrative Service, N Rhodesia, 1947; Private Secretary to Governor of Northern Rhodesia, 1950–53; seconded to Colonial Office, 1954–56; Administrative posts, Northern Rhodesia, 1956–60; Administrator, Cayman Islands (seconded), 1960–63; Assistant to Governor, British Guiana, 1963–64 (Actg Governor and Dep. Governor for periods). Member: Professional and Technical 'A' Whitley Council for Health Services, 1965–75 (Chm., 1973–75); Gen. Whitley Council for Health Services, 1973–75. Secretary: Chartered Soc. of Physiotherapy, 1965–75; Salmon and Trout Assoc., 1975–79 (Vice-Pres., 1980–). Chm., Burford Charity Trustees, 1994–2002. *Address:* The Little House, 178 The Hill, Burford, Oxon OX18 4QY. *T:* (01993) 822553.

ROSE, Prof. Jacqueline Susan, PhD; FBA 2006; Professor of English, Queen Mary, University of London, since 1992; *b* 19 May 1949; *d* of Leslie David Stone and Lynne Rose; one *d*. *Educ:* St Hilda's Coll., Oxford (BA Hons English 1971); Paris-Sorbonne (MA Comparative and Gen. Lit. 1972); PhD London 1979. Lectr, 1976–88, Sen. Lectr, 1988–91, Reader, 1991–92, in English, Univ. of Sussex. Writer and presenter, TV prog., Dangerous Liaisons: Israel and America, 2002. *Publications:* The Case of Peter Pan, or, The Impossibility of Children's Fiction, 1984, 2nd edn 1993; Sexuality in the Field of Vision, 1986, 2nd edn 2005; The Haunting of Sylvia Plath, 1991, 2nd edn 1996; Why War?: psychoanalysis, politics and the return to Melanie Klein, 1993; States of Fantasy, 1995; Albertine (novel), 2001; On Not Being Able to Sleep: psychoanalysis in the modern world, 2003; The Question of Zion, 2005; The Last Resistance, 2007. *Address:* School of English and Drama, Queen Mary, University of London, Mile End Road, E1 4NS. *T:* (020) 7882 5014/3356, *Fax:* (020) 7882 3357; *e-mail:* j.rose@qmul.ac.uk.

ROSE, Sir James; *see* Rose, Sir A. J.

ROSE, Jeffrey David, CBE 1991; Chairman of the Royal Automobile Club, 1981–98 (Deputy Chairman, 1979–81); *b* 2 July 1931; *s* of late Samuel and Daisy Rose; *m* 1st, 1958, Joyce (*née* Clompus) (marr. diss. 1999); one *s* two *d*; 2nd, 1999, Helga Maria Wiederschwinger Dusauzay (marr. diss. 2001). *Educ:* Southend High Sch.; London Sch. of Econs and Pol. Science. Nat. Service, RA, 1950–52 (Lieut). Chm., RAC Motoring Services, 1980–98; Vice Chm., British Road Fedn, 1982–98; Vice President: Fédn Internationale de l'Automobile, 1983–93 and 1994–96 (Hon. Vice Pres., 1996–); Inst. of the Motor Industry, 1992–98; RAC Motor Sports Council, 1994–98; Chm., Commonwealth Motoring Conf., 1988–98; Member: Council, Inst. of Advanced Motorists, 1987–94; Adv. Council, Prince's Youth Business Trust, 1992–2000. Chm., Trustees, Brain and Spine Foundn, 1995–2005; Trustee, Brooklands Mus., 1991–2001. FIMI 1989. Liveryman, Worshipful Co. of Coachmakers and Coach Harness Makers, 1981– (Master, 2006–). *Recreations:* walking, dining, music. *Address:* Albany, Piccadilly, W1J 0AX. *Clubs:* Royal Automobile (Vice-Pres., 1998-), Brooks's, MCC.

ROSE, Sir John (Edward Victor), Kt 2003; FRAeS; Chief Executive, Rolls-Royce, since 1996; *b* 9 Oct. 1952; *s* of (Wentworth) Victor Rose and late Doris Rose (*née* Bridge); *m* 1979, Emma Felicity Granville; two *s* one *d*. *Educ:* Charterhouse Sch.; Univ. of St Andrews (MA Hons Psychology). FRAeS 1993. Board Mem., Rolls-Royce, 1992–. Commander, Légion d'Honneur (France), 2008. *Recreations:* ski-ing, sailing, scuba-diving, tennis, theatre, arts. *Address:* Rolls-Royce plc, 65 Buckingham Gate, SW1E 6AT. *T:* (020) 7222 9020. *Club:* Hurlingham.

ROSE, Maj. Gen. John Gordon, MBE 1991; Director General, Intelligence Collection, Ministry of Defence, since 2006; *b* 30 May 1955; *s* of Charles and Yvonne Rose; *m* 1982, Mandie Jones; one *s*. *Educ:* Kitale Primary Sch., Kenya; Lenana Sch., Kenya; Dollar Acad. Royal Marines: joined, 1974, young officer trng; Troop Comdr 40 Commando, 1975–76; Ops Officer, Desert Regt, Sultan of Oman Land Forces (on secondment), 1976–78; Instructor, SNCO Tactics Wing (Army) and RM Officers Trng, 1979–82; Adjutant 40 Commando, 1982–83; SO HQ 3 Commando Bde, 1984–87; Army staff course, Camberley, 1988; COS Logistics HQ UK Mobile Force, 1989–90; Company Comdr 42 Commando, 1990–92; SO Directorate of Naval Staff Duties, MoD, 1992–93; COS 3 Commando Bde, 1994–96; Staff of C-in-C Fleet, 1996; Asst Dir, Middle East, MoD, 1997–98; CO 40 Commando, 1999–2000; Dir, Intelligence Ops, MoD Defence Intelligence Staff, 2000–03; Chief of Defence Staff Liaison Officer, Pentagon, 2003; hcsc, 2004; Comdr 3 Commando Bde, 2004–06. *Recreations:* golf, ski-ing, running. *Address:* c/o Royal Marines Secretary, Whale Island, Portsmouth PO1 3LS.

ROSE, John Raymond; Clerk of Standing Committees, House of Commons, 1987–91; *b* 22 April 1934; *s* of late Arthur Raymond Rose and Edith Mary Rose, Merstham, Surrey and Minehead, Somerset; *m* 1st, 1961, Vivienne (marr. diss. 1991), *d* of late Charles Dillon Seabrooke, IoW; one *s* one *d*; 2nd, 1991, Dr Betty Webb, *d* of late Ernest Julian Webb, Statesville, NC, USA. *Educ:* Marlborough; Trinity Hall, Cambridge (Major Scholar in Classics; Law Tripos 1st Cl. Hons, Pts I and II). 2nd Lieut DCLI, Belize and Jamaica, 1953–55. Clerk's Department, House of Commons, 1958–91: Clerk of Select Cttees on Estimates (Sub-Cttee), Public Accounts, Violence in the Family, Race Relations, Abortion, European Community Secondary Legislation, Foreign Affairs, 1959–87. Vis. Kenan Prof., 1981, Adjunct Prof., 1991–, Meredith Coll., NC, USA. Fellow, Industry and Parlt Trust, 1987. Freeman, City of London, 1959; Liveryman, Salters' Co., 1959. *Recreations:* travel, walking, cycling, gardening, bridge. *Address:* 1612 Oberlin Road, Raleigh, NC 27608, USA. *T:* (919) 8283443; 4 St James's Square, Bath BA1 2TR. *T:* (01225) 481115; *e-mail:* johnrrose34@hotmail.com.

ROSE, Jonathan Lee; His Honour Judge Rose; a Circuit Judge, since 2008; *b* Leeds, 29 Oct. 1958; *s* of Malcolm and Shirley Rose; *m* 1990, Philippa, *d* of Eric and Pearl Green; one *s* one *d*. *Educ:* Roundhay Sch., Leeds; Preston Poly. (BA Hons); Keble Coll., Oxford. Called to the Bar, Middle Temple, 1981; barrister, N Eastern Circuit, 1983–2008; Recorder, 2000–08. Legal Mem., Mental Health Rev. Tribunal, 2002–08. Vice Pres., 2005–06, Pres., 2006–, United Hebrew Congregation, Leeds. *Publication:* Innocents: how justice failed Stefan Kisko and Lesley Molseed, 1997. *Recreations:* music, scuba diving, cycling, natural history, history. *Address:* Bradford Combined Court Centre, Exchange Square, Bradford BD1 1JA. *T:* (01274) 840274, *Fax:* (01274) 840275.

ROSE, Joyce Dora Hester, CBE 1981; JP, DL; Chairman, Council and Executive, Magistrates' Association, 1990–93; *b* 14 Aug. 1929; *d* of late Abraham (Arthur) Woolf and Rebecca Woolf (*née* Simpson); *m* 1953, Cyril Rose; two *s* one *d*. *Educ:* King Alfred Sch., London; Queen's Coll., London; in N America. Chm., Watford Magistrates' Court, 1990–94 (Dep. Chm., Juvenile Panel, 1968–91, Family Proceedings (formerly Domestic) Panel, 1982–99 (Chm., 1979–82)); Member: Herts Magistrates' Courts Cttee, 1973–95; Herts Probation Cttee, 1971–95. Pres., 1979–80, Chm., 1982–83, Liberal Party; Pres. and Chm., Women's Liberal Fedn, 1972, 1973; Mem., Lib Dem Federal Appeals Panel, 1994–2005. Mem., Women's Nat. Commn, 1981–87 (Mem. Exec., 1985–87); former Mem., Nat. Exec., UK Cttee for UNICEF (Vice-Chm., 1968–70). Board Member: Apex Trust, 1994–2004; Herts Care Trust, 1995–99; SW Herts Hospice Charitable Trust (Peace Hospice), 1996–2003; Herts Family Mediation Service, 1996–2002. JP Herts, 1963; DL Herts, 1990. Hon. LLD Hertfordshire, 1992. *Address:* 2 Oak House, 101 Ducks Hill Road, Northwood, Middx HA6 2WQ. *T:* (01923) 821385, *Fax:* (01923) 840515. *Club:* National Liberal.

ROSE, Ven. Judith; *see* Rose, Ven. K. J.

ROSE, Judith Ann; *see* Goffe, J. A.

ROSE, Sir Julian (Day), 4th Bt *cr* 1909, of Hardwick House, and 5th Bt *cr* 1872, of Montreal; *b* 3 March 1947; 3rd and *o* surv. *s* of Sir Charles Henry Rose, 3rd Bt and of Phoebe, *d* of 2nd Baron Phillimore (*d* 1947); *S* father, 1966, and cousin, Sir Francis Cyril Rose, 4th Bt, 1979; *m* 1976, Elizabeth Goode Johnson, Columbus, Ohio, USA; one *s* one *d*. *Educ:* Stanbridge School. Actor/asst dir, Players' Theatre of New England, 1973–79; Co-founder, Inst. for Creative Develt, Antwerp, 1978–83. Co-ordinator, Organic Farming practice, Hardwick Estate, 1984–. Chm., Assoc. of Rural Businesses in Oxfordshire, 1995–; Member: Council, Soil Assoc., 1984–96; Agricl Panel, Intermediate Technology Develt Gp, 1984–87; Bd, UK Register of Organic Food Standards, Food From Britain, 1987–90; BBC Rural and Agricl Affairs Adv. Cttee, 1991–93; Adv. Cttee, Food and Farming, Thames Valley Univ., 1994–; Agricl and Rural Economy Cttee, CLA, 1999–2002. Rural Economy Advr, SE of England Develt Agency, 1999–; Pres., Internat. Coalition to Protect the Polish Countryside, 2000–. Trustee: SAFE Alliance, 1995–; Dartington Trust, 1996–2000. Agricl Correspondent, Environment Now, 1989–90.

Publication: (contrib.) Town and Country, 1999. *Heir: s* Lawrence Michael Rose, *b* 6 Oct. 1986. *Address:* Hardwick House, Whitchurch-on-Thames, Oxfordshire RG8 7RB.

ROSE, Ven. (Kathleen) Judith; Archdeacon of Tonbridge, 1996–2002; *b* 14 June 1937; *d* of Cuthbert Arthur Rose and Margaret Rose; *m* 1991, David Ernest Gwyer (*d* 2000); two step *d. Educ:* Sexey's Grammar Sch., Blackford; Seale Hayne Agricl Coll. (NDD 1960); St Michael's House Theol Coll., Oxford (DipTh 1966); London Bible Coll. (BD(Hons)). Agriculture, 1953–64; Parish Worker, Rodbourne Cheney Parish Church, 1966–71; ordained deaconess, 1976, deacon, 1987, priest, 1994; Parish Worker, then Deaconess, St George's Church, Leeds, 1973–81; Chaplain, Bradford Cathedral, 1981–85; Minister responsible for St Paul's Parkwood, Gillingham, 1986–90; Chaplain to Bishop of Rochester, 1990–95. Rural Dean of Gillingham, 1988–90. *Publications:* Sunday Learning for All Ages, 1982; (contrib.) Women in Ministry, 1991; (contrib.) Women Priests: the first years, 1996; (contrib.) A Time and A Season, 2000; (contrib.) Voices of this Calling, 2002. *Recreations:* gardening, walking, home-making. *Address:* 4 Glebelands Close, Cheddar, Somerset BS27 3XP.

ROSE, Kenneth Vivian, CBE 1997; FRSL; writer; *b* 15 Nov. 1924; *s* of Dr J. Rose, MB, ChB. *Educ:* Repton Sch.; New Coll., Oxford (scholar; MA). Served Welsh Guards, 1943–46; attached Phantom, 1945. Asst master, Eton Coll., 1948; Editorial Staff, Daily Telegraph, 1952–60; founder and writer of Albany column, Sunday Telegraph, 1961–97. *Publications:* Superior Person: a portrait of Curzon and his circle in late Victorian England, 1969; The Later Cecils, 1975; William Harvey: a monograph, 1978; King George V, 1983 (Wolfson Award for History, 1983; Whitbread Award for Biography, 1983; Yorkshire Post Biography of the Year Award, 1984); Kings, Queens and Courtiers: intimate portraits of the Royal House of Windsor, 1985; (contrib.) Founders and Followers: literary lectures on the London Library, 1992; Elusive Rothschild: the life of Victor, Third Baron, 2003; contribs to Dictionary of National Biography. *Address:* 38 Brunswick Gardens, W8 4AL. *T:* (020) 7221 4783. *Clubs:* Beefsteak, Pratt's.

ROSE, Col Lewis John, OBE 1990; Vice Lord-Lieutenant of Bedfordshire, 1991–98; *b* 18 Aug. 1935; *s* of Reginald George Rose and Mary Agnes Rose; *m* 1st, 1964, Aileen Beth Robertson (marr. diss. 1974); two *s*; 2nd, 1978, Gillian Mary King (marr. diss. 2005); one step *s* one step *d. Educ:* Bedford Sch.; College of Law. Served RA, 1954–56; Beds Yeomanry, later Herts & Beds Yeomanry, 1956–67. In practice as solicitor, 1962–. Comdt, Beds ACF, 1976–90; Chm., Beds TA&VR Cttee, 1991–94; Vice Chm. (Mil.), E Anglia TA&VRA, 1994–99. President: Beds Small-bore Shooting Assoc., 1992–2004; Bedford District Scout Council, 1975–2007. DL Bedfordshire, 1981. *Recreations:* shooting, rowing (Pres., Bedford Rowing Club, 1988–91). *Address:* 11 Woodlands Close, Cople, Beds MK44 3UE. *T:* (01234) 838210. *Club:* Leander (Henley on Thames).

ROSE, Martin Tristram; Director, Canada, British Council, since 2006; *b* 3 Dec. 1954; *s* of Geoffrey Rose and Jocelyn Rose (*née* Briggs); *m* 1984, Georgina Benson; one *s* three *d. Educ:* Bradfield Coll.; Magdalen Coll., Oxford (BA Hons Mod. Hist. 1976; MA 1984); St Antony's Coll., Oxford (MPhil Mod. Mid. Eastern Studies 1984). Sub-ed., The Egyptian Gazette, 1976–78; Sales exec., later ELT Sales, Macmillan Press, S Africa and Mid East, 1979–82; Mid East Dept, Mellon Bank NA, 1984–88; British Council, 1988–: Asst Rep., Baghdad, 1989–90; Asst Dir, Rome and founding Dir, Pontignano Conf., 1991–96; Hd, Europ. Series, London, 1996–99; Dir, Brussels and Cultural Counsellor, HM Embassies, Belgium and Luxembourg, 1999–2002; Dir, Counterpoint, 2002–06; Cultural Counsellor, High Commn, Ottawa, 2006–. *Publications:* (with N. Wadham-Smith) Mutuality, Trust and Cultural Relations, 2004; (with M. Leonard) British Public Diplomacy in an Age of Schisms, 2005. *Recreations:* history, literature, language, memory, Middle East, gravestones, friends on many continents. *Address:* 215 North River Road, Ottawa, ON K1L 8B5, Canada. *T:* (613) 3646234, *Fax:* (613) 5691478; *e-mail:* waldenroses@rogers.com.

ROSE, Gen. Sir Michael; *see* Rose, Gen. Sir H. M.

ROSE, Norman John, FRICS, FCIArb; Member, Lands Tribunal, since 1998; *b* 22 Oct. 1943; *s* of late Jack Rose and Margaret Rose (*née* de Groot); *m* 1968, Helena de Mesquita; three *s. Educ:* Christ's Coll., Finchley; Coll. of Estate Management (BSc (Est. Man.); Valuation Prize). FRICS 1976; FCIArb 1977. Gerald Eve & Co., 1964–71; Partner, de Groot Collis, 1971–91; Dir of Valuation, Chesterton, 1992–98. *Address:* Lands Tribunal, Procession House, 55 Ludgate Hill, EC4M 7JW. *T:* (020) 7029 9780.

ROSE, Paul (Bernard); HM Coroner, London Southern District, 1988–2002; *b* 26 Dec. 1935; *s* of Arthur and Norah Rose; *m* 1957, Eve Marie-Thérèse; two *s* one *d. Educ:* Bury Gram. Sch.; Manchester Univ.; Gray's Inn. LLB (Hons) Manch., 1956; Barrister-at-Law, 1957. Legal and Secretarial Dept, Co-op. Union Ltd, 1957–60; Lectureship, Dept of Liberal Studies, Royal Coll. of Advanced Technology, Salford, 1961–63; Barrister-at-Law, 1963–88; Asst Recorder (formerly Dep. Circuit Judge), 1974–88; Immigration Adjudicator (part-time), Hatton Cross, 1987– (Special Adjudicator, 1993–). MP (Lab) Manchester, Blackley, 1964–79; PPS to Minister of Transport, 1967–68; Opposition Front Bench Spokesman, Dept of Employment, 1970–72. Chairman: Parly Labour Home Office Group, 1968–70; Parly Labour Employment Group, 1974–79; Campaign for Democracy in Ulster, 1965–73. Delegate to Council of Europe and WEU, 1968–69; Vice-Chm., Labour Cttee for Europe, 1977–79. Mem., Campaign for Electoral Reform, 1975–. Founder Mem., SDP (Brent Area Sec., 1981–82). Chm., NW Regional Sports Council, 1966–68. Member: Coroners' Soc. (Pres., SE Coroners Soc., 1996–97); Medico-Legal Soc. AIL. *Publications:* Handbook to Industrial and Provident Societies Act, 1960; Guide to Weights and Measures Act 1963, 1965; The Manchester Martyrs, 1970; Backbencher's Dilemma, 1981; The Moonies' Unmasked, 1981; (jt) A History of the Fenian Movement in Britain, 1982; contrib. to many periodicals on political and legal topics. *Recreations:* sport, theatre, languages, travel, computers. *Address:* Lynnden, 70 Amersham Road, Chalfont St Peter, Bucks SL9 0PB.

ROSE, Paul Telfer; QC 2002; *b* 18 Nov. 1958; 3rd *s* of late Ian Alexander Rose and of Pamela Margaret Rose (*née* Paisley); *m* 1986, Sara Jane Herbert; three *s* one *d. Educ:* University Coll. Sch., Hampstead; Reading Univ. (LLB 1980). Called to the Bar, Gray's Inn, 1981; in practice as barrister, specialising in employment law and personal injury law, 1983–. Part-time Chm., Employment Tribunals, 2003–. *Recreations:* travel, Rugby, cricket, golf, walking with friends and family. *Address:* Old Square Chambers, 10–11 Bedford Row, WC1R 4BU. *T:* (020) 7269 0300; *e-mail:* roseqc@oldsquarechambers.co.uk.

ROSE, Prof. Richard, FBA 1992; Director, Centre for the Study of Public Policy, University of Aberdeen (formerly at Strathclyde University), since 1976; Professor of Politics, University of Aberdeen, since 2005; *b* 9 April 1933; *o s* of late Charles Imse and Mary C. Rose, St Louis, Mo, USA; *m* 1956, Rosemary J., *o d* of late James Kenny, Whitstable, Kent; two *s* one *d. Educ:* Clayton High Sch., Mo; Johns Hopkins Univ., BA (Double distinction, Phi Beta Kappa) comparative drama, 1953; London Sch. of Economics, 1953–54; Oxford University, 1957–60, DPhil (Lincoln and Nuffield Colls). Political public relations, Mississippi Valley, 1954–55; Reporter, St Louis Post-Dispatch, 1955–57; Lecturer in Govt, Univ. of Manchester, 1961–66; Prof. of Politics and Public Policy, Strathclyde Univ., 1966–2005; Sen. Fellow, Oxford Internet Inst., 2003–05. Consultant Psephologist, The Times, Independent Television, Daily Telegraph, STV, UTV etc., 1964–. American SSRC Fellow, Stanford Univ., 1967; Vis. Lectr in Political Sociology, Cambridge Univ., 1967; Dir, ISSC European Summer Sch., 1973. Sec., Cttee on Political Sociology, Internat. Sociological Assoc., 1970–85; Founding Mem., European Consortium for Political Res., 1970; Member: US/UK Fulbright Commn, 1971–75; Eisenhower Fellowship Programme, 1971. Guggenheim Foundn Fellow, 1974; Visiting Scholar: Woodrow Wilson Internat. Centre, Washington DC, 1974; Brookings Inst., Washington DC, 1976; Amer. Enterprise Inst., Washington, 1980; Fiscal Affairs Dept, IMF, Washington, 1984; Visiting Professor: European Univ. Inst., Florence, 1977, 1978; Central European Univ., Prague, 1992–95; Instituto Ortega y Gasset, Madrid, 2000; Visitor, Japan Foundn, 1984; Hinkley Prof., Johns Hopkins Univ., 1987; Guest Prof., Wissenschaftsentrum, Berlin, 1988–90, 2006, 2007; Research Associate: UN Eur. Centre for Social Welfare Policy and Res., 1992–; Centre for Study of Democracy, Univ. of Westminster, 1998–2000; Fellow, Max-Planck Transformation Process Gp, Berlin, 1996; Wei Lun Prof., Chinese Univ. of Hong Kong, 2000. Ransone Lectr, Univ. of Alabama, 1990. Consultant Chm., NI Constitutional Convention, 1976; Mem., Home Office Working Party on Electoral Register, 1975–77. Co-Founder: British Politics Gp, 1974–; Global Barometer Survey Network, 2001–05; Convenor, Work Gp on UK Politics, Political Studies Assoc., 1976–88; Mem. Council, Internat. Political Science Assoc., 1976–82; Keynote Speaker, Aust. Inst. of Political Science, Canberra, 1978; Steering Cttee, World Values Study, 1995; Transparency Internat. Index Construction Cttee, 1998–. Technical Consultant: OECD; World Bank; Internat. Inst. for Democracy and Electoral Assistance, Stockholm; Council of Europe; Dir, ESRC (formerly SSRC) Res. Programme, Growth of Govt, 1982–86; UNDP Cons. to Pres. of Colombia, 1990; Scientific Advr, Paul Lazarsfeld Soc., Vienna, 1991–. Mem. Council, Scottish Opera Ltd, 1992–. Hon. Vice-Pres., Political Studies Assoc., UK, 1986. Editor, Jl of Public Policy, 1985–. Foreign Member: Finnish Acad. of Science and Letters, 1985; Amer. Acad. of Arts and Scis, 1994. Hon. Dr Orebrou, 2005. Amex Internat. Econs Prize, 1992; Lasswell Prize for Public Policy, Policy Studies Orgn, USA, 1999; Lifetime Achievement Award, UK Pol Studies Assoc., 2000. Subject of prog. in Man of Action series, BBC Radio 3, 1974. *Publications:* The British General Election of 1959 (with D. E. Butler), 1960; Must Labour Lose? (with Mark Abrams), 1960; Politics in England, 1964, 5th edn 1989; (ed) Studies in British Politics, 1966, 3rd edn 1976; Influencing Voters, 1967; (ed) Policy Making in Britain, 1969; People in Politics, 1970; (ed, with M. Dogan) European Politics, 1971; Governing Without Consensus: an Irish perspective, 1971; (with T. Mackie) International Almanack of Electoral History, 1974, 3rd edn 1991; (ed) Electoral Behavior: a comparative handbook, 1974; (ed) Lessons from America, 1974; The Problem of Party Government, 1974; (ed) The Management of Urban Change in Britain and Germany, 1974; Northern Ireland: a time of choice, 1976; Managing Presidential Objectives, 1976; (ed) The Dynamics of Public Policy, 1976; (ed, with D. Kavanagh) New Trends in British Politics, 1977; (ed with J. Wiatr) Comparing Public Policies, 1977; What is Governing?: Purpose and Policy in Washington, 1978; (ed, with G. Hermet and A. Rouquié) Elections without Choice, 1978; (with B. G. Peters) Can Government Go Bankrupt?, 1978; (ed with W. B. Gwyn) Britain: progress and decline, 1980; Do Parties Make a Difference?, 1980, 2nd edn 1984; (ed) Challenge to Governance, 1980; (ed) Electoral Participation, 1980; (ed with E. Suleiman) Presidents and Prime Ministers, 1980; Understanding the United Kingdom, 1982; (with I. McAllister) United Kingdom Facts, 1982; (ed with P. Madgwick) The Territorial Dimension in United Kingdom Politics, 1982; (ed with E. Page) Fiscal Stress in Cities, 1982; Understanding Big Government, 1984; (with I. McAllister) The Nationwide Competition for Votes, 1984; Public Employment in Western Nations, 1985; (with I. McAllister) Voters Begin to Choose, 1986; (with D. Van Mechelen) Patterns of Parliamentary Legislation, 1986; (ed with R. Shiratori) The Welfare State East and West, 1986; Ministers and Ministries, 1987; (with T. Karran) Taxation by Political Inertia, 1987; The Post-Modern President: the White House meets the world, 1988, 2nd edn 1991; Ordinary People in Public Policy, 1989; (with I. McAllister) The Loyalty of Voters: a lifetime learning model, 1990; Lesson-Drawing in Public Policy: a guide to learning across time and space, 1993; (with P. L. Davies) Inheritance in Public Policy: change without choice in Britain, 1994; What is Europe?, 1996; (with S. White and I. McAllister) How Russia Votes, 1997; (with W. Mishler and C. Haerpfer) Democracy and Its Alternatives, 1998; (ed jtly) A Society Transformed?: Hungary in time-space perspective, 1999; International Encyclopedia of Elections, 2000; The Prime Minister in a Shrinking World, 2001; (with Neil Munro) Elections Without Order: Russia's challenge to Vladimir Putin, 2002; (with Neil Munro) Elections and Parties in New European Democracies, 2003, 2nd edn 2009; Learning from Comparative Public Policy, 2005; (with W. Mishler and Neil Munro) Russia Transformed, 2006; Understanding Transformation, 2009; contribs to academic journals in Europe and America; trans. into eighteen foreign languages; broadcasts on comparative politics and public policy. *Recreations:* architecture, textiles, music, writing. *Address:* Centre for the Study of Public Policy, Department of Politics and International Relations, King's College, The University, Aberdeen AB24 3QY; 1 East Abercromby Street, Helensburgh, Argyll G84 7SP. *T:* (01436) 672164, *Fax:* (01436) 673125. *Clubs:* Reform; Cosmos (Washington DC).

ROSE, Prof. Steven Peter Russell, PhD; Professor of Biology and Director, Brain and Behaviour Research Group, Open University, 1969–2006, now Emeritus Professor; *b* 4 July 1938; *s* of Lionel Sydney Rose and Ruth Rose (*née* Waxman); *m* 1961, Hilary Ann Chantler; two *s. Educ:* Haberdashers' Aske's Sch., Hampstead; King's Coll., Cambridge (BA); Inst. of Psychiatry, Univ. of London (PhD). FIBiol 1970. Beit Meml and Guinness Res. Fellow, New Coll., Oxford, 1961–63; NIH Res. Fellow, Istituto Superiore di Sanita, Rome, 1963–64; MRC Res. Staff, Dept of Biochem., Imperial Coll., London, 1964–69. Vis. Sen. Res. Fellow, ANU, 1977; Vis. Schol., Harvard Univ., 1980; Distinguished Res. Prof., Univ. of Minn, 1992; Osher Fellow, Exploratorium, San Francisco, 1993; Vis. Prof., UCL, 1999–; Jt Gresham Prof. of Physic, 1999–2002. FRSA 1980. Anokhin Medal, Russia, 1990; Sechenov Medal, Russia, 1992; Ariens Kappers Medal, Netherlands Royal Acad. of Sci., Amsterdam, 1999; Biochem. Soc. Prize, 2002; Edinburgh Medal, 2004. *Publications:* The Chemistry of Life, 1966, 4th edn 1999; (with Hilary Rose) Science and Society, 1969; The Conscious Brain, 1973; No Fire No Thunder, 1984; (jtly) Not in our Genes, 1984; The Making of Memory, 1992, new edn 2003 (Science Book Prize, COPUS, 1993); Lifelines, 1997; (ed) From Brains to Consciousness?, 1998; (ed with Hilary Rose) Alas, Poor Darwin, 2000; The 21st Century Brain: explaining, mending and manipulating the mind, 2005; numerous edited books, res. papers and scholarly articles. *Address:* Department of Life Sciences, The Open University, Milton Keynes MK7 6AA.

ROSE, Sir Stuart (Alan Ransom), Kt 2008; Chief Executive, since 2004, and Chairman, since 2008, Marks and Spencer plc; Chairman, British Fashion Council, since 2003; *b* 17 March 1949; *s* of Harry Ransom Rose and Margaret Ransom Rose; *m* 1973, Jennifer Cook; one *s* one *d. Educ:* St. Joseph's Convent, Dar-es-Salaam; Bootham Sch., York. With Marks & Spencer plc, 1971–89, Commercial Exec., Europe; Chief Executive: Multiples, Burton Gp plc, 1989–97; Argos plc, 1998; Booker plc, 1998–2000; Iceland Group plc,

2000; Arcadia plc, 2000–02. Non-executive Director: NSB Retail Systems plc, 2000–04; Land Securities, 2003–. Chm., BITC, 2008–. *Recreations:* flying, wine. *Address:* (office) Waterside House, 35 North Wharf Road, W2 1NW. *Club:* Groucho.

ROSEBERY, 7th Earl of, *cr* 1703; **Neil Archibald Primrose;** DL; Bt 1651; Viscount of Rosebery, Baron Primrose and Dalmeny, 1700; Viscount of Inverkeithing, Baron Dalmeny and Primrose, 1703; Baron Rosebery (UK), 1828; Earl of Midlothian, Viscount Mentmore, Baron Epsom, 1911; *b* 11 Feb. 1929; *o* surv. *s* of 6th Earl of Rosebery, KT, PC, DSO, MC, and Eva Isabel Marian (Eva Countess of Rosebery, DBE) (*d* 1987), *d* of 2nd Baron Aberdare; *S* father, 1974; *m* 1955, Alison Mary Deirdre, *d* of late Ronald William Reid, MS, FRCS; one *s* four *d*. *Educ:* Stowe; New Coll., Oxford. DL Midlothian, 1960. *Heir: s* Lord Dalmeny, *qv*. *Address:* Dalmeny House, South Queensferry, West Lothian EH30 9TQ.

ROSEN, Alan Peter; Headteacher, Aylesbury High School, since 2005 (Deputy Headteacher, 1995–2005); *b* Edgware, Middx, 27 June 1955; *s* of M. and R. Rosen; *m* 1977, Janet; one *s* one *d*. *Educ:* Haberdashers' Aske's Sch., Elstree; Univ. of Wales, Aberystwyth (BSc Hons Maths and Computer Sci. 1976; PGCE 1977); Hatfield Poly. (MEd Classroom Processes 1989). NPQH 2001. Teacher, Hatfield Sch., Hatfield, 1977–83; Hd of IT, Astley Cooper Sch., Hemel Hempstead, 1983–89; Curriculum Manager, Maths, Sci. and Technol., Westfield Sch., Watford, 1989–95. *Recreations:* World Challenge Expedition Leader, orienteering—national and international competitor, controller (referee) of 1999 World Championships and 2005 World Cup. *Address:* c/o Aylesbury High School, Walton Road, Aylesbury, Bucks HP21 7SX. *T:* (01296) 388222, *Fax:* (01296) 388200; *e-mail:* secretary@ahs.bucks.sch.uk.

ROSEN, Charles; pianist; International Chair in Performance and Musicology, Royal Northern College of Music, since 2007; *b* New York, 5 May 1927; *s* of Irwin Rosen and Anita Gerber. *Educ:* studied piano with Mr and Mrs Moriz Rosenthal; Princeton Univ. (PhD). Début, NY, 1951. His many recordings include: first complete recording of Debussy Etudes, 1951; late keyboard works of Bach, 1969; last six Beethoven Sonatas, 1970; Schumann piano works; Diabelli Variations; also works by Liszt, Elliott Carter, Boulez, etc. Eliot Norton Prof. of Poetry, Harvard Univ., 1980; George Eastman Vis. Prof., Oxford Univ., 1987–88; Prof. of Music, Univ. of Chicago, 1991–96. Corresp. FBA 2002. Hon. MusD: Trinity Coll., Dublin, 1976; Cambridge, 1992; Hon. DMus Durham, 1980. *Publications:* The Classical Style, 1971; Schoenberg, 1976; Sonata Forms, 1980; (with H. Zerner) Romanticism and Realism: the mythology of nineteenth century art, 1984; The Romantic Generation, 1995; Piano Notes: the hidden world of the pianist, 2003. *Recreations:* music, books. *Address:* c/o Owen/White Management, Top Floor, 59 Lansdowne Place, Hove, East Sussex BN3 1FL. *T:* (01273) 727127, *Fax:* (01273) 328128.

ROSEN, Rabbi Jeremy, PhD; Professor of Jewish Studies, since 1991, and President, since 1994, Faculty for Comparative Study of Religions, Wilrijk, Belgium; Principal, Yakar Study Centre, London, 1999–2007; *b* 11 Sept. 1942; *s* of Rabbi Kopul Rosen and Bella Rosen; *m* 1st, 1971, Vera Giuditta Zippel (marr. diss. 1987); two *s* two *d*; 2nd, 1988, Suzanne Kaszirer. *Educ:* Carmel Coll.; Pembroke Coll., Cambridge (MA); Mir Academy, Jerusalem. Minister, Bulawayo Hebrew Congregation, Rhodesia, 1966; Minister, Giffnock Hebrew Congregation, Scotland, 1968–71; Headmaster, 1971–84, Principal, 1983–84, Carmel Coll; Minister, Western Synagogue, subseq. (following amalgamation in 1990 with Marble Arch Synagogue) Marble Arch Western Synagogue, 1985–93. Chief Rabbi's Rep. on Inter-Faith Affairs, 1987–91. Scholar in Residence, Jewish Community Center, New York, 2008–. Mem. Bd, Centre Européen Juif d'Information, Brussels, 1991–. Trustee, Yakar Educn Foundn, 1990–2000. *Publications:* Exploding Myths that Jews Believe, 2001; Understanding Judaism, 2003; Beyond the Pulpit, 2005; Kabbalah, 2005. *Address:* 28 Johns Avenue, NW4 4EN. *T:* (020) 8202 4528; *e-mail:* jeremyrosen@msn.com.

ROSEN, Prof. Michael, CBE 1990; FRCA; FRCOG; FRCS; Consultant Anaesthetist, South Glamorgan Health Authority, since 1961; Hon. Professor, University of Wales College of Medicine, 1986–93; President, College of Anaesthetists, 1988–91 (Dean of the Faculty of Anaesthetists, Royal College of Surgeons, 1988); *b* 17 Oct. 1927; *s* of Israel Rosen and Lily Hyman; *m* 1955, Sally Cohen; two *s* one *d*. *Educ:* Dundee High Sch. (Dux, 1944); St Andrews Univ. (MB ChB 1949). FRCA (FFARCS 1957); FRCOG 1989; FRCS 1994. House appts, Bolton, Portsmouth and Bradford, 1949–52; served RAMC, 1952–54; Registrar Anaesthetist, Royal Victoria Infirmary, Newcastle upon Tyne, 1954–57; Sen. Registrar, Cardiff, 1957–60; Fellow, Case Western Reserve Univ., Ohio, 1960–61. Member: GMC, 1989–; Clinical Standards Adv. Gp, 1991–94. Mem. Bd, College (formerly Faculty) of Anaesthetists, RCS, 1978–94; Pres., Assoc. of Anaesthetists of GB and Ire, 1986–88 (Mem. Council, 1972–91; formerly Sec. and Treasurer); Founder Academician, European Acad. of Anaesthesiol., 1972 (Treas., 1985–91; Hon. Mem., 1996); Chairman: Obstetric Anaesthesia Cttee, World Fedn of Socs of Anaesthesia, 1980–88; World Fedn of Socs of Anaesthesia Foundn, 2000–04; Exec. Officer and Treas., World Fedn of Socs of Anesthesiologists, 1992–2000. Hon. Mem., French and Australian Socs of Anaesthetists; Hon. FFARCSI 1990; Hon. Fellow, Acad. of Medicine, Malaysia, 1989. Hon. LLD Dundee, 1996. Sir Ivan Magill Gold Medal, Assoc. of Anaesthetists, 1993. *Publications:* Percutaneous Cannulation of Great Veins, 1981, 2nd edn 1992; Obstetric Anaesthesia and Analgesia: safer practice, 1982; Patient-Controlled Analgesia, 1984; Tracheal Intubation, 1985; Awareness and Pain in General Anaesthesia, 1987; Ambulatory Anaesthesia, 1991; Quality Measures for the Emergency Services, 2001. *Recreations:* family, reading, opera, bridge, exercise. *Address:* 45 Hollybush Road, Cardiff CF23 6TZ. *T:* and *Fax:* (029) 2075 3893; *e-mail:* rosen@mrosen.plus.com.

ROSEN, Michael Wayne, PhD; poet and author; Children's Laureate, 2007–June 2009; BBC Radio presenter, since 1989; *b* 7 May 1946; *s* of Harold Rosen and Connie Ruby Isakofsky; *m* 1st, 1976, Susanna Steele (marr. diss. 1987); one *s* (and one *s* decd); 2nd, 1987, Geraldine Clark (marr. diss. 1997); one *s*, and two step *d*; 3rd, 2003, Emma-Louise Williams; one *s* one *d*. *Educ:* Wadham Coll., Oxford (BA); Reading Univ. (MA); Univ. of N London (PhD 1997). BBC general trainee, 1969–73; freelance, 1973–, incl. BBC Radio 4, World Service, Radio 3; Word of Mouth, Radio 4, 1998–; On Being Selfish, Radio 4, 2004–; Dons and Dragons, Radio 4, 2006; The People in the Playground Revisited, Radio 4, 2008. FEA 2006. DUniv Open, 2005; Hon. DLitt: Exeter, 2007; Tavistock and Portman NHS Foundn Trust/UEL, 2008. Sunday Times NUS Drama Fest. Award for Best New Play, 1968; Glenfiddich Award for Best Radio Programme on subject of food, 1996; Eleanor Farjeon Award for Distinguished Services to Children's Literature, 1997; Sony Radio Acad. Short Form Award for On Saying Goodbye, 2003. Chevalier, Ordre des Arts et des Lettres (France), 2008. *Publications:* include: Backbone, 1968; Mind Your Own Business, 1974; Quick, Let's Get Out of Here, 1983; Don't put Mustard in the Custard, 1985; The Hypnotiser, 1988; We're Going on a Bear Hunt, 1989 (Smarties Award for Best Children's Book of Year, 1990); You Wait Till I'm Older Than You, 1996; Michael Rosen's Book of Nonsense, 1997; (ed) Classic Poetry, 1998; Rover, 1999; Centrally Heated Knickers, 2000; Shakespeare, His Work and His World, 2001; Carrying the Elephant, 2002; Oww!, 2003; This Is Not My Nose, 2004; Howler, 2004; Michael Rosen's Sad Book, 2004 (Exceptional Award, English Assoc.); Shakespeare's Romeo and Juliet, 2004; Totally Wonderful Miss Plumberry, 2006; Mustard, Custard, Grumble Belly and Gravy, 2006; Fighters for Life, 2007; Selected Poems, 2007; What's so Special about Shakespeare?, 2007; What's so Special about Dickens?, 2007; The Bear in the Cave, 2007; Dear Mother Goose, 2008. *Recreations:* Arsenal Football Club, politics, general arts. *Address:* c/o United Agents, 12–26 Lexington Street, W1F 0LE.

ROSEN, Murray Hilary; QC 1993; a Recorder, since 2000; Head of Advocacy Unit, Herbert Smith, since 2005; *b* 26 Aug. 1953; *s* of Joseph and Mercia Rosen; *m* 1975, Lesley Samuels; one *s* three *d*. *Educ:* St Paul's Sch.; Trinity Coll., Cambridge (MA). FCIArb 1999. Called to the Bar, Inner Temple, 1976; Mem., Lincoln's Inn *ad eundem*, Bencher, 2004; Head of Chambers, 11 Stone Buildings, 2000–04; admitted Solicitor, 2006. Chairman: Bar Sports Law Gp, 1998–2001; British Assoc. for Sport and Law, 2003–06. *Recreations:* books, arts, sports. *Address:* Herbert Smith LLP, Exchange House, Primrose Street, EC2A 2HS. *T:* (020) 7374 8000.

ROSENBERG, Michael Anthony; a District Judge (Magistrates' Courts) (formerly Provincial Stipendiary Magistrate), South Yorkshire, since 1993; *b* 6 March 1943; *s* of late Harry Rosenberg and Gertrude Rosenberg (*née* Silver); *m* 1969, Gillian Anne Wolff; two *s*. *Educ:* Hymers Coll., Hull; Law Soc. Joined Myer Wolff & Co., Hull, 1961: articled clerk, 1963–68; qualified as solicitor, 1969; Asst Solicitor, 1970–73; Jt Sen. Partner, 1973–93. *Recreations:* sport, gardening, music, humour. *Address:* The Old School House, Main Road, Scalby, Gilberdyke, E Yorks HU15 2UU. *T:* (Barnsley Magistrates' Court) (01226) 320000.

ROSENBERG, Pierre Max; Member, Académie française, since 1995; President-Director, Louvre Museum, Paris, 1994–2001; *b* Paris, 13 April 1936; *s* of Charles Rosenberg and Gertrude (*née* Nassauer); *m* 1981, Béatrice de Rothschild. *Educ:* Lycée Charlemagne, Paris; Law Faculty, Paris (Licence); Louvre Sch., Paris (Dip.). Chief Curator, Dept of Paintings, Louvre Mus., 1982–94. Member: Hist. of French Art Soc. (Pres., 1982–84); French Hist. of Art Cttee (Pres., 1984–96). *Publications:* Chardin, 1979, 2nd edn 1999; Peyron, 1983; Watteau, 1984; Fragonard, 1987; La Hyre, 1988; Les frères Le Nain, 1993; Poussin, 1994; Watteau: catalogue raisonné des dessins, 1996; Georges de la Tour, 1997; exhibn catalogues. *Address:* 35 rue de Vaugirard, 75006 Paris, France.

ROSENBERG, Richard Morris; Chairman and Chief Executive Officer, BankAmerica Corporation and Bank of America NT&SA, 1990–96; *b* 21 April 1930; *s* of Charles Rosenberg and Betty (*née* Peck); *m* 1956, Barbara C. Cohen; two *s*. *Educ:* Suffolk Univ. (BS 1956); Golden Gate Univ. (MBA 1962; LLB 1966). Served from Ensign to Lieut, USNR, 1953–59. Publicity Assistant, Crocker-Anglo Bank, San Francisco, 1959–62; Wells Fargo Bank: Banking Services Officer, 1962–65; Asst Vice Pres., 1965–68; Vice Pres., Marketing Dept, 1968; Vice Pres., Dir of Marketing, 1969; Sen. Vice Pres., Marketing and Advertising Div., 1970–75; Exec. Vice Pres., 1975–80; Vice Chm., 1980–83; Vice Chm., Crocker Nat. Corp., 1983–85; Pres., Chief Op. Officer and Dir, Seafirst Corp., 1986–87; Pres. and Chief Op. Officer, Seattle-First Nat. Bank, 1985–87; Vice Chm., BankAmerica Corp., 1987–90. Past Director: Airborne Express; Northrop Corp.; SBC Communications; past Chm., Mastercard Internat. Director: Buck Inst. for Age Res.; Health Care Property Investors Inc.; San Francisco Symphony; Naval War Coll. Foundn; Chairman: UCSF Foundn; Exec. Council, Univ. of Calif Med. Center. Member: Bd of Dirs, Marin Ecumenical Housing Assoc.; Bd of Trustees, CIT. Mem., State Bar of Calif. Jewish. *Recreations:* tennis, avid reader, history. *Address:* BankAmerica Corporation, 555 California Street CA5–705–11–01, San Francisco, CA 94104, USA. *T:* (415) 9537963. *Clubs:* Rainier (Seattle); Hillcrest (Los Angeles).

ROSENBROCK, Prof. Howard Harry, DSc; FRS 1976; FREng, FIET, FIChemE; Professor of Control Engineering, 1966–87, now Emeritus, Vice-Principal, 1977–79, University of Manchester Institute of Science and Technology, (UMIST); Science Research Council Senior Fellow, 1979–83; *b* 16 Dec. 1920; *s* of Henry Frederick Rosenbrock and Harriett Emily (*née* Gleed); *m* 1950, Cathryn June (*née* Press); one *s* two *d*. *Educ:* Slough Grammar Sch.; University Coll. London (BSc, PhD; Fellow 1978). Served War, RAFVR, 1941–46. GEC, 1947–48; Electrical Research Assoc., 1949–51; John Brown & Co., 1951–54; Constructors John Brown Ltd, 1954–62 (latterly Research Manager); ADR, Cambridge Univ., 1962–66. Mem. Council, IEE, 1966–70, Vice-Pres., 1977–78; Pres., Inst. of Measurement and Control, 1972–73; Member: Computer Bd, 1972–76; SRC Engineering Bd, 1976–78; SERC/ESRC Jt Cttee, 1981–85. Hon. FInstMC. Hon. DSc Salford, 1987. *Publications:* (with C. Storey) Computational Techniques for Chemical Engineers, 1966; (with C. Storey) Mathematics of Dynamical Systems, 1970; State-space and Multivariable Theory, 1970; Computer-aided Control System Design, 1974; (ed) Designing Human-centred Technology, 1989; Machines with a Purpose, 1990; contribs Proc. IEE, Trans IChemE, Proc. IEEE, Automatica, Internat. Jl Control, etc. *Recreations:* microscopy, photography, 17th and 18th Century literature. *Address:* Linden, Walford Road, Ross-on-Wye, Herefordshire HR9 5PQ. *T:* (01989) 565372.

ROSENCRANTZ, Claudia, (Mrs Daniel Abineri); Director of Television, Virgin Media Television (Director of Programming, Living TV and FTN, 2006); *b* 23 June 1959; *d* of late Alfred Rosenkranz and Leonore (*née* Meyer); *m* 1998, Daniel Abineri; one *d*. *Educ:* Queen's Coll., London; French Inst., London. Picture editor and journalist, The Telegraph Sunday Mag., Sunday Mag., and Elle, 1979–86; TV Researcher, LWT, An Audience with Victoria Wood, Dame Edna Experience, 1986; Producer: Dame Edna Experience, 1989; Incredibly Strange Film Shows, A Late Lunch with Les, An Audience with Jackie Mason, A Night on Mount Etna, 1990 (Golden Rose of Montreux, 1991); Dame Edna's Hollywood, Edna Time, Tantrums and Tiaras; Creator and Producer, Dame Edna's Neighbourhood Watch, 1992; Exec. Producer, Don't Forget Your Toothbrush, 1994; Exec. Producer, BBC, 1994–95; Controller of Entertainment, ITV Network, 1995–2006. Responsible for commissioning over 600 progs a year, incl. Who Wants to be a Millionaire (Best Light Entertainment Prog., BAFTA, 1999 and 2000), Popstars (Silver Rose of Montreux, 2001), Pop Idol (Best Entertainment Prog., TRIC Awards, 2002; Lew Grade Award for Entertainment Prog. or Series, BAFTA 2002), I'm a Celebrity...Get Me Out of Here! (BAFTA 2003), Ant and Dec's Saturday Night Takeaway, The X Factor, Hell's Kitchen, Dancing on Ice, TV Burp. *Address:* (office) 160 Great Portland Street, W1W 5QA. *T:* (020) 7299 5000, *Fax:* (020) 7299 5482.

ROSENFELD, Alfred John, CB 1981; Deputy Secretary, 1979–82, and Principal Finance Officer, 1976–82, Department of Transport; *b* 27 Feb. 1922; *s* of late Ernest Rosenfeld and late Annie Jeanette Rosenfeld (*née* Samson); *m* 1955, Mary Elisabeth (*née* Prudence); two *s* one *d*. *Educ:* Leyton County High Sch. Entered Public Trustee Office, 1938. Served War, Fleet Air Arm, 1942–46. Min. of Civil Aviation, 1947 (later, Min. of Transport, and Dept of Environment); Private Sec. to Jt Parliamentary Sec., 1958–59; Asst Sec., 1967; Under-Sec., 1972. Special Advr to Envmt Cttee, H of C, 1983–96. Mem., Shoreham Port Authority, 1983–92 (Dep. Chm., 1984–89; Chm., 1990–92). *Recreations:* chess, bridge, gardening, cherishing grandchildren. *Address:* 33 Elmfield Road, Chingford, E4 7HT. *T:* (020) 8529 8160.

ROSENKRANZ, Franklin Daniel, (Danny); Chief Executive, BOC Group plc, 1996–99; *b* 28 May 1945; *s* of Manfred and Hendel Rosenkranz; *m* 1990, Catherine Ann Eisenklam. *Educ:* UMIST (BSc Chem. Engrg 1967); Univ. of Waterloo, Canada (MASc 1969); Manchester Business Sch. (DipBA 1970). Plessey Radar, 1970–73; BOC, later BOC Group plc: Monitoring Manager, 1973–74; Business Manager, Industrial, Sparklets, 1974–76; UK Manager, 1976–78, Gen. Manager, 1978–81, BOC Sub Ocean Services; Business Develt Dir, 1982–83, Man. Dir, 1983–90, Edwards High Vacuum; Chief Exec., Vacuum Technology and Distribution Services, 1990–94; Man. Dir, 1994–96; Dir, 1994–99. Non-exec. Dir, 3i, 2000–07. *Recreations:* reading, music, theatre, sport, gardening.

ROSENTHAL, Jim; presenter, ITV Sport, 1980–2008; *b* 6 Nov. 1947; *s* of late Albi and Maud Rosenthal; *m* 1987, Chrissy (*née* Smith); one *s. Educ:* Magdalen College Sch., Oxford. Oxford Mail and Times, 1968–72; BBC Radio Birmingham, 1972–76; BBC Radio Sports Unit, 1976–80; presenter: Sport on Two; Sports Report; World Cup, and Wimbledon, 1978; award-winning Formula One coverage, ITV Sport, 1997–2005; Rugby World Cup, 2003 and 2007; ITV Boxing and World Cup, 2006. Sports Presenter of the Year, TRIC, 1990, RTS, 1997, 1999. *Recreation:* still trying to drag my body round football and cricket pitches! *Address:* c/o ITV Sport, 200 Gray's Inn Road, WC1X 8HF. *T:* (020) 7843 8116; *e-mail:* rosen@globalnet.co.uk. *Clubs:* Lord's Taverners; Oxford United Football.

ROSENTHAL, Maureen Diane, (Mrs J. M. Rosenthal); *see* Lipman, M. D.

ROSENTHAL, Sir Norman Leon, Kt 2007; Exhibitions Secretary, Royal Academy of Arts, 1977–2008; *b* 8 Nov. 1944; *s* of Paul Rosenthal and Kate Zucker; *m* 1989, Manuela Beatriz Mena Marques, *d* of Francisco Mena and Manuela Marques de Mena, Madrid; two *d. Educ:* Westminster City Grammar School; University of Leicester. BA Hons History. Librarian, Thomas Agnew & Sons, 1966–68; Exhibitions Officer, Brighton Museum and Art Gallery, 1970–71; Exhibition Organiser, ICA, 1974–76; organiser of many exhibns including: Art into Society, ICA, 1974; A New Spirit in Painting, RA, 1981; Zeitgeist, West Berlin, 1982; German Art of the Twentieth Century, RA, London and Staatsgalerie, Stuttgart, 1985–86; Italian Art of the Twentieth Century, RA, 1989; Metropolis, Berlin, 1991; American Art in the Twentieth Century, Martin-Gropius Bau, Berlin, and RA, 1993; at Royal Academy: Charlotte Salomon, 1998; Apocalypse, 2000; Frank Auerbach, The Genius of Rome 1592–1628, Botticelli's Dante, 2001; Paris: capital of the arts 1900–1968, Return of the Buddha, The Galleries Show, The Aztecs, 2002; Masterpieces from Dresden, Kircher: expressionism and the city, 2003; Illuminating the Renaissance: the triumph of Flemish manuscript painting in Europe, The Art of Philip Guston 1913–1980, 2004; Turks: a journey of a thousand years 600–1600, Edvard Munch by Himself, China: the three emperors 1662–1795, 2005; Jacob van Ruisdael: master of landscape, Modigliani and His Models, USA Today: new American art from the Saatchi Gallery, 2006; Georg Baselitz Retrospective, 2007. TV and radio broadcasts on contemporary art. Member: Opera Bd, Royal Opera House, 1994–98; Bd, Palazzo Grassi, Venice, 1995–; Comité Scientifique, Réunion des Musées Nationaux, Paris, 2005–; Trustee, Thyssen Bornemisza Foundn, 2002–; Baltic Centre for Contemporary Art, Gateshead, 2004–. Hon. Fellow RCA, 1987. Hon. DLitt: Southampton, 2003; Leicester, 2006. German British Forum Award, 2003. Cavaliere Ufficiale, Order of Merit (Italy), 1992; Cross, Order of Merit (Germany), 1993; Officier, l'Ordre des Arts et des Lettres (France), 2003 (Chevalier, 1987); Order of Aztec Eagle (Mexico), 2006. *Recreation:* music, especially opera. *Address:* The Royal Academy of Arts, Burlington House, Piccadilly, W1J 0BD. *T:* (020) 7300 8000.

ROSENTHAL, Thomas Gabriel, PhD; publisher, writer and broadcaster; Chairman: André Deutsch Ltd, 1984–98 (joined as Joint Chairman and Joint Managing Director, 1984; Chief Executive, 1987–96); Bridgewater Press Ltd, since 1997; *b* 16 July 1935; *o s* of late Dr Erwin I. J. Rosenthal and Elisabeth Charlotte (*née* Marx); *m* Ann Judith Warnford-Davis; two *s. Educ:* Perse Sch., Cambridge; Pembroke Coll., Cambridge (Exhibnr, MA, PhD 2005). Served RA, 1954–56, 2nd Lieut; subseq. Lieut Cambridgeshire Regt (TA). Joined Thames and Hudson Ltd, 1959; Man. Dir, Thames & Hudson Internat., 1966; joined Martin Secker & Warburg Ltd as Man. Dir, 1971; Dir, Heinemann Gp of Publishers, 1972–84; Man. Dir, William Heinemann International Ltd, 1979–84; Chairman: World's Work Ltd, 1979–84; Heinemann Zsolnay Ltd, 1979–84; William Heinemann Ltd, 1980–84; Martin Secker & Warburg Ltd, 1980–84; Kaye & Ward Ltd, 1980–84; William Heinemann, Australia and SA, 1981–82; Frew McKenzie (Antiquarian Booksellers), 1985–93; Pres., Heinemann Inc., 1981–84. Art Critic: The Listener, 1963–66; The New Statesman, 2001. Chm., Soc. of Young Publishers, 1961–62; Member: Cambridge Univ. Appts Bd, 1967–71; Exec. Cttee, NBL, 1971–74; Trans. Panel, Arts Council, 1988–94; Cttee of Management, Amateur Dramatic Club, Cambridge (also Trustee); Council, RCA, 1982–87; Exec. Council, ICA, 1987–99 (Chm., 1996–99); Council, Friends of ENO, 1997–2001; Trustee: Phoenix Trust, 1970–79; Fitzwilliam Mus., Cambridge, 2003–. Mem. Editl Bd, Logos, 1989–93. *Publications:* Monograph on Jack B. Yeats, 1964; (with Alan Bowness) Monograph on Ivon Hitchens, 1973; (with Ursula Hoff) Monograph on Arthur Boyd, 1986; A Reader's Guide to European Art History, 1962; A Reader's Guide to Modern American Fiction, 1963; The Art of Jack B. Yeats, 1993; Sidney Nolan, 2002; Paula Rego: the complete graphic work, 2003; Josef Albers Formulation: articulation, 2006; introdns to paperback edns of Theodore Dreiser's The Financier, The Titan and Jennie Gerhardt; programme essays for Royal Opera House, ENO and WNO; articles in The Times, Guardian, TLS, THES, Punch, Music Magazine, London Magazine, Encounter, New Statesman, Jl of Brit. Assoc. for Amer. Studies, Studio Internat., Modern Painters, Art Rev., DNB, Bookseller, Nature, Prospect, Opera Now, Opera News, Opera-Opera, etc. *Recreations:* opera, bibliomania, looking at pictures, reading other publishers' books, watching cricket. *Address:* Flat 7, Huguenot House, 19 Oxendon Street, SW1Y 4EH. *T:* (020) 7839 3589, *Fax:* (020) 7839 0651. *Clubs:* Garrick, MCC.

ROSER, Air Vice-Marshal Phillip Wycliffe, CB 2003; MBE 1983; Senior Directing Staff, Royal College of Defence Studies, 1999–2003, retired; *b* 11 July 1948; *s* of George Alfred Roser and Margaret Elizabeth Roser; *m* 1974, Andrea Jean Dobbin; one *s* one *d. Educ:* Thetford Grammar Sch.; RAF Coll., Cranwell; RAF Staff Coll., Bracknell. Qualified Weapons Instructor, 1974; Fighter Pilot, Lightning, Phantom, Tornado F3, 1970–94; on staff, MoD, 1979–83; MA to Minister for Armed Forces, MoD, 1983–85; OC 111(F) Sqdn, 1985–87; Operational Staff, Strike Comd, 1987–91; OC RAF Leeming, N Yorks, 1992–94; UK Liaison Officer, HQ US European Comd, Stuttgart, 1994–95; rcds 1996; Air Ops Staff, NATO, Sarajevo, 1996–97; NATO Staff, Heidelberg and Ramstein, Germany, 1997–98; Dep. UK Mil. Rep., HQ NATO, Brussels, 1998–99. Trustee, RAF Benevolent Fund, 2000–03. *Recreations:* golf, hill-walking, home maintenance, gardening, photography, woodwork. *Address:* c/o Lloyds TSB, Cox's and King's, 7 Pall Mall, SW1Y 5NA. *Club:* Royal Air Force (Chm., 2000–03).

ROSEVEARE, Robert William, CBE 1977; Secretary, 1967–83, and Managing Director for administrative affairs, 1971–83, British Steel Corporation; *b* Mandalay, Burma, 23 Aug. 1924; *s* of W. L., (Bill), Roseveare, MC and Marjory Roseveare; *m* 1954, Patricia Elizabeth, *d* of Guy L. Thompson, FRCS, Scarborough; one *s* three *d. Educ:* Gresham's Sch., Holt; University Coll., Oxford (Naval short course, 1943); St John's Coll., Cambridge (BA 1948). Served in Fleet Air Arm (Observer), 1943–46. Entered Home Civil Service, 1949. Asst Private Sec. to Minister of Fuel and Power, 1952–54; Cabinet Office, 1958–60; British Embassy, Washington, 1960–62; Asst Sec., Ministry of Power, 1964; seconded to Organising Cttee for British Steel Corporation, 1966; left Civil Service, 1971; Dir, BSC, 1969–71; Non-exec. Dir, Community Industry Ltd, 1983–91. Mem. Exec. Cttee, Hereford Diocesan Bd of Finance, 1986–95. *Recreations:* hill-walking, bird-watching, music. *Address:* Old Pasture, Hillfield Drive, Ledbury, Herefordshire HR8 1BH. *T:* (01531) 632913.

ROSEWARN, John; Secretary, Royal Institution of Naval Architects, 1989–97; *b* 14 Jan. 1940; *s* of Ernest and Frances Beatrice Rosewarn; *m* 1963, Josephine Rita Mullis; two *s. Educ:* Westminster City Sch. Royal Institution of Naval Architects, 1958–97: Administrator, 1958–65; Chief Clerk, 1965–75; Asst Sec., 1975–84; Sen. Asst. Sec., 1984–89. Freeman, City of London, 1976. *Recreations:* sailing, DIY, reading. *Address:* Little Fisher Farm, South Mundham, Chichester, West Sussex PO20 1ND.

ROSEWELL, Bridget Clare; Chairman, Volterra Consulting, since 1999; *b* 19 Sept. 1951; *d* of Geoffrey Noel Mills and Helen Handescombe Mills; divorced; one *s* one *d. Educ:* Wimbledon High Sch.; St Hugh's Coll., Oxford (MA, MPhil). Tutor and Lectr in Econs, St Hilda's and Oriel Colls, Oxford, 1976–84; Dep. Dir, Econs, CBI, 1984–86; Chief European Economist, Wharton Econometric Forecasting Associates (WEFA), 1986–88; Founder and Chm., Business Strategies Ltd, 1988–2000. Consultant Chief Economist, GLA, 2002–. Non-executive Director: Britannia Building Soc., 1999–; DWP, 2003–05. Member: Forum UK, 1990–; Internat. Women's Forum, 1990–. FRSA 1991. *Publications:* pamphlets and contribs on econs to press and econ. jls. *Recreations:* hill walking, picture framing, yoga, curiosity. *Address:* Volterra Consulting, Sheen Elms, 135C Sheen Lane, SW14 8AE. *T:* (020) 8878 6333, *Fax:* (020) 8878 6685; *e-mail:* brosewell@volterra.co.uk.

ROSIER, Rt Rev. Stanley Bruce, AM 1987; Rector of St Oswald's, Parkside, Diocese of Adelaide, 1987–94, retired; *b* 18 Nov. 1928; *s* of S. C. and A. Rosier; *m* 1954, Faith Margaret Alice Norwood (*d* 2006); one *s* three *d. Educ:* Univ. of WA; Christ Church, Oxford. Asst Curate, Ecclesall, Dio. of Sheffield, 1954; Rector of: Wyalkatchem, Dio. of Perth, 1957; Kellerberrin Dio. of Perth, 1964; Auxiliary Bishop in Diocese of Perth, Western Australia, 1967–70; Bishop of Willochra, 1970–87. *Recreation:* natural history. *Address:* 5A Fowlers Road, Glenunga, SA 5064, Australia. *T:* (8) 83795213.

ROSIN, (Richard) David, FRCS, FRCSE; Consultant in General Surgery and Surgical Oncology, St Mary's Hospital, London, 1980, now Honorary; Professor of Surgery, University of the West Indies, Cavehill Campus, Barbados; *b* 29 April 1942; *s* of late Isadore Rowland Rosin and Muriel Ena Rosin (*née* Wolff); *m* 1971, Michele Shirley Moreton; one *s* two *d. Educ:* St George's Jesuit Coll., Zimbabwe; Westminster Hosp. Sch. of Medicine, Univ. of London (MB, MS); DHMSA 2003. Westminster Hospital: House Physician, subseq. House Surg., 1966–67; Sen. House Officer in Clin. Pathology, 1968, Surgical Rotation, 1969–71; Sen. Registrar, 1975–79; Ship's Surg., P & O Lines, 1967; Sen. House Officer, Birmingham Accident Hosp., 1969; Registrar: Sutton Hosp., Surrey, 1971–73; St Helier's Hosp., Carshalton, 1973–74; Clin. Asst, St Mark's Hosp., London, 1974–75; Sen. Registrar, Kingston Hosp., 1975–77; Vis. Lectr, Univ. of Hong Kong, 1978–79; Clin. Dir of Surgery, St Charles' Hosp., 1990–92; Chm., Div. of Surgery, St Mary's Hosp., London, 1992–96. Consultant Surg., King Edward VII's Hosp. for Officers, 1995–96. Chm. DTI Cttee, Operating Room of Year 2010, 1995–2000. Regl Advr, NW Thames Region, RCSE, 1990–; Member: Council, RCS, 1994–2006 (Vice-Pres., 2004–05; Sen. Vice-Pres., 2005–06; Penrose-May Tutor, 1985–90; Hunterian Prof., 1987; Lectures: Arris and Gale, 1978; Arnott, 1991; Gordon Gordon Taylor, 2005; Vicary, 2006; Stanford Cade, 2006; Zachary Cope, 2008); RSM, 1975 (Pres., Clin. Section, 1982–83, Surgery Section, 1992–93; Mem. Council, 2002–); Surgical Res. Soc., 1980; British Assoc. of Surgical Oncology, 1980 (Hon. Sec., 1983–86, Vice Pres., 2000–01, Pres., 2002–03); British Soc. of Gastroenterology, 1980; Melanoma Study Gp, 1988 (Hon. Sec., 1986–89, Pres., 1989–92); Soc. of Minimally Invasive Gen. Surgs, 1991 (Founder and Hon. Sec.); Hunterian Soc., 1994; Internat. Coll. of Surgs, 1992–. Chm., Intercollegiate Bd of Surgical Examinations, 2003–. Fellow: Assoc. of Surgs of GB and Ire., 1975; Assoc. of Endoscopic Surgs of GB and Ire. (Mem. Council, 1995–); Assoc. of Upper Gastro-Intestinal Surgs of GB and Ire., 1997. Mem. Council, Marie Curie Foundn, 1984–92. Sir Ernest Finch Meml Lectr, Sheffield, 2000; G. B. Ong Lectr, Hong Kong Coll. of Surgeons, 2007; BJS Lectr, 2008. Freeman, City of London, 1972; Liveryman: Soc. of Apothecaries, 1971; Co. of Barber Surgeons, 1978. Series Ed., Minimal Access textbooks, 1993–; Editor-in-Chief, Internat. Jl of Surgery, 2007–. *Publications:* (ed jtly) Cancer of the Bile Ducts and Pancreas, 1989; (ed jtly) Head and Neck Oncology for the General Surgeon, 1991; (ed jtly) Diagnosis and Management of Melanoma in Clinical Practice, 1992; (ed) Minimal Access Medicine and Surgery: principles and practice, 1993; (ed) Minimal Access General Surgery, 1994; (ed) Minimal Access Surgical Oncology, 1995; (co-ed) Minimal Access Thoracic Surgery, 1998; papers in jls and contribs to books. *Recreations:* all sport, particularly golf; opera, music, theatre, history of medicine and surgery, travelling. *Address:* 4 Ledbury Mews North, W11 2AF; 80 Harley Street, W1G 7HL. *T:* (020) 7087 4260, *Fax:* (020) 7224 0645; *e-mail:* rdrosin@uk-consultants.com.uk. *Clubs:* Garrick, MCC, Roehampton; New Zealand Golf (Weybridge).

ROSINDELL, Andrew; MP (C) Romford, since 2001; *b* Romford, 17 March 1966; *s* of Frederick William Rosindell and Eileen Rosina Rosindell (*née* Clark). *Educ:* Rise Park Jun. and Infant Sch.; Marshalls Park Secondary Sch. Researcher and freelance journalist, and Res. Asst to Vivian Bendall, MP, 1986–97; Dir, 1997–99, Internat. Dir, 1999–2005, Eur. Foundn. Mem., London Accident Prevention Council, 1990–95. Mem. (C) Havering BC, 1990–2002 (Vice-Chm., Housing Cttee, 1996–97; Alderman, 2007–); Chm., N Romford Community Area Forum, 1998–2002. Contested (C): Glasgow Provan, 1992; Thurrock, 1997. An Opposition Whip, 2005–07; Shadow Home Affairs Minister and spokesman on Animal Welfare, 2007–; Member: Deregulation and Regulatory Reform Select Cttee, 2001–05; Constitutional Affairs Select Cttee, 2004–05; Jt Cttee on Statutory Instruments, 2002–04; NI Grand Cttee, 2006–; Secretary: Falkland Is and Australia/NZ All Party gps, 2001–; Gibraltar All Party Gp, 2001–02; All Party Parly Liechtenstein Gp, 2005–; All Party Parly British Virgin Is Gp, 2006–; All Party Parly Zoos and Aquariums Gp, 2007–; Vice-Chairman: Iceland All Party Gp, 2005–; All Party Parly Channel Is Gp, 2006–; All Party Parly Madagascar Gp, 2007–; Chairman: Montserrat Gp, 2005–; Anglo-Manx All Party Gp, 2005–; All Party Greyhound Gp, 2005–; All Party Parly St George's Day Gp, 2007–; All Party Parly Flag Gp, 2008–; Jt Treas., All Party Danish Gp, 2001–. Sec., Cons. 92 Gp, 2003–06; Member: Cornerstone Gp of Cons. MPs; No Turning Back Gp. Joined Cons. Party and Young Conservatives, 1981; Chairman: Romford YC, 1983–84 (Pres., 2006–); Gtr London YC, 1987–88; Nat. YC, 1993–94; Eur. YC, 1993–97; Conservative Party: Mem., Nat. Union Exec. Cttee, 1986–88 and 1992–94; Vice-Chm., 2004–05; Pres., Gibraltar Br., 2004–; Chm., Romford Cons.

Assoc., 1998–2001; Chm., Internat. Young Democrat Union, 1998–2002; Pres., Caribbean Young Democrat Union, 2001–. Chm., Cons. Friends of Gibraltar, 2002–. Vice-Pres., Constitutional Monarchy Assoc. Mem. Council, Freedom Assoc., 2005–. Pres., Romford Sqdn ATC, 2002–; Hon. Mem., Romford Lions Club, 2008–. Member: RAFA; RBL. Governor: Bower Park Sch., Romford, 1989–90; Dame Tipping C of E Sch., Havering-atte-Bower, 1990–2002. Vice-Pres., Romford FC; Hon. Mem., Havering-atte-Bower CC. Patron: Justice for Dogs; Remus Meml Horse Sanctuary, 2005–; Assoc. of British Counties, 2007–. Hon. Member: Staffs Bull Terrier Club; E Anglian Staffs Bull Terrier Club. *Publication:* (jtly) Defending Our Great Heritage, 1993. *Recreations:* Staffordshire bull terriers, travel, swimming. *Address:* House of Commons, SW1A 0AA. *T:* (020) 7219 8475; (constituency office) 85 Western Road, Romford, Essex RM1 3LS. *T:* (01708) 766700, 761583, (home) (01708) 761186; *e-mail:* andrew@rosindell.com. *Clubs:* Romford Conservative and Constitutional; Romford Golf (Hon.).

ROSLING, Derek Norman, CBE 1988; FCA; Vice-Chairman, Hanson PLC, 1973–93; *b* 21 Nov. 1930; *s* of Norman and Jean Rosling; *m* 1st (marr. diss. 1982); two *s* one *d*; 2nd, 2000, Julia Catherine Crookston; one step *s*. *Educ:* Shrewsbury Sch. ACA 1955, FCA 1962. Professional practice, 1956–65; Hanson PLC, 1965–94. FRSA 1990. *Recreations:* golf, sailing, theatre. *Address:* South Hayes, Grove Road, Lymington, Hants SO41 3RN. *T:* (01590) 670201. *Clubs:* Royal Yacht Squadron (Cowes); Royal Southampton Yacht; Brokenhurst Manor Golf.

ROSOMAN, Leonard Henry, OBE 1981; RA 1969 (ARA 1960); FSA; Tutor, Royal College of Art, 1957–78; *b* 27 Oct. 1913; *s* of Henry Rosoman; *m* 1st, 1963, Jocelyn (marr. diss. 1969; she *d* 2005), *d* of Bertie Rickards, Melbourne, Australia; 2nd, 1994, Roxanne, *d* of Dr Milton Wruble, Michigan, USA. *Educ:* Deacons Sch., Peterborough; Durham Univ. Teacher of Drawing and Painting, Reimann Sch. of Art, London, 1938–39; Official War Artist to Admiralty, 1943–45; Teacher: Camberwell Sch. of Art, London, 1948–56; (Mural Painting) Edinburgh Coll. of Art, 1948–56; Chelsea School of Art, 1956–57. One Man Shows: St George's Gallery, London, 1946 and 1949; Roland, Browse and Delbanco Gallery, London, 1954, 1957, 1959, 1965 and 1969; Fine Art Soc., 1974, 1978, 1983, 1990, 2003. Works bought by: HM Govt, Arts Council, British Council, York Art Gall., Contemporary Art Soc., Adelaide Art Gallery, V&A Museum, Lincoln Center, NY. Executed large mural paintings for: Festival of Britain, 1951; British Pavilion, Brussels World Fair, 1958; Harewood House, 1959; Lambeth Palace Chapel, 1988, 1992. HRSW; FRPS; Hon. ARCA; Hon. Fellow, Edinburgh Coll. of Art, 2005. *Recreation:* travelling as much as possible. *Address:* 7 Pembroke Studios, Pembroke Gardens, W8 6HX. *T:* (020) 7603 3638. *Clubs:* Arts, Chelsea Arts.

ROSPIGLIOSI, family name of **Earl of Newburgh**.

ROSS, Rt Hon. Lord; Donald MacArthur Ross; PC 1985; a Senator of the College of Justice, Scotland, and Lord of Session, 1977–97; Lord Justice-Clerk and President of the Second Division of the Court of Session, 1985–97; Lord High Commissioner, General Assembly, Church of Scotland, 1990 and 1991; *b* 29 March 1927; *s* of late John Ross, solicitor, Dundee; *m* 1958, Dorothy Margaret (*d* 2004), *d* of late William Annand, Kirriemuir; two *d*. *Educ:* Dundee High School; Edinburgh University. MA (Edinburgh) 1947; LLB with distinction (Edinburgh) 1951. National Service with The Black Watch (RHR), 2nd Lt, 1947–49. Territorial Service, 1949–58, Captain. Advocate, 1952; QC (Scotland) 1964; Vice-Dean, Faculty of Advocates of Scotland, 1967–73; Dean, 1973–76; Sheriff Principal of Ayr and Bute, 1972–73. Dep. Chm., Boundary Commn for Scotland, 1977–85. Member: Scottish Cttee of Council on Tribunals, 1970–76; Cttee on Privacy, 1970; Parole Bd for Scotland, 1997–2002; Chm., Judicial Studies Cttee, Scotland, 1997–2001. Mem. Court, Heriot-Watt Univ., 1978–90 (Chm., 1984–90). FRSE 1988 (Mem. Council, 1997–99, Vice Pres., 1999–2002). Hon. LLD: Edinburgh, 1987; Dundee, 1991; Abertay Dundee, 1994; Aberdeen, 1998. DUniv Heriot-Watt, 1988. *Recreations:* gardening, walking, travelling. *Address:* 7/1 Tipperlinn Road, Edinburgh EH10 5ET. *T:* (0131) 447 6771. *Club:* New (Edinburgh).

ROSS, Rear Adm. Alastair Boyd, CB 1999; CBE 1995; Clerk to Worshipful Company of Drapers, since 2000; *b* 29 Jan. 1947; *s* of Joseph Charles Patrick Ross and Shirley Carlile (*née* Stoddart); *m* 1977, Heather Judy Currie; two *d*. *Educ:* Radley Coll.; BRNC, Dartmouth. Joined RN, 1965; commnd 1968; specialised in aviation; flew as Anti-Submarine Warfare helicopter observer, 1970–80; commanded: HMS Brinton, 1977–79; HMS Falmouth, 1983–85; HMS Edinburgh, 1988–89; RCDS 1990; Capt., HMS Osprey, 1991–93; Comdr, NATO Standing Naval Force, Mediterranean (Adriatic Ops), 1993–94; Dir Overseas (ME and Africa), MoD, 1994–96; Asst Dir Ops, Internat. Mil. Staff, NATO HQ, 1996–99. Mem., RNSA, 1984–. Freeman, City of London. Hon. Fellow, Univ. of Wales, Bangor, 2005. *Recreations:* sailing, golf. *Address:* Drapers' Hall, Throgmorton Avenue, EC2N 2DQ. *Clubs:* Farmers', Royal Navy of 1765 and 1785.

ROSS, Alexander, (Sandy); freelance television producer; Managing Director, Murrayfield Media Ltd; *b* 17 April 1948; *s* of late Alexander Coutts Ross and Charlotte Edwards (*née* Robertson); *m* 1992, Alison Joyce (*née* Fraser); two *s* one *d*. *Educ:* Edinburgh Univ. (LLB); Moray House Coll., Edinburgh (Pres., Students' Union, 1977–78; Cert. Youth and Community Work). Articled Solicitor, 1971; Solicitor, 1971–73; Lectr in Law, Paisley Coll., 1975–77; Researcher and Producer, Granada Television, 1978–86; Scottish Television: Controller Entertainment, 1986–97; Dep. Chief Exec., Scottish TV Enterprises, 1997–98; Controller Regional Production, Scottish TV and Grampian TV, Scottish Media Gp, 1998–2000; Controller, 2000; Man. Dir, 2000–04; Man. Dir, Internat. Develt Div., 2004–07. Councillor, Edinburgh Corp., 1971–74; Mem., Edinburgh DC, 1974–78. Chm., Salford Conf. on Television from Nations and Regions, 2005–. Mem., BAFTA, 1990 (Chm., 2004–08, Vice-Chm., 2008–, BAFTA Scotland). Mem., Scotch Malt Whiskey Soc. *Recreations:* golf, theatre, music, reading, ski-ing. *Address:* 7 Murrayfield Avenue, Edinburgh EH12 6AU. *T:* (0131) 539 1192; *e-mail:* sandy.ross@murrayfieldmedia.com. *Clubs:* The Hallion (Edinburgh); Haunted Major Golf Society (N Berwick); Glen Golf, Prestonfield Golf, Edinburgh Corporation Golf, Rhodes Golf.

ROSS, Amanda; Joint Managing Director, Cactus TV, since 1994; *b* 4 Aug. 1962; *d* of Dorothy Burnett; *m* 1990, Simon Ross. *Educ:* Univ. of Birmingham (BA Hons Drama and Theatre Arts). Freelance TV producer and presenter, 1984–94; Founder, with Simon Ross, Cactus TV, 1994; programmes produced include: Richard and Judy (numerous awards incl. Bookseller Expanding Mkt Award, 2007, for Richard and Judy Summer Read); Saturday Kitchen (Best TV Cookery Show, Olive mag., 2007); British Book Awards; Music and Entertainment Specials. *Publications:* Richard and Judy Wine Guide, 2005; Saturday Kitchen Cookbook, 2007; Saturday Kitchen: best bites, 2008. *Recreations:* my two dogs, Poppet and Bella, house in Italy, eating out and cooking, auctions and design. *Address:* c/o Cactus TV, 373 Kennington Road, SE11 4PS. *T:* (020) 7091 4900. *Club:* Bluebird.

ROSS, Lt-Col Sir Andrew (Charles Paterson), 3rd Bt *cr* 1960, of Whetstone, Middlesex; RM; *b* 18 June 1966; *s* of Sir James Keith Ross, 2nd Bt, RD, FRCS, FRCSE and of Jacqueline Annella Ross (*née* Clarke); *S* father, 2003; *m* 1997, Surg. Comdr Sarah Joanne Murray, RN; one *s* one *d*. *Educ:* Sherborne; Plymouth Poly. (BSc). Joined RM, 1988; left RM 2007. A Security Ops Manager, Royal Dutch Shell. *Recreations:* sailing, fencing, ski-ing. *Heir: s* James Ross, *b* 21 May 1999.

ROSS, Anthony Lee, (Tony); author and illustrator; *b* 10 Aug. 1938; *s* of Eric Turle Lee Ross and Effie Ross (*née* Griffiths); *m* 1st, 1961, Carole D'Arcy (marr. diss. 1971); 2nd, 1971, Joan Spokes (marr. diss. 1976); 3rd, 1979, Zoe Goodwin. *Educ:* Helsby Grammar Sch.; Liverpool Art Sch. (NDD, ATD). Advertising work, 1962–65; Sen. Lectr, Manchester Poly., 1965–86; children's author, illustrator and film-maker, 1972–; TV animated films: Towser, 1985; Horrid Henry, 2006; Little Princess, 2007; books published in UK, Europe, USA, Japan, Australia, Korea and S America. *Publications: picture books include:* Towser (series), 1984; I'm Coming to Get You, 1984; I Want My Potty (series), 1986; Oscar Got The Blame, 1987; Super Dooper Jezebel, 1988; I Want a Cat, 1989; A Fairy Tale, 1991; Don't Do That, 1991; Through the Looking Glass, 1992, and Alice's Adventures in Wonderland, 1993, abridged from Lewis Carroll; The Shop of Ghosts, from G. K. Chesterton, 1994; Three Little Kittens and Other Favourite Nursery Rhymes, 2007; *books illustrated include:* Eric Morcambe, The Reluctant Vampire, 1982; Willis Hall, Vampire Park, 1983; Michael Palin, Limericks, 1985; Roald Dahl, Fantastic Mr Fox, 1988; Simon Brett, How to be a Little Sod, 1992; Michael Morpurgo, Red Eyes at Night, 1998; Oscar Wilde, The Picture of Dorian Gray, 2000; series: Ian Whybrow, Little Wolf, 1985; Jeanne Willis, Dr Xargle, 1988; Richmal Crompton, Meet Just William, 1999; Astrid Lindgren, Pippi Longstocking, 2000; Francesca Simon, Horrid Henry, 2003. *Recreations:* sailing, gentle sports, keeping unfit. *Address:* c/o Andersen Press, 20 Vauxhall Bridge Road, SW1V 2SA. *Club:* Chelsea Arts.

ROSS, Candice Kathleen; *see* Atherton, C. K.

ROSS, David Peter John; Co-Founder, 1991, and Deputy Chairman, since 2003, The Carphone Warehouse (Chief Operating Officer, 1996–2003); *b* 10 July 1965; *s* of John Malcolm Thomas and Linda Susan Ross; one *s*. *Educ:* Univ. of Nottingham (BA Hons Law 1987). Chartered accountant; with Arthur Andersen, 1988–91. Non-exec. Chairman: Nat. Express Gp, 2001–; Gondola Hldgs plc, 2005–06; non-executive Director: Big Yellow Self Storage, 2000–; Wembley Nat. Stadium Ltd, 2002–; Trinity Mirror plc, 2004–07; Cosalt plc, 2005–. Mem., Audit Cttee, Home Office, 2004–. Mem. Council, Sport England, 2001–05. Dir, LOCOG, 2008–. Trustee, NPG, 2006–. Liveryman, Co. of Chartered Accountants. *Recreations:* opera, sport, shooting. *Address:* Kandahar Group, 3rd Floor, Nuffield House, 41–46 Piccadilly, W1J 0DS. *T:* (020) 7534 1547, *Fax:* (020) 7534 1560; *e-mail:* KD@kandahargroup.co.uk. *Club:* Royal Automobile.

ROSS, Donald Grant, OBE 2005; Lord Lieutenant of Dunbartonshire, since 2007; *b* 24 June 1946; *s* of John Sutherland Ross and Catherine Grant Ross; *m* 1974, Doreen Colina; two *s* one *d*. *Educ:* High Sch. of Glasgow; King Edward VI Grammar Sch., Chelmsford; Army Staff Coll., Camberley. Commnd Argyll and Sutherland Highlanders, 1967; i/c British Contingent, Multi-nat. Force and Observers, Sinai, 1987–88; i/c 3/51 Highland Volunteers, 1988–90; COS British Rear Combat Zone, Germany, 1990–93; Comdr, Recruiting and Liaison Staff, Scotland, 1993–96; retd 1996; Comdt, Garelochhead Trng Area, 1996. Member: Exec. Cttee, Erskine Hosp., 1997; C of S Cttee on Chaplains to the Armed Forces, 1996–99. Comdt, Argyll and Sutherland Highlanders Army Cadets, 1998–2003; Hon. Pres., Lennox and Argyll Boys' Bde, 2007. Chm., Grangemouth Br., RBL, 2002; Hon. Pres., Dunbartonshire Br., SSAFA, 2007. Trustee, Tullochan Trust, 2007. *Recreations:* sailing, hill-walking, gardening. *Address:* Carfin House, Shore Road, Clynder, Dunbartonshire G84 0QD. *T:* (01436) 831892, *Fax:* (01436) 810369; *e-mail:* donaldanddoreen@hotmail.com.

ROSS, Rt Hon. Donald MacArthur; *see* Ross, Rt Hon. Lord.

ROSS, Donald Nixon, FRCS; Consultant Thoracic Surgeon, Guy's Hospital, 1958–78, now Emeritus; Consultant Surgeon, National Heart Hospital, 1963–93 (Senior Surgeon, 1967); *b* 4 Oct. 1922; *m* 1st, 1956, Dorothy Curtis (marr. diss. 2001); one *d*; 2nd, 2001, Barbara Cork. *Educ:* Boys' High Sch., Kimberley, S Africa; Univ. of Capetown (BSc, MB, ChB 1st Cl. Hons, 1946). FRCS 1949; FACC 1973; FACS 1976. Sen. Registrar in Thoracic Surgery, Bristol, 1952; Res. Fellow, 1953, Sen. Thoracic Registrar, 1954, Guy's Hosp.; Dir, Dept of Surgery, Inst. of Cardiology, 1970. Introduced: aortic homograft, 1962; Ross procedure (pulmonary autograft), 1967. Hon. FRSocMed 1996; Hon. FRCSI 1984; Hon. FRCS Thailand, 1987. Hon. DSc CNAA, 1982. Clement Price Thomas Award, RCS, 1983; Lifetime Achievement Award, Soc. for Cardiothoracic Surgery in GB and Ireland, 2008. Order of Cedar of Lebanon, 1975; Order of Merit (1st cl.) (West Germany), 1981; Royal Order (Thailand), 1994. *Publications:* A Surgeon's Guide to Cardiac Diagnosis, 1962; (jtly) Medical and Surgical Cardiology, 1968; (jtly) Biological Tissue in Heart Valve Replacement, 1972; contrib. BMJ, Lancet, Proc. RSM, Annals Royal Coll. Surg., Amer. Jl Cardiol. *Recreations:* Arabian horse breeding, horseriding, gardening. *Address:* 35 Cumberland Terrace, Regent's Park, NW1 4HP. *T:* (020) 7935 0756; (office) 25 Upper Wimpole Street, W1G 6NF. *T:* (020) 7935 8805. *Clubs:* Garrick; Kimberley (SA).

ROSS, Prof. Douglas Alan, DPhil; FRS 2005; Professor of Physics, University of Southampton, since 1993; *b* 9 May 1948; *s* of Arnold and Odette Ross; *m* 1973, Jacqueline Nahoum; two *s*. *Educ:* New Coll., Oxford (MA 1969; DPhil 1972). Postdoctoral Fellow: Imperial Coll., London, 1972–74; Rijksuniversiteit Utrecht, 1974–76; Fellow, CERN, 1976–78; Sen. Res. Fellow, CIT, 1978–80; Lectr, Univ. of Southampton, 1980–93. Mem., Southampton Choral Soc. *Publication:* (with J. R. Forshaw) Quantum Chromodynamics and the Pomeron, 1997. *Recreations:* singing in choir (bass), learning modern languages. *Address:* 242 Hill Lane, Southampton SO15 7NT. *T:* (023) 8078 7711; *e-mail:* dar@phys.soton.ac.uk.

ROSS, Duncan Alexander, CBE 1993; CEng, FIET; Chairman, Southern Electric plc (formerly Southern Electricity Board), 1984–93, retired; *b* 25 Sept. 1928; *s* of William Duncan Ross and Mary Ross; *m* 1958, Mary Buchanan Clarke Parsons; one *s* one *d*. *Educ:* Dingwall Academy; Glasgow Univ. (BSc Elec. Engrg). Various engineering posts, South of Scotland Electricity Board, 1952–57; engineering, commercial and management posts, Midlands Electricity Board, 1957–72; Area Manager, South Staffs Area, 1972–75, Chief Engineer, 1975–77; Dep. Chm., 1977–81, Chm., 1981–84, South Wales Electricity Bd. Mem., Electricity Council, 1981–90. CCMI. *Recreations:* golf, ski-ing. *Address:* Winterfold, Dovers Orchard, Hoo Lane, Chipping Campden, Glos GL55 6AZ. *T:* and *Fax:* (01386) 841797.

ROSS, Ernest; *b* Dundee, July 1942; *m*; two *s* one *d*. *Educ:* St John's Jun. Secondary Sch. Quality Control Engineer, Timex Ltd. Mem., MSF (formerly AUEW (TASS)). MP (Lab) Dundee W, 1979–2005. Mem., Select Cttee on Foreign Affairs, 1997–99; Chm., All-Party Poverty Gp, 1997–2005. Chm. Bd of Govs, Westminster Foundn for Democracy, 1997–2002.

ROSS, Prof. Graham Garland, PhD; FRS 1991; Professor of Theoretical Physics, Oxford University, since 1992; Fellow of Wadham College, Oxford, since 1983. *Educ:* Aberdeen Univ. (BSc); Durham Univ. (PhD); MA Oxon. Rutherford Atlas Res. Fellow, Pembroke Coll., Oxford, 1981–83; Lectr, 1983–90, Reader and SERC Sen. Res. Fellow in Theoretical Physics, 1990–92, Oxford Univ. *Address:* Department of Physics, 1 Keble Road, Oxford OX1 3RH. *T:* (01865) 273999; Woodcock Cottage, Lincombe Lane, Boars Hill, Oxford OX1 5DX.

ROSS, Hugh Robert; Chief Executive, Cardiff and Vale NHS Trust, since 2004; *b* 21 April 1953; *s* of Robert James Ross and Marion Bertha Ross (*née* Maidment); *m* 1981, Margaret Catherine Hehir; one *s* one *d*. *Educ:* Univ. of Durham (BA Pol. and Sociol.); London Business Sch. (MBA). Fellow, IHSM, 1987. Admin. Trainee, NHS, 1976–78; Asst Adminr, Princess Margaret Hosp., Swindon, 1978–80; Asst Adminr, 1980–81, Patient Services Officer, 1981–83, Westminster Hosp.; Dep. Adminr, 1983–84, Dir of Operational Services, 1984–86, St Bartholomew's Hosp.; Unit General Manager: City Unit, Coventry, 1986–90; Leicester Gen. Hosp., 1990–92; Chief Executive: Leicester Gen. Hosp. NHS Trust, 1993–95; Utd Bristol Healthcare NHS Trust, 1995–2002; Prog. Dir, Bristol Health Services Plan, 2002–04. *Recreations:* sport, travel, real ale, rock music. *Address:* 40 Alma Road, Clifton, Bristol BS8 2DB. *T:* (0117) 974 4987.

ROSS, James Hood; Deputy Chairman, National Grid Transco plc, 2002–04 (Chairman, National Grid Group plc, 1999–2002); *b* 13 Sept. 1938; *s* of Thomas Desmond Ross and Lettice Ferrier Ross (*née* Hood); *m* 1964, Sara Blanche Vivian Purcell; one *s* two *d*. *Educ:* Sherborne Sch.; Jesus Coll., Oxford (BA Hons Modern Hist.); Manchester Business Sch. (Dip. with distinction). British Petroleum, 1962–92: Gen. Manager, Corporate Planning, 1981–85; Chief Exec., BP Oil Internat., 1986–88; Chm. and Chief Exec., BP America, 1988–91; a Man Dir, BP, 1991–92; Chief Exec. and Dep. Chm., Cable and Wireless, 1992–96; Chm., Littlewoods Orgn, 1996–2002. Non-executive Director: McGraw Hill; Datacard; Schneider Electric; Prudential, 2004–. Chm., Leadership Foundn for Higher Educn; Mem., Marshall Commn. Hon. LLD: Manchester, 2001; Liverpool, 2001. *Recreations:* gardening, travel, swimming, golf.

ROSS, Jane Angharad; *see* Watts, J. A.

ROSS, John Alexander, CBE 1993; FRAgS; Chairman, Dumfries and Galloway NHS Board, 2001–08; *b* 19 Feb. 1945; *m* 1967, Alison Jean Darling; two *s* one *d*. *Educ:* Mahaar Primary Sch., Stranraer; George Watson's Coll., Edinburgh. FRAgS 1993. National Farmers' Union of Scotland: Convener, Hill Farming Sub-cttee, 1984–90; Wigtown Area Pres., 1985–86; Convener, Livestock Cttee, 1987–90; Vice-Pres., 1986–90; Pres., 1990–96. Comr, Meat & Livestock Commn, 1996–2002; Chm., Scotch Quality Beef and Lamb Assoc. Ltd, 1997–2000. Dir, 1996–2007, Chm. Regl Bd, Scotland, 2007–, NFU Mutual Insurance Soc. Dir, Animal Diseases Res. Assoc., 1986–; Chairman: Moredun Res. Inst., 2002–04; Moredun Res. Foundn, 2004–. Chairman: Dumfries and Galloway Health Bd, 1997–2000; Dumfries and Galloway Primary Care NHS Trust 2000–01. Chm., Stranraer Sch. Council, 1980–89. Session Clerk, Portpatrick Parish Church, 1975–80; Elder, C of S. *Recreations:* golf, curling. *Address:* Upper Dinvin Farm, Portpatrick, Stranraer DG9 8TL. *T:* (01776) 810259. *Club:* Farmers'.

ROSS, John Graffin; QC 2001; a Recorder, since 1994; *b* 9 March 1947; *er s* of late James Ross, MRCVS and of Eileen Ross; *m* 1973, Elizabeth Patricia Alexandra Layland. *Educ:* Umtali Boys' High Sch., Southern Rhodesia; University Coll. of Rhodesia and Nyasaland (LLB (ext.) London Univ.); University College London (LLM). Called to the Bar, Inner Temple, 1971, Bencher, 2006; Asst Recorder, 1990–94. Legal Assessor, RCVS, 2007–. Mem., Professional Negligence Cttee, 2006–, London Common Law and Commercial Cttee, 2006–, Bar Assoc. *Publication:* (contrib.) Pittaway and Hammerton, Professional Negligence Cases, 1998. *Recreations:* music, bridge, riding, golf, ski-ing. *Address:* c/o 1 Chancery Lane, WC2A 1LF. *T:* 0845 634 6666. *Clubs:* Denham Golf; Valderrama (Golf).

ROSS, Jonathan Steven, OBE 2005; broadcaster; *b* 17 Nov. 1960; *m* 1988, Jane Goldman; three *c*. *Educ:* Sch. of Slavonic and E European Studies, Univ. of London (BA History). Formerly researcher, Channel 4; founding co-Producer, Channel X. Television includes: chat shows: The Last Resort (deviser and associate producer with Alan Marke), 1987; One Hour with Jonathan Ross, 1990; Tonight with Jonathan Ross, 1990; The Late Jonathan Ross, 1996; Friday Night with Jonathan Ross, 2001–; presenter: The Incredibly Strange Film Show, 1988–89; Jonathan Ross Presents; For One Week Only, 1991; Gag Tag; In Search Of…; The Big Big Talent Show; Film 1999–; Secret Map of Hollywood, 2005; panel games: (host) It's Only TV… But I Like It, 1999–2002; (team mem.) They Think It's All Over, 1999–2006. Radio presenter, 1987–. *Publication:* Why Do I Say These Things?, 2008. *Address:* c/o Off the Kerb Productions, Hammer House, 113–117 Wardour Street, W1F 0UN.

ROSS, Kenneth Alexander; Sheriff of South Strathclyde, Dumfries and Galloway at Dumfries, since 2000; President, Law Society of Scotland, 1994–95 (Vice-President, 1993–94); *b* 21 April 1949; *s* of Alexander Cree Ross and Mary Hamilton Ross (*née* M'Lauchlan); *m* 1972, Morag Laidlaw; one *s* one *d*. *Educ:* Hutcheson's GS, Glasgow; Edinburgh Univ. (LLB (Hons) 1971). Pres., Edinburgh Univ. Union, 1970–71. Partner, M'Gowans, later Gillespie, Gifford & Brown, solicitors, Dumfries, 1975–97. Temp. Sheriff, 1987–97; Sheriff of Lothian and Borders at Linlithgow, 1997–2000. Mem., Scottish Legal Aid Bd, 2004–. Mem. Council, Law Soc. of Scotland, 1987–96. Contested (C): Kilmarnock, Feb. 1974; Galloway, Oct. 1974. *Recreations:* gardening, golf, beekeeping, walking. *Address:* Slate Row, Auchencairn, Castle Douglas, Kirkcudbrightshire DG7 1QL.

ROSS, Leslie Samuel, CB 2006; Managing Director, Business International, Invest Northern Ireland, 2002–05; advisor on economic development, since 2005; *b* 5 July 1944; *s* of Herbert Ross and late Gretta Ross; *m* 1969, Violet Johnston; one *s* one *d*. *Educ:* Portora Royal Sch.; Open Univ. (BA Hons). Dep. Chief Exec. and other sen. positions, 1982–2000, Chief Exec., 2000–02, Industrial Develt Bd, NI. *Recreations:* sport, gardening, travel. *Address:* 5 Belmont Drive, Belfast BT4 2BL.

ROSS, Lt-Col Sir Malcolm; *see* Ross, Lt-Col Sir W. H. M.

ROSS, Margaret Beryl C.; *see* Clunies Ross.

ROSS, Michael David, CBE 2001; FFA; Chief Executive, Scottish Widows plc (formerly Managing Director, then Group Chief Executive, Scottish Widows' Fund and Life Assurance Society), 1991–2003; Joint Deputy Group Chief Executive, Lloyds TSB Group plc, 2000–03; *b* 9 July 1946; *s* of Patrick James Forrest Ross and Emily Janet; *m* 1973, Pamela Marquis Speakman. *Educ:* Daniel Stewart's Coll., Edinburgh. FFA 1969. Joined Scottish Widows', 1964, as Trainee Actuary; Asst Gen. Manager, 1986–88; Actuary, 1988; Gen. Manager, 1988–90; Dep. Man. Dir, 1990–91. Non-executive Director: Pearl Gp Ltd, 2005–; mform Ltd, 2005–; British Islamic Insce Hldgs, 2006–. Chm., Scottish Financial Enterprise, 1999–2004 (Dep. Chm., 1998). Mem., Finance Cttee, 2005–, Investment Cttee, 2005–, Nat. Trust for Scotland. Association of British Insurers: Chm., 2001–03; Chm., Customer Impact Panel, 2006–. CCMI (CBIM 1991). *Publications:* contrib. Trans. Faculty of Actuaries. *Recreations:* golf, curling, ski-ing, gardening. *Clubs:* Caledonian; Mortonhall Golf.

ROSS, Nicholas David, (Nick Ross); broadcaster and journalist; *b* 7 Aug. 1947; *s* of late John Caryl Ross and of Joy Dorothy Ross; *m* 1985, Sarah Caplin; three *s*. *Educ:* Wallington County Grammar Sch.; Queen's Univ., Belfast (BA Hons Psychol). Broadcaster, BBC N Ireland, 1971–72; Radio 4: reporter, Today, World at One, 1972–75; presenter, The World Tonight, Newsdesk, 1972–74, World at One, 1982, Call Nick Ross, 1986–97, Gulf News, 1991, The Commission, 1998–2005; producer and dir, TV documentaries, 1979–81; presenter, BBC TV: Man Alive, Man Alive Debates, Out of Court, 1975–82; Breakfast Time, Fair Comment, Star Memories, 60 Minutes, 1982–85; Watchdog, 1985–86; Crimewatch UK, 1984–2007; Westminster with Nick Ross, 1994–97; political party confs, 1996; Campaign Roadshow, 1997; So You Think You're A Good Driver, 1999–2002; The Syndicate, 2000; Nick Ross debates, 2000; indep. TV incl. A Week in Politics, Ch 4, 1986–88, Crime Museum, 2008. Member: COPUS, 1991–96; Cttee on the Ethics of Gene Therapy, DoH, 1991–93; Gene Therapy Adv. Cttee, DoH, 1993–96; Wider Working Gp on Health of the Nation, DoH, 1992–; Nuffield Council on Bioethics, 1999–2005; NHS Action Team, 2000–01; RCP Cttee on Ethics in Medicine, 2004–; Acad. of Med. Scis inquiry into use of non-human primates in res., 2005–06. Member: Nat. Bd for Crime Prevention, 1993–96; Crime Prevention Agency, 1996–99; Property Crime Task Force, 1999–2002; Victim Support Adv. Bd, 1991–; Crime Concern Adv. Bd, 1991–2003. President: SANEline, 1990–; Tacade, 1996–; Healthwatch, 1990–; Vice-President: Patients' Assoc., 1991–93; London Accident Prevention Council, 2007–; Vice-Chairman: Nat. Road Safety Campaign, RoSPA, 1990–93; Adv. Bd, Wales Cancer Bank. Chm., Rhône-Poulenc, then Aventis, Prize for Sci. Books, 1993, 2006. Guest Dir, Cheltenham Sci. Festival, 2008. Trustee: UK Stem Cell Foundn, 2005–; Crimestoppers, 2007–; Sense About Science, 2008–. Mem. Council, IAM, 2002–. Chm., Jill Dando Inst. of Crime Sci., UCL, 2000–. Vis. Prof. and Hon. Fellow, UCL, 2006. Ambassador, WWF, 2000–. Patron of various charities. FRSA 1994; FRSocMed 1998. Hon. Fellow Acad. of Experimental Criminology. DUniv QUB, 2002. *Recreations:* ski-ing, scuba diving, influencing public policy. *Address:* PO Box 999, London W2 4XT; *e-mail:* nickross@lineone.net; *web:* www.nickross.com.

ROSS, Peter Michael; His Honour Judge Peter Ross; a Circuit Judge, since 2004; *b* 24 June 1955; *s* of Michael and Colleen Ross; *m* 1979, Julie Anna Ibbetson; two *s* one *d*. *Educ:* John Hampden GS, High Wycombe; Venerable English Coll., Gregorian Univ., Rome (PhB 1975); Coll. of Law. Admitted solicitor, 1980; called to the Bar, Inner Temple, 2000. Articles of clerkship, Allan Janes & Co., 1976–79; Court Clerk, High Wycombe Magistrates' Court, 1979–81; Thames Valley Police: Asst Prosecuting Solicitor, 1981–82; Sen. Prosecuting Solicitor, 1982–84; Principal Prosecuting Solicitor, 1984–86; Sen. Crown Prosecutor, 1986–87, Br. Crown Prosecutor, 1987–90, CPS Aylesbury; Br. Crown Prosecutor, N London CPS, 1990–93; Asst Chief Crown Prosecutor (Ops), CPS London, 1993–96; Dir, Office for Supervision of Solicitors, 1996–99; an Asst Recorder, 1999–2000; a Recorder, 2000–04. *Recreations:* shooting, smallholding, gardening, fishing, hedgelaying.

ROSS, Prof. Richard Lawrence; Research Professor, Norwegian Film School, 2001–07; Head of Diploma Course and Deputy to Director, National Film and Television School, 1998–2000; *b* 22 Dec. 1935; *s* of Lawrence Sebley Ross and Muriel Ross; *m* 1957, Phyllis Ellen Hamilton; one *s* one *d*. *Educ:* Westland High School, Hokitika, NZ; Canterbury University College, NZ. Exchange Telegraph, 1958–60; Visnews Ltd, 1960–65; BBC TV News, 1965–80; Prof. of Film and TV, then of Film, RCA, 1980–89; Co-Chm. (with Milos Forman) Grad. Film Dept, Columbia Univ., NY, 1989–90; Chm., Grad. Film Dept, NY Univ., 1990–92; Sen. Lectr in Film, 1995–96, Hd, Curriculum Planning, 1996–98, Nat. Film and TV Sch. Hon. Prof. of Film, Hochschule für Fernsehen und Film, Munich, 1992–2004; Visiting Professor: Jerusalem Film and TV Sch., 1992–2005; Deutsche Film- und Fernsehakad., Berlin, 1993–2003. Consultant Dir, Film Educn, 1986–89; Dir, Nat. Youth Film Foundn, 1988–89. Consultant: Univ. Sains, Penang, Malaysia, 1984–; Calouste Gulbenkian Foundn, Lisbon, 1983–85. Chm., Educn Cttee, British Film Year, 1985–86; Exec. Mem., Centre Internat. de Liaison des Ecoles de Cinéma et de Télévision, 1990–95 (Chm., Short Film Project, 1990–95; Hon. Mem., 2004). Fellow in Fine Arts, Trent Polytechnic, 1970–72. Fellow, RCA, 1981–89. *Publications:* Strategy for Story-Telling (2 vols), 1992; Triangle (The Creative Partnership), vol. 1, 1998, vol. 2, 2001, vol. 3, 2002. *Recreations:* walking in London, eating in France, talking and drinking anywhere. *Address:* *e-mail:* dickross@dircon.co.uk.

ROSS, Richard Y.; *see* Younger-Ross.

ROSS, Robert; *see* Ross, W. R. A.

ROSS, Lt-Gen. Sir Robert (Jeremy), (Sir Robin), KCB 1994 (CB 1992); OBE 1978; Chairman, SSAFA Forces Help, since 2000; *b* 28 Nov. 1939; *s* of Gerald and Margaret Ross; *m* 1965, Sara (*née* Curtis); one *s* one *d*. *Educ:* Wellington Coll.; Corpus Christi Coll., Cambridge (MPhil). Entered RM, 1957; Commando and Sea Service, 1959–69; Army Staff Coll., 1970; Commando Service, 1971–78; Instr, Army Staff Coll., 1978–79; CO 40 Commando RM, 1979–81; RCDS 1982; MoD, 1984–86; Comdr 3 Commando Bde, 1986–88; Maj.-Gen. RM Trng, Reserve and Special Forces, 1988–90; Maj.-Gen. RM Commando Forces, 1990–93; CGRM, 1993–96. Liveryman, Plaisterers' Co., 1996. Comdr, Legion of Merit (USA), 1993. *Recreations:* shooting, fishing, walking. *Club:* Army and Navy.

ROSS, Sandy; *see* Ross, A.

ROSS, Sophie, (Mrs R. P. Ross); *see* Mirman, S.

ROSS, Tessa Sarah; Controller, Film and Drama (formerly Head of FilmFour and Drama), Channel 4, since 2005; *b* 26 July 1961; *d* of E. Leonard Ross and Sharon F. Ross (*née* Kingsley), MBE; *m* 1987, Mark Scantlebury; two *s* one *d*. *Educ:* Somerville Coll., Oxford (BA Hons, MA Oriental Studies (Chinese)). Literary Agent, Anthony Shiel Associates, 1986–88; Script Editor, BBC Scotland, 1988–89; Hd of Develt, British Screen Finance, 1990–93; Independent Commng Exec., 1993–97, Hd of Independent Commng, 1997–2000, BBC TV Drama; Hd of Drama, 2000–03, Hd of FilmFour, 2003–05, Channel 4. *Address:* Channel 4, 124 Horseferry Road, SW1P 2TX. *T:* (020) 7396 4444. *Club:* Groucho.

ROSS, Timothy David M.; *see* Melville-Ross.

ROSS, Victor; Chairman, Reader's Digest Association Ltd, 1978–84; *b* 1 Oct. 1919; *s* of Valentin and Eva Rosenfeld; *m* 1st, 1944, Romola Wallace; two *s*; 2nd, 1970, Hildegard Peiser. *Educ:* schs in Austria, Germany and France; London Sch. of Economics. Served in Army, 1942–45. Journalist and writer, 1945–55; joined Reader's Digest, 1955; Man. Dir and Chief Exec., 1972–81. Dir, Folio Soc., 1985–89. Pres., Assoc. of Mail Order Publishers, 1979–80, 1983–84; Mem., Data Protection Tribunal, 1985–95. Hon. Fellow,

Inst. of Direct Marketing, 1995. Mackintosh Medal for Advertising, Advertising Assoc., 1989. *Publications:* A Stranger in my Midst, 1948; Tightrope, 1952; Basic British, 1956. *Recreations:* collecting books, fishing. *Address:* Worten Mill, Great Chart, Kent TN23 3BS.

ROSS, Lt-Col Sir (Walter Hugh) Malcolm, GCVO 2005 (CVO 1994; KCVO 1999); OBE 1988; JP; Lord-Lieutenant, Stewartry of Kirkcudbright (Dumfries and Galloway Region), since 2006; Master of the Household of the Prince of Wales and Duchess of Cornwall, 2006–08; *b* 27 Oct. 1943; *s* of Col Walter John Macdonald Ross, CB, OBE, MC, TD and Josephine May (*née* Cross); *m* 1969, Susie, *d* of Gen. Sir Michael Gow, *qv*; one *s* two *d*. *Educ:* Eton Coll.; Royal Military Acad., Sandhurst. Served in Scots Guards, 1964–87; Asst Comptroller, 1987–91, Comptroller, 1991–2006, Lord Chamberlain's Office; Management Auditor, The Royal Household, 1987–89. Sec., Central Chancery of the Orders of Knighthood, 1989–91. Chm., Westminster Gp plc, 2007–. An Extra Equerry to the Queen, 1988–. Mem., Queen's Body Guard for Scotland, Royal Company of Archers, 1981– (Brigadier, 2003). Stewartry of Kirkcudbright (Dumfries and Galloway): DL 2003; JP 2006. Freeman, City of London, 1994. CStJ 2007. *Address:* Netherhall, Bridge-of-Dee, Castle-Douglas, Kirkcudbrightshire DG7 2AA. *Clubs:* White's, Pratt's; New (Edinburgh).

See also W. R. A. Ross.

ROSS, (Walter) Robert (Alexander), CVO 2006; FRICS; Secretary and Keeper of the Records, Duchy of Cornwall, since 1997; *b* 27 Feb. 1950; *s* of Col Walter John Macdonald Ross, CB, OBE, MC, TD and Josephine May Ross (*née* Cross); *m* 1985, Ingrid Wieser; one *s* one *d*. *Educ:* Eton Coll.; Royal Agricl Coll., Cirencester. FRICS 1982. Chartered Surveyor, Buccleuch Estates Ltd, Selkirk, 1972–73; joined Savills, 1973: Partner, 1982–86; Dir, 1986–97. *Address:* 10 Buckingham Gate, SW1E 6LA. *T:* (020) 7834 7346. *Clubs:* Boodle's, Farmers.

ROSS, William; *b* 4 Feb. 1936; *m* 1974, Christine; three *s* one *d*. MP (UU) Londonderry, Feb. 1974–83, Londonderry East, 1983–2001 (resigned seat Dec. 1985 in protest against Anglo-Irish Agreement; re-elected Jan. 1986); contested (UU) Londonderry E, 2001. *Recreations:* fishing, shooting. *Address:* Hillquarter, Turmeel, Dungiven, Northern Ireland BT47 4SL. *T:* (028) 7774 1428.

ROSS, William Mackie, CBE 1987; TD 1969; DL; MD; FRCS; FRCSE; FRCR; retired; Consultant Radiotherapist, Northern Regional Health Authority, 1953–87; Lecturer in Radiotherapy, University of Newcastle upon Tyne, 1973–87; *b* 14 Dec. 1922; *s* of Harry Caithness Ross and Catherine Ross; *m* 1948, Mary Burt; one *s* two *d*. *Educ:* Durham and Newcastle. MB, BS 1945; MD 1953. FRCS 1956; FRCR 1960; FRCSE 1994. Trainee in Radiotherapy, 1945–51; National Service, 1951–53; RAMC TA, 1953–72; Col, CO 201 Gen. Hosp., 1967–72, Hon. Col, 1977–82. President: Section of Radiology, RSM, 1978; British Inst. of Radiology, 1979; North of England Surgical Soc., 1983; Royal Coll. of Radiologists, 1983–86. Hon. FACR, 1986. DL Northumberland, 1971–74, Tyne and Wear, 1974. *Publications:* articles on cancer, its causation and treatment. *Address:* 62 Archery Rise, Durham City DH1 4LA. *T:* (0191) 3869256.

ROSS-MUNRO, Colin William Gordon; QC 1972; *b* 12 Feb. 1928; *s* of late William Ross-Munro and of Adela Chirgwin; *m* 1958, Janice Jill Pedrana; one step *d*. *Educ:* Lycée Français de Londres; Harrow Sch.; King's Coll., Cambridge. Served in Scots Guards and in Army Education Corps. Called to the Bar, Middle Temple, 1951 (Master of the Bench, 1983). *Recreations:* tennis and travel. *Address:* (home) 28 St Maur Road, SW6 4DP; Blackstone Chambers, Blackstone House, Temple, EC4Y 9BW.

ROSS RUSSELL, Graham; Chairman, UK Business Incubation, since 1997; *b* 3 Jan. 1933; *s* of Robert Ross Russell and Elizabeth Ross Russell (*née* Hendry); *m* 1963, Jean Margaret Symington; three *s* one *d*. *Educ:* Loretto; Trinity Hall, Cambridge (BA; Hon. Fellow, 2001); Harvard Business School (MBA; Frank Knox Fellow, 1958–60). Sub Lieut, RNVR, 1951–53 (Mediterranean Fleet). Merchant banking: Morgan Grenfell & Co. and Baring Brothers, 1956–58; Philip Hill Higginson Erlanger, 1960–63; Stockbroker, Laurence Prust & Co., 1963–90, Partner, 1965; Chm., Laurence Prust & Co. Ltd, 1986–88. Chairman: Braham Miller Group, 1981–84; C. C. F. Hldgs, 1988–90; EMAP, 1990–94 (Dir, 1970–94); Tunnel Services Ltd, 1991–2002; Securities Inst., 1992–2000; F & C Capital and Income (formerly F & C Pep and Isa) Investment Trust plc, 1993–2005; Advent, then Foresight 3, Venture Capital Trust plc, 1996–2005; Enterprise Panel, 1997–; non-executive Director: UK Select Investment Trust (formerly Investment Trust of Guernsey) plc, 1995–; Fordath, 1971–84; Foster Braithwaite, 1988–96; Nasdaq (Europe) (formerly EASDAQ) SA, 1995–98 (Pres., 2000–01, Mem., Market Authy, 1999–2003); Barloworld plc, 1998–2003; Bamboo Investments plc, 2000–06; Barloworld Ltd, 2001–03. Dir, SIB, 1989–93; Mem. Council, Internat. Stock Exchange, subseq. London Stock Exchange, 1973–91 (Dep. Chm., 1984–88; Chairman: Pre-emption Gp, 1987–2000; Rev. Cttee on Initial Public Offers, 1989–90). Comr, Public Works Loan Bd, 1980–95; Chm., Domestic Promotions Cttee, British Invisible Exports Council, 1987–91. Chm. Trustees, F & C Asset Mgt Pension Fund, 2004–07; Mem., Investment Cttee, RBK&C Pension Fund, 2004–. Trustee, NESTA, 2001–07. Mem. Council, Crown Agents Foundn, 1997–2002. Chm. Govs, Sutton's Hosp., Charterhouse, 1996–2006. Pres., Trinity Hall Assoc., 1994–95. *Publications:* occasional articles in esoteric financial and fiscal jls. *Recreations:* tennis, golf, reading. *Address:* 30 Ladbroke Square, W11 3NB. *T:* (020) 7727 5017. *Clubs:* Athenæum; Hawks (Cambridge); Woodpeckers (Oxford and Cambridge).

ROSS-WAWRZYNSKI, Dana; Headmistress, Altrincham Grammar School for Girls, since 1999; *b* 24 March 1951; *d* of Richard and Pauline Ross; *m* 1974, Jack Wawrzynski; two *s*. *Educ:* Glasgow Univ. (BSc Hons 1975); Strathclyde Univ. (MSc 1976); Manchester Univ. (NPQH 1999). Teacher, Loreto Sixth Form Coll., Manchester, 1977–81; Hd of Lower Sch. Sci., Central High Sch. for Boys, Manchester, 1981–82; Hd of Sci., St Joseph's High Sch. for Girls, Manchester, 1982–84; Dep. Headteacher, Abraham Moss High Sch. and N Manchester Coll., 1984–90; Dep. Headteacher, All Hallows High Sch., Macclesfield, 1990–98. *Publications:* sex educn booklet, papers. *Recreations:* classical music, hill walking, reading, ski-ing. *Address:* Altrincham Grammar School for Girls, Cavendish Road, Bowdon, Altrincham, Cheshire WA14 2NL. *T:* (0161) 912 5912.

ROSSANT, Dr Janet, FRS 2000; FRSC; Professor, Department of Molecular and Medical Genetics, since 1988, University Professor, since 2001, University of Toronto; Chief of Research, Hospital for Sick Children, Toronto, since 2005; *b* 13 July 1950; *d* of Leslie and Doris Rossant; *m* 1977, Alex Bain; one *s* (one *d* decd). *Educ:* St Hugh's Coll., Oxford (BA, MA 1972); Darwin Coll., Cambridge (PhD 1976). Beit Meml Fellow, Univ. of Oxford, 1975–77; Asst Prof., 1977–82, Associate Prof., 1982–85, Brock Univ., St Catharines, Ont.; Associate Prof., Univ. of Toronto, 1985–88; Sen. Scientist, 1985–2005, and Co-head, 1998, Prog. in Devel and Fetal Health, Samuel Lunenfeld Res. Inst., Toronto. FRSC 1996. Hon. LLD Dalhousie, 2005. *Publications:* (with R. A. Pedersen) Experimental Approaches to Mammalian Development, 1986; (with P. L. M. Tam) Mouse Development, 2002; contrib. numerous articles to peer-reviewed jls. *Recreations:* walking, cooking, theatre. *Address:* Hospital for Sick Children, 555 University Avenue, Toronto, ON M5G 1X8, Canada.

ROSSDALE, Rt Rev. David Douglas James; *see* Grimsby, Bishop Suffragan of.

ROSSDALE, Peter Daniel, OBE 1996; PhD; FRCVS; Editor, Equine Veterinary Journal, since 1979, Editor-in-Chief, Equine Veterinary Education, since 1991, and Chairman, Equine Veterinary Journal Ltd, since 1985; *b* 8 Sept. 1927; *s* of George and Kate Rossdale; *m* 1st, 1954, Jillian Ruth Clifton (*d* 1999); two *s* one *d*; 2nd, 2003, Mary Annette Sharkey (*née* Lawrence). *Educ:* Egerton House; Stowe Sch.; Trinity Coll., Cambridge (MA, PhD 1985); RVC. FRCVS 1967. Founding Partner, Rossdale and Partners, Newmarket, 1959–2002, now Consultant. British Equine Veterinary Association: Treas., 1960–65; Pres., 1976–77; Chm., BEVA Trust, 1978–82; Chm., 1980–84, Treas., 1984–90, Internat. Equine Reproduction Symposia Cttee; Member: Veterinary Adv. Cttee, Wellcome Trust, 1975–79; Sci. Adv. Cttee, Animal Health Trust, 1978–90; Veterinary Adv. Cttee, Horserace Betting Levy Bd, 1983–96; Chm., Internat. Veterinary Perinatology Soc., 1992–95. Mem., 1957–2003, Hon. Mem., 2003–, Neonatal Soc. (Vickers Lecture); Frank Milne Lecture, American Assoc. of Equine Practitioners, 2004. FACVSc 1973; Dip. of Equine Stud Medicine, 1986. Dr *hc* Berne, 1987; Edinburgh, 2001; Sydney, 2007. William Hunting Prize, Vet. Record, 1973; George Fleming Prize, British Vet. Jl, 1974; John Henry Steel Meml Medal, RCVS, 1978; Hochmoor Prize, Tierklinik Hochmoor, 1987; Equestrian Award, Animal Health Trust, 1992; Darymple Champneys Award, BVA, 1996; Duke of Devonshire Award, 2004; Merial Lifetime Achievement Award, World Equine Veterinary Assoc., 2008. *Publications:* (jtly) The Practice of Equine Stud Medicine, 1974, revd edn 1980; (jtly) The Horse's Health from A–Z, 1974, revd edn 1998; The Horse from Conception to Maturity, 1975, revd edn 2003; Inside the Horse, 1975; Seeing Equine Practice, 1976; Horse Ailments Explained, 1979; Horse Breeding, 1981 (trans. French, Japanese, German, Swedish); (ed) Veterinary Notes for Horse Owners, 1987; contrib. peer reviewed jls inc. Vet. Rec., EVJ, Jl Reprod. Fert., Res. Vet. Sci., Lancet, Nature, etc and jls of educn. *Recreations:* contract bridge, music, opera, horseracing and breeding, photography, travel. *T:* (01638) 663639; *e-mail:* pd.rossdale@btinternet.com.

ROSSE, 7th Earl of, *cr* 1806; **(William) Brendan Parsons;** Bt 1677; Baron Oxmantown 1792; *b* 21 Oct. 1936; *s* of 6th Earl of Rosse, KBE, and Anne (*d* 1992), *o d* of Lt-Col Leonard Messel, OBE; *S* father, 1979; *m* 1966, Alison Margaret, *er d* of Major J. D. Cooke-Hurle, Startforth Hall, Barnard Castle, Co. Durham; two *s* one *d*. *Educ:* Aiglon Coll., Switzerland; Grenoble Univ.; Christ Church, Oxford (BA 1961; MA 1964). 2nd Lieut, Irish Guards, 1955–57. UN Official 1963–80, appointed successively to Ghana, Dahomey, Mid-West Africa, Algeria, as first UN Volunteer Field Dir (in Iran) and UN Disaster Relief Co-ordinator (in Bangladesh). Govt of Ireland: Mem., Adv. Council on Devolt Co-operation, 1984–89; Dir, Agency for Personal Service Overseas, 1986–90. Founder and Dir, Birr Scientific and Heritage Foundn (resp. for creation of Ireland's Historic Science Centre), 1985–; Director: Historic Irish Tourist Houses and Gardens Assoc., 1980–91; Lorne House Trust, 1993–2001; Trustee, The Tree Register, 1989–. Lord of the Manor: Womersley and Woodhall, Yorks; Newtown, Parsonstown and Roscomroe, Ireland. FRAS; Hon. FIEI. Hon. LLD Dublin, 2005. *Heir: s* Lord Oxmantown, *qv*. *Address:* (home) Birr Castle, Co. Offaly, Ireland. *T:* (57) 912 0023.

See also Earl of Snowdon.

ROSSER, family name of **Baron Rosser**.

ROSSER, Baron *cr* 2004 (Life Peer), of Ickenham in the London Borough of Hillingdon; **Richard Andrew Rosser;** JP; General Secretary, Transport Salaried Staffs' Association, 1989–2004; *b* 5 Oct. 1944; *s* of Gordon William Rosser and Kathleen Mary (*née* Moon); *m* 1973, Sheena Margaret (*née* Denoon); two *s* one *d*. *Educ:* St Nicholas Grammar Sch., Northwood. BScEcon London (external degree), 1970. CMILT (MCIT 1968). Clerk, London Transport, 1962–65; PA to Operating Man. (Railways), LTE, 1965–66; joined full staff of TSSA, 1966: Res. Officer, 1966–74; Asst, London Midland Div. Sec., 1974–76; Finance and Organising Officer, 1976–77; London Midland Region Div. Sec., 1977–82; Asst Gen. Sec., 1982–89. Non-exec. Dir, Nat. Offender Mgt Bd (formerly Correctional Services Bd), 2000–; non-exec. Chm., National Offender Management Service (formerly Prison Service) Audit Cttee, 2003–. Councillor, London Bor. of Hillingdon, 1971–78 (Chm., Finance Cttee, 1974–78); contested (Lab) Croydon Central, Feb. 1974. Mem., NEC, Labour Party, 1988–98; Vice-Chair, 1996–97, Chair, 1997–98, Labour Party. Mem. General Council, TUC, 2000–04. JP Middlesex, 1978 (Chm., Uxbridge Bench, 1996–2000). *Recreations:* walking, music, reading The Guardian, and watching non-league football. *Address:* House of Lords, SW1A 0PW.

ROSSI, Sir Hugh (Alexis Louis), Kt 1983; farmer and arboriculturist, Dordogne, since 1991; consultant in environmental law with Simmons and Simmons, solicitors, 1991–97; *b* 21 June 1927; *m* 1955, Philomena Elizabeth Jennings; one *s* four *d*. *Educ:* Finchley Catholic Gram. Sch.; King's Coll., Univ. of London (LLB; FKC 1986). Solicitor with Hons, 1950. Member: Hornsey Borough Coun., 1956–65; Haringey Council, 1965–68; Middlesex CC, 1961–65. MP (C) Hornsey, 1966–83, Hornsey and Wood Green, 1983–92; Govt Whip, Oct. 1970–April 1972; Europe Whip, Oct. 1971–1973; a Lord Comr, HM Treasury, 1972–74; Parly Under-Sec. of State, DoE, 1974; opposition spokesman on housing and land, 1974–79; Minister of State: NI Office, 1979–81; for Social Security and the Disabled, DHSS, 1981–83. Chm., Select Cttee on the Environment, 1983–92. Dep. Leader, UK Delegn to Council of Europe and WEU, 1972–73 (Mem., 1970–73). Non-exec. Dir, Iveco NV, 1989–2003; Consultant, Wimpey Environmental Ltd, 1993–95. Vice President: (UK), Adv. Cttee on Protection of the Seas, 1992–2002; Nat. Soc. for Clean Air, 1985–. Chairman: UNA (UK), 1992–96; Italian Hosp., London, 1988–89, Italian Hosp. Fund, 1990–2002; Assoc. of Papal Orders in GB of Pius IX, St Gregory and St Sylvester, 1989–99; Historic Chapels Trust, 1992–2002 (Hon. Pres., 2002–); Trustee, Trusthouse Charitable Foundn (formerly Mem., Forte Council), 1992–. Pres., KCL Assoc., 2004–06 (Vice Pres., 2003). Hon. FCIWEM 1990; Hon. Fellow, Inst. Wastes Management, 1993. Knight of Holy Sepulchre, 1966; KCSG 1985. *Publications:* Guide to the Rent Act, 1974; Guide to Community Land Act, 1975; Guide to Rent (Agriculture) Act, 1976; Guide to Landlord and Tenant Act, 1987; Guide to Local Government Acts 1987 and 1988, 1988. *Club:* Athenæum.

See also M.-L. E. Rossi.

ROSSI, Marie-Louise Elizabeth; Head of Insurance and Risk Management and Member of Advisory Board, New Security Foundation, since 2007; *b* 18 Feb. 1956; *d* of Sir Hugh Rossi, *qv*. *Educ:* St Paul's Girls' Sch.; St Anne's Coll., Oxford (BA Hons Lit. Hum., MA; Treas., Oxford Union, 1978). Hogg Robinson Gp plc, 1979–87; Asst Dir, Sedgwick Gp plc, 1987–90; Consultant, Tillinghast-Towers Perrin, mgt consultants and actuaries, 1990–93; Chief Executive: London Internat. Insurance and Reinsurance Market Assoc., 1993–98; Internat. Underwriting Assoc. of London, 1998–2005; Dep. Chm., 2004–06, Acting Chm., 2006, Chm., 2006–07, European Movement UK. Member: Lloyd's, 1985–97 (Underwriting Mem., 1985–91); Gen. Cttee, Lloyd's Register of Shipping, 2000–04. Mem. (C), Westminster CC, 1986–94 (Chm., Educn Cttee, 1989–92).

Chairman: Bow Gp, 1988–89 (Trustee, 1996–99); Foreign Affairs Forum, Conservative Party, 1993–96; Chm. Orgn Cttee, Pro Euro Cons. Party, 1999–2001. Liberal Democrats: Chm., The Peel Gp, 2005– ; Member: Federal Exec., 2005, 2007–08; Internat. Relns Cttee, 2005–. Trustee and Director: Foundn for Young Musicians, 1990–2005; Orch. of St John's Ltd, 1995–99. Mem., LSC London Central, 2000–04. Mem. Governing Council, Nottingham Univ., 2001–05. Contested (Lib Dem) Cities of London and Westminster, 2005. MIEx 1991; FIRM 2004. FRSA 1993. Hon. Citizen, City of Baltimore, Md, 1994. *Clubs:* Athenæum, Special Forces.

ROSSINGTON, (Timothy) David; Director, Local Democracy, Department for Communities and Local Government, since 2007; *b* 9 Feb. 1958; *s* of Peter Gilman Rossington and Freda Elizabeth (*née* Moseley); *m* 1989, Sarah Jane Lee; one *s* one *d*. *Educ:* Balliol Coll., Oxford (BA 1980); Kennedy Sch. of Govt, Harvard (Masters Public Policy 1982); Birkbeck Coll., London (MSc Econ 1985). Joined Civil Service, 1982; Private Sec. to Lord Belstead, 1986; seconded to UK Repn, Brussels, and EC, 1988–91; Private Sec. to Minister of Agriculture, 1991–93; Hd of Div., MAFF, 1993–2000 (Project Dir, IT system to trace cattle in GB, 1996–99); e-Business Dir, DEFRA, 2000–04 (Ops Dir in Cumbria during foot and mouth outbreak, 2001); Dir, Efficiency Team, OGC, 2004–07. *Recreations:* hill walking, gardening, music, history, running. *Address:* Department for Communities and Local Government, Eland House, Bressenden Place, SW1E 5DU. *T:* (020) 7944 6970; *e-mail:* david.rossington@communities.gsi.gov.uk.

ROSSITER, Ann Helen; Director, Social Market Foundation, since 2005; *b* 18 May 1966; *d* of Charles and Averil Rossiter; partner, Lucy Burns. *Educ:* Birkbeck Coll., Univ. of London (BA Philosophy). Researcher, BBC Political Res. Unit, 1988–90; Asst Producer, BBC/C4, 1990–92; Researcher: John Denham, MP, 1992–94; Glenda Jackson, MP, 1994–96; Consultant, 1996–99, Dir, 1999–2001, Fishburn Hedges; Dir, Lexington Communications, 2001–02; Dir of Res. and Dep. Dir, Social Mkt Foundn, 2003–05. FRSA. *Publications:* The Future of the Private Finance Initiative, 2004; Choice: the evidence, 2004; News Broadcasting in the Digital Age, 2005; Road User Charging: a map, 2007; The Future of Healthcare, 2007; (contrib.) Public Matters: the renewal of the public realm, ed Patrick Diamond, 2007. *Recreations:* exploring Cornwall, contemporary art, bending the ear of politicians, gardening, serial music, film. *Address:* Social Market Foundation, 11 Tufton Street, SW1P 3QB. *T:* (020) 7222 7060; *e-mail:* arossiter@smf.co.uk.

ROSSITER, Rt Rev. (Anthony) Francis, OSB; Abbot President of the English Benedictine Congregation, 1985–2001 (Second Assistant, 1976–85); *b* 26 April 1931; *s* of Leslie and Winifred Rossiter. *Educ:* St Benedict's, Ealing; Sant Anselmo, Rome (LCL). Priest, 1955; Second Master, St Benedict's School, 1960–67; Abbot of Ealing, 1967–91; Vicar for Religious, Archdiocese of Westminster, 1969–88; Pres., Conf. of Major Religious Superiors of England and Wales, 1970–74; Pro-Primate, Benedictine Confedn, 1995–96 (Mem., Abbot Primate's Council, 1988–98). Hon. DD St Vincent Coll., Pa, 1988. *Address:* Ealing Abbey, W5 2DY. *T:* (020) 8862 2100.

ROSSLYN, 7th Earl of, *cr* 1801; **Peter St Clair-Erskine;** Bt 1666; Baron Loughborough, 1795; Commander, Royalty and Diplomatic Protection Department, Metropolitan Police, since 2003; *b* 31 March 1958; *s* of 6th Earl of Rosslyn, and of Athenais de Mortemart, *o d* of late Duc de Vivonne; *S* father, 1977; *m* 1982, Helen, *e d* of Mr and Mrs C. R. Watters, Christ's Hospital, Sussex; two *s* two *d*. *Educ:* Eton; Bristol Univ. (BA); Univ. of Cambridge (MSt). Metropolitan Police, 1980–94; Thames Valley Police, 1994–2000; a Comdr, Metropolitan Police, 2000–. Elected Mem., H of L, 1999. Mem., Queen's Body Guard for Scotland, Royal Company of Archers, 2005–. Trustee, Dunimarle Museum. Dir, Ludgrove Sch. Trust (Chm. of Govs). *Heir:* *s* Lord Loughborough, *qv*. *Address:* House of Lords, SW1A 0PW. *Club:* White's.

ROSSMORE, 7th Baron *cr* 1796; **William Warner Westenra;** *b* 14 Feb. 1931; *o s* of 6th Baron Rossmore and Dolores Cecil (*d* 1981), *d* of late Lieut-Col James Alban Wilson, DSO, West Burton, Yorks; *S* father, 1958; *m* 1982, Valerie Marion, *d* of Brian Tobin; one *s*. *Educ:* Eton; Trinity Coll., Cambridge (BA). 2nd Lieut, Somerset LI. Co-founder, Coolemine Therapeutic Community, Dublin. *Recreations:* drawing, painting. *Heir:* *s* Hon. Benedict William Westenra, *b* 6 March 1983. *Address:* Rossmore Park, Co. Monaghan, Eire. *T:* 81947.

ROSSOR, Prof. Martin Neil, MD, FRCP, FMedSci; Professor of Neurology, since 1998, and Chairman, Division of Neurology, since 2002, Institute of Neurology, University College London; Professor of Clinical Neurology, Division of Neurosciences, Imperial College London, since 2000; Hon. Consultant Neurologist: National Hospital for Neurology and Neurosurgery, since 1998; St Mary's Hospital, London, since 2000 (Consultant Neurologist, 1986); *b* 24 April 1950; *s* of late Bruce Rossor and of Eileen Rossor; *m* 1973, Eve Lipstein; two *s* one *d*. *Educ:* Watford Boys' Grammar Sch.; Jesus Coll., Cambridge (MA, MD); King's College Hosp. Med. Sch. (MB BChir). FRCP 1990. Clinical Scientist, MRC Neurochemical Pharmacology Unit, 1978–82; Registrar, 1982–83, Sen. Registrar, 1983–86, Nat. Hosp. for Nervous Diseases and King's Coll. Hosp.; Clinical Dir, Medical Specialities, St Mary's Hosp., 1989–92; Sen. Lectr, Inst. of Neurology, 1992–98; Clin. Dir for Neurology, Nat. Hosp. for Neurology and Neurosurgery, 1994–98. Dir, DoH UK Clin. Res. Network for Dementia and Neurodegenerative Diseases, 2005–. FMedSci 2002. Liveryman, Soc. of Apothecaries, 1978– (Mem., Ct of Assistants, 1999–). Ed., Jl of Neurology, Neurosurgery and Psychiatry, 2004–. *Publications:* Unusual Dementias, 1992; (with J. Growdon) Dementia, 1998, 2007; papers on Alzheimer's disease and related dementias. *Recreations:* English literature, equestrian sports, sailing. *Address:* The National Hospital for Neurology and Neurosurgery, Queen Square, WC1N 3BG. *T:* (020) 7829 8773. *Club:* Athenæum.

ROSSWALL, Prof. Thomas; Executive Director, International Council for Science, since 2002; *b* 20 Dec. 1941; *s* of Axel Rosswall and Britta (*née* Lindroth). *Educ:* Univ. of Uppsala (BSc 1966). Asst, Dept of Biochemistry, Univ. of Uppsala, 1967–70; Res. Asst, Dept of Microbiol., Swedish Univ. of Agricl Scis, 1970–76; Programme Officer, Swedish Council for Planning and Co-ordination of Research, 1976–80; Researcher, 1980–82, Asst Prof., 1982–84, Associate Prof., 1984, Dept of Microbiol., Swedish Univ. of Agricl Research; Prof., Dept of Water and Envmtl Studies, Univ. of Linköping, 1984–92; Exec. Dir, Internat. Geosphere-Biosphere Prog., 1987–94; Rector, 1994–2000, Prof., 2000–, Swedish Univ. of Agricl Scis. Prof., Stockholm Univ., 1992–2000; Dir, Internat. Secretariat, System for Analysis, Res. and Trng, Washington, 1992–93; Dir, Internat. Foundn for Science, Stockholm, 2000–01. MAE 1989; Fellow: Royal Swedish Acad. of Scis, 1989; Royal Swedish Acad. of Agric. and Forestry, 1995; Royal Acad. of Arts and Scis of Uppsala, 1999; World Acad. of Arts and Scis, 2005; Associate Fellow, Acad. of Scis for the Developing World (formerly Third World Acad. of Sci.), 2002. *Publications:* edited: Systems Analysis in Northern Coniferous Forests, 1971; (jtly) IBP Tundra Biome Procs 4th International Meeting on Biological Productivity of Tundra, 1971; Modern Methods in the Study of Microbial Ecology, 1973; (jtly) Structure and Function of Tundra Ecosystems, 1975; Nitrogen Cycling in West African Ecosystems, 1980; (jtly) Terrestrial Nitrogen Cycles: processes, ecosystems strategies and management impacts, 1981; (jtly) Nitrogen Cycling in South-East Asian Wet Monsoonal Ecosystems, 1981; (jtly) The Nitrogen Cycle, 1982; (jtly) Nitrogen Cycling in Ecosystems of Latin America and the Caribbean, 1982; (jtly) Scales and Global Change: spatial and temporal variability of biospheric and geospheric processes, 1988; (jtly) Ecology of Arable Land: the role of organism in carbon and nitrogen cycling, 1989; 100 papers in scientific jls. *Address:* (office) 51 boulevard de Montmorency, 75016 Paris, France.

ROST, Peter Lewis; energy consultant; *b* 19 Sept. 1930; *s* of Frederick Rosenstiel and Elisabeth Merz; *m* 1961, Hilary Mayo; two *s* two *d*. *Educ:* various primary schs; Aylesbury Grammar Sch. National Service, RAF, 1948–50; Birmingham Univ. (BA Hons Geog.), 1950–53. Investment Analyst and Financial Journalist with Investors Chronicle, 1953–58; firstly Investment Advisor, 1958, and then, 1962, Mem. London Stock Exchange, resigned 1977. MP (C) Derbys SE, 1970–83, Erewash, 1983–92. Secretary: Cons. Parly Trade and Industry Cttee, 1972–73; Cons. Parly Energy Cttee, 1974–77; Select Cttee on Energy, 1979–92. Treasurer, Anglo-German Parly Gp, 1974–92; Jt Chm., Alternative and Complementary Medicine Parly Gp, 1989–92. Chairman: Major Energy Users' Council, 1992–95; Utility Buyers' Forum, 1995–98; Vice-Pres., Combined Heat and Power Assoc. (Hon. Life Mem.). FRGS (Mem. Council, 1980–83); Fellow, Industry and Parlt Trust, 1987; Companion, Inst. of Energy, 1992. Freeman, City of London. Grand Cross, Order of Merit, Germany, 1979. *Publications:* papers on energy. *Recreations:* tennis, ski-ing, gardening, antique map collecting. *Address:* Norcott Court, Berkhamsted, Herts HP4 1LE. *T:* (01442) 866123, *Fax:* (01442) 865901.

ROSTRON, Martin Keith; Principal, Greenhead College, Huddersfield, since 2002; *b* 10 Sept. 1953; *s* of Harold and Lucy Rostron; *m* 1976, Linda Potts; two *s* one *d*. *Educ:* Liverpool Univ. (BA Hons English 1974; PGCE 1977). Teacher: Knutsford High Sch., 1977–84; Priestley Coll., Warrington, 1984–91; Vice Principal, Greenhead Coll. (Sixth Form Coll.), 1991–2002. FRSA 2005. *Recreations:* slow holidays, interesting walks, gardening, reading, listening to classical music, friendly football games. *Address:* Greenhead College, Greenhead Road, Huddersfield HD1 4ES. *T:* (01484) 422032, *Fax:* (01484) 518025.

ROTA, Anthony Bertram; Chairman, Bertram Rota Ltd, antiquarian booksellers, since 2003 (Managing Director, 1967–2003); *b* 24 Feb. 1932; *s* of Cyril Bertram Rota and Florence Ellen Rota (*née* Wright); *m* 1957, Jean Mary Foster Kendall; two *s*. Entered family business, 1952. Vis. Distinguished Fellow, Univ. of Tulsa, 1988. President: Antiquarian Booksellers' Assoc., 1971–72; Internat. League of Antiquarian Booksellers, 1988–91. DeGolyer Medal, Southern Methodist Univ., 1988. *Publications:* Points at Issue, 1984; Life in a London Bookshop, 1989; The Changing Face of Antiquarian Bookselling 1950–2000 AD, 1995; Apart from the Text, 1998; Books in the Blood: memoirs, 2002; articles on book-collecting and bibliography in British and American jls. *Recreations:* cinema, opera, theatre, concerts, watching cricket, walking. *Address:* 31 Long Acre, WC2E 9LT. *T:* (020) 7836 0723. *Clubs:* Garrick; Grolier (NY).

ROTH, Andrew; Director, Parliamentary Profiles, since 1955; *b* NY, 23 April 1919; *s* of Emil and Bertha Roth; *m* 1st, 1941, Renee Knitel (marr. annulled 1949); 2nd, 1949, Mathilda Anna Friederich (marr. diss. 1984); one *s* one *d*; 3rd, 2004, Antoinette Putnam. *Educ:* City Coll. of NY (BSS); Columbia Univ. (MA); Harvard Univ. Reader, City Coll., 1939; Res. Associate, Inst. of Pacific Relations, 1940; US Naval Intell., 1941–45 (Lieut, SG); Editorial Writer, The Nation, 1945–46; Foreign Corresp., Toronto Star Weekly, 1946–50; London Corresp., France Observateur, Sekai, Singapore Standard, 1950–60; Political Correspondent: Manchester Evening News, 1972–84; New Statesman, 1984–97. Editor: Parliamentary Profiles, 1953–; Westminster Confidential, 1955–; Obituarist, Guardian, 1996–. DUniv Open, 1993. *Publications:* Japan Strikes South, 1941; French Interests and Policies in the Far East, 1942; Dilemma in Japan, 1945 (UK 1946); The Business Background of MPs, 1959, 7th edn 1980; The MPs' Chart, 1967, 5th edn 1979; Enoch Powell: Tory Tribune, 1970; Can Parliament Decide…, 1971; Heath and the Heathmen, 1972; Lord on the Board, 1972; The Prime Ministers, Vol. II (Heath chapter), 1975; Sir Harold Wilson: Yorkshire Walter Mitty, 1977; Parliamentary Profiles, 4 vols, 1984–85, 6th series 2003–; New MPs of '92, 1992; Mr Nice Guy and His Chums, 1993; New MPs of '97, 1997; New MPs of '01, 2001. *Recreation:* sketching. *Address:* 34 Somali Road, NW2 3RL. *T:* (office) (020) 7435 6673, *T:* (020) 7794 5884, *Fax:* (020) 7794 5774; 25 rue des Sabotiers, Lanrivain, Bretagne 22480, France.

ROTH, Prof. Klaus Friedrich, FRS 1960; Emeritus Professor, University of London; Hon. Research Fellow, Department of Mathematics, University College London, since 1996; *b* 29 Oct. 1925; *s* of late Dr Franz Roth and Mathilde Roth; *m* 1955, Melek Khairy, BSc, PhD (*d* 2002). *Educ:* St Paul's Sch.; Peterhouse, Cambridge (BA 1945; Hon. Fellow, 1989); University College, London (MSc 1948; PhD 1950; Fellow, 1979). Asst Master, Gordonstoun School, 1945–46. Member of Dept of Mathematics, University College, London, 1948–66; title of Professor in the University of London conferred 1961; Prof. of Pure Maths (Theory of Numbers), 1966–88, Vis. Prof. in Dept of Maths, 1988–96, Fellow, 1999, Imperial College, London. Visiting Lecturer, 1956–57, Vis. Prof., 1965–66, at Mass Inst. of Techn., USA. Foreign Hon. Mem., Amer. Acad. of Arts and Scis, 1966. Hon. FRSE 1993. Fields Medal awarded at International Congress of Mathematicians, 1958; De Morgan Medal, London Math. Soc., 1983; Sylvester Medal, Royal Soc., 1991. *Publications:* papers in various mathematical jls. *Recreations:* chess, cinema, ballroom dancing. *Address:* Colbost, 16A Drummond Road, Inverness IV2 4NB.

ROTH, Peter Marcel; QC 1997; a Recorder, since 2000; *b* 19 Dec. 1952; *s* of Stephen Jeffery Roth and Eva Marta Roth. *Educ:* St Paul's Sch.; New Coll., Oxford (Open Schol.; BA 1974; MA 1986); Law Sch., Univ. of Pennsylvania (Thouron Fellow; LLM 1977). Called to the Bar, Middle Temple, 1977 (Harmsworth Schol.), Bencher, 2008; in practice at the Bar, 1979–. Vis. Associate Prof., Law Sch., Univ. of Pennsylvania, 1987; Vis. Prof., KCL, 2003–. Jt Chair, Bench and Bar Cttee, United Jewish Israel Appeal, 1997–2003. Chair, Competition Law Assoc., 2003–. Trustee, British Inst. of Internat. and Comparative Law, 2006–. Chair, Insurance Wkg Party, Terrence Higgins Trust, 1989–94. *Publications:* (Gen. Ed.) Bellamy & Child's European Community Law of Competition, 5th edn 2001, 6th edn 2008; articles in legal jls. *Recreations:* travel, music. *Address:* Monckton Chambers, 1 & 2 Raymond Buildings, Gray's Inn, WC1R 5NR.

ROTHERMERE, 4th Viscount *cr* 1919, of Hemsted, co. Kent; **Jonathan Harold Esmond Vere Harmsworth;** Bt 1910; Baron 1914; Chairman, Daily Mail and General Trust plc, since 1998; *b* 3 Dec. 1967; *s* of 3rd Viscount Rothermere and his 1st wife, Patricia Evelyn Beverley (*née* Matthews; *d* 1992); *S* father, 1998; *m* 1993, Claudia, *d* of T. J. Clemence; one *s* three *d*. *Heir:* *s* Hon. Vere Richard Jonathan Harold Harmsworth; *b* 20 Oct. 1994. *Address:* (office) Northcliffe House, 2 Derry Street, W8 5TT.

ROTHERWICK, 3rd Baron *cr* 1939, of Tylney, Southampton; **Herbert Robin Cayzer;** Bt 1924; *b* 12 March 1954; *s* of 2nd Baron Rotherwick and Sarah-Jane (*d* 1978), *o d* of Sir Michael Nial Slade, 6th Bt; *S* father, 1996; *m* 1st, 1982, Sara Jane (marr. diss. 1994), *o d* of Robert James McAlpine; two *s* one *d*; 2nd, 2000, Tania, *d* of Christopher Fox; one *s* one *d* (and one *s* decd). *Educ:* Harrow; RAC, Cirencester. Lieut, Life Guards. Elected Mem.,

H of L, 1999; Opposition Whip, H of L, 2001–05; Opposition spokesperson for Educn and Skills, Work and Pensions, 2001–03, for DEFRA, 2003–05. Mem., Council of Europe, 2000–01. Fellow, Industry and Parlt Trust, 2005. Mem. Exec. Cttee, PFA, 1997–2001, 2005– (Vice Chm., 1999–2001). Pres., Gen. Aviation Awareness Council, 1997–. Director: Cayzer Continuation PCC Ltd, 2004–; Cornbury Estates Co. Ltd, 2006–. Non-exec. Dir, Air Touring Ltd, 2006–. *Heir: s* Hon. Herbert Robin Cayzer, *b* 10 July 1989. *Address:* Cornbury Park, Charlbury, Oxford OX7 3EH.

ROTHES, 22nd Earl of, *cr* before 1457; **James Malcolm David Leslie;** Lord Leslie 1445; Baron Ballenbreich 1457; *b* 4 June 1958; *s* of 21st Earl of Rothes and of Marigold, *o d* of Sir David Evans Bevan, 1st Bt; *S* father, 2005. *Educ:* Eton. Graduated Parnham House, 1990. *Heir: b* Hon. Alexander John Leslie [*b* 18 Feb. 1962; *m* 1990, Tina Gordon; *m* 2008, Mrs Francesca Clare MacManaway]. *Address:* Littlecroft, West Milton, Bridport, Dorset DT6 3SL.

ROTHNIE, Iain Andrew; Global Head of Real Estate, Herbert Smith LLP, international law firm, since 2006; *b* 14 Nov. 1955; *s* of Norman George Rothnie and Margaret Venables Rothnie; *m* 2003, Julie Fewtrell. *Educ:* Reading Sch.; Pembroke Coll., Cambridge (BA 1978). Admitted solicitor, 1981; Herbert Smith: Partner, 1988–; Hd, Real Estate, 2000–02; Exec. Partner, subseq. Chief Operating Officer, 2002–06. *Recreations:* travel, art, theatre. *Address:* Herbert Smith LLP, Exchange House, Primrose Street, EC2A 2HS. *T:* (020) 7374 8000, *Fax:* (020) 7374 0888; *e-mail:* iain.rothnie@herbertsmith.com.

ROTHSCHILD, family name of **Baron Rothschild.**

ROTHSCHILD, 4th Baron *cr* 1885; **Nathaniel Charles Jacob Rothschild,** Bt 1847; OM 2002; GBE 1998; Chairman: Five Arrows Ltd, since 1980; RIT Capital Partners plc; Deputy Chairman, BSkyB Group plc, since 2003; *b* 29 April 1936; *e s* of 3rd Baron Rothschild, GBE, GM, FRS and Barbara, *o d* of St John Hutchinson, KC; *S* father, 1990; *m* 1961, Serena Mary, *er d* of late Sir Philip Gordon Dunn, 2nd Bt; one *s* three *d*. *Educ:* Eton; Christ Church, Oxford (BA 1st cl. hons History; Hon. Student, 2006). Chairman: Bd of Trustees, Nat. Gallery, 1985–91; Nat. Heritage Meml Fund, 1992–98, administering Heritage Lottery Fund, 1995–98. Fellow, Ashmolean Mus., Oxford, 2006; Hon. Fellow, Courtauld Inst. of Art, 2008; Hon. FKC 2002; Hon. FBA 1998; Hon. FRIBA 1998; Hon. FRAM 2002. Hon. PhD Hebrew Univ. of Jerusalem, 1992; Hon. DLitt: Newcastle, 1998; Warwick 2003; Hon. LLD Exeter, 1998; DUniv Keele, 2000; Hon. DCL Oxon, 2002; Hon. DSc (Econs) London, 2004. Hon. Fellow, City of Jerusalem, 1992. Weizmann Award for Humanities and Scis, 1997. Comdr, Order of Henry the Navigator (Portugal), 1985. *Heir: s* Hon. Nathaniel Victor James Rothschild, *b* 12 July 1971. *Address:* The Pavilion, Eythrope, Aylesbury, Bucks HP18 0HS. *T:* (01296) 748337.

See also E. Rothschild.

ROTHSCHILD, Edmund Leopold de, CBE 1997; TD; VMH; Partner, N M Rothschild & Sons Limited, 1946–70 (Senior Partner, 1960–70, Chairman, 1970–75); *b* 2 Jan. 1916; *s* of late Lionel Nathan de Rothschild and Marie Louise Beer; *m* 1st, 1948, Elizabeth Edith Lentner (*d* 1980); two *s* two *d*; 2nd, 1982, Anne, JP, *widow* of J. Malcolm Harrison, OBE. *Educ:* Harrow Sch.; Trinity Coll., Cambridge. Major, RA (TA). Served France, North Africa and Italy, 1939–46 (wounded). Deputy Chairman: Brit. Newfoundland Corp. Ltd, 1963–69; Churchill Falls (Labrador) Corp. Ltd, 1966–69. Mem., Asia Cttee, BNEC, 1970–71, Chm., 1971. Pres., Exbury Gardens Ltd, 2000–. Trustee, Queen's Nursing Inst.; Founder, Res. into Ageing. Pres., Assoc. of Jewish Ex-Servicemen and Women; Vice-Pres., Council of Christians and Jews. Governor, Tech. Univ. of Nova Scotia. Hon. LLD Memorial Univ. of Newfoundland, 1961; Hon. DSc Salford, 1983. VMH 2005. Order of the Sacred Treasure, 1st Class (Japan), 1973. *Publications:* Window on the World, 1949; A Gilt-Edged Life: memoir, 1998. *Recreations:* gardening, fishing. *Address:* Exbury House, Exbury, Southampton SO45 1AF. *Clubs:* White's, Portland, Cavalry and Guards.

See also L. D. de Rothschild.

ROTHSCHILD, Emma, CMG 2000; Fellow, since 1988, and Co-Director, Centre for History and Economics, since 1991, King's College, Cambridge; Knowles Professor of History, Harvard University, since 2008 (Professor of History, 2007–08); *b* 16 May 1948; *d* of 3rd Baron Rothschild, GBE, GM, FRS and of Lady Rothschild, MBE (*née* Teresa Mayor); *m* 1991, Prof. Amartya Kumar Sen, *qv*. *Educ:* Somerville Coll., Oxford (MA); Massachusetts Inst. of Technology (Kennedy Schol. in Econs). Associate Professor: of Humanities, MIT, 1978–80; of Science, Technology and Society, MIT, 1979–88; Dir de Recherches Invité, Ecole des Hautes Etudes en Sciences Sociales, Paris, 1981–82. Mem., OECD Gp of Experts on Science and Technology in the New Socio-Economic Context, 1976–80; OECD Sci. Examiner, Aust., 1984–85. Member: Govg Bd, Stockholm Internat. Peace Res. Inst., 1983–93; Govg Bd, Stockholm Envmt Inst., 1989–93; Bd, Olof Palme Meml Fund (Stockholm), 1986–2007; Royal Commn on Environmental Pollution, 1986–94; Bd, British Council, 1993–98; Bd, UN Foundn, 1998–; Council for Sci. and Technol., 1998–2001; Chairman: UN Res. Inst. for Social Develt, 1999–2005; Kennedy Meml Trust, 2000–. Foreign Mem., Amer. Philosophical Soc., 2002. *Publications:* Paradise Lost: the Decline of the Auto-Industrial Age, 1973; Economic Sentiments, 2001; articles in learned and other jls. *Address:* King's College, Cambridge CB2 1ST.

ROTHSCHILD, Baron Eric Alain Robert David de; Chairman, Rothschild Bank AG, since 2000; Partner, Rothschild et Compagnie Banque, since 1982; *b* NY, 3 Oct. 1940; French nationality; *m* 1983, Maria Béatrice Caracciolo di Forino; two *s* one *d*. *Educ:* Ecole Polytechnique Fédérale, Zürich (Engr 1963). Chairman: Paris Orléans, 1974; Soc. du Château Rieussec, 1999; Managing Partner: Soc. Civile de Château Lafite Rothschild, 1974; Soc. Civile de Duhart Milon Rothschild, 1975; Partner, Rothschild et Cie Gestion, 1998; Board Member: N. M. Rothschild & Sons (London), 1978; SIACI, 1983; Los Vascos, 1993; Christie's France, 1994. Chairman: Fondation de Rothschild, 1982; Centre de Documentation Juive Contemporaine, 1984; Mémorial du Martyr Juif Inconnu, 1984; Fondation Casip-Cojasor, 1988; Fondation Nat. des Arts Graphiques et Plastiques, 1989; Fondation Rothschild, 1993; Rothschild Private Mgt Ltd, 2003; Vice Chm., Fondation pour la Mémoire de la Shoah, 2001; Bd Mem., Alliance Israélite Universelle, 1994. *Address:* (office) 3 rue de Messine, 75008 Paris, France. *T:* (1) 40744006, *Fax:* (1) 40749816.

ROTHSCHILD, Sir Evelyn de, Kt 1989; Chairman, Concordia BV; *b* 29 Aug. 1931; *s* of late Anthony Gustav de Rothschild; *m* 1973, Victoria Schott (marr. diss. 2000); two *s* one *d*; *m* 2000, Lynn Forester. *Educ:* Harrow; Trinity Coll., Cambridge. Chm., N. M. Rothschild and Sons Ltd, 1976–2003. Chairman: Economist Newspaper, 1972–89; United Racecourses Ltd, 1977–94. Chm., British Merchant Banking and Securities Houses Assoc. (formerly Accepting Houses Cttee), 1985–89. *Recreations:* art, racing.

ROTHSCHILD, Leopold David de, CBE 1985; Director, N M Rothschild & Sons Limited, since 1970 (Partner, 1956–70); *b* 12 May 1927; *yr s* of Lionel de Rothschild and Marie Louise Beer. *Educ:* Bishops Coll. Sch., Canada; Harrow; Trinity Coll., Cambridge. Director of Bank of England, 1970–83. Chm., Exbury Gdns Ltd, 1989–. Chairman: Anglo Venezuelan Soc., 1975–82; English Chamber Orchestra and Music Soc. Ltd, 1963–2001 (Pres., 2001–); Bach Choir, 1976–99 (Pres., 2002–); Music Adv. Cttee, British Council, 1986–93; Council, RCM, 1988–99 (FRCM 1977). Trustee, Science Mus., 1987–98; Mem. Council, Winston Churchill Meml Trust, 1990–2000. DUniv York, 1991. Order of Francisco de Miranda, 1st cl. (Venezuela), 1978; Gran Oficial, Order of Merit (Chile), 1993; Ordem Nacional do Cruzeiro do Sul (Brazil), 1993; Order of Aztec Eagle, Encomienda (Mexico), 1994. *Recreations:* music, walking, industrial archaeology. *Address:* New Court, St Swithin's Lane, EC4P 4DU. *T:* (020) 7280 5000. *Clubs:* Brooks's; Royal Yacht Squadron.

See also E. L. de Rothschild.

ROTHWELL, Margaret Irene, CMG 1992; HM Diplomatic Service, retired; Ambassador to Côte d'Ivoire, 1990–97, and concurrently to the Republic of Niger, the People's Democratic Republic of Burkina and Liberia; *b* 25 Aug. 1938; *d* of Harry Rothwell and Martha (*née* Goedecke). *Educ:* Southampton Grammar School for Girls; Lady Margaret Hall, Oxford (BA LitHum). Foreign Office, 1961; Third, later Second Secretary, UK Delegn to Council of Europe, Strasbourg, 1964; FO, 1966; Second Sec. (Private Sec. to Special Representative in Africa), Nairobi, 1967; Second, later First Sec., Washington, 1968; FCO, 1972; First Sec. and Head of Chancery, Helsinki, 1976; FCO, 1980; Counsellor and Hd of Trng Dept, FCO, 1981–83; Counsellor, Consul-Gen. and Head of Chancery, Jakarta, 1984–87; Overseas Inspectorate, FCO, 1987–90. Reviewer, Quinquennial Review of the Marshall Aid Commemoration Commn, 1998; UK Rep., Jt US/UK Commn on Student Travel Exchanges, 1998; voluntary work for Govt of Rwanda, 2001. Lay Rep., Council of Inns of Court, 2004–. Vice-Chm., FCO Assoc., 1993–07. Chm., Ampfield Parish Council, 1993–. Trustee, Pimpernel Trust, 2007–. Hon. LLD Southampton, 1994. *Recreations:* travel, gardening, cooking, tennis. *Address:* Hill House, Knapp, Ampfield, Romsey, Hants SO51 9BT.

ROTHWELL, Dame Nancy (Jane), DBE 2005; PhD, DSc; FMedSci; FRS 2004; FIBiol; MRC Professor of Physiology, since 1994, and Deputy President and Deputy Vice-Chancellor, since 2007, University of Manchester (Vice President for Research, 2004–07). *Educ:* Univ. of London (BSc, PhD, DSc). Royal Soc. Res. Fellow, 1987, then Reader in Physiol Scis, and formerly Res. and Graduate Dean for Biol Scis, Univ. of Manchester. Chm., MRC Neurosci. and Mental Health Bd, 2002–04; Member, Council: MRC, 2000–04; BBSRC, 2005–; Cancer Res. UK, 2002–08; NESTA, 2002–06. Chm., Wellcome Trust Public Engagement Strategy Gp, 2005–08. President: British Neurosci. Assoc., 2000–03; Bioscis Fedn, 2008–. Royal Instn Christmas Lectures, 1998. FMedSci 1999; Hon. FRCP 2006; FRSA. *Publications:* over 250 research papers and several books. *Address:* Faculty of Life Sciences, Michael Smith Building, University of Manchester, Oxford Road, Manchester M13 9PT.

ROUCH, Peter Christopher; QC 1996; *b* 15 June 1947; *s* of Rupert Trevelyan Rouch and Doris Linda Rouch; *m* 1980, Carol Sandra Francis; one *s* one *d*. *Educ:* UCW, Aberystwyth (LLB). Called to the Bar, Gray's Inn, 1972. *Recreations:* golf, ski-ing, fishing, cinema, music. *Address:* Church View, 9 Mayals Road, Mayals, Swansea SA3 5BT; 20 Archery Close, W2 2BE.

ROUGIER, Maj.-Gen. Charles Jeremy, CB 1986; FICE; Director, Royal Horticultural Society's Garden, Rosemoor, 1988–95; *b* 23 Feb. 1933; *s* of late Lt-Col and Mrs C. L. Rougier; *m* 1964, Judith Cawood Ellis; three *s* one *d*. *Educ:* Marlborough Coll.; Pembroke Coll., Cambridge (MA). FICE 1986. Aden, 1960; Instructor, RMA Sandhurst, 1961–62; psc 1963; MA to MGO, 1964–66; comd 11 Engineer Sqn, Commonwealth Bde, 1966–68; jssc 1968; Company Comd, RMA Sandhurst, 1969–70; Directing Staff, Staff Coll., Camberley, 1970–72; CO 21 Engineer Regt, BAOR, 1972–74; Staff of Chief of Defence Staff, 1974–77; Commandant, Royal Sch. of Military Engineering, 1977–79; RCDS 1980; COS, Headquarters Northern Ireland, 1981; Asst Chief of General Staff (Trng), 1982–83; Dir of Army Training, 1983–84; Chm., Review of Officer Training and Educn Study, 1985; Engr-in-Chief (Army), 1985–88, retd. Col Comdt, RE, 1987–92. Mem. (part-time), Lord Chancellor's Panel of Ind. Inspectors, 1988–2003. Gold Veitch Meml Medal, RHS, 1995. *Recreations:* hill walking, DIY, gardening. *Address:* c/o Lloyds TSB, 5 High Street, Bideford, Devon EX39 2AD.

ROULSTONE, Brig. Joan Margaret; Director, Women (Army), 1992–94; Aide-de-Camp to the Queen, 1992–95; *b* 7 Nov. 1945; *d* of Eric Laurie Frank Tyler and Jessie Tyler (*née* Louise); *m* 1971, Peter John Roulstone. *Educ:* seven schools worldwide. Commnd, WRAC, 1964; UK and BAOR, 1965–78; resigned 1978, reinstated, 1980; UK, 1980–86; Corps Recruiting and Liaison Officer, WRAC, 1986–87; Chief G1/G4 NE Dist and 2nd Inf. Div., 1988–89; Comd WRAC, UKLF, 1990–92. *Address:* c/o Barclays Bank, Priestpopple, Hexham, Northumberland NE46 1PE.

ROUND, Prof. Nicholas Grenville, FBA 1996; Hughes Professor of Hispanic Studies, University of Sheffield, 1994–2003, now Emeritus; *b* 6 June 1938; *s* of Isaac Eric Round and Laura Christabel (*née* Poole); *m* 1966, Ann Le Vin; one *d*. *Educ:* Boyton CP Sch., Cornwall; Launceston Coll.; Pembroke Coll., Oxford. BA (1st cl. Hons, Spanish and French) 1959; MA 1963; DPhil 1967. MITI 1990. Lecturer in Spanish, Queen's Univ. of Belfast, 1962–71, Reader, 1971–72; Warden, Alanbrooke Hall, QUB, 1970–72; Stevenson Prof. of Hispanic Studies, Glasgow Univ., 1972–94. Mem., Exec. Cttee, Strathclyde Region Labour Party, 1986–94; Chm., Cornwall Labour Party, 2007–. Pres., Assoc. Internat. de Galdosistas, 1999–2001. Officer, Order of Isabel the Catholic (Spain), 1990. *Publications:* Unamuno: Abel Sánchez: a critical guide, 1974; The Greatest Man Uncrowned: a study of the fall of Alvaro de Luna, 1986; trans., Tirso de Molina, Damned for Despair, 1986; (ed) Re-reading Unamuno, 1989; On Reasoning and Realism: three easy pieces, 1991; Libro llamado Fedrón, 1993; (ed) Translation Studies in Hispanic Contexts, 1998; (ed) New Galdo's Studies, 2003; contribs to: Mod. Lang. Review, Bulletin Hispanic Studies, Proc. Royal Irish Academy, etc. *Recreations:* reading, music, all aspects of Cornwall. *Address:* 10 King's Road, Penzance, Cornwall TR18 4LG. *Club:* (Hon. Life Mem.) Students' Union (Belfast).

ROUNDS, Helen; *see* Edwards, H.

ROUNTREE, His Honour Peter Charles Robert; a Circuit Judge, 1986–2001; *b* 28 April 1936; *s* of late Francis Robert George Rountree, MBE and Mary Felicity Patricia Rountree, MBE (*née* Wilson); *m* 1st, 1968, Nicola Mary (*née* Norman-Butler) (marr. diss. 1996); one *s*, and one step *d*; 2nd, 2004, Shirley Murray (*née* Arbuthnot); one step *s* one step *d*. *Educ:* Uppingham School; St John's College, Cambridge (MA). Called to the Bar, Inner Temple, 1961; a Recorder, April–July 1986. *Recreations:* sailing, golf, tennis. *Clubs:* Boodle's, Pratt's, Royal Yacht Squadron; Rye Golf, New Zealand Golf.

ROUQUIER, Prof. Raphaël Alexis Marcel, PhD; Waynflete Professor of Pure Mathematics, University of Oxford, since 2007; Fellow of Magdalen College, Oxford, since 2007; *b* Etampes, France, 9 Dec. 1969; *s* of Pierre Rouquier and Danièle Rouquier (*née* Raynaud); *m* 2003, Dr Meredith Cohen. *Educ:* Lycée Saint-Louis, Paris; Ecole

Normale Supérieure, Paris; Université Paris 7 (PhD 1992). Chargé de Recherches, 1992–2002, Dir de Recherches, 2002–05, CNRS; Prof. of Representation Theory, Univ. of Leeds, 2005–06. *Address:* Magdalen College, Oxford OX1 4AU; *e-mail:* rouquier@maths.ox.ac.uk.

ROUS, family name of **Earl of Stradbroke**.

ROUS, Matthew James; HM Diplomatic Service; Deputy Head of Mission, since 2005 and Consul General, since 2008, Jakarta; *b* 29 June 1964; *s* of Ronald Frank Rous and Florence Mary (*née* Woodward); *m* 1989, Beryl Ann Scott; one *s* two *d*. *Educ:* Churchill Coll., Cambridge (BA 1986; MA 1989). Chugai Pharmaceutical Co. Ltd, Tokyo, 1986–88; Asahi Shimbun European Gen. Bureau, London, 1989–91; joined HM Diplomatic Service, 1991; First Secretary: (Chancery), Peking, 1994–97; (Commercial), Tokyo, 1998–2001; Dep. Hd of Mission and Consul-Gen., Brussels, 2002–05. *Recreations:* globetrotting, star gazing, tracing obscure ancestors, raising the next generation. *Address:* c/o Foreign and Commonwealth Office, King Charles Street, SW1A 2AH.

ROUSE, Jonathan Mark; Chief Executive, London Borough of Croydon, since 2007; *b* 23 May 1968; *s* of James Clement Rouse and Barbara Jean Rouse (*née* Fowler); *m* 1991, Heulwen Mary Evans. *Educ:* Univ. of Manchester (LLB); Univ. of Nottingham (MBA Finance Dist.); Univ. of N London (MA Dist.). Principal Policy Officer, Ealing BC, 1992–93; Policy Analyst, Energy Saving Trust, 1993–94; Private Sec. to Housing Minister, 1994–95; Policy and Communications Manager, English Partnerships, 1995–98; Sec., Govt Urban Task Force, 1998–99; Chief Executive: CABE, 2000–04; Housing Corp., 2004–07. Non-exec. Dir, English Partnerships, 2004–07. Trustee, Homeless Internat., 2005–. FA Referee, 2004–. Hon. RIBA 2001; Hon. RTPI 2002. DUniv Oxford Brookes, 2003. *Recreations:* tennis, golf, hiking. *Address:* London Borough of Croydon, Taberner House, Park Lane, Croydon CR9 3JS. *Club:* Queen's Park Rangers Football.

ROUSE, Ruth Elizabeth; Permanent Representative of Grenada to the United Nations, New York (with personal rank of Ambassador), 2004–07; *b* 30 Jan. 1963. *Educ:* German Foundn for Internat. Develt, Berlin (Dip. Internat. Relns and Econ. Co-operation 1987); Diplomatic Acad. of London, PCL, (Post-Grad. Prog. in Diplomacy, Practice, Procedures, Dynamics 1989); Carleton Univ., Canada (BA French and Spanish 1996); Univ. of Westminster, London (MA Diplomatic Studies 2002). Ministry of Foreign Affairs, Grenada: Desk Officer (Africa and ME Affairs), Political and Economic Affairs Div., 1982–83; Protocol Officer, Protocol and Consular Div., 1983–90; Second Sec. (Protocol, Culture and Develt), Orgn of Eastern Caribbean States, High Commn, Ottawa, 1990–96; Chief of Protocol, 1996–99; High Comr in UK, 1999–2004; High Comr (non resident) to S Africa, 2000–05; Ambassador Designate to France, 2001–04. Perm Rep., IMO, 2000–. Mem., Nat. Celebrations Cttee, Grenada, 1996; Governor: Commonwealth Inst., 1999–; Commonwealth Foundn, 1999–. Independence Award for Exemplary Public Service, 1998. *Recreations:* reading, travelling, Caribbean cooking, tennis, designing (art), photography, meeting people of different cultures, communications (radio/television), music (piano). *Address:* Westerhall, St David's, Grenada. *T:* 4435316; *e-mail:* ruthelizabethrouse@hotmail.com. *Clubs:* Royal Over-Seas League, Royal Commonwealth Society.

ROUSSEAU, Prof. George Sebastian, PhD; Professor, Faculty of History and Co-Director, Centre for the History of Childhood, since 2003, University of Oxford; *b* 23 Feb. 1941; *s* of Hyman Victoire Rousseau and Esther (*née* Zacuto). *Educ:* Amherst Coll., USA (BA 1962); Princeton Univ. (MA 1964; PhD 1966). Princeton University: Osgood Fellow in English Lit., 1965–66; Woodrow Wilson Dissertation Fellow, 1966; Instructor, then Asst Prof., Harvard Univ., 1966–68; University of California, Los Angeles: Asst Prof. of English, 1968–69; Associate Prof., 1969–76; Prof., 1976–94; Regius Prof. of English Lit. and Dir, Thomas Reid Inst., Aberdeen Univ., 1994–98; Res. Prof. of English, De Montfort Univ., 1999–2003, now Prof. Emeritus. Fulbright Res. Prof., W Germany, 1970; Cambridge University: Hon. Fellow, Wolfson Coll., 1974–75; Overseas Fellow, 1979; Vis. Fellow Commoner, Trinity Coll., 1982; Sen. Fulbright Res. Schol., Sir Thomas Browne Inst., Netherlands, 1983; Vis. Exchange Prof., King's Coll., Cambridge, 1984; Clark Liby Prof., Univ. of Calif, 1985–86; Sen. Fellow, NEH, 1986–87; Vis. Fellow and Waynflete Lectr, Magdalen Coll., Oxford, 1993–94. Book reviewer, NY Times (Sunday), 1967–82. FRSocMed 1967; FRSA 1973. Dr *hc* Bucharest, 2007. *Publications:* (with M. Hope Nicolson) This Long Disease My Life: Alexander Pope and the sciences, 1968; (with N. Rudenstine) English Poetic Satire, 1969; (ed jtly) The Augustan Milieu: essays presented to Louis A. Landa, 1970; (ed jtly) Tobias Smollett: bicentennial essays presented to Lewis M. Knapp, 1971; (ed) Organic Form: the life of an idea, 1972; Goldsmith: the critical heritage, 1974; (with R. Porter) The Ferment of Knowledge: studies in the historiography of science, 1980; The Letters and Private Papers of Sir John Hill, 1981; Tobias Smollett: essays of two decades, 1982; (ed) Science and the Imagination: the Berkeley Conference, 1987; (with R. Porter) Sexual Underworlds of the Enlightenment, 1987; (with P. Rogers) The Enduring Legacy: Alexander Pope Tercentenary Essays, 1988; (with R. Porter) Exoticism in the Enlightenment, 1990; The Languages of Psyche: mind and body in enlightenment thought, 1990; Perilous Enlightenment: pre- and post-modern discourses - sexual, historical, 1991; Enlightenment Crossings: pre- and post-modern discourses - anthropological, 1991; Enlightenment Borders: pre- and post-modern discourses - medical, scientific, 1991; (jtly) Hysteria Before Freud, 1993; (with Roy Porter) Gout: the patrician malady, 1998; Framing and Imagining Disease in Cultural History, 2003; Yourcenar: a biography, 2004; Nervous Acts: essays on literature, culture and sensibility, 2004; Children and Sexuality: the Greeks to the Great War, 2007; contrib. numerous articles to learned jls and mags. *Recreations:* chamber music, opera, walking, hiking. *Address:* Magdalen College, Oxford OX1 4AU; *e-mail:* george.rousseau@ntlworld.com.

ROUSSEL, (Philip) Lyon, OBE 1974; Controller, Arts Division, British Council, 1979–83; retired; *b* 17 Oct. 1923; *s* of late Paul Marie Roussel and Beatrice (*née* Cuthbert; later Lady Murray); *m* 1959, Elisabeth Mary (*d* 2007), *d* of Kenneth and Kathleen Bennett; one *s* one *d*. *Educ:* Hurstpierpoint Coll.; St Edmund Hall, Oxford (MA, Cert. Public and Social Admin); Chelsea Sch. of Art. Served Indian Army in Parachute Regt, 1942–46 (Major); Parachute Regt (TA), 1946–50. Sudan Political Service, 1950–55; Principal, War Office, 1955–56; Associated Newspapers, 1956–57; British Council, 1960–83: India, 1960–67 (Regional Rep., Western and Central India, 1964–67); Dir, Scholarships, 1967–71; Rep. and Cultural Attaché, British Embassy, Belgium and Luxembourg, 1971–76; Europalia-Great Britain Festival Cttee, 1973; Cultural Attaché (Counsellor), British Embassy, Washington, 1976–79. Sponsorship Consultant, National Theatre, 1983–84. Member: Fest. of India Cttee, 1981–82; British Adv. Cttee, Britain Salutes New York, 1981–83; Bd, The Hanover Band, 1984–87; Common Room, Wolfson Coll., Oxford, 1988 (Chm., Arts Soc., 2000–). Hon. Organiser, Poppy Appeal, Woodstock Br., Royal British Legion, 1991–97 (Cert. of Appreciation, 1997). FRGS 1981; FRSA 1979. *Recreations:* painting, looking at pictures, travel, tennis, golf and a barn in France. *Address:* 26 High Street, Woodstock, Oxford OX20 1TG. *Clubs:* Athenæum; Oxford Union; Woodstock Tennis; North Oxford Golf.

ROUSSOS, Stavros G.; Secretary General, Ministry of Foreign Affairs, Greece, 1980–82, retired; *b* 1918; *m*; two *s* one *d*. *Educ:* Univ. of Lyons (LèsL); Univ. of Paris (LèsL, LèsScPol, LLD). Entered Greek Diplomatic Service as Attaché, Min. of Foreign Affairs, 1946; Mem., Greek Delegn to Gen. Assembly of UN, 1948 and 1954–55; Sec. to Permanent Mission of Greece to UN in New York, 1950; Consul, Alexandria, 1955; i/c Greek Consulate General, Cairo, 1956; Counsellor, 1959; Min. of Foreign Affairs, 1959–61; Mem., Perm. Delegn of Greece to EEC, Brussels, 1962; Perm. Rep. to EEC, 1969; Dir-Gen., Econ. and Commercial Affairs, Min. of Foreign Affairs, 1972; Ambassador of Greece to UK, 1974–79; Alternate Sec. Gen., Min. of Foreign Affairs, 1979–80. Grand Comdr, Order of Phoenix; Commander: Order of Belgian Crown; Order of Merit of Egypt. *Publication:* The Status of Dodecanese Islands in International Law, 1940 (Paris).

ROUT, Leslie; Director General, National Kidney Research Fund and Kidney Foundation, 1992–97; *b* 5 Dec. 1936; *s* of James Rout and Ada Elizabeth Rout; *m* 1957, Josephine Goodley; one *s* one *d*. *Educ:* Queens, Wisbech. Police cadet, 1952–54; Nat. Service, 1954–56; Police Service, 1956–89: served in all depts; attained rank of Comdr Ops; awarded 6 commendations. FCMI. *Recreations:* music, history, travel.

ROUT, Owen Howard, FCIB; Executive Director (UK Operations), Barclays PLC and Barclays Bank PLC, 1987–90; Chairman: Barclays Financial Services Ltd, 1988–90; Starmin plc, 1990–93 (Deputy Chairman, 1993–94); *b* 16 April 1930; *s* of Frederick Owen and Marion Rout; *m* 1954, Jean (*née* Greetham); two *d*. *Educ:* Grey High Sch., Port Elizabeth, SA. ACIS. Dir, Barclays Bank UK Ltd, 1977–87; Gen. Man., Barclays PLC and Barclays Bank PLC, 1982–87. Chairman: Barclays Insurance Services Co. Ltd, 1982–85; Barclays Insurance Brokers International Ltd, 1982–85; Mercantile Gp, 1989–92; Director: Spreadeagle Insurance Co. Ltd, 1983–85; Baric Ltd, 1982–84; Albaraka Internat. Bank, 1990–93. Chartered Institute of Bankers: Mem. Council, 1985–90; Treas., 1986–90. Mem., Supervisory Bd, Banking World Magazine, 1986–90. Mem., Bd of Govs, Anglia Polytechnic Univ., 1993–2001. *Recreations:* watching sport—Rugby and cricket, playing golf, listening to music, gardening. *Club:* Aldeburgh Golf.

ROUTH, Donald Thomas; Under Secretary, Department of the Environment, 1978–90; *b* 22 May 1936; *s* of Thomas and Flora Routh; *m* 1961, Janet Hilda Allum. *Educ:* Leeds Modern Sch. Entered WO, Northern Comd, York, as Exec. Officer, 1954; Nat. Service, RN, 1954–56; Higher Exec. Officer, Comd Secretariat, Kenya, 1961–64; Asst Principal, Min. of Housing and Local Govt, 1964–66; Asst Private Sec. to Minister, 1966–67; Principal, 1967; on loan to Civil Service Selection Bd, 1971; Asst Sec., DoE, 1972; Under Sec., 1978; Regional Dir, West Midlands, 1978–81; Hd of Construction Industries Directorate, 1981–85; Dir of Senior Staff Management, 1985–86; Controller, The Crown Suppliers, 1986.

ROUTLEDGE, (Katherine) Patricia, CBE 2004 (OBE 1993); actress; *b* 17 Feb. 1929; *d* of Isaac Edgar Routledge and Catherine (*née* Perry). *Educ:* Birkenhead High Sch.; Univ. of Liverpool; Bristol Old Vic Theatre Sch.; Guildhall Sch. of Music. *Theatre* appearances include: A Midsummer's Night Dream, Liverpool Playhouse, 1952; The Duenna, Westminster, 1954; musical version, The Comedy of Errors, Arts, 1956; The Love Doctor, Piccadilly, 1959; revue, Out of My Mind, Lyric, Hammersmith, 1961; Little Mary Sunshine, Comedy, 1962; Virtue in Danger, Mermaid, transf. Strand, 1963; How's the World Treating You?, Hampstead Theatre Club, 1965, New Arts, transf. Wyndham's, Comedy and Broadway, 1966; Darling of the Day, George Abbott, NY, 1967 (Antoinette Perry Award); The Caucasian Chalk Circle, The Country Wife, and The Magistrate, Chichester Fest., 1969; Cowardy Custard, Mermaid, 1972; Dandy Dick, Chichester Fest., transf. Garrick, 1973; 1600 Pennsylvania Avenue, Mark Hellinger, NY, 1976; Pirates of Penzance, NY, 1980; Noises Off, Savoy, 1981; When the Wind Blows, Whitehall, 1983; Richard III, RSC, 1984–85; Candide, Old Vic, 1988–89 (Laurence Olivier Award); Come for the Ride (one-woman show), Playhouse, 1989; Carousel, NT, 1992; The Rivals, Albery, 1994; Beatrix, Chichester, 1996, transf. Greenwich, 1997; The Importance of Being Earnest, Chichester, transf. Haymarket, 1999, Savoy, 2001; Wild Orchids, Chichester, 2002; The Solid Gold Cadillac, Garrick, 2004; The Best of Friends, Hampstead, 2006; Office Suite, Chichester, 2007; *television* appearances include: Doris and Doreen, 1978; A Woman of No Importance, 1982; Victoria Wood As Seen on TV, 1983–86; Marjorie and Men, 1985; A Lady of Letters, 1988; Keeping Up Appearances (5 series), 1990–95; Hetty Wainthropp Investigates (4 series), 1996–98; Miss Fozzard finds her Feet, 1998; many radio plays. *Address:* c/o Penny Wesson Management, 26 King Henry's Road, NW3 3RP.

ROUTLEDGE, Air Vice-Marshal Martin John; Chief of Staff Strategy, Policy and Plans, Headquarters Air Command, High Wycombe, since 2007; *b* 22 Nov. 1954; *s* of James Routledge and Pamela Routledge (*née* Bangor-Ward); *m* 1981, Annette Powell; one *s* one *d*. *Educ:* St John's Sch., Episkopi; Glyn Sch.; Portsmouth Poly. (BSc Elec. Engrg); RAF Coll., Cranwell. Front-line service as navigator on Phantoms, 1977–89; commanded 29 (F) Sqdn equipped with Tornadoes, 1995–97; Comdr, British Air Forces Italy, 1999; Dep. Principal SO to Chief of Defence Staff, 1999–2001; AO Scotland and Comdr RAF Leuchars, 2001–03; staff duties, MoD, 2003–05; Nat. Mil. Rep. to SHAPE, 2006. *Recreations:* watching wildlife, ornithology, walking, fighting the lawn, thinking about learning to dive, playing atrocious golf. *Address:* Headquarters Air Command, RAF High Wycombe HP14 4UE. *Club:* Royal Air Force.

ROUX, Michel André, Hon. OBE 2002; Director and Chef de Cuisine, since 1967; *b* 19 April 1941; *s* of late Henry Roux and Germaine Triger; *m* 1984, Robyn (Margaret Joyce); one *s* two *d* by previous marr. *Educ:* Ecole Primaire, Saint Mande; Brevet de Maîtrise (Pâtisserie). Apprenticeship, Pâtisserie Loyal, Paris, 1955–57; Commis Pâtissier-Cuisinier, British Embassy, Paris, 1957–59; Commis de Cuisine with Miss Cécile de Rothschild, Paris, 1959–60; Military service, 1960–62, at Versailles and Colomb Bechar, Sahara; Chef with Miss Cécile de Rothschild, 1962–67; came to England, 1967; restaurants opened: Le Gavroche, 1967; Le Poulbot, 1969; Waterside Inn, 1972; Gavvers, 1981. Mem., UK Br., Académie Culinaire de France, 1984–. TV series, At Home with the Roux Brothers, 1988. Numerous French and British prizes and awards, including: Médaille d'Or, Cuisiniers Français, 1972; Restaurateur of the Year, Caterer & Hotelkeeper, 1985; Personnalité de l'Année, Gastronomie dans le Monde, Paris, 1985; Culinary Trophy, Assoc. of Maîtres-Pâtissiers La Saint Michel, 1986; (with Albert Roux) Men of the Year (Radar), 1989; (with Albert Roux) Lifetime Achievement Award, Restaurant Magazine, 2006. Chevalier, National Order of Merit (France), 1987; Officer, Order of Agricultural Merit (France), 1987; Chevalier, Order of Arts and of Letters (France), 1990; Chevalier, Legion of Honour (France), 2004. *Publications:* Desserts: a lifelong passion, 1994; Sauces, 1996; Life is a Menu (autobiog.), 2000; Only the Best, 2002; Eggs, 2006; Pastry, 2008; with Albert Roux: New Classic Cuisine, 1983 (French edn, 1985); The Roux Brothers on Pâtisserie, 1986; At Home with the Roux Brothers, 1988; French Country Cooking, 1989; Cooking for Two, 1991. *Recreations:* shooting, walking, ski-ing. *Address:* The

Waterside Inn, Ferry Road, Bray, Berks SL6 2AT. *T:* (01628) 620691; 1 Bettoney Vere, Bray, Berks SL6 2BA. *Club:* The Benedicts.

ROVE, Rev. Sir Ikan, KBE 2005; Spiritual Authority of the Christian Fellowship Church, Solomon Islands, since 1990; *b* 13 Sept. 1942; *s* of late Silas Eto (Founder and Holy Mama, Christian Fellowship Ch) and Mary Nanasabe; *m* 1981, Marama Elesi Lupaqula; four *s* one *d*. Began church work at age 14; ordained minister, 1960; succeeded father to take control of tasks and responsibilities, Christian Fellowship Ch, 1983. Encourages and engages rural community participation in socio-econ. develt. *Address:* Christian Fellowship Church, Duvaha Village, PO Box 974, Honiara, Solomon Islands; *e-mail:* ocksi@hotmail.com.

ROWALLAN, 4th Baron *cr* 1911; **John Polson Cameron Corbett;** Director: Rowallan Holdings, since 1991; Rowallan Activity Centre Ltd, since 1991; Rowallan Asset Management, since 2002; *b* 8 March 1947; *s* of 3rd Baron Rowallan and of his 1st wife, Eleanor Mary Boyle; *S* father, 1993; *m* 1st, 1971, Jane Green (marr. diss. 1983); one *s* one *d*; 2nd, 1984, Sandrew Bryson (marr. diss. 1994); one *s* one *d*; 3rd, 1995, Claire Dinning; one step *s* one step *d*. *Educ:* Cothill House; Eton Coll.; RAC, Cirencester. Chartered Surveyor, 1972–; farmer, 1975–; equestrian centre owner. British Show Jumping Association: Area Rep., 1982–2007; Judge, 1982–; Dir, 1998–; FEI Jumping Judge, 2000–. Commentator at equestrian events. Contested (C): Glasgow, Garscadden, Oct. 1974; Kilmarnock, 1979. Former Member All Party Groups on: Mental Health; Clinical Depression; Arts and Heritage; Alternative Medicine; Racing and Bloodstock; Rwanda and Genocide; Conservation; Advertising; Epilepsy; introduced Mental Health (Amendment) Act 1998 to H of L. Mem., Greenway Cttee. Dir, SANE, 1996–2007. Patron, Depression Alliance, 1998–. Chm., Lochgoin Covenanters Trust, 1977–. *Recreations:* commentating, ski-ing. *Heir:* *s* Hon. Jason William Polson Cameron Corbett [*b* 21 April 1972; *m* 2000, Anna, *d* of Chris Smedley; two *s*]. *Address:* Meiklemosside, Fenwick, Ayrshire KA3 6AY. *T:* (01560) 600769.

ROWAN, David; Editor, Wired magazine, since 2008; *b* 8 April 1965; *s* of Nigel Rowan and Iris Rowan; *m* 1995, Sarah Harris; two *s* one *d*. *Educ:* Haberdashers' Aske's Sch. for Boys; Gonville and Caius Coll., Cambridge (BA Hist. 1988). Trainee journalist, The Times, 1988–89; The Guardian, 1990–2000: Editor: EG and Education magazines, 1990–93; Outlook, Saturday section, 1993–94; Comment and letters, 1994–97; Analysis page, 1997–98; The Editor magazine, 1998–99; Guardian Unlimited websites, 1999–2000; freelance journalist and broadcaster, 2000–06: columnist, The Times; interviewer for Evening Standard; magazine writer, Sunday Times and Telegraph; film maker, Channel 4 News and More4 News; Editor, The Jewish Chronicle, 2006–08. *Publication:* A Glossary for the Nineties, 1998. *Recreations:* cycling past traffic, family adventures, accumulating newsprint. *Address:* Wired, Condé Nast Publications, 6–8 Old Bond Street, W1S 4PH. *T:* (020) 7499 9080; *e-mail:* david.rowan@condenast.co.uk.

ROWAN, Patricia Adrienne, (Mrs Ivan Rowan); journalist; Editor, The Times Educational Supplement, 1989–97; *d* of late Henry Matthew Talintyre and Gladys Talintyre; *m* 1960, Ivan Settle Harris Rowan; one *s*. *Educ:* Harrow County Grammar School for Girls. Time & Tide, 1952–56; Sunday Express, 1956–57; Daily Sketch, 1957–58; News Chronicle, 1958–60; Granada Television, 1961–62; Sunday Times, 1962–66; TES, 1972–97. Mem. Bd of Trustees, Nat. Children's Bureau, 1997–2003; Trustee, Stroud Valleys Project, 2001– (Chm., 2002–). Hon. Fellow, Inst. of Educn, London Univ., 1997. Hon. FRSA 1989. *Publications:* What Sort of Life?, 1980; (contrib.) Education—the Wasted Years?, 1988. *Recreations:* cookery, gardening. *Club:* Reform.

See also D. G. Talintyre.

ROWAN-ROBINSON, Prof. (Geoffrey) Michael, PhD; FInstP; Professor of Astrophysics, Blackett Laboratory, since 1993, and Head, Astrophysics Group, 1993–2007, Imperial College, University of London; *b* 9 July 1942; *s* of John Christopher Rowan-Robinson and Audrey Christine (*née* Wynne); *m* 1978, Mary Lewin (*née* Tubb); one *d*, and two step *s*. *Educ:* Eshton Hall Sch., Gargrave, Yorks; Pembroke Coll., Cambridge (BA 1963); Royal Holloway Coll., London (PhD 1969). FInstP 1992. Queen Mary, later Queen Mary and Westfield College, London: Asst Lectr in Maths, QMC, 1967–69; Lectr, 1969–78; Reader in Astronomy, 1978–87; Prof. of Astrophysics, 1987–93. Royal Soc. and Academia dei Lincei Vis. Res. Fellow, Univ. of Bologna, 1969, 1971, 1976; Vis. Res. Fellow, Univ. of Calif, Berkeley, 1978–79. Member: Exec. Cttee, IAU Commn 47 on Cosmology, 1976–79; Sci. Team for Infrared Astronomical Satellite, 1977–84; Astronomy Wkg Gp, ESA, 1985–88; Space Sci. Prog. Bd, BNSC, 1988–91. Chm., Time Allocation Cttee, Isaac Newton Gp, 1988–91; Member, Time Allocation Committee: ESA's Infrared Space Observatory mission, 1993–96; Hubble Space Telescope, 1995 and 2000. Co-investigator, Infrared Space Observatory Photometer, ESA, 1996–99; Principal Investigator, European Large Area ISO Survey, 1995–2000. Chm., Res. Assessment Panel for Astronomy, PPARC, 1994–97. Mem., RAS, 1965– (Pres., 2006–08). Mem., Scientists for Global Responsibility, 1992–; Vice-Chm., Scientists Against Nuclear Arms, 1988–92. Chm., Hornsey Lab. Party, 1971–72. Governor: Creighton Comp. Sch., 1971–78; Fortismere Comp. Sch., 1985–88. Daiwa Adrian Prize, Daiwa Anglo-Japanese Foundn, 2004; Hoyle Medal, Inst. of Physics, 2008. *Publications:* Cosmology, 1977, 4th edn 2004; Cosmic Landscape, 1979; The Cosmological Distance Ladder, 1985; Fire and Ice: the nuclear winter, 1985; Our Universe: an armchair guide, 1990; Ripples in the Cosmos, 1993; Nine Numbers of the Cosmos, 1999; numerous research papers in astronomical jls, articles and book reviews. *Recreations:* poetry, politics, going to the theatre, music, especially Liszt, golf. *Address:* Astrophysics Group, Blackett Laboratory, Imperial College, Prince Consort Road, SW7 2AZ. *T:* (020) 7594 7530.

ROWBOTHAM, Prof. Sheila; Professor of Gender and Labour History, University of Manchester, since 2003; *b* 27 Feb. 1943; *d* of Lancelot and Jean Rowbotham; one *s* with Paul Atkinson. *Educ:* Hunmanby Hall Sch.; St Hilda's Coll., Oxford (BA Hons Hist. 1964); Chelsea Coll., London Univ. Lectr in Liberal Studies, Chelsea Coll. of Advanced Technol. and Tower Hamlets Coll. of Further Educn, 1964–68; Extra-mural Lectr, WEA, 1968–80; Vis. Prof. in Women's Studies, Univ. of Amsterdam, 1981–83; Res. Officer, Industry and Employment Dept, GLC, 1983–86; Course Tutor, MA Women's Studies, Univ. of Kent, 1987–89; Res. Advr, World Inst. for Develt and Econ. Res., Helsinki, UN Univ., 1987–91; Sociology Department, Manchester University: Simon Res. Fellow, 1993–94; Sen. Res. Fellow, 1995–2000; Sen. Lectr, 2000–01; Reader, 2001–03. FRSA. Hon. DSSc N London, 1994. *Publications:* Women, Resistance and Revolution, 1973; Woman's Consciousness, Man's World, 1973; Hidden from History, 1973; Socialism and the New Life, 1977; A New World for Women: Stella Browne, Socialist Feminist, 1977; (jtly) Beyond the Fragments: Feminism and the Making of Socialism, 1980; Dreams and Dilemmas: collected writings, 1983; Friends of Alice Wheeldon, 1986; The Past is Before Us: feminism in action since the 1960s, 1989; Women in Movement: feminism and social action, 1993; Homeworkers Worldwide, 1993; A Century of Women, 1999; Threads Through Time, 1999; Promise of a Dream, 2000; *edited jointly:* Dutiful Daughters: women talk about their lives, 1977; Dignity and Daily Bread: new forms of economic organisation among poor women, 1994; Women Encounter Technology, 1995; Women Resist Globalization, 2001; Looking at Class, 2001. *Recreations:* cinema, reading, swimming. *Address:* 4 High Lane, Chorlton, Manchester M21 9DF.

ROWE, Prof. Adrian Harold Redfern; Professor of Conservative Dentistry, University of London, at Guy's Hospital, 1971–91, now Professor Emeritus; Dean of Dental Studies, 1985–89, Dean of Dental Sch., 1989–91, and Head of Department of Conservative Dental Surgery, 1967–91, United Medical and Dental Schools of Guy's and St Thomas' Hospitals (Hon. Fellow, 1997); *b* 30 Dec. 1925; *y s* of late Harold Ridges Rowe and Emma Eliza (*née* Matthews), Lymington, Hants; *m* 1951, Patricia Mary Flett; three *s*. *Educ:* King Edward VI Sch., Southampton; Guy's Hosp. Dental Sch., London Univ. (BDS 1948, distinguished in Surgery, Op. Dental Surgery, Dental Surgery and Orthodontics; distinguished in Dental Anatomy, 2nd BDS, 1946); MDS London, 1965. FDSRCS 1954; MCCDRCS 1989. Nat. Service, RADC, 1949–50. Guy's Hospital Dental School: part-time practice and teaching, 1950–63; Sen. Lectr, 1963–67; Hon. Consultant, 1966–; Univ. Reader, 1967–71; London University: Chm., Bd of Studies in Dentistry, 1980–83; Mem., Senate, 1981–83. Member: Lewisham and N Southwark DHA, 1986–90; Special HA, 1986–90. Member: Dental Sub-Cttee, UGC, 1974–83; Council, Medical Defence Union, 1977–96; Specialist Adv. Cttee in Restorative Dentistry, 1979–85; Bd, Faculty in Dental Surgery, RCS, 1980–93 (Vice Dean, 1987); Faculty Advr for SE Thames reg., RCS, 1983–89; President: British Endodontic Soc., 1964 (Hon. Mem., 1974); British Soc. for Restorative Dentistry, 1978 (Hon. Mem., 1991). Past examiner in dental surgery in Univs of Belfast, Birmingham, Cardiff, Colombo, Dublin, Dundee, Edinburgh, Lagos, London, Malaysia, Malta, Manchester, Nairobi, Newcastle and Singapore; Statutory Exam. of GDC; Examnr for Licence and Fellowship exams of RCS and for Fellowship of RCSI. Dir, Medical Sickness Annuity and Life Assce Soc., 1987–95. Governor: UMDS of Guy's and St Thomas' Hosps, 1985–91; Eastman Dental Hosp., 1986–90. First Pres., GKT Dental Alumni Assoc., 2003–05. Governor: Walmer Sci. Coll., 1997–; Kingsdown and Ringwood C of E Primary Sch., 1997–. Freeman, City of London, 1990; Liveryman, Soc. of Apothecaries, 1995–. Hon. FKC 1998. Colyer Gold Medal, Faculty of Dental Surgery, RCS, 1993. *Publications:* (Ed. in Chief) Companion to Dental Studies, vol. I: Book I, Anatomy, Biochemistry and Physiology, 1982; Book II, Dental Anatomy and Embryology, 1981; vol. II, Clinical Methods, Medicine, Pathology and Pharmacology, 1988; vol. III, Clinical Dentistry, 1986; contrib. to British and foreign dental jls. *Recreations:* DIY, gardening. *Address:* Manor Lodge, Manor Mews, Ringwould, Deal, Kent CT14 8HT. *T:* (01304) 375487.

See also O. J. T. Rowe.

ROWE, Andrew John Bernard; DL; *b* 11 Sept. 1935; *s* of John Douglas Rowe and Mary Katharine Storr; *m* 1st, 1960, Alison Boyd (marr. diss.); one *s*; 2nd, 1983, Sheila L. Finkle, PhD; two step *d*. *Educ:* Eton Coll.; Merton Coll., Oxford (MA). Sub Lt RNVR, 1954–56. Schoolmaster, 1959–62; Principal, Scottish Office, 1962–67; Lectr, Edinburgh Univ., 1967–74; Consultant to Voluntary Services Unit, Home Office, 1974; Dir, Community Affairs, Cons. Central Office, 1975–79; self-employed consultant and journalist, 1979–83. MP (C) Mid Kent, 1983–97, Faversham and Mid Kent, 1997–2001. PPS to Minister for Trade, 1992–95. Chm., Parly Panel for Personal Social Services, 1986–92; Member: Public Accounts Cttee, 1995–97; Internat. Develt Cttee, 1997–2001. Chm. Steering Cttee, UK Youth Parlt, 1998–2001. Pres., Kent Youth. *Publications:* Democracy Renewed, 1975; pamphlets and articles incl. Somewhere to Start. *Recreations:* fishing, reading, theatre. *Address:* Knowle Cottage, The Green, Bearsted, Maidstone, Kent ME14 4DN.

ROWE, Bridget; Content Director, Yava, since 2000; *b* 16 March 1950; *d* of late Peter and Myrtle Rowe; *m*; one *s*. *Educ:* St Michael's School, Limpsfield. Editor, Look Now, 1971–76; Editor, Woman's World, 1976–81; Asst Editor, The Sun, 1981–82; Editor: Sunday Magazine, 1982–86; Woman's Own, 1986–90; TV Times, 1990–91; Sunday Mirror, 1991–92; Editor, 1992–96, Man. Dir, 1995–98, The People; Man. Dir, 1995–98, and Editor, 1997–98, Sunday Mirror; Dir of Communications, Nat. Magazines, 1998–99. *Recreations:* football, shopping.

ROWE, Crispin; Headmaster, St Paul's School, São Paulo, Brazil, since 2008; *b* 28 May 1955; *s* of Peter Whitmill Rowe, *qv*; *m* 1977, Jillian Highton; two *s* one *d*. *Educ:* Univ. of Newcastle upon Tyne (BA Hons; PGCE). Assistant Teacher: Watford Boys' Grammar Sch., 1978–80; Royal Grammar Sch., Newcastle upon Tyne, 1980–92; Dep. Hd, 1992–2004, Headmaster, 2004–08, King Edward's Sch., Bath. *Recreations:* sport, running, golf, music. *Address:* St Paul's School, Rua Juquia 166, J. Paulistano CEP 01440–903, São Paulo, Brazil.

ROWE, Jennifer, (Mrs J. Ellis); Chief Executive Designate, UK Supreme Court, since 2008; *b* 2 Oct. 1955; *d* of Caryl Rowe and Beryl Rose Florence Rowe; *m* 1993, John Richard Ellis. *Educ:* Sir James Smith's Sch., Camelford; King's Coll., London (BA Hons Hist. 1977); Coll. of Law, Lancaster Gate; Birkbeck Coll., London (MSc Policy Admin 1984). Principal Private Sec. to Lord Chancellor, 1990–93; Principal Estabt and Finance Officer, Serious Fraud Office, 1993–95; Lord Chancellor's Department: Hd, Criminal Policy, 1995–97; Principal Private Sec. to Lord Chancellor, 1997–99; Dir, Corporate Services, 1999–2002; Dir, Finance and Corporate Affairs, 2002–03; Sec., Butterfield Rev., 2003; Dir, Policy Admin, Attorney General's Office, 2004–08. Trustee, RBL, 2005–. *Recreations:* reading, theatre, opera, gardening, cricket. *Address:* Judicial Office, House of Lords, SW1A 0PW. *T:* (020) 7219 3146, *Fax:* (020) 7271 2433; *e-mail:* rowej@parliament.uk. *Clubs:* Royal Over-Seas League, Middlesex CC, Surrey CC.

ROWE, Judith May; QC 2003; a Recorder, since 1999; a Deputy High Court Judge, since 2005; *b* 7 Aug. 1957; *d* of David and Eileen Rowe; *m* 1989, Bill Waite; two *d*. *Educ:* Rednock Sch., Dursley; UCL (LLB Hons). Called to the Bar: Gray's Inn, 1979, Bencher, 2007; Lincoln's Inn, 1988. *Recreations:* playing with the children, ski-ing, scuba diving. *Address:* 1 Garden Court, Temple, EC4Y 9BJ. *T:* (020) 7797 7900, *Fax:* (020) 7797 7929; *e-mail:* clerks@1gc.com.

ROWE, Owen John Tressider, MA; retired; *b* 30 July 1922; *e s* of late Harold Ridges Rowe and Emma E. Rowe (*née* Matthews), Lymington, Hampshire; *m* 1946, Marcelle Ljufliny Hyde-Johnson (*d* 1986); one *s* one *d*. *Educ:* King Edward VI School, Southampton; Exeter College, Oxford (Scholar, MA); 1st Cl. Hons in Classical Hon. Mods, 1942. Served War of 1939–45, Lieut in Roy. Hampshire Regt, 1942–45. 1st Cl. Hons in Lit Hum, Dec. 1947; Assistant Master: Royal Grammar School, Lancaster, 1948–50; Charterhouse, 1950–60 (Head of Classical Dept); Officer Comdg Charterhouse CCF, 1954–60; Headmaster: Giggleswick School, 1961–70; Epsom College, 1970–82; Head of Classics, St John's Sch., Leatherhead, 1982–87. *Recreations:* Rotary, gardening, playing the recorder. *Address:* 8 Pine Hill, Epsom KT18 7BG. *Club:* Rotary (Epsom).

See also A. H. R. Rowe.

ROWE, Rear-Adm. Sir Patrick (Barton), KCVO 2002 (LVO 1975); CBE 1990; Deputy Master and Chairman of the Board, Trinity House, 1996–2002; Chairman, General Lighthouse Authority, 1996–2002; *b* 14 April 1939; *e s* of Captain G. B. Rowe, DSC, RN and Doreen Rowe (*née* Robarts), Liphook, Hants; *m* 1964, Alexandra, *e d* of

Alexander Mellor, OBE; one *s* one *d*. *Educ:* Wellington College; RNC Dartmouth. Served Far East Fleet, 1960–65; specialised in Navigation, 1966; navigation appts, 1966–70; Comd, HMS Soberton, 1970–71; Army Staff Coll., 1972; Navigation Officer, HM Yacht Britannia, 1973–75; Comd, HMS Antelope, 1977–79; Naval Staff appts, 1979–82; Comd, HMS Keren, 1983; Comd, HMS Liverpool, 1983–85; RN Presentation Team, 1985–86; Commodore, Clyde, 1986–88; RCDS 1989; Mil. Deputy, Defence Export Services, 1990–92; Clerk to the Worshipful Co. of Leathersellers, 1993–96. Liveryman: Shipwrights' Co., 1993–2008; Leathersellers' Co., 1996–. *Recreations:* sailing, ski-ing. *Address:* Juniper Cottage, Meonstoke, Southampton, Hampshire SO32 3NA. *Clubs:* Army and Navy; Royal Yacht Squadron; Hornet Sailing, Ocean Cruising.

ROWE, Prof. Peter John, PhD; Professor of Law, since 1995, and Head of School of Law, 1995–2000 and 2003–05, Lancaster University; *s* of late Major Dennis Rowe and Anne Rowe; *m* 1970, Anne Murland, *d* of D. A. White, OBE and J. C. White; one *s* one *d*. *Educ:* Methodist Coll., Belfast; Queen's Univ. Belfast (LLB); University College London (LLM); Univ. of Liverpool (PhD). Called to the Bar, Lincoln's Inn, 1979. Appts at Anglia Poly., 1970–77 and Lancashire Poly., 1977–79; University of Liverpool, 1979–95: Prof. of Law, 1988–95; Head of Dept of Law, 1988–93. Dir of Legal Studies, Cayman Islands Law Sch., 1982–84; Sir Ninian Stephen Vis. Scholar, Faculty of Law, Univ. of Melbourne, 2003. Chm., Ind. Tribunal Service, subseq. Tribunals Service, 1988–2008. Chm., UK Gp, Internat. Soc. for Mil. Law and Law of War, 1990–98. Mem., Governing Body, St Martin's Coll., Lancaster, 2005–07. *Publications:* (with S. Knapp) Evidence and Procedure in the Magistrates' Court, 1983, 3rd edn 1989; (ed with C. Whelan) Military Intervention in Democratic Societies, 1985; Defence: the legal implications, military law and the laws of war, 1987; (ed) The Gulf War 1990–91, in International and English Law, 1993; (ed jtly) The Permanent International Criminal Court, 2004; The Impact of Human Rights Law on Armed Forces, 2006; contrib. on War and Armed Conflict to vol. 49 (i) and on Legal Position of the Armed Forces to vol. 2 (ii), Halsbury's Laws of England; articles in learned jls. *Recreations:* sailing, hill-walking, buying at auction. *Address:* Lancaster University Law School, Lancaster LA1 4YN.

ROWE, Prof. Peter Noël, DSc(Eng); FREng, FIChemE; Ramsay Memorial Professor of Chemical Engineering, and Head of Department, University College London, 1965–85, now Professor Emeritus; *b* 25 Dec. 1919; *e s* of Charles Henry Rowe and Kate Winifred (*née* Storry); *m* 1952, Pauline Garmirian; two *s*. *Educ:* Preston Grammar Sch.; Manchester Coll. of Technology; Imperial Coll., London. Princ. Scientific Officer, AERE, Harwell, 1958–65. Crabtree Orator, 1980. Vis. Prof., Univ. Libre de Bruxelles, 1988, 1995. Advr, HEFCE, 1992– (Chm., Assessment Panel, 1992, 1996). Non-exec. Dir, Bentham Fine Chemicals, 1985–; Consultant, SERC, 1990–. Pres., IChemE, 1981–82; Hon. Sec., Fellowship of Engrg, 1982–85. FCGI 1983. Hon. Fellow, UCL, 1993. Hon. DSc Brussels, 1978. *Publications:* scientific articles in Trans IChemE, Chem. Eng. Science, etc. *Address:* Pamber Green, Upper Basildon, Reading, Berks RG8 8PG. *T:* (01491) 671382.

ROWE, Peter Whitmill, MA; Schoolteacher at Kent College, Canterbury, 1983–90, retired; *b* 12 Feb. 1928; British; *s* of Gerald Whitmill Rowe, chartered accountant, one-time General Manager of Morris Commercial Cars Ltd; *m* 1952, Bridget Ann Moyle; two *s* one *d*. *Educ:* Bishop's Stortford College; St John's College, Cambridge. BA 1950; MA (Hons) 1956. VI Form History Master, Brentwood School, Essex, 1951–54; Senior History Master, Repton School, Derbys, 1954–57; Headmaster: Bishop's Stortford Coll., Herts, 1957–70; Cranbrook Sch., Kent, 1970–81; teacher, Williston-Northampton Sch., Mass, USA, 1981–83. JP Bishop's Stortford, 1968–70, Cranbrook, 1971–81. *Recreations:* literature, music, woodland restoration, golf.
See also C. Rowe.

ROWE, Robert Stewart, CBE 1969; Director, Leeds City Art Gallery and Temple Newsam House, 1958–83 (and also of Lotherton Hall, 1968–83); *b* 31 Dec. 1920; *s* of late James Stewart Rowe and late Mrs A. G. Gillespie; *m* 1953, Barbara Elizabeth Hamilton Baynes; one *s* two *d*. *Educ:* privately; Downing Coll., Cambridge; Richmond Sch. of Art. Served RAF, 1941–46. Asst Keeper of Art, Birmingham Museum and Art Gallery, 1950–56; Dep. Dir, Manchester City Art Galls, 1956–58. Pres., Museums Assoc., 1973–74; Member: Adv. Council, V&A Mus., 1969–74; Arts Council of GB, 1981–86; Fine Arts Adv. Cttee, British Council, 1972–84; Chm., Bar Convent Museum Trust, York, 1986–91; Trustee, Henry Moore Sculpture Trust, 1983–95. Liveryman, Worshipful Co. of Goldsmiths. Hon. LittD Leeds, 1983. *Publications:* Adam Silver, 1965; articles in Burlington Magazine, Museums Jl, etc. *Recreations:* gardening, reading. *Address:* Grove Lodge, Shadwell, Leeds LS17 8LB. *T:* (0113) 265 6365.

ROWE, Dr Roy Ernest, CBE 1977; FREng; consultant; Director General, Cement and Concrete Association, 1977–87; *b* 26 Jan. 1929; *s* of Ernest Walter Rowe and Louisa Rowe; *m* 1954, Lillian Anderson; one *d*. *Educ:* Taunton's Sch., Southampton; Pembroke Coll., Cambridge (MA, ScD). FICE, FIStructE; FREng (FEng 1979). Cement and Concrete Association: later British Cement Association: Research Engineer, 1952–57; Head, Design Research Dept, 1958–65; Dir, R&D, 1966–77. Chm., Engrg Res. Commn, SERC, 1991–93. President: IStructE, 1983–84; Comité Euro-Internat. du Béton, 1987–98. Hon. Mem., Amer. Concrete Inst., 1978; For. Associate, Nat. Acad. of Engineering, USA, 1980. Hon. DEng Leeds, 1984. *Publications:* Concrete Bridge Design, 1962, 3rd impr. 1972; numerous papers in technical and professional jls. *Recreations:* fell walking, listening to music, playing bridge. *Address:* 15 Hollesley Road, Alderton, Woodbridge, Suffolk IP12 3BX. *T:* (01394) 411096.

ROWE-BEDDOE, family name of **Baron Rowe-Beddoe**.

ROWE-BEDDOE, Baron *cr* 2006 (Life Peer), of Kilgetty in the County of Dyfed; **David Sydney Rowe-Beddoe,** Kt 2000; DL; Chairman, Wales Millennium Centre, since 2001; *b* 19 Dec. 1937; *s* of late Sydney Rowe-Beddoe and Dolan Rowe-Beddoe (*née* Evans); *m* 1st, 1962, Malinda Collison (marr. diss. 1982); three *d*; 2nd, 1984, Madeleine Harrison. *Educ:* Cathedral Sch., Llandaff; Stowe Sch.; St John's Coll., Cambridge (MA); Harvard Univ. Grad. Sch. of Business Admin (PMD). Served RN, Sub-Lt, RNVR, 1956–58, Lieut, RNR, 1958–66. Thomas de la Rue & Company, 1961–76: Chief Executive, 1971–76; Exec. Dir, De la Rue Co. plc, 1974–76; Revlon Inc., NY, 1976–81; President: Latin America and Caribbean, 1976–77; Europe, ME and Africa, 1977–81; Pres. and Chief Exec. Officer, Ges. für Trendanalysen, 1981–87; Director: Morgan Stanley-GFTA Ltd, 1983–91; Development Securities plc, 1994–2000; EHC International Ltd and subsidiaries, 2001–; Newport Networks Gp plc, 2004–; Chairman: Victoria Capital (UK) Ltd, 2004–07; GFTA Analytics Ltd, 2005–; Dep. Chm., Toye Gp plc, 2003–. Dep. Chm., UK Statistics Authority, 2008–; Chairman: Welsh Development Agency, 1993–2001; Develt Bd for Rural Wales, 1994–98; N Wales Econ. Forum, 1996–2001; Mid Wales Partnership, 1996–2001; SE Wales Econ. Forum, 1999–2001; Wales N America Business Council, 1999–2004 (Pres., 2004–05); Cardiff Business Club, 2002–06 (Pres., 2006–); Member: Welsh Economic Council, 1994–96; UK Regl Policy Forum, 1999–2002; Chm., Rep. Body, Church in Wales, 2002–; Pres., Welsh Centre for Internat. Affairs, 1999–2005. Director: Welsh Internat. Film Fest. Ltd, 1998–2000; Cardiff Internat. Festival of Musical Theatre Ltd, 2000–04; City of London Sinfonia, 2000–03;

President: Celtic Film Festival, 2000; Llangollen Internat. Musical Eisteddfod, 2000–05; Johnian Soc., Cambridge Univ., 2007. Mem., Prince of Wales' Cttee, 1994–97; Patron: Prince's Trust Bro, 1997–; Menuhin Competition, 2008. Pro-Chancellor, Glamorgan Univ., 2007–. Pres., RWCMD (formerly WCMD), 2004– (Gov., 1993–2004; Chm., 2000–04). Liveryman, 1993–. Mem. Ct of Assts, 2002–, Broderers' Co. DL Gwent, 2003. CCMI; FRSA 1993. Hon. Fellow: Univ. of Wales Coll. Newport, 1998; Cardiff Univ., 1999; UWIC, 2002. DUniv Glamorgan, 1997; Hon. DScEcon Wales, 2004. *Recreations:* music, theatre, country pursuits. *Address:* Wales Millennium Centre, Bute Place, Cardiff CF10 5AL. *T:* (029) 2063 6400, *Fax:* (029) 2063 6401. *Clubs:* Garrick; Cardiff & County; Brook (New York); Automobile (Monaco).

ROWE-HAM, Sir David (Kenneth), GBE 1986; chartered accountant, since 1962; Lord Mayor of London, 1986–87; Consultant to Touche Ross & Co., 1984–93; *b* 19 Dec. 1935; *o s* of late Kenneth Henry and Muriel Phyllis Rowe-Ham; *m* Sandra Celia (*née* Nicholls), *widow* of Ian Glover; three *s*. *Educ:* Dragon School; Charterhouse. FCA. Commnd 3rd King's Own Hussars. Mem., Stock Exchange, 1964–84; Sen. Partner, Smith Keen Cutler, 1972–82. Chairman: Asset Trust plc, 1982–89; Jersey General Investment Trust Ltd, 1988–89; Olayan Europe Ltd, 1989–; Brewin Dolphin Hldgs PLC, 1992–2003; APTA Healthcare PLC, 1994–96; Coral Products PLC, 1995–2006; Peninsular S Asia Investment Co. (formerly BNP Paribas South Asia Investment Co.) Ltd, 1995–2008; Arden Partners PLC, 2006–; Jt Chm., Gradus Group PLC, 1995–97; Regional Dir (London), Lloyds Bank plc, 1985–91; Director: W. Canning plc, 1981–86; Savoy Theatre Ltd, 1986–98; Williams PLC, 1992–2000; CLS Hldgs plc, 1994–99; Chubb plc, 2000–03; Hikma Pharmaceuticals plc, 2005–. Pres., Crown Agents Foundn, 1996–2002. Chm., Adv. Panel, Guinness Flight Unit Trust Managers Ltd, 1987–99. Alderman, City of London, Ward of Bridge and Bridge Without, 1976–2004; Sheriff, City of London, 1984–85; HM Lieut, City of London, 1987–2004. Liveryman: Worshipful Co. of Chartered Accountants in England and Wales (Master, 1985–86); Worshipful Co. of Wheelwrights; Hon. Mem., Worshipful Co. of Launderers. Mem. Ct, 1981–86, Chancellor, 1986–87, City Univ. Gov., Royal Shakespeare Co., 1988–2003; former Trustee, Friends of D'Oyly Carte. Pres., Black Country Mus. Develt Trust. Chm., Birmingham Municipal Bank, 1970–72; Mem., Birmingham CC, 1965–72. Chm., Political Council, Junior Carlton Club, 1977; Dep. Chm., Political Cttee, Carlton Club, 1977–79; Chm., 1900 Club, 2003–08. Member: Lord's Taverners; Pilgrims. JP City of London, 1976 (Chief Magistrate, 1986–87; Supp. List, 1994–). Hon. DLitt City Univ., 1986. KJStJ 1986. Commandeur de l'Ordre Mérite, France, 1984; Commander, Order of the Lion, Malaŵi, 1985; Order of the Aztec Eagle (Cl. II), Mexico, 1985; Order of King Abdul Aziz (Cl. 1), 1987; Grand Officer, Order of Wissam Alouite, Morocco, 1987; Order of Diego Losada, Caracas, Venezuela, 1987; Pedro Ernesto Medal, Rio de Janeiro, 1987. *Recreation:* theatre. *Address:* 140 Piccadilly, W1J 7NS. *Club:* Carlton.

ROWELL, Anthony Aylett, CMG 1992; Senior Consultant, since 2006 and Member Advisory Council, since 2007, Good Governance Group (G3 UK); *b* 10 Jan. 1937; *s* of Geoffrey William and Violet Ella Aylett Rowell; *m* 1st, 1965, Bridget Jane Reekie (marr. diss. 1985); one *s* one *d*; 2nd, 1985, Caroline Anne Edgcumbe. *Educ:* Marlborough. With British American Tobacco, 1959–65; HM Diplomatic Service, 1966–93: 2nd Sec., Lusaka, 1968–69; 1st Secretary: FCO, 1969; Bucharest, 1970–73; FCO, 1974–78; Nicosia, 1979–80; FCO, 1981–85; Counsellor: Nairobi, 1985–90; Pretoria, 1990–93. Pol Advr (Southern Africa), Racal Radio Group UK, 1993; Dir, Racal Electronics SA Ltd, 1994; Pol Advr (Southern Africa), Racal Electronics PLC, 1996–97; Consultant (Africa), Kroll Associates, 1998–2005. *Recreations:* tennis, badminton, hiking, photography, fine wines. *Address:* Bracken Cottage, Devauden, Monmouthshire NP16 6NS. *Club:* Muthaiga Country (Nairobi).

ROWELL, Rt Rev. Dr (Douglas) Geoffrey; *see* Gibraltar in Europe, Bishop of.

ROWELL, Jack, OBE 1998; Chairman, Celsis plc, 1997–98 and since 2000 (Director, 1995; Chief Executive, 1998–2000); President, Bath Rugby Football Club, since 2007 (Director, 2002–07); *s* of late Edwin Cecil Rowell and Monica Mary Rowell (*née* Day); *m* 1969, Susan, *d* of Alan Cooper; two *s*. *Educ:* West Hartlepool Grammar Sch.; St Edmund Hall, Oxford (MA). FCA 1964. With Procter & Gamble to 1976; Finance Dir, then Chief Exec., Lucas Ingredients, Bristol, 1976–88; Chief Exec., Golden Wonder, 1988–92; Exec. Dir, Dalgety, 1993–94; Chairman: Lyon Seafoods Ltd, 1994–2003; Marlar Bennetts Internat. Ltd, 1994–99; Dolphin Computer Services Ltd, 1994–99; OSI Ltd, 1995–99; Pilgrim Foods Ltd, 1995–2004; Coppice Ltd, 2002–04; Ukrproduct Gp, 2004–; Dir, Oliver Ashworth Gp, 1997–98. Played for Gosforth RFC, later Newcastle Gosforth (Captain, later coach; Cup winners, 1976); coach, Bath RFC, 1977–94: Cup winners 8 times, League winners 5 times, Middlesex Sevens winners, 1994; Manager, England RFU Team, 1994–97; Dir, 1998–2000, Man. Dir, 2000–02, Bristol Rugby Ltd. Member: Bd, Sport England, 2006–; Council, Prince's Trust (SW), 2008–. Hon. LLD Bath, 1994.

ROWELL, Prof. John Martin, DPhil; FRS 1989; Visiting Professor, Arizona State University, since 2002; *b* 27 June 1935; *s* of Frank L. and P. E. Rowell; *m* 1959, Judith A. Harte; two *s* one *d*. *Educ:* Wadham Coll., Oxford (BSc, MA; DPhil 1961). Bell Telephone Labs, 1961–84; Bell Communications Research, 1984–89; Conductus Inc., 1989–95; Prof., Materials Res. Inst., Northwestern Univ., 1997. Member: Acad. of Scis, 1994; Acad. of Engrg, 1995. Fellow, Amer. Physical Soc., 1974. Fritz London Meml Low Temperature Physics Prize, 1978. *Publications:* about 100 pubns in jls. *Address:* 102 Exeter Drive, Berkeley Heights, NJ 07922, USA. *T:* (908) 4646994.

ROWEN, Paul John; MP (Lib Dem) Rochdale, since 2005; *b* 11 May 1955. *Educ:* Bishop Henshaw RC Meml High Sch., Rochdale; Univ. of Nottingham (BSc 1976); PGCE 1977; NPQH 2004. Teacher of sci., Kimberley Comprehensive Sch., Nottingham, 1977–80; Hd of Chemistry, St Albans RC High Sch., Oldham, 1980–86; Hd of Sci., Our Lady's RC High Sch., Oldham, 1986–90; Dep. Headteacher, Yorkshire Martyrs Catholic Coll., Bradford, 1990–2005. Mem. (Lib Dem), Rochdale MBC, 1983–2006. Contested (Lib Dem) Rochdale, 2001. *Address:* (office) 144 Drake Street, Rochdale, Lancs OL16 1PS; House of Commons, SW1A 0AA.

ROWLAND, Rev. Prof. Christopher Charles; Dean Ireland's Professor of the Exegesis of Holy Scripture, and Fellow of Queen's College, University of Oxford, since 1991; *b* Doncaster, 21 May 1947; *s* of late Eric Rowland and Frances Mary Lawson; *m* 1969, Catherine Rogers; three *s* one *d*. *Educ:* Doncaster Grammar Sch.; Christ's Coll., Cambridge; Ridley Hall, Cambridge; BA 1969, PhD 1975, Cantab. Ordained deacon, 1975, priest 1976. Lectr in Religious Studies, Univ. of Newcastle upon Tyne, 1974–79; Curate: St James', Benwell, 1975–78; All Saints', Gosforth, 1978–79; Asst Lectr in Divinity, 1983–85, Lectr in Divinity, 1985–91, Univ. of Cambridge; Fellow and Dean, Jesus Coll., Cambridge, 1979–91. Canon Theologian, Liverpool Cathedral, 2005–. *Address:* Queen's College, Oxford OX1 4AW.

ROWLAND, Sir David; *see* Rowland, Sir J. D.

ROWLAND, David Powys; Stipendiary Magistrate, Mid Glamorgan (formerly Merthyr Tydfil), 1961–89, retired; *b* 7 Aug. 1917; *s* of late Henry Rowland, CBE, Weston-super-Mare; *m* 1st, 1946, Joan (*d* 1958), *d* of late Group Capt. J. McCrae, MBE, Weston-super-Mare; one *s* one *d*; 2nd, 1961, Jenny (marr. diss. 1977), *d* of late Percival Lance, Swanage, and *widow* of Michael A. Forester-Bennett, Alverstoke; one *s* one *d*, and one step *d*; 3rd, 1980, Diana, *d* of late W. H. Smith, Cannock, and *widow* of Lt-Col W. D. H. McCardie, S Staffs Regt; two step *d*. *Educ:* Cheltenham Coll.; Oriel Coll., Oxford (BA). Lieut, Royal Welch Fusiliers, 1940–46. Called to Bar, Middle Temple, 1947. Deputy Chairman: Glamorgan QS, 1961–71; Breconshire QS, 1964–71. Mem. Nat. Adv. Council on Training of Magistrates, 1964–73. *Recreations:* fly-fishing, gardening. *Address:* Holmdale, Cwmdu, Crickhowell, Powys NP8 1RY. *T:* (01874) 730635.

ROWLAND, Prof. F(rank) Sherwood, PhD; Donald Bren Research Professor of Chemistry, University of California at Irvine, since 1994 (Professor of Chemistry, since 1964); *b* 28 June 1927; *m* 1952, Joan Lundberg; one *s* one *d*. *Educ:* Ohio Wesleyan Univ. (AB 1948); Univ. of Chicago (MS 1951; PhD 1952). Chemistry Instr, Princeton Univ., 1952–56; Asst Prof., 1956–58, Associate Prof., 1958–63, Prof., 1963–64, of Chemistry, Univ. of Kansas; Chm. of Chemistry Dept, 1964–70, Daniel G. Aldrich, Jr Prof. of Chemistry, 1985–89, Donald Bren Prof. of Chemistry, 1989–94, Univ. of Calif at Irvine. Discovered (with Dr Mario J. Molina) that chlorofluorocarbon gases deplete the ozone layer of the stratosphere. Mem., Acid Rain Peer Review Panel, US Office of Science and Tech., 1982–84. International Association of Meteorology and Atmospheric Physics: Member: Commn on Atmospheric Chemistry and Global Pollution, 1979–91; Ozone Commn, 1980–88 (Hon. Life Mem., 1996); Jt Chm., Dahlem Conf. on Our Changing Atmosphere, Germany, 1987. Member: Amer. Acad. of Arts and Scis, 1977; NAS, 1978 (Foreign Sec., 1994–2002); AAAS (Pres., 1992; Chm. Bd, 1993; Fellow); Amer. Philosophical Soc., 1995–; Founding Mem., Academia Bibliotheca Alexandrinae, Egypt, 2004–; Fellow: APS; Amer. Geophysical Union. For. Mem., Royal Soc., 2004. Numerous hon. degrees and awards; (jtly) Nobel Prize for Chemistry, 1995. *Publications:* on atmospheric chemistry, radio-chemistry and chemical kinetics. *Address:* Department of Chemistry, University of California, 571 Rowland Hall, Irvine, CA 92697–2025, USA. *T:* (949) 8246016, *Fax:* (949) 8242905.

ROWLAND, Geoffrey Robert; Bailiff of Guernsey, since 2005; President, Court of Appeal of Guernsey, since 2005; a Judge of the Court of Appeal of Jersey, since 2005; *b* 5 Jan. 1948; *s* of late Percy George Rowland and of Muriel Florence (*née* Maunder); *m* 1972, Diana Janet Caryl; two *s*. *Educ:* Elizabeth Coll., Guernsey; Univ. of Southampton; Univ. of Caen. Called to the Bar, Gray's Inn, 1970; called to the Guernsey Bar, 1971; QC (Guernsey) 1993. In private practice as advocate, Guernsey, 1971–91; Sen. Partner, Collas Day and Rowland, 1984–91; Solicitor General for Guernsey, 1992–99; Attorney-General for Guernsey, 1999–2002; HM Receiver General for Guernsey, 1999–2002; Dep. Bailiff of Guernsey, 2002–05. Vice-Chm., Guernsey Financial Services Commn, 1988–92. Chairman: Guernsey Press Co. Ltd, 1990–92; TSB Foundn for CI, 1990–92. Provincial Grand Master, Guernsey and Alderney, United Grand Lodge of Freemasons of England, 2000–07. Hon. Fellow, Soc. for Advanced Legal Studies, 2001–. Hon. LLD Bournemouth, 2006. *Recreations:* ski-ing, reading history, international travel. *Address:* Armorica, L'Ancresse, Guernsey, CI GY3 5JR. *T:* (01481) 247494; *e-mail:* bailiff@gov.gg. *Club:* United (Guernsey).

ROWLAND, Sir (John) David, Kt 1997; President, Templeton College, Oxford, 1998–2003, Hon. Fellow 2003; Chairman and Chief Executive, National Westminster Bank plc, 1999–2000 (Joint Deputy Chairman, 1998–99); *b* 10 Aug. 1933; *s* of Cyril Arthur Rowland and Eileen Mary Rowland; *m* 1st, 1957, Giulia Powell (marr. diss. 1991); one *s* one *d*; 2nd, 1991, Diana Louise Matthews (*née* Dickie). *Educ:* St Paul's School; Trinity College, Cambridge (MA Natural Sciences). Joined Matthews Wrightson and Co., 1956, Dir, 1965; Dir, Matthews Wrightson Holdings, 1972; Dep. Chm., 1978–81, Chm., 1981–87, Stewart Wrightson Holdings plc; Dep. Chm., Willis Faber plc, 1987–88; Chief Exec., 1988–92, Chm., 1989–92, Sedgwick Gp plc; Chm. of Lloyd's, 1993–97. Chm., Westminster Insurance Agencies, 1981–88; Dir, Sedgwick Lloyd's Underwriting Agencies, 1988–92. Director: Project Fullemploy, 1973–88; Fullemploy Gp Ltd, 1989–90; non-executive Director: Royal London Mutual Insurance Soc., 1985–86; S. G. Warburg Gp, 1992–95; Somerset House Ltd, 1997–2003; NatWest Gp, 1998–2000. Mem. Council, Lloyd's, 1987–90; Mem., President's Cttee, Business in the Community, 1986–92 (Mem., City of London section, 1983–86). Vice-Pres., British Insurance and Investment Brokers' Assoc. (formerly British Insurance Brokers' Assoc.), 1980–; Member of Council: Industrial Soc., 1983–88; Contemporary Applied Arts, subseq. British Crafts Centre, 1985–92; Council of Industry and Higher Educn, 1990–92. Chm. Develt Bd, Th. Royal Bury St Edmunds, 2003–07. Member: Council, Templeton Coll. (Oxford Centre for Management Studies), 1980–2003 (Chm., 1985–92); Governing Bd, City Res. Project, 1991–92; Governor: Coll. of Insurance, 1983–85; St Paul's Schs, 1991–2007 (Dep. Chm., St Paul's Sch., 2001–07). Hon. FIA 2000; Hon. Fellow, Cardiff Univ., 1999. Hon. MA Oxford, 1993; Hon. DPhil London Guildhall, 1996; Hon. DSc City, 1997. Lloyd's Gold Medal, 1996. *Recreations:* family, admiring my wife's garden, golf, running slowly. *Address:* 44 Boss House, SE1 2PS; Giffords Hall, Wickhambrook, Newmarket, Suffolk CB8 8PQ. *T:* (01440) 820221. *Clubs:* Brooks's, MCC; Royal and Ancient Golf (St Andrews), Royal St George's (Sandwich), Royal Worlington and Newmarket Golf.

ROWLAND, John Peter; QC 1996; barrister; *b* 17 Jan. 1952; *s* of Peter Rowland and Marion Rowland (*née* Guppy); *m* 1979, Juliet Hathaway; three *s* two *d*. *Educ:* Univ. of Western Australia (BEc Hons); King's Coll., London (LLB Hons). Pilot Officer, RAAF (Reserves), 1970–72; Sen. Tutor and Lectr in Econs, Univ. of Western Australia, 1973–74; Lectr in Economics, WA Inst. of Technology, 1974–75; called to the Bar, Middle Temple, 1979; admitted to practice, NSW, 2001, Victoria, 2001. *Recreations:* cricket, walking, ski-ing. *Address:* 4 Pump Court, Temple, EC4Y 7AN. *T:* (020) 7842 5555. *Club:* Theberton Cricket.

ROWLAND, Mark; Social Security Commissioner and Child Support Commissioner, since 1993; *b* 20 July 1953; *s* of late Sqdn Leader Bernard Rowland and Elizabeth Rowland (*née* Cuerden); *m* 1977, Eileen Cleary; two *d*. *Educ:* Ampleforth Coll.; Univ. of Warwick (LLB Hons). Called to the Bar, Gray's Inn, 1975; Welfare rights adviser, CPAG, 1975–78; private practice at the Bar, 1979–93; part-time Chm., social security, medical and disability appeal tribunals, 1988–93; Dep. Social Security Comr, 1992–93; Chairman: registered homes tribunal, 1995–2002; care standards tribunal, 2002–. *Publications:* (ed jtly) Rights Guide to Non-means-tested Benefits, 2nd edn 1978, 14th edn 1991; The Industrial Injuries Scheme, 1983; Medical and Disability Appeal Tribunals: the Legislation, 1993, 3rd edn 1998; (ed jtly) Social Security Legislation, 2000, 9th edn 2009; papers on social security law. *Recreations:* railways, military history, social history. *Address:* Commissioners' Office, Third Floor, Procession House, 55 Ludgate Hill, EC4M 7JW.

ROWLAND, Rev. Mgr Phelim Christopher; Rector, St Mary's, Holly Place, Hampstead, since 2006; *b* 9 Dec. 1949; *s* of Hugh and Ann Rowland. *Educ:* Tyburn Sch.; St George's Sch., London; Campion House; St Edmund's Coll., Ware. Ordained priest, 1975; Asst Priest, Holy Trinity, Brook Green, Hammersmith, 1975–79; commnd RN Chaplaincy Service, 1979–86: served in various estabts, incl. BRNC Dartmouth; served in Falkland Is, 1982; transf. RAChD, 1986: served Germany, NI, Cyprus, Bosnia, Kosovo and RMA Sandhurst; Principal RC Chaplain and VG for HM Land Forces, 2002–06. QHC 2004–06. Gov., St Edmund's Coll., Ware, 2001–. *Recreations:* cinema, military history. *Address:* 4 Holly Place, Hampstead, NW3 6QU. *T:* (020) 7435 6678. *Club:* Army and Navy.

ROWLAND, His Honour Robert Todd; QC 1969; County Court Judge of Northern Ireland, 1974–90; President, Lands Tribunal for Northern Ireland, 1983–90; part-time Chairman, Value Added Tax Tribunals, 1990–94; *b* 12 Jan. 1922; *yr s* of late Lt-Col Charles Rowland and Jean Rowland; *m* 1952, Kathleen (*d* 1991), *er d* of late H. J. Busby, Lambourn, Berks; two *s*. *Educ:* Crossley and Porter Sch., Halifax, Yorks; Ballyclare High Sch.; Queen's Univ. of Belfast (LLB 1948). Called to Bar of N Ireland, 1949; Mem., Bar Council, 1967–72. Served 2nd Punjab Regt, IA, in India, Assam, Burma, Thailand, Malaya, 1942–46. Counsel to Attorney-Gen. for N Ireland, 1966–69; Sen. Crown Prosecutor for Co. Tyrone, 1969–72; Vice-Pres., VAT Tribunal for N Ireland, 1972–74. Served on County Court Rules Cttee, 1965–72; Chairman: War Pensions Appeal Tribunal, 1962–72; Commn of Inquiry into Housing Contracts, 1978; Member: Bd of Governors, Strathearn Sch., 1969–89; Legal Adv. Cttee, Gen. Synod of Church of Ireland, 1975–89. Chancellor, dioceses of Armagh, and Down and Dromore, 1978–89. *Recreations:* fly-fishing, golf, hill-walking. *Address:* The Periwinkle, 25 Back Lane, South Luffenham, Oakham, Rutland LE15 8NQ. *Clubs:* Flyfishers'; Rutland County Golf.

ROWLAND-JONES, Prof. Sarah Louise, (Mrs R. T. Walton), DM; FRCP; Professor of Immunology, University of Oxford, since 2000; Director of Research, MRC Laboratories, The Gambia, since 2004; Research Student, Christ Church, Oxford, since 1997; *b* 8 Nov. 1959; *d* of Timothy Louis Rowland-Jones and Kathleen Norah Rowland-Jones; *m* 1988, Dr Robert Thompson Walton. *Educ:* Girton Coll., Cambridge (BA 1st Cl. Hons 1980; MA 1984); Green Coll., Oxford (BM BCh 1983; DM 1995). MRCP 1986, FRCP 1999. Postgrad. med. trng in gen. medicine and infectious diseases, Oxford, London (St George's and Brompton Hosps) and Sheffield, 1983–89; Molecular Immunology Group, Oxford: MRC Trng Fellow, 1989–92; MRC clinician scientist, 1992–95; MRC Sen. Fellow, 1995–2000; Dir, Oxford Centre for Tropical Medicine, 2001–04. Hon. Consultant in Infectious Diseases, Churchill Hosp., Oxford, 1995–. FMedSci 2000. Elizabeth Glaser Scientist Award, Paediatric Aids Foundation, 1997. *Publications:* (ed with A. J. McMichael) Lymphocytes: a practical approach, 2000; contrib. papers to Nature, Nature Medicine, Immunity, The Lancet, Jl Exptl Medicine, Jl Immunology, Jl Virology, etc. *Recreations:* scuba diving, travel, gardening, collecting art deco, good wine and good company. *Address:* MRC Human Immunology Unit, Weatherall Institute of Molecular Medicine, John Radcliffe Hospital, Headington, Oxford OX3 9DS. *T:* (01865) 222316; 53 Jack Straw's Lane, Headington, Oxford OX3 0DW; MRC Laboratories, PO Box 273, Banjul, The Gambia.

ROWLANDS, family name of **Baron Rowlands**.

ROWLANDS, Baron *cr* 2004 (Life Peer), of Merthyr Tydfil and of Rhymney in the County of Mid-Glamorgan; **Edward Rowlands,** CBE 2002; *b* 23 Jan. 1940; *e s* of W. S. Rowlands; *m* 1968, Janice Williams (*d* 2004), Kidwelly, Carmarthenshire; two *s* one *d*. *Educ:* Rhondda Grammar Sch.; Wirral Grammar Sch.; King's Coll., London. BA Hons History (London) 1962. Research Asst, History of Parliament Trust, 1963–65; Lectr in Modern History and Govt, Welsh Coll. of Adv. Technology, 1965–66. MP (Lab): Cardiff North, 1966–70; Merthyr Tydfil, April 1972–1983, Merthyr Tydfil and Rhymney, 1983–2001. Parliamentary Under-Secretary of State: Welsh Office, 1969–70, 1974–75; FCO, 1975–76; Minister of State, FCO, 1976–79; Opposition spokesman on energy, 1980–87; Mem., Select Cttee on Foreign Affairs, 1987–2001; Chm., Jt Cttee (inquiring into strategic export controls) of Select Cttees on Defence, Internat. Develt, and Trade and Industry, 1999–2001. Trustee, History of Parliament Trust, 1991– (Chm., 1993–2001). Member: Governing Body, Commonwealth Inst., 1980–92; Academic Council, Wilton Park, 1983–92. A Booker Prize Judge, 1984. *Publications:* various articles. *Recreations:* music, golf. *Address:* 110 Duncan House, Dolphin Square, Pimlico, SW1V 3PW. *T:* (020) 7798 5647; House of Lords, SW1A 0PW; 42 Station Road, Kidwelly, Carms SA17 4UT.

ROWLANDS, Prof. Brian James, MD; Professor of Gastrointestinal Surgery, Queen's Medical Centre and University of Nottingham, since 1997; *b* 18 March 1945; *s* of Arthur Leslie Rowlands and Lilian Grace Allan; *m* 1971, Judith Thomas; one *d*. *Educ:* Wirral Grammar Sch. for Boys; Guy's Hosp., Univ. of London (MB BS 1968); Univ. of Sheffield (MD 1978). Surgical trng, Sheffield Hosps, 1971–77; Associate Prof. of Surgery, Univ. of Texas Health Sci. Center, Houston, 1977–86; Prof. of Surgery and Hd, Dept of Surgery, QUB, and Consultant Surgeon, Royal Victoria Hosp., Belfast, 1986–97. Pres., Assoc. of Surgeons of GB and Ireland, 2007–08. *Publications:* Critical Care for Post Graduate Trainees, 2005; numerous peer-reviewed contribs on surgical clinical practice, res., educn and trng. *Recreations:* the mountains and the sea, anything Greek, music and theatre. *Address:* Section of Surgery, Queen's Medical Centre/University Hospital, Nottingham NG7 2UH. *T:* (0115) 823 1149, *Fax:* (0115) 823 1160; *e-mail:* bjr.surgery@nottingham.ac.uk.

ROWLANDS, Christopher John, FCA; Chief Operating Officer and Deputy Chairman, Apace Media plc, 2006–07; *b* 29 Aug. 1951; *s* of late Wilfrid John Rowlands and of Margaretta (*née* Roberts); *m* 1978, Alison Mary Kelly; twin *d*. *Educ:* Roundhay Sch., Leeds; Gonville and Caius Coll., Cambridge (MA Econ). FCA 1975. Peat Marwick Mitchell: articled clerk, 1973–75; CA, 1975; Manager, 1981; seconded as Partner, Zambia, 1981–83; Sen. Manager, London, 1983–85; Asda Group plc: Controller, business planning, Asda Stores, 1985–86; Divl Dir, Gp Finance, 1986–88; Dep. Man. Dir and Finance Dir, Asda Gp/Property Develt and Investment cos, 1988–92; Gp Finance Dir, 1992–93, Chief Exec., 1993–97, HTV Gp plc; Chief Exec., The Television Corporation, 1998–2001. Non-executive Director: iTouch plc, 2002–05; Standard Life (formerly Deutsche) Equity Investment Trust plc, 2003–; Bristol & London plc, 2003–04. Mem. Council, ITVA, 1993–97 (Chm., Engrg Policy Gp, 1993–96). CCMI (CIMgt 1995); FRSA 1995. *Recreations:* family, theatre, church, reading, ski-ing, tennis, travel.

ROWLANDS, Sir David, KCB 2006 (CB 1991); Permanent Secretary, Department for Transport, 2003–07; *b* 31 May 1947; *s* of George and Margaret Rowlands; *m* 1975, Louise Marjorie Brown; two *s*. *Educ:* St Mary's Coll., Crosby; St Edmund Hall, Oxford. Entered Civil Service, 1974; Private Sec. to Minister of State for Industry, 1978–80; Principal, Dept of Trade, then of Transport, 1980–84; Asst Sec., 1984–90, Under Sec., 1990–93, Dept of Transport; Dep. Sec. (Dir Gen.), Dept of Transport, later DETR, then DTLR, then DfT, 1993–2003. *Address:* 22 Lyon Close, Chelmsford, Essex CM2 8NY.

ROWLANDS, Rev. Chancellor John Henry Lewis; Team Rector, Rectorial Benefice of Whitchurch, since 2001 (Vicar, 1997–2001); Chaplain of Whitchurch Hospital, since 1997; Chancellor, Llandaff Cathedral, since 2002; *b* 16 Nov. 1947; *s* of William Lewis and Elizabeth Mary Rowlands; *m* 1976, Catryn Meryl Parry Edwards; one *s* two *d*. *Educ:*

Queen Elizabeth Grammar Sch., Carmarthen; St David's University Coll., Lampeter (BA); Magdalene Coll., Cambridge (MA); Durham Univ. (MLitt); Wescott House, Cambridge. Ordained deacon, 1972, priest, 1973 (St David's Cathedral); Curate, Rectorial Benefice of Aberystwyth, 1972–76; Chaplain, St David's University Coll., Lampeter, 1976–79; Youth Chaplain, dio. of St David's, 1976–79; Dir, Academic Studies, St Michael's Coll., Llandaff, 1979–84, Sub-Warden, 1984–88, Warden, 1988–97. Lectr, Faculty of Theology, University Coll., Cardiff, later Univ. of Wales Coll. of Cardiff, then Univ. of Wales, Cardiff, 1979–97, Asst Dean, 1981–83; Dean, Faculty of Divinity: Univ. of Wales, 1991–95; Univ. of Wales, Cardiff, 1993–97. Diocesan Dir of Ordinands, Dio. Llandaff, 1985–88; Exmng Chaplain to Archbishop of Wales, 1987–91; Sec., Doctrinal Commn of the Church in Wales, 1987–94. Hon. Canon, 1990–97, Residentiary Canon, 1997–2002, Llandaff Cathedral. Chaplain, Whitchurch Br., RBL, 1997–. Pres., Diwinyddiaeth (Soc. of Theol. Grads, Univ. of Wales), 1989–92. Member: (ex officio) Governing Body of the Church in Wales, 1988–97; Court, Univ. of Wales, 1988–94; Court, Univ. of Wales Coll. of Cardiff, 1988–97; Academic Bd, Univ. of Wales, 1991–94; Council, Llandaff Cathedral Sch., 1991–. Fellow, Woodard Corp., 1993. Publications: (ed) Essays on the Kingdom of God, 1986; Church, State and Society 1827–45, 1989; Doing Theology, 1996. Recreations: beachcombing, auctioneering, antique markets. Address: The Rectory, 6 Penlline Road, Whitchurch, Cardiff CF14 2AD. T: and Fax: (029) 2062 6072; e-mail: rector@ beneficeofwhitchurch.org.uk.

ROWLANDS, John Kendall, FSA; Keeper, Department of Prints and Drawings, British Museum, 1981–91; b 18 Sept. 1931; s of Arthur and Margaret Rowlands; m 1st, 1957, Else A. H. Bachmann (marr. diss. 1981); one s two d; 2nd, 1982, Lorna Jane Lowe; one d. Educ: Chester Cathedral Choir Sch.; King's Sch., Chester; Gonville and Caius Coll., Cambridge (MA Cantab 1959); MA Oxon. FSA 1976. Asst Keeper, Dept of Art, City Mus. and Art Gall., Birmingham, 1956–60; Editor, Clarendon Press, Oxford, 1960–65; Asst Keeper, 1965–74, Dep. Keeper, 1974–81, Dept of Prints and Drawings, British Museum. Mem. Adv. Cttee, Collected Works of Erasmus, 1979–. Collaborated on film, Following the Trail of a Lost Collection, Amsterdam, 1995. Publications: David Cox Centenary Exhibition Catalogue, 1959; Graphic Work of Albrecht Dürer, 1971; Bosch, 1975; Rubens: drawings and sketches…, 1977; Urs Graf, 1977; Hercules Segers, 1979; Bosch, the Garden of Earthly Delights, 1979; German Drawings from a Private Collection, 1984; Master Drawings and Watercolours in the British Museum: from Fra Angelico to Henry Moore, 1984; The Paintings of Hans Holbein the Younger, 1985; The Age of Dürer and Holbein, 1988; Drawings by German Artists in the British Museum: 15th century, and 16th century by artists born before 1530, 1993; contribs to specialist journals, Festschriften. Recreation: music making. Address: Brant House, Brant Broughton, Lincs LN5 0SL. T: (01400) 272184. Club: Beefsteak.

ROWLATT, Amanda, (Mrs T. Heymann); Associate, Oxera, since 2007; b 21 Dec. 1962; d of Charles Rowlatt and Penelope Anne Rowlatt, qv; m 1995, Tim Heymann; two s one d. Educ: University Coll., Oxford (MA Maths); St Antony's Coll., Oxford (MPhil Econs). Economist, FCO and ODA, 1987–91; Econ. Advr, HM Treasury, 1991–95; Chief Economist: ONS, 1998–2002; Competition Commn, 2002–05; Dir, Internat. Finance and Europe (formerly Europe, Trade and Internat. Financial Instns), DFID, 2005–08. Vice Chair, Care Internat. UK, 2003–05; Treasurer: Co-operation for Develt, 1996–2004; Charities Evaluation Service, 1999–2002. Mem. Council, REconS, 2003–.

ROWLATT, Penelope Anne, PhD; economist; b 17 May 1936; d of Theodore Alexander Maurice Ionides and Anne Joyce Ionides (née Cooke); m 1961, Charles Rowlatt; one s three d. Educ: King Alfred Sch.; Somerville Coll., Oxford (BA 1959); Imperial Coll., London (PhD 1963); London Sch. of Economics (MSc 1973). Chief Economist, Economic Models Gp of Cos, 1975–76; Economist, NIESR, 1976–78; Economic Advr, HM Treasury, 1978–86; Sen. Economic Advr, Dept of Energy, 1986–88; Director: Nat. Economic Res. Associates, 1988–98; Europe Economics, 1998–2001. Publisher, Medicine Today, 2000–03. Member: Retail Prices Adv. Cttee, 1991–94; Royal Commn on Envmtl Pollution, 1996–2000; Steering Gp, Performance and Innovation Unit Project, Cabinet Office, 1999; Better Regulation Commn (formerly Task Force), 2000–07. Treas., REconS, 1999–. Publications: Group Theory and Elementary Particles, 1966; Inflation, 1992; papers in learned jls on nuclear physics and economics. Recreations: walking, sailing, bridge, eating and drinking. Address: 10 Hampstead Hill Gardens, NW3 2PL.
See also A. Rowlatt.

ROWLEY, Frederick Allan, CMG 1978; OBE 1959; MC 1945; Major (retd); HM Diplomatic Service, retired; b 27 July 1922; m 1951, Anne Crawley; one s three d. Educ: Haig Sch., Aldershot. Served War of 1939–45: Ranks, 8th Worcs Regt (TA), 1939–40; Emergency Commnd Officer, 5th Bn, 10th Baluch Regt (KGVO), Jacob's Rifles, Indian Army, Burma Campaign (MC), June 1941–Nov. 1948. At partition of India, granted regular commn (back-dated, 1942) in Worcestershire Regt, but retd (wounded), sub. Major. Joined HM Diplomatic Service, Nov. 1948: served (with brief periods in FO) in: Egypt; Ethiopia; Turkey; Burma; Singapore; Australia; Malaysia; FCO 1971–72; Under-Sec., N Ireland Office (on secondment), 1972–73; Counsellor, FCO, 1973–79. Joint Services Staff College (jssc), 1959. Recreations: cricket, golf. Clubs: Army and Navy; MCC.

ROWLEY, Geoffrey William, CBE 1989; Town Clerk, City of London, 1982–91; b 9 Sept. 1926; s of George Frederick Rowley and Ellen Mary Rowley; m 1950, Violet Gertrude Templeman; one s one d. Educ: Owens School. FCIPD (FIPM 1974). Served War, Royal Marines, 1944–47. Corporation of the City of London, 1947–: Head, Personnel Sect., 1965–74; Dep. Town Clerk, 1974–82. Trustee, Jubilee Walkway Trust, 1992–. Liveryman, Basketmakers' Co. (Prime Warden, 1990–91). Hon. Fellow, City of London Poly., subseq. London Guildhall Univ., 1991. DCL hc City, 1989. Order of White Rose, Finland, 1969; Order of Orange Nassau, Holland, 1982; Légion d'Honneur, France, 1985. OStJ 1987. Recreations: sport: badminton, cricket and soccer as a spectator. Address: 3 Wensley Avenue, Woodford Green, Essex IG8 9HE. T: (020) 8504 6270.

ROWLEY, (John) James; QC 2006; a Recorder, since 2002; b 24 June 1964; s of late John Rowley and of Gillian E. M. Rowley; m 1990, Clare Louise Brown; three s. Educ: Stonyhurst Coll.; Emmanuel Coll., Cambridge (BA Hons Classics 1985); Dip. Law. Called to the Bar, Lincoln's Inn, 1987 (Hardwicke Scholar); in practice as a barrister, Manchester, 1987–; Counsel to Royal Liverpool Children's Inq., 2000–01. Treas., Personal Injuries Bar Assoc., 2006–. Publications: (contrib.) Personal Injuries Handbook, 1997, 3rd edn 2007; contrib. articles to Jl Personal Injuries Litigation. Recreations: cricketer, gardener, cook. Address: Byrom Street Chambers, 12 Byrom Street, Manchester M3 4PP. T: (0161) 829 2100.

ROWLEY, Keith Nigel; QC 2001; s of James and Eva Rowley; m 1986, Chantal Anna Mackenzie; one s one d. Educ: King's Coll., London (LLB). Called to the Bar, Gray's Inn, 1979; in practice at Chancery Bar, 1980–. Chm., Consumer Credit Appeals Tribunal. Recreations: classical music, gardening, theatre, wine. Address: Radcliffe Chambers, 11 New Square, Lincoln's Inn, WC2A 3QB. T: (020) 7831 0081. Club: Hurlingham.

ROWLEY, Sir Richard (Charles), 8th Bt cr 1836, of Hill House, Berkshire, and 9th Bt cr 1786, of Tendring Hall, Suffolk; Partner, PRW LLP, since 2006; b 14 Aug. 1959; s of Sir Charles Robert Rowley, 7th and 8th Bt and of Astrid Pennington Cleife, d of Sir Arthur Massey, CBE; S father, 2008; m 1989, Elizabeth Alison (marr. diss. 1999), d of late Henry Bellingham; two s. Educ: Exeter Coll., Oxford (BA Metallurgy and Material Scis 1982); Open Univ. (BSc Psychol. 2005); Nottingham Univ. (MSc Occupational Psychol. 2006). Director: Prolantic, 2001–; Flemprat Ltd, 2007–; Mansley Travel Apartments (International) Ltd, 2008–. Heir: s Joshua Andrew Rowley, b 5 Dec. 1989. Address: 21 Tedworth Square, SW3 4DR; Lodge Farm, Pickworth, Stamford, Rutland, PE9 4DJ.

ROWLEY-CONWY, family name of **Baron Langford.**

ROWLING, Joanne Kathleen, OBE 2000; FRSL; writer of children's books; b 31 July 1965; d of Peter John Rowling and late Anne Rowling; m 1st, 1992 (marr. diss.); one d; 2nd, 2001, Dr Neil Murray; one s one d. Educ: Univ. of Exeter (BA 1986). FRSL 2002. Author of the Year, British Book Awards, 2000. Publications: Harry Potter and the Philosopher's Stone, 1997 (Smarties Prize, 1997; filmed, 2001); Harry Potter and the Chamber of Secrets, 1998 (Smarties Prize, 1998; Children's Book Award, Scottish Arts Council, 1999; filmed, 2002); Harry Potter and the Prisoner of Azkaban, 1999 (Smarties Prize, 1999; Whitbread Children's Book of the Year, 2000; filmed, 2004); Harry Potter and the Goblet of Fire, 2000 (WH Smith Children's Book of the Year, Children's Book Award, Scottish Arts Council, 2001; filmed, 2005); Harry Potter and the Order of the Phoenix, 2003 (filmed, 2007); Harry Potter and the Half-Blood Prince, 2005; Harry Potter and the Deathly Hallows, 2007; The Tales of Beedle the Bard, 2008. Address: c/o Christopher Little Literary Agency, Ten Eel Brook Studios, 125 Moore Park Road, SW6 4PS.

ROWLING, Sir John (Reginald), Kt 2003; educational consultant; Headteacher, Nunthorpe School, Middlesbrough, 1984–2003; b 8 Jan. 1941; m 1977, Sheila Elizabeth; one s one d. Educ: Durham Univ. (BSc Maths 1962; MSc Applied Maths 1963). Teacher, Royal GS, Newcastle, 1963–74; teacher, later Dep. Head, Hirst High Sch., Ashington, 1974–84. Vis. Prof., St Mary's UC, Twickenham. Publications: Heading Towards Excellence, 2002, 2nd edn 2003; Changing Towards Excellence, 2003; Climbing Towards Excellence, 2006. Recreations: golf, photography, walking, gardening. Address: Cromwell House, 38 College Square, Stokesley TS9 5DW. T: (01642) 712095; e-mail: therowlings@hotmail.com.

ROWLINSON, Sir John (Shipley), Kt 2000; DPhil; FRS 1970; FREng, FRSC, FIChemE; Dr Lee's Professor of Physical Chemistry, Oxford University, 1974–93, now Emeritus; Fellow of Exeter College, Oxford, since 1974; b 12 May 1926; er s of late Frank Rowlinson and Winifred (née Jones); m 1952, Nancy Gaskell; one s one d. Educ: Rossall School (Scholar); Trinity College, Oxford (Millard Scholar; BSc, MA, DPhil; Hon. Fellow, 1992). Research Associate, Univ. of Wisconsin, USA, 1950–51; ICI Research Fellow, Lecturer, and Senior Lecturer in Chemistry, University of Manchester, 1951–60; Prof. of Chemical Technology, London Univ. (Imperial Coll.), 1961–73. Mary Upson Prof. of Engrg, 1988, Andrew D. White Prof.-at-large, 1990–96, Cornell Univ. Lectures: Liversidge, Chem. Soc., 1978; von Hofmann, Gesell. Deutscher Chem., 1980; Faraday, 1983, Lennard-Jones, 1985, Priestley, 2004, RSC; Guggenheim, Reading Univ., 1986; T. W. Leland, Rice Univ., Houston, Texas, 1990; Rossini, IUPAC, 1992; Dreyfus, Dartmouth Coll., 1993; Birch, ANU, 1994. Pres., Faraday Div., Chem. Soc., 1979–81; Hon. Treas., Faraday Society, 1968–71; Vice-Pres., Royal Instn of GB, 1974–76, 1993–95; Physical Sec. and Vice-Pres., Royal Soc., 1994–99. Member, Sale Borough Council, 1956–59. FREng (FEng 1976). Hon. FCGI 1987. Hon. For. Mem., Amer. Acad. of Arts and Scis, 1994. Meldola Medal, Roy. Inst. of Chemistry, 1954; Marlow Medal, Faraday Soc., 1957; Leverhulme Medal, Royal Soc., 1993; Edelstein Award, ACS, 2008. Publications: Liquids and Liquid Mixtures, 1959, (jtly) 3rd edn, 1982; The Perfect Gas, 1963; Physics of Simple Liquids (joint editor), 1968; (trans. jtly) The Metric System, 1969; (jtly) Thermodynamics for Chemical Engineers, 1975; (jtly) Molecular Theory of Capillarity, 1982; (ed) J. D. van der Waals, On the Continuity of the Gaseous and Liquid States, 1988; (jtly) Record of the Royal Society 1940–1989, 1993; (jtly) Van der Waals and Molecular Science, 1996; Cohesion: a scientific history of intermolecular forces, 2002; papers in scientific journals. Recreation: hill walking. Address: 12 Pullens Field, Headington, Oxford OX3 0BU. T: (01865) 767507; Physical and Theoretical Chemistry Laboratory, South Parks Road, Oxford OX1 3QZ. T: (01865) 275157. Club: Alpine.

ROWNTREE, Timothy John; Director General Air Support, Defence Equipment and Support, Ministry of Defence, since 2007; b 13 Sept. 1956; s of George Arthur and Cicely Beryl Rowntree; m 1982, Susan Margaret Jones; two d. Educ: Strenshall Primary Sch.; Joseph Rowntree Secondary Modern Sch.; Univ. of Bradford (BTech Hons Electrical Engrg). Systems Analyst, Army Electro Magnetic Compatibility Agency, Blandford, 1980–84; Sen. Engr, RAE, Farnborough, 1984–87; Attack and Identification System Manager, NATO Eur. Fighter Aircraft Mgt Agency, Munich, 1987–92; Head, RAF Signal Engrg Labs, RAF Henlow, 1992–96; Head, Tornado Mission Systems Support Authy, 1996–99; Dep. Tornado Integrated Project Team Leader, 1999–2001, RAF Wyton; Lynx Helicopter Integrated Project Team Leader, Yeovilton, 2001–04; Dep. Ops Dir, Air Systems, Defence Procurement Agency, Bristol, 2004–07. Recreations: more than I can fit in my busy lifestyle, involving family, friends and the family dog, including walking, gardening, theatre, music, boating, fishing, vintage motorcycles and tractors. Address: Defence Equipment and Support, Walnut 2c # 1232, MoD Abbey Wood, Bristol BS34 8JH. Club: Royal Air Force.

ROWSELL, Edmund Charles P.; see Penning-Rowsell.

ROWSON, John Anthony; Director, Royal & Sun Alliance Insurance Group, 1996–2000; b 6 May 1930; s of Thomas Herbert Rowson and Hilda Elizabeth Rowson; m 1st, 1955, Elizabeth Mary (née Fiddes) (marr. diss. 1980); two s one d; 2nd, 1989, Molly Lesley (née Newman). Educ: Beckenham Grammar Sch.; College of Law. Admitted Solicitor, 1959. Partner, Herbert Smith, 1960, Sen. Partner, 1988–93. Director: Glaxo Trustees Ltd, 1992–96 (Chm., 1994–96); Royal Insurance Holdings, 1994–96. Master, Solicitors' Co., and Pres., City of London Law Soc., 1992–93. FRSA 1992. Recreations: tennis, golf, ski-ing, music. Address: 112 Rivermead Court, Ranelagh Gardens, SW6 3SB. Clubs: Athenæum, Royal Automobile; Hurlingham; New Zealand Golf.

ROWSON, Martin George Edmund; cartoonist, illustrator, writer, poetaster and broadcaster; b 15 Feb. 1959; adopted s of late K. E. K. Rowson, MD, PhD; m 1987, Anna Victoria Clarke; one s one d. Educ: Merchant Taylors' Sch., Northwood; Pembroke Coll., Cambridge (BA 1982). Cartoons contributed regularly to: New Statesman, 1982–84, 1985–86, 1995–98; One Two Testing/Making Music, 1983–91; Chartist, 1985–; Financial Weekly, 1985–90; Today, 1986–92; Sunday Today, 1986–87; Guardian, 1987–89, 1991–93, 1994–; Sunday Correspondent, 1989–91; Independent, 1989–; Time Out, 1990–2002; Sunday Tribune, 1991–2000; Independent on Sunday, 1991–; European, 1991–92; Modern Review, 1993–95; Tribune, 1994–; Daily Mirror, 1995–; Observer, 1996–98; Scotsman, 1998–; TES, 1998–2005; Irish Times, 1999–2000; Daily

Express, 1999–2001; Red Pepper, 1999–; Erotic Review, 1999–; Index on Censorship, 2000–; The Times, 2001–05; Scotland on Sunday, 2002–04; New Humanist, 2002–; Spectator, 2007–; Morning Star, 2007–. Book reviews, Independent on Sunday, 1994–; Cult Books Expert, Mark Radcliffe Show, Radio 1, 1996–97; columnist, Tribune, 1998–; Dir, Tribune Publications, 2000–04. Chm., British Cartoonists' Assoc., 2000. Vice-Pres., Zool Soc. of London, 2002–05 (Council Mem., 1991–2005, 2007–). Hon. Associate, Nat. Secular Soc. Cartoonist Laureate to Mayor of London (in return for 1 pint of London Pride Ale per annum), 2001–. Political Cartoonist of the Year, Cartoon Arts' Trust, 2000, 2003; Political Cartoon of the Year, Political Cartoon Soc., 2002, 2007; Premio Satira Politica Award, Italy, 2007. Hon. DLitt Westminster, 2007. *Publications:* Scenes from the Lives of the Great Socialists, 1983 (with Kevin Killane); Lower than Vermin: an anatomy of Thatcher's Britain, 1986; The Waste Land, 1990; (with Anna Clarke) The Nodland Express, 1994; (with Chris Scarre) Imperial Exits, 1995; (with Will Self) Sweet Smell of Psychosis, 1996; The Life and Opinions of Tristram Shandy, Gentleman, 1996; (with John Sweeney) Purple Homicide, 1997; Mugshots, 2005; Snatches, 2006; Stuff, 2007; The Dog Allusion, 2008; Fuck: the human odyssey, 2008. *Recreations:* cooking, drinking, ranting, atheism, zoos, collecting taxidermy. *Address:* 46 Vicar's Hill, SE13 7JL. *T:* (020) 8244 7576, *Fax:* (020) 8244 7577; *e-mail:* martin.rowson1@ntlworld.com. *Clubs:* Soho House, Chelsea Arts, Academy; Zoological.

ROWTHORN, Prof. Robert Eric; Professor of Economics, Cambridge University, 1991–2006; Fellow, King's College, Cambridge, since 1991; *b* 20 Aug. 1939; *s* of Eric William Rowthorn and Eileen Rowthorn; *m* 1981, Amanda Jane Wharton; one *s* one *d.* *Educ:* Newport High Sch. for Boys; Jesus Coll., Oxford (BA, BPhil, MA). University of Cambridge: Res. Fellow, Churchill Coll., 1964–65; College Lectr, King's Coll., 1965–66; Asst Lectr, 1966–71; Lectr, 1971–82; Reader in Economics, 1982–91. *Publications:* International Big Business, 1971; Capitalism, Conflict and Inflation, 1980; (with J. Wells) De-industrialisation and Foreign Trade, 1987; (with N. Wayne) Northern Ireland: the political economy of conflict, 1988; (ed jtly) The Role of the State in Economic Change, 1995; (ed jtly) Democracy and Efficiency in the Economic Enterprise, 1996; (ed jtly) Transnational Corporations and the Global Economy, 1998; (ed with Antony Dnes) The Law and Economics of Marriage and Divorce, 2002. *Recreations:* swimming, reading, scuba-diving. *Address:* King's College, Cambridge CB2 1ST.

ROXBURGH, Iain Edge; consultant in local governance and public service management, since 2001; Director, Warwick Research Consortium, since 2003; *b* 4 Nov. 1943; *s* of John and Irene Roxburgh; *m* 1965, Tessa Breddy; two *s.* *Educ:* William Hulme's Grammar Sch., Manchester; Imperial Coll., London (BSc Eng, MSc, DIC). ACGI; CEng; MICE. Civil Engineer and transport planner, 1965–80; Greater London Council: Dep. Head of Personnel Services, 1981–83; Dir of Admin, 1983–85; Dep. Sec., AMA, 1985–89; Chief Exec. and Town Clerk, Coventry City Council, 1989–2001. Chm., New Local Govt Network, 2007–. Sen. Associate Fellow, Warwick Business Sch., 1998–. *Recreations:* photography, motor cycling, walking, ski-ing. *Address:* Hill Rise, Leys Lane, Meriden, Coventry CV7 7LQ. *T:* (01676) 522496.

ROXBURGH, Prof. Ian Walter; Research Professor of Astronomy, since 2001 (Professor of Mathematics and Astronomy, 1987–2001), Queen Mary and Westfield (formerly Queen Mary) College, London; *b* 31 Aug. 1939; *s* of Walter McRonald Roxburgh and Kathleen Joyce (*née* Prescott); *m* 1960, Diana Patricia (*née* Dunn); two *s* one *d.* *Educ:* King Edward VII Grammar Sch., Sheffield; Univ. of Nottingham (BSc Mathematics 1st Cl. Hons); Univ. of Cambridge (PhD); Elected Res. Fellow, Churchill Coll., Cambridge, 1963; Asst Lectr, Mathematics, 1963–64, Lectr, 1964–66, KCL; Reader in Astronomy, Univ. of Sussex, 1966–67; Queen Mary, later Queen Mary and Westfield College, London University: Prof. of Applied Maths, 1967–87; Hd, Dept of Applied Maths, 1978–84; Dir, Astronomy Unit, 1983–2001; Hd, Sch. of Math. Scis, 1984–95; Pro-Principal, 1987. Chm., Cttee of Heads of Univ. Depts of Maths and Stats, 1988–93. Chercheur associé, Observatoire de Paris, 2000–. ESA scientist on COROT mission. Contested: (L) Walthamstow W, 1970; (SDP) Ilford N, 1983. *Publications:* articles in Monthly Notices RAS, Astrophys. Jl, Astronomy and Astrophysics, Jl Geophysical Res., Phil. Trans Royal Soc., Gen. Relativity and Gravitation, Jl Physics A., Foundations of Physics, Nature, Solar Physics, Brit. Jl for the Philosophy of Science. *Recreations:* politics, economics, philosophy. *Address:* 37 Leicester Road, Wanstead, E11 2DW. *T:* (020) 8989 7117.

ROXBURGH, Karen Elizabeth; *see* Pierce, K. E.

ROXBURGHE, 10th Duke of, *cr* 1707; **Guy David Innes-Ker;** Baron Roxburghe 1600; Earl of Roxburghe, Baron Ker of Cessford and Cavertoun, 1616; Bt (NS) 1625; Viscount Broxmouth, Earl of Kelso, Marquis of Bowmont and Cessford, 1707; Earl Innes (UK), 1837; *b* 18 Nov. 1954; *s* of 9th Duke of Roxburghe, and Margaret Elisabeth (*d* 1983) (who *m* 1976, Jocelyn Olaf Hambro, MC); *d* of late Frederick Bradshaw McConnel; *S* father, 1974; *m* 1st, 1977, Lady Jane Meriel Grosvenor (*see* Lady J. M. Dawnay) (marr. diss. 1990); two *s* one *d*; 2nd, 1992, Virginia, *d* of David Wynn-Williams; one *s* one *d.* *Educ:* Eton; RMA Sandhurst (Sword of Honour, June 1974); Magdalene Coll., Cambridge (BA (Land Economy) 1980; MA 1984). Commnd into Royal Horse Guards/1st Dragoons, 1974; RARO 1977. Mem., Jockey Club. Mem., Fishmongers' Co.; Freeman of City of London, 1983. *Recreations:* shooting, fishing, golf, racing, ski-ing. *Heir:* *s* Marquis of Bowmont and Cessford, *qv.* *Address:* Floors Castle, Kelso TD5 7RW. *T:* (01573) 224288. *Clubs:* Turf, White's.

ROY, Frank; MP (Lab) Motherwell and Wishaw, since 1997; a Lord Commissioner of HM Treasury (Government Whip), since 2006; *b* 29 Aug. 1958; *s* of James Roy and Esther McMahon; *m* 1977, Ellen Foy; one *s* one *d.* *Educ:* St Joseph's High Sch.; Our Lady's High Sch., Motherwell; Motherwell Coll. (HNC Mktg); Glasgow Caledonian Univ. (BA Consumer and Mgt Studies 1994). Steelworker, Ravenscraig Steelworks, Motherwell, 1977–91; PA to Helen Liddell, MP, 1994–97. An Asst Govt Whip, 2005–06. *Recreations:* gardening, reading, football. *Address:* House of Commons, SW1A 0AA. *T:* (020) 7219 3000.

ROY, Lindsay Allan, CBE 2004; Rector, Kirkcaldy High School, since 2008; *b* 19 Jan. 1949; *s* of John and Margaret Roy; *m* 1972, Irene Patterson; two *s* one *d.* *Educ:* Univ. of Edinburgh (BSc 1970). Principal Teacher of Mod. Studies, Queen Anne High Sch., 1974–83; Asst Rector, Kirkcaldy High Sch., 1983–86; Depute Rector, Glenwood High Sch., 1986–89; Rector, Inverkeithing High Sch., 1990–2008. Associate Assessor, HM Inspectorate of Educn, 1996–. Pres., Headteachers' Assoc. of Scotland, 2004–05; Member: Jt Adv. Cttee, Scottish Credit and Qualifications Framework, 2003–; Nat. Qualifications Steering Gp, 2003–. Chm., Curriculum and Student Affairs Cttee, Lauder Coll., 1997–2006. Internat. Confederation of Principals, 2006–. FRSA 2004. *Recreations:* angling, mountain biking. *Address:* Inverkeithing High School, Hillend Road, Inverkeithing, Fife KY11 1PL. *T:* (01383) 313404, *Fax:* (01383) 313596; *e-mail:* lindsay.roy@fife.gov.uk. *Club:* Inverkeithing and Dalgety Bay Rotary.

ROY, Paul David; Partner, NewSmith Capital Partners LLP, since 2003; Chairman, British Horseracing Authority, since 2007; *b* 8 May 1947; *s* of Vernon Alfred Roy and Elsie Florence Roy; *m* 1985, Susan Mary Elkies; five *s* one *d.* *Educ:* Trinity Sch., Croydon; Liverpool Univ. (BA Hons Econs). Partner: Morton Bros (Stockbrokers), 1974–77; Kemp-Gee & Co., 1977–87; Jt Man. Dir, Citicorp Scrimgeour Vickers, 1987–89; Man. Dir, Smith New Court (UK), 1989–95; Chief Exec., Smith New Court plc, 1995; Merrill Lynch & Co: Man. Dir Equities, Europe, Middle East and Africa, 1995–98; Sen. Vice-Pres. and Head of Global Equities, 1998–2001; Exec. Vice-Pres. and Co-Pres., Investment Banking and Global Markets, 2001–03. Non-executive Director: Benfield plc, 2003–; Cenkos Securities plc, 2006–. *Recreations:* art, golf, tennis, fishing, watching school matches. *Address:* NewSmith Capital Partners LLP, Lansdowne House, 57 Berkeley Square, W1J 6ER. *Club:* City of London.

ROY, Sheila; Group Director of Healthcare Services, Westminster Health Care, 2000–05; *b* 27 Feb. 1948; *d* of late Bertie and of Dorothy Atkinson; *m* 1970, Robert Neil Roy. *Educ:* BA Open Univ.; RGN; DN (London); Cert Ed Leeds Univ.; RNT; PMD Harvard Business Sch. Milton Keynes Health Authority: Dir, Nursing Studies, 1983–86; Actg Chief Nursing Officer and Dir, Nursing Studies, Feb.–May 1986; Dist Nursing Advr and Dir, Nurse Educn, Hillingdon HA, 1986–88; Dir of Nursing Management and Res., NW Thames RHA, 1988–91; Dir, Newchurch & Co., 1991–96; owner, Sheila Roy & Associates, 1996–2000. Non-exec. Dir, Meditech Gp Ltd, 1996. *Recreations:* riding, tennis, sailing.

ROYALL OF BLAISDON, Baroness *cr* 2004 (Life Peer), of Blaisdon in the County of Gloucestershire; **Janet Anne Royall;** PC 2008; Leader of the House of Lords, since 2008; *b* 20 Aug. 1955; *d* of Basil Oscar Royall and Myra Jessie (*née* Albutt); *m* 1980, Stuart Henry James Hercock; two *s* one *d.* *Educ:* Westfield Coll., Univ. of London (BA Hons). Flower importer, Covent Garden, 1978; Gen. Sec., British Labour Gp, European Parlt, 1979–85; Policy Advr/PA, 1985–92, Researcher/Press Officer, 1992–95, to Rt Hon. Neil Kinnock, MP; Mem., Cabinet of Mr Kinnock as Comr, then Vice-Pres., EC, 1995–2001; Parly Co-ordinator, Directorate Gen., Press and Communication, EC, 2001–03; Hd, EC Office in Wales, 2003–05; a Baroness in Waiting (Govt Whip), 2005–08; Captain of the Hon. Corps of Gentlemen at Arms (Govt Chief Whip in H of L), 2008. *Recreations:* reading, gardening, cooking, swimming. *Address:* House of Lords, SW1A 0PW.

ROYCE, David Nowill; Director-General, Institute of Export, 1980–85; *b* 10 Sept. 1920; *s* of late Bernard Royce and Ida Christine (*née* Nowill); *m* 1942, Esther Sylvia Yule (*d* 2001); two *s* one *d.* *Educ:* Reading School; Vienna University. Served HM Forces, 1940–46. Major, Intelligence Corps, 1946; Asst Principal, Foreign Office, German Section, 1948; Foreign Service, 1949; First Secretary: Athens, 1953; Saigon, 1955; Foreign Office, 1957; Head of Chancery, Caracas, 1960; Counsellor (Commercial), Bonn, 1963; Counsellor (Commercial) and Consul-Gen., Helsinki, 1967–68; Commercial Inspector, FCO, 1969–71; Dir for Co-ordination of Export Services, DTI, 1971–73; Under-Secretary: Overseas Finance and Planning Div., Dept of Trade, 1973–75; CRE 3 and Export Develt Divs, Dept of Trade, 1975–77; Export Develt Div., Dept of Trade, 1977–80. Hon. Fellow, Inst. of Export, 1985. *Publication:* Successful Exporting for Small Businesses, 1990. *Recreation:* gardening. *Address:* 5 Sprimont Place, SW3 3HT. *T:* (020) 7589 9148. *Club:* Hurlingham.

ROYCE, Hon. Sir (Roger) John, Kt 2002; **Hon. Mr Justice Royce;** a Judge of the High Court, Queen's Bench Division, since 2002; a Presiding Judge, Western Circuit, since 2006; *b* 27 Aug. 1944; *s* of late J. Roger Royce and Margaret A. Royce (*née* Sibbald); *m* 1979, Gillian Wendy Adderley; two *s* one *d.* *Educ:* The Leys Sch., Cambridge; Trinity Hall, Cambridge (BA). Qualified as Solicitor, 1969; called to the Bar, Gray's Inn, 1970, Bencher, 1997; a Recorder, 1986–2002; QC 1987; a Dep. High Ct Judge, QBD, 1993–2002; Leader, Western Circuit, 1998–2001. Master, St Stephen's Ringers, 2002. Cambridge Hockey Blue, 1965, 1966; Captain Somerset Hockey, 1976; Austrian qualified ski instructor. Commandeur, Commanderie de Bordeaux (Bristol). *Recreations:* cricket, ski-ing, golf, collecting corkscrews. *Address:* Royal Courts of Justice, Strand, WC2A 2LL. *Clubs:* Hawks (Cambridge); St Enodoc Golf.

ROYDEN, Sir Christopher (John), 5th Bt *cr* 1905; *b* 26 Feb. 1937; *s* of Sir John Ledward Royden, 4th Bt, and Dolores Catherine (*d* 1994), *d* of late Cecil J. G. Coward; *S* father, 1976; *m* 1961, Diana Bridget, *d* of Lt-Col J. H. Goodhart, MC; two *s* (one *d* decd). *Educ:* Winchester Coll.; Christ Church, Oxford (MA). Duncan Fox & Co. Ltd, 1960–71; Spencer Thornton & Co., 1971–88: Partner, 1974–86; Dir, 1986–88; Associate Dir, Gerrard Vivian Gray Ltd, 1988–96. *Recreations:* fishing, shooting, gardening. *Heir:* *s* John Michael Joseph Royden [*b* 17 March 1965; *m* 1989, Lucilla, *d* of J. R. Stourton; two *d*]. *Address:* Flat 2, 8 Nevern Square, SW5 9NW. *Club:* Boodle's.

ROYDS, Rev. John Caress, MA Cantab; *b* 1920; 3rd *s* of Rev. Edward Thomas Hubert Royds, BA. *Educ:* Monkton Combe School, Bath; Queens' College, Cambridge (BA II 1 hons History, 1947). Military service with British and Indian Armies, 1940–46. Assistant master, Bryanston School, Dorset, 1947–61, House-master, 1951–61; Headmaster: General Wingate School, Addis Ababa, 1961–65; Uppingham Sch., 1965–75. Deacon, 1974; Priest, 1975; Dir of Educn for Peterborough diocese, 1976–81; Vicar of St James's, Northampton, 1981–85; with CMS, Peshawar, Pakistan, 1985–86. *Address:* 16B Donaldson Road, Salisbury SP1 3DA.

ROYLE, Catherine Jane; HM Diplomatic Service; Ambassador to Venezuela, since 2007; *b* 17 Aug. 1963; *d* of Peter and Anne Royle; *m* 1991, Dr Marcelo Camprubi; two *s.* *Educ:* Somerville Coll., Oxford (MA 1985; Hon. Fellow 2007); Univ. of Wales, Aberystwyth (MScEcon 1990). Joined FCO, 1986; Third, then Second Sec., Chile, 1988–91; First Sec., FCO, 1992–97; First Sec., Dublin, 1997–2001; Policy Advr on European Constitution, FCO, 2001–03; Dep. Hd of Mission, Buenos Aires, 2003–06. *Recreations:* reading, riding, sailing, cinema, politics, travelling. *Address:* c/o Foreign and Commonwealth Office, King Charles Street, SW1A 2AH; *e-mail:* catherine.royle@fco.gov.uk.

ROYLE, Rev. Canon Roger Michael; freelance broadcaster and writer, since 1979; Chaplain, Southwark Cathedral, since 1993; *b* 30 Jan. 1939; *s* of Reginald and Agnes Royle. *Educ:* St Edmund's Sch., Canterbury; King's Coll. London (AKC 2nd Class Hons). Curate, St Mary's, Portsea, Portsmouth, 1962–65; Sen. Curate, St Peter's, Morden, 1965–68; Succentor, Southwark Cathedral, 1968–71; Warden of Dorney Parish, Eton Coll. Project, 1971–74; Conduct, Eton Coll., 1974–79; Chaplain, Lord Mayor Treloar Coll., 1990–92. MA Lambeth, 1990. Hon. Fellow, Harris Manchester Coll., Oxford, 2006. *Publications:* A Few Blocks from Broadway, 1987; Royle Exchange, 1989; To Have and to Hold, 1990; Picking up the Pieces, 1990; Mother Teresa: her life in pictures, 1992; Between Friends, 2001. *Recreations:* theatre, music, patience, cooking. *Address:* Southwark Cathedral, Montague Close, SE1 9DA.

ROYLE, Timothy Lancelot Fanshawe, FCIM; Director, Wellmarine Reinsurance Brokers, 1976–2002; *b* 24 April 1931; *s* of Sir Lancelot Carrington Royle, KBE, and Barbara Rachel Royle; *m* 1958, Margaret Jill Stedeford; two *s* one *d.* *Educ:* Harrow; Mons

Mil. Acad. FCIM (FInstM 1977). Commnd 15th/19th King's Royal Hussars, 1949, Inns of Court Regt, TA, 1951–63. Joined Hogg Robinson Gp, 1951; Man. Dir, 1980–81. Chairman: Control Risks Group, 1975–91; Berry Palmer & Lyle, 1984–91; Hemotex Holdings, 1991–93; Director: Imperio Reinsurance Co. (UK), 1989–97; Imperio Holdings Ltd, 1995–97. Mem., Insce Brokers Regulatory Council, 1989–94. Member: Church Assembly of C of E, 1965–70; Gen. Synod of C of E, 1985–2005; Church Comr, 1966–83. Director: Christian Weekly Newspapers, 1975–2002 (Chm., 1979–97); Lindley Educn Trust, 1970–2002 (Chm., 1970–98); Chm., Cotswold Assistance, 2005–. Trustee: Ridley Hall, Cambridge, 1976–2003; Wycliffe Hall, Oxford, 1976–2003; Charinco, 1977–2002; Charishare, 1977–2002; Intercontinental Church Soc., 1977–2001. Freeman, City of London, 1976; Member: Marketors' Co., 1977; Insurers' Co., 1979. Councillor (C) Cotswold DC, 1999–2007 (Chm. Council, 2001–04). *Recreations:* country pursuits, ski-ing. *Address:* Icomb Place, near Stow on the Wold, Cheltenham, Glos GL54 1JD. *Clubs:* Cavalry and Guards, MCC; St Moritz Tobogganing (St Moritz).

ROZARIO, Patricia Maria, OBE 2001; soprano; *b* Bombay; *m* Mark Troop; two *c. Educ:* Guildhall Sch. of Music (Gold Medal; Maggie Teyte Prize). Performances include: Werther, Opera North, 1985; Idomeneo, Royal Opera House, 1985; Coronation of Poppea, Kent Opera, 1986; Golem, 1989; title rôle, world première, Mary of Egypt, Aldeburgh, 1992; The Duel of Tancredi and Clorinda, 1993; Depart in Peace (tour), 1998; première, The Veil of the Temple, Temple Ch, 2003; numerous concerts and recitals in UK, France and Germany. Recordings include Schubert songs, Tavener's Akhmatova songs. *Address:* c/o Stafford Law, Candleway, Broad Street, Sutton Valence, Kent ME17 3AT. *T:* (01622) 840038.

ROZENBERG, Joshua Rufus; legal journalist and commentator; *b* 30 May 1950; *s* of late Zigmund and Beatrice Rozenberg; *m* 1974, Melanie Phillips, *qv;* one *s* one *d. Educ:* Latymer Upper Sch., Hammersmith; Wadham Coll., Oxford (MA 1976). Solicitor's articled clerk, 1972; admitted Solicitor, 1976; trainee journalist, BBC, 1975; Legal Affairs Correspondent, 1985–97, Legal and Constitutional Affairs Correspondent, 1997–2000, BBC News; Legal Editor, Daily Telegraph, 2000–07. Hon. Bencher, Gray's Inn, 2003. Hon. LLD Hertfordshire, 1999. *Publications:* Your Rights and the Law (with Nicola Watkins), 1986; The Case for the Crown, 1987; The Search for Justice, 1994; Trial of Strength, 1997; Privacy and the Press, 2004. *Recreations:* reading, writing and wrestling with my computer. *Address:* The Daily Telegraph, 111 Buckingham Palace Road, SW1W 0DT; *e-mail:* joshua@rozenberg.net. *Club:* Garrick.

ROZENBERG, Melanie; *see* Phillips, M.

ROZENTAL, Andrés; President: Rozental y Asociados, since 1997; Mexican Council on International Affairs, since 2001; Retired Eminent Ambassador of Mexcico; *b* 27 April 1945; *s* of Leonid Rozental and Neoma Gutman; *m* 1971, Vivian Holzer; two *d. Educ:* Univ. of Bordeaux (Dip. French 1962); Univ. of the Americas (BA 1965); Univ. of Pennsylvania (MA 1966). Joined Foreign Service, 1967; Alternate Perm. Rep. to OAS, Washington, 1971–74; Counsellor, London, 1974–76; Prin. Advr to the Minister, 1977–79; Dir-Gen. of Diplomatic Service, 1979; Dir-Gen. for N American Affairs, 1979–82; Ambassador: to UN, Geneva, 1982–83; to Sweden, 1983–88; Sen. Vice-Pres., Banco Nacional de México, 1988; Dep. Foreign Minister, 1988–94; Amb. to Court of St James's, 1995–97; Amb. at Large, Mexico, 2000–01. Chm. Bd, Mittal Steel Mexico. Sen. Non-resident Fellow, Brookings Instn. Gov., Internat. Develt Res. Centre, Canada. Orders include: Polar Star (Sweden), 1983; Civil Merit (Spain), 1991; Order of Merit (France), 1993. *Publications:* (jtly) Paradoxes of a World in Transition, 1993; (jtly) The United Nations Today: a Mexican vision, 1994; Mexican Foreign Policy in the Modern Age, 1994; (jtly) Foreign Ministries: change and adaptation, 1997; (jtly) Mexico under Fox, 2004. *Recreations:* swimming, sailing, hiking. *Address:* (home) Virreyes 1360, Col. Lomas de Chapultepec, 11000 México DF, México. *T:* (55) 52025347; *e-mail:* mexconsult@gmail.com.

ROZHDESTVENSKY, Gennadi Nikolaevich; Founder, Artistic Director and Chief Conductor, State Symphony Orchestra of Ministry of Culture, Russia (New Symphony Orchestra), 1983–92; Chief Conductor, Royal Stockholm Philharmonic Orchestra, 1991–95; Professor of Conducting, Moscow State Conservatoire, since 1965; *b* 4 May 1931; *m* Victoria Postnikova, concert pianist. Studied piano at Moscow Conservatoire; started conducting at 18. Bolshoi Theatre: Asst Conductor, 1951; Conductor, 1956–60; Principal Conductor, 1965–70; Artistic Dir, 2000–01. Chief Conductor, USSR Radio and Television Symphony Orchestra, 1960–74; Chief Conductor: Stockholm Philharmonic Orchestra, 1974–77; BBC Symphony Orchestra, 1978–81; Moscow Chamber Opera, 1974–83; Vienna Symphony Orchestra, 1981–83. Guest conductor, Europe, Israel, America, Far East, Australia. Lenin Prize, 1970; People's Artist, USSR, 1972; Order of Red Banner of Labour, 1981. *Recreation:* music. *Address:* c/o Allied Artists Agency, 42 Montpelier Square, SW7 1JZ. *Club:* Athenæum.

RUANE, Caitríona; Member (SF) South Down, Northern Ireland Assembly, since 2003; Minister for Education, since 2007; *b* 19 July 1962; *d* of Michael Ruane and Nuala Gilmartin; *m* Brian McAteer; two *d. Educ:* St Angela's Nat. Sch., Mayo; St Joseph's Secondary Sch., Mayo. Former professional tennis player; human rights and develt worker, US aid foundn, Central America, 1983–87; Latin Amer. Project Officer, Trocaire, Dublin, 1987–88; Co-ordinator, Human Rights Centre, Centre for Res. and Documentation, Belfast, 1988–96; Dir, Féile an Phobail, W Belfast, 1997–2001. *Address:* Northern Ireland Assembly, Parliament Buildings, Belfast BT4 3XX.

RUANE, Christopher Shaun; MP (Lab) Vale of Clwyd, since 1997; *b* 18 July 1958; *s* of late Michael Ruane, labourer, and of Esther Ruane, dinner lady; *m* 1994, Gill, *d* of Joe and Phyl Roberts; two *d. Educ:* Blessed Edward Jones Comp. Sch., Rhyl; UCW Aberystwyth (BSc); Liverpool Univ. (PGCE). Teacher, Ysgol Mair RC Primary Sch., Rhyl, 1982–97 (Dep. Hd, 1991–97). Mem. (Lab) Rhyl Town Council, 1988–98. Contested (Lab) Clwyd NW, 1992. PPS to Sec. of State for Wales, 2002–07, to Minister of State, DWP, 2007–08, to Minister for Housing, DCLG, 2008–. Mem., Welsh Affairs Select Cttee, 1999–2002; Vice-Chm., PLP Welsh Regl Gp, 2007–. Chairman: N Wales Gp of Labour MPs, 2002–; All Party Gp on Heart Disease, 2002–. *Address:* House of Commons, SW1A 0AA.

RUAUX, Gillian Doreen, (Mrs W. D. Partington); Her Honour Judge Ruaux; a Circuit Judge, since 1993; *b* 25 March 1945; *d* of late Charles Edward Ruaux and Denise Maud Ruaux (*née* Le Page); *m* 1968, William Derek Partington; one *d. Educ:* Bolton Sch.; Univ. of Manchester (LLB Hons, LLM). Called to the Bar, Gray's Inn, 1968; practised at the Bar, Manchester, 1968–93. *Recreations:* theatre, opera, horse-racing, cookery. *Address:* Bolton Combined Court Centre, Blackhorse Street, Bolton, Greater Manchester BL1 1SU. *Club:* Bolton Old Links Golf.

RUBBIA, Prof. Carlo; physicist; Senior Physicist, European Organisation for Nuclear Research, since 1993 (Director-General, 1989–93); Professor of Physics, University of Pavia, since 1997; *b* 31 March 1934; *s* of Silvio and Bice Rubbia; *m* Marisa; one *s* one *d. Educ:* Scuola Normale Superiore, Pisa; Univ. of Pisa (Dr 1957). Research Fellow,

Columbia Univ., 1958–59; Lectr, Univ. of Rome, 1960–61; CERN, 1960– (head of team investigating fundamental particles on proton-antiproton collider); scientist, Fermi Nat. Accelerator Lab., USA, 1969–73; Higgins Prof. of Physics, Harvard Univ., 1971–88. Pres., Agency for New Technology, Energy and the Envmt, Rome, 1999–2005. Member: Papal Acad. of Science, 1985–; Amer. Acad. of Arts and Sciences, 1985; Accademia dei XL; Accademia dei Lincei; European Acad. of Sciences; Ateneo Veneto; Foreign Member: Royal Soc.; Soviet Acad. of Scis, 1988; US Nat. Acad. of Scis; Polish Acad. of Scis. Hon. Doctorates: Boston, Chicago, Geneva, Genoa, Northwestern, Udine, Carnegie-Mellon, Loyola, Sofia, Moscow, Chile, Padova, Madrid, Rio de Janeiro, La Plata and Oxford Universities. Gold Medal, Italian Physical Soc., 1983; Lorenzo il Magnifico Prize for Sciences, 1983; Achille de Gasperi Prize for Sciences, 1984; Nobel Prize for Physics (jtly), 1984; Leslie Prize for exceptional achievements, 1986. Knight Grand Cross, Italy; Officer, Legion of Honour, France, 1989. *Publications:* papers on nuclear physics: weak force quanta (W−, W+ and Z particles, intermediate vector bosons); proton-antiproton collision; sixth quark. *Address:* CERN, 1211 Geneva 23, Switzerland.

RUBEN, Prof. David-Hillel; Director, New York University in London, 1999–2008; *b* 25 July 1943; *s* of Blair S. Ruben and Sylvia G. Ruben; *m* 1968, Eira (*née* Karlinsky); one *s* two *d. Educ:* Dartmouth Coll. (BA); Harvard Univ. (PhD). Tutor in Philosophy, Univ. of Edinburgh, 1969; Lecturer in Philosophy: Univ. of Glasgow, 1970–75; Univ. of Essex, 1975–79; Lectr, 1979–82, Sen. Lectr, 1982–84, City Univ.; Prof. of Philosophy, LSE, 1984–98; Dir, Jews' Coll., London, later London Sch. of Jewish Studies, 1998–99; part-time Professor of Philosophy: SOAS, London, 2000–04; Birkbeck Coll., Univ. of London, 2004–. Phi Beta Kappa, 1964. *Publications:* Marxism and Materialism, 1977, 2nd edn 1979; Metaphysics of the Social World, 1985; Explaining Explanation, 1990; (ed) Explanation, 1994; Action and its Explanation, 2003; articles in phil. jls.

RUBENS, Prof. Robert David, MD; FRCP; Professor of Clinical Oncology, Guy's, King's and St Thomas' School of Medicine of King's College London (formerly United Medical and Dental Schools of Guy's and St Thomas' Hospitals), University of London, 1985–2003; Consultant Physician in Medical Oncology, Guy's Hospital, 1975–2003; *b* 11 June 1943; *s* of Joel Rubens and Dinah Rubens (*née* Hasseck); *m* 1970, Margaret Chamberlin; two *d. Educ:* King's Coll., London (BSc); St George's Hosp. Med. Sch. (MB, BS); MD London. FRCP 1984. House and Registrar appts, St George's, Brompton, Hammersmith and Royal Marsden Hosps, 1968–72; Clin. Res. Fellow, ICRF Labs, 1972–74; Dir, ICRF Clinical Oncology Unit, Guy's Hosp., 1985–97. Chm., EORTC Breast Cancer Co-op. Gp, 1991–94. Examr, RCP, 1987–93. Pres., Assurance Medical Soc., 2003–05. Editor-in-Chief, Cancer Treatment Reviews, 1993–2001. *Publications:* A Short Textbook of Clinical Oncology, 1980; Bone Metastases: diagnosis and treatment, 1991; Cancer and the Skeleton, 2000; ed and contrib. books and papers on cancer and other med. subjects. *Recreations:* golf, bridge. *Address:* 5 Currie Hill Close, Wimbledon, SW19 7DX. *Club:* Royal Wimbledon Golf.

RUBERY, Dr Eileen Doris, CB 1998; Senior Research Fellow and Registrar of the Roll, Girton College, Cambridge, since 2000 (Visiting Senior Fellow, 1997–2000); Tutor in Art History, Institute of Continuing Education, University of Cambridge, since 2004; Senior Associate, Judge Business School (formerly Judge Institute of Management Studies), University of Cambridge, since 2004; *b* 16 May 1943; *d* of James and Doris McDonnell; *m* 1969, Philip Huson Rubery; one *d. Educ:* Westcliff High Sch. for Girls; Sheffield Univ. Med. Sch. (MB ChB Hons); PhD Cambridge 1973; MA Art Hist. London Univ. 2004. FRCR 1976; FRCPath 1986; FFPH (FFPHM 1993). Royal Infirmary, Sheffield, 1966–67; MRC Res. Fellow, Dept of Biochem., Cambridge, 1967–71; Meres' Sen. Student, St John's Coll., Cambridge, 1971–73; Addenbrooke's Hospital, Cambridge: Registrar in Radiotherapy and Oncology, 1973–76; Sen. Registrar, 1976–78; Wellcome Sen. Clinical Res. Fellow, 1978–83; Hon. Consultant, 1978–83; Sen. Res. Fellow and Dir of Med. Studies, Girton Coll., 1981–83; SMO (Toxicology), DHSS, 1983–88; Department of Health: PMO, 1988–89; SPMO and Hd of Med. Div., Communicable Disease and Immunisation, 1989–91; SPMO and Hd of Health Promotion Med. Div., 1991–95; Under Sec. and Hd of Health Aspects of Envmtl and Food Div., 1995–97; Under Sec. and Hd of Protection of Health Div., 1996–99. Lectr in Public Policy, 1997–2004, and Course Dir, Masters in Community Enterprise, 1997–2001, Judge Inst. of Mgt Studies, Cambridge Univ. Advr to Food Standards Agency and other public sector bodies on public health and public policy issues, 2000–07. Mem., Professional Conduct Cttee, 2000–06, Professional Performance Cttee, 2003–06, GMC. QHP, 1993–96. *Publications:* (ed) Indications for Iodine Prophylaxis following a Nuclear Accident, 1990; (ed) Medicine: a degree course guide, 1974–83; papers on art history, public health, food safety, health promotion, professionals and public sector incl. policy making, the management of uncertainty and leadership in community enterprise, in professional jls. *Recreations:* visiting Rome, reading Proust, Byzantine and Medieval art, opera, Wagner, Ruskin. *Address:* Girton College, Huntingdon Road, Cambridge CB3 0JG. *T:* (01223) 337025; *e-mail:* edr1001@cam.ac.uk.

RUBERY, Prof. Jill Christine, PhD; FBA 2006; Director, European Work and Employment Centre, since 1994, Professor of Comparative Employment Systems, since 1995, and a Deputy Dean, since 2007, Manchester Business School, University of Manchester (formerly University of Manchester Institute of Science and Technology); *b* 4 Nov. 1951; *d* of Austin Rubery and late Gladys Mary Rubery (*née* Clueit); *m* 1974, Andrew Wilson; one *d. Educ:* Wintringham Grammar Sch., Grimsby; Newnham Coll., Cambridge (BA 1973, MA 1976); New Hall, Cambridge (PhD 1987). Res. Asst, Queen Elizabeth House, Oxford, 1973–75; Jun. Res. Officer, Res. Officer, then Sen. Res. Officer, Dept of Applied Econs, Univ. of Cambridge, 1978–89; Fellow and Dir of Studies in Econs, New Hall, Cambridge, 1977–89, Emeritus Fellow, 2006; Lectr, then Sen. Lectr, Manchester Sch. of Mgt, UMIST, 1989–95. Vis. Associate Prof., Univ. of Notre Dame, 1989; Visiting Fellow: Wissenschaftszentrum für Sozialforschung, Berlin, 1993; Inst. Industrial Relns, Univ. of Calif, Berkeley, 2002. Member: Bd of Arbitrators, ACAS, 1989–; Adv. Forum on Employment Regulations, DTI, 2005–. Co-ordinator, expert gp on gender and employment, EC, 1991–96, 2000–03 and 2004–07. *Publications:* (jtly) Labour Market Structure, Industrial Organisation and Low Pay, 1982; (ed) Women and Recession, 1988; (jtly) Women and European Employment, 1988; (ed) Equal Pay in Europe, 1988; (ed jtly) International Integration and Labour Market Organisation, 1992; (ed with F. Wilkinson) Employer Strategy and the Labour Market, 1994; (ed jtly) Occupation and Skills, 1994; (jtly) Women's Employment in Europe: trends and prospects, 1999; (jtly) Managing Employment Change: the new realities of work, 2002; (with D. Grimshaw) The Organization of Employment: an international perspective, 2003; (ed jtly) Systems of Production: markets, organizations and performance, 2003; (jtly) Fragmenting Work: blurring organisational boundaries and disordering hierarchies, 2005; contribs to jls in econs, mgt, industrial relns and sociology. *Recreations:* cooking, holidays, reading. *Address:* Manchester Business School, University of Manchester, Booth Street West, Manchester M15 6PB. *T:* (0161) 306 3406, *Fax:* (0161) 306 3505; *e-mail:* Jill.Rubery@manchester.ac.uk.

RUBERY, Reginald John; His Honour Judge Rubery; a Circuit Judge, since 1995; *b* 13 July 1937; *s* of Reginald Arthur Rubery and Phyllis Margaret (*née* Payne); *m* 1st, 1961, Diana Wilcock Holgate (marr. diss.); one *s*; 2nd, 1974, Frances Camille Murphy; one step *d*. *Educ*: Wadham House, Hale, Cheshire; King's Sch., Worcester. Admitted Solicitor, 1963; Partner: Whitworths, Manchester, 1966–72; Taylor Kirkman & Mainprice, 1972–78; County Court and Dist Registrar, then District Judge, 1978–95; Asst Recorder, 1987–91; a Recorder, 1991–95; Judge, St Helena Court of Appeal, 1997–; Justice of Appeal, Falkland Is, British Indian Ocean Territory, British Antarctic Territory. Chm. (pt-time) Immigration Appeal Tribunal, 1998–2005; Mem., Mental Health Review Tribunal, 2001–. Mem., Manchester City Council, 1968–71. Hon. Sec., Manchester Law Soc., 1974–78. *Recreations*: golf, swimming, gardening. *Address*: Birkby, Charnes Road, Ashley, Market Drayton, Shropshire TF9 4LQ. *Clubs*: Lansdowne; Hale Golf, Nefyn Golf, Market Drayton Golf.

RUBIN, Prof. Peter Charles, DM; FRCP; Professor of Therapeutics, University of Nottingham, since 1987 (Dean, Faculty of Medicine and Health Sciences, 1997–2003); *b* 21 Nov. 1948; *s* of late Woolf Rubin and Enis Rubin; *m* 1976, Dr Fiona Logan (marr. diss. 2006); one *s* one *d*. *Educ*: Redruth Grammar Sch.; Emmanuel Coll., Cambridge (MA); Exeter Coll., Oxford (DM 1980). FRCP 1989. Jun. hosp. posts, Stoke on Trent, 1974–77; American Heart Assoc. Fellow, Stanford Med. Center, 1977–79; Sen. Registrar (Medicine and Clinical Pharmacology), Glasgow, 1979–82; Wellcome Trust Sen. Fellow in Clinical Sci., Glasgow, 1982–87; University of Nottingham: Chairman: Dept of Medicine, 1991–97; Veterinary Sch. Project Bd, 2002–06. Mem., Nottingham HA, 1998–2002; Chairman: Specialist Adv. Cttee in Clinical Pharmacol. and Therapeutics, RCP, 1992–95; Steering Cttee, MAGPIE trial, MRC, 1998–2004; GMC Educn Cttee, 2002–08; Postgrad. Med. Educn and Trng Bd, 2005–; Co-Chm., Dental Jt Implementation Gp, 2005–Aug. 2009; Member: Physiol Medicine and Infections Grants Cttee, MRC, 1992–96; Bd, HEFCE, 2003–Aug. 2009. FMedSci 1999. *Publications*: Lecture Notes on Clinical Pharmacology, 1981, 7th edn 2006; Prescribing in Pregnancy, 1987, 4th edn 2007; Hypertension in Pregnancy, 1988, 2nd edn 2000. *Recreations*: sport, walking, music. *Address*: Division of Therapeutics, Queen's Medical Centre, Nottingham NG7 2UH. *T*: (0115) 823 1063; *e-mail*: peter.rubin@nottingham.ac.uk. *Club*: Oxford and Cambridge.

RUBIN, Robert E(dwin); Chairman of the Executive Committee, Citigroup, since 1999; Secretary of the United States Treasury, 1995–99; *b* 29 Aug. 1938; *s* of Alexander Rubin and Sylvia Rubin (*née* Seiderman); *m* 1963, Judith Leah Oxenberg; two *s*. *Educ*: Harvard (AB *summa cum laude* 1960); LSE, London Univ.; Yale Univ. (LLB 1964). Admitted to NY Bar, 1965; Associate, Cleary, Gottlieb, Steen & Hamilton, 1964–66; Goldman, Sach & Co.: Associate, 1966–70; Partner, 1971; Mem. Mgt Cttee, 1980; Vice Chair and Co-Chief Operating Officer, 1987–90; Sen. Partner and Co-Chair, 1990–93; Asst to the Pres. on econ. policy and Head, Nat. Econ. Council, Exec. Office of US President, 1993–95. Member, Board of Directors: Chicago Bd of Options Exchange, Inc., 1972–76; NY Futures Exchange, 1979–85; Center for Nat. Policy, 1982–93 (Vice Chair, 1984); NY Stock Exchange, Inc., 1991–93 (Mem., Regulatory Adv. Cttee, 1988–90); NYC Partnership Inc., 1991–93 (also Partner). Member: Adv. Cttee on Tender Offers, 1983, Adv. Cttee on Market Oversight and Financial Services, 1991–93, Securities and Exchange Commn; NY Adv. Cttee on Internat. Capital Markets, Federal Reserve Bank, 1989–93; Mayor's Council of Econ. Advrs, 1990. Trustee: Amer. Ballet Theatre Foundn, 1969–93; Mt Sinai Hosp., 1977 (Vice-Chm., 1986); Collegiate Sch., 1978–84; Station WNET-TV, 1985–93; Carnegie Corp., NY, 1990–93; Harvard Mgt Co. Inc., 1990–93. Hon. DHL Yeshiva, 1996. Nat. Assoc. of Christians and Jews Award, 1977; Dist. Leadership in Govt Award, Columbia Business Sch., 1996; Finance Minister of the Year Award, Euromoney mag., 1996. *Publication*: (with J. Weisberg) In an Uncertain World (memoirs), 2003. *Recreation*: fly fishing. *Address*: Citigroup Inc., 399 Park Avenue, New York, NY 10043, USA. *Clubs*: Harvard (NYC); Century Country (Purchase).

RUBIN, Stephen Charles; QC 2000; a Recorder, since 2004; *b* 14 March 1955; *s* of Joseph Rubin and Shirley Rubin (*née* Dank); *m* 1985, Jayne Anne Purdy; two *s* two *d*. *Educ*: Merchant Taylors' Sch., Northwood; Brasenose Coll., Oxford (Open Exhibnr; MA Jurisp.). Called to the Bar, Middle Temple, 1977; in practice at the Bar, 1979–. Member: Professional Conduct and Complaints Cttee, Bar Council, 1994–99; Cttee, London Common Law and Commercial Bar Assoc. *Recreations*: contemporary art, tennis, ski-ing, golf. *Address*: Fountain Court Chambers, Temple, EC4Y 9DH.

RUBINS, Jack, FIPA; Chairman, Osprey Communications plc, 1993–2002 (non-executive Chairman, 1999–2000; Chief Executive, 1993–95); *b* 4 Aug. 1931; *m* 1962, Ruth Davids; three *s*. *Educ*: Northern Polytechnic (Architecture). Chm. and Chief Exec., DFS Dorland Advertising, 1976–87; Chm. and Chief Exec., McCann Erickson Gp UK, 1990–91; Chm., SMS Communications, 1991–93. *Recreations*: philately, golf. *Address*: 8 Portman Hall, Old Redding, Harrow Weald, Middx HA3 6SH.

RUBINSTEIN, Hilary Harold; Chairman, Hilary Rubinstein Books (Literary Agents), since 1992; *b* 24 April 1926; *s* of H. F. and Lina Rubinstein; *m* 1955, Helge Kitzinger; three *s* one *d*. *Educ*: Cheltenham Coll.; Merton Coll., Oxford (MA). Editorial Dir, Victor Gollancz Ltd, 1952–63; Special Features Editor, The Observer, 1963–64; Dep. Editor, The Observer Magazine, 1964–65. Partner, later Director, 1965–92, Chm. and Man. Dir, 1983–92, A. P. Watt Ltd. Mem. Council, ICA, 1976–92; Trustee, Open Coll. of the Arts, 1987–96. Founder-editor, The Good Hotel Guide (published in USA as Europe's Wonderful Little Hotels and Inns), 1978–2000. *Publications*: The Complete Insomniac, 1974; Hotels and Inns, an Oxford anthology, 1984. *Recreations*: hotel-watching, reading in bed. *Address*: 32 Ladbroke Grove, W11 3BQ. *T*: (020) 7727 9550; *e-mail*: hilaryrubinstein@pobox.com.

RUCK-KEENE, John Robert, CBE 1977 (MBE 1946); TD 1950; Secretary General, Royal Society of Chemistry, 1980–81; *b* 2 Jan. 1917; *s* of late Major Robert Francis Ruck Keene, OBE, and Dorothy Mary (*née* Chester); *m* 1951, Beryl M Manistre (*d* 2004); two *s*. *Educ*: Eton; Trinity Coll., Cambridge (BA 1938, MA 1955). Commissioned TA, Oxford and Bucks LI, 1939; served UK and NW Europe, 1939–45 (Major 1944, MBE 1946). First appointment with Chemical Society, 1946; General Secretary, 1947–80, when the Royal Society of Chemistry was formed by unification under Royal Charter of The Chemical Society and The Royal Institute of Chemistry, 1 June 1980. Hon. FRSC, 1982. *Address*: Flat 28, Archer Court, 43 Chesham Road, Amersham, Bucks HP6 5UL. *T*: (01494) 727123.

RUCKER, (Belinda) Christian; Founder, The White Company, since 1994; *b* 6 Nov. 1968; *d* of Anthony Rucker and Rosemary Calcutt; *m* 1995, Nicholas Charles Tyrwhitt Wheeler, *qv*; one *s* three *d*. *Educ*: Combe Bank Sch., Sevenoaks. Various asst roles, Condé Nast Pubns, 1987–90; PR Asst, Clarins UK Ltd, 1991; Asst Health and Beauty Asst, Harpers & Queen magazine, 1992–94. *Recreation*: looking after four children in every spare moment! *Address*: The White Company, Unit 30, Perivale Park, Horsenden Lane South, Greenford UB6 7RJ.

RUCKER, His Honour Jeffrey Hamilton; a Circuit Judge, 1988–2007; a Resident Judge, Truro Crown Court, 2001–07; *b* 19 Dec. 1942; *s* of late Charles Edward Sigismund Rucker and Nancy Winifred Hodgson; *m* 1965, Caroline Mary Salkeld; three *s*. *Educ*: St Aubyn's, Rottingdean; Charterhouse. Called to the Bar, Middle Temple, 1967; a Recorder, 1984; a Circuit Judge, assigned to SE Circuit, 1988, transf. W Circuit, 2001. Mem. Council of Govs, UMDS of Guy's and St Thomas', 1991–98. *Recreations*: sailing, ski-ing, music.

RUDD, Sir (Anthony) Nigel (Russell), Kt 1996; DL; Chairman, BAA plc, since 2007; Deputy Chairman, Barclays Bank plc, since 2004 (non-executive Director, since 1996); *b* 31 Dec. 1946; *m* 1969, Lesley Elizabeth (*née* Hodgkinson); two *s* one *d*. *Educ*: Bemrose Grammar Sch., Derby. FCA. Qualified Chartered Accountant 1968; Divl Finance Dir, London & Northern Group, 1970–77; Chairman: C. Price & Son Ltd, 1977–82; Williams Holdings (later Williams plc), 1982–2000; Dep. Chm., Raine Industries, 1992–94 (non-exec. Chm., 1986–92); non-executive Chairman: Pendragon PLC, 1989–; East Midlands Electricity, 1994–97 (Dir, 1990–97); Pilkington plc, 1995–2006 (Dir, 1994–2006); Kidde, 2000–03; The Boots Co. plc, subseq. Alliance Boots plc, 2003–07 (non-exec. Dir, 1999–2007; Dep. Chm., 2001–03). Member: European Round Table of Industrialists 1996–2001; Council, CBI, 1999–. Freeman, City of London; Mem., Chartered Accountants' Co. DL Derbys, 1996. Hon. DTech Loughborough, 1998; DUniv Derby, 1998. *Recreations*: golf, ski-ing, theatre, field sports. *Address*: Barclays Bank plc, 1 Churchill Place, E14 5HP. *Clubs*: Brooks's, Royal Automobile.

RUDD, Dominic; Chief Executive Officer, Samaritans, since 2007; *b* 4 Oct. 1958; *s* of William Rudd and Primrose (*née* Saddler Phillips; now Lady Lewis, widow of Adm. Sir Andrew Lewis, KCB); *m* 2004, Helena Clayton; two *s*. *Educ*: Bedford Sch. Midshipman, RN, 1976–77; Officer, RM, 1977–89. Partner, Holley, Hextall & Associates, 1989–99; Manager for Wales, 1999–2001, Dir of Ops, 2001–07, RSPCA. FRSA. *Recreations*: rock climbing, Alpine mountaineering. *Address*: c/o Samaritans, The Upper Mill, Kingston Road, Ewell, Surrey KT17 2AF. *T*: (020) 8394 8300, *Fax*: (020) 8394 8301.

RUDD, Hon. Kevin Michael; MP (ALP) Griffith, Queensland, since 1998; Prime Minister of Australia, since 2007; *b* Nambour, Qld, 21 Sept. 1957; *s* of Bert and Margaret Rudd; *m* 1981, Thérèse Rein; two *s* one *d*. *Educ*: Marist Coll., Ashgrove; Nambour State High Sch.; Australian Nat. Univ. (BA 1st cl. Hons Asian Studies 1981). Diplomat, Aust. Dept of Foreign Affairs, 1981–88: served Stockholm, later First Sec., Beijing; Counsellor, 1988; COS to Hon. Wayne Goss, Leader of the Opposition, later Premier, of Qld, 1988–91; Dir-Gen., Office of the Cabinet, Qld, 1991–95; Sen. China Consultant, KPMG Australia, 1996–98. Contested (ALP) Griffith, Qld, 1996. Chm., Parly ALP Cttee on Nat. Security and Trade, 1998; Shadow Minister: for Foreign Affairs, 2001–06; for Internat. Security, 2003–06; for Trade, 2005–06; Leader of the Opposition, Australia, 2006–07. Leader, ALP, 2006–. *Publications*: articles on Chinese politics, Chinese foreign policy, Australia-Asia relations and globalisation. *Address*: Parliament House, Canberra, ACT 2600, Australia.

RUDD, His Honour Norman Julian Peter Joseph; a Circuit Judge, 1988–2004; *b* 12 May 1943; *s* of Norman Arthur Rudd and Winifred Rudd; *m* 1968, Judith Margaret Pottinger; three *s*. *Educ*: Paston Sch., N Walsham, Norfolk; University Coll. London (LLB, LLM). Called to the Bar, Inner Temple, 1969; Asst Recorder, 1982–87, Head of Chambers, 1982–87; a Recorder, 1987. Trustee, New Forest Commoning Trust, 1993– (Chm., 1993–98); Chm., Northern Commoners Assoc. (New Forest), 1999–. *Recreation*: farming.

RUDD-JONES, Derek, CBE 1981; PhD; Director, Glasshouse Crops Research Institute, Littlehampton, Sussex, 1971–86; *b* 13 April 1924; 2nd *s* of late Walter Henry Jones and late Doris Mary, *er d* of H. Rudd Dawes; *m* 1948, Joan, 2nd *d* of late Edward Newhouse, Hong Kong, and Malvern, Worcs; two *s* one *d*. *Educ*: Whitgift; Repton; Emmanuel Coll., Cambridge. BA, MA, PhD (Cantab); FIBiol; FIHort. Agricultural Research Council, postgrad. student, Botany Sch., Univ. of Cambridge, 1945–48; Plant Pathologist, E African Agric. and Forestry Research Orgn, Kenya, 1949–52; Nat. Research Council, Postdoctoral Fellow, Univ. of Saskatchewan, Saskatoon, Canada, 1952–53. ICI Ltd, Akers Research Laboratory, The Frythe, Welwyn, Herts, 1953–56; Jealott's Hill Research Station, Bracknell, Berks, 1956–59; Scientific Adviser to Sec., Agricl Research Council, 1959–71; Foundn Chm., 1968–72, Managing Editor, 1986–93, British Crop Protection Council (Mem., 1968–86); Pres., Section K, BAAS, 1981–82; Mem., Scientific Cttee, RHS, 1985–96; formerly Mem., Adv. Cttee on Pesticides and Other Toxic Chemicals. Vis. Fellow, Univ. of Southampton, 1975–86. Governor, Chichester (formerly W Sussex) Inst. of Higher Educn, 1980–95; Trustee, Thomas Phillips Price Trust, 1988–93. *Publications*: papers in scientific journals. *Recreations*: gardening, riding, fly-fishing. *Address*: Corner Cottage, Austin Street, Stamford PE9 2QP. *Club*: Farmers'.

RUDDEN, Prof. Bernard (Anthony), LLD; FBA 1995; Professor of Comparative Law, University of Oxford, 1979–99, now Emeritus; Fellow of Brasenose College, Oxford, 1979–99, now Emeritus; *b* 21 Aug. 1933; *s* of John and Kathleen Rudden; *m* 1957, Nancy Campbell Painter; three *s* one *d*. *Educ*: City of Norwich Sch.; St John's Coll., Cambridge. LLD Cantab; DCL Oxon; PhD Wales. Solicitor. Fellow and Tutor, Oriel Coll., Oxford, 1965–79. Hon. LLD McGill, 1991. *Publications*: Soviet Insurance Law, 1966; The New River, 1985; Basic Community Cases, 1987, 2nd edn 1997; co-author or editor of: The Law of Mortgages, 1967; Source-Book on French Law, 1973, 3rd edn 1991; Basic Community Laws, 1980, 7th edn 1999; The Law of Property, 1982, 3rd edn 2002; Comparing Constitutions, 1995; contrib. periodical pubns. *Address*: 15 Redinnick Terrace, Penzance TR18 4HR. *T*: (01736) 360395. *Club*: Oxford and Cambridge.

RUDDOCK, Alan Stephen Dennis; columnist, Sunday Independent, since 2006; *b* 21 July 1960; *s* of John and Doreen Ruddock; *m* 1986, Jacqueline Kilroy; three *s*. *Educ*: Coll. of St Columba, Dublin; TCD (BA 1983). Reporter: Business Day, Johannesburg, 1984–86; Today newspaper, 1986–89; Business Editor, Sunday Tribune, Dublin, 1989–92; Sunday Times, 1992–96; Man. Editor, Sunday Express, 1996; Projects Editor, Mirror Gp Newspapers, 1996–98; Editor, The Scotsman, 1998–2000; columnist, The Sunday Times, 2004–06. *Publication*: Michael O'Leary: a life in full flight, 2007. *Recreations*: watching sport, ski-ing, tennis. *Address*: Rathmore Park, Tullow, Co. Carlow, Ireland. *T*: (5991) 61179.

RUDDOCK, Rev. Canon Bruce; see Ruddock, Rev. Canon R. B.

RUDDOCK, Joan Elizabeth, CBE 2004 (OBE 1995); Parliamentary Boundary Commissioner for Northern Ireland, 2003–08; Independent Assessor for Public Appointments, 2004–09; *b* 22 May 1948; *d* of Robert John Boyle and Bertha Irene Boyle (*née* Johnston); *m* 1968, Alvin Ruddock. *Educ*: Trinity Coll., Dublin (BA 1970); Univ. of Ulster (Postgrad. DMS 1977); Open Univ. (BSc 1st Cl. Hons 2002). FCIM 1997. Mktg Manager, Conf. Div., FT, London, 1972–74; Redevelt Team Leader, NI Housing Exec., 1975–76; Corp. Finance Exec., NI Develt Agency, 1976–79; Mgt Consultant, Coopers & Lybrand, 1979–82; Sen. Exec., Industrial Develt Bd NI, 1982–84; Advr to European Pres.

and Dir of Res., AVX Ltd, 1984–86; Gen. Manager, European Special Products Div., 1986–90; Man. Dir, Educational Company Ltd, 1990–99. Director: LEDU, 1984–98; Investment Belfast Ltd, 2000–06. Ind. Bd Mem., Dept of Agric. and Rural Develt, 2006–08. Chm., Belfast City Hosp. HSS Trust, 1999–2007; Dep. Chm., Gtr Village Regeneration Trust, 2000–06; Member: NIHEC, 1998–2005; Central Investment Trust for Charities, 1998–2004.

RUDDOCK, Joan Mary; MP (Lab) Lewisham, Deptford, since 1987; Parliamentary Under-Secretary of State, Department of Energy and Climate Change, since 2008; *b* 28 Dec. 1943; *d* of Ken and Eileen Anthony. *Educ:* Pontypool Grammar Sch. for Girls; Imperial Coll., Univ. of London (BSc; ARCS). Worked for Shelter, national campaign for the homeless, 1968–73; Dir, Oxford Housing Aid Centre, 1973–77; Special Programmes Officer with unemployed young people, MSC, 1977–79; Organiser, CAB, Reading, 1979–86. Chairperson, CND, 1981–85, a Vice Chairperson, 1985–86. Opposition spokesperson: on transport, 1989–92; on home affairs, 1992–94; on envmtl protection, 1994–97; Parliamentary Under-Secretary of State: for Women, DSS, 1997–98; DEFRA, 2007–08. Active in politics and pressure groups, and mem. of anti-racist concerns, throughout working life. Bd Mem., Trinity Laban, 2005–. Hon. Fellow: Goldsmiths Coll., Univ. of London, 1996; Laban Centre, 1996. Frank Cousins' Peace Award, TGWU, 1984. *Publications:* CND Scrapbook, 1987; co-author of pubns on housing; (contrib.): The CND Story, 1983; Voices for One World, 1988. *Recreations:* music, travel, gardening. *Address:* c/o House of Commons, SW1A 0AA.

RUDDOCK, Paul Martin; Chief Executive and Co-Founder, Lansdowne Partners Ltd, since 1998; *b* 28 Aug. 1958; *s* of William Frederick Ruddock and Mary Eileen Ruddock; *m* 1991, Jill Ann Shaw; two *d*. *Educ:* King Edward's Sch., Birmingham; Mansfield Coll., Oxford (BA 1st Cl. Law 1980, MA 1984; Bancroft Fellow, 2008). Goldman Sachs, 1980–84; Man. Dir, Hd of Internat., Schroder & Co. Inc., 1984–98. Trustee: V&A Mus., 2002– (Chm., 2007–; Chm., Finance Cttee, 2002–; Chm., Develt Cttee, 2002–; Mem., Collections Cttee, 2002–); Burlington Mag. *Recreations:* tennis, mountain walking, medieval art, theatre. *Address:* c/o Lansdowne Partners Ltd, 15 Davies Street, W1K 3AG. *T:* (020) 7290 5500, *Fax:* (020) 7409 1122; *e-mail:* pruddock@lansdownepartners.com. *Club:* Lansdowne.

RUDDOCK, Air Vice-Marshal Peter William David, CBE 2001; Director General, Saudi Armed Forces Project, since 2006; *b* 5 Feb. 1954; *s* of William Ruddock and Evelyn (*née* Besanson); *m* 2001, Joanna Elizabeth Milford; one *s* one *d*. *Educ:* Grosvenor High Sch., Belfast. FRAeS 2004. Joined RAF, 1974; Fighter Pilot, Qualified Weapons Instructor, to 1990; Advanced Staff Coll., Bracknell, 1990; Wing Comdr, MoD, 1991–93; OC Ops Wg, RAF Coningsby (Display Pilot, Battle of Britain Meml Flight), 1993–96; Gp Capt., MoD, 1996–99; Station Comdr, RAF Coningsby, 1999–2000; Air Cdre Defence Ops, HQ 1 Gp, 2000–02; Dir of Air Staff, 2002–04; Air Sec., 2004–06. Officer, American Legion of Merit, 2003. *Recreations:* gliding, sailing, equestrian activities, most sports, military history. *Address:* (office) Castlewood House, 77–91 New Oxford Street, WC1A 1DT. *Club:* Royal Air Force.

RUDDOCK, Rev. Canon (Reginald) Bruce; Residentiary Canon and Precentor of Peterborough Cathedral, and Diocesan Liturgical Officer, Peterborough, since 2004; Chaplain to the Queen, since 2008; *b* 17 Dec. 1955; *s* of Reginald and Hilary Ruddock; *m* 1983, Vivien Chrismas. *Educ:* Hurstpierpoint Coll., Sussex; Guildhall Sch. of Music and Drama (AGSM); Chichester Theol Coll.; Southampton Univ. (Cert. Theol.). Ordained deacon, 1983, priest, 1984; Asst Curate, St Mary's, Felpham with St Nicholas, Middleton-on-Sea, 1983–86; Priest-in-Charge, St Wilfrid's Church, Parish of St Mary, Portsea, 1986–88; Vicar, St Michael's, Barnes, 1988–95; Dir, Anglican Centre in Rome, and Archbishop of Canterbury's Counsellor for Vatican Affairs, 1995–99; Residentiary Canon, Worcester Cathedral, 1999–2004. Hon. Canon, Amer. Cathedral, Paris, 1996. *Recreations:* music, cricket, art, theatre, visiting Italy. *Address:* Cathedral Office, Minster Precincts, Peterborough, Cambs PE1 1XS. *T:* (01733) 355310.

RUDENSTINE, Neil Leon; Chairman, ARTstor, since 2001; President Emeritus, Harvard University, since 2001; *b* 21 Jan. 1935; *s* of Harry Rudenstine and Mae Esperito Rudenstine; *m* 1960, Angelica Zander; one *s* two *d*. *Educ:* Princeton Univ. (BA 1956); New Coll., Oxford (BA 1959; MA 1963; Hon. Fellow, 1992); Harvard Univ. (PhD 1964). Instructor, English and American Lit. and Lang., Harvard Univ., 1964–66, Asst Prof. 1966–68; Princeton University: Associate Prof., English Dept, 1968–73; Dean of Students, 1968–72; Prof. of English, 1973–88; Dean of College, 1972–77; Provost, 1977–88, Provost Emeritus, 1988–; Exec. Vice-Pres., Andrew W. Mellon Foundn, 1988–91; Pres., and Prof. of English and Amer. Lit. and Lang., Harvard Univ., 1991–2001. Hon. Fellow, Emmanuel Coll., Cambridge, 1991. Hon. DPhil: Princeton, 1989; Yale, 1992. Hon. DCL: Harvard, 1992; Oxford, 1998. *Publications:* Sidney's Poetic Development, 1967; (ed with George Rousseau) English Poetic Satire: Wyatt to Byron, 1972; (with William Bowen) In Pursuit of the PhD, 1992; Pointing Our Thoughts, 2001. *Address:* ARTstor, 151 E 61st Street, New York, NY 10065, USA.

RUDERS, Poul; full-time composer, since 1991; *b* Ringsted, Denmark, 27 March 1949; *s* of late Poul Ruders and Inge Ruders; *m* 1995, Annette Gerlach. *Educ:* Royal Danish Conservatory (Organist's degree 1975). Self-taught composer. Guest Prof., Yale Music Sch., 1991; Distinguished Internat. Vis. Prof. of Composition, RAM, London, 2002–04. Composer in Residence, Aspen Music Fest., Colorado, 2003. Principal *compositions:* Symphony No 1, 1989; Listening Earth, 2002; Final Nightshade, 2003; *operas:* The Handmaid's Tale, 1996–98; Kafka's Trial, 2001–03. *Publications:* Tundra (orch.), 1990; Violin Concerto No 2, 1991; Anima (2nd 'cello concerto), 1993; Symphony No 2, 1997; Oboe Concerto, 1998; Horn Trio, 1998; Fairytale (orch.), 1999; Paganini Variations (2nd guitar concerto), 2000; The Handmaid's Tale, vocal score 2002, full score 2003; Kafka's Trial, 2004. *Recreations:* reading, DIY activities. *Address:* c/o Edition Wilhelm Hansen, 1 Bornholmsgade, 1266 Copenhagen K, Denmark. *T:* 33117888; *e-mail:* ewh@ewh.dk; *web:* www.PoulRuders.net.

RUDGE, Sir Alan (Walter), Kt 2000; CBE 1995 (OBE 1987); PhD; FRS 1992; FREng; Chairman: ERA Technology Ltd, 1997–2003; ERA Foundation, since 2001; President, MSI Cellular, 2002–04 (Chief Executive Officer, 2001–02); *b* 17 Oct. 1937; *s* of Walter Thomas Rudge and Emma (*née* McFayden); *m* 1969, Jennifer Joan Minott; one *s* one *d*. *Educ:* Hugh Myddelton Sch.; London Polytechnic; Univ. of Birmingham (PhD ElecEng). FIET, FIEEE; FREng (FEng 1984). Res. Engr, Illinois Inst. of Technol. Res. Inst., 1968–71; Lectr, Electronic and Elec. Engrg Dept, Univ. of Birmingham, 1971–74; Engrg Adviser, Illinois Inst. of Technol. Res. Inst., 1974–79; Man. Dir, Era Technology Ltd, 1979–86; BT (formerly British Telecom): Dir, Research and Technology, 1987–89; Group Technology and Develt Dir, 1989–90; Mem. Main Bd, 1989–97; Man. Dir, Develt and Procurement, 1990–95; Dep. Gp Man. Dir, 1995–96; Dep. Chief Exec., 1996–97; Chm., WS Atkins plc, 1997–2001. Non-executive Director and Member Board: British Maritime Technology Ltd, 1984–89; Ricardo Consulting Engrs PLC, 1985–89; BT&D Technologies Ltd, 1987–93; Telecom Securicor Cellular Radio, 1989–90; MCI (USA), 1995–96; LucasVarity plc, 1997–99; GEC, subseq. Marconi, plc, 1997–2002; GUS plc, 1997–2006; MSI Cellular Investment Hldgs BV, 1998–2002; Experian, 2006–; non-exec. Chm., Metapath Software Internat. Inc., 1999–2000. Vis. Prof., Queen Mary and Westfield Coll. (formerly QMC), Univ. of London, 1985–. Pres., AIRTO, 1986. Pres., IEE, 1993–94 (Vice Chm., 1989–91; Dep. Pres., 1991; Mem., Electronics Divl Bd, 1980–89, Chm., 1984; Faraday Medal, 1991); Chairman: Learned Soc. Bd, 1989–91; EPSRC, 1994–99; Senate, Engrg Council, 1996–99; Member: Systems and Electronics Bd, MoD Defence Scientific Adv. Council, 1981–87; CBI Res. and Technol. Cttee, 1980–86; ACOST, 1987–90; Council, DRA, then DERA, MoD, 1991–96; Council for Sci. and Technology, 1993–97. Chairman: Bd of Trustees, British Retinitis Pigmentosa Soc., 1996–; Bd of Mgt, Royal Commn for Exhibn of 1851, 2001– (Mem., 1997–). Member, Council: QMW, 1991–93; Royal Instn, 1992–95. Pro-Chancellor, Univ. of Surrey, 2002–07. Freeman, City of London; Liveryman, Engineers' Co., 1998–. Hon. FIEE 2000. Hon. Fellow, UCL, 1998. Hon. DEng: Birmingham, 1991; Bradford, Portsmouth, 1994; Nottingham Trent, 1995; Hon. DSc: Strathclyde, 1992; Bath, Loughborough, 1995; Westminster, 1996; DUniv Surrey, 1994. Duncan Davies Meml Medal, R&D Soc., 1998; Founder's Medal, IEEE, 1998; Millennium Medal, IEEE, 2000. *Publications:* The Handbook of Antenna Design, vol. 1 1982, vol. 2 1983; papers in sci. and tech. jls on antennas, microwaves and satellite communications. *Recreations:* sailing, cycling, reading. *Address:* ERA Foundation, Cleeve Road, Leatherhead, Surrey KT22 7SA. *Clubs:* Athenæum, Royal Automobile, Royal Ocean Racing; Royal Southampton Yacht, Royal Southern Yacht.

RUDGE, Christopher John, FRCS; Managing and Transplant Director, UK Transplant, since 2005; National Clinical Director for Transplants, Department of Health, since 2008; *b* 1 Oct. 1948; *s* of Ben Rudge, DFC and Joan Rudge; *m* 1973, Elizabeth Mary Jameson; two *s*. *Educ:* Guy's Hosp. Medical Sch. (BSc 1969, MB BS 1972). FRCS 1976. Consultant Transplant Surgeon: Guy's Hosp., London, 1981–85; St Peter's Hosps, London, 1985–95; Royal London Hosp., 1995–2001; (pt-time) Royal London Hosp., 2001–; Med. Dir, UK Transplant, 2001–05. Gov., Tonbridge School, 2007–. *Recreations:* Rugby Union, music, gardening, travel, cricket. *Address:* Pennis Farm, Fawkham, Kent DA3 8LZ. *T:* and *Fax:* (01474) 707522; *e-mail:* cjrudge@btinternet.com. *Club:* MCC.

RUDIN, Toni Richard Perrott; Secretary, Magistrates' Association, 1986–93; *b* 13 Oct. 1934; *s* of Richard William Rudin and Sarah Rowena Mary Rudin (*née* Perrott); *m* 1958, Heather Jean (*née* Farley); one *s* three *d*. *Educ:* Bootham Sch.; Millfield Sch.; RMA Sandhurst; Army Staff Coll.; Coll. of Law, Guildford. Commissioned Royal Artillery, 1954; served BAOR, Cyprus (1957–60), UK; MoD, 1967–69; Battery Comdr and 2 i/c 26th Field Regt, RA, BAOR, 1969–72; MoD, 1972–75; retired, 1975. Solicitor, 1978; private practice as solicitor, 1978–80; Press and Public Relations, Law Soc., 1980–86. Pt-time Legal Chm., Pensions Appeal Tribunals, 1994–2007. Gen. Comr of Income Tax, 1995–97. Mem. Cttee, Rutland and Leics Army Benevolent Fund, 1997–2001. *Recreations:* 19th century history, house renovation, France, woodwork, bridge. *Address:* 2 Chapel Walk, Adderley Street, Uppingham, Rutland LE15 9NE. *T:* (01572) 822999. *Club:* Army and Navy.

RUDKIN, Duncan Hugh; Chief Executive and Registrar, General Dental Council, since 2006; *b* 2 Aug. 1966; *s* of Philip Rudkin and Peggy Rudkin (*née* Watts). *Educ:* Queen's Coll., Oxford (BA Mod. Langs 1989). Solicitor, City of London; General Dental Council: Dir, Legal Services, 1998; Dir, Professional Standards, 2001; Dep. Chief Exec., 2005. *Address:* General Dental Council, 37 Wimpole Street, W1G 8DQ.

RUDKIN, (James) David; playwright; *b* 29 June 1936; *s* of David Jonathan Rudkin and Anne Alice Martin; *m* 1967, Alexandra Margaret Thompson; one *s* two *d* (and one *s* decd). *Educ:* King Edward's Sch., Birmingham; St Catherine's Coll., Oxford (MA). Judith E. Wilson Fellow, Cambridge Univ., 1984; Vis. Prof., Middlesex Univ., 2004–; Hon. Prof., Univ. of Wales, 2006–. *Screenplays:* Testimony, 1987; December Bride, 1991; The Woodlanders, 1996; *opera libretti:* Broken Strings, 1992; (with Jonathan Harvey) Inquest of Love, 1993; Black Feather Rising, 2008; *radio plays:* The Lovesong of Alfred J. Hitchcock, 1993; The Haunting of Mahler, 1994; The Giant's Cause..., 2005. *Publications:* plays: Afore Night Come, 1963; (trans.) Moses and Aaron (opera libretto), 1965; The Grace of Todd (orig. opera libretto), 1969; Cries from Casement as his Bones are Brought to Dublin (radio), 1974; Penda's Fen (film), 1975; Burglars (for children), 1976; Ashes, 1978; (trans.) Hippolytus, 1980; The Sons of Light, 1981; The Triumph of Death, 1981; (trans.) Peer Gynt, 1983; The Saxon Shore, 1986; (trans.) When We Dead Waken, 1989; (trans.) Rosmersholm, 1990; Vampyr (monograph), 2005; articles, reviews etc. for Encounter, Drama, Tempo, Theatre Res. Internat. *Recreations:* piano, geology, anthropology, languages, swimming, bridge. *Address:* c/o Casarotto Ramsay Ltd, Waverley House, 7–12 Noel Street, W1F 8GQ. *T:* (020) 7287 4450, *Fax:* (020) 7287 9128.

RUDKIN, Walter Charles, CBE 1981; Director of Economic Intelligence, 1973–81, of Economic and Logistic Intelligence, 1982, Ministry of Defence; retired; *b* 22 Sept. 1922; *e s* of Walter and Bertha Rudkin; *m* 1950, Hilda Mary Hope; two *s*. *Educ:* Carre's Grammar Sch., Sleaford; UC Hull. BSc (Econ) London. Served with RAF, 1942–46. Lectr, Dept of Econs and Econ. History, Univ. of Witwatersrand, 1948–52. Entered Min. of Defence, 1954; appts incl. Hong Kong, 1956–59; Junior Directing Staff, Imperial Defence Coll., 1962–64; Cabinet Office, 1968–71. *Recreation:* fishing. *Club:* Royal Commonwealth Society.

RUDLAND, Margaret Florence; Headmistress, Godolphin and Latymer School, 1986–2008; *b* 15 June 1945; *d* of Ernest George and Florence Hilda Rudland. *Educ:* Sweyne School, Rayleigh; Bedford College, Univ. of London (BSc); Inst. of Education (PGCE). Asst Mathematics Mistress, Godolphin and Latymer Sch., 1967–70; VSO, Ilorin, Nigeria, 1970–71; Asst Maths Mistress, Clapham County Sch., 1971–72; Asst Maths Mistress and Head of Dept, St Paul's Girls' Sch., 1972–83; Deputy Headmistress, Norwich High Sch., GPDST, 1983–85. Pres., GSA, 1996 (Chm., Educn Cttee, 1993–94). Member: UCAS Bd, 2002–06; Gen. Teaching Council, 2002–06. Member Council: Nightingale Fund, 1989– (Chm., 1998–); UCL, 1998–2006. Governor: St Margaret's Sch., Bushey, 1997–; Merchant Taylors' Sch., Northwood, 2000–; Redcliffe Sch., 2001–; Glendower Prep. Sch., 2003–; St Mary's, Ascot, 2003–; British Sch. at Paris, 2007–; English Coll., Prague, 2008–. Gov., ESU, 2008–. *Recreations:* opera, cinema, travel. *Address:* 3 Langham Place, Chiswick, W4 2QL.

RUDLAND, Martin William; His Honour Judge Rudland; a Circuit Judge, Northern Circuit, since 2002; *b* 13 March 1955; *s* of Maurice Rudland and Patricia Rudland (*née* Crossley); *m* 1st, 1980, Norma Jane Lee (marr. diss. 1989); two *s*; 3rd, 1997, Linda Sturgess Jackson (*née* Potter); one step *s* one step *d*. *Educ:* Rowlinson Sch., Sheffield; Sheffield Univ. (LLB Hons 1976). Called to the Bar, Middle Temple, 1977 (Harmsworth Schol. 1977); in practice at the Bar, North Eastern Circuit, 1977–2002; Circuit Jun., 1985; Asst Recorder, 1992–96; a Recorder, 1996–2002. *Recreations:* books, music, cinema, travel. *Address:* Manchester Crown Court, Courts of Justice, Crown Square, Manchester M3 3FL.

RUDMAN, Michael Edward; theatre director and producer; Artistic Director, Sheffield Theatres (Crucible and Lyceum), 1992–94; *b* Tyler, Texas, 14 Feb. 1939; *s* of M. B.

Rudman and Josephine Davis; *m* 1963, Veronica Anne Bennett (marr. diss. 1981); two *d*; *m* 1983, Felicity Kendal, *qv* (marr. diss. 1994); one *s*. *Educ:* St Mark's Sch., Texas; Oberlin Coll. (BA *cum laude* Govt); St Edmund Hall, Oxford (MA). Pres., OUDS, 1963–64. Asst Dir and Associate Producer, Nottingham Playhouse and Newcastle Playhouse, 1964–68; Asst Dir, RSC, 1968; Artistic Director: Traverse Theatre Club, 1970–73; Hampstead Theatre, 1973–78 (Theatre won Evening Standard Award for Special Achievement, 1978); Associate Dir, Nat. Theatre, 1979–88; Dir, Lyttelton Theatre (National), 1979–81; Dir, Chichester Festival Theatre, 1990. Mem., Bd of Dirs, Hampstead Theatre, 1979–89. *Plays directed* include: *Nottingham Playhouse:* Changing Gear, Measure for Measure, A Man for All Seasons, 1965; Julius Caesar, She Stoops to Conquer, Who's Afraid of Virginia Woolf, Death of a Salesman, 1966; Long Day's Journey into Night, 1967; Lily in Little India, 1968; *RSC Theatregoround:* The Fox and the Fly, 1968; *Traverse Theatre:* Curtains (transf. Open Space, 1971), Straight Up (transf. Piccadilly, 1971), A Game called Arthur (transf. Theatre Upstairs, 1971), Stand for my Father, (with Mike Wearing) A Triple Bill of David Halliwell plays, 1970; The Looneys, Pantagleize, 1971; Caravaggio Buddy, Tell Charlie Thanks for the Truss, The Relapse, 1972; *Hampstead Theatre:* Ride across Lake Constance (transf. Mayfair), A Nightingale in Bloomsbury Square, 1973; The Black and White Minstrels, The Show-off, The Connection, The Looneys, 1974; Alphabetical Order (transf. Mayfair), 1975; Clouds, 1977 (transf. Duke of York's, 1978); Cakewalk, Beyond a Joke, Gloo-Joo (transf. Criterion), 1978; Making it Better (transf. Criterion), 1992; Benchmark (also co-writer), 2002; *National Theatre:* For Services Rendered (televised, 1980), Death of a Salesman, 1979; Thee and Me, The Browning Version/ Harlequinade, Measure for Measure, 1980; The Second Mrs Tanqueray, 1981; Brighton Beach Memoirs (transf. Aldwych), The Magistrate, 1986; Six Characters in Search of an Author, Fathers and Sons, Ting Tang Mine, Waiting for Godot, 1987; *Chichester:* The Merry Wives of Windsor, Rumours, 1990; Mansfield Park, 1996; The Admirable Crichton, 1997; Tallulah!, 1997; Our Betters, 1997; *Sheffield:* A Midsummer Night's Dream, 1992; Donkeys' Years, (with Robert Delamere) Jane Eyre, Hamlet, Mansfield Park, 1993; The Grapes of Wrath, 1994; *West End:* Donkeys' Years, Globe, 1976; Taking Steps, Lyric, 1980; Camelot, 1982; The Winslow Boy, 1983; The Dragon's Tail, Apollo, 1985; Exclusive, Strand, 1989; Fallen Angels, Apollo, 2000; A Man for all Seasons, Th. Royal, Haymarket, 2005; *Gate Theatre, Dublin:* The Heiress, 1997; *New York:* The Changing Room, 1973 (Drama Desk Award); Hamlet, 1976; Death of a Salesman, 1984 (Tony Award for Best Revival); Measure for Measure, 1993; Have you spoken to any Jews lately?, 1995. *Address:* c/o Nick Marsten, Curtis Brown Group, 162–168 Regent Street, W1R 5TA. *T:* (020) 7396 6600. *Clubs:* Royal Automobile; Royal Mid-Surrey Golf, Richmond Golf.

RUDOE, Wulf, CB 1975; *b* 9 March 1916; *m* 1942, Ellen Trilling; one *s* one *d*. *Educ:* Central Foundation School; Peterhouse, Cambridge (Open Schol. and Research Schol.). Mathematics Tripos Pt III, 1938, Distinction. Royal Aircraft Establishment, 1939. Operational Research, RAF, 1939–45. Operational Research in Building Industry, Min. of Works, 1946–48, Principal Scientific Officer 1948; Board of Trade, Statistician 1948, Chief Statistician 1952; Dir of Statistics and Research, DHSS (formerly Min. of Health), 1966–76; Asst Sec., Price Commn, 1976–79; Adviser to Govt of Ghana, 1980–81. Fellow Inst. of Statisticians; Mem. Council, 1962–78, Hon. Treasurer, 1965–74, Vice-Pres., 1974–75 and 1976–77, Royal Statistical Soc. *Recreations:* walking, travel, languages. *Address:* 72 North End Road, NW11 7SY. *T:* (020) 8455 2890.

RUDWICK, Prof. Martin John Spencer, PhD, ScD; FBA 2008; Professor of History, University of California, San Diego, 1988–98, now Emeritus; Affiliated Research Scholar, History and Philosophy of Science, University of Cambridge, since 1998; *b* 26 March 1932; *er s* of Joseph Spencer Rudwick and Olivia Grace Rudwick (*née* Western); *m* 1st, 1965, Gillian Yendell (marr. diss. 1972); 2nd, 1974, Tricia MacColl (marr. diss. 1995). *Educ:* Harrow Sch.; Trinity Coll., Cambridge (BA 1953; PhD 1958; ScD 1976). University of Cambridge: Demonstrator, 1955–59; Sen. Asst in Res., 1960–65; Lectr, in Geol., 1965–67, in Hist. of Sci., 1967–74; Fellow, Trinity Coll., 1956–60, Corpus Christi Coll., 1962–74, Cambridge; Prof. of Hist. and Social Aspects of the Natural Scis, Vrije Univ., Amsterdam, 1974–80; Fellow-Commoner, Trinity Coll., Cambridge, 1983–85; Prof. of Hist., and Hist. of Sci., Princeton Univ., 1985–87. Vis. Fellow, Clare Hall, Cambridge, 1994–95. Visiting Professor of History of Science: Princeton Univ., 1981; Hebrew Univ., Jerusalem, 1982; Mem., Inst. for Advanced Study, Princeton, 1982–84; Maître de Recherche Associé, École des Mines de Paris, 1985; Vis. Prof. of Hist. of Scis Rijksuniversiteit Utrecht, 1993. Guggenheim Foundn Fellow, 1994–95. Tarner Lectr, Trinity Coll., Cambridge, 1994–97. Mem., Doctrine Commn, C of E, 1982–85. Mem., Acad. Internat. d'Histoire des Scis, 1980–; Pres., Hist. of Earth Scis Soc., 2005–06. Scientific Medal, Zool Soc. of London, 1973; Hist. of Geol. Award, Geol Soc. of America, 1987; Friedman Medal, Geol Soc. of London, 1988; Founder's Medal, Soc. for Hist. of Natural Hist., 1988; Bernal Prize, Soc. for Social Studies of Sci., 1999; Sarton Medal, Hist. of Sci. Soc., 2007; Prix Wegmann, Soc. Géologique de France, 2008. *Publications:* Living and Fossil Brachiopods, 1970; The Meaning of Fossils, 1972, 2nd edn 1985; The Great Devonian Controversy, 1985; Scenes from Deep Time, 1992; Georges Cuvier, 1997; The New Science of Geology, 2004; Lyell and Darwin Geologists, 2005; Bursting the Limits of Time, 2005; Worlds before Adam, 2008; contrib. articles to learned jls on paleontology and hist. of earth scis. *Recreations:* early music, hill walking, wood-turning, vernacular architecture. *Address:* Department of History and Philosophy of Science, University of Cambridge, Free School Lane, Cambridge CB2 3RH.

RUFFLE, Mary, (Mrs Thomas Ruffle); *see* Dilnot, M.

RUFFLES, Philip Charles, CBE 2001; RDI 1997; FRS 1998; FREng, FRAeS, FIMechE; Technical Advisor, Rolls-Royce plc, 2001–04; *b* 14 Oct. 1939; *s* of Charles Richard Ruffles and Emily Edith Ruffles; *m* 1967, Jane Connor; two *d*. *Educ:* Sevenoaks Sch.; Bristol Univ. (BSc 1st Cl. Mech. Engrg 1961). FRAeS 1985; FREng (FEng 1988); FIMechE 1989. Rolls-Royce: trainee, 1961–63; technical appts, 1963–77; Chief Engr, RB211, 1977–81; Head of Engrg, Small Engines, 1981–84; Dir, Technol. & Design Engrg, 1984–89; Technical Dir, 1989–91; Dir of Engrg, Aerospace Gp, 1991–96; Dir, Engrg and Technol., 1997–2001. Non-exec. Dir, Domino Printing Science plc, 2001–. Member: Defence Scientific Adv. Council, 1990–93; Technol. Foresight Defence and Aerospace Panel, 1994–97; LINK Bd (OST), 1995–98; Council for Central Lab. of Res. Councils, 1998–2004; Council for Sci. and Technol., 2007–. Member Council: Royal Acad. Engrg, 1994–97, 2002–; RAeS, 1995–2004. FRSA 1998. Liveryman, Engineers' Co., 1998. Hon. FIC 2002. Hon. DEng: Bristol, 1995; Birmingham, 1998; Sheffield, 1999; Hon. DSc City, 1998. Ackroyd Stuart Prize, 1987, Gold Medal, 1996, RAeS; MacRobert Award, 1996, Prince Philip Medal, 2001, Royal Acad. of Engrg; James Clayton Prize, IMechE, 1998; Duncan Davies Meml Medal, R & D Soc., 2000; François-Xavier Bagnoud Aerospace Prize, Univ. of Michigan, 2001; R. Tom Sawyer Award, ASME, 2002; Premio Internazionale Barsanti e Matteucci, 2002. *Publications:* contrib. to numerous learned jls on engrg and technol. topics. *Recreations:* Rugby, D-I-Y. *Address:* 5 Ford Lane, Allestree, Derby DE22 2EX.

RUFFLEY, David Laurie; MP (C) Bury St Edmunds, since 1997; *b* 18 April 1962; *s* of Jack Laurie Ruffley, solicitor. *Educ:* Bolton Boys' Sch.; Queens' Coll., Cambridge (Exhibnr, 1981, Foundn Scholar, 1983; Histl Tripos pt 1, Law Tripos pt 2, BA 1985, MA 1988). Articled clerk and Solicitor with Coward Chance, then Clifford Chance, 1985–91; Special Advr to Sec. of State for Educn and Science, 1991–92, to Home Sec., 1992–93, to Chancellor of the Exchequer, 1993–96; Economic Consultant, Cons. Party, 1996–97; Vice-Pres., Small Business Bureau, 1996–. An Opposition Whip, 2004–05; Shadow Minister: for Work and Pensions, 2005–07; for Police Reform, 2007–. Member: Select Cttee on Public Admin, 1997–99; Select Cttee on Treasury Affairs, 1998–2004; Exec., 1922 Cttee, 2003–04; Secretary: Cons. Backbench Finance Cttee, 1999–2001; Cons. Backbench Econ. and Social Affairs Policy Gp, 2002–03; Parly Gp on Wholesale Financial Mkts and Services, 2003–; Vice-Chairman: All Party Small Business Gp, 2001–05; All Party BBC Gp, 2002–06; All Party Kazakhstan Gp, 2005–. Mem., Adv. Council, Centre for Policy Studies, 2004–. Governor: Marylebone Sch., 1992–94; Pimlico Sch., 1994–96; Bolton Boys' Sch., 1997–99. Patron: Bury St Edmunds Town Trust; W Suffolk Voluntary Assoc. for the Blind. US State Dept Internat. Visitor, res. prog. on econ. develt and trade, 2003; Fellow, British-American Project, 2002. *Recreations:* football, golf, film, thinking. *Address:* House of Commons, SW1A 0AA. *Clubs:* Farmers' (Bury St Edmunds); Bury St Edmunds Golf.

RUGBY, 3rd Baron *cr* 1947, of Rugby, Co. Warwick; **Robert Charles Maffey;** farmer; *b* 4 May 1951; *s* of 2nd Baron Rugby and of Margaret Helen, *d* of late Harold Bindley; *S* father, 1990; *m* 1974, Anne Penelope, *yr d* of late David Hale; two *s*. *Educ:* Brickwall House Sch., Northiam. *Recreations:* shooting, woodwork and metal work. *Heir: s* Hon. Timothy James Howard Maffey, *b* 23 July 1975.

RUGG, Prof. Michael Derek, PhD; Professor of Neurobiology and Behavior, since 2003 and Director, Center for the Neurobiology of Learning and Memory, since 2004, University of California, Irvine; *b* 23 Sept. 1954; *s* of Derek and Brenda Rugg; *m* 1976, Elizabeth Jackson; one *s*. *Educ:* Univ. of Leicester (BSc Psychol; PhD 1979). FRSE 1996. Res. Fellow, Dept of Psychology, Univ. of York, 1978–79; University of St Andrews: Lectr in Psychology, 1979–88; Reader, 1988–92; Prof., 1992–98; Head, Sch. of Psychology, 1992–94; Prof. of Cognitive Neurosci. and Wellcome Trust Principal Res. Fellow, UCL, 1998–2003. Hon. Res. Fellow, Inst. of Neurology, 1994–98. Member: DoH Wkg Gp on Organophosphates, 1998–99; Govt Ind. Expert Gp on Mobile Phones, 1999–2000; Prog. mgt cttee, mobile telecomm. and health res. prog., 2000–03 and 2005–; Adv. gp on non-ionising radiation, NRPB, 2001–03; CP Study Section, NIH. *Publications:* (ed with A. D. Milner) Neuropsychology of Consciousness, 1991; (ed with M. G. H. Coles) Electrophysiology of Mind, 1995; (ed) Cognitive Neuroscience, 1996; numerous articles in cognitive neuroscience and related fields in learned jls. *Recreations:* rock climbing, ski-ing, mountaineering, 20th century novels, music. *Address:* Center for the Neurobiology of Learning and Memory, University of California at Irvine, Irvine, CA 92697–3800, USA.

RUGGIERO, Renato, Hon. KCMG 1980; Senior Adviser and Member of European Advisory Board, Citigroup; *b* Naples, 9 April 1930; *s* of Antonio Ruggiero and Lucia (*née* Rubinacci); *m* 1956, Paola Tomacelli Filomarino; two *s* one *d*. *Educ:* Univ. of Naples (degree in law 1953). Joined Italian diplomatic service; served Sao Paulo, Moscow, Washington, Belgrade and Brussels; Chef de Cabinet of Pres., 1969–73, Dir-Gen. for Regional Policies, 1973–77, Spokesman of the Pres., 1977–78, EC; Foreign Ministry, Rome, 1978–80; Ambassador to EEC, 1980–84; Dir-Gen. for Econ. Affairs, 1984–85, Sec. Gen., 1985–87, Foreign Ministry; Foreign Trade Minister, 1987–91; Dir-Gen., WTO, 1995–99; Vice-Chm., Salomon Smith Barney Internat., 2000–01; Foreign Minister, Italy, 2001–02; Chm., Citigroup in Switzerland, and Vice-Chm., Citigroup European Investment Bank, 2002. Dir and adviser, various Italian, European and American cos, 1991–95. KCSG 1997. Cavalierato di Gran Croce (Italy), 1985; Grand Cordon, Order of the Sacred Treasure (Japan), 1991. *Recreations:* sailing, hiking. *Address:* Citigroup, Foro Buonaparte 16, 20121 Milan, Italy.

RUGGLES-BRISE, Sir Timothy (Edward), 3rd Bt *cr* 1935, of Spains Hall, Finchingfield; owner, Spains Hall estate, since 1966; proprietor, The Stables, Spains Hall, wedding venue and conference centre, since 2006; *b* 11 April 1945; *s* of Guy Edward Ruggles-Brise, TD and Elizabeth Ruggles-Brise (*née* Knox); *S* uncle, 2007; *m* 1975, Rosemary Elizabeth (*née* Craig); three *s* two *d*. *Educ:* Eton Coll.; Regent St Polytechnic; RAC Cirencester. DipCE; DipAgr; CDipAF. CEng, MICE, now retired. 1964–78: Sen. Engr, Livesey & Henderson then Rendel Palmer & Tritton; civil engrg consultant. Sen. Partner, Whitehouse Farms Partnership, 1974–2001; estab. and Sen. Partner, Spains Hall Forest Nursery, 1979–. Chm., Forestry Gp, Horticultural Trades Assoc., and E Anglian Br., Timber Growers Assoc., 1993–97. Trustee: Perry Watlington Trust; Finchingfield Guildhall Trust. Jt Master, East Essex Foxhounds, 1980–83. Mem., Finchingfield PCC. Mem. Ct of Assts, Armourers' and Brasiers' Co., 2005–. *Recreations:* country pursuits, food and wine. *Heir: s* Archibald Edward Ruggles-Brise [*b* 9 Dec. 1979; *m* 2007, Anna French]. *Address:* Spains Hall Farmhouse, Finchingfield, Braintree, Essex CM7 4NJ. *T:* (01371) 810232; *e-mail:* spainshall@btinternet.com. *Clubs:* Farmers; Essex.

RÜHE, Volker; Member of Bundestag, 1976–2005; Minister of Defence, Germany, 1992–98; *b* 25 Sept. 1942; *m*; three *c*. *Educ:* Univ. of Hamburg. School teacher, Hamburg, 1968–76. Joined CDU, 1963; Mem., Hamburg City Council, 1970–76; Gen. Sec., CDU, 1989–92.

RUHFUS, Dr Jürgen, Officer's Cross, Order of Merit, Federal Republic of Germany, 1983; Hon. KBE 1978; State Secretary, Federal Foreign Office, Germany, 1984–87; *b* 4 Aug. 1930; three *d*. *Educ:* Universities of Munich, Münster and Denver, USA. Joined Federal Foreign Office, Bonn, 1955; Consulate General: Geneva, 1956–57; Dakar, 1958–59; Embassy, Athens, 1960–63; Dep. Spokesman of Federal Foreign Office, 1964, Official Spokesman, 1966; Ambassador to Kenya, 1970–73; Asst Under-Secretary, Federal Foreign Office, 1973–76; Adviser on Foreign Policy and Defence Affairs to Federal Chancellor Helmut Schmidt, 1976–80; Ambassador to UK, 1980–83; Head of Political Directorate-General (dealing with Third World and other overseas countries), Federal Foreign Office, Dec. 1983–June 1984; Ambassador to USA, 1987–92; Chm., Deutsch-Englische Ges., 1993–98; Mem., Supervisory Bd, Adam Opel AG, 1993–2001. *Recreations:* golf, tennis, ski-ing, shooting. *Address:* Ettenhausener Strasse 23a, 53229 Bonn, Germany.

RUHNAU, Heinz; consultant in strategic planning, since 1991; Professor of Business Administration, Technical University, Dresden, since 1990; *b* Danzig, 5 March 1929; *m* Edith Loers; three *d*. *Educ:* Dip. in Business Administration, 1954. Asst to Chm., IG-Metall, Frankfurt; Regional Dir, IG-Metall, Hamburg, 1956–65; Mem., Senate of Free Hanseatic City of Hamburg (responsible for security and city admin.), 1965–73; Mem., Exec. Bd, COOP, 1973; State Sec., Ministry of Transport, 1974–82; CEO, Deutsche Lufthansa, 1982–91. Chairman: IATA, 1985; Assoc. of European Airlines, 1988. Federal Grand Cross of Merit, 1980, with Star, 1989, FRG; Officer, Légion d'Honneur (France), 1989; Cross of Merit (Spain), 1990. *Address:* Elsa Brändström Straße 213, 53227 Bonn, Germany.

RUIZ, Cristina; Editor, The Art Newspaper, since 2003; *b* 16 Oct. 1971; *d* of Grazia and Domenico Ruiz. *Educ:* University Coll. London (BA Hons Ancient and Medieval Hist.); Courtauld Inst. of Art (MA Classical Art). Mem., British Drawings and Watercolours Dept, Christie's, London, 1994–95; The Art Newspaper: joined as staff reporter, 1995; Dep. Editor, 2000–03. *Recreations:* trash television, scuba-diving. *Address:* The Art Newspaper, 70 South Lambeth Road, SW8 1RL. *T:* (020) 7735 3331.

RULE, Brian Francis; Director General of Information Technology Systems, Ministry of Defence, 1985–94; Chairman, Emeritus Plus Ltd, 1994–98; *b* 20 Dec. 1938; *s* of late Sydney John Rule and Josephine Rule, Pen-y-ffordd, near Chester; *m* 1993, Irene M. Rees, Pembs. *Educ:* Daniel Owen Sch., Mold; Loughborough Univ. of Technology (MSc). Engineer, de Havilland Aircraft Co., 1955–59; Res. Assistant, Loughborough Univ., 1963–65; Lectr, Univ. of Glasgow, 1965–67; University of Aberdeen: Lectr, 1967–70; Sen. Lectr, 1970–72; Dir of Computing, 1972–78; Dir, Honeywell Information Systems Ltd, 1978–79; Dir of Scientific Services, NERC, 1979–85. *Publications:* various papers in scientific jls. *Recreations:* Boxer dogs, antique clocks. *Address:* c/o Lloyds TSB, 14 Castle Street, Cirencester, Glos GL7 1QJ.

RULE, Margaret Helen, (Mrs A. W. Rule), CBE 1983; FSA; Consultant, Mary Rose Trust, 1994–98 (Research Director, 1983–94); *b* 27 Sept. 1928; *d* of Ernest Victor and Mabel Martin; *m* 1949, Arthur Walter Rule; one *s*. *Educ:* Univ. of London. FSA 1967. Dir of Excavations, Chichester Civic Soc., 1961–79; Hon. Curator, Fishbourne Roman Palace and Museum, 1968–79; Archaeol Dir, Mary Rose Trust, 1979–82. Hon. Fellow, Portsmouth Polytechnic, 1982. Hon. DLitt Liverpool, 1984; Hon. DSc Portsmouth, 1999. Reginald Mitchell Medal, Stoke-on-Trent Assoc. of Engrs, 1983. *Publications:* Chichester Excavations 1, 1967; The Mary Rose, 1982; A Gallo-Roman Trading Vessel from Guernsey, 1993; Life at Sea: Tudors and Stuarts, 1994; many papers in jls in Britain and USA. *Recreations:* anything in or on the water. *Address:* Crofton, East Bracklesham Drive, Bracklesham Bay, W Sussex PO20 8JW.

RUMALSHAH, Rt Rev. Munawar Kenneth, (Mano); Bishop of Peshawar, 1994–98 and since 2003; *b* 16 June 1941; *s* of Ven. Inayat and Mrs Akhtar Rumalshah; *m* 1st, 1966, Rosalind Andrews; two *d*; 2nd, 1984, Sheila Benita Biswas; one *d*. *Educ:* Punjab Univ. (BSc 1960); Serampur Univ. (BD 1965); Karachi Univ. (MA 1968); Cambridge Univ. (PGCE 1986). Ordained deacon, 1965, priest, 1966; Curate: Holy Trinity Cathedral, Karachi, 1965–69; St Edmund Roundhay, Leeds, 1970–73; Area Sec., and Asst Home Sec., CMS, 1973–78; Educn Sec., BCC, 1978–81; Priest-in-charge, St George, Southall, 1981–88; Presbyter, St John's Cathedral, and Lectr, Edwarde's Coll., Peshawar, 1989–94; Gen. Sec., USPG, 1998–2003, and an Asst Bp, Southwark Dio., 1999–2003. Mem., Archbp of Canterbury's Commn on Urban Priority Areas, 1984–86. Ramsden Preacher, Cambridge Univ., 2003; Vis. Prof., Gen. Theol Seminary of Episcopal Church, NY. Jt Ed., Lambeth Conf., 1998. *Publications:* Focus on Pakistan, 1989, 4th edn 1999; Being a Christian in Pakistan, 1998. *Recreations:* watching cricket, music, reading, travel. *Address:* Diocesan Centre, 1 Sir Syed Road, Peshawar 25000, NWFP, Pakistan. *T:* (91) 5279094.

RUMBELOW, Arthur Anthony; QC 1990; **His Honour Judge Rumbelow;** a Circuit Judge, since 2002; a Deputy High Court Judge (Family Division), since 2001; *b* Salford, Lancs, 9 Sept. 1943; *er s* of Arthur Rumbelow and Theresa (*née* Lucketti); *m*; three *d*. *Educ:* Salford Grammar Sch.; Queens' Coll., Cambridge (Squire Schol.; BA 1966). Called to the Bar, Middle Temple, 1967 (Harmsworth Exhibnr, Astbury Schol.). A Recorder, 1988–2002. Chairman: Medical Appeal Tribunal, 1988–2002; Mental Health Rev. Tribunal, 2001–. Mem., Rochdale MBC, 1982–84. *Recreations:* wine, theatre, gardening. *Address:* Manchester County Court, Manchester Civil Justice Centre, 1 Bridge Street, Manchester M3 3FX.

RUMBELOW, (Roger) Martin, CEng; non-executive director and consultant, since 1996; *b* 3 June 1937; *s* of Leonard Rumbelow and Phyllis (*née* Perkins); *m* 1965, Marjorie Elizabeth Glover. *Educ:* Cardiff High Sch.; Bristol Univ. (BSc); Cranfield Inst. of Technol. (MSc). CEng 1966. National Service, RAF Pilot, 1955–57. British Aircraft Corporation, 1958–74: Dep. Prodn Controller, 1967–73; Concorde Manufg Project Manager, 1973–74; Department of Trade and Industry, 1974–96: Principal, 1974–78; Asst Sec., 1978–86; Under Sec., 1987–96; Services Management Div., 1987–92; Head, Electronics and Engrg Div., 1992–96. *Recreations:* singing, opera, theatre, tennis. *Club:* Royal Air Force.

RUMBLE, Peter William, CB 1984; Chief Executive, Historic Buildings and Monuments Commission, (English Heritage), 1983–89; Director-General, Union of European Historic Houses Associations, 1991–94; *b* 28 April 1929; *s* of Arthur Victor Rumble and Dorothy Emily (*née* Sadler); *m* 1953, Joyce Audrey Stephenson; one *s* one *d*. *Educ:* Harwich County High Sch.; Oriel Coll., Oxford (MA). Entered Civil Service, 1952; HM Inspector of Taxes, 1952; Principal, Min. of Housing and Local Govt, 1963; Asst Sec., 1972, Under Sec., 1977, DoE. Member: Architectural Heritage Fund, 1984–98 (Vice-Chm., 1992–98); Cttee, Southern Region, NT, 1990–96; Churches Conservation Trust (formerly Redundant Churches Fund), 1991–99; Rep., Church Heritage Forum, 1997–99. Trustee, Amer. Friends of English Heritage, 1988–94. *Recreations:* music, pottery. *Address:* 11 Hillside Road, Cheam, Surrey SM2 6ET. *T:* (020) 8643 1752.

RUMBLES, Michael John; Member (Lib Dem) West Aberdeenshire and Kincardine, Scottish Parliament, since 1999; *b* 10 June 1956; *s* of Samuel and Joan Rumbles; *m* 1985, Pauline Sillars; two *s*. *Educ:* Univ. of Wales (MSc Econ). Commissioned RAEC, 1979–94 (Major); Team Leader in Business Management, Aberdeen Coll., 1995–99. *Recreations:* family, hill walking. *Address:* Kinloch House, Birse, Aboyne, Aberdeenshire AB34 5BY. *T:* (01339) 886841.

RUMBOLD, Rt Hon. Dame Angela (Claire Rosemary), DBE 1992 (CBE 1981); PC 1991; a Vice Chairman, Conservative Party, 1995–97 (a Deputy Chairman, 1992–95); *b* 11 Aug. 1932; *d* of late Harry Jones, FRS; *m* 1958, John Marix Rumbold; two *s* one *d*. *Educ:* Perse Sch. for Girls; Notting Hill and Ealing High Sch.; King's Coll., London. Founder Member, National Assoc. for the Welfare of Children in Hospital, and National Chairman, 1974–76. Councillor, Royal Borough of Kingston upon Thames, 1974–83; Chm., Council, Local Educn Authorities, 1979–80. Mem., Doctors and Dentists Review Body, 1979–81. Co-Chm., Women's Nat. Commn, 1986–90. MP (C) Merton, Mitcham and Morden, June 1982–1983, Mitcham and Morden 1983–97; contested (C) Mitcham and Morden, 1997. PPS to Financial Sec. to the Treasury, 1983, to Sec. of State for Transport, 1983–85; Parly Under Sec. of State, DoE, 1985–86; Minister of State, DES, 1986–90, Home Office, 1990–92. Mem., Social Services Select Cttee, 1982–83. Chairman: Minerva Fund, GDST, 1993–2001; GBGSA, 2001–; United Learning Trust, 2002–; Co-Chm., Assoc. of Governing Bodies of Indep. Schs, 2001–07; Dir, United Church Schs Trust (formerly Church Schs Co.), 2000–. Chairman of Governors: Mill Hill Sch. Foundn, 1995–2004; Wimbledon High Sch., 1999–2005; Governor: Danes Hill Prep. Sch., 1998– (Chm., Vernon Educn Trust, 2005); More House Sch., 2000–02; Chm., Surbiton High Sch., 2006–. Freeman, City of London, 1988. *Recreations:* swimming, cinema, reading, ballet.

RUMBOLD, Sir Henry (John Sebastian), 11th Bt *cr* 1779; Partner, Dawson Cornwell, 1991–2004; *b* 24 Dec. 1947; *s* of Sir Horace Anthony Claude Rumbold, 10th Bt, KCMG, KCVO, CB, and Felicity Ann Rumbold (*née* Bailey); *S* father, 1983; *m* 1978, Frances Ann (*née* Hawkes, formerly wife of Julian Berry). *Educ:* Eton College; College of William and Mary, Virginia, USA (BA). Articled Stileman, Neate and Topping, 1975–77; admitted solicitor, 1977; asst solicitor, Stileman, Neate and Topping, 1977–79; Partner, 1979–81; joined Stephenson Harwood, 1981, Partner, 1982–91. *Recreations:* hunting, shooting, reading. *Heir: cousin* Charles Anton Rumbold [*b* 7 Feb. 1959; *m* 1967, Susan, *er d* of J. M. Tucker]. *Address:* 19 Hollywood Road, SW10 9HT. *T:* (020) 7352 9148; Hatch House, Tisbury, Wilts SP3 6PA. *T:* (01747) 870622. *Clubs:* Boodle's, Brooks's, Groucho.

RUMFITT, Nigel John; QC 1994; a Recorder, since 1995; *b* 6 March 1950; *s* of late Alan Regan Rumfitt and Dorothy Rumfitt (*née* Ackroyd); *m* 1984, Dorothy Pamela Pouncey. *Educ:* Leeds Modern Sch.; Pembroke Coll., Oxford (MA, BCL). Teaching Associate, Northwestern Univ. Sch. of Law, Chicago, 1972–73; called to the Bar, Middle Temple, 1974; Asst Recorder, 1991–95. *Recreations:* ski-ing, travel, sailing, Francophilia. *Address:* 7 Bedford Row, WC1R 4BU. *T:* (020) 7242 3555.

RUMSFELD, Hon. Donald Henry; Secretary of Defense, USA, 1975–77 and 2001–06; *b* Chicago, 9 July 1932; *s* of George Donald Rumsfeld and Jeannette Rumsfeld (*née* Husted); *m* 1954, Joyce Pierson; one *s* two *d*. *Educ:* New Trier High Sch., Ill; Princeton Univ. (AB 1954). Served US Navy, 1954–57. Admin. Asst, US House of Reps, 1957–59; investment broker, A. G. Becker & Co., Chicago, 1960–62. Mem., House of Reps, 1963–69; Dir, Office of Econ. Opportunity, and Asst to US Pres., 1969–70; Dir, Econ. Stabilization Prog., and Counsellor to the Pres., 1971–72; US Ambassador and Perm. Rep. to NATO, 1973–74; Chief of Staff, White House, and Asst to the Pres., 1974–75. Pres. and CEO, then Chm., G. D. Searle & Co., Ill, 1977–83 and 1984–85; special envoy to ME, 1983–84; Sen. Advr, William Blair & Co., 1985–90; Chm. and CEO, General Instrument Corp., Chicago, 1990–93; in private business, 1996–97; Chm., Gilead Sciences Inc., Calif, 1997–2000. US Presidential Medal of Freedom, 1977.

RUNACRES, Mark Alastair; HM Diplomatic Service; Senior Visiting Fellow, The Energy and Resources Institute, New Delhi, since 2006; *b* 19 May 1959; *s* of John and Coral Runacres; *m* 1989, Shawn Reid; two *s* one *d*. *Educ:* St John's Coll., Cambridge (BA Hons). Entered FCO, 1981; FCO, 1981–83; New Delhi, 1983–86; Trade Relations Dept, 1986–88, and News Dept, 1988–90, FCO; First Sec. (Chancery), Paris, 1991–95; SE Asia Dept, FCO, 1995–97; Dir, Trade for S Asia and Africa, DTI, 1997–99 (on secondment); Counsellor (Economic and Social Affairs), UKMIS to UN, NY, 1999–2002; Minister and Dep. High Comr, New Delhi, 2002–06. Dir, Sheffield and Vermark Consultants Private Ltd, 2007–; Mem. of Bd., Business and Community Foundn (Delhi), 2006–; non-executive Director: Mind Tree Ltd, 2006–; G4S (India) Ltd, 2006–; Elara Capital (India) Pvt Ltd, 2007–; Advisory Board: Xyanni Pvt Ltd, 2008–; Avian Media Pvt Ltd, 2008–; Chm., Chase India, 2008–. *Address:* c/o Foreign and Commonwealth Office, King Charles Street, SW1A 2AH; *e-mail:* markr@teri.res.in. *Club:* MCC.

RUNCIMAN, family name of **Viscount Runciman of Doxford**.

RUNCIMAN OF DOXFORD, 3rd Viscount, *cr* 1937; **Walter Garrison Runciman, (Garry),** CBE 1987; FBA 1975; Bt 1906; Baron Runciman, 1933, of Shoreston; President, British Academy, 2001–05; Chairman, Runciman Investments Ltd, since 1990; Fellow, Trinity College, Cambridge, since 1971; *b* 10 Nov. 1934; *o s* of 2nd Viscount Runciman of Doxford, OBE, AFC, AE and Katherine Schuyler (*d* 1993), *y d* of late William R. Garrison, New York; *S* father, 1989; *m* 1963, Ruth (*see* Viscountess Runciman of Doxford); one *s* two *d*. *Educ:* Eton (Oppidan Schol.); Trinity Coll., Cambridge (Schol.; Fellow, 1959–63, 1971–). National Service, 1953–55 (2/Lt, Grenadier Guards); Harkness Fellow, 1958–60; part-time Reader in Sociology, Univ. of Sussex, 1967–69; Vis. Prof., Harvard Univ., 1970; Vis. Fellow, Nuffield Coll., Oxford, 1979–87 (Hon. Fellow, 1998). Lectures: Radcliffe-Brown, British Acad., 1986; Spencer, Oxford Univ., 1986; Chorley, London Univ., 1993; ESRC, 1993; T. H. Marshall, Southampton Univ., 1994; British Acad., 1998; Walters, Univ. of Bath, 2006. Chairman: Walter Runciman plc, 1976–90; Andrew Weir & Co. Ltd, 1991–2005. Treas., Child Poverty Action Gp, 1972–97; Member: SSRC, 1974–79; Securities and Investments Board, 1986–97 (a Dep. Chm., 1990–97); British Library Bd, 1999–2002; Dep. Chm., FSA, 1997–98. Pres., Gen. Council of British Shipping, 1986–87 (Vice-Pres., 1985–86). Chm., Royal Commn on Criminal Justice, 1991–93. Hon. Foreign Mem., Amer. Acad. of Arts and Sciences, 1986. Hon. DSc (SocScis) Edinburgh, 1992; DUniv York, 1994; Hon. DLitt Oxford, 2000; Hon. DSc (Soc Sci) London, 2007. *Publications:* Plato's Later Epistemology, 1962; Social Science and Political Theory, 1963, 2nd edn 1969; Relative Deprivation and Social Justice, 1966, 2nd edn 1972; Sociology in its Place, and other essays, 1970; A Critique of Max Weber's Philosophy of Social Science, 1972; A Treatise on Social Theory: vol. I, 1983, vol. II, 1989, vol. III, 1997; Confessions of a Reluctant Theorist, 1989; The Social Animal, 1998; articles in academic jls. *Heir: s* Hon. David Walter Runciman, PhD [*b* 1 March 1967; *m* 1997, Beatrice, (Bee), *yr d* of A. N. Wilson, *qv* and Katherine Duncan-Jones, *qv*; one *s* one *d*]. *Address:* 44 Clifton Hill, NW8 0QG. *Club:* Brooks's.

RUNCIMAN OF DOXFORD, Viscountess; Ruth Runciman, DBE 1998 (OBE 1991); Chairman, Central and North West London NHS Foundation Trust (formerly Central and North West London Mental Health NHS Trust), since 2001; *b* 9 Jan. 1936; *o d* of Joseph Hellmann and Dr Ellen Hellmann; *m* 1st, 1959, Denis Mack Smith, *qv* (marr. diss. 1962); 2nd, 1963, Viscount Runciman of Doxford, *qv*; one *s* two *d*. *Educ:* Roedean Sch., Johannesburg; Witwatersrand Univ. (BA 1956); Girton Coll., Cambridge (BA 1958; Hon. Fellow, 2001). Chairman: Mental Health Act Commn, 1994–98; Ind. Inquiry into Misuse of Drugs Act 1971, 1997–2000; Member: Adv. Council on Misuse of Drugs, 1974–95; Press Complaints Commn, 1998–2001 (Mem., Charter Compliance Panel, 2004–06). Council Mem., Nat. Assoc. of CAB, 1978–83; Outreach advice worker, Kensington CAB, 1988–2000; Chairman: Nat. AIDS Trust, 2000–06 (Trustee, 1989–93); UK Drug Policy Commn, 2007–; Dep. Chm., Prison Reform Trust, 1981–. Trustee: Prince's Trust Volunteers, 1989–94; Mental Health Foundn, 1990–96; Pilgrim Trust, 1999–; Sainsbury Centre for Mental Health, 2001–03. Dir, ENO, 1978–83. Hon. Fellow, Univ. of Central Lancs, 2000. Hon. LLD De Montfort, 1997. *Recreations:* tennis, gardening. *Address:* 44 Clifton Hill, NW8 0QG.

RUNDELL, Richard John; His Honour Judge Rundell; a Circuit Judge, since 2001; *b* 29 July 1948; *s* of Norman Henry Rundell and Pamela Anne Rundell; *m* 1969, Yvonne Doreen Lipinski; two *s*. *Educ:* Chelmsford Tech. High Sch.; Mid Essex Tech. Coll., Chelmsford (LLB London). Called to the Bar, Gray's Inn, 1971; barrister in practice, S Eastern Circuit, 1972–2001; a Recorder, 1996–2001. *Recreations:* golf, cricket, choral music, opera, gardening. *Address:* c/o Midland Circuit, Regional Director's Office, PO Box 11772, 6th Floor, Temple Court, Bull Street, Birmingham B4 6WF. *T:* (0121) 681 3206. *Club:* Farmers.

RUNDLE, Hon. Anthony Maxwell; Chairman, Australian Fisheries Management Authority, since 2004; Treasurer, 1993–98, and Premier, 1996–98, Tasmania; *b* 5 March 1939; *s* of M. J. Rundle; *m* Caroline Watt; two *d*. *Educ:* Launceston Church Grammar Sch. Journalist, Australian Associated Press, London, 1961–62; Eric White & Associates Public Relns, London, 1963–68; journalist, Tasmanian TV, 1979. MHA (L) Braddon, Tasmania, 1986–2002; Govt Whip, 1986; Speaker, House of Assembly, 1988–89; Shadow Minister for Tourism and for Transport, 1989–92; Minister: for Forests and for Mines, 1992–93; assisting Premier on Econ. Develt, 1992–93; for Public Sector Mgt, 1993–96; for Finance, 1993–95; for Employment and for Racing and Gaming, 1993–95; assisting Premier on State Develt and Resources, 1993–96; for Energy, 1995–96; Leader of the Opposition, 1998–99; Shadow Minister: for Energy, 1998–2002; for Tourism, for Nat. Parks & Public Lands, and for Planning & Inland Fisheries, 1999–2001; for Small Business, 2001; for Planning, 2001–02. Chm., Port Devonport Authy, 1982–87. *Recreations:* yachting, tennis, fishing. *Address:* 8a Reid Road, Wongaling Beach, Qld 4852, Australia.

RUNDLE, Christopher John Spencer, OBE 1983; HM Diplomatic Service, retired; Research Counsellor, Foreign and Commonwealth Office, 1991–98; *b* 17 Aug. 1938; *s* of late Percy William and Ruth Rundle (*née* Spencer); *m* 1970, Qamar Said; one *d*. *Educ:* Cranbrook Sch.; St John's Coll., Cambridge (MA). Served HM Forces, 1957–59. Central Asian Res. Centre, 1962–63; joined Diplomatic Service, 1963; Tehran, 1967–68; Oriental Sec., Kabul, 1968–70; FCO, 1970–75; seconded to Cabinet Office, 1975–77; First Secretary: FCO, 1977–81; Tehran, 1981–84; FCO, 1985. Member Council, British Inst. of Persian Studies, 1990–2003. Hon. Fellow, Inst. for Middle Eastern and Islamic Studies, Durham Univ., 2001. *Publications:* From Colwyn Bay to Kabul: an unexpected journey, 2004; papers in academic jls, incl. Durham Middle East Papers. *Recreations:* sports, foreign films and literature.

RUNDLE, John Louis, AM 1981; JP; Agent-General for South Australia, 1980–85; *b* 11 Jan. 1930; *s* of late J. A. Rundle; *m* Elizabeth Phillipa, *d* of John P. Little, Melbourne; one *s* one *d*. *Educ:* Rostrevor Coll. Formerly Senior Partner, J. C. Rundle & Co., and Rundle, Parsons & Partners; Former Chairman: J. C. Rundle Holdings Pty Ltd; Seacliff Investments Pty Ltd; Thevenard Hotel Pty Ltd; former Director: Commonwealth Accommodation & Catering Service Ltd; Mallen & Co. Ltd; Commercial & Domestic Finance Ltd. Former Member: Nat. Employers Ind. Council (Dep. Chm., 1979–80); Confed. of Aust. Industry (Mem. Bd, 1978–80); State Develt Council, SA; Ind. Relations Adv. Council, SA; Adv. Curriculum Bd, SA; Council, Royal AA of SA. Pres., Junior Chambers, Adelaide, 1957, SA, 1958, Australia, 1959; Vice-Pres., JCI, 1960, 1963, Exec. Vice-Pres., 1964, World Pres., 1965, Pres. Senate, 1966; Councillor, Adelaide Chamber of Commerce, 1956–57, 1961–72, Vice-Pres., 1968–70, Dep. Pres., 1970–72; Vice-Pres., Chamber of Commerce & Industry, SA, 1973–75, Dep. Pres., 1975–77, Pres. 1977–79 (Chm., Commerce Div., 1973, 1974; Chm., Ind. Matters Cttee); Exec. Mem., Aust. Chamber of Commerce, 1980. Councillor: Red Cross Soc., SA Div., 1957–63 (Chm., Junior Red Cross, 1961–62); Burnside City Council, 1962–64; President: Assoc. of Ind. Schools of SA, 1972–75; Nat. Council of Ind. Schools, 1975–77; Chm., Bd of Governors, Rostrevor Coll., 1967–77. Mem. Central Council, Royal Over-Seas League, 1988–93. Freeman, City of London, 1981. JP SA, 1956. KHS 1989. *Address:* 230 Victoria Grove, 254 Greenhill Road, Glenside, SA 5065, Australia. *Clubs:* East India; Naval Military and Air Force (Adelaide).

RUPERT'S LAND, Metropolitan of; *see* Athabasca, Archbishop of.

RUPERT'S LAND, Bishop of, since 2000; **Rt Rev. Donald David Phillips;** *m* Nancy. *Educ:* Univ. of Western Ontario (BSc 1976, MSc 1979); Huron Coll., Univ. of Western Ontario (MDiv 1981; Hon. DD 2002). Ordained deacon, 1981, priest, 1981; incumbent, Lac La Biche, Alberta, 1981–84; Priest in charge, St Thomas Ch, Fort McMurray and St Paul's Ch, Fort Chipewyan, Alberta, 1984–87; incumbent, St Michael and All Angels, Moose Jaw, Sask, 1987–92; Ministries Develt Co-ordinator, 1992–96, Exec. Officer, 1997–2000, Dio. Qu'Appelle. Hon. Asst, Parish of St Matthew, Regina, Sask, 1992–2000. *Address:* (office) 935 Nesbitt Bay, Winnipeg, MB R3T 1W6, Canada. *T:* (204) 9924212, *Fax:* (204) 9924219; *e-mail:* dphillips@rupertsland.anglican.ca.

RUSBRIDGE, Brian John, CBE 1984; exhibition and training consultant, since 1998; *b* 10 Sept. 1922; *s* of late Arthur John and Leonora Rusbridge, Appleton, Berks; *m* 1951, Joyce, *d* of late Joseph Young Elliott, Darlington; two *s*. *Educ:* Willowfield Sch., Eastbourne; Univ. of Oxford Dept of Social and Admin. Studies (Dip. Social Admin.). Served War of 1939–45, Lieut RNVR. Personnel Manager, Imperial Chemical Industries (Teesside), 1949; British Railways Board: Dir of Industrial Relations, 1963; Divisional Manager, London, 1970; Dir, LACSAB (advising on human relations for Local Govt in UK), 1973–87. Ed., Municipal Year Book, 1987–94; Dir, Newman Books Ltd, 1991–94. Dir, Assoc. of Exhibition Organisers, 1992–98. Freeman, City of London, 1976. CCIPD; CMILT. FRSA. *Recreations:* walking, travel, local politics. *Address:* 19 Beauchamp Road, East Molesey, Surrey KT8 0PA. *T:* (020) 8979 4952.

RUSBRIDGE, Christopher Anthony, CEng; Director, Digital Curation Centre, University of Edinburgh, since 2005; *b* 25 Feb. 1946; *s* of Charles Edward Rusbridge and Elma May Rusbridge; *m* 1973, Sheila Margaret Stuart; one *s* two *d*. *Educ:* Imperial Coll., Univ. of London (BSc; ARCS). Programmer and Manager, ICT/ICL, 1967–74; Asst Dir, ADP, S Australian Public Service Hosps Dept, 1974–75; Programming Services Manager, 1975–83, Acad. Computing Services Manager, 1983–92, SA Inst. of Technol., then Univ. of S Australia; Dir, IT Services, Univ. of Dundee, 1992–94; Liby IT Co-ordinator, Univ. of S Australia, 1994; Dir, Jt Inf. Systems Cttee Electronic Libraries Prog., Univ. of Warwick, 1995–2000; Dir, Inf. Services, Glasgow Univ., 2000–05. *Recreations:* walking, music. *Address:* University of Edinburgh, Appleton Tower, Crichton Street, Edinburgh EH8 9LE. *T:* (0131) 651 3823; *e-mail:* c.rusbridge@ed.ac.uk.

RUSBRIDGER, Alan Charles; Editor, The Guardian, since 1995; *b* 29 Dec. 1953; *s* of late G. H. Rusbridger and B. E. Rusbridger (*née* Wickham); *m* 1982, Lindsay Mackie; two *d*. *Educ:* Cranleigh Sch.; Magdalene Coll., Cambridge (MA). Reporter, Cambridge Evening News, 1976–79; reporter, columnist and feature writer, The Guardian, 1979–86; TV Critic, The Observer, 1986–87; Washington Corresp., London Daily News, 1987; Editor, Weekend Guardian, 1988–89; The Guardian: Features Editor, 1989–93; Dep. Editor, 1993–95; Exec. Ed., The Observer, 1997–. Director: Guardian Newspapers Ltd, 1994–; Guardian Media Gp, 1999–. Vis. Fellow, Nuffield Coll., Oxford, 2004–; Vis. Prof., QMC, London Univ. Mem., The Scott Trust, 1997–. Chairman: Photographer's Gall., 2001–04; NYO of GB, 2004–. Co-author (with Ronan Bennett), Fields of Gold, BBC TV, 2002. Editor of the Year: Granada TV What the Papers Say Awards, 1996 and 2001; Newspaper Focus Awards, 1996; Nat. Newspaper Editor, Newspaper Industry Awards, 1996; Freedom of the Press Award, London Press Club, 1998; Judges Award, Granada TV What the Papers Say, 2005. *Publications: for children:* Coldest Day at the Zoo, 2004; Wildest Day at the Zoo, 2004. *Recreations:* music, painting, golf. *Address:* The Guardian, Kings Place, 90 York Way, N1 9AG. *Clubs:* Garrick, Soho House; Broadway Golf.

RUSBY, Vice-Adm. Sir Cameron, KCB 1979; LVO 1965; *b* 20 Feb. 1926; *s* of late Captain Victor Evelyn Rusby, CBE, RN, and Mrs Irene Margaret Rusby; *m* 1948, Marion Elizabeth Bell; two *d*. *Educ:* RNC, Dartmouth. Midshipman 1943; specialised in communications, 1950; CO HMS Ulster, 1958–59; Exec. Officer, HM Yacht Britannia, 1962–65; Dep. Dir, Naval Signals, 1965–68; CO HMS Tartar, 1968–69; Dep. ACOS (Plans and Policy), staff of Allied C-in-C Southern Europe, 1969–72; Sen. Naval Officer, WI, 1972–74; Rear-Adm. 1974; ACDS (Ops), 1974–77; Vice-Adm. 1977; Flag Officer Scotland and N Ireland, 1977–79; Dep. Supreme Allied Comdr, Atlantic, 1980–82. Chief Exec., Scottish SPCA, 1983–91; former Chm., British Wildlife Rehabilitation Council. Dir, World Soc. for the Protection of Animals, 1986–98 (Hon. Vice Pres., 1998–2005). Dir, Freedom Food Ltd, 1994–2000. Vice Pres., King George's Fund for Sailors, 1996–. *Recreations:* sailing, country pursuits. *Club:* New (Edinburgh).

RUSE, David John; Director of Libraries (formerly Assistant Director, Lifetime, then Lifelong, Learning), Westminster City Council, since 1999; *b* 24 Aug. 1951; *s* of Ronald Frank and Betty Irene Ruse; *m* 1975, Carole Anne Lawton; two *d*. *Educ:* Birmingham Coll. of Commerce. MCLIP (ALA 1973). Bath Municipal Libraries, 1969–70; Asst Librarian, London Borough of Havering, 1972–77; Branch Librarian, London Borough of Barking and Dagenham, 1977–81; Asst Dir, Library Assoc., 1981–89; Head, Planning and Review, Berks CC, 1989–93; Asst Dir, Leisure and Libraries, Westminster CC, 1993–99. Member: Bd, Lifelong Learning UK, 2005–; Adv. Council on Libraries, 2006–. Mem., Inst. of Leisure and Amenity Mgt. *Publications:* chapters in various librarianship books; various articles in professional library press. *Recreations:* social history of railways, reading, music, countryside matters. *Address:* Management Suite, 3rd Floor, Westminster Reference Library, 35 St Martins Street, WC2H 7HP. *T:* (020) 7641 2496.

RUSEDSKI, Gregory; professional tennis player, retired 2007; media commentator; *b* Montreal, 6 Sept. 1973; *s* of Tom and Helen Rusedski; *m* 1999, Lucy Connor; one *d*. *Educ:* Lower Canada Coll. Mem., British Davis Cup Team, 1995–2007. Winner of 15 career titles including: singles: Newport, Rhode Is., 1993, 2004, 2005; Paris Indoor Open, 1998; Compaq Grand Slam Cup, 1999; Vienna Indoor Open, 1999; Sybase Open, San Jose, 2001; Indianapolis Open, 2002; Auckland, 2002. Recorded world record serve of 149 mph, 1998. LTA Talent Ambassador. Sports Personality of the Year, BBC, 1997. *Recreations:* golf, chess, Arsenal Football Club, cinema, James Bond. *Address:* Ructions, PO Box 31369, SW11 3GH; *e-mail:* sharon@park54.fsnet.co.uk.

RUSH, Ann Patricia; consultant, Archam, since 2002; *b* 17 March 1948; *d* of Peter Deshaw and Hanni Adele Gray; *m* 1969, Charles Anthony Rush; one *s* one *d*. *Educ:* Ursuline Convent; LSE (MSc). The Observer, 1966–68; RABI, 1969–76; CR Associates, 1974–89; Dep. Dir, 1990–92, Dir, Migraine Trust, 1992–2002. Trustee, Neurological Alliance, 1999–2001. *Publication:* Migraine, 1996. *Recreations:* family, reading, sailing. *Address:* 36 Mayfield Road, Weybridge, Surrey KT13 8XB.

RUSH, Geoffrey Roy; actor; *b* Toowoomba, Qld, 6 July 1951; *s* of Roy Baden Rush and Merle Rush (*née* Kiehne); *m* 1988, Jane Manelaus; one *s* one *d*. *Educ:* Everton Park High Sch., Brisbane; Univ. of Queensland (BA); Jacques Lecoq Sch. of Mime, Movement and Th., Paris. Stage début in Wrong Side of the Moon, 1971; Mem., Qld Th. Co., 1971–74; Mem., Lighthouse State Th. Co., SA, 1982–83; Dir, Magpie Th., SA, 1984–86; Associate Artist, Qld Arts Council, 2003–. *Theatre* includes: The Diary of a Madman, 1989; The Government Inspector, 1991; Uncle Vanya, The Importance of Being Earnest, 1992; Hamlet, 1994; The Alchemist, 1996; The Marriage of Figaro, 1998; The Small Poppies, 1999; Exit the King, 2007; also dir numerous prodns. *Films* include: Hoodwink, 1981; Twelfth Night, 1987; Children of the Revolution, Shine, 1996 (Academy, Golden Globe, BAFTA and Aust. Film Inst. Awards for Best Actor); Oscar and Lucinda (voice), 1997; Les Misérables, Elizabeth, Shakespeare in Love (BAFTA Award for Best Supporting Actor), 1998; Mystery Men, House on Haunted Hill, 1999; The Tailor of Panama, Lantana, Quills, 2001; The Banger Sisters, Frida, Ned Kelly, Intolerable Cruelty, Pirates of the Caribbean: The Curse of the Black Pearl, Finding Nemo (voice), 2003; The Life and Death of Peter Sellers, 2004 (Golden Globe, Screen Actors and Emmy Awards, 2005); Swimming Upstream, 2005; Munich, Pirates of the Caribbean: Dead Man's Chest, 2006; Pirates of the Caribbean: At World's End, Elizabeth: The Golden Age, 2007; *television* includes: Menotti, 1981; Mercury, 1996; Frontier, 1997. *Publications:* (jtly) The Popular Mechanicals (play), 1992; (adapted with J. Clarke) Aristophanes' Frogs; (trans. jtly) The Government Inspector. *Address:* c/o Shanahan Management, PO Box 1509, Darlinghurst, NSW 1300, Australia.

RUSHDIE, Sir (Ahmed) Salman, Kt 2007; FRSL; writer; *b* 19 June 1947; *s* of Anis Ahmed Rushdie and Negin Rushdie (*née* Butt); *m* 1976, Clarissa Luard (marr. diss. 1987); one *s*; *m* 1988, Marianne Wiggins (marr. diss. 1993); *m* 1997, Elizabeth West (marr. diss. 2002); one *s*; *m* 2004, Padma Lakshmi. *Educ:* Cathedral Sch., Bombay; Rugby Sch.; King's Coll., Cambridge (MA (Hons) History). Hon. Prof., MIT, 1993; Dist. Fellow in Lit., UEA, 1995. Pres., PEN America Center, 2004–. Hon. DLitt Bard Coll., 1995; Hon. Dr: Amherst, Tromsø, 1997; Torino, UEA, Liège, Free Univ. of Berlin, 1999; Sorbonne, Albion Coll., 2003. Arts Council Literature Bursary Award; Kurt Tucholsky Prize, Sweden, 1992; Prix Colette, Switzerland, 1993; Austrian State Prize for European Literature, 1994; EU Aristeion Prize for Literature, 1996; London Internat. Writers' Award, 2002. Freedom of Mexico City, 1999. Commandeur, Ordre des Arts et des Lettres (France), 1999. *Films for TV:* The Painter and the Pest, 1985; The Riddle of Midnight, 1988. *Publications:* Grimus, 1975; Midnight's Children, 1981 (Booker Prize for Fiction, 1981; James Tait Black Meml Book Prize; ESU Literary Award; Booker of Bookers Prize, 1993; Best of the Booker award, 2008) (adapted for stage, 2003); Shame, 1983 (Prix du Meilleur Livre Etranger, 1984); The Jaguar Smile: a Nicaraguan journey, 1987; The Satanic Verses, 1988 (Whitbread Novel Award; German Author of the Year Award, 1989); Haroun and the Sea of Stories, 1990 (Writers' Guild Award); Imaginary Homelands (essays), 1991; The Wizard of Oz, 1992; East, West, 1994; The Moor's Last Sigh (Whitbread Novel Award; British Book Awards Author of the Year), 1995; (ed with Elizabeth West) The Vintage Book of Indian Writing, 1947–97, 1997; The Ground Beneath Her Feet, 1999; Fury, 2001; Step Across This Line: collected non-fiction 1992–2002, 2002; Shalimar the Clown, 2005; The Enchantress of Florence, 2008; contribs to many journals. *Address:* c/o Wylie Agency (UK) Ltd, 17 Bedford Square, WC1B 3JA.

RUSHFORD, Antony Redfern, CMG 1963; consultant on constitutional, international and commonwealth law; *b* 9 Feb.; *m* 1975, June Jeffrey, *widow* of Roy Eustace Wells; one step *s* one step *d*. *Educ:* Taunton Sch.; Trinity Coll., Cambridge (BA 1948; LLM (LLB 1948); MA 1951). FRSA. RAFVR, 1942 (active service, 1943–47, reserve, 1947–59); Sqdn Ldr, 1946. Solicitor, 1944–57 (distinction in Law Soc. final exams, 1942); Called to the Bar, Inner Temple, 1983. Asst Solicitor, E. W. Marshall Harvey & Dalton, 1948. Home Civil Service, Colonial Office, 1949–68; joined HM Diplomatic Service, 1968; CO, later FCO, retd as Dep. Legal Advr (Asst Under-Sec. of State), 1982. Crown Counsel, Uganda, 1954; Principal Legal Adviser, British Indian Ocean Territory, 1983; Attorney-Gen., Anguilla, and St Helena, 1983; Legal Adviser for Commonwealth Sec.-Gen. to Governor-Gen. of Grenada, Mem. Interim Govt, Attorney-Gen., and JP,

Grenada, 1983; consultancies: FCO (special duties), 1982; Commonwealth Sec.-Gen., St Kitts and Nevis independence, 1982–83, St Lucia treaties, 1983–85; E Caribbean courts, 1983; maritime legislation for Jamaica, Internat. Maritime Orgn, 1983 and 1985; constitutional advr, Govt of St Kitts and Nevis, and Govt of St Lucia, 1982–85. Has drafted many constitutions for UK dependencies and Commonwealth countries attaining independence; presented paper on constitutional develt to meeting of Law Officers from Smaller Commonwealth Jurisdictions, IoM, 1983. UK deleg. or advr at many constitutional confs and discussions; CO Rep., Inst. of Advanced Legal Studies; participant, Symposium on Federalism, Chicago, 1962; Advr, Commonwealth Law Ministers Conf., 1973. Lectr, Overseas Legal Officers Course, 1964; Special Examnr, London Univ., 1963, 1987; a dir of studies, RIPA (Overseas Services Unit), and also associate consultant on statute law, 1982–86. Mem. Editl Bd, Inst. of Internat. Law and Econ. Develt, Washington, 1977–82. Co. Sec., Forwardstrike Ltd, 1997–. Foundn Mem. Exec. Council, Royal Commonwealth Soc. for the Blind, 1969–81, 1983–99 (Hon. Legal Counsellor, 1984–2001; Indiv. Mem., 1998–); Hon. Sec., Services Race Club, Hong Kong, 1946–47. Member: Glyndebourne Fest. Soc., 1950–96; Inst. of Advanced Motoring, 1959–73; Commonwealth Lawyers Assoc., 1982–90; Commonwealth Assoc. of Legislative Counsel, 1984–; Commonwealth Magistrates and Judges Assoc., 1986–90; Anglo-Arab Assoc., 1990–; Saudi-British Soc., 1990–. Governor, Taunton Sch., 1948–. CStJ 1989 (Hon. Legal Counsellor, 1978–93; Mem., Chapter-Gen., 1983–94). *Address:* Flat 5, 50 Pont Street, Knightsbridge, SW1X 0AE. *T:* (020) 7589 4235; (chambers) 12 King's Bench Walk, Temple, EC4Y 7EL. *T:* (020) 7353 5692/6. *Clubs:* Royal Commonwealth Society; Polish Air Force Association.

RUSHFORTH, Philip Christopher; Director of Music, Chester Cathedral, since 2007; *b* Chester, 31 Dec. 1972; *s* of Christopher and Gillian Rushforth; *m* 2001, Louise Walker; two *s* one *d*. *Educ:* Abbey Gate Coll., Chester; Trinity Coll., Cambridge (BA 1994). ARCO 1993. Asst Organist, Southwell Minster, 1994–2002; Asst Dir of Music, Chester Cath., 2002–07. *Recreations:* Olympic class ships, horology, biography. *Address:* Chester Cathedral Office, 12 Abbey Square, Chester CH1 2HU. *T:* (01244) 500974; *e-mail:* philip.rushforth@chestercathedral.com.

RUSHTON, Ian Lawton, FIA, FCII, FSS; Chairman, Hackney Empire Ltd, 1994–2004; Vice Chairman, Royal Insurance Holdings plc, 1991–93 (Group Chief Executive, 1989–91); *b* 8 Sept. 1931; *s* of Arthur John and Mabel Lilian Rushton; *m* 1st, 1956, Julia Frankland (decd); one *d*; 2nd, 1986, Anita Spencer; one step *s* one step *d*. *Educ:* Rock Ferry High Sch., Birkenhead; King's Coll., London (BSc Mathematics). FIA 1959; FCII 1961. Served RAF, 1953–56 (Flt-Lieut). Royal Insurance, 1956–93: Dep. Gen. Man. (UK), 1972; Exec. Vice Pres., Royal US, 1980; Gen. Man. Royal UK, 1983; Exec. Dir and Gp Gen. Man., Royal Insurance plc, 1986. Chairman: Fire Protection Assoc., 1983–87; Assoc. of British Insurers, 1991–93; Vice Pres., Inst. of Actuaries, 1986–89. FRSA. *Recreations:* gardening, theatre, music. *Address:* Flat 136, 4 Whitehall Court, SW1A 2EP.

RUSHTON, Prof. Julian Gordon, DPhil; West Riding Professor of Music, University of Leeds, 1982–2002, now Emeritus; *b* 22 May 1941; *s* of Prof. William A. H. Rushton and Marjorie Rushton; *m* 1968, Virginia S. M. Jones (marr. diss. 2000); two *s*. *Educ:* Trinity Coll., Cambridge (BA 1963; BMus 1965; MA 1967); Magdalen Coll., Oxford (DPhil 1970). Lecturer in Music: UEA, 1968–74; and Fellow, King's Coll., Cambridge, 1974–81. Chm., Editl Bd, Musica Britannica, 1993–. Pres., Royal Musical Assoc., 1994–99. Corres. Mem., Amer. Musicol Soc., 2000. *Publications:* W. A. Mozart: Don Giovanni, 1981, 2nd edn 1990; The Musical Language of Berlioz, 1983; Classical Music: a concise history, 1986; W. A. Mozart: Idomeneo, 1993; Berlioz: Roméo et Juliette, 1994; Elgar: Enigma Variations, 1999; The Music of Berlioz, 2001; (ed with D. M. Grimley) The Cambridge Companion to Elgar, 2004; Mozart: an extraordinary life, 2005; Mozart (Master Musicians series), 2006; (ed with J. P. E. Harper-Scott) Elgar Studies, 2007; contrib. to Music & Letters, Music Analysis, Cambridge Opera Jl, Musical Times, Elgar Soc. Jl. *Recreations:* literature, walking, gardening, preserving. *Address:* School of Music, University of Leeds, Leeds LS2 9JT. *T:* (0113) 343 2583; *e-mail:* j.g.rushton@leeds.ac.uk; 362 Leymoor Road, Golcar, Huddersfield HD7 4QF.

RUSHTON, Prof. Neil, MD; FRCS; FIMMM; Professor of Orthopaedics, University of Cambridge, since 2003; Fellow of Magdalene College, Cambridge, since 1984; *b* 16 Dec. 1945; *s* of John Allen Rushton and Iris Rushton; *m* 1971, Sheila Margaret Johnson; two *s* one *d*. *Educ:* Middlesex Hosp., London (MB BS 1970); Magdalene Coll., Cambridge (MA 1979; MD 1984). LRCP 1970; MRCS 1970, FRCS 1975; FIMMM 2008. Pre-Registration Sen. House Officer, Orsett Hosp., 1971–75; Registrar in Trauma and Orthopaedics, Royal Northern, Royal Free and Heatherwood Hosps, 1975–77; University of Cambridge: Sen. Registrar Orthopaedics, 1977–79; Clinical Lectr in Surgery, Cambridge and Black Notley, 1979–83; Lectr in Surgery, 1983–2000; Sen. Lectr, 2000–01, Reader, 2001–03, in Orthopaedics; Hon. Consultant in Orthopaedics, Addenbrooke's Hosp., 1983–. Dep. Ed. (Res.), Jl of Bone and Joint Surgery, 1996–2006; Ed., British Orthopaedic News, 2002–06. *Publications:* Surgical Exposures of the Limbs, 1984; Classification of Limb Fractures in Adults, 2002; chapters in 8 books; articles on biocompatibility of materials used in orthopaedics, tissue engrg bone and cartilage, fractures of the proximal femur and the bone response to arthroplasty, in Jl of Bone and Joint Surgery, Acta Orthopaedica Scandinavica, Biomaterials and Jl of Materials Sci.: Materials in Medicine. *Recreations:* sailing, ski-ing, scuba diving, music, cycling, wine. *Address:* 37 Bentley Road, Cambridge CB2 8AW. *T:* (01223) 353624, *Fax:* (01223) 365889; Orthopaedic Research Unit, Box 180, Addenbrooke's Hospital, Cambridge CB2 2QQ. *T:* (01223) 217551, *Fax:* (01223) 214094; *e-mail:* nr10000@cam.ac.uk. *Clubs:* Athenæum, Ski Club of Great Britain.

RUSHWORTH, Dr (Frank) Derek; Headmaster, Holland Park School, London, 1971–85; *b* 15 Sept. 1920; *s* of late Frank and Elizabeth Rushworth, Huddersfield; *m* 1941, Hamidah Begum, *d* of late Justice S. Akhlaque Hussain, Lahore, and Edith (*née* Bayliss), Oxford; three *d*. *Educ:* Huddersfield Coll.; St Edmund Hall, Oxford (Schol.; BA 1942, MA 1946); Doctorate of Univ. of Paris (Lettres), 1947. Served 6th Rajputana Rifles, Indian Army, 1942–45 (Major); began teaching, 1947; Head of Modern Languages: Tottenham Grammar Sch., 1953; Holland Park Sch., 1958; Head of Shoreditch Sch., London, 1965. Chairman: Associated Examining Board, French Committee, 1964–74; Schools Council, 16+ Examination Feasibility Study (French), 1971–75; Pres., London Head Teachers' Assoc., 1985. Governor, Holland Park Sch., 1990–95. *Publications:* Our French Neighbours, 1963, 2nd edn 1966; French text-books and language-laboratory books; articles in French Studies, Modern Languages, also educnl jls. *Recreation:* photography. *Address:* 25c Lambolle Road, NW3 4HS. *T:* (020) 7794 3691.

RUSKELL, Mark Christopher; Communications Manager, Scottish Renewables Forum; *b* 14 May 1972; *s* of David and Brenda Ruskell; *m* 1999, Melinda McEwen. *Educ:* Edinburgh Acad.; Stevenson Coll., Edinburgh; Univ. of Stirling (BSc Hons Envmtl Sci. with Biol.); Scottish Agricl Coll., Univ. of Aberdeen (MSc Sustainable Agric.). Develt Worker, Falkirk Voluntary Action Resource Centre, 1997–2000; Regeneration Officer, Midlothian Council, 2000–02; Project Officer, Soil Assoc., 2002–03; MSP (Green) Scotland and Mid Fife, 2003–07. Dir, LETSlink Scotland, 1996–99. *Recreations:* cycling, growing and cooking food.

RUSSELL; *see* Hamilton-Russell, family name of Viscount Boyne.

RUSSELL, family name of **Duke of Bedford**, **Earl Russell**, **Baron Ampthill**, **Baron de Clifford** and **Baron Russell of Liverpool**.

RUSSELL, 6th Earl *cr* 1861; **Nicholas Lyulph Russell;** Viscount Amberley 1861; *b* 12 Sept. 1968; *s* of 5th Earl Russell, FBA and Elizabeth Franklyn Russell (*née* Sanders); *S* father, 2004. *Heir:* *b* Hon. John Francis Russell [*b* 19 Nov. 1971; *m* 2002, Jane Elizabeth Swann; one *d*].

RUSSELL OF LIVERPOOL, 3rd Baron *cr* 1919; **Simon Gordon Jared Russell;** *b* 30 Aug. 1952; *s* of Captain Hon. Langley Gordon Haslingden Russell, MC (*d* 1975) (*o s* of 2nd Baron), and of Kiloran Margaret, *d* of late Hon. Sir Arthur Jared Palmer Howard, KBE, CVO; *S* grandfather, 1981; *m* 1984, Dr Gilda Albano, *y d* of late Signor F. Albano and of Signora Maria Caputo-Albano; two *s* one *d*. *Educ:* Charterhouse; Trinity Coll., Cambridge; INSEAD, Fontainebleau, France. *Heir:* *s* Hon. Edward Charles Stanley Russell, *b* 2 Sept. 1985.

RUSSELL, Alan Keith, OBE 2000; DPhil; Chairman, Dresden Trust, since 1993; charity administrator, consultant and writer; *b* 22 Oct. 1932; *s* of late Keith Russell and Gertrude Ann Russell; *m* 1959, Philippa Margaret Stoneham; two *s* one *d*. *Educ:* Ardingly Coll.; Lincoln Coll., Oxford (BA; MA Econ and Pol Sci. 1956); Nuffield Coll., Oxford (DPhil 1962); Oxford Brookes Univ. (Cert. in Architectural Hist., 1997; Dip. in Historic Conservation, 1998). Colonial Office, ODM, FCO, 1959–69, 1972–75; CS Coll., 1969–71; Dir, Inter University Council for Higher Educn Overseas, 1980–81; sen. official, Commn of EC, 1976–79, 1981–86, 1988–89; Fellow, Lincoln Coll., Oxford and Sen. Res. Associate, Queen Elizabeth House, 1986–88; manager of civic improvement trust, 1990–92. Vice Chm., British-German Assoc., 2007–. Medal of Honour, City of Dresden, 2006; Erich Kästner Prize, Dresden Journalists' Club, 2006. Order of Merit (FRG), 1997, 2006. *Publications:* (ed) The Economic and Social History of Mauritius, 1962; Liberal Landslide: the General Election of 1906, 1973; (contrib.) Edwardian Radicalism, 1974; The Unclosed Eye (poems), 1987; (ed and contrib.) Dresden: a city reborn, 1999; (ed and contrib.) Why Dresden?, 2000; (ed and contrib.) Kulturelle Beziehungen zwischen Sachsen und Grossbritannien, 2002; (contrib.) Firestorm: the bombing of Dresden, 2006; articles on: internat. relations and development; Dresden, Germany and Europe; conservation. *Recreations:* conservation and town planning, German and European history, services for the mentally handicapped. *Address:* Dresden House, 30 Stirling Road, Chichester, W Sussex PO19 7DS.

RUSSELL, Sir (Alastair) Muir, KCB 2001; DL; FRSE; FInstP; Principal and Vice-Chancellor, University of Glasgow, since 2003; *b* 9 Jan. 1949; *s* of Thomas Russell and Anne Muir; *m* 1983, Eileen Alison Mackay, *qv*. *Educ:* High Sch. of Glasgow; Univ. of Glasgow (BSc Nat. Phil.). FInstP 2003. Joined Scottish Office, 1970; seconded as Sec. to Scottish Development Agency, 1975–76; Asst Sec., 1981; Principal Private Sec. to Sec. of State for Scotland, 1981–83; Under Sec., 1990; seconded to Cabinet Office, 1990–92; Under Sec. (Housing), Scottish Office Envmt Dept, 1992–95; Dep. Sec., 1995; Sec. and Hd of Dept, Scottish Office Agric., Envmt and Fisheries Dept, 1995–98; Permanent Under-Sec. of State, Scottish Office, 1998–99; Permanent Sec., Scottish Exec., 1999–2003. Non-exec. Dir, Stagecoach Hldgs, 1992–95. Dir, UCAS, 2005–; Mem. Council, ACU, 2006–; Convener, Universities Scotland, 2006–08; Mem. Bd, Univs Superannuation Scheme, 2007–. Council Mem., Edinburgh Festival Soc., 2004–. Freeman, City of London, 2006. DL Glasgow, 2004. FRSE 2000; CCMI (CIMgt 2001). Hon. FRCPSGlas 2005. Hon. LLD Strathclyde, 2000; DUniv Glasgow, 2001. *Recreations:* music, food, wine. *Address:* University of Glasgow, Glasgow G12 8QQ. *T:* (0141) 330 5995, 4250. *Clubs:* Royal Commonwealth Society, Caledonian; New (Edinburgh).

RUSSELL, (Albert) Muir (Galloway), CBE 1989; QC (Scot.) 1965; Sheriff of Grampian, Highland and Islands (formerly Aberdeen, Kincardine and Banff) at Aberdeen and Stonehaven, 1971–91; *b* 26 Oct. 1925; *s* of Hon. Lord Russell; *m* 1954, Margaret Winifred, *o d* of T. McW. Millar, FRCSE, Edinburgh; two *s* two *d*. *Educ:* Edinburgh Academy; Wellington College; Brasenose College, Oxford (BA (Hons) 1949); LLB Edinburgh, 1951. Lieut, Scots Guards, 1944–47. Member of Faculty of Advocates, 1951–. *Recreation:* golf. *Address:* Tulloch House, Aultbea, Ross-shire IV22 2JA. *T:* (01445) 731325.

RUSSELL, Alexander William, (Sandy), CB 1996; Commissioner, 1985–98, and Deputy Chairman, 1993–98, HM Customs and Excise; *b* 16 Oct. 1938; *s* of late William and Elizabeth W. B. Russell (*née* Russell); *m* 1st, 1962, Elspeth Rae (*d* 1996); *m* 2nd, 1999, Patricia Sebbelov. *Educ:* Royal High Sch., Edinburgh; Edinburgh Univ. (MA Hons); Manitoba Univ. (MA). Assistant Principal, Scottish Development Dept, 1961–64; Private Sec. to Parliamentary Under Secretary of State, Scottish Office, 1964–65; Principal, Regional Development Div. and Scottish Development Dept, 1965–72; Principal Private Sec. to Secretary of State for Scotland, 1972–73; Asst Secretary: Scottish Development Dept, 1973–76; Civil Service Dept, 1976–79; Under-Secretary: Management and Personnel Office (formerly CSD), 1979–82; Hd of Treasury MPO Financial Management Unit, 1982–85; Dir Orgn, HM Customs and Excise, 1985–90, Dir Customs, 1990–93, HM Customs and Excise. Advr on efficiency matters to Cabinet Sec., 1999–2002. Mem., Council on Tribunals, 2002–05. Chm., Europro, 1999–2001 (Mem. Council, 2001–); Dir and Mem. Bd, SITPRO, 1999–; Mem., Steering Gp, Tax Mgt Res. Network (Univs of Nottingham and Bath, and UK Revenue Depts), 2000–03. *Address:* 1/18 Fidra Road, North Berwick EH39 4NG.

RUSSELL, Alison Hunter; QC 2008; barrister, since 1983; a Recorder, since 2004; *b* Harrogate, 17 June 1958; *d* of Alexander Law Macpherson Russell and Margaret Erskine Russell; partner, Julian Francis. *Educ:* Wellington Sch., Ayr; Poly. of South Bank (BA Hons 1982). Called to the Bar, Gray's Inn, 1983; in practice as barrister specialising in family law, human rights and internat. family law. *Address:* Coram Chambers, 9–11 Fulwood Place, WC1V 6HG. *T:* (020) 7092 3700, *Fax:* (020) 7092 3777; *e-mail:* clerks@coramchambers.co.uk.

RUSSELL, Andrew Victor Manson; Chief Executive (formerly Executive Director), Association for Spina Bifida and Hydrocephalus, since 1991; *b* 7 Dec. 1949; *s* of Manson McCausland Russell and Margaret Ivy Russell; *m* 1974, Susan Elizabeth Aykroyd; one *s* one *d*. *Educ:* Dartington Hall; Fitzwilliam Coll., Cambridge Univ. (MA). NSMHC, 1974–85; General Manager, Eastern Div., Royal MENCAP Soc., 1985–91. *Recreations:* sailing, music. *Address:* c/o ASBAH House, 42 Park Road, Peterborough PE1 2UQ. *T:* (01733) 555988.

RUSSELL, Rt Rev. Anthony John; *see* Ely, Bishop of.

RUSSELL, Anthony Patrick; QC 1999; **His Honour Judge Russell;** a Circuit Judge, since 2004; a Senior Circuit Judge and Resident Judge, Preston Combined Court Centre, since 2006; *b* 11 April 1951; *s* of late Dr Michael Hibberd Russell and of Pamela Russell (*née* Eyre). *Educ:* King's Sch., Chester; Pembroke Coll., Oxford (MA). Called to the Bar, Middle Temple, 1974; in practice at the Bar, Northern Circuit, 1974–2004; Junior, Northern Circuit, 1977; Standing Counsel to Inland Revenue, 1994–96; a Recorder, 1993–96, 2001–04; Hon. Recorder of Preston, 2006–. Mem., Gen. Council of the Bar, 1987–94. Hon. FGCM 2001 (Vice-Pres., 2005–). *Recreations:* music, especially singing, the countryside. *Address:* Law Courts, Openshaw Place, Ringway, Preston PR1 2LL. *T:* (01772) 844700. *Club:* Oxford and Cambridge.

RUSSELL, Sir (Arthur) Mervyn, 8th Bt *cr* 1812, of Swallowfield, Berkshire; *b* 7 Feb. 1923; *s* of Sir Arthur Edward Ian Montagu Russell, 6th Bt, MBE, and his 2nd wife, Cornélie, *d* of Maj. Jacques de Bruijn, Amsterdam; *S* half brother, 1993, but his name does not appear on the Official Roll of the Baronetage; *m* 1st, 1945, Ruth Holloway (marr. diss.); one *s*; 2nd, 1956, Kathleen Joyce Searle (*d* 2005); one *s*. *Heir: s* Stephen Charles Russell [*b* 12 Jan. 1949; *m* 1974, Dale Frances Markstein; one *d*].

RUSSELL, Ven. Brian Kenneth, PhD; Archdeacon of Aston, since 2005; *b* 1 Aug. 1950; *s* of William George Russell and Joan Russell; *m* 1976, Pamela Jean Gillard; one *s* one *d*. *Educ:* Bristol Grammar Sch.; Trinity Hall, Cambridge (BA 1973, MA 1976); Cuddesdon Coll., Oxford; Birmingham Univ. (MA 1977; PhD 1983). Ordained deacon, 1976, priest, 1977; Curate, St Matthew, Redhill, 1976–79; Priest-in-charge, St John, Kirk Merrington, and Dir of Studies, NE Ordination Course, 1979–83; Dir of Studies and Lectr in Christian Doctrine, Lincoln Theol Coll., 1983–86; Sec. to Cttee for Theol Educn, and Selection Sec., ACCM, subseq. ABM, 1986–93; Bishop's Dir for Ministries, Dio. Birmingham, 1993–2005. Hon. Canon, Birmingham Cathedral, 1999–. Mem., Bishops' Inspections Wkg Pty, 2003–. Gov., Queen's Foundn for Theol Educn, Birmingham, 1994–. *Publications:* (ed jtly) Leaders for the 21st Century, 1993; (ed) Formation in a Changing Church, 1999; articles on theol educn in Theology and British Jl of Theol Educn, and reviews in Theology. *Recreations:* theatre, literature, National Hunt racing, links with Nordic and Baltic Churches. *Address:* Birmingham Diocesan Office, 175 Harborne Park Road, Harborne, Birmingham B17 0BH. *T:* (0121) 426 0428, *Fax:* (0121) 428 1114; *e-mail:* Archdeaconofaston@birmingham.anglican.org.

RUSSELL, Cecil Anthony Francis; Director of Intelligence, Greater London Council, 1970–76; *b* 7 June 1921; *s* of late Comdr S. F. Russell, OBE, RN retd and late Mrs M. E. Russell (*née* Sneyd-Kynnersley); *m* 1950, Editha May (*née* Birch); no *c*. *Educ:* Winchester Coll.; University Coll., Oxford (1940–41, 1945–47). RNVR, 1941–45. Civil Service, 1949–70: Road Research Lab., 1949–50; Air Min., 1950–62; Dep. Statistical Adviser, Home Office, 1962–67; Head of Census Div., General Register Office, 1967–70. FSS. *Recreation:* ocean sailing. *Address:* Pagan Hill, Whiteleaf, Princes Risborough, Bucks HP27 0LQ. *T:* (01844) 343655. *Clubs:* Cruising Association; Ocean Cruising.

RUSSELL, Sir Charles (Dominic), 4th Bt *cr* 1916, of Littleworth Corner, Burnham, co. Buckingham; antiquarian bookseller, trading as Russell Rare Books, since 1978; *b* 28 May 1956; *o s* of Sir Charles Ian Russell, 3rd Bt and Rosemary Lavender Russell (*née* Prestige) (*d* 1996); *S* father, 1997; *m* 1st, 1986, Sarah Chandor (marr. diss. 1995); one *s*; 2nd, 2005, Wandee Ruanrakrao. *Educ:* Worth Sch. *Heir: s* Charles William Russell, *b* 8 Sept. 1988. *Club:* Chelsea Arts.

RUSSELL, Christine Margaret; JP; MP (Lab) City of Chester, since 1997; *b* 25 March 1945; *d* of John Alfred William Carr and Phyllis Carr; *m* 1971, Dr James Russell (marr. diss. 1991); one *s* one *d*. *Educ:* Spalding High Sch.; London Sch. of Librarianship (ALA). PA to Brian Simpson, MEP, 1992–94. Mem. (Lab) Chester CC, 1980–97 (Chair, Develt). Co-ordinator, Mind Advocacy Scheme, 1995–97. JP 1980. *Recreations:* film, visual arts, walking, football. *Address:* House of Commons, SW1A 0AA.

RUSSELL, Christopher; *see* Russell, R. C. G.

RUSSELL, Clare Nancy; Lord-Lieutenant for Banffshire, since 2002 (Vice Lord-Lieutenant, 1998–2002); estate owner and rural land manager, Ballindalloch, since 1979; *b* 4 Aug. 1944; *d* of Sir Ewan Macpherson-Grant, 6th Bt, and Lady Macpherson-Grant; *m* 1967, Oliver Henry Russell; two *s* one *d*. *Educ:* in Scotland. Professional florist, Head Decorator, Constance Spry, 1962–65; Sec. to Fourth Clerk at the Table, H of C, 1965–67; Dir, Craigo Farms Ltd, 1970–; living at Ballindalloch, 1978–; opened Ballindalloch Castle to public, 1993. Mem., Moray Health Council, 1986–91. Mem. Council, NT for Scotland, 1985–88; Dist Organiser, Moray and Banff, 1980–93; Mem. Exec. Cttee, 1987–93, Scotland's Garden Scheme. Chm., Queen Mary's Clothing Guild, 1990–93 (started Queen Mary's Clothing Guild in Scotland, 1986). Mem. Bd, Children's Hospice Assoc., Scotland, 1995–2002. Sunday Sch. teacher, Inveraven Ch, 1982–94. DL Banffshire, 1991–98. JP Aberdeenshire, 2003. *Publications:* Favourite Recipes, Dried Flowers and Pot Pourri from Ballindalloch Castle, 1993; Favourite Puddings from Ballindalloch Castle, 1995; Favourite First Courses from Ballindalloch Castle, 1996; Favourite Recipes from Ballindalloch Castle, 1998; I Love Food, 2004. *Recreations:* dog-handling, gardening, flower arranging, piano, tapestry, knitting, cooking, historic houses, antiques. *Address:* Ballindalloch Castle, Banffshire AB37 9AX. *T:* (01807) 500206. *Club:* Sloane.

RUSSELL, Dan Chapman; Sheriff of South Strathclyde, Dumfries and Galloway at Hamilton, 1992–2004; *b* 25 Dec. 1939; *s* of William Morris Russell and Isabella Ritchie Stein Scott; *m* 1969, Janet McNeil; three *d*. *Educ:* Airdrie Acad.; Glasgow Univ. (MA 1960; LLB 1963). Qualified as Solicitor, 1963; in private practice, 1963–92; Partner, Bell, Russell & Co., Solicitors, Airdrie, 1965–92; Temp. Sheriff, 1976–78 and 1985–92. Reporter, Airdrie Children's Panel, 1972–75. Mem. Council, Law Soc. of Scotland, 1975–84; Dean, Airdrie Soc. of Solicitors, 1986–88. *Recreations:* golf, bridge, walking.

RUSSELL, Rt Rev. David Hamilton; Bishop of Grahamstown, 1987–2004; *b* 6 Nov. 1938; *s* of James Hamilton Russell and Kathleen Mary Russell; *m* 1980, Dorothea Madden; two *s*. *Educ:* Diocesan College, Rondebosch; Univ. of Cape Town (BA, PhD); Univ. of Oxford (MA). Assistant Priest, 1965–75; Chaplain to migrant workers, 1975–86; banned and house arrested by SA Government, 1977–82; Suffragan Bishop, Diocese of St John's, 1986. *Address:* 3 Pillans Road, Rosebank, Cape Town 7700, South Africa. *T:* and *Fax:* (21) 6862721.

RUSSELL, Rev. David Syme, CBE 1982; MA, DD, DLitt; President, Baptist Union of Great Britain and Ireland, 1983–84 (General Secretary, 1967–82); *b* 21 Nov. 1916; second *s* of Peter Russell and Janet Marshall Syme; *m* 1943, Marion Hamilton Campbell; one *s* one *d*. *Educ:* Scottish Baptist Coll., Glasgow; Trinity Coll., Glasgow; Glasgow Univ. (MA, BD, DLitt, Hon. DD); Regent's Park Coll., Oxford Univ. (MA, MLitt; Hon. Fellow, 1995). Minister of Baptist Churches: Berwick, 1939–41; Oxford, 1943–45; Acton, 1945–53. Principal of Rawdon Coll., Leeds, and lectr in Old Testament languages and literature, 1953–64; Joint Principal of the Northern Baptist College, Manchester, 1964–67. Moderator, Free Church Federal Council, 1974–75. Pres., European Baptist Fedn, 1979–81. Mem., Central Cttee, WCC, 1968–83; Vice-Pres., BCC, 1981–84. Hon. DD McMaster, 1991. *Publications:* Between the Testaments, 1960; Two Refugees (Ezekiel and Second Isaiah), 1962; The Method and Message of Jewish Apocalyptic, 1964; The Jews from Alexander to Herod, 1976; Apocalyptic: Ancient and Modern, 1978; Daniel (The Daily Study Bible), 1981; In Journeyings Often, 1982; From Early Judaism to Early Church, 1986; The Old Testament Pseudepigrapha: patriarchs and prophets in early Judaism, 1987; Daniel: an active volcano, 1989; Poles Apart: the Gospel in creative tension, 1990; Divine Disclosure: an introduction to Jewish apocalyptic, 1992; Prophecy and the Apocalyptic Dream: protest and promise, 1994; contrib. to Encyc. Britannica, 1963. *Recreation:* woodwork. *Address:* Avenue House, 5 Cotham Park North, Bristol BS6 6BH. *T:* (0117) 989 2048.

RUSSELL, Prof. Donald Andrew Frank Moore, FBA 1971; Fellow, St John's College, Oxford, 1948–88, now Emeritus; Professor of Classical Literature, Oxford, 1985–88; *b* 13 Oct. 1920; *s* of Samuel Charles Russell (schoolmaster) and Laura Moore; *m* 1967, Joycelyne Gledhill Dickinson (*d* 1993). *Educ:* King's College Sch., Wimbledon; Balliol Coll., Oxford (MA 1946); DLitt Oxon 1985. Served War: Army (R Signals and Intelligence Corps), 1941–45. Craven Scholar, 1946; Lectr, Christ Church, Oxford, 1947; St John's College, Oxford: Tutor, 1948–84; Dean, 1957–64; Tutor for Admissions, 1968–72; Reader in Class. Lit., Oxford Univ., 1978–85. Paddison Vis. Prof., Univ. of N Carolina at Chapel Hill, 1985; Vis. Prof. of Classics, Stanford Univ., 1989, 1991. Co-editor, Classical Quarterly, 1965–70. *Publications:* Commentary on Longinus, On the Sublime, 1964; Ancient Literary Criticism (with M. Winterbottom), 1972; Plutarch, 1972; (with N. G. Wilson) Menander Rhetor, 1981; Criticism in Antiquity, 1981; Greek Declamation, 1984; (ed) Antonine Literature, 1990; Commentary on Dio Chrysostom, Orations, 7, 12, 36, 1992; (trans.) Plutarch: selected essays and dialogues, 1993; (trans.) Libanius, Imaginary Speeches, 1996; (trans. and ed) Quintilian, 2001; (ed with D. Konstan) Heraclitus: Homeric problems, 2005; articles and reviews in classical periodicals. *Address:* 35 Belsyre Court, Oxford OX2 6HU. *T:* (01865) 556135.

RUSSELL, Edwin John Cumming, FRBS 1978; sculptor; *b* 4 May 1939; *s* of Edwin Russell and Mary Elizabeth Russell; *m* 1964, Lorne McKean; two *d*. *Educ:* Brighton Coll. of Art and Crafts; Royal Academy Schs (CertRAS). *Works:* Crucifix, limewood, pulpit, St Paul's Cathedral, 1964; St Catherine, lead, Little Cloister, Westminster Abbey, 1966; St Michael, oak, Chapel of St Michael and St George, St Paul's Cath., 1970; Bishop Bubwith, W Front Wells Cath., 1980; sundials: Jubilee Dolphin Dial, bronze, Nat. Maritime Mus., Greenwich, 1978; 3m, Sultan Qaboos Univ., Oman, 1986; Botanical Armillery, Kew Gardens, 1987; 5m, bronze, Parliament Square, Dubai, 1988; Forecourt sculpture, Rank Xerox Internat. HQ, 1989; shopping centre sculpture: Mad Hatter's Tea Party play sculpture, granite, Warrington, 1984; Lion and Lamb, teak, Farnham, 1986; public works: Suffragette Meml, 1968; 1st Gov. of Bahamas, Sheraton Hotel, Nassau, 1968; Lewis Carroll commemorative sculpture, Alice and the White Rabbit, Guildford, 1984; Panda, marble, WWF Internat. HQ, 1988; private collections: Goodwood House; Sir Robert McAlpine & Sons Ltd; Rosehaugh Stanhope Developments; Arup Associates; Bovis; YRM International; Trafalgar House plc; Cementation International; John Laing Construction; John Mowlem & Co.; ARC; Worshipful Co. of Stationers; City of London Grammar Shool. Royal Academy Gold Medal for Sculpture, 1960; Otto Beit Medal for sculpture, RBS, 1991. *Recreation:* philosophy. *Address:* Lethendry, Polecat Valley, Hindhead, Surrey GU26 6BE. *T:* (01428) 605655.

RUSSELL, Eileen Alison, (Lady Russell); *see* Mackay, E. A.

RUSSELL, Frank; *see* Russell, J. F. B.

RUSSELL, Sir George, Kt 1992; CBE 1985; Deputy Chairman: Granada plc, 2002–04; ITV plc, since 2004; *b* 25 Oct. 1935; *s* of William H. Russell and Frances A. Russell; *m* 1959, Dorothy Brown; three *d*. *Educ:* Gateshead Grammar Sch.; Durham Univ. (BA Hons). ICI, 1958–67 (graduate trainee, Commercial Res. Officer, Sales Rep., and Product Sales Man.); Vice President and General Manager: Welland Chemical Co. of Canada Ltd, 1968; St Clair Chemical Co. Ltd, 1968; Man. Dir, Alcan UK Ltd, 1976; Asst Man. Dir, 1977–81, Man. Dir, 1981–82, Alcan Aluminium (UK) Ltd; Man. Dir and Chief Exec., British Alcan Aluminium, 1982–86; Chief Exec., 1986–92, Chm., 1989–93, non-exec. Chm., 1993–97, Marley plc; Dir, 1992–2001, Chm., 1993–2001, 3i Gp plc; Chm., Camelot Gp plc, 1995–2002. Chairman: Luxfer Holdings Ltd, 1976–78; Alcan UK Ltd, 1978–82; Northern Develt Co., 1994–99; Director: Alcan Aluminiumwerke GmbH, Frankfurt, 1977–82; Northern Rock plc (formerly Bldg Soc.), 1985–2006; Alcan Aluminium Ltd, 1987–2000; Taylor Woodrow, 1992–2004; British Alcan plc, 1997–2001. Chairman: ITN, 1987–88; IBA, 1988–92 (Mem., 1979–86); ITC, 1991–96; Cable Authy, 1989–90; Dep. Chm., Channel Four TV, 1987–88. Visiting Professor, Univ. of Newcastle upon Tyne, 1978. Chm., IPPR North Commn on Public Sector Reform in NE, 2007–; Member: Board, Northern Sinfonia Orchestra, 1977–80; Northern Industrial Development Board, 1977–80; Washington Development Corporation, 1978–80; Board, Civil Service Pay Research Unit, 1980–81; Megaw Inquiry into Civil Service Pay, 1981; Widdicombe Cttee of Inquiry into Conduct of Local Authority Business, 1985. Dir, Wildfowl and Wetlands Trust, 2002–08. Trustee, Beamish Develt Trust, 1985–90. Hon. DEng Newcastle upon Tyne, 1985; Hon. DBA Northumbria, 1992; Hon. LLD: Sunderland, 1995; Durham, 1997. *Recreations:* tennis, bird watching. *Address:* ITV plc, 200 Gray's Inn Road, WC1X 8HF. *Club:* Garrick.

RUSSELL, Gerald Francis Morris, MD; FRCP, FRCPE, Hon. FRCPsych; Professor of Psychiatry, Institute of Psychiatry, University of London, and Physician, Bethlem Royal and Maudsley Hospital, 1979–93, now Professor Emeritus; Consultant Psychiatrist, Eating Disorders Unit, The Priory Hospital Hayes Grove, since 1993 (Director, 1993–2001); *b* Grammont, Belgium, 12 Jan. 1928; 2nd *s* of late Maj. Daniel George Russell, MC, and late Berthe Marie Russell (*née* De Boe); *m* 1950, Margaret Taylor, MB, ChB; three *s*. *Educ:* Collège St Jean Berchmans, Brussels; George Watson's Coll., Edinburgh (Dux); Univ. of Edinburgh (Mouat Schol. in Practice of Physic). MD (with commendation), 1957; DPM; FRCPE 1967; FRCP 1969; Hon. FRCPsych (FRCPsych 1971). RAMC Regimental Med. Off., Queen's Bays, 1951–53; Neurological Registrar, Northern Gen. Hosp., Edin., 1954–56; MRC Clinical Res. Fellow, 1956–58; Inst. of Psychiatry, Maudsley Hospital: 1st Asst, 1959–60; Senior Lectr, 1961–70; Dean, 1966–70; Bethlem Royal and Maudsley Hospital: Physician, 1961–70; Mem. Bd of Governors, 1966–70; Mem., Special Health Authority, 1979–90; Prof. of Psychiatry, Royal Free Hosp. Sch. of Medicine, 1971–79. Chairman: Educn Cttee, Royal Medico-Psychological Assoc., 1970 (Mem. Council, 1966–71); Sect. on Eating Disorders, World Psychiatric Assoc., 1989–99; Assoc. of Univ. Teachers of Psychiatry, 1991–94; Sec. of Sect. of Psychiatry, Roy. Soc. Med., 1966–68 (Pres., 1998–99); Special Interest Gp on Eating Disorders, RCPsych, 1995–99; Mem., European Soc. for Clinical Investigation, 1968–72; Pres., Soc. for Psychosomatic Res., 1989–91. Corr. Fellow, Amer. Psychiatric Assoc., 1967–2000. Member Editorial Boards: British Jl of Psychiatry, 1966–71; Psychological Medicine, 1970–2000; Jl Neurology, Neurosurgery and Psychiatry, 1971–75; Medical Education, 1975–84; Internat. Jl of

Eating Disorders, 1981–2002. Mem., 1942 Club, 1978–. *Publications:* contrib. to Psychiatrie der Gegenwart, vol. 3, 1975; (ed jtly with L. Hersov and contrib.) Handbook of Psychiatry, vol. 4, The Neuroses and Personality Disorders, 1984; (contrib. and ed jtly) Anorexia Nervosa and Bulimic Disorders: current perspectives, 1985; (contrib.) Oxford Textbook of Medicine, 2nd edn, 1987; (contrib.) Handbook of Treatment for Eating Disorders, 2nd edn, 1997; (contrib.) New Oxford Textbook of Psychiatry, 2000; articles in med. jls on psychiatry, disorders of eating, dyslexia, education and neurology. *Recreations:* art galleries, language, photography. *Address:* The Priory Hospital Hayes Grove, Prestons Road, Hayes, Kent BR2 7AS.

RUSSELL, Graham; *see* Russell, R. G. G.

RUSSELL, Graham R.; *see* Ross Russell.

RUSSELL, Ven. (Harold) Ian (Lyle); Archdeacon of Coventry, 1989–2000; Chaplain to the Queen, 1997–2004; *b* 17 Oct. 1934; *s* of Percy Harold and Emma Rebecca Russell; *m* 1961, Barbara Lillian Dixon; two *s* one *d. Educ:* Epsom College; London Coll. of Divinity (BD, ALCD). Shell Petroleum Co., 1951–53; RAF, Jan. 1953; RAF Regt, Nov. 1953–1956; London Coll. of Divinity, 1956–60; ordained, 1960; Curate of Iver, Bucks, 1960–63; Curate-in-charge of St Luke's, Lodge Moor, Parish of Fulwood, Sheffield, 1963–67; Vicar: St John's, Chapeltown, Sheffield, 1967–75; St Jude's, Mapperley, Nottingham, 1975–89. *Recreations:* walking, photography, sport, gardening. *Address:* 5 Old Acres, Woodborough, Nottingham NG14 6ES. *T:* (0115) 965 3543.

RUSSELL, Prof. Ian John, FRS 1989; Professor of Neurobiology, Sussex University, since 1987; *b* 19 June 1943; *s* of Philip William George Russell and Joan Lillian Russell; *m* 1968, Janice Marion Russell (marr. diss. 2006); one *s* one *d. Educ:* Chatham Technical Sch.; Queen Mary Coll., London (BSc Zoology); Univ. of British Columbia (NATO Student; MSc Zool.); Univ. of Cambridge (SRC Student; Trinity Hall Res. Student; PhD Zool.). Res. Fellowship, Magdalene Coll., Cambridge, 1969–71; SRC Res. Fellowship, Cambridge, 1969–71; Royal Soc. Exchange Fellowship, King Gustav V Res. Inst., Stockholm, 1970–71; University of Sussex: Lectr in Neurobiology, 1971–79; Reader in Neurobiology, 1979–80 and 1982–87; MRC Sen. Res. Fellow, 1980–82, 1995–98. *Publications:* on the neurobiology of hearing, in learned jls. *Recreations:* hockey, windsurfing, reading, music, gardening, walking. *Address:* Little Ivy Cottage, Waldron, Heathfield, East Sussex TN21 0QX. *T:* (01435) 813382.

RUSSELL, Ian Simon MacGregor, CBE 2007; CA; Chairman, Remploy Ltd, since 2007; *b* 16 Jan. 1953; *s* of James MacGregor Russell and Christine Russell (*née* Clark); *m* 1975, Fiona Brown; one *s* one *d. Educ:* George Heriot's Sch., Edinburgh; Univ. of Edinburgh (BCom). Mem., ICAS, 1977. Auditor, Thomson McLintock, 1974–78; accountant, Mars Ltd, 1978–81; Controller, Pentos plc, 1981–83; Finance Dir, HSBC, 1983–90; Financial Controller, Tomkins plc, 1990–94; Finance Dir, 1994–99, Dep. Chief Exec., 1999–2001, Chief Exec., 2001–06, Scottish Power plc. Non-exec. Dir, Johnston Press plc, 2007–. Chm., Seeing is Believing Network, BITC. Chm., Russell Commn, 2004–05.

RUSSELL, Jack; *see* Russell, R. C.

RUSSELL, His Honour James Francis Buchanan, (Frank); QC (NI) 1968; County Court Judge of Northern Ireland, 1978–97; *b* 7 July 1924; *e s* of John Buchanan Russell and Margaret Bellingham Russell; *m* 1946, Irene McKee; two *s* one *d* (and one *d* decd). *Educ:* King's Sch., Worcester; St Andrews Univ.; Queen's Univ., Belfast (LLB). Served Royal Air Force, 1941–47. Called to Bar, NI, 1952; Crown Prosecutor: Co. Fermanagh, 1970; Co. Tyrone, 1974; Co. Londonderry, 1976; Recorder of Belfast, 1995–97. Bencher, Inn of Court, N Ireland, 1972–78 and 1988–, Treasurer, 1977. Member, Standing Advisory Commn on Human Rights, 1974–78; Chairman, Pensions Appeal Tribunal, N Ireland, 1970–99. *Recreations:* golf, gardening. *Address:* 5 Grey Point, Helen's Bay, Co. Down, Northern Ireland BT19 1LE. *T:* (028) 9185 2249. *Clubs:* Royal Air Force; Royal Belfast Golf.

RUSSELL, Jeremy Jonathan; QC 1994; *b* 18 Dec. 1950; *s* of Sidney Thomas Russell and Maud Eugenie Russell; *m* 1987, Gillian Elizabeth Giles; one *s* one *d. Educ:* Watford Boys' GS; City of London Poly. (BA); LSE (LLM). Lectr in Law, City of London Poly., 1973–80; called to the Bar, Middle Temple, 1975; in practice, 1977–. Lloyd's Salvage Arbitrator, 2000–05. CEDR accredited mediator, 2001. *Recreations:* reading, gliding, classic cars. *Address:* Quadrant Chambers, Quadrant House, 10 Fleet Street, EC4Y 1AU.

RUSSELL, John Harry; Chairman and Chief Executive, Duport plc, 1981–86; *b* 21 Feb. 1926; *s* of Joseph Harry Russell and Nellie Annie Russell; *m* 1951, Iris Mary Cooke; one *s* one *d. Educ:* Halesowen Grammar Sch. FCA. War Service, RN. Joseph Lucas Ltd, 1948–52; Vono Ltd (Duport Gp Co.), 1952–59; Standard Motors Ltd, 1959–61; rejoined Duport Gp, 1961: Man. Dir, Duport Foundries Ltd, 1964; Dir, Duport Parent Bd, 1966; Chm., Burman & Sons Ltd (formerly part of Duport), 1968–72; Chief Exec., Duport Engrg Div., 1972–73; Dep. Gp Man. Dir, 1973–75; Gp Man. Dir, 1975–80, Dep. Chm., 1976–81, Duport plc. Chm., Blagg plc, 1994–95; non-exec. Dir, Birmingham Local Bd, Barclays Bank Ltd, 1976–88. Chm., Black Country Museum Trust Ltd, 1988–99. CCMI. Liveryman, Worshipful Co. of Glaziers and Freeman and Citizen of London, 1976. *Recreations:* reading, music, antiques. *Address:* 442 Bromsgrove Road, Hunnington, Halesowen, West Midlands B62 0JL.

RUSSELL, Ken; film director, since 1958; *b* 3 July 1927; *m* Shirley Kingdom (marr. diss. 1978; she *d* 2002); four *s* one *d; m* 1984, Vivian Jolly; one *s* one *d; m* 1992, Hetty Baines (marr. diss. 1997); one *s; m* 2001, Elize Tribble. Merchant Navy, 1945; RAF, 1946–49. Ny Norsk Ballet, 1950; Garrick Players, 1951; free-lance photographer, 1951–57; Film Director, BBC, 1958–66; free-lance film director, 1966–; started new film movt on mini-DV, Les Garagistes, 2004. Vis. Prof. of Film Studies, Southampton Solent Univ. (formerly Southampton Inst.), 1996–. *Films for TV:* Elgar; Bartok; Debussy; Henri Rousseau; Isadora Duncan; Delius; Richard Strauss; Clouds of Glory; The Planets; Vaughan Williams; ABC of British Music (Emmy award); The Mystery of Dr Martinù; The Secret Life of Arnold Bax; Classic Widows; Elgar: fantasy on a composer on a bicycle, 2002; *television serial:* Lady Chatterley, 1993; *films:* French Dressing, 1964; The Billion Dollar Brain, 1967; Women in Love, 1969; The Music Lovers, 1970; The Devils, 1971; The Boy Friend, 1971; Savage Messiah, 1972; Mahler, 1973; Tommy, 1974; Lisztomania, 1975; Valentino, 1977; Altered States, 1981; Crimes of Passion, 1985; Gothic, 1987; (jtly) Aria, 1987; Salome's Last Dance, 1988; Lair of the White Worm, 1989; The Rainbow, 1989; Whore, 1991; Lion's Mouth, 2000; Fall of the Louse of Usher, 2001; Hot Pants: 3 Sexy Shorts (Revenge of the Elephant Man, The Mystery of Mata Hari, The Good Ship Venus), 2005; *opera:* The Rake's Progress, Florence, 1982; Madam Butterfly, Spoleto, 1983; La Bohème, Macerata, 1984; Faust, Vienna, 1985; Princess Ida, ENO, 1992; Salome, Bonn, 1993. Screen Writers Guild Award for TV films Elgar, Debussy, Isadora and Dante's Inferno; Achievement Awards: Telluride Film Fest., 2001; Dallas Film Fest., 2002; Belgrade Film Fest., 2003; Istanbul Film Fest., 2003; Mar del Plata Film Fest., 2004. *Publications:* A British Picture

(autobiog.), 1989; Fire Over England, 1993; Mike and Gaby's Space Gospel (novel), 1999; Directing Film: the director's art from script to cutting room, 1999; Violation (novel), 2006; Elgar: the erotic variations, 2006; Delius: a moment with Venus, 2006; Beethoven Confidential and Brahms Gets Laid, 2006. *Recreations:* music, walking.

RUSSELL, Mark Kenneth; Chief Executive, Church Army, since 2006; *b* 25 June 1974; *s* of Kenneth and Elizabeth Russell. *Educ:* Portadown Coll.; Queen's Univ., Belfast (LLB 1995). Proj. Exec., W. D. Irwin & Sons Ltd, 1995–97; Youth Pastor, Lurgan Methodist Ch, 1997–2000; Youth Minister, Christ Ch, Chorleywood, 2000–06. Member: Conf. of Methodist Ch in Ireland, 1996–98; Gen. Synod of C of E, 2005–; Archbishops' Council, 2005–; C of E Bd of Educn, 2006–; Marylebone Project Bd, 2006–; Coll. of Evangelists, 2008–. Member: Christian Socialist Movement; Amnesty Internat. *Recreations:* theatre, cinema, supporter of Tottenham Hotspur FC and U2 (Irish rock group). *Address:* Church Army, Marlowe House, 109 Station Road, Sidcup, Kent DA15 7AD. *T:* (020) 8309 3505, *Fax:* (020) 8309 3500; *e-mail:* m.russell@churcharmy.org.uk.

RUSSELL, Sir Mervyn; *see* Russell, Sir (Arthur) M.

RUSSELL, Prof. Michael Anthony Hamilton, FRCP, FRCPsych; Hon. Consultant and Head of Tobacco Research Section, National Addiction Centre, Institute of Psychiatry, University of London, 1997–2002, now Emeritus Consultant (Professor of Addiction, 1992–98, now Emeritus); *b* 9 March 1932; *s* of late James Hamilton Russell and of Hon. Kathleen Mary (*née* Gibson); *m* 1962, Audrey Ann Timms; two *s. Educ:* Diocesan Coll., Cape Town; University Coll., Oxford (BA Physiol. 1954; MA); Guy's Hosp., London (BM BCh 1957). FCP (SA) 1963; MRCP 1964, FRCP 1982; DPM 1968; FRCPsych 1980. Junior hospital appointments: Guy's Hosp., 1957–58; in Medicine, Cardiology and Pathology, Groote Schuur Hosp., Cape Town and King Edward VII Hosp., Durban, 1959–63; Sen. Med. Registrar, Groote Schuur Hosp., 1963–64; travel, incl. 6 months as Med. Registrar, Ruttonjee TB Sanatorium, Hong Kong, 1964–65; Trainee Registrar in Psychiatry, 1965–68, Sen. Registrar, 1968–69, Maudsley Hosp.; Institute of Psychiatry: Res. Worker, 1969–71; Lectr, 1971–73; Sen. Lectr, 1973–85; Reader, 1985–92. Hon. Consultant Psychiatrist: Maudsley Hosp., 1973–2002; UCH, 1996–2002. Mem., Ext. Scientific Staff, MRC, 1978–98; built up ICRF Health Behaviour Unit at Inst. of Psychiatry, 1988–96, moved to UCL, 1996, Hon. Dir, 1988–97, Hon. Consultant, 1997–2002. Invited Lect., Royal Stat. Soc., 1974; Robert Philip Lect., RCPE, 1978. No-tobacco Medal, WHO, 1989; Alton Oschner Award, Amer. Coll. Chest Physicians, 1996; Ove Ferno Award, Soc. Res. on Nicotine and Tobacco, 1998. *Publications:* numerous contribs to scientific books and jls on: nicotine psychopharmacology, pharmacokinetics and dependence; regulation of nicotine intake by smokers; motivational typologies of smoking; effect of cigarette prices on consumption; smoking in children; passive smoking; less harmful cigarettes; nicotine replacement and other treatments in clinic, workplace, primary care and medical practice settings. *Recreations:* reading, travel, watersports, oil paintings. *Address:* 10 Alphen Drive, Constantia, 7806 Cape Town, South Africa.

RUSSELL, Michael William; Member (SNP) Scotland South, Scottish Parliament, 1999–2003 and since 2007; Minister for Environment, since 2007; *b* 9 Aug. 1953; *s* of late Thomas Stevenson Russell and Jean Marjorie Russell (*née* Haynes); *m* 1980, Cathleen Ann Macaskill; one *s. Educ:* Marr Coll., Troon; Edinburgh Univ. (MA 1974). Creative Producer, Church of Scotland, 1974–77; Dir, Cinema Sgire, Western Isles Islands Council, 1977–81; Founder and Dir, Celtic Film and Television Fest., 1981–83; Exec. Dir, Network Scotland Ltd, 1983–91; Dir, Eala Bhan Ltd, 1991–; Chief Exec., SNP, 1994–99. Opposition front bench spokesman for Parlt, 1999–2000, for children, educn and culture, 2000–03, Scottish Parlt. Contested (SNP): Clydesdale, 1987; Cunninghame South, Scottish Parlt, 2003. FRSA 2007. *Publications:* (ed) Glasgow: the book, 1990; (ed) Edinburgh: a celebration, 1992; A Poem of Remote Lives: the enigma of Werner Kissling, 1997; In Waiting: travels in the shadow of Edwin Muir, 1998; A Different Country, 2002; (ed) Stop the World, 2004; (with Dennis MacLeod) Grasping the Thistle, 2006; The Next Big Thing, 2007; (with Iain McKie) The Price of Innocence, 2007. *Recreation:* tending my Argyll garden. *Address:* Scottish Parliament, Edinburgh EH99 1SP; Feorlean, Glendaruel, Argyll PA22 3AH.

RUSSELL, Muir; *see* Russell, A. M. G.

RUSSELL, Sir Muir; *see* Russell, Sir A. M.

RUSSELL, Ven. Norman Atkinson; Archdeacon of Berkshire, since 1998; *b* 7 Aug. 1943; *s* of Norman Gerald Russell and Olive Muriel Russell (*née* Williamson); *m* 1974, Victoria Christine Jasinska; two *s. Educ:* Royal Belfast Academical Instn; Churchill Coll., Cambridge (BA 1965; MA 1969); London Coll. of Divinity (BD London 1970). Articled Clerk, Coopers & Lybrand, 1966–67; ordained deacon, 1970, priest, 1971; Curate: Christ Church with Emmanuel, Clifton, Bristol, 1970–74; Christ Church, Cockfosters, and pt-time Chaplain, Middx Poly., 1974–77; Rector, Harwell with Chilton, 1977–84; Priest in Charge: St James, Gerrards Cross, 1984–88; St James, Fulmer, 1985–88; Rector, Gerrards Cross and Fulmer, 1988–98; RD, Amersham, 1996–98. Vice-Chm., Ecumenical Council for Corporate Responsibility, 1999–2002. Member: Gen. Synod, C of E, 2002–; Archbishops' Council, C of E, 2005–. Prolocutor, Lower House of the Convocation of Canterbury, 2005–. *Publication:* Censorship, 1972. *Recreations:* downland walking, watching Rugby football. *Address:* Foxglove House, Love Lane, Donnington, Newbury, Berks RG14 2JG. *T:* (01635) 552820.

RUSSELL, Pam; *see* Ayres, P.

RUSSELL, Prof. Philip St John, DPhil; FRS 2005; Professor of Physics, University of Bath, since 1996; Director and Alfried Krupp von Bohlen und Halbach Professor in Max Planck Research Group, University of Erlangen-Nuremberg, since 2005; *b* 25 March 1953; *s* of Edward Augustine Russell and Emily Frances Russell (*née* Stevenson); *m* 1981, Alison Rosemary Bennett; two *s. Educ:* Royal Belfast Academical Instn; Magdalen Coll., Oxford (BA 1976; MA, DPhil 1979). Hayward Jun. Res. Fellow, Oriel Coll., Oxford, 1978–81; Alexander von Humboldt Fellow, Technische Universität Hamburg-Harburg, 1981–83; World Trade Vis. Scientist, IBM TJ Watson Res. Center, NY, 1983, 1985; Professeur Associé, Univ. de Nice, 1985, 1986; Lectr, then Reader, Univ. of Southampton, 1986–89, 1991–96; Reader, Univ. of Kent, 1989–90. Chief Tech. Officer and Founder, BlazePhotonics Ltd, 2000–04. Fellow, Optical Soc. of America, 2000 (Joseph Fraunhofer Award, Robert M. Burley Prize, 2000). Wolfson Res. Merit Award, Royal Soc., 2004–; Dist. Lectr, IEEE Lasers and Electro-Optics Soc., 2004–06. Applied Optics Div. Prize, 2002, Thomas Young Prize, 2005, Inst. of Physics; Körber Prize for Europ. Sci., 2005. *Publications:* approaching 600 papers in learned jls and scientific confs. *Recreations:* classical and jazz piano playing, music composition and improvisation, art, reading. *Address:* Institute of Optics, Information and Photonics, University of Erlangen-Nuremberg, Guenther-Scharowsky-Strasse 1, 91058 Erlangen, Germany.

RUSSELL, Most Rev. Philip Welsford Richmond; *b* 21 Oct. 1919; *s* of Leslie Richmond Russell and Clarice Louisa Russell (*née* Welsford); *m* 1945, Violet Eirene, *d* of Ven. Dr O. J. Hogarth, sometime Archdeacon of the Cape; one *s* three *d*. *Educ:* Durban High Sch.; Rhodes Univ. College (Univ. of South Africa), BA 1948; LTh 1950. Served War of 1939–45; MBE 1943. Deacon, 1950; Priest, 1951; Curate, St Peter's, Maritzburg, 1950–54; Vicar: Greytown, 1954–57; Ladysmith, 1957–61; Kloof, 1961–66; Archdeacon of Pinetown, 1961–66; Bishop Suffragan of Capetown, 1966–70; Bishop of Port Elizabeth, 1970–74; Bishop of Natal, 1974–81; Archbishop of Cape Town and Metropolitan of Southern Africa, 1981–86, now Archbishop Emeritus. *Recreation:* walking. *Address:* Roselin Court, 251 Payneham Road, Joslin, SA 5070, Australia.

RUSSELL, Robert Charles, (Jack), MBE 1996; cricketer; international artist; *b* 15 Aug. 1963; *s* of late Derek John Russell and of Jennifer Russell; *m* 1985, Aileen Ann Dunn; two *s* three *d*. *Educ:* Uplands Co. Primary Sch.; Archway Comprehensive Sch. Played for Glos CCC, 1981–2004; internat. début, England *v* Pakistan, 1987; played 54 Test Matches and 40 One-day Internationals; world record (11) for dismissals in a Test Match, England *v* SA, Johannesburg, 1995; record for dismissals (27) in a Test series for England, England *v* SA, 1995–96; retd from internat. cricket, 1998. Opened Jack Russell Gall., Chipping Sodbury, 1992; paintings sold and displayed in mus and collections worldwide; commissions include: We Will Remember Them, for RRF, in Tower of London; The Ten Field Marshals of the British Army, for Army Benevolent Fund, in Nat. Army Museum; Cricket World Cup Final, 1999, Australia *v* Pakistan, for NatWest Bank; Ashes Series 2005; Legal London series; portraits include: Duke of Edinburgh; Duke of Kent; Eric Clapton; Sir Norman Wisdom. *Publications:* A Cricketer's Art: sketches by Jack Russell, 1988; (illustr.) Sketches of a Season, 1989; Jack Russell's Sketch Book, 1996; Jack Russell: unleashed (autobiog.), 1997; The Art of Jack Russell: a collection of paintings, 1999; New Horizons: a collection of paintings, 2006. *Address:* Jack Russell Gallery, 41 High Street, Chipping Sodbury, S Glos BS37 6BA. *T:* (01454) 329583, *Fax:* (01454) 329683.

RUSSELL, Robert Christopher Hamlyn, CBE 1981; formerly Director, Hydraulics Research Station, Department of the Environment (formerly Ministry of Technology), 1965–81; *b* Singapore, 1921; *s* of late Philip Charles and Hilda Gertrude Russell; *m* 1950, Cynthia Mary Roberts; one *s* two *d*. *Educ:* Stowe; King's Coll., Cambridge. Asst Engineer: BTH Co., Rugby, 1944; Dunlop Rubber Co., 1946; Sen. Scientific Officer, later PSO, then SPSO, in Hydraulics Research Station, 1949–65. Visiting Prof., Univ. of Strathclyde, 1967. *Publications:* Waves and Tides, 1951; papers on civil engineering hydraulics. *Address:* 29 St Mary's Street, Wallingford, Oxfordshire OX10 0ET. *T:* (01491) 837323.

RUSSELL, Robert Edward, (Bob); MP (Lib Dem) Colchester, since 1997; *b* 31 March 1946; *s* of late Ewart Russell and Muriel Russell (*née* Sawdy); *m* 1967, Audrey Blandon; twin *s* one *d* (and one *d* decd). *Educ:* Myland Primary Sch., Colchester; St Helena Secondary Modern Sch., Colchester; NE Essex Technical Coll. Reporter, Essex County Standard and Colchester Gazette, 1963–66; News Editor, Braintree & Witham Times, 1966–68; Editor, Maldon & Burnham Standard, 1968–69; Sub-Editor, London Evening News, 1969–72; Sub-Editor, London Evening Standard, 1972–73; Press Officer, Post Office Telecommunications, subseq. British Telecom (Eastern Reg.), 1973–85; Publicity Officer, Univ. of Essex, 1986–97. Mem., Colchester BC, 1971–2002 (Lab 1971–81, SDP 1981–88, Lib Dem 1988–2002) (Mayor, 1986–87). *Recreations:* promoting the interests of the town of Colchester, watching Colchester United. *Address:* Magdalen Hall, Wimpole Road, Colchester CO1 2DE. *Clubs:* Colchester United Football; Colchester Gala Bingo.

RUSSELL, Prof. (Robert) Graham (Goodwin), PhD, DM; FRCP, FRCPath, FMedSci; FRS 2008; Professor of Musculoskeletal Pharmacology, Nuffield Department of Orthopaedic Surgery, University of Oxford, since 2006 (Norman Collisson Professor of Musculoskeletal Science, 2000–06); Fellow of St Peter's College, Oxford, 2001–07, now Emeritus; *b* 16 Feb. 1941; *s* of Charles Chambers Russell and Mary (*née* Goodwin); *m* 1960, Diana Mary (*née* Allfrey); one *s* three *d*. *Educ:* Clare Coll., Cambridge (BA 1962; MA 1966; MB BChir 1971); PhD Leeds 1967; DM Oxon 1975. MRCP 1974, FRCP 1981; MRCPath 1974, FRCPath 1986. MRC Unit, Leeds, 1962–65; Res. Fellow, Swiss Res. Inst., Davos, 1965–67; Med. Student, Clinical Sch., Oxford Univ., 1967–71; House Officer posts, Radcliffe Infirmary, Oxford, 1972–73; Med. Res. Fellow, St Peter's Coll., Oxford, 1973–76; Sen. Lectr, 1976–77, Prof. and Head of Dept of Human Metabolism and Clin. Biochemistry, 1977–2000, Sheffield Univ.; Dir, Botnar Res. Centre (Oxford Univ. Inst. of Musculoskeletal Scis), 2002–07; Head, Nuffield Dept of Orthopaedic Surgery, Oxford Univ., 2003–06. Sen. Lectr, Univ. Bern, 1970–71; Asst Prof. of Medicine, Harvard Med. Sch., 1974–75. Chm., Nat. Osteoporosis Soc., 2000–02 (Kohn Award, 2000). Pres., Internat. Bone and Mineral Soc., 1998–2001 (Gaillard Award, 2007). FMedSci 2001. Hon. MD Sheffield, 2003. John B. Johnson Award, Paget's Foundn, USA, 1997; Neuman Award, Amer. Soc. of Bone and Mineral Metabolism, 2000. *Publications:* contribs to learned jls and books. *Recreations:* fishing, ski-ing, nature, third generation. *Address:* Oxford University Institute of Musculoskeletal Sciences, Botnar Research Centre, Nuffield Department of Orthopaedic Surgery, Nuffield Orthopaedic Centre, Windmill Road, Headington, Oxford OX3 7LD; 20 Feilden Grove, Headington, Oxford OX3 0DU; *e-mail:* graham.russell@ndos.ox.ac.uk.

RUSSELL, (Ronald) Christopher (Gordon), FRCS; Consultant Surgeon: Middlesex Hospital, 1975–2005; King Edward VII Hospital, since 1985; *b* 15 May 1940; *s* of Rognvald Gordon Russell, OBE and Doris Isa Russell (*née* Troup); *m* 1965, Mary Ruth Pitcher; two *s* (and one *s* decd). *Educ:* Epsom College; Middlesex Hosp. Med. Sch. (MB BS, MS). Sen. Lectr in Surgery, St Mary's Hosp., 1973–75. Medical Advr, Nuffield Hosps, 1988–2003; Civilian Medical Advr, RN, 2002–08. Member Council: Med. Defence Union, 1996–; RCS, 1999–2008 (Chm., Ct of Examnrs, 1997–99; Vice-Pres., 2006–08); Pres., Assoc. of Upper Gastrointestinal Surgeons, 1998–2000; Pres., Assoc. of Surgeons of GB and Ire., 2001–02. Chm., Jt Cttee on Inter-Collegiate Examinations, 2000–04. Chm., British Jl of Surgery Soc. Ltd, 1996–04; Associate Editor, 1978, Co-Editor, 1986–91, British Jl of Surgery; Gen. Editor, Operative Surgery, 1986–. *Publications:* (ed) Recent Advances in Surgery, vol. XI 1982, vol. XII 1985, vol. XIII 1991; (ed jtly) Bailey & Love Textbook of Surgery, 1991–2005; numerous contribs to surgical and gastroenterological jls. *Recreation:* travel. *Address:* Little Orchards, 6 Layters Way, Gerrards Cross SL9 7QY. *T:* (01753) 882264. *Club:* Royal Society of Medicine.

RUSSELL, Rudolf Rosenfeld; a Recorder of the Crown Court, 1980–97; *b* 5 Feb. 1925; *s* of Robert and Johanna Rosenfeld; *m* 1952, Eva Maria Jaray; one *s*. *Educ:* Bryanston Sch.; Worcester Coll., Oxford (MA). Service in RAF, 1943–46. Called to the Bar, Middle Temple, 1950. *Recreations:* walking, music, ski-ing. *Address:* 197 Roehampton Lane, SW15 4HN. *T:* (020) 8788 9925.

RUSSELL, Sally Joy; *see* Feldman, S. J.

RUSSELL, Stephen George; Chief Executive, The Boots Co., 2000–03; *b* 13 March 1945; *s* of Llandel and Olive Russell; *m* 1969, Elizabeth Jane Brook; one *s* one *d*. *Educ:* Tiffin Sch., Kingston upon Thames; Trinity Hall, Cambridge (BA Hons Classics). Joined Boots 1967; Dir of Merchandise, Boots The Chemists, 1988–92; Managing Dir, Do It All Ltd, 1992–95; Man. Dir, Boots The Chemists, 1995–2000; Jt Gp Man. Dir, Boots Co., 1997–2000. Non-executive Director: Woolwich plc, 1998–2000; Barclays Bank plc, 2000–; Business Control Solutions Gp, 2005–. Trustee, Tommy's the Baby Charity, 2003–. Mem. Council, Nottingham Univ., 2003–. *Recreations:* sport, classical music, opera, reading. *Address:* c/o Barclays Corporate Secretariat, Barclays PLC, 1 Churchill Place, E14 5HP. *Club:* Hawks (Cambridge).

RUSSELL, Terence Francis; Sheriff of North Strathclyde at Kilmarnock, 1983–2002; *b* 12 April 1931; *s* of Robert Russell and Catherine Cusker Russell; *m* 1965, Mary Ann Kennedy; two *d*. *Educ:* Glasgow Univ. (BL). Qualified as Solicitor, 1955; practised in Glasgow, 1955–58 and 1963–81; Solicitor in High Court, Bombay, 1958–63. Sheriff of N Strathclyde, and of Grampian, Highland and Islands, 1981–83. *Recreations:* gardening, travel.

RUSSELL, Thomas, CMG 1980 CBE 1970 (OBE 1963); HM Overseas Civil Service, retired; Representative of the Cayman Islands in UK, 1982–2000; *b* 27 May 1920; *s* of late Thomas Russell, OBE, MC and Margaret Thomson Russell; *m* 1951, Andrée Irma Désfossés (*d* 1989); one *s*. *Educ:* Hawick High Sch.; St Andrews Univ.; Peterhouse, Cambridge. MA St Andrews; Dip. Anthrop. Cantab. War Service, Cameronians (Scottish Rifles), 1941; 5th Bn (Scottish), Parachute Regt, 1943: served in N Africa and Italy; POW, 1944; Captain 1945; OC Parachute Trng Company, 1946. Cambridge Univ., 1946–47. Colonial Admin. Service, 1948; District Comr, British Solomon Is Protectorate, 1948; Asst Sec., Western Pacific High Commn, Fiji, 1951; District Comr, British Solomon Is Protectorate, 1954–56; seconded Colonial Office, 1956–57; Admin. Officer Class A, 1956; Dep. Financial Sec., 1962; Financial Sec., 1965; Chief Sec. to W Pacific High Commn, 1970–74; Governor of the Cayman Islands, 1974–81. Member Council: Pacific Islands Soc. of UK and Ire., 1986–2000 (Chm., 1982–86); Royal Commonwealth Ex Services League (formerly British Commonwealth Ex Services League), 1982– (Chm., Welfare Cttee, 1993–2005); Chm., Dependent Territories Assoc., 1997–98. FRAI. *Publication:* I Have The Honour To Be, 2003. *Recreations:* anthropology, archæology. *Address:* Hassendean, Gattonside, Melrose TD6 9NA. *Clubs:* Royal Commonwealth Society, Caledonian.

RUSSELL, William Martin, (Willy); author, since 1971; *b* 23 Aug. 1947; *s* of William and Margery Russell; *m* 1969, Ann Seagroatt; one *s* two *d*. *Educ:* St Katharine's Coll. of Educn, Liverpool, 1970–73 (Cert. of Educn). Ladies' Hairdresser, 1963–69; Teacher, 1973–74; Fellow in Creative Writing, Manchester Polytechnic, 1977–78. Founder Mem., and Dir, Quintet Films; Hon. Dir, Liverpool Playhouse. *Theatre:* Blind Scouse (3 short plays), 1971–72; When the Reds (adaptation), 1972; John, Paul, George, Ringo and Bert (musical), 1974; Breezeblock Park, 1975; One for the Road, 1976; Stags and Hens, 1978; Educating Rita, 1979; Blood Brothers (musical), 1983; Our Day Out (musical), 1983; Shirley Valentine, 1986; *television plays:* King of the Castle, 1972; Death of a Young, Young Man, 1972; Break In (for schools), 1974; Our Day Out, 1976; Lies (for schools), 1977; Daughters of Albion, 1978; Boy with Transistor Radio (for schools), 1979; One Summer (series), 1980; *radio play:* I Read the News Today (for schools), 1976; *screenplays:* Band on the Run, 1979 (not released); Educating Rita, 1981; Shirley Valentine, 1988; Dancing Through the Dark, 1989. Hon. MA Open Univ., 1983; Hon. DLit Liverpool, 1990. *Publications:* Breezeblock Park, 1978; One for the Road, 1980, rev. edn 1985; Educating Rita, 1981; Our Day Out, 1984; Stags and Hens, 1985; Blood Brothers, 1985 (also pubd as short non-musical version for schools, 1984); Shirley Valentine, 1989; The Wrong Boy (novel), 2000; several other plays included in general collections of plays; songs and poetry. *Recreations:* playing the guitar, composing songs, gardening, cooking. *Address:* c/o Casarotto Company Ltd, Waverley House, 7–12 Noel Street, W1F 8GQ. *T:* (020) 7287 4450. *Club:* Athenæum (Liverpool).

RUSSELL BEALE, Simon; *see* Beale.

RUSSELL FLINT, Simon Coleridge; QC 2003; a Recorder of the Crown Court, since 2000; *b* 8 Oct. 1957; *s* of late Francis Murray Russell Flint and of Susan Mary Russell Flint (*née* Sumner); *m* 1983, Jacqueline Ann Verden; one *s* one *d*. *Educ:* Cranleigh Sch.; Polytechnic of Central London (BA Hons Law). Called to the Bar, Inner Temple, 1980; Asst Recorder, 1998–2000. Chm., Police Discipline Appeals Tribunal, 2003–. Chm., Kent Bar Mess, 2004–. Gov., St George's Sch., Wrotham, 1996–. *Recreations:* tennis, ski-ing, armchair sport. *Address:* 23 Essex Street, WC2R 3AA. *T:* (020) 7413 0353, *Fax:* (020) 7413 0374; *e-mail:* simonrussellflint@23es.com.

RUSSELL-JONES, Maj. Gen. (Peter) John, OBE 1988; Army Adviser to BAE Systems, since 2001; *b* 31 May 1948; *s* of Peter Rathbone Russell-Jones and Margaret Silis Russell-Jones; *m* 1976, Stella Margaret Barrett; one *s* one *d*. *Educ:* Wellington Coll.; RMCS (BScEng Hons 1972). Commnd RE, 1968; Regtl duty, 1972–79; Army Staff Coll., 1979–80; MA to Master Gen. of the Ordnance, 1986–88; CO 23 Engr Regt, 1988–90; Col, Defence Policy, MoD, 1990–91; Comdt, Royal Mil. Sch. of Engrg, 1992–95; rcds, 1995; Dir, Internat. Orgns, MoD, 1996–97; ACDS, Operational Requirements (Land Systems), MoD, 1997–99; Capability Manager (Manoeuvre), MoD, 1999–2001. *Recreations:* sport, military history, travel, rock and roll, family. *Address:* Regimental HQ RE, Brompton Barracks, Chatham, Kent ME4 4UG.

RUSSELL-SMITH, Penelope, CVO 2007 (LVO 2000); Director of External Relations, AQ Research; *b* 22 Oct. 1956; *d* of Denham William Russell-Smith and Barbara Cynthia Russell-Smith. *Educ:* Sherborne Sch. for Girls; Girton Coll., Cambridge (MA). Dep. Editor, Whitaker's Almanack, 1980–81; Editor of Navy and Army publications, MoD, 1982–84; MoD Press Office (incl. Falkland Is, 1986), 1984–88; Chief Press Officer, Dept of Transport, 1988–90; EU Desk, News Dept, FCO, 1990–93; Asst Press Sec., 1993–97, Dep. Press Sec., 1997–2000, Press Sec., 2000–02, Communications and Press Sec., 2002–07, to the Queen. *Address:* Tarnwood, Chargrove Lane, Up Hatherley, Glos GL51 3LP.

RUSSELL VICK, Arnold Oughtred; *see* Vick.

RUSSILL, Patrick Joseph; Director of Music, London Oratory, since 1999; Head of Choral Conducting (formerly Choral Direction and Church Music), since 1997, and Professor of Organ, since 1999, Royal Academy of Music; *b* 9 Sept. 1953; *e s* of John Leonard Russill and Vera Mary Russill (*née* Clarke); *m* 1979, Jane Mary Rogers; two *s* three *d*. *Educ:* Shaftesbury Grammar Sch.; New Coll., Oxford (Organ Schol.; BA 1st Cl. Hons 1975; MA). ARCO 1971. Asst Organist, 1976–77, Organist, 1977–99, London Oratory; Dir, Oxford Chamber Choir, 1976–79; organist for Papal Mass, Wembley Stadium, 1982; Prof. of Acad. Studies, 1982–87, Hd of Ch Music, 1987–97, RAM; Director: London Oratory Jun. Choir, 1984–2003; Europa Singers of London, 1985–89. RFH recital début, 1986; appearances as organist and conductor in UK, Europe, Near East and Asia; has made recordings. Visiting Lecturer: St George's Coll., Jerusalem, 1994–95; Malmö Coll. of Music, Sweden, 1994; Vis. Lectr, 1999, Vis. Prof. of Choral Conducting, 2001–, Leipzig Hochschule für Musik und Theater. External Examiner: UEA, 1991–97; Univ. of Leeds, 2003–05; Ext. Moderator, Archbps' Cert., Guild of Ch Musicians,

1997–2002; Chief Examnr, RCO, 2005–. Mem. Council, RCO, 1996–. Member Committee: Ch Music Soc., 1990–; Organists' Benevolent League, 1994–. Trustee, Nicholas Danby Trust, 1998–. Organ restoration consultant, incl. St Dominic's Priory, London, 1992, Ely Cathedral, 1997–2001. Vice-Pres., Herbert Howells Soc., 2007 (Hon. Patron, 1993). Hon. RAM 1993 (Hon. ARAM 1989); Hon. FGCM 1997; Hon. FRCO 2002. *Publications:* (musical ed.) The Catholic Hymn Book, 1998; (contrib.) The Cambridge Companion to the Organ, 1998; (ed) Sweelinck and Howells choral works; contrib. articles and reviews in Gramophone, Musical Times, Organists' Rev., Choir and Organ, British Inst. Organ Studies Jl, RCO Year Book. *Recreations:* family photography, rural open air. *Address:* 65 Sandford Avenue, Wood Green, N22 5EJ.

RUSSON, David, CPhys, FInstP; Deputy Chief Executive, British Library, 1996–2001; *b* 12 June 1944; *s* of Thomas Charles Russon and Violet Russon (*née* Jarvis); *m* 1967, Kathleen Mary Gregory; one *s* two *d*. *Educ:* Wellington Grammar Sch.; University College London (BSc); Univ. of York. CPhys, FInstP 2000. Various appts, Office for Scientific and Technical Information, DES, 1969–74; British Library: R & D Dept, 1974–75; Lending Div., 1975–85; Dir, Document Supply Centre, 1985–88; Dir Gen., Sci., Technol. and Industry, later Boston Spa, 1988–96; Mem., British Liby Bd, 1988–2001. Pres., Internat. Council for Scientific and Technical Information, 1995–2001 (Vice Pres., 1992–95). FCLIP. *Publications:* contribs to professional jls of library and inf. science. *Recreations:* golf, village tennis and badminton. *Address:* March House, Tollerton, York YO61 1QQ. *T:* (01347) 838253.

RUST, Susan Esther; *see* Golombok, S. E.

RUSTON, Rt Rev. John Harry Gerald, OGS; Bishop of St Helena, 1991–99; *b* 1 Oct. 1929; *s* of late Alfred Francis Gerald Ruston and Constance Mary (*née* Symonds). *Educ:* Berkhamsted Sch.; Sidney Sussex Coll., Cambridge (BA 1952; MA 1956); Ely Theol Coll. Ordained deacon 1954, priest 1955; joined OGS, 1955; Asst Curate, St Andrew's, Leicester, 1954–57; Tutor, Cuddesdon Coll., Oxford, 1957–61; Asst Curate, All Saints, Cuddesdon, 1957–61; Asst Priest, St Francis, Sekhukhuniland, Transvaal, dio. of Pretoria, 1962–70; Principal, St Francis's Coll., Sekhukhuniland, 1967–70; Canon, Pretoria, 1968–76; Sub-Dean, Pretoria, 1970–76; Archdeacon of Bloemfontein, 1976–83; Warden, Community of St Michael and All Angels, and Chaplain, St Michael's Sch., Bloemfontein, 1976–83; consecrated Bishop, 1983; Bishop Suffragan, Pretoria, 1983–91. *Recreation:* music (composition and adaptation for 3-part singing). *Address:* The College of St Barnabas, Blackberry Lane, Lingfield, Surrey RH7 6NJ.

RUTHERFORD, Andrew; His Honour Judge Rutherford; DL; a Circuit Judge, since 1995; *b* 25 March 1948; *s* of late Robert Mark Rutherford and Alison Wellington (*née* Clark); *m* 1994, Lucy Elizabeth Bosworth; two *d*. *Educ:* Clifton Coll.; Exeter Univ. (LLB). Called to the Bar, Middle Temple, 1970; Asst Recorder, 1990–93; Recorder, 1993–95. Chm., Fees Adv. Commn, Gen. Synod of C of E, 2006–. DL Somerset, 2000. *Address:* c/o Lord Chancellor's Department, Western Circuit Office, 5th Floor, Greyfriars, Lewins Mead, Bristol BS1 2NR. *Club:* Bath and County.

RUTHERFORD, Derek Thomas Jones, CBE 1994; FCA; financial and management accounting consultant, 1990–96; *b* 9 April 1930; *s* of late Sydney Watson Rutherford and Elsie Rutherford; *m* 1956, Kathleen Robinson; one *s* four *d*. *Educ:* Doncaster Grammar School. Practising accountant and auditor, 1955–59; Company Sec./Accountant, P. Platt & Sons, 1959–61; Retail Accountant, MacFisheries, 1961–63; Factory Management Accountant, then Company Systems Manager, T. Wall & Son (Ice Cream), 1963–70; Dir of Finance, Alfa-Laval Co., 1970–74; Group Financial Dir, Oxley Printing Group, 1974; HMSO: Chief Accountant, Publications Group, 1975–76; Dir, Management Accounting Project, 1976–77; Dir of Finance and Planning Div., 1977–83; Principal Estabt and Finance Officer, 1983–84; Comr for Admin and Finance, Forestry Commn, 1984–90. *Recreations:* reading, gardening, home computing. *Address:* 3 Berkeley Gardens, Bury St Edmunds, Suffolk IP33 3JW. *T:* (01284) 767279. *Club:* Royal Air Force.

RUTHERFORD, Frederick John; District Judge (Magistrates' Courts), Humberside, since 2001; *b* Kelso, 6 Aug. 1954; *s* of late Frederick George Rutherford and Isabella Rutherford; *m* 1997, Jayne Louise Curry; one *s* two *d*. *Educ:* Heckmondwike Grammar Sch.; Leicester Univ. (LLB Hons). Articled Clerk, 1976–78, Asst Solicitor, 1978–80, Partner, 1980–89, Inesons, Solicitors, Cleckheaton; Partner, Jordans, Solicitors, Dewsbury, 1989–2000. *Recreations:* reading, walking, gardening, fly fishing.

RUTHERFORD, Jessica Marianne Fernande, FSA; Head of Libraries and Museums, and Director of the Royal Pavilion (Brighton and Hove), 1996–2005; *b* 7 Feb. 1949; *d* of Raymond Denys Rutherford and Simone Genvieve (*née* Michaud). *Educ:* Brighton and Hove High Sch.; Manchester Univ. (BA Hons Hist. of Art); Sussex Univ. (PGCE). V&A Mus., 1974; Royal Pavilion, Art Gallery and Museums, Brighton: Keeper of Decorative Art, 1974–85; Principal Keeper, Royal Pavilion, 1985–87; Asst Dir (Collections), 1987–92; Head of Mus and Dir, Royal Pavilion, 1992–96. Member: Steering Cttee, Nat. Report on Mus. Educn, Dept of Nat. Heritage, 1994–97; Bd, SE Museums Agency, 2001–02; Libraries, Museums & Archives Expert Panel, Heritage Lottery Fund, 2002–05 (Advr, Heritage Lottery Fund, 2005–). Decorative Arts Society: Sec., 1975–85; Trustee, 1992–2004; Mem. Council, Charleston Trust, 1992–2005; Sec. to Trustees and Governors, Friends of Royal Pavilion, Art Gall. and Museums, 1992–2004. Sussex University: Mem. Council, 1995–2001; Mem. Ct, 2002–; Dir, Gardner Arts Centre, 1996–98; Trustee, The Barlow Collection, 1996–2001. FRSA 1998. Hon. DLit Sussex, 2005. *Publications:* Art Nouveau, Art Deco and the Thirties: the furniture collections at Brighton Museum, 1983; (jtly) Art Nouveau, Art Deco and the Thirties: the ceramic, glass and metalwork collections at Brighton Museum, 1986; The Royal Pavilion: the palace of George IV, 1995; A Prince's Passion: the life of the Royal Pavilion, 2003; *chapters in:* James Tissot, 1984; The Crace Firm of Royal Decorators 1768–1900, 1990; Country House Lighting, 1992; articles and reviews for learned jls. *Recreations:* Spain, historic houses, film. *Address:* 24 Clifton Hill, Brighton, E Sussex BN1 3HQ. *T:* (01273) 326718.

RUTHERFORD, John Alexander; Chief Executive, Sea Fish Industry Authority, since 2002; *b* 5 Dec. 1948; *s* of John and Pamela Gordon Rutherford; *m* 1970, Judith Ann Lodge; three *s*. *Educ:* Univ. of Birmingham (BCom). FCA 1972. Accountant, Cooper Bros & Co., 1969–72; Mgt Accountant, Procter & Gamble Ltd, 1972–75; Finance Dir, West of England Farmers Ltd, 1986–91; West Midland Farmers Ltd, subseq. WMF Ltd: Finance Dir, 1991–96; Man. Dir, 1996–99; Dep. Man. Dir, Countrywide Farmers, 1999–2001. *Recreations:* helping wife build garden in Scottish hills, classic sports cars. *Address:* Sea Fish Industry Authority, 18 Logie Mills, Logie Green Road, Edinburgh EH7 5HS. *T:* (0131) 524 8675; *e-mail:* J_Rutherford@seafish.co.uk. *Clubs:* Farmers'; Morgan Sports Car.

RUTHERFORD, Thomas, CBE 1982; Chairman, North Eastern Electricity Board, 1977–89, retired; *b* 4 June 1924; *s* of Thomas and Catherine Rutherford; *m* 1950, Joyce Foreman; one *s* one *d*. *Educ:* Tynemouth High Sch.; King's Coll., Durham Univ. BSc(Hons); CEng, FIET. Engrg Trainee, subseq. Research Engr, A Reyrolle & Co. Ltd, Hebburn-on-Tyne, 1943–49; North Eastern Electricity Bd: various engrg and commercial appts, 1949–61; Personal Asst to Chm., 1961–63; Area Commercial Engr, then Area Engr, Tees Area, 1964–69; Dep. Commercial Man., 1969–70; Commercial Man., 1970–72; Chief Engr, 1972–73; Dep. Chm., 1973–75; Chm., SE Electricity Board, 1975–77. *Address:* 76 Beach Road, Tynemouth, Northumberland NE30 2QW. *T:* (0191) 257 1775.

RUTHERFORD-JONES, Maj. Gen. David John; Commandant, Royal Military Academy Sandhurst, since 2007; *b* Steamer Point, Aden, 11 Aug. 1958; *s* of Arthur and Penelope Rutherford-Jones; *m* 1985, Sarah Jane McNish; one *s* one *d*. *Educ:* Lancing Coll.; RMA Sandhurst. Commnd 15th/19th Hussars, 1977; COS 1st Mechanized Bde, 1993–95; Balkan Planning, HQ Allied Powers Europe, 1995–97; Comd Light Dragoons, 1997–2000; COS 3rd UK Div., 2000; Comd 20 Armoured Bde, Kosovo and Iraq, 2001–04; Dir Land Studies, UK Defence Acad., 2004–05; Dir RAC, 2005–07. *Recreations:* sailing, ski-ing, fishing, reading, walking, Newcastle United FC.

RUTHNASWAMY, Elizabeth Kuanghu; *see* Han Suyin.

RUTHVEN; *see* Hore-Ruthven, family name of Earl of Gowrie.

RUTHVEN OF CANBERRA, Viscount; Patrick Leo Brer Hore-Ruthven; Operations Director, Camphor Ltd; *b* 4 Feb. 1964; *s* and *heir* of 2nd Earl of Gowrie, *qv*; *m* 1990, Julie Goldsmith; one *s*. *Heir:* *s* Hon. Heathcote Patrick Cornelius Hore-Ruthven, *b* 28 May 1990.

RUTHVEN, Prof. Kenneth Borthwick Howard, PhD; Professor of Education, University of Cambridge, since 2005; Fellow, Hughes Hall, Cambridge, since 1983; *b* 1 Feb. 1952. *Educ:* Corpus Christi Coll., Oxford (BA Hons Maths 1973, MA 1977); Moray House Coll., Edinburgh (PGCE 1974); Univ. of Edinburgh (DipEd 1974); Univ. of Stirling (PhD Educn 1980); MA Cantab 1983. Teacher of Maths and Computing, 1974–83: Broughton High Sch., Edinburgh; Brighton Hove & Sussex Sixth Form Coll.; Hills Road Sixth Form Coll., Cambridge; Lectr, 1983–98, Reader, 1998–2005, in Educn, Univ. of Cambridge. Mem., British Soc. for Res. into Learning Maths, 1983– (Chm., 2006–). Trustee, Sch. Mathematics Proj., 1996– (Dep. Chm., 2004–05, Chm., 2006–, of Trustees). Adv. Editor, Educnl Studies in Maths, 2001– (Ed., 1994–95, Ed.-in-Chief, 1996–2000). *Publications:* Society and the New Technology, 1983; The Maths Factory, 1989; Learning from Computers: mathematics education and technology, 1993; The Didactical Challenge of Symbolic Calculators: turning a computational device into a mathematical instrument, 2005; around 50 res. papers in peer-reviewed jls. *Address:* University of Cambridge Faculty of Education, 184 Hills Road, Cambridge CB2 8PQ. *T:* (01223) 767600, *Fax:* (01223) 767602; *e-mail:* kr18@ cam.ac.uk.

RUTHVEN, Hon. Malise Walter Maitland Knox Hore, PhD; writer; *b* 14 May 1942; *s* of late Major Hon. Alexander Hardinge Patrick Hore-Ruthven and Pamela Margaret Hore-Ruthven (*née* Fletcher); *m* 1967, Ianthe Hodgkinson; two *d*. *Educ:* Eton Coll.; Trinity Coll., Cambridge (BA Eng. Lit. 1964; MA 1994; PhD Social and Pol Scis 2000). Writer and ed., BBC External Services, 1966–70, 1976–86; Lectr, Dept of Divinity with Religious Studies, Univ. of Aberdeen, 1994–99. Visiting Professor: Dartmouth Coll., NH, 1989–90; UCSD, 1990–91, 1999–2000; Colorado Coll., Colorado Springs, 2000–01. *Publications:* Torture: the grand conspiracy, 1978; Islam in the World, 1984, 3rd edn, 2006; Traveller Through Time: a photographic journey with Freya Stark, 1986; The Divine Supermarket, 1989; A Satanic Affair: Salman Rushdie and the wrath of Islam, 1990; Islam: a very short introduction, 1997, 2nd edn 2000; A Fury for God: the Islamist attack on America, 2002; Fundamentalism: the search for meaning, 2004; Children of Time: the Aga Khan and the Ismailis, 2008. *Recreation:* walking. *Address:* Hameau Travers, St Jacques de Néhou, 50390, France. *T:* (02) 33013849; *e-mail:* mhruthven@aol.com.
See also Earl of Gowrie.

RUTLAND, 11th Duke of, *cr* 1703; **David Charles Robert Manners;** Marquess of Granby 1703; Earl of Rutland 1525; Baron Manners of Haddon 1679; Baron Roos of Belvoir 1896; *b* 8 May 1959; *er s* of 10th Duke of Rutland, CBE and of Frances Helen (*née* Sweeny); *S* father, 1999; *m* 1992, Emma, *d* of John Watkins; two *s* three *d*. Mem. Civilian Cttee, ATC Sqdn, Grantham; Pres., Trent Wing ATC. Member: CLA Cttee for Leicestershire/Rutland; HHA (Chm., E Midlands Area, 1995–99). President: Notts Rifle Assoc.; Ex-Aircrew Assoc., Grantham and Dist Br.; Vice Pres., Buckminster Gliding Club, 2006–; Patron, Grantham to Nottingham Canal Preservation Trust. Freeman, City of London; Liveryman, Gunsmiths' Co. *Recreations:* shooting, fishing, flying when I can. *Heir:* *s* Marquis of Granby, *qv*. *Address:* Belvoir Castle, Grantham, Lincs NG32 1PE. *T:* (01476) 870246. *Clubs:* Turf, Annabel's.

RUTOVITZ, Jeanne Elisabeth; *see* Bell, J. E.

RUTT, Rev. Canon (Cecil) Richard, CBE 1973; MA; *b* 27 Aug. 1925; *s* of Cecil Rutt and Mary Hare Turner; *m* 1969, Joan Mary Ford (*d* 2007). *Educ:* Huntingdon Grammar School; Kelham Theol. Coll.; Pembroke Coll., Cambridge. RNVR, 1943–46. Deacon, 1951; Priest, 1952. Asst Curate, St George's, Cambridge, 1951–54; Dio. of Korea, 1954; Parish Priest of Anjung, 1956–58; Warden of St Bede's House Univ. Centre, Seoul, 1959–64; Rector of St Michael's Seminary, Oryu Dong, Seoul, 1964–66; Archdeacon, West Kyonggi (Dio. Seoul), 1965–66; Asst Bishop of Taejon, 1966–68; Bishop of Taejon, 1968–74; Bishop Suffragan of St Germans, 1974–79; Hon. Canon, St Mary's Cathedral, Truro, 1974–79; Bishop of Leicester, 1979–90. Received into RC Ch, 1994, ordained priest, 1995; Hon. Asst, St Mary Immaculate, Falmouth; Hon. Canon, Plymouth Cathedral Chapter, 2001–. Associate Gen. Sec., Korean Bible Soc., 1964–74; Episcopal Sec., Council of the Church of SE Asia, 1968–74; Commissary, dio. of Taejon, 1974–90; Pres., Roy. Asiatic Soc., Korea Br., 1974. Chairman: Adv. Council on Relations of Bishops and Religious Communities, 1980–90; Bishop of Truro's Adv. Gp on Services in Cornish, 1975–79 and Ecumenical Adv. Gp (formerly Adv. Gp on Services in Cornish), 1990–2005; Mem., Anglican/Orthodox Jt Doctrinal Discussions, 1983–89. Bard of the Gorsedd of Cornwall, Cornwhylen, 1976 (Chaplain, 1993–97). Hon. Fellow, Northumbrian Univs' E Asia Centre, 1990. Hon. DLitt Confucian Univ., Seoul, 1974. Tasan Cultural Award (for writings on Korea), 1964. ChStJ 1978. Order of Civil Merit, Peony Class (Korea), 1974. *Publications:* (ed) Songgonghoe Songga (Korean Anglican Hymnal), 1961; Korean Works and Days, 1964; P'ungnyu Han'guk (in Korean), 1965; (trans.) An Anthology of Korean Sijo, 1970; The Bamboo Grove, an introduction to Korean Sijo poetry, 1971; James Scarth Gale and his History of the Korean People, 1972; The Green People (translations of Korean poet, Yi Unsang), 1973; Virtuous Women, three masterpieces of traditional Korean fiction, 1974; A History of Handknitting, 1987; The Book of Changes (Zhouyi): a Bronze Age document translated with introduction and notes, 1996; (with K. L. Pratt) Korea: an historical and cultural dictionary, 1999; The Song of a Faithful Wife: Ch'unhyang, 1999; (contrib.) The Path to Rome, ed D. Longenecker, 1999; Martyrs of Korea, 2002; contribs on Korean classical poetry and history to Trans Royal Asiatic Soc. (Korea Br.) and various Korean publications. *Address:* 3 Marlborough Court, Falmouth, Cornwall TR11 2QU. *T:* (01326) 312276.

RUTTER, Prof. Arthur John; Emeritus Professor, Imperial College, University of London (Professor of Botany, 1967–79 and Head of Department of Botany and Plant Technology, 1971–79); *b* 22 Nov. 1917; *s* of late W. Arthur Rutter, CBE, FRIBA and Amy, *d* of William Dyche, BA, Cardiff; *m* 1944, Betsy Rosier Stone (*d* 1978); two *s* one *d*. *Educ:* Royal Grammar Sch., Guildford; Imperial Coll. of Science and Technology. ARCS, BSc, PhD, FIBiol. Mem., ARC team for selection of oil-seed crops and develt selective herbicides, 1940–45; Asst Lectr, Imperial Coll., 1945, Lectr 1946; Reader in Ecology, Univ. of London, 1956. Vis. Prof., Univ. of the Panjab, Pakistan, 1960–61. *Publications:* papers, mainly in Annals of Botany, Jl of Ecology, Jl of Applied Ecology on water relations of plants, forest hydrology and effects of atmospheric pollution on trees. *Recreations:* gardening, walking. *Address:* 10 Thursby Road, Woking, Surrey GU21 3NZ. *T:* (01483) 765009.

RUTTER, Barrie Thomas; Founder and Artistic Director, Northern Broadsides Theatre Co., since 1992; *b* 12 Dec. 1946; *s* of Edward and Annie Rutter; *m* 1978, Carol Chillington (marr. diss. 1997); two *d* (one *s* decd). *Educ:* Newton Hall, Hull; Royal Scottish Acad. of Music and Drama; Nat. Youth Th. Professional actor, 1968–, mostly in theatre, but occasional TV, film and radio; *theatre* includes: Napoleon, in Animal Farm, 1984, and Silenus, in The Trackers of Oxyrhynchus, 1990, NT; Northern Broadsides Theatre Co., director: Richard III (also title rôle), 1992; A Midsummer Night's Dream (Shakespeare's Globe, Tyrone Guthrie Award for Best Production), 1995; Antony and Cleopatra (also title rôle), 1995; Samson Agonistes (also title rôle), 1998; King Lear (also title rôle), 1999; Alcestis (Ted Hughes' final play), 2000; Antigone, 2003; The Merchant of Venice (also title rôle), 2004; Sweet William (Fat Jack), Comedy of Errors (Egeon), 2005; Wars of the Roses (also edited and acted, Duke of York), 2006; The Tempest (Prospero), 2007. Hon. DLitt: Hull, 2001; Bradford, 2005; Huddersfield, 2006. TMA Award for best dir, 1995; Overall Winner, Creative Briton Awards, Arts & Business/ Prudential, 2000; Sam Wanamaker Award, Shakespeare's Globe, 2003. *Recreations:* food and drink, sport, poetry. *Address:* Northern Broadsides, Dean Clough, Halifax HX3 5AX. *T:* (01422) 369704, *Fax:* (01422) 383175; *e-mail:* rutter@northern-broadsides.co.uk. *Club:* East India.

RUTTER, Dr (James) Michael, CBE 2002; Consultant, JMR Consultancy, since 2002; Director of Veterinary Medicines, 1989–2002, and Chief Executive, Veterinary Medicines Directorate, 1990–2002, Department for Environment, Food and Rural Affairs (formerly Ministry of Agriculture, Fisheries and Food); *b* 20 Aug. 1941; *s* of late James and Lily Rutter; *m* 1967, Jacqueline Patricia Watson; one *d*. *Educ:* Kendal Grammar Sch.; Univ. of Edinburgh (BVM&S 1964; BSc 1965; PhD 1967). MRCVS 1964. Res. Schol., 1964–67, Res. Asst, 1967–69, Univ. of Edinburgh; Institute for Research on Animal Diseases, later Institute for Animal Health: Vet. Res. Officer, 1969–73; Principal Vet. Res. Officer, 1973–84 (on secondment to DES, 1975–78); Head: Dept of Microbiol., 1984–89; Compton Lab., 1986–89. Expert Consultant: ODA; FAO; WHO. Member: Cttee for Vet. Medicinal Products, EC, 1991–99; Mgt Bd, Eur. Medicines Evaluation Agency, 1996–2002; Assessor, Animal Medicines Trng Regulatory Authy, 2007–. Dir, 2004–, Sec., 2006–, Vet. Benevolent Fund; Pres., Vet. Res. Club, 2007–08. FRSocMed 1985. *Publications:* Perinatal Ill Health in Calves, 1973; Pasteurella and Pasteurellosis, 1989; contrib. numerous papers to scientific jls. *Recreations:* gardening, outdoor sports, theatre, ballet, music.

RUTTER, Jill Kathleen; Director, Strategy and Sustainable Development, Department for Environment, Food and Rural Affairs, since 2004; *b* 30 Oct. 1956; *d* of Derek John Rutter and June Kathleen Rutter. *Educ:* Somerville Coll., Oxford (BA PPE 1978). HM Treasury, 1978–97; BP plc, 1998–2004. *Address:* Department for Environment, Food and Rural Affairs, Nobel House, 17 Smith Square, SW1P 3JR; *e-mail:* jill.rutter@defra.gsi.gov.uk.

RUTTER, His Honour John Cleverdon; a Circuit Judge, 1972–92 (a Senior Circuit Judge, 1990–92); *b* 18 Sept. 1919; 2nd *s* of late Edgar John Rutter; *m* 1951, Jill (*d* 1993), *d* of late Maxwell Duncan McIntosh; one *s* one *d*. *Educ:* Cardiff High Sch.; Univ. Coll., of SW of England, Exeter (Open Schol.); Keble Coll., Oxford. MA Oxon; LLB London. Royal Artillery, 1939–46; commnd 1941; served overseas. Called to the Bar, Lincoln's Inn, 1948; practised Wales and Chester Circuit, 1948–66, Stipendiary Magistrate for City of Cardiff, 1966–71. A Legal Member, Mental Health Review Tribunal for Wales Region, 1960–66. An Assistant Recorder of: Cardiff, 1962–66; Merthyr Tydfil, 1962–66; Swansea, 1965–66; Dep. Chm., Glamorgan QS, 1969–71. *Recreations:* reading, bridge. *Address:* Law Courts, Cardiff CF1 3PG. *T:* (029) 2041 4400.

RUTTER, John Milford, CBE 2007; composer and conductor; *b* 24 Sept. 1945; *s* of Laurence Frederick and Joan Mary Rutter; *m* 1980, JoAnne Redden; one *s* (and one *s* decd), and one step *d*. *Educ:* Highgate Sch.; Clare Coll., Cambridge (MA, MusB; Hon. Fellow, 2001). Fellow and Director of Music, Clare Coll., Cambridge, 1975–79; Founder and Director, Cambridge Singers, 1981–. Hon. FGCM 1988; Hon. Fellow, Westminster Choir Coll., Princeton, 1980. DMus Lambeth, 1996; Hon. Dr: Anglia Ruskin, 2004; Leicester, 2005; Hull, 2008. *Publications:* compositions include choral pieces, anthems and carols, 1969–. *Address:* Old Laceys, St John's Street, Duxford, Cambridge CB22 4RA. *T:* (01223) 832474, *Fax:* (01223) 836723.

RUTTER, Michael; *see* Rutter, J. M.

RUTTER, Sir Michael (Llewellyn), Kt 1992; CBE 1985; MD; FRCP, FRCPsych, FMedSci; FRS 1987; Professor of Child Psychiatry, 1973–98, Professor of Developmental Psychopathology, since 1998, University of London Institute of Psychiatry; *b* 15 Aug. 1933; *s* of Llewellyn Charles Rutter and Winifred Olive Rutter; *m* 1958, Marjorie Heys; one *s* two *d*. *Educ:* Moorestown Friends' Sch., USA; Wolverhampton Grammar Sch.; Bootham Sch., York; Birmingham Univ. Med. Sch. (MB ChB 1955, MD Hons 1963). MRCS 1955; LRCP 1955, MRCP 1958, FRCP 1972; FRCPsych 1971. Training in paediatrics, neurology and internal medicine, 1955–58; Maudsley Hosp., 1958–61; Nuffield Med. Travelling Fellow, Albert Einstein Coll. of Medicine, NY, 1961–62; Mem., Sci. Staff, MRC Social Psych. Res. Unit, 1962–65; University of London Institute of Psychiatry: Sen. Lectr, then Reader, 1966–73; Hon. Dir, MRC Child Psychiatry Unit, 1984–98; Dir, Social, Genetic and Develtl Psychiatry Res. Centre, 1994–98. Fellow, Center for Advanced Study in Behavioral Scis, Stanford, Calif, 1979–80. Lectures: Goulstonian, RCP, 1973; Salmon, NY Acad. of Medicine, 1979; Adolf Meyer, Amer. Psych. Assoc., 1985; Maudsley, RCPsych, 1986. Pres., Soc. for Res. in Child Develt, 1999–2001 (Pres.-elect, 1997–99). Gov., 1996–2003, Dep. Chm., 1999–2003, Wellcome Trust; Trustee: Nuffield Foundn, 1992–; Jacobs Foundn, 1998–2004; Novartis Foundn, 1999–; One Plus One, 2001–. Founding Mem., Acad. Europaea, 1988; Founder FMedSci 1998; Foreign Associate Member: Inst. of Medicine, Nat. Acad. of Scis, USA, 1988; US Nat. Acad. of Educn, 1990; Foreign Hon. Mem., Amer. Acad. of Arts and Scis, 1989. FKC 1998. Hon. Prof., Amsterdam Univ., 2001. Hon. FBPsS 1978; Hon. Fellow: Amer. Acad. of Pediatrics, 1981; RSocMed 1996; Hon. FRCPCH 1996; Hon. FBA 2002. Hon. DSSc Univ. of Leiden, 1985; Hon. Dr Leuven, 1990; Hon. DSc: Birmingham, 1990; Chicago, 1991; Minnesota, 1993; Ghent, 1994; Warwick, 1999; E Anglia, 2000; Oxon, 2005; Hon. MD Edinburgh, 1990; Hon. DPsych Jyväskylä, Finland, 1996; DUniv: N London, 2000; York, 2005. Numerous awards, UK and USA. *Publications:* Children of Sick Parents, 1966; (jtly) A Neuropsychiatric Study in Childhood, 1970; (ed jtly) Education, Health and Behaviour, 1970; (ed) Infantile Autism, 1971; Maternal Deprivation Reassessed, 1972, 2nd edn 1981; (ed jtly) The Child with Delayed Speech, 1972; Helping Troubled Children, 1975; (jtly) Cycles of Disadvantage, 1976; (ed jtly) Child Psychiatry, 1977, 2nd edn as Child and Adolescent Psychiatry, 1985, 4th edn, 2002; (ed jtly) Autism, 1978; Changing Youth in a Changing Society, 1979; (jtly) Fifteen Thousand Hours: secondary schools and their effects on children, 1979; (ed) Scientific Foundations of Developmental Psychiatry, 1981; A Measure of Our Values: goals and dilemmas in the upbringing of children, 1983; (jtly) Lead Versus Health, 1983; (jtly) Juvenile Delinquency, 1983; (ed) Developmental Neuropsychiatry, 1983; (ed jtly) Stress, Coping and Development, 1983; (ed jtly) Depression in Young People, 1986; (jtly) Treatment of Autistic Children, 1987; (ed jtly) Language Development and Disorders, 1987; (jtly) Parenting Breakdown: the making and breaking of inter-generational links, 1988; (ed jtly) Assessment and Diagnosis in Child Psychopathology, 1988; (ed) Studies of Psychosocial Risk: the power of longitudinal data, 1988; (ed jtly) Straight and Devious Pathways from Childhood to Adulthood, 1990; (ed jtly) Biological Risk Factors for Psychosocial Disorders, 1991; (jtly) Developing Minds: challenge and continuity across the life span, 1993; (ed jtly) Development Through Life: a handbook for clinicians, 1994; (ed jtly) Stress, Risk and Resilience in Children and Adolescents: processes, mechanisms and interventions, 1994; (ed jtly) Psychosocial Disorders in Young People, 1995; (jtly) Behavioural Genetics, 3rd edn, 1997; (jtly) Antisocial Behaviour by Young People, 1998; (jtly) Sex Differences in Antisocial Behaviour: conduct disorder, delinquency and violence in the Dunedin longitudinal study, 2001; (ed jtly) Ethnicity and Causal Mechanisms, 2005; Genes and Behaviour, 2006. *Recreations:* fell walking, tennis, wine tasting, theatre, family. *Address:* 190 Court Lane, Dulwich, SE21 7ED. *Club:* Royal Society of Medicine.

RUTTER, Trevor John, CBE 1990 (OBE 1976); Assistant Director General, British Council, 1990–91, retired; *b* 26 Jan. 1934; *s* of Alfred Rutter and Agnes Rutter (*née* Purslow); *m* 1959, Josephine Henson; one *s*. *Educ:* Monmouth Sch.; Brasenose Coll., Oxford (BA). National Service, Army, 1955–57. British Council, Indonesia, W Germany (Munich), London, 1959–66; First Secretary, Foreign Office, 1967; British Council, 1968–91: Representative: Singapore, 1968–71; Thailand, 1971–75; various appointments, London, 1975–85, including: Head, Home Div., 1980; Asst Dir Gen., 1981–85; Rep. in W Germany, 1986–90. *Address:* 7 Grove Mews, Totnes, Devon TQ9 5GT.

RUTTLE, (Henry) Stephen (Mayo); QC 1997; *b* 6 Feb. 1953; *s* of His Honour Henry Samuel Jacob Ruttle and Joyce Mayo Ruttle (*née* Moriarty); *m* 1985, Fiona Jane Mitchell-Innes; two *s* two *d*. *Educ:* Westminster Sch. (Queen's Schol.); Queens' Coll., Cambridge (BA Hons Eng. Lit. and Law). Called to the Bar, Gray's Inn, 1976, Bencher, 2004; in practice at the Bar, 1976–; practising as commercial and community mediator, 2000– (CEDR accredited mediator, 1998). A Lieut Bailiff of Guernsey, 2008–. Fellow, Internat. Acad. of Mediators, 2005–. *Recreations:* Church, fly-fishing, the countryside, mountains, oak furniture. *Address:* Brick Court Chambers, 7–8 Essex Street, WC2R 3LD. *T:* (020) 7379 3550, *T:* (020) 7520 9871. *Club:* Flyfishers'.

RYAN, Prof. Alan James, FBA 1986; Fellow, since 1969, Warden, 1996–Aug. 2009, New College, Oxford; Professor of Politics, University of Oxford, since 1997; *b* 9 May 1940; *s* of James William Ryan and Ivy Ryan; *m* 1971, Kathleen Alyson Lane; one *d*. *Educ:* Christ's Hospital; Balliol Coll., Oxford (Hon. Fellow, 2004). Lectr in Politics, Univ. of Keele, 1963–66, Univ. of Essex, 1966–69; Lectr in Politics, 1969–78, Reader, 1978–87, Univ. of Oxford; Prof. of Politics, Princeton Univ., 1988–96; Dir, Rothermere Amer. Inst., Univ. of Oxford, 1999–2002. Visiting Professor in Politics: City University of New York, 1967–68; Univs of Texas, 1972, California, 1977, the Witwatersrand, 1978; Vis. Fellow, ANU, 1974, 1979; Mellon Fellow, Inst. for Advanced Study, Princeton, 1991–92; Fellow, Center for Advanced Study, Stanford, 2002–03; de Carle Lectr, Univ. of Otago, 1983. Official Mem., CNAA, 1975–80. Delegate, Oxford Univ. Press, 1983–87. *Publications:* The Philosophy of John Stuart Mill, 1970, 2nd edn 1987; The Philosophy of the Social Sciences, 1970; J. S. Mill, 1975; Property and Political Theory, 1984; (ed jtly) The Blackwell Encyclopaedia of Political Thought, 1987; Property, 1987; Bertrand Russell: a political life, 1988; John Dewey and the High Tide of American Liberalism, 1995; Liberal Anxieties and Liberal Education, 1998. *Recreations:* dinghy sailing, long train journeys. *Address:* Warden's Lodgings, New College, Oxford OX1 3BN; *e-mail:* alan.ryan@new.ox.ac.uk. *Club:* Oxford and Cambridge.

RYAN, Prof. Anthony John, OBE 2006; PhD, DSc; Professor of Physical Chemistry, since 1997, and Pro Vice Chancellor (Faculty of Science), since 2008, University of Sheffield (ICI Professor of Physical Chemistry, 2002–08); *b* 20 March 1962; *s* of Anthony Ryan and Margaret Ryan; *m* 1990, Angela Potts; two *d*. *Educ:* Univ. of Manchester (BSc Hons 1983; PhD 1988); DSc UMIST 2004. Lectr, 1985–88 and 1990–94, Sen. Lectr, 1994–95, Reader, 1995–97, in Polymer Sci. and Technol., UMIST; NATO Res. Fellow, Univ. of Minnesota, 1988–89; Hd, Chemistry Dept, Univ. of Sheffield, 1998–2003. Christmas Lectr, Royal Instn, 2002. *Publications:* Polymer Processing: structure development, 1998; Emerging Themes in Polymer Science, 2000. *Recreations:* mountaineering, cycling, eating, drinking and being merry. *Address:* Faculty of Pure Science, University of Sheffield, Sheffield S3 7HF. *T:* (0114) 222 9409, *Fax:* (0114) 222 9389.

RYAN, (Christopher) Nigel (John), CBE 1977; freelance writer; Chairman, TV-am News, 1989–92 (Director, 1985–92); *b* 12 Dec. 1929; *s* of late Brig. C. E. Ryan, MC, RA; *m* 1984, Susan Anne Crewe, *qv* (marr. diss.). *Educ:* Ampleforth Coll.; Queen's Coll., Oxford (MA). Joined Reuters, London, 1954; Foreign Corresp., 1957–60; joined Independent Television News, 1961, Editor, 1968–71, Editor and Chief Executive, 1971–77; Vice-Pres., NBC News, America, 1977–80; Dir of Progs, Thames Television, 1980–82. Silver Medal, Royal Television Soc., 1970; Desmond Davis Award, 1972. *Publications:* A Hitch or Two in Afghanistan, 1983; (jtly) The Scholar and the Gypsy, 1992; trans. novels from French by Georges Simenon and others. *Address:* 4 Cleveland Square, W2 6DH. *T:* (020) 7723 8552. *Club:* Beefsteak.

RYAN, David, CBE 2003; Area Director Designate, Crime, London Region, HM Courts Service, 2004–05; *b* 7 Dec. 1948; *s* of Christopher and Ellen Ryan; *m* 1971, Anna Maria Scumaci; one *s* one *d*. *Educ:* City Grammar Sch., Lincoln. Personnel and Finance Officer, Midland and Oxford Circuit, 1987–92; Courts Administrator, Winchester, 1992–97; Circuit Administrator: Western Circuit, 1997–2003; S Eastern Circuit, 2003–04. *Recreations:* supporting Aston Villa and spectating sports generally, drinking the odd glass of red wine, holidays in Calabria. *Address:* 1 The Paddocks, Ampfield, Romsey, Hants SO51 9BG; *e-mail:* daveandanna123@aol.com. *Club:* Hampshire Cricket.

RYAN, Maj.-Gen. Denis Edgar, CB 1987; Director of Army Education, 1984–87; *b* 18 June 1928; *s* of late Reginald Arthur Ryan and of Amelia (*née* Smith); *m* 1955, Jean Mary Bentley; one *s* one *d*. *Educ:* Sir William Borlase School, Marlow; King's College, London (LLB). Commissioned RAEC, 1950; served BAOR, 1950–54; Instr, RMA Sandhurst,

1954–56; Adjt, Army Sch. of Educn, 1957–59; Staff Coll., 1960; served in Cyprus, Kenya and UK, 1961–67; CAES, HQ 4 Div., BAOR, 1968–70; Cabinet Office, 1970–72; TDA, Staff Coll., 1972–75; Col GS MoD, 1976–78; Chief Education Officer: HQ SE Dist, 1978–79; HQ BAOR, 1979–82; Comd, Education, UK, 1982–84. Col Comdt, RAEC, 1990–92; Dep. Col Comdt, AGC, 1992–93. *Recreations:* cricket, tennis, Rugby, music, theatre. *Club:* Army and Navy.

RYAN, Sir Derek (Gerald), 4th Bt *cr* 1919, of Hintlesham, Suffolk; architect; *b* 25 March 1954; *s* of Sir Derek Gerald Ryan, 3rd Bt and of Penelope Anne Hawkings; *S* father, 1990; *m* (marr. diss.); *m* 1997, Roberta Tonn. *Educ:* Univ. of California at Berkeley (BAED 1977). Washington State Architect License #4296, 1984; NCARB Certificate #32,269, 1984; Idaho State Architect License #AR-2623. NBBJ architects and planners, Seattle, WA, 1980–99; Williams Partners Architects (formerly Jeffrey Charles Williams Architects), Ketchum, ID, 1999–. *Recreations:* ski-ing, guitar. *Heir: cousin* Desmond Maurice Ryan [*b* 16 Sept. 1918; *m* 1942, Margaret Catherine, *d* of A. H. Brereton; three *s*]. *Address:* PO Box 6966, Ketchum, ID 83340, USA. *T:* (208) 7204153; *e-mail:* derek@williams-partners.com.

RYAN, Gerard Charles; QC 1981; a Recorder of the Crown Court, 1984–98; *b* 16 Dec. 1931; *er s* of Frederick Charles Ryan, Hove, and Louie Violet Ryan (*née* Ball); *m* 1960, Sheila Morag Clark Cameron, *qv*; two *s. Educ:* Clayesmore Sch.; Brighton Coll.; Pembroke Coll., Cambridge (Exhibnr; MA). Served RA, 1955–57 (Lieut). Called to the Bar, Middle Temple, 1955, Bencher, 1988; Harmsworth Scholar, 1956; in practice at Common Law Bar, 1957–65, at Parly Bar and Planning and Envmt Bar, 1965–2001. Chm., Tribunal of Inquiry into Loscoe (Derbyshire) gas explosion, 1986–87. Chairman: Soc. of Sussex Downsmen, 1977–80; Murray Downland Trust, 1993–2001. *Publication:* (with A. O. B. Harris) Outline of the Law of Common Land, 1967. *Recreations:* conservation, growing trees and other plants, walking.

RYAN, Joan Marie; MP (Lab) Enfield North, since 1997; Special Representative to Cyprus, since 2007; *b* 8 Sept. 1955; *d* of late Michael Joseph Ryan and of Dolores Marie Ryan (*née* Joyce); *m* 1998, Martin Hegarty; one *s* one *d*, and one step *s* one step *d. Educ:* City of Liverpool Coll. of Higher Educn (BA Hons 1993); South Bank Poly. (MSc 1983); Avery Hill Coll. (PGCE 1984). Sociology, Soc. Sci., Religious Studies and Eur. Politics Teacher, and Hd of Year, Hurlingham and Chelsea Secondary Sch., Fulham, 1984–89; Head of Pastoral Educn, Hawksmoor Sixth Form Coll., Fulham, 1989–94; Hd of Humanities, William Morris Acad., Hammersmith, 1994–97. Mem. (Lab), Barnet LBC, 1990–98. An Asst Govt Whip, 2002–03; a Lord Comr of HM Treasury (Govt Whip), 2003–06; Parly Under-Sec. of State, Home Office, 2006–07. Oral history interviewer, Imperial War Mus., 1984–86. *Recreations:* visiting historic buildings, swimming, cinema, ski-ing. *Address:* House of Commons, SW1A 0AA. *T:* (020) 7219 6502.

RYAN, Michael James, CBE 2005; Vice President and General Manager, Bombardier Aerospace, Belfast, since 2004; *b* 14 Aug. 1959; *s* of Patrick and Maeve Ryan; *m* 1986, Mary Gibson; two *s* one *d. Educ:* Queen's Univ., Belfast (BSc Hons Aeronautical Engrg). CEng 1992; FRAeS 2003. Joined Short Brothers, 1981: Develt Engr, 1981–84; Prodn Engr, 1985–87; Prodn Engrg Manager, 1988–89; Bombardier Aerospace: Ops Manager, 1990–93; Dir of Manufg, 1993–97; Procurement Dir, 1997–99; Gen. Manager Procurement, Montreal, 1999–2000. Chm., Maydown Precision Engrg, 2000–. Council Mem., SBAC, 2000–. Chm., Business in the Community, NI, 2005–; Bd Mem., Centre for Competitiveness, 2000–. Pres. NI Br., RAeS, 2004–05. *Recreations:* keeping fit, reading, music, art, travel. *Address:* Bombardier Aerospace, Belfast, Airport Road, Belfast BT3 9DZ. *T:* (028) 9073 3553, *Fax:* (028) 9073 3143; *e-mail:* michael.ryan@aero.bombardier.com.

RYAN, Nigel; *see* Ryan, C. N. J.

RYAN, Peter James, QPM 1991; management consultant; Principal Security Advisor: International Olympic Committee, since 2000; Athens 2004 Olympic Games, 2002–04; *b* 18 May 1944; *s* of late Lawrence Joseph Ryan and of Margaret Jane (*née* Stephenson); *m* 1985, Adrienne Margaret Butterworth; two *d. Educ:* Newman Coll., Preston; Univ. of Lancaster (BA Hons); Preston Poly. (DMS); Open Univ. (MSc). FIPM 1994. Lancs Constabulary, 1963–83; Metropolitan Police, 1983–84; Asst Chief Constable, N Yorks Police, 1984–88; Dep. Chief Constable, Durham Constabulary, 1988–90; Chief Constable, Norfolk, 1990–93; Nat. Dir of Police Trng and Comdt Police Staff Coll., 1993–96; Comr of Police for NSW, 1996–2002. Advr, Bd, Canadian Centre for Emergency Preparedness, 2002–04. Sec., 1991–92, Chm., 1992–93, Personnel & Trng Cttee, ACPO. Mem., BTEC, 1985–88. Vis. Fellow, UEA Sch. of Educn, 1993–; Grad., FBI Nat. Exec. Inst., 1994. Pres., Assoc. of Eur. Police Colls, 1996; Vice Pres., Police Mutual Assurance Soc., 1994–96. Asst Dir Gen., St John Ambulance, 1995. FCMI (FIMgt 1980); FCIPD 1990; MAICD 2002. FRSA 1992. Hon. LLD Macquarie, 2000. OStJ 1995. *Publications:* contrib. Police Jl and similar professional jls. *Recreations:* occasional golf, reading. *Address:* St Mary's Cottage, St Mary's Road, Shoreham by Sea, W Sussex BN43 5ZA. *Clubs:* Royal Air Force; Royal Sydney Yacht Squadron.

RYAN, Sheila Morag Clark, (Mrs G. C. Ryan); *see* Cameron, S. M. C.

RYAN, Prof. Terence John, DM; FRCP; Clinical Professor of Dermatology, Oxford University, 1992–97, now Emeritus Professor; Fellow, Green College, 1979–97, now Emeritus Fellow; *b* 24 July 1932; *s* of Gerald John Ryan and Kathleen May (*née* Knight); *m* 1968, Trudie Anne Merry; one *s* one *d. Educ:* numerous schs including: Michael Hall (Rudolf Steiner); Brickwall Sch., Northiam; Worcester Coll., Oxford (BM, BCh 1957; DM 1977). FRCP 1975. Capt. RAMC, 1955–60: Officer i/c Dept of Dermatol. and ENT Surgery, Colchester Mil. Hosp.; Radcliffe Infirmary, Oxford: Hse Officer, 1958; Registrar and Sen. Registrar in Dermatol., 1962–68; Lectr and Sen. Lectr, Inst. of Dermatol., London Univ., 1967–71; Dept of Dermatol., RPMS, 1968–71; Lectr in Dermatology, Oxford Univ., 1971–92. Cons. Dermatologist, 1969–97, Hon. Cons., 1997–, Oxon HA. Vis. Prof., Brookes Univ., Oxford, 1991–; Adjunct Professor: Jefferson Univ., Philadelphia, 1988–; Univ. of Limerick, 2007–; Hon. Prof., Nanjing, 2003–. Med. Advr, St Francis Leprosy Guild, 1987–; Advr, Morbidity Control, Global Alliance to Eliminate Lymphatic Filariasis, 2003–. Promoter, Sine Lepra and Healthy Skin for All programmes, Internat. League of Dermatologists, 1987–2002; Dir, Fuel Initiatives Resources Strategies Technologies, 1998–. Pres., Section of Dermatol., RSocMed, 1990. Mem., Internat. Ctee of Dermatol., 1987–2002; Pres., Internat. Soc. for Dermatol., 1994–99 (Hon. Pres., 1999); Chm., Internat. Foundn for Dermatol., 1997–2002. Trustee: Oxford Internat. Biomedical Centre, 1999–; Arts Dyslexia Trust, 1999–; British Skin Foundn, 1999. Hon. Mem., various foreign nat. socs of dermatol. Hon. DM Martin Luther Univ., Halle-Wittenberg, 2007. Gold Medal: Eur. Tissue Repair Soc., 1995; Brit. Assoc. Dermatology, 1997; Curatorium Angiologiae Internationalis, 2002; Brazilian Acad. Medicine, 2003. KStJ 1984 (County Surgeon Comr, then Comdr, SJAB, Oxon). *Publications:* (contrib.) Oxford Textbook of Medicine, 3rd edn 1995 to 5th edn 2002; contrib. textbooks of dermatology and numerous in field of blood supply and lymphatics,

dermatology and internat. dermatological policy. *Recreations:* painting water-colours, flowers, piano playing, foreign travel. *Address:* Hill House, Abberbury Road, Iffley, Oxford OX4 4EU. *T:* (01865) 777041.

RYAN, Prof. William Francis, DPhil; FSA; FBA 2000; Librarian, 1976–2002, Emeritus Professor, 2003, and Hon. Fellow, since 2003, Warburg Institute, and Professor of Russian Studies, School of Advanced Study, 2000–02, University of London; *b* 13 April 1937; *s* of William Gerard Ryan and Marjorie Ellen Ryan; *m* 1st, 1963, Marina Guterman (marr. diss. 1970); two *d*; 2nd, 1986, Janet Margaret Hartley; one *s* one *d. Educ:* Bromley GS for Boys; Oriel Coll., Oxford (MA; DPhil 1970). FSA 1972. Editor, Clarendon Press, Oxford, 1963–65; Asst Curator, Mus. of Hist. of Science, Oxford, 1965–67; Lectr in Russian Lang. and Lit., SSEES, London Univ., 1967–76. President: Folklore Soc., 2005–08; Hakluyt Soc., 2008–. *Publications:* (with Peter Norman) The Penguin Russian Dictionary, 1995; The Bathhouse at Midnight: an historical survey of magic and divination in Russia, Stroud and University Park PA, 1999. *Address:* Warburg Institute, Woburn Square, WC1H 0AB; *e-mail:* wfr@sas.ac.uk.

RYCROFT, Matthew John, CBE 2003; HM Diplomatic Service; Director, European Union, Foreign and Commonwealth Office, since 2008; *b* 16 June 1968; *s* of Prof. Michael John Rycroft, *qv*; *m* 1997, Alison Emma Victoria Semple; three *d. Educ:* Merton Coll., Oxford (BA Maths and Philos. 1989). Joined FCO, 1989; Third Sec., Geneva, 1990; Then second, Sec. (Chancery), Paris, 1991–95; First Sec., FCO, 1995–98; First Sec. (Political), Washington, 1998–2002; Private Sec. for Foreign Affairs to the Prime Minister, 2002–04; Ambassador to Bosnia and Herzegovina, 2005–08. *Address:* c/o Foreign and Commonwealth Office, King Charles Street, SW1A 2AH; *e-mail:* matthew.rycroft@fco.gov.uk.

RYCROFT, Prof. Michael John, PhD; Proprietor, Cambridge Atmospheric, Environmental and Space Activities and Research Consultancy, since 1998; Professor, International Space University, France, since 1995 (part-time, since 1998); *b* 15 July 1938; *s* of late John Lambert Rycroft and Molly Elizabeth Rycroft (*née* Riglen); *m* 1967, Mary Cheeseright; three *s. Educ:* Merchant Taylors' School, Northwood; Imperial Coll., London (BSc Hons Physics); Churchill Coll., Cambridge (PhD Met. Physics). CPhys, MInstP; CMath, FIMA; CSci; FRAS. Lectr, Dept of Physics, Univ. of Southampton, 1966–79; Head, Atmospheric Scis Div., NERC British Antarctic Survey, Cambridge, 1979–90; Prof. of Aerospace, 1990–94, Hd, Coll. of Aeronautics, 1990–92, Cranfield Inst. of Technol., subseq. Cranfield Univ. Visiting Professor: Dept. of Physics, Univ. of Houston, 1974–75; Cranfield Univ., 1995–; De Montfort Univ., 1998–2003; Vis. Sen. Fellow, Univ. of Bath, 2005–. Gen. Sec., Eur. Geophysical Soc., 1996–2003. Mem., Internat. Acad. of Astronautics, 1986; MAE 2000. Editor-in-Chief, Jl of Atmospheric and Solar-Terrestrial Physics, 1989–99; Man. Editor, Surveys in Geophysics, 2001–. Hon. DSc De Montfort, 1998. *Publications:* (with D. Shapland) Spacelab: research in Earth orbit, 1984; (ed) Cambridge Encyclopedia of Space, 1990; (with G. Genta) Space, the Final Frontier?, 2003; (with V. Y. Trakhtengerts) Whistler and Alfvén Mode Cyclotron Masers in Space, 2008; 250 pubns on atmospheric and space sci. and related fields. *Recreations:* music, gardening, wining and dining. *Address:* Bassett Mead, 35 Millington Road, Cambridge CB3 9HW. *T:* (01223) 353839, *Fax:* (01223) 303839; *e-mail:* michaelrycroft@btinternet.com.

See also M. J. Rycroft.

RYCROFT, Philip, DPhil; Director-General of Education, Scottish Government (formerly Scottish Executive), since 2007; *b* 22 May 1961; *s* of John and Shirley Rycroft; *m* 1989, Kate Richards; two *s. Educ:* Leys Sch., Cambridge; Wadham Coll., Oxford (MA; DPhil 1988). Scottish Office: Res. Div., Agric. Dept, 1989–90; Private Sec. to Scottish Office Agric. and Fisheries Minister, 1990–91; Principal: European Support Unit, Industry Dept, 1992–94; Fisheries Gp, Fisheries Policy Branch, 1994; Cabinet of Sir Leon Brittan, EC, 1995–97; Scottish Office: Hd, Agricl Policy Co-ordination and Rural Develt Div. and IT Support Div., Agric., Envmt and Fisheries Dept, 1997–98; Hd, Mgt Gp Support Staff Unit, 1998–99; Dep. Hd, Scottish Exec. Policy Unit, 1999–2000; Public Affairs Manager, Scottish & Newcastle plc, 2000–02; Hd, Schs Gp, Scottish Exec. Educn Dept, 2002–06; Hd of Scottish Exec. Enterprise, Transport and Lifelong Learning Dept, 2006–07. *Recreations:* hill-walking, woodwork, triathlon. *Address:* Scottish Government, Victoria Quay, Edinburgh EH6 6QQ; *e-mail:* philip.rycroft@scotland.gsi.gov.uk.

RYCROFT, Sir Richard (John), 8th Bt *cr* 1784, of Calton, Yorkshire; *b* 15 June 1946; *s* of Cdre Henry Richard Rycroft, OBE, DSC, RN, 4th *s* of 5th Bt, and Penelope Gwendoline Rycroft (*née* Evans-Combe); *S* cousin, 1999. *Educ:* Sherborne. Dep. Launching Authority, Burnham-on-Crouch RNLI Lifeboat. *Recreations:* sailing, listening to jazz, Burmese cats. *Heir: cousin* Francis Edward Rycroft [*b* 4 Aug. 1950; *m* 1975, Cherry Willmott; one *s* one *d*]. *Club:* Royal Corinthian Yacht.

RYDER, family name of **Earl of Harrowby** and of **Baron Ryder of Wensum**.

RYDER OF WENSUM, Baron *cr* 1997 (Life Peer), of Wensum in the co. of Norfolk; **Richard Andrew Ryder,** OBE 1981; PC 1990; Chairman, Board of Management, Institute of Cancer Research, since 2005; *b* 4 Feb. 1949; *s* of Richard Stephen Ryder, JP, DL, and Margaret MacKenzie; *m* 1981, Caroline Mary, CVO, MBE, *o d* of Sir David Stephens; one *d* (one *s* decd). *Educ:* Radley; Magdalene Coll., Cambridge (BA Hons History, 1971). Journalist. Chm., Eastern Counties Radio, 1997–2001; Vice-Chm., Bd of Govs, BBC, 2002–04 (Acting Chm., 2004). Dir, Great Bradley Farms Co. and other family businesses, 2002–. Political Secretary: to Leader of the Opposition, 1975–79; to Prime Minister, 1979–81. Contested (C) Gateshead E, Feb. and Oct., 1974. MP (C) Mid Norfolk, 1983–97. Parliamentary Private Secretary: to Financial Sec. to the Treasury, 1984; to Sec. of State for Foreign and Commonwealth Affairs, 1984–86; an Asst Govt Whip, 1986–88; Parly Under-Sec. of State, MAFF, 1988–89; Econ. Sec. to HM Treasury, 1989–90; Paymaster General, 1990; Parly Sec. to HM Treasury and Govt Chief Whip, 1990–95. Chm., Cons. Foreign and Commonwealth Council, 1984–89. *Address:* House of Lords, SW1A 0PW.

RYDER, Edward Alexander, CB 1992; HM Chief Inspector of Nuclear Installations, Health and Safety Executive, 1985–91; Joint Chairman and Head of UK Delegation, Channel Tunnel Safety Authority, 1992–97; *b* 9 Nov. 1931; *s* of Alexander Harry and Gwendoline Gladys Ryder; *m* 1956, Janet (*d* 2006); one *s* one *d. Educ:* Cheltenham Grammar School; Bristol University (BSc). CPhys; FInstP. Flying Officer, RAF, 1953–55; Engineer, GEC Applied Electronics Labs, 1955–57; Control Engineer, Hawker Siddeley Nuclear Power Co., 1957–61; Sen. Engineer, CEGB, 1961–71; Principal Inspector, then Superintending Inspector, HM Nuclear Installations Inspectorate, 1971–80; Head of Hazardous Installations Policy Branch, 1980–85, Head of Nuclear Installations Policy Branch, 1985, HSE. Sec., Adv. Cttee on Major Hazards, 1980–85. Chairman: HSC Working Gp on Ionising Radiations, 1987–91; IAEA Nuclear Safety Standards Adv. Gp, 1988–93; Mem., Intergovtl Commn for Channel Tunnel, 1992–97. Organiser, Shiplake and Dunsden Area, RBL Poppy Appeal, 1996–2003. Mem., Shiplake Parish Council, 1999– (Vice-Chm., 2000–03 and 2007–; Chm., 2003–05). *Recreations:* golf—or is it nature study, concertgoing, bridge. *Address:* Pinewood, Baskerville Lane, Lower Shiplake, Henley on Thames, Oxon RG9 3JY.

RYDER, Hon. Sir Ernest (Nigel), Kt 2004; TD 1996; **Hon. Mr Justice Ryder;** a Judge of the High Court of Justice, Family Division, since 2004; *b* 9 Dec. 1957; *s* of Dr John Buckley Ryder, TD and Constance Ryder; *m* 1990, Janette Lynn Martin; one *d*. *Educ:* Bolton Sch.; Peterhouse, Cambridge (MA 1983). Merchant banker, Grindley Brandt & Co., 1979; called to the Bar, Gray's Inn, 1981; QC 1997; Asst Recorder, 1997–2000; a Recorder, 2000–04; a Dep. High Court Judge, 2001–04; Northern Circuit. Counsel, N Wales Tribunal of Inquiry, 1996–99. Asst Boundary Comr, 2000–04. Commnd Duke of Lancaster's Own Yeomanry, 1981; Sqdn Leader, 1990; Sqdn Leader, Royal Mercian and Lancastrian Yeomanry, 1992. *Recreations:* listening, walking. *Address:* Royal Courts of Justice, Strand, WC2A 2LL. *Club:* Royal Commonwealth Society.

RYDER, Janet; Member (Plaid Cymru) North Wales, National Assembly for Wales, since 1999; *b* Sunderland, 21 June 1955; *m* 1977, Peter Ryder (marr. diss. 2005); two *s* one *d*. *Educ:* Northern Counties Coll. of Educn (Teacher's Cert. (Dist.)); Open Univ. (BA Hist./Arts). Teacher: Little Weighton Co. Primary Sch., E Riding of Yorks, 1980–83; St Bede's Catholic Primary Sch., Hull, 1987–88; Coleford Primary Sch., Hull (i/c Religious and Moral Educn), 1988–89; Bransholme Youth Club, Hull. Member: N Wales Fire Authy, 1995–99; Bd, Denbighshire Voluntary Services Council, 1995–99. Mem., voluntary gps, incl. Strategic Planning Gp for People with a Learning Difficulty. Member (Plaid Cymru): Rhuthun Town Council, 1992–2003 (Mayor, 1998–2000); Denbighshire CC, 1994–99 (mem., various cttees; Chairman: Children and Families Sub-cttee, 1995–98; Denbigh Early Years Partnership, 1996–98; Denbigh Plan Partnership). National Assembly for Wales: Plaid Cymru spokesperson on local govt, planning, housing, envmt and transport, 1999–2001, on local govt and finance, 2001–03, on educn and life-long learning, 2003–. Mem., Nat. Exec., Plaid Cymru, 1993–99, 2006–. *Address:* National Assembly for Wales, Cardiff Bay, Cardiff CF99 1NA. *T:* (029) 2089 8250; (constituency) 65 Stryd y Ffynnon, Rhuthun, Denbighshire LL15 1AG. *T:* (01824) 704625; *e-mail:* janet.ryder@wales.gov.uk.

RYDER, John; QC 2000; a Recorder, since 2000; *m* 1989, Carolyn Espley; one *d*. *Educ:* Monmouth Sch. Called to the Bar, Inner Temple, 1980; Asst Recorder, 1997–2000. *Recreations:* riding, ski-ing, opera. *Address:* 6 King's Bench Walk, Temple, EC4Y 7DR. *Club:* Travellers.

RYDER, Dr Peter, CB 1994; FRMets; consultant in environmental information services, since 1996; General Secretary, Royal Meteorological Society, 2001–06; *b* 10 March 1942; *s* of Percival Henry Sussex Ryder and Bridget (*née* McCormack); *m* 1965, Jacqueline Doris Sylvia Rigby; two *s* one *d*. *Educ:* Yorebridge Grammar Sch., Askrigg; Univ. of Leeds (BSc 1963; PhD 1966). FRMets 2004. Research Asst, Physics Dept, Univ. of Leeds, 1966–67; Meteorological Office, 1967–96: Asst Dir, Cloud Physics Res., 1976–82; Asst Dir, Systems Develt, 1982–84; Dep. Dir, Observational Services, 1984–88; Dep. Dir, Forecasting Services, 1988–89; Dir of Services, 1989–90; Dep. Chief Exec. and Dir of Ops, then Man. Dir (Ops), 1990–96. Royal Meteorological Society: Mem. Council, 1980–83; Mem., Qly Jl Editing Cttee, 1981–84. Chairman: Thames Regl Flood Defence Cttee, EA, 2003–July 2009 (Mem., 1997–2003); EuroGOOS, 2003–08. William Gaskell Meml Medal, RMetS, 1981; L. G. Groves Meml Prize for Meteorology, MoD, 1982. *Publications:* papers in learned jls on experimental atmospheric physics and meteorology. *Recreations:* gardening, walking, fishing, photography. *Address:* 8 Sherring Close, Bracknell, Berks RG42 2LD.

RYDER, Dr Richard Hood Jack Dudley; author, campaigner; *b* 3 July 1940; *s* of late Major D. C. D. Ryder, JP and Vera Mary (*née* Cook); *m* 1974, Audrey Jane Smith (marr. diss. 1999); one *s* one *d*. *Educ:* Sherborne Sch.; Cambridge Univ. (MA; PhD 1993); Edinburgh Univ. (DCP); Columbia Univ., NY (Fellow). AFBPsS; FZS. Sen. Clinical Psychologist, Warneford Hosp., Oxford, 1967–84; Principal Clin. Psychologist, St James Hosp., Portsmouth, 1983–84. Chm., Oxford Div. of Clin. Psych., 1981–83. Member: Oxford Regional Adolescent Service, 1971–84; DHSS Health Adv. Service, 1977–78. Royal Society for Prevention of Cruelty to Animals: Mem. Council, 1972– (Chm., 1977–79 and 2002–03; Vice Chm., 1990–91); Dep. Treas., 2000–01; Chairman: Political Cttee, 1979–80; Animal Experimentation Adv. Cttee, 1983–85; Public Relns and Campaign Cttee, 1990–91; Scientific Cttee, 1992–; Internat. Cttee, 1999–. Dep. Chm., Cttee on Welfare of Animals in Psychology, BPsS, 2001–. Political Consultant, 1991–93, Dir, 1993–97, Political Animal Lobby Ltd. Founder Mem., Gen. Election Co-ordinating Cttee on Animal Protection, 1978; Founder, Eurogroup for Animal Welfare, 1979; Pres., British Union for Abolition of Vivisection, 1980; Prog. Organiser, 1984–91, Dir of Animal Welfare Studies, 1997–2000, IFAW; UK Delegate, Eurogroup, 1980, 2002. Chm., Liberal Animal Welfare Gp, 1981–88; Member: Liberal Party Council, 1983–87; Liberal Party Policy Panels on defence, health, home affairs, Eur. affairs, foreign affairs, environment, 1981–88; contested (L): Buckingham, 1983; Teignbridge, 1987. Pres., Lib. Democrats Animal Protection Gp, 1989–91. Chairman: Teignbridge NSPCC, 1984–87; Teignbridge Home Start, 1987–89. Mellon Prof., Tulane Univ., New Orleans, 1996. Broadcaster and writer on psychological, ethical, political and animal protection subjects. Trustee, NT, 2001–04. Mem. Cttee, British Conifer Soc., 2005–. Co-founder of business, Psychoprofiles, 2005. FRSA 1992. *Publications:* Speciesism, 1970; Victims of Science, 1975, 2nd edn 1984; (ed) Animal Rights—a Symposium, 1979; Animal Revolution: changing attitudes to speciesism, 1989, 2nd edn 2000; Painism, 1990; (ed) Animal Welfare and the Environment, 1992; The Political Animal, 1998; Painism: a modern morality, 2001; The Calcrafts of Rempstone Hall, 2005; Putting Morality Back into Politics, 2006. *Recreations:* trees, opera, philosophy. *Address:* 11 The Imperial, Exeter EX4 4AJ. *T:* (01392) 426727. *Clubs:* National Liberal, Royal Over-Seas League.

RYDILL, Prof. Louis Joseph, OBE 1962; FREng; RCNC; Consultant in Naval Ship Design, since 1986; Professor of Naval Architecture, University College London, 1981–85, now Emeritus Professor; *b* 16 Aug. 1922; *s* of Louis and Queenie Rydill; *m* 1949, Eva (*née* Newman); two *d*. *Educ:* HM Dockyard Sch., Devonport; RNEC Keyham; RNC Greenwich; Royal Corps of Naval Constructors. FRINA (Gold Medallist); FREng (FEng 1982). Asst Constructor, 1946–52; Constructor, 1952–62, incl. Asst Prof. of Naval Architecture, RNC Greenwich, 1953–57; Chief Constructor, 1962–72, incl. Prof. of Naval Architecture, RNC Greenwich and UCL, 1967–72; Asst Dir Submarines, Constructive, 1972–74; Dep. Dir Submarines (Polaris), 1974–76; Dir of Ship Design and Engrg (formerly Warship Design), MoD, 1976–81. Hon. Fellow, UCL, 2008; Vis. Prof., US Naval Acad., Annapolis, Md, 1985–86. Silver Jubilee Medal, 1977. *Publication:* (jtly) Concepts in Submarine Design, 1993. *Recreations:* literature, theatre, jazz and other music. *Address:* The Lodge, Entry Hill Drive, Bath BA2 5NJ. *T:* (01225) 427888.

RYDSTRÖM, Marilyn; Director General, People's Dispensary for Sick Animals, 1999–2008; *b* 24 Oct. 1947; *d* of Kenneth Oberg and Averil Irene Oberg (*née* Harding); *m* 1985, Björn Lennart Rydström. *Educ:* Guildford Co. Tech. Coll.; Bedford Coll., London Univ. (BSc Hons Sociol.). Churchill Fellow, 1984. Probation Officer, Surrey Probation Service, 1971–72; Social Worker, Surrey CC, 1972–74; Sen. Social Worker, Borough of Hillingdon, 1974–77; Hd of Community Projects, Capital Radio Plc, 1977–87; Dir, Fundraising, RNID, 1987–89; Consultant, Chapter One Ketchum Fundraising, 1989–92; Mktg/Commercial Dir, Stowe Sch., 1992–95; Dir, Client Services, Guide Dogs for the Blind, 1995–99. Mem., Crime Prevention Adv. Cttee, NACRO, 1979–83. Member: Grants Cttee, Help a London Child, 1977–84; Mgt Cttee, Piccadilly Advice Centre, 1978–82; Mgt Cttee, Alone in London, 1979–82. The Prince's Trust: Member: NW London Cttee, 1982–90 (Chm., 1987–90); Council, 1986–88; Strategy Gp for London, 1989–90. Founding Trustee and Mem., Mgt Cttee, Artsline, 1983–85; voluntary fundraising: Royal GS for Boys, High Wycombe, 1994–95; Mildmay Mission Hospital, 1998–2003. Dir, Severn Hospice Ltd, 2007–. CCMI 2007. *Publications:* various articles/features of social/health interest in women's press. *Recreations:* reading, walking, diving. *Address:* *e-mail:* brydstrom@aol.com.

RYKWERT, Prof. Joseph, MA (Cantab), DrRCA; Paul Philippe Cret Professor of Architecture, University of Pennsylvania, 1988–98, now Emeritus; *b* 5 April 1926; *s* of Szymon Rykwert and Elizabeth Melup; *m* 1st, 1960 (marr. diss. 1967); 2nd, 1972, Anne-Marie Sandersley; one *s* one *d*. *Educ:* Charterhouse; Bartlett Sch. of Architecture; Architectural Assoc. Lectr, Hochschule für Gestaltung, Ulm, 1958; Librarian and Tutor, Royal Coll. of Art, 1961–67; Prof. of Art, Univ. of Essex, 1967–80; Lectr on Arch., 1980–85, Reader, 1985–88, Univ. of Cambridge. Bollingen Fellow, 1966; Inst. for Arch. and Urban Studies, NY, 1969–71; Sen. Fellow, Council of Humanities, Princeton Univ., 1971; Visiting Professor: Institut d'Urbanisme, Univ. of Paris, 1974–76; Princeton Univ., 1977; Andrew Mellon Vis. Prof., Cooper Union, NY, 1977; Slade Prof. of Fine Art, Cambridge Univ., 1979–80; Vis. Fellow, Darwin Coll., Cambridge, 1979–80; Mem., Trinity Hall, Cambridge, 1980–; Sen. Fellow, Center for the Advanced Studies in the Visual Arts. Nat. Gall. of Art, Washington; Vis. Prof., Univ. of Louvain, 1981–84; George Lurcy Vis. Prof., Columbia, 1986; Sen. Schol., Getty Res. Inst. in Hist. of Art and Humanities, 1992–93; British Acad. Vis. Prof., Univ. of Bath, 1998–99. Pres., Comité Internat. des Critiques d'Architecture, 1996–. Mem. Commn, Venice Biennale, 1974–78. Consultant, Min. of Urban Develt and Ecology, Republic of Mexico, 1986–88. Co-ed., RES (Anthropology and Aesthetics), 1981–. Member: Accademia Clementina, 1992; Accademia di S Luca, 1993; Polish Acad. of Arts and Scis, 1998. Hon. DSc: Edinburgh, 1995; Bath, 2000; Hon. Dr: Córdoba, Argentina, 1998; Rome, 2005; Toronto, 2005; Trieste 2008. Alfred Jurzykowski Foundn Award, 1990. Chevalier des Arts et des Lettres, 1984. *Publications:* The Golden House, 1947; (ed) The Ten Books of Architecture, by L. B. Alberti (annotated edn of Leoni trans. of 1756), 1955, new translation from Latin, as On the Art of Building in Ten Books, 1988; The Idea of a Town, 1963, 3rd edn 1988; Church Building, 1966; On Adam's House in Paradise, 1972, 2nd edn 1982; (ed) Parole nel Vuoto, by A. Loos, 1972; The First Moderns, 1980; The Necessity of Artifice, 1981; (with Anne Rykwert) The Brothers Adam, 1985; The Dancing Column, 1996; The Seduction of Place, 2000, 2nd edn 2004; The Judicious Eye, 2008; contrib. Arch. Rev., Burlington Mag., Lotus. *Recreations:* rare. *Address:* 26A Wedderburn Road, NW3 5QG. *Club:* Savile.

RYLANCE, John Randolph Trevor; His Honour Judge Rylance; a Circuit Judge, since 2003; *b* 26 Feb. 1944; *s* of late Dr Ralph Curzon Rylance and Margaret Joan Clare Rylance (*née* Chambers); *m* 1974, Philippa Anne Bailey; two *d*. *Educ:* Shrewsbury Sch. Called to the Bar, Lincoln's Inn, 1968; Parly Res. Asst to Sir Edward Gardner, QC, MP, 1971–73; Asst Recorder, 1989–93; a Recorder, 1993–2003. Gov., Fulham Cross Sch., 1977–88. Chm., Fulham Palace Mus. Trust, 1996–. *Address:* Guildford County Court, The Law Courts, Mary Road, Guildford, Surrey GU1 4PS. *T:* (01483) 405300. *Club:* Hurlingham.

RYLAND, His Honour Timothy Richard Godfrey Fetherstonhaugh; a Circuit Judge, 1988–2008; a Judge at Central London Civil Trial Centre (formerly Central London County Court), 1994–2008; *b* 13 June 1938; *s* of late Richard Desmond Fetherstonhaugh Ryland and Frances Katharine Vernon Ryland; *m* 1991, Jean Margaret Muirhead. *Educ:* St Andrew's Coll.; TCD (BA (Moderatorship), LLB). Called to Bar, Gray's Inn, 1961. Dep. Circuit Judge, 1978; a Recorder, 1983–88. *Recreations:* opera, wine. *Clubs:* Lansdowne; Kildare Street and University (Dublin).

RYLE, Evelyn Margaret; consultant and author; *b* 26 March 1947; *d* of Paul McConnell Cassidy and Emily Margaret Cassidy (*née* Wright); *m* 1975, Anthony E. Ryle, OBE; one *s* one *d*. *Educ:* King's Park Sch., Glasgow; Univ. of Glasgow (MA Hons; Dip. Management Studies). Dexion-Comino Internat., 1969; commnd WRAF; Flight Lieut, accountant officer, 1973; financial systems analyst: Dexion Gp, 1975; Southern Electricity, 1976; Departments of Trade and Industry, 1977–96; British Steel Corp. Finance; Commercial Relations and Exports; Consumer Affairs; Vehicles Div.; Dep. Dir, IT Services, 1987; Head, Educn and Trng Policy, 1990; seconded to Design Council as Dir-Gen., 1993; Dir, Business Competitiveness, Govt Office for London, 1995–96; Mem., CSSB Panel of Chairs, 1996–99. Mem., Finance Cttee, 1996–2002 (Chair, 2001–02), Mem., Exec., 1999–2002, Charter 88. Mem. Cttee, Romantic Novelists' Assoc., 2003– (Hon. Treasurer, 2004–). FRSA. *Recreations:* family, music, gardening, needlework, walking. *Address:* *e-mail:* emryle@waitrose.com. *Club:* Royal Air Force.

RYLE, Michael Thomas; Clerk of Committees, House of Commons, 1987–89, retired; *b* 30 July 1927; *s* of Peter Johnston Ryle and Rebecca Katie (*née* Boxall); *m* 1952, Bridget Moyes; one *s* two *d*. *Educ:* Newcastle upon Tyne Royal Grammar Sch.; Merton Coll., Oxford (1st Cl. Hons PPE, 1951; MA). Served RA, 1946–48 and TA, 1950–57. Entered Clerk's Dept, House of Commons, 1951; served in various offices; Clerk of Overseas Office, 1979–83; Principal Clerk, Table Office, 1983–84; Clerk of the Journals, 1985–87; attached Nova Scotia Legislature, 1976. Consultant/advr, Belarus, Slovakian, Ukrainian and other parlts in E Europe, 1995–97. Chm., Lib Dem Wkg Gp on Reform of H of C, 1996. Member: Study of Parlt Gp, 1964– (Founding Mem.; Chm., 1975–78; Pres., 1986–94); Council, Hansard Soc., 1974–94 (Mem. and Sec., Commn on the Legislative Process, 1991–93); Council, RIPA, 1982–88; Lambeth HMC, 1960–64. Governor, St Thomas' Hosp., 1964–74. Hon. Res. Fellow, Univ. of Exeter, 1990–. Mem., Exec. Cttee, 1991–2005, Vice-Chm., 2000–05, Exmoor Soc. *Publications:* (ed with S. Walkland) The Commons in the Seventies, 1977, 2nd edn, as The Commons Today, 1981; (contrib.) The House of Commons in the Twentieth Century, 1979; (ed with P. G. Richards) The Commons Under Scrutiny, 1988; (with J. A. G. Griffith) Parliament, 1989, (contrib.) 2nd edn (ed R. Blackburn and A. Kennon), 2003; (contrib.) The Future of Parliament, 2006; contrib. to books on parly practice and procedure; articles in Pol Qly, Parly Affairs, The Table, etc. *Recreations:* watching cricket, golf, birds, playing bridge. *Address:* Jasmine Cottage, Winsford, Minehead, Somerset TA24 7JE. *T:* and *Fax:* (01643) 851317; *e-mail:* michaelryle@tiscali.co.uk.

RYMAN, John; *b* 7 Nov. 1930. *Educ:* Leighton Park; Pembroke College, Oxford. Inns of Court Regt (TA), 1948–51. Called to the Bar, Middle Temple, 1957. Harmsworth Law Scholar. MP (Lab): Blyth, Oct. 1974–1983; Blyth Valley, 1983–87. Mem. Council, Assoc. of the Clergy, 1976. *Recreation:* Horses.

RYRIE, Sir William (Sinclair), KCB 1982 (CB 1979); Chairman, Baring Emerging Europe Trust plc, 1994–2002; *b* 10 Nov. 1928; *s* of Rev. Dr Frank Ryrie and Mabel Moncrieff Ryrie (*née* Watt); *m* 1st, 1953, Dorrit Klein (marr. diss. 1969); two *s* one *d*; 2nd, 1969, Christine Gray Thomson; one *s*. *Educ:* Mount Hermon Sch., Darjeeling; Heriot's Sch., Edinburgh; Edinburgh Univ. (MA 1st cl. hons History, 1951). Nat. Service, 1951–53: Lieut, Intell. Corps, Malaya, 1952–53 (despatches). Colonial Office, 1953; seconded to Uganda, 1956–58; Principal 1958; transf. to Treasury, 1963; Asst Sec., internat. monetary affairs, 1966–69; Principal Private Sec. to Chancellor of Exchequer, 1969–71; Under-Sec., Public Sector Gp, HM Treasury, 1971–75; Econ. Minister, Washington, and UK Exec. Dir, IMF and IBRD, 1975–79; 2nd Perm. Sec. (Domestic Economy Sector), HM Treasury, 1980–82; Permanent Sec., ODA, FCO, 1982–84; Exec. Vice-Pres. and Chief Exec., IFC at World Bank, 1984–93; Dir, Commonwealth Develt Corp., 1994–98 (Dep. Chm., 1995–98). Vice Chm., ING Barings Hldg Co., 1995–98. Director: Barings plc, 1994–95; First NIS Regl Fund, 1994–99; W. S. Atkins plc, 1994–2001; Ashanti Goldfields Co. Ltd, 1995–2000. Dir, CARE Britain, 1994–2001. Pres., Edinburgh Univ. Develt Trust, 1994–99. Mem., Gp of 30, 1992–98. FRSA 1993. *Publication:* First World, Third World, 1995. *Recreations:* photography, walking. *Address:* Hawkwood, Hawkwood Lane, Chislehurst, Kent BR7 5PW. *Club:* Reform.

S

SAAKASHVILI, Mikheil; President of Georgia, since 2004; *b* 21 Dec. 1967; *s* of Nokoloz Saakashvili and Giuli Alasania; *m* Sandra Elizabeth Roelofs; one *s*. *Educ:* Nat. Law Center, George Washington Univ.; Columbia Univ. (LLM); Internat. Inst. of Human Rights, France (Dip.); Dept of Internat. Law, Kiev State Univ. (law degree). Hd, Dept of Ethnic Relns, Georgian Cttee for Human Rights and Ethnic Relns, 1992–94; Foreign Lawyer, Patterson, Belknap, Webb & Tyler, NY, 1994–95; MP, Georgia, 1995–98; Chm., Cttee for Constitnl, Legal Affairs and Rule of Law, Parlt of Georgia, 1995–98; Co-Chm., Council of Justice, Georgia, 1998; Vice-Pres., Parly Assembly of Council of Europe, 2000; Minister of Justice, 2000–01; Chm., Tbilisi City Council, 2002–03. Chm., Majority Faction of Union of Citizens, Parlt of Georgia, 1998. *Address:* Office of the President, 7 Ingorokva Street, Tbilisi 0134, Georgia. *T:* (32) 990070, *Fax:* (32) 998887; *e-mail:* secretariat@admin.gov.ge.

SAATCHI, family name of **Baron Saatchi**.

SAATCHI, Baron *cr* 1996 (Life Peer), of Staplefield in the county of West Sussex; **Maurice Saatchi;** Partner, M & C Saatchi plc, since 1995; *b* 21 June 1946; *s* of late Daisy and Nathan Saatchi; *m* 1984, Josephine Hart; one *s*, and one step *s*. *Educ:* London School of Economics and Political Science (1st class BSc Econ). Co-Founder of Saatchi & Saatchi Co., 1970, Chm., 1985–94. Chm., Finsbury Food Gp (formerly Megalomedia) PLC, 1995–2008. Opposition spokesman, H of L, on Treasury affairs, 1999–2003, on Cabinet Office affairs, 2001–03. Co-Chm., Conservative Party, 2003–05. A Trustee, Victoria and Albert Mus., 1988–96; Mem. Council, RCA, 1997–2000; Director: Centre for Policy Studies, 1999–; Mus. of Garden History, 2001–. Governor, LSE, 1996–. *Publications:* The Science of Politics, 2001; *pamphlets:* The War of Independence, 1999; Happiness Can't Buy Money, 1999; The Bad Samaritan, 2000; Poor People! Stop Paying Tax!, 2001; If This is Conservatism, I am a Conservative, 2005; In Praise of Ideology, 2006; Sleeping Beauty, 2007. *Address:* (office) 36 Golden Square, W1F 9EE. *T:* (020) 7543 4510.
See also C. Saatchi.

SAATCHI, Charles; Founder, Saatchi & Saatchi Co., 1970–93; Partner, M & C Saatchi plc, since 1995; *b* 9 June 1943; *m* 2003, Nigella Lucy Lawson, *qv*. *Educ:* Christ's Coll., Finchley. *Address:* (office) 36 Golden Square, W1F 9EE. *T:* (020) 7543 4500.

SABAPATHY, Paul Chandrasekharan, CBE 2004 (OBE 1995); Lord Lieutenant of West Midlands, since 2007; *b* Madras, 26 Sept. 1942; *s* of John and Catherine Sabapathy; *m* 1969, Win White; one *s* one *d*. *Educ:* Lawrence Sch., Lovedale, India; Madras Christian Coll. (BSc Phys 1963); Aston Univ., Birmingham (MSc Industrial Admin 1968). ACMA 1994. IMI plc: Accountant, Eley Ltd, 1968–72; Cost Accountant, Enots Ltd, 1972–74; Finance Dir, IMI Refiners Ltd, 1974–88; IMI Gp Corporate Services Manager, 1988–92; Asst Man. Dir, IMI Titanium Ltd, 1992–96. Member Board: Black Country Develt Corp., 1987–89; Birmingham Heartland Develt Corp., 1992–98; Pres., Walsall Chamber of Commerce, 1988; Chm., W Midlands Industrial Develt Adv. Bd, 1997–2002. Chief Exec., N Birmingham Community NHS Trust, 1996–2000; Member Board: Nat. Blood Authy, 2000–05; N Birmingham PCT, 2001–03; Chairman: E Birmingham PCT, 2004–06; Birmingham E and N PCT, 2006–; Vice Chm., NHS Confederation PCT Network, 2007–. Trustee: New Walsall Art Gall., 1997–2003; Refugee Council, 2002–03; Bournville Village Trust, 2006–. Chm., Birmingham City Univ., 2002–; Dep. Chm., Cttee of Univ. Chairmen, 2004–05. FRSA; FRSocMed 2006. *Recreations:* travelling, gardening. *Address:* West Midlands Lieutenancy, The Coach House, Wood Lane, Barston, West Midlands B92 0JL. *T:* (01675) 442921, *Fax:* (01675) 442934; *e-mail:* wmlty@btinternet.com.

SABATINI, Lawrence John; retired; Assistant Under Secretary of State, Ministry of Defence, 1972–79; *b* 5 Dec. 1919; *s* of Frederick Laurence Sabatini and Elsie May Sabatini (*née* Friggens); *m* 1947, Patricia Dyson; one *s* one *d*. *Educ:* Watford Grammar School. Joined HM Office of Works, 1938. Army service, 1940–46: commnd in RTR, 1943: service in NW Europe with 5 RTR. Asst Principal, Min. of Works, 1947; Asst Private Sec. to Minister of Works, 1948–49; Principal, 1949; Principal Private Sec. to Ministers of Defence, 1958–60; Asst Sec., MoD, 1960; Defence Counsellor, UK Delegn to NATO, on secondment to Diplomatic Service, 1963–67. *Recreations:* gardening, photography, music. *Address:* 44a Batchworth Lane, Northwood, Middx HA6 3DT. *T:* (01923) 823249. *Club:* MCC.

SABBEN-CLARE, James Paley; Headmaster, Winchester College, 1985–2000; *b* 9 Sept. 1941; *s* of late Ernest Sabben-Clare and Rosamond Dorothy Mary Scott; *m* 1969, Geraldine Mary Borton, LLB; one *s* one *d*. *Educ:* Winchester College (Scholar); New College, Oxford (Scholar; 1st Class Classical Hon. Mods and Greats, 1964; MA). Asst Master, Marlborough College, 1964–68; Vis. Fellow, All Souls College, Oxford, 1967–68; Winchester College, 1968–2000: Head of Classics Dept, 1969–79; Second Master, 1979–85. Chm., HMC, 1999. Governor: Oundle Sch., 2001–; British Sch., Paris, 2001–; Gordonstoun Sch., 2002–06. Member, Advisory Board: Global Educn Mgt Systems (GEMS), 2003–07; VT Educn and Skills, 2004–06. Mem., Steering Gp, Prince of Wales Educn Summer Sch., 2002–. *Publications:* Caesar and Roman Politics, 1971, 2nd edn 1981; Fables from Aesop, 1976; The Culture of Athens, 1978, 2nd edn 1980; Winchester College, 1981, 2nd edn 1988; (contrib.) Winchester: history and literature, 1992; contribs to educnl and classical jls. *Recreations:* Italian opera, mountains, furniture making, living in Dorset. *Address:* Sandy Hill Barn, Corfe Castle, Dorset BH20 5JF. *T:* (01929) 481080.

SABIN, Paul Robert; DL; Chief Executive, Leeds Castle Foundation and Leeds Castle (Enterprises) Ltd, 1998–2003; Chairman, Folkestone and Dover Water Company, since 2007 (non-executive Director, 1988–98); *b* 29 March 1943; *s* of Robert Reginald and Dorothy Maude Sabin; *m* 1965, Vivien Furnival; one *s* two *d*. *Educ:* Oldbury Grammar Sch. DMS Aston Univ.; CPFA (IPFA 1966). West Bromwich CBC, 1959–69; Redditch Develt Corp., 1969–81, Chief Finance Officer, 1975–81; City of Birmingham, 1981–86: City Treas., 1982–86; Dep. Chief Exec., 1984–86; Chief Exec., Kent CC, 1986–97. Hon. Citizen, City of Baltimore, Md, USA, 1985. FCMI (MBIM 1967); FTS 2000. DL Kent, 2001. *Recreations:* fine books, music.

SABINE, Peter Aubrey, DSc; FRSE; FIMMM; CEng, CGeol, CSci, FGS; Deputy Director (Chief Scientific Officer, Chief Geologist), British Geological Survey (formerly Institute of Geological Sciences), 1977–84; *b* 29 Dec. 1924; *s* of late Bernard Robert and Edith Lucy Sabine; *m* 1946, Peggy Willis Lambert, MSc, FBCS, CITP, FRSA, FSS; one *s*. *Educ:* Brockley County Sch.; Chelsea Polytechnic; Royal Coll. of Science, Imperial Coll., London (BSc, ARCS (1st Cl. Geol.; Watts medal) 1945); PhD 1951, DSc 1970, London. Apptd Geological Survey of Gt Britain as Geologist, 1945; Geological Museum, 1946–50; in charge Petrographical Dept, Geol Survey and Museum, 1950, Chief Petrographer, 1959; Asst Dir, S England and Wales, 1970; Chief Geochemist, 1977; Dep. Dir, 1977–84. Sec., Geol Soc. of London, 1959–66, Vice-Pres., 1966–67, 1982–84 (Lyell Fund, 1955; Sen. Fellow, 1994); International Union of Geological Sciences: Mem. Commn on Systematics of Igneous Rocks, 1969–2002; Mem. Commn on Systematics in Petrology, 1980–96 (Chm., 1984–92; Vice-Chm., 1992–96); Chief UK Deleg., 1980–84; Mem. Council, 1980–92; Member Council: Geologists' Assoc., 1966–70; Mineralogical Soc., 1950–53; Instn of Mining and Metallurgy, 1976–80; Mineral Industry Res. Orgn, 1983–86; Member: DTI Chem. and Mineral Research Requirements Bd, 1973–82; Minerals, Metals Extraction and Reclamation Cttee, 1981–84; EEC Cttees on minerals and geochemistry; Cttee of Dirs of W European Geolog. Surveys, 1978–84; Chm., Sub-Cttee on geochem. and cosmochem. of British Nat. Cttee for Geology, 1977–86. Royal Institution: Visitor, 1979–82; Mem., Audit Cttee, 1987–90 (Chm., 1989–90). Fellow, Mineralogical Soc., 1999; FMSA 1959 (Sen. Fellow, 2003); FBCartS 1996. FRSA. *Publications:* Chemical Analysis of Igneous Rocks (with E. M. Guppy), 1956; (with D. S. Sutherland) Petrography of British Igneous Rocks, 1982; (jtly) Classification of Igneous Rocks, 1989, 2nd edn 2002 (trans. Chinese and Russian); numerous scientific contribs in Mem. Geol. Surv., Qly Jl Geol. Soc., Mineral. Mag., Phil. Trans Roy. Soc., etc. *Recreations:* gardening, genealogy. *Address:* Malmsmead, 12 Orchehill Avenue, Gerrards Cross, Bucks SL9 8PX. *T:* (01753) 891529. *Clubs:* Athenæum; Geological Society (Sen. Hon. Mem.).

SACHRAJDA, Prof. Christopher Tadeusz Czeslaw, PhD; FRS 1996; Professor of Physics, University of Southampton, since 1990; *b* 15 Nov. 1949; *s* of Czeslaw Sachrajda and Hanna Teresa Sachrajda (*née* Grabowska); *m* 1974, Irena Czyzewska; two *s* one *d*. *Educ:* Finchley GS; Univ. of Sussex (BSc); Imperial Coll. of Sci. and Technol. (PhD 1974). CPhys, FInstP 1989. Harkness Fellow, Stanford Linear Accelerator Center, Stanford Univ., 1974–76; Fellow and Staff Mem., CERN, 1976–79 (Scientific Associate, 1986–87, 1995–96 and 2002); Department of Physics, University of Southampton: Lectr, 1979–86; Sen. Lectr, 1986–88; Reader, 1988–89; Hd of Dept of Physics and Astronomy, 1997–99. Sen. Fellow, SERC and PPARC, 1991–96. Mem. Council, PPARC, 1998–2004. *Publications:* numerous research and review articles on theory of elementary particles. *Recreations:* family, tennis, philately (early Polish), walking. *Address:* Department of Physics and Astronomy, University of Southampton, Southampton SO17 1BJ. *T:* (023) 8059 2105; *e-mail:* cts@phys.soton.ac.uk; (home) 20 Radway Road, Southampton SO15 7PW. *Club:* Portswood Lawn Tennis (Southampton).

SACHS, Andrew; actor and writer; *b* 7 April 1930; *s* of Hans and Katharina Sachs; *m* 1962, Melody Good; two *s* one *d*. *Educ:* Zinnowald Sch., Berlin; William Ellis Sch., London. Nat. service, RAC, 1949–51. Started acting career in rep., 1948–49, 1951–56; *theatre* includes: as actor: Whitehall farces, 1958–61; A Voyage Round My Father, Haymarket, 1971; Habeas Corpus, Lyric, 1973; Jumpers, Aldwych, 1985; Kafka's Dick, Royal Court, 1986; Wild Oats, RNT, 1995; Enoch Arden, Steinway Hall, London, NY, 1998 and arts fests, 1998–; Life After Fawlty (tour), 2001; pantomimes, UK and Canada; writer, Made in Heaven, Chichester Fest., 1975; *television* includes: as actor: The Tempest, 1979; History of Mr Polly (serial), 1979; series: Fawlty Towers, 1975, 1979; Every Silver Lining, 1993; Jack of Hearts, 1999; Attachments, 2000, 2001; Single Voices, 2002; commentaries for TV documentaries; as actor and co-writer of series: The Galactic Garden, 1984; When in Spain, 1987; Berliners, 1988; *radio* includes: as actor, Heart of a Dog, 1988 (Sony Best Actor Award, 1989); as writer: numerous plays and series, incl. The Revenge, 1978 (Ondas Prize, Radio Barcelona, 1979); audio-cassettes (Talkies Award, for best actor, 1999); *films:* Nicholas Nickleby, 1946; Hitler - the Last Ten Days, 1972; Taxandria, 1989; Mystery of Edwin Drood, 1992; Nowhere in Africa, 2003; Speer and Hitler: The Devil's Architect, 2005. *Address:* c/o Richard Stone Partnership, 2 Henrietta Street, WC2E 8PS. *T:* (020) 7497 0849.

SACHS, Prof. Leo, PhD; FRS 1997; Otto Meyerhof Professor of Molecular Biology, Weizmann Institute of Science, Rehovot, Israel, since 1968; *b* 14 Oct. 1924; *s* of Elias and Louise Sachs; *m* 1970, Pnina Salkind; one *s* three *d*. *Educ:* City of London Sch.; Univ. of Wales, Bangor (BSc 1948; Hon. Fellow, 1999); Trinity Coll., Cambridge (PhD 1951). Research Scientist in Genetics, John Innes Inst., 1951–52; Weizmann Institute of Science, Rehovot, Israel: Res. Scientist, 1952–; estabd Dept of Genetics and Virology, 1960; Head, Dept of Genetics, 1962–89; Dean, Faculty of Biol., 1974–79. Fogarty Internat. Scholar, US NIH, 1972; Harvey Lecture, Rockefeller Univ., 1972; Ham-Wasserman Lecture, Amer. Soc. of Hematology, 2000. Member: EMBO, 1965; Israel Acad. of Scis and Humanities, 1975. Foreign Associate, NAS, 1995; Foreign MAE, 1998; Hon. Life Mem., Internat. Cytokine Soc., 2001. Hon. Dr Bordeaux, 1985; Hon. DrMed Lund, 1997. Israel Prize for Natural Scis, 1972; Rothschild Prize in Biol Scis, 1977; Wolf Prize in Medicine, 1980; Bristol-Myers Award for Distinguished Achievement in Cancer Res., 1983;

Wellcome Foundn Prize, Royal Soc., 1986; Alfred P. Sloan Prize, General Motors Cancer Res. Foundn, 1989; Warren Alpert Foundn Prize, Harvard Med. Sch., 1997; EMET Prize for Life Scis, AMN Foundn, Israel, 2002. *Publications:* published papers on stem cells, blood cells, develt and cancer res. in various scientific jls. *Recreations:* music, museums. *Address:* Department of Molecular Genetics, Weizmann Institute of Science, Rehovot 76100, Israel. *T:* (8) 9344068, *Fax:* (8) 9344108.

SACKLER, Dame Jillian (Lesley), DBE 2005; President, AMS Foundation for the Arts, Sciences and Humanities, since 1980; *b* 17 Nov. 1948; *d* of Kenneth Herbert Tully and Doris Queenie Gillman Smith; *m* 1980, Arthur Mitchell Sackler (*d* 1987). *Educ:* Bromley Girls' High Sch.; New York Univ. Bd Mem., US Cttee for UNICEF, 1988–97. Chm., Cttee, Edinburgh Internat. Fest., 1985–90; Member: Vis. Cttee for Art Mus of Harvard Univ., 1983–; Bd, Metropolitan Opera, NY, 1986–2001; President's Circle, NAS, 1989–; Nat. Bd, Smithsonian Instn, 1989–; Bd, New York City Ballet, 1992–2001; Trustee: RA, 1988–; Council, Nat. Gall. of Art, Washington, 1986–94; American Film Inst., 1986–; Tufts Univ., 1986–98; Foundn for NIH, 2000–. Patron and Hon. Dir, Arthur M. Sackler Mus. of Art and Archaeol., Peking Univ., 1994–. Dame with Crown, Order of Malta, 1994. *Address:* 666 Park Avenue, New York, NY 10021, USA. *T:* (212) 5178880, *Fax:* (212) 6282879. *Clubs:* Queen's; Pilgrims, Cosmopolitan, Town Tennis (New York).

SACKLER, Dr Mortimer David, Hon. KBE 1999; philanthropist; Co-Chairman, Purdue Pharma Inc., Stamford, Connecticut, 1952–2007; *b* NYC, 7 Dec. 1916; *s* of Isaac Sackler and Sophie Greenberg; *m* 1980, Theresa Rowling; one *s* two *d*; one *s* three *d* (and one *s* decd) from a previous marriage. *Educ:* Anderson Coll. of Medicine, Glasgow Univ.; Middlesex Univ. Sch. of Medicine, USA (MD 1944). FAPA 1952. Co-Founder and Associate Dir, Creedmoor Inst. for Psychobiologic Studies, NY, 1950–53. Mem., Chancellor's Court of Benefactors, Oxford Univ., 1993–; Benefactor, Univ. of Edinburgh, 2005. Fellow, Ashmolean Mus., Univ. of Oxford, 2006. Hon. Senator, Univ. of Salzburg, 1981; Hon. Fellow: KCL, 2001; UCL, 2003. Hon. PhD Tel Aviv, 1980; Hon. DSc Glasgow, 2001. Philanthropies include: universities and educational institutes: (jtly) Sackler Sch. for Biomed. Scis, Tufts Univ., Boston, 1980; (jtly) Sackler Inst. of Grad. Biomed. Scis, NY Univ. Sch. of Medicine, 1981; Sackler Inst. of Pulmonary Pharmacol., King's Coll. Sch. of Medicine and Dentistry, 1993; Sackler Liby of Humanities, Oxford Univ., 1996; Sackler Musculo-Skeletal Res. Centre, UCL, 2000; Sackler Labs, Reading Univ., 2000; Sackler Inst. of Psychobiological Res., Edinburgh and Glasgow Univs, 2003; galleries and museums: (jtly) Sackler Gall., Metropolitan Mus. of Art, NYC, 1985; Sackler Res. Fellowship at Ashmolean Mus., Worcester Coll., Oxford, 1993; Sackler Centre for Arts Education: Serpentine Gall., 1995; Dulwich Picture Gall., 1998; Guggenheim Mus., NY, 1995; Sackler Octagon, Tate Gall., 1990; Sackler Room, National Gall., London, 1992; Sackler Wing of Oriental Antiquities, Louvre Mus., 1995; Jewish Mus., Berlin, 2003; Sackler Seminar Rooms, Sadlers Wells Th., 1998; Sackler Sculpture Hall, National Gall. of Scotland, Edinburgh, 2001; (jtly) Educn Centre, V&A Mus., 2004; Sackler Crossing, Royal Botanic Gdns, 2006; Darwin Centre, Natural Hist. Mus., 2006; (jtly) Mus. of London, 2006. Hon. Mention for Scientific Res., Med. Soc. of State of NY, 1952. Officier, Légion d'Honneur, 1997 (Chevalier 1989). *Publications:* scientific papers. *Recreation:* tennis. *Clubs:* Eagle Ski (Gstaad); Gstaad Yacht.

SACKS, The Chief Rabbi Sir Jonathan (Henry), Kt 2005; PhD; Chief Rabbi of the United Hebrew Congregations of the Commonwealth, since 1991; *b* 8 March 1948; *s* of late Louis David Sacks and Louisa (*née* Frumkin); *m* 1970, Elaine (*née* Taylor); one *s* two *d*. *Educ:* Christ's Coll., Finchley; Gonville and Caius Coll., Cambridge (MA 1972; Hon. Fellow, 1993); New Coll., Oxford; PhD London, 1981. Rabbinic Ordination: Jews' Coll., London, 1976; Yeshivat Etz Hayyim, London, 1976. Lectr in Moral Philosophy, Middlesex Polytechnic, 1971–73; Jews' College, London: Lectr in Jewish Philosophy, 1973–76; Lectr on the Talmud and in Phil., 1976–82; apptd (first) Sir Immanuel (now Lord) Jakobovits Prof. of Modern Jewish Thought, 1982–90; Dir, Rabbinic Faculty, 1983–90; Principal, 1984–90; Rabbi: Golders Green Synagogue, 1978–82; Marble Arch Synagogue, 1983–90. Member (Univ. of London): Bd of Phil., 1985–90; Bd of Studies in Oriental Languages and Literature, 1985–90; Bd of Studies in Theology and Religious Studies, 1986–90. Member: Theol. and Religious Studies Bd, CNAA, 1984–87; Central Religious Adv. Cttee, BBC and IBA, 1987–90. Visiting Professor: Univ. of Essex, 1989–90; Hebrew Univ. in Jerusalem, 1999–; KCL, 1999–. BBC Reith Lectr, 1990. Associate Pres., Conf. of European Rabbis, 2000–. Editor, L'Eylah: A Journal of Judaism Today, 1984–90. FKC 1993. DD Lambeth, 2001; Hon. DD Cantab, 1993; DUniv Middlesex, 1993; Hon. PhD: Haifa, 1996; Glasgow, 2001; Hon. LLD Liverpool, 1997; Hon. Dr: Yeshiva, NY, 1997; St Andrews, 1997; Bar-Ilan, 2004. Jerusalem Prize, 1995; Grawemayer Award, 2003. *Publications:* Torah Studies, 1986; (ed) Tradition and Transition: essays presented to Sir Immanuel Jakobovits, 1986; Traditional Alternatives, 1989; Tradition in an Untraditional Age, 1990; The Persistence of Faith, 1991; Argument for the Sake of Heaven, 1991; (ed) Orthodoxy Confronts Modernity, 1991; Crisis and Covenant, 1992; One People? Tradition, Modernity and Jewish Unity, 1993; Will we have Jewish grandchildren?, 1994; Faith in the Future, 1995; Community of Faith, 1996; The Politics of Hope, 1997; Morals and Markets, 1999; Celebrating Life, 2000; Radical Then, Radical Now, 2001; The Dignity of Difference, 2002, 2nd edn 2003; The Passover Haggadah, 2003; From Optimism to Hope, 2004; To Heal a Fractured World, 2005; The Authorised Daily Prayer Book, 4th edn (new trans. and commentary), 2007; The Home We Build Together: recreating society, 2007; articles, booklets and book reviews. *Address:* (office) 735 High Road, N12 0US. *T:* (020) 8343 6301, *Fax:* (020) 8343 6310; *e-mail:* info@chiefrabbi.org.

SACKS, Oliver Wolf, CBE 2008; neurologist and writer; Professor of Clinical Neurology, Columbia University, since 2007; *b* London, 9 July 1933; *s* of Samuel Sacks and Muriel Elsie Landau Sacks. *Educ:* St Paul's Sch.; Queen's Coll., Oxford (BA 1954; BM BCh 1958; Hon. Fellow, 1999); Middlesex Hosp. Med. Sch. (MA 1956). Jun. med. posts, Middlesex Hosp., 1959–60, Mount Zion Hosp., San Francisco, 1961–62; Resident in Neurology and Neuropathology, UCLA, 1962–65; Fellow, Neurology and Neurochemistry, 1965–66, Instructor in Neurology, 1966–75, Albert Einstein Coll. of Medicine, NY; Consulting Neurologist: Headache Unit, Montefiore Hosp., NY, 1966–68; Bronx Psychiatric Center, NY, 1966–91; Beth Abraham Hosp., NY, 1966–; Little Sisters of the Poor Hosp., NY, 1971–; Asst Prof., 1975–78, Associate Prof., 1978–85, in Neurology, Clinical Prof. of Neurology, 1985–2007, Albert Einstein Coll. of Medicine; Adjunct Prof. of Neurology, NY Univ. Med. Center, 1992–2007. Member: Amer. Acad. of Neurology, 1962– (Presidential Citation, 1991); NY Inst. for the Humanities, 1984–; Soc. for Neurosci., 1992–. Guggenheim Fellow, 1989; Fellow: Amer. Acad. of Arts and Letters, 1996; NY Acad. of Scis, 1999. Hon. Fellow, Cowell Coll., Univ. of Calif, 1987; Hon. Mem. Amer. Neurological Assoc., 1992. Hon. DHumLit: Georgetown Univ., Washington, DC, 1990; Coll. of Staten Island, NY, 1991; Hon. DSc: Tufts Univ., Mass, 1991; NY Med. Coll., 1991; Bard Coll., NY, 1992; Hon. LLD Queen's Univ. at Kingston, Ont, 2001; Hon. MD Karolinska Inst., Stockholm, 2003; Hon. DCL Oxon, 2005. Oskar Pfisker Award, Amer. Psychiatric Assoc., 1988; Harold D. Vursell Meml Award, Amer. Acad. and Inst. of Arts and Letters, 1989; Communicator of the Year Award, RNID, 1991; George S. Polk Award, 1994; Lewis Thomas Prize, Rockefeller Univ., 2002. *Publications:* Migraine, 1970, 2nd edn 1993; Awakenings, 1973, 2nd edn 1990 (Hawthornden Prize, 1975; filmed, 1990); A Leg to Stand On, 1984, 2nd edn 1993; The Man Who Mistook His Wife For a Hat, 1985; Seeing Voices: a journey into the world of the deaf, 1989; An Anthropologist on Mars: seven paradoxical tales, 1995; The Island of the Colorblind, and Cycad Island, 1996; Uncle Tungsten: memories of a chemical boyhood, 2001; Oaxaca Journal, 2002; Musicophilia: tales of music and the brain, 2007; papers, contribs to books and jls chiefly on neurology and neuroscience. *Address:* 2 Horatio Street #3G, New York, NY 10014, USA. *T:* (212) 6338373, *Fax:* (212) 6338928; *e-mail:* mail@oliversacks.com.

SACKUR, Stephen John; Presenter, Hardtalk, BBC Television, since 2005; *b* 9 Jan. 1964; *s* of Robert Neil Humphrys Sackur and Sallie Caley; *m* 1992, Zina Sabbagh; two *s* one *d*. *Educ:* Emmanuel Coll., Cambridge (BA Hons Hist. 1985). Reporter, Hebden Bridge Times, 1981–82; Henry Fellow, Harvard Univ., 1985–86; BBC: Producer, Current Affairs, 1986–89; Foreign Affairs Corresp., 1989–92; ME Corresp., Cairo, 1992–95; Jerusalem Corresp., 1995–97; Washington Corresp., 1997–2002; Europe Corresp., 2002–05. *Publication:* On the Basra Road, 1991. *Recreations:* books, films, sports, family adventures. *Address:* c/o BBC News, BBC TV Centre, W12 7RJ. *T:* (020) 8743 8000.

SACKVILLE, family name of **Earl De La Warr**.

SACKVILLE, 7th Baron *cr* 1876; **Robert Bertrand Sackville-West;** *b* 10 July 1958; *s* of Hugh Rosslyn Inigo Sackville-West, MC and Bridget Eleanor (*née* Cunliffe); *S* uncle, 2004; *m* 1st, 1985, Catherine Dorothea Bennett (marr. diss. 1992); 2nd, 1994, Margot Jane MacAndrew; one *s* two *d*. *Heir: s* Hon. Arthur Sackville-West, *b* 25 Feb. 2000.

SACKVILLE, Hon. Thomas Geoffrey, (Tom); Chief Executive, International Federation of Health Plans (formerly International Federation of Health Funds), since 1998; *b* 26 Oct. 1950; 2nd *s* of 10th Earl De La Warr (*d* 1988) and of Anne Rachel, *o d* of Geoffrey Devas, MC, Hunton Court, Maidstone; *m* 1979, Catherine Theresa, *d* of Brig. James Windsor Lewis; one *s* one *d*. *Educ:* St Aubyn's, Rottingdean, Sussex; Eton Coll.; Lincoln Coll., Oxford (BA). Deltec Banking Corp., New York, 1971–74; Grindlays Bank Ltd, London, 1974–77; Internat. Bullion and Metal Brokers (London) Ltd, 1978–83. MP (C) Bolton West, 1983–97; contested (C) same seat, 1997. PPS to Minister of State at the Treasury, 1985, to Minister for Social Security, 1987–88; an Asst Govt Whip, 1988–90; a Lord Comr of HM Treasury (Govt Whip), 1990–92; Parliamentary Under-Secretary of State: DoH, 1992–95; Home Office, 1995–97. Sec., All-Party Cttee on Drug Misuse, 1984–88. Chairman: Renal Services plc, 2007–; Family Survival Trust, 2007–. *Address:* (office) 35–37 Grosvenor Gardens, SW1W 0BS; *e-mail:* tom@ifhp.com.

SACKVILLE-WEST, family name of **Baron Sackville**.

SACRANIE, Sir Iqbal (Abdul Karim Mussa), Kt 2005; OBE 1999; Secretary General, The Muslim Council of Britain, 2002–06; *b* 6 Sept. 1951; *s* of Abdul Karim Mussa and Mariam Mussa; *m* 1976, Yasmin; three *s* two *d*. *Educ:* Kennington Coll.; Walbrook Coll. Fellow, Inst. of Financial Accountants, 1978; MInstAM 1978. Man. Dir, Global Traders and Exporters Ltd (family business). Chm., Muslim Council of Britain Charitable Foundn, 2000–; Chm. Bd of Trustees, Memon Assoc. UK, 1998–; Dep. Pres., World Memon Org., 2002–; Vice Pres., Assoc. of Family Welfare, 1998–; Member: Inner Cities Religious Council, 1992–2001; Rev. of Coroners' System, 2001–03; Higher Council, Islamic Educnl Scientific and Cultural Org., 2001–; Race Equality Adv. Panel, 2003–05; Bd, World Islamic Economic Forum, 2005–. Chairman Board of Trustees: Balham Mosque, 1986–; Al Risalla Sch. Trust, 2002–. Trustee, Muslim Aid, 1995–. Hon. DLaws Leeds Metropolitan, 2006. Award for Excellence, Muslim News, 2000; Award for commitment and dedication to community work, Memon Assoc. UK, 2001. *Publications:* joint author and contributor: Need for Reform, 1992; Election 1997 and British Muslims, 1997; The Quest for Sanity, 2003; contrib. to Muslim News, News Internat., Daily Jang, Nation, Asian News and other ethnic media. *Recreations:* golf, cricket, volleyball. *T:* (020) 8974 2780, *Fax:* (020) 8974 2781; *e-mail:* isacranie@glotex.co.uk.

SADEQUE, Shahwar; educational and ICT consultant, since 1996; a Governor, BBC, 1990–95; *b* 31 Aug. 1942; *d* of late Ali Imam and of Akhtar Imam; *m* 1962, Pharhad Sadeque; one *s* one *d*. *Educ:* Dhaka Univ., Bangladesh (BSc 1st Cl. Hons Physics); Bedford Coll., London (MPhil Physics); Kingston Poly. (MSc Inf. Technol.). MBCS 1991. Computer Programmer with BARIC Services Ltd, 1969–73; Teacher, Nonsuch High Sch., Sutton, 1974–84; research in computer integrated manufacture incorporating vision systems and artificial intelligence, Kingston Univ. (formerly Poly.), 1985–92. Associate Hosp. Manager, SW London and St George's Mental Health NHS Trust, 2004–. Member: Commn for Racial Equality, 1989–93; VAT Tribunals (England and Wales), 1991–; (pt-time) Income and Corporation Tax Tribunals, 1992–; SCAA, 1993–97; NCET, 1994–97; Metropolitan Police Cttee, 1995–2000; Cttee on Ethical Issues in Medicine, RCP, 1998–2007; Wkg Gp on operational and ethical guidelines (tissue collections), MRC, 1998–2001; Good Practice in Consent Adv. Gp, DoH, 2000–01; Wkg Pty on Healthcare-related Res. in Developing Countries, Nuffield Council on Bioethics, 2000–02; Patient Inf. Adv. Gp, DoH, 2001–04; Patient and Carer Network, RCP, 2004–07; Lord Chancellor's Adv. Council on Public Records, subseq. on Nat. Records and Archives, 1999–2004. Foreign and Commonwealth Office: Member: Panel 2000, 1998; Marshall Aid Commemoration Commn, 1998–2004; Special Rep. of Sec. of State, FCO, 1998–. Vice-Chm., Immigration Adv. Service, 2000–07. Member: Bd, Waltham Forest HAT, 1991–2002; Council, C&G, 1995–; Bd of Govs, Kingston Univ., 1995–2002; Panel of Ind. Persons, UCL, 2003–. Gov., Res. into Ageing, 1998–2001; Trustee, Windsor Leadership Trust, 1998–2005. FRSA 1994–2000. Hon. FCGI 2008. *Publications:* papers (jointly): Education and Ethnic Minorities, 1988; Manufacturing—towards the 21st Century, 1988; A Knowledge-Based System for Sensor Interaction and Real-Time Component Control, 1988. *Recreations:* collecting thimbles and perfume bottles, cooking Indian-style, passion for keeping up-to-date with current affairs. *Address:* *e-mail:* shahwar.sadeque@btinternet.com.

SADGROVE, Very Rev. Michael; Dean of Durham, since 2003; *b* 13 April 1950; *s* of late Ralph and Doreen Sadgrove; *m* 1974, (Elizabeth) Jennifer Suddes; one *s* three *d*. *Educ:* UCS; Balliol Coll., Oxford (BA (Maths and Philosophy, Theology) 1972; MA 1975); Trinity Coll., Bristol. Ordained, deacon, 1975, priest, 1976; Lectr in OT studies, 1977–82, Vice-Principal, 1980–82, Salisbury and Wells Theol College; Vicar, Alnwick, Northumberland, 1982–87; Canon Residentiary, Precentor and Vice-Provost, Coventry Cathedral, 1987–95; Provost, subseq. Dean, Sheffield, 1995–2003. Bishops' Inspector of Theol Colls and Courses, 1982– (Sen. Inspector, 1997–). Mem., General Synod, 2003–. Chairman: Precentors' Conf. of England and Wales, 1991–94; Church Men in the Midlands, 1991–95; Pastoral Cttee, Dio. of Sheffield, 1996–2001; Sheffield DAC, 2001–03; Ethics Adv. Cttee, Univ. of Durham, 2004–; Durham DAC, 2005–; Mem., Cathedrals Fabric Commn for England, 1996–2006. Chm., Sheffield Common Purpose, 1996–99. Mem. Council, Univ. of Durham, 2003–; Visitor, St Chad's Coll., Durham, 2003–. President: St Cuthbert's Hospice, Durham, 2003–; MUSICON, Univ. of Durham, 2003–. FRSA 1997. *Publications:* A Picture of Faith, 1995; The Eight Words of Jesus, 2006; contributor to: Studia Biblica, 1978; Reflecting the Word, 1989; Lion

Handbook of the World's Religions, 1982, 2nd edn 1994; Rethinking Marriage, 1993; Coventry's First Cathedral, 1994; The Care Guide, 1995; Calling Time, 2000; Creative Chords, 2001; Dreaming Spires?, 2006; Wisdom and Ministry, 2008; articles and reviews in theol jls. *Recreations:* music, arts, classical literature, walking the north-east of England, railways and trams, travels in Burgundy, European issues, photography. *Address:* The Deanery, Durham DH1 3EQ. *T:* (0191) 384 7500, *Fax:* (0191) 386 4267; *e-mail:* michael.sadgrove@durhamcathedral.co.uk. *Club:* Royal Over-Seas League.

SADLER, Ven. Anthony Graham; Archdeacon of Walsall, 1997–2004, now Emeritus; *b* 1 April 1936; *s* of Frank and Hannah Sadler; unmarried. *Educ:* Bishop Vesey's Grammar Sch.; The Queen's Coll., Oxford (MA); Lichfield Theol Coll. Ordained deacon, 1962, priest, 1963; Asst Curate, St Chad, Burton upon Trent, 1962–65; Vicar: All Saints, Rangemore and St Mary, Dunstall, 1965–72; St Nicholas, Abbots Bromley, 1972–79; St Michael, Pelsall, 1979–90; Rural Dean of Walsall, 1982–90; Priest-in-charge of Uttoxeter, Bramshall, Gratwich, Marchington Kingstone, Marchington Woodlands, Checkley, Stramshall and Leigh, and Leader of the Uttoxeter Area of Ministry Develt, 1990–97; Rector of Uttoxeter, 1997. Prebendary of Whittington, 1987–97, Hon. Canon, 1997–, Lichfield Cathedral. *Recreations:* music, painting. *Address:* Llidiart Newydd, Llanrhaeadr-ym-Mochnant, Oswestry, Powys SY10 0ED. *T:* (01691) 780276.

SADLER, Anthony John, CBE 2004; Archbishops' Appointments Secretary, 1996–2003; *b* 2 Oct. 1938; *s* of David James Sadler and Joan Sybil (*née* Alt); *m* 1966, Marie-José Lucas; three *d. Educ:* Bedford Sch.; Magdalene Coll., Cambridge (MA). Personnel Manager, Hawker Siddeley Aviation, Hatfield, 1964–75; Asst Personnel Controller, Rank Orgn, 1975–78; Employee Relns Manager, Lloyds Bank Internat., 1978–83; Dir, Gp Human Resources, Minet plc, 1983–92. Vice-Pres., Internat. IPM, 1981–83; Chm., Staff Mgt Assoc., 1989–91. Chm., Southwark Welcare Centenary Appeal Cttee, 1993–95. Chm., S London Industrial Mission, 1980–82. Church Warden, St Luke, Kew, 1976–88. CCIPD (CIPM 1983). *Publication:* Human Resource Management: developing a strategic approach, 1995. *Recreations:* cycling, bird-watching, classical music. *Address:* 14 Venelle de la Clef des Champs, 17590 Ars en Ré, France. *T:* (5) 46424518. *Clubs:* Lansdowne, MCC.

SADLER, Joan; Principal, Cheltenham Ladies' College, 1979–87; *b* 1 July 1927; *d* of Thomas Harold Sadler and Florence May Sadler. *Educ:* Cambridgeshire High Sch.; Univ. of Bristol (BA Hons (History); DipEd; MEd 1998); Univ. of Glos (PhD 2006). Downe House, Cold Ash, Newbury, Berks: Asst History teacher, 1950–56; Head of History Dept, 1956–58; Heriots Wood School, Stanmore, Middx: Head of History Dept, 1958–68; Sen. Mistress, 1966–68; Headmistress, Howell's School, Denbigh, 1968–79. Chairman: Boarding Schools' Assoc., 1983–85; Independent Schools' Curriculum Cttee, 1986; Trustee: Central Bureau for Educnl Visits and Exchanges; Common Entrance Examination for Girls' Schools. Hon. Freewoman: City of London; Drapers' Co., 1979. FRSA. *Recreations:* music, theatre, travel, reading. *Address:* Locke's Cottage, Caudle Green, Cheltenham, Glos GL53 9PR.

SADLER, John Stephen, CBE 1982; Chairman, Argent Group PLC, 1997–2001; *b* 6 May 1930; *s* of late Bernard and Phyllis Sadler; *m* 1952, Ella (*née* McCleery); three *s. Educ:* Reading Sch.; Corpus Christi Coll., Oxford (MA 1st cl. PPE). Board of Trade, 1952–54; Treasury, 1954–56; Board of Trade, 1956–60; British Trade Commissioner, Lagos, Nigeria, 1960–64; Board of Trade, 1964–66. John Lewis Partnership Ltd, 1966–89: Finance Dir, 1971–87; Dep. Chm., 1984–89. Chairman: Water Res. Centre, subseq. WRC, 1989–93; West End Bd, Royal & Sun Alliance (formerly Sun Alliance) Insurance Gp, 1991–2001; UK Bd, Australian Mutual Provident Soc. and London Life, 1991–96; Pearl Gp PLC, 1994–96; Dir, Debenham Tewson & Chinnock Hldgs plc, 1987–2000. Dir, IMRO, 1987–94; Chm., Authorised Conveyancing Practitioners Bd, 1991–93; Mem., Monopolies and Mergers Commn, 1973–85. Special Advr, Ofgem, 1996–2001. Trustee, British Telecommunications Staff Superannuation Scheme, 1983–98. *Publication:* report of enquiry into media promotion. *Recreation:* boating. *Address:* Riverlea, The Warren, Caversham, Reading RG4 7TQ. *Clubs:* Oriental, Lansdowne.

SADLER, Kevin Ian; Strategic Planning and Performance Director, Ministry of Justice, since 2008; *b* 18 March 1962; *s* of Colin and Brenda Sadler; *m* 2004, Gillian (*née* Hazlehurst); two *d. Educ:* Leicester Polytechnic (BA Hons Law). DSS, 1984–93; Cabinet Office, 1993–95; DSS, subseq. DWP, 1995–2002; Dir, Tribunals, Unified Admin and Magistrates' Courts, LCD, subseq. DCA, 2002–05; Dir, Corporate Mgt, then Change Dir, DCA, subseq. MoJ, 2005–08. *Address:* Ministry of Justice, 8th Floor, Selborne House, 54–60 Victoria Street, SW1E 6QW. *T:* (020) 7210 8020, *Fax:* 0870 739 4486.

SADLER, Prof. Peter John, DPhil; FRS 2005; FRSE; Professor of Chemistry and Head of Department of Chemistry, University of Warwick, since 2007; *b* 6 April 1946; *s* of Alfred George and Louisa Elsie Sadler; *m* 1972, Dr Tessa Elizabeth Halstead; two *s* one *d. Educ:* City of Norwich Sch.; Magdalen Coll., Oxford (MA 1972; DPhil Chemistry 1972). CChem, FRSC 1987; CSci 2004. MRC Res. Fellow, Univ. of Cambridge and NIMR, Mill Hill, 1971–73; Birkbeck College, London: Lectr in Chemistry, 1973–85; Reader in Biol Inorganic Chemistry, 1985–91; Prof. of Chemistry, 1991–96; Crum Brown Prof. of Chemistry, Univ. of Edinburgh, 1996–2007. FRSE 1999. *Publications:* res. papers in jls, inc. Jl of ACS, Angewandte Chemie, Inorganic Chemistry, Chemical Communications, Dalton Transactions, Nature, Structural Biology, Science, Jl of Medicinal Chemistry, Biochemical Jl, Biochemistry and Procs of the NAS. *Recreations:* gardening, amateur dramatics and musical theatre, playing clarinet, guitar and piano. *Address:* Department of Chemistry, University of Warwick, Gibbet Hill Road, Coventry CV4 7AL. *T:* (024) 7652 3818, *Fax:* (024) 7652 3819.

SAGE, Stephen Paul; Director, Trading Fund Programme, Foreign and Commonwealth Office, since 2006; *b* 3 June 1953; *s* of late Ivor John Sage and Kathleen Gwendoline Sage (*née* Jeffrey); *m* 1982, Anne Jennifer Mickleburgh; two *s* one *d. Educ:* Bristol Grammar Sch.; Peterhouse, Cambridge (BA Hons Classics 1974; MA). MCIPS 1993. John Henderson Sports, 1976–78; Crown Agents, 1978–80; Department of the Environment, 1980–93: Private Sec. to Housing Minister, 1984–85; Controller, Merseyside Task Force, 1989–93; Chief Exec., The Buying Agency, 1993–2000; Chief Exec., FCO Services, FCO, 2000–06. Mem. Cttee, Pierhead Housing Assoc., 1994–2000. Trustee, Lancs W and Wigan (formerly Lancs W) Groundwork Trust, 2005–. *Recreations:* reading, music, Alfa Romeos, tennis, golf. *Address:* Foreign and Commonwealth Office, King Charles Street, SW1A 2AH. *Club:* Bristol City Football.

SAGOVSKY, Rev. Canon Nicholas, PhD; Canon Theologian, Westminster Abbey, since 2004; *b* 13 Aug. 1947; *s* of Vladimir Sagovsky and Hilary Douglas Sagovsky (*née* Taylor); *m* 1974, Ruth Scott; one *s* one *d. Educ:* Oundle Sch.; Corpus Christi Coll., Oxford (BA (English Lang. and Lit.) 1969); St John's Coll., Nottingham and Nottingham Univ. (BA (Theol.) 1973); St Edmund's Coll., Cambridge (PhD 1981). Ordained deacon, 1974, priest, 1975; Curate: St Gabriel's, Heaton, 1974–77; Gt St Mary's, Cambridge, 1981–82; Vice Principal, Edinburgh Theol Coll., 1982–86; Dean, Clare Coll., Cambridge, 1986–97; William Leech Prof. of Applied Christian Theol., Newcastle Univ., 1997–2002; Liverpool Prof. of Theol. and Public Life, Liverpool Hope UC, 2002–04. Hon. Prof., Durham Univ., 1997–2000; Vis. Prof., Liverpool Hope Univ. (formerly University Coll.), 2004–. Mem., ARCIC, 1992–. *Publications:* Between Two Worlds: George Tyrrell's relationship to the thought of Matthew Arnold, 1983; On God's Side: a life of George Tyrrell, 1990; Ecumenism, Christian Origins and the Practice of Communion, 2000. *Recreations:* rough gardening and other Northumbrian pursuits. *Address:* c/o Chapter Office, Dean's Yard, Westminster Abbey, SW1P 3PA. *T:* (020) 7654 4808; *e-mail:* nicholas.sagovsky@westminster-abbey.org.

SAINI, Pushpinder Singh; QC 2008; barrister; *b* Nairobi, 26 Feb. 1968; *s* of Surinder Jit Singh Saini and late Janak Dulari; *m* 1996, Gemma White; one *s* one *d. Educ:* Dormers Wells High Sch., Southall; Corpus Christi Coll., Oxford (MA, BCL). Called to the Bar, Gray's Inn, 1991; barrister, Blackstone Chambers, 1992–. *Address:* Blackstone Chambers, Temple, EC4Y 9BW. *T:* (020) 7583 1770.

SAINSBURY, family name of **Barons Sainsbury of Preston Candover** and **Sainsbury of Turville**.

SAINSBURY OF PRESTON CANDOVER, Baron *cr* 1989 (Life Peer), of Preston Candover in the county of Hampshire; **John Davan Sainsbury,** KG 1992; Kt 1980; President, J Sainsbury plc, since 1992 (Vice-Chairman, 1967–69; Chairman, 1969–92; Director, 1958–92); *b* 2 Nov. 1927; *e s* of Baron Sainsbury; *m* 1963, Anya Linden, *qv*; two *s* one *d. Educ:* Stowe School; Worcester College, Oxford (Hon. Fellow 1982). Director: Royal Opera House, Covent Garden, 1969–85 (Chm., 1987–91); Rambert Sch. of Ballet and Contemporary Dance, 2003–05; Chairman: Friends of Covent Garden, 1969–81; Benesh Inst. of Choreology, 1986–87; Bd of Trustees, Dulwich Picture Gall., 1994–2000 (Patron, 2004–); Govs, Royal Ballet, 1995–2003 (Gov., 1987–2003); Trustees, Royal Opera House Endowment Fund, 2001–05; Gov., Royal Ballet Sch., 1965–76, and 1987–91. Director: The Economist, 1972–80; Royal Opera House Trust, 1974–84 and 1987–97; Jt Hon. Treas., European Movt, 1972–75; Pres., British Retail Consortium, 1993–97 (Mem. Council, Retail Consortium, 1975–79); Member: Nat. Cttee for Electoral Reform, 1976–85; President's Cttee, CBI, 1982–84; Jt Parly Scrutiny Cttee on Draft Charities Bill, 2004–05. Vice Patron, Contemporary Arts Soc., 1984– (Hon. Sec., 1965–71; Vice Chm., 1971–74); Patron, Sir Harold Hillier Gardens and Arboretum, 2005–; Trustee: Nat. Gall., 1976–83; Westminster Abbey Trust, 1977–83; Tate Gall., 1982–83; Rhodes Trust, 1984–98; Saïd Business Sch. Foundn, 2003–. Visitor, Ashmolean Mus., 2003–. Dir, Friends of the Nelson Mandela Children's Fund, 1996–2000. Pres., Sparsholt Coll., Hants, 1993–2000. Hon. Bencher, Inner Temple, 1985. FIGD 1973. Hon. Fellow, British Sch. at Rome, 2002. Hon. DScEcon London, 1985; Hon. DLitt South Bank, 1992; Hon. LLD Bristol, 1993; Hon. DEconSc Cape Town, 2000. Albert Medal, RSA, 1989. *Address:* c/o 33 Holborn, EC1N 2HT. *T:* (020) 7695 6000. *Clubs:* Garrick, Beefsteak.

See also Rt Hon. Sir T. A. D. Sainsbury.

SAINSBURY OF PRESTON CANDOVER, Lady; *see* Linden, Anya.

SAINSBURY OF TURVILLE, Baron *cr* 1997 (Life Peer), of Turville in the co. of Buckinghamshire; **David John Sainsbury;** Parliamentary Under-Secretary of State, Department of Trade and Industry, 1998–2006; *b* 24 Oct. 1940; *s* of Sir Robert Sainsbury and of Lisa Ingeborg (*née* Van den Bergh); *m* 1973, Susan Carroll Reid; three *d. Educ:* King's Coll., Cambridge (BA); Columbia Univ., NY (MBA). Joined J. Sainsbury, 1963; Finance Dir, 1973–90; Dep. Chm., 1988–92; Chm., 1992–98; Chief Exec., 1992–97. Member: Cttee of Review of the Post Office (Carter Cttee), 1975–77; IPPR Commn on Public Policy and British Business, 1995–97. Trustee, Social Democratic Party, 1982–90; Mem. Governing Body, London Business Sch., 1985–98 (Chm., 1991–98); Chm. Transition Bd, Univ. for Industry, 1998–99. Hon. FREng (Hon. FEng 1994); Hon. FRS 2008. Hon. LLD Cambridge, 1997. *Publications:* Government and Industry: a new partnership, 1981; (with Christopher Smallwood) Wealth Creation and Jobs, 1987.

SAINSBURY, Jeffrey Paul, FCA; chartered accountant; Executive Vice-President, Computershare Ltd (formerly General Manager, Computershare Investor Services plc), since 2000; Lord Mayor of Cardiff, 1991–92; *b* 27 June 1943; *s* of Capt. Walter Ronald Sainsbury and Joan Margaret Slamin; *m* 1967, Janet Elizabeth Hughes; one *s* one *d. Educ:* Cardiff High Sch. FCA 1966. Partner, Pannell Kerr Forster, 1969–94; Man. Dir, Exchange Registrars Ltd, 1994–2000. Mem., Cardiff CC, 1969–96. Member: S Glamorgan HA, 1987–91; Bd, Cardiff Bay Develt Corp., 1991–2000. Chm., New Theatre, Cardiff, 1983–87. Chm., S Glam TEC, 1996–99; Dep. Chm., TEC SE Wales, 1999–2000. Gov., WCMD, 1995–2001. FRSA 1997. OStJ 1997. *Recreations:* computing, cooking, music, theatre, sport. *Address:* 6 Druidstone House, Druidstone Road, St Mellons, Cardiff CF3 6XF. *Club:* Cardiff & County.

SAINSBURY, Prof. (Richard) Mark, FBA 1998; Professor of Philosophy, University of Texas at Austin, since 2002; *b* 2 July 1943; *s* of Richard Eric Sainsbury and Freda Margaret Sainsbury (*née* Horne); *m* 1st, 1970, Gillian McNeill Rind (marr. diss. 2000); one *s* one *d*; 2nd, 2000, Victoria Goodman. *Educ:* Sherborne Sch.; Corpus Christi Coll., Oxford (MA, DPhil). Lecturer in Philosophy: Magdalen Coll., Oxford, 1968–70; St Hilda's Coll., Oxford, 1970–73; Brasenose Coll., Oxford, 1973–75; Univ. of Essex, 1975–78; Bedford Coll., Univ. of London, 1978–84; King's College London: Lectr in Philosophy, 1984–87; Reader in Philosophy, 1987–89; Stebbing Prof. of Philosophy, 1989–2008. Leverhulme Sen. Res. Fellow, 2000–02. Editor of Mind, 1990–2000. *Publications:* Russell, 1979; Paradoxes, 1988, 2nd edn 1995; Logical Forms, 1991, 2nd edn 2000; Departing From Frege, 2002; Reference Without Referents, 2005. *Recreation:* baking bread. *Address:* Department of Philosophy, University of Texas, Austin, TX 78712, USA; *e-mail:* marksainsbury@mail.utexas.edu.

SAINSBURY, Rt Rev. Dr Roger Frederick; Chairman, National Youth Agency, 2002–08; an Assistant Bishop, diocese of Bath and Wells, since 2003; *b* 2 Oct. 1936; *s* of Frederick William Sainsbury and Lillian Maude Sainsbury; *m* 1960, Jennifer Marguerite Carey. *Educ:* High Wycombe Royal Grammar School; Jesus Coll., Cambridge (MA); Clifton Theological Coll.; Seabury-Western Theol Seminary (DMin). Curate, Christ Church, Spitalfields, 1960–63; Missioner, Shrewsbury House, Liverpool, 1963–74; Warden, Mayflower Family Centre, Canning Town, 1974–81; Priest-in-Charge, St Luke, Victoria Dock, 1978–81; Vicar of Walsall, 1981–87; Rector, Walsall Team Ministry, 1987–88; Archdeacon of West Ham, 1988–91; Area Bp of Barking, 1991–2002. Alderman, London Borough of Newham, 1976–78. Moderator, Churches' Commn for Racial Justice, 1999–2003; Chairman: Frontier Youth Trustees, 1987–92; Barking Area Church Leaders Gp, 1994–2002; Urban Bishops Panel, 1996–2001; London Churches Gp, 1998–2002; Trustees, Children in Distress, 1998–2000; Centre for Youth Ministry, 2004–07; UK Urban Congress Exec., 2005–; Co-Chair, Urban Mission Develt Adv. Project, 2004–. Member: Coll. of Preachers, 2002–; Coll. of Evangelists, 2003–. Pres., Frontier Youth Trust, 2002–. Tutor, Trinity Coll., Bristol, 2006–. *Publications:* From a Mersey Wall, 1970; Justice on the Agenda, 1985; Lifestyle, 1986; Rooted and Grounded in Love, 1988; God of New Beginnings, 1990; Barking Mad Letters, 1999; Young People as Prophets, 2006. *Recreations:* geology, art, gardening. *Address:* (home) Abbey Lodge,

Battery Lane, Portishead, Bristol BS20 7JD; (office) National Youth Agency, 17–23 Albion Street, Leicester LE1 6GD.

SAINSBURY, Rt Hon. Sir Timothy (Alan Davan), Kt 1995; PC 1992; Chairman: Pendennis Shipyard (Holdings) Ltd, 1999–2007; Marlborough Tiles Ltd, since 1999; *b* 11 June 1932; *y s* of Baron Sainsbury; *m* 1961, Susan Mary Mitchell; two *s* two *d*. *Educ:* Eton; Worcester Coll., Oxford (MA; Hon. Fellow 1982). Dir, J. Sainsbury, 1962–83; non-exec. Dir, J. Sainsbury plc, 1995–99. Chm., Council for the Unit for Retail Planning Information Ltd, 1974–79. MP (C) Hove, Nov. 1973–1997. PPS to Sec. of State for the Environment, 1979–83, to Sec. of State for Defence, 1983; a Govt Whip, 1983–87; Parly Under-Sec. of State for Defence Procurement, 1987–89; Parly Under-Sec. of State, FCO, 1989–90; Minister of State, DTI, 1990–94 (Minister for Trade, 1990–92, for Industry, 1992–94). Pres., Cons. Friends of Israel, 1997–2005 (Parly Chm., 1994–97). Chm., Somerset House Ltd, then Somerset House Trust, 1997–2002. Mem. Council, RSA, 1981–83. Visitor, Ashmolean Mus., Oxford, 2000–06; Trustee, V&A Mus., 2004–. Hon. FRIBA 1994.

See also Baron Sainsbury of Preston Candover, Rt Hon. S. Woodward.

SAINT, Prof. Andrew John; General Editor, Survey of London, since 2006; *b* 30 Nov. 1946; *s* of late Arthur James Maxwell Saint and Elisabeth Yvetta Saint (*née* Butterfield); three *d*. *Educ:* Christ's Hosp.; Balliol Coll., Oxford. Part-time Lectr, Univ. of Essex, 1971–74; Architectural Editor, Survey of London, 1974–86; Historian, London Div., English Heritage, 1986–95; Prof. of Architecture, Univ. of Cambridge, 1995–2006. Hon. FRIBA 1993. *Publications:* Richard Norman Shaw, 1976; The Image of the Architect, 1983; Towards a Social Architecture, 1987; (ed with D. Keene and A. Burns) St Paul's: the cathedral church of London 604–2004, 2004. *Address:* Survey of London, c/o English Heritage, 138–142 Holborn, EC1N 2ST. *T:* (020) 7973 3638; *e-mail:* ajs61@cam.ac.uk; (home) 14 Denny Crescent, SE11 4UY. *T:* (020) 7735 3863.

SAINT, Dora Jessie, MBE 1998; (*pen name* Miss Read); writer, since 1950; *b* 17 April 1913; *d* of Arthur Gunnis Shafe and Grace Lilian Shafe; *m* 1940, Douglas Edward John Saint; one *d*. *Educ:* Bromley County Sch.; Homerton Coll., Cambridge. Teaching in Middlesex, 1933–40; occasional teaching, 1946–63. *Publications:* Village School, 1955, reissue, 2005; Village Diary, 1957, reissue, 2005; Storm in the Village, 1958, reissue, 2005; Thrush Green, 1959; Fresh from the Country, 1960; Winter in Thrush Green, 1961; Miss Clare Remembers, 1962; Chronicles of Fairacre, 1963; Over the Gate, 1964; Market Square, 1965; Village Christmas, 1966; Fairacre Festival, 1968; News from Thrush Green, 1970; Tiggy, 1971; Emily Davis, 1971; Tyler's Row, 1972; The Christmas Mouse, 1973; Farther Afield, 1974; Battles at Thrush Green, 1975; No Holly for Miss Quinn, 1976; Village Affairs, 1977; Return to Thrush Green, 1978; The White Robin, 1979; Village Centenary, 1980; Gossip from Thrush Green, 1981; Affairs at Thrush Green, 1983; Summer at Fairacre, 1984; At Home in Thrush Green, 1985; The School at Thrush Green, 1987; The World of Thrush Green, 1988; Mrs Pringle, 1989; Friends at Thrush Green, 1990; Celebrations at Thrush Green, 1992; Farewell to Fairacre, 1993; Tales from a Village School, 1994; Early Days, 1995; The Year at Thrush Green, 1995; A Peaceful Retirement, 1996; Christmas at Fairacre, 2005; *for children:* Hobby Horse Cottage, 1958; Hob and the Horse-Bat, 1965; The Red Bus Series, 1965; *non-fiction:* Country Bunch (anthology), 1963; Miss Read's Country Cooking, 1969; *autobiography:* A Fortunate Grandchild, 1982; Time Remembered, 1986. *Recreations:* theatre-going, reading. *Address:* c/o Michael Joseph Ltd, Penguin Group (UK), 80 Strand, WC2R 0RL.

ST ALBANS, 14th Duke of, *cr* 1684; **Murray de Vere Beauclerk;** Earl of Burford, Baron of Heddington, 1676; Baron Vere of Hanworth, 1750; Hereditary Grand Falconer of England; Hereditary Registrar, Court of Chancery; Partner, Burford & Partners LLP (formerly Burford & Co.), chartered accountants, since 1981; *b* 19 Jan. 1939; *s* of 13th Duke of St Albans, OBE and Nathalie Chatham, *d* of P. F. Walker (later Mrs Nathalie C. Eldrid, *d* 1985); *S* father, 1988; *m* 1st, 1963, Rosemary Frances Scoones (marr. diss. 1974); one *s* one *d*; 2nd, 1974, Cynthia Theresa Mary (marr. diss. 2002; she *d* 2002), *d* of late Lt-Col W. J. H. Howard, DSO and formerly wife of Sir Anthony Robin Maurice Hooper, 2nd Bt; 3rd, 2002, Gillian Anita, *d* of late Lt-Col C. G. R. Northam and *widow* of Philip Nesfield Roberts. *Educ:* Tonbridge. Chartered Accountant, 1962. Gov.-Gen., Royal Stuart Soc., 1989–. Pres., Beaufort Opera, 1991–; Patron: Bestwood Male Voice Choir, 2001–; Old Sessions House Charitable Trust, 2008–. Liveryman, Drapers' Co., 1971–. *Heir: s* Earl of Burford, *qv*. *Address:* 16 Ovington Street, SW3 2JB.

ST ALBANS, Bishop of, 1995–2009; **Rt Rev. Christopher William Herbert;** *b* 7 Jan. 1944; *s* of Walter Meredith Herbert (who *m* 1950, Dorothy Margaret Curnock) and late Hilda Lucy (*née* Dibbin); *m* 1968, Janet Elizabeth Turner; two *s*. *Educ:* Monmouth School; St David's Coll., Lampeter (BA); Univ. of Bristol (PGCE); Wells Theol Coll.; Univ. of Leicester (MPhil 2002; PhD 2008). Asst Curate, Tupsley, Hereford, 1967–71; Asst Master, Bishop's Sch., Hereford, 1967–71; Adv in Religious Educn, 1971–76, Dir of Educn, 1976–81, Dio. of Hereford; Vicar, St Thomas on the Bourne, Farnham, Surrey, 1981–90; Archdeacon of Dorking, 1990–95. Dir, Post-ordination Training, Dio. of Guildford, 1984–90; Hon. Canon of Guildford, 1984–95. Hon. DLitt Hertfordshire, 2003; Hon. DArts, Bedfordshire, 2008. *Publications:* The New Creation, 1971; A Place to Dream, 1976; St Paul's: A Place to Dream, 1981; The Edge of Wonder, 1981; Listening to Children, 1983; On the Road, 1984; Be Thou My Vision, 1985; This Most Amazing Day, 1986; The Question of Jesus, 1987; Alive to God, 1987; Ways into Prayer, 1987; Help in your Bereavement, 1988; Prayers for Children, 1993; Pocket Prayers, 1993; The Prayer Garden, 1994; Words of Comfort, 1994; Pocket Prayers for Children, 1999; Pocket Words of Comfort, 2004; Seeing and Believing, 2008. *Recreations:* walking, cycling, reading, gardening, writing unpublished novels. *Address:* (until Jan. 2009) Abbey Gate House, St Albans, Herts AL3 4HD. *T:* (01727) 853305; (from Jan. 2009) 1 Beacon Close, Boundstone, Farnham, Surrey, GU10 4PA. *T:* (01252) 7895600.

ST ALBANS, Dean of; *see* John, Very Rev. J. P. H.

ST ALBANS, Archdeacon of; *see* Smith, Ven. J. P.

ST ALDWYN, 3rd Earl *cr* 1915; **Michael Henry Hicks Beach;** Bt 1619; Viscount St Aldwyn 1906; Viscount Quenington 1915; Managing Director, International Fund Marketing (UK) Ltd, since 1994; *b* 7 Feb. 1950; *s* of 2nd Earl St Aldwyn, GBE, TD, PC and Diana Mary Christian Smyly (*d* 1992), *o d* of Henry C. G. Mills; *S* father, 1992; *m* 1982, Gilda Maria, *o d* of Barão Saavedra, Copacabana, Rio de Janeiro (marr. diss. 2005); two *d*; *m* 2005, Louise Wigan. *Educ:* Eton; Christ Church, Oxford (MA). *Heir: b* Hon. David Seymour Hicks Beach [*b* 25 May 1955; *m* 1993, Kate, *d* of Michael Henriques; one *s* two *d*]. *Address:* 23 Orbel Street, SW11 3NX. *T:* (020) 7978 6056; Williamstrip Park, Coln St Aldwyns, Cirencester, Glos GL7 5AT; International Fund Marketing (UK) Ltd, 5th Floor, Suite 7A, Berkeley Square House, Berkeley Square, W1J 6BY. *T:* (020) 7616 7400, *Fax:* (020) 7616 7411.

ST ANDREWS, Earl of; George Philip Nicholas Windsor; *b* 26 June 1962; *s* of HRH the Duke of Kent and HRH the Duchess of Kent; *m* 1988, Sylvana Tomaselli; one *s* two *d*. *Educ:* Eton (King's Scholar); Downing College, Cambridge. Attached to FCO, 1987–88. Specialist, Christie's (Books and Manuscripts Dept), 1996–98. Trustee: GB-Sasakawa Foundn, 1995– (Chm., 2005–); SOS Children's Villages UK, 1999–; Golden Web Foundn, 2003– (Chm., 2006–); Prince George Galitzine Meml Library, 2005–. Patron: Assoc. for Internat. Cancer Res., 1995–; Princess Margarita of Romania Trust, 1997–. *Heir: s* Lord Downpatrick, *qv*. *Address:* York House, St James's Palace, SW1A 1BQ.

See under Royal Family.

ST ANDREWS AND EDINBURGH, Archbishop of, (RC), since 1985; **His Eminence Cardinal Keith Michael Patrick O'Brien;** *b* Ballycastle, Co. Antrim, 17 March 1938; *s* of late Mark Joseph O'Brien and Alice Mary (*née* Moriarty). *Educ:* St Patrick's High Sch., Dumbarton; Holy Cross Acad., Edinburgh; Edinburgh Univ. (BSc 1959, DipEd 1966); St Andrew's Coll., Drygrange; Moray House Coll. of Education, Edinburgh. Ordained priest, 1965; pastoral appointments: Holy Cross, Edinburgh, 1965–66; St Bride's, Cowdenbeath, 1966–71 (while Chaplain and teacher of Maths and Science, St Columba's High Sch., Cowdenbeath and Dunfermline); St Patrick's, Kilsyth, 1972–75; St Mary's, Bathgate, 1975–78; Spiritual Dir, St Andrew's Coll., Drygrange, 1978–80; Rector, St Mary's Coll., Blair, Aberdeen, 1980–85. Apostolic Adminr, Dio. Argyll and the Isles, 1996–99. Cardinal Priest, 2003. Hon. LLD Antigonish, Nova Scotia, 2004; Hon. DD: St Andrews, 2004; Edinburgh, 2004. KGCHS 2003 (Grand Prior, Scottish Lieutenancy, 2001–); Bailiff Grand Cross of Honour and Devotion, SMO Malta, 2005. *Recreations:* music, hill walking. *Address:* Archbishop's House, 42 Greenhill Gardens, Edinburgh EH10 4BJ. *T:* (0131) 447 3337, *Fax:* (0131) 447 0816; *e-mail:* cardinal@staned.org.uk.

ST ANDREWS, DUNKELD AND DUNBLANE, Bishop of, since 2005; **Rt Rev. David Robert Chillingworth;** *b* 23 June 1951; *s* of David Andrew Richard Chillingworth and Sheila Margaret (*née* Bateman); *m* 1975, Alison Penney; two *s* one *d*. *Educ:* Portora Royal Sch., Enniskillen; Royal Belfast Academical Instn; Trinity Coll., Dublin (BA Classics 1973); Oriel Coll., Oxford (BA Theol. 1975, MA 1981); Ripon Coll., Cuddesdon. Ordained deacon, 1976, priest, 1977; Curate-Asst, Holy Trinity, Joanmount, 1976–79; C of I Youth Officer, 1979–83; Curate-Asst, Bangor Abbey, 1983–86; Rector, Seagoe Parish Ch, Portadown, 1986–2005; Dean of Dromore, 1995–2002; Archdeacon of Dromore, 2002–05. *Recreations:* music, reading, cycling, sailing, travel. *Address:* 4 Newbigging Grange, Coupar Angus, Blairgowrie PH13 9GA. *T:* (01738) 580426; *e-mail:* bishop@standrews.anglican.org; *web:* www.bishopdavid.net.

ST ANDREWS, DUNKELD AND DUNBLANE, Dean of; *see* Rathband, Very Rev. K.

ST ASAPH, Bishop of; *no new appointment at time of going to press.*

ST ASAPH, Dean of; *see* Potter, Very Rev. C. N. L.

ST AUBIN de TERÁN, Lisa Gioconda; writer; *b* London, 2 Oct. 1953; *d* of Cuthbert Jan Alwin Rynveld Carew and late Joan Mary St Aubin; *m* 1st, 1970, Jaime Terán (marr. diss. 1981); one *d*; 2nd, 1982, George Mann Macbeth (marr. diss. 1989; he *d* 1992); one *s*; 3rd, 1989, Robbie Charles Duff-Scott (marr. diss. 2004); one *d*; partner, Mees van Deth. *Educ:* James Allen's Girls' Sch., Dulwich. Sugar farmer and plantation manager, Venezuelan Andes, 1971–78. Founder, Teran Foundn, 2004; voluntary worker, Community Coll. of Tourism and Agriculture, Teran Foundn, Mossuril Dist, N Mozambique, 2005–. Writer of 3 film screenplays. John Llewellyn Rhys Prize, 1983; Eric Gregory Award for Poetry, 1983. *Publications:* Keepers of the House, 1982 (Somerset Maugham Award, 1983); The Slow Train to Milan, 1983; The Tiger, 1984; High Place (poetry), 1985; The Bay of Silence, 1986; Black Idol, 1987; Indiscreet Journeys, 1989; The Marble Mountain (short stories), 1989; Off the Rails: memoirs of a train addict, 1989; Joanna, 1990; Venice: the four seasons (essays), 1992; Nocturne, 1992; A Valley in Italy: confessions of a house addict, 1994; Distant Landscapes, 1995; The Hacienda (memoirs), 1997; The Palace, 1997; (ed) The Virago Book of Wanderlust and Dreams, 1998; Southpaw (short stories), 1999; Memory Maps (memoirs), 2001; Otto, 2005; Mozambican Mysteries, 2006. *Address:* c/o Maggie Phillips, Ed Victor Ltd, 6 Bayley Street, WC1B 3HB.

ST AUBYN, family name of **Baron St Levan**.

ST AUBYN, Nicholas Francis; *b* 19 Nov. 1955; *yr s* of late Hon. Piers St Aubyn, MC, and Mary St Aubyn (*née* Bailey-Southwell); *m* 1980, Jane Mary Brooks; two *s* three *d*. *Educ:* Eton Coll.; Trinity Coll., Oxford (MA PPE). With J. P. Morgan, 1977–86; Kleinwort Benson, 1986–87; American Internat. Gp, 1987–89; Gemini Clothescare, 1989–93; Chm., Fitzroy Gp, 1993–. Contested (C) Truro, March 1987, gen. elecn 1987 and 1992. MP (C) Guildford, 1997–2001; contested same seat, 2001. Mem., Select Cttee on Educn and Employment, 1997–2001. Dir, Arab British Council, 2005–. Director: Project Trust, 2001–; Zebra Housing Assoc., 2001–. MInstD. *Recreations:* riding, shooting, swimming, sailing. *Address:* 66 Westminster Gardens, SW1P 4JG. *T:* (020) 7828 2804. *Club:* Brooks's.

ST AUBYN, Major Thomas Edward, CVO 1993; DL; FRGS; Lieutenant, HM Body Guard of Honourable Corps of Gentlemen at Arms, 1990–93 (Clerk of the Cheque and Adjutant, 1986–90); *b* 13 June 1923; *s* of Hon. Lionel Michael St Aubyn, MVO, and Lady Mary St Aubyn; *m* 1953, Henrietta Mary, *d* of Sir Henry Studholme, 1st Bt; three *d*. *Educ:* Eton. Served in King's Royal Rifle Corps, 1941–62; Italian Campaign, 1944–45; Adjt 1st KRRC, 1946–48; seconded to Sudan Defence Force in rank of Bimbashi, 1948–52; leader of Tibesti Mountain Expedn in Chad, 1957; Bde Adjt Green Jackets Bde, 1960–62. Mem., HM Body Guard, 1973–93. High Sheriff of Hampshire, 1979–80; DL Hampshire, 1984. FRGS 1959. *Recreations:* shooting, fishing. *Address:* West Leigh House, Nether Wallop, Stockbridge, Hants SO20 8EY. *T:* (01264) 782914. *Club:* Army and Navy.

ST AUBYN, Sir William M.; *see* Molesworth-St Aubyn.

ST CLAIR, family name of **Lord Sinclair**.

ST CLAIR, William Linn, FBA 1992; FRSL; author; Senior Research Fellow: Institute of Advanced Study, University of London, since 2006; Centre for History and Economics, University of Cambridge, since 2007; Chairman, Open Book Publishers, since 2008; *b* 7 Dec. 1937; *s* of late Joseph and Susan St Clair, Falkirk; two *d*. *Educ:* Edinburgh Acad.; St John's Coll., Oxford. FRSL 1973. Admiralty and MoD, 1961–66; First Sec., FCO, 1966–69; transferred to HM Treasury, 1969, Under Sec., 1990–92; Consultant to OECD, 1992–95, to EC, 1997. Visiting Fellow: All Souls Coll., Oxford, 1981–82; Huntington Library, Calif, 1985; Fellow: All Souls Coll., Oxford, 1992–96; Trinity Coll., Cambridge, 1998–2006. Member: Cttee, London Liby, 1996–2000; Council, British Acad., 1996–2000. Internat. Pres., Byron Soc. Thalassa Forum award for culture, Greece, 2000. *Publications:* Lord Elgin and the Marbles, 1967, 3rd edn 1998; That Greece Might Still Be Free, 1972 (Heinemann prize); Trelawny, 1978; Policy Evaluation: a guide for managers, 1988; The Godwins and the Shelleys, 1989 (Time Life prize and Macmillan silver pen);

Executive Agencies: a guide to setting targets and measuring performance, 1992; (ed with Irmgard Maassen) Conduct Literature for Women 1500–1640, 2000; Conduct Literature for Women 1640–1710, 2002; (ed with Peter France) Mapping Lives: the uses of biography, 2002; The Reading Nation in the Romantic Period, 2004; The Grand Slave Emporium: Cape Coast Castle and the British slave trade, 2006; The Door of No Return, 2007. *Recreations:* old books, Scottish hills. *Address:* 52 Eaton Place, SW1X 8AL. *Clubs:* Athenæum, PEN.

ST CLAIR-ERSKINE, family name of **Earl of Rosslyn**.

ST CLAIR-FORD, Sir James (Anson), 7th Bt *cr* 1793, of Ember Court, Surrey; *b* 16 March 1952; *s* of Capt. Sir Aubrey St Clair-Ford, 6th Bt, DSO, RN and of Anne, *o d* of Harold Cecil Christopherson; *S* father, 1991; *m* 1st, 1977, Jennifer Margaret (marr. diss. 1984), *yr d* of Commodore Robin Grindle, RN; 2nd, 1987, Mary Anne, *er d* of His Honour Nathaniel Robert Blaker, QC. *Educ:* Wellington; Bristol Univ. *Heir: cousin* Colin Anson St Clair-Ford [*b* 19 April 1939; *m* 1964, Gillian Mary, *er d* of Rear Adm. Peter Skelton, CB; two *d*].

ST CYRES, Viscount; Thomas Stafford Northcote; *b* 5 Aug. 1985; *s* and *heir* of Earl of Iddesleigh, *qv*. *Educ:* Oratory Sch., Reading; Univ. of Exeter. *Recreations:* cricket, Real tennis, cooking, shooting, Rugby. *Address:* Hayne Barton, Newton St Cyres, Exeter, Devon EX5 5AH. *Clubs:* East India, MCC, Tennis and Rackets Assoc.

ST DAVIDS, 3rd Viscount *cr* 1918; **Colwyn Jestyn John Philipps;** Baron Strange of Knokin, 1299; Baron Hungerford, 1426; Baron de Moleyns, 1445; Bt 1621; Baron St Davids, 1908; *b* 30 Jan. 1939; *s* of 2nd Viscount St Davids and Doreen Guinness (*d* 1956), *o d* of late Captain Arthur Jowett; *S* father, 1991; *m* 1965, Augusta Victoria Correa Larrain, *d* of late Don Estanislao Correa Ugarte; two *s*. *Educ:* Haverfordwest Grammar Sch.; Sevenoaks Sch.; King's Coll., London (Cert. Advanced Musical Studies, 1989). Nat. Service, 1958–60; commnd 2nd Lt Welsh Guards. Securities Agency Ltd, 1960–65; Mem., Stock Exchange, 1965–93; Maguire Kingsmill and Co., 1965–68; Partner, Kemp-Gee and Co., later Scrimgeour Kemp-Gee and Co., 1971; Director: Citicorp Scrimgeour Vickers (Securities) Ltd, 1985–88; Greig Middleton & Co. Ltd, 1989–90, 1994–99. Mem. Bd, Milford Haven Port Authority, 1997–2007. A Lord in Waiting (Govt Whip), 1992–94; a Dep. Speaker, H of L, 1995–99. Mem., Baden-Powell Fellowship, 1985–. Mem. Council, Univ. of Wales, Lampeter, 1995–99; Gov., WCMD, 1996–2000. Liveryman: Musicians' Co., 1971–; Welsh Livery Guild, 1997–2006. *Recreations:* music, literature, natural history. *Heir: s* Hon. Rhodri Colwyn Philipps [*b* 16 Sept. 1966; *m* 2003, Sarah, *o d* of late Dr Peter Butcher]. *Club:* Garrick.

ST DAVIDS, Bishop of; *no new appointment at time of going to press.*

ST DAVIDS, Dean of; *see* Evans, Very Rev. J. W.

ST DAVIDS, Archdeacon of; *see* Holdsworth, Ven. Dr J. I.

ST EDMUNDSBURY, Dean of; *see* Collings, Very Rev. N.

ST EDMUNDSBURY AND IPSWICH, Bishop of, since 2007; **Rt Rev. (William) Nigel Stock;** *b* 29 Jan. 1950; *s* of Ian Heath Stock and Elizabeth Mary Stock; *m* 1973, Carolyne Grace (*née* Greswell); three *s*. *Educ:* Durham Sch.; Durham Univ. (BA Hons Law and Politics); Ripon Coll., Cuddesdon (Oxford Univ. DipTh). Ordained deacon, 1976, priest, 1977; Asst Curate, Stockton St Peter, Durham, 1976–79; Priest-in-charge, Taraka St Peter, Aipo Rongo, PNG, 1979–84; Vicar, St Mark, Shiremoor, Newcastle, 1985–91; Team Rector, North Shields Team Ministry, 1991–98; RD, Tynemouth, 1992–98; Hon. Canon, Newcastle Cathedral, 1997–98; Residentiary Canon, Durham Cathedral, 1998–2000; Bishop Suffragan of Stockport, 2000–07. Commissary for Archbp of PNG, 1986–. *Recreations:* walking, photography, travel. *Address:* Bishop's House, 4 Park Road, Ipswich IP1 3ST. *T:* (01473) 252829.

ST GEORGE, Sir John (Avenel Bligh), 10th Bt *cr* 1766 (Ire.), of Athlone, co. Westmeath; *b* 18 March 1940; *s* of Sir George Bligh St George, 9th Bt and of Mary Somerville St George (*née* Sutcliffe); *S* father, 1995; *m* (marr. diss.); two *d*; *m* 1981, Linda, *d* of Robert Perry; two *s*. *Heir: s* Robert Alexander Bligh St George, *b* 17 Aug. 1983. *Address:* 2 Curzon Street, Ibstock, Leics LE67 6LA.

ST GEORGE-HYSLOP, Prof. Peter Henry, MD; FRCPC; FRS 2004; FRSC 2002; Professor of Experimental Neuroscience, University of Cambridge, since 2007; University Professor, since 2003, Director, Centre for Research in Neurodegenerative Diseases, since 1995, University of Toronto; Consultant in Neurology, University Health Network, since 1990; *b* 10 July 1953; *s* of Noel St George-Hyslop and Daphne Bower Hyslop (*née* Tinker); *m* 1985, Veronika Andrea Fried; three *d*. *Educ:* Wellington Sch., Somerset; Univ. of Ottawa (MD *primum cum laude* 1976); Univ. of Toronto; Harvard Univ. FRCPC 1989. Instructor, Dept of Neurology, Harvard Med. Sch., 1987–90; Asst Prof., 1990–95, Prof., 1995–2003, Dept of Medicine, Univ. of Toronto. Dir, Toronto Western Hospital Res. Inst., 2004–. *Publications:* more than 280 peer-reviewed scientific articles and 20 book chapters. *Recreation:* vintage sports car racing. *Address:* Cambridge Institute of Medical Research, Wellcome Trust/MRC Building, Addenbrooke's Hospital, Hills Road, Cambridge CB2 0XY; *e-mail:* phs22@cam.ac.uk; Centre for Research in Neurodegenerative Diseases, Tanz Neuroscience Building, University of Toronto, 6 Queen's Park Crescent, Toronto, ON M5S 3H2, Canada. *T:* (416) 978 7461, *Fax:* (416) 978 1878; *e-mail:* CRND.secr@utoronto.ca.

ST GERMANS, 10th Earl of, *cr* 1815; **Peregrine Nicholas Eliot;** Baron Eliot 1784; *b* 2 Jan. 1941; *o s* of 9th Earl of St Germans, and Helen Mary (*d* 1951), *d* of late Lieut-Col Charles Walter Villiers, CBE, DSO, and Lady Kathleen Villiers; *S* father, 1988; *m* 1st, 1964, Hon. Jacquetta Jean Frederika Lampson (marr. diss. 1989), *d* of 1st Baron Killearn and Jacqueline Aldine Lesley (*née* Castellani); two *s* (and one *s* decd); 2nd, 1992, Elizabeth Mary Williams (marr. diss. 1996); 3rd, 2005, Catherine Elizabeth Wilson. *Educ:* Eton. *Recreation:* mucking about. *Heir: g s* Lord Eliot, *qv*. *Address:* Port Eliot, St Germans, Cornwall PL12 5ND. *Clubs:* Pratt's; Cornish Club 1768.

ST GERMANS, Bishop Suffragan of, since 2000; **Rt Rev. Royden Screech;** *b* 15 May 1953; *s* of Raymond Kenneth Screech and Gladys Beryl Screech; *m* 1988, Angela May Waring; no *c*. *Educ:* Cotham Grammar Sch.; King's Coll. London (BD 1974, AKC 1974); St Augustine's Coll., Canterbury. Ordained deacon, 1976, priest, 1977; Curate, St Catherine, Hatcham, 1976–80; Vicar, St Antony, Nunhead, 1980–87; Priest-in-charge, St Silas, Nunhead, 1982–87; Rural Dean, Camberwell, 1984–87; Vicar, St Edward, New Addington, 1987–94; Selection Sec., 1994–97, Sen. Selection Sec., 1997–2000, ABM, subseq. Ministry Div., Archbishops' Council. *Recreations:* opera, holidays in Italy, Coronation Street. *Address:* 32 Falmouth Road, Truro, Cornwall TR1 2HX. *T:* (01872) 273190.

ST HELENA, Bishop of, since 1999; **Rt Rev. John William Salt,** OGS; *b* 30 Oct. 1941; *s* of William Edward and Jenny Salt. *Educ:* Kelham Theol Coll.; London Univ. (DipTh). Ordained deacon, 1966, priest, 1967; Curate, St Matthew's, Barrow-in-Furness, 1966–69; dio. of Lesotho, 1970–77; dio. of Kimberley and Kuruman, 1977–89; Dean of Zululand, 1989–99. *Recreations:* music, walking, reading. *Address:* Bishopsholme, PO Box 62, Island of St Helena, South Atlantic Ocean. *T:* 4471, *Fax:* 4330.

ST HELENS, 2nd Baron *cr* 1964; **Richard Francis Hughes-Young;** *b* 4 Nov. 1945; *s* of 1st Baron St Helens, MC, and Elizabeth Agnes (*d* 1956), *y d* of late Captain Richard Blakiston-Houston; *S* father, 1980; *m* 1983, Mrs Emma R. Talbot-Smith; one *s* one *d*. *Educ:* Nautical College, Pangbourne. *Heir: s* Henry Thomas Hughes-Young, *b* 7 March 1986.

ST JOHN, family name of **Earl of Orkney** of **Viscount Bolingbroke** and of **Baron St John of Bletso**.

ST JOHN, Lord; Michael John Paulet; *b* 31 Aug. 1999; *s* and *heir* of Earl of Wiltshire, *qv*.

ST JOHN OF BLETSO, 21st Baron *cr* 1558; **Anthony Tudor St John;** Bt 1660; financial consultant to Merrill Lynch, London, since 1989; Chairman: Eurotrust International, since 1993; Spiritel plc, since 2004; Equest Balkan Properties plc, since 2005; Chairman, Governing Board, Certification International, since 1995; solicitor; *b* 16 May 1957; *s* of 20th Baron St John of Bletso, TD, and of Katharine, *d* of late A. G. von Berg; *S* father, 1978; *m* 1994, Dr Helen Westlake; two *s* two *d*. *Educ:* Diocesan College, Rondebosch, Cape; Univ. of Cape Town (BSocSc 1977, BA (Law) 1978); Univ. of S Africa (BProc 1982); London Univ. (LLM 1983). Man. Dir, Globix Corp., 1998–2002; Consultant to Globix Europe. Non-exec. Dir, Regal Petroleum plc, 2003–. An Extra Lord-in-Waiting to the Queen, 1998–. Cross-bencher in House of Lords, specific interests foreign affairs, envmtl protection, sport, financial services, European monetary union, IT. Vice Chm., Parly South Africa Gp; Member: EU Select Cttee A on Trade, Finance and Foreign Affairs, 1996–99, 2001–; EU Sub Cttee B, 2003–; elected Mem., H of L, 1999. Pres., Friends of Television Trust for the Envmt. Trustee: Tusk; M'Afrika Tikkun; Citizens online, 2000–. *Recreations:* golf, tennis and ski-ing; bridge. *Heir: s* Hon. Oliver Beauchamp St John, *b* 11 July 1995. *Address:* c/o House of Lords, SW1A 0AA. *Clubs:* Hurlingham; Royal Cape Golf, Sunningdale Golf.

ST JOHN OF FAWSLEY, Baron *cr* 1987 (Life Peer), of Preston Capes in the County of Northamptonshire; **Norman Antony Francis St John-Stevas;** PC 1979; FRSL 1966; Master, Emmanuel College, Cambridge, 1991–96, Life Fellow, 1996; Chairman: Royal Fine Art Commission, 1985–99; Royal Fine Art Commission Educational Trust, since 1985; Sky Arts, since 2007; Grand Bailiff and Head of the Military and Hospitaller Order of St Lazarus of Jerusalem in England and Wales, since 2000; author, barrister and journalist; *b* London, 18 May 1929; *o s* of late Stephen S. Stevas, civil engineer and company director, and late Kitty St John O'Connor; unmarried. *Educ:* Ratcliffe; Fitzwilliam, Cambridge (Hon. Fellow 1991); Christ Church, Oxford; Yale. Scholar, Clothworkers Exhibnr, 1946, 1947; BA (Cambridge) (1st cl. hons in law), 1950, MA 1954; President, Cambridge Union, 1950; Whitlock Prize, 1950; MA 1952, BCL 1954 (Oxon); Sec. Oxford Union, 1952; DLitt Oxon 1994; LittD Cantab, 1994. Barrister, Middle Temple, 1952; Blackstone and Harmsworth schol., 1952; Blackstone Prize, 1953. Lecturer, Southampton University, 1952–53, King's Coll., London, 1953–56, tutored in jurisprudence, Christ Church, 1953–55, and Merton, 1955–57, Oxford. Founder member, Inst. of Higher European Studies, Bolzano, 1955; PhD (Lond.) 1957; Yorke Prize, Cambridge Univ., 1957; Fellow Yale Law School, 1957; Fulbright Award, 1957; Fund for the Republic Fellow, 1958; Dr of Sc. of Law (Yale), 1960; Lecture tours of USA, 1958–68. Regents' Prof., Univ. of California at Santa Barbara, 1969; Regents' Lectr, Univ. of Calif at La Jolla, 1984. Legal Adviser to Sir Alan Herbert's Cttee on book censorship, 1954–59; joined The Economist, 1959, to edit collected works of Walter Bagehot and became legal, ecclesiastical and political correspondent. Contested (C) Dagenham, 1951; MP (C) Chelmsford, 1964–87. Mem. Shadow Cabinet, 1974–79, and Opposition Spokesman on Educn, 1975–78, Science and the Arts, 1975–79; Shadow Leader of the House, 1978–79; Parly Under-Sec. of State, DES, 1972–73; Min. of State for the Arts, DES, 1973–74; Chancellor of the Duchy of Lancaster, Leader of the House of Commons and Minister for the Arts, 1979–81. Sec., Cons. Parly Home Affairs Cttee, 1969–72; Vice-Chm., Cons. Parly N Ireland Cttee, 1972–74; Mem. Executive, Cons. Parly 1922 Cttee, 1971–72 and 1974; Vice Chm., Cons. Group for Europe, 1972–75; Member: Cons. Nat. Adv. Cttee on Policy, 1971; Fulbright Commission, 1961; Parly Select Cttee: on Race Relations and Immigration, 1970–72; on Civil List, 1971–73; on Foreign Affairs, 1983–89; Deleg., Council of Europe and WEU, 1967–71; Head, British delegn to Helsinki Cultural Forum, Budapest, 1985. Chm., New Bearings for the Re-Establishment, 1970–. Dir, Sky TV, 1991. Hon. Sec., Fedn of Cons. Students, 1971–73, Hon. Vice-Pres. 1973. Chm., Booker McConnell Prize, 1985. Mem. Council: RADA, 1983–88; Nat. Soc. for Dance, 1983–; Nat. Youth Theatre, 1983– (Patron, 1984–); RCA, 1985–; Mem., Pontifical Council for Culture, 1987–92; Patron, Medieval Players, 1984–89; Dir, N. M. Rothschild Trust, 1990–98; Trustee: Royal Philharmonic Orch., 1985–88; Philharmonic Orch., 1988–; Royal Soc. of Painters in Watercolours, 1984; Decorative Arts Soc., 1984–. Editor The Dublin (Wiseman) Review, 1961. Vice Pres., Les Amis de Napoléon III, 1974; Mem., Académie du Second Empire, 1975. Hon. FRIBA 1990; Presidential Fellow, Aspen Inst., 1980; Hon. Fellow, St Edmund's College, Cambridge, 1985. Romanes Lectr, Oxford, 1987. DD (*hc*) Univ. of Susquehanna, Pa, 1983; DLitt (*hc*): Schiller Univ., 1985; Bristol Univ., 1988; Hon. LLD: Leicester, 1991; Notre Dame, 1999; Hon. DArts De Montfort, 1996. Silver Jubilee Medal, 1977. SBStJ. Gran Ufficiale, Order of Merit (Italian Republic), 1989 (Commendatore, 1965). GCLJ 1976 (KLJ 1963). *Publications:* Obscenity and the Law, 1956; Walter Bagehot, 1959; Life, Death and the Law, 1961; The Right to Life, 1963; Law and Morals, 1964; The Literary Works of Walter Bagehot, vols I, II, 1966, The Historical Works, vols III, IV, 1968, The Political Works, vols V, VI, VII and VIII, 1974, The Economic Works, vols IX, X and XI, 1978, Letters and Miscellany, vols XII, XIII, XIV and XV, 1986; The Agonising Choice, 1971; Pope John Paul II, his travels and mission, 1982; The Two Cities, 1984; contrib. to: Critical Quarterly, Modern Law Review, Criminal Law Review, Law and Contemporary Problems, Twentieth Century, Times Lit. Supp., Dublin Review. *Recreations:* reading, talking, listening (to music), travelling, walking, appearing on television, sleeping. *Address:* Chacombe House, Chacombe Park, Banbury, Oxon OX17 2SL; The Penthouse, 15 North Court, Great Peter Street, SW1P 3LL. *T:* (020) 7222 1066; Emmanuel College, Cambridge CB2 3AP; House of Lords, SW1A 2PW. *T:* (020) 7219 3199. *Clubs:* White's, Garrick, Pratt's, Arts (Hon. Mem., 1980), The Other; Hawks (Cambridge) (Hon. Mem., 1993); Emmanuel Boat (Pres., 1993–2006).

ST JOHN, Rt Rev. Andrew Reginald; Rector, Church of the Transfiguration, New York, since 2005; *b* 16 Feb. 1944; *s* of Reginald and Leila St John. *Educ:* Wesley Coll., Melbourne; Melbourne Univ. (LLB 1966); Trinity Coll., Melbourne (ThSchol 1971); Gen. Theol Seminary, New York (STM 1984). Barrister and solicitor, Supreme Court of Victoria, 1967. Ordained priest, 1972; Precentor, St Paul's Cathedral, Melbourne, 1975–78; Vicar: St Mary's, E Chadstone, 1978–84; Holy Trinity, Kew, 1984–95; an Asst Bp, dio. of Melbourne (Bp of the Western Region), 1995–2001. Hon. DD Gen. Theol

Seminary, NY, 1995. *Recreations:* reading, gardening, opera. *Address:* 1 East 29th Street, New York, NY 10016, USA. *T:* (212) 6843275. *Clubs:* Melbourne, Melbourne Cricket (Melbourne); Players (NY).

ST JOHN, Lauren; freelance writer, since 1987; *b* 21 Dec. 1966; *d* of Errol Antonie Kendall and Margaret May Dutton Kendall. *Educ:* Roosevelt High Sch., Harare, Zimbabwe; Harare Poly. (Dip. Journalism). Sub-editor, Resident Abroad magazine, 1987; journalist, Today's Golfer, 1988–89; Golf Correspondent, Sunday Times, 1994–98. Mem., Assoc. of Golf Writers, 1989–. *Publications:* Shooting at Clouds: inside the European golf tour, 1991; Seve: the biography, 1993, 2nd edn 1997; Out of Bounds: inside professional golf, 1995; Greg Norman: the biography, 1998; Walkin' After Midnight: a journey to the heart of Nashville, 2000; Hardcore Troubadour: the life and near death of Steve Earle, 2002; articles in Sunday Times, Independent. *Recreations:* music, art, literature, golf, horse riding, green issues.

ST JOHN, Oliver Beauchamp, CEng, FRAeS; Chief Scientist, Civil Aviation Authority, 1978–82; *b* 22 Jan. 1922; 2nd *s* of late Harold and Ella Margaret St John; *m* 1945, Eileen (*née* Morris); three *s*. *Educ:* Monkton Combe Sch.; Queens' Coll., Cambridge (MA); London Univ. (External) (BSc). Metropolitan Vickers, Manchester, 1939; Royal Aircraft Estabt, Farnborough, from 1946, on automatic control of fixed-wing aircraft and helicopters; Supt, Blind Landing Experimental Unit, RAE, Bedford, 1966; Director of Technical Research & Development, CAA, 1969–78. Queen's Commendation for Valuable Services in the Air, 1956. *Publication:* A Gallimaufry of Goffering: a history of early ironing implements, 1982. *Recreations:* mountaineering, early music, familiy history research. *Address:* The Old Stables, Manor Farm Lane, East Hagbourne OX11 9ND. *T:* (01235) 818437.

See also P. R. T. St John.

ST JOHN, Peter Rowland Tudor; Partner, Caruso St John Architects, since 1991; *b* 27 June 1959; *s* of Oliver St John, *qv*; *m* 1988, Siw Thomas; two *s* one *d*. *Educ:* University Coll. London (BSc Hons); AA Dip. Hons 1984. Major projects include: New Art Gall., Walsall, 2000; extn to Hallfield Sch., Paddington, 2005; Gagosian Gall., King's Cross, 2005; extn to V&A Mus. of Childhood, 2006; Tate Britain improvements, 2006–; Chiswick House regeneration, 2006–. Sen. Lectr, Poly. of N London, 1990–97; Course Tutor, Grad. Sch. of Design, Harvard Univ., 2005–06. Visiting Professor: Acad. of Architecture, Mendrisio, 1999–2001; Dept of Architecture and Civil Engrg, Univ. of Bath, 2001–04; Guest Prof., ETH Zurich, 2007–June 2009. Hon. DDes Wolverhampton, 2001. *Recreations:* architecture, walking, visiting exhibitions of contemporary art, visiting landscape gardens. *Address:* Caruso St John Architects, 1 Coate Street, E2 9AG.

ST JOHN-MILDMAY, Sir Walter (John Hugh), 11th Bt *cr* 1772, of Farley, Southampton; *b* 3 Sept. 1935; *s* of Michael Paulet St John-Mildmay (*d* 1993), *gggs* of Sir Henry Paulet St John-Mildmay, 3rd Bt, and Joan Elizabeth (*née* Stockley; *d* 1977); *S* kinsman, Rev. Sir (Aubrey) Neville St John-Mildmay, 10th Bt, who *d* 1955, after which Btcy was dormant until revived, 1998. *Educ:* Wycliffe Coll.; Emmanuel Coll., Cambridge (BA 1958); Hammersmith Coll. of Art and Building; RAC Cirencester. *Heir: b* Michael Hugh Paulet St John-Mildmay [*b* 28 Sept. 1937; *m* 1965, Mrs Crystal Margaret Ludlow; two *s* one *d*]. *Address:* 9 Lansdown Crescent, Bath BA1 5EX.

ST JOHN PARKER, Michael, MA (Cantab); Headmaster, Abingdon School, Oxfordshire, 1975–2001; *b* 21 July 1941; *s* of Rev. Canon J. W. Parker; *m* 1965, Annette Monica Ugle; two *s* two *d*. *Educ:* Stamford Sch.; King's Coll., Cambridge. Asst Master: Sevenoaks Sch., 1962–63; King's Sch., Canterbury, 1963–69; Winchester Coll., 1969–75; Head of History Dept, Winchester Coll., 1970–75. Schoolmaster Student, Christ Church, Oxford, 1984. Member: Council, Hansard Soc., 1972–2003 (Exec. Cttee, 2001–03); Marsh Cttee on Politics and Industry, 1978–79. Chm., Midland Div., HMC, 1984; Member: Exec. Cttee, Assoc. of Governing Bodies of Ind. Schs., 2002–08; Council, Nat. Trust, 2008– (Mem., Stowe Adv. Cttee, 2002–). Governor: St Helen's Sch., 1975–83; Christ Church Cathedral Sch., 1981–; Cokethorpe Sch., 1985– (Chm., 1990–); Josca's Sch., 1988–98; Hatherop Castle Sch., 2002– (Chm., 2003–); Walsall Acad. (formerly Walsall City Acad.), 2003–; Midhurst Acad., 2008–. Fellow, Winchester Coll., 2006. Dir, Bampton Classical Opera, 2005–. Master, Civic Guild of Old Mercers, 2004–05. *Publications:* The British Revolution—Social and Economic History 1750–1970, 1972; The Martlet and the Griffen, 1997; contributing ed., Attain mag.; various pamphlets and articles, incl. contribs to Oxford DNB. *Recreations:* old buildings, music, books, gardens. *Address:* Exeter House, Cheapside, Bampton, Oxfordshire OX18 2JL. *Clubs:* Athenæum; Leander.

ST JOHNSTON, Colin David; Director, Ocean Transport and Trading Ltd, 1974–88; *b* 6 Sept. 1934; *s* of Hal and Sheilagh St Johnston; *m* 1958, Valerie Paget; three *s* one *d*. *Educ:* Shrewsbury Sch.; Lincoln Coll., Oxford. Booker McConnell Ltd, 1958–70; Ocean Transport and Trading Ltd, 1970–88: Dep. Gp Chief Exec., 1985–88; Man. Dir, Ocean Cory, 1976–85; Non-exec. Dir, FMC plc, 1981–83; Man. Dir, PRO NED, 1989–95. Mem. Council: Royal Commonwealth Society for the Blind, 1967–95; Industrial Soc., 1981–96; Trustee, Frances Mary Buss Foundn, 1981–95; Governor: Camden Sch., 1974–96; Arnold House Sch., 1993–2005 (Chm., 1995–2004). FRSA. *Recreations:* music, Real and lawn tennis. *Address:* 30 Fitzroy Road, NW1 8TY. *T:* (020) 7722 5932. *Club:* MCC.

See also R. D. St Johnston.

ST JOHNSTON, Daniel; *see* St Johnston, R. D.

St JOHNSTON, Prof. (Robert) Daniel, PhD; FRS 2005; Professor of Developmental Genetics, University of Cambridge, since 2003; Bye Fellow, Peterhouse, Cambridge, since 1995; Wellcome Trust Principal Fellow, Wellcome Trust/Cancer Research UK Institute of Cancer and Developmental Biology, since 1997; *b* 24 April 1960; *s* of Colin St Johnston, *qv*; partner, Bénédicte Sanson; one *s* one *d*. *Educ:* Christ's Coll., Cambridge (BA 1st cl. (Natural Scis) 1981); Harvard Univ. (PhD (Cellular and Develtl Biol.) 1988). EMBO Post-doctoral Fellow, Max-Planck Inst., Tübingen, Germany, 1988–91; Wellcome Trust Sen. Fellow, Wellcome/CRC Inst. of Cancer and Develtl Biol., and Dept of Genetics, Cambridge Univ., 1991–97. Loeb Fellow, Woods Hole Marine Biol. Lab., 1982; Fellow, EMBO, 1997 (Gold Medal, 2000). Member, Editorial Advisory Board: Development, 1999–; EMBO Jl, 1999–. *Publications:* numerous papers in jls on anterior-posterior axis formation in Drosophila, how cells become polarized, and mechanism of messenger RNA localization. *Recreations:* cryptic crosswords, hill walking, cooking. *Address:* Wellcome Trust/Cancer Research UK Gurdon Institute, Tennis Court Road, Cambridge CB2 1QR. *T:* (01223) 334127.

ST LEGER, family name of **Viscount Doneraile**.

ST LEVAN, 4th Baron *cr* 1887; **John Francis Arthur St Aubyn,** OBE 2004; DSC 1942; DL; Bt 1866; Vice Lord-Lieutenant of Cornwall, 1992–94; *b* 23 Feb. 1919; *s* of 3rd Baron St Levan, and Hon. Clementina Gwendolen Catharine Nicolson (*d* 1995), *o d* of 1st Baron Carnock; *S* father, 1978; *m* 1970, Susan Mary Marcia (*d* 2003), *d* of late Maj.-Gen. Sir John Kennedy, GCMG, KCVO, KBE, CB. *Educ:* Eton Coll.; Trinity Coll., Cambridge (BA). Served RNVR, 1940–46 (Lieut). Admitted a Solicitor, 1948. Administrator for Nat. Trust, St Michael's Mount, 1976–2003. President: Friends of Plymouth City Museums and Art Gallery, 1985–2000; St Ives Soc. of Artists, 1979–; Penwith NT Assoc., 1987–2007; Penwith and Isles of Scilly Dist Scout Council, 1991–; W Cornwall Br., STA, 1994–; Vice President: Royal Bath and West and Southern Counties Soc., 1984– (Pres., 1983); Royal Cornwall Agricl Assoc., 1980– (Pres., 1979); Minack Theatre, 1989–; London Cornish Assoc., 1997– (Pres., 1987–97); Jt Pres., Cornwall Community Foundn, 2005–; Patron: Penzance YMCA; Cornwall Br., Normandy Veterans' Assoc.; Truro Naval Assoc., 1995–; West Country Writers' Assoc., 1999–; Nat. Coastwatch Instn, 2000–; Penlee Lifeboat Station, 2008–; former Hon. Patron, Penzance Sea Cadet Corps. High Sheriff of Cornwall, 1974; DL Cornwall, 1977. Bard of Cornwall, 1995. FRSA 1974. KStJ 1998. *Publication:* Illustrated History of St Michael's Mount, 1974. *Recreation:* sailing. *Heir: nephew* James Piers Southwell St Aubyn [*b* 6 June 1950; *m* 1981, Mary Caroline, *yr d* of late Peter Ward Bennett, OBE; two *s* two *d*]. *Address:* 8 St Mary's Terrace, Penzance, Cornwall TR18 4DZ. *Clubs:* Brooks's; Royal Yacht Squadron.

See also N. F. St Aubyn.

ST OSWALD, 6th Baron *cr* 1885, of Nostell, co. York; **Charles Rowland Andrew Winn;** DL; landowner; *b* 22 July 1959; *s* of 5th Baron St Oswald and of Charlotte Denise Eileen Winn, *d* of Wilfred Haig Loyd; *S* father, 1999; *m* 1985, Louise Alexandra, *yr d* of Stewart Mackenzie Scott; one *s* one *d*. *Educ:* New Sch., King's Langley. DL W Yorks, 2004. *Recreations:* shooting, walking. *Heir: s* Hon. Rowland Charles Sebastian Henry Winn, *b* 15 April 1986. *Address:* Nostell Priory Estate Office, Doncaster Road, Nostell, Wakefield, W Yorkshire WF4 1AB. *T:* (01924) 862221.

ST PAUL'S, Dean of; *see* Knowles, Rt Rev. G. P.

ST VINCENT, 8th Viscount *cr* 1801; **Edward Robert James Jervis;** *b* 12 May 1951; *er s* of 7th Viscount St Vincent and of Phillida (*née* Logan); *S* father, 2006; *m* 1977, Victoria Margaret, *o d* of Wilton Joseph Oldham; one *s* one *d*. *Educ:* Radley. *Heir: s* Hon. James Richard Anthony Jervis, *b* 1982.

SAINTY, Sir John Christopher, KCB 1986; Clerk of the Parliaments, 1983–90, retired; *b* 31 Dec. 1934; *s* of late Christopher Lawrence Sainty and Nancy Lee Sainty (*née* Miller); *m* 1965, (Elizabeth) Frances Sherlock; three *s*. *Educ:* Winchester Coll.; New Coll., Oxford (MA). FSA; FRHistS. Clerk, Parlt Office, House of Lords, 1959; seconded as Private Sec. to Leader of House and Chief Whip, House of Lords, 1963; Clerk of Journals, House of Lords, 1965; Res. Asst and Editor, Inst. of Historical Research, 1970; Reading Clerk, House of Lords, 1974. Mem., Royal Commn on Historical MSS, 1991–2002. Institute of Historical Research: Sen. Res. Fellow, 1994; Hon. Fellow, 2000–. *Publications:* Treasury Officials 1660–1870, 1972; Officials of the Secretaries of State 1660–1782, 1973; Officials of the Boards of Trade 1660–1870, 1974; Admiralty Officials 1660–1870, 1975; Home Office Officials, 1782–1870, 1975; Colonial Office Officials 1794–1870, 1976; (with D. Dewar) Divisions in the House of Lords: an analytical list 1685–1857, 1976; Officers of the Exchequer, 1983; A List of English Law Officers, King's Counsel and Holders of Patents of Precedence, 1987; The Judges of England 1272–1990, 1993; (with R. O. Bucholz) Officials of the Royal Household 1660–1837, vol. 1 1997, vol. 2 1998; Peerage Creations 1649–1800, 1998; articles in Eng. Hist. Rev., Bull. Inst. Hist. Research. *Address:* 22 Kelso Place, W8 5QG. *T:* (020) 7937 9460. *Club:* Brooks's.

SAINZ MUÑOZ, Most Rev. Faustino; Apostolic Nuncio to the Court of St James's, since 2005; *b* 5 June 1937; *s* of Manuel Sainz and Luisa Muñoz. *Educ:* Colegio de Nuestra Señora del Prado, Ciudad-Real; Colegio de Nuestra Señora del Pilar, Madrid; Univ. Central de Madrid (Lic. in Law 1958); Pontifical Univ., Salamanca (Lic. in Theology 1965); Pontifical Lateran Univ. (DCnL 1969). Ordained priest, 1964; priest, dio. of Madrid, 1965–67: parish priest, Somosierra, 1965–66; Prof. of Religion, Faculty of Law, 1965–67; asst priest, Parish of Conception of Our Lady, Madrid, 1966–67; Counsellor to young Catholic students at the univ., 1966–67; trng, Pontifical Ecclesiast. Acad., Rome, 1967–69; entered Diplomatic Service of Holy See, 1970; served in: Senegal, for French speaking W Africa, 1970–72; Denmark, and other countries of Scandinavia, 1972–75; Secretariat of State, 1975–88; Titular Archbishop of Novaliciana and Apostolic Pro-Nuncio to Cuba, 1988–92; Apostolic Nuncio: Zaire, 1992–97, then Dem. Rep. of Congo, 1997–99; EC, Brussels, 1999–2004. *Address:* The Apostolic Nunciature, 54 Parkside, Wimbledon, SW19 5NE. *T:* (020) 8944 7189, *Fax:* (020) 8947 2494; *e-mail:* nuntius@globalnet.co.uk.

SAKER, Andrew Stephen G.; *see* Gordon-Saker.

SAKMANN, Prof. Bert, MD; Director, Department of Cell Physiology, Max-Planck-Institut für medizinische Forschung, Heidelberg, 1989–2008; Group Leader, Max-Planck-Institut für Neurobiologie, Martinsried, since 2008; Professor of Physiology, Medical Faculty, University of Heidelberg, 1990; *b* Stuttgart, 12 June 1942; *m* 1970, Dr Christiane Wülfert; two *s* one *d*. *Educ:* Univ. of Tübingen; Univ. of Munich; University Hosp., Munich; Univ. of Göttingen (MD). Research Asst, Max-Planck-Institut für Psychiatrie, Munich, 1969–70; British Council Fellow, Dept of Biophysics, UCL, 1971–73; Max-Planck-Institut für biophysikalische Chemie, University of Göttingen: Res. Asst, 1974–79; Res. Associate, Membrane Biology Gp, 1979–82; Head, Membrane Physiology Unit, 1983–85; Dir 1985–87, Prof. 1987–89, Dept of Cell Physiology. Lectures: Yale, 1982; Washington Univ., Seattle, 1986, 1990; Univ. of Miami, 1989; Liverpool Univ., 1990; Univ. of Rochester, NY, 1991. Foreign Member: Royal Soc., 1994; Nat. Acad., USA, 1993. Numerous prizes and awards; (jtly) Nobel Prize for Physiology, 1991. *Publications:* (contrib.) The Visual System: neurophysiology, biophysics and their clinical applications, 1972; (contrib.) Advances in Pharmacology and Therapeutics, 1978; (contrib. and ed with E. Neher) Single Channel Recording, 1983; (contrib.) Membrane Control of Cellular Activity, 1986; (contrib.) Calcium and Ion Channel Modulation, 1988; (contrib.) Neuromuscular Junction, 1989; numerous articles in jls incl. Annual Rev. Physiol., Jl Physiol., Nature, Proc. Nat. Acad. Scis, Pflügers Archiv., Jl Exptl Physiol., Neuron, FEBS Lett., Science, Eur. Jl Biochem., Proc. Royal Soc., Jl Cell Biol. *Recreations:* tennis, ski-ing, music, reading. *Address:* Max-Planck-Institut für Neurobiologie, Am Klopferspitz 18, 82152 Planegg-Martinsried, Germany.

SAKO, Prof. Mari, PhD; Professor of Management Studies, University of Oxford, since 1997; Fellow, New College, Oxford, since 2007; *b* Japan, 12 June 1960; *d* of Kanzo Sako and Akemi Sako; *m* 1983, Sumantra Chakrabarti (*see* Sir S. Chakrabarti); one *d*. *Educ:* Lady Margaret Hall, Oxford (BA Hons); London Sch. of Econs (MSc); PhD London 1990. Researcher, Technical Change Centre, London, 1984–86; London School of Economics and Political Science: Lectr in Modern Japanese Business, 1987–92; Lectr in Industrial Relns, 1992–94; Reader, 1994–97; Fellow, Templeton Coll., Oxford, 1997–2007. Fellow, Japanese Soc. for Promotion of Sci., Kyoto Univ., 1992; Japan Foundn Fellow, Tokyo Univ., 1997. *Publications:* (with R. Dore) How the Japanese Learn to Work, 1989, rev. edn 1998; Prices, Quality and Trust: inter-firm relations in Britain and Japan, 1992;

(ed with H. Sato) Japanese Labour and Management in Transition, 1997; (jtly) Are Skills the Answer?, 1998; Shifting Boundaries of the Firm, 2006. *Recreation:* music. *Address:* Saïd Business School, University of Oxford, Park End Street, Oxford OX1 1HP. *T:* (01865) 288925.

SALAS, Dame Margaret Laurence, (Dame Laurie), DBE 1988; QSO 1982; *b* 8 Feb. 1922; *d* of Sir James Lawrence Hay, OBE and late Davidina Mertel (*née* Gunn); *m* 1946, Dr John Reuben Salas, FRCSE, FRACS; two *s* four *d*. *Educ:* Christchurch; Univ. of New Zealand (BA). Teacher, audiometrist in Med. practice. National Council of Women of NZ: legislative and parly work; Nat. Sec., 1976–80; Nat. Vice-Pres., 1982–86; Vice-Convener, Internat. Council, Women's Cttee on Develt, 1985–94; Nat. Sec., Women's Internat. League for Peace and Freedom, 1985–90; Pres., UNA, NZ, 1988–92; Vice-Pres., World Fedn of UNAs, 1993–2000; Member: Public Adv. Cttee, Disarmament and Arms Control, 1987–96; Nat. Cons. Cttee on Disarmament (Chair, 1979–90); Adv. Cttee, External Aid and Develt, 1986–88; Educn Cttee, Alcoholic Liquor Adv. Council, 1976–81; Nat. Review Cttee on Social Studies, Educn Dept; Cttee, SCF, 1970–76; Nat. Commn, UN Internat. Year of the Child, 1978–80; UN Internat. Year of Peace, Aotearoa Cttee (Vice-Chair, 1986); NZ Cttee, Council for Security and Co-operation in Asia and Pacific, 1994–2007. Hon. Vice-Pres., NZ Inst. of Internat. Affairs, 1994–. Pres., Wellington Branch, NZ Fedn of Univ. Women, 1970–72; repr. NZ, overseas meetings. Silver Jubilee Medal, 1977; NZ Commemoration Medal, 1990. *Publication:* Disarmament, 1982. *Recreations:* choral and classical music, enjoying extended family. *Address:* 2 Raumati Terrace, Khandallah, Wellington 4, New Zealand. *T:* (4) 4793415.

See also Sir David Hay, Sir Hamish Hay.

SALEM, Daniel Laurent Manuel; Chairman, The Condé Nast Publications Ltd, London, 1968–97; *b* 29 Jan. 1925; *s* of Raphael Salem and Adriana Gentili di Giuseppe; *m* 1950, Marie-Pierre Arachtingi. *Educ:* Harvard Univ., Cambridge, Mass (BA, MA). Served Free French Forces, 1943–45. Exec. Asst, Lazard Frères & Co., New York, 1946–50; exec. positions, The Condé Nast Publications Inc., New York, 1950–60, Vice-Pres., 1965–86, Dep. Chm., 1986–92; Vice Pres., Banque Paribas, Paris, 1961–65; Chm., Condé Nast International Inc., 1971–91. Chairman: Mercury Selected Trust, 1974–96; Mercury Offshore Selected Trust, 1979–96; Philharmonia Trust Ltd, 1985–92. Officier, Legion of Honour (France), 1997; Commendatore, Order of Merit (Italy), 1988. *Recreations:* music, bridge, chess, golf. *Clubs:* White's, Portland, Beefsteak; Harvard (New York City).

SALES, (Donald) John; gardens consultant; Chief Gardens Adviser, then Head of Gardens, The National Trust, 1974–98; *b* 1 May 1933; *s* of Frederic Donald Sales and Alice Elizabeth (*née* Burrell); *m* 1958, Lyn Thompson; three *s*. *Educ:* Westminster City Sch.; Kent Horticultural Coll.; Royal Botanic Gardens, Kew. MHort (RHS) 1957; FIHort 1984. Lectr in Horticulture, Writtle Agricl Coll., Chelmsford, 1958–70 (Fellow, 1998); Horticulturist (Asst to Gardens Advr), NT, 1971–74. Vice-President: Garden History Soc., 2004–; RHS, 2008–. Medal of Honour, Internat. Castles Inst., 1991; VMH, RHS, 1992; Inst. of Horticulture Award for Outstanding Services to Horticulture, 1996. *Publications:* West Country Gardens, 1980; A Year in the Garden, 2001; contrib. articles in Country Life. *Recreations:* gardening, photography, walking, music, ballet, the arts generally. *Address:* Covertside, Perrott's Brook, Cirencester, Glos GL7 7BW. *T:* (01285) 831537, *T:* and *Fax:* (office) (01285) 831116.

SALES, Hon. Sir Philip James, Kt 2008; **Hon. Mr Justice Sales;** a Judge of the High Court of Justice, Chancery Division, since 2008; *b* 11 Feb. 1962; *s* of Peter and Janet Sales; *m* 1988, Miranda Wolpert; one *s* one *d*. *Educ:* Royal Grammar Sch., Guildford; Churchill Coll., Cambridge (BA 1983); Worcester Coll., Oxford (BCL 1984). Called to the Bar, Lincoln's Inn, 1985; barrister, 1986–2008; First Treasury Jun. Counsel (Common Law), 1997–2006; Asst Recorder, 1999–2001; Recorder, 2001–08; Dep. High Court Judge, 2004–08; QC 2006; First Treasury Counsel (Common Law), 2006–08. Mem., Panel of Chairmen, Competition Appeal Tribunal, 2008–. *Publications:* (Asst Ed) Halsbury's Laws of England, Vol. I (I), Administrative Law, 4th edn 1989; articles in Cambridge Law Jl, Oxford Jl of Legal Studies, Law Qly Rev., Public Law, Judicial Rev. *Recreations:* theatre, film, reading. *Address:* Royal Courts of Justice, Strand, WC2A 2LL.

SALFORD, Bishop of, (RC), since 1997; **Rt Rev. Terence John Brain;** *b* 19 Dec. 1938; *s* of Reginald John Brain and Mary Cooney. *Educ:* Cotton Coll., North Staffordshire; St Mary's Coll., Oscott, Birmingham. Ordained priest, 1964; Asst Priest, St Gregory's, Longton, 1964–65; mem. of staff, Cotton Coll., 1965–69; Hosp. Chaplain, St Patrick's, Birmingham, 1969–71; Archbishop's Secretary, Birmingham, 1971–82; Parish Priest: Bucknall, Stoke-on-Trent, 1982–88; St Austin's, Stafford, 1988–91; Auxiliary Bishop of Birmingham, 1991–97. RC Bishop for Prisons, 1994–. Chm., RC Bishops' Social Welfare Cttee, 1992–2002. Episcopal Advr, Nat. Council of Lay Assocs, 1993–2006. *Recreations:* crossword puzzles, water colour painting. *Address:* Wardley Hall, Worsley, Manchester M28 2ND.

SALINGER, Jerome David; American author; *b* New York City, 1 Jan. 1919; *m* 1953, Claire Douglas (marr. diss. 1967); one *s* one *d*; *m* Colleen O'Neill. *Educ:* Manhattan public schools; Military Academy, Paris. Served with 4th Infantry Division, US Army, 1942–46 (Staff Sergeant). Travelled in Europe, 1937–38. Started writing at age of 15; first story published, 1940. *Publications:* The Catcher in the Rye, 1951; For Esme-with Love and Squalor, 1953; Franny and Zooey, 1962; Raise High the Roof Beam, Carpenters and Seymour: an Introduction, 1963. *Address:* c/o Harold Ober Associates, 425 Madison Avenue, New York, NY 10017–1110, USA.

SALISBURY, 7th Marquess of, *cr* 1789; **Robert Michael James Gascoyne-Cecil;** PC 1994; DL; Baron Cecil, 1603; Viscount Cranborne, 1604; Earl of Salisbury, 1605; Baron Gascoyne-Cecil (Life Peer), 1999; *b* 30 Sept. 1946; *s* of 6th Marquess of Salisbury and of Marjorie Olein, (Molly), *d* of Captain Hon. Valentine Wyndham-Quin, RN; *S* father, 2003; *m* 1970, Hannah Ann, *er d* of Lt-Col William Joseph Stirling of Keir; two *s* three *d*. *Educ:* Eton; Oxford. MP (C) Dorset South, 1979–87. Summoned to the Upper House of Parliament, 1992, as Baron Cecil, of Essendon in the County of Rutland; Parly Under-Sec. of State for Defence, MoD, 1992–94; Lord Privy Seal and Leader of H of L, 1994–97; Leader of the Opposition, H of L, 1997–98. Chm. Council, RVC, 1998–2007; Chancellor, Univ. of Herts, 2005–. DL Herts, 2007. *Heir: s* Viscount Cranborne, *qv*. *Address:* Hatfield House, Hatfield, Herts AL9 5NF.

SALISBURY, Bishop of, since 1993; **Rt Rev. David Staffurth Stancliffe,** FRSCM; *b* 1 Oct. 1942; *s* of late Very Rev. Michael Staffurth Stancliffe; *m* 1965, Sarah Loveday Smith; one *s* two *d*. *Educ:* Westminster School; Trinity College, Oxford (MA; Hon. Fellow 2003); Cuddesdon Theological College. Assistant Curate, St Bartholomew's, Armley, Leeds, 1967–70; Chaplain to Clifton Coll., Bristol, 1970–77; Canon Residentiary of Portsmouth Cathedral, Diocesan Director of Ordinands and Lay Ministry Adviser, 1977–82; Provost of Portsmouth, 1982–93. Member: Gen. Synod, 1985–; Liturgical Commn, 1986–2005 (Chm., 1993–2005); Cathedrals' Fabric Commn, 1991–2001. Pres., Council, Marlborough Coll., 1994–. FRSCM 2001. Hon. DLitt Portsmouth, 1993; DD Lambeth, 2004. *Publications:* God's Pattern: shaping our worship, ministry and life, 2003; The Pilgrim Prayer Book, 2003; Celebrating Daily Prayer, 2005; The Lion Companion to Church Architecture, 2008. *Recreations:* old music, Italy. *Address:* South Canonry, 71 The Close, Salisbury, Wilts SP1 2ER. *T:* (01722) 334031; *e-mail:* dsarum@salisbury.anglican.org.

See also M. J. Stancliffe.

SALISBURY, Dean of; *see* Osborne, Very Rev. J.

SALISBURY, David Maxwell, CB 2001; FRCP, FRCPCH, FFPH; Director of Immunisation (formerly Principal Medical Officer), Department of Health, since 1986; *b* 10 Aug. 1946; *s* of Dr Steven Salisbury and Judith Grace Vivien Salisbury; *m* 1974, Anne Harvey; one *s* one *d*. *Educ:* Epsom Coll.; Royal London Hosp., Univ. of London (MB BS 1969). FRCP 1992; FRCPCH 1997; FFPH (FFPHM 1998). Sir William Coxen Res. Fellow, Dept of Paediatrics, Univ. of Oxford, 1973–75; Paediatric Registrar, John Radcliffe Hosp., Oxford, 1976–77; Sen. Registrar, Great Ormond Street Hosp. for Children, 1977–85; Consultant Paediatrician, New Cross Hosp., Wolverhampton, 1985–86. Vis. Prof., Dept of Infectious Disease Epidemiology, Imperial Coll., London, 2007–. Chairman: Strategic Adv. Gp of Experts on Immunization, WHO, 2005–; Commn for Certification of Poliomyelitis Eradication, European Region, WHO, 2007–; Co-Chm., Pandemic Influenza Preparedness, G7 Global Health Security Action Gp, 2004–. Freeman, City of London, 1980; Liveryman, Soc. of Apothecaries, 1980–. *Publications:* contrib. jls and textbooks on immunisation, infectious disease, paediatrics and neonatology. *Recreations:* destructive gardening (lawns, logs and hedges), sailing. *Address:* Pound Cottage, Brightwell-cum-Sotwell, Wallingford OX10 0QD. *T:* (01491) 837209.

SALISBURY, David Murray; Head of European Operations, Dimensional Fund Advisors, since 2002 (Director, 1991–96); *b* 18 Feb. 1952; *s* of Norman Salisbury and Isobel Sutherland Murray; *m* 1977, Lynneth Mary Jones; two *d*. *Educ:* Harrow Sch.; Trinity Coll., Oxford (MA). Joined J. Henry Schroder Wagg & Co. Ltd, 1974; Chief Exec., Schroder Capital Management International Inc., 1986–97; Jt Chief Exec., 1995–97, Chm., 1997–2000, Schroder Investment Management Ltd; Dir, Schroders PLC, 1998–2001; Chief Exec., Schroders, 2000–01. Gov., Harrow Sch., 1996–99, 2002–. *Recreations:* tennis, ski-ing. *Address:* The Dutch House, West Green, Hartley Wintney, Hants RG27 8JN.

SALISBURY, John; *see* Caute, J. D.

SALISBURY, Sir Robert (William), Kt 1998; educational consultant, Northern Ireland; consultant to Department for Education and Skills, since 2001; Director of Partnerships, University of Nottingham, 1999–2004; *b* 21 Oct. 1941; *s* of Ernest Arthur Salisbury and Vera Ellen Salisbury; *m* 1975, Rosemary D'Arcy (former Principal, Drumragh Coll., Omagh, NI, now nat. educnl consultant); three *s*. *Educ:* Henry Mellish Sch., Nottingham; Kesteven Trng Coll., Lincs (Teacher's Cert.); Nottingham Univ. (CFPS); Loughborough Univ. (MA). Geography teacher, Holgate Sch., Hucknall, Notts, 1962–64; study in Europe, 1964–66; Second in English, Kimberley Comp. Sch., Notts, 1973–77; Head of Humanities and of 6th Form, Gedling Comp. Sch., Notts, 1977–83; Dep. Head, Alderman White Comp. Sch., Notts, 1983–89; Headteacher, Garibaldi Sch., Mansfield, 1989–99. Vis. Prof., Sch. of Educn, Nottingham Univ., 1998. Chief Examr, JMB/NEAB, 1979–90; tutor, Professional Qualification for Headship, 2000–; Co-Leader, Nat. Coll. of Sch. Leadership (Trainee Heads Scheme), 2000–. Formerly Ind. Chm., NE Lincs Educn Action Zone, 1998–99. Chm., Sherwood Partnership, 1998–2002; Vice-Chair, Integrated Educn Fund, NI, 2003–05. Associate Advr, Industrial Soc., 1992–; Mem. Adv. Council, Carlton Television, 2000–02; Educational Advisor: Centre for British Teaching, 1996–; CfBT Educn Trust, 2003–; QUB, 2006–. Regl Chairman: Teaching Awards Trust, 1998–; Literacy and Numeracy Task Force, NI, 2008–; Chairman, Trustees: Fathers Direct, 1998–2005; Sherwood Coalfield Develt Trust, 1999–2003. Patron, Drugs Abuse Resistance Educn, 2002–. Nat. and internat. speaker, 1992–. FRSA 1998. *Publications:* Series Ed., Humanities textbooks, 1988; Marketing for Schools Guide, 1993; contrib. numerous articles on educational issues, also on fishing and country matters; freelance articles for The Times and TES. *Recreations:* trout and salmon fishing, travel, gardening. *Address:* The Fod, 46 Drumconnelly Road, Omagh, Co. Tyrone BT78 1RT.

SALJE, Prof. Ekhard Karl Hermann, PhD; FRS 1996; FInstP, FGS; Professor of Mineralogy and Petrology, since 1994, and Head of Department of Earth Sciences, since 1998, Cambridge University (Professor of Mineral Physics, 1992–94); President, Clare Hall, Cambridge, 2001–08; *b* Hanover, Germany, 26 Oct. 1946; *s* of Gerhard Salje and Hildegard (*née* Drechsler); *m* 1980, Elisabeth Démaret; one *s* four *d*. *Educ:* Univ. of Hanover (PhD 1972); MA Cantab 1986. FInstP 1996; FGS 1997. University of Hanover: Lectr in Physics, 1972–75; Habilitation in Crystallography, 1975; Prof. of Crystallography, 1978–86; Hd, Dept of Crystallography and Petrology, 1983–86; Mem., Senate, 1980–82; Lectr, Cambridge Univ., 1987–92; Fellow, Darwin Coll., Cambridge, 1987–2001, Hon. Fellow, 2002. Programme Dir, Cambridge-MIT Inst., 2001–03; Chairman: Cambridge Envmtl Initiative, 2003–08; Mgt Cttee, Isaac Newton Inst., Cambridge, 2007–. Chm., Eur. Network on Mineral Transformations, 1997–2001; Mem., Royal Soc. Cttee on Nuclear Waste, 2002. Associate Prof. of Physics, Univ. of Paris, 1981; Prof. invité in Physics, Grenoble Univ., 1990–91; Mombushu Vis. Prof., Nagoya, Japan, 1996; Visiting Professor: Le Mans Univ., France, 1998, 2000; Bilbao Univ., Spain, 1999; Leipzig, 2008. Advr to British, French, German and EU scientific orgns incl. to Max Planck Soc., 1998–. Member: Wissenschaftsrat and German Sci. Foundn, 2006–; Steering Cttee, Eur. Academies Adv. Council, 2006–; Pres., Alexander von Humboldt Assoc., 2004–08. Member Board: Univ. of Hamburg, 2000–08; Max Planck Inst. of Maths, Leipzig, 2001–. Fellow, Leopoldina German Acad. of Natural Sci., 1994. Schlumberger Medal, 1988; G. Werner Medal, 1995, Agricola Medal, 2006, Mineralogical Soc., Germany; Humboldt Prize, Humboldt Foundn, Germany, 1999; Ernst Ising Prize for Physics, Univ. of Hamburg, 2002; Gold Medal for Internat. Relns, Univ. of Hamburg, 2002. Chevalier, Ordre des Palmes Académiques (France), 2003. FRSA 1996. Cross, Order of Merit (Germany), 2007. *Publications:* Physical Properties and Thermodynamic Behaviour of Minerals, 1987; Phase Transitions in ferroelastic and co-elastic crystals, 1991; Application of Landau Theory for the Analysis of Phase Transitions in Minerals, 1992; numerous res. papers in solid state physics, crystallography and mineralogy. *Recreations:* painting, music. *Address:* 59 Glisson Road, Cambridge CB1 2HG.

SALLON, Christopher Robert Anthony; QC 1994; a Recorder, since 1996; *b* 3 May 1948; *s* of late Alexander and Alice Sallon; *m* 1971, Jacqueline Gould; two *s*. Called to the Bar: Gray's Inn, 1973, Bencher, 2002; Eastern Caribbean, 1994; Trinidad and Tobago, 2008. Bar Council: South Eastern Circuit Rep., 1992–94; Member: Professional Conduct Cttee, 1992–93; Public Affairs Cttee, 1994–97; Dir, Public Affairs, 1995–. Fellow, American Bd of Criminal Lawyers, 1997. Mem. Bd, Counsel Magazine, 1995–. *Recreations:* swimming, cycling, music. *Address:* Doughty Street Chambers, 11 Doughty Street, WC1N 2PG. *T:* (020) 7404 1313.

SALMON, Maj. Gen. Andrew, OBE 2004; Commander UK Amphibious Forces, since 2008; *b* Wellington, Shropshire, 2 July 1959; *s* of Gordon John Grant Salmon and Margaret Salmon; *m* 1986, Elizabeth Jane Bolt; one *s* two *d.* *Educ:* Royal Grammar Sch., Guildford; Godalming Sixth Form Coll.; Univ. of Warwick (BA Hons Mod. Hist. 1980); King's Coll. London (MA Defence Studies 1993). Joined RM, 1977; Troop Comdr, 40 Cdo, 1981–83; Platoon Comd, RMA, 1985–87; Batch Officer, Officer Trng Wing, 1987–88; Company Comdr, 45 Cdo, 1989–91; psc 1993; COS Secretariat, MoD, 1997–99; CO, 42 Cdo, 2000–01; Dir Balkans, MoD, 2001–03; Dir Plans, Coalition Mil. Adv. Trng Team, Iraq, 2003; RCDS 2004; ACOS Plans and Resources, Fleet Comd, 2004–06; HCSC 2006; Comdt, Cdo Trng Centre, RM, 2006–08; Comdr, Multi Nat. Div. (SE), Iraq, 2008–. Special Advr, Human Security Study Gp, 2004–. Vis. Sen. Fellow, LSE, 2008–. Vice President: RNRU, 2006–; RNLTA, 2007–; Pres., C Group, 2008–. QCVS 2000. Bronze Star (USA), 2006. *Recreations:* music, walking, cycling, swimming, mountains, ski-ing. *Club:* Tavistock Rugby Football (Vice Pres.).

SALMON, Charles Nathan; QC 1996; *b* 5 May 1950; *s* of His Honour Judge Cyril Salmon, QC and of Patrice Salmon; *m* 1981, Vanessa Clewes; one *s.* *Educ:* Carmel Coll.; University Coll. London (LLB Hons 1971). Travelled through Asia and SE Asia, 1971–73, worked as rubber tapper in Malaysia; called to the Bar, Middle Temple, 1972; volunteer, ME war, 1973; in practice as barrister, 1974–. *Recreations:* reading about Middle East history, 2nd World War and Italian Risorgimento, travel, collecting 18th century Japanese woodcuts and contemporary European paintings. *Address:* 2 Hare Court, Temple, EC4Y 7BH. *T:* (020) 7353 5324, *Fax:* (020) 7353 0667.

SALMON, Michael John; Vice Chancellor, Anglia Polytechnic University, 1992–95, now Emeritus Professor; Chairman, Essex Rivers Healthcare NHS Trust, 1995–2005; *b* 22 June 1936; *o s* of Arthur and May Salmon; *m* 1st, 1958, Angela Cookson (marr. diss. 1973); one *s*; 2nd, 1973, Daphne Bird (*d* 1996); one *s*; 3rd, 1998, Sheila Frances Sisto. *Educ:* Roundhay Sch., Leeds; Leeds Univ.; Leicester Univ. Served RAF, 1957–62; commnd 1957. Teaching posts: Letchworth Coll. of Technology, 1962–65; Leeds Coll. of Technology, 1965–68; Barking Regional Coll., 1968–71; Head of Dept, NE London Poly., 1971–77; Dep. Dir, Chelmer Inst., 1977–83; Dir, Essex Inst., 1983–89; Director: Anglia HEC, 1989–91; Anglia Poly., 1991–92. Member: CNAA, 1970–92; IBA Educn Adv. Council, 1973–81; Electricity Industry Trng Council, 1971–74; PCFC, 1989–93; CBI (Eastern Region) Council, 1990–93; Gen. Optical Council, 1999– (Vice-Chm., 2002–05). Dir, Essex TEC, 1990–93. Member: Court, Essex Univ., 1987–2006; Acad. Cttee, RCM, 1994–2000; Governor: Norwich Sch. of Art and Design, 1996–2001 (Chm. Govs, 1998–2001); King Edward VI GS, Chelmsford, 1995–2001. Director: Proshare, 1991–93; Mid-Essex NHS Hosp. Trust, 1993–95. Mem., Disciplinary Cttee, Royal Pharmaceutical Soc., 2005–. Chm., Tendring Community Develt Forum, 1998–2001. Vice Patron, Helen Rollason Cancer Appeal, 2001–. Mem., Spectacle Makers' Co., 2005–. FCMI (FBIM 1983); FRSA 1984. Hon. Fellow: Limburg Poly., Netherlands, 1993; Fachhochschule für Wirtschaft, Berlin, 1994.

SALMON, Nicholas Robin, FREng, FIMechE; Chief Executive, Cookson Group, since 2004; *b* 13 June 1952; *s* of Keneth Salmon and Winifred Elsie Salmon (*née* Martin); *m* 1976, Deirdre Ann Thompson Hardy; two *d.* *Educ:* Bristol Univ. (BSc (Hons) Mech. Engrg 1973). Grad. trainee, 1969–74, Project Engr, 1974–77, CEGB; Project Manager, China Light and Power Co. Ltd (Hong Kong), 1977–88; Dir and Gen. Manager, Power Station Projects Div., GEC Turbine Generators Ltd, 1988–89; Dep. Man. Dir, Power Stn Projects Div. and Gas Turbine and Diesel Div., GEC Alsthom, 1989–93; Chief Exec., Babcock Internat. Gp plc, 1993–97; Man. Dir, Power Generation Div., GEC Alsthom, 1997–99; Exec. Vice Pres., ABB ALSTOM, subseq. ALSTOM Power, then ALSTOM, 1999–2004. FREng (FEng 1995). *Recreations:* sailing, ski-ing, bridge. *Address:* Cookson Group plc, 165 Fleet Street, EC4A 2AE. *Club:* Royal Hong Kong Yacht.

SALMON, Paul Raymond, FRCPE, FRCP; independent consultant Physician and Gastroenterologist, 1989–2004; *b* 11 July 1936; *s* of late Harold William Salmon and Blanche Percy Salmon (*née* Piper); *m* 1st, 1962 (marr. diss. 1980); one *s* one *d*; 2nd, 1984, Diana Frances Lawrence. *Educ:* Epsom Coll.; Middx Hosp. Sch. of Medicine, Univ. of London (BSc Hons Anatomy 1958). MRCS 1961; MRCPE 1966, FRCPE 1977; MRCP 1967, FRCP 1978. House Physician and House Surgeon, 1962, Casualty MO, 1963–64, Middlesex Hosp.; House Physician, London Chest Hosp., 1963; Sen. House Physician, Ipswich and E Suffolk Hosp., 1964–65; Med. Registrar, Princess Margaret Hosp., Swindon, 1965–66; Res. Registrar in Gastroenterology, Bristol Royal Infirmary, 1967–68; Lectr in Medicine, 1969–73, Sen. Lectr in Medicine, 1974–79, Univ. of Bristol; Hon. Sen. Registrar, United Bristol Hosps, 1969–73; Hon. Consultant Physician, Bristol Health Dist, 1974–79; Consultant Physician, UCH, and Sen. Clin. Lectr in Gastroenterology, Sch. of Medicine, UCL, 1978–89; Consultant Physician, Middlesex Hosp., 1985–89. Annual Foundn Lectr, British Soc. for Digestive Endoscopy, 1979; Poona Orator, Indian Gastroenterology Soc., 1984. FDS Examr, RCS, 1982–88. Pres., Eur. Laser Assoc., 1981–85; Member: British Soc. of Gastroenterology, 1969–2004; Chelsea Clin. Soc., 1986– (Mem. Council, 2000–04); Independent Doctors Forum, 1989–. FRSocMed 1986. Freeman, City of London, 1985; Liveryman: Co. of Farriers, 1986; Soc. of Apothecaries, 1993. Privilegiate *hc* St Hilda's Coll., Oxford, 1996. Several teaching films (Dip., Marburg Film Fest., 1977, Silver Award, BMA Film Competition, 1983). *Publications:* Fibreoptic Endoscopy, 1974; (ed) Topics in Modern Gastroenterology, 1976; (jtly) Radiological Atlas of Biliary and Pancreatic Disease, 1978; (ed) Ranitidine, 1982; (ed) Advances in Gastrointestinal Endoscopy, 1984; (ed) Key Developments in Gastroenterology, 1988; 200 contribs to books, scientific papers and review articles. *Recreations:* golf, music, ski-ing, travel, angling. *Address:* 2d Melbury Road, W14 8LP. *T:* (020) 7602 3311, *Fax:* (020) 7602 2562; *e-mail:* paulsalmon@btinternet.com. *Clubs:* Athenæum, Roehampton; Sunningdale.

SALMON, Peter; Chief Creative Officer, BBC Vision Studios, since 2006; *b* 15 May 1956; *s* of Patrick and Doreen Salmon; three *s*; *m* 2001, Sarah Jane Abigail Lancashire, *qv*; one *s.* *Educ:* Univ. of Warwick (BA English and European Lit.). VSO, 1977; Min. of Overseas Develt, 1978; Chatham News, 1979–81; BBC, 1981–93: Series Producer, Crimewatch UK; Editor, Nature; Exec. Producer, 999, and The Wrong Trousers; Head of TV Features, BBC Bristol; Controller of Factual Programmes, Channel 4, 1993–96; Dir of Programmes, Granada TV, 1996–97; Controller, BBC 1, 1997–2000; Dir of Sport, BBC, 2000–05; Chief Exec., Television Corp., 2005–06. *Recreations:* music, football, cycling, museums. *Address:* BBC Vision Studios, Wood Lane, W12 7RJ.

SALMON, Sarah Jane Abigail; *see* Lancashire, S. J. A.

SALMON, Very Rev. Thomas Noel Desmond Cornwall; Dean of Christ Church, Dublin, 1967–88; *b* Dublin, 5 Feb. 1913; *s* of Francis Allen Cornwall Salmon, BDS, and Emma Sophia, *d* of Dr Hamilton Jolly, Clonroche, Co. Wexford; unmarried. *Educ:* privately; Trinity College, Dublin; BA 1935, MA, BD. Deacon 1937; Priest 1938. Curate Assistant: Bangor, Co. Down, 1937–40; St James' Belfast, 1940–42; Larne, Co. Antrim, 1942–44; Clerical Vicar, Christ Church Cathedral, 1944–45; Curate Assistant, Rathfarnham, Dublin, 1945–50; Incumbent: Tullow, Carrickmines, 1950–62; St Ann, Dublin, 1962–67. Asst Lectr in Divinity School, TCD, 1945–63; Examining Chaplain to Archbishop of Dublin, 1949–96. *Recreations:* in younger days Rugby football (Monkstown FC Dublin) and swimming; now walking, gardening and reading. *Address:* Brabazon House, Gilford Road, Sandymount, Dublin 4, Ireland. *T:* 2800101.

SALMOND, Rt Hon. Alexander Elliot Anderson; PC 2007; MP (SNP) Banff and Buchan, since 1987; Member (SNP) Gordon, Scottish Parliament, since 2007; First Minister, since 2007; Leader, Scottish National Party, 1990–2000 and since 2004; *b* 31 Dec. 1954; *s* of Robert F. F. Salmond and late Mary S. Milne; *m* 1981, Moira F. McGlashan. *Educ:* Linlithgow Acad.; St Andrews Univ. (MA Hons). Govt Econ. Service, 1980; Asst Agricl and Fisheries Economist, DAFS, 1978–80; Energy Economist, Royal Bank of Scotland plc, 1980–87. Scottish National Party: Mem. Nat. Exec., 1981–; Vice-Chair (Publicity), 1985–87; Sen. Vice-Convener (Dep. Leader) (formerly Sen. Vice-Chair), 1987–90. SNP parly spokesperson on energy, treasury and fishing, 1987–88, on economy, energy, environment and poll tax, 1988–97, on constitution and fishing, 1997–2005. Mem. (SNP) Banff & Buchan, Scottish Parlt, 1999–2001; Ldr of the Opposition, 1999–2000. Vis. Prof of Economics, Univ. of Strathclyde, 2003–. *Publications:* articles and conference papers on oil and gas economics; contribs to Scottish Government Yearbook, Fraser of Allander Economic Commentary, Petroleum Review, Opec Bulletin, etc. *Address:* House of Commons, SW1A 0AA; Scottish Parliament, Edinburgh EH99 1SP; 17 Maiden Street, Peterhead, Aberdeenshire AB42 1EE.

SALMOND, Dame Anne; *see* Salmond, Dame M. A.

SALMOND, Prof. George Peacock Copland, PhD; Professor of Molecular Microbiology, University of Cambridge, since 1996; Fellow, Wolfson College, Cambridge, since 2000; *b* 15 Nov. 1952; *s* of John Brown Salmond and Joan Tennant Lambie Salmond (*née* Copland); *m* 1975, Christina Brown Adamson (marr. diss. 1985); partner, Carolyn Ann Alderson; one *d.* *Educ:* Whitburn Primary Sch.; Bathgate Acad.; Whitburn Acad.; Univ. of Strathclyde (BSc 1st cl. Hons Microbiology); Univ. of Warwick (PhD Bacterial Genetics); MA Cantab. Postdoctoral Res. Fellow, Dept of Molecular Biology, Univ. of Edinburgh, 1977–80; Lectr in Microbiology, Biological Lab., Univ. of Kent at Canterbury, 1980–83; Lectr in Microbiology, 1983–89, Sen. Lectr, 1989–93, Prof., 1993–96, Dept of Biological Scis, Univ. of Warwick. Biotechnology and Biological Sciences Research Council: Member: Plants and Microbial Scis Cttee, 1999–2002; Integration Panel, BBSRC Inst. Sci. Quality Assessment, 2001; Cross Cttee Gp on Antimicrobial Res., 2001; Sequencing Panel, 2002–; Plant and Microbial Metabolomics Initiative Sift Panel, 2002; Chairman: Plant and Microbial Scis Cttee 'Natural Products Biology' Steering Gp, 2000–02; Res. Equipment Initiative Cttee, 2002–04; Mem., Plant Panel, 2002, Integration Panel, 2002, and Chm., Plant Panel for Scottish Res. Insts, 2002, Quality of Sci. Assessment Panels, Scottish Exec. Envmt and Rural Affairs Dept; Member: Adv. Bd, NSC Technologies, USA, 1996–2000; Panel for Jt Res. Councils Equipment Initiative, 2001; Pathogen Sequencing Adv. Gp, Wellcome Trust Sanger Inst., 2002–06. Society for General Microbiology: Mem. Council, 1997–2001, 2004–; Convener, Physiol., Biochem. and Molecular Genetics Gp Cttee, 2002–07; Internat. Sec., 2004–; Member Council: Fedn of Eur. Microbiol Socs, 2004–; Sci. Unions Cttee, Royal Soc., 2005–. Member, Governing Body: Wolfson Coll., Cambridge, 2000–; Scottish Crop Res. Inst., 2003– (Sci. Cttee, 2006–); Mem. Governing Council, Dir and Trustee, John Innes Centre, Norwich, 2003–. UK Sen. Ed., Jl of Molecular Microbiology and Biotechnology, 1998–2008; Member Editorial Board: Molecular Microbiology, 1988–97; Molecular Plant Pathology-On Line, 1996–99; Microbiology, 1999–2000; Molecular Plant Pathology, 1999–2002; Associate Editor: European Jl of Plant Pathology, 1992–98; Molecular Plant-Microbe Interactions, 1993–98; Editl Adv. Panel, Future Microbiology, 2006–. Member: Biochem. Soc.; Genetics Soc.; Amer. Soc. of Microbiol.; Soc. for Industrial Microbiol., USA; Soc. for Applied Microbiol.; British Soc. for Antimicrobial Chemotherapy; British Soc. for Plant Pathology. FRSA 2001; Founding Fellow, Inst. of Contemp. Scotland, 2001; Fellow, Cambridge Phil Soc. *Publications:* many res. articles on molecular microbiology and bacterial genetics, incl. studies on bacterial cell div., molecular phytopathology, carbapenem antibiotics, quorum sensing, bacterial virulence and protein secretion in learned jls. *Recreations:* driving, poetry, philosophy, comedy; avoiding hysterical media spins. *Address:* Department of Biochemistry, University of Cambridge, Tennis Court Road, Cambridge CB2 1QW. *T:* (01223) 333650.

SALMOND, Dame (Mary) Anne, DBE 1995 (CBE 1988); PhD; FRSNZ; Distinguished Professor of Social Anthropology and Maori Studies, since 2001, and Pro Vice-Chancellor (Equal Opportunity), since 1997, University of Auckland (Professor of Socal Anthropology and Maori Studies, 1992–2001); *b* 16 Nov. 1945; *d* of Jack Thorpe and Joyce Thorpe; *m* 1971, Jeremy Salmond; two *s* one *d.* *Educ:* Univ. of Auckland (BA 1966; MA 1st cl. 1966); Univ. of Pennsylvania (PhD 1972). FRSNZ 1990. Post-grad. Schol., Univ. of Auckland, 1968; Fulbright Schol., 1969; Nuffield Fellow, 1980–81; Capt. James Cook Fellow, RSNZ, 1987; Caird Fellow, Nat. Maritime Mus., 2004. Henry Myers Lectr, RAI, 1996. Chm., NZ Historic Places Trust, 2002–. Corresp. FBA 2008. Founding Fellow, NZ Acad. of the Humanities, 2007. Elsdon Best Meml Gold Medal, Polynesian Soc., 1976; Wattie Book of Year Awards, 1977, 1981, 1991; Nat. Book Award (non-fiction), 1991, 2004; Ernest Scott Prize, Melbourne Univ., 1992, 1997; NZ Prime Minister's Award for Literary Achievement, 2004. *Publications:* Hui: a study of Maori ceremonial gatherings, 1975, 7th edn 1994; Amiria: the life story of a Maori woman, 1976, 3rd edn 1994; Eruera: the teachings of a Maori Elder, 1980; Two Worlds: first meetings between Maori and Europeans 1642–1772, 1991, 2nd edn 1993; Between Worlds: early Maori-European exchanges 1773–1815, 1997; The Trial of the Cannibal Dog: Captain Cook in the South Seas, 2003. *Recreations:* gardening, tennis, reading, family and friends. *Address:* 14 Glen Road, Devonport, Auckland, New Zealand. *T:* (9) 4452573.

SALOLAINEN, Pertti Edvard; Grand Cross, Order of the Lion of Finland, 1994; MP (C), Helsinki, Parliament of Finland, since 2007; *b* 19 Oct. 1940; *s* of Edvard Paavali Salolainen and Ella Elisabet Salolainen; *m* 1964, Anja Sonninen (*d* 2005); one *s* one *d.* *Educ:* Helsinki Sch. of Economics (MSc Econ 1969). TV newsreader and editor, then producer, 1962–66, London Correspondent, 1966–69, Finnish Broadcasting Co.; London Editor, BBC Finnish Sect., 1966; Head of Dept, Finnish Employers' Confedn, 1969–89. Ambassador of Finland to UK 1996–2004. MP (C), Helsinki, 1970–96; Minister for Foreign Trade, Finland, 1987–95; Dep. Prime Minister of Finland, 1991–95; Ministerial Chm., Finland-EU membership negotiations, 1991–95; Chm., Foreign Affairs Cttee, 2007–. Leader, Conservative Party of Finland, 1991–94. Hon. Founder, WWF Finland, 1972 (Pres., 2006). Major, Mil. Reserve. Freeman, City of London, 1998. Liveryman: Co. of Hackney Carriage Drivers; Co. of Homers. Internat. Conservation Award, WWF, 1990. Grand Cross, Nordstjerna Order (Sweden), 1996; Grand Cross, nat. orders of Germany, Austria, Hungary and Estonia. *Recreations:* nature conservation, nature photography, tennis. *Address:* Parliament of Finland, 00100 Helsinki, Finland. *Clubs:* Athenæum, Travellers.

SALONEN, Esa-Pekka; conductor and composer; Music Director, Los Angeles Philharmonic Orchestra, 1992–Sept. 2009; Principal Conductor and Artistic Adviser,

Philharmonia Orchestra, London, since 2008; *b* 30 June 1958; *s* of Raimo Salonen and Pia Salonen; *m* 1991, Jane Price; one *s* two *d*. *Educ*: Sibelius Acad., Helsinki. Principal Conductor, Swedish Radio Symphony Orch., 1985–95; Artistic Dir, Helsinki Fest., 1995–96. Principal Guest Conductor, Philharmonia Orch., 1985–94. Mem., Royal Swedish Music Acad., 1991; FRCM 1995. Opera Award, 1995, Conductor Award, 1997, Royal Philharmonic Soc.; numerous record and composition awards. Pro Finlandia Medal (Finland), 1992; Litteris et Artibus Medal (Sweden), 1996; Officier de l'ordre des Arts et des Lettres (France), 1998. *Compositions include*: Saxophone Concerto, 1980; Floof, 1982; Giro, 1982–97; YTA I, 1982, II, 1985 and III, 1986; MIMO II, 1992; LA Variations, 1996; Gambit, 1998; Five Images after Sappho, 1999; Mania, 2000; Concert Etude, 2000; Two Songs to Poems of Ann Jäderlund, 2000; Dichotomie, 2000; Foreign Bodies, 2001; Insomnia, 2002; Wing on Wing, 2004; Piano Concerto, 2007. *Address*: Van Walsum Management, The Tower Building, 11 York Road, SE1 7NX. *T*: (020) 7902 0520.

SALOP, Archdeacon of; *see* Hall, Ven. J. B.

SALSBURY, Peter Leslie; Chairman, TR Property Investment Trust, since 2004 (Director, since 1997); Deputy Chairman and Senior Independent Director, Highway Insurance plc, since 2006; Consultant Director, Praesta LLP (formerly The Change Partnership), since 2002; *b* 20 June 1949; *s* of Joseph Leslie Salsbury and Sylvia Olive (*née* Cook); *m* 1987, Susan Elizabeth Gosling; one *s* from previous *m*. *Educ*: Bancroft Sch.; London Sch. of Econs (BSc Econ). Joined Marks & Spencer, 1970: mgt trainee in stores, 1970–73; merchandiser, Head Office, 1973–76; Merchandise Manager, 1976–82; Exec., 1982–85; Sen. Exec., 1985–86; Divisional Director: Homeware Gp, 1986–88; Ladieswear Gp, 1988–90; Dir, Personnel, 1990–93, and Store Ops, 1993–94; Man. Dir, 1994–98; Chief Exec., 1998–2000. Non-exec. Dir, NORWEB plc, 1992–95. Mem., Govt Better Regulation Task Force, 1997–99. Member Council: Inst. of Employment Studies, 1995–2005; C&G, 1997–. *Address*: TR Property Investment Trust, 51 Berkeley Square, W1J 5BB.

SALT, Rear-Adm. James Frederick Thomas George, CB 1991; Director of UK Ship Sales, Vosper Thornycroft, then VT Shipbuilding, 2001–05; *b* 19 April 1940; *s* of Lieut Comdr George Salt (lost in 1939–45 War in command HMS Triad, 1940) and Lillian Bridget Lamb; *m* 1975, Penelope Mary Walker; three *s* (and one *s* decd). *Educ*: Wellington College; RNC Dartmouth (1958–59). Served Far East, Mediterranean, South Atlantic and home waters; commanded HM Sub. Finwhale, 1969–71; 2 i/c HM Sub. Resolution (Polaris), 1973–74; Comd HM Nuclear Sub. Dreadnought, 1978–79; Comd HMS Sheffield, 1982 (sank Falklands); Comd HMS Southampton, 1983; ACOS Ops C-in-C Fleet, 1984–85; Dir, Defence Intell., 1986–87; Sen. Naval Mem., Directing Staff, RCDS, 1988–90; ACNS (Gulf War), 1990–91; Mil. Dep., Defence Export Services, 1992–97. Hd of Marketing, Colebrand Ltd, 1998–2000. Master, Cordwainers' Co., 2000–01. *Recreations*: sailing, stone engraving, painting, gardening. *Address*: Salterns, Birdham Pool, Chichester, West Sussex PO20 7BB.

SALT, Rt Rev. John William; *see* St Helena, Bishop of.

SALT, Sir Michael; *see* Salt, Sir T. M. J.

SALT, Sir Patrick (Macdonnell), 7th Bt *cr* 1869, of Saltaire, Yorkshire; *b* 25 Sept. 1932; *s* of Sir John Salt, 4th Bt and Stella Houlton Jackson (*d* 1974); *S* brother, 1991; *m* 1976, Ann Elizabeth Mary Kilham Roberts, *widow* of Denys Kilham Roberts, OBE. *Educ*: Summer Fields, Oxford; Stowe Sch. Dir, Cassidy Davis Members Agency Ltd, 1983–92. *Recreation*: fishing. *Heir*: cousin Daniel Alexander Salt [*b* 15 Aug. 1943; *m* 1968, Merchide, *d* of Dr Ahmad Emami; two *d*]. *Address*: Hillwatering Farmhouse, Langham, Bury St Edmunds, Suffolk IP31 3ED. *T*: (01359) 259367.

SALT, Sir (Thomas) Michael (John), 4th Bt *cr* 1899; *b* 7 Nov. 1946; *s* of Lt-Col Sir Thomas Henry Salt, 3rd Bt, and of Meriel Sophia Wilmot, *d* of late Capt. Berkeley C. W. Williams and Hon. Mrs Williams, Herringston, Dorchester; *S* father, 1965; *m* 1971, Caroline, *er d* of Henry Hildyard; two *d*. *Educ*: Eton. *Recreations*: cricket, shooting. *Heir*: *b* Anthony William David Salt [*b* 5 Feb. 1950; *m* 1978, Olivia Anne, *yr d* of Martin Morgan Hudson; two *s*]. *Address*: Shillingstone House, Shillingstone, Blandford Forum, Dorset DT11 0QR. *Club*: Boodle's.

SALTER, Ian George; Director, Tilney Private Wealth Management (formerly Tilney Investment Management), 2003–07; *b* Hobart, Tasmania, 7 March 1943; *s* of Desmond and Diane Salter. *Educ*: Hutchins Sch., Hobart, Tasmania. AASA. Member: Hobart Stock Exchange, 1965–69; London Stock Exchange, 1970–2000; Principal, Strauss Turnbull, subseq. Société Générale Strauss Turnbull (Investment Advisers Ltd), then SG (formerly Socgen) Investment Management Ltd, 1978–2003, Man. Dir, 2001–03; Chm., EmdexTrade, subseq. CCH International plc, 2001–; non-executive Director: Plus Markets Gp plc, 2007–; Pan Hldgs, 2008–. Mem., Stock Exchange Council, 1980–91, subseq. London Stock Exchange Bd, 1991–2004, a Dep. Chm., 1990–2004. DTI Inspector, 1984–87. Mem., Bd, British Youth Opera, 1998–2000. *Recreations*: opera, travel, gardening. *Address*: c/o Tilney Private Wealth Investment Management, Winchester House, 1 Great Winchester Street, EC2N 2DB.

SALTER, Martin John; MP (Lab) Reading West, since 1997; *b* 19 April 1954; *s* of Raymond and Naomi Salter. *Educ*: Univ. of Sussex. Co-ordinator, Reading Centre for Unemployed, 1986; Regl Manager, Co-operative Home Services Housing Assoc., 1987–96. Mem., Reading BC, 1984–96 (Dep. Leader, 1987–96). Contested (Lab) Reading E, 1987. *Address*: House of Commons, SW1A 0AA.

SALTER, Patience Jane; *see* Wheatcroft, P. J.

SALTER, Richard Stanley; QC 1995; a Recorder, since 2000; *b* 2 Oct. 1951; *s* of late Stanley James Salter and Betty Maud Salter (*née* Topsom); *m* 1991, Shona Virginia Playfair Cannon. *Educ*: Harrow County Sch. for Boys; Balliol Coll., Oxford (MA). Inns of Court Sch. of Law. Called to the Bar, Inner Temple, 1975, Bencher, 1991; pupil to Sir Henry Brooke, 1975–76; in practice at Commercial Bar, 1976–; an Asst Recorder, 1997–2000. Chm., London Common Law and Commercial Bar Assoc., 2004–05 (Mem. Cttee, 1986–2001; Vice-Chm., 2001–03). Member: Council of Legal Educn, 1990–96; Advocacy Studies Bd, 1996–2000; (ex-officio) 2004–05, (elected) 2006–, Bar Council; Chairman: Bd of Examnrs for Bar Vocational Course, 1992–93; Scholarships Cttee, Inner Temple, 2002–. Gov., Inns of Court Sch. of Law, 1996–2001; Mem. Adv. Bd, City Univ. Inst. of Law, 2001–. Consulting Ed., All England Commercial Cases, 1999–; Legislation Ed., Encyclopedia of Insurance Law, 2001–04. *Publications*: (contrib.) Banks, Liability and Risk, 1991, 3rd edn 2001; (contrib.) Banks and Remedies, 1992, 2nd edn 1999; Guarantee and Indemnity, Halsbury's Laws of England, Vol. 20, 4th edn 1993; (ed) Legal Decisions Affecting Bankers, vols 12–14, 2001. *Recreations*: books, music, theatre, cricket. *Address*: 3 Verulam Buildings, Gray's Inn, WC1R 5NT. *T*: (020) 7831 8441. *Clubs*: Savile; Shoscombe Village Cricket.

SALTHOUSE, Edward Charles, PhD; CEng, FIET; Master of University College, Durham University, 1979–98; *b* 27 Dec. 1935; *s* of Edward Salthouse, MBE, and Mrs Salthouse (*née* Boyd); *m* 1961, Denise Kathleen Margot Reid; two *s*. *Educ*: Campbell Coll., Belfast; Queen's University of Belfast (BSc, PhD). Lecturer in Electrical Engrg, Univ. of Bristol, 1962–67; University of Durham: Reader in Elec. Engrg Science, 1967–79; Chairman, Board of Studies in Engrg Science, 1976–79; Dean, Faculty of Science, 1982–85; First Chm., School of Applied Science and Engrg, 1985–87; Pro-Vice-Chancellor, 1985–88. Sec., Scottish Industrial Heritage Soc., 1998–. *Publications*: papers on electrical insulation in Proc. IEE and other appropriate jls. *Recreations*: industrial archaeology, photography. *Address*: Shieldaig, Hume, Kelso TD5 7TR.

SALTHOUSE, Leonard; Assistant Under Secretary of State, Ministry of Defence, 1977–87; *b* 15 April 1927; *s* of late Edward Keith Salthouse and Dorothy Annie (*née* Clark); *m* 1950, Kathleen May (*née* Spittle); one *s* one *d*. *Educ*: Queen Elizabeth Grammar Sch., Atherstone, Warwickshire; University Coll. London (BScEcon). Home Civil Service: Asst Principal, Min. of Fuel and Power, 1950–55; Principal, Air Min., then Min. of Defence, 1955–66; Asst Sec., 1966–77. *Recreations*: gardening, music. *Address*: Highfield, 115 Cross Oak Road, Berkhamsted, Herts HP4 3HZ. *T*: (01442) 877809.

SALTON, Prof. Milton Robert James, FRS 1979; Professor and Chairman of Microbiology, New York University School of Medicine, 1964–90, now Emeritus Professor; *b* 29 April 1921; *s* of Robert Alexander Salton and Stella Salton; *m* 1951, Joy Marriott; two *s*. *Educ*: Univ. of Sydney (BSc Agr. 1945); Univ. of Cambridge (PhD 1951, ScD 1967). Beit Meml Res. Fellow, Univ. of Cambridge, 1950–52; Merck Internat. Fellow, Univ. of California, Berkeley, 1952–53; Reader, Univ. of Manchester, 1956–61; Prof. of Microbiology, Univ. of NSW, Australia, 1962–64. Hon. Mem., British Soc. for Antimicrobial Chemotherapy, 1983. Docteur en Médecine, D*hc*, Université de Liège, 1967. *Publications*: Microbial Cell Walls, 1960; The Bacterial Cell Wall, 1964; Immunochemistry of Enzymes and their Antibodies, 1978; β-Lactam Antibiotics, 1981; (ed jtly) Antibiotic Inhibition of Bacterial Cell Surface Assembly and Function, 1988. *Address*: Department of Microbiology, New York University School of Medicine, 550 First Avenue, New York, NY 10016, USA. *Club*: Oxford and Cambridge.

SALTOUN, Lady (20th in line) *cr* 1445, of Abernethy (by some reckonings 21st in line); Flora Marjory Fraser; Chief of the name of Fraser; *b* 18 Oct. 1930; *d* of 19th Lord Saltoun, MC, and Dorothy (*d* 1985), *e d* of Sir Charles Welby, 5th Bt; *S* father, 1979; *m* 1956, Captain Alexander Ramsay of Mar, Grenadier Guards retd (*d* 2000), *o s* of late Adm. Hon. Sir Alexander Ramsay, GCVO, KCB, DSO, and The Lady Patricia Ramsay, CI, VA, CD; three *d*. Elected Mem., H of L, 1999. *Heiress*: *d* Hon. Katharine Ingrid Mary Isabel Fraser [*b* 11 Oct. 1957; *m* 1980, Captain Mark Malise Nicolson, Irish Guards; one *s* two *d*].

SALUSBURY-TRELAWNY, Sir John Barry; *see* Trelawny.

SALVADOR PINHEIRO, João de Deus; *see* Pinheiro.

SALVAGE, Jane Elizabeth; author and international healthcare consultant; *b* 6 Aug. 1953; *d* of Robert Salvage and Patricia Grutchfield; *m* 1995, Nareman Taha Wahab. *Educ*: Newnham Coll., Cambridge (BA Hons); Royal Holloway and Bedford New Coll., London (MSc). RGN 1978: Staff Nurse, London Hosp., 1978–80; worked on British nursing jls, and Ed., Sen. Nurse, 1980–88; Dir, Nursing Develt Prog., King's Fund, London, 1988–91; Regl Advr for Nursing and Midwifery, European Reg., WHO, 1991–95; Editor, 1996–97, Editor-in-Chief, 1997–99, Nursing Times; Nursing Dir, Emap Healthcare, 2000–02. Mem. Bd, Geneva Initiative on Psychiatry, 2001–04. Associate, Newnham Coll., Cambridge, 1993–2004; Visiting Professor: Sheffield Univ., 1999–2004; Florence Nightingale Sch. of Nursing and Midwifery, KCL, 2007–. First Hon. Mem., Romanian Nurses Assoc., 1992. Hon. LLD Sheffield, 1996. *Publications*: The Politics of Nursing, 1985; (ed) Models for Nursing, Vol. 1 1986, Vol. 2 1990; Nurses at Risk, 1988, 2nd edn 1999; (ed) Nurse Practitioners, 1991; (ed) Nursing in Action, 1993; (ed) Nursing Development Units, 1995; (ed) Nursing in Europe, 1997; contrib. numerous articles. *Recreations*: friendship, travel, reading, swimming, cooking and eating, walking, theatre, watching football. *Address*: 2 Church Cottages, Piddinghoe, near Newhaven, E Sussex BN9 9AP.

SALVESEN, (Charles) Hugh, PhD; Ambassador to Uruguay, 2005–08; *b* 10 Sept. 1955; *s* of late John and Eelin Salvesen; *m* 1983, Emilie Maria Ingenhousz; two *s* (one *d* decd). *Educ*: Loretto Sch., Musselburgh; Christ's Coll., Cambridge (MA, PhD). Joined Diplomatic Service, 1982; FCO, 1982–84; First Sec., BMG, Berlin, 1984–85; Bonn, 1985–88; FCO, 1988–93; Argentina, 1993–96; Dep. High Comr, NZ, 1996–2000; Dep. Hd, Econ. Policy Dept, FCO, 2000–02; Hd, Mgt Consultancy, FCO, 2002–05.

SALVIDGE, Paul; Member, Consumer Panel, Financial Services Authority, 2000–06; *b* 22 Aug. 1946; *s* of Herbert Stephen and Winifred Alice Elisabeth Salvidge; *m* 1972, Heather Margaret (*née* Johnson); one *d*. *Educ*: Cardiff High School; Birmingham Univ. (LLB). Ministry of Power, 1967; Dept of Trade and Industry, 1972–2000: Asst Secretary, 1982; Under Sec., 1989; Dir, Employment Relations, 1998–2000; Acting Legal Services Ombudsman, 2002–03.

SALWAY, Francis William; Chief Executive, Land Securities Group plc, since 2004 (Director, since 2001; Chief Operating Officer, 2003–04); *b* 5 Oct. 1957; *m* 1985, Sarah Peplow; one *s* one *d*. *Educ*: Rugby Sch.; Christ's Coll., Cambridge (BA 1979). FRICS. Richard Ellis, 1979–82; Abacus Develts Ltd, 1982–85; Coll. of Estate Management, 1985–86; Standard Life, 1986–2000; Land Securities Gp plc, 2000–. *Publication*: Depreciation of Commercial Property, 1986. *Recreations*: walking, tennis. *Address*: Land Securities Group plc, 5 Strand, WC2N 5AF. *T*: (020) 7413 9000, *Fax*: (020) 7925 0202; *e-mail*: francis.salway@landsecurities.com.

SALZ, Anthony Michael Vaughan; Executive Vice Chairman, N. M. Rothschild & Sons Ltd, since 2006; *b* 30 June 1950; *s* of Michael H. Salz and Veronica Edith Dorothea Elizabeth Salz (*née* Hall); *m* 1975, Sally Ruth Hagger; one *s* two *d*. *Educ*: Summerfields Sch., Oxford; Radley Coll.; Exeter Univ. (LLB Hons). Admitted Solicitor, 1974; Kenneth Brown Baker Baker, 1972–75; joined Freshfields, 1975, Partner, 1980, Sen. Partner, 1996–2000; seconded to Davis Polk & Wardwell, NY, 1977–78; Jt Sen. Partner, Freshfields Bruckhaus Deringer, 2000–06. Vice-Chm., Bd of Govs, BBC, 2004–06. Member: Tate Gall. Corporate Adv. Gp, 1997– (Chm., 1997–2002); Adv. Panel, Swiss Re Centre for Global Dialogue, 2006–. Director: Tate Foundn, 2000–; Habitat for Humanity GB, 2004–. Trustee: Eden Project, 2001–; Paul Hamlyn Foundn, 2005–; Conran Foundn, 2007–; Media Standards Trust, 2007–; SHINE: Support and Help in Educn, 2008–. Chm., London Higher Skills Bd, 2008–. FRSA 1996. Hon. LLD, Exeter, 2003. *Publications*: contrib. to various legal books and jls. *Recreations*: golf, fly-fishing, watching sports (including Southampton FC), tennis, walking, theatre, contemporary art. *Address*: N. M. Rothschild & Sons Ltd, 1 King William Street, EC4N 7AR. *Clubs*: Walbrook, MCC; Berkshire Golf, Trevose Golf.

SAMARANCH, Juan Antonio; Marqués de Samaranch, 1991; President, International Olympic Committee, 1980–2001 (Member, 1966; Hon. Life President, 2001); *b* 17 July 1920; *s* of Francisco Samaranch and Juana Torello; *m* 1955, Maria Teresa Salisachs Rowe (*d* 2000); one *s* one *d. Educ:* Instituto Superior Estudios de Empresas, Barcelona; German College; Higher Inst. of Business Studies, Barcelona. Industrialist, Bank Consultant; Pres., Barcelona Diputacion, 1973–77; Ambassador to USSR and to People's Republic of Mongolia, 1977–80. Mem., Spanish Olympic Cttee, 1954 (Pres., 1967–70); Nat. Deleg. for Physical Educn and Sport. Hon. Pres., Caja de Ahorros y de Pensiones de Barcelona. Holds numerous decorations and various honorary degrees from different univs. *Publications:* Deporte 2000, 1967; Olympic Message, 1980; Memorias Olímpicas, 2002; Olympic Review. *Recreation:* philately. *Address:* Diagonal 520-bajos, 08006 Barcelona, Spain.

SAMBLES, Prof. John Roy, PhD; FRS 2002; FInstP; Professor of Physics, Exeter University, since 1991; *b* 14 Oct. 1945; *s* of Charles Henry Sambles and Georgina (*née* Deeble); *m* 1966, Sandra Elizabeth Sloman; two *s* one *d. Educ:* Callington Grammar Sch., Cornwall; Imperial Coll., London Univ. (BSc 1st Cl. Hons Physics 1967; ARCS; PhD 1970; DIC). FInstP 1988. Res. Fellow, Imperial Coll., London, 1970–72; Exeter University: Lectr in Physics, 1972–85; Sen. Lectr, 1985–88; Reader, 1988–91. Mem., EPSRC, 2008–. George Gray Medal, British Liquid Crystal Soc., 1998; Thomas Young Medal and Prize, Inst. of Physics, 2003. *Publications:* numerous papers in learned scientific jls, incl. works on liquid crystals, diffractive optics, melting, electron microscopy, resistivity of thin samples, molecular electronics and surface plasmons. *Recreations:* writing poetry, local Methodist preacher. *Address:* School of Physics, University of Exeter, Exeter, Devon EX4 4QL. *T:* (01392) 264103.

SAMBROOK, Prof. Joseph Frank, PhD; FRS 1985; FAA; Distinguished Fellow, Peter MacCallum Cancer Institute, Melbourne, since 2003 (Director of Research, 1995–2000; Director, Familial Cancer Centre, 2000–05); Executive Scientific Director, Australian Stem Cell Centre, 2006–07; *b* 1 March 1939; *s* of Thomas Sambrook and Ethel Gertrude (*née* Lightfoot); *m* 1st, 1960, Thelma McGrady (marr. diss. 1984); two *s* one *d*; 2nd, 1986, Mary-Jane Gething; one *d. Educ:* Liverpool Univ. (BSc 1962); Australian Nat. Univ. (PhD 1965). FAA 2000. Res. Fellow, John Curtin Sch. of Med. Res., ANU, 1965–66; Postdoctoral Fellow, MRC Lab. of Molecular Biol., 1966–67; Jun. Fellow, Salk Inst. for Biol Studies, 1967–69; Sen. Staff Investigator, 1969–77, Asst Dir, 1977–85, Cold Spring Harbor Lab.; Prof. and Chm., Dept of Biochemistry, Southwestern Medical Center, Dallas, 1985–91; Dir, McDermott Center for Human Growth and Develt, Southwestern Med. Sch., Dallas, 1991–94. Hon. DSc: Watson Sch. of Biol Scis, 2007; Liverpool, 2007. *Publications:* contribs to learned jls. *Recreation:* music. *Address:* Peter MacCallum Cancer Institute, St Andrews Place, East Melbourne, Vic 3002, Australia. *T:* (3) 96561513, *Fax:* (3) 96561411; PO Box 3254, East Melbourne, Vic 3002, Australia.

SAMBROOK, Richard Jeremy; Director, BBC Global News, since 2004; *b* 24 April 1956; *s* of Michael Sambrook and Joan Sambrook (*née* Hartridge); *m* 1987, Susan Fisher; one *s* one *d. Educ:* Maidstone Sch. for Boys; Reading Univ. (BA); Birkbeck Coll., London Univ. (MSc). Trainee journalist, Thomson Newspapers, 1977–80; joined BBC, 1980: Radio News, 1980–84; TV News, 1984–87; Dep. Ed., Nine O'Clock News, 1988–92; News Editor, BBC News, 1992–96; Head, Newsgathering, 1996–99; Dep. Dir, 1999–2001, Dir, 2001–04, BBC News. FRTS 1992; FRSA. *Recreations:* walking, golf, music. *Address:* BBC, Bush House, PO Box 76, WC2B 4PH.

SAMMONS, Prof. Pamela, PhD; Professor of Education, University of Nottingham, since 2004; *b* 6 April 1956; *d* of Albert Edward Henry Sammons and Violet Ruth Sammons; *m* 1984, David Michael Greet (*d* 2003); two *d. Educ:* Nower Hill High Sch.; Harrow County Girls' Sch.; Univ. of Bristol (BSocSci Geog. with Econs); CNAA (PhD 1986). Sen. Res. Officer, Res. and Stats Br., ILEA, 1981–90; Res. Fellow, Centre for Educnl Res., LSE, 1990–93; Institute of Education, London: Sen. Researcher, 1993–98; Reader in Educn, 1998; Prof. of Educn, and Co-ordinating Dir, Internat. Sch. Effectiveness and Improvement Centre, 1999–2004. *Publications:* (jtly) School Matters: the junior years, 1988; (jtly) Forging Links: effective schools and effective departments, 1997; School Effectiveness: coming of age in the 21st century, 1999; (jtly) Teachers Matter, 2007; many articles, etc in area of school effectiveness. *Recreations:* walking, visiting museums and art galleries. *Address:* School of Education, University of Nottingham, The Dearing Building, Jubilee Campus, Wollaton Road, Nottingham NG8 1BB. *T:* (0115) 951 4434, *Fax:* (0115) 951 4436; *e-mail:* pam.sammons@nottingham.ac.uk.

SAMPAIO, Jorge Fernando Branco de, Hon. GCMG 2002; Hon. GCVO 1993; Special Envoy of the UN Secretary-General to Stop Tuberculosis, since 2006; High Representative of the UN Secretary-General for the Alliance of Civilisations, since 2007; Counsellor of State, Portugal, since 2006; *b* Lisbon, 18 Sept. 1939; *s* of António Arnaldo de Carvalho Sampaio and Fernanda Bensaúde Branco de Sampaio; *m* Maria José Ritta; one *s* one *d. Educ:* Law Sch., Univ. of Lisbon. Practised as a lawyer, specialising in defending political prisoners. Sec. of State for External Co-operation, 1975; MP, Lisbon, 1979–84; Speaker, Socialist Parly Gp, 1987–88; Mem., Council of State, 1989–92; Mayor of Lisbon, 1989–95; Pres. of Portugal, 1996–2006. Founder, Intervenção Socialista, 1975; joined Socialist Party, 1978: Mem., Nat. Secretariat, 1979–92; Dir, Internat. Dept, 1986–87; Sec. Gen., 1989–92. Mem., European Human Rights Commn, Council of Europe, 1979–84. Numerous decorations, including: Grand Officer, Order of Prince Henry (Portugal), 1983; Grand Collar, Orders of the Tower and Sword, of Loyalty, of Merit, and of Liberty (Portugal), 2006; Grand Cross, Order of Orange Nassau (Netherlands), 1990. *Publications:* A Festa de um Sonho, 1991; A Look on Portugal, 1995; Os Portugueses, vols I-IX, 1997–2005; Com os Portugueses: dez anos na Presidência da República, 2005; numerous articles on political issues. *Recreations:* music, golf. *Address:* Casa do Regalo, Tapada das Necessidades, 1350–213 Lisbon, Portugal.

SAMPLES, Reginald McCartney, CMG 1971; DSO 1942; OBE 1963; HM Diplomatic Service, retired; *b* 11 Aug. 1918; *o s* of late William and Jessie Samples; *m* 1947, Elsie Roberts Hide (*d* 1999); two *s* one step *d. Educ:* Rhyl Grammar Sch.; Liverpool Univ. (BCom). Served, 1940–46; RNVR (Air Branch); torpedo action with 825 Sqn against German ships Scharnhorst, Gneisenau and Prinz Eugen in English Channel (wounded, DSO); Lieut (A). Central Office of Information (Economic Editor, Overseas Newspapers), 1947–48. CRO (Brit. Inf. Services, India), 1948; Economic Information Officer, Bombay, 1948–52; Editor-in-Chief, BIS, New Delhi, 1952; Dep.-Dir, BIS, New Delhi, 1952–56; Dir, BIS, Pakistan (Karachi), 1956–59; Dir, BIS, Canada (Ottawa), 1959–65, OBE; Counsellor (Information) to Brit. High Comr, India, and Dir, BIS, India (New Delhi), 1965–68; Asst Under-Sec. of State, Commonwealth Office, 1968; Head of British Govt Office, and Sen. British Trade Comr, Toronto, 1969; Consul-Gen., Toronto, 1974–78. Asst Dir, Royal Ontario Museum, 1978–83. Volunteer recording books for the blind, Canadian Nat. Inst. for the Blind, 1983–. *Recreations:* watching tennis, ballet. *Address:* 514W Belmont House, 55 Belmont Street, Toronto, ON M5R 1R1, Canada. *Clubs:* Naval; Queens (Toronto).

SAMPRAS, Peter; tennis player; *b* 12 Aug. 1971; *s* of Sam and Georgia Sampras; *m* 2000, Bridgette Wilson; two *s.* Professional tennis player, 1988–2003; won US Open, 1990 (youngest winner), 1993, 1995, 1996, 1999, 2002; Australian Open, 1994, 1997; Wimbledon, 1993, 1994, 1995, 1997, 1998, 1999, 2000; ATP World Champion, 1991, 1994, 1996, 1997, 1999; Davis Cup player. Member: American Cancer Soc. Public Awareness Council; Board, Tim and Tom Gullikson Foundation; Founder, Aces for Charity Fund. *Recreations:* golf, basketball, Formula 1 racing. *Address:* c/o 200 ATP Tour Boulevard, Ponte Vedra Beach, FL 32082, USA. *T:* (904) 2858000.

SAMPSON, Adam; Chief Executive (formerly Director), Shelter, since 2003; *b* 13 June 1960; *s* of Derek and Janet Sampson; *m* 2000, Siobhan Grey; one *s* one *d. Educ:* Brasenose Coll., Oxford (BA; MSc). Jun. Dean, Brasenose Coll., Oxford, 1986–87; Probation Officer, Tottenham, 1987–89; Dep. Dir, Prison Reform Trust, 1989–94; Asst Prisons Ombudsman, Home Office, 1994–97; CEO, RAPt, 1998–2002. *Publication:* Acts of Abuse, 1993. *Recreation:* sleeping. *Address:* c/o Shelter, 88 Old Street, EC1V 9HU. *T:* 0844 515 2124; *e-mail:* adam_sampson@shelter.org.uk.

SAMPSON, Sir Colin, Kt 1993; CBE 1988; QPM 1978; DL; HM Chief Inspector of Constabulary for Scotland, 1991–93; *b* 26 May 1929; *s* of James and Nellie Sampson; *m* 1953, Kathleen Stones; two *s. Educ:* Stanley Sch., Wakefield; Wakefield Technical Coll.; Univ. of Leeds (Criminology). Joined Police Force, 1949; served mainly in the CID (incl. training of detectives), at Dewsbury, Skipton, Doncaster, Goole, Wakefield, Huddersfield, Rotherham, Barnsley; Comdt, Home Office Detective Trng Sch., Wakefield, 1971–72; Asst Chief Constable, West Yorks, 1973; Dep. Chief Constable, Notts, 1976; Chief Constable, W Yorks, 1983–89; HM Inspector of Constabulary, 1989–90 (for NE England, 1990). Advr on police matters to govt of Namibia, 1989–93. Vice Pres., Yorkshire Soc., 1983–. Freeman, City of London, 1990. DL West Yorks, 1994. DUniv Bradford, 1988; Hon. LLD Leeds, 1990. KStJ 1998. *Recreations:* choral music, walking, gardening. *Address:* 3 Castle Hill, Woodacre Lane, Bardsey, Wetherby, W Yorks LS17 9BT.

SAMPSON, Nicholas Alexander, MA; Master of Marlborough College, since 2004; *b* 27 Aug. 1958; *s* of Charles and Patricia Sampson; *m* 1981, Nancy Threlfall; two *d. Educ:* Gillingham Grammar Sch.; Howard Sch., Kent; Selwyn Coll., Cambridge (MA); Westminster Coll., Oxford (PGCE). Teacher of English and Housemaster, Wells Cathedral Sch., 1984–94; Headmaster, Sutton Valence Sch., 1994–2000; Principal, Geelong Grammar Sch., Australia, 2001–04. Member: Bd, Assoc. of Ind. Schs of Vic, 2003–04; Council, Marcus Oldham Coll., 2001–04; Council, Janet Clarke Hall, 2002–04. Governor: King's Sch., Rochester, 2006–; St Andrew's Sch., Pangbourne, 2006–; Swindon Acad., 2007–. *Recreations:* family, literature, history, sport. *Address:* Marlborough College, Marlborough, Wilts SN8 1PA. *Clubs:* Athenæum, East India, Lansdowne.

SAMS, Craig Lynn; Chairman, Soil Association Certification Ltd, since 2007; President, Green & Black's, since 1999; *b* 17 July 1944; *s* of Kenneth Sams and Margaret Sams; *m* 1991, Josephine Fairley; one *s* one *d* by a previous marriage. *Educ:* Wharton Sch., Univ. of Pennsylvania (BSc Econs). Co-founded Whole Earth Foods, 1967; estd Ceres Bakery, 1972; co-founded Green & Black's Chocolate, 1991, created Maya Gold Chocolate, 1993. Hon. Treas., 1990–2001, Chm., 2001–07, Soil Assoc. Co-Publisher, Seed: the jl of organic living, 1972–77. *Publications:* About Macrobiotics, 1972; The Macrobiotic Brown Rice Cookbook, 1993; The Little Food Book, 2003; (with Jo Fairley) Sweet Dreams: the story of Green & Black's, 2008. *Recreations:* allotment gardening, orchardist, cliff walking, propcycling. *Address:* 106 High Street, Hastings, E Sussex TN34 3ES. *T:* (01424) 430016; *e-mail:* craig@craigsams.com. *Club:* Groucho.

SAMS, Jeremy Charles; composer, translator, director; *b* 12 Jan. 1957; *s* of late Eric Sams and Enid Sams (*née* Tidmarsh); one *s. Educ:* Magdalene Coll., Cambridge (BA); Guildhall Sch. of Music. Freelance pianist, 1977–82; director: *theatre* includes: Entertaining Mr Sloane, Greenwich, 1992; Wind in the Willows, Tokyo, 1993, Old Vic, 1995; Neville's Island, Apollo, 1994; Wild Oats, RNT, 1995; Passion, Queen's, 1996; Marat/Sade, RNT, 1997; Enter the Guardsman, Donmar, 1997; Two Pianos, Four Hands, Birmingham Rep., and Comedy, 1999; Spend! Spend! Spend!, Piccadilly, 1999; Noises Off, RNT, 2000, transf. Piccadilly and NY, 2001; What the Butler Saw, Theatre Royal, Bath, and tour, 2001; Benefactors, Albery, and tour, 2002; The Water Babies, Chichester, 2003; Little Britain, UK tour, 2005; Donkeys' Years, Comedy, 2006; The Sound of Music, Palladium, 2006; *opera:* The Reluctant King, Opera North, 1994; *translations* include: The Rehearsal, Almeida and Garrick, 1991 (Time Out Award); Becket, Theatre Royal Haymarket, 1991; The Miser, NT; Les Parents Terribles, RNT and NY, 1990; Mary Stuart, RNT, 1996; Merry Widow, Royal Opera, 1997; A Fool and His Money, Nottingham Playhouse and Birmingham Rep., 1998; Colombe, Salisbury Playhouse, 1999; Twilight of the Gods (The Rhinegold, The Valkyrie, Siegfried), 2001, Così fan tutte, 2002, and The Magic Flute, Macbeth, Figaro's Wedding, La Bohème, in repertory, ENO; Scapino, Chichester, 2005; Arms and the Cow, Opera North, 2006; *adaptations* include: Waiting in the Wings, NY, 1999; Chitty Chitty Bang Bang, Palladium, 2002, transf. NY; Amour, NY, 2002; composer of numerous scores: *theatre* includes: Kean, Old Vic, 1990; for RSC: Temptation, The Tempest, Measure for Measure, Merry Wives of Windsor, Midsummer Night's Dream; for RNT: Ghetto (also lyrics); Wind in the Willows (also lyrics); Arcadia; Honour, 2003; *television:* Persuasion, 1996 (Award for Original TV Music, BAFTA); Have Your Cake, 1997; *films:* The Mother, 2003; Enduring Love (Ivor Novello Award), 2004. *Publications:* (ed) Wild Oats, 1995; *translations:* Molière, The Miser, 1991; Anouilh, The Rehearsal, 1991; Cocteau, Les Parents Terribles, 1995; Schiller, Mary Stuart, 1996; Anouilh, Becket, 1997; Lehár, The Merry Widow, 2000; Antigone, 2002; Eric Emmanuel Schmitt, Plays: 1, 2002; Enigma Variations, 2003. *Address:* c/o The Agency, 24 Pottery Lane, W11 4LZ.

SAMSON, Prof. Thomas James, (Jim), PhD; FBA 2000; Professor of Music, Royal Holloway, University of London, since 2002; *b* 6 July 1946; *s* of Edward Samson and Matilda Jayne (*née* Smyth). *Educ:* Queen's Univ., Belfast (BMus); UC, Cardiff, (MMus; PhD 1972). LRAM. Res. Fellow in Humanities, Univ. of Leicester, 1972–73; University of Exeter: Lectr in Music, 1973–87; Reader in Musicology, 1987–92; Prof. of Musicology, 1992–94; Stanley Hugh Badock Prof. of Music, Univ. of Bristol, 1994–2002. Order of Merit, Ministry of Culture (Poland), 1990. *Publications:* Music in Transition: a study of tonal expansion and early atonality 1900–1920, 1977, 3rd edn 1993; The Music of Szymanowski, 1980; The Music of Chopin, 1985, 2nd edn 1994 (trans. German 1991); (ed) Chopin Studies, 1988; (ed) The Late Romantic Era: Vol. VII, Man and Music, 1991; Chopin: the Four Ballades, 1992; (ed) The Cambridge Companion to Chopin, 1992; (ed with J. Rink) Chopin Studies 2, 1994; Chopin, 1996; (ed) The Cambridge History of Nineteenth-Century Music, 2002; (ed with Bennett Zon) Nineteenth Century Music: selected proceedings of the Tenth International Conference, 2002; Virtuosity and the Musical Work: the Transcendental Studies of Liszt, 2003 (Royal Philharmonic Bk Prize, 2004); (ed with P. J. E. Harper-Scott) Introduction to Music Studies, 2008. *Recreation:* astronomy. *Address:* 81 Gainsborough Road, Kew, Richmond TW9 2ET; Department of Music, Royal Holloway, University of London, Egham, Surrey TW20 0EX.

SAMSON-BARRY, Hilary Alice; Head of Children, Families and Maternity, Department of Health, since 2004; *b* 16 Aug. 1958; *d* of Dr Mattanja Erasmus Richard Samson and Dr Margaret Noel Samson (*née* Williams); *m* 1989, Desmond Neville Barry; one *s* one *d*. *Educ:* Sch. of St Mary and St Anne, Abbots Bromley; Ellesmere Coll.; Univ. of Exeter (BA Hons (Econs and Geog.) 1980); Cranfield Univ. (MBA 1986). Personnel Manager, Securiguard Services Ltd, 1980–85; Mgt Consultant, Towers Perrin, 1986–91; Project Manager, London Implementation Gp, DoH, 1992–95; Dir, Camden and Islington HA, 1995–96; Head: Health Develt, NHS London Region, 1997–2000; Policy Integration and Health, GLA, 2000–01; Dir, Productivity and Diversity, Women and Equality Unit, Cabinet Office and DTI, 2001–04. Gov., Francis Combe Sch. and Community Coll., 2003–. Hon. DSc Greenwich, 2001. *Recreations:* family, horse riding, community, personal development. *Address:* Highclere, 34 Abbots Road, Abbots Langley, Herts WD5 0AZ; *e-mail:* HSamsonBarry@aol.com.

SAMSOVA, Galina; producer; Teacher with the company in the Royal Ballet; *b* Stalingrad, 1937; *d* of a Byelorussian; *m* 1st, Alexander Ursuliak; 2nd, André Prokovsky. *Educ:* the Ballet Sch., Kiev (pupil of N. Verekundova). Joined Kiev Ballet, 1956 and became a soloist; Canadian Ballet, 1961; created chief rôle in Cendrillon, Paris 1963 (Gold Medal for best danseuse of Paris Festival). Ballerina, Festival Ballet, 1964–73; headed the group of André Prokovsky, The New London Ballet, (disbanded in 1977, revived for 3 new productions, The Theatre Royal, York, 1979); a Principal Dancer, Sadler's Wells Royal Ballet, subseq. Birmingham Royal Ballet, 1980–91; Artistic Dir, Scottish Ballet, 1991–97; has danced principal rôles in Sleeping Beauty, Nutcracker, Giselle, Swan Lake, Anna Karenina, and other classical ballets; danced in Europe, Far East and USA. Produced: Sequence from Paquita, Sadler's Wells, 1980; (with Peter Wright) Swan Lake, Sadler's Wells, 1983, Covent Garden, 1991, Royal Swedish Ballet, 2001; Giselle, London City Ballet, 1986; Les Sylphides, Birmingham Royal Ballet, 1992; Sleeping Beauty, Scottish Ballet, 1994, Tulsa Ballet, USA, 2000; Swan Lake, Scottish Ballet, 1995, Rome Opera House, 2003, NBA Ballet Co., Japan, 2006.

SAMUEL, family name of **Viscounts Bearsted** and **Samuel**.

SAMUEL, 3rd Viscount *cr* 1937, of Mount Carmel and of Toxteth, Liverpool; **David Herbert Samuel,** OBE 1996; Professor of Physical Chemistry, Weizmann Institute of Science, Rehovot, Israel, 1967–87, now Emeritus; *b* 8 July 1922; *s* of 2nd Viscount Samuel, CMG, and Hadassah (*d* 1986), *d* of Judah Goor (Grasovsky); *S* father, 1978; *m* 1st, 1950, Esther Berelowitz; one *d*; 2nd, 1960, Rinna Dafni (*née* Grossman); one *d*. *Educ:* Balliol Coll., Oxford (MA 1948); Hebrew Univ. (PhD 1953). Served War of 1939–45 (despatches); Captain RA, in India, Burma and Sumatra. Weizmann Institute of Science, Rehovot, Israel: Member of Scientific Staff, 1949–, of Isotope Dept, 1949–86, of Dept of Neurobiology, 1986–; Dir, Center for Neurosciences and Behavioural Research, 1978–87; Head, Chemistry Gp, Science Teaching Dept, 1967–83; Dean, Faculty of Chemistry, 1971–73; Chm., Bd of Studies in Chemistry, Feinberg Grad. Sch., 1968–74. Post-doctoral Fellow, Chem. Dept, UCL, 1956; Res. Fellow, Chem. Dept, Harvard Univ., 1957–58; Res. Fellow, Lab. of Chemical Biodynamics (Lawrence Radiation Lab.), Univ. of California, Berkeley, 1965–66; Vis. Prof., Sch. of Molecular Scis, Univ. of Warwick, 1967; Royal Soc. Vis. Prof., MRC Neuroimmunology Unit, Zoology Dept, UCL, 1974–75; Vis. Prof., MIT, 1982; Vis. Prof., Pharmacol. Dept, Yale Sch. of Medicine, 1983–84; McLaughlin Prof., Sch. of Medicine, McMaster Univ., 1984; Vis. Prof., Dept of Chemistry, Univ. of York, 1995–96, 1997. Member: Adv. Bd, Bat-Sheva de Rothschild Foundn for Advancement of Science in Israel, 1970–83; Bd, US-Israel Educnl (Fulbright) Foundn, 1969–74 (Chm., 1974–75); Bd, Israel Center for Scientific and Technol Information, 1970–74; Scientific Adv. Cttee and Bd of Trustees of Israel Center for Psychobiol., 1973–; Acad. Adv. Cttee, Everyman's (Open) Univ., 1976–83; Bd of Govs, Bezalel Acad. of Arts and Design, 1977–; Council, Israel Chemical Soc., 1977–83; Internat. Brain Res. Org. (IBRO), 1977–; Israel Exec. Cttee, America-Israel Cultural Foundn, 1978–89 (Chm., 1986–89); Bd of Governors, Tel Aviv Museum of Art, 1980–; Cttee on Teaching of Chemistry, IUPAC, 1981–89; Anglo-Israel Assoc., 1985– (Chm., Colloquia, 1997–); British Israel Arts Foundn, 1986–98; Bd of Trustees, Menninger Foundn, USA, 1988–; Soc. of Manufacturing Engrs, 1989–94; Fibre Soc., 1990–94. Pres., Shenkar Coll. of Textile Technology and Fashion, 1987–94. Former Member, Editorial Board: Jl of Labelled Compounds & Radiopharmaceuticals; Alzheimer Disease and Associated Disorders; Brain Behaviour and Immunity. Hon. Fellow, Shenkar Coll. of Engrg and Design, 2002. Scopus Award, Hebrew Univ. of Jerusalem, 2000; Tercentenary Medal, Yale Univ., 2001. *Publications:* Memory: how we use it, lose it and can improve it, 1999; more than 300 papers, reviews and parts of collective volumes on isotopes, physical chemistry, reaction mechanisms, neurochemistry, psychopharmacology, animal behavior, education and the history and teaching of science. *Heir: b* Hon. Dan Judah Samuel [*b* 25 March 1925; *m* 1st, 1957, Nonni (Esther) (marr. diss. 1977), *d* of late Max Gordon, Johannesburg; one *s* two *d*; 2nd, 1981, Heather, *d* of Angus and Elsa Cumming, Haywards Heath; one *s* one *d*]. *Address:* Department of Environmental Sciences and Energy Research, Weizmann Institute of Science, Rehovot 76100, Israel. *T:* (8) 9344229.

SAMUEL, Adrian Christopher Ian, CMG 1959; CVO 1963; *b* 20 Aug. 1915; *s* of late George Christopher Samuel and Alma Richards; *m* 1942, Sheila, *er d* of late J. C. Barrett, Killiney, Co. Dublin; three *s* one *d*. *Educ:* Rugby Sch.; St John's Coll., Oxford. Entered HM Consular Service, 1938; served at Beirut, Tunis and Trieste. Served War, 1940–44, in Royal Air Force. Returned to HM Foreign Service and served at HM Embassies in Ankara, Cairo and Damascus; First Secretary, 1947; Counsellor, 1956; Principal Private Secretary to the Secretary of State for Foreign Affairs, Oct. 1959–63; Minister at HM Embassy, Madrid, 1963–65; resigned 1965. Director: British Chemical Engrg Contractors Assoc., 1966–69; British Agrochemicals Assoc., 1972–78; Dir-Gen., Groupement Internat. des Assocs Nats de Fabricants de Pesticides (GIFAP), 1978–79. *Publication:* An Astonishing Fellow: a life of Sir Robert Wilson, KMT, MP, 1986. *Recreation:* reading. *Address:* 6 The Meadows, St George's Park, Ditchling Common, Ditchling, East Sussex RH15 0SF. *Club:* Garrick.

SAMUEL, Gillian Patricia; JP; Director (formerly General Manager) of Corporate Communications, P&O Nedlloyd Ltd, 1998–2005; *b* 19 Oct. 1945; *d* of Harry Martin Samuel and Kathleen Joyce Samuel (*née* Drake). *Educ:* Edmonton Co. Grammar Sch.; Exeter Univ. (BA Hons Hist.). Current Affairs Gp, BBC TV, 1968–70; Plessey Co., 1970–72; Department of: Nat. Savings, 1972–75; Industry, later DTI, 1975–87; Dir of Information, Dept of Transport, 1987–92; Press Sec. and Chief of Information, 1992–97, Sen. Advr, Internal Communications Develt, 1997–98, MoD. JP, 2008. *Recreations:* walking, modern jazz.

SAMUEL, Sir John (Michael Glen), 5th Bt *cr* 1898; Chairman: Synergy Management Services Ltd, since 1983; RE-Fuel Technology Ltd, since 2008; *b* 25 Jan. 1944; *o s* of Sir John Oliver Cecil Samuel, 4th Bt, and Charlotte Mary, *d* of late R. H. Hoyt, Calgary, Canada; *S* father, 1962; *m* 1st, 1966, Antoinette Sandra, *d* of late Captain Antony Hewitt, RE, 2nd SAS Regt, and of Mrs K. A. H. Casson, Frith Farm, Wolverton, Hants; two *s*; 2nd, 1982, Mrs Elizabeth Ann Molinari, *y d* of late Major R. G. Curry, Bournemouth, Dorset. *Educ:* Radley; London Univ. Director: Enfield Automotive, 1967–70; Advanced Vehicle Systems Ltd, 1971–78; Chm., Electric Auto Corp. (USA), 1978–83. *Recreation:* motor racing. *Heir: s* Anthony John Fulton Samuel [*b* 13 Oct. 1972; *m* 2004, Gemma Chloe Rose Gubbins; one *s*].

SAMUEL, Martin; Columnist, since 2002, Chief Football Correspondent, since 2007, The Times; *b* 25 July 1964; *s* of Arthur Samuel and Rita Samuel; *m* 1994, Deborah Edmead; three *s*. *Educ:* Fairlop Jun. Sch.; Ilford Co. High Sch. Hayters Sports Agency, 1982–84; The People, 1984–87; The Sun, 1987–97, Chief Football Writer, 1994–97; The Express: Football Editor, 1997–2000; Chief Sports Writer and Columnist, 2000–02; Chief Sports Writer, News of the World, 2002–07. Sports Writer of the Year: What the Papers Say, 2002, 2005, 2006; Sports Journalists' Assoc., 2005, 2006, 2007. *Recreations:* cooking, the occasional glass of wine, unpopular music. *Address:* News International Newspapers, 1 Virginia Street, E98 1XY. *T:* (020) 7782 4000.

SAMUEL, Richard Christopher, CMG 1983; CVO 1983; HM Diplomatic Service, retired; Ambassador to Latvia, 1991–93; *b* Edinburgh, 8 Aug. 1933; *m* 1986, Frances Draper (*d* 2007); one *s* one *d*. *Educ:* Durham Sch.; St John's Coll., Cambridge (BA). Royal Navy, 1952–54. FO, 1957–58; Warsaw, 1958–59; Rome, 1960–63; FO, 1963; Private Sec. to Parly Under-Sec. of State, 1965–68; Hong Kong, 1968–69; 1st Sec. and Head of Chancery: Singapore, 1969–71; Peking, 1971–73; Counsellor, Washington, 1973–76; Head of Far Eastern Dept, FCO, 1976–79; Counsellor (Commercial), Moscow, 1980–82; Minister and Dep. High Comr, New Delhi, 1982–85; Under-Sec. for Asia and the Oceans, ODA, FCO, 1986–88; on loan to Inter-Amer. Develt Bank, Washington, as Exec. Dir for UK/Western Europe, 1988–91. Hd, CSCE Resident Mission, Moldova, 1994; Head, OSCE Resident Mission: Estonia, 1995; Latvia, 1997–98. Diplomatic Adviser: to UN Special Envoy, Inter-Tajik negotiations in Ashkhabad, 1995–96; to EU Justice and Home Affairs Mission to Central Asia, 1997; Consultant to OSCE, Vienna, 2002–03. Chm., British-Latvian Assoc., 2004–. Comdr, Order of the Three Stars (Latvia), 1999. *Address:* 36 Northumberland Place, W2 5AS. *T:* and *Fax:* (020) 7229 8357.

SAMUELS; *see* Turner-Samuels.

SAMUELS, Rev. Canon Christopher William John; Rector of St Mary without-the-walls, Handbridge, Chester, 1983–2005; Chaplain to the Queen, since 2001; *b* 8 Oct. 1942; *s* of John Bernard Boniface Samuels and Ethel Samuels (*née* Bamford); *m* 1967, Sarah Parry (*née* Irving); one *s* one *d*. *Educ:* Denstone Coll., Uttoxeter; KCL (AKC 1966); St Boniface, Warminster. Ordained deacon, 1967, priest, 1968; Curate, St Thomas, Kirkholt, Rochdale, 1967–72; Priest i/c, St Thomas, Parkside, Houghton Regis, 1972–76; Rector, St Helen's, Tarporley, 1976–83. Hon. Canon, Chester Cathedral, 1997–2005, now Emeritus. Nat. Chaplain, Dunkirk Veterans' Assoc., 1996–2000. Chm. of Trustees, Children in Distress, 2007–. Chm. of Govs, King's Sch., Chester, 2002–05. Freeman, City of London, 1996. Paul Harris Fellow, Rotary Club, 1997. *Recreations:* book collecting, Scottish islands, travel. *Address:* Riversleigh House, Station Road, Rossett, Wrexham LL12 0HE. *Club:* Rotary (Chester).

SAMUELS, His Honour John Edward Anthony; QC 1981; a Circuit Judge, 1997–2006; a Deputy Circuit Judge, since 2006; *b* 15 Aug. 1940; *s* of late Albert Edward Samuels, solicitor, Reigate, Surrey; *m* 1967, Maxine (*née* Robertson), JP; two *s*. *Educ:* Charterhouse; Perugia; Queens' Coll., Cambridge (MA). Commnd, Queen's Royal Regt (TA), 1959; Lieut, Queen's Royal Surrey Regt (TA), 1961–67. Chairman, Cambridge Univ. United Nations Assoc., 1962. Called to Bar, Lincoln's Inn, 1964 (Mansfield Schol., 1963; Bencher, 1990); South Eastern Circuit; a Dep. High Court Judge, 1981–97; a Recorder, 1985–97. Asst Parly Boundary Comr, 1992–95. Judicial Mem., Parole Bd, 2005–. Member: Senate of the Inns of Court and the Bar, 1983–86; Bar Council, 1992–97; Council of Legal Educn, 1983–90; Trustee, Centre for Crime and Justice Studies, 2002–; Chm., Jt Regulations Cttee, Inns' Council and Bar Council, 1987–90. Mem. Cttee, Council of HM Circuit Judges, 2001– (Chm., Criminal Sub-Cttee, 2002–06). Co-opted Mem., ILEA Education Cttee, 1964–67; Jt Chm., ILEA Disciplinary Tribunals, 1977–87; Alternate Chm., Burnham Cttee, 1981–87; Lay Chm., NHS Complaints Panels, 1996–97; Dep. Chm., Disciplinary Cttee, RPSGB, 2006–; Mem., Criminal Injuries Compensation Appeal Panel, 1997. Member: Richmond, Twickenham and Roehampton HA, 1982–85; Kingston and Richmond FPC, 1982–86. Trustee: Richmond Parish Lands Charity, 1986–96 (Chairman: Educn Cttee, 1987–89; Property Cttee, 1987–95); Prisoners' Educn Trust, 2000– (Chm., 2006–); Howard League for Penal Reform, 2007–. Vice-Pres., Unlock (Nat. Assoc. for Reformed Offenders), 2006–. *Publications:* Action Pack: counsel's guide to chambers' administration, 1986, 2nd edn 1988; contributor to Halsbury's Laws of England, 4th edn. *Recreations:* conservation, restoration, serendipity. *Address:* c/o Treasury Office, Lincoln's Inn, WC2A 3TL. *T:* (020) 7405 1393.

SAMUELS, Prof. Michael Louis, FRSE; Professor of English Language, University of Glasgow, 1959–89; *b* 1920; *s* of late Harry Samuels, OBE, MA, barrister-at-law, and Céline Samuels (*née* Aronowitz), London; *m* 1950, Hilary, *d* of late Julius and Ruth Samuel, Glasgow; one *d*. *Educ:* St Paul's School; Balliol College, Oxford. Domus Exhibitioner in Classics, Balliol College, Oxford, 1938–40 and 1945–47; MA 1947 (First Class Hons English Lang. and Lit.). Worked for Air Ministry (Maintenance Command), 1940–45. Research Fellow, University of Birmingham, 1947–48; Assistant in English Language, University of Edinburgh, 1948–49; Lecturer in English Language, Univ. of Edinburgh, 1949–59. Chm., Scottish Studentships Selection Cttee, 1975–88. FRSE 1989. Hon. DLitt Glasgow, 2006. *Publications:* Linguistic Evolution, 1972; (ed jtly) A Linguistic Atlas of Late Medieval English, 1987; (jtly) Middle English Dialectology, 1989; (with J. J. Smith) The English of Chaucer, 1989; contribs to: Approaches to English Historical Linguistics, 1969; So Meny people Longages and Tonges (presented to A. McIntosh), 1981; Middle English Studies (presented to N. Davis), 1983; Proc. 4th Internat. Conf. on English Historical Linguistics, 1985; Explanation and Linguistic Change, 1987; A Companion to Piers Plowman, 1988; articles and reviews in linguistic and literary jls.

SAMUELSON, Sir (Bernard) Michael (Francis), 5th Bt *cr* 1884; *b* 17 Jan. 1917; *s* of Sir Francis Henry Bernard Samuelson, 4th Bt, and Margaret Kendall (*d* 1980), *d* of H. Kendall Barnes; *S* father, 1981; *m* 1952, Janet Amy, *yr d* of Lt-Comdr L. G. Elkington, RN retd, Chelsea; two *s* two *d*. *Educ:* Eton. Served War of 1939–45 with RA and Leicestershire Regt (despatches). *Heir: s* James Francis Samuelson [*b* 20 Dec. 1956; *m* 1987, Caroline Anne Woodley; two *d*]. *Address:* Harborne, Hailsham Road, Stone Cross, Pevensey, East Sussex BN24 5AS. *T:* (01323) 760487.

SAMUELSON, Prof. Paul Anthony; Institute Professor, Massachusetts Institute of Technology, 1966–86, now Emeritus; Shinsei Bank (formerly Long-Term Credit Bank of Japan) Visiting Professor of Political Economy, Center for Japan-US Business and Economic Studies, New York University, since 1987; *b* Gary, Indiana, 15 May 1915; *m* 1st, 1938, Marion Crawford (*d* 1978); four *s* (incl. triplets) two *d*; 2nd, 1981, Risha Claypool. *Educ:* Univs of Chicago (BA) and Harvard (MA, PhD). SSRC Predoctoral

Fellow, 1935–37; Soc. of Fellows, Harvard, 1937–40; Guggenheim Fellow, 1948–49; Ford Faculty Research Fellow, 1958–59; Hoyt Vis. Fellow, Calhoun Coll., Yale, 1962; Carnegie Foundn Reflective Year, 1965–66. MIT: Asst Prof. of Econs, 1940; Assoc. Prof. of Econs, 1944; Staff Mem., Radiation Lab., 1944–45; Prof. of Econs, 1947; Prof. of Internat. Economic Relations (part-time), Fletcher Sch. of Law and Diplomacy, 1945. Consultant: to Nat. Resources Planning Bd, 1941–43; to Rand Corp., 1948–75; to US Treasury, 1945–52, 1961–74; to Johnson Task Force on Sustained Prosperity, 1964; to Council of Econ. Advisers, 1960–68; to Federal Reserve Bd, 1965–; to Congressional Budget Office, 1974–. Economic Adviser to Senator, Candidate and President-elect John F. Kennedy, informal adviser to President Kennedy. Member: War Prodn Bd and Office of War Mobilization and Reconstruction, 1945; Bureau of the Budget, 1952; Adv. Bd of Nat Commn on Money and Credit, 1958–60; Research Adv. Panel to President's Nat. Goals Commn, 1959–60; Research Adv. Bd Cttee for Econ. Develt, 1960; Nat. Task Force on Econ. Educn, 1960–61; Sen. Advr, Brookings Panel on Econ. Activity. Contrib. Editor and Columnist, Newsweek, 1966–81. Vernon F. Taylor Vis. Dist. Prof., Trinity Univ., Texas, 1989. Lectures: Stamp Meml, London, 1961; Wicksell, Stockholm, 1962; Franklin, Detroit, 1962; Gerhard Colm Meml, NYC, 1971; Davidson, Univ. of New Hampshire, 1971; 12th John von Neumann, Univ. of Wisconsin, 1971; J. Willard Gibbs, Amer. Mathematical Soc., 1974; 1st Sulzbacher, Columbia Law Sch., 1974; John Diebold, Harvard Univ., 1976; Alice Bourneauf, Boston Coll., 1981; Horowitz, Jerusalem and Tel Aviv, 1984; Marschak Meml, UCLA, 1984; Olin, Univ. of Virginia Law Sch., 1989; Joseph W. Martin Commemorative, Stonehill Coll., 1990; Lionel Robbins Meml, Claremont Coll., 1991. Corresp. Fellow, British Acad., 1960; Fellow: Amer. Philosoph. Soc.; Econometric Soc. (Mem. Council; Vice-Pres. 1950; Pres. 1951); Member: Amer. Acad. Arts and Sciences; Amer. Econ. Assoc. (Pres. 1961; Hon. Fellow, 1965); Phi Beta Kappa; Commn on Social Sciences (NSF), 1967–70; Internat. Econ. Assoc. (Pres. 1965–68; Hon. Pres. 1968–); Nat. Acad. of Sciences, 1970–; Omicron Delta Epsilon, Bd of Trustees (Internat. Honor Soc. in Econ.). Hon. Fellow: LSE; Peruvian Sch. of Economics, 1980. Hon. LLD: Chicago, 1961; Oberlin, 1961; Boston Coll., 1964; Indiana, 1966; Michigan, 1967; Claremont Grad. Sch., 1970; New Hampshire, 1971; Seton Hall, 1971; Keio, Tokyo, 1971; Harvard, 1972; Gustavas Adolphus Coll., 1974; Univ. of Southern Calif, 1975; Univ. of Rochester, 1976; Univ. of Pennsylvania, 1976; Emmanuel Coll., 1977; Stonehill Coll., 1978; Widener, 1982; Indiana Univ. of Pennsylvania, 1993; Hon. DLitt: Ripon Coll., 1962; Northern Michigan Univ., 1973; Valparaiso Univ., 1987; Columbia Univ., 1988; Hon DSc: E Anglia, 1966; Massachusetts, 1972; Rhode Is., 1972; City Univ. of London, 1980; Tufts Univ., 1988; Rensselaer Poly. Inst., 1998; Hon. LHD Williams Coll., 1971; *Dhc*: Université Catholique de Louvain, 1976; Catholic Univ. at Riva Aguero Inst., Lima, 1980; Universidad Nacional de Educación a Distancia, Madrid, 1989; Universidad Politécnica de Valencia, 1991; DUniv New Univ. of Lisbon, 1985; Hon. DSS Yale, 2005. David A. Wells Prize, Harvard, 1941; John Bates Clark Medal, Amer. Econ. Assoc., 1947; Medal of Honor, Univ. of Evansville, 1970; Nobel Prize in Econ. Science, 1970; Albert Einstein Commemorative Award, 1971; Alumni Medal, Chicago Univ., 1983; Britannica Award, 1989; Medal and Hon. Mem., Club of Economics and Management, Valencia, Spain, 1990; Gold Scanno Prize in Economy, Naples, Italy, 1990; Nat. Medal of Science, USA, 1996. *Publications:* Foundations of Economic Analysis, 1947, enlarged edn 1982; Economics, 1948, (with William D. Nordhaus) 12th edn 1985 to 18th edn 2005 (trans. 40 langs, 1948); (jtly) Linear Programming and Economic Analysis, 1958 (trans. French, Japanese); Readings in Economics, 1955; The Collected Scientific Papers of Paul A. Samuelson (ed J. E. Stiglitz), vols I and II, 1966, vol. III (ed R. C. Merton), 1972, vol. IV (ed H. Nagatani and K. Crowley), 1977, vol. V (ed K. Crowley), 1986; co-author, other books in field, papers in various jls, etc. *Recreation:* tennis. *Address:* Department of Economics, Massachusetts Institute of Technology E52–383C, 50 Memorial Drive, Cambridge, MA 02142, USA. *T:* (617) 2533368, *Fax:* (617) 2530560.

SAMUELSON, Sir Sydney (Wylie), Kt 1995; CBE 1978; first British Film Commissioner, 1991–97; President, 1990–95, Senior Consultant, 1998–2000, Samuelson Group PLC (Chairman and Chief Executive, 1966–90); *b* 7 Dec. 1925; 2nd *s* of G. B. and Marjorie Samuelson; *m* 1949, Doris (*née* Magen); three *s*. *Educ:* Irene Avenue Council Sch., Lancing, Sussex. Served RAF, 1943–47. From age 14, career devoted to various aspects of British film industry: cinema projectionist, 1939–41; asst film editor, 1942–43; asst film cameraman, cameraman and dir of documentary films and television, 1947–59; founded Samuelson Gp, company to service film, TV and, later, audio-visual prodn organisations, supplying cameras and other technical equipment, with purchase of first camera, 1954; continued filming as technician on locations throughout world until 1959, when activities concentrated on developing the company. Trustee, BAFTA, 1973– (Vice-Chm. Film, 1971–73; Chm. of Council, 1973–76; Chm., Bd of Mgt, 1976–2001; Mem., Business Bd, 1994–2001; Michael Balcon Award, 1985; Fellow, 1993); Chm., BAFTA-Shell UK Venture, 1988–91; Member: BECTU History Project, 1995–2002; Exec. Cttee, Cinema and Television Veterans (Pres., 1980–81); Council and Exec. Cttee, Cinema and TV Benevolent Fund, 1969–92 (Trustee, 1982–89; Pres., 1983–86). Pres., Projected Picture Trust, 2002–. Hon. Mem., Brit. Soc. of Cinematographers (Governor, 1969–79; 1st Vice-Pres., 1976–77; award for Outstanding Contribution to Film Industry, 1967; special award for services to UK film prodn sector as British Film Comr, 1997); Associate Mem., Amer. Soc. of Cinematographers, 1981–96; Hon. Life Mem., BECTU, 1990 (Mem., ACTT, 1947); Fellow, BFI, 1997; Hon. Life Fellow, BKSTS - The Moving Image Soc., 1995 (Patron, 1997–; Award of Merit, 2003); Hon. Mem., Guild of British Camera Technicians (Trustee, 1993–). Hon. Technical Advr, Royal Naval Film Corp.; Member: Adv. Bd, Northern Media Sch., 1996–2001; Assoc. of Film Comrs Internat., 1999–. Pres., UK Friends of Akim (Israel Assoc. for Mentally Handicapped); Vice Pres., Muscular Dystrophy Campaign; Patron, Young Persons Concert Foundn. Dr (*hc*) Sheffield Hallam, 1996. Award of Merit, Guild of Film Prodn Execs, 1986; Lifetime achievement award, Birmingham Internat. Film and TV Festival, 1997; Howard Dutch Horton Award, Assoc. of Film Comrs Internat., 1997. *Recreations:* listening to music, vintage motoring, veteran jogging (finished a mere 13,006 places behind the winner, London Marathon 1982). *Address:* 31 West Heath Avenue, NW11 7QJ. *T:* (020) 8455 6696, *Fax:* (020) 8458 1957; *e-mail:* sydney.samuelson@zen.co.uk.

SAMUELSSON, Prof. Bengt Ingemar; Professor of Medical and Physiological Chemistry, Karolinska Institutet, Stockholm, 1972–99, now Emeritus; Chairman, Nobel Foundation, Stockholm, 1993–2005; *b* Halmstad, Sweden, 21 May 1934; *s* of Anders and Stina Samuelsson; *m* 1958, Inga Karin Bergstein; one *s* one *d* (and one *d* decd). *Educ:* Karolinska Institutet (DMedSci 1960, MD 1961). Res. Fellow, Harvard Univ., 1961–62; Asst Prof. of Med. Chemistry, Karolinska Inst., 1961–66; Prof., Royal Vet. Coll., Stockholm, 1967–72; Chm., Dept of Chemistry, 1973–83, Dean of Med. Faculty, 1978–83, Pres., 1983–95, Karolinska Inst., Stockholm. Vis. Prof., Harvard, 1976; T. Y. Shen Vis. Prof. in Med. Chem., MIT, 1977; Walker-Ames Prof., Washington Univ., 1987. Lectures include: Shirley Johnson Meml, Philadelphia, 1977; Sixth Annual Marrs McLean, Houston, 1978; Harvey, NY, 1979; Lane Medical, Stanford Univ., 1981; Eighth Annual Sci. in Med., Univ. of Washington, 1981; Arthur C. Corcoran Meml, Cleveland, Ohio, 1981; Kober, Assoc. of Amer. Physicians, 1982; Brown-Razor, Rice Univ., Houston, 1984; Solomon A. Berson Meml, Mount Sinai Sch. of Medicine, NY, 1984; Angelo Minich, Venice, 1988; Hans Neurath, Univ. of Washington, 1990; Dunham, Harvard Med. Sch., 1990; First Fogarty Internat., NIH, 1992. Member: Nobel Assembly, Karolinska Inst., 1972–99 (Chm., 1990); Nobel Cttee for Physiol. or Medicine, 1984–89 (Chm., 1987–89); Swedish Govt Res. Adv. Bd, 1985–88; Nat. Commn on Health Policy, 1987–90; ESTA, 1995–97. Member: Royal Swedish Acad. of Scis, 1981–; Mediterranean Acad., Catania, 1982–; US Nat. Acad. of Scis, 1984; French Acad. of Scis, 1989; Royal Soc., 1990; Royal Nat. Acad. of Medicine, Spain, 1991; Hon. Prof., Bethune Univ. of Med. Scis, China, 1986; Hon. Member: Amer. Soc. of Biological Chemists, 1976; Assoc. of American Physicians, 1982; Swedish Med. Assoc., 1982; Italian Pharmacological Soc., 1985; Acad. Nac. de Medicina de Buenos Aires, 1986; Internat. Soc. of Haematology, 1986; Spanish Soc. of Allergology and Clinical Immunology, 1989; Foreign Hon. Member: Amer. Acad. of Arts and Scis, 1982–; Internat. Acad. of Science, ICSD; Founding Mem., Academia Europaea, 1988. Hon. DSc: Chicago, 1978; Illinois, 1983; DUniv: Rio de Janeiro, 1986; Buenos Aires, 1986; Complutense, Madrid, 1991; Milan, 1993; Louisiana State, 1993; Uppsala, 2007. Nobel Prize in Physiology or Medicine (jtly), 1982; numerous awards and prizes. *Publications:* papers on biochemistry of prostaglandins, thromboxanes and leukotrienes. *Address:* Department of Medical Biochemistry and Biophysics, Karolinska Institutet, 17177 Stockholm, Sweden. *T:* (8) 52487600.

SAMWORTH, David Chetwode, CBE 1985; DL; President, Samworth Brothers (Holdings) Ltd (formerly Gorran Foods Ltd), since 2005 (Director since 1981; Chairman, 1984–2005); *b* 25 June 1935; *s* of Frank and Phyllis Samworth; *m* 1969, Rosemary Grace Cadell; one *s* three *d*. *Educ:* Uppingham Sch. Chm., Pork Farms Ltd, 1968–81; Director: Northern Foods Ltd, 1978–81; Imperial Gp, 1983–85; (non-exec.) Thorntons plc, 1988–93. Chm., Meat and Livestock Commn, 1980–84. Member: Leicester No 3 HMC, 1970–74; Trent RHA, 1974–78, 1980–84. President: RASE, 2000–01; Leics Agricl Soc., 1996–99; Young Enterprise, Leics, 2001–04. Chm. Trustees, Uppingham Sch., 1995–99. DL Leics, 1984, High Sheriff, Leics, 1997. *Recreation:* fishing. *Address:* Samworth Brothers (Holdings) Ltd, Chetwode House, Samworth Way, Melton Mowbray, Leics LE13 1GA.

SANBERK, Özdem; Member, Foreign Relations Board, TESEV (Turkish economic and social studies foundation), 2003 (Director, 2000–03); *b* 1938; *m* Sumru Sanberk; one *d*. *Educ:* Faculty of Law, Univ. of Istanbul. Joined Turkish Ministry of Foreign Affairs, 1963; Dep. Perm. Deleg. to OECD, Paris, and to UNESCO, Paris, 1980–83; Dep. Dir-Gen. for Bilateral Economic Affairs, Min. of Foreign Affairs, 1983–85; Advr for external relations to Prime Minister, 1985–87; Ambassador and Perm Deleg. to EC, 1987; Under-Sec., Min. of Foreign Affairs, 1991; Ambassador to UK, 1995–2000. Numerous foreign orders. *Address:* c/o TESEV, Bankalar Cad. No 2, Kat 3, Minerva Han, Karakoy 80020, Istanbul, Turkey. *T:* (212) 2928903, *Fax:* (212) 2439509.

SANCTUARY, Gerald Philip; Secretary, National Union of Journalists Provident Fund, 1984–95; *b* 22 Nov. 1930; *s* of late John Cyril Tabor Sanctuary, MD and Maisie Toppin Sanctuary (*née* Brooks); *m* 1956, Rosemary Patricia L'Estrange, Dublin; three *s* two *d*. *Educ:* Bryanston Sch.; Law Soc.'s Sch. of Law. National Service Pilot, 1953–55; Asst Solicitor, Kingston, 1955–56; Partner in Hasties, Solicitors, Lincoln's Inn Fields, 1957–62; Field Sec., Nat. Marriage Guidance Council, 1963–65, Nat. Secretary 1965–69; Exec. Dir, Sex Information and Educn Council of US, 1969–71; Sec., Professional and Public Relations, The Law Soc., 1971–78; Exec. Dir, Internat. Bar Assoc., 1978–79; Legal Adviser and Regional and Local Affairs Dir, Mencap, 1979–84. Regl PR Consultant, E of England Reg., Prince's Trust, 2000–. Hon. Treas., GAPAN, 1986–. Editor, Law Soc. series, It's Your Law, 1973–79. Regular broadcaster on radio. *Publications:* Marriage Under Stress, 1968; Divorce—and After, 1970, 2nd edn 1976; Before You See a Solicitor, 1973, 2nd edn 1983; After I'm Gone—what will happen to my Handicapped Child?, 1984, 2nd edn 1991; contrib., Moral Implications of Marriage Counselling, 1971; Vie Affective et Sexuelle, 1972; Loss Prevention Manual, 1978; The English Legal Heritage, 1979; booklets: Fishpool Street—St Albans, 1984; Tudor St Albans; St Albans and the Wars of the Roses, 1985; The Romans in St Albans, 1986; The Monastery at St Albans, 1987; Shakespeare's Globe Theatre, 1992; Abbey Theatre, St Albans, 1993. *Recreations:* amateur drama, organising murder mystery weekends. *Address:* 99 Beechwood Avenue, St Albans, Herts AL1 4XU. *T:* (01727) 842666.

SANDARS, Christopher Thomas; Director General (Central Budget) (formerly Assistant Under-Secretary of State (General Finance)), Ministry of Defence, 1997–2002; *b* 6 March 1942; *s* of late Vice-Adm. Sir Thomas Sandars, KBE, CB and Lady Sandars; *m* 1966, Elizabeth Anne Yielder; three *s* one *d*. *Educ:* Oundle Sch.; Corpus Christi Coll., Cambridge (Trevelyan Schol.; Foundation Schol.). Joined MoD, 1964; Asst Private Sec. to Minister of State, 1967–69; Central Policy Review Staff, Cabinet Office, 1971–74; Private Sec. to Minister of State, 1975–77; Hd, General Finance Div. 1, 1977–80; Hd, Defence Secretariat 13, 1980–84; RCDS, 1985; Hd, Secretariat 9 (Air), 1986–90; Asst Under-Sec. of State, MoD, 1990–95; Fellow, Center for Internat. Affairs, Harvard Univ., 1995–96. *Publication:* America's Overseas Garrisons: the leasehold empire, 2000. *Recreations:* painting, gardening, theatre. *Address:* 10 Crescent Grove, SW4 7AH.

SANDARS, Nancy Katharine, FBA 1984; FSA; archaeologist; *b* 29 June 1914; *d* of Edward Carew Sandars and Gertrude Annie Sandars (*née* Phipps). *Educ:* at home; Wychwood School, Oxford; Inst. of Archaeology, Univ. of London (Diploma 1949); St Hugh's College, Oxford (BLitt 1957). Archaeological research and travel in Europe, 1949–69; British School at Athens, 1954–55; Elizabeth Wordsworth Studentship, St Hugh's College, Oxford, 1958–61; travelled in Middle East, 1957, 1958, 1962, 1966; conferences, lectures (Prague, Sofia, McGill Univ.); excavations in British Isles and Greece. *Publications:* Bronze Age Cultures in France, 1957; The Epic of Gilgamesh, an English version, 1960; Prehistoric Art in Europe, 1967, rev. edn 1985; Poems of Heaven and Hell from Ancient Mesopotamia, 1971; The Sea-Peoples: warriors of the ancient Mediterranean, 1978; Grandmother's Steps: poems, 2001; articles on David Jones, painter and poet. *Recreations:* walking, translating, looking at pictures. *Address:* The Manor House, Little Tew, Chipping Norton, Oxford OX7 4JF. *Club:* University Women's.

SANDARS, Prof. Patrick George Henry; Professor of Experimental Physics and Student of Christ Church, Oxford University, 1978–2000; *b* 29 March 1935; *s* of late P. R. and A. C. Sandars; *m* 1959, P. B. Hall; two *s*. *Educ:* Wellington Coll.; Balliol Coll., Oxford (MA, DPhil). Oxford University: Weir Junior Research Fellow, University Coll., and ICI Research Fellow, Clarendon Laboratory, 1960–63; Tutorial Fellow, Balliol Coll., and Univ. Lectr, 1964–72; Reader in Physics, 1972–77; Head of Clarendon Lab., 1987–90; Hd, Atomic and Laser Physics, 1990–95; Junior Proctor, 1971–72. *Address:* 3 Hawkswell Gardens, Oxford OX2 7EX. *T:* (01865) 558535.

SANDBANK, Charles Peter, FREng; Deputy Director of Engineering, BBC, 1985–91; Broadcasting Technology Adviser, Department of Trade and Industry, 1993–2007; *b* 14 Aug. 1931; *s* of Gustav and Clare Sandbank; *m* 1955, Audrey Celia; one *s* two *d*. *Educ:* Bromley Grammar Sch.; London Univ. (BSc, DIC). FREng (FEng 1983); FIET, FInstP. Prodn Engr, 1953–55, Develt Engr, 1955–60, Brimar Valve Co.; Develt Section Head, STC Transistor Div., 1960–64; Head of Electron Devices Lab., 1964–68, Manager,

Communication Systems Div., 1968–78, Standard Telecommunication Laboratories; Head of BBC Research Dept, 1978–84; Asst Dir of Engrg, 1984–85, Asst to Dir of Engrg, 1991–93, BBC. Mem. Council: IEE, 1978–81, 1989–92 (Chairman: Electronics Divisional Bd, 1979–80; London Centre, 1991–92); Royal TV Soc., 1983–86, 1989–92; Chairman: EBU New Systems and Services Cttee, 1984–89; EBU High Definition TV Cttee, 1981–84; EUREKA High Definition Television Project Adv. Bd, 1988–94; Jt Technical Cttee, EBU/Eur. Telecommunications Standards Inst., 1990–93; DTI Cttee for Enhanced Definition TV, 1990–2007; DCMS/DTI Electronic Cinema Cttee, 2000; Founding Co-Chm., European Digital Cinema Forum, 2001–; Bureau mem., EBU Tech. Cttee, 1989–93. Ext. Examr, London Univ., 1982–89. Royal Acad. of Engrg Vis. Prof. of Information Systems Design, Univ. of Bradford, 1995–. Dir, Snell and Wilcox Ltd, 1993–97. Chm., Internal Cttee of Inquiry into Legionnaires Disease Outbreak at Broadcasting House, London, 1988. Liveryman, Scientific Instrument Makers' Co., 1988–. Fellow, SMPTE, 1989; FBKSTS 1991; FRTS; FRSA. DUniv Surrey, 1994; Hon. DEng Bradford, 2004. *Publications:* Optical Fibre Communication Systems, 1980; Digital Television, 1990; papers and patents (about 200) on semiconductor devices, integrated circuits, solid-state bulk effects, compound semiconductors, micro-waves, electron-phonon interactions, navigational aids, electro-optics and broadcasting technology. *Recreations:* boatbuilding, sailing, film-making, music, garden-watching. *Address:* Grailands, 30 Beech Road, Reigate, Surrey RH2 9NA. *Club:* Royal Norfolk and Suffolk Yacht.

SANDBERG, family name of **Baron Sandberg.**

SANDBERG, Baron *cr* 1997 (Life Peer), of Passfield in the co. of Hampshire; **Michael Graham Ruddock Sandberg,** Kt 1986; CBE 1982 (OBE 1977); Chairman: The Hongkong and Shanghai Banking Corporation, 1977–86; The British Bank of the Middle East, 1980–86; *b* 31 May 1927; *s* of Gerald Arthur Clifford Sandberg and Ethel Marion Sandberg; *m* 1954, Carmel Mary Roseleen Donnelly; two *s* two *d. Educ:* St Edward's Sch., Oxford. 6th Lancers (Indian Army) and First King's Dragoon Guards, 1945. Joined The Hongkong and Shanghai Banking Corp., 1949. Director: Winsor Properties Hldgs Ltd, HK; Winsor Industrial Corp. Ltd, HK; Green Island Cement Hldgs Ltd, HK; New World Develt Co. Ltd, HK. Mem. Exec. Council, Hong Kong, 1978–86. Steward, Royal Hong Kong Jockey Club, 1972–86, Chm., 1981–86; Treasurer, Univ. of Hong Kong, 1977–86. FCIB (FIB 1977; Vice Pres. 1984–87); FRSA 1983. Freeman, City of London, 1988. Hon. LLD: Hong Kong, 1984; Pepperdine, 1986. *Publication:* The Sandberg Watch Collection, 1998. *Recreations:* horse racing, bridge, cricket, horology. *Address:* Field House, Wheatsheaf Enclosure, Liphook, Hants GU30 7EJ. *Clubs:* White's, Garrick, MCC; Surrey CC (Pres. 1988), Hampshire CC.

SANDBY-THOMAS, Rachel Mary; Solicitor and Director General, Legal Services, Department for Business, Enterprise and Regulatory Reform, since 2008; *b* 25 May 1963; *d* of Dr Paul and Mary Sandby-Thomas; *m* 1999, Richard Gough; two *s. Educ:* St Catharine's Coll., Cambridge (BA Law (double 1st) 1985). Admitted solicitor, 1989; Linklaters & Paines, 1987–92; Legal Adviser: Legal Advrs, HM Treasury, 1993–95; Legal Advrs, Cabinet Office, 1995–97; Attorney General's Chambers, 1997–99; DoH, 1999–2004; Legal Advrs, Cabinet Office, 2004; Dir, Legal Services B, DTI, 2004–07; Dir, Tax Law Gp, HMRC, 2007–08. *Recreations:* reading, socialising, family. *Address:* Department for Business, Enterprise and Regulatory Reform, 1 Victoria Street, SW1H 0ET. *T:* (020) 7215 3039; *e-mail:* Rachel.Sandby-Thomas@berr.gsi.gov.uk.

SANDELL, Terence, (Terry), OBE 1991; Director, Ukraine, British Council, and Cultural Counsellor, British Embassy, Kyiv, since 2005; *b* 8 Sept. 1948; *s* of James William Sandell and Helen Elizabeth McCombie; *m* 1984, Kate Ling; two *s. Educ:* Watford Grammar Sch. for Boys; Univ. of Nottingham (BA Hons); Univ. of Edinburgh; City Univ. (MA). VSO, Berber, N Sudan, 1970–72. Joined British Council, 1974: Asst Rep. Dir, Omdurman Centre, Sudan, 1974–78; Regional Officer, Soviet Union and Mongolia, London, 1978–81; 1st Sec. (Cultural), British Embassy, Moscow, 1981–83; Asst Rep., Vienna, 1983–86, Rep. 1986–89; Projects Manager, Soviet Union, London, 1989; Dir, Soviet Union/CIS, and Cultural Counsellor, British Embassy, Moscow, 1989–92; attachment to Dept of Arts Policy and Management, City Univ., 1992–93; Consultant, Arts Policy Develt, British Council, 1993–94; Dir, Visiting Arts Office of GB and NI, subseq. Visiting Arts, 1994–2005. Chairman, Council of Europe Review of Cultural Policy: Russian Fedn, 1995–96; Romania, 1998–99; Georgia, 2000–02; Azerbaijan, 2000–02; Armenia, 2003; Ukraine, 2005–07. *Recreations:* walking, literature, theatre, travel. *Address:* c/o British Council, 10 Spring Gardens, SW1A 2BN.

SANDER, Her Honour Audrey Olga Helen; a Circuit Judge, 1995–2003; *b* 10 Nov. 1936; *d* of Ernest Sander and Marian Sander; *m* 1963, Prof. Adrian Gale; one *s* two *d. Educ:* St Paul's Girls' Sch.; Somerville Coll., Oxford (MA Jurisprudence). Called to the Bar, Gray's Inn, 1960; in practice at the Bar, 1960–77; Editl Asst, Legal Action Gp, 1978–83; admitted solicitor, 1986; practised as solicitor, 1986–95 (at Gill Akaster, 1989–95); Asst Recorder, 1990–94; Recorder, 1994–95. Legal Mem., Mental Health Rev. Tribunals, 1992–; Mem., Parole Bd of England and Wales, 2000–06. *Address:* c/o Plymouth Combined Court Centre, Armada Way, Plymouth, Devon PL1 2ER.

SANDERLING, Kurt; conductor; *b* 19 Sept. 1912; *m* 1st, 1941, Nina Bobath; one *s*; 2nd, 1963, Barbara Wagner; twin *s. Educ:* privately. Conductor: Leningrad Philharmonic Orch., 1941–60; East Berlin Symphony Orch., 1960–95; Philharmonia, 1980, now Conductor Emeritus. Guest conductor of many orchs in Europe and N America. *Address:* Am Iderfenngraben 47, 13156 Berlin, Germany.

SANDERS, Adrian Mark; MP (Lib Dem) Torbay, since 1997; *b* 25 April 1959; *s* of late John Sanders and Helen Sanders; *m* 1992, Alison Nortcliffe. *Educ:* Torquay Boys' Grammar Sch. Vice Pres., Nat. League of Young Liberals, 1985. Campaigns Officer, Assoc. of Liberal Councillors, 1986–89; Parly Officer, Lib Dem Whips' Office, 1989–90; Res. Officer, Assoc. of Lib Dem Councillors, 1990–92; Project Officer, Paddy Ashdown, MP, 1992–93; Policy Officer, NCVO, 1993–94; Grants Advr, Southern Assoc. of Voluntary Action Gps for Europe, 1994. Mem. (L) Torbay BC, 1984–86. Contested (Lib Dem): Torbay, 1992; Devon and Plymouth East, EP elecn, 1994. Lib Dem spokesman: on local govt and housing (on housing, 1997–2001, and on local govt, 1999–2001); on tourism, 2001–05; a Lib Dem Whip, 1997–2001; Lib Dem Dep. Chief Whip, 2006–. Mem., DCMS Select Cttee, 2005–. Chm., All Pty Diabetes Gp, 1997–. *Address:* House of Commons, SW1A 0AA.

SANDERS, Prof. Dale, PhD, ScD; FRS 2001; Professor of Biology, since 1992 and Head of Department, since 2004, University of York; *b* 13 May 1953; *s* of Leslie G. D. Sanders and Daphne M. Sanders; *m* 1983, Marcelle Mekies (marr. diss. 2002); three *d. Educ:* Hemel Hempstead Grammar Sch.; Univ. of York (BA); Darwin Coll., Cambridge (PhD 1978, ScD 1993). James Hudson Brown Res. Fellow, 1978–79, Post-doctoral Res. Associate, 1979–83, Sch. of Medicine, Yale Univ.; University of York: Lectr, 1983–89; Reader, 1989–92. Nuffield Foundn Sci. Res. Fellow, 1989–90; Royal Soc./Leverhulme Trust Sen. Res. Fellow, 1997–98. President's Medal, Soc. for Exptl Biol., 1987; Körber Eur. Sci.

Award, 2001. *Publications:* numerous refereed articles in learned jls. *Recreations:* talking and walking with family and friends. *Address:* Biology Department (Area 6), PO Box 373, University of York, York YO10 5YW. *T:* (01904) 328555.

SANDERS, Prof. David John, PhD; FBA 2005; Professor of Government, University of Essex, since 1993; *b* 19 Dec. 1950; *s* of John Sanders and Nora Sanders; *m* 2001, Gillian Wills; three *s* one *d. Educ:* John Port Sch., Etwall; Loughborough Univ. (BSc); Univ. of Essex (MA; PhD). University of Essex: Lectr, 1975–88, Sen. Lectr, 1988–90, Reader, 1990–93, in Government; Pro Vice Chancellor for Res., 1997–2001. Vis. Prof., Univ. of Wisconsin-Madison, 1981–82. *Publications:* Patterns of Political Instability, 1981; Lawmaking and Co-operation in International Politics, 1986; Losing an Empire, Finding a Role, 1990; (jtly) On Message, 1997; Political Choice in Britain, 2004; over 50 articles in learned jls. *Recreations:* playing folk music in pubs, walking. *Address:* Department of Government, University of Essex, Wivenhoe Park, Colchester CO4 3SQ. *T:* (01206) 872759; *e-mail:* sanders@essex.ac.uk.

SANDERS, Donald Neil, AO 1994; CB 1983; Chief Executive, 1987–92 and Managing Director, 1991–92, Commonwealth Bank of Australia; *b* Sydney, 21 June 1927; *s* of L. G. and R. M. Sanders; *m* 1952, Betty Elaine, *d* of W. B. and E. M. Constance; four *s* one *d. Educ:* Wollongong High Sch.; Univ. of Sydney (BEc). Commonwealth Bank of Australia, 1943–60; Australian Treasury, 1956; Bank of England, 1960; Reserve Bank of Australia, 1960–87: Supt, Credit Policy Div., Banking Dept, 1964–66; Dep. Manager: Banking Dept, 1966–67; Res. Dept, 1967–70; Aust. Embassy, Washington DC, 1968; Chief Manager: Securities Markets Dept, 1970–72; Banking and Finance Dept, 1972–74; Adviser and Chief Manager, Banking and Finance Dept, 1974–75; Dep. Governor and Dep. Chm., 1975–87; Man. Dir, Commonwealth Banking Corp., 1987–91. Chm., H-G Ventures Ltd, 1995–2000; Director: Queensland Investment Corp., 1992–98; Lend Lease Corp. Ltd, 1992–99; Australian Chamber Orch. Ltd, 1993–99; MLC Ltd, 1994–99 (Chm., 1998–99). *Address:* Somerset, Taralga Road, via Goulburn, NSW 2580, Australia.

SANDERS, Prof. Ed Parish, FBA 1989; Arts and Sciences Professor of Religion, Duke University, 1990–2005; *b* 18 April 1937; *s* of Mildred Sanders (née Parish) and Eula Thomas Sanders; *m* 1st, 1963, Becky Jill Hall (marr. diss. 1978); one *d*; 2nd, 1996, Rebecca N. Gray. *Educ:* Texas Wesleyan College (BA); Southern Methodist Univ. (BD); Union Theological Seminary, NY (ThD). Asst Prof. of Religious Studies, McMaster Univ., 1966–70, Associate Prof., 1970–74, Prof., 1974–88; Dean Ireland's Prof. of Exegesis of Holy Scripture, Oxford Univ., 1984–89. Visiting Professor: Jewish Theol. Seminary, 1980; Chair of Judeo-Christian Studies, Tulane Univ., 1980; Walter G. Mason Dist. Vis. Prof., Coll. of William and Mary in Virginia, 1981; Vis. Fellow Commoner, Trinity Coll., Cambridge, 1982; Kraft-Hiatt Vis. Prof., Brandeis Univ., 1999. Donnellan Lectr, TCD, 1982. Fellow, Amer. Acad. of Arts and Scis, 2003. *Publications:* The Tendencies of the Synoptic Tradition, 1969; Paul and Palestinian Judaism, 1977, 2nd edn 1981; (ed) Jewish and Christian Self-Definition, vol. I, The Shaping of Christianity in the Second and Third Centuries, 1980, vol. II, Aspects of Judaism in the Graeco-Roman Period, 1981, vol. III, Self-Definition in the Graeco-Roman World, 1982; Paul, The Law and the Jewish People, 1983; Jesus and Judaism, 1985, 3rd edn 1987; (ed) Jesus, The Gospels and the Church, 1987; (with Margaret Davies) Studying the Synoptic Gospels, 1989; Jewish Law from Jesus to the Mishnah, 1990; Paul, 1991; Judaism: practice and belief 63 BCE to 66 BCE, 1992; The Historical Figure of Jesus, 1993; Paul: a very short introduction, 2001; articles in NT Studies, Jl of Biblical Literature, Harvard Theol. Review, Jewish Quarterly Review.

SANDERS, Prof. Jeremy Keith Morris, FRS 1995; Professor, Department of Chemistry, since 1996, Head, School of Physical Sciences, since 2009, and Deputy Vice-Chancellor, since 2006, Cambridge University; Fellow of Selwyn College, Cambridge, since 1976; *b* 3 May 1948; *s* of Sidney Sanders and Sylvia (née Rutman); *m* 1972, Louise Elliott; one *s* one *d. Educ:* Imperial Coll., London (BSc, ARCS Chem. 1969); PhD 1972, MA 1974, ScD 2001, Cantab. FRSC, CChem. Junior Res. Fellow, Christ's Coll., Cambridge, 1972; NATO/EMBO Fellow, Stanford Univ., 1972–73; Cambridge University: Demonstrator, 1973–78; Lectr in Chemistry, 1978–92; Reader in Chemistry and Asst Hd, Dept of Chemistry, 1992–96; Dep. Hd, 1998–2000, Hd, 2000–06, Dept of Chem.; Mem. Council, 1999–2002; Chm., Allocations Cttee, 1999–2000; Chm., Bd of Mgt, Cambridge Prog. for Industry, 2003–07. Chm., Chem. sub-panel, 2008 RAE, 2004–08. Trustee, Cambridge Foundn, 2007–. FRSA 1997. Associate Ed., New Jl of Chemistry, 1998–2000; Chm. Editl Bd, Chem. Soc. Reviews, 2000–02. Pfizer Awards, Pfizer plc, 1984, 1988; Royal Society of Chemistry: Meldola Medal, 1975; Hickinbottom Award, 1981; Josef Loschmidt Prize, 1994; Pedler Lect. and Medal, 1996; Fellow, Japan Soc. for the Promotion of Science, 2002; Izatt-Christensen Award for Macrocyclic Chemistry, USA, 2003. *Publications:* (with B. K. Hunter) Modern NMR Spectroscopy, 1987, 2nd edn 1993; contribs to chem. and biochem. jls. *Recreations:* family, cooking, music, walking. *Address:* University Chemical Laboratory, Lensfield Road, Cambridge CB2 1EW. *T:* (01223) 336411, *Fax:* (01223) 336017; *e-mail:* jkms@cam.ac.uk. *Club:* Athenæum.

SANDERS, Rear-Adm. Jeremy Thomas, CB 1994; OBE 1982; Commander British Forces, Gibraltar, 1992–94; *b* 23 Nov. 1942; *s* of late Thomas Sanders and Pauline (née Woodfield-Smith); *m* 1st, 1966, Judith Rosemary Jones (*d* 2003); two *d*; 2nd, 2005, Jane Elizabeth Cambrook. *Educ:* Norwood Sch., Exeter; Pangbourne Coll. BRNC, Dartmouth, 1960; appts include: Lieut i/c HMS Chilcompton and Kellington, 1968–69; long communications course, HMS Mercury, 1970; Lt Comdr on staff of Flag Officer, Submarines, 1974–76; Comdr i/c HMS Salisbury, 1977–78; ndc 1979; SO Ops to Flag Officer, 1st Flotilla, 1981–83; Capt., 8th Frigate Sqdn and i/c HMS Andromeda, 1985–87; Dir, Maritime Tactical Sch., 1987–89; Chief Naval Signal Officer, 1989–90; Dir, Naval Warfare, 1990–92. Trustee: Falkland Islands Memorial Chapel, 2003– (Chm., 2006–); RN Submarine Mus., 2004–06. JP S Hants 1997–2006 (Dep. Chm. Bench, 2003, 2004). *Recreations:* rambling and hill walking, cabinet making, growing vegetables, cricket. *Club:* MCC.

SANDERS, John Leslie Yorath; HM Diplomatic Service, retired; *b* 5 May 1929; *s* of late Reginald Yorath Sanders and Gladys Elizabeth Sanders (née Blything); *m* 1953, Brigit Mary Lucine Altounyan (*d* 1999); one *s* two *d. Educ:* Dulwich Coll. Prep. Sch.; Cranleigh School. Higher Dip. in Furniture Prodn and Design, London Coll. of Furniture, 1982. Nat. Service in HM Forces (RA), 1948–50; entered HM Foreign Service, 1950; FO, 1950–52; MECAS, Lebanon, 1953; Damascus, 1954–55; Bahrain, 1955–56; Vice-Consul, Basra, 1956–60; Oriental Sec., Rabat, 1960–63; FO, 1964–67; 1st Sec., Beirut, 1968–70; 1st Sec. and Head of Chancery, Mexico City, 1970–73; Counsellor, Khartoum, 1973–75; Counsellor, Beirut, 1975–76; Dir of Res., FCO, 1976–78; Ambassador to Panama, 1978–80. *Publication:* contrib. to Archaeologia Aeliana. *Recreations:* genealogy, music.

SANDERS, Sir John Reynolds M.; *see* Mayhew-Sanders.

SANDERS, Kate Emily Tyrrell, (Mrs C. W. Sanders); *see* Boyes, K. E. T.

SANDERS, Michael David, FRCS, FRCP, FRCOphth; Consultant Ophthalmologist, National Hospital for Neurology and Neurosurgery, 1969–99; *b* 19 Sept. 1935; *s* of Norris Manley Sanders and Gertrude Florence Sanders (*née* Hayley); *m* 1969, Thalia Margaret Garlick; one *s* one *d*. *Educ:* Tonbridge Sch.; Guy's Hosp., Univ. of London (MB BS). DO RCS/RCP; FRCS 1967; FRCP 1977; FRCOphth 1990 (Hon. FRCOphth 2001). Guy's Hosp., 1954–60; Moorfields Eye Hosp., 1964–67; Univ. of California, San Francisco, 1967–68; Consultant Ophthalmologist, St Thomas' Hosp., 1972–96. Civilian Consultant, RAF, 1975–2000; Dep. Hospitallier, St John Ophthalmic Hosp., Jerusalem, 1992. Visiting Professor: Mayo Clinic, 1979; Univ. of New South Wales, 1982; NY Eye and Ear Infirmary, 1995. Lectures: Middlemore, Birmingham and Midlands Eye Hosp., 1985; Percival J. Hay Meml, N of England Ophthalmol Soc., 1986; Ida Mann, Oxford Univ., 1987; Sir Stewart Duke Elder, Ophthalmol. Soc. UK, 1987; Lettsomian, Med. Soc. London, 1988; Sir William Bowman, RCOphth, 1996; Montgomery, Irish Coll. of Ophthalmologists, 1997. Trustee, Frost Charitable Trust, 1974–96 (Chm., 1996–); Med. Advr, Iris Fund for Prevention of Blindness, 1982–97 (Mem. Council, 1997–2003); Pres., Internat. Neuro-Ophthalmology Soc., 1990– (Mem. Council, 1974–). *Publications:* Topics in Neuro-Ophthalmology, 1978; Computerised Tomography in Neuro-Ophthalmology, 1982; Common Problems in Neuro-Ophthalmology, 1997. *Recreations:* golf, collecting. *Address:* Chawton Lodge, Chawton, near Alton, Hants GU34 1SL. *T:* (01420) 86681. *Clubs:* Royal Air Force; Hankley Common Golf (Farnham).

SANDERS, Nicholas John, CB 1998; PhD; Higher Education Adviser, Department for Education and Skills, 2004–05; *b* 14 Sept. 1946; *s* of Ivor and Mollie Sanders; *m* 1971, Alison Ruth Carter; one *s* one *d*. *Educ:* King Edward's Sch., Birmingham; Magdalene Coll., Cambridge (MA, PhD). Joined DES, 1971, subseq. Dept for Educn, then DFEE, then DFES; Principal Private Sec. to Sec. of State, 1974–75; Private Sec. to Prime Minister, 1978–81; Prin. Finance Officer, 1989–93; Hd, Teachers Br., 1993–95; Dir, Teachers, Funding and Curriculum, 1995–99; Dir for Higher Education, 1999–2003. Mem. Council, Univ. of Warwick, 2004–. Hon. LLD Manchester, 2004.

SANDERS, Nicholas Paul Martin; a District Judge (Magistrates' Courts), Wirral, Merseyside, since 2004, and Chester, Cheshire, since 2007; *b* 25 Feb. 1958; *s* of late Oswald Sanders and Betty Sanders (*née* Hooper); *m* 1981, Alexandra (*née* Langham); two *d*. *Educ:* Exeter Sch.; Britannia Royal Naval Coll.; Univ. of Exeter (LLB Hons). RN officer, 1976–89. Called to the Bar, Middle Temple, 1987; admitted solicitor, 1990; Solicitor: Linford Brown, Exmouth, 1989–94; Rundle Walker, Exeter, 1994–2001; Sen. Magistrate and HM Coroner, Falkland Is and British Antarctic Territory, 2001–04; Sen. Magistrate, Ascension Is., 2004–06. Mem., Shropshire Union Canal Soc. *Recreations:* sailing, English canals, golf, motor cycles. *Address:* c/o Wirral Magistrates' Court, The Sessions Court, Chester Street, Birkenhead CH41 5HW. *Club:* Royal Over-Seas League.

SANDERS, Peter Basil, CBE 1993; Chief Executive, Commission for Racial Equality, 1988–93 (Director, 1977–88); *b* 9 June 1938; *s* of Basil Alfred Horace Sanders and Ellen May Sanders (*née* Cockrell); *m* 1st, 1961, Janet Valerie (*née* Child) (marr. diss. 1984); two *s* one *d*; 2nd, 1988, Anita Jackson. *Educ:* Queen Elizabeth's Grammar Sch., Barnet; Wadham Coll., Oxford (MA, DPhil). Administrative Officer, Basutoland, 1961–66; Research in Oxford for DPhil, 1966–70; Officer, Min. of Defence, 1971–73; Race Relations Bd: Principal Conciliation Officer, 1973–74; Dep. Chief Officer, 1974–77. *Publications:* Lithoko: Sotho Praise-Poems (ed jtly and trans. with an Introd. and Notes), 1974; Moshoeshoe, Chief of the Sotho, 1975; The Simple Annals: the history of an Essex and East End family, 1989; (ed jtly) Race Relations in Britain: a developing agenda, 1998; The Last of the Queen's Men: a Lesotho experience, 2000; (with C. Murray) Medicine Murder in Colonial Lesotho: the anatomy of a moral crisis, 2005. *Address:* 31D Church Street, Saffron Walden, Essex CB10 1JW. *T:* (01799) 520411.

SANDERS, Sir Robert (Tait), KBE 1980; CMG 1974; HMOCS; Secretary to the Cabinet, Government of Fiji, 1970–79; Treaties Adviser, Government of Fiji, 1985–87; *b* 2 Feb. 1925; *s* of late A. S. W. Sanders and Charlotte McCulloch; *m* 1951, Barbara, *d* of G. Sutcliffe; two *s* (and one *s* decd). *Educ:* Canmore Public Sch., Dunfermline; Dunfermline High Sch.; Fettes Coll., Edinburgh; Cambridge Univ. (Major Open Classical Schol., Pembroke Coll., 1943; John Stewart of Rannoch Schol. in Latin and Greek, 1947; 1st cl. Hons, Pts I and II of Classical Tripos); London Sch. of Economics, 1949–50; SOAS, 1949–50. Served War, 1943–46: Lieut, 1st Bn the Royal Scots, India and Malaya. Sir Arthur Thomson Travelling Schol., 1948; Sir William Browne Medal for Latin Epigram, 1948; MA (Cantab) 1951. Joined HM Overseas Civil Service, Fiji, as Dist Officer, 1950; Sec. to Govt of Tonga, 1956–58; Sec., Coconut Commn of Enquiry, 1963; MLC, Fiji, 1963–64; Sec. for Natural Resources, 1965–67; Actg Sec. Fijian Affairs, and Actg Chm. Native Lands and Fisheries Commn, 1967; MEC, Fiji, 1967; Sec. to Chief Minister and to Council of Ministers, 1967; apptd Sec. to Cabinet, 1970, also Sec. for Foreign Affairs, 1970–74, Sec. for Home Affairs, 1972–74 and Sec. for Information, 1975–76. Mem., Internat. Cttee, Stirling Univ., 1991–93. Fiji Independence Medal, 1970; 25th Anniversary of Fiji's Independence Medal, 1995. *Publications:* Interlude in Fiji, 1963; Fiji Treaty List, 1987; articles in Corona, jl of HMOCS. *Recreations:* languages, travel, golf, music, sailing. *Address:* 6 Park Manor, Crieff PH7 4LJ. *Club:* Royal Scots (Edinburgh).

SANDERS, His Honour Roger Benedict; a Circuit Judge, 1987–2005; Resident Judge, Harrow Crown Court, 1999–2005; *b* 1 Oct. 1940; *s* of late Maurice and Lilian Sanders; *m* 1st, 1969, Susan Brenner (marr. diss. 1992); two *s* (one *d* decd); 2nd, 1998, Dee Connolly, *e d* of John and Mary Connolly. *Educ:* Highgate School. Co-founder, Inner Temple Debating Soc., 1961, Chm. 1962. Called to the Bar, Inner Temple, 1965; South Eastern Circuit. Metropolitan Stipendiary Magistrate, 1980–87; a Recorder, 1986–87. A Chm., Inner London Juvenile Courts, 1980–87; Chm., Legal Cttee, Inner London Juvenile Panel, 1983–86; First Chm., No 1 (London S) Regional Duty Solicitor Cttee, 1984–85; Chm., NW London Adv. Cttee (Magistrates), 2008– (Dep. Chm., 2004–08); Member: Inner London Magistrates' Training Panel, 1983–87; Mental Health Review Tribunal, 1990–2000, 2006–; Middx Probation Cttee, 1999–2001. Chairman, Walker School Assoc. (Southgate), 1976, 1977; Schools' Debating Assoc. Judge, 1976–93. Mem., Haringey Schools Liaison Group, 1979. Mem., N Gauge Soc. Hon. Fellow, Univ. of E London, 1993.

SANDERS, Sir Ronald (Michael), KCMG 2002 (CMG 1997); KCN 2001; international consultant; Senior Ambassador with Ministerial rank, Antigua and Barbuda, 1999–2004; High Commissioner for Antigua and Barbuda in London, 1984–87, and 1995–2004; non-resident Ambassador to France and Germany, 1996–2004; *b* Guyana, 26 Jan. 1948; *m* 1975, Susan Indrani (*née* Ramphal). *Educ:* Sacred Heart RC Sch., Guyana; Boston Univ., USA; Sussex Univ. Gen. Man., Guyana Broadcasting Service, 1973–76; Communication Cons. to Pres., Caribbean Develt Bank, Barbados, 1977; Cons. to Govt of Antigua, 1977–81; Advr to For. Minister of Antigua and Barbuda, 1981–82; Dep. Perm. Rep. to UN, 1982–83; Ambassador to UNESCO and EEC, 1983–87, to FRG, 1986–87; Vis. Fellow, Oxford Univ., 1988–89. Director: Swiss Amer. Nat. Bank, Antigua, 1990–97; Guyana Telephone and Telegraph Co., 1991–97; Innovative Communications Corp., USA, 1998–; US Virgin Islands Telephone Co., 2003–; Belize Telephone Ltd, 2004–05; consultant, Internat. Relns, Atlantic Tele Network, USA, 1989–97. Dep. Chm., 2002–03, Chm., 2003–04, Caribbean Financial Action Task Force; Ambassador to WTO, 2002–04. Member: Inter-Govtl Council, Internat. Prog. for Develt of Communications, UNESCO, 1983–87; Exec. Bd, UNESCO, 1985–87; RIIA, 1987–; Internat. Inst. of Communications, 1984–; Caribbean Adv. Bd to FCO, 2007–. *Publications:* Broadcasting in Guyana, 1977; Antigua and Barbuda: transition, trial, triumph, 1984; (ed) Inseparable Humanity—an anthology of reflections of Shridath Ramphal, Commonwealth Secretary-General, 1988; (ed) Antigua Vision, Caribbean Reality: perspectives of Prime Minister Lester B. Bird, 2002; Crumbled Small: the Commonwealth Caribbean in world politics, 2005; several contribs to internat. jls on the Commonwealth, the Caribbean, and the Small States, also political commentaries. *Recreations:* reading, cinema. *Clubs:* Royal Automobile, St James's.

SANDERS, Prof. Roy, FRCS; consultant plastic surgeon, 1974–2006; former Consultant: Mount Vernon Centre for Plastic Surgery; BUPA Hospital Harpenden; BUPA Hospital Bushey; Humana Hospital; Bishops Wood Hospital, Northwood; *b* 20 Aug. 1937; *s* of Leslie John Sanders and Marguerite Alice (*née* Knight); *m* 1st, 1961, Ann Ruth Costar (marr. diss.); two *s* one *d*; 2nd, 1984, Fleur Annette Chandler, Baroness von Balajthy. *Educ:* Hertford Grammar Sch.; Charing Cross Hosp. Med. Sch. (BSc Hons Anatomy, MB, BS). LRCP 1962; FRCS 1967. Various hosp. appts; Sen. Lectr in Plastic Surgery, London Univ. and Hon. Cons. Plastic Surgeon, Mt Vernon Centre for Plastic Surgery, 1972–74; Cons. Plastic Surgeon, St Andrew's Hosp., Billericay and St Bart's Hosp., 1974–76; Hon. Sen. Lectr, London Univ., 1976–93; Hd, Service Dept, Plastic Maxillo-Facial and Oral Surgery, Mt Vernon Hosp., 1986–2003; Hon. Prof., UCL, 1993–. Sec., Brit. Assoc. Aesthetic Plastic Surgeons, 1984–87; Pres., Brit. Assoc. Plastic Surgeons, 1993 (Sec., 1987–90). OC Light Cavalry, HAC, 1996–2004. *Publications:* scientific pubns in med. jls and textbooks. *Recreations:* equestrian pursuits, watercolour painting, books. *Address:* 77 Harley Street, W1G 8QN. *T:* (020) 7935 7417; Upper Rye Farmhouse, Moreton-in-Marsh, Glos GL56 9AB. *T:* (01608) 650542. *Clubs:* Garrick, Honourable Artillery Company, Royal Society of Medicine.

SANDERS, Sebastian; Stable Jockey to Sir Mark Prescott, since 1997; *b* 25 Sept. 1971; *s* of Kevin Sanders and Jean Sanders (now Cooper); *m* 1998, Leona Robertson; one *d*. *Educ:* Lakeside Sch., Tamworth, Staffs. Champion Apprentice, 1995; winner: July Cup, on Compton Place, 1997; Irish 2000 Guineas, on Bachelor Duke, 2004; Preis von Europa, on Albanova, 2004; Nunthorpe, on Bahamian Pirate, 2004; French Prix de Diane Hermes, on Confidential Lady, 2006. (Jt) Champion Flat Jockey, 2007. *Recreations:* golf, scuba diving.

SANDERS, William George, CB 1991; CEng, FRINA; RCNC; Head of Royal Corps of Naval Constructors, 1986–91; Director General, Submarines, Ministry of Defence (PE), 1985–91; *b* 22 Jan. 1936; *s* of George and Alice Irene Sanders; *m* 1956, Marina Charlotte Burford; two *s* one *d*. *Educ:* Public Secondary Sch., Plymouth; Devonport Dockyard Tech. Coll.; RN Coll., Greenwich. Asst Constructor, Ship Dept, Admiralty, 1961–68; FNCO Western Fleet, 1968–70; Constructor, Ship Dept, MoD (Navy), 1970–77; Principal Naval Overseer, Scotland, 1977–79; Marconi Space and Defence Systems, 1979–81; Project Director, Type 23, 1981–83; DG Future Material Projects (Naval), MoD (PE), 1983–85. *Recreations:* golf, painting, gardening. *Address:* 3 Peel Court, Melksham, Wilts SN12 6DB.

SANDERSON, family name of **Baron Sanderson of Bowden**.

SANDERSON OF AYOT; 2nd Baron *cr* 1960, title disclaimed by the heir, Dr Alan Lindsay Sanderson, 1971.

SANDERSON OF BOWDEN, Baron *cr* 1985 (Life Peer), of Melrose in the District of Ettrick and Lauderdale; **Charles Russell Sanderson,** Kt 1981; Chairman, Clydesdale Bank PLC, 1998–2004 (Director, 1986–87 and since 1994; Deputy Chairman, 1996–98); Vice Lord-Lieutenant, Borders Region (Roxburgh, Ettrick and Lauderdale), 2003–08; *b* 30 April 1933; *s* of Charles Plummer Sanderson and Martha Evelyn Gardiner; *m* 1958, Frances Elizabeth Macaulay; one *s* two *d* (and one *s* decd). *Educ:* St Mary's Sch., Melrose; Trinity Coll., Glenalmond; Scottish Coll. of Textiles, Galashiels; Bradford Coll. (now Bradford Univ.). Commnd Royal Signals, 1952; served: 51 (Highland) Inf. Div. Signal Regt TA, 1953–56, KOSB TA, 1956–58. Partner, Chas P. Sanderson, Wool and Yarn Merchants, Melrose, 1958–87; Chairman: Edinburgh Financial Trust (formerly Yorkshire & Lancashire Investment Trust), 1983–87; Shires Investment Trust, 1984–87; Hawick Cashmere Co., 1991–; Scottish Mortgage & Trust, 1993–2003 (Mem. Bd, 1991–); Scottish Pride plc, 1994–97; Director: United Auctions, 1992–99; Edinburgh Woollen Mills, 1993–97; Watson & Philip, 1993–99; Morrison Construction Group, 1995–2000; Nat. Australia Gp Europe, 1998–2004; Develica Deutschland plc, 2006–; Accsys Technologies plc, 2007–. Minister of State, Scottish Office, 1987–90. Chairman, Roxburgh, Selkirk and Peebles Cons. and Unionist Assoc., 1970–73; Scottish Conservative Unionist Association: Chm. Central and Southern Area, 1974–75; Vice-Pres. 1975–77; Pres. 1977–79; Vice-Chm. Nat. Union of Cons Assocs, 1979–81 (Mem. Exec. Cttee, 1975–); Chm. Exec. Cttee, Nat. Union of Cons. Assocs, 1981–86; Member: Cons. Party Policy Cttee, 1979–86; Standing Adv. Cttee of Parly Candidates, 1979–86 (Vice-Chm. with responsibility for Europe, 1980–81); Chm., Scottish Cons. Party, 1990–93. Chm., Scottish Peers Assoc., 1998–2000. Pres., RHASS, 2002–03. Deacon, Galashiels Manufrs Corp., 1976; Chm., Eildon Housing Assoc., 1978–82. Chm., Abbotsford Trust, 2008–. Mem. Court, Napier Univ., 1994–2001; Governor, St Mary's Sch., Melrose, 1977–87 (Chm., 1998–2004); Mem. Council, Trinity Coll., Glenalmond, 1982–2000 (Chm., 1994–2000). Comr, Gen. Assembly of Ch. of Scotland, 1972. Mem. Court, Framework Knitters' Co., 2000– (Master, 2005–06). DL Roxburgh, Ettrick and Lauderdale, 1990. *Recreations:* golf, fishing, amateur operatics (Past Pres., Producer and Mem. Melrose Amateur Operatic Soc.). *Address:* Becketts Field, Bowden, Melrose, Roxburgh TD6 0ST. *T:* (01835) 822736. *Clubs:* Caledonian; Hon. Co. of Edinburgh Golfers (Muirfield).

SANDERSON, Prof. Alexis Godfrey James Slater; Spalding Professor of Eastern Religions and Ethics, and Fellow of All Souls College, Oxford University, since 1992; *b* 28 June 1948; *e s* of J. J. Sanderson, Houghton-le-Spring. *Educ:* Royal Masonic Sch., Watford; Balliol Coll., Oxford (BA 1971). Oxford University: Domus Sen. Schol., Merton Coll., 1971–74; Platnauer Jun. Res. Fellow, Brasenose Coll., 1974–77; Univ. Lectr in Sanskrit, 1977–92; Fellow of Wolfson Coll., 1977–92, Fellow Emeritus, 1992. *Address:* All Souls College, Oxford OX1 4AL.

SANDERSON, Bryan Kaye, CBE 1999; Chairman, Northern Rock plc, 2007–08; *b* 14 Oct. 1940; *s* of Eric and Anne Sanderson; *m* 1966, Sirkka Kärki; one *s* one *d*. *Educ:* Dame Allan's Sch., Newcastle upon Tyne; LSE (BSc Econ.); Dip. Business Studies, IMEDE Lausanne, 1973. VSO Peru, 1962–64; British Petroleum, 1964; Sen. BP rep., SE Asia and China, 1984–87; Chief Exec. Officer, BP Nutrition, 1987–90; CEO, BP Chemicals, then Chief Exec., BP Amoco Chemicals, 1990–2000; Man. Dir, British Petroleum, then BP Amoco, 1992–2000. Chairman: BUPA, 2001–06; Standard Chartered plc, 2003–06 (non-exec. Dir, 2002–06); non-executive Director: Corus (formerly British Steel), 1994–2001; Six Continents plc, 2001–03; Sunderland FC plc, 1997–2006 (Chm., 1998–2004); Chm., Sunderland Area Regeneration Co., 2001–. Chm., LSC, 2000–04. Member: Adv. Gp to the Labour Party on industrial competition policy, 1997–98; DTI Co. Law Steering Gp, 1998–2001. Mem., Cttee of Mgt, King's Fund, 1999–2006. Dir, Durham CCC, 2005–. Gov., LSE, 1997– (Vice-Chm. Govs, 1998–2003). Trustee, Economist, 2006–. Hon. FIChemE 2002. Hon. DBA: Sunderland, 1998; York, 1999. *Recreations:* reading, golf, walking, gardening. *Address:* 42 Brook Street, W1K 5DB. *T:* (020) 3178 4132, *Fax:* (020) 3178 4130. *Club:* Buckinghamshire Golf.

SANDERSON, Charles Denis; HM Diplomatic Service, retired; Fellow, St Peter's College, Oxford, 1985–96, now Emeritus; *b* 18 Dec. 1934; *s* of Norman and Elsie Sanderson; *m* 1960, Mary Joyce Gillow; one *s* two *d*. *Educ:* Bishopshalt Sch., Hillingdon, Middx; Pembroke Coll., Oxford (MA). National Service, 1953–55; Oxford, 1955–58; British Petroleum Co. Ltd, 1958–64; Second, later First Secretary, Commonwealth Relations Office, 1964–67; First Sec., Kingston, and concurrently, Haiti, 1967–70; Acting Consul, Port au Prince, 1969; First Sec., Head of Chancery and Consul, Panama, 1970–73; First Sec., FCO, 1973–75; Consul (Commercial), British Trade Development Office, New York, 1975–77; Dep. Consul General and Director Industrial Development, New York, 1977–79; Counsellor, Caracas, 1979–84; Hd, W Indian and Atlantic Dept, FCO, 1984–85. Domestic Bursar, 1985–92, Bursar, 1992–96, St Peter's Coll., Oxford. *Address:* Reskajeage Farm, Gwithian, Hayle, Cornwall TR27 5EF. *T:* (01209) 712512.

SANDERSON, Eric Fenton; Chairman, Marylebone Warwick Balfour plc, since 2005 (non-executive Director, since 2002); *b* 14 Oct. 1951; *s* of Francis Kirton Sanderson and Margarita Shand (*née* Fenton); *m* 1975, Patricia Ann Shaw; three *d*. *Educ:* Morgan Acad., Dundee; Univ. of Dundee (LLB); Harvard Business Sch. (AMP). FCIBS (MCIBS 1991). Touche Ross & Co., CA, 1973–76; CA 1976; British Linen Bank Group Ltd, 1976–97: Corporate Finance Div., 1976–84; Dir, British Linen Bank and Head, Corporate Finance Div., 1984–89; Chief Exec., 1989–97; Chief Exec., Bank of Scotland Treasury Services PLC, 1997–99; Chm., Kwik-Fit Insurance Services Ltd, 2002– (Dir, 1999–2002; Man. Dir, 2000–01). Non-executive Director: MyTravel Group (formerly Airtours) plc, 1987–2004 (Dep. Chm., 2001–02; Chm., 2002–04); DLR Ltd, 1999–2001 (Chm., Quality Panel, 2001–05); First Milk Ltd, 2006–. Mem., BRB, 1991–94. Graduates Assessor and Mem. Court, Univ. of Dundee, 2005–. *Recreations:* tennis, photography, gardening. *Address: e-mail:* ericsanderson@blueyonder.co.uk. *Club:* New (Edinburgh).

SANDERSON, Sir Frank (Linton), 3rd Bt *cr* 1920, of Malling Deanery, South Malling, Sussex; OBE 2005; *b* 21 Nov. 1933; *s* of Sir Bryan Sanderson, 2nd Bt and Annette Korab Laskowska (*d* 1967); *S* father, 1992; *m* 1961, Margaret Ann, *o d* of late John Cleveland Maxwell, New York, USA; two *s* three *d* (incl. twin *d*). *Educ:* Stowe; Univ. of Salamanca. RNVR, 1950–65. J. H. Minet & Co. Ltd, 1956–93 (Dir, 1985); Dir, Knott Hotels Co. of London, 1965–75; Dir and Chm., Humber Fertilisers plc, 1972–88. Underwriting Mem. of Lloyd's, 1957–88. Mem., Chichester Dio. Synod, 1980–93. Chm., Thiepval Project., 1999–2006. Master, Worshipful Co. of Curriers, 1993–94. *Heir: s* David Frank Sanderson [*b* 26 Feb. 1962; *m* 1990, Fiona Jane Ure]. *Address:* Grandturzel Farm, Fontridge Lane, Burwash, Etchingham, East Sussex TN19 7DE. *Clubs:* Naval, City of London, Farmers'.

SANDERSON, Lt-Gen. John Murray, AC 1994 (AO 1991; AM 1985); AUSTCARE Ambassador for Cambodia, since 2006; Governor of Western Australia, 2000–05; *b* 4 Nov. 1940; *s* of John Edward, (Jack), Sanderson and (Dorothy) Jean Sanderson; *m* 1962, Viva Lorraine; one *s* two *d*. *Educ:* Bunbury High Sch., WA; Royal Mil. Coll., Duntroon; Royal Melbourne Inst. of Technol. (FRMIT 1964). Australian Army: Comdr of Sqdn, Vietnam, 1970–71; Sen. Instructor, Sch. of Mil. Engrg, 1972; Instructor, Staff Coll., Camberley, UK, 1976–78; Comdr, 1st Field Engrg Regt, 1979–80; MA to CGS, 1982; Dir of Army Plans, 1982–85; Comdr, 1st Bde, 1986–88; Chief of Staff, Land HQ, 1989; Asst Chief, Defence Forces Develt, 1989–91; Mil. Comdr, UN Transitional Authy, Cambodia, 1992–93; Comdr, Jt Forces Aust., 1993–95; CGS, 1995–97; Chief of Aust. Army, 1997–98. Hon. FIEAust 2000. Comdr, Legion of Merit, USA, 1997; Grand Cross, Royal Cambodian Order, 2006. *Club:* Commonwealth.

SANDERSON, Dr Michael David; Managing Director, Technical Qualifications Validation Ltd, since 2005; *b* 7 June 1943; *s* of Arthur Joseph Sanderson and Betty (*née* Potter); *m* 1967, Mariana Welly Madinaveitia; one *s* one *d*. *Educ:* Strode's Sch., Egham; Univ. of Reading (BSc Hons Chem. 1964); Univ. of Leeds (PhD 1968). With Wilkinson Sword: Research Scientist, 1968–71; Technical Manager, 1971–73; Technical Dir, 1973–79; Internat. Marketing Dir, 1979–82; Engrg Dir, AMF Legg, 1982–84; with Lansing Bagnall: Export Dir, 1984–87; Gp Dir, UK Market, 1987–89; Jt Man. Dir, Lansing Linde, 1989–90; Man. Dir, AWD Bedford, 1990–91; Chief Executive: BSI, 1991–93; Nat. Assoc. of Goldsmiths and Sec. Gen., Internat. Confedn of Jewellers, 1994–95; Engrg and Marine Trng Authy, subseq. Sci., Engrg and Manufacturing Technologies Alliance, 1995–2004. Pres., Inst. of Supervision and Mgt, 1995–99; Chairman: Action for Engrg, Task Force 3, 1995–96; Output Standards Adv. Cttee, Engrg Professors Council, 2000–05; Res. Div., Inst. of Continuing Professional Develt, 2004–06; Nat. Chm., Women into Sci. and Engrg Campaign, 2001–03; Dep. Nat. Chm., Inst. Materials Management, 1991–93; Member Council: Inst. of Materials, 1993–96; Inst. of Logistics, 1988–94; Inst. of Quality Assurance, 1997–2001; Foundn for Sci. and Technol., 2000–04; Dir, Engrg and Technol. Bd, 2001–02. Consultant, Engrg Council, 2005–. Mem., Benchmarking Forum, Amer. Soc. for Trng and Develt, 1999–2004. Trustee: Enterprise Education Trust (formerly Understanding Industry, subseq. Business Dynamics), 1998–; Scottish Council of NTOs, 1999–2004; EdExcel Foundn, 2001–04; Sci., Engrg Technol. and Math. Network, 1999–2004; E Midlands Leadership Centre, 2004–. Chm. and Trustee, Young Electronic Designer of the Year Award, 2002–05; Trustee, Nat. Exam. Bd for Occupational Health and Safety, 2005–. Member Court: Cranfield Univ., 1996–2005; Imperial Coll. London, 2002–; City Univ., 2004–. Mem., Editorial Bd, TQM Magazine, 1993–. Chm., Childs Hill Allotment Soc., 2006–07 (Dep. Chm., 2005–06). Freeman: City of London, 1995; City of Glasgow, 2001; Incorp. of Hammermen of City of Glasgow, 2001; Freeman, 1994–96, Liveryman, 1996–, Mem. Court, 2000–, Master, 2008–, Clockmakers' Co.; Freeman, 2002–03, Liveryman, 2003–, Engrs Co. Hon. FIET (Hon. FIIE 2003). *Publications:* contribs to learned jls on surface chemistry, thin surface films, materials management, quality and general management topics. *Recreation:* books. *Address:* 31 Murray Mews, NW1 9RH. *T:* (020) 7284 3155, *Fax:* (020) 7267 9453; *e-mail:* sandersonmm@netscape.net. *Clubs:* Athenæum, Carlton, St Stephen's.

SANDERSON, Rev. Canon Peter Oliver; Canon, St Paul's Cathedral, Desmoines, Iowa, since 2004; Interim Priest-in-Charge, Lincoln County, Diocese of the Rio Grande, New Mexico, since 2008; *b* 26 Jan. 1929; *s* of Harold and Doris Sanderson; *m* 1956, Doreen Gibson; one *s* one *d* (and one *s* decd). *Educ:* St Chad's College, Durham Univ. (BA, DipTh). Asst Curate, Houghton-le-Spring, Durham Diocese, 1954–59; Rector, Linstead and St Thomas Ye Vale, Jamaica, 1959–63; Chaplain, RAF, 1963–67; Vicar, Winksley-cum-Grantley and Aldfield-with-Studley, Ripon, 1967–74; Vicar, St Aidan, Leeds, 1974–84; Provost of St Paul's Cathedral, Dundee, 1984–91; Vicar, All Saints' Episcopal Ch., Storm Lake, Iowa, 1991–2000; Interim Dean, Trinity Cathedral, Davenport, Iowa, 2005–06. *Recreations:* gardening, music, reading. *Address:* 410 Brentwood Drive, Alamogordo, NM 88310, USA.

SANDERSON, Roy, OBE 1983; National Secretary, Federation of Professional Associations Section, Amalgamated Engineering and Electrical Union, 1992–93; *b* 15 Feb. 1931; *s* of George and Lillian Sanderson; *m* 1951, Jean (*née* Booth); two *s* (and one *s* decd). *Educ:* Carfield Sch., Sheffield. Electrical, Electronic Telecommunication & Plumbing Union: Convenor, Lucas Aerospace, Hemel Hempstead, 1952–67; Asst Educn Officer, 1967–69; Nat. Officer, 1969–87; Nat. Sec., Electrical and Engrg Staff Assoc., 1987–92. Non-exec. Dir, UKAEA, 1987–96. Member: Armed Forces Pay Review Body, 1987–95; Economic and Social Cttee, EU, 1990–98; Industrial Tribunals, 1992–99; Employment Appeal Tribunal, 1995–2002. *Recreations:* golf, snooker; supporter of Watford Football Club. *Address:* 24 Harborough Road North, Kingsthorpe, Northampton NN2 8LU.

SANDERSON, Theresa Ione, (Tessa), CBE 2004 (OBE 1998; MBE 1985); Ambassador for London 2012, since 2005; Head of Talent Development for 2012, Newham Council, since 2005; former athlete; *b* 14 March 1956. *Educ:* Wards Bridge Comprehensive Sch., Wednesfield, Wolverhampton; Bilston Coll. of Further Educn. Javelin thrower; represented GB, 1974–96: Olympic Games: Gold Medal, Los Angeles, 1984 (Olympic record); finalist, Barcelona, 1992; competitor, Atlanta, 1996 (record 6th Olympic Games); Gold Medal, Commonwealth Games, 1978, 1986, 1990; Silver Medal, European Championships, 1978; Gold Medal, World Cup, Cuba, 1992. Set UK record, javelin, 1976 and 1983; UK record, heptathlon, 1981. Sports presenter, Sky News, 1989–92; presenter of own Sunday radio show for Colourful Radio. Mem., 1998–2005, Vice-Chm., 1999–2005, Sport England; Mem., Sports Honours Cttee, 2005–. Patron, Disabled Olympics. *Publication:* Tessa: my life in athletics (autobiog.), 1985. *Address:* Abingdon Management and Consulting, Rosedale House, Rosedale Road, Richmond, Surrey TW9 2SZ.

SANDFORD, 2nd Baron *cr* 1945, of Banbury; **Rev. John Cyril Edmondson,** DSC 1942; *b* 22 Dec. 1920; *e s* of 1st Baron Sandford; *S* father, 1959; *m* 1947, Catharine Mary Hunt; two *s* two *d*. *Educ:* Eton Coll.; Royal Naval Coll., Dartmouth; Westcott House, Cambridge. Served War of 1939–45: Mediterranean Fleet, 1940–41; Home Fleet, 1942; Normandy Landings, 1944 (wounded); Mediterranean Fleet, HMS Saumarez, 1946 (wounded). Staff of RN Coll., Dartmouth, 1947–49; HMS Vengeance, 1950; HMS Cleopatra, 1951–52; Staff Commander-in-Chief Far East, 1953–55; Commander of Home Fleet Flagship, HMS Tyne, 1956; retired 1956. Ordained in Church of England, 1958; Parish of St Nicholas, Harpenden, 1958–63; Exec. Chaplain to Bishop of St Albans, 1965–68. Conservative Peer in H of L, 1959–99; Opposition Whip, 1966–70; Parly Sec., Min. of Housing and Local Govt, June–Oct. 1970; Parliamentary Under-Secretary of State: DoE, 1970–73; DES, 1973–74. Dir, Ecclesiastical Insce Office, 1977–89. Chairman: Cttee to review the condition and future of National Parks in England and Wales, 1971; Standing Conf. of London and SE Regl Planning Authorities, 1981–89. A Church Comr, 1982–89. Chairman: Hertfordshire Council of Social Service, 1969–70; Church Army, 1969–70; Community Task Force, 1975–82; Redundant Churches Cttee, 1982–88; Founder Chm., Pilgrims Assoc., 1982–88; Mem., Adv. Council on Penal Reform, 1968–70. President: Anglo-Swiss Soc., 1974–84; Council for Environmental Educn, 1974–84; Assoc. of District Councils, 1980–86; Offa's Dyke Assoc., 1980–84; Countrywide Holidays Assoc., 1982–86; Vice-Pres., YHA, 1979–90. Founder Trustee, WaterAid, 1981 (Council Mem., 1984; Vice Pres., 1991). Founder, Sandford Award for Heritage Educn, 1978; inaugurated Heritage Educn Trust, 1982. Hon. Fellow, Inst. of Landscape Architects, 1971. *Heir: s* Hon. James John Mowbray Edmondson [*b* 1 July 1949; *m* 1st, 1973, Ellen Sarah, *d* of Jack Shapiro, Toronto; one *d*; 2nd, 1986, Linda, *d* of Mr and Mrs Wheeler, Nova Scotia; one *s*]. *Address:* 27 Ashley Gardens, Ambrosden Avenue, Westminster, SW1P 1QD. *T:* (020) 7834 5722. *Clubs:* Ski of Great Britain, Camping and Caravan.

SANDFORD, Arthur; DL; Chairman, Trent Strategic Health Authority, 2002–06; *b* 12 May 1941; *s* of Arthur and Lilian Sandford; *m* 1963, Kathleen Entwistle; two *d*. *Educ:* Queen Elizabeth's Grammar Sch., Blackburn; University Coll., London (LLB Hons (Upper 2nd Class)). Preston County Borough Council: Articled Clerk to Town Clerk, 1962–65; Asst Solicitor, 1965–66; Sen. Asst Solicitor, 1966–68; Asst Solicitor, Hants CC, 1969–70; Nottinghamshire County Council: Second Asst Clerk, 1970–72; First Asst Clerk, 1972–74; Dep. Dir of Admin, 1973–75; Dir of Admin, 1975–77; Dep. Clerk and County Sec., 1977–78; Clerk and Chief Exec., 1978–89; Chief Executive: Football League, 1990–92; Manchester CC, 1992–98. Chm., Christie Hosp. NHS Trust, 1999–2002. Consultant: Pannone & Partners, 1998–2002; Amey plc, 1998–2002. DL Notts, 1990. *Recreations:* watching sport, gardening. *Address:* 33 Manor Close, Edwalton, Nottingham NG12 4BH. *T:* (0115) 914 9854.

SANDFORD, Rear-Adm. Sefton Ronald, CB 1976; *b* 23 July 1925; *s* of Col H. R. Sandford and Mrs Faye Sandford (*née* Renouf); *m* 1st, 1950, Mary Ann Prins (*d* 1972); one *s*; 2nd, 1972, Jennifer Rachel Newell; two *d*; 3rd, 2001, Susan Elizabeth Capstick. *Educ:* St Aubyns, Rottingdean, 1934–38; Royal Naval Coll., Dartmouth, 1939–42. Served War: went to sea, July 1942; commanded HMMTB 2017, Lieut, 1946–47; ADC to Comdr British Forces, Hong Kong (Lt-Gen. Sir Terence Airey), 1952–53; commanded HMS Teazer (rank Comdr), 1958; Staff of Imperial Defence Coll., 1963–65; comd HMS Protector, Captain, 1965–67; Naval Attaché, Moscow, 1968–70; comd HMS Devonshire, 1971–73; ADC to the Queen, 1974; Flag Officer, Gibraltar, 1974–76. A Younger Brother of Trinity House, 1968. *Recreations:* cricket, messing about in boats, fishing, photography. *Address:* Rozel, Le Bourg, 47700 Anzex, France. *T:* (5) 53846839. *Clubs:* MCC; Royal Yacht Squadron (Cowes).

SANDHURST, 6th Baron; *see* Mansfield, G. R. J.

SANDIFORD, Rt Hon. Sir Lloyd Erskine, KA 1999; PC (Barbados); PC 1989; JP; Prime Minister of Barbados, 1987–94; *b* 24 March 1937; *s* of Cyril and Eunice Sandiford; *m* 1963, Angelita P. Ricketts; one *s* two *d*. *Educ:* Coleridge/Parry Sec. Sch.; Harrison Coll.; Univ. of WI, Jamaica (BA Hons English); Univ. of Manchester (MAEcon). Assistant Master: Modern High Sch., Barbados, 1956–57; Kingston Coll., Jamaica, 1960–61; Asst Master, 1963–64, Sen. Graduate Master, 1964–66, Harrison Coll., Barbados; part-time Tutor and Lectr, Univ. of the WI, Barbados, 1963–65; Asst Tutor, Barbados Community Coll., 1976–86. Democratic Labour Party, Barbados: Mem., 1964–; Asst Sec., 1966–67; Gen. Sec., 1967–68; (first) Vice-Pres., 1972–74; Pres., 1974–75; Vice-Pres., 1975–76; Founder, Acad. of Politics. Member: Senate, 1967–71; House of Assembly, St Michael South, 1971–99; Personal Asst to the Prime Minister, 1966–67; Minister: of Educn, 1967–71; of Educn, Youth Affairs, Community Develt and Sport, 1971–75; of Health and Welfare, 1975–76; Dep. Leader of Opposition, 1978–86; Dep. Prime Minister and Minister of Educn and Culture, 1986–87; Minister: for Civil Service, 1987–94; of Finance and Economic Affairs, 1987–93; of Economic Affairs, 1993–94; of Tourism and Internat. Transport, 1994. Dist. Fellow, Univ. of WI, Barbados. Order of the Liberator (Venezuela),

1987. *Publications:* Books of Speeches 1987–1994; The Essence of Economics, 1997; Politics and Society in Barbados and the Caribbean, 2000; *poems:* Ode to the Environment; When She Leaves You; (contrib.) Business, Government and Society, ed Monya Anyadike-Danes. *Address:* Hillvista, Porters, St James, Barbados, West Indies.

SANDIFORD, Peter, OBE 1992; Director, Spain, British Council, 1999–2003; *b* 23 May 1947; *s* of Jack Sandiford and Joan Mary Sandiford; *m* 1st, 1970, Yvonne Kay Haffenden (marr. diss. 2005); one *s* one *d*; 2nd, 2006, Victoria Francesca Cornwell-García. *Educ:* Watford Grammar Sch. for Boys; University College London (BSc Hons Anthropology 1969). VSO Volunteer, Malawi, 1965–66; Archaeologist, MPBW, 1969–70; British Council: Asst Dir, Singapore, 1971–75; Regl Dir, Munich, 1975–82; Dir, Mgt Services Dept, London, 1982–86; Dir, Israel, 1986–94; Regl Dir, East and Southern Europe, 1994–96, Americas, 1996–98, London. *Recreations:* amateur radio, sailing, hiking.

SANDILANDS, family name of **Baron Torphichen**.

SANDIS, Alexandros C.; Director, Diplomatic Office of the Prime Minister, Athens (with rank of Ambassador), since 2004; *b* Alexandria, Egypt, 29 Aug. 1947; *s* of Constantinos and Maria Sandis; *m* 1969, Anastasia Tsagarakis; one *s* one *d*. *Educ:* Univ. of Athens (BA Pol and Econ. Scis). Joined Ministry of Foreign Affairs, Athens, 1971: Attaché, 1971–73; 2nd Sec., New Delhi, 1973–77; Counsellor, Nicosia, 1977–83; Counsellor, Perm. Delegn to EC, Brussels, 1983–88; Dir, EU Affairs Dept, Athens, 1989–91; Ambassador to: Zimbabwe, 1991–93; Cyprus, 1993–97; Italy, 1997–2000; UK, 2000–03. Greek Govt Rep. at Cyprus Talks, 1997–2001. Grand Cross: Order of Makarios III (Cyprus), 1993; Norwegian Order of Merit (Norway), 2004; Order of the Phoenix (Greece), 2005; Order of the Honour in Gold, First Class (Austria), 2007; Comdr, Order of Greek Orthodox Patriarchate of Alexandrea, 1995; Grand Comdr, Order of Dannebrog (Denmark), 2006. *Recreations:* history, music, theatre, football.

SANDISON, Alexander, (Alec), FCCA; charity governance and finance consultant, since 1994; *b* 24 May 1943; *s* of late Alexander Sandison and Mary Roscoe. *Educ:* Cambs High Sch.; Trinity Sch. of John Whitgift, Croydon. FCCA 1975 (ACCA 1970). Commercial Union Assce Co., 1962–63; John Mowlem PLC, 1964–71 (Gp Financial Accountant, 1970–71); Chief Accountant: and Co. Sec., J. E. Freeman & Co., 1972–73; Wings Ltd, 1973–78; Divl Financial Dir, Doulton Glass Inds, 1978–80; Sec. for Finance and Corporate Controller, RICS, 1980–90; Chief Exec., Surveyors Holdings Ltd, 1985–89; Chm., Imaginor Systems Ltd, 1989–90; Director: Cruse-Bereavement Care, 1990–91; Finance and Admin, Prince's Trust and Royal Jubilee Trusts, 1992–94; Co. Sec., Who Cares? Trust, 1995–2008. Mem. Charities Panel, Chartered Assoc. of Certified Accountants. Trustee: Chartered Certified Accountants Benevolent Fund (formerly ACCA Benevolent Assoc.), 1999–; Islington Volunteer Centre, 1999–2002; Charity Appointments, 2002–; Co-Founder, SpeakersBank, 2002–05. *Publications:* People to People: course notes, 1985; Watton-at-Stone Village Guide, 1989; contribs to learned jls, brainteasers and poetry. *Recreations:* voluntary social work; reading, writing; avoiding involvement with and conversations about sport. *Address:* 38 Grange Rise, Codicote, Hitchin, Herts SG4 8YR. *T:* 07958 643472.

SANDISON, James Sinclair, FCA; freelance financial and management consultant, 1998–2000; *b* 22 June 1936; *s* of William Robert Sandison and Evelyn Gladys Sandison; *m* 1978, Jeannette Avery Keeble; one *s* one *d*. *Educ:* John Lyon Sch., Harrow. FCA 1958. Nat. Service, 2nd Lt, 1958–60. Franklin, Wild & Co., 1953–58; Touche Ross & Co., 1960–62; British Relay Wireless and Television Ltd, 1962–66; joined Dexion Gp, 1966: Gp Controller, 1975–76; Finance Dir, Dexion Ltd, 1977–91; Royal Society for Encouragement of Arts, Manufactures and Commerce: Dir of Finance and Admin, 1991–96; Acting Dir, 1996–97. Treas., London Soc., 2005–. FRSA 1998. *Recreations:* reading, tennis, cinema, London, film noir. *Address:* 33 Montagu Road, Highcliffe, Christchurch, Dorset BH23 5JT.

SANDLE, Prof. Michael Leonard, DFA; RA; FRBS 1994; sculptor; Professor of Sculpture, Akademie der Bildenden Künste, Karlsruhe, Germany, 1980–99; *b* 18 May 1936; *s* of Charles Edward Sandle and Dorothy Gwendoline Gladys (*née* Vernon); *m* 1971, Cynthia Dora Koppel (marriage annulled 1974); *m* 1988, Demelza Spargo (marriage annulled 2004); one *s* one *d*. *Educ:* Douglas High Sch., IOM; Douglas Sch. of Art and Technol.; Slade Sch. of Fine Art (DFA 1959). ARA 1982, RA 1989, resigned 1997, rejoined 2004. Studied painting and printmaking, Slade Sch. of Fine Art, 1956–59; changed to sculpture, 1962; various teaching posts in Britain, 1961–70, including Lectr, Coventry Coll. of Art, 1964–68; resident in Canada, 1970–73; Vis. Prof., Univ. of Calgary, Alberta, 1970–71; Vis. Associate Prof., Univ. of Victoria, BC, 1972–73; Lectr in Sculpture, Fachhochschule für Gestaltung, Pforzheim, W Germany, 1973–77, Prof., 1977–80. Sen. Res. Fellow, De Montfort Univ., 1996–2001; Fellow, Kenneth Armitage Foundn, 2004–06. Has participated in exhibns in GB and internationally, 1957–, including: V Biennale, Paris, 1966; Documenta IV, Kassel, W Germany, 1968 and Documenta VI, 1977. Work in public collections, including: Arts Council of GB, Tate Gall.; Australian Nat. Gall., Canberra; Met. Mus., NY; Stzüki Mus., Lodz; Nat. Gall., Warsaw; Wilhelm Lehmbruck Mus., Duisburg, W Germany. Designed: Malta Siege Bell Meml, Valetta, 1992; Seafarers Meml, for Internat. Maritime Orgn's HQ, London, 2001. Nobutaka Shikanai Special Prize, Utsukushi-Ga-Hara Open-Air Mus., Japan, 1986; Henry Hering Meml Medal, Nat. Sculpture Soc. of Amer., 1995. *Address:* c/o The Royal British Society of Sculptors, 108 Brompton Road, SW7 3RA.

SANDLER, Prof. Merton, MD; FRCP, FRCPath, FRCPsych; Professor of Chemical Pathology, Royal Postgraduate Medical School, Institute of Obstetrics and Gynaecology, University of London, 1973–91, Professor Emeritus, since 1991; Consultant Chemical Pathologist, Queen Charlotte's Maternity Hospital, 1958–91; *b* 28 March 1926; *s* of late Frank Sandler and Edith (*née* Stein), Salford, Lancs; *m* 1961, Lorna Rosemary, *d* of late Ian Michael and Sally Grenby, Colindale, London; two *s* two *d*. *Educ:* Manchester Grammar Sch.; Manchester Univ. (MB ChB 1949; MD 1962). FRCPath 1970 (MRCPath 1963); FRCP 1974 (MRCP 1955); FRCPsych 1986. Jun. Specialist in Pathology, RAMC (Captain), 1951–53. Research Fellow in Clin. Path., Brompton Hosp., 1953–54; Lectr in Chem. Path., Royal Free Hosp. Sch. of Med., 1955–58. Visiting Professor: Univ. of New Mexico, 1983; Chicago Med. Sch., 1984; Univ. of S Fla, 1988. Recognized Teacher in Chem. Path., 1960–91; extensive examining experience for various Brit. and for. univs and Royal Colls; Mem. Standing Adv. Cttee, Bd of Studies in Path., Univ. of London, 1972–76 (also Mem. Chem. Path. Sub-Cttee, 1973–91); Chm., Academic Bd, 1972–73, Bd of Management, 1975–84, Inst. of Obst. and Gyn.; Governor: Brit. Postgrad. Med. Fedn, 1976–78; Queen Charlotte's Hosp. for Women, 1978–84; Council Mem. and Meetings Sec., Assoc. of Clin. Pathologists, 1959–70; Mem. Council, Collegium Internat. Neuro-Psychopharmacologicum, 1982–90. Various offices in: RSM, incl. Hon. Librarian, 1987–93, and Pres. Section of Med. Exper. Med. and Therapeutics, 1979–80; Brit. Assoc. for Psychopharm., incl. Pres., 1980–82 (Hon. Mem., 1993); British Assoc. for Postnatal Illness (Pres., 1980–); office in many other learned socs and grant-giving bodies, incl. Med. Adv. Councils of Migraine Trust, 1975–80 (Chm., Scientific Adv. Cttee, 1985–91; Trustee, 1987–91), Schizophrenia Assoc. of GB, 1975–78, Parkinson's Disease Soc., 1981–97 (Trustee, 1994–97); Chm. of Trustees, Nat. Soc. for Res. into Mental Health, 1983–. Pres., W London Medico-Chirurgical Soc., 1996–97. Chm. and Sec., Biol Council Symposium on Drug Action, 1979; Sec., Mem. Bd of Management and Chm. Awards Subcttee, Biological Council, 1983–91; Member, Executive Committee: Marcé Soc., 1983–86; Med. Council on Alcoholism, 1987–90; Sec. and Mem. Council, Harveian Soc. of London, 1979–89 (Vice Pres., 1990; Pres., 1991–92); Mem. Council of Management and Patron, Helping Hand Orgn, 1981–87. Organiser or Brit. rep. on org. cttees of many nat. and internat. meetings incl. Internat. Chm., 6th Internat. Catecholamine Congress, 1987. For. Corresp. Mem., Amer. Coll. of Neuropsychopharm., 1975; Hon. Member: Indian Acad. of Neuroscis, 1982; Hungarian Pharmacological Soc., 1985. Jt Editor: British Jl of Pharmacology, 1974–80; Clinical Science, 1975–77; Jl of Neural Transmission, 1979–82; Jt Editor-in-Chief, Jl of Psychiatric Research, 1982–93, and present or past Mem. Editorial Bds of 17 other sci. jls; eponymous lectures to various learned socs incl. 1st Cumings Meml, 1976, James E. Beall II Meml, 1980, Biol Council Lecture and Medal, 1984; F. B. Smith Meml, 1995; Jane Chomet Meml, 1997; Marcia Wilkinson, 2001; provision of Nat. Monoamine Ref. Laboratory Service, 1976–91. Dr *hc* Semmelweis Univ. of Medicine, Budapest, 1992. Anna Monika Internat. Prize (jtly), for Res. on Biol Aspects of Depression, 1973; Gold Medal, Brit. Migraine Assoc., 1974; Senator Dr Franz Burda Internat. Prize for Res. on Parkinson's Disease, 1988; Arnold Friedman Distinguished Clinician Researcher Award, 1991; British Assoc. for Psychopharmacology/Zeneca Lifetime Achievement Award, 1999; Pfizer Pioneer in Psychopharmacology Award, Collegium Internat. Neuro-Psychopharmacologicum, 2006. *Publications:* Mental Illness in Pregnancy and the Puerperium, 1978; The Psychopharmacology of Aggression, 1979; Enzyme Inhibitors as Drugs, 1980; Amniotic Fluid and its Clinical Significance, 1980; The Psychopharmacology of Alcohol, 1980; The Psychopathology of Anticonvulsants, 1981; Nervous Laughter, 1990; Parkinson's Disease, 1993; *jointly:* The Adrenal Cortex, 1961; The Thyroid Gland, 1967; Advances in Pharmacology, 1968; Monoamine Oxidases, 1972; Serotonin—New Vistas, 1974; Sexual Behaviour: Pharmacology and Biochemistry, 1975; Trace Amines and the Brain, 1976; Phenolsulphotransferase in Mental Health Research, 1981; Tetrahydroisoquinolines and β-Carbolines, 1982; Progress towards a Male Contraceptive, 1982; Neurobiology of the Trace Amines, 1984; Psychopharmacology and Food, 1985; Neurotransmitter Interactions, 1986; Progress in Catecholamine Research, 1988; Design of Enzyme Inhibitors as Drugs, Vol. 1, 1989, Vol. 2, 1994; Migraine: a spectrum of ideas, 1990; 5-Hydroxytryptamine in Psychiatry, 1991; Monoamine Oxidase: basic and clinical aspects, 1993; Genetic Research in Psychiatry, 1992; Migraine-Pharmacology and Genetics, 1996; Wine: a scientific exploration, 2003; numerous research pubns on aspects of biologically-active monoamine metabolism. *Recreations:* reading, listening to music, travel. *Address:* 33 Park Road, Twickenham, Middlesex TW1 2QD. *T:* (020) 8892 9085, *Fax:* (020) 8891 5370. *Club:* Athenæum.

SANDLER, Ronald Arnon, Hon. CBE 2004; non-executive Chairman: Paternoster, since 2006; Ironshore Inc., since 2007; Northern Rock, since 2008 (Executive Chairman, 2008); *b* 5 March 1952; *s* of Bernard Maurice Sandler and Carla Sandler; *m* 1977, Susan Lee; two *s*. *Educ:* Milton Sch., Bulawayo; Queens' Coll., Cambridge (MA); Stanford Univ., USA (MBA). Boston Consulting Gp Inc., 1976–84, Dir 1983–84; Sen. Vice Pres., Booz Allen & Hamilton Inc., 1984–88; Chm., Chalcon Ltd, 1989–93; Chm. and Chief Exec., Martin Bierbaum Gp plc, 1990–93; Chief Executive: Exco plc, 1993–94; Lloyd's of London, 1995–99; Chief Operating Officer, NatWest Gp, 1999–2000. Non-executive Chairman: Computacenter plc, 2001–08; Kyte Gp, 2000–08; Oxygen Gp plc, 2004–08; non-executive Director: Greenalls Gp plc, 1998–2000; Fortis, 2004–. Pres., CIB, 2004–05. Mem., Partnership Council, Herbert Smith, 2001–06. Chm., Personal Finance Educn Gp, 2003–. Trustee, Royal Opera House, 1999–2001. *Recreations:* golf, ski-ing, guitar playing. *Address:* 5 Southside, Wimbledon, SW19 4TG. *T:* (020) 8946 1179. *Clubs:* MCC; Sunningdale.

SANDON, Viscount; Dudley Anthony Hugo Coventry Ryder; *b* 5 Sept. 1981; *s* and *heir* of Earl of Harrowby, *qv*. *Educ:* Eton Coll.; Edinburgh Univ. (MA). *Address:* Sandon Estate Office, Sandon, Stafford ST18 0DA.

SANDS, John Robert; Chairman, Invesco English and International Trust, since 2006 (Director, since 2004); *b* 8 Oct. 1947; *s* of John Sands and Jane Caroline Sands (*née* Reay); *m* 1969, Susan Elizabeth McCulloch; two *s* two *d*. J. W. Cameron & Co. Ltd: Trng and Develt Manager, 1980–81; Tied Trade Dir, 1981–84; Trade Dir, 1984–85; Managing Director: Cameron Inns, 1985–88; and CEO, Tollemache & Cobbold Breweries Ltd, 1988–89; Brent Walker Inns and Retail, 1989–91; Man. Dir, 1991–96, Chief Exec., 1996–2002, Exec. Chm., 2002–04, Pubmaster Ltd. Non-exec. Dir, Jennings Brothers, 2004–. *Recreations:* ski-ing, keep fit, playing guitar and banjo, playing mahjong, watching Newcastle United FC.

SANDS, Jonathan Peter; Chairman, Elmwood Design, brand design consultancy, since 1989; *b* 27 March 1961; *s* of Peter and Viveanne Sands; *m* 1983, Carolyn Fletcher; two *s* one *d*. *Educ:* Normanton Boys' Sch.; Stockport Coll. of Technol. Council Mem., Design Council, 2000–; non-exec. Dir, Networking for Industry. Former Mem., Arts Council Yorkshire. Regular speaker at internat. confs on design worldwide. FRSA (Council Mem., 1997–2000). Hon. DSc Huddersfield, 2002. *Publications:* regular contribs to design jls and media. *Recreation:* long-suffering Derby County supporter. *Address:* Elmwood, Elmwood House, Ghyll Royd, Guiseley, Leeds LS20 9LT. *Clubs:* Groucho; Harrogate Golf, Gullane Golf.

SANDS, Peter Alexander; Group Chief Executive Officer, Standard Chartered plc, since 2006 (Group Finance Director, 2002–06); *b* 8 Jan. 1962; *s* of Martin and Susan Sands; *m* 1989, Mary Elizabeth, (Betsy), Tobin; one *s* three *d*. *Educ:* Brasenose Coll., Oxford (BA PPE); Kennedy Sch. of Govt, Harvard Univ. (MPA). Asst Desk Officer for Afghanistan and Pakistan, and Desk Officer for Libya, FCO, 1984–86; McKinsey & Co.: Associate, 1988–96; Principal, 1996–2000; Dir, 2000–02. *Recreations:* reading, music, riding. *Address:* Standard Chartered plc, 1 Aldermanbury Square, EC2V 7SB. *T:* (020) 7280 7019, *Fax:* (020) 7600 2546; *e-mail:* Peter.sands@uk.standardchartered.com.

SANDS, Prof. Philippe Joseph; QC 2003; Professor of Laws, and Director, Centre on International Courts and Tribunals, University College London, since 2002; *b* 17 Oct. 1960; *s* of Alan Sands and Ruth (*née* Buchholz); *m* 1993, Natalia Schiffrin; one *s* two *d*. *Educ:* Corpus Christi Coll., Cambridge (BA 1982; LLM 1983). Res. Fellow, St Catharine's Coll., Cambridge, 1984–88; called to the Bar, Middle Temple, 1985; Lectr, Faculty of Law, KCL, 1988–92; Lectr, then Reader, subseq. Prof. of Internat. Law, SOAS, 1993–2001. *Publications:* Chernobyl: law and communication, 1988; (ed and contrib.) Greening International Law, 1993; Principles of International Environmental Law, 1995, 2nd edn 2003; Manual of International Courts and Tribunals, 1999; (jtly) Bowett's Law of International Institutions, 5th edn 2001; From Nuremburg to The Hague, 2003; Lawless World, 2005; Torture Team: deception, cruelty and the compromise of law, 2008. *Address:* Matrix Chambers, Gray's Inn, WC1R 5LN. *T:* (020) 7404 3447, *Fax:* (020) 7404 3448; *e-mail:* philippesands@matrixlaw.co.uk.

SANDS, Sir Roger (Blakemore), KCB 2006; Clerk and Chief Executive of the House of Commons, 2003–06; *b* 6 May 1942; *s* of late Thomas Blakemore Sands and Edith Malyon (Betty) Sands (*née* Waldram); *m* 1966, Jennifer Ann Cattell; one *d* (and one *d* decd). *Educ:* University Coll. Sch., Hampstead; Oriel Coll., Oxford (scholar; MA LitHum). A Clerk, House of Commons, 1965–2006; Sec. to H of C Commn and Clerk to H of C (Services) Cttee, 1985–87; Clerk of Overseas Office, 1987–91; Clerk of Select Cttees and Registrar of Members' Interests, 1991–94; Clerk of Public Bills, 1994–97; Clerk of Legislation, 1998–2001; Clerk Asst, 2001–02. Chm., Study of Parlt Group, 1993–95. Chm., Standards Cttee, Mid Sussex DC, 2007–. *Recreations:* listening to music, walking, incompetent golf. *Address:* No 4 (Ashurst Suite), Woodbury House, Lewes Road, East Grinstead, W Sussex RH19 3UD. *T:* (01342) 302245. *Clubs:* Commonwealth; Holtye Golf.

SANDS SMITH, David, CBE 2002; development administrator; *b* 19 April 1943; *s* of late Arthur S. Smith and Eileen Annie Smith; *m* 1966, Veronica Harris; one *s* one *d*. *Educ:* Brighton Coll. of Technology, Dept of Technical Co-operation, 1963–71. 2nd Sec., British High Commn, Kuala Lumpur, 1971–75; Overseas Development Administration: Principal: European Community Dept, 1975–80; Zimbabwe Desk, 1980–85; Asst Head, 1985–88, Head, 1988–90, European Community Dept; Head, British Develt Div. in Eastern Africa, 1990–93; UK Perm. Rep., FAO, World Food Programme and IFAD, 1993–97; Head: Procurement, Appts and NGOs Dept, DFID, 1997–99; Develt Policy Dept, DFID, 1999–2001. Consultant to FAO, 2003–06. Trustee, Sightsavers Internat., 2006–. *Recreations:* running, cycling.

SANDWICH, 11th Earl of, *cr* 1660; **John Edward Hollister Montagu;** Viscount Hinchingbrooke and Baron Montagu of St Neots, 1660; editor and researcher; *b* 11 April 1943; *er s* of (Alexander) Victor (Edward Paulet) Montagu and Rosemary Peto; *S* to disclaimed Earldom of father, 1995; *m* 1968, Caroline, *o d* of late Canon P. E. C. Hayman, Beaminster, Dorset; two *s* one *d*. *Educ:* Eton; Trinity College, Cambridge. Inf. Officer, 1974–85, Res. Officer, 1985–86, Mem., Bd, 1999–2004, Christian Aid; Editor, Save the Children Fund, 1987–92; Consultant, CARE Britain, 1987–93; Mem. Council, Anti-Slavery Internat., 1997–2006. Chm., Britain Afghanistan Trust, 1995–2000; Trustee, TSW Telethon Trust, 1987–91; Gov. Beaminster Sch., 1996–2004. Pres., Earl of Sandwich, 2001–. Jt Administrator, Mapperton Estate, 1982–. Crossbencher, H of L, 1995–; elected Mem., H of L, 1999; Member: Information Cttee, 2001–04; Constitution Cttee, 2004–06; Ind. Asylum Commn, 2006–08. Pres., Samuel Pepys Club, 1985–. *Publications:* The Book of the World, 1971; Prospects for Africa's Children, 1990; Children at Crisis Point, 1992; (ed jtly) Hinch: a celebration of Viscount Hinchingbrooke, MP 1906–1995, 1997. *Heir:* *s* Viscount Hinchingbrooke, *qv*. *Address:* Mapperton House, Beaminster, Dorset DT8 3NR.

SANDYS, 7th Baron *cr* 1802; **Richard Michael Oliver Hill;** DL; Captain of the Yeomen of the Guard (Deputy Government Chief Whip, House of Lords), 1979–82; Landowner; *b* 21 July 1931; *o s* of 6th Baron Sandys, Lt-Col, RE, and Cynthia Mary (*d* 1990), *o d* of late Col F. R. T. T. Gascoigne, DSO; *S* father, 1961; *m* 1961, Patricia Simpson Hall, *d* of late Captain Lionel Hall, MC. *Educ:* Royal Naval College, Dartmouth. Lieutenant in The Royal Scots Greys, 1950–55. A Lord in Waiting, 1974; an Opposition Whip, H of L, 1974–79. FRGS. DL Worcestershire, 1968. *Heir:* Marquess of Downshire, *qv*. *Address:* Ombersley Court, Droitwich, Worcestershire WR9 0HH. *T:* (01905) 620220. *Club:* Cavalry and Guards.

SANÉ, Pierre Gabriel; Assistant Director-General for Social and Human Sciences, UNESCO, since 2001; *b* 7 May 1948; *s* of Nicolas Sané and Therese Carvalho; *m* 1981, Ndeye Sow; one *s* one *d*. *Educ:* LSE (MSc in Public Admin and Public Policy); Ecole Supérieure de Commerce, Bordeaux (MBA); Carleton Univ., Canada (doctoral studies in pol scis). Regl Dir, Internat. Develt Research Centre, Ottawa, Canada, 1978–92; Sec.-Gen., Amnesty Internat., 1992–2001. *Address:* UNESCO, 1 rue Miollis, 75732 Paris Cedex 15, France.

SANGER, David John, FRAM, FRCO; organ recitalist, composer, teacher; *b* 17 April 1947; *s* of Stanley Charles Sanger and Ethel Lillian Florence Sanger (*née* Woodgate). *Educ:* Eltham Coll.; Royal Acad. of Music, London (FRAM). ARCM; FRCO. Royal Academy of Music: Prof. of Organ, 1982–89; Chm., Organ Dept, 1987–89; Vis. Prof. of Organ, 1989–96; freelance teaching at Cambridge and Oxford Univs, 1976–. Guest Prof., Royal Danish Acad. of Music, 1991–93; Vis. Tutor in Organ Studies, RNCM, 1991–. Perfs at the Proms and RFH; internat. tours as soloist, notably in Scandinavia; masterclasses, lectures and seminars. Jury Mem., internat. organ competitions in St Albans, Paisley, Speyer, Biarritz, Alkmaar and Odense. Consultant: new organ, Exeter Coll., Oxford; restoration of Usher Hall organ, Edinburgh. Numerous recordings. Winner, international organ competition: St Albans, 1969; Kiel, 1972. *Publications:* Play the Organ, vol. 1, 1990, vol. 2, 1993; (ed) organ works of Willan, 1990, Pepusch, 1994, and Lefébure-Wély, 2 vols, 1994; numerous compositions for organ and choir; articles for Organists' Review, The Organ. *Recreations:* racquet sports, swimming, fell-walking. *Address:* Old Wesleyan Chapel, Embleton, Cumbria CA13 9YA. *T:* (01768) 776628; *e-mail:* david.sanger@virgin.net.

SANGER, Frederick, OM 1986; CH 1981; CBE 1963; PhD; FRS 1954; on staff of Medical Research Council, 1951–83; *b* 13 Aug. 1918; *s* of Frederick Sanger, MD, and Cicely Sanger; *m* 1940, M. Joan Howe; two *s* one *d*. *Educ:* Bryanston; St John's College, Cambridge. BA 1939; PhD 1943. From 1940, research in Biochemistry at Cambridge University; Beit Memorial Fellowship for Medical Research, 1944–51; at MRC Lab. of Molecular Biol., Cambridge, 1961–83; Fellowship at King's College, Cambridge, 1954. (Hon. Fellow 1983). For. Hon. Mem., Amer. Acad. of Arts and Sciences, 1958; Hon. Mem. Amer. Society of Biological Chemists, 1961; Foreign Assoc., Nat. Acad. of Sciences, 1967. Hon. DSc: Leicester, 1968; Oxon, 1970; Strasbourg, 1970; Cambridge, 1983. Corday-Morgan Medal and Prize, Chem. Soc., 1951; Nobel Prize for Chemistry, 1958, (jointly) 1980; Alfred Benzon Prize, 1966; Royal Medal, Royal Soc., 1969; Sir Frederick Gowland Hopkins Meml Medal, 1971; Gairdner Foundation Annual Award, 1971, 1979; William Bate Hardy Prize, Cambridge Philosophical Soc., 1976; Hanbury Meml Medal, 1976; Copley Medal, Royal Soc., 1977; Horwitz Prize, Albert Lasker Award, 1979; Biochem. Analysis Prize, German Soc. Clin. Chem., 1980; Gold Medal, RSM, 1983. *Publications:* papers on Chemistry of Insulin and Nucleic Acid Structure in Biochemical and other journals. *Address:* Far Leys, Fen Lane, Swaffham Bulbeck, Cambridge CB25 0NJ.

SANGSTER, Nigel; QC 1998; a Recorder, since 2000; *s* of Dr H. B. Singh and Irene Singh (*née* Carlisle), JP. *Educ:* Repton; Leeds Univ. (LLB Hons). Called to the Bar, Middle Temple, 1976, Bencher, 2008; criminal defence barrister specialising in fraud cases; Head of Chambers, St Pauls Chambers, Leeds, 1995–2005; Asst Recorder, 1997–2000. Member: Bar Council, 1994–2004; Criminal Bar Assoc. *Address:* 25 Bedford Row, WC1R 4HD. *T:* (020) 7067 1500; St Pauls Chambers, St Pauls House, Park Square, Leeds LS1 2ND. *T:* (0113) 245 5866; *e-mail:* mail@nigelsangster.qc.com.

SANKEY, John Anthony, CMG 1983; PhD; HM Diplomatic Service, retired; Secretary General, Society of London Art Dealers, 1991–96; *b* 8 June 1930; *m* 1958, Gwendoline Putman; two *s* two *d*. *Educ:* Cardinal Vaughan Sch., Kensington; Peterhouse, Cambridge (Classical Tripos Parts 1 and 2, Class 1; MA); Univ. of Leeds (PhD). 1st (Singapore) Regt, RA (2nd Lieut), 1952. Colonial Office, 1953–61; UK Mission to United Nations, 1961–64; Foreign Office, 1964–68; Guyana, 1968–71; Singapore, 1971–73; NATO Defence Coll., Rome, 1973; Malta, 1973–75; The Hague, 1975–79 (Gov., British Sch. in the Netherlands); FCO, 1979–82; High Comr, Tanzania, 1982–85; UK Perm. Rep. to UN Office, Geneva, 1985–90. Leader, British Govt Delegn to Internat. Red Cross Conf., 1986. Dir, Internat. Art and Antiques Loss Register Ltd, 1993–96. Chm., Tanzania Develt Trust, 1997–2004. Sir Evelyn Wrench Lectr, ESU, 1990. KCHS 2003 (KHS 1996). *Publications:* (contrib.) The United Kingdom—the United Nations, 1990; The Conscience of the World, 1995; Sir Thomas Brock, sculptor, 2002. *Address:* 108 Lancaster Gate, W2 3NW.

SANKEY, Vernon Louis; Chairman, Photo-Me International plc, 2005–07 (Deputy Chairman, 2000–05); *b* 9 May 1949; *s* of late Edward Sankey and Marguerite Elizabeth Louise (*née* van Maurik); *m* 1976, Elizabeth, *d* of Tom Knights; three *s* one *d* (of whom one *s* one *d* are twins). *Educ:* Harrow School; Oriel Coll., Oxford (MA Mod. Langs). Joined Reckitt & Colman, 1971: Mgt Trainee, 1971–74; Asst Manager, Finance and Planning, 1974–76; Dir, Planning and Develt, Europe, 1976–78; General Manager, Denmark, 1978–80; PA to Chm. and Chief Exec., 1980–81; Man. Dir, France, 1981–85; Man. Dir, Colman's of Norwich, 1985–89; Chm. and Chief Exec. Officer, Reckitt & Colman Inc., USA, 1989–92; Chief Exec., 1992–99. Chairman: The Really Effective Develt Co. Ltd, 2000–05; Thomson Travel Gp, 2000; Gala Gp Holdings, 2000–03; Dep. Chm., Beltpacker plc, 2000–04; non-executive Director: Pearson, 1993–2006; Allied Zurich plc, 1998–2000; Zurich Allied AG, 1998–2000; Zurich Financial Services AG, 2000–; Cofra AG, 2001–07; Taylor Woodrow plc, 2004–07; Zurich Insurance Co. AG, 2004–; Atos Origin SA, 2005–; Vividas plc, 2005–; Firmenich SA, 2005–. Member: Internat. Adv. Bd, Korn/Ferry Internat., 1994–2005; Adv. Bd, Proudfoot UK, 2000–06; Adv. Bd, MCC Inc., 2000–; Adv. Bd, GLP LLP, 2005–. Mem. Bd, Grocery Manufacturers of Amer., 1995–99. Member: Listed Cos Adv. Cttee, London Stock Exchange, 1997–99; Bd, Food Standards Agency, 2000–05. FRSA 2000. *Recreations:* jogging, tennis. *Address:* c/o Board Secretariat, Zurich Financial Services AG, Mythenquai 2, 8002 Zurich, Switzerland. *Club:* Leander (Henley).

SANKEY, William Patrick F.; *see* Filmer-Sankey.

SANSOM, Bruce Edward; Director, Central School of Ballet, since 2006; *b* 8 Sept. 1963; *s* of Dr Bernard Sansom and Prudence Sansom. *Educ:* Royal Ballet Sch. Joined Royal Ballet Co., 1982; Soloist, 1985; Principal Dancer, 1987–2000; also danced with San Francisco Ballet Co., 1991–92 season. Has danced principal rôles in all major ballets, incl. La Fille Mal Gardée, Swan Lake, Giselle, The Nutcracker, Manon, Sleeping Beauty, La Bayadère, Cinderella, The Dream, Romeo and Juliet, Scènes de Ballet, Manon; leading rôles created for him in a number of ballets including Galanteries, Still Life at the Penquin Café, Pursuit, Piano, Prince of the Pagodas, Tombeaux. Vice Chair, Cecchetti Soc. Trust, 2007–; Mem., Exec. Cttee, Dance UK, 2004–. Time Out Award for performances with Royal Ballet, 1990. *Recreations:* shooting, opera, contemporary art, Parson Jack Russell terriers.

SANT, Hon. Dr Alfred; MP (Lab) Malta, since 1987; Leader of the Opposition, Malta, 1998–2008; *b* 28 Feb. 1948; *s* of Joseph and Josephine Sant; one *d*. *Educ:* Univ. of Malta (BSc, MSc); Inst. Internat. d'Admin Publique, Paris (Dip.); Boston Univ. (MBA); Harvard Univ. (DBA). Res. Fellow, Harvard Business Sch. First Sec., Malta Mission to EEC, Brussels, 1970–75; Man. Dir, Medina Consulting Gp, 1979–80; Dep. Chm., Malta Develt Corp., 1980–82. Leader, Labour Party, 1992–2008; Prime Minister of Malta, 1996–98. *Publications:* Memoires: confessions of a European Maltese, 2003; *novels:* L-Ewwel Weraq tal-Bajtar, 1968; Silg fuq Kemmuna, 1982; Bejgħ u Xiri, 1984; La Bidu, La Tmiem, 2001; *dramas:* Min hu Evelyn Costa?, 1982; Fid-Dell tal-Katidral, 1994. *Recreations:* listening to classical music, walking. *Address:* 18A Victory Street, B'Kara, Malta.

SANTANA CARLOS, António Nunes; Ambassador of Portugal to the Court of St James's, since 2006; *b* Lisbon, 20 March 1945; *s* of Victor Santana Carlos and Maria N. C. Santana Carlos; *m* 1982, Maria Pena Escudeiro; one *s*. *Educ:* Univ. of Lisbon (Soc. and Pol Scis). Joined Foreign Service, 1971, Attaché of Embassy; Third Sec., 1973–74; Second Sec., Tokyo, 1974–76; Hd, Cipher Dept, Foreign Office, 1976–79; First Sec., Dept of Internat. Econ. Orgns, Foreign Office, 1979–82; Perm. Mission of Portugal in Geneva, 1982–86; Minister Counsellor, Portuguese Embassy, Luanda, 1986–90; Dir, Multilateral Affairs Dept, Foreign Office, 1990–93; Minister Plenipotentiary and Dep.-Dir Gen. of Pol and Econ. Affairs, 1993–94; Dir, Office of Econ. Affairs, 1994, Chargé de Mission to the Minister of Foreign Affairs for promotion of Expo 98, Lisbon World Exhibn, 1995; Sen. Rep. to Sino-Portuguese Jt Liaison Gp and Pres., Interministerial Commn on Macau, 1996–2000; rank of Ambassador, 2000; Chargé de Mission to Minister of Foreign Affairs for East Timor Affairs, 2000; Dir-Gen. of Foreign Policy (Pol Dir), 2000–02; Ambassador to the People's Republic of China, 2002–06. Grand Cross, Order of Christ (Portugal); Grand Cross, Order of Merit (Portugal); Grand Officer, Order of Infante Dom Henrique (Portugal); Grand Officer, Order of Wissan Alouite (Morocco); Knight, Order of Rio Branco (Brazil). *Recreations:* golf, sailing, cinema. *Address:* Portuguese Embassy, 11 Belgrave Square, SW1X 8PP. *T:* (020) 7235 5331, *Fax:* (020) 7245 1287; *e-mail:* amb@portembassy.co.uk. *Clubs:* Athenæum, Travellers, Royal Automobile; Royal Mid-Surrey Golf.

SANTER, Jacques; Chairman, CLT-UFA, since 2004; Member of the Board, RTL Group, since 2004; Chairman, UniCredit International Bank, Luxembourg, since 2005; *b* 18 May 1937; *m* Danièle Binot; two *s*. *Educ:* Athénée de Luxembourg; Paris Univ.; Strasbourg Univ.; Inst. d'Etudes Politiques, Paris. DenD. Advocate, Luxembourg Court of Appeal, 1961–65; Attaché, Office of Minister of Labour and Social Security, 1963–65; Govt Attaché, 1965–66; Christian Socialist Party: Parly Sec., 1966–72; Sec.-Gen., 1972–74; Pres., 1974–82; Sec. of State for Cultural and Social Affairs, 1972–74; Mem., Chamber of Deputies, 1974–79; MEP, 1975–79 (a Vice-Pres., 1975–77); Minister of Finance, Labour and Social Security, Luxembourg, 1979–84; Prime Minister of Luxembourg, 1984–94; Pres. of Govt, Minister of State and Minister of Finance, 1984–89; Minister for Cultural Affairs, 1989–94; Pres., EC, 1995–99; MEP (EPP), 1999–2004.

SANTER, Rt Rev. Mark; Bishop of Birmingham, 1987–2002; Hon. Assistant Bishop: diocese of Worcester, since 2002; diocese of Birmingham, since 2003; *b* 29 Dec. 1936; *s* of late Rev. Canon Eric Arthur Robert Santer and Phyllis Clare Barlow; *m* 1st, 1964, Henriette Cornelia Weststrate (*d* 1994); one *s* two *d*; 2nd, 1997, Sabine Böhmig Bird. *Educ:* Marlborough Coll.; Queens' Coll., Cambridge (MA; Hon. Fellow, 1991); Westcott House, Cambridge. Deacon, 1963; priest 1964; Asst Curate, Cuddesdon, 1963–67; Tutor, Cuddesdon Theological Coll., 1963–67; Fellow and Dean of Clare Coll., Cambridge, 1967–72 (and Tutor, 1968–72; Hon. Fellow, 1987); Univ. Asst Lectr in Divinity, 1968–72; Principal of Westcott House, Cambridge, 1973–81; Hon. Canon of Winchester

Cathedral, 1978–81; Area Bishop of Kensington, 1981–87. Co-Chm., Anglican Roman Catholic Internat. Commn, 1983–98. Hon. DD Birmingham, 1998; DD Lambeth, 1999; DUniv UCE, 2002. *Publications:* (contrib.) The Phenomenon of Christian Belief, 1970; (with M. F. Wiles) Documents in Early Christian Thought, 1975; Their Lord and Ours, 1982; (contrib.) The Church and the State, 1984; (contrib.) Dropping the Bomb, 1985; contrib. Jl of Theological Studies, Ecclesiology, Theology. *Address:* 81 Clarence Road, Birmingham B13 9UH. *T:* (0121) 441 2194.

SANTOMARCO, Oona Tamsyn; *see* King, O. T.

SANTS, Hector William Hepburn; Chief Executive, Financial Services Authority, since 2007; *b* 15 Dec. 1955; *s* of Hector John Sants and Elsie Ann Watt Sants (*née* Hepburn); *m* 1987, Caroline Jane Mackenzie; three *s*. *Educ:* Clifton Coll.; Corpus Christi Coll., Oxford (MA PPP). Phillips & Drew, stockbrokers: joined as grad. trainee res., 1977; Partner, 1984–89; Hd, European Equities, Union Bank of Switzerland, 1989–97; Hd, Internat. Equities, Donaldson, Lufkin and Jenrette, 1997–2000; European Chief Exec., Credit Suisse First Boston, 2001–04; Man. Dir., Wholesale and Instnl Mkts, FSA, 2004–07. Non-executive Director: London Stock Exchange, 1996–2001; LCH.Clearnet, 2003–04. Member: Adv. Bd, Oxford Business Sch., 2001–; Bd, Nuffield Orthopaedic Centre, 2002–. *Address:* Financial Services Authority, 25 The North Colonnade, Canary Wharf, E14 5HS. *T:* (020) 7066 1000.

SAOUMA, Edouard; Director-General of the Food and Agriculture Organization of the United Nations, Rome, 1976–93; agricultural engineer and international official; *b* Beirut, Lebanon, 6 Nov. 1926; *m* Inés Forero; one *s* two *d*. *Educ:* St Joseph's University Sch. of Engineering, Beirut; École Nat. Supérieure d'Agronomie, Montpellier, France. Director: Tel Amara Agric. Sch., 1952–53; Nat. Centre for Farm Mechanization, 1954–55; Sec. Gen., Nat. Fedn of Lebanese Agronomists, 1955; Dir-Gen., Nat. Inst. for Agricl Res., 1957–62; Mem. Gov. Bd, Nat. Grains Office, 1960–62; Minister of Agric., Fisheries and Forestry, 1970. Food and Agric. Organization of UN: Dep. Regional Rep. for Asia and Far East, 1962–65; Dir, Land and Water Develt Div., 1965–75; Dir-Gen., 1976, re-elected 1981, 1987. Hon. Prof. of Agronomy, Agricl Univ. of Beijing, China. Said Akl Prize, Lebanon; Chevalier du Mérite Agricole, France; Grand Cross: Order of the Cedar, Lebanon; Ordre National du Chad; Ordre Nat. du Ghana; Ordre National de Haute Volta; Mérito Agrícola of Spain; Orden Nacional al Mérito, Colombia; Kt Comdr, Order of Merit, Greece; Order of Agricl Merit, Colombia; Gran Oficial, Orden de Vasco Nuñez de Balboa, Panamá; Orden al Mérito Agrícola, Peru; Order of Merit, Egypt; Order of Merit, Mauritania; Grand Officier: Ordre de la République, Tunisia; Ordre National, Madagascar; Ordre de Commandeur, Ouissan Alouite, Morocco. Dr (*hc*): Univ. of Bologna, Italy; Agric. Univ. La Molina, Peru; Univ. of Seoul, Republic of Korea; Univ. of Uruguay; Univ. of Jakarta, Indonesia; Univ. of Warsaw; Univ. of Los Baños, Philippines; Punjab Agricultural Univ., India; Faisalabad Agricultural Univ., Pakistan; Univ. of Agricl Scis of Gödöllö, Hungary; Univ. Nacional Autónoma, Nicaragua; Univ. of Florence, Italy; Univ. of Gembloux, Belgium; Univ. of Prague, Czechoslovakia; Catholic Univ. of America; Univ. of Bologna, Italy; Agricl Inst., Mongolia. Accademico Corrispondente, Accademià Nazionale di Agricultura, Bologna, Italy. *Publications:* technical publications on agriculture. *Address:* POB 40210, Baabda, Lebanon.

SAPERSTEIN, Rabbi Prof. Marc Eli, PhD; Principal, Leo Baeck College, London, since 2006; *b* 5 Sept. 1944; *s* of Harold Irving Saperstein and Marcia Belle Saperstein (*née* Rosenblum); *m* 2007, Tamar de Vries Winter; two *d* from former marriage. *Educ:* Harvard Coll. (AB English Lit. 1966); Hebrew Univ. of Jerusalem (MA Jewish Hist. 1971); Hebrew Union Coll.-Jewish Inst. of Religion, NY (MA 1972); Harvard Grad. Sch. of Arts and Scis (PhD Jewish Hist., Lit. and Thought 1977). Ordained Rabbi, 1972; Lectr on Hebrew Lit., Harvard Faculty of Arts and Scis, 1977–79; Asst Prof. of Jewish Studies, 1979–83, Associate Prof. of Jewish Studies, 1983–86, Harvard Divinity Sch.; Goldstein Prof. of Jewish Hist. and Thought, Washington Univ. in St Louis, 1986–97; Charles E. Smith Prof. of Jewish Hist. and Dir of Prog. in Judaic Studies, George Washington Univ., 1997–2006. Visiting Professor: Columbia Univ., 1980; Univ. of Pennsylvania, 1995; Revel Grad. Sch., Yeshiva Univ., 2002; Visiting Fellow: Inst. for Advanced Studies, Jerusalem, 1989; Center for Advanced Judaic Studies, Univ. of Pennsylvania, 1995–96; Centre for Jewish-Christian Relns, Cambridge, 2002; Harvard Center for Jewish Studies, 2005. Mem. Bd of Dirs, Assoc. for Jewish Studies, 1983–99; Vice Pres., Amer. Acad. for Jewish Res., 2004–06. Book Rev. Ed., Assoc. for Jewish Studies Rev., 1997–2002. *Publications:* Decoding the Rabbis: a thirteenth-century commentary on the Aggadah, 1980; Jewish Preaching 1200–1800, 1980; Moments of Crisis in Jewish-Christian Relations, 1989; Your Voice Like a Ram's Horn: themes and texts in traditional Jewish preaching, 1996; Exile in Amsterdam: Saul Levi Morteira's sermons to a congregation of New Jews, 2005; Jewish Preaching in Times of War 1800–2001, 2008; editor: Essential Papers on Messianic Movements and Personalities in Jewish History, 1992; Harold I. Saperstein: Witness from the Pulpit: topical sermons 1933–1980, 2000; articles and reviews on Jewish hist., lit. and thought. *Recreation:* classical piano. *Address:* Leo Baeck College, 80 East End Road, N3 2SY. *T:* (020) 8349 5600; *e-mail:* marc.saperstein@lbc.ac.uk.

SAPHIR, Nicholas Peter George; Chairman: OMSCo, The Organic Milk Suppliers Co-operative, since 2003; Coressence, since 2006; *b* 30 Nov. 1944; *s* of Emanuel Saphir and Ann (*née* Belikoff); *m* 1971, Ena Bodin; one *s*. *Educ:* City of London Sch.; Manchester Univ. (LLB Hons). Called to the Bar, Lincoln's Inn, 1967. Chm., Hunter Saphir, 1987–97; Director: Bodin & Nielsen Ltd, 1975–; Albert Fisher Gp PLC, 1993–97; non-executive Director: Dairy Crest Ltd, 1987–93; San Miguel SA (Argentina), 1993–98, 2001–07. Chairman: CCAHC, 1980–83; Agricultural Forum, 2001–04; Rural Revival, 2004–07; Founder Chm., Food From Britain, 1983–87; Mem., Food and Drink EDC, 1984–87; Chm., British Israel Chamber of Commerce, 1991–94. Pres., Fresh Produce Consortium, 1997–2000. *Recreation:* sailing. *Address:* Combe Manor Farm, Coombe Lane, Wadhurst, E Sussex TN5 6NU. *T:* (01892) 785111, *Fax:* (01892) 785222. *Club:* Farmers.

SAPIN, Michel Marie; Mayor, Argenton-sur-Creuse (Indre), since 1995; Deputy (Soc.) for Indre, National Assembly, France, since 2007; *b* 9 April 1952; *m* 1982, Yolande Millan; three *s*. *Educ:* Ecole Normale Supérieure de la rue d'Ulm (MA Hist., post-grad. degree Geog.); Institut d'Etudes Politiques de Paris; Ecole Nationale d'Administration. Joined Socialist Party, 1975; National Assembly: Socialist Deputy of the Indre, 1981–86, of Hauts-de-Seine, 1986–91; Sec., 1983–84; Vice-Pres., 1984–85, 1988; Vice-Chm., Socialist Gp, 1987–88; Pres., Commn of Law, 1988–91. Minister-Delegate of Justice, 1991–92; Minister of the Economy and Finance, 1992–93, for the Civil Service and Admin. Reform, 2000–02. Mem., Monetary Policy Council, Bank of France, 1994–95. City Cllr, Nanterre, 1989–94; Regl Cllr, Ile de France, 1992–94; Gen. Cllr of the Indre, 1998–2004; Pres., 1998–2000, 2004–07, Vice-Pres., 2000–01, Centre Regl Council. First Vice-Pres., Assoc. of Regions of France, 1998–2000. *Address:* 9 bis rue Dupertuis, 36200 Argenton-sur-Creuse, France.

SARAMAGO, José; writer; *b* Azinhaga, Portugal, 16 Nov. 1922; *s* of José de Sousa and Maria da Piedade; *m* 1st, 1944, Ilda Reis (marr. diss. 1970; she *d* 1998); one *c*; 2nd, 1998, Pilar de Río. Formerly car mechanic, admin. civil servant, and metal co. worker; with Estúdios Cor until 1971; translator of Colette, Tolstoy, Maupassant, Baudelaire, etc, 1955–81; political commentator and cultural editor, Diário de Lisboa, 1972–75; Asst Ed., Diário de Notícias, 1975. Nobel Prize for Literature, 1998. *Publications: fiction:* Terra do Pecado, 1947; Manual de Pintura e Caligrafia, 1977 (trans. Manual of Painting and Calligraphy); Objecto Quase (short stories), 1978; Levantado do Chão, 1980; Memorial do Convento, 1982 (trans. Baltasar and Blimunda); O Ano da Morte de Ricardo Reis, 1984 (The Year of the Death of Ricardo Reis); A Jangada de Pedra, 1986 (The Stone Raft); História do Cerco de Lisboa, 1989 (The History of the Siege of Lisbon); O Evangelho Segundo Jesus Cristo, 1991 (The Gospel According to Jesus Christ); Ensaio Sobrea a Cegueira, 1995 (Blindness); O Conto da ilha desconhecida, 1996 (The Tale of the Unknown Island); Todos os Nomes, 1997 (All the Names); El Amor Posible, 1998; La Caverna (The Cave, 2002); El Hombre Duplicado (The Double, 2004); Ensaio Sobre a Lucidez, 2004 (Seeing, 2006); As Intermitências da Morte, 2005 (Death at Intervals, 2008); *poetry:* Os Poemas Possíveis, 1966; Provavelmente Alegria, 1970; O Ano de 1993, 1975; *plays:* A Noite, 1979; Que Farei com este Livro?, 1980; A Segunda Vida de Francisco de Assisi, 1987; In Nomine Dei, 1993; *essays:* Deste Mundo e do Outro, 1971; A Bagagem do Viajante, 1973; Os Opiniões que o D. L. Teve, 1974; Os Apontamentos, 1976; Viagem a Portugal, 1981; *journals:* Cadernos de Lanzarote, 5 Vols, 1994–. *Address:* Los Topes 3, 35572 Tias, Lanzarote, Canary Islands.

SARDAR, Ziauddin; writer, critic, broadcaster; *b* 31 Oct. 1951; *s* of late Salahuddin Sardar and of Hamida Bagum; *m* 1978, Saliha Basit; two *s* one *d*. *Educ:* Brooke House Sec. Sch., London; City Univ., London (BSc Hons 1974, MSc Inf. Sci. 1975). Inf. Consultant, Hajj Res. Centre, King Abdul Aziz Univ., Jeddah, 1975–79; Reporter, LWT, 1981–83; Dir, Centre for Policy and Future Studies, East West Univ., Chicago, 1985–88; Advr to Dep. Prime Minister of Malaysia, 1988–97. Mem., Commn for Equality and Human Rights, 2006–. Editor, Futures, 1997–; Co-editor, Third Text, 1999–. *Publications:* Science, Technology and Development in the Muslim World, 1977; (jtly) Hajj Studies, 1978; Muhammad: aspects of his biography, 1978; Science Policy and Developing Countries, 1978; Islam: outline of a classification scheme, 1979; The Future of Muslim Civilization, 1979, 1987; Science and Technology in the Middle East, 1982; (ed) Touch of Midas: science values and environment in Islam and the West, 1984, 1999; Islamic Futures: the shape of ideas to come, 1986; (ed) The Revenge of Athena: science, exploitation and the Third World, 1988; Information and the Muslim World: a strategy for the twenty-first century, 1988; (ed) Building Information Systems in the Islamic World, 1988; (ed) An Early Crescent, 1989; Explorations in Islamic Science, 1989; (jtly) Distorted Imagination: lessons from the Rushdie affair, 1990; (jtly) Christian-Muslim Relations: yesterday, today, tomorrow, 1991; (ed) How We Know, 1991; Introducing Islam, 1992; Barbaric Others, 1993; (ed jtly) Muslim Minorities in the West, 1995; (ed jtly) Cyberfutures, 1996; Postmodernism and the Other, 1998; (ed) Futures Studies; Orientalism, 1999; Introducing Muhammad, 1999; Introducing Mathematics, 1999; The Consumption of Kuala Lumpur, 2000; Thomas Kuhn and the Science Wars, 2000; Introducing Media Studies, 2000; Introducing Chaos, 2001; Introducing Cultural Studies, 2001; (jtly) Introducing Learning and Memory, 2002; Introducing Science, 2002; Aliens R Us, 2002; The A to Z of Postmodern Life, 2002; (jtly) Why Do People Hate America?, 2002; (ed jtly) The "Third Text" Reader on Art, Culture and Theory, 2002; (jtly) The No-Nonsense Guide to Islam, 2003; Islam, Postmodernism and other Futures, 2003; Desperately Seeking Paradise, 2004; (jtly) American Dream, Global Nightmare, 2004; (jtly) What is British?, 2004; American Terminator: myths, movies and global power, 2004; How Do We Know?: reading Ziauddin Sardar on Islam, science and cultural relations, 2005; What Do Muslims Believe?, 2006; Balti Britain: a journey through the British Asian experience, 2008. *Recreation:* smoking Havana cigars. *Address: e-mail:* mail@ziasardar.com. *Club:* Athenæum.

SAREI, Sir Alexis Holyweek, Kt 1987; CBE 1981; PhD; Premier of North Solomons Provincial Government, Papua New Guinea, 1976–80 and 1985–88; *b* 25 March 1934; *s* of late Joseph Nambong and Joanna Mota; *m* 1972, Claire Dionne; three *s* three *d* (all adopted). *Educ:* PNG Primary to Tertiary, 1949–66; Rome Univ., 1968–71 (PhD Canon Law). RC Priest, 1966–72; Secretary to Chief Minister, PNG, 1972–73; District Comr, 1973–75; Advisor to Bougainville people, 1975–76; High Comr in UK, 1980–83. Following revolution on Bougainville, went to USA, 1990; Security Guard, 1992–93; retired 1994. PNG Independence Medal 1977; CBE for work in Provincial Govt, pioneering work in the system in PNG. Successor to his uncle, Gregory Moah, as Chief of Clan, Petisuun. *Publication:* The Practice of Marriage Among the Solos, Buka Island, 1971. *Recreations:* music, sketching, golf, swimming, sports. *Address:* Gagan Village — 2008, PO Box 28, Buka Island, Bougainville Region, Papua New Guinea.

SARGEANT, Carl; Member (Lab) Alyn and Deeside, National Assembly for Wales, since 2003; *b* 1968; *s* of Malcolm and Sylvia Sargeant; *m* Bernie; one *s* one *d*. Trained industrial fire fighter; quality and envmtl auditor; process operator, manufacturing co., N Wales. Mem. (Lab) Connah's Quay Town Council. Chief Whip and Dep. Business Minister, Nat. Assembly for Wales, 2007. Gov., Deeside Coll. *Address:* (office) Deeside Enterprise Centre, Rowley's Drive, Shotton, Deeside, Flintshire CH5 1PP; National Assembly for Wales, Cardiff CF99 1NA.

SARGEANT, Rt Rev. Frank Pilkington; an Hon. Assistant Bishop, Diocese of Manchester, since 1999, and Diocese of Liverpool, since 2007; *b* 12 Sept. 1932; *s* of John Stanley and Grace Sargeant; *m* 1958, Sally Jeanette McDermott; three *s* two *d*. *Educ:* Boston Grammar School; Durham Univ., St John's Coll. and Cranmer Hall (BA, Dip Theol); Nottingham Univ. (Diploma in Adult Education). National Service Commission, RA (20th Field Regt), 1955–57. Assistant Curate: Gainsborough Parish Church, 1958–62; Grimsby Parish Church, and Priest-in-Charge of St Martin's, Grimsby, 1962–67; Vicar of North Hykeham and Rector of South Hykeham, 1967–73; Residentiary Canon, Bradford Cathedral, 1973–77; Archdeacon of Bradford, 1977–84; Bishop Suffragan of Stockport, 1984–94; head of the Archbishop of Canterbury's staff (with title of Bishop at Lambeth), 1994–99, and Asst Bishop, dio. of Canterbury, 1995–99; retired 1999. Hon. Asst Bishop, Dio. in Europe, 1999–2008. Pres., Actors' Church Union, 1995–2007; Chm., Retired Clergy Assoc., 2003–07. *Address:* 32 Brotherton Drive, Trinity Gardens, Salford M3 6BH. *T:* (0161) 839 7045; *e-mail:* franksargeant68@hotmail.com.

SARGENT, Anthony; *see* Sargent, D. A.

SARGENT, Dick; *see* Sargent, J. R.

SARGENT, (Donald) Anthony; General Director, The Sage Gateshead (formerly Music Centre Gateshead) and North Music Trust, since 2000; *b* 18 Dec. 1949; *s* of Sir Donald Sargent, KBE, CB and Mary (*née* Raven); *m* 1st, 1978, Sara Gilford (marr. diss.); 2nd, 1986, Caroline Gant; one *d*. *Educ:* King's Sch., Canterbury; Oriel Coll., Oxford (Open Exhibnr; MA Hons PPE); Magdalen Coll., Oxford (Choral Schol.); Christ Church, Oxford (Choral Schol.). Various prodn and presentation posts, BBC Radio and TV, 1974–86 (Manager, Concert Planning, 1982–86); Artistic Projects Dir, S Bank Centre, London, 1986–89; Hd of Arts, Birmingham CC, 1989–99; Partnerships and Prog. Develt Manager, BBC Music Live, 1999–2000. Mem. Bd, Internat. Soc. for Performing Arts,

2005. FRSA 1999. Hon. Fellow: Birmingham Conservatoire, 1999; Sunderland Univ., 2005. *Publications:* contrib. miscellaneous periodical and professional articles. *Recreations:* problem solving, fresh air, laughing. *Address:* (home) 6 Winchester Terrace, Summerhill Square, Newcastle upon Tyne NE4 6EH; The Sage Gateshead, St Mary's Square, Gateshead Quays, Gateshead NE8 2JR.

SARGENT, Prof. John Reid, PhD; FRSE; Professor of Biological Science, University of Stirling, 1986–2001, now Emeritus; Director, Natural Environment Research Council Unit of Aquatic Biochemistry, University of Stirling, 1986–98; *b* 12 Oct. 1936; *s* of Alex and Annie Sargent; *m* 1961, Elizabeth Jean Buchan; two *d. Educ:* Buckie High Sch.; Robert Gordon's Coll., Aberdeen; Aberdeen Univ. (BSc 1st Cl. Hons, PhD). FRSE 1986. Res. Fellow, Middlesex Hosp. Med. Sch., 1961–64; Lectr, Biochem. Dept, Univ. of Aberdeen, 1964–69; PSO, then SPSO, then Dir, NERC Inst. of Marine Biochem., 1970–85; Stirling University: Head of Dept of Biol Science, 1985–89; Head of Sch. of Natural Scis, 1989–93. Bond Gold Medal, Amer. Oil Chemists' Soc., 1971. *Publications:* numerous research pubns in biochem. and marine biol., esp. on marine lipids and polyunsaturated fatty acids. *Recreations:* sailing, ski-ing. *Address:* 5 Rosebery View, Dalgety Bay, Fife, KY11 9YH; c/o Institute of Aquaculture, Faculty of Natural Sciences, University of Stirling, Stirling FK9 4LA. *T:* (01786) 473171.

SARGENT, John Richard, (Dick); *b* 22 March 1925; *s* of John Philip Sargent and Ruth (*née* Taunton); *m* 1st, 1949, Anne Elizabeth Haigh (marr. diss. 1980); one *s* two *d;* 2nd, 1980, Hester Mary Campbell (*d* 2004). *Educ:* Dragon Sch., Oxford; Rugby Sch.; Christ Church, Oxford (MA). Fellow and Lectr in Econs, Worcester Coll., Oxford, 1951–62; Econ. Consultant, HM Treasury and DEA, 1963–65; Prof. of Econs, Univ. of Warwick, 1965–73 (Pro-Vice-Chancellor, 1971–72), Hon. Prof., 1974–81 and 2007–. Vis. Prof. of Econs, LSE, 1981–82; Gp Economic Adviser, Midland Bank Ltd, 1974–84; Houblon-Norman Res. Fellow, Bank of England, 1984–85. Member: Doctors and Dentists Rev. Body, 1972–75; Armed Forces Pay Rev. Body, 1972–86; Channel Tunnel Adv. Gp, 1974–75; SSRC, 1980–85; Pharmacists Review Panel, 1986–; Pres., Société Universitaire Européenne de Recherches Financières, 1985–88. Editor, Midland Bank Rev., 1974–84. *Publications:* British Transport Policy, 1958; (ed with R. C. O. Matthews) Contemporary Problems of Economic Policy, 1983; To Full Employment: the Keynesian Experience and After, 2007; articles in various economic jls, and in vols of conf. papers etc. *Recreation:* work. *Address:* 38 The Leys, Chipping Norton, Oxon OX7 5HH. *T:* (01608) 641773. *Club:* Reform.

SARGENT, Prof. Roger William Herbert, FREng; Courtaulds Professor of Chemical Engineering, Imperial College, 1966–92, now Emeritus; Senior Research Fellow, Imperial College, since 1992; *b* 14 Oct. 1926; *s* of Herbert Alfred Sargent and May Elizabeth (*née* Gill); *m* 1951, Shirley Jane Levesque (*née* Spooner); two *s. Educ:* Bedford Sch.; Imperial Coll., London (FIC 1994). BSc, ACGI, PhD, DScEng, DIC; FIChemE, FIMA; FREng (FEng 1976). Design Engineer, Société l'Air Liquide, Paris, 1951–58; Imperial College: Sen. Lectr, 1958–62; Prof. of Chem. Engrg, 1962–66; Dean, City and Guilds Coll., 1973–76; Head of Dept of Chem. Engrg and Chem. Technology, 1975–88; Dir of Interdisciplinary Res. Centre in Process Systems Engrg, 1989–92. Member: Engrg and Technol. Adv. Cttee, British Council, 1976–89 (Chm., 1984–89); Technol. Subcttee, UGC, 1984–88. Pres., Instn of Chem. Engrs, 1973–74; For. Associate, US Nat. Acad. of Engrg, 1993. FRSA 1988. Hon. FCGI 1977. D*hc:* Institut Nat. Polytechnique de Lorraine, 1987; Univ. de Liège, 1996; Hon. DSc Edinburgh, 1993. *Publications:* contribs to: Trans Instn Chem. Engrs, Computers and Chemical Engrg, Jl of Optimization Theory and Applications, SIAM Jl of Optimization, Mathematical Programming, Internat. Jl of Control, etc. *Address:* Mulberry Cottage, 291A Sheen Road, Richmond, Surrey TW10 5AW. *T:* (020) 8876 9623.

SARGENT, Prof. Wallace Leslie William, FRS 1981; Ira S. Bowen Professor of Astronomy, California Institute of Technology, since 1981; *b* 15 Feb. 1935; *s* of Leslie William Sargent and Eleanor (*née* Denniss); *m* 1964, Anneila Isabel Cassells, PhD; two *d. Educ:* Scunthorpe Tech. High Sch. (first pupil to go to univ., 1953); Manchester Univ. (BSc Hons, MSc, PhD). Research Fellow in Astronomy, California Inst. of Tech., 1959–62; Sen. Research Fellow, Royal Greenwich Observatory, 1962–64; Asst Prof. of Physics, Univ. of California, San Diego, 1964–66; California Institute of Technology: Asst Prof. of Astronomy, 1966–68, Associate Prof., 1968–71, Professor, 1971–81; Executive Officer for Astronomy, 1975–81 and 1996–97; Dir, Palomar Observatory, 1997–2000. Lectures: George Darwin, RAS, 1987; Thomas Gold, Cornell Univ., 1995; Sackler Dist., Harvard Univ., 1995; Sackler Prize, Univ. of California, Berkeley, 1996; Henry Norris Russell, AAS, 2001; Icko Iben, Univ. of Illinois, 2002. Vice-Pres., American Astronomical Soc., 2004–07. Mem., Nat. Acad. of Scis, USA, 2005; Fellow, American Acad. of Arts and Sciences, 1977; Associate, RAS, 1998. Warner Prize, American Astronomical Soc., 1968; Dannie Heineman Prize, 1991; Bruce Gold Medal, Astronomical Soc. of the Pacific, 1994. *Publications:* many papers in learned jls. *Recreations:* reading, gardening, mountain walking, watching sports. *Address:* Astronomy Dept 105–24, California Institute of Technology, Pasadena, CA 91125, USA. *T:* (626) 3954055; 400 South Berkeley Avenue, Pasadena, CA 91107, USA. *T:* (626) 7956345. *Club:* Athenæum (Pasadena).

SARGESON, Prof. Alan McLeod, FRS 1983; Professor of Inorganic Chemistry, Australian National University, 1978–95, now Emeritus; *b* 13 Oct. 1930; *s* of late H. L. Sargeson; *m* 1959, Marietta, *d* of F. Anders; two *s* two *d. Educ:* Maitland Boys' High Sch.; Sydney Univ. (BSc, PhD, DipEd). FRACI; FAA. Lectr, Chem. Dept, Univ. of Adelaide, 1956–57; Res. Fellow, John Curtin Sch. of Med. Research, ANU, 1958, Fellow 1960; Sen. Fellow, then Professorial Fellow, 1969–78, Res. Sch. of Chemistry, ANU. For. Mem., Royal Danish Acad. of Science, 1976; Mem., Royal Physiographic Soc., Lund, 2002; For. Hon. Mem., Amer. Acad. of Arts and Sci., 1998; For. Associate, US Nat. Acad. of Science, 1996. DSc *hc:* Sydney, 1990; Copenhagen, 1996; Bordeaux, 1997. *Address:* Research School of Chemistry, Australian National University, Canberra, ACT 0200, Australia.

SARIN, Arun; Chief Executive, Vodafone plc, 2003–08; *b* 21 Oct. 1954; *s* of Lt Col Krishan Sarin and Romilla Sarin; *m* 1980, Rummi Anand; one *s* one *d. Educ:* Indian Inst. of Technol., Kharagpur (BS Engrg); Univ. of California, Berkeley (MS Engrg; MBA). Various positions, Pacific Telesis Gp Inc., 1984–94; Vice Pres., Human Resources, Corporate Strategy and Develt, AirTouch Communications, 1994–95; Pres. and Chief Exec., AirTouch Internat., 1995–97; Pres. and Chief Operating Officer, AirTouch Communications, 1997–99; Chief Executive Officer: US/Asia Pacific Reg., Vodafone AirTouch, 1999–2000; Infospace, 2000; Accel-KKR Telecom, 2001–03. Non-exec. Dir, Bank of England, 2005–. *Recreations:* golf, tennis, running. *Address:* c/o Vodafone Group plc, Vodafone House, 1 The Connection, Newbury, Berks RG14 2FN. *T:* (01635) 33251, *Fax:* (01635) 686111.

SARK, Seigneur of; see Beaumont, J. M.

SARKIS, Angela Marie, CBE 2000; National Secretary, YMCA England, 2006–08; Board Member, Capacitybuilders, since 2008; *b* 6 Jan. 1955; *d* of Rupert Sadler and Hazel Sadler (*née* McDonald); *m* 1980, Edward Tacvor Sarkis; one *s* one *d. Educ:* Cottesmore Sch., Nottingham; Clarendon Coll. of Further Educn, Nottingham; Leeds Univ. (BA Theol./Sociol.); Leicester Univ. (Dip. Social Work and CQSW). Probation Officer, Middx Probation Service, 1979–89; Unit Manager, Brent Family Services Unit, 1989–91; Asst Dir, Intermediate Treatment Fund, 1991–93; Dir, DIVERT Trust, 1993–96; Chief Exec., Church Urban Fund, 1996–2001; a Governor, BBC, 2002–06. Advr, Social Exclusion Unit, Cabinet Office, 1997–; Mem., H of L Appts Commn, 2000–. Mem. Council, Howard League for Penal Reform, 1998–. Mem., Housing and Neighbourhood Cttee, Joseph Rowntree Foundn, 1997–. Mem. Council, Evangelical Alliance, 1995–99; Vice-Pres., African and Caribbean Evangelical Alliance, 1996; Mem., Leadership Team, Brentwater Evangelical Ch, NW2, 1990–94. Mem. Cttee, Assoc. Charitable Foundns, 1995–99; Trustee: BBC Children in Need, 1995–2002; Inst. Citizenship Studies, 1995–97; Notting Hill Housing Trust, 1995–97. Trustee: Single Homeless Housing Project, NW10, 1980–87; Learie Constantine Youth Club, NW2, 1980–90; Single Mothers Project, NW10, 1984–90; Tavistock Youth Club, NW10, 1985–90. *Recreations:* gardening, family, singing.

SARKÖZY DE NAGY-BOCSA, Nicolas Paul Stéphane; Hon. GCB 2008; President of the French Republic, since 2007; *b* 28 Jan. 1955; *s* of Paul Sarközy de Nagy-Bocsa and Andrée (*née* Mallah); *m* 1996, Cécilia Ciganer-Albeniz (marr. diss. 2007); one *s*, and two *s* from previous marriage; *m* 2008, Carla Bruni. *Educ:* Maîtrise de droit privé, 1978; Cours St-Louis de Monceau; Inst d'Études Politiques, Paris (Cert d'aptitude à la profession d'avocat, 1981); Univ. Paris X-Nanterre. Lawyer, 1981–87. Neuilly-sur-Seine: Municipal Councillor, 1977–83; Mayor, 1983–2002; Dep. Mayor, 2002; Conseil Général des Hauts-de-Seine: Mem., 1985–88 and 2004; Vice-Pres., 1986–88; Pres., 2004; Deputy (RPR) Hauts-de-Seine, 1988, re-elected 1993, 1995, 1997, 2002. Minister: of the Budget, 1993–95; of Communication, 1994–95; of the Interior, Interior Security and Local Freedom, 2002–04; of State, and Minister of the Economy, Finance and Industry, 2004; of the Interior and Regional Develt, 2005–07. Rassemblement pour la République: Nat. Sec., 1988–92; Dep. Sec.-Gen., 1990–93; Mem., Political Office, 1993; Sec. Gen., then interim Pres., 1998–99; Pres., Deptl Cttee, Hauts-de-Seine, 2000; Pres., UMP, 2004–. Chevalier de la Légion d'Honneur, 2005. *Publications:* Georges Mandel: le moine de la politique, 1994; (with M. Denisot) Au bout de la passion, l'équilibre, 1995; Libre, 2001; La République, les Réligions, l'Espérance, 2004. *Address:* Palais de l'Elysée, 75008 Paris, France.

SARMADI, Morteza; Deputy Foreign Minister for European and American Affairs, Iran, since 2004; *b* July 1954; *m* 1982, Fatemeh Hosseini; four *d. Educ:* Sharif Univ. (BS Metallurgy); Tehran Univ. Joined Ministry of Foreign Affairs, Tehran, 1981: Dir Gen., Press and Inf., 1982–89; Deputy Foreign Minister: for Communication, 1989–97; Eur. and American and CIS Countries' Affairs, 1997–2000; Iranian Ambassador to UK, 2000–04. Special Rep. to Caspian Sea Legal Regime; Sen. Mem., Delegn for Iran and Iraq Peace Negotiation. Has participated in numerous confs internationally. Trustee Member: Islamic Thought Foundn; Islamic Republic News Agency; Islamic High Council of Propagation Policy; Inst. for Political and Internat. Studies. *Recreations:* reading, watching TV, swimming, spending time with the family. *Address:* c/o Ministry of Foreign Affairs, Ebn e Sina Street, Emam Khomeini SQ, Tehran, Iran.

SARNAK, Prof. Peter, PhD; FRS 2002; Eugene Higgins Professor of Mathematics, Princeton University, since 2002; Professor, Courant Institute of Mathematical Sciences, New York University, since 2001; *b* Johannesburg, 18 Dec. 1953. *Educ:* Univ. of Witwatersrand (BSc 1975); Stanford Univ. (PhD 1980). Asst Prof., 1980–83, Associate Prof., 1983–84, Courant Inst. of Math. Scis, NY Univ.; Associate Prof., 1984–87, Prof., 1987–91, Stanford Univ.; Princeton University: Prof., 1991–; H. Fine Prof., 1995–96; Chm., Dept of Maths, 1996–99; Mem., Inst. for Advanced Study, 1999–2002. *Publications:* Some Applications of Modular Forms, 1990; (jtly) Extremal Riemann Surfaces, 1997; (ed jtly) Random Matrices, Frobenius Eigenvalues and Monodromy, 1998; articles in jls. *Address:* Department of Mathematics, Princeton University, Fine Hall, Washington Road, Princeton, NJ 08544–1000, USA.

SAROOP, Narindar, CBE 1982; Senior Adviser, Gow & Partners, 2005–07; *b* 14 Aug. 1929; *e s* of Chaudhri Ram Saroop, Ismaila, Rohtak, India and late Shyam Devi; *m* 1st, 1952, Ravi Gill (marr. diss. 1967), *o* surv. *c* of the Sardar and Sardarni of Premgarh, India; two *d* (one *s* decd); 2nd 1969, Stephanie Denise, *yr d* of Alexander and Cynthia Amie Cronopulo, Zakynthos, Greece. *Educ:* Aitchison Coll. for Punjab Chiefs, Lahore; Indian Military Acad., Dehra Dun. Served as regular officer, 2nd Royal Lancers (Gardner's Horse) and Queen Victoria's Own The Poona Horse; retired, 1954. Management Trainee, Yule Catto, 1954; senior executive and Dir of subsidiaries of various multinationals, to 1976; Hon. Administrator, Oxfam Relief Project, 1964; Director: Devi Grays Insurance Ltd, 1981–84; Capital Plant International Ltd, 1982–86. Adviser: Develt, Clarkson Puckle Gp, 1976–87; Banque Belge, 1987–91; Cancer Relief Macmillan Fund, 1992–95; Nat. Grid plc, 1993; Coutts & Co., 1995–98. Mem., BBC Adv. Council on Asian Programmes, 1977–81. Pres., Indian Welfare Soc., 1983–92. Member Council: Freedom Assoc., 1978–86; Internat. Social Services, 1981–91; Inst. of Directors, 1983–93; Founder Mem., Tory Asians for Representation Gp, 1984–85; Mem. Adv. Council, Efficiency in Local Govt, 1984. Contested (C) Greenwich, 1979 (first Asian Tory Parliamentary candidate this century); Founder and 1st Chm., UK Anglo Asian Cons. Soc., 1976–79, 1985–86; Vice Chm., Cons. Party Internat. Office, 1990–92. Councillor (C), Kensington and Chelsea, 1974–82; initiated Borough Community Relations Cttee (Chm., 1975–77, 1980–82); Chm., Working Party on Employment, 1978; Founder and Chm., Durbar Club, 1981–. Mem., V & A Mus. Appeal Cttee, 1994–95. Patron, Conservative World, 2003–05. Hon. Mem., Clan Moncreiffe, 2000. *Publications:* In Defence of Freedom (jtly), 1978; A Squire of Hindoostan, 1983; The Last Indian (autobiog.), 2005. *Recreations:* keeping fools, boredom and socialism at bay. *Clubs:* Beefsteak, Cavalry and Guards, Pratt's, Turf; Puffin's (Edinburgh); Imperial Delhi Gymkhana; Royal Bombay Yacht, Royal Calcutta Golf.

SARUM, Archdeacon of; see Jeans, Ven. A. P.

SARWAR, Mohammad; MP (Lab) Glasgow Central, since 2005 (Glasgow Govan, 1997–2005); *b* 18 Aug. 1952; *s* of Mohammed and Rashida Abdullah Sarwar; *m* 1976, Perveen Sarwar; three *s* one *d. Educ:* Univ. of Faisalabad (FSC; BA). Shopkeeper, 1976–83; Dir, United Wholesale Ltd, 1983–97. Member (Lab): Glasgow DC, 1992–96; Glasgow CC, 1995–97. First ethnic minority MP in Scotland; first Muslim MP in Britain. *Recreation:* relaxing with family and friends. *Address:* House of Commons, SW1A 0AA. *T:* (020) 7219 3000; (constituency) 247 Paisley Road West, Glasgow G51 1NE. *T:* (0141) 427 5250, *Fax:* (0141) 427 5938; *e-mail:* sarwar@sarwar.org.uk.

SASKATCHEWAN, Bishop of, since 1993; **Rt Rev. Anthony John Burton;** *b* 11 Aug. 1959; *s* of Peter and Rachel Burton; *m* 1989, Anna Kristine Erickson; one *s* one *d. Educ:* Trinity Coll., Toronto Univ. (BA (Hons) 1982); King's Coll., Dalhousie Univ.;

Wycliffe Hall, Oxford (BA, MA). Ordained deacon, 1987, priest, 1988; Curate, St John the Baptist, N Sydney, Nova Scotia, 1987–88; Rector, Trinity Church, Sydney Mines, 1988–91; Rector and Canon Residentiary, Cathedral Church of St Alban the Martyr, Saskatchewan, 1991–93; Dean of Saskatchewan, 1991–94. Anglican-Roman Catholic Bps' Dialogue, Canada, 1994–97, 2000–02, Co-Chm., 2007–. Mem. Bd, Scholarly Engagement with Anglican Doctrine, USA, 2003–04. Chair, Council of the North, 2004–07; Vice-Chm., Prayer Book Soc. of Canada, 1999–. Episcopal Visitor, S American Missionary Soc., Canada, 2002–. Hon. DD King's Coll., Halifax, 1994. *Publications:* (contrib.) Anglican Essentials: reclaiming faith in the Anglican Church of Canada, 1995; contrib. to Machray Rev. *Recreations:* walking, fighting ignominiously in last ditches. *Address:* Synod Office, 1308 Fifth Avenue East, Prince Albert, SK S6V 2H7, Canada. *T:* (306) 7632455, *Fax:* (306) 7645172.

SASKATOON, Bishop of, since 2004; **Rt Rev. Rodney Osborne Andrews;** *b* 11 Nov. 1940; *s* of George William Andrews and Mary Isabel (*née* Smith); *m* 1990, Jacqueline Plante; one *s* one *d. Educ:* Univ. of Saskatchewan (BA 1963); Coll. of Emmanuel and St Chad, Saskatoon (BTh 1965; MDiv 1981). Ordained deacon, 1964, priest, 1965; parish work and native ministry, Dio. Calgary, 1965–84; parish work and military chaplaincy, Dio. Montreal, 1984–87; parish work, Dio. Ottawa, 1988–91; Exec. Archdeacon, Dio. Algoma, 1991–2000; Rector of St Alban's, Richmond, and Univ. Chaplain, UBC, Dio. New Westminster, BC, 2000–03. Columnist, Country Guide, Canada's nat. farm mag., 1994–. Holds airline transport pilot's licence, Canada. Medal commemorating 100th anniv. of treaty betw. southern Alberta native tribes and Queen Victoria, 1977; Saskatchewan Centennial Medal, 2006. *Recreations:* flying, curling, camping. *Address:* (office) Unit 1, 505–23 Street East, PO Box 1965, Saskatoon, SK S7K 3S5, Canada. *T:* (306) 2445651, *Fax:* (306) 9334606; *e-mail:* anglicansynod@sasktel.net.

SASSOON, Adrian David; dealer in 18th century French porcelain and contemporary British studio ceramics, glass and silver, since 1992; *b* 1 Feb 1961; *s* of Hugh Meyer Sassoon and Marion Julia Sassoon (*née* Schiff). *Educ:* Sunningdale Sch.; Eton Coll.; Inchbald Sch. of Design, London; Christie's, London (fine arts diploma). Asst Curator of Decorative Arts, J. Paul Getty Mus., Malibu, 1980–84; ind. researcher, 1984–87; Dir, Alexander & Berendt Ltd, London, 1987–92; private dealer and art advr, 1992–. Trustee: UK Friends of Hermitage Mus., St Petersburg, 2006–; Wallace Collection, 2007–. *Publications:* Decorative Arts: a handbook catalogue of the collection of the J. Paul Getty Museum (with Gillian Wilson), 1986; Catalogue of Vincennes and Sèvres Porcelain in the J. Paul Getty Museum, Malibu, 1991; Vincennes and Sèvres Porcelain from a European Private Collector, 2001. *Recreations:* museums, beaches. *Address:* *e-mail:* email@adriansassoon.com. *Clubs:* Brooks's; Lyford Cay (Nassau).
See also Sir J. M. Sassoon.

SASSOON, Prof. Donald, PhD; Professor of Comparative European History, Queen Mary, University of London, since 1997; *b* 25 Nov. 1946; *s* of Joseph Isaac Sassoon and Doris Sassoon (*née* Bardak); *m* 1973, Anne Showstack (marr. diss. 1987); one *d. Educ:* schools in Paris, Milan and Tunbridge Wells; University Coll. London (BSc Econ 1969); Pennsylvania State Univ. (MA 1971); Birkbeck Coll., Univ. of London (PhD 1977). Lectr in Hist., 1979–89, Reader in Hist., 1989–97, Westfield Coll., then QMW, Univ. of London. Nuffield Social Sci. Fellow, 1997–98; Vis. Prof., Univ. of Trento, 1999; Leverhulme Maj. Res. Fellow, 2000–03; Sen. Res. Fellow, New York Univ., 2001. Literary Ed., Political Qly, 2000–. *Publications:* The Strategy of the Italian Communist Party, 1981; Contemporary Italy: politics, economy and society since 1945, 1986, 2nd edn 1997; One Hundred Years of Socialism: the West European Left in the Twentieth Century, 1996 (Deutscher Meml Prize 1997); Mona Lisa: the history of the world's most famous painting, 2001; Leonardo and the Mona Lisa Story, 2006; The Culture of the Europeans, 2006; Mussolini and the Rise of Fascism, 2007; contribs to jls. *Recreations:* travel, classical music, country walking. *Address:* Department of History, Queen Mary, University of London, Mile End Road, E1 4NS; *e-mail:* d.sassoon@qmul.ac.uk.

SASSOON, Sir James Meyer, Kt 2008; FCA; Chancellor's Representative for Promotion of the City, HM Treasury, 2006–08; *b* 11 Sept. 1955; *s* of Hugh Meyer Sassoon and Marion Julia Sassoon (*née* Schiff); *m* 1981, Sarah Caroline Ray Barnes, *d* of Sir (Ernest) John Ward Barnes; one *s* two *d. Educ:* Eton Coll.; Christ Church, Oxford (MA). ACA 1980, FCA 1991. Thomson McLintock & Co., 1977–86; SG Warburg & Co. Ltd, 1987–95 (Dir, 1991–95); Warburg Dillon Read, subseq. UBS Warburg: Man. Dir, 1995–2002; Vice Chm., Investment Banking, 2000–02; Man. Dir, Finance, Regulation and Industry, HM Treasury, 2002–06. Pres., Financial Action Task Force, 2007–08. Director: Partnerships UK, 2002–06; Merchants Trust, 2006–; Nuclear Liabilities Fund, 2008–. Dir, Hackney Business Venture, subseq. HBV Enterprise, 2000–02. Trustee: Gerald Coke Handel Foundn, 2001–; Nat. Gall. Trust, 2002–; Governor, Ashdown House Sch., 2001–06. *Publications:* articles in art and financial jls. *Recreations:* travel, the arts, watching sport. *Address:* *e-mail:* james.sassoon@sassoon.co.uk. *Club:* MCC.
See also A. D. Sassoon.

SATCHELL, Keith; Group Chief Executive, Friends Provident plc (formerly Friends Provident Life Office), 1997–2007; *b* 3 June 1951; *s* of Dennis Joseph Satchell and Joan Betty Satchell; *m* 1972, Hazel Burston; two *s* one *d. Educ:* Univ. of Aston (BSc). FIA 1976. With Duncan C. Fraser, 1972–75; UK Provident, 1975–86; Friends Provident, 1986–2007: Gen. Manager, 1987–97; Dir, 1992–2007. Chairman: ABI, 2005–07; Rothesay Life, 2007–. *Recreations:* soccer, golf, ski-ing, theatre.

SATCHWELL, Sir Kevin (Joseph), Kt 2001; Headmaster, Thomas Telford School, since 1991; *b* 6 March 1951; *e s* of late Joseph and Pauline Satchwell; *m* 1975, Maria Bernadette Grimes; one *s* one *d. Educ:* Wodensborough High Sch.; Wednesbury Boys' High Sch.; Shoreditch Coll. of Technology (Cert Ed London Univ. 1973); Open Univ. (BA 1977; AdvDip Educn Mgt 1978). Teacher, Cantril High Sch., Liverpool, 1973–79; Dep. Head, Brookfield Sch., Liverpool, 1979–87; Headteacher, Moseley Park Sch., Wolverhampton, 1987–90. Dir, London Qualifications, 2003–05. Member: NCET, 1994–96; City Technology Colls Principals' Forum, 1991– (Chm., 1997); Chm., W Midlands Consortium for School Centred Initial Teacher Trng, 1993–. FRSA 2005. *Recreations:* family, football coaching, tennis, golf. *Address:* Thomas Telford School, Old Park, Telford TF3 4NW. *T:* (01952) 200000.

SATOW, Rear-Adm. Derek Graham, CB 1977; *b* 13 June 1923; *y s* of late Graham F. H. Satow, OBE, and Evelyn M. Satow (*née* Moore); *m* 1944, Patricia E. A. Penaligon; two *d. Educ:* Oakley Hall Sch.; Haileybury Coll.; Royal Naval Engineering Coll. CEng, FIMechE, FIMarEST. HMS Ceylon, 1945–46; RNC, Greenwich, 1946–48; HMS Duke of York, 1948–49; RAE Farnborough, 1949–51; HMS Newcastle, 1951–53 (despatches, 1953); Naval Ordnance and Weapons Dept, Admiralty, 1953–59; Dir of Engineering, RNEC, 1959–62; HMS Tiger, 1962–64; Asst and Dep. Dir of Marine Engineering, MoD, 1964–67; IDC, 1968; Captain, RNEC, 1969–71; Dir, Naval Officer Appointments (Eng), MoD, 1971–73; Chief Staff Officer, Technical, later Engineering, to C-in-C Fleet, 1974–76; Dep. Dir-Gen., Ships, MoD, 1976–79; Chief Naval Engr Officer, 1977–79. Comdr, 1955; Captain, 1964; Rear-Adm., 1973.

SATTERTHWAITE, Christopher James; Group Chief Executive, Chime Communications plc, since 2003; *b* 21 May 1956; *s* of Col Richard George Satterthwaite and Rosemary Ann Satterthwaite; *m* 1988, Teresa Mary Bailey; two *s* one *d. Educ:* Ampleforth Coll.; Lincoln Coll., Oxford (MA Mod. Hist.). Graduate trainee, H. J. Heinz, 1978–81; IMP Ltd, 1981–98, Chief Exec., 1990–98; Chief Executive: HHCL Ltd, 1998–2000; Bell Pottinger Ltd, 2000–02. *Recreations:* Parson Woodforde Society, marathon running, bombology. *Address:* Tuesley Manor, Tuesley Lane, Godalming, Surrey GU7 1UD. *T:* (01483) 429336; *e-mail:* csatterthwaite@chime.plc.uk.

SATTERTHWAITE, Rt Rev. John Richard, CMG 1991; Bishop of Gibraltar in Europe, 1980–93; an Assistant Bishop, diocese of Carlisle, since 1994; *b* 17 Nov. 1925; *s* of William and Clara Elisabeth Satterthwaite. *Educ:* Millom Grammar Sch.; Leeds Univ. (BA); Coll. of the Resurrection, Mirfield. History Master, St Luke's Sch., Haifa, 1946–48; Curate: St Barnabas, Carlisle, 1950–53; St Aidan, Carlisle, 1953–54; St Michael Paternoster Royal, London, 1955–59, Curate-in-Charge, 1959–65; Guild Vicar, St Dunstan-in-the-West, City of London, 1959–70. Gen. Sec., Church of England Council on Foreign Relations, 1959–70 (Asst Gen. Sec., 1955–59); Gen. Sec., Archbp's Commn on Roman Catholic Relations, 1965–70; Bishop of Gibraltar and Bishop Suffragan of Fulham, 1970, known as Bishop of Fulham and Gibraltar until creation of new diocese, 1980. Hon. Canon of Canterbury, 1963–71; ChStJ 1972 (Asst ChStJ 1963); Hon. Canon of Utrecht, Old Catholic Church of the Netherlands, 1969. Holds decoration from various foreign churches. *Recreations:* fell walking, music. *Address:* 25 Spencer House, St Paul's Square, Carlisle, Cumbria CA1 1DG. *T:* (01228) 594055. *Club:* Athenæum.

SATYANAND, Anand, PCNZM 2006 (DCNZM 2005); QSO 2007; Governor-General of New Zealand, since 2006; *b* 22 July 1944; *s* of Dr Mutyala Satyanand and Tara Satyanand; *m* 1970, Susan Jean Sharpe; one *s* two *d. Educ:* Univ. of Auckland (LLB). Barrister and solicitor, 1970–82; Dist Court Judge with Jury Trial Warrant, 1982–2005; Parly Ombudsman, 1995–2005. Registrar, Pecuniary Interests of MPs, 2005. Chm., Confidential Forum for Former In Patients of Psychiatric Hosps, 2005–06. Hon. LLD Auckland, 2006. KStJ 2006. *Publications:* contrib. jls and legal pubns on legal educn, trial skills enhancement and ombudsman studies. *Recreations:* reading, writing, sport, sporting administration. *Address:* Government House, Wellington, New Zealand. *T:* (4) 3896055; *e-mail:* anand.satyanand@govthouse.govt.nz. *Clubs:* Wellington, Royal Commonwealth (Wellington); Northern (Auckland).

SAUER, Fernand Edmond; Honorary Director General, European Commission, since 2006; Member, High Council for Public Health (France), since 2007; *b* 14 Dec. 1947; *s* of Ferdinand Sauer and Emilie Scherer Sauer; *m* 1971, Pamela Sheppard; one *s* two *d. Educ:* Univ. of Strasbourg (pharmacist, 1971); Paris II Univ. (Masters in European Law, 1977). Hosp. Pharmacist, Reunion Island, 1972–73; Pharmaceutical Insp., Health Min., France, 1974–79; European Commission: Adminr, 1979–85; Head of Pharmaceuticals, 1986–94; Exec. Dir, Eur. Agency for the Evaluation of Medicinal Products, 1994–2000; Dir, Public Health Policy, DG for Health and Consumer Protection, EC, 2000–05. Mem., Faculty of Pharmacy, London Univ., 1996–. Hon. Fellow, RPSGB, 1996. Chevalier de l'Ordre du Mérite (France), 1990; Chevalier de la Légion d'Honneur (France), 1998. *Publications:* various articles and publications on pharmaceutical regulation. *Recreation:* jogging. *Address:* 12 avenue de la Marne, 13260 Cassis, France.

SAUL, Berrick; *see* Saul, S. B.

SAUL, Christopher Francis Irving; Senior Partner, Slaughter and May, since 2008; *b* Carlisle, 1955; *s* of Irving and Greta Saul; *m* 1985, Anne Cartier; one *s* one *d. Educ:* Tiffin Sch.; St Catherine's Coll., Oxford (BA Juris.). Joined Slaughter and May, 1977; Partner, 1986–. *Recreations:* motor cars, contemporary music, reading, cinema. *Address:* 11 Chepstow Villas, W11 3EE. *T:* (020) 792 2514; *e-mail:* christopher.saul@slaughterandmay.com.

SAUL, Hon. David John; JP; PhD; financial consultant; President, Fidelity International Bermuda Ltd, 1984–99, retired; Premier of Bermuda, 1995–97; *b* 27 Nov. 1939; *s* of late John Saul and Sarah Saul; *m* 1963, Christine Hall; one *s* one *d. Educ:* Queen's Univ., Canada (BA); Univ. of Toronto (MEd, PhD); Nottingham Univ. (CertEd); Loughborough Univ. of Tech. (DipEd). Perm. Sec. for Educn, 1972–76, Financial Sec., 1976–81, Bermuda Govt; Chief Admin Officer, Edmund Gibbons Ltd, 1982–84; MP (United Bermuda Party) Devonshire South, 1989–97; Minister of Finance, Bermuda, 1989–95. Pres., Fidelity Internat. Ltd, 1984–95; Exec. Vice Pres., Fidelity Investments, Worldwide, 1990–95; Director: Fidelity Internat. Ltd, 1984–; Lombard Odier (Bermuda) Ltd, 1995–. Director: Bermuda Monetary Authority, 1987–89, 1998–99; Bermuda Track and Field Assoc., 1987–; London Steamship Owners Mutual Assoc., 1989–; Odyssey Marine Exploration Inc., 2001–. Trustee, Bermuda Underwater Exploration Inst., 1992–99 (Life Trustee, 1999). *Recreations:* running, scuba, fishing, kayaking, stalking, collecting Bermuda stamps, Bermuda currency notes, and sea shells. *Address:* Rocky Ledge, 18 Devonshire Bay Road, Devonshire DV 07, Bermuda. *T:* 2367338; *e-mail:* davidjsaul@aol.com. *Clubs:* Explorers' (New York); Mid Ocean, Royal Hamilton Amateur Dinghy (Bermuda).

SAUL, Prof. Nigel Edward, DPhil; FSA, FRHistS; Professor of Medieval History, Royal Holloway, University of London, since 1997; *b* 20 June 1952; *s* of Edward Thomas Saul and Marion Saul (*née* Duffy); *m* 1983, Jane Melanie Nichols; one *s* one *d. Educ:* King Edward VI Sch., Stratford-upon-Avon; Hertford Coll., Oxford (BA 1974; MA, DPhil 1978). FRHistS 1984; FSA 1988. Royal Holloway, University of London: Lectr in Medieval Hist., 1978–88; Reader in Medieval Hist., 1988–97; Hd, Dept of History, 2002–05. Vice-Pres., Monumental Brass Soc., 2002– (Pres., 1995–2002). Series Editor, Hambledon and London Books, 1998–2007; Mem., Editorial Adv. Bd, History Today, 1987–. *Publications:* Knights and Esquires: the Gloucestershire gentry in the fourteenth century, 1981; Scenes from Provincial Life: knightly families in Sussex 1280–1400, 1986; (ed and contrib.) Historical Atlas of Britain: prehistoric to medieval, 1994; Richard II, 1997; (ed and contrib.) Oxford Illustrated History of Medieval England, 1997; Companion to Medieval England 1066–1400, 2000; (ed) Fourteenth Century England, vol. I, 2000; Death, Art and Memory: the Cobham family and their monuments 1300–1500, 2001; The Three Richards, 2005; (ed) St George's Chapel, Windsor, in the Fourteenth Century, 2005; Fourteenth Century England, vol. V, 2008; English Church Monuments in the Middle Ages: history and representation, 2009; articles in learned jls. *Recreations:* visiting country churches, lepidoptera, gardening. *Address:* Gresham House, Egham Hill, Egham, Surrey TW20 0ER; *e-mail:* n.saul@rhul.ac.uk.

SAUL, Roger John; Director, Monty's, since 2004; Owner: Charlton House Hotel, since 1997; Sharpham Park, since 2004; Kilver Court Gardens, since 2008; *b* 25 July 1950; *s* of Michael and Joan Saul; *m* 1977, Monty Cameron; three *s. Educ:* Kingswood Sch., Bath; Westminster Coll., London. Founded Mulberry Co., 1971 (Queen's Award to Industry for Export, 1979, 1989 and 1996); Chm. and Chief Exec., 1971–2002; Pres., 2002–03; launched Mulberry at Home, 1991; opened Charlton House Hotel and Mulberry Restaurant, 1997 (Michelin Star, annually, 1998–2005); launched Sharpham Park (rare breed meat) and Spelt Flour (bread, pasta and cereal range), 2005; built first organic spelt flour mill in UK, 2006. Chm., London Designer Collections, 1976–80. Trustee and Chm., Bottletop, 2003–. Mem., RHS. Gov., Kingswood Sch., 2006–. Classic Designer of Year, British Fashion Council, 1992. *Publication:* Mulberry at Home, 1992. *Recreations:* gardening, tennis, ski-ing, historic car racing (Mem., Vintage Sports Car Club; winner: Brooklands Trophy, 2006; Porto GP, Irish GP, Donnington Legends, 2006; Brighton Speed Trials Pre '59 Trophy, 2007), 6m yacht racing. *Address:* Charlton House Hotel, Shepton Mallet, Somerset BA4 4PR. *Club:* Mark's.

SAUL, Prof. (Samuel) Berrick, CBE 1992; PhD; Executive Chairman, Universities and Colleges Admissions Service, 1993–97; Vice Chancellor, University of York, 1979–93; *b* 20 Oct. 1924; *s* of Ernest Saul and Maud Eaton; *m* 1953, Sheila Stenton; one *s* one *d*. *Educ:* West Bromwich Grammar Sch.; Birmingham Univ. (BCom 1949, PhD 1953). National Service, 1944–47 (Lieut Sherwood Foresters). Lectr in Econ. History, Liverpool Univ., 1951–63; Edinburgh University: Prof. of Econ. History, 1963–78; Dean, Faculty of Social Sciences, 1970–75; Vice Principal, 1975–77; Actg Principal, 1978. Rockefeller Fellow, Univ. of Calif (Berkeley), and Columbia Univ., 1959; Ford Fellow, Stanford Univ., 1969–70. Vis. Prof., Harvard Univ., 1973. Chairman: Central Council for Educn and Trng in Social Work, 1986–93; Standing Conf. on Univ. Entrance, 1986–93; Vice-Chm., Commonwealth Scholarship Commn, 1993–2000. Hon. LLD York, Toronto, 1981; Hon. Dr *hc* Edinburgh, 1986; DUniv York, 1994. *Publications:* Studies in British Overseas Trade 1870–1914, 1960; The Myth of the Great Depression, 1969; Technological Change: the US and Britain in the 19th Century, 1970; (with A. S. Milward) The Economic Development of Continental Europe 1780–1870, 1973; (with A. S. Milward) The Development of the Economies of Continental Europe 1850–1914, 1977. *Recreations:* fell walking, travel, music. *Address:* 39 Drome Road, Copmanthorpe, York YO23 3TG. *T:* (01904) 701011.

SAULL, Rear-Adm. (Keith) Michael, CB 1982; Chairman, New Zealand Ports Authority, 1984–88; *b* 24 Aug. 1927; *s* of Harold Vincent Saull and Margaret Saull; *m* 1952, Linfield Mabel (*née* Barnsdale); two *s* one *d*. *Educ:* Altrincham Grammar Sch.; HMS Conway. Royal Navy, 1945–50; transferred to Royal New Zealand Navy, 1951; commanded HMNZ Ships: Kaniere, Taranaki, Canterbury, 1956–71; Naval Attaché, Washington DC, 1972–75; RCDS 1976; Commodore, Auckland, 1978; Chief of Naval Staff, RNZN, 1980–83. Vice Patron, Royal NZ Coastguard Fedn, 1987–2000.

SAULTER, Paul Reginald; Managing Director, Heritage of Industry (formerly Cornwall of Mine) Ltd, since 1989; *b* 27 Aug. 1935; *s* of Alfred Walter Saulter and Mabel Elizabeth Oliver. *Educ:* Truro Sch.; University Coll., Oxford (MA). Admin. Asst, Nat. Council of Social Service, 1960–63; Sen. Asst and Principal, CEGB, 1963–65; Dep. Head, Overseas Div., BEAMA, 1965–69; Dir, Internat. Affairs, ABCC, 1969–73; Sec.-Gen., British Chamber of Commerce in France, 1973–81; Chief Executive: Manchester Chamber of Commerce and Industry, 1981–85; Assoc. of Exhibn Organisers, 1985–86; Administrator, St Paul's, Knightsbridge, 1987–95. Mgt consultant, 1986–89; Exhibn Advr, London Chamber of Commerce, 1986–88. Secretary: For. Trade Working Gp, ORGALIME, 1967–69; Council of British Chambers of Commerce in Continental Europe, 1977–80; Member: Export Promotion Cttee, CBI, 1983–86; Bd, Eur. Fedn of Assocs of Industrial and Technical Heritage, 1999– (Vice-Pres., 2002–). Member: RHS; Trevithick Soc., 1986–; Assoc. for Industrial Archaeology; Newcomen Soc., 1995– (Mem. Council, 1995–98, 1999–2002). *Recreations:* walking, music, theatre, researching Cornish mining history, industrial archaeology. *Address:* Rye, Sussex.

SAUMAREZ, family name of **Baron de Saumarez**.

SAUMAREZ SMITH, Dr Charles Robert, CBE 2008; FSA; Secretary and Chief Executive, Royal Academy of Arts, since 2007; *b* 28 May 1954; *s* of late William Hanbury Saumarez Smith, OBE and of Alice Elizabeth Harness Saumarez Smith (*née* Raven); *m* 1979, Romilly Le Quesne Savage; two *s*. *Educ:* Marlborough Coll.; King's Coll., Cambridge (BA 1st cl. History of Art 1976; MA 1978); Henry Fellow, Harvard, 1977; Warburg Inst. (PhD 1986). FSA 1997. Christie's Res. Fellow in Applied Arts, Christ's Coll., Cambridge, 1979–82 (Hon. Fellow, 2002); Asst Keeper with resp. for V&A/RCA MA course in history of design, 1982–90, Head of Res., 1990–94, V & A; Dir, NPG, 1994–2002; Slade Prof., Univ. of Oxford, 2001–02; Dir, National Gallery, 2002–07. Vis. Fellow, Yale Center for British Art, 1983; Benno Forman Fellow, Winterthur Mus., 1988; South Square Fellow, RCA, 1990; Vis. Prof., QMUL, 2007–. Member, Executive Committee: Design History Soc., 1985–89; Soc. of Architectural Historians, 1987–90; Assoc. of Art Historians, 1990–94; London Library, 1992–96; Member, Advisory Council: Paul Mellon Centre for British Studies, 1995–99; Warburg Inst., 1997–2003; Inst. of Historical Research, 1999–2003; Sch. of Advanced Study, 2003–07; Mem. Council, Museums Assoc., 1998–2001 (Vice-Pres., 2002–04; Pres., 2004–06). Gov., Univ. of the Arts, London (formerly London Inst.), 2001–. Trustee: Soane Monuments Trust, 1988–; Charleston, 1993–; Prince's Drawing Sch., 2003–; Public Catalogue Foundn, 2003–. FRSA 1995. Hon. Fellow, RCA, 1991; Hon. FRIBA 2000. Hon. DLitt: UEA, 2001; Westminster, 2002; London, 2003; Sussex, 2003; Essex, 2005. *Publications:* The Building of Castle Howard, 1990 (Alice Davis Hitchcock Medallion); Eighteenth Century Decoration, 1993; The National Portrait Gallery, 1997. *Address:* Royal Academy of Arts, Burlington House, Piccadilly, W1J 0BD. *T:* (020) 7300 8006; *e-mail:* chiefexecutive@royalacademy.org.uk.

SAUNDERS, Albert Edward, CMG 1975; OBE 1970; HM Diplomatic Service, retired; Ambassador to the United Republic of Cameroon and the Republic of Equatorial Guinea, 1975–79; *b* 5 June 1919; *s* of late Albert Edward and Marie Marguerite Saunders; *m* 1945, Dorothea Charlotte Mary Whittle (*d* 1985); one *s* one *d*. *Educ:* yes. Westminster Bank Ltd, 1937. Royal Navy, 1942–45: last appt, Asst Chief Port Security Officer, Middle East. Apptd to British Embassy, Cairo, 1938 and 1945; Asst Information Officer, Tripoli, 1949; Asst Admin. Officer, Athens, 1951; MECAS, 1952; Third Sec., Office of UK Trade Comr, Khartoum, 1953; Third Sec. (Information), Beirut, 1954; POMEF, Cyprus, 1956; FO, 1957; Second Sec. (Oriental), Baghdad, 1958; FO, 1959; Vice-Consul, Casablanca, 1963; Second Sec. (Oriental), Rabat, 1963; Consul, Jerusalem, 1964; First Sec., FO, 1967; Chancery, Baghdad, 1968; Head of Chancery and Consul, Rabat, 1969; Counsellor and Consul General in charge British Embassy, Dubai, 1972; Chargé d'Affaires, Abu Dhabi, 1972 and 1973; RN War Coll., Greenwich, 1974, sowc, 1975. *Recreation:* iconoclasm (20th Century). *Address:* 3 Deanhill Road, SW14 7DQ.

SAUNDERS, Andrew Downing; Chief Inspector of Ancient Monuments and Historic Buildings, Department of the Environment, then English Heritage, 1973–89; Hon. Curator, Cranbrook Museum, since 2004; *b* 22 Sept. 1931; *s* of Lionel Edward Saunders; *m* 1st, 1961, Hilary Jean (*née* Aikman) (marr. diss. 1980); two *s* one *d*; 2nd, 1985, Gillian Ruth Hutchinson; one *d*. *Educ:* Magdalen Coll. Sch., Oxford; Magdalen Coll., Oxford (MA). FSA, FRHistS, FSAScot, MIFA. Joined Ancient Monuments Inspectorate, 1954; Inspector of Ancient Monuments for England, 1964. President: Cornwall Archaeol Soc., 1968–72; Royal Archaeol Inst., 1993–96; Vice-Pres., Hendon and Dist Archaeol Soc.; Chairman: Internat. Fortress Council, 1995–98; Fortress Study Gp, 1995–2001; Member: Exec. Cttee, Council for British Archaeology, 1996–2002; Scientific Council, Europa Nostra/Internat. Castles Inst. Chm. Adv. Panel, Defence of Britain Project, Council for British Archaeology, 1996–2002. Hon. Res. Fellow, Exeter Univ., 2000–01. Editor, Fortress: the Castles and Fortifications Qly, 1989–94. *Publications:* ed jtly and contrib., Ancient Monuments and their Interpretation, 1977; Fortress Britain, 1989; Devon and Cornwall, 1991; Channel Defences, 1997; Fortress Builder: Bernard de Gomme, Charles II's military engineer, 2004; Excavations at Launceston Castle, Cornwall, 2006; excavation reports on various Roman and Medieval sites and monuments, papers on castles and artillery fortification in various archæological and historical jls; guidebooks to ancient monuments. *Address:* The Crest, The Hill, Cranbrook, Kent TN17 3AH. *Club:* Athenæum.

SAUNDERS, Andrew William, CB 1998; Director, Communications-Electronics Security Group, 1991–98; *b* 26 Oct. 1940; *s* of late Joseph and Winifred Saunders; *m* 1964, Josephine Sharkey; one *s* two *d*. *Educ:* Wolverhampton Grammar Sch.; Christ Church, Oxford (MA). Joined Civil Service, GCHQ, 1963: Principal, 1968; Asst Sec., 1978; Counsellor, Washington, 1983–86 (on secondment); Under Sec., 1991. *Recreations:* outdoor pleasures and practicalities, genealogy. *Address:* c/o Barclays Bank PLC, 128 High Street, Cheltenham, Glos GL50 1EL.

SAUNDERS, Ann Loreille, MBE 2002; PhD; FSA; historian; Lecturer in History of London, University of Connecticut Programme, City University, London, 1982–2007; *b* 23 May 1930; *d* of George and Joan Cox-Johnson; *m* 1960, Bruce Kemp Saunders; one *s* (and one *d* decd). *Educ:* Henrietta Barnett Sch., London; Queen's Coll., London; UCL (BA); Leicester Univ. (PhD 1965). FSA 1975. Asst, City of York Art Gall., 1951–52; Dep. Librarian, Lambeth Palace, 1952–55; Temp. Asst Keeper, BM, 1955–56; Borough Archivist, Marylebone Public Library, 1956–63; freelance writing, lecturing and editing, 1965–; Lectr in Hist. of London, Richmond Coll., London, 1979–94; Fellow and Hon. Res. Fellow, UCL, 1992–. Mem. Council, Soc. of Antiquaries of London, 1989–91; President: Camden History Soc., 1984–89; St Marylebone Soc., 1985–89; Regent's Park DFAS, 1989–95. Governor, Bedford Coll., 1982–85. Asst to Hon. Editor, Jl of British Archaeol Assoc., 1963–75; Honorary Editor: Costume Soc., 1967–2008; London Topographical Soc., 1975–. *Publications:* Regent's Park: a study of the development of the area from 1066 to the present day, 1969, 2nd edn 1981; (ed) Arthur Mee's London North of the Thames, 1972; (ed) Arthur Mee's London: the City and Westminster, 1975; The Art and Architecture of London: an illustrated guide (Specialist Guide Book of the Year Award, London Tourist Bd), 1984, 3rd edn 1992; (ed and contrib.) The Royal Exchange, 1997; St Paul's: the story of the cathedral, 2001; (jtly) The History of the Merchant Taylors' Company, 2004; (ed) The London County Council Bomb Damage Maps, 2005; Historic Views of London from the Collection of B. E. C. Howarth-Loomes, 2008; contribs to Burlington Mag., London Jl, Geographical Mag., Dome, LAMAS, etc. *Recreations:* reading, walking, embroidery, cooking, studying London, going to exhibitions and theatres, visiting churches. *Address:* 3 Meadway Gate, NW11 7LA. *T:* (020) 8455 2171.

SAUNDERS, Christopher John, MA; Headmaster, Lancing College, 1993–98; *b* 7 May 1940; *s* of R. H. Saunders and G. S. Saunders (*née* Harris); *m* 1973, Cynthia Elizabeth Stiles; one *s* one *d*. *Educ:* Lancing Coll.; Fitzwilliam Coll., Cambridge (MA); PGCE Wadham Coll., Oxford. Assistant Master, Bradfield College, 1964–80 (Housemaster, 1972–80); Headmaster, Eastbourne Coll., 1981–93. Vice-Pres., FA, 2002–. *Recreations:* music, bridge, theatre, gardening, soccer (Oxford Blue 1963), cricket (Oxford Blue 1964), golf, people. *Address:* Folly Bottom, Scottalls Lane, Hampstead Norreys, Thatcham, Berks RG18 0RT. *T:* (01635) 200222. *Clubs:* MCC; Hawks (Cambridge).

SAUNDERS, David, DPhil; Keeper of Conservation, Documentation and Science, British Museum, since 2005; *b* 10 Oct. 1959; *s* of Morris and Gwen Saunders; *m* 1984, Alison Hesketh. *Educ:* Harrow Co. Sch. for Boys; Univ. of York (BSc Chem. 1981; DPhil Chem. 1984). Post-doctoral Researcher, Univ. of Bristol, 1984–85; Scientist, Nat. Gall., London, 1985–2005. Dir, Pubns, Internat. Inst. for Conservation, 2003–. Editor, Studies in Conservation, 1990–. *Publications:* 100 articles incl. in Nat. Gall. Technical Bulletin, Studies in Conservation and Jl of Chemical Soc. *Recreations:* cooking for friends, Italian and Scandinavian cities, hill-walking, orienteering, selected opera, other people's museums. *Address:* British Museum, Great Russell Street, WC1B 3DG.

SAUNDERS, Air Vice-Marshal David John, CBE 1986; FIMechE; FRAeS; FILog; Senior Vice President, Airinmar Group, since 1999 (Director of Logistics, 1997–99); *b* 12 June 1943; *s* of John Saunders and Nina Saunders (*née* Mabberley); *m* 1966, Elizabeth Jane Cairns; one *s* one *d*. *Educ:* Commonweal Grammar Sch.; RAF College; Cranfield Inst. of Technology. BSc, MSc; CEng, FRAeS 1993; FILog 1997. Joined RAF 1961; management appts, 1966–85; Station Comdr, RAF Sealand, 1983; ADC to HM the Queen, 1984–86; Command Mechanical Engineer, HQ RAF Germany, 1986; Dir of Engineering Policy (RAF), MoD, 1989–91; ACDS (Logistics), 1991–93; Hd of RAF Mobility Study, 1993; AO Engrg and Supply, 1993–97. Director: Airinmar Gp, 2000–; Airinmar Ltd, 2000–. *Recreations:* hill walking, cross country ski-ing, off-road cycling, fishing. *Address:* St John's Coach House, St John's Street, Lechlade, Glos GL7 3AT. *Club:* Royal Air Force.

SAUNDERS, David John; Director, Consumer and Competition Policy, Department for Business, Enterprise and Regulatory Reform (formerly Department for Trade and Industry), since 2004; *b* 4 Aug. 1953; *s* of James and Margaret Saunders; *m* 1975, Elizabeth Jean Hodgson; two *s* two *d*. *Educ:* Royal Grammar Sch., Guildford; Kingston Poly. (BSc Chemistry and Business Studies); Aston Univ. (PhD Applied Business Studies 1978). Joined DTI, 1978; Private Sec. to Sec. of State, 1981–82, to Parly Under Sec. of State, 1982–84; seconded to OFT, 1984–87; British Steel privatisation, 1987–88; Export Promotion, 1988–95; Sec., BOTB, 1990–95; Director: Nuclear Power Privatisation Team, 1995–96; Oil and Gas Directorate, 1996–98; Regl Dir, Govt Office for SE, 1998–2002; Dir, Business Support, DTI, 2002–04. *Recreations:* swimming, cycling, surfing, diving, cinema. *Address:* (office) 1 Victoria Street, SW1H 0ET. *T:* (020) 7215 0310.

SAUNDERS, David Martin St George; HM Diplomatic Service, retired; *b* 23 July 1930; *s* of late Hilary St George Saunders and Helen (*née* Foley); *m* 1960, Patricia, *d* of James Methold, CBE; one *s* one *d*. *Educ:* Marlborough Coll.; RMA Sandhurst; Staff Coll., Quetta, Pakistan. Commnd Welsh Guards, 1950; Staff Captain Egypt, 1954–56; Asst Adjt, RMA Sandhurst, 1956–58; Adjt 1st Bn Welsh Guards, 1958–60; GSO III War Office, 1960–62; sc Quetta, Pakistan, 1963; Company Comdr 1st Bn Welsh Guards, 1964; GSO II British Defence Liaison Staff, Canberra, 1965–67; Guards Depot, Pirbright, 1967–68; joined Foreign Service, 1968; Consul (Economic), Johannesburg, 1970–73; First Secretary: FCO, 1973–74; Dakar, 1974–76; FCO, 1976–77; Pretoria, 1977–79; The Hague, 1979–83; Counsellor, FCO, 1983–90. *Recreations:* military history, shooting, cinema, bridge, the wines of Burgundy. *Address:* 18 Garfield Road, SW11 5PN.

SAUNDERS, David William, CB 1989; Counsel to the Chairman of Committees, House of Lords, 1999–2005; *b* 4 Nov. 1936; *s* of William Ernest Saunders and Lilian Grace (*née* Ward); *m* 1963, Margaret Susan Rose Bartholomew. *Educ:* Hornchurch Grammar Sch.; Worcester Coll., Oxford (MA). Admitted solicitor, 1964. Joined Office of Parly Counsel, 1970; Dep. Parly Counsel, 1978–80; Parly Counsel, 1980–94 and 1996–99; Second Parly Counsel, 1994–96; with Law Commn, 1972–74, 1986–87. *Recreations:* golf, bridge. *Address:* Highfields, High Wych, Sawbridgeworth, Herts CM21 0HX. *T:* (01279) 724736. *Club:* Oxford and Cambridge.

SAUNDERS, Ernest Walter, MA; President, Stambridge Management (formerly Associates), since 1992; *b* 21 Oct. 1935; *m* 1963, Carole Ann Stephings; two *s* one *d. Educ:* Emmanuel Coll., Cambridge (MA). Man. Dir, Beecham Products Internat., and Dir, Beecham Products, 1966–73; Chm., European Div., Great Universal Stores, 1973–77; Pres., Nestlé Nutrition SA, and Mem. Worldwide Management Cttee, Nestlé SA, Vevey, Switzerland, 1977–81; Chm., Beechnut Corp., USA, 1977–81; Chief Exec., 1981–87, Chm., 1986–87, Arthur Guinness & Sons plc, later Guinness PLC; Chairman: Arthur Guinness Son & Co. (Great Britain), 1982–87; Guinness Brewing Worldwide, 1982–87. Dir, Brewers' Soc., 1983. Dir, Queens Park Rangers Football & Athletic Club, 1983. *Recreations:* ski-ing, tennis, football.

SAUNDERS, Jennifer; actress, writer; *b* 6 July 1958; *m* Adrian Edmondson; three *d. Educ:* Central Sch. of Speech and Drama. *Theatre:* An Evening with French and Saunders (nat. tour), 1989; Me and Mamie O'Rourke, Strand, 1993; French and Saunders Live - 2000, Apollo Hammersmith, 2000; French and Saunders: Still Alive (nat. tour), 2008; *television:* Ab Fab The Last Shout, 1996; Mirrorball, 2000; *series:* The Comic Strip Presents…, 1982–90; Girls on Top, 1985–87; French and Saunders (5 series); Absolutely Fabulous, 1992–96, 2001–03 (Emmy Award, 1993); Let Them Eat Cake, 1999; Jam and Jerusalem, 2006, 2008; The Life and Times of Vivienne Vyle, 2007; *films:* The Supergrass, 1984; Muppet Treasure Island, 1996; In the Bleak Midwinter, 1996; Fanny and Elvis, 1999. *Publications:* (with Dawn French) A Feast of French and Saunders, 1992; Absolutely Fabulous: the scripts, 1993; Absolutely Fabulous: Continuity, 2001. *Address:* c/o United Agents, 12–26 Lexington Street, W1F 0LE.

SAUNDERS, Hon. Sir John Henry Boulton, Kt 2007; **Hon. Mr Justice Saunders;** a Judge of the High Court of Justice, Queen's Bench Division, since 2007; *b* 15 March 1949; *s* of Kathleen Mary Saunders and Henry G. B. Saunders; *m* 1975, Susan Mary Chick; one *s* two *d. Educ:* Uppingham School; Magdalen College, Oxford (BA). Called to the Bar, Gray's Inn, 1972; a Recorder, 1990–2004; QC 1991; a Senior Circuit Judge, 2004–07; Recorder of Birmingham, 2004–07. *Publication:* (ed) Paterson's Licensing Acts, 2004–. *Recreations:* music, sailing. *Address:* Royal Courts of Justice, Strand, WC2A 2LL.

SAUNDERS, Prof. Kenneth Barrett, MD, DSc; FRCP; Professor of Medicine, St George's Hospital Medical School, 1980–95, now Emeritus; *b* 16 March 1936; *s* of Harold N. Saunders and Winifred F. Saunders (*née* Gadge); *m* 1961, Philippa Mary Harrison; one *s* one *d. Educ:* Kingswood Sch., Bath; Trinity Hall, Cambridge (MB BChir 1961; MA 1966; MD 1966); St Thomas's Hosp. Med. Sch.; DSc London 1995. FRCP 1978. Sen. Lectr, then Reader in Medicine, Middx Hosp. Med. Sch., 1972–80; Dean, Fac. of Medicine, London Univ., 1990–94. Member: GMC, 1992–95; Jt Planning and Adv. Cttee, 1990–94; Jt Cttee on Higher Med. Trng, 1990–94. Hon. Consultant Physician to the Army, 1994–97. Chm., Assoc. of Clinical Profs of Medicine, 1993–95. Royal College of Physicians: Tudor Edwards Lectr, 1987; Procensor, 1986–87; Censor, 1987–88. Member: Governing Body, BPMF, 1990–96; Council, Sch. of Pharmacy, London Univ., 1990–96. Vice-Pres., Hellenic Soc., 2005– (Hon. Treas., 1998–2005). *Publications:* Clinical Physiology of the Lung, 1977; various papers on respiratory science and medicine, and on Homer. *Recreations:* English, classical and Egyptian literature, gardening, golf. *Address:* 77 Lee Road, Blackheath, SE3 9EN. *T:* (020) 8852 8138. *Clubs:* Royal Automobile, Academy, Royal Society of Medicine; Royal Blackheath Golf.

SAUNDERS, Matthew John, MBE 1998; FSA; Secretary, Ancient Monuments Society, since 1977; *b* 12 April 1953; *s* of John William Saunders and Joyce Mary Saunders. *Educ:* Latymer Sch., Edmonton; Corpus Christi Coll., Cambridge (MA Hist. and Hist. of Architecture 1974). FSA 1980. Editorial Asst, Whitaker's Almanack, 1975; Sec., SAVE Britain's Heritage, 1976–77; Asst Sec., Ancient Monuments Soc., 1976. Sec., Jt Cttee of Nat. Amenity Socs, 1982–2005; Hon. Dir, Friends of Friendless Churches, 1993–; Trustee: Historic Chapels Trust, 1993–95; Heritage Lottery Fund, 2005– (Member: Places of Worship Adv. Cttee, 1995–98; Historic Bldgs and Land Panel, 1999–2005); Mem., Fabric Adv. Cttee, St Paul's Cathedral, 2001–03. Vice President: Ecclesiological Soc., 1994–; Men of the Stones, 2000–; Enfield Preservation Soc., 1999–. IHBC 1998. *Publications:* (contrib.) Railway Architecture, 1979; (contrib.) The Architectural Outsiders, 1985; The Historic Home Owner's Companion, 1987; (contrib.) Concerning Buildings, 1996. *Recreations:* music, travel, photography, good food. *Address:* (office) St Ann's Vestry Hall, 2 Church Entry, EC4V 5HB. *T:* (020) 7236 3934.

SAUNDERS, Nigel James, MD; FRCSE, FRCOG; Consultant Obstetrician, Southampton University Hospitals, since 1992; *b* 9 May 1955; *s* of Peter St John and Eileen Saunders; *m* 1988, Deborah Sanderson; three *d. Educ:* Manchester Grammar Sch.; Manchester Univ. (MB ChB; MD 1989). FRCSE 1983; FRCOG 1983. Lectr in Obstetrics and Gynaecol., Sheffield Univ., 1985–89; Consultant and Sen. Lectr, St Mary's Med. Sch., Paddington, 1989–92; Med Dir, Southampton Univ. Hosps NHS Trust, 2001–07. *Publications:* articles and editorials relating to labour ward mgt and minimally invasive surgery in BMJ, Lancet. *Recreations:* cycling, reading, songwriting, blues guitar. *Address:* Southampton University Hospitals NHS Trust, Southampton General Hospital, Tremona Road, Southampton SO16 6YD. *T:* (023) 8081 4285; *e-mail:* Nigel.Saunders@suht.swest.nhs.uk.

SAUNDERS, Peter Gordon; Editor, The Birmingham Post, 1986–90; *b* 1 July 1940; *s* of late Gordon and Winifred Saunders; *m* 1964, Teresa Geraldine Metcalf; two *d. Educ:* Newport High Sch. for Boys, Gwent; London Sch. of Econs and Pol Science (BScEcon 1961). Reporter, Gloucestershire Echo, 1961–63; Sports Reporter, Sunderland Echo, 1963–64; Sub-Editor: Yorkshire Post, 1964; The Birmingham Post, 1964–69; Lectr in Journalism, Cardiff Coll. of Commerce, 1969–70; The Birmingham Post, 1971–90: successively Dep. Chief Sub-Editor, Chief Sub-Editor, Asst Editor, Exec. Editor; media consultant, 1991–2005. *Recreations:* Rugby Union, reading, rhythm and blues, golf. *Address:* 3 Carpenter Close, Langstone, Newport, South Wales NP18 2LF. *T:* and *Fax:* (01633) 411688; *e-mail:* petesaund@dsl.pipex.com. *Club:* Newport High School Old Boys.

SAUNDERS, Raymond; Secretary, British Museum (Natural History), 1976–87; *b* 24 July 1933; *s* of late Herbert Charles Saunders and Doris May (*née* Kirkham-Jones); *m* 1959, Shirley Marion (*née* Stringer); two *s. Educ:* Poole Grammar Sch. WO, 1950; Air Min., 1956; Min. of Land and Natural Resources, 1966; Land Commn, 1967; Treasury, 1968; CSD, 1969. *Recreations:* reading biographies, gardening, sport (now as spectator). *Address:* High Trees, 24 Landguard Manor Road, Shanklin, Isle of Wight PO37 7HZ.

SAUNDERS, Richard; Partnership Consultant, Christ's Hospital, 1993–96; *b* 4 July 1937; *s* of late Edward E. Saunders and Betty Saunders; *m* 1st, 1961, Suzannah Rhodes-Cooke (marr. diss.); one *s*; 2nd, 1970, Alison Fiddes. *Educ:* St Edmund's Sch., Hindhead; Uppingham. FRICS 1965. National Service, commnd The Life Guards, 1958–60. Jun. Partner, Richard Ellis, Chartered Surveyors, 1966–69; formed Richard Saunders & Partners, 1969; Baker Harris Saunders, 1977; Chm., Baker Harris Saunders Group, 1986–92; Director: Herring Baker Harris, 1992–93; (non-exec.) Herring Baker Harris Gp, 1992–93. Chm., City Br., RICS, 1979–80; Pres., Associated Owners of City Properties, 1985–87; Member: Council, British Property Fedn, 1974–90 (Hon. Treas., 1974–85); Bd, Gen. Practice Finance Corp., 1984–89. Chairman: Barbican Residential Cttee, 1979–81; Barbican Centre Cttee, 1983–86; Metropolitan Public Gardens Assoc., 1984–90; Governor: Bridewell Royal Hosp. and King Edward's Sch., Witley, 1976–93; St Edmund's Sch., Hindhead, 1979–93 (Chm., 1979–87); (also Almoner), Christ's Hosp., 1980–93; Royal Star and Garter Home, 1984–2007. Mem., Court of Common Council, Corp. of London, 1975–2000; Deputy for Ward of Candlewick, 1983–2000; Liveryman: Clothworkers Co., 1960– (Warden, 1989; Master, 2001–02); Co. of Chartered Surveyors, 1979–93; Church Warden, St Lawrence Jewry-by-Guildhall, 1984–2004; Sheriff, City of London, 1987–88. *Recreations:* instant gardening, music, golf, tennis. *Address:* The Old Rectory, Bagendon, Cirencester, Glos GL7 7DU. *Clubs:* City Livery, MCC.

SAUNDERS, Prof. William Philip, PhD; Professor of Endodontology, and Dean of Dentistry, University of Dundee, since 2000; *b* 12 Oct. 1948; *s* of William Walton and Elva Doreen Saunders; one *s* one *d. Educ:* RAF Changi Grammar Sch., Singapore; Maidstone Grammar Sch.; Royal Dental Hosp. of London (BDS 1970); Univ. of Dundee (PhD 1986). FDSRCSE 1982; FDSRCPSGlas 1993; MRD 1994; FDSRCS *ad hominem* 2001; FHKAM 2007. Dental Officer, RAF, 1971–75; gen. dental practice, 1975–81; Lectr, Dept of Conservative Dentistry, Univ. of Dundee, 1981–88; University of Glasgow: Sen. Lectr in Clinical Practice, 1988–93; Personal Chair in Clinical Practice, 1993–95; Personal Chair in Endodontology, 1995–2000. Postgrad. Dental Hosp. Tutor, Glasgow Dental Hosp., 1992–95. Chm., Council of Heads and Deans of Dental Schs, 2008–. Pres., British Endodontic Soc., 1997–98; Chm., Assoc. of Consultants and Specialists in Restorative Dentistry, 1999–2002; Mem., Dental Council, 2000–, Chm., Speciality Adv. Bd in Restorative Dentistry, 2006–, RCSE. Chm. Educn Cttee, 1996–, Congress Pres., 2007–09, Europ. Soc. of Endodontology. FHEA (ILTM 2000). Consulting Ed., Internat. Endodontic Jl, 1999– (Ed., 1992–98); mem. editl bds of a number of dental jls. *Publications:* chapters in textbooks; res. papers on endodontics and applied dental materials. *Recreations:* ornithology (a lapsed bird ringer), natural history, golf (badly), Scottish art, endodontics. *Address:* University of Dundee Dental School, Park Place, Dundee DD1 4HN. *T:* (01382) 635977, *Fax:* (01382) 225163; *e-mail:* w.p.saunders@dundee.ac.uk. *Club:* Royal Air Force.

SAUNDERS WATSON, Comdr (Leslie) Michael (Macdonald), CBE 1993; RN (retired); DL; Chairman: British Library Board, 1990–93; Kettering General Hospital NHS Trust, 1993–99; *b* 9 Oct. 1934; *s* of Captain L. S. Saunders, DSO, RN (retd), and Elizabeth Saunders (*née* Culme-Seymour); *m* 1958, Georgina Elizabeth Laetitia, *d* of Adm. Sir William Davis, GCB, DSO; two *s* one *d. Educ:* Eton; BRNC, Dartmouth. Joined Royal Navy, 1951; specialised in Communications (Jackson Everett Prize); Comdr 1969; retired, 1971, on succession to Rockingham Castle Estate. Pres., Historic Houses Assoc., 1982–88 (Dep. Pres., 1978–82; Chm., Tax and Parly Cttee, 1975–82); Chairman: Northamptonshire Assoc. Youth Clubs, 1977–91 (Pres., 1997–); Heritage Educn Year, 1977; Corby Community Adv. Gp, 1979–86; Ironstone Royalty Owners Assoc., 1979–91; Nat. Curriculum History Wkg Gp, 1988–90; Heritage Educn Trust, 1988–99; Modern Records Centre Adv. Cttee, Warwick Univ., 1993–98; Public Affairs Cttee, ICOMOS UK, 1994–98; Friends of British Library, 1994–2000; Vice-Chm., Northamptonshire Small Industries Cttee, 1974–79; Member: British Heritage Cttee, BTA, 1978–88; Northamptonshire Enterprise Agency, 1986–90; Country Landowners' Association: Member: Taxation Cttee, 1975–90; Exec. Cttee, 1977–82, 1987–92; Legal and Land Use Cttee, 1982–87; F and GP Cttee, 1994–98; Chairman: Northamptonshire Branch, 1981–84; Game Fair Local Cttee, 1997. Director: Lamport Hall Preservation Trust, 1978–91; English Sinfonia, 1981–2000. Trustee: Royal Botanic Gdns, Kew, 1983–91 (Chm., Bldgs and Design Cttee, 1985–91); Nat. Heritage Meml Fund, 1987–96. Chm., Governors Lodge Park Comprehensive Sch., 1977–82; Trustee, Oakham Sch., 1975–77. FSA 2001; FRSA 1986. High Sheriff, 1978–79, DL 1979–, Northamptonshire. Hon. DLitt: Warwick, 1991; Leicester, 1997. *Publication:* I Am Given A Castle: a memoir, 2008. *Recreations:* sailing, music, gardening, painting. *Address:* The Manor House, Ashley Road, Stoke Albany, Market Harborough, Leicestershire LE16 8PL. *Club:* Brooks's (Manager, 1994–99).

SAUVAIN, Stephen John; QC 1995; *b* 3 June 1949; *s* of Alan Sauvain and Norah Sauvain; *m* 1980, Christine McLean; two *s*, and one step *s. Educ:* King Edward VII Grammar Sch., King's Lynn; Sidney Sussex Coll., Cambridge (MA, LLB). Lectr in Law, Univ. of Manchester, 1971–78; called to the Bar, Lincoln's Inn, 1977; in practice as barrister, 1978–. *Publications:* Highway Law, 1988, 3rd edn 2004; (ed) Encyclopedia of Highway Law and Practice. *Address:* Kings Chambers, 36 Young Street, Manchester M3 3FT. *T:* (0161) 832 9082.

SAUVEN, John Bernard; Executive Director, Greenpeace, since 2007; *b* London, 6 Sept. 1954; *s* of Maurice Oswald Sauven and Helen Mary Orpin; *m* 1990, Janet Helene Convery; two *s. Educ:* University Coll., Cardiff (BSc Econ). Actg Gen. Sec., CND, 1989; Campaign and Communications Dir, Greenpeace, 2001–07. *Recreations:* photography, poetry, sailing. *Address:* Greenpeace, Canonbury Villas, N1 2PN. *T:* 07929 638296; *e-mail:* john.sauven@uk.greenpeace.org.

SAVAGE, Caroline Le Quesne; *see* Lucas, C.

SAVAGE, Francis Joseph, CMG 1996; LVO 1986; OBE 1989; HM Diplomatic Service, retired; Adviser to Foreign and Commonwealth Office, since 2003; *b* Preston, Lancs, 8 Feb. 1943; *s* of Francis Fitzgerald Savage and late Mona May Savage (*née* Parsons); *m* 1966, Veronica Mary McAleenan; two *s. Educ:* Holy Cross Convent, Broadstairs; St Stephen's Sch., Welling, Kent; NW Kent Coll., Dartford. Joined FO, 1961; served in: Cairo, 1967–70; Washington, 1971–73; Vice-Consul, Aden, 1973–74; FCO, 1974–78; Vice-Consul, then Consul (Commercial), Düsseldorf, 1978–82; Consul, Peking, 1982–86; First Sec. (Consular), Lagos, and Consul for Benin, 1987–90; First Sec., FCO, 1990–93; Counsellor, FCO, 1993; Governor: Montserrat, 1993–97; British Virgin Islands, 1998–2002. Member: Catenian Assoc., 1991–; Montserrat Nat. Trust, 1993–97; Montserrat Cricket Assoc., 1993–97; London Soc. of Ragamuffins, 2002– (Pres., 2008–). Trustee: Virgin Islands Search and Rescue, UK, 2002; Montserrat Foundn, 2008–. Chm., Friends of the BVI, 2005. Montserrat Badge of Honour, 2001. KCSG 2002. *Recreations:* cricket, volcano watching, hurricane dodging, travel, meeting people. *Address:* c/o Foreign and Commonwealth Office, SW1A 2AH. *Clubs:* Royal Over-Seas League; Kent CC; Peking Cricket; Royal British Virgin Islands Yacht (Life Mem.).

SAVAGE, Prof. (Richard) Nigel, PhD; Chief Executive, College of Law of England and Wales, since 1996; *b* 27 May 1950; *s* of Jack and Joan Savage; *m* 1976, Linda Jane Sherwin; two *s*. *Educ:* Edward Cludd Sch., Southwell; Newark Tech. Coll.; Manchester Poly. (BA 1st cl. 1972); Univ. of Sheffield (LLM 1974); Univ. of Strathclyde (PhD 1980). Lectr, Univ. of Strathclyde, 1974–83; Principal Lectr, Nottingham Poly., 1983–85; Prof., 1985–96, and Dean and Founding Man. Dir, 1989–96, Nottingham Law Sch. Mem., HEFCE, 2002–. *Publications:* Business Law, 1987, 2nd edn (with R. Bradgate) 1993; (with R. Bradgate) Commercial Law, 1991; articles in business and legal jls. *Recreation:* cricket. *Address:* 14 Nantwich Road, Tarporley, Cheshire CW6 9UW. *Club:* Reform.

SAVAGE, Thomas Hixon, CBE 1990; Chairman: North American Trust Co., 1992–95; A. G. Simpson Automotive Inc., 1996–2000; Director, Samuel Manu-Tech Inc., since 1994; *b* Belfast, 21 Nov. 1928; *s* of Thomas Hixon Savage and Martha Foy Turkington; *m* 1st, 1950, Annie Gloria Ethel Gilmore (marr. diss. 1975); one *s* two *d*; 2nd, 1976, Evelyn Phyllis Chapman. *Educ:* Belfast High Sch.; Indian Army Officers' Trng Coll.; Univ. of Toronto Dept of Extension (Indust. Management). Supervisor, Methods & Standards, W. J. Gage, 1953–58; Manager, Process Engrg, Hallmark Greeting Cards, 1958–63; Manager, Ops Improvemts, Union Carbide (Canada) 1963–68; ITT Canada Ltd: Dir, Ops Staffs, 1968–73; Chm. and Pres., 1973–93; Sen. Officer (Canada), ITT Corp., NY, 1984–93. Chm., Abbey Life Insurance Co., Canada; formerly Chief Industrial Engineer: Dunlop Canada; Electric Reduction Co.; Dir, Acklands; Mem. Adv. Bd, Accenture (formerly Andersen Consulting). Former Mem., Policy Cttee, Business Council on Nat. Issues; Business Co-Chm., Canadian Labour Market & Productivity Center, 1990. Director: Nat. Retinitis Pigmentosa Eye Res. Foundn, Canada; Ireland Fund of Canada, 1979–95 (Chm., 1996–98). Mem., Bd of Trustees, 1995–99, Heritage Gov., 2000–05, Royal Ontario Mus. Chairman: Bd of Govs, West Park Hosp., 1991–94; Adv. Bd, Canadian Inst. of Management, 1971 (Life Mem.); Adv. Bd, Boys' and Girls' Clubs of Canada; NI Partnership in Canada. *Recreation:* golf. *Address:* c/o Samuel Manu-Tech Inc., 185 The West Mall, Suite 1500, Toronto, ON M9C 5LS, Canada; (home) 64 Royal Oak Drive, Barrie, ON L4N 7S5, Canada. *Clubs:* Ontario (Toronto); Lambton Golf and Country (Islington).

SAVAGE, (Thomas) William, CMG 1993; HM Diplomatic Service, retired; Senior Duty Officer, Cabinet Office, 1996–2001; *b* Knockloughrim, Co. Derry, 21 Nov. 1937; *s* of late Hugh Murray Savage and Anna Mary Savage (*née* Whyte); *m* 1966, Gloria Jean Matthews; three *d*. *Educ:* Sullivan Upper Sch., Holywood, Co. Down; Queen's Univ., Belfast (BA (Hons), DipEd); LSE. Vice-Pres. and Sec., 1961–64, Pres., 1964–66, Nat. Union of Students; journalist, ITN, 1967; joined Diplomatic Service, 1968; Dar es Salaam, 1970–73; First Sec., FCO, 1973; Counsellor, on loan to Cabinet Office, 1981; Counsellor, FCO, 1984–93. *Recreations:* amateur drama, golf, topiary. *Clubs:* Royal Over-Seas League; Wimbledon Park Golf, Tanganyika Golfing Society.

SAVAGE, Wendy Diane, FRCOG; Senior Lecturer in Obstetrics and Gynaecology, St Bartholomew's and the Royal London School of Medicine and Dentistry, Queen Mary and Westfield College (formerly London Hospital Medical College), University of London, 1977–2000; *b* 12 April 1935; *d* of William George Edwards and Anne (*née* Smith); *m* 1960, Miguel Babatunde Richard Savage (marr. diss. 1973); two *s* two *d*. *Educ:* Croydon High School for Girls; Girton Coll., Cambridge (BA); London Hosp. Med. Coll. (MB BCh); London Sch. of Hygiene and Tropical Medicine (MSc (Public Health) 1997). MRCOG 1971, FRCOG 1985. Res. Fellow, Harvard Univ., 1963–64; MO, Nigeria, 1964–67; Registrar: Surgery and Obst. and Gynaec., Kenya, 1967–69; Obst. and Gynaec., Royal Free Hosp., 1969–71; venereology, abortion work, family planning, Islington, 1971–73; Specialist in obst. and gynaec., family planning and venereology, Gisborne, NZ 1973–76; Lectr, London Hosp., 1976–77. Queen Mary, University of London: Hon. Sen. Clinical Lectr, Wolfson Inst. of Preventive Medicine, Bart's and The London Sch. of Medicine and Dentistry, 2002–05; Hon. Sen. Res. Fellow, Centre for Envmtl and Preventative Medicine and Dentistry, 2005–. Hon. Vis. Prof., Middx Univ., 1991–. Contract as Hon. Cons. suspended for alleged incompetence, April 1985 - reinstated by unanimous vote of DHA after exoneration by HM61/112 Enquiry, July 1986. Mem., GMC, 1989–2005. Hon. DSc Greenwich, 2001. *Publications:* Hysterectomy, 1982; (with Fran Reader) Coping with Caesarean Section and other difficult births, 1983; A Savage Enquiry - who controls childbirth?, 1986; (jtly) Caesarean Birth in Britain, 1993; (jtly) Birth and Power, 2008; papers on abortion, sexually transmitted disease, ultrasound, sex in pregnancy, cervical cytology, medical education. *Recreations:* playing piano duets, reading. *Address:* 19 Vincent Terrace, N1. *T:* and *Fax:* (020) 7837 7635; *e-mail:* wd.savage@qmul.ac.uk, wdsavage@doctors.org.uk.

SAVAGE, William; *see* Savage, T. W.

SAVARESE, Signora Fernando; *see* Elvin, Violetta.

SAVERNAKE, Viscount; Thomas James Brudenell-Bruce; *b* 11 Feb. 1982; *s* and *heir* of Earl of Cardigan, *qv*. *Educ:* Radley Coll.; Univ. of Edinburgh. *Address:* Savernake Lodge, Savernake Forest, Marlborough, Wilts SN8 3HP.

SAVIDGE, Malcolm Kemp; *b* 9 May 1946; *s* of late David Gordon Madgwick Savidge and Jean Kirkpatrick Savidge (*née* Kemp). *Educ:* Wallington County Grammar Sch., Surrey; Aberdeen Univ. (MA); Aberdeen Coll. of Educn (Teaching Cert.). Production Control and Computer Asst, Bryans Electronics Ltd, 1970–71; Teacher: Greenwood Dale Secondary Sch., Nottingham, 1971; Peterhead Acad., 1972–73; Teacher of Maths, Kincorth Acad., Aberdeen, 1973–97. Mem. (Lab) Aberdeen City Council, 1980–96 (Dep. Leader, 1994–96). Contested (Lab) Kincardine and Deeside, Nov. 1991 and 1992. MP (Lab) Aberdeen N, 1997–2005. Convener, All Party Parly Gp on Global Security and Non-Proliferation, 2000–05. Vice-Pres., UNA (UK), 2003–. Governor: Robert Gordon's Inst. of Technol., 1980–88; Aberdeen Coll. of Educn, 1980–87. Hon. Fellow, Robert Gordon Univ., 1997. *Recreation:* exploring "life, the Universe and everything". *Address:* 13F Belmont Road, Aberdeen AB25 3SR.

SAVILE, family name of **Earl of Mexborough**.

SAVILE, 4th Baron *cr* 1888; **John Anthony Thornhill Lumley-Savile;** *b* 10 Jan. 1947; *s* of late Hon. Henry Leoline Thornhill Lumley-Savile and of Presiley June, *o d* of Geoffrey Herbert Elliot Inchbald; *S* uncle, 2008; *m* 1986, Barbara Ann Holmes, *d* of Anthony Henry Toms. *Educ:* Aiglon Coll., Switzerland. *Heir: half b* James George Augustus Lumley-Savile [*b* 30 April 1975; *m* 2005, Stephanie, *d* of Dr A. Barba Mendoza].

SAVILE, Sir James (Wilson Vincent), Kt 1990; OBE 1971; TV and radio personality; *b* 31 Oct. 1926. *Educ:* St Anne's, Leeds. Presenter: Radio One Weekly Show, 1969–89; Independent Radio weekly show, 1989–; television: Jim'll Fix It, making dreams come true, No 1 in the ratings every year, 1975–94; Jim'll Fix It Strikes Again, 2007; Mind How You Go, road safety show; Top of the Pops. Man of many parts but best known as a voluntary helper at Leeds Infirmary, Broadmoor Hospital, and Stoke Mandeville where he raised twelve million pounds to rebuild the National Spinal Injuries Centre. Fellow of Cybernetics, Reading Univ., 1990. Hon. FRCR 1997. Hon. LLD Leeds, 1986. Hon. KCSG (Holy See), 1982; Bronze and Gold medals, SMO, St John of Jerusalem. *Publications:* As It Happens (autobiog.), 1975; Love is an Uphill Thing (autobiog.), 1975; God'll Fix It, 1978. *Recreations:* running, cycling, wrestling. *Address:* General Infirmary at Leeds, Great George Street, Leeds LS1 3EX. *T:* (0113) 392 2620; National Spinal Injuries Centre, Stoke Mandeville Hospital, Aylesbury, Bucks HP21 8AL. *Club:* Athenæum.

SAVILL, His Honour David Malcolm; QC 1969; a Senior Circuit Judge and Resident Judge, Leeds Combined Court Centre, 1991–96 (a Circuit Judge, 1984–91); *b* 18 Sept. 1930; *s* of late Lionel and of Lisbeth Savill; *m* 1955, Mary Arnott (*née* Eadie), JP, *d* of late Lady Hinchcliffe and step *d* of late Hon. Sir (George) Raymond Hinchcliffe; one *s* two *d*. *Educ:* Marlborough Coll. (Pres., Marlburian Club, 1996–97); Clare Coll., Cambridge. 2nd Lieut Grenadier Guards, 1949–50. BA (Hons) Cambridge, 1953. Called to the Bar, Middle Temple, 1954 (Bencher, 1977); Mem., Senate of Inns of Court and the Bar, 1976, 1980–83. A Recorder, 1972–84 (Hon. Recorder, Leeds, 1993–96); Chancellor: diocese of Bradford, 1976–99; diocese of Ripon, 1987–92; Leader, NE Circuit, 1980–83. Chairman: Adv. Cttee on Conscientious Objectors, 1978–91; W Yorks Criminal Justice Liaison Cttee, 1992–96. *Recreations:* travel, golf, gardening. *Address:* Priory Cottage, Abbey Road, Knaresborough, N Yorks HG5 8HX. *Clubs:* MCC; Aldwoodley Golf.

SAVILL, Sir John Stewart, Kt 2008; PhD; FRCP, FRCPE, FMedSci, FRSE; Professor of Experimental Medicine, since 2005, and Vice-Principal and Head of College of Medicine and Veterinary Medicine, since 2002, University of Edinburgh (Professor of Medicine, 1998–2005); Hon. Consultant Physician in Renal and General Medicine, Royal Infirmary of Edinburgh, since 1998; Chief Scientist, Scottish Government Health Directorates, since 2008; *b* 25 April 1957; *s* of Peter Edward Savill and Jean Elizabeth Savill (*née* Garland); *m* 1979, Barbara Campbell; two *s*. *Educ:* St Catherine's Coll., Oxford (BA 1st cl. Hons Physiol Scis 1978); Sheffield Univ. Med. Sch. (MB ChB Hons 1981); Royal Postgrad. Med. Sch., London (PhD 1989). MRCP 1984, FRCP 1994; FRCPE 2000; FRSE 2005. Jun. med. posts in Sheffield, Nottingham and London, 1981–85; Department of Medicine, Royal Postgraduate Medical School, Hammersmith Hospital: Registrar in Renal Medicine, 1985–86; MRC Training Fellow, 1986–89; Sen. Registrar in Renal Medicine 1989–90; Wellcome Trust Sen. Res. Fellow in Clin. Sci., Hon. Sen. Lectr and Consultant Physician, 1990–93; Prof. in Medicine and Hd, Div. of Renal and Inflammatory Disease, 1993–98, Hd of Sch., 1997–98, Sch. of Med. and Surgical Scis, Univ. of Nottingham Faculty of Medicine and Health Scis; Dir, Univ. of Edinburgh/MRC Centre for Inflammation Res., 2000–02. Mem., MRC, 2002–08 (Chair: Physiol Med. and Infections Bd, 2002–04; Physiol Systems and Clinical Scis Bd, 2004–08). Founder FMedSci 1998 (Chm., Wkg Party on Career Structure and Prospects for Clinical Scientists in UK, 1999–2000); Fellow, Amer. Soc. of Nephrology, 2004. Presidential Award, Soc. of Leukocyte Biology of USA, 1989, 1990; Milne-Muehrcke Award, Nat. Kidney Foundn, USA, 1992; Lifetime Achievement Award, European Cell Death Orgn, 2004. *Publications:* papers on cell death in inflammation. *Recreations:* hockey, cricket, real ale. *Address:* College of Medicine and Veterinary Medicine, University of Edinburgh, Queen's Medical Research Institute, Edinburgh EH16 4TJ. *T:* (0131) 242 9313. *Clubs:* West Bridgford Hockey, Wilson's Cricket.

SAVILL, Peter David; Chairman, British Horseracing Board, 1998–2004; *b* 30 July 1947; *s* of Harry and Betty Savill; *m* 1996, Ruth Pinder; two *s* four *d*. *Educ:* Ampleforth Coll.; Downing Coll., Cambridge (LLB 1969). Trainee, Doyle Dane Bernbach, Advertising Agency, 1969–70; Special Projects Manager, Admaster Corp., 1970–71; Asst to Chm., Barclay Securities, 1971–75; President: P & D International, 1975–91; International Voyager Publications, 1980–91; Shorex International, 1991–95; Chm., North South Net, 1985–98. Chm., Plumpton Racecourse, 1998–. Director: Horserace Totalisator Bd, 1998–2002; Horserace Betting Levy Bd, 1998–99; Attheraces, 2001–04. *Recreations:* golf, horse racing, sport. *Club:* Turf.

SAVILL, Rosalind Joy, CBE 2000; FBA 2006; FSA; Director, The Wallace Collection, since 1992; *b* 12 May 1951; *d* of late Dr Guy Savill and of Lorna (*née* Williams); one *d*. *Educ:* Wycombe Abbey Sch.; Châtelard Sch., sur-Montreux; Univ. of Leeds (BA Hons 1972); Study Centre, London (Dip in Fine and Decorative Arts 1973). Ceramics Dept, V&A Mus., 1973–74; The Wallace Collection: Museum Asst, 1974–78; Asst to Dir, 1978–92. Guest Scholar, J. Paul Getty Mus., 1985. Mem. Council, Attingham Trust, 1980–92; Member: Nat. Trust Arts Panel, 1995–; Art Adv. Cttee, Nat. Mus and Galls of Wales, 1997–2003; Museums and Collections Adv. Cttee, English Heritage, 1998–2003; Accreditation Panel, MLA (formerly Registration Cttee, Museums and Galls Commn), 1999–; Adv. Cttee, Royal Mint, 1999–2007. Trustee: Somerset House Trust, 1997–2004; Campaign for Museums, 1999–; Samuel Courtauld Trust, 2008–. Pres., French Porcelain Soc., 1999– (Chm., 1988–94). Gov., Camden Sch. for Girls, 1996–. Vis. Prof., Univ. of Arts, London, 2008. FSA 1990; FRSA 1990. Hon. PhD Bucks and Chiltern UC, 2005. Nat. Art Collections Award for Scholarship, 1990; European Woman of Achievement Arts and Media Award, EUW, 2005. *Publications:* The Wallace Collection Catalogue of Sèvres Porcelain, 3 vols, 1988; (contrib.) Treasure Houses of Britain, 1985; Boughton House, 1992; Versailles: tables royales, 1993; articles in Apollo, Burlington Mag., Antologia di Belle Arti, J. Paul Getty Mus. Jl, Ars Ceramica, Antique Collector. *Recreations:* music, birds, wildlife, the collections of the 2nd Earl of Lonsdale (1787–1872). *Address:* The Wallace Collection, Hertford House, Manchester Square, W1U 3BN. *T:* (020) 7563 9512, *Fax:* (020) 7224 2155.

SAVILLE, family name of **Baron Saville of Newdigate**.

SAVILLE OF NEWDIGATE, Baron *cr* 1997 (Life Peer), of Newdigate in the co. of Surrey; **Mark Oliver Saville,** Kt 1985; PC 1994; a Lord of Appeal in Ordinary, since 1997; *b* 20 March 1936; *s* of Kenneth Vivian Saville and Olivia Sarah Frances Gray; *m* 1961, Jill Gray; two *s*. *Educ:* St Paul's Primary Sch., Hastings; Rye Grammar Sch.; Brasenose Coll., Oxford (BA, BCL; Hon. Fellow, 1998). Nat. Service, 2nd Lieut Royal Sussex Regt, 1954–56; Oxford Univ., 1956–60 (Vinerian Schol. 1960); called to Bar, Middle Temple, 1962 (Bencher, 1983); QC 1975; Judge of the High Court, QBD, 1985–93; a Lord Justice of Appeal, 1994–97. Hon. LLD London Guildhall, 1997. *Recreations:* sailing, flying, computers. *Address:* House of Lords, SW1A 0PW. *Club:* Garrick.

SAVILLE, Clive Howard; Chief Executive, UKCOSA: Council for International Education, 1997–2004; *b* 7 July 1943; *m* 1967, Camille Kathleen Burke. *Educ:* Bishop Gore Grammar Sch., Swansea; University Coll., Swansea (BA). Joined DES as Asst Principal, 1965; Grade 3, DES, then DFE, later DFEE, 1987–97. Vis. Associate, Center for Studies in Higher Educn, Univ. of California, Berkeley, 1987. Member: Exec. Cttee, Nat. Literary Trust, 1997–2007; British Accreditation Council for Ind. Further and Higher Educn, 1998–2004; Adv. Panel, Office of Immigration Services Comr, 2001–05. Governor: Morley Coll., 1999–2002; UCL Hosps Foundn Trust, 2004–. *Address:* *e-mail:* savilleclive@aol.com.

SAVILLE, Prof. John; Emeritus Professor of Economic and Social History, University of Hull; *b* 2 April 1916; *o s* of Orestes Stamatopoulos, Volos, Greece, and Edith Vessey (name changed by deed poll to that of step-father, 1937); *m* 1943, Constance Betty Saunders (*d* 2007); three *s* one *d*. *Educ:* Royal Liberty Sch.; London Sch. of Economics. 1st Cl. Hons BSc (Econ) 1937. Served War, RA, 1940–46; Chief Scientific Adviser's Div., Min. of Works, 1946–47; Univ. of Hull, 1947–82, Prof. of Economic and Social History, 1972–82. Leverhulme Emeritus Fellow, 1984–86. Mem., British Communist Party, 1934–56; Chm., Oral Hist. Soc., 1976–87; Convenor, Northern Marxist Historians Gp, 1986–95; Vice-Chm., and then Chm., Soc. for Study of Labour Hist., 1974–82; Mem. Exec. Cttee and Founder-Mem., Council for Academic Freedom and Democracy, 1971–81, Chm. 1982–89; Chm., Economic and Social Hist. Cttee, SSRC, 1977–79. Trustee, Michael Lipman Trust, 1977–93. Vice-Chm., Friends of the Brynmor Jones Library, Hull Univ., 1988–2000. FRHistS 1973. *Publications:* Ernest Jones, Chartist, 1952; Rural Depopulation in England and Wales 1851–1951, 1957; 1848, The British State and the Chartist Movement, 1987; The Labour Movement in Britain: a commentary, 1988; The Politics of Continuity: British Foreign Policy and the Labour Government 1945–46, 1993; The Consolidation of the Capitalist State, 1994; Memoirs from the Left, 2003; numerous articles; Co-Editor: (with E. P. Thompson) Reasoner and New Reasoner, 1956–59; (with Asa Briggs) Essays in Labour History, 1960, 1971, 1977; (with Ralph Miliband) Socialist Register (annual, 1964–90); (with Joyce M. Bellamy) Dictionary of Labour Biography, 1972–2000. *Recreations:* working for socialism, looking at churches. *Address:* 152 Westbourne Avenue, Hull HU5 3HZ. *T:* (01482) 343425.

SAVILLE, John Donald William; HM Diplomatic Service; High Commissioner to Brunei, since 2005; *b* 29 June 1960; *s* of Donald and Elizabeth Saville; *m* 1992, Fabiola Moreno de Alboran; one *d*. *Educ:* Hitchin Boys' Grammar Sch.; Jesus Coll., Oxford (MA). Joined FCO, 1981; Third, then Second Sec., Jakarta, 1982–85; FCO, 1985–88; Second, then First Sec., Warsaw, 1988–91; First Secretary: FCO, 1991–95; Vienna, 1995–98; Hd, Commonwealth and Burma Section, SE Asia Dept, FCO, 1998–2000; Dep. Hd of Mission, Havana, 2000–03; Hd, Weapons of Mass Destruction Review Unit (Butler Review of Iraq Intelligence), FCO, 2004. *Recreations:* fishing, pulling sofas from the River Wandle, jungle trekking. *Address:* c/o Foreign and Commonwealth Office, SW1A 2AH. *Club:* Travellers.

SAVILLE, Peter Andrew; designer; *b* 9 Oct. 1955; *s* of Lionel Stuart Saville and Dorothy Mabel Saville (*née* Foley). *Educ:* St Ambrose Coll., Altrincham; Manchester Poly. (BA 1st Cl. Hons Graphic Design 1978). FCSD 1992. Founding Partner, Factory Records, 1979, created album covers for Joy Division and New Order, etc; Art Dir, Dindisc Records, 1979–82; founded Peter Saville Associates design studio, 1983; Partner, Pentagram, 1990–92; Art Dir, Frankfurt Balkind, LA, 1993–94; founded: The Apartment, with Meiré and Meiré, advertising and design agency, 1995; with Nick Knight, SHOWstudio.com, 1999; Consultant Creative Dir to Manchester CC, 2004–. Vis. Prof., Univ. of the Arts, London, 2008. *Exhibitions* include: major retrospective, Design Mus., London, 2003, transf. Tokyo and Manchester; ESTATE, Migros Mus., Zurich, 2005. MInstD. Hon. DArts Manchester Metropolitan, 2005. *Publications:* Designed by Peter Saville, 2003; Peter Saville Estate, 2007. *Address:* Peter Saville, Export House, 25–31 Ironmonger Row, EC1V 3QN. *T:* (020) 7253 4334, *Fax:* (020) 7336 7992; *e-mail:* peter@petersavillestudio.com. *Club:* Groucho.

SAVORY, Sir Michael Berry, Kt 2006; Chief Executive, Young Enterprise, since 2006; Lord Mayor of London, 2004–05; *b* 10 Jan. 1943; *s* of late Claude Berry Savory and Irene Anne Parker; *m* 1992, Fiona Anne Macrae; two *d*. *Educ:* Whitestones, Bulawayo, Zimbabwe; Harrow Sch. ASIP; FSI. Partner, Foster & Braithwaite Stockbrokers, 1967–89; Chm., BT Batsford, 1981–90; Dir, Terrafix, 1985–90. Chairman: HSBC Bank plc Stockbroker Services, 2001–05; ProShare, 2003–05. Partner, Muckleburgh Collection, 1989–. Mem. Council, SSAFA-Forces Help, 1972–2006; Treas., Royal Nat. Mission to Deep Sea Fishermen, 1985–2006; Trustee: Hull Fishermen's Widows and Orphans Trust, 1985–2006; John Rice Charity, 1991–2003; Adm. Arthur Phillip Meml Trust, 1996–; Lord Mayor's 800th Anniversary Trust, 2000–; Britain-Australia Bicentennial Trust, 2001–; John Carpenter Trust, 2002. Hon. Col, London Regt, TA, 2007–. Churchwarden, St Margaret, Lothbury, 1987–2003; Freeman, City of London, 1964; Corporation of London: Mem., Court of Common Council, 1981–96; Alderman, 1996–; Sheriff, 2001–02; Freeman, Co. of Goldsmiths, 1984; Liveryman: Co. of Poulters (Master, 1996); Co. of Clockmakers (Master, 1998); Co. of Information Technologists, 2004. *Recreations:* field sports, military vehicle collection. *Address:* 133 Regent Street, W1B 4HX. *T:* 0845 5852051; *e-mail:* mbsavory@aol.com.

SAVOURS; *see* Campbell-Savours, family name of Baron Campbell-Savours.

SAVULESCU, Prof. Julian, PhD; Uehiro Professor of Practical Ethics, University of Oxford, and Fellow of St Cross College, Oxford, since 2002; *b* 22 Dec. 1963; *s* of Radu Ion and Valda Jean Savulescu. *Educ:* Monash Univ., Australia (BMedSci 1st cl. Hons 1985; MB BS 1st cl. Hons 1988; PhD 1994). Sir Robert Menzies Med. Scholar, Oxford Univ., 1994–97; Clinical Ethicist, Oxford Radcliffe Hosps, 1995–97; Logan Res. Fellow, Monash Univ., 1997–98; Director: Bioethics Prog., Centre for Study of Health and Society, Univ. of Melbourne, 1998–2002; Ethics of Genetics Prog., Murdoch Children's Res. Inst., Royal Children's Hosp., Melbourne, 1998–2002. Chm., Dept of Human Services, Victoria Ethics Cttee, 1998–2002. Editor, Jl of Med. Ethics, 2001–. *Publications:* (jtly) Medical Ethics and Law: the core curriculum, 2003; over 100 articles in BMJ, Lancet, Australasian Jl of Philosophy, Bioethics, Jl of Med. Ethics, American Jl of Bioethics, Med. Jl of Australia, Philosophy, Psychiatry and Psychology and New Scientist. *Recreations:* skiing, surfing, cycling, swimming, roller blading, film, wine. *Address:* Oxford Uehiro Centre for Practical Ethics, Littlegate House, St Ebbe's Street, Oxford OX1 1PT. *T:* (01865) 286888, *Fax:* (01865) 286886; *e-mail:* ethics@philosophy.ox.ac.uk.

SAWARD, Rev. Canon Michael John; Treasurer and Canon Residentiary of St Paul's Cathedral, 1991–2000, Canon Emeritus, since 2001; *b* 14 May 1932; *s* of late Donald and Lily Saward; *m* 1956, Jackie, *d* of late Col John Atkinson, DSO, OBE, TD, and Eileen Atkinson, MBE; one *s* three *d*. *Educ:* Eltham Coll.; Bristol Univ. (BA Theology). 2nd Lieut, RA, 1950–52, RWAFF (Nat. Service). Deacon 1956, priest 1957; curacies in Croydon, 1956–59, and Edgware, 1959–64; Sec., Liverpool Council of Churches, 1965–67; C of E Radio and Television Officer, 1967–72; Vicar: St Matthew, Fulham, 1972–78; Ealing, 1978–91; Prebendary of St Paul's Cathedral, 1985–91. Canon Theologian, St Michael Sanibel, Florida, 2001–02. Mem., General Synod, 1975–95 (Mem., House of Clergy Standing Cttee, 1981–86); a Church Comr, 1978–93 (Member: Redundant Churches Cttee, 1978–81; Houses Cttee, 1981–88; Bd of Govs, 1986–93; Pastoral Cttee, 1988–93); Chairman: C of E Pensions Measure Revision Cttee, 1987–88; Care of Cathedrals (Supplementary Provisions) Measure Revision Cttee, 1992–93; Billy Graham Mission '89 Media Task Gp, 1988–89; Member: Lambeth Conf., Preparatory Cttee, 1967–68; Archbishops' Council on Evangelism, 1975–78; C of E Evangelical Council, 1976–93; Nat. Partners in Mission Wkg Party, 1979–81; Dioceses Commn, 1981–89; Council, CPAS, 1992–98; Cttee, Hymn Soc., 2000–08. Sec., Gen. Synod Broadcasting Commn, 1970–73. Trustee: Hartlebury Castle Trust, 1983–88; Church Urban Fund, 1989–90; Christian Evidence Soc., 1992–98. Mem. Council, Trinity Theol Coll., 1974–78; Mem., RTS, 1970–72. Gov., St Paul's Cathedral (formerly Choir) Sch., 1991–2000. Chm., Jubilate Hymns Ltd, 1999–2001. Religious Advr, Cromwell (film), 1971. Journalist, broadcaster (650 progs), lectr, reviewer. Winston Churchill Travelling Fellowship, 1984. Freeman, City of London, 1993; Liveryman, Co. of Gardeners, 1997–2001. Words Editor: Hymns for Today's Church, 1974–82; Sing Glory, 1997–99; Sing to the Lord, 2000; Contemporary Hymns, 2009. Chairman, Panel of Judges: St Paul's Cathedral Millennium Hymn Competition, 1997–99; The Times Preacher of the Year Comp., 2000. Prizewinner: Southern TV Hymn for Britain competition, 1966; BBC-TV Songs of Praise new hymn competition, 1985; Polly Bond journalism award (USA), 1990. *Publications:* Leisure, 1963 (Norwegian edn 1971); Christian Youth Groups, 1965; Cracking the God-Code, 1974, 3rd edn 1989 (USA edn 1974, Chinese and Swedish edns 1976); And So To Bed?, 1975; God's Friends, 1978; All Change, 1983; Evangelicals on the Move, 1987; These Are The Facts, 1997; A Faint Streak of Humility, 1999; Jubilate Everybody, 2003; Signed, Sealed, Delivered, 2004; Christ Triumphant (hymns), 2006; contribs to books including: Broadcasting, Society and the Church, 1973; Christian Initiation, 1991; Prayers for Today's World, 1993; Has Keele Failed?, 1995; The Post Evangelical Debate, 1997; 366 Graces, 1999, and to 247 hymnbooks worldwide; author of 109 hymns. *Recreations:* reading (esp. military history), music, cricket, travel, food and drink, writing hymns. *Address:* 6 Discovery Walk, E1W 2JG. *T:* (020) 7702 1130. *Clubs:* Athenæum (Mem., General Cttee, 1997–2000); Sion College.

SAWDY, Peter Bryan; Director: Griffin International Ltd, since 1988; Yule Catto PLC, 1990–2002; Lazard Birla Indian Investment Fund plc, 1994–2002; *b* 17 Sept. 1931; *s* of Alfred Eustace Leon Sawdy and Beatrice Sawdy; *m* 1st, 1955, Anne Stonor (marr. diss. 1989; she *d* 1995); two *d*; 2nd, 1989, Judith Mary Bowen. *Educ:* Ampleforth Coll.; Regent St Polytechnic; LSE. Trainee, Brooke Bond Ltd, 1952; Chm., Brooke Bond Ceylon Ltd, 1962–65; Director: Brooke Bond Ltd, 1965–68; Brooke Bond Liebig Ltd, 1968–75; Brooke Bond Group: Man. Dir, 1975–77; Gp Chief Exec., 1977–81; Dep. Chm. and Gp Chief Exec., 1981–85. Chm., Costain Gp, 1990–93; Dep. Chm., Hogg Gp, 1992–94 (Dir, 1986–). *Recreations:* golf, opera, collecting modern first editions. *Address:* 20 Smith Terrace, SW3 4DL. *Clubs:* Naval and Military; Royal Mid-Surrey Golf (Richmond).

SAWERS, David Richard Hall; environmental campaigner and writer; *b* 23 April 1931; *s* of late Edward and Madeline Sawers; unmarried. *Educ:* Westminster Sch.; Christ Church, Oxford (MA). Research Asst to Prof. J. Jewkes, Oxford Univ., 1954–58; Journalist, The Economist, 1959–64; Vis. Fellow, Princeton Univ., 1964–65; Econ. Adviser, Min. of Aviation and of Technology, 1966–68; Sen. Econ. Adviser, Min. of Technology, Aviation Supply, and DTI, 1968–72; Under-Sec., Depts of Industry, Trade and Prices and Consumer Protection, 1972–76; Under-Sec., Depts of Environment and Transport, 1976–83; Principal Res. Fellow, Technical Change Centre, 1984–86. *Publications:* (with John Jewkes and Richard Stillerman) The Sources of Invention, 1958; (with Ronald Miller) The Technical Development of Modern Aviation, 1968; Competition in the Air, 1987; Should the Taxpayer Support the Arts, 1993; (contrib.) Markets and the Media, 1996; (contrib.) Does the Past Have a Future?: the political economy of heritage, 1998; articles in daily press and journals. *Recreations:* listening to music, looking at pictures, gardening. *Address:* 10 Seaview Avenue, Angmering-on-Sea, Littlehampton BN16 1PP. *T:* (01903) 779134.

SAWERS, Sir (Robert) John, KCMG 2007 (CMG 1996); HM Diplomatic Service; UK Permanent Representative to the United Nations, since 2007; *b* 26 July 1955; *s* of Colin Simon Hawkesley Sawers and Daphne Anne Sawers; *m* 1981, Avril Helen Shelley Lamb; two *s* one *d*. *Educ:* Beechen Cliff Sch., Bath; Univ. of Nottingham (BSc Hons Physics and Philosophy). FCO 1977; served Sana'a, 1980; Damascus, 1982; FCO, 1984; Pretoria/ Cape Town, 1988; Head, EU Presidency Unit, 1991; Principal Private Sec. to Sec. of State for Foreign and Commonwealth Affairs, 1993–95; Career Develt Attachment, Harvard Univ., 1995–96; Counsellor, Washington, 1996–99; For. Affairs Private Sec. to the Prime Minister, 1999–2001; Ambassador to Egypt, 2001–03; Special Rep. for Iraq, 2003; Political Dir, FCO, 2003–07. Gov., Ditchley Foundn. *Recreations:* riding, theatre, tennis. *Address:* c/o Foreign and Commonwealth Office, SW1A 2AH.

SAWFORD, Philip Andrew; *b* 26 June 1950; *s* of John and Audrey Sawford; *m* 1971, Rosemary Stokes; two *s*. *Educ:* Ruskin Coll., Oxford (Dip. Soc.); Univ. of Leicester (BA Hons). Manager, training orgn, Wellingborough, 1985–97. Member (Lab): Desborough Town Council, 1977–97; Kettering BC, 1979–83, 1986–97, 1991–97 (Leader). Contested (Lab): Wellingborough, 1992; Kettering, 2005. MP (Lab) Kettering, 1997–2005. *Recreations:* playing guitar, reading. *Address:* 46 Federation Avenue, Desborough, Northants NN14 2NX.

SAWKO, Prof. Felicjan, DSc; Professor of Civil Engineering and Head of Department at the Sultan Qaboos University, Oman, 1986–95, now Emeritus Professor; *b* 17 May 1937; *s* of Czeslaw Sawko and Franciszka (*née* Nawrot); *m* 1960, Genowefa Stefania (*née* Bak); four *s* one *d*. *Educ:* Leeds Univ. (BSc Civil Engrg, 1958; MSc 1960; DSc 1973). Engr, Rendel Palmer & Tritton, London, 1959–62; Lectr, 1962–67, Reader, 1967, Leeds University; Prof. of Civil Engrg, Liverpool Univ., 1967–86. Henry Adams Award, IStructE, 1980. *Publications:* (ed) Developments in Prestressed Concrete, Vols 1 and 2, 1968; (with Cope and Tickell) Numerical Methods for Civil Engineers, 1981; some 70 papers on computer methods and structural masonry. *Recreations:* travel, bridge, numismatics. *Address:* 23 Floral Wood, Liverpool L17 7HR. *T:* (0151) 727 0913; *e-mail:* fsawko@hotmail.com.

SAWYER, Baron *cr* 1998 (Life Peer), of Darlington in the co. of Durham; **Lawrence Sawyer, (Tom);** *b* 12 May 1943. *Educ:* Eastbourne Sch., Darlington; Darlington Tech. Sch. Dep. Gen. Sec., NUPE, later UNISON, 1981–94; Gen. Sec., Labour Party, 1994–98. Mem., NEC, Labour Party, 1981–94 and 1999–2001; Chm., Labour Party, 1990–91. Non-exec. Chm., Reed Health Gp, 2001–03; Chm., Royal Mail Partnership Bd, 2001–07; non-exec. Dir, Investors in People UK, 1998–2005. Chairman: Notting Hill Housing Gp, 1998–2005; Supervisory Bd, Thompsons, Solicitors, 2001–. Vis. Prof., Cranfield Sch. of Mgt, 1999. Chancellor, Univ. of Teesside, 2005–. *Address:* House of Lords, SW1A 0PW.

SAWYER, Anthony Charles, CB 1999; fiscal expert, International Monetary Fund, since 1999 (expert missions to Bulgaria, Egypt, Jordan, Kenya, Kyrgyzstan, Nigeria, Pakistan, Romania, Tajikistan, Tanzania and the Philippines); *b* 3 Aug. 1939; *s* of Charles Bertram and Elizabeth Sawyer; *m* 1962, Kathleen Josephine McGill; two *s* one *d*. *Educ:* Redhill Tech. Coll., Surrey. Nat. Service, RA, 1960. Underwriter, Northern Assurance Group, 1962; Customs and Excise, 1964–99: Collector, Edinburgh, 1984; Dep. Dir, 1988; Comr, 1991–99; Director: Outfield, 1991–94; Enforcement, 1994–99. Dir, Customs Annuity and Benevolent Fund, 1998–2004. Non-exec. Dir, Retail Banking Bd, Royal Bank of Scotland, 1994–97; fiscal adviser: Kyrgyzstan, 2000; Egypt, 2003. FRSA 1994; FCMI (FIMgt 1996); FInstD 1997; FRMetS 2001. *Recreations:* walking, cricket, sailing. *Clubs:* National Liberal; Royal Scots (Edinburgh).

SAWYER, Rt Hon. Dame Joan (Augusta), DBE 1997; PC 2004; President, Bahamas Court of Appeal, since 2001; *b* 26 Nov. 1940; *m* 1962, Geoffrey Sawyer (*d* 2004); one *s*. *Educ:* London Univ. (LLB 1973). Clerk, 1958–68; HEO (Public Service), 1968–73; called to the Bar, Gray's Inn, 1973; Asst Crown Counsel, 1973–78; acting Stipendiary and Circuit Magistrate, 1978; Sen. Counsel, 1979–83; acting Dir, Legal Affairs, 1983; Counsel, Central Bank of the Bahamas, 1984–88; Justice, 1988–95, Sen. Justice, 1995–96, Supreme Court of Bahamas; Chief Justice of the Bahamas, 1996–2001. *Publications:* articles in Bahamian Review. *Recreations:* reading, sewing, serious theatre, gardening, embroidering. *Address:* Bahamas Court of Appeal, PO Box N-3209, Nassau, Bahamas. *T:* 3285400/1.

SAXBEE, Rt Rev. John Charles; *see* Lincoln, Bishop of.

SAXBY, Sir Robin (Keith), Kt 2002; FREng; Chairman, ARM Holdings plc (formerly Advanced RBC Machines Ltd), 2001–06, now Emeritus Chairman (Chief Executive Officer, 1991–2001); *b* 4 Feb. 1947; *s* of Keith William Saxby and Mary Saxby; *m* 1970, Patricia Susan Bell; one *s* one *d*. *Educ:* Univ. of Liverpool (BEng Electronics 1968). R&D engr, Rank Bush Murphy, 1968–72; Sen. Engr, Pye TMC, 1972–73; Sales Engr, then System Strategy Manager, Europe, Motorola Semiconductors, 1973–84; Chief Exec., Henderson Security Systems, 1984–86; Man. Dir, ES2 Ltd, 1986–91. Non-exec. Dir, Glotel, 1999–. Vis. Prof., Dept of Electronics, Univ. of Liverpool. Pres., IET, 2006–07. Trustee, IEF. FREng 2002. FRSA; CCMI. Hon. FIET. Hon. DEng Liverpool, 2000; Hon. DTech Loughborough, 2001; DU Essex. *Publications:* (contrib.) Electronic Engineers' Reference Book, 1983; Microcomputer Handbook, 1985; (contrib.) Advances in Information Technology, 1998. *Recreations:* tennis, ski-ing, music, swimming, astronomy, genealogy, old technology. *Address:* ARM Holdings plc, Liberty House, Moorbridge, Maidenhead, Berks SL6 8LT.

SAXON, Prof. David Harold, OBE 2005; DPhil, DSc; CPhys, FInstP; FRSE; Kelvin Professor of Physics, 1990–2008, now Professor Emeritus, Dean, Physical Sciences, 2002–08, University of Glasgow; *b* 27 Oct. 1945; *s* of late Rev. Canon Eric Saxon and Ruth (*née* Higginbottom); *m* 1968, Margaret Flitcroft; one *s* one *d*. *Educ:* Manchester Grammar Sch.; Balliol Coll., Oxford (MA, DSc); Jesus Coll., Oxford (DPhil). CPhys 1985; FInstP 1985; FRSE 1993. Jun. Res. Fellow, Jesus Coll., Oxford, 1968–70; Res. Officer, Nuclear Physics Dept, Oxford, 1969–70; Res. Associate, Columbia Univ., NY, 1970–73; Rutherford Appleton Laboratory, Oxford: Res. Associate, 1974–75; SSO, 1975–76; PSO, 1976–89; Grade 6, 1989–90; Glasgow University: Hd, Dept of Physics and Astronomy, 1996–2001; Vice-Dean, Physical Scis, 2000–02. Member, SERC Committees: Particle Physics Experiment Selection Panel, 1989–92; Particle Physics, 1991–94 (Chm., 1992–94); Nuclear Physics Bd, 1992–93; Particles, Space & Astronomy Bd, 1993–94. Member Council: PPARC, 1997–2001 (Chairman: Particle Physics Cttee, 1994–95; Public Understanding of Sci. Panel, 1997–2001); CCLRC, 2000–01, 2005–07 (Chm., Particle Physics Users Adv. Cttee, 1998–2004). Chairman: 27th Internat. Conf. on High Energy Physics, 1994; Scottish Univs Summer Schs in Physics, 1997–2003; Member: Scientific Policy Cttee, 1993–98, External Rev. Cttee, 2001–02, CERN, Geneva; Physics Res. Cttee, Deutsches Elektronen Synchrotron, Hamburg, 1993–99; MRC Scientific Adv. Gp on Technology, 1999; MRC Discipline Hopping Panel, 2000–01 and 2006; Eur. Cttee on Future Accelerators, 2003–05; Commn C11, Internat. Union of Pure and Applied Physics, 2006–08. Member: Physics Panel, 1996 RAE, HEFC; Physics Benchmarking Panel, QAA, 2000–01; Res. Exchange Panel, British Council, 2006–. Mem. Council, 2001–04, Res. Convener, 2002–05, RSE; Chm., Inst. of Physics in Scotland, 2003–05. Mem., Scientific Adv. Panel, Univ. Trento, Italy, 2001–05. FRSA 1997. *Recreation:* staying close to home. *Address:* Department of Physics and Astronomy, University of Glasgow, Glasgow G12 8QQ. *T:* (0141) 330 5890.
See also R. G. Saxon.

SAXON, Richard Gilbert, CBE 2001; RIBA; Client Advisor for construction projects, Consultancy for the Built Environment, since 2005; *b* 14 April 1942; *s* of late Rev. Canon Eric Saxon and of Ruth Saxon (*née* Higginbottom); *m* 1968, Elizabeth Anne Tatton. *Educ:* Univ. of Liverpool (BArch 1st cl. Hons 1965; MCD 1966). RIBA 1970. Joined Building Design Partnership, 1966: Partner, 1977–2005; Mem., Mgt Gp, 1984–86; Project Dir, J. P. Morgan HQ, AELTC Masterplan, Adam Opel HQ, 1986–93; Chm., London Office, 1993–99; Practice Chm., 1996–2002; Dir, Strategic Marketing, 1999–2005. Pres., British Council for Offices, 1995–96; Vice-Pres., RIBA, 2002–08. Chairman: Reading Construction Forum, 1999–2002; Be (Collaborating for the Built Environment), 2002–04; Mem., Ind. Dispute Avoidance Panel for the London Olympics, 2008–. MCIM 1990. FRSA 1987. Liveryman, Co. of Chartered Architects, 1988 (Master, 2005–06). *Publications:* Atrium Buildings: development and design, 1983, 2nd edn 1986 (also USA, Japan, Russia); The Atrium Comes of Age, 1993 (also USA, Japan); Be Valuable, 2005; articles in Building Res. and Inf., Architects Jl, Building Design and Building. *Recreations:* travel, early music, theatre, film, birds, enjoying London. *Address:* Consultancy for the Built Environment, 9 Whistlers Avenue, SW11 3TS. *T:* (020) 7585 1976; *e-mail:* Richard@saxoncbe.com.
See also D. H. Saxon.

SAXTON, Jonathon Hugh Christopher, (Joe); Driver of Ideas, nfpSynergy, since 2003 (Head, Not for Profit, Future Foundation, 2000–03); *b* Bristol, 6 Feb. 1962; *s* of Hugh Michael Saxton and Barbara Bevil Saxton; *m* 1990, Julie Margaret Evans; two *s* one *d*. *Educ:* Leigh Prim. Sch.; Downsend Sch.; Bedales Sch.; Robinson Coll., Cambridge (BA Nat. Sci. 1984); Univ. of E Anglia (MA Develt Studies 1986); Henley Management Coll. (MBA 1995). Co-ordinator, Harambee Centre, Cambridge, 1986–88; Fundraising Dept, Oxfam, Oxford, 1988–91; Account Dir and Dep. Client Services Dir, Brann Ltd, Cirencester, 1991–96; Dir of Communications, RNID, 1997–2000. Trustee: RSPCA, 1994–2001; Inst. of Fundraising, 2002–08 (Chm., 2005–08); Chm. and Co-founder, CharityComms, 2007–; Chm., People & Planet, 2005–. *Publications:* It's Competition, but not as we know it?, 1997; What are Charities For?, 1998; Polishing the Diamond, 2002; Mission Impossible, 2004; The 21st Century Volunteer, 2005; The 21st Century Donor, 2007. *Recreations:* DIY, reading, sports training with my kids, fell walking, kayaking, snuggling with my wife. *Address:* nfpSynergy, 2–6 Tenter Ground, Spitalfields, E1 7NH. *T:* (020) 7426 8888; *e-mail:* joe.saxton@nfpsynergy.net.

SAXTON, Robert Louis Alfred, DMus; FGSM; University Lecturer, Oxford University, and Tutor and Fellow in Music, Worcester College, Oxford, since 1999; Director, University of York Music Press, since 2004; *b* 8 Oct. 1953; *s* of Jean Augusta Saxton (*née* Infield) and Ian Sanders Saxton; *m* 2005, Teresa Cahill, *qv*. *Educ:* Bryanston Sch.; St Catharine's Coll., Cambridge (MA); Worcester Coll., Oxford (BMus; DMus 1992). FGSM 1987. Lectr, Bristol Univ., 1984–85; Fulbright Arts award, 1985; Vis. Fellow, Princeton Univ., 1986; Head of Composition: GSMD, 1990–98; RAM, 1998–99; Vis. Fellow in Composition, Bristol Univ., 1995–2001. Artistic Dir, Opera Lab, 1994–2000; Associate Dir, Performing Arts Labs, 1998–2001; Pres., Brunel Ensemble, 1995–. Hon. Pres., Assoc. of English Singers and Speakers, 1997–. Dir, South Bank Centre, 1998– (Mem., Site Develt Bd, 1997–). Patron: Bristol Univ. Music Soc., 1998–; Sounds Underground, 2005–. Trustee, Orchestra Europe, 2006–. Finalist, BBC Young Composers' Comp., 1973; First Prize, Gaudeamus Music Fest., Holland, 1975; early works at ISCM Fest., Bonn, 1977, Royan Fest., 1977; later works, majority recorded, include: The Ring of Eternity, 1983; Concerto for Orchestra, 1984; The Circles of Light, 1985; The Child of Light (carol), 1985; The Sentinel of the Rainbow, 1984; Viola Concerto, 1986; Night Dance, 1986–87; I Will Awake the Dawn, 1987; In the Beginning, 1987; Elijah's Violin, 1988; Chacony, 1988; Music to celebrate the Resurrection of Christ, 1988; Violin Concerto, Leeds Fest., 1990; Caritas (opera with libretto by Arnold Wesker), 1990–91; Paraphrase on Mozart's Idomeneo, 1991; At the Round Earth's Imagined Corners (anthem), 1992; 'Cello Concerto, 1992; Psalm—a song of ascents, 1992; O Sing unto the Lord a new song (anthem), 1993; Fantazia, 1993; Canticum Luminis, 1994; A Yardstick to the Stars, 1994; Ring, Time, 1994; Songs, Dances, Ellipses, 1997; Prayer before Sleep, 1997; Music for St Catharine, 1998; Miniature Dance for a Marionette Rabbi, 1999; Sonata for solo 'cello on a theme of Sir William Walton, 1999; The Dialogue of Zion and God, 2000; Alternative Canticles, 2002; Five Motets, 2003; Was It Winter? (carol), 2005; Song Without Words, 2005; There and Back, 2005; works commissioned by: Fires of London, London Sinfonietta, BBC, LSO, ECO, Aldeburgh Fest., Cheltenham Fest., Opera North, LPO, RPO, City of London Fest./St Paul's Cathedral, Leeds Fest. *Publications:* contributor to: Composition-Performance-Reception, 1998; Cambridge Companion to the Orchestra, 2003; Composing Music for Worship, 2003; all compositions; contribs TLS, Musical Times, etc. *Recreations:* reading, theatre, cinema, studying history, watching cricket. *Address:* c/o Music Sales, 14/15 Berners Street, W1T 3LJ. *T:* (020) 7612 7400; University of York Music Press, Department of Music, University of York, Heslington, York YO10 5DD. *T:* (01904) 432434, *Fax:* (01904) 432450.

SAYCE, Elizabeth; Chief Executive, Royal Association for Disability and Rehabilitation, since 2007; *b* 12 Jan. 1954; *d* of Dr Richard Sayce and Dr Olive Sayce; partner, Dr Rachel Perkins. *Educ:* Kent Univ. (BA English and French 1976); Bedford Coll., London Univ. (MSc Soc. Work and Soc. Policy, CQSW, 1985). Policy Dir, Mind, 1990–98; Director: Lambeth, Southwark and Lewisham Health Action Zone, 1998–2000; Policy and Communications, Disability Rights Commn, 2000–07. Harkness Fellow, Washington, 1995–96. Member: Mental Health Task Force, 1994; Disability Rights Task Force, 1997–99; Commn for Health Improvement Investigation Team, N Lakeland NHS Trust, 2000; Mental Health Media Adv. Gp, 2002–07; NICE Cttee on Confidential Inquiries, 2003–04; DWP Images of Disability Steering Gp, 2003–05; EU Steering Gp on Anti-Discrimination Campaigns, 2003–06; Healthcare Commn Expert Ref. Gp, 2005–07; Disability Cttee, Equality and Human Rights Commn, 2007–; UK Commn for Employment and Skills, 2007–. FRSA. Trustee, Stonewall, 2005–. *Publications:* From Psychiatric Patient to Citizen, 2000; contrib. numerous chapters; papers in disability and mental health jls, reports pubd by Mind, Research and Develt for Psychiatry. *Recreations:* walking the Thames and other waterways. *Address:* Royal Association for Disability and Rehabilitation, 12 City Forum, 250 City Road, EC1V 8AF. *T:* (020) 7566 0125; *e-mail:* liz.sayce@radar.org.uk.

SAYE AND SELE, 21st Baron *cr* 1447 and 1603; **Nathaniel Thomas Allen Fiennes;** DL; *b* 22 Sept. 1920; *s* of Ivo Murray Twisleton-Wykeham-Fiennes, 20th Baron Saye and Sele, OBE, MC, and Hersey Cecilia Hester, *d* of late Captain Sir Thomas Dacres Butler, KCVO; *S* father, 1968; *m* 1958, Mariette Helena, *d* of Maj.-Gen. Sir Guy Salisbury-Jones, GCVO, CMG, CBE, MC; two *s* one *d* (and two *s* decd). *Educ:* Eton; New College, Oxford. Served with Rifle Brigade, 1941–49 (despatches twice). Chartered Surveyor. Partner in firm of Laws and Fiennes. Regl Dir, Lloyds Bank, 1982–90. Trustee, Ernest Cook Trust, 1960–95 (Chm. Trustees, 1965–92). DL Oxfordshire, 1979. Fellow, Winchester Coll., 1967–83. *Heir:* *s* Hon. Martin Guy Fiennes [*b* 27 Feb. 1961; *m* 1996, Pauline Kang Chai Lian, *o d* of Kang Tiong Lam; three *s*]. *Address:* Broughton Castle, Banbury, Oxon OX15 5EB. *T:* (01295) 262624.
See also Very Rev. Hon. O. W. Fiennes.

SAYEED, Jonathan; Chairman, Ranelagh International Ltd, since 2005; *b* 20 March 1948; *m* 1980, Nicola Anne Parkes Power; two *s*. *Educ:* Britannia Royal Naval Coll., Dartmouth; Royal Naval Engrg Coll., Manadon. Chairman, Ranelagh Ltd, 1992–96; Trng Div., Corporate Services Group plc, 1996–97. MP (C) Bristol E, 1983–92; contested (C) same seat, 1992; MP (C) Mid Bedfordshire, 1997–2005. PPS to Paymaster General and Minister of State for NI, 1991–92; Opposition frontbench spokesman on the environment, 2001–03. Vice-Chm., 1987–91, Chm., 1991–92, Cons. Backbench Shipping and Shipbuilding Cttee; Dep. Chm., All Party Maritime Group, 1987–92; Member: Environment Select Cttee, 1987–92; Defence Select Cttee, 1988–91; Chairman's Panel, 1999–2001, 2003–05. Pres., Bristol E Cons. Assoc., 1995–. Pres., Bristol West Indian Cricket Club, 1986–. Member: RYA; RNSA. *Recreations:* golf, yachting, riding, classical music, architecture. *Clubs:* Carlton, Home House; Highgate Golf.

SAYER, Guy Mowbray, CBE 1978; JP; retired banker; *b* 18 June 1924; *yr s* of late Geoffrey Robley and Winifred Lily Sayer; *m* 1951, Marie Anne Sophie, *o d* of late Henri-Marie and Elisabeth Mertens; one *s* two *d*. *Educ:* Mill Mead Prep. Sch.; Shrewsbury School. FCIB (FIB 1971). Royal Navy, 1942–46. Joined Hongkong & Shanghai Banking Corp., 1946; Gen. Man. 1969; Exec. Dir 1970; Dep. Chm. 1971; Chm., 1972–77. Treas., Hong Kong Univ., 1972–77. Mem., Exchange Fund Adv. Cttee, Hong Kong, 1971–77. MLC, 1973–74, MEC, 1974–77, Hong Kong. JP Hong Kong, 1971. Hon. LLD Hong Kong, 1978. Liveryman, Innholders' Co., 1963– (Master, 2000–01). *Recreations:* golf, walking. *Address:* 5 Pembroke Gardens, W8 6HS. *T:* (020) 7602 4578. *Clubs:* Oriental, MCC; Royal Wimbledon Golf; West Sussex Golf; Hong Kong, Shek O Country (Hong Kong).

SAYER, John Raymond Keer, MA; Director and Hon. Secretary, Developing Services for Teaching in Europe, 1997–2005; Research Fellow, Department of Educational Studies, University of Oxford, since 1991; *b* 8 Aug. 1931; *s* of Arthur and Hilda Sayer; *m* 1955, Ilserose (*née* Heyd); one *s* one *d*. *Educ:* Maidstone Grammar Sch.; Brasenose Coll., Oxford (Open Scholar; MA). Taught languages, 1955–63; Dep. Head, Nailsea Sch., Somerset, 1963–67; Headmaster, Minehead Sch., Somerset, 1967–73; Principal, Banbury Sch., 1973–84; Vis. Fellow, Univ. of London Inst. of Educn, 1985–92 (Dir, Educn Management Unit, 1987–90); Dir, E. C. Tempus Projects: Developing Schs for Democracy in Europe, Oxford Univ., 1991–2000; Co-Dir, European Sch. of Educnl Mgt, 1991–96. Chairman: Reform of Assessment at Sixteen-Plus, 1972–75; External Relations Cttee, Headmasters' Assoc., 1974–77; Secondary Heads Association: Mem. Exec., 1978–86; Press and Publications Officer, 1978–79, 1982–84; Pres., 1979–80. Chm., Jt Council of Heads, 1981; Member: Exec., UCCA, 1975–84; Schools Panel, CBI, 1975–82; Heads Panel, TUC, 1975–80; National Adv. Council on Educn for Industry and Commerce, 1974–77; Adv. Cttee on Supply and Educn of Teachers, 1982–85. Hon. Sec., 1990–94, Vice-Chm., 1994–2000, Chm., 2000–02, GTC (England and Wales) Trust. Trustee and Mem. Exec., Education 2000, 1983–89 (Hon. Sec., 1987–89); Mem. Exec., Schools Curriculum Award, 1986–91. Hon. Prof., Russian Fedn Min. of Educn (Perm State Pedagogical Univ.), 1998–. *Publications:* (ed) The School as a Centre of Enquiry,

1975; (ed) Staffing our Secondary Schools, 1980; (ed) Teacher Training and Special Educational Needs, 1985; What Future for Secondary Schools?, 1985; Secondary schools for All?, 1987, 2nd edn 1994; (ed) Management and the Psychology of Schooling, 1988; Schools and External Relations, 1989; Managing Schools, 1989; Towards the General Teaching Council, 1989; The Future Governance of Education, 1993; Developing Schools for Democracy in Europe, 1995; (ed) Developing Teaching for Special Needs in Russia, 1999; (ed with K. Van der Wolf) Opening Schools to All, 1999; (ed with J. Vanderhoeven) School Choice, Equity and Social Exclusion, 2000; (ed with J. Vanderhoeven) Reflection for Action, 2000; The General Teaching Council, 2000; (ed) Opening Windows to Change, 2002; Jean Racine: life and legend, 2006; frequent contribs on educnl topics to learned jls and symposia. *Recreation:* postal history. *Address:* 8 Northmoor Road, Oxford OX2 6UP. *T:* (01865) 556932.

SAYER, Robert; Senior Partner, Sayer Moore & Co., since 1983; President, Law Society, 1999–2000 (Vice-President, 1995–96 and 1998–99); *b* 16 Jan. 1952; *s* of Kenneth Albert Ernest Sayer and Ellen Sayer; *m* 1997, Cathy Hunt. *Educ:* Salvatorian Coll., Harrow Weald, Middx; Swansea Univ. (BA Hons). Admitted Solicitor, 1979. Law Society: Dep. Vice Pres., 1997–98; Treas., 1997–99. Hon. Mem., Inst. of Advanced Legal Studies, 2000. *Publications:* numerous articles in legal jls. *Recreations:* sailing, walking. *Address:* (office) 190 Horn Lane, W3 6PL. *T:* (020) 8993 7571. *Club:* Naval and Military.

SAYERS, Michael Patrick; QC 1988; a Recorder of the Crown Court, 1986–2005; *b* 28 March 1940; *s* of Major Herbert James Michael Sayers, RA (killed on active service, 1943) and late Joan Sheilah de Courcy Holroyd (*née* Stephenson); *m* 1976, Mrs Moussie Brougham (*née* Hallstrom); one *s* one *d*, and one step *s*. *Educ:* Harrow School; Fitzwilliam College, Cambridge (Evelyn Rothschild Scholar; MA). Called to the Bar, Inner Temple, 1970, Bencher, 1994; Junior, Central Criminal Court Bar Mess, 1975–78; Supplementary Prosecuting Counsel to the Crown, Central Criminal Court, 1977–88; a Dep. Circuit Judge, 1981–82; Asst Recorder, 1982–86. Mem. Cttee, Barristers' Benevolent Assoc., 1991–2007. Vice-Pres., Harrow Assoc., 1999– (Chm., 1992–97). Hon. Sec., Anglo-Swedish Soc., 2006–. *Recreations:* shooting, stalking, theatre, Sweden. *Address:* 2 King's Bench Walk, Temple, EC4Y 7DE. *T:* (020) 7353 1746; 41 Chelsea Crescent, Chelsea Harbour, SW10 0XB. *T:* (020) 7351 6003. *Clubs:* Garrick, Pratt's; Swinley Forest Golf.

SAYLE, Alexei David; actor, comedian, writer; *b* 7 Aug. 1952; *s* of Joseph Henry Sayle and Malka Sayle; *m* 1974, Linda Rawsthorn. *Educ:* Alsop GS, Liverpool; Southport Coll. of Art; Chelsea Sch. of Art (DipAD); Garnett Coll. (CertEd). Compère: Comedy Store Club, 1979–80; Comic Strip Club, 1980–81; *television series:* Young Ones, 1982–84; Alexei Sayle's Stuff (also writer), 1988–89, 1991; The Gravy Train, 1990; All New Alexei Sayle Show (also writer), 1994–95; Alexei Sayle's Merry-go-round, 1998; Arabian Nights, 2000; Alexei Sayle's Liverpool, 2008; *films include:* Gorky Park, 1983; Indiana Jones and the Last Crusade, 1989; Swing, 1998. Columnist: Independent; formerly on Observer, Time Out, Car, Sunday Mirror. Hon. Prof., Thames Valley Univ., 1995. *Publications:* Train to Hell, 1982; Geoffrey the Tube Train and the Fat Comedian, 1987; Great Bus Journeys of the World, 1988; Barcelona Plates (short stories), 2000; The Dog Catcher (short stories), 2001; Overtaken (novel), 2003; The Weeping Women Hotel (novel), 2006; Mister Roberts (novel), 2008. *Recreation:* walking. *Address:* c/o Cassie Mayer, 5 Old Garden House, The Lanterns, Bridge Lane, SW11 3AD. *T:* (020) 7350 0880. *Club:* Chelsea Arts.

SCACCHI, Greta; actress. *Films* include: Heat and Dust, 1983; The Coca Cola Kid, 1985; Burke & Wills; Defence of the Realm, 1986; Good Morning Babylon, 1987; A Man in Love, 1988; White Mischief, 1988; Love and Fear (Les Trois Soeurs), 1990; Presumed Innocent, 1990; Fires Within, 1991; Shattered, 1991; Turtle Beach, 1992; The Player, 1992; Salt on our Skin; The Browning Version, 1994; Jefferson in Paris, 1994; Country Life, 1994; Emma, 1996; The Serpent's Kiss; The Red Violin, 1999; Cotton Mary, 1999; Tom's Midnight Garden, 2000; Beyond the Sea, 2004; *television:* The Ebony Tower, 1984; Dr Fischer of Geneva; Waterfront (Best Actress, Penguin and Golden Logie Awards, Australia); Rasputin (Emmy for best-supporting actress), 1996; The Odyssey, 1997; Macbeth, 1997; Daniel Deronda, 2002; Miss Austen Regrets, 2008; *stage:* Cider with Rosie, Phoenix Arts, Leicester, 1982; Times Like These, Bristol Old Vic, 1985; Airbase, Oxford Playhouse, 1986; Uncle Vanya, Vaudeville, 1988; The Doll's House, Fest. of Perth, 1991; Miss Julie, 1992, Simpatico, 1996, Sydney Theatre Co.; The Guardsman, Albery, 2000; The True Life Fiction of Mata Hari Palace Theatre, Watford, 2002; Private Lives, Th. Royal, Bath, 2005; The Deep Blue Sea, Vaudeville, 2008. *Address:* c/o Conway van Gelder Grant Ltd, 3rd Floor, 18–21 Jermyn Street, SW1Y 6HP.

SCADDING, Dr John William, FRCP; Consultant Neurologist, National Hospital for Neurology and Neurosurgery, since 1982 (Medical Director, 1993–96); *b* 17 June 1948; *s* of late Prof. John Guyett Scadding, FRCP. *Educ:* University College London and UCH Med. Sch. (BSc 1st Cl. Hons, MB BS, MD). Jun. hosp. posts at UCH, Hammersmith, Brompton, Royal Free and National Hosps, 1972–82; Res. Fellow, UCL and Royal Free Hosp. Sch. of Medicine, 1978–80. Hon. Sen. Lectr, Inst. of Neurology, 1982–. Consultant Neurologist, Whittington Hosp., 1982–2003; Hon. Neurologist: St Luke's Hosp. for the Clergy, 1983–2002; Royal Soc. of Musicians, 1996–; Civilian Consultant Adviser, MoD, 1989–; Civilian Consultant Neurologist to RN, 1993–2003, to RAF, 1997–2003. Associate Dean, 2002–06, Dean, 2006–, RSocMed. *Publications:* research papers on mechanisms of pain in neurological disease; contribs to learned jls. *Recreations:* music (pianist), mountain walking. *Address:* National Hospital for Neurology and Neurosurgery, Queen Square, WC1N 3BG. *T:* (020) 7837 3611.

SCALES, Neil, OBE 2005; Chief Executive and Director General, Merseytravel, since 1999; *b* 24 June 1956; *s* of Gordon and Joyce Scales; *m* 1983, June Bradley; one *s* one *d*. *Educ:* Sunderland Poly. (BSc 1981; MSc 1984; DMS 1986); Open Univ. (MBA 1991). Apprentice, Sunderland Corp. Transport, 1972–76; engrg posts, Tyne & Wear PTE, 1976–86; Chief Engr, 1986–88, Dir of Engrg, 1988–90, Greater Manchester Buses; Man. Dir, Northern Counties, 1990–96; Greater Manchester PTE, 1996; consultant, private sector, 1997–99; Dir of Customer Services, Merseytravel, 1999. *Recreations:* Sunderland FC, tutoring with Open University. *Address:* Merseytravel, 24 Hatton Garden, Liverpool L3 2AN. *T:* (0151) 330 1101.

SCALES, Prunella, (Prunella Margaret Rumney West), CBE 1992; actress; *d* of John Richardson Illingworth and Catherine Scales; *m* 1963, Timothy Lancaster West, *qv*; two *s*. *Educ:* Moira House, Eastbourne; Old Vic Theatre School, London; Herbert Berghof Studio, New York (with Uta Hagen). Repertory in Huddersfield, Salisbury, Oxford, Bristol Old Vic, etc; seasons at Stratford-on-Avon and Chichester Festival Theatre; plays on London stage include: The Promise, 1967; Hay Fever, 1968; It's a Two-Foot-Six-Inches-Above-The-Ground-World, 1970; The Wolf, 1975; Breezeblock Park, 1978; Make and Break, 1980; An Evening with Queen Victoria, 1980; The Merchant of Venice, 1981; Quartermaine's Terms, 1981; Big in Brazil, 1984; When We Are Married, 1986; Single Spies (double bill), 1988; The School for Scandal, 1990; Long Day's Journey into Night, 1991; Mother Tongue, 1992; The Birthday Party, 1999; A Day in the Death of Joe Egg, 2001; A Woman of No Importance, 2003; regional theatre: Happy Days, Leeds, 1993; The Matchmaker, Chichester, 1993; Staying On, nat. tour, 1997; The Cherry Orchard, Oxford Playhouse, 2000; Gertrude's Secret, nat. tour, 2006–08; *films include:* Howard's End, 1992; Second Best, 1993; Wolf, 1994; An Awfully Big Adventure, 1994; An Ideal Husband, 1999; Ghost of Greville Lodge, 2001; *television:* Fawlty Towers (series), 1975, 1978; Grand Duo, The Merry Wives of Windsor, 1982; Mapp and Lucia (series), 1985–86; Absurd Person Singular, 1985; The Index Has Gone Fishing, What the Butler Saw, 1987; After Henry (series), 1988, 1990; The Rector's Wife, Fair Game, 1994; Dalziel & Pascoe, 1996; Signs and Wonders, Lord of Misrule, Breaking the Code, 1997; Midsomer Murders, 2001; Looking for Victoria, 2003; Casualty, 2004; Where the Heart Is, 2005; frequent broadcasts, readings, poetry recitals and fringe productions. Has directed plays at Bristol Old Vic, Arts Theatre, Cambridge, Billingham Forum, Almost Free Theatre, London, Nottingham Playhouse, Palace Theatre, Watford, W Yorks Playhouse, Leeds, Nat. Theatre of WA, Perth, and taught at several drama schools. Pres., CPRE, 1997–2002. Hon DLitt: Bradford, 1995; East Anglia, 1996. *Publication:* (with Timothy West) So You Want to be an Actor?, 2005. *Recreation:* gardening. *Address:* c/o Jeremy Conway, 18–21 Jermyn Street, SW1Y 6HP.

See also S. A. J. West.

SCALES, Sheila Lesley, (Mrs Roger Harris); Director, Early Years, Extended Schools and Special Educational Needs Group, Department for Children, Schools and Families (formerly Department for Education and Skills), since 2006; *b* Leeds, 22 Aug. 1949; *d* of Lesley and Hilda Scales; *m* 1973, Dr Roger Harris; three *s* one *d*. *Educ:* New Hall, Cambridge (BA 1970). Joined CS, 1970; Private Sec. to Perm. Under-Sec. of State, DES, 1973–75; Devlt Planner, Kiribati, 1977–79; Asst Chief Exec., Surrey CC, 1997–98; Dir, Local Transformation Gp, DfES, 2004–06. Gov., City Acad., Hackney, 2008–. *Address:* Department for Children, Schools and Families, Sanctuary Buildings, SW1 3BT. *T:* 07990 541514; *e-mail:* sheila.scales@dcsf.gsi.gov.uk.

SCALIA, Antonin; Associate Justice, United States Supreme Court, since 1986; *b* 11 March 1936; *s* of S. Eugene Scalia and Catherine Louise (*née* Panaro); *m* 1960, Maureen McCarthy; five *s* four *d*. *Educ:* Georgetown Univ. (AB 1957); Fribourg Univ., Switzerland; Harvard (LLB 1960; Sheldon Fellow, 1960–61). Admitted to Ohio Bar, 1962, to Virginia Bar, 1970. Associate, Jones, Day, Cockley & Reavis, Cleveland, 1961–67; Associate Prof., 1967–70, Prof., 1970–74, Univ. of Virginia Law Sch.; Gen. Counsel, Office of Telecommunications, Exec. Office of Pres., 1971–72; Chm., Admin. Conf. US, Washington, 1972–74; Asst Attorney Gen., US Office of Legal Counsel, Justice Dept, 1974–77; Prof., Law Sch., Chicago Univ., 1977–82; Judge, US Court Appeals (DC Circuit), 1982–86. American Bar Association: Mem. Council, 1974–77, Chm., 1981–82, Section Admin. Law; Chm., Conf. Section, 1982–83. Jt Editor, Regulation Magazine, 1979–82. *Address:* US Supreme Court, 1 First Street NE, Washington, DC 20543, USA.

SCALLY, Dr Gabriel John, FFPH; Regional Director of Public Health, South West Region, Department of Health, since 1996; *b* 24 Sept. 1954; *s* of Bernard Gabriel Scally and Maureen Scally (*née* Hopkins); *m* 1990, Rona Margaret Campbell; two *d*. *Educ:* St Mary's Grammar Sch., Belfast; Queen's Univ., Belfast (MB, BCh, BAO 1978); London Sch. of Hygiene and Tropical Medicine, Univ. of London (MSc 1982). MFPHM 1984, FFPH (FFPHM 1991); MFPHMI 1992; MRCGP 1993; FRCP 2004. Trainee in Gen. Practice, 1980–81; Sen. Tutor, Dept of Community Medicine, QUB, 1984–86; Consultant in Public Health Medicine, 1986–88, Chief Admin. MO and Dir of Public Health, 1989–93, Eastern Health and Social Services Bd, Belfast; Regional Director of Public Health: SE Thames RHA, 1993–94; South and West RHA, 1994–96. Member: NI Bd for Nursing, Health Visiting and Midwifery, 1988–93; Council, BMA, 1985–86, 1988–89 (Chm., Jun. Mems Forum, 1988–89); GMC, 1989–99. *Publications:* papers on med. res. and health policy in med. jls. *Recreations:* sailing, traditional and contemporary Irish music, London Irish RFC. *Address:* 11 Dowry Square, Bristol BS8 4SH. *T:* (0117) 926 8510.

SCAMPION, John, CBE 2001; DL; Chairman, Determinations Panel, Pensions Regulator, since 2005; *b* 22 Aug. 1941; *s* of John William and Rosa Mary Scampion; *m* 1995, Jennifer Mary Reeves; two *s*, and two step *d*. *Educ:* Queen Elizabeth's Grammar Sch., Alford, Lincs; Downing Coll., Cambridge (MA). Admitted solicitor, 1966; Town Clerk and Chief Exec., Solihull MBC, 1977–95; Social Fund Comr for GB and NI, 1995–2000; Comr for Immigration Services, 2000–05; Chm., Immigration Adv. Service, 2007–. Member: Criminal Injuries Compensation Appeals Panel, 1997–; Healthcare Commn (formerly Commn for Health Audit and Improvement), 2003–. DL W Midlands, 1992. *Recreations:* theatre-going, directing plays - occasionally, watching football, reading, hill walking, music listening. *Address:* Pensions Regulator, Napier House, Trafalgar Place, Brighton BN1 4DW.

SCANLAN, Dorothy, (Mrs Charles Denis Scanlan); *see* Quick, Dorothy.

SCANLAN, Prof. John Oliver, PhD, DSc; FIEEE, FIET, FIMA, FIEI; Professor of Electronic Engineering, University College Dublin, 1973–2002, now Emeritus; President, Royal Irish Academy, 1993–96; *b* 20 Sept. 1937; *s* of John and Hannah Scanlan; *m* 1961, Ann Weadock. *Educ:* University Coll. Dublin (BE, ME); Leeds Univ. (PhD); NUI (DSc). FIMA 1971; FIET (FIEE 1972); FIEEE 1976; FIEI 1980. Lectr, 1963–68, Prof. of Electronic Engrg, 1968–73, Univ. of Leeds. Dir, Telecom Eireann, 1984–97. MRIA 1977 (Sec., 1981–89). Editor, Internat. Jl of Circuit Theory and Applications, 1973–. *Publications:* Analysis and Synthesis of Tunnel Diode Circuits, 1966; Circuit Theory, vol. I, 1970, (with R. Levy) vol. II, 1973; numerous contribs to learned jls. *Recreations:* golf, music. *Address:* Department of Electronic and Electrical Engineering, University College Dublin, Dublin 4, Ireland. *T:* 7161909.

SCANLAN, Michael; Senior Partner, Russells Gibson McCaffrey (formerly Russells), Solicitors, Glasgow, since 1982; President, Law Society of Scotland, 1999–2000 (Vice-President, 1998–99); *b* 6 June 1946; *s* of William Scanlan and Agnes (Nancy) Scanlan; *m* 1971, Margaret Denvir (OBE 2006); one *s*. *Educ:* St Aloysius Coll., Glasgow; Glasgow Univ. Apprentice, T. F. Russell & Co., 1965–71; admitted solicitor, 1971; Asst, 1971–73, Partner, 1973–82, T. F. Russell & Co., subseq. Russells. Lectr in Evidence and Procedure, Strathclyde Univ., 1979–85. Ext. Examr in Evidence and Procedure, Glasgow Univ., 1982–85. Temp. Sheriff, 1986–96. Mem., Judicial Appts Bd for Scotland, 2002–08. *Recreations:* golf, reading, music. *Address:* Russells Gibson McCaffrey, 13 Bath Street, Glasgow G2 1HY; Willowfield, Kirkintilloch Road, Lenzie, Glasgow G66 4LW.

SCANLON, Mary Elizabeth; Member (C) Highlands and Islands, Scottish Parliament, 1999–2006 and since 2007; *b* 25 May 1947; *d* of John Charles Campbell and Anne Campbell (*née* O'Donnell); *m* 1970, James Scanlon; one *s* one *d*. *Educ:* Univ. of Dundee (MA Econ/Pol 1982). Civil Service Administrator; Lecturer: Dundee Inst. of Technology, 1982–85; Perth Coll., 1985–88; Lectr in Econs, Dundee Coll. of Technology, 1988–94; Lectr in Econs and Business Studies, Inverness Coll., 1994–99. Contested (C) Moray, Scottish Parlt, April 2006. *Recreations:* hill walking, swimming, gardening. *Address:* 25 Miller Street, Inverness IV2 3DN. *T:* (01463) 718951; (constituency office) 14 Ardross Street, Inverness IV3 5NS.

SCARBOROUGH, Vernon Marcus; HM Diplomatic Service, retired; Deputy High Commissioner, Tarawa, Republic of Kiribati, 2000–04; *b* 11 Feb. 1940; *s* of George Arthur Scarborough and Sarah Florence Scarborough (*née* Patey); *m* 1966, Jennifer Bernadette Keane; three *d*. *Educ:* Brockley County Grammar Sch.; Westminster Coll. Passport Office, FO, 1958–61, CRO 1961; served Dacca, Karachi, Brussels, Bathurst, later Banjul, FCO, Muscat, Lagos and El Salvador; Kuala Lumpur, 1983–86 (First Sec., 1984); FCO, 1986; Chargé d'Affaires, San Salvador, 1987–90; Dep. Consul Gen. and Trade Comr, Auckland, 1990–94; Dep. High Comr, Suva, and Ambassador to Palau, Federated States of Micronesia and Marshall Is, 1995–2000. Mem. Council, Pacific Is Soc. of UK, 2000–. *Recreations:* photography, golf. *Address:* Broadoaks, 29 Erica Way, Copthorne, W Sussex RH10 3XG. *Clubs:* Royal Commonwealth Society; Fiji, Defence, Returned Servicemen's and Ex-Servicemen's Association (Suva).

SCARBROUGH, 13th Earl of, *cr* 1690; **Richard Osbert Lumley;** Viscount Lumley (Ire.), 1628; Baron Lumley, 1681; Viscount Lumley, 1690; *b* 18 May 1973; *s* of 12th Earl of Scarbrough, and of Lady Elizabeth Ramsay, LVO, *d* of 16th Earl of Dalhousie, KT, GCVO, GBE, MC; S father, 2004; *m* 2007, Mrs Henrietta Elfrida Helen Scherman (*née* Boyson).

SCARD, Dennis Leslie; General Secretary, Musicians' Union, 1990–2000; *b* 8 May 1943; *s* of late Charles Leslie Scard and Doris Annie (*née* Farmer); *m* 1st (marr. diss.); two *s*; 2nd, 1993, Linda Perry. *Educ:* Lascelles Co. Secondary Sch.; Trinity Coll. of Music, London (Hon. Fellow, 1997). Professional horn player, 1962–85, performed with leading symphony and chamber orchestras. Part-time instrumental teacher, London Borough of Hillingdon, 1974–85. Musicians' Union: Chm., Central London Br., 1972–85; Mem., Exec. Cttee, 1979–85; full-time Official, Birmingham, 1985–90. Mem., TUC Gen. Council, 1990–2001. Bd Mem., 2002–, Dep. Chm., 2003–06, Chm., 2007–, Shoreham Port Authy. Worker Rep., DTI Central Arbitration Cttee, 2002–; Lay Mem., Employment Tribunal Service, 2005–. Member Board: Symphony Hall and Town Hall (formerly Symphony Hall), Birmingham, 1996–; Trinity Coll. of Music, 1998–2006. Chair, Music Students Hostel Trust, 2003–. FRSA 1992. *Recreations:* music, walking, theatre. *Address:* 6 Cranborne Avenue, Meads, Eastbourne BN20 7TS. *T:* (01323) 648364.

SCARDINO, Dame Marjorie (Morris), DBE 2002; DJur; Chief Executive, Pearson plc, since 1997; *b* 25 Jan. 1947; *d* of Robert Weldon and Beth Morris (*née* Lamb); adopted dual American-British nationality, 2002; *m* 1974, Albert James Scardino; two *s* one *d*. *Educ:* Baylor Univ. (BA); Univ. of San Francisco (DJur). Partner, Brannen Wessels & Searcy, 1976–85; Pres., Economist Newspaper Gp Inc., 1985–93; Chief Exec., Economist Gp, 1993–97. Trustee: V&A Mus., 2003–; Carter Center, 2003–; MacArthur Foundn, 2005–. *Address:* Pearson plc, 80 Strand, WC2R 0RL.

SCARFE, Gerald, CBE 2008; RDI 1989; artist; *b* 1 June 1936; *m* Jane Asher, *qv*; two *s* one *d*. *Educ:* scattered (due to chronic asthma as a child). Punch, 1960; Private Eye, 1961; Daily Mail, 1966; Sunday Times, 1967–; cover artist to illustrator, Time Magazine, 1967; animation and film directing for BBC, 1969–; artist, New Yorker, 1993–. Has taken part in exhibitions: Grosvenor Gall., 1969 and 1970; Pavillon d'Humour, Montreal, 1967 and 1971; Expo '70, Osaka, 1970; six sculptures of British Character, Millennium Dome, 2000. One-man exhibitions of sculptures and lithographs: Waddell Gall., New York, 1968 and 1970; Grosvenor Gall., 1969; Vincent Price Gall., Chicago, 1969; National Portrait Gall., 1971; retrospective exhibn, Royal Festival Hall, 1983; drawings: Langton Gall., 1986; Chris Beetles Gall., 1989; Gerald Scarfe Meets Walt Disney, MOMI, 1997; Gerald Scarfe, The Art of Hercules, Z Gall., NY, 1997; Nat. Portrait Gall., 1998, 2003; Cleveland Gall., 1998; Millennium Galls, Sheffield, 2005; Fine Arts Soc., London, 2005; Portcullis House, Westminster, 2008. Animated film for BBC, Long Drawn Out Trip, 1973 (prizewinner, Zagreb); Dir, Scarfe by Scarfe, BBC (BAFTA Award, 1987); Designer and Dir, animated sequences in film, The Wall, 1982; designer: Who's A Lucky Boy?, Royal Exchange, Manchester, 1984; Orpheus in the Underworld, ENO, 1985; Born Again, Chichester, 1990; The Magic Flute, Los Angeles, 1993, Houston, Texas, 1997, Seattle, 1999, San Francisco, 2007; An Absolute Turkey, Globe, 1994 (Olivier Award for best costumes); Mind Millie For Me, Haymarket, 1996; Fantastic Mr Fox, Los Angeles Opera, 1998; The Nutcracker, English Nat. Ballet, 2002; production designer, Hercules (Walt Disney film), 1995–97; costume designer, Peter and the Wolf, Holiday on Ice and world tour, 2000; animation sequence, Miss Saigon, UK tour, 2004. Hon. DLitt Kent, 2003; Hon. DArts Liverpool, 2005; Hon. LLD Dundee, 2007. *Publications:* Gerald Scarfe's People, 1966; Indecent Exposure (ltd edn), 1973; Expletive Deleted: the life and times of Richard Nixon (ltd edn), 1974; Gerald Scarfe, 1982; Father Kissmass and Mother Claws, 1985; Scarfe by Scarfe (autobiog), 1986 (televised, 1987); Scarfe's Seven Deadly Sins, 1988; Scarfe's Line of Attack, 1988; Scarfeland: a lost world of fabulous beasts and monsters, 1989; Scarfe on Stage, 1992; Scarfeface, 1993; Hades: the truth at last, 1997; Heroes and Villains, 2003; Gerald Scarfe: drawing blood - 40 years of Scarfe uncensored, 2005; Monsters, 2008. *Recreations:* drawing, painting and sculpting. *Address:* c/o 24 Cale Street, SW3 3QU.

SCARFE, Jane; *see* Asher, J.

SCARGILL, Arthur; General Secretary, Socialist Labour Party; Honorary President, National Union of Mineworkers, since 2002 (General Secretary, 1992; President, 1981–2002); *b* 11 Jan. 1938; *o c* of Harold and Alice Scargill; *m* 1961, Anne, *d* of Elliott Harper; one *d*. *Educ:* Worsbrough Dale School; White Cross Secondary School; Leeds Univ. Miner, Woolley Colliery, 1953; Mem., NUM branch cttee, 1960; Woolley branch deleg. to Yorks NUM Council, 1964; Mem., Nat. Exec., 1972, Pres., 1973, Yorks NUM. Mem., TUC Gen. Council, 1986–88. Member: Young Communists' League, 1955–62; Co-op Party, 1963; Labour Party, 1966–95; Socialist Labour Party, 1996; CND. Contested (Socialist Lab): Newport East, 1997; Hartlepool, 2001. *Address:* Socialist Labour Party, 9 Victoria Road, Barnsley, S Yorks S70 2BB.

SCARLETT, family name of **Baron Abinger**.

SCARLETT, Sir John (McLeod), KCMG 2007 (CMG 2001); OBE 1987; Chief, Secret Intelligence Service, since 2004; *b* 18 Aug. 1948; *s* of late Dr James Henri Stuart Scarlett and Clara Dunlop Scarlett; *m* 1970, Gwenda Mary Rachel Stilliard; one *s* three *d* (and one *s* decd). *Educ:* Epsom Coll.; Magdalen Coll., Oxford (MA). Secret Intelligence Service, 1971–2001: Nairobi, 1973–74; lang. student, 1974–75; Second, later First, Sec., Moscow, 1976–77; First Secretary: London, 1977–84; Paris, 1984–88; London, 1988–91; Counsellor: Moscow, 1991–94; London, 1994–2001 (Dir of Security and Public Affairs, 1999–2001); Chm., Jt Intelligence Cttee, and Intelligence Co-ordinator, then Head of Intelligence and Security Secretariat, Cabinet Office, 2001–04. *Recreations:* history, medieval churches, family. *Address:* PO Box 1300, London SE1 1BD. *Club:* Oxford and Cambridge.

SCARONI, Paolo; Chief Executive, Eni, since 2005; *b* 28 Nov. 1946; *s* of Bruno and Clementina Boniver Scaroni; *m* 1974, Francesca (*née* Zanconato); two *s* one *d*. *Educ:* Luigi Bocconi Commercial Univ., Milan (Dr Econs 1969); Columbia Univ., NY (MBA). Chevron, 1968–71; Associate, McKinsey & Co., 1972–73; Saint-Gobain, 1973–85: Financial Dir, Italy, 1973–78; General Delegate: Venezuela, Colombia, Equador, and Peru, 1978–81; Italy, 1981–84; Pres., Flat Glass Div. (world-wide), France, 1984–85; Exec. Vice-Pres., Techint, Italy, 1985–96; Pilkington plc: Pres., Automotive Products Worldwide, 1996–98; Gp Chief Exec., 1997–2002; Dep. Chm., 2002; Chief Exec., Enel SpA, 2002–05. Non-executive Director: Burmah Castrol plc, 1998–2000; BAE SYSTEMS, 2000–04; Alliance UniChem, 2003–06 (Chm., 2005–06); Mem., Supervisory Bd, ABN AMRO Bank NV, 2003–. Mem., Bd of Overseers, Columbia Business Sch., 1996–. *Publication:* (jtly) Professione Manager, 1985. *Recreations:* reading, ski-ing, golf. *Address:* Eni, Piazzale Mattei 1, 00144 Rome, Italy. *Club:* Royal Automobile.

SCARSDALE, 4th Viscount *cr* 1911; **Peter Ghislain Nathaniel Curzon;** Bt (Scot.) 1636, (Eng.) 1641; Baron Scarsdale 1761; *b* 6 March 1949; *s* of 3rd Viscount Scarsdale and his 1st wife, Solange Yvonne Palmyre Ghislaine Curzon (*née* Hanse); *S* father, 2000; *m* 1st, 1983, Mrs Karen Osborne (marr. diss. 1996); one *d*; 2nd, 1996, Michelle Reynolds. *Educ:* Ampleforth. *Heir:* *b* Hon. David James Nathaniel Curzon [*b* 3 Feb. 1958; *m* 1981, Ruth Linton; one *s* one *d*].

SCHAFF, Alistair Graham; QC 1999; *b* 25 Sept. 1959; *s* of John Schaff and Barbara Schaff (*née* Williams); *m* 1991, (Marie) Leona Burley; one *s* one *d*. *Educ:* Bishop's Stortford Coll.; Magdalene Coll., Cambridge (MA 1st Cl. Jt Hons History and Law). Called to the Bar, Inner Temple, 1983; in practice at the Bar, 1983–. *Recreations:* family life, foreign travel, history, spectator sport. *Address:* 7 King's Bench Walk, Temple, EC4Y 7DS. *T:* (020) 7583 0404.

SCHALLER, George Beals; Vice President, Wildlife Conservation Society, New York, since 2001; *b* 26 May 1933; *m* 1957, Kay Morgan; two *s*. *Educ:* Univ. of Alaska (BA, BS 1955); Univ. of Wisconsin (PhD 1962). Fellow, Center for Advanced Study in the Behavioral Sciences, Stanford Univ., 1962–63; Res. Associate, Johns Hopkins Univ., 1963–66; Wildlife Conservation (formerly NY Zoological) Society, 1966–: Dir of Internat. Progs, 1972–88; Dir for Sci., 1988–2001. *Publications:* The Mountain Gorilla, 1963; The Year of the Gorilla, 1964; The Deer and the Tiger, 1967; The Serengeti Lion, 1972; Serengeti: a kingdom of predators, 1972; Golden Shadows, Flying Hooves, 1973; Mountain Monarchs: wild sheep and goats of the Himalaya, 1977; Stones of Silence, 1980; (with Chinese co-authors) The Giant Pandas of Wolong, 1985; The Last Panda, 1993; Tibet's Hidden Wilderness, 1997; Wildlife of the Tibetan Steppe, 1998; (ed jtly) Antelopes, Deer and Relatives, 2000. *Recreations:* watching wildlife, photography. *Address:* Wildlife Conservation Society, 185th Street and Southern Boulevard, Bronx, NY 10460, USA.

SCHALLY, Dr Andrew Victor; Distinguished Medical Research Scientist, Veterans Affairs Department, and Chief of Endocrine, Polypeptide and Cancer Institute, Veteran Affairs Medical Center, Miami, since 2006; Professor, University of Miami, Miller School of Medicine, since 2006; *b* Wilno, Poland, 30 Nov. 1926; US Citizen (formerly Canadian Citizen); *s* of Casimir and Maria Schally; *m* 1st, 1956, Margaret White (marr. diss.); one *s* one *d*; 2nd, 1976, Ana Maria Comaru (*d* 2004). *Educ:* Bridge of Allan, Scotland (Higher Learning Cert.); London (studied chemistry); McGill Univ., Montreal, Canada (BSc Biochem., 1955; PhD Biochem., 1957). Res. Assistant: Dept of Biochem., Nat. Inst. for Med. Res., MRC, Mill Hill, 1949–52; Endocrine Unit, Allan Meml Inst. for Psych., McGill Univ., Montreal, 1952–57; Baylor University Coll. of Medicine, Texas Med. Center: Res. Associate, Dept of Physiol., 1957–60; Asst Prof. of Physiol., Dept of Physiol., and Asst Prof. of Biochem., Dept of Biochem., 1960–62; Chief, Endocrine, Polypeptide and Cancer Inst., Veterans Admin Hosp., then Veterans Affairs Med. Center, New Orleans, 1962–2006, Sen. Med. Investigator, 1973–99; Tulane University School of Medicine, New Orleans: Associate Prof., 1962–67; Prof. of Medicine, 1967–2006; Head, Section of Experimental Medicine, 1978–2006. Member: Endocrine Soc., USA; AAAS; Soc. of Biol Chemists; Amer. Physiol Soc.; Soc. for Experimental Biol. and Med.; Amer. Assoc. for Cancer Res.; Amer. Soc. for Reproductive Medicine; Internat. Brain Res. Org.; Nat. Acad. of Medicine, Mexico; Nat. Acad. of Medicine, Brazil; Nat. Acad. of Medicine, Venezuela; Nat. Acad. of Scis (US); Hungarian Acad. of Scis; Acad. of Scis, Russia, 1991; Acad. of Medicine, Poland, 1995; Royal Acad. of Medicine, Spain, 2004. Hon. Member: Chilean Endocrine Soc.; Mexican Soc. of Nutrition and Endocrinol.; Acad. of Med. Sciences of Cataluna and Baleares; Endocrine Soc. of Madrid; Polish Soc. of Internal Med.; Endocrine Soc. of Ecuador; Endocrine Soc. of Peru. Dr *hc* State Univ. of Rio de Janeiro, 1977; Rosario, Argentina, 1979; Univ. Peruana Cayetano Heredia, Lima, 1979; Univ. Nat. de San Marcos, Lima, 1979; MD *hc*: Tulane, 1978; Cadiz, 1979; Univ. Villareal-Lima, 1979; Copernicus Med. Acad., Cracow, 1979; Chile, 1979; Buenos Aires, 1980; Salamanca, 1981; Complutense Univ., Madrid, 1984; Pécs Univ., 1986; Autónoma, Madrid, 1994; Alcala, Madrid, 1996; Malaga, 2002; Milan, 2005; Hon. DSc McGill, 1979; Hon. Dr Université René Descartes, Paris, 1987; Hon. Dr rer. nat. Regensburg Univ., 1992; Hon. Dr Nat. Sci. Salzburg, 1997; Hon. Dr: Federal Univ. Porto Alegre, Brazil, 1998; Univ. Nacional Autónoma de México, 2001; Rio de Janeiro, 2003; Athens, 2003. Nobel Prize in Physiology or Medicine, 1977. Veterans Administration: William S. Middleton Award, 1970; Exceptional Service Award and Medal, 1978. Van Meter Prize, Amer. Thyroid Assoc., 1969; Ayerst-Squibb Award, US Endocrine Soc., 1970; Charles Mickle Award, Faculty of Med., Univ. of Toronto, 1974; Gairdner Foundn Internat. Award, Toronto, 1974; Edward T. Tyler Award, 1975; Borden Award, Assoc. of Amer. Med. Colls, 1975; Albert Lasker Basic Med. Res. Award, 1975; Spanish Pharmaceutical Soc., 1977; Laude Award, 1978; Heath Meml Award from M. D. Anderson Tumour Inst., 1989. Member Editorial Board: Life Sciences, 1980–; Peptides, 1980–; The Prostate, 1985–. *Publications:* (compiled and ed with William Locke) The Hypothalamus and Pituitary in Health and Disease, 1972; over 2200 other pubns (papers, revs, books, abstracts). *Address:* Research Service (151), Veterans Administration Medical Center, 1201 NW 16th Street, Miami, FL 33125, USA. *T:* (305) 5753126.

SCHAMA, Prof. Simon Michael, CBE 2001; University Professor, Department of History, Columbia University, since 1997; art critic, New Yorker, since 1995; *b* 13 Feb. 1945; *s* of Arthur Osias Schama and Gertrude Steinberg Schama; *m* 1983, Virginia Papaioannou; one *s* one *d*. *Educ:* Christ's Coll., Cambridge (BA 1966; MA 1969; Hon. Fellow, 1995). Fellow and Dir of Studies in History, Christ's Coll., Cambridge, 1966–76; Fellow and Tutor in Modern History, Brasenose Coll., Oxford, 1976–80; Mellon Prof. of History, 1980–90, and Kenan Prof., 1990–93, Harvard Univ.; Old Dominion Foundation Prof. in the Humanities, Columbia Univ., 1993–96. Writer and presenter: A History of Britain, BBC TV Series, 2000, 2001, 2002; Simon Schama's Power of Art, BBC2, 2006; The American Future: A History, 2008. *Publications:* Patriots and Liberators: revolution in the Netherlands 1780–1813, 1978; Two Rothschilds and the Land of Israel, 1979; The Embarrassment of Riches: an interpretation of Dutch culture in the Golden Age, 1987; Citizens: a chronicle of the French Revolution, 1989; Dead Certainties (Unwarranted Speculations), 1991; Landscape and Memory, 1995; Rembrandt's Eyes, 1999; A History of Britain, vol. 1, 3000 BC–AD 1603, 2000, vol. 2, The British Wars 1603–1776, 2001, vol. 3, The Fate of Empire 1776–2000, 2002; Hang-Ups: essays on painting (mostly), 2004; Rough Crossings, 2005; Power of Art, 2006; The American Future: a history, 2008.

Recreations: Bordeaux wine, gardening, Brazilian music. *Address:* Department of History, Fayerweather Hall, Columbia University, New York, NY 10027, USA. *T:* (212) 8544593. *Club:* Century (New York).

SCHAPIRA, Prof. Anthony Henry Vernon, MD; DSc; FRCP, FMedSci; Chairman, and Professor of Neurology, University Department of Clinical Neurosciences, Royal Free and University College Medical School, and Professor of Neurology, Institute of Neurology, University College London, since 1990; *b* 3 Sept. 1954; *s* of Markus and Constance Schapira; *m* 2003, Laura Jean Johnson; one *d. Educ:* Bradford Grammar Sch.; Westminster Med. Sch., London Univ. (BSc Hons, AKC; MB BS, MD, DSc). MRCP, FRCP 1992; FMedSci 1999. House Physician to Chief Physician to the Queen, 1979; med. trng, Hammersmith and Whittington Hosps, Nat. Hosp. for Neurology and Neurosurgery and St Thomas' Hosp., 1980–84; trng in neurology, Royal Free Hosp. and Nat. Hosp. for Neurology and Neurosurgery, 1983–88; Wellcome Res. Fellow, 1985–87; Sen. Lectr and Consultant in Neurology, Royal Free Hosp. and UC Med. Sch., and Inst. of Neurology, London, 1988–90; Consultant Neurologist, Royal Free Hosp. and Nat. Hosp. for Neurology and Neurosurgery, 1988–. Hon. Prof. of Neurology, Mount Sinai Med. Sch., NY, 1995. Member: Movement Disorders Soc., 1992–; Harveian Soc., 1994–. Queen Square Prize, Inst. of Neurology, 1986; Graham Bull Prize for Clinical Sci., RCP, 1995; European Prize for Clinical Sci., Eur. Soc. Clin. Sci., 1998; Buckston Browne Medal, Harveian Soc., 1995; Opprecht Prize, Neurol. Soc. Switzerland, 1999; Duchenne Prize, German Neurol. Soc., 2005. *Publications:* (ed jtly) Mitochondrial Disorders in Neurology, 1994, 2nd edn 2002; Mitochondria: DNA, protein and disease, 1994; (ed jtly) Muscle Diseases, 1999; (ed jtly) Clinical Cases in Neurology, 2001; (ed) Mitochondrial Function and Dysfunction, 2002; Treatment of Parkinson's Disease, 2005; Understanding Parkinson's Disease, 2005; Neurology and Clinical Neuroscience, 2007. *Recreations:* chess (Yorkshire champion, 1966), European history, international affairs. *Address:* University Department of Clinical Neurosciences, Royal Free and University College Medical School, Rowland Hill Street, NW3 2PF. *T:* (020) 7830 2012, *Fax:* (020) 7431 1577; *e-mail:* anthony.schapira@royalfree.nhs.uk.

SCHAPIRO, Isabel Margaret; *see* Madariaga, I. M. de.

SCHARPING, Rudolf; Member, Bundestag, 1994–2005; Deputy Chairman, Social Democratic Party of Europe, 2001 (Chairman, 1994–2001); *b* Niederelbert, Westerwald, 2 Dec. 1947. *Educ:* Univ. of Bonn. State Chm. and Nat. Dep. Chm., Jusos (Young Socialists), 1966; joined SPD, 1966; Rhineland-Palatinate: Mem., State Parlt, 1975–94; Leader, SPD, 1985–91; Leader of Opposition, 1985–91; Minister-Pres., 1991–94; Leader of Opposition, 1994–98; Dep. Chm., SPD, 1995–2003 (Chm., 1993–95); Minister of Defence, 1998–2002. *Address:* c/o Bundeshaus, Platz der Republik, 11011 Berlin, Germany.

SCHÄUBLE, Dr Wolfgang; Member of Bundestag, since 1972; Federal Minister of the Interior, since 2005; Deputy Chairman, CDU/CSU Parliamentary Group, Germany, 2002–05 (Chairman, 1991–2000); *b* 18 Sept. 1942; *s* of Karl Schäuble and Gertrud (*née* Göhring); *m* 1969, Ingeborg Hensle; one *s* three *d. Educ:* Univ. of Freiburg; Univ. of Hamburg (Dr jur 1971). Tax Revenue Dept, State of Baden-Württemberg, 1971–72; solicitor, 1978–84; Parly Sec., CDU/CSU, 1981–84; Federal Minister with special responsibility and Head of Federal Chancellery, 1984–89; Federal Minister of the Interior, 1989–91. Chm., 1998–2000, Mem. Governing Bd, 2000–, CDU, Germany. Chairman: CDU Cttee on Sports, 1976–84; Working Gp, European Border Regions, 1979–82. Grosskreuz des Verdienstordens der Bundesrepublik Deutschland, 1990. *Publications:* Der Vertrag, 1991; Und der Zukunft zugewandt, 1994; Mitten im Leben, 2000; Scheitert der Westen?, 2003. *Recreation:* classical music. *Address:* (office) c/o Deutscher Bundestag, Platz der Republik 1, 11011 Berlin, Germany; *e-mail:* wolfgang.schaeuble@bundestag.de; *web:* www.wolfgang-schaeuble.de.

SCHAUFUSS, Peter; ballet dancer, producer, choreographer, director; *b* 26 April 1950; *s* of late Frank Schaufuss and Mona Vangsaae, former solo dancers with Royal Danish Ballet. *Educ:* Royal Danish Ballet School. Apprentice, Royal Danish Ballet, 1965; soloist, Nat. Ballet of Canada, 1967–68; Royal Danish Ballet, 1969–70; Principal, London Festival Ballet, 1970–74; NY City Ballet, 1974–77; Principal, National Ballet of Canada, 1977–83; Artistic Dir, London Fest. Ballet, later English Nat. Ballet, 1984–90; Dir of Ballet, Deutsche Oper, Berlin, 1990–93; Ballet Dir, Royal Danish Ballet, 1994–95; Founder Dir, Peter Schaufuss Ballet, 1997–. Guest appearances in Austria, Canada, Denmark, France, Germany, Greece, Israel, Italy, Japan, Norway, S America, Turkey, UK, USA, USSR; Presenter, Dancer, BBC, 1984; numerous TV appearances. Roles created for him in: Phantom of the Opera; Orpheus; Verdi Variations; The Steadfast Tin Soldier; Rhapsodie Espagnole. Produced ballets: La Sylphide (London Fest. Ballet, Stuttgart Ballet, Roland Petit's Ballet de Marseille, Deutsche Oper Berlin, Teatro Comunale, Florence, Vienna State Opera, Opernhaus Zurich, Teatro dell' Opera di Roma, Hessisches Staatstheater, Wiesbaden, Ballet du Rhin, Royal Danish Ballet, Ballet West); Napoli (Nat. Ballet of Canada, Teatro San Carlo, English Nat. Ballet); Folktale (Deutsche Oper Berlin); Dances from Napoli (London Fest. Ballet); Bournonville (Aterballetto); The Nutcracker (English Nat. Ballet, Deutsche Oper, Berlin); Giselle, Sleeping Beauty, Swan Lake, Tchaikovsky Trilogy (Deutsche Oper, Berlin). Staging for Ashton's Romeo and Juliet, and prod. and choreog. Hamlet, Royal Danish Ballet, 1996; produced and/or choreographed, for Peter Schaufuss Ballet, new versions of: Swan Lake, Sleeping Beauty, The Nutcracker, 1997; Hamlet, Romeo and Juliet, 1998; The King, Manden der Onskede Sig en Havudsigt, 1999; Midnight Express, The Three Presents, 2000; Hans Christian Andersen, 2001; Satisfaction, 2007; Divas, 2008. Solo award, 2nd Internat. Ballet Competition, Moscow, 1973; Star of the Year, Munich Abendzeitung, 1978; Evening Standard and SWET ballet award, 1979; Manchester Evening News theatre award, 1986; Lakerolprisen, Copenhagen, 1988; Berlin Co. award, Berlinerzeitung, 1991; Edinburgh Festival Critics' Prize, 1991. Knight of the Dannebrog (Denmark), 1988; Officier de l'Ordre de la Couronne (Belgium), 1995. *Recreation:* boxing. *Address:* c/o Peter Schaufuss Ballet, Den Roede Plads 10, 7500 Holstebro, Denmark.

SCHEEL, Walter; Grand Cross First Class of Order of Merit of Federal Republic of Germany; President of the Federal Republic of Germany, 1974–79; *b* 8 July 1919; *m* 1942, Eva Kronenberg (*d* 1966); one *s*; *m* 1969, Dr Mildred Wirtz (*d* 1985); one *s* two *d*; *m* 1988, Barbara Wiese. *Educ:* Real Gymnasium, Solingen. Served in German Air Force, War of 1939–45. Founder and Partner, Interfinanz, and Intermarket, 1946–61. Mem. of Bundestag, 1953–74; Federal Minister for Economic Co-operation, 1961–Oct. 1966, Vice-President of Bundestag, 1967–69; Vice-Chancellor and Foreign Minister, 1969–74. Mem., Landtag North Rhine Westphalia, 1950–54; Mem. European Parlt, 1958–61 (Vice-Chm., Liberal Gp; Chm., Cttee on Co-operation with Developing Countries). Free Democratic Party: Mem., 1946; Mem. Exec. Cttee for North Rhine/Westphalia, 1953–74; Mem. Federal Exec., 1956–74; Chm., 1968–74; Hon. Pres., 1979. Member, Supervisory Board: Thyssen AG, 1979–99; Thyssen Stahl, 1983–99. Hon. Chm., Deutsche Investitions und Entwicklungs GmbH, 1998–. Holds numerous hon. degrees and foreign decorations. *Publications:* Konturen einer neuen Welt, 1965; Formeln deutscher Politik, 1968; Warum Mitbestimmung und wie - eine Diskussion, 1970; Reden und Interviews, 1969–79; Vom Recht des anderen, 1977; Die Zukunft der Freiheit, 1979; Wen schmerzt noch Deutschlands Teilung?, 1986. *Address:* Persönliches Büro, Postfach 08 06 62, 10006 Berlin, Germany.

SCHEELE, Sir Nicholas Vernon, KCMG 2001; President, Ford Motor Company, 2001–05 (Chief Operating Officer, 2001–04); Chairman, Key Safety Systems Inc., USA, since 2007; *b* 3 Jan. 1944; *s* of late Werner James Scheele and Norah Edith Scheele (*née* Gough); *m* 1967, Rosamund Ann Jacobs; two *s* one *d. Educ:* Durham Univ. (BA). Purchasing, Supply, Procurement, Ford of Britain, 1966–78; Ford of US: Purchasing, Supply, Procurement Management, 1978–83; Dir, Supply Policy and Planning, 1983–85; Dir, Body and Chassis Parts Purchasing, 1985–88; Pres., Ford of Mexico, 1988–91; Vice-Chm., Jan.–April 1992, Chm. and Chief Exec., 1992–99, Jaguar Cars; Sen. Vice-Pres., April–July 1999, Chm., July 1999–2001, Ford of Europe; Mem. Supervisory Bd, Ford Werke AG, 1999–2001; Vice-Pres. for N America, Ford Motor Co., 2001. Dir, W Midlands Radio, 2000–. Member Council: Midlands Region, Inst. of Dirs, 1994–99; SMMT, 1992–99; President: Motor and Allied Trades Benevolent Fund, 1996–97; Coventry and Warwicks Partnership; Midlands Business of the Year, 1996; Chm., Business in the Arts, West Midlands, 1997–99. Chairman: Prince of Wales Business and Envmt Cttee, 1999–2006; Manufacturing Theme Gp, Foresight, 2020, 1999–2002; (non-exec.) CMI (Cambridge/MIT jt commercial venture), 2005–. Non-executive Director: BAT, 2005–; Grupo Proeza (Mexico), 2005–; Pegasus Gp Hldgs (USA), 2005–; Caparo Gp Ltd, 2006–. Member, Advisory Board: British American Chamber of Commerce, 1995–99; Fulbright Commn, 1995–99. Member, Board of Advisors: Coventry Univ., 1995–; Durham Univ., 1996–. Chancellor, Warwick Univ., 2002–. Pres., Coventry Mus. of Transportation, 2006–. Life Mem., NSPCC (Chm., Coventry Centenary Appeal, 1994–96); mem. charity bds and cttees devoted to children's welfare, community relns and indust. regeneration. Hon. RCM. Hon. FIMechE 2000. Gold Medal: IMI Castrol, 1999; IMechE, 2000; Carmen's Co., 2000. 6 hon. doctorates. *Publications:* articles on manufg efficiency, quality, envmtl affairs, and youth employment and trng. *Recreations:* reading, classical music, golf, tennis, squash. *Clubs:* Royal Automobile; Catawba Island (Great Lakes); Bloomfield Hills Country (Bloomfield Hills); Loblolly (Florida).

SCHELLING, Prof. Thomas Crombie, PhD; Distinguished University Professor, University of Maryland, 1990–2003, now Professor Emeritus; *b* 14 April 1921; *s* of John M. Schelling and Zelda Ayres Schelling; *m* 1989, Alice Coleman; four *s. Educ:* Univ. of Calif, Berkeley (AB 1944); Harvard Univ. (PhD 1951). US Bureau of the Budget, 1945–46; ECA, Europe, 1948–51; White House and Exec. Office of the President, 1951–53; Associate Prof., then Prof. of Econs, Yale Univ., 1953–58; RAND Corp., 1958–59; Prof. of Econs, 1959–90, Lucius N. Littauer Prof. of Political Econ., 1969–90, now Emeritus, Harvard Univ. (Jtly) Nobel Prize for Econs, 2005. *Publications:* National Income Behavior, 1951; International Economics, 1958; The Strategy of Conflict, 1960; (with Morton H. Halperin) Strategy and Arms Control, 1961; Arms and Influence, 1966; Micromotives and Macrobehavior, 1978; Thinking Through the Energy Problem, 1979; Choice and Consequence, 1984; Strategies of Commitment, 2006. *Recreation:* hiking. *Address:* 4506 Wetherill Road, Bethesda, MD 20816, USA. *T:* (301) 3209411, *Fax:* (301) 3206698; *e-mail:* tschelli@umd.edu.

SCHELLNHUBER, Prof. Hans Joachim, (John), Hon. CBE 2004; PhD; Director, Potsdam Institute for Climate Impact Research, and Professor for Theoretical Physics, Potsdam University, since 1993; Distinguished Science Advisor, Tyndall Centre for Climate Change Research, since 2005; *b* 7 June 1950; *s* of Gottlieb and Erika Schellnhuber; *m* 1981, Petra (*d* 2001); *m* 2003, Margret Boysen; one *s. Educ:* Regensburg Univ. (MSc; PhD); Univ. of California, Santa Barbara and Santa Cruz; Oldenburg Univ. (Habitation). Heisenberg Fellow, 1987–89; Prof. for Theoretical Physics, Oldenburg Univ., 1989–93; Res. Dir, Tyndall Centre for Climate Change Res., and Prof. for Envmtl Scis, UEA, 2001–05. Vis. Prof. of Physics, Oxford Univ., 2005–. Mem., German Adv. Council on Global Change, 1992–; Chm., Global Change Adv. Gp, EC, 2002–06; Chief Govt Advr on Climate to German EU/G8 Presidency, 2007; Mem., High-Level Adv. Gp on Energy and Climate to Pres. EU Commn, 2007–. Scientific Mem., Max Planck Soc., 2002–. Member: NAS, 2005; German Nat. Acad. (formerly German Acad. of Scis) Leopoldina, 2007. Wolfson Res. Merit Award, Royal Soc., 2002; German Envmt Prize, Deutsche Bunderstsftung Umwelt, 2007. *Publications:* author or editor of about 40 books on complex systems theory and environmental analysis; about 200 articles in Nature, Science, Physical Rev. Letters, etc. *Recreations:* Romanesque art, philosophy of science, reading about history, mountain hiking. *Address:* Potsdam Institute for Climate Impact Research, PO Box 601203, 14412 Potsdam, Germany. *T:* (331) 2882501, *Fax:* (331) 2882600; *e-mail:* john@pik-potsdam.de.

SCHERER, Paul Joseph; Managing Director, 1982–95, Chairman, 1995–96, Transworld Publishers Ltd; *b* 28 Dec. 1933; *s* of François Joseph Scherer and Florence (*née* Haywood); *m* 1959, Mary Fieldus; one *s* three *d. Educ:* Stonyhurst Coll. National Service, commnd BUFFS (Royal E Kent Regt), 1952–54. Bailey Bros & Swinfen, 1954–56; Jun. Editor, G. Bell & Sons, 1956–58; Sales Man., Penguin Books, 1958–63; Gp Sales Dir, Paul Hamlyn, 1963–68; William Collins Sons & Co.: Man. Dir, Internat. Div., 1968–77; Pres., Collins & World USA, 1974–75; Man. Dir, Mills & Boon, 1977–82; Sen. Vice Pres., Bantam Doubleday Dell Publishing Gp Inc., 1990–98; Chm., Curtis Brown Gp, 1996–2004. Director: Bloomsbury Publishing plc, 1993–2006 (Vice-Chm., 2004–06); Book Tokens Ltd, 1995–2002. Member Board: Book Develt Council, 1971–74; Book Marketing Council, 1977–84 (Chm., 1982–84); British Library, 1996–2000; Mem. Council, Publishers Assoc., 1982–84 and 1989–94 (Pres., 1991–93); Pres., Book Trade Benevolent Soc., 1995–99. Trustee, Whizz-Kidz, 1996–2001 (Chm., 1998–2000). Founding Chm., Unicorn Sch., Kew, 1970–73; Gov., Worth Sch., 1993–96. *Recreation:* laughing at my own jokes. *Address:* 18 Carlyle Mansions, Cheyne Walk, SW3 5LS. *T:* (020) 7376 7570. *Clubs:* Garrick, Hurlingham.

SCHIEMANN, Rt Hon. Sir Konrad Hermann Theodor, Kt 1986; PC 1995; a Judge of the Court of Justice of the European Communities, since 2004; *b* 15 Sept. 1937; *s* of Helmuth and Beate Schiemann; *m* 1965, Elisabeth Hanna Eleonore Holroyd-Reece; one *d. Educ:* King Edward's Sch., Birmingham; Freiburg Univ.; Pembroke Coll., Cambridge (Schol.; MA, LLB; Hon. Fellow, 1998). Served Lancs Fusiliers, 1956–58 (commnd, 1957). Called to Bar, Inner Temple, 1962 (Bencher, 1985; Reader, 2002; Treas., 2003); Junior Counsel to the Crown, Common Law, 1978–80; QC 1980; a Recorder of the Crown Court, 1985–86; a Justice of the High Court, QBD, 1986–95; a Lord Justice of Appeal, 1995–2004. Chairman of panels conducting Examinations in Public of: North-East Hants and Mid Hants Structure Plans, 1979; Merseyside Structure Plan, 1980; Oxfordshire Structure Plan, 1984. Mem., Parole Bd, 1990–92 (Vice-Chm., 1991–92). Member Advisory Board: Centre for Eur. Legal Studies, Cambridge Univ., 1996–; Eur. Competition Jl, 2005–; Eur. Law Rev., 2007–. Mem. Council of Mgt, British Inst. of Internat. and Comparative Law, 2000–06. Patron, Busoga Trust, 1999– (Chm., 1989–99); Trustee, St John's, Smith Square, 1990– (Chm., 1994–2004). Dir, Acad. of Ancient Music, 2001–04; Gov., English Nat. Ballet, 1995–2001. *Publications:* contrib. English and

German legal books and jls. *Recreations:* music, reading. *Address:* Court of Justice of the European Communities, Plateau du Kirchberg, 2925 Luxembourg.

SCHIFF, András; concert pianist and conductor; *b* Budapest, 21 Dec. 1953; *s* of Odon Schiff and Klara Schiff (*née* Csengeri); *m* 1987, Yuuko Shiokawa. *Educ:* Franz Liszt Academy of Music, Budapest; with Prof. Pal Kadosa, Ferenc Rados and Gyorgy Kurtag; private study with George Malcolm. Artistic Dir, September Chamber Music Fest., Mondsee, Austria, 1989–98; Co-founder, Ittinger Pfingstkonzerte, Switzerland, 1995; Founder, Homage to Palladio Fest., Vicenza, Italy, 1998; Artist in Residence, Kunstfest, Weimar, 2004–. Concerts as soloist with orchestras including: NY Philharmonic, Chicago Symphony, Vienna Phil., Concertgebouw, Orch. de Paris, London Phil., London Symph., Philharmonia, Royal Phil., Israel Phil., Philadelphia, Washington Nat. Symph.; orchestras conducted include: Baltimore Symphony, Chamber Orch. of Europe, City of Birmingham Symphony, Danish Radio, LA Philharmonic, Philadelphia and Philharmonia; major festival performances include: Salzburg, Lucerne, Edinburgh, Aldeburgh, Tanglewood, Feldkirch Schubertiade, Lucerne. Created Cappella Andrea Barca orch., 1999. Recordings include: extensive Bach repertoire (Grammy Award for recording of English Suites, 1990); all Mozart Piano Sonatas; all Mozart Piano Concertos; all Schubert Sonatas; all Bartok Piano Concertos; all Beethoven Piano Concertos; Lieder records with Peter Schreier, Robert Holl and Cecilia Bartoli. Hon. Mem., Beethoven House, Bonn, 2006. Prizewinner, Tchaikovsky competition, Moscow, 1974 and Leeds comp., 1975; Liszt Prize, 1977; Premio, Accademia Chigiana, Siena, 1987; Wiener Flotenuhr, 1989; Bartok Prize, 1991; Instrumentalist of the Year, Internat. Classical Music Awards, 1993; Claudio Arrau Meml Medal, 1994; Instrumentalist of the Year, Royal Philharmonic Soc., 1994; Kossuth Prize, 1996; Deutsche Schallplattenkrik, 1996; Leonie Sonnings Music Prize, Copenhagen, 1997; Palladio d'Oro, Citta di Vicenza, 2003; Musikfest Preis, Bremen, 2003; Abbiati Prize, 2007; Bach Prize, RAM, 2007. *Recreations:* literature, languages, soccer, theatre, art, cinema. *Address:* c/o Terry Harrison Artists Management, The Orchard, Market Street, Charlbury, Oxon OX7 3PJ.

SCHIFF, Heinrich; conductor; 'cellist; *b* Gmunden, Austria, 18 Nov. 1951. Studied with Tobias Kühne and André Navarra; attended Hans Swarovsky's conducting class. Joined professional orchestras, 1986; Chief Conductor and Guest Conductor of numerous orchestras in Austria, Finland, Germany, Holland, Sweden, Switzerland, UK, USA; also opera director. Principal Conductor: Musikcollegium, Winterthur, 1995–; Copenhagen Philharmonic Orchestra, 1995–. Numerous recordings. *Address:* Intermusica Artists' Management, 16 Duncan Terrace, N1 8BZ.

SCHIFFRIN, Prof. David Jorge, PhD; FRSC; Brunner Professor of Physical Chemistry, University of Liverpool, 1990–2004, now Emeritus; *b* 8 Jan. 1939; *s* of Bernardo Schiffrin and Berta Kurlat Schiffrin; *m* 1965, Margery Watson; one *s* one *d*. *Educ:* Univ. of Buenos Aires (BSc); Univ. of Birmingham (PhD). FRSC 1997. Lectr in Physical Chemistry, Univ. of Buenos Aires, 1966; Asst Technical Manager, CIABASA, Buenos Aires, 1967; Lectr in Physical Chemistry, Chemistry Dept, Univ. of Southampton, 1968–72; Head of Applied Electrochemistry Div., Nat. Inst. of Technology, Buenos Aires, 1972–77; Manager and Dir, Wolfson Centre for Electrochemical Science, 1979–90, Sen. Lectr, Chemistry Dept, 1988–90, Univ. of Southampton. Vis. Prof., Helsinki Univ. of Technol., 2004–. Foreign Mem., Finnish Soc. of Scis and Letters, 1996. Electrochemistry Medal and Prize, RSC, 2001. Member: Editorial Bd, Jl of Electroanalytical Chemistry, 1997–; Advisory Editorial Board: PhysChemComm, 2002–03; Physical Chemistry Chemical Physics, 2005–. *Publications:* numerous articles in jls; chapters in books. *Recreations:* hill walking, music, photography. *Address:* Chemistry Department, University of Liverpool, Liverpool L69 7ZD. *T:* (0151) 794 3574.

SCHILD, Geoffrey Christopher, CBE 1993; PhD, DSc; FRCPath, FRCPE, FMedSci; FIBiol; Director, National Institute for Biological Standards and Control, 1985–2002; Chief Scientific Officer, InB:Biotechnologies Inc., USA, since 2006; *b* 28 Nov. 1935; *s* of Christopher and Georgina Schild; *m* 1961, Tora Madland; two *s* one *d*. *Educ:* High Storrs Sch., Sheffield; Univ. of Reading (BSc Hons 1954; DSc 1993); Univ. of Sheffield (PhD 1963). FIBiol 1978; FRCPath 1993; FRCPE 1998. Hon. FRCP 1995. Res. Fellow 1961–63, Lectr in Virology 1963–67, Univ. of Sheffield; National Institute for Medical Research: Mem., Scientific Staff of MRC, 1967–75; Dir, World Influenza Centre, 1970–75; Hd, Div. of Virology, Nat. Inst. for Biol Standards, 1975–85; Dir, MRC Directed Prog. of AIDS Res., 1987–95. Professional Affairs Officer, Soc. for Gen. Microbiol., 2002–. Chm., WHO Steering Cttee on Biomed. Res. on AIDS, 1987–90; Member: WHO Scientific Adv. Gp on Vaccine Develt, 1991–; Strategic Planning Task Force, Internat. Children's Vaccine Initiative, 1996; Bd, UK Health Protection Agency, 2003–. Chm., Steering Cttee, Acad. Med. Scis Forum on safety assessment of medicinal products, 2004–; Actg Chm., Internat. Soc. for Influenza and other Respiratory Viruses, 2006–. Mem. Council, RVC, Univ. of London, 2005–. Vice Chm. Bd of Trustees, UNDP Internat. Vaccine Inst., Seoul, 1995–. Freeman, City of London, 1989. FMedSci 2001. Hon. DSc Sheffield, 2002. *Publications:* Influenza, the Virus and the Disease, 1975, 2nd edn 1985; some 300 original res. papers on virology in learned jls. *Recreations:* hill walking, music, ornithology. *Address:* e-mail: the.schilds@btinternet.com.

SCHINDLER, Prof. David William, DPhil; FRS 2001; FRSC 1983; Killam Memorial Professor of Ecology, University of Alberta, since 1989. *Educ:* N Dakota State Univ. (BSc 1962); St Catherine's Coll., Oxford (Rhodes Schol.; DPhil 1966). Asst Prof., Trent Univ., 1966–68; Prog. Leader, then Res. Scientist, Experimental Limnology Prog., Freshwater Inst., and Founder and Dir, Experimental Lakes Project, Dept of Fisheries and Oceans, Canada, 1968–89. Adjunct Prof., Univ. of Manitoba, 1971–89. *Publications:* contrib. learned jls. *Address:* Department of Biological Sciences, University of Alberta, Edmonton, AB T6G 2E9, Canada.

SCHLAGMAN, Richard Edward; Chairman and Publisher, Phaidon Press Ltd, since 1990; *b* 11 Nov. 1953; *s* of Jack Schlagman and late Shirley Schlagman (*née* Goldston). *Educ:* University Coll. Sch., Hampstead; Brunel Univ. Co-Founder, Jt Chm., and Man. Dir, Interstate Electronics Ltd, 1973–86; purchased Bush from Rank Orgn, renamed IEL Bush Radio Ltd, 1981, floated on London Stock Exchange, 1984; sold as Bush Radio Plc, 1986; acquired Phaidon Press Ltd, 1990; President: Phaidon Press Inc., 1998–; Phaidon SARL, 1999–; Phaidon Verlag, 2000–; Phaidon KK, 2004–. Mem., Exec. Cttee, Patrons of New Art, Tate Gall., 1994–97. Mem., Judd Foundn, Marfa, Texas, 1999– (Pres., 1999–2001); Jury Mem., City of Ascona Concert Hall Architecture Comp., 2004. Member: Royal Opera House Trust; Glyndebourne Fest. Soc.; British Design and Art Direction; Freunde der Bayreuther Festspiele; Freunde der Salzburger Festspiele. Patron: Bayreuther Festspiele; Salzburger Festspiele; Whitechapel Art Gall.; Schubertiade; supporter, Fest. and Acad. de Verbier. FRSA 1994. *Recreations:* music, art, architecture. *Address:* Phaidon Press Ltd, 18 Regent's Wharf, All Saints Street, N1 9PA. *T:* (020) 7843 1100, (020) 7843 1212; *e-mail:* richard@phaidon.com.

SCHLESINGER, David Adam; Editor-in-Chief, Reuters, since 2006 (Global Managing Editor, 2003–06); *b* 15 April 1960; *s* of Ernest Carl and Gabriella Pintus Schlesinger; *m* 1987, Rachel Shiu-Ping Wong. *Educ:* Oberlin Coll. (BA 1982); Harvard Univ. (AM 1986). Freelance journalist, 1986–87; Reuters: correspondent, Hong Kong, 1987–89; Bureau Chief: Taiwan, 1989–91; China, 1991–94; Ed., Greater China, 1994–95; Financial Ed., 1995–97, Man. Ed., 1997–2000, Ed., 2000–03, Americas. Board Mem., Internat. News Safety Inst., 2005–. Director: Danenberg Oberlin-in-London Prog., 2007–; Reuters Foundn, 2008–. *Address:* Reuters, 30 South Colonnade, Canary Wharf, E14 5EP. *T:* (020) 7542 8380; *e-mail:* david.schlesinger@reuters.com. *Clubs:* Blacks; Frontline.

SCHLUTER, Prof. Dolph, PhD; FRS 1999; FRSC 2001; Professor of Zoology, University of British Columbia, since 1996 (Director, Biodiversity Research Centre, 2003–07); *b* 22 May 1955; *s* of Antoine Schluter and Magdalena Schluter; *m* 1993, Andrea Lawson; one *d*. *Educ:* Univ. of Guelph, Ont (BSc Wildlife Biol. 1977); Univ. of Michigan (PhD Ecol. and Evolution 1983). NSERC Postdoctoral Fellow, Zool. Dept, UBC and Univ. of Calif, Davis, 1983–85; Zoology Department, University of British Columbia: NSERC Univ. Res. Fellow, 1985–89; Asst Prof., 1989–91; Associate Prof., 1991–96. E. W. R. Steacie Meml Fellow, NSERC, 1993; Izaak Walton Killam Meml Faculty Res. Fellow, UBC, 1996; Scholar-in-Residence, Peter Wall Inst. of Advanced Studies, UBC, 1999; Canada Res. Chair, 2001–; Guggenheim Fellow, 2003. Vice-Pres., American Soc. Naturalists, 1999 (President's Award, 1997). Charles A. McDowell Medal, UBC, 1995. *Publications:* (ed with R. Ricklefs) Species Diversity in Ecological Communities: historical and geographical perspectives, 1993; The Ecology of Adaptive Radiation, 2000; contrib. chapters in books; contrib. numerous articles to Science, Nature, Evolution, American Naturalist, Ecology, Proc. Royal Soc., Philosophical Trans Royal Soc. *Address:* Zoology Department, University of British Columbia, 6270 University Boulevard, Vancouver, BC V6T 1Z4, Canada. *T:* (604) 8222387, *Fax:* (604) 8222416; *e-mail:* schluter@zoology.ubc.ca.

SCHMIDHUBER, Peter Michael; Member, Commission of the European Communities, 1987–94; lawyer; *b* 15 Dec. 1931; *s* of Jakob Schmidhuber and Anna (*née* Mandlmayr); *m* 1960, Elisabeth Schweigart; one *d*. *Educ:* Univ. of Munich (MA Econs 1955). Qualified as lawyer, 1960. Mem. Bd, Deutsche Bundesbank, 1995–. Member: Bundestag, 1965–69 and 1972–78; Bundesrat, Bavarian Parliament, 1978–87 (Bavarian Minister of State for Federal Affairs). Mem., CSU. *Address:* Wiesengrund 1b, 81243 Munich, Germany.

SCHMIDT, Benno Charles, Jr; Vice Chairman of the Board, Edison Schools, since 2007 (Chairman 1998–2007; President and Chief Executive, The Edison Project, 1992–98); *b* 20 March 1942; *s* of Benno Charles Schmidt and Martha Chastain; *m* 2001, Anne McMillen; one *s* two *d* from previous marriage. *Educ:* Yale Univ. (BA 1963; LLB 1966). Mem., DC Bar, 1968; Law Clerk to Chief Justice Earl Warren, 1966–67; Special Asst Atty Gen., Office of Legal Counsel, US Dept of Justice, Washington, 1967–69; Harlan Fiske Stone Prof. of Constitutional Law, Columbia Univ., 1969–86, Dean of Law School, 1984–86; Professor of Law, and President, Yale Univ., 1986–92. Hon. Bencher, Gray's Inn, 1988. Hon. degrees: LLD Princeton, 1986; DLitt Johns Hopkins, 1987; LLD Harvard, 1987. Hon. AM, 1989. *Publications:* Freedom of the Press Versus Public Access, 1974; (with A. M. Bickel) The Judiciary and Responsible Government 1910–1921, 1985. *Address:* Edison Schools, 521 5th Avenue, New York, NY 10175, USA. *T:* (212) 4191611.

SCHMIDT, Helmut H. W.; Chancellor, Federal Republic of Germany, 1974–82; Member of Bundestag, Federal Republic of Germany, 1953–61, and 1965–87; Publisher, Die Zeit, since 1983; *b* 23 Dec. 1918; *s* of Gustav Lentfält Schmidt and Ludovica Schmidt; *m* 1942, Hannelore Glaser; one *d*. *Educ:* Univ. of Hamburg. Diplom-Volkswirt, 1949. Manager of Transport Administration, State of Hamburg, 1949–53; Social Democratic Party: Member, 1946–; Mem. Federal Executive, 1958–83; Chm., Parly Gp, 1967–69; Vice-Chm. of Party, 1968–84; Senator (Minister) for Domestic Affairs in Hamburg, 1961–65; Minister of Defence, 1969–72; Minister of Finance and Economics, 1972; Minister of Finance, 1972–74. Hon. LLD: Newberry Coll., S Carolina, 1973; Johns Hopkins Univ., 1976; Cambridge, 1976; Hon. DCL Oxford, 1979; Hon. Doctorate: Harvard, 1979; Sorbonne, 1981; Georgetown, 1986; Scranton, Pennsylvania, 1987; Bergamo, 1989; Keio, Tokyo, 1991; Nat. Chung-Hsing, Taipei, 1992; Potsdam, Haifa, 2000. Athinai Prize for Man and Mankind, Onassis Foundn, Greece, 1986. *Publications:* Defence or Retaliation, 1962; Beiträge, 1967; Balance of Power, 1971; Auf dem Fundament des Godesberger Programms, 1973; Bundestagsreden, 1975; Kontinuität und Konzentration, 1975; Als Christ in der politischen Entscheidung, 1976; (with Willy Brandt) Deutschland 1976—Zwei Sozialdemokraten im Gespräch, 1976; Der Kurs heisst Frieden, 1979; Freiheit verantworten, 1980; Pflicht zur Menschlichkeit, 1981; A Grand Strategy for the West, 1985; Menschen und Mächte, 1987 (trans. as Men and Powers, 1989); Die Deutschen und ihre Nachbarn, 1990; Handeln fur Deutschland, 1993; Das Jahr der Entscheidung, 1994; Weggefährten, 1996; Jahrhundertwende, 1998; Allgemeine Erklärung der Menschenpflichten, 1998; Globalisierung, 1998; Auf der Suche nach einer öffentlichen Moral, 1998; Die Selbstbehauptung Europas, 2000; Hand aufs Herz, 2002; Die Mächte der Zukunft, 2004; Auf dem Weg zur deutschen Einheit, 2005. *Recreations:* sailing, chess, playing the organ. *Address:* c/o Deutscher Bundestag, Platz der Republik 1, 11011 Berlin, Germany.

SCHMIDT, Prof. Michael Norton, OBE 2006; FRSL; Professor of Poetry, Glasgow University, since 2006; Founder, and Editorial and Managing Director, Carcanet Press Ltd, since 1969; *b* 2 March 1947; *s* of Carl Bernhardt Schmidt and Elizabeth Norton Schmidt (*née* Hill); *m* 1979, Claire Harman (marr. diss. 1989); two *s* one *d*. *Educ:* Harvard Univ.; Wadham Coll., Oxford (BA 1969; MA). Manchester University: Gulbenkian Fellow of Poetry, 1970–73; Special Lectr, Poetry, 1973–92; Sen. Lectr in Poetry, 1992–98; Dir, Writing Sch., 1998–2005, and Prof. of English, 2000–05, Manchester Metropolitan Univ. Founder and Ed., PN Rev. (formerly Poetry Nation), 1971–; Poetry Ed., Grand Street (NY), 1998–2000. FRSL 1994. Hon. Dr Bolton, 2006. *Publications: criticism:* Fifty Modern British Poets: an introduction, 1979; Fifty English Poets 1300–1900: an introduction, 1979; Reading Modern Poetry, 1989; Lives of the Poets, 1998; The Story of Poetry: from Caedmon to Caxton, 2001; The Story of Poetry: from Skelton to Dryden, 2002; The First Poets: lives of the ancient Greek poets, 2004; The Story of Poetry: from Pope to Burns, 2007; *translations:* (with E. Kissam) Flower and Song: Aztec poetry, 1977; On Poets and Others, by Octavio Paz, 1986; *poetry anthologies* include: Eleven British Poets, 1980; The Harvill Book of 20th Century Poetry in English, 1999; The Great Modern Poets, 2006; *fiction:* The Colonist, 1983; The Dresden Gate, 1988; *poetry* includes: New and Selected Poems, 1997; The Resurrection and the Body, 2007. *Address:* Carcanet Press Ltd, Alliance House, 30 Cross Street, Manchester M2 7AQ; Department of English Literature, University of Glasgow, 5 University Gardens, Glasgow G12 8QQ. *Club:* Savile.

SCHNEIDER, Dr William George, OC 1977; FRS 1962; FRSC 1951; Research Consultant, National Research Council of Canada, Ottawa, since 1980 (President, 1967–80); *b* Wolseley, Saskatchewan, 1 June 1915; *s* of Michael Schneider and Phillipina Schneider (*née* Kraushaar); *m* 1940, Jean Frances Purves; two *d*. *Educ:* University of Saskatchewan; McGill University; Harvard University. BSc 1937, MSc 1939, University of Saskatchewan; PhD (in physical chem.), 1941, McGill Univ. Research physicist at Woods Hole Oceanographic Inst., Woods Hole, Mass, USA, 1943–46 (US Navy Certificate of Merit, 1946). Joined Nat. Research Council, Division of Pure Chemistry, Ottawa, 1946; Vice-President (Scientific), 1965–67. Pres., Internat. Union of Pure and Applied Chemistry, 1983–85. Chemical Inst. of Canada Medal, 1961, Montreal Medal, 1973; Henry Marshall Tory Medal, RSC, 1969. Hon. DSc: York, 1966; Memorial, 1968; Saskatchewan, 1969; Moncton, 1969; McMaster, 1969; Laval, 1969; New Brunswick, 1970; Montreal, 1970; McGill, 1970; Acadia, 1976; Regina, 1976; Ottawa, 1978; Hon. LLD: Alberta, 1968; Laurentian, 1968. *Publications:* (with J. A. Pople and H. J. Bernstein) High Resolution Nuclear Magnetic Resonance, 1959; scientific papers in chemistry and physics research jls. *Recreations:* tennis, ski-ing. *Address:* 200 Rideau Terrace, Apt 809, Ottawa, ON K1M 0Z3, Canada.

SCHOFIELD, Prof. Andrew Noel, MA, PhD (Cantab); FRS 1992; FREng, FICE; Professor of Engineering, Cambridge University, 1974–98, now Professor Emeritus; Fellow of Churchill College, Cambridge, 1963–66 and since 1974; *b* 1 Nov. 1930; *s* of late Rev. John Noel Schofield and Winifred Jane Mary (*née* Eyles); *m* 1961, Margaret Eileen Green; two *s* two *d*. *Educ:* Mill Hill Sch.; Christ's Coll., Cambridge. John Winbolt Prize, 1954. Asst Engr, in Malawi, with Scott Wilson Kirkpatrick and Partners, 1951. Cambridge Univ.: Demonstrator, 1955, Lectr, 1959, Dept of Engrg. Research Fellow, California Inst. of Technology, 1963–64. Univ. of Manchester Inst. of Science and Technology: Prof. of Civil Engrg, 1968; Head of Dept of Civil and Structural Engrg, 1973. Chm., Andrew N. Schofield & Associates Ltd, 1984–2000. Rankine Lecture, ICE British Geotechnical Soc., 1980. Chm., Tech. Cttee on Centrifuge Testing, Int. Soc. for Soil Mech. and Foundn Engrg, 1982–85. FREng (FEng 1986). James Alfred Ewing Medal, ICE, 1993. US Army Award, Civilian Service 1979. *Publications:* (with C. P. Wroth) Critical State Soil Mechanics, 1968; (ed with W. H. Craig and R. G. James and contrib.) Centrifuges in Soil Mechanics, 1988; (ed with J. R. Gronow and R. K. Jain and contrib.) Land Disposal of Hazardous Waste, 1988; Disturbed Soil Properties and Geotechnical Design, 2005; papers on soil mechanics and civil engrg. *Address:* 9 Little St Mary's Lane, Cambridge CB2 1RR. *T:* (01223) 314536; *e-mail:* ans@eng.cam.ac.uk.

SCHOFIELD, Derek; Hon. Mr Justice Schofield; Chief Justice of Gibraltar, 1996; a Recorder, since 2000; *b* 20 Feb. 1945; *s* of John Schofield and Ethelena Schofield (*née* Calverley); *m* 1st, 1967, Judith Danson (marr. diss.); one *s* one *d*; 2nd, 1983, Anne Wangeci Kariuki; one *s* one *d*. *Educ:* Morecambe Grammar Sch.; NAJCA Dip. in Magisterial Law, 1966. English Magisterial Service, 1961–74; called to the Bar, Gray's Inn, 1970; Kenya: Resident Magistrate, 1974–78; Sen. Resident Magistrate, 1978–82; Puisne Judge, 1982–87; Judge of Grand Court, Cayman Islands, 1988–96; Asst Recorder, 1997–2000. *Recreations:* travel, reading. *Address:* Supreme Court, Gibraltar. *T:* 78808. *Club:* Royal Gibraltar Yacht.

SCHOFIELD, Grace Florence; Regional Nursing Officer to the South West Thames Regional Health Authority, 1974–82, retired; *b* 24 Feb. 1925; *d* of Percy and Matilda Schofield. *Educ:* Mayfield Sch., Putney; University College Hosp. (SRN, SCM); Univ. of London (Dip. in Nursing); Royal College of Nursing (Dip. in Nursing Admin. (Hosp.)). Asst Matron, Guy's Hosp., 1960–61; Dep. Matron, Hammersmith Hosp., 1962–66; Matron, Mount Vernon Hosp. Northwood, and Harefield Hosp., Harefield, 1966–69; Chief Nursing Officer, University Coll. Hosp., 1969–73.

SCHOFIELD, John Allen, PhD; FSA; Curator, Architecture, Museum of London, since 1998; *b* 23 Aug. 1948; *s* of Jack and Edna Schofield. *Educ:* Christ Church Coll., Oxford (BA 1970); Univ. of Edinburgh (MPhil 1974); Royal Holloway Coll., Univ. of London (PhD 1989). FSA 1981; MIFA 1983. Museum of London: Field Officer, Dept of Urban Archaeol., 1977–87; Actg Chief Urban Archaeologist, 1987–90; Hd of Pubns, Archaeol. Service, 1991–98. Cathedral Archaeologist, St Paul's Cathedral, 1990–. Chm., Assoc. of Diocesan and Cathedral Archaeologists, 2000–06; Hon. Sec., City of London Archaeol. Trust, 1989–. *Publications:* Building of London from the Conquest to the Great Fire, 1984, 3rd edn 1999; (with A. Vince) Medieval Towns, 1994, 2nd edn 2003; Medieval London Houses, 1995, rev. edn 2003; (with R. Lea) Holy Trinity Priory Aldgate, City of London, 2005. *Recreations:* travel, jazz. *Address:* Museum of London, London Wall, EC2Y 5HN. *T:* (020) 7814 5740, *Fax:* (020) 7600 1058.

SCHOFIELD, Kenneth Douglas, CBE 1996; Executive Director, European Golf Tour, Professional Golfers' Association, (PGA European Tour), 1975–2004, now Consultant; *b* 3 Feb. 1946; *s* of late Douglas Joseph and Jessie Schofield (*née* Gray); *m* 1968, Evelyn May Sharp; two *d*. *Educ:* Auchterarder High Sch. Associate, Savings Bank Inst., 1966. Joined Trustee Savings Bank, Perth, 1962, Br. Manager, Dunblane, 1969–71; Media and PR Exec. to Dir-Gen., PGA Tournament, 1971–74; Sec., PGA European Tour, 1975. Order of Merit, Royal Spanish Golf Fedn, 1993; Christer Lindberg Award, PGA of Europe, 2002. *Publication:* Pro Golf: the official PGA European Tour Media Guide, 1972–1975. *Recreations:* golf, cricket, soccer, walking. *Address:* European Tour, Wentworth Drive, Virginia Water, Surrey GU25 4LX. *T:* (01344) 840452. *Clubs:* Caledonian; Wentworth Golf; Crieff Golf; Auchterarder Golf; Royal and Ancient Golf (St Andrews).

SCHOFIELD, Prof. Malcolm, FBA 1997; Professor of Ancient Philosophy, University of Cambridge, since 1998; Fellow, St John's College, Cambridge, since 1972; *b* 19 April 1942; *er s* of Harry Schofield and Ethel Schofield (*née* Greenwood); *m* 1970, Elizabeth Milburn (*d* 2005); one *s*. *Educ:* St Albans Sch.; St John's Coll., Cambridge; Balliol Coll., Oxford. Asst Prof. of Classics, Cornell Univ., 1967–69; Dyson Res. Fellow in Greek Culture, Balliol Coll., Oxford, 1970–72; Cambridge University: Lectr in Classics, 1972–89; Reader in Ancient Philosophy, 1989–98; Mem., Gen. Bd, 1991–94 and 1999–2003; Chm. Council, Sch. of Arts and Humanities, 1993–94; Chm. Faculty Bd of Classics, 1997–98; Mem., Univ. Council, 1997–2003; Chm., Liby Syndicate, 1998–2003; St John's College: Dean, 1979–82; Tutor, 1982–89; Pres., 1991–95. Chm., Benchmarking Gp for Classics and Ancient History, QAA, 1999–2000. Editor, Phronesis, 1987–92. Hon. Sec., Classical Assoc., 1989–2003 (Pres., 2006–07). Hon. Citizen, Rhodes, 1992. *Publications:* (ed jtly) Articles on Aristotle, 4 vols, 1975–79; (ed jtly) Doubt and Dogmatism, 1980; An Essay on Anaxagoras, 1980; (ed with M. Nussbaum) Language and Logos, 1982; (ed jtly) Science and Speculation, 1982; (with G. S. Kirk and J. E. Raven) The Presocratic Philosophers, 2nd edn, 1983; (ed with G. Striker) The Norms of Nature, 1986; The Stoic Idea of the City, 1991; (ed with A. Laks) Justice and Generosity, 1995; Saving the City, 1999; (ed jtly) The Cambridge History of Hellenistic Philosophy, 1999; (ed with C. J. Rowe) The Cambridge History of Greek and Roman Political Thought, 2000; Plato: political philosophy, 2006. *Address:* St John's College, Cambridge CB2 1TP. *T:* (01223) 338644.

SCHOFIELD, Michael, CBE 1999; Chairman, Dorset Community NHS Trust, 1996–2001; *b* 30 Jan. 1941; *s* of Edward Ronald Schofield and Edna Schofield (*née* Davies); *m* 1st, 1971, Patricia Ann Connell (marr. diss. 1982); two *s*; 2nd, 1989, Angela Rosemary Tym. *Educ:* Manchester Grammar Sch.; Exeter Coll., Oxford (BA Mod. Hist. 1962); Manchester Univ. (Dip. Social Admin). Asst House Gov., General Infirmary, Leeds, 1969–72; Asst Sec., United Liverpool Hosps, 1972–74; Dep. Dist Administrator, Liverpool Central and Southern NHS Dist, 1974–76; Area Administrator, 1976–86, and Chief Exec., 1985–86, Rochdale HA; Dir, Health Services Mgt Unit, Univ. of Manchester, 1987–95; Chm., Bradford Community NHS Trust, 1992–96. Vis. Prof., Bournemouth Univ., 1999–2007. Mem., EOC, 1997–2000. Chm., Nat. Assoc. of Health Authorities and Trusts, 1995–97. Pres., IHSM, 1990–91; Mem. Council, RPSGB, 1999–2007. *Publications:* (jtly) The Future Healthcare Workforce, First Report, 1996, Second Report, 1999, Final Report, 2002. *Recreations:* golf, music, gardening. *Address:* 8 Gravel Lane, Charlton Marshall, Blandford Forum, Dorset DT11 9NS. *T:* (01258) 450588. *Clubs:* Broadstone Golf, Ferndown Golf (Dorset).

SCHOFIELD, Neill; consultant in vocational education and training, since 1996. DoE, 1970–78; Dept of Energy, 1978–82; Department of Employment, later Department for Education and Employment, 1982–96: Director: Business and Enterprise, 1990–92; Quality Assurance, 1992–93; Training, Infrastructure and Employers Div., 1994–96. *Recreations:* walking, theatre.

SCHOFIELD, Peter Hugh Gordon; Director, Enterprise and Growth Unit, HM Treasury, since 2008; *b* Redhill, 27 April 1969; *s* of John Michael Stuart Schofield and Bridget Merrilyn Schofield; *m* 2001, Sarah-Louise Prime; two *s* one *d*. *Educ:* Whitgift Sch.; Gonville and Caius Coll., Cambridge (BA 1991). HM Treasury: Public Enterprises Team, 1991–93; Educn Team, 1993–94; Privatisation Team, 1994–96; Private Sec. to Chief Sec., 1996–98; Hd of Public Enterprises, 1998–2002; Investment Exec., London Buy-out Team, 3i Gp plc, 2002–04 (on secondment); Dir, Shareholder Exec., 2004–08. Non-exec. Dir, Partnerships UK, 2006–. *Address:* HM Treasury, 1 Horse Guards Road, SW1A 2HQ. *T:* (020) 7270 5000.

SCHOFIELD, Dr Roger Snowden, LittD; FRHistS; FBA 1988; FSS; Senior Research Associate, Cambridge Group for the History of Population and Social Structure, Economic and Social Research Council, 1994–98 (Director, 1974–94); Fellow of Clare College, Cambridge, since 1969; *b* 26 Aug. 1937; *s* of Ronald Snowden Schofield and Muriel Grace Braime; *m*; one *d*. *Educ:* Leighton Park Sch., Reading; Clare Coll., Cambridge (BA (History); PhD 1963); LittD Cantab 2005. FRHistS 1970; FSS 1987. Hon. Reader in Historical Demography, Univ. of Cambridge, 1991–98. Vis. Prof., Div. of Humanities and Social Scis, CIT, 1992–94. Member: Computing Cttee, SSRC, 1970–75; Stats Cttee, SSRC, 1974–78; Software Provision Cttee, UK Computer Bd, 1977–79. Mem., Population Investigation Cttee, 1976–97 (Treas., 1981–85; Pres., 1982–87); British Society for Population Studies: Mem., Council, 1979–87; Treas., 1981–85; Pres., 1985–87. *Publications:* (with E. A. Wrigley) The Population History of England 1541–1871: a reconstruction, 1981, repr. with introd. essay, 1993; (ed with John Walter) Famine, Disease, and the Social Order in Early Modern Society, 1989; (jtly) English Population History from Family Reconstitution 1580–1837, 1997; Taxation under the early Tudors, 2004; contrib. to Population Studies, Jl of Interdisciplinary Hist., Jl of Family Hist. *Address:* Clare College, Cambridge CB2 1TL. *T:* (01223) 333189.

SCHOLAR, Sir Michael (Charles), KCB 1999 (CB 1991); President, St John's College, Oxford, since 2001; Pro-Vice-Chancellor, University of Oxford, since 2005; *b* 3 Jan. 1942; *s* of Richard Herbert Scholar and Mary Blodwen Scholar; *m* 1964, Angela Mary (*née* Sweet); three *s* (one *d* decd). *Educ:* St Olave's Grammar School, Bermondsey; St John's College, Cambridge (PhD, MA; Hon. Fellow, 1999); Univ. of California at Berkeley. ARCO. Loeb Fellow, Harvard Univ., 1967; Asst Lectr in Philosophy, Leicester Univ., 1968; Fellow, St John's College, Cambridge, 1969; HM Treasury, 1969; Private Sec. to Chief Sec., 1974–76; Barclays Bank International, 1979–81; Private Sec. to Prime Minister, 1981–83; Under Secretary, HM Treasury, 1983–87, Dep. Sec., 1987–93; Permanent Secretary: Welsh Office, 1993–96; DTI, 1996–2001. Non-exec. Dir, Legal & Gen. Investment Mgt (Hldgs), 2002–07. Chm., Civil Service Sports Council, 1998–2001 (Chm., Staff Pension Fund, 2006–); Mem., Council of Mgt, NIESR, 2001–05. Chm., UK Statistics Authy, 2008–. Chm., Benton Fletcher Trust, 2004–. Fellow: Univ. of Wales, Aberystwyth, 1996; Cardiff Univ., 2003. Hon. Dr Glamorgan, 1999. *Recreations:* playing the piano and organ, making long journeys by foot. *Address:* St John's College, Oxford OX1 3JP.

See also T. W. Scholar.

SCHOLAR, Thomas Whinfield; Managing Director, International and Finance Directorate, HM Treasury, since 2008; *b* 17 Dec. 1968; *s* of Sir Michael Charles Scholar, *qv*. *Educ:* Trinity Hall, Cambridge (MA); LSE (MSc). HM Treasury, 1992–2007: Principal Private Sec. to Chancellor of the Exchequer, 1997–2001; UK Exec. Dir, IMF and World Bank, and Minister (Econ.), British Embassy, Washington, 2001–07; Chief of Staff and Principal Private Sec. to the Prime Minister, 2007–08. *Address:* HM Treasury, 1 Horse Guards Road, SW1A 2HQ.

SCHOLEFIELD, Susan Margaret, CMG 1999; Director General for Cohesion and Resilience, Department for Communities and Local Government, since 2007; *b* 9 May 1955; *d* of John and Millicent Scholefield; *m* 1977 (marr. diss. 1981); one *s*. *Educ:* Blackheath High Sch.; Somerville Coll., Oxford (MA); Univ. of Calif, Berkeley (MA). Joined MoD, 1981; on secondment to Ecole Nationale d'Admin, Paris, 1985–86; Principal, MoD, 1986–92 (Private Sec. to Chief of Defence Procurement, 1990–92); Asst Sec., Efficiency Unit, Cabinet Office (on secondment), 1992–95; Head, Balkans Secretariat, MoD, 1995–98; Asst Sec., NI Office (on secondment), 1998–2000; Under Sec., 2000, Exec. Dir., 2000–02, Defence Procurement Agency, MoD; Head, Civil Contingencies Secretariat, Cabinet Office (on secondment), 2002–04; Comd Sec., Permt Jt HQ, Northwood, MoD, 2004–07; Dir Gen. for Equalities, DCLG, 2007. *Recreations:* reading, music, theatre, gardening. *Address:* c/o Department for Communities and Local Government, Eland House, Bressenden Place, SW1E 5DU.

SCHOLES, Hon. Gordon Glen Denton, AO 1993; MHR for Corio (Victoria), Australia, 1967–93; *b* 7 June 1931; *s* of Glen Scholes and Mary Scholes; *m* 1957, Della Kathleen Robinson; two *d*. *Educ:* various schs. Loco-engine driver, Victorian Railways, 1949–67. Councillor, Geelong City, 1965–67; Pres., Geelong Trades Hall Council, 1965–66. House of Representatives: Chm. cttees, 1973–75; Speaker, 1975–76; Shadow Minister for Defence, 1977–83; Minister for Defence, 1983–84; Minister for Territories, 1984–87. Amateur Boxing Champion (Heavyweight), Vic, 1949. *Recreations:* golf, reading. *Address:* 20 Stephen Street, Newtown, Vic 3220, Australia.

SCHOLES, Mary Elizabeth, (Mrs A. I. M. Haggart), OBE 1983; SRN; Chief Area Nursing Officer, Tayside Health Board, 1973–83; *b* 8 April 1924; *d* of late John Neville Carpenter Scholes and Margaret Elizabeth (*née* Hines); *m* 1983, Most Rev. Alastair Iain Macdonald Haggart (*d* 1998). *Educ:* Wyggeston Grammar Sch. for Girls, Leicester; Leicester Royal Infirmary and Children's Hosp. (SRN 1946); Guy's Hosp., London (CMB Pt I Cert. 1947); Royal Coll. of Nursing, London (Nursing Admin (Hosp.) Cert. 1962). Leicester Royal Infirmary and Children's Hospital: Staff Nurse, 1947–48; Night Sister, 1948–50; Ward Sister, 1950–56; Night Supt, 1956–58; Asst Matron, 1958–61; Asst Matron, Memorial/Brook Gen. Hosp., London, 1962–64; Matron, Dundee Royal Infirm. and Matron Designate, Ninewells Hosp., Dundee, 1964–68; Chief Nursing Officer, Bd of

Management for Dundee Gen. Hosps and Bd of Man. for Ninewells and Associated Hosps, 1968–73. Pres., Scottish Assoc. of Nurse Administrators, 1973–77. Member: Scottish Bd, Royal Coll. of Nursing, 1965–70; Gen. Nursing Council for Scotland, 1966–70, 1979–; Standing Nursing and Midwifery Cttee, Scotland, 1971–74 (Vice-Chm., 1973–74); UK Central Council for Nursing, Midwifery and Health Visiting, 1980–84; Management Cttee, State Hosp., Carstairs, 1983–92; Scottish Hosp. Endowments Res. Trust, 1986–96; Chm., Scottish National Bd for Nursing, Midwifery and Health Visiting, 1980–84. *Recreations:* travel, music. *Address:* 14/2 St Margaret's Place, Edinburgh EH9 1AY. *Club:* Royal Over-Seas League.

SCHOLES, Prof. Myron Samuel, PhD; Chairman, Oak Hill Platinum Partners, since 1999; Managing Partner, Oak Hill Capital Management, since 1999; Frank E. Buck Professor of Finance, Graduate Business School, Stanford University, 1983–95, now Emeritus; *b* 1 July 1941; *m*; two *d*; *m* 1998, Jan Blaustein. *Educ:* McMaster Univ.; Univ. of Chicago. Instr, Univ. of Chicago Business Sch., 1967–68; Asst Prof., 1968–72, Associate Prof., 1972–73, MIT Mgt Sch.; University of Chicago: Associate Prof., 1973–75; Prof., 1975–79; Dir, Center for Res. in Security Prices, 1975–81; Edward Eagle Brown Prof. of Finance, 1979–82; Prof. of Law, 1983–87, and Sen. Res. Fellow, Hoover Inst., 1988–93, Stanford Univ. Man. Dir, Salomon Bros, 1991–93; Partner, Long-Term Capital Management, 1994–98. (Jtly) Nobel Prize for Economics, 1997. *Publication:* (jtly) Taxes and Business Strategy: a planning approach, 1992. *Address:* Oak Hill Platinum Partners, 1100 King Street, Bldg 4, Rye Brook, NY 10573, USA.

SCHOLES, Rodney James; QC 1987; *b* 26 Sept. 1945; *s* of late Henry Scholes and Margaret Bower; *m* 1977, Katherin Elizabeth (*née* Keogh); two *s* (and one *s* decd). *Educ:* Wade Deacon Grammar Sch., Widnes; St Catherine's Coll., Oxford (scholar) (BA; BCL); Univ. of Cape Town (MPhil Criminology 2007). Lincoln's Inn: Hardwicke Schol., 1964; Mansfield Schol., 1967; called to the Bar, 1968, Bencher, 1997; a Recorder, 1986–2004. Mem., Northern Circuit, 1968–. *Recreations:* watching Rugby football, gazing at Table Mountain. *Address:* 706 Witsand, Beach Boulevard, Bloubergrand, Cape Town 7441, S Africa. *T:* (21) 5575442; *e-mail:* rjsqc@scholes.co.za.

SCHOLEY, Sir David (Gerald), Kt 1987; CBE 1976; Senior Advisor, UBS Investment Bank (formerly SBC Warburg, later Warburg Dillon Read, then UBS Warburg), since 1997; Director, Anglo-American, 1999–2005; *b* 28 June 1935; *s* of Dudley and Lois Scholey; *m* 1960, Alexandra Beatrix, *d* of Hon. George and Fiorenza Drew, Canada; one *s* one *d*. *Educ:* Wellington Coll., Berks; Christ Church, Oxford (Hon. Student, 2003). Nat Service, RAC, 9th Queen's Royal Lancers, 1953–55; TA Yorks Dragoons, 1955–57; 3/4 CLY (Sharpshooters), 1957–61; Metropolitan Special Constabulary (Thames Div.), 1961–65. Thompson Graham & Co. (Lloyd's brokers), 1956–58; Dale & Co. (Insce brokers), Canada, 1958–59; Guinness Mahon & Co. Ltd, 1959–64; joined S. G. Warburg & Co. Ltd, 1965, Dir, 1967–95, Dep. Chm., 1977, Jt Chm., 1980–84, Chm., 1985–95; Chm., SBC Warburg, July–Nov. 1995; Sen. Advr, IFC, Washington, 1996–2005. Director: Mercury Securities plc, 1969–86 (Chm., 1984–86); Orion Insurance Co. Ltd, 1963–87; Stewart Wrightson Holdings Ltd, 1972–81; Union Discount Co. of London, Ltd, 1976–81; Bank of England, 1981–98; British Telecom plc, 1986–94; Chubb Corp. (USA), 1991–2008; General Electric Co., 1992–95; J. Sainsbury plc, 1996–2000; Vodafone Group (formerly Vodafone Airtouch) plc, 1998–2005; Close Bros, 1999–2006 (Chm., 1999–2006); Broadreach Advrs Ltd, 2005–07. Mem., Export Guarantees Adv. Council, 1970–75 (Dep. Chm. 1974–75); Chm., Construction Exports Adv. Bd, 1975–78; Member: Inst. Internat. d'Etudes Bancaires, 1976–94 (Pres., 1988); Cttee on Finance for Industry, NEDO, 1980–87; Council, IISS, 1984–93 (Hon. Treas., 1984–90); Industry and Commerce Gp, 1989–95, Lord Mayor's Appeal Cttee, 2002–03, SCF; President's Cttee, BITC, 1988–91; Ford Foundn Adv. Gp on UN Financing, 1992–93; London First, 1993–96; Bd of Banking Supervision, 1996–98; Fitch Internat. Services Adv. Cttee, 2001–; Mitsubishi Internat. Adv. Cttee, 2001–07; Sultanate of Oman Financial Adv. Gp, 2002–. Dir, INSEAD, 1989–2005 (Chairman: UK Council, 1994–97; Internat. Council, 1995–2003 (Hon. Chm., 2005); Hon. Alumnus, 2000). A Gov., BBC, 1994–2000; Mem. Adv. Council, LSO, 1998–2004. Trustee: Glyndebourne Arts Trust, 1989–2002; Nat. Portrait Gallery, 1992–2005 (Chm., 2001–05). Governor: Wellington Coll., 1978–88, 1996–2004 (Vice-Pres., 1998–2004); NIESR, 1984–; LSE, 1993–96. FRSA. Hon. DLitt London Guildhall, 1993; Hon. BSc UMIST, 1999. *Address:* (office) 1 Finsbury Avenue, EC2M 2PP.

SCHOLEY, Dr Keith Douglas; Controller, Content Production and Deputy Chief Creative Officer, BBC Vision Studios, since 2006; *b* 24 June 1957; *s* of Douglas and Jeannie Scholey; *m* 1985, Elizabeth Sara Potter; two *s*. *Educ:* Reed's Sch., Surrey; Univ. of Bristol (BSc Hons; PhD 1982). Postgrad. res., Bristol Univ., 1978–81; joined BBC, 1982: researcher, 1982–85; TV asst producer, 1985–88; TV producer, 1989–93; editor, TV series, Wildlife on One and Wildlife specials, 1993–98; Head, Natural Hist. Unit, 1998–2002; Controller: Specialist Factual, 2002–06; Factual Production, 2006. Hon. DSc Bristol, 2001. *Recreations:* flying (private pilot's licence), scuba diving, sailing, photography. *Address:* BBC, White City, 201 Wood Lane, W12 7TS. *T:* (020) 8752 6790.

SCHOLEY, Sir Robert, Kt 1987; CBE 1982; FREng; Chairman, British Steel plc (formerly British Steel Corporation), 1986–92; *b* 8 Oct. 1921; *s* of Harold and Eveline Scholey; *m* 1946, Joan Methley; two *d*. *Educ:* King Edward VII Sch. and Sheffield Univ. Associateship in Mech Engrg; FREng (FEng 1990). United Steel Companies, 1947–68; British Steel Corporation, 1968–92: Dir and Chief Executive, 1973–86; Dep. Chm., 1976–86. Dir, Eurotunnel Bd, 1987–94. Mem., HEFCE, 1992–95. Pres., Eurofer, 1985–90. Chm., Internat. Iron and Steel Inst., 1989–90; Pres., Inst. of Metals, 1989–90. Hon. DEng Sheffield, 1987; Hon. DSc Teesside, 1995. *Recreations:* outdoor life, history.

SCHOLL, Andreas; countertenor; *b* Germany, 1967. *Educ:* Schola Cantorum Basiliensis, Switzerland (Dip. in Ancient Music). Former chorister, Kiedricher Chorbuben, Germany. Début internat. recital, Théâtre de Grévin, Paris, 1993; opera début in Handel's Rodelinda, Glyndebourne, 1998; appears regularly in recitals and concerts at all major European venues, and in N America. Teaches at Schola Cantorum Basiliensis. Composes and records pop music; prizewinning recordings include works by Vivaldi and Caldara, and English folk and lute songs. *Address:* c/o HarrisonParrott Ltd, 12 Penzance Place, W11 4PA.

SCHOLL, Prof. Anthony James, DPhil; Kuwait Professor of Number Theory and Algebra, University of Cambridge, since 2001; *b* 18 Dec. 1955; *s* of late William Howard Scholl and of Barbara Russell Beilby; *m* 1st, 1980, Caroline Somerville-Large (marr. diss. 2000); three *s*; 2nd, 2002, Gülsin Onay. *Educ:* Worth Sch., Sussex; Christ Church, Oxford (MA, MSc; DPhil 1980). University of Oxford: SRC Res. Fellow, 1980–81; Jun. Lectr, 1981–84; University of Durham: Lectr, 1984–89; Prof. of Pure Mathematics, 1989–2001. Mem., Inst. for Advanced Study, Princeton, 1989–90; Prof. Associé, Univ. Paris-Sud, 1992; Leverhulme Trust Res. Fellow, 2001–02. *Recreation:* music (listening, playing and composing). *Address:* Department of Pure Mathematics and Mathematical Statistics, Centre for Mathematical Sciences, Wilberforce Road, Cambridge CB3 0WB. *T:* (01223) 765889; *e-mail:* a.j.scholl@dpmms.cam.ac.uk.

SCHOLTE, Nicholas Paul; Chief Executive, NHS Business Services Authority, since 2006; *b* 6 May 1959; *s* of Christiaan and Sylvia Joyce Scholte; one *s* one *d* by Iris Esters (decd); *m* 2006, Claire Louise Emmerson. *Educ:* Chesterfield Grammar Sch.; Manchester Univ. (BA Hons Politics). Law Society: Exec. Officer, 1981–85; Sen. Exec. Officer, 1985–86; Finance Manager, 1986–89; Legal Aid Board: Gp Manager (NE), 1990–96; Business Systems Dir, 1996–99; Chief Exec., Prescription Pricing Authy, 1999–2006. *Recreations:* sailing, ballet, literature, football. *Address:* NHS Business Services Authority, Bridge House, 152 Pilgrim Street, Newcastle upon Tyne NE1 6SN. *T:* (0191) 203 5209.

SCHOLTENS, Sir James (Henry), KCVO 1977 (CVO 1963); Director, Office of Government Ceremonial and Hospitality, Department of the Prime Minister and Cabinet, Canberra, 1973–80, retired; Extra Gentleman Usher to the Queen, since 1981; *b* 12 June 1920; *s* of late Theo F. J. Scholtens and late Grace M. E. (*née* Nolan); *m* 1945, Mary Maguire, Brisbane; one *s* five *d*. *Educ:* St Patrick's Marist Brothers' Coll., Sale, Vic. Served War, RAAF, 1943–45. Joined Aust. Public Service, 1935; PMG's Dept, Melbourne, 1935; Dept of Commerce, Melb., 1938; transf. to Dept of Commerce, Canberra, 1941; Dept of Prime Minister, Canberra: Accountant, 1949; Ceremonial Officer, 1954; Asst Sec., Ceremonial and Hospitality Br., 1967. Dir of visits to Australia by the Sovereign and Members of the Royal Family, Heads of State, Monarchs and Presidents, and by Heads of Govt and Ministers of State. *Address:* 34 Teague Street, Cook, Canberra, ACT 2614, Australia. *T:* (2) 62510125. *Clubs:* Canberra, Southern Cross (Canberra).

SCHOLZ, Prof. Dr Rupert; Professor of Public Law, Institut für Politik und öffentliches Recht, University of Munich, 1981–2005, now Emeritus; Of Counsel, Gleiss Lutz, since 2005; *b* 23 May 1937; *s* of Ernst and Gisela Scholz (*née* Merdas); *m* 1971, Dr Helga Scholz-Hoppe. *Educ:* Abitur, Berlin; studied law and economics, Berlin and Heidelberg; Dr Jur., Univ. of Munich. Prof., Univ. of Munich, taught in Munich, Berlin, Regensburg, Augsburg; Public Law Chair, Berlin and Munich, 1978. Senator of Justice, Land Berlin, 1981; Acting Senator for Federal Affairs; Mem., Bundesrat, 1982; Mem., N Atlantic Assembly, 1982; Senator for Federal Affairs, Land Berlin, 1983; MHR, Berlin, and Senator for Justice and Federal Affairs, 1985; Federal Minister of Defence, FRG, 1988–89; Mem. (CDU), German Bundestag, 1990–2002. *Publications:* numerous papers in jurisp., German policy, foreign policy, economic policy. *Address:* Gleiss Lutz, Friedrichstrasse 71, 10112 Berlin, Germany.

SCHOPPER, Prof. Herwig Franz; Professor of Physics, University of Hamburg, 1973–89, now Emeritus; *b* 28 Feb. 1928; *s* of Franz Schopper and Margarete Hartmann; *m* 1949, Dora Klara Ingeborg (*née* Stieler); one *s* one *d*. *Educ:* Univ. of Hamburg. Dip. Phys. 1949, Dr rer nat 1951. Asst Prof. and Univ. Lectr, Univ. of Erlangen, 1954–57; Prof., Univ. of Mainz, 1957–60; Prof., Univ. of Karlsruhe and Dir of Inst. for Nuclear Physics, 1961–73; Chm., Scientific Council, Kerforschungszentrum, Karlsruhe, 1967–69; Chm., Deutsches Elektronen Synchrotron particle physics Lab., Hamburg, 1973–80; European Organisation for Nuclear Research (CERN): Res. Associate, 1966–67; Head, Dept of particle physics and Mem., Directorate for experimental prog., 1970–73; Chm., Intersecting Storage Ring Cttee, 1973–76; Mem., Sci. Policy Cttee, 1979–80; Dir-Gen., 1981–88. Chm., Assoc. of German Nat. Research Centres, 1978–80; Mem., Scientific Council, IN2P3, Paris; Advr, UNESCO, 1994–. President: German Physical Soc., 1992–94; European Physical Soc., 1995–97; Council, Synchrotron-light for Exptl Sci. and Applications in Middle East, 2003–. Member: Akad. der Wissenschaften Leopoldina, Halle; Joachim Jungius Gesellschaft, Hamburg; Sudetendeutsche Akad. der Wissenschaft, 1979; Acad. Scientiarium et Artium, Vienna, 1993; MAE 1992; Corresp. Mem., Bavarian Acad. of Scis, 1981; Hon. Mem., Hungarian Acad. of Scis, 1995. Fellow, APS, 2006; Foreign FInstP 1996. Dr *hc*: Univ. of Erlangen, 1982; Univ. of Moscow, 1989; Univ. of Geneva, 1989; Univ. of London, 1989; Jt Inst. of Nuclear Res., Dubna, 1998; Inst. of High Energy Physics, Russia, 1999. Physics Award, Göttinger Akad. der Wissenschaft, 1957; Carus Medal, Akad. Leopoldina, 1958; Ritter von Gerstner Medal, 1978; Sudetendeutscher Kulturpreis, 1984; Golden Plate Award, Amer. Acad. of Achievement, 1984; Gold Medal, Weizmann Inst., 1987; Wilhelm Exner Medal, Gewerbeverein, Austria, 1991; Purkyne Meml Medal, Czech Acad. of Scis, 1994; 650 Years Jubilee Medal, Charles Univ., Prague, 1998; Tate Medal, Amer. Inst. Physics, 2004; Einstein Gold Medal, UNESCO, 2004; Bohr Gold Medal, UNESCO-Denmark, 2005. Grosses Bundesverdienstkreuz (FRG), 1989; Friendship Order of Russian Pres., 1996; Grand Cordon, Order of Independence (Jordan), 2003. *Publications:* Weak Interactions and Nuclear Beta Decay, 1966; Matter—Antimatter, 1989; papers on elementary particle physics, high energy accelerators, relation of science and society. *Recreations:* music, gardening. *Address:* c/o CERN, 1211 Geneva 23, Switzerland. *T:* (22) 7675350.

SCHORI, Most Rev. Katharine J.; *see* Jefferts Schori.

SCHOUVALOFF, Alexander, MA; Founder Curator, Theatre Museum, Victoria & Albert Museum, 1974–89; *b* 4 May 1934; *s* of Paul Schouvaloff (professional name Paul Sheriff) and Anna Schouvaloff (*née* Raevsky); *m* 1st, Gillian Baker; one *s*; 2nd, 1971, Daria Chorley (*née* de Mérindol). *Educ:* Harrow Sch.; Jesus Coll., Oxford (MA). Asst Director, Edinburgh Festival, 1965–67; Dir, North West Arts Assoc., 1967–74. Director: Rochdale Festival, 1971; Chester Festival, 1973. Sec. Gen., Société Internat. des Bibliothèques et des Musées des Arts du Spectacle, 1980–90; Committee Member: for Jerome Robbins Dance Div., NY Public Liby for Performing Arts, 1993–; Scientific Cttee, Inst nat. d'histoire de l'art, Paris, 2002–06. Trustee, London Archives of the Dance, 1976–2008. BBC Radio plays: Summer of the Bullshine Boys, 1981; No Saleable Value, 1982. Cross of Polonia Restituta, 1971. *Publications:* Place for the Arts, 1971; Summer of the Bullshine Boys, 1979; (with Victor Borovsky) Stravinsky on Stage, 1982; (with April FitzLyon) A Month in the Country, 1983; (with Catherine Haill) The Theatre Museum, 1987; Theatre on Paper, 1990; Léon Bakst: The Theatre Art, 1991; catalogues: Thyssen-Bornemisza Collection (set and costume designs), 1987; The Art of Ballets Russes (the Serge Lifar collection of theater designs, costumes, and paintings at the Wadsworth Atheneum), 1998. *Recreations:* France, Italy. *Address:* 10 Avondale Park Gardens, W11 4PR. *T:* (020) 7727 7543. *Club:* Garrick.

SCHRAM, Prof. Stuart Reynolds; Professor of Politics (with reference to China) in the University of London, School of Oriental and African Studies, 1968–89, now Emeritus; Research Associate, Harvard University, since 1989; *b* Excelsior, Minn, 27 Feb. 1924; *s* of Warren R. Schram and Nada Stedman Schram; *m* 1972, Marie-Annick Lancelot; one *s*. *Educ:* West High Sch., Minneapolis, Minn; Univ. of Minnesota (BA, 1944); Columbia Univ. (PhD 1954). Dir, Soviet and Chinese Section, Centre d'Etude des Relations Internationales, Fondation Nationale des Sciences Politiques, Paris, 1954–67; Head, Contemporary China Inst., SOAS, 1968–72. *Publications:* Protestantism and Politics in France, 1954; The Political Thought of Mao Tse-Tung, 1963, rev. edn 1969; Le marxisme et l'Asie 1853–1964, 1965, rev. and enl. English edn 1969; Mao Tse-tung, 1966; Ideology and Policy in China since the Third Plenum, 1978–84, 1984; (ed) The Scope of State Power in China, 1985; (ed) Foundations and Limits of State Power in China, 1987; The Thought of Mao Tse-tung, 1989; (ed) Mao's Road to Power: Revolutionary Writings 1912–1949, vol. I 1992, vol. II 1994, vol. III 1995, vol. IV 1997, vol. V 1999, vols VI and

VII, 2004. *Recreations:* concert- and theatre-going, walking in the country, fishing. *Address:* John King Fairbank Center for East Asian Research, Harvard University, 1737 Cambridge Street, Cambridge, MA 02138, USA.

SCHRAMEK, Sir Eric (Emil) von; *see* von Schramek.

SCHREIBER, family name of **Baron Marlesford**.

SCHREIER, Sir Bernard, Kt 2000; mechanical engineer; Chairman, CP Holdings Ltd; Pres., IIC Industries Inc., NY. Chm., Danubius Hotels RT, Hungary; Dep. Chm., Bank Leumi (UK) plc. Hon. Fellow, UCL. Queen's Award for Export, 1976; Jubilee Award, Israel, 1998. Officer's Cross, Order of Hungarian Republic, 1998; Third Class, Order of White Two-Arm Cross (Slovak Republic). *Address:* CP Holdings Ltd, CP House, Otterspool Way, Watford, Herts WD25 8JP.

SCHREMPP, Jürgen E.; Chairman, Board of Management, DaimlerChrysler AG, 2000–05 (Joint Chairman, 1998–2000); *b* 15 Sept. 1944; *m* 2000, Lydia Deininger; one *s* one *d*, and two *s* from previous marriage. *Educ:* Univ. for Applied Scis, Offenburg. Apprentice motor mechanic, Mercedes-Benz Dealership, Freiburg, 1961–64; joined Daimler-Benz AG, 1967; Mercedes-Benz of South Africa: Manager, Service Div., 1974–80; Mem., Bd of Mgt, 1980–82, 1984–87; Vice Pres., 1984; Pres., 1985–87; Pres., Euclid Inc., USA (subsidiary of Daimler-Benz AG), 1982–84; Daimler-Benz Board of Management: Dep. Mem., 1987–89; Mem., 1989–95; Chm., 1998; Pres. and CEO, Daimler-Benz Aerospace AG, 1989–95. Non-executive Director: Sasol Ltd, 1997–; Vodafone Gp plc, 2000–; Cie Financière Richemont SA, 2003–. Partner, Cie Financière Rupert, 2006–. Cross, Order of Merit (Germany). *Address:* PO Box 200651, 80006 Munich, Germany.

SCHREUDER, Prof. Deryck Marshall, DPhil; FAHA; FRHistS; historian and educationalist; Visiting Professor, Faculty of Education and Social Work (formerly College of Humanities and Social Sciences), University of Sydney, since 2004; Adjunct Professor, Australian National University, since 2005; *b* 19 Jan. 1942; *s* of Peter Jurian and Jean Margaret Schreuder; *m* 1965, Patricia Anne Pote; three *s*. *Educ:* Llewellin High Sch., Zambia; Univ. of Rhodes, S Africa (BA Hons); DPhil Oxon 1964. FAHA 1985; FRHistS 1988. Rhodes Schol. from Central Africa, 1964–67; Kennedy Fellow of Modern Hist., New Coll., Oxford, 1967–69; Prof. of Hist., and Hd of Dept, Trent Univ., Ontario, 1970–79; Challis Prof. of Hist., Univ. of Sydney, 1980–93 (Dep. Chm., Acad. Bd, 1984–85); on secondment as Associate Dir, Humanities Res. Centre, ANU, 1992–93; Dep. Vice-Chancellor (Acad.), Macquarie Univ., 1993–95; Vice-Chancellor, Univ. of Western Sydney, 1995–98; Emeritus Prof., Macquarie Univ. and Univ. of Western Sydney, 1998; Vice-Chancellor, and Principal, subseq. Pres., Univ. of WA, 1998–2004. Res. Fellow, Res. Sch. of Social Scis, ANU, 1976–77. Pres., Aust. Vice-Chancellors' Cttee, 2002–03; Chm., Aust. Univs Quality Agency, 2004–; Member: Aust. Res. Grants Cttee, 1986–92; Commn on Commonwealth Studies, 1995–97. President: Aust. Hist. Assoc., 1985–86; Aust. Acad. Humanities, 1992–95 (Vice-Pres., 1989–90). Associate Ed., Oxford DNB, 1995–2000. Hon. LLD Rhodes, 2004. *Publications:* Gladstone and Kruger: Liberal Government and Colonial Home Rule (1880–85), 1969; The Scramble for Southern Africa (1877–95), 1981; (jtly) The Rise of Colonial Nationalism: Australia, New Zealand, Canada and South Africa first assert their nationality 1880–1914, 1988; (ed jtly) The Commonwealth and Australia in World Affairs, 1990; (ed jtly) History and Social Change: the G. A. Wood Memorial Lectures 1949–91, 1991; (ed) Imperialisms, 1991; A Letter from Sydney: history and the post-Colonial society (J. M. Ward Memorial Lecture), 1991; (ed jtly) History at Sydney, 1992; (ed) The Humanities and the Creative Nation, 1995; (ed jtly) Africa Today, 1997; (ed jtly) The State and the People: Australian federation 1870–1901, 2002; (ed jtly) Sir Graham Bower's Secret History of the Jameson Raid and the South African Crisis 1895–1902, 2002; (ed jtly) Australia's Empire, 2008, in The Oxford History of the British Empire Companion Series. *Recreations:* gardening, jogging, writing history. *Address:* Faculty of Education and Social Work, University of Sydney, Sydney, NSW 2006, Australia.

SCHREYER, Rt Hon. Edward Richard, CC 1979; CMM 1979; CD 1979; PC 1984; High Commissioner for Canada in Australia, and concurrently Ambassador to Vanuatu, 1984–88; *b* Beausejour, Man., 21 Dec. 1935; *s* of John and Elizabeth Schreyer, a pioneer family of the district; *m* 1960, Lily, *d* of Jacob Schulz, MP; two *s* two *d*. *Educ:* Beausejour, Manitoba; United Coll., Winnipeg; St John's Coll., Winnipeg, Univ. of Manitoba (BA, BEd, MA). While at university served as 2nd Lieut, COTC, Royal Canadian Armored Corps, 1954–55. Member, Legislative Assembly of Manitoba, 1958; re-elected, 1959 and 1962; MP: for Springfield, 1965; for Selkirk, 1968; chosen as Leader of New Democratic Party in Manitoba, 1969, and resigned seat in House of Commons; MLA for Rossmere and Premier of Manitoba, 1969–77; Minister of: Dominion-Provincial Relns, 1969–77; Hydro, 1971–77; Finance, 1972–74; re-elected MLA, 1977; Governor-Gen. and C-in-C of Canada, 1979–84. Prof. of Political Science and Internat. Relns, St John's Coll., Univ. of Manitoba, 1962–65. Distinguished Vis. Prof., Univ. of Winnipeg, 1989–90; Vis. Prof., Simon Fraser Univ., Vancouver, 1991; Distinguished Fellow, Inst. for Integrated Energy Systems, Univ. of Victoria, 1992–94; Univ. of BC, 1995–. Director: Perfect Pacific Investments, 1989–; China International Trade and Investment Corp., Canada, 1991–; Saskatchewan Energy Conservation and Develt Authy, 1993–; Alternate Fuel Systems Inc. (Calgary), 1994–; Cephalon Oil & Gas Resource Corp. (Calgary), 1994–. Chancellor, Brandon Univ., 2002–. Chm., Canadian Shield Foundn, 1984–; Member: Internat. Assoc. of Energy Economists; CPA; IPU. Hon. LLD: Manitoba, 1979; Mount Allison, 1983; McGill, 1984; Simon Fraser, 1984; Lakehead, 1985; Hon. Dr Sci. Sociale Ottawa, 1980. *Recreations:* reading, golf, sculpting, woodworking. *Address:* 250 Wellington Center, Unit 401, Winnipeg, MB R3M 0B3, Canada. *T:* (204) 9897580, *Fax:* (204) 9897581. *Clubs:* Rideau (Ottawa); York, Upper Canada (Toronto).

SCHREYER, Michaele, PhD; Member, European Commission, 1999–2004; *b* Cologne, 9 Aug. 1951. *Educ:* Univ. of Cologne (Dip. Econs and Sociology 1976); Univ. of Berlin (PhD 1983). Research Assistant: Inst. for Public Finances and Social Policy, Free Univ. of Berlin, 1977–82; Green Party, Bundestag, 1983–87; Researcher, Inst. for Econ. Res., 1987–88. Mem., Green Party, 1987–; Minister for Urban Develt and Envmtl Protection, State Govt (Senate) of Berlin, 1989–90; Mem., State Parlt of Berlin (Green Party), 1991–99 (Chair, Green Party Gp, 1998–99). Vice-Pres., European Movt, Germany, 2006–. Lectr on European Politics, Free Univ. of Berlin, 2004–. Member, Advisory Council: Transparency Internat., Germany, 2005–; Heinrich Böll Stiftung, Germany, 2007–.

SCHRIEFFER, Prof. John Robert, PhD; University Professor, Florida State University, and Chief Scientist, National High Magnetic Field Laboratory, since 1992; University Eminent Scholar Professor, State of Florida University System, since 1995; *b* Oak Park, Ill, 31 May 1931; *s* of John Henry Schrieffer and Louise Anderson; *m* 1960, Anne Grete Thomsen; one *s* two *d*. *Educ:* MIT (BS); Univ. of Illinois (MS, PhD). Nat. Sci. Foundn Fellow, Univ. of Birmingham, and Niels Bohr Inst. for Theoretical Physics, Copenhagen, 1957–58; Asst Prof., Univ. of Chicago, 1957–59; Asst Prof., Univ. of Illinois, 1959–60, Associate Prof., 1960–62; Univ. of Pennsylvania: Mem. Faculty, 1962–79; Mary Amanda Wood Prof. of Physics, 1964–79; University of California, Santa Barbara: Prof. of Physics, 1980–91; Chancellor's Prof., 1984–91; Dir, Inst. for Theoretical Physics, 1984–89. Guggenheim Fellow, Copenhagen, 1967. Member: Nat. Acad. Scis; Amer. Acad. of Arts and Scis; Amer. Philos. Soc.; Amer. Phys Soc. (Vice-Pres., 1994; Pres.-elect, 1995; Pres., 1996); Danish Royal Acad. Sci.; Acad. of Sci. of USSR, 1989. Hon. ScD: Technische Hochschule, Munich, 1968; Univ. of Geneva, 1968; Univ. of Pennsylvania, 1973; Illinois Univ., 1974; Univ. of Cincinnati, 1977; Hon. DSc Tel-Aviv Univ., 1987. Buckley Prize, Amer. Phys Soc., 1968; Comstock Prize, Nat. Acad. Scis, 1968; (jtly) Nobel Prize for Physics, 1972; John Ericsson Medal, Amer. Soc. of Swedish Engineers, 1976; Nat. Medal of Science, USA, 1985. *Publications:* Theory of Superconductivity, 1964; articles on solid state physics and chemistry. *Recreations:* painting, gardening, wood working. *Address:* NHMFL/FSU, 1800 E Paul Dirac Drive, Tallahassee, FL 32310, USA.

SCHROCK, Prof. Richard Royce, PhD; Frederick G. Keyes Professor of Chemistry, Massachusetts Institute of Technology, since 1989; *b* Berne, Indiana, 4 Jan. 1945; *s* of late Noah J. Schrock and Martha A. Schrock (*nee* Habegger); *m* 1971, Nancy F. Carlson; two *s*. *Educ:* Mission Bay High Sch.; Univ. of Calif, Riverside (AB 1967); Harvard Univ. (PhD 1971). Postdoctoral Fellow, Univ. of Cambridge, 1971; Res. Chemist, Central Res. and Develt Dept, E. I. duPont de Nemours and Co., Wilmington, Delaware, 1972–75; joined MIT, 1975, Prof., 1980–89. Foreign Mem., Royal Soc., 2008. (Jtly) Nobel Prize for Chemistry, 2005. *Publications:* articles in jls. *Address:* Department of Chemistry, Massachusetts Institute of Technology, 77 Massachusetts Avenue, Cambridge, MA 02139–4307, USA.

SCHRÖDER, Gerhard; Member, Bundestag, 1980–86 and 1998–2005; Chancellor, Federal Republic of Germany, 1998–2005; Chairman, Social Democratic Party, Germany, 1999–2004; *b* Mossenberg, 7 April 1944; *m* 1997, Doris Köpf. *Educ:* Univ. of Göttingen. Apprentice retailer, 1959–61; qualified as lawyer, 1976; in practice, Hannover, 1978–90. Joined SPD, 1963; Mem. for Hannover Bezirk, 1977, Lower Saxony Landtag, 1986–98; Chm., SPD Gp, 1986–90; Prime Minister, Lower Saxony, 1990–98. Sozialdemokratische Partei Deutschlands: Chm., Young Socialists, Göttingen, 1969–70; Nat. Chm., Young Socialists, 1978–80; Member: Exec. Cttee, Hannover, 1977 (constituency Chm., 1983–93); Party Council, 1979–2005; NEC, 1986–2005; Presiding Council, 1989–2005; Chm., Lower Saxony Br., 1994–98. *Address:* c/o Deutscher Bundestag, Unter den Linden 50, 10117 Berlin, Germany.

SCHUBERT, Sir Sydney, Kt 1985; Chief Executive, Daikyo Group Australia, 1988–2000; *b* 22 March 1928; *s* of Wilhelm F. Schubert and Mary A. Price; *m* 1961, Maureen Kistle; two *d*. *Educ:* Univ. of Queensland; Univ. of Durham. Queensland Government: Civil Engr, 1950; Dep. Chief Engr, Main Roads Dept, 1965–69; Chief Engr Dept., 1969–72; Dep. Co-ordinator Gen., 1972–76, Co-ordinator Gen. and Permanent Head, 1982–88, Dir Gen., 1987–88, Premier's Dept. Director: Jupiters, 1988–92 (Dep. Chm., 1990–92); Coffey Internat., 1990–96; APN Hldgs, 1992–; Victoria Hotels Pty Ltd (Christchurch), 1990–; Premier Hotels Pty Ltd (Christchurch), 1990–; Christchurch Casinos Pty Ltd, 1992–. Chancellor, Bond Univ., 1987–89. Mem., Gt Barrier Reef Marine Park Authy, 1978–88; Deputy Chairman: Brisbane Exposition and S Bank Redevelt Authy, 1984–88; Qld Cultural Centre Trust, 1986–88. Member: Bd of Management, Graduate Sch. of Management, Univ. of Queensland, 1985–88; Exec. Council, Australia Japan Assoc. Qld, 1988–90. Eisenhower Fellow, Aust., 1972. FIE(Aust); Hon. Fellow, Aust. Instn of Engrs. *Recreation:* golf. *Address:* 15 Apex Street, Clayfield, Brisbane, Qld 4011, Australia. *Clubs:* Queensland, Royal Queensland Golf.

SCHÜELEIN-STEEL, Danielle Fernande, (Danielle Steel); writer; *b* 14 Aug. 1947; *d* of John and Norma Schüelein-Steel; *m*; one *d*; *m* 1977, Bill Toth; (one *s* decd); *m* 1981, John Traina (marr. diss.); one *s* four *d*. *Educ:* Lycée Français, NYC; Parsons Sch. of Design, NY; Univ. of New York. Vice-Pres. of Public Relations and New Business, Supergirls Ltd, 1968–71; copywriter, Grey Advertising Agency, 1973–74. Officier, Ordre des Arts et des Lettres (France), 2002. *Publications: fiction:* Going Home, 1973; Now and Forever, 1978; The Promise, 1978; Golden Moments, 1979; Season of Passion, 1980; Summer's End, 1980; The Ring, 1980; To Love Again, 1981; Palomino, 1981; Loving, 1981; Remembrance, 1981; A Perfect Stranger, 1982; Once in a Lifetime, 1982; Crossings, 1982; Changes, 1983; Thurston House, 1983; Full Circle, 1984; Secrets, 1985; Family Album, 1985; Wanderlust, 1986; Fine Things, 1987; Kaleidoscope, 1987; Zoya, 1988; Star, 1989; Daddy, 1989; Message from Nam, 1990; Heartbeat, 1991; No Greater Love, 1991; Jewels, 1992; Mixed Blessings, 1992; Vanished, 1993; Accident, 1994; The Gift, 1994; Wings, 1994; Lightning, 1995; Five Days in Paris, 1995; Malice, 1996; Silent Honor, 1996; The Ranch, 1997; The Ghost, 1997; Special Delivery, 1997; The Long Road Home, 1998; The Klone and I, 1998; Mirror Image, 1998; Bittersweet, 1999; Granny Dan, 1999; Irresistible Forces, 1999; The Wedding, 2000; The House on Hope Street, 2000; Journey, 2000; Lone Eagle, 2001; Leap of Faith, 2001; The Kiss, 2002; The Cottage, 2003; Sunset in St Tropez, 2002; Answered Prayers, 2002; Dating Game, 2003; Johnny Angel, 2003; Safe Harbour, 2003; Ransom, 2004; Second Chance, 2004; Miracle, 2005; Coming Out, 2006; Bungalow 2, 2006; The House, 2007; Amazing Grace, 2007; Rogue, 2008; *non-fiction:* (contrib.) Having a Baby, 1984; His Bright Light: the story of Nick Traina, 1998; *poetry:* Love, 1981; several children's books. *Address:* c/o Dell Publishing, 1540 Broadway, New York, NY 10036, USA.

SCHULTZ, Rt Rev. Bruce Allan, Bishop of Grafton, NSW, 1985–98; *b* 24 May 1932; *s* of Percival Ferdinand and Elsie Amelia Schultz; *m* 1962, Janet Margaret Gersbach; two *s* two *d* (and one *s* decd). *Educ:* Culcairn High School; St Columb's Hall and St John's Coll., Morpeth. ThL (ACT) 1960. Sheep and wheat property, Manager-Owner, 1950–57. Theolog. student, 1957–60; deacon 1959, priest 1960, dio. Riverina; Asst Priest, Broken Hill, 1961–63; Priest-in-charge, Ariah Park, Ardlethan and Barellan with Weethalle, 1964–67; Rector: Deniliquin, 1967–73; Gladstone, dio. Rockhampton, 1973–79; Archdeacon and Commissary of Rockhampton, 1975–79; Rector of Grafton and Dean of Christ Church Cathedral, 1979–83; Asst Bishop of Brisbane (Bishop for the Northern Region), 1983–85. Nat. Chm., Anglican Boys' Soc. in Australia, 1987–94; Episcopal overseer, Cursillo Movement in Australia, 1987–95; Chm., NSW Provincial Commn on Christian Educn, 1988–94; Bd Mem., Australian Bd of Missions, 1988–95; Chm., Nat. Home Mission Fund, 1999–2002. *Recreations:* family, fishing, gardening. *Address:* 11 Carwoola Crescent, Mooloolaba, Qld 4557, Australia. *Clubs:* Mooloolaba Surf Life Saving, Mooloolaba Bowls (Mooloolaba).

SCHULTZ, Prof. Wolfram, MD; Wellcome Trust Principal Research Fellow and Professor of Neuroscience, University of Cambridge, since 2001; *b* 27 Aug. 1944; *s* of Robert and Herta Schultz; *m* 1972, Gerda Baumann; two *s* one *d*. *Educ:* Heidelberg (MD 1972); Univ. of Fribourg (Habilitation 1981). Postdoctoral work, 1973–77: MPI, Goettingen; NY State Univ., Buffalo, NY; Karolinska Inst., Stockholm; Asst, Associate, then full Prof. of Neurophysiology, Univ. of Fribourg, 1977–2001. Sabbaticals: Univ. of Cambridge, 1993; Tokyo Metropolitan Inst. for Neurosci., 1997; CIT, Pasadena, 2004, 2005, 2007, 2008. *Publications:* articles in learned jls. *Recreations:* sailing, snowboarding.

Address: Department of Physiology, Development and Neuroscience, University of Cambridge, Downing Street, Cambridge CB2 3DY. *T:* (01223) 333779; *e-mail:* ws234@cam.ac.uk.

SCHUMACHER, Diana Catherine Brett; Director, Work Structuring Ltd, since 2002; *b* 8 April 1941; *d* of Clarence Edward Brett Binns and Phyllis Mary Brett Binns; *m* 1966, Christian Schumacher; two *d*. *Educ:* St Hilda's Coll., Oxford (MA Mod. Hist.). British Council, 1964–66; Internat. Survey Res., Univ. of Chicago, 1969–73; Partner, Schumacher Projects Consultancy, 1979–2002; Co-Founder, Green Books, 1986. Founder Mem. and Trustee, Schumacher Soc., 1978– (Pres., 1991–2000); Advr, Schumacher Coll., 1991–93; Founder Mem., Schumacher Inst., 2005. Member: Exec. Cttee, Green Alliance, 1982–92; Mgt Bd, Centre for Internat. Peacebuilding, 1985–; Founder Member and Trustee: Gandhi Foundn, 1983–98; New Econs Foundn, 1986–98; Founder Member: Envmtl Law Foundn, 1987– (Vice Chm., 1987–95; Life Vice-Pres., 1995–); SPES Forum, 2005–; Trustee: India Develt Gp, 1980–2005; Ecological Action Gp for Europe, 1984– (Vice Pres., 2005–); Themba Trust, 2005–. Patron: UK Social Investment Forum; Green Network; Peace Child Internat.; Tree Aid; Member: PRASEG; Soil Assoc. Gov., St Stephen's C of E and Middle Sch., S Godstone, 1970–90. FRSA. *Publications:* (jtly) Going Solar, 1977, 2nd edn 1979; (jtly) Solar Flatplate Collectors for Developing Countries, 1979; Energy: crisis or opportunity, 1985; Our Human Shelter Within the Global Shelter, 1987; Ten Principles for an Organic Energy Policy, 1992; Small is Manageable: from theory to practice, 2003; *contributions to:* Habitat un ambiente per Vivere, 1994; This I Believe, 1997; Cuba Verde, 1999; The Council of Europe as the Conscience of Europe, 1999; Spirituality as a Public Good, 2007; contribs to jls incl. European Business Review, Resurgence, etc. *Recreations:* walking, the arts, organic gardening and food, making incomprehensible lists. *Address:* Church House, Godstone, Surrey RH9 8BW. *Club:* Royal Over-Seas League.

SCHUMACHER, Michael; professional racing driver, 1983–2006; *b* 3 Jan. 1969; *s* of Rolf and late Elisabeth Schumacher; *m* 1995, Corinna Betsch; one *s* one *d*. Formula 3, 1983–90; European and World Champion, 1990; Formula 1, 1991–2006; Benetton-Ford team, 1991–95; Ferrari team, 1996–2006; Drivers' World Champion, 1994, 1995, 2000, 2001, 2002, 2003, 2004. *Publications:* (jtly) Formula for Success, 1996; (jtly) Michael Schumacher: driving force, 2003. *Address:* c/o Weber Management GmbH, Traenkenstrasse 11, 70597 Stuttgart, Germany. *T:* (711) 726460.

SCHÜSSEL, Dr Wolfgang; MP (People's Party), Austria, since 1979; Chancellor of Austria, 2000–07; *b* Vienna, 7 June 1945; *m;* two *c*. *Educ:* Vienna Univ. (DJur). Sec., Austrian People's Party, 1968–75; Sec.-Gen., Austrian Econ. Fedn, 1975–89. Minister of Econ. Affairs, Austria, 1989–95; Vice-Chancellor and Minister of Foreign Affairs, 1996–2000. Chm., 1995–2006, Leader, Parly Gp, 2006–, Austrian People's Party. *Address:* Parlamentsklub der ÖVP, Dr-Karl-Renner-Ring 1–3, 1017 Vienna, Austria.

SCHWAB, Dr Klaus, Hon. KCMG 2006; Founder and Executive Chairman, World Economic Forum, since 1971; *b* 30 March 1938; *s* of Eugen and Erika Schwab; *m* 1971, Hilde Stoll; one *s* one *d*. *Educ:* Humanistisches Gymnasium, Ravensburg; Swiss Fed. Inst. of Technology (Dip. ing 1962; Dr ing 1966); Univ. of Fribourg (Lic.ès.sc.écon 1963; Dr rer. pol. 1967); John F. Kennedy Sch. of Govt, Harvard (MPA 1967). Experience on shop floor of several cos, 1958–62; Asst to Dir Gen. of German Machine-building Assoc., Frankfurt, 1963–65; Mem., Managing Bd, Sulzer Escher Wyss AG, Zurich, 1967–70. Prof., Geneva Univ., 1973–2003. Co-founder and Mem. Foundn Bd, Schwab Foundn for Social Entrepreneurship, Geneva, 1998–. Trustee, Peres Center for Peace, Tel Aviv, 1997–; Mem. Adv. Bd, Foreign Policy, Washington, 1997–. Mem. Vis. Cttee, JFK Sch. of Govt, Harvard Univ., 1996–; Hon. Prof., Ben-Gurion Univ. of the Negev, Israel, 2003–; Mem. President's Council, Univ. of Tokyo, 2006–. Mem. Bd, Lucerne Fest., 2007–. Freedom, City of London, 2006. Six hon. doctorates. Grand Cross, Nat. Order of Merit (Germany), 1995; Knight, Légion d'Honneur (France), 1997; Golden Grand Cross, Nat. Order (Austria), 1997; Medal of Freedom (Slovenia), 1997; Comdr's Cross with Star, Nat. Order (Poland), 2002; Decoration of 1st Degree for Outstanding Giving (Jordan), 2005. *Publications:* Global Competitiveness Report (annually), 1979–; numerous articles. *Recreations:* cross-country ski marathon, high mountain climbing. *Address:* (office) World Economic Forum, 91–93 route de la Capite, 1223 Cologny, Switzerland. *T:* (22) 8691212, *Fax:* (22) 7862744; *e-mail:* contact@weforum.org.

SCHWARTE, Maria; *see* Adebowale, M.

SCHWARTZ, Prof. Steven, PhD; Vice-Chancellor and President, Macquarie University, Sydney, since 2006; *b* New York, 5 Nov. 1946; *s* of Robert and Frances Schwartz; *m* 2001, Claire Mary Farrugia; two *s* three *d*. *Educ:* Brooklyn Coll., City Univ. of New York (BA); Syracuse Univ., New York (MSc, PhD). FASSA 1991; FAICD 2001; FAIM 2001. Res. Scientist, Dept of Psychiatry, Community and Public Health, Med. Br., Univ. of Texas, 1975–79; Sen. Lectr, Dept of Psychology, Univ. of Western Australia, Perth, 1978–79; University of Queensland: Prof. and Hd, Dept of Psychology, 1980–90; Pres., Academic Bd, 1991–93; Exec. Dean, Faculty of Medicine and Dentistry, Univ. of WA, 1994–95; Vice-Chancellor and Pres., Murdoch Univ., 1996–2001; Vice-Chancellor and Principal, Brunel Univ., 2002–05. Royal Soc. Anglo-Australian Exchange Fellow, ICRF Labs, London, 1988. Leader, Admissions to Higher Educn Review, 2003–04; Member: Adv. Bd, Centre for Ind. Studies, 1997–; Bd, Council for Internat. Educn Exchange, 1997–; Chm., Bologna Process Steering Gp, Dept of Educn, Employment and Workplace Relns, 2007–. Mem., London Production Industries Commn, 2004–05; Dir, Australia-America Fulbright Commn, 2007–. Gov., Richmond, Amer. Internat. Univ. in London, 2004–05; Australian Govt Rep., Council, Univ. of South Pacific, 2007–. Mem. Adv. Council, Reform, 2004–. *Publications:* (jtly) Psychopathology of Childhood, 1981, 2nd edn 1995; Measuring Reading Competence, 1984; Classic Studies in Psychology, 1986 (trans. German 1991); (with T. Griffin) Medical Thinking: the psychology of medical judgement and decision-making, 1986; Pavlov's Heirs, 1987; Classic Studies in Abnormal Psychology, 1993; Abnormal Psychology, 2000; *edited:* (jtly) Human Judgement and Decision Processes, 1975; (jtly) Human Judgement and Decision Processes in Applied Settings, 1977; Language and Cognition in Schizophrenia, 1978; Case Studies in Abnormal Psychology, 1992; contrib. books and learned jls. *Recreations:* rambling, reading, writing. *Address:* Macquarie University, North Ryde, Sydney, NSW 2109, Australia; Apartment 802, 45 Bowman Street, Pyrmont, Sydney, NSW 2009, Australia.

SCHWARTZMAN, Arnold Martin, OBE 2002; RDI 2006; President, Arnold Schwartzman Productions, Los Angeles, since 1985; *b* London, 6 Jan. 1936; *s* of David and Rose Schwartzman; *m* 1st, 1958, Marilyn Bild (marr. diss. 1979); one *d;* 2nd, 1980, Isolde Weghofer. *Educ:* Thanet Sch. of Art and Crafts, Margate; Canterbury Coll. of Art (NDD 1955). Served Royal Sussex Regt, Germany and Korea, 1955–57. Graphic Designer: Southern TV, Southampton, 1959–60; Associated-Rediffusion Television, London, 1960–66; Concept Planning Executive, Erwin Wasey Advertising, London, 1966–69; Dir, Conran Design Gp, 1969; Principal, Arnold Schwartzman Prodns, London, 1970–78; Design Dir, Saul Bass & Associates, LA, 1978–79; Producer/Dir, Genocide, 1981 (Acad. Award for Best Documentary Feature); Dir of Design, 1984 Los Angeles Olympic Games,

1982. Other documentary feature films include: Building a Dream, 1989; Echoes that Remain, 1991; Liberation, 1994. First Co-Chm., 1997–98, Chm. Bd, 1999–2000, Gov., 2000–, BAFTA/LA; Chm. Documentary Exec. Cttee, Acad. of Motion Picture Arts and Scis, 2000–01. Mem., Bd of Govs, Univ. for the Creative Arts, 2008–. Mem., AGI, 1974–. *Publications:* Airshipwreck (with Len Deighton), 1978; Graven Images, 1993; Phono-Graphics, 1993; Liberation, 1994; Designage, 1998; (with Michael Webb) It's a Great Wall, 2000; Flicks: how the movies began, 2000; Deco Landmarks, 2005; London Art Deco, 2007. *Recreations:* cinema, photography. *Address:* 317½ North Sycamore Avenue, Los Angeles, CA 90036, USA. *T:* (323) 9381481, *Fax:* (323) 9314741; *e-mail:* arnold@schwartzmandesign.com.

SCHWARZ, Cheryl Lynn; *see* Studer, C. L.

SCHWARZ, Gerard; conductor; Music Director: Seattle Symphony Orchestra, since 1985; Royal Liverpool Philharmonic Orchestra, 2001–06; *b* NJ, 19 Aug. 1947; *m* 1984, Jody Greitzer; two *s* two *d*. *Educ:* Juilliard Sch., NYC. Conductor, 1966–; Music Director: Erick Hawkins Dance Co., 1967–72; SoHo Ensemble, 1969–75; Eliot Field Dance Co., NYC, 1972–78; NY Chamber SO, 1977–2002; LA Chamber Orch., 1976–86; Music Advr, 1983–84, Principal Conductor, 1984–85, Seattle SO. Estabd Music Today, 1981, Music Dir, 1981–89; Music Advr, Mostly Mozart Fest., NYC, 1982–84 (Music Dir, 1984–2001); Artistic Advr, Tokyo Bunkamura's Orchard Hall, 1994–97; operatic conducting début with Washington Opera, 1982, with Seattle Opera, 1986. Guest Conductor with major orchestras in N America, Europe, Australia and Japan. Has made numerous recordings. Hon. DMus: Juilliard Sch.; Puget Sound; Hon. DFA: Farleigh Dickinson; Seattle. Ditson Conductor's Award, Columbia Univ., 1989; Conductor of Year, Musical America Internat. Directory of Performing Arts, 1994. *Address:* c/o Seattle Symphony, 200 University Street, Seattle, WA 98101, USA.

SCHWARZENEGGER, Arnold Alois; actor; Governor of California, since 2003; *b* Graz, Austria, 30 July 1947; *s* of late Gustav Schwarzenegger and Aurelia Schwarzenegger (*née* Jedrny); arrived in USA 1968, naturalized citizen of USA, 1983; *m* 1986, Maria Owings Shriver; two *s* two *d*. *Educ:* Univ. of Wisconsin-Superior (BA 1980). Weightlifter and bodybuilder, 1965–75; Jun. Mr Europe, 1965; Best Built Man of Europe, 1966; Mr Europe, 1966; Internat. Powerlifting Champion, 1966; Mr Universe, Nat. Amateur Body Builders' Assoc. (amateur) 1967, (professional) 1968, 1969, 1970; German Powerlifting Champion, 1968; Mr International, 1968, Mr Universe (amateur), 1969, Mr Olympia, annually, 1970–75, 1980, Internat. Fedn of Body Building; Mr World, 1970. *Films include:* Stay Hungry, 1976; Pumping Iron, 1977; The Villain, 1979; The Jayne Mansfield Story, 1980; Conan the Barbarian, 1982; Conan the Destroyer, 1983; The Terminator, 1984; Commando, 1985; Raw Deal, 1986; Predator, Running Man, 1987; Red Heat, Twins, 1988; Total Recall, Kindergarten Cop, 1990; Terminator 2: Judgement Day, 1991; The Last Action Hero (also prod.), 1993; True Lies, Junior, 1994; Jingle All the Way, Eraser, 1996; Batman and Robin, With Wings of Eagles, 1997; End of Days, 1999; The Sixth Day (also prod.), 2000; Collateral Damage, 2002; Terminator 3: Rise of the Machines, 2003. Chm., US President's Council on Physical Fitness and Sports, 1990–93. *Publications:* (jtly) Arnold: the education of a bodybuilder, 1977; Arnold's Bodyshaping for Women, 1979; Arnold's Bodybuilding for Men, 1981; Arnold's Encyclopedia of Modern Bodybuilding, 1985, 2nd edn 1998; (jtly) Arnold's Fitness for Kids, 1993. *Address:* State Capitol, Sacramento, CA 95814, USA.

SCHWARZKOPF, Gen. H. Norman, Hon. KCB 1991; Commander, Allied Forces, Gulf War, Jan.–Feb. 1991; Commander in Chief, US Central Command, MacDill Air Force Base, Florida, 1988–91; *b* 22 Aug. 1934; *s* of Herbert Norman Schwarzkopf and Ruth (*née* Bowman); *m* 1968, Brenda Holsinger; one *s* two *d*. *Educ:* Bordentown Mil. Inst.; Valley Forge Mil. Acad. (football schol.); US Mil. Acad., West Point; Univ. of S Calif (MME 1964). Commnd 2nd Lieut. Inf. and airborne trng, Fort Benning, Ga; 101st Airborne Div., Fort Campbell, Ky; Teacher, Mil. Acad., West Point, 1964 and 1966–68; Task-Force Advr, S Vietnamese Airborne Div., 1965; Comdr, 1st Bn, 6th Inf., 198th Inf. Bde, Americal Div., 1969–73; Dep. Comdr, 172nd Inf. Bde, Fort Richardson, Alaska, 1974–76; Comdr, 1st Bde, 9th Inf. Div., Fort Lewis, Wash, 1976–78; Dep. Dir of Plans, US Pacific Comd, Camp Smith, Hawaii, 1978–80; Asst Div. Comdr, 8th Mechanized Inf. Div., W Germany, 1980–82; Dir, Military-Personnel Management, Office of Dep. Chief of Staff for Personnel Management, Office of Dep. Chief of Staff for Personnel, Washington, DC, 1982–83; Comdr, 24th Mechanized Inf. Div., Fort Stewart, Ga, 1983–85; Comdr, US Ground Forces and Dep. Comdr, Jt Task Force, Grenada op. Oct. 1983; Asst Dep. Chief of Staff, Army Ops, Washington DC, 1985–86; Comdr, I Corps, Fort Lewis, Wash, 1986–87; Dep. Chief for Ops and Plans, Washington, DC, 1987–88. DSM with oak leaf cluster; DFC; Silver Star with 2 oak leaf clusters; Bronze Star with 3 oak leaf clusters; Purple Heart with oak leaf cluster; Congressional Gold Medal, 1991. *Publication:* (with Peter Petre) It Doesn't Take a Hero (autobiog.), 1992. *Address:* c/o Marvin Josephson, International Creative Management, 40 West 57th Street, New York, NY 10019–4001, USA.

SCHWEBEL, Stephen Myron; President, Administrative Tribunal, International Monetary Fund, since 1994; arbitrator and mediator; *b* 10 March 1929; *s* of Victor Schwebel and Pauline Pfeffer Schwebel; *m* 1972, Louise Killander; two *d*. *Educ:* Harvard Coll. (BA); Trinity Coll., Cambridge (Frank Knox Meml Fellow; Hon. Fellow, 2005); Yale Law Sch. (LLB). Attorney, White & Case, 1954–59; Asst Prof. of Law, Harvard Law Sch., 1959–61; Asst Legal Advr, State Dept, 1961–66; Exec. Dir, Amer. Soc. of Internat. Law, 1967–73; Dep. Legal Advr, State Dept, 1973–81; Judge, 1981–2000, Pres., 1997–2000, Internat. Court of Justice. Burling Prof. of Internat. Law, Sch. of Advanced Internat. Studies, Johns Hopkins Univ., 1967–81. Member: UN Internat. Law Commn, 1977–81; Panel of Arbitrators and Panel of Conciliators, ICSID, 2001–08; Perm. Court of Arbitration, The Hague, 2006–; Admin. Tribunal, World Bank, 2007–. Hon. Bencher, Gray's Inn, 1998. Weill Medal, NY Univ. Sch. of Law, 1992; Medal of Merit, Yale Law Sch., 1997; Manley O. Hudson Medal, Amer. Soc. of Internat. Law, 2000. *Publications:* The Secretary-General of the United Nations, 1952; International Arbitration: three salient problems, 1987; Justice in International Law, 1994. *Recreations:* music, walking. *Address:* (office) 1501 K Street NW, Washington, DC 20005, USA. *T:* (202) 7368328; Cady Brook Farm, PO Box 356, South Woodstock, Vermont 05071, USA. *T:* (802) 4571358. *Clubs:* Athenæum; Harvard (New York); Cosmos, Metropolitan (Washington).

SCHWEITZER, Louis; Chairman, Renault, since 1992 (Chief Executive Officer, 1992–2005); *b* Geneva, 8 July 1942; *s* of late Pierre-Paul Schweitzer; *m* 1972, Agnès Schmitz; two *d*. *Educ:* Institut d'Etudes Politiques, Paris; Faculté de Droit, Paris; Ecole Nationale d'Administration, Paris. Inspectorate of Finance, 1970–74; special assignment, later Dep. Dir, Min. of Budget, 1974–81; Chief of Staff: to Minister of Budget, 1981–83; of Industry and Research, 1983; to Prime Minister, 1984–86; Régie Renault: Vice-Pres. for Finance and Planning, 1986–90; Chief Finance Officer, 1988–90; Exec. Vice-Pres., 1989–90; Pres. and Chief Operating Officer, 1990–92. Prof., Inst. d'Etudes Politiques de Paris, 1982–86. Director: Inst Français des Relations Internats, 1989–; BNP, 1993–; Philips, 1997–; EDF, 1999–; Volvo, 2001–; Veolia Environnement, 2003–; L'Oréal,

2005–; non-exec. Chm., AstraZeneca, 2005–. Chm., Haute Autorité de Lutte contre les Discriminations et pour l'Égalité, 2005–. Grand Officier, Ordre National du Mérite (France), 2007 (Officier, 1992, Comdr, 2002); Commandeur, Légion d'Honneur (France), 2005 (Officier, 1998). *Address:* Renault, 860 Quai de Stalingrad, 92109 Boulogne-Billancourt cedex, France.

SCHWEITZER, Prof. Miguel; Dean, Finisterrae University Law School, since 2003; *b* 22 July 1940; *s* of Miguel Schweitzer and Cora Walters; *m*; two *s* one *d*. *Educ:* The Grange School, Santiago (preparatory and secondary schooling); Law School, Univ. of Chile (law degree). Doctorate in Penal Law, Rome, 1964–65; Professor of Penal Law: Law Sch., Univ. of Chile, 1966; High Sch. of Carabineros (Police), 1968, 1970 and from 1974; Director, Dept of Penal Sciences, Univ. of Chile, 1974–76; Chile's Alternate Representative with the Chilean Delegn to UN, 1975, 1976, 1978; Ambassador on special missions, 1975–80; Chilean Delegate to OAS, 1976–78; Ambassador to UK, 1980–83; Minister for Foreign Affairs, Chile, 1983. *Publications:* El Error de Derecho en Materia Penal (Chile), 1964; Sull elemento soggettivo nel reato di bancarotta del l'imprenditore (Rome), 1965; Prospectus for a Course on the Special Part of Penal Law (USA), 1969. *Recreations:* music, reading, golf, tennis, Rugby. *Address:* Floor 15, Miraflores 178, Santiago, Chile; *e-mail:* msw@schweitzer.cl. *Clubs:* Union; Prince of Wales Country (Santiago).

SCICLUNA, Martin Anthony, FCA; Chairman, Deloitte & Touche LLP, 1995–2007; *b* 20 Nov. 1950; *s* of late William Scicluna and Miriam Scicluna; *m* 1979 (marr. diss. 2000); two *s* one *d*. *Educ:* Berkhamsted Sch., Herts; Univ. of Leeds (BCom). FCA 1983 (ACA 1977). Joined Deloitte & Touche (formerly Touche Ross & Co.), 1973; Partner, 1982–2008; Head, London Audit, 1990–95; Mem., Bd of Partners, 1991–2007; Mem. Bd Dirs and Governance Cttee, 1999–2007, Managing Partner, Global Strategic Clients, 2001–03, Deloitte Touche Tohmatsu. Chm., Accounting and Reporting Working Gp, and Mem., Steering Gp, Company Law Review, 1999–2001. Chm., London Soc. Chartered Accountants in England and Wales, 1989–90; Institute of Chartered Accountants in England and Wales: Mem. Council, 1990–95; Chm., Auditing Cttee, 1990–95. Chm., Chairmen's Business Forum, Leeds Univ. Bus. Sch., 2002–06; Mem. Council, Leeds Univ., 2008–. Trustee, Understanding Industry, 1999–2003; Mem. Bd of Trustees, WellBeing, 2000–03. Vice Patron, businessdynamics, 2003–06. Member: Sailability Develt Bd, RYA, 2000–03; Adv. Council, Cancer Res. UK (formerly CRC), 1999–2003; Finance Cttee, V&A Mus., 2007–. Governor: NIESR, 2002–; Berkhamsted Collegiate Sch., 2008–. Freeman, City of London, 1993; Liveryman, Co. of Chartered Accountants in England and Wales, 1993. FRSA 1996. CCMI (CIMgt 1996). Hon. LLD Leeds, 2008. *Recreations:* Arsenal FC, tennis, gardening, wine. *Address:* Parkways, Little Heath Lane, Potten End, Herts HP4 2RX.

SCICLUNA, Martin Leonard Andrew; Director General, Today Public Policy Institute, since 2007; Adviser on Illegal Immigration to Minister of Justice and Home Affairs, Malta, since 2005; Vice-President, Din l-Art Helwa (National Trust of Malta), since 2005 (Executive President, 2001–05); *b* 16 Nov. 1935; *s* of Richard Hugh Scicluna and Victoria Mary (*née* Amato-Gauci); *m* 1st, 1960, Anna Judith Brennand (marr. diss. 1988); one *s*; 2nd, 1989, Loraine Jean Birnie; two step *d*. *Educ:* St Edward's Coll., Cottonera, Malta; RMA, Sandhurst. Royal Malta Artillery, 1953–65 (commnd 1955); transferred to RA, 1965–74 (Army Staff Coll., 1965). Joined Civil Service, MoD, 1974; Principal: Naval Personnel Div., 1974–76; Naval and Army Defence Secretariats, 1976–80; Asst Sec., 1980; Hd, Air Force Logistics Secretariat, 1980–83; Dep. Chief, Public Relns, 1983–85; Hd, Gen. Staff Secretariat, 1985–89; RCDS, 1989; Hd, Manpower Resources and Progs, 1990–91; Hd, Resources and Progs (Management Planning), 1991; Asst Under Sec. of State (Adjt Gen.), MoD, 1992; on secondment to FCO, UK delegn to NATO, 1993–95; Ambassador of Malta to NATO, 1996; Advr on Defence Policy to the PM of Malta, 1996–99; Dir of Finance and Infrastructure, PricewaterhouseCoopers, Malta, 1999–2002. Dir, HSBC Cares for Heritage Fund, 2007–. 1992–93: Chm. of Comrs, Duke of York's Royal Mil. Coll.; Comr, Royal Hosp., Chelsea; Commissioner: Queen Victoria Sch., Dunblane; Welbeck Coll., Notts; Chm., of Trustees, Army Welfare Fund; Trustee: Nat. Army Mus.; Army Benevolent Fund. Member: Council, Europa Nostra, 2003–; Cttee of Guarantee of Malta's Cultural Heritage, 2003–05; Nat. Commn for Sustainable Develt, 2003–; Bd, Internat. Nat. Trusts Orgn, 2005–; Pres., European Network of Nat. Heritage Orgns, 2003–04. Chm. Bd of Govs, St Edward's Coll., 2000–05; Trustee, Lady Strickland's Trust for St Edward's Coll., 2000–. *Recreations:* painting, theatre, watching sport, other sedentary pursuits. *Address:* c/o Barclays Bank plc, 212 Regent Street, W1A 4BP; Dar San Martin, Triq Il-Bali Guarena, Qrendi ZRQ 07, Malta. *T:* 21689532.

SCLATER, Prof. John George, PhD; FRS 1982; Professor of Marine Geophysics, Scripps Institution of Oceanography, University of California at San Diego, since 1991; *b* 17 June 1940; *s* of John George Sclater and Margaret Bennett Glen; *m* 1st, 1968, Fredrica Rose Felcyn; two *s*; 2nd, 1985, Paula Ann Edwards (marr. diss. 1991); 3rd, 1992, Naila Gloria Cortez; one *d*. *Educ:* Carlekemp Priory School; Stonyhurst College; Edinburgh Univ. (BSc); Cambridge Univ. (PhD 1966). Research Scientist, Scripps Instn of Oceanography, 1965; Massachusetts Institute of Technology: Associate Prof., 1972; Professor, 1977; Dir, Jt Prog. in Oceanography and Oceanographic Engrg with Woods Hole Oceanographic Instn, 1981; Prof., Dept of Geol Scis, and Associate Dir, Inst. for Geophysics, 1983–91, Shell Dist. Prof., 1983–88, Univ. of Texas at Austin. Guggenheim Fellow, 1998–99. Fellow Geological Soc. of America; Fellow Amer. Geophysical Union; Mem., US Nat. Acad. of Scis, 1989. Rosenstiel Award in Oceanography, Rosenstiel Sch., Univ. of Miami, 1979; Bucher Medal, Amer. Geophysical Union, 1985. *Recreations:* running, swimming, golf. *Address:* Scripps Institution of Oceanography, 9500 Gilman Drive, La Jolla, CA 92093–0220, USA.

SCLATER, John Richard, CVO 1999; Trustee, The Grosvenor Estate, 1973–2005; Chairman: Foreign & Colonial Investment Trust PLC, 1985–2002 (Director, 1981–2002); Graphite (formerly Foreign & Colonial) Enterprise Trust Plc, since 1986; *b* 14 July 1940; *s* of late Arthur William Sclater and Alice Sclater (*née* Collett); *m* 1st, 1967, Nicola Mary Gloria Cropper (marr. diss.); one *s* (one *d* decd); 2nd, 1985, Grizel Elizabeth Catherine Dawson, MBE. *Educ:* Charterhouse; Gonville and Caius Coll., Cambridge (schol., 1st Cl. Hons History Tripos, BA, MA); Commonwealth Fellow, 1962–64; Yale Univ. (MA 1963); Harvard Univ. (MBA 1968). Glyn, Mills & Co., 1964–70; Dir, Williams, Glyn & Co., 1970–76; Man. Dir, Nordic Bank, 1976–85 (Chm., 1985); Dir, 1985–87, Jt Dep. Chm., 1987, Guinness Peat Gp PLC; Dir and Dep. Chm., 1985–87, Chm., 1987, Guinness Mahon & Co. Ltd; Chairman: Foreign & Colonial Ventures Ltd, 1989–98; Berisford plc, 1990–2000 (Dir, 1986–2000); Hill Samuel Bank Ltd, 1992–96 (Dir, 1990–96; Vice-Chm., 1990–92); Graphite (formerly Foreign & Colonial) Private Equity Trust PLC, 1994–2002; Union (formerly Union Discount Co. of London) plc, 1996 (Dir, 1981–96, Dep. Chm., 1986–96); Biotech Growth Trust plc (formerly Reabourne Merlin, then Finsbury, Life Sciences Investment Trust, subseq. Finsbury Emerging Biotechnology Trust Plc), 1997–; Argent Group Europe Ltd, 1998–; Berner, Nicol & Co. Ltd, 2002–04, 2005– (Dir, 1968–2004); Pres., Equitable Life Assce Soc., 1994–2001 (Dir, 1985–2002); Deputy Chairman: Yamaichi International (Europe) Ltd, 1985–97; Millennium & Copthorne Hotels PLC, 1996–2007; Grosvenor Gp Ltd (formerly Grosvenor Estate Hldgs), 1999–2005 (Dir, 1989–); Director: James Cropper PLC, 1972–; Holker Estates Co. Ltd, 1974–; F & C Group (Hldgs) Ltd, 1989–2001; Fuel Tech (Europe), 1990–98; Angerstein Underwriting Trust PLC, 1995–96; Wates Group Ltd, 1999–2004; Member, London Bd of Halifax Building Soc., 1983–90. Mem., City Taxation Cttee, 1973–76. Chm., Assoc. of Consortium Banks, 1980–82. Mem., City Adv. Gp, CBI, 1988–99. Mem. Council, Duchy of Lancaster, 1987–2000. First Church Estates Comr, 1999–2001; Mem., Archbishops' Council and Gen. Synod, C of E, 1999–2001. Governor: Internat. Students House, 1976–99; Brambletye Sch. Trust, 1976–2006. Freeman, City of London, 1992; Liveryman, Goldsmiths' Co., 1992–. *Recreations:* country pursuits. *Address:* Sutton Hall, Barcombe, near Lewes, Sussex BN8 5EB. *T:* (01273) 400450, *Fax:* (01273) 401086. *Clubs:* Brooks's; University Pitt (Cambridge); Sussex.

SCLATER-BOOTH, family name of **Baron Basing**.

SCOBIE, Kenneth Charles, CA; Chairman, Chemring, since 1997; *b* 29 July 1938; *s* of Charles Scobie and Shena (*née* Melrose); *m* 1973, Adela Jane Hollebone; one *s* one *d*. *Educ:* Daniel Stewart's Coll., Edinburgh; Edinburgh Univ. CA 1961. Romanes-Munro, CA, 1956–61; BMC (Scotland) Ltd, 1961–63; Rolls-Royce Ltd, 1963–66; Robson Morrow & Co., 1966–70; Black & Decker, 1971–72; Vavasseur South Africa Ltd, 1972–76; H. C. Sleigh Ltd, 1979–83; Blackwood Hodge plc, 1984–90; Dep. Chm. and Chief Exec., Brent Walker Group, 1991–93; Chairman: Lovells Confectionery Ltd, 1991–98; William Hill Group, 1992–93; Allied Leisure, 1994–2000; Dep. Chm., Addis, 1993–94; Dir, Postern Exec. Gp., 1991–97. Non-exec. Director: Albrighton plc., 1990–93; Gartmore Venture Capital, 1993–98. Chm. Exec. Bd, Scottish Rugby Union, 2000–03. CCMI (CBIM 1987). *Recreations:* sport, Bridge. *Address:* Path Hill House, Path Hill, Goring Heath, Oxon RG8 7RE. *T:* (0118) 9842417. *Clubs:* London Scottish Football (Pres., 1997–2001); Huntercombe Golf; Durban (S Africa).

SCOBLE, Christopher Lawrence; Assistant Under-Secretary of State, Home Office, 1988–95; *b* 21 Nov. 1943; *s* of Victor Arthur Oliphant Scoble and Mabel Crouch; *m* 1972, Florence Hunter; one *s* one *d*. *Educ:* Kent Coll., Canterbury; Corpus Christi Coll., Oxford. Asst Principal, Home Office, 1965; Private Sec. to Minister of State, Welsh Office, 1969–70; Home Office: Principal, 1970; Sec. to Adv. Council on the Penal System, 1976–78; Asst Sec., 1978; Asst Under-Sec. of State, Broadcasting and Miscellaneous Dept, 1988–91, Establishment Dept, 1991–94, Police Dept, 1994–95. Vice-Chm., Media Policy Cttee, Council of Europe, 1985–87. CS (Nuffield and Leverhulme) Travelling Fellowship, 1987–88. *Publications:* Fisherman's Friend: a life of Stephen Reynolds, 2000; (ed) A Poor Man's House, by Stephen Reynolds, 2001; Colin Blythe: lament for a legend, 2005. *Address:* The School House, Church Lane, Sturminster Newton, Dorset DT10 1DH. *T:* (01258) 473491.

SCOBLE, Malcolm John, PhD, DSc; Keeper of Entomology, Natural History Museum, since 2006; *b* Buckfastleigh, Devon, 6 July 1950; *s* of George Luis Evan, (Dick), Scoble and Edith Maud, (Babs), Scoble; *m* 1982, Theresa Jean Smuts. *Educ:* Kelly Coll., Tavistock; Portsmouth Poly. (BSc Zool., London ext., 1972; MPhil 1974); Rhodes Univ. (PhD 1982); DSc London 2002. MIBiol 1982; CBiol 1982; FLS 1995; FRES 1987. Res. Asst, Portsmouth Poly., 1972–74; Professional Officer, then Sen. Professional Officer in Entomol., Transvaal Mus., Pretoria, 1975–82; Asst Curator/Actg Curator, Hope Entomological Collections, University Mus., Univ. of Oxford, 1982–85; Res. Entomologist, 1985–2002, Associate Keeper, 2002–06, Natural Hist. Mus. Member Council: Systematics Assoc., 1986–89; Linnean Soc. of London, 1995–98, 2007– (Vice-Pres., 1997–98); Brit. Entomol and Natural Hist. Soc., 1997–98 (Vice Pres., 1994–95, 1996–97; Pres., 1995–96). Karl Jordan Medal, Amer. Lepidopterists' Soc., 2002. *Publications:* The Lepidoptera: form, function and diversity, 1992; (ed) A taxonomic catalogue to the Geometridae of the world (Insecta: Lepidoptera), 1999; (ed) ENHSIN: the European natural history specimen information network, 2003; (ed jtly) Digital Imaging of Biological Type Specimens: a manual of best practice, 2005; articles in learned jls on Lepidoptera taxonomy (incl. Linnaeus's butterflies), natural history museum resources and information access, biodiversity informatics, esp. internet-based taxonomy. *Recreations:* natural history, music, theatre, Devon. *Address:* Department of Entomology, Natural History Museum, Cromwell Road, SW7 5BD. *T:* (020) 7942 5469, *Fax:* (020) 7942 5229; *e-mail:* m.scoble@nhm.ac.uk.

SCOLES, Prof. Giacinto, FRS 1997; Donner Professor of Science, Princeton University, since 1987 (fall term only, since 2004); Professor of Biophysics and Condensed Matter Physics, International School for Advanced Studies, Trieste, since 2004; *b* 2 April 1935; *m* 1964, Giok-Lan Lim; one *d*. *Educ:* Univ. of Genova (DChem 1959; Libera docenza 1968). Asst Prof., 1960–61 and 1964–68, Associate Prof., 1968–71, Physics Dept, Univ. of Genova; Res. Associate, Kamerlingh-Onnes Lab., Univ. of Leiden, 1961–64; Prof. of Chemistry and Physics, Univ. of Waterloo, Canada, 1971–86. Hon. DPhys Genova, 1996. *Publications:* Atomic and Molecular Beam Methods, vol. 1, 1988, vol. 2, 1992; The Chemical Physics of Atomic and Molecular Clusters, 1990; contribs to learned jls. *Address:* (fall term) Department of Chemistry, Frick Laboratory, Princeton University, Princeton, NJ 08544–1009, USA. *T:* (609) 2585570; International School for Advanced Studies, Via Beirut 2–4, Trieste, Italy.

SCOON, Sir Paul, GCMG 1979; GCVO 1985; OBE 1970; Governor General of Grenada, 1978–92; *b* 4 July 1935; *m* 1970, Esmai Monica McNeilly (*née* Lumsden); two step *s* one step *d*. *Educ:* St John's Anglican Sch., Grenada; Grenada Boys' Secondary Sch.; Inst. of Education, Leeds; Toronto Univ. BA, MEd. Teacher, Grenada Boys' Secondary Sch., 1953–67. Chief Educn Officer, 1967–68, Permanent Sec., 1969, Secretary to the Cabinet, 1970–72, Grenada; Dep. Director, Commonwealth Foundn, 1973–78. Governor, Centre for Internat. Briefing, Farnham Castle, 1973–78; Vice-Pres., Civil Service Assoc., Grenada, 1968; Co-founder and former Pres., Assoc. of Masters and Mistresses, Grenada. *Publication:* Survival for Service, 2003. *Recreations:* reading, tennis. *Address:* PO Box 180, St George's, Grenada. *T:* 4402180.

SCOPELITIS, Anastase; Special Adviser to Minister of Foreign Affairs, Greece, since 2006; *b* Port Said, 1944; *s* of Evangelos Scopelitis and late Rhodesia Scopelitis (*née* Antoniadis); *m* 1971, Hélène Lolos; three *s*. *Educ:* Univ. of Athens (Master in Politics and Econs). Lectr in Public Finance, Univ. of Athens, 1969–71; Ministry of Foreign Affairs: Attaché, 1971; Third Sec., Cairo, 1973; Second Sec., 1976–79, First Sec., 1979, London; Dep. Hd of Mission, The Hague, 1980; Second Counsellor, 1982; First Counsellor, 1985; Hd, EC Ext. Relns and EC New Policies Units, 1987; European Correspondent and Actg Dir of European Political Cooperation, 1989; Minister Plenipotentiary 2nd Cl. and Dir of European Political Cooperation, 1991; Minister and Dep. Hd of Mission, London, 1993, Minister Plenipotentiary 1st Cl., 1994; Ambassador to Denmark, 1996–99; Dir Gen. for Political Affairs and Political Dir, 1999, promoted to Ambassador, 2001; Sec. Gen., 2002–03; Ambassador to Court of St James's, 2003–06. Grand Cross, Order of Phoenix (Greece), 2003. Commander: Order of Merit (Egypt), 1976; Order of Oranje-Nassau (Netherlands), 1987; Grand Cross: Order of White Star (Estonia), 1999; Order of Dannebrog (Denmark), 1999; Order of Merit (Germany), 2001; Order of Leopold II

(Belgium), 2001; Order of Infante Dom Henrique (Portugal), 2002; Order of Merit (Italy), 2003; Order of Merit (Cyprus), 2003; Grand Cross, Order of Phoenix (Greece), 2003. *Address:* 6 Panagouli Street, 190 09 Rafina, Greece.

SCORSESE, Martin; American film director; *b* 17 Nov. 1942; *s* of Charles Scorsese and Catherine (*née* Cappa); *m* 1st, 1965, Laraine Marie Brennan (marr. diss.); one *d*; 2nd, Julia Cameron (marr. diss.); one *d*; 3rd, 1979, Isabella Rosellini (marr. diss. 1983); 4th, 1985, Barbara DeFina; *m* 1999, Helen Morris; one *d*. *Educ:* Univ. of New York (BS 1964; MA 1966). Faculty Asst, 1963–66, Lectr, 1968–70, Dept of Film, Univ. of New York; dir and writer of documentaries, incl. No Direction Home - Bob Dylan, 2005. *Films* include: Who's That Knocking At My Door? (also writer), 1968; Mean Streets (also co-writer), 1973; Alice Doesn't Live Here Any More, 1974; Taxi Driver (Palme d'Or, Cannes Film Fest.), 1976; New York, New York, 1977; The Last Waltz (also actor), 1978; Raging Bull, 1980; After Hours, 1985 (Best Dir Award, Cannes Film Fest., 1986); The Color of Money, 1986; acted in 'Round Midnight, 1986; The Last Temptation of Christ, 1988; Goodfellas, 1990; Cape Fear, 1992; The Age of Innocence, 1993; Bringing out the Dead, 1999; Gangs of New York, 2002; The Aviator, 2005; The Departed, 2006 (Acad. Award, Best Dir, 2007); Shine a Light, 2008; producer: Mad Dog and Glory, 1993; Naked in New York, 1994; Casino, 1996; Kundun, 1998. *Address:* c/o The Firm, 9465 Wilshire Boulevard, 6th Floor, Beverly Hills, CA 90212, USA.

SCOTFORD, Garth Barrie, OBE 1994; QFSM 1982; County Manager, Berkshire County Council, 1993–96; *b* 28 Oct. 1943; *s* of Albert Edward Scotford and Louisa Emily Jane Scotford (*née* Leach); *m* 1st, 1964, Gillian Avril Patricia Constable (*d* 1999); one *s* two *d*; 2nd, 2000, Caroline Susan James. *Educ:* Reading Grammar Sch. Joined Fire Service, 1961: served in Reading, Liverpool, Hants and Gtr Manchester; Chief Fire Officer, Berks, 1984–93, retd. FIFireE 1977 (Pres., 1985). *Recreations:* opera, bridge, golf. *Address:* 9 Tarbenian Way, Brigadoon, WA 6069, Australia. *T:* (8) 92961497.

See also J. E. Scotford.

SCOTFORD, John Edward, CBE 1993; Treasurer, Hampshire County Council, 1983–97; *b* 15 Aug. 1939; *s* of Albert and Louisa Scotford; *m* 1st, 1962, Marjorie Clare Wells (marr. diss. 2001); one *s*; 2nd, 2001, Alison Cawley. *Educ:* Reading Grammar Sch. CPFA. Reading County Borough Council, 1955–62; Coventry County Borough Council, 1962–65; Hampshire CC, 1965–97; Dep. County Treasurer, 1977–83. Public Works Loan Comr, 1992–96. Pres., CIPFA, 1996–97. Freeman, City of London, 1995. *Address:* 265 Boulonnais Drive, Brigadoon, WA 6069, Australia.

See also G. B. Scotford.

SCOTHERN, Mark Francis; Director, Cornwall Foundation of Promise, since 2006; *b* 2 July 1960; *s* of late Norman Scothern and of Joan Scothern; *m* 1998, Caroline Fiske. *Educ:* Austin Friars Sch., Carlisle; MBA Warwick Univ. Business Sch., 2000. Co-ordinator, Thamesdown Housing Link, 1984–88; Policy Officer, CHAR (Housing Campaign for Single People), 1988–91; Dir, Crisis (formerly Crisis at Christmas), 1991–96; Develt Man., Shelter, 1997–98; Associate, Rho Delta, mgt consultancy, 1998–99; Dir, Derby CVS, 1999–2005. *Recreations:* film, contemporary music, food, biographies, cycling.

SCOTLAND OF ASTHAL, Baroness *cr* 1997 (Life Peer), of Asthal in the co. of Oxfordshire; **Patricia Janet Scotland;** PC 2001; QC 1991; Attorney General, since 2007; *m* 1985, Richard Mawhinney; two *s*. *Educ:* London Univ. (LLB). Called to the Bar, Middle Temple, 1977, Bencher, 1997; Mem., Antigua Bar; a Recorder, 2000. Parly Under-Sec. of State, FCO, 1999–2001; Parly Sec., LCD, 2001–03; Minister of State (Minister for Criminal Justice System and Law Reform, subseq. for Criminal Justice and Offender Mgt), Home Office, 2003–07. Former Mem., Commn for Racial Equality; Mem., Millennium Commn, 1994. *Address:* House of Lords, SW1A 0PW.

SCOTLAND, Alastair Duncan, FRCSE, FRCP, FFPH; Medical Director, National Clinical Assessment Service, since 2005; *b* 19 Aug. 1951; *s* of James Scotland and Jean (*née* Cowan). *Educ:* Glasgow High Sch., Aberdeen Grammar Sch.; Aberdeen Univ. (MB ChB 1975). FRCSE 1980; MFPHM 1987, FFPH (FFPHM 1993); FRCP 1999. House Surgeon/House Physician, Aberdeen Royal Infirmary, 1975–76; training prog. in surgery specialising in plastic surgery, Aberdeen, Inverness, Dundee and Perth Hosps, 1976–83; training prog. in public health medicine, SE and NW Thames RHAs, 1983–88; Consultant in Public Health Medicine, then Regl MO, NE Thames RHA, 1988–94; Trust Unit Med. Dir, N Thames RHA, 1994–96; Dir of Med. Educn and Res. and Postgrad. Clinical Tutor, Chelsea and Westminster Hosp., 1996–2001; Chief Exec. and Med. Dir, Nat. Clin. Assessment Authy, NHS, 2001–05. Hon. Senior Lecturer in Public Health Medicine: ICSM, 2000–01; KCL Sch. of Medicine (formerly GKT), 2001–; Vis. Prof. in Public Health, KCL Sch. of Medicine (formerly GKT), 2004–. Advr, Med. Educn, Training and Staffing, London Implementation Gp, 1993–95; Chm., Clinical Disputes Forum for England and Wales, 1996–2002; Member: Ministerial Gp on Jun. Doctors' Hours of Work, 1990–95; Jt Cttee, Funding of Postgrad. Med. and Dental Educn in NHS, 1991–96; CMO's Cttee on Specialist Med. Training, 1992–95; Jt Cttee, NHS Consultant Appointment Procedures, 1992–94. FRSocMed 1981. FRSA 1992. Member Editorial Boards: Hospital Medicine, 1989–; Clinical Risk, 2000–. *Publications:* (with L. Swift) Disciplining and Dismissing Doctors in the NHS, 1995; (ed) Clinical Governance One Year On, 2000; orig. papers on medical professional and public health issues. *Recreations:* theatre, music. *Address:* National Clinical Assessment Service, 9th Floor, Market Towers, 1 Nine Elms Lane, SW8 5NQ. *T:* (020) 7084 3840, *Fax:* (020) 7084 3851; *e-mail:* ncas@ncas.npsa.nhs.uk. *Club:* Reform.

SCOTT; *see* Hepburne-Scott, family name of Lord Polwarth.

SCOTT; *see* Montagu Douglas Scott, family name of Duke of Buccleuch.

SCOTT, family name of **Earl of Eldon, Baron Scott of Foscote** and **Baroness Scott of Needham Market**.

SCOTT OF FOSCOTE, Baron *cr* 2000 (Life Peer), of Foscote in the county of Buckinghamshire; **Richard Rashleigh Folliott Scott,** Kt 1983; PC 1991; a Lord of Appeal in Ordinary, 2000–Oct. 2009; *b* 2 Oct. 1934; *s* of Lt-Col C. W. F. Scott, 2/9th Gurkha Rifles and Katharine Scott (*née* Rashleigh); *m* 1959, Rima Elisa, *d* of Salvador Ripoll and Blanca Korsi de Ripoll, Panama City; two *s* two *d*. *Educ:* Michaelhouse Coll., Natal; Univ. of Cape Town (BA); Trinity Coll., Cambridge (BA, LLB). Bigelow Fellow, Univ. of Chicago, 1958–59. Called to Bar, Inner Temple, 1959, Bencher, 1981. In practice, Chancery Bar, 1960–83; QC 1975; Attorney Gen., 1980–83, Vice-Chancellor, 1987–91, Duchy and County Palatine of Lancaster; Judge of the High Court of Justice, Chancery Div., 1983–91; a Lord Justice of Appeal, 1991–94; Vice-Chancellor, Supreme Court, 1994–2000; Head of Civil Justice, 1995–2000; a non-permanent Judge, Hong Kong Court of Final Appeal, 2003–. Inquiry into defence related exports to Iraq and related prosecutions, 1992–96. Chm. of the Bar, 1982–83 (Vice-Chm., 1981–82). Editor-in-Chief, Supreme Court Practice, 1996–2000. Hon. Member: Amer. Bar Assoc., 1983; Canadian Bar Assoc., 1983. Hon. LLD: Birmingham, 1996; Buckingham, 1999. *Publications:* articles in legal jls. *Recreations:* hunting, tennis, bridge, twelve grandchildren, formerly Rugby (Cambridge Blue, 1957). *Address:* House of Lords, SW1A 0PW. *Club:* Hawks (Cambridge).

SCOTT OF NEEDHAM MARKET, Baroness *cr* 2000 (Life Peer), of Needham Market in the co. of Suffolk; **Rosalind Carol Scott;** *b* 10 Aug. 1957; *d* of Kenneth Vincent and Carol Jane Leadbeater; *m* (marr. diss.); one *s* one *d*. *Educ:* Whitby Grammar Sch.; Univ. of East Anglia. Member (Lib Dem) Mid Suffolk DC, 1991–94; Suffolk CC, 1993–2005 (Gp Leader, 1997–2000). Member: UK delegn to EU Cttee of the Regions, 1998–2002; Commn for Integrated Transport, 2001–. Chm., Transport Cttee, LGA, 2002–04 (Vice-Chair, 1996–2002). Contested (Lib Dem) Eastern Region, EP elecns, 1999. Non-executive Director: Entrust, 2000–; Anglia TV, 2002–05; Lloyds Register, 2004–. *Recreations:* walking, travel. *Address:* House of Lords, SW1A 0PW. *Club:* Royal Commonwealth Society.

SCOTT, Alan James, CVO 1986; CBE 1982; Governor, Cayman Islands, 1987–92; *b* 14 Jan. 1934; *er s* of Rev. Harold James Scott and Mary Phyllis Barbara Scott; *m* 1st, 1958, Mary Elizabeth Ireland (*d* 1969); one *s* two *d*; 2nd, 1971, Joan Hall; one step *s* two step *d*. *Educ:* King's Sch., Ely; Selwyn Coll., Cambridge Univ. Suffolk Regt, Italy and Germany, 1952–54. HMOCS, 1958–87: Fiji: Dist Officer, 1958; Estabts Officer, 1960; Registry of Univ. of S Pacific, 1968; Controller, Organisation and Estabts, 1969; Hong Kong: Asst Financial Sec., 1971; Prin. Asst Financial Sec., 1972; Sec. for CS, 1973; MLC, 1976–85; Sec. for Housing, and Chm. Hong Kong Housing Authy, 1977; Sec. for Information, 1980; Sec. for Transport, 1982; Dep. Chief Sec., 1985–87. President: Fiji AAA, 1964–69; Hong Kong AAA, 1978–87. *Recreations:* boules, dilatory travel, writing.

SCOTT, Hon. Alexander; *see* Scott, Hon. W. A.

SCOTT, Allan; *see* Shiach, A. G.

SCOTT, Andrew John, CBE 2006; FMA; CEng; Director (formerly Head), National Railway Museum, since 1994; *b* 3 June 1949; *s* of late Cyril John Scott and of Gertrude Ethel (*née* Miller); *m* 1972, Margaret Anne Benyon, JP, BA. *Educ:* Bablake Sch., Coventry; Univ. of Newcastle upon Tyne (BSc Civil Engrg 1970; MSc Mining Engrg 1971). CEng, MICE 1976. AMA 1987, FMA 1993. Practising civil engr, 1972–84; Actg Dir, W Yorks Transport Mus., 1984–86; Keeper of Technol., Bradford City Museums, 1986–87; Dir, London Transport Mus., 1988–94. Mem., North Eastern Locomotive Preservation Gp, 1967– (Cttee Mem., 1972–84); Council Member: Assoc. of Indep. Museums, 1991–2003; Internat. Assoc. of Transport Museums, 1992– (Vice Pres., 1999–); Vice-Chm., Assoc. of British Transport and Engrg Museums, 1992–. Dir, York Tourism Bureau, 1995–2008 (Chm., 1999–2008). Trustee, Friends of London Transport Mus., 1994–; Exec. Mem., Friends of Nat. Railway Mus., 1994–; Pres., London Underground Railway Soc., 1995–96. *Publications:* North Eastern Renaissance, 1991; (with C. Divall) Making Histories in Transport Museums, 2001; contrib. to railway and museological jls and books. *Recreations:* travel, railways, ecclesiastical architecture. *Address:* National Railway Museum, Leeman Road, York YO26 4XJ. *T:* (01904) 686200; 14 New Walk Terrace, York YO10 4BG; *e-mail:* andrew.scott@nrm.org.uk.

SCOTT, Anthony Douglas, TD 1972; chartered accountant in public practice, 1988–2005; *b* 6 Nov. 1933; *o s* of Douglas Ernest and Mary Gladys Scott; *m* 1962, Irene Robson; one *s* one *d*. *Educ:* Gateshead Central Technical Secondary Sch. Articled to Middleton & Middleton, also J. Stanley Armstrong, Chartered Accountants, Newcastle upon Tyne, 1952–57; National Service, WO Selection Bd, 1957–59; Accountant with Commercial Plastics Ltd, 1959; joined ICI Ltd (Agricl Div), 1961; seconded by ICI to Hargreaves Fertilisers Ltd, as Chief Accountant, 1966; ICI Ltd (Nobel Div.) as Asst Chief Acct, 1970; seconded by ICI to MoD as Dir-Gen. Internal Audit, 1972–74. Dir of Consumer Credit, Office of Fair Trading, 1974–80. Chief Exec. and Dir, CoSIRA, 1981–88. Chm., Teesside Soc. of Chartered Accts, 1969–70; Mem. Cttee, London Chartered Accountants, 1974–79. Chm., Jt Working Party on Students' Societies (ICAE&W), 1979–80. Mem., Smaller Firms Council, CBI, 1983–86. TA (17th (later 4th) Bn Para. Regt (9 DLI) TA, 44 Para. Bde (TA) and 6th (V) Bn Royal Anglian Regt), 1959–91, Major. *Publications:* Accountants Digests on Consumer Credit Act 1974, 1980; Accountants Digest on Estate Agents Act 1979, 1982. *Recreations:* antiquary, walking, gardening. *Address:* 2 Oakfield Road, Harpenden, Herts AL5 2NE. *T:* (01582) 763067.

SCOTT, Sir Anthony (Percy), 3rd Bt *cr* 1913; *b* 1 May 1937; *s* of Sir Douglas Winchester Scott, 2nd Bt, and of Elizabeth Joyce, *d* of W. N. C. Grant; *S* father, 1984; *m* 1962, Caroline Theresa Anne, *er d* of Edward Bacon; two *s* one *d*. *Educ:* Harrow; Christ Church, Oxford. Barrister, Inner Temple, 1960. *Recreation:* racing. *Heir:* *s* Henry Douglas Edward Scott [*b* 26 March 1964; *m* 1993, Carole Ruth Maddick]. *Address:* Chateau La Coste, 81140 Larroque, France.

SCOTT, Brough; *see* Scott, J. B.

SCOTT, Dame Catherine Margaret Mary; *see* Scott, Dame M.

SCOTT, Charles Thomas, FCA; Chairman, William Hill, since 2004; *b* 22 Feb. 1949. FCA 1979. Binder Hamlyn, 1967–72; ITEL Internat. Corp., 1972–77; IMS Internat. Inc., 1978–89; Saatchi & Saatchi Co. plc, later Cordiant plc, 1990–97: Chief Exec., 1993–95; Chm., 1995–97; Chm., Cordiant Communications Group plc, 1997–2003. *Recreations:* golf, tennis, sport in general. *Address:* William Hill, Greenside House, 50 Station Road, Wood Green, N22 7TP.

SCOTT, Prof. Clive, DPhil; FBA 1994; Professor of European Literature, University of East Anglia, 1991–2007, now Emeritus; *b* 13 Nov. 1943; *s* of Jesse Scott and Nesta Vera Scott (*née* Morton); *m* 1st, 1965, Elizabeth Anne (*née* Drabble) (marr. diss.); one *s* one *d*; 2nd, 1984, Marie-Noëlle Guillot; two *s*. *Educ:* St John's Coll., Oxford (MA, MPhil, DPhil). University of East Anglia: Asst Lectr, 1967–70; Lectr, 1970–88; Reader, 1988–91; Hd, Sch. of Literature and Creative Writing, 2004–05. *Publications:* French Verse-Art: a study, 1980; Anthologie Eluard, 1983; A Question of Syllables: essays in nineteenth-century French verse, 1986; The Riches of Rhyme: studies in French verse, 1988; Vers Libre: the emergence of free verse in France 1886–1914, 1990; Reading the Rhythm: the poetics of French free verse 1910–1930, 1993; The Poetics of French Verse: studies in reading, 1998; The Spoken Image: photography and language, 1999; Translating Baudelaire, 2000; Channel Crossings: French and English poetry in dialogue 1550–2000, 2002 (R. H. Gapper Book Prize, Soc. for French Studies, 2004); Translating Rimbaud's Illuminations, 2006; Street Photography: from Atget to Cartier-Bresson, 2007. *Address:* School of Literature and Creative Writing, University of East Anglia, University Plain, Norwich NR4 7TJ. *T:* (01603) 592135.

SCOTT, Rt Rev. Colin John Fraser; Bishop Suffragan of Hulme, 1984–98; Hon. Assistant Bishop of Leicester, since 1999; *b* 14 May 1933; *s* of late Kenneth Miller Scott and Marion Edith Scott; *m* 1958, Margaret Jean MacKay; one *s* two *d*. *Educ:* Berkhamsted

School; Queens' College, Cambridge (MA); Ridley Hall, Cambridge. Curate: St Barnabas, Clapham Common, 1958–61; St James, Hatcham, 1961–64; Vicar, St Mark, Kennington, 1964–71; Vice-Chm., Southwark Diocesan Pastoral Cttee, 1971–77; Team Rector, Sanderstead Team Ministry, 1977–84. Chm., Council for the Care of Churches, 1994–98. *Address:* The Priest House, Prior Park Road, Ashby de la Zouch, Leics LE65 1BH. *T:* (01530) 564403.

SCOTT, Prof. Dana Stewart, FBA 1976; Hillman University Professor of Computer Science, Philosophy and Mathematical Logic, Carnegie Mellon University, 1981–2003, now Emeritus; *b* Berkeley, Calif, 11 Oct. 1932; *m* 1959, Irene Schreier; one *d. Educ:* Univ. of Calif, Berkeley (BA); Princeton Univ. (PhD). Instructor, Univ. of Chicago, 1958–60; Asst Prof., Univ. of Calif, Berkeley, 1960–63; Associate Prof. and Prof., Stanford Univ., 1963–69; Prof., Princeton, 1969–72; Prof. of Mathematical Logic, Oxford Univ., 1972–81. Visiting Professor: Amsterdam, 1968–69; Linz, 1992–93; Guggenheim Fellow, 1978–79. Mem., US Nat. Acad. of Scis, 1988. *Publications:* papers on logic and mathematics in technical jls. *Address:* 1149 Shattuck Avenue, Berkeley, CA 94707–2609, USA.

SCOTT, Sir David (Aubrey), GCMG 1979 (KCMG 1974; CMG 1966); HM Diplomatic Service, retired 1979; *b* 3 Aug. 1919; *s* of late Hugh Sumner Scott and Barbara E. Scott, JP; *m* 1941, Vera Kathleen, *d* of late Major G. H. Ibbitson, MBE, RA; three *c. Educ:* Charterhouse; Birmingham University (Mining Engrg). Served War of 1939–45, Royal Artillery, 1939–47; Chief Radar Adviser, British Military Mission to Egyptian Army, 1945–47, Major. Appointed to CRO, 1948; Asst Private Secretary to Secretary of State, 1949; Cape Town/Pretoria, 1951–53; Cabinet Office, 1954–56; Malta Round Table Conf., 1955; Secretary-General, Malaya and Caribbean Constitutional Confs, 1956; Singapore, 1956–58; Monckton Commn, 1960; Dep. High Comr, Fedn of Rhodesia and Nyasaland, 1961–63; Imperial Defence College, 1964; Dep. High Comr, India, 1965–67; British High Comr to Uganda, and Ambassador (non-resident) to Rwanda, 1967–70; Asst Under-Sec. of State, FCO, 1970–72; British High Comr to New Zealand, and Governor, Pitcairn Is., 1973–75; HM Ambassador to Republic of S Africa, 1976–79. Chairman: Ellerman Lines plc, 1982–83; Nuclear Resources Ltd, 1984–88; Director: Barclays Bank International Ltd, 1979–85; Mitchell Cotts plc, 1980–86; Delta Metal Overseas Ltd, 1980–83; Bradbury Wilkinson plc, 1984–86; Consultant, Thomas De La Rue & Co. Ltd, 1986–88. Pres., Uganda Soc. for Disabled Children, 1984–2000; Vice-Pres., UK South Africa Trade Assoc., 1980–85. Mem., Manchester Olympic Bid Cttee, 1989–93. Gov., Sadler's Wells Trust, 1984–89. Trustee, John Ellerman Foundn, 1979–2000 (Chm., 1997–2000). Freeman, City of London, 1982; Liveryman, Shipwrights' Co., 1983. *Publications:* Ambassador in Black and White, 1981; Window into Downing Street, 2003; contrib. DNB. *Recreations:* music, birdwatching. *Address:* 4 Birtley Mews, Birtley Road, Bramley, Guildford, Surrey GU5 0LB. *Club:* Royal Over-Seas League (Chm., 1981–86; Vice-Pres., 1986–98, 2005–; Pres., 1998–2002).
See also Sir R. D. H. Scott, Sir J. B. Unwin.

SCOTT, David Gidley; Registrar of the High Court in Bankruptcy, 1984–96; *b* 3 Jan. 1924; *s* of late Bernard Wardlaw Habershon Scott, FRIBA and Florence May Scott; *m* 1948, Elinor Anne, *d* of late Major Alan Garthwaite, DSO, MC, and Mrs Garthwaite; two *s* two *d. Educ:* Sutton Valence School (scholarship); St John's College, Cambridge (exhibnr, MA, LLM). Army service, 1942–47, Royal Engineers; Assault RE European theatre, 1944–45 (wounded); Acting Major, Palestine. Called to the Bar, Lincoln's Inn, 1951; practised Chancery Bar, 1951–84. *Recreation:* choral singing. *Address:* 45 Benslow Lane, Hitchin, Herts SG4 9RE. *T:* (01462) 434391.

SCOTT, David Gordon Islay, MD; FRCP, FRCPE; Consultant Rheumatologist, Norfolk and Norwich University Hospital NHS Trust, since 1988; *b* Elgin, 8 July 1948; *s* of Gordon Islay Scott and Mora Joan Scott (née Craig); *m* 1976, Daphne Bellworthy, (Dee); three *s. Educ:* Trinity Coll., Glenalmond; Univ. of Bristol Med. Sch. (MB ChB 1973; MD 1982). MRCP 1977, FRCP 1994; FRCPE 2007. Lectr in Rheumatol., Univ. of Birmingham, 1981–88. Hon. Sen. Lectr in Rheumatol., Royal London Hosp. Med. Sch., 1988–96; Hon. Sen. Lectr in Rheumatol., 1995–98, Hon. Prof., Sch. of Medicine, Health Policy and Practice, 1998–, UEA. Pres., British Soc. for Rheumatol., 2002–04; Chief Med. Advr, Nat. Rheumatoid Arthritis Soc., 2007–; Patient Involvement Officer, RCP, 2007–; Clinical Dir, Norfolk and Suffolk Comp. Local Res. Network, 2007–. *Publications:* contrib. chapters in medical textbooks on clinical aspects, epidemiology and outcome of systemic vasculitis; over 250 reviews, editorials and papers. *Recreations:* hockey—(ex) player, now watching, running—marathons/half marathons (Great North Run x 13 so far). *Address:* Department of Rheumatology, Norfolk and Norwich University Hospital, Colney Lane, Norwich NR4 7UY. *T:* (01603) 286766, *Fax:* (01603) 287004; *e-mail:* David.Scott@nnuh.nhs.uk.

SCOTT, David Ian; Group Human Resources Director, United Utilities PLC, 1998; *b* 2 May 1953; *s* of Daniel McAlees and Jean Scott; *m* 1999, Ingrid Ann Blackford-Swaries. *Educ:* Lancaster Univ. (BA Hons English and French). Pilot Officer, RAF, 1971–74. Post Office Telecommunications, later British Telecommunications: Personnel Manager, 1975–80; Ops Manager, 1980–87; Personnel Manager, 1987–89; Gp Industrial Relns Manager, 1989–95; Personnel Dir, Gp HQ, 1995; Dir of Personnel, HM Prison Service, 1995–98. Non-executive Director: Your Communications Ltd; Whitehall and Industry Gp; Unity Th., Liverpool. Trustee, United Utilities Gp, Electricity Supply Pension Scheme. Chm., NW Reg., Duke of Edinburgh's Award; Mem. Council, NW Reg., Prince's Trust. MIPD 1992. *Recreations:* sport, motoring.

SCOTT, David Richard Alexander, CBE 2006; FCA; Chief Executive, Digital UK (formerly SwitchCo) Ltd, since 2008 (Director, since 2005); *b* 25 Aug. 1954; *s* of R. I. M. Scott, OBE and Daphne Scott (née Alexander); *m* 1981, Moy Barraclough; one *s* one *d. Educ:* Wellington Coll. FCA 1979. Chartered Accountant, Peat Marwick Mitchell & Co., 1972–81; Channel Four Television, subseq. Channel Four Television Corporation: Controller of Finance, 1981–88; Dir of Finance, 1988–97; Man. Dir, 1997–2005; Dep. Chief Exec., 2002–05; Consultant, 2005–08. Director: Digital 3 and 4 Ltd, 1998–2008; Digital Television Gp Ltd, 2006–; Digital Network, subseq. Digital Multiplex Operators Ltd, 2007–08. *Recreations:* sailing, walking, film, opera, bridge. *Address:* 25 Moreton Place, Pimlico, SW1V 2NL. *Club:* Guards' Polo.

SCOTT, Derek John; Managing Consultant, Europe Economics, since 2005; *b* 17 Jan. 1947; *s* of John William Scott and Alice Isabel Scott (née Heal); *m* 1985, Elinor Mary Goodman, *qv* (marr. diss.). *Educ:* Liverpool Univ. (BA Hons); London Sch. of Econs (MSc Econ); Birkbeck Coll., Univ. of London (MSc Econ). Special Advr to Denis Healey, 1977–79; Econ. Advr to James Callaghan, 1979–81; Internat. Policy Advr, Shell Internat., 1982–86; Dir, European Economics, Barclays de Zoete Wedd, 1986–97; Econ. Advr to Prime Minister, 1997–2003; Economic Consultant, KPMG, 2004–06. *Publication:* Off Whitehall, 2004. *Address:* 80 Denbigh Street, SW1V 2EX.

SCOTT, Dermot; *see* Scott, W. D.

SCOTT, Sir Dominic James M.; *see* Maxwell Scott.

SCOTT, Douglas Andrew Montagu-Douglas-, OBE 1994; Chief Executive and Director, Cancer Relief Macmillan Fund, 1987–95; *b* 21 June 1930; *s* of late Col C. A. Montagu-Douglas-Scott, DSO and Lady Victoria Haig, *d* of Field Marshal 1st Earl Haig, KT, GCB, OM, GCVO, KCIE; *m* 1st, 1954, Bridget George (marr. diss. 1976), *d* of Air Vice-Marshal Sir Robert George, KCMG, KCVO, KBE, CB, MC; two *d* (one *s* decd); 2nd, 1977, Daphne Shortt (marr. diss. 2000), *d* of Dr Cyril Shortt, Winchcombe; 3rd, 2005, Monica, Lady Bernard. *Educ:* Eton; RMA, Sandhurst. Commnd Irish Guards, 1950. ADC to Gov. of S Australia, 1953–55; Tubemakers of Australia, 1955–63; TI Group, 1963–83: Dir, Accles & Pollock Ltd, 1966–76; Man. Dir, TI Chesterfield Ltd, 1976–81; Dir, TI Gp Overseas Ops, 1981–83; Recruitment Consultant, PE Internat. plc, 1984–87. Director: S Warwicks Gen. Hosps NHS Trust, 1995–97; Global Cancer Concern, 1995–2000; CLIC, 1997–2000; Compton Hospice, 1995–99. Douglas Haig Fellow, 2004. *Publication:* (ed) The Preparatory Prologue: Douglas Haig, diaries and letters 1861–1914, 2006. *Recreations:* painting, gardening, fishing, opera. *Address:* Stonefield, Bemersyde, Melrose TD6 9DP. *T:* (01835) 824123. *Clubs:* Pratt's, MCC; New (Edinburgh).

SCOTT, Douglas Keith, (Doug Scott), CBE 1994; *b* Nottingham, 29 May 1941; *s* of George Douglas Scott and Edith Joyce Scott; *m* 1962, Janice Elaine Brook (marr. diss. 1988); one *s* two *d; m* 1993, Sharavati, (Sharu), Prabhu; two *s; m* 2007, Patricia Lang. *Educ:* Cottesmore Secondary Modern Sch.; Mundella Grammar Sch., Nottingham; Loughborough Teachers' Trng Coll. (Teaching Certificate). Began climbing age of 12; first ascent, Tarso Teiroko, Tibest Mts, Sahara, 1965; first ascents, Cilo Dag Mts, SE Turkey, 1966; first ascent, S face Koh-i-Bandaka (6837 m), Hindu Kush, Afghanistan, 1967; first British ascent, Salathé Wall, El Capitain, Yosemite, 1971; 1972: Spring, Mem., European Mt Everest Expedn to SW face; Summer, first ascent, E Pillar of Mt Asgard, Baffin Island Expedn; Autumn, Mem., British Mt Everest Expedn to SW face; first ascent, Changabang (6864 m), 1974; first ascent, SE spur, Pic Lenin (7189 m), 1974; reached summit of Mt Everest, via SW face, with Dougal Haston, as Members, British Everest Expedn, 24th Sept. 1975 (first Britons on summit); first Alpine ascent of S face, Mt McKinley (6226 m), via new route, British Direct, with Dougal Haston, 1976; first ascent, East Face Direct, Mt Kenya, 1976; first ascent, Ogre (7330 m), Karakoram Mountains, 1977; first ascent, N Ridge route, Kangchenjunga (8593 m), without oxygen, 1979; first ascent, N Summit, Kussum Kangguru, 1979; first ascent, N Face, Nuptse, 1979; Alpine style, Kangchungtse (7640 m), 1980; first ascent Shivling E Pillar, 13-day Alpine Style push, 1981; Chamlang (7366 m) North Face to Central Summit, with Rheinhold Messner, 1981; first ascent, Pungpa Ri (7445 m), 1982; first ascent Shishapangma South Face (8046 m), 1982; first ascent, Lobsang Spire (Karakoram), and ascent Broad Peak (8047 m), 1983; Mt Baruntse (7143 m), first ascent, East Summit Mt Chamlang (7287 m), and traverse over unclimbed central summit Chamlang, Makalu SE Ridge, Alpine Style, to within 100 m of summit, 1984; first Alpine style ascent, Diran (7260 m), 1985; first ascent of rock climbs in S India, 1986; first ascent of rock climbs, Wadi Rum, Jordan, 1987; Mt Jitchu Drake (Bhutan) (6793 m), South face first ascent of peak, Alpine style, 1988; first ascent, Indian Arete Latok III, 1990; first ascent, Hanging Glacier Peak South (6294 m), via South Ridge, 1991; first British ascent of Chimtarga (5482 m), Fanskiye Mountains, Tadzhikistan, 1992; first ascent, Central Mazend Peaks (6970m) of Nanga Parbat, 1992; first ascent, Mt Pelagic (2000m), Tierra del Fuego, 1993; first ascent Carstensz Pyramid North Face, 1995; first ascent, Chombu East (5745m), NE Sikkim, 1996; first ascent Drohmo Central summit (6855 m), via South pillar, Alpine style, with Roger Mear, 1998; first ascent, Targo Ri (6650m), Central Tibet, 2000. Pres., Alpine Climbing Gp, 1976–82; Vice-Pres., British Mountaineering Council, 1994–97. A vegetarian, 1978–. Hon. MA: Nottingham, 1991; Loughborough, 1993; Hon. MEd Nottingham Trent, 1995. *Publications:* Big Wall Climbing, 1974; (with Alex MacIntyre) Shishapangma, Tibet, 1984; Himalayan Climber, 1992; contrib. to Alpine Jl, Amer. Alpine Jl, Mountain Magazine and Himal Magazine. *Recreations:* rock climbing, photography, organic gardening. *Address:* Warwick Mill, Warwick Bridge, Carlisle CA4 8RR. *T:* (01228) 564488; *e-mail:* info@catreks.com. *Clubs:* Alpine (Pres., 1999–2001); Alpine Climbing Group; Nottingham Climbers'.

SCOTT, Edward McM.; *see* McMillan-Scott.

SCOTT, Eleanor Roberta; Member (Green) Highlands and Islands, Scottish Parliament, 2003–07; *b* 23 July 1951; *d* of late William Ettles and of Roberta Ettles (née Reid); *m* 1977, David Scott (marr. diss. 1995); one *s* one *d; partner, Robert McKay Gibson, *qv. Educ:* Bearsden Acad.; Glasgow Univ. (MB ChB 1974). Jun. doctor posts, 1974–80; Clin. Med. Officer, Community Paediatrics, Inverness, 1980–87; Sen. Clin. Med. Officer, Community Paediatrics, Dingwall, Ross-shire, 1987–2003. *Recreations:* traditional music, gardening. *Address:* Tir Nan Oran, 8 Culcairn Road, Evanton IV16 9YT. *T:* (01349) 830388; *e-mail:* eleanorsco@googlemail.com.

SCOTT, Esme, (Lady Scott), CBE 1985; WS; Chair, Volunteer Centre UK, 1993–96; *b* 7 Jan. 1932; *d* of David Burnett, SSC and Jane Burnett (née Thornton); *m* 1st, 1956, Ian Macfarlane Walker, WS (*d* 1988); one *s*; 2nd, 1990, Sir Kenneth Scott, *qv*; one step *s* one step *d. Educ:* St George's School for Girls, Edinburgh; Univ. of Edinburgh (MA, LLB). NP; Vice-Pres., Inst. of Trading Standards Admin. Lectr in Legal Studies, Queen Margaret College, Edinburgh, 1977–83. Voluntary worker, Citizens' Advice Bureau, 1960–85; Chm., Scottish Assoc. of CABx, 1986–88. Comr, Equal Opportunities Commn, 1986–90. Chm., Scottish Consumer Council, 1980–85; Vice-Chm., Nat. Consumer Council, 1984–87; Chm., Volunteer Development Scotland, 1989–92; Member: Expert Cttee, Multiple Surveys and Valuations (Scotland), 1982–84; Working Party on Procedure for Judicial Review of Admin. Action, 1983–84; Cttee on Conveyancing, 1984; Scottish Cttee, Council on Tribunals, 1986–92; Social Security Adv. Cttee, 1990–96; Direct Mail Services Standards Bd, 1990–95; Privacy Adv. Cttee, Common Services Agency, 1990–95; SIB, 1991–93; Monopolies and Mergers Commn, 1992–95; Exec. Cttee, NCVO, 1993–95. Member: Court, Edinburgh Univ., 1989–92; Council, St George's Sch. for Girls, 1989–96. FRSA. *Recreation:* crosswords. *Address:* 13 Clinton Road, Edinburgh EH9 2AW. *T:* (0131) 447 5191.

SCOTT, Finlay McMillan, TD 1984; Chief Executive and Registrar, General Medical Council, since 1994; *b* 25 May 1947; *s* of Finlay McMillan Scott and Anne Cameron Robertson Coutts Scott; *m* 1st, 1969, Eileen Frances Marshall (marr. diss. 2001); one *s* one *d*; 2nd, 2002, Prof. Elizabeth Susan Perkins. *Educ:* Greenock High Sch.; Open Univ. (BA Hons; LLB Hons); Durham Univ. (MSc). Department of Education and Science, subseq. Department for Education, 1975–94: Head of Pensions Br. and Controller, Darlington, 1983–86; Head of Inf. Systems Br., 1986–90; on secondment: to UFC, 1990–93; to PCFC, 1992–93; to HEFCE, 1992–94; Under Sec., 1990–94. Lt-Col, RAOC, 1989–93, RLC, 1993–95, RARO, 1995–, TA. Member: NIHEC, 1993–2001; Medical Workforce Standing Adv. Cttee, 1996–2001; Postgrad. Med. Educn and Trng Bd, 2003–. Governor: London Guildhall Univ., 1996–2002; London Metropolitan Univ., 2003–. *Recreations:* hill walking, horse riding. *Address:* General Medical Council, Regents Place, 350 Euston Road, NW1 3JN. *T:* (020) 7189 5291; *e-mail:* finlayscott@gmc-uk.org.

SCOTT, Sir (George) Peter, Kt 2007; Vice-Chancellor, Kingston University, since 1998; *b* 1 Aug. 1946; *s* of George Edward Grey Scott and Evelyn Mary Scott (*née* Robb); *m* 1968, Cherill Andrea Williams; one *d*. *Educ:* Merton Coll., Oxford (BA 1st cl. Hons Modern History 1967). Journalist: TES, 1967–69; The Times, 1969–71; Dep. Editor, THES, 1971–73; Vis. Scholar (Harkness Fellow), Grad. Sch. of Public Policy, Univ. of Calif at Berkeley, 1973–74; leader writer, The Times, 1974–76; Editor, THES, 1976–92; Prof. of Education, 1992–97, Pro-Vice-Chancellor, 1996–97, Univ. of Leeds. Mem. Bd, HEFCE, 2000–06. Hon. Fellow, UMIST, 1992. Hon. LLD Bath, 1992; Hon. DLitt: CNAA, 1992; Grand Valley State Univ., 1999; Hon. PhD Anglia Polytech. Univ., 1998. *Publications:* The Crisis of the University, 1986; Knowledge and Nation, 1990; The New Production of Knowledge, 1994; The Meanings of Mass Higher Education, 1995; Governing Universities, 1996; Re-thinking Science, Knowledge and the Public in an age of uncertainty, 2001. *Address:* Kingston University, River House, 53–57 High Street, Kingston-upon-Thames KT1 1LQ. *T:* (020) 8547 7010.

SCOTT, Dr Graham Alexander; Deputy Chief Medical Officer, Scottish Home and Health Department, 1975–89; *b* 26 Nov. 1927; *s* of Alexander Scott and Jessie Scott; *m* 1951, Helena Patricia Margaret Cavanagh; two *s* one *d*. *Educ:* Daniel Stewart's Coll., Edinburgh; Edinburgh Univ. (MB, ChB). FRCPE, FFPH, DPH. RAAMC, 1951–56 (Dep. Asst Dir, Army Health, 1st Commonwealth Div., Korea, 1953–54). Sen. Asst MO, Stirling CC, 1957–62, Dep. County MO, 1962–65; Scottish Home and Health Department: MO, 1965–68; SMO, 1968–74; PMO, 1974–75. Consultant in Public Health Medicine, Borders Health Board, 1990–93. QHP 1987–90. *Recreations:* gardening, walking. *Address:* 5 Eildon Bank, Eildon, Melrose TD6 9HH.

SCOTT, Prof. Hamish Marshall, PhD; FBA 2006; FRSE; Professor of International History, University of St Andrews, since 2000; *b* 12 July 1946; *s* of James Donaldson Scott and Elizabeth Levack Scott (*née* Dalrymple); *m* 2005, Julia M. H. Smith. *Educ:* George Heriot's Sch., Edinburgh; Univ. of Edinburgh (MA 1968); London Sch. of Econs (PhD 1978). Lectr, Univ. of Birmingham, 1970–78; Lectr, then Sen. Lectr, Univ. of St Andrews, 1979–2000. FRSE 2008. *Publications:* (with D. McKay) The Rise of the Great Powers 1648–1815, 1983; British Foreign Policy in the Age of the American Revolution, 1990; (ed) Enlightened Absolutism: reform and reformers in eighteenth-century Europe, 1990; (ed) The European Nobilities in the Seventeenth and Eighteenth Centuries, 2 vols, 1995, 2nd edn 2007; (ed jtly) Royal and Republican Sovereignty in Early Modern Europe: essays in memory of Ragnhild Hatton, 1997; The Emergence of the Eastern Powers 1756–1775, 2001; The Birth of a Great Power System 1740–1815, 2006; (ed jtly) Cultures of Power in Europe during the Long Eighteenth Century, 2007; contrib. to learned jls and collected vols. *Recreations:* music, sport, hill-walking, cooking. *Address:* 39 Winton Drive, Glasgow G12 0QB. *T:* (0141) 339 8452; *e-mail:* hms3@st-and.ac.uk.

SCOTT, Hilary; independent development consultant; *b* 9 June 1954; *d* of Stephen and late June Scott. *Educ:* Camden Sch. for Girls; Poly. of Central London (BA Hons Social Sci. 1978); Poly. of South Bank (MSc Sociol. of Health and Illness 1986); DipHSM 1983. Nat. Admin. Trainee, NHS, 1978–81; Asst House Gov., St Stephen's Hosp., 1981–83; Dep. Administrator, Brook Gen. Hosp., 1983–86; Outpatient and Diagnostic Services Manager, Northwick Park Hosp., 1986–89; Chief Exec., Enfield & Haringey FHSA, 1989–93; Project Dir, City and E London Family and Community Health Services, 1993–95; Chief Exec., Tower Hamlets Health Care NHS Trust, 1995–99; Dep. Health Service Ombudsman, 1999–2003; Complaints and Clin. Negligence Prog. Manager, DoH, 2003–04. Chm., Action of Elder Abuse, 2004–07. Vis. Prof., 2002–07, Associate Prof., 2007–, Middx Univ. Business Sch.; Vis. Sen. Fellow, Birmingham Univ., 2004–. Mem. Ct of Govs, Univ. of Westminster, 2002–. FIHM 1997. *Recreations:* family, friends, films, flowers. *Address:* 4 St Agnes Close, E9 7HS.

SCOTT, (Ian) Jonathan, CBE 1995; FSA; Deputy Chairman, 1997–2003 and Trustee, 1996–2003, Victoria & Albert Museum; *b* 7 Feb. 1940; *s* of late Col Alexander Brassey Jonathan Scott, DSO, MC and Rhona Margaret Scott; *m* 1965, Annabella Constance Loudon; two *s* one *d*. *Educ:* Harrow Sch.; Balliol Coll., Oxford (BA). FSA 1980. Director: Charterhouse Japhet, 1973–80; Barclays Merchant Bank, subseq. Barclays de Zoete Wedd, 1980–92. Chairman: Reviewing Cttee on Export of Works of Art, 1985–95; Acceptance in Lieu Panel, 2000–. Trustee, Imperial War Mus., 1984–98. *Publications:* Piranesi, 1975; Salvator Rosa, 1995; The Pleasures of Antiquity, 2003. *Recreations:* horses, trees. *Address:* Lasborough Manor, Tetbury, Glos GL8 8UF. *Club:* Brooks's.

SCOTT, Prof. Ian Richard, PhD; Barber Professor of Law, 1978–2000, Professor of Law (personal chair), 2001–05, University of Birmingham, Emeritus Professor, since 2006; *b* 8 Jan. 1940; *s* of Ernest and Edith Scott; *m* 1971, Ecce Cole; two *d*. *Educ:* Geelong Coll.; Queen's Coll., Univ. of Melbourne (LLB); King's Coll., Univ. of London (PhD). Barrister and Solicitor, Supreme Court of Victoria; called to Bar, Gray's Inn, 1995. Dir, Inst. of Judicial Admin, 1975–82. Exec. Dir, Victoria Law Foundn, 1982–84; Dean, Faculty of Law, Univ. of Birmingham, 1985–94. Member: Lord Chancellor's Civil Justice Review Body, 1985–88; Policy Adv. Gp, NHS Litigation Authy, 1996–2000; Alternative Dispute Resolution sub-cttee, Civil Justice Council, 1998–2002; Chm., N Yorks Magistrates' Courts Inquiry, 1989. Non-exec. Dir, Royal Orthopaedic Hosp. NHS Trust, 1995–2000. Hon. Bencher, Gray's Inn, 1988. Life Mem., Aust. Inst. of Judicial Admin, 1990. An Ed., 1989–2006, Gen. Ed., 2007–, Civil Procedure (the White Book). *Recreation:* law. *Address:* School of Law, University of Birmingham, Birmingham B15 2TT. *T:* (0121) 414 3637.

SCOTT, Irene Elizabeth; Chief Operating Officer, University Hospitals of Bristol NHS Foundation Trust, since 2008; *b* 1 Oct. 1954; *d* of Bernard and Eilene Rowlinson; *m* 1984, George Scott (marr. diss.); two *s*; partner, Malcolm Gray. *Educ:* S Manchester HA (RN); Nottingham Univ. (MSc). Ward Sister, 1976–83, Dep. Dir of Nursing, 1983–86, Withington Hosp., Manchester; Director of Nursing: Christie Hosp., Manchester, 1986–94; Leicester Royal Infirmary, 1994–99; Regl Dir of Nursing, W Midlands NHS Exec., 1999–2001; Dir of Nursing, Guy's Hosp. and St Thomas' Hosp., 2001–04; CEO, Nurse Dirs Assoc. UK, 2004–05; Dir of Nursing, Surrey and Sussex Healthcare NHS Trust, 2005–08. Vis. Prof. of Nursing, De Montfort Univ., 1992–2003; Hon. Professor of Nursing: Wolverhampton Univ., 2000–; South Bank Univ., 2002–; KCL, 2002–. Trustee and Dir, Royal Hosp. for Neurol Diseases, 2001–07. *Publication:* (with W. Bishop) Challenges in Clinical Practice, 2000. *Recreations:* gardening, keep fit, reading for relaxation. *Address:* 33 Chatsworth Drive, Manor Gardens, Market Harborough, Leics LE16 8BS. *T:* (01858) 433018; *e-mail:* iscotty90@hotmail.com.

SCOTT, Prof. James, FRCP; FRS 1997; Professor of Medicine, since 1997 and Deputy Principal for Research, since 2000, Imperial College London (Deputy Vice-Principal, 1997–2000); Director, Imperial College Genetics and Genomics Research Institute, since 2000; *b* 13 Sept. 1946; *s* of Robert Bentham Scott and Iris Olive Scott (*née* Hill); *m* 1976, Diane Marylin Lowe; two *s* one *d*. *Educ:* London Univ. (BSc 1968); London Hosp. Med. Coll. (MB, BS 1971; MSc Biochem. 1978). MRCP 1974, FRCP 1986. House Officer: London Hosp., 1971–72; Hereford Co. Hosp., 1972; Sen. House Officer, Midland Centre for Neurosurgery and Neurol., and Queen Elizabeth Hosp., Birmingham, 1972–73; Registrar in Medicine: General Hosp., Birmingham, 1973–74; Acad. Dept of Medicine, Royal Free Hosp., 1975–76; MRC Res. Fellow and Hon. Sen. Registrar, RPMS and Hammersmith Hosp., 1977–80; European Molecular Biol. Fellow, Dept of Biochem., Univ. of Calif, San Francisco, 1980–83; MRC Clinical Scientist and Hon. Consultant Physician, MRC Clinical Res. Centre and Northwick Park Hosp., 1983–91; Prof. and Chm. of Medicine, RPMS, 1992–97; Dir of Medicine and Chief of Service Med. Cardiology, Hammersmith Hosps NHS Trust, 1994–97; Hon. Consultant Physician, Hammersmith Hosp., 1992–; Hon. Dir, MRC Molecular Medicine Gp, 1992–. Member: RCP Res. Cttee, 1988–91; Assoc. of Physicians of GB and Ireland, 1987; European Molecular Biol. Orgn, 1993–; RSocMed Adv. Cttee, 1999–; Chm., N Thames Higher Merit Award Adv. Cttee, 1996–2000. Lectures include: Humphrey Davy Rolleston, RCP, 1989; Simms, RCP, 1995; Pfizer, Clin. Res. Inst., Montreal; Guest, Japan Atherosclerosis Soc., 1992. Founder FMedSci 1998. Graham Bull Prize, RCP, 1989; Squibb Bristol Myers Award for Cardiovascular Res., 1993. *Publications:* numerous on molecular medicine, molecular genetics, atherosclerosis, RNA modification, RNA editing and gene expression. *Recreations:* family and friends, the twentieth century novel, British Impressionists and modern painting, long distance running, swimming. *Address:* Genetics and Genomics Research Institute, Imperial College London, The Flowers Building, Armstrong Road, South Kensington, SW7 2AZ.

SCOTT, James Alexander, OBE 1987; FCA; Partner, Binder Hamlyn, Chartered Accountants, 1969–98; *b* 30 April 1940; *s* of Douglas McPherson Scott and Mabel Mary (*née* Skepper); *m* 1965, Annette Goslett; three *s* two *d*. *Educ:* Uppingham Sch.; Magdalene Coll., Cambridge (Schol.; MA); London Business Sch. (MSc). Joined Binder Hamlyn, 1961; Man. Partner, London Region, 1980–88; Nat. Man. Partner, 1988–89. Director: Vestey Group Ltd, 1992–; Schroder Exempt Property Unit Trust, 1994–. Chm. Trustees, Lonmin Superannuation Scheme, 2000–. Mem., Agricl Wages Bd for England and Wales, 1971–86; Sec., Review Bd for Govt Contracts, 1969–98; Member: NHS Pharmacists Remuneration Review Panel, 1982; Restrictive Practices Court, 1993–2000. DTI Inspector, Atlantic Computers plc, 1990. *Recreations:* walking, golf, tennis, ski-ing. *Clubs:* Berkshire Golf; St Enodoc Golf.

SCOTT, James Archibald, CB 1988; LVO 1961; FRSE; Deputy Spokesman on trade and industry, Scottish National Party, 1997–99; *b* 5 March 1932; *s* of late James Scott, MBE, and Agnes Bone Howie; *m* 1957, Elizabeth Agnes Joyce Buchan-Hepburn; three *s* one *d*. *Educ:* Dollar Acad.; Queen's Univ. of Ont.; Univ. of St Andrews (MA Hons). FRSE 1993. RAF aircrew, 1954–56. Asst Principal, CRO, 1956; served in New Delhi, 1958–62, and UK Mission to UN, New York, 1962–65; transf. to Scottish Office, 1965; Private Sec. to Sec. of State for Scotland, 1969–71; Asst Sec., Scottish Office, 1971; Under-Sec., Scottish Economic Planning Dept, later Industry Dept for Scotland, 1976–84; Sec., Scottish Educn Dept, 1984–87; Sec., Industry Dept for Scotland, 1987–90; Chief Exec., SDA, 1990–91; Exec. Dir, Scottish Financial Enterprise, 1991–94. Non-exec. Director: Scottish Power plc, 1992–96; Dumyat Investment Trust plc, 1995–2000. Fellow, SCOTVEC, 1990. Chevalier, Ordre National du Mérite (France), 1995. *Recreations:* travel, golf. *Address:* 38 Queen's Crescent, Edinburgh EH9 2BA. *T:* (0131) 667 8417.

SCOTT, Prof. James Floyd, PhD; FRS 2008; Professor of Ferroics, University of Cambridge, since 1999 (Symetrix Professor of Ferroics, 1999–2004); *b* 4 May 1942; *s* of William Burgess Scott and Isabel Miles; *m* 1982, Galina Alexeevna Dergilyova; one *d*. *Educ:* Harvard (AB 1963); Ohio State Univ. (PhD 1966). Prof. (Physics) and Asst Vice Chancellor, Univ. of Colorado, 1971–92; Professor and Dean: RMIT, Melbourne, 1992–95; Univ. of New South Wales, 1995–99. Chm. Bd, 1986–90, Dir, 1986–99, Symetrix Corp., USA. Fellow, APS, 1974. Humboldt Prize, Germany, 1997; Monkasho Prize, Japan, 2001. *Publications:* Ferroelectric Memories, 2000; over 400 articles in learned jls. *Recreations:* travel, gardening. *Address:* Thorndyke, Huntingdon Road, Cambridge CB3 0LG. *T:* (01223) 277793, *Fax:* (01223) 333450; *e-mail:* jsco99@esc.cam.ac.uk.

SCOTT, Sir James (Jervoise), 3rd Bt *cr* 1962, of Rotherfield Park, Alton, Hants; farmer and landowner; *b* 12 Oct. 1952; *e s* of Lt-Col Sir James Walter Scott, 2nd Bt, and Anne Constantia (*née* Austin); *S* father, 1993; *m* 1982, Judy Evelyn, *d* of Brian Trafford and Hon. Mrs Trafford; one *s* one *d*. *Educ:* Eton; Trinity Coll., Cambridge (MA). Agricultural journalist, 1977–88. Mem., Hampshire CC, 2001–05. High Sheriff, Hants, 2004–05. *Recreation:* shooting. *Heir: s* Arthur Jervoise Trafford Scott, *b* 2 Feb. 1984. *Address:* Estate Office, Rotherfield Park, East Tisted, Alton, Hampshire GU34 3QN. *T:* (01420) 588207. *Clubs:* White's, Travellers.

SCOTT, Janet Howard; *see* Darbyshire, J. H.

SCOTT, Janys Margaret; QC (Scot.) 2007; Advocate, since 1992; part-time Sheriff, since 2005; *b* Radcliffe, 28 Aug. 1953; *d* of John and Dylys Allen; *m* 1974, Dr Kevin F. Scott; two *s* one *d*. *Educ:* Newnham Coll., Cambridge (BA 1974). Articled clerk, Oxford, 1974–76; Asst Lectr, Sulaimaniyah Univ., Iraq, 1976–78; Solicitor, Oxford, 1978–86, Edinburgh, 1987–91. Hon. Lectr, Dundee Univ., 1989–94. Convener, Scottish Child Law Centre, 1992–97; Chairman: Stepfamily Scotland, 1998–2002; Scottish Legal Gp, Brit. Assoc. for Adoption and Fostering, 2004–. *Publication:* Education Law in Scotland, 2003. *Recreations:* growing vegetables, cooking, reading.

SCOTT, Jean Grant, (Mrs Donald Macleod); Chairman, Independent Schools Council, 2001–06; Headmistress, South Hampstead High School GDST, 1993–2001; *b* 7 Oct. 1940; *d* of Dr Duncan W. D. MacLaren and Etta M. MacLaren (*née* Speirs); *m* 1st, 1964, John Scott (*d* 1979); two *s*; 2nd, 2000, Donald Macleod. *Educ:* George Watson's Ladies' Coll., Edinburgh; Wellington Sch., Ayr; Univ. of Glasgow (BSc Hons Zool.); Univ. of London Inst. of Educn (PGCE). Research Biologist: Glaxo Labs Ltd, 1962–65; ICI, Alderley Edge, 1966–67; part-time Lectr in Biol., Newcastle-under-Lyme Coll. of FE, 1969–70; Teacher of Biology: (part-time) Dr Challoner's High Sch., 1970–76; Northgate Grammar Sch., Ipswich, 1976–77; Hd of Biol. and Sen. Mistress, Ipswich High Sch. (GPDST), 1977–86; Headmistress, St George's Sch. for Girls, Edinburgh, 1986–93. *Recreations:* concerts, theatre, film, swimming, ski-ing, loch fishing, travel abroad. *Address:* 3 Merton Rise, NW3 3EN.

SCOTT, Sir John; *see* Scott, Sir P. J. and Scott, Sir W. J.

SCOTT, John; *see* Scott, W. J. G.

SCOTT, (John) Brough; Director, Racing Post, since 1986; Sports Writer, Sunday Telegraph, since 1995; *b* 12 Dec. 1942; *s* of Mason Hogarth Scott and Irene Florence Scott, Broadway, Worcs; *m* 1973, Susan Eleanor MacInnes; two *s* two *d*. *Educ:* Radley College; Corpus Christi, Oxford (BA History). Amateur, then professional, Nat. Hunt jockey, 1962–71 (100 winners, incl. Imperial Cup and Mandarin Chase). ITV presenter, sports programmes and documentaries, 1971–; chief racing presenter, ITV, 1979–85; chief presenter, Channel 4 Racing, 1985–2001. Evening Standard sports correspondent, 1972–74; sports journalist: Sunday Times, 1974–90, 1993–94; The Independent on Sunday, 1990–92. Vice-Pres., Jockeys' Assoc., 1969–71; Trustee, Injured Jockeys Fund,

1978– (Chm., 2007–); Trustee, Moorcroft Racehorse Welfare Centre, 2003–. Lord Derby Award, 1978 (racing journalist of the year); Clive Graham Trophy, 1982; Sports Feature Writer of the Year, 1985, 1991, 1992. *Publications:* World of Flat Racing, 1983; On and Off the Rails, 1984; Front Runners, 1991; Up Front—Willie Carson, 1994; Racing Certainties, 1995; Galloper Jack, 2003. *Recreation:* making bonfires. *Address:* Willow House, 35 High Street, Wimbledon Common, SW19 5BY. *T:* (020) 8946 9671.

SCOTT, Prof. John Donald, PhD; FRS 2003; Senior Scientist, Vollum Institute, Oregon Health and Sciences University, since 1997; Investigator, Howard Hughes Medical Institute, 2004 (Associate Investigator, 1997–2003); *b* 13 April 1958; *m* Shonnie; one *s* one *d. Educ:* Heriot-Watt Univ., Edinburgh (BSc Hons (Biochem.) 1980); Univ. of Aberdeen (PhD Biochem.). Med. Endowments Hon. Scholar, Univ. of Aberdeen, 1980–83; NIH Postdoctoral Fellow, Dept of Pharmacol., 1983–86, Res. Asst Prof., Dept of Biochem., 1986–88, Univ. of Washington, Seattle; Sen. Associate, Howard Hughes Med. Inst., 1986–88; Asst Prof., Dept of Physiol. and Biophysics, Univ. of Calif, Irvine, 1988–89; Asst Scientist, 1990–92, Scientist, 1993–96, Vollum Inst., Oregon Health and Sciences Univ. Consultant, ICOS Corp., Seattle, 1992–2000; Scientific Adv. Bd, Upstate Biotechnology, Lake Placid, 1995–; Trellis Bioscience Inc., Mountain View, 2003–. Member NIH Study Section: Med. Biochem., 1993–96; Biochem., 1998–2002. Member: Biochemical Soc., 1981–; Amer. Soc. for Biochem. and Molecular Biol., 1990– (Mem. Program Cttee, 2000–); Endocrine Soc., 1997– (Ernst Oppenheimer Award, 2001); Amer. Soc. for Pharmacol. and Experimental Therapeutics, 1997– (Mem., 1999–2001, Chm., 2001–, John Jacob Abel Award Selection Cttee; John J. Abel Award in Pharmacol., 1996). Mem. Editl Bd, Jl of Biological Chemistry, 1993–98; Review Ed., Biochemical Jl, 2002–. D'Agrosa Meml Lecture, St Louis Univ., 2001. Discovery Award, Med. Res. Foundn, 2003. *Publications:* many articles in learned jls. *Address:* Howard Hughes Medical Institute, Vollum Institute, Oregon Health and Sciences University, 3181 SW Sam Jackson Park Road, L474, Portland, OR 97239, USA. *T:* (503) 494 4652, *Fax:* (503) 494 0519; *e-mail:* scott@ohsu.edu.

SCOTT, Rev. Prof. John Fraser, AO 1990; Vice-Chancellor, La Trobe University, Melbourne, 1977–90; Associate Priest, St George's, Malvern, since 1992; *b* 10 Oct. 1928; *s* of Douglas Fraser Scott and Cecilia Louise Scott; *m* 1956, Dorothea Elizabeth Paton Scott; one *s* three *d. Educ:* Bristol Grammar Sch.; Trinity Coll., Cambridge (MA); Melbourne Coll. of Divinity (BD 1994). FIS. Research Asst, Univ. of Sheffield, 1950–53; Asst, Univ. of Aberdeen, 1953–55; Lectr in Biometry, Univ. of Oxford, 1955–65; University of Sussex: Reader in Statistics, 1965–67; Prof. of Applied Statistics, 1967–77; Pro-Vice-Chancellor, 1971–77. Adv. Prof., E China Normal Univ., 1988. Visiting Consultant in Statistics: Nigeria, 1961, 1965; Sweden, 1969; Kuwait, 1973, 1976; Iraq, 1973; Malaysia, 1976. Reader, Church of England, 1971–77; Examining Chaplain to Bp of Chichester, 1974–77; Diocesan Lay Reader, Anglican Dio. of Melbourne, 1977–90; ordained deacon, then priest, 1990; Asst Curate, St George's, E Ivanhoe, 1990–91. Chairman: Jt Cttee on Univ. Statistics, 1978–86; Cttee of Review of Student Finances, 1983; Aust. Univs Industrial Assoc., 1986–88; AVCC, 1986–88 (Dep. Chm., 1986, Chm., Wkg Party on Attrition, 1981–86); Council for Chaplains in Tertiary Instns, 1990–94; Member: Grad. Careers Council of Aust., 1980–86; Council, 1986–89, Exec. Cttee, 1986–88, ACU; ABC Victorian State Adv. Cttee, 1978–81; Ethics Cttee, Victorian State Dept of Health, 1990–2004; Pres., Victorian State Libraries Bd, 1990–96. Dir, La Trobe Univ. Credit Union, 2001–05. Chieftain, Ringwood Highland Games, 2003. Editor, Applied Statistics, 1971–76; Mem., Editl Bd, The Statistician, 1987–. DUniv La Trobe, 1990. *Publications:* The Comparability of Grade Standards in Mathematics, 1975; Report of Committee of Review of Student Finances, 1983; papers in JRSS, Lancet, BMJ, Chemistry and Industry, Statistician, etc. *Recreations:* wine, women and song; canals. *Address:* 1/18 Riversdale Road, Hawthorn, Victoria 3122, Australia. *T:* (3) 98191862. *Club:* Melbourne.

SCOTT, John Gavin, LVO 2004; FRCO; Organist and Director of Music, St Thomas, Fifth Avenue, New York City, since 2004; *b* 18 June 1956; *s* of Douglas Gavin Scott and Hetty Scott (*née* Murphy); *m* 1979, Carolyn Jane Lumsden; one *s* one *d. Educ:* Queen Elizabeth Grammar Sch., Wakefield; St John's Coll., Cambridge (MA, MusB). Asst Organist, Wakefield Cath., 1970–74; Organ Scholar, St John's Coll., Cambridge, 1974–78; Asst Organist, Southwark Cath., 1978–85; St Paul's Cathedral: Asst Organist, 1978–85; Sub-Organist, 1985–90; Organist and Dir of Music, 1990–2004. Prof., Royal Acad. of Music, 1988–91. Accompanist, Bach Choir, 1979–91. Hon. RAM 1990; Hon. FGCM 1996; Hon. FTCL 2002; Hon. FRSCM 2005. Hon. DMus Nashotah House, 2007. First Prizewinner: Manchester Internat. Organ Fest., 1978; Leipzig Internat. J. S. Bach Competition, 1984. *Recreations:* reading, travel, ecclesiastical architecture. *Address:* 202 West 58th Street, New York, NY 10019, USA.

SCOTT, John Hamilton; Lord-Lieutenant for Shetland, since 1994; farming in Bressay and Noss; *b* 30 Nov. 1936; *s* of Dr Thomas Gilbert Scott and Elizabeth M. B. Scott; *m* 1965, Wendy Ronald; one *s* one *d. Educ:* Bryanston; Cambridge Univ.; Guy's Hosp., London. Shepherd, Scrabster, Caithness, 1961–64. Chm., Woolgrowers of Shetland Ltd, 1981–. Pres., Shetland NFU, 1976; Chairman: Shetland Crofting, Farming and Wildlife Adv. Gp, 1984–95; Shetland Arts Trust, 1993–98; Sail Shetland Ltd, 1997–2002; Belmont Trust, 1997–; Member: Nature Conservancy Council Cttee for Scotland, 1984–91; NE Regl Bd, Nature Conservancy Council for Scotland, 1991–92, Scottish Natural Heritage, 1992–97. *Recreations:* mountain climbing, Up-Helly-Aa, music. *Address:* Keldabister Banks, Bressay, Shetland ZE2 9EL. *T:* (01595) 820281. *Club:* Alpine.
See also T. H. Scott.

SCOTT, John James, PhD; medical research consultant, since 2003; *b* 4 Sept. 1924; *s* of late Col John Creagh Scott, DSO, OBE and Mary Elizabeth Marjory (*née* Murray of Polmaise); *m* 1st, Katherine Mary (*née* Bruce); twin *d*; 2nd, Heather Marguerite (*née* Douglas Brown); 3rd, June Rose (*née* Mackie); twin *s. Educ:* Radley (Schol.); Corpus Christi Coll., Cambridge (Schol.); National Inst. for Medical Research, London. War Service, Captain, Argyll and Sutherland Highlanders, 1944–47. BA 1st cl. hons Nat. Sci. Tripos, Pts I and II, 1950, MA 1953, Cantab; PhD London 1954. Senior Lectr in Chem. Pathology, St Mary's Hosp., 1955–61; Mem. Editorial Bd, Biochem. Jl, 1956–61; Mem. Cttee of Biochem. Soc., 1961; Vis. Scientist, Nat. Insts of Health, Bethesda, Md, 1961. Joined Govt Service: Singapore, 1961–66; London, 1966–71; Rio de Janeiro and Brasilia, 1971–74; NI (Stormont), 1974–76; London, 1976–80. Asst Managing Dir, later Commercial Dir, Industrial Engines (Sales) Ltd, Elbar Group, 1980; Man. Dir, Dudmass Ltd, 1983–93; Associate: Trident Life, 1984–85; Save & Prosper Group, 1985–95; Financial Advr, Allied Dunbar, 1995–96. Sir Nicholas Bacon Prize, Cambridge, 1950. *Publications:* papers in Biochem. Jl, Proc. Royal Soc. and other learned jls. *Recreations:* botany, photography, music. *Address:* Moat Cottage, Northbeck, Scredington, Sleaford, Lincs NG34 0AD. *Clubs:* Carlton, Institute of Directors; Leander (Henley-on-Thames); Hawks (Cambridge); Ski Club of GB.

SCOTT, (John) Michael, CMG 2003; rural livelihoods consultant, since 2003; *b* 18 Feb. 1943; *s* of late Harold Scott and of Joan Winifred Scott (*née* Holroyd); *m* 1967, Pauline Rachel Wright; one *d. Educ:* Boston Grammar Sch., Lincs; Royal Veterinary Coll., London Univ. (BVetMed 1967); Royal (Dick) Sch. of Vet. Studies, Univ. of Edinburgh. MRCVS 1967. Vet. Surgeon, Whittle, Taylor and Chesworth, Rochdale, 1967–69; Vet. Officer, Govt of Botswana, Mahalapye and Francistown, 1969–71; Veterinary Investigation Officer (funded as UK Government Technical Co-operation Officer): Ethiopia, 1972–77; El Salvador, 1977–79; Overseas Development Administration: Animal Health and Prodn Advr, 1979–82; Sen. Animal Health and Prodn Advr, 1982–86; Sen. Natural Resources Advr, Fiji, 1987–90; Hd, Natural Resources Policy and Adv. Dept, 1990–97; Hd, Rural Livelihoods Dept, 1997–2003, Chief Natural Resources Advr, 2002–03, DFID. *Publications:* contrib. learned jls on animal trypanosomiasis and fascioliasis. *Recreations:* international affairs, running, cricket, ornithology, wildlife. *Address:* 63 Oxford Road, Wokingham, Berks RG41 2YH. *T:* (0118) 978 6603; *e-mail:* jm.vets@btinternet.com.

SCOTT, Prof. John Peter, PhD; FBA 2007; Professor of Sociology, University of Plymouth, since 2008; *b* 8 April 1949; *s* of Philip Charles Scott and Phyllis Scott (*née* Bridges); *m* 1971, Gillian Wheatley; one *s* one *d. Educ:* Kingston Coll. of Technol. (BScSoc London 1971); London Sch. of Econs; Univ. of Strathclyde (PhD 1976). Lectr in Sociol., Univ. of Strathclyde, 1972–76; University of Leicester: Lectr, 1976, Reader, 1987–91, in Sociol.; Prof. of Sociol., 1991–94; Prof. of Sociol., Univ. of Essex, 1994–2008. Adjunct Prof., Bergen Univ., Norway, 1997–2005. British Sociological Association: Mem., 1970–; Chm., 1992–93; Pres., 2000–02; Hon. Vice Pres., 2002–. AcSS 2003; FRSA 2005. Editor: Network, 1984–87; Sociology Review, 1986–2002; European Societies, 2006–. *Publications:* Corporations, Classes and Capitalism, 1979, 2nd edn 1985; The Anatomy of Scottish Capital, 1980; The Upper Classes: property and privilege in Britain, 1982; (with C. Griff) Directors of Industry, 1984; (ed jtly) Networks of Corporate Power, 1985; Capitalist Property and Financial Power, 1986; A Matter of Record: documentary sources in social research, 1990; (ed) The Sociology of Elites, three vols, 1990; Who Rules Britain?, 1991; Social Network Analysis, 1992, 2nd edn 2000; (ed jtly) Reviewing Sociology, 1993; (with M. Nakata and H. Hasegawa) Kigyo to kanri no kokusai hikaku (An International Study of Enterprise and Administration), 1993; Poverty and Wealth: citizenship, deprivation and privilege, 1994; (ed) Power, three vols, 1994; Sociological Theory: contemporary debates, 1995; Stratification and Power: structures of class, status and domination, 1996; (ed) Class, four vols, 1996; Corporate Business and Capitalist Classes, 1997; (with Masao Watanabe and John Westergaard) Kaikyu genron no genzai igirisu to Nihon (Debates on Class in Contemporary Britain and Japan), 1998; (with James Fulcher) Sociology, 1999, 3rd edn 2007; (with José López) Social Structure, 2000; (ed jtly) Renewing Class Analysis, 2000; Power, 2001; (ed) Social Networks: critical concept, four vols, 2002; (ed jtly) Rethinking Class: culture, identities, and lifestyle, 2004; (ed jtly) Models and Methods in Social Network Analysis, 2005; (ed with G. Marshall) Oxford Dictionary of Sociology, 3rd edn 2005; Social Theory: central issues in sociology, 2006; (ed) Documentary Research, four vols, 2006; (ed) Sociology: the key concepts, 2006; (ed) Fifty Key Sociologists: the formative theorists, 2007; (ed) Fifty Key Sociologists: the contemporary theorists, 2007; contribs to many learned jls inc. British Jl of Sociol., Sociol Rev., Sociology, Sociol Analysis and Theory, etc. *Recreations:* listening to music, reading. *Address:* School of Law and Social Science, University of Plymouth, Drake Circus, Plymouth PL4 8AA. *T:* (01752) 233220; *e-mail:* john.scott@plymouth.ac.uk.

SCOTT, Jonathan; *see* Scott, I. J.

SCOTT, Judith Margaret, CEng, FBCS; Chief Executive, British Computer Society, 1995–2002; *b* 4 Oct. 1942; *d* of Robert Wright and Marjorie Wood; *m* 1972, Gordon Robert Scott; two *d. Educ:* St Andrews Univ. (BSc Hons); Cambridge Univ. (Dip. Computer Sci.). Various posts, Computel Systems Ltd (Canada), 1968–79; seconded to Computer/Communications Policy Task Force, Govt of Canada, 1971–72; Manager, Product Mktg, Gandalf Data Inc. (Canada), 1979–82; Dir Corporate Planning, Gandalf Technologies Inc. (Canada), 1982–87; Man. Dir, Gandalf Digital Communications Ltd, UK, 1987–95. Mem., PPARC, 2001–06. Vice Pres., Reading Univ., 2007–. DUniv Staffs, 2002. *Recreation:* orchid growing. *Address:* 4 Crescent Road, Wokingham, Berks RG40 2DB.

SCOTT, Sir Kenneth (Bertram Adam), KCVO 1990; CMG 1980; an Extra Equerry to the Queen, since 1996; *b* 23 Jan. 1931; *s* of late Adam Scott, OBE, and Lena Kaye; *m* 1st, 1966, Gabrielle Justine (*d* 1977), *d* of R. W. Smart, Christchurch, New Zealand; one *s* one *d*; 2nd, 1990, Esme Walker (*see* Esme Scott); one step *s. Educ:* George Watson's Coll., Edinburgh; Edinburgh Univ. MA Hons 1952. Foreign Office, 1954; served in Moscow, Bonn, Washington and Vientiane; Counsellor and Head of Chancery, Moscow, 1971; Sen. Officers' War Course, RNC, Greenwich, 1973; Dep. Head, Personnel Ops Dept, FCO, 1973; Counsellor and Head of Chancery, Washington, 1975; Head of E European and Soviet Dept, FCO, 1977; Minister and Dep. UK Perm. Rep. to NATO, 1979–82; Ambassador to Yugoslavia, 1982–85; Asst Private Sec. to the Queen, 1985–90; Dep. Private Sec. to the Queen, 1990–96. Vice-Chm., Provisional Election Commn for Bosnia and Herzogovina, Sarajevo, 1996. Trustee: Hopetoun House Preservation Trust, 1998–2007; Develt Trust, Edinburgh Univ., 1999–2007. Gov., George Watson's Coll., 1997–2002. *Address:* 13 Clinton Road, Edinburgh EH9 2AW. *Clubs:* Royal Over-Seas League (Vice Chm., 2000–02; Vice-Pres., 2002–); New (Edinburgh).

SCOTT, Lee; MP (C) Ilford North, since 2005; *b* 6 April 1956; *s* of late Sidney and Renne Scott; *m* 1987, Estelle Dombey; two *s* three *d. Educ:* Clarks Coll., Ilford; Coll. of Distributive Trades, London. Worked for: Scott & Fishell (Leather Goods); Selfridges, 1975–80; Tatung, 1980–82; Toshiba, 1982–84; ITT, 1984–86; NFR Office Furniture, 1986–88; Campaign Dir, Utd Jewish Israel Appeal, 1988–98; Scott Associates (consultancy working with charities), 1998–2005. Contested (C) Waveney, 2001. *Recreations:* music, travel, football (Leyton Orient supporter), tennis. *Address:* House of Commons, SW1A 0AA. *T:* (020) 7219 8326; *e-mail:* scottlee@parliament.uk.

SCOTT, Linda Valerie; *see* Agran, L. V.

SCOTT, Malcolm Charles Norman; QC (Scot.) 1991; *b* 8 Sept. 1951; *s* of James Raymond Scott and Marjorie Stewart Simpson. *Educ:* Trinity Coll., Glenalmond; Gonville and Caius Coll., Cambridge (BA 1972); Glasgow Univ. (LLB 1975). Advocate 1978. Dir, Mid Wynd International Investment Trust plc, 1990–. *Recreations:* fishing, skiing, hill walking. *Club:* New (Edinburgh).

SCOTT, Dame Margaret, (Dame Catherine Margaret Mary Denton), AC 2005; DBE 1981 (OBE 1977); Founding Director of the Australian Ballet School, 1964–90, retired; *b* 26 April 1922; *d* of John and Marjorie Douglas-Scott; *m* 1953, Derek Ashworth Denton, *qv*; two *s. Educ:* Parktown Convent, Johannesburg, S Africa; Graduate Dip. in Visual and Performing Arts, RMIT, 2000. Sadler's Wells Ballet, London, 1940–43; Principal: Ballet Rambert, London and Australia, 1944–49; National Ballet, Australia, 1949–50; Ballet Rambert, and John Cranko Group, London, 1951–53; private ballet teaching, Australia, 1953–61; planned and prepared the founding of the Aust. Ballet Sch., 1962–64. Hon. Life Mem., Australian Ballet Foundn, 1988. Hon. LLD Melbourne, 1989;

Hon. DEd RMIT, 2001. Life Time Achievement Award: Green Room Awards Assoc., 1998; Aust. Dance Awards, 1998; JC Williamson Award, Live Performance Australia, 2007. *Recreations:* music, theatre, garden. *Address:* 816 Orrong Road, Toorak, Melbourne, Vic 3142, Australia. *T:* (3) 98272640. *Club:* Alexandra (Melbourne).

SCOTT, Matthew Paul Noy; composer and musician; Head of Music, National Theatre, since 2006; *b* 19 Sept. 1956; *s* of David and Elizabeth Scott. *Educ:* Eton Coll.; Epsom Coll.; City Univ./Guildhall Sch. of Music and Drama (BSc 1979). Freelance composer, 1979–; Tutor, RADA, 1984–; Lecturer: Univ. of Southampton, 1996–; Univ. of Reading, 1996–2000; Associate Artist, Birmingham Rep Th., 1997–; Associate Composer, Chichester Fest. Th., 2006–. Many theatre and television credits as composer incl. Drop the Dead Donkey, 1990; films including: Lord of Misrule, 1996; The Landgirls (co-composer), 1998. *Publications:* A New Orpheus, 1985; *composition:* Four Bars of Agit, 1983. *Recreations:* architecture, surrealism, surrealist architecture, stationery and gadgets, detecting scepticism in others and comparing. *Address:* Music Department, National Theatre, SE1 9PX. *T:* (020) 7452 3390; *e-mail:* mscott@nationaltheatre.org.uk.

SCOTT, Maurice FitzGerald, FBA 1990; Official Fellow in Economics, Nuffield College, Oxford, 1968–92, now Emeritus Fellow; *b* 6 Dec. 1924; *s* of Colonel G. C. Scott, OBE and H. M. G. Scott; *m* 1953, Eleanor Warren (*née* Dawson) (*d* 1989); three *d. Educ:* Wadham Coll., Oxford (MA); Nuffield Coll., Oxford (BLitt). Served RE, 1943–46. OEEC, Paris, 1949–51; Paymaster-General's Office (Lord Cherwell), 1951–53; Cabinet Office, 1953–54; NIESR, London, 1954–57; Tutor in Economics and Student of Christ Church, Oxford, 1957–68; NEDO, London, 1962–63; OECD, Paris, 1967–68. *Publications:* A Study of U.K. Imports, 1963; (with I. M. D. Little and T. Scitovsky) Industry and Trade in Some Developing Countries, 1970; (with J. D. MacArthur and D. M. G. Newbery) Project Appraisal in Practice, 1976; (with R. A. Laslett) Can We get back to Full Employment?, 1978; (with W. M. Corden and I. M. D. Little) The Case against General Import Restrictions, 1980; A New View of Economic Growth, 1989; Peter's Journey, 1998. *Recreation:* walking. *Address:* 11 Blandford Avenue, Oxford OX2 8EA. *T:* (01865) 559115.

SCOTT, Michael; *see* Scott, J. M.

SCOTT, Maj.-Gen. Michael Ian Eldon, CB 1997; CBE 1987; DSO 1982; Complaints Commissioner, Bar Council, 1997–2006; *b* 3 March 1941; *s* of Col Eric Scott and Rose-Anne Scott; *m* 1968, Veronica Daniell; one *s* one *d. Educ:* Bradfield Coll. Commnd Scots Guards, 1960; Regtl service in UK, E Africa, N Ireland, BAOR; Staff Coll., Camberley, 1974; 2nd MA to CGS, 1975; COS Task Force Delta, 1979; Armed Forces Staff Coll., USA, 1981; CO, 2nd Bn Scots Guards, London, Falklands War and Cyprus, 1981–84; Comd 8th Inf. Bde, N Ireland, 1984–86; RCDS 1987; Dep. Mil. Sec., 1988–93; GOC Scotland and Gov., Edinburgh Castle, 1993–95; Mil. Sec., 1995–97. Pres., Third Guards Club, 1999–. *Recreations:* travel, visual arts, outdoor pursuits. *Clubs:* Pratt's, Garrick.

SCOTT, Sir Oliver (Christopher Anderson), 3rd Bt *cr* 1909 of Yews, Westmorland; Radiobiologist, Richard Dimbleby Cancer Research Department, St Thomas' Hospital, 1982–88; Radiobiologist, 1954–66, Director, 1966–69, British Empire Cancer Campaign Research Unit in Radiobiology; *b* 6 Nov. 1922; *s* of Sir Samuel H. Scott, 2nd Bt and Nancy Lilian (*née* Anderson); *S* father, 1960; *m* 1951, Phoebe Ann Tolhurst; one *s* two *d. Educ:* Charterhouse; King's College, Cambridge. Clinical training at St Thomas' Hosp., 1943–46; MRCS, LRCP, 1946; MB, BCh, Cambridge, 1946; MD Cambridge, 1976; Surgeon-Lieutenant RNVR, 1947–49. Dir, Provincial Insurance Co., 1955–64. Hon. Consultant, Inst. of Cancer Res., Sutton, 1974–82. Pres., Section of Oncology, RSM, 1987–88. Mem. Council, Cancer Res. Campaign, 1978–91. Mem., BIR, 1999. Hon. FRCR 1998. High Sheriff of Westmorland, 1966. *Publications:* contributions to scientific books and journals. *Recreations:* music, walking. *Heir: s* Christopher James Scott [*b* 16 Jan. 1955; *m* 1988, Emma, *o d* of Michael Boxhall; two *s* two *d*]. *Address:* 31 Kensington Square, W8 5HH. *T:* (020) 7937 8556. *Club:* Brooks's.

SCOTT, Oliver Lester Schreiner; Emeritus Consultant: Skin Department, Charing Cross Hospital, since 1985 (Physician-in-Charge, 1956–84); South West Metropolitan Regional Hospital Board, since 1985 (Consultant Dermatologist, 1951–84); *b* London, 16 June 1919; *s* of Ralph Lester Scott, FRCSE, and Ursula Hester Schreiner; *m* 1943, Katherine Ogle Branfoot (*d* 1987); two *d. Educ:* Diocesan College, Cape Town; Trinity College, Cambridge; St Thomas's Hospital, London. MRCS, LRCP 1942; MA, MB, BChir, (Cantab) 1943; MRCP (London) 1944. FRCP 1964. Med. Specialist, RAF Med. Branch, 1943–46 (Sqn Leader). Consultant, Medical Insurance Agency, 1976–93; Hon. Consultant: Dispensaire Français, 1960–86; King Edward VII Hosp. for Officers, London, 1975–84. Hon. Treas., RSocMed, 1978–82 (Pres., Dermatology Section, 1977–78); Vice-Pres., Royal Medical Foundn of Epsom Coll., 1992– (Hon. Treas., 1978–93); Hon. Mem., British Assoc. of Dermatologists (Pres., 1982–83). Chevalier, l'Ordre National du Mérite, France. *Publications:* section on skin disorders in Clinical Genetics, ed A. Sorsby; medical articles in Lancet, British Journal of Dermatology, etc. *Recreations:* fishing, gardening. *Address:* South Lodge, 7 South Side, Wimbledon Common, SW19 4TL. *T:* (020) 8946 6662.

SCOTT, Paul Henderson, CMG 1974; writer; HM Diplomatic Service, retired 1980; *b* 7 Nov. 1920; *s* of Alan Scott and Catherine Scott (*née* Henderson), Edinburgh; *m* 1953, Beatrice Celia Sharpe; one *s* one *d. Educ:* Royal High School, Edinburgh; Edinburgh University (MA, MLitt). HM Forces, 1941–47 (Major RA). Foreign Office, 1947–53; First Secretary, Warsaw, 1953–55; First Secretary, La Paz, 1955–59; Foreign Office, 1959–62; Counsellor, Havana, 1962–64; Canadian National Defence College, 1964–65; British Deputy Commissioner General for Montreal Exhibition, 1965–67; Counsellor and Consul-General, Vienna, 1968–71; Head of British Govt Office, 1971, Consul-Gen., 1974–75, Montreal; Research Associate, IISS, 1975–76; Asst Under Sec., FO (negotiator on behalf of EEC Presidency for negotiations with USSR, Poland and East Germany), 1977; Minister and Consul-General, Milan, 1977–80. Chairman: Adv. Council for the Arts in Scotland, 1981–98; Steering Cttee for a Scottish Nat. Theatre, 1988–; Mem., Constitutional Steering Cttee, which drew up A Claim of Right for Scotland, published 1988; Pres., Saltire Soc., 1996–2002 (Dep. Chm., 1981–95; Hon. Pres., 2004; Vice-Convenor, 2005–); Member: Council, Nat. Trust for Scotland, 1981–87; Assoc. for Scottish Literary Studies, 1981–; Scots Language Soc., 1981–; Cockburn Assoc., 1982–; Council, Edinburgh Internat. Fest., 1984–87; Chm., Friends of Dictionary of Older Scottish Tongue, 1984–2002; President: Andrew Fletcher Soc., 1988–96; Scottish Centre, PEN Internat., 1992–97. Scottish National Party: Mem., NEC, 1989–97; spokesman on educn and the arts, 1991–97; Vice-Pres., 1992–97; dep. spokesman on Europe and external affairs, 1997–99; contested (SNP): Eastwood, 1992; Lothians, Scottish Parlt, 1999. Convener, Scottish Centre for Econ. and Social Res., 1990–95. Rector, Dundee Univ., 1989–92. Hon. Fellow, Glasgow Univ., 1996. Grosse Goldene Ehrenzeichen, Austria, 1969. *Publications:* 1707: The Union of Scotland and England, 1979; (ed with A. C. Davis) The Age of MacDiarmid, 1980; Walter Scott and Scotland, 1981; (ed) Walter Scott's Letters of Malachi Malagrowther, 1981; (ed) Andrew Fletcher's United and Separate Parliaments, 1982; John Galt, 1985; In Bed with an Elephant, 1985; (ed with George Bruce) A Scottish Postbag, 1986; The Thinking Nation, 1989; Towards Independence, 1991; Andrew Fletcher and the Treaty of Union, 1992; Scotland in Europe: a dialogue with a sceptical friend, 1992; (ed) Scotland: a concise cultural history, 1993; Defoe in Edinburgh and Other Papers, 1995; (ed) Scotland's Ruine: Lockhart of Carnwath's Memoirs, 1995; Scotland: an unwon cause, 1997; Still in Bed with an Elephant, 1998; The Boasted Advantages, 1999; A Twentieth Century Life (autobiog.), 2002; Scotland Resurgent, 2003; (ed) The Saltoun Papers, 2003; (ed) Spirits of the Age: Scottish self-portraits, 2005; The Union of 1707: why and how, 2006; The Age of Liberation, 2008; The New Scotland: a 21st century sequel, 2008; articles and book reviews esp. in Economist, Sunday Herald and other periodicals. *Recreation:* ski-ing. *Address:* 33 Drumsheugh Gardens, Edinburgh EH3 7RN. *T:* (0131) 225 1038. *Clubs:* New, Scottish Arts (Edinburgh).

SCOTT, Sir Peter; *see* Scott, Sir G. P.

SCOTT, Peter Anthony; Managing Director, Peel Holdings plc, since 1985; *b* 24 April 1947; *s* of Barclay and Doris Scott; *m* 1969, Lynne Smithies; one *s* one *d. Educ:* Heywood Grammar Sch.; Littleborough High Sch.; Manchester Poly. ACCA 1979. Financial Accountant: Fothergill & Harvey Ltd, 1962–75; Crane Fruehauf Trailers (Oldham) Ltd, 1975–77; Co. Sec., 1977–81, Financial Dir, 1981–85, Peel Hldgs plc. *Address:* Peel Holdings plc, Peel Dome, Trafford Centre, Manchester M17 8PL; (home) 6 Bowling Green Way, Bamford, Rochdale, Lancs OL11 5QQ.

SCOTT, Peter Denys John, CBE 2008; QC 1978; Chairman, City Panel on Takeovers and Mergers, since 2000; *b* 19 April 1935; *s* of John Ernest Dudley Scott and Joan G. Steinberg. *Educ:* Monroe High Sch., Rochester, NY, USA; Balliol Coll., Oxford (MA). Second Lieut, RHA, Lieut (TA), National Service, 1955. Called to the Bar, Middle Temple (Harmsworth Scholar), 1960, Bencher, 1984; Standing Counsel: to Dir, Gen. of Fair Trading, 1973–78; to Dept of Employment, 1974–78. Member: Home Sec.'s Cttee on Prison Disciplinary System, 1984; Interception of Communications Tribunal, 1986–2002; Lord Chancellor's Adv. Cttee on Legal Educn and Conduct, 1991–94; Investigatory Powers Tribunal, 2000–; Investigatory Powers Guernsey Tribunal, 2006–; conducted Attorney Gen.'s rev. of Northern Irish judicial proceedings, 2006–07; Chm., Appeal Bd, Inst. of Actuaries, 1995–2001; a Judicial Tribunal Chm., City Disputes Panel, 1997–. Vice-Chm., Senate of the Inns of Court and the Bar, 1985–86; Chm., General Council of the Bar, 1987; Mem., Senate and Bar Council, 1981–87; Chm., London Common Law Bar Assoc., 1983–85. Mem. Adv. Council, Centre for Commercial Law Studies, QMW, 1990–2006; former Chm., Dame Colet House and Tower Hamlets Law Centre. Chm., Bd of Trustees, Nat. Gall., 2000–08. Chairman: N Kensington Amenity Trust, 1981–85; Kensington Housing Trust, 1999–2002. *Recreations:* gardening, theatre. *Address:* 4 Eldon Road, W8 5PU. *T:* (020) 7937 3301, *Fax:* (020) 7376 1169; Château Bellegarde, 32140 Masseube, France. *T:* (5) 62660027, *Fax:* (5) 62661683.

SCOTT, Peter Francis, CBE 1982; retired; *b* 21 Sept. 1917; *s* of Francis C. Scott and Frieda Jager; *m* 1953, Prudence Mary Milligan (marr. diss. 1974); one *s* three *d. Educ:* Winchester; Oriel Coll., Oxford (BA). Commnd 1st Bn, KRRC; Capt.; served War, 1939–46: with 8th Army in N Africa, Sicily and Italy; with 21st Army Gp in NW Europe. Joined Provincial Insurance Co. Ltd, 1946: Dir, 1946–77; Chm., 1957–77; Pres., 1977; Pres., Sand Aire Ltd, 1997. Former Member: Northern Econ. Planning Council; Careers Res. Adv. Council; Standing Cttee on Museums and Galleries. Former Chairman: Trustees, Brathay Hall; Lake Dist Art Gall. Trust; Kendal Brewery Arts Centre Trust; Mem., Lake Dist Mus. Trust. Chm., Lake Dist Cttee, NT. Dir, National Theatre (Mem., Exec. Cttee); Mem., Council, Northern Arts Assoc. DL, High Sheriff 1963, Westmorland. Freeman of Kendal. Hon. LLD Lancaster. *Clubs:* Brooks's, Garrick, Royal Automobile.

SCOTT, Air Vice-Marshal Peter John, CB 2003; CEng, FIMechE; Air Officer Logistics and Communications Information Systems, HQ Strike Command, 1998–2004; *b* 4 April 1949; *s* of John and Kathleen Scott; *m* 1973, Carolyn Frances, (Chips), Barrett; one *d. Educ:* Bromley Grammar Sch.; RAF Coll. Cranwell (BSc Hons 1971); Cranfield Inst. of Technol. (MSc 1979). Joined RAF, 1967; OC Engineering and Supply Wing, RAF Germany Wildenrath, 1985–87; OC Engineering Wing, Falkland Islands, 1987–88; rcds 1995; Station Comdr and AO Wales, RAF St Athan, and ADC to the Queen, 1995–97. Patron, Univ. of Wales Air Sqn, 2004–. *Recreation:* golf (9 handicap). *Address:* Princes Risborough. *Clubs:* Royal Air Force; Ellesborough Golf; Aero Golf Soc.

SCOTT, Sir (Philip) John, KBE 1987; FRCP; FRACP; FRSNZ; Professor of Medicine, University of Auckland, 1975–97, now Emeritus; *b* 26 June 1931; *s* of Horace McD. Scott and Doris A. Scott (*née* Ruddock); *m* 1st, 1956, Elizabeth Jane MacMillan (*d* 2002); one *s* three *d*; 2nd, 2003, Margaret Fernie Wann (*d* 2007). *Educ:* Univ. of Otago (BMedSci; MB, ChB); Univ. of Birmingham (MD). Qual. in medicine, Dunedin, 1955; hosp. and gen. practice experience, Auckland, 1956–58; postgrad. trng, RPMS, London, 1959–60; Queen Elizabeth Hosp. and Univ. of Birmingham, 1960–62; Med. Res. Fellowships, Auckland, 1962–68; Sen. Lectr, Univ. of Otago, based on Auckland Hosp., 1969–72; University of Auckland: Sen. Lectr, 1970–72; Associate Prof., 1973–75; Hd, Dept of Medicine, the Univ.'s Sch. of Medicine, 1979–87. Pres., Royal Soc. of NZ, 1998–2000. Res. interests in lipoprotein metabolism, arterial disease, human nutrition, med. econs and educn, professional ethics. *Publications:* (first author/co-author) articles in sci./med. jls and in press, on aspects of coronary artery disease, atherosclerosis, lipoprotein metabolism, human nutrition, ethical issues, medical history and educn, health service orgn. *Recreations:* music, pottery, gardening. *Address:* 64 Temple Street, Meadowbank, Auckland 1072, New Zealand. *T:* (9) 5215384.

SCOTT, Primrose Smith; Head of Quality Review, Institute of Chartered Accountants of Scotland, 1999–2002; Senior Partner, The McCabe Partnership (formerly Primrose McCabe & Co.), 1987–99; *b* 21 Sept. 1940. *Educ:* Ayr Acad. Trained with Stewart Gilmour, Ayr; qualified as CA, 1963; joined Romanes & Munro, Edinburgh, 1964; progressed through manager ranks to Partner, Deloitte Haskins & Sells, 1981–87; set up own practice, Linlithgow, 1987; moved practice to Edinburgh, 1997. Dep. Chm., Dunfermline Building Soc., 1998–2006; non-exec. Dir, Northern Venture Trust PLC, 1995–. Pres., Institute of Chartered Accountants of Scotland, 1994–95. Trustee, New Lanark Conservation Trust, 2002–06. Comr, Queen Victoria Sch., Dunblane, 1998–2006. Hon. Treas., Hospitality Industry Trust Scotland, 1994–2002; Treasurer: Age Concern Scotland, 2004–; Borders Youth Th., 2007–. Fellow, SCOTVEC, 1994. *Recreation:* walking dogs in Scottish Borders. *Address:* The Cleugh, Redpath, Earlston, Berwicks TD4 6AD. *T:* (01896) 849042.

SCOTT, Richard John Dinwoodie; Sheriff of Lothian and Borders at Edinburgh, 1986–2004; *b* 28 May 1939; *s* of late Prof. Richard Scott and Mary Ellen Maclachlan; *m* 1969, Josephine Moretta Blake; two *d. Educ:* Edinburgh Academy; Univ. of Edinburgh (MA, LLB) (Vans Dunlop Schol. in Evidence and Pleading, 1963). Lektor in English, British Centre, Sweden, 1960–61; Tutor, Faculty of Law, Univ. of Edinburgh, 1964–72; admitted to Faculty of Advocates, 1965; Standing Jun. Counsel to Min. of Defence (Air) in Scotland, 1968–77. Sheriff of Grampian, Highland and Islands, at Aberdeen and

Stonehaven, 1977–86. Mem., Parole Bd for Scotland, 2003–. Convenor, Additional Support Needs Tribunals for Scotland, 2005–. Chm., Scottish Assoc. for Study of Delinquency, 1996–2001 (Chm., Aberdeen Branch, 1978–86, Edinburgh Branch, 1993–96); Mem., Working Party on Offenders aged 16–18, 1991–93; Chm., Grampian Victim Support Scheme, 1983–86; Pres., Sheriffs' Assoc., 2002–04 (Mem. Council, 1979–82 and 1994–2004; Vice-Pres., 2001–02); Mem., Sheriff Court Rules Council, 1995–98. Hon. Lectr, Univ. of Aberdeen, 1980–86. *Publications:* various articles in legal jls. *Recreations:* golf, curling, traditional music of Scotland. *Address:* c/o Sheriff Court House, 27 Chambers Street, Edinburgh EH1 1LB.

SCOTT, Sir Ridley, Kt 2003; film director and producer; *b* S Shields, 30 Nov. 1937. *Educ:* Royal Coll. of Art. *Films include:* The Duellists, 1976; Alien, 1978; Blade Runner, 1980; Someone to Watch over Me, 1987; Black Rain, 1989; Thelma and Louise, 1991; 1492: Conquest of Paradise, 1992; White Squall, 1996; GI Jane, 1997; Gladiator, 2000; Hannibal, 2001; Black Hawk Down, 2002; Matchstick Men, 2003; Kingdom of Heaven, 2005; A Good Year, 2006; American Gangster, 2007; *for television:* Churchill - The Gathering Storm, 2002. *Address:* Scott Free, 42–44 Beak Street, W1R 3DA. *T:* (020) 7437 3163.

SCOTT, Robert Avisson, CBE 2002; Chairman, Yell Group plc, since 2003; *b* 6 Jan. 1942; *s* of Robert Milligan Scott and Phyllis Winifred Scott; *m* 1979, Joanne Rose Adams; two *d*. *Educ:* Scots Coll., Wellington, NZ. Associate: Australian Ins. Inst.; Ins. Inst. NZ; FCIBS 2004. South British Insurance Co. Ltd, later NZI Corp. Ltd, then General Accident plc, subseq. CGU plc, then CGNU plc, 1959–2001: Asst Gen. Manager, NZ, 1981–83; Australia: Asst Gen. Manager, 1983–85; Gen. Manager, 1985–87; Chief Gen. Manager, 1987–90; Dep. Gen. Manager, UK, 1990–91, Gen. Manager, 1991–94; Dep. Chief Exec., 1994–96; Gp Chief Exec., 1996–2001. Director: Royal Bank of Scotland Gp, 2001–; Swiss Reinsurance Co., Zürich, 2002–; Pension Insce Corp. Hldgs LLP, 2006–; Advr, Duke Street Capital Private Equity, 2006–. Hon. FCII 2005. *Recreations:* sporting interests, walking, do it yourself. *Address:* Axford Lodge, Axford, Basingstoke, Hants RG25 2DZ. *T:* (01256) 389259.

SCOTT, Sir Robert (David Hillyer), Kt 1994; Chairman, Trinity Laban, since 2005; International Ambassador, Liverpool Culture Company, since 2005 (Chief Executive, 2000–03; Chairman, 2003–05); *b* 22 Jan. 1944; *s* of Sir David (Aubrey) Scott, *qv*; *m* 1st, 1972, Su Dalgleish (marr. diss. 1995); two *s* one *d*; 2nd, 1995, Alicia Tomalino; two step *d*. *Educ:* Haileybury; Merton Coll., Oxford (Pres., OUDS, 1965–66). Actor, 1966–67; Administrator: 69 Theatre Co., Manchester, 1968–74; Royal Exchange Theatre Trust, 1974–77; Man. Dir, Manchester Theatres Ltd, 1978–96; Chairman: Manchester Olympic Bid Cttee, 1985–93; Manchester Commonwealth Games Bid Cttee, 1993–95; Chief Exec., Greenwich Millennium Trust, 1995–2001. Mem., Central Manchester Develt Corp., 1988–96. Special Projects Dir, Apollo Leisure Gp, 1994–99. Chairman: Cornerhouse Manchester, 1984–95; Granada Foundn, 1993–; Piccadilly Radio, 1993–2001; Tour East London, 1998–2001; S London Business (formerly S London Econ. Develt Alliance), 1999–; City Bars and Restaurants, 1999–2003; Greenwich Theatre, 1999–; Bexley Heritage Trust, 1999–2007; Greenwich Peninsula Partnership, 2001–08; City Screen Ltd, 2006–; Director: Royal Exchange Theatre, 1976–94; Hallé Concerts Soc., 1989–94; White Horse Fast Ferries, 1998–2002; London First, 1999–2003. Mem. Cttee, Whitworth Art Gall., 1989–95. DL Greater Manchester, 1988–97. Hon. RNCM 1990. Hon. Fellow: Manchester Poly., 1987; UMIST, 1989; Liverpool John Moores Univ., 2003. Hon. MA: Manchester, 1988; Salford, 1991; Hon. LLD Greenwich, 2003. Officier de l'Ordre des Arts et des Lettres (France), 1991. *Publication:* The Biggest Room in the World, 1976. *Recreations:* food, travel, talking, sport, theatre. *Address:* Liverpool Culture Company, Millennium House, 60 Victoria Street, Liverpool L1 3JD.

SCOTT, Prof. Roger Davidson, PhD; CPhys, FInstP; FRSE; Director, Scottish Universities Research and Reactor Centre, 1991–98; Professor of Nuclear Science, University of Glasgow, 1994–98; *b* 17 Dec. 1941; *s* of Alexander N. Scott and Jessie H. Scott (*née* Davidson); *m* 1965, Marion S. McCluckie; two *s* one *d*. *Educ:* Anderson Inst., Lerwick; Univ. of Edinburgh (BSc 1st Cl. Hons Physics; PhD Nuclear Physics). University Demonstrator, Univ. of Edinburgh, 1965–68; Lectr, 1968–88, Depute Dir, 1988–91, Scottish Univs Res. and Reactor Centre. Non-exec. Dir, Nuclear Decommissioning Authy, 2004–. FRSE 1995. *Publications:* articles on nuclear physics and envmtl radioactivity; contribs to learned jls. *Recreations:* watching football, walking wife and dogs, home maintenance. *Address:* 6 Downfield Gardens, Bothwell, Glasgow G71 8UW. *T:* (01698) 854121.

SCOTT, Roger Martin; His Honour Judge Scott; a Circuit Judge, since 1993; *b* 8 Sept. 1944; *s* of Hermann Albert and Sarah Margaret Scott; *m* 1966, Diana Elizabeth Clark; two *s* one *d*. *Educ:* Mill Hill Sch.; St Andrews Univ. (LLB). Called to the Bar, Lincoln's Inn, 1968. *Recreations:* golf, cricket, walking, theatre. *Address:* North Eastern Circuit Administrator's Office, West Riding House, Albion Street, Leeds LS1 5AA. *T:* (0113) 244 1841. *Club:* Yorkshire County Cricket (Leeds).

SCOTT, Sheila Margaret, OBE 2007; Chief Executive, National Care Association (formerly National Care Homes Association), since 1993; *b* 18 Dec. 1948; *d* of G. W. Brownlow and late Audrey Brownlow (*née* Louth); *m* 1973, A. L. Scott (marr. diss. 1996); one *s* one *d*. *Educ:* Wisbech High Sch.; Addenbrooke's Hosp., Cambridge (RGN 1971). Sister, Springdene Gp, N London, 1975–83; care home proprietor, N London, 1983–88; with Nat. Care Homes Assoc., 1988–; Office Manager/Company Sec., 1988–93; on secondment to DoH, 1992–93. *Recreations:* travel, cinema, cycling, gardening. *Address:* 6 Nansicles Road, Orton Longueville, Peterborough PE2 7AS; *e-mail:* sheilamscott@hotmail.com.

SCOTT, Stuart Lothian, JD; Chairman, Jones Lang LaSalle (formerly LaSalle Partners Inc.), 1990–2004 (Chief Executive Officer, 1990–2001); *b* 21 Aug. 1938; *s* of David G. Scott and Jean Lothian Scott; *m* 1st, 1961, Penelope Spare; four *d*; 2nd, 1971, Elizabeth Love; one *s* one *d*; 3rd, 1982, Anne O'Laughlin; one *d*. *Educ:* Hamilton Coll. (AB 1961); Northwestern Univ. Sch. of Law (JD 1964). Attorney, US Securities and Exchange Commn, 1964–67; Sen. Vice-Pres. and Dir, Arthur Rubloff & Co., 1967–73; Pres., LaSalle Partners Inc., 1973–90. *Recreations:* golf, shooting, fishing (fly), theatre, reading. *Address:* c/o Jones Lang LaSalle, 200 East Randolph Drive, Chicago, IL 60601, USA. *Clubs:* Royal Troon (Scotland); Wisley (Surrey); Pine Valley (NJ); Seminole (Florida); Old Elm (Chicago); Shoreacres (Illinois).

SCOTT, Tavish Hamilton; Member (Lib Dem) Shetland, Scottish Parliament, since 1999; farmer; *b* 6 May 1966; *s* of John Hamilton Scott, *qv*; *m* 1990, Margaret MacDonald (marr. diss.); two *s* one *d*; *m* 2008, Kirsten Campbell. *Educ:* Napier Coll., Edinburgh (BA Hons Business Studies). Research Asst to J. R. Wallace, MP, 1989–90; Press Officer, Scottish Lib Dem Party, 1990–92. Mem. (Lib Dem) Shetland Islands Council, 1994–99. Scottish Executive: Dep. Minister for Parlt, 2000–01, for Parly Business and for Finance and Public Services, 2003–05; Minister for Transport, 2005–07; Opposition front bench spokesman on finance and sustainable growth, Scottish Parlt, 2007–. Leader, Scottish Lib Dems, 2008–. Chm., Lerwick Harbour Trust, 1996–99. *Recreations:* cinema, golf, Up Helly Aa. *Address:* Scottish Parliament, Edinburgh EH99 1SP. *T:* (0131) 348 5815.

SCOTT, Timothy John Whittaker; QC 1995; a Recorder, since 1999; *b* 19 July 1949; *s* of late John Dick Scott and Helen Scott (*née* Whittaker); *m* 1982, Clare, *d* of Baron Renton, KBE, TD, PC, QC; one *s* two *d*. *Educ:* Westminster Sch. (Queen's Schol.); New Coll., Oxford (Exhibnr; MA). Journalist, 1970–72; called to the Bar, Gray's Inn, 1975; Asst Recorder, 1995–99. *Publications:* articles on family law topics in specialist jls. *Recreations:* fishing, reading, travel. *Address:* 29 Bedford Row, WC1R 4HE. *T:* (020) 7404 1044. *Club:* Garrick.

SCOTT, Sir (Walter) John, 5th Bt *cr* 1907, of Beauclerc, Bywell St Andrew, Northumberland; countryside campaigner, farmer, author, columnist and broadcaster; *b* 24 Feb. 1948; *s* of Sir Walter Scott, 4th Bt and Diana Mary (*d* 1985), *d* of J. R. Owen; *S* father, 1992; *m* 1st, 1969, Lowell Patria (marr. diss. 1971), *d* of late Gp Capt. Pat Vaughan Goddard, Auckland, NZ; one *d*; 2nd, 1977, Mary Gavin, *d* of Alexander Fairly Anderson, Gartocharn, Dunbartonshire; one *s* one *d*. Chm., N Pennine Hunt; Co-Pres., Union of Country Sports Workers, 2000–; Pres., Tay Valley Wildfowlers' Assoc., 2001–; Member Board: Heather Trust, 2004–; Eur. Squirrel Fedn, 2004–; Patron: Sporting Lucas Terrier Assoc., 2004–; Nat. Orgn of Beaters and Pickers Up; Wildlife Ark Trust; Centenary Patron, British Assoc. for Shooting and Conservation. Writer and co-presenter with Clarissa Dickson Wright, Clarissa and the Countryman, TV series, 2000–03. Founder Mem., Cholmondeley Coursing Club, 1995. *Publications:* (with Clarissa Dickson Wright): Clarissa and the Countryman, 2000; Clarissa and the Countryman Sally Forth, 2001; A Sunday Roast, 2002; The Game Cookbook, 2004; A Greener Life, 2005. *Recreations:* field sports. *Heir:* *s* Walter Samuel Scott, *b* 6 Dec. 1984. *Address:* The Hermitage Farmhouse, Newcastleton, Roxburghshire TD9 0LY.

SCOTT, Prof. William, RSA 1984; FRBS; Post-Graduate Course Leader, Edinburgh College of Art, 1997–2000 (Head of Sculpture, 1989–97); *b* 16 Aug. 1935; *s* of George Barclay Scott and Jeanie Stuart Scott (*née* Waugh); *m* 1961, Phyllis Owen Fisher; one *s* two *d*. *Educ:* Edinburgh Coll. of Art (DA 1959); Ecole des Beaux Arts, Paris. FRBS 1994. Prof., Heriot-Watt Univ., 1994–2000, now Prof. Emeritus. Contributor to: annual exhibns in Scotland; British Art Show, 1979–80; Fifth Biennial of Small Sculptures, Budapest, 1981; Chelsea Harbour Show, 1993; Städtische Gal. im Park, Viersen, 1999; Transistors, Iwate Arts Fest., 1999, Trondheim, 2000; Sudbahnhof Gall., Krefeld, 2000; Internat. Medaillen Kunst, Weimar, 2000; Kunst Transfer Heinsberg, 2003; Insiders: Boxart, Oriel Davies Gall., 2003; Canterbury Mus., 2005; *one-person exhibitions* in galleries and museums, 1971–, including: New 57 Gall., Edinburgh, 1979; Kirkcaldy Mus. and Gall., 1985; Talbot Rice Gall., Edinburgh Univ., 1994; Fettes Coll. Gall., 2002; Demarco Roxy Gall., 2003; Kunst Verein, Heinsberg, 2004; RBS Gall., London. 2005; *commissions* include: public sculptures, St Andrews, 1970, Cumbernauld, 1980, Glasgow, 1985 and 1998; sculpture for Sir Alec Douglas-Home at The Hirsel, Coldstream, 1998; Elizabeth Crichton Sculpture, Crichton campus, Dumfries, 2000; portrait of Sorley Maclean, Edinburgh Park, 2003; sculptures and drawings in *public collections*, including: Aberdeen Art Gall.; Royal Scottish Acad.; Kirkcaldy Gall. and Mus.; Leeds City; Edinburgh City; also work in private collections. Mem., Bd of Dirs, Fruit Mkt Gall., Edinburgh, 1981–92; Chm., Edinburgh Sculpture Workshop, 1998–. Mem., Selection Cttee for British Sch. at Rome, 1985–90; Chm., Scottish Arts Council Awards Panel, 1990–93. Sec., RSA, 1998–. *Recreations:* walking, reading, travel. *Address:* 45 St Clair Crescent, Roslin, Midlothian EH25 9NG. *T:* (0131) 440 2544.

SCOTT, Hon. (William) Alexander; JP; MP (PLP) Warwick South East, since 2003; Premier of Bermuda, 2003–06; *b* 12 June 1940; *s* of Willard Alexander Scott and Edith Lucille Scott; *m* 1972, Olga Lawrence; one *s* one *d*. *Educ:* Temple Univ., Philadelphia (BA Fine Arts). Graphic designer and design consultant; owner, Scotts Crafts Ltd, 1964–97. Founding Mem. and former Chm., Big Brothers. Mem., Pitt Commn, 1978. Mem. (PLP), 1985–93, and Leader of the Opposition, 1989–93, Senate, Bermuda; MP (PLP) Warwick E, 1993–2003; Minister of Works and Engrg, 1998–2003. JP Bermuda, 1985. *Address:* House of Assembly, Parliament Street, Hamilton HM12, Bermuda.

SCOTT, (William) Dermot; Director, European Parliament Office for the United Kingdom, since 2002; *b* 19 Sept. 1943; *s* of Rev. Dr Eric Scott and Bee Scott (*née* Knight); *m* 1970, Susan Burdon Davies; one *s* one *d*. *Educ:* Campbell Coll., Belfast; Trinity Coll., Dublin (BA Mod., MSc Econ); Sch. of Public Admin, Dublin. Institute of Public Administration, Dublin: Editor: Léargas, 1967–73; European Community Directory and Diary, 1974–76; Manager, Develt Co-opn, 1977–79; European Parlt Office in Ireland, 1979–98 (Actg Hd, 1990); Hd, European Parlt Office in Scotland, 1998–2002. Mem., Exec. Cttee, European Movement Ireland, 1989–98; Life Mem., Irish Inst. of European Affairs (Mem. Council, 1990–98). Mem., Nat. Parents' Council, 1986–88. Mem., Chatham House, 2003–. Mem. Council, Dublin Orch. for Young Players, 1986–89. Life Mem., NUJ. Mem., Royal Dublin Soc. *Publications:* Caisléan Eireannacha, 1972; (contrib.) Ireland and EU Membership Evaluated, 1991; Ireland's Contribution to the European Union, 1994; Ireland and the IGC, 1996; numerous articles on European affairs. *Recreations:* trout fishing, putting on recitals, looking at ruins. *Address:* European Parliament Office for the United Kingdom, 2 Queen Anne's Gate, SW1H 9AA. *T:* (020) 7227 4300, *Fax:* (020) 7227 4302; *e-mail:* eplondon@europarl.europa.eu. *Club:* Reform.

SCOTT, (William) John (Graham); Member (C) Ayr, Scottish Parliament, since March 2000; *b* 7 June 1951; *s* of William Scott and Elizabeth Haddow Scott; *m* 1975, Charity Nadine Mary Bousfield (*d* 2000); one *s* one *d*. *Educ:* Barhill Primary Sch.; George Watson's Coll.; Edinburgh Univ. (BSc Civil Engrg 1973). Farming in family partnership, 1973–; Partner, family catering business, 1985–2000. Founder Dir, Ayshire Country Lamb Ltd, 1988–93; created Ayrshire Farmers' Mkts, 1999 (Chm., 1999–). Convenor, Hill Farming Cttee, NFU Scotland, 1993–99; Chairman: S of Scotland Regl Wool Cttee, 1996–2000; Ayrshire and Arran Farming Wildlife Adv. Gp, 1993–99. Scottish Parliament: Cons. Shadow Cabinet Sec. for Rural Affairs and Envmt, 2007–; Member: Transport and Envmt Cttee, 2001–03; Corporate Body, 2003–07; Vice-Chm., Petitions Cttee, 2003–07 (Mem., 2000–01); Vice Chm., Rural Affairs and Envmt Cttee, 2007–. Chm., Hill Sheep and Native Woodland Project, Scottish Agricl Coll., 1999–. Founder Chm., Scottish Assoc. of Farmers' Markets, 2001–05. JP Girvan, 1997–99. Elder, Ballantrae Ch, 1985–. *Recreations:* curling, geology, bridge. *Address:* Scottish Parliament, George IV Bridge, Edinburgh EH99 1SP. *T:* (0131) 348 5664, *Fax:* (0131) 348 5617; (constituency office) 1 Wellington Square, Ayr KA7 1EN. *T:* (01292) 286251, *Fax:* (01292) 280480.

SCOTT, Rev. Preb. William Sievwright; Sub-Dean of Her Majesty's Chapels Royal, Deputy Clerk of the Closet and Sub-Almoner, since 2007; Prebendary, St Paul's Cathedral, since 2000; Chaplain to the Queen, since 2003; *b* 1 Feb. 1946; *s* of David Anderson Harper Scott and Amelia Scott (*née* Sievwright). *Educ:* Harris Acad., Dundee; Edinburgh Theol Coll. Ordained deacon 1970, priest 1971; Curate: St Ninian's, Glasgow, 1971–73; St Francis, Bridgwater, 1973–77; Rector: Shepton Beauchamp, Barrington, Puckington and Stocklinch, 1977–82; Woolavington and Cossington, 1982–84; Chaplain, Community of All Hallow's, Ditchingham, 1984–91; Vicar, St Mary's, Bourne St, SW1,

1991–2002; Chaplain of the Queen's Chapel of the Savoy and of the Royal Victorian Order, 2002–07. Chaplain, Priory of Our Lady of Walsingham, 1991–2007. Area Dean of Westminster (St Margaret), 1997–2004. *Recreations:* music making and listening, reading novels and poetry, conducting retreats. *Address:* Chapel Royal, St James's Palace, SW1A 1DH. *Clubs:* National Liberal, Garrick.

SCOTT, William Wootton, CB 1990; Under Secretary, Industry Department for Scotland, 1985–90; *b* 20 May 1930; *s* of Dr Archibald C. Scott and Barbara R. Scott; *m* 1958, Margaret Chandler, SRN; three *s* one *d*. *Educ:* Kilmarnock Academy; Dollar Academy; Glasgow Univ. (MA, 1st Cl. Hons History). National Service in Royal Artillery, 1952–54. Assistant Principal, 1954, Principal, 1958, Min. of Transport and Civil Aviation; Principal Private Sec. to Minister of Transport, 1965–66; Asst Sec., 1966; Regional Controller (Housing and Planning), Northern Regional Office of DoE, 1971–74; joined Scottish Development Dept, 1974, Under Sec., 1978. *Publications:* occasional historical notes. *Recreations:* historical research, music, gardening, reading. *Address:* Whitethorn, Hardgate, Castle Douglas, Kirkcudbrightshire DG7 3LD. *T:* (01556) 660200.

SCOTT-BOWDEN, Maj.-Gen. Logan, CBE 1972 (OBE 1964); DSO 1944; MC 1944 and Bar 1946; farmer; *b* 21 Feb. 1920; *s* of late Lt-Col Jonathan Scott-Bowden, OBE, TD, and Mary Scott-Bowden (*née* Logan); *m* 1950, Helen Jocelyn, *d* of late Major Sir Francis Caradoc Rose Price, 5th Bt, and late Marjorie Lady Price; three *s* three *d*. *Educ:* Malvern Coll.; RMA Woolwich. Commissioned Royal Engineers, 1939; served in War of 1939–45: Norway, 1940; Adjt, 53rd (Welsh) Div. RE, 1941; Liaison Duties in Canada and USA, 1942; Normandy Beach Reconnaissance Team (Major), 1943; OC 17 Fd Co RE, NW Europe, 1944; psc 1945; Singapore, Burma (Bde Maj. 98 Indian Inf. Bde), Palestine, Libya, 1946–51; Korea, 1953; jssc 1956; Arabia, 1958–60 (Lt-Col 1959); CRE 1st Div., BAOR, 1960; Head, UK Land Forces Planning Staff, 1963; Asst Dir, Def. Plans MoD (Col), 1964; Comd Trg Bde RE (Brig.), 1966; Nat. Defence Coll. (India), 1969; Comd Ulster Defence Regiment, 1970–71; Head of British Defence Liaison Staff, India, 1971–74, retd 1974. Col Comdt RE, 1975–80. *Recreations:* ski-ing, travel.

SCOTT-GALL, Anthony Robert Gall; His Honour Judge Scott-Gall; a Circuit Judge, since 1996; *b* 30 March 1946; *s* of Robert and Daphne Scott-Gall; *m* 1973, Caroline Anne Scott; one *s* one *d*. *Educ:* Stowe Sch.; New Coll., Oxford (BA). Called to the Bar, Middle Temple, 1971; Recorder, 1993. *Recreations:* cricket, Rugby football, gardening, travel, ornithology, history, music. *Address:* 3 Temple Gardens, Temple, EC4Y 9AU. *T:* (020) 7353 3102. *Clubs:* Richmond Football; Armadillos Cricket.

SCOTT-JAMES, Anne Eleanor, (Lady Lancaster); author and journalist; *b* 5 April 1913; *d* of R. A. Scott-James and Violet Brooks; *m* 1st, 1939, Derek Verschoyle (marr. diss.); 2nd, 1944, Macdonald Hastings (marr. diss.; he *d* 1982); one *s* one *d*; 3rd, 1967, Sir Osbert Lancaster, CBE (*d* 1986). *Educ:* St Paul's Girls' Sch.; Somerville Coll., Oxford (Class. Schol.). Editorial staff of Vogue, 1934–41; Woman's Editor, Picture Post, 1941–45; Editor, Harper's Bazaar, 1945–51; Woman's Editor, Sunday Express, 1953–57; Woman's Adviser to Beaverbrook Newspapers, 1959–60; Columnist, Daily Mail, 1960–68; freelance journalist, broadcasting, TV, 1968–. Member: Council, RCA, 1948–51, 1954–56; Council, RHS, 1978–82. *Publications:* In the Mink, 1952; Down to Earth, 1971; Sissinghurst: The Making of a Garden, 1975; (with Osbert Lancaster) The Pleasure Garden, 1977; The Cottage Garden, 1981; (with Christopher Lloyd) Glyndebourne—the Gardens, 1983; The Language of the Garden: a personal anthology, 1984; (introd.) Our Village, by Mary Russell Mitford, 1987; The Best Plants for your Garden, 1988; (with Ray Desmond) The British Museum Book of Flowers, 1989; (with Clare Hastings) Gardening Letters to My Daughter, 1990; Sketches from a Life (autobiog.), 1993. *Recreations:* reading, gardening, travelling, looking at churches and flowers.

See also Sir M. M. Hastings.

SCOTT-JOYNT, Rt Rev. Michael Charles; *see* Winchester, Bishop of.

SCOTT-LEE, Sir Paul (Joseph), Kt 2007; QPM 1997; DL; Chief Constable, West Midlands Police, since 2002; *b* 25 July 1953; *s* of Hubert George Scott-Lee and Decima Florence Scott-Lee (*née* Hancorn); *m* 1975, Rosemary Susan Hargreaves. *Educ:* Whitley Abbey Comprehensive Sch., Coventry; Police Staff Coll., Bramshill. Joined Warwickshire and Coventry Constabulary from Cadet Corps, 1972; Sergeant to Chief Inspector, W Midlands Police, 1978–88; Superintendent to Chief Superintendent, Northants Police, 1988–92; Asst Chief Constable, Kent Co. Constabulary, 1992–94; Dep. Chief Constable, 1994–98, Chief Constable, 1998–2002, Suffolk Police. DL W Midlands, 2003. *Recreations:* fly fishing, golf, reading. *Address:* West Midlands Police, Lloyd House, Colmore Circus, Queensway, Birmingham B4 6NQ.

SCOTT-MANDERSON, Marcus Charles William; QC 2006; *b* 10 Feb. 1956; *s* of late Dr William Scott-Manderson, MB ChB, MRCGP and of Pamela Scott-Manderson; *m* 2003, Melinda Penelope Tillard. *Educ:* Harrow Sch.; Christ Church, Oxford (BCL, MA); Hague Acad. of Internat. Law; Glasgow Univ. Called to the Bar, Lincoln's Inn, 1980; in practice, specialising in internat. cases relating to children. *Recreations:* archaeology, travel. *Address:* 4 Paper Buildings, Temple, EC4Y 7EX. *T:* (020) 7583 0816. *Club:* Lansdowne.

SCOTT THOMAS, Kristin, OBE 2003; actress; *b* 24 May 1960; *m* 1981, François Olivennes; two *s* one *d*. *Educ:* Cheltenham Ladies' Coll.; Central Sch. of Speech and Drama; École Nat. des Arts et Technique de Théâtre, Paris. *Theatre includes:* Bérénice, Paris, 2001; The Three Sisters, 2003, As You Desire Me, 2005, Playhouse Th.; The Seagull, Royal Court, 2007 (Best Actress, Laurence Olivier Award, 2008). *Films include:* Under the Cherry Moon, 1986; Djamel et Juliette, Agent Trouble, 1987; La Méridienne, A Handful of Dust, 1988; Force Majeure, Bille en Tête, 1989; The Bachelor, Bitter Moon, 1992; Four Weddings and a Funeral, 1994; Angels and Insects, 1995 (Best Actress Award, BAFTA); Richard III, The Confessional, Mission Impossible, 1996; The English Patient, Amour et Confusions, 1997; The Horse Whisperer, 1998; Random Hearts, The Revengers' Comedies, 1999; Up at the Villa, Play, 2000; Gosford Park, Life as a House, 2002; Petites Coupures, 2003; Man to Man, The Adventures of Arsène Lupin, Keeping Mum, 2005; The Walker, 2007. *Television includes:* Mistral's Daughter, 1984; Tricheuse, Sentimental Journey, 1987; The Tenth Man. 1988; Endless Game, Framed, 1990; Titmuss Regained, 1991; Look At It This Way, 1992; Body and Soul, 1994.

SCOTT WHYTE, Stuart; *see* Whyte.

SCOULLER, (John) Alan; Head of Industrial Relations, Midland Bank Group, 1975–88; Visiting Professor in Industrial Relations, Kingston University (formerly Kingston Polytechnic), 1988–95; Senior Visiting Fellow, City University Business School, 1989–92; *b* 23 Sept. 1929; *e s* of late Charles James Scouller and Mary Helena Scouller; *m* 1954, Angela Geneste Ambrose; two *s* five *d*. *Educ:* John Fisher Sch., Purley. Army service, Queen's Own Royal W Kent Regt, 1948–58 (Captain). Joined Unilever as management trainee, 1958; Personnel Man., Wall's Ice Cream, 1959–62; Domestos, 1963–66; Holpak, 1966–68; Commercial Plastics and Holpak, 1968–69; left Unilever to join Commn on Industrial Relations, 1969; Dir of Industrial Relations until 1973, full-time Comr, 1973–74. Member: Employment Appeal Tribunal, 1976–2000; Educn Commn, RC Dio. of Westminster, 1990–2006. FIPD. Chm., Letchworth Garden City Heritage Foundn, 2004– (Gov., 1995–). KSG 1996. *Recreations:* reading political biographies, walking, listening to music, looking after grandchildren, cricket. *Address:* Walnut Cottage, 33 Field Lane, Letchworth, Herts SG6 3LD. *T:* (01462) 682781.

SCOURSE, Rear-Adm. Frederick Peter, CB 1997; MBE 1972; FREng, FIET; Acting Controller of the Navy, 1996–97; *b* 23 June 1944; *s* of late Frederick David John Scourse and Margaret Elaine Scourse; *m* 1967, Nicolette Jean Somerville West; one *s*. *Educ:* Wells Cathedral Sch.; RN Coll., Dartmouth; Churchill Coll., Cambridge (MA Mech Sci, Elect. Sci). Served HM Ships: Dido, 1963–64; Warspite, 1969–72; Renown, 1974–77; MoD (PE), 1979–82; NDC, 1982–83; MoD (PE), 1983–89; Dir-Gen., Surface Weapons (Navy), 1989–94; Dir-Gen., Surface Ships, 1994–97. Nuclear Weapons Safety Advr, MoD, 1997–2003. Industry Advr, Churchill Coll., Cambridge, 1998–. Dir, Wild Trout Trust, 2002–04. Vice Chm., Regular Forces Employment Assoc., 1998–2002. FREng 2000. *Recreations:* fly fishing, singing. *Address:* Valley View, 278a Turleigh, Bradford on Avon BA15 2HH. *Club:* Royal Commonwealth Society.

SCOWCROFT, Gen. Brent, Hon. KBE 1993; President: Forum for International Policy, since 1993; Scowcroft Group, since 1993; *b* 19 March 1925; *s* of James Scowcroft and Lucile (*née* Ballantyne); *m* 1951, Marian (Jackie) Horner (*d* 1995); one *d*. *Educ:* Ogden City Schs; US Mil. Acad.; Columbia Univ. (MA 1953; PhD 1967); Lafayette Coll.; Georgetown Univ. Joined Army 1943; qualified pilot 1948; Prof. of Russian History, US Mil. Acad., 1953–57; service in Washington, Yugoslavia, Colorado, Western Hemisphere Region; with Jt Chiefs of Staff, 1970; MA to President, 1972–73; Dep. Asst, 1973–75, and Asst 1975–77 and 1989–93, to successive Presidents, for Nat. Security Affairs; retired from mil. service, 1975; Dir, Council on Foreign Relations, 1983–89; served on major US cttees, commns and bds, 1977–89. Vice-Chm., Kissinger Associates, 1982–89. Chm., CSIS/Pacific Forum, 1993–. Mem. Bd of Visitors, USAF Acad., 1993–99. US Medal of Freedom, 1991; numerous Service medals and awards. *Recreation:* ski-ing.

SCRAFTON, Douglas, CMG 1998; Member, St Blaise Town Council, since 2007; *b* 14 July 1949; *s* of late Douglas Scrafton and Irene Hilda Kirk (formerly Scrafton, *née* Hammett); *m* 1975, Carolyn Patricia Collison; one *s* one *d*. HM Diplomatic Service, 1967–2001: Mem., UK Delegn (later UK Perm. Repn) to EC, 1970–73; Kampala, 1973–74; Mbabane, 1975–77; FCO, 1977–80; Jedda, 1980–82; British Liaison Office, Riyadh, 1982–84; Cairo, 1984–85; FCO, 1985–87; on loan to Cabinet Office, 1987–88; Ottawa, 1989–92; FCO, 1992–94; Ambassador: to Yemen Republic, 1995–97; to Democratic Republic of the Congo, 1998–2000; Foreign Sec.'s Special Rep. for the Great Lakes region, 2000–01. Volunteer, CAB, 2003–. *Recreations:* photography, reading, gardening. *Address:* Reynards Rest, The Mount, Par, Cornwall PL24 2BZ.

SCRASE-DICKINS, Mark Frederick Hakon, CMG 1991; DL; HM Diplomatic Service, retired; *b* 31 May 1936; *s* of late Alwyne Rory Macnamara Scrase-Dickins and Ingeborg Oscara Frederika Scrase-Dickins; *m* 1969, Martina Viviane Bayley; one *s* one *d* (and one *d* decd). *Educ:* Eton Coll.; RMA, Sandhurst. Commnd Rifle Bde (later Royal Green Jackets), 1956; Malaya, 1956–57 (despatches); ADC to GOC Ghana Army, 1958–59; ADC to Chief of Imperial Gen. Staff, 1959–60; SE Asia, 1962–65; Army Staff Coll., 1967; Hong Kong, 1968–70; transferred to FCO, 1973; Vientiane, 1975; Muscat, 1976; Counsellor: Jakarta, 1983; Riyadh, 1990. Pres., St John Ambulance Sussex, 2005. Chm., John Bodley Trust, 2004; Trustee, Lodge Hill Trust, 2006. High Sheriff, 2003–04, DL 2004, West Sussex. SBStJ 2008. *Recreation:* field sports. *Address:* Coolhurst Grange, Horsham, West Sussex RH13 6LE. *T:* (01403) 252416. *Clubs:* White's, Beefsteak, Special Forces.

SCREECH, Rev. Prof. Michael Andrew, FBA 1981; FRSL; Fellow and Chaplain, All Souls College, Oxford, 2001–03, now Emeritus Fellow (Senior Research Fellow, 1984–93); Assistant Curate (non-stipendiary), St Giles with St Philip, and St James with St Margaret, Oxford, since 1993; *b* 2 May 1926; 3rd *s* of Richard John Screech, MM and Nellie Screech (*née* Maunder); *m* 1956, Anne (*née* Reeve); three *s*. *Educ:* Sutton High Sch., Plymouth; University Coll. London (BA (1st cl. Hons) 1950; Fellow, 1982); University of Montpellier, France; Oxford Ministry Course; DLitt Birmingham, 1959; DLit London, 1982; DLitt Oxon 1990. Other Rank, Intelligence Corps (mainly Far East), 1944–47. Asst, UCL, 1950–51; Birmingham Univ.: Lectr, 1951–58; Sen. Lectr., 1959–61; UCL: Reader, 1961–66; Personal Chair of French, 1966–71; Fielden Prof. of French Language and Lit., London Univ., 1971–84; Extraordinary Fellow, 1993–2001, Hon. Fellow, 2001, Wolfson Coll., Oxford. Ordained deacon, 1993, priest, 1994. Visiting Professor: Univ. of Western Ontario, 1964–65; Univ. of New York, Albany, 1968–69; Johnson Prof., Inst. for Research in the Humanities, Madison, Wisconsin, 1978–79; Vis. Fellow, All Souls, Oxford, 1981; Edmund Campion Lectr, Regina, 1985; Wiley Vis. Prof., N Carolina, 1986; Professeur, Collège de France, 1989; Prof. Associé, Paris IV (Sorbonne), 1990; Leverhulme Emeritus Fellow, 1995–98. Member: Cttee, Warburg Inst., 1970–84; Comité d'Humanisme et Renaissance, 1971–; Comité de parrainage des Classiques de l'Humanisme, 1988–; Corresponding Member: Société Historique de Genève, 1988; Acad. des Inscriptions et Belles Lettres, Paris, 2000. Hon. DLitt Exeter, 1993; Hon. D(Th.) Geneva, 1998. Chevalier dans l'Ordre National du Mérite, 1983; Médaille de la Ville de Tours, 1984; Chevalier, Légion d'Honneur, 1992. *Publications:* The Rabelaisian Marriage, 1958, rev. edn trans. French, 1992; L'Evangélisme de Rabelais, 1959, rev. edn trans. English, 1992; Tiers Livre de Pantagruel, 1964; Les épistres et évangiles de Lefèvre d'Etaples, 1964; (with John Jollife) Les Regrets et autres oeuvres poëtiques (Du Bellay), 1966; Marot évangélique, 1967; (with R. M. Calder) Gargantua, 1970; La Pantagrueline Prognostication, 1975; Rabelais, 1980, rev. edn trans. French, 1992; Ecstasy and the Praise of Folly, 1981, rev. edn trans. French, 1991; Montaigne and Melancholy, 1983, rev. edn trans. French, 1992; (prefaces) Erasmus' Annotations on the New Testament (ed Anne Reeve): The Gospels, 1986, Acts, Romans, I and II Corinthians, 1990, Galatians—Revelation, 1993; (ed trans.) Montaigne, An Apology for Raymond Sebond, 1987; (with Stephen Rawles *et al.*) A New Rabelais Bibliography: editions before 1626, 1987; (ed trans.) The Essays of Montaigne, 1991; Some Renaissance Studies, ed. M. Heath, 1992; Clément Marot: a Renaissance poet discovers the Gospel, 1994; Monumental Inscriptions in All Souls College, Oxford, 1997; Laughter at the Foot of the Cross, 1998; Montaigne's Copy of Lucretius, 1998; (ed trans.) Rabelais, Gargantua and Pantagruel, 2006; *edited reprints:* Le Nouveau Testament de Lefèvre d'Etaples, 1970; F. de Billon: Le Fort inexpugnable de l'Honneur du Sexe Femenin, 1970; Opuscules d'Amour par Héroët et autres divins poëtes, 1970; Amyot: Les œuvres morales et meslées de Plutarque, 1971; Warden Mocket of All Souls: Doctrina et Politia Ecclesiae Anglicanae, 1995. *Recreation:* walking. *Address:* 5 Swanston-field, Whitchurch-on-Thames RG8 7HP. *T:* and *Fax:* (0118) 984 2513. *Clubs:* Athenæum; Pangbourne Working Men's.

SCREECH, Rt Rev. Royden; *see* St Germans, Bishop Suffragan of.

SCRIVEN, Rt Rev. Henry William; Assistant Bishop of Pittsburgh, USA, since 2002; *b* 30 Aug. 1951; *s* of late William Hamilton Scriven and Jeanne Mary Edwards; *m* 1975,

Catherine Rose Ware; one *s* one *d*. *Educ*: Repton Sch.; Sheffield Univ. (BA Hons); St John's Theol Coll., Nottingham. Ordained deacon, 1975, priest, 1976; Asst Curate, Holy Trinity, Wealdstone, Harrow, 1975–79; Missionary with S American Missionary Soc., N Argentina, 1979–82; Educn Associate Rector, Christ Church, Little Rock, Arkansas, 1982–83; Missionary, S American Missionary Soc., Spain, 1984–90; Chaplain, British Embassy Church of St George, Madrid, 1990–95; Suffragan Bp of Gibraltar in Europe, 1995–2002. *Recreations*: reading, walking, tennis, music. *Address*: 1437 Greystone Drive, Pittsburgh, PA 15206, USA; (office) 900 Oliver Building, 535 Smithfield Street, Pittsburgh, PA 15222, USA. *T*: (412) 2816131; *e-mail*: scriven@pgh.anglican.org.

SCRIVEN, Pamela; QC 1992; a Recorder, since 1996; *b* 5 April 1948; *d* of Maurice Scriven and Evelyn Scriven (*née* Stickney); *m* 1973; two *s*. *Educ*: University College London (LLB Hons). Called to the Bar, Inner Temple, 1970 (Bencher, 1995). Chm., Family Law Bar Assoc., 1999–2001. *Address*: 1 King's Bench Walk, Temple, EC4Y 7DB. *T*: (020) 7583 6266.

SCRIVENER, Anthony Frank Bertram; QC 1975; a Recorder of the Crown Court, 1976–92; *b* 31 July 1935; *s* of late Frank Bertram Scrivener and of Edna Scrivener; *m* 1964, Irén Becze (marr. diss.); one *s* one *d*; *m* 1993, Ying Hui Tan. *Educ*: Kent Coll., Canterbury; University Coll. London (LLB). Called to Bar, Gray's Inn, 1958 (Holt Scholar); Bencher, Lincoln's Inn, 1985. Lectr in Law, Ghana, 1959–61; practice as Junior, 1961–75. Chm., Gen. Council of Bar, 1991 (Vice-Chm., 1990). *Recreations*: tennis, chess, cricket, car racing, taking the dog for a walk. *Address*: 2–3 Gray's Inn Square, WC1R 5JH.

SCRIVENER, Christiane; Commandeur de la Légion d'Honneur, 2001 (Officier, 1995); Médiateur, Société Générale, since 1996; Member, Commission of the European Communities, 1989–95; *b* 1 Sept. 1925; *m* 1944, Pierre Scrivener; one *s* decd. *Educ*: Lycée de Grenoble; Faculté de lettres et de droit de Paris. Dip. Psychol.; Dip. Harvard Business Sch. Directeur Général: l'Assoc. pour l'organisation des Stages en France, 1958–69; l'Assoc. pour l'organisation des missions de coopération technique, 1961–69; l'Agence pour la coopération technique industrielle et économique, 1969–76; Sec. d'Etat à la Consommation, 1976–78; Pres., la Commission chargée d'étudier les problèmes éthiques de la publicité, 1978; Sec. Gen. Adj. du parti républicain, 1978–79; Mem., Parlement européen (UDF), 1978–89; Mem., Conseil d'admin des Assurances Générales de France, 1986–89. Alumni Achievement Award (Harvard Business Sch.), 1976. Officier, Polonia Restituta, 1968; Médaille d'Or du Mérite Européen, 1990; Grand Croix de l'Ordre de Léopold II (Belgium), 1995; Grand Croix de Mérite du Grand Duché de Luxembourg, 1996. *Publications*: L'Europe, une bataille pour l'avenir, 1984; (pour les enfants) L'histoire du Petit Troll, 1986. *Recreations*: ski-ing, tennis, classical music. *Address*: 21 avenue Robert-Schumann, 92100 Boulogne-Billancourt, France.

SCRIVER, Prof. Charles Robert, CC 1997 (OC 1986); GOQ 1997; FRS 1991; FRSC 1973; Alva Professor of Human Genetics, 1994–2002, Professor of Pediatrics, Faculty of Medicine, and Professor of Biology, Faculty of Science, 1969–2002, McGill University, Montreal, now Professor Emeritus; *b* 7 Nov. 1930; *s* of Walter DeMoulpied Scriver and Jessie Marion (*née* Boyd); *m* 1956, Esther Katherine Peirce; two *s* two *d*. *Educ*: McGill Univ., Montreal (BA *cum laude* 1951, MD, CM *cum laude* 1955). Intern, Royal Victoria Hosp., Montreal, 1955–56; Resident: Royal Victoria and Montreal Children's Hosps, 1956–57; Children's Med. Center, Boston, 1957–58; McLaughlin Travelling Fellow, UCL, 1958–60; Chief Resident in Pediatrics, Montreal Children's Hosp., 1960–61; Asst. Associate Prof., Pediatrics, 1961–69, Markle Schol., 1962–67, McGill Univ. Rutherford Lectr, RSCan, 1983. Associate, 1968–95, Dist. Scientist, 1995–, MRC; Dir, MRC Gp (Med. Genetics), 1982–94; Associate Dir, Can. Genetic Diseases Networks (Centers of Excellence), 1989–98. President: Can. Soc. Clinical Investigation, 1974–75; Soc. Pediatric Res., 1975–76; Amer. Soc. Human Genetics, 1986–87; Amer. Pediatric Soc., 1994–95. FAAAS 1992; Member: Amer. Soc. Clinical Investigation; Assoc. Amer. Physicians; Hon. Member: Brit. Paediatric Assoc.; Soc. Française de Pédiatrie. Hon. DSc: Manitoba, 1992; Glasgow, 1993; Montreal, 1993; Utrecht, 1999; UBC, 2002; Western Ontario, 2007; McGill, 2007. Wood Gold Medal, McGill Univ., 1955; Mead Johnson Award, 1968; Borden Award 1973, Amer. Acad. Pediatrics; Borden Award, Nutrition Soc. Can., 1969; Allan Award, 1978, Excellence in Human Genetics Educn Award, 2001, Amer. Soc. Human Genetics; G. Malcolm Brown Award, Can. Soc. Clin. Invest., 1979; Gairdner Internat. Award, Gairdner Foundn, 1979; McLaughlin Medal, RSC, 1981; Ross Award, Can. Pediatric Soc., 1990; Award of Excellence, Genetic Soc. of Canada, 1992; Prix du Québec (Wilder Penfield), 1995; Lifetime Achievement Award in Genetics, Birth Defects Foundn, 1997; Querci Prize, Italy, 2001. *Publications*: (jtly) Amino Acid Metabolism and its Disorders, 1973; (ed) The Metabolic Basis of Inherited Disease, 6th edn 1986, 7th edn as The Metabolic and Molecular Bases of Inherited Disease, 1995, 8th edn 2001; numerous res. pubns. *Recreations*: history, music, photography, literature. *Address*: McGill University—Montreal Children's Hospital Research Institute, 2300 Tupper Street, Montreal, QC H3H 1P3, Canada. *T*: (514) 4124417, *Fax*: (514) 9344329; *e-mail*: charles.scriver@mcgill.ca; (home) 232 Strathearn N, Montreal West, QC H4X 1Y2, Canada. *T*: (514) 4860742.

SCROGGS, Cedric Annesley; Chief Executive, Fisons plc, 1992–93; *b* 2 Jan. 1941; *s* of Richard B. H. Scroggs and Vera Wesley Shutte (*née* Coombs); *m* 1964, Patricia Mary Sutherland Ogg; two *s* one *d*. *Educ*: Reading Sch.; St John's Coll., Oxford (Sir Thos White Scholar; BA 1962). Marketing posts: AEI-Hotpoint Ltd, 1962–67; General Foods Ltd, 1967–73; Cadbury Ltd, 1973–76 (Mkting Dir, 1974–76); Mkting Dir, Leyland Cars, 1976–78; Fisons plc: Man. Dir, Scientific Equipment Div., 1979–81; Dir and Div. Chm., 1981. Dep. Chm., Sarginsons plc, 1999–; non-executive Director: Caradon plc, 1988–89; Montpellier Group plc (formerly Y. J. Lovell (Hldgs) plc, then YJL plc), 1990–2004 (Chm., 1999–2004); Hillingdon Hosp. NHS Trust, 1991–92; Genus plc, 1994–2000 (Dep. Chm., 1995–2000); Huntsworth (formerly Holmes & Marchant Gp) plc, 1997–2000. Advr, Müller Gp, 1997–2003. Director: Oxfordshire Mental Healthcare NHS Trust, 1995–2001; Oxon & Bucks Mental Health NHS Foundn Trust (formerly Oxon & Bucks Mental Health Partnership NHS Trust), 2006– (Vice Chm., 2008–); Chm., SE Oxon Primary Care Trust, 2001–02. President: BEAMA, 1991–92; CBI Nat. Mfg Council, 1992–94; Mem., Milk Mktg Bd, 1991–94. Vis. Fellow, Nuffield Coll., Oxford, 1993–2001. *Recreations*: boating, golf, diving. *Address*: Sotwell Priory, Wallingford, Oxon OX10 0RH. *Clubs*: Leander (Henley); Huntercombe Golf (Oxon).

SCRUBY, Ven. Ronald Victor, MA; Archdeacon of Portsmouth, 1977–85, now Emeritus; *b* 23 Dec. 1919; 6th *s* of late Thomas Henry Scruby and late Florence Jane Scruby, Norwood Green, Southall, Middx; *m* 1955, Sylvia Tremayne Miles (*d* 1995), *e d* of late Rear-Adm. Roderic B. T. Miles, Trotton, Sussex; two *s* one *d*. *Educ*: Southall Technical Coll.; Trinity Hall, Cambridge. Engineering Apprentice, London Transport, 1936–39. Royal Engineers, 1939–45; Capt. 1943. Trinity Hall, Cambridge, 1945–48; Cuddesdon Coll., Oxford, 1948–50. Asst Curate, Rogate, Sussex, 1950–53; Chaplain, King Edward VII Hosp., Midhurst, 1950–53; Chaplain, Saunders-Roe, Osborne, E Cowes, 1953–58; Vicar of Eastney, Portsmouth, 1958–65; Rural Dean of Portsmouth,

1960–65; Archdeacon of the Isle of Wight, 1965–77. *Address*: Church House, Rogate, Petersfield, Hants GU31 5EA. *T*: (01730) 821784.

SCRUTON, Prof. Roger Vernon, FBA 2008; writer and philosopher; *b* 27 Feb. 1944; *s* of John Scruton and Beryl C. Haynes; *m* 1st, 1973, Danielle Laffitte (marr. diss. 1979); 2nd, 1996, Sophie Jeffreys; one *s* one *d*. *Educ*: Jesus Coll., Cambridge (MA, PhD). Called to the Bar, Inner Temple, 1978. Res. Fellow, Peterhouse, 1969–71; Lectr in Philosophy, Birkbeck Coll., London, 1971–79, Reader, 1979–85, Prof. of Aesthetics, 1985–92; Prof. of Philosophy, Boston Univ., Mass, 1992–95. Founder and Dir, The Claridge Press, 1987–. Editor, Salisbury Review, 1982–2000. *Publications*: Art and Imagination, 1974, 2nd edn 1982; The Aesthetics of Architecture, 1979; The Meaning of Conservatism, 1980, 3rd edn 2001; From Descartes to Wittgenstein, 1981, 2nd edn 1995; Fortnight's Anger (novel), 1981; The Politics of Culture, 1981; Kant, 1982; A Dictionary of Political Thought, 1982, 2nd edn 1996; The Aesthetic Understanding, 1983; (with Baroness Cox) Peace Studies: A Critical Survey, 1984; Thinkers of the New Left, 1985; (jtly) Education and Indoctrination, 1985; Sexual Desire, 1986; Spinoza, 1986; A Land held Hostage, 1987; Untimely Tracts, 1987; The Philosopher on Dover Beach (essays), 1990; Francesca (novel), 1991; A Dove Descending and Other Stories, 1991; (ed) Conservative Texts: an anthology, 1992; Xanthippic Dialogues (novel), 1993; Modern Philosophy, 1994; The Classical Vernacular, 1994; An Intelligent Person's Guide to Philosophy, 1996; The Aesthetics of Music, 1997; On Hunting, 1998; (ed with Anthony Barnett) Town and Country, 1998; An Intelligent Person's Guide to Modern Culture, 1998; Animal Rights and Wrongs, 2000; England: an elegy, 2000; The West and the Rest: globalisation and the terrorist threat, 2002; Death-devoted Heart: sex and the sacred in Wagner's Tristan and Isolde, 2004; News from Somewhere, 2004; Gentle Regrets, 2005; A Political Philosophy, 2006; contribs to The Times, Guardian, etc. *Recreations*: music, architecture, literature, hunting. *Address*: Sunday Hill Farm, Brinkworth, Wilts SN15 5AS.
See also E. Hodder.

SCRYMGEOUR, family name of **Earl of Dundee**.

SCRYMGEOUR, Lord; Henry David Wedderburn of that Ilk; *b* 20 June 1982; *s* and heir of 12th Earl of Dundee, *qv*; *m* 2005, Eloise, *d* of Ludovic van der Heyden, Fontainebleau; one *s*. *Heir*: *s* Tassilo Alexander Robert Scrymgeour, Master of Scrymgeour, *b* 16 Dec. 2005.

SCUDAMORE, Prof. James Marfell, CB 2004; consultant, since 2004; Professor of Livestock and Veterinary Public Health, University of Liverpool, since 2004; *b* 24 March 1944; *s* of Leonard John Scudamore and Joan Kathleen Scudamore; *m* 1968, Alison Ceridwen Foulkes. *Educ*: Chester City Grammar Sch.; Liverpool Univ. (BVSc 1967; BSc 1st cl. Hons 1968). Qualified as vet. surg., 1967; Dist Vet. Officer, Kenya, 1968–71; Vet. Res. Officer, Kenya, 1971–74; joined MAFF, 1974: Vet. Investigation Service, 1974–80; Divl Vet. Officer, Tolworth, 1980–84, Taunton, 1984–87; Regl Vet. Officer, S Scotland, 1987–90; Asst Chief Vet. Officer, Edinburgh, 1990–96, Tolworth (Meat Hygiene), 1996–97; Chief Vet. Officer, 1997–2004, and Dir Gen., Animal Health and Welfare, 2001–04, MAFF, subseq. DEFRA. *Recreations*: reading, swimming, gardening. *Address*: 56 Horseshoe Lane East, Guildford, Surrey GU1 2TL. *T*: (01483) 572706.

SCUDAMORE, Peter Michael, MBE 1990; National Hunt jockey, 1979–93; Trainer at Bromsash, Herefordshire, with Michael Scudamore, since 2003; *b* 13 June 1958; *s* of Michael and Mary Scudamore; *m* 1980, Marilyn Linda Kington; two *s*. *Educ*: Belmont Abbey, Hereford. Champion Jockey, 1981–82 and annually, 1986–93; rode for British Jump Jockeys; winners in Australia, Belgium, Germany, New Zealand, Norway; Leading Jockey, Ritz Club Charity Trophy, Cheltenham Festival, 1986; leading jockey, Cheltenham, 1986, 1987; set new record for number of winners ridden in career, 1989, for number in one season (221), 1989; rode 1,500th winner, 1992; record 1,678 wins on retirement. Asst Trainer to Denis Caro, 2002–03. Racing journalist, Daily Mail, 1993–; Commentator for Nat. Hunt racing, Grandstand, BBC TV, 1993–. *Publication*: Scu: the autobiography of a champion, 1993. *Recreations*: golf, watching sport. *Fax*: (01989) 750281; *e-mail*: Peter.Scu@ic24.net.

SCUDAMORE, Richard Craig; Chief Executive, Football Association Premier League, since 1999; *b* 11 Aug. 1959; *s* of late Kenneth Ronald Scudamore and of Enid Doreen Scudamore (*née* Selman); *m* 1999, Catherine Joanne Ramsey; three *s* two *d*. *Educ*: Kingsfield Sch., Bristol; Nottingham Univ. Regl Dir, BT Yellow Pages, ITT World Directories, 1981–89; Man. Dir, Newspaper and Media Sales Ltd, Ingersoll Publications, 1989–90; Thomson Corporation: Newspaper Gp Sales and Mktg Dir, 1991–94; Asst, then Man. Dir, Scotsman Publications, 1994–95; Sen. Vice Pres., N America, 1995–98; Chief Exec. and Dir, Football League Ltd, 1998–99. *Recreations*: golf, music, children, and of course football. *Address*: FA Premier League, 30 Gloucester Place, W1U 8PL. *T*: (020) 7864 9107.

SCULLARD, Geoffrey Layton, OBE 1971; HM Diplomatic Service, retired; *b* 5 July 1922; *s* of late William Harold Scullard and late Eleanor Mary Scullard (*née* Tomkin); *m* 1945, Catherine Margaret Pinington (*d* 2003); three *d*. *Educ*: St Olave's Grammar Sch. Joined Foreign Office, 1939. Served War (RAF Signals), 1942–46. Diplomatic service at Stockholm, Washington, Baghdad, Los Angeles, Moscow and in FCO. *Recreation*: birdwatching. *Address*: Braemar Court, 16 Sydney Road, Guildford, Surrey GU1 3LJ. *T*: (01483) 539915. *Clubs*: Civil Service; Bramley Golf.

SCULLY, Prof. Crispian Michael, CBE 2000; MD, PhD; FDSRCPSGlas, FFDRCSI, FDSRCS, FDSRCSE, FRCPath, FMedSci; Dean and Director of Studies and Research, Eastman Dental Institute, University of London, 1994–2008; Professor of Oral Medicine, Pathology and Microbiology, University of London, since 1993; Professor of Special Needs Dentistry, University College London, since 1998; *b* 24 May 1945; *s* of Patrick and Rosaleen Scully; *m* Zoitsa Boucoumani; one *d*. *Educ*: Univ. of London (BSc, BDS, PhD); Univ. of Glasgow; Univ. of Bristol (MD, MDS). MRCS; LRCP; LDS RCS; FDSRCPSGlas 1979; FFDRCSI 1983; FDSRCS 1988; FDSRCSE 1998; FRCPath 1998. MRC Research Fellow, Guy's Hosp., 1975–78; Lectr, 1979–81, Sen. Lectr, 1981–82, Univ. of Glasgow; Prof. of Stomatology, 1982–93, and Dean, 1982–92, Univ. of Bristol. Hon. Consultant: Inst. of Dental Surgery, subseq. Eastman Dental Inst., London Univ., 1993–; Great Ormond St Hosp., 1998–; Nuffield Orthopaedic Centre, Oxford, 1998–2002; John Radcliffe Hosp., Oxford, 1998–2002. Clinical Dir, UC London Hosps NHS Trust, 1995–96. Visiting Professor: Middx Univ., 1998–; UWE, 1998–; Univ. of Edinburgh, 2006–08; Univ. of Athens, 2008–; Adjunct Prof., Univ. of Helsinki, 2005–. Consultant Adviser in Dental Research, DHSS, 1986–98. Member: GDC, 1984–94, 2000–03; Adv. Council for Misuse of Drugs, 1985–89; Chm., Central Examining Bd for Dental Hygienists, 1989–94; Member: Medicines Control Agency Cttee on Dental and Surgical Materials, 1990–93; Standing Dental Adv. Cttee, 1992–99; Adv. Cttee on Infected Health Care Workers, 1991–2002; Expert Adv. Cttee on Antimicrobial Resistance, 2001–02. Chm. Jt Adv. Cttee, Additional Dental Specialities, 1993–99. Pres., Europ. Assoc. for Oral Medicine, 2002–04 (Sec.-Gen., 1993–2002; Vice-Pres., 2000–02; Past Pres., 2004–06); Sec.-Gen., Internat. Acad. of Oral Oncology, 2005–08 (Vice-Pres.,

2007–09). Founder FMedSci 1998; FHEA. Founder, Internat. Fedn of Oral Medicine, 1998. Hon. DSc Athens, 2006; Hon. DChD Granada; Hon. DMed Pretoria. *Publications:* Medical Problems in Dentistry, 1982, 5th edn 2004; (jtly) Multiple Choice Questions in Dentistry, 1985; Handbook for Hospital Dental Surgeons, 1985; (jtly) Slide Interpretation in Oral Disease, 1986; Dental Surgery Assistants' Handbook, 1988; Colour Atlas of Stomatology, 1988, 2nd edn 1996; Colour Aids to Oral Medicine, 1988, 3rd edn 1998; The Dental Patient, 1988; The Mouth and Perioral Tissues, 1989; Patient Care: a dental surgeon's guide, 1989; (jtly) Occupational Hazards in Dentistry, 1990; (jtly) Clinic Virology in Oral Medicine and Dentistry, 1992; (jtly) Medicine and Surgery for Dentistry, 1993, 2nd edn 1999; (jtly) Colour Atlas of Oral Diseases in Children and Adolescents, 1993, 2nd edn 2001; (jtly) Colour Atlas of Oral Pathology, 1995; (jtly) Oxford Handbook of Dental Patient Care, 1998, 2nd edn 2005; Handbook of Oral Disease, 1999; (jtly) Dermatology of the Lips, 2000; ABC of Oral Health, 2000; (jtly) Patologiae Medicina del Cavo Orale, 2001; (jtly) Periodontal Manifestations of Systemic Disease, 2002; (jtly) Oxford Handbook of Applied Dental Sciences, 2003; (jtly) Orofacial Disease: a guide for the dental clinical team, 2003; Oral and Maxillofacial Medicine, 2004, 2nd edn 2008; (jtly) Atlas of Oral and Maxillofacial Diseases, 2004; (jtly) Key Topics in Human Disease, 2005; (jtly) Periodontal Manifestations of Systemic Disease, 2006; (jtly) Culturally Sensitive Oral Health Care, 2006; (jtly) Oral Medicine—Update for the Dental Practitioner, 2006; (jtly) Medicinary Patologia Oral, 2006; (jtly) Peridontology and Oral Medicine Interactions, 2006; (jtly) Special Care Dentistry: handbook of oral health care, 2007; 800 contribs to learned jls. *Recreations:* music, ski-ing, cycling, walking, windsurfing, sailing. *Address:* Eastman Dental Institute, 256 Gray's Inn Road, WC1X 8LD. *T:* (020) 7915 1038.

SCULLY, Sean Paul; artist; *b* Dublin, 30 June 1945; *s* of John Anthony Scully and Holly Scully; *m* Catherine Lee. *Educ:* Croydon Coll. of Art; Newcastle Univ.; Harvard Univ. Lecturer: Harvard Univ., 1972–73; Chelsea Sch. of Art, and Goldsmiths' Sch. of Art, 1973–75; Princeton Univ., 1978–83; Parsons Sch. of Design, NY, 1983–. *Solo exhibitions* include: Rowan Gall., London, 1973, 1975, 1977, 1979, 1981; Tortue Gall., Calif, 1975–76; Nadin Gall., NY, 1979; Mus. für (Sub-) Kultur, Berlin, 1981; retrospective, Ikon Gall., Birmingham, and tour, 1981; David McKee Gall., NY, 1983, 1985–87, 1989–91; Art Inst. of Chicago, 1987; University Art Mus., Univ. of Calif at Berkeley, 1987; Paintings and Works on Paper 1982–88, Whitechapel Art Gall., Neubachhaus, Munich, Palacio Velásquez, Madrid, 1989; Waddington Gall., 1992, 1995; The Catherine Paintings, Mus. of Modern Art, Fort Worth, 1993, Palais de Beaux-Arts, Belgium, 1995, Galérie Nat. de Jeu de Paume, Paris, 1996; Abbot Hall Gall., Cumbria, 2005; *works in public collections* include: Mus. of Modern Art, NY; Tate Gall.; V & A Mus.; Aust. Nat. Gall., Canberra. *Address:* c/o Mayor Rowan Gallery, 31A Bruton Place, W1X 7AB; c/o Diane Villani Editions, 285 Lafayette Street, New York, NY 10012, USA.

SCURR, Dr Cyril Frederick, CBE 1980; LVO 1952; FRCS, FRCA; Hon. Consulting Anaesthetist, Westminster Hospital, since 1985 (Consultant Anaesthetist, 1949–85); Hon. Anaesthetist, Hospital of SS John and Elizabeth, 1952–94, now Emeritus; *b* 14 July 1920; *s* of Cyril Albert Scurr and Mabel Rose Scurr; *m* 1947, Isabel Jean Spiller; three *s* one *d*. *Educ:* King's Coll., London; Westminster Hosp. MB, BS. Served War of 1939–45: RAMC, 1942–47, Major, Specialist Anaesthetist. Faculty of Anaesthetists: Mem. Bd, 1961–77; Dean, 1970–73; Mem. Council, RCS, 1970–73; Pres., Assoc. of Anaesthetists of GB and Ireland, 1976–78; Mem. Health Services Bd, 1977–80; Chm., Scientific Programme, World Congress of Anaesthetists, London, 1968; Pres., 1978–79, Hon. Mem., 1988, Anaesthetics Section, RSocMed; Mem. Adv. Cttee on Distinction Awards, 1973–84; Vice-Chm., Jt Consultants Cttee, 1979–81; past Member: Cttee, Competence to Practise; Standing Med. Adv. Cttee, DHSS. Mem. d'Honneur, Société Française d'Anesthésie et de Réanimation, 1978; Academician, European Acad. of Anaesthesiology, 1978. Frederick Hewitt Lectr, RCS, 1971; Magill Centenary Oration, RCS, 1988. Dudley Buxton Prize, RCS, 1977; Gold Medal, Faculty of Anaesthetists, 1983; John Snow Medal, Assoc. of Anaesthetists of GB and Ireland, 1984. Hon. FFARCSI 1977. *Publications:* Scientific Foundations of Anaesthesia, 1970, 4th edn 1990; (jtly) Drug Mechanisms in Anaesthesia, 1987, 2nd edn 1993. *Recreations:* photography, gardening. *Address:* 16 Grange Avenue, Totteridge Common, N20 8AD. *T:* (020) 8445 7188.

SEABECK, Alison Jane; MP (Lab) Plymouth Devonport, since 2005; *b* 20 Jan. 1954; *d* of Michael John Ward, *qv*; *m* 1975 (separated 2006); two *d*. *Educ:* North East London Polytechnic. Parly Asst to Rt Hon. Roy Hattersley, MP, 1987–92; Advr to Rt Hon. Nick Raynsford, MP, 1992–2005; PPS to Minister of State for Europe, 2006–07; an Asst Govt Whip, 2007–08. Member: Select Cttee for Communities and Local Govt, 2005–06; Regulatory Reform Select Cttee, 2005–; Chm., All Party Gp for Local Govt, 2006–. *Recreations:* reading, walking, swimming, gardening. *Address:* House of Commons, SW1A 0AA. *T:* (020) 7219 6431; *e-mail:* seabecka@parliament.uk.

SEABORN, Hugh Richard; Chief Executive Officer and Agent to the Trustees, The Portman Estate, since 2000; *b* 24 May 1962; *s* of Richard Anthony Seaborn and Wendy Nora Seaborn (*née* Punt); *m* 2000, Michaela Louise Scanlon; two *s*. *Educ:* Pocklington Sch.; Newcastle upon Tyne Poly. (BSc 1984). FRICS 1999. Landmark Property Consultants, Cape Town, 1985–88; Richard Ellis Fleetwood-Bird, Gaborone, 1988–91; Dir and Hd, Investment Mgt Dept, Richard Ellis, 1991–2000. Mem. Council and Audit Cttee, Duchy of Lancaster, 2005–. Chm., Westminster Property Owners Assoc., 2008– (Dep. Chm., 2006–08). Non-exec. Dir, TR Property Investment Trust, 2007–. *Recreations:* family, running, reading. *Address:* c/o The Portman Estate, 38 Seymour Street, W1H 7BP. *T:* (020) 7563 1400. *Clubs:* Oriental, Home House.

SEABROOK, Air Vice-Marshal Geoffrey Leonard, CB 1965; *b* 25 Aug. 1909; *s* of late Robert Leonard Seabrook; *m* 1949, Beryl Mary (*née* Hughes); one *s* one *d*. *Educ:* King's Sch., Canterbury. Commissioned in RAF (Accountant Branch), 1933; served in: Middle East, 1935–43; Bomber Command, 1943–45; Transport Command, 1945–47; Iraq, 1947–49; Signals Command, 1949–51; Air Ministry Organisation and Methods, 1951–53; Home Command Group Captain Organisation, 1953–56; Far East Air Force, 1957–59; idc 1960; Director of Personnel, Air Ministry, 1961–63; Air Officer Administration, HQ, RAF Tech. Trg Comd, 1963–66; retired June 1966. Air Cdre 1961; Air Vice-Marshal, 1964. Head of Secretarial Branch, Royal Air Force, 1963–66. FCA 1957 (Associate, 1932). *Recreations:* sailing, golf. *Address:* Long Pightle, Piltdown, Uckfield, E Sussex TN22 3XB. *T:* (01825) 722322. *Clubs:* Royal Air Force; Piltdown Golf.

SEABROOK, Graeme; Director (non-executive): P. Cleland Enterprises Ltd, Australia, 1997–2003; Country Road Ltd, 1997–2003; *b* 1 May 1939; *s* of Norman and Amy Winifred Seabrook; *m* 1967, Lorraine Ellen Ludlow; one *s* one *d*. G. J. Coles & Co. (later Coles Myer), Australia, 1955; Chief Gen. Manager, G. J. Coles, 1982; acquisition of Myer, 1985; Man. Dir, Discount Stores Group, 1985; Jt Man. Dir, Coles Myer, 1987, resigned 1988; joined Dairy Farm International, Hong Kong and seconded to Kwik Save Group, 1988: Man. Dir, 1988–93, Chief Exec., 1989–93, non-exec. Dir, 1993–96; Man. Dir, Dairy Farm Internat., Hong Kong, 1993–96. Non-exec. Dir, Woolworths Hldgs Ltd, S Africa, 1997–2000. *Recreations:* tennis, photography.

SEABROOK, Peter John, MBE 2005; VMH; consultant horticulturist, since 1971; *b* 2 Nov. 1935; *s* of Robert Henry Seabrook and Emma Mary Seabrook (*née* Cottey); *m* 1960, Margaret Ruth Risbey; one *s* one *d*. *Educ:* King Edward VI Grammar Sch., Chelmsford; Essex Inst. of Agric., Writtle (Dip. Hort, MHort). Cramphorn Ltd, 1952–66; Bord Na Mona, 1966–70; Gardening Corresp., Sun, 1977–; Director: Wm Strike Ltd, 1972–95; Roger Harvey Ltd, 1981–99. TV presenter: WGBH TV, Boston, USA, 1975–97; Pebble Mill At One, 1975–86; Gardeners' World, 1976–79; Chelsea Flower Show, (annually) 1976–89; Gardeners' Direct Line, 1982–90; Peter Seabrook's Gardening Week, 1996. Hon. Fellow, Writtle Coll., 1997. Pearson Meml Medal, Horticultural Trades Assoc., 1985; Associate of Honour, 1996, VMH 2003, RHS. *Publications:* Shrubs for Your Garden, 1973, 10th edn 1991; Plants for Your Home, 1975; Complete Vegetable Gardener, 1976, 4th edn 1981; Book of the Garden, 1979, 2nd edn 1984; Good Plant Guide, 1981; Good Food Gardening, 1983; Shrubs for Everyone, 1997. *Recreation:* gardening. *Address:* (office) 212A Baddow Road, Chelmsford, Essex CM2 9QR. *T:* (01245) 490201. *Club:* Farmers'.

SEABROOK, Robert John; QC 1983; a Recorder, 1985–2007; a Deputy High Court Judge, since 1991; *b* 6 Oct. 1941; *s* of late Alan Thomas Pertwee Seabrook, MBE and Mary Seabrook (*née* Parker); *m* 1965, Liv Karin Djupvik, Bergen, Norway (marr. diss. 2008); two *s* one *d*. *Educ:* St George's Coll., Salisbury, Southern Rhodesia; University Coll., London (LLB). Called to the Bar, Middle Temple, 1964, Bencher, 1990, Treas., 2007. Leader, SE Circuit, 1989–92; Chm., Bar Council, 1994. Member: Criminal Justice Consultative Council, 1995–2003; Interception of Communications Tribunal, 1996–2000; Investigatory Powers Tribunal, 2000–; Regulation of Investigatory Powers Tribunal for Guernsey, 2006–. Member: Brighton Fest. Cttee, 1976–86; Court, Univ. of Sussex, 1988–93. Vice Pres., Brighton Coll., 2005– (Gov., 1993–2004; Chm. of Govs, 1998–2004). Liveryman, Curriers' Co., 1972– (Master, 1995–96). *Recreations:* travel, walking, listening to music, wine. *Address:* (chambers) 1 Crown Office Row, Temple, EC4Y 7HH. *T:* (020) 7797 7500. *Clubs:* Athenæum, Les Six.

SEAFIELD, 13th Earl of, *cr* 1701; **Ian Derek Francis Ogilvie-Grant;** Viscount Seafield, Baron Ogilvy of Cullen, 1698; Viscount Reidhaven, Baron Ogilvy of Deskford and Cullen, 1701; *b* 20 March 1939; *s* of Countess of Seafield (12th in line), and Derek Studley-Herbert (who assumed by deed poll, 1939, the additional surnames of Ogilvie-Grant; he *d* 1960); *S* mother, 1969; *m* 1st, 1960, Mary Dawn Mackenzie (marr. diss. 1971), *er d* of Henry Illingworth; two *s*; 2nd, 1971, Leila, *d* of Mahmoud Refaat, Cairo. *Educ:* Eton. *Recreations:* shooting, fishing, tennis. *Heir:* *s* Viscount Reidhaven, *qv*. *Address:* Old Cullen, Cullen, Banffshire AB56 4XW. *T:* (01542) 840221. *Club:* White's.

SEAFORD, 6th Baron *cr* 1826, of Seaford, co. Sussex; **Colin Humphrey Felton Ellis;** *b* 19 April 1946; *o s* of Major William Felton Ellis and Edwina (*née* Bond); *S* to Seaford Barony of cousin, 9th Baron Howard de Walden, 1999; *m* 1st, 1971, Susan Magill (marr. diss. 1992); two *s* two *d*; 2nd, 1993, Penelope Mary Bastin. *Educ:* Sherborne; RAC, Cirencester (MRAC 1968). MRICS (ARICS 1970). *Heir:* *s* Hon. Benjamin Felton Thomas Ellis, *b* 17 Dec. 1976. *Address:* Bush Farm, West Knoyle, Warminster, Wilts BA12 6AE.

SEAFORD, Very Rev. John Nicholas Shtetinin; Dean of Jersey and Rector of St Helier, 1993–2005; *b* 12 Sept. 1939; *s* of Nicholas Shtetinin Seaford and Kathleen Dorothy (*née* Longbotham); *m* 1967, Helen Marian Webster; two *s* one *d*. *Educ:* Radley Coll.; St Chad's Coll., Durham Univ. (BA 1967; DipTh 1968). Ordained deacon, 1968, priest, 1969; Assistant Curate: St Mark, Bush Hill Park, Enfield, 1968–71; St Luke, Winchester, 1971–73; Vicar: Chilworth and North Baddesley, 1973–78; Highcliffe and Hinton Admiral, 1978–93. Hon. Canon, Winchester Cathedral, 1993–2005, now Canon Emeritus. Chaplain, HM Prison La Moye, Jersey, 2003–05. Religious Broadcasting Advr, Channel TV, 1993–2005. Mem., States of Jersey, 1993–2005. *Recreation:* walking.

SEAGA, Most Hon. Edward Philip George; PC 1982; ON 2002; Distinguished Fellow, University of the West Indies, 2005; Leader of the Jamaica Labour Party, 1974–2005; *b* 28 May 1930; *s* of late Philip Seaga and of Erna (*née* Maxwell); *m* 1965, Marie Elizabeth (marr. diss. 1995) (*née* Constantine) (Miss Jamaica, 1964); two *s* one *d*; *m* Carla Frances Vendryes, MPA; one *d*. *Educ:* Wolmers Boys' Sch., Kingston, Jamaica; Harvard Univ., USA (BA Social Science, 1952). Did field research in connection with Inst. of Social and Econ. Res., University Coll. of the West Indies (now Univ. of the WI), Jamaica, on develt of the child, and revival spirit cults, by living in rural villages and urban slums; proposed estabt of Unesco Internat. Fund for Promotion of Culture, 1971, and was founding mem. of its Administrative Council. Nominated to Upper House (Legislative Council), 1959 (youngest mem. in its history); Asst Sec., Jamaica Labour Party, 1960–62; MP for Western Kingston, 1962–2005; Minister of Develt and Social Welfare, 1962–67; Minister of Finance and Planning, 1967–72, and 1980–89; Leader of Opposition, 1974–80, 1989–2004; Prime Minister, 1980–89. Director: Consulting Services Ltd, to 1979; Capital Finance Co. Ltd, to 1979. Hon. LLD: Miami, 1981; Tampa, 1982; S Carolina, 1983; Boston, 1983; Hartford, 1987. Grand Collar, and Golden Mercury Internat. Award, Venezuela, 1981; Grand Cross, Order of Merit of Fed. Rep. of Germany, 1982. Gold Key Award, Avenue of the Americas, NYC, 1981; Environment Leadership Award, UN, 1987; Golden Star Caribbean Award Man of the Year, 1988. Religion Anglican. *Publications:* The Development of the Child; Revival Spirit Cults. *Recreations:* classical music, reading, sport. *Address:* Office of the Distinguished Fellow, University of the West Indies, Main Library, Mona Campus, Kingston 7, Jamaica. *Clubs:* Kingston Cricket, Jamaica Gun (Jamaica).

SEAGER, family name of **Baron Leighton of Saint Mellons**.

SEAGER BERRY, Thomas Henry Seager; Deputy Costs Judge, since 2005; Master (Costs Judge) of the Supreme Court Costs (formerly Taxing) Office, 1991–2005; *b* 29 Jan. 1940; *s* of late Thomas Geoffrey Seager Berry, CBE and Ann Josephine Seager Berry; *m* 2002, Agnes Christine Thomson. *Educ:* Shrewsbury Sch. Admitted solicitor, 1964; Sherwood & Co., 1964–69 (Partner, 1966–69); Partner, Boodle Hatfield, 1969–91. Pres., London Solicitors Litigation Assoc., 1982–84; Mem. Cttee, Media Soc., 1985–91; Mem. Council, Feathers Clubs Assoc., 1986–2007. Liveryman, Merchant Taylors' Co., 1967. *Publication:* Longman's Litigation Practice, 1988. *Recreations:* tennis, gardening, wine-tasting, walking. *Clubs:* Hurlingham, MCC.

SEAGROATT, Hon. Conrad; a Judge of the Court of First Instance of the High Court (formerly a Judge of the High Court), Hong Kong, 1995–2003; a Recorder of the Crown Court, 1980–2004; *s* of late E. G. Seagroatt, Solicitor of the Supreme Court and Immigration Appeals Adjudicator, and of Gray's Inn, and of Barbara C. Seagroatt; *m* Cornelia Mary Anne Verdegaal; five *d*. *Educ:* Solihull Sch., Warwicks; Pembroke Coll., Oxford (MA Hons Modern History). ACIArb 2006. Admitted Solicitor of the Supreme Court, 1967; called to the Bar, Gray's Inn, 1970, Bencher, 1991; QC 1983; Dep. High Court Judge, 1993–2004; Judge i/c of Personal Injury List, 1998–2003. Member: Senate of the Inns of Court and the Bar, 1980–83; Criminal Injuries Compensation Bd, 1986–94. Mem., Chief Justice's Wkg Party on Civil Reform Process, 2000–03. Mem., Editl Adv.

Bd, Hong Kong Court Forms, 2000–03; Adv. Ed., Hong Kong Civil Procedure, (The White Book), 2000–03. *Publications:* (contrib.) The Reform of the Civil Process in Hong Kong, 1999; contrib. Hong Kong Law Jl. *Recreations:* running, fairweather ski-ing. *Club:* Garrick.

SEAGROVE, Jennifer Ann; actress, since 1979; Trustee, Born Free, since 2002; *b* 4 July 1957; *d* of Derek and Pauline Seagrove; *m* 1984, Madhav Sharma (marr. diss. 1988); partner, William Kenwright, *qv*. *Educ:* St Hilary's Sch., Godalming; Queen Anne's Sch., Caversham; Kirby Lodge, Cambridge; Bristol Old Vic Theatre Sch. *Theatre* includes: Jane Eyre, Chichester, 1986; King Lear in New York, Chichester, 1992; Present Laughter, Globe, 1993; The Miracle Worker, Comedy, 1994; Dead Guilty, Apollo, 1995; Hurlyburly, Queen's, 1997; Brief Encounter, Lyric, 2000; The Female Odd Couple, Apollo, 2001; The Constant Wife, Apollo, 2002; The Secret Rapture, Lyric, 2003; The Night of the Iguana, Lyric, 2005; The Letter, Wyndhams, 2007; Absurd Person Singular, Garrick, 2007; *films* include: Local Hero, 1982; A Shocking Accident, 1982; Savage Islands, 1982; Appointment with Death, 1987; A Chorus of Disapproval, 1988; The Guardian, 1989; Miss Beatty's Children, 1992; Don't Go Breaking My Heart, 1997; Zoe, 1999; *television* includes: The Woman in White, 1982; A Woman of Substance, 1984; Diana, 1984; Judge John Deed, 2000–07. FRSA. Michael Elliott Award for Best Actress, 2006. *Recreations:* dog walking, tennis, running, cycling, promoting organic farming and animal welfare, trying to save the planet! *Address:* c/o MF Management, 55 Newman Street, W1T 3EB. *T:* (020) 3291 2929, *Fax:* (020) 3003 6303.

SEAL, Dr Barry Herbert; Chairman, Bradford District Care Trust, since 2007; *b* 28 Oct. 1937; *s* of Herbert Seal and Rose Anne Seal; *m* 1963, Frances Catherine Wilkinson; one *s* one *d*. *Educ:* Heath Grammar Sch., Halifax; Univ. of Bradford (MSc, PhD); European Business Sch., Fontainebleau. CEng. Served RAF, 1955–58. Trained as Chem. Engr, ICI Ltd, 1958–64; Div. Chem. Engr, Murex Ltd, 1964–68; Sen. Engr, BOC Internat., 1968–71; Principal Lectr in Systems, Huddersfield Polytechnic, 1971–79. Contested (Lab) Harrogate, Oct. 1974; Leader, Bradford MDC Labour Gp, 1976–79. MEP (Lab) Yorks W, 1979–99. European Parliament: Leader, British Lab. Gp, 1988–89; Chm., Econ., Monetary and Industrial Policy Cttee, 1984–87; Chm., delegn to USA, 1998–99. Chm., N Kirklees PCT, 2002–07. Hon. Freeman, Borough of Calderdale, 2000. *Publications:* papers on computer and microprocessor applications. *Recreations:* walking, reading, films, bridge. *Address:* Brookfields Farm, Brookfields Road, Wyke, Bradford, West Yorks BD12 9LU; *e-mail:* barryseal@aol.com.

SEAL, (Karl) Russell; Joint Managing Director, British Petroleum Co. plc, 1991–97; *b* 14 April 1942; *m* 1966, Pauline Hilarie (*née* Edwards); three *s*. *Educ:* Keele Univ. Joined BP, 1964; NY, 1970–72; Rotterdam, 1976–78; Asst Gen. Manager, Gp Corporate Planning, 1978–80; Chief Exec., Mktg and Refining, Singapore, Malaysia, and Hong Kong, and Sen. Rep., SE Asia, 1980–84; Gen. Manager, BP Oil Trading & Supply Dept, 1984; Chief Exec. and Man. Dir, BP Oil, 1988–95. Non-executive Director: Commonwealth Develt Corp., 1996–2001; Blue Circle plc, 1996–2001. Sen. Exec. Prog., Stanford Univ., 1984. Pro-Chancellor and Chm. Council, Exeter Univ., 2005–. *Recreations:* jogging, walking, golf.

SEAL, Richard Godfrey, FRCO; FRSCM; Organist of Salisbury Cathedral, 1968–97; *b* 4 Dec. 1935; *s* of late William Godfrey Seal and of Shelagh Seal (*née* Bagshaw); *m* 1975, Dr Sarah Helen Hamilton; two *s*. *Educ:* New Coll. Choir Sch., Oxford; Cranleigh Sch., Surrey; Christ's Coll., Cambridge (MA). FRCO 1958; FRSCM 1987; FGCM 2008. Assistant Organist: Kingsway Hall, London, 1957–58; St Bartholomew the Great, London, 1960–61; Chichester Cathedral (and Dir of Music, Prebendal Sch.), Sussex, 1961–68. DMus Lambeth, 1992. *Address:* The Bield, Flamstone Street, Bishopstone, Salisbury, Wilts SP5 4BZ. *Club:* Crudgemens (Godalming).

SEALE, Sir (Clarence) David, Kt 2000; JP; Chairman and Managing Director, R. L. Seale & Co., since 1969; *b* 11 Dec. 1937; *m* 1961, Margaret Anne Farmer; one *s* three *d*. *Educ:* Harrison Coll., Barbados. Airline Clerk, 1956–62; Gen. Manager, R. L. Seale & Co., 1962–69. JP Bridgetown, 1978. *Recreation:* horse racing. *Address:* Hopefield Manor, Hopefield, Christ Church, Barbados. *T:* 4280065. *Club:* Barbados Turf (Bridgetown).

SEALE, Sir John Henry, 5th Bt *cr* 1838; RIBA; *b* 3 March 1921; *s* of Sir John Seale, 4th Bt; *S* father, 1964; *m* 1953, Ray Josephine, *d* of Robert Gordon Charters, MC, Christchurch, New Zealand; one *s* one *d*. *Educ:* Eton; Christ Church, Oxford. Served War of 1939–45: Royal Artillery, North Africa and Italy; Captain, 1945. ARIBA 1951. *Heir: s* John Robert Charters Seale [*b* 17 Aug. 1954; *m* 1996, Michelle, *d* of K. W. Taylor]. *Address:* Slade, Kingsbridge, Devon TQ7 4BL. *T:* (01548) 550226.

SEALEY, Barry Edward, CBE 1990; Director, Archangel Informal Investments Ltd, since 2000; *b* 3 Feb. 1936; *s* of Edward Sealey and Queenie Katherine Sealey (*née* Hill); *m* 1960, Helen Martyn; one *s* one *d*. *Educ:* Dursley GS; St John's Coll., Cambridge (BA 1958; MA 1991); Harvard Business Sch. (PMD 1968). Christian Salvesen plc, 1958–90: Dir, 1969–90; Man. Dir, 1981–89; Chm., Optos plc (formerly Besca Ltd), 1992–2006. Director: Scottish American Investment Co. plc, 1983–2001; Morago Ltd, 1989–; Queen's Hall (Edinburgh) Ltd, 1990–99; Caledonian Brewing Co. Ltd, 1990–2004; Wilson Byard plc, 1992–2003; Interface Graphics Ltd, 1992–99; Stagecoach Hldgs plc, 1992–2001; Scottish Equitable Policy Holders Trust Ltd, 1993–2006; Scottish Equitable, 1993–99; ESI Investors Ltd, 1999–2008; Northern 3 VCT plc, 2001–07; CXR Biosciences Ltd, 2001–; Scottish Health Innovations Ltd, 2002–07 (Chm., 2002–07); Lab 901 Ltd, 2002–08 (Chm., 2002–08); Dundas Commercial Property (Gen. Partner), Ltd, 2002–; Earlsgate Hldgs Ltd, 2004–06; Indigo Lighthouse Gp, 2004–; EZD Ltd, 2005–; Landmark Trustee Co. Ltd, 2006–. Chairman: Edinburgh Healthcare NHS Trust, 1993–99; Lothian Univ. Hosps NHS Trust, 1999–2002. Dir, Lothian Health Bd, 1999–2001. Mem. Council and Policy Cttee, Industrial Soc., 1990–2001. Dep. Chm. of Court, Napier Poly., subseq. Univ., 1987–98. *Recreations:* walking, music. *Address:* Flat 5, 2 The Cedars, Colinton Road, Edinburgh EH13 0PL. *T:* (0131) 441 2802; *e-mail:* bes@morago.co.uk. *Club:* New (Edinburgh).

SEALY, Austin Llewellyn; Managing Partner, A. Sealy & Co., international business consultancy and management services, since 1996; *b* 17 Sept. 1939; *s* of Kenneth Llewellyn Sealy and Gerdsene Elaine Sealy (*née* Crawford); *m* 1964, Rita Anita Pilgrim; three *s*. *Educ:* St Mary's Boys' Sch., Barbados; Harrison Coll., Barbados. Banker, 1958–93: Sen. Mgt Official with Barclays Bank PLC in Caribbean; High Comr for Barbados in UK, and Ambassador to Israel, 1993–94. Pres., Nat. Olympic Cttee of Barbados, 1982–96; Hon. Treas., Commonwealth Games Fedn, 1986–; Member: IOC, 1994–; Exec. Council, Assoc. of Nat. Olympic Cttees, 1995–2002. Silver Crown of Merit (Barbados), 1985. *Recreations:* cricket, tennis, golf. *Address:* Crestview, 35 Highgate Gardens, St Michael, Barbados. *T:* 4272256; A. Sealy & Co., Leamington House, 4th Avenue, Belleville, St Michael, Barbados; *e-mail:* austinsealy@sealygroup.com.

SEALY, Prof. Leonard Sedgwick, PhD; S. J. Berwin Professor of Corporate Law, University of Cambridge, 1991–97, now Emeritus; Life Fellow, Gonville and Caius College, Cambridge, since 1997 (Fellow, 1959–97); *b* 22 July 1930; *s* of Alfred Desmond Sealy and Mary Louise Sealy, Hamilton, NZ; *m* 1960, Beryl Mary Edwards; one *s* two *d*. *Educ:* Stratford High Sch.; Auckland Univ. (MA, LLM); Gonville and Caius Coll., Cambridge (PhD). Barrister and solicitor, NZ, 1953; in practice at NZ Bar, 1953–55 and 1958–59. Faculty of Law, University of Cambridge: Asst Lectr, 1959–61; Lectr, 1961–91; Tutor, 1961–70, Sen. Tutor, 1970–75, Gonville and Caius Coll. *Publications:* Cases and Materials in Company Law, 1971, 8th edn (with S. Worthington) 2007; Company Law and Commercial Reality, 1984; Disqualification and Personal Liability of Directors, 1986, 5th edn 2000; (with D. Milman) Guide to the 1986 Insolvency Legislation, 1987, 10th edn as Guide to the Insolvency Legislation, 2007; (with R. Hooley) Cases and Materials in Commercial Law, 1994, 4th edn 2008; (ed with A. G. Guest *et al.*) Benjamin's Sale of Goods, 1974, 7th edn 2006; (General Editor): British Company Law and Practice, 1989; International Corporate Procedures, 1992–2005; Commonwealth Editor, Gore-Browne on Companies, 1997–2005. *Address:* Gonville and Caius College, Cambridge CB2 1TA. *T:* (01223) 332400.

SEAMAN, Christopher; international conductor; Music Director, Rochester Philharmonic Orchestra, New York, since 1998; *b* 7 March 1942; *s* of late Albert Edward Seaman and Ethel Margery Seaman (*née* Chambers). *Educ:* Canterbury Cathedral Choir Sch.; The King's Sch., Canterbury; King's Coll., Cambridge. MA, double first cl. Hons in Music; ARCM, ARCO. Principal Timpanist, London Philharmonic Orch., 1964–68 (Mem., LPO Bd of Dirs, 1965–68); Asst Conductor, 1968–70, Principal Conductor, 1971–77, BBC Scottish Symphony Orchestra; Princ. Conductor and Artistic Dir, Northern Sinfonia Orch., 1974–79; Principal Guest Conductor, Utrecht Symphony Orch., 1979–83; Principal Conductor, BBC Robert Mayer concerts, 1978–87; Conductor-in-Residence, Baltimore SO, 1987–98; Music Dir, Naples Phil. Orch., Florida, 1993–2004; also works widely as a guest conductor, and appears in America, Holland, France, Germany, Belgium, Italy, Norway, Spain, Portugal, Czechoslovakia, Israel, Hong Kong, Japan, Australia, New Zealand and all parts of UK. FGSM 1972. *Recreations:* people, reading, walking, theology. *Address:* 25 Westfield Drive, Glasgow G52 2SG.

SEAMAN, Gilbert Frederick, AO 1981; CMG 1967; Chairman, State Bank of South Australia, 1963–83; Deputy Chairman, Electricity Trust of SA, 1970–84; Trustee, Savings Bank of SA, 1973–81; *b* 7 Sept. 1912; *s* of Eli S. Seaman, McLaren Vale, South Australia; *m* 1935, Avenal Essie Fong; one *s* one *d*. *Educ:* University of Adelaide. BEc, Associate of University of Adelaide, 1935, High School Teacher, Port Pirie and Unley, 1932–35; South Australian Public Service, 1936–41; Seconded to Commonwealth of Australia as Assistant Director of Manpower for SA, 1941–46; Economist, SA Treasury, 1946–60; Under Treasurer for SA, 1960–72. *Address:* 27 William Street, Hawthorn, SA 5062, Australia. *T:* (8) 82714271.

See also Sir K. D. Seaman.

SEAMAN, Sir Keith (Douglas), KCVO 1981; OBE 1976; Governor of South Australia, 1977–82; *b* 11 June 1920; *s* of late E. S. and E. M. Seaman; *m* 1946, Joan, *d* of F. Birbeck; one *s* one *d*. *Educ:* Unley High Sch.; Univ. of Adelaide (BA, LLB); Flinders Univ. (MA, DipHum). South Australian Public Service, 1937–54; RAAF Overseas HQ, London, 1941–45, Flt-Lieut. Entered Methodist Ministry, 1954: Renmark, 1954–58; Adelaide Central Methodist Mission, 1958–77 (Supt, 1971–77). Sec., Christian Television Assoc. of S Australia, 1959–73; Mem. Executive, World Assoc. of Christian Broadcasting, 1963–70; Director, 5KA, 5AU and 5RM Broadcasting Companies, 1960–77; Chm., 5KA, 5AU and 5RM, 1971–77. Mem., Australian Govt Social Welfare Commn, 1973–76. KStJ 1978. *Recreations:* reading, gardening. *Address:* 93 Rosetta Village, Maude Street, Victor Harbor, SA 5211, Australia.

See also G. F. Seaman.

SEAMER, Lydia Akrigg; *see* Brown, L. A.

SEAMMEN, Diana Jill; *see* Hansen, D. J.

SEAR, Prof. John William, PhD; Professor of Anaesthetics, University of Oxford, since 2002; Fellow, Green Templeton College (formerly Green College), Oxford, since 1982; *b* 3 Sept. 1947; *e s* of late Lionel and Ethel Alice Moore, and adoptive *s* of late Frederick Carl William Sear; *m* 1978, Yvonne Margaret Begley; three *s*. *Educ:* Enfield Grammar Sch.; London Hosp. Med. Coll. (BSc, MBBS); Univ. of Bristol (PhD); MA Oxford. FFARCS, FANZCA. Posts in London Hosp., 1972–75; Registrar in Anaesthetics, Royal Devon & Exeter Hosp. and United Bristol Hosps, 1975–77; University of Bristol: MRC Res. Training Fellow and Hon. Sen. Registrar, 1977–80; Lectr in Anaesthetics, 1980–81; University of Oxford: Clin. Reader in Anaesthetics, 1982–2002; Dir of Clinical Studies, 1995–98; Vice Warden, Green Coll., Oxford, 2002–07. Hon. Consultant Anaesthetist, Oxford Radcliffe Hosp. NHS Trust, 1982–; non-exec. Dir, Nuffield Orthopaedic Centre NHS Trust, 1993–2002. Member, Editorial Board: British Jl of Anaesthesia, 1989–; Jl of Clinical Anesthesia, USA, 1989–; Anesthesia and Analgesia, 2006–. *Publications:* papers in learned jls. *Recreations:* sport, music, writing. *Address:* 6 Whites Forge, Appleton, Abingdon, Oxon OX13 5LG. *T:* (01865) 863144.

SEARBY, Richard Henry, AO 2006; QC (Aust.) 1971; Deputy Chairman, Times Newspapers Holdings Ltd, since 1981; *b* 23 July 1931; *s* of late Henry and Mary Searby; *m* 1962, Caroline (*née* McAdam); three *s*. *Educ:* Geelong Grammar Sch., Corio, Vic; Corpus Christi Coll., Oxford Univ. (MA Hons). Called to Bar, Inner Temple, London, 1956; admitted Barrister and Solicitor, Victoria, Aust., 1956; called to Victorian Bar, 1957; Associate to late Rt Hon. Sir Owen Dixon, Chief Justice of Aust., 1956–59; commenced practice, Victorian Bar, 1959; Independent Lectr in Law relating to Executors and Trustees, Univ. of Melbourne, 1961–72. Director: Equity Trustees Executors & Agency Co. Ltd, 1975–2000 (Chm., 1980–2000); CRA Ltd, then Rio Tinto Ltd, 1977–97; Rio Tinto PLC, 1995–97; Shell Australia Ltd, 1977–98; News Corp. Ltd, 1977–92 (Chm., 1981–91; Dep. Chm., 1991–92); News Ltd, 1977–92 (Chm., 1981–92); News International plc, 1980–92 (Chm., 1981–89); South China Morning Post Ltd, 1986–92 (Chm., 1987–92); Reuters Founders Share Co. Ltd, 1987–93; BRL Hardy Ltd, 1992–2003; Amrad Corp. Ltd, 1992–2001; Tandem Australian Ltd, 1992–98; Woodside Petroleum Ltd, 1998–2004; Chairman: Bowater Trust, 2006–; Hearing CRC Ltd, 2007–. Member Council: Nat. Library of Australia, 1992–95; Mus. of Victoria, 1993–98. President: Medico-Legal Soc. of Vic, 1986–87; Aust. Inst. of Internat. Affairs, 1993–97. Chancellor, Deakin Univ., 1997–2005. Chm., Geelong Grammar Sch., 1983–89. Hon. LLD Deakin, 2005. *Publication:* (jtly) report on Conciliation and Arbitration Act, 1981. *Recreations:* reading, music, tennis, fishing. *Address:* Milton House, 25 Flinders Lane, Melbourne, Vic 3000, Australia. *T:* (3) 96668975. *Club:* Melbourne (Melbourne).

SEARBY, Maj. Gen. Robin Vincent, CB 2002; UK Defence Co-ordinator for Libya, 2004; *b* 20 July 1947; *s* of late John Henry Searby and Eva Searby; *m* 1976, Caroline Angela Beamish; one *s* two *d*. *Educ:* Leasam House; RMA Sandhurst. Commissioned 9th/12th Royal Lancers, 1968; Directing Staff, Camberley, 1984–87; CO, 9th/12th Royal Lancers, 1987–89; COS to HQ Dir, RAC, 1989–91; Comdr, Armoured 1st (Br) Corps, 1991–93;

Comdr, British Forces Bosnia-Hercegovina, 1993; Pres., Regular Commissions Bd, 1994; Chief, Jt Ops (Bosnia), HQ Allied Forces Southern Europe, 1995; GOC 5th Div., 1996–2000; Sen. British Loan Service Officer, Sultanate of Oman, 2000–04. Hon. Col, 9th/12th Lancers, 2003–. Distinguished Service Medal for Gallantry, Sultanate of Oman, 1975; QCVS 1994. *Recreations:* walking, country sports, reading. *Club:* Cavalry and Guards.

SEARLE, Prof. Geoffrey Russell, PhD; FBA 2005; FRHistS; Professor of Modern British History, University of East Anglia, 1993–2001, now Emeritus; *b* 3 Oct. 1940; *s* of George William, (Bill), Searle and Winifred Alice Searle (*née* Chapman); *m* 1994, Barbara Elisabeth Caroline Rahn. *Educ:* St Dunstan's Coll., Catford; Peterhouse, Cambridge (BA 1962; PhD 1966). FRHistS 1977. Lectr in Hist., 1962–81, Sen. Lectr, 1981–93, Univ. of East Anglia. *Publications:* The Quest for National Efficiency 1899–1914, 1971; Eugenics and Politics in Britain 1900–1914, 1976; Corruption in British Politics 1895–1930, 1987; The Liberal Party: triumph and disintegration 1886–1929, 1992, 2nd edn 2001; Entrepreneurial Politics in Mid-Victorian Britain, 1993; Country Before Party 1885–1987, 1995; Morality and the Market in Victorian Britain, 1998; A New England?: peace and war 1886–1918, 2004. *Recreations:* music, art, literature, supporter of local football team. *Address:* School of History, University of East Anglia, Norwich, Norfolk NR4 7TJ; *e-mail:* g.searle@uea.ac.uk.

SEARLE, Ronald William Fordham, CBE 2004; RDI 1988; AGI; artist; *b* Cambridge, 3 March 1920; *m* 1st, Kaye Webb (marr. diss. 1967; she *d* 1996); one *s* one *d*; 2nd, 1967, Monica Koenig. *Educ:* Cambridge School of Art. Served with 287 Field Co. RE, 1939–46; captured by the Japanese at fall of Singapore, 1942; Prisoner of War in Siam and Malaya, 1942–45; Dept of Psychological Warfare, Allied Force HQ Port Said Ops, 1956. Creator of the schoolgirls of St Trinian's, 1941 (abandoned them in 1953); Cartoonist to Tribune, 1949–51; to Sunday Express, 1950–51; Special Feature artist: News Chronicle, 1951–53; Life Mag., 1955–62; Weekly Cartoonist, News Chronicle, 1954; Punch Theatre artist, 1949–62; Contributor: New Yorker and New York Times, 1966–; Le Monde, 1995–. Designer of commemorative medals for: the French Mint, 1974–; British Art Medal Soc., 1983–. FRSA 1990. DUniv Anglia Ruskin, 2007. Chevalier de la Légion d'Honneur (France), 2006. *One man exhibitions include:* Leicester Galls, 1948, 1950, 1954, 1957; New York, 1959, 1963, 1969, 1976; Galerie La Pochade, Paris, 1966, 1967, 1968, 1969, 1971; Galerie Gurlitt, Munich, 1967, 1968, 1969, 1970, 1971, 1973, 1976; Grosvenor Gall., London, 1968; Bibliothèque Nat., Paris, 1973; Galerie Carmen Cassé, Paris, 1975, 1976, 1977; Staatliche Mus., Berlin, 1976; Rizzoli Gall., NY, Gal. Bartsch & Chariau, Munich, 1981; Cooper-Hewitt Museum, NY, 1984; Neue Galerie Wien, 1985, 1988; Imperial War Museum, BM, 1986; Fitzwilliam Museum, Cambridge, 1987; Mus. of Fine Arts, San Francisco, 1987–88; Heineman Galls, NY, 1994; Wilhelm-Busch Mus., Hanover, 1996, (with Monica Searle), 2001; Galerie Martine Gossieaux, Paris, 2000; Chris Beetles Gall., 2003; Forbes Galls, NY, 2007. *Works in permanent collections:* V&A, BM, Imperial War Museum, Tate Gall.; Bibliothèque Nat., Paris; Wilhelm-Busch Museum, Hanover; Staatlische Mus., Berlin; Cooper-Hewitt Museum, NY; Univ. of Texas, Austin; Mus. of Fine Arts, San Francisco; Liby of Congress, Washington, DC. *Films based on the characters of St Trinian's:* The Belles of St Trinian's, 1954; Blue Murder at St Trinian's, 1957; The Pure Hell of St Trinian's, 1960; The Great St Trinian's Train Robbery, 1966; The Wildcats of St Trinian's, 1980; St Trinian's, 2007. *Films designed:* John Gilpin, 1951; On the Twelfth Day, 1954 (Acad. Award Nomination); Energetically Yours (USA), 1957; Germany, 1960 (for Suddeutschen RTV); The King's Breakfast, 1962; Those Magnificent Men in their Flying Machines (Animation Sequence), 1965; Monte Carlo or Bust (Animation Sequence), 1969; Scrooge (Animation Sequence), 1970; Dick Deadeye, 1975. *Publications:* Forty Drawings, 1946; Le Nouveau Ballet Anglais, 1947; Hurrah for St Trinian's!, 1948; The Female Approach, 1949; Back to the Slaughterhouse, 1951; John Gilpin, 1952; Souls in Torment, 1953; Rake's Progress, 1955; Merry England, etc, 1956; A Christmas Carol, 1961; Which Way Did He Go?, 1961; Searle in the Sixties, 1964; From Frozen North to Filthy Lucre, 1964; Pardong M'sieur, 1965; Searle's Cats, 1967; The Square Egg, 1968; Take one Toad, 1968; Baron Munchausen, 1960; Hello—where did all the people go?, 1969; Hommage à Toulouse-Lautrec, 1969; Secret Sketchbook, 1970; The Addict, 1971; More Cats, 1975; Drawings from Gilbert and Sullivan, 1975; The Zoodiac, 1977; Ronald Searle (Monograph), 1978; The King of Beasts, 1980; The Big Fat Cat Book, 1982; Illustrated Winespeak, 1983; Ronald Searle in Perspective (monograph), 1984; Ronald Searle's Golden Oldies 1941–61, 1985; To the Kwai—and Back, 1986, facsimile edn 2006; Something in the Cellar, 1986; Ah Yes, I Remember It Well …, 1987; Ronald Searle's Non-Sexist Dictionary, 1988; Slightly Foxed—but still desirable, 1989; Carnet de Croquis: le plaisir du trait, 1992; The Curse of St Trinian's, 1993; Marquis de Sade meets Goody Two-Shoes, 1994; Ronald Searle dans Le Monde, 1998; The Scrapbook Drawings, 2005; More Scraps & Watteau Revisited, 2008; *in collaboration:* (with D. B. Wyndham Lewis) The Terror of St Trinian's, 1952; (with Geoffrey Willans) Down with Skool, 1953; How to be Topp, 1954; Whizz for Atomms, 1956; The Compleet Molesworth, 1958; The Dog's Ear Book, 1958; Back in the Jug Agane, 1959; (with Kaye Webb) Paris Sketchbook, 1950 and 1957; Looking at London, 1953; The St Trinian's Story, 1959; Refugees 1960, 1960; (with Alex Atkinson) The Big City, 1958; USA for Beginners, 1959; Russia for Beginners, 1960; Escape from the Amazon!, 1964; (with A. Andrews & B. Richardson) Those Magnificent Men in their Flying Machines, 1965; (with Heinz Huber) Haven't We Met Before Somewhere?, 1966; (with Kildare Dobbs) The Great Fur Opera, 1970; (with Irwin Shaw) Paris! Paris!, 1977; (with Sarah Kortum) The Hatless Man, 1995; (with Simon Rae) The Face of War, 1999; Le théâtre à Paris (1954–1962), 2000; (with Monica Searle) Searle & Searle, 2001; (with Robert L. Forbes) Beastly Feasts, 2007; *relevant publications:* Ronald Searle: a biography, by Russell Davies, 1990; Ronald Searle: monograph, ed Gisela Vetter-Liebenow, 1996. *Address:* Sayle Literary Agency, 1 Petersfield, Cambridge CB1 1BB. *T:* (01223) 303035, *Fax:* (01223) 301638. *Club:* Garrick.

SEARS, David; *see* Sears, R. D. M.

SEARS, Hon. Raymond Arthur William; Judge of the Court of First Instance of the High Court (formerly a Judge of the Supreme Court), Hong Kong, 1986–99; Commissioner of the Supreme Court of Brunei Darussalam, 1987–99; *b* 10 March 1933; *s* of William Arthur and Lillian Sears; *m* 1960 (marr. diss. 1981); one *s* one *d*. *Educ:* Epsom Coll.; Jesus Coll., Cambridge. BA 1956. Lieut RA (TA) Airborne, 1953. Called to Bar, Gray's Inn, 1957. QC 1975; Recorder of the Crown Court, 1977–86. Vice-Chm., Judges' Forum, Internat. Bar Assoc., 1993. Dir, South China Financial Hldgs Ltd (formerly South China Brokerage Ltd), 2000–. *Recreations:* watching horse-racing, music. *Address:* PO Box 10156, GPO, Hong Kong. *Clubs:* Hong Kong, Hong Kong Jockey (Hong Kong); Sydney Turf (Sydney).

SEARS, (Robert) David (Murray); QC 2003; barrister; *b* 13 Dec. 1957; *s* of Robert Murray and Janet Leslie Sears; *m* 1984, Victoria Morlock (marr. diss. 2007); one *s* one *d*. *Educ:* Eton Coll.; Trinity Coll., Oxford (MA Jurisprudence 1979). Called to the Bar, Middle Temple, 1984; in practice, specialising in professional negligence and construction law, 1985–. *Recreations:* sailing, motorcycling, supporting Ipswich Town FC, watching and working with heavy horses. *Address:* Atkin Chambers, Gray's Inn, WC1R 5AT. *T:* (020) 7404 0102, *Fax:* (020) 7405 7456; *e-mail:* dsears@atkinchambers.com. *Club:* Leander (Henley-on-Thames).

SEATON, Andrew James; HM Diplomatic Service; Consul General, Hong Kong, since 2008; *b* 20 April 1954; *s* of Albert William Seaton and Joan Seaton (*née* Mackenzie); *m* 1983, Helen Elizabeth Pott; three *s*. *Educ:* Royal Grammar Sch., Guildford; Univ. of Leeds (BA Hons); Beijing Univ. Joined FCO, 1977: Third, later Second, Sec., Dakar, 1979–81; Hd, China Trade Unit, British Trade Commn, Hong Kong, 1982–86; FCO, 1987–92; Asst Hd, Aid Policy Dept, ODA, 1992–95; Trade Counsellor, British Trade Commn, Hong Kong, 1995–97; Dep. Consul-Gen., Hong Kong, 1997–2000; Hd, China Hong Kong Dept, FCO, 2000–03; Consul-Gen., Chicago, 2003–07. *Recreations:* family, wine, walking. *Address:* c/o Foreign and Commonwealth Office, King Charles Street, SW1A 2AH.

SEATON, Prof. Anthony, CBE 1997; MD; FRCP, FRCPE, FFOM, FMedSci; Professor of Environmental and Occupational Medicine, Aberdeen University, 1988–2003, now Emeritus; Hon. Consultant, Institute of Occupational Medicine, Edinburgh, since 2003; *b* 20 Aug. 1938; *s* of late Douglas Ronald Seaton and of Julia Seaton; *m* 1962, Jillian Margaret Duke; two *s*. *Educ:* Rossall Sch.; King's Coll., Cambridge (BA, MB, MD); Liverpool Univ. FRCP 1977; FFOM 1982; FRCPE 1985. Jun. med. posts, Liverpool and Stoke-on-Trent, 1962–69; Asst Prof. of Medicine, W Virginia Univ., 1969–71; Consultant Chest Physician, Cardiff, 1971–77; Dir, Inst. of Occupational Medicine, Edinburgh, 1978–90. Chairman: Expert Panel on Air Quality Standards, DoE, 1992–2002; Res. Adv. Cttee, NERC, 2006–; Member: Cttee on Med. Effects of Air Pollution, DoH, 1992–2003; Wkg Gp on Nanotechnol., Royal Soc./Royal Acad. Engrg, 2003–04. Lectures: Tudor Edwards, RCP, 1996; Baylis, PPP, 1997; Warner, British Occupational Hygiene Soc., 1998; Hunter, FOM, 2000; Gehrmann, Amer. Coll. of Occupational and Envmtl Medicine, 2001. President: British Thoracic Soc., 1999; Harveian Soc., 2007. Founder FMedSci 1998. Editor, Thorax, 1977–81. Hon. DSc Aberdeen, 2007. Medal, British Thoracic Soc., 2006. *Publications:* jointly: Occupational Lung Diseases, 1975, 3rd edn 1995; Crofton and Douglas's Respiratory Diseases, 1989, 2nd edn 2000; Practical Occupational Medicine, 1994, 2nd edn 2004; papers in med. literature. *Recreations:* opera, painting. *Address:* 8 Avon Grove, Cramond, Edinburgh EH4 6RF. *T:* (0131) 336 5113. *Club:* St Andrew Boat.

SEAWARD, Colin Hugh, CBE 1987; HM Diplomatic Service, retired; *b* 16 Sept. 1926; *s* of late Sydney W. Seaward and Molly W. Seaward; *m* 1st, 1949, Jean Bugler (decd); three *s* one *d*; 2nd, 1973, Judith Margaret Hinkley; two *d*. *Educ:* RNC, Dartmouth. Served Royal Navy, 1944–65. Joined HM Diplomatic Service, 1965; served: Accra, 1965; Bathurst (Banjul), 1966; FO, 1968; Rio de Janeiro, 1971; Prague, 1972; FCO, 1973; RNC, Greenwich (sowc), 1976; Counsellor (Econ. and Comm.), Islamabad, 1977–80; Consul-General, Rio de Janeiro, 1980–86, retd; re-employed in FCO, 1987–91. Sec., Anglo-Brazilian Soc., 1992–95 (Hon. Sec., 1986–91). Freeman, City of London, 1987. *Address:* Brasted House, Brasted, Westerham, Kent TN16 1JA.

SEBAG-MONTEFIORE, Harold Henry; Barrister-at-law; Deputy Circuit Judge, 1973–83; *b* 5 Dec. 1924; *e s* of late John Sebag-Montefiore and Violet, *o c* of late James Henry Solomon; *m* 1968, Harriet, *o d* of late Benjamin Harrison Paley, New York; one *d*. *Educ:* Stowe; Lower Canada Coll., Montreal; Pembroke Coll., Cambridge (MA). Served War of 1939–45, RAF. Called to Bar, Lincoln's Inn, 1951. Mem., Disciplinary Tribunal, Bar Council. Contested (C) North Paddington, Gen. Elec., 1959; Chm., Conservative Parly Candidates Assoc., 1960–64. Member: LCC, 1955–65 (last Alderman, Co. of London, 1961–65); GLC, for Cities of London and Westminster, 1964–73, First Chm., GLC Arts and Recreation Cttee, 1968–73; Sports Council, 1972–74. Pres., Anglo-Jewish Assoc., 1966–71; Jt Pres., Barkingside Jewish Youth Centre, 1988–94; Mem. Council, Anglo-Netherlands Soc., 1988–2001. Freeman, City of London, and Liveryman, Spectacle Makers' Co. Trustee: Royal Nat. Theatre Foundn; Internat. Festival of Youth Orchestras; Whitechapel Art Gall.; Touro National Heritage, RI; Mem., Cttee of Honour: RAH Centenary; "Fanfare for Europe"; William and Mary Tercentenary; Centenary of Montefiore Hosp., NY. Rode winner of Bar Point-to-Point, 1957 and 1959; Pres., Greater London Horse Show, 1970–73. Chevalier, Légion d'Honneur, 1973. *Publications:* obituaries; book reviews and articles on Polo under *nom-de-plume* of "Marco II". *Recreations:* theatre, travel, collecting conductors' batons. *Clubs:* Garrick, Hurlingham, Pegasus (Pres., 1979).

See also Sir M. W. Hanham, Bt.

SEBAG-MONTEFIORE, Simon Jonathan, FRSL; writer; historian; *b* London, 27 June 1965; *s* of Dr Stephen Sebag-Montefiore and April Jaffe; *m* 1998, Santa Palmer-Tomkinson; one *s* one *d*. *Educ:* Harrow Sch.; Gonville and Caius Coll., Cambridge (BA Hist. 1987). *Publications:* Catherine the Great and Potemkin, 2000; Stalin: court of the Red Tsar, 2003 (History Book of the Yr, British Book Awards, 2004); Young Stalin (Costa Biography Prize; LA Times Book Prize in Biography; Bruno Kreisky Prize for Political Lit.), 2007; 101 World Heroes: great men and women for an unheroic age, 2007; Monsters: history's most evil men and women, 2008; *novels* (as Simon Montefiore): King's Parade, 1991; My Affair With Stalin, 1997; Sashenka, 2008. *Recreations:* walking, reading, gardening. *Address:* c/o Georgina Capel, Literary Agent, Capel & Land, 29 Wardour Street, W1D 6PS. *T:* (020) 734 2414; *web:* www.simonsebagmontefiore.com. *Club:* Literary Society.

SEBASTIAN, Sir Cuthbert (Montraville), GCMG 1996; OBE 1970; MD; Governor-General, St Christopher and Nevis, since 1996; *b* 22 Oct. 1921. *Educ:* Mount Allison Univ., Canada (BSc 1953); Dalhousie Univ., Canada (MD, CM 1958). Pharmacist and Lab. Technician, Cunningham Hosp., St Kitts, 1942–43; RAF, 1944–45; Captain Surg., St Kitts Nevis Defence Force, 1958–80; Medical Superintendent: Cunningham Hosp., 1966; Joseph N. France Gen. Hosp., 1967–80; CMO, St Christopher and Nevis, 1980–83; private medical practitioner, 1983–95. Hon. FRCS 2000; Hon. FRCSE 2002. Hon. LLD Dalhousie, 1998. *Publication:* 100 Years of Medicine in St Kitts, 2001. *Recreations:* farming, reading, dancing. *Address:* Government House, Basseterre, St Kitts, W Indies; #6 Cayon Street, Basseterre, St Kitts, West Indies. *T:* 4652315. *Club:* Rotary of St Kitts.

SEBASTIAN, Timothy; freelance writer, broadcaster and consultant; *b* 13 March 1952; *s* of Peter Sebastian, CBE and late Pegitha Saunders; *m* 1977, Diane Buscombe; one *s* two *d*. *Educ:* Westminster School; New College, Oxford. BA (Hons) Mod. Lang. BBC Eastern Europe correspondent, 1979–82; BBC TV News: Europe correspondent, 1982–84; Moscow correspondent, 1984–85; Washington correspondent, 1986–89. Presenter, Hardtalk, BBC TV, 1997–2004. Chm., Doha Debates, 2004–. TV journalist of the year, 1982, Interviewer of the Year, 2000, 2001, RTS; Richard Dimbleby Award, BAFTA, 1982. *Publications:* Nice Promises, 1985; I Spy in Russia, 1986; *novels:* The Spy in Question, 1988; Spy Shadow, 1989; Saviour's Gate, 1990; Exit Berlin, 1992; Last Rights, 1993; Special Relations, 1994; War Dance, 1995; Ultra, 1997.

SEBER, Andrew James, CBE 2004; consultant in leadership, education and public services, since 2006; *b* 18 Sept. 1950; *s* of Philip George Seber and Helen Kathleen Seber (*née* Medhurst); *m* 1972, Sally Elizabeth Tyrrill; one *s* one *d*. *Educ:* East Barnet Grammar Sch.; Hertford Coll., Oxford (MA Biochemistry); Univ. of York; Middlesex Poly. (PGCE dist. 1977). Science Teacher: City of Leeds Sch., 1973–74; Hayes Manor Sch., 1974–79; Education Officer: Ealing LBC, 1979–81; Bucks CC, 1981–83; Hants CC, 1983–98; City Educn Officer, Portsmouth CC, 1998; County Educn Officer, Hants CC, 1998–2005; Dir, Andrew Seber Ltd Consultancy, 2006–. Director: Southern Careers Ltd, 1996–2005; South Central Connexions, 2001–05; Chm., Hants and Portsmouth Learning Partnership, 2002–04; Advr, Service Children's Educn, 2000–02; Mem., local LSC, 2001–05. Mem., Nat. Council, Soc. of Educn Officers, 2000–02; Pres., Confedn of Educn Service Managers, 2002–04. Member: Governing Council, Nat. Coll. for Sch. Leadership, 2006–; Bd, Training and Develt Agency for Schs, 2007–. *Publications:* contribs to educnl jl. *Recreations:* cycling, rambling, cake baking, ukulele. *Address: e-mail:* andrewseber@yahoo.co.uk.

SEBRIGHT, Sir Rufus Hugo Giles, 16th Bt *cr* 1626, of Besford, Worcestershire; *b* 31 July 1978; *s* of Sir Peter Giles Vivian Sebright, 15th Bt and his 1st wife, Regina Maria (*née* Clarebrough); *S* father, 2003, but his name does not appear on the Official Roll of the Baronetage.

SECCOMBE, family name of **Baroness Seccombe**.

SECCOMBE, Baroness *cr* 1991 (Life Peer), of Kineton in the County of Warwickshire; **Joan Anna Dalziel Seccombe,** DBE 1984; Deputy Opposition Chief Whip, House of Lords, since 2001; an Extra Baroness in Waiting to the Queen, since 2004; *b* 3 May 1930; *d* of Robert John Owen and Olive Barlow Owen; *m* 1950, Henry Lawrence Seccombe (*d* 2008); two *s*. *Educ:* St Martin's Sch., Solihull. Member: Heart of England Tourist Bd, 1977–81 (Chm., Marketing Sub-Cttee, 1979–81); Women's Nat. Commn, 1984–90; Chm., Lord Chancellor's Adv. Cttee, 1975–93. Mem. Exec., 1975–97, Vice-Chm., 1984–87, Chm., 1987–88, Nat. Union of Cons. and Unionist Assocs; Chairman: W Midlands Area Cons. Women's Cttee, 1975–78; Cons. Women's Nat. Cttee, 1981–84; Cons. Party Social Affairs Forum, 1985–87; Dep. Chm., W Midlands Area Cons. Council, 1979–81; Vice-Chm., with special responsibility for women, Cons. Party, 1987–97. Mem., W Midlands CC, 1977–81 (Chm., Trading Standards Cttee, 1979–81). An Opposition Whip, H of L, 1997–2001. Governor, 1988–2001, Dep. Chm., 1994–2001, Nuffield Hosps; Chm. Trustees, Nuffield Hosps Pension Scheme, 1992–2000. Pres., Govs of St Martin's Sch., Solihull, 1990–. Patron, W Midlands Youth Ballet, 1998–. JP Solihull, 1968–2000 (Chm., 1981–84). *Recreations:* golf, ski-ing, needlework. *Address:* House of Lords, SW1A 0PW. *Club:* St Enedoc Golf (Pres., 1992–).

See also Hon. Sir J. A. D. Owen.

SECCOMBE, Sir (William) Vernon (Stephen), Kt 1988; JP; Chairman, Plymouth Hospitals NHS Trust, 1993–98; former electrical contractor; *b* 14 Jan. 1928; *s* of Stephen Seccombe and Edith Violet (*née* Smith); *m* 1950, Margaret Vera Profit; four *s*. *Educ:* Saltash Grammar Sch.; Plymouth and Devonport Tech. Coll. Mem., E Cornwall Water Bd, 1960–74 (Vice-Chm., 1963–66; Chm., 1966–69); Chairman: Cornwall and Isles of Scilly DHA, late AHA, 1981–82; S Western RHA, 1983–90; Plymouth HA, 1990–93; Dep. Comr, 1970–79, Comr, 1979–82, Western Area Traffic Comrs. Member: Saltash BC, 1953–74 (Chairman: Works Cttee, 1956–62; Finance and Estabs Cttee, 1963–74; Mayor, 1962–63); Caradon DC, 1973–79 (Vice-Chm., 1973–76; Chm., 1976–78). Governor, Saltash Comprehensive Sch., 1970–81 (Chm., 1974–78). JP SE Cornwall, 1970. *Recreations:* industrial and local archaeology, genealogy (Pres., Cornwall Family History Soc., 1995–). *Address:* Hawks Park House, Hawks Park, Saltash, Cornwall PL12 4SP.

SECKER-WALKER, Prof. Lorna Margaret, PhD; Professor of Cancer Cytogenetics, Royal Free Hospital School of Medicine, 1993–97, Emeritus since 1997; *b* 17 Nov. 1933; *d* of late William Elmer Lea and Margaret Violet Lea (*née* Rees); *m* 1957, David Secker-Walker; one *s* three *d*. *Educ:* numerous schs; St Anne's Coll., Oxford (BA 1955; MA 1959); Inst. of Orthopaedics, London Univ. (PhD 1961). FRCPath 1996. Res. Fellow, MRC Unit for bone seeking isotopes, Oxford, 1955–56; Post-grad. Scholarship, Louvain Univ., Belgium, 1956–57; Royal Marsden Hospital, 1967–84; Non-clinical Lectr in cytogenetics of leukaemia; Gordon Jacobs, MRC and Leukaemia Res. Fund Fellowhips; Royal Free Hospital School of Medicine: Lectr, 1984–85; Sen. Lectr, 1985–93. Member Editorial Board: Acta Haematologica, 1988–2000; Cancer Genetics and Cytogenetics, 1987–97; Leukemia, 1994–2001. Chm., UK Cancer Cytogenetics Gp, 1988–97; Dir, Leukaemia Res. Fund Leukaemia Cytogenetics Gp and UK Cancer Cytogenetics Gp Karyotype Database in Acute Lymphoblastic Leukaemia, 1992–97; Mem. Fac., European Sch. of Haematol., 1986–95. Advr to MRC on cytogenetics of leukaemia, 1985–97. Member: Brit. Soc. Haematol., 1975–97; Internat. Soc. Hematol., 1976–97; Genetical Soc., 1976–97; RSocMed, 1984–; Assoc. of Clin. Cytogeneticists, 1984–97; Amer. Soc. Hematol., 1994–97; European Haematol. Assoc., 1994–97; European Soc. Human Genetics, 1994–97. *Publications:* Chromosomes and Genes in Acute Lymphoblastic Leukemia, 1997; chapters in: Postgraduate Haematology, 3rd edn 1989, 4th edn 1998; Haematological Oncology, 1994; over 100 articles in scientific and med. jls. *Recreations:* theatre, opera, travel, jigsaw puzzles. *Address:* 18 Pavilion Court, Frognal Rise, NW3 6PZ. *T:* (020) 7722 6467.

SECKERSON, Edward Stuart; music critic, writer and broadcaster; Chief Music Critic, The Independent, since 1991; *b* 27 July 1947; *s* of William Douglas Seckerson and Daphne Lilian (*née* Beard). *Educ:* Spender Park Sch.; private studies music and drama. BBC Gramophone Liby, 1966–69; Marketing Assistant, Decca Record Co., 1969–72; professional actor, 1972–80; music journalist, 1980–; contributor to: music mags incl. Classical Music, Hi-Fi News & Record Rev., BBC Music Mag., Gramophone; newspapers: The Guardian; The Times; Chief Music Critic, Sunday Correspondent, 1989–90. Radio and TV: contrib. BBC Radio 2, 3, 4 and World Service; commentator, Cardiff Singer of the World, BBC TV, 1991, 1993, 1995, 1997, 2004, 2007. *Publications:* Mahler: his life and times, 1984; Viva Voce: conversations with Michael Tilson Thomas, 1994. *Recreations:* music, literature, cinema, theatre.

SECONDÉ, Sir Reginald (Louis), KCMG 1981 (CMG 1972); CVO 1968 (MVO 1957); HM Diplomatic Service, retired; Ambassador to Venezuela, 1979–82; *b* 28 July 1922; *s* of late Lt-Col Emile Charles Secondé and Doreen Secondé (*née* Sutherland); *m* 1951, Catherine Penelope (*d* 2004), *d* of late Thomas Ralph Sneyd-Kynnersley, OBE, MC and late Alice Sneyd-Kynnersley; one *s* two *d*. *Educ:* Beaumont; King's Coll., Cambridge. Served, 1941–47, in Coldstream Guards: N Africa and Italy (despatches); Major. Entered Diplomatic Service, 1949; UK Delegn to the UN, New York, 1951–55; British Embassy: Lisbon, 1955–57; Cambodia, 1957–59; FO, 1959–62; British Embassy, Warsaw, 1962–64; First Secretary and later Political Counsellor, Rio de Janeiro, 1964–69; Head of S European Dept, FCO, 1969–72; Royal Coll. of Defence Studies, 1972–73; Ambassador to Chile, 1973–76, to Romania, 1977–79. *Address:* Stowlangtoft Hall, Stowlangtoft, Bury St Edmunds, Suffolk IP31 3JY. *T:* (01359) 230927. *Club:* Cavalry and Guards.

SECRETAN, Lance Hilary Kenyon; corporate adviser, author and keynote speaker; Founder and President, The Secretan Center Inc., since 1972; Founder, The Higher Ground Community; President, Thaler Resources Ltd, since 1981; *b* 1 Aug. 1939; *s* of late Kenyon Secretan and Marie-Therese Secretan (*née* Haffenden); *m* 1st, 1961, Gloria Christina (marr. diss. 1990; she *d* 2000); two *d* (and one *d* decd); 2nd, 1993, Patricia Edith Sheppard. *Educ:* Los Cocos, Argentina; Italia Conti, London; St Peters, Bournemouth; Univ. of Waterloo, Canada; Univ. of Southern California (MA in International Relations, *cum laude*, 1980); LSE (PhD in International Relations 1984). Emigrated to Canada, 1959; Sales Manager, J. J. Little and Ives, Toronto, 1959–60; Analyst, Toronto Stock Exchange, 1960; Sales Manager, Office Overload Co. Ltd, 1960–67; Man. Dir, Manpower Ltd Gp of Cos, UK, Ireland, Middle East and Africa, 1967–81. Prof. of Entrepreneurship, McMaster Univ., 1981–82; Vis. Prof., York Univ., Toronto, 1983–84; Special Goodwill Ambassador for Canada, UNEP, 1989–93; Chm. Adv. Bd, 1997 Special Olympics World Winter Games. Internat. Caring Award, US Senate, 1999; McFreely Award, Internat. Mgt Council, 2002. *Publications:* How to be an Effective Secretary, 1972; From Guns to Butter, 1983; Managerial Moxie, 1986, rev. edn 1993; The State of Small Business in Ontario, 1986; The Masterclass, 1988; The Way of the Tiger, 1989; The Personal Masterclass, 1992; Living the Moment, 1992; Reclaiming Higher Ground, 1996; Inspirational Leadership, 1999; Spirit@Work Cards, 2002; !Inspire! What Great Leaders Do, 2004; One: the art and practice of conscious leadership, 2006. *Recreations:* life, music, ski-ing, Mother Earth. *T:* (Canada) (519) 9275213, *Fax:* (519) 9273909; *e-mail:* info@secretan.com. *Club:* Mensa.

SEDAT, Elizabeth Helen, (Mrs J. W. Sedat); *see* Blackburn, E. H.

SEDCOLE, Cecil Frazer, FCA; a Vice Chairman, Unilever PLC, 1982–85; *b* 15 March 1927; *s* of late William John Sedcole and Georgina Irene Kathleen Bluett (*née* Moffatt); *m* 1962, Jennifer Bennett Riggall; one *s* one *d*. *Educ:* Uppingham Sch., Rutland. FCA 1952; CBIM 1982. Joined Unilever Group of Cos, 1952: Dir, Birds Eye Foods, 1960–66; Vice-Chairman: Langnese-Iglo, Germany, 1966–67; Frozen Products Gp, Rotterdam, 1967–71; Dir, Unilever PLC and Unilever NV, 1974–85; Chm., UAC International, 1976–79; Mem., 1971–75, Chm., 1979–85, Overseas Cttee, Unilever; Dir, Tate & Lyle, 1982–90; Dep. Chm., Reed International, 1985–87. Mem., BOTB, 1982–86; Mem. Bd, Commonwealth Devlt Corp., 1984–88. Trustee, Leverhulme Trust, 1982–97. Governor: Bedales Sch., 1983–90; Queen Elizabeth's Foundn for Disabled People, 1993–2002. *Recreation:* golf. *Address:* Beeches, Tyrrell's Wood, Leatherhead, Surrey KT22 8QH. *Club:* Royal Air Force.

SEDGEMORE, Brian Charles John; *b* 17 March 1937; *s* of Charles John Sedgemore, fisherman; *m* 1964, (Mary) Audrey Reece (marr. diss.; remarried 2002); one *s*. *Educ:* Newtown Primary Sch.; Heles Sch.; Oxford Univ. (MA). Diploma in public and social administration. Called to Bar, Middle Temple, 1966. RAF, 1956–58; Oxford, 1958–62. Administrative Class, Civil Service, Min. of Housing and Local Govt, 1962–66 (Private Sec. to R. J. Mellish, MP, then junior Minister of Housing, 1964–66). Practising barrister, 1966–74. MP (Lab): Luton West, Feb. 1974–1979; Hackney South and Shoreditch, 1983–2005. PPS to Tony Benn, MP, 1977–78. Researcher, Granada TV, 1980–83. *Publications:* The How and Why of Socialism, 1977; Mr Secretary of State (fiction), 1979; The Secret Constitution, 1980; Power Failure (fiction), 1985; Big Bang 2000, 1986; Pitiless Pursuit (fiction), 1994; Insider's Guide to Parliament, 1995; one time contributor to Britain's top satirical magazine. *Recreations:* art, Mozart. *Address:* 17 Sutton Square, E9 6EQ. *Club:* National Liberal.

SEDGMAN, Francis Arthur, AM 1980; Lawn Tennis Champion: Australia, 1949, 1950; USA, 1951, 1952; Wimbledon, 1952; Italy, 1952; Asia, 1952; Professional Tennis Player since 1953; *b* Victoria, Australia, 29 Oct. 1927; *m* 1952, Jean Margaret Spence; four *d*. *Educ:* Box Hill High School, Vic, Australia. First played in the Australian Davis Cup team, 1949; also played in winning Australian Davis Cup team, 1950, 1951, 1952. With John Bromwich, won Wimbledon doubles title, 1948; with Kenneth McGregor, won the Australian, French, Wimbledon and American doubles titles in the same year (1951), the only pair ever to do so; with Kenneth McGregor also won Australian, French and Wimbledon doubles titles, 1952; with Doris Hart, won French, Wimbledon and US mixed doubles titles, 1952. Last male player to win three titles at Wimbledon in one year, 1952. Director of many private companies. USA Hall of Fame, 1987; Australian Hall of Fame, 1988. *Publication:* Winning Tennis, 1955. *Recreations:* golfing, racing. *T:* (3) 95986341. *Clubs:* All England Lawn Tennis and Croquet, Queen's; Melbourne Cricket (Melbourne); Kooyong Tennis; Grace Park Tennis; Victoria Amateur Turf, Victoria Racing; Royal Melbourne Golf, Carbine (Melbourne); Mornington Racing (Mem. Cttee).

SEDGMORE, Lynne, CBE 2004; Chief Executive, Centre for Excellence in Leadership, since 2004; *b* 23 Oct. 1955; *d* of Mansel Sedgmore and Vera Sedgmore; *m* 1975, John Capper; one *d*, and two step *d*. *Educ:* Clayton Hall Grammar Sch.; Univ. of Kent (BA Hons); Madeley Coll. (PGCE 1980); Univ. of Surrey (MSc 1995). Lectr in further educn colls, 1979–86; Hd of Dept, Hackney Coll., 1986–88; Croydon College: Dir of Mktg, 1988–90; Hd, Croydon Business Sch., 1990–94; Vice Principal, 1994–98; Principal, Guildford Coll., 1998–2004. Non-exec. Dir of several Bds. MCIM 1989; MInstD 1998; FRSA 2002. *Publication:* Marketing for College Managers, 1992. *Recreations:* comparative religion, travel to Far East/India. *Address:* 9 Greencroft, Merrow, Guildford, Surrey GU1 2SY. *T:* (01483) 821961; *e-mail:* lynne.sedgmore@centreforexcellence.org.uk.

SEDGWICK, (Ian) Peter; Chairman, Schroders, 2000–02 (Deputy Chairman, 1995–2000); *b* 13 Oct. 1935; *m* 1956, Verna Mary Churchward; one *s* one *d*. National Westminster Bank, 1952–59; Ottoman Bank, 1959–69; J. Henry Schroder Wagg & Co., 1969–89; Chief Exec., Schroder Investment Management, 1985–95; Schroders, 1987–2002; Pres. and CEO, Schroders Inc., NY, 1996–2000; Chm., Schroder & Co. Inc., NY, 1996–2000; Vice Pres., Equitable Life Assurance Soc., 1995–2001. Chm., Queen Elizabeth's Foundn for disabled people, 2006–. *Recreations:* golf, theatre, grandchildren.

SEDGWICK, Peter; *see* Sedgwick, I. P.

SEDGWICK, Rev. Canon Peter Humphrey, PhD; Principal, St Michael's College, Llandaff, since 2004; Metropolitan Canon, Province of Wales, Llandaff Cathedral, since 2006; *b* 13 Dec. 1948; *s* of Oliver George Humphrey Sedgwick and Cathleen Winifred Sedgwick; *m* 1st, 1973, Helena Elizabeth Cole (marr. diss. 1995); one *s* two *d*; 2nd, 1996, Rev. Janet Gould. *Educ:* Trinity Hall, Cambridge (BA (Hist.) 1970; BA (Theol.) 1973); Durham Univ. (PhD 1983). Ordained deacon, 1974, priest, 1975; Curate, St Dunstan's, Stepney, 1974–77; Priest-in-charge, St Lawrence, Pittington, Durham, 1977–79; Lectr in Theol., Birmingham Univ., 1979–82; Theol Consultant, NE Churches, 1982–88; Lectr in Theol., Hull Univ., 1988–94; Fellow, Center for Theol Inquiry, Princeton, 1991; Vice Principal, Westcott House, Cambridge, 1994–95; Policy Officer (Home Affairs), C of E Bd for Social Responsibility, 1996–2004. *Publications:* Mission Impossible?: a theology of the local church, 1990; The Enterprise Culture, 1992; (ed) The Weight of Glory: the future of liberal theology, 1992; (ed) God in the City, 1996; The Market Economy and

Christian Ethics, 1999; (ed) The Future of Criminal Justice, 2002; (with A. Britton) Economic Theory and Christian Belief, 2003; (ed) Rethinking Sentencing, 2004. *Recreations:* gardening, walking, Bedlington Terriers. *Address:* St Michael's College, Llandaff, Cardiff CF5 2YJ. *T:* (029) 2056 3379; *e-mail:* ps@stmichaels.ac.uk.

SEDGWICK, Peter Norman; Vice-President, and Member of Management Committee, European Investment Bank, 2000–06; Director, European Investment Fund, 2002–06; Chairman, 3i Infrastructure Ltd, since 2007; *b* 4 Dec. 1943; *s* of late Norman Victor Sedgwick and of Lorna Clara (*née* Burton); *m* 1984, Catherine Jane, *d* of Mr and Mrs B. D. T. Saunders; two *s* two *d*. *Educ:* Westminster Cathedral Choir Sch.; Downside; Lincoln Coll., Oxford (MA PPE, BPhilEcon). HM Treasury: Economic Asst, 1969; Economic Adviser, 1971; Sen. Economic Adviser, 1977; Under Sec., 1984; Hd of Internat. Finance Gp, 1990–94; Hd of Educn, Trng and Employment Gp, 1994–95; Dep. Dir, Public Services (formerly Public Spending) Directorate, 1995–99. Chm. 1979–84, Mem. Develt Cttee 1984–, London Symphony Chorus; Dir, Dyslexia Action, 2007–. *Recreations:* singing, walking, gardening. *Address:* 20 Skeena Hill, SW18 5PL.

SEDLEY, Prof. David Neil, PhD; FBA 1994; Laurence Professor of Ancient Philosophy, University of Cambridge, since 2000; Fellow, Christ's College, Cambridge, since 1976; *b* 30 May 1947; *s* of William Sedley and Rachel Sedley (*née* Seifert); *m* 1973, Beverley Anne Dobbs; two *s* one *d*. *Educ:* Westminster Sch.; Trinity Coll., Oxford (BA Lit. Hum. 1969; MA 1973; Hon. Fellow 2003); University Coll. London (PhD 1974). Dyson Jun. Res. Fellow in Greek Culture, Balliol Coll., Oxford, 1973–75; University of Cambridge: Asst Lectr in Classics, 1975–78; Lectr, 1978–89; Reader in Ancient Philosophy, 1989–96; Prof. of Ancient Philosophy, 1996–2000. Townsend Lectr, Cornell Univ., 2001; Sather Prof., Univ. of California, Berkeley, 2004. Foreign Hon. Mem., Amer. Acad. of Arts and Scis, 1998. Editor: Classical Qly, 1986–92; Oxford Studies in Ancient Philosophy, 1998–2007. *Publications:* (with A. A. Long) The Hellenistic Philosophers, 2 vols, 1987; Lucretius and the Transformation of Greek Wisdom, 1998; (ed) The Cambridge Companion to Greek and Roman Philosophy, 2003; Plato's Cratylus, 2003; The Midwife of Platonism: text and subtext in Plato's Theaetetus, 2004; Creationism and its Critics in Antiquity, 2007; articles in classical and philosophical jls and collaborative vols. *Recreations:* cinema, vegetable growing. *Address:* Christ's College, Cambridge CB2 3BU. *T:* (01223) 334910; 97 Hills Road, Cambridge CB2 1PG. *T:* (01223) 368845.

See also Rt Hon. Sir S. J. Sedley.

SEDLEY, Rt Hon. Sir Stephen (John), Kt 1992; PC 1999; **Rt Hon. Lord Justice Sedley;** a Lord Justice of Appeal, since 1999; *b* 9 Oct. 1939; *s* of William and Rachel Sedley; *m* 1st, 1968, Ann Tate (marr. diss. 1995); one *s* two *d*; 2nd, 1996, Teresa, (Tia) (*née* Chaddock). *Educ:* Mill Hill Sch. (entrance schol.); Queens' Coll., Cambridge (open schol./exhibnr; BA Hons 1961). Musician, translator, 1961–64; called to the Bar, Inner Temple, 1964, Bencher, 1989; QC 1983; a Judge of the High Court of Justice, QBD, 1992–99; Pres., Nat. Reference Tribunals for the Coalmining Industry, 1983–88. Chm., Sex Discrimination Cttee, Bar Council, 1992–95. Pres., British Inst. of Human Rights, 2000–. *Ad hoc* judge, European Court of Human Rights, 2000. Vis. Professorial Fellow, Warwick Univ., 1981; Vis. Fellow, 1987, Vis. Prof., 1997, Osgoode Hall Law Sch., Canada; Distinguished Visitor, Hong Kong Univ., 1992; Hon. Professor: Univ. of Wales, Cardiff, 1993–; Univ. of Warwick, 1994–; Vis. Fellow, Victoria Univ. of Wellington, NZ, 1998; Judicial Visitor, UCL, 1999–. Lectures: Bernard Simons Meml, 1994; Paul Sieghart Meml, 1995; Radcliffe (with Lord Nolan), 1996; Laskin, 1997; Hamlyn, 1998; Lord Morris of Borth-y-Gest, 1999; MacDermott, 2001; Atkin, 2001; Pilgrim Fathers, 2002; Leicester Univ., 2004; Holdsworth, 2005; Blackstone, 2006; Mishcon, 2007. A Dir, Public Law Project, 1989–93; Hon. Vice-Pres., Administrative Law Bar Assoc., 1992–. Mem., Internat. Commn on Mercenaries, Angola, 1976. Chm., British Council Adv. Cttee on Governance, 2002–05. Sec., Haldane Soc., 1964–69. Hon. Fellow, Inst. for Advanced Legal Studies, 1997. Hon. Dr N London, 1996; Hon. LLD: Nottingham Trent, 1997; Bristol, 1999; Warwick, 1999; Durham, 2001; Hull, 2002; Southampton, 2003; Exeter, 2004; Essex, 2007. *Publications:* (trans.) From Burgos Jail, by Marcos Ana and Vidal de Nicolas, 1964; (ed) Seeds of Love (anthology), 1967; Whose Child? (report of inquiry into death of Tyra Henry), 1987; (ed) A Spark in the Ashes: writings of John Warr, 1992; (with Lord Nolan) The Making and Remaking of the British Constitution (Radcliffe Lectures), 1997; Freedom, Law and Justice (Hamlyn Lectures), 1999; contributed: Orwell: inside the myth, 1984; Civil Liberty, 1984; Police, the Constitution and the Community, 1986; Challenging Decisions, 1986; Public Interest Law, 1987; Civil Liberties in Conflict, 1988; Law in East and West, 1988; Citizenship, 1991; Administrative Law and Government Action, 1994; Frontiers of Legal Scholarship, 1995; Law Society and Economy, 1997; Human Rights for the 1990s, 1997; The Golden Metwand and the Crooked Cord (essays for Sir William Wade), 1998; Freedom of Expression and Freedom of Information (essays for Sir David Williams), 2000; Judicial Review in International Perspective (essays for Lord Slynn of Hadley), 2000; Discriminating Lawyers, 2000; The New Brain Sciences, 2004; Le Conseil d'Etat et le Code Civil, 2004; Liber amicorum (essays for Luzius Wildhaber), 2007; contrib. DNB: Missing Persons; Oxford DNB; London Review of Books, Public Law, Modern Law Review, Jl of Law and Soc., Civil Justice Qly, Law Qly Review, Industrial Law Jl, Eur. Human Rights Law Rev., NI Law Qly, Jl of Legal Ethics, Aust. Jl of Administrative Law. *Recreations:* carpentry, music, cycling, walking, changing the world. *Address:* c/o Royal Courts of Justice, Strand, WC2A 2LL.

See also D. N. Sedley.

SEDWILL, Mark Philip, CMG 2008; HM Diplomatic Service; Director, International Group, UK Border Agency, since 2008; *b* 21 Oct. 1964; *s* of late Edward Peter Sedwill and of Mary June Sedwill; *m* 1999, Sarah-Jane Lakeman; one *d*. *Educ:* Univ. of St Andrews (BSc Hons); St Edmund Hall, Oxford (MPhil). Joined FCO, 1989; Second Secretary: Security Coordination Dept, FCO, 1989–91; Cairo, 1991–94; First Secretary: Resource Mgt Dept, 1994–96, ME Dept, 1996–98, FCO; Nicosia, 1998–2000; Press Sec., FCO, 2000; Private Sec. to Sec. of State for Foreign and Commonwealth Affairs, 2000–03; Dep. High Comr, Islamabad, 2003–05; Dep. Dir, Middle East and N Africa, FCO, 2005; Dir, UK Visas, 2006–08. UK Dir, American Acad. of Overseas Studies, 1987. *Recreations:* golf, squash, scuba diving, windsurfing, hill-walking, history, bridge, family and friends. *Address:* Foreign and Commonwealth Office, King Charles Street, SW1A 2AH. *T:* (020) 7008 8350, *Fax:* (020) 7008 3198; *e-mail:* mark.sedwill@fco.gov.uk. *Clubs:* Special Forces; Kate Kennedy (St Andrews); Vincent's (Oxford).

SEED, John Junior, CEng, FIET; Chief Executive, South Western Electricity plc, 1992–95; *b* 25 Oct. 1938; *s* of John Seed and Elizabeth (*née* Earley); *m* 1961, Maureen Syder; two *d*. *Educ:* City of Norwich Grammar Sch.; Norwich City Coll. CEng 1972; FIET (FIEE 1986). Eastern Electricity: Dist Manager, Bury St Edmunds, 1976–80; Area Manager, Suffolk, 1980–82; Dir of Engrg, 1982–86; Dep. Chm., S Western Electricity Bd, 1986–90; Man. Dir, S Western Electricity plc, 1990–92. Director: Royal United Hosp. Trust, 1991–97; United Utilities plc, 1996–2005; British Smaller Companies VCT plc, 1996–2004; Prism Rail plc, 1996–2000; Rebus Gp plc, 1997–99; Weston Attenas Ltd, 2001–02; Frazer-Nash Consultancy Ltd, 2002–04; Chairman: Great Western Assured Growth plc, 1991–97; Windelectric Ltd, 1996–99; Warren Associates Ltd, 1998–2001. CCMI (FBIM 1980). *Recreations:* golf, walking, bridge.

SEED, Rev. Michael Joseph Steven, SA; STD; Chaplain of Westminster Cathedral, since 1985; Secretary, Ecumenical Commission (formerly Ecumenical Officer), Archdiocese of Westminster, since 1988; on sabbatical, 2008–Sept. 2009; *b* Manchester, 16 June 1957; *né* Godwin; adopted *s* of late Joseph Seed and Lillian Seed (*née* Ramsden). *Educ:* St Mary's Coll., Aberystwyth; St Joseph's Coll., Cork; Missionary Inst., Mill Hill; Washington Theol Inst., Md; Catholic Univ. of America, Washington (MDiv. 1984); Heythrop Coll.; Pontifical Lateran Univ., Rome (STL 1987; STD 1989); Polish Univ., London (PhD 1991). Entered Franciscan Friars of the Atonement, 1979; final profession, 1985; ordained deacon, 1985, priest, 1986; Chaplain, Westminster Hosp., 1986–90; Officiating Chaplain to the Forces, Wellington Barracks, 1990–2000. Chaplain, Soc. of Useless Information, 1998. For. Corresp. Academician, Historical Inst. of Dom Luiz I (Portugal), 1998. Freeman, City of London, 2005. Cross of Merit in Gold (Poland), 1988; Order of Orthodox Hospitallers (Cyprus), 1988; Ecclesiastical Kt Comdr of Grace, Sacred and Mil. Constantinian Order of St George (Naples), 1989; Cross Pro Ecclesia et Pontifice (Holy See), 2004; Three Faiths Forum Interfaith Gold Medallion, 2006. *Publications:* I Will See You in Heaven, 1991; (contrib.) Sons and Mothers, 1996; (contrib.) Faith, Hope and Chastity, 1999; Will I See You in Heaven?, 1999; Assurance, 2000; Letters from the Heart, 2000; (contrib.) Catholic Lives, 2001; The Gift of Assurance, 2003; Nobody's Child (autobiog.), 2007; (contrib.) C4 x 25, 2007; Memoirs of a Turbulent Priest (autobiog.), 2009; contribs to various publications. *Recreations:* politicians, pasta, Zwinglianism. *Address:* The Friary, 47 Francis Street, SW1P 1QR. *T:* (020) 7828 4163. *Club:* Beefsteak.

SEED, Nigel John; QC 2000; a Recorder, since 2000; *b* 30 Jan. 1951; *s* of Thomas Robinson Seed and Joan Hall Seed (*née* Evison). *Educ:* Ellesmere Port Grammar Sch. for Boys; St Chad's Coll., Durham (BA 1972). Called to the Bar, Inner Temple, 1978, Bencher, 2008; Mem., Western Circuit, 1981–; Asst Recorder, 1995–2000. Special Adjudicator, Immigration and Asylum Appeals, 1997–98. Chancellor: Dio. of Leicester, 1989–2002; Dio. of London, 2002–; Deputy Chancellor: Dio. of Salisbury, 1992–97; Dio. of Norwich, 1992–98. *Recreations:* walking, cooking, eating and drinking. *Address:* 3 Paper Buildings, Temple, EC4Y 7EU. *T:* (020) 7583 8055. *Club:* Athenæum.

SEED, Ven. Richard Murray Crosland; Archdeacon of York, since 1999; Rector of Micklegate and Bishophill Junior, since 2000; *b* 9 May 1949; *s* of Denis Briggs Seed and Mary Crosland Seed (*née* Barrett); *m* 1974, Jane Margaret Berry; one *s* three *d*. *Educ:* St Philip's Sch., Burley-in-Wharfedale; Edinburgh Theol Coll.; Leeds Univ. (MA). Deacon 1972, priest 1973; Asst Curate, Christ Church, Skipton, 1972–75, Baildon, 1975–77, Dio. Bradford; Team Vicar, Kidlington, Oxford, 1977–80; Chaplain, HM Detention Centre, Campsfield House, 1977–80; Vicar of Boston Spa, Dio. York, 1980–99; Priest-in-charge: Clifford, 1989–99; Thorp Arch with Walton, 1998–99. Mem., Gen. Synod of C of E, 2000–. Chairman: Diocesan Redundant Churches Cttee, 1999–; Diocesan Pastoral Cttee, dio. York, 2003–. Founder Chm. and Chaplain, Martin House Hospice for Children, 1980–. *Publication:* (contrib.) Appointed for Growth, 1994. *Recreations:* swimming, travel, Byzantine studies, monastic spirituality, walking dogs. *Address:* Holy Trinity Rectory, Micklegate, York YO1 6LE. *T:* (01904) 623798, *Fax:* (01904) 628155.

SEEISO, HRH Prince Seeiso Bereng; High Commissioner of Lesotho to the United Kingdom, since 2005; *b* 16 April 1966; *s* of HM King Bereng Seeiso; *m* HRH Princess Imabereng Seeiso; one *s* one *d*. *Educ:* Gilling Castle; Ampleforth Coll.; Nat. Univ. of Lesotho; Birmingham Univ.; Guyana. Principal Chief, Matsieng, 1991. Member: Nat. Constituent Assembly, 1993–; Senate. *Recreations:* horse-riding, theatre, reading, football, Rugby. *Address:* High Commission for Lesotho, 7 Chesham Place, Belgravia, SW1X 8HN. *T:* (020) 7285 5686, *Fax:* (020) 7235 5023; *e-mail:* hicom@lesotholondon.org.uk.

SEEL, Derek, FDSRCS; FRCS; FRCA; Dental Postgraduate Dean, University of Bristol, 1986–98; *b* 2 April 1932; *s* of William Alfred and Olive Seel; *m* 1960, Gillian Henderson. *Educ:* Stockport Sch.; Manchester Univ. Inst. of Dental Surgery (BDS). MOrthRCS; FRCS 1994; FRCA 1995. General dental practice, 1956–62; orthodontic trainee, 1962–68; Lectr in Orthodontics, Bristol Univ., 1967–69; Consultant Orthodontist, Univ. of Wales Coll. of Medicine, 1969–94; Consultant in Orthodontics, Welsh RHA, 1969–94. Dean, Faculty of Dental Surgery, RCS, 1990–92. LRPS 1991. Hon. Diploma in Gen. Dental Practice, RCS 1994. C. F. Ballard Medal, Consultant Orthodontists' Gp, 1992; Colyer Gold Medal, RCS, 1994. *Recreations:* golf, music, reading, photography. *Address:* 20 Blenheim Road, Bristol BS6 7JP. *T:* (0117) 973 6635; *e-mail:* seel@which.net.

SEELEY, Rev. Canon Martin Alan; Principal, Westcott House, Cambridge, since 2006; *b* 29 May 1954; *s* of Alan and Joyce Seeley; *m* 1st, 1980, Cynthia McLean (marr. diss. 1989); 2nd, 1999, Jutta Brueck; one *s* one *d*. *Educ:* Jesus Coll., Cambridge (BA 1976, MA 1979); Ripon Coll., Cuddesdon, Oxford; Union Theol Seminary, NYC (STM 1978). Ordained deacon 1978, priest 1979; Curate: Bottesford with Ashby, Scunthorpe, 1978–80; Ch of the Epiphany, NYC, 1980–85; Asst Dir, Trinity Inst., Wall St, NYC, 1981–85; Exec. Dir, Thompson Center, St Louis, Mo, 1985–90; Sec. for Contg Ministerial Educn and Selection Sec., ABM, Gen. Synod of C of E, 1990–96; Vicar, Isle of Dogs, 1996–2006. Hon. Canon, Ely Cathedral, 2007. *Recreations:* cooking, playing tenor saxophone, cinema. *Address:* Principal's Lodge, Westcott House, Jesus Lane, Cambridge CB5 8BP. *T:* (01223) 741010, *Fax:* (01223) 741002; *e-mail:* mas209@cam.ac.uk.

SEELY, family name of **Baron Mottistone**.

SEELY, Sir Nigel (Edward), 5th Bt *cr* 1896; Dorland International; *b* 28 July 1923; *s* of Sir Victor Basil John Seely, 4th Bt and of Sybil Helen, *d* of late Sills Clifford Gibbons; *S* father, 1980; *m* 1949, Loraine (marr. diss.; she *d* 2007), *d* of late W. W. Lindley-Travis; three *d*; *m* 1984, Trudi Pacter, *d* of Sydney Pacter. *Educ:* Stowe. *Heir: half-b* Victor Ronald Seely [*b* 1 Aug. 1941; *m* 1972, Annette Bruce, *d* of Lt-Col J. A. D. McEwen; one *s* one *d*]. *Address:* 3 Craven Hill Mews, W2 3DY. *Clubs:* Buck's; Royal Solent.

SEENEY, Leslie Elon Sidney, OBE 1978; Director General (formerly General Secretary), National Chamber of Trade, 1971–87; *b* 19 Jan. 1922; *s* of Sidney Leonard and Daisy Seeney, Forest Hill; *m* 1947, Marjory Doreen Greenwood, Spalding; one *s*. *Educ:* St Matthews, Camberwell. RAFVR, 1941–46 (Flt Lt, Pilot). Man. Dir, family manufrg business (clothing), 1946–63, with other interests in insce and advertising. Mem., West Lewisham Chamber of Commerce, 1951, subseq. Sec. and Chm.; Delegate to Nat. Chamber of Trade, 1960; joined NCT staff, 1966. Mem., Home Office Standing Cttee on Crime Prevention, 1971–87. Council Member: (founding) Retail Consortium, 1971–87; Assoc. for Prevention of Theft from Shops, 1976–87. Fellow, Soc. of Assoc. Executives, 1970. *Publications:* various articles. *Recreations:* genealogy, travel, photography.

SEETO, Sir (James Hip) Ling, Kt 1988; MBE 1975; Managing Director, Lingana Pty Ltd, Port Moresby, Papua New Guinea, since 1965; Director and part owner, Kwila Insurance Corp., Port Moresby, since 1978; *b* 19 June 1933; *s* of Yeeying Seeto and

Kamfoung Mack; *m* 1960, Anna Choiha Peng; two *s*. *Educ:* Rabaul Public Sch., PNG; Mowbray House Sch., Sydney, Australia; Trinity Grammar Sch., Sydney. Pings Co., Rabaul, PNG, 1954–58; Shell Co., Rabaul, 1958–62; Rabaul Metal Industries, Rabaul, 1962–64. Former Board Member: Nat. Investment and Develt Authy, PNG; PNG Develt Bank; Harbors Board; Water Resources Bd of PNG; Salvation Army Adv. Bd, PNG. A Youth Leader, Rabaul Methodist Ch., 1954–60. Silver Jubilee Medal, 1977; PNG Independence Medal, 1986. *Recreations:* golf, swimming, gardening, cooking. *Address:* PO Box 1756, Boroko, National Capital District, Papua New Guinea. *T:* (office) 3254966, (home) 3211873. *Club:* Cathay (Port Moresby) (Patron).

SEEYAVE, Sir René (Sow Choung), Kt 1985; CBE 1979; Chairman: Altima Group, since 2004; Happy World Foods (formerly Mauritius Farms) Ltd, since 1974; *b* 15 March 1935; *s* of late Antoine Seeyave, CBE and Lam Tung Ying; *m* 1961, Thérèse How Hong; one *s* four *d*. *Educ:* Royal College, Port Louis, Mauritius. Gp Man. Dir, 1968–86, Gp Chm., 1986–2004, Happy World Ltd. Chm., Electricity Adv. Cttee, 1972–76. Vice Chairman: Mauritius Employers' Fedn, 1972; Mauritius Broadcasting Corp., 1980–81. Director: Mauritius Development Investment Trust Ltd, 1968–2000; Swan Insurance Co. Ltd, 1969–2003; Mauritius Marine Authority, 1980–95. Mauritius Res. Council, 1997–2000; Vice-Chm. Council, Univ. of Mauritius, 1985–87. Chm., Sui Loong Elders Centre, 1997–. Hon. Pres., Heen Foh Soc., 1991–. *Address:* Altima Ltd, Level 3 Happy World Foods Building, Caudan, Port Louis, Mauritius. *T:* 2103003, *Fax:* 2132828; *e-mail:* rene.seeyave@intnet.mu. *Clubs:* Royal Over-Seas League; Mauritius Gymkhana, Port Louis City.

SEFI, Michael Richard, FCA; FRPSL; Keeper of the Royal Philatelic Collection, since 2003 (Deputy Keeper, 1996–2002); *b* 11 Dec. 1943; *s* of Antony Michael Sefi and Judith Sefi (*née* Hull); *m* 1968, Harriet Mary Davidson; one *s* two *d*. *Educ:* Downside Sch. Chartered Accountant 1970; FCA 1975. Partner, Mann Judd, then Touche Ross, 1975–83; Dir, Noble Lowndes Personal Financial Services Ltd, then Noble Lowndes & Partners Ltd, 1983–92. FRPSL 1990 (Council Mem., 1990–2005); Pres., GB Philatelic Soc., 1998–2000. *Publications:* contrib. to London Philatelist, GB Jl, Crosspost. *Recreations:* philately, ski-ing, diving, naval history. *Address:* Royal Philatelic Collection, Buckingham Palace, SW1A 1AA; *e-mail:* michael.sefi@royal.gov.uk. *Club:* Army and Navy.

SEFTON, Dr Allan Douglas; non-executive Director, Angel Trains Group, since 2006; Director, Rail Safety, and HM Chief Inspector of Railways, Health and Safety Executive, 2001–05; *b* 15 April 1945; *s* of James and Alice Sefton; *m* 1968, Jennifer Elizabeth Pratt; two *s*. *Educ:* UCNW, Bangor (BSc; PhD 1970). FIOSH 1990. Trainee, HM Insp. of Factories, Dept of Employment, Scotland, 1969–73; HM Insp. of Factories, Dept of Employment and HSE, Scotland, 1973–81; Health and Safety Executive: HM Insp., Hazardous Substances Div., 1981–86; Principal Insp., Field Ops Div., 1986–87; Hd, Hazardous Installation Nat. Interest Gp, 1987–90; Dir, W and N Yorks, 1990–92; Dir of Ops, 1992–96, Hd, 1996–2000, Off-shore Safety Div.; Dir, Scotland, 2000–01. *Recreations:* fishing, game shooting. *Address:* 4 Barnfield, Common Lane, Hemingford Abbots, Cambs PE28 9AX.

SEGAL, Prof. Anthony Walter, MD; PhD, DSc; FRCP, FMedSci; FRS 1998; Charles Dent Professor of Medicine, University College London, since 1986; *b* 24 Feb. 1944; *s* of Cyril Segal and late Doreen (*née* Hayden); *m* 1966, Barbara Miller; three *d*. *Educ:* Univ. of Cape Town (MB, ChB; MD 1974); PhD 1979, DSc 1984, London. FRCP 1987. Internship, Groote Schuur Hosp., SA, 1968–69; Sen. House Officer, Registrar and Sen. Registrar in Medicine, Hammersmith Hosp., 1970–76; Registrar and Clinical Scientist, Northwick Park Hosp. and Clinical Res. Centre, 1971–79; Wellcome Trust Sen. Clinical Fellow, UCL, 1979–86; Hon. Consultant Physician, UCH, 1979–. Fellow, UCL, 2002. Founder FMedSci 1998. *Publications:* contribs on biochemistry, cell biology, immunology and gastroenterology. *Recreations:* golf, sculpture, painting, theatre, music, dining. *Address:* Department of Medicine, Rayne Institute, 5 University Street, WC1E 6JJ. *T:* (020) 7679 6175. *Clubs:* Garrick; Highgate Golf.

SEGAL, Prof. Erich; Adjunct Professor of Classics, Yale University, 1981–88; *b* 16 June 1937; *s* of Samuel M. Segal, PhD, DHL and Cynthia Shapiro Segal; *m* 1975, Karen James; two *d* (one *s* decd). *Educ:* Harvard (Boylston Prize 1957, Bowdoin Prize 1959; AB 1958, AM 1959, PhD 1965; Guggenheim Fellowship, 1968). Teaching Fellow, Harvard, 1959–64; Lectr in Classics, Yale, 1964, Asst Prof., 1965–68, Associate Prof., 1968–73; Vis. Prof. in Classics: Munich, 1973; Princeton, 1974–75; Tel Aviv, 1976–77; Vis. Prof. in Comp. Lit., Dartmouth, 1976–78; Wolfson College, Oxford: Vis. Fellow, 1979–80; Supernumerary Fellow, 1982–88; Mem. Common Room, 1984–; Hon. Fellow, 1999. Member: Acad. of Literary Studies, USA, 1981; Nat. Adv. Council, 1970–72, Exec. Cttee, 1971–72, Peace Corps, USA (Presidential Commendation for Service to Peace Corps, 1971). Lectures: Amer. Philological Assoc., 1971, 1972; Amer. Comparative Lit. Assoc., 1971; German Classical Assoc., 1974; Boston Psychoanalytic Inst., 1974; Istituto Nazionale del Dramma Antico, Sicily, 1975; Brit. Classical Assoc., 1977; William Kelley Prentice Meml, Princeton, 1981; Inaugural Andrea Rosenthal Meml, Brown Univ., 1992. Author and narrator, The Ancient Games, 1972; TV commentator, ABC-TV, US, radio commentator in French, RTL Paris, Olympic Games, 1972 and 1976. Screenplays include: The Beatles' Yellow Submarine, 1968; The Games, 1969; Love Story, 1970 (Golden Globe Award, 1970); Oliver's Story, 1978; Man, Woman and Child, 1983. Mem., Authors Guild, 1970–. (With Mother Teresa and Peter Ustinov) Premio San Valentin di Terni, 1989. Chevalier de l'Ordre des Arts et des Lettres (France), 1998. *Publications:* Roman Laughter: the comedy of Plautus, 1968, rev. edn 1987; (ed) Euripides: a collection of critical essays, 1968; (ed and trans.) Plautus: Three Comedies, 1969, rev. edn 1985; (ed) Oxford Readings in Greek Tragedy, 1983; (ed with Fergus Millar) Caesar Augustus: seven aspects, 1984; (ed) Plato's Dialogues, 1985; Oxford Readings in Aristophanes, 1996; (ed and trans.) Plautus: Four Comedies, 1996; Death of Comedy, 2001; Oxford Readings in Menander, Plautus and Terence, 2002; *novels:* Love Story, 1970; Fairy Tale (for children), 1973; Oliver's Story, 1977; Man, Woman and Child, 1980; The Class, 1985 (Prix Deauville, France, and Premio Bancarella Selezione, Italy, 1986); Doctors, 1988; Acts of Faith, 1992; Prizes, 1995; Only Love, 1997; articles and reviews in Amer. Jl of Philology, Classical World, Harvard Studies in Classical Philology, Classical Review, Greek, Roman and Byzantine Studies, TLS, New York Times Book Review, New Republic, The Independent, Washington Post. *Recreations:* swimming, walking. *Address:* Wolfson College, Oxford OX2 6UD. *T:* (01865) 274100. *Club:* Athenæum.

SEGAL, Graeme Bryce, DPhil; FRS 1982; Senior Research Fellow, All Souls College, Oxford, since 1999; *b* 21 Dec. 1941; *s* of Reuben Segal and Iza Joan Harris; *m* 1962, Desley Rae Cheetham (marr. diss. 1972). *Educ:* Sydney Grammar School; Univ. of Sydney (BSc 1962); Univ. of Cambridge; Univ. of Oxford (MA, DPhil 1967). Oxford University: Junior Res. Fellow, Worcester Coll., 1964–66; Junior Lectr in Mathematics, 1965–66; Fellow, St Catherine's Coll., 1966–90; Reader in Maths, 1978–89; Prof. of Maths, 1989–90; Lowndean Prof. of Astronomy and Geometry, and Fellow, St John's Coll., Cambridge, 1990–99. Mem., Inst. for Advanced Study, Princeton, 1969–70. Editor, Topology, 1970–90. *Publications:* (with A. Pressley) Loop Groups, 1986; articles in learned jls. *Address:* All Souls College, Oxford OX1 4AL. *T:* (01865) 279379; 1 Beechcroft Road, Oxford OX2 7AY. *T:* (01865) 558016.

SEGAL, Hanna Maria, FRCPsych; psycho-analyst in private practice, retired; teacher; *b* Poland, 20 Aug. 1918; *d* of Czeslaw and Isabella Poznanski; *m* 1946, Paul Segal (*d* 1996); three *s*. *Educ:* Warsaw and Geneva; Polish Medicine Sch. in Edinburgh. Vis. Prof., Freud Meml Chair, UCL, 1987–88. Pres., 1977–80, Actg Pres., 1981–82, British Soc. Psycho-Analysis; Vice-Pres., Internat. Psychoanalytical Assoc. Founder Member: Psychoanalysts for Prevention of Nuclear War, 1983; Internat. Psychoanalysts Against Nuclear Weapons, 1985. Sigourney Award for Services to Psychoanalysis, 1992. *Publications:* Introduction to the Work of Melanie Klein, 1964, repr. 1988; Melanie Klein, 1979; The Work of Hanna Segal (collected papers), 1981, repr. 1986; (contrib.) Do I Dare Disturb the Universe? A Memorial to Wilfrid R. Bion, ed James S. Grotstein, 1981; (contrib.) Models of the Mind: their relationships to clinical work, ed Arnold Rothstein, 1985; Dream, Phantasy and Art, 1990; (contrib.) Psychoanalysis, Mind and Art: Perspectives on Richard Wollheim, 1992; (contrib.) Psychoanalysis in Contexts: paths between theory and modern culture, 1995; Psychoanalysis, Literature and War (collected papers, ed John Steiner); (contrib.) Terrorism and War: unconscious dynamics of political violence, 2002; Yesterday, Today and Tomorrow (collected papers, ed N. Abel-Hirsch), 2007; contribs to jls incl. Internat. Jl Psycho-Analysis, Internat. Rev. Psycho-Analysis, Psychoanalysis in Europe, Jl Amer. Psychoanalytic Soc., Jl de la psychoanalyse de l'enfant. *Recreations:* swimming and snorkelling, family, politics and aesthetics. *Address:* c/o Melanie Klein Trust, 21 Goodwyns Vale, N10 2HA. *T:* (020) 8883 1700; *e-mail:* KleinTrust@aol.com.

See also M. G. Segal.

SEGAL, Michael Giles, PhD; Director, Food and Farming Group, Department for Environment, Food and Rural Affairs, since 2007; *b* 31 July 1950; *s* of late Paul and of Hanna Maria Segal, *qv*; *m* 1972, Agnes Henderson; one *s* (and one *s* decd). *Educ:* St Paul's Sch.; King's Coll., Cambridge (BA 1972; PhD 1975). MRSC; CChem. Res. Officer, CEGB, 1978–88; Civil Servant: MAFF, 1988–99, variously Hd, Food Safety (Radiation) Unit, Hd, Radiological Safety Div. and Chief Nuclear Inspector, and Hd, Radiological Safety and Nutrition Div.; Dir of Corporate Strategy and Sec. to the Bd, Food Standards Agency, 2000–01; Department for Environment, Food and Rural Affairs: Hd, Livestock Strategy Div., 2001–04; Dir, Food Chain Analysis and Farming Regulation, 2004–06; Dir, Sustainable Farming Strategy, 2006–07. *Publications:* approx. 70 articles in learned jls, conf. procs, etc. *Recreations:* sports—cricket, badminton, ski-ing and scuba diving, photography (incl. underwater), dancing. *Address:* Department for Environment, Food and Rural Affairs, 9 Millbank, c/o 17 Smith Square, SW1P 3JR. *T:* (020) 7238 3064, *Fax:* (020) 7238 4980; *e-mail:* michael.segal@defra.gsi.gov.uk.

SEGAL, Michael John; District Judge (formerly Registrar), Principal Registry, Family Division, since 1985; *b* 20 Sept. 1937; *s* of Abraham Charles Segal and Iris Muriel (*née* Parsons); *m* 1963, Barbara Gina Fluxman; one *d*. *Educ:* Strode's Sch., Egham. Served 7th RTR, 1955–56. Called to the Bar, Middle Temple, 1962. Practised at Bar, Midland and Oxford Circuit, 1962–84. Mem., Civil and Family Cttee, Judicial Studies Bd, 1990–94. Editor, Family Div. section, Butterworth's Cost Service, 1987–2008; Jt Editor, Supreme Court Practice, 1991–94; contributor: Protecting Children Update, 2003–; Education Law Update, 2006–. FLS 2004. *Publications:* Costs Advocacy, 2002; contribs to New Law Jl, Family Law. *Recreation:* living in the past. *Address:* 28 Grange Road, N6 4AP. *T:* (020) 8348 0680. *Clubs:* Garrick, Savage.

SEGAL, Prof. Naomi Dinah, PhD; Director, Institute of Germanic & Romance Studies, School of Advanced Study, University of London, since 2004; *b* 6 Oct. 1949; *d* of Prof. Judah Benzion Segal, FBA and Leah Segal (*née* Seidemann); marr. diss.; one *d* one *s*. *Educ:* Newnham Coll., Cambridge (BA 1972); King's Coll. London (PhD 1978). Fellow, Tutor and Lectr, Queens' Coll., Cambridge, 1980–86; Fellow, Tutor and Lectr, St John's Coll., Cambridge, 1986–93; Prof. of French Studies, Univ. of Reading, 1993–2004. Convenor, Panel 5, Advanced Res., and Mem. Bd, AHRB, 1999–2005; UK Rep., Standing Cttee for Humanities, ESF, 2005–. Chevalier, l'Ordre des palmes académiques, 2005. *Publications:* The Banal Object, 1981; The Unintended Reader, 1986; Narcissus and Echo, 1988; (ed jtly) Freud in Exile, 1988; The Adulteress's Child, 1992; André Gide: pederasty and pedagogy, 1998; (ed jtly) Coming Out of Feminism, 1998; Le Désir à l'œuvre, 2000; (ed jtly) Indeterminate Bodies, 2003; Consensuality, 2008; contrib. numerous articles. *Recreation:* friendship. *Address:* Institute of Germanic and Romance Studies, School of Advanced Study, University of London, Senate House, Malet Street, WC1E 7HU. *T:* (020) 7862 8739, *Fax:* (020) 7862 8672; *e-mail:* naomi.segal@sas.ac.uk.

SEGALL, Anne Celia, (Mrs D. H. Evans); freelance journalist; Economics Correspondent, Daily Telegraph, 1985–2001; *b* 20 April 1948; *d* of John Segall and Marsha (*née* Greenberg); *m* 1973, David Howard Evans, *qv*; two *s*. *Educ:* St Paul's Girls' Sch., London; St Hilda's Coll., Oxford (BA Hons PPE 1969). Banking correspondent: Investors' Chronicle, 1971–76; The Economist, 1976–80; Daily Telegraph, 1981–85. Wincott Award for Financial Journalism, 1975. *Recreations:* swimming, reading, theatre. *Address:* 24 Pembroke Gardens, W8 6HU. *Club:* Lansdowne.

SEGAR, Christopher Michael John, CMG 2004; HM Diplomatic Service, retired; Energy Analyst, Europe, Middle East and North Africa, International Energy Agency, Paris, since 2008; *b* 25 Nov. 1950; *s* of Cyril John Segar and Margery (*née* Angliss). *Educ:* Sevenoaks Sch.; Sidney Sussex Coll., Cambridge (BA Hons). VSO, Cameroun, 1969; joined FCO, 1973; MECAS, 1974–76; Third, later Second Sec., Dubai, 1976–79; FCO, 1979–84; Head of Chancery and Consul, Luanda, 1984–87; UK Delgn to OECD, Paris, 1987–90; Dep. Head of Mission and Consul Gen., Baghdad, 1990–91; on secondment to MoD, 1991–94; Commercial Counsellor: Riyadh, 1994–97; Peking, 1997–2001; Head of Aviation, Maritime, Sci. and Energy Dept, subseq. Aviation, Maritime and Energy Dept, FCO, 2001–03; Head of British Office, Baghdad, 2003–04. Dep. Dir, Centre for Studies in Security and Diplomacy, Univ. of Birmingham, 2006–08. Trustee: Foundn for Relief and Reconciliation in the Middle East, 2006–; Arab-British Centre, 2006–. *Recreations:* music, travel. *Club:* Royal Over-Seas League.

SEGARS, Joanne, OBE 2003; Chief Executive, National Association of Pension Funds, since 2006 (Director of Policy, 2005–06); *b* 5 Dec. 1964; *d* of Terry and Jean Segars; partner, David Coats. *Educ:* Liverpool Poly. (BA Hons Econs 1986); Univ. of Warwick (MA Industrial Relns 1987). Sen. Policy Officer (Pensions), TUC, 1987–2001; Hd, Pensions and Savings, ABI, 2001–05. Mem. Bd, Occupational Pensions Regulatory Authy, 1987–2002. Mem. Council and Gov., Pensions Policy Inst., 2001–. *Recreations:* travel, ski-ing, gardening. *Address:* National Association of Pension Funds, NIOC House, 4 Victoria Street, SW1H 0NX. *T:* (020) 7808 1300, *Fax:* (020) 7222 7585; *e-mail:* napf@napf.co.uk.

SEIFTER, Pavel, PhD; Ambassador of the Czech Republic to the Court of St James's, 1997–2003; Distinguished Visiting Fellow, Centre for the Study of Global Governance, London School of Economics, since 2003; *b* 27 May 1938; *s* of Karel and Anna Seifter; *m*

1st, 1966, Jana Macenauerová; one *d*; 2nd, 1986, Lenka Urbanová; 3rd, 1999, Lesley Chamberlain. *Educ:* Charles Univ., Prague (Hist., Czech Lang. and Lit. degree 1961; PhD Hist. 1968); Centre Universitaire Européen, Nancy, France (postgrad. study). Lectr in Hist., Charles Univ., Prague, 1964–68; translator, window cleaner, editor of dissident histl publications, 1969–89; Deputy Director: Inst. of Contemporary Hist., Prague, 1990–91; Inst. of Internat. Relns, Prague, 1991–92; Dir, Foreign Policy Dept, Office of Pres. of Czech Republic, 1993–97. Visiting Fellow: CISAC, Stanford Univ., 1992; Uppsala Univ., 1992. *Address:* Centre for the Study of Global Governance, Houghton Street, WC2A 2AE.

SEIPP, Walter, Dr jur; Chairman, Supervisory Board, Commerzbank AG, 1991–99, now Hon. Chairman; *b* 13 Dec. 1925. *Educ:* Univ. of Frankfurt (Law studies); final legal examination and doctorate in Law, 1950–53. Military Service, 1943–45. Deutsche Bank AG, 1951–74: Exec. Vice Pres., 1970–74; Vice Chm., UBS-DB Corp., New York, 1972–74; Westdeutsche Landesbank Girozentrale, 1974–81: Mem. Bd, 1974–81, and Dep. Chm. of the Bd, 1977–81; Chm., Bd of Man. Dirs, Commerzbank AG, 1981–91. Pres., Internat. Monetary Conf., 1987–88. *Publications:* multiple. *Address:* (office) Kaiserplatz, 60311 Frankfurt/Main, Germany. *T:* (69) 13620.

SEITLER, Jonathan Simon; QC 2003; barrister; *b* 11 June 1961; *s* of Benjamin and Sandra Seitler; *m* 1988, Sarah Anticoni; one *s* one *d*. *Educ:* Stand Grammar Sch., Whitefield, Manchester; Pembroke Coll., Oxford (BA Hons PPE); City Univ., London (Dip Law). Called to the Bar, Inner Temple, 1985; in practice, specialising in law of property and related professional negligence. *Publications:* Property Finance Negligence: claims against solicitors and valuers, 1995; Commercial Property Disputes: law and practice, 1999. *Address:* Wilberforce Chambers, 8 New Square, Lincoln's Inn, WC2A 3QP. *T:* (020) 7306 0102; *e-mail:* JSeitler@wilberforce.co.uk.

SEITZ, Raymond George Hardenbergh; Vice Chairman, Lehman Brothers, 1996–2003 (a Senior Managing Director, 1995–96); *b* Hawaii, 8 Dec. 1940; *s* of Maj.-Gen. John Francis Regis Seitz and Helen Johnson Hardenbergh; two *s* one *d*; *m* 1985, Caroline Richardson. *Educ:* Yale University (BA History 1963). Joined Foreign Service, Dept of State, 1966; served Montreal, Nairobi, Bukavu, Zaire, 1966–72; Staff Officer, later Director, Secretariat Staff, Washington, Special Asst to Dir Gen., Foreign Service, 1972–75; Political Officer, London, 1975–79; Dep. Exec. Sec., Washington, 1979–81; Senior Dep. Asst Sec., Public Affairs, Washington, 1981–82; Exec. Asst to Secretary George P. Shultz, Washington, 1982–84; Minister and Dep. Chief of Mission, US Embassy, London, 1984–89; Asst Sec. for European and Canadian Affairs, State Dept, Washington, 1989–91; Ambassador to UK, 1991–94. Trustee: Nat. Gall., 1996–2001; Royal Acad., 1996–. Benjamin Franklin Medal, RSA, 1996. Kt Comdr's Cross (Germany), 1991. *Publication:* Over Here (memoir), 1998. *Address:* 10 Pembridge Place, W2 4XB; 39 East Battery, Charleston, SC 29401, USA.

SEKERS, David Nicholas Oliver, OBE 1986; FMA; consultant for heritage, museums and charities; *b* 29 Sept. 1943; *s* of Sir Nicholas Sekers, MBE and Lady Sekers; *m* 1965, Simone, *er d* of late Moran Caplat, CBE; one *d*. *Educ:* Eton; Worcester College, Oxford (BA). Dir, Gladstone Pottery Museum (Museum of the Year 1976), 1973–78; Museum Dir, Quarry Bank Mill (Museum of the Year 1984), 1978–89; Dir, Southern Reg., 1989–98, Dir of the Regions, 1998–2001, Nat. Trust; Specialist Advr, DCMS Select Cttee, 2005–. *Recreations:* growing vegetables, fell-walking. *Address:* Cross House, Henstridge BA8 0QZ. *Club:* Garrick.

SELBORNE, 4th Earl of, *cr* 1882; **John Roundell Palmer,** KBE 1987; FRS 1991; DL; Baron Selborne, 1872; Viscount Wolmer, 1882; Chairman of Trustees, Royal Botanic Gardens, Kew, since 2003 (Trustee, 1993–98); *b* 24 March 1940; *er s* of William Matthew, Viscount Wolmer (killed on active service, 1942), and of Priscilla (who *m* 1948, Hon. Peter Legh, later 4th Baron Newton (*d* 1992); she *m* 1994, Frederick Fryer), *d* of late Captain John Egerton-Warburton; *S* grandfather, 1971; *m* 1969, Joanna Van Antwerp, PhD, *yr d* of Evan Maitland James, *qv*; three *s* one *d*. *Educ:* Eton; Christ Church, Oxford (MA). Chm., AFRC, 1983–90 (Mem., 1975–90; Vice-Chm., 1980–83); Vice-Chm., Apple and Pear Develt Council, 1969–73; Mem., Hops Mktg Bd, 1972–82 (Chm., 1978–82); Pres., British Crop Protection Council, 1977–80; Chm., SE Regl Panel, MAFF, 1979–83. Member: Royal Commn on Environmental Pollution, 1993–98; Govt Panel on Sustainable Develt, 1994–97. Chm., UK Chemical Stakeholder Forum, 2000–04. Chairman: H of L Select Cttee on Sci. and Technol., 1993–97; Sub-Cttee D (Agric. and Food), H of L Select Cttee on European Communities, 1991–93; Sub-Cttee D (Agric., Food, Envmt and Consumer Affairs), H of L Select Cttee on EU, 1999–2003; elected Mem., H of L, 1999; Pres., Parly and Scientific Cttee, 1997–2000. Director: Agricl Mortgage Corp., 1990–2002 (Chm., 1995–2002); Lloyds Bank, 1994–95; Lloyds TSB Gp, 1995–2004. Chm., Jt Nature Conservation Cttee, 1991–97. President: South of England Agric. Soc., 1984; RASE, 1988; Royal Bath & West Agricl Soc., 1995; RGS (with IBG), 1997–2000; Vice-Pres., RSPB, 1996–2007; Chm., Foundn for Sci. and Technol., 2006– (Vice-Pres., 1994–2006). Chancellor, Southampton Univ., 1996–2006. Treas., Bridewell Royal Hosp. (King Edward's Sch., Witley), 1972–83. Mem., Hampshire County Council, 1967–74. FIBiol 1984; FRAgS 1986; FLS, 1994. Master, Mercers' Co., 1989–90. JP Hants 1971–78; DL Hants 1982. Hon. LLD Bristol, 1989; Hon. DSc: Cranfield, 1991; UEA, 1996; Southampton, 1996; Birmingham 2000. *Heir: s* Viscount Wolmer, *qv*. *Address:* Temple Manor, Selborne, Alton, Hants GU34 3LR. *T:* (01420) 473646. *Club:* Travellers.

SELBOURNE, David Maurice; author; *b* 4 June 1937; *s* of Hugh Selbourne, MD and Sulamith Amiel; *m* 1963, Hazel Savage; one *s* one *d*. *Educ:* Manchester Grammar Sch.; Balliol Coll., Oxford (Winter Williams Law Schol., Hon. Exhibnr, Paton Studentship, Jenkins Law Prize, BA Hons, MA). Called to the Bar, Inner Temple, 1960. British Commonwealth Fellow, Univ. of Chicago, 1959; Tutor, Ruskin Coll., Oxford, 1966–86 (Mem. Governing Body, 1973–75). Freelance journalist, 1975–: New Society, New Statesman, Spectator, Independent, Guardian, Tribune, The Times, Sunday Times, Daily Telegraph, Sunday Telegraph, India Today (Delhi), Sunday (Calcutta), *etc.* Member: Chief Minister's Cttee on Human Rights in Sri Lanka, Madras, 1984; Steering Cttee on Ethnic Violence, Dutch Inst. of Human Rights, 1984–85. Vis. Fellow, Europa Inst., Univ. of Leiden, 1964; Aneurin Bevan Meml Fellow, Govt of India, 1975–76; Indian Council of Social Sci. Res. Fellow, New Delhi, 1979–80. Lectures: The Times-Dillon's, LSE, 1994; Geraldine Aves Meml, H of C, 1994; Visiting Lectures, 1975–2005: RIIA; Inst. Commonwealth Studies, Oxford; Jawaharlal Nehru Univ., New Delhi; Aligarh Muslim Univ.; Czech Underground Univ., Prague and Bratislava, 1987, 1989; Berkeley; UCSD; Notre Dame Univ., Indiana, *etc.* Mem., Accademia Rubiconia, Savignano, Italy, 1993. *Plays* performed, 1968–83: Traverse Th., Edinburgh; Everyman Th., Liverpool; Northcott Th., Exeter; Crucible Th., Sheffield; Soho Th., London; People's Th., Calcutta, *etc.* Officer, Order of Merit of the Italian Republic, 2001. *Publications:* The Play of William Cooper and Edmund Dew-Nevett, 1968; The Two-backed Beast, 1969; Samson, 1971; The Damned, 1971; An Eye to China, 1975, 2nd edn 1978; An Eye to India, 1977; Through the Indian Looking-Glass, 1982; The Making of A Midsummer Night's Dream, 1982, 2nd edn 1984; (ed) In Theory and in Practice, 1985; Against Socialist Illusion, 1985; Left Behind: journeys into British politics, 1987; (ed) A Doctor's Life: the diaries of Hugh Selbourne, MD 1960–64, 1989; Death of the Dark Hero: Eastern Europe 1987–1990, 1990; The Spirit of the Age, 1993; Not an Englishman: conversations with Lord Goodman, 1993; The Principle of Duty: an essay on the foundations of the civic order, 1994, 3rd edn 1997; Moral Evasion, 1998; The City of Light, 1997, 2nd edn 1998, other edns in translation, incl. Catalan, Chinese, French, German, Hebrew, Hungarian, Korean, Norwegian, Polish, Portuguese and Spanish, 1997–2002; The Losing Battle with Islam, 2005; contribs to learned jls, incl. Bull. Concerned Asian Scholars, Critique, Electoral Studies, Hist. Workshop Jl, Monthly Review, Social Scientist and Third World Qly. *Recreations:* listening to music, reading, walking, talking. *Address:* c/o Christopher Sinclair-Stevenson, 3 South Terrace, SW7 2TB. *Club:* Oxford and Cambridge.

SELBY, 6th Viscount *cr* 1905, of the City of Carlisle; **Christopher Rolf Thomas Gully;** *b* 18 Oct. 1993; *s* of 5th Viscount Selby and of his 1st wife, Charlotte Cathrine Brege; *S* father, 2001. *Heir: great-uncle* Hon. James Edward Hugh Grey Gully [*b* 17 March 1945; *m* 1971, Fiona Margaret Mackenzie; two *s*].

SELBY, Bishop Suffragan of, since 2003; **Rt Rev. Martin William Wallace;** *b* 16 Nov. 1948; *s* of Derek Philip William Wallace and Audrey Sybil Wallace (*née* Thomason); *m* 1971, Diana Christine Pratt; one *s* one *d*. *Educ:* Varndean Grammar Sch., Brighton; Tauntons Sch., Southampton; King's Coll., London (BD (Hons); AKC; Winchester Schol.); St Augustine's Theol Coll., Canterbury. Ordained deacon, 1971, priest, 1972; Assistant Curate: Attercliffe, Sheffield, 1971–74; New Malden, Surrey, 1974–77; Vicar, St Mark's, Forest Gate, 1977–93 and Priest-in-charge, Emmanuel, 1985–89, All Saints, 1991–93, Forest Gate; Chaplain, Forest Gate Hosp., 1977–80; Rural Dean, Newham, 1982–91; Chelmsford Diocesan Urban Officer, 1991–93; Priest-in-charge, Bradwell and St Lawrence, 1993–97; Industrial Chaplain, Maldon and Dengie, 1993–97; Archdeacon of Colchester, 1997–2003. Hon. Canon, Chelmsford Cathedral, 1989–97. *Publications:* Healing Encounters in the City, 1987; City Prayers, 1994; Pocket Celtic Prayers, 1996; Celtic Resource Book, 1998; (contrib.) Worship: window of the urban Church, 2007. *Recreations:* local history, garden design. *Address:* Bishop's House, Barton-le-Street, Malton, N Yorks YO17 6PL. *T:* (01653) 627191, *Fax:* (01653) 627193; *e-mail:* bishselby@clara.net.

SELBY, Dona Pamela; *d* of Donald and Sybil Davis; *m* 1981, Peter Selby. *Educ:* Bexleyheath Technical High Sch. Royal Mail: Marketing Asst, 1971–76; Marketing Exec., 1976–81; Marketing Manager, 1981–86; Sen. Corporate Manager, WWF, 1989–92; Great Ormond Street Hospital Children's Charity: Head of Commercial and Direct Marketing, then Dir of Fundraising, 1992–2001; Exec. Dir, 2001–06; Dir of Fundraising, Jeans for Genes, 2006–08; Exec. Fundraiser, 2007–08, Trustee 2008–, Orchid. *Recreations:* keep fit, travel, motor racing.

SELBY, Prof. Peter John, CBE 2001; MD; Professor of Cancer Medicine, and Consultant Physician, St James's University Hospital, Leeds, since 1988; Director, Cancer Research UK Clinical Centre (formerly ICRF Cancer Medicine Research Unit), Leeds, since 1993; Joint Director, UK Clinical Research Network, since 2005; *b* 10 July 1950; *s* of Joseph Selby and Dorothy Selby (*née* Cross); *m* 1972, Catherine Elisabeth, *d* of Peter Thomas; one *s* one *d*. *Educ:* Lydney Grammar Sch.; Christ's Coll., Cambridge (MA; MB BChir; MD 1980). FRCP 1990; FRCR 1994. Registrar, Fellow and Sen. Lectr (Consultant), Royal Marsden Hosp. and Inst. Cancer Res., 1977–88; Dir, Clin. Res., ICRF, 1997–2001; Lead Clinician, then Clin. Dir, Leeds Cancer Centre, 1997–2005. Dir, Nat. Cancer Res. Network, 2001–05; Foundn Dir, Leeds Inst. of Molecular Med. and Cancer Res., 2003–06. President: British Oncol Soc., 1992–94; Assoc. of Cancer Physicians, 2008. FMedSci 1998. Pfizer Prize for Excellence in Oncology, British Oncol Soc., 2008. *Publications:* Hodgkin's Disease, 1987; Confronting Cancer: Care and Prevention, 1993; Cancer in Adolescents, 1995; Malignant Lymphomas, 2000; Cell and Molecular Biology of Cancer, 2005. *Recreations:* reading, music, jogging, watching sport. *Address:* 17 Park Lane, Roundhay, Leeds LS8 2EX.

SELBY, Rt Rev. Peter Stephen Maurice, PhD; Bishop of Worcester, 1997–2007; President, National Council for Independent Monitoring Boards, since 2008; *b* 7 Dec. 1941. *Educ:* St John's Coll., Oxford (BA 1964; MA 1967); Episcopal Theol Sch., Cambridge, Mass (BD 1966); Bishops' Coll., Cheshunt; PhD London, 1975. Asst Curate, Queensbury, 1966–68; Associate Dir of Training, Southwark, 1969–73; Asst Curate, Limpsfield with Titsey, 1969–77; Vice-Principal, Southwark Ordination Course, 1970–72; Asst Missioner, Dio. Southwark, 1973–77; Canon Residentiary, Newcastle Cathedral, 1977–84; Diocesan Missioner, Dio. Newcastle, 1977–84; Suffragan Bishop, 1984–91, Area Bishop, 1991–92, of Kingston-upon-Thames; William Leech Professorial Fellow in Applied Christian Theol., Univ. of Durham, 1992–97; Hon. Asst Bishop, dios of Durham and Newcastle, 1992–97, dio. of Portsmouth, 2008–; Bishop to HM Prisons, 2001–07. Visitor Gen., Community of Sisters of the Church, 1991–2001. Vis. Prof., Dept of Theol. and Religious Studies and Internat. Centre for Prison Studies, KCL, 2008–. Charles Gore Lectr, Westminster Abbey, 2006. Mem., Doctrine Commn, 1991–2003. President: Modern Churchpeople's Union, 1990–96; Soc. for Study of Theology, 2003–04. *Publications:* Look for the Living, 1976; Liberating God, 1983; BeLonging, 1991; Rescue, 1995; Grace and Mortgage, 1997.

SELDON, Anthony Francis, PhD; FRHistS; Master of Wellington College, since 2006; *b* 2 Aug. 1953; *s* of late Arthur Seldon, CBE and of (Audrey) Marjorie Seldon (*née* Willett); *m* 1982, Joanna Pappworth; one *s* two *d*. *Educ:* Tonbridge Sch.; Worcester Coll., Oxford (MA 1980); London School of Economics (PhD 1981); KCL (PGCE 1983); MBA Poly. of Central London 1989. FRHistS 1992. Res. Fellow and Tutor, London School of Economics, 1980–81; Consultant Historian, Rio Tinto Zinc, 1981–83; Head of Politics, Whitgift Sch., 1983–86; Co-founder, 1987, and first Dir, 1987–89, Inst. of Contemporary British History; Head of History and Gen. Studies, Tonbridge Sch., 1989–92; Dep. Headmaster, 1993–97, acting Headmaster, 1997, St Dunstan's Coll.; Headmaster, Brighton Coll., 1997–2005. FRSA 1990. Series Ed., Making Contemporary Britain, 1988. Co-founder: Contemporary Record, 1987 (Ed., 1987–95); Modern Hist. Rev., 1988 (Ed., 1989–92); Twentieth Century British Hist., 1989 (Consulting Ed., 1989–91); Contemp. European Hist., 1989 (Consulting Ed., 1989–90). Hon. DLitt Brighton, 2004. *Publications:* Churchill's Indian Summer, 1981; (jtly) By Word of Mouth, 1983; (ed) Contemporary History, 1987; (ed jtly) Ruling Performance, 1987; (ed) Political Parties since 1945, 1988; (ed jtly) Thatcher Effect, 1989; (jtly) Politics UK, 1991; (ed jtly) Conservative Century, 1994; (ed jtly) Major Effect, 1994; (ed jtly) The Heath Government 1970–74, 1996; (ed jtly) Contemporary History Handbook, 1996; (ed jtly) Ideas That Shaped Postwar Britain, 1996; (ed) How Tory Governments Fall: the Conservative Party in power since 1783, 1996; Major: a political biography, 1997; 10 Downing Street: the illustrated history, 1999; (jtly) Britain under Thatcher, 1999; (jtly) The Powers Behind the Prime Minister, 1999; The Foreign Office: an illustrated history of the place and the people, 2000; (ed) The Blair Effect, 2001; (jtly) A New Conservative Century?, 2001; Public and Private Education, 2001; Brave New City, 2002; Partnership not Paternalism, 2002; Blair: the biography, 2004; (ed jtly) Governing or New Labour,

2004; (jtly) The Conservative Party: an illustrated history, 2004; (ed jtly) Recovering Power: the Conservatives in Opposition since 1867, 2005; (ed) The Blair Effect 2, 2001–05: a wasted term?, 2005; Blair Unbound: 2001–07, 2007; (ed) Blair's Britain 1997–2007, 2007; The Future of Independent Schools, 2008. *Recreations:* drama, sport, writing, old sports cars. *Address:* Master's Lodge, Wellington College, Crowthorne, Berks RG45 7PU. *T:* (01344) 444000; *e-mail:* afs@wellingtoncollege.org.uk. *Club:* East India.

SELF, Deborah Jane; *see* Orr, D. J.

SELF, William Woodard; writer, since 1990; *b* 26 Sept. 1961; *s* of late Prof. Peter John Otter Self and of Elaine Self (*née* Rosenbloom); *m* 1st, 1989, Katharine Sylvia Chancellor (marr. diss. 1997); one *s* one *d*; 2nd, 1997, Deborah Jane Orr, *qv*; two *s*. *Educ:* Exeter Coll., Oxford (BA Hons). Freelance cartoonist, 1982–88; Publishing Dir, Cathedral Publishing, 1988–90; contributing editor, London Evening Standard mag., 1993–95; columnist: Observer, 1995–97; The Times, 1998–99; Independent on Sunday, 1999–2001; London Evening Standard, 2002–. *Publications:* The Quantity Theory of Insanity, 1991; Cock & Bull, 1992; My Idea of Fun, 1993; Grey Area, 1994; Junk Mail, 1995; The Sweet Smell of Psychosis, 1996; Great Apes, 1997; Tough Tough Toys for Tough Tough Boys, 1998; Sore Sites, 2000; How the Dead Live, 2000; Perfidious Man, 2000; Feeding Frenzy, 2001; Dorian, 2002; Dr Mukti and Other Tales of Woe, 2004; The Book of Dave, 2006; PsychoGeography, 2007; The Butt, 2008. *Recreation:* walking. *Address:* The Wylie Agency, 17 Bedford Square, WC1B 3JA. *T:* (020) 7908 5900. *Clubs:* Groucho, Colony Room.

SELIGMAN, Sir Peter (Wendel), Kt 1978; CBE 1969; BA; FIMechE; *b* 16 Jan. 1913; *s* of late Dr Richard Joseph Simon Seligman and of Hilda Mary Seligman; *m* 1st, 1937, Elizabeth Lavinia Mary Wheatley (*d* 2005); two *s* three *d* (and one *d* decd); 2nd, 2006, Joan Bruins. *Educ:* King's Coll. Sch., Wimbledon; Harrow Sch.; Kantonschule, Zürich; Caius Coll., Cambridge. Joined APV Co. Ltd, as Asst to Man. Dir, 1936; appointed Dir, 1939; Man. Dir, 1947; Dep. Chm., 1961; Chm., APV Holdings Ltd, 1966–77. Director: St Regis International Ltd, 1973–83 (Vice-Chm., 1981–83); EIBIS International Ltd, 1980–90; Bell Bryant Pty Ltd, 1976–80; St Regis ACI Pty Ltd, 1980–84. Mem., Engineering Industries Council, 1975–77. Mem., Retired Chartered Engrs Assoc., 2003–05. Chm., Nat. Ski Fedn of GB, 1977–81. *Recreation:* travelling. *Address:* Church View, The Street, Thakehan, W Sussex RH20 3EP. *T:* (01798) 815726. *Clubs:* Athenæum; Hawks (Cambridge); Ski of Great Britain (Invitation Life Mem.); Kandahar Ski (Chm., 1972–77; Hon. Mem.).

SELKIRK, Earldom of (*cr* 1646); title disclaimed by 11th Earl (*see under* Selkirk of Douglas, Baron).

SELKIRK OF DOUGLAS, Baron *cr* 1997 (Life Peer), of Cramond in the City of Edinburgh; **James Alexander Douglas-Hamilton;** PC 1996; QC (Scot.) 1996; Member (C) Lothians, Scottish Parliament, 1999–2007; *b* 31 July 1942; 2nd *s* of 14th Duke of Hamilton, and *b* of 15th Duke of Hamilton, *qv*; disclaimed Earldom of Selkirk, 1994, prior to succession being determined in his favour, 1996; *m* 1974, Hon. Priscilla Susan Buchan, *d* of 2nd Baron Tweedsmuir, CBE, CD, and late Baroness Tweedsmuir of Belhelvie, PC; four *s* (incl. twins). *Educ:* Eton College; Balliol Coll., Oxford (MA, Mod. History; Oxford Boxing Blue, 1961; Pres., Oxford Univ. Cons. Assoc., 1963; Pres., Oxford Union Soc., 1964); Edinburgh Univ. (LLB, Scots Law). Cameronian Officer, 6th/7th Bn of Cameronians (Scottish Rifles), 1961–66; 2nd Bn of Lowland Vols, 1971–74, Capt., 1973. Advocate at Scots Bar and Procurator Fiscal Depute, 1968–72. Town Councillor, Murrayfield-Cramond, Edinburgh, 1972–74. MP (C) Edinburgh West, Oct. 1974–1997; contested (C) same seat, 1997. Scottish Conservative Whip, 1977; a Lord Comr of HM Treasury, and Govt Whip for Scottish Cons. Mems, 1979–81; PPS to Foreign Office Minister, 1983–86, to Sec. of State for Scotland, 1986–87; Parly Under-Sec. of State for Home Affairs and the Envmt, 1987–92, for Educn and Housing, 1992–95, Scottish Office; Minister of State for Home Affairs and Health, Scottish Office, 1995–97. Scottish Parliament: Business Manager and Chief Whip, Conservative Gp, 1997–2000; spokesman on home affairs, 2000–03, on education, 2003–07. Captain Cameronian Co., 2 Bn Low Vols RARO, 1972–92. Hon. Air Cdre, No 2 (City of Edinburgh) Maritime HQ Unit, 1994–99; Hon. Air Cdre, 603 (City of Edinburgh) Sqn, RAAF, 1999–; Pres., Internat. Rescue Corps, 1995. Hon. Pres., Scottish Amateur Boxing Assoc., 1975–99; President: Royal Commonwealth Soc. in Scotland, 1979–87; Scottish Council, UNA, 1981–87. Mem. Royal Co. of Archers, Queen's Body Guard for Scotland. Patron, Hope and Homes for Children, 2002– (Chm., Edinburgh Support Gp, 2002–07); Pres., Scottish Veterans Garden City Assoc. Inc., 2003–. *Publications:* Motive for a Mission: The Story Behind Hess's Flight to Britain, 1971; The Air Battle for Malta: the diaries of a fighter pilot, 1981, 2nd edn 1990; Roof of the World: man's first flight over Everest, 1983; The Truth About Rudolf Hess, 1993. *Recreations:* golf, forestry. *Heir: (to Earldom of Selkirk): s* Hon. John Andrew Douglas-Hamilton, Master of Selkirk, *b* 8 Feb. 1978. *Address:* House of Lords, SW1A 0PW. *Clubs:* Pratt's; New (Edinburgh); Hon. Company of Edinburgh Golfers.

SELL, Rev. Prof. Alan Philip Frederick, DD, DLitt, PhD; FRHistS; philosopher-theologian and ecumenist; *b* 15 Nov. 1935; *s* of Arthur Philip Sell and Freda Marion Sell (*née* Bushen); *m* 1959, Dr Karen Elisabeth Lloyd; one *s* two *d*. *Educ:* Pewley Sch., Guildford; Univ. of Manchester (Cert Biblical Knowledge 1954; BA, BD, MA; DD 1998); Univ. of Nottingham (PhD 1967; DLitt 2006). LTCL 1981, FTCL 1983; LGSM (Public Speaking) 1981, LGSM (Speech and Drama) 1982; LLAM 1982; FRHistS 1980. Ordained, Congregational Ch, 1959; Minister: Sedbergh and Dent, 1959–64; Angel St, Worcester with Hallow and Ombersley, 1964–68; Lectr, Sen. Lectr, then Prin. Lectr, 1968–83, Coll. Counsellor, 1970–83, W Midlands Coll. of Higher Educn; Tutor, Open Univ., 1970–73; Theol Sec., World Alliance of Reformed Churches (Presbyterian and Congregational), Geneva, 1983–87; Chair of Christian Thought, Univ. of Calgary, 1988–92; Prof. of Christian Doctrine and Philosophy of Religion, United Theol Coll., Aberystwyth, 1992–2001. Visiting Professor: Acadia Divinity Coll., 1996–2006; Phillips Theol Seminary, 1998; Hon. Prof., Sárospatak Theol. Acad., Hungary, 1996. External examiner at numerous univs. Lectures include: Simpson, Acadia, 1989; Staley, Union Coll., Ky, 1991; Congregational, London, 1991; Alfred Stocks, Liverpool, 1993; Ingram, Memphis, 1996; Davies, Wales, 2001; Protestant Dissenting Deputies, 2001; Christianity and Culture, St Francis Xavier Univ., 2003; Didsbury, Manchester, 2006. Dist. Fellow, Acadia Divinity Coll., 2005. Chairman: World Church and Mission Dept and Dir of Auxiliary Trng, W Midlands Province, URC; Worcester Council of Churches; Pres., Worcester and Dist Free Church Fed. Council. Member: Exec. Cttee, and County Sec. for Youth and Educn, Worcs Congregational Union; Doctrine and Worship Cttee, URC, 1980–83, 1993–96, 2004–07; Doctrine Cttee, Presbyterian Church of Wales, 1993–2001. Founder: Eighteenth Century Studies Gp, Univ. of Calgary, 1988; Centre for Study of British Christian Thought, United Theol Coll., Aberystwyth, 1993; Assoc. of Denominational Historical Socs and Cognate Libraries, 1993. Vice-Pres., Friends of Dr Williams's Liby, 1983; Chm., Friends of the Congregational Liby, 2006–. Member: Amer. Theol Soc.; Soc. for the Study of Theol. Member: Sedburgh Rural DC; Yorks Rural Churches Commission. Hon. DD: Ursinus Coll., USA, 1988; Acadia, Canada, 2002; Hon. DrTheol: Debrecen, Hungary, 1995; Cluj, Romania, 2003. *Publications:* Alfred Dye, Minister of the Gospel, 1974; Robert Mackintosh, Theologian of Integrity, 1977; God Our Father, 1980; The Great Debate: Calvinism, Arminianism and Salvation, 1983; Church Planting: a study of Westmorland Nonconformity, 1986; Theology in Turmoil: the roots, course and significance of the Conservative-Liberal debate in modern theology, 1986; Saints: Visible, Orderly and Catholic: the Congregational idea of the Church, 1986; Defending and Declaring the Faith: some Scottish examples 1860–1920, 1987; The Philosophy of Religion 1875–1980, 1988; Aspects of Christian Integrity, 1990; Dissenting Thought and the Life of the Churches: studies in an English tradition, 1990; A Reformed, Evangelical, Catholic Theology: the contribution of the World Alliance of Reformed Churches 1875–1982, 1991; Commemorations: studies in Christian thought and history, 1993; Philosophical Idealism and Christian Belief, 1995; John Locke and the Eighteenth-Century Divines, 1997; Mill and Religion: contemporary responses to Three Essays on Religion, 1997; Christ Our Saviour, 2000; The Spirit Our Life, 2000; Confessing and Commending the Faith: historic witness and Apologetic Method, 2002; Philosophy, Dissent and Nonconformity 1689–1920, 2004; Mill on God: the pervasiveness and elusiveness of Mill's religious thought, 2004; Testimony and Tradition: studies in reformed and dissenting thought, 2005; Enlightenment, Ecumenism, Evangel: theological themes and thinkers 1550–2000, 2005; Nonconformist Theology in the Twentieth Century, 2006; Hinterland Theology: a stimulus to theological construction, 2008; *Festschrift*: Ecumenical and Eclectic, ed Anna M. Robbins, 2007; Series Editor: Philosophy and Christian Thought 1700–1900, 1998–2000; Studies in Christian History and Thought, 2004–; Christian Doctrines in Historical Perspective, 2004–; Protestant Nonconformist Texts, 4 vols, 2006–07; edited books; dictionary articles, and articles and reviews in theol, philosophical and historical jls. *Recreations:* music, dissenting and university history, British dance bands 1930–50. *Address: e-mail:* alan@theolsing.co.uk.

SELLAPAN, Ramanathan, (S R Nathan); President, Republic of Singapore, since 1999; *b* 3 July 1924; *s* of V. Sellapan and Madam Abirami; *m* 1958, Urmila, (Umi), Nandey; one *s* one *d*. *Educ:* Anglo-Chinese Primary and Middle Sch.; Rangoon Rd Afternoon Sch.; Victoria Sch.; Univ. of Malaya in Singapore (Dip. Social Studies with Dist. 1954). Clerical Service, Johore Govt (Malaya), 1945–55; Almoner, Medical Dept, Gen. Hosp., Singapore, 1955–56; Seamen's Welfare Officer, Min. of Labour, 1956–62; Asst Dir, 1962–63, Dir, 1964–66, Labour Res. Unit; Ministry of Foreign Affairs, Singapore: Asst Sec., 1966; Principal Asst Sec., 1966–67; Dep. Sec., 1967–71; Perm. Sec. (Actg), Min. of Home Affairs, 1971; Dir, Security and Intelligence Div., MoD, 1971–79; First Perm. Sec., Min. of Foreign Affairs, 1979–82; Exec. Chm., Straits Times Press, 1982–88; High Comr to Malaysia, 1988–90; Ambassador to USA, 1990–96; Ambassador-at-Large, Min. of Foreign Affairs, 1996–99; Dir, Inst. of Defence and Strategic Studies, Nanyang Technol Univ., 1996–99. Chm., Mitsubishi Singapore Heavy Industries (Pte) Ltd, 1973–86; Director: Singapore Nat. Oil Co. (Pte), 1980–88; Singapore Mint Pte, 1983–88; Singapore Press Hldgs, 1984–88; Marshall Cavendish, London, 1985–88; Singapore Internat. Media Pte, 1996–99. Chm., Hindu Endowments Bd, 1983–88; Mem. Bd of Trustees, NTUC Res. Unit, 1983–88; Founding Mem. and Trustee, Singapore Indian Develt Assoc., 1997–99. Pro-Chancellor, National Univ. of Singapore, 1996–99. Mem., Bd of Govs, CS Coll., 1997–99. Public Service Star (Singapore), 1964; Public Admin Medal (Silver) (Singapore), 1967; PJG (Meritorious Service Medal) (Singapore), 1974. *Recreations:* walking, reading. *Address:* President's Office, Istana, Orchard Road, Singapore 238823. *T:* 67375522.

SELLAR, W(illiam) David H(amilton); Lord Lyon King of Arms and Secretary of the Order of the Thistle, since 2008; *b* Burnside, Rutherglen, 27 Feb. 1941; *s* of William and Esther Sellar; *m* 1981, Susan Bonar (*née* Sainsbury); three *s*, and one step *s*. *Educ:* Kelvinside Acad.; Fettes Coll.; Univ. of Oxford (BA Hons Hist.); Univ. of Edinburgh (LLB). Legal Assessor, Scottish Land Court, 1967–68; Lectr, Sen. Lectr and Hon. Fellow, Faculty of Law, Univ. of Edinburgh, 1968–. Mem., Ancient Monuments Bd for Scotland, 1991–98. Sec., Co. of Scottish Hist. Ltd, 1972–77; Literary Dir, Stair Soc., 1979–84; Pres., Scottish Soc. for Northern Studies, 1984–87; Chm. Council, Scottish Hist. Soc., 1998–2001; Vice-Pres., Soc. of Antiquaries of Scotland, 1999–2002. Bute Pursuivant of Arms, 2001–08. *Publications:* articles and contribs on genealogy, history, law and legal history. *Recreations:* genealogy, golf, island hopping, numismatics. *Address:* The Court of the Lord Lyon, HM New Register House, Edinburgh EH1 3YT. *T:* (0131) 556 7255, *Fax:* (0131) 557 2148.

SELLARS, John Ernest, CBE 1994; Chief Executive, Business and Technology (formerly Business and Technician) Education Council, 1983–94; *b* 5 Feb. 1936; *s* of late Ernest Buttle Sellars and Edna Grace Sellars; *m* 1958, Dorothy Beatrice (*née* Morrison); three *d*. *Educ:* Wintringham Grammar Sch., Grimsby; Manchester Univ. (BSc, MSc). Research Engineer, English Electric (GW) Ltd, 1958–61; Lectr, Royal College of Advanced Technology (now Univ. of Salford), 1961–67; Head of Mathematics, Lanchester College of Technology, Coventry, 1967–71; Head of Computer Science, Lanchester Polytechnic, Coventry/Rugby, 1971–74; Chief Officer, Business Educn Council, 1974–83. Member: Bd, Nat. Adv. Body for Public Sector Higher Educn, 1982–88; BBC School Broadcasting Council for UK, 1982–87; City Technology Colls Trust, 1989–94; Engrg and Technol. Adv. Cttee, British Council, 1990–95; Engrg Council, 1994–95 (Mem., Standing Cttee for Engrg Profession, 1994–95); British Accreditation Council for Indep., Further and Higher Educn, 1999–2002. Mem. Exec. Cttee, RoSPA, 1994–2002. Governor, London Guildhall Univ., 1994–2000. Trustee, Gatsby Technical Educn Projects, 1999–2005. Hon. FCP 1989. DUniv Sheffield Hallam, 1994; Hon. DTech London Guildhall, 2001. *Publications:* papers on mathematics, computer science and business educn. *Recreation:* walking. *Clubs:* Reform, MCC.

SELLARS, Peter; American opera and theatre director; *b* 27 Sept. 1957. *Educ:* Phillips Acad., Mass; Harvard Univ. (BA 1980). Artistic Director: Boston Shakespeare Co., 1983–84; American Nat. Theater at Kennedy Center for the Performing Arts, 1984; LA Fest., 1990, 1993. Prof. of World Arts and Cultures, UCLA. *Productions* include: Armida, Monadnock Music Fest., 1981; The Mikado, Lyric Opera of Chicago, 1983; Così fan tutte, Castle Hill Fest., Mass, 1984; The Electrification of the Soviet Union, Glyndebourne Touring Opera, 1987; Nixon in China, Houston, 1987, ENO, 2000; Die Zauberflöte, Glyndebourne, 1990; The Persians, Edinburgh Fest., 1993; Pelléas and Mélisande, Amsterdam, 1993; The Merchant of Venice, Barbican, 1994; Mathis der Maler, Royal Opera House, 1995; Theodora, Glyndebourne, 1996; The Rake's Progress, 1996, El Niño, 2000, L'Amour de Loin, 2001, Châtelet, Paris; Idomeneo, Glyndebourne, 2003; Tristan und Isolde, Opéra Nat. de Paris, 2005; Zaïde, Barbican, 2006.

SELLARS, Wendy Jane; *see* Lloyd, W. J.

SELLERS, Ann H.; *see* Henderson-Sellers.

SELLERS, Basil Alfred, AM 2003; Chairman, Sellers Group, since 1987; *b* 19 June 1935; *s* of William Alfred Sellers and Irene Ethel Sellers (*née* Freemantle); *m* 2nd, 1980, Gillian Clare Heinrich; two *s* one *d* from previous marr. *Educ:* King's College, Adelaide, SA.

Clerk, State Bank of SA, 1952; Clerk, Cutten & Harvey, Adelaide, 1954–69 (Investment Advr, 1969); owner, Devon Homes, SA, 1970; bought Ralph Symonds Ltd, 1975 (Man. Dir); Chm., Gestetner plc, 1987–94. *Recreations:* cricket, art, music. *Address:* 43 William Street, Double Bay, NSW 2028, Australia. *Clubs:* MCC, Cricketers'; University (Australia).

SELLERS, Geoffrey Bernard, CB 1991; Parliamentary Counsel, since 1987; *b* 5 June 1947; *s* of late Bernard Whittaker Sellers and Elsie (*née* Coop); *m* 1971, Susan Margaret Faulconbridge (*d* 1995); two *s* two *d*. *Educ:* Manchester Grammar Sch. (Scholar); Magdalen Coll., Oxford (Mackinnon Scholar; BCL 1st Cl. Hons; MA). Called to the Bar, Gray's Inn, 1971 (Macaskie Scholar). Legal Assistant: Law Commn, 1971; Commn on Industrial Relations, 1971–74; joined Office of Parly Counsel, 1974; with Law Commn, 1982–85, and 1991–93; with Inland Revenue, 1996–99. *Address:* (office) 36 Whitehall, SW1A 2AY. *Club:* Royal Automobile.

See also J. M. Sellers.

SELLERS, John Marsland, CB 2005; Parliamentary Counsel, since 1998; on secondment to Tax Law Rewrite Project, since 2007; *b* 15 July 1951; *s* of late Bernard Whittaker Sellers and Elsie (*née* Coop); *m* 1975, Patricia Susan Burns; two *s*. *Educ:* Manchester Grammar Sch.; Magdalen Coll., Oxford (BA, BCL). Lecturer: Lincoln Coll., Oxford, 1973–75; LSE, 1975–77; Articled Clerk, 1977–80, Solicitor, 1980–83, Freshfields; Asst Parly Counsel, 1983–88; Sen. Asst Parly Counsel, 1988–91; Dep. Parly Counsel, 1991–98; on secondment to Law Commn, 1998–2001. *Address:* Office of the Parliamentary Counsel, 36 Whitehall, SW1A 2AY. *T:* (020) 7438 6676.

See also G. B. Sellers.

SELLERS, Philip Edward, CBE 2001; Advisor, Nomura Asset Management, since 2002; Chairman, Nuclear Decommissioning Programme Board, Department of Trade and Industry, 2003–05; *b* 20 March 1937; *s* of George Edward and Helen Sellers; *m* 1962, Brenda Anne Bell; two *s*. *Educ:* Ernest Bailey Grammar School, Matlock; CIPFA. Local Govt, 1953–72; Controller of Audit, British Gas Corp., 1972–76; Finance Dir, North Thames Gas, 1976–80; Dir of Finance and Planning, British Rail Board, 1980–84; Board Mem. for Corporate Finance and Planning, Post Office, 1984–89. Mem., Postel Property Cttee, 1992–94; non-exec. Dir, Postel Investment Management, 1994–95; Trustee, Post Office Pension Funds, 1985–99; Chm., Audit Cttee, DTI, 1994–2003. Non-executive Chairman: CSL Group, 1989–93; ICL Outsourcing Ltd (formerly CFM Group Ltd, then ICL/CFM), 1989–99; Pegasus Group plc, 1992–2000; Inner City Enterprises, 1992–98; Powerleague Soccer Centres Ltd (formerly Powerplay Supersoccer Ltd), 1995–99; Workplace Technologies plc, 1995–99; Alexander Mann Associates Ltd, 1997–; Dep. Chm., Powerleague Ltd, 1999–2001; non-exec. Dir, Etam Gp, 1991–98. UK rep., IFAC Public Sector Cttee, 1987–90; Philip Sellers Communications and Consultancy, 1989–. Mem., NCC Impact Adv. Bd, 1989–92. Pres., CIPFA, 1985–86; Chm., Nationalised Industries Finance Panel, 1986–89. Non-exec. Dir, London Festival Orch., 1994–98. *Recreations:* tennis, ski-ing. *Address:* Yarrimba, 31 Howards Thicket, Gerrards Cross, Bucks SL9 7NT. *T:* (01753) 893489.

SELLERS, Robert Firth, ScD; FRSE; MRCVS; consultant on foreign animal diseases; *b* 9 June 1924; *s* of Frederick Sellers and Janet Walkinshaw Shiels; *m* 1951, Margaret Peterkin; one *s* one *d*. *Educ:* Christ's Hospital; Gonville and Caius Coll., Cambridge (MA, ScD); Royal (Dick) School of Veterinary Studies, Edinburgh (PhD, BSc). FIBiol. Served War, Royal Artillery, 1943–46. Research Institute (Animal Virus Diseases), Pirbright, 1953–58; Wellcome Research Laboratories, Beckenham, 1958–62; Instituto Venezolano de Investigaciones Cientificas, Venezuela, 1962–64; Animal Virus Research Institute, Pirbright, 1964–84, Dep. Dir, 1964–79, Dir, 1979–84; Consultant, Foreign Animal Disease Unit, Agriculture, Canada, 1985–88. J. T. Edwards Meml Medal, 1976. *Publications:* papers on animal viruses in scientific jls. *Recreation:* archaeology. *Address:* 4 Pewley Way, Guildford, Surrey GU1 3PY.

SELLIER, Robert Hugh, FICE; Chief Executive, Y. J. Lovell, 1991–95; *b* 15 Nov. 1933; *s* of Major Philip Joseph Sellier and Lorna Geraldine Sellier (*née* Luxton); *m* 1st, 1963, Cynthia Ann Dwelly (*d* 1985); one *d*; 2nd, 1987, Gillian Dalley (*née* Clark). *Educ:* St Joseph's Coll., Oxford; King's Coll., Durham Univ. (BScCivEng). FIHT. Man. Dir, New Ideal Homes, 1972–74; Dep. Man. Dir, Cementation International, 1974–79; Man. Dir, Cementation Construction, 1979–83; Chm., Cementation Gp of Companies, 1983–86; Gp Man. Dir, George Wimpey, 1986–91. Non-exec. Dir, Hyder plc, 1993–2000. *Recreations:* ski-ing, shooting, scuba, flying. *Address:* Mullions, 4 Trulls Hatch, Argos Hill, Rotherfield, Crowborough, E Sussex TN6 3QL. *T:* (01892) 853752.

SELLORS, Sir Patrick (John) Holmes, KCVO 1999 (LVO 1990); FRCS, FRCOphth; Surgeon-Oculist to the Queen, 1980–99; Ophthalmic Surgeon, King Edward VIIth Hospital for Officers, 1975–99; *b* 11 Feb. 1934; *s* of Sir Thomas Holmes Sellors, DM, MCh, FRCP, FRCS; *m* 1961, Gillian Gratton Swallow; two *s* one *d*. *Educ:* Rugby Sch.; Oriel Coll., Oxford (MA; BM, BCh 1958); Middlesex Hosp. Med. Sch. FRCS 1965; FRCOpthth 1990. Registrar, Moorfields Eye Hosp., 1962–65; recognised teacher in Ophthalmology, St George's Hosp., 1966; Ophthalmic Surgeon: St George's Hosp., 1965–82 (Hon., 1983); Croydon Eye Unit, 1970–94; Surgeon-Oculist to HM Household, 1974–80; Hon. Consultant Ophthalmic Surgeon, St Luke's Hosp. for the Clergy, 1983–96. Sec. to Ophthalmic Soc. of UK, 1970–72; Examr for Diploma of Ophthalmology, 1974–77; Pres., Ophthalmology Section, RSocMed, 1992–94; Vice-Pres., Coll. of Ophthalmologists, 1992–96 (Mem. Council, 1988–96); Member, Council: Faculty of Ophthalmologists, 1977–88; Med. Defence Union, 1977–2003; Gen. Optical Council, 1978–96. Dep. Master, Oxford Congress, 1991. *Publications:* (jtly) Outline in Ophthalmology, 1985, 2nd edn 1994; articles in BMJ and Trans OSUK. *Recreations:* gardening, golf. *Address:* The Summer House, Sandy Lane, West Runton, Cromer, Norfolk NR27 9NB.

SELLS, Oliver Matthew; QC 1995; a Recorder of the Crown Court, since 1991; *b* 29 Sept. 1950; *s* of late Sir David Perronet Sells and Beryl Cecilia Sells (*née* Charrington); *m* 1986, Lucinda Jane, *d* of late Gerard William Mackworth-Young and Lady Eve Mackworth-Young; one *s* one *d*. *Educ:* St Peter's, Seaford; Wellington Coll.; Coll. of Law, London. Mem., Hon. Soc. of Inner Temple, 1969–; called to the Bar, Inner Temple, 1972, Bencher, 1996; SE Circuit, 1974–; Supplementary Counsel to the Crown, 1981–86. Chm., SE Circuit Liaison Cttee, 1998–2007. Member: Gen. Council of the Bar, 1977–80 and 1986–91; Commonwealth Law Assoc.; Hon. Mem., Amer. Bar Assoc.; Dir, Music for Charity. Trustee, Breckland Soc. *Recreations:* shooting, cricket, fishing. *Address:* 5 Paper Buildings, Temple, EC4Y 7HB. *T:* (020) 7583 6117. *Clubs:* Boodle's, MCC; Norfolk (Norwich); Royal West Norfolk Golf.

SELLS, Robert Anthony, FRCS, FRCSE; Consultant Surgeon, Royal Liverpool University Hospital (formerly Liverpool Royal Infirmary), 1970–2005; *b* 13 April 1938; *s* of Rev. William Blyth Sells and Eleanor Mary Sells; *m* 1st, 1964, Elizabeth Lucy Schryver (marr. diss. 1976); two *s* one *d*; 2nd, 1977, Pauline Gilchrist Muir; two *s*. *Educ:* Christ's Hosp. Sch., Horsham; Guy's Hosp. Med. Sch., Univ. of London (MB BS). FRCS 1966; FRCSE 1966. Lecturer, Department of Surgery: Guy's Hosp. Med. Sch., 1966–67; Univ. of Cambridge, 1967–69; MRC Travelling Schol., Univ. of Harvard, 1969–70; Dir of Transplantation, 1970–97, Dir of Surgery, 1997–99, Royal Liverpool Univ. Hosp.; Hon. Prof. of Surgery and Immunology, Univ. of Liverpool, 1998–. Vis. Professor: Detroit Univ., 1977; Adelaide Univ., 1984; Minnesota Univ., 1984–85; London Univ., 1998. Gen. Sec. and Pres., British Transplantation Society, 1978–86; Mem. Council, Chm. of Ethics Cttee and Vice Pres., The Transplantation Soc., 1986–94; Vice Pres., Inst. of Med. Ethics, 1986–; Co-Founder and Chm., Internat. Forum for Transplant Ethics, 1995–; Pres., Liverpool Med. Instn, 1997–98 (Mem., 1972–). Principal Conductor and Musical Dir, Crosby SO, 1982–; Hon. Pres., Aberwheeler Show, 1995. Hon. Fellow, Amer. Soc. of Transplant Surgeons, 1978–. *Publications:* (ed jtly) Transplantation Today, 1983; (ed jtly) Organ Transplantation: Current Clinical and Immunological Concepts, 1989; papers on transplantation and bioethics in med. jls. *Recreations:* collecting Victorian pickle jars, orchestral and choral conducting. *Address:* Cil Llwyn, Bodfari, Denbighshire LL16 4HY. *T:* (01745) 710296. *Clubs:* Moynihan Chirurgical Travelling (Pres., 2000–01), Twenty (Liverpool).

SELLWOOD, Philip Henry George; Chief Executive Officer, Energy Saving Trust, since 2003; *b* 10 Jan. 1954; *s* of Albert Edward Sellwood and Irene Sellwood; *m* 1977, Lynn Ann Harris (marr. diss. 2005); one *s* one *d*; partner, Susan Hollis; one *d*. *Educ:* Nottingham Univ. (BEd); Univ. of Westminster (MBA Dist.). Marks & Spencer plc, 1977–2000: Commercial Exec.; Dir, Gp Strategy, 1998–2000; Man. Dir, Thresher Gp, 2000–02. Non-executive Director: Veos plc, 1999–2002; Marks & Spencer Financial Services, 1998–2001; Criminal Records Bureau, 2000–03; Improvement and Develt Agency, 2002–. Member: Adv. Bd, Nat. Consumer Council, 2003–; Sustainable Bldgs Task Force, 2004–05; UK Energy Res. Council, 2005–; LGA Climate Commn, 2007–. FCMI; FRSA. *Recreations:* reading, wine, cricket, theatre. *Address:* The Beach House, 30 Val Prinseps Road, Pevensey Bay, E Sussex BN24 6JG. *T:* (01323) 762064, 07831 829888; *e-mail:* philip_sellwood@hotmail.com. *Club:* London Cricket.

SELOUS, Andrew Edmund Armstrong; MP (C) Bedfordshire South West, since 2001; *b* 27 April 1962; *s* of late Gerald M. B. Selous, OBE, VRD, and Miranda Selous (*née* Casey); *m* 1993, Harriet Marston; three *d*. *Educ:* London Sch. of Econs (BSc Econ). ACII 1993. Great Lakes Re (UK) PLC, 1991–2001. Served TA, HAC and RRF, 1981–94. *Recreation:* family life. *Address:* House of Commons, SW1A 0AA. *Clubs:* Leighton Buzzard Conservative, Dunstable Conservative.

SELSDON, 3rd Baron *cr* 1932, of Croydon; **Malcolm McEacharn Mitchell-Thomson;** Bt 1900; banker; *b* 27 Oct. 1937; *s* of 2nd Baron Selsdon (3rd Bt, *cr* 1900), DSC; *S* father, 1963; *m* 1st, 1965, Patricia Anne (marr. diss.), *d* of Donald Smith; one *s*; 2nd, 1995, Gabrielle Tesseron (*née* Williams). *Educ:* Winchester College. Sub-Lieut, RNVR. Deleg. to Council of Europe and WEU, 1972–78. C. T. Bowring Gp, 1972–76; Midland Bank Group, 1976–90: EEC Advr, 1979–85; Public Finance Advr, 1985–90. Dir of various companies. Chm., Committee for Middle East Trade (COMET), 1979–86; Member: BOTB, 1983–86; E European Trade Council, 1985–87. Pres., British Exporters Assoc., 1990–98. Elected Mem., H of L, 1999. Chm., Greater London and SE Regional Council for Sport and Recreation, 1977–83. *Recreations:* rackets, squash, tennis, lawn tennis, ski-ing, sailing. *Heir:* *s* Hon. Callum Malcolm McEacharn Mitchell-Thomson [*b* 7 Nov. 1969; *m* 1999, Vanessa, *d* of Stefan Glasmacher]. *Address:* c/o House of Lords, SW1A 0PW. *Club:* MCC.

SELTEN, Prof. Reinhard J., PhD; Professor of Economics, University of Bonn, 1984–96, now Emeritus; Research Co-ordinator, Laboratory for Experimental Research in Economics, University of Bonn, since 1984; *b* 5 Oct. 1930; *s* of Adolf Selten and Käthe Selten; *m* 1959, Elisabeth. *Educ:* Univ. of Frankfurt (Dip. Maths; PhD Maths 1961). Asst posts in econs, Frankfurt, 1975–67; Vis. Prof., Schs of Business Admin, Univ. of Calif., Berkeley, 1967–68; privat docent, econs, Frankfurt, 1968–69; Professor of Economics: Berlin, 1969–72; Bielefeld, 1972–84. Fellow: Econometric Soc.; European Economic Assoc. Hon. PhD (Economics): Bielefeld, 1989; Frankfurt, 1991; Graz, 1996; Breslau, 1996; UEA, 1997; Hon. Dr: Ecole Normale Supérieure de Cachan, Paris, 1998; Innsbruck, 2000; Chinese Univ. of Hong Kong, 2003; Osnabruck, 2006. (Jtly) Nobel Prize in Economics, 1994. Bundesverdienstkreuz am Band mit Stern (Germany); Verdienstorden für Wissenschaft und Kunst (Germany), 2006. *Publications:* Preispolitik der Mehrproduktenunternehmung in der Statischen Theorie, 1970; (with T. H. Marschak) General Equilibrium with Price Making Firms, 1974; Models of Strategic Rationality, 1988; (with John C. Harsanyi) A General Theory of Equilibrium Selection in Games, 1988. *Recreation:* hiking. *Address:* Hardtweg 23, 53639 Königswinter, Germany. *T:* (2223) 23610.

SELVANAYAGAM, Rev. Dr Israel; Principal, United Theological College, Bangalore, since 2007; *b* 10 March 1951; *s* of Samuel and Nallathai Selvanayagam; *m* 1977, Gnana Leelal; two *d*. *Educ:* Kerala Univ. (MA); Serampore Coll. (BD 1978; DTh 1990); Tamilnadu Theol Seminary. Probationer in church ministry, Kanyakumari dio., Ch of S India, 1969–73; ministerial training, 1973–77; on staff of Tamilnadu Theol Seminary, Madurai, S India, teaching religions, mission and inter-faith dialogue with special responsibilities in lay theol educn, prog. on dialogue and editing Tamil theol books, 1977–96; ordained deacon, 1980, presbyter, 1981; World Ch Tutor, World Ch in Britain Partnership, Wesley Coll., Bristol, 1996–2000; Principal, United Coll. of the Ascension, Birmingham, 2001–06; Interfaith Consultant, Heartlands Team of Elandon Circuit, Birmingham Dist of Methodist Ch, 2006. Advr for Inter-faith Dialogue, WCC, 1991–98. *Publications:* A Dialogue on Dialogue, 1995; The Dynamics of Hindu Religious Traditions, 1996; Gospel and Culture in Tamilnadu, 1996; Vedic Sacrifice, 1996; A Second Call, 2000; (ed) Moving Forms of Theology, 2002; Relating to People of Other Faiths, 2004; contribs to learned jls incl. Asian Jl Theol., Current Dialogue. *Recreations:* music, composing Tamil songs, swimming.

SELVARATNAM, Vasanti Emily Indrani, (Mrs P. Capewell); QC 2001; a Recorder, since 2000; *b* 9 April 1961; *d* of late George H. Selvaratnam and Wendy L. Selvaratnam (*née* Fairclough); *m* 1989, Phillip Capewell; one *s*. *Educ:* King's Coll., London (AKC 1982; LLB Hons 1982, LLM 1st Cl. 1984); Inns of Court Sch. of Law. Called to the Bar, Middle Temple, 1983; in practice as barrister, specialising in commercial and shipping law, 1985–; Asst Recorder, Western Circuit, 1999–2000. *Recreations:* fine dining, foreign travel, horse riding. *Address:* (chambers) Stone Chambers, 4 Field Court, Gray's Inn, WC1R 5EF. *T:* (020) 7440 6900. *Clubs:* Royal Automobile; Phyllis Court (Henley-on-Thames).

SELVEY, Michael Walter William; Cricket Correspondent, The Guardian, since 1987; *b* 25 April 1948; *s* of late Walter Edwin Selvey and of Edith Milly Selvey; *m* 1st, 1970, Mary Evans (marr. diss. 1991); one *d*; 2nd, 1992, Sarah (*née* Taylor); two *s* one *d* (triplets). *Educ:* Battersea Grammar Sch.; Univ. of Manchester (BSc Geog.); Emmanuel Coll., Cambridge (Cert Ed). Professional cricketer: Middlesex, 1972–82; Glamorgan, 1983–84 (Capt.); played 3 Tests for England: two *v* West Indies, 1976; one *v* India, 1977. Journalist, Guardian, 1985–. *Publication:* The Ashes Surrendered, 1989. *Recreations:* golf, fitness, cooking, real ale, crosswords, garden, children, guitar. *Address:* c/o The Guardian, Kings Place, 90 York Way, N1 9AG. *Club:* Woburn Golf and Country.

SELWAY, Mark Wayne; Chief Executive, Weir Group plc, since 2001; *b* Adelaide, Australia, 2 June 1959; *s* of Vernon and Dawn Selway; *m* 1985, Catherine Piper; twin *s* one *d*. *Educ:* Westminster Sch., Adelaide. Pres., Britax Rainsfords Inc., USA, 1989–94; Board Member: Britax Rear Vision Systems, 1995–96; Britax Internat. Plc, 1996–2000; Shefenacker Internat. AG, 2000–01. Non-exec. Dir, Lend Lease. Mem., Efficient Govt Adv. Bd, Scottish Enterprise, 2003–06. *Address:* Weir Group plc, Clydesdale Bank Exchange, 20 Waterloo Street, Glasgow G2 6DB. *T:* (0141) 308 3700, *Fax:* (0141) 221 3778; *e-mail:* m.selway@weir.co.uk.

SELWOOD, His Honour Maj.-Gen. David Henry Deering; a Circuit Judge, 1992–2004; Resident Judge, Portsmouth Crown Court, 1996–2004; *b* 27 June 1934; *s* of late Comdr George Deering Selwood, RN, and Enid Marguerite Selwood (*née* Rowlinson); *m* 1973, Barbara Dorothea (*née* Hütter); three *s* one *d*. *Educ:* Kelly Coll., Tavistock; University College of the South-West; Law Society's School of Law. Articled to G. C. Aldhouse, Esq., Plymouth, 1952–57; admitted Solicitor 1957; National Service, RASC 2/Lieut, 1957–59; private practice, Plymouth, 1959–61; TA 4 Devons, Lieut, 1959–61; commnd Army Legal Services Staff List, 1961; service on legal staffs, MoD, Headquarters: BAOR, MELF, FARELF, UKLF, Land Forces Cyprus, 1961–85; Brig., Legal, HQ BAOR, 1986–90; Dir of Army Legal Services, MoD, 1990–92. Asst Recorder, SE Circuit, 1980, Recorder, 1985–92. Dep. Col Comdt, AGC, 1996–2003. Hon. Advocate, US Court of Military Appeals, 1972. *Publications:* (jtly) Criminal Law and Psychiatry, 1987; (ed jtly) Crown Court Index, 1996–2004.

SELWOOD, Prof. Sara Michel, PhD; Professor and Head of Department of Cultural Policy and Management, City University, since 2005; *b* 3 Aug. 1953; *d* of Maurice David Selwood and Cordelia Selwood; *m* 1994, Russell Southwood. *Educ:* Putney High Sch.; Univ. of Newcastle (BA 1st cl. Hons Fine Arts 1974); Univ. of Essex (MPhil Hist. and Theory of Art 1979); Univ. of Westminster (PhD 2005). Director: AIR Gall., London, 1986–89; Art & Society, London, 1989–91; Res. Fellow, 1991–95, Hd of Cultural Prog., 1995–98, Policy Studies Inst.; Quintin Hogg Res. Fellow, then Principal Lectr, Sch. of Media, Arts and Design, Univ. of Westminster, 1998–2005. Trustee, NPG, 2002–; Bd Mem., MLA, 2006–. Editor, Cultural Trends, 1996–. *Publications:* The Benefits of Public Art: the polemics of permanent art in public places, 1995; The UK Cultural Sector: profile and policy issues, 2001; frequent contribs to learned jls incl. Cultural Trends. *Recreations:* food, films, visiting museums and galleries, travel. *Address:* Department of Cultural Policy and Management, School of Arts, City University, Northampton Square, EC1V 0HB. *T:* (020) 7040 4182; *e-mail:* s.selwood@city.ac.uk.

SEMKEN, John Douglas, CB 1980; MC 1944; Legal Adviser to the Home Office, 1977–83; *b* 9 Jan. 1921; *s* of Wm R. Semken and Mrs B. R. Semken (*née* Craymer); *m* 1952, Edna Margaret, *yr d* of T. R. Poole; three *s*. *Educ:* St Albans Sch.; Pembroke Coll., Oxford (MA, BCL). Solicitor's articled clerk, 1938–39. Commnd in Sherwood Rangers Yeo., 1940; 1st Lieut 1941, Captain 1942, Major 1944; 8th Armd Bde, N Africa, 1942–43; Normandy beaches to Germany, 1944. Called to Bar, Lincoln's Inn, 1949; practised at Chancery Bar, 1949–54; joined Legal Adviser's Br., Home Office, 1954; Mem., Criminal Law Revision Cttee, 1980–83. Silver Star Medal (USA), 1944. *Address:* 4 Mariner's Court, Victoria Road, Aldeburgh IP15 5EH. *T:* (01728) 453754.

SEMMENS, Victor William; Partner, Eversheds Solicitors, until 2002 (Chairman, 1989–96; Director of International Business, 1998–2002); *b* 10 Oct. 1941; *s* of Ronald William Semmens and Cecile Maude Semmens; *m* 1964, Valerie Elizabeth Norton; two *s*. *Educ:* Blundell's. Qualified Solicitor, 1964; Partner, Wells & Hind, subseq. Eversheds, Nottingham, 1968–2002. *Recreations:* golf, tennis, ski-ing. *Address:* 12 Park Valley, Nottingham NG7 1BQ. *Club:* Combined Services (Notts).

SEMPER, Very Rev. Colin (Douglas); Canon of Westminster, 1987–97; House for Duty Priest, Parish of Frensham, 2003–06; *b* 5 Feb. 1938; *s* of William Frederick and Dorothy Anne Semper; *m* 1962, Janet Louise Greaves; two *s*. *Educ:* Lincoln School; Keble College, Oxford (BA); Westcott House, Cambridge. Curate of Holy Trinity with St Mary, Guildford, 1963–66; Recruitment and Selection Sec., ACCM, 1966–69; Head of Religious Programmes, BBC Radio, and Deputy Head of Religious Broadcasting, BBC, 1969–82; Provost of Coventry Cathedral, 1982–87. Hon. Chaplain, 1985–, Freeman, 1991, Liveryman, 1991–, Feltmakers' Co. *Recreations:* travel, reading modern novels, canals, golf. *Address:* Beech House, 1 Twycross Road, Godalming, Surrey GU7 2HH; *e-mail:* sempers@freezone.co.uk.

SEMPILL, family name of **Baron Sempill**.

SEMPILL, 21st Baron *cr* 1489; **James William Stuart Whitemore Sempill;** Marketing Consultant, since 2006; Director, The Gathering 2009 Ltd, since 2007; *b* 25 Feb. 1949; *s* of Lady Sempill (20th in line), and Lt-Col Stuart Whitemore Chant-Sempill (*d* 1991); *S* mother, 1995; *m* 1977, Josephine Ann Edith, *e d* of J. Norman Rees, Kelso; one *s* one *d*. *Educ:* The Oratory School; St Clare's Hall, London (BA Hons History, 1971); Hertford Coll., Oxford. Gallaher Ltd, 1972–80; PA to Man. Dir, Sentinel Engineering Pty Ltd, Johannesburg, 1980–81; Manager, TWS Public Relations Company, Johannesburg, 1981–83; investment manager, Alan Clarke and Partners, 1982–83; Marketing Manager, S African Breweries, 1983–86; Account Director: Bates Wells (Pty), 1986; Partnership in Advertising, Johannesburg, 1988–90; Client Service Dir, Ogilvy & Mather, Cape Town, 1990–92; Trade Marketing Dir, 1993–95, Dir, Special Projects, 1995, Scottish & Newcastle; Sales and Marketing Manager, Angus Distillers plc, 2001–03; Dir of Marketing, Caledonian Brewing Co. Ltd, Edinburgh, 2003–06. Chm., Edinburgh N and Leith Cons. Assoc., 1999–2001. Contested (C) Edinburgh N and Leith, Scottish Parly elecn, 1999; Prosp. Scottish Parly Cand. (C) Edinburgh Central, 2006–07. Mem., Standing Council of Scottish Chiefs, 1996– (Vice-Convenor, 2005–). *Heir:* *s* Master of Sempill, *qv*.

SEMPILL, Master of; Hon. Francis Henry William Forbes Sempill; Investment Manager, Walter Scott & Partners Ltd, Edinburgh, since 2001; *b* 4 Jan. 1979; *s* and *heir* of Baron Sempill, *qv*. *Educ:* Western Province Prep. Sch., Cape Town; Merchiston Castle Sch., Edinburgh; Napier Univ., Edinburgh. *Recreations:* cricket, golf, travel. *Address:* 3F3 83 McDonald Road, Edinburgh EH7 4NA.

SEMPLE, Prof. Andrew Best, CBE 1966; VRD 1953; Professor of Community and Environmental Health (formerly of Public Health), University of Liverpool, 1953–77, now Professor Emeritus; *b* 3 May 1912; *m* 1941, Jean (*née* Sweet); one *d*. *Educ:* Allan Glen's School, Glasgow; Glasgow Univ. MB, ChB 1934, MD 1947, DPH 1936, Glasgow. FFCM 1972. Various hospital appointments, 1934–38; Asst MOH and Deputy Medical Superintendent, Infectious Diseases Hosp., Portsmouth, 1938–39; Asst MOH and Asst School Medical Officer, Blackburn, 1939–47 (interrupted by War Service); Senior Asst MOH, Manchester, 1947–48; Deputy MOH, City and Port of Liverpool, 1948–53, MOH and Principal Sch. Med. Officer, 1953–74; Area MO (teaching), Liverpool AHA, 1974–77. Served War of 1939–46; Surgeon Commander, RNVR; Naval MOH, Western Approaches, Malta and Central Mediterranean. Chm. Council and Hon. Treasurer, RSH, 1963. QHP 1962. *Publications:* various regarding infectious disease, port health, hygiene, etc.

SEMPLE, Andrew Greenlees; *b* 16 Jan. 1934; *s* of late William Hugh Semple and Madeline, *d* of late E. H. Wood, Malvern, Worcs; *m* 1st, 1961, Janet Elizabeth Whates (*d* 1993); one *s* one *d*; 2nd, 2000, Susan Lucy Jacobs. *Educ:* Winchester Coll.; St John's Coll., Cambridge (MA). Entered Min. of Transport and Civil Aviation, 1957; Private Sec. to Permanent Sec., 1960–62; Principal, 1962; Asst Sec., 1970; Private Sec. to successive Secs of State for the Environment, 1972–74; Under Sec., DoE, 1976; Principal Finance Officer, PSA, DoE, 1980–83; Sec., Water Authorities Assoc., 1983–87; Man. Dir, Anglian Water Authority, 1987–89; Gp Man. Dir, 1989–90, Vice-Chm., 1990–92, Anglian Water plc. Mem., Bd, Eureau, 1983–92. Chm., Huntingdonshire Enterprise Agency, 1990–2001. Governor: Huntingdonshire Regl Coll., 1992–2002; Kimbolton Sch., 2001–08. Chm., Plumstead Almshouses, 2001–. Hon. Mem., IWO (AWO, 1988). FCIWEM 1994. *Recreations:* reading, gardens, watching cricket. *Address:* 14 Druce Road, SE21 7DW. *T:* (020) 8693 8202; 3 Church Lane, Covington, Cambs PE28 0RT. *T:* (01480) 860497. *Club:* Surrey CC.

SEMPLE, Sir John (Laughlin), KCB 2000 (CB 1993); Head of Northern Ireland Civil Service, 1997–2000; Director, Northern Ireland Affairs for Royal Mail Group (formerly Consignia), 2001–06; *b* 10 Aug. 1940; *s* of late James E. Semple and Violet E. G. Semple; *m* 1970, Maureen Anne Kerr; two *s* one *d*. *Educ:* Campbell Coll., Belfast; Corpus Christi Coll., Cambridge (MA); BScEcon London. Joined Home CS as Asst Principal, Min. of Aviation, 1961; transf. to NI CS, 1962; Asst Principal, Mins of Health and Local Govt, Finance, and Health and Social Services, 1962–65; Dep. Principal, Min. of Health and Social Services, 1965; Principal: Min. of Finance, 1968; Min. of Community Relations, 1970–72; Asst Sec. (Planning), Min. of Develt, 1972; Asst Sec. (Housing), DoE, 1977–79; Under Sec. (Housing), DoE for N Ireland, 1979–83; Under Sec., 1983–88, Permanent Sec., 1988–97, Dept of Finance and Personnel for NI; Second Perm. Under-Sec. of State, NI Office, 1998–99; Sec. to Exec. Cttee, NI Assembly, 1999–2000. *Recreations:* golf, tennis, gardening.

SEMPLE, Margaret Olivia, (Maggie), OBE 2000; Chief Executive and Director, The Experience Corps, since 2001; *b* 30 July 1954; *d* of Robert Henry Semple and Olivia Victorine Semple. *Educ:* Shelborne High Sch. for Girls; Worcester Coll. of Higher Educn (BEd); Univ. of London (Advanced Dip.); Univ. of Sussex (MA). Teacher, Hd of Performing Arts, Inspector, ILEA, 1975–88; Dir, Educn and Trng, Arts Council of GB, 1989–97; Dir, Learning Experience, New Millennium Experience Co., 1997–2001. Civil Service Comr, Cabinet Office, 2001–07. Non-exec. Dir, HM Court Service, 2007–08. Member: DfES Nat. Curriculum PE Working Gp, 1989–90; DfES Widening Participation Cttee, 1995–97; DfES Lifelong Learning Cttee, 2001–02; DfES e-learning Task Gp, 2002–03. Fellow, British American Project, 1992; Expert: EC Cttee, 1994–97; European Cultural Centre, Delphi, 1997–2000; Council of Europe Young People's Cttee, 1998–2000. Member: Commonwealth Inst. Educn Cttee, 1992–94; All Souls Educn Gp, All Souls Coll., Oxford, 1994–; TTA, 2000–03; Women's Liby, 2000–04; De Montfort Univ., 2000–; Inst. of Educn, London, 2003–; Adv. Bd, Arts Council London, 2003–06; Council, C&G, 2006–; Pres., Laban Guild, 1994–2000; Chairman: Nat. Youth Music Th., 2002–; Nat. Res. and Develt Centre, 2004–; Wolfson Welcome Dana Centre, 2004–. Ext. Examnr, Liverpool Inst. for Performing Arts, 1997–2000. Trustee: Barnardo's, 1997–2000; RSA, 1998–2003 (Council Mem., 1992–98); Rambert Dance Th., 1998–2006; Roundhouse Trust, 2000–06; Arts Educnl Schs Trust, 2000–; Nat. Mus of Sci. and Ind., 2003–; Balance Foundn for Unclaimed Assets, 2004–07; British Library, 2007–. Sen. Associate, King's Fund, 2001–04. Governor: Brit Sch., 2000–; Sadlers Wells Th., 2005–. FCGI 2005. Hon. DEd De Montfort, 2000. *Recreations:* member of Gorilla Club, reading. *Address:* The Experience Corps Ltd, Waterloo Business Centre, 117 Waterloo Road, SE1 8UL. *T:* (020) 7921 0561, *Fax:* (020) 7681 2649; *e-mail:* maggie.semple@experience-corps.co.uk.

SEMPLE, Prof. Stephen John Greenhill, MD, FRCP; Emeritus Professor, University College London, since 1991; Visiting Professor of Medicine, Imperial College School of Medicine (at Charing Cross Hospital), since 1991; *b* 4 Aug. 1926; *s* of late John Edward Stewart and Janet Semple; *m* 1961, Penelope Ann, *y d* of Sir Geoffrey Aldington, KBE, CMG; three *s*. *Educ:* Westminster; London Univ. MB, BS, 1950, MD 1952, FRCP 1968. Research Asst, St Thomas' Hosp. Med. Sch., 1952; Jun. Med. Specialist, RAMC, Malaya, 1953–55; Instr, Med. Sch., Univ. of Pennsylvania, USA, 1957–59; St Thomas' Hosp. Medical Sch.: Lectr, 1959; Sen. Lectr, 1961; Reader, 1965; Prof. in Medicine, 1969; Prof. of Medicine, The Middlesex Hosp. Medical Sch., 1970–87; Prof. of Medicine, and Head, Dept of Medicine, UCL, 1987–91. Hon. Consultant Physician, Hammersmith Hosps NHS Trust, 1991–2005. *Publications:* Disorders of Respiration, 1972; articles in: Lancet, Jl Physiol. (London), Jl Applied Physiol. *Recreations:* tennis, music. *Address:* White Lodge, 3 Claremont Park Road, Esher, Surrey KT10 9LT. *T:* (01372) 465057. *Club:* Queen's.

SEN, Prof. Amartya Kumar, Bharat Ratna, 1999; Hon. CH 2000; FBA 1977; Lamont University Professor, Harvard University, 1988–98 and since 2004 (Emeritus, 1998–2003); Fellow, Trinity College, Cambridge (Master, 1998–2004); *b* 3 Nov. 1933; *s* of late Dr Ashutosh Sen, Dhaka, and of Amita Sen, Santiniketan, India; *m* 1st, 1960, Nabaneeta Dev (marr. diss. 1975); two *d*; 2nd, 1978, Eva Colorni (*d* 1985); one *s* one *d*; 3rd, 1991, Emma Rothschild, *qv*. *Educ:* Calcutta Univ.; Trinity Coll., Cambridge (MA, PhD; Hon. Fellow, 1991). Prof. of Economics, Jadavpur Univ., Calcutta, 1956–58; Trinity Coll., Cambridge: Prize Fellow, 1957–61; Staff Fellow, 1961–63; Professor of Economics: Delhi Univ., 1963–71 (Chm., Dept of Economics, 1966–68, Hon. Prof., 1971–); LSE, 1971–77; Oxford Univ., 1977–80; Fellow, Nuffield College, Oxford, 1977–80 (Associate Mem., 1980–89; Hon. Fellow, 1998); Drummond Prof. of Political Economy, and Fellow, All Souls Coll., Oxford, 1980–88 (Distinguished Fellow, 2005); Prof. of Economics and Philosophy, Harvard Univ., 1987–97; Sen. Fellow, Harvard Soc. of Fellows, 1989–98. Hon. Dir, Agricultural Economics Research Centre, Delhi, 1966–68 and 1969–71. Res. Advr, World Inst. for Develt Econ. Res., Helsinki, Finland, 1985–93; Special Advr to Sec. Gen. of UN, 2001–. Vis. Professor: MIT, 1960–61; Univ. of Calif at Berkeley, 1964–65; Harvard Univ., 1968–69; Andrew D. White Professor-at-large, Cornell Univ., 1978–84. Chm., UN Expert Gp Meeting on Role of Advanced Skill and Technology, New York, 1967. President: Develt Studies Assoc., 1980–82; Econometric Soc., 1984 (Fellow 1968–, Vice-Pres. 1982–83); Internat. Economic Assoc., 1986–89 (Hon. Pres., 1989); Indian Econ. Assoc., 1989; Amer. Econ. Assoc., 1994; Soc. for Social Choice and Welfare, 1993–94; Vice-Pres., Royal Economic Soc., 1988– (Mem. Council, 1977–87); Hon. Advr, Oxfam, 2002– (Hon. Pres., 2000–02); Trustee, Inst. for Advanced Study, Princeton, 1987–94. Member: Accademia Nazionale dei Lincei; Amer. Philos. Assoc.; Foreign Hon. Mem., Amer. Acad. of Arts and Sciences, 1981; Hon. Mem., Amer. Econ. Assoc., 1981. Hon. FRSE; Hon. FMedSci; Hon. Fellow: Inst. of Social Studies, The Hague, 1982; LSE, 1984; IDS, Sussex Univ., 1984; SOAS, London Univ., 1998; Darwin

Coll., Cambridge, 1998; LSHTM; St Edmund's Coll., Cambridge, 2004; Frances Perkins Fellow, Amer. Acad of Political and Social Sci., 2003. Hon. DLitt: Saskatchewan, 1980; Visva-Bharati, 1983; Georgetown, 1989; Jadavpur, Kalyani, 1990; Williams Coll., City of London Poly., 1991; New Sch. for Social Res., NY, 1992; Calcutta, 1993; Syracuse, 1994; Oxford, 1996; Bard Coll., 1997; Leicester, Kingston, Columbia, Chhatrapati Shahu Ji Maharaj, 1998; UEA, Nottingham, Heriot-Watt, 1999; Allahabad, Assam, Strathclyde, Kerala, 2000; Mumbai, 2002; N Bengal, 2002; Hon. DHumLit: Oberlin Coll., 1993; Wesleyan, 1995; McGill, 1998; Mass, Lowell, 2006; Hon. DSc: Bath, 1984; Edinburgh, 1995; Dhaka, 1999; Assam Agricl, Birmingham, London, 2000; Sussex, 2003; Michigan, 2006; Hon. DSocSc: Chinese Univ. of HK, 1999; Yale, 2003; DU: Essex, 1984; Rabindra Bharati, 1998; Dr *hc* Caen, 1987; Bologna, 1988; Univ. Catholique de Louvain, 1989; Athens Univ. of Econs and Business, 1991; Valencia, Zurich, 1994; Antwerp, 1995; Stockholm, 1996; Kiel, 1997; Padua, 1998; Athens, Méditerranée (Marseille), Delhi, 1999; Tech. Univ. of Lisbon, Univ. Jaume I de Castellón, Spain, 2001; Tokyo, Clark Univ. (Worcester, USA), Southampton, 2002; Univ. Pierre Mendès France, Grenoble, 2002; Santa Clara Univ., Calif, 2002; Bidhan Chandra Krishi Viswavidyalaya, 2003; Ritsumeikan, Japan, 2003; York, 2004; Koc, Turkey, 2004; Rhodes, S Africa, 2004; York, Canada, 2004; Rovira I Virgili, Tarrogona, 2004; Simmons Coll., Boston, 2005; Gottingen, 2005; Hon. LLD: Tulane, 1990; Queen's Univ., Kingston, Ont., 1993; Harvard, 2000; Mount Holyoke Coll., USA, 2003; Toronto, 2004; Connecticut, 2006; Hon. Dr Ph Jawaharlal Nehru, 1998; Hon. DSc Econs: London, 2000; Cape Town, 2006; Laurea *hc*: Florence, 2000; Turin, 2004; Pavia, 2005; DUniv Open, 2002; Hon. DCL Durham, 2002. Mahalanobis Prize, 1976; Frank E. Seidman Dist. Award in Pol Econ., 1986; Agnelli Internat. Prize, 1990; Alan Shawn Feinstein World Hunger Award, 1990; Jean Mayer Global Citizenship Award, 1993; Indira Gandhi Gold Medal Award, Asiatic Soc., 1994; Edinburgh Medal, 1997; Catalonia Internat. Prize, 1997; Nobel Prize for Economics, 1998; Leontief Prize, 2000; Ayrton Senna Grand Prix of Journalism, 2002; Medal of Distinction, Barnard Coll., USA, 2005; Silver Banner, Florence, 2005; George C. Marshall Award, USA, 2005. Eisenhower Medal, USA, 2000; Presidency of Italian Republic Medal, 2000. Grand Cross, Order of Scientific Merit (Brazil), 2000. *Publications:* Choice of Techniques, 1960, 3rd edn 1968; Growth Economics, 1970; Collective Choice and Social Welfare, 1971; On Economic Inequality, 1973; Employment, Technology and Development, 1975; Poverty and Famines: an essay on entitlement and deprivation, 1981; (ed with Bernard Williams) Utilitarianism and Beyond, 1982; Choice, Welfare and Measurement, 1982; Resources, Values and Development, 1984; Commodities and Capabilities, 1985; On Ethics and Economics, 1987; The Standard of Living, 1987; (with Jean Drèze) Hunger and Public Action, 1989; (ed with Jean Drèze) The Political Economy of Hunger, 3 vols, 1990–91; Inequality Re-examined, 1992; (with Jean Drèze) India: economic development and social opportunity, 1995; Development as Freedom, 1999 (Bruno-Kreisky Award for Political Book of the Year, 2001; European Economics Book Prize, 2002); Rationality and Freedom, 2002; The Argumentative Indian, 2005; Identity and Violence: the illusion of destiny, 2006; articles in various jls in economics, philosophy, political science, decision theory, demography and law. *Address:* Harvard University, University Hall, Cambridge, MA 02138, USA.

SEN, Emma; *see* Rothschild, Emma.

SEN, Ranendra, (Ronen); Ambassador for India to the United States of America, since 2004; *b* 9 April 1944; *s* of late Satyendra Mohan Sen and Shrimati Suniti Rani; *m* 1970, Kalpana Chowdhury; one *d.* *Educ:* Calcutta Univ. (BA Hons). Joined Indian Foreign Service, 1966; served: Moscow, 1968–71; San Francisco, 1972–74; Dhaka, 1974–77; Dep. Sec., Min. of External Affairs, 1977; Dep. Sec., Dept of Atomic Energy, and Sec., Atomic Energy Commn, 1978–80; Counsellor, then Minister, Moscow, 1981–84; Jt Sec., Min. of External Affairs, 1984–85; Jt Sec. to Prime Minister of India, 1986–91; Ambassador: to Mexico, 1991–92; to Russia, 1992–98; to Germany, 1998–2002; High Comr in UK, 2002–04. *Recreations:* music, reading, travel. *Address:* Embassy of India, 2107 Massachusetts Avenue NW, Washington, DC 20008, USA. *Clubs:* Delhi Gymkhana; Cosmos (Washington).

SENDAK, Maurice Bernard; writer and illustrator of children's books; theatrical designer; Artistic Director, The Night Kitchen, national children's theater; *b* 10 June 1928; *yr s* of Philip Sendak and Sarah (*née* Schindler). *Educ:* Lafayette High School, Brooklyn; Art Students' League, NY. Worked part-time at All American Comics; window display work with Timely Service, 1946–48, F. A. O. Schwartz, 1948–50; illustrated over 50 books by other writers, 1951–. Retrospective one-man exhibitions: Sch. of Visual Arts, NY, 1964; Ashmolean, Oxford, 1975; Amer. Cultural Center, Paris, 1978. *Stage designs:* The Magic Flute, Houston, 1980; The Cunning Little Vixen, NY, 1981; The Love of Three Oranges, Glyndebourne, 1982; Where the Wild Things Are, NT, 1984; L'enfant et les sortilèges, L'Heure espagnole, Glyndebourne, 1987. Hon. RDI 1986. *Publications:* Kenny's Window, 1956; Very Far Away, 1957; The Sign on Rosie's Door, 1960; Nutshell Library set, 1962; Where the Wild Things Are, 1963 (Amer. Liby Assoc. Caldecott Medal, 1964; opera, by Oliver Knussen, Glyndebourne, 1984); Higglety Pigglety Pop!, 1967; Hector Protector, 1967; In the Night Kitchen, 1971; (with Charlotte Zolotow) Rabbit and the Lovely Present, 1971; Pictures, 1972; Maxfield Parrish Poster Book, 1974; (with Matthelo Margolis) Some Swell Pup, 1976; Charlotte and the White Horse, 1977; (ed) Disney Poster Book, 1977; Seven Little Monsters, 1977; (with Doris Orgel) Sarah's Room, 1977; Very Far Away, 1978; Outside Over There, 1981; (with Frank Corsaro) The Love for Three Oranges, 1984; (with Ralph Manheim) Nutcracker, 1984; Dear Mili, 1988; Caldecott and Company (essays), 1989; We are all in the Dumps with Jack and Guy, 1993; (illus.) Swine Lake, 1999; (with T. Kushner) Brundibar, 2003; (with J. Sendak) The Happy Rain, 2004; (with R. Krauss) Bears, 2005; (with A. Yorinks) Mommy?, 2006. *Address:* c/o HarperCollins Children's Books, 1350 Avenue of the Americas, New York, NY 10019, USA.

SENEWIRATNE, Kshenuka Dhireni; High Commissioner for Sri Lanka in the United Kingdom, 2005–08; *b* 20 July 1960; *d* of late Deutram de Silva and of Githa de Silva; *m* 1998, Surendra Senewiratne. *Educ:* Univ. of Salford (BSc Econs 1982); Corpus Christi Coll., Oxford (Chevening Schol.; Foreign Affairs Study Prog.); Univ. of Colombo (MA Internat. Relns 1992). Asst Dir, Bureau of the Minister of Foreign Affairs, Min. of Foreign Affairs, Sri Lanka, 1985–88; diplomatic posting, Perm. Mission of Sri Lanka to the UN, NY, 1988–90; Ministry of Foreign Affairs: Deputy Director: Publicity Div., 1990–91; UN and Multilateral Affairs Div., 1991–93; diplomatic posting, Brussels, 1993–96; Ministry of Foreign Affairs: Dir, UN and Multilateral Div., 1997–98; Dir, 1998–2001, Actg Dir Gen., 2001–02, Econ. Affairs Div.; Dep. High Comr, London, 2002–04; Additional Dir Gen., Econ. Affairs Div., Min. of Foreign Affairs, 2004–05. *Recreations:* reading, cycling, music, travelling.

SENIOR, Olive Edith; JP; MPhil; SRN; consultant in clinical risk, 1995–2000; Regional Nursing Officer, Trent Regional Health Authority, 1973–86; Fellow, Nottingham University, 1988–95; *b* 26 April 1934; *d* of Harold and Doris Senior, Mansfield, Notts. *Educ:* Harlow Wood Orthopaedic Hosp., 1949–52; St George's Hosp., Hyde Park Corner, 1952–56; City Hosp., Nottingham (Pt I, CMB 1956); Nottingham Univ. (HV Cert. 1957, MPhil 1978). Health Visitor, Notts CC, 1958–60; St George's Hosp., London (Ward Sister), 1960–63; S Africa, June–Dec. 1963; Forest Gate Hosp., London (SCM), 1964; St Mary's Hosp., Portsmouth (Asst Matron/Night Supt), 1964–66; NE Metropolitan Regional Hosp. Bd (Management Services), 1966–71; Chief Nursing Officer, Nottingham and Dist. HMC, 1971–73. Member: Local Res. Ethics Cttee, N Notts HA, 1998–; N Notts CHC, 2001–03. Secretary of State Fellow, 1973. JP Nottingham Guildhall, 1973. *Publications:* An Analysis of Nurse Staffing Levels in Hospitals in the Trent Region (1977 Data), 1978; Dependency and Establishments, 1979; contrib. to Nursing Times (Determining Nursing Establishments). *Address:* 94 Oak Tree Lane, Mansfield, Notts NG18 3HL. *Club:* Nottingham University (Nottingham).

SENNITT, His Honour John Stuart; a Circuit Judge, 1994–2007; *b* Cambridge, 5 March 1935; *s* of late Stuart Osland Sennitt and Nora Kathleen Sennitt; *m* 1966, Janet Ann; one *s* two *d.* *Educ:* Culford Sch., Bury St Edmunds; St Catharine's Coll., Cambridge (MA, LLB). Admitted Solicitor, 1961; Partner, Wild, Hewitson & Shaw, Cambridge, 1963–83; County Court Registrar, then Dist Judge, 1983–94; Asst Recorder, 1988–92; a Recorder, 1992–94. *Address:* c/o Cambridge County Court, 197 East Road, Cambridge CB1 1BA.

SENTAMU, Most Rev. and Rt Hon. John Tucker Mugabi; *see* York, Archbishop of.

SENTANCE, Dr Andrew William; Member, Monetary Policy Committee, Bank of England, since 2006; Professorial Fellow, University of Warwick, since 2006; *b* 17 Sept. 1958; *s* of William Thomas Wulfram Sentance and Lillian Sentance (*née* Bointon); *m* 1985, Anne Margaret Penfold; one *s* one *d.* *Educ:* Eltham Coll., London; Clare Coll., Cambridge (BA Hons, MA); London Sch. of Econs (MSc Econ; PhD 1988). Manager, Petrocell Ltd, 1980–81; with NCB, 1982–83; Confederation of British Industry: Head, Econ. Policy, 1986–89; Dir, Econ. Affairs, 1989–93; London Business School: Sen. Res. Fellow, 1994–95; Dir, Centre for Economic Forecasting, 1995–98; British Airways: Chief Economist, 1998–2006; Head of Envmtl Affairs, 2003–06. Chief Economic Advr, British Retail Consortium, 1995–98. Member: HM Treasury Panel of Independent Forecasters, 1992–93; various statistical adv. cttees, 1988–99. Comr, Commn for Integrated Transport, 2006–. Vis. Prof. of Econs, Royal Holloway, Univ. of London, 1998–; Vis. Prof., Cranfield Univ., 2001–. Fellow, Soc. of Business Economists (Mem. Council, 1991–2003; Chm., 1995–2000; Dep. Chm., 2000–03). Trustee: Anglo-German Foundn, 2001–; British Airways Pension Funds, 2002–06. Ed., London Business Sch. Econ. Outlook, 1994–98. FRAeS 2004. *Publications:* numerous articles in books and jls on current economic issues. *Recreations:* playing piano, guitar and organ, listening to music. *Address:* Bank of England, Threadneedle Street, EC2R 8AH. *T:* (020) 7601 5189; *e-mail:* andrew.sentance@bankofengland.co.uk.

SEOKA, Rt Rev. Johannes Thomas; *see* Pretoria, Bishop of.

SEPHTON, Craig Gardner; QC 2001; a Recorder, since 2002; *b* 7 Dec. 1957; *s* of Bruce and Betty Sephton; *m* 1985, Colette (marr. diss.); three *s.* *Educ:* Ecclesbourne Sch., Duffield; Lincoln Coll., Oxford (MA, BCL). Called to the Bar, Middle Temple, 1981. *Recreations:* swimming, mountaineering, music. *Address:* 24 St John Street, Manchester M3 4DF. *T:* (0161) 214 6000.

SEPÚLVEDA, Bernardo, Hon. GCMG 1985; Judge, International Court of Justice, The Hague, since 2006; *b* 14 Dec. 1941; *s* of Bernardo Sepúlveda and Margarita Amor; *m* 1970, Ana Yturbe; three *s.* *Educ:* Univ. of Mexico (Law Degree *magna cum laude*, 1964); Queens' Coll., Cambridge (LLB 1966; Hon. Fellow, 1990). Prof. of Internat. Law, El Colegio de México, 1967–81; Dep. Dir Gen. for Legal Affairs to Secretary of the Presidency, 1968–70; Asst Sec. for Internat. Affairs, Min. of the Treasury, 1976–80; Principal Advisor on Internat. Affairs to the Minister of Planning and Budget, 1981; Ambassador to USA, 1982; Minister of Foreign Relations, Mexico, 1982–88; Ambassador to UK, 1989–93; Foreign Affairs Advr to Pres. of Mexico, 1993. Mem., UN Internat. Law Commn, 1996–2006. Dr *hc*: Univ. of San Diego, Calif, 1982; Univ. of Leningrad, 1987. Princípe de Asturias Prize, Spain, 1984; Simón Bolívar Prize, UNESCO, 1985. Grand Cross, Order of: Civil Merit (Spain), 1979; Isabel the Catholic (Spain), 1983; Southern Cross (Brazil), 1983; Boyacá (Colombia), 1984; Merit (FRG), 1984; Liberator San Martín (Argentina), 1984; Vasco Núñez de Balboa (Panama), 1984; Manuel Amador Guerrero (Panama), 1985; Christ (Portugal), 1985; Crown (Belgium), 1985; Quetzal (Guatemala), 1986; Prince Henry the Navigator (Portugal), 1986; Sun (Peru), 1987; Rio Branco (Brazil), 1988; Grand Officier, Nat. Order of Legion of Honour (France), 1985; also orders and decorations from Korea, Venezuela, Poland, Yugoslavia, Greece, Japan, Egypt and Jamaica. *Publications:* The United Nations: dilemma at 25, 1970; Foreign Investment in Mexico, 1973; Transnational Corporations in Mexico, 1974; articles on internat. law in prof. jls. *Recreations:* reading, music. *Address:* International Court of Justice, Peace Palace, 2517 KJ The Hague, The Netherlands. *Clubs:* Brooks's, Travellers.

SERAFÍN, David; *see* Michael, I. D. L.

SERENY, Gitta, Hon. CBE 2003; writer; *b* 13 March 1921; *d* of Gyula and Margit Serényi; *m* 1948, Donald Honeyman; one *s* one *d.* *Educ:* Vienna Realgymnasium Luithlen; Stonar House Sch., Sandwich, Kent; Reinhardt-Seminar, Vienna; Sorbonne, Univ. of Paris. *Publications:* The Medallion (novel), 1957; *non-fiction:* The Case of Mary Bell, 1972; Into That Darkness, 1974; The Invisible Children, 1984; Albert Speer, His Battle With Truth, 1995; Cries Unheard, 1998; The Healing Wound: experiences and reflections 1938–2001, 2001; contrib. features and series to newspapers and periodicals, incl. The Times, Sunday Times and The Independent, Die Zeit, Dagens Nyheter, and NY Review of Books. *Recreations:* swimming, hiking, reading. *Address:* c/o Sayle Literary Agency, 1 Petersfield, Cambridge CB1 1BB.

SERGEANT, Emma; artist; *b* 9 Dec. 1959; *d* of Sir Patrick John Rushton Sergeant, *qv*; *m* 2001, Count Adam Zamoyski. *Educ:* Channing Sch.; Camden High Sch.; Camberwell Sch. of Arts and Crafts; Slade Sch. of Fine Art. Commnd by NPG to paint portraits of Lord David Cecil and Lord Olivier, 1981; Official Royal Tour Artist to Prince of Wales: Egypt and Morocco, 1995; Ukraine and Central Asian Republics of Turkmenistan, Kazakhstan, Kyrgyzstan and Uzbekistan, 1996. Exhibitions include: Drinks at Milapote: friends and family, 1984, Afghanistan, in aid of UNICEF, 1986, Faces from Four Continents, 1988, Orpheus and the Underworld, 1994, Agnew's, London; Retour en Afghanistan, in aid of Médecins du Monde, Mona Bismarck Foundn, Paris, 1987; Gods, Newhouse Gall., NY, and Agnew's, London, 1996; Dolphins, 1998, From the Sea, 1999, Shades of Grey, 2004, Fine Art Soc.; Scenes from a Hittite Court, Prince's Foundn, 2001; portrait commissions include: the Duke of York, Sir Christopher Cockerell, Lord Carrington, Imran Khan, Lord Todd, Sir William Deacon, Paul Dacre, Padraic Fallon, Lord Rothermere, Trudie Styler, Earl of Radnor, Sir Rocco Forte, Jeremy Paxman, Michael Portillo, Jerry Hall. NPG Award, 1981. *Recreations:* horses, polo, hacking with Adam. *Address:* Fine Art Society plc, 148 New Bond Street, W1Y 0JT. *T:* (020) 7629 5116; *e-mail:* art@faslondon.com.

SERGEANT, John; freelance writer, broadcaster and after-dinner speaker; Political Editor, ITN, 2000–02; *b* 14 April 1944; *s* of Ernest Sergeant and late Olive Sergeant (then Stevens); *m* 1969, Mary Smithies; two *s*. *Educ:* Millfield Sch., Street; Magdalen Coll., Oxford (BA Hons PPE). Appeared in On the Margin, BBC TV, 1966–67; Reporter, Liverpool Daily Post and Echo, 1967–70; BBC: Reporter, 1970–81: reported from 25 countries, incl. conflicts in Vietnam, Cyprus, Israel, Lebanon, Rhodesia and NI; acting Corresp., Dublin, Paris and Washington; Presenter, current affairs progs, Radio 4, incl. Today, World at One, PM; Political Corresp., 1981–88; Chief Political Corresp., 1988–2000; Lobby Chm., 2000–01. Mem., Hansard Soc. Commn on Communication of Parly Democracy, 2004–05. Has appeared on numerous TV and radio progs, incl. Have I Got News for You, Room 101, Call My Bluff, News Quiz, Quote Unquote, etc.; UK theatre tour, An Audience with John Sergeant, 2003–. Pres., Johnson Soc., 2003–04. Most Memorable TV Broadcast award, BPG, 1991; Best Individual TV Contributor, Voice of the Listener and Viewer, 1999. *Publications:* Give Me Ten Seconds (memoirs), 2001; Maggie: her fatal legacy, 2005. *Recreations:* sailing, listening to classical music. *Address:* c/o Capel and Land, 29 Wardour Street, W1D 6PS.

SERGEANT, Sir Patrick (John Rushton), Kt 1984; City Editor, Daily Mail, 1960–84; Founder, 1969, and Chairman, 1985–92, Euromoney Publications (Managing Director, 1969–85); *b* 17 March 1924; *s* of George and Rene Sergeant; *m* 1952, Gillian Anne Wilks, Cape Town; two *d*. *Educ:* Beaumont Coll. Served as Lieut, RNVR, 1945. Asst City Editor, News Chronicle, 1948; Dep. City Editor, Daily Mail, 1953. Director: Associated Newspapers Group, 1971–83; Daily Mail General Trust, 1983–2004; (non-exec.) Euromoney Institutional Investor plc (formerly Euromoney Publications), 1992–. Domus Fellow, St Catherine's Coll., Oxford, 1988. Freeman, City of London, 1987. Wincott Award, Financial Journalist of the Year, 1979. *Publications:* Another Road to Samarkand, 1955; Money Matters, 1967; Inflation Fighters Handbook, 1976. *Recreations:* tennis, swimming, talking. *Address:* One The Grove, Highgate Village, N6 6JU. *T:* (020) 8340 1245. *Clubs:* Royal Automobile; All England Lawn Tennis and Croquet, Queen's.
See also E. Sergeant.

SERJEANT, Graham Roger, CMG 1981; MD; FRCP; Chairman, Sickle Cell Trust of Jamaica, since 1986; *b* 26 Oct. 1938; *s* of Ewart Egbert and Violet Elizabeth Serjeant; *m* 1965, Beryl Elizabeth, *d* of late Ivor Edward King, CB, CBE. *Educ:* Sibford Sch., Banbury; Bootham Sch., York; Clare Coll., Cambridge (BA 1960, MA 1965); London Hosp. Med. Sch.; Makerere Coll., Kampala. MB BChir 1963, MD 1971, Cantab. MRCP 1966, FRCP 1977. House Physician: London Hosp., 1963–64; Royal United Hosp., Bath, 1965–66; RPMS, 1966; Med. Registrar, University Hosp. of WI, 1966–67; Wellcome Res. Fellow, Dept of Medicine, Univ. of WI, 1967–71; Medical Research Council: Mem., Scientific Staff, Abnormal Haemoglobin Unit, Cambridge, 1971–72; Epidemiology Res. Unit, Jamaica, 1972–74; Dir, MRC Labs, Jamaica, 1974–99. Hon. Prof. of Clin. Epidemiology, Univ. of WI, 1981–99, now Emeritus. Pres., Caribbean Orgn of Sickle Cell Assocs, 1997–2000. Gold Musgrave Medal, Inst. of Jamaica, 1995; Pelican Award, Univ. of WI, 1995; Vice-Chancellor's Award for Excellence, 1999. Dist. Res. Award, Caribbean Health Res. Council, 1999. Hon. CD (Jamaica), 1996; Commander, Mérite Congolais, 2005. *Publications:* The Clinical Features of Sickle Cell Disease, 1974; Sickle Cell Disease, 1985, 3rd edn 2001; Guide to Sickle Cell Disease, 2001; approx. 400 papers on the nat. hist. of sickle cell disease, in med. jls. *Recreations:* theatre, art. *Address:* Sickle Cell Trust, 14 Milverton Crescent, Kingston 6, Jamaica, WI. *T:* 9272300, *Fax:* 9700074; *e-mail:* grserjeant@cwjamaica.com.

SERJEANT, William Ronald, FRHistS; County Archivist, Suffolk, 1974–82, retired; Vice-President, Society of Archivists, since 1988 (President, 1982–88); Hon. Archivist to Lord Tollemache, and to the British Association for Local History, since 1982; *b* 5 March 1921; *s* of Frederick William and Louisa (*née* Wood); *m* 1961, Ruth Kneale (*née* Bridson); one *s*. *Educ:* Univ. of Manchester (BA Hons History); Univ. of Liverpool (Dip. Archive Admin. and Study of Records). Archivist/Librarian: Univ. of Sheffield, Sheffield City Library, Liverpool Record Office, 1952–56; Librarian/Archivist, Manx Nat. Library and Archives, Dep. Dir, Manx Mus. and Nat. Trust, 1957–62; County Archivist, Notts, 1962–70; Jt County Bor. and County Archivist, Ipswich and E Suffolk, 1970–74; Hon. Archivist to Lord de Saumarez, 1982–2007. Member: Lord Chancellor's Adv. Council on Public Records, 1982–88; Suffolk Heraldry Soc., 1982–; Member, Executive Committee: Suffolk Local History Council, 1970–2001; Ipswich Film Soc., 1974–; Council Member: Suffolk Inst. of Archeology and History, 1970–90; Suffolk Records Soc., 1970–; British Records Soc., 1974–2001; Ipswich Building Preservation Trust, 1988–; British Assoc. for Local History, 1994–97 (Mem. Publications Cttee, 1982– (Chm., 1988–92)); Trustee, 1983–2005, Patron, 2005–, Leiston Long Shop (formerly Steam) Museum, 1983–. Editor: Jl of the Manx Museum, 1957–62; The Suffolk Review, 1970–82; The Blazon (Suffolk Heraldry Soc.), 1984–88. *Publications:* The History of Tuxford Grammar School, 1969; (ed) Index to the Probate Records of the Court of the Archdeacon of Suffolk 1444–1700, 1979–80; (ed) Index to the Probate Records of the Court of the Archdeacon of Sudbury 1354–1700, 1984; articles in county and other local history periodicals. *Recreations:* walking, participation in local historical and heraldic studies and activities, theatre and cinema going; any gaps filled by reading novels. *Address:* 23 Dalton Road, Ipswich, Suffolk IP1 2HT. *T:* (01473) 221219.

SERMON, (Thomas) Richard, FCIS; Chairman, Gryphon Corporate Counsel, since 1996; *b* 25 Feb. 1947; *s* of Eric Thomas Sermon and Marjorie Hilda (*née* Parsons); *m* 1970, Rosemary Diane, *yr d* of Thomas Smith; one *s* one *d*. *Educ:* Nottingham High Sch. FCIS 1972. Crest Hotels, 1969–74; Good Relations Gp, 1974–79; Co-founder and Chief Exec., 1979–87, Chm., 1987–90, 1996–2000, Shandwick Consultants; Man. Dir, Shandwick Consulting Gp, 1987–88; Chief Executive: Shandwick Europe, 1988–90; Shandwick International, 1990–96; public relns advr, Goldman Sachs Internat., 1992–96. Director: Gryphon Partners (formerly Wrightson Wood Associates), 1994–; Jardine Lloyd Thompson Gp, 1996–; Newmond, 1997–2000; MoD Defence Storage and Distributions Agency, 1999–; Mgt Bd, Defence Acad. of UK, 2007–; China Eastsea Business Software Ltd, 2008–; Appointed Mem., PPP, 1993–98. Mem., Nat. Adv. Council on Employment of People with Disabilities, 1994–98. Mem. Council, C & G, 1993– (Mem. Exec. Cttee, 1999–; Hon. Mem., 1999; Jt Hon. Sec., 2005–). Vice-President: RADAR, 1987–; Providence Row, 1999–; Mem. Exec. Cttee, Fedn of London Youth Clubs (formerly London Fedn of Clubs for Young People), 1994– (Hon. Treas., 1995–96; Chm., 1996–2008; Dep. Chm., 2008–). Dir, City of London Sinfonia, 1995–2001. Chm., The Home Improvement Trust, 1997–. Freeman, City of London, 1968; Member, Court of Assistants: Wheelwrights' Co., 1990– (Master, 2000–01); Chartered Secretaries and Administrators' Co., 1991– (Master, 2006–07). Hon. FCGI 2004. *Address:* Friars Well, Roundtown, Aynho, Banbury, Oxon OX17 3BG. *T:* (01869) 810284. *Clubs:* City of London, City Livery, Walbrook.

SEROTA, Daniel; QC 1989; **His Honour Judge Serota;** a Circuit Judge, since 1999; *b* 27 Sept. 1945; *s* of Louis and N'eema Serota; *m* 1970; two *d*. *Educ:* Carmel Coll.; Jesus Coll., Oxford (MA). Called to the Bar, Lincoln's Inn, 1969; a Recorder, 1989–99. Consulting Ed., Civil Practice Law Reports. *Address:* Milton Keynes County Court, 351 Silbury Boulevard, Witan Gate East, Milton Keynes MK9 2DT. *T:* (01908) 668855.

SEROTA, Sir Nicholas (Andrew), Kt 1999; Director of the Tate Gallery, since 1988; *b* 27 April 1946; *s* of Stanley Serota and Beatrice Serota (Baroness Serota, DBE); *m* 1st, 1973, Angela Beveridge (marr. diss. 1995); two *d*; 2nd, 1997, Teresa Gleadowe; two step *d*. *Educ:* Haberdashers' Aske's Sch., Hampstead and Elstree; Christ's Coll., Cambridge (BA; Hon. Fellow, 2003); Courtauld Inst. of Art, London (MA). Regional Art Officer and Exhibn Organiser, Arts Council of GB, 1970–73; Dir, Museum of Modern Art, Oxford, 1973–76; Dir, Whitechapel Art Gallery, 1976–88. Mem. Bd, Olympic Delivery Authy, 2006–. Chm., Visual Arts Adv. Cttee, British Council, 1992–98 (Mem., 1976–98); Comr, Commn for Architecture and the Built Envmt, 1999–2006. Trustee: Public Art Develt Trust, 1983–87; Architecture Foundn, 1991–99; Little Sparta Trust, 1995–2007; Chinati Foundn, 1999–. Sen. FRCA 1996. Hon. Fellow: QMC 1988; Goldsmiths' Coll., Univ. of London, 1994. Hon. FRIBA 1992. Hon. DLitt: Keele, 1994; South Bank, 1996; Surrey, 1997; Exeter, 2000; London Inst., 2001; Hon. Dr Arts: City of London Polytechnic, 1990; Plymouth, 1993; DU Essex, 2002. Officier de l'Ordre des Arts et des Lettres (France), 2003. *Publication:* Experience or Interpretation: the dilemma of museums of modern art, 1996. *Address:* Tate, Millbank, SW1P 4RG. *T:* (020) 7887 8003.

SERVICE, Alastair Stanley Douglas, CBE 1995; MVO 2007; writer, historian and campaigner; *b* 8 May 1933; *s* of late Douglas William Service and Evelyn Caroline (*née* Sharp); *m* 1st, 1959, Louisa Anne Hemming (*see* L. A. Service) (marr. diss. 1984); one *s* one *d*; 2nd, 1992, Zandria Madeleine Pauncefort. *Educ:* Westminster Sch.; Queen's Coll., Oxford. Midshipman, RNR, 1952–54. Trainee, Lazard Bros, 1956–58; Director: McKinlay, Watson and Co. Ltd, Brazil, USA and London, 1959–64 (export finance); Seeley, Service and Co. Ltd (publishers), 1965–79; Municipal Journal Ltd, 1970–78. Hon. Parly Officer: Abortion Law Reform Assoc., organising MPs' and Peers' support of Abortion Act, 1964–67; Divorce Law Reform Union, organising support of Divorce Reform Act, 1967–69; Chm., Birth Control Campaign, organising support of NHS (Family Planning) Amendment Act, 1972, and NHS Reorganisation Act, 1973 (made vasectomy and contraception available free from NHS); involved in other parly campaigns, incl.: Town and Country Amenities Act, 1974; Children's Act, 1975; Public Lending Right for Authors; One-Parent Families. Nat. Chm., 1975–80, Gen. Sec., 1980–89, FPA; Vice-Chm., Health Educn Council, 1976–87; Dep. Chm. (Sec. of State appointee), Health Educn Authy, 1987–89. Chairman: Wilts and Bath Health Commn, 1992–96; Wessex RHA, 1993–94 (non-exec. Dir, 1989–93; Vice-Chm., 1992–93); Wilts HA, 1996–2000; Wilts NHS and Local Govt Strategic Forum, 1996–2000. Vice-Pres., Interact World Wide (formerly Population Concern), 2004– (Mem., Nat. Cttee, 1973–2004; Chm., 1975–79); Mem., Adv. Panel, Optimum Population Trust, 2005–. Mem., Nat. Cttee, Victorian Soc., 1975–95 (Chm., Publications Cttee, 1982–89); Co-Founder, Action for River Kennet, 1991– (Hon. Sec., 1991–2002). Trustee, Prince of Wales's Foundn, 1999–2002; Chm., Prince's Regeneration Through Heritage Gp, 2000–02. Chm., Avebury Soc., 2002–. Mem. Judging Panel, Patron's Award, Almshouse Assoc., 2000–05; Chm., Judging Cttee, Prince of Wales' Craft Scholarships, 2000–07. Life Member: FPA; SPAB; Victorian Soc. *Publications:* A Birth Control Plan for Britain (with Dr John Dunwoody and Dr Tom Stuttaford), 1972; The Benefits of Birth Control—Aberdeen's Experience, 1973; Edwardian Architecture and its Origins, 1975; Edwardian Architecture, 1977; The Architects of London from 1066 to Present Day, 1979; London 1900, 1979; (with Jean Bradbery) Megaliths of Europe, 1979; Lost Worlds, 1981; Edwardian Interiors, 1982; series editor, The Buildings of Britain, 1981–84, and author, Anglo-Saxon and Norman Buildings vol., 1982; Victorian and Edwardian Hampstead, 1989; The Standing Stones of Europe, 1993; Sky Speaker (opera libretto; music by James Harpham), 1999; An Avebury Carol (Christmas carol; music by Robin Nelson), 2002; The Angel Cantata (cantata; music by Robin Nelson), 2003; Brunel's Kingdom (cantata; music by Robin Nelson), 2005; articles in Arch. Rev., Guardian, Independent, Oldie, etc. *Recreations:* Italy, Greece, Scotland, looking at buildings (old, new and megalithic), opera (esp. Verdi and Bellini), cycling, Dalmatian dogs, et al. *Address:* Swan House, Avebury, Wilts SN8 1RA. *Club:* Garrick.

SERVICE, Louisa Anne, OBE 1997; Joint Chairman: The Hemming Group (formerly The Municipal Group) of Companies, since 1976; Hemming Publishing Ltd, since 1987; *d* of late Henry Harold Hemming, OBE, MC, and Alice Louisa Weaver, OBE; *m* 1959, Alastair Stanley Douglas Service, *qv* (marr. diss. 1984); one *s* one *d*. *Educ:* private and state schs, Canada, USA and Britain; Ecole des Sciences Politiques, Paris; St Hilda's Coll., Oxford (BA and MA, PPE). Export Dir, Ladybird Appliances Ltd, 1957–59; Municipal Journal Ltd and associated cos: Financial Dir, 1966; Dep. Chm., 1974; Chm., Merchant Printers Ltd, 1975–80; Dir, Brintex Ltd, 1965–; Dir, Glass's Information Services Ltd, 1971, Dep. Chm. 1976–81, Chm., 1982–95. Member: Dept of Trade Consumer Credit Act Appeals Panel, 1981–2006; Cttee of Magistrates, 1985–88; FIMBRA Appeals Panel, 1988–92; Solicitors Complaints Bureau, 1992–93. JP Inner London Juvenile Courts, 1969–2001; Chm., Hackney Youth Court, 1975–82, Westminster Juvenile Ct, 1982–88, Hammersmith and Fulham Juvenile Court, 1988–94, Camden Youth and Family Proceedings Ct, 1994–2002; JP Inner London (5) PSD, 1980–; Chairman: Exec. Cttee, Inner London Juvenile Courts, 1977–79; Inner London Juvenile Liaison Cttee, 1986–88 (Mem., 1980–86); Member: working party on re-org. of London Juvenile Courts, 1975; Inner London Family Proceedings Courts, 1991–2002; Inner London Youth Courts, 1992–2002; Inner London Magistrates' Cts Cttee, 1995–2001; Vice-Chm., Paddington Probation Hostel, 1976–86. Corres. mem., SDP Policy Gp on Citizens' Rights, 1982–89. Mem., St Hilda's Coll. Develt Adv. Cttee, 1996–; Dir, 1997–, Chm., 2001–06, Jacqueline du Pré Music Building Ltd. Dir, Opera Circus Ltd, 2000–04. Chm. Council, Mayer-Lismann Opera Workshop, 1976–91; Hon. Sec., Women's India Assoc. of UK, 1967–74. Dir, Arts Club Ltd, 1981–84; Member Council: Friends of Covent Garden, 1982–2005; Haydn-Mozart Soc., 1988–93; Chm., Youth & Music, 1990–2001 (Dir, 1988–90); Mem., E-SU Music Cttee, 1984–91, 1997–2001. Mem. Adv. Bd, Rudolf Kempe Soc., 2000–03. Trustee, Performing Arts Labs, 1996–99. *Publications:* articles on a variety of subjects. *Recreations:* travel, and attractive and witty people including my family. *Address:* c/o Hemming Publishing Ltd, 32 Vauxhall Bridge Road, SW1V 2SS. *T:* (020) 7973 6404. *Club:* Athenæum (Mem. Gen. Cttee, 2003–, Mem. Exec. Cttee, 2004–).
See also J. H. Hemming.

SERVICE, Prof. Robert John, PhD; FBA 1998; Professor of Russian History, Oxford University, since 2002; Fellow, St Antony's College, Oxford, since 1998; *b* 29 Oct. 1947; *s* of Matthew Service and Janet Service (*née* Redpath); *m* 1975, Adele Biagi; two *s* two *d*. *Educ:* Northampton Town and County Grammar Sch. for Boys; King's Coll., Cambridge (Douton Open Schol. in Classics; BA 1970; MA 1971); Univ. of Essex (MA Govt and Politics 1971; PhD 1977). British Council Exchange Res. Student, Leningrad, 1973–74; Lectr in Russian Studies, Univ. of Keele, 1975–84; School of Slavonic and East European Studies, University of London: Lectr in Hist., 1984–87; Reader in Soviet Hist. and Politics, 1987–91; Prof. of Russian Hist. and Politics, 1991–98; Chairman: Hist. Dept, 1987–90; Acad. Assembly, 1990–92; Grad. Studies, 1993–97; Oxford University: Dir, Grad. Studies in Russian and E European Studies, 2000–02; Dean, St Antony's Coll.,

2003. *Publications:* The Bolshevik Party in Revolution, 1979; Lenin: a political life, Vol. 1 1985, Vol. 2 1991, Vol. 3 1995; The Russian Revolution 1900–1927, 1986, 3rd rev. edn 1999; A History of Twentieth-Century Russia, 1997; Lenin: a biography, 2000; Russia: experiment with a people, from 1991 to the present, 2002; A History of Modern Russia from Nicholas II to Putin, 2003; Stalin: a biography, 2004; Comrades: Communism, a world history, 2007. *Recreations:* walking, bicycling, singing. *Address:* 6 Braydon Road, N16 6QB. *T:* (020) 8809 1800; St Antony's College, Oxford OX2 6JF. *T:* (01865) 284747.

SERWOTKA, Mark Henryk; General Secretary, Public and Commercial Services Union, since 2002 (General Secretary elect, 2001–02); *b* 26 April 1963; *s* of Henryk Josef Serwotka and Audrey Phylis Serwotka; *m* 2001, Ruth Louise Cockroft; one *s* one *d*. *Educ:* St Margaret's RC Primary Sch., Aberdare; Bishop Hedley RC Comprehensive Sch., Merthyr Tydfil. Admin Officer, DHSS, subseq. DSS, 1980–2001. *Recreations:* sport (golf, football), reading, walking. *Address:* (office) 160 Falcon Road, SW11 2LN; 87 Woodlands Grove, Coulsdon, Surrey CR5 3AP. *T:* (01737) 554545.

SESHADRI, Prof. Conjeevaram Srirangachari, PhD; FRS 1988; Director, Chennai Mathematical Institute (formerly Dean, School of Mathematics, SPIC Science Foundation, then SPIC Mathematic Institute), since 1989; *b* 29 Feb. 1932; *s* of C. Srirangachari and Chudamani; *m* 1962, Sundari; two *s*. *Educ:* Loyola College, Madras (BA Hons Maths Madras Univ. 1953); PhD Bombay Univ. 1958. Tata Institute of Fundamental Research: Student, 1953; Reader, 1961; Professor, 1963; Senior Professor, 1975–84; Sen. Prof., Inst. of Math. Scis, Madras, 1984–89. *Publications:* Fibres Vectorials sur les courtes algébriques, Asterisque, 96, 1982; Introduction to the Theory of Standard Monomials, 1985. *Recreation:* south Indian classical music. *Address:* Chennai Mathematical Institute, Plot H1, SIPCOT IT Park, Padur PO, Siruseri 603103, India.

SESSIONS, John; see Marshall, J. G.

SESSIONS, His Honour John Lionel; a Circuit Judge, 1992–2007; Judge Advocate of the Fleet, 1995–2007; *b* 8 Jan. 1941; *s* of Geoffrey and Anita Sessions; *m* 1st, 1967, Patrizia Corinna Sanminiatelli (*d* 2005); one *s* two *d*; 2nd, 2006, Averil Harrison. *Educ:* King Edward's Sch., Birmingham; BRNC, Dartmouth. Joined RN, 1959; served in HM Ships incl. Venus, Roebuck, Protector, Agincourt and Leopard; Naval interpreter in Italian, 1966; Comdr, 1976; retd 1981. Called to the Bar, Middle Temple, 1972; in practice (Common Law), 1981–92; Recorder, 1989–92. Mem., Parole Bd, 2005–. Member: Civil and Family Cttee, 1996–99, Criminal Cttee, 2002–06, Judicial Studies Bd; Civil Justice Council, 1998–2000; Assoc. of Italian-Speaking Jurists, 1989–. Grand Registrar, United Grand Lodge of England, 1996–98. Chm., Arun Choral Soc., 2007–. *Publication:* Naval Interpreters' Handbook (Italian), 1974. *Recreations:* sailing, music. *Address:* Henderson Chambers, 2 Harcourt Buildings, Temple, EC4Y 9DB. *Clubs:* Anchorites; Bar Yacht; Royal London Yacht (Cowes); Itchenor Sailing.

SETCHELL, Marcus Edward, CVO 2004; FRCSE, FRCS, FRCOG; Surgeon-Gynaecologist to the Queen, since 1990; Consultant Obstetrician and Gynaecologist, Whittington Hospital NHS Trust, since 2000; *b* 4 Oct. 1943; *s* of late Eric Hedley Setchell and Barbara Mary (*née* Whitworth); *m* 1973, Dr Sarah French; two *s* two *d*. *Educ:* Felsted Sch.; Gonville and Caius Coll., Cambridge (MA, MB BChir); St Bartholomew's Hosp. Consultant Obstetrician and Gynaecologist, St Bartholomew's and Homerton Hosps, 1975–2000, now Hon. Consultant; Hon. Consultant Gynaecologist: King Edward VII Hosp. for Officers, 1982– (Chm. Med. Cttee, 1998–2005); St Luke's Hosp. for Clergy, 1983–. Advr in Gynaecology, Nat. Patient Safety Agency, 2003–06. Convener, Scientific Meetings, 1989–92, Mem. Council, 1994–2000, Chm., Consumers' Forum, 1995–98, RCOG; Mem., Council, 1990–94, Pres., Section of Obstetrics and Gynaecology, 1994–95, RSocMed. Chm. of Govs, Voluntary Hosp. of St Bartholomew, 2007–. Trustee, WellBeing of Women, 2004–. *Publications:* (with R. J. Lilford) Multiple Choice Questions in Obstetrics and Gynaecology, 1985, 3rd edn 1996, 4th edn (with B. Thilaganathan) 2001; (contrib.) Ten Teachers in Obstetrics and Gynaecology, 13th edn 1980 to 16th edn 1995; (with E. E. Philipp) Scientific Foundations of Obstetrics and Gynaecology, 1991; (with C. N. Hudson Shaw) Shaw's Textbook of Operative Gynaecology, 5th edn, 2001. *Recreations:* tennis, ski-ing, gardening, walking. *Address:* 5 Devonshire Place, W1G 6HL. *T:* (020) 7935 4444. *Clubs:* Royal Society of Medicine, St Albans Medical, Soho House; All England Lawn Tennis.

SETH, Vikram, Hon. CBE 2001; writer; *b* 20 June 1952; *s* of Premnath and Leila Seth. *Educ:* Doon Sch., Dehradun, India; Tonbridge Sch., Kent; Corpus Christi Coll., Oxford (MA Hons PPE; Hon. Fellow 1994); Stanford Univ., Calif (MA Econs); Nanjing Univ., China. Sen. Editor, Stanford Univ. Press, 1985–86. Trustee, British Mus., 2004–08. Chevalier, Ordre des Arts et des Lettres (France), 2001; Padma Shri (India), 2007. *Publications:* Mappings (poems), 1982; From Heaven Lake: travels through Sinkiang and Tibet, 1983; The Humble Administrator's Garden (poems), 1985; The Golden Gate (novel in verse), 1986; All You Who Sleep Tonight (poems), 1990; Three Chinese Poets: translations of Wang Wei, Li Bai and Du Fu, 1992; Beastly Tales From Here and There (fables in verse), 1992; A Suitable Boy (novel), 1992; Arion and the Dolphin (libretto), 1994; An Equal Music (novel), 1999; Two Lives (memoir), 2005. *Recreations:* music, Chinese calligraphy, swimming. *Address:* c/o David Goodwin Associates, 55 Monmouth Street, WC2H 9DG.

ŠETINC, Marjan; Ambassador Responsible for Relations with Multi-Lateral Economic Organisations, Ministry of Foreign Affairs, Slovenia, since 2006; *b* 15 May 1949; *s* of late Martin Šetinc and Ana Šetinc; *m* 1973, Marta Bartol; one *s* one *d*. *Educ:* Atlantic Coll., S Wales; Univ. of Ljubljana (BA Psychol.); London Sch. of Econs (MSc). Researcher, TUC of Slovenia, 1974–80; Sen. Researcher, Educnl Res. Inst., Ljubljana, 1980–92. MP (Liberal Democracy) Brezice, Slovenia, 1992–96; Mem., Culture and Educn, Sci. and Technol. and Foreign Affairs Select Cttees; Chm., EU Affairs Select Cttee. Rep. of Slovenia, OSCE Parly Delegn, IPU Delegn and Delegn to EU Parlt; Chm., Parly delegns to various bilateral confs; Ambassador to UK and to Ireland, 1998–2002; Dir Gen., Develt Co-operation, Min. of Foreign Affairs, 2002–06. Member: Gen. Assembly for Slovenia, Internat. Assoc. for Evaluation of Educnl Achievement, 1989–96; Exec. Cttee, Eur. Educnl Res. Assoc., 1996–2001; Nat. Stats Council, 1996–2000. Mem., London Diplomatic Assoc., 1998. Founder Ed., Theory and Res. in Educn jl (formerly School Field), 1989–. *Publications:* Social Conflicts and Strikes, 1975; Public Opinion on Political Decision-Making, 1980; The Averageachieving Curriculum: comparative assessment of pre-university mathematics in Slovenia, 1991; (jtly) Knowledge for Entering the 21st Century, Maths and Natural Sciences: comparison of the achievements of school children aged 14 to 15, in 45 countries, 1997; contrib. numerous articles and papers to scientific jls. *Recreations:* tennis, mountain walking, chess. *Address:* Ministry of Foreign Affairs, Prešernova cesta 25, 1000 Ljubljana, Slovenia.

SETON, Sir Charles Wallace, 13th Bt *cr* 1683 (NS), of Pitmedden, Aberdeenshire; *b* 25 Aug. 1948; *s* of Charles Wallace Seton (*d* 1975) and of Joyce (*née* Perdunn); *S* uncle, 1998, but his name does not appear on the Official Roll of the Baronetage; *m* 1st, 1974, Rebecca

(marr. diss. 1994), *d* of Robert Lowery; one *d*; 2nd, 2000, Cindy, *d* of Billy Lee Smith. *Heir:* *b* Bruce Anthony Seton [*b* 29 April 1957; *m* 1991, Paula Harper; one *s* one *d*].

SETON, Sir Iain (Bruce), 13th Bt *cr* 1663 (NS), of Abercorn; *b* 27 Aug. 1942; *s* of Sir (Christopher) Bruce Seton, 12th Bt and Joyce Vivien (*d* 2005), *d* of late O. G. Barnard; *S* father, 1988; *m* 1963, Margaret Ann, *d* of Walter Charles Faulkner; one *s* one *d*. *Educ:* Colchester and Chadacre. Farming until 1972; mining, 1972–2004. *Heir:* *s* Laurence Bruce Seton [*b* 1 July 1968; *m* 1990, Rachel, *d* of Jeffery Woods; one *s* two *d*]. *Address:* 16 Radiata Drive, Albany, WA 6330, Australia. *T:* (8) 98415667.

SETON, Lady, (Julia), OBE 1989; VMH; (Julia Clements, professionally); author, speaker, international floral art judge; flower arrangement judge for RHS and National Association of Flower Arrangement Societies; *b* 10 April 1906; *d* of late Frank Clements; *m* 1962, Sir Alexander Hay Seton, 10th Bt, of Abercorn (*d* 1963); no *c*. *Educ:* Isle of Wight; Zwicker College, Belgium. Organised and conducted first Judges' School in England at Royal Horticultural Society Halls; has since conducted many other courses for judges all over Europe. VMH, RHS, 1974. *Publications:* Fun with Flowers; Fun without Flowers; 101 Ideas for Flower Arrangement; Party Pieces; Flower Arranging for All Occasions, 1993; Flower Arrangements in Stately Homes; Julia Clements' Gift Book of Flower Arranging; Flowers in Praise; The Art of Arranging a Flower, etc; My Life with Flowers, 1993. *Address:* 122 Swan Court, SW3 5RU.

SETTRINGTON, Lord; Charles Henry Gordon-Lennox; *b* 20 Dec. 1994; *s* and heir of Earl of March and Kinrara, *qv*.

SEVER, (Eric) John; *b* 1 April 1943; *s* of Eric and Clara Sever; *m* Patricia; one *d*. *Educ:* Sparkhill Commercial School. Travel Executive with tour operator, 1970–77. MP (Lab) Birmingham, Ladywood, Aug. 1977–1983; PPS to the Solicitor General, 1978–79. Contested (Lab) Meriden, 1983. *Recreations:* theatre, cinema, reading. *Address:* 16 The Chase, Sutton Coldfield, West Midlands B761JS.

SEVERIN, Prof. Dorothy Virginia Sherman, Hon. OBE 2003; PhD; FSA; Gilmour Professor of Spanish, University of Liverpool, 1982–2008; *b* 24 March 1942; *d* of Wilbur B. and Virginia L. Sherman; marr. diss.; one *d*. *Educ:* Harvard Univ. AB 1963; AM 1964; PhD 1967. FSA 1989. Teaching Fellow and Tutor, Harvard Univ., 1964–66; Vis. Lectr, Univ. of W Indies, 1967–68; Asst Prof., Vassar Coll., 1968; Lectr, Westfield Coll., London Univ., 1969–82; Pro-Vice-Chancellor, Univ. of Liverpool, 1989–92. Member: NI Higher Educn Council, 1993–2001; Res. Panel, British Acad. Humanities Res. Council, 1994–96; Iberian sub-panel, 2008 RAE, HEFCE, 2005–08; Peer Review Coll., AHRC, 2006–09. Vis. Associate Prof., Harvard Univ., 1982; Visiting Professor: Columbia Univ., 1985; Yale Univ., 1985; Univ. of Calif, Berkeley, 1996. Past Pres., British Br., Internat. Courtly Lit. Soc.; Member: Cttee, Asociación Hispánica de Literatura Medieval, 1997–99; Cttee, Asociación Internacional de Hispanistas, 2004–; Cttee, Convivio, 2004–; Trustee, MHRA, 1998–. Editor, Bulletin of Hispanic Studies, 1982–2008; Mem. Editl Bd, Hispanic Rev., Celestinesca. *Publications:* (ed) de Rojas, La Celestina, 1969; Memory in La Celestina, 1970; (ed) Diego de San Pedro, La pasión trobada, 1973; (ed) La Lengua de Erasmo romançada por muy elegante estilo, 1975; The Cancionero de Martínez de Burgos, 1976; (ed with K. Whinnom) Diego de San Pedro, Poesía (Obras completas III), 1979; (ed with Angus MacKay) Cosas sacadas de la Historia del rey Juan el Segundo, 1982; (ed) Celestina, trans. James Mabbe (Eng./Spanish text), 1987; (ed) Celestina (Spanish edn), 1987; Tragicomedy and Novelistic Discourse in Celestina, 1989; Cancionero de Oñate-Castañeda, 1990; ADMYTE: The Paris Cancioneros, 1993, 2nd edn 1999 (PN2 with M. Garcia, PN9, PN13 with F. Maguire); Witchcraft in Celestina, 1995; Animals in Celestina, 1999; Two Spanish Songbooks (The Colombina (LB3) and Egerton (SV2), 2000; Del manuscrito a la imprenta en la época de Isabel la Católica, 2004; Religious Parody and the Spanish Sentimental Romance, 2005; An Electronic Corpus of 15th Century Castilian Cancionero Manuscripts, 2007; contribs to learned jls incl. Hispanic Rev., Romance Philology, Medium Aevum, MLR and THES. *Address:* School of Cultures, Languages and Area Studies, Modern Languages Building, The University, Chatham Street, Liverpool L69 7ZR.

SEVERIN, (Giles) Timothy; author, traveller and historian; *b* 25 Sept. 1940; *s* of Maurice Watkins and Inge Severin; *m* 1966, Dorothy Virginia Sherman (marr. diss. 1979); one *d*. *Educ:* Tonbridge School; Keble Coll., Oxford. MA, BLitt. Commonwealth Fellow, USA, 1964–66. Expeditions: led motorcycle team along Marco Polo route, 1961; R Mississippi by canoe and launch, 1965; Brendan Voyage from W Ireland to N America, 1977; Sindbad Voyage from Oman to China, 1980–81; Jason Voyage from Iolkos to Colchis, 1984; Ulysses Voyage from Troy to Ithaca, 1985; first Crusade route by horse to Jerusalem, 1987–88; travels by horse in Mongolia, 1990; N Pacific voyage by bamboo sailing raft, 1993; Moluccan Islands voyage by traditional sailing prahu, 1996; Pacific and Indonesian island travels, 1998; Caribbean rim travels, 2000. Hon. DLitt Dublin, 1997; Hon. LLD NUI, 2003. Founders Medal, RGS; Livingstone Medal, RSGS; Sykes Medal, RSAA. *Publications:* Tracking Marco Polo, 1964; Explorers of the Mississippi, 1967; The Golden Antilles, 1970; The African Adventure, 1973; Vanishing Primitive Man, 1973; The Oriental Adventure, 1976; The Brendan Voyage, 1978; The Sindbad Voyage, 1982; The Jason Voyage, 1985; The Ulysses Voyage, 1987; Crusader, 1989; In Search of Genghis Khan, 1991; The China Voyage, 1994; The Spice Islands Voyage, 1997; In Search of Moby Dick, 1999; Seeking Robinson Crusoe, 2002; *fiction:* Viking trilogy: Odinn's Child; Sworn Brothers; King's Man, 2005; Corsair, 2007; Buccaneer, 2008. *Address:* Timoleague, Co. Cork, Eire. *T:* (23) 46127, *Fax:* (23) 46233.

SEVERN, Viscount; James Alexander Philip Theo Mountbatten-Windsor; *b* 17 Dec. 2007; *s* of TRH the Earl and Countess of Wessex.
See under Royal Family.

SEVERN, David; see Unwin, David Storr.

SEVERN, Prof. Roy Thomas, CBE 1992; FREng, FICE; Professor of Civil Engineering, Bristol University, 1968–95, now Emeritus; *b* 6 Sept. 1929; *s* of Ernest Severn and Muriel Woollatt; *m* 1957, Hilary Irene Saxton; two *d*. *Educ:* Deacons School, Peterborough; Imperial College (DSc). Lectr, Imperial College, 1949–54; Royal Engineers (Survey), 1954–56; Bristol University: Lectr, 1956–65; Reader, 1965–68; Dean of Faculty of Engrg, 1970–73 and 1991–94; Pro-Vice Chancellor, 1981–84. Pres., ICE, 1991. FREng (FEng 1981). *Publications:* (ed) Engineering Structures: developments in the twentieth century, 1983; contribs to Procs of ICE, Jl Earthquake Eng. and Structural Dynamics. *Recreations:* sailing, gardening, cricket. *Address:* 49 Gloucester Road, Rudgeway, Bristol BS35 3SF. *T:* (01454) 412027.

SEVERNE, Air Vice-Marshal Sir John (de Milt), KCVO 1988 (LVO 1961); OBE 1968; AFC 1955; Extra Equerry to the Queen, since 1984; *b* 15 Aug. 1925; *s* of late Dr A. de M. Severne, Wateringbury, Kent; *m* 1951, Katharine Veronica, *d* of late Captain V. E. Kemball, RN (Retd); three *d*. *Educ:* Marlborough. Joined RAF, 1944; Flying Instr, Cranwell, 1948; Staff Instr and PA to Comdt CFS, 1950–53; Flt Comdr No 98 Sqdn,

Germany, 1954–55; Sqdn Comdr No 26 Sqdn, Germany, 1956–57; Air Min., 1958; Equerry to Duke of Edinburgh, 1958–61; psa 1962; Chief Instr No 226 Operational Conversion Unit (Lightning), 1963–65; jssc 1965; Jt HQ, ME Comd, Aden, and Air Adviser to the South Arabian Govt, 1966–67; DS, JSSC, 1968; Gp Captain Organisation, HQ Strike Comd, 1968–70; Stn Comdr, RAF Kinloss, 1971–72; RCDS 1973; Comdt, Central Flying School, RAF, 1974–76; Air Cdre Flying Trg, HQ RAF Support Comd, 1976–78; Comdr, Southern Maritime Air Region, Central Sub-Area Eastern Atlantic Comd, and Plymouth Sub-Area Channel Comd, 1978–80; retd 1980; recalled as Captain of the Queen's Flight, 1982–89. ADC to The Queen, 1972–73. Hon. Air Cdre, No 3 (Co. of Devon) Maritime HQ Unit, RAuxAF, 1990–95. President: SW Area, RAFA, 1981–95; Queen's Flight Assoc., 1990–2000; CFS Assoc., 1993–98; Taunton and dist Br., ESU, 1996–. Won King's Cup Air Race, British Air Racing Champion, 1960. Pres., RAF Equitation Assoc., 1976–79 (Chm. 1973); Chm., Combined Services Equitation Assoc., 1977–79 (Vice-Chm., 1976). DL Somerset, 1991–2001. *Address:* Ashley House, Alhampton, Shepton Mallet, Somerset BA4 6PY. *Club:* Royal Air Force.

SEVILLE, Prof. Jonathan Peter Kyle, PhD; CEng, FREng, FIChemE; Dean of Engineering, University of Warwick, since 2008; *b* 5 Feb. 1956; *s* of Peter Linton Seville and Joan Kathleen Seville (*née* Monks); *m* 1984, Elizabeth Jane Pope; two *d. Educ:* Gonville and Caius Coll., Cambridge (BA 1979, MA 1983; MEng 1994); Univ. of Surrey (PhD 1987). FIChemE 1997; FREng 2004. Chemical engr, Courtaulds Ltd, 1979–81; Lectr, 1984–91, Sen. Lectr, 1991–94, Univ. of Surrey; Prof. of Chemical Engrg, 1994–2008, Hd, Dept of Chemical Engrg, 1998–2008, Univ. of Birmingham. Visiting Professor: Univ. of BC, 1989; Tech. Univ. of Denmark, 1997. Ed.-in-Chief, Powder Technol., 1995–. Mem. Council, IChemE, 2003–. *Publications:* (ed jtly) Gas Cleaning at High Temperatures, 1993; (jtly) Processing of Particulate Solids, 1997; (ed) Gas Cleaning in Demanding Applications, 1997; (ed jtly) Granulation, 2007. *Recreation:* theatre. *Address:* 46 Kingscote Road, Birmingham B15 3JY. *T:* (0121) 455 9435; *e-mail:* j.p.k.seville@warwick.ac.uk.

SEWARD, Guy William; QC 1982; *b* 10 June 1916; *s* of late William Guy Seward and Maud Peacock; *m* 1946, Peggy Dearman (*d* 2003). *Educ:* Stationers' Sch. Called to the Bar, Inner Temple, 1956. FRVA 1948. Chairman: Medical Service Cttee, 1977–81; Examination in Public, Devon Structure Plan, 1980; E Herts Health Authority, 1982–90; Member: Mid-Herts HMC, 1966–70; Napsbury HMC, 1970–74 (Chm., 1972–74); Bd of Governors, UCH, 1970–74; Herts AHA, 1974–82 (Vice Chm., 1980–82); Herts FPC, 1974–82; Council, Rating and Valuation Assoc., 1983. Freeman, City of London, 1949. Grand Officer, United Grand Lodge of England. *Publications:* (jtly) Enforcement of Planning Control, 1956; (jtly) Local Government Act, 1958; Howard Roberts Law of Town and Country Planning, 1963; (jtly) Rent Act, 1965; (jtly) Land Commission Act, 1967; (jtly) Leasehold Reform, 1967. *Recreations:* travel, gardening. *Address:* Stocking Lane Cottage, Ayot St Lawrence, Welwyn, Herts AL6 9BW. *Club:* Garrick.

SEWARD, Dame Margaret (Helen Elizabeth), DBE 1999 (CBE 1994); Chief Dental Officer, Department of Health, 2000–02; *b* 5 Aug. 1935; *d* of Dr Eric Oldershaw and Gwen Oldershaw; adopted, 1938, by John Hutton Mitchell and Marion Findlay Mitchell; *m* 1962, Prof. Gordon Seward, CBE; one *s* one *d. Educ:* Latymer Sch., Edmonton; London Hosp. Med. Coll. Dental Sch. (BDS Hons 1959; MDS 1970). FDSRCS 1962; MCCDRCS 1989. Dental practice: Highlands Hosp., 1962–64; Cheshunt Community Clinic, 1969–75; Royal London Hosp., 1980–94. Sen. Res. Fellow, BPMF, Univ. of London, 1975–77. Member: GDC, 1976–99; Bd, Faculty of Dental Surgery, RCS, 1980–94 (Vice-Dean, 1990). President: Section of Odontology, RSM, 1991; BDA, 1993–94; GDC, 1949–99. Editor: Brit. Dental Jl, 1979–92; Internat. Dental Jl, 1990–2000. Dir, Teamwork Project, DoH, 1991–95; Ind. Dir, Quality Assessment Agency, 1997–2000. Chm., Communication Cttee, FDI, 1984–89. Hon. Pres., Women in Dentistry, 1989–92; Hon. Member: Amer. Dental Assoc., 1992; Amer. Coll. of Dentists, 1994. Chm. Govs, Latymer Sch., 1984–94. Hon. FDSRCSE 1995; Hon. Fellow, QMW, 1997. Hon. DDSc: Newcastle, 1995; Sheffield, 2002; Hon. DDS Birmingham, 1995; Hon. DSc Portsmouth 2005. *Publications:* Disturbances Associated with the Eruption of the Primary Dentition, 1969; Provision of Dental Care by Women Dentists in England and Wales, 1975, 2nd survey 1985; Better Opportunities for Women Dentists, 2001; Open Wide: memoir of a dental dame, 2009; numerous articles in learned jls, UK and internationally. *Recreations:* cooking, entertaining, house-work! *Address:* 1 Wimpole Street, W1G 0AE. *Club:* Royal Society of Medicine.

SEWEL, family name of **Baron Sewel**.

SEWEL, Baron *cr* 1995 (Life Peer), of Gilcomstoun in the District of the City of Aberdeen; **John Buttifant Sewel,** CBE 1984; PhD; *b* 15 Jan. 1946; *s* of late Leonard Buttifant Sewel and of Hilda Ivy Sewel (*née* Brown). *Educ:* Hanson Boys' Grammar Sch., Bradford; Univ. of Durham (BA 1967); UC, Swansea (MSc (Econ) 1970); Univ. of Aberdeen (PhD 1977). Res. Asst, Dept of Sociology and Anthropology, UC, Swansea, 1967–69; University of Aberdeen: Res. Fellow, Dept of Politics, 1969–72, Depts of Educn and Political Economy, 1972–75; Lectr, 1975; Sen. Lectr, 1988; Prof., Regl Centre for Study of Econ. and Social Policy, 1991–97; Dean: Econ. and Social Scis, 1988–95; Social Scis and Law, 1995–96; Vice-Principal, 1994–96 and 1999–2001; Sen. Vice-Principal, 2001–04. Mem., City of Aberdeen DC, 1974–84 (Leader, 1977–80). Parly Under-Sec. of State, Scottish Office, 1997–99. Pres., COSLA, 1982–84. Member: Accounts Commn for Scotland, 1987–96; Scottish Constitutional Commn, 1994–95. *Publications:* Colliery Closure and Social Change, 1975; Education and Migration, 1976; (with F. W. Bealey) The Politics of Independence: a study of a Scottish town, 1981; (jtly) The Rural Community and the Small School, 1983; articles and chapters on sociology and politics. *Recreations:* hill walking, ski-ing, watching cricket. *Address:* House of Lords, SW1A 0PW.

SEWELL, Prof. Herbert Fitzgerald, PhD; FRCP, FRCPGlas, FRCPath; Professor of Immunology, and Consultant Immunologist, Faculty of Medicine, since 1990, and Pro-Vice-Chancellor Research, since 2002, University of Nottingham; *b* 19 May 1949; *s* of late Wilfred Sewell and Maud Sewell; two *s. Educ:* King Edward's Grammar Sch., Birmingham; Univ. of Birmingham (BDS 1973, MSc 1975, PhD 1978); Univ. of Leicester (MB ChB 1983). MRCPath 1980, FRCPath 1992; MRCPGlas 1987, FRCPGlas 1989; FRCP 1998. Jun. dental posts, Birmingham Dental and Gen. Hosp., 1974–75; MRC Student and Res. Fellow, Dept Exptl Pathol., Univ. of Birmingham, 1974–78; jun. med. posts, East Birmingham Hosp., 1983–84; Consultant Immunologist, Glasgow Royal Infirmary, 1984–85; Sen. Lectr and Hon. Consultant, Dept of Pathology, Univ. of Aberdeen, 1985–90. Member: UK Xenotransplantation Interim Regulatory Authy, 1997–2001; UK Medicines Commn, 1998–2004; Nuffield Council on Bioethics, 1999–; Medical Research Council: Council Mem., 2004–; Member: Clinical Trng and Career Develt Panel, 1998–2001; subgp on Inflammatory Bowel Disease and Autism, Strategy Develt Gp, 1998–2000. Founder FMedSci 1998. Hon. DDS Birmingham 2001; Hon. DSc West Indies, 2003. *Publications:* papers on mechanisms in allergy and on basic and clinical immunology. *Recreations:* road running, Chinese and African cultural studies, sampling rums of the world. *Address:* Pro-Vice-Chancellor's Office, University of Nottingham, B Floor Foyer, Medical School, Queen's Medical Centre, Notts NG7 2UH. *T:* (0115) 875 4659, *Fax:* (0115) 875 7658; *e-mail:* herb.sewell@nottingham.ac.uk.

SEWELL, James Reid, OBE 2001; FSA; City Archivist (formerly Deputy Keeper of Records), Corporation of London, 1984–2003; *b* 12 April 1944; *s* of late James Campbell Sewell and Iris Eveleen Sewell (*née* Reid). *Educ:* High Sch., Glasgow; Univ. of Glasgow (MA Hons Hist.); University Coll. London (Dip. Archive Admin). FSA 1979. Asst Archivist, Durham Co. Record Office, 1967–70; Asst Dep. Keeper, Corp. of London Records Office, 1970–84. Chm. and Pres., Section of Municipal Archives, Internat. Council on Archives, 1992–2000 (Mem. Cttee, 1986–92). Fellow, Guildhall Wine Acad., 1993. *Publications:* (with W. A. L. Seaman) The Russian Journal of Lady Londonderry 1836–37, 1973; The Artillery Ground and Fields in Finsbury, 1977; contrib. articles to various professional jls. *Recreations:* tennis, orchid growing, wine. *Address:* 120 Addiscombe Road, Croydon, Surrey CR0 5PQ. *T:* (020) 8656 4046. *Club:* Shirley Park Lawn Tennis (Hon. Sec., 1983–98).

SEWELL, Rufus Frederick; actor; *b* 29 Oct. 1967; *s* of late Bill Sewell and of Jo Sewell; *m* 1999, Yasmin Abdallah (marr. diss.); partner, Amy Gardener; one *s. Theatre includes:* As You Like It, The Government Inspector, The Seagull, Crucible, Sheffield, 1989; Royal Hunt of the Sun, Comedians, Compass, 1989; Pride and Prejudice, Royal Exchange, Manchester, 1991; Making It Better, Hampstead and Criterion, 1992; Arcadia, NT, 1993; Translations, Plymouth Th., NY, 1995; Rat in the Skull, Duke of York's, 1995; Macbeth, Queen's, 1999; Luther, NT, 2001; Rock 'n' Roll, Royal Court, 2006 (Best Actor: London Evening Standard Th. Awards, 2006; Critics' Circle Th. Awards, 2006; Laurence Olivier Awards, 2007). *Films include:* Twenty-One, 1991; Dirty Weekend, 1993; A Man of No Importance, 1994; Carrington, Victory, 1995; Hamlet, 1997; Dark City, The Woodlanders, At Sachem Farm, Martha Meet Frank Daniel and Laurence, Illuminata, 1998; The Honest Courtesan, In a Savage Land, 1999; Bless the Child, A Knight's Tale, 2001; Extreme Ops, 2003; The Legend of Zorro, 2005; Tristan & Isolde, The Holiday, 2006; The Illusionist, Amazing Grace, 2007. *Television includes:* The Last Romantics, 1991; Gone to Seed, 1992; Dirty Something, 1993; Citizen Locke, Middlemarch, 1994; Cold Comfort Farm, Henry IV, 1995; Arabian Nights, 2000; She-Creature, 2001; Helen of Troy, 2003; Charles II: The Power and the Passion, 2003. *Address:* c/o Julian Belfrage Associates, Adam House, 14 New Burlington Street, W1S 3BQ.

SEWELL, Thomas Robert McKie; HM Diplomatic Service, retired; Contributing Editor, Informa Group Publishing plc, since 1991; international grains consultant; *b* 18 Aug. 1921; *s* of late O. B. Fane Sewell and late Frances M. Sewell (*née* Sharp); *m* 1955, Jennifer Mary Sandeman; one *d* (and one *d* decd). *Educ:* Eastbourne Coll.; Trinity Coll., Oxford (Schol., Heath Harrison Prize, MA); Lausanne and Stockholm Univs (Schol.). HM Forces, 1940–46 (despatches), Indian Armoured Corps; Major. Entered Foreign Service, 1949; Second Sec., Moscow, 1950–52; FO, 1952–55; First Sec., 1954; Madrid, 1955–59; Lima, 1959–61; Chargé d'Affaires, 1960; FO, 1961–63; Counsellor and Head of Chancery, Moscow, 1964–66; Diplomatic Service Rep. at IDC, 1966; Head of Associated States, West Indies and Swaziland Depts, Commonwealth Office, 1967–68; accompanied Sec. of State to Swazi Independence Celebrations, 1968; Head of N American and Caribbean Dept, FCO, 1968–70; Asst Sec., MAFF, 1970–81; UK Rep. to Internat. Wheat Council, 1972–81. Chm., World Grain Conf., Brussels, 1984–92. Contested: (C) Greater Manchester Central, EP elecn, 1984; (Referendum) Weston-super-Mare, 1997. Vis. Fellow, Hubert H. Humphrey Inst. of Public Affairs and Dept of Agricl and Applied Econs, Univ. of Minnesota, 1985; Leverhulme Res. Fellow, 2003. Chm., 1987–2001, Pres., 2001–, Training the Teachers of Tomorrow Trust. *Publications:* Famine and Surplus (with John de Courcy Ling), 1985; The World Grain Trade, 1992; Grain-Carriage by Sea, 1998, 2nd edn 2002 (trans. Japanese, 2002); The Global Grain Market, 2000, 2nd edn 2004; What Did You Do in the Cold War, Daddy?, 2006. *Recreations:* international trail riding, inland waterways cruising. *Clubs:* Farmers', Airborne.

SEWELL, Maj.-Gen. Timothy Patrick T.; *see* Toyne Sewell.

SEXTON, David Howard; Literary Editor, Evening Standard, since 1997; *b* 2 Aug. 1958; *s* of late Richard Herbert Sexton and of Margaret Laura Sexton (*née* Page); *m* 1988, Emma Crichton-Miller (marr. diss. 1997); one *d* by Catherine Bennett. *Educ:* Colchester Royal Grammar Sch.; Trinity Coll., Cambridge (BA 1980). Literary Ed., Sunday Correspondent, 1990–91; columnist, TLS, 1991–97; radio critic, Sunday Telegraph, 1991–2007. *Publication:* The Strange World of Thomas Harris, 2001. *Recreations:* food, wine, books, trees, France. *Address:* Evening Standard, Northcliffe House, 2 Derry Street, W8 5EE; *e-mail:* David.Sexton@standard.co.uk; Saint Caprais, 82110 Bouloc, France. *T:* (5) 63957269.

SEYCHELLES, Bishop of, since 1979; **Rt Rev. French Kitchener Chang-Him;** Archbishop of the Indian Ocean, 1984–95; *m* 1975, Susan Talma; twin *d. Educ:* Lichfield Theol Coll.; St Augustine's Coll., Canterbury; Trinity Coll., Univ. of Toronto (LTh 1975). Deacon, Sheffield, 1962; priest, Seychelles, 1963; Curate of Goole, 1962–63; Rector of Praslin, Seychelles, 1963–66 and 1969–71; Asst Priest, St Leonard's, Norwood, Sheffield, 1967–68; Vicar General, Seychelles, 1972–73; Rector, S Mahé Parish, 1973–74; Archdeacon of Seychelles, 1973–79; Priest-in-charge, St Paul's Cathedral, Mahé, 1977–79; Dean, Province of the Indian Ocean, 1983–84. DD (*hc*) Trinity Coll., Toronto, 1991. *Address:* Box 44, Victoria, Mahé, Seychelles. *T:* 224242, *Fax:* 224296; *e-mail:* angdio@seychelles.net.

SEYFRIED HERBERT, family name of **Baron Herbert**.

SEYMOUR, family name of **Marquess of Hertford** and **Duke of Somerset**.

SEYMOUR, Lord; Sebastian Edward Seymour; *b* 3 Feb. 1982; *s* and *heir* of 19th Duke of Somerset, *qv*; *m* 2006, Arlette Lafayeedney. *Educ:* Marlborough Coll. *Address:* Berry Pomeroy, Totnes, Devon TQ9 6NJ.

SEYMOUR, Anya; *see* Hindmarch, A.

SEYMOUR, Prof. Carol Anne, (Mrs Carol Seymour-Richards), PhD; FRCP, FRCPath, FFFLM; Professor of Clinical Biochemistry and Metabolic Medicine, St George's Hospital Medical School, 1991–2004, now Emeritus; Medico-legal Adviser, Medical Protection Society, since 2003; *b* 19 March 1945; *d* of Raymond and Erica Seymour; *m* 1987, Prof. Peter Richards, *qv*. *Educ:* Badminton Sch.; St Anne's Coll., Oxford (MA, BM BCh); RPMS (MSc, PhD); Holborn Coll., Univ. of Wolverhampton (Postgrad. DipLaw 1998); Inns of Court Sch. of Law (Postgrad. DipLS 2001). MRCP 1972, FRCP 1985; FRCPath 1993; FFFLM 2006. Lectr in Medicine and Hon. Consultant Physician, Univ. of Cambridge Sch. of Clinical Medicine/Addenbrooke's Hosp., 1977–91; Fellow, and Dir of Med. Studies, Trinity Coll., Cambridge, 1981–91. Dir of Med. Advice to Parly and Health Service Comr, 1997–2003; Royal College of Physicians: Academic Registrar, 1987–2008; Examiner for MRCP, 1991–; Mem. Council, 1996–2000, 2003–05; Examiner for MRCPath, RCPath, 1993–2005; Mem., GMC, 1987–91 (Lead Performance Assessor, 1999–2003). Called to the Bar, Gray's Inn,

2001. *Publications:* (contrib.) Oxford Textbook of Medicine, 1983, 3rd edn 1995; Clinical Clerking, 1984, (jtly) 3rd edn 2003; many articles on liver disease and metabolic aspects of clinical medicine. *Recreations:* music (clarinet and organ), walking, cycling. *Address:* Barefords, 78 Commercial End, Swaffham Bulbeck, Cambs CB25 0NE. *T:* (01223) 812007; *e-mail:* carol.seymour@mps.org.uk.

SEYMOUR, David, CB 2005; Legal Adviser to the Home Office and Northern Ireland Office, since 2000; *b* 24 Jan. 1951; *s* of Graham Seymour and late Betty (*née* Watson); *m* 1972, Elisabeth Huitson; one *s* two *d. Educ:* Trinity Sch., Croydon; Queen's Coll., Oxford (Open Exhibn; BA Jurisprudence 1972; MA 1977); Fitzwilliam Coll., Cambridge (LLB 1974). Law clerk, Rosenfeld, Meyer & Susman (Attorneys), Beverly Hills, Calif, 1972–73; called to the Bar: Gray's Inn (Holt Schol.), 1975, Bencher, 2001; NI, 1997; pupillage, 1975–76; Legal Advr's Br., Home Office, 1976–97; Principal Asst Legal Advr, 1994; Dep. Legal Advr, 1996; Legal Sec. to the Law Officers, 1997–2000. Vis. Lectr in European Human Rights Law, Univ. of Conn Sch. of Law, 1986. Mem., Review of Criminal Justice System in NI, 1998–2000. *Recreations:* watching cricket, gardening, squash, walking. *Address:* c/o Home Office, 2 Marsham Street, SW1P 4DF. *Club:* MCC.

SEYMOUR, Julian Roger, CBE 2001; Director, New Star European Hedge Fund, since 2002; *b* 19 March 1945; *s* of Evelyn Roger Seymour and Rosemary Evelyn Seymour (*née* Flower); *m* 1984, Diana Elizabeth Griffith; one *s* one *d. Educ:* Eton. Director: Collett, Dickinson, Pearce Ltd, 1969–79; Robert Fox Ltd, 1980–85; Dir, Corporate Finance, Lowe Gp PLC, 1985–91; Dir, Lady Thatcher's Private Office, 1991–2000. Non-exec. Dir, Chime Communications PLC, 1990–2007. Comr, English Heritage, 1992–98; Chm., Margaret Thatcher Archive Trust, 2005–. *Recreations:* gardening, shooting. *Address:* 37 Surrey Lane, SW11 3PA.

SEYMOUR, Prof. Leonard William, PhD; Professor of Gene (formerly Genetic) Therapies, University of Oxford, since 2002; *b* 4 Sept. 1958; *s* of Percy and Daisy Seymour. *Educ:* Plymouth Coll.; Univ. of Manchester (BSc Hons 1980); Keele Univ. (PhD 1985). Lectr, 1993–99, Reader in Molecular Therapy, 1999–2002, CRC Inst. for Cancer Studies, Univ. of Birmingham. Pres. (first), British Soc. for Gene Therapy, 2004–. *Publications:* over 100 primary scientific papers in fields of gene therapy and virotherapy of cancer. *Recreations:* all forms of music, playing keyboard, hill walking and trekking through remote areas. *Address:* Institute for Cancer Medicine, Churchill Hospital, Oxford OX3 7XB. *T:* (01865) 617040.

SEYMOUR, Lynn, CBE 1976; ballerina; *b* Wainwright, Alberta, 8 March 1939; *d* of E. V. Springbett; *m* 1st, 1963, Colin Jones, photo-journalist (marr. diss.); 2nd, 1974, Philip Pace; three *s*; 3rd, 1983, Vanya Hackel (marr. diss.). *Educ:* Vancouver; Sadler's Wells Ballet School. Joined Sadler's Wells Ballet Company, 1957; Deutsche Oper, Berlin, 1966; Artistic Director: Ballet of Bavarian State Opera, Munich, 1979–80; Greek National Opera Ballet, 2006–07; has danced with Royal Ballet, English Nat. Ballet, Berliner Ballet, and Adventures in Motion Pictures. *Roles created:* Adolescent, in The Burrow, Royal Opera House, 1958; Bride, in Le Baiser de la Fée, 1960; Girl, in The Invitation, 1960; Young Girl, in Les Deux Pigeons, 1961; Principal, in Symphony, 1963; Principal, in Images of Love, 1964; Juliet, in Romeo and Juliet, 1964; Albertine, BBC TV, 1966; Concerto, 1966; Anastasia, 1966; Flowers, 1972; Side Show, 1972; A Month in the Country, 1976; Five Brahms Waltzes in the manner of Isadora Duncan, 1976; mother, in Fourth Symphony, 1977; Mary Vetsera, in Mayerling, 1978; Take Five, 1978. *Other appearances include:* Danses Concertantes; Solitaire; La Fête Etrange; Sleeping Beauty; Swan Lake; Giselle (title-role); Cinderella; Das Lied von der Erde; The Four Seasons; Voluntaries; Manon, Sleeping Beauty, Dances at a Gathering, The Concert, Pillar of Fire, Romeo and Juliet (Tudor, Nureyev and Cranko), Las Hermañas, Moor's Pavane, Auriole, Apollon, Le Corsaire, Flower Festival, La Sylphide (Sylph and Madge), A Simple Man, Onegin. *Choreography for:* Rashomon, for Royal Ballet Touring Co., 1976; The Court of Love, for SWRB, 1977; Intimate Letters, 1978 and Mac and Polly, for Commonwealth Dance Gala, 1979; Boreas, and Tattoo, for Bavarian State Opera Ballet, 1980; Wolfi, for Ballet Rambert, 1987; Bastet, for SWRB, 1988. A Time to Dance (film), 1986. *Publication:* Lynn: leaps and boundaries (autobiog.), 1984.

SEYMOUR, Sir Michael Patrick Culme-, 6th Bt *cr* 1809, of Highmount, co. Limerick and Friery Park, Devonshire; Regional Vice-President, Asia, Pacific and India, Swissair, since 1998; *b* 28 April 1962; *s* of Major Mark Charles Culme-Seymour and of his 3rd wife, Patricia June, *d* of Charles Reid-Graham; *S* cousin, 1999; *m* 1986, Karin Fleig (marr. diss. 2007); two *s. Heir: s* Michael Culme-Seymour, *b* 5 Oct. 1986. *Address:* Kronprinzenstrasse 56, 53173 Bad Godesberg, Germany. *Club:* British (Singapore).

SEYMOUR, Richard William; QC 1991; **His Honour Judge Seymour;** a Senior Circuit Judge, since 2000; *b* 4 May 1950; *e s* of late Albert Percy and of Vera Maud Seymour; *m* 1971, Clare Veronica, BSS, MSc, *d* of Stanley Victor Peskett, *qv*; one *s* one *d. Educ:* Brentwood Sch.; Royal Belfast Academical Instn; Christ's Coll., Cambridge (schol.; BA 1971; MA 1975). Holker Jun. Exhibn, 1970, Holker Sen. Schol., 1972, Gray's Inn; called to the Bar, Gray's Inn, 1972. Asst Recorder, 1991–95; Recorder, 1995–2000; a Judge of the Technology and Construction Court, 2000–05; assigned to Queen's Bench Div. of High Court, 2005–. Pres., Mental Health Review Tribunals, 2000. *Publications:* (ed jtly) Kemp and Kemp, The Quantum of Damages, 4th edn 1975; legal chapters in: Willis and Willis, Practice and Procedure for the Quantity Surveyor, 8th edn 1980; Willis and George, The Architect in Practice, 6th edn 1981; (with Clare Seymour) Courtroom Skills for Social Workers, 2007. *Recreations:* archaeology, walking, foreign travel. *Address:* Royal Courts of Justice, Strand, WC2A 2LL. *T:* (020) 7947 6331.

SEYMOUR, Richard William; Founder and Director, Seymour Powell, since 1984; *b* 1 May 1953; *s* of Bertram Seymour and Annie Irene (*née* Sherwood); *m* 1980, Anne Margaret Hart; one *s* one *d. Educ:* Central Sch. of Art & Design (BA); Royal Coll. of Art (MA; Sen. Fellow, 2005). Advertising Creative Dir, Blazelynn Advertising, London, 1978–81; film prodn designer, with Anton Furst, later Seymour Furst, 1981–83; freelance designer working on advertising and new product develt projects, 1982–83; Founder, with D. Powell, Seymour Powell (product and transportation design consultancy), 1984 (clients incl. Nokia, Ford, Aqualisa). Vis. Prof. of Product and Transportation Design, RCA, 1995–. Trustee, Design Mus., London, 1994–. Contrib. to TV progs and children's progs featuring design and future thinking. Pres., D&AD, 1999 (Mem., Exec. Cttee, 1997–). FRSA 1993; FCSD 1993. Hon. DDes Centre of Creative Studies, Michigan, 2002. Awards include: Best Overall Design and Product Design (for Norton F1 motorcycle), Design Week Awards, 1990; Silver Awards (for Technophone Cellular Phone), 1991, and (for MuZ Scorpion motorcycle), 1993, and President's Award (for outstanding contribn to design), 1995, D&AD; Product Design Award, BBC Design Awards, 1994; Design Effectiveness Award, Design Business Assoc. (for SEB appliances), 1995, 2002, 2003; Special Commendation, Prince Philip Designers Prize, 1997; Janus award, France, 2002; Gerald Frewer Meml Trophy, Inst. of Engrg Designers, 2003; Star Pack Award, 2003; Best Corporate Film, Golden Camera Awards: for Samsung European Premium Design, 2003; for Unilever, 2005. *Publication:* (with M. Palin) The Mirrorstone (Smarties Design Award, Hatchard's Top Ten Author's Award), 1986. *Recreations:* Early English music, cello, motorcycling. *Address:* Seymour Powell, 327 Lillie Road, SW6 7NR. *T:* (020) 7381 6433. *Clubs:* Bluebird, Chelsea Arts.

SEYMOUR, Urmila; *see* Banerjee, U.

SEYMOUR-JACKSON, Ralph; Chief Executive Officer, Student Loans Company Limited, since 2003; *b* 11 May 1963; *s* of Alan and Arabella Seymour-Jackson; *m* 1993, Angela Fenn; one *s* one *d. Educ:* Wadham Coll., Oxford (BA Maths 1984). FIA 1991. Pilot, RAF, 1980–88; Actuary, Norwich Union, 1988–92; Chief Exec., Scoplife Insce Co., Athens, 1992–96; Scottish Provident Institution (Mutual Life Insurer): Gp Corporate Develt and Mktg Manager, Gp Hd Office, Edinburgh, 1996–98; Hd, UK Ops, 1998–2000; IT Dir, Abbey National Finance and Investment Services, 2001–03. *Recreations:* skydiving, cooking, children. *Address:* (office) 100 Bothwell Street, Glasgow G2 7JD. *T:* (0141) 306 2011, *Fax:* (0141) 306 2006.

SEYMOUR-RICHARDS, Carol Anne; *see* Seymour, C. A.

SEYS LLEWELLYN, Anthony John, QC 2003; **His Honour Judge Seys Llewellyn;** a Senior Circuit Judge and Designated Civil Judge for Wales, since 2008; *b* 24 April 1949; *s* of late His Honour John Desmond Seys-Llewellyn and Hilda Elaine (*née* Porcher); *m* 1975, Helen Mary Manson; two *s* two *d. Educ:* King's Sch., Chester; Jesus Coll., Oxford (1st cl. Hons Law 1970; BCL 1st cl. Hons 1971). Called to the Bar, Gray's Inn, 1972 (scholarships; Bencher, 2006); Recorder of the Crown Court, Wales and Chester Circuit, 1990–2008. Asst Comr, Parly Boundary Commns for England and Wales, 1991–. *Recreations:* sports including rowing (now viewed from river banks), art, music, family man. *Address:* Cardiff Civil Justice Centre, 2 Park Street, Cardiff CF10 1ET.

SHACKLE, Prof. Christopher, PhD; FBA 1990; Professor of Modern Languages of South Asia, University of London, 1985–2007, now Emeritus; *b* 4 March 1942; *s* of late Francis Mark Shackle and Diana Margaret Shackle (*née* Harrington, subseq. Thomas); *m* 1st, 1964, Emma Margaret Richmond (marr. diss.); one *s* two *d*; 2nd, 1988, Shahrukh Husain; one *s* one *d. Educ:* Haileybury and ISC; Merton College, Oxford (BA 1963); St Antony's College, Oxford (DipSocAnthrop 1965; BLitt 1966); PhD London, 1972. School of Oriental and African Studies, University of London: Fellow in Indian Studies, 1966; Lectr in Urdu and Panjabi, 1969; Reader in Modern Languages of South Asia, 1979; Pro-Dir for Academic Affairs, 1997–2002 (Acting Dir, Jan.–April 2001); Pro-Dir, 2002–03; Res. Prof., 2007–08. British Academy: Mem. Council, 1995–96, 2001–04; Chm., Sect. H3 Oriental and African Studies, 1999–2003. Medal, Royal Asiatic Soc., 2006. Sitara-i-Imtiaz (Pakistan), 2005. *Publications:* Teach Yourself Punjabi, 1972; (with D. J. Matthews) An Anthology of Classical Urdu Love Lyrics, 1972; The Siraiki Language of Central Pakistan, 1976; Catalogue of the Panjabi and Sindhi Manuscripts in the India Office Library, 1977; A Guru Nanak Glossary, 1981; An Introduction to the Sacred Language of the Sikhs, 1983; The Sikhs, 1984; (with D. J. Matthews and S. Husain) Urdu Literature, 1985; (with R. Snell) Hindi and Urdu since 1800, 1990; (with Z. Moir) Ismaili Hymns from South Asia, 1992; (with R. Snell) The Indian Narrative, 1992; (with S. Sperl) Qasida Poetry in Islamic Asia and Africa, 1996; (with J. Majeed) Hali's Musaddas, 1997; (with N. Awde) Treasury of Indian Love Poetry, 1999; (with G. Singh and A. Mandair) Sikh Religion, Culture and Ethnicity, 2001; (with D. Arnold) SOAS Since the Sixties, 2003; (with A. Mandair) Teachings of the Sikh Gurus, 2005; (with L. Lewisohn) Attar and the Persian Sufi Tradition, 2006 (Iran Book Prize, 2008); (trans.) Mazhar ul Islam, The Season of Love, Bitter Almonds and Delayed Rains, 2006; numerous articles.

SHACKLETON, Fiona Sara, LVO 2006; Personal Solicitor to Prince William of Wales and Prince Harry of Wales, since 1996; Partner, Payne Hicks Beach, since 2001; *b* 26 May 1956; *d* of late Jonathan Philip Charkham, CBE and of Moira Elizabeth Frances Charkham; *m* 1985, Ian Ridgeway Shackleton; two *d. Educ:* Francis Holland Sch.; Benenden Sch.; Univ. of Exeter (LLB 1977). Articled Clerk, Herbert Smith, 1978–80; admitted solicitor, 1980; Partner, Brecher & Co., 1981–84; Farrer & Co., 1984–2000 (Partner, 1987–2000); Personal Solicitor to Prince of Wales, 1996–2005. Inaugural Mem., Internat. Acad. of Matrimonial Lawyers, 1986–. Gov., Benenden Sch., 1986–2007. *Publication:* (with Olivia Timbs) The Divorce Handbook, 1992. *Recreations:* listening to music, particularly opera, cooking, calligraphy, bridge. *Address:* 10 New Square, Lincoln's Inn, WC2A 3QG. *T:* (020) 7465 4300.

SHACKLETON, Keith Hope; artist and naturalist; President, Society of Wildlife Artists, 1978–83; Chairman, Artists League of Great Britain; *b* 16 Jan. 1923; *s* of W. S. Shackleton; *m* 1951, Jacqueline Tate; two *s* one *d. Educ:* Oundle. Served RAF, 1941–46. Civil Pilot and Dir, Shackleton Aviation Ltd, 1948–63; natural history programmes for television, 1964–68; joined naturalist team aboard MS Lindblad Explorer, 1969. Pres., Royal Soc. of Marine Artists, 1973–78. Member: RGS; Zool Soc. of London; NZ Antarctic Soc. Vice Pres., Wildfowl and Wetlands Trust, 1994–. Trustee, UK Antarctic Heritage Trust, 1997–. Hon. LLD Birmingham, 1983. *Publications:* Tidelines, 1951; Wake, 1953; Wild Animals in Britain, 1959; Ship in the Wilderness, 1986; Wildlife and Wilderness, 1986; Keith Shackleton: an autobiography in paintings, 1998; Shakewell Afloat, 2004; illustrations for books. *Recreations:* small Boat Sailing, exploration field work. *Address:* Wood Farm, Woodleigh, Devon TQ7 4DR. *Club:* Itchenor Sailing.

SHADBOLT, Prof. Nigel Richard, PhD; CEng, FREng; CPsychol; Professor of Artificial Intelligence, and Deputy Head, School of Electronics and Computer Science, University of Southampton, since 2000; *b* 9 April 1956; *s* of Douglas William Robert and Audrey Shadbolt; *m* 1992, Beverly Saunders; one *s* one *d. Educ:* Univ. of Newcastle upon Tyne (BA 1st cl. Hons Philosophy and Psychol.); Univ. of Edinburgh (PhD Artificial Intelligence 1983). CPsychol 1990; CITP 2004; CEng 2005, FREng 2006. Res. Fellow, Univ. of Edinburgh, 1982–83; University of Nottingham: Lectr, 1983–90; Reader, 1990–92; Allan Standen Prof. of Intelligent Systems, 1992–99. Dir, Epistemics Ltd, 1993–; Chief Technol. Officer, Garlik Ltd, 2006–. FBCS 2002 (Vice Pres., 2003–05; Dep. Pres., 2005–06; Pres., 2006–07). *Publications:* (jtly) POP-11 Programming for Artificial Intelligence, 1987; Research and Development in Expert Systems VI, 1989; (jtly) Advances in Knowledge Acquisition, 1996; (jtly) Knowledge Engineering and Management, 2000; (jtly) The Spy in the Coffee Machine: the end of privacy as we know it, 2008; articles on facets of artificial intelligence, psychology and computing. *Recreations:* my family, sailing, reading, collecting - ranging from space memorabilia to fossils! *Address:* School of Electronics and Computer Science, University of Southampton, Southampton SO17 1NJ; *e-mail:* nrs@ecs.soton.ac.uk.

SHAFER, Prof. Byron Edwin, PhD; Glenn B. and Cleone Orr Hawkins Professor of Political Science, University of Wisconsin, Madison, since 2001; *b* 8 Jan. 1947; *s* of Byron Henry Shafer and Doris Marguerite (*née* Von Bergen); *m* 1981, Wanda K. Green; one *s. Educ:* Yale Univ. (BA Magna Cum Laude, Deptl Hons in Pol. Sci. with Excep. Dist. 1968); Univ. of California at Berkeley (PhD Pol. Sci. 1979). Resident Scholar, Russell Sage Foundn, USA, 1977–84; Associate Prof. of Pol. Sci., Florida State Univ., 1984–85; Andrew W. Mellon Prof. of American Govt, Univ. of Oxford, 1985–2001; Fellow, 1985–2001, now Emeritus, and Actg Warden, 2000–01, Nuffield Coll., Oxford. Hon.

MA Oxford, 1985. E. E. Schattschneider Prize, 1980, Franklin L. Burdette Prize, 1990, Jack L. Walker Award, 1997, Amer. Pol. Sci. Assoc.; V. O. Key Award, 2007. *Publications:* Presidential Politics, 1980; Quiet Revolution: the struggle for the Democratic Party and the shaping of post-reform politics, 1983; Bifurcated Politics: evolution and reform in the National Party Convention, 1988; Is America Different?, 1991; The End of Realignment?: interpreting American electoral eras, 1991; The Two Majorities: the issue context of modern American politics, 1995; Postwar Politics in the G-7, 1996; Present Discontents: American politics in the very late twentieth century, 1997; Partisan Approaches to Postwar American Politics, 1998; Contesting Democracy: substance and structure in American political history 1775–2000, 2001; The State of American Politics, 2002; The Two Majorities and the Puzzle of Modern American Politics, 2003; The End of Southern Exceptionalism, 2006; articles in learned jls. *Recreations:* furniture restoration, gardening, livestock management. *Address:* Department of Political Science, University of Wisconsin, 110 North Hall, 1050 Bascom Mall, Madison, WI 53706, USA.

SHAFFER, Elinor Sophia, PhD; FBA 1995; Senior Research Fellow, School of Advanced Study, Institute of Germanic and Romance Studies (formerly of Germanic Studies), University of London, since 1998 (Fellow, 1997–98); *b* 6 April 1935; *d* of Vernon Cecil Stoneman and Helene Dorothy Stoneman (*née* Nieschlag); *m* 1964, Brian M. Shaffer; two *s*. *Educ:* Chicago Univ. (BA 1954); St Hilda's Coll., Oxford (BA 1958; MA 1962); PhD Columbia Univ., NY, 1966; MA Cantab 1968. Fellow, Columbia Univ., 1961–63; Instr, 1963–64, Asst Prof., 1964–65, Dept of English, Univ. of Calif, Berkeley; Res. Fellow, Clare Hall, Cambridge, 1968–71; Lectr, 1971–77, Reader in English and Comparative Lit., 1977–97, UEA. Visiting Professor: Brown Univ., 1983–84; Zurich Univ., 1986; Stanford Univ., 1988; Vis. Lectr, Free Univ., Berlin, 1979; Study Fellow, ACLS, 1971; Leverhulme Fellowship, 1976; Research Fellow: Humanities Res. Centre, ANU, 1982; Humanities Res. Inst., Univ. of Calif, 1991; Dist. Fellow, Eur. Humanities Res. Centre, Oxford, 1995–; Vis. Fellow, All Souls Coll., Oxford, 1996. Editor: Comparative Criticism, 1979–2004; inaugural issue (with A. Brady), 2004, special issue on reception studies, 2006, Comparative Critical Studies; Series Editor, The Reception of British and Irish Authors in Europe (contrib. preface or introduction to all vols), 1997–. *Publications:* 'Kubla Khan' and The Fall of Jerusalem: the mythological school in Biblical criticism and secular literature 1770–1880, 1975; Erewhons of the Eye: Samuel Butler as painter, photographer and art critic, 1988; The Third Culture: literature and science, 1998; (ed jtly and introd.) The Reception of S. T. Coleridge in Europe, 2007; Coleridge's Literary Theory, 2009; *chapters in:* The Coleridge Connection, 1990; Romanticism and the Sciences, 1990; Aesthetic Illusion: theoretical and historical approaches, 1990; Reflecting Senses: perception and appearance in literature, culture and the arts, 1994; Milton, the Metaphysicals and Romanticism, 1994; Apocalypse Theory and the Ends of the World, 1995; Boydell's Shakespeare Gallery, 1996; Transports: imaginative geographies 1600–1830, 1996; (contrib.) Oxford Encyclopedia of Aesthetics, 1998; The Cambridge History of Literary Criticism, vol. V, Romanticism, 2000; Coleridge and the Science of Life, 2001; Mapping Lives: the uses of biography, 2001; Goethe in the English-speaking World, 2002; (contrib.) Oxford Companion to Photography, 2003; Anglo-German Affinities and Antipathies in the Nineteenth Century, 2004; Samuel Butler: Victorian against the grain, 2007; Oxford Handbook of Coleridge, 2008; contrib. to Oxford DNB; catalogues for exhibns about Samuel Butler, 1989, 2002; many lectures, reviews and contribs to learned jls. *Recreations:* theatre, travelling, photography, wine. *Address:* 9 Cranmer Road, Cambridge CB3 9BL. *T:* (01223) 357406.

SHAFFER, Sir Peter (Levin), Kt 2001; CBE 1987; FRSL; playwright; *b* 15 May 1926; *s* of Jack Shaffer and Reka Shaffer (*née* Fredman). *Educ:* St Paul's School, London; Trinity College, Cambridge. Literary Critic, Truth, 1956–57; Music Critic, Time and Tide, 1961–62. Cameron Mackintosh Vis. Prof. of Contemporary Theatre, and Fellow, St Catherine's Coll., Oxford Univ., 1994. Mem., European Acad. of Yuste (Cervantes Seat), 1998. Hon. DLitt St Andrews, 1999. Hamburg Shakespeare Prize, 1989; William Inge Award for Distinguished Achievement in the American Theatre, 1992. *Stage Plays:* Five Finger Exercise, prod. Comedy, London, 1958–60, NY, 1960–61 (Evening Standard Drama Award, 1958; NY Drama Critics Circle Award (best foreign play), 1959–60); (double bill) The Private Ear (filmed 1966) and The Public Eye, produced, Globe, London, 1962, NY, 1963 (filmed 1972); It's About Cinderella (with Joan Littlewood and Theatre Workshop) prod. Wyndham's Theatre, Christmas, 1963; The Royal Hunt of the Sun, Nat. Theatre, Chichester Festival, 1964, The Old Vic, and Queen's Theatres, 1964–67, NY, 1965–66 (filmed 1969), Nat. Theatre, 2006; Black Comedy, Nat. Theatre, Chichester Fest., 1965, The Old Vic and Queen's Theatres, 1965–67; as double bill with White Lies, NY, 1967, Shaw, 1976; The White Liars, Lyric, 1968; The Battle of Shrivings, Lyric, 1970; Equus, Nat. Theatre, 1973, NY, 1974, Albery Theatre, 1976 (NY Drama Critics' and Antoinette Perry Awards) (filmed 1977), Gielgud, 2007; Amadeus, Nat. Theatre, 1979 (Evening Standard Drama Award, Plays and Players Award, London Theatre Critics Award), NY, 1980 (Antoinette Perry Award, Drama Desk Award), Her Majesty's, 1981 (filmed 1984, Acad. Award, Golden Globe Award, Los Angeles Film Critics Assoc. Award, Premi David di Donatello, 1985), Old Vic, 1998, NY, 1999, Wilton's Music Hall, 2006; Yonadab, Nat. Theatre, 1985; Lettice and Lovage, Globe, 1987, Barrymore Theatre, NY, 1990 (Evening Standard Drama Award for Best Comedy, 1988); The Gift of the Gorgon, Barbican, 1992, transf. Wyndhams, 1993; Whom Do I Have the Honour of Addressing?, Chichester, 1996. Plays produced on television and sound include: The Salt Land (ITV), 1955; Balance of Terror (BBC TV), 1957; Whom Do I Have the Honour of Addressing? (radio), 1989, etc. *Recreations:* music, architecture. *Address:* c/o Macnaughton Lord Ltd 2000, 19 Margravine Gardens, W6 8RL. *T:* (020) 8741 0606. *Club:* Garrick.

SHAFIK, Nemat, (Minouche), DPhil; Permanent Secretary, Department for International Development, since 2008; *b* 13 Aug. 1962; *d* of Dr Talaat Shafik and Maissa Hamza; *m* 2002, Dr Raffael Jovine; one *s* one *d*, and three step *c*. *Educ:* Univ. of Massachusetts, Amherst (BA *summa cum laude* Pols and Econs 1983); London Sch. of Econs (MSc Econs 1986); St Antony's Coll., Oxford (DPhil Econs 1989). World Bank: joined 1990, as economist in Res. Dept; Country Economist, Central Europe, 1992–94; Dir, Private Sector and Finance, ME and N Africa, 1997–99; Vice-Pres., Private Sector and Infrastructure, 1999–2004; Dir Gen., Country (formerly Regl) Progs, DFID, 2004–08. Adjunct Prof., Econs, Georgetown Univ., 1989–94; Vis. Associate Prof., Wharton Business Sch., Univ. of Pennsylvania, 1996. Non-exec. Dir, Mgt Bd, DFID, 2002–04. Chairman: Consultative Gp to Assist the Poorest, 1999–2004; Infodev, 1999–2004; Global Water and Sanitation Prog., 1999–2004; Private Participation in Infrastructure Adv. Facility, 1999–2004; Treas., Our Place DC, 2001–04; Bd Mem., Operating Council, Global Alliance for Workers and Communities, 1999–2003. Bd Mem., Middle East Jl, 1996–2002. *Publications:* Reviving Private Investment in Developing Countries, 1992; Globalization Regionalism and Growth, 1996; Challenges Facing Middle Eastern and North African Countries: alternative futures, 1998; Prospects for Middle East and North African Economies: from boom to bust and back?, 1998; articles in Jl of Develt Economics, Oxford Economic Papers, World Develt, Columbia Jl of World Business, Middle East Jl. *Recreations:* family, friends, museums, theatre, occasionally reading, walking and yoga. *Address:* Department for International Development, 1 Palace Street, SW1E 5HE. *T:* (020) 7023 0674, *Fax:* (020) 7023 0371.

SHAFTESBURY, 12th Earl of, *cr* 1672; **Nicholas Edmund Anthony Ashley-Cooper;** Bt 1622; Baron Ashley 1661; Baron Cooper 1672; *b* 3 June 1979; *yr s* of 10th Earl of Shaftesbury and of Christina Eva (*née* Montan); *S* brother, 2005.

SHAGARI, Alhaji Shehu Usman Aliyu, GCFR 2000; President of Nigeria and Commander-in-Chief of the Armed Forces, 1979–83; *b* Feb. 1925; *s* of Magaji Aliyu; *m* 1946; two *s* three *d* (and one *s* decd). *Educ:* Middle Sch., Sokoto; Barewa Coll., Kaduna; Teacher Trg Coll., Zaria. Teacher of science, Sokoto Middle Sch., 1945–50; Headmaster, Argungu Sen. Primary Sch., 1951–52; Sen. Visiting Teacher, Sokoto Prov., 1953–58. Entered politics as Mem. Federal Parl., 1954–58; Parly Sec. to Prime Minister, 1958–59; Federal Minister: Economic Develt, 1959–60; Establishments, 1960–62; Internal Affairs, 1962–65; Works, 1965–66; Sec., Sokoto Prov. Educl Develt Fund, 1966–68; State Comr for Educn, Sokoto Province, 1968–70; Fed. Comr for Econ. Develt and Reconstruction, 1970–71; for Finance, 1971–75. Mem., Constituent Assembly, Oct. 1977–83; Mem., Nat. Party of Nigeria. *Publications:* (poetry) Wakar Nijeriya, 1948; Dun Fodia, 1978; (collected speeches) My Vision of Nigeria, 1981. *Recreations:* Hausa poetry, reading, farming, indoor games.

SHAH, Dipesh Jayantilal, OBE 2007; Chairman: Hg Capital Renewable Power Partners LLP, since 2006; Jetion Holdings Ltd, since 2007; *b* 11 May 1953; *s* of Jayantilal S. Shah and Sumati J. Shah; *m* 1983, Annie Therese Duchesne; one *s* one *d*. *Educ:* Warwick Univ. (BA Hons Econs); Birkbeck Coll., London (MSc Distn Econs); Harvard Business Sch. (Prog. for Mgt Develt). Various roles in planning, Shell-Mex and BP, 1974–75; BP plc, 1976–2002: Chief Economist, BP Oil UK, 1977–79; Commercial Dir, Natural Resources, NZ, 1985–87; Man. Dir and CEO, BP Solar Internat., 1991–97; Chief Exec., Forties Pipeline System, and Gen. Manager, Grangemouth, 1998–99; Vice Pres. and Gen. Manager, Acquisitions and Divestments, 2000–02; Chief Exec., and Bd Mem., UKAEA, 2003–06. Non-exec. Chm., IT Power Ltd, 2002–05; Chm., Viridian Gp plc, 2005–06 (non-exec. Dir, 2003–04); non-executive Director: Babcock Internat. Gp plc, 1999–; Thames Water and Kemble Gp of Cos, 2007–; Lloyd's of London Franchise Bd, 2008–. Mem., Renewable Energy Adv. Cttee, DTI, 1994–2002. Chm., European Photovoltanics Industry Assoc., Brussels, 1992–97; Mem., UK Panel, European Awards for Envmt, 2000. MInstD; FRSA. *Recreations:* sports, travel (with family), reading. *Address:* (office) 2 More London Riverside, SE1 2AP. *Club:* Harvard Business School Alumni (London).

SHAH, Monisha; Director, Emerging Markets, 2005–08 and from July 2009, Director, Developed Markets, 2008–July 2009, BBC Worldwide; *b* Bombay, 11 Sept. 1969; *d* of Amrit Shamji Shah and Rekha Shah; partner, Mark Young. *Educ:* Univ. of Bombay (BA Pol Sci. 1989); Sch. of Oriental and African Studies, Univ. of London (MSc Politics of Asia and Africa 1991); London Business Sch. (MBA 2002). Director: BBC World India, 2001–. BBC Worldwide Bd Rep., Radio Mid-Day West, India, 2006–; Dir, Worldwide Media, India, 2008–. Trustee, Tate, 2007–; non-exec. Dir, Tate Enterprises, 2008–. *Recreations:* travelling, cooking for friends and family, walking the dogs, collecting contemporary Indian art, watching copious amounts of television, reading (anything). *Address:* BBC Worldwide, 45 Marchmont Street, WC1N 1AP; *e-mail:* monisha.shah@bbc.co.uk.

SHAH, Samir, OBE 2000; DPhil; Chief Executive, Juniper, since 2006 (Managing Director, 1998–2006); *b* 29 Jan. 1952; *s* of Amrit Shah and Uma Bakaya (*née* Chaudhary); *m* 1983, Belkis Bhegani; one *s*. *Educ:* Latymer Upper Sch.; Univ. of Hull (BSc Hons 1973); St Catherine's Coll., Oxford (DPhil 1978). Sen. Res. Officer, Home Office, 1978–79; London Weekend Television, 1979–87: Producer, Eastern Eye, 1982–84; Editor: Credo, 1984–86; The London Programme, 1986–87; British Broadcasting Corporation, 1987–98: Head: Current Affairs, TV, 1987–94; Political Programming, TV and Radio, 1994–98. Non-exec. Dir, BBC, 2007–. Trustee, V&A Mus., 2005–. Special Prof., Centre for Study of Post Conflict Cultures, Univ. of Nottingham, 2006–. Chm., Runnymede Trust, 1999–; Trustee, Med. Foundn for Victims of Torture, 2004–06. FRTS 2002; FRSA 2008. *Recreations:* Manchester United, movies, music. *Address:* Juniper, 52 Lant Street, SE1 1RB. *T:* (020) 7407 9292. *Club:* Groucho.

SHAKER, Mohamed Ibrahim, PhD; Order of the Arab Republic of Egypt (Second Grade), 1976; Order of Merit (Egypt) (First Grade), 1983; Advisor, Regional Technology & Software Engineering Centre, Cairo, since 1997; Vice Chairman, Egyptian Council for Foreign Affairs, since 2003 (Chairman, 1999–2003); Chairman, Sawiris Foundation for Social Development, since 2001; *b* 16 Oct. 1933; *s* of Mahmoud Shaker and Zeinab Wasef; *m* 1960, Mona El Kony; one *s* one *d*. *Educ:* Cairo Univ. (Lic. en Droit); Inst. of Internat. Studies, Geneva (PhD). Representative of Dir-Gen. of IAEA to UN, New York, 1982–83; Amb. and Dep. Perm. Rep. of Egypt to UN, New York, 1984–86; Amb. to Austria, 1986–88; Hd of Dept of W Europe, Min. of For. Affairs, Cairo, 1988; Ambassador of the Arab Republic of Egypt to UK, 1988–97. President: Third Review Conf. of the Parties to the Treaty on Non-Proliferation of Nuclear Weapons, Geneva, 1985; UN Conf. for the Promotion of Internat. Co-operation in the Peaceful Uses of Nuclear Energy, Geneva, 1987; Member: UN Sec. General's Adv. Bd on Disarmament, 1993–98 (Chm., 1995); Core Gp of Prog. for Promotion of Non-Proliferation of Nuclear Weapons, 1987–97; Higher Council on Policies, Nat. Democratic Party, 2002–; Court on Values, Arab Rep. of Egypt, 2004–06. *Publications:* The Nuclear Non-Proliferation Treaty: origin and implementation 1959–1979, 1980; The Evolving Regime of Nuclear Non-proliferation, 2006; several articles. *Recreations:* tennis, music. *Address:* 9 Aziz Osman Street, Zamalek, Cairo, Egypt; Regional Technology and Software Engineering Centre, 11A Hassan Sabry Street, Zamalek, Cairo, Egypt; Egyptian Council for Foreign Affairs, Osman Towers No 2, 12th Floor, Kornish El Nile, Maadi, Cairo, Egypt; Sawiris Foundation, 22 Montazah Street, Zamalek, Cairo, Egypt. *Clubs:* Royal Automobile; Guizera Sporting (Cairo).

SHAKERLEY, Sir Geoffrey (Adam), 6th Bt *cr* 1838; Chairman, Photographic Records Ltd, since 1972; *b* 9 Dec. 1932; *s* of Sir Cyril Holland Shakerley, 5th Bt, and Elizabeth Averil (MBE 1955; *d* 1990), *d* of late Edward Gwynne Eardley-Wilmot; *S* father, 1970; *m* 1st, 1962, Virginia Elizabeth (*d* 1968), *d* of W. E. Maskell; two *s*; 2nd, 1972, Lady Elizabeth Georgiana, *d* of late Viscount Anson and Princess Georg of Denmark; one *d*. *Educ:* Harrow; Trinity College, Oxford. *Publications:* Henry Moore Sculptures in Landscape, 1978; The English Dog at Home, 1986. *Heir: s* Nicholas Simon Adam Shakerley, *b* 20 Dec. 1963. *Address:* Brent House, North Warnborough, Hants RG29 1BE.

SHAKESPEARE, John William Richmond, CMG 1985; LVO 1968; HM Diplomatic Service, retired; *b* 11 June 1930; *s* of late Dr W. G. Shakespeare; *m* 1955, Lalage Ann, *d* of late S. P. B. Mais; three *s* one *d*. *Educ:* Winchester; Trinity Coll., Oxford (Scholar, MA). 2nd Lieut Irish Guards, 1949–50. Lectr in English, Ecole Normale Supérieure, Paris, 1953–54; on editorial staff, Times Educational Supplement, 1955–56 and Times, 1956–59; entered Diplomatic Service, 1959; Private Sec. to Ambassador in Paris, 1959–61; FO,

1961–63; 1st Sec., Phnom-Penh, 1963–64; 1st Sec., Office of Polit. Adviser to C-in-C Far East, Singapore, 1964–66; Dir of British Information Service in Brazil, 1966–69; FCO, 1969–73; Counsellor and Consul-Gen., Buenos Aires, 1973–75; Chargé d'Affaires, Buenos Aires, 1976–77; Head of Mexico and Caribbean Dept, FCO, 1977–79; Counsellor, Lisbon, 1979–83; Ambassador to Peru, 1983–87, to Kingdom of Morocco, 1987–90. Mem., Sensitivity Review Unit, FCO, 1991–2002. Chm., Morgan Grenfell Latin American Cos Trust, 1994–2000; Latin Amer. Consultant, Clyde & Co., 1991–2002. Chm., Anglo-Portuguese Soc., 1994–97. Hon. Vice Pres., Anglo-Peruvian Soc., 1991–. Officer, Order of Southern Cross (Brazil), 1968. *Recreations:* tennis, gardening, music (light), travel. *Address:* Townsend Wood, Sutton Mandeville, Salisbury SP3 5ND. *Club:* Garrick.

See also N. W. R. Shakespeare.

SHAKESPEARE, Nicholas William Richmond; author and journalist; *b* 3 March 1957; *s* of J. W. R. Shakespeare, *qv*; *m* 1999, Gillian Johnson; two *s*. *Educ:* Dragon Sch., Oxford; Winchester Coll.; Magdalene Coll., Cambridge (MA English). BBC TV, 1980–84; Dep. Arts and Literary Editor, The Times, 1985–87; Literary Editor: London Daily News, 1987–88; Daily Telegraph, 1988–91; Sunday Telegraph, 1989–91; film critic, Illustrated London News, 1989. Work for TV includes: writer and narrator: The Evelyn Waugh Trilogy; Mario Vargas Llosa; Iquitos; For the Sake of the Children (Christopher Award, USA); Return to the Sacred Ice; In the Footsteps of Bruce Chatwin; The Private Dirk Bogarde (BAFTA and RTS awards, 2001); presenter, Cover to Cover. FRSL 1999. *Publications:* The Men who would be King, 1984; Londoners, 1986; The Vision of Elena Silves, 1989 (Somerset Maugham Prize, Betty Trask Award, 1990); The High Flyer, 1993; The Dancer Upstairs, 1995 (American Liby Assoc. Award, 1997; adapted for film, 2002); Bruce Chatwin, 1999; Snowleg, 2004; In Tasmania, 2004; Secrets of the Sea, 2007. *Recreations:* travelling, drawing. *Address:* Miles Cottage, Sutton Mandeville, Wilts SP3 5LX. *Club:* Beefsteak.

SHAKESPEARE, Sir Thomas William, 3rd Bt *cr* 1942, of Lakenham, City of Norwich; (known professionally as Dr Tom Shakespeare); Research Fellow, Policy, Ethics and Life Sciences Research Institute, Newcastle University, since 2005 (Director of Outreach, 1999–2005); *b* 11 May 1966; *er s* of Sir William Geoffrey Shakespeare, 2nd Bt and of Susan Mary Shakespeare (*née* Raffel); *S* father, 1996; one *d* by Lucy Ann Broadhead; one *s* by Judy Brown; *m* 2002, Caroline Emily (*née* Bowditch). *Educ:* Pembroke Coll., Cambridge (BA (Hons) 1987); King's Coll., Cambridge (PhD 1994). Printer, Cambridge Free Press, 1987–88; Administrator, The Works Theatre Co-operative, 1988–89; Lectr, Univ. of Sunderland, 1993–95; Res. Fellow, Univ. of Leeds, 1996–99. Mem., Working Party on the ethics of res. on genes and behaviour, Nuffield Council on Bioethics, 2000–02. Vice-Chair, Gateshead Voluntary Orgns Council, 1993–96; Chair, Northern Disability Arts Forum, 1993–95. Vice-Chm., Northern Arts Bd, 1998–99 (Mem., 1995–99 and 2000–02); Member: Tyneside Cinema Bd, 1995–97; Arts Council England, 2004– (Chm., NE Regl Arts Council, 2004–). *Publications:* (jtly) The Sexual Politics of Disability, 1996; The Disability Reader, 1998; (jtly) Exploring Disability, 1999; Help, 2000; (jtly) Disability and Postmodernism, 2002; (jtly) Genetic Politics, 2002; Disability Rights and Wrongs, 2006; various articles in academic jls. *Recreations:* film appreciation and production, reading, gardening. *Heir: b* James Douglas Geoffrey Shakespeare [*b* 12 Feb. 1971; *m* 1996, Alison (*née* Lusby)]. *Address:* 22 Derby Crescent, Hebburn, Tyne and Wear NE31 2TP.

SHALIKASHVILI, Gen. John Malchase David; Chairman, Joint Chiefs of Staff, USA, 1993–97; *b* Poland, 27 June 1936; *s* of Dimitri Shalikashvili and Maria Shalikashvili (*née* Ruediger); *m* 1st, 1963, Gunhild Bartsch (*d* 1965); 2nd, 1966, Joan Zimpelman; one *s*. *Educ:* Bradley Univ. (BS Mech Eng 1958); George Washington Univ. (MS Internat. Affairs 1970); Officer Candidate Sch. Commissioned Artillery, 1959; served USA, Germany, Vietnam, Korea, Italy; Office of DCS for Ops, 1981–84 and 1986–87; Asst Div. Comdr, 1st Armd Div., 1984–86; Commanding Gen., 9th Inf. Div., 1987–89; Dep. C-in-C, US Army Europe and 7th Army, 1989–91; Asst to Chm., Jt Chiefs of Staff, 1991–92; Supreme Allied Comdr, Europe, and C-in-C, US European Command, 1992–93. *Address:* 55 Chapman Loop, Steilacoom, WA 98388, USA.

SHALLICE, Prof. Timothy, PhD; FRS 1996; Professor of Psychology, University College London, 1990–2005 (Director, Institute of Cognitive Neuroscience, 1996–2004); *b* 11 July 1940; *s* of Sidney Edgar Shallice and Doris Dronsfield Shallice; *m* 1987, Maria Anna Tallandini. *Educ:* St John's Coll., Cambridge (BA 1961); University Coll. London (PhD 1965). Asst Lectr in Psychol., Univ. of Manchester, 1964–65; Lectr in Psychol., UCL, 1966–72; Sen. Res. Fellow in Neuropsychol., Inst. Neurology, London, 1972–77; Scientist, MRC Applied Psychol. Unit, 1978–90. Prof. of Cognitive Neurosci., Scuola Internazionale Superiore di Studi Avanzati, Trieste, 1994–. MAE 1996. Founder FMedSci 1998. Hon. Dr: Univ. Libre de Bruxelles, 1992; London Guildhall, 1999; Trinity Coll., Dublin, 2005. President's Award, BPsS, 1991. *Publications:* From Neuropsychology to Mental Structure, 1988; (with D. Plaut) Connectionist Modelling in Cognitive Neuropsychology, 1994. *Recreations:* e-mail chess, mountain walking, cinema, theatre. *Address:* Cognitive Neuroscience Sector, Scuola Internazionale Superiore di Studi Avanzati, 2–4 via Beirut, 34014 Trieste, Italy.

SHAMS-UD DOHA, Aminur Rahman; Minister for Foreign Affairs, Government of the People's Republic of Bangladesh, 1982–84; Publisher and Editor-in-Chief: Dialogue Publications Ltd, Dhaka; Dialogue, international English weekly, since 1988; *b* 24 Jan. 1929; *m*; two *s*; *m* 1981, Wajiha Moukaddem. *Educ:* Calcutta and Dacca Univs (BSc Hons; BA). Commnd 2nd Lieut, Pakistan Artillery, 1952; Sch. of Artillery and Guided Missiles, Ft Sill, Okla, USA, 1957–58; Gen. Staff Coll., Quetta, 1962; GS Inf. Bde HQ, 1963; RMCS, Shrivenham, 1964–65; Sen. Instr, Gunnery, 1965; GS GHQ, 1965–66; retired, 1968 (Major). Editor and Publisher, Inter-Wing, Rawalpindi, 1968–71; Gen. Sec., Awami League, Rawalpindi, 1969–71, and Mem. Working Cttee; Ambassador of Bangladesh to: Yugoslavia and Roumania, 1972–74; Iran and Turkey, 1974–77; High Comr for Bangladesh in UK, 1977–82; Minister for Information, Bangladesh, March–June 1982. Member and Leader of Bangladesh delegns to numerous internat., Islamic and Commonwealth meetings. Associate Mem., Inst. of Strategic Studies, London. C-in-C's Commendation, 1964; several military awards and decorations. Order of the Lance and Flag, Cl. 1 (Yugoslavia); Order of Diplomatic Service, Gwanghwa Medal (S Korea). *Publications:* Arab-Israeli War, 1967; The Emergence of South Asia's First Nation State; Aryans on the Indus (MS); In the Shadow of the Eagle and the Bear (MS). *Recreations:* sport (selected for all India Trials, London Olympics, 1948), writing, gardening. *Address:* e-mail: amindoha@aol.com. *Clubs:* English-Speaking Union, Royal Over-Seas League.

SHAND, Rt Rev. David Hubert Warner; Assistant Bishop and Bishop in Geelong, Diocese of Melbourne, Archbishop's Provincial Assistant, 1985–88; *b* 6 April 1921; *s* of late Rev. Canon Rupert Warner Shand and Madeleine Ethel Warner Shand; *m* 1946, Muriel Jean Horwood Bennett; one *s* three *d*. *Educ:* The Southport Sch., Queensland; St Francis' Theological Coll., Brisbane (ThL, 2nd Cl. Hons); Univ. of Queensland (BA, 2nd Cl. Hons). Served War, AIF, 1941–45: Lieut, 1942. St Francis' Coll., Brisbane, 1946–48. Deacon, 1948; priest, 1949; Asst Curate, Lutwyche. Served in Parishes: Moorooka, Inglewood, Nambour, Ipswich; Org. Sec., Home Mission Fund, 1960–63; Rural Dean of Ipswich, 1963–66; Dio. of Brisbane: Chaplain CMF, 1950–57; Vicar, Christ Church, South Yarra, 1966–69; St Andrew's, Brighton, 1969–73; Rural Dean of St Kilda, 1972–73; Dio. of Melbourne: consecrated Bishop, St Paul's Cathedral, Melbourne, Nov. 1973; Bishop of St Arnaud, 1973–76 (when diocese amalgamated with that of Bendigo); Vicar of St Stephen's, Mt Waverley, 1976–78; Bishop of the Southern Region, 1978–85. Chm., Gen. Bd of Religious Educn, 1974–84. *Recreation:* carpentry. *Address:* 27 Weerona Way, Mornington, Vic 3931, Australia.

SHAND, His Honour John Alexander Ogilvie; DL; a Circuit Judge, 1988–2005; *b* 6 Nov. 1942; *s* of late Alexander Shand and Marguerite Marie Shand; *m* 1st, 1965, Patricia Margaret (*née* Toynbee) (marr. diss.); two *s* one *d*; 2nd, 1990, Valerie Jean (*née* Bond). *Educ:* Nottingham High Sch.; Queens' Coll., Cambridge (MA, LLB; Chancellor's Medal for Law 1965). Called to the Bar, Middle Temple, 1965 (Harmsworth Scholarship); practised on Midland and Oxford Circuit (Birmingham), 1965–71 and 1973–81 (Dep. Circuit Judge, 1979); a Recorder, 1981–88. Chm. of Industrial Tribunals (Birmingham Reg.), 1981–88. Fellow and Tutor, Queens' Coll., Cambridge, 1971–73. Chancellor: Dio. Southwell, 1981–2004; Dio. Lichfield, 1989–2005. DL Staffs, 1998. *Publications:* (with P. G. Stein) Legal Values in Western Society, 1974; contrib. various articles in Cambridge Law Jl. *Address:* c/o Stafford Combined Court Centre, Victoria Square, Stafford ST16 2QQ. *T:* (01785) 610801.

SHAND, Lesley Munro, (Mrs T. G. Reid); QC (Scot.) 2005; *b* 9 Feb. 1960; *d* of Alexander Dewar Shand and Isabella Shand (*née* Irving); *m* 1988, Thomas Graham Reid; two *s* one *d*. *Educ:* Lenzie Acad.; Edinburgh Univ. (LLB Hons; DipLP). Admitted solicitor, 1985; in practice, 1985–89; Advocate, 1990–. *Recreations:* reading, cycling, walking. *Address:* Advocates' Library, Parliament House, Edinburgh EH1 1RQ. *T:* (0131) 226 5071; *e-mail:* lesley.shand@advocates.org.uk.

SHAND, William Stewart, MD; FRCS, FRCSE; Hon. Consulting Surgeon to St Bartholomew's Hospital and Royal London Hospital, since 1997; *b* 12 Oct. 1936; *s* of William Paterson Shand and Annabella Kirkland Stewart Shand (*née* Waddell); *m* 1972, (Anne) Caroline Dashwood (*née* Charvet) (*d* 2005); two *s*, and one step *s* two step *d*. *Educ:* Repton Sch.; St John's Coll., Cambridge (BA 1958, MA 1962; MB BChir 1962; MD 1970); Medical Coll. of St Bartholomew's Hosp. LRCP; MRCS; FRCS 1970; FRCSE 1970. Consultant Surgeon: St Bartholomew's, Hackney and Homerton Hosps, London, 1973–96; King Edward VII's Hosp. for Officers, London, 1995–97. Hon. Consultant Surgeon: St Luke's Hosp. for the Clergy, London, 1982–97; St Mark's Hosp. for Diseases of Colon and Rectum, London, 1986–96. Senior Fellow: Assoc. of Surgeons of GB and Ireland, 2001–; Assoc. of Coloproctology of GB and Ireland, 2001–. Penrose May Tutor, 1980–85, Penrose May Teacher, 1985–, RCS. Member: Ct of Examrs, RCS, 1985–91; Bd of Examrs, RCSE, 1986–96; Examiner: Professional and Linguistic Assessment Bd for GMC, 1983–98; Univ. of London, 1990–96; Univ. of Liverpool, 1991–96. FRSocMed 1967. Fellow: Hunterian Soc., 1971–; Harveian Soc. of London, 1972–. Vice-Pres., Phyllis Tuckwell Hospice, Farnham, 2001– (Trustee, 1995–2000). Governor: Med. Coll. of St Bartholomew's Hosp., 1987–96; Sutton's Hosp. in Charterhouse, 1989–; BPMF, 1991–96. Member: Ct of Assts, Soc. of Apothecaries, 1990 (Master, 2004–05); Ct of Assts, Barbers' Co., 1992 (Master, 2001–02); Travelling Surgical Soc. of GB and NI, 1982 (Pres., 1994–97). Member: Cambridge Med. Graduates' Club, subseq. Cambridge Graduates' Med. Soc. (Pres., 1993–); Hon. Med. Panel, Artists' Gen. Benevolent Instn, 1979–. Chm., Homerton Hosp. Art Work Cttee, 1988–92; Hon. Curator of Ceramics, RCS, 1980–. NACF Award, 1992. *Publications:* (jtly) The Art of Dying: the story of two sculptors' residency in a hospice, 1989; contribs to books and articles in jls on surgery, colorectal disease, chronic inflammatory bowel disease in children and oncology. *Recreations:* maker of stained glass windows, water-colour painting, ski-ing, dry-fly fishing, walking. *Address:* Fennel Cottage, 25 Station Road, Nassington, Peterborough PE8 6QB. *T:* (01780) 782933.

SHANKAR, Ravi, Hon. KBE 2001; Presidential Padma Vibhushan Award, 1980; Bharat Ratna, 1999; musician and composer; MP (Member of Rajya Sabha) India, since 1986; *b* 7 April 1920; *m* 1989, Sukanya Rajan; one *d*, and one *d* by Sue Jones (one *s* decd). *Educ:* Studied with brother Uday Shankar in Paris, 1930, with Ustad Allaudin Khan in Maihar, 1938–. Music Dir, All-India Radio, 1949–56; music and choreography for ASIAD 82 (Asian Games, New Delhi, 1982). Fellow, Sangeet Natak Akademi, 1977 (President's Award, 1962); Member, Nat. Acad. for Recording Arts and Sciences, 1966. Over 50 recordings, including recordings with Yehudi Menuhin, Jean-Pierre Rampal, Philip Glass, and others. Has received 14 hon. doctorates in letters and arts including Harvard Univ., Univ. of Calcutta, Deshikottam Award, 1982. Praemium Imperiale, 1997. *Compositions:* Indian ragas; music for ballet, and films incl. Gandhi, 1983; Concertos for sitar and orch., No 1, 1971, No 2, 1981; Ghanashyam—A Broken Branch, 1989. *Publications:* My Music My Life, 1968; Raga Mala (autobiog.), 1997. *Recreations:* films, people, music, theatre. *Address:* c/o Sulivan Sweetland, 1 Hillgate Place, Balham Hill, SW12 9ER; Ravi Shankar Institute of Performing Arts, New Delhi.

SHANKS, Duncan Faichney, RSA 1990 (ARSA 1972); RGI 1982; RSW 1987; artist; *b* 30 Aug. 1937; *s* of Duncan Faichney Shanks and Elizabeth Clark; *m* 1966, Una Brown Gordon. *Educ:* Glasgow School of Art; DA (Post Diploma) 1960. Travelling scholarship to Italy, 1961; part-time teacher, Glasgow Sch. of Art, 1963–79; full-time artist, 1979–. *Recreations:* classical and contemporary music.

SHANKS, Ian Alexander, PhD; FRS 1984; FREng; FRSE; Vice President, Physical and Engineering Sciences (formerly Head of Engineering Sciences), Unilever plc, 2001–03; *b* 22 June 1948; *s* of Alexander and Isabella Affleck (*née* Beaton); *m* 1971, Janice Smillie Coulter; one *d*. *Educ:* Dumbarton Acad.; Glasgow Univ. (BSc); Glasgow Coll. of Technology (PhD). CEng, MIEE 1983, FIET (FIEE 1990); FREng (FEng 1992). Projects Manager, Scottish Colorfoto Labs, 1970–72; Research Student, Portsmouth Polytechnic, 1972–73 (liquid crystal displays); RSRE, Malvern, 1973–82 (displays and L-B films); Unilever Research, 1982, Principal Scientist, 1984–86 (electronic biosensors); Chief Scientist, THORN EMI plc, 1986–94; Divl Sci. Advr, Unilever Res., 1994–2000. Vis. Prof. of Electrical and Electronic Engrg, Univ. of Glasgow, 1985–. Chm., Inter-Agency Cttee for Marine Sci. and Technol., 1991–93; Member: Opto-electronics Cttee, Rank Prize Funds, 1985–; Science Consultative Gp, BBC, 1989–91; ABRC, 1990–93; Sci. Adv. Gp, NPL, 1998–2007 (Chair, 2008–); Sci. Adv. Bd, Inst. of Nanotechnology, 2001–06. A Vice-Pres. and Mem. Council, Royal Soc., 1989–91. FRSA 1993; FRSE 2000. Hon. Fellow, Inst. of Nanotechnology, 2005. Hon. DEng Glasgow, 2002. Paterson Medal and Prize, Inst. of Physics, 1984; Best Paper Award, Soc. for Inf. Display, 1983. *Publications:* numerous sci. and tech. papers; numerous patents. *Recreations:* music, horology, Art Deco sculpture. *Address:* 23 Reres Road, Broughty Ferry, Dundee DD5 2QA.

SHANKS, Prof. Robert Gray, (Robin), CBE 1997; MD, DSc; FRCP, FRCPI, FRCPE, FACP; Whitla Professor of Therapeutics and Pharmacology, 1977–98, now Emeritus, and Pro-Vice-Chancellor, 1991–98, Queen's University, Belfast; *b* 4 April 1934; *s* of Robert Shanks and Mary Anne Shanks (*née* Gray); *m* 1st, 1960, Denise Isabelle

Sheila Woods (*d* 1998); four *d*; 2nd, 2000, Mary Carson; one step *s* one step *d*. *Educ:* Queen's Univ., Belfast (MD; DSc). FRCPE 1977; FRCP 1987; FRCPI 1987; FACP 1998. MRIA. RMO, Royal Victoria Hosp., Belfast, 1958–59; Res. Fellow, Medical Coll. of Georgia, 1959–60; Lectr in Physiology, QUB, 1960–62; Pharmacologist, ICI, 1962–66; Queen's University, Belfast: Sen. Lectr, Therapeutics and Pharmacology, 1967–72; Prof., Clinical Pharmacology, 1972–77; Dean, Faculty of Medicine, 1986–91; Consultant Physician, Belfast City and Royal Victoria Hosps, 1967–98. Hon. LLD QUB, 1999. *Publications:* papers in scientific jls. *Recreations:* golf, gardening, cooking. *Address:* Whitla Lodge, 15 Lenamore Park, Lisburn, Northern Ireland BT28 3NJ. *Club:* Royal County Down Golf.

SHANNON, 9th Earl of, *cr* 1756; **Richard Bentinck Boyle;** Viscount Boyle, Baron of Castle-Martyr, 1756; Baron Carleton (GB), 1786; late Captain Irish Guards; Director of companies; *b* 23 Oct. 1924; *o s* of 8th Earl of Shannon; *S* father, 1963; *m* 1st, 1947, Catherine Irene Helen (marr. diss. 1955), *d* of the Marquis Demetrio Imperiali di Francavilla; 2nd, 1957, Susan Margaret (marr. diss. 1979), *d* of late J. P. R. Hogg; one *s* two *d*; 3rd, 1994, Almine, *d* of late Rocco Catorsia de Villiers, Cape Town. *Educ:* Eton College. A Dep. Speaker and Dep. Chm. of Cttees, House of Lords, 1968–78; Chm., British-Armenian All-Party Parly Gp, 1992–99. Dir, Cttee of Dirs of Res. Assocs, 1969–85; Sec. and Treas., Fedn of Eur. Indust. Co-operative Res. Orgns, 1971–86; President: Architectural Metalwork Assoc., 1966–74; Kent Br., BIM, 1970–87; Vice-President: Aslib, 1974; British Hydromechanics Res. Assoc., 1975–87; Foundn for Sci. and Tech. (founding Chm., 1977–83); IWA. FRSA, FCMI, FBHI. Provincial Grand Master, Masonic Province of Surrey, 1967–99. Patron, Freemen of England and Wales, 2000–. *Heir: s* Viscount Boyle, *qv*. *Address:* Pimm's Cottage, Man's Hill, Burghfield Common, Berks RG7 3BD. *Club:* White's.

SHANNON, Alan David; Permanent Secretary, Department for Social Development, Northern Ireland, since 2003; *b* 11 Jan. 1949; *s* of Samuel and Florence Shannon; *m* 1972, Christine Montgomery; one *s* two *d*. *Educ:* Belfast Royal Acad.; Queen's Univ., Belfast (BA Hons 1971). Joined NI Civil Service as Asst Principal, 1971; Min. of Agriculture (NI), 1971–82; Cabinet, British Mem. of European Court of Auditors, Luxembourg, 1982–85; Hd of Efficiency Scrutiny, Health Service, NI Dept of Finance and Personnel, 1985–86; Northern Ireland Office: Hd of Police Div., 1986–90; Hd of Probation, Juveniles and Compensation Div., 1990–92; Chief Exec., NI Prison Service, 1992–98; Principal Estabt and Finance Officer, NI Office, 1998–99; Perm. Sec., Dept of Higher and Further Educn, Training and Employment, subseq. Dept for Employment and Learning, NI, 1999–2003. *Recreations:* tennis, gardening, local history, music. *Address:* (office) The Lighthouse Building, 1 Cromac Place, Gasworks, Ormeau Avenue, Belfast BT7 2JB. *T:* (028) 9082 9002.

SHANNON, David William Francis, PhD; Chief Scientist, Department of Environment, Food and Rural Affairs (formerly Ministry of Agriculture, Fisheries and Food), 1986–2001; *b* 16 Aug. 1941; *s* of late William Francis Shannon and Elizabeth (*née* Gibson); *m* 1967, Rosamond (*née* Bond); one *s* one *d*. *Educ:* Wallace High Sch., Lisburn, NI; Queen's Univ., Belfast (BAgr, PhD); DMS Napier Coll., Edinburgh, 1976. Poultry Res. Centre, ARC, Edinburgh, 1967; study leave; Dept of Animal Science, Univ. of Alberta, Edmonton, 1973–74; Hd of Nutrition Sect., Poultry Res. Centre, AFRC, 1977, Dir, 1978. Member: AFRC, 1986–94; BBSRC, 1995–2001; NERC, 1995–2001; Pres., UK Br., World's Poultry Science Assoc., 1986–90. Chm., Exec. Council, CAB Internat., 1988–91. Director: The Perry Foundn, 2002–; David Shannon Ltd, 2002–. Mem. Court, Cranfield Univ., 1996–2001. FRSA 1996. *Publications:* contribs to learned jls on poultry science and animal nutrition. *Recreations:* golf, bridge. *Address:* 4 Old Court, Ashtead, Surrey KT21 2TS. *T:* (01372) 813096.

SHANNON, (Richard) James; Member (DemU) Strangford, Northern Ireland Assembly, since 1998; *b* Omagh, 25 March 1955; *s* of Richard James Shannon and Mona Rebecca Rhoda Shannon; *m* 1987, Sandra George; three *s*. *Educ:* Ballywalter Primary Sch.; Coleraine Academical Instn. Served UDR, 1974–75 and 1976–77; 102 Light Air Defence Regt, RA, 1978–89. Ards Borough Council: Mem. (DemU), 1985–; Mayor, 1991–92; Alderman, 1997–. Mem., NI Forum, 1996–98. GSM (NI) 1974. *Recreations:* field sports, football. *Address:* Strangford Lodge, 40 Portaferry Road, Kircubbin, Co. Down BT22 2RY. *T:* (028) 9178 8581.

SHANT, Nirmal Kanta; QC 2006; a Recorder, since 2001; *b* 2 July 1962; *d* of Chaman Lal Shant and Santosh Lakhanpal; *m* 1992, Narinder Sharma; two *d*. *Educ:* Univ. of Leicester (LLB Hons 1983); Council of Legal Educn. Called to the Bar, Gray's Inn, 1984; in practice as a barrister specialising in criminal law. *Recreations:* tennis, theatre, reading, cooking. *Address:* Barristers Chambers, 1 High Pavement, Nottingham NG1 1HF. *T:* (0115) 941 8218.

SHAPCOTT, Jo A.; poet; *b* 24 March 1953; *d* of Frank William Gordon Shapcott and Josephine Cann; *m* 1995, Simon Andrew James Hainault Mundy. *Educ:* Cavendish Sch., Hemel Hempstead; TCD (BA 1st cl. Hons, MA); Bristol Univ. (DipEd); Harvard Univ. (Harkness Fellowship). Lectr in English, Rolle Coll., Exmouth, 1981–84; Educn Officer, South Bank Centre, 1986–92. Judith E. Wilson Vis. Fellow, Cambridge Univ., 1991; Penguin Writers' Fellow, BL, 1996–97; Northern Arts Literary Fellow, 1998–2000; Visiting Professor: Newcastle Univ., 2000–; Univ. of the Arts, London (formerly London Inst.), 2003–; Royal Literary Fund Fellow, Oxford Brookes Univ., 2003–05. Mem., Yr Academi Cymreig (Welsh Acad.). FRSL. First Prize, Nat. Poetry Competition, 1985, 1991. *Publications: poetry:* Electroplating the Baby, 1988 (Commonwealth Poetry Prize); Phrase Book, 1992; (ed with Matthew Sweeney) Emergency Kit: poems for strange times, 1996; Motherland, 1996; Penguin Modern Poets 12, 1997; My Life Asleep, 1998 (Forward Poetry Prize); (ed with Don Paterson) Last Words: poetry for the new century, 1999; Her Book: poems 1988–1998, 2000; Tender Taxes, 2002; The Transformers, 2007; *essay collection:* (ed with Linda Anderson) Elizabeth Bishop: poet of the periphery, 2002. *Address:* c/o Faber & Faber, 3 Queen Square, WC1N 3AU.

SHAPER, Prof. (Andrew) Gerald, FRCP; FRCPath; FFPH; Professor of Clinical Epidemiology and Head of Department of Public Health and Primary Care, Royal Free Hospital School of Medicine, University of London, 1975–92, now Professor Emeritus; *b* 9 Aug. 1927; *s* of Jack and Molly Shaper; *m* 1952, Lorna June Clarke; one *s*. *Educ:* Univ. of Cape Town (MB ChB); DTM&H with Milne Medal (Liverpool). Ho. Phys./Surg., Harare, 1952; SHO, Trop. Diseases Unit, Sefton Gen. Hosp., Liverpool, and Res. Asst, Liverpool Sch. of Trop. Med., 1953–54; Registrar: Clatterbridge Gen. Hosp., 1954–55; Hammersmith Hosp. and Post Grad. Med. Sch., 1955–56; Lectr, Sen. Lectr, Reader in Medicine and Prof. of Cardiovascular Disease, Makerere Univ. Med. Sch., Kampala, 1957–69; Mem. Sci. Staff, MRC Social Medicine Unit, LSHTM, 1970–75; Hon. Cons. Phys. (Cardiology), UCH, 1975–87; Hon. Consultant in Community Medicine, subseq. Public Health Medicine, Hampstead HA, 1975–92. RCP Milroy Lectr, 1972; Pickering Lectr, British Hypertension Soc., 1993. Chm., Jt Wkg Party of RCP and Brit. Cardiac Soc. on Prevention of Coronary Heart Disease, 1976; Member: DHSS Cttee on Med. Aspects of Water Quality, 1978–84; DHSS Cttee on Med. Aspects of Food Policy, 1979–83; Chairman: MRC Health Services Res. Panel, 1981–86; Heads of Academic Depts of Public Health (formerly Community) Medicine, 1987–90; Vice-Chm., Nat. Heart Forum, 1995–98; Member: WHO Expert Adv. Panel on Cardiovascular Disease, 1975–; DHSS Central Health Monitoring Unit Steering Gp, 1989–91. Elected Mem., Commonwealth Caribbean MRC, 1986–98. Alwyn Smith Prize Medal, FPHM, 1991. *Publications:* (ed) Medicine in a Tropical Environment, 1972; (ed) Cardiovascular Disease in the Tropics, 1974; Coronary Heart Disease: risks and reasons, 1988. *Recreations:* walking, second-hand/antiquarian books, theatre, golf. *Address:* 12 Greenholme Farm, Leatherbank, Burley in Wharfdale, Ilkley, W Yorks LS29 7HP. *T:* (01943) 865675.

SHAPIRO, Dr Bernard Jack, OC 1999; Principal and Vice-Chancellor, McGill University, Montreal, 1994–2002, now Emeritus; first Ethics Commissioner of Canada, 2004–07; *b* 8 June 1935; *s* of Maxwell Shapiro and Mary Tafler; *m* 1957, Dr Phyllis Schwartz; one *s* one *d*. *Educ:* McGill Univ. (Schol.; BA Hons Econs and Pol Sci. 1956); Harvard Univ. (MAT Social Sci.; EdD Measurement and Stats 1967). Vice-Pres., William Barbara Corp., 1956–61; Res. Fellow, Educnl Testing Service, 1963; Res. Asst/Associate, Educnl Res. Council of America, 1965–67; Boston University: Asst Prof., 1967–71; Associate Prof., 1971–76; Chm., Dept of Humanistic and Behavioral Studies, 1971–74; Associate, Sch. of Educn, 1974–76; University of Western Ontario: Dean, Faculty of Educn and Prof. of Educn, 1976–78; Vice-Pres. (Academic) and Provost, 1978–80; Dir, Ont Inst. for Studies in Educn, 1980–86; Deputy Minister, Ontario: of Educn, 1986–89; of Skills Develt, 1988–89; Dep. Sec. of Cabinet, Ont, 1989–90; Deputy Minister: and Sec., Mgt Bd, 1990–91; of Colls and Univs, 1991–93; Prof. of Educn and Public Policy, Univ. of Toronto, 1992–94. Co-Chm., Nat. Adv. Cttee on Educn Stats, 1987–89. Chm., Governing Bd, OECD Centre for Educnl Res. and Innovation, 1984–86. President: Canadian Soc. for Study of Educn, 1983–84; Social Sci. Fedn of Canada, 1985–86; Conf. of Rectors and Principals of Quebec Univs, 1997–99. Hon. LLD: McGill, 1988; Toronto, 1994; Ottawa, 1995; Yeshiva, 1996; McMaster, 1997; Montreal, 1998; Edinburgh, 2000; Glasgow, 2001; Bishop's, 2001.

SHAPIRO, Dr Harold Tafler; Professor of Economics and Public Affairs, Woodrow Wilson School, and President Emeritus, Princeton University, since 2001; *b* Montreal, 8 June 1935; *m* Vivian; four *d*. *Educ:* McGill Univ. (Lieut Governor's Medal; BA 1956); Graduate Sch., Princeton (PhD Econ 1964). University of Michigan: Asst Prof. of Economics, 1964; Associate Prof., 1967; Prof., 1970–88; Vice-Pres. for Acad. Affairs and Chm., Cttee on Budget Admin, 1977; President, 1980–88; President, Princeton Univ., 1988–2001. Dir, Nat. Bureau of Economic Research. Member: Conference Board Inc.; Govt-Univ.-Industry Res. Round-table; Inst. of Medicine, Nat. Acad. of Scis; Council of Advrs to Pres. Bush on Sci. and Technology, 1990–92; Bd, Robert Wood Johnson Med. Sch., 2000–; Bd, DeVry Inst., 2001–; Bd, Hastings Center, 2001–; Knight Foundn Cttee on Intercollegiate Athletics, 2004–; Merck Vaccine Adv. Bd, 2004–; Stem Cell Inst. of NJ Jt Bd Managers, 2005–; Adv. Cttee, Human Embryonic Stem Cell Res., 2006–; Reading is Fundamental. Mem., Amer. Philosophical Soc.; Fellow, Amer. Acad. of Arts and Scis. Trustee: Alfred P. Sloan Foundn; Univs Res. Assoc.; Univ. of Pa Med. Center; Educnl Testing Service; Amer. Jewish Cttee, 2002–; Princeton Healthcare Systems, 2006–; Univ. of Med. and Dentistry of NJ, 2006–. William D. Carey Lectureship Award, 2006. *Publications:* (ed jtly) Universities and their Leadership, 1998; A Larger Sense of Purpose: higher education and society, 2005; (ed jtly) Belmont Revisited: ethical principles for research with human subjects, 2005. *Address:* Woodrow Wilson School, Princeton University, 355 Wallace Hall, Princeton, NJ 08544, USA.

SHAPIRO, Leonard Melvyn, MD; FRCP, FACC; Consultant Cardiologist, Papworth Hospital, Cambridge, since 1988; *b* 9 March 1951; *s* of Joseph and Stella Shapiro. *Educ:* Manchester Univ. (BSc 1st Cl.; MB ChB Hons 1976). MD 1981; FRCP 1994; FACC 1994. Senior Registrar: Brompton Hosp., 1982–84; Nat. Heart Hosp., 1984–88. Medical Advr, FA, 1997–. Founding Pres., British Soc. of Echocardiography, 1994–96. *Publications:* (jtly) A Colour Atlas of Hypertension, 1985, 2nd edn 1992; (jtly) A Colour Atlas of Angina Pectoris, 1986; (jtly) A Colour Atlas of Heart Failure, 1987, 2nd edn 1995; (jtly) A Colour Atlas of Physical Signs in Cardiovascular Disease, 1988; (jtly) A Colour Atlas of Palpitations and Syncope, 1990; (jtly) A Colour Atlas of Congenital Heart Disease in the Adult, 1990; A Colour Atlas of Coronary Atherosclerosis, 1992, 2nd edn 1993; (jtly) Mitral Valve Disease Diagnosis and Treatment, 1995; (jtly) An Atlas of Cardiac Ultrasound, 1998. *Recreations:* sport, triathlon. *Address:* Papworth Hospital, Cambridge CB23 3RE. *T:* (01480) 364353, *Fax:* (01480) 831035; *e-mail:* lms@lmshapiro.com; *web:* www.lmshapiro.com.

SHAPLAND, Prof. Joanna Mary, DPhil; Professor of Criminal Justice, since 1993 and Director, Centre for Criminological Research, since 2005, University of Sheffield; *b* 17 Feb. 1950; *d* of late Brig. John C. C. Shapland and Mary W. Shapland (*née* Martin, now Moberly); *m* 1978, Dr John Patrick George Mailer; one *s*. *Educ:* Croydon High Sch.; St Hilda's Coll., Oxford (BA 1971); Darwin Coll., Cambridge (Dip. Criminol. 1972); Wolfson Coll., Oxford (DPhil 1975). CPsychol 1989; Chartered Forensic Psychologist, 1993. Home Office Res. Fellow in Criminology, KCL, 1975–78; Res. Fellow, Centre for Criminol. Res., Oxford Univ., 1978–88; Jun. Res. Fellow, 1979–83, Res. Fellow, 1983–88, Wolfson Coll., Oxford; Sheffield University: Sen. Res. Fellow, Centre for Criminol. and Socio-Legal Studies, 1988–89; Lectr, 1989–91, Sen. Lectr, 1991–93, Dept of Law. Cons. Expert, Select Cttee on Victim and Criminal and Social Policy, Council of Europe, 1982–87; Dir, Inst. for the Study of the Legal Profession, 1993–2005; Indep. Assessor, Review of Criminal Justice in NI, 1998–2000. Co-Ed., 1989–2002, Exec. Ed., 2002–, Internat. Review of Victimology; Ed., British Jl of Criminology, 1990–98. *Publications:* Between Conviction and Sentence: the process of mitigation, 1981; Justice, Community and Civil Society, 2008; *jointly:* Victims in the Criminal Justice System, 1985; Policing by the Public, 1988; Developing Vocational Legal Training for the Bar, 1990; Violent Crime in Small Shops, 1993; Arson in Schools, 1993; Studying for the Bar, 1995; Drug Usage and Drugs Prevention, 1993; Organising UK Professions: continuity and change, 1994; Starting Practice, 1995; Pupillage and the Vocational Course, 1995; Milton Keynes Criminal Justice Audit: the detailed report, 1996; Professional Bodies' Communications with Members and Clients, 1996; Affording Civil Justice, 1998; Good Practice in Pupillage, 1998; Social Control and Policing: the public/private divide, 1999; A Civil Justice Audit, 2002; The Informal Economy: threat and opportunity in the City, 2003; Evaluation of Statutory Time Limit Pilot Scheme in the Youth Court, 2003; The Junior Bar in 2002, 2003; Restorative Justice in Practice, 2006. *Recreations:* gardening, music, tapestry. *Address:* Centre for Criminological Research, University of Sheffield, Bartolomé House, Winter Street, Sheffield S3 7ND. *T:* (0114) 222 6712.

SHAPPS, Grant; MP (C) Welwyn Hatfield, since 2005; *b* 14 Sept. 1968; *s* of Tony and Beryl Shapps; *m* 1997, Belinda Goldstone; two *s* one *d* (of whom one *s* one *d* are twins). *Educ:* Watford Grammar Sch.; Cassio Coll., Watford (business and finance); Manchester Polytech. (HND Business and Finance). Founded Printhouse Corp. (design, web and print co.), 1990, Chm., 2000–. Contested (C) Welwyn Hatfield, 2001. Shadow Housing Minister, 2007–. Mem., Public Admin Select Cttee, 2005–07. Vice Chm. (Campaigning), Cons. Party, 2005–07. *Recreation:* private pilot with IMC and night qualifications. *Address:*

House of Commons, SW1A 0AA. *T:* (020) 7219 8497, *Fax:* (020) 7219 0659; *e-mail:* grant@shapps.com.

SHAPS, Simon; Director of Television, ITV, 2005–08; *b* 10 Sept. 1956; *m. Educ:* Magdalene Coll., Cambridge (BA 1979). Researcher, Thames TV, 1982–83; London Weekend Television: researcher, 1983–90; Head of Current Affairs, 1990–93; Controller, Factual Progs, 1993–96; Dir of Progs, 1996–97; Dir of Progs, Granada TV, 1997–2000; Managing Director: Granada Prodns, 2000; Granada Broadband, 2000–01; Man. Dir, then Chief Exec., Granada Content, 2001–04; Chief Exec., Granada, 2004–05. *Address:* c/o ITV, 200 Gray's Inn Road, WC1X 8HF.

SHARIF, Mohammad Nawaz; Prime Minister of Pakistan, 1990–93, and 1997–99; *b* 25 Dec. 1949; *m* Kalsoom Nawaz Sharif; two *s* two *d. Educ:* St Anthony Sch., Lahore; Government Coll., Lahore; University Law Coll., Lahore. Finance Minister, Govt of Punjab, 1981–85; Chief Minister, Punjab, 1985–90; Leader of the Opposition, Nat. Assembly of Pakistan, 1993–97. *Recreations:* sports, especially cricket.

SHARLAND, (Edward) John; HM Diplomatic Service, retired; High Commissioner, the Seychelles, 1992–95; *b* 25 Dec. 1937; *s* of late William Rex Sharland and Phyllis Eileen Sharland (*née* Pitts); *m* 1970, Susan Mary Rodway Millard; four *d. Educ:* Monmouth Sch.; Jesus Coll., Oxford. BA Hons History; MA. FO, 1961–62; Bangkok, 1962–67; Far Eastern Dept, FCO, 1967–69; Dep. Perm. Rep. to UNIDO and Dep. Resident Rep. to IAEA, Vienna, 1969–72; Bangkok, 1972–75; Montevideo, 1976–79; Cultural Relations Dept, FCO, 1979–82; Consul-Gen., Perth, 1982–87; Consul-Gen., Cleveland, 1987–89; High Comr, PNG, 1989–91. *Recreations:* bridge, stamp collecting.

SHARLAND, Susan Margaret, (Mrs D. Woodwark), PhD; Chief Executive, Transport Research Foundation and TRL Ltd, since 2001; *b* 26 Aug. 1961; *d* of Ian and Margaret Sharland; *m* 2005, Dr David Woodwark. *Educ:* St Swithun's Sch., Winchester; New Hall, Cambridge (BA (Maths) 1983); Imperial Coll., London (PhD 1988). Res. Scientist/Dept Manager, UKAEA, 1983–96; Gen. Manager, AEA Technology plc, 1996–98; Man. Dir, AEA Technology Consulting/Engineering Software, 1998–2001. Non-exec. Dir, MGM Assurance, 2003–. *Recreations:* gardening, travelling, walking, gym. *Address:* TRL Ltd, Crowthorne House, Nine Mile Ride, Wokingham, Berks RG40 3GA. *T:* (01344) 770001, *Fax:* (01344) 770761; *e-mail:* ssharland@trl.co.uk.

SHARMA, Kamalesh; Commonwealth Secretary-General, since 2008; *m* Babli; one *s* one *d. Educ:* St Stephen's Coll., Delhi; King's Coll., Cambridge (Eng. Lit.). Lectr in English, Delhi Univ.; Indian Foreign Service, 1965–2002: Hd of Divs, Technical Co-opn, Econ. Relns, Internat. Orgns and Policy Planning, Min. of External Affairs; Oil Sector and Develt Assistance from Europe, Treasury; served in Bonn, Hong Kong, Saudi Arabia and Turkey; Ambassador: to GDR; to Republics of Kazakhstan and Kyrgyzstan; Ambassador and Perm. Rep. of India to the UN, Geneva, 1988–90, NY, 1997–2002; Special Rep. of Sec.-Gen. of the UN to E Timor, as Under-Sec.-Gen., 2002–04; High Commr for India in the UK, 2004–08. Formerly Mem. Bd, Internat. Peace Acad., NY. Fellow, Weatherhead Center for Internat. Affairs, Harvard Univ. Medal, Foreign Policy Assoc. of US, 2001. *Publications:* (ed) Imagining Tomorrow: rethinking the global challenge, 1999; (ed) Mille Fleurs: poetry from around the world, 2000. *Recreations:* literature, religious and mystical traditions, cosmology, development, global affairs, human society, cricket, Indian classical music, jazz. *Address:* Commonwealth Secretariat, Marlborough House, Pall Mall, SW1Y 5HX.

SHARMA, Murari Raj; Ambassador of Nepal to the Court of St James's, since 2007; *b* Dingla, Bhojpur, Nepal, 16 April 1951; *s* of Dina Raj Adhikari and Padma K. Adhikari; *m* 1989, Nila Adhikari Koirala; two *s. Educ:* Univ. of Pittsburgh (MPIA 1983); Tribhuvan Univ. (MA Econs 1975; MCom 1978; BL 1990). Asst Lectr, Tribhuvan Univ., 1974–76; Jt Accounts Officer, Nat. Commercial Bank, Nepal, 1976–77; Officer, Nepal Food Corp., 1977–78; Section Officer, Min. of Finance, 1978–83; Under Sec., Min. of Gen. Admin., 1983–88; Under Sec., Min. of Home, 1988–90; Jt Sec. (Dir-Gen.), Ministries of Finance and of Foreign Affairs, 1991–97; Foreign Sec., 1997–2000; Ambassador of Nepal to the UN, NY, 2000–04; Mem., Adv. Cttee on Admin. and Budgetary Questions, UN, 2004–06. Consultant, Admin. Reform Commn, 1991; Convener, High-level Foreign Policy Rev. Cttee of Nepal, 2006. Gorkha Dakchhin Bahu (Nepal), 1999. *Publications:* Murari Adhikari's Short Stories, 2000; (jtly) Reinventing the United Nations, 2007; papers and articles on topical issues in reputed daily newspapers, weekly magazines and e-magazines. *Recreations:* reading, writing, travel, volleyball, tennis. *Address:* 110/49 Janasahayog Marg, New Baneshwar, Kathmandu–34, Nepal. *T:* 4474048; *e-mail:* murari.sharma@gmail.com; Nepal Embassy, 12A Kensington Palace Gardens, W8 4QU. *Club:* Lions (Dingla, Bhojpur).

SHARMA, Surinder Mohan; JP; Director General, Equality and Human Rights, Department of Health, since 2004; *s* of Daulat Ram Sharma and Raksha Vati Sharma; *m* 1976, Vijay; one *s* one *d. Educ:* Univ. of Kent, Canterbury (BA Hons Law). Joined CRE, 1978; work at BBC; Corporate Equal Opportunities Manager, Littlewoods, until 2000; Dir, Diversity, Ford of Europe, 2000–04. Mem., EOC, 2000–07; Chm., Leicester Racial Equality Council. Mem., Leicester CC, 1983–91. Trustee, Nat. Space Centre, 2003–. JP Leicester, 1983. Hon. Dr Central England, 2006; Hon. DLitt De Montfort, 2007. *Recreations:* gardening, holidays, playing cricket.

SHARMA, Virendra; MP (Lab) Ealing and Southall, since July 2007; *b* 5 April 1947; *s* of Dr Lekh Raj Sharma and R. P. Sharma; *m* 1968, Nirmala; one *s* one *d. Educ:* London Sch. of Econs (MA 1979). Started working life as bus conductor; subseq. in voluntary sector; Day Services Manager for people with learning disabilities, Hillingdon, 1996–2007. Mem. (Lab) Ealing BC, 1982–. Nat. Ethnic Minorities Officer, Lab Party, 1986–92. Governor: Three Bridges Sch., 1998–; Wolf Field Sch., 1998–. *Recreations:* reading, walking. *Address:* House of Commons, SW1A 0AA. *T:* (020) 7219 6080; *e-mail:* sharmav@parliament.uk.

SHARMAN, family name of **Baron Sharman.**

SHARMAN, Baron *cr* 1999 (Life Peer), of Redlynch in the county of Wiltshire; **Colin Morven Sharman,** OBE 1979; FCA; Chairman: Aegis Group plc, since 2000 (Deputy Chairman, 1999–2000); Aviva plc, since 2006; *b* 19 Feb. 1943; *s* of late Col Terence John Sharman and of Audrey Emmiline Sharman (*née* Newman); *m* 1966, Angela M. Timmins; one *s* one *d. Educ:* Bishops Wordsworth Sch., Salisbury. FCA 1977. Qualified as Chartered Accountant with Woolgar Hennel & Co., 1965; joined Peat Marwick Mitchell, later KPMG Peat Marwick, then KPMG, 1966; Manager, Frankfurt office, 1970–72; The Hague, 1972–81 (Partner 1973, Partner i/c, 1975); London, 1981–99; Sen. Partner (Nat. Mkting and Industry Gps), 1987–90; Sen. Mgt Consultancy Partner, 1989–91; Sen. Regl Partner (London and SE), 1990–93; Sen. Partner, 1994–98; Chm., KPMG International, 1997–99. Chm., Securicor plc, then Group 4 Securicor, 2003–05; non-executive Director: BG Gp plc, 2000–; Reed Elsevier plc, 2001–; Supervisory Dir, ABN Amro NV, 2003–; Chm., Le Gavroche Restaurant. Conducted review of audit and accountability for Central Govt (report published, 2001). Mem., Lib Dem Business Adv. Forum. Mem.,

Industrial Soc. CCMI. Liveryman, Co. of Gunmakers, 1992. *Publication:* (jtly) Living Culture, 2001. *Recreations:* shooting, sailing, opera, wine and food. *Address:* House of Lords, SW1A 0PW. *Clubs:* Reform, Flyfishers'; Royal Yacht Squadron.

SHARMAN, Maj.-Gen. Alan George, CBE 2002; CEng, FIMechE; Director General, Defence Manufacturers Association, 1997–2007; *b* 14 May 1942; *s* of late Major Frederick Sharman and Margaret (*née* Watkins); *m* 1st, 1967, Caroline Anne Lister (marr. diss.); one *d*; 2nd, 1977, Juanita Jane Lawson; one *s* one *d. Educ:* Hutton Grammar Sch.; Welbeck Coll.; RMA, Sandhurst; Army Staff Coll. CEng, FIMechE 1989. Commnd REME, 1962; served Aden and Oman, 1963; Elec. and Mech. Engr, The Life Guards, Singapore, 1967–68; Comd Allied Comd Europe Mobile Force (Land) Workshop, 1978–79; Mil. Sec's Dept, MoD, 1979–80; Comdr Maintenance, 1 (Br) Corps Troops, 1984; Col Elec. and Mech. Engr 7, 1985–87; Project Manager, Logistic Vehicles, MoD (PE), 1987–89; Prog. Dir, Tank Systems, MoD (PE), 1991–95; Dir Gen. Land Systems, MoD (PE), 1995–96. Non-exec. Dir, Aspire Defence Ltd, 2006–. Member: DTI Defence and Aerospace Cttee, 1998–2002; Defence Industries Council, 1997–2007. Non-exec. Dir, MIRA, 2006–. Col Comdt, REME, 1996–2002. Chm., Auto. Div., IMechE, 1996. *Recreations:* sailing, photography, family. *Address:* c/o Regimental HQ REME, Isaac Newton Road, Arborfield, Reading, Berks RG2 9NJ. *Clubs:* Army and Navy; Royal Southern Yacht (Southampton).

SHARMAN, Evelyn Janet, (Jane), CBE 1998; *b* 5 July 1943; *d* of Kenneth Blair Austin Dobson and Evelyn Barbara Dobson (*née* Phillips); *m* 1972, John Matthew Reid Sharman; two *s. Educ:* St Andrews Univ. (MA 1st Cl. Hons Mod. and Med. History); Bryn Mawr Coll., USA. Asst Principal, MPBW then DoE, 1968–72; Principal, DoE, 1972–85 (incl. secondment to Cabinet Office and Royal Commn on Envmtl Pollution); English Heritage: Head, Ancient Monuments Div., 1985–89; Actg Dir of Conservation, 1989–91; Dir of Conservation, 1991–96; Acting Chief Exec., 1996–97. Sec., Historic Buildings Council, 1981–84. Chm., Architectural Heritage Fund, 2001–07. Trustee: Chatham Historic Dockyard Trust, 1997–2008; Royal Artillery Museums, 1998–; Bexley Heritage Trust, 2001–; Greenwich Foundn for Old Royal Naval Coll., 2002–. *Recreations:* reading, travelling.

SHARMAN, Mark Brian; Director (formerly Controller), Sport, since 2005, and Director, News, since 2007, ITV; *b* 2 Jan. 1950; *s* of Stanley Sharman and Beryl Sharman; *m* 1981, Patricia; two *s. Educ:* John Port Grammar Sch., Etwall, Derby. Reporter, Derby Evening Telegraph, 1967–71; Sports Sub-Editor, Birmingham Evening Mail, 1971–76; Asst Producer, ATV Birmingham, 1976–77; Prog. Ed., Sport, LWT, 1977–81; Controller of News and Sport, TVS, Southampton, 1981–88; Man. Dir, Chrysalis Television, 1988–92; Dir of Progs, London News Network, 1992–94; Dep. Man. Dir, Sky Sports, 1994–98; Controller of Sport, Channel 4, 1998–2000; Dir of Broadcasting, 2000–03; Dep. Man. Dir, 2003–04, Sky Networks, BSkyB Ltd. *Address:* ITV Network Ltd, 200 Gray's Inn Road, WC1X 8HF. *T:* (020) 7843 8113.

SHARMAN, Peter William, CBE 1984; Director, 1974–95 and Chief General Manager, 1975–84, Norwich Union Insurance Group; *b* 1 June 1924; *s* of William Charles Sharman and Olive Mabel (*née* Burl); *m* 1946, Eileen Barbara Crix; one *s* two *d. Educ:* Northgate Grammar Sch., Ipswich; Edinburgh Univ. MA 1950; FIA 1956. War service as Pilot, RAF. Joined Norwich Union Insce Gp, 1950; Gen. Man. and Actuary, 1969. Chairman: Life Offices' Assoc., 1977–78; British Insurance Assoc., 1982–83. *Recreation:* golf. *Address:* 28B Eaton Road, Norwich NR4 6PZ. *T:* (01603) 451230.

SHARON, Maj. Gen. Ariel; Prime Minister of Israel and Minister of Immigrant Absorption, 2001–06; Leader, Likud Party, 1999–2005; founded Kadima Party, 2005; Member, Knesset, 1973–74 and 1977–2006; *b* 27 Feb. 1928; *s* of Schmuel and Devorah Sharon; *m* 1st (*d* 1961); 2nd, Lili (*d* 2000); two *s. Educ:* Hebrew Univ.; Tel Aviv Univ. (LLB). Joined Haganah, 1942; Instructor, Haganah Police units, 1947; Platoon Comdr, Alexandroni Bde, 1948; Regtl Intelligence Officer, Israeli Army, 1948; Co. Comdr, 1949; Comdr, Bde Reconnaissance Unit, 1949–50; Intelligence Officer, Central and Northern Comds, 1951–52; Hd, Commando Unit 101, 1953–57; Comdr, Paratroopers Bde 202, Sinai Campaign, 1956; staff coll., Camberley, UK, 1957–58; Trng Comdr, Gen. Staff and Hd, Infantry Sch., 1958–62; Comdr, Armoured Bde, 1962; Chief of Northern Comd, 1964; Chief of Gen. HQ Trng Dept, 1966; Comdr, Armoured Reserve Div. 138, Six-Day War, 1967; Chief of Southern Comd, 1969; resigned from Army, 1973; recalled as Comdr, Armd Reserve Div. 143, Yom Kippur War, 1973. Founder Mem., Likud Front, 1973; Security Advr to Prime Minister of Israel, 1975–77. Minister: of Agriculture, 1977–81; of Defence, 1981–83; without portfolio, 1983–84; of Trade and Industry, 1984–90; of Construction and Housing, 1990–92; of Nat. Infrastructure, 1996–99; of Foreign Affairs, 1998–99. Mem., Foreign Affairs and Defence Cttee, Knesset, 1992–96. *Publications:* Warrior (autobiog.), 1989; articles in newspapers. *Address:* c/o Office of the Prime Minister, PO Box 187, 3 Rehov Kaplan, Kiryat Ben-Gurion, Jerusalem 91919, Israel.

SHARP, family name of **Baroness Sharp of Guildford.**

SHARP OF GUILDFORD, Baroness *cr* 1998 (Life Peer), of Guildford in the co. of Surrey; **Margaret Lucy Sharp;** *b* 21 Nov. 1938; *d* of Osmund and Sydney Mary Ellen Hailstone; *m* 1962, Thomas Sharp, *qv;* two *d. Educ:* Tonbridge Girls' Grammar Sch.; Newnham Coll., Cambridge (BA 1960; MA 1962). Asst Principal, Bd of Trade and HM Treasury, 1960–63; Lectr in Economics, LSE, 1963–72; (pt-time) Guest Fellow, Brookings Instn, Washington, DC, 1973–76; Econ. Advr, NEDO, 1977–81; Res. Fellow, Sussex European Res. Centre, 1981–84, Sen. Fellow, Sci. Policy Res. Unit, 1984–99, Vis. Fellow, 1999–, Univ. of Sussex. Mem., Lib Dem Federal Policy Cttee, 1992–2003. Contested: (SDP/Alliance) Guildford, 1983 and 1987; (Lib Dem) Guildford, 1992 and 1997. Lib Dem front bench spokesman on educn, H of L, 2000–. Chm., Age Concern Surrey, 2004–. Hon. FCGI 2004. Hon. Fellow, Birkbeck Coll., London, 2006. Hon. LLD Sussex, 2005. *Publications:* The State, the Enterprise and the Individual, 1974; The New Biotechnology: European Governments in search of a strategy, 1985; (ed) Europe and the New Technologies, 1985; (with Geoffrey Shepherd) Managing Change in British Industry, 1986; (ed with Peter Holmes) Strategies for New Technologies, 1987; (with Claire Shearman) European Technological Collaboration, 1987; (ed jtly) Technology and the Future of Europe, 1992; (with John Peterson) Technology Policy in the European Union, 1998; many articles in learned jls dealing with science and technology policy. *Recreations:* reading, walking, theatre. *Address:* House of Lords, SW1A 0PW. *T:* (020) 7219 3121; *e-mail:* sharpm@parliament.uk.

SHARP, Sir Adrian, 4th Bt *cr* 1922, of Warden Court, Maidstone, Kent; *b* 17 Sept. 1951; *s* of Sir Edward Herbert Sharp, 3rd Bt and of Beryl Kathleen, *d* of Leonard Simmons-Green; *S* father, 1986; *m* 1st, 1976, Hazel Patricia Bothwell (marr. diss. 1986), *o d* of James Trevor Wallace; 2nd, 1994, Denise, *o d* of Percy Edward Roberts; one *s. Heir: s* Hayden Sean Sharp, *b* 27 Aug. 1994. *Address:* 33 Calder Crescent, Whitby, ON L1N 6M2, Canada.

SHARP, Christopher Francis; QC 1999; a Recorder, since 2005; *b* 17 Sept. 1952; *s* of late (Charles Vyvyan) Peter Sharp and (Lilian) Corona Sharp (*née* Bradshaw); *m* 1978, Sarah Margot Cripps, LLB, JP; one *s* one *d*. *Educ:* Canford Sch., Dorset; Worcester Coll., Oxford (MA). Called to the Bar, Inner Temple, 1975; Mem., Western Circuit; founder mem., St John's Chambers, Bristol, 1978 (Dep. Hd, 1988–2000, Hd of Chambers, 2000–08). Founder Chm., Bristol Family Law Bar Assoc., 1990–96. Vis. Fellow, Faculty of Law, UWE, 2003–. Mem. Adv. Council, Worcester Coll., Oxford, 2006–. *Publications:* articles in legal jls. *Recreations:* family holidays, Real tennis, ski-ing, sailing. *Address:* St John's Chambers, 101 Victoria Street, Bristol BS1 6PU. *Clubs:* Bar Yacht, Bristol and Bath Tennis.

SHARP, Isobel Nicol; Partner, Deloitte & Touche LLP, since 2002; President, Institute of Chartered Accountants of Scotland, 2007–08; *d* of Alexander and Catherine Sharp. *Educ:* Kirkcaldy High Sch.; Univ. of Edinburgh (BSc 1976). CA 1980; ACIS 1986. Member: Financial Reporting Rev. Panel, 1994–99; Accounting Standards Bd, 2000–05. *Publications:* Stock Exchange Reporting, 1994; Financial Statements for Smaller Companies, 1997, 4th edn 2002; Financial Statements for UK Listed Groups, 2004, 4th edn 2007. *Address:* c/o Deloitte & Touche LLP, 2 New Street Square, EC4A 3BZ.

SHARP, James Lyall; HM Diplomatic Service; Regional Director Asia-Pacific, UK Border Agency, Hong Kong, since 2008; *b* 12 April 1960; *s* of Sir Richard Lyall Sharp, KCVO, CB; *m* 1992, Sara Essam El-Gammal; two *s*. *Educ:* Queen Elizabeth's Boys' Sch., Barnet; Durham Univ. (BA Hons Modern Middle Eastern Studies 1982). Customer Relations, British Aerospace, Riyadh, 1983–86; entered FCO, 1987; S America Dept, 1987–88; lang. trng, 1988–89, 2nd Sec., Chancery/Inf., 1989–92, Cairo; Hd of Section, Eastern Dept, 1992–95, Hong Kong Dept, 1995–96, FCO; 1st Sec., OSCE, Vienna, 1996–98; Hd of Section, NE Asia and Pacific Dept, FCO, 1998–2000; Dep. Hd, Security Policy Dept, FCO, 2000–01; lang. trng, 2002; Ambassador to Kazakhstan, 2002–05; Hd, Western Mediterranean/JHA Gp, FCO, 2006–08. *Address:* c/o Foreign and Commonwealth Office, King Charles Street, SW1A 2AH.

SHARP, Sir Kenneth (Johnston), Kt 1984; TD 1960; Partner, Baker, Tilly & Co. (formerly Howard, Tilly), Chartered Accountants, 1983–89; *b* 29 Dec. 1926; *s* of late Johnston Sharp and Ann Sharp (*née* Routledge); *m* 1955, Barbara Maud Keating; one *s*. *Educ:* Shrewsbury Sch.; St John's Coll., Cambridge (MA). ACA 1955, FCA 1960. Partner, Armstrong, Watson & Co., Chartered Accountants, 1955–75; Head, Govt Accountancy Service and Accountancy Advr to DoI, 1975–83. Indian Army, 1945–48; TA, 251st (Westmorland and Cumberland Yeo.) Field Regt RA, 1948–62; 2nd-in-Comd, 1959–62. Inst. of Chartered Accountants: Mem. Council, 1966–83; Vice-Pres., 1972–73; Dep. Pres., 1973–74; Pres., 1974–75. Master, Co. of Chartered Accountants in England and Wales, 1979–80. Mem., Governing Body, Shrewsbury Sch., 1976–95. JP Carlisle, 1957–73. *Publications:* The Family Business and the Companies Act 1967, 1967; articles in professional accountancy press. *Recreation:* gardening. *Address:* Lower Bohella House, The Square, St Mawes, Truro TR2 5AG.

SHARP, Sir Leslie, Kt 1996; QPM 1986; Chief Constable of Strathclyde Police, 1991–95; *b* 14 May 1936; *s* of George James Sharp and Lily Mabel (*née* Moys); *m* 1st, 1956, Maureen (*née* Tyson) (decd); two *d*; 2nd, 1985, Audrey (*née* Sidwell); two *d*. *Educ:* University Coll. London (LLB). MRC, 1952–54; Nat. Service, Middx Regt, 1954–56; Metropolitan Police, 1956–80; Asst Chief Constable, 1980–83, Dep. Chief Constable, 1983–88, W Midlands Police; Chief Constable, Cumbria Constab., 1988–91. Hon. LLD Strathclyde, 1995. *Recreations:* angling, genealogy, home computing, gardening. *Address:* Top Copse, Tile Barn, Woolton Hill, Newbury, Berks RG20 9XE.

SHARP, Dr Lindsay Gerard; Director, National Museum of Science & Industry, 2000–05; *b* 22 Aug. 1947; *s* of Clifford Douglas Sharp and late Olive Dora Sharp; *m* 1st, 1968, Margaret Mary Sommi (marr. diss. 1979); one *s*; 2nd, 1981, Robyn Catherine Peterson; one *d*. *Educ:* Wadham Coll., Oxford (BA 1st cl. Hons 1969); Queen's Coll., Oxford (DPhil 1976). Clifford Norton Res. Fellow, Queen's Coll., Oxford, 1972–75; Asst Keeper, Pictorial Collection, Science Mus., 1976–78; Dep. Dir, then Dir, Mus. of Applied Arts and Scis, Sydney, 1978–88; Director: Entertainment and Leisure, Merlin Internat. Properties, Sydney, 1988–90; The Earth Exchange, Sydney, 1990–93; consultant, Asia and Australasia, 1990–93; Sen. Mus. Consultant and Dep. Dir, Mus. of Creativity Project, Milken Family Foundn, Santa Monica, 1993–96; Pres. and CEO, Royal Ontario Mus., Toronto, 1996–2000. *Recreations:* reading, garden design, music, opera, film, wine collection, travel, cultural and architectural history, bio-diversity, sustainability and cultural diversity issues. *Address:* Magdalene House, High Street, Templecomb, Som BA8 0JD.

SHARP, Prof. Phillip Allen, PhD; Institute Professor, David H. Koch Institute for Integrative Cancer Research (formerly Center for Cancer Research), Massachusetts Institute of Technology, since 1999 (Salvador E. Luria Professor, 1992–99); *b* 6 June 1944; *s* of Joseph W. Sharp and Katherin (*née* Colvin); *m* 1964, Ann Christine Holcombe; three *d*. *Educ:* Union Coll., Barbourville, Ky (BA 1966); Univ. of Illinois (PhD 1969). NIH Postdoctoral Fellow, CIT, 1969–71; Sen. Res. Investigator, Cold Spring Harbor Lab., NY, 1972–74; Massachusetts Institute of Technology: Associate Prof., 1974–79; Prof. of Biol., 1979–86; Class of '41 Prof., 1986–87; John D. MacArthur Prof., 1987–92; Associate Dir, 1982–85, Dir, 1985–91, Center for Cancer Res.; Hd, Dept of Biol., 1991–99; Dir, McGovern Inst., 2000–04. Co-founder, and Mem. Director Bd, 1978–; Chm., Scientific Bd, 1987–2002, Biogen IDEC (formerly Biogen, Inc.); Co-founder, and Mem., Scientific and Director Bds, Alnylam Pharmaceuticals Inc., 2002–; Mem., Scientific Adv. Bd and Bd of Dirs, Magem BioSciences Inc., 2006–. Chm., General Motors Cancer Res. Foundn Awards Assembly, 1994–2006. Member: Cttee on Sci., Engrg and Public Policy, 1992–95; President's Cttee of Advrs on Sci. and Technol., 1994–97; Scientific Cttee, Ludwig Inst. for Cancer Res., 1998–; Bd of Scientific Govs, Scripps Res. Inst., 1999–; Bd of Advrs, Polaris Venture Partners, 2002–. Mem., Alfred P. Sloan Foundn, 1995–2004; Mem. Bd of Trustees, Massachusetts Gen. Hosp., 2002–. Member: American Acad. of Arts and Scis, 1983; NAS, 1983; Inst. of Medicine, NAS, 1991; American Philosophical Soc., 1991 (Benjamin Franklin Medal, 1999). FAAAS 1987. Hon. FRSE 2002. Hon. Mem., NAS, Republic of Korea, 2004. Hon. Dr: Union Coll., Ky, 1991; Univ. of Ky, 1994; Bowdoin Coll., Maine, 1995; Univ. of Tel Aviv, 1996; Albright Coll., Penn, 1996; Univ. of Glasgow, 1998; Thomas Moore Coll., Ky, 1999; Uppsala Univ., 1999; Univ. of Buenos Aires, 1999; Northern Ky Univ., 2001; Rippon College, Wis, 2006. Alfred P. Sloan Jr Prize for Cancer Res., Gen. Motors Res. Foundn, 1986; Gairdner Foundn Internat. Award, Canada, 1986; Albert Lasker Basic Med. Res. Award, 1988; Nobel Prize in Physiology or Medicine, 1993; Nat. Medal of Sci., 2004; Double Helix Medal for Sci. Res., Cold Spring Harbor Lab., NY, 2006. *Publications:* numerous scientific articles in jls and other pubns. *Address:* The Koch Institute, Room E17–529, Massachusetts Institute of Technology, 40 Ames Street, Cambridge, MA 02139–4307, USA. *T:* (617) 2536421.

SHARP, Robert Charles, CMG 1971; Director of Public Works, Tasmania, 1949–71; *b* 20 Sept. 1907; *s* of Robert George Sharp and Gertrude Coral (*née* Bellette); *m* 1st, 1935, Margaret Fairbrass Andrewartha (*d* 1975); one *d*; 2nd, 1978, Marie, *widow* of Alan C. Wharton, St Albans, Herts. *Educ:* Univ. of Tasmania. BE 1929. Bridge Engr, Public Works, 1935. Enlisted RAE (Major): comd 2/4 Aust. Field Sqdn RAE, 1942; 1 Aust. Port Mtce Co. RAE, 1943; HQ Docks Ops Gp, 1944. Chief Engr, Public Works, 1946; State Co-ordinator of Works, 1949–71. *Address:* The Coach House, Wickwood Court, Sandpit Lane, St Albans, Herts AL1 4BP; 594 Sandy Bay Road, Hobart, Tasmania 7005, Australia. *Club:* Athenæum.

SHARP, Robin; *see* Sharp, Sir S. C. R.

SHARP, Robin John Alfred, CB 1993; Director, Global Environment, Department of the Environment, 1994–95; *b* 30 July 1935; *s* of Robert Arthur Sharp and Yona Maud (*née* Brazier); *m* 1963, Anne Elizabeth Davison. *Educ:* Brentwood Sch.; Brasenose Coll., Oxford (MA); Wesley House, Cambridge (BA). Methodist Minister, West Mersea, 1960–62; Theol Colls Sec., SCM, 1962–65; Minister, Paddington, 1965–66. Principal, Min. of Housing and Local Govt and DoE, 1966–72; Asst Sec., 1972; Special Advr to Chancellor of Duchy of Lancaster, Cabinet Office, 1972; Department of the Environment: Road Safety Div., 1972–75; Housing Div., 1975–81; Under Sec., 1981; Public Housing and Right to Buy, 1981–86; Local Govt, 1986–91; Dir of Rural Affairs, 1991–94. Chairman: European Sustainable Use Gp, IUCN, 1997–2007, now Emeritus; New Renaissance Gp, 1997–2002; Vice Pres., BTCV, 1997–2007. Trustee, Fauna and Flora Internat., 1995–2004 (Company Sec., 2000–04). Harry Messel Award for Conservation Leadership, IUCN Species Survival Commn, 2006. *Publications:* (jtly) Preparing for the Ministry of the 1970's, 1964; (jtly) Worship in a United Church, 1964; (contrib.) British Environmental Policy and Europe, 1998; (jtly) Freshwater Fisheries in Central and Eastern Europe, 2004; (contrib.) Recreational Hunting: conservation and livelihoods, 2008. *Recreations:* bird-watching, walking, concert-going, travel. *Address:* 30 Windermere Avenue, NW6 6LN. *T:* (020) 8969 0381.

SHARP, Prof. Roy Martin, DPhil; Vice-Chancellor, University of Canterbury, New Zealand, since 2003; *b* 3 April 1946; *s* of Leonard and Freda Sharp; *m* 1971, Beverley Davison; two *s* one *d*. *Educ:* Dame Allan's Sch., Newcastle-on-Tyne; St Peter's Coll., Oxford (MA; DPhil). Dist. FIPENZ (FIPENZ 1992); FNZIM 2003. University of Auckland: Lectr, 1973–75; Sen. Lectr, 1975–89; Prof., 1989–97; Dean of Engrg, 1992–97; Asst Vice-Chancellor, 1993–94; Dep. Vice-Chancellor, 1995–96; Dep. Vice-Chancellor, Victoria Univ. of Wellington, 1997–2003. *Recreations:* walking, music. *Address:* University of Canterbury, Private Bag 4800, Christchurch 8040, New Zealand. *T:* (3) 3642495, *Fax:* (3) 3642856; *e-mail:* roy.sharp@canterbury.ac.nz.

SHARP, Sir Sheridan (Christopher Robin), 4th Bt *cr* 1920, of Heckmondwike, co. York, (known as **Mr Robin Sharp**); independent writer and consultant, since 1992; *b* 25 April 1936; *s* of Reginald Sharp (*d* 1969), 3rd *s* of Sir Milton Sheridan Sharp, 1st Bt and Doris Eve (*née* Faulder; *d* 1985); *S* cousin, 1996; *m* 1st, 1958, Sheila Aileen Moodie (marr. diss. 1967); 2nd, 1969, Anna Maria, *d* of N. H. Saverio Rossi, Rome; one *s* one *d*. *Educ:* Rugby Sch. News Ed., United Press, Montreal, 1956–58; Reuters, London, 1959–60; Correspondent, Australian Broadcasting Corp., 1961–71; Head of Public Affairs, Oxfam, London, 1973–77; Dir of Information, Soc. for Internat. Develt, Rome, 1978–81; Sec. Gen., World Food Assembly, 1983–86; Internat. Inst. for Envmt and Develt, 1986–92; freelance consultant and Dir of Res., Right Livelihood Award, 1993–2003. FRSA. *Publications:* Whose Right to Work?, 1976; (with C. Whittemore), Europe and the World Without, 1977; Burkina Faso: new life for the Sahel?, 1990; Senegal: a state of change, 1994; All About Elcombe: the intimate history of a Cotswold hamlet, 2003. *Heir: s* Fabian Alexander Sebastian Sharp, *b* 5 Nov. 1973.

SHARP, Thomas, (Tom), CBE 1987; retired; General Manager, Names' Interests, Lloyd's of London, 1987–91; *b* 19 June 1931; *s* of late William Douglas Sharp and Margaret Sharp (*née* Tout); *m* 1962, Margaret Lucy Hailstone (*see* Baroness Sharp of Guildford); two *d*. *Educ:* Brown Sch., Toronto; Abbotsholme Sch., Derbs; Jesus Coll., Oxford. BoT and DTI (with short interval HM Treasury), 1954–73; Counsellor (Commercial), British Embassy, Washington, 1973–76; Dept of Trade, 1976–79; Dept of Industry, 1979–83; DTI, 1983–87. Member (Lib Dem): Surrey CC, 1989–2005 (Chm., Social Services Cttee, 1993–95); Guildford BC, 1991–99. Chm., Guildford CAB, 2004–07. *Address:* 96 London Road, Guildford, Surrey GU1 1TH. *T:* (01483) 572669; *e-mail:* tomsharp96@ntlworld.com.

SHARP, Hon. Victoria Madeleine; QC 2001; a Recorder, since 1998; *b* 8 Feb. 1956; *d* of Lord Sharp of Grimsdyke, CBE and of Marion (*née* Freedman); *m* 1986, Olivier Chappatte; three *s* one *d*. *Educ:* N London Collegiate Sch.; Univ. of Bristol (LLB). Called to the Bar, Inner Temple, 1979, specialising in libel and media law. *Recreations:* reading, cooking, my children. *Address:* 1 Brick Court, Temple, EC4Y 9BY. *T:* (020) 7353 8845, *Fax:* (020) 7583 9144.

SHARPE, Prof. David Thomas, OBE 1986; FRCS; Consultant Plastic Surgeon, St Luke's Hospital, Bradford, Bradford Royal Infirmary, Royal Halifax Infirmary and Huddersfield Royal Infirmary, since 1985; Director, Plastic Surgery and Burns Research Unit, since 1986, and Professor in Plastic and Reconstructive Surgery, since 1996, University of Bradford; *b* 14 Jan. 1946; *s* of Albert Edward Sharpe and Grace Emily Sharpe; *m* 1st, 1971, Patricia Lilian Meredith (marr. diss. 2002); one *s* two *d*; 2nd, 2004, Tracey Louise Bowman. *Educ:* Grammar School for Boys, Gravesend; Downing Coll., Cambridge (MA); Clin. Med. Sch., Oxford (MB BChir); FRCS 1975. Ho. Surg., Radcliffe Inf., Oxford, 1970–71; Senior House Officer: Plastic Surgery, Churchill Hosp., Oxford, 1971–72; Accident Service, Radcliffe Inf., 1972; Pathology, Radcliffe Inf., 1972–73; Gen. Surgery, Royal United Hosp., Bath, 1973–75; Plastic Surgery, Welsh Plastic Surgery Unit, Chepstow, 1976; Registrar, Plastic Surgery: Chepstow, 1976–78; Canniesburn Hosp., Glasgow, 1978–80; Sen. Registrar, Plastic Surgery, Leeds and Bradford, 1980–84; Visiting Consultant Plastic Surgeon: Yorkshire Clinic, Bradford, 1985–; BUPA Hosp., Elland, W Yorks, 1985–; Cromwell Hosp., London, 1985–. Chm., Breast Special Interest Gp, British Assoc. of Plastic Surgeons, 1997–. Pres., British Assoc. of Aesthetic Plastic Surgeons, 1997–99. Chm., Yorks Air Ambulance, 2001–03. Inventor and designer of med. equipment and surgical instruments and devices; exhibitor, Design Council, London, 1987. British Design Award, 1988; Prince of Wales Award for Innovation and Production, 1988. *Publications:* chapters, leading articles and papers on plastic surgery topics, major burn disaster management, tissue expansion and breast reconstruction. *Recreations:* painting, shooting, flying. *Address:* Hazelbrae, Calverley, Leeds LS28 5QQ. *T:* (0113) 257 0027; *e-mail:* profsharpe@hotmail.com.

SHARPE, John Herbert S.; *see* Subak-Sharpe.

SHARPE, Prof. Richard, PhD; FBA 2003; FSA, FRHistS; Professor of Diplomatic, University of Oxford, since 1998, and Fellow, Wadham College, Oxford, since 1990; *b* 17 Feb. 1954; *s* of John Maden Sharpe and Dorothy Sharpe (*née* Lord). *Educ:* St Peter's Sch., York; Trinity Coll., Cambridge (BA, MA, PhD). FRHistS 1988; FSA 1990. Asst Warden, YHA Lakeland Reg., 1973; Asst Editor, Dictionary of Medieval Latin from British Sources, 1981–90; University of Oxford: Reader in Diplomatic, 1990–98; Sen.

Tutor, Wadham Coll., Oxford, 1997–2000; Jun. Proctor, 2000–01. O'Donnell Lectr in Celtic Studies, Oxford, 2004. Res. Assoc., Sch. of Celtic Studies, Dublin Inst. of Adv. Studies, 1988–; Mem., Sch. of Historical Studies, IAS, Princeton, 1997. Mem., Oxford CC, 1987–95. Member: Oxford Archaeol Adv. Cttee, 1987–2000 (Chm., 1995–2000); Council, Oxford Historical Soc., 1990–; Pres., Surtees Soc., 2002–. Gen. Editor, Corpus of British Medieval Library Catalogues, 1990–. *Publications:* Raasay: a study in island history, vol. 1 1977, vol. 2 1978, 2nd edn 1982; (with M. Lapidge) A Bibliography of Celtic-Latin Literature 400–1200, 1985; (contrib. with D. R. Howlett) Dictionary of Medieval Latin from British Sources, fasc. III 1986, fasc. IV 1989, fasc. V 1997; Medieval Irish Saints' Lives, 1991; (with J. Blair) Pastoral Care before the Parish, 1992; Adomnán of Iona: Life of St Columba, 1995; (with R. G. Eales) Canterbury and the Norman Conquest, 1995; (jtly) English Benedictine Libraries, 1996; A Handlist of the Latin Writers of Great Britain and Ireland before 1540, 1997; (with A. T. Thacker) Local Saints and Local Churches in the Early Medieval West, 2002; Titulus: identifying Medieval Latin texts, 2003; Norman Rule in Cumbria 1092–1136, 2006; contribs to books and learned jls. *Recreations:* exploring Britain, working out, piano. *Address:* History Faculty Library, Broad Street, Oxford OX1 3BD; *e-mail:* richard.sharpe@history.ox.ac.uk.

SHARPE, Robert James, FRCO; Director of Music, York Minster, since 2008; *b* 14 Nov. 1971; *s* of Nigel and Carole Sharpe; *m* 1998, Mary, (Polly), Proctor; one *s* one *d*. *Educ:* Lincoln Christ's Hosp. Sch.; Exeter Coll., Oxford (Organ Schol.; BA Music 1994; MA 1998). FRCO 1993. Asst Organist, Lichfield Cathedral, 1994–2002. Asst Conductor, Birmingham Bach Choir, 1996–2002; Dir of Music, Truro Cath., 2002–08; Conductor, Three Spires Singers and Orch., 2002–08. FRSA. Hon. FGCM 2008. Cornish Gorsedd Cornwhylen Cross, 2008. *Recreations:* interesting wines, cooking, entertaining, engravings, old furniture, architecture, technology. *Address:* 1 Minster Court, York YO1 7JJ; *e-mail:* robert@robertsharpe.org.uk.

SHARPE, Samuel John; Finance Director, Department for International Development, since 2007; *b* London, 4 May 1962; *s* of Anthony John Sharpe and late Monica Margaret Sharpe (*née* Vincent); *m* 1997, Tansy Stephané Jessop; two *s*. *Educ:* University Coll., Oxford (BA Classics 1985); Birkbeck Coll., Univ. of London (MSc Econs 1988). CPFA 2008. Various posts, ODA, 1985–97; Department for International Development: India, 1997–2000; South Africa, 2000–04; Policy Div., 2004–07. *Address:* Department for International Development, 1 Palace Street, SW1E 5HE; *e-mail:* s-sharpe@dfid.gov.uk.

SHARPE, Thomas Anthony Edward; QC 1994; *b* 21 Dec. 1949; *e s* of late James Sharpe, MC, Maxwelltown, Dumfriesshire and Lydia de Gegg, Donauworth, Germany; *m* 1st, 1974, Sheena M. Carmichael (marr. diss. 1987), *o d* of Lord Carmichael of Kelvingrove, and of Catherine McIntosh Carmichael, *qv*; one *s* one *d*; 2nd, 1988, Phillis M. Rogers, *y d* of late W. P. Rogers; one *s* one *d*. *Educ:* Trinity Hall, Cambridge (MA). Called to the Bar: Lincoln's Inn, 1976 (Bencher, 2004); St Kitts and Nevis, 2002; Fellow in Law, Wolfson and Nuffield Coll., Oxford, 1979–88; in practice at the Bar, 1987–. Exec. Dir (part-time), Inst. for Fiscal Studies, 1981–87. Chm., New London Orch., 1998–2000; Trustee, Musicians' Benevolent Fund, 1999–. FRSA. *Publications:* monographs and articles in law jls on competition law, utility regulation and EC law. *Recreations:* opera, ballet, children, furniture. *Address:* 1 Essex Court, Temple, EC4Y 9AR. *T:* (020) 7583 2000, *Fax:* (020) 7583 0118. *Clubs:* Reform, Beefsteak.

SHARPE, Thomas Ridley; novelist; *b* 30 March 1928; *s* of Rev. George Coverdale Sharpe and Grace Egerton Sharpe; *m* 1969, Nancy Anne Looper; three *d*. *Educ:* Lancing College; Pembroke Coll., Cambridge (MA). National service, Royal Marines, 1946–48. Social worker 1952, teacher 1952–56, photographer 1956–61, in S Africa; Lecturer in History, Cambridge Coll. of Arts and Technology, 1963–71; full time novelist, 1971–. Lauréat, Le Grand Prix de l'Humour Noir, Paris, 1986; Légion de l'Humour, Assoc. for Promotion of Humour in Internat. Affairs, Paris, 1986. *Publications:* Riotous Assembly, 1971; Indecent Exposure, 1973; Porterhouse Blue, 1974 (televised, 1987); Blott on the Landscape, 1975 (televised, 1985); Wilt, 1976 (filmed, 1989); The Great Pursuit, 1977; The Throwback, 1978; The Wilt Alternative, 1979; Ancestral Vices, 1980; Vintage Stuff, 1982; Wilt on High, 1984; Grantchester Grind, 1995; The Midden, 1996; Wilt in Nowhere, 2004. *Recreations:* gardening, photography. *Address:* 38 Tunwells Lane, Great Shelford, Cambridge CB2 5LJ.

SHARPE, Prof. William Forsyth; STANCO 25 Professor of Finance, Stanford University, 1995–99, now Emeritus (Timken Professor of Finance, 1970–89; Professor of Finance, 1993–95); *b* 16 June 1934; *s* of Russell Thornley Sharpe and Evelyn Jillson Maloy; *m* 1st, 1954, Roberta Ruth Branton; one *s* one *d*; 2nd, 1986, Kathryn Peck. *Educ:* UCLA (AB 1955; MA 1956; PhD 1961). Economist, Rand Corp., 1957–61; University of Washington: Asst Prof. of Economics, 1961–63; Associate Prof., 1963–67; Prof., 1967–68; Prof., Univ. of California, Irvine, 1968–70. Pres., William F. Sharpe Associates, 1986–92. Chm., Financial Engines Inc., 1996–2003. Hon. DHumLit De Paul, 1997; Dr *hc* Alicante, 2003; Dr Econs *hc* Vienna, 2004. Graham and Dodd Award, 1972, 1973, 1986, 1988, 1998, 2007, Nicholas Molodovsky Award, 1989, Financial Analysts Fedn; (jtly) Nobel Prize in Economics, 1990; UCLA Medal, 1998. *Publications:* Economics of Computers, 1969; Portfolio Theory and Capital Markets, 1970; Investments, 1978, 6th edn 1999; Fundamentals of Investments, 1989, 3rd edn 2000; Investors and Markets, 2007. *Recreations:* sailing, opera, music. *Address:* Graduate School of Business, Stanford University, Stanford, CA 94305–5015, USA. *T:* (4650) 7254876.

SHARPLES, family name of **Baroness Sharples**.

SHARPLES, Baroness *cr* 1973 (Life Peer); **Pamela Sharples;** Director, TVS, 1981–90 and 1991–93; *b* 11 Feb. 1923; *o d* of late Lt-Comdr K. W. Newall and of Violet (who *m* 2nd, Lord Claud Hamilton, GCVO, CMG, DSO); *m* 1st, 1946, Major R. C. Sharples, MC, Welsh Guards (later Sir Richard Sharples, KCMG, OBE, MC, assassinated 1973); two *s* two *d*; 2nd, 1977, Patrick D. de Laszlo (*d* 1980); 3rd, 1983, Robert Douglas Swan (*d* 1995). *Educ:* Southover Manor, Lewes; Florence. WAAF, 1941–46. Mem., Review Body on Armed Forces Pay, 1979–81. Trustee, Wessex Med. Trust, 1997–. *Recreations:* gardening, golf. *Address:* 60 Westminster Gardens, SW1P 4JG. *T:* (020) 7821 1875; Well Cottage, Higher Coombe, Shaftesbury, Dorset SP7 9LR. *T:* (01747) 852971.

See also Hon. C. J. Sharples.

SHARPLES, Adam John, CB 2007; Director General, Work, Welfare and Equality Group, Department for Work and Pensions, since 2004; *b* 1 Feb. 1954; *s* of Frederick Sharples and Margaret (*née* Robertson); *m* 1982, Barbara Bleiman; one *s* one *d*. *Educ:* Corpus Christi Coll., Oxford (BA PPE 1975); Queen Mary Coll., London Univ. (MSc Econs 1977). Economist, Labour Party, 1978–83; Head of Res., NUPE, 1983–88; HM Treasury: Principal, 1988; Head: Tax Policy Team, 1992–96; Transport Team, 1996–97; Public Enterprise Partnerships Team, 1997–98; Dep. Dir, Public Services Directorate, then Dir, Public Spending, 1998–2003; Dir, Internat., Bd of Inland Revenue, 2003–04. FRSA 2000. *Recreations:* family, football, guitar, cooking. *Address:* Department for Work and Pensions, The Adelphi, 1–11 John Adam Street, WC2N 6HT. *T:* (020) 7962 8011; *e-mail:* adam.sharples@dwp.gsi.gov.uk.

SHARPLES, Hon. Christopher John; Director: Unigestion (UK) Ltd, since 2000; Grandeye Ltd, since 2004; Seeker Wireless, since 2006; *b* 24 May 1947; *s* of Sir Richard Sharples, KCMG, OBE, MC and of Baroness Sharples, *qv*; *m* 1975, Sharon Joanne Sweeny, *d* of late Robert Sweeny, DFC and Joanne Sweeny; one *s* two *d*. MSI 1992. VSO, India, 1965–66; C. Czarnikow Ltd (commodity brokers), 1968–72; Co-founder and Dir, Inter-Commodities Ltd, 1972 (renamed GNI Ltd, 1984; Chm., 1994–96); Director: GNI Holdings Ltd, 1984–2000; GNI Wallace Ltd, 1986–97; Founder Director and Chairman: ICV Ltd, 1981–98; Intercom Data Systems (renamed RoyalBlue Ltd), 1982–90; Chairman: GH Asset Management Ltd, 1991–94; Datastream Internat. Ltd, 1996–98; Lombard Street Research, 1997–2000; Membertrack Ltd, 1999–2000; Director: Gerrard Vivian Gray, 1994–98; Hiscox Dedicated Insurance Fund, 1995–96; Digital River Inc., 1998–2000. Member: Adv. Panel to SIB, 1986–87; City Panel on Takeovers and Mergers, 1991–95; Association of Futures Brokers and Dealers, 1987–92: Chairman: Rules Cttee, 1987–91; F and GP Cttee, 1987–91; Chm., Securities and Futures Authority, 1991–95 (Chairman: Exec. Cttee, 1991–95; Capital Rules Cttee, 1991–95; Finance Cttee, 1991–95). International Petroleum Exchange: Dir, 1981–87; Dep. Chm., 1986–87; Mem., Public Relns Cttee, 1981–87; Member: Public Relns Cttee, London Commodity Exchange, 1983–96; Clearing Cttee, LIFFE, 1982–87; Taxation Cttee, British Fedn of Commodity Assocs, 1985–87; London Markets Adv. Gp on Regulation, 1986–87. Chm., Air Sqdn, 1998–2005. *Recreations:* sailing, tennis, flying. *Address:* Unigestion Ltd, 105 Piccadilly, W1J 7NJ. *Clubs:* Pratt's, White's; Royal Yacht Squadron; Royal Bermuda Yacht.

SHARPLES, Florence Elizabeth; Executive Director, Young Women's Christian Association of Great Britain, 1987–93 (National General Secretary, 1978–87); *b* 27 May 1931; *d* of late Flying Officer Albert Sharples, RAFVR, and Kathleen (*née* Evans). *Educ:* Alice Ottley Sch., Worcester; Homerton Coll., Cambridge (Teachers' Cert.); King's Coll., London (Cert. Prof. in Religious Knowledge). Head of Religious Education: Bruton Sch. for Girls, Somerset, 1953–57; Loughton High Sch., Essex, 1957–60; Housemistress, Headington Sch., Oxford, 1960–66; Headmistress, Ancaster House, Bexhill, Sussex, 1966–78. Vice Pres., World YWCA, 1995–99. Reader, dio. of Oxford, 1994–. Former Mem., New Philharmonia Chorus. *Recreation:* the theatre.

SHARPLES, Sir James, Kt 1996; QPM 1989; DL; Chief Constable, Merseyside Police, 1989–98. Lancashire Constabulary, 1964–74; Greater Manchester Police, 1974–82; Asst Chief Constable, 1982–85, Dep. Chief Constable, 1985–88, Avon and Somerset Constabulary; Dep. Chief Constable, Merseyside Police, 1988–89. Mem., ESRC, 1996–98. Non-exec. Chm., Countess of Chester NHS Trust, 2005– (non-exec. Dir, 2001–). DL Merseyside, 1997. *Address:* c/o Merseyside Police HQ, PO Box 59, Liverpool L69 1JD.

SHARPLESS, Prof. K. Barry, PhD; W. M. Keck Professor of Chemistry, The Scripps Research Institute, since 1990, and Skaggs Institute for Chemical Biology, La Jolla, California, since 1996; *b* 28 April 1941; *m* 1965, Jan Dueser; two *s* one *d*. *Educ:* Dartmouth Coll. (BA 1963); Stanford Univ. (PhD 1968). Postdoctoral Associate: Stanford Univ., 1968; Harvard Univ., 1969; Chemistry Faculty, MIT, 1970–77; Stanford Univ., 1977–80; Prof., 1980–90, Arthur C. Cope Prof., 1987–90, Chemistry Faculty, MIT. Fellow: Nat. Sci. Foundn, 1963; NIH, 1968; Foundation Fellow: A. P. Sloan, 1973; Camille and Henry Dreyfus, 1973; Sherman Fairchild, CIT, 1987; Simon Guggenheim, 1987. FAAAS 1984; Fellow: American Acad. Arts and Sci., 1984; NAS, 1985 (Chemical Scis Award, 2000); Hon. MRSC 1998. Honorary Doctorate: Dartmouth Coll., 1995; Royal Inst. of Technology, Stockholm, 1995; Technical Univ., Munich, 1995; Catholic Univ. of Louvain, 1996; Wesleyan Univ., 1999. Janssen Prize, 1986; Chemical Pioneer Award, Amer. Inst. of Chemists, 1988; Prelog Medal, ETH, Zurich, 1988; Scheele Medal, Swedish Acad. of Pharm. Scis, 1991; Tetrahedron Prize, 1993; King Faisal Prize for Sci., 1995; Microbial Chemistry Medal, Kitasato Inst., Tokyo, 1997; Harvey Sci. and Tech. Prize, Israel Inst. of Tech., 1998; Chirality Medal, Italian Chemical Soc., 2000; (jtly) Nobel Prize for Chemistry, 2001; Wolf Prize in Scis, Israel, 2001; Rhône Poulenc Medal, UK, 2001; Benjamin Franklin Medal, 2001, John Scott Prize and Medal, 2001, Philadelphia. American Chemical Society: Award for Creative Work in Organic Synthesis, 1983; Arthur C. Cope Scholar, 1986; Arthur C. Cope Award, 1992; Roger Adams Award in Organic Chemistry, 1997. *Address:* The Scripps Research Institute, 10550 North Torrey Pines Road, La Jolla, CA 92037, USA. *T:* (858) 784 7505, *Fax:* (858) 784 7562; *e-mail:* sharples@scripps.edu.

SHARPLEY, Ven. Roger Ernest Dion; Archdeacon of Hackney and Vicar of Guild Church of St Andrew, Holborn, 1981–92; *b* 19 Dec. 1928; *s* of Frederick Charles and Doris Irene Sharpley; unmarried. *Educ:* Dulwich College; Christ Church, Oxford (MA); St Stephen's House, Oxford. Deacon, 1954; Priest, 1955; Curate of St Columba, Southwick, 1954–60; Vicar of All Saints', Middlesbrough, 1960–81; Curate-in-charge, St Hilda with St Peter, Middlesbrough, 1964–72; RD of Middlesbrough, 1970–81; Canon and Prebendary of York Minster, 1974–81; Priest-in-charge, St Aidan, Middlesbrough, 1979–81. Chaplain, Grey Coll., Durham Univ., 1996–98. *Address:* 2 Hill Meadows, High Shincliffe, Durham DH1 2PE. *T:* (0191) 386 1908.

SHARPSTON, Eleanor Veronica Elizabeth; QC 1999; Advocate General, Court of Justice of the European Communities, since 2006; Fellow in Law, King's College, Cambridge, since 1992; Senior Fellow, Centre for European Legal Studies, Cambridge, since 1998; *b* 13 July 1955; *d* of Charles Sharpston and Pauline Sharpston (*née* Bryant); *m* 1991, David John Lyon (*d* 2000). *Educ:* St Paul's Girls' Sch. (Schol.); Bedales Sch. (Schol.); Konservatorium der Stadt Wien, Vienna; King's Coll., Cambridge (BA 1st Cl. Hons 1976; MA 1979); Inns of Court Sch. of Law; Corpus Christi Coll., Oxford (Squash Blue, 1978; Rowing Blue, 1978, 1979, 1980; Pres., Oxford Univ. Women's Boat Club, 1978–79 and 1979–80). Called to the Bar: Middle Temple, 1980 (Bencher, 2005); Republic of Ireland, 1986; Gibraltar, 1999; Hong Kong, 2001; in practice as barrister, specialising in EU and ECHR law, Brussels, 1981–87, London, 1990–2005; référendaire (judicial asst) to Advocate Gen. (later Judge) Sir Gordon Slynn at Court of Justice of EC, Luxembourg, 1987–90; Lectr and Dir of Eur. Legal Studies, UCL, 1990–92; Univ. Lectr, 1992–98, Affiliated Lectr, 1998–2006, Yorke Dist. Vis. Lectr, 2006–, Cambridge. *Publications:* Interim and Substantive Relief in Claims Under Community Law, 1993; contrib. articles to Eur. Law Rev. and Common Market Law Rev. *Recreations:* theatre, classical music, European literature, sailing square riggers, rowing, squash, scuba diving, ski-ing, karate. *Address:* Court of Justice of the European Communities, 2925 Luxembourg. *T:* 43032215; King's College, Cambridge CB2 1ST. *T:* (01223) 331436. *Clubs:* Athenæum; Leander (Henley).

SHATTOCK, David John, CBE 1995; QPM 1985; Personal Advisor to Prime Minister of Mauritius, 1998–2000; Chief Constable, Avon and Somerset Constabulary, 1989–98; *b* 25 Jan. 1936; *s* of Herbert John Shattock and Lucy Margaret Shattock; *m* 1973, Freda Thums; three *s*. *Educ:* Sir Richard Huish's Sch., Taunton. Joined as Constable, final post Asst Chief Constable, Somerset and Bath, later Avon and Somerset Constabulary, 1956–82; Deputy Chief Constable: Wilts Constab., 1983–85; Dyfed-Powys Police,

1985–86; Chief Constable, Dyfed-Powys Police, 1986–89. Hon. MA Bristol, 1998; Hon. LLD UWE, 1999. OStJ 1989. *Recreations:* racket sports, particularly badminton, antique restoration, keeping fit, horse riding. *Clubs:* Bristol Shakespeare, Bristol Savages (Bristol).

SHATTOCK, Sir Gordon, Kt 1985; Vice-Chairman, VDC plc, since 1990 (Director, 1982–98); Divisional Bursar, Western Division, and Hon. Fellow, Woodard Schools, since 1988; *b* 12 May 1928; *s* of Frederick Thomas and Rose May Irene Shattock; *m* 1952, Jeanne Mary Watkins (*d* 1984); one *s* one *d*; *m* 1988, Mrs Wendy Sale. *Educ:* Hele's Sch., Exeter; Royal Veterinary Coll., London. MRCVS. Senior Partner, St David's Vet. Hosp., Exeter, 1954–84. Mem., Exeter HA, 1987–93. Fellow of Woodard Corp., 1973–88; Executive Member: Animal Health Trust, 1978–99; GBA, 1986–89; Mem. of Council, Guide Dogs for the Blind, 1985–97; Chairman: Grenville Coll., 1982–88; Exeter Cathedral Music Foundn Trust, 1987–2004 (Trustee, 2004–). Pres., Old Heleans' Soc., 1999–2008. FRSocMed 1987; FRSA 1990. Hon. FRVC 1994; Hon. Mem., BVA, 1989. Farriers' Company: Liveryman, 1978–; Mem. Ct of Assistants, 1986–; Master, 1992. Jun. Grand Warden, United Grand Lodge of England, 1997–98. *Publications:* contrib. to Jl Small Animal Practice; papers to British Veterinary Assoc. *Recreation:* gardening. *Address:* Bowhill, Riverside Road, Topsham, Exeter EX3 0LR. *T:* (01392) 876655, *Fax:* (01392) 875588.

SHAUGHNESSY, family name of **Baron Shaughnessy**.

SHAUGHNESSY, 5th Baron *cr* 1916 of Montreal and of Ashford, Limerick; **Charles George Patrick Shaughnessy;** actor; *b* 9 Feb. 1955; *s* of late Capt. Alfred James Shaughnessy and of Jean Margaret (*née* Lodge); *S* cousin, 2007; *m* 1983, Susan Rachael, *d* of Sydney Fallender; two *d*. *Educ:* Eton; Magdalene Coll., Cambridge (BA Hons Law 1977); Central Sch. of Speech and Drama. Theatre includes Salisbury Repertory, 1981–83 and stage appearances in USA; television in UK and USA incl. Days of Our Lives (series), 1984–91; The Nanny (series), 1992–99; also many film credits. Co-Founder, Bus Stop 31 Prodns, 2005. *Heir: b* David James Bradford Shaughnessy [*b* 3 March 1957; *m* 1985, Anne-Marie, *d* of Thomas Schoettle; three *d*]. *Address:* PO Box 705, Santa Monica, CA 90406, USA. *T:* (310) 7491551; *e-mail:* chucker22@mac.com.

SHAVE, Alan William, CVO 1994; OBE 1991; HM Diplomatic Service, retired; businessman; Representative for Bolivia, British Consultancy Charitable Trust, since 2005; *b* 3 Nov. 1936; *s* of late William Alfred Shave and Emily Shave; *m* 1961, Lidia Donoso Bertolotto; one *s* one *d*. *Educ:* George Green's Grammar Sch., Poplar. Cert., Nat. Council of Journalists. Journalist, E London Advertiser, 1953–57; Nat. Service, RAF, 1957–59; Journalist: Greenock Telegraph, 1960; Bristol Evening World, 1961; Asst Information Officer, COI, 1961; joined CRO, 1961; Salisbury, Rhodesia, 1961–62; Dar es Salaam, 1962–64; Sydney, 1964–66; La Paz, 1966–70; FCO, 1970–72; Santiago, 1972–76; Consul (Commercial): Barcelona, 1977–81; Milan, 1981–84; First Sec., FCO, 1984–88; Dep. Hd of Mission and Consul, La Paz, 1988–92; Governor of Anguilla, 1992–95. Rep. for Bolivia, BESO, 1996–2005. *Recreations:* cycling, ornithology, travel. *Address:* Casilla 3–35183, San Miguel (Calacoto), La Paz, Bolivia; *e-mail:* awshave@acelerate.com, awshave@unete.com.

SHAW, family name of **Barons Craigmyle** and **Shaw of Northstead**.

SHAW OF NORTHSTEAD, Baron *cr* 1994 (Life Peer), of Liversedge in the County of West Yorkshire; **Michael Norman Shaw,** Kt 1982; JP; DL; *b* 9 Oct. 1920; *e s* of late Norman Shaw; *m* 1951, Joan Mary Louise, *o d* of Sir Alfred L. Mowat, 2nd Bt; three *s*. *Educ:* Sedbergh. Chartered Accountant. MP (L and C) Brighouse and Spenborough, March 1960–Oct. 1964; MP (C) Scarborough and Whitby, 1966–74, Scarborough, 1974–92. Mem., UK Delegn to European Parlt, 1974–79. FCA. JP Dewsbury, 1953; DL W Yorks, 1977. *Address:* Duxbury Hall, Liversedge, W Yorkshire WF15 7NR. *T:* (01924) 402270. *Club:* Carlton.

SHAW, Andrew Jeremy; a District Judge (Magistrates' Courts), since 2004; *b* 2 Feb. 1956; *s* of late Geoffrey James Shaw and of Noelle Shaw; *m* 2004, Miriam Jane Taylor; one *s*. *Educ:* Bromsgrove Sch.; Berkhamsted Sch.; Staffordshire Univ. (BA Hons Law). Admitted solicitor, 1981; joined Walker Smith & Way, 1981; Partner and Hd of Criminal Dept; Higher Courts Advocate (Criminal), 1999–2004. *Recreations:* golf, ski-ing, mountaineering.

SHAW, Angela Brigid L.; *see* Lansbury, A. B.

SHAW, Maj.-Gen. Anthony John, CB 1988; CBE 1985; Director General, Army Medical Services, 1988–90, retired; *b* 13 July 1930; *s* of late Lt Col W. A. Shaw, MC and Mrs E. Shaw (*née* Malley); *m* 1961, Gillian Shaw (*née* Best); one *s* one *d*. *Educ:* Epsom College; Clare College, Cambridge (MA; MB BChir); Westminster Hosp. MRCS; LRCP 1954; D(Obst)RCOG 1956; DTM&H 1961; FFCM 1983; FRCP 1989. Casualty Officer, Westminster Hosp.; House Surgeon and Obst. House Officer, Kingston Hosp., 1955–56; Commissioned Lieut RAMC, 1956; Staff College, 1963; served in UK, Malta, Berlin, BAOR, MoD, Malaya, Nepal, Penang, Cameron Highlands; CO 28 Field Ambulance, 1969–70; Chief Instructor, RAMC Training Centre, 1970–72; Nat. Defence Coll., 1973; ADGMS, MoD, 1973–76; CO Cambridge Mil. Hosp., 1977–79; Comdr Med. 2 Armd Div., BAOR, 1979–81; Comdr Med. SE Dist., 1981; Dir of Med. Supply, MoD, 1981–83; DDGAMS, 1983–84; Dir, Army Community and Occupational Medicine, 1983–87; Comdr Medical Servs, UKLF, 1984–87. QHP 1983–90. Member: BMA; Board of Faculty of Community Medicine, 1983–87. Pres., Standing Med. Bd, Aldershot, 1995–2005. Fellow, Med. Soc. of London, 1988. Freeman, City of London, 1990. CStJ 1989. *Recreations:* gardening, military history. *Club:* Army and Navy.

SHAW, Antony Michael Ninian; QC 1994; a Recorder, since 2000; *b* 4 Oct. 1948; *s* of Harold Anthony Shaw and Edith Beatrice Sandbach (*née* Holmes); *m* 1983, Louise Göta Faugust (*d* 2006); one *s* two *d*. *Educ:* King's Sch., Canterbury; Trinity Coll., Oxford (Schol.; BA Juris. 1969). Researcher in Law, Bedford Coll., London, 1972–74; called to the Bar, Middle Temple, 1975 (Astbury Scholar, 1975; Bencher 2003); an Asst Recorder, 1997–2000. Head of Chambers, 4 Brick Court, 1988–99. Major cases: Guinness; Eagle Trust; Polly Peck; BCCI; Butte Mining; Alliance. Vice Chm., Fees and Legal Aid Cttee, Gen. Council of the Bar, 1995–97. Gov., Internat. Students House, 1999–2003. *Publications:* contrib. Halsbury's Laws of England, 1977; (ed jtly) Archbold: Criminal Pleading, Evidence and Practice, 1991–; contrib. various law jls. *Recreations:* history, most literature. *Address:* 18 Red Lion Court, EC4A 3EB. *T:* (020) 7520 6000.

SHAW, Sir Barry; *see* Shaw, Sir C. B.

SHAW, Prof. Bernard Leslie, FRS 1978; Professor of Chemistry, 1971–94, Research Professor, 1995– 2005, now Emeritus Professor, University of Leeds; *b* Springhead, Yorks, 28 March 1930; *s* of Thomas Shaw and Vera Shaw (*née* Dale); *m* 1951, Mary Elizabeth Neild; two *s* (and one *s* decd). *Educ:* Hulme Grammar Sch., Oldham; Univ. of Manchester (BSc, PhD). Sen. DSIR Fellow, Torry Research Station, Aberdeen, 1953–55; Scientific Officer, CDEE, Porton, 1955–56; Technical Officer, ICI Ltd, Akers Research Labs, Welwyn, 1956–61; Lectr, Reader, and Prof., Univ. of Leeds, 1962–. Visiting Professor: Univ. of Western Ontario, 1969; Carnegie Mellon Univ., 1969; ANU, 1983; Univ. of Auckland, 1986; Univ. of Strasbourg, 1993. Liversidge Lectr, 1987–88, Ludwig Mond Lectr, 1992–93, Sir Edward Frankland Prize Lectr, 1996, RSC. Member: Royal Soc. Cttees; RSC Cttees; SERC (formerly SRC) Chem. Cttee, 1975–78, 1981–84 (and Inorganic Panel, 1977–78, Co-operative Grants Panel, 1982–84); Tilden Lectr and Prizewinner, 1975; Chem. Soc. Medal and Prize for Transition Metal Chem., 1975. *Publications:* Transition Metal Hydrides, 1967; (with N. Tucker) Organotransition Metal Chemistry, and Related Aspects of Homogeneous Catalysis, 1973; numerous original papers and reviews in chem. jls, several patents. *Recreations:* pottery, music, walking, gardening. *Address:* Department of Chemistry, The University of Leeds, Leeds LS2 9JT. *T:* (0113) 343 6454.

SHAW, Brian Hamilton; Director and Chief Executive, Britannic Group plc (formerly Britannic Assurance plc), 1997–2001; *b* 26 April 1942; *s* of late Dennis Hamilton Shaw and Peggy Shaw (later Dolan). *Educ:* King Edward's Sch., Birmingham. FIA 1966. Nat. Farmers' Union Mutual Insurance Soc., 1960–63; joined Britannic Assurance, 1963: Dir and Gen. Manager, 1979–86; Dir, Gen. Manager and Actuary, 1986–97. *Recreation:* sports. *Address:* Vicarage Farmhouse, Pillerton Hersey, Warwicks CV35 0QA. *T:* (01789) 740423. *Club:* Royal Automobile.

SHAW, Sir Brian (Piers), Kt 1986; Chairman, Port of London Authority, 1993–2000 (Member, 1987–2000); *b* 21 March 1933; *s* of Percy Augustus Shaw and Olive Shaw (*née* Hart); *m* 1962, Penelope Reece; three *s*. *Educ:* Wrekin Coll.; Corpus Christi Coll., Cambridge (MA). National Service (2nd Lieut, Cheshire Regt), 1951–53. Called to Bar, Gray's Inn, 1957, Bencher, 1992. Joined Pacific Steam Navigation Co., Liverpool, 1957; Company Secretary, 1960; Company Sec., Royal Mail Lines, London, 1961; Dir, Royal Mail Lines, 1968–87; Furness Withy & Co.: Manager, 1969; Dir, 1973; Man. Dir, 1977–87; Chm., 1979–90; Chairman: Shaw Savill & Albion Co., 1973–87; ANZ Grindlays Bank, 1987–95; Director: Overseas Containers Ltd, 1972–80; Nat. Bank of NZ, 1973–77 (London Board, 1977–80; Chm., London Adv. Cttee, 1980–84); New Zealand Line, 1974–79; Grindlays Bank, 1977–85; Orient Overseas (Holdings), 1980–91; ANZ Holdings (UK), 1985–87; Enterprise Oil, 1986–98; Walter Runciman, 1988–90; Andrew Weir, 1991–2003; Henderson plc, 1998–2000; Centrica plc, 1999–2003. Mem., Gen. Cttee, Lloyd's Register of Shipping, 1974–2000; Chairman: Internat Chamber of Shipping, 1987–92; Council of European and Japanese Nat. Shipowners' Assocs (CENSA), 1979–84; Pres., Gen. Council of British Shipping, 1985–86. Automobile Association: Mem. Cttee, 1988–99; Treas., 1990–93; Vice-Chm., 1992–95; Chm., 1995–99; Chm., Motoring Trust, 2002–05. Pres., New Zealand Soc., 1979–80; Chm., Cook Soc., 1995. Pres., Seamen's Hosp. Soc., 2003–. Prime Warden, Shipwrights' Co., 1993–94; Freeman, Watermen and Lightermen's Co., 1994; Elder Brother, Trinity House, 1989–. *Recreations:* golf, music, theatre, cricket. *Address:* The Coach House, Biddestone, Wilts SN14 7DQ. *T:* (01249) 713112; 3A Lansdowne Road, W11 3AL. *T:* (020) 7221 4066. *Clubs:* Brooks's, MCC; Denham Golf.

SHAW, Carolyn Janet; Headmistress, Roedean School, 2003–08; *b* 24 April 1947; *d* of Norman and Mary Carey; *m* 1974, Dr Charles Drury Shaw; one *s* one *d*. *Educ:* Goldsmiths' Coll., Univ. of London (BA Hons 1970); Liverpool Univ. (PGCE 1971). English Teacher, La Sainte Union Convent, Bath, 1972–74; Head of English, Mount Saint Agnes Acad., Bermuda, 1974–77; English Teacher and Univ. Advr, Cheltenham Ladies' Coll., 1989–96; Headmistress, St Mary's Sch., Calne, 1996–2003. *Recreations:* reading, walking, travel. *Club:* University Women's.

SHAW, Sir (Charles) Barry, Kt 1980; CB 1974; QC 1964; DL; Director of Public Prosecutions for Northern Ireland, 1972–89; *b* 12 April 1923; *s* of late Ernest Hunter Shaw and Sarah Gertrude Shaw, Mayfield, Balmoral, Belfast; *m* 1964, Jane (*née* Phillips). *Educ:* Inchmarlo House, Belfast; Pannal Ash Coll., Harrogate; The Queen's Univ. of Belfast (LLB). Served War: commissioned RA, 97 A/Tk Regt RA, 15th (Scottish) Div., 1942–46. Called to Bar of Northern Ireland, 1948, Bencher 1968; called to Bar, Middle Temple, 1970, Hon. Bencher, 1986. DL Co. Down, 1990. *Address:* c/o Royal Courts of Justice, Belfast, Northern Ireland BT1 3NX.

SHAW, Sir Charles (de Vere), 8th Bt *cr* 1821, of Bushy Park, Dublin; Managing Director, Goodman (formerly Arlington) Property Services, since 2005; *b* 1 March 1957; *s* of John Frederick de Vere Shaw, *yr s* of 6th Bt and of Penelope Ann Shaw (*née* Milbank, now Mills); *S* uncle, 2002; *m* 1985, Sonia (*née* Eden); one *s* one *d*. *Educ:* Michaelhouse, Natal; RMA Sandhurst. Officer, 5th Royal Inniskilling Dragoon Guards, 1976–87 (Major, retd). Dir, Safetynet plc, 1987–94; Gp Man. Dir, Morgan Lovell plc, 1994–2000; CEO, IntelliSpace, 2001–05. Non-exec. Dir, Shaw Travel Co. Ltd, 2002–. Expedition leader: Geographic North Pole, Aconcagua, Kilimanjaro, Himalayas, South China Seas. FRGS 2003. *Recreations:* shooting, fishing, photography, active Rugby supporter. *Heir: s* Robert Jonathan de Vere Shaw, *b* 7 Aug. 1988. *Address:* Pigeon Farmhouse, Greenham, Newbury, Berkshire RG19 8SP. *T:* (01635) 35117; *e-mail:* charles@leadershipdynamics.co.uk. *Club:* Army and Navy.

SHAW, Prof. C(harles) Thurstan, CBE 1972; FBA 1991; Professor of Archaeology, University of Ibadan, 1963–74; *b* 27 June 1914; 2nd *s* of late Rev. John Herbert Shaw and Grace Irene (*née* Woollatt); *m* 1st, 1939, Gilian Ione Maud (*d* 1992), *e d* of late Edward John Penberthy Magor and Gilian Sarah (*née* Westmacott); two *s* three *d*; 2nd, 2004, Pamela Jane Smith, PhD, *d* of Loren Reed Smith and Agnes (*née* Palmer). *Educ:* Blundell's Sch.; Sidney Sussex Coll., Cambridge (1st cl. hons Arch. and Anthrop. Tripos 1936; MA; PhD; Hon. Fellow 1994); Univ. of London Inst. of Education (DipEd). FRAI 1938; FSA 1947. Curator, Anthropology Museum, Achimota Coll., Gold Coast, 1937–45; Cambs Educn Cttee, 1945–51; Cambridge Inst. of Educn, 1951–63; Dir of Studies, Archaeol. and Anthrop., Magdalene Coll., Cambridge, 1976–79. Vis. Fellow, Clare Hall, Cambridge, 1973; Vis. Prof., Northwestern Univ., USA, 1969; Vis. Res. Prof., Ahmadu Bello Univ., 1975–78; Visiting Lecturer: Harvard, 1975; Yale, 1979; Calgary, 1980; Hans Wolff Meml Lectr, Indiana Univ., 1984. Founder and Editor: W African Archaeological Newsletter, 1964–70; W African Jl of Archaeology, 1971–75. Mem. Perm. Council, Internat. Union of Pre- and Proto-historic Sciences, 1965–74; Vice-Pres., Panafrican Congress on Prehistory and Study of Quaternary, 1966–77; Dir, and Mem. Exec. Cttee, World Archaeol Congress, 1986–89. Founder, and Chm., Icknield Way Assoc., 1984–89, Pres., 1989–; Pres., Prehistoric Soc., 1986–90. Mem. Council, Univ. of Ibadan, 1969–71. Hon. DSc: Univ. of Nigeria, 1982; Ibadan, 1989. Amaury Talbot Prize, Royal Anthrop. Inst., 1970 and 1978; Gold Medal, Soc. of Antiquaries, 1990. Onuna-Ekwulu Ora of Igbo-Ukwu, 1972; Onyofuonka of Igboland, 1989; Onuna Ekwulu Nri, 1989; Olokun-Ayala of Ife, 1991. *Publications:* Excavation at Dawu, 1961; Archaeology and Nigeria, 1964; (with J. Vanderburg) Bibliography of Nigerian Archaeology, 1969; (ed) Nigerian Prehistory and Archaeology, 1969; Igbo-Ukwu: an account of archaeological discoveries in eastern Nigeria, 2 vols, 1970; Discovering Nigeria's Past, 1975; Why 'Darkest' Africa?, 1975; Unearthing Igbo-Ukwu, 1977; Ancient People and Places: Nigeria, 1978; (with S. G. H. Daniels) Excavations at Iwo Eleru, Ondo State, Nigeria, 1988; (with K. D.

Aiyedun) Prehistoric Settlement and Subsistence in the Kaduna Valley, Nigeria, 1989; (ed jtly) The Archaeology of Africa, 1993; *festschrift:* (ed jtly) Africa: the challenge of archaeology, 1998; numerous articles on African archaeology and prehistory in jls. *Recreations:* walking, music, calligraphy. *Address:* 3 Brooklyn Court, Cherry Hinton Road, Cambridge CB1 7HF. *T:* (01223) 413669. *Clubs:* Athenæum; Explorers' (New York).

SHAW, Prof. Charles Timothy, CEng; Professor of Mining, Imperial College, London, 1980–2000, now Emeritus (Head of Department of Mineral Resources Engineering, 1980–85; Dean, Royal School of Mines, 1991–95); *b* 4 Oct. 1934; *s* of Charles John and Constance Olive Shaw (*née* Scotton); *m* 1962, Tuulike Raili Linari-Linholm; one *s* two *d. Educ:* Univ. of Witwatersrand (BSc (Mining) 1956); McGill Univ. (MSc(Applied) (Mineral Exploration) 1959). Mine Manager's, Mine Overseer's and Mine Surveyor's Certs of SA; Chartered Engineer. Johannesburg Consolidated Investment Co. Ltd (JCI): numerous positions at various levels, 1960–67; Head of Computer Div., 1967–70; Manager, 1970–72 (as such an appointed dir of 14 cos incl. Consolidated Murchison Ltd and Alternate Dir of 9 cos); Consulting Engr, Consolidated Murchison Ltd, Randfontein Estates Gold Mining Co. (Wits.) Ltd and Shangani Mining Corp. (Zimbabwe), 1972–74; Consulting Engr and Alternate Dir, Rustenburg Platinum Mines Ltd, 1974–76; Chief Consulting Engr and Alternate Dir, Johannesburg Consolidated Investment Co. Ltd, also Man. Dir, Western Areas Gold Mining Co. Ltd, 1976–77; Associate Prof., Virginia Polytechnic Inst. and State Univ., 1977–80. Rep. for JCI on Technical Adv. Cttee of SA Chamber of Mines, 1974–77; Alternate Mem. for Gold Producers Cttee, 1976–77. Sec. Gen., Soc. of Mining Professors, 1990–; Member Council: InstnMM, 1981–88; IMinE, 1989– (Pres., S Counties Br., 1988–89). Hon. Prof., Inst. of Archaeol., London. Hon. PhD Miskolc, Hungary, 1995; Hon. Dr Moscow State Mining Univ., 1999. *Publications:* (with J. R. Lucas) The Coal Industry: Industry Guides for Accountants, Auditors and Financial Executives, 1980; papers both in technical literature and in house at Johannesburg Consolidated Investment Co. Ltd. *Recreations:* golf, mining history. *Address:* Department of Earth Science and Engineering, Imperial College, SW7 2AZ.

SHAW, Prof. Christopher Edward Dennistoun, MD; FRCP, FRACP; Professor of Neurology and Neurogenetics, King's College London, since 2004; *b* 27 March 1960; *s* of Roger and Helen Shaw; *m* 1988, Pinar Bagci; one *s* one *d. Educ:* Burnside High Sch.; Otago Medical Sch. (MB ChB 1984); MD 1997. FRACP 1993; FRCP 2000. Med. trng, Northland Hosp., 1985, and Wellington Hosp., 1986–92; Wellcome Trust-HRCNZ Res. Fellow, Univ. of Cambridge, 1992–95; Institute of Psychiatry, King's College London: Lectr, 1995–98; Sen. Lectr, 1998–2004; Actg Dir, Clinical Neuroscience Inst., 2006–. *Publications:* 70 scientific articles; res. interest includes genetic and molecular basis of motor neuron disorders, use of cloning technologies in discovery of novel therapies. *Recreations:* house building, watching old films, dancing with family, slow meals with extended family, holidays in Turkey. *Address:* Clinical Neuroscience PO 43, Institute of Psychiatry, De Crespigny Park, SE5 8AF. *T:* (020) 7848 5180, *Fax:* (020) 7848 0988; *e-mail:* Chris.shaw@iop.kcl.ac.uk.

SHAW, Christopher Thomas; Senior Programme Controller, Five (formerly Channel 5), since 2000; *b* 19 June 1957; *s* of John Denis Bolton Shaw and Isabel Shaw (*née* Löewe); *m* 2001, Martha Catherine Kearney, *qv. Educ:* Westminster Sch.; Balliol Coll., Oxford (BA Hons Modern Hist.). Independent Radio News, 1980–85; ITN, 1985–89; Sen. Prog. Ed., Sky News, 1989–91; Foreign Ed., Channel 4 News, 1991–93; Programme Ed., News At Ten, 1993–95; Exec. Producer, ITN Factual, 1995–96; Ed., Channel 5 News, 1996–98; Controller, News, Current Affairs and Documentaries, Channel 5, 1998–2000. Dir, Edinburgh TV Fest., 2006–. FRTS 2008. *Recreations:* travel, watching football, archaeology. *Address:* c/o Five, 22 Long Acre, WC2E 9LY. *T:* (020) 7421 7123.

SHAW, Colin Don, CBE 1993; writer and lecturer; Director, Broadcasting Standards Council, 1988–96; *b* 2 Nov. 1928; *s* of late Rupert M. Shaw and Enid F. Shaw (*née* Smith); *m* 1955, Elizabeth Ann, *d* of late Paul Bowker; one *s* two *d. Educ:* Liverpool Coll.; St Peter's Hall, Oxford (MA). Called to the Bar, Inner Temple, 1960. Nat. Service, RAF, 1947–49. Joined BBC as Radio Drama Producer, North Region, 1953; Asst, BBC Secretariat, 1957–59; Asst Head of Programme Contracts Dept, 1959–60; Sen. Asst, BBC Secretariat, 1960–63; special duties in connection with recruitment for BBC2, 1963; Asst Head of Programmes, BBC North Region, 1963–66; various posts in TV Programme Planning, ending as Head of Group, 1966–69; Secretary to the BBC, 1969–72, Chief Secretary, 1972–76; Dir of Television, IBA, 1977–83; Dir, Programme Planning Secretariat, ITCA, 1983–87. Vis. Fellow, Europ. Inst. for the Media, Düsseldorf, 1985–98; Vis. Lectr, Annenberg Sch. of Communications, Univ. of Pa, 1988; Manchester University: Hon. Lectr in Educn, 1994–96; Hon. Prof., 1996–99. Member: Arts Council of GB, 1978–80 (Chairman: Arts Council Research Adv. Gp, 1978–80; Housing the Arts Cttee, 1979–80; Touring Cttee, 1980); Home Office Working Party on Fear of Crime, 1990. Trustee, Internat. Inst. of Communications, 1983–89; Chm., Voice of the Listener Trust, 2004–05. Governor, E-SU of the Commonwealth, 1976–83; Chm., Bd of Governors, Hampden House Sch., 1972–77. FRTS 1987. *Publications:* Deciding what we watch: taste, decency and media ethics in the UK and the USA, 1999; several radio plays and a stage-play for children. *Recreations:* going to the theatre, reading. *Address:* Lesters, Little Ickford, Aylesbury, Bucks HP18 9HS. *T:* (01844) 339225.

SHAW, David, PhD; Executive Director, International Badminton Federation, 1992–98; *b* 19 Oct. 1936; *s* of Thomas Young Boyd Shaw and Elizabeth Shaw; *m* 1961, Margaret Esmé Bagnall; one *s* one *d. Educ:* Univ. of Birmingham (BA (Hons) Geography); Univ. of Sussex (Adv. Dip. Educnl Technology); Univ. of Leicester (PhD 2003). Education Officer in Royal Air Force, final rank Sqn Ldr, 1960–76; Training Adviser to North Western Provincial Councils, 1976–78; Gen. Sec., British Amateur Athletic Bd, 1978–81; Gen. Sec., ITCA, then Dir, Indep. Television Assoc., 1981–92. Represented Great Britain in Athletics (3000 metres steeplechase), 1958; British Universities Cross-Country Champion, 1959. *Recreations:* reading, walking, theological research. *Club:* Royal Air Force.

SHAW, Prof. David Aitken, CBE 1989; FRCP, FRCPE; Professor of Clinical Neurology, University of Newcastle upon Tyne, 1976–89, now Emeritus; *b* 11 April 1924; *s* of John James McIntosh Shaw and Mina Draper; *m* 1960, Jill Parry; one *s* two *d. Educ:* Edinburgh Academy; Edinburgh Univ. MB ChB (Edin) 1951; FRCPE 1968; FRCP (Lond.) 1976. Served as Lieut RNVR, 1943–46. Hospital appts, Edinburgh Royal Infirmary, 1951–57; Lectr, Inst. of Neurology, Univ. of London, 1957–64; Mayo Foundation Fellow, 1962–63; University of Newcastle upon Tyne: Sen. Lectr, 1964–76; Public Orator, 1976–79; Dean of Medicine, 1981–89. Mem., GMC, 1979–94. Hon. FRCSLT (Hon. FCST 1988). *Publications:* (with N. E. F. Cartlidge) Head Injury, 1981; chapters in books and scientific articles in medical jls. *Recreations:* golf and fishing. *Address:* The Coach House, 82 Moor Road North, Newcastle upon Tyne NE3 1AB. *T:* (0191) 285 2029.

SHAW, David Lawrence, FCA; chartered accountant; Founder, Chairman and Director, Sabrelance Ltd, corporate finance advisers, since 1983; *b* 14 Nov. 1950; *m* 1986, Dr Lesley Brown; one *s* one *d. Educ:* King's Sch., Wimbledon; City of London Polytechnic. FCA 1974. Coopers & Lybrand, 1971–79; County Bank, 1979–83. Chairman: RRI PLC, 1994–2000; 2020 Strategy Ltd, 1997–; Dep. Chm., The Adscene Group PLC, 1986–99; Dir, Nettec plc, 2003–05. Mem., Political, Communications and Marketing Cttee, Quoted Cos Alliance (formerly City Gp for Smaller Quoted Cos), 1997–. Mem., Royal Borough of Kingston upon Thames Council, 1974–78. Contested (C) Leigh, 1979; MP (C) Dover, 1987–97; contested (C) same seat, 1997; contested (C) Kingston and Surbiton, 2001. Chm., Bow Gp, 1983–84 (Founder, Transatlantic Conf., 1982); Mem., Social Security Select Cttee, 1991–97; Jt Chm., All Party Cttee on Dolphins, 1989–97; Chm., Cons. Backbench Smaller Businesses Cttee, 1990–97 (Sec., 1987–90); Vice Chm., Cons. Backbench Finance Cttee, 1991–97 (Hon. Sec., 1990–91). Vice-Chm., Kingston and Malden Cons. Assoc., 1979–86. Mem., Bd of Sen. Advrs, Center for Global Econ. Growth, Washington DC, 2005–. Founder and Dir, David Shaw Charitable Trust, 1994–. Vice-Pres., Inst. of Patentees and Inventors, 1996–. *Address:* 66 Richborne Terrace, SW8 1AX; *e-mail:* david@davidshaw.net.

SHAW, Maj.-Gen. Dennis, CB 1991; CBE 1983 (OBE 1978); FIMechE; Director General Electrical and Mechanical Engineering (Army), 1988–91; *b* 11 May 1936; *s* of Nathan Shaw and Frances Ellen (*née* Cookson); *m* 1955, Barbara Tate; two *d. Educ:* Humberstone Foundn Sch.; Scunthorpe Grammar Sch.; Royal Military Coll. of Science. BScEng 1st Cl. Hons, London. Commd into REME, 1956; served in Cyprus, 1957–58, and with 3 Commando Bde, Far East, 1963–66; sc Shrivenham and Camberley, 1967–68; Staff of High Commn, Ottawa, 1969–70; comd 1 Corps Troops Workshop, W Germany, 1971–72; Dep. Asst Adjt Gen., MoD, 1972–74; NDC Latimer, 1974–75; comd Commando Logistic Regt, RM, 1975–78; Instr, Ghana Armed Forces Staff Coll., Accra, 1978–80; ACOS in Comd HQ, 1981–83; served Logistic Executive (Army), 1983; RCDS 1984; ACOS, HQ UKLF, 1985–87. Col Comdt, REME, 1991–95. Dir, Greig Fester Group Services Ltd, 1994–96 (Gp Advr, 1992–96). Liveryman, Turners' Co., 1990– (Clerk, 1996–97). Freeman, City of London, 1990. *Recreations:* golf, motoring. *Address:* c/o Royal Bank of Scotland, Laurie House, Victoria Road, Farnborough, Hants GU14 7NR. *Club:* Gainsborough Golf.

SHAW, Dr Dennis Frederick, CBE 1974; Fellow, 1957, Professorial Fellow, 1977, Emeritus Fellow, 1992, Keble College, Oxford; Keeper of Scientific Books, Bodleian Library, Oxford, 1975–91; *b* 20 April 1924; 2nd *s* of Albert Shaw and Lily (*née* Hill), Teddington; *m* 1949, Joan Irene, *er d* of Sidney and Maud Chandler; one *s* three *d. Educ:* Harrow County Sch.; Christ Church, Oxford. BA 1945, MA 1950, DPhil 1950. FInstP 1971, CPhys; FZS. Jun. Sci. Officer, MAP, 1944–46; Res. Officer in Physics, Clarendon Lab., Oxford, 1950–57, Sen. Res. Officer 1957–64; Univ. Lectr in Physics, Oxford, 1964–75. Vis. Prof. of Physics and Brown Foundn Fellow, Univ. of the South, Tennessee, 1974. Hon. Mem., Internat. Assoc. of Technol Univ. Libraries, 1992 (Sec., 1983–85; Pres., 1986–90); International Federation of Library Associations: Chm., Cttee for Sci. and Technol. Libys, 1987–91 (Mem., 1985–87); Finance Officer, Special Libraries Div., 1991–93; Mem., Press Cttee, ICSU, 1991–2002. Mem., Oxford City Council, 1963–67; Chm., Oxford City Civil Emergency Cttee, 1966–67; Member: Home Office Sci. Adv. Council, 1966–78; Home Defence Sci. Adv. Cttee, 1978–95; Hebdomadal Council, 1980–89; Chairman: Oxford Univ. Delegacy for Educnl Studies, 1969–73; Home Office Police Equipment Cttee, 1969–70; Home Office Police Sci. Develt Cttee, 1971–74. Member: Amer. Phys. Soc., 1957; NY Acad. of Scis, 1981. Gov., Christ's Hosp., 1980– (Almoner, 1980–98). Freeman, City of London, 1997. *Publications:* An Introduction to Electronics, 1962, 2nd edn 1970; A Review of Oxford University Science Libraries, 1977, 2nd edn 1981; (ed) Information Sources in Physics, 1985, 3rd edn 1994; (ed jtly) Electronic Publishing in Science, 1996; papers in sci. jls. *Recreations:* gardening, enjoying music. *Address:* Keble College, Oxford OX1 3PG. *T:* (01865) 272727. *Club:* Oxford and Cambridge.

SHAW, Donald, WS; Managing Partner, Dundas & Wilson, since 2006; *b* 14 Jan. 1956; s of D. B. Shaw, DSc, NP and P. E. Shaw; *m* Susan; two *d. Educ:* Univ. of Aberdeen (LLB 1977). WS 1984. Dundas & Wilson: joined 1979; Partner, 1985–; Real Estate Industry Leader, 2003–06. Leader Real Estate Law, Andersen Legal, 1998–2002. FSALS 1999. *Recreations:* history, music, travel, walking, wine. *Address:* Dundas & Wilson, Bush House, Northwest Wing, Aldwych, WC2B 4EZ; *e-mail:* donald.shaw@dundas-wilson.com.

SHAW, Rev. Douglas William David; Professor of Divinity, 1979–91, and Principal, St Mary's College, 1986–92, University of St Andrews; *b* 25 June 1928; *s* of William David Shaw and Nansie Smart. *Educ:* Edinburgh Acad.; Loretto; Ashbury Coll., Ottawa; Univs of Cambridge and Edinburgh. MA (Cantab), BD (Edin.), LLB (Edin.). WS. Practised law as Partner of Davidson and Syme, WS, Edinburgh, 1953–57. Ordained Minister of Church of Scotland, 1960; Asst Minister, St George's West Church, Edinburgh, 1960–63; Official Observer of World Alliance of Reformed Churches at Second Vatican Council, Rome, 1962. University of Edinburgh: Dean, Faculty of Divinity, and Principal, New College, 1974–78; Lectr in Divinity, 1963–79; Dean, Faculty of Divinity, Univ. of St Andrews, 1983–86. Croall Lectr, New Coll., Edinburgh, 1983; Alexander Robertson Lectr, Univ. of Glasgow, 1991–92. Editor, Theology in Scotland, 1994–2002. Hon. DD: Glasgow, 1991; St Andrews, 2005. *Publications:* Who is God? 1968, 2nd edn 1970; The Dissuaders, 1978; trans. from German: F. Heyer: The Catholic Church from 1648 to 1870, 1969; (ed) In Divers Manners—a St Mary's Miscellany, 1990; Dimensions—Literary and Theological, 1992; various articles in theological jls. *Recreations:* squash (Scottish Amateur Champion, 1950–51–52), golf. *Address:* 4/13 Succoth Court, Edinburgh EH12 6BZ. *T:* (0131) 337 2130. *Clubs:* New (Edinburgh); Royal and Ancient (St Andrews); Luffness New; Edinburgh Sports.

SHAW of Chapelverna, Very Rev. Duncan; JP; PhD; Representer of Clan and Name of MacGilleChainnich of Dalriada (Shaw of Argyle and the Isles); Minister Emeritus of the parish of Craigentinny, Edinburgh; *b* 27 Jan. 1925; *e s* of Neil Shaw (Mac Gille Chainnich), master carpenter, and Mary Thompson Borthwick; *m* 1st, 1955, Ilse (*d* 1989), *d* of Robert Peiter and Luise Else Mattig, Dusseldorf; one *s* two *d*; 2nd, 1991, Prof. Anna Libera, DrPhil, *d* of Prof. Luigi Dallapiccola and Dr Laura Coen Luzzatto, Florence. *Educ:* Univ. of Edinburgh (PhD). Served REME, TA(WR), 1943–47 (Warrant Officer, cl. I 1946). Minister of parish: of St Margaret, Dumbiedykes, Edinburgh, 1951–59, of Craigentinny, Edinburgh, 1959–97. Scottish Rep. of Aktion Sühnezeichen, Berlin, 1966–71; Chm. of Bd, St Andrew Press, 1967–74; Editorial Dir, 1974–2000, Man Dir, 2000–, Edina Press, Edinburgh; Chm., IMS Trust and Instant Muscle (Scotland) plc, 1988–92; Dir, Instant Muscle plc, London, 1988–95. Dir, Centre for Theological Exploration Inc. USA, 1989–95. Trustee: Nat. Museum of Antiquities of Scotland, 1974–85; Edinburgh Old Town Charitable Trust, 1989–2005; Luigi and Laura Dallapiccola Foundn, 1997–. Pres., Scottish Record Soc., 1998– (Treas., 1964–97); Founder and Chm. of Council, Scottish Soc. for Reformation History, 1980–2000. University of Edinburgh: Sec. of Gen. Council, 1965–93; Sen. Hume Brown Prizeman for Scottish History, 1965; Visiting Fellow, Inst. for Advanced Studies in the Humanities, 1975; part-time Lectr in Theological German, Faculty of Divinity, 1975–81; Sec., Gen. Council Trust, 1982–90; Dr *hc* 1990. Guest Prof., Lancaster Theolog. Seminary and Vis. Lectr, Princeton Theolog. Seminary, USA, 1967; Hastie Lectr in Divinity, Univ. of Glasgow, 1968–71; Visiting Lecturer: Univ. of Munich, 1980; Univ. of Heidelberg, 1983;

McGill Univ., Montreal, 1984; Univ. of Mainz, 1991; St Andrew's Coll., Laurenburg, USA, 1999. Member of Advisory Committee: Christian Peace Conf., Prague, 1960–68; Conf. of European Churches, 1970–86 (acted as Gen. Sec., 1971). Hon. Mem., United Church of Berlin Brandenburg, 1969; Mem. of Cons. Cttee, Selly Oak Colls, Birmingham, 1976–87; Moderator, Presbytery of Edinburgh, 1978; Moderator, Gen. Assembly of Church of Scotland, 1987–88. Freeman, City of London, 1990; Liveryman, Scriveners' Co., 1990. JP 1974; Chm., City of Edinburgh Justices Cttee, 1984–87; Burgess, City of Edinburgh, 2007. KStJ 1983 (Mem., Chapter Gen., 1984–93, Chancellor of Scotland, 1986–92, Order of St John). ThDr *hc* Comenius Faculty of Theology, Charles Univ., Prague, 1969. Patriarchal Cross, 1978, for Hierarchs, 1988, Romanian Orthodox Church; Bundesverdienstkreuz, 1st cl. (Germany), 1980; Com. al Merito Melitense (SMO Malta), 1987; Order of St Sergius, 1987, Order of St Vladimir, 1997, Russian Orthodox Church. *Publications:* The General Assemblies of the Church of Scotland 1560–1600: their Origins and Development, 1964; (contrib. and ed) Reformation and Revolution: Essays presented to Principal Emeritus Hugh Watt, 1967; Inauguration of Ministers in Scotland 1560–1600, 1968; (contrib. and ed) John Knox: A Quartercentenary Reappraisal, 1975; Knox and Mary, Queen of Scots, 1980; (contrib. foreword and supervised translation) Zwingli's Thought: New Perspectives (by G. W. Locher), 1981; (contrib. and ed with I. B. Cowan) The Renaissance and Reformation in Scotland: Essays in Honour of Gordon Donaldson, 1983; A Voice in the Wilderness, 1995; Valedictory Address, 1997; (contrib.) Die Zürcher Reformation: Ausstrahlungen und Rückwirkungen, 2001; (ed) Acts and Proceedings of the General Assemblies of the Church of Scotland 1560–1618, 3 vols, 2004; Zwingli's Influence on Scotland: collected papers, 2008; contrib. Oxford DNB; contribs to learned jls. *Address:* 4 Sydney Terrace, Edinburgh EH7 6SL. *T:* (0131) 669 9155; 12 Castelnau Gardens, Arundel Terrace, SW13 8DU. *T:* (020) 8746 3087. *Club:* Highland (Inverness).

SHAW, Elizabeth Angela; Director, Musikansky Theatre Company, 1998–2003; *b* 5 June 1946; *d* of John Edward Comben and Irene (*née* Thomson); *m* 1st, 1970, Graham Shaw (marr. diss. 1985); two *s* one *d*; 2nd, 1993, Adrian Carter. *Educ:* Sydenham High School. Executive Officer: Home Office, 1965–68; FCO, 1968–70; DSS, 1970–72; Department of Health and Social Security: HEO (Develt), 1972–77; Principal, 1977–84; Asst Sec., 1984–87; Dir of Finance, Planning and Marketing, Civil Service Coll., 1987–90; Head of Staff Develt, DoH, 1990–91; Exec. Dir, Charity Commn, 1991–96. Chair: COMPAID Trust, 1997–99; St Michael's Fellowship, 1997–99. *Recreations:* music, literature, walking, riding, family.

SHAW, Fiona Mary, Hon. CBE 2001; actress; *b* 10 July 1958; *d* of Dr Denis Joseph Wilson and Mary Teresa Wilson (*née* Flynn), MSc; adopted Shaw as stage name. *Educ:* University Coll. Cork (BA); Royal Acad. of Dramatic Art (Hons Dip.; Bancroft Gold medal; Tree Prize; Ronson Award). *Theatre* includes: The Rivals, 1983; RSC, 1985–88: Philistines; As You Like It; Les Liaisons Dangereuses; Mephisto; Much Ado About Nothing; The Merchant of Venice; Hyde Park; The Taming of the Shrew; New Inn; Electra (title rôle); Mary Stuart, Greenwich, 1988; As You Like It, Old Vic, 1989; The Good Person of Sichuan, NT, 1989; Hedda Gabler (title rôle), Dublin and Playhouse, 1991; Machinal, NT (Best Actress, Evening Standard Awards), 1993; Footfalls, Garrick, 1994; Richard II, The Way of the World, RNT, 1995; The Waste Land, Brussels and Dublin Fests, NY, 1996, Wilton's Music Hall, London, 1997, Adelaide, 1998; The Prime of Miss Jean Brodie, RNT, 1998; Medea, Abbey Th., Dublin, 2000, Queen's (Best Actress, Evening Standard Awards), 2001, NY 2002; The PowerBook, NT, 2002; The Seagull, Edinburgh, 2004; Julius Caesar, Barbican, 2005; Woman and Scarecrow, Royal Ct, 2006; Happy Days, NT, 2007; *films* include: My Left Foot, 1988; The Mountains of the Moon, 1988; Three Men and a Little Lady, 1990; London Kills Me, 1991; Super Mario Brothers, 1993; Undercover Blues, 1993; Jane Eyre, 1994; Anna Karenina, 1996; The Butcher Boy, 1996; The Avengers, 1997; The Last September, 2000; Harry Potter and the Philosopher's Stone, 2001; Harry Potter and the Chamber of Secrets, 2002; The Triumph of Love, 2004; The Black Dahlia, 2006; Catch and Release, 2007; Fracture, 2007; Harry Potter and the Order of the Phoenix, 2007; *television* includes: Fireworks for Elspeth, 1983; Persuasion, 1994; The Waste Land, 1995; Gormenghast, 2000; Mind Games, 2000. Hon. Prof. of Drama, TCD, 1997. Hon. LLD NUI, 1996; DUniv Open, 1998; Hon. DLitt: TCD, 2001; Ulster, 2004. London Theatre Critics' Award, 1989, 1992; Best Actress, Olivier Awards, 1989, 1994. Officier, Ordre des Arts et des Lettres (France), 2003. *Publications:* contributor to: Players of Shakespeare, 1987; Clamorous Voices, 1988; Conversations with Actresses, 1990. *Recreations:* travel, reading, walking, thinking, snorkling. *Address:* c/o Independent Talent Group Ltd, Oxford House, 76 Oxford Street, W1D 1BS.

SHAW, Rev. Canon Geoffrey Norman; Hon. Canon Emeritus of Christ Church Cathedral, Oxford, since 1989 (Hon. Canon, 1985–89); *b* 15 April 1926; *s* of Samuel Norman Shaw and Maud Shaw; *m* 1st, 1948, Cynthia Brown (*d* 1997); one *s* two *d*; 2nd, 1998, Margaret Dorothy Thurlow. *Educ:* Holgate Grammar Sch., Barnsley; Jesus Coll., Oxford (MA); Wycliffe Hall, Oxford. Asst Curate, St Mary, Rushden, 1951–54; Vicar of St Paul, Woking, 1954–62; Rector of St Leonards-on-Sea, Sussex, 1962–68; Asst Master, Ecclesfield Grammar Sch., Sheffield, 1968–69; Head of Religious Educn and Classics, Silverdale Sch., Sheffield, 1969–72; Vice-Principal, Oak Hill Theol Coll., Southgate, 1972–79; Principal, Wycliffe Hall, Oxford, 1979–89. Hon. Asst Chaplain, Kingham Hill Sch., 1992–. *Recreations:* bird watching, walking, golf, music. *Address:* 15A West Street, Kingham, Oxon OX7 6YQ. *T:* (01608) 658006; *e-mail:* canonshaw@aol.com.

SHAW, Geoffrey Peter; QC 1991; *b* 19 April 1944; *s* of late James Adamson Shaw and Hilda Gargett Shaw (*née* Edwards); *m* 1985, Susan Cochrane. *Educ:* Worksop College, Notts; Worcester College, Oxford (BA, BCL). Teaching Fellow, Univ. of Chicago Law Sch., 1966; Arden Scholar of Gray's Inn, 1967; called to the Bar, Gray's Inn, 1968; defamation specialist. CEDR accredited mediator, 2003. *Recreations:* walking, travel, gardening. *Address:* 1 Brick Court, Temple, EC4Y 9BY. *T:* (020) 7353 8845; *e-mail:* gs@onebrickcourt.com.

SHAW, Sir (George) Neville B.; *see* Bowman-Shaw.

SHAW, Sir John (Calman), Kt 1995; CBE 1989; CA; FRSE; Governor, Bank of Scotland, 1999–2001 (non-executive Director, 1990–2001; Deputy Governor, 1991–99); *b* 10 July 1932; *m* 1960, Shirley Botterill; three *d*. *Educ:* Strathallan Sch.; Edinburgh Univ. BL; FCMA, MBCS, JDipMA. National Service, RAF, 1955–57. Partner in Graham, Smart & Annan (later Deloitte, Haskins & Sells), 1960, Sen. Edinburgh Partner, 1980–87. Pres., Inst. of Chartered Accountants of Scotland, 1983–84. Johnstone Smith Prof. of Accountancy (pt-time appt), 1977–82, Vis. Prof., 1986–, Glasgow Univ. Chairman: Scottish American Investment Co. PLC (formerly Trust), 1991–2001 (Dir, 1986–2003); US Smaller Cos Investment Trust, 1991–99 (Dir, 1991–2000); TR European Growth Trust PLC, 1998–2002 (Dir, 1992–2002); Director: Scottish Metropolitan Property plc, 1994–2000; Scottish Mortgage and Trust PLC, 1982–2001; Templeton Emerging Markets Investment Trust plc, 1994–2003. Chairman: SHEFC, 1992–98; Scottish Financial Enterprise, 1995–99 (Exec. Dir, 1986–90); Scottish Science Trust, 1998–2002; Edinburgh Technology Fund, 1999–2001; Member: Bd, Scottish Enterprise, 1990–98; Financial Reporting Council, 1990–96. Chm., David Hume Inst., 1995–2002. Dep. Chm., Edinburgh Fest. Soc., 1991–2000. Mem. Court, Univ. of Edinburgh, 1998–2003. Dr *hc* Edinburgh, 1998; Hon. LLD: Glasgow, 1998; Abertay Dundee, 1998; St Andrews, 1999; Hon. DEd Napier, 1999. Receiver General, The Priory of Scotland of Most Venerable Order of St John, 1992–2002; KStJ 1992. *Publications:* (ed) Bogie on Group Accounts (3rd edn), 1973; The Audit Report, 1980; (jtly) Information Disclosure and the Multinational Corporation, 1984; numerous articles in accountancy and res. jls. *Recreations:* opera, theatre, walking. *Address:* Tayhill, Dunkeld PH8 0BA. *Clubs:* Caledonian; New (Edinburgh).

SHAW, John Campbell; Managing Director: Amberton Shaw, 1997–2004; Stannifer Group Holdings, 1998–2004; *b* 2 Aug. 1949; *s* of late John C. B. Shaw and of May B. Shaw; *m*; two *d*. *Educ:* Grosvenor High Sch., Belfast; QUB (BSc Hons in Urban Geography); Heriot-Watt Univ. (MSc in Town & Country Planning). Lanarkshire CC, 1973–75; Motherwell DC, 1975–78; East Kilbride Development Corporation, 1978–95: Head of Planning, 1982; Tech. Dir, 1986; Man. Dir, 1990–95; Bd Mem., Lanarkshire Develt Agency, 1991–95. *Recreation:* sport.

SHAW, John Frederick, CB 1996; Director of Corporate Affairs, National Health Service Executive, 1993–96; *b* 7 Dec. 1936; *s* of James Herbert and Barbara Shaw; *m* 1964, Ann Rodden; two *s* one *d*. *Educ:* Loretto Sch., Musselburgh; Worcester Coll., Oxford (MA). National Service, 2/Lieut KOYLI, 1955–57. Church Comrs, 1960–62; Industrial Christian Fellowship, 1962–63; HQ Staff, VSO, 1963–73; Principal (Direct Entry), DHSS, 1973, Asst Sec. 1978; Under Sec., DHSS, then DoH, 1987–93. Chairman: REACH, 1988–92; Nat. Family Mediation, 1996–2001; Rickmansworth Waterways Trust, 1997–2006; UK Transplant Support Services Authority, 1998–2001; Nat. Centre for Volunteering, 1999–2004 (Trustee, 1996–2004, Chm. Trustees, 1998–2004); Member Council: Patients' Assoc., 1996–99 (Vice-Chm., 1996–98); British Assoc. of Day Surgery, 1998–2005; Lay Mem., 1996–2003, Associate Mem., 2003–06, GMC; Lay Mem., Jt Cttee on Postgrad. Training for General Practice, 1997–2005. *Recreations:* church activities, singing, gardening. *Address:* Hyde House, West Hyde, Rickmansworth, Herts WD3 9XH.

SHAW, Sir John Michael Robert B.; *see* Best-Shaw.

SHAW, Jonathan Rowland; MP (Lab) Chatham and Aylesford, since 1997; Parliamentary Under-Secretary of State, Department for Work and Pensions, since 2008; Minister for the South East, since 2007; *b* 3 June 1966; *s* of Alan James Shaw and Lesbia Virginia Percival Shaw; *m* 1990, Susan Lesley Gurmin; one *s* one *d*. *Educ:* Vinters Boys' Sch., Maidstone; Bromley Coll., Kent (Cert. in Social Services). Social Worker, Kent Social Services, 1990–97. An Asst Govt Whip, 2006–07; Parly Under-Sec. of State, DEFRA, 2007–08. *Recreations:* walking, cooking, reading. *Address:* c/o House of Commons, SW1A 0AA; 411 High Street, Chatham, Kent ME4 4NU.

SHAW, Kenneth Martin, MD, FRCP; Clincial Lead (Metabolic and Endocrine), Hampshire and Isle of Wight Comprehensive Local Research Network, since 2008; *b* 20 April 1943; *s* of late Frank Shaw and Gwen (*née* Mosson); *m* 1968, Phyllis Dixon; two *s*. *Educ:* City of Norwich Sch.; Downing Coll., Cambridge (BA 1965, MA 1969; BChir 1968, MB 1969; MD 1979); University Coll. Hosp., London. FRCP 1985. MRC Res. Fellow, Dept of Clin. Pharmacol., UCH Med. Sch., 1971–72; Sen. Registrar, 1973–77, Resident Asst Physician, 1977–78, UCH, London; Portsmouth and SE Hants Health Dist, later Portsmouth Hosps NHS Trust: Associate Clin. Dir, Medicine, and Dir, 1979, Clin. Dir, then Hd of Service, 1979–2008, Dept of Diabetes and Endocrinol.; Sen. Consultant Physician, 1979–2008; Hon. Consultant, 2008–; Postgrad. Clin. Tutor, Univ. of Southampton, 1983–90; Dir, R&D, Portsmouth Hosps NHS Trust, and R&D Support Unit and Portsmouth R&D Consortium, Sch. of Postgrad. Medicine, Univ. of Portsmouth (at Queen Alexandra Hosp.), 1995–2008. Vis. Prof., 1996, Emeritus Prof. of Medicine, 2008, Portsmouth Univ. Editor-in-Chief, Practical Diabetes Internat., 1992–. Royal College of Physicians: Hon. Sec., Jt Specialty Cttee for Endocrinol. and Diabetes, 2001– (Mem., 1998–); Mem., Adv. Panel for Service Rev. Visits, 2000–; Diabetes UK (formerly British Diabetic Association): Mem., Med. Adv. Cttee, 1982–86; Vice Chm., Specialist Care Cttee, 1998–2002; Mem., 2002–, Mem. Exec., 2006–, Professional Adv. Council; Chm., Professional Support and Develt Cttee, 2006–; Chm., Wessex Diabetes and Endocrinol. Assoc., 1989–96; Mem., Med. Panel (Diabetes), DVLA, 2005–. Member: Eur. Assoc. for Study of Diabetes, 1980–; Amer. Diabetes Assoc., 1995–; Internat. Diabetes Fedn, 1995–; Founding Mem. and Trustee, Assoc. of British Clin. Diabetologists, 1996– (Hon. Treas., 1996–2006; Hon. Chm., 2006–08). FRSocMed 1972; Scientific FZS 1974. Mem., Harveian Med. Soc. of London, 1969–. UK Hosp. Diabetes Team Award, 1998. *Publications:* Complications of Diabetes, 1996, 2nd edn 2005; contrib. chapters in books; contrib. numerous rev. articles and peer-reviewed original scientific articles. *Recreations:* golf, opera. *Address:* Castle Acre, Hospital Lane, Portchester, Hants PO16 9QP; *web:* www.profkenshaw.com.

SHAW, Prof. Malcolm Nathan; QC 2002; PhD; Sir Robert Jennings Professor of International Law, University of Leicester, since 1994; *b* 8 July 1947; *s* of late Benjamin Shaw, CBE, and of Paulette Shaw; *m* 1974, Judith Freeman; one *s* two *d*. *Educ:* Liverpool Univ. (LLB Hons); Hebrew Univ., Jerusalem (LLM with distinction); Keele Univ. (PhD). Called to the Bar, Gray's Inn, 1988; Lectr, then Principal Lectr, Liverpool Poly., 1972–81; Sen. Lectr and Reader in Law, 1981–89, Founder, Human Rights Centre, 1983, Essex Univ.; Ironsides, Ray and Vials Prof. of Law, Leicester Univ., 1989–94. Forcheimer Vis. Prof., Hebrew Univ. of Jerusalem, 1986–87; Vis. Fellow, Lauterpacht Res. Centre for Internat. Law, Cambridge Univ., 2000–01 and 2005. Mem., Law Assessment Panel, 1996 and 2001 RAE, HEFCE. *Publications:* International Law, 1977, 5th edn 2003 (trans. Polish, Hungarian, Chinese, Portuguese, Kurdish); Title to Territory in Africa, 1986; contrib. British Yr Book of Internat. Law, Finnish Yr Book of Internat. Law, Internat. and Comparative Law Qly, European Jl of Internat. Law. *Recreations:* reading, listening to music, watching TV, maps. *Address:* Faculty of Law, University of Leicester, Leicester LE1 7RH. *T:* (0116) 252 2648, *Fax:* (0116) 252 5023; *e-mail:* mns2@le.ac.uk; Essex Court Chambers, 24 Lincoln's Inn Fields, WC2A 3ED.

SHAW, Mark Richard; QC 2002; *b* 6 June 1962; *s* of Dennis Ronald Shaw and Jill Merilyn Shaw; *m* 1991, Elisabetta Ladisa. *Educ:* St Peter's Sch., Bournemouth; Durham Univ. (BA 1984); Gonville and Caius Coll., Cambridge (LLM 1985). Called to the Bar, Inner Temple, 1987; in practice, specialising in public law and human rights; Jun. Counsel to the Crown, Common Law, 1992–2002; Special Advocate, 1998–. Mem., Adv. Bd, Judicial Rev., 1996–. *Publications:* (jtly) Immigration and Nationality, in Halsbury's Laws of England: vol. 4, 1992; (contrib.) Human Rights Law and Practice, 1999, and Supplement, 2000. *Recreations:* golf, scuba diving, running, travel (especially in Italy). *Address:* Blackstone Chambers, Temple, EC4Y 9BW. *T:* (020) 7583 1770. *Clubs:* Athenæum; Royal St George's Golf.

SHAW, Dr Mark Robert, FRSE; Keeper of Geology and Zoology, 1996–2005, now Hon. Research Associate, National Museums of Scotland; *b* 11 May 1945; *s* of William Shaw and Mabel Courtenay Shaw (*née* Bower); *m* 1970, Francesca Dennis Wilkinson; two *d. Educ:* Dartington Hall Sch.; Oriel Coll., Oxford (BA 1968; MA, DPhil 1972). FRSE 2004. Res. Assistant, Manchester Univ., 1973–76; Univ. Res. Fellow, Reading Univ., 1977–80; Asst Keeper, Dept of Natural History, 1980–83, Keeper of Natural History, 1983–96, Royal Scottish Mus., subseq. Nat. Museums of Scotland. *Publications:* contribs (mainly on parasitic wasps) to entomological jls. *Recreations:* field entomology, family life. *Address:* 48 St Albans Road, Edinburgh EH9 2LU. *T:* (0131) 667 0577.

SHAW, Martin; actor; *b* 21 Jan. 1945; two *s* one *d. Educ:* Great Barr Sch., Birmingham; LAMDA. *Stage* includes: appearances at Royal Court and National Theatre; West End: Are You Lonesome Tonight, Phoenix, 1985; The Big Knife, Albery, 1987; Other People's Money, Lyric 1990; Betrayal, 1991; An Ideal Husband, Globe, 1992, Haymarket, 1996 (Best Actor Award, NY Drama Desk, 1996), 1997, transf. Gielgud, and Albery, 1998, Haymarket, and Lyric, 1999; Rough Justice, Apollo, 1994; A Man for All Seasons, Haymarket, 2006; *television* includes, 1968–: The Professionals; The Chief, 1994; title rôle in Rhodes, 1996; The Scarlet Pimpernel, 1999; Always and Everyone, later A & E, 1999–; Judge John Deed, 2001–; Death in Holy Orders, 2003; The Murder Room, 2004; Cranford, 2007. *Recreation:* flies own antique biplane.

SHAW, Rt Rev. Martin; *see* Argyll and the Isles, Bishop of.

SHAW, Group Captain Mary Michal, RRC 1981; Director and Matron-in-Chief, Princess Mary's Royal Air Force Nursing Service, and Deputy Director, Defence Nursing Services (Operations and Plans), 1985–88; *b* 7 April 1933; *d* of Ven. Archdeacon Thorndike Shaw and Violet Rosario Shaw. *Educ:* Wokingham Grammar School for Girls. SRN 1955, Royal Berkshire Hosp., Reading; SCM 1957, Central Middlesex Hosp., London and Battle Hosp., Reading; PMRAFNS, 1963–88; QHNS, 1985–88. OStJ 1974. *Recreations:* gardening, home crafts.

SHAW, Michael Hewitt, CMG 1990; foreign affairs adviser and consultant; HM Diplomatic Service, retired; *b* 5 Jan. 1935; *s* of late Donald Shaw and Marion (*née* Hewitt); *m* 1963, Elizabeth Rance; three *d* (and one *d* decd). *Educ:* Sedbergh; Clare College, Cambridge (MA); UCL (MA 1992). HM Forces, 1953–55. HMOCS Tanganyika, 1959–62; joined Diplomatic Service, 1963; served The Hague, FCO and Vientiane, 1964–68; First Sec., FCO, 1968–72, Valletta, 1972–76, FCO, 1976–82, Brussels, 1982–84; Counsellor, Brussels, 1984–86, FCO, 1986–95. *Recreations:* cricket, theatre, travel, historical research. *Address:* The Close, Marley Common, Haslemere, Surrey GU27 3PT; *e-mail:* mhshaw@supanet.com. *Clubs:* Army and Navy, MCC.
See also R. O. Shaw.

SHAW, Sir Neil (McGowan), Kt 1994; Chairman: Tate & Lyle PLC, London, 1986–98 (Director, 1975–98; Chief Executive, 1986–92); Tate & Lyle Holdings, 1981–98; Tate & Lyle Industries, 1981–98; Tunnel Refineries, 1982–98 (Director, 1981–98); Vice-Chairman: Redpath Industries, 1981–98 (Director, 1972–98); A. E. Staley Manufacturing Co., 1988–98; *b* 31 May 1929; *s* of late Harold LeRoy Shaw and Fabiola Marie Shaw; *m* 1952, Audrey Robinson (marr. diss.); two *s* three *d*; *m* 1985, Elizabeth Fern Mudge-Massey. *Educ:* Knowlton High Sch.; Lower Canada Coll., Canada. Trust Officer, Crown Trust Co., Montreal, 1947–54; Exec. Asst, Redpath Industries, 1954–58; Merchandising Manager, 1958–63, Vice Pres. and Gen. Manager, 1967–72, Canada & Dominion Sugar Co., Toronto; Export Sales Manager, Tate & Lyle PLC, 1963–68; Pres., Redpath Industries Ltd, 1972–80; Gp Man. Dir, Tate & Lyle PLC, 1980–86. Director: Americare Corp., 1980–96; G. R. Amylum NV, Brussels, 1982–91; Alcantara, 1983–98; Canadian Imperial Bank of Commerce (Toronto), 1986–2000; United Biscuits (Hldgs), 1988–97; M & G Investment Income Trust, 1991–95; Medcan (Toronto), 2001. Non-executive Director: Texaco Canada Inc., 1974–89; Smiths Industries, 1986–96; Scottish and Newcastle Breweries, 1986–92. Dir, World Sugar Res. Orgn, 1982–97 (Chm., 1994–96); Gov., World Food and Agro Forum, 1988–96. Chairman: BITC, 1991–94; Assoc. of Lloyd's Members, 1992–94; E London Partnership, 1989–91; Member: Food Assoc., 1989–95; Church Urban Fund Council, 1989–91; Canadian Univs Soc. of GB, 1989–2001; Adv. Council, PYBT, 1990–98; Listed Cos Adv. Cttee, Stock Exchange, 1991–97. Trustee, Royal Botanic Gardens, Kew, 1990–98 (Chm., Trustees and Friends, 1994–2000). Dir, Inst. of Dirs, 1986–97. Dir and Gov., United World Coll. of Atlantic, 1997–2000. Gov., Montreal Gen. Hosp. Jt Chm., Percent Club, 1992–97. CIMgt, 1981–98; Fellow, Inst of Grocery Distribn, 1989–2000 (Mem., British N American Cttee, 1991–97). Hon. Fellow, RHBNC, 1995. Hon. LLD E London, 1997. *Recreations:* dogs, ski-ing, golfing. *Clubs:* Toronto, Toronto Golf (Toronto).

SHAW, Sir Neville B.; *see* Bowman-Shaw.

SHAW, Nicholas Glencairn B.; *see* Byam Shaw.

SHAW, Peter Alan, CB 2000; Partner, Praesta Partners, since 2005; *b* 31 May 1949; *s* of late Frank Shaw and Ursula Lister Shaw (*née* Dyson); *m* 1975, Frances Willcox; two *s* one *d. Educ:* Bridlington Sch.; Durham Univ. (BSc Geography); Bradford Univ. (MSc Traffic Eng. and Planning); Regent Coll., Univ. of British Columbia (Master in Christian Studies). FIHT. Department of Education and Science, subseq. Department for Education, then Department for Education and Employment, then Department for Education and Skills, 1972–2003: Private Sec. to Perm. Sec., 1975–76; Principal Private Sec. to Sec. of State, 1979–81; Asst Sec., 1981–91; on loan to HM Treasury, 1985–86; Press Sec. to DES Sec. of State, 1988–89; Grade 3, 1991–98; on loan to Depts of the Envmt and Transport as Regl Dir, Northern Reg., 1991–93; Dir of Estabts and Personnel, 1993–94; Dir of Services (personnel, analytical and inf. systems), 1994–95; Leader, Sen. Mgt Review, 1995; Dir, Sch. Places, Buildings and Governance, 1995–97; Dir, Finance, 1997–98; Grade 2, 1998–2003; Director-General: Finance and Analytical Services, 1998–2000; Employment, Equality and Internat. Relations, 2000–01; Youth Policy, 2001–03; Partner, Change Partnership, 2003–05. Hon. Vis. Prof., Educn Dept, Univ. of Durham, 1997–2000. Trustee, Christian Assoc. of Business Execs, 2005–. Member: Council, St John's Coll., Durham Univ., 1993–; Ct, Univ. of Newcastle upon Tyne, 2005–; Governing Body, Godalming Sixth Form Coll., 1996–2008. Anglican Lay Reader, 1972–, Chm. of Selectors for Lay Readers in Trng, 1999–, Mem., Ministerial Adv. Council, 1999–2004, dio. of Guildford. FRSA. *Publications:* Mirroring Jesus as Leader, 2004; Conversation Matters, 2005; The Vs of Leadership: vision, values, value added and vitality, 2006; Finding Your Future: the second time around, 2006; (with Robin Linnecar) Business Coaching: achieving practical results through effective engagement, 2007; Making Difficult Decisions: how to be decisive and get the business done, 2008; The Christian Leader in the Secular World of Work, 2009; articles on exec. coaching, leadership and spirituality. *Recreations:* walking, travelling. *Address:* Praesta Partners, 83 Pall Mall, SW1Y 5ES. *T:* (020) 7478 3107.

SHAW, Captain Peter Jack, CBE 1990; RN (retd); General Secretary, British Group Inter-Parliamentary Union, 1979–90; Consultant to President, Interparliamentary Council, 1991–93; *b* Geelong, Australia, 27 Oct. 1924; *s* of late Jack and Betty Shaw; *m* 1951, Pauline, *e d* of Sir Frank Madge, 2nd Bt, and Lady (Doris) Madge, East Grinstead; one *s* one *d. Educ:* Watford Grammar School; RNC Dartmouth; RN Staff Coll. Greenwich; NATO Defence Coll., Paris. FCIL (FIL 1957). War service in HM Ships Kenya, Resolution, Quadrant, Kelvin, incl. Malta and Russian Convoys and D-Day landings; comd HM Ships Venus, Carron, Vigilant, 1958–61; Staff, C-in-C Portsmouth and MoD, 1961–65; SHAPE, Paris and Mons, 1966–68; Comdr, RN Coll. Greenwich, 1968–70; Defence and Naval Attaché, The Hague, 1971–73; Captain of Port and Queen's Harbourmaster, Plymouth, 1973–76; Captain of Port, Chatham, 1976–79. *Recreations:* international relations, foreign languages, domestic pursuits. *Address:* Woodside, Rogate, Petersfield, Hants GU31 5DJ. *T:* (01730) 821344.

SHAW, Dr Richard Oliver; Chief Executive, Surrey County Council, since 2005; *b* 20 Jan. 1949; *s* of Donald Smethurst Shaw and Marion Clarissa Shaw; *m* 1983, Poorna Charles; three *s. Educ:* Sedbergh Sch.; Univ. of Sussex (BA 1st cl. Hons); Univ. of Exeter (PGCE 1973); UCL (PhD 1981). Teacher: Lycée el Hourriya, Algeria, 1971–72; Rishi Valley Sch., India, 1974–76; Sen. Educn Officer, then Field Dir, PNG, VSO, 1976–81; Head Teacher, Pahadi Sch., India, 1981–87; teacher, ILEA, 1987–88; Hd, Rural Affairs, then Hd, Global Atmosphere, DoE, 1988–97; Dir for the Envmt, Surrey CC, 1997–2001; Chief Exec., Oxfordshire CC, 2001–04. Mem. Council, Univ. of Surrey. *Publications:* English lang. school textbooks for India. *Recreations:* tennis, swimming, walking, travel, my family, music. *Address:* Surrey County Council, County Hall, Penrhyn Road, Kingston upon Thames, Surrey KT1 2DN. *T:* (020) 8541 8018, *Fax:* (020) 8541 8968; *e-mail:* Richard.Shaw@surreycc.gov.uk.
See also M. H. Shaw.

SHAW, Prof. Richard Wright, CBE 1997; Vice-Chancellor and Principal, University of Paisley, 1992–2001 (Principal, Paisley College, 1987–92); *b* 22 Sept. 1941; *s* of late George Beeley Shaw and Bella Shaw; *m* 1965, Susan Angela Birchley; two *s. Educ:* Lancaster Royal Grammar Sch.; Sidney Sussex Coll., Cambridge (MA). Leeds University: Asst Lectr in Management, 1964–66; Lectr in Econs, 1966–69; Stirling University: Lectr in Econs, 1969–75; Sen. Lectr, 1975–84; Head of Dept of Econs, 1982–84; Paisley College: Head, Dept of Econs and Management and Prof., 1984–86; Vice Principal, 1986–87. Convenor, Cttee of Scottish Higher Educn Principals, 1996–98. Member: Scottish Economic Council, 1995–98; Scottish Business Forum, 1998–99; Chm., Lead Scotland, 2001–07. Fellow, SCOTVEC, 1995; FRSA. DUniv Glasgow, 2001. *Publications:* (with C. J. Sutton) Industry and Competition, 1976; articles in Jl Industrial Econs, Scottish Jl Pol Econ., Managerial and Decision Econs. *Recreations:* walking, listening to music, sketching and painting. *Address:* Drumbarns, 18 Old Doune Road, Dunblane, Perthshire FK15 9AG.

SHAW, Prof. Robert Wayne, CBE 2002; MD; FRCSE, FRCOG; Professor of Obstetrics and Gynaecology, Nottingham University, since 2002; *b* 25 June 1946; *s* of Arthur Stanley Shaw and Margery Maude Shaw (*née* Griffiths); *m* 1980, Mary Philomena McGovern; one *s* one *d. Educ:* Priory Grammar Sch., Shrewsbury; Birmingham Univ. Med. Sch. (MB ChB 1969; MD 1975). FRCSE 1978; MRCOG 1977, FRCOG 1993. Lectr, 1975–79, and Sen. Lectr, 1979–81, in Obstetrics and Gynaecology, Birmingham Univ.; Sen. Lectr, Edinburgh Univ., 1981–83; Prof., Royal Free Hosp. Sch. of Medicine, 1983–92; Prof. and Head of Acad. Dept of Obstetrics and Gynaecology, Univ. of Wales Coll. of Medicine, 1992–2001; Postgrad. Dean, Med. and Dental Educn, Eastern Deanery, Univ. of Cambridge, 2001–02. Vice-Pres., 1995–98, Pres., 1998–2001, RCOG. Chm. Bd, Nat. Collaborating Centre for Women's and Children's Health, 2007. Founder FMedSci 1998; FRCPI 2000; FACOG 2000. Hon. FFFP 2002; Hon. Fellow, Finnish Gynaecological Soc., 1992. *Publications:* (ed jtly) Gynaecology, 1992, 3rd edn, 2003; (ed) Endometriosis: current management, 1995; over 300 articles on gynaecological reproductive medicine. *Recreations:* sailing, hill walking. *Address:* Academic Division of Obstetrics & Gynaecology, Medical School, Derby City General Hospital, Uttoxeter Road, Derby DE22 3DT. *Club:* Athenæum.

SHAW, Prof. Rory James Swanton, MD; FRCP; Medical Director, Royal Berkshire NHS Foundation Trust, since 2007; *b* 5 Jan. 1954; *s* of late Dr James Brian Shaw, OBE and of Irma Valerie Shaw, JP; *m* 1991, Sarah Margaret Foulkes; two *d. Educ:* Bedford Sch.; St Bartholomew's Hosp. Med. Sch. (BSc 1974; MB BS 1977); MD 1985, MBA 1995, London. MRCP 1979, FRCP 1993. Sen. Lectr, St Mary's Hosp. Med. Sch., Imperial Coll., and Consultant Physician in Respiratory Medicine, 1989–97; Prof. of Respiratory Med., Imperial Coll. Sch. of Med., 1997–; Med. Dir, Hammersmith Hosps NHS Trust, 1998–2006. Chm., Nat. Patient Safety Agency, 2001–03; non-exec. Dir, NHS Litigation Authy, 2007–. *Publications:* articles on tuberculosis and asthma in learned jls. *Address:* Medical Director's Office, Royal Berkshire NHS Foundation Trust, Level 4, Main Entrance, Craven Road, Reading RG1 5AN. *T:* (0118) 322 8224.

SHAW, Sir Roy, Kt 1979; Secretary General of the Arts Council of Great Britain, 1975–83; *b* 8 July 1918; *s* of Frederick and Elsie Shaw; *m* 1946, Gwenyth Baron; five *s* two *d. Educ:* Firth Park Grammar School, Sheffield; Manchester Univ. BA(Hons). Newspaper printing department 'copy-holder', 1937; newspaper publicity, 1938; Library Asst, Sheffield City Library, 1939; Cataloguer, Manchester Univ. Library, 1945; Organizing Tutor, WEA, 1946; Adult Educn Lectr, Leeds Univ., 1947; Warden, Leeds Univ. Adult Educn Centre, Bradford, 1959; Professor and Dir of Adult Educn, Keele Univ., 1962. Vis. Prof., Centre for Arts, City Univ., London, 1977–83. Theatre critic, The Tablet, 1990–2000. Hon. DLitt: City, 1978; Southampton, 1984; DUniv Open, 1981. *Publications:* The Arts and the people, 1987; (ed) The Spread of Sponsorship, 1993; contrib. chapters to: Trends in English Adult Education, 1959; The Committed Church, 1966; Your Sunday Paper, 1967; over 170 articles and book chapters on cultural policy, adult education and the mass media. *Recreations:* reading, theatre, opera, films, concerts and art galleries, swimming, watching the best of television—and sometimes, for clinical reasons, the worst. *Address:* Flat Four, 6 Grand Avenue, Hove BN3 2LF. *T:* (01273) 724051. *Club:* Arts.

SHAW, Roy Edwin, OBE 1991; Council Member, London Borough of Camden, since 1964; Mayor of Camden, 1999–2000; *b* 21 July 1925; *s* of Edwin Victor and Edith Lily Shaw. Hampstead Borough Council, 1956–62; St Pancras Borough, 1962–65; Camden Borough Council: Chm., Planning Cttee, 1967–68; Chm., Finance Cttee, 1971–74; Chief Whip and Dep. Leader, 1965–73; Leader, 1975–82; Dep. Leader, 1990–94. Vice-Chm., AMA, 1979–83; Dep. Chm. and Leader of Labour Party, London Boroughs Assoc.; Dep. Leader, London Fire and Civil Defence Authy, 1999–2000; Mem., London Fire and Emergency Planning Authy, 2000– (Vice Chm., 2000–03; Dep. Chm., 2003–04). Part-time Mem., London Electricity Bd, 1977–83; Member: Transport Users Consultative Cttee for London, 1974–80; Adv. Cttee on Local Govt Audit, 1979–82; Audit Commn, 1983–91; Consult. Council on Local Govt Finances, 1978–84. Chm., Camden Trng Centre, 1990–99. *Recreations:* listening to music; entertaining attractive women. *Address:* Town Hall, Euston Road, NW1 2RU. *T:* (020) 7278 4444.

SHAW, Sir Run Run, Kt 1977; CBE 1974; Founder and Chairman, Shaw Organisation, since 1963; Founder and Chairman, Shaw Foundation, since 1973; *b* 14 Oct. 1907; *m* 1st,

1932, Lily Wong Mee Chun (decd); two s two d; 2nd, 1997, Lee Mong-lan (Mona Fong). Left China for Singapore and began making films and operating cinemas, 1927; left Singapore for Hong Kong and built Shaw Movietown, making and distributing films, 1959. Pres., Hong Kong Red Cross Soc., 1972–98. Chairman: Hong Kong Arts Festival, 1974–88; Bd of Governors, Hong Kong Arts Centre, 1978–88; Television Broadcasts Ltd, 1980–. Chinese University of Hong Kong: Mem. Council, 1977–92; Chm., Bd of Trustees, United Coll., 1983–92; Founder, Shaw Coll., 1986. Appointed by Govt of People's Republic of China, Hong Kong Advr, 1992–97, Mem., Preparatory Cttee, 1995–98. Est. Shaw Prize, 2003. Hon. LLD Hong Kong Univ., 1980; Hon. Dr Soc. Scis: Chinese Univ. of Hong Kong, 1981; Univ. of E Asia, Macau, 1985; Hon. DLitt: Sussex, 1987; Hong Kong Baptist Coll., 1990; Hon. DSc City Poly., Hong Kong, 1988; Hon. DHL SUNY at Stony Brook, 1989; Hon. DCL Oxford, 1992; Hon. DBA Hong Kong Poly., 1991. Queen's Badge, Red Cross, 1982; Montblanc de la Culture Award, 1993. Comdr, Order of the Crown of Belgium, 1989; Chevalier, Légion d'Honneur (France), 1991. Address: Shaw House, Lot 220 Clear Water Bay Road, Kowloon, Hong Kong. T: 27198371.

SHAW, Stephen Arthur, CBE 2004; PhD; Prisons and Probation Ombudsman, since 2001; b 26 March 1953; s of late Walter Arthur Shaw and of Gwendolyn Primrose Shaw (née Cottrell); m 1977, Christine Elizabeth Robinson; partner, Jane Angela Skinner; two s. Educ: Rutlish Sch., Merton; Univ. of Warwick (BA 1974); Univ. of Leeds (MA 1976); Univ. of Kent (PhD 1979). Lectr in Further Educn, Mid-Kent Coll. of Technology, 1977–79; Researcher, NACRO, 1979–80; Research Officer, Home Office, 1980–81; Dir, Prison Reform Trust, 1981–99; Prisons Ombudsman, 1999–2001. Publications: numerous contribs to jls. Recreations: family, sport, watching Fulham FC. Address: Prisons and Probation Ombudsman's Office, Ashley House, 2 Monck Street, SW1P 2BQ. T: (020) 7035 2876.

SHAW, Thurstan; see Shaw, C. T.

SHAW, Prof. Timothy Milton, PhD; Director and Professor, Institute of International Relations, University of the West Indies, since 2007; b 27 Jan. 1945; s of Arnold and Margaret Shaw; m 1983, Jane Little Parpart; one s one d, and two step d. Educ: Univ. of Sussex (BA 1967); Univ. of East Africa (MA Internat. Relns 1969); Princeton Univ. (MA Politics 1971, PhD Politics 1975). Teaching Fellow, Dept Political Sci., Makerere UC, Kampala, 1968–70; Dalhousie University, Canada, 1971–2001: Asst Prof., then Assoc. and Full Prof. of Political Sci.; Dir, Centre for African Studies, 1977–78, 1983–89; Exec. Dir, Pearson Inst. for Internat. Develt, 1985–88; Prof. in Internat. Develt Studies, 1990–2000; Dir, Centre for Foreign Policy Studies, 1993–2000; Dir, Inst. of Commonwealth Studies and Prof. of Commonwealth Governance and Develt, Sch. of Advanced Study, Univ. of London, 2001–06. Vis. Lectr, Univ. of Zambia, 1973–74; Vis. Assoc. Prof., Carleton Univ., 1978–80; Vis. Sen. Lectr, Univ. of Ife, Nigeria, 1979–80; Visiting Professor: Univ. of Zimbabwe, 1989; Univs of Stellenbosch and Western Cape, South Africa, 1998–; Aalborg Univ., Denmark, 2000–01; Makerere Univ. Business Sch., 2006–; Bank of Uganda Vis. Prof., Mbarara Univ. of Sci. and Tech., 2000–. Publications: (contrib. and ed jtly) Africa's Challenge to International Relations Theory, 2001; (contrib. and ed jtly) Crises of Governance in Asia and Africa, 2001; (contrib. and ed jtly) Theories of New Regionalism, 2003; (contrib. and ed jtly) Twisting Arms and Flexing Muscles: humanitarian intervention and peacebuilding in perspective, 2005; (contrib. and ed jtly) The Political Economy of Regions and Regionalisms, 2005; Commonwealth, 2008. Recreations: jogging, swimming, tennis, cycling, travelling, cooking. Address: Institute of Internatonal Relations, University of the West Indies, St Augustine Campus, Port of Spain, Trinidad and Tobago.

SHAW, Prof. William V., MD; Professor of Biochemistry, 1974–97, of Chemical Microbiology, 1997–98, Leicester University, now Professor Emeritus; b Philadelphia, Pennsylvania, 13 May 1933. Educ: Williams Coll., Williamstown, Mass (BA Chemistry 1955); Columbia Univ., New York (MD 1959). Diplomate: Amer. Bd of Med. Examrs, 1960; Amer. Bd of Internal Med., 1968 (Examiner, 1970). Appts, Presbyterian Hosp., New York, Nat. Heart Inst., Bethesda, Maryland, and Columbia Univ., New York, until 1966; Asst Prof. of Medicine, Columbia Univ., New York, 1966–68; University of Miami School of Medicine, Miami, Florida: Associate Prof. of Medicine and Biochemistry, 1968–73; Chief, Infectious Diseases, 1971–74; Prof. of Medicine, 1973–74. Hon. Prof. of Biochemistry, Univ. of Glasgow, 1998–2001. Founder, 1998, Chief Scientific Officer, 1998–2000, Sen. Consultant, 2000–, PanTherix Ltd. Vis. Scientist, MRC Lab. of Molecular Biology, Cambridge, Eng., 1972–74. Member: MRC Cell Biology and Disorders Bd, 1976–80 (Bd Chm. and Mem. Council, 1978–80); Science Council, Celltech Ltd, 1980–89 (Chm., 1983–89); Lister Inst. Sci. Adv. Cttee, 1981–85 (Chm., 1997–2000); AFRC, 1990–94. Member: Amer. Soc. for Clinical Investigation, 1971; Infectious Disease Soc. of Amer., 1969; Amer. Soc. of Biol Chemists; Biochem. Soc. (UK); Amer. Soc. for Microbiology; Soc. for Gen. Microbiology (UK). Publications: contribs to professional works and jls in microbial biochemistry and molecular enzymology. Address: PO Box 83, Sunset, ME 04683, USA. T: (207) 3482588, Fax: (207) 3482717; e-mail: bill.shaw@rcn.com.

SHAW STEWART, Sir Ludovic (Houston), 12th Bt cr 1667 (NS), of Greenock and Blackhall, Renfrewshire; b 12 Nov. 1986; s of Sir Houston Shaw-Stewart, 11th Bt, MC, TD and of Lucinda Victoria (née Fletcher); S father, 2004. Educ: Belhaven; Eton; Edinburgh Univ. Recreation: finding silver linings of clouds and promptly unthreading them.

SHAWCROSS, His Honour Roger Michael; a Circuit Judge, 1993–2008; Deputy Designated Family Judge, Hampshire and Isle of Wight, 2006–08; b 27 March 1941; s of Michael and Friedel Shawcross; m 1969, Sarah Broom; one s one d. Educ: Radley Coll.; Christ Church, Oxford (MA). Called to the Bar, Gray's Inn, 1967; a Recorder, 1985–93; Res. Judge, Newport, IoW, 1994–99. Member: Ancillary Relief Adv. Cttee, Family Justice Council, 1994–2005; Family Appeals Review Gp, 1998–2005; Magistrates' Area Trng Cttee (Hants and IoW), 2005–08; Chm., Hants and IoW Family Justice Council, 2006–08. Recreations: playing tennis, following most other sports, history, literature, music, cinema, travel, admiring my wife's gardening skills.

SHAWCROSS, Valerie, CBE 2002; Member (Lab) Lambeth and Southwark, London Assembly, since 2000; b 9 April 1958; d of Alfred and Florence Shawcross; m 1st, 1983, Alan Frank Neil Parker, qv (marr. diss. 2002); 2nd, 2005, Michael John Anteney. Educ: Univ. of Liverpool (BA Hons Pol Theory and Instns 1980); Inst. of Education, Univ. of London (MA Educn 1986). Sabbatical Officer, Liverpool Univ. Guild of Undergraduates, 1980–81; UK Council for Overseas Students' Affairs, 1981–84; ILEA, 1984–86; World Univ. Service (UK), 1986; Commonwealth Secretariat, 1987–91; freelance appointments, 1992–; NFWI, Labour Party, Westminster Foundn for Democracy, Body Shop Internat., Public Policy Unit, Infolog. Mem. (Lab), Croydon LBC, 1994–2000 (Chair of Educn, 1995, Dep. Leader, 1997, Leader, 1997–2000). Mem., Labour Party, 1979–. Chm., Transport Cttee, London Assembly, GLA, 2008–May 2009. Chm., London Fire and Emergency Planning Authy, 2000–08. Recreation: poetry. Address: Greater London

Authority, City Hall, Queen's Walk, SE1 2AA. T: (020) 7983 4371; e-mail: valerie.shawcross@london.gov.uk.

SHAWCROSS, Hon. Mrs William; see Polizzi, Hon. Olga.

SHAWCROSS, Hon. William (Hartley Hume); writer and broadcaster; b 28 May 1946; s of Baron Shawcross, GBE, PC, QC; m 1st, 1971, Marina Sarah Warner, qv; one s; 2nd, 1981, Michal Levin; one d; 3rd, 1993, Hon. Olga Polizzi, qv. Educ: Eton; University Coll., Oxford. Chm., Article 19, Internat. Centre on Censorship, 1986–96; Mem. Bd, Internat. Crisis Gp, 1995–2006; Member: Informal Adv. Gp, High Comr for Refugees, 1996–2001; BBC Govs World Service Consultative Gp, 1997–2004; Council, Disasters Emergency Cttee, 1998–2002. Presenter and Assoc. Producer, Queen and Country, BBC TV, 2002. Publications: Dubcek, 1970; Crime and Compromise, 1974; Sideshow: Kissinger, Nixon and the destruction of Cambodia, 1979; The Quality of Mercy: Cambodia, holocaust and modern memory, 1984; The Shah's Last Ride, 1989; Kowtow: a plea on behalf of Hong Kong, 1989; Murdoch, 1992; Cambodia's New Deal, 1994; Deliver Us from Evil, 2000; Queen and Country, 2002; Allies, 2003. Recreations: walking, sailing. Address: Friston Place, East Dean, E Sussex BN20 0AH. T: (020) 7289 8089. Club: St Mawes Sailing.

SHAWE-TAYLOR, Desmond Philip; Surveyor of the Queen's Pictures, since 2005; b 30 Sept. 1955; s of late Brian Newton Shawe-Taylor and Jocelyn Cecilia Shawe-Taylor; m 1987, Rosemary Gillian North; two s one d. Educ: Shrewsbury Sch.; University Coll., Oxford; Courtauld Inst. of Art, London. Lectr, History of Art Dept, Nottingham Univ., 1979–96; Dir, Dulwich Picture Gall., 1996–2005. Publications: Genial Company: the theme of genius in eighteenth-century British portraiture, 1987; The Georgians: eighteenth-century portraiture and society, 1990; Dramatic Art: theatrical paintings from the Garrick Club, 1997; Rembrandt to Gainsborough: masterpieces from Dulwich Picture Gallery, 1999; Shakespeare in Art, 2003; Breugel to Rubens: masters of Flemish painting, 2007. Recreation: playing the piano. Address: 1 Frogmore Cottages, Frogmore, Windsor, Berks SL4 2JG. T: (01753) 852742. Club: Garrick.

SHAWYER, Eric Francis, CBE 1998; FICS; Chairman, E. A. Gibson Shipbrokers Ltd, 1988–2000; Chairman, Baltic Exchange, 1996–98 (Director, 1991–98); b 17 July 1932; m 1956, Joyce Patricia Henley; one s one d. Joined E. A. Gibson Shipbrokers, 1948; Dir, 1963–; Man. Dir, 1969–98. Chairman: Worldscale Assoc. (London) Ltd, 1979–96; London Tanker Brokers Panel Ltd, 1990–96; Director: Maersk Air Ltd, 1994–2003; Maersk Air Hldg Ltd, 1994–2003; Corda, 2003. Gov., George Green's Sch., 2000. FICS 1994 (Pres., 1996). Freeman, City of London, 1980; Liveryman, Co. of Shipwrights, 1981 (Mem., Ct of Assts); Freeman, Co. of Watermen and Lightermen, 1989. Address: Souvenir, Woodlands Road, Bromley, Kent BR1 2AE.

SHAWYER, Peter Michael, FCA; Chairman: British International Ltd, since 2006; Ingenious Media plc, since 2007; b 11 Sept. 1950; s of Edward William Francis Shawyer and Marjorie Josephine Shawyer; m 1979, Margot Bishop; one s one d. Educ: Enfield GS; Univ. of Sheffield (BA Hons). FCA 1975. Touche Ross & Co., subseq. Deloitte & Touche, 1972–2004: admitted Partner, 1982; Tax Partner, 1982–84; Group Partner, a Tax Group, 1984–93; Partner in charge of Tax Dept, 1993–95; Partner in charge of London Office, 1995–99; Man. Partner, 1999–2004; Mem. Bd, Deloitte & Touche, UK. Non-executive Director and Member, Audit Committee: HSBC Bank, 2004–; HSBC France, 2005–; Silverjet plc, 2006–. Recreation: golf. Address: c/o Janice Aminoff, Deloitte & Touche, Stonecutter Court, 1 Stonecutter Street, EC4A 4TR. Clubs: Hadley Wood Golf; Brocket Hall Golf.

SHCHASNY, Uladzimir; Chairman, National Commission of Republic of Belarus for UNESCO, since 2001; Ambassador at Large, Ministry of Foreign Affairs, Belarus, since 2001; b 25 Nov. 1948; s of Ryhor and Nadzeya Shchasny; m 1972, Lyudmila Kazakova (marr. diss. 1993). Educ: Minsk State Linguistic Univ. (grad. 1972). Interpreter for USSR Min. of Geology, Pakistan, 1969–70, 1972–74; Lectr, Minsk State Inst. of Foreign Languages, 1975–77; Translation Service, UN Secretariat, NY, 1978–82; joined Min. of Foreign Affairs, Belarus, 1983; Press Dept and Dept of Internat. Orgns, 1983–91; Asst to Minister for Foreign Affairs, 1991–92; Dir, Dept of Bilateral Co-operation, 1992–93; Chargé d'Affaires, 1993–94; Counsellor Minister, 1994–95, Lithuania; Ambassador of the Republic of Belarus to the UK and to the Republic of Ireland, 1995–2000; Dir, Dept of Bilateral Relations with CIS Countries, Min. of For. Affairs, 2000–01; Belarus Rep., Exec. Bd, UNESCO, 2001–05. Publications: numerous translations of works of English and Urdu writers into Belarusian; articles in Belarusian jls. Recreation: antique map collecting. Address: Ministry of Foreign Affairs, ul. Lenina 19, Minsk, Belarus.

SHEA, Michael Sinclair MacAuslan, CVO 1987 (LVO 1985); DL; PhD; author and broadcaster; b 10 May 1938; s of late James Michael Shea and Mary Dalrymple Davidson MacAuslan, North Berwick; m 1968, Mona Grec Stensen, Oslo; two d. Educ: Gordonstoun Sch.; Edinburgh Univ. (MA, PhD Econs). FO, 1963; Inst. of African Studies, Accra, Ghana, 1963; FO, 1964; Third, later Second Sec., CRO, 1965; Second, later First Sec. (Econ.), Bonn, 1966; seconded to Cabinet Office, 1969; FO, 1971; Head of Chancery, Bucharest, 1973; Dep. Dir Gen., Brit. Inf. Services, New York, 1976; Press Sec. to the Queen, 1978–87. Dir of Public Affairs, Hanson PLC, 1987–92; Chairman: Connoisseurs Scotland, 1992–98; Scottish Nat. Photography Centre, subseq. Hill Adamson Centre, 2002–; non-executive Director: Caledonian Newspaper Publishing, 1993–96. Scottish Mem., ITC, 1996–2003. Vis. Prof., Strathclyde Univ. Grad. Business Sch., 1991–99. Trustee, Nat. Galls of Scotland, 1992–99; Chm., Royal Lyceum Theatre Co., 1998–2004. Gov., Gordonstoun Sch., 1988–99. Vice-Chm., Foundn for Skin Res., 1993–2004. DL Edinburgh, 1996. Publications: Britain's Offshore Islands, 1981; Maritime England, 1981; Tomorrow's Men, 1982; Influence: how to make the system work for you, 1988; Leadership Rules, 1990; Personal Impact: the art of good communication, 1993; Spin Doctor, 1995; To Lie Abroad, 1996; The British Ambassador, 1996; State of the Nation, 1997; Berlin Embassy, 1998; The Primacy Effect, 1998; Spin off, 2000; A View from the Sidelines, 2003; The Freedom Years, 2006; (as Michael Sinclair): Sonntag, 1971; Folio Forty-One, 1972; The Dollar Covenant, 1974; A Long Time Sleeping, 1976; The Master Players, 1978; (with David Frost): The Mid-Atlantic Companion, 1986; The Rich Tide, 1986. Recreations: writing, sailing. Address: 1A Ramsay Garden, Edinburgh EH1 2NA. Club: Garrick.

SHEAR, Graham Julian; Managing Partner, Teacher Stern solicitors; b London, 19 June 1963; s of Ronald and Frula Shear; m 1991, Dalya; three s. Educ: Seaford Coll., Sussex; City of London Sch. for Boys; London Metropolitan Univ. (LLB Hons); Lancaster Gate Coll. of Law. Admitted Solicitor, 1989; joined Teacher Stern Selby, subseq. Teacher Stern as trainee solicitor, 1986; specialised in commercial entertainment and music law, 1986–91; Litigation Dept, 1991–; founder, Media and Reputation Protection practice gp, 1999; established Sports practice gp, 2000. Mem., Law Panel, The Times. Publications: contrib. The Times Law Supplement. Recreations: contemporary and modern art, Latin music and culture, especially Cuban, lifelong fan of West Ham United FC. Address:

Teacher Stern LLP, 37–41 Bedford Row, WC1R 4JH. *T:* (020) 7242 3191, *Fax:* (020) 7197 8166; *e-mail:* g.shear@teacherstern.com. *Clubs:* Soho House, Ivy.

SHEARD, Rodney Kilner; Senior Principal, HOK sport architecture, since 1999; *b* 11 Sept. 1951; *s* of Saville Kilner Sheard and Margaret Helen Sheard; *m* 1989, Catherine Elisabeth Nouqueret; two *s. Educ:* Queensland Univ. of Technol. (DipArch 1975). RIBA 1977; ARAIA 1979. Partner, LOBB Architectural Practice, 1981; changed from partnership to co., 1993; merged with HOK, 1999. *Architect for:* Alfred McAlpine Stadium, Huddersfield, 1996; Millennium Stadium, Cardiff, 1998; Telstra Stadium (Sydney Olympic Stadium), 2000; Ascot Racecourse, 2006; Emirates Stadium, 2006; Wembley Stadium, 2007; *current projects include:* Wimbledon Centre Court; London Olympic Stadium. Initiator of concept 'Generations of Stadia'. FRSA. Hon. DSc Luton, 2002. *Publications:* Stadia: a design and development guide, 1998 (jtly); Sport Architecture, 2000; numerous articles in sports jls. *Recreations:* flyfishing, tennis, sailing (all poorly). *Address:* HOK sport architecture, 14 Blades Court, 121 Deodar Road, Putney, SW15 2NU. *T:* (020) 8874 7666, *Fax:* (020) 8874 7470; *e-mail:* rod.sheard@hok.com. *Club:* Royal Automobile.

SHEARER, Alan, OBE 2001; football commentator; BBC Television; *b* 13 Aug. 1970; *s* of Alan Shearer and Anne Shearer (*née* Collins); *m* Lainya; one *s* two *d. Educ:* Gosforth High Sch. Professional footballer, scoring 409 goals, with: Southampton FC, 1988–92; Blackburn Rovers, 1992–96; Newcastle United FC, 1996–2006, Captain, 1997–2006; played for England, 1992–2000, Captain, 1996–2000 (63 caps; 30 goals). *Publication:* The Story So Far (autobiog.), 1998. *Address:* c/o Wasserman Media Group, 5th Floor, 33 Soho Square, W1D 3QU.

SHEARER, Anthony Presley; Chairman, Abbey Protection, since 2007; *b* 24 Oct. 1948; *s* of Francis and Judy Shearer; *m* 1st, 1972, Jenny Dixon (marr. diss. 2007); two *d;* 2nd, 2007, Pam Mapes. *Educ:* Rugby Sch. FCA 1971. Partner, Deloitte Haskins & Sells, 1967–88; Commercial Dir, Harland & Wolff, 1987; Chief Operating Officer, M&G Gp, 1988–96; Dep. Chief Exec., Old Mutual Internat., 1997–2000; consultant to Old Mutual and other cos, 2000–02; Singer & Friedlander Group plc: Gp Finance Dir, and Chief Operating Officer, 2003–05; Chief Exec., 2004–05. Director: Wogen, 2005–; Alba plc, 2008–. Chairman: Uruguay Mineral Exploration, 2002–; Caxton FX, 2006–; UK Wealth Management, 2007–. *Recreations:* ski-ing, tennis, rock 'n roll, Elvis Presley. *Address:* 10 Napier Road, W14 8LQ. *T:* (020) 7602 1570; *e-mail:* tony@tonyshearer.com. *Club:* Brooks's.

SHEARING, Sir George (Albert), Kt 2007; OBE 1996; jazz pianist and composer; *b* 13 Aug. 1919; *s* of James Philip Shearing and Ellen Amelia Shearing (*née* Brightman); *m* 1st, 1941, Beatrice Bayes (marr. diss.); one *d;* 2nd, Eleanor Geffert. *Educ:* Linden Lodge Sch. for the Blind, London. Founded George Shearing Quintet, 1949; has also led other jazz ensembles. Composed Lullaby of Birdland, 1952, and many other popular songs. Has made many recordings, 1939–. Hon. DMus: Westminster Coll., Salt Lake City, 1975; Hamilton Coll., NY, 1994; DePauw, 2002. Golden Plate Award, American Acad. of Achievement, 1968. *Publication:* Lullaby of Birdland, 2003. *Address:* c/o IVI Management, 25864 Tournament Road, Suite L, Valencia, CA 91355, USA.

SHEARLOCK, Very Rev. David John; Dean and Rector of St Mary's Cathedral, Truro, 1982–97, now Dean Emeritus; *b* 1 July 1932; *s* of Arthur John Shearlock and Honora Frances Hawkins; *m* 1959, Jean Margaret Marr; one *s* one *d. Educ:* Univ. of Birmingham (BA); Westcott House, Cambridge. Assistant Curate: Guisborough, Yorks, 1957–60; Christchurch Priory, Hants, 1960–64; Vicar: Kingsclere, 1964–71; Romsey Abbey, 1971–82; Diocesan Director of Ordinands (Winchester), 1977–82; Hon. Canon of Winchester, 1978–82. Chm., Beaminster Arts Festival, 1998–2003. FRSA 1991; FRGS 1992; ARSCM 1998. *Publications:* The Practice of Preaching, 1990; When Words Fail: God and the world of beauty, 1996. *Address:* 3 The Tanyard, Shadrack Street, Beaminster, Dorset DT8 3BG. *T:* (01308) 863170; *e-mail:* dshearlock@toucansurf.com.

SHEARMAN, Donald Norman; *b* 6 Feb. 1926; *s* of late S. F. Shearman, Sydney; *m* 1952, Stuart Fay, *d* of late Chap. F. H. Bashford; three *s* three *d. Educ:* Fort St and Orange High Schools; St John's Theological College, Morpeth, NSW. Served War of 1939–45: air crew, 1944–46. Theological College, 1948–50. Deacon, 1950; Priest, 1951. Curate: of Dubbo, 1950–52; of Forbes, and Warden of St John's Hostel, 1953–56; Rector of Coonabarabran, 1957–59; Director of Promotion and Adult Christian Education 1959–62; Canon, All Saints Cathedral, Bathurst, 1962; Archdeacon of Mildura and Rector of St Margaret's, 1963; Bishop of Rockhampton, 1963–71; Chairman, Australian Board of Missions, Sydney, 1971–73; Bishop of Grafton, 1973–85; Asst Bishop, dio. of Brisbane, 1989–91; resigned Holy Orders, 2003. *Address:* PO Box 241, Deception Bay, Qld 4508, Australia.

SHEARMAN, Martin James, CVO 2003; HM Diplomatic Service; High Commissioner, Uganda, since 2008; *b* 7 Feb. 1965; *s* of John Christopher Shearman and Barbara Wendy Shearman; *m* 1996, Miriam Elizabeth Pyburn; two *s. Educ:* Skinners' Sch., Tunbridge Wells; Trinity Coll., Oxford (BA Hons). Joined FCO, 1989; Third, then Second Sec., FCO, 1989–91; Second, then First, Sec., Tokyo, 1993–96; on secondment to DTI, 1996–98, to Cabinet Office, 1998; NATO Secretariat, 1999; FCO, 1999–2003; Dep. High Comr, Abuja, 2003–06; Hd, Common Foreign and Security Policy Gp, Europe Directorate, FCO, 2006–08.

SHEARS, Beverley; Director General Human Resources, Ministry of Justice (formerly Director of Human Resources, Department of Constitutional Affairs), since 2007; *m;* two *c. Educ:* Brunel Univ. London Underground Ltd: HR Manager Engrg Ops, 1990–94; HR Manager Engrg, 1994–95; Gen. Manager, Strategic Employee Relns, 1995–97; Gen. Manager HR, 1997–99; Dep. Man. Dir and HR Dir, South West Trains Ltd; HR consultancy co., 2006–07. *Address:* Ministry of Justice, 6th Floor, Clive House, SW1H 9EX; *e-mail:* beverley.shears@justice.gsi.gov.uk.

SHEARS, Philip Peter; QC 1996; a Recorder, since 1990; *b* 10 May 1947; *m* 1990, Sarah; two *s* one *d* by previous marriage. *Educ:* Leys Sch., Cambridge; Nottingham Univ. (LLB); St Edmund's Coll., Cambridge (LLB). Called to the Bar, Middle Temple, 1972; Mem., Midland and Oxford Circuit. *Recreations:* sailing, France. *Address:* 7 Bedford Row, WC1R 4BU. *T:* (020) 7242 3555. *Club:* Royal London Yacht.

SHEBBEARE, Sir Thomas Andrew, (Sir Tom), KCVO 2003 (CVO 1996); Director of Charities to the Prince of Wales, since 2004; *b* 25 Jan. 1952; *s* of late Robert Austin Shebbeare and Frances Dare Graham; *m* 1976, Cynthia Jane Cottrell; one *s* one *d. Educ:* Malvern Coll.; Univ. of Exeter (BA Politics). World University Service (UK), 1973–75; Gen. Sec., British Youth Council, 1975–80; Administrator, Council of Europe, 1980–85; Exec. Dir, European Youth Foundn, 1985–88; Exec. Dir, The Prince's Trust and Sec., The Royal Jubilee Trusts, 1988–99; Chief Exec., The Prince's Trust, 1999–2004. Trustee: Nations Trust (S Africa), 1995–; Sentebale—The Princes' Fund for Lesotho, 2005–; Turquoise Mountain Foundn (Kabul), 2005–; Dir, Gifts in Kind UK. Hon. LLD Exeter,

2005. *Recreations:* family, cooking, garden, food and drink. *Address:* (office) Clarence House, SW1A 1BA.

SHEDDEN, Alfred Charles; Chairman, Halladale Group plc, 2001–07; *b* 30 June 1944; *s* of Alfred Henry Shedden and Jane Murray Shedden; *m* 1st, 1968, Rosalyn Terris; one *s;* 2nd, 1978, Irene McIntyre; one *d. Educ:* Aberdeen Univ. (MA, LLB). Mem., Law Soc. of Scotland. McGrigor Donald: apprentice, 1967; Partner, 1971; Managing Partner, 1985–92; Sen. Partner, 1993–2000. Non-executive Director: Standard Life Assurance Co., 1992–99; Scottish Financial Enterprise, 1988–99; Martin Currie Japan Investment Trust plc, 1996–2005; Scottish Metropolitan Property plc, 1998–2000; Burn Stewart Distillers plc, 2000–03; Iomart Group plc, 2000–; Murray Internat. Trust plc, 2000–; Equitable Life Assurance Soc., 2002–. Mem., Scottish FEFC, 1999–2005. Mem., Mgt Cttee, Glasgow Housing Assoc., 2003–. Gov., Glasgow Sch. of Art, 2002–. *Recreations:* Scottish art, wine, travel. *Address:* 17 Beaumont Gate, Glasgow G12 9ED. *T:* (0141) 339 4979.

SHEDDEN, Rev. John, CBE 1998; Minister, Fuengirola, Costa del Sol, 2005–08; *b* 23 June 1943; *s* of Robert Blair Arnott Shedden and Grace Roberts (*née* Henderson); *m* 1965, Jeannie Lillian Gilling; one *s* one *d. Educ:* Johnstone High Sch.; Univ. of St Andrews (BD Hons; Dip. in Pastoral and Social Studies). Asst Minister, Paisley Abbey, 1970–72; ordained 1971; Parish Minister, Thornhill, Dumfries, 1972–75; Social Welfare Officer, Salisbury, Rhodesia, 1975–76; Chaplain, RN, 1977–84; Minister, St Mark's, Moose Jaw, Sask., 1984–86; Chaplain, RAF, 1986–98; Principal Chaplain, Church of Scotland and Free Churches, RAF, 1994–98; Minister: Hawick Wilton with Teviothead, 1998–2001; Glenorchy Innishael with Strathfillan, 2001–05. QHC 1994–98. *Recreations:* hill-walking, D-I-Y, reading, radio.

SHEEHAN, Albert Vincent; Sheriff of Tayside, Central and Fife, 1983–2005; *b* 23 Aug. 1936; *s* of Richard Greig Sheehan and May Moffat; *m* 1965, Edna Georgina Scott Hastings (*d* 2000); two *d. Educ:* Bo'ness Acad.; Edinburgh Univ. (MA 1957; LLB 1959). Admitted as Solicitor, 1959. 2nd Lieut, 1st Bn The Royal Scots (The Royal Regt), 1960; Captain, Directorate of Army Legal Services, 1961. Depute Procurator Fiscal, Hamilton, 1961–71; Sen. Depute Procurator Fiscal, Glasgow, 1971–74; Depute Crown Agent for Scotland, 1974–79; Asst Solicitor, Scottish Law Commn, 1979–81; Sheriff of Lothian and Borders, 1981–83. Leverhulme Fellow, 1971. *Publications:* Criminal Procedure in Scotland and France, 1975; Criminal Procedure, 1990, 2nd edn 2003. *Recreations:* naval history, travel, legal history.

SHEEHAN, Prof. Antony; Chief Executive, Leicestershire Partnership NHS Trust, since 2007; *b* 10 Sept. 1964; *s* of late Thomas Sheehan and of Mary Kerr Sheehan; *m* 2001, Andrea Coleman; one *s* one *d. Educ:* Manchester Metropolitan Univ. (BEd Hons 1992); Nottingham Univ. (MPhil 1998); RN 1986. Nurse Manager; Chief Exec., Nat. Inst. for Mental Health in England, 2001–03; Dir Gen. for Care Services, 2003–06, for Health and Care Partnerships, 2006–07, DoH; Prof. of Health and Social Care Strategy, Univ. of Central Lancs, 2006–. Chm., Internat. Initiative for Mental Health Leadership, 2005–. Patron, AS-IT (IT consultancy for people with Asperger Syndrome), 2007–. Hon. DSc Wolverhampton, 2003; DUniv Staffordshire, 2006. *Publications:* more than 50 articles and book chapters. *Recreations:* walking (with two very big labradors), Manchester United, travel (in particular the USA), goalkeepers' gloves (and other paraphernalia), coffee (especially latte). *Address:* 30 Highfield Road, Heath Hayes, near Cannock, Staffs WS12 2DX; *e-mail:* Anthony.Sheehan@leicspart.nhs.uk.

SHEEHAN, Gerald; Chief Executive (Deputy Master and Comptroller), Royal Mint, 2001–06; *b* 20 March 1950; *s* of Edmund and Morfydd Sheehan; *m* 1987, Jacqueline Marian; two *s* one *d. Educ:* Univ. of Nottingham (BSc Hons); Univ. of Sheffield (MSc); Harvard Business Sch. (AMP). ASW Holdings plc, 1981–2001: Bd Mem., 1996–2001; Ops Dir, 1999–2001. Mem. Business Leaders Gp, Princes' Trust. *Recreations:* squash, boating, fishing.

SHEEHAN, Gen. John Joseph, USMC; Senior Vice President for Europe, Africa, Middle East and Southwest Asia, Bechtel Group Inc., since 2001; Supreme Allied Commander, Atlantic and Commander-in-Chief, US Atlantic Command, 1994–97; *b* 23 Aug. 1940; *s* of John J. Sheehan and Ellen Sheehan; *m* Margaret M. Sullivan; one *s* three *d. Educ:* Boston Coll. (BA English 1962); Georgetown Univ. (MA Govt 1985). Joined USMC, 1960; various postings, incl. Vietnam; Amphibious Warfare Sch., 1969–70; Airborne Corps, 1970–71; 2nd Marine Div., 1971–73; Naval War Coll., 1974–75; HQ USMC, 1975–78; 1st Marine Air Wing, 1978–79; Nat. War Coll., 1979–80; 1st Marine Bde, 1980–83; Jt Staff, 1983–84; Office of Sec. of Defense, 1984–86; 2nd Marine Div., 1986–88; 4th Marine Exped. Bde, 1988–89; HQ USMC, 1989–91; US Naval Forces Central Comd, 1991; US Atlantic Comd, 1991–93; Jt Staff, 1993–94. Joined Bechtel Gp Inc., 1998. Numerous gallantry and other Service awards. Grand Cross, Norwegian Order of Merit, 1996. *Publications:* contribs to Joint Forces Qly. *Recreations:* golf, tennis, gardening. *Address:* Bechtel Group Inc., 50 Beale Street, San Francisco, CA 94105–1895, USA. *Clubs:* Military Order of the Carabao, Ancient and Honorable Artillery Company of Massachusetts.

SHEEHAN, Maurice James, CMG 2004; consultant lawyer; *b* 30 Dec. 1937; *s* of Maurice Patrick Sheehan and Winifred Ellen Sheehan; *m* 1974, Janice Marie; two *s* four *d. Educ:* Marist Bros High Sch., Invercargill; Otago Univ., Dunedin (LLB). NZ Antarctic Prog., 1962–64; Judiciary, Fiji: Magistrate, 1970; Judge of Supreme Court, 1982; NZ Broadcasting Tribunal, 1988; Judge of Supreme Court, Judiciary, PNG, 1989–2002. Polar Medal, 1967. *Recreations:* boating, golf, part-time ambulance driver. *Address:* PO Box 57, Gordons, Papua New Guinea. *T:* 3082628, *Fax:* 3203266, *T:* and *Fax:* 3200370. *Clubs:* Royal Papua Yacht; Port Moresby Golf.

SHEEHY, Rev. Jeremy Patrick, DPhil; Rector, Swinton and Pendlebury, since 2006; *b* 31 Oct. 1956; *s* of Eric Sheehy and Noreen Patricia Sheehy. *Educ:* Trinity Sch. of John Whitgift; Bristol Grammar Sch.; King Edward's Sch., Birmingham; Magdalen Coll., Oxford (BA (Jurisprudence Cl. 1)); St Stephen's House, Oxford (BA (Theol. Cl. 1)); MA 1981, DPhil 1990, Oxon. Ordained deacon 1981; priest 1982; Assistant Curate: St Barnabas, Erdington, 1981–83; St Gregory, Small Heath, 1983–84; Dean of Divinity, Chaplain and Fellow, New Coll., Oxford, 1984–90; Vicar, St Margaret, Leytonstone, 1990–96; Priest in charge, St Andrew, Leytonstone, 1993–96; Principal, St Stephen's House, Oxford, 1996–2006. Chm., Oxford Partnership for Theol Educn and Trng, 1999–2001. Examining Chaplain to Bishop of Manchester, 2008–. Vis. Lectr, Nashotah House, Wis, USA, 2006. Guardian, Shrine of Our Lady of Walsingham, 1997–. Gov., Quainton Hall Sch., Harrow, 1998–2007. Hon. DD Grad. Theol Foundn, Indiana, 2004. *Recreations:* hill-walking, cooking. *Address:* St Peter's Rectory, Vicarage Road, Swinton, Manchester M27 0WA. *T:* (0161) 794 1578.

SHEEHY, Sir Patrick, Kt 1991; Chairman, B.A.T Industries, 1982–95; *b* 2 Sept. 1930; *s* of Sir John Francis Sheehy, CSI and Jean Newton Simpson; *m* 1964, Jill Patricia Tindall; one *s* one *d. Educ:* Australia; Ampleforth Coll., Yorks. Served Irish Guards, 1948–50; rank on leaving 2nd Lieut. Joined British-American Tobacco Co., 1950, first appt in Nigeria; Ghana, 1951; Reg. Sales Manager, Nigeria, 1953; Ethiopian Tobacco Monopoly, 1954; Marketing Dir, Jamaica, 1957; Barbados, 1961; Marketing Advr, London, 1962; Gen. Man., Holland, 1967; Mem., Gp Bd, 1970; Mem., Chm.'s Policy Cttee, and Chm., Tobacco Div. Bd, 1975; Dep. Chm., 1976–81, Vice-Chm., 1981–82, B.A.T Industries; Chm., British-American Tobacco Co., 1976–82. *Address:* 11 Eldon Road, W8 5PU. *T:* (020) 7937 6250.

SHEERMAN, Barry John; MP (Lab) Huddersfield, since 1983 (Huddersfield East, 1979–83); *b* 17 Aug. 1940; *s* of late Albert William Sheerman and Florence Sheerman (*née* Pike); *m* 1965 Pamela Elizabeth (*née* Brenchley); one *s* three *d*. *Educ:* Hampton Grammar Sch.; LSE (BSc (Econs) Hons; MSc Hons). Lectr, Univ. Coll. of Swansea, 1966–79. An opposition front bench spokesman on: employment, dealing with training, small business and tourism, 1983–88; home affairs, dealing with police, prisons, crime prevention, drugs, civil defence and fire service, 1988–92; disabled people's rights, 1992–94. Mem., Public Accounts Cttee, 1981–83; Co-Chm., Educn and Employment Select Cttee, 1999–2001 (Chm., Sub-Cttee on Educn, 1999–); Chm., Select Cttee on Educn and Skills, 2001–; Chairman: Parly Adv. Council on Transport Safety, 1981–; Labour Campaign for Criminal Justice, 1989–92; Co-Chm., Parly Manufg Industry Gp, 1993–; Vice-Chm., Parly Univ. Gp, 1994–. Chm. Parly Gps for Sustainable Waste Mgt, 1995–, and for Manufg, Design and Innovation, 1999–; Chm., Cross-Party Adv. Gp on Preparation for EMU, 1998–, on European Economic Reform, 2005–. Mem., Sec. of State for Trade and Industry's Manufg Task Force, 1999–2002. Chairman: World Bank Business Partnerships for Develt Cttee, 2001–03; Global Road Safety Partnership, 2001–. FRSA; FRGS 1989; FCGI 2005. Hon. Dr: Kingston, 2007; Bradford, 2007. *Publications:* (jtly) Harold Laski: a life on the Left, 1993; pamphlets on education and training, tourism, and justice. *Address:* House of Commons, SW1A 0AA. *Club:* Royal Commonwealth Society.

SHEFFIELD; 8th Baron.
See under Stanley of Alderley, 8th Baron.

SHEFFIELD, Bishop of; *no new appointment at time of going to press.*

SHEFFIELD, Dean of; *see* Bradley, Very Rev. P. E.

SHEFFIELD, Graham Edward; Artistic Director, Barbican Centre, since 1995; *b* 12 Feb. 1952; *s* of Gordon and Jacqueline Sheffield; *m* 1979, Ann Roberta Morton; two *s*. *Educ:* Tonbridge Sch.; Edinburgh Univ. (BMus Hons 1975). Producer, then Sen. Producer, Music Dept, BBC Radio 3, 1976–90; Music Dir, South Bank Centre, 1990–95. Dir, City Arts and Culture Forum, 2007–; Consultant, Luminato Fest., Toronto, 2007–. Mem. Council, Arts Council England (London), 2002–08. Mem. Council, 1999–, Chm., 2006–, Royal Philharmonic Soc.; Chm., Internat. Soc. for Performing Arts, 2004–06 (Sec., 2000–01; Chm.-elect, 2002–03). Hon. DArts City, 2004. Chevalier, Tastevin de Bourgogne, 2005. Chevalier, Ordre des Arts et des Lettres (France), 2005. *Recreations:* piano, golf, ski-ing, travel, fine wine. *Address:* 42 Woodland Gardens, N10 3UA. *T:* (020) 8883 0213. *Club:* MCC.

SHEFFIELD, (John) Julian (Lionel George); DL; Chairman: Henry Smith (formerly Henry Smith's) Charity, since 1997 (Trustee, since 1971); North Hampshire Medical Trust, since 2002; *b* 28 Aug. 1938; *s* of late John Vincent Sheffield, CBE; *m* 1961, Carolyn Alexander Abel Smith; three *s* one *d*. *Educ:* Eton Coll.; Christ's Coll., Cambridge. Joined Portals Ltd, 1962; Dir, 1969–95, Chm., 1979–95, Portals Hldgs, then Portals Gp. Director: Norcros, 1974–96 (Chm., 1989–93); Tex Hldgs, 1985–93; Guardian Royal Exchange, 1981–99 (Dep. Chm., 1988–99); Newbury Racecourse, 1988–2005; Inspec, 1994–99. Chm., Axa UK Gp Pension Scheme, 1993–2008. Mem., Economic and Commercial Cttee, EEF, 1974–90. Member: Council, St John's Sch., Leatherhead, 1966–96; Bd of Govs, N Foreland Lodge, 1987–97 (Chm., 1992–97). Trustee: Henry Smith's, subseq. Henry Smith Charity, 1971–2007 (Chm., 1997–2007); Winchester Cathedral Trust, 1984–; Hosp. of St Cross and Almshouse of Noble Poverty, 1996– (Chm., 2005–06). High Sheriff, 1998, DL 2001, Hants. *Recreations:* outdoor sports, collecting. *Address:* Spring Pond, Laverstoke Lane, Whitchurch, Hants RG28 7PD. *T:* (01256) 895130. *Clubs:* White's, MCC.

SHEFFIELD, Sir Reginald (Adrian Berkeley), 8th Bt *cr* 1755; DL; Director, Normanby Estate Co. Ltd, since 1983, and other companies; *b* 9 May 1946; *s* of Edmund Charles Reginald Sheffield, JP, DL (*d* 1977) and Nancie Miriel Denise (*d* 1997), *d* of Edward Roland Soames; *S* uncle, 1977; *m* 1st, 1969, Annabel Lucy Veronica (marr. diss.), *d* of late T. A. Jones; two *d*; 2nd, 1977, Victoria Penelope, *d* of late R. C. Walker, DFC; one *s* two *d*. *Educ:* Eton. Member of Stock Exchange, 1973–75. Vice-Chm., S Humberside Business Advice Centre Ltd, 1984–. Pres., S Humberside CPRE, 1985–96; Member: Cttee, Lincs Br., CLA, 1987–99; Taxation Cttee, CLA, 1989–95; Central Transport Consultative Cttee (NE Reg.), 1988–94; Rail Users Consultative Cttee for NE England, 1994–97. Mem. (C) for Ermine Ward, Humberside County Council, 1985–93. Chm., Brigg and Goole Cons. Assoc., 2007–. Pres., Scunthorpe United Football Club, 1982–94. Pres., Scunthorpe and Dist, Victim Support Scheme, 1989–2003; Vice-Pres., Victim Support Humber, 2003–08. DL Humberside, now Lincs, 1985. *Heir: s* Robert Charles Berkeley Sheffield, *b* 1 Sept. 1984. *Address:* Estate Office, Normanby, Scunthorpe, N Lincs DN15 9HS. *T:* (01724) 720618; *e-mail:* norestate@btconnect.com. *Clubs:* Beefsteak, White's, Pratt's; Lincolnshire (Sleaford).

SHEFFIELD AND ROTHERHAM, Archdeacon of; *see* Blackburn, Ven. R. F.

SHEFTON, Prof. Brian Benjamin, FBA 1985; FSA 1980; Professor of Greek Art and Archaeology, 1979–84, now Emeritus, and Hon. Fellow 2005, University of Newcastle upon Tyne; *b* 11 Aug. 1919; *yr s* of late Prof. I. Scheftelowitz (Cologne, Germany, until 1933 and Oxford) and Frieda (*née* Kohn); *m* 1960, Jutta Ebel of Alingsås, Sweden; one *d*. *Educ:* Apostelgymnasium, Cologne; St Lawrence Coll., Ramsgate; Magdalen Coll. Sch., Oxford; Oriel Coll., Oxford (Open Scholar, 1938; Hon. Mods Greek and Latin Lit. 1940; Lit Hum 1947, Class I). War service, HM Forces (change of name), 1940–45. Sch. Student, British Sch. at Athens, 1947; Derby Scholar, Oxford, 1948; Bishop Fraser Scholar, Oriel Coll., Oxford, 1949, in Aegean to 1950; excavated at Old Smyrna; Lectr in Classics, University Coll., Exeter, 1950–55; Lectr in Greek Archaeology and Ancient History, 1955, Sen. Lectr, 1960, Reader, 1974–79, King's Coll., Univ. of Durham (later Univ. of Newcastle upon Tyne). Established and directed Univ.'s Greek Museum (renamed Shefton Mus. of Greek Art and Archaeology, 1994), 1956–84, Hon. Advr, 1985–; Trustee, Oriental Mus., Durham Univ., 1989–93. Vis. Res. Fellow, Merton Coll., Oxford, 1969; British Acad. Vis. Scholar to Albania, 1973; Munro Lectr, Edinburgh Univ., 1974; British Acad. European Exchange Fellow, Marburg Univ., 1975; German Academic Exchange Fellow, Marburg and Cologne, 1976; Leverhulme Res. Fellow, 1977; Webster Meml Lectr, Stanford Univ., 1981; Vis. Prof. of Classical Archaeology, Vienna Univ. (winter), 1981–82; British Council Vis. Scholar to Soviet Union, 1982, to Spain, 1985; Jackson Knight Meml Lectr, Exeter Univ., 1983; Leverhulme Emeritus Fellow, 1984–86; Balsdon Sen. Fellow, British Sch. at Rome, 1985; Vis. Scholar, J. Paul Getty Museum, 1987; British Academy Exchange Fellow, Jerusalem, 1993. Mem., German Archaeological Inst., 1961; Foreign Mem., Inst. of Etruscan and Italic Studies, Florence, 1990. Hon. Dr.phil Cologne, 1989. Aylwin Cotton Award, 1977; Kenyon Medal, British Acad., 1999. *Publications:* History of Greek Vase Painting (with P. Arias and M. Hirmer), 1962; Die rhodischen Bronzekannen, 1979; *chapters in:* Perachora II, 1962; Phoenizier im Westen, 1982; The Eye of Greece, 1982; Das Kleinaspergle, 1988; Cyprus and the East Mediterranean in the Iron Age, 1989; The Rogozen Treasure, 1989; Kotinos, 1992; Cultural Transformations and Interactions in Eastern Europe, 1993; The Archaeology of Greek Colonization, 1994; Social Complexity and the Development of Towns in Iberia, 1995; Italy in Europe: economic relations 700BC–AD50, 1995; Sur les traces des Argonautes, 1996; Céramique et peinture grecques: modes d'emploi, 1999; I Piceni, 1999; Periplous, 2000; Heuneburg XI, 2000; Piceni e l'Italia medio-adriatica, 2003; Die Hydria von Grächwil 1851–2001, 2004; articles in British and foreign periodicals. *Recreations:* music, travel. *Address:* 24 Holly Avenue, Jesmond, Newcastle upon Tyne NE2 2PY. *T:* (0191) 281 4184.

SHEGOG, Rev. Preb. Eric Marshall; media consultant, since 2002; *b* 23 July 1937; *s* of late George Marshall Shegog and Helen (*née* Whitefoot); *m* 1961, Anne Thomas; two *s* one *d*. *Educ:* Leigh Grammar School; College of St Mark and St John; Whitelands College; Lichfield Theol College; City Univ. (MA). CertEd London; DipTh London. Asst Master, Holy Trinity Primary Sch., Wimbledon, 1960–64; Asst Curate, All Saints, Benhilton, 1965–68; Asst Youth Adviser, Dio. of Southwark, 1968–70; Vicar, St Michael and All Angels, Abbey Wood, 1970–75; Town Centre Chaplain, Sunderland, 1976–83; Head of Religious Broadcasting, IBA, 1984–90; Dir of Communications, C of E, 1990–97; Dir of Communications, 1997–2000 and Acting Gen. Sec., 1999–2000, Dio. of London; Communications Advr, Dio. of Europe, 2000–02; Prebendary, St Paul's Cathedral, 1997–2000, now Emeritus. Chairman: BBC Adv. Cttee for NE, 1980–83; Mgt Cttee, Churches TV Centre, 1997–2007; Dir, World Assoc. for Christian Communication, 1990–93 (Vice-Chm., Eur. Region, 1990–93). Chm., Age Concern Sunderland, 1980–83. *Publications:* (jtly) Religious Television: controversies and conclusions, 1990; (jtly) Religious Broadcasting in the 90s, 1991; (contrib.) Elvy, Opportunities and Limitations in Religious Broadcasting, 1991; (contrib.) The Communication of Values, 1993. *Recreations:* gardening, opera, caravanning. *Address:* 9 Colbron Close, Ashwell, Baldock, Herts SG7 5TH. *T:* (01462) 743251.

SHEHADIE, Sir Nicholas (Michael), AC 1990; Kt 1976; OBE 1971; Managing Director, Nicholas Shehadie Pty Ltd, 1959; *b* 15 Nov. 1926; *s* of Michael and Hannah Shehadie; *m* 1957, Prof. Marie Roslyn Bashir, *qv*; one *s* two *d*. *Educ:* Sydney. Elected Alderman, City of Sydney, Dec. 1962; Dep. Lord Mayor, Sept. 1969–73; Lord Mayor of Sydney, Sept. 1973–75. Chm., Special Broadcasting Services, to 2000. Rugby Union career: Captained NSW and Australia; played 30 Internationals and 6 overseas tours; Mem., Barbarians'. Chm., Sydney Cricket Ground, 1990–2001. *Recreations:* Rugby, surfing, horse racing, bowls. *Club:* Randwick Rugby.

SHEIKH, Baron *cr* 2006 (Life Peer), of Cornhill in the City of London; **Mohamed Iltaf Sheikh;** Chairman and Chief Executive, Camberford Law plc; *b* 13 June 1941; *s* of late Mohamed Abdullah Sheikh and of Kalsum Ara Sheikh; *m* 1986, Shaida Begum Thantrey; one *d* from previous *m*. *Educ:* Mbale Secondary Sch., Uganda; Holborn Coll.; City of London Coll. FCII 1968. With Sun Alliance Insurance Co., 1962–66; Household and General Insurance Co., 1966–69; Guardian Royal Exchange, 1969–78; Camberford Law plc, 1978–. Chairman: Conservative Muslim Forum, 2003–; Conservative Ethnic Diversity Council, 2005–. Freeman, City of London, 1995. *Recreations:* keeping fit, hill-walking, gardening, playing squash. *Address:* House of Lords, SW1A 0PW. *Club:* Carlton.

SHEIKHOLESLAMI, Prof. Ali Reza, PhD; Soudavar Professor of Persian Studies, Oxford University, 1990–2006; Fellow, Wadham College, Oxford, 1990–2006; *b* 21 July 1941; *s* of Ali Soltani Sheikholeslami and Shah-Zadeh Mansouri; *m* 1996, Scheherezade Vigeh. *Educ:* Columbia Univ., NY (BA); Northwestern Univ. (MA); UCLA (PhD). Asst Prof. of Pol Sci., Univ. of Washington, Seattle, 1975–85; Res. Fellow, Harvard Univ., 1987–88; Iranian Fellow, St Antony's Coll., Oxford, 1988–90. *Publications:* Political Economy of Saudi Arabia, 1984; The Structure of Central Authority in Qajar Iran 1876–1896, 1996; articles on 19th and 20th Century Persia in jls and book chapters. *Recreations:* reading, travelling. *Address:* Wadham College, Oxford OX1 3PN. *T:* (01865) 278200.

SHEIL, Brenda Margaret Hale, (Lady Sheil); barrister; Member, Radio Authority, 1994–99; *o d* of late Rev. Forde Patterson and Elizabeth Bell Patterson (*née* Irwin); *m* 1979, John Joseph Sheil (*see* Rt Hon. Sir J. J. Sheil); one *s*. *Educ:* Armagh Girls' High Sch.; Trinity Coll., Dublin (BA (Mod) Legal Science; LLB 1966; MA 1990). Called to the Bar, NI, 1976, Ireland, 1995; Government Service (Legal): Min. of Home Affairs, NI, 1967–72; NI Office, 1972–79; Head, Legal Div., NI Court Service, Lord Chancellor's Dept, 1979–80. Chm. (part time), Industrial Tribunals, 1984–87. Member: Secretariat of Anglo-Irish Law Commn, 1973–74; Indep. Commn for Police Complaints, 1988–90. Mem., Gen. Consumer Council, NI, 1985–88. Mem., Standing Cttee, Gen. Synod of Church of Ireland, 1988– (Lay Hon. Sec., 1999–); Lay Rep., Ch of Ireland, ACC, 1994–2000. Governor, Royal Sch., Armagh, 1992–. *Recreations:* horses (Hon. Sec., Tynan and Armagh Hunt, 1973–), gardening, travel, golf. *Address:* Bar Library, Royal Courts of Justice, Belfast BT1 3JF.

SHEIL, Rt Hon. Sir John (Joseph), Kt 1989; PC 2005; a Lord Justice of Appeal, Supreme Court of Judicature, Northern Ireland, 2004–06; *b* 19 June 1938; *yr* twin *s* of late Hon. Mr Justice (Charles Leo) Sheil and Elizabeth Josephine Sheil (*née* Cassidy); *m* 1979, Brenda Margaret Hale Patterson (*see* B. M. H. Sheil); one *s*. *Educ:* Clongowes Wood Coll.; Queen's Univ. Belfast (LLB); Trinity Coll., Dublin (MA). Called to Bar: NI, 1964 (Bencher 1988), QC 1975; Gray's Inn, 1974 (Hon. Bencher, 1996); Ireland, 1976. A Judge of the High Court, NI, 1989–2004. Chairman: Mental Health Rev. Tribunal, 1985–87; Fair Employment Appeals Bd, 1986–89; Mem., Standing Adv. Commn on Human Rights, 1981–83. Mem., NI Cttee, British Council, 2002–. Senator, QUB, 1987–99. Hon. Bencher, Middle Temple, 2005. *Recreations:* golf, travel. *Address:* c/o Royal Courts of Justice, Belfast BT1 3JY.

SHEINWALD, Sir Nigel (Elton), KCMG 2001 (CMG 1999); HM Diplomatic Service; Ambassador to the United States of America, since 2007; *b* 26 June 1953; *s* of late Leonard Sheinwald and of Joyce Sheinwald; *m* 1980, Dr Julia Dunne; three *s*. *Educ:* Harrow Co. Sch. for Boys; Balliol Coll., Oxford (BA Classics 1976). Joined HM Diplomatic Service, 1976; Japan Desk, FCO, 1976–77; Russian lang. trng, 1977–78; Third, later Second Sec., Moscow, 1978–79; Rhodesia/Zimbabwe Dept, FCO, 1979–81; E European and Soviet Dept, FCO, 1981–83; First Sec., Washington, 1983–87; Deputy Head: Policy Planning Staff, FCO, 1987–89; European Community Dept (Internal), FCO, 1989–92; Counsellor and Hd of Chancery, UK Perm. Rep. to EU, Brussels, 1993–95; Hd of News Dept, FCO, 1995–98; Dir, EU, FCO, 1998–2000; Ambassador and UK Perm. Rep. to EU, Brussels, 2000–03; Foreign Policy and Defence Advr to the Prime Minister, 2003–07. *Recreations:*

reading, music. *Address:* c/o Foreign and Commonwealth Office, King Charles Street, SW1A 2AH.

SHELDON, family name of **Baron Sheldon**.

SHELDON, Baron *cr* 2001 (Life Peer), of Ashton-under-Lyne in the County of Greater Manchester; **Robert Edward Sheldon;** *b* 13 Sept. 1923; *m* 1st, 1945, Eileen Shamash (*d* 1969); one *s* one *d*; 2nd 1971, Mary Shield. *Educ:* Elementary and Grammar Schools; Engineering Apprenticeship; Technical Colleges in Stockport, Burnley and Salford; WhSch 1944. Engineering diplomas; external graduate, London University. Contested (Lab) Withington, Manchester, 1959; MP (Lab) Ashton-under-Lyne, 1964–2001. Chm., Labour Parly Economic Affairs and Finance Group, 1967–68; Opposition front bench spokesman on Civil Service and Machinery of Govt, also on Treasury matters, 1970–74; Minister of State, CSD, March–Oct. 1974; Minister of State, HM Treasury, Oct. 1974–June 1975; Financial Sec. to the Treasury, 1975–79; Opposition front bench spokesman on Treasury matters, 1981–83; Chairman: Public Accounts Cttee, 1983–97 (Mem., 1965–70, 1975–79); Standards and Privileges Cttee, 1997–2001; Liaison Cttee, 1997–2001; Public Accounts Commn, 1997–2001; Dep. Chm., All Party Arts and Heritage Gp, 1997–2001; Member: Public Expenditure Cttee (Chm. Gen. Sub-Cttee), 1972–74; Select Cttee on Treasury and Civil Service, 1979–81 (Chm., Sub-Cttee); Econ. Affairs Cttee, 2003–. Mem., Fulton Cttee on the Civil Service, 1966–68. Chm., NW Gp of Labour MPs, 1970–74. *Address:* 2 Ryder Street, SW1Y 6QA.

SHELDON, Harold; Chairman, Batley Sports Development Council, 1965–2000; Vice Chairman, Kirklees District Sports Council, 1974–2000; *b* 22 June 1918; *s* of Charles Edwin Sheldon and Lily Sheldon (*née* Taylor); *m* 1941, Bessie Sheldon (*née* Barratt); two *s* one *d*. HM Forces, 1939–45 (Sgt; wounded D Day landings). Local Government: elected Batley Borough Council, 1953; Mayor of Batley, 1962–63; W Yorkshire County Council, 1973–86 (Chm., 1976–77), re-elected 1977, 1981; Mem., Kirklees MDC, 1987–98 (Mayor, 1994–95). Mem., W Yorks Police Authy, 1989–95 (Vice-Chm., 1992–95). Mem., Yorks and Humberside Council for Sport and Recreation, 1977–86 and 1991–98; President: Batley Boys' Club (Founder Mem.), 1975–2000; Batley CAB, 1987–92; Batley Sports for the Disabled Assoc., 1987–96.

SHELDON, John Denby, OBE 2000; Joint General Secretary, Public and Commercial Services (formerly Public Services, Tax and Commerce) Union, 1996–2000; *b* 31 Jan. 1941; *s* of Frank and Doreen Sheldon; *m* 1976; two *s*. *Educ:* Wingate County Primary Sch.; West Leeds High Sch.; Oxford Univ. Diploma in Social Studies. Post Office Engineer, 1957–68; student, Ruskin Coll., 1968–70; full time Trade Union Official, Instn of Professional Civil Servants, 1970–72; Civil Service Union: National Officer, 1972–78; Deputy Gen. Sec., 1978–82; Gen. Sec., 1982–88; Dep. Gen. Sec., 1988–93, Gen. Sec., 1993–96, Nat. Union of Civil and Public Servants. *Recreations:* cricket, Rugby League as spectator, family. *Address:* 20 Clifton Park Road, Caversham, Reading, Berks RG4 7PD.

SHELDON, Mark Hebberton, CBE 1997; President of The Law Society, 1992–93; Senior Partner, 1988–91, Joint Senior Partner, 1991–93, Linklaters & Paines; *b* 6 Feb. 1931; *s* of late George Hebberton Sheldon and Marie Sheldon (*née* Hazlitt); *m* 1971, Catherine Ashworth; one *s* one *d*. *Educ:* Wycliffe Coll.; Corpus Christi Coll., Oxford (BA Jurisprudence (Hons), MA; Hon. Fellow, 1995). National Service, 1949–50, TA, 1950–54, Royal Signals (Lieut). Linklaters & Paines: articled clerk, 1953–56; Asst Solicitor, 1957–59; Partner, 1959–93; Resident Partner, NY, 1972–74; Consultant, 1994–96. Dir, Coutts & Co., 1996–98; Chm., PPP healthcare medical trust, subseq. PPP Foundn, 1999–2001 (Gov., 1998–2002). Mem. Council 1978–96, Treas. 1981–86, Vice-Pres., 1991–92, Law Soc.; Mem. Court 1975–, Master 1987–88, City of London Solicitors' Co.; Pres., City of London Law Soc., 1987–88. Bar Council: Mem., Collyear Cttee on Educn and Trng for the Bar, 1998–2000; Indep. Chm., Working Party on Barristers' Rights to Conduct Litigation, 1999–2000; Glidewell Working Pty on Judicial Appts and Silk, 2002–03. Nominated Mem., Council of Corp. of Lloyd's, 1989–90 (Chm., Wkg Party on Members' Voting Rights, 1993); Member: Financial Reporting Council, 1990–98; Cadbury Cttee on Financial Aspects of Corporate Governance, 1991–95; Financial Law Panel, 1993–98; Council, Justice, 1993–2005; Sen. Salaries Rev. Body, 1994–99; Panel of Conciliators, Internat. Centre for Investment Disputes, 1995–2003; Adv. Panel, Centre for Socio-Legal Studies, Univ. of Oxford, 1995–2003. Hon. Bencher, Inner Temple, 1993; Hon. Member: Canadian Bar Assoc., 1993–; SLS (formerly SPTL), 1993–. Trustee/Director: Oxford Inst. of Legal Practice, 1993–2008; Court Based Personal Support, Royal Courts of Justice, 2002–. Gov., Yehudi Menuhin Sch., 1996–. Chm., Corpus Assoc., 1983–89. *Recreations:* music, English water-colours, wine, swimming. *Address:* 5 St Albans Grove, W8 5PN. *T:* (020) 7460 7172, *Fax:* (020) 7938 4771. *Clubs:* Travellers, City of London, Hurlingham.

SHELDON, Peter; JP; FCA; Chairman, BATM Advanced Communications Ltd, since 1999 (Director, 1998–99); *b* 11 June 1941; *s* of Izydor Schuldenfrei and Regina Schuldenfrei; surname changed to Sheldon by Deed Poll, 1964; *m* 1965, Judith Marion Grunberger; two *s* one *d*. *Educ:* Kilburn Grammar Sch. FCA 1969. Partner: Alfred N. Emanuel & Co., Chartered Accountants, 1963–70; Bright, Grahame Murray, Chartered Accountants, 1970–71; Director: UDS Gp Plc, 1971–83; Hambros Bank, 1983–85; World of Leather Plc, 1985–97; Geo Interactive Media Gp Ltd, 1996–98. Chairman: Stirling Gp Plc, 1990–94; Video Domain Technologies Ltd, 2001–07; Dir, Kindertec Ltd, 1994–2000. Pres., United Synagogue, 1999–2005. JP Haringey, 1979–90 and 1997–. *Recreations:* theatre, travel, walking, grandchildren. *Address:* Flat 8, Denver Court, 132 Hendon Lane, N3 3RH. *T:* (020) 8349 9462.

SHELDON, Richard Michael; QC 1996; *b* 29 Sept. 1955; *s* of Ralph Maurice Sheldon and Ady Sheldon (*née* Jaudel); *m* 1983, Helen Mary Lake; two *s* one *d*. *Educ:* Maidenhead Grammar Sch.; Jesus Coll., Cambridge (MA). Called to the Bar, Gray's Inn, 1979, Bencher, 2004. *Publication:* contrib. Halsbury's Laws of England. *Recreations:* music, bassoon. *Address:* 3/4 South Square, Gray's Inn, WC1R 5HP. *T:* (020) 7696 9900.

SHELDRAKE, Prof. Philip Farnsworth; Moulsdale Fellow, St Chad's College, University of Durham, since 2003; *b* 22 Nov. 1946; *s* of Archibald Douglas Farnsworth Sheldrake, MC and Ann Mary Sheldrake (*née* Fitzgibbon). *Educ:* Heythrop Pontifical Athenaeum (Phil. Bac. 1969); Campion Hall, Oxford (MA 1976; BD 1995); Univ. of London (PGDPT 1977; MTh 1977). Dir, Inst. of Spirituality, Heythrop Coll., London, 1983–92; Dir of Pastoral Studies, Westcott House, Cambridge, 1992–97; Sen. Res. Fellow, Queen's Foundn, Birmingham, 1997–98; Academic Dir and Vice-Principal, Sarum Coll., Salisbury, 1998–2003; William Leech Professorial Fellow in Applied Christian Theol., Univ. of Durham, 2003–08. Sen. Mem., St Edmund's Coll., Cambridge, 1993–; Hulsean Lectr, Univ. of Cambridge, 1999–2000. Visiting Professor: Univ. of Notre Dame, Indiana, 1995–; Boston Univ., 2002; Boston Coll., Chestnut Hill, 2005–; Joseph Vis. Prof., Boston Coll., 2008–09. Hon. Prof., Univ. of Wales, Lampeter, 1999–. FRSA 1998; FRHistS 2005. *Publications:* Images of Holiness, 1987; Spirituality and History, 1991, 2nd edn 1996; Befriending our Desires, 1994, 2nd edn 2001; Living Between Worlds: place and journey in Celtic Christianity, 1995; Spirituality and Theology, 1998; Love Took My Hand: the spirituality of George Herbert, 2000; Spaces for the Sacred: place, memory, identity, 2001; (ed) New Dictionary of Christian Spirituality, 2005; A Brief History of Spirituality, 2006; Spirituality in Public, 2009. *Recreations:* music, art, contemporary literature, international affairs, wine (Mem., Wine Soc.), travel, history and culture of Italy, family and friends. *Address:* 18 North Bailey, University of Durham, St Chad's College, Durham DH1 3RH. *T:* 07712 671966; *e-mail:* philip.sheldrake@durham.ac.uk. *Clubs:* Commonwealth, Oxford and Cambridge.

SHELDRICK, Dame Daphne (Marjorie), DBE 2006 (MBE 1989); Chairman, David Sheldrick Wildlife Trust, since 1977; *b* 14 June 1934; *d* of Bryan and Marjorie Jenkins; *m* 1960, David Leslie William Sheldrick (*d* 1977); two *d*. *Educ:* Nakuru Primary Sch.; Kenya Girls' High Sch., Nairobi. Wildlife conservation, 1955–, initially alongside David Sheldrick, founder Warden of Tsavo Nat. Park, then as Chairman of David Sheldrick Wildlife Trust, estbd in his memory; she is a recognised internat. authy on rearing of wild creatures and first person to perfect milk formula and necessary husbandry for infant milk-dependent elephants and rhinos. Hon. DVMS Glasgow, 2000. Global 500 Roll of Honour, UNEP, 1992; Lifetime Achievement Award, BBC, 2002. Mem., Burning Spear (Kenya), 2002. *Publications:* The Orphans of Tsavo, 1966; The Tsavo Story, 1973; My Four Footed Family, 1970; An Elephant Called Eleanor, 1980. *Recreation:* nature. *Address:* Box 15555, 00503 Mbagathi, Nairobi, Kenya. *T:* (20) 891996, (20) 890125, (20) 890335, *Fax:* (20) 890053; *e-mail:* RC-H@africaonline.co.ke.

SHELDRICK, Prof. George Michael, PhD; FRS 2001; Professor of Structural Chemistry, University of Göttingen, since 1978; *b* 17 Nov. 1942; *s* of George and Elizabeth M. Sheldrick; *m* 1968, Katherine E. Herford; two *s* two *d*. *Educ:* Huddersfield New Coll.; Jesus Coll., Cambridge (MA; PhD 1966). University of Cambridge: Demonstrator, 1966–71, Lectr, 1971–78, Dept of Inorganic, Organic and Theoretical Chm.; Fellow, Jesus Coll., 1966–78. Mem., Akademie der Wissenschaften zu Göttingen, 1989. Mineral Sheldrickite named after him, 1996. Meldola Medal, 1970, Corday-Morgan Medal, 1978, Award for Structural Chem., 1981, RSC; Leibniz Prize, Deutsche Forschungsgemeinschaft, 1987; Patterson Prize, Amer. Crystallographic Assoc., 1993; Carl-Hermann Medal, Deutsche Ges. für Kristallographie, 1999; Hodgkin Prize, British Crystallographic Assoc., 2004; Perutz Prize, Eur. Crystallographic Assoc., 2004. *Publications:* numerous papers in scientific jls. *Recreations:* tennis, chess. *Address:* Lehrstuhl für Strukturchemie, Tammannstrasse 4, 37077 Göttingen, Germany. *T:* (551) 393021; *e-mail:* gsheldr@shelx.uni-ac.gwdg.de.

SHELFORD, William Thomas Cornelius; *b* 27 Jan. 1943; *s* of late Cornelius William Shelford and of Helen Beatrice Hilda (*née* Schuster); *m* 1971, Annette Heap Holt; two *s* one *d*. *Educ:* Eton Coll.; Christ Church, Oxford (MA Jurisprudence). Partner, 1970–2002, Sen. Partner, 1990–2002, Cameron Markby Hewitt, later Cameron McKenna; Consultant, CMS Cameron McKenna, 2002–07. Chm. Govs, Chailey Heritage Sch., 2005–. *Recreations:* gardening, walking, ski-ing. *Club:* City of London.

SHELLAM, Fiona Juliet; *see* Stanley, F. J.

SHELLARD, Maj.-Gen. Michael Francis Linton, CBE 1989; Comptroller, Royal Artillery Institution, 2001–08; *b* 19 Aug. 1937; *s* of Norman Shellard and Stella (*née* Linton); *m* 1960, Jean Mary Yates; one *s* one *d*. *Educ:* Queen's Coll., Taunton; RMA, Sandhurst. Commnd, RA, 1957; Staff Coll., Camberley, 1969; NDC, Latimer, 1974; GSO1 MO4, MoD, 1975–76; CO 22 AD Regt, 1977–79; Col, 1983; Brig., 1985; Comd 1st Artillery Bde and Dortmund Garrison, 1985–88; Comdr Artillery, 1st British Corps, 1990–92. Dir, NATO Area, Short Brothers plc, 1992–94; Chief Exec., Regular Forces Employment Assoc., 1994–2001. Col Comdt, RA, 1993–2002; Hon. Col 22nd Regt, RA, 1993–2000. Chairman: RA Historical Affairs Cttee, 1994–2002; RA Historical Trust, 1994–2002. Dir, RA Museums Ltd, 1997–2004. Mem., Army Benevolent Fund Grants Cttee, 2002–. Chm., Confedn of British Service and Ex-Service Orgns, 2003–06. Gov., Queen's Coll., Taunton, 1989–. *Recreations:* golf, gardening, Hawk Conservancy Trust. *Address:* c/o HSBC, High Street, Amesbury, Wilts SP4 7DN. *Club:* Army and Navy (Chm., 2000–03; Trustee, 2004–).

SHELLEY, Dr Alan John; Senior Partner, Knight, Frank & Rutley, 1983–92; *b* 7 Aug. 1931; *s* of Stanley and Ivy Shelley; *m* 1958, Josephine Flood, MBE (*d* 2007); one *s* one *d*. *Educ:* People's College, Nottingham; SOAS, London (MA 1994); PhD Nottingham Trent Univ. 2006. FRICS. Senior Partner, Knight, Frank & Rutley (Nigeria), 1965. General Commissioner of Income Tax, 1984–2007. Chairman: W Africa Cttee, 1985–97; Mansfield Settlement, 1992–2000; Vice-Chm., Aston Mansfield, 2000–. Mem. Ct of Governors, Royal Shakespeare Theatre, 1990–2001. *Publications:* The Colour was Red: a novel, 2008; Athol Fugard: his plays, people and politics, 2008. *Recreations:* theatre, squash. *Address:* Thatch Farm, Glaston, Rutland LE15 9BX. *T:* (01572) 822396. *Clubs:* Oriental, MCC.

SHELLEY, Howard Gordon; concert pianist and conductor; *b* 9 March 1950; *s* of Frederick Gordon Shelley and Katharine Anne Taylor; *m* 1975, Hilary Mary Pauline Macnamara; one *s*, and one step *s*. *Educ:* Highgate Sch.; Royal College of Music (ARCM Hons 1966; Foundn Schol. 1967–71); Boise Schol. 1971–72; ARCO 1967. Studied with Vera Yelverton, Harold Craxton, Kendall Taylor, Lamar Crowson and Ilona Kabos. Recital début, Wigmore Hall, 1971; televised Henry Wood Prom début, 1972; conducting début, London Symphony Orch., Barbican, 1985; Associate Conductor, 1990–92, Principal Guest Conductor, 1992–98, London Mozart Players; Music Dir and Principal Conductor, Uppsala Chamber Orch., Sweden, 2000–03. Internat. solo career extending over five continents; performed world's first complete exposition of solo piano works of Rachmaninov, Wigmore Hall, 1983; soloist, 100th anniv. of Henry Wood Proms, 1995. Discography includes: Rachmaninov solo works (8 vols), Rachmaninov two-piano works, Rachmaninov Complete Piano Concertos, Mozart, Hummel (3 vols) and Mendelssohn Piano Concertos, and Moscheles, Herz and Cramer (conductor/soloist), Chopin, Schumann recitals, Schubert recital on fortepiano, piano concertos of Alwyn, Gershwin, Tippett, Vaughan Williams, Howard Ferguson, Szymanowski, Korngold, Rubbra, Carwithen, Balakirev, Messiaen and Peter Dickinson; Mozart and Schubert symphonies (conductor). 2 piano partnership with Hilary Macnamara, 1976–. Presenter, conductor and pianist, TV documentary on Ravel (Gold Medal, NY Fests Awards), 1998. Chappell Gold Medal and Peter Morrison Prize, 1968, Dannreuther Concerto Prize, 1971, RCM; Silver Medal, Co. of Musicians, 1971. *Address:* c/o Caroline Baird Artists, Pinkhill House, Oxford Road, Eynsham, Oxon OX29 4DA; *e-mail:* caroline@cbartists.sol.co.uk.

SHELLEY, James Edward, CBE 1991; Secretary to Church Commissioners, 1985–92; *b* 1932; *s* of Vice-Adm. Richard Shelley and Eve Cecil; *m* 1956, Judy Grubb; two *s* two *d*. *Educ:* Eton; University College, Oxford (MA). Joined Church Commissioners' staff, 1954; Under Secretary General, 1976–81; Assets Secretary, 1981–85. Dir, Save & Prosper, 1987–94. *Recreations:* country pursuits. *Address:* Mays Farm House, Ramsdell, Tadley, Hants RG26 5RE. *T:* (01256) 850770.

SHELLEY, Sir John (Richard), 11th Bt *cr* 1611; (professionally Dr J. R. Shelley); general medical practitioner; farmer; *b* 18 Jan. 1943; *s* of John Shelley (*d* 1974), and of Dorothy, *d* of Arthur Irvine Ingram; *S* grandfather, 1976; *m* 1965, Clare, *d* of late Claud Bicknell, OBE; two *d. Educ:* King's Sch., Bruton; Trinity Coll., Cambridge (BA 1964, MA 1967); St Mary's Hosp., London Univ. MB, BChir 1967; DObstRCOG 1969; MRCGP 1978. Mem., Exeter Diocesan Synod for South Molton Deanery, 1976–79, for Cadbury Deanery, 2002–. Member: BMA; CLA; NFU. *Heir: b* Thomas Henry Shelley [*b* 3 Feb. 1945; *m* 1970, Katherine Mary Holton (marr. diss. 1992); three *d*]. *Address:* Shobrooke Park, Crediton, Devon EX17 1DG. *T:* (01769) 573101.

SHELTON, Gen. Henry Hugh; Chairman, Joint Chiefs of Staff, USA, 1997–2001; *b* 2 Jan. 1942; *s* of late Hugh Shelton and of Sarah Shelton (*née* Laughlin); *m* 1963, Carolyn L. Johnson; three *s. Educ:* N Carolina State Univ. (BS Textiles 1963); Auburn Univ., Alabama (MS Pol Sci.); Harvard Univ.; Air Comd and Staff Coll., Alabama; Nat. War Coll., Washington. Entered US Army, 1963: active duty assignments in US, Hawaii and Vietnam (2 tours), 1963–87; Dep. Dir for Ops, Nat. Mil. Comd Center, Jt Chiefs of Staff, Washington, 1987–88; Chief, Current Ops, Jt Chiefs of Staff, 1988–89; Assistant Division Commander, 101st Airborne Division (Air Assault): Fort Campbell, Kentucky, 1989–90; Operations Desert Shield and Desert Storm, Saudi Arabia, 1990–91; Fort Campbell, March–May 1991; Commanding General: 82nd Airborne Div., Fort Bragg, NC, 1991–93; XVIII Airborne Corps and Fort Bragg, 1993–96 (i/c Jt Task Force, Operation Uphold Democracy, Haiti, 1994); Lt-Gen. 1993; Gen. 1996; C-in-C, US Special Ops Comd, MacDill Air Force Base, Fla, 1996–97. Mem., Council on Foreign Relns, 1998–. Mem., Assoc. of US Army, 1983–. Gov., American Red Cross, 1998–. Purple Heart, 1967; Bronze Star Medal: (with V device), 1967; (with three Oak Leaf Clusters), 1968, 1969, 1991; MSM (with two Oak Leaf Clusters), 1979, 1982, 1983; Legion of Merit (with Oak Leaf Cluster), 1985, 1991; DSM 1994; Defense DSM (with two Oak Leaf Clusters), 1989, 1994, 1997. *Publications:* contrib. to Harvard Internat. Rev., Armed Forces Jl, Nat. Defense, Special Warfare, Jt Force Qly, Qly Mil. Rev. *Recreations:* jogging, woodworking, reading, playing guitar. *Address:* c/o The Pentagon, Room 2E872, Washington, DC 20318–9999, USA. *T:* (703) 6979121.

SHELTON, Shirley Megan, (Mrs W. T. Shelton); Editor, Home & Freezer Digest, 1988–90; *b* 8 March 1934; *d* of Lt-Col T. F. Goodwin; *m* 1960, William Timothy Shelton; one *s* two *d. Educ:* various schs. Home Editor 1970–75, Assistant Editor, 1975–78, Editor, 1978–82, Woman and Home magazine. *Address:* 59 Croftdown Road, NW5 1EL.

SHELVEY, (Elsie) Miriam; a District Judge (Magistrates' Court) (formerly Provincial Stipendiary Magistrate), Greater Manchester, since 1999; *b* 23 Aug. 1955; *d* of Francis James Dunn and Edith Elsie Dunn; *m* 1977, Peter Anthony Shelvey; one *d. Educ:* Liverpool Univ. (LLB). Admitted Solicitor, 1979; Partner, Silverman Livermore, 1980–99. *Recreation:* gardening. *Address:* Liverpool City Magistrates' Court, 107 Dale Street, Liverpool L2 2JQ. *T:* (0151) 243 5597.

SHENKIN, Prof. Alan, PhD; FRCP, FRCPath, FRCPGlas; Professor of Clinical Chemistry, University of Liverpool, 1990–2007, now Emeritus; Hon. Consultant and Clinical Director, Royal Liverpool and Broadgreen University Hospitals NHS Trust, 1990–2007 (Director of Research and Development, 1998–2004); *b* 3 Sept. 1943; *m* 1967, Leonna Estelle Delmonte; one *s* two *d. Educ:* Hutchesons Boys' Grammar Sch.; Univ. of Glasgow (BSc Hons 1965; MB ChB 1969; PhD 1974). FRCPath 1990; FRCPGlas 1990; FRCP 1993. Lectr in Biochem., Univ. of Glasgow, 1970–74; Sen. Registrar in Clinical Biochem., Glasgow Royal Infirmary, 1974–78; Royal Soc. Eur. Exchange Fellow, Karolinska Inst., Stockholm, 1976–77; Consultant in Clinical Biochem., Glasgow Royal Infirmary, 1978–90. Chm., Specialty Adv. Cttee on Chemical Pathology, RCPath, 1995–98; Chairman: Royal Med. Colls Intercollegiate Gp on Nutrition, 1996–2006; Sub-Cttee on Metabolic Medicine, Jt Cttee on Higher Med. Trng, 2001–04. Pres., Assoc. Clinical Biochemists, 2000–03; Hon. Treas., Eur. Soc. Parenteral and Enteral Nutrition, 1988–92 (Vice-Pres., 2002–03); Scientific Vice-Pres., British Nutrition Foundn, 2005–. Hon. Associate, British Dietetic Assoc., 1989; Hon. Member: Czechoslovakian Med. Soc., 1990; Czechoslovakian Soc. for Parenteral and Enteral Nutrition, 1990. Mem., Scotch Malt Whisky Soc. 650th Anniversary Jubilee Medal, Charles Univ., 1998. *Publications:* contrib. res. papers, book chapters and conf. proc. on trace elements and vitamins in nutritional support, and metabolic response to illness. *Recreations:* golf, word games, malt whisky, travel. *Address:* Duncan Building, University of Liverpool, Liverpool L69 3GA. *Club:* Lee Park Golf (Liverpool).

SHENNAN, Robert Duncan James; Director of Radio, Channel 4, since 2008; *b* 18 March 1962; *s* of Joseph and Margaret Shennan; *m* 1987, Joanne Margaret Melford; two *s* one *d. Educ:* Lancaster Royal Grammar Sch.; Corpus Christi Coll., Cambridge (BA Hons English Lit. 1984). Journalist, Hereward Radio, 1984–87; BBC: Radio Sport: Producer, 1987–90; Asst Editor, 1990–92; Editor, 1992–94; Head, 1994–97; Head of Sport (TV and Radio), 1997–2000; Controller: BBC Radio Five Live, 2000–08; Five Live Sports Extra and BBC Asian Network, 2002–08. *Recreations:* sport, literature, my children. *Address:* Channel 4, 124 Horseferry Road, SW1P 2TX; Fairbanks, 30 Amersham Road, High Wycombe, Bucks HP13 6QU. *T:* (01494) 459216.

SHENNAN, Prof. Stephen James, PhD; FBA 2006; Professor of Theoretical Archaeology, since 1996, and Director, Institute of Archaeology, since 2005, University College London; *b* 9 May 1949; *s* of James Francis Shennan and Martha Shennan (*née* Elias); partner, Lúcia Nagib; one *s* one *d* from former marriage. *Educ:* Becket Sch., Nottingham; Fitzwilliam Coll., Cambridge (BA 1971, MA 1974; PhD 1977). University of Southampton: Lectr in Archaeol., 1978–90; Reader, 1990–95; Prof. of Archaeol., 1995–96. *Publications:* (ed with C. Renfrew) Ranking, Resource and Exchange, 1982; (jtly) Prehistoric Europe, 1984; The East Hampshire Survey, 1985; Quantifying Archaeology, 1988, 2nd edn 1997; (ed) Archaeological approaches to Cultural Identity, 1989; (with C. W. Beck) Amber in Prehistoric Britain, 1991; Bronze Age Copper Producers of the Eastern Alps, 1995; (ed with J. Steele) The Archaeology of Human Ancestry: power, sex and tradition, 1996; Genes, Memes and Human History: Darwinian archaeology and cultural evolution, 2002; (ed jtly) The Explanation of Culture Change, 2004; (ed jtly) The Evolution of Cultural Diversity: a phylogenetic approach, 2005; (ed jtly) Mapping Our Ancestors: phylogenetic methods in anthropology and prehistory, 2006; (ed jtly) A Future for Archaeology: the past in the present, 2006; monographs; contrib. numerous acad. papers. *Recreations:* rock climbing, walking, opera, classical music, cinema, occasional ski-ing, sailing. *Address:* Institute of Archaeology, University College London, 31–34 Gordon Square, WC1H 0PY. *T:* (020) 7679 7483, *Fax:* (020) 7387 2572; *e-mail:* s.shennan@ucl.ac.uk.

SHEPHARD OF NORTHWOLD, Baroness *cr* 2005 (Life Peer), of Northwold in the county of Norfolk; **Gillian Patricia Shephard;** PC 1992; JP; DL; *b* 22 Jan. 1940; *d* of Reginald and Bertha Watts; *m* 1975, Thomas Shephard; two step *s. Educ:* North Walsham High Sch. for Girls; St Hilda's Coll., Oxford (MA Mod. Langs; Hon. Fellow, 1991). Educn Officer and Schools Inspector, 1963–75; Lectr, Cambridge Univ. Extra-Mural Bd, 1965–87. Councillor, Norfolk CC, 1977–89 (Chm. of Social Services Cttee, 1978–83, of Educn Cttee, 1983–85); Chairman: W Norfolk and Wisbech HA, 1981–85; Norwich HA, 1985–87; Co-Chm., Women's Nat. Commn, 1990–91. MP (C) SW Norfolk, 1987–2005. PPS to Economic Sec. to the Treasury, 1988–89; Parly Under Sec. of State, DSS, 1989–90; Minister of State, HM Treasury, 1990–92; Sec. of State for Employment and Minister for Women, 1992–93; Minister of Agric., Fisheries and Food, 1993–94; Sec. of State for Educn, later Educn and Employment, 1994–97; Shadow Leader, H of C, 1997; Opposition front bench spokesman on the envmt, transport and the regions, 1997–99. Dep. Chm., Cons. Party, 1991–92 and 2002–03; Chm., Assoc. of Conservative Peers, 2007–. Mem., Cttee on Standards in Public Life, 2003–08; Pres., Video Standards Council, 2006–. Vice Pres., Hansard Soc., 1997–2004. Mem., Franco-British Council, 1997–2006; Chairman: Cons. Friends of Israel, 1997–2001; E of England Bio-Fuels Forum, 2004–; Franco-British Soc., 2005–; Trustee, WEA, 2006–. Comr, Fawcett Soc., 2005–. Mem. Council, Univ. of Oxford, 2000–06; Chm. Council, RVC, 2008–. Pres., Royal Norfolk Agricl Assoc., 2000–01. JP Norwich, 1973; DL Norfolk, 2003. *Publications:* The Future of Local Government, 1999; Shephard's Watch, 2000; Knapton Remembered, 2007. *Recreations:* music, gardening, France. *Address:* House of Lords, SW1A 0PW.

See also N. Shephard.

SHEPHARD, Jonathan; Chief Executive, PPA, since 2008; *b* 20 March 1949; twin *s* of Grey and Mollie Shephard; *m* 1985, Penelope Guest (marr. diss. 2000); two *s* one *d. Educ:* Sir Thomas Rich's Sch., Gloucester; St Catherine's Coll., Oxford (BA (English) 1971; BA (Law) 1973; Chancellor's English Essay Prize, Matthew Arnold Meml Prize). Called to the Bar, Inner Temple, 1977; with Which?, 1979–94: Financial Researcher, 1979–83, Res. Manager, 1983–86; Editor: Holiday Which?, 1986–90; Health Which?, 1988–90; Project Dir, 1990–92; Dir of Mgt Inf., 1992–94; Mktg Dir, 1994–95; Man. Dir, 1995–97; Newhall Gp; Man. Dir, Southern Magazines, 1997–2002; Gen. Sec., subseq. Chief Exec., Independent Schs Council, 2004–08. *Publication:* (ed) Which? Book of Tax, 1986. *Recreations:* music, architecture, writing novels. *Address:* PPA, Queens House, 28 Kingsway, WC2B 6JR. *T:* (020) 7404 4166.

SHEPHARD, Prof. Neil, PhD; FBA 2006; Professor of Economics, since 2006, and Research Director, Oxford-Man Institute, since 2007, University of Oxford; Professorial Fellow, Nuffield College, Oxford, since 2006; *b* 8 Oct. 1964; *s* of Dr Thomas F. Shephard (who *m* 1975, Gillian Watts (*see* Baroness Shephard of Northwold)) and late Tydfil Shephard; *m* 1998, Dr Heather Bell; one *d. Educ:* Univ. of York (BA Hons Econs and Stats 1986); London Sch. of Economics (MSc Stats 1987; PhD 1990). Lectr, LSE, 1988–93; Gatsby Res. Fellow in Econometrics, 1991–93, Official Fellow in Econs, 1993–2006, Nuffield Coll., Oxford; Titular Prof. of Econs, Univ. of Oxford, 1999–2006. Fellow, Econometric Soc., 2004. *Recreations:* reading, cricket, psephology. *Address:* Department of Economics, Manor Road, Oxford OX1 3UQ. *T:* (01865) 616600, *Fax:* (01865) 616601; *e-mail:* neil.shephard@economics.ox.ac.uk.

SHEPHEARD ROGERS, Patricia Maureen; Chief Executive, Jubilee Debt Campaign, 2005–08; *b* Colchester, 18 May 1947; *d* of Maj. Gen. Joseph Kenneth Shepheard, CB, DSO, OBE and Maureen E. H. Shepheard (*née* Bowen-Colthurst); *m* 1969, David Rogers (marr. diss. 2004); two *s. Educ:* New Hall, Cambridge (BA Hons 1968); Inst. of Educn, London Univ. (PGCE); Univ. of Greenwich (DMS). Lecturer in Mathematics: West Kent Coll., 1968–69; Univ. of Lagos Coll. of Educn, 1969–71; King's Coll., Lagos, 1971–72; Foreman Christian Coll., Univ. of Punjab, 1975–78; broadcaster and newspaper columnist, S Korea, 1985–89; develt educn researcher and writer, 1981–90; Chief Executive: Council for Educn in World Citizenship, 1990–99; Pestalozzi Internat. Village, 1999–2005. Director: RIIA (Mem., 1990–); UN Assoc.-UK; British Humanist Assoc. *Publications:* Sand Harvest, 1985; Let's Visit South Korea, 1988. *Address:* 27 River Court, Upper Ground, SE1 9PE. *T:* (020) 7928 3667; *e-mail:* trisha_rogers@yahoo.com.

SHEPHERD, family name of **Baron Shepherd**.

SHEPHERD, 3rd Baron *cr* 1946, of Spalding, co. Lincoln; **Graeme George Shepherd;** *b* 6 Jan. 1949; *er s* of 2nd Baron Shepherd, PC and Allison (*née* Redmond); *S* father, 2001; *m* 1971, Eleanor Philomena, *d* of Patrick Glynn; one *s. Heir: s* Hon. Patrick Malcolm Shepherd [*b* 10 July 1980; *m* 2007, Laura, *d* of Tim Street].

SHEPHERD, Alan Arthur, CBE 1984; PhD; FREng, FInstP; Director, Ferranti plc, 1981–94; *b* 6 Sept. 1927; *s* of Arthur and Hannah Shepherd; *m* 1953, Edith Hudson; two *d. Educ:* Univ. of Manchester (BSc, MSc, PhD). FREng (FEng 1986). Lectr, Physics Dept, Univ. of Keele, 1950–54; Ferranti Ltd: Chief Engineer, Electronic Components Div., 1954–67; Gen. Manager, Instrument Dept, 1967–70; Gen. Manager, Electronic Components Div., 1970–78; Man. Dir, Ferranti Electronics, 1978–87; Dep. Man. Dir, Ops, Ferranti, then Ferranti Internat. Signal plc, 1987–89; Chm., Ferranti California Group of Cos, 1978–87. Hon. Fellow, UMIST, 1988. J. J. Thomson Medal, IEE, 1985. *Publication:* The Physics of Semiconductors, 1957. *Recreations:* golf, swimming, photography. *Address:* 6 Southern Crescent, Bramhall, Cheshire SK7 3AH. *T:* (0161) 439 2824. *Club:* St James's (Manchester).

SHEPHERD, Archie; HM Diplomatic Service, retired; Counsellor and Head of Migration and Visa Department, Foreign and Commonwealth Office, 1977–80; *b* 2 Nov. 1922; *s* of William Shepherd and Edith (*née* Browning); *m* 1959, Dorothy Annette Walker; one *s. Educ:* Torquay Grammar Sch. Prison Commission, 1939; served War, RAF, 1942–46. Foreign Office, 1949; Asst Political Agent and Vice Consul, Muscat, 1951–53; FO, 1954–55; Second Sec., UK Delegn to United Nations, Geneva, 1956–57; HM Consul: Warsaw, 1958–60; Rabat, 1960–62; FO, 1963–67; Consul, Cape Town, 1968–72; First Sec. (Commercial), Beirut, 1973–75. *Recreations:* tennis, gardening. *Address:* 9 Oaks Way, Kenley, Surrey CR8 5DT. *T:* (020) 8660 1299. *Clubs:* Civil Service, Royal Commonwealth Society.

SHEPHERD, Sir Colin (Ryley), Kt 1996; Director, Haigh Engineering Company Ltd, since 1963; Director of Parliamentary Studies, Centre for Political and Diplomatic Studies, since 1999; *b* 13 Jan. 1938; *s* of late T. C. R. Shepherd, MBE; *m* 1966, Louise, *d* of late Lt-Col E. A. M. Cleveland, MC; three *s. Educ:* Oundle; Caius Coll., Cambridge; McGill Univ., Montreal. RCN, 1959–63. MP (C) Hereford, Oct. 1974–1997; contested (C) same seat, 1997. PPS to Sec. of State for Wales, 1987–90. Jt Sec., Cons. Parly Agr. Fish. and Food Cttee, 1975–79, Vice-Chm., 1979–87, 1991–92; Member: Select Cttee on H of C Services, 1979–92; Select Cttee on H of C Finance and Services, 1993–97; Sec., Cons. Parly Hort. Sub-Cttee, 1976–87; Chairman: Library Sub-Cttee, 1983–91; Catering Cttee, 1991–97. Chm., UK Br., CPA, 1991–94 (Mem. Exec. Cttee, 1986–97; Treas., 1991–93, Chm., 1993–96, Internat. Exec. Cttee). Council Mem., RCVS, 1983–99 (Hon. ARCVS 2001); Governor, Commonwealth Inst., 1989–97. Fellow, Industry and Parlt Trust, 1985. *Address:* Manor House, Ganarew, Monmouth NP25 3SU. *T:* (01600) 890220. *Clubs:* Naval, Royal Commonwealth Society.

SHEPHERD, David; *see* Shepherd, R. D.

SHEPHERD, Prof. James, PhD; FRCPath, FRCPGlas, FMedSci; FRSE; Professor, and Head of Department of Pathological Biochemistry, University of Glasgow and Glasgow Royal Infirmary, 1988–2006, now Professor Emeritus; *b* 8 April 1944; *s* of James Bell Shepherd and Margaret McCrum Shepherd (*née* Camick); *m* 1969, Janet Bulloch Kelly; one *s* one *d.* *Educ:* Hamilton Acad.; Glasgow Univ. (BSc Hons 1965; MB ChB Hons 1968; PhD 1972). MRCPath 1982, FRCPath 1994; FRCPGlas 1990. Lectr in Biochemistry, Univ. of Glasgow, 1969–72; Lectr, 1973–77, Sen. Lectr and Hon. Consultant, 1977–88, Dept of Pathological Biochemistry, Univ. of Glasgow and Glasgow Royal Infirmary; Clin. Dir, Labs, Glasgow Royal Infirmary, 1993–2004. Asst Prof. of Medicine, Methodist Hosp., Houston, Texas, 1976–77; Vis. Prof. of Medicine, Cantonal Hosp., Geneva, 1984. Dir, W Scotland Coronary Prevention Study, 1989–96; Chairman: European Atherosclerosis Soc., 1993–96 (Chm., Congress, 2001); Prospective Study of Pravastatin in the Elderly at Risk, 1997–2002; Exec. Cttee, Treating to New Targets Study, 2001–06; UK Principal Investigator, Justification for the Use of Statins in Primary Prevention, 2005–08; Mem., Internat. Atherosclerosis Soc., 1977–. FRSE 1996; Founder FMedSci, 1998. *Publications:* (jtly) Lipoproteins in Coronary Heart Disease, 1986; (jtly) Atherosclerosis: developments, complications and treatment, 1987; Lipoprotein Metabolism, 1987; (ed jtly) Coronary Risks Revisited, 1989; (ed jtly) Human Plasma Lipoproteins, 1989; (ed jtly) Preventive Cardiology, 1991; (ed jtly) Lipoproteins and the Pathogenesis of Atherosclerosis, 1991; (ed jtly) Cardiovascular Disease: current perspectives on the Asian-Pacific region, 1994; (jtly) Clinical Biochemistry, 1995, 4th edn 2008; (jtly) Lipoproteins in Health and Disease, 1999; (jtly) Statins in Perspective, 1999, 2nd edn 2004; (jtly) Atherosclerosis Annual, 2001; Lipids and Atherosclerosis Annual, 2003. *Recreations:* travel, walking, art appraisal. *Address:* (home) 17 Barriedale Avenue, Hamilton ML3 9DB. *T:* (01698) 428259; (office) Institute of Biochemistry, Royal Infirmary, Glasgow G4 0SF. *T:* (0141) 552 0689.

SHEPHERD, James Rodney; Under-Secretary, Department of Trade and Industry (formerly Department of Industry), 1980–89, retired; *b* 27 Nov. 1935; *s* of Richard James Shepherd and Winifred Mary Shepherd. *Educ:* Blundell's; Magdalen Coll., Oxford (PPE; Diploma in Statistics). National Inst. of Economic and Social Res., 1960–64; Consultant to OECD, 1964; HM Treasury, 1965–80 (Under-Sec., 1975–80). *Publications:* articles in technical jls.

SHEPHERD, Sir John (Alan), KCVO 2000; CMG 1989; Director, Global Leadership Foundation, since 2007; *b* 27 April 1943; *s* of William (Mathieson) Shepherd and (Elsie) Rae Shepherd; *m* 1969, Jessica Mary Nichols; one *d.* *Educ:* Charterhouse; Selwyn Coll., Cambridge (MA); Stanford Univ., Calif (MA). Merchant Navy, 1961; HM Diplomatic Service, 1965–2003: CO, 1965–66; MECAS, Lebanon, 1966–68; 3rd Sec., Amman, 1968–70; 2nd Sec., Rome, 1970–73; 1st Secretary: FCO, 1973–76; The Hague, 1977–80; First Sec., 1980–82, Counsellor and Hd of Chancery, 1982–84, Office of UK Rep. to EEC, Brussels; Head of European Community Dept (External), FCO, 1985–87; Ambassador to Bahrain, 1988–91; Minister, Bonn, 1991–96; Dir, Middle East and North Africa, FCO, 1996–97; Dep. Under-Sec. of State, FCO, 1997–2000; Ambassador to Italy, 2000–03; Sec.-Gen., Global Leadership Foundn, 2003–06. Chm., Norbert Brainin Foundn, 2003–; Dep. Chm. Trustees, Prince's Sch. of Traditional Arts, 2004–. *Recreations:* hills, birds, tennis. *Club:* Oxford and Cambridge.

SHEPHERD, John Dodson, CBE 1979; Regional Administrator, Yorkshire Regional Health Authority, 1977–82, retired; *b* 24 Dec. 1920; *s* of Norman and Elizabeth Ellen Shepherd; *m* 1948, Marjorie Nettleton (decd); one *s* two *d.* *Educ:* Barrow Grammar School. RAF, 1940–46: N Africa, Italy, Middle East, 1943–46. Asst Sec., Oxford RHB, 1956–58; Dep. Sec., Newcastle upon Tyne HMC, 1958–62; Sec., East Cumberland HMC, 1962–67; Sec., Liverpool RHB, 1967–73; Reg. Administrator, Mersey RHA, 1973–77. Pres., Inst. of Health Service Administrators, 1974–75 (Mem. Council, 1969–78). Trustee, Leonard Cheshire Foundn, 1989–95. *Recreations:* reading, music. *Club:* Harrogate Golf.

SHEPHERD, Prof. John Graham, PhD; FRS 1999; CMath, FIMA; Professor of Marine Sciences, since 1994 and Director, Earth System Modelling Initiative, since 1999, University of Southampton; *b* 24 Aug. 1946; *s* of Ian Alastair Shepherd and Eileen Alice Mary Shepherd; *m* 1968, Deborah Mary Powney; two *s.* *Educ:* Pembroke Coll., Cambridge (MA); Cavendish Lab., Cambridge (PhD 1971). FIMA 1989; CMath 1991. Res. Officer, CEGB, 1970–74; MAFF Fisheries Lab., Lowestoft, 1974–94, Dep. Dir and Hd, Fish Stock Mgt Div., 1989–94; Dir, Southampton Oceanography Centre, NERC, 1994–99. Vis. Sen. Res. Associate, Lamont-Doherty Geol Observatory, Columbia Univ., NY, 1978–79. FRGS 1994; Pres., Challenger Soc., 2000–02. *Publications:* numerous professional articles on marine science, climate change, fish stock assessment and fishery mgt. *Recreations:* rowing, music, walking. *Address:* National Oceanography Centre, European Way, Southampton SO14 3ZH. *T:* (023) 8059 6256. *Club:* Lowestoft Rowing.

SHEPHERD, Prof. John Henry, FRCS, FRCOG, FACOG; Professor of Surgical Gynaecology, Barts and the London, Queen Mary's School of Medicine and Dentistry (formerly St Bartholomew's and the Royal London Hospital School of Medicine and Dentistry), since 1999; *b* 11 July 1948; *s* of Dr Henry Robert Shepherd, DSC and Mimika Matarki; *m* 1972, Alison Brandram Adams; one *s* two *d.* *Educ:* Blundell's Sch., Tiverton; St Bartholomew's Hosp. Med. Coll. (MB BS 1971). LRCP 1971; FRCS 1976; MRCOG 1978 (Gold Medal), FRCOG 1996; FACOG 1981. Fellow in Gynaecol Oncology, Univ. of S Florida, Tampa, 1979–81; Sen. Registrar, Queen Charlotte's Hosp., 1978–79; Consultant Surgeon and Gynaecological Oncologist: St Bartholomew's Hosp., 1981–2008; Royal Marsden Hosp., London, 1983–; Consultant Surgeon, Chelsea Hosp. for Women, 1983–84; Consultant: London Clinic, 1994–; King Edward VII Hosp., London, 1995–. Hunterian Prof., RCS, 2006–07. *Publications:* (jtly) Gynaecological Oncology, 1985, 2nd edn 1990; (jtly) Ovarian Cancer, 2002; numerous articles on gynaecol cancer and pelvic surgery. *Recreations:* sailing (offshore ocean racing), ski-ing, opera. *Address:* London Clinic Consulting Rooms, 5 Devonshire Place, W1G 6HE. *T:* (020) 7935 4444, *Fax:* (020) 7935 6224. *Clubs:* MCC, Royal Ocean Racing.

SHEPHERD, Prof. Jonathan Paul, CBE 2008; PhD, DDSc; FDSRCS, FMedSci; Professor of Oral and Maxillofacial Surgery, Cardiff University (formerly University of Wales College of Medicine, later Wales College of Medicine, Cardiff University), since 1991; Vice Dean, Cardiff University, since 2004; *b* 25 Sept. 1949; *s* of Paul Richard Shepherd and Heather Mary Shepherd (*née* Gifford); *m* 1980, Daphne Elizabeth Bird; three *s* one *d.* *Educ:* Bideford Grammar Sch.; King's Coll. London (BDS); Wolfson Coll., Oxford (MSc); PhD Bristol 1988; DDSc Wales 2000. FDSRCS 1977; FFAEM 2001. House Surgeon: KCH, 1974; Queen Victoria Hosp., E Grinstead, 1974–75; Registrar, Royal Infirmary, Oxford, 1975–80; Res. Fellow, Univ. of Oxford, 1978–79; Sen. Registrar in Oral and Maxillofacial Surgery, Yorks RHA, and Hon. Lectr, Univ. of Leeds, 1980–83; Sen. Lectr in Oral and Maxillofacial Surgery, 1983–88, Reader, 1988–91, Univ. of Bristol; Hd, Dept of Oral Surgery, Medicine and Pathol., UWCM, Cardiff Univ., 1991–2004. Hon. Consultant Oral and Maxillofacial Surgeon: Bristol and Weston HA, 1983–91; University Hosp. of Wales/Cardiff and Vale NHS Trust, 1991–. King James IV Prof., RCSE, 2006–. Chm., WHO Violent Crime Task Gp, 1996–. Dir, Violence and Society Res. Gp. Trustee, Victim Support, 1998–2006 (Vice Chair, 2000–03). FMedSci 2002. Hon. FDSRCSE 1996; Hon. FFPH 2001; Hon. FRCPsych 2008; Hon. FFGDP 2008. Hon. Dr Odontol Malmö, 2005. Stockholm Criminology Prize, 2008. *Publications:* Slide Interpretation in Oral Diseases and the Oral Manifestations of Systemic Diseases, 1986; Violence in Healthcare, 1994, 2nd edn 2001; contributions: on decision-making and cost effectiveness in surgery and anaesthesia to surgery, dentistry, anaesthesia and clin. decision-making jls; on psycho-social causes and sequelae and epidemiol. of violence to med. and social sci. jls; series of randomised controlled expts in epidemiol., psychiatry and emergency medicine jls; res. discoveries to BMJ and Lancet editls. *Recreations:* industrial archaeology, building blast furnaces, walking. *Address:* Department of Oral and Maxillofacial Surgery, School of Dentistry, Cardiff University, Heath Park, Cardiff CF14 4XY. *T:* and *Fax:* (029) 2074 2442; *e-mail:* shepherdjp@cardiff.ac.uk.

SHEPHERD, Sister Margaret Ann; Member, and Provincial of UK/Ireland Province, Religious Congregation (RC) of Our Lady of Sion; Director, Council of Christians and Jews, 1999–2006; *b* 26 April 1944; *d* of Alfred and Alice Shepherd. *Educ:* Maria Assumpta Coll. of Educn (DipEd); Open Univ. (BA); Leo Baeck Coll. (Dip. Jewish Studies 1980); King's Coll., London (MTh Biblical Studies). Teacher of English (part time) during noviciate period; teacher, English and religious studies: Our Lady of Sion Boarding Sch., Shropshire, 1969–70; Our Lady of Sion Sen. Sch., Worthing, 1970–77; full time rabbinical studies, 1977–80; Study Centre for Christian Jewish Relations: Team Mem., 1980–86; Dir, 1986–89; Council of Christians and Jews: Educn Officer, 1989–93; Dep. Dir, 1993–98; Mem. Exec. Bd, Internat. CCJ, 2002–. *Publications:* (contrib.) Dialogue with a Difference, ed Tony Bayfield and Marcus Braybrooke, 1992; (contrib.) Splashes of Godlight, ed Terence Copley, 1997; The Holocaust and the Christian World, 2000; Jews and Christians: making theological space for each other, 2000; He Kissed Him and They Wept: towards a theology of Jewish-Catholic partnership, ed Tony Bayfield, Sidney Brichto and Eugene Fisher, 2002; Public Life and the Place of the Church, ed Michael Brierley, 2006; contrib. to The Month. *Recreations:* visiting art galleries and exhibitions, music, painting, poetry, browsing in second hand bookshops, spending time with friends. *Address:* 35 Gilbert Close, Shooters Hill Road, SE18 4PT. *T:* (020) 8319 1930; *e-mail:* margaret@apcomm.net.

SHEPHERD, Philip Alexander; QC 2003; a Recorder of the Crown Court, since 2000; *b* 1 May 1950; *s* of John and Eve Shepherd; *m* 1984, Amanda Robin Clezy; two *s.* *Educ:* St George's Coll., Weybridge; Monash Univ., Melbourne; LSE (BSc Econ). Called to the Bar, Gray's Inn, 1975; barrister specialising in commercial litigation and aviation law. MCIArb 1997; Member: Commercial Bar Assoc.; British-Italian Law Assoc.; Internat. Bar Assoc. *Recreations:* pub walking, marmalade making, Rugby, motorcycles, ballet. *Address:* 24 Old Buildings, Lincoln's Inn, WC2A 3UP. *T:* (020) 7404 0946, *Fax:* (020) 7405 1360; *e-mail:* philip.shepherd@xxiv.co.uk. *Club:* Royal Automobile.

SHEPHERD, Richard Charles Scrimgeour; MP (C) Aldridge-Brownhills, since 1979; *b* 6 Dec. 1942; *s* of late Alfred Reginald Shepherd and Davida Sophia Wallace. *Educ:* LSE; Johns Hopkins Univ. (Sch. of Advanced Internat. Studies). Director: Shepherd Foods (London) Ltd, 1970–; Partridges of Sloane Street Ltd, 1972–. Mem., SE Econ. Planning Council, 1970–74. Underwriting Mem. of Lloyds, 1974–94. Member: Treasury and Civil Service Select Cttee, 1979–83; Modernisation Select Cttee, 1997–; Jt Cttee on Human Rights, 2001–; Secretary: Cons. Parly Industry Cttee, 1980–81; Cons. Parly European Cttee, 1980–81. Parly Co-Vice Chm., Campaign for Freedom of Inf., 1989–. Sponsor, Liberty, 2001–. Mem., Court of Govs, LSE, 1996–. Backbencher of the Year, Spectator, 1987; Special Award, Campaign for Freedom of Information, 1988; Parliamentarian of the Year, Spectator, 1995. *Recreations:* book collecting; searching for the Home Service on the wireless. *Address:* House of Commons, SW1A 0AA. *Clubs:* Garrick, Beefsteak, Chelsea Arts.

SHEPHERD, (Richard) David, CBE 2008 (OBE 1980); artist; *b* 25 April 1931; *s* of Raymond Oxley Shepherd and Margaret Joyce Shepherd (*née* Williamson); *m* 1957, Avril Shirley Gaywood; four *d.* *Educ:* Stowe. Art trng under Robin Goodwin, 1950–53; started career as aviation artist (Founder Mem., Soc. of Aviation Artists). Exhibited, RA, 1956; began painting African wild life, 1960. First London one-man show, 1962; painted 15 ft reredos of Christ for army garrison church, Bordon, 1964; 2nd London exhibn, 1965; Johannesburg exhibns, 1966 and 1969; 3rd London exhibn, 1971; exhibn, Tryon Gall., London, 1978. Painted: HE Dr Kaunda, President of Zambia, 1967; HM the Queen Mother for King's Regt, 1969; HE Sheikh Zayed of Abu Dhabi, 1970; HH Shaikh Khalifa Bin Sulman Al Khalifa, Prime Minister of Bahrain, 2001. Auctioned 5 wildlife paintings in USA and raised sufficient to purchase Bell Jet Ranger helicopter to combat game poaching in Zambia, 1971; painted Tiger Fire, for Operation Tiger, 1973; presented with 1896 steam locomotive by Pres. Kenneth Kaunda of Zambia (its return to Britain subject of BBC TV documentary, Last Train to Mulobezi); purchased 2 main line steam locomotives from BR, 1967 (92203 Black Prince, 75209 The Green Knight); Founder Chm., E Somerset Railway. BBC made 50-minute colour life documentary, The Man Who Loves Giants, 1970; series, In Search of Wildlife, in which he is shown tracking down and painting endangered species, Thames TV, 1988. Established The David Shepherd Conservation, subseq. Wildlife, Foundn, 1984. Mem. of Honour, World Wildlife Fund, 1979. FRGS 1989; FRSA 1986. Freeman, City of London, 2004. Hon. DFA, Pratt Inst., New York, for services to wildlife conservation, 1971; Hon. DSc Hatfield Polytechnic, 1990. OStJ 1996. Order of the Golden Ark, Netherlands, for services to wildlife conservation (Zambia, Operation Tiger, etc), 1973. *Publications:* Artist in Africa, 1967; (autobiog.) The Man who Loves Giants, 1975; Paintings of Africa and India, 1978; A Brush with Steam, 1983; David Shepherd: the man and his paintings, 1985; An Artist in Conversation, 1992; David Shepherd: my painting life, 1995; Painting with David Shepherd, 2004. *Recreations:* driving steam engines, raising money for wildlife. *Address:* Brooklands Farm, Hammerwood, East Grinstead, West Sussex RH19 3QA. *T:* (01342) 302480; *e-mail:* david@davidshepherdartist.co.uk.

SHEPHERD, Richard Thorley, FRCPath; Senior Lecturer in Forensic Medicine and Head of Forensic Medicine Unit, St George's Hospital Medical School, since 1996; Hon. Consultant, Forensic Pathology, Royal Liverpool Hospital, since 2007; *b* 20 Sept. 1952; *s* of George and Lucy Shepherd; *m* 1978, Jane Caroline Malcolm (marr. diss. 2007); one *s* one *d.* *Educ:* University Coll. London (BSc Hons); St George's Hosp. Med. Sch. (MB BS 1977). DMJ 1984; FRCPath 1997; FFFLM 2006. Lectr in Forensic Medicine, St George's Hosp. Med. Sch., 1981–86; Lectr in Forensic Medicine, 1986–88, Sen. Lectr, 1988–96, UMDS of Guy's and St Thomas' Hosps. Vis. Prof., City Univ., 2007–. Civilian Consultant to RAF, 2006–. Asst Ed., Medico-Legal Jl, 1986–97. President: Sect. of Clin. Forensic and Legal Medicine, RSocMed, 2003–05; British Assoc. in Forensic Medicine, 2004–06. Mem., Criminal Injuries Compensation Appeals Panel, 2000–. Expert Advisor: Bloody Sunday Inquiry, 1998–2002; Operation Paget (inquiry into the death of Diana, Princess of Wales), 2004–08. Presenter, Death Detective (BBC TV series), 2006. *Publications:* (contrib.) A Physician's Guide to Clinical Forensic Medicine, 2000; Simpson's

Forensic Medicine, 12th edn 2003. *Recreation:* flying light aircraft. *Address:* Forensic Pathology Unit, Royal Liverpool Hospital, Liverpool L69 3GA. *Club:* Athenæum.

SHEPHERD, Rt Rev. Ronald Francis; Hon. Assisting Bishop for the Development of Mission in the Borrego Region, Diocese of San Diego, California, 2000; *b* 15 July 1926; *s* of Herbert George Shepherd and Muriel Shepherd (*née* Grant); *m* 1952, Ann Alayne Dundas, *d* of Rt Hon. R. S. Dundas; four *s* two *d*. *Educ:* Univ. of British Columbia (BA Hons 1948); King's Coll., London (AKC 1952). Fellow, Coll. of Preachers, Washington, DC, 1972. Curate, St Stephen's, Rochester Row, London SW, 1952–57; Rector: St Paul's, Glanford, Ont, 1957–59; All Saints, Winnipeg, 1959–65; Dean and Rector: All Saints Cathedral, Edmonton, 1965–69; Christ Church Cathedral, Montreal, 1970–83; Rector, St Matthias, Victoria, 1983–84; Bishop of British Columbia, 1985–92. Hon. DDiv. St John's Coll., Winnipeg, 1988. *Recreations:* reading, gardening, walking. *Address:* Easter Hill, 110 Ensilwood, Salt Spring Island, BC V8K 1N1, Canada. *T:* (604) 5371399.

SHEPHERD-BARRON, John Adrian, OBE 2005; Chairman, Ross and Cromarty Enterprise, 1990–95; *b* 23 June 1925; *s* of Wilfrid and Dorothy Shepherd-Barron; *m* 1953, (Jane Patricia) Caroline Murray; three *s*. *Educ:* Stowe Sch.; Trinity Coll., Cambridge. Served War, 159 Parachute Light Regt, 6th Airborne Div. and 2nd Indian Airborne Div. (Captain). Mgt trainee, De La Rue, 1950; set up original op. in USA, 1957–59; Chm., Security Express, 1963 (took co. into Courier Express, Britain's first overnight parcels co.); Man. Dir, De La Rue Instruments, 1964, led team that invented the cash-dispenser (Automated Teller Machine); Dir N America, De La Rue, 1979–85, retired. *Recreations:* shooting, fishing. *Address:* Mains of Geanies, Portmahomack, Ross-shire IV20 1TW. *T:* and *Fax:* (01862) 871443; *e-mail:* geaniesmains@hotmail.uk. *Clubs:* Sloane; All England Lawn Tennis.

See also N. I. Shepherd-Barron.

SHEPHERD-BARRON, Prof. Nicholas Ian, PhD; FRS 2006; Professor of Algebraic Geometry, University of Cambridge, since 2000; Fellow, Trinity College, Cambridge, since 1990; *b* 17 March 1955; *s* of John Adrian Shepherd-Barron, *qv*; *m* 1988, Michelle Stern; one *d*. *Educ:* Winchester; Jesus Coll., Cambridge (BA 1976); Warwick Univ. (PhD 1981). Asst Prof., Columbia Univ., NY, 1982–86; Asst, then Associate, Prof., Univ. of Illinois, Chicago, 1986–93; University of Cambridge: Lectr, 1990–97; Reader, 1997–2000. *Publications:* papers in mathematical jls. *Recreation:* learning the piano. *Address:* Department of Pure Mathematics and Mathematical Statistics, University of Cambridge, CB3 0WB. *T:* (01223) 337925, *Fax:* (01223) 337920; *e-mail:* nisb@dpmms.cam.ac.uk.

SHEPHERDSON, Prof. John Cedric, ScD; FBA 1990; FIMA; H. O. Wills Professor of Mathematics, Bristol University, 1977–91, now Emeritus; *b* 7 June 1926; *s* of Arnold Shepherdson and Elsie (*née* Aspinall); *m* 1957, Margaret Smith; one *s* two *d*. *Educ:* Manchester Grammar Sch.; Trinity Coll., Cambridge (BA, MA, ScD). Asst Experimental Officer, Aerodynamics and Maths Div., NPL, 1946; Bristol University: Asst Lectr in Maths, 1946–49; Lectr, 1949–55; Reader, 1955–63; Prof. of Pure Maths, 1964–77. Mem., Inst. for Advanced Study, Princeton, 1953–54; Vis. Associate Prof., 1958–59, Vis. Prof., 1966–67, Univ. of Calif at Berkeley; Vis. Prof., Monash Univ., 1971, 1986, 1991, 1992, 1994, 1996; Vis. Scientist, IBM Res. Labs, Yorktown Heights, NY, 1973, 1975, 1979; Guest, Technische Hochschule, Zürich, 1988. *Publications:* papers in mathematical, logical and computer sci. jls. *Recreations:* walking, ski-ing, cycling. *Address:* Oakhurst, North Road, Leigh Woods, Bristol BS8 3PN. *T:* (0117) 973 5410; *e-mail:* john.shepherdson@bris.ac.uk. *Clubs:* Fell & Rock Climbing (Lake District); Bristol Corinthian Yacht.

SHEPLEY, Christopher John, CBE 2002; Principal, Chris Shepley Planning Consultancy; *b* 27 Dec. 1944; *s* of George Frederick Shepley and Florence Mildred Shepley (*née* Jepson); *m* 1st, 1967, Jennifer Webber (marr. diss. 1992); one *s* one *d*; 2nd, 1998, Janet Winifred Molyneux. *Educ:* Stockport Grammar Sch.; LSE (BA Hons Geography); Univ. of Manchester (DipTP). MRTPI. Manchester City Council, 1966–73; Greater Manchester County Council, 1973–85 (Dep. County Planning Officer, 1984–85); Plymouth City Council: City Planning Officer, 1985–92; Dir of Develt, 1992–94; Chief Planning Inspector and Chief Exec., Planning Inspectorate Agency, DoE, then DETR, then DTLR, then ODPM and Welsh Office, then Nat. Assembly for Wales, 1994–2002. Mem., Architecture Adv. Gp, Arts Council England (formerly Arts Council of England), 1992–2003. Chm., Bath Festivals Trust, 2003–06. Pres., RTPI, 1989. Honorary Visiting Professor: Univ. of Manchester Dept of Planning and Landscape, 1990–94; Univ. of Westminster, 2007–. FRSA. Hon. DSc West of England, 2001. *Publications:* The Grotton Papers, 1979; (contrib.) Plymouth: a maritime city in transition, 1990; articles in planning and local govt jls. *Recreations:* music, watching sport, travel, walking. *Address:* Greenleas, Perrymead, Bath BA2 5AX. *T:* (01225) 834499.

SHEPPARD OF DIDGEMERE, Baron *cr* 1994 (Life Peer), of Roydon in the County of Essex; **Allen John George Sheppard,** KCVO 1998; Kt 1990; Chairman, Grand Metropolitan plc, 1987–96 (Chief Executive, 1986–93); *b* 25 Dec. 1932; *s* of John Baggott Sheppard and Lily Marjorie Sheppard (*née* Palmer); *m* 1st, 1959, Peggy Damaris (*née* Jones) (marr. diss. 1980); 2nd, 1980, Mary (*née* Stewart). *Educ:* Ilford County School; London School of Economics (BSc Econ). FCMA, FCIS, ATII. Ford of Britain and Ford of Europe, 1958–68; Rootes/Chrysler, 1968–71; British Leyland, 1971–75; Grand Metropolitan, 1975–96. Non-exec. Dir, later Chm., UBM Group, 1981–85; Chm., Mallinson-Denny Group, 1985–87. Chairman: McBride Ltd, 1993–2007; Group Trust (formerly Group Development Capital Trust) PLC, 1994–2001; Unipart, 1996–; GB Railways, 1996–2004; OneClickHR PLC (formerly Visual Business Tools), 1999–; Namibian Resources Ltd, 2004–; Deputy Chairman: Meyer Internat., 1992–94 (non-exec. Dir, 1989–94); Brightreasons Group PLC, 1994–96; part time Mem., BR Board, 1985–90; Director: Bowater, 1993–94; High-Point Rendel Gp plc, 1997–2003; Gladstone PLC, 1999–2001; Nyne (formerly Zolon) plc, 1999–2007; Transware plc, 2001–03. Chm., Adv. Bd, British American Chamber of Commerce, 1991–94; Vice-Pres., BITC (Dep. Chm., 1989–94; Chm., 1994–97); Dep. Chm., Internat. Business Leaders Forum, 1990–95; Member: Nat. Trng Task Force, 1989–92; NEDC, 1990–92. Chairman: Bd of Trustees, Prince's Youth Business Trust, 1990–94; Prince's Trust Council, 1995–98; Mem. Exec. Cttee, Animal Health Trust. Pres., London First, 2002– (Chm., 1992–2002); Co-Chair, London Pride Partnership, 1994–99; Dir, London Develt Partnership, 1997–2000. Vice-President: Blue Cross; United Response; Brewers & Licensed Retailers' Assoc. Mem., Bd of Management, Conservative Party, 1993–98. Governor, LSE, 1989–; Chancellor, Middlesex Univ., 2000–. CCMI (CBIM 1982; Gold Medal, 1994); FRSA. Hon. FCGI 1993; Hon. Fellow, London Business Sch., 1993. Hon. Dr: Internat. Management Centre, 1989; South Bank Univ., 1994; Brunel, 1994; East London, 1997; Westminster, 1998; Middlesex, 1999; LSE, 2001. *Publications:* Your Business Matters, 1958; Maximum Leadership, 1995; articles in professional jls. *Recreations:* gardens, reading, red setter dogs. *Address:* House of Lords, SW1A 0PW.

SHEPPARD, Andy; jazz saxophonist and composer; *b* 20 Jan. 1957; *s* of Philip Charles Sheppard and Irene Sheppard (*née* Rhymes); *m* Rebecca Sian, *d* of Rod Allerton; one *s* one *d*. *Educ:* Bishop Wordsworth Grammar Sch. Performances with bands incl. Urban Sax, In Co Motion, Big Co Motion, Inclassificables, Moving Image (tours of UK, Europe, world). Composer for TV, film, theatre and dance. Recordings incl. Introductions in the Dark, Soft on the Inside, In Co Motion, Rhythm Method, Inclassifiables, Songs with Legs, Moving Image, Delivery Suite, Learning to Wave, Nocturnal Tourist, Music for a New Crossing, PS. *Address:* c/o Serious Ltd, 51 Kingsway Place, Sans Walk, EC1R 0LU.

SHEPPARD, Francis Henry Wollaston; General Editor, Survey of London, 1954–82, retired; *b* 10 Sept. 1921; *s* of late Leslie Alfred Sheppard; *m* 1st, 1949, Pamela Gordon Davies (*d* 1954); one *s* one *d*; 2nd, 1957, Elizabeth Fleur Lees; one *d*. *Educ:* Bradfield; King's Coll., Cambridge (MA); PhD London. FRHistS. Asst Archivist, West Sussex CC, Chichester, 1947–48; Asst Keeper, London Museum, 1948–53. Mayor of Henley on Thames, 1970–71; Pres., Henley Symphony Orchestra, 1973–76. Visiting Fellow, Leicester Univ., 1977–78; Alice Davis Hitchcock Medallion of Soc. of Architectural Historians of Gt Britain, 1964. *Publications:* Local Government in St Marylebone 1688–1835, 1958; London 1808–1870: The Infernal Wen, 1971; Brakspear's Brewery, Henley on Thames, 1779–1979, 1979; The Treasury of London's Past, 1991; London: a history, 1998; (ed) Survey of London, Vols XXVI–XLI, 1956–83. *Address:* 10 Albion Place, West Street, Henley on Thames, Oxon RG9 2DT. *T:* (01491) 574658.

SHEPPARD, Maurice Raymond, RWS; painter; President, Royal Society of Painters in Water-Colours, 1984–87; *b* 25 Feb. 1947; *s* of late Wilfred Ernest Sheppard and of Florence Hilda (*née* Morris). *Educ:* Loughborough; Kingston upon Thames (Dip AD Hons 1970); Royal College of Art (MA 1973). ARWS 1974, RWS 1977, Vice-Pres., 1978–83, Trustee, 1983–95, Hon. Retired Mem., 2002; NEAC 2000. One man exhibitions: New Grafton Gallery, 1979; Christopher Wood Gall., 1989; inaugural exhibn of L'Institut Europ. de l'Aquarelle, Brussels, 1986; Casgliad Maurice Sheppard Collection, Nat. Library of Wales, 2007; works in: Royal Library, Windsor; BM; Contemporary Art Soc. for Wales; V&A; Nat. Museum of Wales; Beecroft Museum and Art Gallery, Southend; Birmingham City Mus. and Art Gallery; Glynn Vivian Mus., Swansea; Nat. Library of Wales; Tullie House, Carlisle; Topsham Mus., Devon; watercolour: The Golden Valley (for film, Shadowlands, 1993). British Instn Award, 1971; David Murray Landscape Award, 1972; Geoffrey Crawshay Meml Travelling Schol., Univ. of Wales, 1973. *Publications:* articles and essays in jls and catalogues; *relevant publication:* Maurice Sheppard, RWS, by Felicity Owen (Old Watercolour Society Club, vol. 59, 1984). *Recreations:* cycling, a small garden, the pursuit of quiet. *Address:* 33 St Martins Park, Haverfordwest, Pembrokeshire SA61 2HP. *T:* (01437) 762659.

SHEPPARD, Prof. Michael Charles, PhD; FRCP; William Withering Professor of Medicine, since 2000 (Professor of Medicine, since 1986), and Pro-Vice-Chancellor, since 2008, University of Birmingham; *b* 24 Jan. 1947; *s* of Kenneth Alfred and Eileen Maude Sheppard; *m* 1973, Judith Elaine James; two *s* one *d*. *Educ:* Univ. of Cape Town (MB, ChB; PhD 1979). MRCP 1974, FRCP 1985. University of Birmingham: Wellcome Trust Sen. Lectr, Dept of Medicine, 1982–86; Hd, Dept of Medicine, 1992; Vice Dean, 2000–07, Dean and Hd, 2007, Med. Sch.; Hon. Consultant Physician, Queen Elizabeth Hosp., Birmingham, 1982–. Founder FMedSci, 1998; Sir Arthur Sims RCS Commonwealth Travelling Professor, 1999. *Publications:* numerous contribs to learned jls and works on clinical and experimental endocrinology. *Recreations:* coastal walking, sport, glass and porcelain collecting. *Address:* University of Birmingham, Edgbaston, Birmingham B15 2TT. *T:* (0121) 414 5938. *Club:* Edgbaston Priory (Birmingham).

SHEPPARD, Prof. Norman, FRS 1967; Professor of Chemical Sciences, University of East Anglia, Norwich, 1964–86, now Emeritus; *b* 16 May 1921; *s* of Walter Sheppard and Anne Clarges Sheppard (*née* Finding); *m* 1949, Kathleen Margery McLean (*d* 2005); two *s* one *d* (and one *s* decd). *Educ:* Hymers Coll., Hull; St Catharine's Coll., Cambridge. BA Cantab 1st cl. hons 1943; PhD and MA Cantab 1947. Vis. Asst Prof., Pennsylvania State Univ., 1947–48; Ramsay Memorial Fellow, 1948–49; Senior 1851 Exhibn, 1949–51; Fellow of Trinity Coll., Cambridge and Asst Dir of Research in Spectroscopy, Cambridge Univ., 1955–64. *Publications:* scientific papers on spectroscopy and surface chemistry in Proc. Roy. Soc., Faraday Trans., Jl Chem. Soc., Spectrochimica Acta, etc. *Recreations:* architecture, classical music, philosophy of science, walking. *Address:* 5 Hornor Close, Norwich NR2 2LY. *T:* (01603) 453052; *e-mail:* kandnsheppard@dsl.pipex.com.

SHEPPARD, Maj.-Gen. Peter John, CB 1995; CBE 1991 (OBE 1982); Controller (Chief Executive), Soldiers, Sailors, Airmen and Families Association—Forces Help, 1996–2004; *b* 15 Aug. 1942; *s* of Kenneth Wescombe Sheppard and Margaret Sheppard; *m* 1964, Sheila Elizabeth Bell; one *s* one *d*. *Educ:* Welbeck Coll.; RMA Sandhurst; RMCS (BScEng 1st Class Hons London Univ.). Commnd Royal Engineers, 1962; Staff Coll., 1974 (psc); British Embassy, Washington, 1975; OC 29 Field Sqn, 1977 (despatches 1978); GSO1 Mil. Ops, MoD, 1980; CO 35 Engineer Regt, 1982; ACOS, HQ 1st (BR) Corps, 1984; Comdr Corps RE, 1st (BR) Corps, 1986; Dir, Army Plans and Programmes, MoD, 1989; COS HQ BAOR, 1991; Dir Gen. Logistic Policy (Army), MoD, 1993; COS HQ QMG, 1994. Special Advr, H of C Defence Select Cttee, 1997–2001. Dir, Army Charitable Adv. Co., 2004–08. Chm., RE Officers Widows Soc., 2000–06. Trustee, Army Benevolent Fund, 2006–. Gov., Royal Sch., Hampstead, 1997–2004 (Chm., Bd of Govs, 1999–2004). *Publications:* contribs to RE Jl, NATO's 16 Nations, Officer mag. *Recreations:* golf, philately, travel. *Address:* c/o Lloyds TSB, 3 Allendale Place, Tynemouth, Tyne and Wear NE30 4RA. *Club:* Army and Navy.

SHEPPERSON, Prof. George Albert, CBE 1989; William Robertson Professor of Commonwealth and American History, University of Edinburgh, 1963–86, now Emeritus; *b* 7 Jan. 1922; *s* of late Albert Edward Shepperson and Bertha Agnes (*née* Jennings); *m* 1952, Joyce Irene (*née* Cooper) (*d* 2006); one *d*. *Educ:* King's Sch., Peterborough; St John's Coll., Cambridge (Schol.; 1st Class Hons: English Tripos, Pt I, 1942; Historical Tripos, Pt II, 1947); 1st Cl. CertEd (Cantab), 1948. Served War, commnd Northamptonshire Regt, seconded to KAR, 1942–46. Edinburgh University: Lectr in Imperial and American History, 1948, Sen. Lectr, 1960, Reader, 1961; Dean of Faculty of Arts, 1974–77. Visiting Professor: Roosevelt and Chicago Univs, 1959; Makerere Coll., Uganda, 1962; Dalhousie Univ., 1968–69; Rhode Is Coll., 1984; Vis. Scholar, W. E. B. DuBois Inst. for Afro-American Res., Harvard Univ., 1986–87; Lectures: Herskovits Meml, Northwestern Univ., 1966 and 1972; Livingstone Centenary, RGS, 1973; Soc. of the Cincinnati, State of Virginia, 1976; Sarah Tryphena Phillips, in Amer. Lit. and Hist., British Acad., 1979; Rhodes Commem., Rhodes Univ., 1981; Alan Graham Meml, Queen's Univ., Belfast, 1992. Chairman: British Assoc. for American Studies, 1971–74; Mungo Park Bicentenary Cttee, 1971; David Livingstone Documentation Project, 1973–89; Commonwealth Inst., Scotland, 1973–89; Mem., Marshall Aid Commemoration Commn, 1976–88. FEIS 1990. DUniv: York, 1987; Edinburgh, 1991; Hon. DLitt Malaŵi, 2002. Jt Editor, Oxford Studies in African Affairs, 1969–85. *Publications:* Independent African: John Chilembwe, 1958, 6th edn 2000; David Livingstone and the Rovuma, 1964; many articles and chapters in learned jls, collaborative vols and encycs. *Recreations:* reading, music. *Address:* 15 Farleigh Fields, Orton Wistow, Peterborough PE2 6YB. *T:* (01733) 238772.

SHER, Sir Antony, KBE 2000; actor, writer; *b* 14 June 1949; *s* of late Emmanuel and Margery Sher; civil partnership 2005, Gregory Doran, *qv*. *Educ:* Sea Point Boys' Junior and

High Schools, Cape Town; Webber-Douglas Acad. of Dramatic Art, London, 1969–71. Repertory seasons at Liverpool Everyman, Nottingham Playhouse and Royal Lyceum, Edinburgh; John, Paul, George, Ringo and Bert; Teeth and Smiles; Goose-Pimples; Torch Song Trilogy, Albery, 1985; National Theatre: True West; The Trial, The Resistible Rise of Arturo Ui, 1991; Uncle Vanya, 1992; Stanley, 1996 (also NY, 1997); Primo, 2004 (also Cape Town, and NY, 2005); Royal Shakespeare Co.: Associate Artist, 1982–; Richard III, Merchant of Venice, Twelfth Night, King Lear, The Revenger's Tragedy, Molière, Tartuffe, Hello and Goodbye, Maydays, Red Noses, Singer, Tamburlaine the Great, Travesties, Cyrano de Bergerac, The Winter's Tale, Macbeth, The Roman Actor, The Malcontent, Othello, (dir) Breakfast with Mugabe; Titus Andronicus, Johannesburg and RNT, 1995; Mahler's Conversion, Aldwych, 2001; (also writer) I.D., Almeida, 2003; Kean, Apollo, 2007; *films:* Shadey, 1986; The Young Poisoner's Handbook, 1995; Alive and Kicking, 1996; Mrs Brown, 1997; Shakespeare in Love, 1999; Churchill the Hollywood Years, 2004; Three and Out, 2008; *television series:* The History Man, 1980; The Jury, 2002; *television films:* The Land of Dreams, 1990; Genghis Cohen, 1994; Macbeth, 2001; Home, 2003; Primo, 2007. Hon. DLitt: Liverpool, 1998; Exeter, 2003; Warwick, 2007. Best Actor Awards: Drama Magazine, 1984; Laurence Olivier, 1985, 1997; Evening Standard, 1985; TMA, 1995; Evening Standard Peter Sellers Film Award, 1998; Best Solo Performance Awards, NY Drama Desk and Outer Critics Circle, 2006. *Publications:* Year of the King, 1985; Middlepost (novel), 1988; Characters (paintings and drawings), 1989; Changing Step (TV filmscript), 1989; The Indoor Boy (novel), 1991; Cheap Lives (novel), 1995; (with Greg Doran) Woza Shakespeare!, 1996; The Feast (novel), 1998; Beside Myself (memoir), 2001; I. D. (stageplay), 2003; Primo (stageplay), 2005; Primo Time, 2005; The Giant (stageplay), 2007. *Address:* c/o Paul Lyon-Maris, Independent Talent Group Ltd, Oxford House, 76 Oxford Street, W1D 1BS. *T:* (020) 7636 6565.

SHER, Samuel Julius, (Jules); QC 1981; a Deputy High Court Judge, since 1990; *b* 22 Oct. 1941; *s* of Philip and Isa Phyllis Sher; *m* 1965, Sandra Maris; one *s* two *d*. *Educ:* Athlone High Sch., Johannesburg; Univ. of the Witwatersrand (BComm, LLB); New Coll., Oxford (BCL). Called to the Bar, Inner Temple, 1968, Bencher, 1988; Hd of Chambers, Wilberforce Chambers, 2006–. *Recreation:* tennis. *Address:* 12 Constable Close, NW11 6TY. *T:* (020) 8455 2753.

See also V. H. Sher.

SHER, Victor Herman, (Harold), CA (SA); Chief Executive, Amalgamated Metal Corporation Plc, since 1992 (Group Managing Director, 1988–92); *b* 13 Jan. 1947; *s* of Philip Sher and Isa Phyllis Sher; *m* 1979, Molly Sher; one *s* three *d*. *Educ:* King Edward VII Sch., Johannesburg; Univ. of the Witwatersrand, Johannesburg (BComm). Chartered Accountant, Fuller, Jenks Beechcroft, 1972–73; Amalgamated Metal Corporation: Taxation Manager, 1973; Finance Manager, 1977; Dir of Corporate Finance, 1978; Dir of Corporate Treasury, 1981; Finance Dir, 1983; Finance and Trading Dir, 1986. Chm. of Trustees, Amalgamated Metal Corp. Pension Scheme, 1983–91 (Trustee, 1978). *Recreation:* tennis.

See also S. J. Sher.

SHERATON, Kenneth Frederick; a District Judge (Magistrates' Courts) for Cambridgeshire, since 2006; *b* 23 July 1955; *s* of Antony and Marian G. Sheraton; *m* 2003, Jayne Claire, *d* of Peter and Audrey Bustin; one *s* one *d* from a previous marriage. *Educ:* Kingsbury County Grammar Sch.; Bristol Poly. (Dip Magisterial Law 1980); Inns of Court Sch. of Law. Called to the Bar, Gray's Inn, 1983; admitted solicitor, 1991. Magistrates' Court Clerk, then Principal Court Clerk, 1976–90; Solicitor, Messrs Hodders, London, 1990–2000; freelance solicitor, 2000–06. Committee Member: Central and S Middx Law Soc., 1994–96; London Criminal Courts Solicitors Assoc., 2003–06. *Recreations:* most sports, watching Queen's Park Rangers Football Club, travel, sunbathing, walking. *Address:* c/o Peterborough Magistrates' Court, The Court House, Bridge Street, Peterborough PE1 1ED. *T:* 0845 310 0575, *Fax:* (01733) 313749; *e-mail:* kensheraton@aol.com. *Club:* St James's.

SHERBOK, Dan. C.; *see* Cohn-Sherbok.

SHERBORNE, Area Bishop of; *no new appointment at time of going to press.*

SHERBORNE, Archdeacon of; *see* Taylor, Ven. P. S.

SHERBORNE, Montague; QC 1993; *b* 2 Dec. 1930; *s* of Abraham and Rose Sherborne; *m* 1963, Josephine Valerie Jay; two *s* one *d*. *Educ:* East Ham Grammar Sch.; New Coll., Oxford (BA Hons PPE); London Univ. (PGCE). Teaching, E London, 1954–58; called to the Bar, Middle Temple, 1960 (Harmsworth Schol.). *Recreations:* bridge, Chinese food, singing, amateur dramatics.

SHERBOURNE, Sir Stephen (Ashley), Kt 2006; CBE 1988; communications consultant; Chief of Staff to Leader of the Opposition, 2003–05; *b* 15 Oct. 1945; *s* of late Jack and Blanche Sherbourne. *Educ:* Burnage Grammar Sch., Manchester; St Edmund Hall, Oxford (BA PPE). Hill Samuel, 1968–70; Conservative Research Dept, 1970–75: Head of Economic Section, 1973–74; Asst Dir, 1974–75; Head of Rt Hon. Edward Heath's Office, 1975–76; Gallaher, 1978–82; Special Adviser to Rt Hon. Patrick Jenkin, (then) Sec. of State for Industry, 1982–83; Political Sec. to the Prime Minister, 1983–88; Sen. Corporate Communications Consultant, Lowe Bell Communications, 1988–92; Man. Dir, Lowe Bell Consultants, subseq. Bell Pottinger Consultants, 1992–99; Chm., Lowe Bell Political, subseq. Bell Pottinger Public Affairs, 1994–2001; Director: Chime Communications plc, 2001–03; Newscounter; Smithfield Consultants, 2006–. Mem., Policy Adv. Bd, Social Mkt Foundn, 2007–. Trustee, China Oxford Scholarship Fund, 2006–. *Recreations:* cinema, tennis, music. *Club:* Reform.

SHERBROOKE, Archbishop of, (RC), since 1996; **Most Rev. Mgr André Gaumond;** *b* 3 June 1936. *Educ:* Ste Anne de la Pocatière, PQ (BA); St Paul's Seminary, Ottawa (LTh); Institut Catholique, Paris (LPh). Teacher of Philosophy: Ste Anne de la Pocatière, 1966–69; Coll. d'Enseignment Général et Professionel de la Pocatière, 1969–80; Parish Priest, St Pamphile and St Omer, PQ, 1980–85; Bishop of Ste Anne de la Pocatière, 1985–95; Coadjutor Archbishop of Sherbrooke, 1995–96. *Recreation:* golf. *Address:* 130 rue de la Cathédrale, Sherbrooke, QC J1H 4M1, Canada.

SHERCLIFF, Simon, OBE 2004; HM Diplomatic Service; First Secretary, Washington, since 2006; *b* 23 Dec. 1972; *s* of Robin Frank Shercliff and Judith Shercliff; *m* 2002, Emma Louise Cole. *Educ:* High Ham Primary Sch.; Wells Cathedral Sch.; St Catharine's Coll., Cambridge (BA Hons Nat. Scis 1995). Chemistry teacher, VSO, Tanzania, 1995–97; FCO, 1998; Pol Officer, Tehran, 2000–03; Private Sec. to Prime Minister's Special Rep. for Iraq, Baghdad, 2003–04; Press Officer, FCO, 2004–06; Actg Press Sec. for Foreign Sec. and Dir Commns, 2006; Pol Officer, Kabul, 2007–08. Trustee, Orphans in the Wild charity, Tanzania, 2005–. *Recreations:* mountains, cricket, Rugby, Tanzania. *Address:* c/o Foreign and Commonwealth Office, King Charles Street, SW1A 2AH. *T:* (202) 5886527, *Fax:* (202) 5887870; *e-mail:* simon.shercliff@fco.gov.uk. *Clubs:* Hawks' (Cambridge); 1890.

SHERFIELD, 3rd Baron *cr* 1964, of Sherfield-on-Loddon, Southampton; **Dwight Wiliam Makins;** Chairman, Just Ice (UK) Ltd, since 2005; *b* 2 March 1951; *yr s* of 1st Baron Sherfield, GCB, GCMG, FRS and Alice Brooks (*d* 1985), *e d* of Hon. Dwight Davis; *S* brother, 2006; *m* 1983, Penelope Massy Collier (separated). *Educ:* Winchester; Christ Church, Oxford (MA). Man. Dir, John Govett & Co. Ltd, 1984–88; Chairman: Cadiz Inc., 1992–2002; Greenway plc, 1997–99. *Recreation:* National Hunt racing. *Heir:* none. *Club:* Boodle's.

SHERGOLD, Peter Roger, AC 2007 (AM 1996); PhD; Chief Executive, Centre for Social Impact, University of New South Wales, since 2008; *b* 27 Sept. 1946; *s* of Archibald Amos Shergold and Kathleen Dora Shergold; *m* Carol Green; one *d*. *Educ:* Univ. of Hull (BA 1967); Univ. of Illinois (MA 1968); LSE (PhD 1976). Hd, Dept of Econ. Hist., Univ. of NSW, 1985–87; Dir, Office of Multicultural Affairs, 1987–90; Chief Executive Officer: Aboriginal and Torres Strait Islander Commn, 1991–94; Comcare Australia, 1994–95; Comr, Public Service and Merit Protection Commn, 1995–98; Secretary: Dept of Employment, Workplace Relns and Small Business, 1998–2002; Dept of Educn, Sci. and Trng, 2002–03; Dept of the Prime Minister and Cabinet, 2003–08. Sen. Vis. Fellow, Singapore Civil Service Coll. Dir, AMP Ltd. Chm., Australian Rural Leadership Foundn. FASSA 2005. Centenary Medal, Australia, 2003. *Publication:* Working Class Life, 1982. *Recreations:* history, native plant gardening, tennis, cross-country ski-ing. *T:* (2) 9385 9702; *e-mail:* p.shergold@unsw.edu.au. *Club:* Commonwealth.

SHERIDAN, Christopher Julian; Chairman, Yorkshire Building Society, 2001–06 (non-executive Director, 1995–2006); *b* 18 Feb. 1943; *s* of late Mark Sheridan and Olive Maud Sheridan (*née* Hobbs); *m* 1972, Diane Virginia (*née* Wadey); one *d*. *Educ:* Berkhamsted School. Joined Samuel Montagu & Co., 1962; Dir, 1974; Managing Dir, 1981; Chief Exec., 1984–94; Dep. Chm., 1988–94. Mem., Internat. Exec. Cttee, Lovells (formerly Lovell White Durrant), 1996–2006. Non-executive Director: Hanover Acceptances Ltd, 1995–; Prudential Bache International Bank, 1996–2004; Minerva plc, 1996–2008; Willmott Dixon Ltd, 1999–2003; Standard Bank Ltd, 1999–; Alpha Bank London, 2004–; Willmott Dixon Hldgs Ltd, 2008–; Dep. Chm., Inspace plc, 2005–08. *Recreations:* theatre, travel, tennis.

SHERIDAN, Prof. Desmond John, MD, PhD; FRCP; Professor of Clinical Cardiology, Imperial College London Faculty of Medicine (formerly St Mary's Hospital School of Medicine), and Consultant Cardiologist, St Mary's Hospital and The Royal Brompton Hospital, since 1985; *b* 10 Feb. 1948; *s* of Bernard Sheridan and Maureen Sheridan (*née* Kelly); *m* 1971, Jacqueline Hirschfeld; two *s*. *Educ:* Patrician Coll., Ballyfin; Trinity Coll. Dublin (MB, BAO, BCh 1971; MD 1974); Univ. of Newcastle upon Tyne (PhD 1982). MRCP 1974, FRCP 1987. British-American Fellow, Washington Univ., St Louis, 1978–79; Sen. Lectr in Cardiology, Univ. of Wales Coll. of Medicine, 1981–85; Consultant Cardiologist, UCH, Cardiff, 1981–85; Clinical Dean, ICSM, 1998–2001. Member: Nat. Forum for Prevention of Coronary Heart Disease, 1991–98; Physiology, Medicine and Infections Bd, MRC, 1997–2001. Principal Advr, Cardiovascular Science, Global R&D, Pfizer, 2002–05. John Banks Medal and Travelling Fellow, 1974. *Publications:* (contrib.) Early Arrhythmias from Myocardial Ischaemia, 1982; (contrib.) Autonomic Failure, 1988; (contrib.) Clinical Aspects of Cardiac Arrhythmias, 1989; (contrib.) Cerebrovascular Ischaemia: investigation and management, 1996; Left Ventricular Hypertrophy, 1998; Innovation in the Biopharmaceutical Industry, 2007; peer reviewed articles relating to disturbances in heart rhythm and normal and abnormal growth of heart muscle. *Recreations:* country walking, making furniture, letter writing. *Address:* Academic Cardiology Unit, St Mary's Hospital, W2 1NY. *T:* (020) 7886 6129, *Fax:* (020) 7886 6732; *e-mail:* d.sheridan@imperial.ac.uk.

SHERIDAN, James; MP (Lab) Paisley and Renfrewshire North, since 2005 (West Renfrewshire, 2001–05); *b* 24 Nov. 1952; *s* of Frank and Annie Sheridan; *m* 1977, Jean McDowell; one *s* one *d*. *Educ:* St Pius Secondary Sch., Drumchapel, Glasgow. Worked in manufacturing industry since leaving school, 1967; full-time Trade Union Official, TGWU, 1998–99. *Recreations:* leisure activities, current affairs. *Address:* 31 Park Glade, Erskine, Renfrewshire PA8 7HH. *T:* (0141) 561 3892.

SHERIDAN, Prof. Lionel Astor, PhD, LLD; Professor of Law, University College, Cardiff, 1971–88 (Acting Principal, 1980 and 1987); retired; *b* 21 July 1927; *s* of Stanley Frederick and Anne Agnes Sheridan; *m* 1948, Margaret Helen (*née* Béghin); one *s* (one *d* decd). *Educ:* Whitgift Sch., Croydon; University College London (LLB 1947; LLD 1969); Queen's Univ., Belfast (PhD 1953). Called to the Bar, Lincoln's Inn, 1948. Part-time Lectr, Univ. of Nottingham, 1949; Lectr, QUB, 1949–56; Prof. of Law, Univ. of Singapore (formerly Univ. of Malaya in Singapore), 1956–63; Prof. of Comparative Law, QUB, 1963–71. Hon. LLD Univ. of Singapore, 1963. *Publications:* Fraud in Equity, 1957; Constitutional Protection, 1963; Rights in Security, 1974; Injunctions and Similar Orders, 1999; *jointly:* The Cy-près Doctrine, 1959; Constitution of Malaysia, 1961, 5th edn 2004; Malaya, Singapore, The Borneo Territories, 1961; Equity, 1969, 3rd edn 1987; Survey of the Land Law of Northern Ireland, 1971; The Modern Law of Charities, 1971, 4th edn 1992; The Law of Trusts, 10th edn 1974, 12th edn 1993; The Comparative Law of Trusts in the Commonwealth and the Irish Republic, 1976; Digest of the English Law of Trusts, 1979; papers in jls. *Recreations:* reading, theatre-going. *Address:* 9 Warwick House, Westgate Street, Cardiff CF10 1DH. *Club:* Athenæum.

SHERIDAN, Roderick Gerald, OBE 1978; MVO 1968; HM Diplomatic Service, retired; Consul-General, Barcelona and Andorra, 1977–80; *b* 24 Jan. 1921; *s* of late Sir Joseph Sheridan; *m* 1942, Lois Mary (*née* Greene); one *s* one *d*. *Educ:* Downside Sch.; Pembroke Coll., Cambridge. Served War, Coldstream Guards, N Africa and Italy, 1940–46. HM Overseas Colonial Service: Zanzibar and Cyprus, 1946–60; retd as District Comr, Nicosia; HM Diplomatic Service, 1960–80: First Sec., Cyprus, 1960–63; Foreign Office, 1964–66; First Sec., Brasilia, 1966–69; FO, 1969–70; Head of Chancery, Oslo, 1970–73; Consul, Algeciras, 1973–77. Hon. Vice-Consul, Menorca, 1983–93. *Recreations:* tennis, golf, ski-ing.

SHERIDAN, Susan Elizabeth; *see* Norman, S. E.

SHERIDAN, Tommy; Member for Glasgow, Scottish Parliament, 1999–2007 (Scot Socialist, 1999–2006, Solidarity Group, 2006–07); Co-Convenor, Solidarity (Scotland), since 2006; *b* 1964; *m* 2000, Gail; one *d*. *Educ:* Lourdes Secondary Sch., Glasgow; Univ. of Stirling. Former Columnist: Daily Record; Sunday Herald; Scottish Socialist Voice. Mem. (Scot Mil Lab) Glasgow Council, 1992–2007. Nat. Convenor, Scottish Socialist Party, 1999–2004. Contested (Scot Mil Lab) Glasgow Pollok, 1992. Pres., Anti-Poll Tax Fedn, 1989–92. *Publications:* (jtly) A Time to Rage, 1994; (with Alan McCombes) Imagine, 2000. *Address:* 2005 Paisley Road West, Glasgow G52 3TD.

SHERINGHAM, Prof. Michael Hugh Tempest, PhD; Marshal Foch Professor of French Literature, University of Oxford, since 2004; Fellow, All Souls College, Oxford, since 2004; *b* 2 June 1948; *s* of late John Guy Tempest Sheringham and Yvette Agnès (*née* Habib); *m* 1974, Priscilla Monique Duhamel; one *s* one *d*. *Educ:* Univ. of Kent at Canterbury (BA; PhD 1993); MA Oxon 2004. Lectr in French, NUI, 1973–74; University of Kent at Canterbury: Lectr, 1974–87; Sen. Lectr, 1987–92; Prof. of French Lit., 1992–95; Prof. of French, Royal Holloway, Univ. of London, 1995–2004; Associate Dir, Inst. of Romance Studies, Univ. of London, 1999–2003. Visiting Professor: Univ. Paris VII, 1995–96; Univ. Paris IV Sorbonne, 2002; Collège de France, 2006; ENS Ulm, 2007; Pajus Dist. Vis. Prof., Univ. of Calif, Berkeley, 2006. Lectures: Roy Knight Meml, Univ. of Wales, Swansea, 2002; Saintsbury, Univ. of Edinburgh, 2005; Vinaver Meml, Univ. of Manchester, 2006. Gen. Ed., Cambridge Studies in French, 1996–2001. Pres., Soc. for French Studies, 2002–04. Officier, Ordre des palmes académiques (France), 2006 (Chevalier, 1998). *Publications:* André Breton: a bibliography, 1971; Samuel Beckett: Molloy, 1986; French Autobiography: devices and desires, 1993; (ed) Parisian Fields, 1996; (ed with J. Gratton) The Art of the Project, 2005; Everyday Life: theories and practices from Surrealism to the present, 2006; contribs to learned jls and collective works. *Address:* All Souls College, Oxford OX1 4AL. *T:* (01865) 279347; *e-mail:* michael.sheringham@all-souls.ox.ac.uk.

SHERLOCK, Barry; *see* Sherlock, E. B. O.

SHERLOCK, David Christopher, CBE 2006; FCGI; Director, Beyond Standards Ltd, since 2007; *b* 6 Nov. 1943; *s* of Frank Ernest Sherlock and Emily Edna (*née* Johnson); *m* 1st, 1970, Jean Earl; 2nd, 1976, Cynthia Mary (*née* Hood); one *s* one *d*. *Educ:* Rutlish Sch., Merton; Newcastle upon Tyne College of Art and Industrial Design; Univ. of Nottingham (BA, MPhil). Nottingham Coll. of Art, 1966–70; Trent Polytechnic, 1970–74; Dep. Dir, Nat. College of Art and Design, Dublin, 1975–80; Principal, Winchester Sch. of Art, 1980–87; Exec. Chm., Hampshire Consortium for Art, Design and Architecture, 1985–87; Head of Central Saint Martin's Coll. of Art and Design and Asst Rector, London Inst., 1988–91; Dir of Develt, RCA, 1991–93; Sen. Inspector, Art, Design and Performing Arts, and for SE England, FEFCE, 1993–97; Chief Inspector and Chief Exec., Training Standards Council, 1997–2001; Chief Inspector of Adult Learning and Chief Exec., Adult Learning Inspectorate, 2000–07. Mem., QCA (Mem., Audit Cttee). Pres., NIACE, 2007–. FRSA; MInstD. Award for Services to Lifelong Learning, Assoc. of Coll. Mgt, 2007. *Publication:* (with N. Perry) Quality Improvement in Adult Vocational Education and Training: transforming skills for the global economy, 2008. *Recreations:* sailing, mountain biking. *Address:* Poplar Farm, West Tytherley, Salisbury SP5 1NR. *Club:* Royal Southern Yacht (Hamble).

SHERLOCK, (Edward) Barry (Orton), CBE 1991; Chairman, Life Assurance and Unit Trust Regulatory Organisation, 1986–96; *b* 10 Feb. 1932; *s* of Victor Edward and Irene Octavia Sherlock; *m* 1955, Lucy Trerice Willey; two *d*. *Educ:* Merchant Taylors' School; Pembroke College, Cambridge (MA 1st cl. Hons Maths). Joined Equitable Life Assurance Society, 1956; qualified actuary, 1958; Asst Actuary, 1962; Asst Gen. Manager, 1968; Gen. Manager and Actuary, 1972–91; Dir, 1972–94. Director: USS Ltd, 1978–96 (Dep. Chm., 1993–96); M & G Group, 1994–96; Medical Defence Union Ltd, 1994–96. Institute of Actuaries: Hon. Sec., 1978–80; Vice-Pres., 1981–84. Chairman: Life Offices' Assoc., 1985; Life Insurance Council, Assoc. of British Insurers, 1985–86. Trustee, Harvest Help, 1993–96. *Recreations:* music, gardening.

SHERLOCK, Kathryn Jane; *see* Parminter, K. J.

SHERLOCK, Maeve Christina Mary, OBE 2000; Member, Equality and Human Rights Commission, since 2007; Chair, National Student Forum, since 2008; *b* 10 Nov. 1960; *d* of William and Roisin Sherlock. *Educ:* Our Lady's Convent, Abingdon; Univ. of Liverpool (BA Hons Sociol. 1984); Open Univ. (MBA 1997); Durham Univ. (MA 2007). Treas., Univ. of Liverpool Guild, 1984–85; National Union of Students: Exec. Officer, 1985–86; Treas., 1986–88; Pres., 1988–90; Dep. Dir, 1990–91, Dir, 1991–97, UKCOSA; Dir, NCOPF, 1997–2000; Advr to the Chancellor of the Exchequer, 2000–03; Chief Exec., Refugee Council, 2003–06. Member: Adv. Bd on Naturalisation and Integration, 2004–; Nat. Refugee Integration Forum, 2006–. Mem., Bd, Financial Ombudsman Service. Mem., Exec. Bd, Eur. Assoc. for Internat. Educn, 1994–97. Dir, Endsleigh Insce, 1986–90. Member: Court, Univ. of Warwick, 1993–95; Assembly, Greenwich Univ., 1995–97; Gov., Sheffield Hallam Univ., 1997–2000. Trustee: Nat. Family and Parenting Inst., 1999–2000; Demos, 2004–07. Hon. Fellow, St Chad's Coll., Durham. DUniv Sheffield Hallam, 2000. *Recreations:* politics, books, restaurants, films.

SHERLOCK, Nigel, OBE 2003; JP; Lord-Lieutenant, County of Tyne and Wear, since 2000; *b* 12 Jan. 1940; *s* of late Horace Sherlock and Dorothea Sherlock (*née* Robinson); *m* 1966, Helen Diana Frances Sigmund; two *s* one *d*. *Educ:* Barnard Castle Sch.; Univ. of Nottingham (BA Law). Chief Exec., 1993–2002, Chm., 2002–05, Wise Speke; Director: Ockham Hldgs, 1993–98; Brewin Dolphin Holdings plc, 1998–2002; Brewin Dolphin Securities, 1998–2005; non-executive Director: London Stock Exchange, 1995–2001; Skipton Bldg Soc., 1998–2007. Mem. Bd, Assoc. of Private Client Investment Managers and Stockbrokers, 1993–2003 (non-exec. Dep. Chm., 1995–2003). Mem. Council, NE Regl Chamber of Commerce, 1997–2004 (Pres., 2000–01). Member: Council, Nat. Assoc. of Pension Funds, 1988–90; C of E Pension Bd, 1998–. Mem., Bishop's Council, Dio. Newcastle, 1975–94; Hon. Financial Advr to Dean and Chapter of Durham Cathedral, 1997–; Chairman: Council, Newcastle Cathedral, 2002–05 (Hon. Lay Canon, 2007–); Crown Nominations Commn for appt of Archbp of York, 2005. Patron, Northumbrian Coalition Against Crime, 2001– (Vice-Patron, 1995–2001). Founder Mem., Community Foundn of Tyne and Wear, 1988 (Vice-Pres., 2001–). Member: Council, 1984–2002 (Pro Chancellor and Chm., 1993–2002), Court, 2002–, Univ. of Newcastle upon Tyne; Council, St John's Coll., Univ. of Durham, 1984–95 (Hon. Fellow, 1997); Bd of Govs, Royal GS, Newcastle upon Tyne, 1998–2006 (Chm., 2000–05). Member: Bd, N Music Trust, 2000–05 (Chm., Fundraising Cttee, 2000–05); Bd, Northern Sinfonia Orchestral Soc., 1974–95 (Chm., 1990–95); Northern Sinfonia Develt Trust, 1980–2001 (Trustee, 1980–2001; Chm., 1981–2001). Pres., Northumberland Co. Scouts, 2000– (Mem. Council, 1980–98, Chm., 1990–97; Silver Wolf, 2007). Co-Pres., RFCA, N of England, 2001–. Jt Pres., St John Ambulance, Northumbria, 2001–. Trustee: Bede Monastery Mus. Trust, 1980–90 (Chm., 1985–90); William Leech Charity, 1990–. Hon. Brother, Trinity House, Newcastle upon Tyne, 1995–. FSI 1999; CCMI (CIMgt 2000). High Sheriff, 1990–91, DL, 1995–2000, Tyne and Wear. Hon. Colonel: Royal Marines Reserve Tyne, 2003–; Northumbrian Univs OTC, 2003–. Freeman, City of London, 2000; Liveryman, Scriveners' Co., 2000–; Freeman, City of Newcastle, 1985. Hon. DCL: Newcastle, 2002; Northumbria, 2006. KStJ 2002. *Recreations:* family, the countryside, listening to music, theatre. *Address:* 14 North Avenue, Gosforth, Newcastle upon Tyne NE3 4DS. *T:* (0191) 285 4379. *Clubs:* Brooks's; Northern Counties (Newcastle upon Tyne).

SHERMAN, Prof. Lawrence William, PhD; Wolfson Professor of Criminology, University of Cambridge, since 2007; Director, Jerry Lee Center of Criminology, since 2000, and Professor of Criminology, since 2003, University of Pennsylvania; *b* 25 Oct. 1949; *s* of Donald L. and Margaret H. Sherman; *m* 1973, Eva Fass (separated 2005); one *s* one *d*; partner, Heather Strang. *Educ:* Denison Univ. (BA High Hons Political Sci. 1970); Univ. of Chicago (MA Social Sci. 1970); Darwin Coll., Cambridge (Dip. Criminol. 1973); Yale Univ. (PhD Sociol. 1976); Univ. of Pennsylvania (MA Hons 1999). Sloan Foundn Urban Fellow, Office of the Mayor, NYC, 1970–71; Prog. Res. Analyst, NYC Police Dept, 1971–72; Ford Foundn Fellow, Cambridge Univ., 1972–73; Associate-in-Res., Yale Univ., 1974–76; Asst to Associate Prof. of Criminal Justice, SUNY at Albany, 1976–82; University of Maryland, College Park: Associate Prof., 1982–84; Prof., 1984–98; Dist. Univ. Prof., 1998–99; Chair, Dept of Criminol. and Criminal Justice, 1995–99; Albert M. Greenfield Prof. of Human Relns and Prof. of Sociol., 1999–2007, and Chair, Dept of Criminol., 2003–07, Univ. of Pennsylvania. Seth Boyden Dist. Vis. Prof., Rutgers Univ., 1987; Adjunct Prof., Regulatory Institutions Network, ANU, 1994–. Dir of Res., Police Foundn, Washington, 1979–85; Pres., Crime Control Inst., Washington, 1985–95; Scientific Dir, Reintegrative Shaming Experiments, Australian Fed. Police, 1995–2000; Co-Dir, Justice Res. Consortium, UK, 2001–. Founding Pres., Acad. Exptl Criminol., 1998 (Fellow 1999); President: Internat. Soc. of Criminol., 2000–05; Amer. Soc. of Criminol., 2001–02 (Fellow 1994); Amer. Acad. Political and Social Sci., 2001–05. FRSA. *Publications:* Scandal and Reform: controlling police corruption, 1978; Policing Domestic Violence: experiments and dilemmas, 1992; (jtly) Preventing Crime: what works, what doesn't, what's promising, 1997; (ed jtly) Evidence-Based Crime Prevention, 2002; (with Heather Strang) Restorative Justice: the evidence, 2007; contribs to learned jls incl. Amer. Sociol. Rev., Criminology, Jl Amer. Med. Assoc. *Recreation:* walking the coast to coast. *Address:* Institute of Criminology, University of Cambridge, Sidgwick Avenue, Cambridge CB3 9DT. *Club:* Cosmos (Washington).

SHERR, Prof. Avrom Hirsh, PhD; Woolf Professor of Legal Education, since 1995, and Director, since 2004, Institute of Advanced Legal Studies, University of London; *b* 28 March 1949; *s* of Louis Julian Sherr and Charlotte Maissel; *m* 1974, Lorraine Isaacs; three *s* one *d*. *Educ:* Carmel Coll. (Sch. Bursary); London Sch. of Econs (LLB 1971); Sch. of Law, Univ. of Warwick (PhD 1992). Admitted solicitor, 1974; University of Warwick: Lectr in Law, Sch. of Law, 1974–90; Dir, Legal Practice, 1976–90; University of Liverpool: Alsop-Wilkinson Prof. of Law, 1990–95; Dir, Centre for Business and Professional Law, 1991–95. Vis. Professor: Sch. of Law, Univ. of San Francisco, 1981; Sch. of Law, UCLA, 1984–85; Univ. of Essex, 1995–; Penn State Dickinson Sch. of Law, 2004–05; summer schools: Sch. of Law, Univ. of Bridgeport, 1984; New York Law Sch., 1985; Law Sch., Touro Coll., 1987; William Mitchell Law Sch., 1987, 1988; Hon. Prof., UCL, 1995–. Chm., Adv. Bd and Strategy Cttee, UK Centre for Legal Educn, 2007–. Member: Exec. Cttee, Law Centres Fedn, 1979–83; Lord Chancellor's Adv. Cttee on Legal Educn and Conduct, 1995–2000; Exec. Cttee, Soc. of Advanced Legal Studies, 1997–; Consumer Adv. Bd, Legal Services Complaints Comr, 2005–. Law Society of England and Wales: Member: Internat. Human Rights Gp, 1987–90; Trng Contracts Cttee, 1992–94; Equal Opportunities Cttee, 1994–2002; Ethics Forum, 2004. Trustee, Jewish Law Pubn Fund, 1990–. Minister, Coventry Hebrew Congregation, 1976–90; Hon. Minister, Wembley United Synagogue, 1986–87. Chm., Ner Yisrael Community, 2005–07 (Gabay, 2002–05). Founder Ed., Internat. Jl of Legal Profession, 1993–. *Publications:* Client Interviewing for Lawyers: an analysis and guide, 1986, 2nd edn as Client Care for Lawyers: an analysis and guide, 1999; Freedom of Protest, Public Order and the Law, 1989; (jtly) Transaction Criteria: quality assurance standards in legal aid, 1992; (jtly) Lawyers—The Quality Agenda, vol. 1, Assessing and Developing Competence and Quality in Legal Aid: the report of the Birmingham Franchising Pilot, vol. 2, Assessing and Developing Competence and Quality in Legal Aid—Transaction Criteria, 1994; (ed with I. Manley) Advising Clients with AIDS/HIV—A Guide for Lawyers, 1998; (jtly) Quality and Cost, Final Report on the Contracting of Civil, Non-Family Advice and Assistance Pilot, 2001; (jtly) Evaluation of the Public Defender Service in England and Wales, 2007; numerous articles on legal profession, legal ethics, legal services and legal aid in learned jls. *Recreations:* wadi walking in Eilat mountains, tennis, scuba diving. *Address:* Institute of Advanced Legal Studies, Charles Clore House, 17 Russell Square, WC1B 5DR. *T:* (020) 7862 5849, *Fax:* (020) 7862 5850. *Club:* Kiddush.

SHERRARD, Michael David, CBE 2003; QC 1968; Director, Middle Temple Advocacy, 1994–2004, now Emeritus; a Recorder of the Crown Court, 1974–93; *b* 23 June 1928; *er s* of late Morris and Ethel Sherrard; *m* 1952, Shirley (artist), *d* of late Maurice and Lucy Bagrit; two *s*. *Educ:* King's Coll., London. LLB 1949. Called to Bar, Middle Temple, 1949 (Bencher 1977; Treas., 1996); Mem., Inner Temple, 1980; Mem. Senate, 1977–80. Mem., SE Circuit, 1950. Mem., Winn Cttee on Personal Injury Litigation, 1966; Mem. Council, Justice, British Section, Internat. Commn of Jurists, 1974–2000; Dept of Trade Inspector, London Capital Group, 1975–77; Chm., Normansfield Hosp. Inquiry, 1977–78; Comr for trial of local govt election petitions (under Representation of the People Act 1949), 1978–80. Mem., Bar Assoc. of NYC, 1986–94. FRSA 1991. *Recreations:* oriental art, travel, listening to opera. *Address:* 26 Eton Avenue, Hampstead, NW3 3HL. *T:* (020) 7431 0713.

SHERRARD, Simon Patrick; Chairman, Port of London Authority, since 2001 (Member, since 2000); *b* 22 Sept. 1947; *s* of Patrick Sherrard and Angela Beatrice Sherrard (*née* Stacey); *m* 1975, Sara Anne Stancliffe; one *s* three *d*. *Educ:* Eton Coll. Samuel Montagu & Co. Ltd, 1968–74; Jardine Matheson & Co. Ltd, 1974–85; Bibby Line Group Ltd: Man. Dir, 1985–99; Chm., 1999–; Chairman: Abacus Syndicates Ltd, 1999–2002 (Dir, 1997–2002); A & P Group, 2002–; Johnson Service Gp plc, 2004– (Dir, 2000–); Cooke Bros (Tattenhall) Ltd, 2005 (Dir, 1991–2005). Dir and Trustee, Lloyds Register, 2005– (Dep. Chm., 2002–05); Pres., Chamber of Shipping, 2000–01; UK Rep. on Exec. Cttee, Internat. Chamber of Shipping, 1993–2001 (Vice Chm., 1999–2001). Elder Brother, Corp. of Trinity House, 2001–. Mem. Adv. Bd, Liverpool Business Sch., 1996–2001; Member Council: Liverpool Sch. of Tropical Medicine, 1998–2007 (Dep. Chm., 2002–07); Mission to Seafarers, 2000–; White Ensign Assoc., 2004–. Trustee, Royal Liverpool Philharmonic Hall Diamond Jubilee Foundn, 1996–2005. Liveryman, Co. of Shipwrights, 1993–; Freeman, Co. of Watermen and Lightermen, 2002–. High Sheriff, Cheshire, 2004. *Recreations:* golf, tennis, breeding rare sheep. *Address:* Port of London Authority, Bakers' Hall, 7 Harp Lane, EC3R 6LB. *T:* (020) 7743 7924, *Fax:* (020) 7743 9995; *e-mail:* simon.sherrard@pla.co.uk. *Clubs:* Boodle's, MCC.

SHERRATT, Brian Walter, OBE 1995; PhD; JP; Headmaster, Great Barr School, 1984–2005; *b* 28 May 1942; *er s* of Walter Eric Sherratt and Violet Florence Sherratt (*née* Cox-Smith); *m* 1966, (Pauline) Brenda Hargreaves; two *s* two *d*. *Educ:* Univ. of Leeds (BA Hons 1964, PGCE 1965); Inst. of Educn, Univ. of London (AcDipEd 1973, MA 1976); Univ. of Birmingham (PhD 2004). Asst Master, Normanton GS, 1965–67; Hd, Religious Studies Dept, Selby GS, 1967–70; Avery Hill College of Education: Sen. Lectr in Religious Studies and Warden, 1970–73 (Sen. Warden, 1972–73); Warden, Mile End Teachers' Centre, 1971–73; concurrently Asst Master, Kidbrooke Sch., London, 1970–71; Sen. Master, 1973–76, Dep. Headmaster, 1976–79, Sandown Court Sch., Tunbridge Wells; Headmaster and Warden, Kirk Hallam Sch. and Community Centre, Ilkeston, Derbys, 1979–84. Mem. Court, 1986–90, Hon. Lectr, Sch. of Educn, 1988–, Univ. of

Birmingham; Mem., Academic Adv. Council, Univ. of Buckingham, 2005–. Member: Centre for Policy Studies, 1994–; Politeia, 1995–; Civitas, 2000–; Educn Commn, 2003–05. Chairman: Eco-Schs Adv. Panel, 1997–2001; Green Code for Schs Adv. Panel, 1998–2001; non-executive Director: Going for Green, 1994–98 (Mem., Organising Cttee, 1994–96); Envmtl Campaigns, 1998–2005 (Trustee, Pension Fund, 1999–2005; Mem., Resources Cttee, 2002–03, Audit Cttee, 2003–05; Vice-Chm., 2003–05; Chm., Devolution Cttee, 2004–05). Dir, Nottingham Park Estate Ltd, 2005–. Mem., Magistrates' Assoc., 2006–; Magistrate Trng Observer, Nottingham Bench, 2008–. FCMI (FIMgt 1984); FRSA 1984. Freeman, Guild of Educators, 2003–. JP Notts, 2006. Queen Mother's Birthday Award for the Envmt, 1999; Best Thesis Award, British Educnl Leadership Mgt and Admin Soc., 2005; George Cadbury Prize in Educn, 2005. *Publications:* Gods and Men: a survey of world religions, 1971; Local Education Authorities Project, 1988; Opting for Freedom: a stronger policy on grant-maintained schools, 1994; Grant-Maintained Status: considering the options, 1994; (jtly) A Structured Approach to School and Staff Development: from theory to practice, 1996; (jtly) Headteacher Appraisal, 1997; (jtly) Radical Educational Policies and Conservative Secretaries of State, 1997; (jtly) Policy, Leadership and Professional Knowledge in Education, 1999; contrib. to TES, etc. *Recreations:* opera, buildings, reading, antiques. *Address:* Oakhurst, 17 Lenton Road, The Park, Nottingham NG7 1DQ; *e-mail:* brian.sherratt@ntlworld.com. *Club:* Athenaeum.

SHERRATT, Prof. David John, PhD; FRS 1992; FRSE; Iveagh Professor of Microbiology, since 1994, and Head of Microbiology Unit, University of Oxford; Fellow, Linacre College, Oxford, since 1994; *b* 14 June 1945; *m* 1st, 1968, Susan Bates (marr. diss. 1992); one *s* two *d*; 2nd, 1992, Dr Lidia Kamilla Arciszewska; one *d*. *Educ:* Manchester Univ. (BSc 1st Cl. Biochem. 1966); Edinburgh Univ. (PhD Molecular Biol. 1969). FRSE 1984. Post-doctoral Fellow, Univ. of California, 1969–71; Lectr in Microbial Genetics, Univ. of Sussex, 1971–80; Prof. of Genetics, Inst. of Genetics, Glasgow Univ., 1980–93. Mem., EMBO, 1983. *Publications:* scientific papers and reviews; editor of several jls. *Recreations:* variety of outdoor pursuits. *Address:* Linacre College, Oxford OX1 3JA.

SHERRINGTON, Prof. David, PhD; FRS 1994; FInstP; Wykeham Professor of Physics, University of Oxford, 1989–08; Fellow, New College, Oxford, 1989–2008, now Emeritus (Sub-Warden, 2006–07); *b* 29 Oct. 1941; *s* of James Arthur Sherrington and Elfreda (*née* Cameron); *m* 1966, Margaret Gee-Clough; one *s* one *d*. *Educ:* St Mary's Coll.; Univ. of Manchester (BSc 1st Cl. Hons Physics, 1962; PhD Theoretical Physics, 1966). FInstP 1974. Asst Lectr in Theoretical Physics, 1964–67, Lectr, 1967–69, Univ. of Manchester; Asst Res. Physicist, UCSD, 1967–69, Lectr in Theor. Solid State Phys, 1969–74, Reader in Theor. Solid State Phys, 1974–83, Prof. of Phys, 1983–89, Imperial Coll., Univ. of London; Cadre Supérieur, Inst Laue Langevin, Grenoble, France, 1977–79; Ulam Scholar, Los Alamos Nat. Lab., USA, 1995–96. Bakerian Lect., Royal Soc., 2001. Delegate, OUP, 2001–06. Fellow, Amer. Physical Soc., 1985. Editor, Advances in Physics, 1984–; Hon. Editor, Jl of Physics A: Mathematical and General, 1989–93. Hon. MA Oxford, 1989. Dirac Medal and Prize, Inst. of Physics, 2007. *Publications:* (ed jtly) Phase Transitions in Soft Condensed Matter, 1990; (ed jtly) Spontaneous Formation of Space-Time Structures and Criticality, 1991; (ed jtly) Phase Transitions and Relaxation in Systems with Competing Energy Scales, 1993; (ed jtly) Physics of Biomaterials: fluctuations, self-assembly and evolution, 1995; (ed jtly) Dynamical properties of unconventional magnetic systems, 1998; (ed jtly) Stealing the Gold, 2004; papers in learned jls. *Recreations:* wine tasting, travel, theatre, walking, ski-ing. *Address:* c/o Rudolf Peierls Centre for Theoretical Physics, 1 Keble Road, Oxford OX1 3NP.

SHERRINGTON, Air Vice-Marshal Terence Brian, CB 1997; OBE 1984; Director Welfare, RAF Benevolent Fund, 1998–2006; *b* 30 Sept. 1942; *s* of Thomas and Edna Sherrington; *m* 1969, Anne Everall; one *s* one *d*. *Educ:* Ottershaw Sch.; Westminster Technical Coll. Commnd RAF, 1963; served Aden, Sharjah, Germany and UK, 1963–78; RAF Staff College, 1979; MoD, 1980–81; OC Admin Wing, RAF Leuchars, 1981–83; OC, RAF Hereford, 1983–85; RCDS, 1986; Sen. Officer Admin, HQ 11 Gp, 1987–88; Dir of Personnel (Ground), MoD, 1988–91; AOA and AOC Support Units, RAF Support Comnd, 1992–93; Head, RAF Admin. Br., 1992–97; AO Admin and AOC Directly Administered Units, Strike Comd, 1994–97. Mem. Council, Wycombe Abbey Sch., 1998–; Gov., Duke of Kent Sch., 2003–08. Freeman, City of London, 2002; Liveryman, Tallow Chandlers' Co., 2002. *Recreations:* fishing, golf, Rugby. *Address:* c/o Lloyds TSB, Shipston-on-Stour, Warwicks CV36 4AJ. *Club:* Royal Air Force.

SHERRY, Prof. Norman, FRSL; writer; Mitchell Distinguished Professor of Literature, Trinity University, San Antonio, Texas, since 1983; *b* 6 July 1935; *m* 1st, 1960, Sylvia Brunt (marr. diss. 1990); 2nd, 1990, Carmen Flores (marr. diss. 1996); one *s* one *d*. *Educ:* Univ. of Durham (BA Eng Lit); Univ. of Singapore (PhD). FRSL 1986. Lectr, Univ. of Singapore, 1961–66; Lectr and Sen. Lectr, Univ. of Liverpool, 1966–70; Prof. of English, 1970–83, Hd, Dept of English, 1980–83, Univ. of Lancaster. Exchange Prof., Univ. of Texas, Austin, 1977–78; Vis. Prof., Univ. of Sierra Leone, 1980; Vis. Res. Fellow, Merton Coll., Oxford, 1996. Hon. Res. Fellow, UCL, 1973; Fellow, Humanities Research Center, N Carolina, 1982; Guggenheim Fellow, 1989–90. Mem., Academic Adv. Council, Univ. of Buckingham, 1976–. Pres., Conrad Soc. of GB, 1972–74. UK Ed., Conradiana, 1970–72. *Publications:* Conrad's Eastern World, 1966, 2005; The Novels of Jane Austen, 1966; Charlotte and Emily Bronte, 1969; Conrad's Western World, 1971, 2005; Conrad and his World, 1972; (ed) Conrad: the Critical Heritage, 1973; (ed) An Outpost of Progress and Heart of Darkness, 1973; (ed) Lord Jim, 1974; (ed) Nostromo, 1974; (ed) The Secret Agent, 1974; (ed) The Nigger of Narcissus, Typhoon, Falk and Other Stories, 1975; (ed) Joseph Conrad: a commemoration, 1976; The Life of Graham Greene, vol. I, 1904–1939, 1989, vol. II, 1939–1955, 1994, vol. III, 1955–1991, 2004 (Edgar Allan Poe Award, Britannica Book of the Year, 1990); contribs to Review of English Studies, Notes & Queries, Modern Language Review, TLS, Observer, The Daily Telegraph, The Guardian, Oxford Magazine, Academic American Encyclopedia. *Recreations:* reading, writing, jogging, body building. *Address:* Trinity University, One Trinity Place, San Antonio, TX 78212, USA. *Club:* Savile.

SHERSTON-BAKER, Sir Robert (George Humphrey), 7th Bt *cr* 1796, of Dunstable House, Richmond, Surrey; *b* 3 April 1951; *o s* of Sir Humphrey Sherston-Baker, 6th Bt and Margaret Alice (*m* 2nd, Sir Ronald Leach, GBE; she *d* 1994), *o d* of Henry William Binns; *S* father, 1990; *m* 1991, Vanessa, *y d* of C. E. A. Baird; one *s* one *d*. *Heir:* *s* David Arbuthnot George Sherston-Baker; *b* 24 Nov. 1992.

SHERVAL, Rear-Adm. David Robert, CB 1989; CEng; FIMechE; FIMarEST; Chief Surveyor and Deputy General Manager, The Salvage Association, 1990–98; *b* 4 July 1933; *s* of William Robert Sherval (HMS Hood, 1941), and Florence Margaret Sherval (*née* Luke); *m* 1961, Patricia Ann Phillips; one *s* one *d*. *Educ:* Portsmouth Southern Grammar School. Artificer Apprentice, 1950; BRNC Dartmouth, 1951; Training: at sea, HM Ships Devonshire, Forth and Glasgow, 1951–52 and 1955; RNEC, 1952–54, 1956; served: HM Ships Eagle, Tiger, Hampshire, HM Dockyard Gibraltar and HMY Britannia, 1957–68; BRNC, 1968–70; HMS Juno, 1970–72; NDC, 1972–73; Naval Plans, MoD, 1973–75; Staff of FO Sea Training, 1975–76; Naval Op. Requirements, MoD, 1976–77; NATO Defence Coll., Rome, 1979; ACOS (Intell.) to SACLANT, 1979–82; Fleet Marine Engineer Officer, 1982–84; Dir, Naval Logistic Planning, 1984–85; ADC to the Queen, 1985; CSO (Engrg) to C-in-C Fleet, 1985–87; Dir Gen. Ship Refitting, 1987–89. *Recreation:* music.

SHERWIN, Glynn George; Chairman and non-executive Director, Sheffield International Venues Ltd, since 2005; Head of Corporate Finance, Sheffield City Council, 1998–2001; *b* 27 Feb. 1948; *s* of George Sherwin and Lilian Sherwin (*née* Billingham); *m* 1969, Janet Heather Broomhead Ferguson; one *s* two *d*. *Educ:* Firth Park Grammar Sch., Sheffield; Chesterfield Coll. of Technol. CPFA (Hons Final) 1971. Various posts, Sheffield CBC, 1966–74; Sheffield City Council: Principal Accountant, 1974–79; Chief Develt Officer, 1979–88; Asst City Treas., 1988–94; Dep. City Treas., 1994–98. Project Examr, 1978–83, Sen. Project Examr, 1983–86, Chartered Inst. Public Finance and Accountancy. Non-executive Director: MFH Engrg (Hldgs) Ltd, 2006–; Quoit Assets Ltd, 2006–; Donnagate Ltd, 2006–. Mem., Bd of Govs, Sheffield City Trust Ltd, 2003–. *Recreations:* keep fit, reading, cinema, theatre.

SHERWIN, Sarah Jane; *see* Asplin, S. J.

SHERWOOD, Bishop Suffragan of, since 2006; **Rt Rev. Anthony Porter;** *b* 10 Feb. 1952; *s* of Sydney and Valerie Porter; *m* 1974, Lucille Joyce Roberts; two *s* two *d*. *Educ:* Don Valley High Sch.; Gravesend Sch. for Boys; Hertford Coll., Oxford (BA English 1974, MA); Ridley Hall, Cambridge (BA Theol. 1977). Ordained deacon, 1977, priest, 1978; Curate: Edgware, 1977–80; St Mary, Haughton, 1980–83; Priest-in-charge, Christ Ch, Bacup, 1983–87; Vicar, 1987–91, Rector, 1991–2006, Holy Trinity, Rusholme. *Publications:* Chips, 1979; Super Jack, 1983; Mission Countdown, 1986; Prince of Thieves, 2006. *Recreation:* sport. *Address:* Dunham House, Westgate, Southwell, Notts NG25 0JL. *T:* (01636) 819133, *Fax:* (01636) 819085; *e-mail:* bishopsherwood@southwell.anglican.org.

SHERWOOD, Antony; *see* Sherwood, R. A. F.

SHERWOOD, Dennis Henry, PhD; Managing Director, Silver Bullet Machine Manufacturing Company Ltd, since 1999; *b* 28 April 1949; *s* of Harry Sherwood and Pearl Sherwood (*née* Karp); *m* 1972, Anny Kirkegaard Jensen; two *s*. *Educ:* Westcliff High Sch. for Boys; Clare Coll., Cambridge (BA 1970, MA 1974); Yale Univ. (MPhil 1972); UCSD (PhD 1974); London Business Sch. (Sloan Fellow with Dist. 1988). Consultant and Manager, Deloitte Haskins & Sells, 1975–81; Consulting Partner: Deloitte Haskins & Sells, 1981–89; Coopers & Lybrand, 1989–93; Exec. Dir, Goldman Sachs, 1993–95; Partner, Bossard Consultants, 1995–97; Man. Dir, SRI Consulting, 1997–99. Non-exec. Dir, NHS Inst. for Innovation and Improvement, 2005–06. Vis. Prof. of Systems Theory, Modelling and Innovation, South Bank Univ., London, 2004–. Mem. RSA. *Publications:* Introductory Chemical Thermodynamics, 1971; Crystals, X-Rays and Proteins, 1976; Financial Modelling: a practical guide, 1983; Unlock Your Mind, 1998; Smart Things to Know About Innovation and Creativity, 2001; Seeing the Forest for the Trees: a manager's guide to applying systems thinking, 2002. *Recreations:* music, reading. *Address:* Silver Bullet Machine Manufacturing Company Ltd, Barnsdale Grange, The Avenue, Exton, Rutland LE15 8AH. *T:* (01572) 813690; *e-mail:* dennis@silverbulletmachine.com. *Club:* Oxford and Cambridge.

SHERWOOD, James Blair; Founder and President, Sea Containers Group, Bermuda and London, 1965–2005; Founder, and Director, since 2007, Orient-Express Hotels (Chairman, 1987–2007); *b* 8 Aug. 1933; *s* of William Earl Sherwood and Florence Balph Sherwood; *m* 1977, Shirley Angela Masser Cross; two step *s*. *Educ:* Yale Univ. (BA Economics 1955). Lieut US Naval Reserve, Far East service, afloat and ashore, 1955–58. Manager, French Ports, later Asst General Freight Traffic Manager, United States Lines Co., Le Havre and NY, 1959–62; Gen. Manager, Container Transport Internat. Inc., NY and Paris, 1963–64. In partnership with Mark Birley, established Harry's Bar Club in London, 1979. Restored, and brought into regular service, the Venice Simplon-Orient-Express, 1982. Dir, Save Venice Inc., 2000–. Trustee, Solomon R. Guggenheim Foundn, 1989–. Mem. Internat. Council, Yale Univ., 2002–. Hon. Citizen of Venice, 1995; Grand Master, Nat. Order of the Southern Cross (Brazil), 2004. *Publication:* James Sherwood's Discriminating Guide to London, 1975, 2nd edn 1977. *Recreations:* sailing, tennis, ski-ing. *Address:* Hinton Manor, Hinton Waldrist, Oxon SN7 8SA. *T:* (01865) 820260. *Clubs:* Hurlingham, Pilgrims, Mark's; Carswell Golf & Country (Faringdon).

SHERWOOD, (Peter) Louis (Michael); Chairman, Govett European Technology and Income Trust plc (formerly First Ireland Investment Co.), 1999–2003; Director, HBOS, 2001–04; *b* 27 Oct. 1941; *s* of Peter Louis Sherwood and Mervyn Sherwood (*née* de Toll); *m* 1970, Nicole Dina; one *s* two *d*. *Educ:* New Coll., Oxford (BA 1963; MA 1966); Stanford Univ. (MBA 1965). Morgan Grenfell & Co., Corporate Finance Officer, 1965–68; Asst to Chm., Fine Fare (Supermarkets), 1968–69; Man. Dir, Melias (Fine Fare subsid.), 1969–72; Dir, Anglo-Continental Investment & Finance Co., 1972–79; Sen. Vice-Pres. for Development, Grand Union Co., USA, 1979–85; Pres., Great Atlantic & Pacific Tea Co., USA, 1985–88; Chm. and Chief Exec., Gateway Foodmarkets, 1988–89; Chairman: HTV Gp, 1991–97 (Dir, 1990–97); HTV West, 1997–99. Director: ROK (formerly EBC Gp, then ROK property solutions) plc, 1990–2006; Clerical Medical Investment Group (formerly Clerical Medical & General Life Assurance Soc.), 1990–2004 (Dep. Chm., 1996–2000; Chm., 2000–01); Halifax Bldg Soc., subseq. Halifax Gp plc, 1997–2001; Wessex Water Services Ltd, 1998–2006; Insight Investment Mgt Ltd, 2001–. Master, Soc. of Merchant Venturers, Bristol, 2003–04. *Recreations:* mountain walking, collecting fine wine. *Address:* 10 College Road, Clifton, Bristol BS8 3HZ. *Clubs:* Garrick, Lansdowne.

SHERWOOD, (Robert) Antony (Frank), CMG 1981; Assistant Director-General, British Council, 1977–81, retired; *b* 29 May 1923; *s* of Frank Henry Sherwood and Mollie Sherwood (*née* Moore); *m* 1953, Margaret Elizabeth Simpson; two *s* two *d*. *Educ:* Christ's Hospital; St John's Coll., Oxford (BA 1949, MA 1953). War service, RAF, 1942–46. Apptd to British Council, 1949; served in Turkey, Nigeria (twice), Syria, Uganda, Somalia and at HQ. Help the Aged: Vice-Chm., Internat. Cttee, 1982–88, Chm., 1988–92; Trustee, 1988–94; Mem. Council and Exec. Cttee, HelpAge Internat., 1983–93; Hon. PRO, Surrey Voluntary Service Council, 1982–88. Vice-Chm., Management Cttee, Guildford Inst. of Univ. of Surrey, 1993–97 (Chm., Finance Cttee, 1988–93). *Publication:* (ed) Directory of Statutory and Voluntary Health, Social and Welfare Services in Surrey, 1987. *Recreations:* travel, genealogy and family history, reading. *Address:* 18 Rivermount Gardens, Guildford, Surrey GU2 4DN. *T:* (01483) 538277; *e-mail:* sherwood18@talktalk.net.

SHERWOOD, Prof. Thomas, FRCP, FRCR; Professor of Radiology, 1978–94, Clinical Dean, 1984–96, University of Cambridge, now Professor Emeritus; Fellow of Girton College, Cambridge, since 1982; *b* 25 Sept. 1934; *m* 1961, Margaret Gooch; two *s* one *d. Educ:* Frensham Heights Sch.; Guy's Hospital, London. MA; DCH. Consultant Radiologist, Hammersmith Hospital and St Peter's Hospitals, 1969–77. Chm. Govs, Frensham Heights Sch., 1996–2000. Ombudsman, The Lancet, 1996–2001. *Publications:* Uroradiology, 1980; Roads to Radiology, 1983; Blow the Wind Southerly, 1988; papers in medical and radiological jls, 1964–. *Recreations:* music, reading and writing. *Address:* 19 Clarendon Street, Cambridge CB1 1JU.

SHESTOPAL, Dawn Angela, (Mrs N. J. Shestopal); *see* Freedman, D. A.

SHEVARDNADZE, Eduard Amvrosiyevich, Hon. GCMG 2000; President of Georgia, 1995–2003; *b* Georgia, 25 Jan. 1928; christened Georgi, 1992, but continues to be known as Eduard. *Educ:* Pedagogical Institute, Kutaisi. Mem., CPSU, 1948–91; Sec., Komsomol Cttee in Kutaisi, 1952–56, of Georgia, 1956–61; 1st Sec., Regional Party Cttee, Mtsheta, 1961–63, Tbilisi, 1963–64; Minister of Internal Affairs, Georgia, 1964–72; 1st Sec., Republican Party Cttee, Georgia, 1972–85; Mem., Politburo, 1985–91; Minister of Foreign Affairs, USSR, 1985–90, 1991; founder, Movement for Democratic Reform, 1991; Chm., Georgian State Council, 1992; Chm., Supreme Council and Head of State, Georgia, 1992–95. Hon. doctorates from Harvard, Boston, Emory and Providence, USA and Trieste, Italy. Order of Lenin (five times); Hero of Socialist Labour (twice); Order of Red Banner of Labour. *Publication:* The Future Belongs to Freedom, 1991.

SHEWRY, Prof. Peter Robert, CBiol, FIBiol; Associate Director, Rothamsted Research, since 2003; *b* 19 March 1948; *s* of late Robert Thomas Shewry and Mary Helen Shewry; *m* 1969, Rosemary Willsdon; one *s* one *d. Educ:* Bristol Univ. (BSc, PhD, DSc). Postdoctoral Res. Fellow, Westfield Coll., Univ. of London, 1972; Rothamsted Experimental Station: Res. Scientist, 1974; Head of Biochem. Dept, 1986; Dir, Long Ashton Res. Stn and Prof. of Agricl Scis, Univ. of Bristol, 1989–2003. Rank Prize for Nutrition (with Donald D. Kasarda), 2002. *Publications:* (ed with Steven Gutteridge) Plant Protein Engineering, 1992; (ed) Barley: genetics, biochemistry, molecular biology and biotechnology, 1992; (ed with A. K. Stobart) Seed Storage Compounds, 1993; (ed jtly) Protein Phosphorylation in Plants, 1996; (ed jtly) Engineering Crop Plants for Industrial End Uses, 1998; (ed with R. Casey) Seed Proteins, 1999; (ed with A. S. Tatham) Wheat Gluten, 2000; (ed jtly) Biotechnology of Cereals, 2001; (ed with G. Lookhart) Wheat Gluten Protein Analysis, 2003; (ed jtly) Elastomeric Proteins, 2003; (ed with E. N. C. Mills) Plant Protein Allergies, 2004; numerous papers in sci. jls on plant genetics, biochem. and molecular biol. *Address:* Rothamsted Research, Harpenden, Herts, AL5 2JQ. *T:* (01582) 763133.

SHI JIUYONG; a Judge, International Court of Justice, since 1994 (Vice-President, 2000–03; President, 2003–06); *b* 9 Oct. 1926; *m* 1956, Zhang Guoying; one *s. Educ:* St John's Univ., Shanghai (BA Govt and Public Law 1948); Columbia Univ., NY (MA Internat. Law 1951). Legal Advr, Min. of Foreign Affairs, People's Republic of China, 1980–93; Prof. of Internat. Law, Foreign Affairs Coll., Beijing, 1984–93. Hon. Prof. of Internat. Law, East China Coll. of Law and Political Sci., 2001–. Pres., Xiamen Acad. of Internat. Law, 2005–. Honorary President: Chinese Soc. of Internat. Law, Beijing, 2006–; Coll. of Internat. Law, Univ. of Foreign Relations, Beijing, 2007–. Mem., 1987–93, Chm., 1990, Internat. Law Commn, UN. *Address:* International Court of Justice, Peace Palace, 2517 KJ The Hague, The Netherlands.

SHIACH, Allan George; film writer (as Allan Scott) and producer; Chairman: Macallan-Glenlivet plc, 1980–96; Rafford Films Ltd, since 1983; *b* Elgin; *er s* of late Gordon Leslie Shiach, WS and Lucy Sybil (*née* De Freitas); *m* 1966, Kathleen Swarbreck; two *s* one *d. Educ:* Gordonstoun Sch.; L'Ecole des Roches; McGill Univ. (BA). Writer of TV and radio drama, 1965–72; screenwriter and co-writer of films, including: Don't Look Now, 1975; Joseph Andrews, 1977; Martin's Day, 1980; D.A.R.Y.L., 1984; Castaway, 1985; A Shadow on the Sun, 1987; The Witches, 1989; Cold Heaven, 1990; Two Deaths, 1994; In Love and War, 1996; The Preacher's Wife, 1996; Regeneration, 1997; also Producer or Exec. Producer: Cold Heaven, 1991; Shallow Grave, 1994; Two Deaths, 1995; True Blue, 1996; Grizzly Falls, 1999; The Match, 1999; The Fourth Angel, 2001. Dir, Scottish Media Group plc (formerly Scottish Television plc), 1993–2006. Mem., BBC Broadcasting Council (Scotland), 1987–90; Chairman: Writers' Guild of GB, 1989 and 1990; Scottish Film Council, 1991–97; Scottish Film Prodn Fund, 1992–; Scottish Screen, 1997–98; Governor, BFI, 1993–. Mem., Amer. Acad. of Motion Picture Arts & Scis, 1991–. Mem. Council, Scotch Whisky Assoc., 1983–96. Liveryman, Distillers' Co., 1989–. *Recreations:* writing, cooking, tennis. *Address:* Rafford Films Ltd, 36 Marshall Street, W1F 7EY. *Club:* Savile.

SHIACH, Gordon; Sheriff of Lothian and Borders, at Edinburgh, 1984–97, also at Peebles, 1996–97; *b* 1935; *o s* of late Dr John Shiach, FDS, QHDS; *m* 1962; one *d* (and one *d* decd). *Educ:* Lathallan Sch.; Gordonstoun Sch.; Edinburgh Univ. (MA, LLB 1959); Open Univ. (BA Hons 1979); Rose Bruford Coll. (BA Hons in Opera Studies 2006). Admitted to Faculty of Advocates, 1960; practised as Advocate, 1960–72; Tutor, Dept of Evidence and Pleading, Univ. of Edinburgh, 1963–66; Clerk to Rules Council of Court of Session, 1963–72; Standing Jun. Counsel in Scotland to Post Office, 1969–72; Sheriff of: Fife and Kinross, later Tayside, Central and Fife, at Dunfermline, 1972–79; Lothian and Borders at Linlithgow, 1979–84; Hon. Sheriff at Elgin, 1986–. Mental Welfare Comr for Scotland, 2001–05. Member: Council, Sheriffs' Assoc., 1989–95 (Pres., 1993–95); Bd, Lothian Family Conciliation Service, 1989–93; Standing Cttee on Criminal Procedure, 1989–93; Parole Bd for Scotland, 1990–99 (Vice-Chm., 1995–99); Council, Faculty of Advocates, 1993–95; Shrieval Training Gp, 1994–95; Review Gp on Social Work Nat. Standards for Throughcare, 1994–95. Chairman: The Scottish Soc., 1992–93; Edinburgh Sir Walter Scott Club, 1995–98. FSAScot 1998. *Recreations:* walking, swimming, music, art, theatre, film. *Clubs:* New, Scottish Arts (Edinburgh).

SHIELDS, Elizabeth Lois; Lecturer, Medieval Studies Department, University of York, since 1995; *b* 27 Feb. 1928; *d* of Thomas Henry Teare and Dorothy Emma Elizabeth Roberts-Lawrence; *m* 1961, David Cathro Shields. *Educ:* Whyteleafe Girls' Grammar School; UCL (BA Hons Classics); Avery Hill College of Education (Cert Ed); MA York 1988. Asst Teacher, St Philomena's Sch., Carshalton, 1954–59; Head of Department: Jersey Coll. for Girls, 1959–61; Whyteleafe Girls' Grammar Sch., 1961–62; Trowbridge Girls' High Sch., 1962–64; St Swithun's, Winchester, 1964–65; Queen Ethelburga's, Harrogate, 1967–69; Malton Sch., N Yorks, 1976–86; Univ. of York (on secondment), 1985–86 (Medieval Studies). Mem., Ryedale DC, 1980– (Chm., 1989–2007; Chm., Community Services Cttee; Chm., Overview and Scrutiny Cttee, 2007). Contested (L) Howden, 1979, Ryedale, 1983, 1992; MP (L) Ryedale, May 1986–87. Lib Dem spokesman on envmt, Yorks and Humberside Reg., 1989–; Chm., Yorks and Humberside Lib Dem Candidates' Assoc., 1992–97; President: Lib Dems in Ryedale Constituency, 1995–; Yorks and Humberside Lib Dem Regl Party, 1998–. Chm., Ryedale Housing Assoc., 1990–91; President: Ryedale Motor Neurone Disease Assoc., 1990–; Ryedale Cats' Protection League, 1991–. *Publication:* A Year to Remember, 1996. *Recreations:* gardening, music, travel. *Address:* Firby Hall, Kirkham Abbey, Westow, York YO60 7LH. *T:* (01653) 618474. *Club:* National Liberal.

SHIELDS, Hon. Margaret Kerslake, DCNZM 2008; QSO 1996; Cabinet Minister, New Zealand, 1984–90; *b* Wellington, NZ, 18 Dec. 1941; *d* of (Ernest) Blake Porter and Dorothy Bessie Porter (*née* Levy); *m* 1960, Patrick John Shields; one *d* (and one *d* decd). *Educ:* Victoria Univ., Wellington (BA). Co-founder, Soc. for Res. on Women in NZ, 1966; Researcher, Consumers' Inst., 1966–71; Res. Officer, NZ Dept of Statistics, 1973–81; MP (Lab) Kapiti, 1981–90. Dir, UN Internat. Res. and Trng Inst. for the Advancement of Women, 1991–94. Mem., Wellington Regl Council, 1995–2007; Chm., Gtr Wellington Regl Council, 2001–04. Vice Pres., Local Govt NZ, 1997–2004. *Recreations:* reading, theatre, narrow boating. *Address:* 23 Haunui Road, Pukerua Bay, Porirua 5026, New Zealand. *T:* (4) 2399949; *e-mail:* marg.shields@xtra.co.nz.

SHIELDS, Michael; *see* Shields, R. M. C.

SHIELDS, Sir Robert, Kt 1990; DL; MD, FRCS, FRCSE, FRCPS, FRCPE; Professor of Surgery, University of Liverpool, 1969–96; Consultant Surgeon, Royal Liverpool Hospital and Broadgreen Hospital, 1969–96; President, Royal College of Surgeons of Edinburgh, 1994–97; *b* 8 Nov. 1930; *o s* of late Robert Alexander Shields and Isobel Dougall Shields; *m* 1957, Grace Marianne Swinburn; one *s* two *d. Educ:* John Neilson Institution, Paisley; Univ. of Glasgow. MB, ChB 1953 (Asher-Asher Medal and MacLeod Medal); MD (Hons and Bellahouston Medal) 1965; FRCSE 1959; FRCS 1966; FRCPS 1993; FRCPE 1996. House appts, Western Infirmary, Glasgow, 1953–54; RAMC, Captain attached 1 Bn Argyll and Sutherland Highlanders, 1954–56; RAMC (TA), Major (Surg. Specialist) attached 7 Bn A and SH, 1956–61. Hall Fellow, Univ. of Glasgow, 1957–58; Mayo Foundn Fellow, 1959–60; Lectr in Surgery, Univ. of Glasgow, 1960–63; Sen. Lectr and Reader in Surgery, Welsh Nat. Sch. of Medicine, 1963–69; Dean, Faculty of Medicine, Univ. of Liverpool, 1982–85. Mem., GMC, 1982–94. Royal College of Surgeons: Mem., Ct of Examrs, 1980–86; Mem. Bd, Hunterian Inst., 1986–94; Zachary Cope Lectr, 1992; Vice Chm., Royal Liverpool Univ. Hosp. Trust, 1992–95 (non-exec. Trustee, 1991–95); Member: Liverpool AHA (T) (Chm., Area/Univ. Liaison Cttee), 1974–78; Mersey RHA, 1982–85 (Vice-Chm., 1985; Regl Advr, 1986–94); Liverpool Med. Instn (Vice-Pres., 1983–84; Pres., 1988–89); Council, RCSE, 1985–98 (Regent, 1999–); MRC, 1987–91 (Member: Cell Bd, 1974–77; Strategy Cttee, 1987–91); Exec. Cttee, Council of Military Educn Cttees of Univs of UK, 1990–94; Vice-Chm., Specialist Trng Authy, Med. Royal Colls, 1996–97. Member: Surgical Research Soc. (Hon. Sec. 1972–76 and Pres. 1983–85); British Soc. of Gastroenterology (Mem. Council, 1984–86; Pres., 1990–91; Hon. Mem., 1998–); N of England Gastroent. Soc. (Pres., 1981–83); Internat. Surgical Gp; James IV Assoc. of Surgeons, 1986– (Dir, 1991–96; Pres., 1994–96); Assoc. of Surgs of GB and Ire. (Mem. Council 1966–69; Pres., 1986–87); Council, European Surgical Assoc., 1995–98; Chm., Med. Adv. Cttee, British Liver Trust (formerly British Liver Foundn), 1991–94; Vice-Chm., Brit. Jl of Surgery Soc., 1989–95; Pres., Travelling Surgical Soc., 2002–03. Member: Panel of Assessors, Nat. Health and Med. Res. Council of Commonwealth and Australia, 1983–; List of Assessors for Cancer Grants, Anti-Cancer Council of Vic, Australia, 1986–. Chm., Merseyside, Lancashire and Cheshire Council on Alcoholism, 1992–94. Marjorie Budd Prof., Univ. of Bristol, 1983; Wilson Wang Vis. Prof., Chinese Univ. of Hong Kong, 1990; Wellcome Prof., Coll. of Medicine of S Africa, 1991. Former Visiting Prof., Univs of Toronto, Virginia, Witwatersrand, Rochester (NY), Hong Kong, Calif, Yale, and Examiner in Surgery, Univs of Glasgow, Edinburgh, Dundee, Leicester, Sheffield, Cambridge, Lagos, Amman, Riyadh, Malta; Dist. Lectr, Alpha Omega Alpha Assoc., 1994; Hon. Sen. Res. Fellow, Univ. of Glasgow, 1998–2001. Mem. Bd of Advrs in Surgery, London Univ., 1983–. Member: Editorial Board: Gut, 1969–76; Brit. Jl of Surgery, 1970–85, 1989–95; Internat. Editl Bd, Current Practice in Surgery, 1989–. Hon. Col Liverpool Univ. OTC, 1994–2001. DL Merseyside, 1991. Founder FMedSci 1998. Hon. FACS 1990; Hon. FCSSA 1991; Hon. FCSHK 1995; Hon. FRCSI 1996; Hon. FRACS 1997; Hon. Fellow: Amer. Surgical Assoc., 1993; Acad. Medicine of Singapore, 1996; Japanese Council for Med. Trng, 2002; Hon. Mem., Indian Assoc. of Surgeons, 1993. Hon. DSc Wales, 1990. Moynihan Medal, Assoc. of Surgs of GB and Ire., 1966. *Publications:* (ed jtly): Surgical Emergencies II, 1979; Textbook of Surgery, 1983; Gastrointestinal Emergencies, 1992; contribs to medical and surgical jls relating to surgery and gastroenterology. *Recreations:* sailing, walking. *Address:* 81 Meols Drive, West Kirby, Wirral CH48 5DF. *T:* (0151) 632 3588. *Club:* Army and Navy.

See also G. E. Camm.

SHIELDS, (Robert) Michael (Coverdale), CBE 2002; Principal, URC Associates, since 2003; Associate, AMION Consulting, since 2004; Chairman, Liverpool Land Development Company, 2005–08 (Deputy Chairman, 2004–05); *b* 23 Jan. 1943; *s* of Thomas and Dorothy Shields; *m* 1965, Dorothy Jean Dennison; two *s* one *d. Educ:* Durham Johnston Grammar Tech. Sch.; Durham Univ. (BSc Hons); Newcastle Univ. (DipTP). MRTPI. Planning Departments: Newcastle upon Tyne, 1964–65; Durham CC, 1965–69; Nottingham, 1969–73; Dep. Dir of Planning, Leeds City Council, 1973–78; City Tech. Services Officer and Dep. Chief Exec., Salford City Council, 1978–83; Chief Executive: Trafford BC, 1983–87; Trafford Park Develt Corp., 1987–98; Northwest (formerly NW Regl) Develt Agency, 1998–2003; Manchester Knowledge Capital, 2003–05. Dir, Innvotec North West Trust Ltd, 1998–2001. Chm., United Utilities Trust Fund, 2005–. Salford University: Pro Chancellor, 1993–99; Chm. Council, 1997–99 (Dep. Chm., 1999–2003); Trustee, Manufacturing Inst., 2006– (Dep. Chm., 2007–). Gov., Altrincham Grammar Sch., 1988–98 (Chm., 1988–93). Hon. DSc Salford, 2000; Hon. DLit UMIST, 2004; Hon. LLD Manchester, 2004. Howorth Medal for Enterprise and Innovation, RSA, 2004. *Recreations:* family, books. *Address:* Neston, Delamer Road, Bowdon, Altrincham, Cheshire WA14 2NT; *e-mail:* mike.shields@urca.co.uk.

SHIERLAW, Norman Craig; Senior Partner, N. C. Shierlaw & Associates (Stock and Sharebrokers), 1968–87; Chairman, Swiss Partners (Stock and Sharebrokers), 1987–91; *b* 17 Aug. 1921; *s* of Howard Alison Shierlaw and Margaret Bruce; *m* 1944, Patricia Yates (*d* 1987); two *d*; *m* 1989, Barbara Jean Lacey. *Educ:* Pulteney Grammar Sch., Adelaide; St Peter's Coll., Adelaide; Univ. of Adelaide (BE). Mem. Australian Inst. Mining and Metallurgy; FSASM; Mining Manager's Certificate. War Service, AIF, 1941–45 (War Service medals). Mining Engr with North Broken Hill Ltd, 1949–58; Sharebroker's Clerk, 1959–60; Partner, F. W. Porter & Co. (Sharebrokers), 1960–68. Chairman: Australian Development Ltd, 1981–83 (Dir, 1959–81); Burmine Ltd, 1990–92 (Dir, 1985–90); Director: Poseidon Ltd, 1968–77; North Flinders Mines Ltd, 1969–77; Nobelex NL, 1974–80; Palm Springs Ltd, 1987–2001; Gympie Eldorado Gold Mines, 1993–97; Cooper's Brewery Ltd, 1995–97. FAIM 1971. *Recreations:* golf, tennis. *Clubs:* Naval, Military and Air Force, Kooyonga Golf (Adelaide); Victoria Racing (Melbourne).

SHIFFNER, Sir Henry David, 8th Bt *cr* 1818; company director; *b* 2 Feb. 1930; *s* of Major Sir Henry Shiffner, 7th Bt, and Margaret Mary (*d* 1987), *er d* of late Sir Ernest Gowers, GCB, GBE; *S* father, 1941; *m* 1st, 1949, Dorothy Jackson (marr. diss. 1956); one *d* (and one *d* decd); 2nd, 1957, Beryl (marr. diss. 1970), *d* of George Milburn, Saltdean, Sussex; one *d*; 3rd, 1970, Joaquina Ramos Lopez. *Educ:* Rugby; Trinity Hall, Cambridge. *Heir: cousin* George Frederick Shiffner [*b* 3 August 1936; *m* 1961, Dorothea Helena Cynthia, *d* of late T. H. McLean; one *s* one *d*].

SHIFFNER, Rear-Adm. John Robert, CB 1995; DL; Consultant, Newton Industrial Consultants, 2002–07; *b* 30 Aug. 1941; *s* of late Captain John Scarlett Shiffner, RN and Margaret Harriet Shiffner (*née* Tullis); *m* 1969, Rosemary Tilly; two *s* one *d*. *Educ:* Sedbergh Sch.; BRNC Dartmouth; RNEC Manadon; RNC Greenwich (BSc). CEng, FIMarEST. Joined RN, 1959; served in HM Ships Centaur, Glamorgan, Andromeda, Zulu; Staff Marine Engineer Officer, CBNS Washington, 1980; RCDS 1983; MoD Procurement Executive: Project Manager, Type 42 Destroyer/Aircraft Carrier, 1984–86; Dir, Mechanical Engineering, 1987–88; Captain, Britannia RNC, Dartmouth, 1989–91; ADC to the Queen, 1989–91; COS to C-in-C Naval Home Comd, 1991–93; Dir Gen. Fleet Support (Equipment and Systems), MoD, 1993–95. Director: MSI-Defence Systems Ltd, 1996–2001; GEC Marine, 1996–98; Marconi Electronic Systems, 1997–99; Internat. Festival of the Sea Ltd, 2000–02. Chairman: Britannia Assoc., 2004–07; Dartmouth RNLI, 2007–. MInstD. DL Devon, 2005. *Recreations:* golf, sailing, country pursuits, garden taming, picture restoration. *Address:* Westholme, Redlap, Dartmouth, S Devon TQ6 0JR. *Club:* Royal Yacht Squadron (Cowes).

SHIGEHARA, Kumiharu; President, International Economic Policy Studies Association (formerly Head, International Economic Policy Studies Group), since 2001; *b* 5 Feb. 1939; *s* of Seizaburo Shigehara and Rutsu (*née* Tanabe); *m* 1965, Akiko Yoshizawa; one *s* one *d*. *Educ:* Law Sch., Univ. of Tokyo (Hozumi Hon. Award, 1960). Joined Bank of Japan, 1962; joined OECD, 1970: Principal Administrator, 1971–72; Hd, Monetary Div., 1972–74; Councillor on policy planning, and Advr on Internat. Finance, Bank of Japan, 1974–80; Dep. Dir, Gen. Econs Br., OECD, 1980–82; Manager of Res., Inst. for Monetary and Econ. Studies, Bank of Japan, 1982–87, Dep. Dir, 1987; Dir, Gen. Econs Br., OECD, 1987–89; Dir, Inst. for Monetary and Econ. Studies, Bank of Japan, 1989–92; Hd, Econs Dept and Chief Economist, OECD, 1992–97; Dep. Sec.-Gen., OECD, 1997–99. Hon. Dr Econs Liège, 1998. *Publications:* The Role of Monetary Policy in Demand Management (with Niels Thygesen), 1975; Stable Economic Growth and Monetary Policy, 1991; New Trends in Monetary Theory and Policy, 1992. *Recreations:* art, hiking, classical music. *Address: e-mail:* office.shigehara@online.fr.

SHILLING, (Hugh) David (V.); artist, designer; President, David Shilling, since 1976; *b* 27 June 1954; *s* of late Ronald and Gertrude Shilling. *Educ:* Colet Court; St Paul's Sch., Hammersmith. Founded David Shilling, 1976. Sen. Consultant on design, ITC, UNCTAD and GATT, 1990. One person shows in UK and worldwide, 1979–, including: NT and Crafts Council, 1979; Ulster, Worthing, Plymouth, Leeds, Cheltenham, Durham, Salisbury, Chester and Edinburgh Museums; LA Co. Mus., 1982; Moscow, 1989; Sotheby's, Stockholm, 1992; Salama-Caro Gall., London, 1993; Rio de Janeiro, 1993; Manila, 1994; Brit. Embassy, Paris, 1995; British Council, Cologne, 1995, and Delhi and Bombay, 1996; War Child/Pavarotti, Modena, 1995; Royal Shakespeare Theatre, Stratford upon Avon, 1996; Dubai, 1999; Hatworks Mus., Stockport, 2001; Nat. Horseracing Mus., Newmarket, 2001; Internat. Mus. of the Horse, Lexington, Ky, 2002; Newmarket Racecourse, 2002; Nat. Mus. of Scotland Dumfries, 2003; Musée Chapeau, Lyon, 2004–05; Ferrero Gall., Nice, 2004, 2005; Regent's Park, London, 2005; Holdenby, Northampton, 2006; Museu da Chapeleria, Portugal, 2008; work in permanent collections: Metropolitan Mus., NY, LA Co. Mus., Philadelphia Mus. of Art, Musée de l'Art Decoratif, Paris, V&A Mus. Pres. for Life, Valdivia, Ecuador, 1993. Freeman, Gold and Silver Wyre Drawers, 1975. *Publication:* Thinking Rich, 1986. *Address:* 2 rue Basse, Monaco, MC 98000. *T:* 97770137. *Clubs:* City Livery; City Livery Yacht.

SHILLINGFORD, (Romeo) Arden (Coleridge), MBE 1977; Permanent Secretary, Ministry of Immigration and Labour, Commonwealth of Dominica, 1994–97; *b* 11 Feb. 1936; *s* of Stafford Shillingford and Ophelia Thomas, step *d* of Hosford Samuel O'Brien and *d* of Clarita (*née* Hunt), Roseau, Dominica; *m* 1st, Evelyn Blanche Hart; one *s* one *d*; 2nd, Maudline Joan Green; three *s*, and one adopted *d*. *Educ:* Wesley High Sch., Roseau Boys' Sch., Dominica; grammar school; School of Law. Member, Hon. Soc. Inner Temple. Joined Dominican Civil Service, 1957, after brief period as solicitor's clerk; junior clerk, various Govt Depts, Dominica, 1957–59; Clerk of Court, then Chief Clerk, Magistrates' Office, 1960–61; joined staff, Eastern Caribbean Commn, London, on secondment from Dominican CS, 1965; served variously as Migrants' Welfare Officer, Students' Officer, Asst Trade Sec. and PA to Comr, 1968–71; Admin. Asst, Consular and Protocol Affairs, 1973–78 (actg Comr, several occasions, 1975–78); High Comr in UK, 1978–85 (concurrently non-resident Ambassador to France, Spain, Belgium, Sweden, Luxemburg, Holland, Italy, W Germany and EEC, Brussels, and Perm. Rep. to UNESCO); Perm. Sec., Min. of Community Develt and Social Affairs, 1985–92, Min. of Legal Affairs, 1992–94, Min. of Communication, Works and Housing, Dominica, 1993–94. Mem., Bd of Trustees, Dominica Conservation Assoc., 1989–92. Past Member, numerous cttees and *ad hoc* bodies for West Indian Immigrant Welfare and Education; Dep. Chm., Bd of Governors, W Indian Students' Centre, 1970–75, Chm., 1976–79; Mem. Bd of Govs, Wesley High Sch., 2000–; Member, West India Cttee (Vice-Pres. 1979). Liaison Officer, Victoria League for Commonwealth Friendship; Founder-Mem. and Vice-Chm., Jaycees (Dominica Jun. Chamber of Commerce); Chm., Nat. Emblems Cttee, 1998–; Member: Nat. Scouts Council Assoc.; Nat. Exec. Council, Girl Guides Assoc., 1988–95. *Recreations:* listening to classical and authentic folk music, reading. *Address:* Hibiscus Street, Elmshall, near Roseau, Commonwealth of Dominica, West Indies. *T:* 4485851.

SHILSON, Stuart James, LVO 2004; Management Consultant, McKinsey & Co.; *b* 12 Feb. 1966. *Educ:* St Paul's Sch.; Balliol Coll., Oxford (BA 1st Cl. Hons 1988, MSc 1989); St John's Coll., Cambridge (MPhil 1990). Called to the Bar, Middle Temple, 1992; in practice at the Bar, 1992–97; McKinsey & Co., 1997–2001; Sen. Civil Servant, Cabinet Office, 1999–2000 (on leave of absence); Asst Pvte Sec. to the Queen, 2001–04, and Asst Keeper of the Queen's Archives, 2002–04; rejoined McKinsey & Co., 2005. FRGS 1989; FRSA 1996. *Address:* McKinsey & Co., 1 Jermyn Street, SW1Y 4UH.

SHILTON, Peter, OBE 1991 (MBE 1986); footballer; *b* 18 Sept. 1949; *s* of Les and May Shilton; *m* 1970, Sue. *Educ:* King Richard III Sch., Leicester. Goalkeeper; started playing, 1964, for Leicester City; scored a goal, 1967; Stoke City, 1974; Nottingham Forest, 1977; Southampton, 1982; Derby County, 1987; Plymouth Argyle, 1992–95 (player-manager); Leyton Orient, 1996; 1,000 League appearances (record), 1996; first played for England, 1970; 125 England caps (record); final appearance, World Cup, 1990. PFA Footballer of the Year, 1978. *Publication:* Peter Shilton: the autobiography, 2004.

SHIMMON, Ross Michael, OBE 2000; FCLIP; Secretary General, International Federation of Library Associations and Institutions, 1999–2004; *b* 10 Jan. 1942; *s* of late John Ross Shimmon and Eileen Margaret Shimmon; *m* 1967, Patricia, *d* of late Ronald George Hayward, CBE; one *s* two *d*. *Educ:* St John's Coll., Southsea; Poly. of North London; Coll. of Librarianship, Wales. FLA 1972; Hon. FCLIP (Hon. FLA 2000). Liby Assistant, Portsmouth City Libraries, 1960; Asst Librarian, 1962, Area Librarian, Havant, 1964, Hants County Liby; Lectr, Southampton Coll. of Technol., 1964; Librarian (Tech. Assistant), London Bor. of Bexley, 1966; Professional Assistant to Library Advisers, DES, 1968; Lectr, Coll. of Librarianship, Wales, 1970; Services Librarian, Preston Poly., 1975; Head, Liby Studies Dept, Admin. Coll. of PNG, 1979; Library Association: Sec. for Manpower and Educn, 1984; Dir, Professional Practice, 1988; Chief Exec., 1992–99. Member: Adv. Council, 1992–99, Adv. Cttee, 1994–99, British Council; BookAid Internat. Council, 1994–99; Adv. Cttee, Liby and Inf. Stats Unit, Univ. of Loughborough, 1997–99; Cttee on Freedom of Access to Information and Freedom of Expression, IFLA, 1998–99; Adv. Council on Libraries, 1999; Design Gp, Museums, Libraries and Archives Council, 1999. President: Eur. Bureau of Liby, Inf. and Documentation Assocs, 1992–95; Internat. Cttee of Blue Shield, 2003. Hon. Mem. PNG Liby Assoc., 1983; Hon. Life Mem., Liby and Inf. Assoc. of S Africa, 2007. Hon. Fellow, Univ. of Central Lancs, 2002. Trustee, Activity for Health, 2005–. Member: Adv. Cttee, Internat. Jl on Recorded Information, 2001–03; Editl Adv. Bd, Information Develt, 2005–07; Ed., The Colonel, 2004–. *Publications:* Reader in Library Management, 1976; conf. papers and contribs to liby jls. *Recreations:* cricket, photography, railways (prototype and model). *Address:* 7 Nobel Court, Faversham, Kent ME13 7SD; *e-mail:* pandrshimmon@btinternet.com.

SHIN, Prof. Hyun Song, DPhil; FBA 2005; Professor of Economics, Princeton University, since 2005; *b* 9 Aug. 1959. *Educ:* Magdalen Coll., Oxford (BA 1985); Nuffield Coll., Oxford (MPhil 1987); DPhil Oxon 1988. Lectr in Econs, Univ. of Oxford and Fellow, University Coll., Oxford, 1990–94; Prof. of Econs, Univ. of Southampton, 1994–96; Lectr in Public Econs, Univ. of Oxford and Fellow, Nuffield Coll., Oxford, 1996–2000; Prof. of Finance, LSE, 2000–05. *Publications:* articles in learned jls. *Address:* Bendheim Center for Finance, Princeton University, 26 Prospect Avenue, Princeton, NJ 08540–5296, USA.

SHINER, Janice, CB 2005; Chief Executive, Tertiary Education Commission, New Zealand, since 2005. PGCE. Private sector advertising; human resource and communication mgt in various cos incl. WH Smith and Chase Manhattan Bank; Vice-Pres. Human Resources, Chase Manhattan, 1987; Vice Principal, Yeovil Coll., 1989–93; Sen. Inspector, 1993–97, Dir of Educn and Instns, 1997–99, FEFC; Principal, Leicester Coll., 1999–2002; Dir Gen. for Lifelong Learning, DfES, 2002–05. *Address:* Tertiary Education Commission, 44 The Terrace, PO Box 27-048, Wellington, New Zealand.

SHINER, Philip Joseph; Principal, Public Interest Lawyers, since 1999; *b* Coventry, 25 Dec. 1956; *s* of Peter and Patricia Shiner; *m* 2004, Rachel Cooney; one *s* three *d*. *Educ:* Univ. of Birmingham (LLB 1978); Coll. of Law; Univ. of Warwick (LLM (by res.) 1985). Articled clerk, Needham and James, 1979–81; Solicitor: Robin Thompson and Partners, 1981–82; Small Heath Community Law Centre, 1982–84; Birmingham Council Estates Project, 1985–89; Thompsons, 1989–90; Community develt worker, Barnardos, 1990–92; Solicitor, Birkenhead Resource Unit, 1992–95; Partner, Tyndallwoods, Solicitors, 1995–99. Hon. Prof. of Law, London Metropolitan Univ., 2005–; Hon. Research Fellow, School of Law: Univ. of Warwick, 1998–2003; LSE, 2005–. *Publications:* (ed with A. Williams) The Iraq War and International Law, 2008; contrib. Eur. Human Rights Law Rev., Local Econ., Judicial Rev., Mineral Planning, Legal Action Jl, Planning, Local Govt Chronicle. *Recreations:* running, cycling, contemporary music, comedy, hill walking, current affairs, religious affairs. *Address:* Public Interest Lawyers, 8 Hylton Street, Birmingham B18 6HN. *T:* (0121) 515 5069, *Fax:* (0121) 515 5129; *e-mail:* phil_shiner@publicinterestlawyers.co.uk.

SHINGLES, Godfrey Stephen, (Geoff), CBE 1987; CEng, FIET; FBCS; Chairman, Imagination Technologies (formerly VideoLogic) Group PLC, since 1995; *b* 9 April 1939; *s* of Sidney and Winifred Shingles; *m*; two *s*; *m* 1997, Frances Margaret Mercer; one *d*. *Educ:* Paston Sch., N Walsham; Leeds Univ. (BSc). Joined Digital UK, 1965; Chm., Digital Equipment Co. Ltd, 1991–94 (Man. Dir, 1983–91; Chief Exec., 1991–93). Vice-Pres., Digital Equipment Corp., 1981–92. Chm. and CEO, speed-trap.com, 2004–; non-exec. Chm., Sarantel, 2006–; non-exec. Dir, Prevx, 2004–. FInstD. Freeman, City of London. *Recreations:* sailing, cricket, Rugby, golf, ski-ing. *Address:* Imagination Technologies Group PLC, Home Park Estate, Kings Langley, Herts WD4 8LZ. *Clubs:* Royal Ocean Racing, MCC.

SHINWELL, Sir Adrian; *see* Shinwell, Sir M. A.

SHINWELL, Anne Hilary, (Mrs K. Middle); Headteacher, Parkstone Grammar School, Poole, since 2001; *b* 21 March 1952; *d* of late Louis Shinwell and of Sylvia Shinwell; *m* 2002, Keith Middle; one step *s* one step *d*. *Educ:* Univ. of Glasgow (MA; PGCE). John Kelly Girls' School, Brent, London: Teacher of Hist., 1973–80; responsible for teaching Econs, 1975–86; Hd of Careers, 1980–86; Dep. Dir, Sixth Form, 1983–86; Tiffin Girls' School, Kingston, London: Sen. Teacher, 1986–88; Hd, Middle Sch. and Careers, 1986–88; Dep. Headteacher, 1988–95; Headteacher, Queen Elizabeth Girls' Sch., Barnet, London, 1995–2001. Pres., Assoc. of Maintained Girls' Schs, 2004–05. *Recreations:* golf, reading, travel, antiques. *Address:* Parkstone Grammar School, Sopers Lane, Poole, Dorset BH17 7EP. *T:* (01202) 605605, *Fax:* (01202) 605606; *e-mail:* anne.shinwell@parkstone.poole.sch.uk. *Club:* Dorset Golf and Country (Bere Regis).

SHINWELL, Sir (Maurice) Adrian, Kt 1996; DL; NP; solicitor; Senior Partner, Kerr Barrie (formerly Kerr, Barrie & Duncan), Glasgow, since 1991; *b* 27 Feb. 1951; *s* of late Maurice Shinwell and Andrina (*née* Alexander); *m* 1973, Lesley McLean; two *s* one *d*. *Educ:* Hutchesons' Boys' Grammar Sch.; Glasgow Univ. (LLB). NP 1976. MCIArb 1999 (ACIArb 1990). Admitted solicitor, 1975; Solicitor-Mediator, 1994–2004. Mem., Children's Panel, 1973–77. Part-time Tutor, Law Faculty, Glasgow Univ., 1980–84. Dir, Digital Animations Gp plc, 2002–07. Dir, Nat. Th. of Scotland, 2007–. Scottish Conservative & Unionist Association: Mem., 1975–; Mem., Scottish Council, 1982–98; Chairman: Eastwood Assoc., 1982–85; Cumbernauld & Kilsyth Assoc., 1989–91; Scottish Cons. Candidates' Bd, 1997–2000; Vice-Pres., 1989–92; Pres., 1992–94; Member: Gen. Purposes Cttee, 1993–98; Scottish Exec. and Scottish Council, 1998–2000. Mem., Central Adv. Cttee on Justices of the Peace, 1996–99; Vice Chm., JP Adv. Cttee, E Renfrewshire, 2000–06. Dir, St Leonards Sch., St Andrews, 2000–03. DL Renfrewshire, 1999. *Address:* Sarona, South Road, Busby, Glasgow G76 8JB. *T:* (office) (0141) 221 6844.

SHIPLEY, Debra Ann; writer and lecturer; *b* 22 June 1957. *Educ:* Oxford Poly. (BA Hons); MA London. Writer and lecturer, history, critical studies and architecture. MP (Lab) Stourbridge, 1997–2005. Chm., Drinkaware, 2007. *Publications:* 17 books on subjects including architecture, museums, heritage, travel. *Recreations:* walking, reading, cooking.

SHIPLEY, Jane; Her Honour Judge Shipley; a Circuit Judge, since 2000; *b* 5 Jan. 1952; *m* 1977, David; two *d*. *Educ:* Maltby Grammar Sch. (Head Girl); St Hugh's Coll., Oxford (Pres., Law Soc.; MA). Called to the Bar, Gray's Inn, 1974; in practice, Leeds, NE Circuit, 1974–2000. Asst Recorder, 1991–95; Recorder, 1995–2000. *Recreation:* gardening. *Address:* Sheffield Combined Court Centre, 50 West Bar, Sheffield S3 8PH.

SHIPLEY, Rt Hon. Jennifer (Mary), DCNZM 2003; PC 1998; Managing Director, Jenny Shipley New Zealand Ltd, since 2002; Chairman, Seniors Money International Ltd, since 2007; Prime Minister of New Zealand, 1997–99; *b* 4 Feb. 1952; *d* of Rev. Len

Robson and Adele Robson; *m* 1973, Burton Shipley; one *s* one *d*. *Educ:* Marlborough Coll., NZ; Christchurch Coll. of Educn (Dip. Teaching). Primary Sch. Teacher, 1972–77; farmer in partnership, 1973–88. MP (Nat.) Ashburton, then Rakaia, NZ, 1987–2002; MEC, NZ, 1990–99; Minister: of Social Welfare, 1990–93; of Women's Affairs, 1990–99; of Health, 1993–96; of State Services, of Transport, i/c Accident Rehabilitation and Compensation Insurance, for State Owned Enterprises, and i/c Radio NZ, 1996–97; i/c Security Intelligence Service, 1997–99; Chair, Security and Intelligence Cttee, 1997–99; Leader of the Opposition, 1999–2001. Chm., Mainzeal Property and Construction Ltd, 2004–; Director: Richina Pacific, 2004–; Momentum, 2005–; China Construction Bank, 2007–. *Recreations:* gardening, walking, water sports.

SHIPLEY DALTON, Duncan Edward; Member (UU) Antrim South, Northern Ireland Assembly, 1998–2003; barrister-at-law; *b* 7 Nov. 1970; *s* of Kenneth Shipley and Susan Iris Dalton, BSc, MA, PhD. *Educ:* Carisbrooke, Isle of Wight; Univ. of Essex (LLB Hons); Queen's Univ., Belfast (CPLS 1996); BL Inn of Court of NI 1996. Called to the Bar, N Ireland, 1996. 7th (City of Belfast) Bn, Royal Irish Regt, 1994–98. *Recreations:* reading (history and politics), karate, computers.

SHIPPERLEY, (Reginald) Stephen; Chief Executive, Connells Group, since 1989; *b* 31 Oct. 1958; *s* of Reginald Scott Shipperley and Elizabeth May Shipperley; *m* Janet Frances; three *d*. *Educ:* Brill Primary Sch.; Aylesbury Grammar Sch. Connells Estate Agents, 1977–; Founding Dir, 2000, non-exec. Dir, 2006–, Rightmove plc. *Recreations:* cricket (player and spectator), all other sports as spectator, golf.

SHIPSTER, Michael David, CMG 2003; OBE 1990; HM Diplomatic Service, retired; Director, International, Rolls-Royce, since 2008; *b* 17 March 1951; *s* of late Col John Neville Shipster, CBE, DSO and Cornelia Margaretha Shipster (*née* Arends); *m* 1974, Jackie, *d* of late Norman Mann, SA Springbok cricketer; one *s* two *d*. *Educ:* Ratcliffe Coll., Leicester; St Edmund Hall, Oxford (MA 1972); Sch. of Develt Studies, UEA (MA 1977). Nuffield Fellow, ODI, in Botswana, 1972–74; worked for Botswana Develt Corp., 1972–75; joined HM Diplomatic Service, 1977: Second Sec., FCO, 1977–79; Army Sch. of Languages, Beaconsfield, 1979–80; First Sec. (Econ.), Moscow, 1981–83; FCO, 1983–86; First Secretary: New Delhi, 1986–89; Lusaka, 1990; Consul (Political), Johannesburg, 1991–94; Counsellor: FCO, 1994–2004; Washington, 2004–06. *Recreations:* music, military history, messing about on bikes and boats. *Address:* c/o Rolls-Royce plc, 65 Buckingham Gate, SW1E 6AT. *Clubs:* Vincent's (Oxford); Royal Naval Sailing Association.

SHIRAKAWA, Prof. Hideki, PhD; Professor, Institute of Materials Science, University of Tsukuba, 1982–2000, now Emeritus; *b* Tokyo, Aug. 1936; *s* of Hatsutarou and Fuyuno Shirakawa; *m* 1966, Chiyoko Shibuya; two *s*. *Educ:* Tokyo Inst. of Technol. (PhD 1966). Res. Associate, Tokyo Inst. of Technol., 1966–79; Associate Prof., Inst. of Materials Sci., Univ. of Tsukuba, 1979–82. Pioneered work on conductive polymers. (Jtly) Nobel Prize for Chemistry, 2000. Order of Culture (Japan), 2000. *Address:* c/o Institute of Materials Science, University of Tsukuba, Sakura-mura, Ibaraki 305, Japan.

SHIRE, Rabbi Dr Michael Jonathan; Vice-Principal, Leo Baeck College (formerly Leo Baeck College - Centre for Jewish Education), since 2002; *b* 15 Dec. 1957; *s* of Dr Heinz Shire and Ruth Shire; *m* 1991, Rabbi Marcia Plumb; one *s* one *d*. *Educ:* George Dixon Sch., Birmingham; University Coll. London (BA Hons 1981); Hebrew Union Coll., USA (MA 1983; PhD 1996); Leo Baeck Coll. (MA 1995). Dir of Educn, Temple Beth Hillel, Calif, 1983–88; Dep. Dir, 1988–90, Dir, 1990–2002, Centre for Jewish Educn. Ordained, 1996. *Publications:* The Illuminated Haggadah, 1998; L'Chaim, 2000; The Jewish Prophet, 2002; Mazal-Tov, 2003. *Recreations:* theatre, contemporary architecture, the men's movement, modern fiction. *Address:* Leo Baeck College, 80 East End Road, N3 2SY. *T:* (020) 8349 5600.

SHIRLEY, family name of **Earl Ferrers**.

SHIRLEY, Malcolm Christopher, CEng; Secretary, Royal Commission for the Exhibition of 1851, since 2002; *b* 10 April 1945; *s* of late Leonard Noel Shirley and Edith Florence Shirley (*née* Bullen); *m* 1970, Lucilla Rose Geary Dyer; three *s*. *Educ:* Churcher's Coll., Petersfield; BRNC Dartmouth; RNEC Plymouth (BSc 1969). CEng 1973; FIMarEST (FIMarE 1981). Royal Navy: served HMS Manxman, HMS Triumph, HMS Zulu, HMS Rapid, HMS Eastbourne, 1970–74; Sen. Engr, HM Yacht Britannia, 1975–77; RNSC Greenwich, 1977; Staff, Dir Gen. Ships, 1977–79; HMS Coventry, 1980–82; Asst Naval Attaché, Paris, 1982–84; staff appts, MoD Naval Staff, 1984–86, 1990–92; Nat. Rep. SHAPE, NATO, 1992–94; Cdre, 1994; Naval Manpower Study Leader, 1994–95; CO HMS Sultan, 1995–98. Dir Gen., Engrg Council, 1998–2001. Member: RNSA, 1967; Assoc. of Cape Horners, 1974–. Freeman, City of London, 1999; Liveryman, Engineers' Co., 1999. FRSA 2002. *Recreations:* sailing, music. *Address:* Greyhound Cottage, Freshford, Bath BA2 7TT. *T:* (01225) 722424. *Club:* Royal Yacht Squadron.

SHIRLEY, Dame (Vera) Stephanie, (Steve), DBE 2000 (OBE 1980); FREng; FBCS CITP; philanthropist; *b* 16 Sept. 1933; *d* of late Arnold Buchthal and Mrs Margaret Brook (formerly Buchthal, *née* Schick); name changed to Brook on naturalisation, 1951; *m* 1959, Derek George Millington Shirley; (one *s* decd). *Educ:* Sir John Cass Coll., London. BSc (Spec.) London 1956. FBCS CITP 2003 (FBCS 1971); CEng 1990. PO Res. Stn, Dollis Hill, 1951–59; CDL (subsid. of ICL), 1959–62; F International Group, later F.I. Group, 1962–93 (Founder and Chief Exec., 1962–87; Settlor Xansa Employee (formerly FI Shareholders') Trust, 1981); Life Pres., Xansa (formerly F.I. Gp plc), 1993; Director: AEA Technology Plc, 1992–2000; Tandem Computers Inc., 1992–97; John Lewis Partnership plc, 1999–2001; European Adv. Bd, Korn/Ferry Internat., 2001–04; CSR Adv. Bd, Steria, 2008–. Member: Computer, Systems and Electronics Requirements Bd, 1979–81; Electronics and Avionics Requirements Bd, 1981–83; Open Tech, MSC, 1983–86; Council, Industrial Soc., 1984–90; NCVQ, 1986–89; Dir, Strategy Bd, Oxford Internet Inst., 2000–. Pres., British Computer Soc., 1989–90; Vice Pres., C&G, 2000–05. Consulting Editor on information processing, J. Wiley & Sons, 1978–87. Member: Council, Duke of Edinburgh's Seventh Commonwealth Study Conf., 1991–92; British-N American Cttee, 1992–2001. Chm., Women of Influence, 1993. Chm., Autism Speaks (formerly Nat. Alliance for Autism Res. (UK)), 2006–; Trustee: Help The Aged, 1987–90; Nat. Alliance for Autism Res. (USA), 2004–06. Patron: Disablement Income Gp, 1989–2001; Centre for Tomorrow's Co., 1997–; Mem., Oxford Univ. Ct of Benefactors, 2001–; Companion, Guild of Cambridge Benefactors, 2006–. Founder: The Kingwood Trust, 1993; The Shirley Foundn, 1996; Prior's Court Foundn, 1998; Autism Cymru, 2001. Master, Information Technologists' Co., 1992 (Liveryman, 1992); Freeman, City of London, 1987. CCMI (CBIM 1984); FREng 2001. Hon. FCGI 1989. Hon. Fellow: Manchester Metropolitan Univ. (formerly Poly.), 1989; Staffordshire Univ. (formerly Poly.), 1991; Sheffield Hallam Univ., 1992; IMCB, 1999; Birkbeck, 2002; New Hall, Cambridge, 2002; Foundn Fellow, Balliol Coll., Oxford, 2001. Hon. DSc: Buckingham, 1991; Aston, 1993; Nottingham Trent, 1994; Southampton Inst., 1994; Southampton, 2003; Brunel, 2005; Hon. DTech: Loughborough, 1991; Kingston, 1995; DUniv: Leeds Metropolitan, 1993; Derby, 1997; London Guildhall, 1998; Stirling, 2000; Hon. DLitt de Montfort, 1993; Hon. DBA: West of England, 1995; City, 2000; Hon. Dr Edinburgh, 2003; Hon. LLD: Leicester, 2005; Bath, 2006. Recognition of Information Technology Achievement Award, 1985; Gold Medal, Inst. of Mgt, 1991; Mountbatten Medal, IEE, 1999; Beacon Prize for Startups, Beacon Fellowship Charitable Trust, 2003; Lifetime Achievement Award, BCS, 2004. US Nat. Women's Hall of Fame, 1995. *Publication:* The Art of Prior's Court School, 2002. *Recreation:* wishful thinking. *Address:* 47 Thames House, Phyllis Court Drive, Henley-on-Thames, Oxon RG9 2NA. *T:* (01491) 579004, *Fax:* (01491) 574995; *e-mail:* steve@steveshirley.com. *Club:* Royal Society of Medicine.

SHIRLEY-QUIRK, John Stanton, CBE 1975; bass-baritone singer; Member, Voice Faculty, Peabody Conservatory, Baltimore, since 1991; *b* 28 Aug. 1931; *s* of Joseph Stanley and Amelia Shirley-Quirk; *m* 1st, 1955, Patricia Hastie (*d* 1981); one *s* one *d*; 2nd, 1981, Sara V. Watkins (*d* 1997); one *s* one *d* (and one *d* decd). *Educ:* Holt School, Liverpool; Liverpool University. Violin Scholarship, 1945; read Chemistry, Liverpool Univ., 1948–53; BSc (Hons), 1952; Dipl. in Educn 1953; became professional singer, 1961. Officer in Education Br., RAF, 1953–57. Asst Lectr in Chemistry, Acton Technical Coll., 1957–61; Lay-clerk in St Paul's Cathedral, 1961–62. First Appearance Glyndebourne Opera in Elegy for Young Lovers, 1961; subseq. 1962, 1963. Sang in first performance of Curlew River, 1964, The Burning Fiery Furnace, 1966, The Prodigal Son, 1968, Owen Wingrave, 1970, Death in Venice, 1973, Confessions of a Justified Sinner, 1976, The Ice Break, 1977. Has sung world wide. First American tour, 1966; Australian tour, 1967; first appearance Metropolitan Opera, NY, 1974. Has made numerous recordings: operas, songs, cantatas, etc. Mem. Voice Faculty, Carnegie-Mellon Univ., Pittsburgh, 1994–98. Mem. Court, Brunel Univ., 1977–81. Hon. RAM 1972; Hon. DMus Liverpool, 1976; DUniv Brunel, 1981. Liverpool Univ. Chem. Soc. Medal, 1965; Sir Charles Santley Meml Gift, Worshipful Co. of Musicians, 1969. *Recreations:* trees, canals, clocks. *Address:* 6062 Red Clover Lane, Clarksville, MD 21029–1272, USA; *e-mail:* jssq@peabody.jhu.edu.

SHIRRAS, Ven. Edward Scott; Priest-in-charge, Marcham with Garford, diocese of Oxford, since 2002; *b* 23 April 1937; *s* of Edward Shirras and Alice Emma Shirras (*née* Morten); *m* 1962, Pamela Susan Mackenzie; two *s* two *d*. *Educ:* Sevenoaks School; St Andrews Univ. (BSc); Union Coll., Schenectady, NY, USA; Clifton Theolog. Coll., Bristol. Curate: Christ Church, Surbiton Hill, 1963–66; Jesmond Parish Church, Newcastle upon Tyne, 1966–68; Church Pastoral Aid Society: Youth Sec., 1968–71; Publications Sec., 1971–74; Asst Gen. Sec., 1974–75; Vicar of Christ Church, Roxeth, dio. London, 1975–85; Area Dean of Harrow, 1982–85; Archdeacon of Northolt, 1985–92; Vicar, Christ Church, Winchester, 1992–2001. *Recreations:* transport photography (Scottish), Aberdeen FC. *Address:* 1 All Saints Close, Marcham, Abingdon, Oxon OX13 6PE. *T:* (01865) 391319; *e-mail:* epshirras@aol.com.

SHIRREFF, Lt-Gen. Alexander Richard David, CBE 2001; Commander Allied Rapid Reaction Corps, since 2007; *b* 21 Oct. 1955; *s* of Alexander David Shirreff, MC and Dione Hilary Shirreff (*née* Wood-White); *m* 1980, Sarah-Jane Patrick; one *s* one *d*. *Educ:* Oundle Sch.; Exeter Coll., Oxford (BA, MA Mod. Hist.). Commnd 14th/20th King's Hussars, 1978; sc 1986–87; COS HQ 33 Armoured Bde, 1988–89; MA to C-in-C BAOR and Comdr Northern Army Gp, 1992–94; Comdg King's Royal Hussars, 1994–96; Col, Army Plans, MoD, 1996–98; Comdr 7th Armoured Bde, 1999–2000; Principal SO to CDS, 2000–02; rcds 2003; COS HQ Land Comd, 2003–05; GOC 3rd (UK) Div., 2005–07. *Recreations:* ski-ing, game shooting, history, reading. *Address:* c/o Home HQ (South), King's Royal Hussars, Peninsula Barracks, Winchester, Hants SO23 8TS. *T:* (01962) 828539. *Club:* Cavalry and Guards.

SHIRREFS, Richard; Executive Vice-President, RHJ International SA, since 2006; *b* 7 May 1955; *s* of William R. and Patricia W. Shirrefs; *m* (marr. diss.); one *s*. *Educ:* Univ. of Birmingham (BSc Hons 1977). ACCA 1981, FCCA 1986. Financial analyst, Tube Investments, 1977–79; Mgt Accountant, El Paso, Paris, 1979–83; Analyst, 1983–86, Finance Dir, Aftermarket Div., 1986–90, Gp Controller, 1990–93, Bendix Europe; Finance and Logistics Dir, Catteau (Tesco), 1993–96; Chief Financial Officer, 1996–2001, Chief Exec., 2002–04, Eurotunnel.

SHIVAS, Mark; film and television producer; Chairman, Headline Pictures, since 2004; *b* 24 April 1938; *s* of James Dallas Shivas and Winifred Alice Lighton (*née* Bristow). *Educ:* Whitgift School; Merton College, Oxford (MA Law). Asst Editor, Movie Magazine, 1962–64; freelance journalist; joined Granada TV, 1964, Director-Producer, 1965–68; Producer of Drama, 1969–88, Head of Drama, 1988–93, Head of Films, 1993–97, BBC TV; Creative Dir, Southern Pictures, 1979–81. Productions include: The Six Wives of Henry VIII (BAFTA awards, Prix Italia), The Evacuees (BAFTA and Emmy awards), Casanova, The Glittering Prizes, Rogue Male, Professional Foul (BAFTA award), Telford's Change, On Giant's Shoulders (Emmy award), Talking Heads 2, Telling Tales, Cambridge Spies; for Channel 4: The Price, What if it's Raining?, The Storyteller (Emmy award); feature films include: Moonlighting, 1982; A Private Function, 1984; The Witches, 1988; Truly, Madly, Deeply, 1991; Enchanted April, 1991; The Snapper, 1993; Priest, 1995; Small Faces, 1996; Jude, 1996; Regeneration, 1997; Hideous Kinky, 1998; I Capture the Castle, 2002. *Publications:* articles in art jls. *Recreations:* Italy, gardens, swimming, cycling, moviegoing. *Address:* 38 Gloucester Mews, W2 3HE. *T:* (020) 7723 4678, *Fax:* (020) 7262 1415.

SHLAIM, Prof. Avi, PhD; FBA 2006; Professor of International Relations, University of Oxford, since 1996; Fellow, St Antony's College, Oxford, since 1987; *b* Baghdad, 31 Oct. 1945; *s* of Joseph and Aida Shlaim; *m* 1973, Gwyneth Daniel; one *d*. *Educ:* Jesus Coll., Cambridge (BA Hist. 1969); London Sch. of Econs (MSc(Econ.) Internat. Relns 1970); Reading Univ. (PhD Politics 1980). Lectr, 1970–86, Reader in Politics, 1986–87, Univ. of Reading; University of Oxford: Alastair Buchan Reader in Internat. Relns, 1987–96; Dir, Grad. Studies in Internat. Relns, 1993–95 and 1998–2001; Dir, Middle E Centre, St Antony's Coll., Oxford, 2007–08. Fellow, Woodrow Wilson Internat. Center for Scholars, Washington, 1980–81; British Acad. Res. Reader, 1995–97; British Acad. Res. Prof., 2003–06. *Publications:* (jtly) British Foreign Secretaries since 1945, 1977; The United States and the Berlin Blockade 1948–49: a study in crisis decision-making, 1983; Collusion across the Jordan: King Abdullah, the Zionist Movement, and the partition of Palestine, 1988; The Politics of Partition, 1990; War and Peace in the Middle East: a concise history, 1995; (ed jtly) The Cold War and the Middle East, 1997; The Iron Wall: Israel and the Arab world, 2000; (ed jtly) The War for Palestine: rewriting the history of 1948, 2001; Lion of Jordan: the life of King Hussein in war and peace, 2007. *Recreation:* walking and talking. *Address:* St Antony's College, Oxford OX2 6JF. *T:* (01865) 274460, *Fax:* (01865) 274529; *e-mail:* avi.shlaim@sant.ox.ac.uk.

SHOCK, Sir Maurice, Kt 1988; Rector, Lincoln College, Oxford, 1987–94, Hon. Fellow, 1995; *b* 15 April 1926; *o s* of Alfred and Ellen Shock; *m* 1947, Dorothy Donald (*d* 1998); one *s* three *d*. *Educ:* King Edward's Sch., Birmingham; Balliol Coll., Oxford (MA); St Antony's Coll., Oxford. Served Intell. Corps, 1945–48. Lectr in Politics, Christ Church and Trinity Coll., Oxford, 1955–56; Fellow and Praelector in Politics, University Coll.,

Oxford, 1956–77, Hon. Fellow, 1986; Estates Bursar, 1959–74; Vice-Chancellor, Leicester Univ., 1977–87. Sen. Treasurer, Oxford Union Soc., 1954–72 (Trustee, 1988–); Member: Franks Commn of Inquiry into the University of Oxford, 1964–66; Hebdomadal Council, Oxford Univ., 1969–75; Chairman: Univ. Authorities Panel, 1980–85; CVCP, 1985–87. Vis. Prof. of Govt, Pomona Coll., 1961–62, 1968–69. Member: ESRC, 1981–85; GMC, 1989–94; RAND Health Bd, 2000–; a Governing Trustee, 1980–2003, Chm., 1988–2003, Nuffield Trust. Trustee, Age Concern, Oxon, 2000–. Hon. Vice-Pres., Political Studies Assoc., 1989. Review Panel on Machinery of Government of Jersey, 1999–2000. Hon. FRCP 1989. Hon. LLD Leicester, 1987. *Publications:* The Liberal Tradition; articles on politics and recent history. *Recreations:* gardening, theatre. *Address:* 4 Cunliffe Close, Oxford OX2 7BL.

SHOEBRIDGE, Michele Indianna; Director, Academic Services, University of Exeter, since 2006; *b* 7 Nov. 1954; *d* of Charles William Shoebridge and Maisie Indianna Shoebridge (*née* Wissenden); partner, Phillip Reed; one *d*. *Educ:* Maidstone Tech. High Sch. for Girls; Univ. of Birmingham (BA Hons Medieval and Mod. Hist. 1976); Univ. of Central England (Postgrad DipLib 1977); Wolverhampton Univ. (MA 1982). University of Birmingham: various posts, University Library, 1979–95, Information Services, 1995–2002; Dir, Inf. Services, 2002–06. *Publications:* Women in Sport: a select bibliography, 1988; Union Catalogue of Periodicals in Sport and Recreation, 1988; Information Sources in Sport and Leisure, 1991; (jtly) A History of the Birmingham Athletic Institute, 1992; articles in jls on aspects of inf. mgt, teaching and learning. *Recreations:* family, cinema, allotment. *Address:* Information Services, University of Exeter, Main Library, Stocker Road, Exeter EX4 4PT.

SHONE, Very Rev. John Terence; Team Vicar, Cullercoats Team, Marden St Hilda, Diocese of Newcastle, 1989–2000; retired; *b* 15 May 1935; *s* of late Arthur Shone and E. B. Shone; *m* 1st, 1958, Ursula Ruth Buss (marr. diss.); three *s*; 2nd, 1987, Annette Simmons, *d* of late William Caterer and Ada Caterer. *Educ:* St Dunstan's College; Selwyn Coll., Cambridge (BA 1958, MA 1962); Lincoln Theological Coll.; Newcastle Univ. (MA 1992). Deacon 1960, priest 1961, London; Curate, St Pancras Parish Church, 1960–62; Chaplain, St Andrew's Cathedral, Aberdeen, 1962–65; Chaplain to Anglican Students, Aberdeen, 1962–68; Lectr, Aberdeen Coll. of Education, 1965–68; Exam. Chaplain to Bishop of Aberdeen, 1966–68; Vicar, St Andrew and St Luke, Grimsby, 1968–69; Rector, St Saviour, Bridge of Allan, 1969–86; Chaplain, Stirling Univ., 1969–80; Priest i/c, St John's, Alloa, 1977–85, and St James', Dollar, 1981–86; Canon, St Ninian's Cathedral, Perth, 1980–82; Dean, 1982–89, Dean Emeritus, 2000, United Dio. of St Andrews, Dunkeld and Dunblane; Diocesan R & D Officer, 1986–89. *Address:* Carnoch Croft, 33d Grange Road, Alloa, Clackmannanshire FK10 1LR. *T:* (01259) 721388.

SHONE, Richard Noel; Editor, The Burlington Magazine, since 2003; *b* Doncaster, 8 May 1949; *s* of Dr Godfrey Noel Shone and Eleanor May Shone (*née* Clough). *Educ:* Wrekin Coll.; Clare Coll., Cambridge (BA 1971). Associate Ed., The Burlington Mag., 1979–2003. Exhibition Curator: Portraits by Duncan Grant, Arts Council, 1969; Duncan Grant: designer, 1980; Portraits by Walter Sickert, 1990; Sickert (co-selector), RA and Van Gogh Mus., Amsterdam, 1992–93; Head First, Arts Council tour, 1998–99; The Art of Bloomsbury, Tate Gall., London, Huntington Liby, San Marino, Calif, Yale Center for British Art, New Haven, Conn, 1999–2000. Mem., Adv. Cttee, Govt Art Collection, 1990–94. Member: Charleston Trust, 1981–; Jury, Turner Prize, 1988. *Publications:* Bloomsbury Portraits: Vanessa Bell, Duncan Grant and their circle, 1976, 2nd edn 1993; The Century of Change: British art since 1900, 1977; The Post-Impressionists, 1980; Walter Sickert, 1988; Rodrigo Moynihan, 1988; Alfred Sisley, 1992; Damien Hirst, 2001; numerous catalogue introductions. *Address:* c/o The Burlington Magazine, 14–16 Duke's Road, WC1H 9SZ; 87 High Street, Hastings, E Sussex TN34 3ES. *Club:* Cranium.

SHOOTER, Prof. Eric Manvers, FRS 1988; Professor of Neurobiology, Stanford University, 1975–2004, now Emeritus; *b* 18 April 1924; adopted US nationality, 1991; *s* of Fred and Pattie Shooter; *m* 1949, Elaine Staley Arnold; one *d*. *Educ:* Gonville and Caius Coll., Cambridge (BA 1945; MA 1950; PhD 1950; ScD 1986); DSc London 1964. Senior Scientist, Brewing Industry Research Foundn, 1950–53; Lectr in Biochem., University Coll. London, 1953–63; Stanford University: Associate Prof. of Genetics, 1963–68; Prof. of Genetics and Prof. of Biochem., 1968–75; Chm. of Neurobiol., 1975–87. Macy Faculty Scholar, Univ. of Geneva, 1974–75. Member: Inst. of Medicine, Nat. Acad. of Scis, USA, 1989; Nat. Acad. of Scis, 2000; Amer. Philos. Soc., 2002. Fellow: American Acad. of Arts and Scis, 1993; AAAS, 1998. Wakeman Award, 1988; Ralph W. Gerard Prize in Neuroscience, 1995; Bristol-Myers Squibb Award for Dist. Achievement in Neurosci. Res., 1997. *Publications:* (associate editor) Annual Review of Neuroscience, vols 6–24, 1983–2001; numerous papers in sci jls. *Address:* Department of Neurobiology, Stanford University School of Medicine, Stanford, CA 94305–5125, USA. *T:* (650) 7237559.

SHOOTER, Michael Stanhope, CBE 2005; FRCPsych; President, Royal College of Psychiatrists, 2002–05; *b* 19 Sept. 1944; *s* of Arnold Shooter and Audrey Frances Shooter (*née* Stanhope); *m* 1967, Mary Davies; three *s* one *d*. *Educ:* Lady Manners Sch., Bakewell; St Catharine's Coll., Cambridge (MA Hist./Law); Clare Coll., Cambridge (MB BChir). FRCPsych 1994. Consultant: Child and Adolescent Psychiatry, S Glamorgan, 1982–94; and Clinical Dir, Child Psychiatry Service, Gwent Healthcare NHS Trust, 1994–2002. Dir of Public Educn, 1994–2002, Registrar, 1997–2002, RCPsych. Chairman: Young Minds, 2006–; Children in Wales, 2006–; Mental Health Foundn, 2008–. *Publications:* contrib. books and jls on all aspects of psychiatry and paediatric liaison in UK, USA and elsewhere. *Recreations:* horse-racing, poetry, late-night cards in isolated country pubs. *Address:* Royal College of Psychiatrists, 17 Belgrave Square, SW1X 8PG. *T:* (020) 7235 2352, *Fax:* (020) 7245 1231; *e-mail:* mshooter@rcpsych.ac.uk; Ty Boda, Upper Llanover, Abergavenny, Gwent NP7 9EP. *Club:* East India.

SHOOTER, Prof. Reginald Arthur, CBE 1980; Emeritus Professor of Medical Microbiology, London University, since 1981; *b* 4 April 1916; *s* of Rev. A. E. Shooter, TD and M. K. Shooter; *m* 1946, Jean Wallace, MB, ChB; one *s* three *d*. *Educ:* Mill Hill Sch.; Caius Coll., Cambridge; St Bartholomew's Hosp. BA 1937; MB, BChir 1940; MRCS, LRCP 1940; MA 1941; MD 1945; MRCP 1961; FRCP 1968; FRCS 1977; FRCPath 1963 (Vice-Pres., 1971–74). After various Hosp. appts became Surgeon Lieut, RNVR. Appointments at St Bartholomew's Hospital from 1946; Rockefeller Travelling Fellow in Medicine, 1950–51; Reader in Bacteriology, 1953–61, Prof. of Medical Microbiology, 1961–81, Univ. of London; Bacteriologist to St Bartholomew's Hosp., 1961–81 and Dean, Medical Coll., 1972–81. Member: City and E London AHA (T), 1974–81; Gloucester HA, 1981–85; Chm., Regional Computing Policy Steering Gp, SW RHA, 1983–85. Mem., Public Health Lab. Service Bd, 1970–82; Chm., Dangerous Pathogens Adv. Gp, 1975–81. Mem., Scientific Adv. Council, Stress Foundn, 1981–90. Governor: St Bartholomew's Hosp., 1972–74; Queen Mary Coll., 1972–81; Trustee: Mitchell City of London Trust, 1958–82; Jenner Trust, 1989–2001 (Smallpox Archivist, 2001–). Mem. Court, City Univ., 1972–81. Pybus Medal, N of England Surg. Soc., 1979. Asst Editor, British Jl of Exp. Pathology, 1953–58; Hon. Editor, RSocMed, 1960–65. *Publications:* books, and articles in medical journals. *Recreations:* archaeology, gardening, fishing. *Address:* Eastlea, Back Edge Lane, The Edge, Stroud, Glos GL6 6PE. *T:* (01452) 812408.

SHORE OF STEPNEY, Lady; *see* Shore, E. C.

SHORE, Dr Elizabeth Catherine, CB 1980; Chairman, St Ives University of the Third Age, 2004–07; *b* 19 Aug. 1927; *d* of Edward Murray Wrong and Rosalind Grace Smith; *m* 1948, Peter David Shore (later Baron Shore of Stepney, PC; he *d* 2001); one *s* two *d* (and one *s* decd). *Educ:* Newnham Coll., Cambridge; St Bartholomew's Hospital; BA Hons Open 1999. MRCP, FRCP; MRCS, FFCM, DRCOG. Joined Medical Civil Service, 1962; Dep. Chief Medical Officer, DHSS, 1977–85. Dean of Postgrad. Medicine, NW Thames Reg., 1985–93; Assoc. Dean of Postgrad. Med. Educn, N Thames Reg., 1993–95. Hon. Sen. Lectr, Charing Cross and Westminster Med. Sch., 1993–97. Mem., GMC, 1989–94 (Member: Standards Cttee, 1989–91; Professional Conduct Cttee, 1991–93; Educnl Cttee, 1992–93; Prelim. Proceeding Cttee, 1993). Pres., Med. Women's Fedn, 1990–92 (Chm., Careers Cttee, 1989–95); Chair: BMA Career Progress Cttee, 1994–96; BMA Working Party on Exodus of Doctors, 1996–97. Mem. Council, PSI, 1992–2001; Chm., Mgt Cttee, St Ives Archive Centre, 2005–07. Trustee, Child Accident Prevention Trust, 1985–91 (Chm., Council and Professional Cttee, 1985–90). Editor, Medical Woman, 1992–98. *Recreations:* reading, cookery, swimming in rough seas. *Address:* 3 Barnaloft, St Ives, Cornwall TR26 1NJ.

SHORE, Jack; President, Royal Cambrian Academy of Art, 1977–83; *b* 17 July 1922; *s* of Frank and Maggie Shore; *m* 1970, Olive Brenda Williams; one *s* one *d*. *Educ:* Accrington and Manchester Schools of Art. Lectr, Blackpool School of Art, 1945–60; Head, Chester Sch. of Art, 1960–81. Paintings in public and private collections, including USA. RCamA 1962–2003 (ARCamA 1961). Jubilee Medal, 1977. *Recreations:* gardening, enjoyment of music. *Address:* 11 St George's Crescent, Queens Park, Chester CH4 7AR. *T:* (01244) 675017.

SHORLEY, Deborah Catherine, FCLIP; Director of Library Services, Imperial College London, since 2007; President, Chartered Institute of Library and Information Professionals, 2005–06; *b* 28 May 1950; *d* of Dennis Randall and Monica (*née* Wilson); *m* 1976, Christopher Shorley. *Educ:* Univ. of Durham (BA Hons French 1972); Queen's Univ., Belfast (DLIS 1977). FCLIP 2004. Librarian: Central Liby, Belfast, 1977–80; Ulster Polytechnic, subseq. Univ. of Ulster, 1980–2000; Univ. of Sussex, 2000–07. *Publications:* contrib. articles on liby and information issues to professional jls. *Recreations:* photography, cycling, cooking, travelling. *Address:* Imperial College London Library, Imperial College London, South Kensington, SW7 2AZ. *T:* (020) 7594 8881, *Fax:* (020) 7584 3763; *e-mail:* d.shorley@imperial.ac.uk.

SHORROCK, (John) Michael; QC 1988; a Recorder of the Crown Court, since 1982; *b* 25 May 1943; *s* of late James Godby Shorrock and Mary Patricia Shorrock (*née* Lings); *m* 1971, Marianne (*née* Mills); two *d*. *Educ:* Clifton College, Bristol; Pembroke College, Cambridge. MA. Called to the Bar, Inner Temple, 1966, Bencher, 1995; practising on Northern Circuit, 1966–: Junior, 1968; Sec., Exec. Cttee, 1981–85. Member: Criminal Injuries Compensation Bd, 1995–2000; Criminal Injuries Compensation Appeals Panel, 1996–. Gov., William Hulme's Grammar Sch., 1999–2005. *Recreations:* walking, gardening, opera, theatre, cinema. *Address:* 2 Harcourt Buildings, Temple, EC4Y 9DB. *T:* (020) 7353 2112; Peel Court Chambers, Sunlight House, Quay Street, Manchester M3 3JZ. *T:* (0161) 832 3791.

SHORT, family name of **Baron Glenamara**.

SHORT, Alan; *see* Short, C. A.

SHORT, Bernard David, CBE 1995; Head of Further Education Support Unit, Department for Education and Employment (formerly Department for Education), 1993–96; *b* 9 June 1935; *s* of late Bernard Charles and of Ethel Florence Short; *m* 1960, Susan Yvonne Taylor; two *s* one *d*. *Educ:* St Edmund Hall, Oxford (MA). Served The Royal Scots, 1953–56 (commnd 1954). Taught at Ingiliz Erkek Lisesi, Istanbul, Turkey, 1960–63; Lectr, Univ. of Kyushu, Japan, 1963–65; Asst Lectr, Garretts Green Technical Coll., Birmingham, 1966–67; Lectr, Bournville Coll. of Further Educn, Birmingham, 1967–71; Sen. Lectr, Henley Coll. of Further Educn, Coventry, 1971–73; Head, Dept of Gen. Studies, Bournville Coll., Birmingham, 1973–76; HM Inspectorate of Schools, 1976–93: Inspector, 1976; Staff Inspector, 1984; Chief Inspector, Further Education, 1986. Chm. of Govs, Bournville Coll., Birmingham, 2000–06. FRSA 1991. *Publications:* A Guide to Stress in English, 1967; Humour, 1970. *Recreations:* music, gardening, boats.

SHORT, Prof. (Charles) Alan, RIBA; Professor of Architecture, University of Cambridge, since 2001 (Head, Department of Architecture, 2001–04); Fellow, Clare Hall, Cambridge, since 2002; Principal, Short & Associates, since 1997; *b* 23 March 1955; *s* of C. R. and D. H. Short; *m* 2003, Slaine Catherine Campbell; one *d*. *Educ:* Trinity Coll., Cambridge (MA, DipArch). RIBA 1981. Exchange Fellow, Harvard Grad. Sch. of Design, 1979–80; Partner: Edward Cullinan Architects, 1980–86; Peake Short and Partners, 1986–92; Short Ford & Associates, 1992–97; Dean, Faculty of Art and Design, De Montfort Univ., 1997–2001. FRSA 1998. Major projects include: Simonds Farsons Cisk Brewery, Malta (High Architecture, Low Energy Award, Architecture Today jl, 1994); Queen's Building, Leicester (Green Building of the Year Award, Independent/RIBA, 1995); Coventry Univ. Library (Public Building of Year award, Building mag., 2001); Poole Arts Centre, Dorset, 2002 (Project of Year Award, CIBSE, 2003); Lichfield Garrick Theatre, 2003 (Project of Year Award, CIBSE, 2004); new SSEES for UCL, 2005 (RIBA Award, 2006; Envmntl Initiative of the Year Award, CIBSE, 2006; Public Building of the Year, BDA, 2006); Braunstone Integrated Health and Social Care Centre, 2005. RIBA President's Award for Res., 2007. *Publications:* contrib. various professional jls, UK, China, USA, Italy and Germany. *Recreations:* restoration of family home and gardens in Lincolnshire, historical and contemporary landscape. *Address:* Department of Architecture, University of Cambridge, 1–4 Scroope Terrace, Trumpington Road, Cambridge CB2 1PX. *T:* (01223) 332958, *Fax:* (01223) 307443; *e-mail:* post@short-assoc.demon.co.uk. *Clubs:* Chelsea Arts, Oxford and Cambridge.

SHORT, Rt Hon. Clare; PC 1997; MP for Birmingham, Ladywood, since 1983 (Lab, 1983–2006, Ind, since 2006); *b* 15 Feb. 1946; *d* of late Frank Short and Joan Short; *m* 1981, Alexander Ward Lyon (*d* 1993), sometime MP for York; one *s* by previous marriage. *Educ:* Keele Univ.; Leeds Univ. (BA Hons Political Sci.). Home Office, 1970–75; Dir, All Faiths for One Race, Birmingham, 1976–78; Dir, Youth Aid and the Unemployment Unit, 1979–83. Chm., All Party Parly Gp on Race Relations, 1985–86; Mem., Home Affairs Select Cttee, 1983–85; front bench spokesperson on employment, 1985–88, on social security, 1989–91, on envmtl protection, 1993, on women, 1993–95, on transport, 1995–96, on overseas develt, 1996–97; Sec. of State for Internat. Develt, 1997–2003. Mem., Labour Party NEC, 1988–98. *Publications:* Talking Blues: a study of young West Indians' views of policing, 1978; Handbook of Immigration Law, 1978; Dear Clare … this is what women think about Page 3, 1991; An Honourable Deception?, 2004. *Recreations:*

family and friends, swimming. *Address:* House of Commons, SW1A 0AA. *T:* (020) 7219 3000.

SHORT, Maj. Gen. James Henderson Terry, CB 2005; OBE 1994; Director, Joint Warfare Centre (formerly Joint Headquarters North), Norway, 2002–05; *b* 20 March 1950; *s* of Frederick Gordon Terry Short and Verona Margaret Terry Short (*née* Peters); *m* 1975, Claire Elizabeth Hedley (*née* Hooper); two *s*. *Educ:* Wellington Coll., Berks; RMCS, Shrivenham (BSc Hons Applied Sci.). Regtl Service, 9th/12th Royal Lancers, 1970–82; army staff course, 1982–83; Cabinet Office Assessments Staff, 1984–85; MA to Comdr 1 (BR) Corps, 1985–87; Directing Staff, Staff Coll., Camberley, 1988–90; Procurement Exec., MoD, 1991–92; CO 9th/12th Royal Lancers, 1992–94; Comdr 39 Infantry Bde, Belfast, 1995–97; Dir, RAC, 1997–2000; Special Advr to Macedonian Govt, 2000–02. Col, 9th/12th Royal Lancers, 2008–. Chm., Jesse May Trust, 2008–. FCMI (FIMgt 1997). *Recreations:* sailing, ski-ing, tennis, windsurfing. *Address:* 11 Tansy Lane, Portishead, N Somerset BS20 7JL. *T:* (01275) 848991; *e-mail:* courtshortfamily@hotmail.com. *Club:* Cavalry and Guards.

SHORT, Rt Rev. Kenneth Herbert, AO 1988; Dean of Sydney (St Andrew's Cathedral), 1989–92; *b* 6 July 1927; *s* of Cecil Charles Short and Joyce Ellen Begbie; *m* 1950, Gloria Noelle Funnell; one *s* two *d*. *Educ:* Moore Theological Coll. (ThL and Moore Coll. Dipl.). Commissioned AIF, 1946; with BCOF, 1946–48; theological training, 1949–52; ordained Anglican Ministry, 1952; Minister in Charge, Provisional Parish of Pittwater, 1952–54; with CMS in Tanzania, E Africa, 1955–64; Chaplain, Tabora 1955, Mwanza 1955–59; founding Principal, Msalato Bible School, 1961–64; Gen. Secretary, CMS NSW Branch, 1964–71, including Sec. for S America; Canon of St Andrew's Cathedral, Sydney, 1970–75; Exam. Chaplain to Archbishop of Sydney, 1971–82; Rector of St Michael's, Vaucluse, 1971–75; Bishop of Wollongong, Dio. of Sydney, 1975–82 (Acting Bishop, 1993 and 1999); Archdeacon of Wollongong and Camden, 1975–79; Chaplain Gen. (CE), Australian Army, 1979–81; Anglican Bishop to Aust. Defence Force (Army, Navy and Air Force), 1979–89; Bishop of Parramatta, Dio. of Sydney, 1982–89; Assistant, St John's Shaughnessy, Vancouver, Dio. of New Westminster, 1992–93 and 1995–96. Acting Gen. Sec., CMS Victoria, 1997, NSW, 1998. ChStJ 1989. *Publications:* Guidance, 1969; (contrib.) Evangelism and Preaching in Secular Australia, 1989. *Recreations:* reading, walking. *Address:* 2/5 Brown Street, Kiama, NSW 2533, Australia. *T:* (2) 42321261.

SHORT, Nigel David, Hon. MBE 1999; professional chess player; *b* 1 June 1965; *s* of David Malcolm Short and Jean Short (*née* Gaskell); *m* 1987, Rhea Argyro, *d* of Nikolaos Karageorgiou; one *s* one *d*. *Educ:* Bolton Sch. British chess champion: 1979 (equal first), 1984, 1987, 1998; English Chess Champion, 1991; internat. master 1980; grandmaster 1984; world championship candidate, 1985–93 (finalist, 1992, defeating Anatoly Karpov in semi-final); Commonwealth Champion, 2004, 2006; EU Champion, 2006. Formed Professional Chess Assoc. with Gary Kasparov, 1993, Sec. Gen., 2005–. Chess columnist: Sunday Telegraph, 1996–2005; The Guardian, 2005–06. *Recreations:* olive farming, cricket, swimming, guitar.

SHORT, Peter, BA; IPFA; financial management consultant, since 1995; *b* 21 June 1945; *s* of Christopher John Grewcock Short and Isabella Short; *m* 1967, Eileen Short (*née* Makin); one *s* one *d*. *Educ:* South Shields Grammar Sch.; Univ. of Exeter (2nd Cl. Hons, Div. 1, Modern Economic History). IPFA (1st place Final, 1970). Local Govt Accountant with Manchester City Council, 1967–73; Leeds City Council, 1973–78; Dir of Finance, South Tyneside MDC, 1978–83; City Treas. and Dep. Chief Exec., Manchester CC, 1983–89; Dir of Finance, Greater Manchester Buses Ltd, 1989–93; Man. Dir, Gtr Manchester Buses South Ltd, 1993–95. *Recreations:* reading, walking, avoiding household maintenance, reminiscing about walking the Pennine Way. *Address:* 2 Netherwood Road, Northenden, Manchester M22 4BQ.

SHORT, Robin; *see* Short, W. R.

SHORT, Prof. Roger Valentine, AM 2004; FRCOG; FRS 1974; FRSE; FRCVS; FAA; Professorial Fellow, Faculty of Medicine, University of Melbourne, since 2006; *b* 31 July 1930; *s* of F. A. and M. C. Short, Weybridge; *m* 1st, 1958, Dr Mary Bowen Wilson (marr. diss. 1981); one *s* three *d*; 2nd, 1982, Prof. Marilyn Bernice Renfree; two *d*. *Educ:* Sherborne Sch.; Univs of Bristol (BVSc, MRCVS), Wisconsin (MSc) and Cambridge (PhD, ScD). FRSE 1974; FRCVS 1976; FAA 1984; FRCOG 1991. Mem., ARC Unit of Reproductive Physiology and Biochemistry, Cambridge, 1956–72; Fellow, Magdalene Coll., Cambridge, 1962–72; Lectr, then Reader, Dept of Veterinary Clinical Studies, Cambridge, 1961–72; Dir, MRC Unit of Reproductive Biology, Edinburgh, 1972–82; Prof. of Reproductive Biology, Monash Univ., Australia, 1982–95; Wexler Professorial Fellow, Dept of Perinatal Medicine, subseq. Obstetrics and Gynaecol., Univ. of Melbourne, 1996–2005. Hon. Prof., Univ. of Edinburgh, 1976–82. Chm., Bd of Dirs, Family Health Internat., NC, USA, 1984–90. Fellow, American Acad. of Arts and Scis. Hon. DSc: Guelph, 1988; Bristol, 1997; Edinburgh, 2002. *Publications:* (ed, with C. R. Austin) Reproduction in Mammals, vols 1–8, 1972–80, 2nd edn vols 1–5, 1982–86; (ed, with D. T. Baird) Contraceptives of the Future, 1976; (with M. Potts) Ever Since Adam and Eve, 1999; contrib. Jl Endocrinology, Jl Reproduction and Fertility, Jl Zoology, Lancet, Nature. *Recreations:* gardening, wildlife, history of biology. *Address:* The Dean's Ganglion, Level 4, 766 Elizabeth Street, University of Melbourne, Vic 3010, Australia.

SHORT, Maj.-Gen. William Robert, (Robin), CB 1999; Operations Director, PHC Ltd, 1999–2007; *b* 30 March 1942; *s* of Dr Andrew Galbraith Short and Dr Helen Greig Short (*née* Dunlop); *m* 1967, Annette Pamela Barrow; three *s*. *Educ:* Glasgow High Sch.; Glasgow Univ. (MB ChB). RMO, 1 Black Watch, RHR, 1969–72; 19 Field Ambulance, RAMC, 1972–73; RAMC Trg Centre, 1973–76; Army Staff Coll., 1976–77 (psc); S02, Med. HQ 1 (BR) Corps, 1978–81; CO, 3 Armd Field Ambulance, RAMC, 1981–84; Chief Instr, RAMC Trg Centre, 1984–86; Comdr Med. 1 Armd Div., 1986–88; Col, Ops and Plans, 1988–91, Dir Med. Ops and Logistics, 1991–94, Defence Med. Services Directorate; Comdr, Med. HQ Land Comd, 1994–96; DGAMS, 1996–99. Chm., RAMC Assoc., 1999–2005. QHP, 1996–99. CStJ 1997 (OStJ 1971). *Recreations:* gardening, ski-ing, collecting cigarette cards (cartophily).

SHORTER, Hugo Benedict; HM Diplomatic Service; Counsellor (Global Issues), Paris, since 2007; *b* 11 Aug. 1966; *s* of Gervase Shorter and Charmian Shorter (*née* Stopford-Adams); *m* 2001, Laura Mercedes Lindon; two *s* one *d*. *Educ:* Lycée Molière, Rio de Janeiro; Queen's Coll., Oxford (BA 1988); Ecole Nat. d'Admin, Paris. Entered HM Diplomatic Service, 1990; FCO, 1990–92; Second Sec., on attachment to Ecole Nat. d'Admin, Paris, 1992–93; Second, later First, Sec., UK Delegn to NATO, 1994–98; FCO, 1998; Private Sec to Minister of State, FCO, 2000–01; Dep. Hd, NE Asia and Pacific Dept, FCO, 2001–04; Dep. Hd of Mission, Brasilia, 2004–07. *Recreations:* reading, cooking, travel, sailing. *Address:* c/o Foreign and Commonwealth Office, King Charles Street, SW1A 2AH; *e-mail:* hugo.shorter@fco.gov.uk.

SHORTIS, Maj.-Gen. Colin Terry, CB 1988; CBE 1980 (OBE 1977; MBE 1974); General Officer Commanding North West District, 1986–89; *b* 18 Jan. 1934; *s* of late Tom Richardson Shortis and Marna Evelyn Shortis (*née* Kenworthy); *m* 1957, Sylvia Mary (*d* 2006), *o d* of H. C. A. Jenkinson; two *s* two *d*. *Educ:* Bedford School. Enlisted Army 1951; 2nd Lieut Royal Fusiliers, 1953; transf. to Dorset Regt, 1955; served Hong Kong, Korea, Suez Canal Zone, Sudan, BAOR, Aden, Singapore and British Guiana, 1953–63; Instructor, Sch. of Infantry, 1964–65; Staff Coll., 1966; Co. Comdr, 1st Devonshire and Dorset, 1967–73; served Malta, NI, Belize, Cyprus, BAOR, CO 1974–77; Directing Staff, Staff Coll., 1977; Comdr, 8 Infantry Brigade, 1978–80; RCDS 1981; Comdr, British Mil. Adv. and Training Team, Zimbabwe, 1982–83; Dir of Infantry, 1983–86. Col Comdt, The Prince of Wales Div., 1983–88; Col, Devonshire and Dorset Regt, 1984–90. *Recreation:* sailing. *Address:* Hart House, 52 Fore Street, Topsham, Exeter EX3 0HW. *Club:* Army and Navy.

SHORTRIDGE, Sir Jon Deacon, KCB 2002; Permanent Secretary, Welsh Office, then National Assembly for Wales, later Welsh Assembly Government, 1999–2008; *b* 10 April 1947; *s* of late Eric Creber Deacon Shortridge and Audrey Joan Shortridge (*née* Hunt); *m* 1972, Diana Jean Gordon; one *s* one *d*. *Educ:* Chichester High Sch.; St Edmund Hall, Oxford (MA); Edinburgh Univ. (MSc). Min. of Housing, then Countryside Commn, subseq. DoE, 1969–75; Shropshire County Planning Dept, 1975–84; Welsh Office: Principal, 1984–88, Pvte Sec. to Sec. of State for Wales, 1987–88; Asst Sec., 1988–92; G3, 1992–97; Dir of Economic Affairs, 1997–99; Perm. Sec., 1999. *Recreations:* sailing, tennis, walking, modern history. *Address:* 27 The Cathedral Green, Llandaff, Cardiff CF5 2EB. *T:* (029) 2056 5367.

SHORVON, Prof. Simon David, MD; FRCP; Professor in Clinical Neurology, Institute of Neurology, University College London, since 1995; Hon. Consultant Neurologist, National Hospital for Neurology and Neurosurgery (formerly for Nervous Diseases), since 1983; *b* 17 June 1948; *s* of late Hyam Joseph Shorvon, DPM and of Mary Barbara Shorvon (*née* Bensusan Butt), MRCPsych; *m* 1st, 1984, Penelope Farmer (marr. diss.); 2nd, 1999, Dr Lynne Soon Li Low; one *s*. *Educ:* City of London Sch.; Trinity Coll., Cambridge (BA 1970; MB BChir 1974; MA 1974; MD 1983); St Thomas' Hosp. Med. Sch. MRCP 1975, FRCP 1990. Jun. med. and academic appts, Oxford, Manchester, KCH, Maudsley Hosp., and Nat. Hosp for Nervous Diseases, 1973–83; Vis. Scientist, Univ. of Virginia, 1981; Sen. Lectr, 1983–92, Reader in Neurology, 1992–95, Chm., Dept of Clin. Neurology, 1998–2002, Inst. of Neurology, UCL; Dir, Nat. Neurosci. Inst., Singapore, 2000–03. Med. Dir, Nat. Soc. for Epilepsy, 1989–98. Member: Med. Panel, DVLA, 1987–; Disability Living Allowance Bd, 1994–96. International League Against Epilepsy: Mem., Exec. Cttee; Vice-Pres., 1993–; Information Officer, 1997–, Mem., editl bds, internat. learned jls; Guarantor, Brain, 1998–; Ed.-in-Chief, Epilepsia. *Publications:* Neurological Emergencies, 1989; Status Epilepticus: its clinical form and treatment in children and adults, 1994; (ed jtly) Magnetic Resonance Scanning and Epilepsy, 1994; (ed jtly) Epilepsy, 2nd edn 1995; Clinical Epilepsy, 1995; (ed jtly) The Treatment of Epilepsy, 1996, 2nd edn 2004; Handbook of Epilepsy Treatment, 2000, 2nd edn 2005; contribs to epilepsy, epidemiology and clin. neurology in learned jls. *Recreations:* the liberal arts, human rights and political freedom. *Address:* Department of Clinical Neurology, Institute of Neurology, University College London, Queen Square, WC1N 3BG. *T:* (020) 7837 3611; *e-mail:* s.shorvon@ion.ucl.ac.uk.

SHOSTAK, Raymond Jon, Hon. CBE 2005; Head, Prime Minister's Delivery Unit, since 2007; *b* 2 July 1949; *s* of late Jerome M. Shostak and Alma (*née* Stern); *m* 1980, Gill Rivaz; one *s* one *d*. *Educ:* Nanuet Jun. Sen. High Sch.; Syracuse Univ. (BA Hons); Univ. of Southern Calif (MSc). Teacher: Isbell Jun. High Sch., Santa Paula, Calif, 1971–73; Leggatts Sch., Watford, Herts, 1973–74; Dep. Warden, 1974, Warden, 1975–83, SW Herts Teachers' Centre, Herts CC; Sen. Staff Inspector, Notts CC Adv. Inspection Service, 1983–86; Asst Dir of Educn and Chief Advr, W Sussex CC, 1989–96; Ofsted Inspector, 1993–99; Head, Pupil Performance Team, Sch. Effectiveness Div., DFEE, 1996–97; Dir of Educn, 1997–2001, Dir, Children, Schs and Families Service, 2001–03, Herts CC; Strategic Advr, Children's Services, Improvement and Develt Agency, 2003; Dir, Public Services, HM Treasury, 2003–07. Dir, Herts TEC, 1997–2001; Board Member: QCA, 2001–03; Herts Learning and Skills Council, 2001–03; Chm., Wallenberg Centre for Improvement in Educn, Univ. of Cambridge, 1998–2001. Mem., Eastern Region NHS Children's Task Force, 2001–03. Sec., Soc. of Chief Inspectors and Advrs, 1992–96. Vis. Fellow (part-time), Sussex Univ., 1996–99. FRSA 1993. *Recreations:* family, ski-ing, tennis, photography, woodturning. *Address:* HM Treasury, 1 Horse Guards Road, SW1A 2HQ.

SHOTTER, Very Rev. Edward Frank; Dean of Rochester, 1989–2003, now Dean Emeritus; *b* 29 June 1933; *s* of late Frank Edward Shotter and Minnetta Shotter (*née* Gaskill); *m* 1978, Jane Edgcumbe; two *s* one *d*. *Educ:* Humberstone Foundation School, Clee; Durham Univ. School of Architecture; St David's Coll., Lampeter, Univ. of Wales (BA 1958); St Stephen's House, Oxford. Deacon 1960, priest 1961; Curate of St Peter, Plymouth, 1960–62; Intercollegiate Sec., SCM, London, 1962–66; Dir of Studies, London Medical Group, 1966–89; Dir, Inst. of Medical Ethics, 1974–89 (Amulree Fellow, 1991–; Vice Pres., 1999–); Chaplain to Univ. of London, 1969–89; Prebendary of St Paul's Cathedral, 1977–89. Leverhulme Sen. Educnl Fellowship, 1976–79. Chairman: Cttee on Welfare of Czechoslovak Med. Students in Britain, 1968–69; Educn Sub-Cttee, Faculty of History and Phil. of Medicine, Apothecaries Soc., 1976–81; Church, Commerce and Industry Project, 1991–95: N Kent NHS Chaplaincy Service, 1993–96; Jt Chm., Kent Police Ecumenical Chaplaincy Cttee, 1993–2001; Force Chaplain, Kent Co. Constab., 1996–2001. Member: SCM Trust Assoc. Exec., 1965–79; Univ. Chaplains' Cttee, C of E Bd of Educn, 1968–70; Archbishop of Canterbury's Counsellors on Foreign Relations, 1971–82; BCC East/West Relations Adv. Cttee, 1971–81; Liberal Party Foreign Affairs Panel (Chm. East Europe Sub-Cttee), 1974–81; St Christopher's Hospice Educn Cttee, 1982–89; Wking Party on ethics of med. involvement in torture, 1989–91; Chm., IME working party on ethics of prolonging life and assisting death, 1991–98; Chm., Univ. of Greenwich Res. Ethics Cttee, 1995–2003. Chairman: Medway Enterprise Agency, 1993–98; Medway Business Support Partnership, 1994–96; Medway Business Point Ltd, 1996–98. Dir, Firmstart Medway Ltd, 1991–2000. C of E rep. on Churches Council of Health and Healing, 1975–76. Mem., Gen. Synod of C of E, 1994–2002; Sec., Assoc. of English Cathedrals, 1994–2002; Mem., Church Heritage Forum, 1999–2002. Chm., HMS Cavalier Meml Steering Gp, 2000–07. Chm., Governing Body, King's School, Rochester, 1989–2003; Pres., St Bartholomew's Hosp., Rochester, 1989–2003. Founder, Jl of Medical Ethics, 1975. FRSocMed 1976. Hon. FRCP 2007. Patriarchal Cross (Oeconomos Stavrophor), Romanian Orthodox Church, 1975. *Publications:* (ed) Matters of Life and Death, 1970; (with K. M. Boyd and B. Callaghan, SJ) Life Before Birth, 1986; The Saints of Rochester, 2003; (with L. A. Reynolds and E. M. Tansey) Medical Ethics Education in Britain 1963–93, 2007. *Recreations:* East European affairs, gardening, domestic architecture. *Address:* Hill House, Westhall, Halesworth, Suffolk IP19 8QZ. *T:* (01502) 575364. *Club:* Reform.

SHOTTON, Dr Keith Crawford, CEng, FIET; CPhys, FInstP; Head of Management and Technology Services Division, Department of Trade and Industry, 1994–96; *b* 11 Sept. 1943; *s* of William Crawford Shotton and Mary Margaret Shotton (*née* Smith); *m* 1969, Maria Elizabeth Gonszor; two *d*. *Educ:* Newcastle upon Tyne Royal Grammar Sch.; Trinity Coll., Cambridge (Schol.; MA, PhD). CPhys, FInstP 1982; CEng, FIET (FIEE 1988). Post-doctoral Fellow (laser physics and spectroscopy), NRCC, 1969–71; National Physical Laboratory: mem. team measuring speed of light, 1971–77; Head, Ultrasonics Metrology Unit, 1977–80; Head, Marketing and Inf. Services, 1980–84; DCSO, Supt, Div. of Radiation Sci. and Acoustics, 1984–87; Department of Trade and Industry: Dir, Radio Technology, Radio Communications Div., 1987–90; Hd, IT Div., 1990–92; Hd, Inf. and Manufg Technols Div., 1992–93; Hd, Technol. Progs and Services Div., 1993–94. *Publications:* papers in sci. jls, principally in spectroscopy, laser physics, ultrasonics and instrumentation. *Recreations:* walking, sailing, motor cars, food.

SHOVELTON, Prof. David Scott, FDSRCS; Professor of Conservative Dentistry, University of Birmingham, 1964–89, Professor Emeritus, since 1990; *b* 12 Sept. 1925; *s* of Leslie Shovelton, LDSRCS, and Marion de Winton (*née* Scott); *m* 1949, Pearl Holland; two *s*. *Educ:* The Downs Sch., Colwall; King's Sch., Worcester; Univ. of Birmingham (BSc, LDS, BDS). House Surg., Birmingham Dental Hosp., 1951; gen. dental practice, Evesham, Worcs, 1951; Dental Officer, RAF, 1951–53; Birmingham University: Lectr in Operative Dental Surg., 1953–60; Sen. Lectr, 1960–64; Dir, 1974–78, Dep. Dir, 1982–84, Dental Sch.; Consultant Dental Surgeon, Utd Birmingham Hosps, subseq. Central Birmingham HA, 1960–89. Vis. Asst Prof. of Clin. Dentistry, Univ. of Alabama, 1959–60. Hon. Cons. Dental Surg., Birmingham Reg. Hosp. Bd, 1962–74; Hon. Consultant in Conservative Dentistry, Central Birmingham HA, 1989–2004. Pres., British Soc. for Restorative Dentistry, 1970–71 (Vice-Pres., 1968–70 and 1971–72). Consultant, Commn on Dental Practice, Fédn Dentaire Internat., 1972–79; Consultant Adviser in Restorative Dentistry, DHSS, 1983–89. Member: Gen. Dental Council, 1974–89; Birmingham Area Health Authority (Teaching), 1973–79; Cttee of Management, Sch. for Dental Therapists, 1977–80; Jt Cttee for Higher Trng in Dentistry, 1979–84 (Chm., Specialist Adv. Cttee in Restorative Dentistry, 1979–84); Standing Dental Adv. Cttee, 1982–88; Bd, Faculty of Dental Surgery, RCS, 1983–91; Jt Dental Cttee of MRC, Health Depts and SERC, 1984–87; Cttee of Enquiry into unnecessary dental treatment, 1984–85. Ext. Examnr in dental subjects, univs and colls, 1968–94. *Publications:* Inlays, Crowns and Bridges (jtly), 1963, 5th edn 1993 (trans. Portuguese 1991); articles in med. and dental jls, 1957–89. *Recreations:* music, learning about wine, gardening. *Address:* 86 Broad Oaks Road, Solihull, West Midlands B91 1HZ. *T:* (0121) 705 3026. *Club:* Royal Air Force.

SHOVELTON, Dame Helena, DBE 1999; Chief Executive, British Lung Foundation, since 2002; *b* 28 May 1945; *d* of late Denis George Richards, OBE and Barbara Smethurst; *m* 1968, Walter Patrick Shovelton, *qv*. *Educ:* North London Collegiate Sch.; Regent St Poly. (HND Business Studies); Strathclyde Univ. (MBA 1998). Manager, Tunbridge Wells and Dist CAB, 1987–94; National Association of Citizens Advice Bureaux: Council Mem., 1989–90; Vice-Chm., 1990–94; Chm., 1994–99. Mem., 1995–98, Chair, 1998–2001, Audit Commn; Member: Local Govt Commn, 1995–98 (Dep. Chm., 1996–98); Banking Code Standards Bd (formerly Ind. Review Body for Banking and Mortgage Lending Codes), 1997–2000; Competition (formerly Monopolies and Mergers) Commn, 1997–2004; Better Regulation Task Force, 1997–99; Nat. Lottery Commn, 1999–2000. Chm., Independent Review Panel on Continuing Care, E Sussex, Brighton and Hove HA, 1996–97. Non-exec. Dir, Energy Saving Trust, 1998–. Trustee, RAF Benevolent Fund, 1997–2005. FRSA 1995; CCMI 2001. Hon. FRCP 2006. *Recreation:* reading. *Address:* Garden Lodge, Bayham Abbey, nr Lamberhurst, Kent TN3 8BG.

SHOVELTON, (Walter) Patrick, CB 1976; CMG 1972; FCILT; obituarist; Director-General, General Council of British Shipping, 1978–85; *b* 18 Aug. 1919; *s* of late S. T. Shovelton, CBE, and May Catherine (*née* Kelly), cousin of Patrick and Willie Pearse, Irish patriots; *m* 1st, 1942, Marjorie Lucy Joan Manners (marr. diss. 1967); one *d*; 2nd, 1968, Helena Richards (*see* Dame Helena Shovelton). *Educ:* Charterhouse; Keble Coll., Oxford (scholar of both). Rep. Oxford Univ. at Eton Fives. Served in RA and RHA (HAC), 1940–46; DAAG, War Office, 1945–46. Entered Administrative Civil Service as Asst Principal, Min. of War Transport, 1946; Principal 1947; Admin. Staff College, 1951; Private Sec. to Secretary of State for Co-ordination of Transport, Fuel and Power, 1951–53; Asst Sec., Road Transport, 1957; transferred to Min. of Aviation, 1959; IDC, 1962; Under Secretary, 1966; transferred to Min. of Technology, 1966, and to DTI, 1970; Mem., UK Negotiating Team for entry into EEC, 1970–72; Deputy Secretary: DTI, 1972–74; Dept of Prices and Consumer Protection, 1974–76; Dept of Trade, 1976–78; led UK Negotiating Team for Bermuda 2, 1977 and 2A, 1978; Dir, British Airports Authy, 1982–85. Chm., Birmingham Executive, later European, Airways, 1988–93; Director: Maersk Co., 1985 (Vice-Chm., 1987–95); Kent Line, 1987–90; Maersk Air Ltd, 1993–95. William and Mary Tercentenary Trust: Chairman: Maritime Cttee, 1985–89; Finance and Sponsorship Cttee, 1988–89. Council, CIT, 1982–85; Advr, Inquiries into EEC Maritime Transport Policy H of L, 1985–86, into Merchant Shipping, H of C, 1986–88. Brancker Lectr (civil aviation), 1979; Grout Lectr (shipping), 1985. Founder and Chm., Friends of Tunbridge Wells and Rusthall Commons, 1991–98. Officer, Order of Orange-Nassau (Netherlands), 1989. *Recreations:* formerly golf, bridge, opera, reading. *Clubs:* Brooks's; Jesters; Royal Ashdown Forest Golf, Hampstead Golf, Seniors Golf.

SHOWALTER, Prof. Elaine, PhD; Professor of English and Avalon Foundation Professor of Humanities, Princeton University, 1984–2003, now Emerita; *b* 21 Jan. 1941; *d* of Paul Cottler and Violet Rottenberg; *m* 1963, English Showalter; one *s* one *d*. *Educ:* Bryn Mawr Coll. (BA 1962); Univ. of California, Davis (PhD 1970). Departments of English: Douglass Coll., 1966–78; Rutgers Univ., 1966–84. Pres., Modern Language Assoc. of America, 1998. *Publications:* A Literature of Their Own, 1977; The Female Malady, 1985; Sexual Anarchy, 1990; Sister's Choice: tradition and change in American women's writing, 1991; (jtly) Hysteria Beyond Freud, 1993; Hystories: hysterical epidemics and modern culture, 1997; Inventing Herself: claiming a feminist intellectual heritage, 2001; Teaching Literature, 2002; Faculty Towers, 2005. *Address:* 4620 North Park Avenue #405E, Chevy Chase, MD 20815–4579, USA. *T:* (301) 6563248; 15A St Paul's View, 15 Amwell Street, EC1R 1UP. *T:* (020) 7837 9405. *Clubs:* Princeton (NY); Cosmos (Washington DC).

SHREEVE, Ven. David Herbert; Archdeacon of Bradford, 1984–99, now Emeritus; *b* 18 Jan. 1934; *s* of Hubert Ernest and Ivy Eleanor Shreeve; *m* 1957, Barbara (*née* Fogden); one *s* one *d*. *Educ:* Southfield School, Oxford; St Peter's Coll., Oxford (MA); Ridley Hall, Cambridge. Asst Curate, St Andrew's Church, Plymouth, 1959–64; Vicar: St Anne's, Bermondsey, 1964–71; St Luke's, Eccleshill, 1971–84; RD of Calverley, 1978–84. Mem., Gen. Synod and Proctor in Convocation, 1977–90, 1993–98; Mem., Dioceses Commn, 1988–98. Hon. Canon of Bradford Cathedral, 1983–84. *Recreations:* walking, travel, photography. *Address:* 26 Kingsley Drive, Harrogate, N Yorks HG1 4TJ. *T:* (01423) 886479.

SHRESTHA, Surya Prasad; Ambassador of Nepal to the Court of St James's, 1992–97; *b* 1 March 1937; *s* of late L. P. Shrestha and Mrs G. K. Shrestha; *m* 1958, Ginni Baba Shrestha; two *s* two *d*. *Educ:* Tribhuvan Univ. (MA Pol Sci.); LSE (Dip. Econs and Social Admin). Joined HM Govt service, Nepal, 1958; Section Officer, Parlt Secretariat and Min. of Develt, 1958–63; Under Secretary: Min. of Home and Panchayat, 1963–65; Election Commn, 1965–66; Jt Zonal Comr, 1970–74, Zonal Comr, 1974–78, Bagmati Zone; Actg Sec., Home and Panchayat Min., 1978–79; Sec. of Industry and Commerce, 1979–83; Jt Mem., Nat. Planning Commn, 1983–85; Chief Election Comr, 1985–92. Prabal Gorkha Dakshin Bahu, III Cl. (Nepal), 1966, Prasiddha, II Cl., 1976; Trishakti Patta, Vikhyat, III Cl. (Nepal), 1973, Suvikhyat, II Cl., 1991. FRGS 1996. *Publication:* Democracy Prevails: general election in Nepal, 1991. *Recreations:* reading, gardening. *Address:* PO Box 2482, Jagaran Marg-130, Maharajgung (Chakrapath), Kathmandu, Nepal. *T:* (1) 4720708, 4721135.

SHREWSBURY, Bishop Suffragan of, since 2001; **Rt Rev. Alan Gregory Clayton Smith,** PhD; *b* 14 Feb. 1957; *s* of late Frank Eric Smith and of Rosemary Clayton Smith. *Educ:* Trowbridge Grammar Sch.; Univ. of Birmingham (BA Theol. 1978; MA 1979); Wycliffe Hall, Oxford; Univ. of Wales, Bangor (PhD 2002). Ordained deacon, 1981, priest, 1982; Assistant Curate: St Lawrence, Pudsey, 1981–82; St Lawrence and St Paul, Pudsey, 1982–84; Chaplain, Lee Abbey Community, Devon, 1984–90; Diocesan Missioner, Lichfield, 1990–97; Team Vicar, St Matthew's, Walsall, 1990–97; Archdeacon, Stoke-upon-Trent, 1997–2001. Hon. Canon, Lichfield Cathedral, 1997–. Chm., Shropshire Strategic Partnership, 2005–. *Publications:* Growing Up in Multifaith Britain, 2007; God-Shaped Mission, 2008. *Recreations:* classical music, travel, squash, ski-ing. *Address:* Athlone House, 68 London Road, Shrewsbury SY2 6PG. *T:* (01743) 235867, *Fax:* (01743) 243296; *e-mail:* bishop.shrewsbury@lichfield.anglican.org.

SHREWSBURY, Bishop of, (RC), since 1995; **Rt Rev. Brian Michael Noble;** *b* 11 April 1936; *s* of Thomas Joseph and Cecelia Noble. *Educ:* Ushaw Coll., Durham. Ordained priest for RC Diocese of Lancaster, 1960; parish appts, 1960–72; Chaplain, Lancaster Univ., 1972–80; Lectr, Pontificio Collegio Beda, Rome, 1980–87; Parish Priest, St Benedict's, Whitehaven, and Dean of West Cumbria, 1987–95. Canon of Lancaster Cath. Chapter, 1994; Ecumenical Canon, Chester Cathedral, 2003–. *Recreations:* music, poetry, natural history, walking. *Address:* Laburnum Cottage, 97 Barnston Road, Barnston, Wirral CH61 1BW.

SHREWSBURY AND WATERFORD, 22nd Earl of, *cr* 1442 and 1446; **Charles Henry John Benedict Crofton Chetwynd Chetwynd-Talbot;** DL; Baron Talbot, 1733; 7th Earl Talbot, Viscount Ingestre, 1784; Premier Earl on the Rolls of England and Ireland, Hereditary Great Seneschal or Lord High Steward of Ireland; Lord Dungarvan; director and landowner; *b* 18 Dec. 1952; *s* of 21st Earl of Shrewsbury and Waterford, and Nadine (*d* 2003), *yr d* of late Brig.-Gen. C. R. Crofton, CBE; *S* father, 1980; *m* 1974, Deborah, *o d* of late Noel Hutchinson; two *s* one *d*. *Educ:* Harrow. Director: Britannia Building Soc., 1984–92 (Dep. Chm., 1987–89; Jt Dep. Chm., 1989–92); Richmount Enterprise Zone Managers, 1988–94. Mem. Exec. Cttee, 1988–, Chm., 2000–, Staffs Br., Game Conservancy Trust. Pres., Staffordshire Soc., 1989–91; Vice-Pres., Midland & West Assoc. of Building Socs, 1984–92; Pres., BSA, 1993–97. Chairman: Firearms Consultative Cttee, 1994–99; British Shooting Sports Council, 2000–. Chancellor, Univ. of Wolverhampton, 1993–99. Elected Mem., H of L, 1999. President: British Inst. of Innkeeping, 1996–97; Staffs & Birmingham Agricl Soc., 2000–01. Patron, Staffs Br., BRCS, 1989–92. Hon. President: Shropshire Bldg Preservation Trust, 1984–; Lord Roberts Wkshops and SSAFA (Wolverhampton Br.), 1987–; Staffs Small Bore Rifle Assoc., 1988–; Gun Trade Assoc., 2000–; Hon. Vice-Pres., Rugeley Rugby FC. Hon. Pres., Shropshire Hospice, 1983–88. Patron of 11 livings. DL Stafford, 1994. Hon. LLD Wolverhampton, 1994. *Recreations:* shooting, fishing. *Heir: s* Viscount Ingestre, *qv*. *Address:* Wanfield Hall, Kingstone, Uttoxeter, Staffs ST14 8QR.

SHRIBMAN, Sheila Joan, FRCP, FRCPCH; Consultant Paediatrician, Northampton General Hospital, since 1985; National Clinical Director for Children, Department of Health, since 2005; *b* 8 March 1951; *d* of Wilfred and Margaret Norval; *m* 1981, Dr Jonathan Shribman; two *s* one *d*. *Educ:* Girton Coll., Cambridge (BA 1972; MB BChir 1976); St George's Hosp., London. FRCP 1993; FRCPCH 1996. Paediatric trng posts at St George's, Brompton, Queen Charlotte's and Gt Ormond St Hosps; Med. Dir, Northampton Gen. Hosp., 1995–2005. Registrar, RCPCH, 2003–05. *Recreations:* travel, books, cookery, family. *Address:* Stonegables, 3 Harrison Court, Bugbrooke, Northants NN7 3ET. *T:* (01604) 831700; *e-mail:* sheila@shribman.co.uk. *Club:* Royal Society of Medicine.

SHRIMPLIN, John Steven; consultant, since 1994; Member, European Space Agency Appeals Board, since 2000; *b* 9 May 1934; *s* of late John Reginald Shrimplin and Kathleen Mary (*née* Stevens); *m* 1957, Hazel Baughen; two *s*. *Educ:* Royal Grammar Sch., Colchester; King's Coll., London (BSc Maths). Joined RAE, Farnborough, 1956; Defence Operational Analysis Estabt, 1966; JSSC, 1970; Weapons Dept, RAE, 1971; Defence R&D Staff, British Embassy, Washington, 1972; Asst Dir, Future Systems, Air Systems Controllerate, MoD PE, 1974; Asst Chief Scientist, RAF, 1978; Head of Weapons Dept, RAE, 1983; Dep. Hd, British Defence Staff, and Minister/Counsellor, Defence Equipment, British Embassy, Washington, DC, 1985–88; Dir, Defence Science (Studies), MoD, 1988–91; Dep. Dir Gen. and Dir, Space Technol., BNSC, 1991–94. UK Rep., Eur. Space Policy Cttee, 1994–99. FRAeS 1993. *Recreations:* travel, camping, walking. *Address:* c/o National Westminster Bank, 2 Alexandra Road, Farnborough, Hants GU14 6BZ.

SHRIMSLEY, Bernard; journalist and novelist; *b* 13 Jan. 1931; *er s* of John and Alice Shrimsley, London; *m* 1952, Norma Jessie Alexandra, *d* of Albert and Maude Porter, Southport; one *d*. *Educ:* Kilburn Grammar School, Northampton. Press Association, 1947–48; Southport Guardian, 1948–49 and 1951–53; RAF, 1949–51; Daily Mirror, 1953–58 and 1961–68; Sunday Express, 1958–61; Editor, Daily Post, Liverpool, 1968–69; Dep. Editor, 1969–72, Editor, 1972–75, The Sun; Editor, News of the World, and Dir, News Group Newspapers Ltd, 1975–80; Editor-designate (subseq. Editor), The Mail on Sunday, and Dir (subseq. Vice-Chm.), The Mail on Sunday Ltd, 1980–82; Asst Editor, 1983–86, Associate Editor, 1986–96, Daily Express; media consultant, Referendum Party, 1996–97; leader writer, Press Gazette, 1999–2002. Member: Press Council, 1989–90 (Jt Vice-Chm., 1990); Defence, Press and Broadcasting Cttee, 1989–93. Mem. judging acad., British Press Awards, 1988–2007. *Publications:* The Candidates, 1968; Lion Rampant, 1984 (US Book of the Month Choice); The Silly Season, 2003. *Club:* Garrick.

SHRIMSLEY, Robert Gideon; News Editor, Financial Times, since 2005; *b* 21 Sept. 1964; *s* of late Anthony Shrimsley and of Yvonne Shrimsley; *m* 1997, Reeve Lewis; one *s* one *d*. *Educ:* St Nicholas Preparatory Sch.; University College Sch.; London Sch. of Economics (BSc Econs 1985). Reporter: Darlington Evening Despatch, 1986; Kentish Times, 1986–88; Sunday Telegraph, 1988–89; Reporter, 1989–92, political staff, 1992–95, Daily Telegraph; Lobby Corresp., Financial Times, 1995–96; Chief Pol Corresp., Daily Telegraph, 1996–2000; Financial Times: Chief Pol Corresp., 2000–02;

UK News Ed., 2002–04; columnist, 2004–05. *Recreations:* cinema, reading, comedy clubs, watching QPR, spending time with my family. *Address:* Financial Times, 1 Southwark Bridge, SE1 9HL. *T:* (020) 7873 3000.

SHRIVER, (Robert) Sargent; Partner, 1971–86, Lawyer Of Counsel, Fried, Frank, Harris, Shriver & Jacobson, since 1986; Chairman, Special Olympics International, 1990–2003, now Emeritus (President, 1984–90); *b* Westminster, Md, 9 Nov. 1915; *s* of Robert Sargent and Hilda Shriver; *m* 1953, Eunice Mary Kennedy; four *s* one *d.* *Educ:* parochial schools, Baltimore; Canterbury School, New Milford, Conn.; Yale College; Yale University. BA (*cum laude*) 1938; LLB 1941; LLD 1964. Apprentice Seaman, USNR, 1940; Ensign, 1941. Served War of 1941–45: Atlantic and Pacific Ocean Areas aboard battleships and submarines; Lt-Comdr, USNR. Admitted to: New York Bar, 1941; Illinois Bar, (retd) 1959; US Supreme Court, 1966; District of Columbia Bar, 1971. With legal firm of Winthrop, Stimson, Putnam & Roberts, NYC, 1940–41; Asst Editor, Newsweek, 1945–46; associated with Joseph P. Kennedy Enterprises, 1946–48; Asst Gen. Man., Merchandise Mart, 1948–61; President: Chicago Bd of Educn, 1955–60; Catholic Interracial Council of Chicago, 1954–59; Dir, Peace Corps, Washington, 1961–66; Dir, Office of Economic Opportunity (resp. for develt of Head Start, Job Corps, VISTA Community Action, Legal Services for the Poor, etc), and Special Asst to Pres. Johnson, 1964–68; US Ambassador to France, 1968–70. Vice-Presidential candidate (Democrat), Nov. 1972. Democrat; Roman Catholic. US Presidential Medal of Freedom, 1994; Franklin D. Roosevelt Freedom From Want Award, 1994. *Address:* 12th Floor, 1133 19th Street NW, Washington, DC 20036, USA.

SHTAUBER, Dr Zvi; Director, The Institute for National Security Studies, Israel (Head, Jaffee Center for Strategic Studies, Tel Aviv University, 2005); company director; *b* 15 July 1947; *m* Nitza Rousso; two *s* one *d.* *Educ:* Fletcher Sch. of Law and Diplomacy; Harvard Business Sch.; Hebrew Univ. of Jerusalem. Brig. Gen., Israel Defence Force, 1970–95; Vice-Pres., Ben Gurion Univ. of Negev, 1996–99; Foreign Policy Advr to Prime Minister of Israel, 1999–2000; Ambassador of Israel to the Court of St James's, 2001–04.

SHUCKBURGH, Sir Rupert (Charles Gerald), 13th Bt *cr* 1660, of Shuckburgh, Warwickshire; *b* 12 Feb. 1949; *s* of Sir Charles Gerald Stewkley Shuckburgh, 12th Bt, TD and Nancy Diana Mary, OBE (*d* 1984), *o d* of late Captain Rupert Lubbock, RN; *S* father, 1988; *m* 1st, 1976, Judith (marr. diss. 1987), *d* of W. G. Mackaness; two *s*; 2nd, 1987, Margaret Ida, *d* of late W. Evans. *Heir: s* James Rupert Charles Shuckburgh, *b* 4 Jan. 1978. *Address:* Shuckburgh Hall, Daventry, Northants NN11 6DT. *Club:* Farmers'.

SHUCKSMITH, Prof. (David) Mark, PhD; Professor of Planning, University of Newcastle upon Tyne, since 2005; *b* 25 Aug. 1953; *s* of Thomas David Shucksmith and Gwladys Inga Shucksmith; *m* 1979, Janet Susan Raper; two *d.* *Educ:* Sidney Sussex Coll., Cambridge (BA 1976); Univ. of Newcastle upon Tyne (MSc; PhD Agricl Econs 1987). University of Aberdeen: Lectr, 1981–87; Sen. Lectr, 1987–89; Reader, Dept of Land Econ., 1989–93; Prof. of Land Economy, 1993–2004; Dir, Arkleton Centre for Rural Develt Res., 1995–2004. Vis. Prof., Univ. of Trondheim, 2006–08. Co-Dir, Scottish Centre for Res. on Social Justice, 2001–04. Joseph Rowntree Foundation: Advr, Action in Rural Areas prog., 1995–; Sec., Rural Housing Policy Forum, 2005–06. Member: Bd, Countryside Agency, 2005–06; Affordable Rural Housing Commn, 2005–06; Bd, Commn for Rural Communities, 2006–. Chm., Cttee of Enquiry on Crofting, 2007–08. Prog. Chm., World Rural Sociol. Congress, 2004; First Vice-Pres., Internat. Rural Sociol. Assoc., 2004–08. *Publications:* No Homes for Locals?, 1981; Rural Housing in Scotland: recent research and policy, 1987; Housebuilding in Britain's Countryside, 1990; (jtly) Rural Scotland Today: the best of both worlds, 1996; Exclusive Countryside?: social inclusion and regeneration in rural Britain, 2000; (jtly) Housing in the European Countryside, 2003; (jtly) Young People in Rural Europe, 2004; (jtly) CAP and the Regions: the territorial impact of the Common Agricultural Policy, 2005; contrib. numerous articles to learned jls. *Recreations:* music, reading novels, hill-walking, finding coffee shops. *Address:* School of Architecture, Planning and Landscape, University of Newcastle upon Tyne, Claremont Tower, Newcastle upon Tyne NE1 7RU. *T:* (0191) 222 6808; *e-mail:* m.shucksmith@ncl.ac.uk.

SHUE, Prof. Vivienne B., PhD; FBA 2008; Leverhulme Professor of Contemporary China, University of Oxford, since 2002; Fellow of St Antony's College, Oxford, since 2002. *Educ:* Vassar Coll., NY (BA 1967); St Antony's Coll., Oxford (BLitt 1969); Harvard Univ. (PhD 1975). Asst Prof., 1976–81, Associate Prof., 1981–82, Dept of Pol Sci., Yale Univ.; Associate Prof., 1982–87, Prof. of Govt, 1987–95, Frank and Rosa Rhodes Prof. of Chinese Govt, 1995–2004, Cornell Univ. *Publications:* Peasant China in Transition, 1980; The Reach of the State, 1988; (ed jtly) State Power and Social Forces, 1994; (with Marc Blecher) Tethered Deer: government and economy in a Chinese county, 1996; (ed with C. Wong) Paying for Progress in China, 2007; contrib. learned jls. *Address:* St Antony's College, Oxford OX2 6JF.

SHUFFREY, Ralph Frederick Dendy, CB 1983; CVO 1981; Deputy Under-Secretary of State and Principal Establishment Officer, Home Office, 1980–84; *b* 9 Dec. 1925; *s* of late Frederick Arthur Shuffrey, MC and Mary Shuffrey (*née* Dendy); *m* 1953, Sheila, *d* of late Brig. John Lingham, CB, DSO, MC, and Juliet Judd; one *s* one *d.* *Educ:* Shrewsbury; Balliol Coll., Oxford. Served Army, 1944–47 (Captain). Entered Home Office, 1951; Private Sec. to Parly Under-Sec. of State, 1956–57; Private Sec. to Home Sec., 1965–66; Asst Sec., 1966–72; Asst Under-Sec. of State, 1972–80. Chairman: The Cranstoun Projects Ltd, 1988–97; Fire Service Res. and Trng Trust, 1989–2004. Hon. Sec., Soc. for Individual Freedom, 1985–89. *Address:* Flat D, Campden House, 29 Sheffield Terrace, W8 7ND. *Club:* Reform.

SHUKLA, Rashmita, CBE 2007; Regional Director of Public Health, since 2004, and Medical Director, since 2006, West Midlands Department of Health; *b* 4 July 1960; *d* of Himatlal Shukla and Mrudula Shukla; *m* 1992, Dr Vinod Patel. *Educ:* Univ. of Southampton Med. Sch. (BM 1984). MRCP 1988; FFPH 2001. Leicestershire Health Authority: Consultant in Communicable Disease/Public Health Medicine, 1994–2001; Actg Dir of Public Health, 2000–01; Director of Public Health: Eastern Leicester PCT, 2001–04; Leicester City West PCT, 2004. Hon. Sen. Lectr, Univ. of Leicester, 2003–. *Publications:* articles in Communicable Disease Review, Sexually Transmitted Infections, Jl of Public Health Medicine and Postgraduate Med. Jl. *Recreations:* cycling, ski-ing, reading, supporting local Rugby team (Leicester Tigers). *Address:* West Midlands Public Health Group, Government Office for West Midlands, 5 St Philip's Place, Birmingham B3 2PW. *T:* (0121) 352 5347, *Fax:* (0121) 352 5312; *e-mail:* Rashmi.Shukla@dh.gsi.gov.uk.

SHUKMAN, David Roderick, FRGS; Environment and Science Correspondent, BBC News, since 2003; *b* 30 May 1958; *s* of Dr Harold Shukman and Rev. Dr Ann Shukman; *m* 1988, Jessica Therese Pryce-Jones; two *s* one *d.* *Educ:* Eton Coll.; Durham Univ. (BA Hons Geog.). Reporter, Coventry Evening Telegraph, 1980–83; joined BBC, 1983: trainee, News, 1983–85; reporter, NI, 1985–87; Defence Corresp., TV News, 1987–95; Europe Corresp., Brussels, 1995–99; World Affairs Corresp., News, 1999–2003. *Publications:* (with B. Brown) All Necessary Means, 1991; The Sorcerer's Challenge: fears and hopes for the weapons of the next millennium, 1995, US edn as Tomorrow's War, 1996; contribs to RUSI Jl, Brassey's Defence Yearbook. *Recreations:* cooking, diving, surfing. *Address:* BBC TV Centre, Wood Lane, W12 7RJ. *T:* (020) 8624 9048; *e-mail:* david.shukman@bbc.co.uk. *Club:* Frontline.

SHULMAN, Alexandra, OBE 2005; Editor, British Vogue, since 1992; *b* 13 Nov. 1957; *d* of late Milton Shulman and of Drusilla Beyfus, *qv*; *m* 1994, Paul (marr. diss. 2005), *s* of late Rev. Dr Robert W. Spike, NY; one *s.* *Educ:* St Paul's Girls' Sch.; Sussex Univ. (BA Social Anthropology). Tatler: Commissioning Editor, 1982–84; Features Editor, 1984–87; Sunday Telegraph: Editor, Women's Page, 1987; Dep. Editor, 7 Days Mag., 1987–88; Features Editor, Vogue, 1988–90; Editor, GQ, 1990–92. Dir, Condé Nast Pubns, 1997–2002. Trustee: Nat. Portrait Gall., 1999–2008; Arts Foundn, 2001–. *Address:* Condé Nast Publications, Vogue House, Hanover Square, W1S 1JU. *T:* (020) 7499 9080.

See also Marchioness of Normanby.

SHULMAN, Drusilla Norman; *see* Beyfus, Drusilla N.

SHULMAN, Neville, CBE 2005 (OBE 1995); Director, British Centre, International Theatre Institute, since 1992; *m* 1970, Emma Broide; two *s* one *d.* ACA 1961, FCA 1971. Chartered Accountant, in private practice, 1961–. Vice Pres., NCH Action for Children, 1989–; Vice Chm., UK UNESCO Culture Cttee, 2005–. Director: Theatre Forum, 2002–; Shepperton Studios Ltd, 2003–. Freeman, City of London, 1992; Liveryman, Co. of Blacksmiths, 1992. FRGS 1990. *Publications:* Exit of a Dragonfly, 1985; Zen in the Art of Climbing Mountains, 1992; On Top of Africa, 1995; Zen Explorations in Remotest New Guinea, 1997; Some Like it Cold, 2001; Climbing the Equator, 2003. *Recreations:* mountaineering, exploring, theatre, film, writing. *Address:* 35A Huntsworth Mews, Gloucester Place, NW1 6DB. *Clubs:* Travellers, Explorers (Fellow, 2002), Rotary.

SHULTZ, George Pratt; Secretary of State, United States of America, 1982–89; Distinguished Fellow, Hoover Institution, since 1989; *b* New York City, 13 Dec. 1920; *s* of Birl E. Shultz and Margaret Pratt; *m* 1946, Helena Maria O'Brien (*d* 1995); two *s* three *d*; *m* 1997, Charlotte Mailliard Swig (Hon. CVO 2007). *Educ:* Princeton Univ., 1942 (BA Econ); Massachusetts Inst. of Technology, 1949 (PhD Industrial Econ). Served War, US Marine Corps, Pacific, 1942; Major, 1945. Faculty, MIT, 1949–57; Sen. staff economist, President's Council of Economic Advisers, 1955–56 (on leave, MIT); Univ. of Chicago, Graduate Sch. of Business: Prof. of Industrial Relations, 1957–68; Dean, 1962–69; Prof. of Management and Public Policy, Stanford Univ., Graduate Sch. of Business, 1974. Secretary of Labor, 1969–July 1, 1970; Dir, Office of Management and Budget, 1970–72; Secretary of the Treasury, 1972–74; Exec. Vice-Pres., Bechtel Corp., 1974–75, Pres. 1975–77; Vice-Chm., Bechtel Corp., 1977–81 (Dir); Pres., Bechtel Group Inc., San Francisco, 1981–82. Chairman: President's Economic Policy Adv. Bd, 1981–82; Internat. Council, J. P. Morgan, 1989–; Adv. Council, Inst. of Internat. Studies, 1989–; Adv. Bd, Accenture Energy, 2002–07. Director: General Motors Corp., 1981–82, 1989–91; Boeing Corp., 1989–93; Bechtel Gp Inc., 1989–; Tandem Computers Inc., 1989–92; Chevron Corp., 1989–93; Gulfstream Aerospace Corp., 1992–99; AirTouch Communications, 1994–98; Gilead Scis, 1996–2006; Charles Schwab & Co. Inc., 1997–2004; Unext, 2000–03; Infrastructure World, 2000–03; Accretive Health Associates, 2004–; Mem., GM Corporate Adv. Council. Chm., State of California Gov's Econ. Policy Adv. Bd, 1995–98, Council of Econ. Advrs, 2004–. US Chm., N American Forum, 2005–; Chairman: Adv. Council, Precourt Inst. for Energy Efficiency, Stanford Univ., 2007–; Ext. Adv. Bd, MIT Energy Initiative, 2007–; Energy Taskforce, Hoover Inst., 2007–. Hon. Dr of Laws: Notre Dame Univ., 1969; Loyola Univ., 1972; Pennsylvania, 1973; Rochester, 1973; Princeton, 1973; Carnegie-Mellon Univ., 1975; Columbia, 2001; Williams Coll., 2008. *Publications:* Pressures on Wage Decisions, 1950; The Dynamics of a Labor Market (with C. A. Myers), 1951; Labor Problems: cases and readings (with J. R. Coleman), 1953; Management Organization and the Computer (with T. L. Whisler), 1960; Strategies for the Displaced Worker (with Arnold R. Weber), 1966; Guidelines, Informal Controls, and the Marketplace (with Robert Z. Aliber), 1966; Workers and Wages in the Urban Labor Market (with Albert Rees), 1970; Leaders and Followers in an Age of Ambiguity, 1975; Economic Policy Beyond the Headlines (with Kenneth W. Dam), 1977, 2nd edn 1998; Turmoil and Triumph: my years as Secretary of State, 1993; (with John Shoven) Putting Our House in Order: a guide to social security and healthcare reform, 2008. *Recreations:* golf, tennis. *Address:* Hoover Institution, Stanford University, Stanford, CA 94305–6010, USA.

SHURMAN, Laurence Paul Lyons; Banking Ombudsman, 1989–96; Member, Executive Board, The Accountancy Investigation and Discipline Board Ltd, since 2004 (a Director, 2001–04); *b* 25 Nov. 1930; *s* of Joseph and Sarah Shurman; *m* 1963, Mary Seamans (*née* McMullan); two *s* one *d.* *Educ:* Newcastle upon Tyne Royal Grammar Sch.; Magdalen Coll., Oxford (MA). Solicitor. Articles, John H. Sinton & Co., Newcastle, 1954–57; Assistant Solicitor: Haswell Croft, Newcastle, 1957–58; Hall Brydon, London, 1958–60; Kaufman & Siegal, London, 1960–61; Partner: Shurman & Bindman, Solicitors, London, 1961–64; Shurman & Co., London, 1964–67; Kingsley Napley, London, 1967–89 (Managing Partner, 1975–89). Legal Mem., Mental Health Review Tribunal, 1976–94; Chm., Portman Gp (drinks industry) Complaints Panel, 1997–2001; Mem. Council, Justice, 1973– (Mem., Exec. Bd, 2003–). Lectures: Gilbart, 1990; Ernest Sykes Meml, 1991. Pres., City of Westminster Law Soc., 1980–81; Chm., British and Irish Ombudsman Assoc., 1993–95. Vice-Chm., Disciplinary Cttee, Assoc. of Chartered Certified Accountants, 1998–2000. Member: Mgt Cttee, Care and Repair England, 1998– (Vice-Chm., 2001–); Council, RSAS Age Care, 1998–2007. Governor: Channing Sch., 1985–2007 (Vice-Chm., 1988–2007); Newcastle upon Tyne Royal Grammar Sch., 1991–2001. Trustee, Highgate Literary and Scientific Inst., 2002– (Pres., 1998–2002). *Publications:* The Practical Skills of the Solicitor, 1981, 2nd edn 1985; contributor on Mental Health Tribunals in Vol. 26 of Atkin's Encyc. of Court Forms, 2nd edn 1985. *Recreations:* reading, fell walking, swimming, law reform. *Address:* 14 Southwood Avenue, N6 5RZ. *T:* (020) 8348 5409. *Club:* Leander (Henley).

SHUTLER, (Ronald) Rex (Barry), CB 1992; FRICS; FAAV; Chairman, Leasehold Valuation Tribunal and Rent Assessment Panel, 1994–2001 (Vice President, 1994–99); *b* 27 June 1933; *s* of Ronald Edgar Coggin Shutler and Helena Emily Shutler (*née* Lawes); *m* 1958, Patricia Elizabeth Longman; two *s.* *Educ:* Hardye's, Dorchester. Articled pupil and assistant, chartered surveyors, Dorchester, 1952–59; joined Valuation Office (Inland Revenue), 1959; District Valuer, Hereford and Worcester, 1970; Superintending Valuer, Wales, 1976; Dep. Chief Valuer, 1984–88; Chief Valuer, then Chief Exec., Valuation Office Agency, 1988–94. FRICS 1972; FAAV 1962; Hon. FSVA 1994. *Recreations:* golf, country pursuits, gardening. *Club:* Bank House Golf & Country.

SHUTT, family name of **Baron Shutt of Greetland**.

SHUTT OF GREETLAND, Baron *cr* 2000 (Life Peer), of Greetland and Stainland in the county of West Yorkshire; **David Trevor Shutt,** OBE 1993; FCA; Consultant, Bousfield Waite & Co., Halifax, 1994–2001 (Partner, 1970–94); *b* 16 March 1942; *s* of

Edward Angus Shutt and Ruth Satterthwaite Shutt (*née* Berry); *m* 1965, Margaret Edith Pemberton; two *s* one *d. Educ:* Pudsey Grammar Sch. FCA 1969. Smithson Blackburn & Co., Leeds: Articled Clerk, 1959–64; Audit Clerk, 1964–66; Taxation Asst, Bousfield Waite & Co., Halifax, 1967–70. Mem. (L then Lib Dem) Calderdale MBC, 1973–90 and 1995–2003 (Mayor, 1982–83). Dir, Joseph Rowntree Reform Trust Ltd, 1975– (Vice Chm., 1987–2005; Chm., 2007–); Trustee, Joseph Rowntree Charitable Trust, 1985–. Treas., Inst. for Citizenship, 1995–2002. Contested: (L): Sowerby, 1970, Feb. and Oct. 1974, 1979; (L/Alliance): Calder Valley, 1983, 1987; (Lib Dem): Pudsey, 1992. House of Lords: Lib Dem Asst Whip, 2001–02, Dep. Chief Whip, 2002–05, Chief Whip, 2005–; spokesman on internat. devel t, 2001–02, on NI, 2001–05. Freeman of Calderdale, 2000. Paul Harris Fellow, Rotary Club, 1999. Citoyen d'honneur, Commune de Riorges (France), 1983. *Recreations:* transport, travel. *Address:* Woodfield, 197 Saddleworth Road, Greetland, Halifax, West Yorkshire HX4 8LZ. *T:* (01422) 375276.

SHUTTLE, Penelope (Diane); writer and poet; *b* 12 May 1947; *d* of Jack Frederick Shuttle and Joan Shepherdess Lipscombe; *m* Peter Redgrove, FRSL (*d* 2003); one *d. Educ:* Staines Grammar Sch.; Matthew Arnold County Secondary Sch., Middx. Radio plays: The Girl who Lost her Glove, 1975 (Jt 3rd Prize Winner, Radio Times Drama Bursaries Comp., 1974); The Dauntless Girl, 1978. Poetry recorded for Poetry Room, Harvard Univ. Arts Council Awards, 1969, 1972 and 1985; Greenwood Poetry Prize, 1972; E. C. Gregory Award for Poetry, 1974. *Publications: novels:* An Excusable Vengeance, 1967; All the Usual Hours of Sleeping, 1969; Wailing Monkey Embracing a Tree, 1974; Rainsplitter in the Zodiac Garden, 1976; Mirror of the Giant, 1979; *poetry:* Nostalgia Neurosis, 1968; Midwinter Mandala, 1973; Photographs of Persephone, 1973; Autumn Piano, 1973; Songbook of the Snow, 1973; Webs on Fire, 1977; The Orchard Upstairs, 1980; The Child-Stealer, 1983; The Lion from Rio, 1986; Adventures with my Horse, 1988; Taxing the Rain, 1992; Building a City for Jamie, 1996; Selected Poems, 1998; A Leaf out of his Book, 1999; Redgrove's Wife, 2006; *with Peter Redgrove:* The Hermaphrodite Album (poems), 1973; The Terrors of Dr Treviles (novel), 1974; The Wise Wound (psychology), 1978, 5th edn 1999; Alchemy for Women, 1995. *Recreations:* listening to music, Hatha Yoga, walking, reading, contemplation. *Address:* c/o David Higham Associates Ltd, 5–8 Lower John Street, Golden Square, W1R 4HA.

SHUTTLEWORTH, 5th Baron *cr* 1902, of Gawthorpe; **Charles Geoffrey Nicholas Kay-Shuttleworth;** JP; Bt 1850; Lord-Lieutenant and Custos Rotulorum of Lancashire, since 1997; *b* 2 Aug. 1948; *s* of 4th Baron Shuttleworth, MC, and Anne Elizabeth (*d* 1991), *er d* of late Col Geoffrey Phillips, CBE, DSO; *S* father, 1975; *m* 1975, Mrs Ann Mary Barclay, *d* of James Whatman, MC; three *s. Educ:* Eton. Trainee Surveyor, Raby Estates, Co. Durham, 1966–70; Vigers, Chartered Surveyors, 1970–77; Partner, Burton, Barnes & Vigers, Chartered Surveyors, 1977–96; National & Provincial Building Society: Dir, 1983–96; Chm., 1994–96; Director: Burnley Bldg Soc., 1978–82 (Vice-Chm., 1982); Rank Foundn, 1993–; Abbey National plc, 1996–2004 (Dep. Chm., 1996–99); Rural Solutions Ltd, 1999–2007 (Chm., 2005–07); Chm., Abbey National Gp Pension Funds Trustee Co., 2002–. Chairman: Rural Develt Commn, 1990–97; Lancs Small Industries Cttee, COSIRA, 1978–83; Lancs Youth Clubs Assoc., 1980–86, Pres., 1986–; Member: Skelmersdale Develt Corp., 1982–85; NW Regional Cttee, National Trust, 1980–89; Council, CBI, 1993–96; Council, Duchy of Lancaster, 1998– (Chm., 2006–). Chm., Assoc. of Lord-Lieutenants, 2008–. President: Royal Lancashire Agricl Soc., 1985–86, 2000–01; Assoc. of Lancastrians in London, 1986–87 and 1997. Vice-Pres., RFCA, NW, 1997–. Chm. of Trustees, Yorkshire Dales Millennium Trust, 2000–05. Mem. Council, Lancaster Univ., 1990–93; Governor, Giggleswick Sch., 1981–2006 (Chm., 1984–97). Hon. Fellow: Univ. of Central Lancs, 1996; Myerscough Coll., 2002. Hon. Colonel: 4th (V) Bn, Queen's Lancs Regt, 1996–99; Lancastrian and Cumbrian Vol., 1999–2005. FRICS, 1983–2002. JP 1997, DL Lancs, 1996. KStJ 1997 (Pres., Council for Lancs, 1997–). *Heir: s* Hon. Thomas Edward Kay-Shuttleworth [*b* 29 Sept. 1976; *m* 2002, Clare Barbara Tozer; one *s* one *d*]. *Address:* Leck Hall, Carnforth, Lancs LA6 2JF. *Clubs:* Brooks's, MCC.

SHUTTLEWORTH, Kenneth Owen; Chief Executive, Make Ltd, since 2004; *b* 10 Sept. 1952; *s* of Owen William Shuttleworth and late Ilene Doris (*née* Peakman); *m* 1987, Seana Ann Brennan; one *s* one *d. Educ:* Leicester Poly. (DipArch 1977). RIBA 1978. Registered architect, 1978; Dir, Foster and Partners, 1984–2003. Projects include: 30 St Mary Axe; City Hall, London; Elephant and Castle. Mem., CABE, 2003–. Hon. DDes De Montfort 1994. *Recreations:* painting, landscape drawing. *Address:* Make Ltd, 55–65 Whitfield Street, W1T 4HE. *T:* (020) 7636 5151, *Fax:* (020) 7636 5252; *e-mail:* kenshuttleworth@makearchitects.com.

SIBBETT, Prof. Wilson, CBE 2001; PhD; FRS 1997; FInstP; FRSE; Wardlaw Professor of Natural Philosophy, School of Physics and Astronomy, University of St Andrews, since 1997 (Professor, since 1985); *b* 15 March 1948; *s* of John Sibbett and Margaret (*née* McLeister); *m* 1979, Barbara Anne Brown; three *d. Educ:* Ballymena Tech. Coll.; Queen's Univ., Belfast (BSc 1st Cl. Hons Physics); Imperial Coll., London (PhD Laser Physics 1973). FInstP 1986. Blackett Laboratory, Imperial College, London: Postdoctoral Res. Asst, 1973–77; Lectr in Physics, 1977–84; Reader, 1984–85; University of St Andrews: Head, Physics Dept, 1985–88; Chm., Sch. of Physics and Astronomy, 1988–94. Mem., EPSRC, 1998–2001; Chm., Scottish Science Adv. Cttee, 2002–. Mem., St Andrews Rotary Club. FRSE 1988; Fellow, Optical Soc. of America, 1998. Hon. LLD Dundee, 2002; Hon. DSc Dublin, 2005. Hubert Schardin Gold Medal for Res. in Ultrafast Lasers and Diagnostics, 1978; C. V. Boys Prize and Medal for Exptl Physics, Inst. of Physics, 1993; Rank Prize for Optoelectronics, 1997; Rumford Medal, Royal Soc., 2000; Quantum Electronics Prize, European Physical Soc., 2002. *Publications:* numerous on laser physics and related diagnostic techniques in internat. scientific jls. *Recreations:* golf, gardening, DIY. *Address:* School of Physics and Astronomy, University of St Andrews, North Haugh, St Andrews, Fife KY16 9SS. *T:* (01334) 463100. *Clubs:* Rotary (St Andrews); Royal and Ancient Golf, New Golf (St Andrews).

SIBERRY, William Richard; QC 1989; a Recorder, since 2000; a Deputy High Court Judge, since 2002; *b* 11 Dec. 1950; *s* of late John William Morgan Siberry; *m* 1976, Julia Christine Lancaster. *Educ:* King's Coll., Taunton; Pembroke Coll., Cambridge (MA, LLB). Fellow, Pembroke Coll., Cambridge, 1973–75. Called to the Bar, Middle Temple, 1974, Bencher, 2002. Asst Recorder, 1997–2000. *Recreations:* music, gardening, walking, photography, North West Highlands of Scotland. *Address:* Essex Court Chambers, 24 Lincoln's Inn Fields, WC2A 3EG. *T:* (020) 7813 8000. *Club:* Royal Automobile.

SIBLEY, Dame Antoinette, (Dame Antoinette Corbett), DBE 1996 (CBE 1973); Prima Ballerina, The Royal Ballet, Covent Garden; President, Royal Academy of Dance (formerly of Dancing), since 1991 (Vice-President, 1989–91); guest coach, Royal Ballet, since 1991; Governor, Royal Ballet Board, since 2000; *b* 27 Feb. 1939; *d* of late Edward G. Sibley and Winifred M. Sibley (*née* Smith); *m* 1964, M. G. Somes, CBE (marr. diss. 1973; he *d* 1994); *m* 1974, Panton Corbett; one *s* one *d. Educ:* Arts Educational Sch. and Royal Ballet Sch. 1st performance on stage as Student with Royal Ballet at Covent Garden, a swan, Jan. 1956; joined company, July 1956; appeared with the company or as guest artist in most opera houses worldwide; dancing partnership with Anthony Dowell spanned three decades. Leading rôle in: Swan Lake, Sleeping Beauty, Giselle, Coppelia, Cinderella, The Nutcracker, La Fille Mal Gardée, Romeo and Juliet, Harlequin in April, Les Rendezvous, Jabez and the Devil (created the rôle of Mary), La Fête Etrange, The Rake's Progress, Hamlet, Ballet Imperial, Two Pigeons, La Bayadère, Symphonic Variations, Scènes de Ballet, Lilac Garden, Daphnis and Chloe, Pas de Quatre (Dolin's), Konservatoriet, A Month in the Country, Raymonda Act III, The Dream (created Titania), Laurentia, Good Humoured Ladies, Aristocrat in Mam'zelle Angot, Façade, Song of the Earth, Monotones (created rôle), Jazz Calendar (created Friday's Child), Enigma Variations (created Dorabella), Thais (created pas de deux), Anastasia (created Kshessinska), Afternoon of a Faun, Triad (created the Girl), Pavanne (created pas de deux), Manon (created title rôle), Soupirs (created pas de deux), L'invitation au voyage (created), Impromptu (created pas de deux), Varii Capricci (created La Capricciosa), Fleeting Figures (created rôle). *Film:* The Turning Point (with Baryshnikov), 1978. *Relevant publications:* Classical Ballet—the Flow of Movement, by Tamara Karsavina, 1962; Sibley and Dowell, by Nicholas Dromgoole and Leslie Spatt, 1976; Antoinette Sibley, 1981, photographs with text by Mary Clarke; Reflections of a Ballerina, by Barbara Newman, 1986. *Recreations:* watching sport, opera, reading. *Address:* c/o Royal Academy of Dance, 36 Battersea Square, SW11 3RA.

SIBSON, Angela Margaret; Chief Executive Officer, National Academy for Parenting Practitioners, since 2007; *b* 1 May 1949; *d* of Robert Sibson, Maryport, Cumbria and Joan Sibson (*née* Stafford); *m* 1971, Tom Ridler (*d* 2001); one *s* one *d. Educ:* Univ. of Birmingham (BA 1970); Queen Mary and Westfield Coll., London (MSc 2000). Chief Exec. Officer, Mothers' Union, 1993–99; Chief Executive: Relate, 2000–06; Commn for the Compact, 2007. *Recreation:* gardening. *Address:* c/o National Academy for Parenting Practitioners, Strand Bridge House, 138–142 Strand, WC2R 1HH.

SIBSON, Prof. Richard Hugh, PhD; FRS 2003; FRSNZ; FGS; Professor of Geology, University of Otago, New Zealand, 1990–2009, now Emeritus (Head, Department of Geology, 1990–96); *b* 28 Nov. 1945; *s* of Richard Broadley Sibson and Joan Winifred Sibson (*née* Fleming); *m* 1999, Prof. Francesca Cancarini Ghisetti, Catania, Italy. *Educ:* King's Coll., Otahuhu, Auckland; Univ. of Auckland (BSc 1st Cl. Hons Geol. 1968); Imperial Coll., London (MSc, DIC Structural Geol. 1970; PhD 1977). Jun. Scientific Officer, Geophysics Div., DSIR, NZ, 1969; Lectr in Structural Geol., Imperial Coll., London, 1973–81; Vis. Scientist, Office of Earthquake Studies, US Geol Survey, Menlo Park, Calif, 1981; Asst Prof., 1982–83, Associate Prof., 1984–87, Prof., 1988–90, Dept of Geol Scis, UCSB. FGS 1973; FRSNZ 1993; FAAAS 2006; Fellow: Geol Soc. of America, 1991; American Geophysical Union, 1999. Dist. Res. Medal, Univ. of Otago, 2003. *Publications:* contrib. numerous scientific res. papers to geol and geophysical jls on earthquake source mechanics in relation to structure, mechanics and mineralisation of crustal fault zones. *Recreations:* recorded music, hill and coastal walking, sea-kayaking, fly-fishing. *Address:* Department of Geology, University of Otago, PO Box 56, Dunedin 9054, New Zealand. *T:* (3) 4797519, *Fax:* (3) 4797527; *e-mail:* rick.sibson@otago.ac.nz; Casa Kotare, 129 Takamatua Bay Road, RD 1 Akaroa 7581, New Zealand. *T:* (3) 3048003.

SIBSON, Prof. Robin, PhD; Chief Executive, Higher Education Statistics Agency, since 2001; *b* 4 May 1944; *o s* of late Robert and Florence Elizabeth Sibson; *m* 1975, Heather Gail Gulliver; two *s. Educ:* Sutton County Grammar Sch.; King's Coll., Cambridge (Schol.; Wrangler, Maths Tripos Pt II, 1965; BA 1966; Smith's Prize, 1968; MA, PhD 1970). CStat 1993. Fellow, King's Coll., 1968–76, Lectr in Math. Stats, 1971–76, Univ. of Cambridge; University of Bath: Prof. of Stats, 1976–94; Head, Sch. of Maths, 1979–82; Pro-Vice-Chancellor, 1989–94; Vice-Chancellor, Univ. of Kent at Canterbury, 1994–2001. Member: various SSRC/ESRC and SERC cttees, 1980–85; Science Bd, SERC, 1986–89; Wildfowl Trust Sci. Adv. Cttee, 1979–83; Bd, Higher Educn Stats Agency, 1996–; UK Acad. Mem., Higher Educn and Res. Cttee, Council of Europe, 1997–2002 (Mem. Bureau, 2000–02). Mem. Corp., Canterbury Coll., 1995–2001. Hon. DCL Kent, 2002. *Publications:* (with N. Jardine) Mathematical Taxonomy, 1971; papers in learned jls. *Recreation:* natural history. *Address:* Higher Education Statistics Agency, 95 Promenade, Cheltenham GL50 1HZ.

SIDAWAY, Ven. Geoffrey Harold; Archdeacon of Gloucester, since 2000; Canon Residentiary, Gloucester Cathedral, since 2007; *b* 28 Oct. 1942; *s* of Harold and Margaret Sidaway; *m* 1970, Margaret Bates; two *s* one *d. Educ:* Kelham Theol Coll. Ordained deacon, 1966, priest, 1967; Curate: Beighton, Derby, 1966–70; St Mary and All Saints, Chesterfield, 1970–72; Vicar, St Bartholomew, Derby, 1972–77; Chaplain to E Midlands Ordination Course, 1974–77; Vicar: St Martin, Maidstone, 1977–86; Bearstead and Thurnham, 1986–2000. Rural Dean, Sutton, 1992–99; Hon. Canon, Canterbury Cathedral, 1994–2000. Mem., Gen. Synod of C of E, 1995–2000, 2005–07. *Recreations:* cooking, gardening, walking, showing labradors. *Address:* Glebe House, Church Road, Maisemore, Gloucester GL2 8EY.

SIDDALL, Jonathan Charles; Chief Executive, LandAid Charitable Trust Ltd, since 2007; *b* 6 July 1954; *s* of John Siddall and Joan Siddall; *m* 1988, Nicola Ann Glover; two *d. Educ:* Rugby Sch.; Univ. of Birmingham (LLB Hons 1976). Called to the Bar, Middle Temple, 1978; Accredited Mediator, CEDR, 1999. Pupillage, 1979–80; in-house Lawyer, Internat. Mgt Gp, 1980–83; Gen. Sec., British Univs Sports Fedn, 1984–86; Sec., Cumberland Lawn Tennis Club, 1987–90; Sec. and Campaign Co-ordinator, Law Aid Trust, 1990–91; Dep. Sec., LTA, 1992–98; Dir, Sports Dispute Resolution Panel Ltd, 1999–2006. *Recreations:* golf, tennis, squash, ski-ing, running, gardening. *Address:* LandAid Charitable Trust Ltd, 1 Warwick Row, SW1E 5ER. *T:* (020) 7802 0117. *Clubs:* Cumberland Lawn Tennis; Jesters; Highgate Golf.

SIDDELEY, family name of **Baron Kenilworth**.

SIDDELEY, Randle; *see* Kenilworth, 4th Baron.

SIDDELL, Peter Graham, DCNZM 2008; QSO 1991; painter (full-time), since 1971; *b* Ngawha, 31 July 1935; *s* of Joseph and Dorothy Siddell; *m* 1960, Sylvia Grace Bartlett; two *d. Educ:* Richmond Road and Newton Central Prim. Schs; Mount Abert Grammar Sch.; Auckland Teachers' Coll. Former electrician and teacher. *Recreations:* reading, exploring bush and beach, mountaineering, snorkelling. *Address:* 27 Fairview Road, Mount Eden, Auckland 1024, New Zealand. *T:* (9) 6301130; *e-mail:* siddell@xtra.co.nz.

SIDDIQ, Irfan, OBE 2005; HM Diplomatic Service; Deputy Head of Mission, Syria, since 2007; *b* London, 27 Jan. 1977; *s* of late Mohammed Siddiq Noor and of Nusrat Siddiq. *Educ:* University Coll., Oxford (BA Hons PPE 1998). Entered FCO, 1998; Second Sec. (Econ.), New Delhi, 1999–2000; Arabic Lang. Trng, 2000–02; Second Sec. (Pol), Cairo, 2002–03; First Sec. (Pol), Coalition Provisional Authy, Baghdad, 2003–04; on secondment to US State Dept, Washington, 2004–05; Private Sec. to Sec. of State for Foreign and Commonwealth Affairs, 2005–07. *Recreations:* football, literature, current affairs, trekking, rock climbing, travel. *Address:* c/o Foreign and Commonwealth Office,

King Charles Street, SW1A 2AH. *T:* (Syria) (11) 3391513, *Fax:* (11) 3921873; *e-mail:* irfan.siddiq@fco.gov.uk.

SIDDIQI, Prof. Obaid, Padma Vibhushan 2006 (Padma Bhushan 1984); FRS 1984; FIASc 1968; FNA 1977; Professor Emeritus, Tata Institute of Fundamental Research, National Centre for Biological Sciences, Bangalore; *b* 7 Jan. 1932; *s* of M. A. Qadeer Siddiqi and Umme Kulsum; *m* 1955, Asiya Siddiqi; two *s* two *d. Educ:* Univ. of Aligarh (MSc); Univ. of Glasgow (PhD). Lecturer, Aligarh Univ., 1954–57; Indian Agricl Res. Inst., 1957–58; Dept of Genetics, Glasgow Univ., 1958–61; Cold Spring Harbor Lab., NY, 1961; Univ. of Pennsylvania, 1961–62; Tata Inst. of Fundamental Research: Fellow, 1962; Prof. of Molecular Biol., 1972–95; Dir, Nat. Centre for Biol Scis, Bangalore, 1992–99. Vis. Associate, Yale Univ., 1966; Vis. Prof., MIT, 1970–71; CIT Gosney Fellow, 1971–72; Sherman Fairchild Distinguished Scholar, 1981–82; Fellow, Third World Acad. of Sciences, Trieste, 1986; Vis. Fellow, 1997, and Life Mem., Clare Hall, Cambridge. Foreign Associate, NAS, USA, 2003. Hon. DSc: Aligarh, 1984; Banaras Hindu, 1986. *Publications:* (co-ed) Development and Neurobiology of Drosophila, 1981; several papers in learned jls on genetics and neurobiology. *Recreations:* music, tennis, photography. *Address:* Tata Institute of Fundamental Research, National Centre for Biological Sciences, GKVK Campus, Bangalore 560065, India. *T:* (80) 3636420, ext. 2110, *Fax:* (80) 3636662; *e-mail:* osiddiqi@ncbs.res.in; (home) 1280 3d Main, 9th Cross, BEL Layout 1st Block, Vidyaranyapura, Bangalore 560097, India. *T:* (80) 3648507.

SIDDIQUI, Prof. Mona, PhD; FRSE; Professor of Islamic Studies and Public Understanding, University of Glasgow, since 2006; *b* 3 May 1963; *d* of Abdul Ali and Hasina Khatoon; *m* 1991, Farhaj Ahmed Siddiqui; three *s. Educ:* Leeds Univ. (BA Hons Arabic and French); Manchester Univ. (MA; PhD 1992). Lectr in Islamic Law, Glasgow Caledonian Univ., 1993–95; University of Glasgow: Sen. Lectr in Arabic and Islamic Studies, 1995–2006; Hd, Dept of Theol. and Religious Studies, 2002–05; Mem. Court, 2004–. Mem., Central Religious Adv. Council, BBC, 1998–2005; Chair, Scottish Religious Adv. Council, BBC, 2005–. FRSE 2005. FRSA 2005. *Publications:* How to Read the Qur'an, 2007; contrib. articles on inter-religious dialogue and Islamic law to various internat. jls. *Recreations:* cooking, interior design. *Address:* Department of Theology and Religious Studies, University of Glasgow, Glasgow G12 8QQ. *T:* (0141) 330 6525, *Fax:* (0141) 330 4943; *e-mail:* msi@arts.gla.ac.uk.

SIDDLE, Prof. Kenneth, PhD; Professor of Molecular Endocrinology, University of Cambridge, since 1990; Fellow, Churchill College, Cambridge, since 1982; *b* 30 March 1947; *s* of Fred and Vera Siddle; *m* 1st, 1971, Yvonne Marie Kennedy (marr. diss. 1994); one *s*; 2nd, 1996, Anne Elizabeth Willis; one *s. Educ:* Morecambe Grammar Sch.; Downing Coll., Cambridge (BA 1969). MA, PhD 1973. Lectr, Dept Medical Biochemistry, Welsh Nat. Sch. Med., Cardiff, 1971–78; Meres Sen. Student for Med. Research, St John's Coll., Cambridge, 1978–81; Wellcome Lectr, Dept Clinical Biochem., Univ. of Cambridge, 1981–90. Vis. Scientist, Joslin Diabetes Center and Harvard Med. Sch., 1989–90. Hon. Treas., Cambridge Univ. CC, 1990–. Chm. Editl Bd, Biochemical Jl, 1995–99. *Publications:* articles in biochem. jls. *Recreations:* mountaineering (especially Munro bagging), cricket, bird watching, gardening. *Address:* 6 Church Street, Wing, Oakham, Rutland LE15 8RS. *T:* (01572) 737675. *Clubs:* MCC; Hawks (Cambridge); Lancashire County Cricket.

SIDDLE, Oliver Richard, CB 1995; OBE 1983; General Manager, Enterprises Group, and Assistant Director-General, British Council, 1992–96; retired; *b* 11 March 1936; *s* of George Siddle and Grace (*née* Hatfield); *m* 1964 (marr. diss. 1995); one *s* one *d. Educ:* Hymers Coll., Hull; Queen's Coll., Oxford (BA 2nd Cl. Hons Mod. Hist. 1959). Joined British Council, 1961: Budget Dept, 1961–63; Poland, 1963–65; Argentina, 1965–68; Nigeria, 1968–70; Mgt Trng, Heriot-Watt Univ., 1970–71; Staff Trng Dept, 1971–74; Dir, Budget Dept, 1974–76; Representative: Peru, 1976–80; Hong Kong, 1980–85; Malaysia, 1985–87; Gen. Manager, Direct Teaching, 1987–92. *Recreations:* hill-walking, gardening, drawing. *Address:* 24320 La Tour Blanche, France.

SIDDONS, Michael Powell; Wales Herald of Arms Extraordinary (Herodr Arbennig Cymru), since 1994; *b* 4 June 1928; *s* of Bertram Siddons and Enid Mary Powell; *m* 1951, Denise Maria Jacqueline Dambre; three *s* (and one *d* decd). *Educ:* Shrewsbury Sch.; Trinity Coll., Cambridge (MA, MB BCh); St Thomas' Hosp. MFOM 1983; Licence en médecine du Travail, Univ. Catholique de Louvain, 1980. Casualty and anaesthetics officer, then house physician, St Thomas' Hosp., London, 1952–53; Nat. Service, RAMC, Malaya, 1953–55; general medical practitioner, Pontypool, 1955–74; Commission of European Communities: MO, Med. Service, Brussels, 1974–78; Head, Medical Service, Brussels Staff, 1978–87. Mem., Académie Internat. d'Héraldique, 2000; FSA 1987; FHS 1996; FSG 1998. Hon. DLitt Wales, 1997. *Publications:* The Development of Welsh Heraldry, vol. I, 1991, vols II and III, 1993, vol. IV, 2006; Welsh Pedigree Rolls, 1996; Visitations by the Heralds in Wales, 1996; Visitation of Herefordshire 1634, 2002; contribs to books on heraldic and genealogical subjects and articles in jls. *Recreations:* gardening especially magnolias, medieval Welsh heraldry, genealogy. *Address:* Castagnon, 32800 Eauze, France.

SIDELL, Ron Daniel; architect; Sidell Gibson Partnership LLP (private practice), since 1970; *b* 20 April 1941; *s* of Daniel Sidell and Dorothy Eady; *m* Sally Hodgson; one *d. Educ:* Canterbury Coll. of Architecture; York Univ. Projects in London and Germany include: Unilever, Lloyds, Cazenove, Prudential, Rothschilds, European Bank and Civic Bldgs; Crown Jewel House and Windsor Castle reconstruction; masterplan, Paddington Central. Winner: Grand Buildings Trafalgar Square Internat. Competition, 1986; City of Winchester Central Redevelt Proposal Comp., 1989. *Recreations:* just about most things. *Address:* (office) Canal Building, 37 Kentish Town Road, NW1 8NX. *T:* (020) 7284 9005.

SIDI, Marianne; *see* Elliott, M.

SIDMOUTH, 8th Viscount *cr* 1805; **Jeremy Francis Addington;** *b* 29 July 1947; *s* of 7th Viscount and Barbara Mary Addington (*née* Rochford); *S* father, 2005; *m* 1st, 1970, Grete Henningsen; one *s* one *d*; 2nd, 1986, Una Coogan; one *s* two *d. Educ:* Ampleforth. *Heir:* *s* Hon. John Addington, *b* 29 Nov. 1990.

SIDNEY, family name of **Viscount De L'Isle.**

SIEFF, Hon. Sir David (Daniel), Kt 1999; Chairman, Newbury Racecourse plc, since 1998 (Member of Board, since 1988); non-executive Director, Benesco Charity Ltd, since 2005; *b* 22 March 1939; *s* of Baron Sieff of Brimpton, OBE, and late Rosalie Cottage; *m* 1962, Jennifer Walton; two *s. Educ:* Repton. Joined Marks & Spencer, 1957: Dir, 1972–97; non-exec. Dir, 1997–2001. Pt-time Mem., NFC, 1972–78; non-exec. Chm., FIBI Bank (UK) Plc (formerly First Internat. Bank of Israel (UK) Ltd), 1994–2004; Chm., ukbetting, 2001–04; non-exec. Dir, GET plc, 2003–06. Chm., British Retail Consortium, 1998–2002. Chairman, North Metropolitan Conciliation Cttee of Race Relations Board, 1969–71; Vice-Chm., Inst. of Race Relations, 1971–72; Member: Policy Studies Inst. (formerly PEP), 1976–84; Bd, Business in the Community; Council, Industrial Soc.,

1975–90. Governor: Weizmann Inst. of Science, Rehovot, Israel, 1978– (Chm. Exec. Cttee, UK Foundn, 1984–2000); Shenkar Coll. of Textile Technology (Israel), 1980–; Hon. Pres., British ORT, 1983–. Trustee, Glyndebourne Arts Trust, 1971–2000. Pres., Racehorse Owners Assoc., 1975–78; Chairman: Racing Welfare Charities, 1988–2000; Nat. Lottery Charities Bd, 1994–99; Member: Jockey Club, 1977–; Horserace Totalisator Bd, 1991–98; British Horseracing Bd, 1998–2001. FRSA 1989. *Address:* c/o Bedford Estates, 29a Montague Street, WC1B 5BL. *Club:* White's.

SIEGERT, Prof. Martin John, PhD; FRSE; Professor of Geosciences, and Head, School of GeoSciences, University of Edinburgh, since 2006; *b* Walthamstow, London, 19 Nov. 1967; *s* of David Alan Siegert and Kathleen May Siegert; *m* 2001, Maggie Robertson. *Educ:* Sudbury Upper Sch.; Univ. of Reading (BSc Geol Geophysics 1989); Pembroke Coll., Cambridge (PhD 1993). Lectr in Phys. Geog., Univ. of Wales, Aberystwyth, 1994–98; University of Bristol: Lectr, 1999–2002, Reader, 2002–03, in Phys. Geog.; Prof. of Phys. Geog., 2003–06. FRSE 2007. *Publications:* Ice Sheets and Late Quaternary Environmental Change, 2001; over 100 papers in scientific jls, incl. Nature and Science, on Antarctic glaciol. and subglacial lake exploration. *Recreations:* running in Holyrood Park, walking in countryside, watching football (especially Leyton Orient), playing golf. *Address:* School of GeoSciences, University of Edinburgh, Grant Institute, King's Buildings, West Mains Road, Edinburgh EH9 3JW. *T:* (0131) 650 7543, 07780 703008, *Fax:* (0131) 650 7340; *e-mail:* m.j.siegert@ed.ac.uk.

SIEGHART, Mary Ann Corinna Howard; writer and broadcaster; *b* 6 Aug. 1961; *d* of Paul Sieghart and Felicity Ann Sieghart (*née* Baer); *m* 1989, David Prichard; two *d. Educ:* Cobham Hall; Bedales Sch.; Wadham Coll., Oxford (MA). Occasional feature and leader writer (part-time), Daily Telegraph, 1980–82; Eurobond Correspondent and Lex Columnist, Financial Times, 1982–86; City Editor, Today, 1986; Political Correspondent, Economist, 1986–88; The Times: Asst Editor, 1988–2007; Opinion Page Editor, 1988–91; Arts Editor, 1989–90; Political Leader Writer, 1990–2007; acting Editor on Sundays, 1997–99; columnist, 1998–2007. Television: presenter: The World This Week; The Brains Trust; The Big Picture Show; Powerhouse; radio: presenter, The Week in Westminster; guest interviewer, Start the Week. Founding Cttee Mem., Women in Journalism, 1995–98; Member: Adv. Council and Steering Cttee, New Europe, 1999–2006; Steering Gp, "No" Campaign, 2000–04. Mem., Social Studies Adv. Bd, Oxford Univ., 1999–2003. Trustee: Nat. Heritage Meml Fund, 1997–2002; The Radcliffe Trust, 2006–. Vice Pres., Nat. Assoc. for Gifted Children, 1996–. Vice-Chair, New Deal for Communities, N Fulham, 2001–06. Laurence Stern Fellow, Washington Post, 1984. Harold Wincott Young Financial Journalist of the Year, 1983; Commended, Young Journalist of the Year, British Press Awards, 1983. *Recreations:* reading, rollerblading, architecture, music, travel to remote places, doodling, singing in choirs, art. *Address:* 11 Campden Hill Towers, Notting Hill Gate, W11 3QW. *T:* 07956 221861; *e-mail:* sieghart@journalist.com. *Club:* Groucho.
See also W. M. T. S. Sieghart.

SIEGHART, William Matthew Timothy Stephen; Director, Forward Group, since 1986; Chairman, Forward Thinking, since 2004; *b* 14 April 1960; *s* of Paul Sieghart and Felicity Ann Sieghart (*née* Baer); *m* 1996, Molly Dineen; one *s* two *d. Educ:* Eton Coll.; St Anne's Coll., Oxford (MA Hons PPE). Founder and Chm., Forward Publishing, 1986–2001. Director: Groucho Club plc, 1995–2001; Hammer Films, 1998–. Vice-Pres., Arts and Business, 2001–; Dir, Index on Censorship, 1999–2000. Founder and Chm., Forward Arts Foundn, 1993–; Chm., Arts Foundn, 2002–. Mem. Council, Arts Council England (formerly Arts Council of England), 2000–06 (Chm., Lottery Panel, 2000–05). Trustee: Citizenship Foundn, 1994–; and Mem. Council, RSA, 1995–99; Esmée Fairbairn Foundn, 1998–; YCTV, 1998–2001; Writer's and Scholar's Educnl Trust, 1999–2000; The Poetry Archive, 2001–05. Sen. Adv. Fellow, UK Defence Acad., 2004–. Gov., British Inst. of Human Rights, 1998–. Founder: Nat. Poetry Day, 1995–; Bedtime Reading Week, 2000–; Big Arts Week, 2001–. *Publications:* (ed) The Forward Book of Poetry, annually 1993–; (ed) Poems of the Decade, 2001; The Swing Factory, 2004. *Recreations:* travelling, playing and watching sport, poetry. *Address:* c/o Forward, 84–86 Regent Street, W1B 5DD. *T:* (020) 7734 2303, *Fax:* (020) 7287 4911; *e-mail:* william.sieghart@theforwardgroup.com. *Clubs:* Brooks's, Groucho, MCC; Queenwood Golf, Aldeburgh Golf.
See also M. A. C. H. Sieghart.

SIGMON, Robert Leland; lawyer; *b* Roanoke, Va, 3 April 1929; *s* of Ottis Leland Sigmon and Aubrey Virginia (*née* Bishop); *m* 1st, 1963, Marianne Rita Gellner (marr. diss.; she *d* 2005); 2nd, 1992, Jean Mary Anderson. *Educ:* Univ. of Virginia; Sorbonne; London Sch. of Economics. BA, DrJur. Member of the Bar: US Supreme Court; Court of Appeals, Second and District of Columbia Circuits; Virginia; District of Columbia. Vice-Pres., Pilgrims Soc. of GB, 1993– (Chm., Exec. Cttee, 1977–93); Founder Member: Associates of the Victoria and Albert Museum, 1976 (Dir, 1976–87); Amer. and Internat. Friends of V&A Mus. (Trustee, 1985–2000). Mem., Council of Management, British Inst. of Internat. and Comparative Law, 1982–2006. Trustee: American Sch. in London, 1977–91; Magna Carta Trust, 1984–94; Vice-Chm., Mid-Atlantic Club of London, 1977–96; Vice-Pres., European-Atlantic Gp, 1978–94; Member: Exec. Cttee, Amer. Soc. in London, 1969– (Chm. 1974); Amer. Soc. of Internat. Law; Selden Soc.; Guild of St Bride's Church, Fleet Street; Ends of the Earth; Gov., E-SU, 1984–90. Chevalier du Tastevin. *Publications:* contribs to legal periodicals. *Recreations:* collecting antiquarian books, oenology. *Address:* 2 Plowden Buildings, Middle Temple, EC4Y 9AS. *T:* (020) 7583 4851. *Club:* Reform.

SIGURDSSON, Niels P.; Ministry of Foreign Affairs, Iceland, 1990–96; *b* Reykjavik, 10 Feb. 1926; *s* of Sigurdur B. Sigurdsson and Karitas Einarsdóttir; *m* 1953, Olafia Rafnsdóttir; two *s* one *d. Educ:* Univ. of Iceland (Law). Joined Diplomatic Service 1952; First Sec., Paris Embassy, 1956–60; Dep. Permanent Rep. to NATO and OECD, 1957–60; Dir, Internat. Policy Div., Min. of Foreign Affairs, Reykjavik, 1961–67; Delegate to UN Gen. Assembly, 1965; Ambassador and Permanent Rep. of Iceland to N Atlantic Council, 1967–71; Ambassador: to Belgium and EEC, 1968–71; to UK, 1971–76; to Fed. Republic of Germany, 1976–78; Ministry of Foreign Affairs, Reykjavik, 1979–84; Ambassador to Norway, 1985–89. *Recreations:* swimming, riding. *Address:* Naustabryggja 55, 110 Reykjavík, Iceland.

SIKORA, Prof. Karol, FRCP, FRCR, FFPM; Dean, Buckingham Medical School, since 2007; *b* 17 June 1948; *s* of Witold Karol Sikora and Thomasina Sikora; *m* 1974, Alison Mary Rice; one *s* two *d. Educ:* Dulwich Coll.; Corpus Christi Coll., Cambridge (MA, MB, BChir, PhD); Middlesex Hospital. FRCR 1980; FRCP 1988; FFPM 2002. Middlesex Hosp., 1972; Hammersmith Hosp., 1973; MRC Clinical Fellow, Lab. for Molecular Biol., Cambridge, 1974–77; Clinical Fellow, Stanford Univ., 1978–79; Dir, Ludwig Inst. for Cancer Research, Cambridge, 1980–86; Prof. of Clin. Oncol., RPMS, then ICSM, Hammersmith Hosp., 1986–2007; Dep. Dir (Clinical Res.), ICRF, 1995–97; Chief, WHO Cancer Prog., Lyon, France, 1997–99. Vis. Prof. of Cancer Medicine, ICSM, 2007–. Med. Dir, Cancer Partners UK, 2006–. Vice Pres., Global Clinical Res.

(Oncology), Pharmacia Corp., 1999–2002; Special Advr on cancer services, HCA Internat., 2002–06. *Publications:* Monoclonal Antibodies, 1984; Interferon, 1985; Cancer: a student guide, 1988; (ed jtly) Treatment of Cancer, 1990, 5th edn 2008; Fight Cancer, 1990; Genes and Cancer, 1990; (with N. Bosanquet) The Economics of Cancer Care, 2006; contrib. Gene Therapy. *Recreations:* boating, travelling, rock climbing. *Address:* 21 Barrett Street, W1U 1BD. *T:* (020) 7518 0780. *Clubs:* Athenæum, Polish Hearth.

SILBER, Dr Evelyn Ann, FMA; Hon. Professorial Research Fellow, University of Glasgow, since 2006; *b* 22 May 1949; *d* of late Martin Helmut Silber and Mavis Evelyn (*née* Giles). *Educ:* Hatfield Girls' Grammar Sch.; New Hall, Cambridge (MA); Univ. of Pennsylvania (MA); Clare Hall, Cambridge (PhD). Guide, Hatfield House, 1965–70; Thouron Fellow, Univ. of Penn., 1972–73; copy-writer and media controller, Associated Book Publishers, 1973–74; publicity manager, Addison Wesley Publishers, 1974–75; Leverhulme Res. Fellow in Hist. of Art, 1975–76; Lectr, Hist. of Art, Glasgow Univ., 1978; Birmingham Museum and Art Gallery: Asst Keeper (Fine Art), 1979–82; Dep. Keeper (Painting and Sculpture), 1982–85; Birmingham Museums and Art Gallery: Asst Dir, Public Services, 1985–94; Head of Central Museums, 1994–95; Director: Leeds Mus and Galls, 1995–2001; Hunterian Mus. and Art Gall., Univ. of Glasgow, 2001–06. Mem. Council, Ikon Gall., 1981–88. Member: Bd, Cultural Heritage NTO (formerly Museums Trng Inst.), 1996–2003; Historic Envmt Adv. Council for Scotland, 2006–May 2009. Chm., Charles Rennie Mackintosh Soc., 2006–. FMA 1996; FRSA 2000. *Publications:* The Sculpture of Epstein, 1986; (with T. Friedman) Jacob Epstein Sculpture and Drawings, 1987; Gaudier-Brzeska: Life and Art, 1996. *Recreations:* travel, music, walking, gardening. *Address:* Department of Art History, University Avenue, Glasgow G12 8QQ. *Club:* Royal Over-Seas League.

SILBER, Hon. Sir Stephen (Robert), Kt 1999; **Hon. Mr Justice Silber;** a Judge of the High Court of Justice, Queen's Bench Division, since 1999; *b* 26 March 1944; *s* of late J. J. Silber and Marguerite Silber; *m* 1982, Lucinda, *d* of Lt-Col David St John Edwards, retd; one *s* one *d*. *Educ:* William Ellis Sch.; University Coll. London; Trinity Coll., Cambridge. Called to Bar, Gray's Inn, 1968, Bencher, 1994. QC 1987; a Recorder, 1987–99; a Dep. High Court Judge, 1995–99. A Judge, Employment Appeal Tribunal, 2004–. Law Comr for England and Wales, 1994–99. Mem., Criminal Law Cttee, Judicial Studies Bd, 1994–99. Mem. Adv. Council, Inst. of Eur. and Comparative Law, Univ. of Oxford, 2004–. Pres., Travel and Tourism Law Assoc., 2002–. *Recreations:* walking, music, watching sport, theatre. *Address:* Royal Courts of Justice, Strand, WC2A 2LL.

SILBERSTON, Prof. (Zangwill) Aubrey, CBE 1987; Professor of Economics, University of London, at Imperial College, 1978–87, now Emeritus, and Head of Department of Social and Economic Studies, 1981–87; Senior Research Fellow, Tanaka Business School (formerly Management School), Imperial College, 1987–2005; *b* 26 Jan. 1922; *s* of Louis and Polly Silberston; *m* 1st, 1945, Dorothy Marion Nicholls, MBE (marr. diss.; she *d* 2006); (one *s* decd and one *d* decd); 2nd, 1985, Michèle Ledić. *Educ:* Hackney Downs Sch., London; Jesus Coll., Cambridge. MA (Cantab); MA (Oxon). Courtaulds Ltd, 1946–50; Kenward Res. Fellow in Industrial Admin, St Catharine's Coll., Cambridge, 1950–53; University Lectr in Economics, Cambridge, 1951–71; Fellow, 1958–71, Dir of Studies in Econs, 1965–71, St John's Coll., Cambridge; Chm., Faculty Bd of Econs and Politics, Cambridge, 1966–70; Official Fellow in Econs, 1971–78, and Dean, 1972–78, Nuffield Coll., Oxford. Rockefeller Fellow, Univ. of Calif, Berkeley, 1959–60; Visiting Professor: Queensland Univ., 1977; Univ. of the South, Sewanee, 1984. Member: Monopolies Commn, 1965–68; Board of British Steel Corp., 1967–76; Departmental Cttee on Patent System, 1967–70; Econs Cttee, SSRC, 1969–73; Royal Commn on the Press, 1974–77; Restrictive Practices Ct, 1986–92; Royal Commn on Environmental Pollution, 1986–96; Biotechnol. Adv. Commn, Stockholm Envmt Inst., 1993–97; Council of Experts, Intellectual Property Inst., 1992–. Sen. Advr, London Economics, 1992–2004; Economic Adviser, CBI, 1972–74; Specialist Advr, Eur. Communities Cttee, H of L, 1993; Chm., Assoc. of Learned Societies in the Social Sciences, 1985–87; President: Section F, British Assoc., 1987; Confedn of European Economic Assocs, 1988–90 (Vice-Pres., 1990–92); Vice-Pres., REconS, 1992– (Sec.-Gen., 1979–92). *Publications:* Education and Training for Industrial Management, 1955; (with G. Maxcy) The Motor Industry, 1959; (jtly) Economies of Large-scale Production in British Industry, 1965; (jtly) The Patent System, 1967; (with C. T. Taylor) The Economic Impact of the Patent System, 1973; (ed) Industrial Management: East and West, 1973; (with A. Cockerill) The Steel Industry, 1974; (jtly) Microeconomic Efficiency and Macroeconomic Performance, 1983; The Multi-Fibre Arrangement and the UK Economy, 1984; (jtly) British Manufacturing Investment Overseas, 1985; The Economic Importance of Patents, 1987; (ed) Technology and Economic Progress, 1989; Patent Policy: is the pharmaceutical industry a special case?, 1989; (with Michèle Ledić) The Future of the Multi-Fibre Arrangement, 1989; (ed with Gianna Boero) Environmental Economics, 1995; (jtly) Beyond the Multifibre Arrangement, 1995; (with C. Raymond) The Changing Industrial Map of Europe, 1996; PR China's Textile and Clothing Sector and its Export Potential, 1999; (with Philip Bentley) Anti-dumping and Countervailing Action: limits imposed by economic and legal theory, 2007; articles in Econ. Jl, Bulletin of Oxford Inst. of Statistics, Oxford Economic Papers, Jl of Royal Statistical Society. *Recreations:* music, ballet. *Address:* Rue Jules Lejeune 2, 1050 Brussels, Belgium. *Club:* Fondation Universitaire (Brussels).

SILCOCK, David Thomas; road safety consultant; Chief Executive, Global Road Safety Partnership, 2002–08; *b* 2 March 1945; *s* of John and Marjorie Silcock; *m* 1st, 1967, Lesley Maureen Reeves (marr. diss. 1994); three *d*; 2nd, 1996, Annette de Villiers Herholdt. *Educ:* Churchill Coll., Cambridge (BA 1966, MA 1970); Imperial Coll., London (MSc 1970). CEng, MICE, 1971. Engr, Canadian Pacific Railway Co. and Consultant, N. D. Lea and Assocs, Vancouver, 1967–69; various transport consultancy assignments, Halcrow Fox and Assocs, UK, 1969–74; Sen. Associate, Halcrow Fox and Assocs (London), and Man. Dir, Halcrow Fox and Assocs (Hong Kong), 1974–79; Dep. Dir, Transport Ops Res. Gp, Univ. of Newcastle upon Tyne, 1979–92; Ross Silcock, subseq. Babtie Group: Partner, Ross Silcock Partnership, 1986–96; Man. Dir, Ross Silcock Ltd, transportation and road safety consultants, 1996–2001; Divl Dir, Babtie Gp Ltd, 2001–02. Mem. Council, 1995–96, Dir, 1996–2001, British Consultants Bureau. Mem. Editl Bd, Transport Reviews (internat. jl), 1989–92. *Publications:* over 90 tech. articles in fields of transport and road safety. *Recreations:* walking, music.

SILJA, Anja; German opera singer; *b* Berlin, 17 April 1940; parents both actors; *m* 1980, Christoph von Dohnányi, *qv*; one *s* two *d*. Started career at age 10; first opera engagement, Staatstheater Braunschweig, 1956; débuts: Stuttgart State Opera, Frankfurt Opera, 1958; Bayreuth Fest. (Senta in The Flying Dutchman), 1960; has appeared widely in USA, Japan and Europe, in all major opera houses, incl. Salzburg, and Glyndebourne Fest. (début, 1989); repertoire includes: all major Wagner rôles, Salome, Lulu, Fidelio, Elektra, Jenůfa, The Makropulos Case, Erwartung, Pierrot Lunaire, Dialogues des Carmélites, etc. Has made recordings and videos. *Address:* c/o Artists Management Zürich/Rita Schütz, Rütistrasse 52, 8044 Zürich-Gockhausen, Switzerland.

SILK, Rt Rev. David; *see* Silk, Rt Rev. R. D.

SILK, Dennis Raoul Whitehall, CBE 1995; MA; Warden of Radley College, 1968–91; Chairman, Test and County Cricket Board, 1994–96; *b* 8 Oct. 1931; 2nd *s* of late Rev. Dr Claude Whitehall Silk and Mrs Louise Silk; *m* 1963, Diana Merilyn, 2nd *d* of W. F. Milton, Pitminster, Somerset; two *s* two *d*. *Educ:* Christ's Hosp.; Sidney Sussex Coll., Cambridge (Exhibr). MA (History) Cantab. Asst Master, Marlborough Coll., 1955–68 (Housemaster, 1957–68). JP Abingdon, 1972–89. *Publications:* Cricket for Schools, 1964; Attacking Cricket, 1965. *Recreations:* antiquarian, literary, sporting (Blues in cricket (Capt. Cambridge Univ. CC, 1955) and Rugby football). *Address:* Sturts Barn, Huntham Lane, Stoke St Gregory, Taunton, Somerset TA3 6EG. *T:* (01823) 490348. *Clubs:* East India, Devonshire, Sports and Public Schools, MCC (Pres., 1992–94); Hawks (Cambridge).

SILK, (Evan) Paul; Director of Strategic Projects, House of Commons, since 2007; *b* 8 Feb. 1952; *s* of late Evan Silk and Joan Silk (*née* King); *m* 1986, Kathryn Barnes; three *s*. *Educ:* Christ Coll., Brecon; Brasenose Coll., Oxford (John Watson Scholar; MA 1st Cl. Hons Lit.Hum.); Princeton Univ. A Clerk in H of C, 1975–77 and 1979–2001: Energy Cttee, 1984–89; Home Affairs Cttee, 1989–93; Foreign Affairs Cttee, 1998–2001; NI Office, 1977–79; occasional work with Council of Europe Parly Assembly, 1976–99; Clerk to Nat. Assembly for Wales, 2001–07. Member, Board of Visitors: HM Prison Ashford, 1981–90; HM Prison Belmarsh, 1991–93. *Publications:* (with R. Walters) How Parliament Works, 1987, 4th edn 1998; (with P. Evans) Parliamentarians Assembly of the Council of Europe: practice and procedure, 10th edn 2008; contribs to other works on Parliament. *Recreations:* living in countryside, Mexicana. *Address:* House of Commons, SW1A 0AA; *e-mail:* silkp@parliament.uk. *Clubs:* Chelsea Arts; Ebbw Vale Rugby Football; Gwernyfed Rugby Football.

SILK, Prof. Joseph Ivor, PhD; FRS 1999; Savilian Professor of Astronomy, Oxford University, since 1999; Fellow, New College, Oxford, since 1999; *b* 3 Dec. 1942; *s* of Philip and Sylvie Silk; *m* 1st, 1968, Margaret Wendy Kuhn (marr. diss. 1998); two *s*; 2nd, 2001, Jacqueline Riffault. *Educ:* Clare Coll., Cambridge (MA 1963); Harvard Univ. (PhD 1968). Research Fellow: Inst. of Astronomy, Cambridge Univ., 1968–69; Princeton Univ. Observatory, 1969–70; University of California at Berkeley: Prof. of Astronomy, 1970–; Miller Res. Prof., 1980–81; Prof. of Physics, 1988–. Alfred P. Sloan Foundn Fellow, 1972–74; Guggenheim Fellow, 1975–76; Leon Lectr, Univ. of Penn, 1984; Hooker Dist. Vis. Prof., McMaster Univ., 1987; Bearden Vis. Prof., Johns Hopkins Univ., 1994; Sackler Fellow, Inst. Astronomy, Cambridge, 1997; Tercentenary Fellow, Emmanuel Coll., Cambridge, 1997; Blaise-Pascal Prof., Inst. d'Astrophysique, Paris, 1997–98; Biermann Lectr, Max-Planck Inst. für Astrophys., Garching, 1997. FAAAS 1987; Fellow, APS, 1996. Hon. Mem., French Physical Soc., 1997. *Publications:* The Big Bang, 1980, 3rd edn 2001; (jtly) Star Formation, 1980; The Left Hand of Creation, 1983, rev. edn 1994; Cosmic Enigmas, 1994; A Short History of the Universe, 1994; contrib. numerous articles to refereed jls. *Recreation:* ski-ing. *Address:* Physics Department (Astrophysics), Denys Wilkinson Building, Keble Road, Oxford OX1 3RH. *T:* (01865) 273300; New College, Oxford OX1 3BN.

SILK, Prof. Michael Stephen, PhD; Professor of Classical and Comparative Literature, King's College, London, since 2006; *b* 11 June 1941; *s* of Norman and Ada Silk; *m* 1964, Laurel Evans; one *s* two *d*. *Educ:* King Edward's Sch., Birmingham; St John's Coll., Cambridge (BA 1964; MA 1967; PhD 1969). Res. Fellow, St John's Coll., Cambridge, 1967–70; King's College, London: Lectr in Classics, 1970–85; Reader in Classics, 1985–91; Head, Dept of Classics, 1993–97; Prof. of Greek Lang. and Lit., 1991–2006. Leverhulme Major Res. Fellowship, 2000–03. Vis. Prof., Greek and Comparative Lit., Boston Univ., 2003, 2005, 2007. Co-founder and co-editor, Dialogos, 1994–99. *Publications:* Interaction in Poetic Imagery, 1974; (with J. P. Stern) Nietzsche on Tragedy, 1981, rev. edn 1983; Homer: the Iliad, 1987, 2nd edn 2004; (ed) Tragedy and the Tragic: Greek theatre and beyond, 1996; Aristophanes and the Definition of Comedy, 2000; (ed with A. Hirst) Alexandria, Real and Imagined, 2004; (ed with A. Georgakopoulou) Standard Languages and Language Standards: Greek, past and present, 2009; articles and reviews in classical and literary jls and collections. *Recreations:* poetry, jazz, standard popular songs, cricket. *Address:* Department of Classics, King's College London, Strand, WC2R 2LS. *T:* (020) 7848 2627.

SILK, Paul; *see* Silk, E. P.

SILK, Rt Rev. (Robert) David; Bishop of Ballarat, 1994–2003; Hon. Assistant Bishop, Diocese of Exeter, since 2004; *b* 23 Aug. 1936; *s* of Robert Reeve Silk and Winifred Patience Silk; *m* 1957, Joyce Irene Bracey; one *s* one *d*. *Educ:* Gillingham Grammar School; Univ. of Exeter (BA Hons Theology 1958); St Stephen's House, Oxford. Deacon 1959, priest 1960, Rochester; Curate: St Barnabas, Gillingham, 1959–63; Holy Redeemer, Lamorbey, 1963–69; Priest-in-Charge of the Good Shepherd, Blackfen, 1967–69; Rector of Swanscombe, 1969–75; Rector of Beckenham, St George, 1975–80; Team Rector, Holy Spirit, Leicester, 1982–88; Archdeacon of Leicester, 1980–94; Priest i/c of Amberley with N Stoke, Parham, Greatham and Wiggonholt, 2003–04. Proctor in Convocation, 1970–94; Prolocutor of Lower House of Convocation of Canterbury, 1980–94; Member of Liturgical Commn, 1976–91; Chm., Leicester Council of Faiths, 1986–93; Moderator, Churches Commn for Inter-Faith Relations (formerly Cttee for Relations with Peoples of Other Faiths), 1990–93; Pres., Victorian Council of Churches, 1995–97; Member: Anglican-Lutheran Commn, 1995–2003 (Chm., 2001–03); Liturgy Commn, 1996–2003; Chm., Leaders of Faith Communities Forum, Victoria, 1996–2003. *Publications:* Prayers for Use at the Alternative Services, 1980; Compline—an Alternative Order, 1980; In Penitence and Faith, 1988. *Recreations:* Richard III Society, Leicester FC, theatre. *Address:* 1 Centenary Way, Torquay TQ2 7SB.

SILK, Robert K.; *see* Kilroy-Silk.

SILKE, William James; Non-Permanent Judge, Court of Final Appeal, Hong Kong, 1997–2006; Judge of the Court of Appeal, Brunei Darusalam, 1998–2005; *b* 21 Sept. 1929; *s* of William Joseph Silke and Gertrude (*née* Delany). *Educ:* Dominican Convent, Wicklow; Xavier Sch., Donnybrook; King's Inns, Dublin. Called to Irish Bar (South Eastern Circuit, Leinster Bar), 1955; Magistrate, North Borneo/Malaysia, 1959; Registrar, High Court in Borneo (Sabah-Sarawak), 1965; Puisne Judge, 1966; retired under compensation scheme during Malaysianisation, 1969; Hong Kong: Magistrate, 1969; President, Tenancy Tribunal, 1971; Acting Asst Registrar, High Court, 1972; President, Lands Tribunal, 1974; Judge, District Court, 1975; Judge of the High Court, 1979; Justice of Appeal, Supreme Court, 1981–94; Vice-Pres., Court of Appeal, 1987–94; Judicial Comr, State of Brunei, 1978–91. Mem., Royal Dublin Soc., 1996–. *Recreations:* horse racing/breeding, music, travel. *Address:* 16 Seabank Court, Marine Parade, Sandycove, Co. Dublin, Ireland. *T:* (1) 2808739, *Fax:* (1) 2808372. *Clubs:* Royal Over-Seas League; Stephen's Green (Dublin); Royal Sabah Turf (Sabah, Malaysia); Hong Kong, Hong Kong Jockey (Hong Kong).

SILKIN, Barony of (*cr* 1950); title disclaimed by 3rd Baron; *see under* Silkin, Christopher Lewis.

SILKIN, Christopher Lewis; *b* 12 Sept. 1947; *s* of Baron Silkin of Dulwich (Life Peer), PC, QC and his 1st wife, Elaine Violet (*née* Stamp); *S* uncle, 2001, as 3rd Baron Silkin, but disclaimed his peerage for life; one *s* one *d* by Carolyn Theobald. *Educ:* Dulwich; LLB London 1974. Admitted solicitor, 1977.

SILLARS, James; management consultant; Assistant to Secretary-General, Arab-British Chamber of Commerce, 1993–2002; *b* Ayr, 4 Oct. 1937; *s* of Matthew Sillars; *m* 1st, 1957; one *s* one *d*; 2nd, 1981, Mrs Margo MacDonald, *qv*. *Educ:* Newton Park Sch., Ayr; Ayr Academy. Former official, Fire Brigades Union; Past Member Ayr Town Council and Ayr County Council Educn Cttee. Head of Organization and Social Services Dept, Scottish TUC, 1968–70. Full-time Labour Party agent, 1964 and 1966 elections. Contested (SNP): Linlithgow, 1987; Glasgow, Govan, 1992. MP: (Lab) South Ayrshire, March 1970–1976, (SLP) 1976–79; (SNP) Glasgow, Govan, Nov. 1988–1992. Among the founders of the Scottish Labour Party, Jan. 1976. Man. Dir, Scoted Ltd, 1980–83. Especially interested in education, social services, industrial relations, development policies. *Publications:* Scotland—the Case for Optimism, 1986; Labour Party pamphlets on Scottish Nationalism; Tribune Gp pamphlet on Democracy within the Labour Party. *Recreations:* reading, golf. *Address:* 97 Grange Loan, Edinburgh EH9 2ED.

SILLARS, Margo; *see* MacDonald, M.

SILLERY, William Moore, OBE 2002; DL; Headmaster, Belfast Royal Academy, 1980–2000; *b* 14 March 1941; *s* of William and Adeline Sillery; *m* 1963, Elizabeth Margaret Dunwoody; two *d*. *Educ:* Methodist Coll., Belfast; St Catharine's Coll., Cambridge. Head of Modern Languages, Belfast Royal Academy, 1968, Vice-Principal 1974, Deputy Headmaster 1976. Educnl Advr, Ulster Television, 1985–94. Chm., Ministerial Working Party on Modern Langs in NI Curriculum, 1991; Member: NI Cttee, UFC, 1989–93; Belfast Educn and Liby Bd, 1994–97; Cttee, HMC, 1998–99; Chm., Irish Div., HMC, 1998–99. Lay Mem., Solicitors' Disciplinary Tribunal, NI, 1999–. Chm., Arion Selection Panel, British Council, 2003–06. Gov., Methodist Coll., Belfast, 2007–. DL Belfast, 1997. *Recreations:* golf, bridge. *Address:* Ardmore, 15 Saintfield Road, Belfast BT8 7AE. *T:* (028) 9064 5260. *Clubs:* East India; Belvoir Park (Belfast).

SILLITO, Prof. Adam Murdin, PhD; Professor of Visual Science, since 1987, and Director, 1991–2006, Institute of Ophthalmology, University College London; *b* 31 March 1944; *s* of Adam Cheswardine Sillito and Jean Mary Sillito, Amington, Tamworth; *m* Sharon Pascoe; one *s* one *d*. *Educ:* Univ. of Birmingham (MRC Schol.; BSc, PhD). Res. Fellow, Dept of Physiol., Univ. of Birmingham, 1968–70; Sir Henry Wellcome Travelling Fellow, Dept of Physiol., Johns Hopkins Med. Sch., Baltimore, 1970–71; Lectr, 1971–79, Wellcome Trust Sen. Lectr, 1979–82, Med. Sch., Birmingham; Prof. and Hd of Dept of Physiol., UC, Cardiff, 1982–87. Mem. Editl Bd, Jl Physiol., 1979–86; Co-Ed., Exptl Brain Res., 1989–; Mem., Adv. Cttee, Plenum Press Cerebral Cortex series, 1991–. Non-exec. Dir, Moorfields NHS Trust, 1994–2006 (Mem. Bd, Moorfields Eye Hosp., 1992–94). Medical Research Council: Member: Neurosci. Grants Cttee, 1982–86; Neurosci. Bd, 1991–95; Non-clinical Trng and Career Develt Panel, 1993–95. Chairman: Res. Cttee, BPMF, 1990–94; Electrophysiol. Panel, Prog. Cttee, ARVO, 1996–99; Member: Surgery Task Force—Technol. Transfer of Minimal Access Surgery, ACOST Med. Res. and Health Cttee, 1992; Human Frontiers Fellowship Panel, 1994–98. Chm., Brain Res. Assoc., 1980–83; Member: Physiol Soc. (Mem. Cttee, 1982–86); IBRO; British Neurosci. Assoc.; Soc. for Neurosci.; Assoc. for Res. in Vision and Ophthalmology (Mem., Prog. Cttee, 1996–99); Eur. Neurosci. Assoc. Founder FMedSci, 1998. Hon. Fellow, UCL. *Publications:* (ed jtly) Progress in Brain Research, 1990; Mechanisms of the GABA Action in the Visual System, 1992; (ed with G. Burnstock) Nervous Control of the Eye, 2000; numerous contribs to learned jls on mechanisms of vision. *Recreations:* dreaming of better things, learning and speculating. *Address:* Institute of Ophthalmology, University College London, Bath Street, EC1V 9EL. *T:* (020) 7608 6805, *Fax:* (020) 7608 6852; *e-mail:* a.sillito@ucl.ac.uk.

SILLITOE, Alan; writer, since 1948; *b* 4 March 1928; *s* of Christopher Sillitoe and Sabina (*née* Burton); *m* 1959, Ruth Fainlight; one *s* one *d*. *Educ:* various elementary schools in Nottingham. Raleigh Bicycle Factory, 1942; air traffic control asst, 1945–46; wireless operator, RAF, 1946–49. Lived in France and Spain, 1952–58. Vis. Prof. of English, De Montfort Univ., 1994–97. FRGS. Hon. Fellow, Manchester Polytechnic, 1977. Hon. DLitt: Nottingham Poly., 1990; Nottingham Univ., 1994; De Montfort Univ., 1998. Freedom, City of Nottingham, 2008. *Publications: novels:* Saturday Night and Sunday Morning, 1958 (Authors' Club Award for best first novel of 1958; filmed, 1960, play, 1964); The General, 1960 (filmed 1967 as Counterpoint); Key to the Door, 1961; The Death of William Posters, 1965; A Tree on Fire, 1967; A Start in Life, 1970; Travels in Nihilon, 1971; Raw Material, 1972; The Flame of Life, 1974; The Widower's Son, 1976; The Storyteller, 1979; Her Victory, 1982; The Lost Flying Boat, 1983; Down from the Hill, 1984; Life Goes On, 1985; Out of the Whirlpool, 1987; The Open Door, 1989; Last Loves, 1990; Leonard's War: a love story, 1991; Snowstop, 1993; The Broken Chariot, 1998; The German Numbers Woman, 1999; Birthday, 2001; A Man of His Time, 2004; *stories:* The Loneliness of the Long Distance Runner, 1959 (Hawthornden Prize; filmed, 1962); The Ragman's Daughter, 1963 (filmed, 1972); Guzman, Go Home, 1968; Men, Women and Children, 1973; The Second Chance, 1981; The Far Side of the Street, 1988; Collected Stories, 1995; Alligator Playground, 1997; New and Collected Stories, 2003; *poetry:* The Rats and Other Poems, 1960; A Falling Out of Love, 1964; Love in the Environs of Voronezh, 1968; Storm and Other Poems, 1974; Snow on the North Side of Lucifer, 1979; Sun before Departure, 1984; Tides and Stone Walls, 1986; Collected Poems, 1993; *for children:* The City Adventures of Marmalade Jim, 1967; Big John and the Stars, 1977; The Incredible Fencing Fleas, 1978; Marmalade Jim at the Farm, 1980; Marmalade Jim and the Fox, 1985; *travel:* Road to Volgograd, 1964; (with Fay Godwin) The Saxon Shore Way, 1983; (with David Sillitoe) Nottinghamshire, 1987; Leading the Blind, 1995; Gadfly in Russia, 2007; *plays:* (with Ruth Fainlight) All Citizens are Soldiers, 1969; Three Plays, 1978; *essays:* Mountains and Caverns, 1975; A Flight of Arrows, 2003; *autobiography:* Life Without Armour, 1994; *miscellaneous:* Every Day of the Week, 1987. *Recreations:* travel, shortwave wireless telegraphy listening. *Address:* 14 Ladbroke Terrace, W11 3PG.

SILLITOE, Prof. Paul, PhD, ScD; FBA 2006; Professor of Anthropology, Durham University, since 1997; *s* of Frank Arthur George Sillitoe and Doris Mary Sillitoe (*née* Graves); *m* 1972, Jacqueline Ann Bryan; two *s*. *Educ:* Durham Univ. (BA, MA Anthropol.); Trinity Coll., Cambridge (PhD 1976, ScD Social Anthropol. 2001); Open Univ. (BA Nat. Scis); Newcastle Univ. (MSc Soil Sci.); Wye Coll., London Univ. (MSc Agricl Scis). Field work in New Guinea and projects in S Asia. Work with internat. develt agencies. *Publications:* Give and Take, 1979; Roots of the Earth, 1983; Made in Niugini, 1988; The Bogaia of the Muller Ranges, 1994; A Place Against Time, 1996; An Introduction to the Anthropology of Melanesia, 1998; Social Change in Melanesia, 2000; (jtly) Horticulture in Papua New Guinea, 2002; Managing Animals in New Guinea, 2003; (jtly) Indigenous Knowledge Inquiries, 2005. *Recreations:* urban peasant occupations. *Address:* Anthropology Department, Durham University, 43 Old Elvet, Durham DH1 3HN. *T:* (0191) 334 6190, *Fax:* (0191) 334 6101; *e-mail:* paul.sillitoe@durham.ac.uk.

SILMAN, Prof. Alan Jonathon, FRCP, FMedSci; ARC Professor of Rheumatic Disease Epidemiology, and Director, ARC Epidemiology Research Unit, University of Manchester, since 1989; *b* 4 Dec. 1951; *m* 1979, Ruth Abrams; two *s* one *d*. *Educ:* Leeds Univ. (MB ChB); LSHTM (MScSocMed 1979); MD London 1985. MRCP 1977, FRCP 1992; MFCM 1980, FFCM 1988; FMedSci 2001. House Surgeon, then House Physician, St James Univ. Teaching Hosp., Leeds, 1974–75; SHO, Professorial Dept of Paediatrics, Royal Liverpool Children's Hosp., 1975–76; SHO/Registrar, N Manchester Gen. Hosp., 1976–77; DHSS Bursary and Hon. Registrar, SE Thames RHA, 1977–79; Lectr, 1979–82, Sen. Lectr, 1982–88, in Clinical Epidemiology, London Hosp. Med. Coll.; Hon. Sen. Registrar, 1979–82, Hon. Consultant, 1982–88, Tower Hamlets Health Dist. *Publications:* (with M. Hochberg) Epidemiology of the Rheumatic Diseases, 2001; (ed jtly) Rheumatology, 3rd edn 2003; articles on rheumatic diseases. *Address:* ARC Epidemiology Research Unit, School of Epidemiology and Health Sciences, Stopford Building, University of Manchester, Oxford Road, Manchester M13 9PT. *T:* (0161) 275 5041, *Fax:* (0161) 275 5043; *e-mail:* alan.silman@man.ac.uk.

SILSOE, 3rd Baron *cr* 1963, of Silsoe, co. Bedford; **Simon Rupert Trustram Eve;** Bt 1943; *b* 17 April 1966; *o s* of 2nd Baron Silsoe, QC and of Bridget Min (*née* Hart-Davis); *S* father, 2005. *Heir: uncle* Hon. Peter Nanton Trustram Eve, OBE [*b* 2 May 1930; *m* 1961, Petronilla Letiere Sheldon (*née* Elliott); two *s*].

SILUNGWE, Hon. Annel Musenga; Hon. Mr Justice Silungwe; Judge of the High Court and acting Judge of the Supreme Court, Namibia, since 1999; Judge, Court of Appeal, Seychelles, 1992; *b* 10 Jan. 1936; *s* of late Solo Musenga Silungwe and Janet Nakafunda Silungwe; *m* 1960, Abigail Nanyangwe; one *s* four *d*. *Educ:* Council of Legal Educn; Univ. of Zambia (LLM 1977). Called to the Bar, Inner Temple, 1966; State Counsel, Zambia, 1974; Judge of the High Court, Zambia, 1971–73; Minister of Legal Affairs and Attorney-General, 1973–75; Chief Justice of Zambia, 1975–92; Dir, Justice Trng Centre, Ministry of Justice, Namibia, 1994–99. Chairman: Judicial Services Commn, 1975–92; Council of Legal Educn, 1975–92; Council of Law Reporting, 1975–92. Award of Merit, Rotary Internat. Dist 9210, 1989. *Publications:* contrib. learned jls. *Recreations:* music, photography, reading, golf. *Address:* High Court, Private Bag 13179, Windhoek, Namibia. *T:* (office) (61) 227927, *Fax:* (61) 221686, *T:* and *Fax:* (home) (61) 242705.

SILVER, Clinton Vita, CBE 1993; Chairman, British Fashion Council, 1994–97; Deputy Chairman, 1991–94, and Managing Director, 1990–94, Marks & Spencer plc; *b* 26 Sept. 1929; *s* of Sidney (Mick) Silver and Mina Silver (*née* Gabriel); *m* 1973, Patricia Ann (Jill) Vernon; one *s* one *d*. *Educ:* Upton House Sch.; Southampton Univ. (BSc Econ). Nat. Service, 1950–52. Joined Marks & Spencer, 1952; Alternate Dir, 1974; Dir, 1978. Director: Hillsdown Hldgs, 1994–98; Pentland Group plc, 1994–99; Tommy Hilfiger Corp., 1994–2006. Member: Bd, Youth and Music, 1987–99 (Patron, 1999–2000); Southampton Univ. Develt Trust, 1992–2002 (Patron, 2002–); Chm., Israel/Diaspora Trust, 1989–2003; Trustee, Jewish Assoc. for Business Ethics, 1995–2006 (Chm. Trustees, 1995–97). CCMI (CBIM 1991); CompTI 1994. Hon. DLitt Southampton, 1997. *Recreations:* gardening, music. *Clubs:* Athenæum; Phyllis Court (Henley-on-Thames).

SILVER, Prof. Ian Adair; Professor of Comparative Pathology, University of Bristol, 1970–93, Emeritus Professor of Pathology, since 1993; Adjunct Professor of Neurology, University of Pennsylvania, 1977–2006; *b* 28 Dec. 1927; *s* of Captain George James Silver and Nora Adair Silver; *m* 1st, 1950, Dr Marian Scrase (*d* 1994), *d* of Dr F. J. Scrase; two *s* two *d*; 2nd, 1996, Prof. Maria Erecińska, *d* of Prof. K Ereciński. *Educ:* Rugby School; Corpus Christi Coll., Cambridge (BA, MA); Royal Veterinary Coll. MRCVS 1952, FRCVS 1990. University of Cambridge: Univ. Demonstrator, Zoology, 1952–57; Univ. Lectr, Anatomy, 1957–70; Official Fellow and Coll. Lectr, Churchill Coll., 1965–70; Sen. Tutor for Advanced Students, Churchill Coll., 1966–70; University of Bristol: Hd, Dept of Path., later Path. and Microbiol., 1982–93; Dean, Faculty of Medicine, 1987–90; Chm., Inst. of Clinical Neuroscience, 2000–; Chm., Burden Neurological Inst., 2006–. Chm., Southmead Health Services NHS Trust, Bristol, 1992–99. Vis. Fellow, Weitzmann Inst., Rehovot, 1963; Vis. Prof., Louisiana Tech. Univ., 1973; Royal Soc. Vis. Prof., Fed. Univ. of Rio de Janeiro, 1977. Mem., SERC Biol. Scis Cttee, 1975–80; President: Internat. Soc. for O_2 Transport to Tissue, 1976 and 1986; RCVS, 1985–86 and 1987 (Sen. Vice-Pres., 1986–87 and 1987–88). RAgS Silver Medal, 1952; Sir Frederick Hobday Meml Medal, British Equine Vet. Assoc., 1982; Dalrymple-Champneys Medal, BVA, 1984. *Publications:* Editor of scientific books, 1971–; numerous articles in scientific jls. *Recreations:* farming, exploring, fishing, DIY. *Address:* Department of Anatomy, School of Veterinary Science, University of Bristol, Southwell Street, Bristol BS2 8EJ. *T:* (0117) 928 8362.

SILVER, Dame Ruth (Muldoon), DBE 2006 (CBE 1998); Principal and Chief Executive Officer, Lewisham College, London, since 1991; *b* 23 Jan. 1945; *d* of Francis Faughnan and Catherine Muldoon; *m* 1970, Anthony Silver (marr. diss. 1985); partner, Andrew Mingay; one *d*. *Educ:* Hamilton Acad.; Univ. of Glasgow (NUM schol.; MA Lit. and Psychol. 1966); Univ. of Southampton (Dip. Educn Psychol. 1968); Tavistock Inst. of Human Relations (clinical trng); Univ. of London (Dip. Educn Mgt 1978); Polytech. of Central London (MA 1983). Teaching in schs, Hackney, and Trng Psychologist, Woodberry Down Child Guidance Clinic, 1968–70; in training and work (pt-time), ILEA, 1970–75; BBC broadcaster and author in community youth develts, 1975–77; ILEA inspectorate, DES, 1977–80; Policy Principal in Youth Develt Team, MSC, 1980–82; academic consultant to MSC, 1982–83; Hd of Faculty, Southwark Coll., 1983–86; Vice Principal and actg Principal, Newham Community Coll., 1986–91. Vis. Scholar, Lucy Cavendish Coll. Centre for Women Leaders, Cambridge, 1988–. Broadcaster, lectr and author on equal opportunities and leading orgnl change. Member: Bd, British Trng Internat., 1997–99; Bd, Council for Ind. and Higher Educn, 1999– (Trustee, 1999–); Post 16 e-Learning Task Force, 2002–04; Standing Conf. of E London Principals, 2003–; Women and Work Commn, 2004–; Strategic Skills Commn, 2004–; Review Gp, students with learning difficulties and disabilities, LSC, 2004–; Nat. Skills Forum, 2005–; London Skills and Employment Bd, 2006–; Dir, Horse's Mouth (online mentoring service), 2005–; Chair, Further Educn Improvement Agency, 2008–; Founder Member: Further Educn NTO, 1999–2001; Higher Educn Policy Inst., 1999–; Centre for Excellence in Leadership, 2001–05; Adv. Forum, Learning and Skills Res. Centre, 2002–; Acad. Adv. Bd, NHSU, 2004–05; EDGE, 2004–; acted as Scrutineer to Cabinet Office's ministerial network on social exclusion, 2000–02; Chm., Wkg Gp on Faiths and Further Educn, LSC/Nat. Ecumenical Agency in Further Educn, 2005–. Chief Assessor, Trng of Principals' Qualifications in England, 2006–08. Trustee: Working Men's Coll., 1995– (Chm. Govs, 1995–); Laban Coll., 2000; Lottie Betts-Priddy Educn Trust, 2004–. Bd Mem., London Internat. Fest. of Theatre, 1999–2004. FRSA 1994; FCGI 2003. Hon. DSocSc Southampton, 2001; Hon. DEd London Southbank, 2005. *Publications:* Making a Living, 1977; Personal Effectiveness and Young People, 1983; Guidance of Young

People, 1984; Changing College Culture, 1984; (with Julian Gravatt) Further Education Re-formed, 2000; regular contribs to TES on further educn. *Recreations:* Martha, cinema, talking, reading, wondering. *Address:* 52 Fortess Road, NW5 2HG. *T:* (office) (020) 8694 3201; *e-mail:* ruth.silver@lewisham.ac.uk. *Club:* Commonwealth.

SILVERMAN, Prof. Bernard Walter, FRS 1997; Master of St Peter's College, Oxford, and Professor of Statistics, University of Oxford, since 2003; *b* 22 Feb. 1952; *s* of Elias and Helen Silverman; *m* 1985, Dr Rowena Fowler; one *s*. *Educ:* City of London Sch.; Jesus Coll., Cambridge (MA, PhD, ScD; Hon. Fellow, 2003); Southern Theol Educn and Trng Scheme (BTh). CStat. Research Fellow, Jesus Coll., Cambridge, 1975–77; Calculator Develt Manager, Sinclair Radionics, 1976–77; Weir Fellow, University Coll., Oxford, and Jun. Lectr, Oxford Univ., 1977–78; University of Bath: Lectr, Reader, and Prof. of Statistics, 1978–93; Head, Sch. of Math. Scis, 1988–91; University of Bristol: Prof. of Stats, 1993–2003, now Emeritus; Henry Overton Wills Prof. of Maths, 1999–2003; Provost, Inst. for Advanced Studies, 2000–03. Various vis. appts at foreign univs, 1978–; Fellow, Center for Advanced Study in Behavioral Scis, Stanford, 1997–98. Ed., Annals of Stats, 2007–. Non-exec. Dir, Defence Analytical Services Agency, MoD, 2003–. Mem., GM Sci. Rev. Panel, 2002–04; Chm., Peer Rev. Panel, Project for Sustainable Develt of Heathrow, 2005–06. Pres., Inst. of Mathematical Stats, 2000–01; Chairman: Jt Mathematical Council of UK, 2003–06; UK Maths Trust, 2004–. MAE 2001. Ordained deacon, 1999, priest, 2000; Hon. Curate, 1999–2003, Associate Parish Priest, 2003–05, St Paul's Clifton, and St Mary's, Cotham, Bristol; Proctor in Convocation, Gen. Synod of C of E, 2000–03. Awards from UK and USA. *Publications:* Density Estimation for Statistics and Data Analysis, 1986; (with P. J. Green) Nonparametric Regression and Generalized Linear Models, 1994; (with J. O. Ramsay) Functional Data Analysis, 1997, 2nd edn 2005; (with J. O. Ramsay) Applied Functional Data Analysis, 2002; numerous papers in learned jls. *Address:* St Peter's College, Oxford OX1 2DL. *Club:* Royal Commonwealth Society.

SILVERMAN, Prof. (Hugh) Richard, OBE 2000; Professor of Architecture, University of Wales, Cardiff (formerly University of Wales College of Cardiff), 1986–99, now Emeritus (Head of Welsh School of Architecture, 1986–97); *b* 23 Sept. 1940; *m* 1963, Kay Sønderskov-Madsen; two *d*. *Educ:* Edinburgh Univ. (MSc Soc. Sci). Lectr, then Sen. Lectr, Univ. of Bristol, 1971–82. Partner, Alec French Partnership, Architects, Bristol, 1984–86. Built project, 1 Bridewell St, Bristol, 1985 (RIBA Regl Award). Mem. Board, Cardiff Bay Develt Corp., 1990–2000; Director: Edward Ware Homes, Bristol, 2002–03; Under the Sky Urban Renewal, 2004–. FRSA 1989.

SILVERSTONE, Daniel William; Chief Executive Officer, London Remade, since 2004; *b* 29 Sept. 1951; *s* of Jack and Liesl Silverstone; *m* 1988, Judith Anne Hunt, *qv*; two step *d*. *Educ:* Univ. of Sussex (BA Hons Politics); Univ. of Manchester (MA Govt). Greater London Council: Prin. Race Relns Advr, 1982–84; Dep. Dir, Personnel, 1984–86; Dep. Dir, Personnel, ILEA, 1986–89; Dep. Dir, Educn, London Bor. of Hackney, 1989–95; Dir, London Boroughs Grants, 1995–2001; Chief Exec., CRE, 2001–04; Principal Associate, Global Diversity Practice, Norman Broadbent, 2004. Mem., Commn for a Sustainable London 2012, 2008–. FRSA 1998. *Publication:* (jtly) The System, 1981. *Recreations:* modern jazz, books, film, tennis, Tottenham Hotspur. *Address:* London Remade, 1 Quality Court, Chancery Lane, WC2A 1HR. *T:* (020) 7061 6370; *e-mail:* daniel@dsilverstone.co.uk.

SILVERSTONE, Judith Anne; *see* Hunt, J. A.

SILVERTON, Kate; broadcaster and journalist with BBC, since 2003; *b* Waltham Abbey, Essex, 4 Aug. 1970; *d* of Terence George and Patricia Ann Silverton. *Educ:* West Hatch High Sch., Chigwell; Univ. of Durham (BSc Psychol.). Volunteer, Operation Raleigh, 1990; Corporate Finance, Barclays de Zoete Wedd, 1994–96; with BBC, 1996–98: travel and traffic reporter, Breakfast Show, Radio Newcastle, 1997–98; reporter and presenter: Look North, 1997–98; Evening News, Tyne Tees Television, 1998–2000; The Wright Stuff, Channel 5, 2000–02; presenter: World Travel, Travel Channel, 2003; Third Degree, BBC 3, 2003; 3D, Sky News, 2003; BBC: co-presenter: Five Live Breakfast Show, Radio 5 Live, 2004; Weekend with Rod Liddle and Kate Silverton, 2004; reporter and presenter, News Channel, 2004–; reporter, Panorama, 2006–; News Foreign Corresp., Iraq, 2006; reporter and presenter, Breakfast News, 2006–; presenter, Ultimate Wild Water, 2007; reporter and presenter: One O'Clock News, 2008–; Six O'Clock News, 2008–; presenter, Big Cat Live, 2008. *Recreations:* outdoor pursuits, adventure sports, swimming, triathlon, travelling. *Address: e-mail:* enquiries@katesilverton.com; *web:* www.katesilverton.com. *Clubs:* The Ivy, Frontline.

SILVESTER, Frederick John; author; Chairman and Managing Director, Advocacy (formerly Advocacy Partnership) Ltd, 1986–2000; *b* 20 Sept. 1933; *s* of William Thomas Silvester and Kathleen Gertrude (*née* Jones); *m* 1971, Victoria Ann, *d* of James Harold and Mary Lloyd Davies; two *d*. *Educ:* Sir George Monoux Grammar Sch.; Sidney Sussex Coll., Cambridge. Called to the Bar, Gray's Inn, 1957. Teacher, Wolstanton Grammar School, 1955–57; Political Education Officer, Conservative Political Centre, 1957–60. Member, Walthamstow Borough Council, 1961–64; Chairman, Walthamstow West Conservative Association, 1961–64. Contested (C) Manchester, Withington, 1987. MP (C): Walthamstow West, Sept. 1967–70; Manchester, Withington, Feb. 1974–1987. An Opposition Whip, 1974–76; PPS to Sec. of State for Employment, 1979–81, to Sec. of State for NI, 1981–83. Member: Public Accounts Cttee, 1983–87; Procedure Cttee, 1983–87; Exec., 1922 Cttee, 1985–87; Vice-Chm., Cons. Employment Cttee, 1976–79. Sen. Associate Dir, J. Walter Thompson, 1970–88. *Publications:* The Northern Briton, 1984; Global Speak: the five untruths, 2005; Rape of democracy, 2008. *Address:* 27 King Edward Walk, SE1 7PR.

SIM, Andrew Fraser; Consultant, Kennedys, solicitors, 1999–2005; *b* 27 Nov. 1948; *s* of Donald Fraser Sim and Pamela Jean Sim; *m* 1975, Antonia Rolfe Tweedie Aitken; two *s* one *d*. *Educ:* Haileybury Coll., Herts; City of London Poly. (BA Business Law). Admitted Solicitor. British Railways Board: Asst Solicitor, 1975; Head of Litigation, 1982; Dep. Solicitor, 1986–93; Solicitor, 1993–99. *Recreations:* cricket, golf, fishing.

SIMEON, Sir Richard (Edmund Barrington), 8th Bt *cr* 1815, of Grazeley, Berkshire; PhD; Professor of Political Science and Law, University of Toronto, since 1990; *b* 2 March 1943; *s* of Sir John Simeon, 7th Bt and of Anne Robina Mary (*née* Dean); *S* father, 1999; *m* 1st, 1966, Agnes Joan Weld (marr. diss. 1990); one *s* one *d*; 2nd, 1992, Maryetta Cheney. *Educ:* Univ. of British Columbia (BA Hons 1964); Yale Univ. (MA 1966; PhD 1968). Queen's University, Kingston, Ont: Asst Prof., 1968; Assoc. Prof., 1972–76; Dir, Inst. of Intergovtl Relns, 1976–83; Prof. of Political Studies, 1976–90; Dir, Sch. of Public Admin, 1985–90. Res. Co-ordinator, Royal Commn on the Econ. Union and Canada's Develt Prospects, 1983–85; Vice Chm., Ontario Law Reform Commn, 1988–96. Vis. Prof., Essex Univ., 1975–76; Vis. Prof. of Public Law, Univ. of Cape Town, 1997 and 2000; William Lyon Mackenzie King Prof. of Canadian Studies, Harvard Univ., 1998. *Publications:* Federal-Provincial Diplomacy: the making of recent policy in Canada, 1972; (jtly) Small Worlds: provinces and parties in Canadian political life, 1983; (jtly) State, Society and the Development of Canadian Federalism, 1991; (jtly) Degrees of Freedom: Canada and the United States in a changing world, 1997; ed numerous other works; contribs to jls. *Recreations:* walking, canoeing. *Heir: s* Stephen George Barrington Simeon [*b* 29 Oct. 1970; *m* 1996, Michelle Owens; one *s* one *d*]. *Address:* (home) #906, 21 Dale Avenue, Toronto, ON M4W 1K3, Canada. *T:* (416) 9618314; *e-mail:* rsimeon@chass.utoronto.ca.

SIMEONE, Reginald Nicola, CBE 1985; FRMetS; Adviser to the Chairman, Nuclear Electric plc, 1990–96; *b* 12 July 1927; *s* of late Nicola Francisco Simeone, FCIS, and Phyllis Simeone (*née* Iles); *m* 1954, Josephine Frances Hope; two *s*. *Educ:* Raynes Park Grammar Sch.; St John's Coll., Cambridge (Schol.; MA). FRMetS 1993. Instructor Lieut (Meteorol), Royal Navy, 1947–50; Admiralty: Asst Principal, 1950–55; Principal, 1955–59; UKAEA: Finance Br., 1959–61; Economics and Programmes Br., 1961–65; Chief Personnel Officer, AWRE, 1965–69; Principal Estabts Officer, 1970–76; Authority Personnel Officer, 1976–84; Comptroller and Bd Mem. for Finance and Administration, 1984–88; Advr to the Chm., 1988–90. Chm., Atomic Energy Constabulary Police Cttee, 1985–90; Exec. Vice Pres., European Atomic Energy Soc., 1987–91. *Recreations:* European travel, theatre, opera, ballet, music, meteorology. *Address:* 31 Portsmouth Avenue, Thames Ditton, Surrey KT7 0RU.

SIMEONS, Charles Fitzmaurice Creighton, MA; formerly Consultant: Environmental Control, Market and Behavioural Studies, Health and Safety at Work, Communications with Government, technical programmes for conferences and annual events in international chemical control, London and Washington; *b* 22 Sept. 1921; *s* of Charles Albert Simeons and Vera Hildegarde Simeons; *m* 1st, 1945, Rosemary (*née* Tabrum) (*d* 1991); one *s* one *d*; 2nd, 1991, Constance Anne Dowson (*née* Restell). *Educ:* Oundle; Queens' Coll., Cambridge. Royal Artillery with 8th Indian Div., 1942–45, HQ RA E African Comd and Northern Comd (Major). Man. Dir, supplier to photographic industry, 1957–70. MP (C) Luton, 1970–Feb. 1974. Dir, Action Learning Trust, 1978–82. Chm., Luton Cons. Assoc., 1960–63. President: Luton, Dunstable and District Chamber of Commerce, 1967–68; Rotary Club of Luton, 1960 (Mem., 1951–91); District Gov., Rotary International, 1967–68; Mem., Rotary Club of Holt, 1992; Advisor, Eastern Area, Prince's Youth Business Trust, 1994–2000; Chm. of cttees raising funds for disabled and cancer research and for National Children's Homes, 1969–78; Chm., Kelling Hosp. Gala, 1996–97, 2000; Member: Nat. Appeals Cttee, Cancer Res. Campaign, 1977–78; Children in Danger Campaign, 1985–90. Chm., Adv. Cttee, Rotary Internat. Bd on Environmental Research and Resources, 1973–74; Vice Pres., Nat. Industrial Material Recovery Assoc., 1972–77; Member: Internat. Cttee, Water Pollution Control Federation, Washington, DC, 1974–77; Customer Consultative Cttee, Anglian Water, 1984–89, Thames Water, 1986–89; Eastern Customer Services Cttee, Water Services, 1990–96; Council, Smaller Business Assoc., 1974–76; ABCC Small Firms Panel; Chm., Central Govt Cttee, Union of Independent Cos. Member: N Norfolk Public Plenary Gp, 1998–2000; N Norfolk Healthwatch, 2000–03; Co-ordinator, Kelling Hosp. Ambulance Appeal, 2003–04. Founder Chm., Friends of Pensthorpe Waterfowl Trust, 1993–95 (Founder Patron of Trust, 1990). Hon. Mem., Inst. of Water Pollution Control, 1973. Liveryman: Co. of Feltmakers (Master, 1987–88); Co. of Water Conservators, 2000 (Mem., 1991). Guild of Freemen of City of London. FIIM; FRSA. Hon. FIWEM. Pres., Old Oundelian Club, 1976–77; Hon. Secretary: 8th Indian Clover Club, 1984–2003; Manchester Artillery 52nd Field Regt RA Officers' Reunion, 1998–2003. Patron, Luton Area, Dunkirk Veterans, 1995–2000 (Pres., 1965–95). JP Luton, 1959–74; DL Beds, 1987. *Publications:* Energy Research in Western Europe, 1976; Coal: its role in tomorrow's technology, 1978; Water as a Source of Energy, 1980; A Review of Chemical Response Data Bases in Europe and the United States, 1985; Studies on Incidents Involving Chemicals on Board Ship, in Port, and at Sea in Europe and the United States, 1985; Data Bases capable of response to Chemical Incidents Worldwide, 1986; Kelling Hospital Centenary Book, 2003. *Recreations:* watching football, cricket, gardening. *Address:* Mill Leet, High Street, Cley-next-the-Sea, Norfolk NR25 7RR. *T:* (01263) 740772; *e-mail:* charles.simeons@btinternet.com. *Clubs:* Achilles, City Livery.

SIMHA, Maj.-Gen. Bharat Kesher; Om Ram Patta, 1st Class; Tri Sakti Patta, 1st Class; Gorkha Dakchhina Bahu, 1st Class; Nepal Kirtimaya Shreepad, 3rd Class; President, World Hindu Federation, since 2003 (Senior Vice President, 1998); *b* 15 Aug. 1934; *s* of Lt-Gen. Dharma Bahadur Simha and Chaitanya Rajya Laxmi Simha; *m* 1955, Teeka Rajya Laxmi Rana; three *s*. *Educ:* Durbar High Sch., Kathmandu; Col Brown's Cambridge Sch., Dehradun; Indian Mil. Acad., Dehradun (grad. 1954). Commnd into Royal Nepalese Army, 1952; appts as Adjt, Co. Comdr, ADC to C-in-C, 1954–55; various courses in England, 1956; attached BAOR, 1956; Instr, Sch. of Inf., 1957–59; GSO 3 Directorate of Mil. Ops and Staff Duties, also ADC to C-in-C, 1960; Mem., Nepal-China Jt Boundary Commn, 1960–63; sc Camberley, 1964 (grad.); Resident Mil. Attaché, UK, with accreditation to France, W Germany, Belgium, Netherlands, Sweden, 1964–67; Dir of Mil. Intelligence, 1967–68; Para Overall Comdr, 1968–70; Dir of Res. and Planning, 1970; Asst Dir of Mil. Ops and Staff Duties, 1971; Dir of Mil. Trng, 1972–73; Officiating Dir of Mil. Ops and Staff Duties, 1974; Master-Gen. of Ordnance, 1975; Comdr, No 4 Bde, 1975–77; Dir, Mil. Ops, Staff Duties, Res. and Planning, 1978–80; Adjt-Gen., 1980; QMG, 1982–83; CGS, 1983–85 (retired); ADC Gen. to King of Nepal, 1986. Ambassador of Nepal to the UK, concurrently accredited to Finland, Iceland, Sweden, Norway and Denmark, 1988–92. Mem. Exec. Cttee, Pashupati Area Develt Trust, 1987–. Army Long Service Medal. Comdr OM (France), 1966; OM (Jugoslavia), 1974; Grand Cross: Order of the Lion of Finland, 1989; Order of the Dannebrog (Denmark), 1989. *Recreations:* hunting, jogging, squash, tennis, trekking. *Address:* Dharma Ashram, Jogi Pakwa Narga, Kaldhara, Pakanajol, Kathmandu 16, PO Box 257, Nepal. *T:* (1) 251472, *Fax:* (1) 419625. *Club:* Tribhuwan Army Officers (Kathmandu).

SIMINOVITCH, Dr Louis, CC 1989 (OC 1980); PhD, FRS 1980; FRSC 1965; Director, Samuel Lunenfeld Research Institute of Mount Sinai Hospital (formerly Mount Sinai Hospital Research Institute), University of Toronto, 1983–94, now Director Emeritus (University Professor Emeritus, 1985); *b* Montreal, PQ, 1 May 1920; *s* of Nathan Siminovitch and Goldie Watchman; *m* 1944, Elinore, *d* of late Harry Faierman; three *d*. *Educ:* McGill Univ. (BSc 1941, PhD 1944; Arts and Sci. schol. 1939, Sir William McDonald schol. 1940, Anne Molson prize in Chem. 1941). With NRC at Ottawa and Chalk River, Ont., 1944–47; NRC Studentship and Fellowship, 1942–44; Canadian Royal Soc. Fellowship, 1947–49; with Centre Nat. de la Recherche Scientifique, Paris, 1949–53; Nat. Cancer Inst. Canadian Fellowships, 1953–55; Connaught Med. Res. Labs, Univ. of Toronto, 1953–56. Sen. Scientist, 1956–69 and Head, Div. of Biolog. Research, 1958–69, Ontario Cancer Inst., Univ. of Toronto; Chm., Dept of Med. Cell Biology, Univ. of Toronto, 1969–72; Chm., Dept of Med. Genetics, 1972–79, Univ. Prof., 1976–85, Special Advr to Dean on Res., 1994–, Toronto Univ.; Geneticist-in-Chief, Hosp. for Sick Children, Toronto, 1976–85. Founding Mem. and Pres., Editorial Bd, Science Forum, 1966–79; Pres., Canadian Cell Biology Soc., 1967. Member: Bd of Dirs, Nat. Cancer Inst. of Canada, 1975–85 (Pres., 1982–84); Nat. Bd of Dirs, Canadian Cancer Soc., 1981–84; Bd, Ontario Cancer Treatment and Res. Foundn, 1979–94; Scientific Adv. Cttee, Connaught Res. Inst., 1980–84; Alfred P. Sloan, Jr, Selection Cttee, General Motors Cancer Res. Foundn, 1980–81, 1983–84; Health Res. and Develt Council of Ont,

1983–86. Chairman: Scientific Advisory Committee: Ontario Cancer Treatment and Res. Foundn, 1985–99; Loeb Inst. for Med. Res., Ottawa, 1988–99; Rotman Res. Inst., Toronto, 1988–; Phagetech, 1998–2005; Scientific Advisory Board: Bioniche Inc., 1996–98; Cytochroma Inc., 1999–2001; Member, Scientific Advisory Committee: Montreal Neurol Inst., 1992– (Mem., Neuro. Adv. Council, 1997–2001); Glycodesign, 1996–2001; Member, Scientific Advisory Board: Apoptogen Inc., 1995–2000; Univ. Medical Discoveries Inc., 1996–2006; GeminX, 1997–2000; Lorus (formerly Genesense) Technologies Inc., 1998–; Ottawa Gen. Hosp. Res. Inst., 1998–2000; Genetic Diagnostics, 2003–. Member: Hybrisens Ltd, 1995–98; Program Adv. and Sci. Adv. Cttee, Tanenbaum Chairs, Univ. of Toronto, 1995–2000; Scientific Adv. Bd, Canadian Med. Discoveries Fund, 1998–2002; Bd, Premier's Res. Excellence Awards Prog., 1998–2005; Bd, Viventia Biotech, 2000–06. Member: Bd of Dirs, Ottawa Civic Hosp. & Loeb Res. Inst. Corp., 1996–2000; Bd, Baycrest Centre for Geriatric Care, Toronto, 1998– (Consultant to Vice-Pres. Res. and Co-Chm. Res. Adv. Cttee, 1994–; Chm., Sci. Adv. Cttee, KLARU, 1997–). Founding Editor: Virology, 1960–80; Cell, 1973–81; Ed., Jl of Molecular and Cellular Biology, 1980–90; Member Editorial Board: Jl Cancer Surveys (London), 1980–89; Somatic Cell and Molecular Genetics, 1984–2005. Foreign Associate, NAS, 1999. Hon. DSc: Meml Univ., Newfoundland, 1978; McMaster Univ., 1978; Hon. Dr: Univ. of Montreal, 1990; McGill Univ., Montreal, 1990; Univ. of Western Ont, London, 1990; Univ. of Toronto, 1995; Univ. of Guelph, 2001. Flavelle Gold Medal, RSC, 1978; Univ. of Toronto Alumni Assoc. Award, 1978; Izaak Walton Killam Meml Prize, 1981; Gairdner Foundn Wightman Award, 1981; Medal of Achievement Award, Institut de Recherches Cliniques de Montreal, 1985; Environmental Mutagen Society Award, Baltimore, Maryland, 1986; R. P. Taylor Award, Canadian Cancer Soc., Nat. Cancer Inst., 1986; Distinguished Service Award, Canadian Soc. for Clinical Investigation, 1990; Toronto Biotechnol. Initiative Community Service Award, 1991; Canadian Medical Hall of Fame, 1997; Canadian Sci. and Engrg Hall of Fame, 2008. Silver Jubilee Medal, 1977; Gov.-Gen.'s Commemorative Medal for 125th Anniversary of Canadian Confedn, 1992; Lifetime Achievement Award, Toronto Biotechnol. Initiative, 2006. Has specialised in the study of bacterial and somatic cell genetics. *Publications:* many contribs to scientific and learned journals. *Address:* c/o Samuel Lunenfeld Research Institute of Mount Sinai Hospital, 600 University Avenue, Room 778D, Toronto, ON M5G 1X5, Canada; Apt 805, 130 Carlton Street, Toronto, ON M5A 4K3, Canada.

SIMITIS, Konstantinos, DJur; MP (PASOK) Piraeus, since 1985; Prime Minister of Greece, 1996–2004; Leader, Panhellenic Socialist Movement, 1996–2004; *b* Athens, 23 June 1936; *s* of George Simitis and Fani Cristopoulou; *m* Daphne Arkadiou; two *d. Educ:* Univ. of Marburg (DJur 1959); LSE. Lawyer of the Supreme Court, 1961; Reader in Law, Univ. of Konstanz, Germany, 1971; Prof. of Commercial Law and Civil Law, Justus Liebig Univ., Germany, 1971–75; Prof. of Commercial Law, Panteion Univ. of Political and Social Scis, Athens, 1977. Member: Nat. Council, Panhellenic Liberation Movt, 1970; PASOK, 1974–. Minister: of Agriculture, 1981–85; of Nat. Econ., 1985–87; of Educn and Religious Affairs, 1989–90; of Industry and Commerce, 1993–95. *Publications:* The Structural Opposition, 1979; Policy for Economic Stabilisation, 1989; Nationalistic Populism or National Strategy?, 1992; Towards a Vigorous Society, Towards a Vigorous Greece, 1995; books and articles on legal and econ. matters.

SIMLER, Ingrid Ann; QC 2006; a Recorder, since 2002; *b* 17 Sept. 1963; *d* of Derek and Judy Simler; *m* 1991, John Bernstein; two *s* two *d. Educ:* Henrietta Barnet Sch.; Sidney Sussex Coll., Cambridge (BA 1985); Europa Inst., Univ. of Amsterdam (Dip. EC Law 1986). Called to the Bar, Inner Temple, 1987, Bencher, 2008; Jun. Counsel to IR, 2002–06. Chm., Equality and Diversity Cttee, Bar Council, 2003–; Mem., Equal Treatment Adv. Cttee, Judicial Studies Bd, 2007–. Gen. Editor, Jordans Employment Law Service, 2007–. *Publications:* (contrib.) Tottel Discrimination Law; (contrib.) Tolley's Employment Law. *Recreations:* theatre, travel, being with my children. *Address:* Devereux Chambers, Devereux Court, WC2R 3JH. *T:* (020) 7353 7534; *e-mail:* simler@devchambers.co.uk.

SIMMERS, Graeme Maxwell, CBE 1998 (OBE 1982); DL; Chairman, Scottish Sports Council, 1992–99; *b* 2 May 1935; *s* of W. Maxwell Simmers and Gwen Simmers; *m* 1965, Jennifer Roxburgh; two *s* two *d. Educ:* Glasgow Acad.; Loretto Sch. CA 1959. National Service, commnd Royal Marines, 1959–61. Sen. Partner, S. Easton Simmers & Co., 1960–86; Dir, Scottish Highland Hotels Gp, 1962–92 (Chm., 1972–92). Mem., Scottish Tourist Bd, 1979–86; British Hospitality Association (formerly British Hotels & Restaurants Association): Chm., Bd of Management, 1987–88; Mem. Nat. Exec., 1991–97. Chm., Forth Valley Acute Hosps NHS Trust, 2002–04; non-exec. Mem., Forth Valley Health Bd, 2002–. Governor: Loretto Sch., 1968–2000 (Chm., 1992–99); Queen's Coll., Glasgow, 1989–93. DL Stirling and Falkirk, 2004. Hon. Col, RM Reserve, Scotland, 2000–06. Treasurer and Elder, Killearn Kirk. *Address:* Kincaple, Boquhan, Balfron, Glasgow G63 0RW. *Clubs:* All England Lawn Tennis; Royal & Ancient Golf (Chm., Championship Cttee, 1988–91; Captain, 2001–02); Prestwick Golf, Loch Lomond Golf, Buchanan Castle Golf, Pine Valley Golf.

SIMMONDS, Andrew John; QC 1999; a Deputy High Court Judge, since 2006; *b* 9 May 1957; *s* of late Ernest Simmonds and of Sybil Simmonds; *m* 1981, Kathleen Moyse; one *d. Educ:* Sevenoaks Sch., Kent; St John's Coll., Cambridge (MA). Called to the Bar, Middle Temple, 1980. *Recreations:* alpine ski-ing, running. *Address:* 5 Stone Buildings, Lincoln's Inn, WC2A 3XT. *T:* (020) 7242 6201.

SIMMONDS, Brigid Mary, OBE 2006; Chief Executive, Business in Sport and Leisure, since 1992; *b* 17 April 1958; *d* of Rev. Dermot Quinlan and Edna Quinlan; *m* 1984, Gavin Simmonds; two *s* one *d. Educ:* St Margaret's Sch., Bushey; WRAC Coll., Camberley. Short Service Commn, WRAC, 1978–86: Hong Kong, 1982–84; MoD, 1984–86. Dir, Mktg and PR, S & P Architects, 1986–91. Mem., then Chm., Lottery Panel, 1994–2000, Mem. Bd, 1998–2004, Sport England; Chm., CCPR, 2005– (Mem. Bd, 2000–); Dir, Tourism Alliance, 2005– (Chm., 2005–06). Non-exec. Dir, Quintus PA, 2006–. Shine Industry Expert of the Year Award, 2007. *Publication:* Developing Partnerships in Sport and Leisure, 1996. *Recreations:* sport (running and tennis), reading, music. *Address:* 17a Chartfield Avenue, Putney, SW15 6DX. *T:* (020) 8780 2377, *Fax:* (020) 8788 2277; *e-mail:* brigid.Simmonds@btconnect.com.

SIMMONDS, John Andrew; Registrar in Bankruptcy, High Court of Justice, since 1993; *b* 8 March 1939; *s* of Frank Andrew Simmonds and Eugenie Marie Alexandra (*née* Longyear); *m*; one *s. Educ:* Holloway Grammar Sch. Admitted solicitor, 1968; Partner, Stafford Clark & Co., 1971–93. Mem., Insolvency Practitioners Tribunal, 1987–. *Publications:* Statutory Demands: use and abuse, 1992; contributions to: Report by Lord Justice Otton, Litigants in Person in the High Court, 1995–96; Report by Mr Justice Ferris, Insolvency Practitioner Renumeration, 1999–2000. *Address:* Parkhill Road, NW3.

SIMMONDS, Rt Hon. Sir Kennedy (Alphonse), KCMG 2004; PC 1984; Prime Minister, Federation of St Christopher (St Kitts) and Nevis, 1983–95; *b* 12 April 1936; *s* of Bronte Clarke and Arthur Simmonds; *m* 1976, Mary Camella (*née* Matthew); three *s* two *d. Educ:* St Kitts and Nevis Grammar School; Leeward Islands Scholar, 1954; Univ. of West Indies (studies in Medicine), 1955–62. Senior Bench Chemist, Sugar Assoc. Res. Lab., St Kitts, 1955; Internship, Kingston Public Hosp., 1963; medical practice, St Kitts, Anguilla and Nevis, 1964–66; postgrad. studies, Princess Margaret Hosp., Bahamas, 1966; Resident in Anaesthesiology, Pittsburgh, 1968–69; medical practice, St Kitts, 1969–80; Premier of St Christopher (St Kitts) and Nevis, 1980–83. Foundn Mem., People's Action Movement Opposition Party, 1965, Pres., People's Action Movement, 1976. Fellow, Amer. Coll. of Anaesthesiology, 1970. Medal of Honour, Anguilla, 2005. *Recreations:* tennis, cricket, football, video taping. *Address:* PO Box 167, Earle Morne Development, Basseterre, St Kitts, West Indies.

SIMMONDS, Mark Jonathan Mortlock; MP (C) Boston and Skegness, since 2001; *b* 12 April 1964; *s* of Neil Mortlock Simmonds and Mary Griffith Simmonds; *m* 1994, Lizbeth Josefina Hanomancin; one *s* two *d. Educ:* Nottingham Poly. (BSc Hons). MRICS 1987. With Savills, 1986–88; Partner, Strutt & Parker, 1988–96; Dir, C. B. Hillier Parker, 1996–98; Man. Dir, 1998–2001, Chm., 2001–, Mortlock Simmonds Brown. Shadow Minister: for Public Services, Health and Educn, subseq. Educn, 2003–04; for Foreign Affairs, 2004–05; for Internat. Develt, 2005–07; for Health, 2007–. *Recreations:* family, Rugby, tennis, history, reading. *Address:* House of Commons, SW1A 0AA. *T:* (020) 7219 6254. *Club:* Naval and Military.

SIMMONDS, Posy, MBE 2002; FRSL; freelance illustrator/cartoonist, since 1969; *b* 9 Aug. 1945; *d* of late Reginald A. C. Simmonds and Betty Cahusac; *m* 1974, Richard Graham Hollis, *qv. Educ:* Queen Anne's Sch., Caversham; L'Ecole des Beaux Arts, Paris; Central Sch. of Art and Design, London (BA Art and Design). Cartoonist: The Guardian, 1977–87, 1988–90, 1992–; The Spectator, 1988–90. Exhibitions: The Cartoon Gall. (formerly the Workshop), 1974, 1976, 1979, 1981, 1982, 1984; Mus. of Modern Art, Oxford, 1981; Manor House Mus. & Art Gall., Ilkley, 1985. TV documentary, Tresoddit for Easter, 1991. FRSL 2005. Hon. DArt Plymouth, 1993; Hon. DLitt Exeter, 2007. Cartoonist of the Year: Granada TV/What The Papers Say, 1980; British Press Awards, 1981; Nat. Art Liby Illustrations Award, 1998. *Publications:* Bear Book, 1969; Mrs Weber's Diary, 1979; True Love, 1981; Pick of Posy, 1982; (illustrator) Daisy Ashford, The Young Visiters, 1984; Very Posy, 1985; Fred, 1987 (filmed as Famous Fred, 1997); Pure Posy, 1987; Lulu and the Flying Babies, 1988; The Chocolate Wedding, 1990; (illustrator) Hilaire Belloc, Matilda, who told such Dreadful Lies, 1991; Mustn't Grumble, 1993; Bouncing Buffalo, 1994; F-Freezing ABC, 1995; (illustrator) Hilaire Belloc, Cautionary Tales, 1998; Gemma Bovery, 1999; (illustrator) Folio Book of Humorous Verse, 2002; Lavender, 2003; Literary Life, 2003; Baker Cat, 2004; Tamara Drewe, 2007. *Address:* c/o United Agents, 12–26 Lexington Street, W1F 0LE. *T:* (020) 3214 0800.

See also R. J. Simmonds.

SIMMONDS, Richard James, CBE 1996; farmer and forester; Chairman, London and Economic Properties, since 2002; *b* 2 Aug. 1944; *s* of late Reginald A. C. Simmonds and Betty Cahusac; *m* 1967, Mary (*née* Stewart); one *s* two *d. Educ:* Trinity Coll., Glenalmond. Councillor, Berkshire CC (Chm. of Environment, Property, Transport, and Development Cttees), 1973–79. National Vice-Chm. of Young Conservatives, 1973–75; Founding Vice-Chm. of Young European Democrats, 1974; Personal Asst to Rt Hon. Edward Heath, 1973–75; MEP (C) Midlands W, 1979–84, Wight and Hampshire E, 1984–94; PPS to Sir James Scott-Hopkins, Leader of European Democratic Gp, European Parlt, 1979–82; Cons. spokesman on youth and educn, European Parlt, 1982–84, on budget control, 1984–87; Whip, 1987–89; Chief Whip, 1992–94. Mem., Agric., Fisheries, Food and Rural Develt Cttee, 1992–94; Expert Advr, Eur. Commn, 1997–. Fellow of Parly & Industry Trust. Chairman: Countryside Commn, 1995–99; Ind. Transport Commn, 1999–2001. Pres., A>B Global Inc., 2005–. Mem. Council, PDSA, 1995–2001. Founding Pres., Mounted Games Assoc. of GB, 1984–; President: Royal E Berks Agricl Assoc., 1995; Jersey Cattle Soc., 1997. Fellow, Waitangi Foundn, NZ, 1996. Chm. of Governors, Berkshire Coll. of Agriculture, 1979–92; Mem. Adv. Cttee, Centre for Agric. Strategy, Reading Univ., 1998–2001. ARAgS 1997. *Publications:* The Common Agricultural Policy—a sad misnomer, 1979; An A to Z of Myths and Misunderstandings of the European Community, 1981, 3rd edn 1993; (jtly) Cork Declaration on Rural Development, 1996; European Parliamentary report on farm animal welfare, 1985, 1987, 1990; report on prodn, processing, politics and potential of NZ meat (P4 report), 1996. *Recreations:* resisting bureaucracy, getting things done. *Address:* Dyars, Cookham Dean, Berkshire SL6 9PJ. *Clubs:* Ancient Britons, Tamworth; OPB Sailing (Hon. Cdre, 1999–).

See also Posy Simmonds.

SIMMONS, His Honour Alan Gerald; a Circuit Judge, 1990–2006; *b* 7 Sept. 1936; *s* of late Maurice Simmons and Sophie Simmons (*née* Lasserson); *m* 1961, Mia, *d* of late Emanuel and Lisa Rosenstein; one *s* one *d. Educ:* Bedford Modern Sch.; Quintin Sch. RAF, 1956–58. Director: Aslon Labs; Record Productions (Surrey); Ashcourt. Called to the Bar, Gray's Inn, 1968 (Lee Essay Prize; Holker Sen Exhibn); SE Circuit; Assistant Recorder, 1985; Recorder, 1989. Mem., Mental Health Rev. Tribunal, 1993–2000. Member: Board of Deputies of British Jews, 1982–88; Council, United Synagogue, 1979–93. *Recreations:* music, reading, (formerly) fencing.

SIMMONS, Sir David (Anthony Cathcart), KA 2001; BCH 2001; QC 1984; Chief Justice of Barbados, since 2002; *b* 28 April 1940; *s* of late Kenneth G. Simmons and of Sybil Louise Simmons; *m* 1966, Marie MacCormack, QC; one *s* one *d. Educ:* London Sch. of Econs and Pol Sci. (LLB Hons 1963; LLM 1965). Called to the Bar, Lincoln's Inn, 1968, Hon. Bencher, 2006; joined law chambers of Henry Forde, QC, Barbados, 1970; private law practice, 1970–85 and 1986–94; Lectr in Law (pt-time), Univ. of WI, 1970–75; Chairman: Nat. Housing Corp., 1976–79; Caribbean Broadcasting Corp., 1979–81; Nat. Sports Council, 1982–85. MP, Barbados, 1976–81, 1985–2001; Mem., Barbados House of Assembly, 1981–85; Attorney General, 1985–86 and 1994–2001. Caribbean Court of Justice: Chairman: Prep. Cttee for establishment, 1999–2001; Regl Judicial Legal Services Cttee, 2003–04; High Level Task Force for inauguration, 2004–05. Mem., Barbados Cricket Assoc. Hon. Fellow, Univ. of WI, 2003. Hon. LLD LSE, 2003. *Recreations:* reading, sports, collecting calypso music, playing trumpet. *Address:* c/o Supreme Court of Barbados, Coleridge Street, Bridgetown, Barbados. *T:* 4264670, *Fax:* 4278917; *e-mail:* chiefjustice@lawcourts.gov.bb. *Club:* Barbados Turf (Appellate Steward).

See also P. P. Simmons.

SIMMONS, Fr Eric, CR; Prior of St Michael's Priory, Burleigh Street, London, 1993–98; *b* 3 Aug. 1930. *Educ:* Univ. of Leeds (BA Phil 1951). Coll. of the Resurrection, Mirfield, 1951; deacon, 1953, priest, 1954; Curate of St Luke, Chesterton, 1953–57; Chaplain, University Coll. of N Staffordshire, 1957–61; licensed to officiate: Dio. Wakefield, 1963–65 and 1967–; Dio. Ripon, 1965–67; Warden and Prior of Hostel of the Resurrection, Leeds, 1966–67; subseq. Novice Guardian, CR, looking after young Community members; Superior, Community of the Resurrection, Mirfield, Yorks, 1974–87; permission to officiate, Dio. London, 1989–98; the Community is an Anglican monastic foundation engaged in evangelism and teaching work, based in Yorkshire. *Address:* House of the Resurrection, Mirfield, W Yorks WF14 0BN.

SIMMONS, Guy Lintorn, LVO 1961; HM Diplomatic Service, retired; *b* 27 Feb. 1925; *s* of late Captain Geoffrey Larpent Simmons, RN and Frances Gladys Simmons (*née* Wright); *m* 1951, Sheila Jacob; three *d. Educ:* Bradfield Coll.; Oriel Coll., Oxford. RAF, 1943–46; CRO, 1949; 2nd Sec., British High Commn: Lahore, 1950; Dacca, 1952; CRO, 1954–58 and 1964–66; 1st Sec.: Bombay, 1958; New Delhi, 1961; Commercial Counsellor: New Delhi, 1966–68; Cairo, 1968–71; Head of Trade Policy Dept, FCO, 1971–73; Diplomatic Service Inspectorate, 1973–76; Commercial Counsellor, Copenhagen, 1976–79; Consul-General: Karachi, 1979–82; Montreal, 1982–84; FCO, 1984–90. Chm., Crouch End Open Space, 1992–94. *Recreations:* the arts, travel. *Address:* 29 Wood Vale, N10 3DJ.

SIMMONS, Prof. Ian Gordon, PhD, DLitt; FSA; FBA 1997; Professor of Geography, University of Durham, 1981–2001, now Emeritus; *b* 22 Jan. 1937; *s* of Charles Frederick Simmons and Christina Mary Simmons (*née* Merrills); *m* 1962, Carol Mary Saunders; one *s* one *d. Educ:* UCL (BSc 1959; PhD 1962); Durham Univ. (DLitt 1990). CGeog 2002. Lectr, 1962–70, Sen. Lectr, 1970–76, Reader, 1976–77, in Geography, Univ. of Durham; Prof. of Geography, Univ. of Bristol, 1977–81. ACLS Postdoctoral Fellow, Univ. of Calif at Berkeley, 1964–65; Churchill Meml Travelling Fellow, 1970–71. Chm., Benchmarking Panel for Geography, QAA, 1999–2001; Mem. Geog. Panel, RAE, 1996–2001. FSA 1980; MAE 1994. Hon. DSc Aberdeen, 2005. *Publications:* Changing the Face of the Earth, 1989, 2nd edn 1996; Earth, Air and Water, 1993; Interpreting Nature, 1993; Environmental History, 1993; The Environmental Impact of Later Mesolithic Cultures, 1996; Humanity and Environment: a cultural ecology, 1997; An Environmental History of Great Britain, 2001; An Environmental History of the Moorlands of England and Wales, 2003; A Global Environmental History, 2008; chapters in edited collections and about 100 papers in learned jls. *Recreations:* music, poetry. *Address:* Department of Geography, Science Laboratories, South Road, Durham DH1 3LE. *T:* (0191) 334 1800, *Fax:* (0191) 334 1801; *e-mail:* i.g.simmons@durham.ac.uk.

SIMMONS, Jean Merilyn, OBE 2003; film actress; *b* London, 31 Jan. 1929; *m* 1950, Stewart Granger (marr. diss. 1960; he *d* 1993); one *d*; *m* 1960, Richard Brooks (marr. diss. 1977; he *d* 1992); one *d. Educ:* Orange Hill Sch.; Aida Foster School of Dancing. First film appearance in Give Us the Moon, 1942; minor parts in Cæsar and Cleopatra, The Way to the Stars, etc., 1942–44; since then has appeared in numerous British films, including: Great Expectations, 1946; Black Narcissus, Hungry Hill, Uncle Silas, 1947; Hamlet, 1948 (Best Actress Award, Venice Film Festival, 1950); The Blue Lagoon, Adam and Evalyn, 1949; So Long at the Fair, Trio, 1950; Clouded Yellow, 1951; The Grass is Greener, 1960; Life at the Top, 1965; Say Hello to Yesterday, 1971; began American film career, 1950; American films include: Androcles and the Lion, 1952; Young Bess, The Actress, 1953; Desirée, 1954; Footsteps in the Fog, Guys and Dolls, 1955; This Could be the Night, 1957; Spartacus, Elmer Gantry, 1960; All the Way Home, 1963; Divorce American Style, 1967; The Happy Ending, 1970; The Thorn Birds, 1982 (Emmy award, 1983); How to Make an American Quilt, 1996; American television includes: Beggarman, Thief, 1979; A Small Killing, 1981; Down at the Hydro, 1982; Murder She Wrote, 1984; North and South, 1985; Perry Mason, Star Trek: The New Generation, 1987; Dark Shadows, 1991; UK television: December Flower, 1984; The Dawning, 1988; Great Expectations, 1989; They Do it with Mirrors, 1991; Daisies in December, 1995; Winter Solstice, 2003. Musical: A Little Night Music, Adelphi, 1975. Outstanding Film Achievement Award, Italy, 1989. Comdr, Order of Arts and Letters (France), 1990.

SIMMONS, John Barry Eves, OBE 1987; VMH 1986; Curator: Castle Howard Arboretum Trust, 1997–2006; Royal Botanic Gardens, Kew, 1972–95; *b* 30 May 1937; *s* of Alfred John and Gladys Enid Simmons; *m* 1958, Valerie Lilian Dugan; two *s* one *d. Educ:* Harrow County Grammar Sch.; Herts Coll. of Agric. and Hort.; Regent Street Polytechnic; Sch. of Horticulture, Kew. MHort 1962, FIHort 1984; FIBiol 1988–2004; FLS 2004. Royal Botanic Gardens, Kew: Supervisor, Tropical Propagation Unit, 1961–64; Asst Curator, Temperate Section, 1964–68; Deputy Curator, 1968–72. Chm., Nat. Council for Conservation of Plants and Gardens, 1994–97 (Mem. Council, 1985–97; Vice-Chm., 1991–94; Pres., Norfolk Gp, 1993–2002); Member: RHS Award and Judging Cttees, 1969–2007; Longwood Gardens (Pennsylvania) Visiting Cttee, 1984–91; Westonbirt Arboretum Consultative Cttee, 1986–2004; Chm., Bedgebury Pinetum Consultative Cttee, 1992–2003; Dir, Flora for Fauna, 1997–2000; Trustee, Stanley Smith (UK) Horticultural Trust, 1994–. Pres., Inst. of Horticulture, 1987–88. Gov., Writtle Agricl Coll., 1990–93. *Publications:* The Life of Plants, 1974, 2nd edn 1990; (series editor) Kew Gardening Guides, 1987–; (gen. editor) Kew Gardens Book of Indoor Plants, 1988; (jtly) The Gardens of William Morris, 1998; (jtly) English Plants for your Garden, 2000; Managing Wet Gardens, 2008; ed and contrib. to learned jls. *Recreations:* photography, walking, gardening (own garden!).

SIMMONS, Air Marshal Sir Michael (George), KCB 1989 (CB 1988); AFC 1976; Member, Air Force Board, Defence Council, 1989–92; *b* 8 May 1937; *s* of George and Thelma Simmons; *m* 1964, Jean Aliwell; two *d. Educ:* Shrewsbury Sch.; RAF Coll., Cranwell. Commissioned 1958; No 6 Squadron, Cyprus, 1959–61; ADC to AOC-in-C FTC, 1961–64; No 39 Sqdn, Malta, 1964–66; No 13 Sqdn, Malta, 1966–67; No 51 Sqdn, Wyton, 1967–69; RN Staff Coll., 1970; MoD, 1971–72; OC No XV Sqdn, Germany, 1973–76; MoD, 1976–79; OC RAF Cottesmore, 1980–82; MoD, 1982–84; SASO, HQ Strike Comd, 1984–85; AOC No 1 Gp, RAF, 1985–87; ACAS, 1987–89; Dep. Controller Aircraft, MoD, 1989–92. ADC to the Queen, 1980–81. Mem. Council, RAF Benevolent Fund, 1994–2006. Chm. Bd of Govs, Duke of Kent Sch., 1994–96. *Recreations:* clock repairing, gardening, golf. *Club:* Royal Air Force.

SIMMONS, Peter Patrick; High Commissioner for Barbados in the United Kingdom, 1995–2003; *b* 13 April 1942; *s* of late Kenneth G. Simmons and of Sybil Louise Simmons; *m* 1968, Rosalind Cecelia Hinds; one *s* one *d. Educ:* London Sch. of Journalism (Diploma); New York State Univ. (BA); Univ. of WI, St Augustine (Cert. Govt Admin). Sub-Editor, Barbados Advocate, 1961–73; Min. of Foreign Affairs, London, NY, Bridgetown, 1963–76; Asst Registrar, Univ. of WI, Cave Hill Campus, 1976–79; Dep. Perm. Rep. and Chargé d'Affaires, Barbados Mission to UN, 1979–82; Chief Develt Planner, Min. of Finance and Planning, 1982–84; Dir of Communications, Barbados, 1984–86; Political Specialist, US Embassy, Bridgetown, 1986–91; Chm., SBG Develt Corp., 1991–94. ITV documentary: The Red Legs of Barbados, 1986. *Publications:* Red Legs: class and colour contradictions in Barbados, 1976; (with Sir Garfield Sobers) The Changing Face of Cricket, 1995. *Recreations:* reading, public affairs, cricket, cooking, walking.

SIMMONS, Richard John, CBE 1995; FCA; Chairman, BDP Media Group Ltd, since 2002; Senior Partner, Andersen (formerly Arthur Andersen), 1996–2001, Senior Adviser, 2002; *b* 2 June 1947; *s* of John Eric Simmons and Joy Mary Simmons (*née* Foat); *m* 1983, Veronica Sinkins; one *s* one *d. Educ:* Moseley GS, Birmingham; London School of Economics (BSc Econs); Haas Business Sch., Univ. of California, Berkeley. FCA 1971. Joined Arthur Andersen, subseq. Andersen, 1968; Partner, 1979–2001. Asst Sec., Internat. Accounting Standards Cttee, 1973–75. Non-executive Director: Cranfield Information Technology Inst., 1987–89; Westminster Forum Ltd, 1999–; Chairman: Atticmedia Ltd, 2007–; Shimmer Productions Ltd, 2008–. Chairman: Bow Gp, 1980–81; CBlu Adv. Council, 2000–02; Member: Shadow Nat. Accounts Commn, 2000–01; Bd of Treasurers, Cons. Party, 2002–03. Mem., Develt Bd, Royal Acad. of Arts, 1995–2002. Dir, Constable Trust, 2003–; Trustee, Foundn for Social and Econ. Thinking, 2003– (Chm., Governing Council, 2005–). Gov., Moat Sch., 2003–. FRSA 2004. *Recreations:* horse racing, tennis, gardening. *Address:* BDP Media, The Leathermarket, Weston Street, SE1 3ER. *Clubs:* Carlton (Hon. Treas., 1995–2001, Hon. Mem., 2006–, Political Cttee), United and Cecil.

SIMMONS, Richard Thomas, PhD; Chief Executive, Commission for Architecture and the Built Environment, since 2004; *b* 17 Feb. 1953; *s* of Laurence and Audrey Simmons; *m* 1976, Elizabeth Mary; two *s* two *d. Educ:* Univ. of Sheffield (BA Hons 1974); South Bank Polytech. (BTP (Postgrad.) 1982); Univ. of Leicester (PhD 1995). MRTPI 1984. Town Planner, London Bor. of Hackney, 1978–85; Sen. Planning Officer, Inner Cities Directorate, DoE, 1985–87; Develt Manager, LDDC, 1987–93; Chief Exec., Dalston City Challenge, 1993–97; Dir of Develt and Envmt, Medway Council, 1997–2004. FRSA. *Recreations:* climbing, scouting, DJing, reading science fiction and detective novels. *Address:* Commission for Architecture and the Built Environment, 1 Kemble Street, WC2B 4AN. *T:* (020) 7070 6700, *Fax:* (020) 7070 6777; *e-mail:* enquiries@cabe.org.uk.

SIMMONS, Prof. Robert Malcolm, FRS 1995; Professor of Biophysics, King's College London, 1983–2001, now Emeritus; *b* 23 Jan. 1938; *s* of Stanley Laurence Simmons and Marjorie Amys; *m* 1967, Mary Ann (Anna) Ross; one *s* one *d. Educ:* King's College London (BSc Physics 1960; FKC 1996); Royal Institution (PhD London 1965); University College London (MSc Physiol. 1967). CBiol, FIBiol 2000. Department of Physiology, University College London: Sharpey Scholar, 1967–70; Lectr, 1970–79; MRC Res. Fellow, 1979–81; King's College London: MRC Cell Biophysics Unit, 1981–83; Associate Dir, 1983–91; Head of Dept of Biophysics, 1983–88; Head of Div. of Biomolecular Scis, 1988–91; Hon. Dir, MRC Muscle and Cell Motility Unit, 1991–2001; Dir, Randall Centre (formerly Randall Inst.), 1995–2001. *Publications:* contribs on physiol. and biophys to learned jls. *Recreations:* music, fishing. *Address:* Edmunds Ground, 1 Woodborough Road, Pewsey, Wilts SN9 5NH.

SIMMONS, Rosemary Ann; freelance artist, writer and curator, since 1975; *b* 19 Oct. 1932; *d* of Donald and Alys Simmons; *m* 1974, Anthony H. Christie (*d* 1994); two step *s* three step *d. Educ:* Chelsea Sch. of Art (NDD and Chelsea Dip. 1955). Graphic Designer, Curwen Press, 1955–58; Dir, Curwen Gall., 1965–71; Man. Dir, Curwen Prints Ltd, 1971–75. Chm., Combe Down Heritage Soc., 2004–. Pres., Bath Artist Printmakers, 2006–. Founder Ed., 1990–98, Consultant Ed., 1998–, Printmaking Today. Hon. RE 1990. *Publications:* Printmaking in Easy Steps, 1977; Collecting Original Prints, 1980; (with Katie Clemson) The Complete Manual of Relief Printmaking, 1988; A Dictionary of Printmaking Terms, 2002; Collecting Original Prints, 2005. *Recreations:* supporting Printmaking Today, art and science, gardens, the company of friends. *Address:* 12 Greendown Place, Combe Down, Bath BA2 5DD. *T:* (01225) 833301; *e-mail:* rosyprint@care4free.net.

SIMMONS, Sir Stanley (Clifford), Kt 1993; FRCS, FRCOG; Consultant Obstetrician and Gynaecologist, Windsor, 1965–92; *b* 28 July 1927; *s* of Lewis Alfred and Ann Simmons; *m* 1956, Ann Wine; one *s* three *d. Educ:* Hurstpierpoint Coll.; St Mary's Hosp., London Univ. (MB BS 1951). FRCS 1957, FRCOG 1971. National Service, Royal West African Frontier Force, 1953–55. Resident MO, Queen Charlotte's Hosp. and Chelsea Hosp. for Women, 1955–56; Registrar, St Mary's Hosp. Paddington, 1957–59; Sen. Registrar, St Thomas' Hosp., 1960–64. Member: GMC, 1975–84; Council, RCOG, 1971–72, 1973–78, 1982– (Vice-Pres., 1986; Sen. Vice-Pres., 1987; Pres., 1990–93); Council, RCS (co-opted), 1984–86; President: Hosp. Consultants and Specialists Assoc., 1972; Windsor Med. Soc., 1983; Section of Obst. and Gyn., RSocMed, 1985. Hon. FRCSE 1994; Hon. FRACOG 1992; Hon. FACOG 1993; Hon. Fellow, Inst. of Gynaecologists, RCPI, 1993. *Publications:* (jtly) General Surgery in Gynaecological Practice, 1974; contribs to med. jls. *Recreations:* flying, sailing, golf, ski-ing, painting. *Address:* 23 Chapel Square, Virginia Park, Virginia Water, Surrey GU25 4SZ. *T:* (01344) 844029. *Clubs:* Royal Society of Medicine, Royal Ocean Racing; Wentworth.

SIMMONS, Timothy Michael John; HM Diplomatic Service; Ambassador to Slovenia, since 2005; *b* 8 April 1960; *m* 1989, Caroline Mary Radcliffe; two *s. Educ:* Univ. of East Anglia (BA Jt Hons 1981). Entered FCO, 1982; Nuclear Energy Dept, FCO, 1982–85; Third, later Second Sec., Warsaw, 1985–87; First Secretary: FCO, 1987–93; UK Mission to UN, Geneva, 1993–97; Price Waterhouse, subseq. PricewaterhouseCoopers, 1997–99 (on secondment); Asst Dir, Personnel Comd, FCO, 1999–2001; Dep. Hd of Mission, Warsaw, 2001–04. *Recreations:* reading, music, miniature wargames. *Address:* c/o Foreign and Commonwealth Office, King Charles Street, SW1A 2AH.

SIMMONS, Tom Christopher; Town Clerk, Corporation of London, 1998–2003; *b* 29 Oct. 1942; *s* of Tom Francis Simmons and Mary Simmons; *m* 1971, Barbara Loxley; one *s. Educ:* Nottingham Univ. (BA Law 1963). Admitted Solicitor, 1968. Borough Sec., Chelmsford BC, 1973–83; Dep. Town Clerk, 1983–95, City Sec., 1996–98, Corp. of London. Sec., Mus. of London, 1990–2003; Clerk: Nat. Crime Squad Authy, 1998–2003; Nat. Criminal Intelligence Service Authy, 1998–2003. Board Member: and Hon. Treas., Mosaic Housing Assoc. (formerly New Islington and Hackney Housing Assoc.), 2003–06; Family Mosaic Housing Assoc., 2006–08. *Recreations:* water colour painting, gardening, walking. *Address:* 20 Great Oaks, Hutton, Brentwood, Essex CM13 1AZ.

SIMMS, Sir Neville (Ian), Kt 1998; FREng, FICE, FCIOB; Chairman, International Power plc, since 2000; *b* 11 Sept. 1944; *s* of late Arthur Neville Simms and of Anne Davidson Simms (*née* McCulloch). *Educ:* Queen Elizabeth's GS, Crediton; Univ. of Newcastle upon Tyne (BSc 1st cl. Hons 1966); Univ. of Glasgow (MEng 1971). CEng 1970; FICE 1995; FCIOB 1995; FREng (FEng 1996). Structural Engr, Ove Arup and Partners, 1966–69; joined Tarmac plc as Sect. Engr, Roads Div., Tarmac Civil Engrg, 1970; Chief Exec., Tarmac Construction Ltd, 1988–92; Gp Chief Exec., 1992–99, Dep. Chm., 1994–99, Tarmac plc; Chief Exec., 1999–2000, Chm., 1999–2005, Carillion plc. Dir, Bank of England, 1995–2002; non-executive Director: Courtaulds, 1994–98; Private Finance Panel Ltd, 1994–99; National Power, 1998–2000; Operating Partner, Duke St Capital, 2006–. Chairman: BITC (W Midlands), 1998–2001; BITC Solent Regl Leadership Team, 2006–; Govt Sustainable Procurement Task Force, 2005–06; Member: Pres.'s Cttee, CBI, 1997–; New Deal Task Force, 1999–2001; Trade Partners UK-Business Adv. Panel, 2001–03. Trustee, BRE Trust (formerly Foundn for Built Envmt), 2002– (Chm., 2006–). Gov., Ashridge Mgt Coll., 2000– (Dep. Chm., 2006–). MInstD 1995; CCMI (CIMgt 1992); FRSA 1992. Hon. DTech Wolverhampton Univ., 1997; Dr *hc* Edinburgh, 2000; Dr Eng Glasgow, 2001. *Address:* International Power plc, 85 Queen Victoria Street, EC4V 4DP.

SIMON, family name of **Viscount Simon**, and of **Simon of Highbury** and **Simon of Wythenshawe**.

SIMON, 3rd Viscount *cr* 1940; **Jan David Simon;** a Deputy Speaker, House of Lords, since 1999; *b* 20 July 1940; *o s* of 2nd Viscount Simon, CMG; *S* father, 1993; *m* 1969, Mary Elizabeth, *d* of late John J. Burns, Sydney, NSW; one *d*. *Educ:* Westminster; Sch. of Navigation, Univ. of Southampton; Sydney Tech. Coll. Dep. Chm. of Cttees, H of L, 1998–; Member, Select Committee: on Procedure of H of L, 1999–2002; on Personal Bills, 2004–; on Standing Orders (Private Bills), 2004–; elected Mem., H of L, 1999. *Heir:* none. *Address:* House of Lords, SW1A 0PW.

SIMON OF HIGHBURY, Baron *cr* 1997 (Life Peer), of Canonbury in the London Borough of Islington; **David Alec Gwyn Simon,** Kt 1995; CBE 1991; *b* 24 July 1939; *s* of late Roger Albert Damas Jules Simon and Barbara (*née* Hudd); *m* 1st, 1964, Hanne (*née* Mohn) (marr. diss. 1987); two *s*; 2nd, 1992, Sarah (*née* Roderick Smith). *Educ:* Christ's Hospital; Gonville and Caius College, Cambridge (MA Hons; Hon. Fellow 2001); MBA INSEAD. Joined BP 1961; a Man. Dir, 1985–97, CEO, 1992–95 and Chm., 1995–97, BP. A Dir, Bank of England, 1995–97. Minister of State, HM Treasury and DTI, 1997–99; Advr, Cabinet Office, 1999–2003. Mem., Prodi Gp advising on Enlargement Implications, EU, 1999. Sen. Advr (formerly Dir), Morgan Stanley Internat., 2000–; Director: Unilever, 2000– (Dep. Chm., 2006–); Suez Group, 2001–; Supervisory Bd, Volkswagen, 2002–05. Member: International Council and UK Adv. Bd, INSEAD, 1985–2008; President's Cttee, CBI, 1992–97; Internat. Adv. Bd, Dana Gas, 2006–; Vice Chm., European Round Table, 1993–97. Mem., Cambridge Univ. Council, 2005–. Hon. DSc(Econ) Hull, 1990; DUniv. of N London, 1995; Hon. LLD Bath, 1998; Hon. DSc Birmingham, 2003. Cadman Medal, Inst. of Petroleum, 1997. Grand Officer, Order of Leopold (Belgium), 2005 (Comdr, 2001). *Recreations:* golf, books, music. *Address:* House of Lords, SW1A 0PW. *Clubs:* Athenæum, Brooks's.

SIMON OF WYTHENSHAWE, 3rd Baron *cr* 1947, of Didsbury, City of Manchester; **Matthew Simon;** Principal Lecturer, Sheffield Hallam University; *b* 10 April 1955; *o s* of 2nd Baron Simon of Wythenshawe and of (Anthea) Daphne (*née* May); *S* father, 2002, but does not use the title; *m* 1987, Sally Mitchell; two *d*. *Educ:* St Paul's Sch.; Balliol Coll., Oxford (BA 1978); Manchester Poly. (PhD 1983). CEng; MIMechE 1991. Sen. Lectr, Dept Mech. Engrg, Manchester Metropolitan Univ. (formerly Manchester Poly.), 1983–98; Univ. of Zimbabwe, Harare, 1988–90. *Heir: cousin* Martin Simon [*b* 29 Nov. 1944; *m*; one *s* one *d*].

SIMON, Jacob Michael Henry, FSA, FMA; Chief Curator, National Portrait Gallery, since 2001; *b* 29 Sept. 1946; *s* of John Eric Henry Simon and Josephine (*née* Sammone); partner, Jenny Bescoby; two *s*. *Educ:* Christ's Coll., Cambridge (BA 1969; MA 1972). FMA 1988; FSA 1992. Trainee Asst, Temple Newsam House, Leeds, 1971–73; Asst Curator, Iveagh Bequest, Kenwood, 1973–83; Curator, 18th century portraits, NPG, 1983–2001. Mem. Council and Cttee, NT, 1969–2000; Trustee, Grimsthorpe and Drummond Castle Trust, 1989–2005. Editor, Walpole Soc., 1981–89. *Publications:* (ed) Handel: a celebration of his life and times 1685–1759, 1985; The Art of the Picture Frame: artists, patrons and the framing of portraits in Britain, 1996. *Recreations:* walking, book collecting. *Address:* National Portrait Gallery, WC2H 0HE. *T:* (020) 7312 2416, *Fax:* (020) 7306 0056; *e-mail:* jsimon@npg.org.uk.

SIMON, Prof. Leon, PhD; FRS 2003; FAA; Robert Grimmett Professor of Mathematics, Stanford University; *b* 6 July 1945. *Educ:* Univ. of Adelaide (BSc 1967; PhD 1971). FAA 1983. Lectr in Math., Flinders Univ., 1972–73; Asst Prof., Stanford Univ., 1973–76; Vis. Prof., Univ. of Adelaide, 1976–77; Associate Prof., Univ. of Minnesota, 1977–78; Professor of Mathematics: Univ. of Melbourne, 1978–81; ANU, 1981. *Address:* Department of Mathematics, Stanford University, 450 Serra Mall, Building 380, Stanford, CA 94305–2125, USA.

SIMON, Neil; playwright; *b* NYC, 4 July 1927; *s* of Irving and Mamie Simon; *m* 1st, 1953, Joan Baim (*d* 1973); 2nd, 1973, Marsha Mason; 3rd, 1987, Diane Lander; 4th, Elaine Joyce. *Educ:* De Witt Clinton High Sch.; entered Army Air Force Reserve training programme as an engineering student at New York University; discharged with rank of corporal, 1946. Went to New York Offices of Warner Brothers Pictures to work in mail room. Hon. LHD Hofstra Univ., 1981; Dr *hc* Williams Coll., 1984. *Screenplays include:* After The Fox (produced 1966); Barefoot in the Park, 1967; The Odd Couple, 1968; The Out-of-Towners, 1970; Plaza Suite, 1971; The Last of the Red Hot Lovers, 1972; The Heartbreak Kid, 1973; The Prisoner of 2nd Avenue, 1975; The Sunshine Boys, 1975; Murder by Death, 1976; The Goodbye Girl, 1977 (and TV film, 2004); The Cheap Detective, 1978; California Suite, 1978; Chapter Two, 1979; Seems Like Old Times, 1980; Only When I Laugh, 1981; I Ought To Be In Pictures, 1982; Max Dugan Returns, 1983; adapt. Lonely Guy, 1984; The Slugger's Wife, 1984; Brighton Beach Memoirs, 1986; Biloxi Blues, 1988; The Marrying Man, 1991; Broadway Bound (TV film), 1992; Lost in Yonkers, 1993; Jake's Women (TV film), 1996; London Suite (TV film), 1996; The Odd Couple II, 1998; Laughter on the 23rd Floor (TV film), 2001; other films based on his stage plays: Come Blow Your Horn, 1963; Sweet Charity, 1969; The Star-Spangled Girl, 1971. *Plays produced:* Come Blow Your Horn, 1961 (publ. 1961); (jtly) Little Me, 1962 (publ. 1979), rev. version 1982, West End 1984; Barefoot in the Park, 1963 (publ. 1964); The Odd Couple, 1965 (publ. 1966), West End 1996, NY revival 2005; (jtly) Sweet Charity, 1966 (publ. 1966), NY revivals 1986 and 2005; The Star-Spangled Girl, 1966 (publ. 1967); Plaza Suite, 1968 (publ. 1969); (jtly) Promises, Promises, 1968 (publ. 1970); Last of the Red Hot Lovers, 1969 (publ. 1970), Criterion, 1979; The Gingerbread Lady, 1970 (publ. 1971); The Prisoner of Second Avenue, 1971 (publ. 1972); The Sunshine Boys, 1972 (publ. 1973); The Good Doctor, 1973 (publ. 1974); God's Favorite, 1974 (publ. 1975); California Suite, 1976 (publ. 1977); Chapter Two, 1977 (publ. 1979), West End 1996; (jtly) They're Playing Our Song, 1979 (publ. 1980); I Ought To Be In Pictures, 1980 (publ. 1981); Fools, 1981 (publ. 1982); Brighton Beach Memoirs, 1983 (publ. 1984), NT, 1986, West End, 1987; Biloxi Blues, 1985 (Tony Award for Best Play, 1985) (publ. 1986); The Odd Couple (female version), 1985 (publ. 1992); Broadway Bound, 1986 (publ. 1988); Rumors, 1988 (publ. 1990), Chichester, 1990; Lost in Yonkers, 1991 (Pulitzer Prize, Tony Award for Best Play, 1991) (publ. 1992), West End, 1992; Jake's Women, 1992 (publ. 1994); (jtly) The Goodbye Girl, 1993; Laughter on the 23rd Floor, 1993 (publ. 1995), West End 1996; London Suite, 1995; Proposals, 1997; The Dinner Party, 2000; Hotel Suite, 2000; 45 Seconds from Broadway, 2001; Oscar and Felix, LA, 2002 (publ. 2004); Rose's Dilemma, 2004 (publ. 2004). *Publications:* Rewrites: a memoir, 1996; The Play Goes On, 1999. *Address:* c/o Gary DaSilva, 111 N Sepulveda Boulevard #250, Manhattan Beach, CA 90266, USA. *T:* (310) 3185665, *Fax:* (310) 3182114; *e-mail:* mail@garydasilva.com.

SIMON, Paul; American singer and songwriter; *b* 13 Oct. 1941; *s* of Louis and Belle Simon; *m* 1st, Peggy Harper (marr. diss.); one *s*; 2nd, 1983, Carrie Fisher (marr. diss.); 3rd, 1992, Edie Brickell; two *s* one *d*. *Educ:* Queens Coll. (BA Eng. Lit.). Mem., Simon and Garfunkel, 1964–71; solo performer, 1971–. *Songs include: with Art Garfunkel:* The Sounds of Silence; Homeward Bound; I Am a Rock; 59th Street Bridge Song (Feelin' Groovy); Scarborough Fair/Canticle; Mrs Robinson; The Boxer; Bridge Over Troubled Water; Cecilia; *solo:* American Tune; Loves Me Like a Rock; Still Crazy After All These Years; 50 Ways to Leave Your Lover; Slip Slidin' Away; Something So Right; Hearts and Bones; Graceland; You Can Call Me Al; Diamonds on the Soles of her Shoes; Under African Skies; The Rhythm of the Saints; albums include: (with Derek Walcott) Songs from The Capeman, 1997; You're the One, 2000; *films:* performer (with Art Garfunkel) and composer of soundtrack, The Graduate, 1967; actor, Annie Hall, 1977; writer of screenplay and score, One-Trick Pony, 1980; musical, The Capeman (lyrics with Derek Walcott), 1998. Numerous Grammy Awards. *Publication:* At the Zoo, 1991. *Address:* c/o C. Vaughn Hazell, Paul Simon Music, Suite 500, 1619 Broadway, New York, NY 10019, USA.

SIMON, Hon. Sir Peregrine (Charles Hugo), Kt 2002; FLS; **Hon. Mr Justice Simon;** a Judge of the High Court, Queen's Bench Division, since 2002; Presiding Judge, North Eastern Circuit, 2006–08; *b* 20 June 1950; *s* of Baron Simon of Glaisdale, PC and of Fay Elizabeth Leicester (*née* Pearson); *m* 1980, Francesca Fortescue Hitchins; two *s* two *d*. *Educ:* Westminster School; Trinity Hall, Cambridge (MA). Called to the Bar, Middle Temple, 1973, Bencher, 1999; QC 1991; a Recorder, 1998–2002; a Dep. High Court Judge, 1999–2002. Mem. Council, Zool Soc., 1992–96 (Vice-Pres., 1995–96). *Address:* Royal Courts of Justice, Strand, WC2A 2LL.

SIMON, Robin John Hughes, FSA; art historian; Founder and Editor, The British Art Journal, since 1999; *b* 23 July 1947; *s* of Most Rev. (William) Glyn (Hughes) Simon, sometime Archbishop of Wales, and Sarah Sheila Ellen (*née* Roberts); *m* 1st, 1971, Jette Margaret Brooke (*see* J. M. Guillebaud) (marr. diss.); one *s* one *d*; 2nd, 1979, Joanna Christine Ross; one *d*. *Educ:* Cardiff High Sch.; Univ. of Exeter (BA Hons English); Courtauld Inst. of Art (MA Hist. European Art). FSA 1998. Lectr in Hist. of Art and English, Univ. of Nottingham, 1972–78; Historic Bldgs Rep., NT, 1979–80; Dir, Inst. European Studies, London, 1980–90; Editor, Apollo, 1990–97; Hd of Publications, NACF, and Ed., Art Qly, Annual Review, 1997–98. Vis. Lectr in Hist. of Art, Univ. of Warwick, 1978; Vis. Prof. in Hist. of Art and Architecture, Westminster Coll., Fulton, Mo, 1989. Arts Corresp., 1987–90, Art Critic, 1990–, Daily Mail; columnist, Tatler, 1994–98. Delmas Foundn Fellow, Venice, 1978. Member: Council, 1991–96, Exec. and Editl Cttee, 1993–96, 2005–, Walpole Soc.; Adv. Council, Paul Mellon Centre for Studies in British Art, 1993–98; Exec. Cttee, Assoc. of Art Historians, 1993–96; Cttee, Courtauld Assoc. (formerly Courtauld Assoc. of Former Students), 1992– (Chm., 1998–); Johnson Club, 1995–; Member, Advisory Committee: Battle of Britain Meml, 2001–02; Thomas Jones (1742–1803) Exhibn, 2001–03; Mem., Centenary Cttee, Nat. Mus. of Wales, 2006–; Trustee, Foundling Mus., 2008–. Writer of commissioned entertainments: Hogarth versus Handel, perf. Middle Temple, 2000; Music and Monarchs, perf. Villa Decius, Cracow, 2002; From Pencerrig to Pozzuoli, perf. Swansea Arts Fest., 2003. Patron, Lord Leighton Centenary Trust, 1994–96. *Publications:* (with Alastair Smart) The Art of Cricket, 1983; The Portrait in Britain and America, 1987; Hogarth, France and British Art, 2007; *edited:* Buckingham Palace: a complete guide, 1993; The King's Apartments, Hampton Court Palace, 1994; (with Gervase Jackson-Stops) The National Trust 1895–1995: 100 great treasures, 1995; Lord Leighton 1830–1896 and Leighton House, 1996; (with Christopher Woodward) A Rake's Progress: from Hogarth to Hockney, 1997; (with Rhian Harris) Enlightened Self-interest: the Foundling Hospital and Hogarth, 1997; Oxford: art and architecture, 1997; Somerset House: the building and collections, 2001; Public Artist, Private Passions: the world of Edward Linley Sambourne, 2001; (with Natasha McEnroe) The Tyranny of Treatment: Samuel Johnson, his friends, and Georgian medicine, 2003; Hogarth's Children, 2007; contrib. Oxford DNB; articles in British Art Jl, Apollo, Burlington Mag., TLS, Papers of Brit. Sch. at Rome, Spectator, Tatler, Opera Now, Country Life, Sunday Times, Mail on Sunday, etc. *Recreations:* cricket (Captain, Poor Fred's XI), music. *Address:* The British Art Journal, 46 Grove Lane, SE5 8ST. *T:* (020) 7787 6944. *Clubs:* Garrick, MCC.

SIMON, Siôn Llewelyn; MP (Lab) Birmingham, Erdington, since 2001; Parliamentary Under-Secretary of State, Department for Innovation, Universities and Skills, since 2008; *b* 23 Dec. 1968; *s* of Jeffrey Simon and Anne Loverini Simon (*née* Jones; now Owen); *m* 1992, Elizabeth Jane Middleton (marr. diss. 2003); one *s* two *d*. *Educ:* Handsworth Grammar Sch., Birmingham; Magdalen Coll., Oxford (BA PPE 1990). Res. Asst to George Robertson, MP, 1990–93; Sen. Manager, Guinness plc, 1993–95; freelance writer, 1995–97; columnist: Daily Telegraph, 1997–2001; News of the World, 2000–01; Associate Ed., The Spectator, 1997–. *Address:* House of Commons, SW1A 0AA.

SIMON, Susannah Kate; HM Diplomatic Service; Head, Climate Change and Energy Group, Foreign and Commonwealth Office, since 2006; *b* 7 June 1964; *d* of Peter and Sheila Simon; *m* 1994, Mikhail Kubekov; one *s*. *Educ:* Lady Eleanor Holles Sch., Hampton; St Hilda's Coll., Oxford (BA Hons Modern Langs). Entered FCO, 1988; Third, later Second Sec., Bonn, 1989–92; Second Sec., Almaty, 1992–93; FCO, 1994–99; First Sec. (EU), Bonn, 1999–2003; Dir, Eur. Policy, Immigration and Nationality Directorate, Home Office (on secondment), 2003–06. *Recreation:* gardening. *Address:* c/o Foreign and Commonwealth Office, King Charles Street, SW1A 2AH; *e-mail:* susannah.simon@fco.gov.uk.

SIMON, Tobias Robert Mark, (Toby); JP; Secretary to London Probation Board, 2002–05; *b* 31 May 1948; *s* of Anthony Percival Warwick, (Tim), Simon and Barbara Mary Simon; *m* 2001, Mrs Margaret Anne McAlpine; two step *s* one step *d*. *Educ:* Bryanston Sch., Dorset; Trinity Hall, Cambridge (MA); BA Open Univ. 1976. Department of Health and Social Security, 1969–87; Sen. Lectr, Civil Service Coll., 1984–87; Sec., Chartered Soc. of Physiotherapy, 1987–96. Gen. Man., Assoc. of Anaesthetists of GB and Ireland, Jan.–Aug. 2000; Interim Chief Exec., 2001–02, Gov., 2004–, Inst. of Optimum Nutrition. Chm. Scrutiny Commn, London Fire and Civil Defence Authy, 1999–2000; Mem., London Fire and Emergency Planning Authy, 2000–02; Member: Regl Legal Services Cttee for London, 2000–04; Investigating Cttee, Inst. of Legal Executives, 2002–. A Gen. Comr of Income Tax, 2001–. Mem. (Lab) Enfield LBC, 1998–2002 and 2006– (Chm., Social Inclusion Scrutiny Panel, 2000–02). Governor: Enfield County Sch., 1996–2004; Edmonton County Sch., 1999–. JP Enfield, 1998. *Address:* 39 Raleigh Road, Enfield EN2 6UD. *T:* (020) 8363 3684.

SIMONDS, Gavin Napier, FCA; Chairman: Craegmoor, since 2006; Apollo, since 2006; *b* 1 Jan. 1955; *s* of Duncan and Monica Simonds; *m* 1980, Venetia Steele; one *s* three *d*. *Educ:* Eton Coll. FCA 1980. Trainee, Peat Marwick Mitchell, 1975–81; Corporate Finance Exec., Rowe & Pitman, 1982–85; Corporate Finance Dir, UBS, 1985–88; Dir, Kleinwort Benson Ltd, 1988–93; Jt Man. Dir, Intercontinental Hotels Gp, 1993–96; Founding Dir, ResidenSea, 1997–2000; Consultant/Dir, various cos, 2000–04; Chairman: Peacock Gp plc, 2004–06; Jessops plc, 2004–07; Club Co., 2004–06; Red Funnel Gp, 2004–07. *Recreations:* family, sailing, tennis. *Address:* Craegmoor, Craegmoor House, Perdiswell Park, Worcs WR3 7NW. *Club:* Seaview Yacht.

SIMONDS-GOODING, Anthony James Joseph; company director; *b* 10 Sept. 1937; *s* of Major and Mrs Hamilton Simonds-Gooding; *m* 1st, 1961, Fiona (*née* Menzies) (marr. diss. 1982); three *s* two *d* (and one *s* decd); 2nd, 1982, Marjorie Anne, *d* of late William and Wendy Pennock; one step *s*. *Educ:* Ampleforth Coll.; BRNC, Dartmouth. Served

RN, 1953–59; Unilever, 1960–73; Marketing Dir, subseq. Man. Dir (UK), finally Gp Man. Dir, Whitbread & Co. plc, 1973–85; Saatchi plc, 1985–87 (Chm. and Chief Exec. of all communication and advertising cos worldwide); Chief Exec., British Satellite Broadcasting, 1987–90. Chairman: Aqueduct Enterprises, 1992–94; Ammirati Puris Lintas, 1994–96; Clark & Taylor (Dir, 1996–99); Pimco Properties, 2002–; OMG plc, 2003–; Director: Robinson and Sons, Chesterfield, 1993–99; Lilliput Group, 1993–94; Community Hosps Gp plc, 1995–2001; Newell & Sorrell, 1996–99; Kunick plc, 1997–2004; Blick plc, 1997–; CLK.MPL, 1999–; Corporate Edge, 1999–. Chairman: D&AD, 1992–; Design Business Assoc., 2003–; Director: ICA, 1992–94; Macmillan Cancer Relief (formerly Cancer Relief Macmillan Fund), 1992–2001; Brixton Prison Bd, 1994–97. Trustee: Rainbow Trust, 2001–04; Sea Cadets Assoc., 2001–03. *Recreations:* family, opera, sport, travel, oil painting. *Clubs:* Garrick, Sloane, Hurlingham.

SIMONET, Sir (Louis Marcel) Pierre, Kt 1985; CBE 1980 (OBE 1972); Director and Proprietor, Pharmacie Simonet, since 1955 (founded by father, 1926); *b* 6 March 1934; *s* of Marcel Simonet and Marguerite Simonet. *Educ:* Collège du St Esprit up to Higher School Certificate. Town Council of Curepipe: Mem., 1960; Vice-Chm., 1962; Chm., 1964; 1st Mem. for Curepipe, Legislative Assembly, 1976. Judge Assessor, Permt Arbitration Tribunal, 1984. Dir, Central Electricity Bd, 1972. Chm., Central Housing Authority, 1986–88. Mem., Ex-servicemen's Assoc., 1977; Pres., Widows and Orphans Pension Fund, 1978; Past Pres., Lions Club of Curepipe; Chm., Centre Culturel d'Expression Française (Founder Mem., 1960). Pres., Soc. of St Vincent de Paul. Testimonial, Royal Humane Soc. for life saving, 1962; Chevalier de l'Ordre National du Mérite (France), 1980. *Address:* Queen Mary Avenue, Floreal, Mauritius. *T:* (office) 6763532, *T:* (residence) 6865240. *Club:* Mauritius Racing.

SIMONS, Joanna Lesley, (Mrs J. L. Robinson); Chief Executive, Oxfordshire County Council, and Clerk to the Lieutenancy, since 2005; *b* 16 Aug. 1959; *d* of late Frank Simons and Philippa Simons; *m* 1987, Richard John Robinson, *qv*. *Educ:* Lady Margaret Sch., Fulham; Open Univ. Business Sch. (MBA 2002). FCIH 1987. Estates Officer, Hammersmith and Fulham LBC, 1980–83; Neighbourhood Manager, Newcastle CC, 1983–87; Dist Housing Officer, Barnet LBC, 1987–89; Asst Dir of Housing, Hounslow LBC, 1989–95; Dir of Housing, Greenwich LBC, 1995–2001; Chief Exec., Sutton LBC, 2001–05. Non-exec. Dir, South London Business, 2003–05. Board Member: London Wildlife Trust, 1981–83, 1988–93; Notting Hill Housing Trust, 1996–2005. Mem. Ct, Oxford Brookes Univ., 2007– (Chm. of Govs, 2008–). FRSA 2006. *Recreations:* travel, cooking, associating with birdwatchers. *Address:* Oxfordshire County Council, County Hall, New Road, Oxford OX1 1ND. *T:* (01865) 815330; *e-mail:* joanna.simons@oxfordshire.gov.uk.

SIMONS, Prof. John Philip, PhD, ScD; FRS 1989; CChem, FRSC; Dr Lee's Professor of Chemistry, Oxford University, 1993–99, now Emeritus; Fellow of Exeter College, Oxford, 1993–99; *b* 20 April 1934; *s* of Mark Isaac Simons and Rose (*née* Pepper); *m* 1st, 1956, Althea Mary (*née* Screaton) (*d* 1989); three *s*; 2nd, 1992, Elizabeth Ann Corps. *Educ:* Haberdashers' Aske's Hampstead Sch.; Sidney Sussex Coll., Cambridge (BA; PhD 1958; ScD 1975). CChem, FRSC 1975. Chemistry Department, University of Birmingham: ICI Fellow, 1959; Lectr, 1961; Reader in Photochemistry, 1977; Prof. of Photochem., 1979; Prof. of Physical Chemistry, Univ. of Nottingham, 1981–93. Erskine Fellow, Univ. of Canterbury, NZ, 1996; Vis. Prof., Univ. of Pittsburgh, 1998; Vis. Miller Prof., Univ. of Calif, Berkeley, 2000. Lectures: Tilden, RSC, 1983; Pimentel, UC Berkeley, 1998; Spiers, RSC, 1999; Burton, KCL, 2001; Humphry Davy, Royal Soc., 2001; Liversidge, RSC, 2007. Vice Pres., and Hon. Sec., 1981–93, Pres., 1993–95, Faraday Div., RSC. Member: Chemistry Cttee, 1983–85, Laser Facility Cttee, 1983–87, SERC; Comité de Direction, CNRS Lab. de Photophysique Moleculaire, Orsay, 1985–90, 2004–05; specially promoted scientific programme panel, NATO, 1985–88; Council, Royal Soc., 1999–2000; Scientific Adv. Cttee, FOM Inst., The Netherlands, 2004–06. Adv. Councillor, Ramsay Meml Fellowship Trust, 1991–2006. Ed., PhysChemComm, 1998–2002. Member Editorial Boards: Molecular Physics, 1980–96; Chemical Physics Letters, 1982–99; Jl Chem. Soc. Faraday Trans, 1990–98; Chemical Physics, 1994–2006; Phys Chem Chem Phys, 1998–. Hon. DSc Birmingham, 2002. Chemical Dynamics Award, 1994, Polanyi Medal, 1996, RSC; Davy Medal, Royal Soc., 2007. Citoyen d'Honneur de la Ville de Toulouse, 1997. *Publications:* Photochemistry and Spectroscopy, 1970; research papers in learned jls of molecular/chemical/biophysics. *Recreations:* writing and reading verse. *Address:* Physical and Theoretical Chemistry Laboratory, South Parks Road, Oxford OX1 3QZ. *T:* (01865) 275400.

SIMONS, Jonathan Michael; Master of Costs Office, (Taxing Master), Supreme Court, since 2001; *b* 15 June 1947; *s* of Eric Louis Simons and Eta Simons; *m* 1972, Judith Priscilla Cohen; one *s* one *d*. *Educ:* Priestmead Primary Sch., Harrow; Hasmonean Grammar Sch., Hendon. Admitted solicitor, 1971; Partner: Hart Fortgang, Solicitors, 1973–92; Simons Platman-Rechnic, Solicitors, 1993–98; Dep. Taxing Master, Supreme Court, 1996–2001. *Recreations:* history, travel, golf, supporting Brentford Football Club. *Address:* Supreme Court Costs Office, Clifford's Inn, Fetter Lane, EC4A 1DQ. *T:* (020) 7947 6459; *e-mail:* Master.Simons@judiciary.gsi.gov.uk. *Clubs:* MCC; Sandy Lodge Golf.

SIMONS, Prof. Peter Murray, PhD; FBA 2004; Professor of Philosophy, University of Leeds, since 1995; *b* 23 March 1950; *s* of Jack Simons and Marjorie Nita Simons (*née* Brown); *m* 1973, Susan Jane Walker; one *s* one *d*. *Educ:* Univ. of Manchester (BSc (Maths) 1971; MA 1973, PhD 1975 (Philos.)); Univ. of Salzburg (Habilitation Philos. 1986). Asst Librarian, Univ. of Manchester, 1975–77; Lectr in Philos., Bolton Inst., 1977–80; Lectr, 1980–95, Hon. Prof., 1996–, in Philos., Univ. of Salzburg. British Acad. Reader, 2004–06. Consultant, Ontek Corp., 1989–2001. MAE 2006. *Publications:* Parts, 1987; Philosophy and Logic in Central Europe from Bolzano to Tarski, 1992; about 200 articles in learned jls. *Recreations:* walking, choral singing, reading history, classical music. *Address:* Department of Philosophy, University of Leeds, Leeds LS2 9JT. *T:* (0113) 343 3298, *Fax:* (0113) 343 3265; *e-mail:* p.m.simons@leeds.ac.uk.

SIMONS, Richard Brian; Managing Director, Banana Split Productions, since 2006; Director, 2entertain Ltd, since 2006; *b* 5 Nov. 1952; *s* of Harry Simons and Ann Lily Simons (*née* Gold); one *s* one *d*; *m* 2001, Lisa, *d* of late Ron Hazlehurst and of Katherine Hazlehurst; one *s*. *Educ:* Royal Grammar Sch., High Wycombe; Exeter Coll., Oxford (BA Hons PPE). Independent Television News Ltd: Trainee TV Journalist, 1974–75; Writer, News at Ten, and Reporter, News at One, 1976–78; Prog. Editor and News Editor, News At One, 1979; Special Progs Producer, Foreign News Editor and Home News Editor, 1980–84; Head of Investigative Unit, and Associate Producer, D-Day: 40 Years On, 1984; Associate Prod., VE Day: 40 Years On, 1985; Sports Editor, and Mem., ITV Sport Network Cttee, 1985; Editor, World Cup Mexico, 1986; News Editor, 'Vote '87', General Election Results Special, 1986; Special Productions Editor, 1988–90; Commissioning Editor, Factual Progs, 1992–94, Head of Features, 1995–96, Carlton TV; Dir of Progs, Meridian Broadcasting, 1994–2000; Develt Dir, New Media Productions, United Broadcasting & Entertainment, 2000; Dir of TV, CSS-Stellar plc, 2001; Hd of Develt, GMTV, 2002–04. *Recreations:* my children, piano, papers and TV for pleasure, tennis.

SIMPKINS, Christopher John; Director General, Royal British Legion, since 2007; *b* Hornchurch, 28 Jan. 1952; *s* of Walter and Constance Simpkins; *m* 1974, Denise Dickens; one *s* one *d*. *Educ:* John Taylor High Sch.; Dovecliff Grammar Sch.; Birmingham Poly.; Stafford Coll. of Further Educn; Local Govt Trng Bd (Dip. Municipal Admin). Dep. Town Clerk, Tamworth BC, 1984–88; Chief Executive: South Holland DC, 1988–2003; Falkland Is Govt, 2003–07. Executive Vice Chairman: Falkland Is Develt Corp., 2003–07; Falkland Hldgs, 2003–07; Director: S Lincs Enterprise Agency and Venture Capital Ltd, 1993–99; Lincs Trng and Enterprise Council, 1996–98; Lincs and Rutland Connexions, 2001–03; Stanley Services, 2003–07; Member: Trent Reg. NHS Modernisation Bd, 2000–02 (Chm., Inequalities Task Force, 2000–02); Nat. Rural Affairs Forum, 2002–03. Chm., Corp., Stamford Coll. of Further Educn, 2000–03. Trustee: Officers' Assoc., 2007–; Nat. Meml Arboretum, 2007–. *Recreations:* good company, good food, good wine, motoring, gardening, rambling, commuting. *Address:* Royal British Legion, 199 Borough High Street, SE1 1AA. *Clubs:* Royal Over-Seas League, Cruising Assoc.

SIMPKINS, Peter B.; *see* Bowen-Simpkins.

SIMPKISS, (Richard) Jonathan; His Honour Judge Simpkiss; a Circuit Judge, since 2004; *b* 21 Oct. 1951; *s* of Dr Michael Simpkiss and Eileen Simpkiss; *m* 1985, Elizabeth Anne Weaver; two *d*. *Educ:* Magdalene Coll., Cambridge (BA 1974). Called to the Bar, Middle Temple, 1975, Bencher of Lincoln's Inn, 2003; a Recorder, 2000–04. *Recreations:* salmon fishing, shooting, gardening, wine. *Club:* Flyfishers'.

SIMPSON, family name of **Baron Simpson of Dunkeld.**

SIMPSON OF DUNKELD, Baron *cr* 1997 (Life Peer), of Dunkeld in Perth and Kinross; **George Simpson,** FCCA; FIMI; FCIT; Chief Executive, Marconi (formerly General Electric Co.) plc, 1996–2001; *b* 2 July 1942; *s* of William Simpson and Elizabeth Simpson; *m* 1964, Eva Chalmers; one *s* one *d*. *Educ:* Morgan Acad., Dundee; Dundee Inst. of Technology. ACIS. Sen. Accountant, Gas Industry, Scotland, 1962–69; Central Audit Man., BLMC, 1969–73; Financial Controller, Leyland Truck and Bus Div., 1973–76; Dir of Accounting, Leyland Cars, 1976–78; Finance and Systems Dir, Leyland Trucks, 1978–80; Managing Director: Coventry Climax Ltd, 1980–83; Freight Rover Ltd, 1983–86; Chief Exec. Officer, Leyland DAF, 1986–88; Man. Dir, 1989–91, Chm., 1991–94, and Chief Exec., 1991–92, Rover Gp; Dep. Chief Exec., BAe, 1992–94 (Dir, 1990–94); Chairman: Ballast Nedam Construction Ltd, 1992–94; Arlington Securities, 1993–94; Chief Exec., Lucas Industries plc, 1994–96. Non-executive Director: Pilkington plc, 1992–99; ICI plc, 1995–2001; Nestlé SA, 1999–2004; Alstom SA, 1998–; Triumph Gp Inc., 2000–; HBOS, 2001–02; Member, Supervisory Board: Northern Venture Capital, 1992–; Pro Share, 1992–94. Member: Exec. Cttee, SMMT, 1986– (Vice Pres., 1986–95, Pres., 1995–96, Council); Senate, Engrg Council, 1996–2002. Industrial Prof., Warwick Univ., 1991–. *Recreations:* golf, squash and Rugby (now spectating). *Address:* c/o House of Lords, SW1A 0PW. *Clubs:* Royal Automobile; Royal Birkdale Golf, New Zealand Golf (Weybridge), Gleneagles Golf, Rosemount Golf (Blairgowrie), Pine Valley Golf (NJ); Kenilworth RFC.

SIMPSON, His Honour Alan; a Circuit Judge, 1985–2000; *b* 17 April 1937; *s* of William Henry Simpson and Gladys Simpson; *m* 1965, Maureen O'Shea; one *s* one *d*. *Educ:* Leeds Grammar Sch.; Corpus Christi Coll., Oxford (MA). Called to the Bar, Inner Temple, 1962; a Recorder, 1975–85. Prosecuting Counsel to DHSS, North Eastern Circuit, 1977–85. Admin. Steward, 1994–, Vice-Chm., 2000–04, Chm., 2004, BBB of C. Mem., Sports Disputes Resolution Panel, 2000–. *Recreations:* music, books, sport (especially cricket and boxing). *Address:* Leeds Combined Court Centre, Oxford Row, Leeds LS1 3BG.

SIMPSON, Alan Francis, OBE 2000; author and scriptwriter since 1951 (in collaboration with Ray Galton, *qv*); *b* 27 Nov. 1929; *s* of Francis and Lilian Simpson; *m* 1958, Kathleen Phillips (*d* 1978). *Educ:* Mitcham Grammar Sch. *Television:* Hancock's Half Hour, 1954–61 (adaptation and trans., Fleksnes, Scandinavian TV, film and stage); Comedy Playhouse, 1962–63; Steptoe and Son, 1962–74 (US TV version, Sanford and Son; Dutch TV, Stiefbeen And Zoon; Scandinavian TV, Albert Och Herbert; Portuguese TV, Camilo & Filho); Galton-Simpson Comedy, 1969; Clochemerle, 1971; Casanova '74, 1974; Dawson's Weekly, 1975; The Galton and Simpson Playhouse, 1976–77; Paul Merton in Galton & Simpson's…, 1996, 1997; Fleksnes Fataliteter (specially written last episode of Hancock), Scandinavian TV, 2002; *films:* The Rebel, 1960; The Bargee, 1963; The Wrong Arm of the Law, 1963; The Spy with a Cold Nose, 1966; Loot, 1969; Steptoe and Son, 1971; Steptoe and Son Ride Again, 1973; Den Siste Fleksnes (Scandinavia), 1974; Skraphandlerne (Scandinavia), 1975; *theatre:* Way Out in Piccadilly, 1966; The Wind in the Sassafras Trees, 1968; Albert och Herbert (Sweden), 1981; Fleksnes (Norway), 1983; Mordet på Skolgatan 15 (Sweden), 1984; *radio:* The Galton & Simpson Radio Playhouse, 1998–99. Awards: Scriptwriters of the Year, 1959 (Guild of TV Producers and Directors); Best TV Comedy Series (Steptoe and Son, 1962, 1963, 1964, 1965 (Screenwriters Guild)); John Logie Baird Award (for outstanding contribution to Television), 1964; Best Comedy Series (Stiefbeen And Zoon, Dutch TV), 1966; Best Comedy Screenplay (Steptoe and Son, Screenwriters Guild), 1972; Best TV Series, Portugal Golden Globe (Camilo & Filho), 1995. *Publications:* (jointly with Ray Galton, *qv*): Hancock, 1961; Steptoe and Son, 1963; The Reunion and Other Plays, 1966; Hancock Scripts, 1974; The Best of Hancock, 1986. *Recreations:* Hampton & Richmond Borough FC (Pres.), gourmet travelling, guest speaking. *Address:* c/o Tessa Le Bars Management, 54 Birchwood Road, Petts Wood, Kent BR5 1NZ. *T:* (01689) 837084.

SIMPSON, Alan John; MP (Lab) Nottingham South, since 1992; *b* 20 Sept. 1948; *s* of Reginald James and Marjorie Simpson; *m* (marr. diss.); one *d* two *s*; *m* 2005, Pascale Quiviger; one *d*. *Educ:* Bootle Grammar Sch.; Nottingham Poly. (BSc Econ). Asst Gen. Sec., Nottingham Council of Voluntary Service, 1970–72; Develt Officer, Home Office Pilot Programme (Non Custodial Treatment of Offenders), 1972–74; Community Worker, Nottingham Areas Project, 1974–78; Res. and Inf. Officer, Nottingham Racial Equality Council, 1979–92. Cllr, Notts CC, 1985–93. Member: CND; Action Aid. *Publications:* (contrib.) Issues in Community Education, 1980; Stacking the Decks: race, inequality and council housing, 1981; I'll Never Forget What's His Name: one year on from the Scarman Report, 1982; (contrib.) The Right to a Home, 1984; Cuckoos in the Nest—Task Forces and urban policy, 1988; (with M. Read, MP) Against a Rising Tide—racism, Europe and 1992, 1991; Beyond the Famished Road—defence and common security, 1994; (contrib.) Football and Commons People, 1994. *Recreations:* tennis, football (lifelong supporter, Everton FC), vegetarian cooking, eclectic interest in music and reading. *Address:* House of Commons, SW1A 0AA. *T:* (020) 7219 4534.

SIMPSON, Prof. (Alfred William) Brian, DCL; FBA 1983; JP; Charles F. and Edith J. Clyne Professor of Law, University of Michigan, since 1987; Professor of Law, University of Kent, 1973–85, now Emeritus; *b* 17 Aug. 1931; *s* of Rev. Canon Bernard W. Simpson and Mary E. Simpson; *m* 1st, 1954, Kathleen Anne Seston (marr. diss. 1968); one *s* one *d*; 2nd, 1969, Caroline Elizabeth Ann Brown; one *s* two *d*. *Educ:* Oakham Sch., Rutland; The Queen's Coll., Oxford (MA 1958, DCL 1976). Nat. Service with Nigeria Regt, RWAFF, 1950–51; E Yorks Regt, TA, 1951–57 (Capt.). Junior Research Fellow, St Edmund Hall, Oxford, 1954–55; Fellow and Tutor, Lincoln Coll., Oxford, 1955–73; Dean: Faculty of Law, Univ. of Ghana, 1968–69; Faculty of Social Sciences, Univ. of Kent, 1975–78; Prof. of Law, Univ. of Chicago, 1984–86. Called to the Bar, Gray's Inn, 1994. Visiting Professor: Dalhousie Univ., 1964; Univ. of Chicago, 1979, 1980, 1982, 1984; Univ. of Michigan, 1985; Goodhart Prof. of Legal Sci., Univ. of Cambridge, 1993–94. Hon. Dep. District Attorney, Denver City, 1982. Member, Deptl Cttee on Obscenity and Film Censorship, 1977–79. Fellow, Amer. Acad. of Arts and Scis, 1993. JP Canterbury and St Augustine's, 1968–. Hon. QC 2001. Hon. Fellow, Lincoln Coll., Oxford, 1995. Hon. DLitt Ghana, 1993; Hon. LLD: Dalhousie, 2003; Kent, 2003. *Publications:* Introduction to the History of the Land Law, 1961, new edn as A History of the Land Law, 1986; (ed) Oxford Essays in Jurisprudence, 2nd Series, 1973; A History of the Common Law of Contract, 1975; Pornography and Politics, 1983; Cannibalism and the Common Law, 1984; (ed) A Biographical Dictionary of the Common Law, 1984; Legal Theory and Legal History: essays on the common law, 1987; Invitation to Law, 1988; In the Highest Degree Odious: detention without trial in wartime Britain, 1992; Leading Cases in the Common Law, 1995; Human Rights and the End of Empire: Britain and the genesis of the European Convention, 2001; articles in legal jls. *Recreations:* sailing, gardening. *Address:* University of Michigan Law School, Hutchins Hall, Ann Arbor, MI 48109–1215, USA. *T:* (734) 7630413, *Fax:* (734) 7639375; 3 The Butchery, Sandwich, Kent CT13 9DL. *T:* (01304) 612783; *e-mail:* bsimpson@umich.edu.

SIMPSON, Anthony Maurice Herbert, TD 1973; Manager, DAPHNE Programme, Justice and Home Affairs Task Force, later Directorate General, Justice and Home Affairs, European Commission, 1996–2000; *b* 28 Oct. 1935; *y s* of late Lt-Col Maurice Rowton Simpson, OBE, TD, DL and Mrs Renée Claire Simpson; *m* 1961, Penelope Gillian, *d* of late Howard Dixon Spackman; one *s* two *d*. *Educ:* Rugby; Magdalene College, Cambridge. BA 1959, LLM (LLB 1961), MA 1963. Leics and Derbys (PAO) Yeomanry, 1956–59; 21st and 23rd SAS Regts (TA), 1959–75, Major 1968. Called to Bar, Inner Temple, 1961; practised Midland and Oxford Circuit, 1961–75; Mem., Legal Service of European Commn, Brussels, 1975–79; MEP (C) Northamptonshire, later Northamptonshire and S Leics, 1979–94; contested (C) Northamptonshire and Blaby, Eur. Parly elecns, 1994; Quaestor of the European Parlt, 1979–87, and 1989–94; EDG spokesman on develt and co-operation, 1987–89; Mem., Inspectorate-Gen. of Services, Eur. Commn, 1994–96. Contested (C) West Leicester, Feb. and Oct. 1974. Treas., Eur. Foundn for Street Children Worldwide, 2003–; Chm., UK Sect., AIACE, 2005–. Mem., Bd of Govs, De Montfort Univ., 2004–08. Common Market Law Editor, Current Law, 1965–72. *Recreations:* walking, travelling. *Address:* 17 Alderney Street, SW1V 4ES. *T:* (020) 7233 9344. *Clubs:* Special Forces, Travellers.

SIMPSON, Prof. Brian; *see* Simpson, A. W. B.

SIMPSON, Brian; Member (Lab) North West England, European Parliament, since 2006; *b* Leigh, Lancs, 6 Feb. 1953; *s* of late John Hartley Simpson and Freda Simpson; *m* 1975, Linda Jane Gwynn; one *s* two *d*. *Educ:* Golborne Comprehensive Sch., Wigan; W Midlands Coll. of Educn, Walsall (Cert Ed). Teacher, City of Liverpool, 1974–89. Member: Merseyside CC, 1981–85; Warrington BC, 1987–91. MEP (Lab) Cheshire E, 1989–99, NW Reg., England, 1999–2004. Campaign Dir, NW Rail Campaign, 1994–; Vice Pres., Heritage Railways Assoc. *Recreations:* Rugby League, cricket, military history, heritage and modern railways. *Address:* (office) Lakeside, Prescott Road, St Helens WA10 3TT. *Club:* Golborne Sports and Social (Wigan).

SIMPSON, Air Vice-Marshal Charles Ednam; Director (Scotland), Royal Air Force Benevolent Fund, 1989–94; *b* 24 Sept. 1929; *s* of Charles and Margaret Simpson; *m* 1955, Margaret Riddell; two *s* one *d*. *Educ:* Stirling and Falkirk High Schools; Univ. of Glasgow (MB ChB); University of London (MSc). FFOM 1986; MFCM. British Defence Staff, Washington DC, 1975; Dep. Dir, Aviation Medicine, RAF, 1978; CO, RAF Hosp., Wegberg, 1981; CO, Princess Alexandra Hosp., Wroughton, 1982; Dir of Health and Research, RAF, 1984; Asst Surgeon General (Envtl Medicine and Res.), 1985; PMO HQ RAF Strike Comd, 1986–89; QHS 1985–89. HM Comr, Queen Victoria Sch., Dunblane, 1990–2000 (Chm. Bd, 1997–2000). *Recreations:* golf, birdwatching. *Address:* 12 Balmyle Grove, Dunblane, Perthshire FK15 0QB. *T:* (01786) 822191. *Club:* Royal Air Force.

SIMPSON, Claire Margaret; *see* Ward, C. M.

SIMPSON, David; District Judge (Magistrates' Courts) (formerly Metropolitan Stipendiary Magistrate), since 1993; *b* 29 July 1947; *s* of Albert Edward Simpson and Lily Simpson; *m* 1975, Jane Richards; one *s*. *Educ:* N Cestrian GS, Altrincham; Worthing High Sch. for Boys; King's Coll., London (LLM 1987). Admitted a solicitor, 1974. British Bank of ME, 1966–67; Court Clerk, Magistrates' Court: Worthing, 1967–74; Mansfield, 1975–76; Dep. Clerk, 1976–82, Clerk, 1982–93, to the Justices, Uxbridge. Part-time Immigration Special Adjudicator, 1996–2000. Vice-Pres., Assoc. of Magisterial Officers, 1981–82; Member: Council, Justices' Clerks' Soc., 1987–93; Magisterial Cttee, Judicial Studies Bd, 1990–93, 2003–; Inner London Magistrates' Courts' Cttee, 1998–2001; Youth Justice Bd, 2004–. Mem., Adv. Panel on Children's Viewing, BBFC, 1999–. Gov., Windsor Boys' Sch., 2002–. FRSA 2007. *Address:* West London Magistrates' Court, 181 Talgarth Road, W6 8DN.

SIMPSON, David; MP (DemU) Upper Bann, since 2005; Member (DemU) Upper Bann, Northern Ireland Assembly, since 2003; *b* 16 Feb. 1959; *m* Elaine Elizabeth; one adopted *s* two adopted *d*. *Educ:* Killicomaine High Sch.; Coll. of Business Studies, Belfast. Businessman. Mem. (DemU), Craigavon BC, 2001–; Mayor of Craigavon, 2004–05. *Address:* (office) 13 Thomas Street, Portadown, Craigavon, Co. Armagh BT62 3NP; House of Commons, SW1A 0AA.

SIMPSON, David Rae Fisher; Economic Adviser, Standard Life Assurance Co., 1988–2001; Deputy Chairman, Water Industry Commission for Scotland, since 2005; *b* 29 Nov. 1936; *s* of late David Ebenezer Simpson and Roberta Muriel Wilson; *m* 1980, Barbara Dianne Goalen, *d* of late N. and Mrs G. Inglis, Edinburgh; one *s* (and one step *s* one step *d*). *Educ:* Skerry's Coll.; Edinburgh and Harvard Univs. MA 1st cl. hons Econs Edinburgh; PhD Econs Harvard. Instr in Econs, Harvard Univ., 1963–64; Assoc. Statistician, UN HQ, NY, 1964–65; Res. Officer, Econ. Res. Inst., Dublin, 1965–67; Lectr in Polit. Economy, UCL, 1967–69; Sen. Lectr in Econs, Univ. of Stirling, 1969–74; University of Strathclyde: Prof. and Dir, Fraser of Allander Inst., 1975–80, Res. Prof., 1980–85; Prof., Dept of Economics, 1985–88. Contested (SNP) Berwick and E Lothian Division, 1970 and Feb. 1974. *Publications:* Problems of Input-Output Tables and Analysis, 1966; General Equilibrium Analysis, 1975; The Political Economy of Growth, 1983; The Challenge of New Technology, 1987; The End of Macro Economics?, 1994; Regulating Pensions, 1996; Re-Thinking Economic Behaviour, 2000; articles in Econometrica, Financial Times, Scientific American, Spectator. *Recreation:* tilting at windmills. *Address:* 24B/6 Polwarth Terrace, Edinburgh EH11 1NA.

SIMPSON, David Richard Salisbury, OBE 1989; Founder and Director, International Agency on Tobacco and Health, since 1991; *b* 1 Oct. 1945; *s* of late Richard Salisbury Simpson and of Joan Margaret Simpson (*née* Braund). *Educ:* Merchiston Castle School, Edinburgh. ACA 1969; FCA 1979 (but resigned from Institute, 1981). Teacher at Cadet College, Hasan Abdal, West Pakistan, 1963–64 (VSO). Peat, Marwick, Mitchell & Co., Chartered Accountants, 1964–72; Scottish Director, Shelter, Campaign for the Homeless, 1972–74; Director: Amnesty International (British Section), 1974–79; ASH, 1979–90. Sundry journalism, broadcasting and public lectures. Hon. Consultant, Clin. Trial Service Unit and Epidemiol Studies Unit, Oxford Univ., 1991–. Vis. Prof., LSHTM, 2000–. News Ed., Tobacco Control, 1993–. Trustee, Pier Arts Centre, Stromness, 1994–. Hon. MFPH (Hon. MFPHM 1991). *Publications:* Doctors and Tobacco: medicine's big challenge, 2000; (with J. Crofton) Tobacco: a global threat, 2002. *Recreations:* friends, reading, music, hill-walking, Orkney. *Address:* Clinical Trial Service Unit, Richard Doll Building, Old Road Campus, Roosevelt Drive, Headington, Oxford OX3 7LF.

SIMPSON, Lt-Col (Retd) David Sackville Bruce, CBE 1990; Chief Executive, Civil Service Catering Organisation, 1981–91, retired; *b* 18 March 1930; *s* of Henry and Violet Simpson; *m* 1956, Margaret Elizabeth Goslin; two *s* three *d*. *Educ:* Brockley Grammar Sch.; Westminster Technical Coll. FIH. Regular Officer, Army Catering Corps (retd in rank of Lt-Col), 1950–75; Principal Education Catering Organiser, Inner London Education Authority, 1975–81. *Recreations:* golf, squash. *Address:* 1 Tavistock Road, Fleet, Hants GU51 4EH. *T:* (01252) 625795.

SIMPSON, Dennis Charles; business consultant and lecturer; Managing Director, Axtel (UK) Ltd, 1986–88; *b* 24 Oct. 1931; *s* of late Arthur and Helen Simpson; *m* 1st, 1964, Margery Bruce Anderson (marr. diss.); three *s* one *d*; 2nd, 1983, Susan Gaynor Conway-Williams. *Educ:* Manchester Univ. (BA). FInstPS. 2nd Lieut Royal Signals, 1952–54; commercial appts, Philips Electrical Industries, 1956–63; Group Purchasing Manager, STC Ltd, 1963–66; Gp Purchasing Controller, Rank Organisation, 1966–69; Gen. Man., Cam Gears (S Wales) Ltd, 1969–72; Industrial Dir for Wales, Dept of Industry, 1972–75; Industrial Dir for Wales, Welsh Office, 1975–76; Business Agent, Welsh Develt Agency, 1983–85. Chairman: Spencer Harris Ltd, 1976–81; Grainger Hydraulics Ltd, 1976–81; Wellfield Engineering, 1976–81; Director: Beechwood Holdings, 1976–81; Gower Technology Ltd, 1983–87; Video Interactive Systems Ltd, 1983–87; Gower Alarms Ltd, 1985–87; Video Interactive Teaching Aids Ltd, 1985–87. *Recreations:* golf, bridge, reading war histories.

SIMPSON, Derek; Joint General Secretary, Unite, since 2007 (General Secretary, Amicus, 2004–07, on merger with Transport and General Workers' Union); *b* 23 Dec. 1944; *m* Freda; three *c*. *Educ:* Sheffield Central Tech. Sch.; Open Univ. (BA 1987). Engrg apprentice, Firth Brown Tools, 1960–66; with Balfour Darwin, 1966–81; full-time official, AEU, 1981–2002; elected Gen. Sec., Amicus-AEEU, 2002; Jt Gen. Sec., Amicus, 2002–04. *Address:* Unite, 35 King Street, Covent Garden, WC2E 8JG.

SIMPSON, Dr Diana, FEI, FFSSoc, FIFST, CEng, FIMMM, EurChem, CSci, CChem, FRSC; Forensic Scientist (civil and criminal); Principal Consultant, Analysis Industry, since 1975; *b* 26 Sept. 1929; *d* of Simon and Leah Caplan; *m* 1960, W. Gordon Simpson (*d* 1999). *Educ:* Oldham Municipal High Sch.; Manchester and Salford Polys; Northern Poly. (MPhil 1970, PhD 1974, London Univ.). CChem, FRSC 1979; FRMS 1987; FIFST 1988; CEng 1989; EurChem 1993; FIM 1997; CSci 2004; FFSSoc 2006. Asst Tech. Officer, ICI Pharmaceutical Div., 1953; Dep. to Control and Develt Dir, Pfizer Ltd, 1953–60; Hd, Analytical Services, Bakelite Xylonite Ltd, 1960–75. Member of Council and Trustee: RSC; Analytical Chem. Trust Fund, RSC; Inst. Food Sci. and Technol.; Soc. Chem. Industry. Life MInstD, 1980. Distinguished Service Award: Soc. Analytical Chem., 1984; RSC, 1994. *Publications:* (with W. G. Simpson) An Introduction to Applications of Light Microscopy to Analysis, 1988; (ed with W. G. Simpson) The COSHH Regulations: a practical guide, 1991; contrib. jls incl. British Plastics, The Analyst, Trends in Analytical Chem., Analysis and Chromatography. *Recreations:* children and animal charities, reading, light microscopy, perpetuance of the use of correct English, attempting to persuade people that English and American are two different languages, word and mathematical puzzles, trying to out-predict the FTSE, watching cricket. *T:* (01206) 851775.

SIMPSON, Edward Alexander, CB 1993; Director, Northern Ireland Court Service, 1987–95; *b* 25 Dec. 1935; *s* of late Robert Simpson and Eva (*née* Graham); *m* 1960, Audrey Gordon; two *s*. *Educ:* Regent House Sch., Newtownards; Queen's Univ., Belfast (BSc Econ). Joined Ministry of Finance, 1953; various posts in Mins of Health and Local Govt and DoE, 1956–77; Asst Sec., Transportation and the Fire Service, 1977–81; Belfast Develt Officer, 1981–87. *Recreations:* golf, bowls, walking, wine. *Address:* 28 Londonderry Avenue, Comber, Newtownards BT23 5ES.

SIMPSON, Edward Hugh, CB 1976; FSS 1947; Visiting Research Fellow, University of Warwick, since 1993; Deputy Secretary, Department of Education and Science, 1973–82, retired; *b* 10 Dec. 1922; *o s* of Hugh and Mary Simpson, of Brookfield, Ballymena, Co. Antrim; *m* 1947, Rebecca, *er d* of Sam and Elizabeth Gibson, Ernevale, Kesh, Co. Fermanagh; one *s* one *d*. *Educ:* Coleraine Academical Institution; Queen's Univ., Belfast (BSc (1st cl. Hons Mathematics), 1942); Mathematical Statistics res., Christ's Coll., Cambridge (Scholar), 1945–47. Foreign Office, Bletchley Park, 1942–45; Min. of Education, 1947–50 and 1952–56; HM Treasury, 1950–52; Commonwealth Fund Fellow, USA, 1956–57; Private Sec. to Lord President of Council and Lord Privy Seal, 1957–60; Dep. Dir, Commonwealth Educn Liaison Unit, 1960–62; Sec., Commonwealth Educn Conf., New Delhi, 1962; Asst Sec., DES, 1962–68; Under-Sec., Civil Service Dept, 1968–71, DES, 1971–73. Sen. Hon. Res. Fellow, Birmingham Univ., 1983–88. Chairman: Nat. Assessment Panel, Schools Curriculum Award, 1983; Educn Grants Adv. Service, 1987; Gov. and Chm., Professional Cttee, Bishop Grosseteste Coll., Lincoln, 1984; Trustee, Educn 2000, 1987. Consultant: Educn Management Information Exchange, 1986–89; Dixons plc, 1987. FRSA 1991. Hon. LLD Hull, 1992. *Publications:* articles in statistical and educn journals. *Address:* 40 Frays Avenue, West Drayton, Middx UB7 7AG. *T:* (01895) 443417. *Club:* Athenæum.

SIMPSON, Prof. Elizabeth, OBE 2004; FMedSci; Professor of Immunogenetics, Imperial College London (formerly Royal Postgraduate Medical School, subsequently Imperial College School, then Faculty, of Medicine, London University), 1994–2004, now Emeritus Professor of Transplantation Biology; Head of Transplantation Biology Group, 1984–2004, and Deputy Director, 1994–2004, MRC Clinical Sciences Centre, Hammersmith Hospital (formerly Clinical Research Centre, Harrow); *b* 29 April 1939; *d* of J. H. G. Browne and O. R. Browne (*née* Wood); *m* 1963 (marr. diss. 1973); one *d* with Prof. Peter Charles Leonard Beverley, *qv*. *Educ:* Old Palace Sch. for Girls, Croydon; Girton Coll., Cambridge (BA Nat. Sci. 1960; VetMB 1963; MA 1964). Vet. Surg., private practice, Canada, 1963–65; Res. Virologist, Ottawa, 1965–66; Univ. Demonstrator in Animal Pathology, Cambridge Univ., 1966–69; Research Scientist: NIMR 1969–71;

Clin. Res. Centre, Harrow, 1971–1984. Visiting Scientist: All India Inst. Med. Res., Delhi, 1971; Nat. Inst. Health, Bethesda, 1972–73; Jackson Lab., Maine, 1976–. FMedSci 1999. *Publications:* (ed) T Cell Receptors, 1995; reviews and scientific papers on transplantation, immunology and genetics in jls. *Recreations:* reading, writing, talking, listening, walking. *Address:* Transplantation Biology Group, Imperial College London, Hammersmith Hospital, Du Cane Road, W12 0NN. *T:* (020) 8383 8282.

SIMPSON, Sir Gilbert, (Sir Gil), KNZM 2000; QSM 1986; Founder and Chief Executive, Jolly Good Software Pty Ltd, since 2006; *b* 5 April 1948; *m* 1998, Joy Reilly. *Educ:* Christchurch Boys' High Sch. Clerk, Nat. Bank of NZ, 1967–71; Sen. Programmer, NZ Aluminium Shelters, 1971–74; Data Processing Manager, Whitcoulls NZ, 1974–78; formed own co., 1978; CEO, Aoraki Corp. Ltd, 1982–2003; Dir, Jade Software Corp., 2003–06. Dir, Reserve Bank of NZ, 1997. Pres., Royal Soc. of NZ, 2000. Fellow: NZ Computer Soc., 1998; NZ Inst. Mgt, 1999; NZ Inst. Dirs, 2000. *Recreations:* tramping, flying, railway enthusiast, following cricket and Rugby.

SIMPSON, Ian; artist and writer; Course Director, Open College of the Arts, 1996–99, now Consultant (East Regional Organizer and Visual Arts Course Leader, 1992–96); *b* 12 Nov. 1933; *s* of Herbert William and Elsie Simpson; *m* 1st, 1958, Joan (*née* Charlton) (marr. diss. 1982); two *s* one *d*; 2nd, 1982, Birgitta Willcocks (*née* Brädde). *Educ:* Bede Grammar Sch., Sunderland; Sunderland Coll. of Art; Royal Coll. of Art. ARCA 1958. Freelance artist and illustrator, 1958–63; Hornsey Coll. of Art: Lectr, 1963–66; Head, Dept of Visual Research, 1966–69; Head, Dept of Co-ordinated Studies, 1969–72; Principal, 1972–86, Head, 1986–88, St Martin's Sch. of Art; Asst Rector, London Inst., 1986–88. Exhibited various exhibns, Britain, USA, etc; one-man exhibn, Cambridge, 1975, Durham, 1977, Blandford, 1985, Chappel, Colchester, 1994. Mem. Council, CNAA, 1974–80 (Chm., Fine Art Bd, 1976–81). Pres., Nat. Soc. for Art Educn, 1976. Consultant, Leisure Study Group Ltd, 1986–87. FSAE 1976; FRSA 1983. *Publications:* Eyeline, 1968; Drawing: seeing and observation, 1973; Picture Making, 1973; Guide to Painting and Composition, 1979; Painters Progress, 1983, repr. as Practical Art School, 1995; Encyclopedia of Drawing Techniques, 1987; The Challenge of Landscape Painting, 1990; The New Guide to Illustration, 1990; Anatomy of Humans, 1991; Collins Complete Painting Course, 1993; Collins Complete Drawing Course, 1994. *Television Programmes:* Eyeline (10 programmes), 1968, 1969; Picture Making (10 programmes), 1973, 1976; Reading the Signs (5 programmes), 1977–78. *Recreations:* reading, music. *Address:* 20A The Paddocks, Bures, Suffolk CO8 5DF.

SIMPSON, Ian Christopher; QC (Scot.) 2005; Sheriff of Lothian and Borders at Edinburgh, 2006; Temporary High Court Judge, 2004–07; *b* 5 July 1949; *s* of David F. Simpson and J. O. S. Simpson (*née* Dickie); *m* 1973, Anne Strang; two *s. Educ:* Glenalmond; Edinburgh Univ. (LLB). Admitted Faculty of Advocates, 1974; Floating Sheriff, 1988–91; Sheriff: at Airdrie, 1991–2003; of Tayside, Central and Fife at Dunfermline, 2003–06. *Recreations:* golf, travel, reading. *Address:* 30 Cluny Drive, Edinburgh EH10 6DP. *T:* (0131) 447 3363. *Clubs:* Royal and Ancient (St Andrews); Luffness Golf.

SIMPSON, James; *see* Simpson, W. J.

SIMPSON, Very Rev. James Alexander; an Extra Chaplain to the Queen in Scotland, since 2004 (Chaplain, 1992–2004); Moderator of the General Assembly of the Church of Scotland, 1994–95; *b* 9 March 1934; *s* of Robert and Marion Simpson; *m* 1960, Helen Gray McCorquodale; three *s* two *d. Educ:* Glasgow Univ. (BSc Hons 1955; BD 1958); Union Seminary, New York (STM 1959). Minister: Grahamston Church, Falkirk, 1960–66; St John's Renfield Church, Glasgow, 1966–76; Dornoch Cathedral, 1976–97; Interim Minister: Almondbank Tibbermore, Perth, 1997–98; Brechin Cathedral, 1998–99. Hon. DD Aberdeen, 1995. *Publications:* There is a Time To, 1971; Marriage Questions Today, 1975; Doubts Are Not Enough, 1982; Holy Wit, 1986, 4th edn 2002; Laughter Lines, 1988, 2nd edn 1991; The Master Mind, 1989; History of Dornoch Cathedral, 1989; More Holy Wit, 1990; Keywords of Faith, 1992; Royal Dornoch Golf Club (a pictorial history), 1992; All about Christmas, 1994; The Laugh shall be First, 1998; Life, Love and Laughter, 2002, 2nd edn 2003; A Funny Way of Being Serious, 2005. *Recreation:* golf. *Address:* Dornoch, Perth Road, Bankfoot, Perth PH1 4ED. *Club:* Royal Dornoch Golf (Captain, 1993).

SIMPSON, James Walter Thorburn, OBE 2007; RIBA; FRIAS; Partner, Simpson & Brown, Architects, since 1977; *b* 27 July 1944; *s* of Robert Alison Crighton Simpson, TD, FRIBA, and Rosemary Euphemia (*née* Morrison); *m* 1968, Ann Mary Bunney; two *d. Educ:* Belhaven Hill Sch.; Trinity Coll., Glenalmond; Edinburgh Coll. of Art (BArch Hons). RIBA 1970; FRIAS 1985. Trained as architect with Ian G. Lindsay and with Sir Bernard Feilden, 1972–77 (work on St Paul's, Norwich and St Giles' Cathedral, Edinburgh); estabd Simpson & Brown, with Stewart Brown, 1977. Building projects in Scotland and NE England, including: St Giles' Cathedral; Alderman Fenwick's House, Newcastle-upon-Tyne; Auchinleck House, Ayrshire; Kinlochmoidart House, Inverness-shire; Rosslyn Castle and Chapel, Midlothian; 26–31 Charlotte Square, Edinburgh. Curator, William Adam Exhibn, Scottish Nat. Portrait Gall., 1989. Surveyor of the Fabric, York Minster, 1994–95. Mem., Ancient Monuments Bd for Scotland, 1984–96. Comr, Royal Commn on Ancient and Historical Monuments of Scotland, 1997–2006. *Publications:* Vitruvius Scoticus, 1980; The Care of Historic Buildings and Ancient Monuments by Government Departments in Scotland, 1995; The British Standard Guide to the Principles of the Conservation of Historic Buildings, 1998. *Recreations:* playing Scottish small pipes, Norfolk Terriers, thinking about architecture, learning Gaelic, India. *Address:* (office) St Ninian's Manse, Quayside Street, Edinburgh EH6 6EJ. *T:* (0131) 555 4678; 40 Raeburn Place, Edinburgh EH4 1HL. *T:* (0131) 332 7294.

SIMPSON, Jane Ann; *see* Plant, J. A.

SIMPSON, Dr Jennifer Linda, (Mrs G. M. M. Thoms), OBE 2000; FRCPE; Founder, and Chief Executive, British Association of Medical Managers, since 1991; *b* 18 April 1953; *d* of Dr I. M. Simpson and Janette Simpson; *m* 1981, Dr Gavin M. M. Thoms; one *s* two *d. Educ:* Univ. of Manchester Med. Sch. (MB ChB, DCH); Sheffield Business Sch. (MBA, DBA). Clinical posts in Manchester and Sheffield, 1976–80; clinical and managerial posts, Sheffield Children's Hosp., 1983–90; Dir, Resource Mgt, Mersey RHA, 1990–94. Clinical Advr, Resource Mgt Team, DoH, 1991–93. Vis. Prof., Centre for Leadership, York Univ.; Vis. Fellow, Cranfield Sch. of Mgt. *Publications:* Clinicians as Managers, 1994; Clinical Governance in the New NHS, 1997; Appraisal in Action, 1998; The Duties of the Medical Director, 2001; Consultant Careers: times of change, 2001; Making Sense: a career framework for medical management, 2003. *Recreations:* music, working with a talented group of musicians running an independent recording label, physical fitness, and sheer enjoyment of my three children. *Address:* British Association of Medical Managers, Petersgate House, St Petersgate, Stockport SK1 1HE. *T:* (0161) 474 1141, *Fax:* (0161) 474 7167; *e-mail:* jenny@bamm.co.uk.

SIMPSON, John Andrew; Chief Editor, Oxford English Dictionary, since 1993; Fellow of Kellogg College (formerly Rewley House), Oxford, since 1991; *b* 13 Oct. 1953; *s* of Robert Morris Simpson and Joan Margaret (*née* Sersale); *m* 1976, Hilary Croxford; two *d. Educ:* Dean Close Sch., Cheltenham; Univ. of York (BA Hons English Literature); Univ. of Reading (MA Medieval Studies). Editorial Asst, Supplement to OED, 1976–79; Editor, Concise Oxford Dictionary of Proverbs, 1979–81; Sen. Editor, Supplement to OED, 1981–84; Editor (New Words), OED, 1984–86; Co-editor, OED, 1986–93. Mem., Faculty of English, Univ. of Oxford, 1993–. Editl Consultant, Australian National Dictionary, 1986–88. Mem. Adv. Cttee, Opera del Vocabolario Italiano, Florence, 2003–. Vis. Asst Prof., Dept of English, Univ. of Waterloo, Ont, Canada, 1985. Mem., Philolog. Soc., 1994–; Founding Mem. and Mem. Exec. Cttee, European Fedn of Nat. Instns for Lang., 2003–. BBC TV series, Balderdash & Piffle, 2006, 2007. FRSA 2007. Hon. LittD ANU, 1999. *Publications:* (ed) Concise Oxford Dictionary of Proverbs, 1982, 3rd edn 1998; (contrib.) Oxford English, 1986; (contrib.) Words, 1989; (ed) Oxford English Dictionary, 2nd edn (with Edmund Weiner) 1989, 3rd edn (online) 2000–; (contrib.) Wörterbücher: ein internationales Handbuch zur Lexikographie, 1990; (ed with John Ayto) Oxford Dictionary of Modern Slang, 1992; (ed with Edmund Weiner) OED Additions series, vols 1 and 2, 1993, (Gen. Ed.) vol. 3, 1997; The First English Dictionary 1604, 2007; articles in Medium Aevum, English Today, and other lexicographical and linguistic publications. *Recreation:* cricket (Holton CC). *Address:* Chestnut Lodge, 7 St Mary's Close, Wheatley, Oxford OX33 1YP. *T:* (office) (01865) 353728; *e-mail:* john.simpson@kellogg.ox.ac.uk.

SIMPSON, John Anthony, CVO 2002; RIBA; architect; Principal, John Simpson & Partners, since 1980; *b* 9 Nov. 1954; *s* of John Simpson and Lydia Simpson; *m* 1990, Erica; two *s* one *d. Educ:* UCL (BSc Hons; DipArch). RIBA 1981. Main commissions: Paternoster Square Develt, City of London, 1990–96 (AIA Honor Award for Urban Design); W Range of Gonville Court, Gonville and Caius Coll., Cambridge, 1993–98 (RICS Conservation Award); Brownsword Market Bldg, Poundbury, 1996–2000; Queen's Gallery, Buckingham Palace, 1998–2002 (RIBA and Royal Fine Art Commn Trust awards, 2003); St Mary's Ch Hall and Vicarage, Old Church St, Chelsea, 1998–2002 (RBKC Envmt Award); masterplan for 4500 new houses, Swindon Southern Develt Area, 2001–05; Cathcart Mansion, 5th Avenue, NY, 2002–05; current major commissions: new range for Gisborne Ct, Peterhouse, Cambridge; redevelt of Royal Worcester Porcelain Wks, Worcester, and of old Rochester Row Police Stn site at 68 Vincent Square, Westminster; Stanhope redevelt, 5th Ave, NY. *Recreations:* music, opera, vintage motor cars. *Address:* 29 Great James Street, WC1N 3ES. *T:* (020) 7405 1285, *Fax:* (020) 7831 1781; *e-mail:* design@johnsimpsonarchitects.com.

SIMPSON, Very Rev. John Arthur, OBE 2001; Dean of Canterbury, 1986–2000, now Emeritus; *b* 7 June 1933; *s* of Arthur Simpson and Mary Esther Simpson; *m* 1968, Ruth Marian (*née* Dibbens); one *s* two *d. Educ:* Cathays High School, Cardiff; Keble Coll., Oxford (BA, 2nd cl. Mod. History 1956, MA 1960); Clifton Theological Coll. Deacon 1958, priest 1959; Curate: Leyton, 1958–59; Christ Church, Orpington, 1959–62; Tutor, Oak Hill Theol Coll., 1962–72; Vicar of Ridge, Herts, 1972–79; Director of Ordinands and Post-Ordination Training, Diocese of St Albans, 1975–81; Hon. Canon of St Albans Cathedral, 1977–79; Residentiary Canon, St Albans, and Priest-in-charge of Ridge, 1979–81; Archdeacon of Canterbury and Canon Res. of Canterbury Cathedral, 1981–86. Dir, Ecclesiastical Insurance Group (formerly Ecclesiastical Insurance Office), 1983–2000. Chm. Govs, King's Sch., Canterbury, 1986–2000. Hon. DD Kent, 1994. *Recreations:* travel, theatre, opera. *Address:* Flat D, 9 Earls Avenue, Folkestone, Kent CT20 2HW.

SIMPSON, John (Cody Fidler-), CBE 1991; World (formerly Foreign) Affairs Editor, BBC, since 1988; *b* 9 Aug. 1944; *s* of Roy Simpson Fidler-Simpson and Joyce Leila Vivienne Cody; *m* 1965, Diane Jean Petteys (marr. diss. 1995), El Cajon, California; two *d*; *m* 1996, Adèle Krüger; one *s. Educ:* St Paul's School; Magdalene Coll., Cambridge (MA; Hon. Fellow, 1999). FRGS 1990. Reporter, BBC Radio News, 1970; BBC correspondent, Dublin, 1972; Common Market correspondent (based in Brussels), 1975; Southern Africa correspondent (based in Johannesburg), 1977; Diplomatic correspondent, BBC Television News, 1978; BBC Political Editor, 1980; Presenter and Correspondent, BBC-TV News, 1981; Diplomatic Editor, BBC-TV, 1982–88. Associate Editor, The Spectator, 1991–96. Chancellor, Roehampton Univ., 2005–. Hon. DLitt: De Montfort, 1995; Nottingham, 2000; Dundee, Southampton, 2003; St Andrews, Roehampton, 2005. RTS Journalist of the Year, 1990, 2000; BAFTA Award, 1992, 2000; Peabody Award, USA, 1998; Internat. Emmy Award for reporting in Afghanistan, 2002; Bayeux War Correspondent's Award, 2002; RTS award for reporting in Afghanistan and Iraq, 2002; Mungo Park Medal, RSGS, 2004. *Publications:* (ed jtly) The Best of Granta, 1966; The Disappeared: voices from a secret war, 1985; Behind Iranian Lines, 1988; Despatches from the Barricades, 1990; From the House of War: Baghdad and the Gulf, 1991; The Darkness Crumbles: the death of Communism, 1992; In the Forests of the Night: drug-running and terrorism in Peru, 1993; (ed) The Oxford Book of Exile, 1995; (jtly) Lifting the Veil: life in revolutionary Iran, 1995; Wars Against Saddam, 2003; *autobiography:* Strange Places, Questionable People, 1998; A Mad World, My Masters: tales from a traveller's life, 2000; News from No Man's Land, 2002; Days from a Different World, 2005; Not Quite World's End, 2007; *novels:* Moscow Requiem, 1981; A Fine And Private Place, 1983. *Recreations:* collecting obscure books, travelling to obscure places, and returning to Suffolk. *Address:* c/o Kruger Cowne Ltd, Unit 18G, Chelsea Wharf, 15 Lots Road, SW10 0QJ. *Clubs:* Garrick, Travellers, Chelsea Arts.

SIMPSON, (John Ernest) Peter, FRCS; Director, Health Management Systems, 1996–99; *b* 30 Jan. 1942; *s* of John and Alice Bewick Simpson; *m* 1st, 1964, Valerie Joan Lamb (marr. diss. 1987); one *s* one *d*; 2nd, 1996, Elizabeth Anne Lang. *Educ:* Jesus Coll., Oxford (MA, BM BCh); St Thomas's Hosp. Med. Sch. (Schol.). MFPHM. Surgical training, St Thomas' and Northwich Park Hosps, 1966–78; Lectr, Community Medicine, St Thomas' Hosp., 1974–75; Tutor, King's Fund Coll., 1975–78; Management, Planning Policy and Internat. Divs, DHSS, 1978–88; Regl MO, Mersey RHA, 1988–93; Med. Advr, London Implementation Gp, 1993–96. Pres., British Assoc. of Day Surgery, 1998–2001. *Publications:* Going Home (from hospital) (ed jtly), 1981; articles on day case surgery and organisation of surgical and other clinical services. *Recreations:* golf, music. *Address:* White Cottage, 21 Clive Road, Esher, Surrey KT10 8PS. *T:* (01372) 463319. *Clubs:* Royal Society of Medicine; Royal Mid Surrey Golf.

SIMPSON, Julia Elizabeth; Head of Corporate Communications, British Airways, since 2007; *b* 15 May 1958; *d* of Jack Victor Simpson and Ellen Kathleen Simpson (*née* Powell); *m* 2002, Graham Hassell; two *d. Educ:* Lady Margaret Sch., Fulham; Royal Acad. of Dancing; Univ. of Warwick (BA Spanish and European Studies); Salamanca Univ. (1978). News reporter, Iberian Daily Sun and Majorca Daily Bulletin, 1982–84; News Ed., Nat. Union of Civil and Public Servants, 1985–93; Hd of Communications, CWU, 1993–96; Asst Chief Exec., London Bor. of Camden, 1996–98; Head of News: DfEE, 1998–2001; Home Office, 2001–02; Dir of Communications, Home Office, 2002–06; Strategic Communications Advr to Prime Minister, 2006–07. Freelance subed. and reviewer, Egon Ronay's Guide: And Baby Comes Too, 1988–89. Gov., Robinsfield Infants Sch. and

Barrow Hill Junior Sch., London, 1992–2001. *Recreations:* tennis, hispanophile, birds, dance, London, my lovely daughters. *Address:* British Airways, Waterside, PO Box 365, Harmondsworth UB7 0GB.

SIMPSON, Keith Robert; MP (C) Mid Norfolk, since 1997; *b* 29 March 1949; *s* of Harry Simpson and Jean Simpson (*née* Day); *m* 1984, Pepita Hollingsworth; one *s*. *Educ:* Thorpe Grammar Sch.; Univ. of Hull (BA Hons 1970). Postgrad. res., KCL, 1970–72; Sen. Lectr in War Studies, RMA Sandhurst, 1973–86; Hd of Oversea and Defence Section, Cons. Res. Dept, 1986–88; Special Advr to Sec. of State for Defence, 1988–90; Dir, Cranfield Security Studies Inst., Cranfield Univ., 1991–97. Opposition front bench spokesman on defence, 1998–99 and 2002–05, on agriculture, 2001–02, on foreign affairs, 2005–; an Opposition Whip, 1999–2001. Mem., DEFRA Select Cttee, 2001–02. Sec., Cons. backbench Defence Cttee, 1997–98; Mem., H of C Catering Cttee, 1997–98; Chm., Cons. History Gp, 2003–. Mem., Lord Chancellor's Adv. Council on Nat. Records and Archives, 2006–. Member: RUSI, 1970–; IISS, 1975–; British Commn for Mil. History, 1980–; Council, SSAFA, 1997–. Trustee, Hist. of Parlt Trust, 2005–. *Publications:* The Old Contemptibles, 1981; (ed) A Nation in Arms, 1985; History of the German Army, 1985; (ed) The War the Infantry Knew 1914–1919, 1987; Waffen SS, 1990. *Recreations:* collecting books, cinema, visiting restaurants, walking battlefields, observing ambitious people. *Address:* House of Commons, SW1A 0AA. *T:* (020) 7219 4053.

SIMPSON, Malcolm Carter; Director of Finance, Leeds City Council, 1978–82, retired; *b* 15 June 1929; *s* of Arthur and Rhoda Simpson; *m* 1st, 1952, Doreen Patricia Wooler; two *d*; 2nd, 1980, Andrea Gillian Blythe. *Educ:* Stanningley Council Sch. DPA; CIPFA. Employed by Leeds CC for whole of working life, 1943–82: Asst Dir of Finance, 1968; Dep. Dir of Finance, 1973. Board Member: Yorks Water Authority, 1983–88; S Yorks Residuary Body, 1985–89. *Recreations:* golf, bridge. *Address:* Swiss Cottage, 44 Millbeck Green, Collingham Bridge, Leeds LS22 5AJ. *T:* (01937) 573917.

SIMPSON, Mark Taylor; QC 2008; barrister; *b* Maidstone, 5 Jan. 1963; *s* of His Honour Keith Taylor Simpson and of Dorothy May Simpson; *m* 1987, Janet McDowell; two *s* one *d*. *Educ:* King's Sch., Canterbury; Oriel Coll., Oxford (BA Hons Classics 1986); Hughes Hall, Cambridge (PGCE 1987); City Univ., London (Dip. Law 1991); King's Coll. London (Dip. Eur. Law 1995). Teacher of Classics, St Paul's Sch., Barnes, 1987–90; called to the Bar, Middle Temple, 1992. *Publications:* (Gen. Ed.) Professional Negligence and Liability, 2000–; (Associate Ed.) Clerk & Lindsell on Torts, 19th edn, 2006. *Recreations:* golf, tennis, travel, reading. *Address:* Fountain Court Chambers, Temple, EC4Y 9DH. *T:* (020) 7583 3335, *Fax:* (020) 7353 0329; *e-mail:* ms@fountaincourt.co.uk. *Club:* Rye Golf.

SIMPSON, Meg; *see* Hillier, M.

SIMPSON, Rear-Adm. Michael Frank, CB 1985; CEng, FIMechE; FRAeS; Chairman, Aircraft Engineering Division, Hunting Aviation Ltd, 1994–98; *b* 27 Sept. 1928; *s* of Robert Michael Simpson and Florence Mabel Simpson; *m* 1973, Sandra MacDonald (*née* Clift); two *s* one *d*. *Educ:* King Edward VI Sch., Bath; RN Engrg Coll., Manadon. CEng, FIMechE 1983; FRAeS 1983. Joined RN, 1944; qual. as Air Engr Officer, 1956; served in FAA Sqdns, cruisers and carriers; served with US Navy on exchange, 1964–66; Air Engr Officer, HMS Ark Royal, 1970–72; MoD appts, 1972–78; Supt, RN Aircraft Yard, Fleetlands, 1978–80; Cdre, RN Barracks, Portsmouth, 1981–83; Dir Gen. Aircraft (Naval), 1983–85; Dir and Gen. Man., 1985–88, Man. Dir, Field, later Hunting, Airmotive Ltd, 1988–94; Chm., Somet Ltd, 1988. Mem. Council and Dir, SBAC, 1994–98. Chairman: RN/RM Children's Home Management Cttee, 1980–83; RN Athletics Assoc., 1981–83. Mem. Court, Cranfield Inst. of Technology, 1983–86. *Publications:* articles on helicopter engrg in Jl of Naval Engrg; symposium paper on helicopter environmental design, 1975. *Recreations:* sailing, ski-ing, shooting, making things, military history, swimming. *Address:* Keppel, Blackhills, Esher, Surrey KT10 9JW. *Clubs:* Army and Navy; Royal Naval Sailing Association (Captain, Portsmouth Br., 1981–83); Royal Navy Ski.

SIMPSON, Morag; *see* Macdonald, M.

SIMPSON, Nicola Catherine; Chief Executive, National Council for One Parent Families, 2004–05; *b* 19 Dec. 1954; *d* of Ian and Susan Simpson; one *s* two *d*. *Educ:* Univ. of NSW (BSW); Univ. of Essex (MA). Various positions, 1981–2003, latterly Dir of Policy and Public Affairs, Nat. Assoc. of CAB; Consultation Champion, DTI, 2003–04.

SIMPSON, Prof. Patricia Ann, DèsSc; FRS 2000; Wellcome Trust Principal Fellow, since 2000, and Professor of Comparative Embryology, since 2003, Department of Zoology, University of Cambridge; Fellow of Newnham College, Cambridge, since 2000; *b* 9 Dec. 1945; *d* of James Alfred Simpson and Peggy Anderson Simpson. *Educ:* Univ. of Southampton (BSc Hons); Univ. Pierre et Marie Curie, Paris (DèsSc). Scientific research at: Inst. d'Embryologie et Tératologie Experimentale, Nogent sur Marne, Paris, 1968–72; Center for Pathobiol., Univ. of Calif, Irvine, 1972–74; Centre de Génétique Moleculaire, Gif sur Yvette, France, 1975–80; Inst. de Génétique et de Biologie Moleculaire et Cellulaire, Univ. Louis Pasteur, Strasbourg (Res. Dir, 1981–2000). Silver Medal, CNRS, France, 1993. *Publication:* The Notch Receptors, 1994. *Recreations:* hiking in remote corners of the world, woodwork, boating. *Address:* Department of Zoology, Downing Street, Cambridge CB2 3EJ. *T:* (01223) 336669.

SIMPSON, Peter; *see* Simpson, J. E. P.

SIMPSON, Sir Peter (Jeffery), Kt 2006; MD; FRCA, FRCP; President, Royal College of Anaesthetists, 2003–06; Consultant Anaesthetist, Frenchay Hospital, Bristol, 1982–2007; *b* 17 Dec. 1946; *s* of Thomas Simpson and Barbara Josephine (*née* Greenwood); *m* 1969, Jane Carpenter-Jacobs; one *s* three *d*. *Educ:* Bryanston Sch., Blandford; St Bartholomew's Hosp. Med. Sch., London (MB BS 1970; MD 1978). MRCS 1970; LRCP 1970; FRCA (FFARCS 1975); FRCP 2005. Registrar and Lectr in Anaesthetics, St Bartholomew's Hosp., 1972–76; Sen. Registrar in Anaesthetics, Oxford, 1976–78; Consultant Sen. Lectr in Anaesthetics, Univ. of Bristol, 1978–82. Chm., Nat. Confidential Enquiry into Patient Outcome and Death (formerly Nat. Confidential Enquiry into Perioperative Deaths), 2002–05; Mem. and Dep. Chm., Postgrad. Medical Educn and Trng Bd, 2004–06. Mem. Council, Royal Coll. of Anaesthetists, 1997–2007 (Vice Pres., 2001–03). Chm. Examination Cttee, European Acad. of Anaesthesiology, 1999–2005; Pres., European Soc. of Anaesthesiology, 2006–07. MRSocMed 1994. Hon. Mem., German Soc. of Anaesthesiology, 2007–. Hon. FCARCSI 2006; Hon. FRCS 2007. *Publications:* Understanding Anaesthesia, 1982, 4th edn 2001; 600 MCQ's in Anaesthesia: basic science, 1985; 600 MCQ's in Anaesthesia: clinical practice, 1986. *Recreations:* golf, walking, photography, classical music, opera. *Address:* 2 St Hilary Close, Stoke Bishop, Bristol BS9 1DA. *T:* (0117) 968 1537, *Fax:* (0117) 904 8725; *e-mail:* pjsimpson@blueyonder.co.uk. *Club:* Bristol and Clifton Golf.

SIMPSON, His Honour Peter Robert; a Circuit Judge, 1989–2008; Second Judge, Mayor's and City of London Court, 1994–2008; *b* 9 Feb. 1936; *o s* of late Surg. Capt. (D) Donald Lee Simpson, RN and of Margaret Olive (*née* Lathan); *m* 1st, 1968, Mary Elizabeth (marr. diss. 1994; she *d* 2003), *y d* of late Thomas Kirton and Frances Florence Cecilia Kirton; two *s*; 2nd, 1995, Megan Elizabeth, *o d* of late Kenneth John Dodd and Melva Dodd. *Educ:* St John's Coll., Southsea, Hants. Admitted Solicitor, 1960; called to the Bar, Inner Temple, 1970, *ad eundem* Lincoln's Inn, 1972. Practised on S Eastern Circuit, then at Chancery Bar, mainly in property and conveyancing matters; a Recorder, 1987–89; London County Courts, 1989–94. Former Mem., Herts and Essex Sessions Bar mess; a Judicial Mem., S Eastern Circuit Bar mess, 2007–08. Freeman, City of London; Liveryman, Fan Makers' Co., 2007–. *Recreations:* playing chess, reading legal and political biographies, dipping into books of history, listening to music, browsing through the law reports, dining out. *Clubs:* Guildhall, Sloane.

SIMPSON, Richard John, FRCPsych; Member (Lab) Scotland Mid and Fife, Scottish Parliament, since 2007; *b* 22 Oct. 1942; *s* of John and Norah Simpson; *m* 1967, Christine McGregor; two *s*. *Educ:* Edinburgh Univ. (MB ChB; DPM). FRCPsych 1994; MRCGP 1996. Pres., Scottish Union of Students, 1967–69. GP, Stirling, 1970–99; psychiatrist, 1970–99; consultant addiction psychiatrist, 2003–07. MSP (Lab) Ochil, 1999–2003; Scottish Executive: Dep. Minister for Justice, 2001–02; Shadow Minister for Public Health. Hon. Prof., Stirling Univ., 1997. *Publications:* numerous papers and articles in medical research. *Recreations:* watching Rugby, golf. *Address:* Scottish Parliament, Edinburgh EH99 1SP.

SIMPSON, Robert Brian; Chairman, Antenna Audio Ltd, 2001–03; *b* 12 Sept. 1944; *s* of Harold and Clara Simpson; *m* 1966, Vivienne Jones; three *s*. *Educ:* Liverpool Inst.; University Coll. London (BA 1966). Asst to Marketing Dir, Holt, Rinehart & Winston (Publishers) Ltd, 1966–68; Asst Develt Manager, later Develt Manager, and Dep. Hd of Inf. Services, Consumers' Assoc., 1968–73; Marketing Manager, Universal News Services Ltd, 1973–74; Marketing Dir, later Man. Dir, University Microfilms Internat. Ltd. 1974–79; Marketing and Develt Manager, later Commercial Manager, Press Assoc., 1979–86; Chief Exec., Universal News Services Ltd, 1986–90; Chm. and Chief Exec., PNA Ltd, 1989–90; Chief Exec., The Press Assoc. Ltd, 1990–2000 (Dir, 1989–2000). Chairman: Two-Ten Communications Ltd, 1990–99; Tellex Monitors Ltd, 1990–99; PA News Ltd, 1994–2000; PA Listings Ltd, 1996–2000; PA WeatherCentre Ltd, 1997–2000; Director: Canada NewsWire, 1986–2000; PA Sporting Life Ltd, 1996–2000; World Assoc. of Newspapers, 1997–2000. Pres., Eur. Alliance of Press Agencies, 1998–99 (Mem., 1990–2000); Mem. Council, CPU, 1995–2000. *Recreations:* music, walking, reading, gardening.

SIMPSON, Robert Watson, (Robin); Director, Brewers and Licensed Retailers Association (formerly Brewers' Society), 1993–98; *b* 14 June 1940; *s* of Robert Simpson and Susan Simpson (*née* Rolland). *Educ:* Perth Academy; University of St Andrews (BSc Hons). Board of Trade (Patent Office), 1962; Dept of Trade (Aviation), 1973; Dept of Industry (Indust. Develt Unit), 1976; Dept of Trade (Shipping), 1979; Department of Trade and Industry: (Management Services and Manpower), 1982; Under Sec., and NE Regl Dir, 1986; Head, Business Task Force Div. (incl. Envmt Unit), 1990–92; Head, Steel, Metals and Minerals Div., 1992. JP W London, 2001–07. *Recreations:* history, commemorative pottery.

SIMPSON, Robin Muschamp Garry; QC 1971; *b* 19 June 1927; *s* of Ronald Maitland Simpson, actor and Lila Maravan Simpson (*née* Muschamp); *m* 1st, 1956, Avril Carolyn Harrisson; one *s* one *d*; 2nd, 1968, Mary Faith Laughton-Scott; one *s* one *d*. *Educ:* Charterhouse; Peterhouse, Cambridge (MA). Called to Bar, Middle Temple, 1951, Bencher, 1979; SE Circuit; former Mem., Surrey and S London Sessions; a Recorder of the Crown Court, 1976–86. Mem., CCC Bar Mess. Appeal Steward, British Boxing Bd of Control. Mem., Friends of Hardwick. *Recreation:* Real tennis (Mem., Dedanists Club). *Address:* 116 Station Road, Barnes, SW13 0NB. *T:* (020) 8878 9898. *Clubs:* Pratt's, MCC.

SIMPSON, Sir Roderick Alexander C.; *see* Cordy-Simpson.

SIMPSON, Prof. Stephen James, PhD; FAA; Federation Fellow, School of Biological Sciences, University of Sydney, since 2005; *b* 26 June 1957; *s* of Arthur Leonard and Patricia Simpson; *m* 1984, Lesley Kathryn Dowie; two *s*. *Educ:* C of E Grammar Sch., Brisbane; Univ. of Queensland (BSc Hons 1978); King's Coll., London (PhD 1982); MA Oxon 1986. FAA 2007. Univ. of Qld Travelling Schol., 1979–82; University of Oxford: MRC post-doctoral res. asst, Dept of Exptl Psychol., 1982–83; Demonstrator, Dept of Zool., 1983–86; Lectr in Entomol., 1986–98 and Curator, 1986–2005, Hope Entomol Collections; Reader in Zool., 1996–98; Prof., 1998–2004; Vis. Prof., 2005–; Associate Hd, Dept of Zool., 2000–04; Principal Curator, Univ. Mus. of Natural Hist., 1989–92; Fellow, Linacre Coll., 1986–88, Jesus Coll., 1988–2004, Oxford. Guest Prof. in Animal Behaviour, Univ. of Basel, 1990; Dist. Vis. Prof., Univ. of Arizona, 1999. Fellow, Wissenschaftskolleg (Inst. for Advanced Study), Berlin, 2002–03. *Publications:* The Right Fly, 1996 (US edn as Angler's Fly Identifier, 1996); Anglers' Flies, 1997; ed books and scientific papers. *Recreations:* fishing, cookery. *Address:* School of Biological Sciences, University of Sydney, NSW 2006, Australia.

SIMPSON, Susan Margaret; *see* Haird, S. M.

SIMPSON, Prof. Thomas James, PhD, DSc; FRS 2001; CChem, FRSC; FRSE; Professor of Organic Chemistry, since 1990, Alfred Capper Pass Professor of Chemistry, since 2005, University of Bristol; *b* 23 Feb. 1947; *s* of Thomas Simpson and Hughina Ross Hay; *m* 1st, 1972, Elizabeth Crosthwaite Nattrass; one *s* one *d*; 2nd, 1987, Prof. Mary Norval. *Educ:* Univ. of Edinburgh (BSc 1st Cl. Hons 1969; Macfarlan-Smith Prize; DSc 1986); Univ. of Bristol (PhD 1973). Sen. Univ. Demonstrator, Dept of Organic Chem., Univ. of Liverpool, 1973–74; Research Fellow: Res. Sch. of Chem., ANU, 1974–76; Dept of Organic Chem., Univ. of Liverpool, 1977–78; Lectr, Dept of Chem., Univ. of Edinburgh, 1978–88; Prof. of Organic Chem., Univ. of Leicester, 1988–89. Mem., Mycotoxins Sub-cttee, MAFF Food Surveillance Gp. Royal Society of Chemistry: Tilden Lectr, 2001; Simonsen Lectr, 2002; Hugo Müller Lectr, 2004; Mem., Perkin Council, 1989–96 (Vice-Pres., 1993–95); Mem., 1989–93, Chm., 1993–96, Perkin Div. Standing Cttee on Meetings; Chm., Editl Bd, Natural Product Reports; Mem., Editl Bd, Chem. in Britain, 1994–2000. FRSE 2006. Corday-Morgan Medal and Prize, 1984, Natural Products Chemistry Medal, 2007, RSC. *Publications:* contrib. numerous original papers and review articles. *Recreations:* mountain walking, food and wine. *Address:* School of Chemistry, University of Bristol, Bristol BS8 1TS. *T:* (0117) 928 7656.

SIMPSON, William George; Director of the John Rylands Library and University Librarian, University of Manchester, 2002–07; *b* 27 June 1945; *s* of William Anion Simpson and Sarah Jane Simpson; *m* 1968, Margaret Lilian Pollard; two *d*. *Educ:* Liverpool Inst.; Univ. of Liverpool (BA 1st class Hons); MA Dublin 1995. MCLIP. Gilroy Scholar in Semitic Languages, Univ. of Aberdeen, 1968; Asst Librarian, Univ. of Durham, 1969–73; Asst Librarian, Sub-Librarian and Senior Sub-Librarian, John Rylands Univ. Library of Manchester, 1973–85; University Librarian: Surrey, 1985–90; London, 1990–94; Librarian and Coll. Archivist, TCD, 1994–2002. Chairman: Guildford Inst., 1987–90; Amer. Studies Library Gp, 1992–94; Mem., Humanities and Social Scis Adv.

Cttee, 1991–92, London Adv. Cttee, 1992–94, British Library; Dir, Consortium of University Res. Libraries, 1992–97 and 2003–05; Curator, Oxford Univ. Libraries, 2002–07. Dir, IRIS, 1994–2003; Member: An Chomhairle Leabharlanna (Liby Council of Ireland), 1995–2002; Council for Library Co-operation, 1995–2002 (Chm., 1998–2000); Nat. Preservation Adv. Cttee, 1994–96; Nat. Preservation Office Mgt Cttee, 1996–2002 (Chm., 1999–2002); Working Gp on UK Literary Heritage, 2005–; Chairman: CONUL, 1997–99; Standing Cttee on Legal Deposit, 1999–2001; Sec., Div. of Library Mgt and Admin, LIBER, 2002–07. Trustee: Worth Library, 1997–; The People's History Mus., 2003–05; Working Class Movement Library, 2007–. Mem., Internat. Editl Bd, Jl of Library Administration, 2004–. FRAS 1994; FRSA 1988. Jubilee Medal, Charles Univ., Prague, 1998. *Publications:* Libraries, Languages and the Interpretation of the Past, 1988; articles in learned and professional jls and press. *Recreations:* astronomy, genealogy, languages, travel. *Address:* White Cottage, 30 New Road, Milford, Godalming, Surrey GU8 5BE.

SIMPSON, Prof. (William) James, PhD; Donald P. and Katherine B. Loker Professor of English and American Literature and Language, Harvard University, since 2006 (Professor of English and American Literature and Language, 2004–06); *b* 16 March 1954; *s* of R. C. Simpson and M. A. Simpson (*née* MacDougall); *m* 1982, Luisella Maria Brunetti; two *s* one *d*. *Educ:* Scotch Coll., Melbourne; Univ. of Melbourne (BA Hons); St Edmund Hall, Oxford (MPhil); Girton Coll., Cambridge (PhD 1996). Lectr in English Lit., Westfield Coll., Univ. of London, 1981–89; University of Cambridge: Fellow, Girton Coll., 1989–2003; Lectr in English, and Lectr, Girton Coll., 1989–99; Prof. of Medieval and Renaissance English, 1999–2003. *Publications:* Piers Plowman: an introduction to the B-text, 1990; Sciences and the Self in Medieval Poetry, 1995; Reform and Cultural Revolution 1350–1547, 2002; Burning to Read: English fundamentalism and its Renaissance opponents, 2007; contrib. articles to Medium Aevum, Rev. English Studies, Speculum, Traditio, Jl Medieval & Early Modern Studies, etc. *Recreations:* conversation, mountain walking. *Address:* Department of English and American Literature and Language, Harvard University, Barker Center, 12 Quincy Street, Cambridge, MA 02138, USA; *e-mail:* jsimpson@fas.harvard.edu.

SIMPSON-JONES, Peter Trevor, CBE 1971; Président d'Honneur, Société Française des Industries Lucas, since 1980 (Président-Directeur Général, 1957–80); *b* 20 March 1914; *s* of Frederick Henry Jones and Constance Agnès Simpson; *m* 1948, Marie-Lucy Sylvain; one *s* one *d*. *Educ:* Royal Navy School. British Chamber of Commerce, France: Vice-Pres., 1967–68 and 1970–72; Pres., 1968–70. Mem., RNSA, 1955–. Chevalier de la Légion d'Honneur, 1948, Officier 1973. *Recreation:* yachting. *Address:* 11 rue Max Blondat, 92 Boulogne-sur-Seine, France. *T:* 48250120. *Clubs:* Special Forces; Polo (Paris).

SIMS, Prof. Andrew Charles Petter, MD; FRCP, FRCPsych, FRCPE; Professor of Psychiatry, 1979–2000, Chairman, Division of Psychiatry and Behavioural Sciences in Relation to Medicine, 1994–97, University of Leeds; Consultant Psychiatrist, St James's University Hospital, 1979–2000; *b* 5 Nov. 1938; *s* of late Dr Charles Henry Sims and of Dr Norah Winifred Kennan Sims (*née* Petter); *m* 1964, Ruth Marie Harvey; two *s* two *d*. *Educ:* Monkton Combe Sch.; Emmanuel Coll., Cambridge (MA; MD 1973); Westminster Hosp. DObstRCOG; FRCPsych 1979; FRCPE 1993; FRCP 1997. House Surgeon, Westminster Hosp., 1963–64; Registrar in Psychiatry, Manchester Royal Infirmary, 1966–69; Consultant Psychiatrist, All Saints Hosp., Birmingham, 1971–76; Sen. Lectr, Univ. of Birmingham, 1976–79; Head of Dept of Psychiatry, Univ. of Leeds, 1980–83, 1986–89, 1994–97. Royal College of Psychiatrists: Sub-Dean, 1984–87; Dean, 1987–90; Pres., 1990–93; Dir, Continuing Professional Develt, 1993–97; Chm., Spirituality and Psychiatry Special Interest Gp, 2003–05. Chairman: Confidential Inquiry into Homicides and Suicides by Mentally Ill People, 1993–96; Schizophrenia Cttee, Clinical Standards Adv. Gp, DoH, 1994–95; Health Adv. Service 2000, 1997–98. Mem., GMC, 1994–99. Hon. FCPS(Pak) 1994; Hon. FCMSA 1997. MD Lambeth, 1995. Editor: Advances in Psychiatric Treatment, 1994–2003; Developing Mental Health, 2002–05. *Publications:* Neurosis in Society, 1983; Psychiatry (Concise Medical Textbooks), 5th edn (with Sir William Trethowan), 1983, 6th edn (with D. Owens), 1993; (with W. I. Hume) Lecture Notes in Behavioural Sciences, 1984; Symptoms in the Mind: introduction to descriptive psychopathology, 1988 (Italian edn 1993, Portuguese edn 2000, Korean edn 2008), 3rd edn 2002; (with R. P. Snaith) Anxiety in Clinical Practice, 1988 (German edn 1993); Speech and Language Disorders in Psychiatry, 1995; (with C. Williams) Disorders of Volition, 1999; Is Faith Delusion?, 2008. *Recreations:* gardening, music, theatre, walking. *Address:* Church Farm House, Alveley, Bridgnorth, Shropshire WV15 6ND. *Clubs:* Athenæum, Christian Medical Fellowship, Royal Society of Medicine.

SIMS, Prof. Geoffrey Donald, OBE 1971; FREng; Vice-Chancellor, University of Sheffield, 1974–90; *b* 13 Dec. 1926; *s* of Albert Edward Hope Sims and Jessie Elizabeth Sims; *m* 1949, Pamela Audrey Richings; one *s* two *d*. *Educ:* Wembley County Grammar School; Imperial College of Science and Technology, London. Research physicist, GEC, 1948–54; Sen. Scientific Officer, UKAEA, 1954–56; Lecturer/Senior Lecturer, University College, London, 1956–63; University of Southampton: Prof. and Head of Dept of Electronics, 1963–74; Dean, Faculty of Engrg, 1967–70; Senior Dep. Vice-Chancellor, 1970–72. Member: Council, British Association for the Advancement of Science, 1965–69 (Chm., Sheffield Area Council, 1974–); EDC for Electronics Industry, 1966–75; Adv. Cttee for Scientific and Technical Information, 1969–74; CNAA Electrical Engineering Bd, 1970–73; Planning Cttee for British Library, 1971–73 (Chm., British Library R&D Adv. Cttee, 1975–81); Adv. Council, Science Museum, 1972–84; British Nat. Cttee for Physics, 1972–78; Royal Soc. Cttee on Sci. Information, 1972–81; Electronics Res. Council, 1973–74; Annan Cttee on Future of Broadcasting, 1974–77; Naval Educn Adv. Cttee, 1974–79; Trent RHA, 1975–84; British Council Engrg and Tech. Adv. Cttee, 1976–84 (Chm.); Interim Action Cttee on British Film Industry, 1977–81; EEC Adv. Cttee on Scientific and Technical Trng, 1977–81; Univs Council for Adult and Continuing Educn, 1978–84 (Chm., 1980–84); CNAA, 1979–83; Liaison Cttee on Highly Qualified Technol Manpower, 1979–82; Council, Nat. Inst. of Adult Educn, 1980–84; SRC, later SERC Engrg Bd, 1980–84; Inter Univ. and Polytechnic Council, 1981–91 (IUC and Exec. Cttee, 1974–81; Vice-Chm., IUPC, 1985–91); Cttee for Internat. Co-operation in Higher Educn, 1981–94 (Vice-Chm., 1985–91); EEC Adv. Cttee on Programme Management, 1981–84; BBC Engrg Adv. Cttee, 1981–90 (Chm.); Council, Fellowship of Engrg, 1986–88; Museums and Galleries Commn, 1983–88; Hong Kong City Polytechnic Sub-cttee, 1984–86, Hong Kong Univ. of Sci. and Technol. Sub-cttee, 1987–91, UPGC, Hong Kong; Mem. of Council and Hon. Dep. Treas., ACU, 1984–90; Chm., Council for Commonwealth Educn, 1991–96. UK rep. on Perm. Cttee of Conf. of European Rectors, 1981–84; *ad personam* rep. on Perm. Cttee and Bureau of Conf. of European Rectors, 1984–94; rep. on Liaison Cttee, Rectors' Confs of EEC Mem. States, 1985–90 (Pres., 1987–89). Chairman of Governors: Southampton College of Technology, 1967–69; Southampton Sch. of Navigation, 1972–74; Sheffield High Sch., 1978–85; Fellow, Midland Chapter, Woodard Schools, 1977–97 (Hon. Fellow, 1997); Custos, Worksop Coll., 1984–92. Trustee, Church Burgesses Trust, Sheffield, 1984– (Capital, 1988–89, 1999–2000; Chm., Educnl Foundn, 1992–). FIET (FIEE 1963); FCGI 1980; FREng (FEng 1980); FRSocMed 2002. Hon. Fellow, Sheffield City Polytechnic, 1990. Hon. DSc: Southampton, 1979; Huddersfield, 2001; Hon. ScD Allegheny Coll., Penn, USA, 1989; Hon. DSc (Eng) QUB, 1990; Hon. LLD: Dundee, 1987; Sheffield, 1991. Symons Medal, ACU, 1991. Co-founder Mem., 1966, Reviews Editor, 1969–91, Chm., 1982–98, Jl of Materials Science Bd. *Publications:* Microwave Tubes and Semiconductor Devices (with I. M. Stephenson), 1963; Variational Techniques in Electromagnetism (trans.), 1965; numerous papers on microwaves, electronics and education in learned jls. *Recreations:* golf, travel, music. *Address:* Ingleside, 70 Whirlow Lane, Sheffield S11 9QF. *T:* (0114) 236 6196, *Fax:* (0114) 236 6196; *e-mail:* geoffreydsims@blueyonder.co.uk. *Club:* Athenæum.

SIMS, Monica Louie, OBE 1971; MA, LRAM, LGSM; Vice President, British Board of Film Classification, 1985–98; *d* of late Albert Charles Sims and Eva Elizabeth Preen, both of Gloucester. *Educ:* Girls' High School, Gloucester; St Hugh's College, Oxford. Tutor in Literature and Drama, Dept of Adult Educn, Hull Univ., 1947–50; Educn Tutor, Nat. Fedn of Women's Institutes, 1950–53; BBC Sound Talks Producer, 1953–55; BBC Television Producer, 1955–64; Editor of Woman's Hour, BBC, 1964–67; Head of Children's Programmes, BBC TV, 1967–78; Controller, BBC Radio 4, 1978–83; Dir of Programmes, BBC Radio, 1983–84; Dir of Prodn, Children's Film and TV Foundn, 1985–97. Chm., Careers Adv. Bd, Univ. of Bristol, 1991–99. Hon. DLitt Bristol, 2000. *Address:* 97 Gloucester Terrace, W2 3HB.

SIMS, Sir Roger (Edward), Kt 1996; JP; *b* 27 Jan. 1930; *s* of late Herbert William Sims and Annie Amy Savidge; *m* 1957, Angela Mathews; two *s* one *d*. *Educ:* City Boys' Grammar Sch., Leicester; St Olave's Grammar Sch., London. MCInstM. National Service, 1948–50. Coutts & Co., 1950–51; Campbell Booker Carter Ltd, 1953–62; Dodwell & Co. Ltd, 1962–90; Dir, Inchcape International Ltd, 1981–90. Contested (C) Shoreditch and Finsbury, 1966 and 1970. MP (C) Chislehurst, Feb. 1974–1997. PPS to Home Sec., 1979–83. Mem., Nat. Commn of Inquiry into the Prevention of Child Abuse, 1995–96. Mem., GMC, 1989–99. Mem., Central Exec. Cttee, NSPCC, 1980–93. Chm., Bromley Voluntary Sector Trust, 1997–2001. Mem. Chislehurst and Sidcup UDC, 1956–62. JP Bromley, 1960–72 (Dep. Chm. 1970–72); Chm., Juvenile Panel, 1971–72. *Recreations:* swimming; music, especially singing (Mem. Royal Choral Soc., 1950–). *Address:* 68 Towncourt Crescent, Petts Wood, Orpington, Kent BR5 1PJ. *Clubs:* Royal Society of Medicine; Bromley Conservative (Bromley).

SIMS, Sonia Lisa; a District Judge (Magistrates' Courts), since 2002; *b* 8 Jan. 1957; *d* of Beryl Leonora Sims (*née* Lang). *Educ:* St John of Jerusalem Primary Sch.; Dalston Co. Grammar Sch.; Kingsway Princeton Coll.; City of London Poly. Trainee legal executive: Richard Sandler & Co., 1975–77; Rance & Co., 1978–81; Legal Exec., then Asst Solicitor, 1981–88, Partner, 1988–98, Whitelock & Storr; Consultant, Traymans, 1998–2002. Dep. Dist Judge, 1998–2002. Mem., London Criminal Courts Cttee, 1999–2003. Mem., Legal Aid Rev. Cttee (formerly Legal Aid Bd), Legal Services Commn, 1989– (Chm., 1995–2002). Mem., Local Cttee, Highbury and City, 1989–2002, Regl Mem., City of London, 1999–2000, Duty Solicitor Schemes. Associate, 1978, and Fellow, 1984, Inst. Legal Execs. *Recreations:* dance, music, travelling, good food, good wine and song, humour, all things of a Latin flavour, friends, children, animals, a challenge. *Address:* c/o Stratford Magistrates' Court, 389–397 High Street, Stratford, E15 4SB. *T:* (020) 8522 5000.

SIMS-WILLIAMS, Prof. Nicholas John, PhD; FBA 1988; Professorial Research Associate, School of Oriental and African Studies, University of London, since 2008 (Research Professor of Iranian and Central Asian Studies, 2004–07); *b* 11 April 1949; twin *s* of late Rev. M. V. S. Sims-Williams; *m* 1972, Ursula Mary Judith, *d* of late Prof. Hugh Seton-Watson, CBE, FBA; two *d*. *Educ:* Trinity Hall, Cambridge (BA, MA; PhD 1978). Res. Fellow, Gonville and Caius Coll., Cambridge, 1975–76; SOAS, University of London: Lectr in Iranian Langs, 1976–89; Reader in Iranian Studies, 1989–94; Prof. of Iranian and Central Asian Studies, 1994–2004. Visiting Professor: Collège de France, 1998–99; Macquarie Univ., 1998–2000; Univ. of Rome 'La Sapienza', 2001. British Acad. Res. Reader, 1992–94; Leverhulme Major Res. Fellow, 2002–04. Corresp. Mem., Austrian Acad. of Scis, 1990; Associé Etranger, Acad. des Inscriptions et Belles Lettres, Inst de France, 2002. Hirayama Prize for Silk Road Studies, 1996. *Publications:* The Christian Sogdian manuscript C2, 1985 (Prix Ghirshman, Inst. de France, 1988); Sogdian and other Iranian Inscriptions of the Upper Indus, vol. I, 1989, vol. II, 1992; (with James Hamilton) Documents turco-sogdiens du IXe–Xe siècle de Touen-houang, 1990; Partita, 1993; Serenade, 1997; New Light on Ancient Afghanistan: the decipherment of Bactrian, 1997; Bactrian Documents from Northern Afghanistan, vol. I, 2001, vol. II, 2007; In Memoriam (string trio), 2002; contrib. on Iranian and Central Asian langs and culture to learned jls. *Recreation:* music. *Address:* 11 Park Parade, Cambridge CB5 8AL; *e-mail:* ns5@soas.ac.uk.

See also P. P. Sims-Williams.

SIMS-WILLIAMS, Prof. Patrick Philip, PhD; FBA 1996; Professor of Celtic Studies, Aberystwyth University (formerly University College of Wales, Aberystwyth, then University of Wales, Aberystwyth), since 1994; *b* 11 April 1949; twin *s* of late Rev. Michael Sims-Williams and Kathleen (*née* Wenborn); *m* 1986, Prof. Marged Haycock; one *s* one *d*. *Educ:* Borden GS, Sittingbourne; Trinity Hall, Cambridge (BA 1972; MA 1975); PhD Birmingham 1980. Cambridge University: Lectr, Dept of Anglo-Saxon, Norse and Celtic, 1977–93; British Acad. Res. Reader, 1988–90; Reader in Celtic and Anglo-Saxon, 1993; Fellow, St John's Coll., 1977–93. O'Donnell Lectr, Oxford Univ., 1981–82, Edinburgh Univ., 1986, Univ. of Wales, 2000–01. Leverhulme Major Res. Fellow, 2003–06. Mem., Royal Commn on Ancient and Historical Monuments of Wales, 1998–2008. Council Member: Irish Texts Soc., 1991–97; Philological Soc., 1997–2000. Editor, Cambrian Medieval Celtic Studies, 1981–. Gollancz Prize, British Acad., 1992; Antiquity Prize, 1998; G. T. Clark Award, 2007. *Publications:* Religion and Literature in Western England 600–800, 1990; Britain and Early Christian Europe, 1995; Ptolemy: towards a linguistic atlas of the earliest Celtic place-names of Europe, 2000; The Celtic Inscriptions of Britain, 2003; New Approaches to Celtic Place-names in Ptolemy's Geography, 2005; Ancient Celtic Place-names in Europe and Asia Minor, 2006; The Iron House in Ireland, 2006; (with Georges Cousin) Additions to Alfred Holder's Celtic Thesaurus, 2006; Studies on Celtic Languages Before the Year 1000, 2007; (with M. E. Raybould) The Geography of Celtic Personal Names in the Latin Inscriptions of the Roman Empire, 2007; (with M. E. Raybould) A Corpus of Latin Inscriptions of the Roman Empire Containing Celtic Personal Names, 2007. *Recreations:* music, sailing, carpentry. *Address:* Department of Welsh, Aberystwyth University, Aberystwyth SY23 2AX. *T:* (01970) 622137.

See also N. J. Sims-Williams.

SIMSON, Michael Ronald Fraser, OBE 1966; Secretary of the National Corporation for the Care of Old People, 1948–73; *b* 9 Oct. 1913; *er s* of Ronald Stuart Fraser Simson and Ethel Alice Henderson; *m* 1939, Elizabeth Joan Wilkinson; one *s*. *Educ:* Winchester Coll.; Christ Church, Oxford. OUAFC 1936 and 1937. Asst Master, West Downs Sch., 1938–40; RNVR, 1941–46; Asst Sec., Nat. Fedn of Housing Socs, 1946–48. Member: Min. of Labour Cttee on Employment of Older Men and Women, 1953–55; Cttee on

Local Authority and Allied Personal Social Services (Seebohm Cttee), 1966–68; Supplementary Benefits Commn, 1967–76; Adv. Cttee on Rent Rebates and Rent Allowances, 1973–75, resigned 1975; Personal Social Services Council, 1973–78. *Recreation:* interested in all forms of sport. *Address:* Beauchamp House, Hatch Beauchamp, Taunton, Somerset TA3 6SG. *T:* (01823) 481508.

SINCLAIR, family name of **Earl of Caithness**, **Viscount Thurso** and **Baron Sinclair of Cleeve**.

SINCLAIR, 18th Lord *cr* 1449 (Scot.); **Matthew Murray Kennedy St Clair;** Director, Saint Property Ltd, since 2001; *b* 9 Dec. 1968; *s* of 17th Lord Sinclair, CVO and of Anne Lettice, *yr d* of Sir Richard Cotterell, 5th Bt, CBE; *S* father, 2004; *m* 2005, Laura Cicely, *y d* of Jonathan Coode, DL; one *s*. *Educ:* Glenalmond; RAC Cirencester. MRICS. *Heir: s* Harry Murray Kennedy St Clair, Master of Sinclair, *b* 6 Oct. 2007. *Address:* Knocknalling, St Johns Town of Dalry, Castle Douglas DG7 3JT; *e-mail:* mstc@saintproperty.com. *Club:* New (Edinburgh).

SINCLAIR OF CLEEVE, 3rd Baron *cr* 1957, of Cleeve, Somerset; **John Lawrence Robert Sinclair;** teacher; Founding Member and Secretary, Hackney Local Economic Trading System, 1992; *b* 6 Jan. 1953; *s* of 2nd Baron Sinclair of Cleeve, OBE, and Patricia, *d* of late Major Lawrence Hellyer; *S* father, 1985; *m* 1997, Shereen Khan. *Educ:* Winchester College; Manchester Univ. Teaching support staff, an Inner London comprehensive sch., 1984–94. Interest in archaeology. *Recreations:* motor cycling, mime, music.

SINCLAIR, Andrew Annandale; author; Managing Director, Timon Films, since 1967; *b* 21 Jan. 1935; *m* 1960, Marianne, *d* of Mr and Mrs Arsène Alexandre; *m* 1972, Miranda, *o d* of Mr and Hon. Mrs George Seymour; one *s*; *m* 1984, Sonia Lady Melchett (*see* S. E. Sinclair), *d* of Dr and Mrs Roland Graham. *Educ:* Eton Coll.; Trinity Coll., Cambridge (BA, PhD); Harvard. Ensign, Coldstream Guards, 1953–55. Harkness Fellow of the Commonwealth Fund, 1959–61; Dir of Historical Studies, Churchill Coll., Cambridge, 1961–63; Fellow of American Council of Learned Societies, 1963–64; Lectr in American History, University Coll., London, 1965–67. FRSL 1973; Fellow Soc. of American Historians, 1974; FRSA 2007. Somerset Maugham Literary Prize, 1966. *Directed films:* Under Milk Wood, 1971; Dylan on Dylan, 2003. *Publications:* The Breaking of Bumbo, 1958; My Friend Judas, 1959; The Project, 1960; Prohibition, 1962; The Hallelujah Bum, 1963; The Available Man: Warren E. Harding, 1964; The Better Half, 1964; The Raker, 1965; Concise History of the United States, 1966; Albion Triptych: Gog, 1967, Magog, 1972, King Ludd, 1988; The Greek Anthology, 1967; Adventures in the Skin Trade, 1968; The Last of the Best, 1969; Guevara, 1970; Dylan Thomas: poet of his people, 1975; The Surrey Cat, 1976; The Savage, 1977; Jack: the biography of Jack London, 1977; A Patriot for Hire, 1978; John Ford, 1979; The Facts in the Case of E. A. Poe, 1979; Corsair, 1981; The Other Victoria, 1981; Sir Walter Raleigh and the Age of Discovery, 1984; Beau Bumbo, 1985; The Red and the Blue, 1986; Spiegel, 1987; War Like a Wasp, 1989; (ed) The War Decade, an anthology of the 1940s, 1989; The Need to Give, 1990; The Far Corners of the Earth, 1991; The Naked Savage, 1991; The Strength of the Hills, 1992; The Sword and the Grail, 1993; Francis Bacon: his life and violent times, 1993; In Love and Anger, 1994; Arts and Cultures: the history of the fifty years of the Arts Council of Great Britain, 1995; Jerusalem: the endless crusade, 1996; Death by Fame: a life of Elisabeth Empress of Austria, 1998; The Discovery of the Grail, 1998; Dylan the Bard: a life of Dylan Thomas, 1999; The Secret Scroll, 2001; Blood & Kin, 2002; An Anatomy of Terror, 2003; Rosslyn, 2005; Viva Che!, 2006; The Grail, 2007; Man and Horse, 2008. *Recreations:* old cities, old movies. *Address:* Flat 20, Millennium House, 132 Grosvenor Road, SW1V 3JY. *Clubs:* Garrick, Chelsea Arts.

SINCLAIR, Angus Hugh; Secretary to the Speaker, House of Commons, since 2005; *b* 4 Nov. 1952; *s* of late Dr Hugh Melville Sinclair and Diana Grieve; *m* 1981 (marr. diss. 2002); one *s* one *d*. *Educ:* Merchiston Castle Sch.; Durham Univ. (BA Hons Geog. 1974). CMILT 2004. Asst Master, Wellingborough Sch., 1975; joined RN, 1975; served submarines and surface ships; Comdr (Trng) Britannia RNC, 1993–95; Sec. C-in-C Fleet, 1995–99; Naval Attaché, Rome, 1999–2002; Defence Attaché, Malta, 2001–02; Dir, RN Logistics, 2002–05. MIH (MHCIMA 2004). Mem., Scottish LTA. Editor: Encyclopaedia Britannia, 1993–95; Norsworthy's Epitome, 1996–97. *Publication:* contrib. to Naval Review. *Recreations:* endeavouring to persevere, striving for parsimony. *Address:* Speaker's Office, House of Commons, SW1A 0AA. *T:* (020) 7219 4000, *Fax:* (020) 7219 6901. *Clubs:* Royal Navy of 1919, Naval; RN Cricket; RN Lawn Tennis; Moffat Rugby.

SINCLAIR, Prof. Anthony Ronald Entrican, DPhil; FRS 2002; FRSC; Professor of Zoology, Centre for Biodiversity Research, University of British Columbia, since 1987; *b* 25 March 1944; *s* of Sir Ronald Ormiston Sinclair, KBE and Ellen Isobelle Sinclair; *m* 1966, Anne Catherine Begbie; two *d*. *Educ:* Pembroke Coll., Oxford (BA 1966, MA 1970; DPhil 1970). Res. Officer, Animal Behaviour Res. Gp, Oxford Univ., 1970; Staff Ecologist, Serengeti Res. Inst., Tanzania, 1970–73; Res. Scientist, Div. of Ecol. and Wildlife, CSIRO, Australia, 1973–75; University of British Columbia: Asst Prof., 1975–81, Associate Prof., 1981–87, Dept of Zool.; Dir, Centre for Biodiversity Res., 1996–2002. FRSC 1996. *Publications:* The African Buffalo, 1977; (ed with M. Norton-Griffiths) Serengeti, 1979, 2nd edn 1995; (with G. Caughley) Wildlife Ecology, 1994; (ed with P. Arcese) Serengeti II, 1995; (ed jtly) Conserving Nature's Diversity, 2000; contrib. scientific papers concerning ecology and conservation to leading jls, incl. Jl Animal Ecol., Ecol., Nature, Science. *Address:* Centre for Biodiversity Research, University of British Columbia, 6270 University Boulevard, Vancouver, BC V6T 1Z4, Canada. *T:* (604) 8224239, *Fax:* (604) 8220653; *e-mail:* sinclair@zoology.ubc.ca.

SINCLAIR, Carolyn Elizabeth Cunningham, (Mrs S. J. Bowen); Director, Constitutional and Community Policy Directorate, and Registrar of the Baronetage, Home Office, 1996–2001; *b* 13 July 1944; *d* of John Archibald Sinclair and Grace Margaret Stuart Sinclair (*née* Cunningham); *m* 1979, Stephen John Bowen. *Educ:* Laurel Bank Sch., Glasgow; Brown Univ., RI; Edinburgh Univ. (MA Hist.); Univ. of E Africa (Leverhulme Schol.; MA Pol Sci.). Joined FCO, 1968; Vienna, 1970–73; Private Sec. to Minister of State, 1977–78; transferred to HM Treasury, 1979; Prime Minister's Policy Unit, 1988–92; transf. to Home Office, as Asst Under-Sec. of State, 1992. *Recreations:* gardening, listening to music, reading, seeing friends.

SINCLAIR, Charles James Francis; Group Chief Executive, Daily Mail and General Trust plc, 1988–2008; *b* 4 April 1948; *s* of Sir George (Evelyn) Sinclair, CMG, OBE; *m* 1974, Nicola Bayliss; two *s*. *Educ:* Winchester Coll.; Magdalen Coll., Oxford (BA). ACA 1974. VSO, Zambia, 1966–67. Dearden Farrow, CA, 1970; joined Associated Newspapers Holdings, 1975; Asst Man. Dir and Mem. Main Bd, 1986; Man. Dir, 1988 (Associated Newspapers Holdings became the wholly-owned operating subsid. of Daily Mail and General Trust, 1988); Director: Euromoney Institutional Investor PLC, 1985–2008; Schroders plc, 1990–2004; Reuters Group plc, 1994–2005; SVG Capital plc, 2005–; Associated British Foods plc, 2008–; Mem., Adv. Bd, Spencer Stuart, 2006–. Chm. of Trustees, Minack Theatre Trust, Porthcurno, Cornwall, 1985–; Mem., UK Cttee, VSO, 2006–. Mem., Adv. Bd, Reuters Inst. for Study of Journalism, Univ. of Oxford, 2007–. *Recreations:* theatre, opera, fishing, ski-ing. *Address:* Northcliffe House, 2 Derry Street, Kensington, W8 5TT. *Clubs:* Athenæum, Flyfishers'; Vincent's (Oxford).

SINCLAIR, Sir Clive (Marles), Kt 1983; Chairman, Sinclair Research Ltd, since 1979; *b* 30 July 1940; *s* of late George William Carter Sinclair and Thora Edith Ella (*née* Marles); *m* 1962, Ann (*née* Trevor Briscoe) (marr. diss. 1985; she *d* 2004); two *s* one *d*. *Educ:* Boxgrove Prep. Sch., Guildford; Highgate; Reading; St George's Coll., Weybridge. Editor, Bernards Publishers Ltd, 1958–61; Chairman: Sinclair Radionics Ltd, 1962–79; Sinclair Browne Ltd, 1981–85; Cambridge Computer Ltd, 1986–90; Dir, Shaye Communications Ltd, 1986–91. Vis. Fellow, Robinson Coll., Cambridge, 1982–85; Vis. Prof., Dept of Elec. Engrg, Imperial Coll. of Science, Technol. and Medicine, London, 1984–92 (Hon. Fellow, 1984). Chm., British Mensa, 1980–97 (Hon. Pres., 2001–). Hon. Fellow UMIST, 1984. Hon. DSc: Bath, 1983; Warwick, 1983; Heriot-Watt, 1983. Mullard Award, Royal Soc., 1984. *Publications:* Practical Transistor Receivers, 1959; British Semiconductor Survey, 1963. *Recreations:* music, poetry, mathematics, science, poker. *Address:* 1A Spring Gardens, Trafalgar Square, SW1A 2BB. *T:* (office) (020) 7839 6868, *Fax:* (020) 7839 6622, *T:* (home) (020) 7839 7744. *Clubs:* National Liberal, Royal Automobile.

SINCLAIR of Freswick, Maj.-Gen. David Boyd A.; *see* Alexander-Sinclair.

SINCLAIR, Prof. David Cecil; Emeritus Professor, University of Western Australia; *b* 28 Aug. 1915; *s* of Norman James Sinclair and Annie Smart Sinclair; *m* 1945, Grace Elizabeth Simondson, Melbourne, Vic.; one *s* one *d*. *Educ:* Merchiston Castle Sch.; St Andrews University. MB, ChB (Commendation) St Andrews, 1937; MD (Hons and Rutherford Gold Medal) St Andrews, 1947; MA Oxon, 1948; DSc Western Australia, 1965. Served in RAMC, 1940–46: AMF, 1943–45; Head of Physiology Sect., Aust. Chem. Warfare Research and Experimental Stn, 1943–44; Dep. Chief Supt, Aust. Field Experimental Stn, 1944–45. Sen. Res. Off., Dept of Human Anatomy, Oxford, 1946–49; Univ. Demonstrator in Anatomy, Oxford, 1949–56; Lectr in Anatomy, Pembroke Coll., Oxford, 1950–56; Lectr in Anatomy, Ruskin Sch. of Fine Art, 1950–56; first Prof. of Anatomy, Univ. of W Australia, 1957–64, Dean of Med. Sch., 1964; Regius Prof. of Anatomy, Univ. of Aberdeen, 1965–75; Dir of Postgrad. Med. Educn, Queen Elizabeth II Med. Centre, WA, 1975–80. FRCSE 1966. Life Governor, Aust. Postgrad. Fedn in Medicine, 1983. *Publications:* Medical Students and Medical Sciences, 1955; An Introduction to Functional Anatomy, 1957 (5th edn 1975); A Student's Guide to Anatomy, 1961; Cutaneous Sensation, 1967, Japanese edn 1969; Human Growth after Birth, 1969 (6th edn 1998); Muscles and Fascia (section in Cunningham's Anatomy), 11th edn, 1972, 12th edn, 1981; Basic Medical Education, 1972; The Nerves of the Skin (section in Physiology and Pathophysiology of the Skin, ed Jarrett), 1973; Growth, section in Textbook of Human Anatomy (ed Hamilton), 1976; Mechanisms of Cutaneous Sensation, 1981; Not a Proper Doctor (autobiog.), 1989; Outside the Dissecting Room, 1989; papers on chemical warfare, neurological anatomy, experimental psychology, and medical education; Editor, Jl of Anatomy, 1970–73. *Recreations:* reading, writing, photography, chess problems. *Address:* Flat 3, Netherby, Netherby Road, Cults, Aberdeen AB15 9HL.

SINCLAIR, Douglas, CBE 2001; Chair, Scottish Consumer Council, since 2006; Member, Accounts Commission for Scotland, since 2007; *b* 28 Jan. 1946; *s* of Douglas Matheson Sinclair and Agnes Jack Sinclair; *m* 1969, Mairi MacPhee; two *d*. *Educ:* Edinburgh Univ. (MA Hons Politics). Admin. Asst, Midlothian, E Lothian and Peebles Social Work Dept, 1969–72; Admin. Officer, Barnardo's, Scotland, 1972–75; Depute Dir of Admin, 1975–78, Dir of Admin, 1978–85, Western Isles Is Council; Chief Executive: Ross and Cromarty Council, 1985–90; Central Regl Council, 1990–95; COSLA, 1995–99; Fife Council, 1999–2006. *Recreations:* Scottish literature, music, gardening, walking. *Address:* Royal Exchange House, 100 Queen Street, Glasgow G1 3DN.

SINCLAIR, Maj.-Gen. George Brian, CB 1983; CBE 1975; Engineer-in-Chief (Army), 1980–83; *b* 21 July 1928; *s* of Thomas S. Sinclair and Blanche Sinclair; *m* 1953, Edna Margaret Richardson; two *s* one *d*. *Educ:* Christ's College, Finchley; RMA Sandhurst. Commissioned, Royal Engineers, 1948; served UK, BAOR, Korea, and Christmas Island, 1948–66; Directing Staff, Staff College, Camberley, 1967–69; CRE, Near East, 1970–71; Col GS, HQ 1st British Corps, 1972–74; Nat. Defence Coll., India, 1975; Commandant Royal School of Military Engineering, 1976–77; BGS, Military Operations, MoD, 1978–80. Col Comdt, RE, 1983–91; Hon. Col, Engineer and Transport Staff Corps, 1988–93. Vice Pres., Red R (formerly Register of Engrs for Disaster Relief), 1985–98; Trustee: Imperial War Mus., 1990–2000; RE Museum Foundn, 1993–2001. Mem., Smeatonian Soc. of Civil Engrs, 1985–. Governor, King's Sch., Rochester, 1984–97. Freeman, City of London, 1981. DL Kent, 1996–97. *Publication:* The Staff Corps: the history of the Engineer and Logistic Staff Corps RE, 2001. *Recreations:* hill walking, bird watching and discussion. *Address:* Brockie's Hole, The Croft, St Boswells, Roxburghshire TD6 0AE. *Club:* Army and Navy (Chm., 1995–97; Trustee, 1999–2006).

SINCLAIR, Rt Rev. (Gordon) Keith; *see* Birkenhead, Bishop Suffragan of.

SINCLAIR, Rt Hon. Ian (McCahon), AC 2001; PC 1977; Chairman, Foundation for Rural and Regional Renewal, since 1999; *b* 10 June 1929; *s* of George McCahon Sinclair and Gertrude Hazel Sinclair; *m* 1st, 1956, Margaret Tarrant (*d* 1967); one *s* two *d*; 2nd, 1970, Rosemary Fenton; one *s*. *Educ:* Knox Grammar Sch., Wahroonga, NSW; Sydney Univ. BA, LLB. Grazier. Mem. Legislative Council, NSW, 1961–63; MP (Nat.) New England, NSW, 1963–98; Minister for: Social Services, 1965–68; Trade and Industry (Minister Assisting Minister), 1966–71; Shipping and Transport, 1968–71; Primary Industry, 1971–72; Leader of House for Opposition, 1974–75; Country Party spokesman for Defence, Foreign Affairs, Law and Agriculture, 1973; Opposition spokesman on primary industry, 1974–75; Leader of House, 1975–79; Minister for: Agriculture and N Territory, Nov.–Dec. 1975; Primary Industry, 1975–79; Special Trade Representations, 1980; Communications, 1980–82; Defence, 1982–83; Leader of the House for the Opposition, 1983–89; Shadow Minister: Defence, 1983–87; Trade and Resources, 1987–89; of State, Jan.–May 1994; Speaker, House of Reps, Australia, 1998. Member Committee: House of Reps Standing Orders, 1974–79, 1980–82, 1983–84; Privileges, 1980–82; Legal and Constitutional Affairs, 1990–98; Jt Foreign Affairs, Defence and Trade, 1990–98 (Chm., 1996–98); Nat. Crime Authority, 1990–98; Member: Jt Standing Cttee on Migration Regulations, 1990–98; Jt Cttee on Corps and Securities, 1990–98; Parly Code of Conduct Working Gp, 1994–96. Perm. Rep., Exec., IPU, 1996–98; Chm., Aust. Parly Gps for UK, PNG, Uruguay and Vietnam, 1996–98. Dep. Leader, 1971–84, Leader, 1984–89, Nat. Party of Australia. Chairman: Australian Constitutional Convention, 1998; Australian Rural Summit, 1999; Co-Chairman: NSW Drugs Summit, 1999; NSW Salinity Summit, 2000; SA Economic Summit, 2003; NSW Health Care Adv. Council, 2005–. Chairman: Good Beginnings (Australia), 2000–; Australia Taiwan Business Council, 2000–. President: Austcare, 2000–; Murray Darling Basin Commn, 2003–; Scouts Australia (NSW), 2003–. Adjunct Prof. of Social Scis (Pol Sci.), Univ. of

New England, 2000–. DUniv New England, 1999; Hon. DLitt Southern Cross, 2005. *Address:* Mulberry Farm, Dumaresq Island, NSW 2430, Australia. *T:* (2) 65538276, *Fax:* (2) 65538358; *e-mail:* iansinclair@ozemail.com.au. *Clubs:* Australian, American, Union (Sydney); Tamworth; Killara Golf.

SINCLAIR, Sir Ian (McTaggart), KCMG 1977 (CMG 1972); QC 1979; Barrister-at-Law, practising public international law, 1984–2005; Visiting Professor of International Law, King's College, London, 1989–93; *b* 14 Jan. 1926; *s* of late John Sinclair, company director; *m* 1954, Barbara Elizabeth (*née* Lenton); two *s* one *d*. *Educ:* Merchiston Castle Sch. (Scholar); King's Coll., Cambridge; BA 1948, LLB 1949 (1st cl. hons). Served Intelligence Corps, 1944–47. Called to the Bar, Middle Temple, 1952; Bencher, 1980. Asst Legal Adviser, Foreign Office, 1950–56; Legal Adviser, HM Embassy, Bonn, 1957–60; Asst Legal Adviser, FO, 1960–64; Legal Adviser, UK Mission to the UN, New York, and HM Embassy, Washington, 1964–67; Foreign and Commonwealth Office: Legal Counsellor, 1967–71; Dep. Legal Advr, 1971–72; Second Legal Advr, 1973–75; Legal Advr, 1976–84. Legal Adviser to UK delegn at numerous internat. confs, incl. Geneva Conf. on Korea and Indo-China, 1954, and Brussels negotiations for UK entry into the EEC, 1961–63; Dep. Chm., UK delegn to Law of Treaties Conf., Vienna, 1968–69; Legal Adviser to UK delegn on negotiations for UK entry into EEC, 1970–72; Member: Bureau of European Cttee on Legal Co-operation, Council of Europe, 1979–81; Panel of Conciliators, Annex to Vienna Convention on Law of Treaties, 1981–; Internat. Law Commn, 1981–86; Panel of Arbitrators, Internat. Centre for Settlement of Investment Disputes, 1988–94; Panel of Legal Experts under INTELSAT Convention, 1990–96; Perm. Ct of Arbitration, 1992–2003. Mem., Committee of Management: British Inst. of Internat. and Comparative Law, 1976–; Inst. of Advanced Legal Studies, 1980–84. Associate Mem., Inst de Droit Internat., 1983, elected Mem., 1987, Emeritus Mem., 2006; Hon. Mem., Amer. Soc. of Internat. Law, 1987. *Publications:* Vienna Convention on the Law of Treaties, 1973, 2nd edn 1984; International Law Commission, 1987; articles in British Yearbook of International Law, International and Comparative Law Qly and other legal jls. *Recreations:* theatre, watching sea-birds. *Address:* Lassington, Chithurst, Petersfield, Hants GU31 5EU. *T:* (01730) 815370.

SINCLAIR, Ven. Jane Elizabeth Margaret; Archdeacon of Stow and Lindsey, since 2007; *b* 1956. *Educ:* St Hugh's Coll., Oxford (BA 1978; MA 1980); St John's Coll., Nottingham (BA 1982). Ordained deaconess, 1983, deacon, 1987, priest, 1994; Deaconess, St Paul's, Herne Hill, London, 1983–86; Chaplain, and Lectr in Liturgy and Pastoral Studies, St John's Coll., Nottingham, 1986–93; Canon Residentiary, 1993–2003, Hon. Canon, 2003–07, Sheffield Cathedral; Vicar, Rotherham, 2003–07. Mem., Gen. Synod of C of E, 1995–. *Address:* Sanderlings, Willingham Road, Market Rasen, Lincs LN8 3RE.

SINCLAIR, Jeremy Theodorson; Chairman, M & C Saatchi plc, since 2004 (Partner, since 1995); *b* 4 Nov. 1946; *s* of Lilian Theodora Sinclair and Donald Alan Forrester Sinclair; *m* 1976, Jacqueline Margaret Metcalfe; two *s* one *d*. *Educ:* Rannoch Sch., Perthshire; Watford Art Sch. Saatchi & Saatchi and Co.: Jt Founder, 1970; Dir, 1973–95; Head of Creative Dept, 1973–86; Chairman: UK Agency, 1982–86; Saatchi & Saatchi International, 1986–95. Pres., D&AD, 1987. Chm., Art Acad., 1999–; Mem., Exec. Cttee, Sch. of Econ. Sci., London, 2003–07; Chm., Ind. Educnl Assoc. Ltd, 2007– (Gov., 1999–). Trustee, Jyotirnidhi Nyasa Trust. *Recreations:* philosophy, economics, Italy. *Address:* M & C Saatchi plc, 36 Golden Square, W1F 9EE. *T:* (020) 7543 4500.

SINCLAIR, Karen; Member (Lab) Clwyd South, National Assembly for Wales, since 1999; *b* 20 Nov. 1952; *m* 1973, Mike Sinclair; one *s* one *d*. *Educ:* Grove Park Girls' Sch., Wrexham. Contracted Care Manager, Wrexham Social Services, 1990–99. CAB Advr, 1995–97. Member (Lab): Glyndwr DC, 1988–95; Denbighshire CC, 1997–99. Minister for Assembly Business, Nat. Assembly for Wales, 2003–05. *Recreations:* family, reading, swimming, horse riding. *Address:* National Assembly for Wales, Cardiff Bay, Cardiff CF99 1NA; (constituency) 6 Oak Mews, Oak Street, Llangollen, Denbighshire LL20 8RP.

SINCLAIR, Rt Rev. Keith; *see* Sinclair, Rt Rev. G. K.

SINCLAIR, Martin John; Assistant Auditor General, National Audit Office, since 1999; *b* 24 April 1957; *s* of late Malcolm Sinclair and of Susan Sinclair; *m* 1996, Joke Pouw; one *s* one *d*. *Educ:* Glasgow Univ. (MPhil Town and Regl Planning). CPFA 1985. Joined Nat. Audit Office, 1981 (Mem., Mgt Bd, 1999–). *Recreations:* hill-walking, ski-ing, reading. *Address:* National Audit Office, 157–197 Buckingham Palace Road, SW1W 9SP. *T:* (020) 7798 7180.

SINCLAIR, Rt Rev. Maurice Walter; Hon. Assistant Bishop, diocese of Birmingham, since 2002; *b* 20 Jan. 1937; *s* of Maurice and Dorothea Sinclair; *m* 1962, Gillian (*née* Spooner); four *s*. *Educ:* Chigwell Sch.; Nottingham Univ. (BSc 1959); Leicester Univ. (PGCE 1960); Tyndale Hall, Bristol. Asst Master, Brays Grove County Secondary Sch., Harlow, Essex, 1960–62. Ordained, 1964; Asst Curate, St John's Church, Boscombe, 1964–67; Missionary, South American Missionary Soc., serving in Argentina, 1967–78; Personnel Sec., 1979–83, Asst Gen. Sec., 1983–84, South American Missionary Soc.; Principal, Crowther Hall, Selly Oak Colls, 1984–90; Bp of Northern Argentina, 1990–2001 and Presiding Bp (Primate), Province of Southern Cone of America, 1995–2001. Dean, All Saints Cathedral, Cairo, 2004–05. Hon. DD Nashotah House Seminary, 2001. Ibo chief, Nigeria, 1987. *Publications:* Green Finger of God, 1980; Ripening Harvest Gathering Storm, 1988; Way of Faithfulness, 1999; To Mend the Net, 2001. *Recreations:* gardening, hill walking, running. *Address:* 55 Selly Wick Drive, Selly Park, Birmingham B29 7JQ. *T:* (021) 471 2617.

SINCLAIR, Michael; *see* Shea, M. S. MacA.

SINCLAIR, Murray Alexander; Solicitor to Scottish Government and Head, Government Legal Service for Scotland, since 2007; *b* Falkirk, 29 May 1961; *s* of late Peter Sinclair and of Kathleen Sinclair; one *s* one *d*. *Educ:* Dollar Acad.; Christ Church, Oxford (MA Hons Juris.); Univ. of Edinburgh (LLB with Dist.; DipLP). Trained, qualified and practised as solicitor with Dundas and Wilson CS, 1985–89; joined Scottish Office, 1989; legal advr to depts incl. Justice Dept, 1989–97; Mem. and legal advr, Constitution Gp, 1997–99; Sen. Civil Service, 1999; Head: Legal Div., 1999–2004; Constitution and Parly Secretariat, 2004–07. *Recreations:* walking, football, reading, staring at the night sky. *Address:* Scottish Government, Victoria Quay, Edinburgh EH6 6QQ. *T:* (0131) 244 0531; *e-mail:* murray.sinclair@scotland.gsi.gov.uk.

SINCLAIR, Sir Patrick (Robert Richard), 10th Bt *cr* 1704 (NS), of Dunbeath, Caithness-shire; barrister; *b* 21 May 1936; s of Alexander Robert Sinclair (Robin) (*d* 1972) (*b* of 8th Bt) and Vera Mabel (*d* 1981), *d* of late Walter Stephings Baxendale; *S* cousin, 1990; *m* 1974, Susan Catherine Beresford Davies, *e d* of Geoffrey Clive Davies, OBE; one *s* one *d*. *Educ:* Winchester; Oriel Coll., Oxford. Nat. Service, RNVR, 1954–56 (Actg Sub-Lieut). Called to the Bar, Lincoln's Inn, 1961, Bencher, 1994; retired Mem., Chancery Bar. *Recreation:* reading. *Heir:* *s* William Robert Francis Sinclair, *b* 27 March 1979. *Address:* 5 New Square, Lincoln's Inn, WC2A 3RJ. *T:* (020) 7404 0404. *Club:* Pin Mill Sailing (Suffolk).

SINCLAIR, Rear-Adm. Peter Ross, AC 1992 (AO (mil.) 1986); Governor of New South Wales, 1990–96; farmer, Flagship Poll Hereford Stud; *b* 16 Nov. 1934; *s* of late G. P. Sinclair; *m* 1957, Shirley, *d* of J. A. McLellan; one *s* two *d*. *Educ:* North Sydney Boys' High Sch.; Royal Aust. Naval Coll.; Royal Coll. of Defence Studies. jssc. Joined RAN 1948; served HM Australian ships Australia, Tobruk, Vengeance, Arunta, Swan, Sydney, Vendetta, Vampire, Penguin, HMS Maidstone, HMS Jutland; CO HMAS Duchess, 1970–72; CO HMAS Hobart, 1974–77; Dir, Naval Plans, 1979–80; Dir-Gen., Mil. Staff Branch, Strategic and Internat. Policy Div., Defence Dept, 1980–82; Chief of Staff, 1983–84; First Comdt, Aust. Defence Force Acad., 1984–86; Maritime Comdr Australia, 1986–90 and Dep. Chief of Naval Staff, 1989. Chm. Council, Order of Australia, 1996–2002. Hon. FIEAust 1994; CPEng 1994. DUniv Sydney, 1992. KStJ 1991. *Recreations:* painting, sketching, whittling, reading, cricket, golf, tennis. *Address:* Post Office, Tea Gardens, NSW 2324, Australia.

SINCLAIR, Sir Robert (John), Kt 2001; Chairman: Lae Builders & Contractors Ltd, since 1974; Lae International Hotel Ltd, since 1977; *b* 21 Nov. 1943; *s* of William Arthur Sinclair; *m* 1985, Phuong Lan; three *s* two *d*. *Educ:* St Mary's Primary High Sch., PNG. Chm., PNG Post Ltd, 2000–. Chm., PNG Apprenticeship Bd, 1996–. *Recreation:* breeding thoroughbred horses. *Address:* PO Box 1730, Lae, Papua New Guinea. *T:* (675) 4724109, *Fax:* (675) 4725494. *Clubs:* Papua (Port Moresby); Royal Yacht (Lae).

SINCLAIR, Sonia Elizabeth, (Mrs A. A. Sinclair); Board Member, Royal Court Theatre, since 1974; *b* 6 Sept. 1928; *d* of Col R. H. Graham; *m* 1st, 1947, Hon. Julian Mond, later 3rd Baron Melchett (*d* 1973); one *s* two *d*; 2nd, 1984, Dr Andrew Annandale Sinclair, *qv*. *Educ:* Royal School, Bath. Board Member: NSPCC, 1960–70; Nat. Theatre, then RNT, 1984–94. JP Marylebone, 1962–72. *Publications:* Tell Me, Honestly, 1964; Someone is Missing, 1987; Passionate Quests, 1991. *Recreations:* reading, walking, swimming, foreign travel. *Address:* Flat 20, Millennium House, 132 Grosvenor Road, SW1V 3JY. *T:* (020) 7976 6958.

See also Baron Melchett.

SINCLAIR, Susan Myraid; Sheriff of North Strathclyde at Paisley, since 2002; *b* 16 Sept. 1958; *d* of William Stevenson Sinclair and Myraid Elizabeth Sinclair; *m* 1983, David Robert Adie. *Educ:* Glasgow Univ. (MA Hons; LLB; DLP). Solicitor, 1983; Advocate, 1988; Pt-time Chm., Appeals Service, 1996–2001; Temp. Sheriff, 1998–99; Pt-time Sheriff, 2000–01; All Scotland Floating Sheriff, 2001–02. Pt-time tutor, Univ. of Glasgow, 1995–97. *Recreations:* sailing, scuba diving, walking, reading, theatre.

SINCLAIR-LOCKHART, Sir Simon (John Edward Francis), 15th Bt *cr* 1636 (NS); *b* 22 July 1941; *s* of Sir Muir Edward Sinclair-Lockhart, 14th Bt, and of Olga Ann, *d* of late Claude Victor White-Parsons, Hawkes Bay, NZ; *S* father, 1985; *m* 1973, Felicity Edith, *d* of late I. L. C. Stewart, NZ; one *s* one *d* (and one *s* decd). *Heir:* *yr* twin *s* James Lachlan Sinclair-Lockhart, *b* 12 Sept. 1973. *Address:* 62 Muritai Crescent, Havelock North, Hawke's Bay, New Zealand.

SINCLAIR-STEVENSON, Christopher Terence; literary agent, since 1995; *b* 27 June 1939; *s* of late George Sinclair-Stevenson, MBE and Gloria Sinclair-Stevenson; *m* 1965, Deborah Susan (*née* Walker-Smith). *Educ:* Eton Coll.; St John's Coll., Cambridge (MA). Joined Hamish Hamilton Ltd, 1961, Dir, 1970, Man. Dir, 1974–89; Man. Dir, Sinclair-Stevenson Ltd, 1989–92; Publisher, Sinclair-Stevenson, and Editor-in-Chief, Reed Consumer Books, 1992–95; Consultant, Sinclair-Stevenson, 1995–96. *Publications:* The Gordon Highlanders, 1968; Inglorious Rebellion, 1971; The Life of a Regiment, 1974; Blood Royal, 1979; That Sweet Enemy, 1987; (ed) Enjoy!, 2000. *Recreations:* music, travel, food, the written word. *Address:* 3 South Terrace, SW7 2TB. *T:* (020) 7584 8087.

SINDALL, Adrian John, CMG 1993; HM Diplomatic Service, retired; Chairman, Council for British Research in the Levant, 1997–2005; *b* 5 Oct. 1937; *s* of Stephen Sindall and Clare Mallet; *m* 1st, 1958; one *s* one *d*; 2nd, 1978, Jill Margaret Cowley. *Educ:* Battersea Grammar Sch. FO, 1956–58; ME Centre for Arab Studies, 1958–60; Third Sec. (Commercial), Baghdad, 1960–62; Second Sec., British Embassy, Rabat, 1962–67; First Secretary: FCO, 1967–70; Beirut, 1970–72; First Sec. and Head of Chancery, British Embassy, Lima, 1972–76; FCO, 1976–79; Counsellor, Head of Chancery and Consul-Gen., Amman, 1979–82; Hd of S America Dept, FCO, 1982–85; Consul-Gen., Sydney, 1985–88; ME Marketing Dir, Defence Export Services Orgn, MoD, on secondment, 1988–91; High Comr, Brunei, 1991–94; Ambassador to Syria, 1994–96. Sen. Diplomatic Consultant, Landair Internat. Chairman: Gtr London Fund for the Blind, 1997–99; Internat. Adv. Panel, Nat. Lottery Charities Bd, 1997–2003; Arab-British Centre, 1997–2001; Vice-Chm., Medical Aid for Palestinians, 1997–99; Mem. Adv. Council, London Middle East Inst., SOAS (formerly Mem. Adv. Bd, Centre for Near and Middle Eastern Studies), 1997–. Mem., RIIA. SPMB (Negara Brunei Darussalam), 1992. *Address:* 2 Midlington House, Swanmore Road, Droxford, Hants SO32 3PT. *Club:* English-Speaking Union.

SINDALL, Barry John; Headmaster, Colyton Grammar School, Devon, 1990–2008; *b* 20 Oct. 1945; *s* of Reginald and Kathleen Sindall; *m* 1975, Margaret Eleanor Barker; one *s* one *d*. *Educ:* Univ. of Exeter (MEd). Teacher of Hist., Duncan Bowen Secondary Mod. Sch., Ashford, Kent, 1967–68; Hd of Humanities, R. M. Bailey High Sch., Nassau, Bahamas, 1968–76; Dir of Studies, Colyton GS, 1976–88; Dep. Headteacher, Torquay Boys' GS, 1988–90. FRSA 1994. *Recreations:* amateur dramatics, cricket, fell-walking, ski-ing.

SINDEN, Sir Donald (Alfred), Kt 1997; CBE 1979; actor; *b* 9 Oct. 1923; *s* of Alfred Edward Sinden and Mabel Agnes (*née* Fuller), Sussex; *m* 1948, Diana (*d* 2004), *d* of Daniel and Muriel Mahony; one *s* (and one *s* decd). First appearance on stage, 1942, in Charles F. Smith's Co., Mobile Entertainments Southern Area; Leicester Repertory Co., 1945; Memorial Theatre Co., Stratford upon Avon, 1946 and 1947; Old Vic and Bristol Old Vic, 1948; The Heiress, Haymarket, 1949–50; Bristol Old Vic, 1950; Red Letter Day, Garrick, 1951. Under contract to Rank Organisation, 1952–60, appearing in 23 films including The Cruel Sea, Doctor in the House, etc. Returned to theatre, appearing in Odd Man In, St Martin's, 1957; Peter Pan, Scala, 1960; Guilty Party, St Martin's, 1961; Royal Shakespeare Co., playing Richard Plantagenet in Henry VI (The Wars of the Roses), Price in Eh!, etc, 1963 and 1964; British Council tour of S America in Dear Liar and Happy Days, 1965; There's a Girl in my Soup, Globe, 1966; Lord Foppington in The Relapse, RSC, Aldwych, 1967; Not Now Darling, Strand, 1968; RSC, Stratford, 1969 and Aldwych, 1970 playing Malvolio; Henry VIII; Sir Harcourt Courtly in London Assurance, revived at New Theatre, 1972, tour of the USA, 1974 (Drama Desk Award); In Praise of Love, Duchess, 1973; Stockmann in An Enemy of the People, Chichester, 1975; Habeas Corpus, USA, 1975; Benedick in Much Ado About Nothing, King Lear, RSC, Stratford, 1976, Aldwych, 1977 (Variety Club of GB Stage Actor of 1976; Evening Standard Drama Award, Best Actor, 1977); Shut Your Eyes and Think of England, Apollo,

1977; Othello, RSC, Stratford, 1979, Aldwych, 1980; Present Laughter, Vaudeville, 1981; Uncle Vanya, Haymarket, 1982; The School for Scandal, Haymarket and Duke of York's (Eur. tour, 1984), 1983; Ariadne auf Naxos, Coliseum, 1983, 1992, 1997; Two Into One, Shaftesbury, 1984; The Scarlet Pimpernel, Chichester transf. to Her Majesty's, 1985; Major Barbara, Chichester, 1988; Over My Dead Body, Savoy, 1989; Oscar Wilde, Playhouse, 1990; Out of Order, Shaftesbury, 1990, nat. tour, 1990–91, Australia, 1992–93; Venus Observed, Chichester, 1992; She Stoops to Conquer, Queen's, 1993; Hamlet, Gielgud, 1994; Quartet, Albery, 1999; The Hollow Crown, RSC, Australia and NZ, 2002, Australia, 2003, Canada, 2004; dir, The Importance of Being Earnest, Royalty, 1987; *television series include:* Our Man at St Mark's; Two's Company; Discovering English Churches; Never the Twain; Judge John Deed; has appeared in many films. Assoc. Artist, RSC, 1967–. Member: Council, British Actors' Equity Assoc., 1966–77 (Trustee, 1988–2004); Council, RSA, 1972; Adv. Council, V&A Museum, 1973–80; Arts Council Drama Panel, 1973–77; Leicestershire Educn Arts Cttee, 1974–2004; BBC Archives Adv. Cttee, 1975–78; London Acad. of Music and Dramatic Art Council, 1976–; Kent and E Sussex Reg. Cttee, National Trust, 1978–82; Arts Council of GB, 1982–86; Chairman: British Theatre Museum Assoc., 1971–77; Theatre Museum Adv. Council, 1973–80; President: Fedn of Playgoers Socs, 1968–93; Royal Theatrical Fund, 1983–; Green Room Benevolent Fund, 1998–2005; Vice-President: London Appreciation Soc., 1960–; Ecclesiological Soc., 2000–. FRSA 1966. Freeman, City of London, 1997. Hon. DLitt Leicester, 2005. *Publications:* A Touch of the Memoirs (autobiog.), 1982; Laughter in the Second Act (autobiog.), 1985; (ed) The Everyman Book of Theatrical Anecdotes, 1987; The English Country Church, 1988; (ed) The Last Word, 1994. *Recreations:* theatrical history, architecture, ecclesiology, genealogy, serendipity. *Address:* Tenterden, Kent TN30 7HX. *Clubs:* Garrick (Trustee, 1980–2000), Beefsteak, MCC.

SINGARES ROBINSON, Ariadne Elizabeth; Ambassador of Panama to the Court of St James's, 2000–04; *b* Panama, 24 Sept. 1961; *m* Andrew Ian Robinson; one *d. Educ:* Knox Sch., Long Island, NY; Le Château Mont-Choisi, Geneva; Stony Brook Univ., NY; Parson Sch. of Design, Manhattan; New York Univ. A designer and personal asst to Gerald Franklin, Canadian designer of haute couture, NY, 1985–88. Member: Breast Cancer Assoc., Race for Life; City Harvest; Meals on Wheels; volunteer, St Lucas Hosp., Manhattan.

SINGER, His Honour Harold Samuel; a Circuit Judge, 1984–2003; *b* 17 July 1935; *s* of Ellis and Minnie Singer; *m* 1966, Adèle Berenice Emanuel; one *s* two *d. Educ:* Salford Grammar School; Fitzwilliam House, Cambridge (MA). Called to the Bar, Gray's Inn, 1957; a Recorder, 1981–84. Governor, Delamere Forest Sch., 1998–. *Recreations:* music, painting, books, photography.

SINGER, Hon. Sir (Jan) Peter, Kt 1993; **Hon. Mr Justice Singer;** a Judge of the High Court of Justice, Family Division, since 1993; *b* 10 Sept. 1944; *s* of late Dr Hanus Kurt Singer and Anita Singer; *m* 1970, Julia Mary Caney (marr. diss. 2006); one *s* one *d. Educ:* King Edward's School, Birmingham; Selwyn College, Cambridge. Called to the Bar, Inner Temple, 1967, Bencher, 1993; QC 1987; a Recorder, 1987–93; NE Circuit Liaison Judge, 1993–2001. Chm., Family Law Bar Assoc., 1990–92 (Sec., 1980–83, Treasurer, 1983–90); Member: Matrimonial Causes Rule Cttee, 1981–85; Senate of Inns of Court and Bar, 1983–86; Law Soc. Legal Aid Cttee, 1984–89; Gen. Council of the Bar, 1990–92. Vice-Pres., European Chapter, Internat. Acad. of Matrimonial Lawyers, 1992–93. Joint Editor: Capitalise (software), 1998–; @eGlance (software), 2001–; Care (software), 2003–07. *Publications:* (ed jtly) Rayden on Divorce, 14th edn, 1983; (ed jtly) At A Glance, annually 1992–; (Consulting Ed.) Essential Family Practice, 2000–02. *Recreations:* walking, travel. *Address:* Royal Courts of Justice, Strand, WC2A 2LL.

SINGER, Norbert, CBE 1990; PhD; FRSC; Vice Chancellor, University of Greenwich (formerly Director, Thames Polytechnic), 1978–93; *b* 3 May 1931; *s* of late Salomon Singer and late Mina Korn; *m* Brenda Margaret Walter, *e d* of Richard and Gladys Walter, Tunbridge Wells, Kent. *Educ:* Highbury County School; Queen Mary Coll., London (BSc, PhD). CChem, FRSC. Research Chemist and Project Leader, Morgan Crucible Co. Ltd, 1954–57; Lecturer, Senior Lectr, Principal Lectr and Dep. Head of Department, Dept of Chemistry, Northern Polytechnic, 1958–70; Head of Dept of Life Sciences 1971–74, Professor of Life Sciences 1972–74, Polytechnic of Central London; Asst Dir, then Dep. Dir, Polytechnic of N London, 1974–78. Vis. Prof., Univ. of Westminster, 1996–. Council for National Academic Awards: Mem., 1982–88; Chm., Reviews Co-ordination Sub-Cttee, 1984–87; Vice Chm., Cttee for Academic and Institutional Policy, 1985–87; Mem., Accreditation Cttee, 1987–89; Chm., Cttee for CATs, 1990–93. Mem., MSC Nat. Steering Gp, TVEI, 1984–88 (Mem., Quality and Standards Gp, 1987–89). Chairman: Bexley HA, 1993–94; Oxleas (formerly Bexley Community Health) NHS Trust, 1994–2001. Chm., Governing Body, Rose Bruford Coll., 1994–99; Governor: London Inst., 1993–99; Nene Coll., Northants, 1993–97; St Peter's C of E Primary Sch., Tunbridge Wells, 1995–2004 (Chm., 2004–). Fellow: QMW, 1993; Nene Coll., 1998. Hon. DSc Greenwich, 1993. *Publications:* research papers in electrochemistry, theoretical chemistry and surface chemistry in scientific jls. *Recreations:* walking, reading. *Address:* Croft Lodge, Bayhall Road, Tunbridge Wells, Kent TN2 4TP. *T:* (01892) 523821.

SINGER, Hon. Sir Peter; *see* Singer, Hon. Sir J. P.

SINGER, Philip Francis; QC 1994; a Recorder, since 1989; *b* 1 Dec. 1940; *s* of late Abraham Singer and of Sylvia (*née* Hyman); *m* 1978, Heather Angela Cutt. *Educ:* Bedford Modern Sch.; Bishop's Stortford Coll.; St John's Coll., Cambridge (MA, LLM). Called to the Bar, Inner Temple, 1964. *Address:* 2 Pump Court, Temple, EC4Y 7AH. *T:* (020) 7353 5597.

SINGER, Sara Catherine; *see* Nathan, S. C.

SINGER, Susan Honor; educational consultant, since 2003; Headmistress, Guildford High School, 1991–2002; *b* 23 Feb. 1942; *d* of late Brig. John James McCully, DSO and of Honor Goad McCully (*née* Ward, now Mrs E. B. Elliott); *m* 1964, Christopher Ronald Morgan Singer; one *s* two *d. Educ:* St Mary's, Calne; Open Univ. (BA); Garnett Coll. (PGCE). Set up and ran pre-school playgroup, E Sheen, 1968–74; St Paul's Girls' School: maths teacher, 1980–91; Head of Middle School, 1988–91; Head of Maths, 1990–91. President: GSA, 2001; Mathematical Assoc., 2005–06. *Recreation:* transatlantic sailing 1907 gaff cutter. *Address:* 39 East Sheen Avenue, SW14 8AR. *T:* (020) 8876 4031.

SINGH, Prof. Ajit, PhD; Professor of Economics, Cambridge University, 1995–2007, now Emeritus; Fellow of Queens' College, Cambridge, since 1965 (Senior Fellow since 1992); *b* 11 Sept. 1940; *s* of Gurbachan Singh and Pushpa Singh; *m* 1993, Josephine Bradley. *Educ:* Punjab Univ. (BA); Howard Univ. (MA); Univ. of California at Berkeley (PhD). Queens' College, Cambridge: Asst Lectr, 1965; Dir of Studies in Econs, 1972–94; Univ. Lectr, then Reader, Econs Faculty, Cambridge Univ. Scholl Vis. Prof. of Internat. Econs, Univ. of Notre Dame, USA, 1987–95. Research Consultant: UN Univ., World Inst. of Develt Econ. Res., 1986–92; ILO, 1988–; UNCTAD, 1988–; IFC, 1989–; South Commn, later South Centre, Geneva, 1990–; other adv. positions in Switzerland, Mexico, Tanzania. Founding Editor, Cambridge Jl of Economics, 1977–. *Publications:* (with G. Whittington) Growth, Profitability and Valuation, 1968; Takeovers, 1971; (ed jtly) The State, Markets and Development, 1994; Corporate Financial Patterns in Industrialising Countries, 1995; (jtly) The Effects of Hyper-Inflation on Accounting Ratios, 1997; (ed with C. Howes) Competitiveness Matters: industry and economic performance in the US, 2000; contribs to learned jls. *Recreations:* table tennis, hiking, travel, friends. *Address:* Queens' College, Cambridge CB3 9ET. *T:* (01223) 335200.

SINGH, Darra, OBE 2004; Chief Executive, Ealing Council, since 2005; *b* 26 July 1959; *s* of Lachsman Singh and Gurmit Kaur; *m* 1995, Monika Singh; one *d. Educ:* Fairfax Secondary Sch., Bradford; Newcastle upon Tyne Poly. (BA Hons Law 1981). Housing caseworker, Tyneside Housing Aid Centre, 1983; Housing Advr, London Housing Aid Centre, 1983–85; housing campaign worker, Housing Campaign for Single People, 1985–88; Sen. Policy and Res. Officer, London Housing Unit, 1988–90; Regl Dir, North British Housing Assoc., 1990–92; Chief Executive: Asra Greater London Housing Assoc., 1992–95; Hexagon Housing Assoc., 1995–2000; Regl Dir, Audit Commn, 2000–01; Chief Exec., Luton BC, 2001–05. Mem., Balance of Funding Review Gp, ODPM, 2004. Chm., Commn of Integration and Cohesion, 2006–07. *Recreations:* motor bikes (Italian especially), guitar-based bands, films. *Address:* Ealing Council, Perceval House, 14–16 Uxbridge Road, Ealing, W5 2HL.

SINGH, Deepak; Director General and Chief Information Officer, HM Revenue and Customs, since 2007; *b* Dessie, Ethiopia, 22 May 1964; *s* of Surjan Singh and Suman L. Singh; *m* 1986, Sally Ruth Westwood; one *s* two *d. Educ:* Avenue Road Jun. Sch., Leicester; Guthlaxton Coll., Leicester; Univ. of York (BA Hons Pols). Team Leader, Jaguar Cars Ltd, 1988–91; Application Services Manager, Facilities Technology Ltd, 1992–95; Sen. Proj. Manager, Astrazeneca plc, 1997–2000; Exec. Vice Pres., T-Mobile, 2001–06. *Recreations:* investing (badly) in the stock market, armchair cricket and football, politics and current affairs, talking in my sleep.

SINGH, Gurbux; Managing Director, Diverse Solutions, Management Consultancy, since 2005; *b* Punjab, India, 4 Dec. 1950; *s* of Parkesh Singh and Shaminder Kaur; *m* 2001, Siobhan Maguire; three *s. Educ:* Univ. of Sussex (BA Hons Pol Sci.). Housing Specialist, CRC, 1972–77; housing and local govt, CRE, 1977–83; Housing Services, GLC, 1983–85; Dep. Dir of Housing, Brent BC, 1985–87; Dir of Housing, 1987–89, Chief Exec., 1989–2000, Haringey BC; Chair, CRE, 2000–02. Mem., Home Sec.'s Race Relns Forum, 1998; Dir, N London TEC, 1990–2000; Mem. Bd, Food Standards Agency, 2000–02; Nat. Dir, Civic Educn and Democracy, Research Triangle Inst., Iraq, 2003–04. *Recreation:* supporting Wolverhampton Wanderers and the Indian cricket team. *Address:* 6 Hollycroft Gardens, Tettenhall, Wolverhampton WV6 8FB. *T:* (01902) 755366, 07810 874189.

SINGH, Indarjit, OBE 1996; JP; CEng; Director, Network of Sikh Organisations (UK), since 1995; *b* 17 Sept. 1932; *s* of Dr Diwan Singh and Kundan K. Singh; *m* 1962, Dr Kanwaljit Kaur; two *d. Educ:* Birmingham Univ. (MCom, MBA). CEng 1967; MIMinE 1967. Worked in sen. positions in mining and civil engrg, 1955–75: NCB, 1955–59, 1965–67; manager of mines, India, 1959–65; with Costain, 1967–75; mgt consultant in various areas of local govt, Gtr London, 1975–; hon. work for Sikh community and in promotion of inter-faith understanding, 1993–. Editor, Sikh Messenger (qly mag.), 1984–. Has made broadcasts on religious and current affairs, incl. Any Questions, Thought for the Day. JP Wimbledon, 1984. UK Templeton Prize for the promotion of inter-faith understanding, 1989; Inter-faith Medallion for services to religious broadcasting, BBC and CCJ, 1991. Hon. DLitt Coventry, 2002; Hon. DLaws Leicester, 2004. *Recreations:* writing, broadcasting. *Address:* 43 Dorset Road, Merton Park, SW19 3EZ. *T:* (020) 8540 4148; *e-mail:* sikhmessenger@aol.com.

SINGH, Kanwar N.; *see* Natwar-Singh.

SINGH, Karamjit Sukhminder, CBE 2000; Northern Ireland Judicial Appointments Ombudsman, since 2006; Member: Electoral Commission, since 2001; Queen's Counsel Selection Panel for England and Wales, since 2005; *b* 11 March 1950; *s* of Tara Singh and Chanan Kaur; *m* 1972, Jaswir Kaur; two *s. Educ:* Univ. of Warwick (MA). Res. Associate, Industrial Relns Res. Unit, Univ. of Warwick, 1971–75; Caseworker, Leicester CRC, 1975–78; Sen. Exec. Officer, CRE, 1978–82; Principal Officer, W Midlands CC, 1982–84; Asst Co. Clerk, Leics CC, 1984–87; Member: Police Complaints Authy for England and Wales, 1987–90 and 1991–94; Parole Bd for England and Wales, 1994–97. Harkness Fellow, US, 1990–91. Member: Data Protection Tribunal, 1997–2003; Criminal Cases Review Commn, 1997–2006; Regulatory Decisions Cttee, FSA, 2002–06. Member: Area Manpower Bd for Coventry and Warwicks, 1984–87; Industrial Tribunals Panel for England and Wales, 1986–96; Complaints Audit Cttee, Immigration and Nationality Dept, Home Office, 1994–97; Judicial Studies Bd, 1994–99; Ind. Mem., W Midlands Police Authy, 1994–96; Mem., CS Commn, 1996–2000. FRSA 1995. Trustee: Citizenship Foundn, 1993–2000; Lloyds TSB Foundn for England and Wales, 2001–06. *Recreations:* family, reading, charity work in India. *Address:* c/o Electoral Commission, Trevelyan House, 30 Great Peter Street, SW1P 2HW. *T:* (020) 7271 0604, *Fax:* (020) 7271 0545; *e-mail:* karamjit@btinternet.com. *Club:* Reform.

SINGH, Khushwant; Padma Bhushan, 1974; Barrister-at-law; writer; Member, Rajya Sabha, India, 1980–86; *b* Feb. 1915; *m* Kaval (*née* Malik); one *s* one *d. Educ:* Univ. of London (LLB); called to Bar. Practising Lawyer, High Court, Lahore, 1939–47; Min. of External Affairs, of India; PRO Ottawa and London, 1947–51; UNESCO, 1954–56. Visiting Lectr: Oxford (Spalding Trust); USA: Rochester, Princeton, Hawaii, Swarthmore; led Indian Delegn to Writers' Conf., Manila, Philippines, 1965; Guest Speaker at Montreal 'Expo 67'. Has written for many nat. dailies and foreign jls: New York Times; Observer and New Statesman (London); Harper's (USA); Evergreen Review (USA); London Magazine. Editor, The Illustrated Weekly of India, Bombay, 1969–78; Chief Editor, New Delhi, 1979–80; increased circulation of Illustrated Weekly of India from 80,000 to 410,000 in 9 yrs; Editor-in-chief, The Hindustan Times and Contour, New Delhi, 1980–83. *Broadcasting and television:* All India Radio, BBC, CBC; LP recordings. Awards include: from Punjab Govt: 5,000 rupees and Robe of Honour, for contrib. to Sikh literature; Mohan Singh Award: 1,500 rupees for trans. of Sikh hymns, etc. *Publications: Sikh history and religion:* The Sikhs, 1953; A History of the Sikhs: vol. i, 1469–1839, 1964; vol. ii, 1839–1964, 1967; Ranjit Singh, Maharajah of the Punjab, 1780–1839, 1963; Fall of the Kingdom of the Punjab; Sikhs Today; (ed) Sunset of the Sikh Empire, by Dr Sita Ram Kohli (posthumous); Hymns of Nanak The Guru; The End of India, 2003; *fiction:* The Mark of Vishnu and other stories, 1951; Train to Pakistan, 1956; I Shall Not Hear the Nightingales, 1961; Delhi; The Company of Women, 2000; Burial at Sea, 2004; *stories:* The Voice of God and other stories; Black Jasmine and other stories; A Bride for the Sahib and other stories; Paradise and other stories, 2004; (*co-author*): Sacred Writing of the Sikhs; (with Arun Joshi) Shri Ram: a biog., 1969; (with Satindra Singh) Ghadr Rebellion; (with Suneet Veer Singh) Homage to Guru Gobind Singh; *miscellaneous:* Love and Friendship (editor of anthology); Khushwant Singh's India—collection of articles (ed Rahul Singh); Shri Ram—a biography; Delhi—a Profile, 1982; The Sikhs,

1984; (with Kuldip Nayar) Punjab Tragedy, 1984; Truth, Love and a Little Malice (autobiog.), 2002; Death at My Doorstep (obituaries), 2005; *translations:* Umrao Jan Ada, Courtesan of Lucknow, by Mohammed Ruswa (with M. A. Husaini); The Skeleton (by Amrita Pritam); Land of the Five Rivers; I Take This Woman, by Rajinder Singh Bedi; Iqbal's Dialogue with Allah (Shikwah and Jawab-e-Shikwah); We Indians. *Recreation:* bird watching. *Address:* 49E Sujan Singh Park, New Delhi 110003, India. *T:* (11) 690159. *Clubs:* Imperial Gymkhana (New Delhi); Bombay Gymkhana (Bombay).

SINGH, Laleshwar Kumar Narayan, CCH 1996; High Commissioner for Guyana in London, since 1993; also non-resident Ambassador to The Netherlands, since 1993, the Republic of France, since 1995, the Russian Federation, since 1995, the Czech Republic, since 1997 and the Holy See, since 1998; *b* 2 April 1941; *s* of late Mr and Mrs Narayan, Windsor Forest, Guyana; *m* 1971, Latchmin Ramrattan; one *s* one *d*. *Educ:* Windsor Forest Govt Sch., Guyana; Indian Educn Trust Coll., Guyana; Univ. of London (ext. student; Intermediate Exam. in Laws); Court Clerk Trng Course. Left Guyana, 1961 to work and study in England; Inner London Magistrates' Courts Service, 1971–93: work in magistrates' courts and Admin Office, Principal Chief Clerk's Office; Personnel Officer, 1988–89. *Address:* Guyana High Commission, 3 Palace Court, Bayswater Road, W2 4LP. *T:* (020) 7229 7684, *Fax:* (020) 7727 9809.

SINGH, Manmohan, DPhil; Member, Rajya Sabha, since 1991; Prime Minister of India, since 2004; *b* 26 Sept. 1932; *m* Gursharan Kaur; three *d*. *Educ:* Punjab Univ.; St John's Coll., Cambridge (BA 1957); Nuffield Coll., Oxford (DPhil 1962). Lectr, Punjab Univ., 1957–69; Prof., Delhi Sch. of Econs, 1969–71; Secretariat, UNCTAD; Econ. Advr, Commerce Min., India, 1971; Chief Econ. Advr, then Sec., Min. of Finance, 1972–76; Dir, 1976–80, Gov., 1982–85, Reserve Bank of India; Dep. Chm., Planning Commn, 1980–82; Sec.-Gen., South Commn, Geneva, 1987–90; Advr to Prime Minister, 1990–91; Finance Minister, 1991–96; Leader of the Opposition, 1998–2004. Chm., Univ. Grants Commn. Hon. DCL Oxon, 2005; Hon. LLD Cantab, 2006. Padma Vibhushan, 1987. *Publication:* India's Export Trends and Prospects for Self-Sustained Growth, 1964. *Address:* Office of the Prime Minister, South Block, New Delhi 110011, India.

SINGH, Margaret Stella, (Mrs Christopher Cook), CBE 1996; Chair, Association of District Councils, 1993–95; *b* 10 Aug. 1945; *d* of Edward Richard Jones and Stella Jones; *m* 1st (marr. diss.); one *s* one *d*; 2nd, 2001, Christopher Cook; one step *d*. Working in and for local govt, 1962–; Mem. (Lab) Reading BC, 1976–95. Lay Mem., W Norfolk Primary Care Trust, 2000–; Indep. Chm., King's Lynn and W Norfolk Standard Bd, 2002–. Bd Mem., Broadlands Housing Assoc., 2004–. *Recreations:* reading, walking the dogs, listening to people. *Address:* Chiswick House, Creake Road, Burnham Market, Norfolk PE31 8EN.

SINGH, Marsha; MP (Lab) Bradford West, since 1997; *b* 11 Oct. 1954; *s* of Harbans Singh and late Kartar Kaur; *m* 1971, Sital Kaur (*d* 2001); one *s* one *d*. *Educ:* Loughborough Univ. (BA Hons Pols and Econs of Modern Europe). With Lloyds Bank, 1976–79; Bradford Community Relations Council, 1979–80; Bradford Law Centre, 1980–83; Directorate of Educn, Bradford Council, 1983–90; Bradford Community Health Trust, 1990–97. *Recreations:* reading, chess, bridge. *Address:* House of Commons, SW1A 0AA.

SINGH, His Honour Mota; QC 1978; a Circuit Judge, 1982–2002; *b* 26 July 1930; *s* of Dalip Singh and Harnam Kaur; *m* 1950, Swaran Kaur; two *s* one *d*. *Educ:* Duke of Gloucester Sch., Nairobi, Kenya; Hon. Soc. of Lincoln's Inn. Called to the Bar, 1956. Left school, 1947; Solicitor's Clerk, Nairobi, 1948–54; Lincoln's Inn, London, 1954–56; Advocate, High Court of Kenya, 1957–65; Alderman, City of Nairobi, 1958–63; Vice-Chm., Kenya Justice; Sec., Law Soc. of Kenya, 1963–64. A Deputy Circuit Judge, 1976–82; a Recorder of the Crown Court, 1979–82; Bencher, Lincoln's Inn, 2002. Member: London Rent Assessment Panel, 1965–67; Race Relations Bd, 1968–77; Chm., Immigration Adv. Service, 2000–. Chm., Statutory Cttee, RPSGB, 2007–. Vice-Pres., Barnardo's. Trustee: St George's Hosp., Tooting; Windsor Leadership Trust. Chairman: Eur. Sect., World Sikh Council, 1998–; Guru Nanak Internat. Educn Fund, Punjab, India, 2006–. Patron: Anne Frank Foundn; World Council of Faiths; Swami Narayan Temple, Neasden; Ben Samuel Trust. Lifetime Achievement Award, Asian Jewels Awards, 2003. Hon. LLD Guru Nanak Dev Univ., Amritsar, 1981. *Recreations:* reading; formerly cricket (represented Kenya). *Club:* MCC.

SINGH, Sir Pritpal, Kt 2005; Head, Drayton Manor High School, since 1994; *b* 22 June 1953; *s* of Dr Gurbuxsh Singh and Vidya Vati; *m* 1983, Elizabeth Szulc; two *s*. *Educ:* Chelsea Coll., Univ. of London (BSc (Hons) Chemistry 1975; PGCE 1979; MA 1986). Head of Chemistry, Feltham Sch., 1982–86; Head of Science, Vyne Sch., 1986–89; Dep. Head, Cranford Community Sch., 1989–94. Non-exec. Dir, E Berks NHS Trust, 1999–2001. Mem., Educn Cttee, Royal Soc., 2003–04. *Recreations:* history, Rugby, sport, travel, music. *Address:* Drayton Manor High School, Drayton Bridge Road, W7 1EU. *T:* (020) 8357 1900, *Fax:* (020) 8357 1901.

SINGH, Rabinder; QC 2002; a Deputy High Court Judge, since 2003; a Recorder, since 2004; *b* 6 March 1964; *s* of late Lakhinder Singh and Swarn Kaur; *m* 1989, Alison Joy Baigent; two *s*. *Educ:* Bristol Grammar Sch.; Trinity Coll., Cambridge (BA Hons 1985); Univ. of Calif, Berkeley (LLM 1986). Lectr in Law, Univ. of Nottingham, 1986–88; called to the Bar, Lincoln's Inn, 1989; in practice as barrister, 1989–. Visitor, Brunel Univ., 2006–. *Publications:* The Future of Human Rights in the United Kingdom, 1997; contrib. articles to Public Law, Judicial Rev. and Eur. Human Rights Law Rev. *Recreations:* walking, drama, film, opera. *Address:* Matrix Chambers, Griffin Building, Gray's Inn, WC1R 5LN. *T:* (020) 7404 3447, *Fax:* (020) 7404 3448; *e-mail:* rabindersingh@matrixlaw.co.uk.

SINGH, Rameshwar, (Ray), CBE 2001; a District Judge, since 1997; *s* of late Brijmohan Singh and Ram Kumari; *m* Gwynneth, BSc; three *s*. *Educ:* Deenbandhu High Sch., Fiji; Council of Legal Educn. In practice as barrister, Wales and Chester Circuit, 1969–97; Dep. Dist Judge, 1992–97. Chm. (pt-time), Child Support Appeals Tribunal, 1993–97; Ind. Chm. (pt-time), Complaints against Nat. Assembly for Wales, 2000. Mem., CRE for England and Wales, 1996–2002. Member: Adv. Cttee on Drugs and Alcohol Abuse to Sec. of State for Wales, 1996–2000; Nat. Assembly for Wales Adv. Cttee, 1999–2000. Mem., S Wales Criminal Justice Cttee, 1996. Chairman: Challenges for the Future, Birmingham, 2000–01; Formal Investigation into the Prison Service, 2000; Stephen Lawrence Inquiry Commn, 2002; Mem., Rees Commn: student support system and tuition fee regime to Wales, 2004–05. Non-exec. Dir, Gwalia Housing, 1999. FLBA. Mem., Hon. Soc. of Middle Temple. Mem., Age Concern, Wales, 1999. Governor: Swansea Inst. for Higher Educn, 2000; Swansea Coll., 2002. *Recreations:* mountain walking, cooking, watching cricket, Rugby. *Address:* Merthyr Tydfil Combined Law Courts, Glebeland Place, Merthyr Tydfil CF47 8TJ; Maranatha, Cilfrew, Neath SA10 8NE. *Clubs:* Neath Cricket; Bonymaen Rugby Football.

SINGH, Reuben; Chairman and Chief Executive Officer, alldayPA, since 2002; Chairman, Reuben Singh Group of Companies, since 2000; *b* 20 Sept. 1976. *Educ:* William Hulme Grammar Sch., Manchester. Founded first company, Miss Attitude, 1994; launched IT Golden Fund, 2001. Member: Competitiveness Council, DTI, 1999–2001; Small Business Council, DTI, 2000–02. British Ambassador for Entrepreneurship, 1999; Chm., Genesis Initiative, 2000–02. British Entrepreneur of the Year, 2002; Asian Entrepreneur of the Year, 2002; World Sikh Personality of the Year, 2003; listed as Youngest Self-made Millionaire, Guinness Book of World Records, 1998. *Recreations:* inspiring future entrepreneurs younger than myself. *T:* 0845 053 1677; *e-mail:* danielle@freedman.alldaypa.com.

SINGH, Simon Lehna, MBE 2003; PhD; writer, journalist and television producer; *b* 19 Sept. 1964; *s* of Mengha and Sawarn Singh. *Educ:* Imperial Coll., London (BSc Physics 1987); Emmanuel Coll., Cambridge (PhD Physics 1990). Joined Science Dept, BBC, 1991, producer, director and broadcaster, radio and TV; Dir, Fermat's Last Theorem (documentary), 1996 (BAFTA Award for best documentary); presenter, Science of Secrecy (series), Channel 4, 2001. Trustee, Science Mus., 2002–06. *Publications:* Fermat's Last Theorem, 1997; The Code Book, 1999; Big Bang, 2004; Trick or Treatment?, 2008. *Recreations:* games of chance, observing solar eclipses. *Address:* PO Box 827, Richmond, Surrey TW9 1QU; *e-mail:* simon@simonsingh.net.

SINGH, Vijay; golfer; *b* Fiji, 22 Feb. 1963; *m* Ardena Seth; one *s*. *Educ:* Univ. of N Carolina. Professional golfer, 1982–; joined PGA Tour, 1983; wins include: Malaysian Championship, 1984; Malaysian Open, 1992, 2001; Buick Classic, 1993, 1995, 2004, 2005; Toyota World Match Play Championship, 1997; Buick Open, 1997, 2004; US PGA Championship, 1998, 2004; US Masters, 2000; Singapore Masters, 2001; Tour Championship, 2002; Pebble Beach Nat. Pro-Am, 2004; Canadian Open, 2004; Sony Open, 2005; Chrysler Championship, 2005. Member: President's Cup Team, 1994, 1996, 1998, 2000, 2003; World Cup Team, 2002. *Address:* c/o IMG Golf, IMG Center, Suite 100, 1360 East 9th Street, Cleveland, OH 44114, USA.

SINGH, Vishwanath Pratap; Prime Minister of India, 1989–90; *b* 25 June 1931; *s* of Raja Bahadur Ram Gopal Singh; *m* 1955, Sita Kumari; two *s*. *Educ:* Poona Univ.; Allahabad Univ. (Vice-Pres., Students Union; LLB); Udip Pratap College, Varanasi (Pres., Students Union). Participated in Bhoodan Movement, 1957, and donated farm, Pasna, Allahabad; Mem. Exec., Allahabad Univ., 1969–71; founded Gopal Vidyalaya, Intermediate Coll., Koraon, Allahabad. Uttar Pradesh appointments: MLA, 1969–71 and 1981–83; Whip, Congress Legislature Party, 1970–71; MLC, 1980–81; Chief Minister, 1980–82; Pres., UP Congress Cttee, 1984. Mem., Lok Sabha, 1971–77, 1980, 1988–89 and 1989–94; Mem., Rajya Sabha, 1983–88; Union Dep. Minister (Commerce), 1974–76; Union Minister of State (Commerce), 1976–77; Union Minister (Commerce), 1983 (also i/c Dept of Supply); Union Finance Minister, 1984–87; Defence Minister, Jan.–April 1987. Founded Jan Morcha, 1987; Pres., Janata Dal, 1988; Convenor, Nat. Front, 1988. *Address:* 1 Teen Murti Marg, New Delhi 110001, India.

SINGLETON, Barry Neill; QC 1989; *b* 12 April 1946; *s* of late Clifford and Moyna Singleton; *m* 1971, Anne Mary Potter; one *s* two *d*. *Educ:* Downside Sch.; Gonville and Caius Coll., Cambridge (MA). Called to the Bar, Gray's Inn, 1968. *Address:* 1 King's Bench Walk, Temple, EC4Y 7DB. *T:* (020) 7936 1500, *Fax:* (020) 7936 1590.

SINGLETON, Sir Roger, Kt 2006; CBE 1997; Chief Executive, Barnardo's, 1984–2006; consultant and government advisor, since 2006; *b* 6 Nov. 1942; *s* of late Malcolm and Ethel Singleton, Nether Edge, Sheffield; *m* 1966, Ann Hasler; two *d*. *Educ:* City Grammar Sch., Sheffield; Durham Univ. (MA); Bath Univ. (MSc); London Univ. (DipSocStud); Leeds (Cert. Ed.). Accredited Mediator. Appts in care and educn of deprived and delinquent young people, 1961–71; professional adviser to Children's Regional Planning Cttee, 1971–74; Dep. Dir, Dr Barnardo's, 1974–84. Non-exec. Dir, Capacitybuilders, 2006–. Chm., Ind. Safeguarding Authy (formerly Ind. Barring Bd), 2007–. Trustee, Nat. Council of Voluntary Child Care Organisations, 1984–2002 (Chm., 1990–92); Member: Central Council for Educn and Training in Social Work, 1984–86; Council, Nat. Children's Bureau, 1982–84; Council, Nat. Youth Bureau, 1986–91. Chair: Princess of Wales Meml Fund, 2006– (Trustee, 2001–); Perennial (Gardeners' Royal Benevolent Soc.), 2006–. Trustee: Inst. for Global Ethics, 2006–; Children's High Level Gp, 2006–. Pres., Friends of St Andrew's Ch, Shalford, 2006–. CCMI (FBIM 1982); FRSA 1991. *Publications:* contribs to professional jls. *Recreation:* timber framed buildings. *Address:* *e-mail:* RandASingleton@aol.com. *Club:* Reform.

SINGLETON, Sarah Louise; QC 2006; a Recorder, since 2000; *b* 9 March 1962; *d* of James and Beryl Singleton; *m* 1991, Bill Hewitt; one *s* one *d*. *Educ:* Goffs Oak Primary Sch., Herts; Roedean; Lancaster Girls' Grammar Sch.; Hertford Coll., Oxford (BA Juris. 1982). Called to the Bar, Middle Temple, 1983; Asst Recorder, 1999–2000. *Recreations:* cycling, running, dogs, enjoying CaniX (running with dogs), cats, reading (member of two book clubs). *Address:* St John's Buildings Chambers, St John's Buildings, 24a–28 St John Street, Manchester M3 4DJ. *T:* (0161) 214 1500, *Fax:* (0161) 835 3929; *e-mail:* clerks@stjohnsbuildings.co.uk.

SINGLETON, Valerie, OBE 1994; television broadcaster, travel writer for newspapers and magazines; with BBC, 1962–93; *b* 9 April 1937; *d* of Wing Comdr Denis G. Singleton, OBE and late Eileen Singleton, LRAM. *Educ:* Arts Educational Sch. (3 times Drama Cup); RADA (schol.). Bromley Rep.; commercial voice-overs; TV advertising magazines; joined BBC as announcer, 1962; presenter: Blue Peter, 1962–71; Blue Peter Special Assignments, covering capital cities, islands, famous houses, 1972–75, and Rivers Niagra and Yukon, 1980; Val Meets the VIPs, 1972–75; Nationwide, 1972–78; Tonight, and Tonight in Town, 1978–79; Echoes of Holocaust, documentary, BBC 2, Midweek, Radio 4, 1980; The Money Programme, BBC 2, 1980–88; Radio 4 PM, 1981–93; (jtly) Travel UK, Central TV, 1992; Backdate, Channel 4, 1996; Playback, History Channel, 2 series, 1998, 1999; numerous other radio and TV progs; corporate videos, business confs. Work for British Wildlife Appeal and Barnardo's. *Recreations:* sailing, ski-ing, water ski-ing, photography, exploring London, travelling anywhere, riding, pottering in museums and antique shops. *Address:* c/o Panmedia, 18 Montrose Crescent, N12 0ED. *Club:* Hurlingham.

SINGLETON, William Brian, CBE 1974; FRCVS; retired; Director, Animal Health Trust, 1977–88; *b* 23 Feb. 1923; *s* of William Max Singleton and Blanche May Singleton; *m* 1947, Hilda Stott; two *s* one *d* (and one *s* decd). *Educ:* Queen Elizabeth Grammar Sch., Darlington; Royal (Dick) Sch. of Vet. Studies, Edinburgh. Vis. Prof. Surgery, Ontario Vet. Coll., Guelph, Canada, 1973–74; Hon. Vet. Advr to Jockey Club, 1977–88. Member: Govt Cttee of Inquiry into Future Role of Veterinary Profession in GB (Chm., Sir Michael Swann), 1971–75; UGC Wkg Pty on Vet. Educn into the 21st Century (Chm., Sir Ralph Riley, FRS), 1987–89. President: British Small Animal Vet. Assoc., 1960–61; RCVS, 1969–70; World Small Animal Vet. Assoc., 1975–77; BEVA, 1988–89. Hon. Diplomate, Amer. Coll. of Vet. Surgeons, 1973; Hon. DVM & S Edinburgh, 1993. Dalrymple-Champneys Award, 1987. *Publications:* (contrib.) Canine Medicine and Therapeutics, 1979; numerous papers on veterinary orthopaedics and comparative medicine. *Recreations:* gardening, sailing, bird watching, horse riding. *Address:* Vine

Cottage, Morston Road, Blakeney, Holt, Norfolk NR25 7BE. *T:* (01263) 740246. *Club:* Farmers'.

SINHA, 6th Baron *cr* 1919, of Raipur; **Arup Kumar Sinha;** *b* 23 April 1966; *er s* of 5th Baron Sinha and of Lolita, *d* of Deb Kumar Das; *S* father, 1999; *m* 1st, 1993, Deborah Jane Tidswell (marr. diss. 1995); 2nd, 2002, Penny. *Heir: b* Hon. Dilip Kumar Sinha, *b* 28 May 1967.

SINKINSON, Philip Andrew, OBE 2006; HM Diplomatic Service; High Commissioner to The Gambia, since 2006; *b* 7 Oct. 1950; *m* 1971, Clare Maria Catherine Jarvis; one *s.* Bd of Inland Revenue, 1967–70; entered FCO, 1970; Warsaw, 1973–74; FCO, 1974; E Berlin, 1974–75; Rome, 1975–76; FCO, 1976–78; Rio de Janeiro, 1978; Quito, 1978–79; Prague, 1979–81; FCO, 1981–82; Blantyre, 1982–85; Lilongwe, 1985–86; FCO, 1986–92; Second Sec. (Commercial), São Paulo, 1992–95; on secondment to British Olympic Assoc., Atlanta, 1995–96; First Sec. (Commercial), Lisbon, 1996–2001; Dep. High Comr, Jamaica, 2001–05. *Address:* c/o Foreign and Commonwealth Office, King Charles Street, SW1A 2AH.

SINNATT, Maj.-Gen. Martin Henry, CB 1984; *b* 28 Jan. 1928; *s* of Dr O. S. Sinnatt and Mrs M. H. Sinnatt (*née* Randall); *m* 1957, Susan Rosemary Clarke; four *d. Educ:* Hitchin Grammar School; Hertford College, Oxford (1 Year Army Short Course); RMA Sandhurst. Commissioned RTR, 1948; served Germany, Korea, UK, Hong Kong, 1948–58; psc 1959; Aden, 1959–62; Germany and UK, 1962–64; MA to C-in-C AFNE, Norway, 1964–66; jssc 1967; Germany and UK, 1967–69; CO 4 RTR, BAOR, 1969–71; Nat. Defence Coll., 1971–72; Comdr RAC, 1 (BR) Corps, BAOR, 1972–74; Dir Operational Requirements MoD, 1974–77; rcds 1978; Dir, Combat Development (Army), 1979–81; Chief of Staff to Live Oak, SHAPE, 1982–84; completed service, 1984. Sen. Exec. and Sec., Kennel Club, 1984–93. *Address:* Meadowside Farmhouse, Tulls Lane, Standford, Bordon, Hants GU35 8RB.

SINNOTT, John Brian; Chief Executive, Leicestershire County Council and Clerk of Lieutenancy, since 1994; *b* 11 March 1949; *s* of William John Sinnott and Mary Josephine Sinnott (*née* Foley); *m* 1970, Helen Mary Turner; two *s* two *d. Educ:* St Mary's Coll., Crosby; Univ. of Liverpool (MA, Dip. Public Admin). Liverpool CC, 1970–74; PA to Chm. and Leader of Council, Head of Leader's office, Merseyside CC, 1974–86; Management Consultant, Coopers and Lybrand Associates, 1986–87; Leicestershire County Council: Asst, then Sen. Asst, County Clerk, 1987–90; Asst Chief Exec., 1990–92; Dir, Corporate Management, 1992–94. Director: Leics TEC, 1994–2001; Leics Business Point (Business Link), 1995–2001; Leics Develt Agency, 1998–2003; Heart of the Nat. Forest Foundn, 1998–2004; Leics and Rutland Sport, 2005–; Leics Econ. Partnership, 2007–. Chm., ACCE, 2001–02. Chairman: Leics Cricket Bd, 2001–06; Everton FC Shareholders' Assoc., 2003–04. *Publications:* papers in local govt jls. *Recreations:* sport, cricket literature, history of rock music. *Address:* County Hall, Glenfield, Leicester LE3 8RA. *T:* (0116) 305 6000. *Club:* Everton Football.

SINTON, William Baldie, OBE 1999; HM Diplomatic Service, retired; Clerk, Committee Office, House of Lords, since 2006; *b* 17 June 1946; *s* of late John William Sinton and Isabella McCrae Sinton (*née* Baldie); *m* 1995, Jane S. B. Aryee. *Educ:* Bristol Cathedral Sch.; Kirkcaldy High Sch.; Edinburgh Univ. (MA 1968). Third Sec., FCO, 1968; Third later Second Sec., Prague, 1970; Second later First Sec., UK Delegn to NATO, Brussels, 1973; FCO, 1977–81; First Sec. (Commercial), Algiers, 1981; FCO, 1985–96; Ambassador to Panama, 1996–99; Ambassador to Algeria, 1999–2001; Ambassador to Bolivia, 2001–05. *Address:* 22 Fairburn Court, St John's Avenue, SW15 2AU. *Clubs:* Reform; Kirkcaldy Golf, Lundin Golf.

SINYOR, Joseph, (Joe); Managing Director, Strategic Value Partners LLP, since 2007; *b* 16 Aug. 1957; *s* of Samuel Joseph Sinyor and Claire Sinyor; *m* 1987, Pamela Caroline Nield Collis; two *s* one *d. Educ:* Jesus Coll., Cambridge; London Business Sch. (MBA). Corporate Finance Exec., J. Henry Schroder Wagg, 1983–85; Sen. Engagement Manager, McKinsey & Co. Inc., 1985–90; Gp Chief Exec., Pepe Gp plc, 1990–93; Man. Dir, Dillon's Bookstores Ltd, 1994–98; Man. Dir, Sony UK Ltd, 1998–2000; Chief Exec., Newspapers, Trinity Mirror plc, 2000–03; Man. Dir, Terra Firma Capital Partners, 2003–06. Non-exec. Dir, Channel 4 TV Corp., 1998–2004. *Recreations:* opera, ski-ing, walking. *Address:* Strategic Value Partners LLP, 5 Savile Row, W1S 3PD. *T:* (020) 7758 7828.

SIONE, Hon. Sir Tomu (Malaefone), GCMG 2001; OBE 1989; MP Niutao and Niulakifa Islands, Tuvalu, since 1970; Chairman of the Caucus, since 2006; *b* 17 Nov. 1941; *m* 1979, Segali Lusia; four *s* two *d.* Journalist, 1962–68. Gov.-Gen., Tuvalu, 1993–94. Speaker, Parlt of Tuvalu, 1998–2006. *Recreation:* fishing. *Address:* Parliament of Tuvalu, Funafuti, Tuvalu. *T:* (688) 20252, *Fax:* (688) 20253; Niutau Island, Tuvalu.

SIRKS, Prof. (Adriaan Johan) Boudewijn; Regius Professor of Civil Law, University of Oxford, and Fellow of All Souls College, Oxford, since 2006. *Educ:* Leyden Univ. (LLM 1972); Univ. of Amsterdam (PhD 1984). Formerly: Lectr, Hist. of Roman Law, Utrecht State Univ.; Associate Prof. of Legal Techniques, Univ. of Amsterdam; Prof. of Legal Hist. and Private Law, Johann Wolfgang Goethe Univ., Frankfurt am Main, 1998–2006. *Publications:* Food for Rome, 1991; (jtly) Ein früh-byzantinisches Szenario für die Amtswechslung in der Sitonie, 1996; The Theodosian Code: a study, 2007. *Address:* All Souls College, Oxford OX1 4AL; *e-mail:* boudewijn.sirks@law.ox.ac.uk.

SIRS, William; JP; General Secretary, Iron and Steel Trades Confederation, 1975–85, retired; *b* 6 Jan. 1920; *s* of Frederick Sirs and Margaret (*née* Powell); *m* 1941, Joan (*née* Clark); one *s* one *d. Educ:* Middleton St Johns, Hartlepool; WEA. Steel Industry, 1937–63; Iron and Steel Trades Confedn: Organiser, 1963; Divisional Officer, Manchester, 1970; Asst Gen. Sec., 1973. Member: Iron and Steel Industry Trng Bd, 1973; TUC Gen. Council, 1975–85; Trade Union Steel Industry Cons. Cttee, 1973– (Chm., 1975–) and Jt Accident Prevention Adv. Cttee, 1973; Employment Appeal Tribunal, 1976–; Jt Sec., Jt Industrial Council for Slag Industry, 1973; Exec. Mem., Paul Finet Foundn, European Coal and Steel Community, 1974; Hon. Sec. (British Section), Internat. Metalworkers Fedn, 1975. Mem., Management Cttee, BSC (Industry) Ltd, 1975–. Pres., Northern Home Counties Productivity Assoc., 1985–; Mem. RIIA, 1973. Mem. Council, Winston Churchill Meml Trust, 1985–90. Director (formerly Governor), Oaklands Coll., Herts, 1991–. JP Hartlepool, Co. Durham, later Knutsford, Cheshire, then Herts, 1963. Freeman, City of London, 1984. *Publication:* Hard Labour (autobiog.), 1985. *Recreations:* sailing, squash, swimming, running. *Address:* Hatfield, Hertfordshire.

SISSON, Rosemary Anne; writer since 1929; *b* 13 Oct. 1923; *d* of Prof. C. J. Sisson, MA, DèsL and Vera Kathleen (*née* Ginn). *Educ:* Cheltenham Ladies' Coll.; University Coll., London (BA Hons English); Newnham Coll., Cambridge (MLit). Served War, Royal Observer Corps, 1943–45. Instr in English, Univ. of Wisconsin, 1949; Lecturer in English: UCL, 1950–53; Univ. of Birmingham, 1953–54; Dramatic Critic, Stratford-upon-Avon Herald, 1954–57; after prodn of first play, The Queen and the Welshman, became full-time writer, 1957. Co-Chm., Writers Guild of GB, 1979 and 1980 (Pres., 1995–98); Hon. Sec., Dramatists' Club, 1984–2008; Mem., BAFTA (Mem. Council, 1995–98). Laurel Award, for service to writers, 1985; Prince Michael of Kent Award, for services to SSAFA, 1987. *Plays:* The Queen and the Welshman, 1957; Fear Came to Supper, 1958; The Splendid Outcasts, 1959; The Royal Captivity, 1960; Bitter Sanctuary, 1963; Ghost on Tiptoe (with Robert Morley), 1974; The Dark Horse, 1978. Contributed to *TV series:* Catherine of Aragon, in The Six Wives of Henry VIII; The Marriage Game, in Elizabeth R; Upstairs, Downstairs; The Duchess of Duke Street; A Town Like Alice; The Young Indiana Jones Chronicles; *TV scripts:* Irish RM; Seal Morning; The Manions of America; The Bretts (creator of series). *Film scripts* include: Ride a Wild Pony; Escape from the Dark; Candleshoe; Watcher in the Woods; The Black Cauldron (full-length animation film) (all for Walt Disney); The Wind in the Willows (animation film), 1983 (also TV series, 1984). *Other scripts:* Heart of a Nation (Son-et-Lumière), Horse Guards Parade, 1983; Dawn to Dusk, Royal Tournament, 1984; Joy to the World, Royal Albert Hall, 1988–97; Royal Military Tattoo, 2000; All the Queen's Horses, 2002; Debt of Honour, Greenwich, 2007. *Publications: children's books:* The Adventures of Ambrose, 1951; The Young Shakespeare, 1959; The Young Jane Austen, 1962; The Young Shaftesbury, 1964; *novels:* The Exciseman, 1972; The Killer of Horseman's Flats, 1973; The Stratford Story, 1975; Escape from the Dark, 1976; The Queen and the Welshman, 1979; The Manions of America, 1982; Bury Love Deep, 1985; Beneath the Visiting Moon, 1986; The Bretts, 1987; Footstep on the Stair, 1999; First Love, Last Love, 2002; Oh My Bonny Blue-eyed Boy! - The Great Gateshead Disaster, 2009; *poetry:* Rosemary for Remembrance, 1995. *Recreations:* travel, walking, riding, writing poetry, being a great-aunt. *Address:* 167 New King's Road, Parson's Green, SW6 4SN.

SISSONS, Prof. (John Gerald) Patrick, MD; FRCP, FRCPath; Professor of Medicine, 1988–2005, Regius Professor of Physic, since 2005, University of Cambridge; Fellow of Darwin College, Cambridge, since 1988; *b* 28 June 1945; *s* of Gerald William Sissons and Georgina Margaret Cockin; *m* 1971, Jennifer Ann Scovell (marr. diss. 1987); two *d. Educ:* Felstead Sch.; St Mary's Hosp. Med. Sch. (MB, MD). FRCP 1983; FRCPath 1995. Hosp. appts, St Mary's, St George's and Hammersmith Hosps, 1968–71; Registrar and Lectr, Dept of Medicine, RPMS, 1972–77; NIH Research Fellow and Asst Mem., Res. Inst. of Scripps Clinic, California, 1977–80; Wellcome Sen. Lectr, Depts of Medicine and Virology, RPMS, 1980–86; Prof. of Infectious Diseases, RPMS, 1987. Hon. Consultant Physician, Cambridge Univ. Hosps (formerly Addenbrooke's) NHS Trust, 1988–. Founder FMedSci 1998. *Publications:* papers on immunology and pathogenesis of virus infections. *Recreation:* travel. *Address:* Department of Medicine, University of Cambridge School of Clinical Medicine, Hills Road, Cambridge CB2 2SP. *T:* (01223) 336738.

SISSONS, Michael; *see* Sissons, T. M. B.

SISSONS, Peter George; presenter, BBC News 24, since 2002; *b* 17 July 1942; *s* of late George Robert Percival Sissons and Elsie Emma Evans; *m* 1965, Sylvia Bennett; two *s* one *d. Educ:* Liverpool Inst. High Sch. for Boys; University College Oxford (MA PPE). Independent Television News: graduate trainee, 1964; general reporter, 1967; industrial corresp., 1970; indust. editor, 1972–78; presenter, News at One, 1978–82; presenter: Channel Four News, 1982–89; BBC TV 6 o'clock news, 1989–93; BBC TV 9 o'clock news, 1993–2000; BBC TV 10 o'clock news, 2000–02; Chm., BBC TV Question Time, 1989–93; occasional presenter, Breakfast with Frost, 2002–05. Hon. Fellow, Liverpool John Moores Univ., 1997. Hon. LLD Liverpool, 2002. Broadcasting Press Guild Award, 1984; RTS Judges' Award, 1988; Newscaster of the Year, TRIC, 2001. *Recreations:* relaxing, supporting Liverpool FC. *Address:* BBC Television Centre, Wood Lane, W12 7RJ. *T:* (020) 8743 8000.

SISSONS, (Thomas) Michael (Beswick); Senior Consultant, The Peters Fraser and Dunlop Group Ltd, since 1999 (Managing Director, 1988–94; Chairman, 1988–99); *b* 13 Oct. 1934; *s* of Captain T. E. B. Sissons (killed in action, 1940) and late Marjorie (*née* Shepherd); *m* 1st, 1960, Nicola Ann Fowler (marr. diss. 1974); one *s* one *d*; 2nd, 1974, Ilze Kadegis (marr. diss. 1992); two *d*; 3rd, 1992, Serena Palmer. *Educ:* Winchester Coll.; Exeter Coll., Oxford (BA 1958, MA 1964). National Service, 2nd Lieut 13/18 Royal Hussars, 1953–55. Lectr in History, Tulane Univ., New Orleans, USA, 1958–59; joined A.D. Peters, Literary Agent, 1959; Dir, 1965, Chm. and Man. Dir, 1973–88, A. D. Peters & Co. Ltd. Pres., Assoc. of Authors' Agents, 1978–81; Director: London Broadcasting Co., 1973–75; Groucho Club plc, 1985–2001; Mem. Council, Consumers Assoc., 1974–77. Board Member: BFSS, 1994–95; Countryside Movt, 1995–97. *Publications:* (ed with Philip French) Age of Austerity, 1963, repr. 1986; (ed) A Countryside for All, 2001. *Recreations:* gardening, cricket, music. *Address:* The White House, Broadleaze Farm, Westcot Lane, Sparsholt, Wantage, Oxon OX12 9PZ. *T:* (01235) 751215, *Fax:* (01235) 751561. *Clubs:* Boodle's, Groucho, MCC (Mem. Cttee, 1984–87, 1993–2000; Chm., Marketing and Public Affairs Sub-Cttee, 1995–2000).

SITWELL, Peter Sacheverell W.; *see* Wilmot-Sitwell.

SITWELL, Sir (Sacheverell) Reresby, 7th Bt *cr* 1808, of Renishaw; DL; *b* 15 April 1927; *s* of Sir Sacheverell Sitwell, 6th Bt, CH and Georgia Louise (*d* 1980), *d* of Arthur Doble; *S* father, 1988; *m* 1952, Penelope, *yr d* of late Col Hon. Donald Alexander Forbes, DSO, MVO; one *d. Educ:* Eton College; King's Coll., Cambridge (schol.). Served Grenadier Guards, 1945–48, mainly as Lieut, 2nd Bn, BAOR. Advertising and PR executive, 1948–63; operated vending machines and wholesale wine business, 1963–73. Took over Renishaw and family estates from late uncle, Sir Osbert, 1965. High Sheriff of Derbyshire, 1983; DL Derbyshire 1984. Freedom of City of London, 1984. Hon. Fellow, Grey Coll., Durham, 2001. Hon. LittD Sheffield, 2004. *Publications:* (with John Julius Norwich and A. Costa) Mount Athos, 1964; Hortus Sitwellianus (epilogue), 1984; Robin Hood's Bow, 2007. *Recreations:* art and architecture, music, travel, photography, racing. *Heir: nephew* George Reresby Sacheverell Sitwell, *b* 22 April 1967. *Address:* Renishaw Hall, Sheffield S21 3WB; 4 Southwick Place, W2 2TN. *T:* (020) 7262 3939. *Clubs:* White's, Brooks's, Pratt's, Society of Dilettanti; Pitt (Cambridge); Derby County.

SIU, Gordon Kwing-Chue, GBS 2002; CBE 1997; JP; Secretary for Planning and Lands, Hong Kong, 1999–2002; *b* 29 Nov. 1945; *s* of Siu Wood-chuen and Chan Shuk-ming; *m* 1999, Cynthia Wong Lok-yee; two *s* by a previous marriage. *Educ:* Birmingham Univ. (MSocSci). Joined Hong Kong Civil Service, 1966; Sec.-Gen., Office of Members of Exec. and Legislative Councils, 1985; Postmaster Gen., 1988; Comr for Transport, 1989; Dir, New Airport Projects Co-ordination Office, 1992; Secretary for: Economic Services, 1993; Transport, 1996; Hd, Central Policy Unit, 1997. *Recreations:* reading, swimming, golf. *Clubs:* Hong Kong Golf, Hong Kong Jockey.

SIZELAND, Paul Raymond, CMG 2006; HM Diplomatic Service, retired; Director, Economic Development, City of London Corporation, since 2008 (Assistant Director, City, European and International Affairs, 2006–08); *b* 19 Feb. 1952; *s* of Raymond Sizeland and Patricia Sizeland (*née* Dudley); *m* 1976, Vasantha, *d* of late James Kanaka and Nancy Jesudasan; two *d. Educ:* Dulwich Coll.; Bradford Univ. (BTech Hons Applied Biol. 1975). MIPD 1995. VSO teacher, St Stephen's Coll., Trinidad, 1970–71; Res. Student,

Rowett Res. Inst., Aberdeen, 1973–74; CMS volunteer teacher, Ida Scudder Sch., Vellore, S India, 1976–78; Med. Rep. for Essex and Suffolk, Merrell Pharmaceuticals, 1978–80; joined HM Diplomatic Service, 1980; Third Sec., UK Delegn to NATO, Brussels, 1981–84; Commercial Attaché, Doha, 1985–86; Second Sec., FCO, 1986–88; First Sec., Political/Develt, Lagos, 1988–91; Private Sec. to Lord Carrington, Chm., EU Conf. on former Yugoslavia, 1991–92; Head, Career Develt Unit, FCO, 1992–95; Dep. Head, Personnel Mgt Dept, FCO, 1995–96; Dep. Hd of Mission, Bangkok, 1996–2000; Consul Gen., Shanghai, 2000–03; Dir, Consular Services, FCO, 2003–06. Trustee, Prisoners Abroad, 2006. *Recreations:* family, Millwall FC supporter, travel, books, music, Kipling Society. *Address:* PO Box 270, Guildhall, EC2P 2EJ.

SKARBEK, Marjorie Shiona, (Countess Skarbek); *see* Wallace, M. S.

SKEA, James Ferguson, OBE 2004; Director, UK Energy Research Centre, since 2004; *b* 1 Sept. 1953; *s* of Colin Hill Skea and Margaret Ferguson Skea; *m* 1976, Jane Howley (marr. diss. 2001); one *s* one *d*; partner, Hilary Ann Ougham. *Educ:* Grove Acad., Broughty Ferry; Univ. of Edinburgh (BSc 1st cl. Hons); Clare Coll., Cambridge (PhD 1979). Res. Asst, Cavendish Lab., 1978–81; Vis. Res. Associate, Carnegie-Mellon Univ., 1981–83; Res. Fellow, 1983–94, Professorial Fellow, 1994–98, Science Policy Res. Unit; Director: Global Envmtl Change Prog., ESRC, 1995–98; PSI, 1998–2004. FRSA 2000. *Publications:* Acid Politics, 1991; Standards, Innovation, Competitiveness and Policy, 1995; Clean and Competitive, 1997; Pollution for Sale, 1998. *Recreations:* walking the South Downs, mountain biking, losing keys. *Address:* 76 Springfield Road, Brighton BN1 6DE. *T:* (01273) 549337; *e-mail:* j.skea@btinternet.com.

SKEAPING, Lucie; musician, singer, broadcaster; Founder and Director of ensembles: The City Waites, since 1978; The Burning Bush, since 1992; *d* of Dr Bernard Finch and Patricia Finch, sculptor; *m* 1979, Roderick Skeaping; one *s*. *Educ:* King Alfred Sch., London; Henrietta Barnett Sch., London; Arts Educnl Sch., London; RCM. Specialist in early and trad. English and Jewish music; presenter: music, travel, and children's programmes, BBC TV, 1980–85; Early Music, BBC Radio 3, 1995–; music and hist. documentaries and features for radio, incl. Early Music Show, Proms, Morning Performance, CD Review. Artistic Dir, Windsor Fest., 1995–1999. Performances with groups incl. English Consort of Viols, Michael Nyman Band, Sadista Sisters, Martin Best Ensemble, Consorte of Musick; producer, historical recordings for Soundalive Music, 1994–96; collaborations include: projects and performances for RNT, Rambert Dance Co., RSC, Cultural Co-operation, Shakespeare's Globe; vocal soundtracks include: History of Britain, BBC TV; The Pianist (film), 2002. Mem. Judging Panel, Live Music Now; contrib. to govt singing in schools initiative 'Sing Up'. Patron, Finchley Children's Music Gp, 1995–. Mem., Samuel Pepys Club, 2006–. *Publications:* Let's Make Tudor Music, 1999; Broadside Ballads, 2005 (Best Classical Music Pubn, Music Industry Awards, 2006); contribs to BBC Music Magazine, BBC History Magazine, The Times, Telegraph, Early Music Today. *Address:* 19 Patshull Road, NW5 2JX. *T:* (020) 7485 3957; *e-mail:* lucieskeaping@hotmail.com.

SKEFFINGTON, family name of **Viscount Massereene and Ferrard**.

SKEGG, Prof. David Christopher Graham, OBE 1990; DPhil; FRSNZ; Vice-Chancellor, University of Otago, since 2004; *b* 16 Dec. 1947; *s* of Donald and Margaret Skegg; *m* 1973, Dr Keren Mary Cargo; two *d*. *Educ:* King's Coll., Auckland; Univ. of Auckland; Univ. of Otago (BMedSc 1970; MB ChB 1972); Univ. of Oxford (DPhil 1979). FAFPHM 1994; FFPHM 1999. Rhodes Scholar, Balliol Coll., Oxford, 1973, 1975–76. House Physician, Waikato Hosp., NZ, 1974; Lectr in Epidemiology, Univ. of Oxford, 1976–79; University of Otago: Prof. of Preventive and Social Medicine, 1980–2004; Fellow, Knox Coll., 1980–. Vis. Fellow, Wolfson Coll., Oxford, 1986. Consultant to WHO, Geneva, 1984–2004 (Chm., various adv. cttees); Chairman: Health Res. Council of NZ, 1991–94; Public Health Commn, 1992–95; BSE Expert Sci. Panel, 1996–. Sec., Rhodes Scholarships in NZ, 2004–. FRSNZ 1992. NZ Commem. Medal, 1990; Sir Charles Hercus Medal, Royal Soc. of NZ, 1999; Dist. Res. Medal, Univ. of Otago, 2003. *Publications:* scientific articles on cancer causes and control, contraceptive and drug safety and epidemiology of multiple sclerosis and AIDS. *Recreations:* books, art history, walking. *Address:* University Lodge, St Leonards, Dunedin, New Zealand. *T:* (3) 4798253.

SKEGGS, Sir Clifford (George), Kt 1987; JP; FNZIM; Chairman and Chief Executive, Skeggs Group; Director of various public and private companies; Mayor, Dunedin City, 1978–89; *b* 19 March 1931; *s* of George Henry Skeggs and Beatrice Hannah (*née* Heathcote); *m* 1952, Marie Eleanor Ledgerwood; three *s*. *Educ:* Southland Technical Coll., New Zealand. Mem., 1968–80, Chm., 1973–77, Otago Harbour Bd. City Councillor, Dunedin, 1972–77. Mem. Council, Univ. of Otago, 1981–89. FNZIM 1985; Mem., Inst. of Dirs, 1984. JP Dunedin, 1978. OStJ 1987. *Publications:* contrib. fishing and general business publications. *Recreations:* yachting, golf, flying, power boating, squash, keen follower of Rugby. *Address:* Skeggs Group, Box 5657, Dunedin, New Zealand. *Club:* Dunedin (Dunedin).

SKEHEL, Sir John (James), Kt 1996; PhD; FRS 1984; Director, MRC National Institute for Medical Research, 1987–2006, now Visiting Scientist; *b* 27 Feb. 1941; *s* of Joseph and Annie Josephine Skehel; *m* 1962, Anita Varley; two *s*. *Educ:* St Mary's Coll., Blackburn; University College of Wales, Aberystwyth (BSc); UMIST (PhD). Post-doctoral Fellow, Marischal Coll., Aberdeen, 1965–68; Fellow, Helen Hay Whitney Foundn, 1968–71; MRC National Institute for Medical Research: Mem., Scientific Staff, 1971–2006; Head of Div. of Virology, 1984–87. Dir, World Influenza Centre, 1975–93. Leeuwenhoek Lecture, Royal Soc., 1990. Hon. Professor: Liverpool John Moores Univ. (formerly Liverpool Poly. Sch. of Nat. Sci.), 1990–; Div. of Virology, UCL, 2003; Vis. Prof. of Virology, Glasgow Univ., 1997–. Founder FMedSci 1998 (Vice-Pres., 2001–07). Hon. Fellow, Univ. of Wales, 2004. Hon. DSc: CNAA, 1990; London, 2004; Liverpool John Moores, 2007. Wilhelm Feldberg prize, Feldberg Foundn, 1986; Robert Koch prize, Robert Koch Foundn, 1987; Prix Louis Jeantet de Médecine, Jeantet Foundn, 1988; Internat. Prize in Virology, ICN Pharmaceuticals, 1992; Royal Medal, Royal Soc., 2003; Ernst Chain Prize, Imperial Coll., London, 2004; Grand Prix, Louis D Foundn, Institut de France, 2007. *Publications:* numerous scientific articles in various jls. *Address:* MRC National Institute for Medical Research, The Ridgeway, Mill Hill, NW7 1AA. *T:* (020) 8816 2256.

SKELLETT, Colin Frank, CChem, FRSC; FCIWEM; Chairman, Wessex Water, since 1999; *b* 13 June 1945; *s* of Harry and Ivy Skellett; *m* 1963, Jennifer Trout (marr. diss.); two *s* one *d*. *Educ:* City Univ. (MSc). CChem 1971, FRSC 1990. Chemist, Nottingham CC, 1961–69; Sen. Chemist, Bath CC, 1970–74; operational and mgt posts, Wessex Water, 1974–88; Chief Exec., Wessex Water plc, 1988–99. Non-executive Chairman: Jarvis plc, 2000–02; Regen South West Ltd, 2002–07; European Connoisseurs Travel, 2006–; Vice-Chm., Azurix Services, 1999–2001; Dir, YTL Utilities UK Ltd, 2002–. Bd Mem., SW RDA, 2001–07. Trustee: WaterAid, 1995–2003; Money Advice Trust, 2000–02. Churchill Fellow, 1983. *Publications:* various technical papers on water and waste water treatment. *Recreations:* walking, theatre, music, charity fundraising. *Address:* (office) Wessex Water, Claverton Down, Bath BA2 7WW. *T:* (01225) 526000.

SKELMERSDALE, 7th Baron *cr* 1828; **Roger Bootle-Wilbraham;** Director, Broadleigh Nurseries Ltd, since 1991 (Managing Director, 1973–81); *b* 2 April 1945; *o s* of 6th Baron Skelmersdale, DSO, MC, and Ann (*d* 1974), *d* of late Percy Cuthbert Quilter; *S* father, 1973; *m* 1972, Christine Joan, *o d* of Roy Morgan; one *s* one *d*. *Educ:* Eton; Lord Wandsworth Coll., Basingstoke; Somerset Farm Institute; Hadlow Coll. VSO (Zambia), 1969–71; Proprietor, Broadleigh Gardens, 1972; Vice-Chm., Co En Co, 1979–81. A Lord in Waiting (Govt Whip), 1981–86; Parly Under-Sec. of State, DoE, 1986–87; Parly Under-Sec. of State, DHSS, 1987–88, Dept of Social Security, 1988–89, NI Office, 1989–90; House of Lords: Dep. Chm. of cttees, 1991–96; Dep. Speaker, 1996–2003; elected Mem., 1999; an Opposition Whip, 2003–05; Opposition spokesman on work and pensions, 2005–. President: Somerset Trust for Nature Conservation, 1980–; British Naturalists Assoc., 1980–85. Chm., Stroke Assoc., 1993–2004. Gov., Castle Sch., Taunton, 1993–97. *Recreations:* gardening, reading, bridge playing. *Heir:* *s* Hon. Andrew Bootle-Wilbraham [*b* 9 Aug. 1977; *m* 2005, Fenella Jane, *yr d* of Jonathan Richmond Edwards; one *s*]. *Address:* c/o House of Lords, SW1A 0PW.

SKELTON, Nicholas David, (Nick); show jumper; *b* 30 Nov. 1957; *s* of David Frank Skelton and Norma Skelton (*née* Brindley); *m* 1982, Sarah Poile; two *s*; partner, Bettina Melliger. Jun. European Champion, 1975; British Champion, 1981, on St James; European Championships: team gold medal, 1985, 1987, 1989, team silver medal, 1991, 1993, 1995, individual bronze medal, 1987; World Championships: team bronze medals, 1982, 1990, 1998, team silver medal, and individual bronze medal, on Apollo, 1986; winner: King George V Gold Cup, on St James, 1984, on Limited Edition, 1993, 1996, on Hopes Are High, 1999; Hickstead Derby, on J Nick, 1987, on Apollo, 1988, 1989; Grand Prix in Britain, Canada, France, Germany, Ireland, USA; Member: Nations Cup team, 1978–; Olympic team, 1988, 1992, 1996. Chef d'équipe, British team, Nations Cup, Lisbon, 2001. *Publication:* Only Falls and Horses (autobiog.), 2001.

SKELTON, Peter John, OBE 1997; Director, Tunisia, 2005–Sept. 2009, and Director, Business Support Services, Near East and North Africa Region, 2008–Sept. 2009, British Council; *b* 24 Sept. 1949; *s* of John Frederick and Gwendoline Mabel Skelton; *m* 1971, Heather Morrison (marr. diss. 2008); one *s* one *d*; *m* 2008, Trupti Desai; one *s*. *Educ:* Queen Elizabeth's Grammar Sch., Barnet; Durham Univ. (BA Hons Modern Arabic Studies 1971); UCNW, Bangor (PGCE (TEFL) 1973). Desk Officer, FCO, 1971; British Council: Asst Rep., Jordan, 1977–81, Peru, 1982–84; Dep. Rep., Wales, 1984–86, Zambia, 1986–88; Dir, Hamburg, 1989–93, E Jerusalem (West Bank and Gaza), 1993–98; Regl Dir, Eastern and Central Africa, and Dir, Kenya, 1998–2000; Dir, Cyprus, 2000–05. *Recreations:* listening to music, playing guitar, playing tennis, hashing, Tottenham Hotspur. *Address:* (until Sept. 2009) British Council, 10 Spring Gardens, SW1A 2BN. *T:* (020) 7930 8466.

SKELTON, Robert William, OBE 1989; Keeper, Indian Department, Victoria and Albert Museum, 1978–88; *b* 11 June 1929; *s* of John William Skelton and Victoria (*née* Wright); *m* 1954, Frances Aird; three *s*. *Educ:* Tiffin Boys' Sch., Kingston-upon-Thames. Joined Indian Section of Victoria and Albert Museum, 1950; Asst Keeper, 1960; Dep. Keeper, 1972; Nuffield Travelling Fellow in India, 1962. Mem. Council: Royal Asiatic Soc., 1970–73, 1975–78, 1988–92; Soc. for S Asian Studies, 1984–94; Trustee: Asia House Trust (London), 1977–; Indian Nat. Trust for Art and Cultural Heritage, UK, 1991–. *Publications:* Indian Miniatures from the XVth to XIXth Centuries, 1961; Rajasthani Temple Hangings of the Krishna Cult, 1973; (jtly) Islamic Painting and Arts of the Book, 1976; (jtly) Indian Painting, 1978; (jtly) Arts of Bengal, 1979; (jtly) The Indian Heritage, 1982; (jtly) Islamic Art in the Keir Collection, 1988; various contribs to art periodicals and conf. proc., 1956–. *Recreations:* chamber music, walking. *Address:* 10 Spencer Road, South Croydon CR2 7EH; *e-mail:* robertskelton@blueyonder.co.uk.

SKEMPTON, Maj. Gen. Keith, CBE 1997; DL; Operations Director, Chester Cathedral, 2007–08; *b* 22 Feb. 1949; *s* of late Dr Ivor Skempton and Leslie Skempton; *m* 1971, Susan Lawrence; one *d*. *Educ:* Birkenhead Sch.; Liverpool Coll. of Building; Mons OCS; Army Staff Coll., Camberley. Commnd Cheshire Regt, 1969; served UK, ME and FE; COS, 33 Armd Bde, 1982–83; MA to GOC NI, 1986–88; CO, 1st Bn, Cheshire Regt, 1988–91 (mentioned in despatches, 1988, 1990, NI); DCS, 1st Armd Div., 1991–93; DACOS, G4 Ops and Plans, HQ Land Comd, 1993–96; COS, HQ British Forces Cyprus, 1996–98; DCS, Support, HQ ARRC, 1998–2001 (QCVS 1999, Kosovo op.); ACOS, HQ AFSOUTH, 2001–03; Col, 22nd (Cheshire) Regt, 1999–2006. Business Develt Dir, Ferrari Gp, 2006–07. FCMI 2003; MInstD 2003. DL Cheshire, 2006. *Recreations:* motor vehicles, travel, walking, shooting, sailing, ski-ing. *Address:* Regimental Headquarters, Cheshire Regiment, The Castle, Chester CH1 2DN. *T:* (01244) 327617. *Clubs:* Army and Navy; Chester City.

SKENE, Alison Jean Katherine; Director, Skene Group, since 1972; Vice Lord-Lieutenant of Aberdeen, since 2007; *b* 26 May 1939; *d* of Alexander Lamont and Alexa Lee Lamont (*née* Will); *m* 1964, Charles Pirie Skene; one *s* two *d*. *Educ:* High Sch. for Girls, Aberdeen; Univ. of Aberdeen (MA); Aberdeen Trng Coll. Teacher of French, 1961–65. Pres., Jun. Chamber Wives Gp, 1970–71; Committee Member: St John Assoc., 1984–90; Queens Cross/Harlaw Community Council, 1987–94; Grampian/Houston Assoc., 1989–2002. Mem., Gen. Council, Business Cttee, 1980–2007, Court, 1990–2002, Aberdeen Univ. Mem. Cttee, Elphinstone Inst. Friends' Assoc., 1996–2005. Burgess of Guild, City of Aberdeen, 1998. DL Aberdeen, 1999. Pres., St Nicholas Probus Club, 2006–07. OStJ 2000 (SSStJ 1987). *Recreations:* spending time with grandsons, Hamish and Cameron, walking, travelling, golfing, reading, crosswords. *Address:* 21 Rubislaw Den North, Aberdeen AB15 4AL. *T:* (01224) 317517; *e-mail:* alison.skene@theskenegroup.com. *Club:* Aberdeen Ladies' Golf.

SKENE, Prudence Patricia, CBE 2000; Chairman, Rambert Dance Company, since 2000; *b* 9 Jan. 1944; *d* of Robert Worboys Skene and Phyllis Monica Skene (*née* Langley); *m* 1986, Brian Henry Wray (*d* 2002); one step *s* one step *d*. *Educ:* Francis Holland Sch., London. Dep. Administrator, The Round House, Chalk Farm, 1973–75; Ballet Rambert: Administrator, 1975–78; Admin. Dir, 1978–84; Exec. Dir, 1984–86; Exec. Producer, English Shakespeare Co., 1987–90 and 1992; Dir, The Arts Foundn, 1993–98. Non-executive Director: Theatre Royal, Bath, 1998–2003; Royal United Hosp. Bath NHS Trust, 1999–2003; Chm., Arvon Foundn, 2000–05. Mem., Arts Council of England (formerly Arts Council of GB), 1992–2000 (Chairman: Dance Panel, 1992–96; Lottery Panel, 1996–2000). Vice-Pres., 1985–89, Pres., 1991–92, Theatrical Management Assoc.; Chm., Dancers Resettlement Trust and Vice-Chm., Dancers Resettlement Fund, 1988–92. Trustee: Cardiff Old Liby Trust, 1996–2000; Stephen Spender Meml Fund, 2000–; Friends of the V&A, 2004–; NESTA, 2006–07. FRSA 1992. *Recreations:* travel, food, the performing arts. *Address:* 19a Eccleston Street, SW1W 9LX.

SKERRIT, Hon. Roosevelt; MHA (Lab) Vieille Case, Dominica, since 2000; Prime Minister of Dominica, since 2004; Minister for Finance and Planning and Caribbean

Affairs, since 2004; *b* 8 June 1972; one *s*. *Educ:* New Mexico State Univ. (Dip. Secondary Educn 1995); Univ. of Mississippi (BA Hons Psychol. and English 1997). Quality Assce Officer, JUC Factory, Dominica; teacher, Portsmouth Secondary Sch.; Supervisor, Student Activity Center, Univ. of Mississippi; Database Manager/Advr, Offshore Firm; Lectr, Dominica State Coll., 1997–99. Minister: for Sports and Youth Affairs, 2000; for Educn, Sports and Youth Affairs, 2000–04. Mem., Exec. Bd, UNESCO. Mem. Council, Univ. of WI (Member: F and GP Cttee; Strategy Cttee). Leader, Dominica Labour Party.

SKEWIS, (William) Iain, PhD; consultant; Chief Executive, Enterprise South West Shropshire, since 1998; Director, Development Consultancy, since 1995; Coordinator, Soccer Destinations, since 2006; *b* 1 May 1936; *s* of John Jamieson and Margaret Middlemass Skewis; *m* 1963, Jessie Frame Weir; two *s* one *d*. *Educ:* Hamilton Academy; Univ. of Glasgow (BSc, PhD). FTS 1987. British Rail, 1961–63; Transport Holding Co., 1963–66; Highlands and Islands Develt Bd, 1966–72; Yorkshire and Humberside Develt, 1973–77; Chief Exec., Develt Bd for Rural Wales, 1977–90. Chm., Regl Studies Assoc., 1990–93. Chairman: British Isles Soccer Tournaments Assoc., 1996–; Football Assoc. of Wales Premier Cup, 1998–. *Recreation:* soccer. *Address:* Rock House, The Square, Montgomery, Powys SY15 6PA. *T:* (01686) 668276.

SKIDELSKY, family name of **Baron Skidelsky**.

SKIDELSKY, Baron *cr* 1991 (Life Peer), of Tilton in the County of East Sussex; **Robert Jacob Alexander Skidelsky,** DPhil; FRSL; FRHistS; FBA 1994; Professor of Political Economy, Warwick University, 1990–2007, now Emeritus; *b* 25 April 1939; *s* of late Boris Skidelsky and Galia Sapelkin; *m* 1970, Augusta Mary Clarissa Hope; two *s* one *d*. *Educ:* Brighton Coll.; Jesus Coll., Oxford (BA and MA Mod. Hist.; DPhil; Hon. Fellow, 1997). FRHistS 1973; FRSL 1978. Res. Fellow: Nuffield Coll., Oxford, 1965–68; British Acad., 1968–70; Associate Prof. of History, Sch. of Advanced Internat. Studies, Johns Hopkins Univ., Washington, DC, 1970–76; Head, Dept of History, Philosophy and Eur. Studies, Polytechnic of N London, 1976–78; Prof. of Internat. Studies, Warwick Univ., 1978–90. Director: Stilwell Financial Inc., 2001–03; Janus Capital, 2003–; Grtr Europe Fund, 2005–; Sistema, 2008. Dir, 1989–91, Chm., 1991–2001, Social Market Foundn; Mem., Policy Cttee, SDP, 1988–90. Opposition Spokesman on: Culture, Media and Sport, H of L, 1997–98; Treasury affairs, 1998–99. Chairman: Charleston Trust, 1987–92; Hands Off Reading Campaign, 1994–98. Member: Adv. Council on Public Records, 1988–93; Schools Examinations and Assessment Council, 1992–93; Council, Royal Economic Soc., 2007–. Mem., Bd of Dirs, Moscow Sch. of Pol Studies, 1999–; Exec. Sec., UK/Russia Roundtable, 2005–. Governor: Portsmouth Univ., 1994–97; Brighton Coll., 1998–2004 (Chm. of Govs, 2004–); Wilton Park Academic Council, 2003–. Hon. DLit Buckingham, 1997. *Publications:* Politicians and the Slump, 1967, 2nd edn 1994; English Progressive Schools, 1969; Oswald Mosley, 1975; (ed) The End of the Keynesian Era, 1977; (ed, with Michael Holroyd) William Gerhardie's God's Fifth Column, 1981; John Maynard Keynes, vol. 1 1883–1920, Hopes Betrayed, 1983, vol. 2 1921–1937, The Economist as Saviour (Wolfson History Prize), 1992, vol. 3 1937–1946, Fighting for Britain (Duff Cooper, Lionel Gelber, James Tait Black Meml and Council on Foreign Relations Prizes), 2000, abridged edn in one vol. 2003; (ed) Thatcherism, 1988; Interests and Obsessions, 1993; The World After Communism, 1995; Keynes, 1996. *Recreations:* music, travelling, sport, conversation. *Address:* Saxon Lodge, Saxon Lane, Seaford, East Sussex BN25 1QL. *T:* (01323) 890941.

SKIDMORE, Jeffrey; Artistic Director and Conductor, Ex Cathedra, since 1969; *b* 27 Feb. 1951; *s* of Ernest and Lily Mary Skidmore; *m* 1974, Janet Mary Moore; two *s* one *d*. *Educ:* Magdalen Coll., Oxford (BA). Head of Music: Hagley Park Sch., Rugeley, 1978–80; John Wilmott Sch., Birmingham, 1980–92. Hon. Res. Fellow, Univ. of Birmingham, 1998–; Hon. Fellow, Birmingham Conservatoire, 2001. Has made recordings. *Address:* Ex Cathedra, 611b The Big Peg, 120 Vyse Street, Birmingham B18 6NF. *T:* (0121) 200 1511, *Fax:* (0121) 200 1522; *e-mail:* info@ex-cathedra.org.

SKILBECK, Diana Margaret; Headmistress, The Queen's School, Chester, 1989–2001; *b* 14 Nov. 1942; *d* of late William Allen Skilbeck and Elsie Almond Skilbeck. *Educ:* Wirral County Grammar School for Girls, Cheshire; Furzedown Coll., London (Teacher's Cert.); BA Hons London (External). Assistant Teacher: Mendell Primary Sch., 1964–67; Gayton Primary Sch., 1967–69; Wirral County Grammar Sch., 1969–74; Head of Geography, Wirral County Grammar Sch., 1974–78; Dep. Headmistress, West Kirby Grammar Sch., 1978–83; Headmistress, Sheffield High School, GPDST, 1983–89. *Recreations:* inland waterways, walking, singing, reading, industrial archaeology.

SKILBECK, Prof. Malcolm; education consultant and writer; *b* 22 Sept. 1932; *s* of Charles Harrison Skilbeck and Elsie Muriel Nash Skilbeck; *m* Helen Connell. *Educ:* Univ. of Sydney (BA); Acad. DipEd London, PhD London; MA Illinois. Secondary school teacher and adult educn teacher, 1958–63; Lectr. Univ. of Bristol, 1963–71; Prof., New Univ. of Ulster, 1971–75; Dir, Australian Curriculum Develt Centre, 1975–81; Dir of Studies, Schs Council for Curriculum and Exams for England and Wales, 1981–83; Prof. of Education, Univ. of London, 1981–85; Prof. and Vice-Chancellor, Deakin Univ., Australia, 1986–91; Dep. Dir (Educn), Directorate of Educn, Employment, Labour and Social Affairs, OECD, 1991–97. Consultancies for Unesco, OECD, etc, intermittently, 1967–; active in voluntary organizations concerned with educn for internat. understanding, eg, Chm., World Educn Fellowship, 1981–85. Hon. DLitt NUI, 2000. *Publications:* John Dewey, 1970; (jtly) Classroom and Culture, 1976; (jtly) Inservice Education and Training, 1977; A Core Curriculum for the Common School 1982; (ed) Evaluating the Curriculum in the Eighties, 1984; School Based Curriculum Development, 1984; Readings in School-Based Curriculum Development, 1984; Curriculum Reform, 1990; The Vocational Quest, 1994; (jtly) Redefining Tertiary Education, 1998; Access and Equity in Higher Education, 2000; Education for All: 2000 assessment, 2000; numerous contribs to jls, project reports, etc. *Recreations:* landcare, winemaking, reading.

SKILTON, Ven. Christopher John; Archdeacon of Lambeth, since 2004; *b* 19 March 1955; *s* of John Hampsheir Skilton and Kathleen Ada Skilton; *m* 1980, Barbara Kilgour; one *s* two *d*. *Educ:* Magdalene Coll., Cambridge (BA 1976, MA 1980); Wycliffe Hall, Oxford; St John's Coll., Nottingham (MA in Mission/Ministry 1996). Ordained deacon, 1980, priest, 1981; Curate: St Mary, Ealing, 1980–84; Newborough and Leigh St John, Wimborne, 1984–88; Team Vicar, St Paul, Great Baddow, 1988–95; Team Rector, Sanderstead, 1995–2003. RD, Croydon S, 2000–03. *Recreations:* gardening, cricket, recent British politics, The Archers. *Address:* 7 Hoadly Road, Streatham, SW16 1AE. *T:* (020) 8769 4384; (office) Kingston Episcopal Area Office, 616–620 Kingston Road, Raynes Park, SW20 8DN. *T:* (020) 8545 2440, *Fax:* (020) 8545 2441; *e-mail:* chris.skilton@southwark.anglican.org.

SKILTON, Prof. David John; Professor of English, since 1988 and Research Professor, since 2002, Cardiff University (formerly University of Wales College of Cardiff); *b* 10 July 1942; *s* of Henry C. S. Skilton and Iris F. M. Skilton (*née* Redfern); *m* 1st, 1976, Marvid E. G. Kennedy-Finlayson (marr. diss.); 2nd, 1984, Joanne V. Papworth; one *s* one *d*. *Educ:* Tollington Grammar Sch., London; King's Coll., Cambridge (MA, MLitt); Univ. of Copenhagen. Lectr, Glasgow Univ., 1970–80; Professor of English: St David's University Coll., Lampeter, 1980–86; UWIST, 1986–88; Head of School of English, Communication and Philosophy, UWCC, then Cardiff Univ., 1988–2002; Pro Vice-Chancellor, UWCC, 1992–96; Dean, Faculty of Humanities, Cardiff Univ., 1997–99. Mem., Nat. Curriculum English Working Group, 1988–89; Trustee, Roald Dahl Arts Project, 1996–. Literary Adviser to Trollope Soc., 1988–; Editor, Trollope Soc. edn of novels of Anthony Trollope, 1988–99; Founding Ed., Jl of Illustration Studies, 2007–. FRSA 2001; FEA 2002. *Publications:* Anthony Trollope and his Contemporaries, 1972, 2nd edn 1996; Defoe to the Victorians, 1977, 2nd edn 1985; The Early and Mid-Victorian Novel, 1993. *Recreations:* music, ruins, Scandinavian culture. *Address:* Cardiff University, Cardiff CF10 3EU. *T:* (029) 2087 4040.

SKINGLE, Diana; HM Diplomatic Service, retired; High Commissioner to Seychelles, 2004–07; *b* 3 May 1947; *d* of Eric Barry Skingle and Joyce Ada Skingle; partner, Christopher John Marshall Carrington. *Educ:* Chatham Grammar Sch. for Girls; Open Univ. (BSc Hons; Dip Env and Dev); Birkbeck Coll., London (MSc Merit Pols and Sociol.). Joined Commonwealth Office, subseq. FCO, 1966; Kampala, 1970; FCO, 1972; Abidjan, 1974; Vila, 1975; Prague, 1977; Casablanca, 1979; Second Secretary: FCO, 1982; (Aid/Commercial) Georgetown, 1985; (Develt) Bridgetown, 1986; First Secretary: (Information) UK Delegn to NATO, Brussels, 1988; FCO, 1993; Dep. Hd of Mission, Addis Ababa, 2001–04. *Recreations:* cats, walking, riding.

SKINGSLEY, Air Chief Marshal Sir Anthony (Gerald), GBE 1992 KCB 1986 (CB 1983); Deputy Commander-in-Chief, Allied Forces Central Europe, 1989–92, retired; *b* 19 Oct. 1933; *s* of Edward Roberts Skingsley; *m* 1957, Lilwen; two *s* one *d*. *Educ:* St Bartholomew's, Newbury; Cambridge Univ. (BA, MA). Commissioned RAFVR 1954, RAF 1955; several flying appointments, then Flt Comdr 13 Sqdn, 1961–62; OC Ops Sqdn, RAF Akrotiri, 1962–63; RAF Staff Coll., Bracknell, 1964; OC 45 Sqdn, RAF Tengah, Singapore, 1965–67; jssc Latimer, 1968; RAF Project Officer for Tornado in MoD, 1968–71; OC 214 Sqdn, RAF Marham, 1972–74; Station Comdr, RAF Laarbruch, Germany, 1974–76; Hon. ADC to the Queen, 1976–78; Asst Chief of Staff, Offensive Ops, HQ 2nd ATAF, 1977; RCDS 1978; Director of Air Staff Plans, MoD, 1978–80; Asst Chief of Staff, Plans and Policy, SHAPE, 1980–83; Comdt, RAF Staff Coll., Bracknell, 1983–84; ACAS, 1985–86; Air Mem. for Personnel, 1986–87; C-in-C RAF Germany, and Comdr, Second ATAF, 1987–89. Mem., Allgemeine Rheinlaendische Industrie Gesellschaft, 1975. Pres., RAFA, Luxembourg, 1992–; Mem. Adv. Council, Atlantic Council, 1993–. *Recreations:* travel, off-shore sailing, music, golf. *Address:* c/o National Westminster Bank, 43 Swan Street, West Malling, Kent ME19 6HF. *Club:* Royal Air Force.

SKINNER, Prof. Andrew Stewart, FBA 1993; FRSE; Adam Smith Professor of Political Economy, University of Glasgow, 1994–97, now Emeritus (Daniel Jack Professor, 1985–94); *b* 11 Jan. 1935; *s* of late Andrew Paterson Skinner and Isabella Bateman (*née* Stewart); *m* 1966, Margaret Mary Dorothy Robertson. *Educ:* Glasgow Univ. (MA 1958; BLitt 1960). FRSE 1988. Tutor and Asst Lectr, QUB, 1959–62; Lectr, Queen's Coll., Dundee, Univ. of St Andrews, 1962–64; University of Glasgow: Lectr, 1964–70; Sen. Lectr, 1970–75; Reader, 1975–77; Prof., 1977–85; Dean, Faculty of Social Scis, 1980–83; Clerk of Senate, 1983–90; Vice-Principal, 1991–96. DUniv Glasgow, 2001. *Publications:* (ed) Sir James Steuart, Principles of Political Economy, 1966; (ed with R. H. Campbell and W. B. Todd) Adam Smith, The Wealth of Nations, 1976; A System of Social Science: papers relating to Adam Smith, 1979, 2nd edn 1996; (with R. H. Campbell) Adam Smith: a short biography, 1982; (ed with P. Jones) Adam Smith Reviewed, 1992; (with K. Haakonssen) Index to Smith's Works, 2001. *Recreation:* gardening. *Address:* Department of Political Economy, The University, Glasgow G12 8RT. *T:* (0141) 330 4657; Glen House, Cardross, Dumbarton, Dunbartonshire G82 5ES. *T:* (01389) 841603. *Club:* Naval.

SKINNER, Angus Mackinnon Cumming; Partner, Care and Health; *b* 4 Jan. 1950; *s* of Dr Theodore Skinner, OBE and Morag Mackinnon Skinner; *m* (separated 1995); one *s* two *d*. *Educ:* Univ. of Edinburgh (BSc 1971); London Univ. (CQSW 1973); Strathclyde Univ. (MBA 1988). Social Worker, Cheshire and Kent, 1971–75; Social Work Manager, Lothian, 1975–87; Depute Dir, Borders, 1987–91; Chief Social Work Advr, Scottish Office, 1991–92; Chief Insp. of Social Work Services for Scotland, Scottish Office, subseq. Scottish Exec. Educn Dept, 1992. *Publication:* Another Kind of Home, 1992. *Recreations:* family, friends, learning.

SKINNER, Charles Edward; Head of Communication, Tower Hamlets Council, since 2007; *b* 27 July 1951; *s* of late Charles John Henry Skinner and Nell Skinner (*née* Seward); *m* 1973, Caroline Mary Gregory; one *d*. *Educ:* Nightingale Sch., Wanstead, London. Editorial Trainee, Industrial Daily News, 1968; Editorial Asst, Maclean-Hunter News Publishing, 1969–71; Asst Ed., IPC Business Press, 1971–75; Central Office of Information: Information Officer, N Amer. Desk, Overseas Press and Radio, 1975; Sen. Press Officer, ME Desk, and Defence Correspondent, 1981; Hd, UK and Overseas Radio, 1985; Dir, Films, Television and Radio, 1988–90; Hd, Mktg and Corporate Communication, Home Office, 1990–97; Dir, Govt Information and Communication Service Develt Centre, Cabinet Office, 1997–99; Hd of Mktg, DETR, 1999–2002; Dir of Communication, DfT, 2002–04; Hd of Communications and Consultation, Haringey Council, 2005–07. Chm., Whitehall Hds of Marketing, 2000–04. FRSA 1993; FCIPR (FIPR 2004). *Publication:* (ed) MI5 - The Security Service, 1993. *Recreations:* opera, political biography, horology, naval history, cycling, motorcycling, old friends. *Address:* Tower Hamlets Council, Town Hall, Mulberry Place, 5 Clove Crescent, E14 2BG; *e-mail:* charles.skinner@towerhamlets.gov.uk. *Clubs:* Royal Automobile, Colony Room.

SKINNER, Prof. Christopher John, PhD; FBA 2004; Professor of Social Statistics, University of Southampton, since 1994; *b* 12 March 1953; *s* of Richard Skinner and Daphne Skinner; *m* 1998, Sheila (*née* Hinchliffe); two *s*. *Educ:* Trinity Coll., Cambridge (BA 1975); LSE (MSc 1976); Univ. of Southampton (PhD 1982). Lectr, 1982–89, Sen. Lectr, 1989–94, Univ. of Southampton. *Publications:* (ed jtly) Analysis of Complex Surveys, 1989; (ed with R. Chambers) Analysis of Survey Data, 2003. *Recreations:* cinema, music. *Address:* Division of Social Statistics, School of Social Sciences, University of Southampton, Southampton SO17 1BJ. *T:* (023) 8059 3216, *Fax:* (023) 8059 3846.

SKINNER, David; Chief Executive, Co-operative Wholesale Society Ltd, 1992–96; *b* 27 Oct. 1931; *s* of late David Skinner and Mary (*née* Davidson); *m* 1st, 1956, Elizabeth Vera Harben (marr. diss. 1976); one *s* one *d*; 2nd, 1996, Morag J. L. Mar (*née* Busby). *Educ:* Gateshead Grammar Sch.; Nottingham Univ. (BSc). Nat. Service, RNVR, 1953–55. Mgt Trainee, Yorkshire Imperial Metals, 1955–57; Productivity Services Manager, Distillers' Co., 1957–60; Mgt Consultant, 1960–68; Food Divl Manager, Scottish CWS, 1969–73; Co-operative Wholesale Society Ltd: Non Food Controller, 1974–83; Retail Controller and Dep. Chief Exec. (Retail & Services), 1983–92. *Recreations:* comfortable travelling, easy gardening. *Address:* Rowan Tree Cottage, Pannal Road, Follifoot, Harrogate HG3 1DR.

SKINNER, David Victor, FRCS, FRCSE, FRCSGlas, FCEM, FIMCRCSE; Consultant, Emergency Department, John Radcliffe Hospital, Oxford, since 1993; Dean, Faculty of Accident and Emergency Medicine, 2000–04; *b* 6 May 1948; *s* of Victor and Joan Skinner; *m* 1975, Alison Rosemary (*née* Earley); one *s* one *d*. *Educ:* Haberdashers' Aske's Sch.; Royal Free Hosp., London (MB BS 1975). FRCSE 1981; FRCS 1990; FRCSGlas 1993; FIMCRCSE 2004. Consultant, Emergency Dept, St Bartholomew's Hosp., London, 1986–93; Med. Dir, Bart's City Lifesaver; Hon. Sen. Lectr, Oxford Med. Sch. Gov., RNLI. Service Medal, OStJ, 2003. *Publications:* (ed jtly) Cambridge Textbook of Accident and Emergency Medicine, 1997; (ed jtly) Trauma Care, 1998; (ed jtly) Trauma (A Companion to Bailey and Love's Short Practice of Surgery), 1999; (ed jtly) ABC of Major Trauma, 3rd edn 2000. *Recreations:* family, home, Portugal, Swan yacht Red Beauty and the Scuderia. *Address:* Northcott, Chiltern Road, Chesham Bois, Amersham, Bucks HP6 5PH; *e-mail:* david.skinner7@virgin.net.

SKINNER, Dennis Edward; MP (Lab) Bolsover, since 1970; *b* 11 Feb. 1932; good working-class mining stock; *m* 1960; one *s* two *d*. *Educ:* Tupton Hall Grammar Sch.; Ruskin Coll., Oxford. Miner, Parkhouse Colliery and Glapwell Colliery, 1949–70. Mem., Nat. Exec. Cttee of Labour Party, 1978–92, 1994–98, 1999–; Vice-Chm., Labour Party, 1987–88, Chm., 1988–89; Pres., Derbyshire Miners (NUM), 1966–70; Pres., NE Derbs Constituency Labour Party, 1968–71; Derbyshire CC, 1964–70; Clay Cross UDC, 1960–70. *Recreations:* tennis, cycling, walking. *Address:* House of Commons, SW1A 0AA. *T:* (01773) 581027. *Clubs:* Miners' Welfares in Derbyshire; Bestwood Working Men's.

SKINNER, Frank; entertainer, since 1987; *b* 28 Jan. 1957; *s* of John and Doris Collins; *né* Chris Collins, changed name to Frank Skinner, 1987. *Educ:* Birmingham Polytech. (BA Hons English 1981); Univ. of Warwick (MA English 1982). Numerous stand-up performances incl. London Palladium, 1996, and Battersea Power Station, 1997; UK tour, 2007; appearances in West End include: Art, 1999; Cooking with Elvis, 2000; Baddiel & Skinner Unplanned, 2001; *television:* Fantasy Football League (with David Baddiel), 5 series, 1994–2005 (VHE Award of Excellence for Top Comedy Prog., 1994); The Frank Skinner Show, 8 series, 1995–2005; Baddiel & Skinner Unplanned (with David Baddiel), 5 series, 2000–05; (writer and star) Shane, 2 series, 2004–05. Number one single (with David Baddiel and The Lightning Seeds), Three Lions, 1996 and 1998. DUniv UCE, 2006. Perrier Comedy Award, 1991; Best Comedy Entertainment Personality, British Comedy Awards, 2001; Variety Club Award for Comedy, 2001; London's Favourite Comedy Act, Capital Awards, 2005. *Publications:* Frank Skinner on Frank Skinner, 2001; Frank Skinner on the Road, 2008. *Recreation:* watching football. *Address:* Avalon Management Group Ltd, 4A Exmoor Street, W10 6BD.

SKINNER, Air Vice-Marshal Graham, CBE 1999 (MBE 1982); CEng, FIMechE, FRAeS; Clerk, Engineers' Company, since 2003; *b* 16 Sept. 1945; *s* of late Frederick and Phyllis Skinner; *m* 1969, Margaret Christine Hacon; one *s* one *d*. *Educ:* Hampton Sch.; RAF Tech. Coll., Henlow; Bristol Univ. (BSc); Loughborough Univ. (MSc). CEng 1972; MRAeS 1980, FRAeS 2003; FIMechE 1990; FCILT (FILT 1997). Commnd Engr Br., RAF, 1964; served at Odiham, Sharjah, Coltishall, Leconfield, Kemble, 1967–78; RAF Staff Coll., Bracknell, 1978; air weapons staff, MoD, London, 1979–83; OC Engrg Wing, RAF Valley, 1983–85; various engrg posts and SO Engrg and Supply, HQ 38 Gp, Strike Comd, 1986–95; Air Cdre, Policy and Plans, HQ Logistics Comd, 1996–97; Dir, Support Mgt (RAF), 1997–99; COS, 1999–2000; last AOC-in-C Logistics Comd, 1999; Mem. Mgt Bd, Defence Logistics Orgn, 1999–2000; retd RAF, 2000. Vis. Prof., Acquisition and Logistics Unit, RMCS, Shrivenham, at Cranfield Univ., 2000–05. Mil. Advr, Marshall Aerospace, Cambridge, 2000–; Defence Advr, Symbia, 2002– (non-exec. Dir, 2003–); non-exec. Dir, Short Bros plc, Belfast, 2000–; Dir, Insider Publishing Ltd, 2003–. Freeman, City of London, 2000–; Liveryman, Engineers' Co., 2000–. Gov., Hampton Sch., Middx, 2001–. *Publications:* contrib. various articles to professional jls on aerospace engrg and defence logistics. *Recreations:* golf, watercolour painting. *Address:* Rokesly, 63 Sandelswood End, Beaconsfield, Bucks HP9 2AA. *T:* (01494) 672350. *Club:* Royal Air Force.

SKINNER, James John; QC; Social Security Commissioner, 1986–96; a Child Support Commissioner, 1993–96; *b* 24 July 1923; *o s* of late William Skinner, Solicitor, Clonmel, Ireland; *m* 1950, Regina Brigitte Reiss; three *s* two *d*. *Educ:* Clongowes Wood Coll.; Trinity Coll., Dublin; King's Inns, Dublin. Called to Irish Bar, 1946; joined Leinster Circuit; called to English Bar, Gray's Inn, 1950; called to Bar of Northern Rhodesia, 1951; QC (Northern Rhodesia) 1964; MP (UNIP) Lusaka East, 1964–68; Minister of Justice, 1964–65; Attorney-General, 1965–69 (in addition, Minister of Legal Affairs, 1967–68); Chief Justice of Zambia, March-Sept. 1969; Chief Justice of Malaŵi, 1970–85. Grand Comdr, Order of Menelik II of Ethiopia, 1965. *Recreation:* reading. *Address:* 12A Ashley Court, Ashley Road, Epsom, Surrey KT18 5AJ. *T:* (01372) 728299.

SKINNER, Joyce Eva, CBE 1975; retired; *b* 5 Sept. 1920; *d* of Matthew and Ruth Eva Skinner. *Educ:* Christ's Hosp.; Girls' High Sch., Lincoln; Somerville Coll., Oxford. BA 1941, MA 1945. Bridlington Girls' High Sch., 1942–45; Perse Girls' Sch., 1946–50; Keswick Sch., 1950–52; Homerton Coll., Cambridge, 1952–64; Vis. Prof., Queen's Coll., NY, 1955–56; Principal, Bishop Grosseteste Coll., Lincoln, 1964–74; Dir, Cambridge Inst. of Educn, 1974–80; Academic Sec., Universities' Council for Educn of Teachers, 1979–84. Fellow: Hughes Hall, Cambridge, 1974–85; Worcester Coll. of Higher Educn, 1985. Hon. FCP 1971. Hon. DEd CNAA, 1989; Hon. DLitt Hull, 1997. *Recreations:* walking, reading, conversation. *Address:* 26 Rasen Lane, Lincoln LN1 3EY. *T:* (01522) 529483.

SKINNER, Sir Keith; *see* Skinner, Sir T. K. H.

SKINNER, Paul David; Chairman: Rio Tinto plc, since 2003; Rio Tinto Ltd, since 2003; *b* 24 Dec. 1944; *s* of William Stanley Skinner and Elizabeth Ann Skinner; *m* 1971, Rita Jacqueline Oldak; two *s*. *Educ:* Pembroke Coll., Cambridge (BA Law). Royal Dutch/Shell Group of Companies, 1963–2003: sen. appts in UK and Greece, 1974–76, Nigeria, 1976–78, NZ, 1984–87, Norway, 1987–91; Gp Man. Dir and Man. Dir, Shell Transport and Trading Co. plc, 2000–03. Non-exec. Director: Rio Tinto plc and Rio Tinto Ltd, 2001–; Standard Chartered plc, 2003–; Tetra Laval Gp, 2005–; Air Liquide SA, 2006–. Pres., UK Chamber of Shipping, 1997–98; Chairman: ICC UK, 2005–08; Commonwealth Business Council, 2007–. Member: Bd, Eur./Asian Business Sch., INSEAD, 1999–; Defence Bd (formerly Mgt Bd), MoD, 2006–. Liveryman, Co. of Shipwrights, 2000–. *Recreations:* opera, ski-ing, fly-fishing, boating. *Address:* Rio Tinto plc, 5 Aldermanbury Square, EC2V 7HR. *T:* (020) 7781 2000; *e-mail:* paul.skinner@riotinto.com. *Clubs:* Royal Automobile; Roehampton; Hawks (Cambridge).

SKINNER, Peter William; Member (Lab) South East Region, England, European Parliament, since 1999 (Kent West, 1994–99); *b* 1 June 1959; *s* of William James Skinner and Jean Theresa Skinner; *m* 1st, 1990, Julie Doreen (marr. diss. 2006); one *d*, and one step *s* one step *d*; 2nd, 2006, Kimberly Strycharz. *Educ:* Bradford Univ. (BSc); Warwick Univ. (Post Grad. Cert. in Industl Relns); Greenwich Univ. (PGCE 1992). Industrial Relations Officer, 1982; Trades Union Organiser, 1984; Course Dir for HNC in Business and Finance, North West Kent Coll. of Technol., 1989–94. European Parliament: Member: Employment and Social Affairs Cttee, 1994–; Educn, Culture, Media and Youth Cttee, 1997–; Economic and Monetary Affairs Cttee, 2000–04; Health and Safety Rapporteur, 1995–; Lab. spokesman on employment and social affairs, 1996–2000, on economic and monetary affairs, 2002–. Mem., Educn and Employment Policy Commn, Lab Party, 1995–. *Address:* (office) 99 Kent Road, Dartford, Kent DA1 2AJ. *T:* (01622) 892222; European Parliament, Rue Wiertz, 1047 Brussels, Belgium.

SKINNER, Prof. Quentin Robert Duthie, FRHistS; FBA 1981; Barber Beaumont Professor of the Humanities, Queen Mary, University of London, since 2008; Fellow, Christ's College, Cambridge, since 1962 (Vice Master, 1997–99); *b* 26 Nov. 1940; 2nd *s* of late Alexander Skinner, CBE, and Winifred Skinner (*née* Duthie), MA; *m* 2nd, 1979, Susan Deborah Thorpe James, MA, PhD; one *s* one *d*. *Educ:* Bedford Sch.; Gonville and Caius Coll., Cambridge (BA 1962, MA 1965; Hon. Fellow, 1997). FRHistS 1971. Cambridge University: Lectr in History, 1967–78; Prof. of Political Sci., 1978–96; Chm., Faculty of Hist., 1993–95; Regius Prof. of Modern History, 1996–2008; Pro-Vice-Chancellor, 1999. Visiting Fellow: Research Sch. of Social Science, ANU, 1970, 1994; Humanities Res. Centre, ANU, 1989, 1994, 2006; Institute for Advanced Study, Princeton: Mem., School of Historical Studies, 1974–75; longer-term Mem., School of Social Science, 1976–79; Professeur invité, Collège de France, 1997. Member: Council, British Acad., 1987–90; Res. Council, Eur. Univ. Inst., Florence, 2003–08. Fellow, Wissenschaftskolleg zu Berlin, 2003–04. Foreign Hon. Mem., Amer. Acad. of Arts and Sciences, 1986; Foreign Member: Amer. Phil Soc., 1997; Accademia Nazionale dei Lincei, 2007. MAE 1989. FRSA 1996. Hon. MRIA 1999. Hon. Fellow, QMW, 1999. Hon. LittD: Chicago, East Anglia, 1992; Helsinki, 1997; Leuven, 2004; Harvard, St Andrews, 2005; Aberdeen, Athens, 2007; Hon. DLitt Oxford, 2000. Benjamin Lippincott Award, Amer. Pol Sci. Assoc., 2001; Sir Isaiah Berlin Prize, British Pol Studies Assoc., 2006; Balzan Foundn Prize, 2006; David Easton Award, Amer. Pol Sci. Assoc., 2007. *Publications:* (ed jtly and contrib.) Philosophy, Politics and Society, Series 4, 1972; The Foundations of Modern Political Thought, Vol. 1, The Renaissance, 1978; Vol. 2, The Age of Reformation, 1978 (Wolfson Prize, 1979); Machiavelli, 1981; (ed jtly and contrib.) Philosophy in History, 1984; (ed and contrib.) The Return of Grand Theory in the Human Sciences, 1985; (ed jtly and contrib.) The Cambridge History of Renaissance Philosophy, 1988; Meaning and Context: Quentin Skinner and his critics, ed J. H. Tully, 1988; (ed and introd) Machiavelli: The Prince, 1988; (ed jtly and contrib.) Machiavelli and Republicanism, 1990; (ed jtly and contrib.) Political Discourse in Early-modern Britain, 1992; (ed jtly) Milton and Republicanism, 1995; Reason and Rhetoric in the Philosophy of Hobbes, 1996; Liberty Before Liberalism, 1998; Visions of Politics, Vol. 1, Regarding Method, 2002, Vol. 2, Renaissance Virtues, 2002, Vol. 3, Hobbes and Civil Science, 2002; (ed jtly and contrib.) Republicanism: a shared European heritage, 2 vols, 2002; (ed jtly and contrib.) States and Citizens, 2003; (ed jtly) Thomas Hobbes: writings on common law and hereditary right, 2005; Hobbes and Republican Liberty, 2008. *Address:* Queen Mary, University of London, Mile End Road, E1 4NS.

SKINNER, Robert George; Chief Executive, Banking Code Standards Board, since 2006; *b* 8 Aug. 1955; *s* of George and Mary Patricia Skinner; *m* 1974, Sheila White; one *s* one *d* (and one *d* decd). *Educ:* St Peter's Coll., Oxford (MA Physics). ACIB 1979. Barclays Bank Plc, 1976–2003: Mgt Develt Prog., 1976–80; Assistant Manager: Sunbury Br., 1981–82; Hounslow Br., 1982–84; Manager, Energy Dept, 1984–87; PA to Gp Chm., 1987–89; Man. Dir, Swaziland, 1989–92; Corporate Dir, Energy Finance Team, 1992–93; UK Personal Sector Network Dir, 1993–98; Mktg Dir, Private Banking Div., 1998–2003; Dir Gen., Money Advice Trust, 2003–06. Fellow, Inst. Financial Services, 1998. *Recreations:* running, photography, travel. *Address:* Banking Code Standards Board, Level 12, City Tower, 40 Basinghall Street, EC2V 5DE. *T:* (020) 7012 0081, *Fax:* (020) 7374 4414; *e-mail:* robertskinner@bcsb.org.uk.

SKINNER, Samuel Knox; lawyer; Of Counsel, GreenbergTraurig LLP; *b* 10 June 1938; *m* 1989, Mary Jacobs; two *s* one *d*. *Educ:* Univ. of Illinois (BSc); DePaul Univ. Law School. Served as Lieut and Tank Platoon Leader, US Army, 1960–61. IBM Corp., 1961–68; Illinois Northern District: Office of US Attorney, 1968–75; US Attorney, 1975–77; Partner, Sidley & Austin, 1977–89; President's Cabinet as Sec. of Transportation, 1989–91; Chief of Staff to President of USA, 1991–92; Gen. Chm., Republican Nat. Cttee, USA, 1992–93; Pres., Commonwealth Edison Co., subseq. Unicom Corp., 1993–98; Co-Chm., Hopkins & Sutter, 1998–2000; Chm., Pres., and CEO, US Freightways Corp., 2000–03; Chm., transportation.com, 2000. *Address:* GreenbergTraurig LLP, 77 West Wacker Drive, Suite 2500, Chicago, IL 60601, USA.

SKINNER, Sir (Thomas) Keith (Hewitt), 4th Bt *cr* 1912; Director, Reed International, 1980–90; Chairman and Chief Executive, Reed Publishing and Reed Regional Publishing, 1982–90, and other companies; *b* 6 Dec. 1927; *s* of Sir (Thomas) Gordon Skinner, 3rd Bt, and Mollie Barbara (*d* 1965), *d* of Herbert William Girling; *S* father, 1972; *m* 1959, Jill, *d* of Cedric Ivor Tuckett; two *s*. *Educ:* Charterhouse. Managing Director, Thomas Skinner & Co. (Publishers) Ltd, 1952–60; also Director, Iliffe & Co. Ltd, 1958–65; Director, Iliffe-NTP Ltd; Chairman: Industrial Trade Fairs Holdings Ltd, 1977–92; Business Press Internat., 1970–84. *Recreations:* publishing, shooting, fishing, gardening, golf. *Heir:* *s* Thomas James Hewitt Skinner, *b* 11 Sept. 1962. *Address:* Wood Farm, Reydon, near Southwold, Suffolk IP18 6SL.

SKIPPER, David John; Director: Westminster Centre for Education, Independent Schools Joint Council, 1991–96; Secondary Post Graduate Certificate of Education Course by Distance Learning, South Bank University (formerly Polytechnic), 1991–97; *b* 14 April 1931; *s* of late Herbert G. and Edna Skipper; *m* 1955, Brenda Ann Williams; three *s* one *d*. *Educ:* Watford Grammar Sch.; Brasenose Coll., Oxford (2nd Cl. Hons Nat. Science (Chemistry)). Royal Air Force (Short Service Commn) (Education), 1954–57; Assistant Master: Radley Coll., 1957–63; Rugby Sch., 1963–69; Headmaster: Ellesmere Coll., Shropshire, 1969–81; Merchant Taylors' Sch., Northwood, 1982–91. Chairman: ISJC Special Educnl Needs, 1983–91; Soc. of Schoolmasters, 1985–97; Pres., Soc. of Schoolmasters and Schoolmistresses, 1998–. Trustee: Confide-Shropshire Counselling, 2000– (Chm., 2002–05); Ellesmere Community Care Centre, 2000– (Chm., 2004–); Founding Chm., Ellesmere Patient Gp, 2004–08. Chm. Governors, Quainton Sch., Harrow, 1993–2001. Fellow, Midland Div., Woodard Corp., 1996–2002. Treas., Welshampton PCC, 2000–; Churchwarden, 2007–. Freeman, City of London, 1991; Liveryman, Merchant Taylors' Co., 1991–. *Recreations:* drawing, music, gardening, books. *Address:* 4 St Michael's Green, Lyneal Lane, Welshampton, Ellesmere, Shropshire SY12 0QT. *T:* (01948) 710899.

SKIPWITH, Sir Patrick Alexander d'Estoteville, 12th Bt *cr* 1622; consultant science editor; *b* 1 Sept. 1938; *o s* of Grey d'Estoteville Townsend Skipwith (killed in action, 1942), Flying Officer, RAFVR, and Sofka (*d* 1994), *d* of late Prince Peter Dolgorouky; *S* grandfather, 1950; *m* 1st, 1964, Gillian Patricia (marr. diss. 1970), *d* of late Charles F. Harwood; one *s* one *d*; 2nd, 1972, Ashkhain (marr. diss. 1997; she *d* 2006), *d* of late Bedros Atikian, Calgary, Alta; 3rd, 1997, Martine Sophie, *d* of late Joseph de Wilde, Theillay,

France; twin *s*. *Educ:* Harrow; Dublin (MA); London (DIC, PhD). With Ocean Mining Inc., in Tasmania, 1966–67, Malaysia, 1967–69, W Africa, 1969–70; with Min. of Petroleum and Mineral Resources, Saudi Arabia, 1970–71 and 1972–73. Editor, Bureau de Recherches Géologiques et Minières, Jiddah, 1973–86; consultant editor/translator (trading as GeoEdit), 1986–96; Hd of Translation, BRGM, Orléans, 1996–2003; Man. Dir, Immel Publishing Ltd, 1988–89. *Heir:* *s* Alexander Sebastian Grey d'Estoteville Skipwith [*b* 9 April 1969; *m* 2006, Anne, *d* of late Paul Tolstoy-Miloslavsky; one *s*]. *Address:* 76 rue de Pont-aux-Moines, 45450 Donnery, France. *Club:* Chelsea Arts.

SKITT, Baden Henry, CBE 1997; BEM 1969; QPM 1990; Lay Member, Office for Judicial Complaints Review Body, since 2006; *b* 5 Dec. 1941; *s* of Frederick Albert Skitt and Laura Kathleen (*née* Oakley). *Educ:* Rugeley Grammar Sch., Staffs; St Paul's Coll., Cheltenham (Dip of PE; CertEd). Schoolmaster, Sir Wilfrid Martineau Sch., Birmingham, 1963–67; Constable to Supt, Birmingham City, later W Midlands, Police, 1967–82; Chief Supt, 1982–84, Comdr, 1984–86, Metropolitan Police; Dep. Chief Constable, Northants, 1986–90; Chief Constable, Herts, 1990–94; Asst Comr, Metropolitan Police, 1994–97. Mem., Criminal Cases Review Commn, 1997–2006. Chm., Personnel and Training Cttee, 1993–96, Chm., Internat. Affairs Adv. Cttee, 1996–97, ACPO. Dir, Police Extended Interviews, 1995–97. Member: Police Adv. Bd, 1993–97; Police Trng Council, 1993–97; Police Advr, Police Negotiating Bd, 1994–96. Dir, Educnl Broadcasting Services Trust, 1992–; Advr, Council of Europe Cttee for prevention of torture and inhuman and degrading treatment or punishment, 2001–. Trustee: Police Convalescent Home, 1995–97; Youth Sport Trust, 1995–97. Advr, N London Common Purpose, 1995–97. Patron, Revolving Doors Agency, 1995–97. CCMI 2002. *Publications:* (jtly) In Service Training: a new approach, 1974; (jtly) Education 2000, 1984; contrib. to learned jls. *Recreations:* the history and travelling of inland waterways, Rugby football, music.

SKOTT, Maria; *see* Nikolajeva, M.

SKOU, Prof. Jens Christian, MD; Professor, Institute of Biophysics, Aarhus University, 1978–88; *b* Lemvig, Denmark, 8 Oct. 1918; *s* of Magnus Martinus Skou and Ane Margrethe (*née* Knak); *m* 1947, Ellen-Margrethe Nielsen; two *d*. *Educ:* Univ. of Copenhagen (MD 1944); Univ. of Aarhus (DrMedSci 1954). Intern, 1944–45, Resident, 1945–46, Hjørring Hosp.; Resident, Orthopaedic Hosp., Aarhus, 1946–47; Institute of Physiology, Aarhus University: Asst Prof., 1947–54; Associate Prof., 1954–63; Prof. and Chm., Inst. Physiol., 1963–78. Member: Danish Royal Acad. Scis, 1965; Deutsche Acad. der Naturforscher Leopoldina, 1977; EMBO, 1978; For. Associate, US Nat. Acad. of Scis, 1988; For. Hon. Mem., Amer. Acad. of Arts and Scis, 1999; Hon. Member: Japanese Biochem. Soc., 1988; American Physiol. Soc., 1990; Academia Europaea, 1993; Internat. Acad. of Humanism, 2002. Hon. DrMedSci Copenhagen, 1986. Leo Prize, 1954; Novo Prize, 1965; Consul Carlsen Prize, 1973; A. Retzius Gold Medal, Swedish Med. Assoc., 1977; Fernström Foundn Prize, 1985; Prakash Datta Medal, Fedn European Biochem. Socs, 1985; (jtly) Nobel Prize for Chemistry, 1997. *Recreations:* classical music, yachting, ski-ing, fishing. *Address:* Rislundvej 9, 8240 Risskov, Denmark. *T:* 86177918; (office) Institute of Biophysics, Ole Worms Allé 185, 8000C Aarhus, Denmark. *T:* 89422929, *Fax:* 86129599; *e-mail:* jcs@biophys.au.dk.

SKOURIS, Prof. Vassilios; Judge, since 1999, President, since 2003, Court of Justice of the European Communities; *b* 6 March 1948; *s* of Panagiotis and Katerina Skouris; *m* Vassiliki Papaïoannou; one *s* one *d*. *Educ:* Free Univ. of Berlin; Univ. of Hamburg (Dr jur 1973). Asst Prof. of Constitutional and Admin. Law, Univ. of Hamburg, 1978; Professor of Public Law: Dimokriteio Univ. of Thrace, 1977–80; Bielefeld Univ., Germany, 1980–82; Prof., Aristoteleio Univ. of Thessaloniki, 1982–; Dir of Res., 1985–90, Sec., 1990–97, Centre for Internat. and Eur. Econ. Law, Thessaloniki. Minister for Internal Affairs, Greece, 1989 and 1996. Mem., Higher Selection Bd for Greek Civil Servants, 1994–96. Mem., Acad. Council, Acad. Eur. Law, Trier, 1995–. Pres., Greek Assoc. for Eur. Law, 1992–94. Hon. LLD: Thrace, 2004; Vilnius, 2005; Münster, 2007; Deutsche Hochschule für Verwaltungswissenschaften, 2005. Grand Officier, Ordre of Merit (Italy), 2005; Grand Cross, Order of Makarios III (Cyprus), 2006; Ehrenkreuz für Wissenschaft und Kunst, 1st Cl. (Austria), 2005. *Publications:* (contrib.) Constitutional Review and Legislation: an international comparison, ed C. Landfried, 1988; (contrib.) Advertising and Constitutional Rights in Europe: a study in comparative constitutional law, 1994; (contrib.) Verfassung im Diskurs der Welt, 2004; (contrib.) The Future of the European Judicial System: the constitutional role of European courts, 2005; contribs to Eur. Business Law Rev. *Address:* Court of Justice of the European Communities, Boulevard Konrad Adenauer, 2925 Luxembourg. *T:* 43032210, *Fax:* 43032736; *e-mail:* vassilios.skouris@curia.europa.eu.

SLABAS, Prof. Antoni Ryszard, DPhil; Professor of Plant Sciences, University of Durham, since 1990 (Director of Research, Department of Biological Sciences, 1995–2000); *b* 30 July 1948; *s* of Franciszek Slabas and Wiera Ruban. *Educ:* Bishop Thomas Grant Sch.; QMC, Univ. of London (BSc); St Edmund Hall, Oxford (DPhil). Postdoctoral Fellow: Univ. of Sheffield, 1974–75; UCL, 1975–77; Unilever Research Laboratory, Sharnbrook, Bedford: Mem., Basic Studies Unit, 1977–80; Gp Leader, Lipid Enzymology, 1980–85; Section Manager, Protein Chem., 1985–86; Plant Molecular Biol. Prog. Leader, 1986–87; Sen. Molecular Biologist, 1988; Section Manager, Cell Scis, 1989–90. Mem., EC Seeds of Tomorrow Scientific Steering Cttee, 1990–; Agricultural and Food Research Council: Member: Engrg Bd, 1992–94; Plants and Envmt Res. Cttee, 1992–94; Wkg Gp, Protein Sci., 1992; Bd of Metabolic Regulation, 1992–94. Member: Cttee, Biochem. Soc. Lipid Gp, 1984–88; Health and Life Scis Panel, 1994–99, Food Chain and Crops for Industry Panel, 1999–2001, Technol. Foresight Prog., OST; Management Cttee, Agricl Systems Directorate, BBSRC, 1994–98; Governing Body, Scottish Crops Res. Inst., 1995–2004. Founder, 2000, and Co-Dir, 2000–, Creative Gene Technology. Member, Editorial Board: Biochem. Jl, 1989–2001; Plant Molecular Biol., 1991–2002. *Publications:* various in area of plant and microbial lipid biochem., enzymology and gene cloning; contrib. Science, Jl Biol Chem., Eur. Jl Biochem., Biochim. Biophys. Acta, Biochem. Jl, etc. *Recreations:* book collecting, classical music, walking, feeding swans by hand. *Address:* Department of Biological Sciences, University of Durham, South Road, Durham DH1 3LE. *T:* (0191) 334 1354.

SLABBERT, Dr Frederik Van Zyl; political consultant; Chairman: Adcorp Holdings, since 1998; Metro Cash&Carry, since 2000; *b* 2 March 1940; *s* of Petrus Johannes and Barbara Zacharia Slabbert; *m* 1965, Marié Jordaan (marr. diss. 1983); one *s* one *d*; *m* 1984, Jane Catherine Stephens. *Educ:* Univ. of Stellenbosch. BA, BA (Hons), MA 1964, DPhil 1967. Lectr in Sociology, Stellenbosch Univ., 1964–68; Senior Lecturer: Rhodes Univ., 1969; Stellenbosch Univ., 1970–71; Cape Town Univ., 1972–73; Prof. of Sociology, Univ. of the Witwatersrand, 1973–74. MP (Progressive Federal Party) Claremont, 1974–86; Leader, Official Opposition, S African Parlt, 1979–86. Founder and Dir, Inst. for a Democratic Alternative for South Africa, 1987; Chm., Open Soc. Initiative for Southern Africa. Vis. Prof., Univ. of the Witwatersrand Business Sch., 1988–. *Publications:* South African Society: its central perspectives, 1972; (jtly) South Africa's Options: strategies for sharing power, 1979; The Last White Parliament (autobiog.), 1986; (jtly) Comrades in Business: post-liberation politics in South Africa, 1998; Afrikaner Afrikaan, 1999; contributions to: Change in Contemporary South Africa, 1975; Explorations in Social Theory, 1976; various SPROCAS (Study Project of a Christian in an Apartheid Society) publications. *Recreations:* jogging, swimming, squash, chess. *Address:* Khula Consulting (Pty) Ltd, PO Box 2817, Houghton, 2041, South Africa.

SLACK, Dr (Charles) Roger, FRS 1989; FRSNZ 1983; Senior Scientist, New Zealand Institute for Crop and Food Research Ltd, 1989–2000, retired; *b* 22 April 1937; *s* of Albert Oram Slack and Eva (*née* Simister); *m* 1963, Pamela Mary Shaw; one *s* one *d*. *Educ:* Audenshaw Grammar Sch., Lancs; Sch. of Agriculture, Univ. of Nottingham (BSc; PhD 1962). Biochemist, David North Plant Res. Centre, CSR Co. Ltd, Brisbane, Australia, 1962–70; Leader, Biochemistry Group, 1970–84, Leader, Crop Physiology Group and Dep. Dir, Plant Physiol. Div., 1984–89, DSIR, NZ; Sen. Scientist, Crop Res. Div., DSIR, NZ, subseq. NZ Inst. for Crop and Food Res. Ltd, 1989. Charles F. Kettering Award for Photosynthesis Res., Amer. Soc. of Plant Physiologists, 1980; Rank Prize for Nutrition, 1981. *Publications:* scientific pubns, mainly on aspects of photosynthesis and plant lipid synthesis. *Recreations:* bird watching, hiking, trout fishing, gardening. *Address:* 30 Ihaka Street, Palmerston North, New Zealand 4410. *T:* (6) 3572966.

SLACK, His Honour John Kenneth Edward, TD 1964; DL; a Circuit Judge, 1977–99; *b* 23 Dec. 1930; *o s* of late Ernest Edward Slack, formerly Chief Clerk Westminster County Court, and late Beatrice Mary Slack (*née* Shorten), Broadstairs; *m* 1959, Patricia Helen, MA Cantab, *o d* of late William Keith Metcalfe, Southport; two *s*. *Educ:* University College Sch., Hampstead; St John's Coll., Cambridge (MA). Captain, RAEC, 1950. Admitted Solicitor, 1957; Partner, Freeborough Slack & Co., 1958–76; Mem. No 1 (later No 14) Legal Aid Area, 1966–69; Deputy Registrar, County Courts, 1969–72; a Recorder of the Crown Court, 1972–77; Pres., Wireless Telegraphy Appeals Tribunal, 1974–77. Captain Club Cricket Conf., 1962–66; Captain Bucks County Cricket Club, 1967–69 (Minor County Champions 1969); Active Vice-Pres., Club Cricket Conf., 1969–77, Pres., 1978. Chm. Council, University Coll. Sch., 1980–87 (Mem., 1974–90). DL Bucks, 1995. *Recreations:* cricket (Cambridge Blue 1954), golf. *Address:* c/o Crown Court, Aylesbury, Bucks HP20 1XD. *Clubs:* Hawks (Cambridge); Beaconsfield Golf.

SLACK, Prof. Jonathan Michael Wyndham, PhD; FMedSci; Professor of Developmental Biology, University of Bath, since 1995; Director, Stem Cell Institute, University of Minnesota, since 2007; *b* 10 Sept. 1949; *s* of Ronald Slack and Pamela Zoe Slack (*née* Gregory); *m* 1980, Janet Elizabeth Blaker; two *d*. *Educ:* Balliol Coll., Oxford (BA 1st. cl. Hons (Biochem.) 1971); Edinburgh Univ. (PhD 1974). Res. Fellow, Middlesex Hosp. Med. Sch., 1974–76; Res. Scientist, later Sen. and Principal Scientist, ICRF, 1976–95; Hd, Dept of Biol. and Biochem., Univ. of Bath, 2000–06. Mem., EMBO, 1993. FMedSci 2004. Waddington Medal, British Soc. Develtl Biol., 2002. *Publications:* From Egg to Embryo, 1983, 2nd edn 1991; Egg and Ego, 1999; Essential Developmental Biology, 2001, 2nd edn 2005; numerous scientific papers. *Recreations:* walking, Morris dancing. *Address:* McGuire Translational Research Facility, 2001 6th Street SE, Mail Code 2873, Minneapolis, MN 55455, USA.

SLACK, Michael Dennis; Founder and Chairman, Temporary Cover Ltd, since 2002; *b* Sudbury, 20 Oct. 1942; *s* of Dennis Slack and Stella Fyfe; one *s*. *Educ:* Kent Coll., Canterbury. Various posts, insce industry, 1960–80; Founder, Stuart Fyfe & Partners Ltd, 1980; Founder and Chm., Road Runner Gp, subseq. Fyfe Gp, 1995–2008. Mem., Insce Brokers' Registration Council, 1989–2002; Founder Dir, Gen. Insce Standards Council, 1999–2003; non-exec. Dir, FSA, 2004–. Dir, Inst. of Insce Brokers, 1992–97; Founder Chm., Assoc. of Insce Intermediaries and Brokers, 1997; Mem. Main Bd, Brit. Insce Brokers' Assoc., 2002–. FCMI. Mem., Co. of Insurers. Mem., RYA. *Recreations:* sailing, boating. *Clubs:* Royal Thames Yacht; City Livery Yacht.

SLACK, Prof. Paul Alexander, DPhil; FBA 1990; FRHistS; Principal of Linacre College, Oxford, since 1996; Titular Professor of Early Modern Social History, University of Oxford, since 1999; *b* 23 Jan. 1943; *s* of Isaac Slack and Helen (*née* Firth); *m* 1965, Diana Gillian Manby (*d* 2003); two *d*. *Educ:* Bradford Grammar Sch.; St John's Coll., Oxford (Casberd Exhibnr and Schol.; 1st cl. Hons Mod. Hist. 1964; MA; DPhil 1972; Hon. Fellow, 1998). FRHistS 1972. A. M. P. Read Schol., Oxford Univ., and Harmsworth Sen. Schol., Merton Coll., Oxford, 1965–66; Jun. Res. Fellow, Balliol Coll., Oxford, 1966–69; Lectr in Hist., York Univ., 1969–72; Oxford University: Fellow and Tutor, 1973–96 (Emeritus Fellow, 1996–), Sub-Rector, 1983, Sen. Tutor, 1984–86 and 1991–92, Exeter Coll.; Reader in Modern Hist., 1990–96; Jun. Proctor, 1986–87; Mem., Hebdomadal Council, 1987–; Chm., Gen. Bd of Faculties, 1995–96; Pro-Vice-Chancellor, 1997–2000; Pro-Vice-Chancellor (Acad. Services and Univ. Collections), 2000–05; Delegate, OUP, 2000–. Vis. Prof., Univ. of S Carolina, 1980; Vis. Res. Associate, Rikkyo Univ., Tokyo, 1988. Ford's Lectr in British History, Oxford, 1994–95; Aylmer Memorial Lectr, York, 2003. Member: Internat. Commn for Hist. of Towns, 1976–; Humanities Res. Bd, 1994–95. Pres., Soc. for Social Hist. of Medicine, 1991; Member, Council: RHistS, 1984–87; British Acad., 1994–95. Editor, Past and Present, 1985–94. DUniv York, 2005. *Publications:* (ed with Peter Clark) Crisis and Order in English Towns 1500–1700, 1972; (ed) Poverty in Early Stuart Salisbury, 1975; (with P. Clark) English Towns in Transition 1500–1700, 1976 (Japanese edn 1989); (ed) Rebellion, Popular Protest and the Social Order in Early Modern England, 1984; The Impact of Plague in Tudor and Stuart England, 1985; Poverty and Policy in Tudor and Stuart England, 1988; The English Poor Law 1531–1782, 1990; (ed with T. Ranger) Epidemics and Ideas, 1992; (ed jtly) Public Duty and Private Conscience in Seventeenth-Century England, 1993; From Reformation to Improvement: public welfare in early modern England, 1999; (ed) Environments and Historical Change, 1999; (ed jtly) Civil Histories: essays presented to Sir Keith Thomas, 2000; (ed jtly) The Peopling of Britain, 2002; contribs to learned jls. *Recreations:* opera, fell-walking. *Address:* Linacre College, Oxford OX1 3JA. *T:* (01865) 271650.

SLACK, Roger; *see* Slack, C. R.

SLACK, Stephen; Head, Legal Office of the Church of England and Chief Legal Adviser to the Archbishops' Council, since 2001; Chief Legal Adviser and Registrar, General Synod of the Church of England, since 2001; Joint Registrar of the Provinces of Canterbury and York, since 2001; *b* 29 Dec. 1954; *s* of Thomas and Ada Genary Slack; *m* 1982, Georgiana Sophia (*née* Shaw); one *s* two *d*. *Educ:* Aylesbury Grammar Sch.; Christ Church, Oxford (MA). Solicitor in private practice, 1979–84; Charity Commission: Sen. Lawyer, Liverpool, 1984–89; Hd, Legal Sect., Taunton, 1989–2001. *Recreations:* gardening, music, history. *Address:* Church House, Great Smith Street, SW1P 3AZ.

SLACK, Timothy Willatt, LVO 1995; MA; Principal, St Catharine's Foundation at Cumberland Lodge, 1985–95; *b* 18 April 1928; *yr s* of late Cecil Moorhouse Slack, MC, and Dora Willatt, Beverley, Yorks; *m* 1st, 1957, Katharine (*d* 1993), 2nd *d* of late Walter Norman Hughes, MA, and Jean Sorsbie, Chepstow, Mon; one *s* three *d*; 2nd, 1996, Shuna Ann Black (marr. diss. 2003; she *d* 2006). *Educ:* Winchester Coll.; New Coll., Oxford. Hons. PPE, 1951. Asst, Lycée de Rennes, France, 1951; Asst master, the Salem School,

Baden, Germany, 1952; Assistant master, Repton School, 1953–59; Headmaster of Kambawsa College, Taunggyi, Shan State, Burma, 1959–62; Headmaster, Bedales Sch., 1962–74. Chairman, Society of Headmasters of Independent Schools, 1968–70. Dep. Dir, 1975–77, Dir, 1977–83, Wiston House FCO Conf. Centre (incorp. Wilton Park Confs), Steyning; Headmaster, Hellenic Coll. of London, 1983–84. Kurt Hahn Meml Lectr, 1982. Dir, Nat. Tenants Resource Centre, 1993–; Chm., Sir Heinz Koeppler Trust, 2001–05. Chm. Governors, The Royal Sch., Windsor Great Park, 1988–95. Chm., Round Table Moot, 1994–2001. Contested (L): Petersfield, Feb. and Oct. 1974; Enfield, Southgate, Dec. 1984; (L/Alliance) Fareham, 1987. *Address:* Greenlands, Stoner Hill, Steep, Petersfield, Hampshire GU32 1AG.

See also Sir W. W. Slack.

SLACK, Sir William (Willatt), KCVO 1990; MA, MCh, BM, FRCS; Consultant Surgeon, Middlesex Hospital, 1962–91, now Emeritus Surgeon; Senior Lecturer in Surgery, 1962–91, and Dean, 1983–87, Middlesex Hospital Medical School; Dean, Faculty of Clinical Sciences, University College and Middlesex School of Medicine, University College London, 1987–91; also Surgeon: Hospital of St John and St Elizabeth, 1970–88; King Edward VII Hospital for Officers, 1975–91; *b* 22 Feb. 1925; *s* of late Cecil Moorhouse Slack, MC, and Dora Slack (*née* Willatt); *m* 1951, Joan, 4th *d* of late Lt-Col Talbot H. Wheelwright, OBE; two *s* two *d*. *Educ:* Winchester Coll.; New Coll., Oxford; Middlesex Hosp. Med. Sch. Ho. Surg., Surgical Registrar and Sen. Surgical Registrar, Middx Hosp., 1950–59; Jun. Registrar, St Bartholomew's Hosp., 1953; Fulbright Scholar, R. & E. Hosp., Univ. of Illinois, Chicago, 1959. Surgeon to the Queen, 1975–83; Serjeant Surgeon to the Queen, 1983–90. Hon. Consultant, RBL, 1984–2007. Hon. Fellow, UCL, 1987. Master, Barbers' Co., 1991–92. *Publications:* various surgical articles in med. jls and textbooks. *Recreations:* ski-ing, gardening; Oxford blue for Association football, 1946. *Address:* Hillside Cottage, Tower Road, Stawell, near Bridgwater, Somerset TA7 9AJ. *T:* (01278) 722719.

See also T. W. Slack.

SLADE, Adrian Carnegie, CBE 1988; marketing consultant, since 1991; *b* 25 May 1936; *y s* of late George Penkivil Slade, KC and Mary Albinia Alice Slade; *m* 1960, Susan Elizabeth Forsyth; one *s* one *d*. *Educ:* Eton Coll.; Trinity Coll., Cambridge (BA Law). Pres., Cambridge Footlights, 1959. Writer, J. Walter Thompson, 1959–64; S. H. Benson, 1964–71, Dir, 1970–71; Co-Founder and Managing Director: Slade Monico Bluff Ltd, 1971–75; Slade Bluff & Bigg Ltd, 1975–86; Slade Hamilton Fenech Ltd, 1986–91. Director: Orange Tree Th., Richmond, 1986–98 (Chm., 1991–98); Adzido, 1998–2004 (Chm., 2001–04). Trustee, One plus One, 1987–97 (Chm., 1990–97). Mem. (L) Richmond, GLC, 1981–86 (Leader, L/SDP Alliance Gp, 1982–86). Contested: (L) Putney, 1966, Feb. and Oct. 1974; (L/SDP Alliance) Wimbledon, 1987. Pres., Liberal Party, 1987–88; Jt Pres., 1988, Vice-Pres., 1988–89, Liberal Democrats. *Recreations:* music, theatre, films, piano playing, photography. *Address:* 28 St Leonard's Road, SW14 7LX. *T:* (020) 8876 8712.

See also Rt Hon. Sir C. J. Slade.

SLADE, Sir Benjamin Julian Alfred, 7th Bt *cr* 1831; Chairman: Shirlstar Container Transport Ltd, since 1973; Wilshaw Plc, since 2005; Director, Shirlstar Holdings Ltd, since 1990; *b* 22 May 1946; *s* of Sir Michael Slade, 6th Bt and Angela (*d* 1959), *d* of Captain Orlando Chichester; *S* father, 1962; *m* 1977, Pauline Carol (marr. diss. 1991), *er d* of Major Claude Myburgh. *Educ:* Millfield Sch. Chm., Pyman Bell (Holding) Ltd. Mem., Worshipful Co. of Ironmongers. Freeman, City of London, 1979. *Recreations:* racing, polo, bridge. *Heir:* none. *Address:* Maunsel House, North Newton, North Petherton, Bridgwater, Somerset TA7 0BU. *T:* (01278) 661076, *Fax:* (01278) 661074; *e-mail:* maunselhouse@btconnect.com. Woodlands Castle, Ruishton, Taunton, Somerset TA3 5LU. *T:* (01823) 444019; *e-mail:* info@woodlandscastle.co.uk. *Clubs:* Turf, White's; Woodlands Castle, Old Somerset Dining (Taunton).

SLADE, Rt Hon. Sir Christopher John, Kt 1975; PC 1982; a Lord Justice of Appeal, 1982–91; *b* 2 June 1927; *e s* of late George Penkivil Slade, KC, and Mary Albinia Alice Slade; *m* 1958, Jane Gwenllian Armstrong Buckley, *d* of Rt Hon. Sir Denys Buckley, PC, MBE; one *s* three *d*. *Educ:* Eton (Scholar); New Coll., Oxford (Scholar). Eldon Law Scholar, 1950. Called to Bar, Inner Temple, 1951; joined Lincoln's Inn *ad eundem*, 1954, Bencher, 1973 (Treas., 1994). In practice at Chancery Bar, 1951–75; QC 1965; Attorney General, Duchy of Lancaster and Attorney and Serjeant Within the County Palatine of Lancaster, 1972–75; a Judge of the High Ct, Chancery Division, 1975–82; a Judge of Restrictive Practices Ct, 1980–82, Pres., 1981–82. Member: Gen. Council of the Bar, 1958–62, 1965–69; Senate of Four Inns of Court, 1966–69; Lord Chancellor's Legal Educn Cttee, 1969–71. Master, Ironmongers' Co., 1973. *Address:* 16 Elthiron Road, SW6 4BN. *Club:* Garrick.

See also A. C. Slade.

SLADE, Hon. Dame Elizabeth Ann, DBE 2008; **Hon. Mrs Justice Slade;** a Judge of the High Court of Justice, Queen's Bench Division, since 2008; *b* 12 May 1949; *d* of late Dr Charles and Henriette Slade; *m* 1975; two *d*. *Educ:* Wycombe Abbey Sch.; Lady Margaret Hall, Oxford (Exhibnr, MA). Called to the Bar, Inner Temple, 1972, Bencher 1990, Master of Staff, 1994–98. QC 1992; Asst Recorder, 1995–98; Recorder, 1998–2008; Dep. High Court Judge, 1998–2008; additional pt-time Judge, Employment Appeal Tribunal, 2000–03. Member, Administrative Tribunal: BIS, 1999– (Vice Pres., 2008–); EBRD, 2008–. Chm., Sex Discrimination Cttee, Bar Council, 2000–02. Hon. Vice Pres., Employment Law Bar Assoc., 1998– (Chm., 1995–97). Trustee, Free Representation Unit, 1998–2002. *Publication:* Tolley's Employment Handbook, 1978, to 7th edn (ed jtly) 1991. *Recreations:* theatre, art, music, walking. *Address:* Royal Courts of Justice, Strand, WC2A 2LL.

SLADE, Laurie George; Insurance Ombudsman, 1994–96 and 1999–2000; *b* Nairobi, 12 Feb. 1944; *yr s* of Humphrey Slade and Constance Laing Gordon. *Educ:* Duke of York's Sch., Nairobi; Magdalen Coll., Oxford (MA); London Univ. Inst. of Educn (PGCE). Called to the Bar, Lincoln's Inn, 1966. Stage management and acting in professional theatre and TV, Kenya and UK, 1967–70; teaching, 1972–75; Advocate, Kenya High Court, 1975–81; Legal Advr, CIArb and Dep. Registrar, London Court of Internat. Arbitration, 1982–88; Dep. Insurance Ombudsman, 1988–94; Independent Investigator, SIB, then FSA, 1996–99. Mem., Insurance Brokers' Registration Council, 1997–98. Chm., FSA Ombudsman Steering Gp, 1998. Voluntary counsellor, Hounslow Social Services, 1988–94; counselling and psychotherapy practice, 1991–; UKCP Registered Psychoanalytic Psychotherapist, 1999; social dreaming practitioner, 2002–. Mem., British and Irish Ombudsman Assoc., 1993–. Mem., Guild of Psychotherapists, 1999–; Founder Mem., Internat. Neuro-Psychoanalysis Soc., 2000–; Mem., Confedn for Analytical Psychology (formerly Confedn of Analytical Psychologists), 2002–. Wrote plays: Out of Africa, 1988 and Karen's Tale, 1996 (both after Karen Blixen); Joe & I, 2005. *Publications:* professional papers and contribs to learned jls. *Recreations:* theatre, painting (2 solo exhibns in Kenya, 1974, 1979).

SLADE, Patrick Buxton M.; *see* Mitford-Slade.

SLADE, William Charles; Vice-Principal, 1998–2000, Consultant, 2000–02, King's College London; *b* 20 June 1939; *s* of late Charles Slade and Phyllis (*née* Littlejohns); *m* 1961, Elizabeth Lyn Roberts; two *d*. *Educ:* St Julian's High Sch., Newport, Gwent; UC of Swansea (BSc; Pres., Students' Union, 1960–61). ACMA 1966. Guest Keen Iron and Steel Ltd, 1961–66; Management Accountant: Tunnel Cement Ltd, 1966–71; Pye TMC Ltd, 1971–75; Finance Officer, 1975–77, Sec., 1977–85, Chelsea Coll., Univ. of London; Sec., 1986–98, Mem. Council, 1998–2000, KCL (FKC 1989). Chm., Univ. of London Purchasing Consortium, 1991–94. Mem. Council, Greenacre Sch. for Girls, 1980–95. Member: NADFAS (Epsom branch), 2002–; Epsom Literary Soc., 2003– (Cttee Mem., 2005–). *Recreations:* theatre, golf, Rugby football. *Address:* Fairway, 1A Links Road, Epsom, Surrey KT17 3PP. *T:* (01372) 742952. *Club:* Royal Automobile.

SLADEN, Teresa; Secretary of the Victorian Society, 1987–93; *b* 16 Sept. 1939; *d* of Robert John Fawcett and Anne (*née* Fairlie Clarke); *m* 1961, David Sladen; one *s* two *d*. *Educ:* Birkbeck Coll., London Univ. (BA Hons Hist. of Art/Italian); Courtauld Inst. (MA Medieval Art and Architecture, 1978). Royal Commn on Historical Monuments, 1978–79; part-time lectr and freelance researcher, 1980–82; Architectural Advr, Victorian Soc., 1983–87. Trustee and Cttee Mem., Mausolea & Monuments Trust, 1997– (Chm., 1998–2000); Vice-Chm., Victorian Soc., 1998–2001; Member: Southwark DAC, 1993–2002; Adv. Bd for Redundant Churches, 1999–. *Publications:* (contrib.) The Albert Memorial, 2000; (contrib.) St Paul's Cathedral, 2004; contrib. to Jl of Garden History. *Recreations:* drawing, 19th century stained glass and painted decoration, 19th century novels.

SLANE, Viscount; Alexander Burton Conyngham; Business Development Manager, Imperative Energy Ltd, Ireland; *b* 30 Jan. 1975; *s* and *heir* of Earl of Mount Charles, *qv*; *m* 2007, Carina Suzanne, *d* of late Nicholas George Bolton. *Educ:* Trinity Coll., Dublin (BA History of Art); Univ. of Cape Town (MBA 2005). Pernod Ricard; Christie's. *Address:* Slane Castle, Co. Meath, Eire.

SLANEY, Prof. Sir Geoffrey, KBE 1984; FRCS; Barling Professor, Head of Department of Surgery, Queen Elizabeth Hospital, Birmingham University, 1971–86, now Emeritus; Hon. Consultant Surgeon: United Birmingham Hospitals and Regional Hospital Board, 1959–2002; Royal Prince Alfred Hospital, Sydney, since 1981; President, Royal College of Surgeons of England, 1982–86; Hon. Consulting Surgeon Emeritus, City of London and Hackney Health Authority, 1983; *b* 19 Sept. 1922; *er s* of Richard and Gladys Lois Slaney; *m* 1956, Josephine Mary Davy; one *s* two *d*. *Educ:* Brewood Grammar Sch.; Univs of Birmingham, London and Illinois, USA. MB, ChB (Birmingham) 1947, FRCS 1953, MS (Ill) 1956, ChM (Birmingham) 1961; Hon. FRCSI 1983; Hon. FRACS 1983; Hon. FCSSL 1984; Hon. FACS 1985; Hon. FCSSA 1986; Hon. FRCSCan 1986; Hon. FRCA (Hon. FFARCS 1987). Ho. Surg. and Surgical Registrar, Gen. Hosp. Birmingham, 1947–48. Captain RAMC, 1948–50. Surgical Registrar, Coventry, London and Hackney Hosps, 1950–53; Surgical Registrar, Lectr in Surgery and Surgical Research Fellow, Queen Elizabeth Hosp., Birmingham, 1953–59; Hunterian Prof., RCS, 1961–62; Prof. of Surgery, Univ. of Birmingham, 1966–87. Non-exec. Dir, St Martins Hosps, 1987–2001. Member: London Adv. Group to Sec. of State, DHSS, 1980–81; Ministerial Adv. Gp on Med. Manpower, 1985–86; Res. Liaison Gp, DHSS, 1979–85; Midlands Med. Appeals Tribunal, 1964–94; Med. Adv. Bd, Internat. Hosp. Gp, 1986–94. Former External Examr in Surgery to Univs of: Newcastle upon Tyne, London, Cambridge, Oxford, Liverpool, Nat. Univ. of Ireland, Lagos, Zimbabwe, and Licentiate Cttee, Hong Kong; Advisor in Surgery, Univs of Bristol and London. Lectures: Richardson Meml, Massachusetts Gen. Hosp., Boston, USA, 1975; Pybus Meml, Newcastle, 1978; Simpson Smith Meml, London, 1979; Legg Meml, KCH, London, 1982; Chesledon, St Thomas' Hosp., London, 1983; Miles Meml, London, 1983; Berrill Meml, Coventry, 1984; Sandblom, Lund, Sweden, 1984; Sir John Frazer Meml, Edinburgh, 1984; Tung Wah Inaugural, Tung Wah Hosp., Hong Kong, 1986; Sir Ernest Finch Meml, Sheffield, 1986; Hunterian Oration, RCS, 1987; Budd Meml, Bristol, 1987; Annual Guest Lecture, Chicago Surgical Soc., 1987; Barney Brooks Meml, Vanderbilt Univ., Tennessee, 1987; Rutherford-Morison, Newcastle, 1987; Walter C. Mackenzie, Edmonton, 1988; Francis C. Moore, Boston, 1988; Joseph C. Finneran, Indianapolis, 1988; Annual Oration, Osler Club, 1988; Qvist Meml, Royal Free Hosp., 1988; Duke Sesquicentennial, NC, 1988; Telford Meml, Manchester, 1989; (first) Bryan Brooke, Ileostomy Assoc., 1990. Visiting Professor: Durban, Cape Town, Witwatersrand, 1970; Sir Logan Campbell and RACS, NZ, 1977; Univ. of Calif and Cedars-Sinai Hosp., LA, 1978; Pearce Gould, Middlesex Hosp., 1980; McIlrath Guest, Sydney, 1981; G. B. Ong, Univ. of Hong Kong, 1983 (Ong Inaugural Lecture); Foundn Culpepper Prof., Univ. of California, 1984; Madras Med. Coll., and Univ. of Istanbul, 1986; Univ. of Alberta, Edmonton, 1988; Harvard, 1988; Uniformed Services Univ., Bethesda, 1988; Duke Univ., 1988; Wernicke-Marks-Elk, Univ. of Zimbabwe, 1989. Mem. Council, RCS, 1975–87; Member: Moynihan Chirurgical Club (Pres., 1986–87); James IV Assoc. of Surgeons (Pres., 1985–86); Internat. Surgical Gp (Pres., 1985–86); Surgical Research Soc.; Internat. Soc. of Cardio-Vascular Surgeons; Vascular Surgical Soc., GB (Pres., 1974–75); Chm., Assoc. of Profs of Surgery of GB and Ireland, 1979–82. Mem. Council, Univ. of Zimbabwe, 1973–82. Fellow: RSM; Assoc. of Surgeons GB and Ire. (Mem. Council, 1966–76, Treasurer, 1970–76); Assoc. Clinical Anatomists; Amer. Surgical Assoc. Hon. Life Member: Los Angeles Surgical Soc.; Chicago Surgical Soc.; Warren H. Cole Surgical Soc.; William H. Scott Surgical Soc.; Hon. Member: Grey Turner Surgical Club; Assoc. of Surgeons of India. Hon. Freeman, Barbers' Co. Jacksonian Prize and Medal, RCS, 1959; Pybus Meml Medal, NE Surgical Soc., 1978; Miles Medal, Royal Marsden Hosp., 1983; Vanderbilt Univ. Medal, 1987; Brooke Medal, Ileostomy Assoc. of GB and Ireland, 1990. Mem. Editl Bd, British Jl of Surgery, 1970–84; Co-Chief Editor, Jl of Cardio-Vascular Surgery, 1988–92. *Publications:* Metabolic Derangements in Gastrointestinal Surgery (with B. N. Brooke), 1967 (USA); (jtly) Cancer of the Large Bowel, 1991; numerous contribs to med. and surg. jls. *Recreations:* fishing, family, sculpture and carving. *Address:* Hill Crest, Collins Green, Worcester WR6 5PT. *T:* (01886) 822024.

SLANEY, (William) Simon (Rodolph) K.; *see* Kenyon-Slaney.

SLATER, Bill; *see* Slater, W. J.

SLATER, Dr David Homfray, CB 1996; Director, Cambrensis Ltd, since 2001; Chairman: RLtec, since 2003; NIREX CLG Ltd, since 2005; *b* 16 Oct. 1940; *m* 1964, Edith Mildred Price; four *d*. *Educ:* University College of Wales Aberystwyth (BSc, PhD). CChem, FRIC, FIChemE, CEng, FInstE. Research Associate, Ohio State Univ., 1966–69; Sen. Res. Fellow, Dept of Chemistry, Univ. of Southampton, 1969–70; Lectr in Combustion, Dept of Chem. Engineering and Chem. Technology, Imperial College London, 1970–75; Cremer and Warner: Sen. Scientist, 1975; Partner, 1979–81; Founding Dir, Technica, 1981–91; Chief Inspector, HM Inspectorate of Pollution, 1991–96; Dir, Pollution Prevention and Control, Envmt Agency, 1996–98; Dir, Oxera Envmtl, 1998–2001; Principal Partner, Acona Gp, 2001–05. Specialist Advr to Envmt, Transport and Regl Affairs Select Cttee, H of C, 1999–2000; Envmtl Advr, Better Regulation Task Force, Cabinet Office, 2000. Chm., Envmtl Gp, Regulatory Policy Inst., Oxford,

2001–03. Associate, Envmtl Change Unit, Oxford Univ., 1999–2001; Royal Acad. of Engrg Vis. Prof., UMIST, 2002–06; Adjunct Prof., Industrial Adv. Panel, KCL, 2002. Hon. Prof. of Life Sciences, Univ. of Wales, Aberystwyth, 1991. Chm. and Trustee, SEE – It Working. Mem. Court, Cranfield Univ., 1997–2001. *Publications:* numerous contribs to sci. jls and conference procs. *Recreations:* music, horses. *Club:* Athenæum.

SLATER, Prof. Edward Charles, ScD; FRS 1975; FAA; Professor of Physiological Chemistry, University of Amsterdam, The Netherlands, 1955–85; *b* 16 Jan. 1917; *s* of Edward Brunton Slater and Violet Podmore; *m* 1940, Marion Winifred Hutley; one *d. Educ:* Melbourne Univ. (BSc, MSc); Cambridge Univ. (PhD, ScD). Biochemist, Australian Inst. of Anatomy, Canberra, Aust., 1939–46; Research Fellow, Molteno Inst., Univ. of Cambridge, UK, 1946–55. Pres., Internat. Union of Biochem., 1988–91. Member: Royal Netherlands Acad. of Science and Letters, 1964; Hollandsche Maatschappij van Wetenschappen, 1970; Hon. Member: Amer. Soc. of Biological Chemists, 1971; Japanese Biochemical Soc., 1973; The Biochemical Soc., 1987; Nederlandse Vereniging voor Biochemie, 1989; For. Mem., Royal Swedish Acad. of Sciences, 1975; Hon. For. Mem., Académie Royal de Méd., Belgium, 1982; Corresponding Member: Acad. Nacional de Ciencias Exactas, Fisicasy Naturales, Argentina, 1973; Australian Acad. of Science, 1985. Hon. DSc Southampton, 1993; Hon. DBiolSci Bari, 1998. Kt, Order of the Netherlands Lion, 1984. *Publications:* Biochimica et Biophysica Acta: story of a biochemical journal, 1986; 475 contribs to learned jls. *Recreation:* yachting. *Address:* Suite 3/1, Richmond Painswick, Stroud Road, Painswick, Glos GL6 6UL. *T:* (01452) 810787.

SLATER, Prof. Gillian Lesley, (Mrs Ian Huntley), DPhil; DL; Vice-Chancellor, Bournemouth University, 1994–2005; *b* 13 Jan. 1949; *d* of Leonard William Henry Filtness and Adeline Mary Filtness; *m* 1st, 1970, John Bruce Slater (marr. diss. 1983); two *d;* 2nd, 1988, Ian David Huntley. *Educ:* Sutton High Sch. for Girls; St Hugh's Coll., Oxford (BA 1970; MSc 1971; MA, DPhil 1973). FIMA 1982; CMath 1991. Lectr, Poly. of South Bank, 1973–79; Sen. Lectr, 1979–84, Prin. Lectr, 1984–86, Sheffield City Poly., 1979–86; Head of Dept of Math. and Physics, 1986–89, Asst Dir and Dean of Science and Engrg, 1989–92, Manchester Poly.; Pro-Vice-Chancellor, Manchester Metropolitan Univ., 1992–94. Governor: UEL, 2006–; Talbot Heath Sch. (Dep. Chm.), 2006–. DL Dorset, 2006. *Publications:* Essential Mathematics for Software Engineers, 1987; (with A. Norcliffe) Mathematics for Software Construction, 1991; numerous articles in learned jls. *Recreation:* listening to classical orchestral music. *Address:* 31 Leven Avenue, Bournemouth BH4 9LH.

SLATER, James Derrick, FCA; Chairman, Salar Properties Ltd, since 1983; Deputy Chairman, Agrifirma Services Ltd, since 2008; *b* 13 March 1929; *o s* of Hubert and Jessica Slater; *m* 1965, Helen Wyndham Goodwyn; two *s* two *d. Educ:* Preston Manor County Sch. Accountant and then Gen. Man. to a gp of metal finishing cos, 1953–55; Sec., Park Royal Vehicles Ltd, 1955–58; Dep. Sales Dir, Leyland Motor Corp. Ltd, 1963; Chm., Slater Walker Securities Ltd, 1964–75; Dir, BLMC, 1969–75. Dep. Chm., Galahad Gold, 2003–08. FCA 1963 (ACA 1953). *Publications:* Return to Go, 1977; The Zulu Principle, 1992; Investment Made Easy, 1994; Pep Up Your Wealth, 1994; Beyond the Zulu Principle, 1996; How to Become a Millionaire, 2000; *for children:* Goldenrod, 1978; A. Mazing Monsters, 1979; Grasshopper and the Unwise Owl, 1979; The Boy Who Saved Earth, 1979. *Recreations:* bridge, salmon fishing.

SLATER, Adm. Sir John Cunningham Kirkwood, (Sir Jock), GCB 1992 (KCB 1988); LVO 1971; DL; First Sea Lord and Chief of Naval Staff, and First and Principal Naval Aide-de-Camp to the Queen, 1995–98; *b* 27 March 1938; *s* of late Dr James K. Slater, OBE, MD, FRCPE and M. C. B. Slater (née Bramwell); *m* 1972, Ann Frances, *d* of late Mr and Mrs W. P. Scott of Orkney; two *s. Educ:* Edinburgh Academy; Sedbergh. BRNC Dartmouth, 1956–58; served HM Ships Troubridge, Yaxham, HM Yacht Britannia, Cassandra, 1959–64; Comd HMS Soberton, 1965; specialised in navigation, HMS Dryad, 1965–66; HM Ships Victorious and Scarborough (Dartmouth Training Sqdn), 1966–68; Equerry to HM the Queen, 1968–71; Comdr 1971; Comd, HMS Jupiter, 1972–73; Directorate of Naval Ops, MoD, 1973–75; Captain 1976; Comd, HMS Kent, 1976–77; RCDS 1978; Asst Dir of Naval Warfare, MoD, 1979–81; Comd, HMS Illustrious, 1982–83; Captain, Sch. of Maritime Ops and Comd, HMS Dryad, 1983–85; Rear Adm. 1985; ACDS (Policy and Nuclear), 1985–87; Vice-Adm., 1987; Flag Officer, Scotland and NI, and NATO Comdr Northern sub area Eastern Atlantic, Comdr Nore sub area Channel and Naval Base Comdr, Rosyth, 1987–89; Chief of Fleet Support (Mem., Admiralty Bd), 1989–91; Adm. 1991; C-in-C, Fleet, Allied C-in-C, Channel, and Eastern Atlantic, 1991–92; VCDS, 1993–95. Non-executive Director: VTGp (formerly Vosper Thornycroft Hldgs) plc, 1999–2004; Lockheed Martin UK Ltd, 2000–; Consultant, Bristow Helicopters, 2001–04. Vice Pres., RUSI, 1995–98 (Vice Chm., 1993–95); Chm., RNLI, 2004– (Council, 1999–; Chm., Ops Cttee, 2001–02; Dep. Chm., 2002–04); Mem., Bd of Mgt, BNSC, 1986–87. Chm., Royal Navy Club of 1765 and 1785, 2001–04; Chm., White Ensign Assoc., 2002–05 (Mem. Council, 1999–); Vice-Pres., British Forces Foundn, 2002– (Vice-Chm., 1999–2002). Chm., Imperial War Mus., 2001–06 (Trustee, 1999–2006); Pres., Amer. Air Mus. in Britain, 2001–06. Mem., Nat. Youth Orchestra of GB, 1955. Gov., Sedbergh Sch., 1997–2002. Elder Brother, Trinity Hse, 1995 (Younger Brother, 1978–95). Freeman, City of London, 1989; Liveryman, Shipwrights' Co., 1991– (Mem. Ct of Assts, 2005–; Fourth Warden, 2008–April 2009). DL Hants, 1999. Hon. DSc: Cranfield, 1998; Southampton, 2008. Comdr Legion of Merit (US), 1997. *Recreations:* outdoor. *Address:* c/o Naval Secretary, Fleet Headquarters, Whale Island, Portsmouth PO2 8BY. *Clubs:* Army and Navy; Liphook Golf.

See also P. J. B. Slater.

SLATER, Dr John Morton; agricultural economic consultant, since 1998; *b* 21 Aug. 1938; *s* of Rev. Percy William Slater and Evelyn Maude Morton Slater; *m* 1972, Susan Mary Black, *d* of Rev. Dr John Ferguson Park and Mary Davis McCaughey Park; two *s* one *d. Educ:* Durham Sch.; Univ. of Nottingham (BSc Agric. Sc 1961); Univ. of Toronto (MS Agric. Econ. 1963); Univ. of Illinois (L. J. Norton Meml Fellow; PhD 1965). Lectr, Univ. of Manchester, 1965–70; Consultant, FAO, 1966–67; Ministry of Agriculture, Fisheries and Food: Economic Advr, 1970–84; Head of Econs and Stats (Food) Div., 1984–92; Head of Econs (Internat.) Div., 1992–96; Head of Econs and Stats Gp, 1996–98. Special Advr, H of L Select Cttee on Science and Technol., 1999–2000. Master, Worshipful Co. of Turners, 1999–2000; Chm., Millennium Masters Assoc., 2003–06. MRI. *Publication:* (ed) Fifty Years of the National Food Survey 1940–1990, 1991. *Recreations:* cricket, golf, bridge. *Address:* 28 Swains Lane, N6 6QR. *T:* (020) 7485 1238, *Fax:* (020) 7485 1268; *e-mail:* j.slater@slaterconsult.demon.co.uk. *Clubs:* City Livery (Hon. Sec., 2002–03), United Wards, MCC.

SLATER, Judith Mary; HM Diplomatic Service; Deputy High Commissioner, Pretoria, since 2007; *b* 26 June 1964; *d* of George Norris Stewart Slater and Valerie Mary Slater (née Pratt); *m* 1998, Philip Frederick de Waal; one *s* one *d. Educ:* Howell's Sch., Denbigh; St John's Coll., Cambridge (BA 1987). Joined HM Diplomatic Service, 1988; Third, then Second Sec. (Political), Canberra, 1989–93; First Sec., FCO, 1993; Private Sec. to

Minister of State, 1994; First Sec. (Press and Public Affairs), New Delhi, 1997–2001; Asst Dir, Personnel Policy, FCO, 2001–04; Consul-Gen., Houston, 2004–07. *Recreations:* golf, tennis, cinema. *Address:* c/o Foreign and Commonwealth Office, King Charles Street, SW1A 2AH.

SLATER, Rt Rev. Keith Francis; see Grafton, NSW, Bishop of.

SLATER, Kenneth Frederick, FREng, FIET; engineering and defence consultant; *b* 31 July 1925; *s* of Charles Frederick and Emily Gertrude Slater; *m* 1965, Marjorie Gladys Beadsworth (*d* 2007), Northampton. *Educ:* Hull Grammar Sch.; Manchester Univ. (BSc Tech (Hons)). Admiralty Signal Estab. Extension, 1943–46; RRE, 1949–63; UK Mem., NATO Air Defence Planning Team, 1964; Supt Radar Div., RRE, 1965–68; Asst Dir of Electronics R&D, Min. of Technology, 1968–70; Dir, 1970–71; Head of various groups, RRE, 1971–76; Dep. Dir, RSRE, 1976–78; Dir, Admiralty Surface Weapons Estabt, Portsmouth, 1978–84; Dir of Engrg, Marconi Underwater Systems Ltd, 1984–88. Vis. Prof., UCL, 1995–. Liveryman, Engineers' Co., 1992–. FREng (FEng 1985). *Publications:* specialist contribs on Radar to Encyclopaedia Britannica and Encyclopaedic Dictionary of Physics; technical articles. *Recreations:* photography, music. *Address:* 21 Sandpiper Court, 8 Thomas More Street, E1W 1AS. *T:* (020) 7702 3770.

SLATER, Prof. Michael Derek, DPhil; Professor of Victorian Literature, Birkbeck College, University of London, 1991–2001, now Emeritus; *b* 29 Dec. 1936; *s* of Jesse Slater and Valentine Blanche (née Clément). *Educ:* Reading Sch.; Balliol Coll., Oxford (Goldsmith Schol., Charles Oldham Schol., MA, DPhil 1965). Birkbeck College, University of London: Res. Asst, 1962–65; Asst Lectr in English, 1965–67; Lectr in English, 1967–79; Sen. Lectr, 1979–83; Reader, 1983–91. Dist. Vis. Prof., Ohio State Univ., 1975–76; Visiting Professor: Univ. of Debrecen, Hungary, 1992; Univ. of Kyoto, Japan, 1995, 2005. Tennyson Soc. annual Lect., 1997. President: Dickens Soc. of America, 1973; Internat. Dickens Fellowship, 1988–90. Chm. Trustees, Dickens House Mus., 1996–99, 2000–02, now Hon. Academic Advr. Hon. Fellow, Birkbeck Coll., 2001; Sen. Res. Fellow, Inst. of English Studies, Univ. of London, 2002. FEA 2004. Editor, The Dickensian, 1968–77. *Publications:* The Catalogue of the Suzannet Charles Dickens Collection, 1975; (ed) Dickens 1970, 1970; Dickens on America and the Americans, 1978; Dickens and Women, 1983, 2nd edn 1986; (with N. Bentley and N. Burgis) The Dickens Index, 1988; (ed) The Dent Uniform Edition of Dickens's Journalism, Vol. 1 1994, Vol. 2 1996, Vol. 3 1998, (with J. Drew) Vol. 4 2000; The Intelligent Person's Guide to Dickens, 2000; Douglas Jerrold 1803–1857, 2002; Biographical Memoir of Kathleen Tillotson, 2006; Charles Dickens, 2007; contrib. Oxford DNB. *Recreations:* theatre, travel, visiting literary museums. *Address:* c/o School of English and Humanities, Birkbeck College, Malet Street, WC1E 7HX. *T:* (020) 7631 6071.

SLATER, Prof. Nigel Kenneth Harry, PhD; FREng, CEng, FIChemE; Professor of Chemical Engineering, Cambridge University, since 2000; Fellow, Fitzwilliam College, Cambridge, 1978–85, and since 2000; *b* 22 March 1953; *s* of Arthur Geoffrey Slater; *m* 1976, Kay Bendle; one *s* two *d. Educ:* Bolton Sch.; Sidney Sussex Coll., Cambridge (MA; PhD). CEng 1990; FREng 2004; FIChemE 1997. Asst Lectr, 1979–82, Lectr, 1982–85, in Chemical Engrg, Cambridge Univ.; Bioprocessing Section Manager, Unilever Research NL, 1985–90; Head of Bioprocess Dept, Wellcome Foundation Ltd, 1990–95; Prof. and Head of Dept of Chem. Engrg and Applied Chemistry, Aston Univ., 1995–2000. Director: Birmingham Technology Ltd, 1995–2000; Cobra Bio-Manufacturing plc, 2002–; Founder, Cobra Biosciences Ltd, 1997. Chm., Chemical and Pharmaceuticals Directorate, BBSRC, 1993–96; Mem. Governing Body, Silsoe Res. Inst., 1996–2000. Governor, King Edward VI Foundn, 1997–2000. *Publications:* numerous articles in learned science and engrg jls. *Recreations:* golf, socialising, outdoor pursuits. *Address:* Shenstone House, 3 St Bernard's Road, Sutton Coldfield, W Midlands B72 1LE. *T:* (0121) 321 2349.

SLATER, Ven. Paul John; Archdeacon of Craven, since 2005; Bishop's Officer for Ministry and Mission, Diocese of Bradford, since 2001; *b* 22 March 1958; *s* of Norman and Jean Slater; *m* 1981, Beverley Louise (née Knight); two *s* (and one *s* decd). *Educ:* Corpus Christi Coll., Oxford (MA (Natural Sci.) 1983); St John's Coll., Durham (BA (Theol.) 1983). Ordained deacon, 1984, priest, 1985; Asst Curate, St Andrew's, Keighley, 1984–88; Priest-in-charge, St John's, Cullingworth, 1988–93; Dir, Lay Trng Foundn Course, 1988–93; PA to Bishop of Bradford, 1993–95; Rector, St Michael's, Haworth, 1995–2001. Mem., Brontë Soc., 1996–. *Recreations:* playing and watching cricket, playing tennis, reading novels. *Address:* Woodlands, Netherghyll Lane, Cononley, Keighley BD20 8PB. *T:* (01535) 635113; *e-mail:* paulj.slater@dial.pipex.com.

SLATER, Prof. Peter James Bramwell, FRSE; Kennedy Professor of Natural History, University of St Andrews, since 1984; *b* 26 Dec. 1942; *s* of Dr James Kirkwood Slater, OBE and Margaret Claire Byrom Slater (née Bramwell); *m* 1968, Elisabeth Priscilla Vernon Smith; two *s. Educ:* Edinburgh Academy; Glenalmond; Univ. of Edinburgh (BSc 1964; PhD 1968; DSc 1983). FIBiol 1986; FRSE 1991. Shaw Macfie Lang Fellow, 1964–66, Demonstrator in Zoology, 1966–68, Univ. of Edinburgh; Lectr in Biology, Univ. of Sussex, 1968–84; University of St Andrews: Head, Sch. of Biol and Med. Scis, 1992–97; Dean, Faculty of Sci., 1998–2002. Chm., Heads of Univ. Biol Scis, 1994–96. Association for Study of Animal Behaviour: Hon. Sec., 1973–78; Hon. Pres., 1986–89; Medallist, 1999. European Editor, Animal Behaviour, 1979–82; Editor: Advances in the Study of Behavior, 1989–2005 (Associate Editor, 1982–88); Science Progress, 1983–89. *Publications:* Sex Hormones and Behaviour, 1978; (ed with T. R. Halliday) Animal Behaviour, 1983; An Introduction to Ethology, 1985; (ed) Collins Encyclopaedia of Animal Behaviour, 1986; (ed with T. R. Halliday) Evolution and Behaviour, 1994; (with C. K. Catchpole) Bird Song: biological themes and variations, 1995, 2nd edn 2008; Essentials of Animal Behaviour, 1999; numerous articles in learned jls. *Recreations:* ornithology, writing, listening to music. *Address:* School of Biology, University of St Andrews, Fife KY16 9TS. *T:* (01334) 463500.

See also Sir J. C. K. Slater.

SLATER, William Bell, CBE 1982; VRD 1959; FCILT; Chairman, The Mersey Docks & Harbour Co., 1987–93; Managing Director, The Cunard Steam-Ship Co. plc, 1974–85 (Director, 1971–85 and 1986–88); Director, Trafalgar House plc, 1975–88; *b* 7 Jan. 1925; *s* of William Bell and Mamie Slater; *m* 1950, Jean Mary Kiernan; two *s. Educ:* Lancaster Royal Grammar Sch. FCILT (FCIT 1970). National Service, RM, 1943–47 (Captain, 3rd Commando Bde); RM Reserve, 1949–63 (Lt-Col and CO Merseyside Unit, 1959–63; Hon. Col, 1986–91). Trainee, Thos & Jno Brocklebank Ltd, 1947, Dir 1966–85, also Chm.; Ops Dir, 1968, Dep. Man. Dir, 1969, Man. Dir, 1971–72, Chm. 1972–85, Cunard Brocklebank Ltd. Director: Atlantic Container Line Ltd, 1968–85 (Chm., 1977–78 and 1982–83); Associated Container Transportation (Australia) Ltd, 1974–85 (Chm., 1982–85); Associated Container Transportation Ltd, 1974–85 (Chm., 1982–85); The Mersey Docks & Harbour Co., 1980–93 (Dep. Chm., 1985–87; Chm., 1987–93). External Dir, British Internat. Freight Assoc., 1989–94. Vice-Pres., CIT, 1984–87; Pres., Inst. of Freight Forwarders Ltd, 1987–88. Gen. Comr of Income Tax, 1987–99. Order of El Istiqlal (2nd Cl.), Jordan, 1972. *Recreations:* Rugby and cricket (formerly Senior Club player). *Address:* Pippins, The Street, Mortimer, Reading RG7 3PE. *T:* (0118) 933 3385. *Club:* Naval.

SLATER, William John, CBE 1998 (OBE 1982); President, British Amateur Gymnastics Association, 1989–2000; Director of National Services, Sports Council, 1984–89; *b* 29 April 1927; *s* of John Rothwell Slater and Ethel May Slater; *m* 1952, Marion Warr; two *s* two *d. Educ:* Clitheroe Royal Grammar Sch.; Carnegie Coll. of Physical Educn; Univ. of Birmingham (BSc 1960). Dir of Phys. Educn, Univ. of Liverpool, 1964–70; Dir of Phys. Educn, Univ. of Birmingham, 1970–83. Member: Central Adv. Council for Educn (Newsom Cttee), 1961–63; Cttee of Enquiry into Association Football (Chester Cttee), 1966–68; Sports Council, 1974–83; Nat. Olympic Cttee, 1990–2000. Chm., Grants Cttee, Sports Aid Foundn, 1978–97. Wolverhampton Wanderers Football Club, 1952–62: FA Championship medal, 1953–54, 1957–58, 1958–59; FA Cup winner's medal, 1960; rep. England in Association Football, 1951–60; Olympic Games, Helsinki, 1952; World Cup (Assoc. Football), Sweden, 1958. Hon. MSc Birmingham, 1990; Hon. DEd Wolverhampton, 2003. Footballer of the Year, 1960.

SLATKIN, Leonard; conductor; music director; Music Director, National Symphony Orchestra, Washington, 1995–2008; Chief Conductor, BBC Symphony Orchestra, 2000–04; *b* Los Angeles, 1 Sept. 1944; *s* of Felix Slatkin and Eleanor Slatkin (*née* Aller); *m* 1986, Linda Hohenfeld; one *s. Educ:* Indiana Univ.; LA City Coll.; Juilliard Sch. of Music. Conducting début as Asst Conductor, Youth Symphony Orch. of NY, Carnegie Hall, 1966; Asst Conductor, Juilliard Opera Theater and Dance Dept, 1967; St Louis Symphony Youth Orchestra: Founder, Music Dir and Conductor, 1969–75; Musical Advr, 1984–96; St Louis Symphony Orchestra: Asst Conductor, 1968–71; Associate Conductor, 1971–74; Music Dir and Conductor, 1979–95; Music Dir, New Orleans Philharmonic Symphony, 1977–78; débuts: with Chicago Symphony, NY Philharmonic, Philadelphia Orch., RPO, 1974; with USSR orchs, 1976–77; Tokyo, 1986; Metropolitan Opera, 1991. Guest conductor with orchs throughout world incl. Concertgebouw, English Chamber Orch., LPO, LSO, Vienna State Opera, Stuttgart Opera; Principal Guest Conductor: Minnesota Orch., 1974–79; Philharmonia, 1997–2000; RPO, 2005–; Los Angeles Philharmonic, 2005–07; Pittsburgh SO, Sept. 2008–; Music Advr, Nashville SO, 2006–. Has made numerous recordings. Mem., Nat. Acad. Recording Arts and Scis, 1985. Holds hon. doctorates. Grammy Awards, 1984, 1991 and 1994. Declaration of Honor (Silver) (Austria), 1986; Nat. Medal of Arts, USA, 2003. *Compositions:* The Raven, 1971; Rhymes and Sonnets, 1974; Dialogue for Two Cellos and Orchestra, 1975; Absurd Alphabed-time Stories, 1976; Extensions, 1, 2, 3 and 4, 1973–75. *Address:* c/o Askonas Holt Ltd, Lincoln House, 300 High Holborn, WC1V 7JH.

SLATTERY, Dr David Antony Douglas, MBE (mil.) 1958; Chief Medical Officer, Rolls-Royce plc, 1973–92; Dean, Faculty of Occupational Medicine, Royal College of Physicians, 1988–91 (Vice-Dean, 1986–88); *b* 28 Jan. 1930; *s* of Rear-Adm. Sir Matthew Slattery, KBE, CB and Mica Mary Slattery (*née* Swain); *m* 1st, 1954, Mary Winifred Miller; two *s* two *d;* 2nd, 1974, Claire Louise McGuinness; one *s. Educ:* Ampleforth Coll.; St Thomas' Hosp., London. MB BS; FFOM RCPI 1977; FFOM RCP 1981; FRCP 1986. Capt., RAMC, 1954–58. MO, E Midlands Gas Bd, 1959–69; Manager, Health and Safety, BSC, Rotherham, 1969–73. Special Lectr, Dept of Community Health, Nottingham Univ., 1978–93; Vis. Prof., Dept of Occupational Health, Univ. of Liverpool, 1992–97. Consultant Advr in occupational medicine, RAF, 1987–96; Advr on occupational health policy, Mersey RHA, 1992–94. Dir, Occupational Health Service, Aintree Hosps NHS Trust, 1993–94. Member: Standing Med. Adv. Cttee, DHSS, 1988–91; Adv. Bd, CS Occupational Health Service, 1988–91. Industrial Health Advr, Derbys Br., BRCS, 1976–93. *Publications:* papers on occupational medicine and the employment of the disabled. *Recreations:* history, fishing, people. *Address:* 99 South Quay, Wapping Dock, Liverpool L3 4BW. *T:* (0151) 707 2022.

SLATYER, Prof. Ralph Owen, AC 1993 (AO 1982); FRS 1975; Visiting Fellow, Australian National University, since 1992; *b* 16 April 1929; *s* of Thomas Henry and Jean Slatyer; *m* 1953, June Helen Wade; one *s* two *d. Educ:* Univ. of Western Australia (DSc (Agric.). CSIRO Res. Scientist, subseq. Chief Res. Scientist, 1951–67; Prof., Inst. of Advanced Studies, 1967–89, Dir, Res. Sch. of Biol Scis, 1984–89, ANU; Chief Scientist, Dept of Prime Minister and Cabinet, Australia, 1989–92; Mem. and Exec. Officer, Prime Minister's Science Council, 1989–92. Aust. Amb. to UNESCO, 1978–81. Vis. Prof., Duke Univ., 1963–64; Ford Foundn Fellow and Vis. Prof., UCSB, 1973–74. Member: Australian Res. Grants Cttee, 1969–72; Nat. Capital Planning Cttee, 1973–76; Aust. Nat. Commn for UNESCO, 1975–78 (Chm., 1976–78); Policy Adv. Council and Bd of Management, Aust. Centre for Internat. Agricl Research, 1981–85; President: Ecol Soc. of Austr., 1969–71; UNESCO Man and the Biosphere Programme, 1977–81; UNESCO World Heritage Cttee, 1981–83; ICSU Sci. Cttee on Problems of the Environment, 1982–85; ANZAAS, 1983; Chairman: Aust. Biol. Resources Study, 1981–84; Australian Science and Technology Council, 1982–87; Co-ordination Cttee on Sci. and Technol., 1989–92; Co-op. Res. Centres Cttee, 1990–93; Co-op. Res. Centre for Rainforest Ecology and Mgt, 1993–2001; Dep. Chm., Nat. Greenhouse Adv. Cttee, 1989–93. FAA 1967; Fellow, Aust. Acad. of Technol Scis and Engrg, 1992. For. Associate, US Nat. Acad. of Sciences, 1976; Hon. For. Mem., Amer. Acad. of Arts and Scis, 1981; For. Mem., Korean Acad. of Scis and Technol., 1996. Hon. DSc: WA, 1983; Duke, 1986; Qld, 1992; Charles Sturt, 1999; James Cook, 2003; Newcastle, 2003. Edgeworth David Medal, Royal Soc. of NSW, 1960; Austr. Medal of Agric. Sci., 1968; ANZAAS Medal, 1991; Centenary Medal, Australia, 2003. *Publications:* (with I. C. McIlroy) Practical Microclimatology, 1961; Plant-Water Relationships, 1967; (ed with R. A. Perry) Arid Lands of Australia, 1969; (ed jtly) Photosynthesis and Photorespiration, 1971; (ed) Plant Response to Climatic Factors, 1974; papers in learned jls. *Recreations:* bushwalking, golf.

SLAUGHTER, Andrew Francis; MP (Lab) Ealing, Acton and Shepherd's Bush, since 2005; *b* 29 Sept. 1960; *s* of Alfred Frederick Slaughter and late Marie Frances Slaughter. *Educ:* Univ. of Exeter; Coll. of Law; Inns of Court Sch. of Law. Called to the Bar, Middle Temple, 1993; barrister, Bridewell Chambers, 1993–2006, Lamb Chambers, 2006–. Mem., Hammersmith and Fulham LBC, 1986–2006 (Dep. Leader, 1991–96; Leader, 1996–2005). *Address:* House of Commons, SW1A 0AA. *T:* (020) 7219 4990.

SLAUGHTER, Audrey Cecelia, (Mrs Denis Lanigan); writer and freelance journalist; *d* of Frederick George Smith and Ethel Louise Smith; *m* 1st, 1949, W. A. Slaughter (marr. diss.); one *s* one *d;* 2nd, 1979, Charles Vere Wintour, CBE (*d* 1999); 3rd, 2002, Denis Lanigan, CBE. *Educ:* Chislehurst High Sch., Stand Grammar Sch., Manchester. Editor, Honey magazine, 1960; founded Petticoat magazine, 1964; columnist, Evening News, 1968; joined National Magazine Co., to edit Vanity Fair, 1969; founded and funded own magazine, Over 21, 1970; after sale to Morgan Grampian, 1972, remained as Dir and Editor until 1979; Associate Editor, Sunday Times, 1979; with husband founded Sunday Express colour magazine, 1981; Founder Editor, Working Woman magazine, 1984–86; Lifestyle Editor, The Independent, 1986–87; Editorial Consultant, Burda Publications, Germany, 1987–88. *Publications:* Every Man Should Have One (with Margaret Goodman), 1969; Getting Through…, 1981; Working Woman's Handbook, 1986; Your Brilliant Career, 1987; Private View (novel), 1990; Blooming (novel), 1992; Unknown Country (novel), 1994. *Recreations:* classical music, theatre, painting.

SLAUGHTER, Giles David, MA; Headmaster, University College School, 1983–96; *b* 11 July 1937; *s* of Gerald Slaughter and Enid Lillian Slaughter (*née* Crane); *m* 1965, Gillian Rothwell Shepherd; three *d. Educ:* Royal Masonic School; King's College, Cambridge. MA. Pierrepont School, Frensham, 1961–65; Campbell College, Belfast, 1965–68; Stockport Grammar School, 1968–70; Housemaster, Ormiston House, Campbell Coll., 1970–73; Headmaster, Solihull School, 1973–82. Non-exec. Dir, Heckett MultiServ plc, 1999–2002. Chm., London and SE, ISIS, 1995–98. Governor: Godolphin and Latymer Sch., 1988–99; Cobham Hall, 1989–2000; Aldwickbury Sch., 1974–2003; King's Coll. Sch., Wimbledon, 1995–; Woodbridge Sch., 1997–2007. JP Solihull, 1977–82. Ch Warden, St Mary's, Ufford, 2007–. *Recreations:* gardening, cricket, golf, theatre. *Address:* 6 Church Lane, Lower Ufford, Woodbridge, Suffolk IP13 6DS.

SLEDGE, Ven. Richard Kitson; Archdeacon of Huntingdon, 1978–96; *b* 13 April 1930; *s* of Sydney Kitson and Mary Sylvia Sledge; *m* 1958, Patricia Henley (*née* Sear); one *s* two *d* (and one *s* decd). *Educ:* Epsom College; Peterhouse, Cambridge (MA). Curate of Emmanuel, Plymouth, 1954–57; Curate-in-charge of St Stephen's, Exeter, 1957–63; Rector: Dronfield, 1963–78; Hemingford Abbots, 1978–89. *Address:* 7 Budge Close, Brampton, Huntingdon, Cambs PE28 4PL. *T:* (01480) 437789.

SLEE, Very Rev. Colin Bruce, OBE 2001; Dean (formerly Provost) of Southwark, since 1994; *b* 10 Nov. 1945; *s* of Herbert Samuel Slee and Miriam Clara May Slee; *m* 1971, Edith Tryon; one *s* two *d,* and one foster *s* one foster *d. Educ:* Ealing Grammar Sch.; King's Coll., London (BD, AKC; FKC 2001); St Augustine's Coll., Canterbury. Ordained deacon, 1970, priest, 1971; Curate, St Francis, Heartsease, 1970–73; Curate, Great St Mary's, Cambridge, and Chaplain, Girton Coll., Cambridge, 1973–76; Chaplain and Tutor, KCL, 1976–82; Sub-Dean and Canon Residentiary, St Alban's Abbey, 1982–94. Member: General Synod, C of E, 1995–; Crown Nominations Cttee, 2006–. Hon. Chaplain, Shakespeare's Globe Theatre, 1997–2000. Mem., Cttee of Visitors, Harvard Univ., 2002–. Chm., Tutu Foundn UK, 2004–. Trustee: Crisis, 1995–2005; Parents for Children, 1995–; Millennium Footbridge, 1996–2001; Borough Market, 2000–. Governor, INFORM, 1985–. Patron: Southwark Fest., 1994–2001; Home Start, 1994–; British Sch. of Osteopathy, 1997–. Winston Churchill Meml Trust Fellowship, 2003. *Publication:* (ed) Honest to God: 40 years on, 2005. *Recreations:* rowing (purple, London Univ., 1967, 1968), gardening, bee keeping. *Address:* Southwark Cathedral, London Bridge, SE1 9DA. *T:* (020) 7367 6731, *Fax:* (020) 7367 6725; Provost's Lodging, 51 Bankside, SE1 9JE. *T:* (020) 7928 6414; *e-mail:* colin.slee@southwark.anglican.org.

SLEE, Prof. Richard; ceramic artist; Principal Lecturer, Camberwell College of Arts, since 1998 and Professor, since 1992, University of the Arts London (formerly The London Institute); *b* 8 May 1946; *s* of Richard and Margaret Slee; *m* 1977, Diana Gill (marr. diss. 1987); one *d. Educ:* Carlisle Coll. of Art and Design; Central Sch. of Art and Design (BA 1st cl. Hons Ceramics 1970); Royal Coll. of Art (MA Design degree by project 1988). Full-time Lectr, Hastings Coll. of Further Educn, 1973–75; Vis. Lectr, Central Saint Martin's Coll. of Art and Design and Brighton Poly., and pt-time Sen. Lectr, Harrow Sch. of Art, 1975–90; Sen. Lectr, Camberwell Coll. of Arts, 1990–98. External Examiner: Department of Ceramics: Camberwell Coll. of Arts, 1985–87; Loughborough Coll. of Art, 1987–1990; Glasgow Sch. of Art, 1998–2002; Dept of Goldsmithing, Silversmithing, Metalwork and Jewellery (MA), RCA, 2007–. Mem., Setting-up Grants Cttee, Crafts Council, 2000–04. Jerwood Prize, 2001. *Recreation:* pottery. *Address:* c/o Barrett Marsden Gallery, 17–18 Great Sutton Street, EC1V 0DN. *T:* (020) 7336 6396, *Fax:* (020) 7336 6391; *e-mail:* barrettmarsden@bmgallery.co.uk.

SLEEMAN, Stuart Philip; His Honour Judge Sleeman; a Circuit Judge, since 1993; Designated Family Judge, Guildford Care Centre, since 2003; *b* 9 May 1947; *s* of His Honour (Stuart) Colin Sleeman; *m* 1973, Elisabeth Nina Brann; one *s* two *d. Educ:* Cranleigh Sch.; Merton Coll., Oxford (BA Jurisprudence 1969; MA 1972). Called to the Bar, Gray's Inn, 1970; a Recorder, 1986–93. Tutor Judge, Civil and Family, Judicial Studies Bd, 2003–. Chm., Old Cranleighan Soc., 1984–97; Gov., Cranleigh Sch., 1989–2005. *Recreations:* hockey (Oxford Occasionals), music, history (in particular the Reformation).

SLEEP, Wayne Philip Colin, OBE 1998; dancer, actor, choreographer; *b* Plymouth, 17 July 1948. *Educ:* Hartlepool; Royal Ballet Sch. (Leverhulme Scholar). Graduated into Royal Ballet, 1966; Soloist, 1970; Principal, 1973; roles in: Giselle; Dancers at a Gathering; The Nutcracker; Romeo and Juliet; The Grand Tour; Elite Syncopations; Swan Lake; The Four Seasons; Les Patineurs; Petroushka (title role); Cinderella; The Dream; Pineapple Poll; Mam'zelle Angot; 4th Symphony; La Fille mal gardée; A Month in the Country; A Good Night's Sleep (gala); Coppelia, English Nat. Ballet, 1994; chor., with Robert North, David & Goliath; also roles in operas, A Midsummer Night's Dream and Aida; roles created for him by Sir Frederick Ashton, Dame Ninette de Valois, Sir Kenneth MacMillan, Rudolf Nureyev, John Neumeier, Joe Layton and many others. *Theatre:* Ariel in The Tempest, New Shakespeare Co.; title role in Pinocchio, Birmingham Rep.; genie in Aladdin, Palladium; soldier in The Soldier's Tale, QEH, 1980 and 1981; Truffaldino in The Servant of Two Masters; chor. and played lead in The Point, Mermaid; Mr Mistoffelees in Cats, New London, 1981; co-starred in Song and Dance, Palace, 1982, Shaftesbury, 1990 (video, 1984); Cabaret, Strand, 1986; chor. Savoy Suite, 1993; The History of Dance, tour, 1995; Chitty Chitty Bang Bang, London Palladium, 2003; Into Thin Air!, New Players, 2005; High Society, tour, 2007. Formed own company, DASH, 1980: Chichester Fest., 1980, national tour and Sadler's Wells, 1982, Apollo Victoria and national tour, Christmas season, Dominion, 1983; danced in and jtly choreographed Bits and Pieces, Dominion, 1989; Hollywood and Broadway tour, 1996–97; World of Classical Ballet tour, 1998; has directed several charity galas including 90 Years of Dance, 1995 and Stars of the Night, 1997. Teaches workshops around the world. *Films:* The Virgin Soldiers; The First Great Train Robbery; The Tales of Beatrix Potter, 1971. Chor. films and television, inc. Adam's Rib, Death on the Nile, and appeared in many television progs inc. Dizzy Feet and series, The Hot Shoe Show, 1983, 1984; Tony Lumpkin in She Stoops to Conquer, radio. Patron: Wheelchair Dance Assoc.; Dance Teachers Benevolent Fund; Benesh Dance Inst. Hon. DLitt Exeter. Show Business Personality of the Year, 1983. *Publications:* Variations on Wayne Sleep, 1983; Precious little Sleep (autobiog.), 1996. *Recreation:* entertaining. *Address:* 22 Queensberry Mews West, SW7 2DY.

SLEIGH, Andrew Crofton, FInstP; Group Chief Technology Officer, QinetiQ plc, since 2007; *b* 4 Nov. 1950; *s* of Arthur Ffennell Crofton Sleigh and Margaret Sleigh; *m* 1986, Christine Mattick; one *s* one *d. Educ:* Portsmouth Grammar Sch.; Maret Sch., Washington; Havant Grammar Sch.; St Catherine's Coll., Oxford (MA Physics). FInstP 2000. Superintendent, Pattern Processing and Machine Intelligence Div., RSRE, 1985–90; Director: of Science, Central Staff, MoD, 1990–93; Operation Studies Sector, DRA, 1993–94; Chief Exec., Defence Operational Analysis Centre, MoD, 1994–95; Man. Dir, Centre for Defence Analysis, DERA, 1995–98; Dir Gen. for Inf. and Communications Services, MoD, 1999–2001; UK Principal, NATO C4I Bd, 1998–2001;

Capability Manager for Information Superiority, MoD Defence Equipment Capability Customer, 1999–2001; QinetiQ plc: Man. Dir, Defence Solutions, 2001–03; Man. Dir, Knowledge and Information Systems Div., 2003–05; Gp Man. Dir, Defence and Technol. Sector, 2005–07. Member: DTI Spectrum Mgt Adv. Gp, 1998–2002; OFCOM Spectrum Mgt Adv. Bd, 2003–; Res. and Develt Gp, NDIC, 2007–; Vice-Chm., Security Adv. Gp, Framework Prog. 7, EC, 2008–. Council Mem., RUSI, 2002–06. Adjunct Prof., Tanaka Business Sch., Imperial Coll. London, 2008–. W Midlands Ambassador, 2005–. Chairman: Malvern Fest. Fringe, 1977–82; Wyvern Trust Ltd, 1984–90. *Publication:* (with O. J. Braddick) The Physical and Biological Processing of Images, 1983. *Recreations:* family, windsurfing, photography, maintaining country cottage and grounds. *Address:* QinetiQ plc, Malvern Technology Centre, Worcs WR14 3PS. *Club:* Savile.

SLEIGHT, Prof. Peter, MD (Cantab), DM (Oxon), FRCP; FACC; Field-Marshal Alexander Professor of Cardiovascular Medicine in the University of Oxford, and Fellow of Exeter College, Oxford, 1973–94, now Emeritus Professor and Fellow; Hon. Consultant Physician, Oxford Radcliffe Hospitals NHS Trust (formerly Oxford Health Authority), since 1964; *b* 27 June 1929; *s* of William and Mary Sleight, Boston Spa, Yorks; *m* 1953, Gillian France; two *s*. *Educ:* Leeds Grammar Sch.; Gonville and Caius Coll., Cambridge; St Bartholomew's Hosp., London. Ho. Phys. and Ho. Surg., Med. and Surg. Professorial Units, Bart's, 1953; Sen. Registrar, St George's Hosp., London, 1959–64; Bissinger Fellow, Cardiovascular Research Inst., Univ. of California, San Francisco, 1961–63; MRC Scientific Officer, Depts of Physiology and Medicine, Univ. of Oxford, 1964–66; Consultant Physician, Radcliffe Infirmary, Oxford, 1966–73. Visiting Prof., Univ. of Sydney (Warren McDonald Sen. Overseas Fellow of Aust. Heart Foundn), 1972–73; Hon. Prof. of Medicine, Federal Univ. of Pernambuco, 1975. Civil Consultant in Medicine, RAF, 1985–94. Co-Chairman: Heartoutcomes Prevention Evaluation Study Gp, 1995–2000; ON TARGET Study Gp, 2000–08; SEARCH, HPS. Vice Pres., ASH, 1994– (Chm., 1982–93); President: British Hypertension Soc., 1993–95; World Hypertension League, 1995–2001; Member Council: Internat. Soc. of Hypertension, 1978–86; European Soc. of Cardiology, 1983–88; Hon. Mem., European Soc. of Hypertension, 2001. Mem. Editorial Bd, British Heart Jl, 1976–83; Editor: Jl of Cardiovascular Res., 1983–92; Jl of Cardiovascular Risk, 1994–2001. Hon. MD Gdansk, 2000. Young Investigators Award, 1963, Bishop Lectr, 2004, Internat. Lecture, 2008, Amer. Coll. of Cardiology; Evian Prize, 1988; Merck Sharp and Dohme Award, Internat. Soc. of Hypertension, 1990; Galen Medal for Therapeutics, Soc. of Apothecaries, 2000; Sen. Internat. Award, Aspirin Foundn, Woking, 2000; MacKenzie Medal, British Cardiac Soc., 2003; Lifetime Achievement Award, European Soc. Hypertension, 2005; Award for Lifetime Res., Russian Fedn Soc. of Cardiology, 2005. *Films:* Control of Circulation; History of Hypertension (Medal, BMA Scientific Film Competition, 1981). *Publications:* Modern Trends in Cardiology, 1976; (ed) Arterial Baroreceptors and Hypertension, 1981; Hypertension, 1982; (ed) Scientific Foundations of Cardiology, 1983; (with D. Eckberg) Human arterial baro reflexes in Health and Disease, 1992; contribs on nervous control of the circulation, hypertension and treatment of myocardial infarction in: Circulation Research; Jl Physiol; Lancet. *Recreations:* sailing, golf, travel. *Address:* Wayside, 32 Crown Road, Wheatley, Oxon OX33 1UL. *Club:* Royal Air Force.

SLEIGHT, Sir Richard, 4th Bt *cr* 1920, of Weelsby Hall, Clee; *b* 27 May 1946; *s* of Sir John Frederick Sleight, 3rd Bt and of Jacqueline Margaret, *o d* of late Maj. H. R. Carter, Brisbane, Queensland; *S* father, 1990; *m* 1978, Marie-Thérèse, *o d* of O. M. Stepan; two *s*. *Heir: s* James Alexander Sleight, *b* 5 Jan. 1981. *Address:* c/o National Westminster Bank, 6 High Street, Teddington, Middlesex TW11 8EP.

SLEVIN, Maurice Louis, MD; FRCP; Consultant Physician, Medical Oncology Department, St Bartholomew's and Homerton Hospitals, since 1982; *b* 2 July 1949; *s* of David Slevin and Nita (*née* Rosenbaum); *m* 1st, 1975, Cherry Jacobsohn (marr. diss. 1987); two *d*; 2nd, 1993, Nicola Jane Harris; one *s* one *d*. *Educ:* Univ. of Cape Town (MB ChB 1973; MD 1984). MRCP 1978, FRCP 1989. Registrar in General Medicine, Groote Schuur Hosp., Cape Town, 1977–78; Registrar in Med. Oncology, St Bartholomew's Hosp., 1978–80, Sen. Registrar, 1980–82. Chm. and Trustee, Cancerbackup (formerly BACUP), 1987–. *Publications:* Randomised Trials in Cancer, 1986; Metastases, 1988; Challenging Cancer: from chaos to control, 1991; Cancer: the facts, 1996; Cancer: how worthwhile is non-curative treatment?, 1998; numerous pubns on clinical oncology, clinical pharmacology and psychosocial oncology. *Address:* Medical Oncology Department, St Bartholomew's Hospital, West Smithfield, EC1A 7BE. *T:* (020) 7606 6662; 95 Harley Street, W1G 6AF. *T:* (020) 7317 2525.

SLIGO, 11th Marquess of, *cr* 1800; **Jeremy Ulick Browne;** Baron Mount Eagle 1760; Viscount Westport 1768; Earl of Altamont 1771; Earl of Clanricarde 1543 and 1800; Baron Monteagle (UK) 1806; *b* 4 June 1939; *s* of 10th Marquess of Sligo and of José Gauche; *S* father, 1991; *m* 1961, Jennifer June, *d* of Major Derek Cooper, Dunlewey, Co. Donegal, and Mrs C. Heber Percy, Pophleys, Radnage; five *d*. *Educ:* St Columba's College, Eire; Royal Agricultural College, Cirencester. *Heir: cousin* Sebastian Ulick Browne [*b* 27 May 1964; *m* 1984, Christina Maria (marr. diss. 1992), *d* of late Luis Suanzbar; one *s* one *d*]. *Address:* Westport House, Co. Mayo, Eire.

SLIM, family name of **Viscount Slim**.

SLIM, 2nd Viscount *cr* 1960, of Yarralumla and Bishopston; **John Douglas Slim,** OBE 1973; DL; Chairman, 1976–91, and non-executive Deputy Chairman, 1991–98, Peek plc (formerly Peek Holdings); Director, Trailfinders Ltd, 1984–2007, and a number of other companies; *b* 20 July 1927; *s* of Field Marshal the 1st Viscount Slim, KG, GCB, GCMG, GCVO, GBE, DSO, MC, and Aileen (*d* 1993), *d* of Rev. J. A. Robertson, MA, Edinburgh; *S* father, 1970; *m* 1958, Elisabeth, *d* of Arthur Rawdon Spinney, CBE; two *s* one *d*. *Educ:* Prince of Wales Royal Indian Military College, Dehra Dun. Indian Army, 6 Gurkha Rifles, 1945–48; Argyll and Sutherland Highlanders, 1948; SAS, 1952; Staff Coll., Camberley, 1961; Brigade Major, HQ Highland Infantry Bde (TA), 1962–64; JSSC 1964; Lt-Col 1967; Comdr, 22 Special Air Service Regt, 1967–70; GSO1 (Special Forces) HQ UK Land Forces, 1970–72; retired 1972. Elected Mem., H of L, 1999. Vice-Pres., Britain-Australia Soc., 1988– (Chm., 1978–84); Vice-Chm., Arab-British Chamber of Commerce and Industry, 1977–96. President: Burma Star Assoc., 1971–; SAS Assoc., 2000–; Trustee, Royal Commonwealth Ex-Services League, 1996–. Patron, Prospect Burma, 1985–. Master, Clothworkers' Co., 1995–96. DL Greater London, 1988. FRGS 1983. *Heir: s* Hon. Mark William Rawdon Slim [*b* 13 Feb. 1960; *m* 1992, Harriet Laura, *yr d* of Jonathan Harrison; three *s*]. *Address:* House of Lords, Westminster, SW1A 0PW. *Clubs:* White's, Special Forces.

SLINGER, Edward; His Honour Judge Slinger; a Circuit Judge, since 1995; *b* 2 Feb. 1938; *s* of Thomas Slinger and Rhoda (*née* Bradshaw); *m* 1965, Rosalind Margaret Jewitt; two *s* two *d*. *Educ:* Accrington Grammar Sch.; Balliol Coll., Oxford (Dist. Law Mods 1956; BA 1958). Admitted solicitor (with Hons), 1961; Partner, Ramsbottom & Co., Solicitors, Blackburn, 1964–95; Dep. Registrar, 1982–88; Asst Recorder, 1988–92; Recorder, 1992–95. Pres., Blackburn Incorporated Law Assoc., 1986; Member: Immigration Law Sub-cttee, Law Soc., 1990–95; Immigration Appeal Tribunal, 1997–2005; Chairperson List, Panel of Arbitrators, Sport Resolution Panel, 2007–. Lancashire County Cricket Club: Captain, 2nd XI, 1967–75; Mem. Cttee, 1969–99; Trustee, 1978–96; Vice-Chm., 1985–98; Vice-Pres., 2000–. Dep. Chm., Discipline Cttee, TCCB (now ECB), 1990–. Governor: Samlesbury C of E Sch., Lancs, 1986–; Westholme Sch., Blackburn, 1985– (Vice-Chm., 2002–). *Recreations:* cricket, gardening. *Address:* c/o Court Administrator's Office, Sessions House, Lancaster Road, Preston, Lancs PR1 2PD. *T:* (01772) 821451. *Clubs:* MCC, Lansdowne.

SLINGO, Prof. Julia Mary, OBE 2008; PhD; Chief Scientist, Meteorological Office, since 2008; *b* 13 Dec. 1950; *d* of late Herbert Walker and Lucy Mary Walker (*née* Hirons); *m* 1978, Anthony Slingo; two *d*. *Educ:* King's High Sch. for Girls, Warwick; Univ. of Bristol (BSc Physics; PhD Atmospheric Physics). Scientist, Meteorol Office, 1972–80; Consultant, European Centre for Medium Range Weather Forecasts, 1981–85; Scientist, Nat. Center for Atmospheric Res., Boulder, Colo, 1986–90; University of Reading: Sen. Scientist, then Dep. Dir, NERC Centre for Global Atmospheric Modelling, 1990–2002; Dir, NERC Centre for Global Atmospheric Modelling, then Dir of Climate Res., Nat. Centre for Atmospheric Sci., 2002–08; Prof. of Meteorology, 2000–08; Founding Dir, Walker Inst. for Climate System Res., 2006–07. Vice-Pres., 2003–05, 2007–08, Pres., 2008–, RMetS. Member, Scientific Committees: of Met Office; of Eur. Centre for Medium-Range Weather Forecasts; of Centre for Ocean-Land-Atmosphere Studies; of Internat. Centre for Theoretical Physics; Mem., Jt Sci. Cttee, World Climate Res. Prog., 2006–. *Publications:* numerous contribs to Qly Jl of RMetS, Proc. Royal Soc., Jl Amer. Meteorol Soc. and others. *Recreations:* choral singing, church music, walking, gardening. *Address:* Meteorological Office, Fitzroy Road, Exeter EX1 3PB.

SLINN, David Arthur, CMG 2008; OBE 2000; HM Diplomatic Service; Head of Office Mitrovica, International Civilian Office, Kosovo, since 2008 (on secondment); *b* 16 April 1959; *s* of Ronald Geoffrey Slinn and Christine Mary Slinn. *Educ:* Univ. of Salford (BA Hons Mod Langs 1981). Joined FCO, 1981; Third Sec., UK Delegn to Conf. on Disarmament, Geneva, 1983–86; Second Secretary: Ulaanbaatar, 1987–89; Pretoria/Cape Town, 1990–93; FCO, 1993–95; Chargé d'Affaires, Tirana, 1995–96; First Sec. (Commercial), 1996–98, (Political), 1998–99, Belgrade; Head, British Liaison Office, Pristina, Kosovo, 1999–2000; HCSC 2001; seconded to EU/NATO, former Yugoslav Rep. of Macedonia, 2001–02; Ambassador, Democratic People's Republic of Korea, 2002–05; UK Regl Co-ordinator, Southern Afghanistan, 2007–08. FRSA 2005. *Recreations:* sport (watching and participating), military history, malt whiskey. *Address:* c/o Foreign and Commonwealth Office, King Charles Street, SW1A 2AH; *e-mail:* david.slinn@fco.gov.uk. *Club:* Frontline.

SLIPMAN, Sue, OBE 1994; Director, Foundation Trust Network, NHS Confederation, since 2004; *b* 3 Aug. 1949; *d* of Marks Slipman and Doris Barham; one *s*. *Educ:* Stockwell Manor Comprehensive School; Univ. of Wales (BA Hons 1st Class English; Post Graduate Cert Ed); Univs of Leeds and London. Sec. and Nat. Pres., Nat. Union of Students, 1975–78; Mem., Adv. Council for Adult and Continuing Educn, 1978–79; Area Officer, Nat. Union of Public Employees, 1979–85; Director: Nat. Council for One Parent Families, 1985–95; London TEC Council, 1995–96; Gas Consumers' Council, 1996–98; Dir for Social Responsibility, 1998–2001, for External Relns and Compliance, 2001–02, Camelot Gp plc; Chm., Financial Ombudsman Service Ltd, 2003–05. Mem. Exec., NCCL, 1974–75; Vice-Chair, British Youth Council, 1977–78; Chair: Women for Social Democracy, 1983–86; Advice Guidance and Counselling Lead Body, 1992–; Member: Exec. and Chair of Training, 300 Group, 1985–86; Exec., London Voluntary Service Council, 1986; Women's Issues Wkg Gp, Dept of Employment, 1990–94; Better Regulation Task Force, 1997–2001. Director: London East TEC, 1990; Social Market Foundn, 1992–93. *Publications:* chapter in The Re-Birth of Britain, 1983; Helping Ourselves to Power: a handbook for women on the skills of public life, 1986. *Address:* NHS Confederation, 29 Bressenden Place, SW1E 5DD.

SLIVE, Prof. Seymour; Gleason Professor of Fine Arts at Harvard University, 1973–91, Emeritus since 1991; Director, Fogg Art Museum, 1975–82, sometime Elizabeth and John Moors Cabot Director of Harvard Art Museums; *b* Chicago, 15 Sept. 1920; *s* of Daniel Slive and Sonia (*née* Rapoport); *m* 1946, Zoya Gregorovna Sandomirsky; one *s* two *d*. *Educ:* Univ. of Chicago (BA 1943; PhD 1952). Served US Navy, Lieut, CO Small Craft, 1943–46. Instructor in Art History, Oberlin Coll., 1950–51; Asst Prof. and Chm. of Art Dept, Pomona Coll., 1952–54; Asst Prof. 1954–57, Assoc. Prof. 1957–61, Prof., 1961–73, Chm. of Dept 1968–71, Fine Arts, Harvard Univ.; Exchange Prof., Univ. of Leningrad, 1961. Ryerson Lectr, Yale, 1962. Slade Prof. of Fine Art, Univ. of Oxford, 1972–73. Trustee, Solomon R. Guggenheim Foundn, 1978–. FAAAS 1964; Corresp. FBA 1995. For. Mem., Netherlands Soc. of Sciences, 1971. Hon. MA Harvard, 1958; Hon. MA Oxford, 1972. Officer, Order of Orange Nassau, 1962. *Publications:* Rembrandt and His Critics: 1630–1730, 1953; Drawings of Rembrandt, 1965; (with J. Rosenberg and E. H. ter Kuile) Dutch Art and Architecture: 1600–1800, 1965, 2nd edn, 1978; Frans Hals, 3 vols, 1970–74; Jacob van Ruisdael, 1981; Frans Hals, 1989; Dutch Painting: 1600–1800, 1995, 2nd edn 1998; Jacob van Ruisdael: a complete catalogue of his paintings, drawings and etchings, 2001; Jacob van Ruisdael: master of landscape, 2005; contribs to learned jls. *Address:* 1 Walker Street Place, Cambridge, MA 02138, USA.

SLOAN, Sir Andrew (Kirkpatrick), Kt 1991; QPM 1983; Chief Constable of Strathclyde, 1985–91; *b* 27 Feb. 1931; *s* of Andrew Kirkpatrick Sloan and Amelia Sarah (*née* Vernon), Kirkcudbright; *m* 1953, Agnes Sofie Storvik, Trondheim, Norway; three *d*. *Educ:* Kirkcudbright Acad.; Dumfries Acad.; Open Univ. (BA). Joined RN as boy seaman, 1947; served at home and abroad in cruisers and submarines, and worked in industry in Norway, 1947–55; joined W Riding Constab., 1955; apptd to CID, 1963; Det. Sgt, Barnsley, 1964; Det. Insp., Reg. Crime Squad, Leeds, 1966; Det. Chief Insp., Goole and Pontefract, 1969; Det. Supt, Reg. Crime Squad, Wakefield, 1970; Chief Supt, Toller Lane Div., Bradford, 1975; Asst Chief Constable, Operations, Lincolnshire Police, 1976–79; National Co-ordinator, Regional Crime Squads of England and Wales, 1979–81; Dep. Chief Constable, Lincs, 1981–83; Chief Constable, Beds, 1983–85. Pres., ACPO (Scotland), 1987–88. *Recreations:* reading, travel, walking, conversation.

SLOANE, Ian Christopher; HM Diplomatic Service, retired; *b* 28 Jan. 1938; *s* of Albert Henry Sloane and Ivy Rose (*née* Dennis); *m* 1968, June Barton; two *s*. *Educ:* Lewes Co. Grammar Sch. for Boys; DMS Poly. of Central London 1971. Joined FO, 1956; RAF, 1957–59; FO, 1959–60; MECAS, 1960–61; Vice-Consul: Khartoum, 1961–64; Algiers, 1964–66; Saigon, 1967; 2nd Secretary: Dacca, 1967; Lahore, 1967–70; FCO, 1970–73; UK Disarmament Delegn, Geneva, 1973–74; 1st Sec., Hd of Chancery and Consul, Seoul, 1974–77; 1st Sec. (Econ.), Bonn, 1978–82; W European Dept, FCO, 1983–85; Cultural Attaché, Moscow, 1985; 1st Sec. (Commercial), Ankara, 1986–88; Overseas Estate Dept, FCO, 1989–90; Counsellor and Dep. Consul-Gen., New York, 1990–93; Ambassador to Mongolia, 1994–96. Chm. Bd of Trustees, Electronic Aids for the Blind, 1997–2002; Exec. Dir, Prospect Burma, 1998–2007; Administrator, British-Egyptian Foundn for Children with Special Needs, 2000–08. *Recreations:* tennis, bridge, collecting antique maps, travelling. *Address:* 4 Nursery Way, Heathfield, East Sussex TN21 0UW.

SLOANE, Peter James, PhD; FRSE; Jaffrey Professor of Political Economy, University of Aberdeen, 1984–2002, now Professor Emeritus; Director, Welsh Economy Labour Market Evaluation and Research Centre, Swansea University (formerly University of Wales, Swansea), since 2002; Research Fellow, Institute for the Study of Labour, Bonn, since 2001; *b* 6 Aug. 1942; *s* of John Joseph Sloane and Elizabeth (*née* Clarke); *m* 1969, Avril Mary Urquhart; one *s*. *Educ:* Cheadle Hulme Sch.; Univ. of Sheffield (BAEcon Hons 1964); Univ. of Strathclyde (PhD 1966). FRSE 1997. Asst Lectr in Pol. Econ., Univ. of Aberdeen, 1966–67, Lectr in Pol. Econ., 1967–69; Lectr in Indust. Econs, Univ. of Nottingham, 1969–75; Economic Adviser, Unit for Manpower Studies, Dept of Employment (on secondment), 1973–74; Prof. of Econs and Management, Paisley Coll., 1975–84; Vice Principal, and Dean of Social Scis and Law, Univ. of Aberdeen, 1996–2002. Vis. Prof. (Commonwealth Fellow), Faculty of Business, McMaster Univ., Canada, 1978; Vis. Prof., Indiana Univ., 1996; Hon. Professorial Fellow, Univ. of Melbourne, 2007–. Member: ESRC (formerly SSRC), 1979–85; Mergers Cttee, SHEFC, 1994–97; Council, Scottish Economic Soc., 1983–2001. Sec., REconS Conf. of Heads of Univ. Depts of Econs, 1990–97. Vice-Pres., Internat. Assoc. of Sports Economists, 2000–. FRSA 1997. *Publications:* (with B. Chiplin) Sex Discrimination in the Labour Market, 1976; (ed) Women and Low Pay, 1980; (with H. C. Jain) Equal Employment Issues, 1981; (with B. Chiplin) Tackling Discrimination, 1982; (with D. Carline *et al*) Labour Economics, 1985; (ed jtly) Low Pay and Earnings Mobility in Europe, 1998; (jtly) Employment Equity and Affirmative Action, 2003; (jtly) The Economics of Sport, 2004; monographs on changing patterns of working hours, discrimination and on sport in the market; articles in learned jls, incl. Econ. Jl, Economica, Econs Letters, Applied Econs, Bull. Econ. Res., Oxford Bull. of Econ. Stats, Scottish Jl of Pol. Econ., British Jl of Indust. Relations, Managerial and Decision Econs, Lab., Lab. Econs, Ind. and Lab. Rels Review, Educn Econs, Nat. Inst. Econ. Review, Jl of Health Econs, Manchester School, Oxford Econs Papers, Regl Studies. *Recreation:* sport. *Address:* 5 Willowbrook Gardens, Mayals, Swansea SA3 5EB. *T:* (01792) 517511. *Club:* Pennard Golf.

SLOBODA, Prof. John Anthony, PhD; FBA 2004; Professor of Psychology, Keele University, since 1991 (part-time, since 2004); Executive Director, Oxford Research Group, since 2004 (part-time); *b* 6 June 1950; *s* of late Mieczyslaw Herman Sloboda and of Mary Edna Sloboda; *m* 1980, Judith Nussbaum (marr. diss. 1991); one *d*. *Educ:* St Benedict's Sch., Ealing; Queen's Coll., Oxford (MA 1st cl. (Psychol. and Philos.) 1971); UCL (PhD (Experimental Psychol.) 1974). Lectr, 1974–87, Sen. Lectr, 1987–91, in Psychol., Keele Univ. Mem. Exec. Council, European Soc. for the Cognitive Scis of Music, 1994–. Associate Researcher and Co-Founder, Iraq Body Count, 2003–. *Publications:* The Musical Mind: the cognitive psychology of music, 1985; Music and Emotion: theory and research, 2001; Exploring the Musical Mind, 2005; Psychology for Musicians, 2007; Beyond Terror, 2007. *Recreation:* choral singing. *Address:* Department of Psychology, Keele University, Newcastle, Staffs ST5 5BG. *T:* (01782) 583381, *Fax:* (01782) 583387; *e-mail:* j.a.sloboda@keele.ac.uk.

SLOCOCK, Caroline Ann, (Mrs C. A. Nightingale); Chief Executive, Refugee Legal Centre, since 2007; *b* 30 Dec. 1956; *d* of Horace Slocock and Florence (Joyce) Slocock (*née* Wheelton); *m* 1990, John Nightingale; two *d*. *Educ:* Talbot Heath Sch., Bournemouth; University Coll. London (BA Hons English Lang. and Lit. 1978). Joined Dept of Employment, 1982; Private Sec. to Sec. of State for Employment, 1985–87; Mem., Next Steps Project Team, Cabinet Office, 1988–89; Private Sec. (Home Affairs) to Prime Minister, 1989–91; HM Treasury: Head: Spending Team Br. on Employment, 1991–92; Treasury Personnel, 1993–96; Sen. Policy Advr on Expenditure, 1997–2000; Jt Hd, Early Years and Childcare Unit, DfES, 2000–02; Chief Exec., Equal Opportunities Commn, 2002–07. *Recreations:* gardening, photography, painting, reading. *Address:* Refugee Legal Centre, Nelson House, 153–157 Commercial Road, E1 2DA.

SLOGGETT, Jolyon Edward, OBE 1995; CEng, Hon. FIMarEST, FRINA, FICS; Secretary, Institute of Marine Engineers, 1986–98; *b* 30 May 1933; *s* of Edward Cornelius Sloggett and Lena May (*née* Norton); *m* 1970, Patricia Marjorie Iverson Ward; two *d*. *Educ:* John Lyon Sch.; Univ. of Glasgow (BSc). CDipAF. William Denny & Brothers Ltd, Leven Shipyard, Dumbarton, 1951–57 and 1959–60. Served, Royal Navy, TA Sub Lieut (E), RNVR, 1957–58; Houlder Brothers & Co. Ltd, 1960–78, Director, 1972–78; Man. Dir, Offshore, British Shipbuilders Corp., 1978–81; Dir, Vickers Shipbuilding Group, 1979–80; Chm., Vickers Offshore (Projects & Development) Ltd, 1979–81; Consultant to Marine and Offshore Industries, 1981–86. Liveryman, Shipwrights' Co. *Publication:* Shipping Finance, 1984, 2nd edn 1998. *Recreations:* sailing, gardening, woodwork. *Address:* Corstone Farm, Broadwoodkelly, Winkleigh, Devon EX19 8EF. *T:* (01837) 851441; *e-mail:* jsloggett@freeuk.com.

SLOMAN, Sir Albert (Edward), Kt 1987; CBE 1980; DPhil; Vice-Chancellor of University of Essex, 1962–1987; *b* Launceston, Cornwall, 14 Feb. 1921; *y s* of Albert Sloman; *m* 1948, Marie Bernadette, *d* of Leo Bergeron, Cognac, France; three *d*. *Educ:* Launceston Coll., Cornwall; Wadham Coll., Oxford (Pope Exhibitioner, 1939; Hon. Fellow, 1982). BA Mediæval and Mod. Langs, 1941; MA (Oxon and Dublin); DPhil (Oxon). Served War of 1939–45 (despatches): night-fighter pilot with 219 and 68 squadrons; Flt-Lieut. Lecturer in Spanish, Univ. of California, Berkeley, USA, 1946–47; Reader in Spanish, in charge of Spanish studies, Univ. of Dublin, 1947–53; Fellow TCD, 1950–53; Gilmour Professor of Spanish, University of Liverpool, 1953–62; Dean, Faculty of Arts, 1961–62. Editor of Bulletin of Hispanic Studies, 1953–62. Reith Lecturer, 1963. Chairman: Dept of Education, subseq. British Acad., Studentship Cttee, 1965–87; Cttee of Vice-Chancellors and Principals of UK Univs, 1981–83 (Vice-Chm., 1979–81); Overseas Research Students Fees Support Scheme, 1980–87; Univs' Council for Adult and Continuing Educn, 1984–86; Inter-Univ. and Polytechnic Council, 1985–88; Cttee for Internat. Co-operation in Higher Educn, 1985–88; Selection Cttee of Commonwealth Scholarship Commn, 1986–; Internat. Bd, United World Colls, 1988–92 (Mem., 1985–92); Bd, Univ. of London Inst. of Latin American Studies, 1990–92; Member: Council of Europe Cttee for Higher Educn and Research, 1963–72; Inter-Univ. Council for Higher Educn Overseas, 1964–81; Conf. of European Rectors and Vice-Chancellors, 1965–85 (Pres., 1969–74); Admin. Bd, Internat. Assoc. of Univs, 1965–75 (Vice-Pres., 1970–75); Economic and Social Cttee, EEC, 1973–82; Council, ACU, 1981–87 (Vice-Chm., 1985–87); Commonwealth Scholarship Commn, 1984–93; Bd, British Council, 1985–88. Chm. Bd of Governors, Centre for Inf. on Lang. Teaching and Res., 1979–87; Member: Bd of Governors, Guyana Univ., 1966–92; Cttee of Management, British Inst. in Paris, 1982–97. Pres., Penzance Library, 1990–97. Director: Isys Ltd, 1987–98; Close Brothers Business Expansion Secure Share Account cos, 1992–99. Hon. Doctorate: Nice, 1974; Essex, 1988; Liverpool, 1989. *Publications:* The Sources of Calderón's El Principe constante, 1950; The Dramatic Craftsmanship of Calderón, 1958; A University in the Making, 1964; articles and reviews in Modern Language Review, Bulletin of Hispanic Studies, Hispanic Review, Romance Philology and other journals. *Recreations:* travel, walking. *Address:* 19 Inglis Road, Colchester CO3 3HU.

SLOMAN, Anne, OBE 2004; Member, Archbishops' Council, since 2003; *b* 24 April 1944; *d* of John Bibby and Kay Bibby (*née* Harvey); *m* 1st, 1966, Andrew Duncan-Jones (marr. diss. 1971); 2nd, 1972, Martyn George Morgan Sloman; two *s*. *Educ:* Farlington; St Hilda's Coll., Oxford (BA (Hons) PPE 1966). BBC journalist, programme maker and policy adviser, 1967–2003: Ed., Gen. Election Results Progs, 1974–92; Dep. Ed., Today Prog., 1981–82; Ed., Special Current Affairs (Radio), 1983–93; Dep. Hd, Weekly Progs (TV and Radio), 1993–96; Chief Political Advr, 1996–2003. Mem. Council, RIIA, 1992–2002. Guest Lectr, Berkeley, Southern Illinois and S Dakota Univs; Faculty, Salzburg Seminar, 2004. Trustee, Norfolk Community Foundn, 2005– (Vice-Chm., 2006–). Press Guild Award for Outstanding Prog., 1986 (The Thatcher Phenomenon), 1988 (My Country Right or Wrong). *Publications:* (with David Butler) British Political Facts, 2nd edn (1900–1968), 1968 to 5th edn (1900–1980), 1980; (with Hugo Young): No Minister, 1982; But Chancellor, 1984; The Thatcher Phenomenon, 1986; (with Simon Jenkins) With Respect Ambassador, 1985. *Recreations:* my garden, travel, looking at pictures, theatre, ballet. *Address:* All Saints Cottage, Bale Road, Sharrington, Norfolk NR24 2PF. *Club:* Fakenham Cricket.

SLOMAN, Mrs (Margaret) Barbara; Under Secretary, Management and Personnel Office (formerly Civil Service Department), 1975–84, retired; *b* 29 June 1925; *d* of Charles and Margaret Pilkington-Rogers; *m* 1950, Peter Sloman (*d* 2003); one *s* one *d*. *Educ:* Cheltenham Ladies' Coll.; Girton Coll., Cambridge (BA Hons Classics). Asst Principal, Treasury, 1947, Principal 1954–65; Asst Sec., DES, 1965–69; Asst Sec., Civil Service Dept, 1970–75. FCMI. *Address:* 11 Lowther Road, SW13 9NX. *T:* (020) 8748 2196.

SLOSS; *see* Butler-Sloss.

SLOT, His Honour Peter Maurice Joseph; a Circuit Judge, 1980–97; *b* 3 Dec. 1932; *s* of Joseph and Marie Slot; *m* 1962, Mary Eiluned Lewis; two *s* three *d*. *Educ:* Bradfield Coll.; St John's Coll., Oxford (MA). Called to Bar, Inner Temple, 1957. A Recorder of the Crown Court, 1974–80. *Recreations:* golf, creating harmony. *Address:* The Red House, Betchworth, Surrey RH3 7DR. *T:* (01737) 842010. *Club:* Walton Heath Golf.

SLYNN OF HADLEY, Baron *cr* 1992 (Life Peer), of Eggington in the County of Bedfordshire; **Gordon Slynn,** Kt 1976; PC 1992; arbitrator and accredited mediator, since 2002; President, Civil Mediation Council, since 2008; a Lord of Appeal in Ordinary, 1992–2002; *b* 17 Feb. 1930; *er s* of John and Edith Slynn; *m* 1962, Odile Marie Henriette Boutin. *Educ:* Sandbach Sch.; Goldsmiths' Coll., Univ. of London (BA; Hon. Fellow, 1993); Trinity Coll., Cambridge (Sen. Schol.; Sub-Lector, 1956–61; MA, LLB; Hon. Fellow, 2001). Called to Bar, Gray's Inn, 1956, Bencher, 1970, Treas., 1988. Junior Counsel: Min. of Labour, 1967–68; to the Treasury (Common Law), 1968–74; QC 1974; Leading Counsel to the Treasury, 1974–76. Recorder of Hereford, 1971; a Recorder, and Hon. Recorder of Hereford, 1972–76; a Judge of the High Ct of Justice, QBD, 1976–81; Pres., Employment Appeal Tribunal, 1978–81; an Advocate Gen., 1981–88, a Judge, 1988–92, Court of Justice of EC, Luxembourg; Pres., Court of Appeal, Solomon Islands, 2001–. Chairman: H of L Select Sub-Cttee on Eur. Law and Instns, 1992–95; H of L Select Cttee on Public Service, 1996–98; Jt Parly Cttee on Corruption Bill, 2003. Dist. Global Fellow, NY Univ., 1999; Singhvi Fellow, Raj Loomba Foundn, India, 1999; Lectures include: Bloomfield, Montreal, 1980; Irvine, Cornell, 1984; Leon Ladner, Univ. of BC, 1987; Hamlyn, 1992; Tanner, 1993, Romanes, 1994, Oxford Univ.; Presidential, Roumania, 1995; M. K. Nambyar, India, 1996; Sakkar, India, 1998; John E. James, Mercer, 2001. Chief Steward of Hereford, 1978–2008 (Freedom of the City, 1996). Chm., Exec. Council, Internat. Law Assoc., 1988–; Hon. Vice-Pres., Union Internat. des Avocats, 1976– (Vice-Pres., 1973–76). Mem., Exec. Cttee, Pilgrims, 1992–98, 1999–2005. Fellow, Internat. Soc. of Barristers, USA; Mem., American Law Inst.; Hon. Member: Canadian Bar Assoc.; Georgia Trial Lawyers' Assoc.; SPTL. Governor: Internat. Students' Trust, 1979–85, and 1992– (Fellow, 1986–); Sadler's Wells Theatre, 1988–95; Chm. Ct of Governors, Mill Hill Sch., 1989–95; Visitor: Mansfield Coll., Oxford, 1995–2002; Univ. of Essex, 1995–2000. President: Bentham Club, 1992; Holdsworth Club, 1993. Master, Broderers' Co., 1994–95. FCIArb 1995. FKC 1995; Hon. Fellow: UC at Buckingham, 1982; St Andrews Coll., Univ. of Sydney, 1991; Amer. Coll. of Trial Lawyers, 1992; Liverpool John Moores, 1993; U C Northampton, 2001. Hon. LLD: Birmingham, Buckingham, 1983; Exeter, 1985; Univ. of Technol., Sydney, 1991; Bristol Poly. (CNAA), Sussex, 1992; Stetson, USA, 1993; Staffordshire, 1994; Pace, NY, 1995; Pondicherry, Kingston, 1997; Strathclyde, London, 1999; Hertfordshire, 2003; Szeged, Hungary, 2003 Hon. DCL: Durham, 1989; City 1994; Hon. Dr Juris Saarlandes, 1994; DUniv: Univ. del Museo Social Argentino, 1994; Essex, 2001; Mercer, Ga, 2001; Münster, 2004. Cordell Hull Medal, Samford Univ., Ala, USA, 1993. Chevalier du Tastevin; Commandeur, Confrérie de St Cunibert; Commandeur d'Honneur, Commanderie du Bon Temps du Médoc et des Graves. KStJ 1998 (OStJ 1992; Prior, England and the Islands, 1999–2004). Grande Croix de l'Ordre de Mérite (Luxembourg), 1998; Knight Cross, Order of Merit (Poland), 1999; Grand Cross, Order of Merit (Malta), 2001; Officer's Cross, Order of Merit (Hungary), 2002; Cross of Solomon Islands, 2007. *Address:* House of Lords, SW1A 0PW. *Clubs:* Beefsteak, Garrick, White's.

SMALE, John Gray; Chairman, Executive Committee of Board of Directors, General Motors Corporation, 1996–2000; *b* 1 Aug. 1927; *s* of Peter John Smale and Vera Gladys (*née* Gray); *m* 1950, Phyllis Anne Weaver; two *s* two *d*. *Educ:* Miami Univ., Oxford, Ohio (BS 1949). Procter & Gamble Company: Pres., 1974–81; Pres. and Chief Exec., 1981–86; Chm. Bd and Chief Exec., 1986–90; Chm., Exec. Cttee of Bd of Dirs, 1990; General Motors: Dir, 1981–92; Chm., 1992–96. Hon. LLD: Kenyon Coll., 1974; Miami, 1979; Xavier, 1986; Hon. DSc DePauw, 1983; Hon. DCL St Augustine's Coll., 1985. *Address:* Procter & Gamble, PO Box 599, Cincinnati, OH 45201–0599, USA. *T:* (513) 9831100. *Clubs:* Queen City, Commercial, Cincinnati Country (Cincinnati).

SMALL, David Purvis, CMG 1988; MBE 1966; HM Diplomatic Service, retired; High Commissioner to Guyana and non-resident Ambassador to Suriname, 1987–90; *b* 17 Oct. 1930; *s* of Joseph Small and Ann (*née* Purvis); *m* 1st, 1957, Patricia Kennedy (*d* 1998); three *s*; 2nd, 2003, Pauline L. Alexander. *Educ:* Our Lady's High Sch., Motherwell. National Service, RAF Transport Comd, 1949–51. Metropolitan Vickers, 1951–53; Clerical Officer, Admiralty, Bath, 1953–55; Exec. Officer, HM Dockyard, Rosyth, 1955–58 and Singapore, 1958–60; Admiralty, London, 1960–61; CRO, 1961; Chief Clerk, Madras, 1962–64; Second Sec., Ibadan, 1964–68; Second, later First Sec. and Head of Chancery, Quito, 1968–73; FCO, 1973–76; Head of Chancery, Dacca, 1976–80; First Sec. (Commercial), Stockholm, 1980–82; Counsellor (Economic and Commercial), Copenhagen, 1982–87. *Recreations:* golf, soccer. *Address:* Linden Lea, 31 Royal Crescent, Dunoon, Argyll PA23 7AQ. *T:* (01369) 702620. *Club:* Innellan Golf.

SMALL, Prof. John Rankin, CBE 1991; Professor of Accountancy and Finance, Heriot-Watt University, 1967–98, now Emeritus; *b* 28 Feb. 1933; *s* of David and Annie Small; *m* 1957, Catherine Wood; one *s* two *d*. *Educ:* Harris Academy, Dundee; Dundee Sch. of Econs. BScEcon London; FCCA, FCMA, JDipMA. Dunlop Rubber Co., 1956–60; Lectr, Univ. of Edinburgh, 1960–64; Sen. Lectr, Univ. of Glasgow, 1964–67; Heriot-Watt University: Head, Dept of Accountancy and Finance, 1967–90; Dean of Faculty of Econ. and Social Studies, 1972–74; Vice-Principal, 1974–78, 1987–90; Dep. Principal, 1990–94. Director: Edinburgh Instruments Ltd, 1976–; Orkney Water Test Centre, Ltd,

1987–96; Environment and Resource Technology Ltd, 1991–99; Petroleum Science and Technology Ltd, 1992–97; Computer Application Services, 1997–; Mem. Bd, Scottish Homes, 1993–2002. Chm., Nat. Appeal Panel for Entry to Pharmaceutical Lists (Scotland), 1987–95. Trustee, Nat. Library of Scotland, 1991–99. Pres., Assoc. of Certified Accountants, 1982 (Mem. Council, 1971–99); Member: Educn Cttee, Internat. Fedn of Accountants, 1978–85 (Chm., 1978–82); Commn for Local Authority Accounts in Scotland, 1982–92 (Chm., 1983–92); Chm., Inst. of Offshore Engrg, 1988–90. Hon. DLitt Heriot-Watt, 1996. *Publications:* (jtly) Introduction to Managerial Economics, 1966; (contrib.) Business and Accounting in Europe, 1973; (jtly) Acccounting, 1991; articles in accounting and financial jls on accounting and financial management. *Recreation:* golf. *Address:* 39 Caiystane Terrace, Edinburgh EH10 6ST. *T:* (0131) 445 2638. *Club:* New (Edinburgh).

SMALL, Jonathan Edwin; QC 2006; *b* 6 Aug. 1967; *s* of late Lensworth Small, E Grinstead, formerly Kingston, Jamaica, and of Marion Small (*née* Hickson). *Educ:* Greenfields Sch., E Sussex; Nottingham Univ. (BA Hist.); City Univ. (Dip. Law). Called to the Bar, Lincoln's Inn, 1990; joined Falcon Chambers, 1992; in practice, specialising in law of real property. Mem., Bar Council, 1994–97 and 2005–08. *Recreations:* polo, hunting, music. *Address:* Falcon Chambers, Falcon Court, Fleet Street, EC4Y 1AA. *T:* (020) 7353 2484.

SMALL, Peter John, CB 1999; Permanent Secretary, Department of Agriculture and Rural Development, Northern Ireland, 1996–2003; *b* 21 July 1946; *s* of John and Kathleen Small; *m* 1971, Pamela Hanna; two *s*. *Educ:* Univ. of London (LLB ext.). Northern Ireland Civil Service: Dept of Finance and Personnel, 1966–94: Treasury Officer of Accounts, 1986–88; Dir of Personnel, 1988–94; Finance Dir, Dept of Health and Social Services, 1994–96. *Recreations:* golf, gardening, reading, music, soccer. *Club:* Farmers'.

SMALLBONE, Graham; Headmaster, Oakham School, 1985–96; *b* 5 April 1934; *s* of Dr E. G. Smallbone and Jane Mann; *m* 1959, Dorothea Ruth Löw; two *s* two *d*. *Educ:* Uppingham School (music scholar); Worcester College, Oxford (Hadow Scholar; MA; Pres., Oxford Univ. Music Club, 1957). ARCO, ARCM. 2nd Lieut, RA, 1952–54. Asst Master, Oundle Sch., 1958–61; Director of Music: Dean Close Sch., 1961–66; Marlborough Coll., 1967–71; Precentor and Director of Music, Eton, 1971–85. Pres., Music Masters' Assoc., 1975; Warden, Music in Educn Section, ISM, 1977; Pres., International Cello Centre, 1985–2000. Conductor: Cheltenham Chamber Orch., 1963–66; N Wilts Orch., 1966–71; Windsor and Eton Choral Soc., 1971–85. Chm., Peterborough Cathedral Fabric Adv. Cttee, 1990–. Chm. of Govs, Purcell Sch., 1998–. FRSA. *Recreations:* music, golf, photography. *Address:* The Old Manse, 56 High Street, Chinnor, Oxon OX39 4DH. *T:* (01844) 354572.

SMALLEY, Very Rev. Stephen Stewart; Dean of Chester, 1987–2001; *b* 11 May 1931; *s* of Arthur Thomas Smalley and May Elizabeth Selina Smalley; *m* 1974, Susan Jane Paterson (*d* 1995); one *s* one *d*. *Educ:* Jesus Coll., Cambridge (MA, PhD); Eden Theological Seminary, USA (BD). Assistant Curate, St Paul's, Portman Square, London, 1958–60; Chaplain of Peterhouse, Cambridge, 1960–63; Lectr and Sen. Lectr in Religious Studies, Univ. of Ibadan, Nigeria, 1963–69; Lectr in New Testament, Univ. of Manchester, 1970–77, Sen. Lectr, 1977 (also Warden of St Anselm Hall, 1972–77); Canon Residentiary and Precentor of Coventry Cathedral, 1977–86, Vice-Provost, 1986. Vis. Prof., Univ. of Chester (formerly Chester Coll., then UC, Chester), 2001–. Mem., C of E Doctrine Commn, 1981–86. Mem., Studiorum Novi Testamenti Soc., 1965–. Manson Meml Lectr, Univ. of Manchester, 1986. Hon. LLD Liverpool, 2001. *Publications:* Building for Worship, 1967; Heaven and Hell (Ibadan), 1968; The Spirit's Power (Achimota), 1972; ed, Christ and Spirit in the New Testament, 1973; John: Evangelist and Interpreter, 1978, USA 1984, 2nd edn 1998; 1, 2, 3 John, 1984, 2nd edn 2007; Thunder and Love, 1994; The Revelation to John, 2005; Hope for Ever, 2005; numerous articles in learned jls, incl. New Testament Studies, Novum Testamentum, Jl of Biblical Lit. *Recreations:* literature, music, drama, travel. *Address:* The Old Hall, The Folly, Longborough, Glos GL56 0QS. *T:* (01451) 830238. *Clubs:* City, Business (Chester), Pitt (Cheshire).

SMALLMAN, Barry Granger, CMG 1976; CVO 1972; HM Diplomatic Service, retired; Founder, Granger Consultancies, 1984; *b* 22 Feb. 1924; *s* of late C. Stanley Smallman, CBE, ARCM, and Ruby Marian Granger; *m* 1952, Sheila Knight; two *s* one *d*. *Educ:* St Paul's School; Trinity College, Cambridge (Major Scholar, MA). Served War of 1939–45, Intelligence Corps, Australia 1944–46. Joined Colonial Office, 1947; Assistant Private Secretary to Secretary of State, 1951–52; Principal, 1953; attached to United Kingdom Delegation to United Nations, New York, 1956–57, 1958, 1961, 1962; seconded to Government of Western Nigeria, Senior Assistant Secretary, Governor's Office, Ibadan, 1959–60; transferred to CRO, 1961; British Deputy High Comr in Sierra Leone, 1963–64; British Dep. High Comr in NZ, 1964–67; Imp. Defence Coll., 1968; FCO, 1969–71; Counsellor and Consul-Gen., British Embassy, Bangkok, 1971–74; British High Comr to Bangladesh, 1975–78; Resident Diplomatic Service Chm., Civil Service Selection Bd, 1978–81; High Comr to Jamaica and non-resident Ambassador to Haiti, 1982–84. Mem. Governing Council: SPCK, 1984–99 (Vice Chm., 1993–99); Leprosy Mission, 1985–97; St Lawrence Coll., Ramsgate, 1984–97 (Vice-Pres., 1997–2005); Benenden Sch., 1985–92 (Chm., 1986–92). Reader, C of E, 1996–. *Recreations:* tennis, golf, making and listening to music, light verse, bird watching. *Address:* Beacon Lodge, Benenden, Kent TN17 4BU. *T:* (01580) 240625.

SMALLMAN, David Leslie, LVO 1990; HM Diplomatic Service, retired; Historical Records Adviser, Foreign and Commonwealth Office, 2000–05; *b* 29 April 1940; *s* of late Leslie Alfred Smallman and of Millicent Jean (*née* Burton); *m* 1st, 1967 (marr. diss.); one *s*; 2nd, 1979, Sandra Jill (*née* Browne); one step *s* one step *d*. *Educ:* St Clement Danes; Kingston upon Hull Univ.; London Business Sch. MIEx. RAFVR/RAF, 1958–60. Nat. Assistance Bd, 1961–66; Colonial, later Foreign and Commonwealth, Office, 1966–67; served Rawalpindi, Islamabad, Nicosia, 1967–72; attached DTI, 1973; Singapore, 1973–77; FCO, 1977; Consul, Aden, 1981–83; Head of Chancery, Rangoon, 1983–87; Head of Royal Matters, FCO, 1987–90; Dep. High Comr, Port of Spain, 1990–94; Gov. and C-in-C, St Helena and Dependencies, 1995–99 (first Gov. to visit Nightingale Is, Inaccessible Is and Gough Is.). Pres., 1995–98, Patron, 1998–99, St Helena Cricket Assoc. (played for Governor's XI, 1996–98); Founder, Governor's Cup internat. yacht race. Promoter, internat. sporting links, Louis Glanville Associates, 1999–. Trustee, Charles Wallace Burma Trust, 2005– (Chm., 2006–). Mem., Towcester PROBUS, 2006–. MCIM. *Publications:* (as Louis Glanville) The BEAM (short stories), 1976; Quincentenary, 2003; articles, incl. on travel (some as Louis Glanville). *Recreations:* riding, walking, tennis, cricket, water-sports. *Address:* Ivy Bank Farmhouse, Maidford, Northamptonshire NN12 8HT. *Clubs:* MCC (Life Mem.); Queen's Park Cricket, Trinidad Union (Trinidad); St Helena Yacht (Hon. Life Mem.).

SMALLMAN, Prof. Raymond Edward, CBE 1992; FRS 1986; FREng; Emeritus Professor of Metallurgy and Materials Science, University of Birmingham, since 2001 (Feeney Professor, 1969–88, Professor, 1988–96; Hon. Professor, 1996–2001); *b* 4 Aug.

1929; *s* of David Smallman and Edith French; *m* 1952, Joan Doreen Faulkner; one *s* one *d*. *Educ:* Rugeley Grammar Sch.; Univ. of Birmingham (BSc, PhD, DSc). FIMMM (FIM 1964); FREng (FEng 1991). AERE Harwell, 1953–58; University of Birmingham: Lectr in Dept of Physical Metallurgy, 1958, Sen Lectr, 1963; Prof. of Phys. Metall., 1964; Head of Dept of Phys. Metall. and Sci. of Materials, 1969–81, of Metallurgy and Materials, 1981–88; Dean of Faculty of Sci. and Eng., 1984–85, of Faculty of Eng., 1985–87; Pro-Vice-Chancellor and Vice-Principal, 1987–92. Visiting Professor: Pennsylvania, 1961; Stanford, 1962; NSW, 1974; Calif, Berkeley, 1978; Cape Town, 1982; Hon. Prof., 1990–, Dist. Lectr, 1999, Univ. of Hong Kong; Van Horn Dist. Lectr, Case Western Reserve Univ., 1978; Edwin Liddiard Lectr, Inst. of Metals, 1991. IUC Consultant, Hong Kong, 1979. Academic Adviser: Ghulam Ishaq Khan Inst. of Engrg Scis and Technol., Topi, Pakistan, 1996–; Hong Kong Univ., 1997–2000. Member: Inter-Services Cttee, MoD, 1965; Metals and Materials Cttee, SRC, 1968–71; Materials Adv. Cttee, MoD, 1971; Cttee, Engrg Profs Conf., 1985; Materials Commn, 1988–91, Council, 1992–94, SERC. President: Birmingham Metallurgical Assoc., 1972–73; Fedn of European Materials Socs, 1994–96 (Vice-Pres., 1992–94); Vice-Pres., Metals Soc., 1980–84 (Chm., Metals Sci Cttee, 1974–84); Member: Council, Inst. of Materials (Vice Pres., 1995–99; Chm., Internat. Affairs Cttee, 1993–96); Lunar Soc., 1991–99; Steering Cttee, Industry '96, W Midlands Festival of Industry and Enterprise, 1993–96. Advr, ACU, 1985–91. Warden, Birmingham Assay Office, 1994–97 (Guardian, 1992–94 and 1997–). Dir, Univ. Hosps Birmingham NHS Trust, 1995–99. Gov., Tettenhall Coll., 1982–. Foreign Associate, NAE, US, 2005. Hon. Foreign Member: China Ordinance Soc., 1992; Czech Soc. for Metal Sci., 1995. Hon. DSc: Wales, 1990; Univ. of Novi Sad, Yugoslavia, 1990; Cranfield, 2001. Sir George Beilby Gold Medal, Inst. of Metals and Chem. Soc., 1969; Rosenhain Medal, Inst. Metals, 1972; Elegant Work Prize, Metals Soc., 1979; Platinum Medal, Inst. of Metals, 1989; Acta Materialia Gold Medal, 2004. *Publications:* Modern Physical Metallurgy, 1962, 4th edn 1985; (jtly) Modern Metallography, 1966; (jtly) Structure of Metal and Alloys, 1969; (jtly) Defect Analysis in Electron Microscopy, 1975; (jtly) Metals and Materials: science, processing and applications, 1994; (jtly) Modern Physical Metallurgy and Materials Engineering, 1999; sci. papers on relationship of microstructure of materials to their properties in learned jls. *Recreations:* writing, travel, friendly golf, bridge. *Address:* Willow End, Foredraught Lane, Tibberton, near Worcester, WR9 7NH; *e-mail:* (home) ray.smallman@btopenworld.com, (office) R.E.Smallman@bham.ac.uk. *Club:* South Staffordshire Golf.

SMALLRIDGE, Peter William, CBE 1995; Chairman, Kent and Medway NHS and Socialcare Partnership Trust, since 2006; *b* 8 Aug. 1943; *s* of William Smallridge and Eileen (*née* Wilson). *m* 1965, Margaret Collis; two *s* one *d*. *Educ:* Sutton High Sch.; Chichester High Sch.; North-Western Polytechnic (CSW 1965); LSE (Dip. Mental Health 1970). Sen. Mental Health Social Worker, W Sussex CC, 1965–71; Area Officer, W Sussex Social Services, 1971–73; Sen. Lectr, Croydon Coll., 1973–75; Divl Manager, Social Services, Norfolk CC, 1975–82; Dep. Dir, 1982–83, Dir, 1983–91, Social Services, Warwicks CC; Dir of Social Services, Kent CC, 1991–98; Chairman: W Kent HA, 1998–2002; Ashford PCT, 2002–06. Dir, Initiatives in Care Ltd, 2002–. Pres., Assoc. of Dirs of Social Services, 1992–93. Nat. Trustee, BRCS, 1997–2004; Trustee, Smith's Charity, 1999–. *Recreations:* reading, walking, golf, travel. *Address:* Maltmans Hill Barn, Maltmans Hill, Smarden, Kent TN27 8RD.

SMALLWOOD, Christopher Rafton; Member, Competition Commission, since 2001; Chairman, Hounslow Primary Care Trust, since 2007; *b* 13 Aug. 1947; *s* of James Rafton Smallwood and Josephine Smallwood (*née* Mortimer); *m* 1979, Ingeborg Hedwig Eva Wiesler; one *s* one *d*. *Educ:* Lancaster Royal Grammar Sch.; Exeter Coll., Oxford (MA 1st Cl. Hons PPE); Nuffield Coll., Oxford (MPhil Econs). Lecturer in Economics: Exeter Coll., Oxford, 1971–72; Edinburgh Univ., 1972–76; Special Advr, Constitution Unit, Cabinet Office, 1974–75; Econ. Advr, HM Treasury, 1976–81; Dir of Policy, SDP, 1981–83; Chief Economist, British Petroleum plc, 1983–86; Econs Ed., Sunday Times, 1986–89; Strategic Develt Dir, TSB Gp and Dir, TSB Bank, 1989–94; Partner: Makinson Cowell Ltd, 1994–98; Brunswick Gp Ltd, 1998–2001; Chief Economic Advr, Barclays plc, 2002–05. Dir, Lombard Street Associates, 2005–. *Recreations:* golf, opera, theatre. *Address:* Competition Commission, Victoria House, Southampton Row, WC1B 4AD. *Club:* Reform.

See also J. D. M. Smallwood.

SMALLWOOD, (James) Douglas (Mortimer); Chief Executive, Diabetes UK, since 2004; *b* 10 June 1955; *s* of James Rafton Smallwood and Josephine Smallwood (*née* Mortimer); *m* 1983, Sally Rayner; one *s* one *d*. *Educ:* Lancaster Royal Grammar Sch.; Exeter Coll., Oxford (MA). FCIH. CEO, Worcestershire Housing Assoc., 1983–87; Dir, Halifax Building Soc., 1987–2001; Man. Dir, HBOS plc, 2001–04. Mem. Bd (non-exec.), Centrepoint, 2002–. Trustee, Long Term Medical Conditions Alliance, 2007–. FRSA. *Recreations:* running, golf, birdwatching. *Address:* Diabetes UK, Macleod House, 10 Parkway, NW1 7AA. *T:* (020) 7424 1100, *Fax:* (020) 7424 1080; *e-mail:* douglas.smallwood@diabetes.org.uk. *Club:* Reform.

See also C. R. Smallwood.

SMALLWOOD, Stuart David, PhD; Headmaster, Bishop Wordsworth's School, Salisbury, since 2002 (Deputy Headmaster, 1998–2002); *b* 21 Feb. 1962; *s* of James Smallwood and Pamela Smallwood; *m* 1988, Charlotte Burlend; two *s* one *d*. *Educ:* Leeds Univ. (BSc Earth Scis 1982); Darwin Coll., Cambridge (PhD Geol 1986); Bristol Univ. (PGCE Geog 1989); NPQH 2002. Head of Geography, then of Humanities, Sir Thomas Rich's Sch., Gloucester, 1989–98. *Recreations:* ornithology, middle distance running. *Address:* Bishop Wordsworth's School, 11 The Close, Salisbury SP1 2EB. *T:* (01722) 333851, *Fax:* (01722) 325899; *e-mail:* sds@bws.wilts.sch.uk.

SMALLWOOD, Trevor, OBE 1995; DL; Chairman: Advanced Transport Systems, since 2000; LDJ Design & Display Ltd, since 2003; Swiftpass Digital, since 2006; UKRD Group, since 2006 (Director, 2001–06); *b* 4 Nov. 1947; *s* of late Eric Smallwood and of Vera Smallwood; *m* 1986, Caroline Mary Ball; two *s* two *d*. *Educ:* Mexborough Grammar Sch. MILT. Mgt Trainee, Yorkshire Traction, 1966; National Bus Co., 1970–80; Traffic Manager, Potteries Motor Traction, 1980–82; Man. Dir, Bristol Country Bus, 1983; purchased Badgerline from Dept of Transport, 1986; developed and floated Badgerline, 1993; merged with GRT to become FirstBus, 1995, renamed FirstGroup, 1997, Exec. Chm., 1995–99; Chm., WestCom Media Ltd, 1999–2001. Director: Bristol Water plc, 1999–; Brandon Hire plc, 2004–06; Chairman: Catalist Ltd, 2002–06; Coull Ltd, 2005–06. Chm., Quartet Community Foundn (formerly Gtr Bristol Foundn), 2000–06. Pres., Confedn of Public Transport, 1994. Gov., Colston's Girls' School, Bristol, 2006. DL Somerset, 2003. *Recreations:* football, cricket.

SMART; see de Bernière-Smart.

SMART, Andrew, CB 1981; defence consultant, retired 1991; Director, Royal Signals and Radar Establishment, Malvern, 1978–84; *b* 12 Feb. 1924; *s* of late Mr and Mrs William S. Smart; *m* 1949, Pamela Kathleen Stephens; two *s* two *d*. *Educ:* Denny; High Sch. of Stirling; Glasgow Univ. MA 1944. TRE Malvern, 1943; Science 2 Air Min., 1950–53;

Guided Weapons Gp, RRE, Malvern, 1953–70 (Head, 1968–70); Dep. Dir (Scientific B), DOAE, 1970; RAE, Farnborough: Head of Weapons Res. Gp, 1972; Head of Weapons Dept, 1973; Dep. Dir (W), 1974–77. *Recreations:* gardening, reading. *Address:* Shelsley, Redland Drive, Colwall, Malvern, Worcs WR13 6ES. *T:* (01684) 540664.

SMART, Prof. (Arthur David) Gerald, CBE 1991; FRTPI; Emeritus Professor of Urban Planning, University of London, since 1984; Professor of Urban Planning at University College London, 1975–84 and part-time, 1984–87 (Head of Bartlett School of Architecture and Planning, University College London, 1975–80); *b* 19 March 1925; *s* of Dr A. H. J. Smart and A. O. M. Smart (*née* Evans); *m* 1955, Anne Patience Smart (*née* Baxter); one *d* (and one *d* decd). *Educ:* King's Coll. Choir Sch., Cambridge (chorister); Rugby Sch.; King's Coll., Cambridge; Regent St Polytechnic. MA, DipTP; MRICS, FRSA. Served in The Rifle Brigade, 1943–47 (Captain). Appts in local govt (planning), London, NE England, E Midlands, 1950–63; County Planning Officer, Hants CC, 1963–75; Member: Planning Adv. Gp, 1964–65, Cttee on Public Participation in Planning, 1968–69, Min. of Housing and Local Govt; Planning and Transportation Res. Adv. Council, DoE, 1975–79; Working Party on alternative uses of Historic Buildings, Historic Bldgs Council and BTA, 1979–81; Council, TCPA, 1983–89; Council, RSPB, 1985–90; Governing Body, British Assoc. for Central and East Europe (formerly GB/E Europe Centre), 1985–96; Council, Solent Protection Soc., 1986– (Soc. rep. on Solent Forum); House Builders' Fedn Commn on Inner Cities, 1986–87; occasional Chm., Structure Plans Exams in Public for DoE; Consultant for review of Areas of Outstanding Natural Beauty, Countryside Commn, 1989–90. Chm., Milford-on-Sea Parish Council, 1989–93 (Councillor, 1987–99); Mem. Cttee, Lymington Choral Soc., 1994–2002. Bowland Award, Nat. Assoc. for Areas of Outstanding Natural Beauty, 1999. *Publications:* (jtly) Landscapes at Risk?, 2001; (jtly) The Future of the South Downs, 2007; articles, conf. papers, chapters in books, professional and other jls, booklets and reports. *Recreations:* sailing, ornithology, music, walking. *Address:* 10 Harewood Green, Keyhaven, Lymington, Hants SO41 0TZ. *T:* (01590) 645475. *Clubs:* Royal Lymington Yacht, Keyhaven Yacht (Lymington).

SMART, Sir Jack, Kt 1982; CBE 1976; JP; DL; Chairman, Wakefield District Health Authority, 1982–88; *b* 25 April 1920; *s* of James and Emily Smart; *m* 1941, Ethel King; one *d. Educ:* Altofts Colliery Sch. Miner, 1934–59; Branch Sec., Glasshoughton Colliery, NUM, 1949–59; Mem., Castleford Municipal Borough Council, 1949–74; Mayor of Castleford, 1962–63; Mem., Wakefield City Council, 1973–86 (Leader, 1973–86). Chm., Assoc. of Metropolitan Authorities, 1977–78, 1980–84; Leader of the Opposition Group, AMA, 1978–80. Chm., Wakefield AHA, 1977–81; Mem., Layfield Cttee of Enquiry into Local Govt Finance, 1974–76. Pres., Yorkshire Soc. (1980), 1988–. Hon. Fellow, Bretton Coll., 1983. Hon. Freeman, City of Wakefield, 1985. JP Castleford, 1960; DL West Yorks, 1987. FRSA. *Recreations:* golf, music. *Address:* Churchside, Weetworth, Pontefract Road, Castleford, West Yorks WF10 4BW. *T:* (01977) 554880.

SMART, John Dalziel Beveridge, CVO 2008; Lord-Lieutenant of Kincardineshire, 1999–2007; *b* Edinburgh, 12 Aug. 1932; *s* of George Beveridge Smart and Christina Mary Ann Smart (*née* MacDonald); *m* 1960, Valerie Bigelow Blaber; two *s. Educ:* Harrow; Admin. Staff Coll. Nat. Service, 2nd Lieut, Black Watch, RHR, Korea, 1952; PA to COS, 1953. With J. & J. Smart (Brechin) Ltd, 1953–64 (Dir, 1954–64); Dir, Don Brothers Buist & Co., 1964–87 (Man. Dir, 1985–87), retd. Chm., British Polyolefin Textile Assoc., 1986–97. Chm., Scottish-American Community Relns Cttee, 1990–93. Mem., Queen's Bodyguard for Scotland (Royal Co. of Archers), 1974–. Mem., St Andrews Mgt Inst., 1989. DL Kincardineshire, 1993–99. Dean, Guildry of Brechin, 1991–93. *Recreation:* looking for the things that I have lost. *Address:* Kincardine, 9a The Glebe, Edzell, Brechin DD9 7SZ. *T:* (01356) 648416; *e-mail:* smart@woodmyre.freeserve.co.uk.

SMART, Kenneth Peter Ross, CBE 1996; Chief Inspector of Air Accidents, Department for Transport (formerly Department of Transport, then Department of Transport, Local Government and the Regions), 1990–2005; *b* 28 April 1946; *s* of Peter Smart and Evelyn Smart (*née* Ross); *m* 1st, 1969, Kathleen Rouse (marr. diss.); one *s* one *d*; 2nd, 1993, Christine Palmer. *Educ:* Coll. of Electronics, Malvern (FTC); Worcester Tech. Coll. (HNC Aero Engrg); Open Univ. (BA). Aircraft Engrg apprentice, Min. of Aviation, 1962–67; Technical Officer, RRE, 1967–75; Inspector of Accidents, Dept of Trade, 1975–82; Principal Inspector of Accidents, 1982–86, Dep. Chief Inspector of Accidents, 1986–90, Dept of Transport. Non-exec. Dir, British Airways, 2005–. *Recreations:* mountaineering, tennis, sailing, classic motorcycle restoration. *Address:* 4 Clandon Drive, Boyatt Wood, Eastleigh, Hants SO50 4QQ.

SMART, Air Vice-Marshal Michael David; DL; Director, Meer Consultants Ltd, since 2000; *b* 18 March 1942; *s* of Gerald Sidney Smart and Keziah Smart (*née* Edwards); *m* 1964, Sheelagh Ann Gent; one *d* (and one *d* decd). *Educ:* Trinity Sch. of John Whitgift, Croydon; BA Open Univ. Joined RAF Secretarial Branch, 1960; ndc 1979; Air Sec.'s Branch, 1980–82 and 1983–85; Comd, Admin Wing, RAF Coltishall, 1982–83; CO RAF Hereford, 1985–88; Sen. Personnel Staff Officer, HQ Strike Command, 1988–89; RCDS, 1990; Dir, Ground Training, 1991–92; Air Cdre, Training Support, 1993; Dir of Personnel, 1994–95; C of S to Air Mem. for Personnel, 1995–98. Dir, Govt Services, Arthur Andersen Business Consulting, 1998–2000. Chm., Herefordshire, SSAFA, 2003–; Vice Chm. (Air), Council of Reserve Forces, 2004–; Council Mem., Forces Pension Soc., 1998–. Trustee, Regular Forces Employment Assoc., 1999–. DL Herefordshire, 2006. *Recreations:* track and field athletics and cross country, travelling, cooking. *Address:* c/o Drummonds Bank, 49 Charing Cross, SW1A 2DX. *Club:* Royal Air Force.

SMART, Rosamund H.; *see* Horwood-Smart.

SMART, William Norman H.; *see* Hunter Smart.

SMEATON, John Joseph; National Director, Society for the Protection of Unborn Children, since 1996; *b* 20 Feb. 1951; *s* of John Henry Smeaton and Marguerite Amy Smeaton; *m* 1984, Josephine Ann Toner (*née* Clarke); one *s* one *d*, and two step *s. Educ:* Salesian Coll., Battersea; Greyfriars Hall, Oxford (MA Eng. Lang. and Lit.); London Univ. (Cert Ed). English Teacher, 1973–75 (full-time), 1976–78 (part-time), Salesian Coll., Battersea; Head of English, Whitefriars, Cheltenham, 1975–76; part-time volunteer worker, 1976–78, Gen. Sec., 1978–96, SPUC. Mem., Nat. Assoc. of Catholic Families. KSC. *Recreations:* reading, enjoying company of my family. *Address:* Society for the Protection of Unborn Children, 3 Whitacre Mews, Stannary Street, SE11 4AB. *T:* (020) 7091 7091. *Club:* New Cavendish.

SMEDLEY, George; *see* Smedley, R. R. G. B.

SMEDLEY, Nicholas John; Research Director, Prince of Wales's Charities Office, since 2006 (on secondment); *b* 23 Nov. 1959; *s* of Albert Glyn Smedley and Barbara Mary (*née* Sansom); partner, 1983, Kate Jennings. *Educ:* UCL (BA 1st cl. Hons (Hist.) 1981); Birkbeck Coll., London (PhD (Hist.) 1992). Lord Chancellor's Department: Admin. trainee, 1981–84; HEO, 1984–86; Grade 7, 1986–88; freelance advr to Dir, BFI, 1988–92; Dir, HR, PRO, 1992–94; Grade 7, Ct Service HQ, 1994–96; Grade 5, Dir Crown Ct Ops, 1996–99; Grade 3, Chief Exec., Public Trust Office, 1999–2001; Dir, Criminal Justice, LCD, then DCA, 2001–04; Dir, Asylum and Diversity, 2004–05, Diversity, 2005–06, DCA. *Publications:* articles on Hollywood film hist.; booklets on British film and TV prodn. *Recreations:* opera, ballet, theatre, cinema, travel. *Address:* c/o Clarence House, SW1A 1BA.

SMEDLEY, (Roscoe Relph) George (Boleyne); Barrister; Counsellor, HM Diplomatic Service, retired; *b* 3 Sept. 1919; *o s* of late Charles Boleyne Smedley and Aimie Blaine Smedley (*née* Relph); *m* 1st, 1947, Muriel Hallaway Murray (*d* 1975), *o d* of late Arthur Stanley Murray; one *s*; 2nd, 1979, Margaret Gerrard Gourlay (*d* 1991), *o c* of late Augustus Thorburn Hallaway and *widow* of Dr John Stewart Gourlay; 3rd, 1993, Marjorie Drummond (*d* 1994), *d* of late John Leonard Haslam and *widow* of David Drummond; 4th, 2004, Margaret Mavis Linton (*d* 2006), *d* of late Alfred Kenneth Loxley Hamilton, and *widow* of William Riddell Linton. *Educ:* King's Sch., Ely; King's Coll., London (LLB). Called to Bar, Inner Temple. Artists Rifles TA; commnd S Lancs Regt, 1940; Indian Army, 1942–46 (Captain); Foreign Office, 1937 and 1946; Foreign Service (subseq. Diplomatic Service): Rangoon, 1947; Maymyo, 1950; Brussels, 1952; Baghdad, 1954; FO, 1958; Beirut, 1963; Kuwait, 1965; FCO, 1969; Consul-Gen., Lubumbashi, 1972–74; British Mil. Govt, Berlin, 1974–76; FCO 1976; Head of Nationality and Treaty Dept, 1977–79. Part-time appointments (since retirement): Adjudicator under Immigration Act 1971; Inspector, Planning Inspectorate, Depts of the Environment and Transport; Dep. Traffic Comr for N Eastern Traffic Area; Legal Mem., Mental Health Review Tribunal; Chm., Rent Assessment Cttee; Mem., No 2 Dip. Service Appeal Bd. Churchwarden; Mem., diocesan and deanery synods. *Recreations:* forestry, reading. *Address:* Garden House, Whorlton, Barnard Castle, Co. Durham DL12 8XQ. *T:* (01833) 627381. *Club:* Royal Over-Seas League.

SMEDLEY, Susan M.; *see* Marsden, S.

SMEE, Clive Harrod, CB 1997; Visiting Professor of Economics, University of Surrey, since 1995; *b* 29 April 1942; *s* of Victor Woolley Smee and Leila Olive Smee (*née* Harrod); *m* 1975, Denise Eileen Sell; one *s* two *d. Educ:* Royal Grammar Sch., Guildford; LSE (BSc Econ); Indiana Univ. (MBA); Inst. of Commonwealth Studies, Oxford. British Council, Nigeria, 1966–68; Economic Advr, ODM, 1969–75; Sen. Economic Advr, DHSS, 1975–82; Nuffield and Leverhulme Travelling Fellow, USA and Canada, 1978–79; Advr, Central Policy Review Staff, 1982–83; Sen. Economic Advr, HM Treasury, 1983–84; Chief Economic Adviser: DHSS, 1984–88; DSS, 1988–89; DoH, 1988–2002; Sen. Policy Advr, NZ Treasury, 2002–04. Consultant: NZ Treasury, 1988; NZ Dept of Health, 1991. Chm., OECD Social Policy Working Party, 1987–90; Member: Internat. Co-ordinating Cttee, Commonwealth Fund, 1998–2004; Economics Adv. Panel, Home Office, 2006–08; Ind. Adv. Cttee on Develt Impact, DFID, 2007–. Trustee, Medicines and People, 2006–. Queen Mother Meml Fellow, Nuffield Trust, 2003–04. *Publications:* Speaking Truth to Power, 2005; articles on economics in learned jls. *Recreations:* painting, walking, gardening; Anna, David and Elizabeth. *Address:* Appletree House, Ockham Road North, East Horsley, Surrey KT24 6PU.

SMEE, John Charles O.; *see* Odling-Smee.

SMETHAM, Andrew James, MA; Headmaster, The Purbeck School, Wareham, Dorset, 1985–2002; *b* 22 Feb. 1937; *s* of Arthur James Smetham and Eunice (*née* Jones). *Educ:* Vaynor and Penderyn Grammar Sch., Cefn Coed, Breconshire; King's Coll., Univ. of London (BA (Hons German) 1959, DipEd 1964, MA (Educn) 1968). Assistant Master: Wandsworth Sch., 1960–66; Sedgehill Sch., 1966–70; Dep. Headmaster, Holloway Sch., 1970–74; Headmaster, Wandsworth Sch., 1974–84. *Recreation:* music. *Address:* The Water Barn, East Burton, Wareham, Dorset BH20 6HL. *T:* (01929) 463727.

SMETHURST, Richard Good, MA; Provost, Worcester College, Oxford, since 1991; Pro Vice-Chancellor, University of Oxford, since 1997; *b* 17 Jan. 1941; *s* of Thomas Good Smethurst and Madeleine Nora Foulkes; *m* 1964, Dorothy Joan (*née* Mitchenall); two *s* two *d*; *m* 2000, Dr Susan Gillingham; two step *d. Educ:* Liverpool Coll.; Worcester Coll., Oxford (Webb Medley Jun. Schol. 1962; BA 1st Cl. 1963; MA); Nuffield Coll., Oxford. Research Fellow: St Edmund Hall, Oxford, 1964–65; Inst. for Commonwealth Studies, Oxford, 1965–66 (Consultant, UN/FAO World Food Program); University of Oxford: Fellow and Tutor in Economics, St Edmund Hall, 1966–67; Fellow and Tutor in Economics, Worcester Coll., and Univ. Lectr in Economics, 1967–76; Dir, Dept for External Studies, and Professorial Fellow, Worcester Coll., 1976–89; Supernumerary Fellow, Worcester Coll., and Chm., Gen. Bd of Faculties, 1989–91; non-exec. Dir, Nuffield Orthopaedic Centre, Oxford, 1992–2000. Economic Adviser, HM Treasury, 1969–71; Policy Adviser, Prime Minister's Policy Unit, 1975–76. Dir, IMRO, 1987–99. Member: Adv. Council for Adult and Continuing Educn, DES, 1977–83; Monopolies and Mergers Commn, 1978–89 (Dep. Chm., 1986–89); UGC/NAB Continuing Educn Standing Cttee, 1984–88; Acad. Consultative Cttee, Open Univ., 1986–92; Adv. Bd, Music at Oxford, 1988–94; Consumer Panel, FSA, 1998–2004. Chm., Unit for Develt of Adult Continuing Educn, 1991–92. Trustee: Eur. Community Baroque Orch., 1986–93; Oxford Philomusica, 2003–. Mem. Council, Templeton Coll., Oxford (formerly Oxford Management Centre), 1982–95; Life Governor, Liverpool Coll., 1968. Foundn Hon. Fellow, Kellogg Coll., Oxford, 1990; Hon. Fellow: St Edmund Hall, Oxford, 1991; St Catharine's Coll., Cambridge, 2002. *Publications:* Impact of Food Aid on Donor Countries (with G. R. Allen), 1967; contribs to New Thinking About Welfare, 1969; Economic System in the UK, 1977, 2nd edn 1979; New Directions in Adult and Continuing Education, 1979; Continuing Education in Universities and Polytechnics, 1982; contrib. Jl of Development Studies, Oxford Rev. of Educn, Studies in Adult Education. *Recreations:* good food, travel. *Address:* The Provost's Lodgings, Worcester College, Oxford OX1 2HB. *T:* (01865) 278362.

SMILEY, Lt-Col Sir John (Philip), 4th Bt *cr* 1903, of Drumalis, Larne, Co. Antrim and Gallowhill, Paisley, Co. Renfrew; *b* 24 Feb. 1934; *s* of Sir Hugh Houston Smiley, 3rd Bt and Nancy Elizabeth Louise Hardy (*née* Beaton) (*d* 1999); *S* father, 1990; *m* 1963, Davina Elizabeth, *e d* of late Denis Charles Griffiths; two *s* one *d. Educ:* Eton Coll.; RMA Sandhurst. Commnd Grenadier Guards, 1954; ADC to Governor of Bermuda, 1961–62; served in Cyprus, BAOR, Hong Kong; Lt-Col, 1981; retired 1986. Russell Reynolds Associates, 1986–89. Governor, Oundle Sch., 1987–99. Mem., Ct of Assts, Worshipful Co. of Grocers, 1987– (Master, 1992–93). *Recreations:* gardening, travel. *Heir: s* Christopher Hugh Charles Smiley [*b* 7 Feb. 1968; *m* 1998, Clare Annabel, *y d* of Maj. Henry Blosse-Lynch; three *s*]. *Address:* Cornerway House, Chobham, Woking, Surrey GU24 8SW. *T:* (01276) 858992. *Club:* Army and Navy.

SMILEY, Prof. Timothy John, PhD; FBA 1984; Knightbridge Professor of Philosophy, University of Cambridge, 1980–98; Fellow of Clare College, Cambridge, since 1955; *b* 13 Nov. 1930; *s* of Prof. M. T. Smiley and Mrs T. M. Smiley (*née* Browne); *m* 1955, Benita Mary Bentley; four *d. Educ:* Ardwyn Grammar Sch., Aberystwyth; Ampleforth Coll.; Fribourg Univ.; Clare Coll., Cambridge (BA 1952, Math. Tripos; MA, PhD 1956). Holt

Scholarship, Gray's Inn, 1954; called to the Bar, 1956. Pilot Officer, RAFVR, 1954. Scientific Officer, Air Min., 1955–56; Clare Coll., Cambridge: Res. Fellow, 1955–59; Asst Tutor, 1959–65; Sen. Tutor, 1966–69; Asst Lectr in Phil., Cambridge Univ., 1957–62, Lectr, 1962–79. Vis. Professor: Cornell Univ., 1964; Univ. of Virginia, 1972; Yale Univ., 1975; Univ. of Notre Dame, 1986; Yale Univ., 1990. Sec. for Postgrad. Studies, 1992–94, Mem., Humanities Res. Bd, 1994–96, British Acad. *Publications:* (with D. J. Shoesmith) Multiple-conclusion Logic, 1978; articles in phil and math. jls. *Recreation:* orienteering. *Address:* Clare College, Cambridge CB2 1TL. *T:* (01223) 352152.

SMILLIE, (William) John (Jones); Managing Director, Gatehouse Records, since 1992; *b* 18 Feb. 1940; *s* of late John Smillie and Emily Mary Caroline (*née* Jones). *Educ:* Lauriston Sch., Falkirk; Territorial Sch., Stirling; Stirling High Sch. Scottish hotel family background; trained in all hotel depts in Scotland and Paris, with extensive kitchen work; progressed to management with Edward R. Barnett & Co. Ltd, industrial caterers (Asst Gen. Man., 1964–67); joined House of Commons Catering Dept as Personnel Manager, 1967: Personnel Manager and Asst to Catering Manager, 1970; Gen. Man., 1971; Head of Dept, 1980–91. Mem., Newbury Community Radio Assoc., 1996–2000. Member: British Inst. of Cleaning Science, 1976–; Hine Soc., 1979–; Craft Guild of Chefs, 1985–; FIH (FHCIMA 1979); Fellow, Cookery and Food Assoc., 1967; Founder Mem., Wine Guild of UK, 1984–; Mem., Restaurateurs Assoc. of GB, 1983–; Hon. Member: Assoc. Culinaire Française, 1972; Conseil Culinaire Française de Grande Bretagne, en Reconnaissance des Services Rendus à l'Art Culinaire, 1987. *Publications:* articles for catering trade papers. *Recreations:* theatre, ballet, music, piano, motoring, boating, radio presenting, travel, gourmandise, intervals at the opera, jazz music. *Address:* The Gatehouse, 90 Wimbledon Parkside, SW19 5LT. *T:* (020) 8780 9232, *Fax:* (020) 7823 8905.

SMIT, Timothy Bartel, Hon. CBE 2002; Chief Executive, Eden Project, since 1999; Director, Lost Gardens of Heligan, since 1990; *b* 25 Sept. 1954; *s* of Jan Adrianus Bartel Smit and Anthea Margaret Smit (*née* Fairclough); *m* 1978, Laura Candace Pinsent; three *s* one *d*. *Educ:* Cranbrook Sch.; Univ. of Durham (BA Hons Archaeol. and Anthropology). Archaeologist, 1977–78; record producer and composer, 1978–90; with John Nelson discovered, 1990, and restored Heligan estate, Cornwall, now open to visitors and known internationally as Lost Gardens of Heligan (Gardener of Year, Country Life, 1995; Garden of Year, Good Guide to Britain, 1999); Co-Founder, Eden Project, 1994 (scientific instn featuring conservatories inside a 34 acre, 200ft deep clay pit near St Austell). Mem. Bd, Prince's Trust Business Div., 1999–2005. Dir, Hurst Lodge Sch. Ltd; Mem., Bd of Trustees, Kneehigh Th. Co. Vice-Pres., Garden History Soc.; Patron: Green Space; Nat. Council for Sch. Leadership; Cornwall Garden Soc. Hon. Fellow, St Catherine's Coll., Oxford, 2003. Hon. MSc Gen. Sci. Plymouth, 1998; Hon. LLD Exeter, 2001; DUniv: UCE, 2005; Open, 2005. Outstanding Contribution to Tourism, English Tourism Council, 2000; Alchemist Award, 2001; Social Entrepreneur of the Year, Southern Region, 2001; Lord Lloyd of Kilgerran Award, Foundn for Sci. & Tech., 2003; Albert Medal, Royal Soc. of Arts, 2003. *Publications:* The Lost Gardens of Heligan, 1997 (Illustrated Book of Year, BCA, 1998); The Complete Works: secrets locked in silence, 1999; (with Philip McMillan Browse) The Heligan Vegetable Bible, 2000; Eden, 2001. *Recreations:* music, reading, film, art, theatre. *Address:* 25 North Street, Fowey, Cornwall PL23 1DB.

SMITH; *see* Darwall Smith.

SMITH; *see* Delacourt-Smith.

SMITH; *see* Dixon-Smith, family name of Baron Dixon-Smith.

SMITH; *see* Gordon-Smith.

SMITH; *see* Hamilton-Smith, family name of Baron Colwyn.

SMITH; *see* Hastie-Smith.

SMITH; *see* Hugh Smith.

SMITH; *see* Llewellyn Smith and Llewellyn-Smith.

SMITH; *see* Mackenzie Smith and McKenzie Smith.

SMITH; *see* Stewart-Smith.

SMITH; *see* Stuart-Smith.

SMITH; *see* Warnock-Smith.

SMITH, family name of **Viscount Hambleden**, **Barons Bicester**, **Kirkhill**, **Smith of Clifton**, **Smith of Kelvin** and **Smith of Leigh**, and **Baroness Smith of Gilmorehill**.

SMITH OF CLIFTON, Baron *cr* 1997 (Life Peer), of Mountsandel, in the co. of Londonderry; **Trevor Arthur Smith,** Kt 1996; FRHistS; Vice-Chancellor, University of Ulster, 1991–99; *b* 14 June 1937; *e s* of late Arthur James Smith and Vera Gladys Smith (*née* Cross); *m* 1st, 1960, Brenda Susan (*née* Eustace) (marr. diss. 1973); two *s*; 2nd, 1979, Julia Donnithorne (*née* Bullock); one *d*. *Educ:* LSE (BSc Econ 1958). Schoolteacher, LCC, 1958–59; temp. Asst Lectr, Exeter Univ., 1959–60; Research Officer, Acton Soc. Trust, 1960–62; Lectr in Politics, Hull Univ., 1962–67; Queen Mary College, later Queen Mary & Westfield College, London: Lectr, then Sen. Lectr, in Political Studies, 1967–83; Prof., Political Studies, 1983–91; Head of Dept, 1972–85; Dean of Social Studies, 1979–82; Pro-Principal, 1985–87; Sen. Pro-Principal, 1987–89; Sen. Vice-Prin., 1989–91; Hon. Fellow, 2003. Vis. Associate Prof., California State Univ., LA, 1969. Director: Job Ownership Ltd, 1978–85; New Society Ltd, 1986–88; Statesman & Nation Publishing Co. Ltd, 1988–90; G. Duckworth & Co., 1990–95. Mem., Tower Hamlets DHA, 1987–91 (Vice Chm., 1989–91); non-exec. Mem., N Yorks HA, 2000–02. Vice Pres., Patients' Assoc. of UK, 1988–97. Chm., Conf. of Rectors in Ireland, 1997. Vice-Pres., Political Studies Assoc. of UK, 1989– (Chm., 1988–89; Pres., 1991–93); Dep. Pres., Inst. of Citizenship Studies, 1991–2001; Member: Admin. Bd, Internat. Assoc. of Univs, 1995–96; Editl Bd, Government and Opposition, 1995–; UK Socrates Council, 1993–99 (Chm., 1996–99). Contested (L) Lewisham W, 1959. House of Lords: Lib Dem Spokesman on NI, 2000–; Chm., Select Cttee on Animals in Scientific Procedures, 2001–02; Member: Select Cttee on Communications, 2004–06; Select Cttee on Constitution, 2005–; Select Sub-Cttee on Lords' Interests, 2006–; Sci. and Technol. Sub-Cttee on Complementary and Alternative Medicine, 1999–2000; EU Sub-Cttee E (Law and Instns), 2000–01. Trustee: Joseph Rowntree Reform (formerly Social Service) Trust, 1975–2006 (Chm., 1987–99); Stroke Assoc., 2002–. Pres., Belfast Civic Trust, 1995–99; Member Board: Taste of Ulster, 1996–99; Opera NI, 1997–99. Governor: Sir John Cass and Redcoats Sch., 1979–84; Univ. of Haifa, 1985–92; Bell Educnl Trust, 1988–93. Hon. Mem. Senate, Fachhochschule Augsberg, 1994. FRHistS 1986; FICPD 1998. CCMI (CBIM 1992); FRSA 1994. AcSS 2000. Hon. LLD: Dublin, 1992; Hull, 1993; Belfast, 1995; NUI, 1996; Hon. DHL Alabama, 1998; Hon. DLitt Ulster, 2002. *Publications:* (with M. Argyle) Training Managers, 1962; (with A. M. Rees) Town Councillors, 1964; Town and County Hall, 1966; Anti-Politics, 1972; (jtly) Direct Action and Democratic Politics, 1972; The Politics of the Corporate Economy, 1979; (with A. Young) The Fixers, 1996; numerous articles. *Address:* House of Lords, SW1A 0PW. *Club:* Reform.

SMITH OF FINSBURY, Baron *cr* 2005 (Life Peer), of Finsbury in the London Borough of Islington; **Christopher Robert Smith;** PC 1997; PhD; Chairman: Advertising Standards Authority, since 2007; Environment Agency, since 2008; *b* 24 July 1951; *s* of Colin Smith and Gladys (*née* Luscombe). *Educ:* Cassiobury Primary Sch., Watford; George Watson's Coll., Edinburgh; Pembroke Coll., Cambridge Univ. (BA 1st Cl. Hons 1972, PhD 1979; Hon. Fellow, 2005); Harvard Univ., Mass (Kennedy Scholar, 1975–76). Develt Sec., Shaftesbury Soc. Housing Assoc., 1977–80; Develt Co-ordinator, Soc. for Co-operative Dwellings, 1980–83. Dir, Clore Leadership Prog., 2003–08. Chm., London Cultural Consortium, 2005–. Sen. Advr, Walt Disney Co., 2001–07; non-exec. Dir, PPL, 2006–. Councillor, London Bor. of Islington, 1978–83 (Chief Whip, 1978–79; Chm., Housing Cttee, 1981–83). MP (Lab) Islington South and Finsbury, 1983–2005. Opposition spokesman on treasury and economic affairs, 1987–92; principal opposition spokesman on environmental protection, 1992–94, on Nat. Heritage, 1994–95, on social security, 1995–96, on health, 1996–97; Sec. of State for Culture, Media and Sport, and Chm., Millennium Commn, 1997–2001. Chairman: Tribune Gp of MPs, 1988–89 (Sec., 1985–88); Labour Campaign for Criminal Justice, 1985–88; Bd, Tribune Newspaper, 1990–93; Bd, New Century Magazine, 1993–96; Pres., Socialist Envmt and Resources Assoc., 1992–2007; Mem. Exec., Fabian Soc., 1990–97 (Chm., 1996–97). Mem., Cttee on Standards in Public Life, 2001–05. Pres., Cambridge Union, 1972; Vice-Chm., Young Fabian Gp, 1974–75; Chm., Charing Cross Br., ASTMS, 1980–83; Member: Exec., NCCL, 1986–88; Bd, Shelter, 1986–92; Exec. Cttee, Nat. Trust, 1995–97; Bd, RNT, 2001–; Bd, Donmar Warehouse, 2001–03 (Chm., 2003–). Chairman: Classic FM Consumer Panel, 2001–07; Man Booker Prize Judges, 2004. Vis. Prof. in Culture and the Creative Industries, Univ. of the Arts, London (formerly London Inst.), 2002–; Vis. Fellow, Ashridge Business Sch., 2007–. Governor: Sadler's Wells Theatre, 1987–97; Univ. of the Arts, 2005–08; Trustee, John Muir Trust, 1991–97; Chm., Wordsworth Trust, 2002–. Pres., Ramblers' Assoc., 2004–08. CCMI 2005. Hon. FRIBA 2000; Hon. Sen. Fellow, RCA, 2007; Hon. FKC 2008. Hon. DArts City, 2003. *Publications:* Creative Britain, 1998; (jtly) Suicide of the West, 2006. *Recreations:* mountaineering, literature, theatre, music. *Address:* House of Lords, SW1A 0PW.

SMITH OF GILMOREHILL, Baroness *cr* 1995 (Life Peer), of Gilmorehill in the City of Glasgow; **Elizabeth Margaret Smith;** DL; *b* 4 June 1940; *d* of Frederick William Moncrieff Bennett and Elizabeth Waters Irvine Shanks; *m* 1967, Rt Hon. John Smith, PC, QC (Scot.), MP (*d* 1994); three *d*. *Educ:* Hutchesons' Girls' Grammar Sch.; Univ. of Glasgow (MA, DipEd). Admin. Asst, 1962–64, Scottish Sec., 1982–88, Great Britain-USSR Assoc.; teacher of French, 1964–68. Mem., Press Complaints Commn, 1995–2001. Chm., Edinburgh Festival Fringe, 1995; non-executive Director: Scottish Media Group plc (formerly Scottish Television), 1995–97; Deutsche Bank (formerly Deutsche Morgan Grenfell) (Scotland), 1996–2003; City Inn Ltd, 2001–; Member: BP Adv. Bd, Scotland, 1996–2004; Adv. Bd, Know How Fund, 1998–99. Member Board: Russo-British Chamber of Commerce, 1996–; Covent Garden Fest., 1997–2001. Pres., Scottish Opera, 1997–. Trustee: John Smith Meml Trust, 1995–; BHF, 1995–98; ESU, 1995–2001; Centre for European Reform, 1996–2003; World Monument Fund, 1996–2000; Hakluyt Foundn, 1998–2001; Mariinsky Theatre Trust, 2001–. Pres., Birkbeck Coll., London, 1998–2003. DL Edinburgh, 1996. Hon. LLD Glasgow, 1998. *Recreations:* family, cinema, music, theatre, travel. *Address:* House of Lords, SW1A 0PW.

SMITH OF KELVIN, Baron *cr* 2008 (Life Peer), of Kelvin in the City of Glasgow; **Robert Haldane Smith,** Kt 1999; CA; FCIBS; Chairman: The Weir Group plc, since 2002; Scottish and Southern Energy plc, since 2005; Commonwealth Games Organising Committee, Glasgow 2014 Ltd; *b* 8 Aug. 1944; *s* of Robert Haldane Smith and Jean Smith (*née* Adams); *m* 1969, Alison Marjorie Bell; two *d*. *Educ:* Allan Glen's Sch., Glasgow. CA 1968; FCIBS 1993. With ICFC, 1968–82; Royal Bank of Scotland plc, 1983–85; Man. Dir, Charterhouse Develt Capital Ltd, 1985–89; Chm., Morgan Grenfell Develt Capital Ltd, 1989–2001 (Chief Exec., 1989–96); Chief Exec., Morgan Grenfell Asset Mgt Ltd, 1996–2000; Vice Chm., Deutsche Asset Mgt, 2000–02. Director: MFI Furniture Gp plc, 1987–2000; Stakis plc, 1997–99 (Chm., 1998–99); Bank of Scotland, 1998–2000; Aegon UK, 2002–; Standard Bank Gp Ltd, 2003–; 3i plc, 2004–. Vice-Pres., China-Britain Business Council, 2003–08. Dir, FSA, 1997–2000. Scottish Gov., BBC, 1999–2004; Bd Mem., British Council, 2002–05. Member: Financial Reporting Council, 2001–04 (Chm., FRC Gp on Guidance to Audit Cttees, 2003); Judicial Appts Bd, 2002–07. Chm. Smith Gp Adv. Gp to Scottish Govt (formerly Scottish Exec.) on young people not in educn, employment or trng, 2006–. Pres., ICA of Scotland, 1996–97. Chm., Bd of Trustees, Nat. Museums of Scotland, 1993–2002 (Trustee, 1985–2002); Mem., Museums and Galls Commn, 1988–98 (Vice Chm., 1996–98). Pres., British Assoc. of Friends of Museums, 1995–2005. Chm., BBC Children in Need, 2003–04. Chancellor, UWS (formerly Paisley Univ.), 2003–. Dr *hc* Edinburgh, 1999; DUniv: Glasgow, 2001; Paisley, 2003. *Publication:* (jtly) Managing Your Company's Finances, 1981. *Recreation:* Inchmarnock Island. *Address:* Inchmarnock, Porthouse, Straad, Rothesay, Bute PA2 0QF. *T:* (01700) 500132.

SMITH OF LEIGH, Baron *cr* 1999 (Life Peer), of Wigan in the county of Greater Manchester; **Peter Richard Charles Smith;** Lecturer, Manchester College of Art and Technology, 1974–2001; *b* 24 July 1945; *s* of Ronald Ernest Smith and Kathleen (*née* Hocken); *m* 1968, Joy Lesley (*née* Booth); one *d*. *Educ:* Bolton Sch.; LSE (BScEcon); Garnett Coll. of Educn (CertEd FE); Salford Univ. (MSc Urban Studies). Lectr, Walbrook Coll., 1969–74. Mem. (Lab) Wigan MBC, 1978– (Chm. Finance, 1982–91; Leader, 1991–). North West Regional Assembly: Vice Chm., 1998–99; Chm., 1999–2000; Chm. Exec. Bd, 2005–. Board Member: Manchester Airport plc, 1986–2001 (Chm., 1989–90); Manchester Airports Gp plc, 2001–. Chm., Assoc. of Gtr Manchester Authorities, 2000–. *Recreations:* gardening, reading political biographies, jazz. *Address:* Mysevin, Old Hall Mill Lane, Atherton, Manchester M46 0RG. *T:* (01942) 676127.

SMITH, Hon. Lady; Anne Smith; a Senator of the College of Justice in Scotland, since 2001; *b* 16 March 1955; *d* of John Mather and Jessica Douglas; *m* 1979, David Alexander Smith, WS; one *s* one *d*. *Educ:* Cheadle Girls' Grammar Sch.; Edinburgh Univ. (LLB Hons). Apprenticeship with Shepherd & Wedderburn WS, 1977–79; pupil of James McGhie, 1979–80; admitted Faculty of Advocates, 1980; QC (Scot.) 1993. Hon. Bencher, Gray's Inn, 2008. *Recreations:* music (piano, flute), aerobics, ski-ing, swimming, gardening, walking. *Address:* Parliament House, Edinburgh EH1 1RF. *T:* (0131) 225 2595.

SMITH, Adrian Charles; His Honour Judge Adrian Smith; a Circuit Judge, since 1996; *b* 25 Nov. 1950; *s* of late Fred Smith and Jenny Smith; *m* 1973, Sallie Ann Palmer (*d* 1994); two *d*. *Educ:* Blackpool Grammar Sch.; Queen Mary Coll., Univ. of London (LLB (Hons)). Called to the Bar, Lincoln's Inn, 1973; in practice on Northern Circuit, 1974–96; a Recorder, 1994–96. Mem., Liverpool Witness Support Mgt Cttee, 1990–93;

Legal Mem., 1994–96, Legal Mem. (Restricted Panel), 2002–, NW Mental Health Review Tribunal. *Recreations:* world travel, theatre, fell walking. *Address:* Crown Court, Crown Square, Manchester M3 3FL. *Club:* Waterloo Rugby Union.

SMITH, Adrian Frederick Melhuish, PhD; FRS 2001; Director General, Science and Research, Department for Innovation, Universities and Skills, since 2008; *b* 9 Sept. 1946; *s* of Claude Herbert Melhuish Smith and late Jean Margaret Eileen Smith (*née* Hunt); one *s. Educ:* Teignmouth Grammar Sch.; Selwyn Coll., Cambridge (MA 1968); University Coll. London (MSc 1969; PhD 1971). Jun. Lectr, 1971–72, Univ. Lectr, 1972–74, in Maths, Univ. of Oxford; Tutorial Fellow in Maths, Keble Coll., Oxford, 1971–74; Lectr in Stats, UCL, 1974–77; Prof. of Mathematical Stats, Univ. of Nottingham, 1977–90; Prof. of Stats, Imperial Coll. of Sci., Technology and Medicine, 1990–98 (Vis. Prof., 1998–); Principal, QMW, subseq. Queen Mary, Univ. of London, 1998–2008. Dir, Imperial College Consultants, 1992–98 (Chm. of Bd, 1996–98). Member: Math. Cttee, SERC, 1985–91 (Chm., 1988–91); Sci. Bd, SERC, 1988–91; Technical Opportunities Panel, EPSRC, 1997–2000; Stats Adv. Cttee, ONS, 1997–99; Chair: UK Inquiry into Post-14 Maths Educn, 2002–03; London Higher, 2004–06; Dep. Chair, UK Statistics Authy, 2008–. Pres., Royal Statistical Soc., 1995–97 (Guy Medal in Bronze, 1977, in Silver, 1993). Member: Governing Body, London Business Sch., 1998–2008; Council, St George's Medical Sch., 2002–04; Dep. Vice-Chancellor, Univ. of London, 2006–08. FIS 1980. Hon. DSc: City, 2003; Loughborough, 2006. *Publications:* (jtly) The Statistical Analysis of Finite Mixture Models, 1985; (jtly) Bayesian Theory, 1994; (jtly) Bayesian Methods for Nonlinear Classification and Regression, 2002; (trans. jtly) Bruno de Finetti, Theory of Probability, vol. I, 1974, vol. II, 1975; papers in statistical jls. *Recreations:* jazz, opera, cooking. *Address:* 58 Camden Square, NW1 9XE. *Club:* Reform.

SMITH, Sir Alan, Kt 1982; CBE 1976; DFC 1941, and Bar 1942; DL; President, Dawson International plc, since 1982; *b* 14 March 1917; *s* of Alfred and Lilian Smith; *m* 1st, 1943, Margaret Stewart Todd (*d* 1971); three *s* one *d* (and one *d* decd); 2nd, 1977, Alice Elizabeth Moncur. *Educ:* Bede College, Sunderland. Self employed, 1931–36; Unilever Ltd, 1937–39; RAF, 1939–45; Man. Dir, Todd & Duncan Ltd, 1946–60; Chm. and Chief Exec., Dawson International, 1960–82. DL Kinross, 1967. *Recreations:* sailing, swimming. *Address:* Ardgairney House, Cleish, by Kinross, Scotland KY13 0LG. *T:* (01577) 850265. *Club:* Lansdowne.

SMITH, Prof. Alan, DPhil; UNESCO Professor of Education, University of Ulster, since 2000; *b* Belfast, 18 Jan. 1954; *s* of Walter Smith and Barbara Smith (*née* Stanex); *m* 1981, Elaine Steele; two *d. Educ:* Univ. of Ulster (BSc Hons; DPhil 1985). Teacher, NI and Zimbabwe, 1978–84; Research Fellow, Centre for Study of Conflict, Univ. of Ulster, 1985–96; Nuffield Foundn nominee to Integrated Educn Fund, 1992–99. Consultant to Dept of Education, NI, DFID, Council of Europe and World Bank, 1997–. Founding Chm., NI Council for Integrated Educn, 1987–89. Member: UNESCO Adv. Cttee on Peace, Human Rights and Democracy, Paris, 2000–04; Internat. Assessment Bd, Postgrad. Scholarship Scheme, Irish Res. Council, 2002–; Civic Engagement Empowerment and Respect for Diversity External Adv. Cttee, World Bank, 2003–. Trustee, Speedwell Envmtl Centre, 1990–96. *Publications:* contribs to acad. jls on educn and conflict in NI, peace, human rights and democracy. *Address:* School of Education, University of Ulster, Coleraine, Northern Ireland BT52 1SA. *T:* (028) 7032 4137.

SMITH, Alan Christopher, CBE 1996; Chief Executive, Test and County Cricket Board, 1987–96; *b* 25 Oct. 1936; *s* of Herbert Sidney and Elsie Smith; *m* 1963, Anne Elizabeth Boddy; one *s* one *d. Educ:* King Edward's Sch., Birmingham; Brasenose Coll., Oxford (BA). Played cricket: Oxford Univ. CC, 1958–60 (Captain, 1959 and 1960); Warwicks CCC, 1958–74 (Captain, 1968–74); rep. England in six Test Matches, Australia and NZ, 1962–63. Gen. Sec., Warwicks CCC, 1976–86; England overseas cricket tours: Asst Manager, Australia, 1974–75; Manager: West Indies, 1981; Fiji, NZ and Pakistan, 1984. Mem., England Cricket Selection Cttee, 1969–73, 1982–86; ICC Referee, 1998–. Director: Royds Advertising and Marketing, 1971–86; Aston Villa Football Club plc, 1972–78. President: Brasenose Soc., 1999–2000; OUCC, 2000–. *Recreations:* both football codes, golf, bridge, motoring. *Address:* The Old Farmhouse, Wyck Rissington, Gloucestershire GL54 2PN. *T:* (01451) 820509. *Clubs:* MCC, I Zingari; Vincent's (Oxford); Warwickshire CC, Worcestershire CC, Glamorgan CC.

SMITH, Alan Frederick; Chairman, Acambis (formerly Peptide Therapeutics) plc, 1999–2006 (non-executive Director, 1995–2006); *b* 21 July 1944; *s* of Frederick Herbert Smith and Winifred Alice Bella (*née* Farthing); *m* 1966, Judith Mary Forshaw (marr. diss. 1991); one *s* one *d. Educ:* Gosfield Sch., Essex. CIPFA. Trainee, Colchester BC, 1961–66; Ipswich County Borough Council: Sen. Accountant, 1966–72; Asst Treas., 1972–74; Principal Accountant, Anglian Water Authy, 1974–75; Asst Dir of Finance, Southern Water Authy, 1975–80; Dir of Finance, Anglian Water Authy, 1980–89; Dep. Man. Dir and Dir of Finance, 1989–90, Gp Man. Dir, 1990–97, Anglian Water PLC. *Recreations:* walking, photography.

SMITH, Rt Rev. Alan Gregory Clayton; *see* Shrewsbury, Bishop Suffragan of.

SMITH, Alan Keith Patrick; non-executive Chairman, Space NK Ltd, 1997; *b* 17 March 1941; *s* of Ernest and Mary Smith; *m* 1st, 1968, Veronica Soskin (marr. diss.); one *s* one *d*; 2nd, 1983, Joan Peregrine; two *s. Educ:* St Michael's Coll., Leeds; Edinburgh Univ. (MA). Marks & Spencer, 1964–93, Dir, 1978–93; Chief Exec., Kingfisher, 1993–95; Dir, Smith Peregrine Ltd, 1996. Non-executive: Chm., Storehouse, then Mothercare, plc, 2000–02; Director: Colefax & Fowler, 1994–; Whitehead Mann Gp, 1997. Governor: South Bank Bd, 1995; Arts & Business, 1999. *Recreations:* family, wine collecting, walking, cooking. *Clubs:* Brooks's, MCC.

SMITH, Alasdair; *see* Smith, M. A. M.

SMITH, Alexander; *b* Kilwinning, 2 Dec. 1943. *Educ:* Irvine Royal Acad. Former gardener. Chm., 1983–87, Trade Union Liaison Officer, 1986–88, Cunninghame S CLP; former Chm., Irvine and District Trades Council. MEP (Lab) Scotland S, 1989–99. Member: TGWU (Mem., Regl, Public Service and Political Cttees); Scottish CND; Anti-Apartheid Movement; Amnesty Internat.; Latin American Solidarity Campaign.

SMITH, Prof. Alexander Crampton, (Alex Crampton Smith); Nuffield Professor of Anaesthetics, Oxford University, and Fellow of Pembroke College, Oxford, 1965–79; now Emeritus Professor; *b* 15 June 1917; *s* of William and Mary Elizabeth Crampton Smith; *m* 1953, Marjorie (*née* Mason); three *s*; two *d* by a former marriage. *Educ:* Inverness Royal Acad.; Edinburgh University; MA Oxon 1961. FFARCS 1953. Medical student, Edinburgh Univ., 1935–41. Served War of 1939–45 (Croix de Guerre, despatches), RNVR, 1942–46. Consultant Anaesthetist, United Oxford Hospitals, 1951–65; Clinical Lectr in Anaesthetics, Oxford Univ., 1961–65. Civilian Consultant Anaesthetist to Royal Navy, 1968–73. Mem. Bd, Faculty of Anaesthetists, 1965–80. Mem. Trustees, Nuffield Medical Benefaction, 1973–92. *Publications:* Clinical Practice and Physiology of Artificial Respiration (with J. M. K. Spalding), 1963; contribs to anaesthetic, medical and

physiological jls. *Recreations:* bird watching, art galleries. *Address:* 1/15 Rawlinson Road, Oxford OX2 6UE. *T:* (01865) 512954.

SMITH, Alexander M.; *see* McCall Smith.

SMITH, Alfred Nicholas Hardstaff L.; *see* Leigh–Smith.

SMITH, Alistair; *see* Smith, E. A.

SMITH, Alwyn; *see* Smith, Ernest A.

SMITH, Alyn; Member (SNP) Scotland, European Parliament, since 2004; *b* 15 Sept. 1973; *s* of Edward and Jane Smith. *Educ:* Univ. of Leeds (LLB Hons 1994); Univ. of Heidelberg; Coll. of Europe, Warsaw (MA European Studies 1995); Nottingham Law Sch. (Dip. Legal Practice 1996). Clifford Chance, Solicitors, 1997–99; Anderson Strathern, Solicitors, 2000–02; Gp Advr, Justice, Business and Europe, SNP Gp, Scottish Parlt, 2002–04. *Address:* c/o SNP HQ, 107 McDonald Road, Edinburgh EH7 4NW; *e-mail:* alyn@alynsmith.net.

SMITH, Andrea Catherine; *see* Catherwood, A. C.

SMITH, Andreas W.; *see* Whittam Smith.

SMITH, Andrew; QC (Scot.) 2002; *b* 22 Jan. 1963; *s* of David Abercrombie Smith and Margaret Smith; *m* Jane Russell; one *s* two *d. Educ:* Eastwood High Sch.; Dundee Univ. (LLB Hons; DipLP); Edinburgh Univ. (Dip. Advanced Legal Studies). Admitted advocate, 1988; called to the Bar, Gray's Inn, 2006. *Recreations:* travel, motorcycling, cycling, running. *T:* (0131) 226 5071.

SMITH, Dr Andrew Benjamin, FRS 2002; FRSE; Senior Research Scientist, Natural History Museum, since 1991; *b* 6 Feb. 1954; *s* of Benjamin Butler Smith and Elsie Marjory (*née* Fleming); *m* 1976, Mary Patricia Cumming Simpson; two *d. Educ:* Univ. of Edinburgh (BSc 1st Cl. Hons Geol. 1976; DSc 1993); Univ. of Exeter (PhD Biol Sci. 1979). Lectr, Dept of Geol., Univ. of Liverpool, 1981–82; Dept of Palaeontol., Natural History Mus., 1982– (Res. Scientist, 1982–91). FRSE 1996. *Publications:* Echinoid Palaeobiology, 1984; Systematics and the Fossil Record, 1994; edited jointly: Echinoderm Phylogeny and Evolutionary Biology, 1988; Fossils of the Chalk, 1988, revd edn 2002; Echinoderm Research 1995, 1996; contrib. numerous scientific papers and monographs. *Address:* Department of Palaeontology, Natural History Museum, Cromwell Road, SW7 5BD. *T:* (020) 7942 5217, *Fax:* (020) 7942 5546; *e-mail:* a.smith@nhm.ac.uk.

SMITH, Hon. Sir Andrew (Charles), Kt 2000; **Hon. Mr Justice Andrew Smith;** a Judge of the High Court of Justice, Queen's Bench Division, since 2000; Judge in charge, Commercial Court, 2008; *b* 31 Dec. 1947; *s* of Charles George Smith and Winifrid Smith; *m* 1986, Indu Nathoo; one *s* two *d. Educ:* Wyggeston Grammar Sch. for Boys, Leicester; Wadham Coll., Oxford (BA). Called to Bar, Middle Temple, 1974, Bencher, 1999. QC 1990; a Recorder, 1996–2000; Presiding Judge, NE Circuit, 2003–06. *Address:* Royal Courts of Justice, Strand, WC2A 2LL.

SMITH, Rt Hon. Andrew (David); PC 1997; MP (Lab) Oxford East, since 1987; *b* 1 Feb. 1951; *m*; one step *s. Educ:* Reading Grammar Sch.; St John's Coll., Oxford. Joined Labour Party, 1973. Mem., Oxford City Council, 1976–87 (Chairman: Recreation Cttee, 1980–83; Planning Cttee, 1984–87). Opposition spokesman on higher and continuing educn, 1988–92, on Treasury and Economic Affairs, 1992–94, on transport, 1996–97; Shadow Chief Sec. to HM Treasury, 1994–96; Minister of State, DFEE, 1997–99; Chief Sec. to HM Treasury, 1999–2002; Sec. of State for Work and Pensions, 2002–04. Contested (Lab) Oxford E, 1983. Chm., Bd, Oxford Brookes Univ. (formerly Oxford Poly.), 1987–93. *Address:* 4 Flaxfield Road, Blackbird Leys, Oxford OX4 5QD; House of Commons, SW1A 0AA.

SMITH, Sir Andrew (Thomas), 5th Bt *cr* 1897, of Stratford Place, St Marylebone, London; Account Director, Mail Marketing Service, New Zealand Post; *b* 17 Oct. 1965; *er s* of Sir Gilbert Smith, 4th Bt and of Patricia Christine Smith (*née* Cooper); *S* father, 2003; one *s* one *d*; *m* 2007, Erin Katrina, *d* of Perry Aspros. *Heir: b* Alistair Blair Smith, *b* 13 July 1969.

SMITH, Angela Christine; MP (Lab) Sheffield Hillsborough, since 2005; *b* 16 Aug. 1961; *d* of Thomas Edward Smith and Patricia Ann Smith; *m* 2005, Steven Wilson; one step *s* one step *d. Educ:* Univ. of Nottingham (BA 1st cl. Hons (English studies) 1990); Newnham Coll., Cambridge. Lectr, Dearne Valley Coll., Wath on Dearne, 1994–2003. Mem., Sheffield CC, 1996–2005 (Chm., Finance, 1998–99; Cabinet Mem. for Educn and Trng, 2002–05). *Recreations:* hill-walking, bird watching, cooking. *Address:* Hillsborough Library, Hillsborough Park, Middlewood Road, Sheffield S6 4HD. *T:* (0114) 231 2889, *Fax:* (0114) 234 3514; House of Commons, SW1A 0AA. *T:* (020) 7219 6713; *e-mail:* smithac@parliament.uk.

SMITH, Angela Evans; MP (Lab and Co-op) Basildon, since 1997; *b* 7 Jan. 1959; *d* of Patrick Joseph Evans and Emily Meikle Evans (*née* Russell); *m* 1978, Nigel J. M. Smith. *Educ:* Chalvedon Comprehensive Sch., Basildon; Leicester Poly. (BA Hons Public Admin). Part-time shop asst, J Sainsbury, 1975–77; Trainee Accountant, Newham LBC, 1981–83; Head of Pol and Public Relations, League Against Cruel Sports, 1983–95; Researcher, Alun Michael, MP, 1995–97. Mem. (Lab) Essex CC, 1989–97. Contested (Lab) Southend W, 1987. PPS to Minister of State, Home Office, 1999–2001; an Asst Govt Whip, 2001–02; Parliamentary Under-Secretary of State: NI Office, 2002–06; DCLG, 2006–07; PPS to Prime Minister, 2007–. *Address:* House of Commons, SW1A 0AA. *T:* (020) 7219 6273.

SMITH, Anne; *see* Smith, Hon. Lady.

SMITH, Anne; Chief Executive, General Practice Airways Group, since 2004; *b* 6 May 1961; *d* of John and Gerry Bradley; *m* 2000, Amahl Smith. *Educ:* Christ's Coll., Cambridge (MA; tennis blue). Product Manager, then Gp Product Manager, Merck Sharp and Dohme Ltd, 1982–89; Allen & Hanburys: Mktg Manager, 1989–94; Business Zone Manager, 1994–96; Glaxo Wellcome UK Ltd, 1989–98: Regl Business Dir, 1994–96; Dir, Respiratory Mktg, 1996–98; Chief Exec., Nat. Asthma Campaign, 1998–2001; management consultant, 2001–04. Mem., Technol. Appraisal Cttee, NICE, 2002–04; Trustee, Long Term Med. Conditions Alliance, 2000–05. *Recreations:* travelling, hill walking, gardening, cycling, tennis. *Address: e-mail:* anne_smith@btconnect.com.

SMITH, Anne Margaret Brearley; *see* Luther, A. M.

SMITH, Annette Dionne K.; *see* Karmiloff-Smith.

SMITH, Lt-Gen. Sir Anthony Arthur D.; *see* Denison-Smith.

SMITH, Anthony David, CBE 1987; President, Magdalen College, Oxford, 1988–2005; *b* 14 March 1938; *s* of Henry and Esther Smith. *Educ:* Brasenose Coll., Oxford (BA; Hon. Fellow, 1994). BBC TV Current Affairs Producer, 1960–71; Fellow, St Antony's Coll., Oxford, 1971–76; Director, BFI, 1979–88 (Fellow 1988). Bd Mem., Channel Four Television Co., 1980–84. Mem., Arts Council, 1990–94. Chairman: Writers and Scholars Educnl Trust, 1989–99 (Mem., 1982–); Jan Hus Educnl Foundn, 1989–2002; Hill Foundn, 1998–; Oxford-Russia Fund, 2004–; Trustee, Cambodia Trust, 1990–99. *Publications:* The Shadow in the Cave: the broadcaster, the audience and the state, 1973, 2nd edn 1976; British Broadcasting, 1974; The British Press since the War, 1976; Subsidies and the Press in Europe, 1977; The Politics of Information, 1978; Television and Political Life, 1979; The Newspaper: an international history, 1979; Newspapers and Democracy, 1980; Goodbye Gutenberg—the newspaper revolution of the 1980's, 1980; The Geopolitics of Information, 1980; The Age of the Behemoths, 1991; From Books to Bytes, 1993; The Oxford Illustrated History of Television, 1995; Software for the Self: culture and technology, 1996. *Address:* Albany, Piccadilly, W1V 9RP. *Clubs:* Grillions, Beefsteak.

SMITH, Prof. (Anthony) David, DPhil; Professor of Pharmacology, 1984–2005, now Emeritus, and Deputy Head, Division of Medical Sciences, 2000–05, University of Oxford; Director, Oxford Project to Investigate Memory and Ageing, since 1988; Fellow, Lady Margaret Hall, Oxford, 1984–2005, now Emeritus Fellow; *b* 16 Sept. 1938; *s* of Rev. William Beddard Smith and Evelyn Smith; *m* 1st, 1962, Wendy Diana Lee (marr. diss. 1974); one *s* one *d*; 2nd, 1975, Dr Ingegerd Östman; one *s*. *Educ:* Kingswood Sch., Bath; Christ Church, Oxford (Bostock Exhibnr; BA 1963, MA 1966, DPhil 1966). Royal Soc. Stothert Res. Fellow, Oxford, 1966–70; Res. Lectr, Christ Church, Oxford, 1966–71; Wellcome Res. Fellow, Oxford, 1970–71; Univ. Lectr in Pharmacology and Student of Christ Church, 1971–84; Hd, Dept of Pharmacol., Univ. of Oxford, 1984–2000. Hon. Dir, MRC Anatomical Neuropharmacology Unit, Oxford, 1985–98, now Hon. Assoc. Dir. Member: Gen. Bd of the Faculties, Oxford, 1980–84; Neurosciences Bd, MRC, 1983–88; Physiol Soc.; Pharmacol Soc.; Chm., Scientific Adv. Bd, Alzheimer's Res. Trust, 1998–2003. Dir of Pubns, IBRO, 1977–95; Editor: Methods in the Neurosciences (IBRO Handbook Series), 1981–; Neuroscience, 1976–2002; Mem., editorial bds of various scientific jls. FMedSci 2000. Mem., Norwegian Acad. of Sci. and Letters, 1996; Hon. Mem., Hungarian Acad. of Sci., 1998. Dr *hc* Szeged Univ., 1993; MD *hc* Lund Univ., 1998. (Seventh) Gaddum Meml Prize, British Pharmacol Soc., 1979. *Publications:* (ed) Handbook of Physiology, Section 7 Vol. 6, 1974; (ed) Commentaries in the Neurosciences, 1980; articles on neuropharmacology in jls. *Recreations:* history, music, travel. *Address:* Department of Physiology, Anatomy and Genetics, South Parks Road, Oxford OX1 3QX; *e-mail:* david.smith@pharm.ox.ac.uk.

SMITH, Anthony Donald Raymond, CMG 2008; Director, European Political Affairs, Foreign and Commonwealth Office, since 2006; *b* 8 Nov. 1958; *s* of Raymond and Flora Smith; *m* 1986, Kerry Rankine; one *s* one *d*. *Educ:* Univ. of Chicago High Sch.; Amherst Coll. (BA); Warwick Univ. (LLB). Joined FCO, 1986; Second, later First Sec., Madrid, 1988–91; First Sec., FCO, 1991–96; Head, EU Dept, then S Africa Dept, DFID, 1996–2006. *Recreations:* tennis, canoeing, pruning. *Address:* c/o Foreign and Commonwealth Office, King Charles Street, SW1A 2AH.

SMITH, Anthony Glen; Director, Health and Education UK (formerly Manager, Local Authority Division, then Director, Children's Services), Cambridge Education, since 2005; *b* 29 July 1955; *s* of Bernard Neil Smith and Jean Margaret Smith; *m* 1978, Anne McLaren; one *s* one *d*. *Educ:* Price's Sch., Fareham; Christ's Coll., Cambridge (BA 1977; MA 1980). Asst Teacher of Geog., Weston Favell Upper Sch., Northampton, 1977–81; Head of Geog., Sir Frank Markham Sch., Milton Keynes, 1981–84; Asst, later Sen. Educn Officer, Wilts CC, 1984–89; Devon County Council: Area Educn Officer, 1989–91; Sen. Educn Officer, 1991–94; Asst Chief Educn Officer, 1994–96; Dep. Chief Educn Officer, 1996–98; Dir of Educn, Arts and Libraries, 1998–2003; Dir of Learning and Culture, 2003–05, Dir for Children's Services, 2005, Torbay Council. *Recreations:* cricket, antique maps, watercolour painting, furniture restoration, gardening, family. *Address:* Trafalgar House, Dawlish Road, Teignmouth, Devon TQ14 8TQ. *T:* (01626) 774289. *Club:* Hawks (Cambridge).

SMITH, Anthony (John Francis); writer, broadcaster; *b* 30 March 1926; 2nd *s* of late Hubert Smith (formerly Chief Agent, National Trust) and Diana Watkin; *m* 1st, 1956, Barbara Dorothy Newman (marr. diss. 1983); one *s* two *d*; 2nd, 1984, Margaret Ann Holloway (marr. diss. 2007); one *s*. *Educ:* Dragon School, Oxford; Blundell's School, Devon; Balliol College, Oxford. MA Oxon., 1951. Served with RAF, 1944–48. Oxford University, 1948–51. Manchester Guardian, 1953 and 1956–57; Drum, Africa, 1954–55; Science Correspondent, Daily Telegraph, 1957–63. Founded British Balloon and Airship Club, 1965 (Pres., 1970–); Chm., Airship Heritage Trust, 1997–. Scientific Fellow of Zoological Society. Glaxo Award for Science Writers, 1977; Cherry Kearton Medal and Award, RGS, 1978. TV series include: Balloon Safari, Balloons over the Alps, Great Zoos of the World, Great Parks of the World, Wilderness; radio series include: A Sideways Look, 1977–89; High Street Africa Revisited, 1983–84; Truth to Tell, 1990–93. *Publications:* Blind White Fish in Persia, 1953, repr. 1990; Sea Never Dry, 1958; High Street Africa, 1961; Throw Out Two Hands, 1963; The Body, 1968, new edn 1985; The Seasons, 1970; The Dangerous Sort, 1970; Mato Grosso, 1971; Beside the Seaside, 1972; Good Beach Guide, 1973; The Human Pedigree, 1975; Animals on View, 1977; Wilderness, 1978; A Persian Quarter Century, 1979; A Sideways Look, 1983; The Mind, 1984; Smith & Son, 1984; Which Animal Are You?, 1988; The Great Rift, 1988; Explorers of the Amazon, 1990; Swaps, 1992; The Free Life, 1994; Sex, Genes and All That, 1997; The Human Body, 1998; Survived, 1998; Ballooning, 1998; The Weather, 2000; Machine Gun, 2002; The Lost Lady of the Amazon, 2003. *Recreations:* travel, lighter-than-air flying. *Address:* 52 Wellington Court, W12 9LU. *T:* 07791 756008; St Aidan's, Bamburgh, Northumberland NE69 7BJ. *T:* (01668) 214253.

SMITH, Ven. (Anthony) Michael P.; *see* Percival Smith.

SMITH, Cdre Anthony Philip M.; *see* Masterton-Smith.

SMITH, Prof. Anthony Terry Hanmer, LLD; Pro Vice-Chancellor, School of Government, and Dean, Faculty of Law, Victoria University of Wellington, since 2007; Fellow, Gonville and Caius College, Cambridge, since 1990; *b* 12 Jan. 1947; *s* of William Duncan Hanmer Smith and Rima Patricia Smith (*née* Donnelly); *m* 1968, Gillian Innes (marr. diss. 1981); one *s*. *Educ:* St Bede's Coll., Christchurch, NZ; Univ. of Canterbury (LLB; LLM). PhD 1985, LLD 1999, Cantab. Barrister and solicitor, High Court of NZ, 1979; called to the Bar, Middle Temple, 1992 (Hon. Bencher, 2001). Asst Lectr, Univ. of Canterbury, 1970–72; Lectr in Law, 1973–81, and Tutor, 1974–81, Gonville and Caius Coll., Cambridge; Reader in Law, 1981–85, and Dean of Faculty, 1984, Univ. of Durham; Prof. of Law, 1986–90, and Head of Dept, 1988–90, Univ. of Reading; Prof. of Criminal and Public Laws, 1996–2006, and Chm., Faculty of Law, 1999–2001, Univ. of Cambridge. *Publications:* Offences Against Public Order, 1987; Property Offences, 1994; (ed jtly) Harm and Culpability, 1996; (with Sir David Eady) The Law of Contempt, 1998,

3rd edn 2005; (ed) Glanville Williams: Learning the Law, 13th edn, 2006. *Recreations:* cookery, travelling, architecture, wine. *Address:* 86 Bolton Street, Wellington, New Zealand. *Club:* Athenæum.

SMITH, Anthony Thomas; QC 1977; *b* 21 June 1935; *s* of Sydney Ernest Smith and Winston Victoria Smith; *m* 1959, Letitia Ann Wheldon Griffith; one *s* two *d*. *Educ:* Northampton, Stafford, and Hinckley Grammar Schs; King's Coll., Cambridge (Exhibnr; MA). Called to the Bar, Inner Temple, 1958, Bencher, 1985; a Recorder, 1977. Flying Officer, RAF, 1958–60. Founder and Chm., Birmingham Free Representation Scheme. *Recreations:* music, reading, the countryside. *Address:* No5 Chambers, Fountain Court, Steelhouse Lane, Birmingham B4 6DR.

SMITH, Arnold Terence, MBE 1963; HM Diplomatic Service, retired; *b* 7 Oct. 1922; *s* of Thomas Smith and Minnie Louisa (*née* Mole); *m* 1st, 1944, Mary James (*d* 1983), Preston, Yorks; one *s* one *d*; 2nd, 1985, Brenda Day (*née* Edwards), Edmonton; one step *s*. *Educ:* Christ Church, Dover; Coll. of Technol., Dover. Enlisted HM Forces, Army, 1939; served War, 1939–45; released, 1947. Joined CRO, 1948; Attaché, Karachi, 1952–56; Second Sec., Madras, 1956–60; CRO, 1960–61; First Sec., Kuala Lumpur, 1961–65; Consul, Oslo, 1965–69; FCO, 1969–73; Head of Chancery, Mbabane, 1973–77; Head of Admin, Nairobi, 1977–78; Counsellor and Consul-Gen., Lagos, Nigeria, 1978–80. *Recreations:* hiking, gardening, golf, swimming. *Address:* Grunters, Cavendish Road, Clare, Suffolk CO10 8PJ. *T:* (01787) 277918.

SMITH, (Arthur) Jeffrey, CEng, FREng; FIMMM; Chairman, Wardell Armstrong (Mining, Minerals Engineering and Environmental Consultants), since 2006 (Partner, since 1983, Managing Partner, 1994–2006); *b* 1 Feb. 1947; *s* of Alfred and Doris Smith; *m* (marr. diss. 2008); one *s* one *d*. *Educ:* Univ. of Newcastle upon Tyne (BSc Engrg (Mech. and Mining) 1968; BSc Hons (Mining Engrg) 1969). CEng 1971; FIMMM 1988. Tech. asst to colliery manager, Golborne, NCB, 1971–73; Sen. Mining Engr, 1973–75, Associate, 1975–82, K. Wardell & Partners, subseq. Wardell Armstrong. Mem. Bd, British Geol Survey, 2000–. Pres., IMMM, 2004–05. Mem. Council, Keele Univ., 2000–. FREng 2001. Freeman, City of London, 1996; Mem., Co. of Engrs, 1999. *Recreations:* golf, boating, classic cars, music (playing guitar (in private!)); opposing: the nanny state; political spin; Federalist Europe; social engineering; red tape. *Address:* Wardell Armstrong, Sir Henry Doulton House, Forge Lane, Etruria, Stoke on Trent ST1 5BD. *T:* 0845 111 7777, *Fax:* 0845 111 8888; *e-mail:* jsmith@wardell-armstrong.com. *Club:* Newcastle Golf.

SMITH, Prof. Austin Gerard, PhD; FRS 2006; FRSE; MRC Professor of Stem Cell Biology, and Director, Wellcome Trust Centre for Stem Cell Research, University of Cambridge, since 2006. *Educ:* Univ. of Oxford (BA). FRSE 2003. University of Edinburgh: Prof. of Stem Cell Biol.; Dir, BBSRC Centre for Genome Res., 1998; Dir, MRC Centre of Develt in Stem Cell Biol.; Chm., Inst. for Stem Cell Res., 2005–06. *Publications:* articles in learned jls. *Address:* Wellcome Trust Centre for Stem Cell Research, University of Cambridge, Tennis Court Road, Cambridge CB2 1QR.

SMITH, Barney; *see* Smith, L. B.

SMITH, Prof. Barry Edward, PhD; Head of Nitrogen Fixation Laboratory, 1987–2000, Associate Research Director, 1994–2000, Emeritus Fellow, 2000–04, John Innes Centre (formerly AFRC Institute of Plant Science Research); *b* 15 Nov. 1939; *s* of late Ernest Smith and Agnes Mary Smith (*née* DeFraine); *m* 1963, Pamela Heather Pullen; one *s* one *d*. *Educ:* Dr Challoner's Grammar Sch., Amersham; Royal Melbourne Tech. Coll., Australia; Hatfield Tech. Coll.; Univ. of Exeter (BSc); Univ. of East Anglia (PhD). Lab. technician, ICIANZ, 1956–59; ICI, 1959–60; res. appts, Univ. of Washington, Seattle, 1966–68, Univ. of Oxford, 1968–69; ARC, subseq. AFRC, Unit of Nitrogen Fixation, 1969–87; Asst Dir, 1986–87. Vis. Prof., Univ. of Essex, 1988–98; Hon. Professorial Fellow, Univ. of Sussex, 1989–95; Hon. Prof., UEA, 1995–. *Publications:* numerous articles in sci. jls and chapters in books on excited state chem., nitrogen fixation and on denitrification. *Address:* 61 Church Lane, Eaton, Norwich NR4 6NY.

SMITH, Bartholomew Evan Eric; Chairman, Amber Foundation, since 1994; *b* 1 Feb. 1955; *s* of Sir John (Lindsay Eric) Smith, CH, CBE and of Christian Margaret Smith, OBE; *m* 1987, Catherine, *d* of Gavin and Mary Rowan Hamilton; three *s* one *d*. *Educ:* Eton Coll.; New Coll., Oxford. Littlemore Scientific Engrg Co., 1976–84; Dir, Lundy Co. Ltd, 1984–; Chairman: Smith Hamilton Ltd, 1989–; Coexis Ltd, 1990–2005 (Dir, 1985–); White Waltham Airfield Ltd, 1992–. Chm., Landmark Trust, 1995–2001. *Recreations:* flying, farming. *Address:* Garden House, Cornwall Gardens, SW7 4BQ; Shottesbrooke Farm, White Waltham, Berks SL6 3SD; *e-mail:* b@rtysmith.com. *Clubs:* Pratt's, MCC; West London Aero (White Waltham).

SMITH, Prof. Bernard Geoffrey Norman, PhD; FDSRCS, FDSRCSE; Professor Emeritus, Guy's, King's and St Thomas' Dental Institute (formerly United Medical and Dental Schools), London University, at Guy's Hospital (Professor, and Head, Division of Conservative Dentistry, 1991–2003); *b* 23 Sept. 1938; *s* of Roland and Dora Smith; *m* 1962, Susan Greenwood; one *s* one *d*. *Educ:* University Coll. London (BDS 1963); Univ. of Michigan (MSc 1968); PhD London Hosp. Dental Sch. 1974. FDSRCS 1970; MRD RCS 1994; FDSRCSE 1995. Lectr, London Hosp. Dental Sch., 1968–75; Senior Lecturer and Hon. Consultant: Royal Dental Hosp., London, 1975–83; UMDS, Guy's Hosp., 1983–91. Hon. Consultant to the Army, 1982–. *Publications:* Planning and Making Crowns and Bridges, 1986, 4th edn 2006; (jtly) Clinical Handling of Dental Materials, 1986, 2nd edn 1995; (jtly) Pickard's Manual of Operative Dentistry, 6th edn 1990 to 8th edn 2003; contrib. papers to restorative and conservative dentistry jls. *Recreations:* rebuilding and restoring old houses, making furniture. *Address:* 175 Clapham Road, SW9 0QE. *T:* (020) 7274 8464, *Fax:* (020) 7924 9447; *e-mail:* bernard.g.smith@talk21.com.

SMITH, Beverley; *see* Smith, Jenkyn B.

SMITH, Sir Brian; *see* Smith, Sir E. B.

SMITH, Sir Brian; *see* Smith, Sir N. B.

SMITH, Brian, CMG 1993; OBE 1975; HM Diplomatic Service, retired; High Commissioner to Trinidad and Tobago, 1991–94; *b* 15 Sept. 1935; *s* of Charles Francis Smith and Grace Amelia (*née* Pope); *m* 1955, Joan Patricia Rivers; one *s* two *d*. *Educ:* Hull Grammar School; BSc Open Univ. 1994. Foreign Office, 1952; HM Forces, 1954–57; Bahrain, 1957; Doha, 1959; Vice-Consul, Luxembourg, 1960, Casablanca, 1962; Tehran, 1964; Berne, 1967; FCO, 1969; Kampala, 1973; Tehran, 1975; FCO, 1977; New York, 1979; Counsellor (Commercial), Bonn, 1982; Overseas Inspector, FCO, 1986; High Comr, Botswana, 1989. *Recreations:* photography, music, handicrafts. *Address:* Bancroft, Castle Walk, Wadhurst, E Sussex TN5 6DB.

SMITH, Brian, CPFA; Chief Executive, Stoke on Trent City Council, 1992–2002; *b* 16 May 1947; *s* of Albert Frederick and Gladys Smith; *m* 1972, Susan Jane Lund; two *s*. *Educ:* Bristol Univ. (BA Hons). Graduate trainee accountant, Derbyshire CC, 1968;

Accountancy Asst, Berkshire CC, 1972; Group Technical Officer, South Yorkshire CC, 1974; Asst County Treasurer, Dorset CC, 1976; Sen. Asst County Treasurer, Avon CC, 1979; Dep. County Treasurer, 1981, County Treasurer, 1983, Staffordshire CC. Chm., Surrey Ambulance NHS Trust, 2004–06 (non-exec. Dir, 2003–04); non-exec. Dir, Surrey PCT, 2006–. Chm., Inst. of Public Finance Ltd, 2004–. Hon. Sec., Soc. of County Treasurers, 1990–92; Hon. Treasurer: CIPFA, 2001–04 (Vice-Pres., 1998–99; Pres., 1999–2000); UNICEF UK, 2002–. *Publications:* various articles in local govt finance jls. *Recreations:* music, gardening, travel.

SMITH, Ven. Brian; Archdeacon of the Isle of Man, since 2005; Vicar, St George, Douglas, since 2005; *b* 15 July 1944; *s* of William Charles Freeman Smith and Frances Smith; *m* 1967, Christine Ann Masterman; one *s* one *d. Educ:* Preston Grammar Sch., Lancs; Barton Peveril Grammar Sch., Eastleigh, Hants; Salisbury and Wells Theol Coll.; Westminster Coll., Oxford (MTh 1995). In commerce and industry, 1960–71. Ordained deacon, 1974, priest, 1975; Curate, St Thomas, Pennywell with St Oswald, Grindon, Sunderland, 1974–77; Chaplain, RAF, 1977–95; Vicar, St John, Keswick, 1995–2005; RD, Derwent, 1998–2005; Priest-in-charge, St Bridget, Bridekirk, 2002–04. Mem., Gen. Synod, C of E, 2005–. Hon. Canon, Carlisle Cathedral, 1999–2005. *Recreations:* walking, golf, DIY. *Address:* St George's Vicarage, 16 Devonshire Road, Douglas, Isle of Man IM2 3RB; *e-mail:* archd-sodor@mcb.net. *Club:* Peel Golf.

SMITH, Rt Rev. Brian Arthur; *see* Edinburgh, Bishop of.

SMITH, Brian Stanley, FSA, FRHistS; Secretary, Royal Commission on Historical Manuscripts, 1982–92; *b* 15 May 1932; *s* of late Ernest Stanley Smith and Dorothy (*née* Palmer); *m* 1963, Alison Margaret Hemming; two *d. Educ:* Bloxham; Keble College, Oxford (Holroyd Scholar). MA 1957. FSA 1972, FRHistS 1980. Archivist, Worcestershire, 1956–58, Essex, 1958–60, Gloucestershire, 1961–68; County Archivist, Gloucestershire, 1968–79; Asst Sec., Royal Commn on Historical Manuscripts, 1980–81. Part-time Editor, Victoria County History of Gloucestershire, 1968–70; Editor, Bristol and Gloucestershire Archaeological Soc., 1971–79 (Pres., 1986–87). Chm., Soc. of Archivists, 1979–80; Vice Pres., British Records Assoc., 1993–2005; Chm., Herefords Victoria County History Trust, 1997–2007; Pres., Woolhope Club, Herefords, 2001–02. Lay Mem., Gloucester Diocesan Synod, 1972–76. *Publications:* History of Malvern, 1964, 2nd edn 1978; (with Elizabeth Ralph) History of Bristol and Gloucestershire, 1972, 3rd edn 1996; The Cotswolds, 1976, 2nd edn 1992; History of Bloxham School, 1978; Manuscript Sources for the History of St Helena, 1996; Herefordshire Maps 1577–1800, 2004; articles in learned jls on local history and archives. *Recreation:* hill-walking. *Address:* Bryn Farm, Vowchurch Common, Hereford HR2 0RL.

SMITH, Brian William, AO 1988; PhD, FIEAust; Vice-Chancellor and Professor, University of Western Sydney, 1989–94; *b* 24 June 1938; *s* of William Lyle Smith and Grace Ellen Smith; *m* 1961, Josephine Peden; two *d* (one *s* decd). *Educ:* Univ. of Melbourne (BEng); Univ. of Cambridge (PhD). Australian Paper Manufacturers Ltd, 1964–70; Consolidated Electronic Industries Ltd, 1971–73; Head, School of Electrical Engineering, 1973–77, Dean, Faculty of Engineering, 1977–79, Dir, 1979–89, Royal Melbourne Inst. of Technology. Chairman of Board: Unisuper Ltd, 1994–2006; Cooperative Res. Centre for Intelligent Manufg Systems and Technologies, 1995–2006. Hon. LLD Hong Kong Baptist Univ., 1999. *Recreations:* music, golf, writing. *Address:* 60 Faraday Street, Carlton, Vic 3053, Australia. *Clubs:* Greenacres Golf, Melbourne Cricket.

SMITH, Dr Bruce Gordon, CBE 1999 (OBE 1992); FREng, FIET; Chairman, Smith Institute for Industrial Mathematics and System Engineering, since 1993; *b* 4 Oct. 1939; *s* of William Francis Smith and Georgina Lucy May Smith (*née* Tompkins); *m* 1964, Rosemary Jane Martineau (*d* 2007); two *s* two *d. Educ:* Dulwich Coll.; Christ Church, Oxford (BA 1st cl. Hons Physics 1961; DPhil 1964; MA 1968). FIET (FIEE 1978; MIEE 1971); FREng (FEng 1998). Res. Associate, Univ. of Chicago, 1964–65; mem., tech. staff, Bellcomm Inc., 1965–68; Prin. Engr, Decca Radar Ltd, 1968–71; Man. Dir, 1971–87, Chm., 1987–97, Smith System Engineering Ltd; Chairman: Industrial Technology Securities Ltd, 1995– (Dir, 1985–95); Univ. of Southampton Hldgs Ltd, 2001–06; Imagineer Systems Ltd, 2002–; Director: Gordon and Co., 1996–; British Maritime Technology Ltd, 1996–99; Southampton Innovations Ltd, 1998–2003; Esys Ltd, 1999–2001; Innovision Res. and Technol. plc, 2001–04; Southampton Asset Mgt Ltd, 2002–03; IPGroup (formerly IP2IPO Gp) plc, 2002– (Chm., 2007–); Orbital Optics Ltd, 2006–. Domus Fellow, St Catherine's Coll., Oxford, 1991–. Chm., ESRC, 1994–2001; Member: Plenary Bd, RAE, 1987–91; BNSC Earth Observation Prog. Bd, 1986–2001 (Chm., 1998–2001); Exec. Cttee, Parly Space Cttee, 1989–97; Industrial R&D Adv. Cttee, EC, 1996–99; Chm., UK Industrial Space Cttee, 1992–94. Chm., Eur. Assoc. of Remote Sensing Cos, 1987–91 (Treas., British Assoc., 1985–95); Pres., Assoc. of Indep. Res. and Technol. Orgns, 1991–93; UK Deleg. and Pres., Eur. Assoc. of Contract Res. Orgns, 1995–97; Member: Council, SBAC, 1992–94; Bd, British Antarctic Survey, 2001–07. Chm., Nat. Space Sci. Centre, 1997–2005. Vice-Chm., Surrey Br., Business Div., Prince's Trust, 1991–2002; Chm., Rainbow Seed Fund, 2002–; Trustee: Gordon Foundn, 1997–; Radio Communications Foundn, 2003–. Vice-Chm. of Council, Southampton Univ., 2001–05 (Mem. Council, 2000–06); Gov., ICSTM, 1999–2005. Hon. DSc Leicester, 2001. *Recreations:* mountain walking, dinghy sailing, cycling, music. *Address:* 11 Oxdowne Close, Cobham, Surrey KT11 2SZ. *T:* (01372) 843526. *Club:* Athenæum.

SMITH, Bryan Crossley, CBE 1982; CEng, FIGEM; Member for Marketing, British Gas Corporation, 1977–82; Chairman: C.S.E. (Wendover) Ltd, Business Consultants, since 1981; Turbine Power Ltd (formerly Power Generation), 1988–2002; *b* 28 Feb. 1925; *s* of Frank Riley Smith and Fanny Smith; *m* 1948, Patricia Mabbott; one *s* one *d. Educ:* Hipperholme Grammar Sch.; Bradford Technical Coll. CEng, FIGEM (FIGasE 1944). Articled pupil to John Corrigan, 1941; Operating Engr, Humphreys & Glasgow, 1944; Works Engr, Middlesbrough Corp. Gas Dept, 1948; N Eastern Gas Board: Asst Works Manager, Huddersfield, 1952; Engr and Man., Dewsbury, 1956; Group Sales Man., Wakefield, 1961; Conversion Man., 1966; Dep. Commercial Man., 1968; Chief Service Man., Gas Council, 1970; Service Dir, British Gas Corp., 1973. Senior Vice-Pres., IGasE, 1980–81. Pres., Wendover Soc., 2002– (Chm., 1985–2002). *Recreations:* golf, gardening. *Address:* Heron Path House, Wendover, Aylesbury, Bucks HP22 6NN. *T:* (01296) 622742.

SMITH, Cecil Raymond Julian H.; *see* Humphery-Smith.

SMITH, Charles; Sheriff of Tayside, Central and Fife at Cupar and Dundee, 1991–97; *b* 15 Aug. 1930; *s* of late Charles Smith and Mary Allan Hunter or Smith; *m* 1959, Janet Elizabeth Hurst; one *s* one *d. Educ:* Kinnoull Primary Sch.; Perth Academy; St Andrews University. MA, LLB. Solicitor 1956. Practised as principal with Campbell Brooke and Myles, Perth, 1961–82; Interim Depute Procurator Fiscal, 1975–82; Temporary Sheriff, 1977–82 and 1997–2002; Sheriff (floating appointment): of Glasgow and Strathkelvin, 1982–86; of Tayside, Central and Fife at Perth, 1986–91. Tutor, Dept of Law, Dundee Univ., 1979–82. Member Council: Law Soc. of Scotland, 1977–82 (Convener, various cttees); Sheriffs' Assoc., 1987–90. Mem., Perth Town Council, 1966–68. *Recreations:* tennis, golf, croquet. *Address:* c/o Brodies, LLP, 15 Atholl Crescent, Edinburgh EH3 8HA. *T:* (0131) 228 3777. *Clubs:* Western (Glasgow); Kinnoull Lawn Tennis.

SMITH, Sir Charles B.; *see* Bracewell-Smith.

SMITH, Charles M.; *see* Miller Smith.

SMITH, (Charles) Philip, MBE 2000; ARCA; book-art maker; Proprietor, Philip Smith Book Arts, since 1961; *b* 10 June 1928; *s* of Henry Mason Smith and Emily Mary Mildon Smith (*née* Pennington); *m* 1957, Dorothy Mary Weighill; three *s. Educ:* Ackworth Sch. (Soc. of Friends), Yorks; Southport Sch. of Art and Crafts; Royal Coll. of Art (ARCA 1st Cl. Hons 1954). Nat. Service, RAF, 1946–49. Teacher of drawing, modelling and bookbinding, Malvern Sch. of Art, 1955–57; Asst to Sydney Cockerell (rare-book conservator), 1957–61. Ed., The New Bookbinder (internat. jl), 1980–95. Dir of Studies in Graphic Design (pt-time), NE London Poly., 1961–71. Inventor: maril (use of leather waste), UK patent, 1969; Lap-Back book structure, US and UK patents, 1992. Mem., BM Team Florence Flood Disaster, 1966–67. Fellow, Designer Bookbinders, 1957 (Pres., 1977–79); Mem., Soc. of Bookbinders, 1991–; MCSD (MSIAD 1972). Mem., Soc. for Study of Normal Psychol., 1955–. Hon. Member: Meister der Einbandkunst, 1971; Center for Book Arts, NY, 1984; Canadian Bookbinders and Book Artists Guild, 1987. Work in exhibns internationally; solo exhibn of works in US/Canadian collections, Portland, Oregon, 2007; *work in collections:* Royal Collection; BL; V&A Mus.; Royal Coll., Holland; NY Public Liby, Spencer Coll.; Harry Ransome Humanities Res. Center, Univ. of Texas; Marriott Liby, Salt Lake City; Lilly Liby, Indiana, and other public and private collections worldwide. 1st Open Prize, Thomas Harrison Meml Comp., 1957; Gold Medals: 2nd Internat. Bienale, São Paulo, 1972; EEC Bookbinding Comp., 1993; Silver Medal: Paris Internat. Comp., 1992; 1st and 2nd Internat. Comps for Book as Art, Italy, 1998 and 2002; 1st Prize, Czech Republic Bookbinding Art, 2004. *Publications:* The Lord of the Rings and Other Bookbindings of Philip Smith, 1970; New Directions in Bookbinding, 1974; The Book: art and object, 1982; contrib. articles and introdns to many books, exhibn catalogues, etc. *Recreations:* non-duality philosophy (Oneness of All), creation of visual metaphors, writing, inventing, painting, table-tennis. *Address:* The Book House, The Street, Yatton Keynell, Chippenham, Wilts SN14 7BH. *T:* and *Fax:* (01249) 782597; *e-mail:* philipsmithbookart@tiscali.co.uk.

SMITH, Charles Robert S.; *see* Saumarez Smith.

SMITH, Christopher Brian P.; *see* Powell-Smith.

SMITH, Rev. Christopher Hughes; Supernumerary Methodist Minister; President of the Methodist Conference, 1985–86; *b* 30 Nov. 1929; *s* of Rev. Bernard Hughes Smith and Dorothy Lucy Smith; *m* 1956, Margaret Jean Smith; three *s* and one foster *s. Educ:* Bolton School; Emmanuel College and Wesley House, Cambridge. MA Cantab. Intercollegiate Sec., SCM, 1955–58; ordained at Methodist Conf., Newcastle upon Tyne, 1958; Leicester South Methodist Circuit, 1958–65; Birmingham South-West Methodist Circuit, 1965–74; Chm., Birmingham Methodist Dist, 1974–87; Lancaster Methodist Circuit, 1987–88; Gen. Sec., Div. of Educn and Youth, Methodist Ch, 1988–95. Pres., Nat. Christian Educn Council, 1995–99. Mem. Court, Univ. of Surrey, Roehampton, 2000–. Hon. Fellow: Selly Oak Colls, 1992; Roehampton Inst., 1997; Southlands Coll., Roehampton Univ., 2004. Hon. MA Birmingham, 1985. *Publications:* (contrib.) Queen's Sermons, 1973; Music of the Heart—Methodist Spirituality, 1991; (contrib.) A Dictionary of Methodism, 2000; (contrib.) Reflections on Ministry, 2004; contribs to Methodist Recorder, Epworth Review. *Recreations:* gardening, music, books, walking. *Address:* 12 Spean Court, Wollaton Road, Nottingham NG8 1GL.

SMITH, Christopher John Addison, FCA; Chief of Staff to Archbishop of Canterbury, since 2003; *b* 30 March 1949; *s* of Rev. Canon Anthony Cecil Addison Smith and Muriel Patricia Addison Smith; *m* 1973, Nina Jane Perry; two *d. Educ:* Univ. of East Anglia (BA Hons). FCA 1980. With Price Waterhouse, London, 1970–93, Human Resources Partner, 1989–93; Gen. Sec., Diocese of London, 1993–99; Gen. Manager, C. Hoare & Co. Bankers, 1999–2003. Mem., Gen. Synod, Church of England, 1995–2000. Vice Chm. Govs, Southwark Coll. of Further Educn, 1987–94; Dep. Chm. Govs, James Allen's Girls' Sch., 1994–2004. Hon. Treas., Holy Trinity Brompton, 1974–91. *Recreations:* theatre, music, reading. *Address:* Lambeth Palace, SE1 7JU. *T:* (020) 7898 1200; *e-mail:* chris.smith@lambethpalace.org.uk. *Club:* Reform.

SMITH, Rev. Canon Christopher Milne; Vicar of the Minster Church of St George, Doncaster, since 2002; Chaplain to the Queen, since 2004; *b* 7 Sept. 1944; *s* of Alastair Gordon Smith and Marjorie Boulton Smith; *m* 1971, Christine Wright; three *s* one *d. Educ:* Selwyn Coll., Cambridge (BA (Theol.) 1966, MA 1970); Cuddesdon Theol Coll. Ordained deacon, 1969, priest, 1970; Curate, Our Lady and St Nicholas, Liverpool, 1969–74; Team Vicar, St Andrew's, Tower Hill, Kirkby, 1974–81; Rector, St Mary's, Walton-on-the-Hill, Liverpool, 1981–91; Canon Residentiary, Sheffield Cathedral, 1991–2002 (Hon. Canon, 2003–). Advr on the Paranormal to Bishop of Sheffield, 1997–2004. *Recreations:* contract bridge, gardening, philately. *Address:* St George's Vicarage, 98 Thorne Road, Doncaster DN2 5BJ. *T:* (01302) 368796; *e-mail:* smith@revcm.fsnet.co.uk.

SMITH, Christopher Shaw G.; *see* Gibson-Smith.

SMITH, Claire Helen; HM Diplomatic Service, retired; non-executive Director, Mott Macdonald Ltd; *b* 23 Dec. 1956; *d* of late Norman Eric Stubbs and Helen Evelyn Stubbs; *m* 1986, Michael Forbes Smith, *qv*; one *s* one *d. Educ:* Queen Mary Coll., London (BA Hons 1979). FCO 1979; Second Sec., Peking, 1983; First Sec., FCO, 1985; Credit Suisse, Zurich, 1990–94; seconded to Auswärtiges Amt, Bonn, 1994–97; First Sec., Bonn, 1997–99; Counsellor, Islamabad, 1999–2001; on loan to Assessments Staff, Cabinet Office, 2001–04; Hd, Whitehall Liaison Dept, FCO, 2004–07. LEA Gov., Curwen Primary Sch. *Recreations:* reading detective novels, recycling. *Club:* Army and Navy.

SMITH, Clive Adrian S.; *see* Stafford Smith.

SMITH, Colin Deverell; Chairman: Poundland Holdings, since 2002; Assured Food Standards, since 2003; *b* 21 May 1947; *m* 1971, Kathy Morgan; two *s. Educ:* All Saints Sch., Bloxham, Banbury; Liverpool Univ. (BCom 1969). FCA 1973. Qualified with Arthur Andersen, Manchester; Argyll Foods: Gp Financial Controller and Co. Sec., 1979–83; Argyll Gp, subseq. Safeway plc: Gp Financial Controller and Co. Sec., 1983–84; Dir, 1984–99; Finance Dir, 1989–93; Gp Chief Exec., 1993–99. Chairman: Blueheath Hldgs (formerly Blue Heath Direct), 2000–06; Masstock Gp Hldgs, 2007–08; non-exec. Dir, McBride plc, 2002–. Trustee, SCF, 2001–05. *Recreations:* theatre, walking, Rugby, interesting vehicles. *Address:* Pyes, Penn Road, Knotty Green, Beaconsfield, Bucks HP9 2TS. *T:* (01494) 675840.

SMITH, Prof. Colin John, CBE 1997; Professor of Oral Pathology, Sheffield University, 1973–2003 (Dean of Dental Studies, School of Clinical Dentistry, 1978–84 and 1988–2000; Deputy Dean, Faculty of Medicine, 2000–02); *b* 7 June 1938; *s* of Rowland William John Smith and Doris Emily Smith; *m* 1st, 1962, Mary Margaret Kathrine MacMahon (marr. diss. 1995); three *d*; 2nd, 1995, Eunice Turner (*née* Acaster). *Educ:* Purley County Grammar Sch. for Boys; Royal Dental Hosp. Sch. of Dental Surgery, Univ. of London (BDS Hons, PhD). FDSRCS, FRCPath. House Surgeon, Royal Dental Hosp., 1961–62; MRC Scientific Asst, 1962–63, Prophit Cancer Res. Student, 1964–68, Dept of Dental Sci., RCS; Wellcome Travelling Res. Fellow, Dept of Oral Path., Royal Dental Coll., Copenhagen, 1968–69; Nuffield Dental Res. Fellow, Dept of Morbid Anatomy, RPMS, 1969–71; Sen. Lectr and Res. Fellow, Dept of Oral Medicine and Path., Guy's Hosp. Dental Sch., 1971–72; Dir, Charles Clifford Dental Hosp., Central Sheffield Univ. Hosps NHS Trust, 1998–2001. Charles Tomes Lectr, RCS, 1987. Member: GDC, 1979–84, 1994–2003 (Chm., Dental Auxiliaries Cttee, 1999–2003; Mem., Fitness to Practise Cttee, 2003–; Co-Chair, Panel of Visitors to Dental Schs, 2003–05); Nuffield Foundn Cttee of Inquiry into Dental Educn, 1978–80; Nuffield Foundn Cttee of Inquiry into Educn and Trng of Personnel Auxiliary to Dentistry, 1992–93; MRC Dental Cttee, 1973–84 (Scientific Sec., 1975–84) and Physiological Systems and Disorders Bd, 1988–92; MRC/DHSS/SERC Joint Dental Cttee, 1988–93 (Vice-Chm.); Council, Odontological Sect., RSocMed, 1973–76 and 1989–92 (Pres., 1990–91); Dental Educn Adv. Council, 1978–2000 (Hon. Sec., 1985–90; Chm., 1990–92); British Soc. for Oral Pathology, 1975– (Pres., 1980–81; Life Mem., 2007); Internat. Assoc. of Oral Pathologists, 1983– (Mem. Council, 1988–2004; Pres., 2000–02; Hon. Life Mem., 2006–); Assoc. for Dental Educn in Europe, 1982– (Sec. Gen., 1984–87; Editor, 1989–92); Internat. Assoc. for Dental Res., 1963–2004 (Internat. Relns Cttee, 1982–84; Ethics Cttee, 1992–95); UGC Dental Sub-Cttee, 1985–89; UGC Dental Review Working Party, 1986–88; UFC Medical Cttee, 1989–92; British Council Medical Adv. Cttee, 1985–91; Standing Dental Adv. Cttee, 1992–96; Clinical Standards Adv. Gp, 1995–99; CVCP Task Force on Clin. Acad. Careers, 1996–98; WHO Expert Adv. Panel on Oral Health, 1989–98. Ed.-in-chief, Jl of Oral Pathology and Medicine, 1993–99. Hon. Treasurer, Alpine Garden Soc., 2003–. Hon. Mem., Hungarian Dental Assoc., 1991. Founder FMedSci 1998. Hon. DSc Sheffield, 2004. Colgate Prize, British Div., Internat. Assoc. for Dental Res., 1964. *Publications:* (jtly) Oral Cancer: epidemiology, etiology and pathology, 1990; (jtly) Histological typing of cancer and precancer of the oral mucosa, 1997; chapters in books and contribs to professional jls. *Recreations:* lawn tennis, walking, gardening, listening to classical music, theatre. *Address:* Hooper House, Playing Fields Lane, Elmley Road, Ashton-under-Hill, Evesham, WR11 7RF. *T:* (01386) 881281. *Club:* Royal Society of Medicine.

SMITH, Colin Milner; QC 1985; **His Honour Judge Colin Smith;** a Circuit Judge, since 1991; *b* 2 Nov. 1936; *s* of late Alan Milner Smith and Vera Ivy Smith; *m* 1979, Moira Soraya, *d* of late Reginald Braybrooke; one *s* one *d*. *Educ:* Tonbridge; Brasenose College, Oxford (MA); Univ. of Chicago (JD). Called to the Bar, Gray's Inn, 1962; a Recorder, 1987–91. *Publication:* (jtly) The Law of Betting, Gaming and Lotteries, 1987. *Recreations:* cricket, ski-ing, reading. *Club:* MCC.

SMITH, Colin Roderick, CVO 1984; CBE 1995; QPM 1987; an appeals commissioner, since 2001; HM Inspector of Constabulary, 1991–2000; *s* of Humphrey and Marie Smith; *m* 1961, Patricia Joan Coppin. *Educ:* Dorking County and Bexhill Grammar Schools; Univ. of Birmingham (BSocSc, Hons Social Admin.); rcds 1981. Royal Army Service Corps (Lieut), 18 Co. (Amph), 1959–62; East Sussex Constabulary, later Sussex Police, from Constable to Chief Supt, 1962–77; Asst Chief Constable, Thames Valley Police, 1977–82; Dep. Asst Comr, Metropolitan Police, 1982–85 (incl. founder, Royalty and Diplomatic Protection Dept); Chief Constable, Thames Valley Police, 1985–91. Caseworker, 2001–, Dorset Chm., 2005–, W of England Regl Rep., and Chm., Nat. Br. Support Cttee, 2006–, SSAFA. *Recreation:* walking.

SMITH, Sir Colin S.; *see* Stansfield Smith.

SMITH, Sir Cyril, Kt 1988; MBE 1966; DL; Managing Director, Smith Springs (Rochdale) Ltd, 1963–87; *b* 28 June 1928; unmarried. *Educ:* Rochdale Grammar Sch. for Boys. Civil Service, 1944–45; Wages Clerk, 1945–48; Liberal Party Agent, Stockport, 1948–50; Labour Party Agent, Ashton-under-Lyne, 1950–53, Heywood and Royton 1953–55; rejoined Liberal Party, 1967; MP Rochdale, Oct. 1972–1992 (L, 1972–88, Lib Dem, 1988–92); Liberal Chief Whip, 1975–76. Newsagent (own account), 1955–58; Production Controller, Spring Manufacturing, 1958–63; founded Smith Springs (Rochdale) Ltd, 1963. Director: Ratcliffe Springs, 1987–90; Robert Riley Springs. Councillor, 1952–66, Alderman, 1966–74, Mayor, 1966–67, Co. Borough of Rochdale (Chm., Education Cttee, 1966–72); Councillor, Rochdale Metropolitan DC, 1973–75. A Dep. Pro-Chancellor, Lancaster Univ., 1978–86. Freeman, Borough of Rochdale, 1992. DL Greater Manchester, 1991. Hon. LLD Lancaster, 1993; Hon. DEd Manchester Metropolitan, 1996. OStJ 1976. *Publications:* Big Cyril (autobiog.), 1977; Industrial Participation, 1977. *Recreations:* music (listener), reading, charitable work, local government. *Address:* 14 Emma Street, Rochdale, Lancs OL12 6QW. *T:* (01706) 648840.

SMITH, Cyril Stanley, CBE 1985; MSc, PhD; Secretary to Economic and Social Research Council (formerly Social Science Research Council), 1975–85; *b* 21 July 1925; *s* of Walter and Beatrice May Smith; *m* 1968, Eileen Cameron; two *d* (by first marr.). *Educ:* Plaistow Municipal Secondary Sch.; London Sch. of Economics. HM Forces, Dorset Regt, 1943–47. Univ. of Birmingham, 1950–51; Univ. of Sheffield, 1951–52; Dulwich Coll. Mission, 1952–56; Nat. Coal Board, 1956–61; Univ. of Manchester, 1961–71; Civil Service Coll., 1971–75. Man. Dir, ReStrat, 1985–90. Visiting Prof., Univ. of Virginia, 1965; Academic Visitor, Nuffield Coll., Oxford, 1980–81, 1985–86; Senior Res. Fellow, Wissenschaftszentrum Berlin für Sozialforschung, 1987. British Nat. Expert, European Poverty Prog., 1977–82. Mem., Sec. of State's Cttee on Inequalities in Health, DHSS, 1977–80. Chm., British Sociological Assoc., 1972–74; Pres., Sociol. Sect., British Assoc., 1979. *Publications:* Adolescence, 1968; (sen. author) The Wincroft Youth Project, 1972; (ed jtly) Society and Leisure in Britain, 1973; numerous articles on youth, leisure and developments in social science.

SMITH, Prof. David; *see* Smith, A. D.

SMITH, Prof. David; *see* Smith, N. J. D.

SMITH, Prof. David, FRS 1988; CPhys, FInstP; Professor, Institute of Science and Technology in Medicine (formerly Department of Biomedical Engineering and Medical Physics), University of Keele, since 1999 (Visiting Professor, 1995–99); Director and Company Secretary, Trans Spectra Ltd, since 2001; *b* 26 Nov. 1935; *s* of J. and F. L. Smith. *Educ:* Keele Univ. (BA 1959); DSc 1975, PhD 1962, Birmingham Univ. FInstP 1973. Res. Fellow, 1962, Prof. of Chemical Physics, 1984–90, Birmingham Univ.; Prof. of Physics, Institut für Ionenphysik der Universität Innsbruck, Austria, 1991–95. Hon. DSc Keele, 1990. *Publications:* numerous res. pubns and review articles in physics, chemistry and astrophysics, for learned jls incl. British Inst. of Physics jls and Amer. Inst. of Physics jls. *Recreations:* classical music, sport. *Address:* 9 The Elms, Porthill, Newcastle-under-Lyme, Staffs ST5 8RP; Institute of Science and Technology in Medicine, University of Keele, Thornburrow Drive, Hartshill, Stoke-on-Trent, Staffs ST4 7QB.

SMITH, David, PhD; FInstPet; consultant; Director, Hampshire Technology Centre, since 1990; formerly Chairman and Managing Director, Esso Chemical Ltd; *b* 18 July 1927; *s* of Walter and Annie Smith; *m* 1951, Nancy Elizabeth (*née* Hawley) (*d* 1999); two *s* three *d*. *Educ:* Burton Grammar School; Univ. of Sheffield. BSc, PhD. Lectr in Fuel Technology and Chemical Engineering, Univ. of Sheffield, 1951–55; Esso Research Ltd, 1955–65; Dir, Products Research Div., Esso Research and Engineering, USA, 1966–68; Marketing Dir and Man. Dir, Esso Chemical Ltd, 1968–71; Vice-Pres., Essochem Europe Inc., Brussels, 1971–73; Vice-Pres., Exxon Chemical Inc., USA, 1973–78. Chm., Assoc. of Hampshire Chambers of Commerce, 1995–97. Chm. Govs, Southampton Inst., 1989–97. *Recreation:* golf. *Address:* Meadowlands, Stockbridge Road, Winchester, Hants SO22 5JH. *T:* (01962) 864880. *Clubs:* MCC; Royal Winchester Golf.

SMITH, David Andrew; Special Adviser, United Nations, since 2006; Director, United Nations Office, Washington, 2004–06; *b* 5 March 1952; *s* of John and Patricia Smith; *m* 1996, Sonia Ruseler; one *s* one *d*, and two *s* from former marriage. *Educ:* Lincoln Coll., Oxford (BA Hons, MA). Reuters Correspondent, Spain and Italy, 1975–78; Africa Correspondent, 1979–81, Middle East Correspondent, 1982–86, ITN; Channel 4 News: Diplomatic Correspondent, 1987–89; Moscow Correspondent, 1989–90; Washington Correspondent, 1991–2003. Vis. Prof., Univ. of Michigan, 1986–87. Hon. Patron, VacProject, Lincoln Coll., Oxford, 2008–. RTS Award, 1983; NY TV Fest. Award, 2000. *Publications:* Mugabe: a biography, 1981; Prisoners of God: conflict of Arab and Israeli, 1987. *Recreations:* coaching soccer, tennis, study of wine. *Address:* 4326 36th Street NW, Washington, DC 20008, USA; *e-mail:* davidsmith.un@gmail.com. *Club:* Reform.

SMITH, His Honour David Arthur; QC 1982; a Circuit Judge, 1986–2004; *b* 7 May 1938; *s* of late Arthur Heber Smith and Marjorie Edith Pounds Smith; *m* 1967, Clementine Smith, JP (*née* Urquhart); two *s*. *Educ:* Lancing College; Merton Coll., Oxford (MA Hons Jurisprudence). Called to Bar, Middle Temple, 1962; Official Principal of Archdeaconry of Hackney, 1973–; a Recorder, 1978–86. Mem., Parole Bd, 1989–94. Wine Treasurer, Western Circuit, 1980–86; Pres., Council of HM Circuit Judges, 2000 (Treas., 1991–98). *Publications:* John Evelyn's Manuscript on Bees from Elysium Britannicum, 1966; (jtly) Bibliography of British Bee Books, 1979; (with David Frimston) Beekeeping and the Law—Swarms and Neighbours, 1993. *Recreations:* acting (Mem., Old Stagers, 1982–), bees (Sec. of Internat. Bee Research Assoc., 1963–), books, canals, Rossini.

SMITH, David Arthur George, OBE 1996; Headmaster of Bradford Grammar School, 1974–96; *b* 17 Dec. 1934; *o s* of Stanley George and Winifred Smith, Bath, Somerset; *m* 1957, Jennifer, *o d* of John and Rhoda Anning, Launceston, Cornwall; one *s* two *d*. *Educ:* City of Bath Boys' Sch.; Balliol Coll., Oxford. MA, Dip. Ed (Oxon). Assistant Master, Manchester Grammar Sch., 1957–62; Head of History, Rossall School, 1963–70; Headmaster, The King's School, Peterborough, 1970–74. Chm., HMC, 1988. Mem., Parole Bd, 1995–2001. JP West Yorks, 1975–2003, Thames Valley, 2003–04. Chm., Woburn Parish Council, 2006–. *Publications:* (with John Thorn and Roger Lockyer) A History of England, 1961; Left and Right in Twentieth Century Europe, 1970; Russia of the Tsars, 1971. *Recreations:* writing, walking. *Club:* East India.

SMITH, David Buchanan, FSAScot; Sheriff of North Strathclyde at Kilmarnock, 1975–2001; *b* 31 Oct. 1936; *s* of William Adam Smith and Irene Mary Calderwood Hogarth; *m* 1961, Hazel Mary Sinclair; one *s* one *d* (and one *s* decd). *Educ:* Paisley Grammar Sch.; Glasgow Univ. (MA); Edinburgh Univ. (LLB). Advocate, 1961; Standing Junior Counsel to Scottish Educn Dept, 1968–75. Tutor, Faculty of Law, Univ. of Edinburgh, 1964–72. Res. Associate, Nat. Mus of Scotland, 2002–. Member Council: Stair Soc., 1994– (Vice Chm. Council, 1998–); Scottish Nat. Dictionary Assoc., 1994–2002; Sheriffs' Assoc., 1998–2001 (Treas., 1979–89; archivist, 1989–); Scottish Language Dictionaries, 2002–; Mem., Scottish Records Adv. Council, 2001–08. Trustee, The Scottish Curling Museum Trust, 1980–; President: Ayr Curling Club, 1995–96; Eglinton County Curling Game, 2000–04. Lifetime Achievement Award, Royal Caledonian Curling Club, 2005. *Publications:* Curling: an illustrated history, 1981; The Roaring Game: memories of Scottish curling, 1985; (contrib.) The Laws of Scotland: Stair Memorial Encyclopedia, vol. 6, 1988; George Washington Wilson in Ayrshire, 1991; (contrib.) Atlas of Scottish History to 1707, 1996; (contrib.) Macphail, Sheriff Court Practice, 2nd edn 1999; (contrib.) Sport, Scotland and the Scots, 2000; (contrib.) Oxford Companion to Scottish History, 2001; (contrib.) Encyclopaedia of Traditional British Rural Sports, 2005; articles in Scots Law Times, Juridical Rev., Jl of Law Soc. of Scotland, Scottish Book Collector, The Medal, Rev. of Scottish Culture, Scottish Curler, Procs of Soc. of Antiquaries of Scotland, and newspapers. *Recreations:* history of the law and institutions of Scotland, curling, collecting curliana, music, architecture, grandchildren. *Address:* 72 South Beach, Troon, Ayrshire KA10 6EG. *T:* (01292) 312130.

SMITH, Sir David C.; *see* Calvert-Smith.

SMITH, Sir David (Cecil), Kt 1986; FRS 1975; FRSE; Principal and Vice-Chancellor, University of Edinburgh, 1987–93; President, Wolfson College, Oxford, 1994–2000; *b* 21 May 1930; *s* of William John Smith and Elva Emily Smith; *m* 1965, Lesley Margaret Mollison Mutch; two *s* one *d*. *Educ:* Colston's Sch., Bristol; St Paul's Sch., London; Queen's Coll., Oxford (Browne Schol., MA, DPhil; Hon. Fellow 2000). Christopher Welch Res. Schol., Oxford, 1951–54; Swedish Inst. Schol., Uppsala Univ., 1951–52; Browne Res. Fellow, Queen's Coll., Oxford, 1956–59; Harkness Fellow, Univ. Calif, Berkeley, 1959–60; Oxford University: Univ. Lectr, Dept Agric., 1960–74; Mem., Linacre Coll., 1962–64, Hon. Fellow, 1988; Royal Soc. Res. Fellow, 1964–71, Tutorial Fellow and Tutor for Admissions, 1971–74, Hon. Fellow, 1987, Wadham Coll.; Melville Wills Prof. of Botany, Bristol Univ., 1974–80; Sibthorpian Prof. of Rural Economy, and Fellow of St John's Coll., Oxford Univ., 1980–87. Vis. Prof., UCLA, 1968. Chairman: NERC Aquatic Life Scis Cttee, 1978–81; Member: AFRC (formerly ARC), 1982–88; Consultative Bd, JCO for Res. in Agric. and Food, 1981–83; SERC Science Board, 1983–85; Co-ordinating Cttee on Marine Sci. and Technology, 1987–91; ABRC, 1989–90; Commn on Scottish Educn, 1994–96. President: British Lichen Soc., 1972–74; British Mycological Soc., 1980; Soc. for Experimental Biol., 1983–85 (Vice-Pres., 1981–83); Internat. Soc. Endocytobiology, 1981–89; Scottish Assoc. for Marine Sci., 1994–2000; Linnean Soc., 2000–03. Royal Society: a Vice-Pres., 1978–80, 1983–87; Biological Sec., 1983–87. Bidder Lecture, Soc. for Experimental Biology, 1985; Sir Joseph Banks Lectures, Australian bicentennial, 1988; L. F. Power Meml Lecture, James Cook Univ., 1988. Editor and Trustee, New Phytologist, 1965–85. FRSE 1988. Hon. FRCPEd 1993; Hon. FRCSEd 1994. Hon. DSc: Liverpool, Exeter, 1986; Hull, 1987; Aberdeen, 1990; Napier, Heriot-Watt, 1993; Oxford Brookes, 1996; Hon. LLD: Pennsylvania, 1990; Queen's Univ., Ontario, 1991; Dr *hc* Edinburgh, 1994. Linnean Medal, Linnean Soc., 1989. Commendatore dell'Ordine al Merito della Repubblica Italiana, 1991; Comdr, Order of Merit, Republic of Poland, 1994. *Publications:* (with A. Douglas) The Biology of

Symbiosis, 1987; various articles on symbiosis, in New Phytol., Proc. Royal Soc., Biol. Rev., etc. *Address:* 13 Abbotsford Park, Edinburgh EH10 5DZ.

SMITH, David Grahame G.; *see* Grahame-Smith.

SMITH, Air Marshal Sir David H.; *see* Harcourt-Smith.

SMITH, David Henry; Economics Editor, since 1989, Policy Adviser, since 1995, Assistant Editor, since 1998, The Sunday Times; *b* 3 April 1954; *s* of Charles Henry Smith and Elizabeth Mary Smith (*née* Williams), Walsall; *m* 1980, Jane Howells, Tenby; two *s* two *d*. *Educ:* West Bromwich Grammar Sch.; UC Cardiff (BSc Econ 1st cl. hons; Tassie Medallion, 1975); Worcester Coll., Oxford; Birkbeck Coll., London (MSc Econ). Economic report writer, Lloyds Bank, 1976–77; economist, Henley Centre for Forecasting, 1977–79; economics and business writer, Now! magazine, 1979–81; Asst Editor, Financial Weekly, 1981–84; Economics Corresp., The Times, 1984–89. Vis. Prof., Cardiff Univ., 2007–. FRSA 1999. Wincott Sen. Financial Journalist of the Year, 2003. *Publications:* The Rise and Fall of Monetarism, 1987; Mrs Thatcher's Economics, 1988; North and South, 1989, 2nd edn 1994; From Boom to Bust, 1992, 2nd edn 1993; Mrs Thatcher's Economics: her legacy, 1992; UK Current Economic Policy, 1994, 2nd edn 1999; Job Insecurity *vs* Labour Market Flexibility, 1996; Eurofutures, 1997; Will Europe Work?, 1999; (ed) Welfare, Work and Poverty, 2000; Free Lunch, 2003; The Dragon and the Elephant: China, India and the new world order, 2007. *Recreations:* squash, golf, music. *Address:* 1 Pennington Street, E98 1ST. *T:* (020) 7782 5750; *e-mail:* david@economicsuk.com. *Club:* Bexley Lawn Tennis and Squash.

SMITH, Sir David (Iser), KCVO 1990 (CVO 1977); AO 1986; BA; Director, Winston Churchill Memorial Trust, since 1999; Official Secretary to the Governor-General of Australia, 1973–90; Secretary of the Order of Australia, 1975–90; *b* 9 Aug. 1933; *s* of late W. M. Smith; *m* 1955, June F., *d* of late M. A. W. Forestier; three *s*. *Educ:* Scotch Coll., Melbourne; Melbourne Univ.; Australian National Univ., Canberra (BA). Commnd CMF, Melb. Univ. Regt, 1956. Entered Aust. Public Service, 1954; Dept of Customs and Excise, Melb., 1954–57; Trng Officer, Dept of the Interior, Canberra, 1957–58; Private Sec. to Minister for the Interior and Minister for Works, 1958–63; Exec. Asst to Sec., Dept of the Interior, 1963–66; Exec. Officer (Govt), Dept of the Interior, 1966–69; Sen. Adviser, Govt Br., Prime Minister's Dept, 1969–71; Sec., Federal Exec. Council, 1971–73; Asst Sec., Govt Br., Dept of the Prime Minister and Cabinet, 1972–73. Attached to The Queen's Household, Buckingham Palace, June-July 1975. Director: FAI Life Insurance Soc. Ltd, 1991–96; FAI Life Ltd, 1991–96. Australian National University: Vis. Fellow in Pol Sci., Res. Sch. of Social Scis, 1991–92; Vis. Fellow, 1998–99, Vis. Scholar, 2000–07, Faculty of Law. Dir, Canberra Symphony Orch., 1976–96 (Chm., 1991–93). Dir, Nat. Heart Foundn of Aust., 1991–97. Pres., Samuel Griffith Soc., 2006–. Vice-Pres., Scout Assoc. of Australia, 1991–99 (Dist Comr, Capital Hill Dist, 1971–74). KStJ 1991 (CStJ 1974). *Publication:* Head of State: the Governor-General, the monarchy, the Republic and the dismissal, 2005. *Recreations:* music, reading. *Address:* 1/36 Shackleton Circuit, Mawson, ACT 2607, Australia. *T:* (2) 62865094. *Club:* Commonwealth (Canberra).

SMITH, Rt Rev. David James; an Hon. Assistant Bishop, Diocese in Europe, and Diocese of York, since 2002; *b* 14 July 1935; *s* of Stanley James and Gwendolen Emie Smith; *m* 1961, Mary Hunter Moult; one *s* one *d*. *Educ:* Hertford Grammar School; King's College, London (AKC; FKC 1999). Assistant Curate: All Saints, Gosforth, 1959–62; St Francis, High Heaton, 1962–64; Long Benton, 1964–68; Vicar: Longhirst with Hebron, 1968–75; St Mary, Monkseaton, 1975–81; Felton, 1982–83; Archdeacon of Lindisfarne, 1981–87; Bishop Suffragan of Maidstone, 1987–92; Bishop to the Forces, 1990–92; Bishop of Bradford, 1992–2002. DUniv Bradford, 2001. *Recreations:* fell walking, reading novels. *Address:* 34 Cedar Glade, Dunnington, York YO19 5QZ. *T:* (01904) 481225; *e-mail:* david@djmhs.force9.co.uk.

SMITH, David John; Executive Chairman, Granada Learning, since 2006; Chairman, Sherston Publishing, since 2006; *b* 4 Oct. 1949; *s* of Frederick and Olive Smith; partner, Julia Stanton; one *s*. *Educ:* Durham Univ. (Teaching Cert.). Wolters Kluwer, NV: Chief Executive Officer: Wayland Publishers, 1995–2001; Stanley Thornes, 1992–2001; Educn/Learning, 1999–2001; Legal, Tax and Business Europe, 2001–02; CEO, Taylor & Francis Gp plc, 2002–04; Chm., T&F Informa plc, 2004–05. *Recreations:* horse-racing, gardening, tennis.

SMITH, David John Harry, CBE 1998; PhD; FRSC; Director, Research and Development, 1994–2001, Board Member, 1995–2001 and Chief Executive Officer, 1996–2001, Whatman plc; *b* 5 Aug. 1941; *s* of Harry Nelson Smith and Mabel Freda Smith (*née* Stanford); *m* 1963, Dorothy Patricia Evans; one *s* one *d*. *Educ:* Univ. of Aston (BSc Chem. 1963); Univ. of Western Ontario (PhD Organic Chem. 1967). FRSC 1982. Univ. Lectr, Chem. Dept, Univ. of Leicester, 1969–80; Res. Dir, Biosynth AG, Zürich, 1978–82; joined BP, 1980; Vice-Pres., R&D, BP America, 1987; Head, BP Gp Res. and Engrg, 1992. Non-exec. Dir, Murphy Oil Corp., 2001–. Member: Strategic Allocations Cttee, Nat. Sci. and Engrg Council, Canada, 1993–96; Technology Foresight Steering Cttee, 1994–96; EPSRC, 1994–2000; Chairman: LINK TCS (formerly LINK) Bd, 1996–2001; LINK Review, 2001–02; Vet. Lab. Agency Ownership Bd, DEFRA, 2006–. *Publications:* numerous scientific papers and patents. *Recreations:* educating palate, golf. *Address:* Iverston House, 20 Fitzroy Road, Fleet, Hants GU51 4JJ.

SMITH, David John Leslie, PhD; CEng, FRAeS; Director of Group Services, Defence Research Agency, 1991–94; *b* 8 Oct. 1938; *s* of Gertrude Mary and late Arthur George Smith; *m* 1962, Wendy Lavinia (*née* Smith); two *d*. *Educ:* Cinderford Tech. Coll.; N Glos Tech. Coll.; Coll. of Aeronautics (MSc); Univ. of London; rcds. Mech. Engrg Apprentice, Rotol Ltd, 1954–59; Nat. Gas Turbine Estabt, Min. of Aviation, 1961, Head of Turbomachinery Dept, 1973; RCDS 1979; Ministry of Defence (PE): Dir, Aircraft Mech. and Elect. Equipment, Controllerate of Aircraft, 1980–81; Head of Aero. Dept, RAE, 1981–84; Dep. Dir (Marine Technology), 1984–85, Dep. Dir (Planning), 1986–87, ARE; Hd, Defence Res. Study Team, MoD, 1988; Asst Under-Sec. of State (Civilian Management) (Specialists), MoD, 1988–91. *Publications:* contribs to learned jls on gas turbine technology and fluid mechanics. *Recreations:* garden (including exhibiting flowers), oil and watercolour painting. *Address:* Michaelchurch Court, St Owens Cross, Hereford, Herefordshire HR2 8LD.

SMITH, David S.; *see* Sands Smith.

SMITH, Dame Dela, DBE 2001; DL; Executive Director, Darlington Education Village, since 2006 (Chief Executive, 2004–06); *b* 10 Oct. 1952; *d* of John Henthorne Wood and Norah Wood (*née* Read); *m* 1976, Colin Smith. *Educ:* schs in York, Bristol and Cambridge; Durham Univ. (AdvDip); Middleton St George Coll. (Cert Ed). Teacher, Dinsdale Park Residential Sch., nr Darlington, 1975–84; Dep. Head Teacher, 1984, Headteacher, 1985–92, Mayfair Special Sch. (Severe Learning Difficulties); Headteacher, Beaumont Hill Special Educnl Needs Centre, subseq. Beaumont Hill Technol. Coll., Primary Sch. and Information, Communication and Technol. Centre, 1992–2004. DL Durham, 2002. *Recreations:* leisure pursuits, caravanning, walking, ski-ing, reading. *Address:* 20 West Green, Heighington, Co. Durham DL5 6RA. *T:* (01325) 314905.

SMITH, Delia, OBE 1995; cookery writer and broadcaster; *m* Michael Wynn Jones. Several BBC TV series; cookery writer, Evening Standard, later the Standard, 1972–85; columnist, Radio Times. Director: Norwich City FC, 1996–; Delia's Canary Catering, 1999–. FRTS 1996. Hon. Fellow, Liverpool John Moores, 2000; Hon. DLitt: Nottingham, 1996; UEA, 1999. Is a Roman Catholic. *Publications:* How to Cheat at Cooking, 1971; Country Fare, 1973; Recipes from Country Inns and Restaurants, 1973; Family Fare, book 1, 1973, book 2, 1974; Evening Standard Cook Book, 1974; Country recipes from "Look East", 1975; More Country Recipes from "Look East", 1976; Frugal Food, 1976; Book of Cakes, 1977; Recipes from "Look East", 1977; Food for our Times, 1978; Cookery Course, part 1, 1978, part 2, 1979, part 3, 1981, The Complete Cookery Course, 1982; A Feast for Lent, 1983; A Feast for Advent, 1983; One is Fun, 1985; (ed) Food Aid Cookery Book, 1986; A Journey into God, 1988; Delia Smith's Christmas, 1990; Delia Smith's Summer Collection, 1993; Delia Smith's Winter Collection, 1995; Delia's Red Nose Collection (Comic Relief), 1997; Delia's How to Cook, Book One, 1998, Book Two, 1999, Book Three, 2001; Delia's Chocolate Collection (Comic Relief), 2001; Delia's Vegetarian Collection, 2002; The Delia Collection: Soup, Chicken, Chocolate, Fish, 2003; Italian, Pork, 2004; Delia's Kitchen Garden, 2004; Baking, 2005; Puddings, 2006; How to Cheat at Cooking, 2008.

SMITH, Denis M.; *see* Mack Smith.

SMITH, Derek; Chief Executive, Hammersmith Hospitals NHS Trust, 2001–07; *b* 26 Sept. 1948; *s* of Arthur Edmund Smith and Hazel Smith (*née* Proudlove); *m* 1st, 1970, Carol Anne Susan Cunio (marr. diss. 2003); one *s* one *d*; 2nd, 2003, Ruth Patricia Harrison; one *s*. *Educ:* Univ. of Wales (BSc Hons Econs); Univ. of Strathclyde (Postgrad. Dip. in Russian Lang.). Gen. Manager, Frenchay Hosp., 1982–87; Dist Gen. Manager, S Beds HA, 1987–90; Chief Exec., King's Healthcare NHS Trust, 1990–99; Man. Dir, 1999–2001, Chm., 2000–01, London Underground Ltd. Chm., NHS Elect, 2004–06. Vis. Hon. Prof. in Strategic Mgt, Univ. of N London, 1994–; Vis. Lectr, Sch. of Econs, Univ. of Stockholm, 1995–98. *Recreations:* tennis, music, sailing, golf. *Address:* c/o Hammersmith Hospital, Du Cane Road, W12 0HS. *Club:* Royal Automobile.

SMITH, Derek B.; *see* Bryce-Smith.

SMITH, Derek Cyril; Under-Secretary, Export Credits Guarantee Department, 1974–87, retired; *b* 29 Jan. 1927; *s* of Albert Cyril and Edith Mary Elizabeth Smith; *m* 1st, 1949, Ursula Kulich (marr. diss. 1967); two *d*; 2nd, 1967, Nina Munday; one *s*. *Educ:* Pinner Grammar Sch.; St Catherine's Soc., Oxford. BA Mod. History 1951. Asst Principal, Min. of Materials, 1952–55; BoT, 1955–57: Asst Private Sec., Minister of State; Private Sec., Parly Sec.; Principal, ECGD, 1958–67; Asst Sec., BoT and DTI, 1967–72: Sec. to Lord Cromer's Survey of Capital Projects Contracting Overseas; Asst Sec., ECGD, 1972–74. *Recreation:* reading. *Address:* 1 Ashcombe Court, Ashcombe Lane, Ilminster, Somerset TA19 0ED.

SMITH, Derek Frank; Alternate Executive Director of the World Bank, and Counsellor (Overseas Develt), Washington, 1979–84; *b* 11 Feb. 1929; *s* of late Frank H. and Rose V. Smith; *m* 1954, Anne Carpenter (*d* 2007); one *s* one *d*. *Educ:* Chatham House Sch., Ramsgate. Served RAF, 1947–49. Colonial Office, 1949–66: Sec., Develt and Welfare Org. in WI, 1956–58; transf. to Min. of Overseas Develt, 1966; Financial Adviser, British Develt Div. in the Caribbean, 1966–68; Principal, India Sect., ODA, 1968–72; Asst Sec., 1972; Head of Southern African Develt Div., 1972–75; Establishment Officer, 1976–78, Head of UN Dept B, 1978–79, ODA. Consultant: ODA, 1985; World Bank, 1986–87. Chairman: Sevenoaks Area NT Association, 1992–96; Probus Club, Sevenoaks, 1997–98. *Address:* 3 The Close, Montreal Park, Sevenoaks, Kent TN13 2HE. *T:* (01732) 452534.

SMITH, Prof. Derek James, PhD; Professor of Infectious Disease Informatics, University of Cambridge, since 2007; *b* 27 Sept. 1959; *s* of Dorothy Mabel Smith. *Educ:* Pensby High Sch.; Univ. of Bradford (BSc); Univ. of New Mexico (MSc; PhD 1997). Software Engr, Texas Instruments, UK, 1982–83; Res. Scientist, Texas Instruments Res. Labs, USA, 1983–92; Graduate Fellow, Santa Fe Inst., 1992–97; Postdoctoral Fellow, Univ. of New Mexico, 1998–99; Res. Scientist, Dept of Virol., Erasmus Med. Centre, Rotterdam, 1999–; Chief Scientist, Popular Power Inc., San Francisco, 2000–01; Scientist, Eatoni Ergonomics, NY, 2001; Res. Associate, Dept of Zool., Univ. of Cambridge, 2003–07. Dir and Mem., Eur. Scientific Wkg Gp on Influenza, 2002– (Vice Pres.. Exec. Cttee, 2007–); Temp. Advr, WHO, 2005–. Dir's Pioneer Award, NIH, 2005. *Publications:* scientific papers in learned jls on evolution, immunol., virol., vaccination, computational biol., bioinformatics, epidemiology, public health, computer sci., computer design, integrated circuit design; patents on computer design and information encoding. *Address:* Department of Zoology, University of Cambridge, Downing Street, Cambridge CB2 3EJ.

SMITH, Desmond; *see* Smith, S. D.

SMITH, Dick K.; *see* King-Smith.

SMITH, Ven. Donald John; Archdeacon of Sudbury, 1984–91, Emeritus, since 1991; Hon. Canon of St Edmundsbury and Ipswich, 1973–91, Emeritus, since 1991; *b* 10 April 1926; *m* 1948, Violet Olive Goss (*d* 1999); two *s* (one *d* decd). *Educ:* Clifton Theological Coll.; Cardiff Law Sch., Univ. of Wales (LLM 1996). Deacon, 1953; priest, 1954; Assistant Curate: Edgware, 1953–56; St Margaret's, Ipswich, 1956–58; Vicar of St Mary, Hornsey Rise, Islington, 1958–62; Rector of Whitton, Ipswich, 1962–75; Rector of Redgrave cum Botesdale with The Rickinghalls, 1975–79; Archdeacon of Suffolk, 1975–84. HCF 1964. *Publications:* A Confirmation Course, 1974; (ed) Tourism and the Use of Church Buildings, 1983; Covenanting for Disunity, 1981; Thank you Lord for Alison, 1987; Straightforward and Simple: a guide for churchwardens, 1989; Fourteen Charges - and The Rest, 2006. *Recreations:* driving, foreign travel, chess, reading, photography, gardening, good food, dining out. *Address:* St Peter's Cottage, Stretton-on-Fosse, Moreton-in-Marsh, Glos GL56 9SE. *T:* (01608) 662790.

SMITH, Douglas Armitage, CB 2005; Chief Executive, Child Support Agency, 2000–05; *b* 8 April 1947; *s* of James and Joan Smith; *m* 1968, Maureen Buckroyd; one *s* one *d*. *Educ:* Leeds Central High Sch. Board of Inland Revenue: Asst Dir, IT, 1989–93; Director: Change, 1993–95; Self Assessment, 1995–98; Business Ops, 1998–2000. Pres., Assoc. of Inspectors of Taxes, 1986–88. *Recreations:* horse-racing, sport, reading, gym. *Club:* Boxmoor Social.

SMITH, Ven. Douglas Leslie B.; *see* Bartles-Smith.

SMITH, Drew; *see* Smith, F. D.

SMITH, Sir Dudley (Gordon), Kt 1983; DL; retired politician and management consultant; *b* 14 Nov. 1926; *o s* of late Hugh William and Florence Elizabeth Smith,

Cambridge; 1st marr. diss.; one *s* two *d*; *m* 2nd, 1976, Catherine Amos, *o d* of late Mr and Mrs Thomas Amos, Liverpool. *Educ:* Chichester High Sch., Sussex. Worked for various provincial and national newspapers, as journalist and senior executive, 1943–66; Asst News Editor, Sunday Express, 1953–59. Vice-Chm. Southgate Conservative Assoc., 1958–59; CC Middlesex, 1958–65; Chief Whip of Majority Group, 1961–63. A Divl Dir, Beecham Group, 1966–70. Contested (C) Camberwell-Peckham, 1955. MP (C) Brentford and Chiswick, 1959–66; Warwick and Leamington, 1968–97; contested (C) Warwick and Leamington, 1997. PPS to Sec. for Tech. Co-operation, 1963–64; an Opposition Whip, 1964–66; an Opposition Spokesman on Employment and Productivity, 1969–70; Parliamentary Under-Secretary of State: Dept of Employment, 1970–74; (Army) MoD, 1974. Vice Chm., Parly Select Cttee on Race Relations and Immigration, 1974–79. UK delegate to Council of Europe and WEU, 1979–97 (Sec.-Gen., European Democratic Group, 1983–96; Chm., WEU Defence Cttee, 1989–93; Pres., WEU Assembly, 1993–97; Hon. Associate, WEU, 1997; Hon. Associate, Council of Europe, 1998); a Founder Mem., CSCE Assembly, 1992. Sen. official observer, elecns in Turkey, Russia, Chile, Bulgaria, Slovenia and Azerbaijan for, variously, Council of Europe, CSCE, then OSCE, and EDG, 1983–. Promoted Town and Country Planning (Amendment) Act, 1977, as a private member. Governor, Mill Hill Sch., 1958–89; Chm., United & Cecil Club, 1975–80. Freeman, City of London. DL Warwickshire, 1988. Order of the Horseman of Madara, 1st cl. (Bulgaria), 1994; Comdr, Order of Isabella la Católica (Spain), 1994. *Publications:* Harold Wilson: A Critical Biography, 1964; etc. *Recreations:* books, travel, music, wild life and wilderness preservation. *Address:* Church Farm, Weston-under-Wetherley, near Leamington Spa, Warwicks CV33 9BY. *T:* (01926) 632352. *Club:* St Stephen's.

SMITH, Dugal N.; *see* Nisbet-Smith.

SMITH, Dr (Edward) Alistair, CBE 1982; Director, University of Aberdeen International Office, 1990–2002; *b* 16 Jan. 1939; *s* of Archibald Smith and Jean Milne Johnston. *Educ:* Aberdeen Grammar Sch.; Univ. of Aberdeen (MA, PhD); Univ. of Uppsala, Sweden. Lectr, Univ. of Aberdeen, 1963–88. Dir, Univ. of Aberdeen Develt Trust, 1982–90; Mem., Grampian Health Bd, 1983–91. Pres., Scottish Conservative and Unionist Assoc., 1979–81; Dep. Chm., Scottish Conservative Party, 1981–85. Member: Exec., Aberdeen and NE Council on Disability; Exec., Grampian ASH; Scottish Cttee, 1989–91, NE Scotland Regl Bd, 1991–92, NCC; SCOTVEC, 1989–92. *Publications:* (with R. E. H. Mellor) Europe: a geographical survey of the Continent, 1979; articles on Scandinavia, Europe and Scotland. *Recreations:* travel, photography, music. *Address:* 68A Beaconsfield Place, Aberdeen AB15 4AJ. *T:* (01224) 642932; *e-mail:* aberdeensmith@aol.com.

SMITH, Prof. Edwin, PhD; FRS 1996; Emeritus Professor, Manchester University School of Materials (formerly Materials Science Centre), since 2004 (Consultant and Hon. Fellow, Manchester University-UMIST Materials Science Centre, 1988–2004); *b* 28 July 1931; *s* of late Albert Edwin Smith and Sarah Ann Smith (*née* Toft); *m* 1958, Patricia Georgina Gale. *Educ:* Chesterfield Grammar Sch.; Nottingham Univ. (BSc); Sheffield Univ. (PhD); MSc Manchester. CEng, FIMMM. AEI Res. Lab., Aldermaston, 1955–61; CEGB Res. Lab., Leatherhead, 1961–68. Manchester University: Prof. of Metallurgy, UMIST Materials Science Centre, 1968–88; Dean, Faculty of Science, 1983–85; Pro-Vice-Chancellor, 1985–88. Vis. Scientist, Battelle Meml Inst., Columbus, Ohio, 1968. Consultant to industrial organisations in UK, USA, Canada. *Publications:* contribs to learned jls on materials science and engineering. *Recreations:* current interest in various sports; when younger, played cricket for Derbyshire Under 21s, ran 14 marathons (personal best, 2 hrs 47 mins, 1957). *Address:* Manchester University School of Materials, Grosvenor Street, Manchester M1 7HS. *T:* (0161) 306 3556.

SMITH, Elaine Agnes; Member (Lab) Coatbridge and Chryston, Scottish Parliament, since 1999; *b* 7 May 1963; *m* 1996, James Vann Smith; one *s*. *Educ:* St Patrick's High Sch., Coatbridge; Glasgow Coll. (BA Hons Social Sci. (Econs and Politics)); St Andrews Teacher Trng Coll. (PGCE); DPSM 1995. Teacher, 1986; work in retail industry, Women's Aid Advice Worker and supply teacher, 1987; Local Authy Homeless Officer and Urban Prog. Asst Co-ordinator, 1988–90; posts in local authy depts, Monklands DC and W Highland Regl Council, 1990–97; Volunteers Manager, 1997–98; Supply Teacher, 1999. *Recreations:* family life, reading, swimming, badminton. *Address:* Scottish Parliament, George IV Bridge, Edinburgh EH99 1SP. *T:* (0131) 348 5824.

SMITH, Elizabeth H.; *see* Hallam Smith.

SMITH, Elizabeth Jane; Member (C) Scotland Mid and Fife, Scottish Parliament, since 2007; *b* 27 Feb. 1960; *d* of James Smith and (Margaret) Thelma Smith (*née* Moncrieff). *Educ:* George Watson's Coll., Edinburgh; Univ. of Edinburgh (MA Hons Econs and Politics 1982; DipEd 1983). Teacher, George Watson's Coll., 1983–98; Schoolteacher Fellow Commoner, Corpus Christi Coll., Cambridge, 1992; Political Advr to Sir Malcolm Rifkind, 1998–2001; Hd, Chairman's Office, Scottish Cons. and Unionist Party, 2001–03; self-employed political consultant, 2003–05; pt-time teacher, George Watson's Coll., 2005–06. *Publications:* Outdoor Adventures, 2003; An Illustrated History of George Watson's Ladies' College, 2006. *Recreations:* cricket, hill-walking, photography, travel. *Address:* Stables Cottage, Woodend, Madderty PH7 3PA; *e-mail:* elizabeth.smith.msp@scottish.parliament.uk. *Club:* New (Edinburgh).

SMITH, Elizabeth Jean, OBE 2004; Secretary-General, Commonwealth Broadcasting Association, since 1994; *b* 15 Aug. 1936; *d* of Lt-Gen. Sir Robert Hay, KCIE; *m* 1960, Geoffrey Smith; one *s* one *d*. *Educ:* St George's Sch., Edinburgh; Univ. of Edinburgh (MA Hons Hist. 1958). BBC Radio: Studio Manager, 1958–61; News Producer, 1961–70; Current Affairs Producer, 1970–78; Producer for BBC Current Affairs TV, 1978–79; Sen. Asst, BBC Secretariat, 1979–81; BBC World Service: Asst Head, Central Talks and Features, 1981–84; Head, Current Affairs, 1984–87; Controller, English Services, 1987–94. Member: Council, RIIA, 1992–97; Bd, Population Communications Internat., 1994–2002; Bd, Internat. Trng and Res. Consultancies, 1994–98; Bd, Westminster Foundn for Democracy, 1998–2001; Communications and Inf. Cttee, UK Nat. Commn for UNESCO, 2006–. Chair, Voice of the Listener and Viewer Trust, 2006–08; Trustee: Oneworld Broadcasting Trust, 1994–2000; Commonwealth Human Rights Initiative, 1998–; Television Trust for the Envmt, 2000–04. Consumer columnist, The Listener, 1978–80. Fellow, Radio Acad., 1996 (Mem. Bd, 1990–94). *Publications:* (as Elizabeth Hay) Sambo Sahib: the story of Helen Bannerman, 1981; Sayonara Sanbo, 1993. *Recreations:* gardening, walking, travelling in the developing world. *Address:* Commonwealth Broadcasting Association, 17 Fleet Street, EC4Y 1AA. *T:* (020) 7583 5550, *Fax:* (020) 7583 5549. *Clubs:* Reform, Royal Commonwealth Society.

SMITH, Emma; author; *b* 21 Aug. 1923; *m* 1951, Richard Stewart-Jones (*d* 1957); one *s* one *d*. *Publications:* Maidens' Trip, 1948 (John Llewellyn Rhys Meml Prize, 1948); The Far Cry, 1949 (James Tait Black Meml Prize, 1949); Emily, 1959; Out of Hand, 1963; Emily's Voyage, 1966; No Way of Telling, 1972; The Opportunity of a Lifetime, 1978;

The Great Western Beach (memoir), 2008. *Address:* c/o Curtis Brown, 28–29 Haymarket, SW1Y 4SP.

SMITH, Sir (Eric) Brian, Kt 1999; PhD, DSc; FRSC; Vice-Chancellor, Cardiff University (formerly Principal, University of Wales College of Cardiff), 1993–2001; *b* 10 Oct. 1933; *s* of Eric Smith and Dilys Olwen (*née* Hughes); *m* 1st, 1957, Margaret Barr (marr. diss. 1978); two *s* one *d*; 2nd, 1983, Regina Arvidson Ball; two step *d*. *Educ:* Alun Grammar Sch., Mold; Wirral Grammar Sch.; Univ. of Liverpool (BSc; PhD 1957); MA Oxon 1960. DSc Oxon 1988. FRSC 1981. Res. Associate, Univ. of Calif, Berkeley, 1957–59; Oxford University: ICI Fellow, 1959–60; Lectr in Physical Chemistry, 1960–88; Member: Gen. Bd of Faculties, 1980–87 (Chm., 1985–87); Hebdomadal Council, 1985–93; St Catherine's College: Fellow, 1960–88; Master, 1988–93; Hon. Fellow, 1993; Dir, Isis Innovation, 1988–97. Vis. Prof., Univ. of Calif, Riverside, 1967; Vis. Lectr, Stanford Univ., 1983, 1984 and 1985; Priestley Lectr, RSC, 1986. Chm., Thermodynamics and Statistical Mechanics Section, RSC, 1979–83; Member Board: WDA, 1998–2002; HEFCW, 2003–; Dir, Higher Aims Ltd, 2002–. Vice-Chm., Oxford Soc. Cttee, 1988–2005; Trustee: Oxford Univ. Soc., 2005–06; Liverpool Sch. of Tropical Medicine, 2004–. Dir, Cardiff Internat. Fest. of Musical Theatre, 2001–07. Mem. Bd, Univ. of Glamorgan, 2002–06. Hon. Fellow, UWCM, 2003. Hon. DSc Glamorgan, 2000; Hon. LLD Wales, 2001. Pott's Medal, Univ. of Liverpool, 1969. *Publications:* (jtly) Virial Coefficients of Pure Gases and Mixtures, 1969, 2nd edn 1980; Basic Chemical Thermodynamics, 1973, 5th edn 2004; (jtly) Intermolecular Forces: origin and determination, 1981; (jtly) Forces between Molecules, 1986; papers in scientific jls. *Recreation:* mountaineering. *Address:* Appletree House, 2 Boults Lane, Old Marston, Oxford OX3 0PW. *Clubs:* Alpine; Gorphwysfa.

SMITH, Eric Norman, CMG 1976; HM Diplomatic Service, retired; British High Commissioner in The Gambia, 1979–81; *b* 28 Jan. 1922; *s* of late Arthur Sidney David Smith; *m* 1955, Mary Gillian Horrocks. *Educ:* Colfe's Sch., London. Served War, Royal Corps of Signals, 1941–46. Foreign Office, 1947–53; HM Embassy, Cairo, 1953–55; UK Delegn to the UN, New York, 1955–57; FO, 1957–60; HM Embassy, Tehran, 1960–64; FO, 1964–68; British Information Services, New York, 1968–71; FCO, 1971–75; Singapore, 1975–79. *Recreations:* music, photography. *Address:* Troodos, Castle Lane, Budleigh Salterton, Devon EX9 7AN.

SMITH, Prof. (Ernest) Alwyn, CBE 1986; PhD; Professor of Epidemiology and Social Oncology, University of Manchester, 1979–90; Chairman, Lancaster Health Authority, 1991–94; *b* 9 Nov. 1925; *s* of Ernest Smith and Constance Barbara Smith; *m* 1950, Doreen Preston; one *s* one *d*. *Educ:* Queen Mary's Sch., Walsall; Birmingham Univ. MB, PhD; FRCP 1970; FRCGP 1973; FFCM 1974. Served War, RM, 1943–46. Res. Fellow in Social Medicine, Birmingham Univ., 1952–55; WHO Vis. Lectr, Univ. of Malaya, 1956–58; Lectr, Univ. of St. Andrews, 1959–61; Sen. Lectr. Univ. of Edinburgh, 1961–66; First Dir, Social Paediatric Res. Gp, Glasgow, 1966–67; Prof. of Community Medicine, Univ. of Manchester, 1967–79. Pres., FCM, 1981–86. *Publications:* Genetics in Medicine, 1966; The Science of Social Medicine, 1968; (ed) Cancer Control, 1979; (ed) Recent Advances in Community Medicine, 1982; papers on epidemiological subjects in Lancet, British Jl of Epidemiol., etc. *Recreations:* music, bird watching, sailing. *Address:* Plum Tree Cottage, Arnside, Cumbria, via Carnforth LA5 0AH. *T:* (01524) 761976.

SMITH, Ewen Dale, FSAScot; Director, Hunterian Museum and Art Gallery, University of Glasgow, since 2006; *b* 14 Sept. 1946; *s* of Norman Smith and Greta Smith (*née* Holton); *m* 1976, Kathleen Ann Kane; two *d*. *Educ:* George Heriot's Sch., Edinburgh; Univ. Nacional Autónoma de México; Univ. of Glasgow (MA, MLitt). MCIPD 1992. Cost clerk, Scottish & Newcastle Breweries Ltd, 1964–69; Investment Analyst, Ivory & Sime, 1969–74; fund-raiser, UNA, 1980–82; Adminr, Open Univ., 1982–85; University of Glasgow: Adminr, CPD Unit, 1985–89; Univ. Staff Develt Service, 1989–94; Planning Unit Adminr, Academic Services, 1994–99; Dep. Dir, Hunterian Mus. and Art Gall., 1999–2006. Mem. Bd, Scottish Museums Council, 2007–. FSAScot 1988. Mem., Assoc. Certificated Field Archaeologists. *Publications:* general articles. *Recreations:* archaeological field surveying, hill-walking, listing things alphabetically, reading, waiting for Aberdeen FC's next European Final. *Address:* Hunterian Museum and Art Gallery, University of Glasgow, University Avenue, Glasgow G12 8QQ. *T:* (0141) 330 3711, *Fax:* (0141) 330 3617; *e-mail:* e.smith@museum.gla.ac.uk.

SMITH, Fiona Mary; *see* Watt, F. M.

SMITH, Sir Francis Graham-, Kt 1986; FRS 1970; Langworthy Professor of Physics, Manchester University, 1987–90, now Emeritus (Professor of Radio Astronomy, 1964–74 and 1981–87); Director, Nuffield Radio Astronomy Laboratories, 1981–88; Astronomer Royal, 1982–90; *b* 25 April 1923; *s* of Claud Henry and Cicely Winifred Smith; *m* 1945, Dorothy Elizabeth (*née* Palmer); three *s* one *d*. *Educ:* Epsom Coll.; Rossall Sch.; Downing Coll., Cambridge. Nat. Sci. Tripos, Downing Coll., 1941–43 and 1946–47; PhD Cantab 1952. Telecommunications Research Estab., Malvern, 1943–46; Cavendish Lab., 1947–64; 1851 Exhibr 1951–52; Warren Research Fellow of Royal Soc., 1959–64; Fellow of Downing Coll., 1953–64, Hon. Fellow 1970; Dir-Designate, 1974–75, Dir, 1976–81, Royal Greenwich Observatory. Vis. Prof. of Astronomy, Univ. of Sussex, 1975. Sec., Royal Astronomical Soc., 1964–71, Pres., 1975–77. Mem. Council and Physical Sec., 1988–94, Vice-Pres., 1990–94, Royal Soc.; For. Associate, RSSAf, 1988. Hon. DSc: QUB, 1986; Keele, 1987; Birmingham, 1989; TCD, 1990; Nottingham, 1990; Manchester, 1993; Liverpool, 2003; Salford, 2003. Royal Medal, Royal Soc., 1987; Glazebrook Medal, Inst. of Physics, 1991. *Publications:* Radio Astronomy, 1960; (with J. H. Thomson) Optics, 1971; Pulsars, 1977; (with Sir Bernard Lovell) Pathways to the Universe, 1988; (with A. G. Lyne) Pulsar Astronomy, 1990, 2nd edn 1998; (with B. F. Burke) Introduction to Radio Astronomy, 1997, 2nd edn 2002; (with T. A. King) Optics and Photonics, 2000, 2nd edn (with T. A. King and Dan Wilkins) 2007; papers in Monthly Notices of RAS, Nature and other scientific jls. *Recreations:* beekeeping, walking. *Address:* Jodrell Bank Observatory, Macclesfield, Cheshire SK11 9DL; Old School House, Henbury, Macclesfield, Cheshire SK11 9PH.

SMITH, Prof. Frank Thomas, FRS 1984; Goldsmid Professor of Applied Mathematics in the University of London, at University College London, since 1984; *b* 24 Feb. 1948; *s* of Leslie Maxwell Smith and Catherine Matilda Smith; *m* 1972, Valerie Sheila (*née* Hearn); three *d*. *Educ:* Bournemouth Grammar Sch.; Jesus Coll., Oxford (BA; DPhil); University College London. Research Fellow in Theoretical Aerodynamics Unit, Southampton, 1972–73; Lectr in Maths Dept, Imperial Coll., London, 1973–78; Vis. Scientist, Applied Mathematics Dept, Univ. of Western Ontario, Canada, 1978–79; Reader in Maths Dept, 1979–83, Prof. in Maths, 1983–84, Imperial Coll., London. Director: Lighthill Inst., 2006–; London TCC, 2007–. *Publications:* on applied mathematics, fluid mechanics, industrial modelling, biomedical modelling, computing and natural sciences, in jls. *Recreations:* the family, reading, music, sport. *Address:* Mathematics Department, University College London, Gower Street, WC1E 6BT. *T:* (020) 7679 2837.

SMITH, Frank William G.; see Glaves-Smith.

SMITH, (Fraser) Drew; Director, Food By Design (formerly Food Factory), since 1991; senior adviser on food strategy, London Docklands Development Corporation, 1995–98; *b* 30 March 1950; *s* of Frank and Beatrice Smith; *m* 1988, Susan Maloney; one *s* one *d.* *Educ:* Westminster School. Worked on Student magazine, 1967; IPC magazines, 1969–72; Westminster Press Newspapers, 1972–81. Editor, Good Food Guide, 1982–89; launched: Good Food Directory, 1985; Budget Good Food Guide, 1986–88; Head of Media Develt, Dir's Office, Consumers' Assoc., 1988–90; Publishing Dir, Alfresco Leisure Publications, 1990–92. Director: Taste Publishing; West India Co. Columnist, Guardian, 1982–; creator, TV Food File, Channel 4. Chm., Guild of Food Writers, 1990. Trustee, Jane Grigson Liby. Chief Judge, British Cheese Awards, 1995, 1996. Restaurant Writer of the Year, 1981, 1988. *Publications:* Modern Cooking, 1990; Food Watch, 1994; Baby Food Watch, 1995; Good Food, 1995; The Circus (novel), 1997; Food Industry and the Internet, 2001. *Recreations:* walking, music, cooking, people.

SMITH, Rt Hon. Sir Geoffrey J.; see Johnson Smith.

SMITH, Geoffrey John; writer and broadcaster; *b* Mich, USA, 23 Aug. 1943; *s* of Earl Willard Smith and Marian Kay Smith (*née* Eisele); *m* 1968, Lenore Ketola (marr. diss. 1985; she *d* 2003); *m* 1995, Janette Grant; one *s.* *Educ:* Central High Sch., Bay City, Mich; Univ. of Michigan (BA English 1966); Univ. of Wisconsin (Woodrow Wilson Fellow; MA English 1967). Musician, 1959–69; Instr in English, Eastern Michigan Univ., 1967–68; NDEA Title IV Fellow, Univ. of Virginia, 1970–73; freelance writer and lectr, 1973–93; Lectr in English and American Lit., City Univ., 1979–91, City Lit., 1986–92. Music Critic and Consultant, Country Life, 1977–; Arts Corresp., The Economist, 1988–; columnist, BBC Music Mag., 2001–; Presenter, BBC Radio 3, 1988–: documentaries, interviews and concerts; series on Gilbert and Sullivan; CD Review; Jazz Record Requests, 1991–. *Publications:* The Savoy Operas, 1983; Stéphane Grappelli, 1987. *Recreations:* tennis, jogging, family outings, 'gaping and dawdling' (Henry James). *Address:* BBC Radio 3, Broadcasting House, W1A 4WW. *T:* (020) 7765 4327, *Fax:* (020) 7765 4378.

SMITH, Prof. Geoffrey Lilley, PhD; FRS 2003; Professor of Virology and Wellcome Trust Principal Research Fellow, since 2000, Chairman, Department of Virology, since 2002, Imperial College London; *b* 23 July 1955; *s* of Irvine Battinson Smith and Kathleen Lilley Smith; *m* 1979, Tessa Marie Trico; two *s* two *d.* *Educ:* Bootham Sch., York; Univ. of Leeds (BSc Hons Microbiol./Biochem. 1977). Nat. Inst. for Med. Res., London (PhD 1981). Wellcome Trust Fellow, Div. of Virology, NIMR, London, 1980–81; Vis. Fellow, Lab. of Viral Diseases, Nat. Inst. of Allergy and Infectious Diseases, NIH, Bethesda, 1981–84; Lectr in Virology, Dept of Pathology, Univ. of Cambridge, 1985–89; Jenner Fellow, Lister Inst. of Preventive Medicine, 1988–92; Reader in Bacteriology, 1989–96, Prof. of Virology, 1996–2000, Sir William Dunn Sch. of Pathology, Univ. of Oxford; EPA Sen. Res. Fellow, Wadham Coll., Oxford, 1989–2000. Chairman: WHO Adv. Cttee for Variola Virus Res., 2004–07; Virology Div., Internat. Union of Microbiol Socs, 2005–08 (Vice-Chm., 2002–05); Mem., MRC Infection and Immunity Bd, 2004–March 2009; Royal Soc. Cttee on Scientific Aspects of Internat. Security, 2005–08; New Agents Cttee, CRUK, 2007–. Gov., Lister Inst. of Preventive Medicine, 2003–. FIBiol 2000; FMedSci 2000. Ed.-in-Chief, Jl of Gen. Virology, 2003–07. *Publications:* editor of several books and author of many book chapters and scientific papers, and several patents. *Recreations:* hockey, cricket, chess, bridge, gardening, carpentry, hill-walking. *Address:* Department of Virology, Faculty of Medicine, Imperial College London, St Mary's Campus, Norfolk Place, W2 1PG. *T:* (020) 7594 3972, *Fax:* (020) 7594 3973; *e-mail:* glsmith@ic.ac.uk.

SMITH, Geoffrey M.; see Maitland Smith.

SMITH, George D.; see Davey Smith.

SMITH, Prof. George David William, DPhil; FRS 1996; FRSC; CEng, FIMMM; CPhys, FInstP; Professor of Materials Science, since 1996 and Head of Department of Materials, 2000–05, University of Oxford; Fellow, Trinity College, Oxford, since 1991; *b* 28 March 1943; *s* of George Alfred William Smith and Grace Violet Hannah Dayton Smith; *m* 1968, Josephine Ann Halford; two *s.* *Educ:* St Benedict's Sch., Aldershot; Salesian Coll., Farnborough; Corpus Christi Coll., Oxford (Scholar; BA Hons Metallurgy 1965; MA, DPhil 1968). CEng 1978; CPhys, FInstP 1996; FIMMM (FIM 1996); FRSC 2003. SRC Res. Fellow, 1968–70; Jun. Res. Fellow, 1968–72, Res. Fellow, 1972–77, Wolfson Coll., Oxford; Oxford University: Res. Fellow, Dept of Metallurgy, 1970–75; Sen. Res. Fellow, 1975–77; Lectr in Metallurgy, 1977–92; George Kelley Reader in Metallurgy, 1992–96; Fellow, St Cross Coll., Oxford, 1977–91, Emeritus Fellow, 1991–. Adv. Prof., Chongqing Univ., China, 2005–; Hon. Prof., Univ of Sci. and Technol., Beijing, 2005–. Man. Dir, Oxford Nanoscience Ltd (formerly Kindbrisk Ltd), 1987–2002 (Chm., 2002–04); Chm., Polaron plc, 2004–06. Councillor (L), W Oxon DC, 1973–76. Co-Chm., UK Materials Congress, 1998. Mem., OST Foresight Panel for Materials, 1999–2003. Pres., Internat. Field Emission Soc., 1990–93; Member: Council, Inst. of Materials, Minerals and Mining (formerly of Materials), 1997–2004 (Vice-Pres., 2002–03); Council, Royal Soc., 2002–04. Freeman, Armourers' and Brasiers' Co., 1998 (Liveryman, 2003). Mem., European Acad. of Scis and Arts, 2006–. FRSA 1997. Sir George Beilby Medal and Prize, SCI, RSC, Inst. Metals, 1985; (jtly) Vanadium Award, 1985, Rosenhain Medal and Prize, 1991, Inst. of Metals; Nat. Innovative Measurement Award, DTI, 2004; Gold Medal, Acta Materialia Inc., 2005; Platinum Medal, IMMM, 2006. *Publications:* (with M. K. Miller) Atom Probe Microanalysis: principles and applications to materials problems, 1989 (trans. Russian 1993, Chinese 1994); (jtly) Atom Probe Field Ion Microscopy, 1996; numerous contribs to scientific jls. *Recreations:* walking, fishing, bird watching, travel. *Address:* Trinity College, Oxford OX1 3BH. *T:* (01865) 273700.

SMITH, Rt Hon. (George) Iain D.; see Duncan Smith.

SMITH, (George) Neil, CMG 1987; HM Diplomatic Service, retired; *b* 12 July 1936; *s* of George Smith and Ena (*née* Hill); *m* 1956, Elvi Vappu Hämäläinen; one *s* one *d.* *Educ:* King Edward VII Sch., Sheffield. Joined HM Foreign (subseq. Diplomatic) Service, 1953; served RAF, 1954–56; Foreign Office, 1957; Rangoon, 1958–61; 2nd Sec., Berne, 1961–65; Diplomatic Service Administration, 1965–66; 1st Sec., CO, 1966–68; British Mil. Govt, Berlin, 1969–73; FCO, 1973–77; Counsellor (Commercial), Helsinki, 1977–80; Consul-Gen., Zürich and Principality of Liechtenstein, 1980–85; Head of Trade Relations and Exports Dept, FCO, 1985–87; RCDS, 1988; Ambassador to Finland, 1989–95. Sec. Gen., Soc. of London Art Dealers, 1996–2001; Sec., British Art Market Fedn, 1996–2001. *Recreations:* music, golf. *Address:* 5 Linton Falls, Linton in Craven, N Yorks BD23 6BQ.

SMITH, Prof. Gerald Stanton, FBA 2001; Professor of Russian, 1986–2003, and Fellow of New College, 1986–2003, now Emeritus, University of Oxford; *b* 17 April 1938; *s* of Thomas Arthur Smith and Ruth Annie Stanton; *m* 1st, 1961, Frances Wetherill (marr. diss. 1981); one *s* one *d;* 2nd, 1982, Barbara Heldt; one step *s* one step *d.* *Educ:* Stretford Grammar Sch.; Sch. of Slavonic and E European Studies, Univ. of London (BA 1964 PhD 1977); DLitt Oxon 1996. Lectr in Russian, Univ. of Nottingham, 1964–71, Univ. of Birmingham, 1971–79; Univ. Research Fellow, Univ. of Liverpool, 1980–82. Visiting Professor: Indiana Univ., 1984; Univ. of California, Berkeley, 1984; Private Scholar, Social Scis and Humanities Res. Council, Canada, 1985; John Simon Guggenheim Meml Fellow, 1986. Pres., MHRA, 2000. *Publications:* (ed) Alexander Galich, Songs and Poems, 1983; Songs to Seven Strings, 1984; Russian Inside and Out, 1989; (ed) D. S. Mirsky, Uncollected Writings on Russian Literature, 1989; Contemporary Russian Poetry: a bilingual anthology, 1993; D. S. Mirsky: Letters to P. P. Suvchinskii, 1995; (co-ed and trans.) M. L. Gasparov, A History of European Versification, 1996; (ed and trans.) Boris Slutsky, Things That Happened, 1999; D. S. Mirsky: a Russian-English life, 2000; Vzglyad izvne: Izbrannye stat'i o russkoi poezii i poetike, 2002; papers in learned jls. *Recreation:* jazz music. *Address:* 15 Dale Close, Oxford OX1 1TU.

SMITH, Geraldine; see Smith, M. G.

SMITH, Gilbert, PhD; writer; Member of Board, National Patient Safety Agency, 2001–05 (Acting Chairman, 2005); Vice Chairman, Northern Stage, 2004 (Board Member, 2002). *Educ:* Brentwood Sch., Essex; Univ. of Leeds (BA Hons 1966); Univ. of Essex (MA 1967); Univ. of Aberdeen (PhD 1973). Research Fellow and Attached Worker, MRC Medical Sociology Unit, Univ. of Aberdeen, 1969–73; Res. Advr, Central Research Unit, Scottish Office, Edinburgh, 1973–75; Sen. Lectr, then Reader, Dept of Social Admin and Social Work, Univ. of Glasgow, 1975–81; University of Hull: Prof. of Social Admin, 1981–96; Head, Dept of Social Admin, 1982–84; Foundn Head, Dept of Social Policy and Professional Studies, 1984–85; Dean, Faculty of Social Scis, 1985–87; Vice-Chancellor and Chief Exec., Univ. of Northumbria at Newcastle, 1996–2001. Sen. Travelling Scholar in Australia, ACU, 1988. Chm., E Yorks HA, then E Riding Health, 1990–93. Dep. Dir, R&D, DoH and NHS Exec., 1993–96. Foundn Trustee, Social Care Inst. for Excellence, 2001–02. Numerous board appts, directorships, commns and adv. posts with univs, res. councils, res. funding agencies, publishers, foundns, arts bodies, Govt depts, ACU, UUK and British Council. Mem., Corbridge with Halton and Newton Hall PCC, 2002–. Mem., Corbridge Allotment Soc., 2001–. Editor, Jl of Social Policy, 1991–93. DUniv Moscow State Univ. of Mgt, 1998. *Publications:* Social Work and the Sociology of Organisations, 1970, 2nd rev. edn 1979 (trans. Japanese and Korean); Social Need: policy practice and research, 1980 (trans. Japanese); (with C. Cantley) Assessing Health Care: a study in organisational evaluation, 1985; numerous book chapters; contrib. articles in professional and academic jls of social policy, sociology, social work and healthcare.

SMITH, Godfrey, FRSL; writer; *b* 12 May 1926; *s* of Reginald Montague Smith and Ada May Smith (*née* Damen); *m* 1951, Mary (*d* 1997), *d* of Jakub Schoenfeld, formerly of Vienna; three *d.* *Educ:* Surbiton County Sch.; Eggar's Grammar Sch.; Worcester Coll., Oxford (MA; Pres. of Oxford Union Soc. 1950). RAF, 1944–47. Joined Sunday Times as PA to Lord Kemsley, 1951; News Editor, 1956; Asst Editor, 1959; Editor, Magazine, 1965–72, Associate Editor, 1972–91; Editor, Weekly Review, 1972–79; columnist, 1979–2004; Director, 1968–81. Regent's Lectr, Univ. of California, 1970. FRSL 1995. *Publications:* novels: The Flaw in the Crystal, 1954; The Friends, 1957; The Business of Loving, 1961 (Book Society Choice); The Network, 1965; Caviare, 1976; *non-fiction:* The English Companion, 1984; The English Season, 1987; The English Reader, 1988; *anthologies:* The Best of Nat Gubbins, 1978; A World of Love, 1982; Beyond the Tingle Quotient, 1982; How it Was in the War, 1989; Take the Ball and Run, 1991. *Recreation:* chums. *Address:* Village Farmhouse, Charlton, Malmesbury, Wilts SN16 9DL. *T:* (01666) 822479; 10 Kensington Park Mews, W11 2EY. *T:* (020) 7727 4155. *Clubs:* Garrick, Savile, Royal Air Force, MCC; Leander.

SMITH, Godric William Naylor, CBE 2004; Director of Communications, Olympic Delivery Authority, since 2006; *b* 29 March 1965; *s* of Eric and Phyl Smith; *m* 1991, Julia Barnes; two *s.* *Educ:* Perse Sch., Cambridge; Worcester Coll., Oxford (MA Lit Hum 1987). Appeals Manager, SANE, 1988–91; Sen. Inf. Officer, 1991–94, Chief Press Officer, 1995, DoH; Prime Minister's Office, 1996–2006: Dep. Press Sec., 1998–2001; Prime Minister's Official Spokesman, 2001–03; Hd of Strategic Communications, 2004–06. *Recreations:* watching Cambridge United, family. *Address:* (office) 23rd Floor, 1 Churchill Place, E14 5LN.

SMITH, Prof. Gordon Campbell Sinclair, MD, PhD; Professor of Obstetrics and Gynaecology, University of Cambridge, since 2001; *b* 11 May 1965; *s* of Robert (Roy) Smith and Peggy Smith; *m* 1986, Nicola Wilkinson; two *d.* *Educ:* Bankhead Primary Sch., Glasgow; Stonelaw High Sch., Glasgow; Univ. of Glasgow (BSc 1st Cl. Hons Physiol. 1986; MB ChB 1990; MD 1995; PhD 2001). MRCOG 1996. House officer and registrar appts, Glasgow, 1990–92 and 1993–96; Wellcome Trust Research Fellow: Dept of Physiol., Univ. of Glasgow, 1992–93; Dept of Physiol., Cornell Univ., Ithaca, NY, 1996–99; trainee in Maternal-Fetal Medicine, Glasgow, 1999–2001. *Publications:* contrib. numerous res. papers on physiol., pharmacol. and obstetrics to learned jls, incl. Lancet, BMJ, New England Jl of Medicine, Jl of Amer. Med. Assoc., Nature. *Recreations:* fly fishing, walking, reading. *Address:* Department of Obstetrics and Gynaecology, Box 223, The Rosie Hospital, Robinson Way, Cambridge CB2 2SW. *T:* (01223) 336871, *Fax:* (01223) 215327; *e-mail:* gcss2@cam.ac.uk.

SMITH, Gordon Edward C.; see Connell-Smith.

SMITH, Gordon James, CBE 2004; Resident Director for Scotland, IBM, since 1997; *b* 17 Dec. 1947; *s* of Stanley and Agnes Smith; *m* 2001, Margaret McKenzie; two *s* two *d.* *Educ:* Univ. of Stirling (BA 2003). IBM: joined 1970; various appts, 1970–97. Chairman: Business Enterprise Trusts, 1996–99; CBI Scotland, 2003–05; Regl Chms Cttee, CBI, 2005–06. Dir, Dunfermline Bldg Soc., 2006–. Board Member: Scottish Qualifications Authy, 2000–04; Young Enterprise Scotland, 2000–04; Trust Bd, Scottish Chamber Orch., 2000–04. *Recreations:* golf, travel, cooking. *Address:* IBM, 21 St Andrew Square, Edinburgh EH2 1AY. *T:* (0131) 558 4311. *Club:* New (Edinburgh).

SMITH, Very Rev. Graham Charles Morell; Dean of Norwich, since 2004; *b* 7 Nov. 1947; *s* of Philip and Helen Smith; *m* 1975, Carys Evans; one *s* two *d.* *Educ:* Whitgift Sch., Croydon; Univ. of Durham (BA Hons Theology 1974); Westcott House, Cambridge. Ordained deacon, 1976, priest, 1977; Asst Curate, All Saints, Tooting Graveney, 1976–80; Team Vicar, St Paul's, Thamesmead, 1980–87; Team Rector, Kidlington with Hampton Poyle, 1987–97; Rural Dean of Oxford, 1988–94; Rector of Leeds, 1997–2004; Hon. Canon, Ripon Cathedral, 1997–2004. *Recreations:* restoring old houses, theatre and cinema, biography, music. *Address:* The Deanery, The Close, Norwich, Norfolk NR1 4EG. *T:* (01603) 218302.

SMITH, Grahame; General Secretary, Scottish Trades Union Congress, since 2006; *b* 8 Jan. 1959; *s* of Thomas Smith and Joyce Smith; partner, Liz Campbell; two *s.* *Educ:* Strathclyde Univ. (BA Hons). Asst Sec., 1986–96, Dep. Gen. Sec., 1996–2006, Scottish

TUC. *Address:* Scottish Trades Union Congress, 333 Woodlands Road, Glasgow G3 6NG. *T:* (0141) 337 8100, *Fax:* (0141) 337 8101; *e-mail:* gsmith@stuc.org.uk.

SMITH, Prof. Hamilton Othanel; Scientific Director, Synthetic Biology and Bioenergy Groups, J. Craig Venter Institute, San Diego, since 2006 (Scientific Director, Institute for Biological Energy Alternatives, 2002–06); *b* 23 Aug. 1931; *s* of Bunnie Othanel Smith and Tommie Harkey Smith; *m* 1957, Elizabeth Anne Bolton; four *s* one *d*. *Educ:* Univ. of Illinois; Univ. of California (AB); Johns Hopkins Univ. Sch. of Medicine (MD). Research Associate, Dept of Human Genetics, Univ. of Michigan, 1964–67; Johns Hopkins University School of Medicine: Asst Prof. of Microbiology, 1967–69; Associate Prof. of Microbiology, 1969–73; Prof. of Microbiology, 1973–81; Prof. of Molecular Biology and Genetics, 1981–2002; Celera Genomics Corp., 1998–2002. During sabbatical leave in Zürich, worked in collaboration with Prof. Dr M. L. Birnstiel, Inst. für Molekularbiologie II der Univ. Zürich, 1975–76; Vis. Prof., Inst. of Molecular Pathol., Vienna, 1990–91. Nobel Prize in Medicine (jtly), 1978. *Publications:* A restriction enzyme from *Hemophilus influenzae:* I. Purification and general properties (with K. W. Wilcox), in Jl Mol. Biol. *51*, 379, 1970; A restriction enzyme from *Hemophilus influenzae:* II. Base sequence of the recognition site (with T. J. Kelly), in Jl Mol. Biol. *51*, 393, 1970. *Recreations:* piano, classical music. *Address:* J. Craig Venter Institute, 10355 Science Center Drive, San Diego, CA 92121, USA.

SMITH, Prof. Harry, CBE 1993; PhD, DSc; FRCPath; FRS 1979; FIBiol; Professor and Head, Department of Microbiology, University of Birmingham, 1965–88, now Emeritus Professor; *b* 7 Aug. 1921; *s* of Harry and Annie Smith; *m* 1947, Janet Mary Holmes; one *s* one *d*. *Educ:* Northampton Grammar Sch.; University Coll. (of London) at Nottingham. BPharm, BScChem (1st Cl. Hons), PhD, DSc London. Analyst, Boots Pure Drug Co., Nottingham, 1942–45; Asst Lectr, then Lectr, Dept of Chemistry, UCL at Nottingham, 1945–47; Microbiological Research Establishment, Porton: Sen. Scientific Officer, 1947; Principal Sci. Officer, 1951; Sen. Prin. Sci. Officer (Research Merit), 1956; Dep. Chief Sci. Officer (Res. Merit), 1964. Visiting Professor: Dept of Bacteriology, Univ. of Calif, Berkeley, USA, 1964, UCLA, 1972; (summer) Dept of Microbiol., Univ. of Washington, Seattle, USA, 1977, Univ. of Michigan, Ann Arbor, 1981, TCD, 1991. Society for General Microbiology: Mem. Council, 1960–64; Meetings Sec., 1964–68; Treas., 1968–75; Pres., 1975–78; Hon. Mem., 1986; Treas., Fedn of Europ. Microbiol Socs, 1975–82; Pres. and Chm., Organising Cttee, 14th (1986) Internat. Congress of Microbiology, Manchester. Member: Adv. Cttee on Dangerous Pathogens, 1985–88; PHLS Bd, 1985–89; Defence Scientific Adv. Council, 1987–93; Council, Royal Soc., 1989–91; NATO Adv. Panel, Security-related Civil Sci. and Tech., 1999–2004; Assessor, AFRC, 1990–94. Lectures: Amer. Soc. for Microbiol., 1984; Australian Soc. for Microbiol., 1985; Fred Griffith, 1989, Jubilee (50 yrs), 1995, Soc. for Gen. Microbiol.; Leeuwenhoek, Royal Soc., 1991. Hon. MRCP 1986; Hon. ARCVS 1993. Hon. DSc: Leicester, 1992; Nottingham, 2001. Bledisloe Vet. Award, RASE, 1992; Stuart Mudd Award, Internat. Union of Microbiol. Socs, 1994. *Publications:* over 350 papers in jls and books, mainly on mechanisms of microbial (bacterial, viral and fungal) pathogenicity. *Recreation:* interest in farming. *Address:* The Medical School, University of Birmingham, Birmingham B15 2TT. *T:* (0121) 414 6920; *e-mail:* hsmithcbefrsbham@btopenworld.com. *Club:* Athenæum.

SMITH, Prof. Harry, FRS 2000; Special Professor in Photobiology, University of Nottingham, since 2001; *b* 19 Sept. 1935; *s* of Joseph and Alice Smith; *m* 1961, Elinor Anne Chandler; one *s* two *d*. *Educ:* Univ. of Manchester (BSc 1959; DSc 1976); Univ. of Wales (PhD 1962). Theresa Seessel Res. Fellow, Yale Univ., 1962–64; Asst Lectr, Birkbeck Coll., London Univ., 1964–65; Lecturer in Botany: Queen Mary Coll., London Univ., 1965–68; Manchester Univ., 1968–71; Prof. of Plant Physiology, Nottingham Univ., 1971–78; Prof. of Botany, Univ. of Leicester, 1978–2001. Miller Foundn Fellow, Univ. of California, Berkeley, 1995. Corresp. Life Mem., Amer. Soc. Plant Physiologists, 1998. Gov., Papworth Hosp. NHS Foundn Trust, 2004–. Hon. DSc: Marseilles, 1978; Teesside, 2001. Chief Ed., Plant, Cell and Envmt, 1975–2001; Founding Editor: Molecular Ecology, 1990–; Global Change Biology, 1995–2002. *Publication:* Phytochrome and Photomorphogenesis, 1975. *Recreations:* garden design, painting in acrylics (abstract). *Address:* c/o Division of Plant Science, University of Nottingham, Sutton Bonington Campus, Loughborough LE12 5RD.

SMITH, Harvey; *see* Smith, R. H.

SMITH, Helen Sylvester, MA; Headmistress, Perse School for Girls, Cambridge, 1989–2001; *b* 7 Jan. 1942; *d* of late S. J. Smith and K. R. Smith. *Educ:* King Edward VI High Sch. for Girls, Birmingham; St Hilda's College, Oxford (BA 1963, MA 1967 Maths); Hughes Hall, Cambridge (PGCE 1964). Cheltenham Ladies' College, 1964–69; International School of Brussels, 1969–71; Perse Sch. for Girls, 1971–2001 (Dep. Head, 1979–82, 1988–89). FRSA. *Recreations:* music, gardening. *Address:* 6A Cavendish Avenue, Cambridge CB1 7US. *T:* (01223) 249200.

SMITH, Prof. Henry Sidney, FBA 1985; Edwards Professor of Egyptology, 1970–86, Head of Department of Egyptology, 1970–88, University College London, now Professor Emeritus; *b* 14 June 1928; *s* of Prof. Sidney Smith, FBA, and of Mary, *d* of H. W. Parker; *m* 1961, Hazel Flory Leeper (*d* 1991). *Educ:* Merchant Taylors' Sch., Northwood; Christ's Coll., Cambridge (MA); DLit London, 1987. Lectr in Egyptology, Univ. of Cambridge, 1954–63; Budge Fellow in Egyptology, Christ's Coll., Cambridge, 1955–63; Reader in Egyptian Archaeology, University Coll. London, 1963–70. Field Dir for Egypt Exploration Soc. in Nubia, 1961, 1964–65, and at Saqqara and Memphis, Egypt, 1970–88. *Publications:* Preliminary Reports of the Egypt Exploration Society's Nubian Survey, 1962; A Visit to Ancient Egypt, 1974; The Fortress of Buhen: the inscriptions, 1976; The Fortress of Buhen: the archaeological report, 1979; (with W. J. Tait) Saqqara Demotic Papyri I, 1983; The Anubieion at Saqqara, Vol. I (with D. G. Jeffreys), 1988, Vol. II (with L. L. Giddy), 1992; (with Sue Davies): The Sacred Animal Necropolis at North Saqqara: the falcon complex and catacomb, the archaeological report, 2005; The Sacred Animal Necropolis at North Saqqara: the main temple complex, 2006; articles in Kush, Jl of Egyptian Arch., Orientalia, Rev. d'Egyptologie, Bull. Inst. Français d'Arch. Or., Z für Äg. Sprache und Altertümskunde, etc.

SMITH, Maj.-Gen. Hugh M.; *see* Macdonald-Smith.

SMITH, Iain-Mór L.; *see* Lindsay-Smith.

SMITH, Iain William; Member (Lib Dem) North East Fife, Scottish Parliament, since 1999; *b* 1 May 1960; *s* of William Smith and Jane Allison Smith (*née* Farmer). *Educ:* Bell Baxter High Sch., Cupar; Newcastle upon Tyne Univ. (BA Hons Politics and Econs). Fife Regional Council: Mem. (Lib Dem), 1982–96; Sec., Alliance Gp, 1982–86; Leader of Opposition, 1986–96; Mem. (Lib Dem), and Leader of Opposition, Fife Council, 1995–99. Dep. Minister for Parlt, Scottish Exec., 1999–2000; spokesman on local govt and transport, 2003–05, on education, 2005–. Scottish Parliament: Convener: Procedures Cttee, 2003–05; Educn Cttee, 2005–07; Mem., Eur. and External Affairs Cttee, 2007–. Convener, Lib Dems Scottish Parly Party, 2007–; Chm., Scottish Lib Dem Gen. Election Cttee, 2007–. *Recreations:* sport (mainly football and cricket), cinema, travel, reading. *Address:* Scottish Parliament, Edinburgh EH99 1SP. *T:* (0131) 348 5817; (office) 16 Millgate, Cupar, Fife KY15 5EG. *T:* (01334) 656361.

SMITH, Prof. Ian Edward, MD; FRCP, FRCPE; Professor of Cancer Medicine, Institute of Cancer Research, University of London, since 2000; Consultant Cancer Physician, since 1978, and Head of Breast Unit, since 2003, Royal Marsden Hospital, London; *b* 16 May 1946; *s* of late David Nicol Smith and Nettie, (Bunty), Thompson Smith (*née* Millar); *m* 1978, Suzanne Dorothy Mackey; three *d*. *Educ:* High Sch. of Dundee; Edinburgh Univ. (BSc Hons 1968; MB ChB 1971; MD 1978). FRCPE 1984; FRCP 1988. House Physician, SHO, then Registrar, Royal Infirmary, Edinburgh, 1971–73; Med. Registrar, Royal Marsden Hosp., London, 1973–75; Res. Fellow, Inst. of Cancer Res., London, 1975–76; UICC Travelling Fellow, Harvard Med. Sch., Boston, 1976–77; Lectr, Royal Marsden Hosp., 1977–78; Head of Section of Medicine, Inst. of Cancer Res., 1994–; Head of Lung Unit, 1994–2001, Med. Dir, 2000–03, Royal Marsden Hosp. Lectures worldwide on breast cancer and new cancer therapies. Chairman: Assoc. of Cancer Physicians, 1995–98; UKCCCR Lung Gp, 1999–; NCRI Lung Clinical Trials Gp, 2000–03; British Breast Gp; UK Breast Intergroup. Member: Amer. Soc. of Clin. Oncology, 1978; British Assoc. for Cancer Res., 1978; Eur. Soc. of Med. Oncology, 1991. *Publications:* (jtly) Autologous Bone Marrow Transplantation, 1984; (jtly) Medical Management of Breast Cancer, 1991; multiple papers, articles and contribs to books on breast cancer. *Recreations:* ski-ing, supporting Chelsea, reading. *Address:* Royal Marsden Hospital, Fulham Road, SW3 6JJ. *T:* (020) 8661 3280; Royal Marsden Hospital, Downs Road, Sutton, Surrey SM2 5PT.

SMITH, Ian Knight; HM Diplomatic Service, retired; Counsellor and Deputy Head of Mission, Berne, 1993–97; *b* 18 June 1938; *m* 1st, 1964, Glenys Audrey Hayter (*d* 1981); one *s*; 2nd, 1989, Ellen Ragnhild Sweet-Escott; one *s* one *d*. FCO, 1962; Mexico City, 1964; Second Secretary: Calcutta, 1967; Caracas, 1969; First Secretary: FCO, 1972; UKREP Brussels, 1982; FCO, 1987; on secondment as Counsellor to EEC, 1989, to DSS, 1991.

SMITH, Ian Richard; Chief Executive, Taylor Woodrow plc, since 2007; *b* 22 Jan. 1954; *s* of Albert and Drusilla Smith; *m* 1989, Caroline Firstbrook; three *c*. *Educ:* St Edmund Hall, Oxford (MA Hons); Univ. of Harvard (MBA high dist.). Gen. Manager, Jordan, Royal Dutch Shell, 1978–86; Chief Exec., Europe, Monitor (strategy consulting), 1986–98; Chief Exec., Europe, Exel (Transportation), 1998–2004; CEO, General Healthcare, 2004–06. *Publication:* Mosquito Pathfinder, 2002. *Recreations:* sports, politics, history. *Address:* Taylor Woodrow plc, 2 Princes Way, Solihull, West Midlands B91 3ES. *Club:* Royal Automobile.

See also Prof. S. K. Smith.

SMITH, Prof. Ian William Murison, PhD; FRS 1995; CChem, FRSC; Senior Research Fellow, Department of Chemistry, University of Cambridge, since 2002; Mason Professor of Chemistry, University of Birmingham, 1991–2002, now Emeritus; *b* 15 June 1937; *s* of William Murison Smith and Margaret Moir Smith; *m* 1961, Susan Morrish; two *s* two *d*. *Educ:* Giggleswick Sch.; Christ's Coll., Cambridge (BA, MA, PhD). Cambridge University: ICI Res. Fellow, 1965–66; Demonstrator, 1966–71, Lectr, 1971–85, in Physical Chem.; Christ's College: Res. Fellow, 1963–66, Fellow, 1966–85; Tutor, 1968–77; Dir of Studies, 1972–85; Fellow Commoner, 2003–; University of Birmingham: Prof. of Chemistry, 1985–2002; Head, Sch. of Chem., 1989–93, 2001. Visiting Professor: Univ. of California, Berkeley, 1980, 1996; Univ. of Rennes I, 1999; Jt Inst. in Lab. Astrophysics Fellow, Univ. of Colorado, 2000. Stauffer Dist. Lectr, USC, 2000; Wilhelm Jost Meml Lectr, Germany, 2003. Royal Society of Chemistry: Liversidge Lectr, 2001–02; Pres., Faraday Div., 2001–03; Special Award for reaction kinetics, 1982; Tilden Medal, 1983; Polanyi Medal, 1990. Hon. Dr rer. nat. Duisburg-Essen. EU Descartes Prize, 2000. *Publications:* Kinetics and Dynamics of Elementary Gas Reactions, 1980; (ed) Physical Chemistry of Fast Reactions: reaction dynamics, 1980; (ed) Modern Gas Kinetics, 1987; (ed) Low Temperatures and Cold Molecules, 2008; numerous contribs to learned jls. *Recreations:* occasional golf, reading, theatre, walking, gardening under instruction. *Address:* University Chemical Laboratories, Lensfield Road, Cambridge CB2 1EW; 36 Grantchester Road, Cambridge CB3 9ED.

SMITH, Prof. Ivor Ramsay, FREng; Professor of Electrical Power Engineering, Loughborough University (formerly Loughborough University of Technology), since 1974; *b* 8 Oct. 1929; *s* of Howard Smith and Elsie Emily Smith; *m* 1962, Pamela Mary Voake; three *s*. *Educ:* Univ. of Bristol (BSc, PhD, DSc), CEng, FIET (FIEE 1974); FREng (FEng 1988). Design and Develt Engr, GEC, Birmingham, 1956–59; Lectr, Sen. Lectr, Reader, Univ. of Birmingham, 1959–74; Loughborough University of Technology: Hd, Dept of Electronic and Electrical Engrg, 1980–90; Dean of Engrg, 1983–86; Pro-Vice-Chancellor, 1987–91. Director: Loughborough Consultants Ltd, 1980–; E Midlands Regl Technology Network, 1989–. Ind. Mem., Defence Scientific Adv. Council, 2003–. *Publications:* (jtly) Magnetocumulative Generators, 2000; Explosively Driven Pulsed Power, 2005; about 400 technical papers and articles on range of power engrg topics, incl. the efficient computation of power supply systems and the prodn, processing and application of large pulses of electrical energy. *Recreations:* gardening, walking, reading. *Address:* Department of Electronic and Electrical Engineering, Loughborough University, Loughborough, Leics LE11 3TU. *T:* (01509) 227005.

SMITH, Jack, ARCA 1952; artist; *b* 18 June 1928; *s* of John Edward and Laura Smith; *m* 1956, Susan Craigie Halkett. *Educ:* Sheffield College of Art; St Martin's School of Art; Royal College of Art. Exhibitions: Whitechapel Art Gallery, 1959, 1971; Beaux Arts Gallery, 1952–58; Matthiesen Gallery, 1960, 1963; Catherine Viviano Gallery, New York, 1958, 1961; Pittsburgh International, 1955, 1957, 1964; Grosvenor Gallery, 1965; Marlborough Gallery, 1968; Konsthallen, Gothenburg, Sweden, 1968; Hull Univ., 1969; Bear Lane Gallery, Oxford, 1970; Whitechapel Gall., 1970; Redfern Gall., 1973 and 1976; Serpentine Gall., 1978; Fischer Fine Art, London, 1981, 1983; British Painting, Museo Municipal, Madrid, 1983; Flowers East Gall., London, 1990, 1991, 1992, 1994, 1996, 2000; Flowers Central, 2003, 2007. Designer, sets and costumes: Carmen Arcadiae Mechanicae Perpetuum, Ballet Rambert, 1986; Pursuit, Royal Ballet, 1987. Guggenheim Award (Nat.), 1960. Work in permanent collections: Tate Gallery; Arts Council of Great Britain; Contemporary Art Society; British Council. *Relevant publications:* Jack Smith: a painter in pursuit of marvels, by Norbert Lynton, 2000; The Art of Jack Smith, by Robert Heller, 2007. *Address:* 29 Seafield Road, Hove, Sussex BN3 2TP. *T:* (01273) 738312.

SMITH, Rt Hon. Jacqueline Jill, (Jacqui); PC 2003; MP (Lab) Redditch, since 1997; Secretary of State for the Home Department, since 2007; *b* 3 Nov. 1962; *d* of Michael and Jill Smith; *m* 1987, Richard James Timney; two *s*. *Educ:* Hertford Coll., Oxford (BA Hons PPE); Worcester Coll. of Higher Education (PGCE). Res. Asst, Terry Davis, MP, 1984–85; Teacher: Arrow Vale High Sch., Redditch, 1986–88; Worcester Sixth Form Coll., 1988–90; Head of Econs, and GNVQ Co-ordinator, Haybridge High Sch., 1990–97. Mem. (Lab) Redditch BC, 1991–97. Contested (Lab) Mid Worcestershire,

1992. Parly Under-Sec. of State, DfEE, 1999–2001; Minister of State: DoH, 2001–03; DTI, 2003–05; Minister of State (Minister for Schs), DfES, 2005–06; Parly Sec. to HM Treasury (Govt Chief Whip), 2006–07. *Recreations:* family, friends, football, theatre. *Address:* House of Commons, SW1A 0AA.

SMITH, James Cadzow, CBE 1989; DRC, FREng, FIMechE, FIET, FIMarEST; FRSE; Chairman, Natural Environment Research Council, 1997–2000; *b* 28 Nov. 1927; *s* of James Smith and Margaret Ann Cadzow; *m* 1954, Moira Barrie Hogg; one *s* one *d*. *Educ:* Bellvue Secondary Sch.; Heriot-Watt Coll.; Strathclyde Univ. FIMechE 1960; FIET (FIEE 1960); FIMarEST (FIMarE 1960); FREng (FEng 1988); FRSE 1981. Engineer Officer, Mercantile Marine, 1948–53; engineering and managerial appts in fossil and nuclear power generation with SSEB and CEGB, 1953–73; Dir of Engineering, N Ireland Electricity Service, 1973–74; Dep. Chm. and Chief Exec., 1975–77; Chm., E Midlands Electricity Bd, 1977–82; Chm. and Chief Exec., Eastern Electricity Bd, 1982–90; Chief Exec., 1990–93, and Chm., 1990–95, Eastern Electricity plc, later Eastern Gp. Pres., IEE, 1989–90. Dir, N. M. Rothschild & Sons Ltd, 1991–97. Freeman, City of London, 1984; Liveryman, 1984, Master, 1997–98, Engineers' Co. Hon. LLD Strathclyde, 1988. *Recreations:* music, drama, mountaineering. *Address:* Rowanlee, Newton Loan, Dunblane, Perthshire FK15 0HF.

SMITH, Prof. James Cuthbert, PhD; FRS 1993; John Humphrey Plummer Professor of Developmental Biology, Cambridge University, since 2001; Chairman, Wellcome Trust/Cancer Research UK Gurdon Institute (formerly Wellcome Trust and Cancer Research UK Institute of Cancer and Developmental Biology), since 2001; Fellow, Christ's College, Cambridge, since 2001; *b* 31 Dec. 1954; *s* of late Leslie Cuthbert Smith and of Freda Sarah (*née* Wragg); *m* 1979, Fiona Mary Watt, *qv*; two *s* one *d*. *Educ:* Latymer Upper Sch.; Christ's Coll., Cambridge (BA 1976; MA 1979); London Univ. (PhD 1979). NATO Postdoctoral Fellow, Sidney Farber Cancer Inst. and Harvard Med. Sch., 1979–81; ICRF Postdoctoral Fellow, 1981–84; National Institute for Medical Research: Mem., Scientific Staff, 1984–2000; Head, Div. of Develtl Biol., 1991–2000; Head, Genes and Cellular Controls Gp, 1996–2000. Chm., British Soc. for Developmental Biol., 1994–99; Mem., EMBO, 1992. Howard Hughes Internat. Res. Scholar, 1993–97. Founder FMedSci 1998. Scientific Medal, Zool Soc. of London, 1989; Otto Mangold Prize, Ges. für Entwicklungsbiologie, 1991; EMBO Medal, 1993; Feldberg Foundn Award, 2000; (jtly) William Bate Hardy Prize, Cambridge Phil Soc., 2001. *Publications:* (ed jtly) The Molecular Basis of Positional Signalling, 1989; (with L. Wolpert and others) Principles of Development, 2nd edn 2001, 3rd edn 2007; scientific articles in various jls. *Recreations:* cycling, running, music, reading. *Address:* Wellcome Trust and Cancer Research UK Gurdon Institute, Tennis Court Road, Cambridge CB2 1QN. *T:* (01223) 334132, *Fax:* (01223) 334134; *e-mail:* jim@gurdon.cam.ac.uk.

SMITH, Jane Caroline Rebecca P.; *see* Parker-Smith.

SMITH, Jane L.; *see* Lewin Smith.

SMITH, Rt Hon. Dame Janet (Hilary), (Dame Janet Mathieson), DBE 1992; PC 2002; **Rt Hon. Lady Justice Smith;** a Lord Justice of Appeal, since 2002; *b* 29 Nov. 1940; *d* of Alexander Roe and Margaret Holt; *m* 1st, 1959, Edward Stuart Smith; two *s* one *d*; 2nd, 1984, Robin Edward Alexander Mathieson. *Educ:* Bolton School. Called to the Bar, Lincoln's Inn, 1972, Bencher, 1992; QC 1986; a Recorder, 1988–92; a Judge of the High Ct of Justice, QBD, 1992–2002; a Judge of the Employment Appeal Tribunal, 1994–2002; Presiding Judge, N Eastern Circuit, 1995–98. Pres., Council, Inns of Court, 2006–. Chm., Shipman Inquiry, 2001–05. Mem., Criminal Injuries Compensation Bd, 1988–92; Chm., Security Vetting Appeals Panel, 2000–. Chm., Civil Cttee, Judicial Studies Bd, 2000–04. Chancellor, Manchester Metropolitan Univ., 2003–. Chm., Buxton Arts Festival, 2007–. Hon. LLD: Manchester Metropolitan, 2002; Lancaster, 2005. *Recreations:* gardening, music. *Address:* Royal Courts of Justice, Strand, WC2A 2LL.

SMITH, Jeffrey; *see* Smith, A. J.

SMITH, Prof. (Jenkyn) Beverley, FRHistS; Research Professor of Welsh History, University of Wales, Aberystwyth, 1995–98 (Emeritus Professor, 1998–2007); Commissioner, 1984–99, Chairman, 1991–99, Royal Commission on Ancient and Historical Monuments for Wales; *b* 27 Sept. 1931; *s* of Cecil Nelson Smith and Hannah Jane (*née* Jenkins); *m* 1966, Llinos Olwen Wyn Vaughan, PhD, FRHistS, medieval historian; two *s*. *Educ:* Gowerton Grammar Sch.; UCW, Aberystwyth (BA, MA). FRHistS 1967. National Service, 1954–56. Researcher, Bd of Celtic Studies, Univ. of Wales, 1956–58; Asst Keeper, Dept of MSS and Records, Nat. Library of Wales, 1958–60; Lectr 1960–67, Sen. Lectr 1967–78, Reader 1978–86, Sir John Williams Prof. of Welsh History, 1986–95, Dept of Welsh History, UCW, Aberystwyth. Sir John Rhys Vis. Fellow, Univ. of Oxford, 1978–79. Member: Court and Council, Nat. Library of Wales, 1974–84; Bd of Celtic Studies, Univ. of Wales, 1965–2007 (Sec., History and Law Cttee, 1979–85, Chm. 1985–91); Ancient Monuments Bd for Wales, 1992–98. Jt Editor, Bulletin of Bd of Celtic Studies, 1972–93; Editor, 1994–96, Chief Editor, 1996–2007, Studia Celtica. *Publications:* Llywelyn ap Gruffudd, Tywysog Cymru, 1986; Llywelyn ap Gruffudd, Prince of Wales, 1998; (ed) Medieval Welsh Society, Selected Essays by T. Jones Pierce, 1972; (ed with G. H. Jenkins) Politics and Society in Wales 1840–1922, 1988; (ed with Llinos Beverley Smith) History of Merioneth, vol. II, The Middle Ages, 2001; articles in English Hist. Review, Welsh Hist. Review, Bulletin Bd of Celtic Studies, Studio Celtica and other jls. *Address:* Department of History and Welsh History, Aberystwyth University, Hugh Owen Building, Penglais, Aberystwyth, Ceredigion SY23 3DY; Erw'r Llan, Llanbadarn Road, Aberystwyth, Ceredigion SY23 1EY.

SMITH, Jennifer A.; Principal, Harrogate Ladies' College, 1993–95; *b* 11 March 1950; *d* of Geoffrey and Elsie Bird; *m* 1974, Michael Smith; one *d*. *Educ:* Leeds Univ. (BSc Hons Physics, PGCE); Open Univ. (BA); Liverpool Univ. (MEd). Asst teacher, Physics, 1973–83, Head of Physics, 1983–85, St Richard Gwyn High Sch., Clwyd; Sen. Project Tutor, Science and Electronics, Bodelwyddau TVEI Centre, 1985–88; Dep. Head Teacher, West Kirby Grammar Sch. for Girls, 1988–93. *Recreations:* ski-ing, climbing, music, theatre, electronics.

SMITH, Hon. Dame Jennifer (Meredith), DBE 2005; JP; MP (Progressive Lab) St George's North, Bermuda, since 1989; Deputy Speaker, House of Assembly, since 2003; *d* of late Eugene Wilberforce Smith and Lillian Edith Godet Smith (*née* De Shields). *Educ:* Bermuda; Art Inst., Pittsburgh. Formerly newspaper and magazine editor, radio and TV promotions manager and choreographer. Mem., Senate of Bermuda, 1980–89; Premier of Bermuda, 1998–2003; Minister of Educn, 1998–99. Dep. Leader, 1994–96, Leader, 1996–2003, Progressive Labour Party. Member: Bd of Trustees, Bermuda Inst. of Ocean Scis; Bd of Trustees, Bermuda Nat. Gall.; Bermuda Heritage Assoc.; Bermuda Musical and Dramatic Soc.; Bermuda Dance Foundn; Masterworks of Bermuda; Boys' and Girls' Club of Bermuda. Hon. DHumLit: Mount St Vincent, Halifax, Canada, 2000; Morris Brown Coll., Atlanta, USA, 2000; Hon. DHum Art Inst. of Pittsburgh, 2003. *Publication:* Voice of Change, 2003. *Address:* c/o House of Assembly, Parliament Street, Hamilton HM12, Bermuda.

SMITH, Jeremy Fox Eric; DL; Chairman, Smith St Aubyn (Holdings) plc, 1973–86, retired; *b* 17 Nov. 1928; *s* of late Captain E. C. E. Smith, MC, and B. H. Smith (*née* Williams); *m* 1953, Julia Mary Rona, DL (*d* 2004), *d* of Sir Walter Burrell, 8th Bt, CBE, TD; two *s* two *d*; *m* 2008, Lady Gillian Moyra Katherine, *d* of 6th Marquess of Exeter, KCMG, DL. *Educ:* Eton; New College, Oxford. Chairman, Transparent Paper Ltd, 1965–76. Chairman, London Discount Market Assoc., 1978–80. Trustee, Henry Smith's Charity, 1971–97. DL 1988, High Sheriff, 1992–93, West Sussex. *Address:* The Old Rectory, Slaugham, Haywards Heath, W Sussex RH17 6AG. *T:* (01444) 400341. *Clubs:* Beefsteak; Pitt; Leander (Henley on Thames).

See also Duchess of Grafton, Earl of Verulam, Countess of Verulam.

SMITH, Jeremy James Russell; Secretary General, Council of European Municipalities and Regions, since 2002; *b* 12 June 1947; *s* of Horace James Smith and Joan Alistair Russell. *Educ:* Peterhouse, Cambridge (BA Law 1968). Called to the Bar, Lincoln's Inn, 1969; Barrister, 1971–78; Sen. Legal Adviser, Brent Community Law Centre, 1978–83; Legal Services Liaison Officer, GLC, 1983–86; Clerk and Legal Advr, ILEA, 1986–89; Dir of Law and Admin, 1989–90, Chief Exec., 1990–95, London Borough of Camden; Dir, Local Govt Internat. Bureau, 1996–2002; Sec. Gen., IULA, 2002–04. *Recreations:* history, current affairs, music, rambling. *Address:* Council of European Municipalities and Regions, 15 rue de Richelieu, 78001 Paris, France.

SMITH, Jock; *see* Smith, John M. M.

SMITH, Dr John, OBE 1945; TD 1950; Deputy Chief Medical Officer, Scottish Home and Health Department, 1963–75, retired; *b* 13 July 1913; *e s* of late John Smith, DL, JP, Glasgow and Symington, and Agnes Smith; *m* 1942, Elizabeth Fleming (*d* 1981), twin *d* of late A. F. Wylie, Giffnock; three *s* one *d* (and one *s* decd). *Educ:* High Sch., Glasgow; Sedbergh Sch.; Christ's Coll., Cambridge; Glasgow Univ. BA 1935; MA 1943; MB, BChir Cantab 1938; MB, ChB Glasgow 1938; MRCPG 1965; FRCPG 1967; FRCPE 1969; FFPH (FFCM 1972). TA (RA from 1935, RAMC from 1940); War Service, 1939–46; ADMS Second Army, DDMS (Ops and Plans) 21 Army Group (despatches); OC 155 (Lowland) Fd Amb., 1950–53; ADMS 52 (Lowland) Div., 1953–56; Hon. Col 52 Div. Medical Service, 1961–67. House appts Glasgow Victoria and Western Infirmaries; joined Dept of Health for Scotland, 1947; Medical Supt, Glasgow Victoria Hosps, 1955–58; rejoined Dept of Health for Scotland, 1958; specialised in hospital planning. QHP 1971–74. Officier, Ordre de Leopold I (Belgium), 1947. *Publications:* articles on medical administration and hospital services in various medical jls. *Recreations:* rifle shooting (shot in Scottish and TA representative teams), hill walking, reading. *Address:* 7 Oswald Road, Edinburgh EH9 2HE.

See also Sir R. C. Smith.

SMITH, Sir John (Alfred), Kt 1994; QPM 1986; Deputy Commissioner of the Metropolitan Police, 1991–95; *b* 21 Sept. 1938; *s* of Ruth Alice and Alfred Joseph Smith; *m* 1960, Joan Maria Smith; one *s* one *d*. *Educ:* St Olave's and St Saviour's Grammar School. Irish Guards, 1959–62. Metropolitan Police, 1962; Head, Scotland Yard drugs squad, 1979; Commander 'P' (Bromley-Lewisham) Dist., 1980; Dep. Chief Constable, Surrey Constabulary, 1981; Metropolitan Police: Dep. Asst Comr, 1984; Inspectorate and Force Reorganisation Team, 1985; Asst Comr, 1987–90; Management Support Dept, 1987–89; Specialist Ops Dept, 1989–90; Inspector of Constabulary for SE England, 1990–91. Dir, Sabrewatch Ltd, 1995–2000. Mem., Ind. Commn on Policing for NI, 1998–99. Pres., ACPO, 1993–94. Consultant, Football Assoc., 1995–98; non-exec. Dir, Brighton and Hove Albion FC, 1997–2000, 2002–07; Member: Cttee, AA, 1996–99; Govt Football Task Force Wkg Gp, 1997–99; Trustee, English Nat. Stadium Trust, 1997–98. *Recreations:* gardening, sport spectating, walking. *Address:* 23 Winterbourne, Horsham, West Sussex RH12 5JW. *T:* (01403) 211076.

SMITH, John Allan Raymond, CBE 2008; PhD; FRCS, FRCSE; Consultant General Surgeon, Northern General Hospital NHS Trust (formerly Northern General Hospital, Sheffield), 1985–2007; President, Royal College of Surgeons of Edinburgh, 2003–06 (a Vice-President, 1997–2000); *b* 24 Nov. 1942; *s* of Alexander Macintyre Smith and Evelyn Joyce Smith; *m* 1979, Valerie Fullalove; two *s* three *d*. *Educ:* Boroughmuir Sch., Edinburgh; Edinburgh Univ. (MB ChB 1966); Aberdeen Univ. (PhD 1979). FRCS 1972; FRCSE 1972. House Officer, Royal Infirmary of Edinburgh, 1966–67; SSC, RAMC, 1967–72; Registrar, Dumfries and Galloway Royal Infirmary, and Royal Infirmary, Aberdeen, 1972–73; Res. Fellow, Lectr in Surgery and Sen. Surgical Registrar, Grampian Health Bd, 1972–78; Sen. Lectr in Surgery and Cons. Surgeon, Royal Hampshire Hosp., Sheffield, 1978–85. Editor, Complications in Surgery series, 1985. *Publications:* (jtly) Wounds and Wound Management, 1992; (ed jtly and contrib.) Pye's Surgical Handicraft. *Recreations:* family, sport. *Address:* Riverside Cottage, Hackthorne, Durrington, Wilts SP4 8AS. *T:* (01980) 551211.

SMITH, John Barry, FCCA; Chief Executive Officer, BBC Worldwide, since 2004; *b* 16 Aug. 1957; *s* of Kenneth William Smith and Elsie Smith (*née* Jackson); *m* 1993, Catherine Esther Heywood Hewetson; two *s* one *d*. *Educ:* South London Coll. (FCCA 1980); Harvard Business Sch. (AMP 1997). Chartered Certified Accountant: Bocock, Bew & Co., Chartered Accountants, 1973–75; BR Gp subsidiaries, 1975–83; BRB, 1983–90; BBC, 1990–: Dir of Finance, 1996–2004; Chief Operating Officer, 2004–05. Director: Vickers PLC, 1999–2000; UK Enterprise Adv. Bd, Zurich Financial Services, 2000–01; Severn Trent PLC, 2003–08. Member: 100 Gp of Finance Dirs, 2000–05; Public Services Productivity Panel, 2000–06; Accounting Standards Bd, 2001–04. FRTS 2001; FRSA 2005. Hon. FRIBA 2004. *Address:* BBC Worldwide, Woodlands, 80 Wood Lane, W12 0TT. *T:* (020) 8433 3533.

SMITH, Air Vice-Marshal John Edward, CB 1979; CBE 1972; AFC 1957; Air Officer Administration, Headquarters Strike Command, 1977–81; retired; *b* 8 June 1924; *m* 1944, Roseanne Margurite (*née* Eriksson); four *s* two *d* (and one *s* decd). *Educ:* Tonbridge Sch. Served in Far East, ME, USA and Germany as well as UK Stations since joining the Service in Nov. 1941. *Recreations:* sailing, travel. *Address:* 1 Butlers Grove, Great Linford, Bucks MK14 5DT.

SMITH, (John) Edward (McKenzie) L.; *see* Lucie-Smith.

SMITH, John Francis Jr; Chairman, Delta Air Lines, 2004–07; *b* 6 April 1938; *s* of John Francis Smith and Eleanor C. Sullivan; *m* 1st, 1962, Marie Roberta Halloway (marr. diss.); two *s*; 2nd, 1988, Lydia G. Sigrist; one step *d*. *Educ:* Univ. of Massachusetts (BBA 1960); Boston Univ. (MBA 1965). General Motors Corporation, 1961–2003: Divisional Manager, 1961–73; Asst Treasurer, NY, 1973–80; Comptroller, Detroit, 1980–81; Dir, Worldwide Planning, 1981–84; Pres. and Gen. Manager, General Motors Canada, 1984–85; Vice-Pres., General Motors Corp. and Pres., General Motors Europe, 1986–88;

Exec. Vice-Pres., Internat. Operations, Detroit, 1988–90; Vice-Chm., 1990; Chief Exec. and Pres., 1992–2000; Chm., 1996–2003.

SMITH, John Frederick; DL; Lord Mayor of Cardiff, 1990–91; *b* 28 Sept. 1934; *s* of Charles Frederick Smith and Teresa Smith (*née* O'Brian); *m* 1962, Irene Rice (*d* 1982); one *s*. *Educ:* St Cuthbert's Jun. Sch.; St Illtyd's Grammar Sch.; Gwent Inst. of Higher Educn, 1981–82 (Dip. Trade Union Studies); University Coll., Cardiff, 1982–85 (BScEcon). Engrg apprenticeship, Edward Curran Engrg, 1951–56; Merchant Navy Engr, Blue Funnel and Andrew Weir, 1956–62; Steel Industry, GKN S Wales, 1964–81; Housing Officer, Adamsdown Housing Assoc. Ltd, 1985–96. Member (Lab), Cardiff City Council, 1972–96, Cardiff County Council, 1995–2004: Chairman: Housing and Public Works Cttee, 1973–75; Land Cttee, 1987–90; Dep. Lord Mayor, 1988–89; Chief Whip, 1995–99; Chair, Economic Develt, 1996–99; Presiding Officer, 1999–2000; Mem., S Glamorgan CC, 1973–81. Chm., S Wales Film Commn, 1996–99. JP Cardiff, 1977–87; DL S Glam, 1999. *Recreations:* music, spectator of Cardiff RFC and Wales RU, Shakespeare, cooking. *Address:* 128 Corporation Road, Grangetown, Cardiff CF1 7AX. *T:* (029) 2033 3193.

SMITH, Sir John Hamilton S.; *see* Spencer-Smith.

SMITH, John Hilary, CBE 1970 (OBE 1964); Secretary, Imperial College, London, and Clerk to the Governors, 1979–89 (Fellow, 1992); *b* 20 March 1928; 2nd *s* of late P. R. Smith, OBE and Edith Prince; *m* 1964, Mary Sylvester Head; two *s* one *d*. *Educ:* Cardinal Vaughan Sch., London; University Coll. London (Fellow, 1987); University Coll., Oxford. BA Hons London 1948; MA Oxon 1991. Mil. service, 1948–50, commnd Queen's Own Royal W Kent Regt. Cadet, Northern Nigerian Administration, 1951; Supervisor, Admin. Service Trng, 1960; Dep. Sec. to Premier, 1963; Dir Staff, Develt Centre, 1964; Perm. Sec., Min. of Finance, Benue Plateau State, 1968; Vis. Lectr, Duke Univ., 1970; Financial Sec., British Solomon Is, 1970; Governor of Gilbert and Ellice Islands, 1973–76, of Gilbert Islands, 1976–78. Procurator, 1990–94, and Fellow, 1991–94, University Coll., Oxford. Public Orator, Univ. of London, 1991–94. Director: Fleming Ventures, 1985–98; Empire Mus. Ltd, 2001–. Mem. Council, Scout Assoc., 1980–98 (Chm., Cttee of Council, 1984–88); Pres., Pacific Is Soc. of UK and Ireland, 1981–85. Governor: St Mary's Coll., Strawberry Hill, 1980–88; Cardinal Vaughan School, 1982–88; Heythrop Coll., 1986–93 (Fellow, 2002); Member, Board of Management: LSHTM, 1989–98 (Treas., 1993–98; Fellow, 1999); St Mary's Sch., Shaftesbury, 1993–2001 (Chm. Govs, 1994–2001). *Publications:* How to Write Letters that get Results, 1965; Colonial Cadet in Nigeria, 1968; (ed) Administering Empire, 1999; articles in S Atlantic Quarterly, Administration, Jl of Overseas Administration, Nigeria. *Recreations:* walking, writing, music. *Address:* Pound House, Dulverton, Som TA22 9HP. *Club:* Athenæum.

SMITH, Sir John Jonah W.; *see* Walker-Smith.

SMITH, John Mitchell Melvin, (Jock), WS; Partner, Masson & Glennie, Solicitors, Peterhead, 1957–94, retired; *b* 5 July 1930; *s* of John Mitchell Smith and Barbara Edda Smith or Glennie; *m* 1958, Elisabeth Marion Slight; two *s* one *d*. *Educ:* Fettes College; Edinburgh Univ. (BL). Pres., Law Soc. of Scotland, 1987–88. *Recreations:* golf, theatre. *Address:* 1 Winton Terrace, Edinburgh EH10 7AP. *Clubs:* Bruntsfield Golf; Luffness Golf.

SMITH, Sir John Rathborne V.; *see* Vassar-Smith.

SMITH, (John) Stephen; QC 2000; a Recorder, since 2004; a Deputy High Court Judge, since 2006; *b* 30 June 1960; *s* of John Slater Smith and Nancy Smith (*née* Clayton); *m* 1982, Lorraine Dunn; four *s* one *d*. *Educ:* Walton High Sch., Nelson; University Coll., Oxford (BA 1st Cl. Jurisprudence). Called to the Bar: Middle Temple, 1983; Eastern Caribbean (BVI), 1994; Bahamas, 2004; Isle of Man, 2007. *Recreations:* family, alpaca farming, deer. *Address:* New Square Chambers, Lincoln's Inn, WC2A 3SW. *T:* (020) 7419 8000; *e-mail:* stephen.smith@newsquarechambers.co.uk.

SMITH, John William Patrick; MP (Lab) Vale of Glamorgan, May 1989–1992 and since 1997; *b* 17 March 1951; *s* of John Henry Smith and Margaret Mary (*née* Collins); *m* 1971, Kathleen Mulvaney; two *s* one *d*. *Educ:* Penarth County Sch.; Gwent Coll. of Higher Educn (Dip. in Indust. Relations and Trade Union Studies); UCW Cardiff (BSc (Econ) Hons). Building worker, 1966–68; RAF, 1967–71; joiner, 1971–76; mature student, 1976–83; University Tutor, 1983–85; Sen. Lectr in Business Studies, 1985–89; Chief Exec., Gwent Image Partnership, 1992–97. Contested (Lab) Vale of Glamorgan, 1992. PPS to Dep. Leader of the Opposition, 1989–92, to Minister of State for the Armed Forces, 1997–98, to Minister of State (Minister of Transport), DETR, 1998–99. Mem., Select Cttee on Welsh Affairs, 1990–92; formerly Parly spokesperson for Vale of Glam. *Recreations:* reading, boating, walking. *Address:* House of Commons, SW1A 0AA. *T:* (constituency office) (01446) 743769. *Clubs:* West End Labour; Sea View Labour (Barry).

SMITH, Jon; Chief Executive Officer, First Artist Corporation plc, since 2001; *b* London, 20 Sept. 1952; *s* of Mick and Rosemary Smith; *m* 1st, 1976, Lee M. (*d* 1981); 2nd, 1986, Janine; two *s*. *Educ:* Orange Hill Grammar Sch.; Kingsway Coll. of Further Educn. Chief Exec., London Monarchs, 1991. Mem., Govt Cttee on Replacement of Tobacco Sponsorship in Sport, 1998. Mem. Bd, Inst. of Child Health, 1987. Trustee, Lee Smith Foundn, 1982–. Patron, British Swimming Assoc., 2004. FInstD. *Recreations:* theatre, most sports, property refurbishment. *Address:* First Artist Corporation plc, 3 Tenterden Street, W1S 1TD. *T:* (020) 7993 0000; *e-mail:* jons@firstartist.com.

SMITH, Jonathan A.; *see* Ashley-Smith.

SMITH, Ven. Jonathan Peter; Archdeacon of St Albans, since 2008; *b* Guildford, 10 Nov. 1955; *s* of John Smith and Dorothea Smith. *Educ:* Ipswich Sch.; King's Coll., London (BD, AKC 1977); Queens' Coll., Cambridge (PGCE 1978); Westcott House, Cambridge. Ordained deacon, 1980, priest, 1981; Assistant Curate: All Saints', Gosforth, 1980–82; Waltham Abbey, 1982–85; Chaplain, City Univ., 1985–88; Rector, Harrold and Carlton with Chellington, 1988–97; Vicar, St John's, Harpenden, 1997–2008. Rural Dean, Wheathampstead, 1999–2004. Chaplain, Bedfordshire Police, 1990–97. *Recreations:* Association Football, travel, opera, proroguing committees, the company of friends. *T:* (01727) 818121, *Fax:* (01727) 844311; *e-mail:* archdeaconstalbans@stalbans.anglican.org. *Club:* Bridgman Bowls (Bedfordshire).

SMITH, Jonathan Simon Christopher R.; *see* Riley-Smith.

SMITH, Dr Joseph, FRHistS; Editor, History: Journal of the Historical Association, since 2000; Reader in American Diplomatic History, University of Exeter, since 1995; *b* 2 May 1945; *m* 1971, Marjorie Rachael Eaves. *Educ:* Grey Coll., Univ. of Durham (BA 1966); UCL (PhD 1970). FRHistS 1979. Research Assistant: UCL, 1969–70; Inst. of Latin American Studies, Univ. of London, 1970–71; Lectr in History, Univ. of Exeter, 1971–95. Visiting Professor of History: Coll. of William and Mary, Va, 1976–77; Univ. of Colorado at Denver, 1990–91. Fulbright Schol., 1990–91. Historical Association: Mem. Council, 1985–2003; Chm. of Pubns, 1995–2000; Vice-Pres., 2002–03. FHA 2007. Ed., The Annual Bull. of Histl Literature, 1990–99. Rio Branco Prize, Casa do Brasil, London, 1971. *Publications:* Illusions of Conflict, 1979; The Cold War, 1989, 2nd edn 1998; Origins of NATO, 1990; Unequal Giants, 1991; The Spanish-American War, 1994; Historical Dictionary of the Cold War, 2000; History of Brazil, 2002; The United States and Latin America, 2005; Historical Dictionary of United States-Latin American Relations, 2007. *Recreations:* travel, tennis. *Address:* 1 California Close, Exeter, Devon EX4 5ET.

SMITH, Prof. Joseph Victor, FRS 1978; Louis Block Professor of Physical Sciences, 1977–2005, now Emeritus, and Co-ordinator of Scientific Programs, since 1992 (Executive Director, 1988–91), Consortium for Advanced Radiation Sources, University of Chicago (Professor of Mineralogy and Crystallography, 1960–76); *b* 30 July 1928; *s* of Henry Victor Smith and Edith (*née* Robinson); *m* 1951, Brenda Florence Wallis; two *d*. *Educ:* Cambridge Univ. (MA, PhD). Fellow, Carnegie Instn of Washington, 1951–54; Demonstrator in Mineralogy and Petrology, Cambridge Univ., 1954–56; Asst then Associate Prof., Pennsylvania State Univ., 1956–60. Editor, Power Diffraction File, 1959–69. Visiting Prof., California Inst. of Technology, 1965; Consultant: Union Carbide Corp., 1956–85; UOP, 1985–99. Member, US Nat. Acad. of Scis, 1986. Murchison Medal, 1980; Roebling Medal, 1982. *Publications:* Feldspar Minerals, Vols 1 and 2, 1975, 2nd edn 1987; Geometrical and Structural Crystallography, 1982; numerous articles on crystallography, inorganic chemistry, mineralogy, petrology and planetology. *Recreations:* music, art. *Address:* Department of the Geophysical Sciences, University of Chicago, 5734 S Ellis Avenue, Chicago, IL 60637–1434, USA. *T:* (773) 7028110.

SMITH, Sir Joseph (William Grenville), Kt 1991; MD; FRCP; FRCPath; FFPH; Director, Public Health Laboratory Service, 1985–92; *b* 14 Nov. 1930; *s* of Douglas Ralph and Hannah Letitia Margaret Smith; *m* 1954, Nira Jean (*née* Davies); one *s*. *Educ:* Cathays High School, Cardiff; Welsh Nat. Sch. of Medicine (MD 1966); Dip. Bact., London Univ., 1960; FRCPath 1975; FFPH (FFCM 1976); FRCP 1987. FIBiol 1978. Lectr, 1960–63, Sen. Lectr, 1963–65, Dept of Bacteriology and Immunology, LSHTM; Consultant Clinical Bacteriologist, Radcliffe Infirmary, Oxford, 1965–69; Gen. Practitioner, Islington, 1970–71; Consultant Epidemiologist, Dep. Dir, Epidemiological Res. Lab., PHLS, 1971–76; Dir, Nat. Inst. for Biological Standards and Control, 1976–85. Consultant on immunisation to British Army, 1985–96. Special Prof., Nottingham Univ., 1989–94. Member: Cttee on Safety of Medicines, 1978–86 (Chm., Biol Sub-Cttee, 1981–86); Jt Cttee on Vaccination and Immunisation, 1976–93 (Chm., Influenza, Measles and Rubella Sub-Cttees, 1979–93); British Pharmacopoeia Commn, 1976–85 (Chm., Immunization Cttee, 1977–85); MRC, 1989–92; Council, RCPath, 1988–90; Adv. Gp on Rabies Quarantine, MAFF, 1997–98; Chairman: Cttee on Vaccination and Immunization Procedures, MRC, 1976–93; Simian Virus Cttee, MRC, 1982–93; Tropical Medicine Res. Bd, MRC, 1989–90; World Health Organisation: Chm., Expert Adv. Gp on Immunization, 1993–95, Chm., Poliomyelitis Commn, 1995–2006, Eur. Reg.; Chm., Global Polio Commn, 2001–03 (Co-Chm., 1998–2001). Mem., Ct of Govs and Bd of Management, LSHTM, 1994–97 (Chm. Bd of Mgt, 1995–97). Hon. DipHIC LSHTM, 1999. *Publications:* (with E. B. Adams and D. R. Laurence) Tetanus, 1969; papers on tetanus, immunization, and epidemiology of infections in scientific and med. jls. *Recreation:* the arts.

SMITH, Julia Clare; *see* Buckingham, J. C.

SMITH, Karen Denise; Director of Programmes, Shine Limited, since 2008; *b* 16 June 1970; *d* of Peter A. Smith and Janet E. Smith; partner, Paul R. Jacobs; one *s* one *d* (twins). *Educ:* Univ. of Liverpool (BA Hons English 1991). Producer, presenter, reporter, BBC Radio York, 1992–95; Producer, NMTV, 1996–97; Producer, 1998, Dep. Editor, 1999, Editor, 2000–01, This Morning, Granada Television; Series Producer, Endemol UK, 2002–04; Exec. Producer, Strictly Come Dancing, BBC, 2003–04 (Rose d'Or Award, 2005); Sen. Editor, BBC Entertainment, 2004–06; Creative Hd, BBC Format Entertainment, 2006; Creative Dir, BBC Entertainment, 2007. *Address:* Shine Limited, 4th Floor, Newcombe House, 45 Notting Hill Gate, W113LQ. *T:* (020) 7985 7000; *e-mail:* karen.smith@shinelimited.com.

SMITH, Hon. Kenneth George, OJ 1973; Justice of Appeal, Bahamas, 1985–90, retired; *b* 25 July 1920; *s* of Franklin C. Smith; *m* 1942, Hyacinth Whitfield Connell; two *d*. *Educ:* Primary schs; Cornwall Coll., Jamaica; Inns of Court Sch. of Law, London. Barrister-at-Law, Lincoln's Inn. Asst Clerk of Courts, 1940–48; Dep. Clerk of Courts, 1948–53; Clerk of Courts, 1953–56; Crown Counsel, 1956–62; Asst Attorney-Gen., 1962–65; Supreme Court Judge, 1965–70; Judge of Appeal, Jamaica, 1970–73; Chief Justice of Jamaica, 1973–85; Judge, Admin. Tribunal, Inter-American Develt Bank, 1987–92 (Pres., 1990–92). *Recreations:* swimming, gardening. *Address:* 5 Wagner Avenue, Kingston 8, Jamaica.

SMITH, Prof. Kenneth George Campbell, PhD; FRCP, FRACP, FRCPA, FMedSci; Genzyme Professor of Experimental Medicine, University of Cambridge, since 2006; Fellow and Director of Studies in Clinical Medicine, Pembroke College, Cambridge, since 1998; *b* 18 April 1963; *s* of Trevor James Sylvester Smith and Margery Leonie Smith (*née* Campbell); one *d*. *Educ:* Bell Post Hill Primary Sch.; Geelong Coll.; Univ. of Melbourne (BMedSc 1985; MB BS 1987; PhD 1996); Pembroke Coll., Cambridge (MA 2000). FRACP 1994; FRCPA 1999; FRCP 2002. Intern, RMO and Med. and Nephrology Registrar, 1988–94, Asst Nephrologist, 1995–96, Royal Melbourne Hosp.; Dir, Studies in Clinical Medicine, and J. Alexander Scott Fellow in Anatomy, Ormond Coll., Univ. of Melbourne, 1992–96; Univ. Lectr, 1996–2004, Reader, 2004–06, in Renal Medicine, Univ. of Cambridge. Hon. Consultant Physician, Addenbrooke's Hosp., Cambridge, 1996–. Khoo Oon Teik Prof. of Nephrology, Univ. of Singapore, 2007–. FHEA (ILTM 2003); FMedSci 2006. Lister Inst. Res. Prize, 2007. *Publications:* articles on immunology and medicine. *Recreations:* Real tennis, reading, natural history. *Address:* Cambridge Institute for Medical Research, Box 139, Addenbrooke's Hospital, Cambridge CB2 0XY. *T:* (01223) 762645, *Fax:* (01223) 762640; *e-mail:* kgcs2@cam.ac.uk. *Clubs:* Melbourne Cricket; Cambridge Real Tennis.

SMITH, Sir Kevin, Kt 2007; CBE 1997; FRAeS; Chief Executive, GKN plc, since 2003; *b* 22 May 1954. *Educ:* Burnley Coll.; Lancashire Poly. (BA Hons). British Aerospace: Contract Officer, 1980–90; Commercial Dir, 1990–91; Dep. Man. Dir, 1991–93, Man. Dir, 1993–95, Mil. Aircraft Div.; British Aerospace plc: Man. Dir, Business Ops, 1995–98; Dep. Gp Man. Dir, New Business, 1998–99; Man. Dir, GKN Aerospace, 1999–2003. Non-exec. Dir, Scottish and Southern Energy plc, 2004–. Dir, SBAC, 2003– (Pres., 2004–05; Dep. Pres., 2005–07). CCMI. FRAeS 1993. *Address:* GKN plc, PO Box 55, Ipsley House, Ipsley Church Lane, Redditch, Worcs B98 0TL.

SMITH, Kingsley Ward, OBE 2007; non-executive Chairman, Newcastle Hospitals NHS Foundation Trust (formerly Newcastle Hospitals Foundation Trust), 2006–07; Chairman, Time for Success, since 2007; Clerk to the Lieutenancy, since 1990; *b* 24 Oct. 1946; *s* of Peter and Doris Evelyn Smith; *m* 1st, 1968, Kathy Rutherford (marr. diss. 1999);

two *s*; 2nd, 2004, Sayoko Barbour. *Educ:* Blue Coat Secondary Sch., Walsall, Staffs; Dame Allan's Boys' Sch., Newcastle upon Tyne. CPFA (IPFA 1970). Trainee Accountant, Gateshead CBC, 1964–67; Durham County Council: Accountant, subseq. Sen. Accountant, 1967–76; Chief Internal Auditor, 1976–79; Sen. Asst County Treasurer, 1979–81; Dep. County Treasurer, 1981–84; County Treasurer, 1984–88; Chief Exec., 1988–2005; Exec. Chm., Co. Durham Develt Co., 2005–07; Interim Chief Exec., Teesdale DC, 2005–06. Non-exec. Dir, Durham Co. Waste Mgt Co., 2005–07. Advr, NSK (Europe), 2004–. Mem., LSC, Co. Durham, 2001–05; Chm., Prince's Trust Regl Council, 1999–2005; formerly: founder Mem., Durham TEC; Chairman: ACCE; Fujitsu Response Gp; E Durham Task Force; Co. Durham Connexions Partnership; Co. Durham Youth Offending Service; Mem., Nat. Coalfields Task Force. *Recreations:* golfing, fishing, walking his labrador (Sam).

SMITH, Kirstie Louise Stewart-; *see* Hamilton, K. L.

SMITH, Laura; *see* Duncan, A. L. A.

SMITH, Lawrence Edward; yachting consultant, since 1971; *b* 19 Feb. 1956; *s* of Harold and Jean Smith; *m* 1991, Penny Jane Smith (*née* Haydock); two *s* two *d* (of whom one *s* one *d* are twins). *Educ:* Bury Grammar Sch. America's Cup: Skipper, British challenger, Lionheart, 1980, Victory, 1983. Winning skipper: Fastnet Race, 1985; Admiral's Cup, 1989. Whitbread Round the World Race: Skipper, Rothmans, 1990 (4th), Intrum Justitia, 1994 (2nd), Silk Cut, 1997–98 (5th). Skipper, UK crew, Soling class, Olympic Games, 1988, 1992 (Bronze medal). *Publications:* Dinghy Helming, 1985; Dinghy Tuning, 1986; Yacht Tuning, 1987; Science of Speed, 1994. *Recreations:* golf, tennis.

SMITH, Lawrence Roger Hines, FSA; Keeper of Japanese Antiquities, 1987–97, and Senior Keeper, 1995–97, British Museum, now Keeper Emeritus; *b* 19 Feb. 1941; *s* of Frank Ernest Smith and Eva Lilian Smith (*née* Hines); *m* 1st, 1965, Louise Geraldine Gallini (marr. diss. 1986); one *s* five *d*; 2nd, 1993, Louise Elaine Woodroff; one *d*. *Educ:* Collyer's Grammar Sch., Horsham; Queens' Coll., Cambridge (Foundn Schol.; BA). British Museum: Asst Keeper, Dept of Manuscripts, 1962; Dept of Oriental Antiquities, 1965; Dep. Keeper, 1976; Keeper, 1977. British Acad. Exchange Fellow, Nihon Gakujutsu Shinkōkai, Kyoto, 1974–75. Academic adviser, Great Japan Exhibn, RA, 1981–82, and contrib. to catalogue. Mem. (Lib Dem), Broadland DC, 2003–07. Uchiyama Prize, Ukiyoe Soc. of Japan, 1986. *Publications:* Netsuke: the miniature sculpture of Japan (with R. Barker), 1976; Flowers in Art from East and West (with P. Hulton), 1979; Japanese Prints: 300 years of albums and books (with J. Hillier), 1980; Japanese Decorative Arts 1600–1900 (with V. Harris), 1982; The Japanese Print since 1900, 1983; Contemporary Japanese Prints, 1985; (ed) Ukiyoe: images of unknown Japan, 1988; (ed) Japanese Art: masterpieces in the British Museum, 1990; Nihonga: traditional Japanese painting, 1991; Japanese Prints 1912–1989: woodblocks and stencils, 1994; Japanese Prints during the Allied Occupation 1945–52, 2002; contribs to BM multi-cultural catalogues; articles and reviews in learned jls; conference and symposium papers. *Recreations:* walking, running, bellringing, music, wine. *Address:* 15 Repton Close, Aylsham, Norfolk NR11 6JE. *T:* (01263) 734499; *e-mail:* lrhsmith@paston.co.uk.

SMITH, Leonard Wayne; QC 2008; *b* Sydney, Australia, 21 July 1959; *s* of Leonard Bryan Smith and Beatrice Wendy Smith (*née* Bawden); *m* 1984, Anne Terese Walker; two *s* one *d*. *Educ:* Univ. of Sydney (BA, LLM). Called to the Bar: NSW, 1986; Australia, 1987; Gray's Inn, 1991; in practice as barrister specialising in criminal law. *Recreations:* cricket, golf, reading. *Address:* No 5 Chambers, Steelhouse Lane, Birmingham B4 6DR. *T:* 0870 203 5555, *Fax:* (0121) 606 1501. *Club:* Kibworth Golf (Kibworth Beauchamp).

SMITH, Prof. Lewis Lauchlan, PhD; FRCPath; FBTS; Director, Syngenta (formerly Zeneca) Central Toxicology Laboratory, since 1998; *b* 21 Aug. 1947; *s* of Lewis Smith and Margaret (*née* Wilson); *m* 1972, Susan Lisbeth Baynes; one *s* two *d*. *Educ:* Hatfield Poly. (BSc, PhD). MRCPath 1990, FRCPath 1997. ICI Central Toxicology Laboratory: Res. Scientist, 1971–80; Sen. Scientist, 1980–85; Hd, Biochem. Toxicology Sect., 1985–91; Dir, Toxicology Unit, 1991–98, and Inst. for Envmt and Health, 1993–98, MRC. *Publications:* numerous in res. jls on mechanisms of toxicity and cellular biochem. *Recreations:* golf, eating, dieting. *Address:* Syngenta Central Toxicology Laboratory, Alderley Park, Macclesfield, Cheshire SK10 4TJ. *T:* (01625) 514848; *e-mail:* lewis.smith@syngenta.com.

SMITH, Llewellyn Thomas; *b* 16 April 1944; *m* 1969, Pamela Williams; two *s* one *d*. *Educ:* Cardiff University. Formerly with Pilkington Glass, George Wimpey and Workers' Educational Assoc. MEP (Lab) SE Wales, 1984–94; MP (Lab) Blaenau Gwent, 1992–2005. Mem., CND. *Address:* The Mount, Uplands, Tynewydd, Newbridge NP11 3RH.

SMITH, Lloyd Barnaby, (Barney), CMG 2002; HM Diplomatic Service, retired; Editor, Asian Affairs, since 2005; *b* 21 July 1945; *s* of Arthur and Zena Smith; *m* 1st, 1972, Nicola Mary Whitehead (marr. diss.); 2nd, 1983, Elizabeth Mary Sumner; one *s* one *d*. *Educ:* Merchant Taylors' Sch., Moor Park; Brasenose Coll., Oxford (MA). Joined Diplomatic Service, 1968; Third, later Second Sec., Bangkok, 1970–74; First Secretary: FCO, 1974–77; Paris, 1977–78; Head of Chancery, Dublin, 1978–81; Ecole Nat. d'Admin, Paris, 1981–82; First Sec., then Counsellor, UK Repn to EEC, Brussels, 1982–86; Counsellor, Bangkok, 1987–90; Dir, Know How Fund for Eastern Europe, 1990–92; Head, S Asia Dept, FCO, 1993–95; Ambassador: to Nepal, 1995–99; to Thailand, also accredited to Laos, 2000–03. Non-exec. Dir, Coastal Energy Co. Ltd, 2006–. *Recreation:* sailing.

SMITH, Prof. Lorraine Nancy, PhD; Professor of Nursing, University of Glasgow, since 1990 (Head, Nursing and Midwifery School, 1999–2001; Head of Department, 1990–99); *b* 29 June 1949; *d* of Geoffrey Leonard Millington and Ida May (*née* Attfield); *m* 1975, Christopher Murray Smith; one *s* one *d*. *Educ:* Univ. of Ottawa (BScN); Univ. of Manchester (MEd, PhD). Staff Nurse, Ottawa, 1971–73; Team Leader, Montreal, 1973–76; Sister, Withington Hosp., Manchester, 1976–77; Lectr, Dept of Nursing Studies, Univ. of Manchester, 1977–90. Member: Clin. Standards Adv. Gp (UK); Standards Cttee, Nat. Bd for Scotland, 1997–2000; RCN UK Rep., Work Gp, Eur. Nurse Researchers, 1999–2008 (Chm., 2005–08). Chair, RCN Res. Soc. Scotland, 1999–2005. *Publications:* articles in Advanced Jl of Nursing, Clinical Rehabilitation, Health Bulletin, Heart, Pain. *Recreations:* ski-ing, sailing, reading, bridge. *Address:* Nursing and Health Care, University of Glasgow, 59 Oakfield Avenue, Glasgow G12 8LW. *T:* (0141) 330 5498. *Clubs:* S Caernarvonshire Yacht, Abersoch Golf (Abersoch, N Wales).

SMITH, Dame Maggie, (Dame Margaret Natalie Cross), DBE 1990 (CBE 1970); actress; Director, United British Artists, since 1982; *b* 28 Dec. 1934; *d* of Nathaniel Smith and Margaret Little (*née* Hutton); *m* 1st, 1967, Robert Graham Stephens (later Sir Robert Stephens) (marr. diss. 1975; he *d* 1995); two *s*; 2nd, 1975, Beverley Cross (*d* 1998). *Educ:* Oxford High School for Girls. Studied at Oxford Playhouse School under Isabel van Beers. First appearance, June 1952, as Viola in OUDS Twelfth Night; 1st New York appearance, Ethel Barrymore Theatre, June 1956, as comedienne in New Faces. Played in Share My Lettuce, Lyric, Hammersmith, 1957; The Stepmother, St Martin's, 1958. Old Vic Co., 1959–60 season: The Double Dealer; As You Like It; Richard II; The Merry Wives of Windsor; What Every Woman Knows; Rhinoceros, Strand, 1960; Strip the Willow, Cambridge, 1960; The Rehearsal, Globe, 1961; The Private Ear and The Public Eye (Evening Standard Drama Award, best actress of 1962), Globe, 1962; Mary, Mary, Queen's, 1963 (Variety Club of Gt Britain, best actress of the year); The Country Wife, Chichester, 1969; Design for Living, LA, 1971; Private Lives, Queen's, 1972, Globe, 1973, NY, 1975 (Variety Club of GB Stage Actress Award, 1972); Peter Pan, Coliseum, 1973; Snap, Vaudeville, 1974; Night and Day, Phoenix, 1979; Virginia, Haymarket, 1981 (Standard Best Actress Award, 1982); The Way of the World, Chichester and Haymarket, 1984 (Standard Best Actress Award, 1985); Interpreters, Queen's, 1985; Lettice and Lovage, Globe, 1987, NY, 1990 (Tony Award, best leading actress, 1990); The Importance of Being Earnest, Aldwych, 1993; Three Tall Women, Wyndham's, 1994, 1995; Talking Heads, Chichester, 1996, Comedy Theatre, 1997, Australian tour, 2004; A Delicate Balance, Haymarket, 1997; Lady in the Van, Queen's, 1999; The Breath of Life, Haymarket, 2002; The Lady from Dubuque, Haymarket, 2007; *at National Theatre:* The Recruiting Officer, 1963; Othello, The Master Builder, Hay Fever, 1964; Much Ado About Nothing, Miss Julie, 1965; A Bond Honoured, 1966; The Beaux' Stratagem, 1970 (also USA); Hedda Gabler, 1970 (Evening Standard Best Actress award); War Plays, 1985; Coming in to Land, 1986; *at Festival Theatre, Stratford, Ontario:* 1976: Antony and Cleopatra, The Way of the World, Measure for Measure, The Three Sisters; 1977: Midsummer Night's Dream, Richard III, The Guardsman, As You Like It, Hay Fever; 1978: As You Like It, Macbeth, Private Lives; 1980: Virginia; Much Ado About Nothing. *Films:* The VIP's, 1963; The Pumpkin Eater, 1964; Young Cassidy, 1965; Othello, 1966; The Honey Pot, 1967; Hot Millions, 1968 (Variety Club of GB Award); The Prime of Miss Jean Brodie, 1968 (Oscar; SFTA award); Oh! What a Lovely War, 1968; Love and Pain (and the Whole Damned Thing), 1973; Travels with my Aunt, 1973; Murder by Death, 1976; California Suite, 1977 (Oscar); Death on the Nile, 1978; Quartet, 1981; Clash of the Titans, 1981; Evil Under the Sun, 1982; The Missionary, 1982; A Private Function, 1984 (BAFTA award, Best Actress, 1985); The Loves of Lily, 1985; A Room with a View, 1986 (Variety Club of GB Award; BAFTA award, Best Actress, 1986); The Lonely Passion of Judith Hearn, 1989 (Evening Standard British Films Award, 1988, and Best Film Actress BAFTA Award, 1988); Hook, 1992; Sister Act, 1992; The Secret Garden, 1993; Sister Act II, 1994; Richard III, 1996; The First Wives Club, 1996; Washington Square, 1998; Tea with Mussolini, 1999 (Best Supporting Actress, BAFTA, 2000); The Last September, 2000; Harry Potter and the Philosopher's Stone, 2001; Gosford Park, 2002; Divine Secrets of the Ya-Ya Sisterhood, 2002; Harry Potter and the Chamber of Secrets, 2002; Harry Potter and the Prisoner of Azkaban, 2004; My House in Umbria, 2004; Ladies in Lavender, 2004; Harry Potter and the Goblet of Fire, 2005; Keeping Mum, 2005; Becoming Jane, Harry Potter and the Order of the Phoenix, 2007; *television:* Talking Heads: Bed Among the Lentils, 1989 (RTS Award); Memento Mori, 1992; Suddenly Last Summer, 1993; All The King's Men, 1999; David Copperfield, 1999; Capturing Mary, 2007. Fellow: BFI; BAFTA. Hon. DLitt: St Andrews, 1971; Cambridge, 1995. Hanbury Shakespeare Prize, 1991. *Recreation:* reading. *Address:* c/o 41 Warbeck Road, W12 8NS.

See also T. Stephens.

SMITH, Malcolm Andrew F.; *see* Ferguson-Smith.

SMITH, Margaret Elizabeth; Lord Provost and Lord-Lieutenant of Aberdeen City, 1999–2003; *b* 10 Aug. 1931. *Educ:* Twickenham Grammar Sch.; Southport High Sch. for Girls; Lady Mabel Coll., Rotherham (DipPE 1953). Physical Education Teacher: Fleetwood Grammar Sch., 1953–58; Blairgowrie High Sch., 1958–67; Youth Officer, Chichester CC, 1967–73; Neighbourhood Worker, Easterhouse, Glasgow, 1973–78; Housing Worker, Scottish Special Housing Assoc., Glasgow, 1978–81; Community Educn Area Officer, Grampian Regl Council, 1981–91. Aberdeen District, now City, Council: Mem. (Lab), 1988–2003; Leader of Council, 1996–99; Mem., Drug Strategy Task Gp, 1996–99; Chair, Community Planning Core Gp; COSLA Rep., 1997–99; Convenor, Women's and Equal Opportunities Cttee, 1992–96. Lord High Adm., Northern Seas, 1999–2003; Vice Adm., Coast of GB and Ireland, 1999–2003. President: World Energy Cities Partnership, 2000–02; Voluntary Service, Aberdeen, 1999–2003; Aberdeen Br., RNLI, 1999–2003; Comr, Northern Lighthouse Bd, 1999–2003; Chair: Froghall Community Project, 1995–99; Aberdeen Alternative Fest. Trust, 1999–2001; Member: Sunnybank Community Educn Mgt Cttee, 1988–2003; NE Scotland Econ. Develt Partnership, 1997–99; Aberdeen Gomel Trust, 1999–2003; Aberdeen Safer Communities Trust, 1999–2003; Aberdeen Bulawayo Trust, 1999–2003; Patron: Mental Health, Aberdeen, 1999; Aberdeen Internat. Youth Fest., 1999. Hon. DL: Robert Gordon, Aberdeen, 1999; Aberdeen, 2004. *Recreations:* walking, theatre and concerts, family and friends, learning Russian, Aberdeen FC. *Address:* 49 Froghall Terrace, Aberdeen AB24 3JP.

SMITH, Margaret Joy; Member (Lib Dem) Edinburgh West, Scottish Parliament, since 1999; *b* 18 Feb. 1961; *d* of late John Murray and of Anna Murray; *m* 1983, Douglas Robert Smith (marr. diss. 2004); one *s* one *d*; civil partnership 2006, Suzanne Main. *Educ:* Edinburgh Univ. (MA Gen. Arts). Pensions Administrator, Guardian Royal Exchange Assurance, 1982–83; Civil Servant (EO), Registers of Scotland, 1983–88; tour guide and freelance journalist, 1988–90; Scottish Officer, UNA, 1990–96; Political Organiser, Edinburgh W Liberal Democrats, 1996–97. Mem. (Lib Dem) Edinburgh CC, 1995–99. Scottish Parliament: Convenor, Health and Community Care Cttee, 1999–2003; Lib Dem spokesperson on justice, 2003–05, on transport and local govt, 2005; Chief Whip (Lib Dem), 2005–07; Lib Dem Shadow Cabinet Sec. for Justice, 2007–. *Recreations:* golf, reading. *Address:* Scottish Parliament, Edinburgh EH99 1SP. *T:* (0131) 348 5786. *Club:* Ravelston Golf (Edinburgh).

SMITH, Margaret Osborne B.; *see* Bickford Smith.

SMITH, (Maria) Geraldine; MP (Lab) Morecambe and Lunesdale, since 1997; *b* 29 Aug. 1961; *d* of John and Ann Smith. *Educ:* Morecambe Bay Primary Sch.; Morecambe High Sch. Postal Administrator, Royal Mail, 1980–97. *Recreations:* chess, walking. *Address:* 79 West End, Morecambe LA4 4DR. *T:* (01524) 425680.

SMITH, Mark Gordon M.; *see* Milliken-Smith.

SMITH, Martin Gregory; Director, New Star Asset Management, since 2000; *b* 2 Feb. 1943; *s* of late Archibald Gregory Smith, OBE, and Mary Eleanor Smith (*née* Malone); *m* 1971, Elise Barr Becket; one *s* one *d*. *Educ:* St Albans Sch.; St Edmund Hall, Oxford (BA, MA); Stanford Univ., Calif (MBA, AM Econ). Brewer, A. Guinness Son & Co. (Dublin) Ltd, 1964–69; McKinsey & Co. Inc., 1971–73; Dir, Citicorp Internat. Bank Ltd, 1974–80; Chm., Bankers Trust Internat., 1980–83; Co-founder, Phoenix Securities, 1983–97; Chairman: Phoenix Partnership, 1990–97; Phoenix Fund Managers, 1990–97; Eur. Investment Banking, Donaldson, Lufkin & Jenrette, 1997–2000; Amerindo Internet Fund PLC, 2000–06; GP Bullhound, 2005–; Finsbury Worldwide Pharmaceutical Ltd, 2008–;

Director: Odgers, Ray & Berndtson, 2001–; Phoenix Equity Partners, 2001–06; Sen. Advr, Bain Capital, 2001–; Mem., Adv. Bd, IDDAS Ltd, 2005–. Chairman: Council (formerly Bd) of Advrs, Orchestra of Age of Enlightenment, 1985–; Bath Mozartfest, 2000–; ENO, 2001–05. Dep. Chm., Science Mus., 1999–; Trustee: IMS Prussia Cove, 1999–; Becket Collection, 1999–; Wigmore Hall, 2000–; Tetbury Music Fest., 2006–; Dir, Glyndebourne Arts Trust, 2007–. Visitor, Ashmolean Museum, 2006–. Gov., RAM, 2006–. Founder, Smith Sch. of Enterprise and the Envmt, Oxford Univ., 2007. Liveryman, Co. of Musicians, 2000–. St Edmund Fellow, St Edmund Hall, Oxford, 2001. Hon. FRAM 2003. *Recreations:* music, conducting, equine pursuits, ski-ing, golf, sailing. *Address:* New Star Asset Management, 1 Knightsbridge Green, SW1X 7NE. *T:* (020) 7225 9200. *Clubs:* Brooks's, Garrick, MCC; Cape Cod National Golf (USA).

SMITH, Maurice John, CB 2007; Diocesan Director of Education, Church of England Manchester Diocese, since 2007; *b* 16 March 1955; *s* of George and Edna Smith; *m* 1980, Alison Mary Jones; two *s*. *Educ:* Quarry Bank Comp. Sch.; Univ. of Wales (BA Hons 1976); Univ. of Manchester (MA Econ 1983); Univ. of Central Lancashire (MBA Dist. 1991); Manchester Metropolitan Univ. (MRes (Educn and Soc.) 2007). Office for Standards in Education: HMI, 1996–2002; Dir, Early Years, 2002–06; HM Chief Inspector, 2006. Pres., Bangor Old Stars on Merseyside, 1982–. *Recreation:* wandering around my garden in the evening. *Address:* Church of England Manchester Diocese, Church House, 90 Deansgate, Manchester M3 2GH.

SMITH, Melvyn Kenneth; actor, writer, director; *b* 3 Dec. 1952; *s* of Kenneth and Vera Smith; *m* 1988, Pamela Gay-Rees. *Educ:* Latymer Upper Sch., Hammersmith; New Coll., Oxford. Asst Dir, Royal Court Th., 1973; freelance Dir, Bristol Old Vic, 1973, Liverpool Everyman, 1974, Bush Th., 1975; Associate Director: Crucible Th., Sheffield, 1975–78; Young Vic, 1978–79; actor: Hairspray (musical), Shaftesbury, 2007; actor/writer, TV series: Not The Nine O'Clock News, Muck and Brass, Alas Smith and Jones, 1979–81; Smith & Jones, 1982–92, 1995, 1997, 1998; appeared in Small Doses (series of short plays), 1989; Milner, 1994. Films: The Tall Guy, 1989 (Dir); Wilt, 1989; Radioland Murders, 1995 (Dir); Twelfth Night, 1996; Bean, 1997 (Dir); High Heels and Low Lifes, 2001 (Dir); Blackball, 2003 (Dir). Director: TalkBack Prodns, 1982–; Playback Training Films, 1987–; Smith Jones Campbell (formerly Smith Jones Brown and Cassie Commercials) Ltd, 1988–99; Lola Prodns, 1998–. *Publications:* Not the book, 1981; Not the Nine O'Clock News Diary, 1982; Alas Smith and Jones Coffee Table Book, 1987; Janet Lives with Mel and Griff, 1988. *Club:* Groucho.

SMITH, Most Rev. Michael; *see* Meath, Bishop of, (RC).

SMITH, Michael A.; *see* Acton Smith.

SMITH, Michael Anthony; Foreign Editor, Daily Telegraph, since 2006; *b* Bristol, 9 March 1968; *s* of Patrick and Frances Smith; *m* 2004, Charlotte Smith; one *s* one *d*. *Educ:* King Edward's Sch., Bath; Univ. of York (BA Hons). Reporter: Western Gazette, 1992–93; The People, 1993–95; Asst News Ed., 1995–97, Associate News Ed., 1997–99, Daily Mail; Asst Ed., 1999–2001, Dep. Ed., 2001–02, Metro; Exec. News Ed., Evening Standard, 2002–04; News Ed., Daily Telegraph, 2005–06. *Recreation:* bagging Betty's in North Yorkshire. *Address:* Daily Telegraph, 111 Buckingham Palace Road, SW1W 0DT. *T:* (020) 931 2000; *e-mail:* mike.smith@telegraph.co.uk. *Clubs:* Glasgow Art; Lyke Wake Walk; Godfrey Evans Cricket.

SMITH, Sir Michael Edward C.; *see* Carleton-Smith.

SMITH, Michael Forbes; Director General, Chartered Institute of Arbitrators, since 2006; Founding Director, The Tempered and True Consultancy (diplomacy skills, international briefing), 2004–06; *b* 4 June 1948; *s* of Forbes Weir Smith and Elizabeth Smith (*née* Mackie); *m* 1st, 1974, Christian Joanna Kersley (marr. diss. 1983, annulled 1986); one *d*; 2nd, 1986, Claire Helen Stubbs (*see* C. H. Smith); one *s* one *d*. *Educ:* Aberdeen Grammar Sch.; Southampton Univ. (BSc Hons Geog.). BoT, 1966–68; commnd Gordon Highlanders, 1971, retd as Captain, 1978. HM Diplomatic Service, 1978–2004: Second Sec., FCO, 1978–79; Second, later First, Sec. and Hd of Chancery, Addis Ababa, 1979–83; Pol Advr to Civil Comr, later Gov., Falkland Is, Port Stanley, 1983–85; First Sec., FCO (SE Asia Dept, later FO Spokesman), 1985–89; Consul (Commercial), Zürich, 1990–94; Hd, Press and Public Affairs, Bonn, 1994–99; Dep. High Comr, Islamabad, 1999–2002; Ambassador to Republic of Tajikistan, 2002–04. Advr, Gulf Internat. Minerals Ltd, 2004–06. Non-exec. Dir, IDRS Ltd, 2007–. FRGS 1971; FRSA 1991; FSAScot 1995; MCIArb 2007; Accredited Mediator 2007. Mem., Appeal Cttee and Church Council, Farm St Ch, Mayfair, 1986–90; Vice-Pres., St Thomas More Parish Council, Bonn, 1996–99. Chm., Bonn Caledonian Soc., 1995–99. *Publications:* contributor: Diplomacy in the 21st Century series, Diplomatic Acad. of London; Piping Times. *Recreations:* music, Scotland, sailing, field and winter sports, entertaining and conviviality. *Address:* The Chartered Institute of Arbitrators, 12 Bloomsbury Square, WC1A 2LP. *Clubs:* Army and Navy; Royal Findhorn Yacht.

SMITH, Michael Gerard A.; *see* Austin-Smith.

SMITH, Michael John W.; *see* Winkworth-Smith.

SMITH, Prof. (Murdo) Alasdair (Macdonald); DL; DPhil; Professor of Economics, University of Sussex, since 1981 (Vice-Chancellor, 1998–2007); *b* 9 Feb. 1949; *s* of late John Smith and Isabella Smith (*née* Mackenzie); *m* Sherry Ferdman; two *d*. *Educ:* Nicolson Inst., Stornoway; Univ. of Glasgow (MA 1969); London Sch. of Econs (MSc 1970); DPhil Oxford 1973. Lecturer: University Coll., Oxford, 1970–72; LSE, 1972–81; Research Fellow, Centre for Econ. Policy Res., 1983–2002. Vis. Prof. of Econs, Coll. of Europe, 1991–98. DL E Sussex, 2001. Hon. DSc(Econ) Warsaw, 2004; Hon. LLD Sussex, 2008. *Publications:* A Mathematical Introduction to Economics, 1982; (ed with P. Krugman) Empirical Studies of Strategic Trade Policy, 1994; articles on international economics in learned jls. *Recreations:* walking, gardening, cooking. *Address:* 11 Gundreda Road, Lewes BN7 1PT. *T:* (01273) 472940; *e-mail:* alasdair@sussex.ac.uk.

SMITH, Neil; *see* Smith, G. N.

SMITH, Prof. Neilson Voyne, FBA 1999; Professor of Linguistics, University College London, 1982–2006, now Emeritus; *b* 21 June 1939; *s* of Voyne Smith and Lilian Freda Smith (*née* Rose); *m* 1966, Saraswati Keskar; two *s*. *Educ:* Trinity College, Cambridge (BA 1961, MA 1964); UCL (PhD 1964). Lectr in W African Languages, SOAS, 1964–70; Harkness Fellow, MIT and UCLA, 1966–68; Lectr in Linguistics and W African Languages, SOAS, 1970–72; University College London: Reader in Linguistics, 1972–81; Hd, Dept of Phonetics and Linguistics, 1983–90; Vice-Dean, 1992–94. Pres., Assoc. of Heads and Profs of Linguistics, 1993–94. Chm., Linguistics Assoc., 1980–86. Hon. Mem., Linguistic Soc. of America, 1999. *Publications:* An Outline Grammar of Nupe, 1967; The Acquisition of Phonology, 1973; (with Deirdre Wilson) Modern Linguistics, 1979; (ed) Mutual Knowledge, 1982; Speculative Linguistics, 1983; The Twitter Machine, 1989; (with Ianthi Tsimpli) The Mind of a Savant, 1995; Chomsky: ideas and ideals, 1999, 2nd edn 2004; Language, Bananas and Bonobos, 2002; Language, Frogs and Savants, 2005; articles in learned jls. *Recreations:* music, walking, travel, playing with children. *Address:* 32 Long Buftlers, Harpenden, Herts AL5 1JE; Department of Phonetics and Linguistics, University College London, Gower Street, WC1E 6BT. *T:* (020) 7580 5928; *e-mail:* smithnv@gmail.com.

SMITH, Nicholas George Edward L.; *see* Loraine-Smith.

SMITH, Nigel Christopher S.; *see* Starmer-Smith.

SMITH, Sir (Norman) Brian, Kt 1998; CBE 1980; Chairman, Cable and Wireless HKT (formerly Hong Kong Telecommunications) Ltd, 1995–97 and 1998–2000 (non-executive Director, 1997–98); *b* 10 Sept. 1928; *s* of late Vincent and Louise Smith; *m* 1955, Phyllis Crossley; one *s* one *d* (and one *s* decd). *Educ:* Sir John Deane's Grammar Sch., Northwich; Manchester Univ. (PhD Phys. Chemistry, 1954). FTI 1981. Joined ICI Ltd, Terylene Council, 1954; Fibres Division: Textile Develt Dir, 1969; Dep. Chm., 1972; Chm., 1975–78; ICI Main Bd, 1978–85; Director: Fiber Industries Inc., 1972–83; Canadian Industries Ltd, 1981–85; Territorial Dir for the Americas, and Chm., ICI Americas Inc., 1981–85 (Dir, 1980–85); Non-Exec. Dir, Carrington Viyella Ltd, 1979–81. Chairman: Metal Box plc, subseq. MB Group, 1986–89 (Dep. Chm., 1985–86); Lister & Co., 1991–94 (Dir, 1985–94; Dep. Chm., 1990–91); BAA plc, 1991–98; Cable and Wireless, 1995–98 (Dir, 1988–95); Hydron Ltd, 1994–2000; Director: Davy Corp., 1986–91; Yorkshire Chemicals, 1990–91; Mercury Communications, 1990–93; Berisford plc, 1990–96. Pres., British Textile Confedn, 1977–79; Chairman: Man-Made Fibres Producers Cttee, 1976–78; EDC for Wool Textile Industry, 1979–81; Priorities Bd for R&D in Agric. and Food, 1987–92; Heatherwood and Wexham Park Hosps Trust, 1991–97; Dir, John Cabot CTC Bristol Trust, 1997–98; Mem., BOTB, 1980–81, 1983–87 (Chm., N American Adv. Group, 1983–87). Chm., Standing Conf. on Schools' Sci. and Technology, 1992–96. Dir, Oxford Dio. Bd of Finance, 1990–2006. CCMI (CBIM 1985); FCIM. Freeman, City of London, 1986; Liveryman, Glovers' Co., 1986. Hon. DBA Buckingham, 1990. *Recreations:* sailing, tennis, gardening.

SMITH, Norman Jack, MA, MPhil; Chairman, Petroleum Venture Management Ltd, 2001–05; *b* 14 April 1936; *s* of late Maurice Leslie and Ellen Dorothy Smith; *m* 1967, Valerie Ann, *o d* of late A. E. Frost; one *s* one *d*. *Educ:* Grammar Sch., Henley-on-Thames; Oriel Coll., Oxford (MA); City Univ. (MPhil); Aberdeen Univ. (PhD). Dexion Ltd, 1957; Vickers Ltd, 1960; Baring Brothers & Co. Ltd, 1969; seconded as Industrial Director, 1977, Dir-Gen., 1978–80, Offshore Supplies Office, Dept of Energy; Chairman: British Underwater Engineering Ltd, 1980–83; Mentor Engineering Consultants, 1987–92; Man. Dir, Smith Rea Energy Associates Ltd, 1981–2000; Director: Smith Rea Energy Analysts, 1985–2000; Smith Rea Energy Aberdeen, 1990–2000; Gas Transmission, 1989–95; Capcis, 1999–2000. Mem., Offshore Energy Technology Bd, 1978–80. Council Mem., Canterbury Archaeol Trust, 2003–07; Chm., Friends of Canterbury Archaeol Trust, 2003–07. Patron, Oriel Coll. Develt Trust, 2003–. Fellow, Soc. of Business Economists; FEI (FInstPet 1978); FInstD. *Publications:* sundry articles in economic and oil industry jls. *Recreations:* walking, swimming, photography, history. *Club:* Oxford and Cambridge.

SMITH, Prof. (Norman John) David, FRCR; Professor of Dental Radiology, University of London, 1978–96, now Emeritus; *b* 2 Feb. 1931; *s* of late Norman S. Smith; *m* 1st, 1954, Regina Eileen Lugg (marr. diss.); one *s*; 2nd, 1983, Mary Christine Pocock; one *d*. *Educ:* King's Coll. Sch., Wimbledon; King's Coll., London; KCH Dental Sch. (BDS 1963; MPhil 1969); Royal Free Hosp. Sch. of Medicine (MSc 1966). FRCR 1997. Apprenticed to Pacific Steam Navigation Co., 1948–51; Officer Service, Royal Mail Lines, 1952–58 (Master Mariner, 1957); part-time posts at KCH Dental Sch., Guy's Hosp. Dental Sch. and in gen. dental practice, 1966–69; Sen. Lectr in Dental Surg., KCH Dental Sch., 1969–72; Hd of Dept of Dental Radiol., KCH Dental Sch., later King's Coll. Sch. of Medicine and Dentistry, 1972–96; Reader in Dental Radiol., Univ. of London, 1973–78; Course DIr, 1996–2002, Project Dir, 2002–04, Unit of Distance Educn, Guy's, King's and St Thomas' (formerly King's) Dental Inst., KCL. Civil Consultant to RAF, 1990–96. Member: Southwark Bor. Council, 1974–78; GLC for Norwood, 1977–86 (Leader of Opposition, ILEA, 1979–86); Thames Water Authority, 1977–83; SE Thames RHA, 1978–86; Council, Open Univ., 1978–81, 1982–91; Court, Univ. of London, 1982–87; Governor, Bethlem Royal and Maudsley Hosps, 1980–82; Mem., Bethlem Royal and Maudsley SHA, 1982–86. Vis. Prof. and lectr worldwide. Gov., King's Coll. Sch., Wimbledon, 1998–2003. Liveryman, Hon. Co. of Master Mariners. Hon. Mem., Polish Radiol Soc., 1989. DUniv Open, 1993. Sir Charlton Briscoe Res. Prize, KCH Med. Sch., 1969. *Publications:* Simple Navigation by the Sun, 1974; Dental Radiography, 1980; articles in dental jls. *Recreations:* sailing, cooking. *Address:* Beechwood, Old Lane, Tatsfield, Westerham, Kent TN16 2LH. *T:* (01959) 577661. *Club:* Athenæum.

SMITH, Patrick J.; *see* Janson-Smith.

SMITH, Paul Adrian; Chairman, Complete Communications Corporation Ltd, since 1986; Chairman and Joint Managing Director, Celador Films Ltd, since 1999; *b* 16 Jan. 1947; *s* of Clifford Bryce Smith and Marjorie Doreen Smith (*née* Walker); *m* 1980, Sarah Anne King; one *s* one *d*. *Educ:* Royal Belfast Academical Instn. Joined BBC TV as Trainee projectionist, 1966, various posts, incl. prodn manager and director, 1966–73; freelance television producer/dir, 1973–82; created It'll Be All Right on the Night, 1977; established: Complete Video Facilities, 1981; Celador Prodns, 1983 (Chm., 1983–2006); Complete Communications Corp., 1986; Celador Films, 1999; launched Who Wants to be a Millionaire? on UK TV, 1998, on US TV, 1999, sold worldwide rights, 2006. Executive Producer (films): Dirty Pretty Things, 2002 (12 industry awards, inc. Best Film, British Ind. Film Awards, 2003, and Evening Standard Film Awards, 2003); The Descent, Separate Lies, 2005. BAFTA Award, 1999; Emmy Award, USA, 2000 and 2001. *Recreations:* photography, cinema, collecting original sixties records, family and home. *Address:* Celador Films Ltd, 39 Long Acre, WC2E 9LG. *T:* (020) 7845 6802, *Fax:* (020) 7836 1117; *e-mail:* psmith@celador.co.uk.

SMITH, Sir Paul (Brierley), Kt 2000; CBE 1994; RDI 1991; fashion designer; Chairman, Paul Smith Ltd; *b* 5 July 1946; *s* of late Harold and Marjorie Smith; *m* 2000, Pauline Denyer. *Educ:* Beeston Fields Grammar Sch. Opened own shop, 1970 (part-time), 1974 (full time); has shops in London, Nottingham, NY, LA, Paris, Milan, Moscow, Hong Kong, Singapore, Taipei, Manila and over 220 in Japan; exporter to numerous other countries; retains Nottingham design room; Queen's Award for Export, 1995. Paul Smith True Brit exhibn, Design Mus., 1995. Freeman, City of Nottingham, 1997. Hon. FRIBA 2007. Hon. MDes Nottingham Trent, 1991. *Address:* Paul Smith Ltd, 20 Kean Street, WC2B 4AS. *T:* (020) 7836 7828. *Club:* Royal Automobile.

SMITH, Paul James; Chief Executive, City and County of Swansea, since 2006; *b* Colchester, 11 Nov. 1955; *s* of late Henry Joseph Smith and Jessie Elizabeth Mackenzie; *m* 1980, Keri Ann Jones; one *s*. *Educ:* Colchester Royal Grammar Sch.; Univ. of Wales Inst. of Science and Technol. (BSc Hons Town Planning; Postgrad. Dip. Town Planning).

Asst Dir (Housing), Cardiff CC, 1988–91; Gloucester City Council: City Housing Officer, 1991–96; Dir, Community Services, 1996–2001; Chief Exec., 2001–06. *Address:* City and County of Swansea, County Hall, Oystermouth Road, Swansea SA1 3SN. *T:* (01792) 637500; *e-mail:* paul.smith@swansea.gov.uk.

SMITH, Paul Jonathan, OBE 1999; Director, Egypt, British Council, and Cultural Counsellor, British Embassy, Cairo, since 2005; *b* 30 May 1956; *s* of late Arthur Godfrey Smith and Constance Mildred Smith (*née* Phelps); *m* 1999, Viveka Kumari; two *s* one *d*. *Educ:* King Edward's Sch., Birmingham; Queens' Coll., Cambridge (BA Hons double 1st 1978, MA 1982). Lectr in Lit., St Stephen's Coll., Univ. of Delhi, 1978–80; British Council: Asst Dir, Kano, 1983–85, Lagos, 1985–87; Dep. Dir, Drama and Dance Dept, 1987–89; Acting Director, Burma, Chile and Berlin, 1989–90; Dep. Dir, Dhaka, 1990–95; Director: NZ, 1995–99; Arts, 1999–2000; W India, 2000–05. *Publications:* (contrib. sections on Shakespeare and Wordsworth) Reference Guide to English Literature, 2nd edn 1991; articles on Shakespeare and Renaissance literature. *Recreations:* directing Shakespeare, all arts, particularly literature, drama and film. *Address:* c/o Foreign and Commonwealth Office, King Charles Street, SW1A 2AH. *T:* (Egypt) (2) 33001805, *Fax:* (2) 33443076; *e-mail:* paul.smith@britishcouncil.org.eg.

SMITH, Prof. Paul Julian, PhD; FBA 2008; Professor of Spanish, Cambridge University, since 1991; Fellow, Trinity Hall, Cambridge, since 1991; *b* 11 Nov. 1956; *s* of Albert Charles Smith and Margaret (*née* Tovey). *Educ:* Cambridge Univ. (BA 1980; MA 1982; PhD 1984). Res. Fellow, Trinity Hall, Cambridge, 1983–84; Lectr, QMC, London Univ., 1984–88; Reader, QMW, 1989–91; Hd, Dept of Spanish and Portuguese, Cambridge Univ., 1991–2001 and 2006–07. *Publications:* Quevedo on Parnassus, 1987; Writing in the Margin: Spanish literature of the Golden Age, 1988; The Body Hispanic: gender and sexuality in Spanish and Spanish American literature, 1989; A Critical Guide to El Buscon, 1991; Representing the Other: race, text and gender in Spanish and Spanish American narrative, 1992; Laws of Desire: questions of homosexuality in Spanish writing and film, 1992; Desire Unlimited: the cinema of Pedro Almodóvar, 1994; Vision Machines: cinema, literature and sexuality in Spain and Cuba, 1996; The Theatre of García Lorca: text, performance and psychoanalysis, 1998; The Moderns: time, space and subjectivity in contemporary Spanish culture, 2000. *Address:* Faculty of Modern and Medieval Languages, University of Cambridge, Sidgwick Avenue, Cambridge CB3 9DA. *T:* (01223) 335005.

SMITH, Penelope R.; *see* Russell-Smith.

SMITH, Peter, FSA; Secretary, Royal Commission on Ancient Monuments in Wales, 1973–91, retired; *b* 15 June; 1926; *s* of late L. W. Smith, HMI, and Mrs H. Smith (*née* Halsted); *m* 1954, Joyce Evelyn, *d* of late J. W. Abbott and of Alice Abbott (*née* Lloyd); two *s* one *d*. *Educ:* King Edward VI Sch., Southampton; Peter Symonds' Sch., Winchester; Oriel Coll. and Lincoln Coll. (Open Scholar), Oxford (BA, Hons Mod. Hist. 1947); Hammersmith Sch. of Building (Inter ARIBA 1950). Royal Commission on Ancient Monuments in Wales: Jun. Investigator, 1949; Sen. Investigator, 1954; Investigator in Charge of Nat. Monuments Record, 1963. President: Cambrian Archaeological Assoc., 1979; Vernacular Architecture Gp, 1983–86. Hon. Mem., Soc. of Architects in Wales, 1993. Hon. DLitt Wales, 1991. G. T. Clark Prize, 1969; Alfred Davis Hitchcock Medallion, Soc. of Architectural Historians of GB, 1978. *Publications:* Houses of the Welsh Countryside, 1975, 2nd edn 1988; contribs to Agrarian History of England; periodical literature on historic domestic architecture. *Recreations:* reading, drawing, learning Welsh. *Address:* Tŷ-coch, Lluest, Llanbadarn Fawr, Aberystwyth, Ceredigion SY23 3AU. *T:* (01970) 623556.

SMITH, Peter Alan, FCA; Director, NM Rothschild & Sons Ltd, since 2001; *b* 5 Aug. 1946; *s* of Dudley Vaughan Smith and Beatrice Ellen (*née* Sketcher); *m* 1971, Cherry Blandford; two *s*. *Educ:* Mill Hill Sch.; Univ. of Southampton (BSc); Wharton Sch., Univ. of Pennsylvania (AMP). FCA 1970. PricewaterhouseCoopers (formerly Coopers & Lybrand), 1967–2000: Partner, 1975–2000 (Senior Partner, 1998–2000); Chm., 1994–98; Mem., Global Leadership Team, 1998–2000. Dir and Dep. Chm., Equitable Life Assce Soc., 2001–; Director: Safeway plc, 2002–04; Savills plc, 2004– (Chm., 2004–); Templeton Emerging Markets Investment Trust plc, 2004– (Chm., 2007–); Associated British Foods plc, 2007–; Chm., RAC plc, 2003–05. Hon. Treas., UK Housing Trust, 1979–83. Member: Finance Cttee, Nat. Trust, 1991–98, 2001–05; Cttee on Corporate Governance, 1996–97; Council, ICAEW, 1997–2003 (Treas., 2001–03); POW Business Leaders Forum, 1994–2000; President's Cttee, 1994–98, F and GP Cttee, 1999–2008, CBI. Liveryman, Chartered Accountants' Co., 1993–. FRSA 1993; CCMI 1994. *Publication:* Housing Association Accounts and Their Audit, 1980. *Recreations:* golf, gardens. *Address:* (office) New Court, St Swithin's Lane, EC4P 4DU. *Clubs:* Carlton, Walbrook; Beaconsfield Golf.

SMITH, Peter Bruce, MA; Head Master, Bradfield College, 1985–2003; *b* 18 March 1944; *s* of Alexander D. Smith and Grace Smith; *m* 1968, Diana Margaret Morgan; two *d*. *Educ:* Magdalen College School, Oxford; Lincoln College, Oxford (Old Members Scholar; MA). Asst Master, Rugby Sch., 1967–85 (Head of Hist. Dept, 1973–77, Housemaster of School Field, 1977–85). Mem. Governing Body, Downe House Sch., 1985–89. Captain Oxfordshire County Cricket Club, 1971–77 (Minor Counties Champions, 1974). *Recreations:* antiquarian, sporting, literary. *Club:* Vincent's (Oxford).

SMITH, Prof. Peter Charles; Professor of Economics, since 1996, and Director, Centre for Health Economics, since 2005, University of York; *b* 29 July 1952; *s* of Dennis John Smith and Evelyn Mary Smith (*née* Rush); *m* 1986, Sally Jane Stone; one *d*. *Educ:* Birkenhead Sch.; Oriel Coll., Oxford (MA Maths 1974). Res. Fellow, Univ. of Cambridge, 1977–82; Lectr, 1984–94, Reader, 1994–96, Univ. of York. Member: DoH Adv. Cttee on Resource Allocation, 1997–2002; Audit Commn, 2003–. Chm., UK Centre for Measurement of Govt Activity, 2005–. Mem., Scientific Peer Rev. Gp, WHO, 2001–02. Council Mem., Royal Statistical Soc., 2002–06. Hon. Professor: Univ. of St Andrews, 1997–; LSE, 2005–; Monash Univ., 2006–. Founding Editor-in-Chief, Health Care Mgt Science, 1997–2005. *Publications:* (ed) Outcome Measurement in the Public Sector, 1996; (ed) Reforming Markets in Health Care, 2000; (ed) Measuring Up: improving health system performance in OECD countries, 2002; Formula Funding of Public Services, 2006; (jtly) Measuring Efficiency in Health Care, 2006; over 100 papers in acad. jls. *Recreations:* bridge, allotment gardening, jazz. *Address:* Centre for Health Economics, University of York, York YO10 5DD. *T:* (01904) 321443; *e-mail:* pcs1@york.ac.uk.

SMITH, Peter Claudius G.; *see* Gautier-Smith.

SMITH, Most Rev. Peter David; *see* Cardiff, Archbishop of, (RC).

SMITH, Peter David V.; *see* Vicary-Smith.

SMITH, Sir Peter Frank Graham N.; *see* Newson-Smith.

SMITH, Prof. Peter George, CBE 2001; Professor of Tropical Epidemiology, London School of Hygiene and Tropical Medicine, since 1989; *b* 3 May 1942; *s* of George Henry Smith and Lily Smith (*née* Phillips); *m* 1999, Jill Margaret Routledge; one *s*, and one step *s* one step *d*. *Educ:* City Univ. (BSc Applied Maths 1st Class 1963; DSc Med. Stats 1983). Statistical Res. Unit, MRC, 1965–67; Clinical and Population Cytogenetics Unit, MRC, 1967–69; Makerere Univ. Med. Sch., Uganda, 1970–71; WHO Internat. Agency for Res. on Cancer, Uganda, 1971–72; Cancer Epidemiology and Clinical Trials Unit, ICRF, Oxford, 1972–79; Dept of Epidemiology, Harvard Sch. of Public Health, 1975; Sen. Lectr, 1979–86, Reader, 1986–89, Hd, Dept of Epidemiol. and Population Scis, 1990–97, Hd, Dept of Infectious and Tropical Diseases, 1997–2002, LSH&TM. WHO Tropical Diseases Res. Prog., Geneva, 1987–88; Member: WHO, MRC, and DoH Cttees, incl. Spongiform Encephalopathy Adv. Cttee, 1996–2004 (Chair, 2001–04); Nuffield Council on Bioethics, 2003– (Dep. Chm., 2006–). Gov., Wellcome Trust, 2004–. FMedSci 1999. Hon. MFPH (Hon. MFPHM 1991). *Publications:* (ed with R. H. Morrow) Field Trials of health interventions in developing countries, 1996; numerous contribs to med. res. literature. *Recreations:* gardening, walking, cycling. *Address:* Department of Epidemiology and Population Health, London School of Hygiene and Tropical Medicine, Keppel Street, WC1E 7HT. *T:* (020) 7927 2246.

SMITH, Peter J.; *see* Jefferson Smith.

SMITH, Peter John, CPFA; Chairman, Gateshead Health NHS Foundation Trust (formerly NHS Trust), since 1998; *b* 31 Dec. 1936; *s* of Frank and Sarah Ann Smith; *m* 1st, Marie Louise Smith (marr. diss. 2001); one *s* one *d*; 2nd, 2001, Judith Anne Brown. *Educ:* Rastrick Grammar Sch., Brighouse, W Yorkshire. Trainee Accountant, Huddersfield CBC, 1953–59; Accountancy Asst, Bradford CBC, 1959–61; Asst Chief Accountant, Chester CBC, 1961–63; Computer Manager, Keighley BC, 1963–66; Asst City Treasurer, Gloucester CBC, 1966–69; Dep. Borough Treasurer, Gateshead CBC, 1969–73; Asst County Treasurer, Tyne and Wear CC, 1973–74, Dep. County Treasurer, 1974–80, County Treasurer, 1980–86. Gen. Manager, Tyne and Wear Residuary Body, 1985–88. Treasurer: NE Regional Airport Jt Cttee, 1980–86; Northumbria Police Authority, 1980–86; Northumbria Probation and After Care Cttee, 1980–86; Mem., Tyne and Wear Passenger Transport Exec. Bd, 1981–86. Director: N American Property Unit Trust, 1982–93; Northern Investors Co., 1983–86; Westgate Trust, 1990–92; Chm., Gateshead Healthcare and Community NHS Trusts, 1992–98. Mem. Bd, NHS Foundn Trust Network, 2006–. *Recreation:* fell walking. *Address:* Wheatsheaf House, 19 Station Road, Beamish, Co. Durham DH9 0QU. *T:* (0191) 370 0481, *Fax:* (0191) 370 2105.

SMITH, Peter John, CBE 1995; HM Diplomatic Service, retired; Governor, Cayman Islands, 1999–2002; *b* 15 May 1942; *s* of late John S. Smith and Irene (*née* Waple); *m* 1964, Suzanne Pauline Duffin; one *s* one *d*. *Educ:* St Dunstan's Coll., London. Joined FO, 1962; Vietnamese lang. student, then 3rd Sec., Saigon, 1964–67; Commercial Attaché, Paris, 1968–69; Commercial Publicity Officer, British Information Services, NY, 1970–73; FCO, 1973–76; 1st Sec., Commercial, Mexico City, 1976–80; Dep. High Comr, Port Louis, Mauritius, 1981–84; FCO, 1984–86; Deputy Consul General: Montreal, 1987–88; Toronto (also Dir, Trade and Investment), 1988–92; RCDS 1992; Ambassador to Madagascar and concurrently Ambassador (non-resident) to The Comoros, 1993–96; High Comr to Lesotho, 1996–99. *Recreations:* golf, cricket, chess, bridge. *Address:* Abbey Gardens, Abbey Street, Cerne Abbas, Dorset DT2 7JQ. *Clubs:* MCC; Somerset County Cricket.

SMITH, Peter Lincoln Chivers, FRCS, FRCP; Consultant Cardiothoracic Surgeon, Imperial College Healthcare NHS Trust (formerly Hammersmith Hospital, then Hammersmith Hospitals NHS Trust), since 1987; *b* 20 Sept. 1948; *s* of Alfred Stanley Chivers Smith and Cynthia Enid (*née* Anstee); *m* 1976, Susan Margaret Evans; one *s* two *d*. *Educ:* St Bartholomew's Hosp., Univ. of London (MB, BS 1975). MRCP 1978, FRCP 1997; FRCS 1980. General surgical trng, St Bartholomew's Hosp., 1976–79; cardiothoracic surgical trng, St Bartholomew's, Royal Brompton, Middlesex, Harefield and Hammersmith Hosps, 1979–86. Hunterian Prof., 1986–87, and Mem. Ct of Examiners, 1995–2003, RCS. FESC 2001; FETCS 2001. *Publications:* (jtly) The Brain and Cardiac Surgery, 1993; numerous scientific pubns on cardiac and thoracic surgical topics. *Recreations:* music, travelling. *Address:* Field House, Ferry Road, Orford, Woodbridge, Suffolk IP12 2NR. *Clubs:* Royal Automobile, Royal Society of Medicine.

SMITH, (Peter) Patrick J.; *see* Janson–Smith.

SMITH, Peter Vivian Henworth, CB 1989; Government legal adviser, 1990–99; Legal Adviser, Broadcasting Standards Council, later Broadcasting Standards Commission, 1989–98; *b* 5 Dec. 1928; *s* of Vivian and Dorothea Smith; *m* 1955, Mary Marjorie, *d* of Frank John Willsher and Sybil Marjorie Willsher; five *d*. *Educ:* Clacton County High Sch.; Brasenose Coll., Oxford (MA, BCL). Called to the Bar, Lincoln's Inn, 1953. HM Overseas Civil Service: Resident Magistrate, Nyasaland, 1955–63; Registrar, High Court, Nyasaland, 1963–64; Sen. Resident Magistrate, Malaŵi, 1964–69; Puisne Judge, Malaŵi, 1969–70; HM Customs and Excise: Legal Asst, 1970–72; Sen. Legal Asst, 1972–76; Asst Solicitor, 1976–82; Prin. Asst Solicitor, 1982–85; Solicitor, 1986–89. Legal Advr, Bldg Socs Commn, 1990–92. Treas., Friends of Malaŵi. *Recreations:* classical music, bridge, computers. *Address:* Likabula, 14 St Albans Road, Clacton-on-Sea CO15 6BA. *T:* (01255) 422053; *e-mail:* pvhsmith@aol.com.

SMITH, Peter William; His Honour Judge Peter Smith; a Circuit Judge, since 1994; *b* 31 Dec. 1945; *s* of late William and Bessie Smith; *m* 1970, Vanessa Mary (*née* Wildash); one *s*. *Educ:* Arnold Sch., Blackpool; Downing Coll., Cambridge (MA). Called to the Bar, Middle Temple, 1969. Practised (as William Smith) on Northern Circuit; a Dep. Judge Advocate, 1983–84; a Recorder, 1991–94. Mem., Mental Health Review Tribunal, 1993–. *Recreation:* weekends in the Lake District. *Address:* c/o The Law Courts, Ring Way, Preston PR1 2LL.

SMITH, Peter William G.; *see* Greig-Smith.

SMITH, Hon. Sir Peter (Winston), Kt 2002; **Hon. Mr Justice Peter Smith;** a Judge of the High Court of Justice, Chancery Division, since 2002; *b* 1 May 1952; *s* of George Arthur Smith and Iris Muriel Smith; *m* 1980, Diane Dalgleish; one *s* two *d*. *Educ:* Selwyn Coll., Cambridge (BA 1974; MA 1976); Coll. of Law. Called to the Bar, Lincoln's Inn, 1975, Bencher, 2000. Lectr, Manchester Univ., 1977–83; practice on Northern Circuit, 1979–2002; QC 1992; Asst Recorder, 1994–97; Actg Deemster, IOM, 1994–2002; a Deputy High Court Judge, 1996–2002; a Recorder, 1997–2002. *Recreations:* Titanic Historical Society, British Titanic Society, Jackie Fisher fan, reading military history, football. *Address:* Royal Courts of Justice, Strand, WC2A 2LL.

SMITH, Philip; *see* Smith, C. P.

SMITH, Philip Andrew B.; *see* Brook Smith.

SMITH, Ralph Andrew; QC (Scot.) 1999; *b* 22 March 1961; *s* of Rev. Ralph Colley Philip Smith and Florence Howat Smith; *m* 1989, Lucy Moore Inglis; one *s* one *d*. *Educ:* Edinburgh Acad.; Kelvinside Acad.; Aberdeen Univ. (LLB 1981; DLP 1982). Admitted to Faculty of Advocates, 1985; in practice, specialising in commercial law and planning; Jun. Counsel to Lord Pres. of Court of Session, 1989–90; Standing Jun. Counsel to DoE (Scotland), 1992–99. *Publications:* contribs to Scots Law Times. *Recreations:* field sports, Scottish Jun. Foil Fencing Champion, 1982. *Address:* Castlemains, Gifford, E Lothian EH41 4PL. *Club:* New (Edinburgh).

SMITH, Rt Rev. Raymond George; Senior Associate Minister, St Philip's, York Street, Sydney, since 2005; *b* 7 March 1936; *s* of Gordon William Smith and Alice Mary (*née* Brett); *m* 1960, Shirley Jeanette Gilmore; three *s*. *Educ:* Australian Coll. of Theology (ThSchol); Univ. of New England (BA, Dip Cont. Ed, MEd). Parish priest, dio. of Armidale, 1959–76; Dir of Christian Educn and Archdeacon, Armidale, 1977–86; Dir of Extension Ministries, Trinity Episcopal Sch. for Ministry, Ambridge, Pa, USA, 1986–90; Rector of Wanniassa, 1990–93, and Archdeacon of S Canberra, 1991–93, dio. of Canberra and Goulburn; Bp of Liverpool, NSW, and an Asst Bp of Sydney, 1993–2001; Sen. Asst Minister, St Clement, Mosman, NSW, 2002–04. *Publication:* People Caring for People, 1990. *Recreations:* swimming, cycling, photography, stamp collecting, Australian history. *Address:* 20/3A Blackwall Point Road, Abbotsford, NSW 2046, Australia.

SMITH, Richard James Crosbie W.; *see* Wilmot-Smith.

SMITH, Richard John, AM 1997; Director-General, Office of National Assessments, Canberra, 1996–98; *b* 14 Dec. 1934; *s* of C. A. Smith and T. A. O'Halloran; *m* 1958, Janet Campbell; two *s* two *d*. *Educ:* Sydney High Sch.; Sydney Univ. (BA, LLB Hons I 1958). Teacher, London, 1958–59; Solicitor, NSW, 1959–61; Foreign Affairs Trainee, 1961; First Sec., Australian Embassy, Washington, 1967–70; Dep. Perm. Rep., Australian Mission to UN, Geneva, 1972–74; Asst Sec., Internat. Legal Branch, 1974–75; Ambassador to Israel, 1975–77; First Assistant Secretary: Legal & Treaties Div., 1977–81; Management & Foreign Service Div., 1981–83; Actg Dep. Sec., Dept of Foreign Affairs, 1983–85; Ambassador to Thailand, 1985–88; Dep. Sec., Dept of Foreign Affairs and Trade, Canberra, 1988–90; High Comr for Australia in the UK, 1991–94; Ambassador to the Philippines, 1994–96. *Recreations:* walking, reading, travel. *Address:* 11 Glebe Street, Edgecliff, NSW 2027, Australia. *T:* (2) 93620504.

SMITH, Prof. Richard John, PhD; FBA 2007; Professor of Econometric Theory and Economic Statistics, University of Cambridge, since 2006; Lecturer in Economics and Fellow of Gonville and Caius College, Cambridge, since 2005; *b* Redhill, 14 May 1949; *s* of John Hayden Smith and Irene Smith (*née* Barlow); *m* 1975, Margaret Veronica Assumpta Breen. *Educ:* Bromley Grammar Sch.; Bournemouth Sch.; Churchill Coll., Cambridge (BA 1972); Univ. of Essex (MA 1976); PhD Cantab 1989. Res. Asst, SSRC Inflation Workshop, 1975–76, Lectr in Econometrics, 1976–89, Univ. of Manchester; Lectr in Econometrics, 1989–95, Reader in Theoretical Econometrics, 1995, Univ. of Cambridge; Coll. Lectr in Econs and Fellow, 1989–95, Dir of Studies in Econs, 1992–94, Gonville and Caius Coll., Cambridge; Professor: of Econs, Univ. of Bristol, 1995–2002; of Econometrics, Univ. of Warwick, 2002–05; Reader in Theoretical Econometrics, Univ. of Cambridge, 2005–06. Visiting Professor: Queen's Univ., Canada, 1983–84; Univ. of Montreal, 1994, 2001, 2006; CREST-INSEE, Paris, 1993, 1996, 2004; Univ. of Calif, Berkeley, 2006; Vis. Fellow, NIESR, 1997–; Centre Fellow, Centre for Microdata Methods and Practice, UCL and IFS, 2001–; 2002 Leverhulme Maj. Res. Fellow, 2003–06. Mem., Academic Econometric Panel, ONS, 1997–2003. Mem., Eur. Standing Cttee, 2002–04, GB and Ireland Regl Consultant, 2003–08, Fellow, 2007, Econometric Soc. Mem., Exec. Cttee, 2007–, Mem. Council, 2007–, REconS. Gov., NIESR, 2004–. Mem., Editl Bd, Rev. of Econ. Studies, 1986–94; Associate Ed., Econometrica, 1995–2007; Co-Ed., Econometric Theory, 2000–08; Man. Ed., Econometrics Jl, 2007– (Founding Ed., 1997–2001). *Publications:* contribs to Biometrika, Econometrica, Econometric Theory, Jl Econometrics, Jl Amer. Statistical Assoc., Rev. Econ. Studies. *Recreations:* fell walking, Manchester United FC, modernist architecture, theatre, film, reading. *Address:* Faculty of Economics, University of Cambridge, Austin Robinson Building, Sidgwick Avenue, Cambridge CB3 9DD. *T:* (01223) 335230, *Fax:* (01223) 335475; *e-mail:* rjs27@econ.cam.ac.uk.

SMITH, Richard Lloyd; QC 2001; a Recorder, since 2000; *b* 28 Jan. 1963; *s* of Lloyd and Dorothy Smith; *m* 1990, Anna Sara Webb; one *s* one *d*. *Educ:* King's Coll. London (LLB). Called to the Bar, Middle Temple, 1986. *Recreations:* Rugby, Leeds United Football Club. *Address:* Guildhall Chambers, 23 Broad Street, Bristol BS1 2HG. *T:* (0117) 927 3366.

SMITH, Prof. Richard Lyttleton, PhD; Mark L. Reed III Distinguished Professor of Statistics, University of North Carolina, since 2004 (Professor of Statistics, 1991–2004 (on leave, 1994–96)); *b* 31 March 1953; *s* of Stanley Lyttleton Smith and Hilary Margaret (*née* James); *m* 2002, Amy Grady; two *s*. *Educ:* Jesus Coll., Univ. of Oxford (BA Maths 1975; MA 1985); Cornell Univ., USA (PhD Ops Res. 1979). Lectr in Stats, Imperial Coll., London, 1979–85; Prof. of Statistics, Univ. of Surrey, 1985–90; Prof. of Statistical Sci., Univ. of Cambridge, 1994–96. Guy Medal in Silver, Royal Statistical Soc., 1991. *Publications:* (jtly) Statistical Analysis of Reliability Data, 1991; (with G. Alastair Young) Essentials of Statistical Inference, 2005; contrib. to Jl Roy. Statistical Soc., Proc. Royal Soc., Biometrika, Annals of Stats, etc. *Recreations:* cross-country and road running, chess, bridge, music. *Address:* 4314 Oak Hill Road, Chapel Hill, NC 27514–9731, USA.

SMITH, Prof. Richard Michael, PhD; FRHistS; FBA 1991; Professor of Historical Geography and Demography, since 2003, and Head, Department of Geography, since 2007, University of Cambridge; Director, Cambridge Group for the History of Population and Social Structure, since 1994; Fellow, since 1994, Vice-Master, since 2004, Downing College, Cambridge; *b* 3 Jan. 1946; *s* of Louis Gordon Smith and Elsie Fanny (*née* Ward); *m* 1971, Margaret Anne McFadden. *Educ:* Earls Colne Grammar Sch.; University Coll. London (BA Hons); St Catharine's Coll., Cambridge (MA 1977; PhD 1974). Lectr in Population Studies, Plymouth Poly., 1973–74; Cambridge University: Asst Lectr in Histl Geography, 1974–76; Sen. Res. Officer, 1976–81, Asst Dir, 1981–83, Cambridge Gp for the Hist. of Population and Social Structure; Fellow, 1977–83, Tutor, 1979–83, Fitzwilliam Coll.; Oxford University: Univ. Lectr in Histl Demography, 1983–89; Fellow, All Souls Coll., 1983–94; Reader in Hist. of Medicine and Dir, Wellcome Unit for Hist. of Medicine, 1990–94; Reader in Historical Demography, Cambridge Univ., 1996–2003. Mem. Council, British Soc. for Population Studies, 1987–91. Sir John Neale Lectr, 1996. Ed., Social Hist. of Medicine, 1986–92. *Publications:* (ed jtly) Bastardy and its Comparative History, 1980; (ed) Land, Kinship and Lifecycle, 1984; (ed jtly) The World We Have Gained: histories of population and social structure, 1986; (ed jtly) Life, Death and the Elderly: historical perspectives, 1991; (ed jtly) Medieval Society and the Manor Court, 1996; contribs to Annales ESC, Jl of Family Hist., Trans RHistS, Ageing and Society, Law and Hist. Rev., Population and Develt Rev. *Recreations:* listening to music, walking in Norfolk. *Address:* Cambridge Group for the History of Population and Social Structure, Sir William Hardy Building, Department of Geography, Downing Place, Cambridge CB2 3EN. *T:* (01223) 333181.

SMITH, Richard Philip Morley R.; *see* Reay-Smith.

SMITH, Richard Sydney William, CBE 2000; Chief Executive, UnitedHealth Europe, since 2004; Visiting Professor, London School of Hygiene and Tropical Medicine, since 1996; *b* 11 March 1952; *s* of Sydney Smith and Hazel Smith (*née* Kirk); *m* 1977, Linda Jean Arnott; two *s* one *d*. *Educ:* Roan Grammar Sch., London; Edinburgh Univ. (BSc 1973; MB ChB 1976); Stanford Univ. (MSc in Management 1990). MFPHM 1992, FFPH (FFPHM 1997); FRCPE 1992; MRCP 1993, FRCP 1995; FRCGP 1997; FRCSE 2000. Hosp. jobs in Scotland and New Zealand, 1976–79; British Medical Journal: Asst Editor, 1979; Sen. Asst Editor, 1984; Editor, and Chief Exec., BMJ Publishing Gp, 1991–2004. BBC Breakfast Time doctor, 1983–87. Founder, 1998, and Vice-Chm., 2001–04, Cttee on Publication Ethics; Member: Internat. Cttee of Med. Jl Editors, 1991–2004; Bd, World Assoc. of Med. Editors, 1994–2000; Editorial Boards: Nat. Med. Jl of India, 1992–2002; Ceylon Med. Jl, 1996–2002; Canadian Med. Assoc. Jl, 1997–2002; Hong Kong Jl of Family Practice, 1998–2002. Prof. of Med. Journalism, Univ. of Nottingham, 1993–2001. Chm., Foresight Wkg Pty on Inf. and Health, 2000; Member: UK Panel for Health and Biomed. Res. Integrity, 2006–; Medicines Partnership Taskforce, Nat. Prescribing Centre, 2006–. Member: Bd, Public Liby of Sci., 2004–; Adv. Bd, Global Trial Bank, 2005–. Mem. Gov. Council, St George's Hosp. Med. Sch., 2004–. Patron: Contact a Family, 1985–; Project Hope UK, 2004– (Mem. Bd, 1996–2002). Founder FMedSci 1998; Fellow, Acad. of Gen. Educn, Karnataka, India, 1993. HealthWatch Award, 2004. *Publications:* Alcohol Problems, 1982; Prison Health Care, 1984; The Good Health Kit, 1987; Unemployment and Health, 1987; (ed) Health of the Nation, 1991; (ed) Rationing in Action, 1993; (ed jtly) Management for Doctors, 1995; (ed jtly) Scientific Basis of Health Services, 1996; The Trouble with Medical Journals, 2006; articles in learned jls; contrib. Guardian. *Recreations:* jazz, cycling, running, wine, talking first and thinking second. *Address:* *e-mail:* Richard_S_Smith@uhc.com.

SMITH, Robert B.; *see* Bettley-Smith.

SMITH, Robert Carr, CBE 1989; PhD; Vice-Chancellor, Kingston University, 1992–97 (Director, Kingston Polytechnic, 1982–92); *b* 19 Nov. 1935; *s* of late Edward Albert Smith and of Olive Winifred Smith; *m* 1960, Rosalie Mary (*née* Spencer) (*d* 2004); one *s* one *d*. *Educ:* Queen Elizabeth's School, Barnet; Southampton Univ. (BSc); London Univ. (PhD). Research Asst, Guy's Hosp. Med. Sch., 1957–61; Lectr, Senior Lectr, Reader, Prof. of Electronics, Southampton Univ., 1961–82. Seconded to DoE, 1973–74. Chairman: Engineering Profs' Conf., 1980–82; Polytechnics and Colls Employers' Forum, 1988–90; Vice-Chm., Cttee of Dirs of Polytechnics, 1988–89; Member: Design Council, 1983–88; Council for Industry and Higher Educn, 1985–97; Council, Inst. for Manpower Studies, 1987–95; PCFC, 1988–93; TEC for Kingston, Merton and Wandsworth, 1989–97; Higher Educn Statistics Agency, 1993–97; Univs and Colls Employers' Assoc., 1994–97. Pt-time Chief Exec., SEARCH (careers service for Kingston, Merton and Wandsworth), 1998; Chm. Bd, Prospect Services Ltd, 2003–08. Chm., Bd of Govs, IoW Further Educn Coll., 1999–2003 and 2007–. Hon. Fellow, St George's Hosp. Med. Sch., 1998. Freeman, Royal Borough of Kingston upon Thames, 1997. *Publications:* research papers on radiation physics, laser physics, new technology. *Recreations:* visual arts, classical music. *Address:* 74 High Street, Fareham, Hampshire PO16 7BB.

SMITH, Sir Robert (Courtney), Kt 1987; CBE 1980; FRSE; MA, CA; Chairman, Alliance and Second Alliance Trust, 1984–96; *b* 10 Sept. 1927; 4th *s* of late John Smith, DL, JP, and Agnes Smith, Glasgow and Symington; *m* 1954, Moira Rose, *d* of late Wilfred H. Macdougall, CA, Glasgow; one *s* two *d* (and one *s* decd). *Educ:* Kelvinside Academy, Glasgow; Sedbergh Sch.; Trinity Coll., Cambridge. BA 1950, MA 1957. Served, Royal Marines, 1945–47, and RMFVR, 1951–57; Hon. Col, RM Reserves Scotland, 1992–96. Partner, Arthur Young McClelland Moores & Co., Chartered Accountants, 1957–78. Director: Standard Life Assurance, 1975–94 (Chm., 1982–88); Sidlaw Gp, 1977–97 (Chm., 1980–88); Wm Collins, 1978–89 (Vice-Chm., 1979–89); Volvo Trucks (GB), later Volvo Truck and Bus, 1979–98; Edinburgh Investment Trust, 1983–98; British Alcan Aluminium, 1983–99; Bank of Scotland, 1985–97. Mem., Scottish Industrial Develt Adv. Bd, 1972–88 (Chm., 1981–88); Pres., Business Archives Council of Scotland, 1986–97; Chancellor's Assessor, Glasgow Univ., 1984–96. Mem., Horserace Betting Levy Bd, 1977–82; Deacon Convener, Trades House of Glasgow, 1976–78; Dir, Merchants House of Glasgow, 1991–96. Mem. Council, Inst. of Chartered Accountants of Scotland, 1974–79. Trustee, Carnegie Trust for Univs of Scotland, 1982–2002. FRSE 1988. Hon. LLD: Glasgow, 1978; Aberdeen, 1991. CStJ 2004. *Address:* The Old Rectory, Cathedral Street, Dunkeld, Perthshire PH8 0AW. *T:* (01350) 727574. *Clubs:* East India; Western (Glasgow); Hawks (Cambridge).

See also John Smith.

SMITH, Robert Daglish, CMG 1998; Executive Director, UK Committee for UNICEF, 1980–99; *b* 2 July 1934; *s* of Robert Ramsay Smith and Jessie Smith (*née* Daglish); *m* 1984, Ursula Schmidt-Brümmer (*née* Stollenwerk). *Educ:* Dulwich Coll.; Queens' Coll., Cambridge (MA). Nat. Service, Royal Signals, 1953–55. Master, King's Sch., Canterbury, 1960–65; Lectr, Newland Park Coll. of Education, 1965–67; Consultant, Wells Management Consultants, 1968–70; freelance mgt consultant in fundraising and arts admin, 1970–74; Dir, East Midlands Arts Assoc., 1974–80. Sec., 1976–78, Chair, 1979–80, Standing Cttee of Regl Arts Assocs; Treas., Council, Children's Rights Alliance for England (formerly Children's Rights Office), 1992–2004. Trustee, NSPCC, 1999–2008; Mem. Council, Shakespeare's Globe, 2005– (Mem. Internat. Cttee, 2000–05); Bd Mem., UNA, 2002–07. FRSA 1990. *Recreations:* music, opera, theatre, travel. *Address:* 37E Westbourne Gardens, W2 5NR. *T:* (020) 7221 0890.

SMITH, (Robert) Harvey; show jumper, farmer; *b* 29 Dec. 1938; *m* 1st, Irene Shuttleworth (marr. diss. 1986); two *s*; 2nd, 1987, Susan Dye. First major win with Farmer's Boy. Leading Show Jumper of the Year; other major wins include: King George V Cup, Royal Internat. Horse Show, 1958; has won the John Player Trophy 7 times, King George V Gold Cup once, and the British Jumping Derby 4 times; Grand Prix and Prix des Nations wins in UK, Ireland, Europe and USA; took part in Olympic Games, 1968 and 1972; best-known mounts: Farmer's Boy, Mattie Brown, Olympic Star, O'Malley, Salvador, Harvester. BBC TV Commentator, Los Angeles Olympics, 1984. Assists wife in training of racehorses. *Publications:* Show Jumping with Harvey Smith, 1979; Bedside Jumping, 1985.

See also R. W. Smith.

SMITH, Prof. Robert Henry Tufrey, AM 1998; PhD; Chancellor, University of Ballarat, Australia, since 2005; *b* 22 May 1935; *s* of late Robert Davidson Smith and Gladys Smith (*née* Tufrey); *m* 1959, Elisabeth Jones; one *s* one *d*. *Educ:* Farrer Memorial Agricultural High Sch., Tamworth, NSW; Univ. of New England, NSW (BA, 1st Cl. Hons Geography); Northwestern Univ. (MA); ANU (PhD). Lectr in Geography, Univ. of Melbourne, 1961–62; University of Wisconsin: Asst Prof. of Geography, 1962–64;

Associate Prof., 1964–67; Prof., 1967–70; Chm., African Studies Programme, 1968–69 (on leave, 1964–66: Associate Res. Fellow, Nigerian Inst. for Social and Econ. Res., and Hon. Vis. Lectr in Geography, Univ. of Ibadan, 1964–65; Vis. Fellow, Dept of Geography, Univ. of Sydney, 1965–66); Prof. of Geography and Head of Dept, Queen's Univ., Kingston, Ontario, 1970–72; Prof. of Geography, Monash Univ., 1972–75 (Chm. of Dept, 1973–75; Associate Dean, Faculty of Arts, 1974–75); University of British Columbia: Prof. of Geography, 1975–85; Head of Dept, 1975–80; Associate Vice-Pres., Academic, 1979–83; Vice-Pres., Academic, 1983–85; Pres. *pro tem*, March–Nov. 1985; Vice-Chancellor, Univ. of WA, 1985–89; Chm., Nat. Bd of Employment, Educn and Trng, Aust., 1989–90; Vice-Chancellor, Univ. of New England, Australia, 1990–93; Exec. Dir, 1994–97, Sen. Consultant, 1997–99, Australian Educn Office, Washington; Dep. Chancellor, Southern Cross Univ., 1998–2002. *Address:* PO Box 5046, Victoria Point, Qld 4165, Australia.

SMITH, Sir Robert Hill, 3rd Bt *cr* 1945, of Crowmallie, Co. Aberdeen; MP (Lib Dem) Aberdeenshire West and Kincardine, since 1997; *b* 15 April 1958; *s* of Sir (William) Gordon Smith, 2nd Bt, VRD, and of Diana (*née* Goodchild); *S* father, 1983; *m* 1993, Fiona Anne Cormack; three *d*. *Educ:* Merchant Taylors' School; King's Coll., Aberdeen Univ. Contested (SDP/Lib Alliance), Aberdeen North, 1987. Mem. (Lib Dem) Aberdeenshire Unitary Council, 1995–97. Vice Chm., Grampian Jt Police Bd, 1995–97. Gen. Council Assessor, Aberdeen Univ. Court, 1994–98. *Heir: b* Charles Gordon Smith, *b* 21 April 1959. *Address:* Crowmallie House, Pitcaple, Inverurie, Aberdeenshire AB51 5HR. *T:* (01330) 820330; *e-mail:* bobsmith@cix.co.uk.

SMITH, Robert Lee, CB 2004; Director General, Regional Development Group, Office of the Deputy Prime Minister, 2004; *b* 9 Feb. 1952; *s* of John Joseph Smith and Joan Margaret Smith (*née* Parry); *m* 1986, Susan Elizabeth Armfield; one *s* one *d*. *Educ:* St Dunstan's Coll., Catford; Magdalene Coll., Cambridge (MA Eng. Lit.). Entered Civil Service as Administrative Trainee, 1974; DES, later DFE, then DFEE, subseq. DfES, 1981–2000: Principal Private Sec. to Sec. of State for Educn and Science, 1985–87; Under Sec., Pupils and Parents Br., 1994; Dir, Pupil Support and Inclusion Gp (formerly Pupils, Parents and Youth), 1995–2000; Dir Gen., Regional Co-ordination Unit, DETR, subseq. Cabinet Office, then ODPM, 2000–04. Public Sector Chm., Inst. of Mgt/CS Network, 1995–2000. Mem., Young People and Families Cttee, Joseph Rowntree Foundn, 1997–2000; Co-Chm., Social Policy Forum, 2003–. *Recreations:* folk dancing and music.

SMITH, Robert Walter; showjumper; *b* 12 June 1961; *e s* of (Robert) Harvey Smith, *qv*, and Irene Smith; *m* 1988, Leanne Carole Alston; one *s* three *d*. Member: GB junior and senior European events teams, 1977–; British Nations Cup Team, 1979–; World Class Performance Squad, 1999–2001, 2003; Gold team medal and Bronze individual medal, Jun. European Championships, 1977; Bronze team medal, European Championships, 1997; King George V Gold Cup winner, 1979, 1988, 1998. British Open Champion, 2005 and 2006. Top ranking rider and owner, BSJA, 2002. *Address:* Brookfurlong Farm, High Cross, Shrewley, Warwickshire CV35 7BD. *T:* (01926) 843886.

SMITH, Robin Anthony, TD 1978; DL; Consultant, DLA Piper (formerly Dibb Lupton Alsop, then DLA), solicitors, 1999–2008; *b* 15 Feb. 1943; *s* of late Tom Sumerfield Smith and Mary Smith; *m* 1967, Jennifer Elizabeth Roslington; one *s* one *d*. *Educ:* St Michael's Coll.; Manchester Univ. (LLB). Solicitor, admitted 1966; joined Dibb Lupton & Co., 1966; Partner, 1966–99; Man. Partner, 1988–93; Sen. Partner, Dibb Lupton & Co., later Dibb Lupton Broomhead, then Dibb Lupton Alsop, 1993–98. Mem. Council, Law Society, 1982–91; Pres., Leeds Law Soc., 1993–94. Director: Leeds (formerly Leeds & Holbeck) Bldg Soc., 1998– (Chm., 2007–); Town Centre Securities plc, 1999–; Local Dir, Coutts & Co., 1999–2006. Gov., Stonyhurst Coll., 1989–98. Commnd 5th Bn LI, TA, 1966; retired 1985, Lt-Col. DL W Yorks, 1991. KSG 2002. *Recreations:* tennis, golf. *Address:* c/o Leeds Building Society, 105 Albion Street, Leeds LS1 5AS. *Clubs:* Army and Navy, MCC; Leeds; Alwoodley Golf; Yorkshire CC (Pres., 2000–04).

SMITH, Robin F.; *see* Field-Smith.

SMITH, Rt Rev. Robin Jonathan Norman; Suffragan Bishop of Hertford, 1990–2001; Hon. Assistant Bishop, diocese of St Albans, since 2001; *b* 14 Aug. 1936; *s* of Richard Norman and Blanche Spurling Smith; *m* 1961, Hon. Lois Jean, *d* of Baron Pearson, CBE, PC; three *s* one *d*. *Educ:* Bedford Sch.; Worcester Coll., Oxford (MA); Ridley Hall, Cambridge. RAF Regiment Commission, 1955–57. Curate, St Margaret's, Barking, 1962–67; Chaplain, Lee Abbey, 1967–72; Vicar, Chesham St Mary, 1972–80; Rector, Great Chesham, 1980–90. Hon. Canon, Christ Church, Oxford, 1988–90. *Recreations:* gardening, walking. *Address:* 7 Aysgarth Road, Redbourn, Herts AL3 7PJ.

SMITH, Prof. Roderick Arthur, PhD, ScD; FREng, FIMechE, FIMMM; Royal Academy of Engineering Research Professor, Imperial College London, since 2006 (Professor and Head of Department of Mechanical Engineering, 2000–05); *b* 26 Dec. 1947; *s* of Eric and Gladys Mary Smith; *m* 1975, Yayoi Yamanoi. *Educ:* Hulme Grammar Sch., Oldham; St John's Coll., Oxford (BA, MA); Queens' Coll., Cambridge (MA; PhD 1975; ScD 1998). CEng 1976; FIMechE 1991; FIMMM (FIM 1992); FREng 1999. Queens' College, Cambridge: Godfrey Mitchell Res. Fellow, 1975–78; Official Fellow, College Lectr and Dir of Studies, 1978–88; Asst Lectr, Engrg Dept, Cambridge Univ., 1977–80, Lectr, 1980–88; Sheffield University: Prof. of Mech. and Process Engrg, 1988–2000; Hd, Dept of Mech. and Process Engrg, 1992–95; Royal Acad. of Engrg/BR Res. Prof., 1995–2000; Chm., Advanced Rly Res. Centre, 1993–2000; Warden, Stephenson Hall, 1992–2000. Sen. Vis. Res. Fellow, St John's Coll., Oxford, 2005–06. Chm., Coll. of Rly Technol., Derby, 1996–97. Consultant to: British Steel plc, 1986–89; BR, 1992–96 (Mem. Bd, Res. and Tech. Cttee, 1992–96). Mem., Res. and Tech. Cttee, AEA Technology, 1997–2006. Mem. Council, 1999–, Trustee, 2006–, IMechE. Trustee, Nat. Mus. of Science and Industry, 2002–. FCGI 2000. *Publications:* Thirty Years of Fatigue Crack Growth, 1986; Innovative Teaching in Engineering, 1991; Engineering for Crowd Safety, 1993; ed books; papers and articles on mech. engrg, design, manufacture, engrg educn and crowd engrg. *Recreations:* mountaineering, reading, history, Japan: its people and technology; conversation, wine. *Address:* Department of Mechanical Engineering, Imperial College London, Exhibition Road, SW7 2AZ. *T:* (020) 7594 7007. *Clubs:* Alpine; Fell and Rock (Lake District).

SMITH, Rodger H.; *see* Hayward Smith.

SMITH, Roger Huntington, FRCP, FRCPE; Joint Vice President, Royal College of Physicians of Edinburgh, 2005–06 (Vice President, 2003–05); *b* 9 April 1945; *s* of John Smith and Evelyn Smith; *m* 1971, Judith Elizabeth Martin; two *s*. *Educ:* Wallasey Grammar Sch.; Univ. of Edinburgh (BSc Hons (Physiol.) 1966; MB ChB 1969). FRCPE 1983; FRCP 1987. Consultant Physician and Cardiologist, Univ. Hosp. of N Tees, 1979–2007; Hon. Clinical Lectr, Univ. of Newcastle, 2000–. Associate Mem., GMC, 2001–08. Royal College of Physicians of Edinburgh: Chm., Collegiate Mems Cttee, 1979; Mem. Council, 1992–93, 1996–2002; Sec., 2001–03. *Publications:* articles on early work in infective endocarditis, pioneering res. in acute thrombolysis (with H. A. Dewar), substantial trialling of thrombolytics in acute infarction. *Recreations:* serious singer (formerly Mem., Edinburgh Festival Chorus, and for 25 years of chamber choir, Michelmas Singers), village politics, gardening, classical music, art, walking in the Lake District. *Address:* The Sheiling, High Street, Wolviston, Stockton on Tees, TS22 5JS. *T:* (01642) 624579, *Fax:* (01642) 624948.

SMITH, Roger John; Chairman: Cotton Spring Farm Ltd (family holding company), since 1975; Harpenden Building Society, since 1999; *b* 20 April 1939; *s* of Horace W. Smith and Marjorie E. Pummery; *m* 1962, Margaret R. Campbell; one *s* two *d*. *Educ:* Bedford School. Nat. Service, Subaltern, RCT, 1958–60. Dir, Family Group business, incl. Lea Heating Merchants (later part of Tricentrol), 1960–70; Man. Dir, Commercial Div., 1971–75, Dir, Special Projects, 1976–78, Tricentrol International; Dir, Group Co-ordination, Tricentrol, 1978–81; Man. Dir, Commercial Div., 1981–83; Dep. Chm., Tricentrol plc, 1983–88; Chm. and Chief Exec., Trimoco plc, 1987–92. Dir, Close Brothers AIM (VCT) plc, and other cos. Chm., European Motor Hlgs plc, 1994–2007. President: Retail Motor Industry Fedn, 1991–93; Internat. Orgn for Motor Trade and Repair, 1998–2000. Sloan Fellow, Stanford Univ., 1976. Chm., Lord's Taverners, 2000–02. Board Mem., Univ. of Herts. Chm., Central Finance Bd, Methodist Church, 2000–. Master, Coachmakers' and Coach Harnessmakers' Co., 2006. *Recreations:* sailing, shooting, tennis, reading. *Address:* Gilvers, Markyate, Herts AL3 8AD. *T:* (01582) 840536. *Clubs:* Royal Automobile, Royal Thames Yacht.

SMITH, Roger John Gladstone, OBE 2008; Director, Justice, since 2001; *b* 20 June 1948; *s* of Kenneth Smith and late Alice Smith; partner, Sue Berger; one *s* one *d*. *Educ:* York Univ. (BA 1970). Admitted solicitor, 1973; Solicitor, Camden Community Law Centre, 1973–75; Dir, W Hampstead Community Law Centre, 1975–79; Solicitor, Child Poverty Action Gp, 1980–86; Director: Legal Action Gp, 1986–98; Legal Educn and Training, Law Soc., 1998–2001. Hon. Prof., Kent Law Sch., 1998–; Vis. Prof., London South Bank Univ., 2008–. Hon. LLD Westminster, 2007. *Publications:* Children and the Courts, 1981; A Strategy for Justice, 1992; Shaping the Future: new directions in legal services, 1995; Achieving Civil Justice, 1996; Justice: redressing the balance, 1997; Legal Aid Contracting: lessons from North America, 1998. *Recreations:* walking, reading, managing an allotment. *Address:* Justice, 59 Carter Lane, EC4V 5AQ. *T:* (020) 7762 6412, *Fax:* (020) 7329 5100; *e-mail:* rsmith@justice.org.uk.

SMITH, Roger L.; *see* Lane-Smith.

SMITH, Roland Hedley, CMG 1994; HM Diplomatic Service, retired; Clerk, Wakefield and Tetley Trust, since 2004; *b* 11 April 1943; *s* of late Alan Hedley Smith and of Elizabeth Louise Smith; *m* 1971, Katherine Jane Lawrence; two *d*. *Educ:* King Edward VII School, Sheffield; Keble College, Oxford (BA 1st cl. hons 1965, MA 1981). Third Sec., Foreign Office, 1967; Second Sec., Moscow, 1969; Second, later First Sec., UK Delegn to NATO, Brussels, 1971; First Sec., FCO, 1974; First Sec. and Cultural Attaché, Moscow, 1978; FCO, 1980; attached to Internat. Inst. for Strategic Studies, 1983; Political Advr and Hd of Chancery, British Mil. Govt, Berlin, 1984–88; Dep. Hd, Sci., Energy and Nuclear Dept, FCO, 1988–90; Hd of Non-Proliferation and Defence Dept, FCO, 1990–92; Minister and Dep. Perm. Rep., UK Delegn to NATO, Brussels, 1992–95; Asst Under-Sec. of State, then Dir, (Internat. Security), FCO, 1995–98; Ambassador to Ukraine, 1999–2002. Dir, St Ethelburga's Centre for Reconciliation and Peace, 2002–04. *Publication:* Soviet Policy Towards West Germany, 1985. *Recreations:* music, esp. choral singing, football (Sheffield United), trams. *Address:* Wakefield and Tetley Trust, Attlee House, 28 Commercial Street, E1 6LR.

SMITH, Prof. Roland Ralph Redfern, DPhil; Lincoln Professor of Classical Archaeology and Art, University of Oxford, since 1995; *b* 30 Jan. 1954; *s* of Rupert and Elinor Smith; *m* 1988, Ingrid Gaitet. *Educ:* Fettes Coll., Edinburgh; Pembroke Coll., Oxford (BA 1977; MPhil 1979); Magdalen Coll., Oxford (DPhil 1983). Fellow, Magdalen Coll., Oxford, 1981–86; Asst Prof. of Classical Archaeology, 1986–90, Associate Prof., 1990–95, Inst. of Fine Arts, NY Univ. Harkness Fellow, Princeton, 1983–85; Alexander von Humboldt Fellow, Munich, 1991–92. Dir, Excavations at Aphrodisias, Caria, 1991–. *Publications:* Hellenistic Royal Portraits, 1988; Hellenistic Sculpture, 1991; The Monument of C. Julius Zoilos, 1993; Roman Portrait Statuary from Aphrodisias, 2006; contrib. learned jls. *Address:* Ashmolean Museum, Oxford OX1 2PH.

SMITH, Ronald Angus; General Secretary, Educational Institute of Scotland, since 1995; *b* 9 June 1951; *s* of William Angus and Daisy Smith; *m* 1976, Mary A. Lambie; one *s* one *d*. *Educ:* Anderson Educnl Inst., Lerwick; Univ. of Aberdeen (MA 1972); Aberdeen Coll. of Educn (PGCE 1973). Teacher, later Principal Teacher, Latin and Modern Studies, Broxburn Acad., W Lothian, 1973–88; Asst Sec., Educnl Inst. of Scotland, 1988–95. Hon. FEIS 2003. *Recreations:* Livingston FC, the Island of Foula. *Address:* (office) 46 Moray Place, Edinburgh EH3 6BH. *T:* (0131) 225 6244.

SMITH, Ronald George; Chief Executive, ESPC Group of Companies (formerly ESPC (UK) Ltd), since 2001; *b* 12 May 1954; *s* of John Hamilton Smith and Jean Lennox Smith (*née* Graeme); *m*, 1978, Elaine Sheila Murdoch (*née* McClure) (marr. diss. 1988); two *s*. *Educ:* George Heriot's Sch., Edinburgh; Edinburgh Univ. (MA Jt Hons Pol. and Mod. Hist., 1976); Queens' Coll., Cambridge (MPhil Internat. Relns, 1988); Kingston Poly. Business Sch. (MBA 1991). Commnd RAF, 1972; RAF Coll., Cranwell, 1976–77 (Queen's Medal); 51 Sqn RAF Regt, 1977–78; 63 Sqn RAF Regt, Gütersloh, 1978–81; HQ RAF Germany, Rheindahlen, 1981–82; RAF Lyneham, 1982–83; Dep. Sqn Ldr II Sqn (Para) RAF Regt, 1983–84; Sqn Ldr, 1984; Staff Officer, HQ 1 Gp, 1984; OC Short Range Air Defence, Belize, 1984–85; OC 1 (Light Armoured) Sqn RAF Regt, RAF Laarbruch, 1985–87; Wing Comdr, 1988; Desk Officer D Air Plans, 1988–92; retd RAF, 1992; Dep. Regl Dir, Corporate Planning, Trent RHA, 1992–93; Chief Executive: Lincs HA/FHSA, 1993–95; Defence Secondary Care Agency, MoD, 1995–98; mgt and consultancy rôles, 1998–2000; Chief Exec., Common Services Agency, NHS, Scotland, 2000–01. Chm., Scottish Solicitors' Property Centres Cttee, 2002–04; Mem., Scottish Archæol Finds Allocation Panel (formerly Treasure Trove Adv. Panel for Scotland), 2004–. Chm., Veterans Scotland, 2006–. Hon. Pres., RAF Regt Assoc. in Scotland, 2007–. Chartered MInstD, 2004; CDir 2004; FCMI 2005; FCIPD 2006. Mem., Merchant Co. of Edinburgh, 2002–. *Publications:* articles in jls. *Recreations:* downhill ski-ing, hillwalking, tennis, philately, fine wine, English landscape paintings. *Address:* c/o New Club, 86 Princes Street, Edinburgh EH2 2BB; *e-mail:* ron.smith@espc.com. *Club:* New (Edinburgh).

SMITH, Ronald Good; Sheriff of North Strathclyde, 1984–99; *b* 24 July 1933; *s* of Adam Smith and Selina Spence Smith; *m* 1962, Joan Robertson Beharrie; two *s*. *Educ:* Glasgow University (BL 1962). Private practice to 1984. *Recreations:* philately, photography, gardening, reading. *Address:* 8 Lomond View, Symington, Ayrshire KA1 5QS. *T:* (01563) 830763.

SMITH, Rosemary Ann, (Mrs G. F. Smith); Headmistress, Wimbledon High School, GPDST, 1982–92; *b* 10 Feb. 1932; *d* of late Harold Edward Wincott, CBE, editor of the Investors Chronicle, and of Joyce Mary Wincott; *m* 1954, Rev. Canon Graham Francis

Smith; two *s* two *d. Educ:* Brighton and Hove High School, GPDST; Westfield College, Univ. of London (BA Hons); London Univ. Inst. of Education (post grad. Cert. in Education). Assistant Teacher: Central Foundation Girls' School, 1964–69; Rosa Bassett Girls' School, 1970–77; Furzedown Secondary School, 1977–80; Deputy Head, Rowan High School, 1980–82. Mem. Council, GDST (formerly GPDST), 1993–2005. *Recreations:* theatre, gardening, reading. *Address:* The Haven, 9 High Street, Syresham, Brackley, Northants NN13 5HL. *T:* (01280) 850421.

SMITH, Air Marshal Sir Roy David A.; *see* Austen-Smith.

SMITH, Gen. Sir Rupert (Anthony), KCB 1996; DSO 1991 (and Bar 1996); OBE 1982; QGM 1978; Deputy Supreme Allied Commander, Europe, 1998–2001; Aide-de-Camp General to the Queen, 2000–01; *b* 13 Dec. 1943; *s* of late Gp Captain Irving Smith, CBE, DFC (and Bar) and Joan Smith (*née* Debenham). Parachute Regt, 1964; Dep. Comdt, Staff Coll., Camberley, 1989–90; Comdr, 1st Armoured Div., BAOR, Gulf, 1990–92; ACDS (Ops), 1992–94; Comdr, UN Protection Force Bosnia-Herzegovina, 1995; GOC and Dir of Military Ops, NI, 1996–98. Lt Col, 1980; Col, 1985; Brig., 1986; Maj.-Gen., 1990; Lt-Gen., 1995. *Publication:* The Utility of Force: the art of war in the modern world, 2005. *Address:* c/o RHQ The Parachute Regiment, Flagstaff House, Napier Road, Colchester CO2 7SW.

SMITH, Sandra Mary; *see* Thomas, S. M.

SMITH, Sandra Melanie, (Mrs K. M. Whittaker); Head of Conservation, Victoria and Albert Museum, since 2003; *b* 28 Oct. 1962; *d* of Anthony Smith and Margaret Smith; *m* 1985, Kenneth Martin Whittaker; one *s* two *d. Educ:* Institute of Archaeology, London (BSc Hons Archaeol Conservation and Material Sci.). Accredited Mem. UKIC 2000; FIIC 2002. British Museum: Hd of Ceramics and Glass Conservation, Dept of Conservation, 1992–97; Hd, Inorganic Materials Gp, 1997–2002; Actg Keeper, Conservation, 2002. Treas., Internat. Inst. for Conservation of Historic and Artistic Works, 2006–. *Publications:* (contrib.) The Art of the Conservator, 1992; (ed jtly) Past Practice, Future Prospects, 2001. *Recreations:* walking, gardening, cycling. *Address:* Department of Conservation, Victoria and Albert Museum, South Kensington, SW7 2RL. *T:* (020) 7942 2132, *Fax:* (020) 7942 2092; *e-mail:* sm.smith@vam.ac.uk.

SMITH, Shaun Malden; QC 2008; a Recorder, since 2001; *b* Sheffield, 3 March 1959; *s* of Jack and Jean Smith; *m* 1991, Janet Wilson. *Educ:* Grenoside Jun. Sch.; Ecclesfield Comp. Sch.; Sheffield Univ. (LLB Law 1980); Inns of Court Sch. of Law. Called to the Bar, Gray's Inn, 1981; in practice as barrister specialising in crime; Figtree Chambers, Sheffield, 1982–90, King Street Chambers, Leicester, 1990–92, 1 High Pavement Chambers, Nottingham, 1992–. Bar Vocational Course Examiner: Nottingham, 2003–06; College of Law, 2006–. *Recreations:* music (particularly Indie bands), reading, running, walking, golf, supporting Sheffield Wednesday. *Address:* 1 High Pavement Chambers, Nottingham NG1 1HF. *T:* (0115) 941 8218, *Fax:* (0115) 941 8240; *e-mail:* shaunsmithqc@highpavement.co.uk.

SMITH, Simon John Meredith; HM Diplomatic Service; Ambassador to Austria, and UK Permanent Representative to international organisations in Vienna, since 2007; *b* 14 Jan. 1958; *s* of Philip and Mary Smith (*née* Williams); *m* 1984, Sian Rosemary Stickings, MBE; two *d. Educ:* Triple C Sch., Grand Cayman; Clifton Coll.; Wadham Coll., Oxford (BA Modern Langs 1980; MA 1984); SOAS, London (Japanese). Dept of Employment, 1981–86, Manager, Unemployment Benefit Office, Tottenham, 1983–84; joined FCO, 1986; Second, then First Sec. (Econ.), Tokyo, 1989–92; Dep. Hd, S European Dept, FCO, 1995–97; Counsellor (Econ./Commercial), Moscow, 1998–2002; Hd, NE Asia and Pacific Dept, 2002–04, Hd, Eastern Dept, 2004–05, Dir, Russia, South Caucasus and Central Asia, 2005–07, FCO. *Recreations:* cooking, cricket, making a bad noise on piano and brass instruments. *Address:* c/o Foreign and Commonwealth Office, King Charles Street, SW1A 2AH.

SMITH, Prof. (Stanley) Desmond, OBE 1998; FRS 1976; FRSE 1972; Chairman, Edinburgh Instruments Ltd, since 1971; Professor of Physics and Head of Department of Physics, Heriot-Watt University, Edinburgh, 1970–96, now Professor Emeritus (Dean of the Faculty of Science, 1981–84); *b* 3 March 1931; *s* of Henry George Stanley Smith and Sarah Emily Ruth Smith; *m* 1956, Gillian Anne Parish; one *s* one *d. Educ:* Cotham Grammar Sch., Bristol; Bristol Univ. (BSc, DSc); Reading Univ. (PhD). SSO, RAE, Farnborough, 1956–58; Research Asst, Dept of Meteorology, Imperial Coll., London, 1958–59; Lectr, then Reader, Univ. of Reading, 1960–70. Member: ACARD, 1985–87; Defence Scientific Adv. Council, 1985–91; Astronomy, Space & Radio Bd, Engrg Bd, SERC, 1985–88; ACOST, 1987–88. Principal Investigator, Scottish Collaborative Initiative in Optoelectronic Scis, 1991–97. Mem. Council, Inst. of Physics, 1984–87; Chm., Scottish Optoelectronics Assoc., 1996–98. Hon. DSc Heriot-Watt, 2003. C. V. Boys Prizeman, Inst. of Physics, 1976; Educn in Partnership with Industry or Commerce Prize, DTI, 1982; Technical or Business Innovation in Electronics Prize, Electronics Weekly, 1986; James Scott Prize, RSE, 1987. *Publications:* Infra-red Physics, 1966; Optoelectronic Devices, 1995; numerous papers on semi-conductor and laser physics, satellite meteorology, nonlinear optics and optical computing. *Recreations:* ski-ing, mountaineering, golf, raising the temperature. *Address:* Tree Tops, 29D Gillespie Road, Colinton, Edinburgh EH13 0NW. *T:* (0131) 441 7225, (office) (01506) 425300, *Fax:* (01506) 425320; *e-mail:* des.smith@edinst.com, desgillsmith@googlemail.com; 106 Corniche du Pinateau, Chaillol 1600, 05260 St Michel de Chaillol, France. *T:* (4) 92500881; *e-mail:* desmond.smith@wanadoo.fr.

SMITH, Stanley Frank, MA; CEng, FIMechE; Vice-President (Technology), Urban Transport Development Company, Kingston, Ontario, 1985–86, retired; *b* 15 Dec. 1924; *s* of Frederick and Edith Maria Smith; *m* 1st, 1946, Margaret (*née* Garrett) (*d* 1984); two *s* three *d*; 2nd, 1987, Catherine Cooke Murphy. *Educ:* Purley Sch.; Hertford Coll., Oxford (MA). Served War, RAF Pilot, 1943–46. Oxford Univ., 1946–49. Rolls-Royce Ltd, 1949–65 (Chief Research Engineer, 1963); British Railways, 1965–71 (Dir of Engineering Research, 1965; Dir of Research, 1966); joined London Transport, 1971: Dir-Gen. of Research and Develt, 1971–72; Chief Mech. Engr, 1972–81, retired; Gen. Manager, Res. Develt, Urban Transport Development Co., 1981–85. *Recreations:* tennis, windsurfing, cycling, walking, ski-ing, sailing. *Address:* Rural Route 1, Bath, ON K0H 1G0, Canada. *T:* (613) 3527429.

SMITH, Stephen; *see* Smith, J. S.

SMITH, Stephen, MA; Headmaster, Bedford Modern School, since 1996; *b* 8 Aug. 1948; *s* of late Joseph Leslie Smith and Audrey May Smith; *m* 1970, Janice Susan Allen; one *s* one *d. Educ:* Loughborough Grammar Sch.; Regent's Park Coll., Oxford (BA Modern History 1969; Cert. Ed. 1970; MA 1974). Loughborough Grammar School: Asst History Master, 1970–87; Junior Housemaster, 1976–79; Head of General Studies, 1983–87; Head of History, 1987–93; Dep. Headmaster, Birkenhead Sch., 1993–96. Chm., HMC/GSA Sports Subcttee, 2001–. *Recreations:* piano, organ, singing, oenology, Church and youth work. *Address:* Bedford Modern School, Manton Lane, Bedford MK41 7NT; Bramble Cottage, Chapel Lane, Colmworth, Beds MK44 2JY. *Club:* East India.

SMITH, Prof. Stephen Kevin, DSc, MD; FRCOG; FMedSci; FIBiol; Principal, Faculty of Medicine, Imperial College London, since 2004; Chief Executive Officer, Imperial College Healthcare NHS Trust, since 2007; *b* 8 March 1951; *s* of Albert and Drusilla Smith; *m* 1978, Catriona Maclean Hobkirk Smith; one *s* two *d. Educ:* Birkenhead Sch.; Westminster Med. Sch., Univ. of London (MB BS 1974; MD 1982); DSc London 2002. FRCOG 1998 (MRCOG 1979); FIBiol 1997. Lecturer: Univ. of Edinburgh, 1979–82; Univ. of Sheffield, 1982–85; Cons. Gynaecologist, MRC Reproductive Biology Unit, Edinburgh, 1985–88; Prof. of Obstetrics and Gynaecol., Univ. of Cambridge Clin. Sch., Rosie Maternity, subseq. Addenbrooke's, Hosp., Cambridge, 1988–2004; Fellow, Fitzwilliam Coll., Cambridge, 1991–2004. Founder FMedSci 1998. FRSA. *Publications:* numerous contribs to sci. and med. pubns on the subject of Reproductive Medicine. *Recreations:* flying, football, music, natural history, politics. *Address:* Faculty of Medicine, Imperial College London, South Kensington Campus, SW7 2AZ.
See also I. R. Smith.

SMITH, Stephen Philip M.; *see* Moverley Smith.

SMITH, Maj.-Gen. Stephen Robert C.; *see* Carr-Smith.

SMITH, Stephen Wynn B.; *see* Boys Smith.

SMITH, Prof. Steven Murray, PhD; AcSS; Vice-Chancellor, University of Exeter, since 2002; *b* 4 Feb. 1952; *s* of William and Doris Smith; partner, Jeannie Forbes. *Educ:* Univ. of Southampton (BSc Soc. Scis 1973; MSc 1974; PhD 1978). Lectr in Politics, Huddersfield Poly., 1976–78; Lectr, 1979–85, Sen. Lectr, 1985–90, Prof., 1990–92, of Internat. Relns, UEA; Prof. of Internat. Politics, 1992–2002, Pro Vice Chancellor, 1999–2002, UCW, Aberystwyth, subseq. Univ. of Wales, Aberystwyth. Hon. Prof., Jilin Univ., China, 2007. Pres., Internat. Studies Assoc., 2003–04. AcSS 2000. Hon. DSc Southampton, 2004. *Publications:* Foreign Policy Adaptation, 1981; (ed with I. Forbes) Politics and Human Nature, 1983; (ed with M. Clarke) Foreign Policy Implementation, 1985; (ed) International Relations, 1985; (ed with R. Crockatt) The Cold War Past and Present, 1987; (ed jtly) British Foreign Policy, 1988; (ed with R. Little) Belief Systems and International Relations, 1988; (with M. Hollis) Explaining and Understanding International Relations, 1990; (jtly) Deciding Factors in British Politics, 1991; (ed with W. Carlsnaes) European Foreign Policy, 1994; (ed with K. Booth) International Relations Theory Today, 1995; (ed jtly) International Theory, 1995; (ed with J. Baylis) The Globalization of World Politics, 1997, 4th edn 2008; (ed jtly) International Relations Theory, 2007; (ed jtly) Foreign Policy, 2008. *Recreations:* Norwich City FC, theatre, music, firework displays, arctophile. *Address:* Vice-Chancellor's Office, University of Exeter, Northcote House, Queen's Drive, Exeter EX4 4QJ. *T:* (01392) 263000; *e-mail:* vice-chancellor@exeter.ac.uk.

SMITH, Stewart Ranson, CBE 1986; Controller, Europe Division, British Council, 1989–90; *b* 16 Feb. 1931; *s* of John Smith and Elizabeth Smith; *m* 1960, Lee Tjam Mui, (Amy), Singapore. *Educ:* Bedlington Grammar Sch., Northumberland; Nottingham Univ. (BA, MA); Yale Univ., USA (MA). British Council: Asst Rep., Singapore, 1957–59; Reg. Officer, Overseas A, 1959–61; Dir, Curitiba, Brazil, 1961–65; Asst Rep., Sri Lanka, 1965–69; Planning Officer, London, 1969–70; seconded Min. of Overseas Develt, 1970–73; Rep., Kenya, 1973–76; Controller, Overseas B, 1976–80; Rep., Spain, 1980–87; Controller, Higher Educn Div., 1987–89. Chm., Consortium for Madrid Capital City of Culture 1992, 1990–92; Consultant, Internat. Relations, Complutense Univ. of Madrid, 1993–95. Cross, Order of Isabella la Católica (Spain). *Recreations:* music, cricket. *Address:* Flat 10, Wellington Place, London Road, Cheltenham, Glos GL52 6EW. *Club:* Athenæum.

SMITH, Stuart Brian, OBE 2004; FMA; Secretary, International Committee for Conservation of Industrial Heritage, since 1986; *b* 19 Aug. 1944; *s* of Jack Fearnly Smith and Edith Dorothy Turner; *m* 1969, Jacqueline Slater; two *s* one *d. Educ:* Rochdale Grammar Sch.; Univ. of Surrey (BSc); Univ. of Manchester (MSc). Curator of Technology, Sunderland Museum, 1968–72; Ironbridge Gorge Museum: Curator of Technology, 1972; Dep. Dir, 1977–83; Dir, 1983–92; Chief Exec., Trevithick Trust, 1993–2002. Hon. Lectr, Univ. of Birmingham, 1981–92. Vice Pres., Assoc. for Industrial Archaeology, 1992– (Asst Sec., 1975–92). Member: Royal Commn on Ancient and Historical Monuments in Wales, 1991–96; Industrial Archaeology Panel, English Heritage, 1993–2002. Pres., Midlands Fedn of Museums and Galls, 1991–92 (Vice-Pres. 1989); Mem. Cttee, Icomos UK, 1987–. Mem. Council, Trevithick Soc., 1993–2002. Freedom of City of London, 1984; Freeman, Pewterers' Co., 2003. *Publications:* A View from the Ironbridge, 1979; (with Michael Sagar-Fenton) Serpentine, 2005; articles in learned jls. *Recreations:* collecting, industrial archaeology. *Address:* Chygarth, 5 Beacon Terrace, Camborne, Cornwall TR14 7BU. *T:* and *Fax:* (01209) 612142.

SMITH, Stuart Graham, FRICS; Director, All England Lawn Tennis Ground plc, since 1997; President, Lawn Tennis Association, since 2006; *b* Paddington, 18 Feb. 1946; *s* of James Pettigrew and Ethel Mary Smith; *m* 1968, Marilyn Lesley; three *s. Educ:* John Ruskin Grammar Sch., Croydon; St Catharine's Coll., Cambridge (BA 1967). FRICS 1982. Partner, Collier & Madge, Chartered Surveyors, 1969–85; Dir, Lambert Smith Hampton, Chartered Surveyors, 1985–2002. *Recreations:* Association Football, gardening, family, tennis. *Address:* Upper Pryors, Cowden, Kent TN8 7HB. *T:* (01342) 850384; *e-mail:* sgscowden@tiscali.co.uk. *Club:* All England Lawn Tennis.

SMITH, Rt Rev. Stuart Meldrum; Assistant Bishop, Diocese of Adelaide, 1992–98; *b* 8 June 1928; *s* of late F. R. and O. E. Smith; *m* 1957, Margaret (*d* 2006), *d* of J. L. F. and D. M. Sando; three *s* two *d. Educ:* Univ. of Adelaide (BA Hons English); St Michael's House, SSM (Scholar in Theol. (Hons), ACT). Ordained 1953; Asst Curate, Glenelg, 1954–56; Mission Chaplain, Meadows, 1956–57; Domestic Chaplain, Bishop of Adelaide, and Precentor, St Peter's Cathedral, 1957–58; Priest-in-charge, Kilburn, 1958–61; Editor, Adelaide Church Guardian, 1959–61 and 1965–76; Rector: Clare, 1961–65; Coromandel Valley (with Blackwood, Eden Hills and Belair), 1965–69; Belair, 1969–72; Unley, 1972–84; Canon of Adelaide, 1974–84; Archdeacon: of Sturt, 1976–84; of Adelaide, 1984–92; Dir of Home Mission and Evangelism, 1984–92. Acting Dean, St Peter's Cathedral, Adelaide, 1998–99; Associate in Ministry, St John's, Adelaide, 2000. Visiting Lecturer: St Barnabas Coll., 1966–81; St Michael's House, 1975–77. Hon. Chaplain, Walford C of E Girls' Grammar Sch., 1973–75. Mem., Gen. Synod and Gen. Synod Standing Cttee, 1979–98. Chm., Council of Govs, Pulteney Grammar Sch., 1973–97. *Recreations:* walking, reading, gardening. *Address:* 4B Eleventh Avenue, St Peters, SA 5069, Australia. *T:* (8) 83625847.

SMITH, Susan Gwynneth; Chair, Local Government Boundary Commission for Wales, 2001–08 (Member, 1996–2001); *b* 18 Dec. 1946; *d* of George Henry David Abbott and Victoria Gwynneth May Abbott; *m* 1969, David Charles Smith. *Educ:* Tiffin Sch. for Girls,

Kingston-upon-Thames; University Coll. London (LLB ext. 1970). Admitted as solicitor, 1970; Asst Solicitor, Hammersmith and Fulham LBC, 1970–73; Sen. Solicitor, then Asst Borough Solicitor, 1973–78, Borough Solicitor, 1978–92, Wandsworth LBC; Dir, Admin. and Legal Services, Cardiff CC, 1992–96. Mem., Parly Boundary Commn for Wales, 1998–2008. Mem., Standing Orders Commn, Nat. Assembly for Wales, 1998–99. Chair, Standards Cttee, Pembrokeshire CC, 2001–. Non-exec. Dir, Cardiff and Vale NHS Trust, 2000–02. Ind. Adjudicator for Local Authorities in Wales, 2003–08. *Recreations:* reading, music, choral singing, visiting Venice. *Address:* c/o Local Government Boundary Commission for Wales, Caradog House, 1–6 St Andrews Place, Cardiff CF10 3BE; *e-mail:* smith.sycamores@btinternet.com.

SMITH, Terence Charles; Chief Executive: Collins Stewart, since 2000; Tullett Prebon, since 2006; *b* 15 May 1953; *s* of Ernest George and Eva Ada Smith; *m* 1974, Barbara Mary George; two *d*. *Educ:* Stratford Grammar Sch.; University Coll., Cardiff (BA); Management Coll., Henley (MBA). Mgt trainee, then Gp Finance Manager, Barclays Bank, 1974–83; Bank Analyst, W. Greenwell & Co., 1984–86; Hd, Financial Desk, BZW, 1986–88; Bank Analyst, James Capel, 1988–89; Hd of Res., UBS Phillips & Drew, 1990–92; Bank Analyst, 1992–96, Dir, 1996–2000, Collins Stewart; Collins Stewart acquired Tullett, 2003 and Prebon, 2004; Collins Stewart Tullett Prebon demerged, 2006. ACIB 1976; Series 24, Nat. Assoc. of Securities Dealers. *Publication:* Accounting for Growth, 1992, 2nd edn 1996. *Recreations:* boxing, shooting. *Address:* Collins Stewart, 9th Floor, 88 Wood Street, EC2V 7QR. *T:* (020) 7523 8443.

SMITH, Thomas C.; *see* Cavalier-Smith.

SMITH, Rt Rev. Timothy D.; *see* Dudley-Smith.

SMITH, Timothy John; Partner, H. M. Williams Chartered Accountants, since 2001; Director, Nevill Hovey & Co. Ltd Chartered Accountants, since 2002; *b* 5 Oct. 1947; *s* of late Captain Norman Wesley Smith, CBE and Nancy Phyllis Smith; *m* 1980, Jennifer Jane Scott-Hopkins, *d* of Sir James Scott-Hopkins; two *s*. *Educ:* Harrow Sch.; St Peter's Coll., Oxford (MA). FCA; CTA. Articled with Gibson, Harris & Turnbull, 1969; Audit Sen., Peat, Marwick, Mitchell & Co., 1971; Company Sec., Coubro & Scrutton (Hldgs) Ltd, 1973. Sec., Parly and Law Cttee, ICA, 1979–82. Pres., Oxford Univ. Conservative Assoc., 1968; Chm., Coningsby Club, 1977–78. MP (C): Ashfield, April 1977–1979; Beaconsfield, May 1982–1997. PPS to Chief Sec. HM Treasury, 1983, to Sec. of State for Home Dept, 1983–85; a Vice Chm. and Treas., Conservative Party, 1992–94; Parly Under-Sec. of State, NI Office, 1994. Member: Public Accts Cttee, 1987–92, 1995–97; Select Cttee on NI, 1994–97; Vice-Chm., Cons. Finance Cttee, 1987–92. Director: Quality South West Ltd, 2003–07; Harbour Centre (Plymouth), 2004–. Mem. Council, ICA, 1992–94. Chm., Launceston Abbeyfield Soc., 2003–; Treas., St Petroc's Soc., 2005–. *Recreations:* theatre, gardening. *Address:* Queen's Acre, Boyton, Launceston, Cornwall PL15 9RJ.

SMITH, Timothy Peter P.; *see* Pigott-Smith.

SMITH, Vanessa Frances H.; *see* Hall-Smith.

SMITH, Prof. Vernon Lomax, PhD; Professor of Economics and Law, Chapman University, Orange, California, since 2008; Professor of Economics and Law, George Mason University, 2001–08, now Emeritus; *b* 1 Jan. 1927; *s* of Vernon Chessman Smith and Lulu Belle Smith (*née* Lomax, then Bougher); *m* Candace C. Smith. *Educ:* North High Sch., Kansas; CIT (BS 1949); Univ. of Kansas (MA 1952); Harvard Univ. (PhD 1955). Purdue University, Indiana: Mem., Mgt Scis Res. Gp, 1955–56; Asst Prof., 1956–58, Associate Prof., 1958–61, Prof. of Econs, 1961–64, Krannert Prof., 1964–67; Professor of Economics: Brown Univ., Rhode Island, 1967–68; Univ. of Mass, Amherst, 1968–75; Prof. of Econs, 1975–88, Regents Prof., 1988–2001, Univ. of Arizona, Tucson. Vis. Associate Prof., Stanford Univ., 1961–62; Fellow, Center for Advanced Study in Behavioral Scis, Calif, 1972–73; Sherman Fairchild Dist. Scholar, CIT, 1973–74; Vis. Prof., USC and CIT, 1974–75; Adjunct Scholar, Cato Inst., Washington, 1983–. (Jtly) Nobel Prize for Econs, 2002. *Publications:* include: (jtly) Economics: an analytical approach, 1958; Investment and Production, 1961; Economics of Natural and Environmental Resources, 1977; (ed) Research in Experimental Economics, vol. 1, 1979, vol. 2, 1982, vol. 3, 1985; (ed) Schools of Economic Thought, 1990; Papers in Experimental Economics, 1991; Experiments in Decision, Organization and Exchange, 1993; Bargaining and Market Behavior: essays in experimental economics, 2000; articles in jls. *Address:* School of Law, Chapman University, One University Drive, Orange, CA 92866, USA.

SMITH, Vincent; Partner, Cohen, Milstein, Hausfeld & Toll LLP, since 2007; *b* 11 Dec. 1962; *m* 1997, Barbara Cross; one *s*. *Educ:* Univ. of Surrey (BSc Hons); Univ. of Liège (licence spécial-droit européen). Admitted solicitor, 1990; Simmons & Simmons, 1988–98; Partner, Pinsent Curtis, 1999–2000; Sen. Legal Advr, Office of Telecommunications, 2000–02; Office of Fair Trading: Dir, Competition Policy Co-ordination, and Dep. Divisional Dir, 2002–03; Dir, Competition Enforcement Div., 2003–06; Sen. Dir for Competition, 2006–07. *Address:* (office) 25 Southampton Buildings, WC2A 1AL. *T:* (020) 3170 7726; *e-mail:* vsmith@cmht.com.

SMITH, Walter Purvis, CB 1982 OBE 1960 (MBE 1945); Director General, Ordnance Survey, 1977–85, retired; *b* 8 March 1920; *s* of John William Smith and Margaret Jane (*née* Purvis); *m* 1946, Bettie Cox; one *s* one *d*. *Educ:* Wellfield Grammar Sch., Co. Durham; St Edmund Hall, Oxford (MA). FRICS 1951. Commnd RE (Survey), 1940; served War, UK and Europe, 1940–46; CO 135 Survey Engr Regt (TA), 1957–60. Directorate of Colonial (later Overseas) Surveys: served in Ghana, Tanzania, Malaŵi, 1946–50; Gen. Man., Air Survey Co. of Rhodesia Ltd, 1950–54; Fairey Surveys Ltd, 1954–75 (Man. Dir, 1969–75); Adviser: Surveying and Mapping, UN, NY, 1975–77; Ordnance Survey Review Cttee, 1978–79. Mem., Field Mission, Argentine-Chile Frontier Case, 1965. 15th British Commonwealth Lectr, RAeS, 1968. Dir, Sys Scan (UK) Ltd, 1985–90. President: Photogrammetric Soc., 1972–73; European Council of Heads of National Mapping Agencies, 1982–84; Eur. Orgn for Photogrammetric Res., 1984–85; Guild of Surveyors, 1985–88; Chm., National Cttee for Photogrammetry and Remote Sensing, 1985–88; Dep. Chm., Govt Cttee of Enquiry into Handling of Geographical Information, 1985–87; Mem., Gen. Council, RICS, 1967–70 (Chm., Land Survey Cttee, 1963–64). Patron's Medal, RGS, 1985. *Publications:* papers and technical jls. *Recreations:* music, walking, woodworking. *Address:* 15 Forest Gardens, Lyndhurst, Hants SO43 7AF. *T:* (023) 8028 2566.

SMITH, Wendy Alison K.; *see* Kenway-Smith.

SMITH, Wilbur Addison; author; *b* 9 Jan. 1933; *m* 1971, Danielle Antoinette Thomas (*d* 1999); *m* 2000, Mokhiniso Rakhimova; two *s* one *d* by former marriages. *Educ:* Michaelhouse, Natal; Rhodes Univ. (BCom). Business executive, 1954–58; factory owner, 1958–64; full-time author, 1964–. *Publications:* When the Lion Feeds, 1964; Dark of the Sun, 1965; Sound of Thunder, 1966; Shout at the Devil, 1968; Gold Mine, 1970; Diamond Hunters, 1971; The Sunbird, 1972; Eagle in the Sky, 1974; Eye of the Tiger, 1975; Cry Wolf, 1976; Sparrow Falls, 1977; Hungry as the Sea, 1978; Wild Justice, 1979; A Falcon Flies, 1980; Men of Men, 1981; The Angels Weep, 1982; The Leopard hunts in Darkness, 1984; The Burning Shore, 1985; Power of the Sword, 1986; Rage, 1987; A Time to Die, 1989; Golden Fox, 1990; Elephant Song, 1991; River God, 1993; The Seventh Scroll, 1995; Birds of Prey, 1997; Monsoon, 1999; Warlock, 2001; Blue Horizon, 2003; A Triumph of the Sun, 2005; The Quest, 2007. *Recreations:* fly fishing, big game angling, wing shooting, ski-ing, scuba diving.

SMITH, Sir William Antony John R.; *see* Reardon Smith.

SMITH, William Austin N.; *see* Nimmo Smith, Rt Hon. Lord.

SMITH, William Jeffrey, CB 1976; Under-Secretary, Northern Ireland Office, 1972–76; *b* 14 Oct. 1916; 2nd *s* of Frederick Smith, Sheffield, and Ellen Hickinson, Ringinglow, Derbyshire; *m* 1942, Marie Hughes (*d* 2007); one *s* one *d*. *Educ:* King Edward VII Sch., Sheffield; University Coll., Oxford (Schol.) (MA). Employed by Calico Printers' Assoc., Manchester, 1938–40 and in 1946. Served War, Army: enlisted Sept. 1939, embodied, 1940; RA and York and Lancaster Regt (Captain), 1940–46. Dominions Office (subseq. CRO), 1946; Principal, 1948; Office of UK High Commissioner in South Africa, 1953–56; Asst Sec., 1959; sundry internat. confs; Dept of Technical Co-operation, 1961–64; Min. of Overseas Development, 1964–70; Overseas Develt Admin., 1970–72; UK Rep. to UNESCO, 1969–72. Sec. to Widgery Tribunal on loss of life in Londonderry, 1972; Northern Ireland Office, 1972. *Recreations:* theatre, walking, bell ringing. *Address:* Lime Tree Cottage, Norris Lane, Chaddleworth, Newbury, Berks RG20 7DZ. *T:* (01488) 638610.

SMITH, (William) Nigel W.; *see* Wenban-Smith.

SMITH, William Peter; *see* Smith, P. W.

SMITH, Zoë Philippa; Her Honour Judge Zoë Smith; a Circuit Judge, since 1999; *b* 16 May 1949; *d* of late Basil Gerrard Smith and of Marjorie Elizabeth Smith (*née* Artz). *Educ:* Queenswood, Hatfield. Called to the Bar, Gray's Inn, 1970; in practice at the Bar, 1970–99; a Recorder, 1991–99. *Recreation:* dining out. *Address:* 15 New Bridge Street, EC4V 6AU.

SMITH-BINGHAM, Col Jeremy David; Director General, British Equestrian Federation, 1994–97; *b* 29 July 1939; *s* of Col Oswald Cyril Smith-Bingham and Vera Mabel Smith-Bingham (*née* Johnson); *m* 1969, Priscilla Mary Incledon-Webber; three *s*. *Educ:* Cheam; Eton; RMA, Sandhurst. Commnd Royal Horse Guards (The Blues), 1959; Lt Col, 1981; jssc, 1982; CO, The Blues and Royals, 1982–85; CO, Tactical Sch., RAC, 1985–87; Col, 1987; Chief Exercise Planner, HQ N Army Gp, 1987–90; Comdr, Household Cavalry, and Silver Stick to the Queen, 1990–93; COS, HQ London Dist, 1993–94. *Recreations:* horses, tennis, rackets, ski-ing, water sports, fishing, shooting, golf. *Address:* St Brannocks House, Braunton, Devon EX33 1HN. *T:* (01271) 812270; *e-mail:* mail@stbrannocks.com. *Clubs:* White's, Cavalry and Guards.

SMITH-CAMERON, Rev. Canon Ivor Gill; Chaplain to the Queen, 1995–99; *b* 12 Nov. 1929; *s* of James Smith-Cameron and Cynthia Smith-Cameron (*née* Fitzgerald). *Educ:* Madras Christian Coll., India (MA Eng. Lang. and Lit.); Coll. of Resurrection, Mirfield, Yorks. Ordained deacon, 1954; priest, 1955; Curate, St George's, Rumboldswyke, Chichester, 1954–58; Chaplain, London Univ., 1958–72; Canon Residentiary and Diocesan Missioner, Dio. Southwark, 1972–92; Asst Curate, All Saints, Battersea, 1992–94; retd 1994; Canon Residentiary Emeritus, 1994. Hon. DD Serampore Coll., India, 2004. *Publications:* Pilgrimage: an exploration into God, 1982; The Church of Many Colours, 1998; New Fire, 2000. *Recreations:* cooking, jam making, reading, walking. *Address:* 24 Holmewood Gardens, SW2 3RS. *T:* (020) 8678 8977; *e-mail:* holmewood24@surefish.co.uk.

SMITH-DODSWORTH, Sir John (Christopher), 8th Bt *cr* 1784; *b* 4 March 1935; *s* of Sir Claude Smith-Dodsworth, 7th Bt, and Cyrilla Marie Louise von Sobbe, (*d* 1984), 3rd *d* of William Ernest Taylor, Linnet Lane, Liverpool; *S* father, 1940; *m* 1st, 1961, Margaret Anne (*née* Jones) (marr. diss. 1971); one *s* one *d*; 2nd, 1972, Margaret Theresa (*d* 1990) (*née* Grey), Auckland, NZ; one *s*; 3rd, 1991, Lolita (marr. diss. 2004), *d* of Romeo Pulante; one *s* one *d*; 4th, 2006, Nerrisa, *d* of Mateo Feratero. *Educ:* Ampleforth Coll., Yorks. Now resident in Coromandel, New Zealand. *Publications:* (jtly) New Zealand Ferns and Allied Plants, 1989; New Zealand Native Shrubs and Climbers, 1991. *Heir: s* David John Smith-Dodsworth [*b* 23 Oct. 1963; *m* 1996, Elizabeth Anne Brady, Thirsk, N Yorks; one *s* one *d*].

SMITH-GORDON, Sir (Lionel) Eldred (Peter), 5th Bt *cr* 1838; engaged in book publishing, since 1960; *b* 7 May 1935; *s* of Sir Lionel Eldred Pottinger Smith-Gordon, 4th Bt, and Eileen Laura (*d* 1979), *d* of late Captain H. G. Adams-Connor, CVO; *S* father, 1976; *m* 1962, Sandra Rosamund Ann, *d* of late Wing Commander Walter Farley, DFC and of Mrs Dennis Poore; one *s* one *d*. *Educ:* Eton College; Trinity College, Oxford. Chm., Smith-Gordon and Co. Ltd; Dir, Dietetic Consultants Ltd. *Heir: s* Lionel George Eldred Smith-Gordon [*b* 1 July 1964; *m* 1993, Kumi, *d* of Masashi Suzuki, Japan; two *s* one *d*]. *Address:* 13 Shalcomb Street, SW10 0HZ. *T:* (020) 7352 8506.

SMITH-LAITTAN, James, CMG 1995; HM Diplomatic Service, retired; *b* 13 May 1939; *s* of James Smith and Etta Smith (*née* Hay); *m* 1969, Mary Susan Messer; three *d*. *Educ:* Buckie High Sch.; North West Poly., London. Nat. Service, 1st Queen's Dragoon Guards, 1958–60; Admiralty, 1961–62; joined CRO, 1963; Dacca, 1964–66; FCO, 1966–68; Brussels, 1968; Rabat, 1969–72; Accra, 1972–75; Rome, 1975–79; Asst Overseas Insp., FCO, 1979–82; Trade Comr, Hong Kong and concurrently Consul, Macao, 1982–86; Asst Head, Migration and Visa Dept, FCO, 1987–90; Commercial Mgt and Exports Dept, FCO, 1990–91; Trade Counsellor and Head of China Trade Unit, Hong Kong, 1991–95; Consul-Gen., Auckland, 1996–99. *Recreations:* crosswords, gardening, European train travel, private flying. *Club:* Hong Kong (Hong Kong).

SMITH-MARRIOTT, Sir Hugh Cavendish, 11th Bt *cr* 1774, of Sydling St Nicholas, Dorset; Public Relations and Marketing Executive Director, since 1987; Director, H.S.M. Marketing Ltd, Bristol, since 1988; *b* 22 March 1925; *s* of Sir Ralph George Cavendish Smith-Marriott, 10th Bt and Phyllis Elizabeth (*d* 1932), *d* of Richard Kemp; *S* father, 1987; *m* 1953, Pauline Anne (*d* 1985), *d* of F. F. Holt; one *d*. *Educ:* Bristol Cathedral School. Man. Dir, Drawing Office Co., 1956; Group Marketing Executive, Bryan Brothers Group, 1976. Dir, Bristol Fest. of Remembrance, RBL, 1966–2006; Mem., Royal Marines Assoc., Bristol. *Recreations:* hockey (county level), cricket, painting, theatre. *Heir: b* Peter Francis Smith-Marriott [*b* 14 Feb. 1927; *m* 1961, Jean Graham Martin, *d* of James Sorley Ritchie; five *s* (including twin *s*)]. *Clubs:* MCC; Gloucestershire CC, Durham CC, Bristol Savages, Bristol RF.

See also D. A. Graveney.

SMITHERS, Prof. Alan George, PhD; CPsychol; author and broadcaster; Professor of Education and Director, Centre for Education and Employment Research, University of Buckingham, since 2004; *b* 20 May 1938; *s* of late Alfred Edward Smithers and Queenie Lilian Smithers; *m* 1962, Angela Grace Wykes (marr. diss. 2003); two *d. Educ:* King's Coll., Univ. of London (BSc, PhD 1966); Bradford Univ. (MSc, PhD 1974). CPsychol 1988. Lecturer in: Biol., Coll. of St Mark and St John, Chelsea, 1962–64; Botany, Birkbeck Coll., Univ. of London, 1964–67; Research Fellow, then Sen. Lectr in Educn, Bradford Univ., 1967–76; Prof. of Educn, Univ. of Manchester, 1977–96; seconded to British Petroleum, 1991–92; Prof. of Educn (Policy Res.), Brunel Univ., 1996–98; Sydney Jones Prof. of Educn, Liverpool Univ., 1998–2004. Member: Nat. Curriculum Council, 1992–93; Beaumont Cttee on Vocational Qualifications, 1995–96; Special Advr, H of C Educn and Employment Cttee, 1997–2001, Educn and Skills Cttee, 2001–07, Children, Schs and Families Cttee, 2007–. Fellow, Soc. for Res. into Higher Educn, 1986. Hon. MEd Manchester, 1981. *Publications:* Sandwich Courses: an integrated education?, 1976; The Progress of Mature Students, 1986; What Employers Want of Higher Education, 1988; Graduates in the Police Service, 1990; Gender, Primary Schools and the National Curriculum, 1991; The Vocational Route into Higher Education, 1991; Every Child in Britain, 1991; Assessing the Value, 1992; All Our Futures: Britain's education revolution, 1993; The New Zealand Qualifications Framework, 1997; Assessment in Primary Schools, 1998; Teacher Qualifications, 2003; England's Education, 2004; Blair's Education: an international perspective, 2007; with Dr Pamela Robinson: The Shortage of Maths and Physics Teachers, 1988; The Growth of Mixed A-Levels, 1988; Increasing Participation in Higher Education, 1989; Teacher Loss, 1990; Trends in Science and Technology Manpower Demands and Mobilities, 1990; Teacher Provision in the Sciences, 1991; Teacher Provision: trends and perceptions, 1991; Staffing Secondary Schools in the Nineties, 1991; Beyond Compulsory Schooling, 1991; Teacher Turnover, 1991; Technology in the National Curriculum, 1992; Technology at A-Level, 1992; General Studies: breadth at A-Level?, 1993; Changing Colleges: further education in the market place, 1993; Technology Teachers, 1994; The Impact of Double Science, 1994; Post-18 Education: growth, change, prospect, 1995; Affording Teachers, 1995; Co-educational and Single-Sex Schooling, 1995; Trends in Higher Education, 1996; Technology in Secondary Schools, 1997; Staffing Our Schools, 1997; Co-educational and Single-Sex Schooling Revisited, 1997; Degrees of Choice, 1998; Teacher Supply: passing problem or impending crisis?, 1998; Teacher Supply: old story or new chapter?, 1999; Further Education Re-formed, 2000; Coping with Teacher Shortages, 2000; Talking Heads, 2000; Attracting Teachers, 2000; Teachers Leaving, 2001; Factors in Teachers' Decisions to Leave the Profession, 2003; The Reality of School Staffing, 2003; Teacher Turnover, Wastage and Movements between Schools, 2005; Physics in Schools and Colleges, 2005; Five Years On, 2006; Patterns and Policies in Physics Education, 2006; The Paradox of Single Sex and Coeducation, 2006; Bucking the Trend, 2007; School Headships: present and future, 2007; book chapters; numerous papers in jls of biology, psychology and educn. *Recreations:* walking, theatre. *Address:* Centre for Education and Employment Research, University of Buckingham, Buckingham MK18 1EG. *T:* (01280) 820270, *Fax:* (01280) 820343; *e-mail:* alan.smithers@buckingham.ac.uk.

SMITHIES, Frederick Albert; General Secretary, National Association of Schoolmasters and Union of Women Teachers, 1983–90; *b* 12 May 1929; *s* of Frederick Albert and Lilian Smithies; *m* 1960, Olga Margaret Yates. *Educ:* St Mary's Coll., Blackburn, Lancs; St Mary's Coll., Twickenham, Middx. Schoolteacher: Accrington, Lancs, 1948–60; Northampton, 1960–76. NAS/UWT (before 1975, NAS): Nat. Executive Member, 1966–76; Chm. of Education Cttee, 1972–76; Vice-President, 1976; Asst Gen. Secretary, 1976–81; Dep. Gen. Secretary, 1981–82; Gen. Sec. Designate, 1982–83. Member: Exec. Bd, European Trade Union Cttee for Educn, 1982–93; TUC Gen. Council, 1983–89; Exec. Bd, Internat. Fedn of Free Teachers' Unions, 1985–93 (Hon. Treas., 1989–93). *Recreations:* reading, music, theatre. *Address:* High Street, Guilsborough, Northampton NN6 8PY.

SMITHIES, His Honour Kenneth (Charles Lester); a Circuit Judge, 1975–90; *b* 15 Aug. 1927; *s* of late Harold King Smithies and Kathleen Margaret (*née* Walsh); *m* 1st, 1950, Joan Winifred (*née* Ellis) (*d* 1983); one *s* two *d*; 2nd, 1996, Kathleen Mary, (Kitty), Floyd (*née* Stevens). *Educ:* City of London Sch. (Corporation Scholar); University College London (LLB). Volunteered 60th Rifles, 1945, later commnd in Royal Artillery, in India; demobilised, 1948. Called to Bar, Gray's Inn, 1955. *Recreations:* music, bridge, pedantry. *Address:* 18 Catharine Place, Bath BA1 2PS. *T:* (01225) 318535. *Clubs:* Athenæum; Bath and County (Bath).

SMITHSON, Rt Rev. Alan; Hon. Assistant Bishop, diocese of Glasgow and Galloway, since 2002, and diocese of Edinburgh, since 2007; Hon. Assistant Curate, All Saints, Challock, since 2002; *b* 1 Dec. 1936; *s* of Herbert and Mary Smithson; *m* 1964, Margaret Jean McKenzie; two *s* two *d. Educ:* Queen's Coll., Oxford (BA 1962; MA 1968); Queen's Coll., Birmingham (DipTh 1964). Deacon 1964, priest 1965; Curate: Christ Church, Skipton, 1964–68; St Mary the Virgin with St Cross and St Peter, Oxford, 1968–72; Chaplain: Queen's Coll., Oxford, 1969–72; Reading Univ., 1972–77; Vicar of Bracknell, 1977–84; Residentiary Canon, Carlisle Cathedral and Dir of Training and Diocesan Training Inst., 1984–90; Bp Suffragan of Jarrow, 1990–2001. External Moderator: Ministry Div., NE Oecumenical Course, 2002–05; Theol Inst. of Scottish Episcopal Ch, 2003–06. Chm., Pastoral Cttee, Mission to Seafarers, 1991–2006. Brigade Chaplain, Church Lads and Church Girls' Bde, 1997–2007. *Recreations:* water colour painting, travel, camping, fell walking, 'cello playing. *Address:* 4 Eskside East, Musselburgh EH21 7RS.

SMITHSON, Michael; Director of Development and Alumni Relations, University of York, 2005–07; Editor, politicalbetting.com, since 2004; *b* 11 May 1946; *s* of late Arthur Smithson and Doris Smithson (*née* Simpson); *m* 1969, Jacqueline Anne Cowan; one *s* two *d. Educ:* Burnage GS, Manchester; London Sch. of Econs (LLB). Thomson Orgn Grad. Trng Scheme, with Newcastle Jl and Evening Chronicle, 1968–71; BBC Radio News: Mem., Editl Staff, 1971–78; Duty Ed., 1978–80; Dep. Hd, BBC TV Licence Campaign, 1980–81; i/c Corporate Publicity Unit, BBC, 1982–84; Dir, Public Relns, RSPCA, 1984–88; Mgt Consultant, 1988–91, Dir, 1990–91, Finite Gp plc; Man. Dir, Pemberley Associates, 1991–94; Dir of Fundraising, LSE, 1994–96; Develt Dir, Univ. of Cambridge, and Fellow of Queens' Coll., Cambridge, 1996–99; Dir of Develt, Univ. of Oxford, 1999–2005; Fellow, Magdalen Coll., Oxford, 2000–05. Councillor (Lib Dem): Beds CC, 1990–96; Bedford BC, 1996–2000. Contested (Lib Dem) N Beds, 1992. *Recreations:* cycling, bridge, enjoying fine teas, my family. *Address:* 5 Devon Road, Bedford, Beds MK40 3DJ.

SMOLIRA, Very Rev. David Richard, SJ; Director, Jesuit Institute for Faith and Culture, Johannesburg, since 2006; Regional Superior, South Africa, since 2008; *b* 9 Sept. 1955; *s* of Mieczyslaw and Eileen Smolira. *Educ:* Manchester Univ. (BSc); Heythrop Coll., London Univ. (BD); Liverpool Univ. (Advanced DipSocSc with CQSW); St Louis Univ., USA (MSocWork); Loyola Chicago Univ., USA (MSc). UKCP Registered Psychotherapist. Entered Society of Jesus, 1978; ordained priest, 1988; Dir, Home & Away Project, Catholic Children's Soc., 1989–94; Provincial Asst for Formation, SJ, 1997–99; Provincial Superior of the British Province, SJ, 1999–2005. *Recreations:* gardening, natural history, photography. *Address:* 493 Marshall Street, Belgravia, Johannesburg, 2094, South Africa.

SMOUHA, Joseph; QC 2003; *b* 20 Jan. 1963; *s* of Brian and Hana Smouha; *m* 1994, Lucy Howard; two *s. Educ:* Harrow Sch.; Magdalene Coll., Cambridge (MA); New York Univ. Sch. of Law (Kenneson Fellow; Fulbright Schol.). Called to the Bar, Middle Temple, 1986; specializes in internat. commercial law. Dir, English Concert, 2003–; Trustee, Young@Now, 2001–. Gov., Royal Sch., Hampstead, 2003–. *Recreations:* opera, ski-ing, walking, tennis, clarinet player. *Address:* Essex Court Chambers, 24 Lincoln's Inn Fields, WC2A 3EG. *T:* (020) 7813 8000, *Fax:* (020) 7813 8080.

SMOUT, Prof. (Thomas) Christopher, CBE 1994; PhD; FBA 1988; FRSE; FSAScot; Director, Institute for Environmental History, University of St Andrews, 1992–2001; Historiographer to the Queen in Scotland, since 1993; *b* 19 Dec. 1933; *s* of Sir Arthur and Lady (Hilda) Smout; *m* 1959, Anne-Marie Schøning; one *s* one *d. Educ:* The Leys Sch., Cambridge; Clare Coll., Cambridge (MA; PhD 1960). FRSE 1975; FSAScot 1991. Dept of Economic History, Edinburgh University: Asst Lectr, 1959; Lectr, 1962; Reader, 1964; Prof. of Econ. History, 1970; University of St Andrews: Prof. of Scottish History, 1980–91; Dir, St John's House Centre for Advanced Histl Studies, 1992–97. Visiting Professor: Strathclyde Univ., 1991–97; Dundee Univ., 1993–2005; York Univ., 1998–99; Hon. Prof., Stirling Univ., 2000–06. Member: Cttee for Scotland, Nature Conservancy Council, 1986–91; Bd, NCC (Scotland), 1991–92; Bd, Scottish Natural Heritage, 1992–98 (Dep. Chm., 1992–97); Royal Commn on Ancient and Historic Monuments of Scotland, 1987–2000 (Vice-Chm., 2000); Bd of Trustees, Nat. Museums of Scotland, 1991–95; Royal Commn on Historical Manuscripts, 1999–2003; Adv. Council on Public and Private Records, 2003–04. Chm., Scottish Coastal Archaeol. and the Problem of Erosion Trust, 2002–; Trustee, Woodland Trust, 1998–2004. Patron, Scottish Native Woods, 2004–. Hon. Fellow, TCD, 1995. Hon. DSSc QUB, 1995; Hon. DSc (SocSci) Edinburgh, 1996; Hon. DLitt: St Andrews, 1999; Glasgow, 2001; DUniv Stirling, 2002. *Publications:* Scottish Trade on the Eve of Union, 1963; A History of the Scottish People, 1969; (with I. Levitt) The State of the Scottish Working Class in 1843, 1979; A Century of the Scottish People, 1986; (with S. Wood) Scottish Voices, 1990; (with A. Gibson) Prices, Food and Wages in Scotland, 1995; Nature Contested, 2000; (jtly) A History of the Native Woodlands of Scotland 1500–1920, 2005. *Recreations:* birdwatching, butterflies, bees. *Address:* Chesterhill, Shore Road, Anstruther, Fife KY10 3DZ. *T:* (01333) 310330; *e-mail:* christopher@smout.org.

SMURFIT, Sir Michael (William Joseph), KBE 2005; Chairman, Smurfit Kappa Group, 2005–07; *b* 7 Aug. 1936; *s* of late Jefferson Smurfit; *m* 1st, Norma Treisman (marr. diss.); two *s* two *d*; 2nd, Birgitta Beimark; two *s.* Joined Jefferson Smurfit & Sons Ltd, Dublin, 1955; founded Jefferson Smurfit Packaging Ltd, Lancs, 1961; Jefferson Smurfit & Sons Ltd, subseq. Jefferson Smurfit Group: Dir, 1964; Jt Man. Dir, 1966–69; Dep. Chm., 1969–77; Chief Exec., 1977–2002; Chm., 1977–2005. Owner of K Club, host to Ryder Cup 2006.

SMYTH, David William; QC (NI) 1989; **His Honour Judge Smyth;** a County Court Judge, Antrim Division, Northern Ireland, since 1997; *b* 12 Nov. 1948; *s* of late William McKeag Smyth and Eva Maud Smyth (*née* Moran); *m* 1977, Anthea Linda Hall-Thompson, DL; one *s* two *d* (and one *d* decd). *Educ:* Methodist Coll., Belfast; Queen's Univ., Belfast (Porter Scholar, 1967; LLB 1971). Called to the NI Bar, 1972, Bencher, 1997; political res., London, 1972–74; called to the Bar, Gray's Inn, 1978, Ireland, 1989; a County Court Judge, Fermanagh and Tyrone Div., NI, 1990–97. Chairman: Legal Aid Adv. Bd, NI, 1994–2005; NI Council on Alcohol, 1996–98; Council of County Court Judges, 2005–; Member: Criminal Justice Wkg Gp on Drugs, 2002; Cttee, Anglo-French Judicial Gp, 2002; Youth Conferencing Adv. Gp, 2003; Pres., NI Community Addiction Service, 1998–. Chm. Bd of Advrs, Inst. of Criminology, QUB, 2002–. Trustee, N Belfast Wkg Men's Club, 1974–. *Publications:* contrib. to NI Legal Qly and Jl of Judicial Studies Bd (Ire.). *Recreations:* cycling, opera, history. *Address:* Royal Courts of Justice, Chichester Street, Belfast BT1 3JE; *e-mail:* dsmyth.rcj@courtsni.gov.uk.

SMYTH, Desmond; *see* Smyth, J. D.

SMYTH, His Honour (James) Robert Staples; a Circuit Judge, 1986–97; *b* 11 July 1926; *s* of late Major Robert Smyth, Gaybrook, Co. Westmeath, and Mabel Anne Georgiana (*née* MacGeough-Bond); *m* 1971, Fenella Joan Mowat; one *s. Educ:* St Columba's, Dublin; Merton Coll., Oxford (BA 1948, MA). Served RAF, 1944–46. Called to Bar, Inner Temple, 1949. Resident Magistrate, Northern Rhodesia, 1951–55; a Dep. Circuit Judge, 1974; Stipendiary Magistrate, W Midlands, 1978–86; a Recorder, 1983–86. Dep. Chm., Agricl Land Tribunal, 1974. *Recreations:* shooting, fishing, English literature. *Address:* Leys, Shelsley Beauchamp, Worcs WR6 6RB.

SMYTH, Joan Rutherford, CBE 1998; Chairman, Progressive Building Society, since 2005 (Director, since 2001); *b* 29 Dec. 1946; *d* of David James Hunter and Kathleen McRoberts (*née* Carson); *m* 1983, John Vernon Smyth. *Educ:* Glenlola Collegiate Sch., Bangor; Dalriada Sch., Ballymoney; Queen's Univ., Belfast (BSc Econ.). Employee Relns Manager, Gallaher Ltd, 1969–89; Partner, Allen & Smyth, 1989–92; Chair and Chief Exec., EOC for NI, 1992–99. Chm., NI Transport Hldg Co., 1999–2005; Dir, Trinity Housing (formerly Choice Housing, then Sanctuary Housing Assoc.), 2002–. Member: Bd, British Council, 1999–2002 (Chm., NI Cttee, 1999–2003); Steering Gp, Women's Nat. Commn, 1999–2002; NI QC Appts Panel, 2005–07; Indep. Assessor of Public Appts, 2005–. Chm., Chief Executives Forum, NI, 2001–08. President: GB and Ireland Fedn, Soroptimist Internat., 2002–03; British Red Cross, NI, 2005–; Confedn of Ulster Socs., 2005–; North Down Guides, 2007–. Trustee, Gender Action for Peace and Security, UK. CIPD 1998. Hon. LLD Ulster, 2000. *Recreations:* golf, drama. *Address:* 12 Shandon Park East, Bangor, Co. Down, Northern Ireland BT20 5HN. *T:* and *Fax:* (028) 9146 9889; *e-mail:* joanrsmyth@btinternet.com.

SMYTH, Prof. John Fletcher, MD; FRCPE, FRCP, FRCSE, FRCR; FRSE; Professor of Medical Oncology, University of Edinburgh, 1979–2008 (Director of Cancer Research Centre, 2002–05); Hon. Director, Cancer Research UK (formerly Imperial Cancer Research Fund) Medical Oncology Unit, Edinburgh, 1980–2005; *b* 26 Oct. 1945; *s* of Henry James Robert Smyth and Doreen Stanger (*née* Fletcher); *m* 1st, 1973, Catherine Ellis; two *d* (marr. diss. 1992); 2nd, 1995, Ann Cull; two step *d. Educ:* Bryanston Sch.; Trinity Coll., Cambridge (BA 1967; MA 1971); St Bartholomew's Hosp. (MB BChir 1970); MD Cantab 1976; MSc London 1975. FRCPE 1981; MRCP 1973, FRCP 1983; FRCSE 1994; FRCR 1995; FRSE 1996. House Officer posts: St Bartholomew's Hosp. and RPMS, London, 1970–72; Asst Lectr, Dept of Med. Oncology, St Bartholomew's Hosp., 1972–73; CRC Res. Fellowship, Inst. Cancer Res., 1973–75; MRC Travelling Fellowship, Nat. Cancer Inst., USA, 1975–76; Sen. Lectr, Inst. Cancer Res., 1976–79. Honorary Consultant Physician: Royal Marsden Hosp. and Brompton Hosp., 1977–79; Lothian Health Bd, 1979–2008; Vis. Prof. of Medicine and Associate Dir for Med. Res., Univ. of Chicago, 1979. Chm., Expert Adv. Gp for Haematol. and Oncology for Commn on Human Medicines, 2006–; Member: Cttee on Safety of Medicines, 1999–2005;

Scientific Adv. Gp for Oncology, EMEA, 2005–07. Member of Council: EORTC, 1990–97; UICC, 1990–94; President: European Soc. of Med. Oncology, 1991–93; Fedn of European Cancer Socs, 2005–07 (Treas., 1992–97). Ed.-in-Chief, European Jl of Cancer, 2000–. *Publications:* Basic Principles of Cancer Chemotherapy, 1980; The Management of Lung Cancer, 1984; more than 300 contribs to various med. and scientific jls on cancer medicine, pharmacology, clinical and exptl cancer therapeutics. *Recreations:* flying and singing (sometimes simultaneously). *Address:* 18 Inverleith Avenue South, Edinburgh EH3 5QA. *T:* (0131) 552 3775. *Club:* Athenæum.

SMYTH, John Jackson; QC 1979; barrister-at-law; legal adviser and media spokesperson, Doctors for Life International, since 2004; Director, Justice Alliance of South Africa, since 2007; *b* 27 June 1941; *e s* of late Col Edward Hugh Jackson Smyth, FRCSEd, and Ursula Helen Lucie (*née* Ross); *m* 1968, Josephine Anne, *er d* of late Walter Leggott and Miriam Moss Leggott, Manor Farm, Burtoft, Lincs; one *s* three *d*. *Educ:* Strathcona Sch., Calgary, Alberta; St Lawrence Coll.; Trinity Hall, Cambridge. MA, LLB (Cantab). Called to Bar, Inner Temple (Major Schol.), 1965. A Recorder, 1978–84. Dir, Zambesi Ministries, Zimbabwe, 1986–2002; Nat. Dir, Christian Lawyers' Assoc. of SA, 2002–03. *Publications:* Discovering Christianity Today, 1985, 2nd edn 2003; Following Christ Today, 1987; Jabulani Bible Reading Notes, 1990–2002. *Recreations:* ski-ing, sailing, trout fishing, tennis. *Address:* 1 Ruskin Road, Bergvliet, Cape Town 7945, South Africa. *T:* and *Fax:* (21) 7133259; *e-mail:* johnsmyth@mweb.co.za; *web:* www.js.za.net.

SMYTH, (Joseph) Desmond, CBE 2000; FCA; Managing Director, Ulster Television, 1983–99; *b* 20 April 1950; *s* of Andrew and Annie Elizabeth Smyth; *m* 1975, Irene Janette (*née* Dale); one *s* one *d*. *Educ:* Limavady Grammar School; Queen's University, Belfast. BSc (Jt Hons Pure Maths and Statistics). Accountancy articles, Coopers and Lybrand, 1971–75; Ulster Television: Chief Accountant, 1975–76; Financial Controller and Company Secretary, 1976–83. Dir, Viridian (formerly NIE) plc, 1996–2005. Pres., NI Chamber of Commerce and Industry, 1991–92. FRTS 1993. *Recreations:* fishing, gardening. *Address: e-mail:* desmondsmyth@yahoo.co.uk.

SMYTH, Liam Cledwyn L.; *see* Laurence Smyth.

SMYTH, Rev. Martin; *see* Smyth, Rev. W. M.

SMYTH, Michael Thomas; Head of Public Policy, Clifford Chance, since 2003; *b* 3 March 1957; 2nd *s* of Rev. Kenneth Smyth and Freda Smyth; *m* 1983, Joyce Anne Young; one *s* one *d*. *Educ:* Royal Belfast Academical Instn; Clare Coll., Cambridge (MA). Admitted solicitor, 1982; Partner, Clifford Chance, 1990–. Chairman: Public Concern at Work, 2001–; Social Welfare Law Coalition, 2006–. Vis. Fellow, Univ. of Essex. FRSA. *Publication:* Business and the Human Rights Act, 2000. *Address:* Clifford Chance, 10 Upper Bank Street, E14 5JJ. *T:* (020) 7006 1000, *Fax:* (020) 7006 5555. *Club:* Reform.

SMYTH, Richard Ian; Headmaster, St Peter's School, York, since 2004; *b* 19 Nov. 1951; *s* of Ronald and Elsa Smyth; *m* 1983, Nicole Adrienne Ryser; one *s* two *d*. *Educ:* Sedbergh Sch.; Emmanuel Coll., Cambridge (BA 1974; PGCE). Asst Master, Christ's Hosp., 1975–77; worked in family baking and confectionery business, 1977–81; Lay Asst to Anglican Vicar of Berne, Switzerland, 1981–82; Asst Master, Gresham's Sch., 1982–85; Housemaster, Wellington Coll., 1985–92; Headmaster, King's Sch., Bruton, 1993–2004. *Recreations:* cricket, golf, Rugby, ski-ing, alpine flowers, roses. *Address:* St Catherine's, 11 Clifton, York YO30 6AA. *T:* (01904) 527334; *e-mail:* r.smyth@st-peters.york.sch.uk. *Clubs:* MCC, East India.

SMYTH, Robert Staples; *see* Smyth, J. R. S.

SMYTH, Prof. Rosalind Louise, MD; FRCPCH, FMedSci; Brough Professor of Paediatric Medicine, since 1999, and Head, Division of Child Health, since 2001, University of Liverpool; *b* 28 Sept. 1958; *d* of Robert Smyth and Louisa Smyth (*née* Noble); *m* 1986, Andrew Richard Bowhay; one *s* one *d*. *Educ:* Down High Sch., Downpatrick; Clare Coll., Cambridge (BA 1980; MA 1984); Westminster Med. Sch. (MB BS 1983; MD 1993). DCH 1985; MRCP 1986; FRCPCH 1997. Jun. posts, Westminster and St Stephen's Hosps, Westminster Children's Hosp. and KCH, 1983–86; Registrar, Ipswich Hosp., 1987–88; Res. Registrar, Papworth Hosp., 1988–90; Sen. Registrar, 1990–93, Consultant Paediatrician, 1994–96, Alder Hey Children's Hosp.; Sen. Lectr, Dept of Child Health, Univ. of Liverpool, 1996–99. Sen. Investigator, NIHR, 2008–. Dir, UK Medicines for Children Res. Network, 2005–; Chm., Paediatric Expert Adv. Gp to Commn on Human Medicines, 2006–. FMedSci 2006. *Publications:* (ed with J. V. Craig) The Evidence-based Manual for Nurses, 2002; (ed jtly) Forfar and Arneil's Textbook of Paediatrics, 6th edn 2003; numerous contribs to med. jls and books. *Recreations:* reading, ski-ing, running, gardening. *Address:* Institute of Child Health, University of Liverpool, Alder Hey Children's Hospital, Eaton Road, Liverpool L12 2AP. *T:* (0151) 252 5693, *Fax:* (0151) 252 5456.

SMYTH, Sir Thomas Weyland Bowyer-, 15th Bt *cr* 1661; *b* 25 June 1960; *s* of Captain Sir Philip Weyland Bowyer-Smyth, 14th Bt, RN, and Veronica Mary, *d* of Captain C. W. Bower, DSC, RN; *S* father, 1978; *m* 1992, Sara Louise Breinlinger (marr. diss. 1997); *m* 1998, Mary Rose Helen Giedroyc; one *s* one *d*, and one step *s*. *Heir: kinsman* John Jeremy Windham [*b* 22 Nov. 1948; *m* 1976, Rachel Mary Finney; one *s* two *d*].

SMYTH, Dr Sir Timothy (John), 2nd Bt *cr* 1956, of Teignmouth, Co. Devon; Health Partner, DLA Phillips Fox (formerly Phillips Fox) Lawyers, since 2000; *b* 16 April 1953; *s* of Julian Smyth (*d* 1974) and of Phyllis, *d* of John Francis Cannon; *S* grandfather, Brig. Rt Hon. Sir John Smyth, 1st Bt, VC, MC, 1983; *m* 1981, Bernadette Mary, *d* of Leo Askew; two *s* two *d*. *Educ:* Univ. of New South Wales. MB, BS 1977; LLB 1987; MBA (AGSM) 1985; FRACMA 1985. Resident Medical Officer, 1977–79; Medical Administrator, Prince Henry Hosp., Prince of Wales Hosp. Gp, Sydney, 1980–86; Chief Exec. Officer, Sydney Health Service, 1986–88; Gen. Man., St George Hosp., Sydney, 1988–91; CEO, Hunter Area Health Service, 1992–97; Dep. Dir-Gen., Policy, DoH, NSW, 1997–2000. *Heir: s* Brendan Julian Smyth, *b* 4 Oct. 1981. *Address:* PO Box A2188, Sydney, NSW 1235, Australia.

SMYTH, Rev. (William) Martin; *b* 15 June 1931; *s* of James Smyth, JP, and Minnie Kane; *m* 1957, Kathleen Jean Johnston, BA; two *d* (and one *d* decd). *Educ:* Methodist Coll., Belfast; Magee University Coll., Londonderry; Trinity Coll., Dublin (BA 1953; BD 1961); Assembly's Coll., Belfast. Assistant Minister, Lowe Memorial, Finaghy, 1953–57; Raffrey Presbyterian Church, Crossgar, 1957–63; Alexandra Presbyterian Church, Belfast, 1963–82. Member, Northern Ireland Convention, 1975; Mem. (UU) Belfast S, NI Assembly, 1982–86 (Chm., Health and Social Services Cttee, 1983–84; Chm., Finance and Personnel Cttee, 1984–86). MP (UU) Belfast South, March 1982–2005 (resigned seat Dec. 1985 in protest against Anglo–Irish Agreement; re-elected Jan. 1986). Chief UU Whip, 1995–2000; Member, Select Committee: for Social Services, 1983–90; on Health, 1990–97; on NI Affairs, 2001–05. Member Executive: UK Branch, IPU, 1985–92, 1995–2005; CPA, 1986–2005. Ulster Unionist Council: Chm. Exec., 1974–76; Vice-Pres. 1974–2000; Hon. Sec., 2000–01; Pres., 2001–03. Governor, Belfast City Mission.

Grand Master, Grand Orange Lodge of Ireland, 1972–96; Grand Master of World Orange Council, 1974–82, Pres., 1985–88; Hon. Past Grand Master, Canada, and Hon. Deputy Grand Master, USA, NZ, NSW, of Orange Order. *Publications:* (ed) Faith for Today, 1961; pamphlets: Why Presbyterian?, 1963; Till Death Us Do Part, 1965; In Defence of Ulster, 1970; The Battle for Northern Ireland, 1972; A Federated People, 1988; occasional papers, and articles in Christian Irishman, Evangelical Quarterly, Biblical Theology. *Recreations:* reading, photography; former Rugby player (capped for Magee University College). *Address:* 6 Mornington, Annadale Avenue, Belfast BT7 3JS. *T:* and *Fax:* (028) 90643816; *e-mail:* wms1690@btinternet.com.

SMYTHE, Brig. Michael, OBE 1989; Clerk to the Vintners' Company, since 1997; *b* 30 April 1948; *s* of Peter and Kay Smythe; *m* 1st, 1976, Sally Paget-Cooke (marr. diss. 2001); one *s* one *d*; 2nd, 2004, Carole James. *Educ:* Ratcliffe Coll. Commnd RA, 1968: Adjt, King's Troop, RHA, 1975–78; psc 1980; CO 94th Regt, RA, 1986–88; MA to C-in-C UKLF, 1988–90; HCSC 1990; COS 2nd Inf. Div., 1990–91; Comdr, RA 1st Armd Div., 1991–93; rcds 1994; Brig., HQ Land, 1995–96. *Recreations:* ski-ing, walking, wine. *Address:* The Vintners' Company, Upper Thames Street, EC4V 3BG. *T:* (020) 7236 1863.

SNAITH, George Robert, FRINA; Partner, Pi-Sigma Technology and Systems Advisers, 1990–97; retired; *b* 9 July 1930; *s* of late Robert and Clara Snaith; *m* 1953, Verna Patricia (*née* Codling); one *s* one *d*. *Educ:* University of Durham. BSc Applied Science (Naval Architecture), 1952. A. Kari & Co., Consulting Naval Architects, Newcastle, 1952–57; Northern Aluminium Co. Ltd, Banbury, 1957–59; Burness, Corlett & Partners, Consulting Naval Architects, Basingstoke, 1959–64; British Ship Research Association, 1964–77, Dir of Research, 1976–77; British Shipbuilders: Dir of Research, 1977–81; Technol. and Systems Adviser (formerly Production Systems Adviser), 1981–85; Consultant, Computervision Ltd, 1985–90. Vis. Prof., 1980–96, Vis. Lectr, 1997–2000, Vis. Fellow, 2000–02, Dept of Marine Technology (formerly Naval Architecture and Shipbldg), Univ. of Newcastle upon Tyne. FNECInst 1992. Member: Council, RINA, 1977–87; Ship and Marine Technol. Requirements Bd, Dept of Industry, 1978–81; Bd, National Maritime Inst., 1978–82. *Recreations:* ships and shipbuilding, technology, education. *Address:* 10 Fieldhouse Close, Hepscott, Morpeth, Northumberland NE61 6LU. *T:* (01670) 515319; *e-mail:* george.snaith1@btinternet.com.

SNAPE, Baron *cr* 2004 (Life Peer), of Wednesbury in the County of West Midlands; **Peter Charles Snape;** transport consultant; *b* 12 Feb. 1942; *s* of late Thomas and of Kathleen Snape; *m* 1st, 1963 (marr. diss. 1980); two *d*; 2nd, 2004, Janet Manley. *Educ:* St Joseph's RC Sch., Stockport; St Winifred's Sch., Stockport. Railway signalman, 1957–61; regular soldier, RE and RCT, 1961–67; goods guard, 1967–70; clerical officer BR, 1970–74. Non-exec. Dir, W Midlands Travel, 1992–97; Chm., Travel W Midlands, 1997–2000. MP (Lab) West Bromwich East, Feb. 1974–2001. An Asst Govt Whip, 1975–77; a Lord Comr, HM Treasury, 1977–79; opposition spokesman for Defence, 1979–82, for Home Affairs, 1982–83, for Transport, 1983–92. Mem., Council of Europe and WEU, May-Nov. 1975. Mem., Bredbury and Romiley UDC, 1971–74 (Chm., Finance Cttee). *Address:* Hildercroft, 281 Highfield Road, Hall Green, Birmingham B28 0BU.

SNAPE, Royden Eric; a Recorder of the Crown Court, 1979–92; *b* 20 April 1922; *s* of John Robert and Gwladys Constance Snape; *m* 1949, Unity Frances Money; one *s* one *d*. *Educ:* Bromsgrove Sch. Served War, Royal Regt of Artillery (Field), 1940–46; Adjt, 80th Field Regt, 1945. Admitted Solicitor, 1949; a Deputy Circuit Judge, 1975. Chairman: Med. Appeal Tribunal, 1985–94; Disability Appeal Tribunal, 1992–94. Governor, St John's Sch., Porthcawl, 1971–88 (Chm., 1971–72). *Recreations:* golf, Rugby Union football, cricket, swimming. *Address:* 7 Cae Rex, Llanblethian, Vale of Glamorgan CF71 7JS. *T:* (01446) 772362. *Club:* Royal Porthcawl Golf.

SNASHALL, David Charles, FRCP; Senior Lecturer and Hon. Consultant in Occupational Medicine, King's College School of Medicine, University of London, since 1982; President, Faculty of Occupational Medicine, Royal College of Physicians, since 2005; *b* 3 Feb. 1943; *s* of Cyril Francis Snashall and Phyllis Mary Snashall; partner, Carolyn Graham; three *d*. *Educ:* Haberdashers' Aske's Sch., Hatcham; Edinburgh Univ. (MB ChB 1968); Univ. of Wales Coll. of Cardiff (LLM 1996); London Sch. of Hygiene and Tropical Medicine (MSc 1979). FFOM 1987; FRCP 1993; FFOMI 2004; FFTM (Glas) 2006. Jun. med. posts, Warwick, Edinburgh, Paris and Vancouver, 1968–73; Chief Medical Officer: Majes Project, Peru, 1975–77; Mufindi Project, Tanzania, 1981–83; Hd of Service, Occupational Health Dept, Guy's & St Thomas' Hosps, 1982–. Chief Medical Adviser: FCO, 1989–98; HSE, 1998–2003. Mem., GMC, 1989–2003. *Publications:* ABC of Work Related Disorders, 1997; (with D. Patel) ABC of Occupational and Environmental Medicine, 2003. *Recreations:* climbing, gardening, European languages, cycling, cooking, jazz. *Address:* 2 Charity Cottages, Petsoe End, Emberton, Bucks MK46 5JL; *e-mail:* dsnashall@lycos.co.uk.

SNEATH, David Rupert, TD 1991; DL; Regional Employment Judge (formerly Regional Chairman, Employment Tribunals), Leeds, since 1998; *b* 7 June 1948; *s* of John and Stella Doreen Sneath; *m* 1st, 1971, Anna Minding (marr. diss. 1984); two *d*; 2nd, 1986, Carol Parsons. *Educ:* Pembroke Coll., Cambridge (MA). Called to the Bar, Inner Temple, 1970; in practice at the Bar, Nottingham, 1971–92; pt-time Chm., 1983–92, full-time Chm., 1992–98, Industrial Tribunals. Commnd TA, 1969; Comd, 3rd Bn Worcestershire and Sherwood Foresters Regt (V), 1991; Col (TA) 1994; Dep. Hon. Col D (WFR) Co., E of England Regt, 1999–2007; Chief Mil. Ops, Office of Staff Judge Advocate, Multinat. Corps, Iraq, 2006. County Vice-Pres., Notts, RBL, 2004–. Trustee: Worcs and Sherwood Foresters Regt, 1996–2007; Sherwood Foresters Mus., 1996–. DL Notts 1998. Bronze Star Medal (USA), 2006. *Publications:* Employment Tribunals, 2005; (jtly) booklet on pensions loss in employment tribunals. *Recreations:* flute playing, choral singing, opera, theatre, ski-ing, scuba diving. *Address:* 7 Kirkby Road, Ravenshead, Nottingham NG15 9HD. *T:* (01623) 456310.

SNEATH, Prof. Peter Henry Andrews, MD; FRS 1995; Professor of Clinical Microbiology, Leicester University, 1975–89, Emeritus Professor, Department of Infection, Immunity and Inflammation (formerly Microbiology and Immunology), since 1989; *b* 17 Nov. 1923; *s* of Rev. Alec Andrews Sneath and Elizabeth Maud Adcock; *m* 1953, Joan Sylvia Thompson; one *s* two *d*. *Educ:* Wycliffe Coll., Stonehouse, Glos; King's Coll., Cambridge (BA 1944; MB BChir 1948, MD 1959); King's Coll. Hosp.; London Sch. of Hygiene and Trop. Med. (Dip. Bact. 1953). MRCS, LRCP 1947. RAMC, Captain and Temp. Major, 1950–52. Mem., Sci. Staff, MRC, 1953–75 and Dir, Microbial Systematics Res. Unit, 1964–75; Hon. Consultant Microbiologist, Leics HA, 1975–89. Hon. mem., microbiol. and bacteriol. socs, UK, France, USA. Hon. DSc Ghent, 1969. *Publications:* (with R. R. Sokal) Principles of Numerical Taxonomy, 1963; Planets and Life, 1970; (with R. R. Sokal) Numerical Taxonomy, 1973; papers in learned jls on microbiology and computing. *Recreations:* reading, gardening, music. *Address:* 22 Barnsdale Close, Great Easton, Leics LE16 8SQ. *T:* (01536) 771071; Department of Infection, Immunity and Inflammation, The University, Leicester LE1 7RH. *T:* (0116) 252 2951.

SNEDDEN, David King, CA; Chairman, Trinity International Holdings, 1994–98 (Chief Executive and Managing Director, 1982–93; Deputy Chairman, 1993–94); Chairman, Liverpool Daily Post and Echo, 1985–96; *b* 23 Feb. 1933; *s* of David King Snedden and Isabella (*née* Martin); *m* 1958; two *s* one *d*. *Educ:* Daniel Stewart's College, Edinburgh. CA 1956. Flying Officer, RAF, 1956–57. Investment Adviser, Guinness Mahon, 1958–59; Chief Accountant, Scotsman Publications Ltd, Thomson British Publications Ltd, Thomson Scottish Associates Ltd, 1959–64; Commercial Controller, The Scotsman Publications Ltd, 1964–66; Managing Director: Belfast Telegraph Newspapers Ltd, 1967–70 (Director, 1979–82); The Scotsman Publications Ltd, 1970–78 (Director, 1970–82). Thomson Regional Newspapers Ltd: Dir, 1974–82; Gp Asst Man. Dir, 1979–80; Jt Man. Dir, 1980–82. Chm., Norcor Holdings PLC, 1994–99; Director: Radio Forth Ltd, 1973–77; BSkyB, 1994–97; Scottish Council Research Inst. Ltd, 1975–77; The Press Association Ltd, 1984–94 (Vice-Chm., 1988; Chm., 1989–94); Reuters Holdings PLC, 1988–94. Pres., Scottish Daily Newspaper Soc., 1975–78; Mem., Press Council, 1976–80. *Recreations:* golf, hill walking, fishing. *Address:* 29 Ravelston Heights, Edinburgh EH4 3LX. *Clubs:* Bruntsfield Links Golfing Society; Grantown-on-Spey Golf; Scarista Golf (Isle of Harris).

SNEDDON, Hutchison Burt, CBE 1983 (OBE 1968); JP; Lord-Lieutenant of Lanarkshire, 1992–99; former Scottish Divisional Director, Nationwide Anglia Building Society (formerly Nationwide Building Society); *b* 17 April 1929; *s* of Robert and Catherine Sneddon; *m* 1960, Elizabeth Jardine; one *s* two *d*. *Educ:* Wishaw High School. Chm., Cumbernauld Develt Corp., 1979–83; Regl Sales Manager (Special Projects), Scottish Gas, 1983–88. Dir, Motherwell Enterprise Develt Co., 1996–. Dir, National Bldg Agency, 1973–82; Vice-Chm., Scottish National Housing and Town Planning Council, 1965–71; Member: Bd, Housing Corp., 1977–83; Consultative Cttee, Scottish Develt Agency, 1979–83; Scottish Adv. Commn on Housing Rents, 1973–74; Anderson Cttee on Commercial Rating, 1972–74; Western Regional Hosp. Bd, 1968–70; Scottish Tourist Bd, 1969–83; Chm., Burns Heritage Trail, 1971–83; Sen. Vice Pres., 1988–89, Pres., 1989–90, World Fedn of Burns Clubs (Jun. Vice Pres., 1987–88). Dep. Pres., Convention of Scottish Local Authorities, 1974–76; Chairman: Gas Higher Managers Assoc., Scotland, 1984–88; Gas Higher Managers Assoc., GB, 1987–88. Motherwell and Wishaw Burgh Council: Councillor, 1958–77; Bailie, 1960–64; Chm., Housing Cttee, 1960–71; Chm., Policy and Resources Cttee, 1974–77; Leader, 1960–77; Chm., Motherwell DC, 1974–77; Provost, Burgh of Motherwell and Wishaw, 1971–75. Pres., Lanarks Multiple Sclerosis Assoc., 1998–. Gov., Erskine Hosp., 1993–. Hon. Pres., Royal Marines, Lanarks, 1993–. JP North Motherwell District, 1974 (Mem. JP Adv. Cttee); DL Motherwell, Hamilton, Monklands, E Kilbride and Clydesdale Districts, 1989. Gold Medal of Schweinfurt, Bavaria, 1977 (Internat. Relations). *Recreations:* football (watching), philately. *Address:* 36 Shand Street, Wishaw, Lanarks ML2 8HN.

SNELGROVE, Anne Christine; MP (Lab) Swindon South, since 2005; *b* 7 Aug. 1957; *d* of Eric and Chris Stamper; *m* 1978, Michael H. Snelgrove. *Educ:* Ranelagh Sch., Bracknell; King Alfred's Coll., Winchester (BEd (Hons) 1979); City Univ. (MA 1986). Teacher of English and Drama, 1979–86; vocational educn curriculum advr, 1986–95, consultant, 1995–97; political office mngr, 1997–99; community relns mngr, 2001–04. *Address:* (office) 7 Little London Court, Old Town, Swindon SN1 3HY; House of Commons, SW1A 0AA.

SNELGROVE, Rt Rev. Donald George, TD 1972; an Assistant Bishop, diocese of Lincoln, since 1995; Bishop Suffragan of Hull, 1981–94; *b* 21 April 1925; *s* of William Henry Snelgrove and Beatrice Snelgrove (*née* Upshell); *m* 1949, Sylvia May Lowe (*d* 1998); one *s* one *d*. *Educ:* Queens' Coll. and Ridley Hall, Cambridge (MA). Served War, commn (Exec. Br.) RNVR, 1943–46. Cambridge, 1946–50; ordained, 1950; Curate: St Thomas, Oakwood, 1950–53; St Anselm's, Hatch End, Dio. London, 1953–56; Vicar of: Dronfield with Unstone, Dio. Derby, 1956–62; Hessle, Dio. York, 1963–70; Archdeacon of the East Riding, 1970–81. Rural Dean of Hull, 1966–70; Canon of York, 1969–81. Chm., Central Church Fund, 1985–2001; Director: Central Bd of Finance, 1975–99; Ecclesiastical Insurance Gp, 1978–94; Church Schools Co., 1981–97; Clergy Stipend Trust, 1985–; Allchurches, 1992–. Chaplain T&AVR, 1960–73. Chm., Linnaeus Centre, 1994–2002. Director: Cornwall Independent Trust Fund, 1998–2003; Cornwall Develt Foundn, 2003–; Mem. Council, Univ. of Hull, 1988–95. Hon. DD Hull, 1997. *Recreation:* travel. *Address:* Kingston House, 8 Park View, Barton on Humber DN18 6AX. *T:* (01652) 634484.

SNELL, John Nicholas B.; *see* Blashford-Snell.

SNELL, Maeve, (Mrs Gordon Snell); *see* Binchy, M.

SNELL, Paul Stephen; Chief Inspector, Commission for Social Care Inspection, since 2006; *b* 29 June 1955; *s* of Bernard Lionel Snell and Gabrielle Irene Snell (*née* Allman). *Educ:* Warwick Univ. (BA Hons Sociology 1976; MA, CQSW 1979). Social Worker, 1977–84, District Manager, 1984–88, Coventry CC; Area Manager, 1988–89, Asst Dir, Social Services, 1989–95, Birmingham CC; Chief Social Services Officer, Bexley LBC, 1995–97; Dir of Social Services, Nottingham CC, 1997–2004; Dir of Inspection, Regulation and Review, Commn for Social Care Inspection, 2004–06. *Recreations:* reading, theatre, French cinema, good food. *Address:* (office) 33 Greycoat Street, SW1P 2QF.

SNELLGROVE, David Llewellyn, LittD, PhD; FBA 1969; Professor of Tibetan in the University of London, 1974–82, now Emeritus Professor (Reader, 1960–74, Lecturer, 1950–60); Founder Director of Institute of Tibetan Studies, Tring, 1966–82; *b* Portsmouth, 29 June 1920; *s* of Lt-Comdr Clifford Snellgrove, RN, and Eleanor Maud Snellgrove. *Educ:* Christ's Hospital, Horsham; Southampton Univ.; Queens' Coll., Cambridge. Served War of 1939–45: commissioned in Infantry, 1942; Intell. Officer in India until 1946. Then started seriously on oriental studies at Cambridge, 1946, cont. Rome, 1949–50. BA Cantab 1949, MA Cantab 1953; PhD London 1954; LittD Cantab 1969. Made expedns to India and the Himalayas, 1953–54, 1956, 1960, 1964, 1967, 1974–75, 1978–80, 1982, continued with regular travel in Indonesia, 1987–94, to Cambodia, 1995–; founded with Mr Hugh E. Richardson an Inst. of Tibetan Studies, 1966. Apptd Consultant to Vatican in new Secretariat for non-Christian Religions, 1967. Many professional visits abroad, mainly to W Europe and USA. Burton Medal, RAS, 2004. *Publications:* Buddhist Himalaya, 1957; The Hevajra Tantra, 1959; Himalayan Pilgrimage, 1961, 2nd edn 1981; Four Lamas of Dolpo, 1967; The Nine Ways of Bon, 1967, repr. 1980; (with H. E. Richardson) A Cultural History of Tibet, 1968, 4th edn 2003; (with T. Skorupski) The Cultural Heritage of Ladakh, vol. I, 1977, vol. II, 1980; (ed) The Image of the Buddha, 1978; Indo-Tibetan Buddhism, 1987, 2nd edn 2003; Asian Commitment, 2000; Khmer Civilization and Angkor, 2001; Angkor Before and After: a cultural history of the Khmers, 2004; Religion as History—Religion as Myth, 2005; articles in Arts Asiatiques (Paris), Bulletin of the Secretariat for non-Christian Religions (Rome), etc. *Address:* Via Matteo Gay 26/7, 10066 Torre Pellice, Italy; Villa Bantay Chah, Krom 11, No 0718, Siem Reap, Cambodia.

SNELSON, Rear Adm. David George, CB 2004; RN retired; Chief Harbour Master, Port of London Authority, since 2007; *b* 27 May 1951; *s* of W. M. Snelson; *m* 1973, Ruth Mary Clayton; two *s*. *Educ:* Alleyne's Grammar Sch., Uttoxeter, Staffs; BRNC, Dartmouth. Comdr, HMS Liverpool, 1987–88; Naval Asst to Controller of Navy, 1989–92; Staff Ops Officer, Comdr UK Task Gp, 1993–95; Comdr, HMS Liverpool, and Captain 3rd Destroyer Sqdn, 1996–98; Dir, Naval Ops, 1998–99, Naval Staff, 1999–2000, MoD; Captain, HMS Ark Royal, 2001–02; Comdr UK Maritime Force, 2002–04; COS (Warfare) to C-in-C Fleet, 2004–06. Younger Brother, Trinity House, 2007–. FNI. Officer, Operation Telic Legion of Merit (USA), 2003. *Recreations:* sailing, ski-ing, reading. *Address:* c/o Port of London Authority, London River House, Royal Pier Road, Gravesend, Kent DA12 2BG.

SNELSON, Rev. William Thomas; General Secretary, Churches Together in England, 1997–2008; *b* 10 March 1945; *s* of Samuel and Dorothy Snelson; *m* 1968, Beryl Griffiths; one *s* one *d*. *Educ:* Exeter Coll., Oxford (BA 1967); Fitzwilliam Coll., Cambridge (BA 1969; MA 1975); Westcott House, Cambridge. Ordained deacon, 1969, priest, 1970; Curate: Godalming, 1969–72; Leeds Parish Church, 1972–75; Vicar: Chapel Allerton, Leeds, 1975–81; Bardsey, Leeds, 1981–93; W Yorks County Ecumenical Officer, 1993–97. *Publication:* Enriching Communion, 2006. *Recreations:* bridge, opera, continental holidays. *Address:* *e-mail:* bill.snelson@btopenworld.com.

SNODDY, (Matthew) Raymond, OBE 2000; freelance journalist, writing for The Independent, since 2004; *b* 31 Jan. 1946; *s* of Matthew and Mary Snoddy; *m* 1970, Diana Elizabeth Jaroszek; one *s* one *d*. *Educ:* Larne Grammar Sch., NI; Queen's Univ., Belfast; BA Hons Open Univ. Reporter: Middx Advertiser, 1966–68; Oxford Mail, 1968–71; Parly staff, The Times, 1971–72; Visnews, 1972–74; Dep. Eur. Editor, LA Times and Washington Post News Service, 1974–78; Financial Times, 1978–97; Media Ed., The Times, 1997–2004. Presenter, Hard News series, Channel 4, 1988–90. FRSA 2004. Chairman's Award, British Press Awards, 1992. *Publications:* The Good, the Bad and the Unacceptable, 1992; Green Finger: the rise of Michael Green and Carlton Communications, 1996; (with J. Ashworth) It Could be You: the untold story of the UK National Lottery, 2000. *Recreations:* opera, tennis, chess, drinking and eating, supporting Queens Park Rangers. *Address:* 30 Bushey Road, Ickenham, Middx UB10 8JP. *T:* (01895) 460832. *Club:* Uxbridge Tennis.

SNODGRASS, Prof. Anthony McElrea, FSA; FBA 1979; Laurence Professor of Classical Archaeology, University of Cambridge, 1976–2001; Fellow of Clare College, Cambridge, since 1977; *b* 7 July 1934; *s* of William McElrea Snodgrass, MC (Major, RAMC), and Kathleen Mabel (*née* Owen); *m* 1st, 1959, Ann Elizabeth Vaughan (marr. diss.); three *d*; 2nd, 1983, Annemarie Künzl; one *s*. *Educ:* Marlborough Coll.; Worcester Coll., Oxford (BA 1959; MA, DPhil 1963; Hon. Fellow, 1999). FSA 1978. Served with RAF in Iraq, 1953–55 (National Service). Student of the British School, Athens, 1959–60; University of Edinburgh: Lectr in Classical Archaeology, 1961; Reader, 1969; Prof., 1975. Sather Classical Vis. Prof., Univ. of California, Berkeley, 1984–85; Geddes-Harrower Vis. Prof., Aberdeen, 1995–96. Sen. Fellow, Harvard Univ. Center for Hellenic Studies, 2001–. Myres Meml Lectr, Oxford, 1981; Context and Human Society Lectr, Boston Univ., 2002. Chm., British Cttee for the Reunification of Parthenon Marbles, 2002–. British Academy: Vice-Pres., 1990–92; Mem., Humanities Res. Bd, 1994–95. Corresp. Mem., German Archaeol. Inst., 1977; Overseas Fellow, Russian Acad. of Scis, 2003. FRSA 2005. *Publications:* Early Greek Armour and Weapons, 1964; Arms and Armour of the Greeks, 1967; The Dark Age of Greece, 1971; Archaic Greece, 1980; Narration and Allusion in Early Greek Art, 1982; An Archaeology of Greece, 1987; Homer and the Artists, 1998; Archaeology and the Emergence of Greece (collected papers), 2006; contrib. Jl of Hellenic Studies, Proc. of Prehistoric Soc., Gnomon, etc. *Recreations:* mountaineering, ski-ing. *Address:* Clare College, Cambridge CB2 1TL. *Clubs:* Alpine, Alpine Ski.

SNOW, Adrian John, MA, MEd; Real Tennis consultant; Hon. Court Development Officer, International Real Tennis Professionals Association, since 2007; Development Officer, Tennis and Rackets Association, 1994–2006; *b* 20 March 1939; *e s* of Edward Percy John Snow and Marjory Ellen Nicholls; *m* 1963 (marr. diss. 1994); one *s* one *d*. *Educ:* Hurstpierpoint Coll.; Trinity Coll., Dublin (BA, MA, HDipEd; Kt of the Campanile; Hon. Sec., Trinity Week); Reading Univ. (MEd). Asst Master, The New Beacon, Sevenoaks, 1958–59; RAF Pilot Officer, 1963; Assistant Master: King's Sch., Sherborne, 1964; High Sch., Dublin, 1964–65 (part-time); Brighton Coll., 1965–66; The Oratory School: Head of Econ. and Pol Studies, 1966–73; Head of Hist., 1967–73; Housemaster, 1967–73; acting Headmaster, Sept. 1972–Mar. 1973; Headmaster, 1973–88. Warden, Oratory Sch. Assoc., 1989–93; Director: Oratory Construction Ltd, 1988–93; Oratory Trading Ltd, 1990–93. Governor: Prior Park Coll., 1981–87 (Mem., Action Cttee, 1980–81); Moreton Hall Prep. Sch., 1984–93; St Mary's Sch., Ascot, 1986–94; St Edward's Sch. and Highlands Sch., Reading, 1987–2001 (Chm., 1990–2001); Rendcomb Coll., 2004–; St Edward's Sch., Cheltenham, 2004–06. Member: Berks Cttee, Prince's Trust, 1989–93 (Vice-Chm., 1990–91); Tennis Cttee, Tennis and Rackets Assoc., 1990–94 (Chm., Court Develt Cttee, 1992–2006). Pres., Old Oratorian CC, 1994–; Chm., Friends of Hardwick Tennis Court, 1996– (Hon. Treas., 1990–97). *Recreations:* athletics (univ. colour), cricket, hockey (Jun. Internat. trialist), Real Tennis, Rugby (Combined Univs), golf, bridge, croquet. *Address:* The Dormer House, Clarks Hay, South Cerney, Glos GL7 5UA.

SNOW, Antony Edmund, MIPA, FCIPR; Chairman, Hill and Knowlton, Europe, Middle East and Africa, Ltd, 1990–98; *b* 5 Dec. 1932; 2nd *s* of Thomas Maitland Snow, CMG; *m* 1961, Caroline Wilson; one *s* two *d*. *Educ:* Sherborne Sch.; New College, Oxford. National Service, commnd in 10th Royal Hussars, 1952–53; Royal Wiltshire Yeomanry, TA, 1953–63. W. S. Crawford, 1958; joined Charles Barker & Sons, 1961, Dep. Chm., 1975, Chm. and Chief Exec., 1983–88; Chm., 1992–98, non-exec. Dir, 1999–2008, Hill and Knowlton (UK). Non-exec. Dir, Hogg Gp plc (formerly Hogg Robinson & Gardner Mountain), 1989–94. Vice-Pres., Market Planning, Steuben Glass, 1976; Dep. Dir, Corning Museum of Glass, 1976 (Trustee, 1983–); Dir, Rockwell Museum, 1979. Member: Cttee of Management, Courtauld Institute of Art, 1984–89; Exec. Cttee, Nat. Art-Collections Fund, 1985–2008; Ancient Monuments Cttee, English Heritage, 1988–91; Design Council, 1989–94. Chm., Fraser Trust, 1996–2002. Trustee: Monteverdi Choir, 1988–2001; V&A Mus., 1996–2002. Mem. Council, RCA, 1994–2002. *Recreations:* English watercolours, fishing. *Address:* Fyfield Hill Barn, Marlborough, Wilts SN8 1PU. *Club:* Cavalry and Guards.

See also T. Snow.

SNOW, Rear Adm. Christopher Allen, CBE 2002; Flag Officer Sea Training, from Feb. 2009; *b* 16 April 1958; *s* of Rear-Adm. Kenneth Arthur Snow, *qv*; *m* 1983, Helen Young; one *s* one *d*. *Educ:* Jun. King's Sch., Canterbury; Churcher's Coll., Petersfield; Durham Univ. (BA Hons Archaeol.). Joined RN, 1976; 2nd Navigator, HM Yacht Britannia, 1982; i/c HM Prize Tiger Bay (ex-ARA Islas Malvinas), 1983; Navigator, HMS Birmingham, 1983–85; PWO(U), HMS Hermione and HMS Jupiter, 1985–87; Torpedo Officer, HMS Tireless, 1987–89; SWO(U) to FOST, 1990–92; i/c HMS Atherstone,

1993, Iron Duke, 1994–96; Mil. Asst to VCDS, 1996–98; i/c HMS Coventry, 1998–99; Asst Dir, Partnerships and Internat. Relns, Navy, MoD, 2002–01; Ops Team Leader, PJHQ Northwood, for UK Response Post 9/11 and for ops in Afghanistan, 2001–02; ACOS, Progs and Resources, Fleet HQ, 2002–04; Dir, Navy Resources and Plans, MoD, 2004–05; i/c HMS Ocean, 2005–06; Sen. Directing Staff (Navy), RCDS, 2007; Dep. Comdr, Naval Striking Forces Southern Europe, 2008–09. Strategic Leadership Consultation, Windsor Leadership Trust, 2007. Mem., Hon. Co. of Master Mariners. *Recreations:* sailing, reading, walking Dartmoor and the coastal footpath. *Club:* Royal Navy.

SNOW, John William, PhD; Chairman, Cerberus Capital Management, LP, since 2006; Secretary of the Treasury, United States of America, 2003–06; *b* 2 Aug. 1939; *s* of William Dean Snow and Catharine Snow (*née* Howard); *m* 1st, 1964, Frederica Wheeler (marr. diss. 1973); two *s*; 2nd, 1973, Carolyn Kalk; one *s*. *Educ:* Univ. of Toledo (BA 1962); Univ. of Virginia (PhD 1965); George Washington Univ. (LLB 1967). Asst Prof. of Econs, Univ. of Maryland, 1965–67; Associate, Wheeler & Wheeler, law firm, 1967–72; US Department of Transportation: Asst Gen. Counsel, 1972–73; Dep. Asst Sec. for Policy, Plans and Internat. Affairs, 1973–74; Asst Sec. for Govtl Affairs, 1974–75; Dep. Under-Sec., 1975–76; Administrator, Nat. Highway Traffic Safety Admin, 1976–77; Vice-Pres., of Govt Affairs, Chessie Systems Inc., 1977–80; CSX Corporation: Sen. Vice-Pres., Corp. Services, 1980–84; Exec. Vice-Pres., 1984–85; Pres. and CEO, Chessie System Railroads, 1985–86, CSX Rail Transport, 1986–87, CSX Transport, 1987–88; Chief Operating Officer, 1988–89; Pres., 1988–2001; CEO, 1989–2003; Chm., 1991–2003. Co-Chm., Nat. Commn on Financial Instn Reform, Recovery and Enforcement, 1992–93; Chm., Business Roundtable, 1994–96. Adjunct Prof. of Law, George Washington Univ., 1972–75; Vis. Prof. of Econs, Univ. of Virginia, 1977. *Publication:* Perspectives in Economics, 1969. *Address:* Cerberus Capital Management, LP, 299 Park Avenue, New York, NY 10171, USA.

SNOW, Jonathan George, (Jon); television journalist; Presenter, Channel Four News, since 1989; *b* 28 Sept. 1947; *s* of late Rt Rev. George Snow and Joan Snow; partner, Madeleine Colvin; two *d*. *Educ:* St Edward's School, Oxford; Liverpool Univ. (no degree; sent down following political disturbances, 1970). VSO, Uganda, 1967–68; Co-ordinator, New Horizon Youth Centre, Covent Garden, 1970–73 (Chm., 1986–); Journalist, Independent Radio News, LBC, 1973–76; Independent Television News: Reporter, 1976–83; Washington Correspondent, 1983–86; Diplomatic Editor, 1986–89; main presenter, Election '92, ITV. Mem., NUJ. Visiting Professor: Broadcast Journalism, Nottingham Trent Univ., 1992–2001; Media Studies, Univ. of Stirling, 2001–. Chairman: Prison Reform Trust, 1992–97; On The Line Steering Gp, 1999–2003; Dep. Chm., Media Trust, 1995–; Trustee: Noel Buxton Trust, 1992–; Chelsea Physic Garden, 1993–2003; Nat. Gallery, 1999–2008; Stephen Lawrence Trust, 1999–2003; Tate Gall., 2000–08; Chm. Council, Tate Modern, 2002–. Dir, Tricycle Theatre, 1995–. Chancellor, Oxford Brookes Univ., 2001–08. Mem., UK-India Round Table, 2002–. Hon. DLitt Nottingham Trent, 1994; DUniv Open, 2001. Monte Carlo Golden Nymph Award, for Eritrea Air Attack reporting, 1979; TV Reporter of the Year, for Afghanistan, Iran and Iraq reporting, RTS, 1980; Valiant for Truth Award, for El Salvador reporting, 1982; Internat. Award, for El Salvador reporting, RTS, 1982; Home News Award, for Kegworth Air Crash reporting, RTS, 1989; RTS Presenter of the Year, 1994, 2002, 2006; Richard Dimbleby Award, BAFTA, 2005; RTS Journalist of the Year, 2005. *Publications:* Atlas of Today, 1987; (contrib.) Sons and Mothers, 1996; Shooting History, 2004. *Address:* Channel Four News, ITN, 200 Gray's Inn Road, WC1X 8HB. *T:* (020) 7430 4237; *e-mail:* jon.snow@itn.co.uk.

SNOW, Rear-Adm. Kenneth Arthur, CB 1987; Deputy High Bailiff of Westminster, 1998–2008; *b* 14 April 1934; *s* of Arthur Chandos Pole Snow and Evelyn (*née* Joyce); *m* 1956, Pamela Elizabeth Terry (*née* Sorrell); one *s* two *d*. *Educ:* St Andrews College, Grahamstown; South African Nautical College. Joined RN, 1952; commanded HMS Kirkliston, 1962; qualified navigation specialist, 1963; commanded: HMS Llandaff, 1970; HMS Arethusa, 1979; HMS Hermes, 1983; Dep. Asst Chief of Staff (Ops), SACEUR, 1984–87, retired. Receiver-Gen. and Chapter Clerk, Westminster Abbey, 1987–98. FNI 1992. *Recreations:* gardening, painting. *Address:* 49B Queens Road, Cowes, Isle of Wight PO31 8BW. *Club:* Army and Navy.

See also Rear Adm. C. A. Snow, Rear-Adm. R. E. Snow.

SNOW, Peter John, CBE 2006; television presenter, reporter and author; *b* Dublin, 20 April 1938; *s* of Brig. John F. Snow, CBE and Peggy Mary Pringle; *m* 1st, 1964, Alison Carter (marr. diss. 1975); one *s* one *d*; 2nd, 1976, Ann MacMillan; one *s* two *d*. *Educ:* Wellington College; Balliol College, Oxford (BA Hons Greats 1962). 2nd Lieut, Somerset Light Infantry, 1956–58, served Plymouth and Warminster. Independent Television News: newscaster and reporter, 1962–66; diplomatic and defence corresp., 1966–79; events covered include: Cyprus, 1964; Vietnam, Laos, Malaysia, 1968–70; China, 1972; Mideast war, 1973; Nigerian civil war, 1969; Oman, 1975; Rhodesia, 1965–79; Britain and EEC, 1970–73; co-presenter, Gen. Elections, Feb. and Oct. 1974, 1979; BBC: television: presenter, Newsnight, 1979–97; events covered or reported include: Zimbabwe independence, 1980; Falklands war, 1982; S Africa, 1986; co-presenter, Gen. Elections, 1983, 1987, 1992, 1997, 2001 and 2005, and US elections; presenter: Tomorrow's World, 1997–2001; (with Dan Snow): Battlefield Britain, 2004; Peter and Dan Snow: 20th Century Battlefields, 2007; radio: Random Edition, 1997–; Mastermind, 1998–2000; Masterteam, 2001–05. Vice-Patron, Jubilee Sailing Trust. Judges Award, RTS, 1998. *Publications:* (jtly) Leila's Hijack War, 1970; Hussein: a biography, 1972; (with Dan Snow) Battlefield Britain, 2004; (with Dan Snow) The World's Greatest Twentieth Century Battlefields, 2007. *Recreations:* sailing (skipper Cerulean, Atlantic Rally crossing, 2001), ski-ing, model railways, photography. *Address:* c/o BBC TV White City, Wood Lane, W12 7TS; *e-mail:* peterpsnow@aol.com. *Clubs:* Athenæum; Royal Cruising.

SNOW, Philip Albert, OBE 1985 (MBE 1979); JP; MA; FRSA; FRAI; author, bibliographer and administrator; *b* 7 Aug. 1915; *s* of William Edward Snow, FRCO and Ada Sophia Robinson; *m* 1940, Anne Harris (*d* 2005); one *d*. *Educ:* Newton's Sch., Leicester; Christ's Coll., Cambridge (MA Hons). FRAI 1952. HM Colonial Administrative Service: Provincial Comr, Magistrate, Establishment and Protocol Officer, and Asst Colonial Sec., Fiji and Western Pacific, 1937–52; ADC to Governor and C-in-C, Fiji and High Comr for Western Pacific, 1939–40; Dep. Sheriff, Fiji, 1940–52; Official Mem., Legislative Council, Fiji, 1951; Fiji Govt Liaison Officer, US and NZ Forces, 1942–44. Bursar, Rugby Sch., 1952–76. Mem., Jt Cttee, Governing Bodies of Schools' Assoc., 1959–65. President: Public Schs Bursars' Assoc., 1962–65 (Vice-Pres., 1959–62); The Worthing Soc., 1983– (Jt Founder); Vice-Pres., Fiji Soc., 1944–52; Trustee, Fiji Museum, 1950–52. Founder Member Committee: Union Club, Suva, 1944; Fiji Arts Club, 1945. Founder, Suva Cricket Assoc., Nadi Cricket Assoc. and six other dist cricket assocs, 1939–49; Founder, Fiji Cricket Assoc., 1946, Vice-Patron, 1952–; Captain, Fiji Cricket Team, NZ first-class tour, 1948; Liaison Officer/Manager, first Fiji Cricket Team in England, 1979; Liaison Officer, Fiji teams in England, 1982–86. International Cricket Conference: Perm. Rep. of Fiji, 1965–90; Mem., first Cricket World Cup Cttee, 1971–75; first Chm., Associate Member Countries, 1982–87; Perm. Rep. of Fiji, Internat. Cricket Council, 1990–94. Organiser, Rugby Sch. 400th anniv. celebrations and visit of the Queen, 1967; designer, Fiji Govt stamps for centenary of Fiji cricket, 1974. Broadcasts on Fiji radio, BBC and in NZ, 1948–; question setter on Pacific, Mastermind, BBC, 1975–. Literary Executor of Lord Snow. JP Warwicks, 1967–76, and W Sussex, 1976–. FRSA 1984. Foreign Specialist Award, USA Govt, 1964; Independence Silver Jubilee Medal, Fiji, 1995. *Publications:* Air Raids Precautions Services, Lautoka, 1943; (ed with G. K. Roth) Sources Describing Fijian Customs for Fijian Examination Candidates, 1944; (ed) Civil Service Journal, 1945; Cricket in the Fiji Islands, 1949; Rock Carvings in Fiji, 1950; Report on the Visit of Three Bursars to the United States of America and Canada in 1964, 1965; Best Stories of the South Seas, 1967; Bibliography of Fiji, Tonga and Rotuma, vol. 1, 1969; (with Stefanie Snow Waine) The People from the Horizon: an illustrated history of the Europeans among the South Sea Islanders, 1979; Stranger and Brother: a portrait of C. P. Snow, 1982; The Years of Hope: Cambridge, colonial administrator in the South Seas and cricket (autobiog.), 1997; A Time of Renewal: clusters of characters, C. P. Snow and coups (autobiog.), 1998; contrib. to books and jls incl. TLS, Sunday Times, Daily Telegraph, The Times, Jls of RAI, RGS, Fiji Museum, Pacific History, Fiji Soc., Polynesian Soc., and Rupert Brooke Soc., Jl de la Société des Océanistes, Amer. Anthropologist, Wisden's Almanack, Barclays World of Cricket, Dictionary of Nat. Biog; numerous reviews of, and introductions to, Pacific and general books. *Recreations:* taming robins; formerly cricket (Capt., Leics 2nd XI, 1936–38, Leics, 1946, Cambridge Crusaders, Googlies, MCC (Capt., 1955–65), Authors, Fiji first-class), chess (half-Blue), table-tennis (half-Blue and Cambs), deck-tennis, tennis. *Address:* 46 Bennett Court, Station Road, Letchworth, Herts SG6 3WA. *T:* (01462) 677556. *Clubs:* MCC (Hon. Life Mem. for services to internat. cricket, 1970), Stragglers of Asia (Hon. Mem.); De Flamingos (Hon. Mem.) (Holland); Mastermind; Hawks (Cambridge).

SNOW, Surg. Rear-Adm. Ronald Edward, CB 1991; LVO 1972; OBE 1977; Surgeon Rear Admiral (Operational Medical Services), 1989–91; *b* 17 May 1933; *s* of Arthur Chandos Pole Snow (formerly Soppitt) and Evelyn Dorothea Snow (*née* Joyce); *m* 1959, Valerie Melian French; two *d*. *Educ:* St Andrew's Coll., Grahamstown, S Africa; Trinity Coll., Dublin (MA, MB, BCh, BAO); FFOM, DA, LMCC. HMS Victorious, 1966; HMS Dolphin, 1967; HMY Britannia, 1970; MoD, 1973 and 1977; Inst. of Naval Medicine, 1975 and 1984; Staff of Surg. Rear Adm. (Naval Hosps), 1980; Staff of C-in-C Fleet, 1982; Asst Surg. Gen. (Service Hosps), 1985; Surg. Rear Adm. (Support Med. Services), 1987. QHP 1984–91. Vice Patron, Cerebral Palsy Centre, Portsmouth, 2003–06. OStJ 1986. *Recreation:* National Hunt racing.

See also Rear-Adm. K. A. Snow.

SNOW, Thomas; Director, Oxford University Careers Service (formerly Secretary, Oxford University Appointments Committee), 1970–96; Fellow, New College, Oxford, 1973–96, then Emeritus; *b* 16 June 1929; *e s* of Thomas Maitland Snow, CMG; *m* 1961, Elena Tidmarsh; two *s* one *d*. *Educ:* Winchester Coll.; New Coll., Oxford. Joined Crittall Manufacturing Co. Ltd as Management Trainee, 1952; Dir 1966; Director: Crittall Hope Ltd, Darlington Simpson Rolling Mills, Minex Metals Ltd, 1968. Marriage Counsellor, 1964–70; Chm., Oxfordshire Relate (formerly Oxford Marriage Guidance Council), 1974–90; Member: Cttee of Management, Oxford Univ. Counselling Service, 1992–94 (Chm., 1994–96); Standing Cttee, Assoc. of Graduate Careers Adv. Services, 1973–77, 1985–89. Trustee: Thomas Wall Trust, 1980–99; Secure Retirement Assoc., 1996–2007 (Dep. Chm., 2002–07); Ethox, 1998–2002; Governor: Harpur Trust, 1996–2001; Bedford Sch., 1996–2001. Fellow, Winchester Coll., 1985–98. Mem. (Lab.), Witham UDC, Essex, 1957–61 (Mem., 1957–61, Chm., 1959–61, Finance Cttee); Mem. (Lib Dem), Oxfordshire CC, 1997–2001. JP Braintree, Essex, 1964–69. *Address:* Flat 9, Murray Court, 80 Banbury Road, Oxford OX2 6LQ.

See also A. E. Snow.

SNOWBALL, Priscilla Deborah, (Cilla); Chairman and Chief Executive, Abbott Mead Vickers Group Ltd, since 2006; Chairman, Abbott Mead Vickers.BBDO Ltd, since 2004; *b* 1 Oct. 1958; *d* of late Rev. Frank Chadwick and of Gwen Chadwick; *m* 1987, Geoff Snowball (marr. diss. 2007); two *s* one *d*. *Educ:* Sch. of St Mary and St Anne, Abbots Bromley; Birmingham Univ. (BA Hons French). Allen Brady and Marsh, 1981–83; Ogilvy and Mather, 1983–92; Abbott Mead Vickers.BBDO Ltd, 1992–: New Business Dir, 1992–94; Hd, Client Service, 1994–99; Man. Dir, 2000–02; Chief Exec., 2002–06. Non-executive Director: Fishburn Hedges, 1996–; Arcadia plc, 1999–2001; BITC, 2005–. Member: D&AD, 2000–; Mktg Gp of GB, 2002–. Non-exec. Dir, Macmillan Cancer Support, 2004–. *Recreations:* children, travel, music. *Address:* Abbott Mead Vickers Group Ltd, 151 Marylebone Road, NW1 5QE. *T:* (020) 7616 3652, *Fax:* (020) 7616 3700. *Clubs:* Thirty, Women's Advertising Club of London (Past Pres.).

SNOWDEN, Prof. Christopher Maxwell, PhD; FRS 2005; FREng, FIEEE, FIET; Vice-Chancellor and Chief Executive, and University Professor, University of Surrey, since 2005; *b* 5 March 1956; *s* of William and Barbara Snowden; *m* 1993, Irena Lewandowska; two *s*. *Educ:* Univ. of Leeds (BSc Hons, MSc; PhD 1982). FIET (FIEE 1993); FIEEE 1996. Applications Engr, Mullard Applications Lab., Surrey, 1977–78; Lectr, Dept of Electronics, Univ. of York, 1982–83; University of Leeds, 1983–2005: Lectr, then Sen. Lectr, Dept of Electronic and Electrical Engrg, 1983–92; on secondment as Sen. Staff Scientist, M/A-COM Inc., Corporate R&D, Mass, 1990–91; Prof. of Microwave Engrg, 1992–2005; Hd, Sch. of Electronic and Electrical Engrg, 1995–98; Dir, Inst. of Microwaves and Photonics, 1997–98. Filtronic plc: Exec. Dir of Technol., 1998–99; Jt CEO, 1999–2001; CEO, Compound Semiconductors, 2001–03; Chief Exec., Filtronic ICS, 2003–05. Non-executive Director: Intense Ltd, 2004–; Cenamps Ltd, 2003–06; SSTL Ltd, 2005–06; Res. Parks Develts Ltd, 2005–; Univ. of Surrey Seed Fund Ltd, 2005–; Engineering Technol. Bd Ltd, 2007–; non-exec. Chm., HERO Ltd, 2006–08. Mem. Bd, UUK (Chm., Employment, Industry and Business Policy Cttee). Distinguished Lectr, IEEE (Electron Devices Soc.), 1996–2006. Member: Electromagnetics Acad., MIT, 1990–; Council, EPSRC, 2006–. Vice-Pres., Eur. Microwave Assoc., 2003–06; Vice-Pres., 2006–07, Dep. Pres., 2007–Sept. 2009, Pres., Sept. 2009–, IET. FREng 2000; FRSA 2000; FCGI 2005. Chm., Daphne Jackson Trust, 2005–; Patron, Surrey Community Develt Trust, 2005–. Microwave Prize, IEEE, 1999; Silver Medal, Royal Acad. of Engrg, 2004. *Publications:* Introduction to Semiconductor Device Modelling, 1986 (trans. Japanese 1988); (ed jtly and contrib.) Semiconductor Device Modelling, 1987; INCA Interactive Circuit Analysis, 1988; Semiconductor Device Modelling, 1988; (ed and contrib.) Semiconductor Device Modelling, 1989; (ed jtly and contrib.) Compound Semiconductor Device Modelling, 1993; (jtly) International Conference on Computational Electronics, 1993; contrib. numerous papers in IEEE, IEE and other learned jls. *Recreations:* photography, painting. *Address:* Vice-Chancellor's Office, University of Surrey, Guildford, Surrey GU2 7XH. *Club:* Athenæum.

SNOWDEN, Richard Andrew; QC 2003; a Recorder, since 2006; *b* 22 March 1962; *s* of late Dr Paul Snowden and of Patricia Snowden; *m* 1988, Kirsti Niinisalo; two *s*. *Educ:* Downing Coll., Cambridge (MA); Harvard Law Sch. (LLM). Called to the Bar, Lincoln's Inn, 1986; Jun. Counsel to the Crown (A Panel), 1999–2003; Mem., Insolvency Rules

Cttee, 2002–. *Publications:* (ed jtly) Company Directors: law and liability, 1997; (ed jtly) Lightman and Moss, The Law of Administrators and Receivers of Companies, 3rd edn 2000, 4th edn 2007. *Recreations:* Rugby, cricket, golf, music. *Address:* Erskine Chambers, 33 Chancery Lane, WC2A 1EN. *T:* (020) 7242 5532, *Fax:* (020) 7831 0125; *e-mail:* rsnowden@erskine-chambers.co.uk.

SNOWDON, 1st Earl of, *cr* 1961; **Antony Charles Robert Armstrong-Jones,** GCVO 1969; RDI 1978; FCSD; Viscount Linley, 1961; Baron Armstrong-Jones (Life Peer), 1999; Constable of Caernarfon Castle since 1963; Provost, Royal College of Art, 1995–2003; *b* 7 March 1930; *s* of Ronald Owen Lloyd Armstrong-Jones, MBE, QC, DL (*d* 1966), and Anne (*d* 1992), *o d* of Lt-Col Leonard Messel, OBE (later Countess of Rosse); *m* 1st, 1960, HRH The Princess Margaret (marr. diss. 1978; she *d* 2002); *one s one d*; 2nd, 1978, Lucy Lindsay-Hogg, *d* of Donald Davies; *one d. Educ:* Eton; Jesus Coll., Cambridge (coxed winning Univ. crew, 1950). Joined Staff of Council of Industrial Design, 1961, continued on a consultative basis, 1962–87, also an Editorial Adviser of Design Magazine, 1961–87; an Artistic Adviser to the Sunday Times and Sunday Times Publications Ltd, 1962–90; photographer, Telegraph Magazine, 1990–94. Designed: Snowdon Aviary, London Zoo, 1965; Chairmobile, 1972. A Vice President: National Fund for Research for Crippling Diseases; Prince of Wales Adv. Cttee on Disability; Patron, Circle of Guide Dog Owners; Chm., Working Party on Integrating the Disabled (Report 1976); Pres. for England, Cttee, International Year for Disabled People, 1981. Vice Pres., Kensington Soc. Founder, Snowdon Award Scheme, 1980. Hon. Fellow: Institute of British Photographers; Royal Photographic Soc.; Manchester College of Art and Design; Hon. Member: North Wales Society of Architects; South Wales Institute of Architects; Royal Welsh Yacht Club; Patron: Welsh Nat. Rowing Club; Metropolitan Union of YMCAs; British Water Ski Federation. President: Contemp. Art Society for Wales; Welsh Theatre Company; Mem. Council, English Stage Co., 1978–82. Senior Fellow, RCA, 1986. FRSA. Dr *hc* Bradford, 1989; Hon. LLD Bath, 1989; Hon. DLitt Portsmouth, 1994. Silver Progress Medal, RPS, 1985. *Television films:* Don't Count the Candles, 1968 (2 Hollywood Emmy Awards); St George Prize, Venice; awards at Prague and Barcelona film festivals); Love of a Kind, 1969; Born to be Small, 1971 (Chicago Hugo Award); Happy being Happy, 1973; Mary Kingsley, 1975; Burke and Wills, 1975; Peter, Tina and Steve, 1977; Snowdon on Camera, BBC (presenter), 1981. *Exhibitions include:* Photocall, London, 1958; Assignments, Cologne, London, Brussels, USA, 1972, Japan, Canada, Denmark, Holland, 1975, Australia, 1976, France, 1977; Serendipity, Brighton, Bradford, 1989, Bath, 1990; Snowdon on Stage, RNT and Prague, 1997; Photographs by Snowdon: a retrospective, Nat. Portrait Gall., 2000; Snowdon, Chris Beetles Gall., 2006. *Publications:* London, 1958; Malta (in collaboration), 1958; Private View (in collaboration), 1965; A View of Venice, 1972; Assignments, 1972; Inchcape Review, 1977; (jtly) Pride of the Shires, 1979; Personal View, 1979; Sittings, 1983; Israel: a first view, 1986; (with Viscount Tonypandy) My Wales, 1986; Stills 1983–1987, 1987; Public Appearances 1987–1991, 1991; Wild Flowers, 1995; (jtly) Hong Kong: portraits of power, 1995; Snowdon on Stage, 1996; Wild Fruit, 1997; London, Sight Unseen, 1999; Photographs by Snowdon 1952–2000, 2000; Snowdon on Russia, 2003. *Heir:* s Viscount Linley, *qv. Address:* 22 Launceston Place, W8 5RL. *Clubs:* Buck's, Oxford and Cambridge; Leander (Henley-on-Thames); Hawks (Cambridge).
See also under Royal Family, and Earl of Rosse.

SNOWDON, Leslie Colin; Editor, Scotland on Sunday, since 2006; *b* RAF Cosford, 23 June 1961; *s* of Alex and Jackie Snowdon; *m* 1984, Fiona Allison MacGregor; *two s one d. Educ:* Annan Acad.; Univ. of Edinburgh (MA Hons). Photographer, Dumfriesshire Newspapers, 1984–89; Photographer and Sub-editor, Dumfries and Galloway Standard, 1989–94; The Scotsman: Sub-ed., 1994–96; Chief Pol Sub-ed., 1996–97; Chief Sports Sub-ed., 1997–98; Dep. Sports Ed., 1998–99; Sports Ed., Sunday Times Scotland, 1999–2000; Dep. Sports Ed., The Sunday Times, 2000–03; Editor, Sunday Times Scotland, 2003–06. *Recreations:* hill-walking accompanied by two terriers: Woody and Max, sport, exercise, music, cooking, wine. *Address:* c/o Scotland on Sunday, Barclay House, 108 Holyrood Road, Edinburgh EH8 8AS. *T:* (0131) 620 8424, *Fax:* (0131) 620 8491.

SNOWLING, (George) Christopher (Edward); Legal Member, Mental Health Review Tribunal, since 1992; *b* 12 Aug. 1934; *s* of George Edward Snowling and Winifred Beryl (*née* Cave); *m* 1961, Flora Skells; *one s one d. Educ:* The Mercers' Sch.; Fitzwilliam House, Cambridge (MA). Served RAF, 1953–55. Admitted Solicitor, 1961; various local govt posts, 1958–71; Law Society: Legal Aid Admin, 1971–78; Secretary: Educn and Trng, 1978–85, Professional Purposes, 1985–86; Dir, Legal Aid, 1986–89; private practice, 1989–92. Mem., Cuckfield UDC, 1971–74; Mid Sussex District Council: Mem. (C), 1973–; Chm., 1981–82, 1986–87, 1987–88; Chm., Policy and Resources Cttee, 1988–91; Leader majority gp, 1991–95; Leader largest minority gp, 1995–99; Leader majority gp, Leader of Council, and Chm. Policy and Resources Cttee, 1999–2001; Chairman: Central Area Planning Cttee, 2001–03; Service Review and Performance Panel, 2001–03; Dep. Leader, 2003–06; Cabinet Mem. for Resources, subseq. Corporate Services, 2003–06, for Health and Community, 2006–. Vice Chm., Brighton and Mid Sussex Res. Ethics Cttee, 2004–07; Alternate Vice Chm., Brighton E Res. Ethics Cttee; Mem., Crawley & Horsham Local Res. Ethics Cttee (Chm., 2003). Member: Council, Assoc. of Dist Councils, 1990–97; cttees, LGA, 1996–98. Member: Mid Downs CHC, 1988–96; Lindfield Parish Council, 1995– (Vice Chm., 1999–2003; Chm., Planning and Traffic Cttee, 2003–); Lindfield Rural Parish Council, 2003–. Pres., Old Mercers' Club, 1998–99 (Trustee, 2008–). *Recreations:* local government, painting. *Address:* Eldon Lodge, Pondcroft Road, Lindfield, West Sussex RH16 2HQ. *T:* (01444) 482172.

SNOWLING, Prof. Margaret Jean, PhD; Professor of Psychology, University of York, since 1994; *b* 15 July 1955; *d* of Walter and Jean Snowling; *m* 1st, 1986, Christopher Parker (marr. diss. 1992); *one s*; 2nd, 1995, Charles Hulme, *qv*; *three step d. Educ:* Univ. of Bristol (BSc Psychol. 1976); University Coll. London (PhD Psychol. 1979). Dip. Clin. Psychol., BPsS, 1988. National Hospital College of Speech Sciences, London: Lectr in Psychology, 1979–88; Sen. Lectr, 1988–89; Principal, 1989–92; Prof. of Psychology, Univ. of Newcastle upon Tyne, 1992–94. Vice-Pres., British Dyslexia Assoc., 1997. Hon. DSc London, 2007. *Publications:* (ed) Children's Written Language Difficulties, 1985; Dyslexia: a cognitive developmental perspective, 1987, 2nd edn 2000; (ed jtly) Dyslexia: integrating theory and practice, 1991; (ed jtly) Reading Development and Dyslexia, 1994; (ed jtly) Dyslexia, Speech and Language: a practitioner's handbook, 1996; (ed jtly) Dyslexia, Biology and Cognition, 1997; (ed jtly) The Science of Reading: a handbook, 2005. *Recreations:* walking, entertaining, music. *Address:* Department of Psychology, University of York, Heslington, York YO10 5DD. *T:* (01904) 433162.

SNOWMAN, (Michael) Nicholas; General Director, Opéra National du Rhin, since 2002; Chairman, Wartski, since 2002 (Co-Chairman, 1997–2002); *b* 18 March 1944; *s* of late Kenneth Snowman and Sallie Snowman (*née* Moghi-Levkine); *m* 1983, Margo Michelle Rouard; *one s. Educ:* Hall Sch., London; Highgate Sch., London; Magdalene Coll., Cambridge (BA Hons Eng. Lit.). Asst to Hd of Music Staff, Glyndebourne Fest., 1967–69; Co-Founder and Gen. Man., London Sinfonietta, 1968–72; Administrator,

Music Th. Ensemble, 1968–71; Artistic Dir, IRCAM, Centre d'Art et de Culture Georges Pompidou, 1972–86; Gen. Dir (Arts), 1986–92, Chief Exec., 1992–98, South Bank Centre, London; Gen. Dir, Glyndebourne, 1998–2000. Co-Founder, 1975, Artistic Advr, 1975–92, Bd Mem., 1992–, Vice-Chm., 1998–, Ensemble InterContemporain, Paris; Mem. Music Cttee, Venice Biennale, 1979–86; Artistic Dir, Projects in 1980 (Stravinsky), 1981 (Webern), 1983 (Boulez), Fest. d'Automne de Paris; Programme Consultant, Cité de la Musique, La Villette, Paris, 1991. Mem. British Sect., Franco-British Council, 1995–2000. Trustee, New Berlioz Edition, 1996–; Bd Mem., Comité Hector Berlioz, 2000–. Gov., RAM, 1998– (Hon. RAM 1999). Officier de l'Ordre des Arts et des Lettres (France), 1990 (Chevalier, 1985); Order of Cultural Merit (Poland), 1990; Chevalier, l'Ordre National du Mérite (France), 1995. *Publications:* (co-ed) The Best of Granta, 1967; (series ed.) The Contemporary Composers; papers and articles on music, architecture, cultural policy. *Recreations:* films, eating, spy novels, France. *Address:* Opéra National du Rhin, 19 place Broglie, BP 320, 67008 Strasbourg cedex, France.

SNOXELL, David Raymond; HM Diplomatic Service, retired; High Commissioner, Mauritius, 2000–04; *b* 18 Nov. 1944; *s* of late Gordon William Snoxell and of Norah Snoxell; *m* 1971, Anne Carter; *two s one d. Educ:* Bishop Vesey's Grammar Sch., Sutton Coldfield; Bristol Univ. (BA Hons Hist. 1966); Aston Univ. (Dip. Personnel Mgt 1967). MIPD. UNA Volunteer, Senegal, 1967–68; joined FCO, 1969; Islamabad, 1973–76; UK Mission to Geneva, 1976–81; FCO, 1981–86; Dir, British Information Services, NY, 1986–91; Dep. Head of Drugs and Internat. Crime Dept, FCO, 1991–94; Dep. Head of Southern Africa Dept, FCO, 1994–96; Ambassador to Senegal and concurrently to Mali, Guinea, Guinea Bissau and Cape Verde, 1997–2000. Trustee, Marine Educn Trust, 2007–. *Recreations:* choral singing, local history, prison visiting. *Address:* Old Mill Cottage, Bassetsbury Lane, High Wycombe, Bucks HP11 1QZ. *T:* (01494) 529318.

SNYDER, Prof. Allan Whitenack, FRS 1990; FAA; FTSE; Director, Centre for the Mind, 150th Anniversary Chair of Science and the Mind, and University Professor, University of Sydney, since 1999; *s* of Edward H. Snyder, philanthropist, and Zelda (*née* Cotton), Broadway actress and psychodramatherapist. *Educ:* Central High Sch., Phil. (AB); Pennsylvania State Univ. (BS); MIT (SM); Harvard Univ. (MS); University Coll. London (PhD); DSc London. Greenland Ice Cap Communications Project, 1961; Gen. Telecom. and Elec. Res. Lab., 1963–67; Cons. to Brit. PO and Standard Telecom. Lab., 1968–70; Nat. Sci. Foundn Fellow, Yale Univ., 1970–71; Professorial Fellow, ANU, 1971–77; John Simon Guggenheim Fellow, Yale Univ. Med. Sch., 1977–78; Australian National University: Prof. of Optical Physics and Visual Scis, 1978–98; Peter Karmel Chair and Dist. Prof., 1999–2006; Hd, Dept of Applied Maths, Inst. for Advanced Studies, 1980–83; Hd, Optical Scis Centre, 1987–2003; Royal Soc. Quest Res. Fellow, Cambridge Univ., 1987. Foundn Dir, Aust. Photonics Cooperative Res. Centre, 1992–95. Associate Editor, Jl of Optical Soc. of America, 1981–83. Fellow, Optical Soc. of Amer., 1980; Foundn Fellow, Nat. Vision Res. Inst. of Aust., 1983. A. E. Mills Meml Orator, RACP, 1996; Harrie Massey Prize and Lect., Inst. of Phys, 1996; Inaug. Edwin Flack Lect., Australian Olympic Cttee, 1998; Clifford Paterson Prize and Lect., Royal Soc., 2001. Research Medal, Royal Soc. Vic, 1974; Edgeworth David Medal, Royal Soc. NSW, 1974; Thomas Rankin Lyle Medal, Aust. Acad. of Sci., 1985; Stuart Sutherland Meml Medal, Aust. Acad. of Technological Sci. and Engrg, 1991; CSIRO External Medal for Research, 1995; Australia Prize, 1997; Marconi Internat. Prize, 2001; Australian Centenary Medal, 2003. *Publications:* Photoreceptor Optics, 1975; Optical Waveguide Theory, 1983; Optical Waveguide Sciences, 1983; What Makes a Champion, 2002; articles on the mind, the visual system of animals and on the physics of light propagation in internat. sci. jls. *Recreations:* art, culture, swimming. *Address:* Centre for the Mind, Main Quadrangle, University of Sydney, NSW 2006, Australia. *T:* (2) 93518533, *Fax:* (2) 93518534; *e-mail:* allan@centreforthemind.com.

SNYDER, Sir Michael John, Kt 2008; FCA; Senior Partner, Kingston Smith LLP, Chartered Accountants, since 1990; *b* 30 July 1950; *s* of Elsworth and Pauline Snyder; *m* 1974, Mary Dickinson; *two d. Educ:* Brentwood Sch.; City of London Coll. FCA 1978. Chairman: Cheviot Capital Ltd, 1983–; Kingston Sorel Internat., 1990–; Kingston Smith Consultants Ltd, 1997–; Blacktower Financial Advisers (formerly Kingston Smith Financial Services) Ltd, 1997–; Devonshire Corporate Finance Ltd, 2001–; HR Insight Ltd, 2005–. Mem., Lee Valley Regl Park Authy, 1993–. Member: Bd, Thames Gateway London Partnership, 2000–; Gateway to London, 2001–. Chm., Assoc. of Practising Accountants, 1992–. Mem., Leaders Cttee, 2003–, Vice Chm., London Councils (formerly Assoc. of London Govt), 2007–; Mem. Bd, Film London, 2004–. Trustee, Academy Sponsor Trust, 2005–. MSI. FInstD 1986. Corporation of London: Mem., Court of Common Council, 1986–; Dep., Ward of Cordwainer; Chm., Policy and Resources Cttee, 2003–08; Member: Finance Cttee, 1992–; City Lands and Bridge House Estates Cttee, 1998–. Liveryman and Member of Court: Co. of Needlemakers, 1980– (Master, 2005–06); Tallow Chandlers' Co., 1990–. Hon. Treas., Bow Bells Assoc. Governor: London Metropolitan Univ., 1999– (Chm., Audit Cttee); City of London Sch. for Girls, 1989–; Brentwood Sch., 1992– (Hon. Treas.; Dep. Chm.). Hon. DSc City, 2001. Grand Cross, Order of Merit (FRG), 1998. *Recreations:* music, bridge, inland waterways. *Address:* Kingston Smith LLP, Devonshire House, 60 Goswell Road, EC1M 7AD. *T:* (020) 7566 4000, *Fax:* (020) 7689 6300; *e-mail:* mjs@kingstonsmith.co.uk. *Clubs:* City Livery, Ward of Cordwainer (Vice Pres.).

SOAME, Sir Charles (John) Buckworth-Herne-, 12th Bt *cr* 1697; *b* 28 May 1932; *s* of Sir Charles Burnett Buckworth-Herne-Soame, 11th Bt, and Elsie May (*d* 1972), *d* of Walter Alfred Lloyd; *S* father, 1977; *m* 1958, Eileen Margaret Mary, *d* of Leonard Minton; *one s. Heir:* s Richard John Buckworth-Herne-Soame, *b* 17 Aug. 1970. *Address:* Sheen Cottage, Coalbrookdale, Telford, Salop TF8 7EQ.

SOAMES, Lady; Mary Soames, LG 2005; DBE 1980 (MBE (mil.) 1945); FRSL; Member of Council, 1978–97, and Chairman of Trustees, 1991–2002, Winston Churchill Memorial Trust; Chairman, Royal National Theatre Board, 1989–95; *b* 15 Sept. 1922; *y d* of late Rt Hon. Sir Winston Churchill, KG, OM, CH, FRS, and late Baroness Spencer-Churchill, GBE; *m* 1947, Captain Christopher Soames, Coldstream Guards, later Baron Soames, GCMG, GCVO, CH, CBE, PC (*d* 1987); *three s two d. Educ:* privately. Served War: Red Cross and WVS, 1939–41; ATS, 1941–46, with mixed anti-aircraft batteries in UK and Europe (Jun. Comdr). Accompanied father on various journeys; campaigned with husband through six elections whilst he was Conservative MP for Bedford, 1950–66; accompanied husband to Paris where he was Ambassador, 1968–72, and to Brussels where he was first British Vice Pres. of Eur. Commn, 1973–76; accompanied husband when he was appointed last British Governor of Southern Rhodesia, Dec. 1979–April 1980. Chm., UK Assoc. for Internat. Year of the Child, 1979. Governor, Harrow Sch., 1980–95. Freeman, City of London, 1994; Hon. Freewoman, Skinners' Co., 1994. JP E Sussex, 1960–74. FRSL 2000. Hon. Fellow, Churchill Coll., Cambridge, 1983. Hon. DLitt: Sussex, 1989; Kent, 1997; Univ. of the South, Tennessee, 2004; Hon. LLD Alberta, 2004. Franklin Delano Roosevelt Freedom Medal, Franklin and Eleanor Roosevelt Inst., 2005. Chevalier de la Légion d'Honneur (France), 1995. *Publications:* Clementine Churchill by Her Daughter Mary Soames, 1979 (a Wolfson Prize for History, and Yorkshire Post Prize for Best First Work, 1979), rev. and updated edn, 2002; A Churchill Family Album—A Personal Anthology Selected by Mary Soames, 1982; The Profligate Duke: George Spencer-Churchill 5th Duke of Marlborough and his Duchess, 1987; Winston Churchill: his Life as a Painter: a memoir by his daughter Mary Soames, 1990; Speaking for Themselves—The Personal Letters of Winston & Clementine Churchill: edited by their daughter Mary Soames, 1998. *Recreations:* reading, sight-seeing, gardening.

See also Earl Peel, Hon. A. N. W. Soames, Hon. E. M. Soames, Hon. R. C. Soames.

SOAMES, Hon. (Arthur) Nicholas (Winston); MP (C) Mid Sussex, since 1997 (Crawley, 1983–97); *b* 12 Feb. 1948; *s* of Baron Soames, GCMG, GCVO, CH, CBE, PC and of Lady Soames, *qv*; *m* 1st, 1981, Catherine Weatherall (marr. diss. 1990); one *s*; 2nd, 1993, Serena, *d* of Sir John L. E. Smith, CH, CBE; one *s* one *d*. *Educ:* Eton. Served 11th Hussars (PAO), 1967–70 (2nd Lieut); Equerry to the Prince of Wales, 1970–72; Asst Dir, Sedgwick Group, 1976–82. PPS to Minister of State for Employment, 1984–85, to Sec. of State, DoE, 1987–89, to Sec. of State, DTI, 1989–90; Parly Sec., MAFF, 1992–94; Minister of State for the Armed Forces, MoD, 1994–97; Shadow Defence Sec., 2003–05. Mem., Commonwealth War Graves Commn, 2003–. *Recreation:* country pursuits. *Address:* House of Commons, SW1A 0AA. *T:* (020) 7219 3000. *Clubs:* White's, Turf, Pratt's.

See also Hon. E. M. Soames, Hon. R. C. Soames.

SOAMES, Hon. Emma (Mary); Editor, Saga magazine, and Editorial Director, Saga Publishing Ltd, since 2002; *b* 6 Sept. 1949; *d* of Baron Soames, GCMG, GCVO, CH, CBE, PC and of Lady Soames, *qv*; *m* 1981, James MacManus (marr. diss. 1989); one *d*. *Educ:* Hamilton House Sch. for Girls; Queen's Coll., London; Sorbonne, Univ. of Paris; Ecole des Sciences Politiques. Journalist, Evening Standard, 1974–81; Editor, Literary Review, 1984–86; Features Editor, Vogue, 1986–88; Editor: Tatler, 1988–90; Evening Standard mag., 1992–94; Telegraph mag., 1994–2002. Editor of Year Award for Gen. Interest and Current Affairs, BSME, 2003. *Recreations:* travel, gardening.

See also Hon. A. N. W. Soames, Hon. R. C. Soames.

SOAMES, Hon. Nicholas; *see* Soames, Hon. A. N. W.

SOAMES, Hon. Rupert Christopher; Chief Executive, Aggreko plc, since 2003; *b* 18 May 1959; *s* of Baron Soames, GCMG, GCVO, CH, CBE, PC and of Lady Soames, *qv*; *m* 1988, Camilla Dunne; two *s* one *d*. *Educ:* Eton; Worcester Coll., Oxford (BA). Pres., Oxford Union, 1981. With GEC plc, 1982–96 (Man. Dir, Avery Berkel UK); Misys plc, 1996–2002 (Chief Exec., Banking and Securities Div., 2000–02). *Recreations:* country sports, food and wine. *Address:* c/o Aggreko plc, 120 Bothwell Street, Glasgow G2 7JS. *Clubs:* White's, Turf, Pratt's.

See also Hon. A. N. W. Soames, Hon. E. M. Soames.

SOAR, Vice Adm. Trevor Alan, OBE 1994; Chief of Materiel (Fleet), Defence Equipment and Support, Ministry of Defence, 2007–May 2009; *b* 21 March 1957; *s* of Colin and Hazel Soar; *m* 1978, Anne Matlock; two *s*. *Educ:* Loughborough Grammar Sch.; BRNC Dartmouth. Joined RN, 1975; qualified submariner, 1978; Captain: HMS Ocelot, 1987–90; HMS Talent, 1991–94; Navy Plans and Prog., MoD, 1996; Captain, HMS Chatham, 1997–98; Asst Dir Warfare, Navy Plans and Prog., then Captain Navy Plans, Navy Resources and Plans, MoD, 1998–2000; Dir Naval Staff responsible for pan-Navy policy across Defence, 2000–02; Captain, HMS Invincible, 2002–04; Rear Adm. 2004; Capability Manager (Precision Attack), 2004–06. Younger Brother, Trinity House, 2002–. FRSA 1996. Freeman, City of London, 2004. Hon. DEng Heriot-Watt, 2005. *Recreations:* golf, Royal Navy Rugby Football Union (Vice Pres.), supporter of Leicester Tigers. *Address:* c/o Naval Secretary, Leach Building, Whale Island, Portsmouth, Hants PO2 8BY; *e-mail:* trevor.soar@virgin.net. *Club:* Army and Navy.

SOARES, Dr Mário Alberto Nobre Lopes; President of Portugal, 1986–96; Member, Council of State, Portugal; *b* 7 Dec. 1924; *s* of João Lopes Soares and Elisa Nobre Soares; *m* 1949, Maria Barroso Soares; one *s* one *d*. *Educ:* Univ. of Lisbon (BA 1951; JD 1957); Faculty of Law, Faculty of History and Philosophy, Sorbonne. LèsL, LenD. Leader, United Democratic Youth Movement and Mem., Central Cttee, 1946–48; Mem. Exec., Social Democratic Action, 1952–60; Democratic Opposition candidate, Lisbon, legis. elections, 1965, 1969; deported to São Tomé, March-Nov. 1968; Rep., Internat. League of Human Rights; imprisoned 12 times; exile, Paris, 1970–74; Founder, Portuguese Socialist Party, 1973, Sec. Gen., 1973–86; elected to Legis. Assembly as Mem. (Socialist Party) for Lisbon, 1974; Minister of Foreign Affairs, 1974–75; Minister without Portfolio, 1975; Deputy, Constituent Assembly, 1975, Legis. Assembly, 1976; Prime Minister of Portugal, 1976–77, 1978, 1983–85; Leader of Opposition, 1978–83. Mem., European Parlt, 1999–2004. Pres., Mário Soares Foundn, 1996–. Joseph Lemaire Prize, 1975; Internat. Prize of Human Rights, NY, 1977; Robert Schuman Prize, Strasbourg, 1987, etc; numerous hon. degrees, decorations and orders. *Publications:* A Juventude Não Está com o Estado Novo, 1946; As ideias político-sociais de Teófilo Braga, 1950; A Justificação Jurídica da Restauração e a Teoria da Origem Popular do Poder Político, 1954; Escritos Políticos, 1969; Le Portugal Baillonné, 1972 (Portuguese edn, Portugal Amordaçado, 1947; also trans. English, Italian, German and Spanish); Destruir o Sistema, Construir uma Vida Nova, 1973; Caminho Difícil, do Salazarismo ao Caetanismo, 1973; Escritos do Exílio, 1975; (with Willy Brandt and Bruno Kreisky) Liberdade para Portugal, 1975; Democratização e Descolonização, 1975; Portugal, que Revolução? (interviews with Dominique Pouchin), 1976 (also French, German, Italian and Spanish edns); Relatório as II Congresso do Partida Socialista, 1976; A Europa Connosco, 1976; Na Posse do I Governo Constitucional, 1976; Na Hora da Verdade, 1976; Na Reestruturação do I Governo Constitucional, 1977; Medidas Económicas de Emergência, 1978; Na Posse do II Governo Constitucional, 1978; Em Defesa do Estado Democrático, 1978; Encarar o Futuro com Esperança, 1978; Existe o Eurocomunismo?, 1978; O Futuro será o Socialismo Democrático, 1979; Partida Socialista, Fronteira da Liberdade, 1979; Confiar no Partida Socialista, Apostar em Portugal, 1979; Soares Responde a Artur Portela, 1980; Apelo Irrecusável, 1981; Resposta Socialista para o Mundo em Crise, 1983; Persistir, 1984; A Árvore e a Floresta, 1985; Intervenções (collected speeches): Vol. I, 1987; Vol. II, 1988; Vol. III, 1989; Vol. IV, 1990; Vol. V, 1991; Vol. VI, 1992; Vol. VII, 1993; Vol. VIII, 1994; Vol. IX, 1995; Vol. X, 1996; Moderador e Árbitro, 1995; Mémoire Vivante; A Incerteza dos Tempos. *Recreations:* bibliophile; collector of contemporary Portuguese paintings. *Address:* Rua Dr João Soares, 2–3°, 1600 Lisboa, Portugal.

SOBER, Phillip, FCA; consultant; non-executive Director: Liberty International (formerly Transatlantic Holdings, then Liberty International Holdings), 1983–2002; Capital and Counties, 1993–2002; Capital Shopping Centres, 1994–2002; *b* 1 April 1931; *s* of Abraham and Sandra Sober; *m* 1957, Vivien Louise Oppenheimer; two *d* (and one *d* decd). *Educ:* Haberdashers' Aske's. Qual. as Chartered Accountant, 1953; FCA 1963. Stoy Hayward, Chartered Accountants: Partner, 1958; Internat. Partner, 1975–90; Sen. Partner, 1985–90. Eur. Regl Dir, Horwath Internat., 1990–94. Crown Estate Comr, 1983–94. Mem. Council, UK Central Council for Nursing, Midwifery and Health Visiting, 1980–83. Pres., Norwood Child Care, 1990–94. Trustee, Royal Opera House Trust, 1985–91. Gov., London Inst. Higher Educn Corp., 1994–2003; Mem. Council, London Univ., 1999–. *Publications:* articles in prof. press on various subjects but primarily on property co. accounting. *Recreations:* interested in all the arts, partic. music; golf main sporting activity. *Address:* 67B Clarendon Road, W11 4JE. *T:* (020) 7221 8545; Amberley Place, Amberley, West Sussex BN18 9NG. *Clubs:* Savile, Royal Automobile, Hurlingham.

SOBERS, Sir Garfield St Auburn, (Sir Garry), Kt 1975; AO 2003; OCC; former cricketer; Consultant, Barbados Tourism Authority; *b* Bridgetown, Barbados, 28 July 1936; *m* 1969, Prudence Kirby; two *s* one *d*. *Educ:* Bay Street Sch., Barbados. First major match, 1953, for Barbados; played in 93 Test Matches for West Indies, 39 as Captain, 1953–74 (made world record Test Match score, Kingston, 1958); captained West Indies and Barbados teams, 1965–74; Captain of Nottinghamshire CCC, 1968–74. On retirement from Test cricket held the following world records in Test Matches: 365 not out; 26 centuries; 235 wickets; 110 catches. *Publications:* Cricket Advance, 1965; Cricket Crusader, 1966; King Cricket, 1967; (with J. S. Barker) Cricket in the Sun, 1967; Bonaventure and the Flashing Blade, 1967; (with Brian Scovell) Sobers: Twenty Years At The Top (autobiog.), 1988; (jtly) The Changing Face of Cricket, 1995; (with Bob Harris) Garry Sobers: my autobiography, 2002. *Address:* Barbados Tourism Authority, Redman Drive, Harbour Road, St Michael, Barbados, West Indies. *Fax:* 4264080.

SOBHI, Mohamed Ibrahim; Order of Merit, 1st Class, Egypt, 1974; Director General, International Bureau of Universal Postal Union, Berne, 1975–84, retired; *b* Alexandria, 28 March 1925; *s* of Gen. Ibrahim Sobhi and Mrs Zenab Affifi; *m* 1950, Laila Ahmed Sobhi; two *s* one *d*. *Educ:* Cairo Univ. (BE 1949). Construction of roads and airports, Engr Corps, 1950; Technical Sec., Communications Commn, Permanent Council for Develt and National Prodn, Cairo, 1954; Fellow, Vanderbilt Univ., Nashville, Tenn (studying transport and communications services in USA), 1955–56; Tech. Dir, Office of Minister of Communications for Posts, Railways and Coordination between means of transp. and communications, Cairo, 1956–61; Dir-Gen., Sea Transp. Authority (remaining Mem. Tech. Cttees, Postal Org.), 1961–64; Under Sec. of State for Communications and Mem. Bd, Postal Org., Cairo, 1964–68; Chm. Bd, Postal Org., and Sec.-Gen., African Postal Union, Cairo, 1968–74. Universal Postal Union: attended Congress, Ottawa, 1957; attended Cons. Council for Postal Studies session, Brussels, 1958; Head of Egyptian Delegn, Tokyo and Lausanne Congresses, and sessions of CCPS (set up by Tokyo Congress), 1969–74; Dir, Exec. Bureau i/c Egyptian projects in Africa, incl. construction of Hôtel de l'Amitié, Bamako, Mali, and roads, Republic of Mali, 1963–74; as Director-General of UPU, acted as Sec.-Gen. of the Congress, Exec. Council, and Cons. Council for Postal Studies; acted as intermediary between UPU and Restricted Unions, UN and internat. orgns; visited member countries and attended many meetings and congresses, inc. those of Restricted Unions, in all continents. Chm., Communications Cttee, Nat. Dem. Party of Egypt, 1985; Mem., Nat. Council of Production and Econ. Affairs of Egypt, 1985. Mem., Acad. of Scientific Res., 1990. Heinrich von Stephan Medal (Germany), 1979; Order of Postal Merit (Gran Placa) (Spain), 1979. *Recreations:* croquet, philately, music. *Address:* 4 Sheik Zakaria El-Ansary Street, Heliopolis, Cairo, Egypt; 18 Burgstrasse, 3700 Spiez, Switzerland.

SODANO, His Eminence Cardinal Angelo, STD, JCD; Secretary of State to His Holiness the Pope, 1990–2006, now Emeritus; Dean, Sacred College of Cardinals, since 2005; *b* Asti, Italy, 23 Nov. 1927; *s* of Giovanni Sodano and Delfina (*née* Brignolo). *Educ:* Seminario di Asti; Pontifical Università Gregoriana (STD); Pontifical Università Lateranense (JCD). Ordained priest, 1950; Titular Archbishop, 1978; Apostolic Nuncio, Chile, 1978–88; Sec., Council for Public Affairs of Church, later Section for Relns of Holy See with States, 1988–90. Several hon. distinctions. *Address:* c/o Secretariat of State, 00120 Vatican City State.

SODOR AND MAN, Bishop of, since 2008; **Rt Rev. Robert Mar Erskine Paterson;** *b* Cardiff, 27 Feb. 1949; *s* of David Donaldson Paterson and Letitia Paterson; *m* 1971, Pauline Anne Laing; one *s* two *d*. *Educ:* St John's Coll., Univ. of Durham (BA 1971; Van Mildert Scholar 1971; DipTh 1972); MA Dunelm 1982. Ordained deacon, 1972, priest, 1973; Assistant Curate: Harpurhey, Manchester, 1972–73; Sketty, Swansea, 1973–78; Rector, Llangattock and Llangynidr, 1978–83; Vicar, Gabalfa, Cardiff, 1983–94; Team Rector, Cowbridge, 1994–2000; Principal Officer, Council for Mission and Ministry, Church in Wales, 2000–06; Chaplain to Archbishop of York, 2006–08. *Publications:* Short, Sharp and Off the Point: a guide to good and bad preaching, 1987; The Monarch Book of Christian Wisdom, 1997; (contrib.) Common Worship Today, 2000; (contrib.) The Book of Common Prayer Worldwide, 2006. *Recreations:* early music, walking, cycling, theatre, reading. *Address:* Thie yn Aspick, The Falls, Tromode Road, Douglas, Isle of Man IM4 4PZ. *T:* (01624) 622108, *Fax:* (01624) 672890.

SOFAT, Janardan, FCA; Director, Addidi Wealth (formerly AJS Wealth Management) Ltd, since 2006; Chairman, Kent Probation Area, National Probation Services, since 2007; *b* 11 May 1958; *s* of Didar Chand Sofat and Ved Kumari Sofat; *m* 1981, Anna Mathur; two *d*. *Educ:* Univ. of Hull (BSc Econ). FCA 1992. Finance Dir, J. S. Hamilton Ltd, 1983–90; Chief Exec., AJS Financial Consultants Ltd, 1990–97; Ops Dir, Business Link London E, 1997–2000; Regional Dir, Small Business Service, 2000–04; Regl Comr for SE, NHS Appts Commn, subseq. Appts Commn, 2004–07. Non-exec. Dir, W Kent HA, 1994–2000; Chm., Medway NHS Trust, 2000–04. Chm., Medway Racial Equality Council, 2001–; Chief Operating Officer, Business Link for London, 2004–05. Trustee, Mencap, 2005–. *Recreations:* family, good food, travel. *Address:* 47 Pilgrims Road, Halling, Kent ME2 1HN; *e-mail:* sofat@mail.com.

SOFER, Mrs Anne Hallowell; Chief Education Officer, London Borough of Tower Hamlets, 1989–97; *b* 19 April 1937; *d* of Geoffrey Crowther (later Baron Crowther) and Margaret Worth; *m* 1958, Jonathan Sofer (*d* 2003); two *s* one *d*. *Educ:* St Paul's Sch.; Swarthmore Coll., USA; Somerville Coll., Oxford (MA); DipEd London. Secretary, National Assoc. of Governors and Managers, 1972–75; Additional Member, ILEA Education Cttee, 1974–77; Chairman, ILEA Schools Sub-Cttee, 1978–81; Mem. (SDP), GLC/ILEA for St Pancras N, Oct. 1981–86 (by-election) (Labour, 1977–81). Dir, Channel Four Television Co. Ltd, 1981–83; Columnist, The Times, 1983–87. Mem., SDP Nat. Cttee, 1982–87. Contested Hampstead and Highgate (SDP) 1983, (SDP/Alliance) 1987. Trustee, Nuffield Foundn, 1990–2005. Chm., Nat. Children's Bureau, 2000–06. *Publications:* (with Tyrrell Burgess) The School Governors and Managers Handbook and Training Guide, 1978; The London Left Takeover, 1987. *Address:* 46 Regent's Park Road, NW1 7SX. *T:* (020) 7722 8970.

SOHLMAN, (Per) Michael (Sverre Rolfsson); Executive Director, Nobel Foundation, since 1992; *b* 24 May 1944; *s* of Rolf Rolfsson Sohlman and Zinaida Sohlman (*née* Yarotskaya); *m* 1965, Margareta Borg-Sohlman (marr. diss. 1980); one *s* two *d*. *Educ:* Univ. of Uppsala (BA 1964). Asst Sec., Commn on Environmental Problems, 1969–70; Min. of Industry, 1972–74; Internat. Div., 1974–76, Budget Dept, 1976, Min. of Finance; Financial Counsellor, Permt Swedish Delegn to OECD, Paris, 1977–80; Res. Dept, Social-Democratic Parly Gp, 1981–82; Head of Planning, Econ. Dept, 1982–84, Dir of Budget, 1985–87, Min. of Finance; Under-Sec. of State, Min. of Agriculture, 1987–89; Under-Sec. of State for Foreign Trade, Min. for Foreign Affairs, 1989–91. Member:

Stockholm Inst. of Transition Econs, 1990–; Swedish Internat. Develt Agency, 1995–98; Chm., Bd of Dirs, Royal Dramatic Theatre, Stockholm, 1993–96. Member: Royal Swedish Acad. of Scis, 1996; Acad. of Engineering Scis, 1995. Hon. DHL Gustavus Adolphus Coll., 1992. *Address:* Nobel Foundation, PO Box 5232, 102 45 Stockholm, Sweden. *T:* (8) 6630920.

SOKOL, Christopher John Francis; QC 2006; *b* 22 April 1953; *s* of Emil Sokol and Madge Sokol (*née* Woolley); four *d. Educ:* Brighton Coll.; Trinity Coll., Cambridge (BA 1974, MA 1977). Called to the Bar, Lincoln's Inn, 1976, Bencher, 2002; in practice, specialising in tax law. *Publications:* contribs to professional jls. *Recreations:* travel, country sports, old books, fencing, wine. *Address:* 15 Old Square, Lincoln's Inn, WC2A 3UE. *T:* (020) 7242 2744, *Fax:* (020) 7629 6536; *e-mail:* csokol@15oldsquare.co.uk. *Clubs:* Lansdowne, Buck's.

SOKOLOV, Dr Avril, FBA 1996; Reader in Russian, University of Durham, 1989–96, Emeritus since 1996; *b* 4 May 1930; *d* of Frederick Cresswell Pyman and Frances Gwenneth Pyman (*née* Holman), MBE; *m* 1963, Kirill Konstantinovich Sokolov (*d* 2004); one *d. Educ:* Newnham Coll., Cambridge (BA Mod. Langs 1951; PhD 1958). FCIL (FIL 1949). British Council post-grad. scholarship to Leningrad, 1959–61; freelance writer on and translator of Russian lit., 1962–75; lived in Moscow, 1963–74; University of Durham: part-time Lectr in Russian Lit., 1975–77; Lectr, 1977–86; Sen. Lectr, 1986–89. Mem., Soc. of Authors (Translators' Section), 1974–. Hon. Mem., Blok Gp, Russian Acad. of Scis, 2002–; Mem. Hon. Cttee, Fondn Centre d'Etudes Vjatcheslav Ivanov, Rome, 2005. Cert. of Merit, Moscow Patriarchate, 1973. *Publications:* as Avril Pyman: The Distant Thunder: a life of Aleksandr Blok, Vol. I, 1979 (trans. Russian, 2005); The Release of Harmony: a life of Aleksandr Blok, Vol. II, 1980 (trans. Russian, 2006); Aleksandr Blok's The Twelve, 1989; A History of Russian Symbolism, 1994 (trans. Russian, 1998); (contrib.) Mapping Lives: the uses of biography, 2002; (trans.) Requiem, by Anna Akhmatova, 2002; ed and trans. works by Blok, Bulgakov, Shvarts; trans. poetry, prose, art books; numerous articles on Russian Symbolism and later 20th century literature. *Recreations:* travelling, art, theatre, cinema. *Address:* 213 Gilesgate, Durham DH1 1QN. *T:* (0191) 384 2482.

SOLA, Maggie; *see* Koumi, M.

SOLANA MADARIAGA, Javier, Hon. KCMG 1999; Secretary-General, and High Representative for Common Foreign and Security Policy, European Union, since 1999; Secretary-General, Western European Union, since 1999; *b* 14 July 1942; *s* of Luis Solana and Obulia Madariaga; *m* 1972, Concepción Giménez; two *c. Educ:* Colegio del Pilar; Univ. Complutense de Madrid (PhD Physics). Fulbright Schol., USA, 1968. Asst to Prof., Univ. of Valencia, 1968–71, then Univ. Autónoma de Madrid; Mem. Exec., Federación Socialista Madrileña and Federación de Trabajadores de la Enseñanza, Unión General de Trabajadores; Prof. of Physical Scis, Univ. Complutense de Madrid. Mem., Congress of Deputies for Madrid; Mem., Fed. Exec. Cttee, PSOE (Press Sec. and Sec. for Res. and Programmes); Minister of: Culture, and Govt Spokesman, 1982–88; Educn and Sci., 1988–92; Foreign Affairs, 1992–95; Sec.-Gen., NATO, 1995–99. *Publications:* several on physics and solid state physics. *Recreations:* swimming, jogging, tennis, paddle tennis. *Address:* Council of the European Union, Rue de la Loi 175, 1048 Brussels, Belgium.

SOLANDT, Jean Bernard; Chairman: Schroder France SA, 1992–97; J. Henry Schroder & Co. Ltd, 1994–97; Director, Woolwich Building Society, 1993–98; *b* 23 Dec. 1936; *s* of Alfred Solandt and Mathilde Braun Solandt; *m* 1966, Sheila Hammill; one *s* one *d. Educ:* Lycée Pasteur, Strasbourg; Collège Technique Commercial, Strasbourg. Société Générale, Strasbourg, Paris, London, 1954–68; Schroder Gp, 1968–97: Director: J. Henry Schroder & Co., 1973; Schroders plc, 1982; IBJ Schroder Bank & Trust Co. Inc., 1984–86; Schroders Japan Ltd, 1984–95; Schroder & Co. Inc., 1986–96; Schroder Wertheim Hldgs Inc., 1986–97; Schroder Wertheim & Co. Inc., 1986–97; Schroders Asia, 1991; Schroders AG, 1992; Chairman: Schroder Securities Ltd, 1985–89; Schroder Structured Investments Inc., 1995–97. Director: Royal Trust Co. of Canada (London) Ltd, 1978–82; Banca Woolwich SpA, 1996–98; Banque Woolwich SA, 1996–98. Mem. Exec. Cttee, BBA, 1990–94. Advr, Royal Trustees Investment Cttee, 1991–96. Hon. FCIB. *Recreations:* ski-ing, walking, driving, music. *Address:* 27 Heathgate, NW11 7AP. *T:* (020) 8458 2950; La Clapière, 84190 Vacqueyras, France.

SOLANKI, Ramniklal Chhaganlal, CBE 2007 (OBE 1999); author; Editor: Garavi Gujarat, newsweekly, since 1968 (US edition, since 1992); Asian Trader, business journal, with controlled circulation in English, Gujarati and Urdu, since 1985; GG2, since 1990; Pharmacy Business, since 1998; Asian Hospitality, since 2002; GG2 Life, since 2006; Correspondent, Janmabhoomi Group, Bombay, since 1968; *b* 12 July 1931; *s* of Chhaganlal Kalidas and Mrs Ichchhaben Solanki, Surat, Gujarat, India; *m* 1955, Mrs Parvatiben, *d* of Makanji Dullabhji Chavda, Nani Pethan, India; two *s* two *d. Educ:* Irish Presbyterian Mission Sch., Surat (Matriculation Gold Medal, 1949); MTB Coll., Gujarat Univ. (BA(Econ)); Sarvajanik Law Coll., Surat, Gujarat (LLB). Pres., Rander Student Union, 1950–54; Sec., Surat Dist Students' Assoc., 1954–55. Sub-Editor, Nutan Bharat and Lok Vani, Surat, 1954–56; freelance columnist for several newspapers, while serving State Govt in India, 1956–63; London correspondent, Gujarat Mitra Surat, 1964–68; European Correspondent, Janmabhoomi Gp of Newspapers, 1968–; Managing Director: Garavi Gujarat Publications Ltd, Garavi Gujarat Property Ltd and Garavi Gujarat Publications (USA) Inc.; Asian Trade Publications Ltd (columnist of thought of the week on Indian philosophy, Garavi Gujarat, newsweekly). Member: Soc. of Editors (formerly Guild of British Newspaper Editors), 1976–; Asian Adv. Cttee, BBC, 1976–80; Nat. Centre for Ind. Language Trng Steering Gp, 1976–; Exec. Cttee, Gujarati Arya Kshtriya Maha Sabha UK, 1979–84; Exec. Cttee, Gujarati Arya Assoc., 1974–84 (Vice-Pres., 1980–81, 1982–83); CPU, 1964–; Foreign Press Assoc., 1984–; Parly Press Gallery, House of Commons; Sec., Indian Journalists Assoc. of Europe, 1978–79. Founder: Asian Trader Awards for Retail Excellence, 1989; (and Mem. Judging Panel), annual GG2 Leadership and Diversity Awards, 1999; Pharmacy Business Awards, 2001. Chm., Asian Forum, 1999–. Trustee, Gandhi Bapu Meml Trust, 1993–. Best Reporter of the Year in Gujarati, 1970. *Publications:* contrib. many articles. *Recreations:* reading, writing. *Address:* 74 Harrowdene Road, N Wembley, Middx HA0 2JF. *T:* (020) 8902 2879; (office) Garavi Gujarat House, 1/2 Silex Street, SE1 0DW. *T:* (020) 7928 1234, *Fax:* (020) 7261 0055; *e-mail:* ram@gujarat.co.uk; (office) 2020 Beaver Ruin Road, Norcross, Atlanta, GA 30071, USA. *T:* (770) 2637728, *Fax:* (770) 2638617; (office) AMG Business Solutions Pvt Ltd, Commerce House II, Satya Marg, Bodakdev, Ahmedabad, 380054, Gujarat, India. *T:* (79) 40005000.

SOLARI TUDELA, Luis; Ambassador of Peru to the Court of St James's, and concurrently to Ireland, 2004–06; *b* 5 Dec. 1935; *s* of Luis Solari Saco and Rosa Tudela Salmón; *m* 1961, Martha Reinoso Castañeda; one *s* one *d. Educ:* Catholic Univ., Lima (graduate in law); Diplomatic Acad., Peru (postgrad. dip.); l'Institut des Hautes Etudes Internationales, Geneva (postgrad. dip.). Third Sec., 1961; Second Sec., 1966; Ambassador to Panama, 1977–82; Prof. of Internat. Law, Central Univ., Panama, 1978–82; Ambassador to Italy, 1986–88; Vice Minister of Foreign Affairs and Sec. Gen. *ad interim*, 1990; Ambassador to the Holy See, and concurrently to Croatia, Cyprus and Malta, 1992–95; Juridical Advr to Min. of Foreign Affairs, 2002; Sec. of Foreign Policy, 2002–03; Vice Minister and Sec. Gen. of Foreign Affairs, 2003–04. Prof. in Public Internat. Law, Univ. of Lima, Villarreal Univ., San Martin de Porres Univ. and Diplomatic Acad. of Peru, 1986–2004. Mem., Internat. Law Commn, 1987–91. Grand Cross: Order of Peruvian Sun, 1985; Order of Merit for Dist. Services (Peru), 2000. Knight, Order of Condor of Andes (Bolivia), 1955; Grand Cross: Order of Vasco Núñez de Balboa (Panama), 1982; Ordo Pianus (Holy See), 1995; SMO Malta, 1995; Order of Rio Branco (Brazil), 2003; Order of Bernado O'Higgins (Chile), 2004. *Publication:* Derecho Internacional Público, 1982, 8th edn 2003. *Address: e-mail:* solaritudela@hotmail.com. *Clubs:* Nacional, Regatas (Lima); Jockey Club del Perú.

SOLBES MIRA, Pedro; Second Deputy Prime Minister and Minister of Economy and Finance, Spain, since 2004; *b* 31 Aug. 1942; *m* 1973, Pilar Castro; one *s* two *d. Educ:* Univ. of Madrid (BL, Dr Pol Scis); Univ. Libre de Bruxelles (Dip. in European Econs). Entered Min. of Foreign Trade, Spain, 1968; Commercial Counsellor, Spanish Mission to EC, 1973–78; Special Advr to Minister for Relns with EC, 1978–79; Dir Gen. of Commercial Policy, Min. of Econs and Trade, 1979–82; Gen. Sec., Min. of Econs and Finance, 1982–85; Sec. of State for Relns with EC, 1985–91; Minister of Agriculture, Food and Fisheries, 1991–93; Minister of Econs and Finance, 1993–96; Deputy (Socialist Party), Cortes, 1996–99; European Comr for Econs and Monetary Affairs, 1999–2004. Chm., EBRD, 1994. *Address:* Ministry of Economy, Alcalá 9, 28071 Madrid, Spain.

SOLESBURY, William Booth; Senior Visiting Research Fellow, King's College London, since 2005; *b* 10 April 1940; *s* of William and Hannah Solesbury; *m* 1966, Felicity Andrew; one *s* two *d. Educ:* Hertford Grammar Sch.; Univ. of Cambridge (BA Hons Geography); Univ. of Liverpool (MCD Town Planning). London County Council, 1961–65; London Borough of Camden, 1965–66; City of Munich, 1966–67; Min. of Housing, 1967–72; NATO Res. Fellow, Univ. of California, Berkeley, 1973; Dept of Environment, 1974–89; Gwilym Gibbon Res. Fellow, Nuffield Coll., Oxford, 1989–90; Sec., ESRC, 1990–95; res. mgt consultant, 1995–2000. Sen. Vis. Res. Fellow, Queen Mary, Univ. of London, 2000–05. *Publications:* Policy in Urban Planning, 1974; articles in Public Administration, Policy and Politics. *Recreations:* home life, films, reading, travel. *Address:* 1 Dolby Road, SW6 3NE. *T:* (020) 7736 2155.

SOLESBY, Tessa Audrey Hilda, CMG 1986; HM Diplomatic Service, retired; Leader, UK Delegation to Conference on Disarmament, Geneva (with personal rank of Ambassador), 1987–92; *b* 5 April 1932; *d* of Charles Solesby and Hilda Solesby (*née* Willis). *Educ:* Clifton High School; St Hugh's College, Oxford. MA; Hon. Fellow, 1988. Min. of Labour and Nat. Service, 1954–55; joined Diplomatic Service, 1956; FO, 1956; Manila, 1957–59; Lisbon, 1959–62; FO, 1962–64; First Sec., UK Mission to UN, Geneva, 1964–68; FO, 1968–70; First Sec., UK Mission to UN, NY, 1970–72; FCO, 1972–75, Counsellor, 1975; on secondment to NATO Internat. Staff, Brussels, 1975–78; Counsellor, East Berlin, 1978–81; temp. Minister, UK Mission to UN, NY, 1981–82; Head of Central African Dept, FCO, 1982–86; Minister, Pretoria, 1986–87. *Recreations:* hill-walking, music. *Address:* c/o Foreign and Commonwealth Office, SW1A 2AH.

SOLEY, Baron *cr* 2005 (Life Peer), of Hammersmith in the London Borough of Hammersmith and Fulham; **Clive Stafford Soley;** Campaign Director, Future Heathrow, since 2005; *b* 7 May 1939. *Educ:* Downshall Sec. Modern School; Newbattle Abbey Coll.; Strathclyde Univ. (BA Hons); Southampton Univ. (Dip. in Applied Social Studies). Various appointments; Probation Officer, 1970–75; Senior Probation Officer, 1975–79. Chairman: Alcohol Educn Centre, 1977–83; Mary Seacole Meml Statue Appeal, 2003–; Arab-Jewish Forum, 2003–. MP (Lab): Hammersmith N, 1979–83; Hammersmith, 1983–97; Ealing, Acton and Shepherd's Bush, 1997–2005. Opposition front bench spokesman on N Ireland, 1981–84, on Home Affairs, 1984–87, on Housing, 1987–92. Chairman: Select Cttee on NI, 1995–97; All Party Parly Gp on Parenting, 1994–96; Intergovtl Orgns Select Cttee, H of L, 2007–. Chm., PLP, 1997–2001; Mem., NEC, Lab. Pty, 1998–2001. *Publication:* (jtly) Regulating the Press, 2000. *Address:* House of Lords, SW1A 0PW.

SOLLEY, Stephen Malcolm; QC 1989; a Recorder, since 1989; *b* 5 Nov. 1946; *s* of late Leslie Solley, sometime MP, and José Solley; *m* 1971, Helen Olivia Cox; four *s. Educ:* University College London (LLB 1968). Called to the Bar, Inner Temple, 1969, Bencher, 1998. The Recorder, South Eastern Circuit, 1984–87. Chm., Bar Human Rights Cttee, 1999–2003. Dir, Hackney Empire Theatre, 1994–. *Recreations:* jazz, opera, wine, football, cooking. *Address:* Charter Chambers, 33 John Street, WC1N 2AT. *T:* (020) 7618 4400. *Club:* Les Six.

SOLOMON, Prof. David Henry, AM 1990; PhD, DSc; FRS 2004; FAA, FRACI, FTSE, FIChemE; Professorial Fellow, Department of Chemical and Biomolecular Engineering, University of Melbourne, since 1996; *b* 19 Nov. 1929; *s* of H. J. Solomon and Mary Solomon; *m* 1954, Harriet Valerie Dawn Newport; three *d. Educ:* Sydney Technical Coll.; NSW Univ. of Technol. (BSc Hons 1952; MSc 1954; PhD 1959); Univ. of NSW (DSc 1968). ASTC; FRACI 1966; FTSE 1975; FIChemE 2007. Joined, 1946, Leader, 1955–63, Resin and Polymer Resin BALM Paints Ltd; Demonstrator and Teaching Fellow, Univ. of NSW, 1953–55; Commonwealth Scientific and Industrial Research Organization (Australia): Div. of Applied Mineralogy, 1963–70; Chief Res. Scientist, Div. of Applied Chemistry, 1970–74; Chief, Div. of Chemicals and Polymers, 1974–89; Dep. Dir, Inst. of Industrial Technol., 1989–90; Hd of Sch. and ICI Aust.–Masson Prof. of Chemistry, Sch. of Chemistry, Univ. of Melbourne, 1990–94. Pres., RACI, 1979–80. FAA 1975. Victoria Prize, Govt of Vic, Australia, 2006. *Publications:* Chemistry of Organic Film Formers, 1967, 2nd edn 1977; (ed) Step–Growth Polymerizations: kinetics and mechanisms, 1972; The Catalytic Properties of Pigments, 1977; Chemistry of Pigments and Fillers, 1983; The Chemistry of Free Radical Polymerization, 1995. *Recreation:* fishing. *Address:* Department of Chemical and Biomolecular Engineering, University of Melbourne, Vic 3010, Australia. *T:* (3) 8344 8200, *Fax:* (3) 8344 4153; *e-mail:* davids@unimelb.edu.au.

SOLOMON, David Joseph; Senior Partner, D. J. Freeman, solicitors, 1992–96; *b* 31 Dec. 1930; *s* of Sydney and Rosie Harriet Solomon; *m* 1959, Hazel Boam; one *s* two *d. Educ:* Torquay Grammar Sch.; Univ. of Manchester (LLB). Admitted as Solicitor, 1955. Partner, Nabarro Nathanson, 1961–1968; Head of Property Dept, 1976–90, Chief Exec., 1990–93, D. J. Freeman. Chm., Oriental Art Fund plc (formerly Carter Asian Arts PLC), 1996–. Trustee: Highgate Literary and Scientific Instn, 1999–2006 (Pres., 1993–98); Public Art Develt Trust, 1996–2002 (Chm., Public Art Develt Trust, 1998–2001). Mem. Council, Oriental Ceramic Soc., 1988–91, 1994–97, 1998–2001, 2003–06. *Recreations:* Chinese ceramics, music, architecture, art, wine, the championing of unjustly neglected writers. *Address:* Russell House, 9 South Grove, N6 6BS. *T:* (020) 8341 6454; Longecourt les Culetre, 21230 Arnay le Duc, France. *T:* 380900555. *Club:* Athenæum.

SOLOMON, Sir Harry, Kt 1991; Director: Falkland Islands Holdings plc, since 1999; Westcity plc, since 2006; *b* 20 March 1937; *s* of Jacob and Belle Solomon; *m* 1962, Judith

Diana Manuel; one *s* two *d*. *Educ:* St Albans School; Law Society School of Law. Qualified solicitor, 1960; in private practice, 1960–75; Hillsdown Holdings: Man. Dir, 1975–84; Jt Chm., 1984–87; Chm., 1987–93; Dir, 1993–97; Chm., Harvey Hldgs, 1994–2000. Pres., Help Medicine, RCP, 1990–. Hon. FRCP 1992. *Recreations:* jogging, tennis, theatre, collector of historical autographed letters. *Address:* Hillsdown House, 32 Hampstead High Street, NW3 1QD.

SOLOMON, Kate Victoria; *see* Branigan, K. V.

SOLOMON, Rabbi Dr Norman; Fellow, Oxford Centre for Hebrew and Jewish Studies, 1995–2000; Lecturer, Faculty of Theology, University of Oxford, 1995–2001; *b* Cardiff, 31 May 1933; *s* of late Phillip Solomon and Esther Solomon (*née* Lewis); *m* 1st, 1955, Devora, (Doris), Strauss (*d* 1998); three *s* one *d*; 2nd, 2000, Dr Hilary Nissenbaum. *Educ:* Cardiff High Sch.; St John's Coll., Cambridge (BA 1954); Univ. of Manchester (PhD 1966). London Univ. (BMus 1958); ARCM 1956. Rabbi: Whitefield Synagogue, Manchester, 1961–66; Greenbank Drive Synagogue, Liverpool, 1966–74; Hampstead Synagogue, 1974–83; Central Synagogue, Birmingham, 1994; Lectr in Judaism, 1983–89, Dir, Centre for Study of Judaism and Jewish/Christian Relations, 1989–94, Selly Oak Colls, Birmingham. Vis. Lectr, Oxford Centre for Postgraduate Hebrew Studies, 1985–94; Koerner Vis. Fellow, Oxford Centre for Hebrew and Jewish Studies, 1994–95; Scholar-in-Residence, Mandelbaum House, Univ. of Sydney, 2004. Editor, Jewish Christian Relations, 1985–91. Adviser, Internat. CCJ, 1988–; Specialist Adviser, CNAA, 1989–92. Vice-Pres., World Congress of Faiths, 1998– (Vice-Chm., 1992–98); President: Birmingham Inter-Faiths Council, 1984–85; British Assoc. for Jewish Studies, 1994; Soc. for Jewish Studies, 2006–. FBIS 1986. 15th Annual Sir Sigmund Sternberg Award, CCJ, 1993; Distinguished Service Medal, Univ. of San Francisco, 2001. *Publications:* Judaism and World Religion, 1991; The Analytic Movement, 1993; Judaism: a very short introduction, 1996; Historical Dictionary of the Jewish Religion, 1998; (ed) Abraham's Children, 2006; articles in learned jls. *Recreation:* playing chamber music. *Address:* The Oriental Institute, Pusey Lane, Oxford OX1 2LE. *T:* (01865) 278200.

SOLOMONS, Anthony Nathan, FCA; Chairman: Singer & Friedlander Ltd, 1976–99 (Chief Executive, 1973–90); Singer & Friedlander Group plc, 1987–99; *b* 26 Jan. 1930; *s* of Leslie Emanuel Solomons and Susie Schneiders; *m* 1957, Jean Golding; two *d*. Qual. as chartered accountant, 1953; FCA 1963. National Service, 1953–54: commnd Dorset Regt. Articled 1952; Accountant, Kennedy & Fox Oldfield & Co., 1955; Asst Accountant, then Chief Accountant, Lobitos Oilfields Ltd, 1955–58; Singer & Friedlander 1958–99: successively Exec. Dir, Man. Dir, and Jt Chief Exec.

SOLOW, Prof. Robert Merton; Professor of Economics, Massachusetts Institute of Technology, 1949–95, then Emeritus; *b* 23 Aug. 1924; *s* of Milton H. Solow and Hannah Solow (*née* Sarney); *m* 1945, Barbara Lewis; two *s* one *d*. *Educ:* New York City schools; Harvard College (BA 1947); Harvard University (MA 1949, PhD 1951). Served US forces, 1942–45 (Bronze Star, 1944). Joined MIT Faculty as Asst Prof. of Statistics, 1949, Inst. Prof. of Economics, 1974–95. Senior Economist, Council of Economic Advisers, 1961–62. Eastman Prof. and Fellow of Balliol Coll., Oxford, 1968–69; Overseas Fellow, Churchill Coll., Cambridge, 1984, 1991. President: Econometric Soc., 1965; Amer. Econ. Assoc., 1976; Member: Amer. Acad. of Arts and Scis, 1963; Nat. Acad. of Sciences, USA, 1972; Accademia dei Lincei, 1984; Corr. Mem., British Acad., 1975; Mem., Amer. Philosophical Soc., 1974–. Hon. degrees: Chicago, 1967; Brown, 1972; Williams, 1974; Paris I, 1975; Warwick, 1976; Lehigh, 1977; Geneva, Wesleyan, 1982; Tulane, 1983; Yale, 1986; Bryant, 1987; Massachusetts at Boston, Boston Coll., 1989; Colgate, Dartmouth, Helsinki, 1990; New York at Albany, 1991; Harvard, Glasgow, Chile, 1992; Conservatoire Nat. des Arts et Métiers, Paris, 1995; Colorado Sch. of Mines, 1996; New York, 2000; Rensselaer Poly. Inst., 2003; New Sch. Univ., NY, 2006; Rochester, 2007; Iowa, 2008. Nobel Prize for Economics, 1987; Nat. Medal of Sci., USA, 1996. Order of Merit (Germany), 1995. *Publications:* Linear Programming and Economic Analysis (with P. Samuelson and R. Dorfman), 1958; Capital Theory and the Rate of Return, 1964; The Sources of Unemployment in the US, 1964; Growth Theory: an exposition, 1970, 2nd edn 1999; The Labor Market as a Social Institution, 1990; (with F. Hahn) A Critical Essay on Modern Macroeconomic Theory, 1995; Learning from Learning by Doing, 1996; (with J. Taylor) Inflation, Unemployment and Monetary Policy, 1998; Monopolistic Competition and Macroeconomic Theory, 1998; Work and Welfare, 1998; articles in learned jls. *Recreation:* sailing. *Address:* 528 Lewis Wharf, Boston, MA 02110, USA. *T:* (617) 2274436.

SOLTI, (Anne) Valerie, (Lady Solti); Chairman, Solti Foundation to assist young musicians, since 1998; President, Sadler's Wells Theatre, since 2002 (Trustee and Governor, since 1995); Hungarian Government Global Ambassador for Culture, since 2007; *b* Leeds, 19 Aug. 1937; *d* of William Pitts and Nancy Pitts; *m* 1st, 1960, James Sargant; 2nd, 1967, Sir Georg Solti, KBE; two *d*. *Educ:* Leeds Girls High Sch.; Royal Acad. of Dramatic Art (Licentiate). (As Valerie Pitts) TV and radio announcer, 1960–70, interviewer, 1960–67, BBC; freelance writer and broadcaster, 1967–97; programmes include: Face the Music, 1971–81, Town and Around, South at Six, BBC; North East Roundabout, Tyne Tees TV; for children: Playschool, BBC, 1967–70; Extraordinary, Gammon and Spinach, Yorkshire TV, 1978–81; contrib. to radio progs in UK and US. Appeared in play, Roseland's Variation on a Theme, W End, 1958–59. Dir, 1998, Trustee, 1999–, Chm., 1999–2006, Mariinsky Th. Trust; Chm., Develt Campaign for rebuilding Sadler's Wells Th., 1990–98. Mem., BBC Adv. Bd (SE), 1975–80. Adviser: Hungarian Cultural Centre; Liszt Acad., Budapest. Jt Pres., Jewish Music Inst., 2000. Trustee: Hampstead Old People's Housing Trust, 1975–83; LPO, 1980–86 (Chm., Friends); Voice of the Listener; Eur. Orgn for Res. Treatment of Cancer. Hon. Trustee, Chicago SO, 1997–. Gov., Brit Sch. for Performing Arts and Technol., 1997–2006. Patron: Longborough Fest. Opera, 2007. Patron, Frankfurt Internat. Conducting Comp., 2000–; Geneva Internat. Comp.; Jeunesse Musicale Suisse; Mem. Jury, Whittaker Prize for Trios. Comdr, Hungarian Cross with Star, 2002; Pro Cultura Hungarica, 2006. *Recreations:* swimming, sailing, walking, travelling by steam train, music and theatre. *Address:* c/o Solti Foundation, PO Box 67, 1410 Waterloo, Belgium; *e-mail:* Soltioffice51@googlemail.com. *Club:* Athenæum.

See also G. T. Solti-Dupas.

SOLTI-DUPAS, Gabrielle Teresa; Head, Junior Department, Notting Hill and Ealing High School, since 2003; *b* London, 25 April 1970; *d* of Sir Georg Solti, KBE and Anne Valerie Solti, *qv*; *m* 1998, Frederic Dupas; one *s*. *Educ:* Francis Holland Sch.; King's Sch., Canterbury; Jesus Coll., Oxford (BA Hons Mod. Hist. 1991); Inst. of Educn, London (PGCE 1997). Intern, EC, 1991–92; Mktg Exec., Nestlé, 1992–94; Teacher, Trevor Roberts Prep. Sch., 1994–96; Teacher, then Dep. Headteacher, Primrose Hill Prim. Sch., 1997–2003. Trustee, Solti Foundn for Young Musicians, 1999–. *Recreations:* classical music, travel, playing with my son, cooking and eating. *Address:* Junior Department, Notting Hill and Ealing High School, 26 St Stephens Road, Ealing, W13 8HH. *T:* (020) 8799 8484; *e-mail:* g.solti@nhehs.gdst.net.

SOLYMAR, Prof. Laszlo, FRS 1995; PhD; Senior Research Fellow, Department of Electrical and Electronic Engineering, Imperial College London, since 2004; Professor of Applied Electromagnetism, University of Oxford, 1992–97, now Emeritus Professor; Professorial Fellow of Hertford College, Oxford, 1986–97, now Emeritus Fellow; *b* 24 Jan. 1930; *s* of Pál and Aranka Solymar; *m* 1955, Marianne Klopfer; two *d*. *Educ:* Technical University, Budapest (Hungarian equivalents of BSc and PhD in Engineering). Lectr, Technical Univ., Budapest, 1952–53; Research Engineer, Res. Inst. for Telecommunications, Budapest, 1953–56; Res. Engineer, Standard Telecom Labs, Harlow, 1956–65; Oxford University: Fellow in Engineering, Brasenose Coll., 1966–86; Lectr, 1971–86, Donald Pollock Reader in Engrg Sci., 1986–92. Visiting Professor: Ecole Normale Supérieure, Paris, 1965–66; Tech. Univ. of Denmark, 1972–73; Univ. Osnabrück, 1987; Tech. Univ., Berlin, 1990; Univ. Autónoma, Madrid, 1993, 1995; Tech. Univ., Budapest, 1994; ICSTM, 2000–. Consultant: Tech. Univ. of Denmark, 1973–76; Thomson-CSF, Orsay, 1984; British Telecom, 1986–88; GEC Wembley, 1986–88; Pilkington Technol. Centre, 1989–90. Faraday Medal, IEE, 1992. Anaxagoras, Archimedes, Hypatia (radio plays with John Wain), 1991. *Publications:* Lectures on the Electrical Properties of Materials (with D. Walsh), 1970, 7th edn 2004; Superconductive Tunnelling and Applications, 1972; (ed) A Review of the Principles of Electrical and Electronic Engineering, 1974; Lectures on Electromagnetic Theory, 1976, 2nd edn 1984; (with D. J. Cooke) Volume Holography and Volume Gratings, 1981; Lectures on Fourier Series, 1988; (jtly) The Physics and Applications of Photorefractive Materials, 1996; Getting the Message: a history of communications, 1999; Waves in Metamaterials, 2008; articles. *Recreations:* history, languages, chess, swimming. *Address:* Department of Engineering Science, University of Oxford OX1 3PJ. *T:* (01865) 273110.

SÓLYOM, László; President, Republic of Hungary, since 2005; *b* Pécs, 3 Jan. 1942; *m* Erzsébet. *Educ:* Univ. of Pécs (grad 1965); Univ. of Jena (Dr 1969); Dr Pol and Legal Scis, Hungarian Acad. Scis, 1981. Asst Lectr, Inst. Civil Law, Friedrich Schiller Univ. of Jena, 1966–69; Fellow, Inst. Political and Legal Scis, Hungarian Acad. Scis, 1969–78; Librarian, Liby of Parlt, 1975; Associate Prof., 1978–83, Prof., 1983–98, Dept of Civil Law, Eötvös Loránd Univ., Budapest; Prof., Faculty of Law, Pázmány Péter Catholic Univ., Budapest, 1995–. Justice, 1989, Dep. Pres., 1990, Pres., three times, 1990–98, Constitutional Court, Hungary. Vis. Prof., Univ. of Cologne, 1999–2000. Corresp. Mem., Hungarian Acad. Scis, 2001. Hon. Dr Cologne, 1999. Humboldt Prize to foreign social scientists, 1998. *Publications:* A polgári jogi felelősség hanyatlása (The Decline of Civil Law Liability), 1977, 1980; Környezetvédelem és polgári jog (Environmental Protection and Civil Law), 1980; A személyiségi jogok elmélete (The Theory of Personality Rights), 1983; Die Persönlichkeitsrechte, 1984; (ed with M. Szabó) A Zöld Hullám: Olvasókönyv a környezetvédelmi társadalmi mozgalmakról (The Green Wave: a reader on environmental social movements), 1988; (with Georg Brunner) Versassungsgerichtsbarkeit in Ungarn, 1995; (with Georg Brunner) Constitutional Judiciary in a New Democracy: the Hungarian Constitutional Court, 2000; Az alkotmánybíráskodás kezdetei Magyarországon (The Beginnings of Constitutional Jurisdiction in Hungary), 2001; Pártok és érdekszervezetek az Alkotmányban (Parties and Interest Organisations in the Constitution), 2004. *Address:* Office of the President, Szent György tér 1, 1014 Budapest, Hungary.

SOMARE, Rt Hon. Sir Michael (Thomas), GCMG 1990; CH 1978; PC 1977; MP; Prime Minister of Papua New Guinea, 1975–80, 1982–85 and since 2002; *b* 9 April 1936; *m* 1965, Veronica Bula Kaiap; three *s* two *d*. *Educ:* Sogeri Secondary Sch.; Admin. Coll. Teaching, 1956–62; Asst Area Educn Officer, Madang, 1962–63; Broadcasts Officer, Dept of Information and Extension Services, Wewack, 1963–66; Journalism, 1966–68. Member for E Sepik Region (Nat. Parl.), PNG House of Assembly, 1968–; Parly Leader, Pangu Pati, 1968–93; First Chief Minister, 1972–75; first Prime Minister, 1975; Leader of Opposition in House of Assembly, 1980–82; Minister for Foreign Affairs, 1988–94; National Alliance Leader. Gov., E Sepik Province, PNG, 1995–2002. Dep. Chm., Exec. Council, 1972–73, Chm., 1973–75. Mem., Second Select Cttee on Constitutional Develt, 1968–72; Mem. Adv. Cttee, Australian Broadcasting Commission. *Publication:* Sana: an autobiography. *Recreations:* golf, fishing, reading. *Address:* Office of the Prime Minister, PO Box 639, Waigani, NCD, Papua New Guinea; (home) Karan, Murik Lakes, East Sepik, Papua New Guinea.

SOMAVIA, Juan O.; Director General, International Labour Organisation, since 1999; *m*; two *c*. *Educ:* Catholic Univ. of Chile; Univ. of Paris. Joined Min. of Foreign Relations, Chile; Mem. Bd. of Dirs and Vice Pres. for Latin America, Inter-Press Service, 1976–87; Sec. Gen., S American Peace Commn, 1987; Perm. Rep. of Chile to UN, NY, 1990–99; former consultant to GATT and UNDP. Founder and Dir, Latin American Inst. for Transnational Studies. Leonidas Proaño Prize, Latin American Human Rights Assoc. *Address:* International Labour Organisation, 4 route des Morillons, 1211 Geneva 22, Switzerland.

SOMERLEYTON, 3rd Baron *cr* 1916; **Savile William Francis Crossley,** GCVO 1999 (KCVO 1994); DL; Bt 1863; farmer; Master of the Horse, 1991–98; *b* 17 Sept. 1928; *er s* of 2nd Baron Somerleyton, MC; *S* father, 1959; *m* 1963, Belinda Maris Loyd (OBE 1997), *d* of late Vivian Loyd and of Mrs Gerald Critchley; one *s* four *d*. *Educ:* Eton Coll. Captain Coldstream Guards, 1948; retired, 1956. Royal Agricultural Coll., Cirencester, 1958–59; farming, 1959–. A Lord in Waiting to the Queen, 1978–91. Dir, Essex & Suffolk Water plc, 1994–97. DL Suffolk, 1964. *Heir: s* Hon. Hugh Francis Savile Crossley, *b* 27 Sept. 1971. *Address:* Blocka Hall Farm, Herringfleet, Lowestoft, Suffolk NR32 5NW. *Club:* White's.

SOMERS, 9th Baron *cr* 1784; **Philip Sebastian Somers Cocks;** Bt 1772; *b* 4 Jan. 1948; *o s* of John Sebastian Somers Cocks, CVO, CBE (*d* 1964), and late Marjorie Olive (*née* Weller); *S* cousin, 1995. *Educ:* abroad; Elston Hall, Newark; Craig-y-Parc, Cardiff. *Recreations:* opera, music generally, foreign travel. *Heir: cousin* Alan Bromley Cocks [*b* 28 May 1930; *m* 1955, Pamela Fay, *d* of A. H. Gourlay, Christchurch, NZ; one *s* three *d*]. *Address:* 19 Kempson Road, SW6 4PX.

See also Hon. A. G. Somers Cocks.

SOMERS COCKS, Hon. Anna Gwenllian, (Hon. Mrs Allemandi), FSA; Group Editorial Director, Giornale dell' Arte and The Art Newspaper, since 2003; *b* 18 April 1950; *d* of late John Sebastian Somers Cocks, CVO, CBE and Marjorie Olive Weller; *m* 1st, 1971, Martin Walker (marr. diss.); 2nd, 1978, John Hardy (marr. diss.); one *s* one *d*; 3rd, 1991, Umberto Allemandi. *Educ:* abroad; Convent of the Sacred Heart, Woldingham; St Anne's College, Oxford (MA); Courtauld Inst., Univ. of London (MA). Asst Keeper, Dept of Metalwork, 1973–85, Dept of Ceramics, 1985–87, Victoria and Albert Museum; Editor: Apollo Magazine, 1987–90; The Art Newspaper, 1990–94, 1996–2003. Chm., Umberto Allemandi Publishing, 1995–96. Member: Mus., New Buildings and Refurbishment Panel, Heritage Lottery Fund, 1996–97; Adv. Council, Sotheby's Inst. of Art, 2002–; Trustee: Gilbert Collection, 1998–; Cass Sculpture Foundn, 2004–. Chm., Venice in Peril, 1999–. Mem. Bd, Attingham Summer Sch., 1998–. Mem., Ateneo Veneto, 2007. Annual Prize, Nat. Art Collections Fund, 1992; European Women of

Achievement Award (Arts and Media), 2006. Commendatore, Ordine della Stella della Solidarietà Italiana (Italy), 2004. *Publications:* The Victoria and Albert Museum: the making of the collection, 1980; (ed and jt author) Princely Magnificence: court jewels of the Renaissance, 1980; (with C. Truman) Renaissance Jewels, Gold Boxes and Objets de Vertu in the Thyssen Collection, 1985; journalism in The Daily Telegraph etc, articles in magazines. *Recreations:* ski-ing, entertaining, travelling, walking. *Address:* via Giulio 6, Turin 10122, Italy.

See also Baron Somers.

SOMERSET, family name of **Duke of Beaufort** and of **Baron Raglan**.

SOMERSET, 19th Duke of, *cr* 1547; **John Michael Edward Seymour;** DL; FRICS; Baron Seymour 1547; Bt 1611; *b* 30 Dec. 1952; *s* of 18th Duke of Somerset and Gwendoline Collette (Jane) (*d* 2005), 2nd *d* of Major J. C. C. Thomas; *S* father, 1984; *m* 1978, Judith-Rose, *d* of J. F. C. Hull, *qv*; two *s* two *d*. *Educ:* Eton. DL: Wilts, 1993, Devon, 2003. *Heir: s* Lord Seymour, *qv*. *Address:* Berry Pomeroy, Totnes, Devon TQ9 6NJ.

SOMERSET, David Henry Fitzroy, FCIB; Chief of Banking Department and Chief Cashier, Bank of England, 1980–88; *b* 19 June 1930; *s* of late Brig. Hon. Nigel Somerset, CBE, DSO, MC and Phyllis Marion Offley (*née* Irwin); *m* 1955, Ruth Ivy, *d* of late W. R. Wildbur; one *s* one *d*. *Educ:* Wellington Coll.; Peterhouse, Cambridge (MA). Entered Bank of England, 1952; Personal Asst to Managing Director, International Monetary Fund, Washington DC, 1959–62; Private Secretary to Governor of Bank of England, 1962–63; Asst Chief Cashier, 1968–69; Asst Chief of Establishments, 1969–73; Dep. Chief Cashier, 1973–80; Fellow and Financial Advr, Peterhouse, Cambridge, 1988–97, Emeritus Fellow, 1997–. Dir, Yamaichi Bank (UK) PLC, 1988–95; Consultant, Bank Julius Baer, 1997–2000 (Chm. London Adv. Bd, 1991–97). Comr, English Heritage, 1988–91. Mem. Council, Friends of Peterhouse, 1982–; Pres., Old Wellingtonian Soc., 2003– (Chm., 1988–97); Gov., Wellington Coll., 1989–2000. *Recreations:* gardening, racing, shooting. *Address:* White Wickets, Boars Head, Crowborough, Sussex TN6 3HE. *T:* (01892) 661111, *Fax:* (01892) 667281. *Club:* Boodle's.

SOMERTON, Viscount; James Shaun Christian Welbore Ellis Agar; *b* 7 Sept. 1982; *s* and *heir* of 6th Earl of Normanton, *qv*. *Educ:* Harrow Sch. *Address:* Somerley, Ringwood, Hants BH24 3PL.

SOMERVILLE, Prof. Christopher Roland, PhD; FRS 1991; Director, Energy Biosciences Institute, and Professor of Plant and Microbial Biology, University of California, Berkeley, since 2007; *b* 11 Oct. 1947; *s* of Hubert Roland Somerville and Teresa Marie (*née* Bond); *m* 1976, Shauna Christine Phimester. *Educ:* Univ. of Alberta, Canada (PhD, BS). Asst Prof. of Genetics, Univ. of Alberta, Canada, 1980–82; Associate Prof. of Botany and Genetics, Michigan State Univ., Mich, 1982–86; Prof. of Botany and Genetics, Michigan State Univ., 1982–93; Dir, Carnegie Instn for Science and Prof. of Biology, Stanford Univ., 1994–2007. (Jtly) Balzan Prize in Plant Molecular Genetics, Internat. Balzan Foundn, Italy, 2006. *Publications:* numerous research articles on genetics, physiology and biochemistry of plants. *Recreation:* sailing. *Address:* Energy Biosciences Institute, Calvin Laboratory MC5230, Berkeley, CA 94720–5230, USA.

SOMERVILLE, Prof. Jane, MD; FRCP; Consultant Cardiologist, Grown-Up Congenital Heart Disease Clinic: Middlesex Hospital, University College London, 1997–2003; Mater Die Hospital, Malta, since 2006; Emeritus Professor of Cardiology, Imperial College School of Medicine, 1999; *b* 24 Jan. 1933; *d* of Joseph Bertram Platnauer and Pearl Ashton; *m* 1957, Dr Walter Somerville, CBE, FRCP (*d* 2005); three *s* one *d*. *Educ:* Queen's Coll., London; Guy's Hosp., London Univ. MB, BS (Treasurer's Gold Medal for Clin. Surg.) 1955; MD 1966. MRCS 1955; FRCP 1973 (LRCP 1955, MRCP 1957). FACC 1972. Med. Registrar, Guy's Hosp., 1956–58; Registrar, Nat. Heart Hosp., 1958–59; First Asst to Dr Paul Wood, 1959–63, Sen. Lectr 1964–74, Inst. of Cardiol.; Hon. Cons. Phys., Nat. Heart Hosp., 1967–74, Hosp. for Sick Children, Gt Ormond St, 1968–88; Consultant Physician: Nat. Heart Hosp., then Royal Brompton & Nat. Heart Hosp., 1974–99; Cardiac Dept, Grown-Up Congenital Heart Disease Clinic, St Bartholomew's Hosp., 1988–92. Lectr in Cardiovascular Disease, Turin Univ., 1973. Vis. Prof. and Guest Lectr, Europe, ME, USA, Mexico, S America, USSR, China; Lectures: St Cyres, Imperial Coll., London, 1976; 6th Mahboubian, NY, 1981; World Congress Gold Medal, Bombay, 1982; Edgar Mannheimer, Hamburg, 1987; John Keith, Montreal, 1988; Tudor Edwards, RCP, 1991; Paul Wood, British Cardiac Soc., 1995; McCue, Washington, 1997; Henry Neufeld, Israel, 1999. Chm., Staff Cttee, 1988–89, Jt Adv. Cttee, 1989–90, Nat. Heart Hosp.; Chm., Cardiol. Cttee, Royal Brompton & Nat. Heart Hosp., 1990–99. Sci. Sec., World Congress, Paed. Cardiol., 1980; Advr on congenital heart disease, Sec. of State's Hon. Med. Adv. Panel on driving and disorders of cardiovascular system, 1986–96; Advr to Florence, Trieste and Baltic States on setting up Grown-up Congenital Heart Disease Services. Founder, 1993, Pres., 2004–, Grown-Up Congenital Heart Patient Assoc. (Chm., 1993–2003); Member: Assoc. Europ. Pæd. Cardiol.; British Cardiac Soc. (Mem., Paediatric Cardiol. Services Sub-cttee, 1987–; Chm., Wkg Pty on Grown-up Congenital Heart Disease, 2002); RSocMed; Harveian Soc.; French Cardiac Soc.; 300 Gp; Sci. Council, Monaco Cardiothoracic Centre. Hon. Member: Argentine Pæd. Soc.; Chilean Cardiac Soc.; Argentine Soc. of Cardiol.; Brazilian Cardiac Soc.; Argentine Cardiac Soc. Founding Fellow, Europ. Soc. of Cardiol. Mem. Council, Stonham Housing Assoc. Gov., Nat. Heart and Chest Hosps, 1977–82, 1988–90; Chm. Council, Queen's Coll., London, 2000–07. Woman of the Year, 1968. Gold Medal, ESC, 2008. *Publications:* numerous contribs to med. lit. on heart disease in children, adolescents and adults, congenital heart disease and results of cardiac surgery; chapters in Paul Wood's Diseases of Heart and Circulation (3rd edn), Oxford Textbook of Medicine, and Perspectives in Pediatric Cardiology, Vols I and II. *Recreations:* collecting, chess, roof gardening, travel, grandchildren. *Address:* 30 York House, Upper Montagu Street, W1H 1FR. *T:* (020) 7262 2144, *Fax:* (020) 7724 2238; 81 Harley Street, W1G 8PP.

SOMERVILLE, Brig. Sir (John) Nicholas, Kt 1985; CBE 1975; self-employed consultant, personnel selection, 1984–2003; *b* 16 Jan. 1924; *s* of Brig. Desmond Henry Sykes Somerville and Moira Burke Somerville; *m* 1951, Jenifer Dorothea Nash; one *s* two *d*. *Educ:* Winchester College. Commissioned, The South Wales Borderers, 24th Regt, 1943; served: France and Germany, D-day—VE day, 1944–45 (despatches 1945); BAOR, War Office, FARELF, Aden, 1967–68 (despatches 1968); Directing Staff, JSSC, 1967–69; Comdt, Junior Div., Staff Coll., 1969–72; Dir of Army Recruiting, 1973–75; retired, 1978. Managing Director, Saladin Security Ltd, 1981–84; voluntary consultant responsible for designing Cons. Party Parly selection board procedure, 1980–92. *Recreations:* sailing, gardening, house designing. *Address:* Deptford Cottage, Deptford Lane, Greywell, Hook, Hants RG29 1BS. *T:* (01256) 702796.

SOMERVILLE, Julia Mary Fownes; broadcaster and journalist; *b* 14 July 1947; *d* of late John Arthur Fownes Somerville, CB, CBE, and of Julia Elizabeth (*née* Payne); *m* 1st, 1970, Stephen Band (marr. diss. 1975); 2nd, 1984, Ray Gowdridge (separated, 1992); one *s* one *d*; partner, Sir Jeremy Dixon, *qv*. *Educ:* Headington Sch., Oxford; Sussex Univ. (BA Hons English 1969). IPC Magazines, 1969–70; ed., company newspaper, ITT Creed, 1970–72; BBC Radio News: journalist, 1972–79; news reporter, 1979–81; labour/industrial correspondent, 1981–84; Newscaster: Nine o'clock News, BBC TV, 1984–87; ITN, 1987–2001. Mem., Marshall Aid Commn, 1998–2000. Chm., Adv. Cttee, Govt Art Collection. Supporter, Advance Housing & Support Ltd, 1995–; Patron: British Brain and Spine Foundn, 1993; Children of Chernobyl Fund, 1993; Friends United Network, 1993; Samantha Dickson Res. Trust, 1997; Barnet Cancer Care, 1998; Vice Patron, Apex Trust, 1995; Companion, Headway. *Recreations:* music, reading, wining, dining, walking. *Club:* Peg's.

SOMERVILLE, Brig. Sir Nicholas; *see* Somerville, Sir J. N.

SOMERVILLE, Philip Douglas Frank; milliner; Managing Director, Philip Somerville, since 1972; *b* Winchester, 12 Feb. 1930; *s* of Ivie Frank Somerville and Elinor Anne Somerville. *Educ:* St Thomas's High Sch., Winchester; afterwards largely self-educated. Work in theatre, Australia, 1950–52; milliner, NZ, 1952–61; milliner/director, London, 1961–72. Royal Warrant Holder to The Queen, 1994–; milliner to: Duchess of Kent; Duchess of Gloucester; Queen Silvia of Sweden; the late Diana Princess of Wales. *Recreations:* theatre, country pursuits, charity functions. *Address:* 38 Chiltern Street, W1U 7QL. *T:* (020) 7224 1517, *Fax:* (020) 7486 5885; Penthouse D, Kingsley Lodge, 23 New Cavendish Street, W1G 9UG. *T:* (020) 7487 4661. *Club:* Bishopsgate Ward.

SOMERVILLE, Sir Quentin Charles Somerville A.; *see* Agnew-Somerville.

SOMERVILLE, Shirley-Anne; Member (SNP) Lothians, Scottish Parliament, since Sept. 2007; *b* 2 Sept. 1974. *Educ:* Kirkcaldy High Sch.; Univ. of Strathclyde (BA Hons Econs and Pol. 1996); Univ. of Stirling (Dip. Housing Studies 1999); Queen Margaret Univ. Coll. (Dip. Public Relns). Policy and Public Affairs Officer, Chartered Inst. of Housing, 2001–04; Media and Campaigns Officer, Royal Coll. of Nursing, 2004–07. *Recreations:* hill-walking, golf. *Address:* Scottish Parliament, Edinburgh EH99 1SP. *T:* (0131) 348 6823, *Fax:* (0131) 348 6825; *e-mail:* shirley-anne.somerville.msp@scottish.parliament.uk.

SOMERVILLE, Most Rev. Thomas David; Archbishop of New Westminster and Metropolitan of Ecclesiastical Province of British Columbia, 1975–80, retired; Anglican Chaplain, Vancouver School of Theology, 1981–84; *b* 11 Nov. 1915; *s* of Thomas Alexander Somerville and Martha Stephenson Scott; *m* 1985, Frances Best (*d* 2007). *Educ:* King George High Sch., Vancouver; Univ. of British Columbia (BA 1937); Anglican Theological Coll. of BC (LTh 1939, BD 1951). Deacon, 1939; priest, 1940; Incumbent of: Princeton, 1940–44; Sardis with Rosedale, 1944–49; Curate of St James, Vancouver, 1949–52, Rector, 1952–60; Chapter Canon, Dio. of New Westminster, 1957; Dean of Residence, Anglican Theological Coll. of BC, 1960–65; Gen. Sec., Gen. Bd of Religious Education, Anglican Church of Canada, 1965–66; Director of Planning and Research, Anglican Church of Canada, 1966–69; Coadjutor Bishop of New Westminster, 1969–71; Bishop of New Westminster, 1971. Hon. DD: Anglican Theol. Coll. of BC, 1969; Vancouver Sch. of Theology, 1981. *Recreations:* music, botany. *Address:* 980 Lynn Valley Road, North Vancouver, BC V7J 3V7, Canada.

SOMJEE, Shamoon; a District Judge (Magistrates' Courts) (formerly Metropolitan Stipendiary Magistrate), since 1995 (Stipendiary Magistrate, Middlesex, 1991–95); *b* 13 Nov. 1943; *s* of Rahim Somjee, former Sessions Judge, Pakistan, and Khairunissah Somjee; *m* 1970, Isabel Fonfria Fernandez; one *s*. *Educ:* St. Lawrence's Sch., Karachi; Univ. of Karachi (BA 1963; LLB 1965). Came to UK, 1965. Called to the Bar, Lincoln's Inn, 1967. Mem., editl team, Halsbury's Statutes of England, and Annotated Legislation Service, Butterworths, 1967–68; Magistrates' Clerk, Inner London, 1968–91: Dep. Chief Clerk: Bow Street, 1968–75; Juvenile Courts, 1976–77; Horseferry Road, 1977–80; Chief Clerk: Wells Street, 1980–84; Old Street, 1984–90; Horseferry Road, 1990–91; Sen. Chief Clerk, S Westminster PSD, 1990–91. Chm., London Magistrates' Clerks Assoc., 1985–87. Member: Home Office Working Party on Magistrates' Courts, 1983–87; Home Office sub-group on Procedure at Substantive Hearings, 1990–91 and Appeals, Warrants and Forms, 1991. *Recreations:* travelling, music. *Address:* c/o Tower Bridge Magistrates' Court, 211 Tooley Street, SE1 2JY. *T:* (020) 7805 6706.

SOMMARUGA, Cornelio; Chairman, Geneva International Centre for Humanitarian De-mining, since 2000; *b* 29 Dec. 1932; *s* of Carlo Sommaruga and Anna-Maria Valagussa; *m* 1957, Ornella Marzorati; two *s* four *d*. *Educ:* schs in Rome and Lugano; Univs of Zürich (LLD 1957), Paris and Rome. Bank trainee, Zürich, 1957–59; joined Swiss Diplomatic Service, 1960: Attaché, Swiss Embassy, The Hague, 1961; Sec., Bonn, 1962–64; Rome, 1965–68; Dep. Hd of Delegn to EFTA, GATT, UNCTAD and ECE/UN, Geneva, 1969–73; Dep. Sec. Gen., EFTA, 1973–75; Minister plenipotentiary, Div. of Commerce, Fed. Dept of Public Economy, Berne, 1976; Amb., 1977; Delegate, Fed. Council for Trade Agreements, 1980–83; State Sec. for External Econ. Affairs, 1984–86. President: Internat. Cttee of the Red Cross, 1987–99 (Hon. Mem., 2000); Initiatives of Change Internat. (formerly Moral Rearmament) Assoc., 2002–06, now Hon. Chm. Member: Panel on UN Peace Operations, 2000; Internat. Commn on Intervention and State Sovereignty, 2001. Hon. Dr: (Political Affairs) Fribourg, 1985; (Internat. Relns) Minho, Braga, 1990; (Medicine) Bologna, 1991; Nice-Sophia Antipolis, 1992; (Law) Seoul Nat. Univ., 1992; (Law) Geneva, 1997. Presidential Award, Tel Aviv Univ., 1995. *Publications:* La posizione costituzionale del Capo dello Stato nelle Costituzioni francese ed italiana del dopoguerra, 1957; numerous articles in jls and periodicals; *relevant publication:* Cornelio Sommaruga: diplomatie im Dienste der Menschlichkeit, by Jürg Bischoff, 2004. *Address:* 16 chemin des Crêts-de-Champel, 1206 Geneva, Switzerland. *T:* (22) 3474552; *e-mail:* cornelio.sommaruga@bluewin.ch.

SOMMER, Peter Michael; Visiting Professor, Information Systems and Innovation Group, Department of Management, London School of Economics and Political Science, since 2008; Managing Director, Virtual City Associates, since 1981; *b* 21 April 1943; *s* of Fritz and Beate Sommer. *Educ:* King Edward VI Five Ways Sch., Birmingham; St Catherine's Coll., Oxford (BA 1965, MA Hons Juris. 1967). Editor: Harrap Books, 1966–73; Paladin Books, 1973–77; Dep. Editl Dir, Granada Paperbacks, 1977–81; Tech. Dir, Data Integrity, 1987–98; Sen. Res. Fellow, Inf. Systems and Innovation (formerly Inf. Systems Integrity) Gp, Dept of Mgt (formerly Inf. Systems Dept), LSE, 1994–Sept. 2009. Specialist Advr, H of C Trade and Industry Select Cttee, 1998–2001. Vis. Sen. Res. Fellow, Faculty of Maths, Computing and Technology (formerly Maths and Computing), Open Univ., 2006–. Jt Lead Assessor, Computing, Council for Registration of Forensic Practitioners, 2005–. Ext. Examnr, Defence Acad. of UK (Cranfield Univ.), 2002–06. Member: Adv. Council, Foundn for Information Policy Res., 2001–; Scientific Adv. Panel for Emergency Response, 2003–; Digital Evidence Specialist Gp, Forensic Sci. Regulator, 2008–. Self-employed expert in digital forensics: major instructions include: Rome Labs hack, 1997; Wonderland Club of internet paedophiles (Op. Cathedral), 2001; DrinkorDie software piracy conspiracy (Op. Blossom), 2005; Op. Crevice terrorism, 2006–07; Sorrell *v* FullSix defamation, 2007. *Publication:* Guide to Electronic Publishing, 1982; The PC Security Guide, 1993, 2nd edn 1994; (contrib.) Fraud: law, procedure and practice, 2004; Digital Evidence: a guide for directors and corporate advisors, 2005; *as Hugo Cornwall*: The Hacker's Handbook, 1985; Data Theft, 1987; The Industrial Espionage Handbook, 1991; articles in learned jls incl. Criminal Law Rev., Telecommunications Law Rev., IEEE Security and Privacy. *Recreations*: reading, book collecting, gardening, jazz, amateur radio, the ethical abuse of technology. *Address*: c/o London School of Economics, Houghton Street, WC2 2AE; *e-mail*: peter@pmsommer.com, p.m.sommer@lse.ac.uk.

SOMMERLAD, Brian Clive, FRCS, FRCPCH; Consultant Plastic Surgeon: St Andrew's Centre, Broomfield Hospital, Chelmsford (formerly St Andrew's Hospital, Billericay), since 1978; The London Hospital, since 1978; Great Ormond Street Hospital for Children, since 1995; *b* 1 Feb. 1942; *s* of Verdun and Winsome Sommerlad; *m* 1971, Gwyneth Watkins; four *s* one *d. Educ*: Newington Coll., Sydney; Sydney Univ. (MB BS 1966). FRCS 1971. Jun. and Sen. MO, Sydney Hosp., 1966–67; Surgical Registrar, UCH, 1969–73; Surgeon, Australian Surgical Team, Bien Hoa, Vietnam, 1971; Sen. Registrar in Plastic Surgery, London, Billericay and Glasgow, 1974–78. Hunterian Prof., RCS, 1999. President: Plastic Surgery Section, RSocMed, 1985–86; Craniofacial Soc. of GB, 1997–98; British Assoc. of Plastic Surgeons, 1998. Hon. FRCSLT 1998; Hon. FRCSE 2001. Active Service Medal (Australia), 1994; Vietnam Logistic and Support Medal (Australia), 1994. *Publications*: co-editor: Recent Advances in Plastic Surgery 3, 1985; Recent Advances in Plastic Surgery 4, 1992; Recent Advances in Plastic Surgery 5, 1996; contrib. papers to several jls on many subjects, but especially cleft lip and palate. *Recreations*: sailing, running (including occasional marathons), ski-ing, theatre, supporting cleft lip and palate services in the developing world. *Address*: The Old Vicarage, 17 Lodge Road, Writtle, Chelmsford, Essex CM1 3HY. *T*: (01245) 422477, *Fax*: (01245) 421901; *e-mail*: brian@sommerlad.co.uk.

SOMOGYI, Prof. Peter, PhD, DSc; FRS 2000; Professor of Neurobiology, University of Oxford, since 1996; Director, MRC Anatomical Neuropharmacology Unit, Oxford, since 1998. *Educ*: Loránd Eötvös Univ., Budapest (PhD); Semmelweis Med. Sch., Budapest; Univ. of Oxford; Flinders Med. Centre, SA, Australia. Associate, later Co-Dir, MRC Anatomical Neuropharmacology Unit, Oxford, 1985–98. FMedSci 2006. *Address*: MRC Anatomical Neuropharmacology Unit, Mansfield Road, Oxford OX1 3TH; 129 Staunton Road, Oxford OX3 7TN.

SONDHEIM, Stephen Joshua; composer-lyricist; *b* 22 March 1930; *s* of Herbert Sondheim and Janet (*née* Fox). *Educ*: Williams Coll. (BA 1950). Lyrics: West Side Story, 1957; Gypsy, 1959; Do I Hear a Waltz?, 1965; (additional lyrics) Candide, 1973; music and lyrics: A Funny Thing Happened on the Way to the Forum, 1962; Anyone Can Whistle, 1964; Company, 1970; Follies, 1971; A Little Night Music, 1973 (filmed, 1976); The Frogs, 1974; Pacific Overtures, 1976; Sweeney Todd, 1979; Merrily We Roll Along, 1981; Sunday in the Park with George, 1984 (Pulitzer Prize, 1985); Into The Woods, 1987; Assassins, 1991; Passion, 1994; Bounce, 2003; incidental music: The Girls of Summer, 1956; Invitation to a March, 1961; Twigs, 1971; film scores: Stavisky, 1974; Reds, 1981; Dick Tracy, 1990; co-author, The Last of Sheila (film), 1973; songs for Evening Primrose (TV), 1966; *play*: co-author, Getting Away with Murder, 1996; anthologies: Side By Side By Sondheim, 1976; Marry Me A Little, 1981; You're Gonna Love Tomorrow, 1983; Putting It Together, 1992. Vis. Prof. of Drama, and Fellow of St Catherine's Coll., Oxford, Jan.–June 1990. Mem. Council, Dramatists Guild, 1963 (Pres., 1973–81); Mem., AAIL, 1983. Hon. Doctorate, Williams Coll., 1971. Tony Awards and New York Drama Critics' Circle Award for Company, Follies, A Little Night Music, Sweeney Todd, Into the Woods, and Passion; London Evening Standard Best Musical Award for Into the Woods; New York Drama Critics' Circle Award for Pacific Overtures and Sunday in the Park with George; London Evening Standard Best Musical Award, 1987, and SWET Laurence Olivier Award, 1988, for Follies. *Publications*: (book and vocal score): West Side Story, 1958; Gypsy, 1960; A Funny Thing Happened on the Way to the Forum, 1963; Anyone Can Whistle, 1965; Do I Hear a Waltz?, 1966; Company, 1971; Follies, 1972; A Little Night Music, 1974; Pacific Overtures, 1977; Sweeney Todd, 1979; Sunday in the Park with George, 1986; Into the Woods, 1989; Assassins, 1991; Passion, 1996. *Address*: c/o John Breglio, Paul, Weiss, Rifkind, Wharton & Garrison, 1285 Avenue of the Americas, New York, NY 10019, USA.

SONDHEIMER, Prof. Ernst Helmut, MA, ScD; Professor Emeritus of Mathematics, University of London; *b* Stuttgart, 8 Sept. 1923; *er s* of late Max and Ida Sondheimer; *m* 1950, Janet Harrington Matthews, PhD (*d* 2007); one *s* one *d. Educ*: Reformrealgymnasium Stuttgart; University College School; Trinity Coll., Cambridge. Smith's Prize, 1947; Fellow of Trinity Coll., 1948–52; Research Fellow, H. H. Wills Physical Lab., University of Bristol, 1948–49; Research Associate, Massachusetts Inst. of Technology, 1949–50; London University: Lecturer in Mathematics, Imperial College of Science and Technology, 1951–54; Reader in Applied Mathematics, Queen Mary Coll., 1954–60; Prof. of Mathematics, Westfield Coll., 1960–82. Vis. Research Asst Prof. of Physics, Univ. of Illinois, USA, 1958–59; Vis. Prof. of Theoretical Physics, University of Cologne, 1967. FKC 1985; Fellow, Queen Mary and Westfield Coll., London, 1989. Editor, Alpine Journal, 1986–91. *Publications*: (with S. Doniach) Green's Functions for Solid State Physicists, 1974, repr. 1998; (with A. Rogerson) Numbers and Infinity, 1981, repr. 2006; papers on the electron theory of metals. *Recreations*: German history, German expressionist painting, mountains, alpine and Himalayan plants. *Address*: 51 Cholmeley Crescent, Highgate, N6 5EX. *T*: (020) 8340 6607. *Club*: Alpine.

SONDHI, Ranjit, CBE 1999; a Civil Service Commissioner, since 2007; *b* 22 Oct. 1950; *s* of Prem Lal Sondhi and Kanta Sondhi; *m* 1979, Anita Bhalla; one *s* one *d. Educ*: Bedford Sch.; Univ. of Birmingham (BSc Hons Physics). Handsworth Action Centre, Birmingham, 1972–76; Dir, Asian Resource Centre, Birmingham, 1976–85; Sen. Lectr, Westhill Coll., Birmingham, 1985–2007. Freelance lectr and researcher, 1975–2003. A Gov., BBC, 1998–2006; Member: IBA, 1987–90; Radio Authority, 1991–94; Chairman: Jt Council of Welfare for Immigrants, West Midlands, 1987–90; Refugee Employment, Trng and Educn Forum, 1990–93; Home Sec.'s Race Equality Adv. Panel, 2003–; Dep. Chm., CRE, 1993–95 (Mem., 1991–93); Member: Digbeth Trust, 1986–90; Prince's Youth Business Trust, Birmingham, 1986–91; Royal Jubilee and Prince's Trust, Birmingham, 1986–88; Admin. Council, Prince's Trust, 1986–88; Council for Educn and Trng in Youth and Community Work, 1987–90; Ethnic Minorities Adv. Cttee, Judicial Studies Bd, 1991–95; John Feeney Charitable Trust, 1991–2003; Glidewell Panel of Enquiry into Immigration and Asylum Bill, 1996; Lord Chancellor's Adv. Cttee on Legal Educn and Conduct, 1997–99; DFEE Task Force on Disability Rights, 1997–99; Civil Service Commn, 2007–. Trustee: Nat. Primary Centre, 1993–2007 (Chm., 2003–07); Nat. Gall., 2000–. Director: Birmingham TEC, 1990–93; Birmingham HA, 1998–2002; Chm., Heart of Birmingham Primary Care Trust, 2002–. FRSA 1988. DUniv UCE, 2003; Hon. DLitt Wolverhampton. *Publications*: (jtly) Race in the Provincial Press, 1977; Divided Families, 1987; contribs to: Ethnicity and Social Work, 1982; Community Work and Racism, 1982; Minorities: community and identity, 1983; Analysing Inter-cultural Communication, 1987; Community Work in the Nineties, 1994; (ed jtly) 20 Years After the RRA76, 1999. (contrib.) Intercultural Europe, 2000; Equality and Diversity in Birmingham, 2005; Navigating Difference, 2006. *Recreations*: Indian classical music, yoga, travel, antiquarian books. *Address*: 89 Hamstead Hall Avenue, Handsworth Wood, Birmingham B20 1JU.

SONENBERG, Prof. Nahum, PhD; FRS 2006; FRSC; James McGill Professor, Department of Biochemistry, McGill University; *b* Wetzlar, Germany, 29 Dec. 1946; *s* of Meyer Sonenberg and Fradl Sonenberg (*née* Kutchinsky); *m* 1972, Yocheved Shrot; two *d. Educ*: Tel-Aviv Univ. (BSc, MSc); Weizmann Inst. of Sci. (PhD 1976). Chaim Weizmann Fellow, Roche Inst. of Molecular Biol., NJ, 1976–79; Asst Prof., 1979–82, Associate Prof., 1983–86, Prof., 1987–, Dept of Biochem., McGill Univ. Internat. Res. Scholar, Howard Hughes Med. Inst.; Dist. Scientist, CIHR. FRSC 1992. Robert L. Noble Prize, Nat. Cancer Inst. of Canada, 2002; Killam Prize for Health Scis, 2005; Gairdner Award, 2008. *Publications*: articles in jls. *Address*: Department of Biochemistry, MacGill University, McIntyre Medical Building, 3655 Promenade Sir William Osler, Montreal, QC H3G 1Y6, Canada.

SONNABEND, Yolanda; painter, portraitist and theatre designer; *b* 26 March 1935; *d* of Dr Henry Sonnabend and Dr Fira Sonnabend (*née* Sandler). *Educ*: Eveline High Sch., Bulawayo; Slade Sch. of Fine Art (Dip.). Lectr in Theatre Design, Slade Sch. of Fine Art, 1989–2001. Fellow, UCL, 2002. *Painting*: *exhibitions* include: Whitechapel Art Gall. (solo), 1975; Serpentine Gall. (solo), 1986; portraits of Stephen Hawking and others, Nat. Portrait Gall.; *theatre design*: *installations*: Japan, Denmark, Poland; *ballet* productions: for Royal Ballet, incl. Swan Lake and works for Kenneth Macmillan (Requiem, My Brother My Sister); for La Scala, Milan; for K Ballet Co., Tokyo: Swan Lake, 2003; The Nutcracker, 2005; Le Corsaire, 2007; The Beethoven, with symphony and symphonic ballet, 2008; Strasbourg; Lisbon; Stuttgart; Hong Kong; Nice; Chicago; Boston; *opera* productions: Aldeburgh; Sadler's Wells; Italy; *theatre* includes: Oxford Playhouse; RSC; Old Vic; *film*: The Tempest, 1980. Garrick Milne Prize for Theatrical Portraiture, 2000. *Recreations*: usual diversions. *Address*: 30 Hamilton Terrace, NW8 9UG. *T*: (020) 7286 9616.

SOOLE, Michael Alexander; QC 2002; a Recorder, since 2000; *b* 18 July 1954; *yr s* of late Brian Alfred Seymour Soole and of Rosemary Una Soole (*née* Salt); *m* 2002, Catherine Gavine Marshall (*née* Gardiner); three step *s* two step *d. Educ*: Berkhamsted Sch. (schol.); University Coll., Oxford (schol.; MA). Pres., Oxford Union, 1974. Called to the Bar, Inner Temple, 1977, Bencher, 2008; practising barrister, 1978–. Contested (SDP), Aylesbury, 1983, 1987. Mem. Bd, Christian Aid, 1991–2002. Trustee, Oxford Literary and Debating Union Trust, 2005–. *Recreation*: conversation. *Address*: 4 New Square, Lincoln's Inn, WC2A 3RJ. *T*: (020) 7822 2000, *Fax*: (020) 7822 2001. *Club*: Buck's.

SOPEL, Jon(athan); Presenter: BBC News Channel (formerly BBC News 24), since 2003; The Politics Show, BBC One, since 2005; *b* 22 May 1959; *s* of late Myer Sopel and Miriam Sopel; *m* 1988, Linda Twissell; one *s* one *d. Educ*: Christ's Coll. Finchley; Univ. of Southampton (BA Politics 1981). BBC: Radio Solent, 1983–87; reporter, World at One, Radio 4, 1987–89; Political Correspondent, 1989–98; Chief Political Correspondent, 1998–99; Paris Correspondent, 1999–2003; reported on war in Afghanistan, 2001, on war in Iraq, 2003, on tsunami, from Sri Lanka, 2004–05; has presented PM and Today progs, Radio 4. Political Journalist of the Year, 2007. *Publications*: Tony Blair: the moderniser, 1994; contrib. widely to newspapers and mags. *Recreations*: travel, tennis, golf, running, cinema, watching football. *Address*: Television Centre, Wood Lane, W12 7RJ. *T*: (020) 8225 6351; *e-mail*: jon.sopel@bbc.co.uk.

SOPER, Andrew Keith; HM Diplomatic Service; High Commissioner, Republic of Mozambique, since 2007; *b* 6 July 1960; *s* of Brian and Doreen Soper; *m* 1987, Kathryn Garrett Stevens; one *s* one *d. Educ*: Cranbrook Sch., Kent; Sidney Sussex Coll., Cambridge (MA, PGCE). Student helper, Flying Angel Club, Fremantle, Australia, 1978–79; Teacher, Woodstock Sch., Uttar Pradesh, India, 1983–84; Admin. Trainee, DES, 1984–85; entered FCO, 1985; Second, later First, Sec. (Chancery), Mexico City, 1987–90; First Secretary: FCO, 1990–95; Washington, 1995–99; FCO, 1999–2001; Counsellor and Dep. Hd of Mission, Brasilia, 2001–04; Hd, Sustainable Develt and Commonwealth Gp, FCO, 2004–07. *Recreations*: tennis, sailing, playing saxophone. *Address*: c/o Foreign and Commonwealth Office, King Charles Street, SW1A 2AH.

SOPER, Rt Rev. (Andrew) Laurence, OSB; STD; General Treasurer, Benedictine Confederation, since 2002; Titular Abbot of St Alban's, since 2000; *b* 17 Sept. 1943; *s* of Alan and Anne Soper. *Educ*: St Benedict's Sch., Ealing; Blackfriars, Oxford; Sant Anselmo, Rome (STD); Strawberry Hill (PGCE; Hon. Fellow, 1996). Banking until 1964; entered Novitiate at Ealing, 1964; St Benedict's School: Master, 1973–83; Bursar, 1975–91; Prior, 1984–91; Asst Chaplain, Harrow Sch., 1981–91; Abbot of Ealing, 1991–2000. Mem. Council, Union of Monastic Superiors, 1994–99 (Chm., 1995–99). Episcopal Vicar for Religious for Westminster (Western Area), 1995–2001. FRSA. *Publications*: (ed with Rev. Peter Elliott) Thoughts of Jesus Christ, 1970; articles and thesis on T. H. Green and 19th century English theology. *Recreations*: reading, hill walking. *Address*: Badia Primaziale S. Anselmo, Piazza Cavalieri di Malta 5, Rome 00153, Italy.

SORABJI, Prof. Richard Rustom Kharsedji, CBE 1999; FBA 1989; Professor of Ancient Philosophy, King's College London, 1981–2000, now Emeritus; Supernumerary Fellow, Wolfson College, Oxford, 1996–2002, now Hon. Fellow; *b* 8 Nov. 1934; *s* of Richard Kaikushru Sorabji and late Mary Katherine (*née* Monkhouse); *m* 1958, Margaret Anne Catherine Taster; one *s* two *d. Educ*: Dragon Sch.; Charterhouse; Pembroke Coll., Oxford (BA Greats; MA, BPhil). CS Commn in Russian Lang. Cornell University: joined Sage Sch. of Philosophy, 1962; Associate Prof., 1968; Sen. Res. Fellow, Soc. of Humanities, 1979; King's College, London, 1970–: Designer and Dir, King's Coll. Centre for Philosophical Studies, 1989–91; FKC 1990; British Acad./Wolfson Res. Prof., 1996–99; Chm., Bd of Philosophical Studies, London Univ., 1979–82; Dir, Inst. of Classical Studies, London, 1991–96. Sen. Fellow, Council of Humanities, Princeton Univ., 1985; Vis. Prof., Indian Council of Philos. Res., 1989 and 2004; Adjunct Prof., Philosophy Dept, Univ. of Texas at Austin, 2000–; Ranieri Vis. Scholar, New York Univ., 2000–03; Vis. Prof., CUNY Graduate Center, 2004–. Member: Common Room, Wolfson Coll., Oxford, 1991–96; Sen. Common Room, Pembroke Coll., Oxford, 1992–. Gresham Prof. of Rhetoric, 2000–04. Lectures: Read-Tuckwell, Bristol, 1985; Simon, Toronto, 1990; Gray, Cambridge, 1991; Townsend, Cornell, 1991–92; Gaisford, Oxford, 1993; Webster, Stanford, 1994; Donnellan, Dublin, 1995; Radhakrishnan Meml, Indian Inst. of Advanced Study, Simla, 1996; Gifford, St Andrews, 1997; Edinburgh, 1997; Prentice, Princeton, 1998. Pres., Aristotelian Soc., 1985–86. Founder and organiser of internat. project for translating the Ancient Commentators on Aristotle, 1985–. For. Hon. Mem., Amer. Acad. of Arts and Scis, 1997. *Publications*: Aristotle on Memory, 1973, 2nd edn 2004; (ed jtly) Articles on Aristotle, 4 vols, 1975–79; Necessity, Cause and Blame, 1980; Time, Creation and the Continuum, 1983; (ed) Philoponus and the Rejection of Aristotelian Science, 1987, 2nd edn 2007; (ed) The Ancient Commentators on Aristotle, first 68 of over 100 vols, 1987–; Matter, Space and Motion, 1988 (Choice Award for Outstanding Academic Book, 1989–90); (ed) Aristotle Transformed, 1990; Animal Minds and Human Morals: the origins of the western debate, 1993; Emotion and Peace of Mind: from Stoic agitation to Christian temptation, 2000; Philosophy of the Commentators

200–600 AD, 3 vols, 2004; (ed jtly) The Ethics of War: shared problems in different traditions, 2005; Self: ancient and modern insights about individuality, life and death, 2006; (ed jtly) Post-Hellenistic Philosophy 100 BC–200 AD, 2007. *Recreations:* architecture, archaeology, occasional verses. *Address:* Wolfson College, Oxford OX2 6UD.

SORBIE, Prof. Kenneth Stuart, DPhil; FRSE; Professor of Petroleum Engineering, Heriot-Watt University, since 1992; *b* Prestwick, 15 Jan. 1950; *s* of late Kenneth Sorbie and of Lucy (*née* Ferguson); *m* 1976, Prof. Sheila Riddell; two *d. Educ:* Strathclyde Univ. (BSc 1st cl. Hons, 1972); Sussex Univ. (DPhil 1975). Res. Fellow, Cambridge Univ., 1975–76; teaching and lecturing, 1976–80; Group leader, oil res. and enhanced oil recovery, AEE Winfrith, 1980–88; Lectr, 1988–90, Reader, 1990–92, Heriot-Watt Univ. Mem., Soc. of Petroleum Engrs, 1985. FRSE 2001. Tech. Achievement Award, Soc. of Core Analysts, 2004; IOR Pioneer Award, Soc. Petroleum Engrs, 2008. *Publications:* Polymer Improved Oil Recovery, 1991; over 250 technical papers on petroleum-related research. *Recreations:* listening to and collecting classical music, particularly Renaissance masses and lute music, guitar and chamber music; hill walking, running, weight training—but also fond of good food and wine, alas! *Address:* Institute of Petroleum Engineering, Heriot-Watt University, Edinburgh EH14 4AS. *T:* (0131) 451 3139, *Fax:* (0131) 451 3127; *e-mail:* ken.sorbie@pet.hw.ac.uk.

SORENSEN, (Kenneth) Eric (Correll); Chief Executive, Thames Gateway London Partnership, since 2003; *b* 15 Oct. 1942; *m* Susan; two *s* one *d. Educ:* Bedford Sch.; Keele Univ. (BA(Hons) Econs and History). Voluntary work, India; joined DoE, 1967; Private Sec. to Sec. of State for Envmt, 1977; NW Regl Dir, Depts of the Envmt and Transport, 1980–81; Dir, Merseyside Task Force, DoE, 1981–84; Dir, Inner Cities Directorate, DoE, 1984–87; Head of Urban Policy Unit, Cabinet Office, 1987–88; Dir of Personnel Management and Trng, Depts of Envmt and Transport, 1988–90; Dep. Sec., Housing and Construction Comd, DoE, 1990–91; Chief Executive: LDDC, 1991–97; Millennium Commn, 1997–98; London Develt Partnership, 1998. Civil Service Comr (part-time), 1992–95. Chm., Royal Docks Trust (London); Dep. Chm., St Katharine and Shadwell Trust. Non-exec. Dir, Homerton Univ. Hosp. NHS Foundn Trust, 2005–. Gov., Museum of London, 2008–.

SORKIN, (Alexander) Michael; Vice-Chairman, N M Rothschild & Sons, since 2001; *b* 2 March 1943; *s* of Jose Sorkin and Hildegard Ruth Sorkin; *m* 1977, Angela Lucille Berman; one *s* two *d. Educ:* St Paul's Sch.; Manchester Univ. (BA (Hons) Econs). Chartered accountant. Joined Hambros, 1968; Dir, 1973–2001, Vice Chm., 1987–2001, SG Hambros (formerly Hambros Bank Ltd); Dep. Chm., Hambros Bank Ltd, 1995–98; Dir, Hambros plc, 1986–98; Man. Dir, SG Hambros, 1998–2001. *Recreations:* golf, tennis, football, opera. *Address:* N M Rothschild & Sons Ltd, New Court, St Swithin's Lane, EC4P 4DU.

SORLEY WALKER, Kathrine; freelance writer; *d* of James Sorley Walker and Edith Jane Sorley Walker (*née* Robertson). *Educ:* St Margaret's Sch. for Girls, Aberdeen; Crouch End Coll., London; King's Coll. London; Univ. of Besançon; Trinity Coll. of Music. Geographical Magazine, 1951–56; Helga Greene Literary Agency, 1961–86; freelance critic and historian; dance critic, Daily Telegraph, 1969–94. *Publications:* (ed) Raymond Chandler Speaking, 1962; Eyes on the Ballet, 1963; Eyes on Mime, 1969; Saladin, Sultan of the Holy Sword, 1971; Dance and its Creators, 1972; (ed) Writings on Dance, by A. V. Coton, 1975; Emotion and Atmosphere (verse), 1975; Ballet for Boys and Girls, 1979; The Royal Ballet: a picture history, 1981; De Basil's Ballets Russes, 1982; (ed) Remembering Helga, 1986; Ninette de Valois: idealist without illusions, 1987; Late Century Poems (verse), 1999; New Century Reflections (verse), 2004; Cyril W. Beaumont: dance writer and publisher, 2006; Impressions and Comments (verse), 2008; contribs to Dancing Times, Dance Chronicle, Dance Now, Dance Expression, Dance International, DanceView, Encyclopedia Britannica, International Encyclopedia of Dance, Enciclopedia dello Spettacolo, Encyclopedia of Dance and Ballet, International Dictionary of Ballet, Oxford DNB. *Recreations:* travel, art exhibitions, theatre-going. *Address:* 1D Sloane Square, SW1W 8EE.

SOROS, Flora; *see* Fraser, F.

SOROS, George; President, Soros Fund Management, since 1973; *b* Budapest, 12 Aug. 1930; *s* of Tivadar Soros and Elisabeth Soros (*née* Szucs); *m* 1960, Annaliese Witschak (marr. diss. 1983); two *s* one *d*; *m* 1983, Susan Weber; two *s. Educ:* LSE, London Univ. (BS 1952). Arbitrage trader, F. M. Mayer, NYC, 1956–59; Economic Analyst, Wertheim & Co., NYC, 1959–63; Vice Pres., Arnhold and S. Bleichroeder, NYC, 1963–73. Member: Exec. Cttee, Helsinki Watch, 1982–; Cttee, Americas Watch, 1982–; Council on Foreign Relations, 1988–. Chm. and Founding Pres., Central European Univ., Prague, Budapest, 1991. Mem., RIIA, 1990. Hon. DCL Oxford, 1990; Hon. DHL Yale, 1991. *Publications:* The Alchemy of Finance, 1987, 2nd edn 1994; Opening the Soviet System, 1990; Underwriting Democracy, 1991; (jtly) Soros on Soros: staying ahead of the curve, 1995; The Crisis of Global Capitalism (Open Society Endangered), 1998; Open Society: reforming global capitalism, 2000; George Soros on Globalisation, 2002; The Bubble of American Supremacy, 2004; The Age of Fallibility: consequences of the war on terror, 2006; The New Paradigm for Financial Markets: the credit crisis of 2008 and what it means, 2008. *Address:* Soros Fund Management, 888 7th Avenue, Suite 3300, New York, NY 10106–0001, USA. *Clubs:* Brooks's; Queen's; NY Athletic, Town Tennis.

SORRELL, Sir John (William), Kt 2008; CBE 1996; Chairman: Sorrell Foundation, since 1999; London Design Festival, since 2002; Commission for Architecture and the Built Environment, since 2004; *b* 28 Feb. 1945; *s* of late John William Sorrell and Elizabeth Jane Sorrell (*née* Taylor); *m* 1974, Frances Mary Newell; two *s* one *d. Educ:* Hornsey Coll. of Art (NDD 1964). Designer, Maine Wolff & Partners, 1964; Partner, Goodwin Sorrell, 1964–71; Design Manager, Wolff Olins, 1971–76; Newell & Sorrell, subseq. Interbrand Newell & Sorrell: Founder, 1976; Partner, 1976–83; Chm., 1983–2000. Chm., Design Council, 1994–2000. A Vice-Pres., CSD, 1989–92; Chm., Design Business Assoc., 1990–92. Chairman: NHS London Design Adv. Gp, 2001–03; UK Trade & Investment Creative Industries Adv. Bd, 2007–; Member: BR Architecture and Design Panel, 1991–93; RSA Design Adv. Gp, 1991–93; Panel 2000, FCO, 1998–2000; Culture and Creativity Adv. Gp, DCMS, 2002–03; Adv. Gp on Sch. Bldgs Design, 2002–04, London Challenge Ministerial Adv. Gp, 2002–06, DfES; Public Diplomacy Strategy Bd, FCO, 2002–06; Design and Technol. Alliance, Home Office, 2007–; Creative Economy Prog. Ministerial Steering Bd, DCMS, 2008–. Gov., Design Dimension, 1991–93. Trustee, RIBA Trust, 2004–05. Hon. Mem., Romanian Design Foundn, 1996. Hon. FRIBA 2002; Hon. Fellow, UC Falmouth, 2006. CCMI 2006. Hon. DDes: De Montfort, 1997; Greenwich, 2007; Hon. Dr: London Inst., 1999; Middlesex, 2006; Hon. PhD London Metropolitan, 2006. Bicentenary Medal, RSA, 1998. *Publications:* Creative Island, 2002; Joined up Design for Schools, 2005. *Recreations:* architecture, Arsenal, art, film. *Clubs:* Chelsea Arts, Groucho.

SORRELL, Sir Martin (Stuart), Kt 2000; Group Chief Executive, WPP Group, since 1986; *b* 14 Feb. 1945; *s* of late Jack and Sally Sorrell; *m* 1971, Sandra Carol Ann Finestone (marr. diss. 2005); three *s. Educ:* Haberdashers' Aske's School; Christ's College, Cambridge (MA); Harvard Graduate School of Business (MBA 1968). Consultant, Glendinning Associates, Conn, 1968–69; Vice-Pres., Mark McCormack Orgn, London, 1970–74; Dir, James Gulliver Associates, 1975–77; Gp Financial Dir, Saatchi & Saatchi, 1977–86. Non-exec. Dir, Colefax & Fowler Gp plc, 1997–2003. Mem. Bd, NASDAQ, 2001–04. Chm., Adv. Gp, KPMG, 2002–; Mem., ATP Mktg Adv. Bd, 2001–; Internat. Adv. Bd, CBI, 2002–; Special Advr, Loyalty Mgt UK Ltd, 2003–. Modern Apprenticeship Taskforce, DfES, 2003–. Mem., Engrg and Technol. Bd, 2002–. Member: Adv. Bd, Internat. Graduate Sch. of Mgt, Univ. of Navarra, Spain, 1989–; Deans Adv. Council, Boston Univ. Sch. of Mgt, 1998–; Bd of Dirs of Associates, Harvard Business Sch., 1998–; Bd, Indian Sch. of Business, 1998–. Mem., Panel 2000, 1998–99. Mem., Council for Excellence in Mgt and Leadership, 1999–. Ambassador for British Business, 1997–. Member: Bd and Cttee, Special Olympics, 2000–05; Corporate Adv. Gp, Tate Gall., 2000–; Bd, Media Center, Mus. of TV and Radio, NY, 2002–. Gov., London Business Sch., 1990– (Dep. Chm., 1998–). Mem. Bd, Nat. Deaf Children's Soc. (Vice-Pres.); Nat. Appeal Bd, NSPCC. Trustee: Cambridge Foundn, 1990–; RCA Foundn, 1999–. Patron: Queen Charlotte's Appeal, Hammersmith Hosp., 1999–; Christ's Coll., Cambridge; Hon. Patron, Cambridge Univ. Jewish Soc., 2002–. *Recreations:* ski-ing, cricket. *Address:* WPP Group, 27 Farm Street, W1J 5RJ. *T:* (020) 7408 2204. *Clubs:* Reform, MCC; Harvard (NY).

SORRIE, George Strath, CB 1993; Medical Adviser and Director, Civil Service Occupational Health Service, 1987–93; *b* 19 May 1933; *s* of Alexander James Sorrie and Florence Edith Sorrie (*née* Strath); *m* 1959, Gabrielle Ann Baird; three *d. Educ:* Woodside Sch., Aberdeen; Robert Gordon's Coll., Aberdeen; Univ. of Aberdeen (MB ChB); Univs of London and Dundee. FFOM, DPH, DIH. Medical Branch, RAF, 1958–61; Lectr in Epidemiology, London Sch. of Hygiene and Tropical Medicine, 1965–67; GP, Rhynie, Aberdeenshire, 1967–72; Health and Safety Exec., 1972, Dep. Dir of Med. Services, 1980–87. *Address:* 30 Irvine Crescent, St Andrews, Fife KY16 8LG. *T:* (01334) 474510.

SOSKICE, Dr Janet Martin; Reader in Philosophical Theology, University of Cambridge, since 2001; Fellow, Jesus College, Cambridge, since 1988; *b* 16 May 1951; *d* of Alison M. Martin and F. Claire Jamieson; *m* 1982, Oliver C. H. Soskice; two *d. Educ:* Cornell Univ. (BA); Sheffield Univ. (MA); Oxford Univ. (DPhil 1982). Gordon Milburn Jun. Res. Fellow, Oxford Univ. and Somerville Coll., 1980–83; Lecturer: Ripon Coll., Cuddesdon, 1983–88; Univ. of Cambridge, 1988–2001. Canada Commonwealth Fellow, 1996; British Acad. Sen. Res. Fellow, 2000–01. Visiting Professor: Univ. of Uppsala, 1992; Univ. of Calgary, 1996; Univ. of Virginia, 2006; Eugene McCarthy Vis. Prof., Gregorian Univ., 1997. Lectures: Stanton, Univ. of Cambridge, 1997–99; Richards, Univ. of Virginia, 2006. Ecumenical Advr to Archbp of Canterbury, 1990–96. Chm. Bd, Margaret Beaufort Inst. of Theol., 1998–2005. Mem., Bd of Dirs, Concilium, 1998–2006 (Ed., some issues of Concilium). President: Catholic Theol Assoc. of GB, 1992–94; Soc. for Study of Theol., 2008–. *Publications:* Metaphor and Religious Language, 1985, Japanese edn 1992; (ed) After Eve, 1990; (ed jtly) Medicine and Moral Reasoning, 1994; (ed with Diana Lipton) Feminism and Theology, 2003; (ed jtly) Fields of Faith, 2005; The Kindness of God, 2007. *Recreations:* ski-ing, travel. *Address:* Jesus College, Cambridge CB5 8BL. *T:* (01223) 339606, *Fax:* (01223) 339313.

SOSKICE, Nicola Mary; *see* Lacey, N. M.

SOUEIF, Ahdaf; writer; Executive Officer, Al-Furqan Islamic Heritage Foundation, London, 1989–2008; *b* 23 March 1950; *d* of Mustapha Soueif and Fatma Moussa; *m* 1st, 1972, Sherif Hosni (marr. diss. 1977); 2nd, 1981, Ian Hamilton (*d* 2001); two *s. Educ:* schs in Cairo and London; Cairo Univ. (BA English Lit. 1971); American Univ. in Cairo (MA English Lit. 1973); Univ. of Lancaster (PhD Linguistics 1978). Cairo University: Associate Lectr, 1971–79; Lectr, 1979–84; Project Leader and Arabic Ed., Cassel Ltd (Macmillan Inc.), London and Cairo, 1978–84; Associate Prof. of Linguistics, King Saud Univ., Riyadh, 1987–89. Member: Amnesty Internat., 1990–; Cttee for Advancement of Arab-British Understanding, 1995–. Member: Egyptian-British Soc., 1990–; Egyptian Writers' Union, Egypt, 1999–; PEN, Egypt, 1999–; PEN, UK, 1999–; Bd, Caine Prize for African Lit., 2002–. Founding Chm., Engaged Events (charity), 2008–. Fellow: Lannan Foundn, USA, 2002; Bogliasco Foundn, Italy, 2002; FRSL 2003. Hon. DLitt: Lancaster, 2004; London Metropolitan, 2004; Exeter, 2008. *Publications: fiction:* Aisha: a collection of short stories, 1983; In the Eye of the Sun, 1992; Sandpiper and Other Stories, 1996; Zīnat al-Ḥayāh wa Qiṣas Ukhrā (collection of stories in Arabic), 1996 (Best Short Stories of the Year Award, Cairo Book Fair); Ahdāf Suwayf: Mukhtārāt min A'māliha (collection of Arabic writings), 1998; The Map of Love, 1999; I Think of You (short stories), 2007; *non-fiction:* Mezzaterra: fragments from the common ground (essays), 2004; *translation:* In Deepest Night (play), 1998; I Saw Ramallah, memoir by Mourid al-Barghouti, 2000. *Recreations:* friends, film, music, cooking. *Address:* c/o Wylie Agency, 17 Bedford Square, WC1B 3JA. *T:* (020) 7908 5900, *Fax:* (020) 7908 5901; *e-mail:* cbuchan@wylieagency.co.uk; *web:* www.ahdafsoueif.com. *Club:* Gezira (Cairo).

SOUHAMI, Mark; Chairman, Codic International SA, 1998–2005 and since 2008, Hon. President, since 2005; *b* 25 Sept. 1935; *s* of late John Souhami and Freda Souhami (*née* Harris); *m* 1964, Margaret Austin; two *d. Educ:* St Marylebone Grammar School. Lieut RA, 1954–60; early career in City and timber industry; joined Dixons, 1970: Group Marketing Dir, 1970; Man. Dir, 1973; Gp Man. Dir, 1986–92, Dep. Chm., 1992–2003, Dixons Gp plc. Dir, Thomson Travel Group plc, 1998–2000. Chm., British Retail Consortium, 1994–98. Mem. Econ. Affairs Cttee, CBI, 1978–94 (Mem. Council, 1978–91 and 1996–2000). Mem., Metropolitan Police Cttee, 1995–99. Trustee, Photographers' Gall., 1978–90. CCMI; FCIM. Founder Mem., Marketors' Co., 1975. *Recreations:* gardening, fishing, shooting. *Clubs:* Savile, Royal Automobile.

See also R. L. Souhami.

SOUHAMI, Prof. Robert Leon, CBE 2004; MD; FRCP, FRCR, FMedSci; Professor of Medicine, University College London, 1997–2001, now Emeritus; Executive Director of Policy and Communications, 2003–05, Director of Clinical Research and Training, 2001–03, Cancer Research UK; *b* 26 April 1938; *s* of John Souhami and Freda Harris; *m* 1966. *Educ:* St Marylebone Grammar Sch.; University Coll. Hosp. Med. Sch. (BSc, MB BS). MD 1975; FRCP 1979; FRCR 1992. Hon. Lectr, St Mary's Hosp. Med. Sch., 1969–71; Sen. Registrar, UCH, 1971–73; Consultant Physician, Poole Gen. Hosp., 1973–75; Consultant Physician and Sen. Lectr, UCH, 1975–87; Kathleen Ferrier Prof. of Clinical Oncology, UCMSM, subseq. UCL Med. Sch., 1987–97; Dean, Faculty of Clinical Scis, 1997–99, Principal, 1999–2001, UCL Med. Sch., subseq. Royal Free and UC Med. Sch., UCL; Hon. Consultant Physician, Whittington Hosp. and Royal Nat. Orthopaedic Hosp., 1976–2001. Chairman: Cancer Therapy Cttee, MRC, 1987–93; Protocol Review Cttee, EORTC, 1994–97; Member, Science Council: Institut Curie, 1999–; Centre Leon Bérard, 2001–; Institut Bergonié, 2003–. Fellow, UCL, 1990. FMedSci 1998. *Publications:* Tutorials in Differential Diagnosis, 1974, 4th edn 2003;

Cancer and its Management, 1986, 5th edn 2005; Textbook of Medicine, 1990, 4th edn 2002; (ed) Oxford Textbook of Oncology, 2001; clinical and scientific articles on aspects of cancer.
See also M. Souhami.

SOULAS, Alain; Chairman, Greenfield Holdings NV, 1999–2003; *b* 3 May 1943; *s* of Raymond Soulas and Denise Noyer; *m* Simone Gallian; two *d*. *Educ:* Stanford Univ. (MSc 1967); Ingénieur du Génie Maritime, Paris, 1966. Cerci, 1969–74; Cellulose du Pin, 1975–81; Socar, 1981–82; Chief Exec., Condat, 1983–85; Chief Exec., Paper Div., Saint Gobain and Chm., Cellulose du Pin, 1985–92; Chief Executive: Arjo Wiggins Appleton, 1992–96; ASW Hldgs plc, 1996–99. French National Order of Merit. *Recreations:* opera, theatre. *Address:* 16 rue de Fourcy, 75004 Paris, France; 3 South House, Rosemoor Street, SW3 2LP. *Club:* Racing Club de France (Paris).

SOULBURY, 3rd Viscount; *see* Ramsbotham, Hon. Sir P. E.

SOULSBY, family name of **Baron Soulsby of Swaffham Prior**.

SOULSBY OF SWAFFHAM PRIOR, Baron *cr* 1990 (Life Peer), of Swaffham Prior in the County of Cambridgeshire; **Ernest Jackson Lawson Soulsby;** Professor of Animal Pathology, University of Cambridge, 1978–93, now Emeritus; Fellow, Wolfson College, Cambridge, 1978–93, Hon. Fellow, 2004; *b* 23 June 1926; *s* of William George Lawson Soulsby and Agnes Soulsby; *m* 1st, 1950, Margaret Macdonald; one *s* one *d*; 2nd, 1962, Georgina Elizabeth Annette Williams. *Educ:* Queen Elizabeth Grammar Sch., Penrith; Univ. of Edinburgh. MRCVS; DVSM; PhD; MA (Cantab). CBiol; FIBiol 1998. Veterinary Officer, City of Edinburgh, 1949–52; Lectr in Clinical Parasitology, Univ. of Bristol, 1952–54; Univ. Lectr in Animal Pathology, Univ. of Cambridge, 1954–63; Prof. of Parasitology, Univ. of Pennsylvania, 1964–78. Ian McMaster Fellow, CSIRO, 1958; Sen. Vis. Fellow, EEC, Poland, 1961; WHO Vis. Worker, USSR, 1962; UN Special Fund Expert, IAEA, Vienna and Zemun, Yugoslavia, 1964; Ford Foundn Visiting Prof., Univ. of Ibadan, 1964; Richard Merton Guest Prof., Justus Liebig Univ., 1974–75; Vis. Prof. Univ. of Qld, 1992. Lectures: Hume Meml, Univ. Fedn Animal Welfare, 1985; Wooldridge Meml, BVA, 1986; Sir Frederick Hobday Meml, British Equine Vet. Assoc., 1986; Richard Turk Meml, Texas A & M Univ., 1991; Harben, RIPH&H, 1991; Stoll Meml, NJ, 1995; Clive Behrens, Leeds Univ., 1996; Stoll-Stunkard, Amer. Soc. Parasitol., 1997; Bourne, St George's Univ., Grenada, 2001; Boyd Orr, Nutrition Soc., 2002; Windref, St George's Univ., Grenada, 2004; Steele Meml, Univ. of Texas, 2005; Garrod, British Soc. Antimicrobial Therapy, 2008. Member: AFRC, 1984–89 (Chm., Animal Res. Grants Bd, 1986–89); Vet. Adv. Cttee, Horserace Betting Levy Bd, 1984–97 (Chm., 1985–97); EEC Adv. Cttee on Vet. Trng, 1981–86; Animal Procedure Cttee, Home Office, 1986–95. Royal College of Veterinary Surgeons: Mem. Council, 1978–93; Jun. Vice-Pres., 1983; Pres., 1984; Sen. Vice-Pres., 1985; Hon. Fellow, 1997. President: World Assoc. Adv. Vet. Parasit., 1963–67 (Hon. Mem., 1985); Helminthol. Soc., Washington, 1970–71 (Hon. Mem., 1990); Cambridge Soc. for Comp. Medicine, 1984–85; Vet. Res. Club, 1985–86; Pet Adv. Cttee, 1997–; RSocMed, 1998–2000 (Pres., Comp. Medicine Section, 1993–95; Hon. Fellow, 1996); RIPH, 2004–; Parly and Sci. Cttee, 2004–08. Council Mem., Amer. Soc. Parasitologists, 1974–78. Corresponding Member: German Parasitology Soc.; Acad. Royale de Médecine de Belgique; Hon. Member: Mexican Parasitology Soc.; Argentinian Parasitological Soc.; BVA; British Soc. for Parasitology; World Innovation Foundn; Hon. Life Member: British Small Animal Vet. Assoc.; British Soc. Antimicrobial Therapy; Expert Advisor and Consultant, and Member, Scientific Groups: various internat. agencies and govts. Chm., Companion Animal Welfare Council, 1999–; Member: Council, Internat. League for Protection of Horses, 1997–2002; Soc. for Protection of Animals Abroad, 1997–2004. Patron: Vet. Benevolent Fund, 1996; Fund for Replacement of Animals in Med. Experiments, 1997–. Founder FMedSci 1998. Hon. FIBiol 2002; Hon. FRCPath 2005. Hon. AM 1972, Hon. DSc 1984, Univ. of Pennsylvania; Hon. DVMS: Edinburgh, 1991; Glasgow, 2001; Hon. DVM: León, 1993; Liverpool, 2004; Hon. DSc Univ. of Peradeniya, Sri Lanka, 1994. R. N. Chaudhury Gold Medal, Calcutta Sch. of Tropical Med., Calcutta, 1976; Behring-Bilharz Prize, Cairo, 1977; Ludwig-Schunk Prize, Justus-Liebig Universität, Giessen, 1979; Diploma and Medal, XXI World Vet. Congress, Moscow, 1979; Distinguished Parasitologist Award, Amer. Assoc. of Vet. Parasitologists, 1987; Friedrich Mussenmeier Medal, Humboldt Univ., 1990; World Assoc. for Advancement of Vet. Parasitology/Pfizer Excellence in Teaching Award, 1993; Chiron Award, BVA, 1998; Equestrian Vet. Achievement Award, Animal Health Trust, 2005; Dist. Service Award and Mike Fisher Meml Award, St George's Univ., Grenada, 2006. *Publications:* Textbook of Veterinary Clinical Parasitology, 1965; Biology of Parasites, 1966; Reaction of the Host to Parasitism, 1968; Helminths, Arthropods and Protozoa of Domesticated Animals, 6th edn 1968, 7th edn 1982; Immunity to Animal Parasites, 1972; Parasitic Zoonoses, 1974; Pathophysiology of Parasitic Infections, 1976; Epidemiology and Control of Nematodiasis in Cattle, 1981; Immunology, Immunopathology and Immunoprophylaxis of Parasitic Infections, Vols I, II, III & IV, 1986; Zoonoses, 1998; articles in jls of parasitology, immunology and pathology. *Recreations:* travel, gardening, photography. *Address:* House of Lords, SW1A 0PW. *Clubs:* Farmers', Oxford and Cambridge.

SOULSBY, Sir Peter (Alfred), Kt 1999; MP (Lab) Leicester South, since 2005; *b* 27 Dec. 1948; *s* of late Robert and of Mary Soulsby; *m* 1969, Alison Prime; three *d*. *Educ:* Minchenden Sch., Southgate; City of Leicester Coll. (BEd Leicester Univ.). Teacher of children with special educational needs, 1973–90. Mem. (Lab), Leicester City Council, 1973–2003 (Leader, 1981–94 and 1995–99). Mem., Audit Commission, 1994–2000. Vice-Chairman: Waterways Trust, 1999–2003; British Waterways Bd, 2000–04 (Mem., 1998–2004). *Address:* House of Commons, SW1A 0AA. *T:* (020) 7219 8332.

SOUNDY, Andrew John; Senior Partner, Ashurst Morris Crisp (Solicitors), 1992–98; *b* 29 March 1940; *s* of Harold Cecil Soundy and Adele Monica Templeton (*née* Westley); *m* 1963, Jill Marion Steiner; one *s* two *d*. *Educ:* Boxgrove Sch.; Shrewsbury Sch.; Trinity Coll., Cambridge (BA, MA). Ashurst Morris Crisp: articled clerk, 1963–66; qualified as solicitor, 1966; Partner, 1969. Non-exec. Dir, EWFact plc, 1994–98 (Chm., 1997–98). Vice Pres., 1998–, Trustee (Dir), 2003–, The Lord Slynn of Hadley Eur. Law Foundn. Director: St Michael's Hospice, Basingstoke, 1996– (Chm., 2007–); Anglo-Russian Opera and Ballet Trust, 2001–. Mem. Bd Govs, De Montfort Univ., 2001–05. Churchwarden, Parish of Mattingley, 2002–. FRSA 1993. *Recreations:* countryside, farming, opera, tennis. *Address:* Bartletts Farm, Mattingley, Hook, Hants RG27 8JU. *T:* (0118) 932 6279. *Clubs:* Cavalry and Guards, City Law, Bishopsgate Ward.

SOUNESS, Graeme James; Manager, Newcastle United Football Club, 2004–06; *b* 6 May 1953; *s* of James and Elizabeth Souness; *m* 1994, Karen; one *s*, and two *s* one *d* from previous marriage. *Educ:* Carrickvale Sch., Edinburgh. Professional football player: Tottenham Hotspur, 1969–73; Middlesbrough FC, 1973–78; Liverpool FC, 1978–84 (3 European Cups, 1978, 1981 and 1984; 5 League Championships, 1979–84 and 4 League Cups, 1981–84); Sampdoria, Italy, 1984–86; played for Scotland, 1975–86 (54 full caps); Manager: Glasgow Rangers, 1986–91 (also player, 1986–90; 4 Scottish League Championships, 1987, 1989, 1990, 1991; 4 Scottish League Cups, 1987–90); Liverpool FC, 1991–94 (FA Cup 1992); Galatasaray, Turkey, 1995–96; Southampton FC, 1996–97; Torino, Italy, 1997–98; Benfica, Portugal, 1998–99; Blackburn Rovers, 2000–04 (Worthington Cup, 2002). *Publications:* (with B. Harris) No Half Measures, 1984; A Manager's Diary, 1990. *Recreations:* gardening, walking.

SOUROZH, Bishop of, (Russian Orthodox), since 2007; **Rt Rev. Elisey Ganaba;** Bishop of Bogorodsk, since 2006; *b* Russia, 1962. Head, Russian Orthodox Dio. in UK, 2007–. *Address:* 67 Ennismore Gardens, SW7 7NH. *T:* (020) 7584 0096, *Fax:* (020) 7584 9864; *e-mail:* sourozh@mail.ru.

SOUTAR, Air Marshal Sir Charles (John Williamson), KBE 1978 (MBE 1958); Director-General, Medical Services (RAF), 1978–81; *b* 12 June 1920; *s* of Charles Alexander Soutar and Mary Helen (*née* Watson); *m* 1944, Joy Dorée Upton; one *s* two *d*. *Educ:* Brentwood Sch.; London Hosp. MB, BS, LMSSA, FFCM, DPH, DIH. Commissioned RAF, 1946. Various appts, then PMO, Middle East Command, 1967–68; Dep. Dir, Med. Organisation, RAF, 1968–70; OC, PMRAF Hosp., Halton, 1970–73; Comdt, RAF Inst. of Aviation Medicine, 1973–75; PMO, Strike Command, 1975–78. QHS 1974–81. CStJ 1972. *Recreations:* sport, gardening, ornithology, music. *Address:* Oak Cottage, High Street, Aldeburgh, Suffolk IP15 5AU. *T:* (01728) 452201. *Club:* Royal Air Force.

SOUTAR, David Strang; Consultant Plastic Surgeon, West of Scotland Regional Plastic Surgery Unit, Canniesburn Hospital, Bearsden, Glasgow, since 1981; *b* 19 Dec. 1947; *s* of Alexander Anderson Soutar and Lizbeth Agnes Bailey Soutar; *m* 1972, Myra (*née* Banks); two *s* one *d*. *Educ:* Univ. of Aberdeen (MB ChB 1972; ChM 1987). Registrar, Gen. Surgery, Grampian Health Bd, 1975–78; Registrar, then Sen. Registrar, Plastic Surgery, W of Scotland Regional Plastic Surgery Unit, 1978–81. Hon. Clinical Sen. Lectr, Univ. of Glasgow, 1981–. Chm., Div. of Trauma and Related Services, N Glasgow Univ. Hosps NHS Div., 2002–06. *Publications:* Practical Guide to Free Tissue Transfer, 1986; Microvascular Surgery and Free Tissue Transfer, 1993; Excision and Reconstruction in Head and Neck Cancer, 1994; contrib. 30 chapters in books and over 80 papers in peer-reviewed jls. *Recreations:* music, travel, golf. *Address:* Canniesburn Plastic Surgery Unit, Jubilee Building, Glasgow Royal Infirmary, Glasgow G4 05X. *T:* (0141) 211 5776, *Fax:* (0141) 211 5859; *e-mail:* david.soutar@northglasgow.scot.nhs.uk.

SOUTAR, (Samuel) Ian; HM Diplomatic Service, retired; Ambassador to Bulgaria, 2001–03; *b* 2 June 1945; *s* of James Soutar and Maud Soutar (*née* McNinch); *m* 1968, Mary Isabella Boyle; one *s* one *d*. *Educ:* Ballymena Acad.; Trinity Coll. Dublin (BA Mod. Langs and Lit.). FCO, 1968–70; UK Delegn to EC, 1970–72; Saigon, 1972–74; First Sec., FCO, 1974–76; Private Sec. to Parly Under-Sec. of State, 1976–77; Washington, 1977–81; FCO, 1981–86; Dep. High Comr, Wellington, 1986–91; RCDS 1991; Head, Inf. Systems Div. (Ops), FCO, 1991–95; Head, Library and Records Dept, FCO, 1995–97; UK Perm. Rep. to Conf. on Disarmament, Geneva, 1997–2001. Mem., Lord Chancellor's Adv. Council on Nat. Records and Archives, 2008–. *Recreations:* walking, listening to music. *Address:* 86 Woodwarde Road, SE22 8UT.

SOUTER, Brian; Chief Executive, Stagecoach Group plc, since 2002 (Chairman, 1980–2002); *b* 1954; *s* of Iain and Catherine Souter; *m* 1988, Elizabeth McGoldrick; three *s* one *d*. *Educ:* Dundee Univ.; Univ. of Strathclyde (BA Accountancy). CA; MCIT. *Address:* Stagecoach Group plc, 10 Dunkeld Road, Perth PH1 5TW.
See also A. H. Gloag.

SOUTER, Carole Lesley; Director, Heritage Lottery Fund, since 2003; *b* 2 May 1957; *d* of Richard Teague and late June Teague; *m* 1979, David Norman Souter; one *s* one *d*. *Educ:* Truro High Sch. for Girls; St Austell 6th Form Coll.; Jesus Coll., Oxford (BA Hons PPE); Birkbeck Coll., London (MA Victorian Studies). Various posts, DHSS, later DSS, 1978–2000; Dir, Planning and Develt, English Heritage, 2000–03. Chair, Capital (formerly SE London) Community Foundn, 2004–. Trustee, London Bombings Relief Charitable Fund, 2005–. MInstD 2006. FRSA 2003. *Recreations:* gardening, horse-riding, visiting historic sites, museums and galleries, theatre. *Address:* Heritage Lottery Fund, 7 Holbein Place, SW1W 8NR. *T:* (020) 7591 6011, *Fax:* (020) 7591 6013; *e-mail:* caroles@hlf.org.uk.

SOUTER, David Hackett; Associate Justice of the Supreme Court of the United States, since 1990; *b* 17 Sept. 1939. *Educ:* Harvard Univ. (LLB); Oxford Univ. (Rhodes Scholar; MA). Admitted to NH Bar; Associate, Orr & Reno, Concord, NH, 1966–68; Asst Attorney-Gen., 1968–71, Dep. Attorney-Gen., 1976, Attorney-Gen., 1976–78, New Hampshire; Associate Justice: NH Superior Court, 1978–83; NH Supreme Court, 1983–90. *Address:* Supreme Court Building, 1 First Street NE, Washington, DC 20543, USA.

SOUTH, William Lawrence, CBE 1988; FIET; Director, Philips Electronics, 1982–94; management consultant, 1991–2002; *b* 3 May 1933; *s* of Laurence and Anne South; *m* 1960, Lesley (*née* Donaldson); one *s* two *d*. *Educ:* Purley County Grammar Sch. FIET (FIEE 1992). RAF, 1951–55 (Pilot, 511 and 220 Sqdns). Director: Pye of Cambridge, 1977–81; Origin Holdings, 1990–92; Greenwich Healthcare NHS Trust, 1995–2003. Member: NPL Supervisory Bd, 1988–96; ITAB, 1988–93; SERC Engrg Bd, 1992–94. Freeman, City of London, 1991; Liveryman, Co. of Information Technologists, 1992–. Hon. DTech Greenwich, 2004. *Recreations:* sailing, music. *Address:* 14 Harbour Way, Emsworth, Hants PO10 7BE. *Club:* Chichester Yacht.

SOUTH AUSTRALIA, Metropolitan of; *see* Adelaide, Archbishop of.

SOUTHALL, Anna Catherine; Vice Chairman, Big Lottery Fund, since 2006 (Member Board, 2004–06); *b* 9 June 1948; *d* of Stephen Readhead Southall and Philippa (Cadbury) Southall; *m* 1st, 1975, Neil Burton (marr. diss. 1978); 2nd, 1983, Christopher Serle (marr. diss. 2003); two *s*. *Educ:* Univ. of E Anglia (BA Hons 1970); Gateshead Tech. Coll. (Post Grad. Dip. 1974). Ecclesiastical Insce Office, 1970; Adv. Bd for Redundant Churches, Church Comrs, 1970–71; teacher, Shoreditch Secondary Sch., ILEA (full and part-time), 1971–74; Conservator, Polychrome Monuments (freelance), 1974–75; Senior Conservator: S Eastern Museums' Service, 1975–81; Tate Gall., London, 1981–96; Asst Dir, 1996–98, Dir, 1998–2002, Nat. Museums and Galls of Wales; Chief Exec., Resource: The Council for Museums, Archives and Libraries, 2002–03. Chm., Barrow Cadbury Trust, 1996–2006. Member: Govt's Spoliation Adv. Panel, 2000–; Adv. Panel on Futurebuilders, 2005–08. *Publications:* numerous contribs on 18th and 19th century British artists' materials and techniques in conf. papers, exhibn catalogues and professional jls. *Recreations:* my small-holding in Wales, family and friends, and sharing their sporting and cultural interests. *Address:* Big Lottery Fund, 1 Plough Place, EC4A 1DE.

SOUTHALL, Kenneth Charles; Under-Secretary, Inland Revenue, 1975–82; *b* 3 Aug. 1922; *s* of Arthur and Margarette Jane Southall; *m* 1947, Audrey Kathleen Skeels; one *s*. *Educ:* Queen Elizabeth's Grammar Sch., Hartlebury, Worcs. Inland Revenue, 1939; RAF, 1942–46; Administrative Staff College, 1962. *Address:* The Green, Brill, Bucks HP18 9RU.

SOUTHAMPTON, 6th Baron *cr* 1780; **Charles James FitzRoy;** *b* 12 Aug. 1928; *o s* of Charles FitzRoy (5th Baron, disclaimed peerage for life, 1964) and Margaret (*d* 1931), *d* of Rev. Preb. Herbert Mackworth Drake; *S* father, 1989; *m* 1st, 1951, Pamela Anne (*d* 1997), *d* of Edward Percy Henniker; one *s* one *d* (and one *s* decd); 2nd, 1997, Alma (*née* Pascual); one *s* one *d*. *Educ:* Stowe. Master: Easton Harriers, 1968–71; Blaikney Foxhounds, 1971–72. *Recreations:* shooting, fishing, golf. *Heir: s* Hon. Edward Charles FitzRoy [*b* 8 July 1955; *m* 1978, Rachel Caroline Vincent, 2nd *d* of Peter John Curnow Millett; one *s* three *d*]. *Address:* Stone Cross, Stone Lane, Chagford, Newton Abbot, Devon TQ13 8JU.

SOUTHAMPTON, Bishop Suffragan of, since 2004; **Rt Rev. Paul Roger Butler;** *b* 18 Sept. 1955; *s* of Denys Michael Butler and Jean Florence Butler; *m* 1982, Rosemary Jean Johnson; two *s* two *d*. *Educ:* Nottingham Univ. (BA Hons (English and History) 1977); Wycliffe Hall, Oxford (BA (Theol.) 1982). Ordained deacon, 1983, priest, 1984; Curate, Holy Trinity, Wandsworth, 1983–87; Inner London Evangelist, 1987–92, Dep. Hd of Missions, 1992–94, Scripture Union; NSM, St Paul, East Ham, 1988–94; Priest-in-charge: St Mary with St Stephen, and St Luke, Walthamstow, 1994–97; St Gabriel, Walthamstow, 1997; Team Rector, Parish of Walthamstow, 1997–2004; Area Dean, Waltham Forest, 2000–04. Hon. Canon, St Paul's Cathedral, Byumba, Rwanda, 2001–. *Publications:* Reaching Children, 1992; Reaching Families, 1994; God's Friends, 1994; Following Jesus, 1994; Want to be in God's Family?, 1998; Growing Up in God's Family, 1998; Temptation and Testing, 2007. *Address:* Ham House, The Crescent, Romsey, Hants SO51 7NG. *T:* and *Fax:* (01794) 516005; *e-mail:* paul.butler@bpsotonoffice.clara.co.uk.

SOUTHAN, Elizabeth Andreas; *see* Evatt, E. A.

SOUTHAN, His Honour Robert Joseph; a Circuit Judge, 1986–2001; *b* 13 July 1928; *s* of late Thomas Southan and of Kathleen Southan; *m* 1960, Elizabeth Andreas Evatt, *qv*; one *d* (one *s* decd). *Educ:* Rugby; St Edmund Hall, Oxford (MA); University Coll., London (LLM). Called to the Bar, Inner Temple, 1953; called to the Bar of NSW, 1976; a Recorder, 1983–86. *Recreations:* theatre, opera, sailing, tennis. *Clubs:* Royal Corinthian Yacht, Bar Yacht; Cumberland Lawn Tennis.

SOUTHBY, Sir John (Richard Bilbe), 3rd Bt *cr* 1937, of Burford, Co. Oxford; non-executive Director, Milton Keynes General NHS Trust, 2001–08; *b* 2 April 1948; *s* of Sir Archibald Richard Charles Southby, 2nd Bt, OBE and Olive Marion (*d* 1991), *d* of late Sir Thomas Bilbe-Robinson; *S* father, 1988; *m* 1971, Victoria Jane, *d* of John Wilfred Sturrock; two *s* one *d*. *Educ:* Peterhouse, Marandellas, Rhodesia; Loughborough Univ. of Technology (BSc Elec. Eng). CEng, MIET. East Midlands Electricity: Graduate Trainee, 1971; Asst Engineer 1973, O & M Engineer 1976, Shepshed, Leics; Senior Asst Engineer 1979, O & M Engineer 1981, Boston, Lincs; District Engineer, Grantham, 1986; Dist Manager, then Gen. Manager, Milton Keynes, 1991; Network Gen. Manager Northampton, 1996–99. Pres., Milton Keynes Business Leaders (formerly Milton Keynes Large Employers Assoc.), 1998– (Chm., 1994–98); Chm., Milton Keynes Police Area Adv. Cttee, 1995–99; Mem. Bd, Milton Keynes Economic Partnership, 1994–99; Dir, Milton Keynes Theatre and Gallery Mgt Co., 1996–2000. Pres., Milton Keynes Rotary Club, 1997–98 (Sen. Vice Pres., 1996–97; Sec., 1999–2004, 2006–); Asst Sec., 1998–99, Sec., 1999–2004, Asst Gov., 2006–, Rotary Dist 1260. FCMI. *Recreations:* ski-ing, gardening, music, DIY, photography. *Heir: s* Peter John Southby [*b* 20 Aug. 1973; *m* 1995, Katherine Margaret, *d* of Dr R. N. Priestland; two *s*]. *Address:* Lomagundi, High Street, Nash, Bucks MK17 0EP.

SOUTHEND, Archdeacon of; *see* Lowman, Ven. D. W.

SOUTHERN, Graham; Co-founder, Haunch of Venison (galleries in London, Zurich, Berlin, New York), 2002; *b* Cornwall, 21 Sept. 1960; *s* of John and Barbara Southern; *m* 1995, Antje Schmitt; two *d*. Christie's London: Specialist, Modern and Impressionist Dept, 1985–88, Modern British Dept, 1988–94; Founding Dir, Post War and Contemporary British Art Dept, 1994–97; Dir, Contemporary Art Dept, 1997–2001; Director: Christie Manson & Wood, 1990–2001; Anthony d'Offay Gall., London, 2001. *Recreation:* squirrelling. *Address:* Haunch of Venison, 6 Haunch of Venison Yard, W1K 5ES. *T:* (020) 7495 5050. *Club:* Chelsea Arts.

SOUTHERN, Rt Rev. Humphrey Ivo John; *see* Repton, Bishop Suffragan of.

SOUTHERN, Paul David; Senior Immigration Judge, Asylum and Immigration Tribunal, since 2006; *b* 3 Feb. 1954; *m* 1987, Anne Prosser; three *s* one *d*. *Educ:* Tetherdown Primary Sch.; William Ellis Grammar Sch.; Lanchester Poly. (BA Hons Business Law 1976). Admitted as solicitor, 1979; Dep. Dist Judge, 2000–; Immigration Adjudicator, 2002–05; Immigration Judge, 2005–06. *Recreation:* being with my family. *Address:* Asylum and Immigration Tribunal, Field House, 15/25 Bream's Buildings, EC4A 1DZ.

SOUTHERN, Dr Peter Campbell David; Head Master, Christ's Hospital, 1996–2007; *b* 28 Feb. 1947; *s* of Sir Richard Southern, FBA; *m* 1972, Dinah Mitchell; two *s*. *Educ:* Dragon Sch., Oxford; Magdalen College Sch., Oxford; Merton Coll., Oxford (MA); Edinburgh Univ. (PhD). Malosa Secondary Sch., Malawi, 1964–65; Tutorial Asst, Edinburgh Univ., 1970–71; Asst Master, Dulwich Coll., 1973–78; Head of History Dept, Westminster Sch., 1978–85; Head Master, Bancroft's Sch., 1985–96. History Awarder and Reviser, Oxford and Cambridge Examn Bd, 1980–90; Sec., Nat. Centre for Cued Speech, 1990–92. Vice-Chm., Redbridge and Waltham Forest Dist HA, 1993–96. *Publications:* articles on P. G. Wodehouse. *Recreations:* sailing, golf. *Address:* 11 Marsh Baldon, near Nuneham, Courtenay, Oxon OX44 9LW.

SOUTHERN, Richard Michael; QC 2006; *b* Yorks, 1964; *s* of Michael and Merle Southern; *m* 2001, Yvette Austin; two *d*. *Educ:* St Catharine's Coll., Cambridge (BA 1986). Called to the Bar, Middle Temple, 1987; in practice as barrister specialising in commercial litigation. Mem., Oxford & Cambridge Sailing Soc. *Recreation:* sailing. *Address:* 7 King's Bench Walk, Temple, EC4Y 7DS. *T:* (020) 7910 8300; *e-mail:* rsouthern@7kbw.co.uk. *Clubs:* Bar Yacht, Royal Corinthian Yacht (Cowes).

SOUTHESK, Earl of; David Charles Carnegie; *b* 3 March 1961; *s* and *heir* of 3rd Duke of Fife, *qv*; held courtesy title Earl of Macduff until 1992; *m* 1987, Caroline, *d* of Martin Bunting, *qv*; three *s*. *Educ:* Eton; Pembroke Coll., Cambridge (BA Law 1982; MA 1986); Royal Agricultural College, Cirencester; Edinburgh Univ. (MBA 1990). Cazenove & Co., 1982–85; Bell Lawrie & Co., 1988–89; chartered accountant, Reeves & Neylan, to 1997. Partner, Southesk Farms. Mem. Council, HHA for Scotland; Gov., Unicorn Preservation Soc.; Vice Chm., Angus Cons. and Unionist Assoc. Hon. President: Montrose and Dist Angling Club; Angus Show; Hon. Patron, Edinburgh Angus Club. *Heir: s* Lord Carnegie, *qv*.

SOUTHGATE, Sir Colin (Grieve), Kt 1992; Chairman, Whitehead Mann Group plc, 2003–06 (non-executive Director, 1997–2006); *b* 24 July 1938; *s* of Cyril Alfred and Edith Isabelle Southgate; *m* 1962, Sally Patricia Mead; two *s* two *d*. *Educ:* City of London Sch. ICT, later ICL, 1960–70; formed Software Sciences, 1970; apptd Chief Exec., BOC Computer Services Div. on sale of Software Sciences to BOC, 1980–82; Chief Executive: THORN EMI Information Technology, 1983; THORN EMI, subseq. EMI Gp plc, 1989–99 (Dir, 1984–99); Dir, 1990–96, Chm., 1993–96, PowerGen; Dir, Bank of England, 1991–99; Chm., Terence Chapman Gp plc, 1999–2003 (non-exec. Dir, 1997–99). Chm., Royal Opera House, Covent Gdn, 1998–2003; Trustee: Nat. Gall., 1998–2005; Music Sound Foundn, 1998–2002. Vice Patron, Home Farm Develt Trust, 1991– (Trustee, 1988–91). *Recreation:* gardening.

SOUTHGATE, Air Vice-Marshal Harry Charles, CB 1976; CBE 1973 (MBE 1950); Director General of Engineering and Supply Policy and Planning, Ministry of Defence (Air), 1973–76, retired; *b* 30 Oct. 1921; *s* of George Harry Southgate and Lily Maud (*née* Clarke); *m* 1945, Violet Louise Davies (*d* 1991); one *s*. *Educ:* St Saviour's Sch., Walthamstow. Entered RAF, 1941; India, 1942–45; HQ 90 Gp, 1946–50; RAF Stafford, 1950–52; Air Min., 1952–53; transf. to Equipment Br., 1953; RAF Tangmere, 1953–55; Singapore, 1955–57; psc 1957; Air Min., 1958–60; jssc 1961; Dirg Staff, RAF Staff Coll., Bracknell, 1961–64; CO 35 MU RAF Heywood, 1965–66; SESO, RAF Germany, 1967–68; idc 1969; Dir Supply Management, MoD Air, 1970–73. Pres., Ripon Arts, 2001– (Chm., 1989–2000); Patron, Yorkshire Air Mus., 1990–. *Recreations:* travel, golf, painting, bird-watching. *Address:* The Rushings, Winksley, near Ripon, North Yorkshire HG4 3NR. *T:* (01765) 658582. *Club:* Royal Air Force.

SOUTHGATE, Dame Lesley (Jill), DBE 1999; FRCP, FRCGP; Professor of Medical Education, St George's, University of London, since 2004; *b* 25 Sept. 1943; *m* Richard Boyd Bennet, GP; three *c*. *Educ:* Liverpool Univ. (MB ChB 1967); Univ. of Western Ontario (MClinSci 1980). MRCGP 1974, FRCGP 1985; FRCP 1997. House surgeon and phys., St Helen's Hosp.; W. K. Kellog Fellow, Univ. of Western Ontario; former GP, Hoddesdon; Sen. Lectr, then Prof. of Gen. Practice, 1992–95, St Bartholomew's Hosp. Med. Coll.; Prof. of Primary Care and Medical Educn, Royal Free and University College Med. Sch. (formerly at UCL), 1995–2004; founder Mem., Centre for Health Informatics and Multiprofessional Educn, UCL. Convenor, Panel of MRCGP Examnrs, 1994–99; Chm., Perf. Assessment Implementation Gp, GMC, 1994–2004; Mem., Postgrad. Med. Educn and Trng Bd, 2003–06. President: RCGP, 2000–03; ASME, 2006–. Founder FMedSci, 1998. *Publications:* (contrib.) The Certification and Recertification of Doctors, 1993; (jtly) Infection, 1997; (contrib.) Teaching Medicine in the Community, 1997; contrib. to learned jls. *Address:* Department of Medical Education, St George's, University of London, Cranmer Terrace, SW17 0RE. *T:* (020) 7288 5209; *e-mail:* lesley.southgate@sgul.ac.uk.

SOUTHGATE, Malcolm John; Deputy Managing Director, Eurostar UK (formerly European Passenger Services Ltd), 1990–2000; *b* 11 Nov. 1933; *s* of Harold Edwin Southgate and Mary (*née* Kelleher); *m* 1959, Anne Margaret Yeoman; two *s*. *Educ:* Royal Grammar Sch., Colchester; Corpus Christi Coll., Cambridge (BA). British Railways: Divl Manager, S Eastern Div., 1972; Chief Operating Manager, 1975, Dep. Gen. Man., 1977, Southern Region; Dir of Ops, 1980, Dir of Policy Unit, 1983, BRB; Gen. Man., LMR, 1983; Dir, Channel Tunnel, BRB, 1986. *Recreations:* Rugby, education administration, transport affairs. *Address:* 4 Langdale Rise, Maidstone, Kent ME16 0EU. *T:* (01622) 753792.

SOUTHGATE, Robert; Chairman, Birmingham Royal Ballet, 2000–04 (Vice-Chairman, 1994–99); *b* 20 Jan. 1934; *s* of Robert Bevis Southgate and Ann Southgate (*née* Boyes); *m* 1st, 1957, Elizabeth Benson; four *s*; 2nd, 2002, Ann Yeandle, *d* of Edward Yeandle and Kate (*née* Walker). *Educ:* Morecambe Grammar Sch. Work on national newspapers, 1954–64; Dep. Northern Editor, The Sun, 1964–68; Reporter and Presenter, ITN, 1969–78; Presenter, Thames TV, 1978–80; Controller, News and Current Affairs: TVS, 1980–84; Central TV, 1984–92; non-executive Director: Meridian TV, 1995–97; Central Broadcasting, 1994–97 (former Dep. Man. Dir and Man. Dir). Mem., Arts Council, 1993–97; Chairman: W Midlands Regl Arts Bd, 1992–97; City of Birmingham Touring Opera, 1992–97; Dir, Birmingham Rep. Th., 1996–2002. *Recreations:* Lyric Theatre, travel, food, wine.

SOUTHGATE, Sir William (David), Kt 1995; conductor and composer; *b* Waipukurau, NZ, 4 Aug. 1941; *s* of Alfred John Southgate and Phyllis (*née* Maden); *m* 1967, (Alison) Rosemary Martin, *d* of (Alexander James) Lloyd Martin and (Gwendolene) Noel (*née* McGeorge). *Educ:* Otago Boys High Sch.; Otago Univ. (MA Hons First Cl.; BMus Hons First Cl.); Guildhall Sch. of Music and Drama (Ricordi Conducting Prize). Worked in UK with variety of musical orgns incl. Phoenix Opera Co., RSC and BBC TV, 1969–74; worked in NZ, 1974–; Musical Dir, then Principal Guest Conductor, Christchurch Symphony Orch., 1986–97, Conductor Laureate, 1997–; Guest Conductor, NZ Symphony Orch., 1975–, and all main NZ orchs and opera cos; Musical Director: Royal NZ Ballet, 1976–93; Wellington Youth Orch., 1978–90; Wellington Regional Orch.; Conductor, Wellington City Opera Co. Has conducted orchs in Europe, NZ and Australia, incl. Hallé, Royal Philharmonic, Berlin Radio Symphony, and Sydney Symphony. Own arts and music progs on TV and radio in NZ. Chm., Adv. Bd, Wellington Conservatorium. Vice Pres., Wellington Youth Orch.; Patron: NZ SO Foundn; Performing Arts Comp. Assoc. of NZ; New Plymouth Orch. Hon. DMus Otago, 1994. Queen's Sesquicentennial Medal, NZ, 1990; Kirk-Burnand and Brown Citation, Composers' Assoc. of NZ, 1993; NZ Music Award, 2003. Internationally accredited as major interpreter of classic/romantic symphonic repertoire in Wand to Furtwangler/German tradition. *Compositions include:* Capital Variations, 1983; Symphony No 1, 1984; Symphony No 2, 1988; Erewhon (for wind quintet), 1989; Cello Concerto, 1991; Psalmody, 1992; Hamlet (ballet), 1992, Hamlet Suite, 1993; Overture: Réjouissance, 1994; Symphony No 3, 1997. *Recreations:* golf, billiards, snooker, sports of all kinds (Otago Univ. soccer blue), dining with friends, gardening. *Address:* Box 10229, The Terrace, Wellington, New Zealand.

SOUTHWARD, Eileen; *see* Cooper, E.

SOUTHWARD, Sir Nigel (Ralph), KCVO 2003 (CVO 1995; LVO 1985); Apothecary to the Queen, Apothecary to the Household and to the Households of Princess Alice Duchess of Gloucester and the Duke and Duchess of Gloucester, 1975–2003; *b* 8 Feb. 1941; *s* of Sir Ralph Southward, KCVO; *m* 1965, Annette, *d* of J. H. Hoffmann; one *s* two *d*. *Educ:* Rugby Sch.; Trinity Hall, Cambridge; Middlesex Hosp. Med. Sch. MA, MB, BChir, 1965; MRCP 1969. Ho. Surg., Middx Hosp., 1965; Ho. Phys., Royal Berkshire Hosp., Reading, 1966; Ho. Phys., Central Middx Hosp., 1966; Casualty MO, Middx Hosp., 1967; Vis. MO, King Edward VII Hosp. for Officers, 1972–. Apothecary to the Households of Princess Margaret Countess of Snowdon, 1975–2002, and of Queen Elizabeth the Queen Mother, 1986–2002. *Recreations:* sailing, golf, ski-ing. *Address:* Drokesfield, Bucklers Hard, Beaulieu, Hants SO42 7XE. *T:* (01590) 616252. *Clubs:* Royal Yacht Squadron, Royal Cruising.

SOUTHWARK, Archbishop of, (RC), since 2003; **Most Rev. Kevin John Patrick McDonald;** *b* 18 Aug. 1947. *Educ:* St Joseph's Coll., Stoke; Birmingham Univ. (BA

Latin); Ven. English Coll., Rome; Gregorian Univ. (STL); Angelicum Univ. (STD). Ordained priest, 1974; Asst Priest, All Saints, Stourbridge, 1975–76; Lectr in Moral Theol., St Mary's Coll., Oscott, 1976–85; official with resp. for Anglican and Methodist relns, Pontifical Council for Promoting Christian Unity, Rome, 1985–93; Parish Priest, English Martyrs, Sparkhill, Birmingham, 1993–98; Rector, Oscott Coll., 1998–2001; Bishop of Northampton, 2001–03. Chairman: Ecumenical Commn, Archdio. Birmingham, 1980–85; Archdiocesan Commn for Inter-Religious Dialogue, 1998–2001; Bishops' Conf. Cttee for Catholic-Jewish Relns, 2001–; Bishops' Conf. Cttee for Other Faiths, 2001–; Bishops' Conf. Dept of Dialogue and Unity, 2004–; Consultor to Holy See Commn for Religious Relns with the Jews. 2008–. Canon, St Chad's Cathedral, Birmingham, 1998–2001. Hon. DD Birmingham, 2005. *Recreations:* music, reading, walking. *Address:* Archbishop's House, 150 St George's Road, Southwark, SE1 6HX.

SOUTHWARK, Bishop of, since 1998; **Rt Rev. Thomas Frederick Butler;** *b* 5 March 1940; *s* of Thomas John Butler and Elsie Butler (*née* Bainbridge); *m* 1964, Barbara Joan Clark; one *s* one *d*. *Educ:* Univ. of Leeds (BSc 1st Cl. Hons, MSc, PhD). CEng. College of the Resurrection, Mirfield, 1962–64; Curate: St Augustine's, Wisbech, 1964–66; St Saviour's, Folkestone, 1966–68; Lecturer and Chaplain, Univ. of Zambia, 1968–73; Acting Dean of Holy Cross Cathedral, Lusaka, Zambia, 1973; Chaplain to Univ. of Kent at Canterbury, 1973–80; Archdeacon of Northolt, 1980–85; Area Bishop of Willesden, 1985–91; Bishop of Leicester, 1991–98. Chairman: Bd of Mission, Gen. Synod of C of E, 1995–2001; C of E Bd for Social Responsibility, 2001–02; Vice-Chm., Council for Mission and Public Affairs, 2002–. Six Preacher, Canterbury Cathedral, 1979–84. Took seat in H of L, 2007. FKC 2008. Hon. LLD: Leicester, 1995; De Montfort, 1998; Hon. DSc Loughborough, 1997; Hon. DD Kent, 2005; Hon. DLit South Bank, 2005. *Publications:* (with B. J. Butler) Just Mission, 1993; (with B. J. Butler) Just Spirituality in a World of Faiths, 1996. *Recreations:* reading, mountain walking. *Address:* Bishop's House, 38 Tooting Bec Gardens, SW16 1QZ. *T:* (020) 8769 3256.

SOUTHWARK, Auxiliary Bishops in, (RC); *see* Hendricks, Rt Rev. P. J; Hine, Rt Rev. J. F. M.

SOUTHWARK, Dean of; *see* Slee, Very Rev. C. B.

SOUTHWARK, Archdeacon of; *see* Ipgrave, Ven. M. G.

SOUTHWELL, family name of **Viscount Southwell**.

SOUTHWELL, 7th Viscount *cr* 1776; **Pyers Anthony Joseph Southwell;** Bt 1662; Baron Southwell, 1717; International Management and Marketing Consultant, now retired; *b* 14 Sept. 1930; *s* of Hon. Francis Joseph Southwell (2nd *s* of 5th Viscount) and Agnes Mary Annette Southwell (*née* Clifford); *S* uncle, 1960; *m* 1955, Barbara Jacqueline Raynes; two *s*. *Educ:* Beaumont Coll., Old Windsor, Berks; Royal Military Academy, Sandhurst. Commissioned into 8th King's Royal Irish Hussars, 1951; resigned commission, 1955. *Recreation:* golf. *Heir:* *s* Hon. Richard Andrew Pyers Southwell [*b* 15 June 1956; *m* 1985, Alison Margaret Huntington; one *d* (one *s* decd)]. *Address:* PO Box 2211, 8062 Paphos, Cyprus. *T:* 6950227. *Clubs:* Army and Navy, MCC.

SOUTHWELL AND NOTTINGHAM, Bishop of, since 1999 (formerly Bishop of Southwell); **Rt Rev. George Henry Cassidy;** *b* 17 Oct. 1942; *s* of Joseph Abram Cassidy and Ethel McDonald; *m* 1966, Jane Barling Stevens; two *d*. *Educ:* Belfast High School; Queen's Univ., Belfast (BSc 1965; Cert. Bib. Studies 1968); University Coll. London (MPhil 1967); Oak Hill Theological College. MRTPI 1969. Civil Servant: N Ireland, 1967–68; Govt of Kenya, 1968–70. Curate, Christ Church, Clifton, Bristol, 1972–75; Vicar: St Edyth, Sea Mills, Bristol, 1975–82; St Paul's, Portman Square, W1, 1982–87; Archdeacon of London and Canon Residentiary, St Paul's Cathedral, 1987–99. Mem., Cathedrals Fabric Commn for England, 2001–05; Chm., Churches Legislation Adv. (formerly Main) Cttee, 2005–. Freeman, Tylers' & Bricklayers' Co., 1988; Hon. Liveryman, Founders' Co., 1994. Hon. DLitt Heriot-Watt, 2005. Entered House of Lords, 2004. *Recreations:* Rugby football, art, chamber music, walking in the Quantocks. *Address:* Bishop's Manor, Southwell, Notts NG25 0JR. *Clubs:* National; Nottingham (Nottingham).

SOUTHWELL, Dean of; *see* Guille, Very Rev. J. A.

SOUTHWELL, Edward; *see* Southwell, R. C. E.

SOUTHWELL, Richard Charles; QC 1977; *s* of late Sir Philip Southwell, CBE, MC and Mary Burnett; *m* Belinda Mary, *d* of late Col F. H. Pownall, MC; two *s* one *d*. Commercial Arbitrator. Treasurer, Inner Temple, 2002. Pres., Lloyd's Appeal Tribunal. Lay Canon, Salisbury Cathedral, 2007–. *Address:* Serle Court, 6 New Square, Lincoln's Inn, WC2A 3QS. *T:* (020) 7242 6105, *Fax:* (020) 7405 4004; *e-mail:* clerks@serlecourt.co.uk.

SOUTHWELL, (Richard Charles) Edward; His Honour Judge Southwell; a Circuit Judge, since 2000; *b* 31 March 1946; *s* of Dr Neville Southwell and Elizabeth Southwell; *m* 1974, Judith Mary Bowdage; one *s* two *d* (and one *s* decd). *Educ:* Charterhouse Sch. Called to the Bar, Inner Temple, 1970. *Recreations:* golf, sailing, ski-ing, motoring. *Address:* c/o Kingston Crown Court, 6–8 Penrhyn Road, Kingston KT1 2BB. *Clubs:* MCC; West Surrey Golf; Royal London Yacht; Bar Yacht.

SOUTHWELL, Robin, OBE 1999; FRAeS; Chief Executive Officer, EADS UK Ltd, since 2005; *b* 10 April 1960; *s* of Peter and Susan Southwell; *m* 1988, Sally Deakin; one *s* one *d*. *Educ:* Univ. of Hull (BA Hons). FRAeS 1998. With British Aerospace, then BAE Systems, 1981–2000 (Gp Man. Dir, Customer Solutions and Support, 1998–2000); Chief Executive Officer: W. S. Atkins plc, 2001–02; AirTanker Ltd, 2002–05. Non-exec. Dir, Chloride Gp Plc, 2002–. *Recreations:* family, football. *Address:* (office) 111 The Strand, WC2R 0AG.

SOUTHWELL, Ven. Roy; Archdeacon of Northolt, 1970–80, Archdeacon Emeritus, since 1980; Warden of the Community of All Hallows, Ditchingham, Norfolk, 1983–89; *b* 3 Dec. 1914; *s* of William Thomas and Lilian Southwell; *m* 1948, Nancy Elizabeth Lindsay Sharp; two *d*. *Educ:* Sudbury Grammar Sch.; King's Coll., London (AKC 1942). Curate: St Michael's, Wigan, 1942–44; St John the Divine, Kennington, 1944–48; Vicar of Ixworth, 1948–51; Vicar of St John's, Bury St Edmunds, 1951–56; Rector of Bucklesham with Brightwell and Foxhall, 1956–59; Asst Director of Religious Education, Diocese of St Edmundsbury and Ipswich, 1956–58, Director, 1959–67. Hon. Canon of St Edmundsbury, 1959–68; Vicar of Hendon, 1968–71. *Recreations:* reading, singing, watching TV. *Address:* 397 Sprowston Road, Norwich NR3 4HY. *T:* (01603) 405977.

SOUTHWOOD, Prof. David John, PhD; Director of Science and Robotic Exploration, European Space Agency, since 2008; Professor of Physics, Imperial College, London University, since 1986; *b* 30 June 1945; *s* of H. H. J. Southwood and H. M. Southwood; *m* 1967, Susan Elizabeth Fricker; two *s* one *d*. *Educ:* Torquay Boys' Grammar Sch.; Queen Mary Coll., London (BA); Imperial Coll., London (PhD, DIC). UCLA 1970; Lectr, 1971–86, Head of Physics Dept, 1994–97, Imperial Coll., London; on leave of absence as Hd, Earth Observation Strategy, ESA, Paris, 1997–2000; Dir of Sci., ESA, 2001–08. Vis. Prof., 1976, Regents' Prof., 2000–, UCLA. Mem., SERC Boards, 1989–94; Chairman: Commn D, COSPAR, 1986–92; Space Sci. Adv. Cttee, ESA, 1990–93; Sci. Prog. Cttee, ESA, 1993–96; Sci. Adv. Cttee, Internat. Space Sci. Inst., 1995–2001. Fellow, Amer. Geophys. Union (James B. Macelwane Award, 1981); Mem., Internat. Acad. of Astronautics, 1999. *Publications:* numerous contribs in solar terrestrial physics and planetary science to learned jls. *Recreations:* reading, theatre, cinema. *Address:* European Space Agency, 8–10 rue Mario-Nikis, 75738 cedex 15 Paris, France. *T:* (1) 53697107, *Fax:* (1) 53697236; *e-mail:* david.southwood@esa.int.

SOUTHWOOD, Sara Michel; *see* Selwood, S. M.

SOUTHWORTH, Helen Mary; MP (Lab) Warrington South, since 1997; *b* 13 Nov. 1956; *m* Edmund Southworth; one *s*. *Educ:* Larkhill Convent Sch., Preston; Univ. of Lancaster (BA Hons). Director: Age Concern, St Helens; Grosvenor Housing Assoc.; St Helens and Knowsley HA. Mem. (Lab) St Helens MBC, 1994–98 (Chm., Leisure Cttee, 1994–96). Contested (Lab) Wirral South, 1992. *Address:* House of Commons, SW1A 0AA.

SOUTHWORTH, Jean May; QC 1973; a Recorder of the Crown Court, 1972–93; *b* 20 April 1926; *o c* of late Edgar and Jane Southworth, Clitheroe. *Educ:* Queen Ethelburga's Sch., Harrogate; St Anne's Coll., Oxford (MA; Hon. Fellow, 2004). Served in WRNS, 1944–45. Called to Bar, Gray's Inn, 1954; Bencher, 1980. Standing Counsel to Dept of Trade and Industry for Central Criminal Court and Inner London Sessions, 1969–73. Fellow, Woodard Corporation (Northern Div.), 1974–90. *Recreations:* music, travel. *Address:* 21 Caroline Place, W2 4AN.

SOWARD, Prof. Andrew Michael, FRS 1991; Professor of Applied Mathematics, University of Exeter, since 1996; *b* 20 Oct. 1943; *s* of Arthur Layton Soward and Sybil Jessica Lilian Soward (*née* Greathurst); *m* 1968, Elaine Celia McCaully; one *s* one *d*. *Educ:* St Edward's Sch., Oxford; Queen's College, Cambridge (BA 1st cl. Hons Maths 1965; PhD 1969; ScD 1984). University of Newcastle upon Tyne: Lectr, 1971, Reader, 1981–86, Dept of Maths and Stats; Head, Div. of Applied Maths, 1985–95; Prof. of Fluid Dynamics, 1986–95. Visiting appointments: Courant Inst. of Mathematical Scis, NY, 1969–70; CIRES, Boulder, Colorado, 1970–71; IGPP, UCLA, 1977–78. Editor, Jl of Geophysical and Astrophysical Fluid Dynamics, 1991–. *Publications:* contribs to learned jls. *Recreations:* rock-climbing, running. *Address:* 2 Springfield, Western Road, Crediton, Devon EX17 3NG.

SOWDEN, Susan, (Mrs Philip Sowden); education consultant, since 2006; Headmistress, St Mary's School, Wantage, 1994–2006; *b* 10 June 1951; *d* of Albert Henry Letley and Ethel May Letley; *m* 1st, 1973, Michael Geoffrey Bodinham (marr. diss. 1990); one *s* two *d*; 2nd, 2000, Philip Sowden. *Educ:* Clarendon House Grammar Sch. for Girls, Ramsgate; King's Coll., London (BSc 2nd Cl. Hons; AKC; PGCE); Open Univ. (Adv. Dip Ed Man). Geography teacher, Peers Upper Comprehensive, Oxford, 1973–77 and 1984–85; Headington School, Oxford: Geog. teacher, 1985–87; Head of Dept, 1987; Housemistress, 1988; Head of Lower Sixth, 1991–93; Dep. Head, 1993–94. Sen. examng posts with EMREB, Southern Examng Gp and Northern Exams and Assessment Bd. Lay Minister (formerly Reader), Church of England, 1993–. *Publications:* articles in Britain and the British (pubd in Poland). *Recreations:* walking, reading, theatre, canoeing, camping, music.

SOWDEN, Terence Cubitt; QC 1989; Relief Stipendiary Magistrate for Jersey, 2000–04; HM's Solicitor General for Jersey, 1986–93; *b* 30 July 1929; *s* of George Henry Sowden, RNR, Master Mariner and Margaret Duncan Cubitt; *m* 1955, Doreen Mary Lucas (*d* 1983); one *s* two *d*; *m* 1999, Jacqueline Carol Ince. *Educ:* Victoria Coll. Prep. Sch.; Victoria Coll.; Hendon Tech. Coll., London. Called to the Bar, Middle Temple, 1951; Advocate, Royal Court of Jersey, 1951; in private practice in Jersey, 1951–85; Deputy for St Helier, States of Jersey, 1960–63; Sen. Partner, Crill Cubitt Sowden & Tomes, Advocates and Solicitors, 1962–83. Juge d'Instruction, 1994–99. Indep. Mem., Temporary Release Assessment Panel, HM Prison, La Moye, Jersey, 2006–. *Publication:* (with Paul Matthews) The Jersey Law of Trusts, 1988, 3rd edn 1994. *Recreations:* writing, walking the low tide.

SOWREY, Air Marshal Sir Frederick (Beresford), KCB 1978 (CB 1968); CBE 1965; AFC 1954; *b* 14 Sept. 1922; *s* of late Group Captain Frederick Sowrey, DSO, MC, AFC; *m* 1946, Anne Margaret, *d* of late Captain C. T. A. Bunbury, OBE, RN; one *s* one *d*. *Educ:* Charterhouse. Joined RAF 1940; flying training in Canada, 1941; Fighter-reconnaissance Squadron, European theatre, 1942–44; Flying Instructors Sch., 1944; trng Airborne Forces (despatches), 1945; No 615 (Co. of Surrey) Squadron, RAuxAF ('Winston Churchill's Own'), 1946–48; Fighter Gunnery Sch., 1949–50, comdg 615 Sqdn, 1951–54; RAF Staff Coll., Bracknell, 1954; Chiefs of Staff Secretariat, 1955–58; comdg No 46 Sqdn, 1958–60; Personal Staff Officer to CAS, 1960–62; comdg RAF Abingdon, 1962–64; IDC 1965; SASO, Middle East Comd (Aden), 1966–67; Comdr, RAF Aden, Nov. 1967; Dir Defence Policy, MoD, 1968–70; SASO, RAF Trng Comd, 1970–72; Comdt, Nat. Defence Coll., 1972–75; Dir-Gen. RAF Training, 1975–77; UK Representative, Permanent Military Deputies Group CENTO, 1977–79. Research Fellow, IISS, 1980–81. Pres., Sussex Indust. Archaeology Soc., 1993– (Chm., 1981–93); Mem., Bd of Conservators, Ashdown Forest, 1984–99; Vice-Pres., Victory Services Assoc., 1994– (Pres., 1989–93; Chm., 1985–89); Life Vice-Pres., RAF Historical Soc., 1996 (Founder Chm., 1986–96); Trustee, Guild of Aviation Artists, 1990–2007. *Publications:* contributed to: D-Day Encyclopaedia, 1994; Oxford Dictionary of National Biography, 2004; articles and book reviews in defence jls. *Recreations:* watching motor-racing (world class records in a supercharged Cooper, 1956), veteran cars (London/Brighton run annually), mechanical devices of any kind and age, working in the Sussex High Weald. *Club:* Royal Air Force.

SOYINKA, Wole; Nigerian writer; *b* 13 July 1934; *s* of Ayo and Eniola Soyinka; *m*; *c*. *Educ:* Univ. of Ibadan, Nigeria; Univ. of Leeds. Res. Fellow in Drama, Univ. of Ibadan, 1960–61; Lectr in English, Univ. of Ife, 1962–63; Sen. Lectr in English, Univ. of Lagos, 1965–67; political prisoner, 1967–69; Artistic Dir and Head of Dept of Theatre Arts, Univ. of Ibadan, 1969–72; Res. Prof. in Dramatic Literature, 1972, Prof. of Comparative Literature, 1976–85, Emeritus Prof., 2004–, Univ. of Ife (later Obafemi Awolowo Univ., Iwe-Ife); Goldwin Smith Prof. of Africana Studies and Theatre, Cornell Univ., 1988–92; Elias Ghanen Chair of Creative Writing, Univ. of Nevada, until 2005. Fellow: Churchill Coll., Cambridge, 1973–74; Dubois Inst., Harvard Univ., 2004–. Reith Lectr, BBC Radio 4, 2004. Hon. DLitt: Leeds, 1973; Yale, 1981; Paul Valéry, 1984; Morehouse Coll., 1988. Nobel Prize for Literature, 1986; AGIP/Enrico Mattei Award for the Humanities, 1986. *Publications: plays:* The Lion and the Jewel, 1959; The Swamp Dwellers, 1959; A Dance of the Forests, 1960; The Trials of Brother Jero, 1961; The Strong Breed, 1962; The Road, 1964; Kongi's Harvest, 1965; Madmen and Specialists, 1971; Before the Blackout, 1971; Jero's Metamorphosis, 1973; Camwood on the Leaves, 1973; The Bacchae of Euripides, 1974; Death and the King's Horsemen, 1975; Opera Wonyosi,

1978; A Play of Giants, 1984; From Zia with Love, 1992; A Scourge of Hyacinths, 1992; The Beatification of Area Boy, 1995; *novels:* The Interpreters, 1964; The Forest of a Thousand Daemons (trans.), Season of Anomy, 1973; *poetry:* Idanre and other poems, 1967; A Shuttle in the Crypt, 1972; (ed) Poems of Black Africa, 1975; Ogun Abibman, 1977; Mandela's Earth and other Poems, 1989; Selected Poems, 2002; Samarkand And Other Markets I Have Known, 2002; *non-fiction:* The Man Died (prison memoirs), 1972; Myth, Literature and the African World (lectures), 1972; Ake, the Years of Childhood (autobiog.), 1982; Art, Dialogue and Outrage (essays), 1988; Isara: a voyage around "Essay" (biog.), 1989; Ibadan (memoir), 1995; The Open Sore of a Continent, 1996; The Burden of Memory, the Muse of Forgiveness (essays), 1999; Climate of Fear: the quest for dignity in a dehumanized world (essays), 2005; You Must Set Forth At Dawn (memoirs), 2006.

SPACEY, Kevin; actor, director and producer; Artistic Director, Old Vic, since 2004 (Trustee, since 2000); *b* Kevin Spacey Fowler, 26 July 1959; *s* of Thomas and Kathleen Fowler. *Educ:* Chatsworth High Sch., LA; Juilliard Drama Sch., NY. Cameron Mackintosh Vis. Prof. of Contemporary Th., St Catherine's Coll., Oxford, 2008–09. *Theatre includes:* Ghosts, NY, 1982; Hurlyburly, 1985; Long Day's Journey into Night, 1986; National Anthems, Long Wharf Th., New Haven, CT, 1988, Old Vic, 2005; Lost in Yonkers, NY (Tony Award), 1991; The Iceman Cometh, Almeida, 1998, NY 1999; The Philadelphia Story, Richard II (Critics' Circle Award), Old Vic, 2005; A Moon for the Misbegotten, Old Vic, 2006, NY 2007; Speed-the-Plow, Old Vic, 2008. *Television includes:* Wiseguy (series), 1988; The Murder of Mary Phagan, 1988; Fall from Grace, 1990; When You Remember Me, 1990; Darrow, 1991. *Films include:* Working Girl, 1988; See No Evil, Hear No Evil, Dad, 1989; A Show of Force, Henry and June, 1990; Glengarry Glen Ross, Consenting Adults, 1992; The Ref, Swimming with Sharks (also co-prod.), 1994; Outbreak, The Usual Suspects (Acad. Award for Best Supporting Actor), Seven, 1995; Looking for Richard, A Time to Kill, 1996; L. A. Confidential, Midnight in the Garden of Good and Evil, 1997; The Negotiator, 1998; The Big Kahuna (also prod.), 1999; American Beauty (Academy, BAFTA and London Film Critics' Circle Awards for Best Actor), Hurlyburly, Ordinary Decent Criminal, 2000; Pay it Forward, 2001; K-PAX, The Shipping News, 2002; The Life of David Gale, 2003; Beyond the Sea (also dir and prod.), 2004; The United States of Leland (also prod.), 2005; Superman, 2006; Fred Claus, 2007; 21, 2008; Dir, Albino Alligator, 1996; Producer: Interstate 84, 2000; Uncle Frank, 2002; Triggerstreet.com, 2004. *Address:* Old Vic, The Cut, Waterloo, SE1 8NB; c/o William Morris Agency, 151 South El Camino Drive, Beverly Hills, CA 90212, USA.

SPACIE, Maj.-Gen. Keith, CB 1987; OBE 1974; Chairman, Sudbury Consultants Ltd, 1989–2000; *b* 21 June 1935; *s* of Frederick and Kathleen Spacie; *m* 1961, Valerie Rich (*d* 2008); one *s.* Commnd Royal Lincolns, 1955; transf. Parachute Regt, 1959; Staff Coll., Camberley, 1966; DAA&QMG 16 Parachute Bde, 1968–70; Staff, RMA, Sandhurst, 1970–72; Comd, 3rd Bn Parachute Regt, 1973–75; SHAPE, 1976–78; Comdr 7 Field Force, 1979–81; RCDS, 1982; Mil. Comr and Comdr, British Forces Falkland Is, 1983–84; Dir of Army Training, 1984–87. *Recreations:* cross-country running, athletics, walking, battlefield touring. *Clubs:* Army and Navy; Thames Hare and Hounds.

SPACKMAN, Christopher John, FCIOB; Chairman, Bovis Construction Ltd, 1989–96 (Managing Director, 1985–93); Director, Bovis Ltd, 1997–99; *b* 21 May 1934; *s* of Eric Dickens Spackman, MB and Kathleen (*née* Crisp); *m* 1967, Marilyn Ann Rowland; one *s* two *d.* *Educ:* Sherborne Sch., Dorset; Brixton Sch. of Building (HND Building 1959); London Business Sch. FCIOB 1980. Commnd RA, 1952–54. Joined Bovis as trainee, 1955; Asst Contract Manager, then Contract Manager, 1959–64; Regl Dir, 1964; i/c Bovis Bristol Office, 1964–69; Harrow Office, 1969–73; Dir, Bovis Construction Ltd, 1973–99; Asst Man. Dir, 1983–85; Man. Dir, Bovis Europe, 1994–96; Vice-Chm., Bovis Construction Gp, 1996–97; retired 2002. Chm., Deregulation Task Force for Construction, 1993. FRSA 1996. *Recreations:* squash, tennis. *Clubs:* Beaconsfield Squash; Knotty Green Cricket.

SPACKMAN, Brig. John William Charles, PhD; Director, LOI Associates BV, since 2000; *b* 12 May 1932; *s* of Lt-Col Robert Thomas Spackman, MBE and Ann (*née* Rees); *m* 1955, Jeanette Vera; two *s* one *d.* *Educ:* Cyfarthfa Castle Grammar School, Merthyr Tydfil; Wellington Grammar School; RMCS. BSc 1st cl. Hons London (external) 1960, PhD 1964; MSc (Management Sci.) UMIST, 1968. Nat. Service, 1950–52; Regular Commission, RAOC, 1952; Regtl appts, 1952–72; Project Wavell, 1969–72; RARDE, 1972–75; Senior Mil. Officer, Chem. Defence and Microbiological Defence Estab., Porton Down, 1975–78; Branch Chief, Inf. Systems Div., SHAPE, 1978–80; Dir, Supply Computer Services, 1980–83; retired from Army, 1983 (Brig.); Under Sec., and Dir, Social Security Operational Strategy, DHSS, 1983–87; Director: Computing and Information Services, BT, 1987–90; Europ. Telecommunications Informatics Services, 1991–93; Management Systems Unit, Govt of Malta, 1993–96; KFKI (CSC), Hungary, 1993–2004; Logan Orviss Internat., 1993; Intelligent Networks Ltd, 1997–98; KC3.net Ltd, 2007. FBCS 1987 (MBCS 1970); CEng 1990; MCMI (MBIM 1970); MInstD 1983. Liveryman, Information Technologists' Co., 1989 (Mem., 1987). Freeman, City of London, 1987. *Recreations:* gardening, hill walking, opera. *Address:* Perrymead, Dilwyn, Hereford HR4 8HN. *T:* (01544) 319085.

SPACKMAN, Michael John; special consultant, NERA Economic Consulting (formerly National Economic Research Associates), since 2007 (special adviser, 1996–2007); Visiting Fellow, Centre for Analysis of Risk and Regulation, London School of Economics, since 2001; *b* 8 Oct. 1936; *s* of late Geoffrey Spackman and Audrey (*née* Morecombe); *m* 1965, Judith Ann Leathem; two *s* two *d.* *Educ:* Malvern Coll.; Clare Coll., Cambridge (MA); Queen Mary Coll., London (MScEcon). Served RA (2nd Lieut), 1955–57; Physicist, UKAEA, Capenhurst, 1960–69; Sen. Physicist/Engr, Nuclear Power Gp Ltd, 1969–71; PSO, then Economic Advr, Dept of Energy, 1971–77; Economic Advr, HM Treasury, 1977–79; Dir of Econs and Accountancy, CS Coll., 1979–80; Hd of Public Services Econs Div., HM Treasury, 1980–85; Under Sec., 1985; Hd of Public Expenditure Econs Gp, HM Treasury, 1985–91 and 1993–95; Chief Economic Advr, Dept of Transport, 1991–93. Gwilym Gibbon Res. Fellow, Nuffield Coll., Oxford, 1995–96. *Recreation:* climbing. *Address:* 44 Gibson Square, Islington, N1 0RA. *T:* (020) 7359 1053.

SPAFFORD, Rev. Christopher Garnett Howsin; Provost and Vicar of Newcastle, 1976–89, retired; *b* 10 Sept. 1924; *s* of late Rev. Canon Douglas Norman Spafford and Frances Alison Spafford; *m* 1953, Stephanie Peel; three *s.* *Educ:* Marlborough Coll.; St John's Coll., Oxford (MA 2nd Cl. Hons Modern History); Wells Theological Coll. Curate of Brighouse, 1950–53; Curate of Huddersfield Parish Church, 1953–55; Vicar of Hebden Bridge, 1955–61; Rector of Thornhill, Dewsbury, 1961–69; Vicar of St Chad's, Shrewsbury, 1969–76. *Recreations:* reading, gardening. *Address:* Low Moor, Elm Close, Leominster, Herefordshire HR6 8JX. *T:* (01568) 614395.

SPALDING, Alistair William; Chief Executive and Artistic Director, Sadler's Wells, since 2004 (Director of Programming, 2000–04); *b* 25 Aug. 1957; *s* of Robert and Pauline Spalding; *m* 2000, Katy McPhee; one *s.* *Educ:* Hatfield Poly. (BA Hons Combined Studies

in Humanities); Edge Hill Coll. (PGCE). Arts Programmer, Hawth Th., Crawley, 1988–94; Hd of Dance and Performance, South Bank Centre, London, 1994–2000. Chm., Dance UK, 2004–. Chevalier des Arts et des Lettres (France), 2005. *Recreations:* swimming, hill walking. *Address:* e-mail: artisticdirector@sadlerswells.com. *Club:* 2 Brydges Place.

SPALDING, Prof. (Dudley) Brian, MA, ScD; FRS 1983; FREng, FIMechE, FInstF; Professor of Heat Transfer, London University, 1958–88, now Emeritus, and Head, Computational Fluid Dynamics Unit, Imperial College of Science, Technology and Medicine, 1981–88; Managing Director, Concentration, Heat & Momentum Ltd, since 1975; *b* New Malden, Surrey, 9 Jan. 1923; *s* of H. A. Spalding; *m* 1st, Eda Ilse-Lotte (*née* Goericke); two *s* two *d*; 2nd, Colleen (*née* King); two *s.* *Educ:* King's College Sch., Wimbledon; The Queen's Coll., Oxford (BA 1944); Pembroke Coll., Cambridge (MA 1948; PhD 1951). Bataafsche Petroleum Matschapij, 1944–45; Ministry of Supply, 1945–47; National Physical Laboratory, 1947–48; ICI Research Fellow at Cambridge Univ., 1948–50; Cambridge University Demonstrator in Engineering, 1950–54; Reader in Applied Heat, Imperial College of Science and Technology, 1954–58. Man. Dir, Combustion, Heat and Mass Transfer Ltd, 1970–75; Chm., CHAM of N America Inc., 1977–91. FREng (FEng 1989). Member: Russian Acad. of Scis, 1994; Ukrainian Nat. Acad. of Scis, 1994. *Publications:* Some Fundamentals of Combustion, 1955; (with E. H. Cole) Engineering Thermodynamics, 1958; Convective Mass Transfer, 1963; (with S. V. Patankar) Heat and Mass Transfer in Boundary Layers, 1967, rev. edn 1970; (co-author) Heat and Mass Transfer in Recirculating Flows, 1969; (with B. E. Launder) Mathematical Models of Turbulence, 1972; GENMIX: a general computer program for two-dimensional parabolic phenomena, 1978; Combustion and Mass Transfer, 1979; (jtly) Heat Exchanger Design Handbook, 1982; Numerical Prediction of Flow, Heat Transfer, Turbulence and Combustion (selected works), 1983; numerous scientific papers. *Recreations:* music, poetry. *Address:* Concentration, Heat & Momentum Ltd, Bakery House, 40 High Street, Wimbledon, SW19 5AU.

SPALDING, Prof. Frances, CBE 2005; PhD; art historian, biographer and critic; Professor of Art History, Newcastle University, since 2007; *b* 16 July 1950; *d* of Hedley Stinston Crabtree and Margaret (*née* Holiday); *m* 1974, Julian Spalding, *qv* (marr. diss. 1991); one *s.* *Educ:* Farringtons Sch.; Univ. of Nottingham (BA Hons 1972); PhD CNAA 1988. Lectr in Art Hist., Sheffield City Poly., 1978–88; ind. scholar, 1989–99; Lectr in Art Hist., 2000–02, Reader in 20th Century British Art, 2002–07, Univ. of Newcastle upon Tyne. Res. co-ordinator, Writers-in-Prison Cttee, 1991–93; Mem. Exec. Cttee, English Centre of Internat. PEN, 1997–2004 (Vice-Chm., 2000). Mem. Council, Charleston Trust, 1990–; Editor, Charleston Mag., 1992–2000. Ashby Lectr, 1997, Vis. Fellow, 1998, Clare Hall, Cambridge; Assoc. Vis. Mem., Darwin Coll., Cambridge, 2002; Paul Mellon Sen. Res. Fellow and Vis. Res. Fellow, Newnham Coll. Cambridge, 2005–06. Trustee, Hampstead Church Music Trust, 1999–. FRSL 1984; Hon. FRCA 1998. *Publications:* Magnificent Dreams: Burne-Jones and the late Victorians, 1978; Whistler, 1979, rev. edn 1994; Roger Fry: art and life, 1980, rev. edn 1999; Vanessa Bell, 1983; British Art since 1900, 1986; Stevie Smith: a critical biography, 1988, rev. edn 2002; A Dictionary of 20th Century British Painters and Sculptors, 1990; Paper Darts: selected letters of Virginia Woolf, 1991; Dance Till the Stars Come Down: a biography of John Minton, 1991, rev. edn 2005; Duncan Grant, 1997; The Tate: a history, 1998; The Bloomsbury Group, 1998, rev. edn 2005; Gwen Raverat: friends, family and affections, 2001; Ravilious in Public, 2003; (with David Fraser Jenkins) John Piper in the 1930s: abstraction on the beach, 2003; contrib. TLS, Sunday Times, Burlington Mag., etc. *Recreation:* music. *Address:* c/o Coleridge & Rogers, 20 Powis Mews, W11 1JN. *T:* (020) 7221 3717; The Flat, 70 Gloucester Crescent, NW1 7EG. *Club:* PEN.

SPALDING, John Oliver, CBE 1988; Chief Executive and Director, Halifax Building Society, 1982–88; *b* 4 Aug. 1924; *m* 1952, Mary Whitworth Hull; one *d* one *s.* *Educ:* William Hulme's Grammar School, Manchester; Jesus College, Cambridge (MA). Served War: Capt. RA, attached IA; served India, Burma, Singapore, Java. Admitted a Solicitor, 1952; service with Manchester Corporation and Hampshire CC, 1952–62; Halifax Building Society, 1962–88. Chm., NHBC, 1988–92. Chm., Future Constitution and Powers of Bldg Socs Working Party (Spalding Cttee), 1981–83; Mem., Farrand Cttee investigating Conveyancing, 1984. *Recreations:* boats and bird-watching. *Address:* Pembroke, 22 Thamesfield Court, Henley-on-Thames, Oxfordshire RG9 2LX.

SPALDING, Julian, FMA; writer and broadcaster; Master, Guild of St George (John Ruskin's Guild), 1996–2005 (Director, 1983–2005; Companion, 1978); *b* 15 June 1947; *s* of Eric Peter Spalding and Margaret Grace Savager; *m* 1st, 1974, Frances (*née* Crabtree) (*see* F. Spalding) (marr. diss. 1991); one *s*; 2nd, 1991, Gillian (*née* Tait), conservation advisor. *Educ:* Chislehurst and Sidcup Grammar Sch. for Boys; Univ. of Nottingham (BA Hons Fine Art). Dip. Museums Assoc., 1973; FMA 1983. Art Assistant: Leicester Museum and Art Gall., 1970; Durham Light Infantry Mus. and Arts Centre, 1971; Sheffield City Art Galleries: Keeper, Mappin Art Gall., 1972–76; Dep. Dir, 1976–82; Dir of Arts, Sheffield City Council, 1982–85; Dir, Manchester City Art Galls, 1985–89; Acting Dir, Nat. Mus. of Labour History, 1987–88; Dir, Glasgow Museums and Art Galls, 1989–98. Res. Fellow, Nat. Mus. of Denmark, Copenhagen, 1999–2000. Art Panel Mem., Arts Council of GB, 1978–82 (Chm., Exhibns Sub-Cttee, 1981–82 and 1986–); Founder: Art Galleries Assoc., 1976 (Mem. Cttee, 1976–89, Chm., 1987–89); Campaign for Drawing, 2000. Member: Crafts Council, 1986–90 (Member: Projects and Orgn Cttee, 1985–87; Purchasing Cttee, 1986–90; Exhibns Cttee, 1986–90); British Council, 1987–96 (Mem., Fine Arts Adv. Cttee, 1987–96). Dir, Niki de Saint Phalle Foundn, 1994. BBC broadcaster (talks and reviews); Third Ear, BBC Radio Three, 1988. *Publications:* L. S. Lowry, 1979; Three Little Books on Painting, 1984; Is There Life in Museums?, 1990; Glasgow Gallery of Modern Art, 1996; The Poetic Museum: reviving historic collections, 2002; The Eclipse of Art: tackling the crisis in art today, 2003; The Art of Wonder: a history of seeing, 2005 (Sir Banister Fletcher Award, Authors' Club, 2006); pamphlets and exhibition catalogues, including: Modern British Painting 1900–1960, 1975; Fragments against Ruin, 1981; Francis Davison, 1983; George Fullard Drawings, 1984; The Forgotten Fifties, 1984; Modern Art in Manchester, 1986; The Art of Watercolour, 1987; L. S. Lowry, 1987; Ken Currie, 1988; Funfair or Church?, RSA, 1989; Glasgow's Great British Art Exhibition, 1990; Clouds and Tigers: the art of Hock Aun Teh, 1996; contrib. Art Newspaper, Museums Jl. *Recreations:* cycling, gardening. *Address:* 90 Grassmarket, Edinburgh EH1 2JR; e-mail: Julian.Spalding@ukgateway.net.

SPALL, Timothy Leonard, OBE 2000; actor, since 1978; *b* 27 Feb. 1957; *s* of Joseph and Sylvia Spall; *m* 1981, Shane Baker; one *s* two *d.* *Educ:* Battersea Co. Comprehensive Sch.; Kingsway and Princeton Coll.; RADA. Birmingham Rep., 1978–79; *theatre includes:* Royal Shakespeare Co., 1978–80: Merry Wives of Windsor; Nicholas Nickleby; The Three Sisters; National Theatre: Saint Joan, 1985; Mandragola, 1985; Le Bourgeois Gentilhomme, 1993; A Midsummer Night's Dream, 1994; This is a Chair, Royal Court, 1996; *television includes:* The Brylcream Boys, 1978; Auf Weidersehen Pet, 4 series, 1983–84, 2002–04; Christmas Special, 2004; Roots, 1993; Frank Stubbs Promotes, 1994–95; Outside Edge, 1994–96; Neville's Island, 1997; Our Mutual Friend, 1997;

Shooting the Past, 1999; The Thing About Vince, 2000; Vacuuming Completely Nude in Paradise, 2001; Perfect Strangers, 2001; Bodily Harm, 2002; Cherished, 2005; Mr Harvey Lights a Candle, 2005; The Street, 2006, 2007; Mysterious Creatures, 2006; A Room with a View, 2007; Oliver Twist, 2007; Gunrush, 2008; *films* include: Quadrophenia, 1978; Gothic, 1986; The Sheltering Sky, 1989; Life is Sweet, 1990; Secrets and Lies, 1996; Hamlet, 1996; The Wisdom of Crocodiles, 1998; Still Crazy, 1998; Topsy Turvy, 1999; Clandestine Marriage, 1999; Love's Labours Lost, 2000; Vatel, 2000; Lucky Break, 2001; Intimacy, 2001; Rock Star, 2002; Vanilla Sky, 2002; All or Nothing, 2002; Nicholas Nickleby, 2003; My House in Umbria, 2003; Gettin' Square, 2003; The Last Samurai, 2003; Harry Potter and the Prisoner of Azkaban, 2004; Lemony Snicket's A Series of Unfortunate Events, 2004; Harry Potter and the Goblet of Fire, 2005; Pierrepoint, 2006; Enchanted, 2007; Death Defying Acts, 2007; Sweeney Todd: The Demon Barber of Fleet Street, 2008. Patron: Horniman Mus., 1999–; ChildHope, 2002–. FRSA 2000. *Recreations:* boating, strolling. *Address:* c/o Markham & Froggatt, 4 Windmill Street, W1P 1HF. *T:* (020) 7636 4412. *Club:* Colony.

SPALTON, David John, FRCS, FRCP, FRCOphth; Consultant Ophthalmic Surgeon, St Thomas' Hospital, London, since 1983; *b* 2 March 1947; *s* of John and Babs Spalton; *m* 1979, Catherine Bompas; three *s*. *Educ:* Buxton Coll., Buxton, Derbys; Westminster Med. Sch., London (MB BS 1970). FRCS 1976; FRCOphth 1989; FRCP 1992. RSO, Moorfields Eye Hosp., 1973–77; Consultant Ophthalmic Surgeon, Charing Cross Hosp., 1980–83. Hon. Consultant Ophthalmic Surgeon: Royal Hosp., Chelsea, 1989–; King Edward VII's Hosp. (Sister Agnes), London, 1998–; Hon. Civilian Advr in Ophthalmology, Metropolitan Police, 1999–. *Publications:* (ed jtly) Atlas of Clinical Ophthalmology, 1985 (Best Med. Textbook of Year, Abbott Prize for Med. Writing), 3rd edn 2004 (BMA prize for Best Med. Textbook of Year); over 140 peer-reviewed scientific papers. *Recreations:* my family and other animals, fly fishing, gardening, ophthalmology. *Address:* Consulting Rooms, King Edward VII Hospital, 37A Devonshire Street, W1G 6QA. *T:* (020) 7935 6174; *e-mail:* spalton@eyepractice.fsnet.co.uk. *Club:* Garrick.

SPALVINS, Janis Gunars, (John); Chairman: Galufo Pty Ltd, since 1991; Westall Pty Ltd, since 1981; *b* 26 May 1936; *s* of Peter Spalvins and Hilda Blumentals; *m* 1961, Cecily Westall Rymill (*d* 1991); two *s*. *Educ:* Concordia College, Adelaide; Univ. of Adelaide (BEc). FCIS 1961; FASA 1967. Camelec Group of Cos, 1955–73 (Group Sec./Dir, subsidiary cos); Adelaide Steamship Co.: Asst Gen. Manager, 1973; Gen. Manager, 1977; Chief Gen. Manager and Dir, 1979; Man. Dir, 1981–91. Dir and Chief Exec., David Jones Ltd, 1980–91. Mem., Business Council of Australia, 1986–91. FAIM; MInstD Australia, 1981. *Recreations:* snow ski-ing, water ski-ing, tennis, sailing. *Address:* Galufo Pty, 2 Brookside Road, Springfield, SA 5062, Australia. *T:* (8) 83792965. *Clubs:* Cruising Yacht Club of SA (Adelaide); Mt Osmond Golf.

SPANIER, Suzy Peta, (Mrs D. G. Spanier); *see* Menkes, S. P.

SPANKIE, (Hugh) Oliver; HM Diplomatic Service, retired; *b* 11 Dec. 1936; *s* of late Col Hugh Vernon Spankie and Elizabeth Ursula (*née* Hills); *m* 1st, 1963, Anne Bridget Colville (marr. diss. 1981); one *s* one *d*; 2nd, 1988, Leena Marjatta Paloheimo. *Educ:* Tonbridge Sch. RM Officer, 1955–66; HM Diplomatic Service, 1967–86: Helsinki, 1968–71; FCO, 1971–74; Helsinki, 1974–77; FCO and CSD, 1977–81; Counsellor, Copenhagen, 1981–85. *Address:* c/o Barclays Bank plc, 1–3 Broad Street, Hereford HR4 8BH.

SPARKE, Andrew Philip; Chief Executive, Dudley Metropolitan Borough Council, since 1999; *b* 22 July 1956; *s* of Philip Aubrey Sparke and Sheila Myrtle Sparke; *m* 1980, Laura Emma Simmons; one *s* one *d*; partner, Elizabeth Mary Bennett; one *s* (and one *s* decd). *Educ:* Manchester Univ. (LLB Hons 1977). Technician and Surveying Asst, S Hams DC, 1974; admitted Solicitor, 1980. Articled Clerk, Derby CC, 1978–80; Printing Asst, BP, 1981; Solicitor, Kingston upon Hull CC, 1981–85; Asst Town Clerk, 1985–90, Dep. Dir of Corporate Services, 1990–94, Enfield LBC; Chief Exec., Lincoln CC, 1994–99; Clerk to W Midlands Police Authy, 1999–2005. *Publications:* The Compulsory Competitive Tendering Guide, 1993, rev. edn 1995; The Practical Guide to Externalising Local Authority Services, 1994; The Butterworths Best Value Manual, 1999. *Recreations:* record collecting, Chelsea FC. *Address:* (office) Council House, Priory Road, Dudley DY1 1HF. *T:* (01384) 815201; 4 Oakleigh Road, Old Swinford, Stourbridge DY8 2JX. *T:* (01384) 390401.

SPARKES, Andrew James, CMG 2007; HM Diplomatic Service; Ambassador, Kosovo, since 2008; *b* 4 July 1959; *s* of Rev. James Reginald Sparkes and Brenda Mary Sparkes (*née* Brown); *m* 1985, Jean Mary Meakin (marr. diss. 2003); one *s* one *d*. *Educ:* King Edward's Sch., Edgbaston; Manchester Grammar Sch.; Trinity Hall, Cambridge (MA Hons). MCIPD 1999. English teacher, Japan, 1981–82; joined HM Diplomatic Service, 1983; Second Sec., Political, Ankara, 1985–88; Hd, Political Section, Bangkok, 1992–95; Asst Dir, Personnel Mgt, FCO, 1996–97; on secondment as Dir, Service Exports, DTI, 1997–99; Dep. Hd of Mission, Jakarta, 1999–2001; Dep. High Comr, S Africa, 2001–04; Ambassador, Congo, 2004–07. *Recreations:* music, writing poetry, sailing, golf. *Address:* c/o Foreign and Commonwealth Office, King Charles Street, SW1A 2AH. *T:* (020) 7270 3000. *Clubs:* Oakland Park Golf (Chalfont St Giles); Tanjung Lesung Sailing (W Java, Indonesia).

SPARKES, Jonathan Winston; Chief Executive, Scope, since 2006; *b* Elston, Notts, 3 March 1968; *s* of late Donald and Mary Sparkes; partner, Annette Walker. *Educ:* Loughborough Univ. (BSc Hons Mgt Sci. 1990). FCIPD 2008. Gp HR Dir, Generics Gp, 1995–2002; Hd of HR, Cambridgeshire CC, 2002–04; HR Dir, Scope, 2004–06. *Publication:* (jtly) Leading HR, 2001. *Recreations:* reading, films, travel. *Address:* Scope, 6 Market Road, N7 9PW. *T:* (020) 7619 7371; *e-mail:* jon. sparkes@scope.org.uk.

SPARKS, Arthur Charles, BSc (Econ); Under-Secretary, Ministry of Agriculture, Fisheries and Food, 1959–74; *b* 1914; *s* of late Charles Herbert and Kate Dorothy Sparks; *m* 1939, Betty Joan (*d* 1978), *d* of late Harry Oswald and Lilian Mary Simmons; three *d*. *Educ:* Selhurst Grammar Sch.; London School of Economics. Clerk, Ministry of Agriculture and Fisheries, 1931; Administrative Grade, 1936; National Fire Service, 1942–44; Principal Private Secretary to Minister of Agriculture and Fisheries, 1946–47; Asst Secretary, Ministry of Agriculture and Fisheries, 1947–49 and 1951–59; Asst Secretary, Treasury, 1949–51. Chm., Internat. Wheat Council, 1968–69. *Recreations:* reading, walking.

SPARKS, Ian Leslie, OBE 1999; Chief Executive, The Children's Society, 1986–2002; *b* 26 May 1943; *s* of Ronald Leslie and Hilda Sparks; *m* 1967, Eunice Jean; one *d*. *Educ:* Whitefield Road Primary School, Liverpool; Holt High School, Liverpool; Brunel Univ. (MA); Kingston Univ. (DMS). AIB. Bank clerk, 1959–68; social worker, Liverpool, 1971–75; Asst Divl Dir, Barnardo's, 1975–80; Social Work Dir, The Children's Soc., 1981–86. Chairman: British Agencies for Adoption and Fostering, 1996–2000; End Child Poverty Campaign, 2002–04; Consultation Organiser, Internat. Anglican Family Network, 2002– (Chm., 1989–2001). Trustee: NCVCCO, 1995–2002; Frontier Youth Trust, 2000– (Chm., 2004–); Haven House Foundn, 2003– (Chm., 2007–); Tyn-y-Nant Christian Centre, 2004–; ChildAid to Russia and the Republics, 2007–. *Recreations:* piano playing, gardening in miniature. *Address:* 16 Frating Crescent, Woodford Green, Essex IG8 0DW.

SPARKS, Leslie Thomas, OBE 1997; RIBA; consultant architect/planner, specialising in conservation and urban design, since 1999; *b* 3 March 1943; *s* of Eric and Dorothy Leonie Sparks; *m* 1967, Yvonne Ann Sawyer; one *s* one *d*. *Educ:* Kingston Coll. of Art (DipArch); Central London Poly. (DipTP). RIBA 1971; MRTPI 1973. Severn Gorge Projects Manager, Telford Develt Corp., 1977–80; Dir, Envmtl Services, Bath CC, 1980–90; Dir, Planning and Architecture, Birmingham CC, 1991–99; Planning Inspector (pt-time), 1999–2002. Vis. Prof., UWE, 1998–2007. Chm., Expert Panel on Historic Buildings and Land, Heritage Lottery Fund, 1999–2001. Commissioner: CABE, 1999–2006; English Heritage, 2001–08 (Chm., Adv. Cttee, Historic Built Envmt, 2002–03); Chairman: English Heritage/CABE Urban Panel, 2003–; West Midlands Design Rev. Panel, 2007–. Hon. Life Mem., English Historic Towns Forum, 1992. Patron, Urban Design Gp, 1997–; Trustee, Birmingham Conservation Trust, 1999–. FRSA 1981. Hon. DDes UWE, 2000. *Recreations:* painting, music, Rugby, cricket, architecture, historic towns. *Address:* 114 Selly Park Road, Birmingham B29 7LH. *T:* (0121) 415 4547.

SPARKS, Prof. (Robert) Stephen (John), FRS 1988; Chaning Wills Professor of Geology, Bristol University, since 1990 (Professor of Geology, since 1989); Natural Environment Research Council Professor of Earth Sciences, 1998–2003; *b* 15 May 1949; *s* of Kenneth Grenfell Sparks and Ruth Joan Rugman; *m* 1971, Ann Elizabeth Talbot; two *s*. *Educ:* Imperial College London (BSc Hons 1971, PhD 1974). Postdoctoral fellowships, Lancaster Univ., 1974–76, Univ. of Rhode Island, 1976–78, studying physics of volcanic eruptions; Cambridge University: Demonstrator, 1978–82; Lectr in Geology, 1982–89; Fellow, Trinity Hall, 1981–89; Chief Scientist, Montserrat Volcano Observatory, 1997–99. Sherman Fairchild Dist. Scholar, Calif Inst. of Technology, 1987; Hon. Res. Fellow, Nat. History Mus., 2002–05. Studies of volcanic eruptions: Heimaey, Iceland, 1973; Etna, 1975; Soufrière, St Vincent, WI, 1979; Mount St Helens, 1980; Soufrière Hills, Montserrat, WI, 1996–. President: Geol Soc. of London, 1994–96; Internat. Assoc. of Volcanology and Chemistry of Earth's Interior, 1999–2003. Bakerian Lectr, Royal Soc., 2000. Fellow, Amer. Geophys. Union, 1999. Hon. DSc: Université Blaise Pascal, Clermont-Ferrand, 1999; Lancaster Univ., 2000; Inst. de Physique du Globe, Paris, 2005. Wager Prize for Volcanology, Internat. Assoc. of Volcanology and Chemistry of Earth's Interior, 1983; Bigsby Medal, 1985, Murchison Medal, 1998, Geol Soc.; Arthur L. Day Medal, Geol Soc. of America, 2000; Arthur Holmes Medal, European Geosciences Union, 2004; Thorarinsson Medal, IAVCEI, 2008. *Publications:* Volcanic Plumes, 1997; numerous papers on physics of volcanic eruptions, geology of young volcanoes and origins of volcanism. *Recreations:* music, cricket, travel, cooking. *Address:* Walnut Cottage, 19 Brinsea Road, Congresbury, Bristol BS49 5JF.

SPARROW, Bryan, CMG 1992; HM Diplomatic Service, retired; Ambassador to Croatia, 1992–94; *b* 8 June 1933; *m* 1958, Fiona Mary Mylechreest; one *s* one *d*. *Educ:* Hemel Hempstead Grammar Sch.; Pembroke Coll., Oxford (BA Hons; MA). Served Army, 1951–53. Belgrade, 1958–61; FO, 1961–64; Moscow, 1964–66; Tunis, 1967–68; Casablanca, 1968–70; FO, 1970–72; Kinshasa, 1972–76; Prague, 1976–78; Counsellor (Commercial), Belgrade, 1978–81; Ambassador, United Republic of Cameroon, 1981–84, and concurrently to Republic of Equatorial Guinea and Central African Republic, 1982–84; Canadian Nat. Defence Coll., 1984–85; Consul-General: Toronto, 1985–89; Lyon, 1989–92. *Recreations:* gardening, travel. *Address:* c/o HSBC, 15 Crescent Road, Windermere, Cumbria LA23 1EF.

SPARROW, Sir John, Kt 1984; Chairman, Horserace Betting Levy Board, 1991–98; *b* 4 June 1933; *s* of Richard A. and Winifred R. Sparrow; *m* 1967, Cynthia Whitehouse. *Educ:* Coldfall Primary Sch.; Stationers' Company's School; London School of Economics (BSc Econ 1954; Hon. Fellow, 1994). FCA 1957–97. With Rawlinson & Hunter, Chartered Accountants, 1954–59; Ford Motor Co. Ltd, 1960; AEI-Hotpoint Ltd, 1960–63; United Leasing Corporation, 1963–64; Morgan Grenfell Group (formerly Morgan Grenfell & Co.), 1964–88; Dir, Morgan Grenfell Gp (formerly Morgan Grenfell Hldgs), 1971–88; Chairman: Morgan Grenfell Asset Management, 1985–88; Morgan Grenfell Laurie Hldgs, 1985–88. National & Provincial Building Society: Mem., London Adv. Bd, 1986–89; Dir, 1989–96; Dep. Chm., 1994–96; Chm., Universities Superannuation Scheme Ltd, 1988–96. Chm., Mather & Platt, 1979–81; Director: Federated Chemicals, 1969–78 (Chm., 1974–78); Harris Lebus, 1973–79; United Gas Industries, 1974–82 (Dep. Chm., 1981–82); Coalite Group plc, 1974–82, 1984–89; Gas and Oil Acreage, 1975–78; Tioxide Gp, 1977–78; Peterborough Develt Corp., 1981–88; Short Brothers plc, 1984–89 (Dep. Chm., 1985–89); ASW Holdings Plc, 1987–93; Regalian Properties PLC, 1990–93. Seconded as Head of Central Policy Review Staff, Cabinet Office, 1982–83. Chm., EDC for Process Plant Industry, 1984–85; Chairman: National Stud, 1988–91; Horseracing Forensic Lab., 1991–98. Gov., LSE, 1984–2003 (Vice-Chm. Govs, 1984–93; Actg Chm., 1987–88); Pres., Old Stationers' Assoc., 1995–96. Hon. Fellow, Wolfson Coll., Cambridge, 1987. *Recreations:* cricket, crosswords, horse-racing, reading, lunching. *Address:* Padbury Lodge, Padbury, Bucks MK18 2AJ. *Club:* MCC.

SPAWFORTH, David Meredith, MA; Headmaster, Merchiston Castle School, Edinburgh, 1981–98; *b* 2 Jan. 1938; *s* of Lawrence and Gwen Spawforth, Wakefield, Yorks; *m* 1963, Yvonne Mary Gude; one *s* one *d*. *Educ:* Silcoates School; Hertford Coll., Oxford (Heath Harrison Travelling Schol.; MA Mod. Langs). Assistant Master: Winchester Coll., 1961–64; Wellington Coll., 1964–80; Housemaster, Wellington Coll., 1968–80. British Petroleum Education Fellow, Keble Coll., Oxford, 1977. FRSA 1994. *Recreations:* gardening, France, history, theatre, walking, sailing, model railways. *Address:* Kimberley, Netherbarns, Galashiels, Selkirkshire TD1 3NW.

SPEAIGHT, Anthony Hugh; QC 1995; *b* 31 July 1948; *s* of late George Victor Speaight and Mary Olive Speaight (*née* Mudd); *m* 1991, Gabrielle Anne Kooy-Lister; two *s* one *d*. *Educ:* St Benedict's Sch., Ealing; Lincoln Coll., Oxford (MA; Sec., Oxford Union Soc., 1970). Called to the Bar, Middle Temple, 1973 (Bencher, 2004). Member: Bar Council, 1986–92, 1998–2000; Bar Working Party on Televising Courts, 1990; Chm., Bar Council Access to the Bar Cttee, 2004–06. Chm., Editl Bd, Counsel, jl of Bar of England and Wales, 1990–94. Schuman Silver Medal, FVS Foundn, Germany, 1976. *Publications:* (with G. Stone) The Law of Defective Premises, 1982; Architects Legal Handbook, (ed jtly) 3rd edn 1982 to 7th edn 2000, (ed) 8th edn 2004; (ed jtly) Butterworths Professional Negligence Service, 2 vols, 2000. *Recreations:* theatre, cricket. *Address:* 4 Pump Court, Temple, EC4Y 7AN. *T:* (020) 7842 5555. *Clubs:* Carlton, Hurlingham.

SPEAKMAN-PITT, William, VC 1951; *b* 21 Sept. 1927; *m* 1st, 1956, Rachel Snitch; one *s*; 2nd, Jill; one *d*. *Educ:* Wellington Road Senior Boys' Sch., Altrincham. Entered Army as Private. Served Korean War, 1950–53 (VC), King's Own Scottish Borderers. *Recreations:* swimming, ski-ing.

SPEARING, Prof. Anthony Colin; William R. Kenan Professor of English, University of Virginia, since 1989 (Professor of English, since 1987); *b* 31 Jan. 1936; *s* of Frederick Spearing and Gertrude Spearing (*née* Calnin); *m* 1961, Elizabeth; one *s* one *d*. *Educ:* Alleyn's Sch., Dulwich; Jesus Coll., Cambridge (BA 1957; MA 1960). University of Cambridge: W. M. Tapp Res. Fellow, Gonville and Caius Coll., 1959–60; Univ. Asst Lectr in English, 1960–64; Supernumerary Fellow, Gonville and Caius Coll., 1960; Official Fellow, Queens' Coll., 1960–87; Univ. Lectr in English, 1964–85; Dir of Studies in English, Queens' Coll., 1967–85; Reader in Medieval English Literature, 1985–87; Life Fellow, Queens' Coll., 1987. Vis. Prof. of English, Univ. of Virginia, 1979–80, 1984. *Publications:* Criticism and Medieval Poetry, 1964, 2nd edn 1972; The Gawain-Poet: a critical study, 1970; Chaucer: Troilus and Criseyde, 1976; Medieval Dream-Poetry, 1976; Medieval to Renaissance in English Poetry, 1985; Readings in Medieval Poetry, 1987; The Medieval Poet as Voyeur, 1993; (trans.) The Cloud of Unknowing, 2001; Textual Subjectivity, 2005; texts, articles in learned jls. *Address:* Department of English, 219 Bryan Hall, University of Virginia, PO Box 400121, Charlottesville, VA 22904–4121, USA.

SPEARING, Nigel John; *b* 8 Oct. 1930; *s* of late Austen and of May Spearing; *m* 1956, Wendy, *d* of Percy and Molly Newman, Newport, Mon; one *s* two *d*. *Educ:* Latymer Upper School, Hammersmith. Ranks and commission, Royal Signals, 1950–52; St Catharine's Coll., Cambridge, 1953–56. Mem., NUT, 1955–. Tutor, Wandsworth School, 1956–68 (Sen. Geography Master, 1967–68); Director, Thameside Research and Development Group, Inst. of Community Studies, 1968–69; Housemaster, Elliott School, Putney, 1969–70. Chairman: Barons Court Labour Party, 1961–63; Hammersmith Local Govt Cttee of the Labour Party, 1966–68. Co-opted Mem. GLC Planning and Transport Cttees, 1966–73. Contested (Lab) Warwick and Leamington, 1964. MP (Lab): Acton, 1970–74; Newham S, May 1974–1997. Introd Private Members Bill, which became Industrial Diseases (Notification) Act 1981. Secretary: Parly Lab. Party Educn Gp, 1971–74; Parly Inland Waterways Gp, 1970–74; Member Select Cttee: Overseas Develt, 1973–74, 1977–79; Members' Interests, 1974–75; Procedure, 1975–79; Sound Broadcasting, 1978–83; European (formerly EEC) Legislation, 1979–97 (Chm., 1983–92); Foreign and Commonwealth Affairs, 1980–87; Chair, Parly Affairs Cttee, PLP, 1989–97. Jt Pres., London Dockland Forum, 1998–; Vice-Pres., River Thames Soc., 1975–2008; Pres., Socialist Envt and Resources Assoc., 1977–86; Chm., British Anti-Common Market Campaign, 1977–83; a Vice-Pres., Campaign for Indep. Britain, 1997–. Mem. Bd, Christian Aid, 1987–91. Mem., Congregational Church and URC, 1947–. *Publication:* The Thames Barrier-Barrage Controversy (Inst. of Community Studies), 1969. *Recreations:* rowing, cycling, reading. *Address:* 92 Boileau Road, SW13 9BP. *T:* (020) 8748 9266.

SPEARMAN, Sir Alexander Young Richard Mainwaring, 5th Bt *cr* 1840; *b* 3 Feb. 1969; *s* of Sir Alexander Bowyer Spearman, 4th Bt, and Martha, *d* of John Green, Naauwpoort, S Africa; *S* father, 1977; *m* 1st, 1994, Anne Stine (marr. diss. 1997), *d* of K. Munch; 2nd, 1997, Theresa Jean, *d* of Dr Thomas Sutcliffe; one *s*. *Heir: s* Alexander Axel Spearman, *b* 9 March 1999.

SPEARMAN, John L.; Operating Partner, Cognetas LLP; Chairman: Playback Ltd, since 1987; FrameStore Group, since 2001; *b* 25 Nov. 1941; *s* of Thomas Spearman and Elizabeth Alexandra Spearman (*née* Leadbeater); *m* 1st, 1966, Susan Elizabeth Henderson Elms (marr. diss. 1986); one *s* one *d*; 2nd, 1988, Angela Josephine van Praag; one *d*. *Educ:* Trinity Coll., Dublin (MA). Unilever Grad. Trng Scheme; Lintas Ltd; London Press Exchange; Collett Dickenson Pearce, 1972–89: Man. Dir, 1982–83; Chm. and Chief Exec., 1983–89; Chief Exec., 1992–97, Dep. Chm., 1996–97, Classic FM. Chm., Laser Sales (LWT), 1990–93. Member: Government Lead Body for Design, 1991–; Arts Council of England, 1996–98. Patron Dir, RIBA. Trustee, World Monuments Fund. FRSA 1996. *Recreations:* music, sailing, ski-ing, walking, gardening. *Address:* c/o Cognetas LLC, Paternoster House, 65 St Paul's Churchyard, EC4M 8AB. *Clubs:* Athenæum, Hurlingham; Royal Irish Yacht (Dublin).
See also T. D. Spearman.

SPEARMAN, Richard; QC 1996; a Recorder, since 2000; *b* 19 Jan. 1953; *s* of late Clement Spearman, CBE and of Olwen Regina Spearman (*née* Morgan); *m* 1983, Sandra Elizabeth Harris; three *d*. *Educ:* Bedales; King's Coll., Cambridge. Called to the Bar, Middle Temple, 1977, Bencher, 2006. An Asst Recorder, 1998–2000. *Publications:* (with F. A. Philpott) Sale of Goods Litigation, 1983, 2nd edn 1994; (contrib.) Information Rights, Coppel, 2004, 2nd edn 2007. *Recreations:* racquet sports, ski-ing, family. *Address:* 4–5 Gray's Inn Square, Gray's Inn, WC1R 5AY. *T:* (020) 7404 5252. *Clubs:* Brooks's, Hurlingham, MCC.

SPEARMAN, Prof. Thomas David, PhD; President, Royal Irish Academy, 1999–2002; *b* 25 March 1937; *s* of Thomas Spearman and Elizabeth Alexandra Spearman (*née* Leadbeater); *m* 1961, Juanita Smale; one *s* two *d*. *Educ:* Greenlanes Sch., Dublin; Mountjoy Sch., Dublin; Trinity Coll., Dublin (BA, MA); St John's Coll., Cambridge (PhD 1961). Res. Fellow, UCL and CERN, Geneva, 1961–62; Res. Associate, Univ. of Ill, 1962–64; Lectr in Theoretical Physics, Univ. of Durham, 1964–66; Univ. Prof. of Natural Philosophy, Univ. of Dublin, 1966–97; Trinity College, Dublin: Fellow, 1969, Sen. Fellow, 1994–97, Fellow Emeritus, 1997; Vice-Provost, 1991–97. Chm., Trustee Savings Bank, Dublin, 1989–92. Mem. Council, Dublin Inst. for Advanced Studies, 1999–2002. MAE 1988 (Treas., 1989–2000); Chm., Eur. Acads' Sci. Adv. Council, 2004–; Vice-Pres., 1983–89, Mem., Governing Council, 1999–2002, ESF; Mem., ESTA, 1994–98. Mem., Rep. Body, C of I, 1968–2001. Gov. and Guardian, Nat. Gall. of Ireland, 1999–2002. *Publications:* (with A. D. Martin) Elementary Particle Theory, 1970; contrib. papers in elementary particle theory, inverse problems and history of science. *Recreations:* walking, reading, gardening, looking at pictures, listening to music. *Address:* St Elmo, Marlborough Road, Glenageary, Co. Dublin, Ireland; Trinity College, Dublin 2, Ireland. *Club:* Kildare Street and University (Dublin).
See also J. L. Spearman.

SPECTOR, Prof. Roy Geoffrey, MD, PhD; FRCP, FRCPath; Professor of Applied Pharmacology, Guy's Hospital Medical School, 1972–89, now Emeritus; Hon. Physician, Guy's Hospital, since 1967; *b* 27 Aug. 1931; *s* of Paul Spector and Esther Cohen; *m* 1st, 1960, Evie Joan Freeman (marr. diss. 1979); two *s* one *d*; 2nd, 1986, Dr Annette Skinner, botanist. *Educ:* Roundhay Sch., Leeds; Sch. of Medicine, Leeds Univ. (MB, ChB, MD); PhD Lond. 1964, Dip. in Biochem. 1966. FRCP 1971; FRCPath 1976. Lectr in Paediatric Res. Unit, Guy's Hosp., 1961–67; Guy's Hosp. Medical School, subseq. United Medical and Dental Schools of Guy's and St Thomas's Hosps: Reader in Pharmacology, 1968–71; Sub Dean for Admissions, 1975–89; Chm., Div. of Pharmacology, 1985–88. Vis. Prof. in Clin. Pharmacology, West China Med. Univ., Chengdu, 1986–87. External Examiner, Hong Kong Univ., 1994–95 and 1996–97. Vice Chm., British Univs' Film Council, 1976–87. FRSocMed. *Publications:* (jtly) The Nerve Cell, 1964, 2nd edn 1986; (jtly) Clinical Pharmacology in Dentistry, 1975, 6th edn 1995; (jtly) Mechanisms in Pharmacology and Therapeutics, 1976; (jtly) Aids to Pharmacology, 1980, 3rd edn 1993; (jtly) Textbook of Clinical Pharmacology, 1981, 2nd edn 1986; (jtly) Aids to Clinical Pharmacology and Therapeutics, 1984, 3rd edn 1993; (jtly) Common Drug Treatments in Psychiatry, 1984; Catechism in Clinical Pharmacology Therapeutics, 1986; (jtly) Drugs and Medicines, 1989; contributor: Textbook of Clinical Pharmacology, 1994; Handbook of Clinical Research, 1994; contribs to jls on pathology, medicine, gen. science, and applied pharmacology. *Recreation:* cookery. *Address:* 3 St Kilda Road, Orpington, Kent BR6 0ES. *T:* (01689) 810069.

SPECTOR, Prof. Timothy David, MD; FRCP; Professor of Genetic Epidemiology, and Director, Twin Research Unit, King's College London, since 1993; Consultant Rheumatologist, St Thomas' Hospital, since 1993; *b* 14 July 1958; *s* of Walter and June Spector; *m* 1988, Veronique Bataille; one *s* one *d*. *Educ:* St Bartholomew's Hosp. Med. Sch. (MB BS 1982); London Sch. of Hygiene and Tropical Medicine (MSc 1986); MD London 1989. FRCP 1995. SHO in Medicine, 2-year Eur. rotation, St Bartholomew's Hosp., UCL and Brussels, 1983–85; Wellcome Res. Fellow in Clin. Epidemiol., London Hosp. Med. Coll., 1985–88; Sen. Registrar in Rheumatol., St Bartholomew's Hosp., 1988–93. *Publications:* An Introduction to General Pathology, 1999; Your Genes Unzipped, 2003; medical articles. *Recreations:* ski-ing, sailing, wine. *Address:* Twin Research Unit, King's College London, St Thomas' Hospital, Lambeth Palace Road, SE1 7EH; *e-mail:* tim.spector@kcl.ac.uk.

SPEDDING, Sir Colin (Raymond William), Kt 1994; CBE 1988; Professor of Agricultural Systems, 1975–90, and Pro-Vice-Chancellor, 1986–90, University of Reading, now Professor Emeritus; *b* 22 March 1925; *s* of Robert Kewley Spedding and Ilynn Spedding; *m* 1952, Betty Noreen George (*d* 1988); one *s* one *d* (and one *s* decd). *Educ:* London Univ. (External) (BSc 1951; MSc 1953; PhD 1955; DSc 1967). FZS 1962; FIBiol 1967, CBiol 1984; FRASE 1984; FIHort 1986; FRAgS 1986; FLS 1995. Ilford Ltd, 1940–43; RNVR, 1943–46; Allen & Hanbury, 1948–49; Grassland Research Institute: joined 1949; Head of Ecology Div., 1967–75; Asst Dir, 1969–72; Dep. Dir, 1972–75; University of Reading: Visiting, then part-time Prof. of Agric. Systems, 1970–75; Head of Dept of Agric. and Horticl., 1975–83; Dean, Faculty of Agriculture and Food, 1983–86; Dir, Centre for Agricl Strategy, 1981–90, Consultant Dir, 1990–99. Commonwealth Prestige Fellow, NZ, 1977; Vis. Prof., Univ. of Guelph, Canada, 1978. Editor, Agricultural Systems, 1976–88. Mem., Programme Cttee, Internat. Livestock Centre for Africa, Addis Ababa, 1976–80, Vice Chm., 1980–83; Chm., Nat. Equine Forum Organising Cttee, 1992–. Special Advr, H of C Select Cttee on Agric., 1980–83; Chairman: UK Register of Organic Food Standards Bd, 1987–99; Farm Animal Welfare Council, 1988–98; Apple and Pear Res. Council, 1989–97; Science Council (formerly CSTI), 1994–2000; Assured Chicken Production Ltd, 2000–04; Dir, Assured Food Standards, 2001–. Dir, Lands Improvement Hldgs PLC (formerly Gp Ltd), 1986–99 (Dep. Chm., 1990–99). Adv. Dir, 1998–2003, Special Scientific Advr to Dir-Gen., 2003, WSPA; Advr, Companion Animal Welfare Council, 1999–; Specialist Advr, H of L Select Cttee on EC, Sub-Cttee D (Agric., Fisheries and Food), 1999; Hd, UK Delegn to Internat. Whaling Commn, Grenada, 1999, Berlin, 2003. President: European Assoc. of Animal Production Study Commn for Sheep and Goat Production, 1970–76; British Soc. for Animal Production, 1979–80; Vice-Pres., Inst. of Biology, 1997–99 (Pres., 1992–94). Governor: Royal Agricl Coll., 1982–88; Inst. of Grassland and Envmtl Res. (formerly Inst. for Grassland and Animal Production), 1987–91; Mem., Council of Management, PDSA, 1988– (Dep. Chm., 1996–2003); Vice Pres., RSPCA, 2002–. Chm. Trustees, FAWT, 2003–. Mem., Inst. of Dirs, 1992–98. FRSA 1988. Hon. Life Mem., BSAS, 1990; Hon. FIBiol 1994; Hon. Associate, RCVS, 1994; Hon. MRSocMed, 1998. Hon. DSc Reading, 1995. George Hedley Award, 1971; Canadian Inst. of Agric. Recognition Award, 1971; Wooldridge Meml Medal, BVA, 1982; Hawkesbury Centenary Medal of Honour, Univ. of Western Sydney, 1991; Massey Ferguson Nat. Agricl Award, 1991; Victory Medal, Central Vet. Soc., 2000. *Publications:* Sheep Production and Grazing Management, 1965, 2nd edn 1970; Grassland Ecology, 1971; (ed with E. C. Diekmahns) Grasses and Legumes in British Agriculture, 1972; The Biology of Agricultural Systems, 1975; An Introduction to Agricultural Systems, 1979, 2nd edn 1988; (ed) Vegetable Productivity, 1981; (with J. M. Walsingham and A. M. Hoxey) Biological Efficiency in Agriculture, 1981; (ed) Fream's Agriculture, 1983; (ed) Fream's Principles of Food and Agriculture, 1992; Agriculture and the Citizen, 1996; Animal Welfare, 2000; The Natural History of a Garden, 2003; The Second Mouse Gets the Cheese: proverbs and their uses, 2005; over 250 sci papers in learned jls. *Address:* Vine Cottage, Orchard Road, Hurst, Berks RG10 0SD. *Clubs:* Athenæum, Farmers'.

SPEDDING, John Henry Fryer F.; *see* Fryer-Spedding.

SPEED, Anthony James, CBE 1999; QPM 1991; DL; Police Adviser on public order: City of London Police Committee, since 1999; Metropolitan Police, since 2004; Singapore Police, since 2006; *b* 23 Feb. 1941; *m* 1961, Patricia Elizabeth Boyle; one *s* three *d*. *Educ:* Thomas Calton Technical Sch., Dulwich. Metropolitan Police, 1957–99: Personal Protection Officer to the Prince of Wales, 1969; Scarman Inquiries into Red Lion Square Disorders, 1974, Brixton Disorders, 1981; Divl Comdr, Brixton, 1981–83; posts in Westminster, 1983–99, Asst Comr, Central Area, 1994–99. Chm., Football Licensing Authy, 2003–. DL Greater London, 1999; Representative DL London Borough of Hounslow, 2000–05, Lambeth, 2005. *Recreation:* horse riding.

SPEED, Sir (Herbert) Keith, Kt 1992; RD 1967; DL; Director, Folkestone & Dover Water Services (formerly Folkestone and District Water Co.), 1986–2007; *b* 11 March 1934; *s* of late Herbert Victor Speed and Dorothy Barbara (*née* Mumford); *m* 1961, Peggy Voss Clarke; two *s* one *d* (and one *s* decd). *Educ:* Greenhill Sch., Evesham; Bedford Modern Sch.; RNC, Dartmouth and Greenwich. Officer, RN, 1947–56; Lt-Comdr RNR, 1964–79. Sales Man., Amos (Electronics) Ltd, 1957–60; Marketing Man., Plysu Products Ltd, 1960–65; Officer, Conservative Res. Dept, 1965–68. MP (C): Meriden, March 1968–Feb. 1974; Ashford, Oct. 1974–1997. An Asst Govt Whip, 1970–71; a Lord Comr of HM Treasury, 1971–72; Parly Under-Sec. of State, DoE, 1972–74; Opposition spokesman on local govt, 1976–77, on home affairs, 1977–79; Parly Under Sec. of State for Defence for RN, 1979–81; Mem., Parly Select Cttee on Defence, 1983–87; UK Rep. to Parly Assembly of Council of Europe and WEU, 1987–97. Parliamentary Consultant: Professional Assoc. of Teachers, 1982–97; Assoc. for Instrumentation, Control and Automation Industry in UK, 1983–87. DL Kent, 1996. *Publications:* Blue Print for Britain, 1965; Sea Change, 1982; contribs to various political and defence jls. *Recreations:* classical music, reading. *Address:* Strood House, Rolvenden, Cranbrook, Kent TN17 4JJ. *Club:* Garrick.
See also J. J. Speed.

SPEED, Jeffery John, CBE 1991; Director of Fundraising and Treasurer's Department, Conservative Central Office, 1995–96; *b* 3 Oct. 1936; *s* of late Herbert Victor Speed and Dorothy Barbara Speed (*née* Mumford); *m* 1985, Hilary Anne Busfield, *d* of late Haley Busfield, Mayfield, Sussex. *Educ:* Bedford Modern Sch. General Motors (Vauxhall), 1955–58; Sales Manager, later Sales Dir, Tompkins Moss Gp, 1959–65; Conservative Party Agent, 1965–78; Dep. Central Office Agent, S Eastern Area, 1978–82; Central Office Agent: E Midlands Area, 1982–88; Greater London Area, 1988–93; Dir, Constituency Services, Cons. Central Office, 1993–95. FInstLM (FISM 1995; MISM

1993). FRSA 1993; FRGS 2003. *Publication:* Tudor Townscapes, 2000. *Recreations:* antique maps (especially those by John Speed, 1552–1629), oenology, travel, musical theatre and film. *Club:* Royal Over-Seas League.

See also Sir H. K. Speed.

SPEED, Sir Keith; *see* Speed, Sir H. K.

SPEED, Malcolm Walter; Chief Executive, International Cricket Council, 2001–08; *b* 14 Sept. 1948; *s* of Walter and Audrey Speed; *m* 1971, Allison Cutter; three *d. Educ:* Melbourne Univ. (LLB). Admitted barrister and solicitor, Melbourne, 1971; called to Victorian Bar, 1981; Solicitor, 1971–81, Barrister, 1981–94, Melbourne; sports consultant, and Exec. Chm., Basketball Australia, 1994–97; Chief Exec., Australian Cricket Bd, 1997–2001. *Recreations:* golf, cricket, walking, reading, Australian history. *Address:* c/o International Cricket Council, PO Box 500070, Dubai, United Arab Emirates. *Clubs:* Wentworth Golf; Australian, Melbourne Cricket.

SPEELMAN, Sir Cornelis Jacob, 8th Bt *cr* 1686; BA; *b* 17 March 1917; *s* of Sir Cornelis Jacob Speelman, 7th Bt and Maria Catharina Helena, Castendijk; *S* father, 1949; *m* 1972, Julia Mona Le Besque (*d* 1978); *m* 1986, Irene Agnes van Leeuwen; two step *c.* Education Dept, Royal Dutch Army, 1947–49; with The Shell Company (Marketing Service Dept), 1950. Student, Univ. of Western Australia, 1952; formerly Master of Modern Languages at Clifton Coll., Geelong Grammar Sch.; Exeter Tutorial Coll.

SPEIGHT, Hon. Sir Graham (Davies), Kt 1983; Judge of the High Court of New Zealand, 1966–98; *b* 21 July 1921; *s* of Henry Baxter and Anna May Speight; *m* 1947, Elisabeth Muriel Booth; one *s* one *d. Educ:* Auckland Grammar Sch.; Univ. of Auckland (LLB). Qualified barrister and solicitor, 1942; served 2nd NZ Expeditionary Force, Middle East and Italy, 1943–46: Lieut Royal NZ Artillery, 1943–46; Aide-de-Camp, General B. C. Freyberg, VC (later 1st Baron Freyberg), 1944–45; practising barrister, 1946–66. Justice of Appeal, Fiji, 1980–87; Chief Justice, Cook Is, 1982–87. Chairman: Eden Park Bd, 1988–94; Rothman Foundn, 1988–95; NZ Sports Drug Agency, 1990–2000. Chancellor, Univ. of Auckland, 1973–79; Hon. LLD Auckland, 1983. *Publication:* (ed jtly) Adams: criminal law in New Zealand, 1986. *Recreations:* golf, yachting. *Clubs:* Auckland Golf, Royal New Zealand Yacht Squadron (Auckland) (Cdre 1961–63).

SPEIRS, John Garrett, CBE 1996; LVO 2003; Member, Royal Commission on Environmental Pollution, 2002–08; *b* 17 June 1937; *s* of William Blair Speirs and Margaret Sarah Garrett Speirs; *m* 1963, Susan Elizabeth Seyler, Dayton, Ohio; two *s. Educ:* Glenalmond Sch.; Exeter Coll., Oxford (MA Lit.Hum.); Cornell Univ., NY (MBA). Tube Investments Gp, 1962–76: industrial engr, British Aluminium Co., Falkirk, 1962–66; corporate planning exec., London, 1966–69; Prodn Manager, Gen. Manager and Dir, TI Stainless Tubes, Walsall, 1969–74; Dir, Ops Secretariat, 1974–76; Divl Dir, NEB, 1976–81; Man. Dir, Norsk Hydro (UK) Ltd, London, 1981–2002. Chm., Merton, Sutton & Wandsworth FHSA, 1989–95. Mem., British Cttee, Det Norsk Veritas, 1987–2001. Advr, Kleinwort Capital Ltd, 1991–2007; Chm., Dramgate Ltd, 1991–. Member: Adv. Cttee on Business and the Envmt, 1991–95; Business in the Envmt, 1991–99; SERC, 1993–94. Mem. Council, Aluminium Fedn, 1992–2003 (Pres., 1997–98); Pres., Nat. Soc. for Clean Air and Envmtl Protection, 2002–03. Non-exec. Dir, Carbon Trust, 2001–07. Chm., UK Faculty, Prince of Wales's Business and Envmt Prog., 1993–2002 (Mem., Mgt Cttee, 1997–2004). *Recreations:* opera, theatre, visual arts and architecture, Munro-bagging, gardening, incompetent golf. *Address:* 20 Dunstall Road, SW20 0HR. *T:* (020) 8879 1308.

SPEIRS, Robert; Chairman, Stagecoach Group plc, since 2002; *b* 23 Oct. 1936; *s* of John and Isabella Speirs; *m* 1958, Patricia Holt; two *s. Educ:* Alleynes Grammar Sch., Uttoxeter. Cooper Bros, London, 1964–68; Tax Administrator, Texaco Ltd, 1968–77; Tax/Finance Dir, BNOC, subseq. Britoil plc, 1977–88; Finance Director: Olympia and York Canary Wharf Ltd, 1988–93; Royal Bank of Scotland Gp plc, 1993–98; Chairman: Miller Gp Ltd, 1999–; Bell Gp plc, 1999–2004; Dir, Canary Wharf Gp plc, 1999–2004. *Recreations:* hill-walking, gardening, military history. *Address:* Arden, Pitts Lane, Pitts Haven, Binstead, Isle of Wight PO33 3AX. *T:* (01983) 568708; *e-mail:* bob.speirs@btopenworld.com.

SPEIRS, William MacLeod; General Secretary, Scottish Trades Union Congress, 1998–2006; *b* 8 March 1952; *s* of late Ronald Speirs and of Mary Speirs (*née* MacKenzie); *m* 1st, 1975, Lynda Speirs (marr. diss. 1990); one *s* one *d*; 2nd, 2002, Patricia Grieve. *Educ:* Univ. of Strathclyde (BA 1st Cl. Hons Politics). Univ. researcher, Strathclyde, 1974–76; Lectr, Cardonald Coll., Glasgow, 1977; bar steward, Paisley, 1977–78; researcher, Paisley Coll. of Technol., 1978–79; Asst Sec., 1979–88, Dep. Gen. Sec., 1988–98, Scottish TUC. Member: Central Arbitration Cttee; Employment Appeal Tribunal; Bd, Scottish Low Pay Unit; Scottish One Fund For All; Bd, Scottish Enterprise Glasgow; Chm. Bd, Workbase Trng (Scotland); TUC nominee, Nat. Employers' Adv. Bd for the Reserve Forces. Mem. Bd, 7:84 Theatre Co. FRSA 1993. DUniv Paisley, 1999. *Publications:* (contrib.) The Manpower Services Commission in Scotland, ed Brown and Fairley, 1989; contrib. to Scottish Trade Union Rev. *Recreations:* folk music, reading, watching St Mirren FC, cricket, losing money on horses. *Club:* Daft Watty's Ramblers (Paisley).

SPELLAR, Rt Hon. John (Francis); PC 2001; MP (Lab) Warley, since 1997 (Warley West, 1992–97); Comptroller of HM Household, since 2008; *b* 5 Aug. 1947; *s* of William David and Phyllis Kathleen Spellar; *m* 1981, Anne Rosalind Wilmot (*d* 2003); one *d. Educ:* Bromley Parish Primary Sch.; Dulwich Coll.; St Edmund's Hall, Oxford (BA PPE). Electrical, Electronic, Telecommunication and Plumbing Union: Res. Officer, 1969–76; Nat. Officer, 1976–92. Contested (Lab) Bromley, 1970. MP (Lab) Birmingham Northfield, 1982–83; contested (Lab) same seat, 1983, 1987. Parly Under-Sec. of State, 1997–99, Minister of State, 1999–2001, MoD; Minister of State (Minister for Transport), DTLR, then DFT, 2001–03; Minister of State, NI Office, 2003–05. *Recreation:* gardening. *Address:* House of Commons, SW1A 0AA. *T:* (020) 7219 5800. *Clubs:* Bromley Labour; Brandhall Labour.

SPELLER, Antony; Senior Associate (Europe), Resource Planning and Management Systems Ltd, 1992–2000; *b* 12 June 1929; *s* of late John and Ethel Speller; *m* 1st, Margaret Lloyd-Jones (marr. diss.); two *s* one *d*; 2nd, 1960, Maureen R. McLellan; one *s* one *d. Educ:* Loreto; Calcutta; Exeter Sch., Devon; Univ. of London (BScEcon); Univ. of Exeter (BA Social Studies). FIH. Nat. Service, Subaltern, Devonshire Regt, 1951; Major, Devonshire and Dorset Regt TA, 1965. Nigerian Produce Marketing Boards, 1952–54; Dir, Atlas Ltd, Nigeria, 1955–61. Chairman: Exeter Photo-Copying, 1963–93; EuroSpeedy Printing Centres UK, 1988–93; Copyshops of SW England, 1989–93. Vice Chairman: E Devon Water Bd, 1965–73; Devon River Authority, 1970–73. Councillor, Exeter CC, 1963–74 (Chairman: Public Works Cttee, 1965–69; Education Cttee, 1971–72). MP (C) N Devon, 1979–92; contested (C) N Devon, 1992. Mem., Select Cttee on Energy, 1982–88; Chairman: All-Party Alternative Energy Gp, 1984–92; W Africa Cttee, 1987–92. Chm., W Country Cons. MPs, 1983–87; Pres., 1996–99, Vice-Pres., 2000–08, N Devon Cons. Assoc.; Vice-Chm., Tiverton and Honiton Cons. Assoc., 1997–99. Mem., Newton St Cyres Parish Council, 2007–. Hon. Pres., Nat. Outdoor Events Assoc., 1992–98; Hon. Commercial Advr, The Keep, Mil. Mus. of Devon and Dorset, 2001–02; Regtl Advr, History Park, Mus. of Barnstaple and N Devon, 2002–08. Vice-Pres., Railway Develt Soc., 1992–. Mem. Cttee, Duke of Edinburgh Award Scheme, Devon, 2000–04. *Address:* 11 Newton House, Newton St Cyres, Exeter, Devon EX5 5BL; *e-mail:* tonyspeller@hotmail.com. *Clubs:* Royal Over-Seas League; Lagos Motor Boat (Nigeria).

SPELLER, John Christopher, MA (Ed); Headteacher, Norton Knatchbull School, since 1997; *b* 10 May 1949; *s* of Sydney and Doris Speller, Woodford Green, Essex; *m* 1981, Jennifer Edgar; twin *s* one *d. Educ:* Forest Sch., London; Hatfield Coll., Univ. of Durham (BA Hons French; PGCE); Open Univ. (MA Educn). Asst Teacher, Davenant Foundn Sch., Essex, 1972–76; Head of Languages, Grahame Park Comp. Sch., Barnet, 1977–80; Head of Upper Sch., Nicholas Comp. Sch., Basildon, 1981–83; Dep. Head, Ilford County High Sch. for Boys, 1983–89; Headteacher, Liverpool Blue Coat Sch., 1989–97. FRSA 1994. *Recreations:* cricket, walking, travel (UK and abroad), DIY, gardening. *Address:* The Norton Knatchbull School, Ashford, Kent TN24 0QJ. *T:* (01233) 620045.

SPELLER, Maj.-Gen. Norman Henry, CB 1976; Government Relations Adviser, ICL, 1976–86, retired; *b* 5 March 1921; *s* of late Col Norman Speller and Emily Florence Speller (*née* Lambert); *m* 1950, Barbara Eleanor (*née* Earle); two *s. Educ:* Wallingford Grammar School. Commnd RA, 1940; War Service N Africa; transf. to RAOC, 1945; psc 1952; DAA&QMG 39 Inf. Bde, 1953–55; Dirg Staff, Staff Coll., 1955–58; OC 20 Ordnance Field Park, 1958–60; Admin. Staff Coll., 1961; AA&QMG N Ireland, 1961–63; D/SPO COD Donnington, 1964–65; Col AQ 54 (EA) Div./District, 1965–66; AAG AG9, MoD, 1967; DDOS 1 British Corps, 1968–69; idc 1970; Dir of Systems Coordination, MoD, 1971–73; Dir of Ordnance Services, MoD, 1973–76, retired. Col Comdt, RAOC, 1978–83. Chm. Management Cttee, The Royal Homes for Officers' Widows and Daughters (SSAFA), 1987–94. *Recreations:* sailing, golf. *Address:* 1 Steeple Close, SW6 3LE. *Club:* Roehampton.

SPELLER, Paul Anthony; HM Diplomatic Service, retired; Director, International Office, Liberal Democrat Party, since 2008; *b* 21 Jan. 1954; *s* of Cecil Edmund Kirby Speller and Shelagh Maureen Clifford Speller; *m* 1998, Jane Hennessy. *Educ:* Wellington Coll.; University Coll. London (BSc Econ 1976). Joined FCO, 1979; Soviet Dept, 1979–83; Nuclear Energy Dept, 1983–86; Second, later First, Sec., Bonn, 1986–89; EU Dept, 1989–91; Private Sec. to Parly Under-Sec. of State, 1991–93; First Sec., UK Repn to EU, Brussels, 1993–96; Southern Eur. Dept, 1996–98; Dep. Governor, Gibraltar, 1998–2002; Dep. Hd of Mission, Jakarta, 2002–05; Hd, SE Asia and Pacific Dept (formerly Gp), FCO, 2005–08. *Recreations:* cricket, tennis, theatre, guitars. *Address:* Liberal Democrat Party Headquarters, 4 Cowley Street, SW1P 3NB; *e-mail:* paul.speller@libdems.org.uk.

SPELLMAN, (Irene) Ruth, OBE 2007; Chief Executive Officer, Institution of Mechanical Engineers, since 2007; *b* 14 Aug. 1951; *d* of Vernon A. Hewlett and Jean Hewlett (*née* Weir); *m* 1979, Dr William Spellman; one *s* two *d. Educ:* Girton Coll., Cambridge (BA Hons Econs and Pol Sci. 1972). FCIPD 1992. National Coal Board: Investment Analyst, Pension Fund, 1972–73; Industrial Relns Asst, Manpower and Industrial Res., 1973–76; Educn and Trng Advr, NEDO, 1976–86 (pt-time, 1978–86); Consultant in HR and Managing Change, then Managing Consultant, Coopers & Lybrand, 1986–91; Dir, HR, NSPCC, 1991–98; Chief Exec., Investors in People UK, 1998–2006. FRSA 2003. *Publications:* Economic Consequences of New Technology, 1981; Perspectives in Managing Change, 1990. *Recreations:* music (violin, singing), literature, politics. *Address:* 3 Balsams Close, Hertford, Herts SG13 8BN. *T:* (home) (01992) 504119, (office) (020) 7973 1240, 07894 424281; *e-mail:* r.spellman@imeche.org. *Club:* Commonwealth.

SPELMAN, Caroline Alice; MP (C) Meriden, since 1997; Chairman, Conservative Party, since 2007; *b* 4 May 1958; *d* of Marshall Cormack and Helen Margaret Greenfield; *m* 1987, Mark Gerald Spelman; two *s* one *d. Educ:* Herts and Essex Grammar Sch. for Girls; Queen Mary Coll., London (BA 1st cl. Hons European Studies). Sugar Beet Advr, NFU, 1981–84; Dep. Dir, European Confedn of Sugar Beet Growers, Paris, 1984–89; Dir, Spelman, Cormack and Associates (food and biotechnology consultancy), 1989–. Contested (C) Bassetlaw, 1992. Shadow Secretary of State: for internat. develt, 2001–03; for envmt, 2003–04; for local and devolved govt affairs, 2004–05; DCLG, 2006–07; Shadow Minister: for women, 2001–04; ODPM, 2005–06. *Publication:* The Non-Food Uses of Agricultural Raw Materials, 1994. *Recreations:* tennis, ski-ing, gardening. *Address:* House of Commons, SW1A 0AA. *T:* (020) 7219 4189.

SPENCE, Prof. Alastair Andrew, CBE 1993; MD; FRCA, FRCSE, FRCPG, FRCPE, FRCS; Professor of Anaesthetics, University of Edinburgh, 1984–98, now Emeritus; *b* 18 Sept. 1936; *s* of James Glendinning Spence and Margaret Macdonald; *m* 1963, Maureen Isobel Aitchison; two *s. Educ:* Ayr Acad.; Glasgow Univ. FRCA (FFARCS 1964); FRCPG 1980; FRCSE 1991; FRCPE 1994; FRCS 1994. Western Infirmary, Glasgow, 1961–65; MRC Res. Fellow, Univ. of Glasgow Dept of Surgery, 1965–66; Steinberg Res. Fellow and Clinical Asst to Prof. of Anaesthesia, Univ. of Leeds, 1966–69; Sen. Lectr and Head of Dept of Anaesthesia, later Reader and Prof., Western Infirmary, Glasgow, 1969–84. Hon. Consultant Anaesthetist, Lothian Health Bd, then Royal Infirmary of Edinburgh Trust, 1984–98. Lewis H. Wright Meml Lect., Amer. Soc. of Anesthesiologists, 2006. Member: Clinical Standards Adv. Gp, 1994–99; Adv. Cttee on Distinction Awards, 1992–2000 (Dir and Med. Vice-Chm., Scottish Sub-Cttee, 1995–98); Scottish Adv. Cttee on Distinction Awards, 1998–2000. Pres., Royal Coll. of Anaesthetists, 1991–94 (Vice-Pres., 1988–91). Hon. FDS 1994; Hon. FCEM (Hon. FFAEM 1997). Editor, British Jl of Anaesthesia, 1973–83 (Chm. Bd, 1983–91). *Publications:* books, chapters and papers on anaesthesia and respiratory care. *Recreations:* golf, gardening. *Address:* Harewood, Kilmacolm, Renfrewshire PA13 4HX. *T:* (01505) 872962.

SPENCE, Prof. (Andrew) Michael, PhD; Philip H. Knight Professor of Management, and Dean, Graduate School of Business, Stanford University, 1990–99, now Professor Emeritus; Affiliate, Oak Hill Investment Management (formerly Oak Hill Venture Partners), since 1999; *b* 7 Nov. 1943; *s* of Ernest John Hamilton Spence and Mary Jane Spence (*née* Gotschal); *m* 1st, Ann Bennett (marr. diss.); one *s* two *d*; 2nd, 1997, Monica Cappuccini (marr. diss.); 3rd, 2006, Giuliana Ferraino; one *s. Educ:* Princeton Univ. (BA Philosophy 1966); Oxford Univ. (Rhodes Schol.; MA Maths 1968); Harvard Univ. (PhD Econs 1972). Asst Prof. of Pol Econ., Kennedy Sch. of Govt, Harvard Univ., 1971–75; Associate Prof. of Econs, Stanford Univ., 1973–75; Harvard University: Hon. Res. Fellow, 1975–76, Vis. Prof., 1976–77, Econs Dept; Prof. of Econs, 1977–83, and Prof. of Business Admin, 1979–83; George Gund Prof. of Econs and Business Admin, 1983–86; Chm., Econs Dept, 1983–84; Dean, Faculty of Arts and Scis, 1984–90. Mem., Econs Adv. Cttee, Sloan Foundn, 1979–. Chm., Commn on Growth and Develt, 2006–. Mem., editl bds of jls incl. Amer. Econs Rev., Bell Jl Econs, Jl of Econ. Theory and Public Policy, at various times. Fellow: Econometric Soc., 1975; Amer. Acad. Arts and Scis, 1983. John Bates Clark Medal, Amer. Econ. Assoc., 1981; (jtly) Nobel Prize for Econs, 2001.

Publications: Market Signaling: informational transfer in hiring and related processes, 1974; (jtly) Industrial Organization in an Open Economy, 1980; (jtly) Competitive Structure in Investment Banking, 1983; contrib. numerous articles to professional jls incl. Bell Jl Econs, Qly Jl Econs, Econometrica. *Recreations:* windsurfing, motorcycle riding, golf. *Address:* Ohana Investors, 899 Northgate Drive, Suite 301, San Rafael, CA 94903, USA; *e-mail:* mspence98@gmail.com.

SPENCE, Christopher Alexander, CBE 2006 (MBE 1992); Chief Executive: National Centre for Volunteering, since 1998; Volunteering England, 2004–07; Hon. President, London Lighthouse, 1996–2000; *b* 24 April 1944; *s* of late Robert Donald Spence and Margaret Summerford Spence; *m* 1990, Nancy Corbin Meadors Kline. *Educ:* Bromsgrove Sch.; South West London Coll. (Dip. in Counselling Skills). Dir, Task Force, 1968–70; Private Sec. to Speaker of House of Commons, 1970–76; freelance organisational develt consultant, 1976–86; Founder and Dir, London Lighthouse, 1986–96. Dir, Oxfordshire Learning Disability NHS Trust, 1996–2002 (Vice-Chm., 1998–2002). Founding Chair, Pan London HIV/AIDS Providers Consortium, 1992–96; Chair, HIV Project, 1997– (Dir, 1995–97). Chm., Diana, Princess of Wales Meml Fund, 1999–2006 (Trustee, 1998–2006; Chair, Grants Cttee, 1998–2006). Pres., Eur. Volunteer Centre, 2002–07. FRSA 1998. Hon. Fellow, Univ. of Wales, Lampeter, 1999. *Publications:* (with Nancy Kline) At Least a Hundred Principles of Love, 1985, revd edn 1994; AIDS: time to reclaim our power, 1986; On Watch: views from the Lighthouse, 1996. *Recreations:* gardening, reading, writing, walking, vegetarian cooking, cats with challenging behaviour. *Address:* Lower Farm Orchard, Preston Crowmarsh, Wallingford, Oxon OX10 6SL. *T:* (01491) 835266.

SPENCE, Christopher John; Chairman, English Trust Co. Ltd, 1991–2002 (Managing Director, 1978–91); *b* 4 June 1937; *s* of late Brig. Ian Fleming Morris Spence, OBE, MC, TD, ADC and Ruth Spence (*née* Peacock); *m* 1st, 1960, Merle Aurelia (marr. diss. 1968), *er d* of Sir Leonard Ropner, Bt; one *d* (one *s* decd); 2nd, 1970, Susan, *d* of late Brig. Michael Morley, MBE; one *s* one *d*. *Educ:* Marlborough. 2nd Lieut, 10 Royal Hussars (PWO), 1955–57; Royal Wilts Yeomanry, 1957–66. Mem., London Stock Exchange, 1959–78. Sen. Steward, Jockey Club, 1998–2003. High Sheriff, Berks, 1996–97. *Recreations:* racing, shooting, golf. *Address:* Chieveley Manor, Newbury, Berks RG20 8UT. *T:* (01635) 248208. *Clubs:* Jockey, Pratt's; Swinley Forest Golf.

SPENCE, David Lane, CA; London Senior Partner, Grant Thornton, 1998–2006; *b* 5 Oct. 1943; *s* of Dr Alex S. Spence and Edith F. Spence; *m* 1966, Beverley Esther Cardale; one *s* two *d*. *Educ:* Fettes Coll., Edinburgh. CA 1967. C. F. Middleton & Co., 1962–67; Grant Thornton (formerly Thornton Baker), 1967–2006: Partner, 1970; Europ. Practice Partner, 1974–80; Exec. Partner, 1983–89. DTI Inspector, 1989 and 1992. Chm., Chartered Accountants Jt Ethics Cttee, 1995–97. Pres., Inst. Chartered Accountants of Scotland, 1998–99 (Vice-Pres., 1996–98). *Recreations:* golf, occasional cycling, tinkering with old MGs. *Address:* Hendred, Hatton Hill, Windlesham, Surrey GU20 6AB. *Clubs:* Caledonian; Sunningdale, Royal and Ancient Golf.

SPENCE, Rt Rev. (David) Ralph; Bishop of Niagara, 1997–2008; *b* 10 March 1942; *m* Carol Anne Spence; one *s* two *d*. *Educ:* Univ. of Guelph (BA 1964); Wycliffe Coll. (LTh 1968). Ordained priest, 1968; Asst Curate, St George's, Guelph, 1968–70; Rector: St Bartholomew, Hamilton, 1970–74; St John, Thorold, 1974–82; St Luke's, Burlington, 1982–97; Archdeacon of Trafalgar, 1992–97. Hon. DD: Wycliffe Coll., 1999; Trinity Coll., Toronto, 2000; Huron Coll., 2004. *Address:* c/o Cathedral Place, 252 James Street N, Hamilton, ON L8R 2L3, Canada. *T:* (905) 5271316, *Fax:* (905) 5271281.

SPENCE, Most Rev. Francis John; Archbishop of Kingston (Ontario), (RC), 1982–2002, now Emeritus; *b* Perth, Ont, 3 June 1926; *s* of William John Spence and Rose Anna Spence (*née* Jordan). *Educ:* St Michael's Coll., Toronto (BA 1946); St Augustine's Seminary, Toronto; St Thomas Univ., Rome (JCD 1955). Ordained priest, 1950; Bishop, 1967; Auxiliary to Mil. Vicar, Canadian Forces, 1967–82; Bishop of Charlottetown, PEI, 1970–82; Mil. Vicar, 1982–88. Pres., Canadian Conf. of Catholic Bishops, 1995–97. *Address:* 390 Palace Road, Kingston, ON K7L 4T3, Canada.

SPENCE, Gabriel John; Under Secretary, Department of Education and Science, retired; *b* 5 April 1924; *s* of G. S. and D. A. Spence, Hope, Flints; *m* 1950, Averil Kingston (*née* Beresford) (*d* 1998); (one *s* decd). *Educ:* Arnold House; King's Sch., Chester (King's Schol., Head of School); Wadham Coll., Oxon (Schol.). MA 1949; Stanhope Prize and Proxime, Gibbs Schol., Oxon, 1947; Haldane Essay Prize, Inst. Public Admin, 1959. Joined Civil Service 1949 (Min. of Works, Science Office, Min. of Housing and Local Govt, DES); Jt Sec., Adv. Council on Scientific Policy, 1959–62; Asst Sec., DES, 1964–73; Sec., Council for Scientific Policy, 1964–67; Under Sec., DES, 1973–81; Dep. Sec., UGC, 1978–81. Admin. Staff Coll., Henley, 1957. Trustee, The Oates Meml and Gilbert White Library and Museum, 1982–. *Recreations:* natural history, photography, golf. *Address:* Old Heath, Hillbrow Road, Liss, Hants GU33 7QD. *T:* (01730) 893235.

SPENCE, Ian Richard; international tax consultant and adviser to developing countries, since 1998; *b* 15 Oct. 1938; *s* of John Jack Spence and Floretta Spence (*née* Bate); *m* 1971, Anne Kiggell; two *d*. *Educ:* Dulwich Coll.; Jesus Coll., Cambridge (BA Hist.). Joined Inland Revenue, 1962; seconded to DEA, 1966; Principal, 1967; seconded to CSSB, 1972; Asst Sec., 1975; Under Sec., and Dir, Internat. Div., Bd of Inland Revenue, 1991–98. Mem., Permanent Scientific Cttee, Internat. Fiscal Assoc., 1993–99. Sen. Res. Fellow, Internat. Tax and Investment Centre, 1999–2002. *Recreations:* theatre, opera, tennis, sailing, golf. *Address:* 98 Burbage Road, SE24 9HE. *T:* and *Fax:* (020) 7274 6198; *e-mail:* Ian_spence@btinternet.com. *Clubs:* Athenæum; Dulwich Sports; Dulwich and Sydenham Golf; Old Fogeys Golfing Soc.

SPENCE, Prof. Jonathan Dermot, CMG 2001; PhD; Sterling Professor of History, Yale University, since 1993; *b* 11 Aug. 1936; *s* of Dermot Gordon Chesson Spence and Muriel Evelyn Crailsham; *m* 1st, 1962, Helen Alexander (marr. diss. 1993); two *s*; 2nd, 1993, Annping Chin; one step *s* one step *d*. *Educ:* Winchester Coll.; Clare Coll., Cambridge (BA 1959; Hon. Fellow, 2006); Yale Univ. (MA 1961; PhD 1965). Yale University: Asst Prof., then Prof., 1966–, Chm., 1984–86, History Dept; George Burton Prof., 1976; Dir, Div. of Humanities, 1981–83; Mem. Bd of Govs, Yale Univ. Press, 1994–. Hon. Prof., Univ. of Nanjing, 1994–; Guggenheim Fellow, 1979–80; MacArthur Fellow, 1988–92. Council of Scholars, Library of Congress, 1988–96. Fellow: Amer. Acad. of Arts and Scis, 1985; Amer. Philosophical Soc., 1993; Corresp. FBA 1997. Hon. degrees from 8 American colls, and Chinese Univ. of Hong Kong, 1996; Hon. DLitt Oxon, 2003. *Publications:* Ts'ao Yin and the K'ang-hsi Emperor: bondservant and master, 1966, 2nd edn 1988; To Change China: Western advisers in China 1620–1960, 1969, 2nd edn 1980; Emperor of China: self-portrait of K'ang-hsi, 1974; The Death of Woman Wang, 1978; (ed with John E. Wills) From Ming to Ch'ing: conquest, region and continuity in seventeenth-century China, 1979; The Gate of Heavenly Peace: the Chinese and their revolution 1895–1980, 1981; The Memory Palace of Matteo Ricci, 1984; The Question of Hu, 1988; The Search for Modern China, 1990, 2nd edn 1999; Chinese Roundabout: essays in history and culture, 1992; God's Chinese Son: the Taiping heavenly kingdom of Hong Xiuquan, 1996; (with Annping Chin) The Chinese Century: a photographic history of the last hundred years, 1996; The Chan's Great Continent: China in Western minds, 1998; Mao Zedong, 1999; Treason by the Book, 2001. *Recreation:* gardening. *Address:* 691 Forest Road, West Haven, CT 06516, USA. *Clubs:* Athenæum; Yale (New York City).

SPENCE, Dr Joseph Arthur Francis; Headmaster, Oakham School, 2002–Aug. 2009; Master, Dulwich College, from Sept. 2009; *b* 18 Dec. 1959; *s* of Joseph Arthur Spence and Lenice Mary Spence (*nee* Woolley); *m* 1985, Angela Margaret Alexander Fiddes; two *s* one *d*. *Educ:* St Philip's Grammar Sch., Edgbaston; Salesian Coll., Battersea; Univ. of Reading (BA Hons Modern History and Politics); Birkbeck Coll., London (PhD 1991). Master in College, Eton Coll., 1992–2002. Governor: Dragon Sch., Oxford; St John's Sch., Cambridge; S Anselm's Sch., Bakewell. *Publications:* (ed) The Sayings of W. B. Yeats, 1993; (ed) The Sayings of G. B. Shaw, 1993; (ed) The Sayings of Jonathan Swift, 1994; contrib. to Oxford DNB, TLS, Irish Historical Studies. *Address:* (until Aug. 2009) Deanscroft, Oakham School, Rutland LE15 6QU; *e-mail:* headmaster@oakham.rutland.sch.uk; (from Sept. 2009) Dulwich College, Dulwich, SE21 7LD.

SPENCE, Malcolm Hugh; QC 1979; a Recorder, 1985–99; a Deputy High Court Judge, 1988–99; barrister-at-law, since 1958; *b* 23 March 1934; *s* of late Dr Allan William and Martha Lena Spence; *m* 1967, Jennifer Jane, *d* of Lt-Gen. Sir George Cole, KCB, CBE; one *s* one *d*. *Educ:* Summer Fields, Oxford; Stowe Sch.; Gonville and Caius Coll., Cambridge (MA, LLM). Gray's Inn: James Mould Schol., Holker Sen. Exhibnr, Lee Prizeman; called to the Bar, 1958; Bencher, 1988. Worcester Regt, First Lieut, 1954. Marshal to Mr Justice McNair, 1957; Pupil to Mr Nigel Bridge (now Lord Bridge of Harwich), 1958; entered chambers of Mr John Widgery, QC, 1958; practises mainly in Town and Country Planning and Compensation for Compulsory Purchase. Chm., Planning and Envmt (formerly Local Govt Planning and Envmtl) Bar Assoc., 1994–98. Chartered Arbitrator, 2003; Accredited Mediator, 2006; FCIArb 1999. Freeman, City of London, 2001; Liveryman, Arbitrators' Co., 2001. Chm., Wagner Soc., 2002–08. *Publications:* (jtly) Rating Law and Valuation, 1961; The Chambers of Marshall Hall: 125 years, 2005. *Recreations:* trout and salmon fishing, forestry, golf (Captain: Cambridge University Stymies, 1957; Old Stoic Golfing Soc., 1972; Semi-finalist, Scandinavian Amateur Championship, 1964), opera. *Address:* (chambers) 2/3 Gray's Inn Square, WC1R 5JH. *T:* (020) 7242 4986; 1 Gray's Inn Square, WC1R 5AA. *T:* (020) 7405 4379; Scamadale, Arisaig, Inverness-shire PH39 4NS. *T:* (01687) 450698. *Clubs:* Caledonian; Hawks (Cambridge).

SPENCE, Michael; *see* Spence, A. M.

SPENCE, Rt Rev. Ralph; *see* Spence, Rt Rev. D. R.

SPENCE, Prof. Robert, FREng; Professor of Information Engineering, Imperial College of Science, Technology and Medicine, 1984–2000, now Emeritus; *b* 11 July 1933; *s* of Robert Whitehair Spence and Minnie Grace Spence (*née* Wood); *m* 1960, Kathleen Potts (*d* 2003); one *s* one *d*. *Educ:* Hymers Coll., Hull; Hull Coll. of Technology (BScEng Hons London External 1954); Imperial College, London (DIC 1955; PhDEng 1959; DScEng 1983); Dr RCA 1997. FIET, FIEEE, FCGI; FREng (FEng 1990). Hull Corp. Telephones, 1950–51; General Dynamics/Electronics, Rochester, NY, 1959–62; Department of Electrical Engineering, Imperial College: Lectr, 1962–68; Reader, 1968–84. Vis. Erskine Fellow, Univ. of Canterbury, NZ, 2002; Vis. Prof., UMIST, 2003–. Hon. Prof., Univ. of Waikato, 2007–. Chm. and Founding Dir, Interactive Solutions Ltd, 1985–90. Officier de l'Ordre des Palmes Académiques (France), 1995 (Chevalier, 1985). *Publications:* Linear Active Networks, 1970; Tellegen's Theorem and Electrical Networks, 1970 (trans. Russian and Chinese); Resistive Circuit Theory, 1974; Modern Network Theory, 1978; Sensitivity and Optimization, 1980; Circuit Analysis by Computer, 1986; Tolerance Design of Electronic Circuits, 1988 (trans. Japanese); Information Visualization, 2001; Information Visualization: design for interaction, 2007; Introductory Circuits, 2008; numerous papers in learned jls. *Recreations:* steel band (bass player), concrete aspects of gardening. *Address:* 1 Regent's Close, Whyteleafe, Surrey CR3 0AH. *T:* (020) 8668 3649.

SPENCE, Ronald Blackwood, CB 1997; Chairman: The Change Alliance, since 2001; Blackwood Enterprises Ltd, since 2001; Probation Board for Northern Ireland, since 2004; *b* 13 July 1941; *s* of Harold Spence and Margaret Spence (*née* McClure); *m* 1st, 1964, Julia Fitton (marr. diss. 1989); one *s* one *d*; 2nd, 1989, Sarah McKnight. *Educ:* Methodist Coll., Belfast; Queen's Univ., Belfast (BA Hons). Entered NICS as Asst Principal, 1963; Principal, Min. of Devel, 1967–74; Asst Sec., DoE, 1974–80; Head, Econ. and Social Div., NI Office, 1980–82; Under Sec., Dept of Finance and Personnel, 1982–85; Head, Central Secretariat, 1985–90; Under Sec., Dept of Econ. Develt, 1990–94; Permanent Secretary: DoE (NI), 1994–99; Dept for Regl Develt (NI), 1999–2001. Chairman: NI Partnership Bd, 1996–2001; NI Events Co., 1997–2002; Mem., NI Legal Services Commn, 2003–. Trustee and Dep. Chm., Nat. Heritage Meml Fund and Heritage Lottery Fund, 2006–. Mem. Council, Univ. of Ulster, 2007–. Hon. Sen. Res. Fellow, Inst. of Governance, QUB, 2001–07. *Recreation:* golf.

SPENCE, His Honour Stanley Brian; a Circuit Judge, 1991–2006; Resident Judge, Reading Crown Court, 1999–2006; *b* 3 May 1937; *s* of George Henry Spence and Sarah Spence (*née* Hoad); *m* 1961, Victoria Rosaleen Tapper; one *s* one *d*. *Educ:* Portsmouth Grammar Sch.; Britannia Royal Naval College, Dartmouth. Commissioned Supply and Secretariat Specialisation, RN, 1958; served: HMS Eagle; Staff of FO2 FEF; Portsmouth; 3rd Frigate Sqdn; HMS St Vincent; legal training, 1966–68; called to the Bar, Middle Temple, 1968; served: HMS Terror, Singapore; Staff of Commander FEF; 8th Frigate Sqdn; Legal Advr to C-in-C Naval Home Command and Flag Officer Spithead; retired from RN, 1975; Office of Judge Advocate General of the Forces (Army and RAF), 1975–90; Recorder of the Crown Court, 1987–91. *Recreations:* maintaining a cottage in France, wine.

SPENCER, family name of **Viscount Churchill** and of **Earl Spencer**.

SPENCER, 9th Earl *cr* 1765; **Charles Edward Maurice Spencer;** DL; Baron and Viscount Spencer 1761; Viscount Althorp 1765; Viscount Althorp (UK) 1905; writer; *b* 20 May 1964; *s* of 8th Earl Spencer, LVO and Hon. Frances Ruth Burke Roche, *yr d* of 4th Baron Fermoy; *S* father, 1992; *m* 1989, Victoria (marr. diss. 1997), *d* of John Lockwood; one *s* three *d* (incl. twin *d*); *m* 2001, Caroline Victoria Freud (*née* Hutton); one *s* one *d*. *Educ:* Maidwell Hall; Eton College; Magdalen Coll., Oxford. Page of Honour to HM the Queen, 1977–79; contributing correspondent, NBC News, 1987–91 and 1993–95; reporter, Granada Television, 1991–93; presenter, NBC Super Channel, 1995–96; writer, Planet Wild, 1998–2000; freelance writer, 2001–. DL Northants, 2005. *Publications:* Althorp: the story of an English home, 1998; The Spencer Family, 1999; Blenheim: battle for Europe, 2004; Prince Rupert: the last cavalier, 2007. *Heir: s* Viscount Althorp, *qv*. *Address:* Althorp, Northampton NN7 4HG.

SPENCER, Raine, Countess; *b* 9 Sept. 1929; *d* of late Alexander George McCorquodale and Dame Barbara Cartland, DBE; *m* 1st, 1948, 9th Earl of Dartmouth (marr. diss. 1976);

three *s* one *d*; 2nd, 1976, 8th Earl Spencer, LVO; 3rd, 1993, Comte Jean-François de Chambrun (marr. diss. 1996). Westminster City Councillor, 1954–65 (served on various cttees); Member: for Lewisham West, LCC, 1958–65 (served on Town Planning, Parks, Staff Appeals Cttees); for Richmond upon Thames, GLC, 1967–73; GLC Gen. Purposes Cttee, 1971–73; Chm., GLC Historic Buildings Bd, 1968–71; Mem., Environmental Planning Cttee, 1967–71; Chm., Covent Garden Develt Cttee, 1971–72; Chm., Govt working party on Human Habitat in connection with UN Conf. on Environment, Stockholm (June 1972), 1971–72 (report: How Do You Want to Live?); Chm., UK Exec., European Architectural Heritage Year, 1975. British Tourist Authority: Member: Infrastructure Cttee, 1972–86; Board, 1982–93; Chairman: Spas Cttee, 1982–83; Accommodation Cttee (formerly Hotels and Restaurants Cttee), 1983–93; Develt Cttee, 1986–93; Commended Hotels Panel, 1986–90; Cttee, Britain Welcomes Japan, 1990–92; Come to Britain Awards, 1990–93; Member: English Tourist Bd, 1971–75; Adv. Council, V&A Museum, 1980–83; Cttee of Honour, Business Sponsorship of the Arts, 1980; Tourism Deptl Adv. Council, Surrey Univ.; Commn de Tourisme Prestige, Nice, 1993–95. Mem. Jury, improvement of Promenade des Anglais, Nice, 1993–95. Formerly LCC Voluntary Care Cttee Worker, Wandsworth and Vauxhall. Director: Harrods International Ltd, 1996–; Harrods (Management) Ltd, 2001–; Harrods Estates, 2006–. Hon. Dr Laws, Dartmouth Coll., USA. *Publications:* What Is Our Heritage?, 1975; The Spencers on Spas (with photographs by Earl Spencer), 1983; Japan and the East (with photographs by Earl Spencer), 1986. *Address:* Sprimont Lodge, 2A Sprimont Place, SW3 3HU. *T:* 07917 000941, *Fax:* (office) (020) 7225 2021; Whiteway House, Chudleigh, Newton Abbot, Devon TQ13 0DY.

SPENCER, Comdt Anne Christine, CBE 1994; Director, Women's Royal Naval Service, 1991–93; *b* 15 Dec. 1938; *d* of late Ernest Spencer and Dora Harrie (*née* Hauxwell). *Educ:* Newlands High Sch.; Yorks Coll. of Housecraft (HCIMA 1959). Direct Entry Officer, WRNS, 1962; commnd 1963; HMS Victory, 1963–64; HMS Dauntless, 1964–66; HMS Terror, Singapore, 1966–68; HMS St Vincent, 1968–69; HMS Nelson, 1969–70; Officer i/c WRNS, HMS Excellent, 1970–73; HMS Pembroke, 1973–74; Mess Manager, RNC, Greenwich, 1974–76; Defence Intelligence Staff, MoD, 1976–78; RNSC, 1978; Directorate of Naval Service Conditions, MoD, 1978–79; Terminology Co-ordinator, NATO HQ Brussels, 1979–81; WRNS Officers Appointer, MoD, 1981–83; Dep. Dir, WRNS, MoD, 1984–86; Naval Dir, NAAFI Bd of Management, 1986–88; Chief Staff Officer (Admin) to Flag Officer, Plymouth, 1988–91. ADC to HM Queen, 1991–93. *Recreations:* theatre, art, food, friends, Yorkshire. *Address:* 6 Wilkinson House, Gunners Row, Marine Gate, Southsea, Hants PO4 9XQ.

SPENCER, Charles Easdale; theatre critic, Daily Telegraph, since 1991; *b* 4 March 1955; *s* of Graham Easdale Spencer and Dorothy Aileen Spencer (*née* Brundan); *m* 1983, Nicola Katrak; one *s*. *Educ:* Charterhouse; Balliol Coll., Oxford (BA Hons Eng. Lang. and Lit.). Surrey Daily Advertiser, 1976–79; Arts Reporter, Evening Standard, 1979–84; Chief Sub-editor, The Stage, 1984–86; Dep. Theatre Critic, London Daily News, 1986–87; Asst Arts Editor and Dep. Theatre Critic, Daily Telegraph, 1987–91. Vice-Pres., Critics' Circle, 2006– (Chm., Drama Section, 2004–). FRSA 2002. Critic of the Year, British Press Awards, 1999, 2008. *Publications:* I Nearly Died, 1994; Full Personal Service, 1996; Under the Influence, 2000. *Recreations:* food, pop music, dossing around. *Address:* 16 Derwent Close, Claygate, Esher, Surrey KT10 0RF. *T:* (01372) 465591; (work) (020) 7538 6413. *Club:* Garrick.

SPENCER, Cyril Charles, CMG 1951; First Deputy Executive Director, International Coffee Organisation, London, 1964–68; *b* 1 Feb. 1912; *s* of late Albert Edward Spencer, CBE, and Elsie Maud Spencer; *m* 1st, 1938; (one *d* decd); 2nd, 1949, Catherine Dewar Robertson (*d* 1995); 3rd, 1998, Phyllis Steele (*née* Rees) (*d* 1999); 4th, 2001, Penny Adames (*née* Salvidge). *Educ:* Royal Grammar Sch., Worcester; St John's Coll., Cambridge (BA 1934). Uganda: Asst Treas., 1935; Asst District Officer, 1937; Asst Financial Sec., 1946; Economic Sec., E Africa High Commission, 1948; Financial Sec., 1948; Acting Chief Sec. at various dates; Acting Governor, July 1951; Chairman: Uganda Lint Marketing Bd; Uganda Coffee Marketing Board; Member: Uganda Electricity Board; Uganda Development Corp.; Comr on Special Duty, Uganda, 1953–61; Sec.-Gen., Inter-African Coffee Organisation, Paris, 1961–64. *Recreations:* golf, fishing.

SPENCER, Sir Derek (Harold), Kt 1992; QC 1980; QC (NI) 1992; a Recorder, 1979–92 and 1998–2001; *b* 31 March 1936; *s* of Thomas Harold Spencer and Gladys Spencer (*née* Heslop); *m* 1st, 1960, Joan (*née* Nutter) (marr. diss.); two *s* one *d*; 2nd, 1988, Caroline Alexandra (*d* 2003), *yr d* of Dr Franziskus Pärn, Hamburg; one *s*. *Educ:* Clitheroe Royal Grammar Sch.; Keble Coll., Oxford (MA, BCL). 2nd Lieut, King's Own Royal Regt, 1954–56; served in Nigeria. Part-time Law Tutor, Keble Coll., Oxford, 1960–64; called to the Bar, Gray's Inn, 1961 (Holt Scholar; Arden Scholar; Bencher, 1991); in practice SE Circuit. Councillor, London Borough of Camden, 1978–83; Dep. Leader, Conservative Party, London Borough of Camden, 1979–81. Contested (C) Leicester South, 1987. MP (C): Leicester South, 1983–87; Brighton Pavilion, 1992–97; contested (C) same seat, 1997. PPS: to Home Office Ministers, 1986; to the Attorney General, 1986–87; Solicitor-Gen., 1992–97. Joint Sec. Cons. Parly Legal Affairs Cttee, 1985–87. Vice-Chm., St Pancras North Cons. Assoc., 1977–78; Treas., City of London and Westminster Cons. Assoc., 1990–91. *Recreations:* reading, swimming, walking. *Address:* 18 Red Lion Court, EC4A 3EB.

SPENCER, Prof. Harrison Clark, MD; President and Chief Executive Officer, Association of Schools of Public Health, Washington, since 2000; *b* 22 Sept. 1944; *s* of Harrison C. and Dorothy M. Spencer; *m* 1977, Christine Michel; two *s*. *Educ:* Haverford Coll. (BA 1965); Johns Hopkins Univ. (MD 1969); Univ. of Calif at Berkeley (MPH 1972); DTM&H London 1972. FACP 1986; FACPM. Intern in Medicine, Vanderbilt Univ., 1969–70; Med. Resident, USPHS Hosp., San Francisco, 1970–71; Epidemic Intelligence Service Officer, CDC Atlanta, 1972–74; Sen. Med. Resident, Univ. of Calif at San Francisco, 1974–75; Med. Res. Officer, Central American Res. Station, El Salvador, 1975–77; MO, Bureau of Tropical Diseases, CDC, 1977–79; SMO and Malaria Res. Co-ordinator, Clin. Res. Center, Kenya Med. Res. Inst., Nairobi, 1979–84; MO, Malaria Action Prog., WHO, Geneva, 1984–87; Chief, Parasitic Diseases Br., CDC, Atlanta, 1987–91; Dean: Sch. of Public Health and Tropical Medicine, Tulane Univ., 1991–95; LSHTM, London Univ., 1996–2000. *Publications:* over 100 articles on epidemiology, malaria, community-based health, internat. health and tropical medicine. *Recreations:* music, ballet, tennis. *Address:* Association of Schools of Public Health, 1101 15th Street NW, Washington, DC 20005, USA.

SPENCER, Isobel; *see* Johnstone, I. T.

SPENCER, Ivor, MBE 2002; DL; professional toastmaster, since 1956; Chairman and Managing Director, Ivor Spencer Enterprises Ltd, since 1965; *b* 20 Nov. 1924; *s* of Barnet and Dora Isaacs; *m* 1948, Estella Spencer; one *s* one *d*. *Educ:* Rochells Sch., London. Principal: Ivor Spencer Sch. for Professional Toastmasters, 1975–; Ivor Spencer Internat. Sch. for Butler Administrators/Personal Assistants, UK and USA, 1981–. Founder and Life President: Guild of Professional Toastmasters, 1967–98; Guild of Internat. Professional Toastmasters, 1990– (Lifetime Achievement Award, 1998; Toastmaster of the Year 2000); President: Toastmasters for Royal Occasions, 1975–; Toastmasters of GB, 1976–; Toastmasters of England, 1978–. Dir, Guild of British Butlers, 1980–; Chief Executive: British Professional Toastmasters Authority, 1995–; Ivor Spencer Professional Toastmasters Authority, 1998–. AMInstD 1997. DL Greater London, 1985. *Publications:* A Toastmaster's Story, 1975; Speeches and Toasts, 1980. *Recreations:* after-dinner speaking, organising special events worldwide. *Address:* 12 and 14 Little Bornes, Dulwich, SE21 8SE. *T:* (020) 8670 5585, *Fax:* (020) 8670 0055; *e-mail:* ivor@ivorspencer.com.

SPENCER, James; QC 1991; **His Honour Judge Spencer;** a Circuit Judge, since 2001; *b* 27 May 1947; *s* of James Henry Spencer and Irene Dulcie (*née* Wilson). *Educ:* The King's Sch., Pontefract; Univ. of Newcastle upon Tyne (LLB). Admitted solicitor, 1971; called to the Bar, Gray's Inn, 1975. A Recorder, 1990–2001. A Pres., Mental Health Review Tribunal, 1999–. Mem., Parole Bd, 2002–. *Recreations:* watching Rugby League, playing golf. *Address:* Combined Court Centre, 1 Oxford Row, Leeds LS1 3BG.

SPENCER, Prof. John Rason; Professor of Law, University of Cambridge, since 1995; Fellow, Selwyn College, Cambridge, since 1970; *b* 19 March 1946; *s* of Donald Edward Spencer and Catherine Mary Spencer (*née* Cozens); *m* 1972, Rosemary Stewartson; one *s* two *d*. *Educ:* Blandford Grammar Sch.; Selwyn Coll., Cambridge (MA, LLB); LLD. Cambridge University: Asst Lectr, Law Faculty, 1973–76; Lectr, 1976–91; Reader, 1991–95; Chm., Law Faculty, 1995–97. Mem., Calcutt Cttee on Privacy and Related Matters, 1990; Consultant, Criminal Courts Review, 2000. Hon. QC 2003; Bencher, Inner Temple, 2003; Hon. Member of Chambers: Hardwicke Bldg, 2003; 15 New Bridge St, 2004. DenD *hc* Poitiers, 2004. Chevalier, Ordre des Palmes Académiques (France), 2000. *Publications:* Jackson's Machinery of Justice, 8th edn 1989; (with Rhona Flin) The Evidence of Children: the law and the psychology, 1990, 2nd edn 1993; La procédure pénale anglaise (Que sais-je?), 1998; (jtly) European Criminal Procedures, 2002; Evidence of Bad Character, 2006; Hearsay Evidence in Criminal Proceedings, 2008. *Address:* Selwyn College, Cambridge CB3 9DQ.

SPENCER, Dr Jonathan Page, CB 2002; Director General, Clients and Policy, Department for Constitutional Affairs (formerly Lord Chancellor's Department), 2003–05 (Director General, Policy, 2002); company director and public policy consultant, since 2006; *b* 24 April 1949; *s* of John Spencer and Doreen (*née* Page); *m* 1976, Caroline Sarah Armitage; one *s* two *d*. *Educ:* Bournemouth Sch.; Downing Coll., Cambridge (BA); Oxford Univ. (DPhil). ICI Res. Fellow, Oxford, 1973–74; joined Department of Trade and Industry, 1974: Principal, 1977; Principal Private Sec. to successive Secs of State, 1982–83; Asst Sec., 1983; Cabinet Office, 1987–89; Under Sec., 1991; Dir, Insurance Div., then Directorate, 1991–97; Director General: Resources and Services, 1997–2000; Business Competitiveness, 2000–02. Member: Admin. Justice & Tribunals Council (formerly Council on Tribunals), 2005–; SRA (formerly Law Soc. Regulation Bd), 2006–. *Recreations:* music, keeping the house up and the garden down. *Address:* Little Eggarton, Godmersham, Canterbury, Kent CT4 7DY.

SPENCER, Martin Benedict; QC 2003; *b* 19 June 1956; *s* of Dr Seymour Spencer and late Margaret Spencer; *m* 1977, Lisbet Steengaard Jensen; two *s* one *d*. *Educ:* Hertford Coll., Oxford (MA, BCL). Called to the Bar, Inner Temple, 1979; in practice, Hailsham Chambers, 1981–. Mem. Exec. Cttee, Professional Negligence Bar Assoc., 1999–. Mem., Editl Bd, Kemp and Kemp, 2004–. *Publications:* (jtly) The Danish Criminal Code, 1999; (jtly) The Civil Procedure Rules in Action, 2000; (contrib.) Risk Management and Litigation in Obstetrics and Gynaecology, ed by R. V. Clements, 2001. *Recreation:* music (Member, St Albans Bach Choir). *Address:* 4 Paper Buildings, Temple, EC4Y 7EX. *Club:* Danish.

See also M. G. Spencer.

SPENCER, Michael Alan; Group Chief Executive, ICAP plc, since 1999; Treasurer, Conservative Party, since 2007; *b* 30 May 1955; *s* of Oscar and Diana Spencer; *m* 1983, Lorraine Geraldine Murphy; two *s* one *d*. *Educ:* Worth Abbey; Corpus Christi Coll., Oxford (MA). Analyst, Simon & Coates, 1976–80; Vice Pres., Drexel Burnham Lambert, 1981–83; Dir, Charles Fulton, 1983–86; Chairman: Intercapital, 1986–; Numis plc, 2003–. *Recreations:* running, riding, shooting, wine, art, politics. *Address:* ICAP plc, 1–2 Broadgate, EC2M 7UR. *T:* (020) 7050 7400, *Fax:* (020) 7050 7116. *Clubs:* Turf, London Capital.

SPENCER, Michael Gerald; QC 1989; a Recorder, 1987–2005; *b* 1 Dec. 1947; *s* of Dr Seymour J. G. Spencer and late Margaret (*née* Behn); *m* 1969, Catherine Helen (*née* Dickinson); three *s*. *Educ:* Ampleforth Coll.; Hertford Coll., Oxford (MA Hons). Called to the Bar, Inner Temple, 1970, Bencher, 1996; Mem., Oxford Circuit, 1971, Midland and Oxford, then Midland, Circuit, 1972–. Dir, Yattendon Investment Trust, 1992–. Member: Hertford Coll. Boat Club Soc.; Ampleforth Soc. Chm. and Trustee, Ampleforth Beagles, 1995–. *Publications:* (contrib.) Medical Negligence, 1990; (contrib.) Doctors, Patients and the Law, 1992. *Recreations:* golf, reading, classical music, beagling, paragliding, ski-ing. *Address:* Crown Office Chambers, Temple, EC4Y 7HJ. *T:* (020) 7797 8100. *Clubs:* Pegasus, Bar Yacht, Chiltern Rugby Football; Beaconsfield Golf, Inner Temple Golf, Bar Golf.

See also M. B. Spencer.

SPENCER, Robin Godfrey; QC 1999; a Recorder, since 1998; a Deputy High Court Judge, since 2001; *b* 8 July 1955; *s* of late Eric Spencer and of Audrey Elaine Spencer (*née* Brown); *m* 1978, Julia Margaret Eileen Burley; three *d*. *Educ:* King's Sch., Chester; Emmanuel Coll., Cambridge (MA). Called to the Bar, Gray's Inn, 1978 (Holker Sen. Award; Colyer Prize), Bencher, 2005; in practice, Wales and Chester Circuit, 1978–, Leader, 2004–06; an Asst Recorder, 1993–98. *Recreations:* music, cricket, football, Methodist history. *Address:* 9–12 Bell Yard, WC2A 2JR. *T:* (020) 7400 1800; 1 Stanley Place, Chester CH1 2LU. *T:* (01244) 348282.

SPENCER, Dame Rosemary (Jane), DCMG 1999 (CMG 1991); HM Diplomatic Service, retired; Ambassador to the Netherlands, 1996–2001; *b* 1 April 1941; *d* of Air Vice-Marshal Geoffrey Roger Cole Spencer, CB, CBE, and Juliet Mary Spencer (*née* Warwick). *Educ:* Upper Chine Sch., Shanklin, IoW; St Hilda's Coll., Oxford (BA Hons Modern Langs). Joined Foreign Office, 1962; FO, 1962–65; Third Secretary, Nairobi, 1965–67; Second Sec., FCO, 1967–70; Second Sec., UK Delegn to EEC, and Private Sec. to Hon. Sir Con O'Neill, Official Leader of UK negotiating team, 1970–71; First Sec., Office of UK Permanent Representative to EEC, Brussels, 1972–73; First Sec. (Economic), Lagos, 1974–77; First Sec., Asst Head of Rhodesia Dept, FCO, 1977–80; RCDS 1980; Counsellor (Agric. and Economic Affairs), Paris, 1980–84; Counsellor (External Relations), Office of UK Perm. Rep. to EEC, 1984–87; Hd of European Community Dept (External), FCO, 1987–89; Asst Under-Sec. of State, FCO, 1989–92; Minister and Hd of British Embassy Berlin Office, 1993–96. Member: Salisbury Cathedral Chapter, 2001–07; Salisbury Cathedral Council, 2002–; Bd, Salisbury Festival, 2003–; Pres., Salisbury Civic Soc., 2007–. Trustee: Heinz Koeppler Trust, 2001– (Chm., 2005–); Magna Carta Trust, 2002–; World Faiths Develt Dialogue, 2002–05. Chm., Nikaean

Club, 2002–. Member: Council and Court, Imperial Coll., London Univ., 2001–05; Council, St Swithun's Sch., 2001–04; Gov., Internat. Coll., Sherborne Sch., 2001–; Patron, Berlin British Sch., 2002–. *Recreations:* country walking, travel, domestic arts. *Address:* c/o FCO Association, Old Admiralty Building, SW1A 2AA. *Clubs:* Oxford and Cambridge; International (Berlin).

SPENCER, Sarah Ann, CBE 2007; Associate Director (formerly Director of Policy Research), Centre on Migration, Policy and Society, University of Oxford, since 2003; Associate Member, Nuffield College, Oxford, since 2004; Chair, Equality and Diversity Forum, since 2002; *b* 11 Dec. 1952; *d* of late Dr I. O. B. Spencer and of Dr Elspeth Wilkinson; *m* 1978, Brian Anthony Hackland, *qv*; two *s*. *Educ:* Nottingham Univ. (BA Hons); University Coll. London (MPhil). Researcher, Law Faculty, UCL, 1977–79; Res. Officer, Cobden Trust (Civil Liberties Charity), 1979–84, Dir 1984–85; Gen. Sec., NCCL, 1985–89; Res. Fellow, 1990–2003, Dir, Citizenship and Governance (formerly Human Rights) Prog., 1994–2003, IPPR. Member: Home Office Task Force on Implementation of the Human Rights Act, 1998–2001; Commn on Future of Multi-Ethnic Britain, 1999–2000; CRE, 2002–06 (Dep. Chm., 2003–05; Chm., Inquiry into site provision for Gypsies and Travellers, 2004–06); DTI Task Force Commn on Equality and Human Rights, 2003–05. Advr, Cabinet Office, 2000 and 2002–03. Vis. Prof., Human Rights Centre, Univ. of Essex, 2002–. Gov., British Inst. of Human Rights, 2002–. Editor, Rights Jl, 1979–84. FRSA. *Publications:* Called to Account: police accountability in England and Wales, 1985; (jtly) The New Prevention of Terrorism Act, 1985; The Role of Police Authorities during the Miners' Strike, 1985; (jtly) A British Bill of Rights, 1990; (jtly) Accountable Policing: effectiveness, empowerment and equity, 1993; (ed) Strangers and Citizens: a positive approach to migrants and refugees, 1994; (ed) Immigration as an Economic Asset: the German experience, 1994; Migrants, Refugees and the Boundaries of Citizenship, 1995; (jtly) A UK Human Rights Commission, 1998; (jtly) Mainstreaming Human Rights in Whitehall and Westminster, 1999; (jtly) Migration: an economic and social analysis, 2001; (jtly) Reluctant Witness, 2001; (jtly) Them and Us? The Public, Offenders and the Criminal Justice System, 2002; (ed) The Politics of Migration: managing opportunity, conflict and change, 2003; (jtly) Age as an Equality Issue: legal and policy perspectives, 2003; (jtly) Age Equality Comes of Age, 2003; (jtly) Fair Enough: Central and East European migrants in low wage employment in the UK, 2006; (contrib.) Blair's Britain, 1997–2007, 2007. *Address:* (office) 58 Banbury Road, Oxford OX2 6QS.

SPENCER, Shaun Michael; QC 1988; **His Honour Judge Shaun Spencer;** a Circuit Judge, since 2002; a Deputy High Court Judge, since 1999; *b* 4 Feb. 1944; *s* of late Edward Michael Spencer, Leeds and Barbara Spencer (*née* Williams); *m* 1971, Nicola, *e d* of F. G. Greenwood, Tockwith, York; three *s* two *d*. *Educ:* Middleton Boys' Sch., Leeds; Cockburn High Sch., Leeds; King's Coll., Newcastle (Univ. of Durham). LLB 1st cl. Hons 1965. Asst Lectr and Lectr in Law, Univ. of Sheffield, 1965–68; called to the Bar, Lincoln's Inn, 1968, Bencher, 1997; a Recorder, 1985–2002. *Recreations:* singing, cookery, books. *Address:* 34A Rutland Drive, Harrogate, N Yorks HG1 2NX; The Courthouse, Oxford Row, Leeds LS1 3BG.

SPENCER, Thomas Newnham Bayley, (Tom); Executive Director, European Centre for Public Affairs, Templeton College, Oxford, 1987–89, then at University of Surrey, then at Brunel University; Visiting Professor of Public Affairs, Brunel University, 2003; *b* 10 April 1948; *s* of Thomas Henry Newnham Spencer and Anne Hester (*née* Readett-Bayley); *m* 1979, Elizabeth Nan Maltby, *er d* of late Captain Ronald Edgar Bath and of Doreen Lester (*née* Bush); two *d* and one step *d*. *Educ:* Nautical Coll., Pangbourne; Southampton Univ. (BSc Social Sciences). Peat, Marwick, Mitchell & Co., 1972–75; Asst to Dir, Britain-in-Europe Campaign, 1975; J. Walter Thompson & Co., 1975–79. Associate Dean, Templeton Coll., Oxford, 1984–89. MEP (C) Derbyshire, 1979–84, contested same seat, 1984; MEP (C) Surrey West, 1989–94, Surrey, 1994–99. European Democratic Group: Dep. Chief Whip, 1989–91; spokesman on: Social Affairs and Employment, 1979–81; External Econ. Relations, 1982–84; Social Affairs, 1993–94; Chm., British Section, EPP Gp, 1994–95; European Parliament: Member: Envmt, Public Health and Consumer Affairs Cttee, 1991–99; Institutional Affairs Cttee, 1991–94; Foreign Affairs Cttee, 1993–99; Chairman: Cttee on Foreign Affairs, Security and Defence Policy, 1997–99; delegn to Czech, Slovene and Slovak Republics, 1993–99; Jt Parly Cttee with Czech Republic, 1995–97. Chm., European Union Cons. and Christian-Democratic Students, 1971–73; Mem. Council, Cons. Gp for Europe, 1999–. Member: Global Legislators for a Balanced Environment, 1989–99; Commn on Globalisation, 2001–. Chm., Counterpart Europe, 2000–02. Vis. Prof., Univ. of Surrey, 2000–03. Senior Advisor: Inst. for Global Envmtl Strategies, Japan, 1997–2001. Pres., Globe Internat., 1994–99; Patron, Global Commons Inst. Trust, 1997–. Member: Bd of Trustees, Friends of Europe, 2000–; Council, Federal Trust, 2003–. Mem. Court, Univ. of Surrey, 1992–; Mem. Adv. Bd, Centre for Corporate and Public Affairs, Manchester Metropolitan Univ., 2000–. Member Editorial Board: Eur. Business Jl, 1991–2003; Jl of Public Affairs, 2000–. Robert Schuman Silver Medal, 1974; Green Ribbon Award for most envmtl MEP, Forum for the Future, 1999. Great Golden Medal for Merit (Republic of Austria), 1995. *Recreations:* gardening, opera, Conservative Party. *Address:* Barford Court, Lampard Lane, Churt, Surrey GU10 2HJ. *Clubs:* Carlton, Brass Monkey.

SPENCER, Timothy John; QC 2001; a Recorder, since 2000; *b* 6 Nov. 1958; *s* of John Spencer and Muriel Spencer (*née* Rowe); *m* 1983, Ann Fiona Rigg; two *s* one *d* (of whom one *s* one *d* are twins). *Educ:* Baines Grammar Sch.; Downing Coll., Cambridge (MA Hons Law). 1st Lieut, 1st RTR, 1978. Called to the Bar, Middle Temple, 1982; Asst Recorder, 1998–2000. *Recreations:* Preston North End, Lancashire County Cricket Club, gardening. *Address:* 7 Bedford Row, WC1R 4BU. *T:* (020) 7242 3555. *Club:* MCC.

SPENCER-CHURCHILL, family name of **Duke of Marlborough.**

SPENCER-NAIRN, Sir Robert (Arnold), 3rd Bt *cr* 1933; Vice Lord-Lieutenant of Fife, since 1996; *b* 11 Oct. 1933; *s* of Sir Douglas Spencer-Nairn, 2nd Bt, TD, and Elizabeth Livingston (*d* 1985), *d* of late Arnold J. Henderson; *S* father, 1970; *m* 1963, Joanna Elizabeth, *d* of late Lt-Comdr G. S. Salt, RN; two *s* one *d*. *Educ:* Eton College; Trinity Hall, Cambridge (MA). Fellow, Game Conservancy, 1993. Mem. Council, Macmillan Cancer Relief, 1997–. DL Fife, 1995. *Heir: s* James Robert Spencer-Nairn [*b* 7 Dec. 1966; *m* 1994, Dominique Jane, *o d* of Michael Williamson and Mrs Charles Newman; two *s*]. *Address:* Barham, Cupar, Fife KY15 5RG. *Clubs:* Royal and Ancient Golf (St Andrews); Falkland Palace Royal Tennis.

SPENCER-SMITH, Sir John Hamilton, 7th Bt *cr* 1804; *b* 18 March 1947; *s* of Sir Thomas Cospatric Hamilton-Spencer-Smith, 6th Bt, and Lucy Ashton, *o d* of late Thomas Ashton Ingram, Hopes, Norton-sub-Hamdon, Somerset; *S* father, 1959; *m* 1980, Christine (marr. diss. 1990), *d* of late John Theodore Charles Osborne, Durrington, Worthing, Sussex; one *d*. *Educ:* Milton Abbey; Lackham College of Agriculture, Wilts. *Heir: cousin* Michael Philip Spencer-Smith, *b* 2 April 1952.

SPENCER WILLS; see Wills.

SPENDLOVE, Peter Roy, CVO 1981; HM Diplomatic Service, retired; consultant in development and public administration; Chairman, East Anglia Regional Ambulance Service NHS Trust, 1993–95; *b* 11 Nov. 1925; *s* of H. A. Spendlove and Florence (*née* Jackson); *m* 1952, Wendy Margaret Valentine; two *s* three *d*. *Educ:* Chichester High Sch.; London Sch. of Economics; Edinburgh and Cambridge Univs. BScEcon Hons 1951. Called to Bar, Middle Temple, 1964. Served HM Forces, 1943–47: commnd, Indian Army/Royal Indian Artillery. LSE, 1948–51; Internat. Law Scholar at The Hague, 1951; Univ. of Cambridge, 1951–52. Apptd District Officer, Kenya, 1952; retired after serving in Provincial Admin and Central Govt, 1964. First Secretary, FCO, 1964; served in E Malaysia, Washington, Manila, FO, Jamaica; Counsellor, Economic, Commercial and Aid, Jakarta, 1977–80; Deputy High Comr, Sri Lanka, 1981–82; Dep. Chief Administrator, Broads Authority (E Anglia), 1983–86. Chm., Norfolk Ambulance Service NHS Trust, 1990–94. *Recreation:* riding. *Address:* 7 Wrenshaw Court, The Downs, Wimbledon, SW20 8HR. *T:* (020) 8946 2767.

SPENS, family name of **Baron Spens.**

SPENS, 4th Baron *cr* 1959, of Blairsanquar, Fife; **Patrick Nathaniel George Spens;** Partner, Copenhagen Capital LLP, since 2005; *b* 14 Oct. 1968; *s* of 3rd Baron Spens and of Barbara Janet Lindsay Spens; *S* father, 2001; *m* 1998, Hon. Philippa Patricia Lennox-Boyd, *yr d* of Viscount Boyd of Merton, *qv*; one *s* two *d*. *Educ:* Rugby. Strauss Turnbull, 1987–93; Merrill Lynch International, 1993–99; Dir, 1999–2005, Man. Dir, 2001–05, Schroder Salomon Smith Barney, subseq. Citigroup. *Recreations:* racing, claret. *Heir: s* Hon. Peter Lathallan Spens, *b* 3 March 2000. *Address:* 33A Pembroke Road, W8 6DP. *Clubs:* Bluebird, Twelve.

SPENS, David Patrick; QC 1995; a Recorder of the Crown Court, since 1994; *b* 2 May 1950; *s* of late Hugh Stuart Spens and Mary Jean Drake (*née* Reinhold); *m* 1979, Danièle Irving (marr. diss. 2003); two *d*. *Educ:* Rugby Sch.; Univ. of Kent at Canterbury (BA). Called to the Bar, Inner Temple, 1973, Bencher, 2005; Junior Treasury Counsel, CCC, 1988–95; Leader, S Eastern Circuit, 2007–. Chm., Criminal Bar Assoc., 2004–05. *Address:* Garden Court Chambers, 57–60 Lincoln's Inn Fields, WC2A 3LS. *T:* (020) 7993 7600, *Fax:* (020) 7993 7700.

SPENS, John Alexander, RD 1970; WS; Partner, Maclay, Murray & Spens, Solicitors, Glasgow and Edinburgh, 1960–91, later Consultant; *b* 7 June 1933; *s* of Thomas Patrick Spens and Nancy F. Spens (*née* Anderson); *m* 1961, Finella Jane, *d* of Donald Duff Gilroy; two *s* one *d* (and one *s* decd). *Educ:* Cargilfield; Rugby School; Corpus Christi College, Cambridge (BA); Glasgow Univ. (LLB). WS 1977. Director: Scottish Amicable Life Assurance Soc., 1963–97 (Chairman, 1978–81); Standard Property Investment PLC, 1977–87. Carrick Pursuivant, 1974–85; Albany Herald, 1985–. *Recreations:* sailing, countryside and opera. *Address:* The Old Manse, Gartocharn, Dunbartonshire G83 8RX. *T:* (01389) 830456. *Clubs:* Naval; Western (Glasgow).

SPENS, Michael Colin Barkley, MA; Headmaster, Fettes College, since 1998; *b* 22 Sept. 1950; *s* of Richard Vernon Spens and (Theodora) Margaret Yuille Spens (*née* Barkley); *m* 1989, Deborah Susan Lane; one *s* two *d*. *Educ:* Marlborough Coll.; Selwyn Coll., Cambridge (BA 1972; MA Natural Scis 1976). Asst Master, Rathkeale Coll., NZ, 1968–69; Mktg Dept, United Biscuits plc, 1973–74; Asst Master, 1974–93, Housemaster, 1984–93, Radley Coll.; Headmaster, Caldicott Sch., 1993–98. Liveryman, Grocers' Co., 1981–. *Recreations:* mountaineering, golf, bridge, crosswords, geology, electronics, wood turning, gardening. *Address:* Headmaster's Lodge, Fettes College, Edinburgh EH4 1QX. *T:* (0131) 311 6701. *Clubs:* Hawks (Cambridge); New (Edinburgh); Denham Golf.

SPERRY, Rt Rev. John Reginald, CM 2002; CD 1987; Bishop of The Arctic, 1974–90; National President, Canadian Bible Society, since 1990; Vice President, United Bible Societies (Americas Region), since 1992; *b* 2 May 1924; *s* of William Reginald Sperry and Elsie Agnes (*née* Priest); *m* 1952, Elizabeth Maclaren (*d* 2001); one *s* one *d* (and one *d* decd). *Educ:* St Augustine's Coll., Canterbury; King's Coll., Halifax (STh). Deacon, 1950; priest, 1951; St Andrew's Mission, Coppermine, NWT, 1950–69; Canon of All Saints' Cathedral, Aklavik, 1957–59; Archdeacon of Coppermine, 1959–69; Rector of St John's, Fort Smith, NWT, 1969–73; Rector of Holy Trinity, Yellowknife, NWT, 1974. Hon. DD: Coll. of Emmanuel, St Chad, 1974; Wycliffe Coll., Toronto, 1979. *Publications:* translations into Copper Eskimo: Canadian Book of Common Prayer (1962), 1969; Four Gospels and Acts of the Apostles, 1972; Igloo Dwellers Were My Church (memoirs), 2001. *Address:* 1 Dakota Court, Yellowknife, NT X1A 2A4, Canada. *T:* (867) 8736163.

SPERRYN, Simon George; Chief Executive, Chartered Institute of Purchasing and Supply, since 2008; *b* 7 April 1946; *s* of George Roland Neville Sperryn and Wendy Sperryn (*née* King); *m* 1993, Jessica Alice Hayes; two *s* one *d*. *Educ:* Rydal School; Pembroke College, Cambridge (MA); Cranfield School of Management (MBA). Birmingham Chamber of Commerce and Industry, 1967–77; Chief Executive: Northants Chamber of Commerce and Industry, 1979–85; Manchester Chamber of Commerce and Industry, 1986–92; London Chamber of Commerce and Industry, 1992–2000; Chief Exec., Lloyd's Market Assoc., 2001–06. Director: Manchester TEC, 1989–92; Manchester Camerata, 1989–92 (Chm.); Business Link London, 1995–2000. British Chambers of Commerce: Mem. Nat. Council, 1986–97; Dir, 1998–2000; Pres., British Chambers of Commerce Executives, 1994, 1995; Administrator, London Chamber of Commerce and Industry Commercial Educn Trust, 1992–2000; Mem. UK Council, ICC, 2000–06. Vice Pres., World Chambers Fedn, 2000. Mem. Council, Chartered Insurance Inst., 2003–06. Chm., City of London Early Years Develt and Childcare Partnership, 1998–2000. Mem., London Regl Cttee, FEFC, 1996–2000. Trustee, UNIAID, 2002–. Gov., UC Salford, 1988–92. Freeman, City of London, 1998. CCMI; FRSA; MIEx. *Address:* Apartment 12, The Belvedere, Homerton Street, Cambridge CB2 0NT.

SPICELEY, Peter Joseph, MBE 1976; HM Diplomatic Service, retired; Ambassador to Costa Rica, 1999–2002; *b* 5 March 1942; *s* of late Robert Joseph Spiceley and Lucy Violet Spiceley; *m* 1965, Cecilia Orozco-Lemus; two *d*. *Educ:* Trinity Sch. of John Whitgift, Croydon. Entered Diplomatic Service, 1961; FCO, 1961–64; Bogotá, 1964–66; DSAO, 1966–69; Lima, 1969–72; Second Sec., Yaoundé, 1972–74; Consul, Douala, 1974–76; Second, later First, Sec., Quito, 1976–81; FCO, 1982–86; Consul, Miami, 1986–90; Asst Head of Aviation Dept, FCO, 1991–94; Dep. Consul-Gen. and Dir of Trade Promotion, Sydney, 1994–98. *Recreations:* travel, reading. *Address:* Flat 41, 2 Tavistock Road, Croydon, Surrey CR0 2AS.

SPICER, Harriet Greville; Member, Judicial Appointments Commission, since 2006; Governor, London School of Economics, since 2008; *b* 24 April 1950; *d* of James Spicer and Patricia Spicer (*née* Palmer); one *s* one *d*. *Educ:* St Anne's Coll., Oxford (BA Hons English Lit.). Virago Press Ltd, 1973–96, Man. Dir, 1990–96. Mem., 1999–2005, Chair, 2001–02, Nat. Lottery Commn. Chm., The Friendly Almshouses, 2002–05. Advr, Piccadilly Dance Orch., 2007–. *Recreations:* friends, reading, music, theatre.

SPICER, Sir James (Wilton), Kt 1988; company director; *b* 4 Oct. 1925; *s* of James and Florence Clara Spicer; *m* 1954, Winifred Douglas Shanks (MBE 2008); two *d*. *Educ:* Latymer. Regular army, 1943–57, retd (Major); commnd Royal Fusiliers, 1944; Para. Regt, 1951–57. Nat. Chm., CPC, 1968–71. Mem. (C) European Parlt, 1975–84 (elected Mem. for Wessex, 1979–84); Chief Whip, European Democratic Gp, 1975–79; Chairman: Cons. Group for Europe, 1975–78 (Dir, 1972–74); Conservatives Abroad, 1986–93. MP (C) Dorset West, Feb. 1974–1997. Mem., Select Cttee on Agriculture, 1984–85. A Vice Chm., Cons. Party Orgn, and Chm., Internat. Office, 1985–92. Chairman: Westminster Foundn for Democracy, 1992–97; Agricl and Rural Parlt Trust, 1998–2000. Chairman: Inglewood Health Hydro, 1999–2001; St James Security, 2003–06. Patron, Dorset/Somerset, Marie Curie Cancer Care, 2000–06 (Chm., Dorset Br., 1998–2000); Chm., Dorset Br., Action Res., 1999–2000. *Recreations:* swimming, tennis. *Address:* Whatley, Beaminster, Dorset DT8 3SB. *T:* (01308) 862337.

SPICER, Sir Michael; *see* Spicer, Sir W. M. H.

SPICER, Sir Nicholas (Adrian Albert), 5th Bt *cr* 1906, of Lancaster Gate, Paddington; general medical practitioner, since 1982; *b* 28 Oct. 1953; *o s* of (Sir) Peter James Spicer (4th Bt, but did not use the title) and of Margaret (*née* Wilson); *S* father, 1993; *m* 1992, Patricia Carol Dye (marr. diss. 2008); two *s*. *Educ:* Eton; Birmingham Univ. (MB ChB 1977). *Recreation:* amateur singing. *Heir: s* James Peter Warwick Spicer, *b* 12 June 1993. *Address:* The Old Rectory, Malvern Road, Stanford Bishop, Bringsty, Worcs WR6 5TT; Lagafater, New Luce, Newton Stewart, Wigtownshire DG8 0BA.

SPICER, Sir (William) Michael (Hardy), Kt 1996; MP (C) West Worcestershire, since 1997 (South Worcestershire, Feb. 1974–1997); *b* 22 Jan. 1943; *s* of late Brig. L. H. Spicer; *m* 1967, Patricia Ann Hunter; one *s* two *d*. *Educ:* Wellington Coll.; Emmanuel Coll., Cambridge (MA Econs). Asst to Editor, The Statist, 1964–66; Conservative Research Dept, 1966–68; Dir, Conservative Systems Research Centre, 1968–70; Man. Dir, Economic Models Ltd, 1970–80. PPS, Dept of Trade, 1979–81; Parly Under Sec. of State, 1984–87, and Minister for Aviation, 1985–87, Dept of Transport; Parly Under Sec. of State (Minister for Coal and Power), Dept of Energy, 1987–90; Minister of State (Minister for Housing and Planning), DoE, 1990. Mem., Treasury Select Cttee, 1997–2001; Chm., Treasury Sub-Cttee, 1991–2001. Chm., 1922 Cttee, 2001– (Mem. Exec., 1997–99). Conservative Party: a Vice-Chm., 1981–83; Dep. Chm., 1983–84; Mem. Bd, 2001–; Chm., Finance & Audit Cttee, 2007–. Chairman: Parly OST, 1990; Parly and Scientific Cttee, 1996–99; European Res. Gp, 1994–2001. Pres., Assoc. of Electricity (formerly Indep. Power) Producers, 1996– (Chm., 1991–96). Gov., Wellington Coll., 1992–2005. Chm. and Captain, Lords and Commons Tennis Club, 1997–2006. *Publications:* A Treaty Too Far, 1992; The Challenge from the East, 1996; *novels:* Final Act, 1981; Prime Minister Spy, 1986; Cotswold Manners, 1989; Cotswold Murders, 1990; Cotswold Mistress, 1992; Cotswold Moles, 1993; contrib. Jl Royal Inst. Public Admin. *Recreations:* painting, tennis, writing, bridge. *Address:* House of Commons, SW1A 0AA. *T:* (020) 7219 3000. *Clubs:* Garrick, Pratt's.

SPICKERNELL, Rear-Adm. Derek Garland, CB 1974; CEng, FIMechE, FIET, FIMarEST; Chairman, Ritec Ltd, 1987–2004; Director General, British Standards Institution, 1981–86 (Technical Director, 1976–81); *b* 1 June 1921; *s* of late Comdr Sidney Garland Spickernell, RN, and Florence Elizabeth (*née* March); *m* 1st, 1946, Ursula Rosemary Sheila Money (*d* 1997); one *s* one *d* (and one *s* decd); 2nd, 1998, Carolyn Mary Jenkins. *Educ:* RNEC, Keyham. Served War, HM Ships Abdiel, Wayland, and Engr Officer HM Submarine Statesman, 1943–45. Engr Officer HM Submarines Telemachus, Tudor and Alcide, 1945–50; Submarine Trials Officer, 1950–51; Engrg Dept, HM Dockyard, Portsmouth, 1951–53; SEO: Portsmouth Frigate Sqdn, 1954–55; 2nd Submarine Sqdn, 1956–57; Supt, ULE, Bournemouth, 1958–59; Dep. Captain Supt, AUWE, Portland, 1959–62; Dep. Manager, Engrg Dept, HM Dockyard, Portsmouth, 1962–64; in command, HMS Fisgard, 1965–66; Dep. Dir, Naval Ship Production, 1967–70; Dep. Chief Exec., Defence Quality Assurance Bd, 1970–71; Dir-Gen., Quality Assurance, MoD (PE), 1972–75. Dir, James Martin Associates PLC, 1986–90; Bd Mem., Southern Water, 1987–89; Chm., Jeniva Landfill, 1987–92. Chm., Nat. Council for Quality and Reliability, 1973–75; A Vice-President: Inst. of Quality Assurance, 1974– (Hon. FCQI); Inst. of Trading Standards Admin, 1986–; Vice-Pres., Internat. Orgn for Standardisation, 1985–87; Bd Mem. for Internat. Affairs, BSI, 1986–87; Dir, Turkish Standards Inst., 1987–90; Member: Internat. Acad. of Quality Assurance, 1977–97; Design Council, 1984–87; Council, Cranfield Inst. of Technol. FRSA; CCMI. *Publications:* papers on Quality Assurance. *Club:* Royal Fowey Yacht.

ŠPIDLA, Dr Vladimír; Member, European Commission, since 2004; *b* Prague, 22 April 1951; *s* of Václav and Dagmar Špidla; *m* 1st; two *s*; 2nd, Viktorie; one *s* one *d*. *Educ:* Charles Univ., Prague (PhD Hist. and Prehist.). Formerly archaeologist, worker at historical monuments, sawmill worker and worker in dairy and livestock industry. Jindřichův Hradec: Vice-Pres. for Educn, Health Service, Social Affairs and Culture, Dist Cttee, 1990–91; Dir, Labour Office, 1991–96; Mem. (CSSD) Chamber of Deps, Czech Republic, 1996–2004; Dep. Prime Minister and Minister of Labour and Social Affairs, 1998–2002; Prime Minister, 2002–04. Czech Social Democratic Party: Founding Mem., S Bohemian Br., 1989; joined party leadership, 1992; Vice-Chm., 1997–2001; Chm., 2001. *Recreations:* care of historical monuments, books, cross-country running, other outdoor sports. *Address:* c/o European Commission, Rue de la Loi 200, 1049 Brussels, Belgium.

SPIEGELHALTER, Prof. David John, OBE 2006; FRS 2005; Winton Professor of the Public Understanding of Risk, University of Cambridge, since 2007; *b* 16 Aug. 1953; *s* of Edmund Spiegelhalter and late Faith Spiegelhalter (*née* Baker); *m* 1978, Eva Sommerschield (marr. diss. 1987); one *d*; partner, 1988, Kate Bull; one *d* (and one *s* decd). *Educ:* Barnstaple Grammar Sch.; Keble Coll., Oxford (BA); University Coll. London (PhD 1978). Lectr, Univ. of Calif, Berkeley, 1977–78; Res. Asst, Univ. of Nottingham, 1978–81; MRC Biostatistics Unit, Cambridge, 1981– (Sen. Scientist, 1986–; Hon. Prof., 2006–). Hon. DSc Aalborg, Denmark, 1994. *Publications:* (jtly) Leucocyte Typing III: White Cell Differentiation Antigens, 1987; (jtly) Machine Learning, Neural and Statistical Classification, 1994; (jtly) Markov Chain Monte Carlo Methods in Practice, 1996; (jtly) Bayesian Analysis in Probabilistic Networks, 1999; (jtly) Bayesian Approaches to Clinical Trials and Health Care Evaluation, 2004; papers in Jl Royal Statistical Soc., etc. *Recreations:* trekking, samba drumming, making stained-glass panels, watching old films with family, talking to Michael Traynor. *Address:* Department of Pure Mathematics and Mathematical Statistics, Centre for Mathematical Sciences, University of Cambridge, Wilberforce Road, Cambridge CB3 0WB.

SPIELBERG, Steven, Hon. KBE 2001; American film director and producer; *b* 18 Dec. 1947; *s* of Arnold Spielberg and Leah (*née* Posner); *m* 1985, Amy Irving (marr. diss. 1989); one *s*; *m* Kate Capshaw; one *s* two *d*, and one adopted *s* one adopted *d*. *Educ:* Calif State Coll. TV Director, Universal Pictures, 1968. Founder: Amblin Entertainment; Dreamworks SKG. Fellow, BAFTA, 1986. *Films include: directed:* Sugarland Express, 1974; Jaws, 1975; Close Encounters of the Third Kind, 1977; 1941, 1979; Raiders of the Lost Ark, 1981; (also produced) E.T., 1982; (also produced) Twilight Zone—the movie, 1983; Indiana Jones and the Temple of Doom, 1984; The Color Purple, 1985; Empire of the Sun, 1988; Indiana Jones and the Last Crusade, 1989; Hook, 1991; Jurassic Park, 1992; Schindler's List, 1994; The Lost World: Jurassic Park, 1997; Amistad, 1998; Saving Private Ryan, 1998; A. I. Artificial Intelligence, 2001; Minority Report, 2002; Catch Me If You Can, 2003; The Terminal, 2004; War of the Worlds, 2005; Munich, 2006; Indiana Jones and the Kingdom of the Crystal Skull, 2008; *produced:* I Wanna Hold Your Hand, 1978; (also co-wrote) Poltergeist, 1982; Gremlins, 1984; Goonies, 1985; Young Sherlock Holmes, 1985; Back to the Future, 1986; Who Framed Roger Rabbit, 1988; Always, 1990; The Flintstones, 1994; Casper, 1995; Men in Black, 1997; The Last Days, 1999; Flags of Our Fathers, 2006. Co-prod., TV series, Band of Brothers, 2001; Exec.-prod., TV series, Into the West, 2006. *Publication:* (jtly) Close Encounters of the Third Kind. *Address:* Amblin Entertainment, 100 Universal City Plaza, Universal City, CA 91608, USA.

SPIERS, Sir Donald (Maurice), Kt 1993; CB 1987; TD 1966; FREng; Director, General Dynamics UK Ltd, since 2001; *b* 27 Jan. 1934; *s* of Harold Herbert Spiers and Emma (*née* Foster); *m* 1958, Sylvia Mary Lowman; two *s*. *Educ:* Raynes Park County Grammar Sch.; Trinity Coll., Cambridge (MA). CEng. Commnd RE, 1952–54. de Havilland Engine Co., Hatfield, 1957–60; joined Air Min. as SSO, 1960; operational res. on deterrence, 1960–63; trials and analysis, Aden and Radfan, 1964; Kestrel evaluation trial, 1965; Scientific Adviser to FEAF, Singapore, 1967–70; Asst Chief Scientist (RAF), MoD, 1972–77; Asst Dir, Mil. Aircraft Projs, MoD (PE), 1978; Dir of Aircraft Post Design Services, MoD (PE), 1979–81; Dir Gen. Aircraft 1, MoD (PE), 1981–84; Dep. Controller Aircraft, MoD (PE), 1984–86; Controller of R&D Estabts, later of Estabts, Res. and Nuclear Programmes, and Hd of Profession Defence Engrg Service, MoD, 1986–89; Controller Aircraft, and Head of Profession Defence Sci. and Engrg, MoD, 1989–94. Chairman: European Helicopter Industries Ltd, 1998–2004; Farnborough Aerospace Consortium, 2003–; Farnborough Enterprise Hub, 2004–; Agusta Westland International, 2004–. Director: Computing Devices Co. Ltd, 1994–2001 (Chm., 1997–2001); Meggitt plc, 1995–2003 (Chm., 1998–2001); Messier-Dowty Internat. Ltd, 1998–2004; TAG Aviation (UK) Ltd, 1999–2005. Hon. FRAeS (Vice Pres., 1993–95; Pres., 1995–96). Pres., Popular Flying Assoc., 1997–2000. Gold Medal, RAeS, 1989. *Recreations:* mending cars, mowing lawns. *Address:* 20 Paddock Close, Camberley, Surrey GU15 2BN. *Club:* Royal Air Force.

SPIERS, Prof. Edward Michael, PhD; FRHistS; Professor of Strategic Studies, University of Leeds, since 1993; *b* 18 Oct. 1947; *s* of Ronald Arthur Spiers, DSC and Margaret Carlisle Laing Spiers (*née* Manson); *m* 1971, Fiona Elizabeth McLeod; one *s* one *d*. *Educ:* Royal High Sch., Edinburgh; Edinburgh Univ. (MA, PhD). FRHistS 1980. University of Leeds: Defence Lectr, 1975–85; Lectr in History, 1985–87; Reader in Strategic Studies, 1987–93; Chm., School of History, 1994–97; Dean, 1999–2002, Pro-Dean, 2006–, of Res. (Arts). Vis. Lectr, Univ. of Alberta, 1987; Leverhulme Res. Fellow, 1991–92. Chief Examiner, Army, 1992–2002; Peer Reviewer, AHRC, 2004–. Mem. (C), Edinburgh DC, 1974. *Publications:* Haldane: an army reformer, 1980; The Army and Society 1815–1914, 1980; Radical General: Sir George de Lacy Evans 1787–1870, 1983; Chemical Warfare, 1986; Chemical Weaponry: a continuing challenge, 1989; The Late Victorian Army 1868–1902, 1992; Chemical and Biological Weapons: a study of proliferation, 1994; (ed) Sudan: the reconquest reappraised, 1998; Weapons of Mass Destruction, 2000; The Victorian Soldier in Africa, 2004; The Scottish Soldier and Empire 1854–1902, 2006. *Recreation:* supporting the Green Bay Packers. *Address:* 170 Alwoodley Lane, Leeds LS17 7PF. *T:* (0113) 268 5493. *Club:* LSI (Leeds).

SPIERS, John Raymond; Chairman, John Spiers Publishing Ltd, since 1988; Visiting (formerly External) Professor, School of Humanities and Social Studies, University of Glamorgan, since 2001 (External Professor, Business School, 1998–2001); independent health policy commentator and consultant; *b* 30 Sept. 1941; *s* of Horace Henry Spiers and Kate Dawson (*née* Root); *m* 1967, Prof. Margaret Ann Boden, *qv* (marr. diss. 1981); one *s* one *d*; *m* 2003, Leigh Richardson (*née* Radford); one step *s* one step *d*. *Educ:* Redhill Sch., E Sutton, Kent; Catford Coll. of Commerce; Univ. of Sussex (BA 1st Cl. Hons Hist. 1968). Writer and publisher, 1960–; Founder: Harvester Press Ltd (Chm., 1969–88); Harvester Press Microform Pubns Ltd (Chm., 1973–87) (Queen's Award for Export Achievement, 1986); Wheatsheaf Books Ltd (Chm., 1980–88). Special Advr to Dep. Chm., Cons. Party, 1989–90; Consultant Dir, Special Services Dept, Cons. Central Office, 1990–94; Mem., Citizens' Charter Adv. Panel to PM, 1994; Dep. Treas., Cons. Party SE England Area, 1990–92 (Mem., SE Area Council, 1990–92); Pres., Brighton Kemp Town Cons. Assoc., 1991–95. Founder and Chm., Brighton Business Gp, 1989–95. Health Policy Advr, Social Market Foundn, 1994–99; Chairman: Brighton HA, 1991–92; Brighton Health Care NHS Trust, 1992–94; National Association of Health Authorities and Trusts: Mem., Nat. Council and Exec. Cttee, 1993–94; Chm., Nat. Conf. Cttee, 1993–94; Co-Chm., S Thames Network, 1994; Vice-Chm., Provider Cttee, 1993–94; Member: NHS Mgt Exec. Adv. Gps, 1991–98; Bd, Nat. Care Standards Commn, 2001–04. Chairman: Patients Assoc., 1995–97 (Actg Chief Exec., 1995–96); Health Policy Cttee, Centre for Policy Studies, 1997–99; Founding Chm., Civitas: Inst. for Study of Civil Soc., 1999–2000; Member: Exec. Bd, Internat. Health Policy and Management Inst., 1994–98; Adv. Council, Health and Welfare Unit, IEA, 1989–92, 1997–99; (co-opted), Nat. Exec., Voluntary Euthanasia Soc., 1997–99. Co-Chm., The Radical Soc., 1991–2001; Mem., Adv. Council, Reform, 2001–. Vice-Chm., Grant Maintained Schools Foundn, 1992–98 (Trustee, 1992–98). Trustee: Choice in Educn, 1990–92; Trident Trust, 1992–99 (Vice Chm., 1993–94; Chm., 1994–97); Brighton Internat. Arts Fest., 1989–96; English Nat. Schs Orch., 1998–2004; League of Mercy, 1999–2004 (Companion, 2002); Shakespeare Authorship Trust, 2002–05 (Associate, 2005–); Ruskin Foundn, 2002–; Pres., Gissing Foundn, 2005–. Chm., Alumni Soc., 1983–2004 (Hon. Fellow, 1998; Vice-Pres., 2002), and Mem. Court, 1989–, Univ. of Sussex. Visiting Fellow: NHS Staff Coll., Wales, 1995–; King's Fund Mgt Coll., 1996–; IEA, 2003–; Ruskin Prog., Univ. of Lancaster, 2005–; Res. Fellow, 1997–98, Sen. Res. Fellow, Health and Welfare Unit, 1998–99, Head of Health Care Studies, 1999–2000, IEA; Adjunct Schol., Cascade Policy Inst., Portland, Oregon, 1999; Sen. Res. Fellow, Inst. of English Studies, Univ. of London, 2003–. Librarian and Mem. Nat. Council, Francis Bacon Soc., 1998–2005 (Vice-Chm., 2003–05). Pres., Hoxton Hawks Vintage Cycling Club, 2006–. Fellow, Progressive Vision, 2007–. Companion, Guild of St George, 1971 (Founding Editor, The Companion, 2000–04; Dir, 2001–04). Freeman, City of London, 2000. FRSA 1994. DUniv Sussex, 1994. JP E Sussex, 1988–90. Companion's Cross, League of Mercy, 2002. Kt Grand Cross, Order of St Stanislaus (Poland), 1998. *Publications:* (with P. Coustillas) The Re-discovery of George Gissing, Novelist, 1971; The Invisible Hospital and the Secret Garden: an insider's commentary on the NHS reforms, 1995; Who Owns Our Bodies?: making moral choices in health care, 1997; (ed) Dilemmas in Modern Health Care, 1997; The Realities of Rationing: priority setting in the National Health Service, 1999; Coming, Ready or Not: the present, future and politics of the NHS, 2003; Patients, Power and Responsibility in British Health Care, 2003; (ed) George Gissing and the City: cultural crisis and the making of books in late-Victorian England, 2005; Serious About Series, 2007; Who Decides Who Decides?, 2008;

(ed) The Culture of the Publisher's Series, 2009; contrib. Health Service Jl, British Jl of Health Management, Health Summary, Healthcare Today, Health Director, Sunday Telegraph, Guardian, Daily Express, Independent, English Literature in Transition, Jl of Printing Historical Soc. *Recreations:* collecting 19th century novels (and reading them), writing, walking, supporting The Arsenal, exploring inland waterways on narrow boat Harvester. *Address: e-mail:* jr.spiers@virgin.net.

SPIERS, Air Cdre Reginald James, OBE 1972; FRAeS; *b* 8 Nov. 1928; *s* of Alfred James Oscar and Rose Emma Alice Spiers; *m* 1956, Cynthia Jeanette Williams; two *d.* *Educ:* Haberdashers' Aske's Sch.; RAF Coll., Cranwell. FRAeS 1975. Commissioned 1949; 247 and 64 Fighter Sqdns, 1950–54; Graduate, Empire Test Pilots' Sch., 1955; Fighter Test Sqdn, A&AEE, 1955–58; CO 4 Fighter Sqdn, 1958–61; PSO to C-in-C RAF Germany, 1961–63; RAF Staff Coll., 1964; FCO, 1965–67; CO RAF Masirah, 1967–68; Chief Test Flying Instructor, ETPS, 1968–71; Air Warfare Course, 1972; Air Secretary's Dept, MoD, 1972–73; MA to Governor of Gibraltar, 1973–75; CO Experimental Flying Dept, RAE Farnborough, 1975–78; Director, Defence Operational Requirements Staff, MoD, 1978–79; Comdt, A&AEE, Boscombe Down, 1979–83, retd. Marketing Exec., Marconi, later GEC, Avionics, 1984–91. *Recreations:* aviation, painting. *Address:* Barnside, Penton Mewsey, near Andover, Hants SP11 0RQ. *T:* (01264) 772376. *Club:* Royal Air Force.

SPIERS, Ronald Ian; consultant on international affairs, since 1992; Under-Secretary-General, Department of Political and General Assembly Affairs and Secretariat Services, United Nations, 1989–92; *b* 9 July 1925; *s* of Tomas H. and Blanca De P. Spiers; *m* 1949, Patience Baker; one *s* three *d.* *Educ:* Dartmouth Coll., New Hampshire (BA); Princeton Univ. (Master in Public Affairs, PhD). Mem., US Delegn to UN, 1956–60; US Department of State: Dir, Office of Disarmament and Arms Control, 1960–62; Dir, Office of NATO Affairs, 1962–66; Political Counsellor, London, 1966–69; Asst Sec. of State, Politico-Military Affairs, 1969–73; Ambassador to the Bahamas, 1973–74; Minister, London, 1974–77; Ambassador to Turkey, 1977–80; Asst Sec. of State, Bureau of Intelligence and Research, Dept of State, 1980–81; Ambassador to Pakistan, 1981–83; Under Sec. of State for Management, 1983–89. *Recreations:* swimming, music, theatre-going, gardening. *Address:* Middletown Road, South Londonderry, VT 05155, USA.

SPIERS, Shaun Mark; Chief Executive, Campaign to Protect Rural England, since 2004; *b* 23 April 1962; *s* of Charles Gordon Spiers and Ann Kathleen Spiers (*née* Hutton). *Educ:* St John's Coll., Oxford (BA Hons PPE); King's Coll. London (MA War Studies). Political Officer, SE Co-op., 1987–94. MEP (Lab Co-op) London SE, 1994–99; contested (Lab) London Region, 1999. Chief Exec., Assoc. of British Credit Unions, 1999–2004. *Recreations:* music, sport. *Address:* (office) 128 Southwark Street, SE1 0SW; *e-mail:* shauns@cpre.org.uk.

SPIGELMAN, Hon. James Jacob, AC 2000; Lieutenant-Governor and Chief Justice, New South Wales, since 1998; *b* 1 Jan. 1946; *s* of Majloch and Gucia Spigelman; *m* 1979, Alice Kalmar; one *s* two *d.* *Educ:* Maroubra Bay Public Sch.; Sydney Boys' High Sch.; Univ. of Sydney (BA, LLB). Sen. Advr and Principal Private Sec. to Prime Minister, 1972–75; Sec., Dept of Media, 1975; called to the Bar, NSW, 1976; in practice at NSW Bar, 1980–98; QC (NSW) 1986; Actg Solicitor Gen., NSW, 1997. Hon. LLD Sydney, 2004. *Publications:* Secrecy: political censorship in Australia, 1972; (jtly) The Nuclear Barons, 1981; Becket and Henry, 2004. *Recreations:* tennis, swimming, recumbency. *Address:* Chief Justice's Chambers, Supreme Court of New South Wales, GPO Box 3, Sydney, NSW 2001, Australia. *T:* (2) 92308218.

SPIKINGS, Barry Peter; Partner, Spikings Entertainment (formerly Pleskow/Spikings Partnership), international production and distribution of feature films, since 1992; *b* Boston, Lincs, 23 Nov. 1939; *m* 1st, 1962, Judith Anne Spikings; one *s* one *d*; 2nd, 1978, Dorothy Spikings; two step *d.* *Educ:* Boston Grammar School. Joint Managing Director: British Lion Films Ltd, 1973–75; EMI Films Ltd, 1975–78; Director, EMI Films Inc., 1975–78; Chm. and Chief Exec. Officer, EMI Film and Theatre Corp., 1978–80; Chm., Elstree Studios, 1978–82; Chm. and Chief Exec., Thorn EMI Films Worldwide, 1980–82; Pres. and Chief Operating Officer, Nelson Entertainment Inc., 1986–91. Oscar award as Producer of Best Picture of the Year, for The Deer Hunter, 1979; elected one of America's Greatest Hundred Movies by Amer. Film Inst., 1999; other films include: as producer: Conduct Unbecoming; The Man Who Fell to Earth; Convoy; Texasville; Beyond Rangoon; as distributor: Close Encounters of the Third Kind; The Deep; City Slickers; When Harry Met Sally; The Last Emperor. *Recreation:* making films. *Club:* Mark's.

SPILLER, John Anthony Walsh, MBE 1979; Technical Adviser to Organisation for Security and Co-operation in Europe/Office for Democratic Institutions and Human Rights Mission, Montenegro, on secondment to Foreign and Commonwealth Office, 1998; *b* 29 Dec. 1942; *s* of C. H. Spiller and Sarah (*née* Walsh), Moycullen, Co. Galway, Eire; *m* 1972, Angela, *d* of Surtees Gleghorn; one *s* one *d.* *Educ:* County Secondary Sch., Bideford; North Devon College. Member Executive, Nat. League of Young Liberals, 1960–61; Organiser, Torrington Constituency Liberal Assoc., 1962–64; Divl Liberal Agent, Cornwall (Northern) Parly Constituency, 1965–71; Northern Regional Organiser (Election Agent, Rochdale By-Elec. 1972 and Berwick-upon-Tweed By-Elec. 1973), 1972–74; Nat. Agent, Liberal Central Assoc., 1974–76; Mem., Liberal Party Gen. Elec. Campaign Cttee, and Press Officer, Gen. Elections Feb. and Oct. 1974; Western Area Agent, 1977–80; Advisor, African Peoples Union, Independence Elections, Zimbabwe, 1980; By-Elec. and Marginal Seats Agent, Liberal Party Org. Headquarters, 1981–82; Sec. Gen., Liberal Party, 1983–85; Co. Liaison Officer, Devonshire PHAB Organisation UK, 1990–92; Sen. Consultant, Western Approaches PR Ltd, 1993–96. Chm., Lib Dem Campaign, Cornwall (Northern), Gen. Election 1992; Advr, Electoral Reform Soc., Democracy Conf., Lithuania, 1992, Estonia, 1995, Croatia, 1997. Conf. Deleg., Moscow, 1995, Armenia, 1995; Observer, Elections: Republic of Georgia, 1995; Bosnia Herzegovina, 1996, Estonia, 1999, on behalf of OSCE. Mem. Bd of Management, Gladstone Benevolent Fund, 1980–98 (Sec. 1980, Hon. Sec., 1993). *Recreations:* golf, walking in Connemara. *Address:* 4 Branksome Dene Road, Westbourne, Bournemouth, Dorset BH4 8JW.

SPINDLER, Susan Mary; Deputy Director, Drama, Entertainment and Children's, BBC, 2005–07; *b* 1 March 1955; *d* of Kenneth Spindler and Elsie Spindler (*née* Knapper); *m* 1980, Peter Guy Brown, two *s* one *d.* *Educ:* Wycombe High Sch.; Newnham Coll., Cambridge (BA Hons English 1977). Grad. trainee, Thomson Newspapers, 1978–80; BBC 1980–: prodn trainee, 1980–82; Asst Producer and Producer, 1983–88; Producer, Doctors to Be, 1988–92; Ed., QED, 1992–94; Dep. Hd, Sci. Dept, 1994–96; Chief Advr, Editl Policy, 1997; Hd of Strategy, Drama, 1998–99; Controller, Drama Production, 1999–2000; Controller, Factual Drama and New Media, 2000–01; Project Dir, Making It Happen, 2002–04; Co-Leader, Creative Future Project, 2005–06. *Publications:* The Tomorrow's World Book of Food, 1984; Doctors to Be, 1992. *Recreations:* travel, cooking, writing. *Address:* 27 Grove Park Gardens, W4 3RY.

SPINK, Andrew John Murray; QC 2003; a Recorder, since 2005; *b* 21 April 1962; *s* of Nigel Spink and Penny Spink; *m* 1994, Susan Katherine Vivien Taylor; one *s* two *d.* *Educ:* Sherborne Sch.; Queens' Coll., Cambridge (MA). Called to the Bar, Middle Temple, 1985; in practice, specialising in law of clinical negligence, pensions, professional negligence and personal injury. *Recreations:* travel, particularly in France and Asia, mountain walking, ski-ing, scuba diving, cricket, opera, wine. *Address:* Outer Temple Chambers, Outer Temple, 222 Strand, WC2R 1BA. *T:* (020) 7353 6381, *Fax:* (020) 7583 1786; *e-mail:* andrew.spinkqc@outertemple.com. *Clubs:* Soho House, MCC; Hawks (Cambridge).

SPINK, Air Marshal Clifford Rodney, CB 2002; CBE 1992 (OBE 1989); FRAeS; Managing Director, Clifford Spink Associates Ltd, since 2003; Chairman: London Ashford Airport Ltd, since 2004; Spitfire Ltd, since 2005; Director, Contingency Planning Associates Ltd, since 2004; *b* 17 May 1946; *s* of Ronald Charles Spink and Beryl Spink (*née* Phillips); *m* 1977, Caroline Anne Smith; one *s* one *d.* *Educ:* Sheerness Sch.; Halton Apprentice, RAF Coll., Cranwell. FRAeS 1997. Commissioned RAF 1968; Sqn Pilot, 111/56 Sqn, 1970–76; Instructor, RMA Sandhurst, 1976–78; Flight Comdr, 111 Sqn, 1979–82; NDC, 1982–83; HQ RAF Germany, 1983–86; OC No 74 (Fighter) Sqn, 1986–89; Stn Comdr and Dep. Comdr British Forces, Falkland Islands, 1989–90; Detachment Comdr, Dhahran, Gulf conflict, 1990–91; Stn Comdr, RAF Coningsby, 1990–93; rcds, 1993; SASO, No 11 Group, 1993–95; COS No 18 Group, 1995–96; AOC No 11/18 Gp, 1996–98; DG, Saudi Armed Forces Project, 1998–2002; retired RAF, 2003. Chm., Atlantic Reconnaissance, 2003–06. President: ROC Assoc., 1996–; Battle of Britain Meml Flight Assoc., 2007. FCMI (FIMgt 1992). Liveryman, GAPAN, 2004– (Warden, 2008–). *Recreations:* vintage aircraft flying, winter sports, golf. *Club:* Royal Air Force.

SPINK, Prof. Ian Walter Alfred; Professor of Music, London University at Royal Holloway College, then Royal Holloway and Bedford New College, 1974–97, now Emeritus; *b* 29 March 1932; *s* of William James Spink and Margaret Hamilton (*née* Anderson); *m* 1960, Margaret Storry Walton; three *s* four *d.* *Educ:* Mercers' Sch.; Trinity Coll. of Music (BMus 1952); Barber Inst. of Fine Arts, Univ. of Birmingham (MA 1957). Nat. Service, 1953–55, 2nd Lieut, RA. Overseas Examiner for Trinity Coll. of Music in Canada, NZ and Australia, 1958–59; Dir of Music, Westlain GS, Brighton, Sussex, 1960–62; Lectr, then Sen. Lectr, Univ. of Sydney, NSW, 1962–69; RHC, later RHBNC, University of London: Head of Music Dept., 1969–92; Sen. Lectr, 1969–72; Reader, 1972–74; Dean, Fac. of Arts, 1973–75 and 1983–85; Dean, Fac. of Music, and Mem. Senate, Univ. of London, 1974–78. Leverhulme Res. Fellowship, 1996. *Publications:* English Song: Dowland to Purcell, 1974, 2nd edn 1986; The Seventeenth Century, Blackwell History of Music in Britain, vol. 3, 1992; Restoration Cathedral Music 1660–1714, 1995; Henry Lawes: Cavalier songwriter, 2000; editions of music in: The English Lute-songs, 2nd series, vol. 17, 1961, 2nd edn 1974, vol. 18, 1962, vol. 19, 1966; Musica Britannica, vol. 33, 1971, 2nd edn 1977, vol. 42, 1978; The Works of Henry Purcell, vol. 2, 1990, vol. 4, 1994, vol. 20, 1998, vol. 22a, 2000, vol. 22b, 2007; (contrib.) The New Grove, 1980, 2nd edn 2001; (contrib.) The New Oxford History of Music, vol. 6, 1986; (contrib.) Purcell Studies, 1995; articles in Acta Musicologica, Music and Letters, Proc. Royal Musical Assoc., Early Music, etc. *Address:* Bridge House, Trumps Green Road, Virginia Water, Surrey GU25 4JA. *T:* (01344) 843039.

SPINK, Dr Robert Michael; MP Castle Point (C, 1992–97 and 2001–08; UK Ind, since 2008); *b* 1 Aug. 1948; *s* of George and Brenda Spink; *m* 1968, Janet Mary Barham (marr. diss. 2002); three *s* one *d.* *Educ:* Manchester Univ. (research and academic prizes; BSc 1st Cl. Hons Eng 1971); Cranfield Inst. of Technology (MSc Indust Eng 1974; PhD, Sch. of Management, 1989). CEng, MIProdE, MIIM, MIMC, CDipAF. Mill labourer, 1962–64; RAF, 1964–66; EMI Electronics, 1966–77 (Engrg Apprentice; EMI Graduate Apprentice of the Year, 1971); Management consultant, 1977–; Dir and Co-Owner, Seafarer Navigation International, 1980–84; industrial engr, 1984–; Dir, Bournemouth Internat. Airport, 1989–93. Dorset County Councillor, 1985–93 (Chm., Educn Policy Cttee, 1989–91); Mem., Dorset Police Authy, 1985–93. Contested (C) Castle Point, 1997. PPS to Minister of State, Dept of Employment, then Home Office, 1994–97. Mem., Educn Select Cttee, 1992–97; Vice Chm., Backbench Employment Cttee, 1993–94; Chm., All Party Parly Gp for Prisoners Abroad, 1995–97. Dep. Chm., Poole Cons. Assoc., 1984–92; Mem. Nat. Exec., Baby Life Support Systems Charity, 1985–92. MCMI. *Recreations:* occasional marathons, gardening, potter. *Address:* c/o House of Commons, SW1A 0AA.

SPINKS, Mary Cecilia, RGN; health services consultant, specialising in risk management, audit and expert opinion on malpractice, since 1993; *b* 20 Sept. 1940; *d* of Francis and Mary Clark; *m* 1st, 1961, Robert Donn (marr. diss. 1975); 2nd, 1992, Leslie Oswald Spinks. *Educ:* St Vincent's Convent, Cork; Student Nurse, Whipps Cross Hosp. (RGN 1962); DipN London; William Rathbone Coll.; Thames Polytechnic (DMS). Post-graduate Staff Nurse, Charing Cross Hosp., 1962; Theatre Sister, St Mary's Hosp., Paddington, 1963–64; Theatre Sister, Nursing Officer, Sen. Nursing Officer, Bromley AHA, 1964–83; Dir, Nursing Services, Lewisham and N Southwark HA, 1983–84; Chief Nursing Officer and Dir, Consumer Affairs, Brighton HA, 1984–90; Regl Nursing Officer, NE Thames RHA, 1990–93. Former chm. and mem., nursing, health, editorial and advisory cttees; Chm., Nat. Assoc. of Theatre Nurses, 1975–78; Member: Maidstone HA, 1985–90; NHS Training Authy, 1988–91. Chm., E Berks Community Trust, 1998–2002. Dir, Florence Nightingale Foundn, 1996–. Vis. Prof., Univ. of Ulster, 2007. MRSM 1992. *Publications:* numerous contribs to professional jls. *Recreations:* horse-racing, cricket, gardening. *Address:* 2 Somerford Close, Maidenhead, Berks SL6 8EJ. *T:* (01628) 675526.

SPINNER, Bruno Max; Ambassador of Switzerland to the Republic of Italy, and to Malta and San Marino, since 2004; *b* 9 Jan. 1948; *s* of Max Spinner and Ruth Spinner-Schaffner; *m* 1976, Madelon Blaser-Giroud; two *s.* *Educ:* Univ. of Zurich (LLM); Univ. of Geneva. Entered Swiss Diplomatic Service, 1976: Attaché, Ankara, 1977; Diplomatic Sec., Mission to EC, Brussels, 1978–82; Dep. Hd of Mission, Ottawa, 1982–85; Hd, Div. of Internat. Law, Federal Dept of Foreign Affairs, Berne, 1985–89 (Legal Advr to Swiss chief negotiator at GATT negotiations (Uruguay Round), 1987–89; Pres., EFTA Cttee of Legal Experts, 1988–89); Minister, Dep. Hd of Mission to EC, Brussels, 1989–91; Mem., Delegn to EEA negotiations, and Vice-Pres., editl cttee, 1990–92; Ambassador and Hd, Integration Office, Federal Dept of Foreign Affairs and Federal Dept of the Economy, Berne, 1992–99; Ambassador to the UK, 2000–04. Hon. Prof. of European Law, Zurich Univ., 1993–2000. FRPSL 2003 (Mem., 2000). *Recreations:* sports, philately, art. *Address:* Embassy of Switzerland, Via Barnaba Oriani 61, 00197 Rome, Italy. *T:* (06) 80957322. *Club:* Garrick.

SPIRO, Prof. Stephen George, MD; FRCP; Professor of Respiratory Medicine, University College London, since 1997; Consultant Physician, since 1977, Head of Department of Thoracic Medicine, since 1993, University College London Hospitals NHS Trust; *b* 24 Aug. 1942; *s* of Ludwig Spiro and late Anna Spiro (*née* Freidmann); *m* 1971, Alison Mary Brown; three *s.* *Educ:* Manchester Univ. (BSc Anatomy 1964; MB

ChB 1967; MD 1975). FRCP 1981. Consultant Physician, Royal Brompton Hosp., 1977–93. Res. Fellow, Hammersmith Hosp., 1971–73; Sen. Registrar, Royal Brompton Hosp., 1973–77; Clin. Dir of Med. Services, 1994–2000, Med. Dir, 2001–03, UCL Hosps NHS Trust. Fulbright-Hayes Travelling Scholarship, Seattle, 1975–76. Visiting Professor: South African Respiratory Soc., 1993; Univ. of Queensland, Australia, 1994. Chairman: London Lung Cancer Clinical Trials Gp, 1997–; N London Cancer Network for Lung Cancer, 1997–; Vice-Chm., NE London Adv. Cttee for Clinical Excellence, 2003–. President: European Respiratory Soc., 1996–97; British Thoracic Soc., 2004. Exec. Ed., Thorax, 1991–95. *Publications*: Drug Treatment of Respiratory Disease, 1994; (jtly) New Perspectives on Lung Cancer, 1994; Carcinoma of the Lung, 1995, 2nd edn 2001; Self-Assessment Colour Review of Respiratory Medicine, 1997, 2nd edn 2002; The Lung in Auto-Immune Disease, 1997; Comprehensive Respiratory Medicine, 1999, 3rd edn as Clinical Respiratory Medicine, 2008. *Recreations*: tennis, flyfishing, worrying about Arsenal, home handyman. *Address*: 66 Grange Gardens, Pinner, Middx HA5 5QF. *Clubs*: Croxley Hall Fly Fishery; Eastcote Tennis.

SPITTLE, Leslie; His Honour Judge Spittle; a Circuit Judge, since 1996; *b* 14 Nov. 1940; *s* of Samuel and Irene Spittle; *m* 1963, Brenda Clayton; three *s*. *Educ*: Teesside Poly. (ACIS); Hull Univ. (LLB). Mgt trainee, Head Wrightson & Co., 1956–62; Lectr in Law, Econs and Accountancy, Bradford Tech. Coll., 1965–66; Sen. Lectr in Law, Teesside Poly., 1966–70. Called to the Bar, Gray's Inn, 1970; in private practice, 1970–96. Pres., N Yorks Magistrates' Assoc. Paul Harris Fellow, Rotary Club. Gov., Teesside Univ. *Recreations*: family, friends. *Address*: Teesside Combined Court Centre, Russell Street, Middlesbrough, Cleveland TS1 2AE. *T*: (01642) 340000.

SPITTLE, Dr Margaret Flora, (Mrs David Hare), OBE 2004; FRCP, FRCR; Consultant Clinical Oncologist: University College Hospital (formerly at Middlesex Hospital), since 1971; St John's Centre for Diseases of the Skin, St Thomas' Hospital, since 1971; *b* 10 Nov. 1939; *d* of Edwin William Spittle and Ada Florence Spittle (*née* Axam); *m* 1st, 1965, Dr Clive Lucas Harmer (marr. diss. 1977); two *d*; 2nd, 1986, David John Hare. *Educ*: King's Coll., London (AKC 1963; MSc 1969); Westminster Hosp. Med. Sch. (MB BS 1963). MRCS 1963; LRCP 1963, MRCP 1993, FRCP 1995; DMRT 1966; FRCR (Rohan Williams Gold Medal) 1968. Sen. Registrar, Radiotherapy Dept, Westminster Hosp., 1969; Instr., Radiation Div., Stanford Univ. Med. Centre, 1970; Hon. Consultant Clinical Oncologist: W Middx Univ. Hosp., 1971–2002; Royal Nat. Throat, Nose and Ear Hosp., 1986–; St Luke's Hosp. for the Clergy, 1993–. Civilian Consultant Advr in Radiation Medicine, RN, 2000–. Member: Nat. Radiation Protection Bd, 1991–98; Govt Adv. Cttee on Breast Screening, 1986–; Govt Cttee on Medicine and Radiation in the Envmt, 1993–; Govt Adv. Gp on Ionizing Radiation, 1995–; DoH Commng Gp for Health of the Nation Projects, 1996; Defence Nuclear Safety Cttee, 2002–; Depleted Uranium Oversight Bd, 2002–. Chairman: Multicentre Cancer Chemotherapy Gp, 1985–; UK AIDS Oncology Gp, 1988–. Vice-President: RSocMed, 1994–96 (Sen. Hon. Treas., 1988–94); Pres., Oncology Sect., 1987, Radiology Sect., 1989); Royal Coll. of Radiologists, 1995–96 (Dean, Faculty of Clin. Oncology, 1994–96); Pres., Assoc. of Head and Neck Oncologists of GB, 1990–92. *Publications*: chapters and articles on cancer of breast, head and neck, skin, and AIDS-related malignancy. *Recreations*: family, flying, golf, ski-ing, gardening. *Address*: Department of Oncology, University College Hospital, 250 Euston Road, NW1 2PG. *T*: (020) 7380 9090. *Clubs*: Royal Automobile, Royal Society of Medicine.

SPITZ, Prof. Lewis, PhD; FRCS, FRCSE, FRCPCH; Nuffield Professor of Paediatric Surgery, and Head of Surgical Unit, Institute of Child Health, London, 1979–2004, now Emeritus Nuffield Professor; Consultant Surgeon, Great Ormond Street Hospital for Children Trust (formerly Hospital for Sick Children, Great Ormond Street), since 1979; *b* 25 Aug. 1939; *s* of Woolf and Selma Spitz; *m* 1972, Louise Ruth Dyzenhaus; one *s* one *d*. *Educ*: Univ. of Pretoria (MB, ChB); Univ. of the Witwatersrand (PhD). FRCS (*ad eundem*) 1980; FRCSE 1969; Hon. FAAP 1987; FRCPCH 1997; Hon. FRCSI 2005. Smith and Nephew Fellow, Liverpool and London, 1971; Paediatric Surgeon, Johannesburg, 1971–74; Consultant Paediatric Surgeon, Sheffield Children's Hosp., 1974–79. Hon. Consultant in Paediatric Surgery to the Army, 1983–2006. Windermere Vis. Prof., Univ. of Melbourne, 1988; Chafin-Snyder Vis. Prof., Children's Hosp., UCLA, 1992; Santuli Vis. Prof., Babies Hosp., Columbia Univ., NY, 1992; Penman Vis. Prof., Red Cross Meml Hosp. and Univ. of Cape Town, 2000; Guttman Vis. Prof., Montreal, 2000; Jewitt Vis. Prof., Children's Hosp. of Buffalo, 2001–; Visiting Professor: Toronto, 1991; Seattle, 1992; Univ. of Hong Kong, 1993; Indianapolis, Pittsburgh, Washington, 1995; Royal Coll. of Surgeons, Thailand, 1995; Ann Arbor, 1997; Royal Coll. of Surgeons, Korea, 1997; Japanese Surgical Soc., 1998; Albert Einstein Coll. of Medicine, NY, 1999; Univ. of Alabama, 2003; Kansas, 2005; Adelaide, 2005; Chile, 2005. Hunterian Prof., RCS, 2001–02; Lectures: Sulamaa, Children's Hosp., Univ. of Helsinki, 1993 (Sulamaa Medal, 1990); Amer. Pediatric Surgical Assoc., 1995; P. Rickham Meml, Liverpool, 2004; J. Grosfeld, Indianapolis, 2005. Member: British Assoc. of Paediatric Surgeons (Pres., 1996–98); Assoc. of Surgeons of GB and Ireland; BPA (Mem. Acad. Bd, 1991–93); British Soc. of Gastroenterology; Med. Bd, Tracheo-oesophageal Support Soc., 1982–; Invited Mem., RCS, 1997–2000; Chm., Specialist Adv. Cttee in Paediatric Surgery, 1994–2004 (RCS Rep., 1991–96); RCS Rep on Intercollegiate Bd of Paediatric Surgery, 1994–97. Television: Your Life in their Hands, BBC TV; The baby who could not swallow, 1984; Siamese Twins, 1986; Separating Twins, BBC TV, 2005. Exec. Editor, Progress in Paediatric Surgery, 1982; Member, Editorial Board: Jl of Paediatric Surgery, 1980–; Archives of Diseases in Childhood, 1984–89; Turkish Jl of Paediatric Surgery, 1987–; Jl of RCSE, 1992–97; Associate Editor, Pediatric Surgery International, 1986–2004; Editorial Consultant: Surgery in Childhood International, 1996–; Annals of College of Surgery of Hong Kong, 1996–. Patron, Children's Wish, 1998. MRSocMed. Hon. FRCPH 2004; Hon. Mem., Paediatric Surgical Assocs of Switzerland, Austria, Greece, Germany, Asia, America and S Africa; Hon. FCSSA; Hon. FCMSA. Hon. MD: Sheffield, 2002; Witwatersrand. Bronze Medal, Nordik Soc. of Paediatric Surgeons, 1990; James Spence Medal, RCPCH, 2004; Denis Browne Gold Medal, Brit. Assoc. of Paediatric Surgeons, 2004; Clement-Price Thomas Award, RCS, 2004; Rehbein Medal, 2008. *Publications*: A Colour Atlas of Paediatric Surgical Diagnosis, 1981; A Colour Atlas of Surgery for Undescended Testes, 1984; Paediatric Surgery, 4th edn 1988 (Rob and Smith Operative Surgery series), 6th edn 2006; (ed jtly) The Great Ormond Street Colour Handbook of Paediatrics & Child Health, 2007; Visual Handbook of Paediatrics and Child Health: the core, 2008; chapters in books on paediatrics and surgery; articles on oesophageal atresia, oesophageal replacement, gastro-oesophageal reflux, neonatal surgical conditions, paediatric oncology, and conjoined twins. *Recreation*: tennis. *Address*: Great Ormond Street Hospital for Children NHS Trust, WC1 3JH. *T*: (020) 7405 9200.

SPOKES, Ann; *see* Spokes Symonds, A. H.

SPOKES, John Arthur Clayton; QC 1973; *b* 6 Feb. 1931; 2nd *s* of late Peter Spencer Spokes and Lilla Jane Spokes (*née* Clayton), Oxford; *m* 1961, Jean, *yr d* of late Dr Robert McLean and Jean Symington McLean (*née* Barr), Carluke; one *s* one *d*. *Educ*: Westminster Sch.; Brasenose Coll., Oxford (BA 1954; MA 1959); Univ. of Southampton (MA 2000).

Nat. Service, Royal Artillery, 1949–51 (commnd 1950). Called to Bar, Gray's Inn, 1955, Bencher, 1985; a Recorder, 1972–93. Chm., Data Protection, subseq. Inf., Tribunal, 1985–2001. Chancellor, Dio. of Winchester, 1985–93. *Recreation*: local history. *Address*: 31 Southgate Street, Winchester, Hants SO23 9EB. *Club*: Leander (Henley-on-Thames).

See also A. H. Spokes Symonds.

SPOKES SYMONDS, Ann (Hazel); Patron, Age Concern England, since 1994 (Chairman, 1983–86; Vice-President, 1987–94); *b* 10 Nov. 1925; *d* of Peter Spencer Spokes and Lilla Jane Spokes (*née* Clayton); *m* 1980, (John) Richard (Charters) Symonds (*d* 2006). *Educ*: Wychwood Sch., Oxford; Masters Sch., Dobbs Ferry, NY, USA; St Anne's Coll., Oxford (BA 1947; MA). Organising Secretary: Oxford Council of Social Service, 1959–74; Age Concern Oxford, 1958–80. Dir, ATV, 1978–81; Mem. W Midlands Bd, Central Indep. Television plc, 1981–92. Mem., Thames Valley Police Authy, 1973–85; Chm., No 5 Police Dist. Authy Cttee, 1982–85; Vice-Chm., Personal Social Services Council, 1978–80; Chm., Social Services Cttee, ACC, 1978–82; Mem. Bd, Anchor Housing Assoc., 1976–83, 1985–94; Member: Prince of Wales' Adv. Gp on Disability, 1983–90; Oftel Adv. Cttee for Disabled and Elderly People, 1985–91; Hearing Aid Council, 1986–89; Trustee, CERT, 1986–89. Member: Oxford City Council, 1957–95 (Lord Mayor, 1976–77; Hon. Alderman, 1995–); Oxfordshire CC, 1974–85 (Chm., 1981–83). Contested (C) NE Leicester, 1959, Brigg, 1966 and 1970. Mem., Soc. of Authors, 1992–. FRSA 1991. *Publications*: Celebrating Age: an anthology, 1987; Havens Across the Sea, 1990; The Great Grosvenor Hotel Scandal, 1993; Storks, Black Bags and Gooseberry Bushes, 1993; The Changing Faces of Wolvercote, Wytham and Godstow, 1997; The Changing Faces of North Oxford, Books One and Two, 1998; The Changing Faces of Iffley, 1999; The Changing Faces of Rose Hill, 2000; Oxfordshire People and the Forgotten War: the Anglo-Boer conflict 1899–1902, 2002; (with Richard Symonds) Follow Me: a dog's view of the gospel story, 2006. *Recreations*: lawn tennis, golf, photography, enjoying cats. *Address*: 43 Davenant Road, Oxford OX2 8BU. *T*: (01865) 515661.

See also J. A. C. Spokes.

SPOONER, Sir James (Douglas), Kt 1981; Director, John Swire & Sons, 1970–2003; *b* 11 July 1932; *s* of late Vice-Adm. E. J. Spooner, DSO, and Megan Spooner (*née* Megan Foster, the singer); *m* 1958, Jane Alyson, *d* of late Sir Gerald Glover; two *s* one *d*. *Educ*: Eton Coll. (Fellow, 1990); Christ Church, Oxford. Chartered Accountant 1962; Partner, Dixon Wilson & Co., Chartered Accountants, 1963–72; Chm., Vantona Viyella, subseq. Coats Viyella, 1969–89. Chm., NAAFI, 1973–86 (Dir, 1968–86); Director: Abingworth, 1973–91; Morgan Crucible, 1978–97 (Chm., 1983–97); J. Sainsbury, 1981–94; Barclays Bank, 1983–94; Hogg Robinson Gp, 1971–85 (Dep. Chm., 1971–85); Dep. Chm., Royal Opera House, Covent Garden, 1992–97 (Dir, 1987–97); Chm. of Trustees, British Telecom Pension Scheme, 1992–98. Chm. Council, King's College London, 1986–98; Gov., RAM, 1997–2006. *Recreations*: music, history. *Address*: The Chapel, High Street, Pytchley, Kettering, Northants NN14 1EN. *Clubs*: Beefsteak, Brooks's.

SPORBORG, Christopher Henry, CBE 2001; Chairman, Countrywide plc (formerly Hambro Countrywide, then Countrywide Assured Group), 1986–2007; *b* 17 April 1939; *s* of late H. N. Sporborg and Mary (*née* Rowlands); *m* 1961, Lucinda Jane (*née* Hanbury); two *s* two *d*. *Educ*: Rugby School; Emmanuel College, Cambridge (BA Hons). Nat. Service, Coldstream Guards, 1957–59 (Lieut). Hambros Bank, 1962–95: Dir, 1970; Dep. Chm., 1983–95; Hambros PLC: Vice-Chm., 1986–90; Dep. Chm., 1990–98. Chairman: United Racecourses (Hldgs), 1994–96; Racecourse Hldgs Trust, 1998–2003 (Dir, 1994–2003); Chesnara plc, 2004–; Dep. Chm., C. E. Heath PLC, 1994–97; Director: Getty Images Inc., 1997–; Cunningham Lindsey Inc. (formerly Lindsay Morden Ltd), 1999–2007. Mem., Jockey Club, 1982–; Dir, Jockey Club Estates, 1985–2002; Mem., Horserace Totalisator Bd, 1993–2005. Trustee: Develt Trust (for the Mentally Handicapped); Nat. Hosp. Develt Foundn; Corporate Action Trust; Sir Jules Thorn Charitable Trust; Fitzwilliam Family Trusts. *Recreations*: hunting (Joint Master, Puckeridge Foxhounds), racing (owner), bridge. *Address*: Brooms Farm, Upwick Green, Albury, Ware, Herts SG11 2JX. *T*: (01279) 771444. *Club*: Boodle's.

SPOTTISWOOD, Air Vice-Marshal James Donald, CB 1988; CVO 1977; AFC 1971; *b* 27 May 1934; *s* of James Thomas Spottiswood and Caroline Margaret Spottiswood; *m* 1957, Margaret Maxwell (*née* Harrison); two *s* one *d*. *Educ*: West Hartlepool Grammar School; Boston Univ., USA (MA). Enlisted RAF, 1951, commissioned, 1952; 617 Sqn, 1962–64; Royal Naval Staff Coll., 1965; PSO to C-in-C Middle East, 1966–67; Commanded 53 Sqn, 1968–70; JSSC, 1970; Commanded: RAF Thorney Island, 1972–75; RAF Benson, 1975–76; Dep. Captain, the Queen's Flight, 1975–76; RCDS, 1978; Secretary to IMS, HQ NATO, 1980–83; DG of Trng, RAF, 1983–85; Air Officer Trng, RAF Support Comd, 1985–89, retired. Man. Dir, Airwork Ltd, Bournemouth Internat. Airport, 1989–97; Vice Pres., Support Services Div., Short's, 1994–97. Chm., British Gliding Assoc., 1989–97. FCMI (FBIM 1983). *Recreations*: gliding, sailing. *Address*: Royal Bank of Scotland, 49–51 Old Christchurch Road, Bournemouth BH1 1EG. *Club*: Royal Air Force.

SPOTTISWOODE, Clare Mary Joan, CBE 1999; Member, Management Group, PA Consulting Group, since 1999; Policyholder Advocate, Aviva, since 2006; *b* 20 March 1953; *d* of late Charlotte and of Tony Spottiswoode; *m* 1977, Oliver Richards; one *s* three *d*. *Educ*: Cheltenham Ladies' Coll.; Clare Coll., Cambridge (MA Maths Pt 1, Economics Pt 2); Yale Univ. (MPhil). HM Treasury, 1977–80; Spottiswoode Trading, 1980–84 (wholesale importing business); Chm. and Chief Exec., Spottiswoode and Spottiswoode (micro computer software), 1984–90; Dir Gen. of Gas Supply, 1993–98; Sen. Vice Pres. of Regulatory Affairs, Europe, Azurix, Enron, 1998–99; Dep. Chm., British Energy, 2001–07. Chm., Gas Strategies Ltd, 2000–; Dir, BioFuels, 2003–07; non-exec. Dir, Tullow Oil plc, 2002–. Hon. DSc Brunel, 1997. *Publications*: Quill, 1984; Abacus, 1984. *Recreations*: children, gardening, theatre.

SPRACKLING, Maj.-Gen. Ian Oliver John, OBE 1977; *b* 3 Oct. 1936; *m* 1959, Ann Vonda (*née* Coote); two *s*. *Educ*: Bristol Grammar School; RMCS (BSc Eng); psc, RCDS. RMA Sandhurst, 1955; 2nd Lieut, Royal Corps of Signals, 1957; RMCS, 1958–61; served Far East, UK, BAOR, 1961–75; Staff Officer, Sultan of Oman's Armed Forces, 1975–77; CO, Electronic Warfare Regt, BAOR, 1977–79; Col, Cabinet Office, 1979–81; Comdr, Catterick Garrison, 1982–84; RCDS 1984; Dir, Mil. Assistance Overseas, 1985–86; Dir Gen., Management and Support of Intelligence, MoD, 1986–89, retired. Defence Advr, 1989–92, Hd of Russian practice, Moscow, 1993–96, Andersen Consulting. Non-exec. Dir, i Ventures Capital, 2000–03; Chm., ITT Defence Ltd, 2004–. Master of Signals, 1997–2003. *Recreations*: bridge, socialising, keep fit, watching Rugby. *Clubs*: Army and Navy; Fadeaways.

SPRAGGS, Rear-Adm. Trevor Owen Keith, CB 1983; CEng, FIET; Chief of Staff to Commander-in-Chief, Naval Home Command, 1981–83; *b* 17 June 1926; *s* of Cecil James Spraggs and Gladys Maude (*née* Morey); *m* 1st, 1955, Mary Patricia Light (*d* 1983); two *s*; 2nd, 1986, Gwynedd Kate (*née* Adams) widow of Reginald A. W. Green, CEng, MIMechE. *Educ*: Portsmouth Grammar Sch.; St John's Coll., Southsea; Imperial College of Science and Technology, London (BScEng, ACGI). Joined Royal Navy, 1945; courses: HM Ships: King Alfred, Leander, Harrier, 1945–47; Admiralty Compass Obs., Slough, 1948; BRNC, Dartmouth, 1948–50; HM Ships: Dryad, Vanguard, Vernon, Collingwood, Ariel, Falcon, 1950–61; AEI, Manchester, 1962; RNEC, 1962–66; HMS Collingwood, 1966–69 and 1972–75; RNEC, 1969–72, and, as Dean, 1979–80; Dean, RNC, Greenwich, 1975–77; Dir of Naval Trng Support, Dir of Naval Educn and Trng Support, 1977–79; Chief Naval Instr Officer, 1981–83. ADC to the Queen, 1979. Member: Nautical Studies Bd of CNAA, 1975–80; Maritime Studies Adv. Cttee of Plymouth Polytech., 1979–80; Cttee of Management, Royal Hosp. Sch., Holbrook, 1981–83; Governor: Fareham Technical Coll., 1972–75; RN Sch. for Officers' Daughters, Haslemere, 1975–77. Pres., Combined Services and RN Amateur Athletic Assocs, 1981–83. *Recreation:* gardening. *Address:* 46 Sinah Lane, Hayling Island, Hants PO11 0HH. *Clubs:* Royal Naval Sailing Association; Hayling Golf.

SPRAGUE, David Keith, MVO 1972; HM Diplomatic Service, retired; High Commissioner, Sierra Leone, 1991–93; *b* 20 Feb. 1935; *m* 1958, Audrey Mellon; two *s* one *d*. *Educ:* King Edward VI Grammar Sch., Camp Hill, Birmingham. Foreign Office, 1953; Nat. Service, 1953–55; FO, 1955, served Addis Ababa, Paris, Belgrade, Budapest, Kuala Lumpur, Abidjan, Sofia, and FCO; Dep. High Comr, Madras, 1986–89; Ambassador to Mongolia, 1989–91. *Recreations:* bridge, heathers. *Address:* 5 Deepdene Drive, Dorking, Surrey RH5 4AD.

SPRAKE, Anthony Douglas; HM Diplomatic Service, retired; Consul-General, Melbourne, 2001–03; *b* 16 July 1944; *s* of Douglas Alfred Sprake and Doris Elizabeth Sprake (*née* Grindley); *m* 1977, Jane Bonner McNeill; one *s* (and one *s* decd). *Educ:* City of Bath Boys' Sch.; Univ. of Keele (BA Hons Maths and Physics). Asst Principal, Min. of Labour, 1968–72; Private Sec. to Parly Under-Sec. of State for Employment, 1972–73; Principal, Dept of Employment, 1973–77; Labour Attaché, British Embassy, Brussels, 1977–79; joined Diplomatic Service, 1980: FCO, 1980–82; Dep. High Comr, Freetown, Sierra Leone, 1982–85; Defence Dept, FCO, 1986–88; MoD (on secondment), 1989; Counsellor (Commercial), The Hague, 1990–94; Head, Cultural Relns Dept, FCO, 1994–96; Minister and Consul Gen., Peking, 1996–2000; Hd, China and Hong Kong Dept, FCO, 2000. *Recreations:* sailing, theatre, bridge. *Address:* 1 Chapel Street, Woodbridge, Suffolk IP12 4NF. *T:* (01394) 380006.

SPRATT, Prof. Brian Geoffrey, CBE 2008; PhD; FMedSci; FRS 1993; Professor of Molecular Microbiology, since 2001, Head of Department of Infectious Disease Epidemiology, since 2004, Imperial College Faculty of Medicine; Wellcome Trust Principal Research Fellow, since 1989; *b* 21 March 1947; *s* of Clarence Albert Spratt and Marjory Alice (*née* Jeffreys); *m* 1st; one *s*; 2nd, 1995, Jiaji Zhou; one *s*. *Educ:* Tonbridge Sch.; University Coll. London (BSc, PhD). Research Fellow: Princeton Univ., 1973–75; Leicester Univ., 1975–80; Sussex University: Lectr in Biochem., 1980–87; Reader in Molecular Genetics, 1987–89; Prof., 1989–98; Prof. of Biology, Oxford Univ., 1998–2001. Founder FMedSci 1998. Fellow, Amer. Acad. of Microbiol., 2003. *Publications:* numerous pubns on microbiol. and genetics in learned jls. *Address:* Department of Infectious Disease Epidemiology, Imperial College Faculty of Medicine, St Mary's Hospital, W2 1PG. *T:* (020) 7594 3398, *Fax:* (020) 7402 3927.

SPRATT, Sir Greville (Douglas), GBE 1987; TD 1962, Bar 1968; DL; JP; Underwriting Member of Lloyd's, 1950–98; Lord Mayor of London, 1987–88; *b* 1 May 1927; *e s* of Hugh Douglas Spratt and Sheelah Ivy (*née* Stace); *m* 1954, Sheila Farrow Wade (*d* 2002); three *d*. *Educ:* Leighton Park; Charterhouse; Sandhurst. Served Coldstream Guards, 1945–46; commnd Oxfordshire and Bucks LI, 1946; seconded to Arab Legion; served Palestine, Trans Jordan and Egypt, 1946–48; GSO III (Ops and Intell.), 1948. Lloyd's, 1948–61; joined J. & N. Wade Gp of Electrical Distributors, 1961; Dir, 1969–76 and Man. Dir, 1972–76. Dir, 1989–92, Chm., 1991–92, City and West End Regl Adv. Bd, National Westminster Bank; Chairman: Forest Mere Ltd, 1993–96 (Dir, 1991–96); Claremount Underwriting Agency, 1994–97; Kingsmead Underwriting Agency, 1997–99; Director: Williams Lea Gp, 1989–96; Charterhouse Enterprises Ltd, 1991–95; Craigie Taylor Internat., 1995–96. Lieut of the City of London, 1972; Life Mem., Guild of Freemen, 1977 (Mem. Court, 1982–90); Liveryman, Ironmongers' Co., 1977– (Mem. Ct, 1982–; Master, 1995–96); Alderman, Castle Baynard Ward, 1978–95; JP 1978, Sheriff, 1984–85, City of London; DL Greater London, 1986; Mem., Police Cttee, 1989–91, Planning and Communications Cttee, 1990–91, Corp. of City of London. Joined HAC Infantry Bn as private, 1950; re-commnd 1950; CO, 1962–65; Regtl Col, 1966–70; Mem., Ct of Assts, HAC, 1960–70 and 1978–95; ADC to the Queen, 1973–78; Mem., City TA&VRA, 1960– (Vice Chm., 1973–77, Chm., 1977–82); Vice Pres., TA&VRA for Greater London, 1994 (Chm., 1991–94; Mem., Exec. and Finance Cttee, 1977–94); Hon. Colonel: City and NE sector, London ACF, 1983–99; 8th Bn, The Queen's Fusiliers (City of London), 1988–92; The London Regt, 1992–95. Church Comr, 1993–96. Chm., Action Res. for the Crippled Child, 1989–99 (Mem. Council, 1982–; Mem. Haslemere Cttee, 1971–82); President: Alzheimer's Soc., Haslemere, 1995–; Royal British Legion, Haslemere (St James Vice Pres., 1991–); London Fedn of Old Comrades Assocs, 1983–; Vice President: Not Forgotten Assoc., 1990–; British Red Cross, 1993– (Dep. Pres., London, 1983–91); Mem. Council, Reserve Forces Assoc., 1981–84. Chm., Anglo Jordanian Soc., 1990–97; Member: Cttee, Guildhall Sch. of Music and Drama, 1978–80 (Hon. Mem., 1988–); Court, City Univ., 1981–88 (Chancellor, 1987–88); Governing Bodies of Girls' Schs Assoc., 1982–90; Governor: St Ives Sch., 1976– (Vice Chm., 1977–86; Chm., 1986–90); King Edward's Sch., Witley, 1978–96 (Vice-Pres., 1989–96); Christ's Hosp., 1978–95; Bridewell Royal Hosp., 1978–96; City of London Sch. for Girls, 1981–82; Malvern Girls' Coll., 1982–90; St Paul's Cathedral Choir Sch., 1985–99; Charterhouse, 1985–99 (Chm. Governing Body, 1989–95); City of London Freemen's Sch., 1992–95; Life Governor, Corp. of the Sons of the Clergy, 1985–; Patron: Internat. Centre for Child Studies, 1985–; Surrey Charity Gp, 1989–; Emily Appeal, 1992–98; Vice Patron, Almshouse Assoc., 1997–; Chm., David Shepherd Conservation Foundn, 1996–2000; Mem., St Paul's Cathedral Court of Advisers, 1993–99. Mem., Surrey Scout Council, 1990–. Blackdown Cttee, Nat. Trust, 1977–87. Trustee: Chichester Theatre; Chichester Cathedral; Endowment of St Paul's Cathedral; Childrens' Research Internat. Carthusian Trust; Charterhouse Soc.; Castle Baynard Educnl Trust; Special Trustee, St Bartholomew's Hosp., 1989–96. FRSA; FRGS. Hon. DLitt City Univ., 1988. KStJ 1987 (OStJ 1985). Chevalier de la Légion d'Honneur, 1961; Commandeur de l'Ordre National du Mérite, 1984; Commander, Order of the Lion, Malaŵi, 1985; Mem., Nat. Order of Aztec Eagle, Mexico, 1985; Order of St Olav, Norway, 1988; Order of Merit, Senegal, 1988. *Recreations:* tennis, music, military history. *Address:* Rowans, Pathfields Close, Haslemere, Surrey GU27 2BL. *T:* (01428) 644367. *Clubs:* City Livery, Guildhall, United Wards.

SPRENT, Prof. Janet Irene, OBE 1996; DSc; FRSE; Professor of Plant Biology, University of Dundee, 1989–98, now Emeritus (Deputy Principal, 1995–98); *b* 10 Jan. 1934; *d* of James William and Dorothy May Findlater; *m* 1955, Peter Sprent. *Educ:* Slough High Sch. for Girls; Imperial Coll. of Science and Technol., London (BSc; ARCS 1954); Univ. of Tasmania (PhD 1958); Univ. of London (DSc 1988). FRSE 1990. Scientific Officer, Rothamsted Expmtl Stn, 1954–55; ICIANZ Res. Fellow, Univ. of Tasmania, 1955–58; Botany Mistress, Rochester Girls' Grammar Sch., 1959–61; Lectr, subseq. Sen. Lectr, Goldsmiths' Coll., London, 1960–67; University of Dundee: successively Res. Fellow, Lectr, Sen. Lectr and Reader, 1967–89; Dean, Faculty of Science and Engrg, 1987–89; Hd, Dept of Biol Scis, 1992–95. Hon. Res. Fellow, Scottish Crop Res. Inst., 1991–. Extensive overseas collaboration, eg Australia, Brazil, Kenya, in nitrogen fixing crop and tree research. Member: Council, NERC, 1991–95; SHEFC, 1992–96; (indep.) JNCC, 1994–2000; Bd, Scottish Natural Heritage, 2001–07; Royal Commn on Envmtl Pollution, 2002–08. Trustee, Royal Botanic Gardens, Edinburgh, 2007–. Mem. Governing Body and Trustee, MacAulay Land Use Res. Inst., 1990–2001 (Chm., 1995–2001). *Publications:* The Biology of Nitrogen Fixing Organisms, 1979; The Ecology of the Nitrogen Cycle, 1987; (with P. Sprent) Nitrogen Fixing Organisms: pure and applied aspects, 1990; (with P. Sprent) Suilven's World, 1995; Nodulation in Legumes, 2001; papers in scientific jls and chapters in books and symposium vols. *Recreations:* hill-walking, gardening, music. *Address:* 32 Birkhill Avenue, Wormit, Newport on Tay, Fife DD6 8PW. *T:* (01382) 541706. *Club:* Farmers'.

SPRIDDELL, Peter Henry; Director: Capital & Counties plc, 1988–94; Capital Shopping Centres plc, 1994–2000; Royal Artillery Museums Ltd, 1990–94; *b* 18 Aug. 1928; *s* of Thomas Henry Spriddell and Eva Florence Spriddell; *m* 1952, Joyce Patricia (*née* Haycock); two *s* one *d*. *Educ:* Plymouth Coll.; Exeter Coll., Oxford (MA); Harvard Business Sch. Marks & Spencer: store management, 1951–68; Sen. Exec. Store Operations, 1968–70; Dir, 1970–88; Alternate Exec. Dir, 1970–72; Exec. Dir Personnel, 1972–75; Exec. Dir Store Operations, Transport, Building and Store Develt, Real Estate, 1975–88; Dir, NFC, 1978–82; non-exec. Mem., British Rail Property Bd, 1986–2001. Mem. Bd, British Council of Shopping Centres, 1983–95 (Pres., 1988–89; Hon. Life Mem., 1998). Mem. Council, 1978–94, Barclay Fellow, 1994–2003, Hon. Life Fellow, 2003, Templeton Coll., Oxford (formerly Oxford Centre for Management Studies). Mem. Cttee, Wine Soc., 1998–2000. FRSA. Freeman, City of London; Liveryman, Worshipful Co. of Paviors, 1984. *Recreations:* music, golf. *Club:* Moor Park Golf.

SPRING, Sir Dryden (Thomas), Kt 1994; dairy farmer and company director; Director, 1983–98, Chairman, 1989–98, New Zealand Dairy Board; *b* 6 Oct. 1939; *s* of Maurice Spring and Violet Grace Spring; *m* 1st, 1960, Christine Margaret McCarthy (marr. diss. 2002); three *s* three *d*; 2nd, 2003, Margaret Skews. *Educ:* Walton Primary Sch.; Matamata Coll. NZ Co-operative Dairy Co. Ltd: Dir, 1973–98; Dep. Chm., 1979–82; Chm., 1982–89. Director: Rural Banking and Finance Corp., 1974–88; Maramarua Coalfields Ltd, 1978–84; Nufarm (formerly Fernz Corp.) Ltd, 1982–2004; Goodman Fielder Ltd, 1989–2003 (Dep. Chm., 2000–03); Nat. Bank of NZ, 1994–2003; Maersk New Zealand Ltd, 1999–2004; Fletcher Building Ltd, 2001–; Sky City Entertainment Group Ltd, 2003–; Port of Tauranga Ltd, 2004–, and other cos; Chairman: WEL Networks Ltd, 1999–2005; Ericsson Communications NZ Ltd, 1999–2003; Tenon (formerly Fletcher Challenge Forests) Ltd, 2001–04; ANZ Nat. Bank, 2006– (Dir, 2003–); Dep. Chm., Ports of Auckland Ltd, 1988–94. Member: Prime Minister's Enterprise Council, 1991–94; Asian Pacific Econ. Co-operation Eminent Persons Gp, 1994–96; Internat. Adv. Bd, Chile Pacific Foundn, 2005–; Chm., Asia 2000 Foundn of NZ, 2001–06. Hon. Chm., NZ/Philippines Business Council, 1992–98. Chm., ASEAN/NZ Combined Business Council, 1998–99; NZ Chm., Business Adv. Council, Asia Pacific Econ. Co-operation, 2000–06; Patron, NZ/Thailand Business Council, 1995–98. Fellow, 1993, Dist. Fellow, 2000, Inst. of Dirs in NZ. Life Mem., Federated Farmers of NZ (Waikato), 1987. Dist. Fellow, Massey Univ. of Agric., 1999. Hon. DSc Massey, 2000. NZ Commemoration Medal, 1990. *Recreations:* sport, reading. *Address:* 124 Burwood Road, Matamata, New Zealand. *Clubs:* Wellington; Te Aroha; Matamata, Matamata United Sport.

SPRING, Richard, (Dick); Executive Vice Chairman, Financial Exchange Co. of Ireland, since 2002; Chairman, Industrial Development Ireland, since 1998; *b* 29 Aug. 1950; *s* of late Daniel and Anne Spring; *m* 1977, Kristi Lee Hutcheson; two *s* one *d*. *Educ:* Mt St Joseph Coll., Roscrea; Trinity Coll., Dublin (BA 1972). Called to the Bar, King's Inns, Dublin, 1975; in practice on Munster Circuit, 1977–81. Mem. Dáil (TD) (Lab), N Kerry, 1981–2002. Minister of State, Dept of Justice, 1981–82; Dep. Prime Minister of Ireland, 1982–87 and 1993–97; Minister for the Environment, 1982–83; Minister for Energy, 1983–87; Minister for Foreign Affairs, 1993–97. Leader of Irish Labour Party, 1982–97. Director: Alder Capital, 2000–; Altobridge Ltd, 2002–; Repak Ltd, 2006–; Chm., Fexco Stockbroking Ltd, 2002–. Chm., Réalta HIV Global Foundn, 2005–. Associate Fellow, Kennedy Sch. of Govt, Harvard, 1998–; Fellow, Salzburg Seminar, 1998–. *Recreations:* swimming, reading, golf. *Address:* Ridge Lodge, The Spa, Tralee, Co. Kerry, Ireland. *T:* (87) 2391200; *e-mail:* dspring@fexco.com.

SPRING, Richard John Grenville; MP (C) West Suffolk, since 1997 (Bury St Edmunds, 1992–97); *b* 24 Sept. 1946; *s* of late H. J. A. Spring and Marjorie (*née* Watson-Morris); *m* 1979, Hon. Jane (marr. diss. 1993), *o d* of 8th Baron Henniker, KCMG, CVO, MC; one *s* one *d*. *Educ:* Rondebosch, Cape; Univ. of Cape Town; Magdalene Coll., Cambridge (MA Econs). Vice-Pres., Merrill Lynch Ltd, 1976–86; Dep. Man. Dir, E. F. Hutton Internat. Associates, 1986–88; Exec. Dir, Shearson Lehman Hutton, 1988–89; Man. Director, Xerox Furman Selz, 1989–92. Contested (C) Ashton-under-Lyne, 1983. PPS to Min. of State, DTI, 1996, to Ministers for the armed forces and for defence procurement, 1996–97; Opposition front bench spokesman on culture, media and sport, 1997–2000, on foreign and Commonwealth affairs, 2000–04; Shadow Financial Services Minister, 2004–05; Shadow Paymaster Gen., 2005. Member: Employment Select Cttee, 1992–94; NI Select Cttee, 1994–97; Health Select Cttee, 1995–97; Vice Chairman: All Party Racing and Bloodstock Cttee, 1997–98; All Party Mobile Telephone Gp, 2004. A Vice Chm., Cons. Party, and Co-Chm., Cons. City Circle, 2006–. Pres., Arts and Heritage Cttee, Bow Gp, 1992–97. European Elections Campaign Co-ordinator, 1989; Chm., Westminster CPC, 1990; Dep.-Chm., Small Business Bureau, 1997– (Chm., Parly Adv. Gp, 1992–). Chm., British-Ukranian Soc., 2007–. Gov., Westminster Foundn for Democracy, 2001–. *Recreations:* country pursuits, English watercolours. *Address:* c/o House of Commons, SW1A 0AA. *Club:* Boodle's.

SPRING, Stephanie, (Stevie), FIPA, FMS; Chief Executive, Future plc, since 2006; *b* 10 June 1957; *d* of William Harold Spring and Marlene Maud Spring (*née* Coleman, now Green). *Educ:* Eggars Grammar Sch., Alton; Univ. of Kent, Canterbury (LLB Hons 1978). FIPA 1996; FMS 2004. Business Dir, Grey Advertising, 1984–88; Dep. Man. Dir, Gold Greenlees Trott, 1988–92; Managing Director: Woollams Moira Gaskin O'Malley, 1992–94; Young & Rubicam, 1994–2000; Chief Exec., Clear Channel UK, 2000–06. Chm., Fedn of Groundwork Trusts, 2001–. Trustee: NABS, 1990–; Arts & Business, 2006–. *Recreations:* travel, entertainment, socialising, swimming, spinning. *Address:* 34 Courtnell Street, W2 5BX; *e-mail:* stevie.spring@futurenet.co.uk. *Clubs:* Soho House, Women's Advertising.

SPRING RICE, family name of **Baron Monteagle of Brandon**.

SPRINGALL, Diana; artist; *b* 16 Sept. 1938; *d* of William Gordon Alexander and Stella Alice Fuller; *m* 1960, Ernest Thomas Springall (marr. diss. 1975); two *s*. *Educ:* Goldsmiths'

Coll. Sch. of Art (NDD Painting 1960; ATC 1961); City and Guilds of London Inst. (Embroidery 1963); Univ. of London (Dip. Hist. of Art 1968). Hd, Art Dept, West Heath Sch., Sevenoaks, 1961–63; Lectr, Fashion Dept, Maidstone Coll. of Art, 1963–68; Principal Lectr and Hd, Dept of Fashion and Textiles, Stockwell Coll. of Educn, Bromley, 1968–80; Panel Lectr, V&A Mus., 1980–. Chm. and Emeritus Mem., Embroiderers' Guild, 1978–85; Chm. and Fellow, Soc. of Designer-Craftsmen, 1987–90. Design consultant, Embroidery (TV series), BBC TV, 1980; Twelve British Embroiderers (exhibn), Tokyo, 1985. FRSA. *Publications:* Canvas Embroidery, 1969; Embroidery, 1980; Twelve British Embroiderers (catalogue), 1985; Design for Embroidery, 1988; Inspired to Stitch, 2005; An Embroiderer's Eye, 2009. *Recreations:* gardening, cooking, travel. *Address:* Oast Cottage, Park Lane, Kemsing, Sevenoaks, Kent TN15 6NU. *T:* and *Fax:* (01732) 761501; *e-mail:* dianaspringall@btinternet.com. *Club:* Club L International.

SPRINGFORD, John Frederick Charles, CBE 1980 (OBE 1970); retired British Council Officer; *b* 6 June 1919; *s* of Frederick Charles Springford and Bertha Agnes Springford (*née* Trenery); *m* 1945, Phyllis Wharton; one *s* two *d*. *Educ:* Latymer Upper Sch.; Christ's College, Cambridge (MA). Served War 1940–46, RAC; seconded Indian Armoured Corps, 1942; Asst Political Agent II in Mekran, 1945. British Council Service, Baghdad and Mosul, Iraq, 1947–51, Isfahan, Iran, 1951–52; British Council Representative: Tanzania, 1952–57; Sudan, 1957–62; Dir, Overseas Students Dept, 1962–66; Representative: Jordan, 1966–69; Iraq, 1969–74; Canada, 1974–79, and Counsellor, Cultural Affairs, British High Commission, Ottawa. Mem. Council, British Sch. of Archaeology in Iraq, 1980–86. Hon. Sec., Sussex Heritage Trust, 1980–83; Chm., Sussex Eastern Sub-Area, 1981–85, Sussex Area, 1985–92, RSCM. Organist: St Mary's Church, Battle, 1986–99; St Laurence Ch, Guestling, 2001–06. *Recreations:* archaeology, music. *Address:* Precinct, Crowhurst, Battle, East Sussex TN33 9AA. *T:* (01424) 830200.

SPRINGFORD, Prof. Michael, PhD; FInstP; H. O. Wills Professor of Physics, 1996–2001, and Director, Physics Laboratory, 1994–2001, University of Bristol, now Emeritus Professor of Physics; *b* 10 Jan. 1936; *s* of Stanley Walter Springford and Lillian Springford (*née* Tyler); *m* 1st, 1958, Kathleen Elizabeth Wyatt (marr. diss. 1983); two *s* one *d*; 2nd, 1991, Maria Sergeevna (*née* Morosova). *Educ:* Durham Univ. (BSc); Hull Univ. (PhD). Nat. Res. Council of Canada, 1962–64; Univ. of Sussex, 1964–89; Prof. of Experimental Physics, Univ. of Bristol, 1989–2001. Mott Prize Lectr, and Charles Vernon Boys Medal and Prize, 1995, Guthrie Medal and Prize, 2003, Inst. of Physics. *Publications:* (ed) Electrons at the Fermi Surface, 1980; (ed) Electron: a centenary volume, 1997; papers on the quantum properties of condensed matter in learned jls. *Recreations:* piano, writing, hill walking, cooking, pursuit of quietness. *Address:* 12A Royal York Crescent, Bristol BS8 4JY; *e-mail:* m.springford@bristol.ac.uk.

SPRINGMAN, Prof. Sarah Marcella, OBE 1997; PhD; CEng, FICE; Professor of Geotechnical Engineering, Department of Civil, Environmental and Geomatic Engineering, Eidgenössische Technische Hochschule (Swiss Federal Institute of Technology), Zurich, since 1997; *b* 26 Dec. 1956; *d* of (Paul) Michael Eyre Springman and late Dame Ann Marcella Springman, DBE. *Educ:* Wycombe Abbey Sch.; Girton Coll., Cambridge (MA; Roscoe Meml Prize 1978); St Catharine's Coll., Cambridge (MPhil); Magdalene Coll., Cambridge (PhD 1989). 11 blues/half blues in lacrosse, tennis, squash, cross country, swimming, athletics. CEng 1993; FICE 2005. Engr, Sir Alexander Gibb & Partners, UK, Australia and Fiji, 1979–83; Cambridge University: Soil Mechanics Group, Engineering Department: Res. Asst, 1984–88; Res. Associate, 1989–90; Asst Lectr, 1990–93; Lectr, 1993–96; Res. Fellow, 1988–90, Lectr and Fellow, 1991–96, Magdalene Coll.; Chm. and Initiator, Lang. Prog. for Engrs, 1992–96. Member: Swisscode Commn Geodesign, 1998–2003; Swiss Natural Hazards Competence Centre, 1998–; Swiss Council for Sci. and Technol., 2000–07; Peer Review Coll., EPSRC, 2005–; Swiss Platform for Natural Hazards, PLANAT, 2008–. MInstRE 1990; Member: Women's Engrg Soc., 1983–; Swiss Soc. of Engrs and Architects, 1999–; Chm., Tech. Cttee on Physical Modelling in Geotechnics, Internat. Soc. for Soil Mechanics and Geotech. Engrg, 2005–Nov. 2009. Mem., British Triathlon Team, 1984–93 (Nat. Champion 11 times, European Champion 3 times, European Team Champion 5 times); Mem., GB World Cup Rowing team, 1997; Vice Pres., Internat. Triathlon Union, 1992–96; Gov., World Masters Games, 1993–2002; Mem., UK (formerly GB) Sports Council, 1993–2001; Exec. Bd, British Triathlon, 2005– (Pres., 2007–); Mem., Nat. Olympic Cttee, British Olympic Assoc., 2008–. Governor: Marlborough Coll., 1991–94; Wycombe Abbey Sch., 1993–96. FRSA 1993 (Life Fellow 2005). *Publications:* (ed) Constitutive and Centrifuge Modelling: two extremes, 2002; (ed jtly) Permafrost, 2003; contrib. geotechnical jls. *Recreations:* sculling/rowing, triathlon. *Address:* Institut für Geotechnik, Eidgenössische Technische Hochschule, Hönggerberg, 8093 Zürich, Switzerland. *T:* (44) 6333805, *Fax:* (44) 6331079. *Clubs:* Rob Roy, Cambridge Triathlon (Cambridge) (Pres., 1996–); Belvoir (Zurich).

SPROAT, Iain Mac Donald; Chairman, European Cultural Foundation–UK, since 2006; *b* Dollar, Clackmannanshire, 8 Nov. 1938; *s* of late William Bigham Sproat and Lydia Bain Sproat (*née* Mac Donald); *m* 1979, Judith Mary Kernot (*née* King); one step *s*. *Educ:* St Mary's Sch., Melrose; Winchester Coll.; Univ. of Aix-en-Provence; Magdalen Coll., Oxford (MA). Served RGJ (4th Bn), 1972–76; TA Volunteers Reserve Course, RMA, 1973. Chm., Milner and Co., 1981, 1983–93, and 1997–; Founder, and Chm., 1980–81, 1983–93, 1997–2005, Cricketers' Who's Who Ltd. Contested (C) Roxburgh and Berwickshire, 1983. MP (C): Aberdeen South, 1970–83; Harwich, 1992–97; contested (C) Harwich, 1997, 2001. PPS to Sec. of State for Scotland, 1973–74; Parly Under-Sec. of State, Dept of Trade, 1981–83 (Minister: of Aviation and Shipping; of Tourism; responsible for: Govt Statistics; Retail Trade; Distributive Trades; Video, Cinema and Film Industry); Parly Under-Sec. of State, 1993–95, Minister of State, 1995–97, DNH (Minister for Sport, 1993–97). Special Advr to Prime Minister, Gen. Election, 1987. Leader, Cons. Gp, Scottish Select Cttee, 1979–81; Chm., Scottish Cons. Cttee, 1979–81; Chm., Soviet and E European Gp, Cons. Foreign Affairs Cttee, 1975–81. Member: British Parly Delegn to oversee S Vietnamese Elections, 1973; British Parly Delegn to Soviet Union, 1974; Leader, British Parly Delegn to Austria, 1980. Dist. Vis. Prof., Texas Univ., 1992. Lecturer: on guerilla warfare, RCDS, 1973; on Kurdish guerilla warfare in Iran/ Iraq, RUSI, 1975; on works of Alexander Pushkin, in Russia, USA and UK, 2002–07; lecture tour in USA on special relationship between UK and USA, 1979. Trustee: African Med. and Res. Foundn (Flying Doctors), 1986–91; Scottish Self-Governing Schools Trust, 1989–2006. Mem., Churchill Archives Cttee, Churchill Coll., Cambridge, 2003–. Chairman, Editorial Board: Oxford Univ. Press Hist. of the British Empire, 1987–92; Complete Works of Pushkin, 1987–93, 1997– (Moscow Internat. Book Fair prize for trans., 1999). Cricket Writer of the Year, Wombwell Cricket Lovers' Soc., 1983. *Publications:* (ed) Cricketers' Who's Who, annually 1980–93; Wodehouse at War, 1981; (contrib.) The British Prime Ministers; contrib. Oxford DNB. *Recreations:* collecting books, Rugby football, cricket. *Address:* c/o Coutts & Co., 2 Lower Sloane Street, SW1W 8BJ. *Clubs:* Cavalry and Guards, Oxford and Cambridge, MCC.

SPROT, Lt-Col Aidan Mark, MC 1944; JP; landed proprietor and farmer (Haystoun Estate); Lord-Lieutenant of Tweeddale, 1980–94; *b* 17 June 1919; *s* of Major Mark Sprot

of Riddell. *Educ:* Stowe. Commissioned Royal Scots Greys, 1940; served: Middle East, 1941–43; Italy, 1943–44; NW Europe, 1944–45, and after the war in Germany, Libya, Egypt, Jordan and UK; Adjt 1945–46; CO, 1959–62, retired. Councillor, Peeblesshire CC, 1963–75; JP 1966, DL 1966–80, Peeblesshire. Member, Royal Company of Archers (Queen's Body Guard for Scotland), 1950–; Pres., Lowlands of Scotland, TAVRA, 1986–89. Vice-Pres., RHASS, 1986; Trustee, Royal Scottish Agricl Benevolent Instn, 1989–98. British Red Cross Society: County Dir, 1966–74, Patron, 1983–98, Tweeddale Br.; Patron, Borders Br., 1998–; County Comr, 1968–73, Chm., 1975–80, Pres., 1980–94, Tweeddale Scout Assoc.; President: Borders Area Scout Assoc., 1994–99; Lothian Fedn of Boys' Clubs, 1988–96. Hon. President: Tweeddale Soc., 1995–; Peebles Br., RBL, Scotland, 1990–; Hon. Mem., Rotary Club, Peebles, 1986–. Hon. Sec., Royal Caledonian Hunt, 1964–74 (Hon. Mem., 2007). Mem., Service Chaplains Cttee, Church of Scotland, 1974–82 and 1985–92. Freeman, Tweeddale Dist, 1994. Scout Medal of Merit, 1994; Badge of Honour, BRCS, 1998. *Publication:* Swifter than Eagles—War Memoirs 1939–1945, 1998. *Recreations:* country pursuits, motor cycle touring. *Address:* Crookston, Peebles EH45 9JQ. *T:* (01721) 740209. *Club:* New (Edinburgh).

SPRY, Christopher John, CBE 2002; Director, OD Partnerships Network, since 2001; *b* 29 Aug. 1946; *s* of late Reginald Charles Spry and Kathleen Edith Spry (*née* Hobart); *m* 1st, Jean Banks (marr. diss. 1989); two *s*; 2nd, 1989, Judith Christina (*née* Ryder). *Educ:* Sir Roger Manwood's Sch., Sandwich; Exeter Univ. (BA 1967). AHSM. Dep. Hosp. Sec., Lewisham Hosp., 1970; Hosp. Sec., Nottingham Gen. Hosp., 1973; Asst Dist Administrator, S Nottingham, 1975, Dist Administrator, 1978; Dist Administrator, 1981, Dist Gen. Manager, 1984, Newcastle HA.; Regl Gen. Manager, SW Thames RHA, 1989–94; Regl Dir, NHS Exec., S Thames, 1994–96; Chief Exec., Gtr Glasgow Health Bd, 1996–2001. Non-exec. Dir, Dorset County Hosp. NHS Federation Trust (formerly W Dorset Gen. Hosps NHS Trust), 2005–. Vis. Prof., Glasgow Univ., 2001–. *Recreations:* keeping fit, photography, books, enjoying townscapes. *Address:* 31 Redwood House, Charlton Down, Dorchester, Dorset DT2 9UH.

SPUFFORD, Prof. (Honor) Margaret, OBE 1996; PhD, LittD; FRHistS; FBA 1995; Research Professor in Social and Local History, University of Roehampton (formerly Roehampton Institute, later University of Surrey, Roehampton), 1994–2001, now Emeritus Professor; *b* 10 Dec. 1935; *d* of Leslie Marshall Clark and Mary (*née* Johnson); *m* 1962, Peter Spufford, qv; one *s* (one *d* decd). *Educ:* Univ. of Leicester (MA with Dist. 1963; PhD 1970); LittD Cantab 1986. FRHistS 1974. Calouste Gulbenkian Res. Fellow, Lucy Cavendish Coll., Cambridge, 1968–72; University of Keele: Hon. Lectr, 1974–79; Sen. Res. Fellow, 1978–79; Sen. Res. Associate, Faculty of Hist., Univ. of Cambridge, 1979–81; Fellow, Newnham Coll., Cambridge, 1980–92. Vis. Res. Fellow, 1992–93, Guest of the Rector, 2005, Netherlands Inst. for Advanced Study; Vis. Prof., Rikkyo Univ., Tokyo, 1994; Guest, Japan Acad., 2003. Earl Lectr, Univ. of Keele, 1993; James Ford Special Lectr, Univ. of Oxford, 1994. Founder and first Dir, British Acad. Hearth Tax Project, Roehampton, 1996–2006. Founder, Bridget's Hostel for Disabled and Chronically Sick Students, Cambridge, 1987 (Chm., Bridget's Trustees, 1999–2000). DUniv Open, 2002; Hon. LittD Keele, 2005. A Woman of the Year, Women of the Year Assembly and Lunch, 1998. *Publications:* (with P. Spufford) Eccleshall: the story of a Staffordshire market town, 1964; A Cambridgeshire Community: Chippenham from settlement to enclosure, 1966; Contrasting Communities: the English villager in the sixteenth and seventeenth centuries, 1974, 2nd edn 2000; Small Books and Pleasant Histories: popular fiction and its readership in seventeenth century England, 1981; The Great Reclothing of Rural England: petty chapmen and their wares in the seventeenth century, 1984; Celebration, 1989 (trans. Dutch, 1994, French, 1995, Slovene, 2001; USA edn, 1996); (ed) The World of Rural Dissenters, 1995; Poverty Portrayed: Gregory King and Eccleshall, Staffordshire, 1995; Figures in the Landscape: rural society in England, 1500–1700, 1999; contrib. chapters in edited books, including: Literacy and Social Development in the West, 1981; Order and Disorder in Early Modern England, 1985; English Rural Society 1500–1800, 1990; A Miracle Mirror'd: the Dutch Republic in European Perspective, 1995; Spiritual Classics of the late Twentieth Century, 1995; Opening the Nursery Door, 1997; The English Rural Landscape, 2000; Cambridge History of Early Modern English Literature, 2002; Christianity: a complete guide, 2004; contrib. articles in learned jls incl. Albion, Econ. Hist. Review, Textile History, Proc. Cambridge Antiquarian Soc., Agricl Hist. Rev., Studies in Church Hist., Jl Eccl Hist., Theology. *Recreations:* Benedictine Anglican oblate, exploring countryside, vernacular architecture, listening to people. *Address:* The Guildhall, North Road, Whittlesford, Cambridge CB2 4NZ.

SPUFFORD, Prof. Peter, PhD, LittD; FSA; FRHistS; FBA 1994; Professor of European History, University of Cambridge, 2000–01, now Emeritus; Fellow, Queens' College, Cambridge, since 1979; *b* 18 Aug. 1934; *s* of late Douglas Henry Spufford and Nancy Gwendoline Spufford (*née* Battagel); *m* 1962, Honor Margaret Clark (*see* H. M. Spufford); one *s* (one *d* decd). *Educ:* Kingswood Sch.; Jesus Coll., Cambridge (BA 1956; MA 1960; PhD 1963; LittD 1990). FRNS 1955; FRHistS 1968; FSG 1969; FSA 1990. Res. Fellow, Jesus Coll., Cambridge, 1958–60; Asst Lectr, Lectr, Sen. Lectr and Reader, Univ. of Keele, 1960–79; University of Cambridge: Lectr, 1979–90; Reader in Econ. History, 1990–2000. Visiting Fellow: Clare Hall, Cambridge, 1969–70; Netherlands Inst. for Advanced Study, 1992–93; Vis. Prof. of Burgundian Studies, 1972–73, Vis. Prof., Econ. Studies, 1993, Leuven; Guest, Japan Acad., 2003; Guest of the Rector, Netherlands Inst. for Advanced Study, 2005 (Ortelius Lecture, 2005). Vice-Pres., Soc. of Genealogists, 1997–; Chm., British Records Soc., 1985–; Mem. Council, Soc. of Antiquaries, 1996–99. Hon. Mem., Koninklijk Genootschap voor Munt-en Penningkunde, 1992–. Medallist, Royal Numismatic Soc., 2005; Van Gelder Medal, Univ. of Leiden, 2006. *Publications:* Origins of the English Parliament, 1967; Monetary Problems and Policies in the Burgundian Netherlands 1433–1496, 1970; Handbook of Medieval Exchange, 1986; (ed with N. J. Mayhew) Later Medieval Mints, 1988; Money and Its Use in Medieval Europe, 1988; (ed with G. H. Martin) Records of the Nation, 1990; (ed) Index to the Probate Accounts of England and Wales, 2 vols, 1999; Power and Profit: the merchant in medieval Europe, 2002; chapters in: Cambridge Economic History of Europe, vol. 3, 1965, vol. 2, 2nd edn, 1987; New Cambridge Medieval History, vi, 1999. *Address:* Queens' College, Cambridge CB3 9ET. *T:* (01223) 335511.

SPUNNER, Maj. Gen. Barney William Benjamin W.; *see* White-Spunner.

SPURGEON, Maj.-Gen. Peter Lester, CB 1980; Chief Executive, Royal Agricultural Benevolent Institution, 1982–91; *b* 27 Aug. 1927; *s* of Harold Sidney Spurgeon and Emily Anne (*née* Bolton); *m* 1959, Susan Ann (*née* Aylward); one *s* one *d*. *Educ:* Merchant Taylors' Sch., Northwood. Commnd, 1946; 1949–66: HMS Glory; Depot, RM Deal; 40 Commando RM; ADC to Maj.-Gen. Plymouth Gp RM; DS Officers' Sch., RM; RAF Staff Coll., Bracknell; Staff of Comdt Gen. RM; 40 Commando RM; Jt Warfare Estab.; GS02 HQ: ME Comd, Aden, 1967; Army Strategic Comd, 1968–69; Second-in-Comd, 41 Commando RM, 1969–71; DS National Defence Coll., Latimer, 1971–73; CO RM Poole, 1973–75; Dir of Drafting and Records, RM, 1975–76; Comdr, Training Gp, RM, 1977–79 and Training and Reserve Forces, RM, 1979–80; retd 1980. Col Comdt, RM,

1987–90. Pres., RM Assoc., 1986–90. *Recreations:* golf, gardening. *Address:* c/o Lloyds TSB, 1 High Street, Oxford OX1 4AA. *Club:* Army and Navy.

SPURLING, (Susan) Hilary, CBE 2007; biographer; *b* 25 Dec. 1940; *d* of Gilbert Alexander Forrest and Emily Maureen Forrest; *m* 1961, John Spurling; two *s* one *d*. *Educ:* Somerville Coll., Oxford (BA; Hon. Fellow, 2006). FRSL. Theatre Critic of the Spectator, 1964–70, Literary Editor, 1966–70. Hon. Mem., Royal Literary Fund, 2008. Hon. Dr Anglia Ruskin, 2007. (Jtly) Heywood Hill Lit. Prize, 2003. *Publications:* Ivy When Young: the early life of I. Compton-Burnett 1884–1919, 1974; Handbook to Anthony Powell's Music of Time, 1977; Secrets of a Woman's Heart: the later life of I. Compton-Burnett 1920–1969, 1984 (Duff Cooper Meml Prize, 1984; Heinemann Literary Award (jtly), 1985); Elinor Fettiplace's Receipt Book, 1986; Paul Scott, A Life, 1990; Paper Spirits, 1992; The Unknown Matisse 1869–1908, vol. i, 1998; La Grande Thérèse, 1999; The Girl from the Fiction Department: a portrait of Sonia Orwell, 2002; Matisse the Master, A Life of Henry Matisse: the conquest of colour 1909–1954 (Whitbread Book of the Year, Los Angeles Times Biography Prize), 2005. *Recreations:* reading, ratting, country walks. *Address:* c/o David Higham Associates, 5–8 Lower John Street, Golden Square, W1R 4HA.

SPURR, Margaret Anne, OBE 1994; DL; Headmistress, Bolton School, Girls' Division, 1979–94; Governor, BBC, 1993–98; *b* 7 Oct. 1933; *m* 1953, John Spurr (*d* 2003); one *s* one *d*. *Educ:* Abbeydale Girls' Grammar Sch., Sheffield; Univ. of Keele. BA (Hons); PGCE. Tutor: Eng. Lit., Univ. of Glasgow, 1971; Eng. Lit. Dept, Adult Educn, Univ. of Keele, 1972–73. Chm., Scholaservices, 1990–. Sen. Examiner, Univ. of London, 1971–80. Pres., GSA, 1985–86. Chairman: Nat. ISIS Cttee, 1987–90; BBC English Nat. Forum, 1994–98; Member: Adv. Cttee, American Studies Resources Centre, Polytechnic of Central London, 1977–90; Scholarship Selection Cttee, ESU, 1983–94; CBI Schools Panel, 1985–89; Exec. Cttee, GBGSA, 1994–99. Vice-Provost, Woodard Corp., 1994–98. Governor: Kent Coll., Tunbridge Wells, 1993–99; John Moores Univ., Liverpool, 1994–98; Colfe's Sch., 1995–; Stafford Coll. of Further Educn, 1996–2000; Newton Prep. Sch., Battersea, 1999–; Univ. of Lincoln, 2008–; Life Gov., Liverpool Coll., 2001; Mem. Governing Council, Keele Univ., 1996–. Trustee: School Fees Trust Fund, 1994–; Raven Mason Collection, Univ. of Keele, 2001–. Dir, SFS Gp, 1999–; Mid-Atlantic Club, 2000–. Pres., Staffs Soc., 1999–2001. Chm., Croxden Parochial Charities Trusts, 2001. Mem., Exec. Cttee, Lichfield Br., Prayer Book Soc., 2002–04. FRSA 1991. DL Staffs, 1998. Hon. DLitt Keele, 1995. *Publications:* (ed) A Curriculum for Capability, 1986; (ed) Girls First, 1987. *Recreations:* theatre, poetry, music. *Address:* 21 Minster Yard, Lincoln LN2 1PY. *Club:* Reform.

SPURR, Dr (Michael) Stephen, DPhil; Head Master, Westminster School, since 2005; *b* 9 Oct. 1953; *s* of (Arthur) Michael (Marshall) Spurr and Patricia (Ann) Spurr (*née* Newall); *m* 1982, Susanna Armani; one *s* one *d*. *Educ:* King's Sch., Canterbury; Sydney Grammar Sch.; Univ. of Sydney (BA 1st cl. Hons Classics 1975); Corpus Christi Coll., Univ. of Oxford (Oxford Ancient History Prize, 1981; DPhil 1984). Rome Scholar, British Sch. at Rome, 1981–82; Lectr in Classics and Ancient History, ANU, 1982–83; Eton College, 1984–2000: Curator, Myers Mus. of Egyptian Art, 1989–2000; Hd of Classics, 1992–96; House Master, 1996–2000; Headmaster, Upper Sch., Clifton Coll., Bristol, 2000–05. *Publications:* Arable Cultivation in Roman Italy, 1986; Egyptian Art at Eton College, 1995; (trans.) Another Sea by Claudio Magris, 1993; (contrib.) The Oxford Classical Dictionary, 1996; various articles and reviews. *Recreations:* Roman archaeology, Egyptology, mountaineering, Mediterranean agriculture. *Address:* Westminster School, Little Dean's Yard, SW1P 3PF.

SPY, James; Sheriff of North Strathclyde at Paisley, since 1988; *b* 1 Dec. 1952; *s* of James Spy and Jean Learmond; *m* 1980, Jennifer Margaret Malcolm; three *d*. *Educ:* Hermitage Acad., Helensburgh; Glasgow Univ. (LLB Hons). Admitted Solicitor, 1976; passed Advocate, 1979. *Recreations:* music, clocks, model ships, model trains. *Address:* St Ann's, 171 Nithsdale Road, Glasgow G41 5QS.

SPYER, Prof. (Kenneth) Michael, PhD, DSc; Sophia Jex-Blake Professor of Physiology, Royal Free and University College Medical School, since 1980, and Vice-Provost (Enterprise), since 2006, University College London; *b* 15 Sept. 1943; *s* of late Harris Spyer and Rebecca Spyer (*née* Jacobs); *m* 1971, Christine Spalton; two *s*. *Educ:* Coopers' Co. Sch.; Univ. of Sheffield (BSc); Univ. of Birmingham (PhD 1969; DSc 1979). Res. Fellow, Univ. of Birmingham Med. Sch., 1969–72; Royal Soc. European Prog. Fellow, Instituto de Fisologia, Pisa, 1972–73; Res. Fellow, 1973–78, Sen. Res. Fellow, 1978–80, Dept of Physiology, Univ. of Birmingham; joined Royal Free Hosp. Sch. of Medicine, 1980; Dir, Neural Control Gp, BHF, 1985–2000; Head, Jt Depts of Physiology, UCL and Royal Free Hosp. Sch. of Medicine, 1994–99; Dir, Autonomic Neurosci. Inst., 1997–; Dean, Royal Free and UC Med. Sch., UCL, 2001–06 (Dean, Royal Free Campus, 1998–2001); Vice-Provost (Biomedicine), UCL, 2002–06. Founder FMedSci 1998. Hon. FRCP 2002. Hon. MD Lisbon, 1991. *Publications:* (ed jtly) Central Regulation of Autonomic Functions, 1990; papers in Jl of Physiology, Neurosci., Brain Res., Amer. Jl of Physiology, Jl of Autonomic Nervous System, Exptl Physiology. *Recreations:* fly fishing, travelling (particularly in Italy), gardening, books, fine arts. *Address:* University College London, Gower Street, WC1E 6BT. *T:* (020) 7679 9851.

SQUAIR, George Alexander; non-executive Chairman, British Approvals Service for Cables, 1993–2002; *b* 26 July 1929; *s* of Alexander Squair and Elizabeth (*née* Macdonald); *m* 1953, Joy Honeybone; two *s* one *d*. *Educ:* Woolwich Polytechnic; Oxford Technical Coll.; Southampton Univ. CEng, FIET (FIEE 1986); CIMgt (CBIM 1984). Gen. distribution engrg posts, 1950–68; Southern, later South Eastern, Electricity Board, subseq. SEEBOARD: 1st Asst Dist Engr, 1968–69; Dist Engr, Swindon, 1969–70; Area Engr, Newbury, 1970–73; Dist Manager, Oxford, 1973–74; Area Manager, Newbury, 1974–78; Mem., Exec. Bd, 1976–78; Dep. Chm., 1978–83; Chm. and Chief Exec., 1983–92. *Recreations:* reading, golf. *Address:* Swallow Grove Farmhouse, Mangrove Lane, Hertford SG13 8QG.

SQUIRE, Dr (Clifford) William, CMG 1978; LVO 1972; HM Diplomatic Service, retired; Chairman, Grenzebach Glier Europe, since 1996; *b* 7 Oct. 1928; *s* of Clifford John Squire and Eleanor Eliza Harpley; *m* 1st, 1959, Marie José Carlier (*d* 1973); one *s* two *d* (and one *s* decd); 2nd, 1976, Sarah Laetitia Hutchison (*see* S. L. Squire); one *s* one *d*. *Educ:* Royal Masonic Sch., Bushey; St John's Coll., Oxford; Coll. of Europe, Bruges. PhD London 1979. British Army, 1947–49. Nigerian Admin. Service, 1953–59; FO, 1959–60; British Legation, Bucharest, 1961–63; FO, 1963–65; UK Mission to UN, New York, 1965–69; Head of Chancery, Bangkok, 1969–72; Head of SE Asian Dept, FCO, 1972–75; Extramural Fellow, Sch. of Oriental and African Studies, London Univ., 1975–76; Counsellor, later Head of Chancery, Washington, 1976–79; Ambassador to Senegal, 1979–82, concurrently to Cape Verde Is, Guinea (Bissau), Guinea (Conakry), Mali and Mauritania; Asst Under-Sec. of State, FCO, 1982–84; Ambassador to Israel, 1984–88. Develt Dir, Univ. of Cambridge, 1988–96; Fellow of Wolfson Coll., Cambridge, 1988–96. *Address:* 11A Chaucer Road, Cambridge CB2 2EB. *Clubs:* Travellers; Cosmos (Washington, DC).

SQUIRE, Peter John; Headmaster, Bedford Modern School, 1977–96; *b* 15 Feb. 1937; *s* of Leslie Ernest Squire and Doris Eileen Squire; *m* 1965, Susan Elizabeth (*née* Edwards); one *s* one *d*. *Educ:* King Edward's Sch., Birmingham; Jesus Coll., Oxford (BA 1960, MA 1964); Pembroke Coll. and Dept of Educn, Cambridge (Cert. in Educn 1961). Asst Master, Monkton Combe Sch., Bath, 1961–65; Haberdashers' Aske's Sch., Elstree, 1965–77: Sen. Boarding Housemaster, 1968–77; Sen. History Master, 1970–77. Reporting Inspector, HMC/ISI Inspections, 1994–2004. Chm., Bedfordshire Victim Support, 1997–2001. Mem., Whitgift Council, 1997–. *Recreations:* foreign travel, gardening, antique collecting. *Address:* 98A Bromham Road, Biddenham, Bedford MK40 4AH. *T:* (01234) 342373.

SQUIRE, Air Chief Marshal Sir Peter (Ted), GCB 2001 (KCB 1997); DFC 1982; AFC 1979; DL; Chief of the Air Staff, 2000–03; Air Aide-de-Camp to the Queen, 1999–2003; *b* 7 Oct. 1945; *s* of late Wing Comdr Frank Squire and Margaret Pascoe Squire (*née* Trump); *m* 1970, Carolyn Joynson; three *s*. *Educ:* King's Sch., Bruton. psc(n). Flying and Staff appts include: commnd 1966; 20 Sqn, Singapore, 1968–70; 4 FTS, Anglesey, 1970–73; 3 (F) Sqn, Germany, 1975–78; OC1 (F) Sqn, 1981–83; Personal Staff Officer to AOC-in-C Strike Comd, 1984–86; Station Comdr, RAF Cottesmore, 1986–88; Dir Air Offensive, 1989–91; SASO, RAF Strike Comd, 1991–93; AOC No 1 Gp, 1993–94; ACAS, 1994–96; DCDS (Progs and Personnel), MoD, 1996–99; AOC-in-C, Strike Comd and Comdr Allied Air Forces NW Europe, 1999–2000. Mem., CWGC, 2003–08 (Vice-Chm., 2005–08). Trustee, Imperial War Mus., 2003– (Chm., 2006–). Liveryman: GAPAN; Coachmakers' Co; Hon. Freeman, Barbers' Co. FRAeS 1995. Gov., King's Sch., Bruton, 1990– (Chm., 2004–). DL Devon, 2008. Hon. DSc Cranfield, 2001. *Recreation:* golf. *Address:* c/o National Westminster Bank, 5 South Street, Wincanton BA9 9DJ. *Club:* Royal Air Force.

SQUIRE, Robin Clifford; Trust Secretary: Veolia Environmental Services Cleanaway Havering Riverside Trust and Veolia Environmental Services Cleanaway Pitsea Marshes Trust, since 2002; *b* 12 July 1944; *s* of late Sidney John Squire and Mabel Alice Squire (*née* Gilmore); *m* 1981, Susan Margaret Fey, OBE (marr. diss. 2007), *d* of late Arthur Frederick Branch and of Mahala Branch (*née* Parker); one step *s* one step *d*. *Educ:* Tiffin School, Kingston-upon-Thames. FCA. Qualified as Chartered Accountant, 1966; joined Lombard Banking Ltd (subsequently Lombard North Central Ltd) as Accountant, 1968, becoming Dep. Chief Accountant, 1972–79. Dir Advocacy Ltd, 1997–2000. Councillor, London Borough of Sutton, 1968–82; Chm., Finance Cttee, 1972–76; Leader of Council, 1976–79. Chm., Greater London Young Conservatives, 1973; Vice-Chm., Nat. Young Conservatives, 1974–75. Personal Asst to Rt Hon. Robert Carr, Gen. Election, Feb. 1974; contested (C) Havering, Hornchurch, Oct. 1974. MP (C) Hornchurch, 1979–97; contested (C) same seat, 1997, 2001. PPS to Minister of State for Transport, 1983–85, to Rt Hon. Chris Patten, Chm. of Cons. Party, 1991–92; Parliamentary Under-Secretary of State: DoE, 1992–93; DFE, later DFEE, 1993–97. Mem., Commons Select Cttee on Environment, 1979–83 and 1987–91, on European Legislation, 1985–88; Sec., Cons. Parly European Affairs Cttee, 1979–80; Vice-Chm., Cons. Parly Trade Cttee, 1980–83; Chm., Cons. Parly Environment Cttee, 1990–91 (Jt Vice-Chm., 1985–89); Originator of Local Govt (Access to Information) Act, 1985. Chm., Cons. Action for Electoral Reform, 1983–86 (Vice-Chm., 1982–83); Dep. Chm., Anglo-Asian Cons. Soc., 1982–83. Comr, Nat. Lottery Commn, 1999; Adjudicator for Schs Orgns and Admissions, 1999. Mem. Bd, Shelter, 1982–91; Dir, Link Assured Homes series of cos, 1988–92. Chm., Assoc. of Distributive Envmtl Bodies, 2005–07. Freeman, City of London, 2003; Liveryman, Co. of Makers of Playing Cards, 2003–. *Publication:* (jtly) Set the Party Free, 1969. *Recreations:* films, bridge, classical music, man's innate spirituality, reiki. *Address:* Flat 3, 63 Millbank, SW1P 4RW.

SQUIRE, Rosemary Anne, OBE 2008; Joint Chief Executive (formerly Executive Director), Ambassador Theatre Group Ltd, since 1997; *b* 27 May 1956; *d* of late Donald Squire and of Mary Squire (*née* Sykes); *m* 1st, 1982, Alan Brodie (marr. diss. 1994); one *s* one *d*; 2nd, 1994, Howard Hugh Panter, *qv*; one *d*. *Educ:* Nottingham High Sch. for Girls; Southampton Univ. (BA 1st Cl. Hons Spanish with Catalan and French 1979); Brown Univ. (Postgrad. Schol. 1979). Gen. Manager, Maybox Gp plc, 1984–88; Gen. Manager, 1988–90, Exec. Dir, 1990–97, Turnstyle Gp Ltd. Pres., SOLT, 2005–. *Recreations:* gardens, walking, reading. *Address:* Ambassador Theatre Group, The Ambassadors, Peacocks Centre, Woking, Surrey GU21 6GQ. *T:* (01483) 545804, *Fax:* (01483) 770477; *e-mail:* rosemarysquire@theambassadors.com. *Club:* Groucho.

SQUIRE, Sara Laetitia, (Sarah); President, Hughes Hall, Cambridge, since 2006; *b* 18 July 1949; *d* of Michael Duncan Hutchison and Margery Betty Hutchison (*née* Martin); *m* 1976, (Clifford) William Squire, *qv*; one *s* one *d*. *Educ:* St Paul's Girls' Sch.; Newnham Coll., Cambridge (BA Hons Hist., MA). Entered HM Diplomatic Service, 1971: FCO, 1971–72; Tel Aviv, 1972–75; SE Asian Dept, FCO, 1975–76; Washington, 1977–79; Falkland Is Dept, FCO, 1982–84; Tel Aviv, 1986–88; Policy Officer, Cambridge CC, 1989–90; Sen. Inf. Officer, COI, 1990–95; Dep. Dir, Know How Fund, FCO, 1995–96; Dep. Hd, Central Eur. Dept, FCO, 1996–99; Ambassador to Estonia, 2000–03; Gp Dir, FCO Services, FCO, 2004–06. *Address:* Hughes Hall, Cambridge CB1 2EW. *T:* (01223) 334890; 11a Chaucer Road, Cambridge CB2 7EB. *T:* (01223) 329547. *Club:* Oxford and Cambridge.

SQUIRE, William; *see* Squire, C. W.

SQUIRES, (Charles) Ian; Managing Director, ITV Central (formerly Central Broadcasting), since 1996; Director of Regional Production, ITV plc, since 2008; *b* 22 April 1951; *s* of Charles Ian Squires and Mary Squires; *m* 1993, Vanessa Marie Sweet; two *d*. *Educ:* Bede Grammar Sch., Sunderland; University Coll. London (BA Hons English). Westminster Press, 1973–75; Current Affairs and Editor, Omnibus, BBC TV, 1975–86; freelance producer, 1986–88; Head of Network TV, North West, BBC, 1988–90; Managing Director: Zenith North, 1990–94; Carlton Studios, 1994–2004; Dir of Regional Production, ITV News Gp, 2004–08. Chm., EMMedia, 2001–05; Director: West Midlands Life, 1999–2003; NEC, 2005–; Birmingham City Univ. (formerly Univ. of Central England), 2005–; Fair Cities (Birmingham), 2005–07; Midland Heart Housing Assoc., 2007–. Chairman: Birmingham City Pride, 2001–04; Marketing Birmingham, 2004–; Birmingham Repertory Theatre, 2005–; Dir, Birmingham Hippodrome Theatre, 2005–. Pres., Birmingham Chamber of Commerce and Industry, 2004–05 (Vice-Pres., 2002–04). BAFTA Award, Best Arts Prog., for A Simple Man (TV ballet on life of L. S. Lowry), 1987. *Recreations:* riding, shooting, running. *Address:* The Old Rectory, Main Street, Burrough-on-the-Hill, Leics LE14 2JQ. *T:* (01664) 454321. *Club:* Royal Automobile.

SRINIVASAN, Krishnan; Deputy Secretary-General, Commonwealth Secretariat, 1995–2002; *b* 15 Feb. 1937; *s* of late Captain C. Srinivasan, Indian Navy, and Mrs Rukmani Chari; *m* 1975, Brinda Mukerjea; one *s*. *Educ:* Bedford Sch.; Christ Church, Oxford (MA; Boxing Blue, 1956; Hon. Mem., SCR). Joined Indian Foreign Service, 1959; Chargé d'Affaires, Tripoli, 1968–71; High Comr to Zambia and Botswana, 1974–77; Consul-Gen., NY, 1977–80; High Comr to Nigeria, and Ambassador to Benin and Cameroon, 1980–83; Ambassador, Netherlands, 1986–89; High Comr, Bangladesh, 1989–92; Perm. Sec., Min. of External Affairs, 1992–94; Foreign Secretary, 1994–95. Visiting Fellow: Wolfson Coll., Cambridge, 2002–05; Centre of Internat. Studies, Cambridge, 2002–08; Sen. Res. Fellow, Inst. of Commonwealth Studies, Univ. of London, 2002–08; Fellow: Azad Inst. of Asian Studies, Calcutta, 2006–; Swedish Collegium, 2008. Dist. Vis. Schol., Netherlands Inst. for Advanced Study, 2003–04; Vis. Prof., Indian Admin. Staff Coll., 2004–. Ramsden Sermon, Oxford, 2002. Hind Ratna, 2001; Chevalier de l'Ordre de la Valeur (Cameroon), 2007. *Publications:* Selections in Two Keys, 1974; The Water's Edge, 1975; The Eccentricity Factor, 1980; The Fourth Profile, 1991; A Fizzle Yield, 1992; Tricks of the Trade, 2000; The Eccentric Effect, 2001; The Ugly Ambassador, 2003; Guesswork, 2005; The Rise, Decline and Future of the British Commonwealth, 2005; The Jamdani Revolution, 2008. *Recreations:* music, watching sports. *Address:* Flat 8, Courtleigh, 126 Earls Court Road, W8 6QL. *Clubs:* Oxford and Cambridge; Vincent's (Oxford); Bengal (Calcutta); International Centre (New Delhi).

SRINIVASAN, Prof. Mandyam Veerambudi, PhD; FRS 2001; FAA; Professor of Visual Neuroscience, Queensland Brain Institute, University of Queensland, since 2007; *b* 15 Sept. 1948; *s* of Mandyam Veerambudi Sundararajan and Mandyam Veerambudi Vedavalli Ammal; *m* Jaishree Srinivasan. *Educ:* Bangalore Univ. (BE 1st Cl. Electrical Engrg 1968); Indian Inst. of Sci., Bangalore (Masters in Applied Electronics and Servomechanisms 1970); Yale Univ. (MPhil 1973, PhD 1976, Engrg and Applied Sci.). Res. Scientist, Dept of Ophthalmol. and Visual Sci., Yale Univ. Sch. of Medicine, 1977–78; Res. Fellow, Depts of Neurobiol. and Applied Maths, ANU, 1978–82; Asst Prof. of Biophysics, Dept of Neurobiol., Univ. of Zurich, 1982–85; Australian National University: Fellow, Visual Sciences, 1985–91, Sen. Fellow, 1992–93, Prof. of Visual Sci., 1994–2006, Res. Sch. of Biol Scis; Dir, Centre for Visual Sci., 1994–96 and 2000–06. Daimler-Benz Fellow, Inst. Advanced Studies, Berlin, 1996–97. FAA 1995. Hon. DSc Neuroethol., ANU, 1994; Dr *hc* Zurich, 2002. *Publications:* (ed with S. Venkatesh) From Living Eyes to Seeing Machines, 1997; contrib. numerous res. articles and rev. chapters, one internat. patent. *Recreations:* reading, music, bicycling, jogging. *Address:* Queensland Brain Institute, Ritchie Building (64A) (C Wing), St Lucia, Qld 4072, Australia; (home) 42 Rosecliffe Street, Highgate Hill, Brisbane, Qld 4101, Australia.

SRISKANDAN, Kanagaretnam, CEng, FICE, FIStructE, FIHT; Divisional Director, Mott, MacDonald Group (formerly Mott, Hay and Anderson), Consulting Engineers, 1988–93; consultant in highway and bridge engineering, 1993–2000; *b* 12 Aug. 1930; *s* of Kathiravelu Kanagaretnam and Kanmanyammal Kumaraswamy; *m* 1956, Dorothy (*née* Harley); two *s* one *d*. *Educ:* Royal College, Colombo; Univ. of Ceylon. BSc Hons London 1952. Junior Asst Engineer, PWD, Ceylon, 1953; Asst Engr, Sir William Halcrow and Partners, Cons. Engrs, London, 1956; Section Engr, Tarmac Civil Engineering Ltd, 1958; Asst Engr, West Riding of Yorkshire CC, 1959, left as Principal Engr; Department of Transport: Superintending Engr, Midland Road Construction Unit, 1968; Asst Chief Engr, 1971; Deputy Chief Highway Engr, 1976; Chief Highway Engr, 1980–87. *Publications:* papers on various engrg topics. *Recreation:* golf.

SRIVASTAVA, Chandrika Prasad, Padma Bhushan 1972; Hon. KCMG 1990; Secretary-General, International Maritime Organization (formerly IMCO), 1974–89, now Emeritus; Founding Chancellor, World Maritime University, 1983–91, now Emeritus; *b* 8 July 1920; *s* of B. B. Srivastava; *m* 1947, Nirmala Salve; two *d*. *Educ:* Lucknow, India. 1st cl. BA 1940, 1st cl. BA Hons 1941, 1st cl. MA 1942, 1st cl. LLB 1944; gold medals for proficiency in Eng. Lit. and Polit. Science. Under-Sec., Min. of Commerce, India, 1948–49; City Magistrate, Lucknow, 1950; Addtl Dist. Magistrate, Meerut, 1951–52; Directorate-Gen. of Shipping, 1953; Dep. Dir-Gen. of Shipping, 1954–57; Dep. Sec., Min. of Transport, and Pvte Sec. to Minister of Transport and Communications, 1958; Sen. Dep. Dir-Gen. of Shipping, 1959–60; Man. Dir, Shipping Corp. of India, 1961–64; Jt Sec. to Prime Minister, 1964–66; Chm. and Man. Dir, Shipping Corp. of India, 1966–73; Director: Central Inland Water Transport Corp., 1967; Central Bd, Reserve Bank of India, 1972–73; Chm., Mogul Line Ltd, 1967–73. Chm., Indian Register of Shipping, 1991. Chm., Cttee on Maritime Educn and Trng, Govt of India, 1992. Vice-Pres., Sea Cadet Council, 1970–73. President: Indian Nat. Shipowners' Assoc., 1971–73; Inst. of Marine Technologists, India, 1972–89 (Hon. Mem., 1981); UN Conf. on Code of Conduct for Liner Confs, 1973–74; Internat. Maritime Lectrs' Assoc., 1980–91; Chm., Cttee of Invisibles, 3rd UN Conf. on Trade and Develt, 1972; Member: Nat. Shipping Bd, 1959–73; Merchant Navy Trng Bd, 1959–73; Nat. Welfare Bd for Seafarers, 1966–73; Amer. Bureau of Shipping, 1969; Governing Body, Indian Inst. of Foreign Trade, 1970; State Bd of Tourism, 1970; Nat. Harbour Bd, 1970–73; Gen. Cttee, Bombay Chamber of Commerce and Ind., 1971; Governing Body, Indian Inst. of Management, 1972–73; Adv. Bd, Seatrade Acad., 1978–89 (Chm. Awarding Body, Seatrade Annual Awards for Achievement, 1988); Europort Internat. Cttee of Honour, 1980–89; Bd, Internat. Maritime Bureau, ICC, 1981–89; Bd of Dirs, ICC Centre for Maritime Co-operation, 1985–89; Hon. Adv. Cttee, Internat. Congress on The Port—an Ecological Challenge, Hamburg, 1989–90; Chairman: Gov. Bd, IMO Internat. Maritime Law Inst., 1989; Gov. Council, Tolani Maritime Inst., Pune, India, 1998, now Emeritus; Chm., Nat. Maritime Day Awards Cttee, India, 2000. Life Gov., Marine Soc., 1984. Vice Pres., Welsh Centre for Internat. Affairs, 1989. FRSA 1981; Fellow: Inst. Marine Engrs, India, 1998; Co. of Master Mariners, India, 1998. Hon. Member: Master Mariners' Co., UK, 1978–89; Royal Inst. of Navigation, 1984; Internat. Fedn of Shipmasters' Assocs, 1985; The Warsash Assoc., 1988; Internat. Maritime Pilots' Assoc., 1988; Hon. Fellow: Plymouth Polytech., 1979; Nautical Inst., 1985. Hon. LLD: Bhopal, 1984; Wales, 1987; Malta, 1988. Admiral Padilla Award, Colombia, 1978; Gran Amigo del Mar Award, Colombia, 1978; Gold Mercury Internat. Award Ad Personam, 1984; Award, Seatrade Acad., 1988; Gold Medal of Honour and Hon. Citizen, Malmö, Sweden, 2003; Lal Bahadur Shastri Nat. Award for Excellence in Public Admin, Academics and Mgt, India, 2005. Commandeur du Mérite Maritime, France, 1982; Comdr, Order of St Olav, Norway, 1982; Grande Ufficiale dell'Ordine al Merito, Italy, 1983; Comdr, Order of Prince Henry the Navigator, Portugal, 1983; Gold Order of Distinguished Seafarers, Poland, 1983; Nautical Medal, 1st cl., Greece, 1983; Gran Cruz Distintivo Blanco, Orden Cruz Peruana al Mérito Naval, Peru, 1984; Gran Cruz, Orden de Manuel Amador Guerrero, Panama, 1985; Grande-Oficial, Ordem do Mérito Naval, Brazil, 1986; Commander's Cross, Order of Merit, Poland, 1986; Silver Medal of Honour, Malmö, Sweden, 1988; Kt Great Band, Order of Humane African Redemption, Liberia, 1989; Comdr's Cross of Order of Merit, FRG, 1989; Comdr Grand Cross, Royal Order of the Star of the North, Sweden, 1989; Order of Merit, First Grade, Egypt, 1990; Encomienda de Numero de la Orden de Isabel la Católica, Spain, 1994; Comendador, Orden Naval Almirante Padilla, Colombia, 2004. *Publications:* Lal Bahadur Shastri: Prime Minister of India 1964–1966—a life of truth in politics, 1995; Corruption: India's Enemy Within, 2001; World Maritime University: first twenty years-background and concept, establishment and progress, 2 vols, 2003; articles on shipping in newspapers and jls. *Recreations:* music, tennis, reading. *Address:* Palazzo Doria, Cabella Ligure, 15060 Allessandria, Italy; International Maritime Organisation, 4 Albert Embankment, SE1 7SR. *Clubs:* Royal Anglo-Belgian; Willingdon Sports (Bombay); Pune (Pune).

STABLE, His Honour (Rondle) Owen (Charles); QC 1963; a Circuit Judge, 1979–95; Senior Circuit Judge, Snaresbrook Crown Court, 1982–95; *b* 28 Jan. 1923; *yr s* of late Rt Hon. Sir Wintringham Norton Stable, MC, and Lucie Haden (*née* Freeman); *m* 1949, Yvonne Brook, *y d* of late Maj. L. B. Holliday, OBE; two *d*. *Educ:* Winchester. Served with Rifle Bde, 1940–46 (Captain). Barrister, Middle Temple, 1948; Bencher, 1969. Dep. Chm., QS, Herts, 1963–71; a Recorder of the Crown Court, 1972–79. Board of Trade Inspector: Cadco Group of Cos, 1963–64; H. S. Whiteside & Co. Ltd, 1965–67; International Learning Systems Corp. Ltd, 1969–71; Pergamon Press, 1969–73. Sec. National Reference Tribunal for the Coal Mining Industry, 1953–64; Chancellor of Diocese of Bangor, 1959–88; Member, Governing Body of the Church in Wales, 1960–88; Licensed Parochial Lay Reader, Diocese of St Albans, 1961–2003; Member: General Council of the Bar, 1962–66; Senate of 4 Inns of Court, 1971–74; Senate of the Inns of Court and the Bar, 1974–75. Chm., Horserace Betting Levy Appeal Tribunal, 1969–74. Mem. Council, Benslow Music Trust, 1995–2001; Chm., Benslow Develt Appeal, 1995–2000. JP Hertfordshire, 1963–71. *Publication:* (with R. M. Stuttard) A Review of Coursing, 1971. *Recreations:* listening to music, playing the flute. *Address:* Buckler's Hall, Much Hadham, Herts SG10 6EB. *T:* (01279) 842604. *Club:* Boodle's.

STACE, Prof. Anthony John, PhD; FRS 2002; FRSC; Professor of Physical Chemistry, University of Nottingham, since 2004. *Educ:* Univ. of Essex (BA, PhD). Univ. of Sussex, 1974–77; Advanced Res. Fellow, SERC, Univ. of Southampton, 1977–83; Lectr, 1984–93, Prof. of Chemistry, 1993–2004, Univ. of Sussex. Tilden Medal and Lectr, RSC, 1995. *Address:* School of Chemistry, University of Nottingham, University Park, Nottingham NG7 2RD.

STACEY, Mary Elizabeth; Employment Judge (formerly Chairman, Industrial Tribunal, then Employment Tribunals), since 2003 (part-time Chairman, 1997–2003); a Recorder, since 2007; *b* 15 May 1961; *d* of Rev. Nicolas David Stacey, *qv*; *m* 2004, Stuart Bell; two *s*. *Educ:* Keble Coll., Oxford (BA Hons English 1982; MA). Admitted solicitor, 1987; solicitor in private practice, 1987–98; Partner and Hd of Equality, 1993–98, Consultant, 1999–2003, Thompsons, Solicitors. Ind. Chair, Jt Negotiating Cttee for Higher Educn Staff, 2001–07. Dep. Chm., Central Arbitration Cttee, 2000–. Mem., Gtr London Magistrates' Courts Authy, 1999–2003 (Chm., Audit Cttee). Mem., CIPD (Law Faculty), 1995–. Chm., Industrial Law Soc., 2006–. Ind. Mem. Council, Goldsmiths, Univ. of London, 2008–. FRSA. *Publications:* Part-time Workers and the Law, 1995; Challenging Disability Discrimination at Work, 2001; Discrimination Law Handbook, 2002, 2nd edn 2006. *Address:* 80 Erlanger Road, SE14 5TH. *T:* (020) 7652 2370.

STACEY, Michael Albert; Chairman: Meggitt plc, 2001–04 (Chief Executive Officer, 1995–2001); McKechnie Group, 2001–05; Dynacast International, 2002–05; Deputy Chairman, Avio SpA, Italy, since 2007; *b* 25 Jan. 1939; *s* of William Robert Stacey and Ivy May Stacey; *m* 1st, 1962, Anne Jenkins (marr. diss. 1970); two *s*; 2nd, 1970, Jean Brymer (marr. diss. 1997); 3rd, 1997, Elizabeth Jane Collins. *Educ:* City of Bath Sch. for Boys; Univ. of Hull (BSc Hons Physics). Res. Officer, Joseph Lucas Res. Centre, 1960–70; prodn engr, mktg, and factory manager, 1970–82; Managing Director: Lucas Automotive Electronics, 1982–87; Lucas Aerospace UK, 1987–90; Meggitt Aerospace, 1990–94. Dir and Chm., Rubicon plc, 1994–99; Director: Sidlaw plc, 1997–98; Vitec plc, 1999–2003; Marshalls plc, 2000–03. Director: Dorset Chamber of Commerce and Industry, 1995–2000; Dorset TEC, 1996–2001. *Recreations:* golf, Rugby, gardening. *Address:* Vines House, Horton, Wimborne, Dorset BH21 7JA. *Club:* Remedy Oak (Dorset).

STACEY, Rear-Adm. Michael Lawrence, CB 1979; private consultant in marine pollution; Member, Advisory Committee on Protection of the Sea, since 1988; Life Vice President, Royal National Lifeboat Institution, since 1997; *b* 6 July 1924; *s* of Maurice Stacey and Dorice Evelyn (*née* Bulling); *m* 1955, Penelope Leana (*née* Riddoch); two *s*. *Educ:* Epsom Coll. Entered RN as Cadet, 1942; Normandy landings, HMS Hawkins, 1944; served in HM Ships Rotherham, Cambrian, Shoreham, Hornet, Vernon, Euryalus, Bermuda, Vigilant; Comdr 1958; staff of RN Staff Coll.; in comd HMS Blackpool, 1960–62; JSSC; Captain 1966; Chief Staff Officer to Admiral Commanding Reserves, 1966–68; in comd HMS Andromeda and Captain (F) Sixth Frigate Sqdn, 1968–70; Dep. Dir of Naval Warfare, 1970–73; in comd HMS Tiger, 1973–75; Asst Chief of Naval Staff (Policy), 1975–76; Flag Officer, Gibraltar, 1976–78. ADC to the Queen, 1975. Dir, Marine Emergency Ops, Marine Div., Dept of Trade, later Dept of Transport, 1979–87. FNI; FCMI. Younger Brother, Trinity House, 1979. Liveryman, Shipwrights' Co., 1991; Mem., Master Mariners' Co., 1999. *Recreations:* fishing, yachting. *Address:* Flat 6, Headon Court, The Close, Tilford Road, Farnham, Surrey GU9 8DR. *T:* (01252) 713032. *Clubs:* Army and Navy, Royal Navy of 1765 and 1785, Royal Naval Sailing Association.

STACEY, Morna Dorothy, (Mrs W. D. Stacey); *see* Hooker, M. D.

STACEY, Rev. Nicolas David; Chairman, East Thames Housing Group (formerly East London Housing Association), 1993–98; *b* 27 Nov. 1927; *s* of late David and Gwen Stacey; *m* 1955, Hon. Anne Bridgeman, *er d* of 2nd Viscount Bridgeman, KBE, CB, DSO, MC; one *s* two *d*. *Educ:* RNC, Dartmouth; St Edmund Hall, Oxford (hons degree Mod. Hist.); Cuddesdon Theol Coll., Oxford. Midshipman, HMS Anson, 1945–46; Sub-Lt, 1946–48. Asst Curate, St Mark's, Portsea, 1953–58; Domestic Chap. to Bp of Birmingham, 1958–60; Rector of Woolwich, 1960–68; Dean of London Borough of Greenwich, 1965–68; Dep. Dir of Oxfam, 1968–70; Director of Social Services: London Borough of Ealing, 1971–74; Kent County Council, 1974–85; Dir, AIDS Policy Unit, sponsored by Citizen Action, 1988–89. Vice-Chm., TV South Charitable Trust, 1988–92. Six Preacher, Canterbury Cathedral, 1984–89. Sporting career: internat. sprinter, 1948–52, incl. British Empire Games, 1949, and Olympic Games, 1952 (semi-finalist 200 metres and finalist 4×400 metres relay); Pres., OUAC, 1951; winner, Oxf. v Cambridge 220 yds, 1948–51; Captain, Combined Oxf. and Camb. Athletic Team, 1951. Cross of St Augustine, 2005. *Publication:* Who Cares (autobiog.), 1971. *Address:* The Old Vicarage, Selling, Faversham, Kent ME13 9RD. *T:* (01227) 752833, *Fax:* (01227) 752889; *e-mail:* nicolas@nstacey.fsnet.co.uk. *Clubs:* Beefsteak; Royal St George's Golf (Sandwich, Kent).
See also M. E. Stacey.

STACEY, Valerie Elizabeth; QC (Scot.) 1999; *b* 25 May 1954; *d* of James and Helen Thom; *m* 1981, Andrew Stacey; two *s*. *Educ:* Elgin Acad.; Edinburgh Univ. (LLB Hons). Solicitor, 1978–86; admitted to Faculty of Advocates, 1987 (Vice Dean, 2004–07); Advocate Depute, 1993–96; Standing Jun. Counsel to Home Office in Scotland, 1996–99; Temp. Sheriff, 1997–99. Member: Sentencing Commn for Scotland, 2003–06; Judicial Appts Bd for Scotland, 2005–07. *Recreation:* listening to music. *Address:* Advocates' Library, Parliament House, Edinburgh EH1 1RF. *T:* (0131) 226 5071.

STACK, (Ann) Prunella, (Mrs Brian St Quentin Power), OBE 1980; President, The Fitness League (formerly Women's League of Health and Beauty), since 1982 (Member of Council, since 1950); *b* 28 July 1914; *d* of Capt. Hugh Bagot Stack, 8th Ghurka Rifles, and Mary Meta Bagot Stack, Founder of The Women's League of Health and Beauty; *m* 1st, 1938, Lord David Douglas-Hamilton (*d* 1944); two *s*; 2nd, 1950, Alfred G. Albers,

FRCS (d 1951), Cape Town, S Africa; 3rd, 1964, Brian St Quentin Power (d 2008). *Educ:* The Abbey, Malvern Wells. Mem. of the National Fitness Council, 1937–39. Vice-Pres., Outward Bound Trust, 1980–. *Publications:* The Way to Health and Beauty, 1938; Movement is Life, 1973; Island Quest, 1979; Zest for Life, 1988; Style for Life, 1990; If I Were to Tell You (poems), 1994; Then and Now (poems), 2003. *Recreations:* poetry, music, travel. *Address:* 14 Gertrude Street, SW10 0JN.

STACK, Rt Rev. George; Auxiliary Bishop of Westminster, (RC), and Titular Bishop of Gemellae in Numidia, since 2001; *b* 9 May 1946; *s* of Gerald Stack and Elizabeth (*née* McKenzie). *Educ:* St Aloysius Coll., Highgate; St Edmund's Coll., Ware; St Mary's Coll., Strawberry Hill. BEd (Hons). Ordained priest, 1972; Curate, St Joseph's, Hanwell 1972–75; Diocesan Catechetical Office, 1975–77; Curate, St Paul's, Wood Green, 1977–83; Parish Priest, Our Lady Help of Christians, Kentish Town, 1983–90; VG, Archdiocese of Westminster, 1990–93; Administrator, Westminster Cathedral, 1993–2001. Hon. Canon Emeritus, St Paul's Cathedral, 2001. Prelate of Honour to HH The Pope, 1993; KHS 2000. *Address:* Archbishop's House, Ambrosden Avenue, SW1P 1QJ. *T:* (020) 7798 9075.

STACK, Neville; international editorial consultant and syndicated political columnist, in South and South East Asia, Africa and the Caribbean, since 1989; *b* 2 Sept. 1933; *m* 1953; one *s* one *d. Educ:* Arnold School. Reporter: Ashton-under-Lyne Reporter, 1948; Express & Star, 1950; Sheffield Telegraph, and Kemsley National Papers, 1955; Northern News Editor, IPC national papers, 1971; Sub-editor, Daily Express, 1973; Editor, Stockport Advertiser, 1974; Editor, Leicester Mercury, 1974–87; Dir, F. Hewitt and Co. (1927) Ltd (Mercury Publishers), 1982–88; Editorial Consultant, Straits Times, Singapore, 1988–89; Consultant: New Paper, Singapore, 1990–; Trinidad Daily Express, 1990–; Independent Newspapers Gp, SA, 1998–99; Columnist: The Hindu, Madras, 1990–2004; Indian Business Leaders mag., Bombay, 1990–; Today, Singapore, 1999–2003; political commentator, Singapore Straits Times, 1990–99. Hon. Press Fellow, Wolfson Coll., Cambridge, 1987–88. Evaluator, RSA journalism qualification, 1992–; Co-organiser and Mem., Wolfson Coll. Regl Seminar for Editors, 1992–. Mem. Court, Leicester Univ., 1999. Hon. MA Leicester, 1988. *Publications:* The Empty Palace, 1976; Editing for the Nineties, 1988. *Recreations:* writing, computers, travel. *Address:* Letter-na-Caight, Donegal Town, Co. Donegal, Ireland.

STACK, Prunella; see Stack, A. P.

STACPOOLE, John Wentworth; Deputy Secretary, Department of Health and Social Security, 1979–82; *b* 16 June 1926; *s* of late G. W. Stacpoole and of Mrs M. G. Butt; *m* 1954, Charmian, *d* of late J. P. Bishop and Mrs E. M. Bishop; one *s* one *d. Educ:* Sedbergh; Magdalen Coll., Oxford (Demy; MA). Army, 1944–47 (Lieut, Assam Regt). Colonial Office, 1951–68, Private Sec. to Sec. of State, 1964–65; transf. to Min. of Social Security, 1968; Under-Sec., DHSS, 1973. Mem., Maidstone HA, 1982–91. Chm., Maidstone Hospice Appeal, 1987–92. *Publication:* (ed) Sedbergh School 1900–2000: a celebration, 2000. *Recreations:* reading, sketching. *Address:* 25 Offham Road, West Malling, Kent ME19 6RB. *T:* (01732) 847162.

STACY, Graham Henry, CBE 1993; FCA; Chairman, Sanctuary Housing Association, since 2004 (Treasurer, 1995–2004); *b* 23 May 1933; *s* of Norman Winny Stacy and Winifred Frances Stacy (*née* Wood); *m* 1958, Mary Fereday; one *s* three *d. Educ:* Stationers' Co.'s Sch. FCA 1955. Articled to Walter Smee Will & Co., 1950–55; Nat. Service, RN (Sub-Lieut), 1955–57; joined Price Waterhouse, 1957: Partner, 1968–93; Dir of Technical Services, 1976–88; Dir of Professional Standards (UK and Europe), 1988–93; Mem., Policy Cttee, 1987–93. Member: Auditing Practices Cttee, 1976–84; Accounting Standards Cttee, 1986–90; Accounting Standards Bd, 1990–94. Mem., Monopolies and Mergers, subseq. Competition, Commn, 1995–2001. Hon. Treas., URC in UK, 1995–2002. *Recreations:* bridge, reading, painting watercolours, DIY.

STADLEN, Hon. Sir Nicholas Felix, Kt 2007; **Hon. Mr Justice Stadlen;** a Judge of the High Court of Justice, Queen's Bench Division, since 2007; *b* 3 May 1950; *s* of late Peter Stadlen and Hedi (*née* Simon); *m* 1972, Frances Edith Howarth, *d* of T. E. B. and Margaret Howarth; three *s. Educ:* St Paul's School (Scholar); Trinity Coll., Cambridge (Open Scholarship and McGill Exhibition; BA Hons Classics Part 1, History Part 2). Pres., Cambridge Union Soc., 1970. First in order of merit, Part 1 Bar Exams, 1975; called to the Bar, Inner Temple, 1976. QC 1991; Asst Recorder, 1997–2000; Recorder, 2000–07. Mem., Bar Council Public Affairs Cttee, 1987; Chm., Bar Caribbean pro bono Cttee, 1999–2007. Chm. of Trustees, Volunteer Reading Help, 2005–08. First Sec., British-Irish Assoc., 1972–74. *Publications:* (with Michael Barnes) Gulbenkian Foundation Reports on National Music and Drama Education, 1974–75; (contrib.) Convention: an account of the 1976 US Democratic Party Presidential Nominating Convention, 1976. *Recreation:* listening to classical music. *Address:* Royal Courts of Justice, Strand, WC2A 2LL.

STAFFORD, Marquis of; James Granville Egerton; *b* 12 Aug. 1975; *s* and *heir* of Duke of Sutherland, *qv; m* 2007, Barbara Ruth, *d* of Dr Graham Schneider, Vienna; one *d. Educ:* Eton Coll., Windsor; Univ. of Edinburgh. *Address:* Ley Farm, Stetchworth, Newmarket, Suffolk CB8 9TX.

STAFFORD, 15th Baron *cr* 1640; **Francis Melfort William Fitzherbert;** DL; *b* 13 March 1954; *s* of 14th Baron Stafford and of Morag Nada, *yr d* of late Lt-Col Alastair Campbell; *S* father, 1986; *m* 1980, Katharine Mary Codrington; two *s* two *d. Educ:* Ampleforth College; Reading Univ.; RAC, Cirencester. Director (non-executive): Tarmac Industrial Products Div., 1987–93; Mid Staffs Mental Health Foundn, 1990–99; Hanley Economic BS, 1992–. Pro-Chancellor, Keele Univ., 1993–2004. Pres., Staffs CCC, 1999–2008; Pres. and Patron various orgns in North Staffs. Governor, Harper Adams University (formerly Agricl) Coll., 1990–2007 (Chm. Govs, 2004–07). DL Stafford, 1994; High Sheriff, Staffs, 2005. DUniv: Keele, 2005; Staffs, 2006. *Recreations:* shooting, cricket, golf. *Heir: s* Hon. Benjamin John Basil Fitzherbert, *b* 8 Nov. 1983. *Address:* Swynnerton Park, Stone, Staffordshire ST15 0QE. *T:* (01782) 796228. *Club:* Lord's Taverners.

STAFFORD, Bishop Suffragan of, since 2005; **Rt Rev. (Alfred) Gordon Mursell;** *b* 4 May 1949; *s* of late Philip Riley Mursell and Sheena Nicholson Mursell; *m* 1989, Anne Muir. *Educ:* Ardingly Coll.; Brasenose Coll., Oxford (MA 1974; BD 1987). ARCM 1975. Ordained deacon, 1973, priest, 1974; Curate, St Mary Walton, Liverpool, 1973–77; Vicar, St John, E Dulwich, 1977–87; Tutor, Salisbury and Wells Theol Coll., 1987–91; Team Rector, Stafford, 1991–99; Provost, subseq. Dean, of Birmingham, 1999–2005. Hon. DD Birmingham, 2005. *Publications:* Theology of the Carthusian Life, 1988; Out of the Deep: prayer as protest, 1989; The Meditations of Guigo I, Prior of the Charterhouse, 1995; The Wisdom of the Anglo-Saxons, 1997; English Spirituality, 2001; (Gen. Ed.) The Story of Christian Spirituality: two thousand years, from East to West, 2001; Praying in Exile, 2005. *Recreations:* music, hill-walking. *Address:* Ash Garth, 6 Broughton Crescent, Barlaston, Stoke-on-Trent, ST12 9DD. *T:* (01782) 373308, *Fax:* (01782) 373705; *e-mail:* bishop.stafford@lichfield.anglican.org. *Club:* Athenæum.

STAFFORD, Andrew Bruce; QC 2000; *b* 30 March 1957; *s* of Cyril Henry Stafford and Audrey Estelle Stafford; *m* 1982, Catherine Anne, *d* of Derek and Kathleen Johnson; one *s* four *d. Educ:* Royal Grammar Sch., Newcastle upon Tyne; Trinity Hall, Cambridge (BA Law, MA). Called to the Bar, Middle Temple, 1980. Part-time Chm., Employment Tribunals, 2000–. *Recreations:* art, theatre, Newcastle United. *Address:* Littleton Chambers, 3 King's Bench Walk North, Temple, EC4Y 7HR.

STAFFORD, David Valentine; Secretary, Economic and Social Research Council, 1988–90; *b* 14 Feb. 1930; *s* of Augustus Everard and Emily Blanche Stafford; *m* 1953, Aileen Patricia Wood; one *s* one *d. Educ:* Rutlish School, Merton. Dept of Educn and Science, 1951–88; Sec., Open Univ. Planning Cttee, 1967–69. Acting Chm., ESRC, Feb.–Sept. 1988. *Recreations:* reading, gardening. *Address:* Vallis, Lyncombe Vale Road, Bath, Som BA2 4LS. *T:* (01225) 312563.
See also N. D. Stafford.

STAFFORD, Godfrey Harry, CBE 1976; PhD; FRS 1979; FInstP; Master of St Cross College, Oxford, 1979–87; *b* 15 April 1920; *s* of Henry and Sarah Stafford; *m* 1950, Helen Goldthorp (*née* Clark) (*d* 2003); one *s* twin *d. Educ:* Rondebosch Boys High Sch., S Africa; Univ. of Cape Town; Gonville and Caius Coll., Cambridge. MSc Cape Town, 1941; Ebden Scholar, PhD Cantab 1950; MA Oxon 1971. South African Naval Forces, 1941–46. Harwell, 1949–51; Head of Biophysics Subdiv., CSIR, Pretoria, 1951–54; Cyclotron Gp, AERE, 1954–57; Rutherford Laboratory: Head of Proton Linear Accelerator Gp, 1957; Head of High Energy Physics Div., 1963; Dep. Dir, 1966; Dir, Rutherford Lab., Chilton, 1969–79; Dir Gen., 1979–81, Hon. Scientist, 1987–, Rutherford Appleton Laboratory; Fellow, St Cross Coll., Oxford, 1971–79 (Hon. Fellow, 1987). CERN appointments: UK deleg. to Council, 1973; Vice-Pres., Council, 1973; Scientific Policy Cttee, 1973, Vice-Chm., 1976, Chm., 1978. Vice-Pres. for meetings, Inst. of Physics, 1976; President: European Physical Soc., 1984–86 (Vice-Pres., 1982–84); Inst. of Physics, 1986–88. Governor: Oxford Centre for Post-Graduate Hebrew Studies, 1983–93; Westminster Coll., 1987–93. Glazebrook Prize and Medal, Inst. of Physics, 1981. Hon. DSc Birmingham, 1980. *Publications:* papers and articles in learned jls on: biophysics, nuclear physics, high energy physics. *Recreations:* walking, foreign travel, music. *Address:* Ferry Cottage, North Hinksey Village, Oxford OX2 0NA. *T:* (01865) 247621.

STAFFORD, Prof. Nicholas David, FRCS; Professor of Head and Neck Surgery and Otolaryngology, since 1995, and Director, Postgraduate Medical Institute (formerly Head, Postgraduate School of Medicine), since 1997, University of Hull; *b* 13 Aug. 1954; *s* of David Valentine Stafford, *qv; m* 1977, Heather Gay Sims; four *d. Educ:* Farnborough Grammar Sch.; Univ. of Leeds (MB ChB 1977). FRCS 1983. Various SHO posts, 1978–82; Registrar in ENT Surgery, RNTNEH, 1982–84; Sen. Registrar in ENT/Head and Neck Surgery, Royal Marsden Hosp. and St Mary's Hosp., London, 1985–89; Consultant Head and Neck/ENT Surgeon, St Mary's, Ealing and Charing Cross Hosps, 1989–95. Résident Etranger, Inst. Gustave-Roussy, Paris, 1987–88. *Publications:* (with R. Youngs) Colour Aids: ENT, 1988, 3rd edn 2006; (ed with J. Waldron) Management of Oral Cancer, 1989; contribs mainly in field of head and neck oncology. *Recreation:* classic cars. *Address:* 10 New Walk, Beverley HU17 7AD. *T:* (01482) 871541. *Club:* XK Car.

STAFFORD, Peter Moore, FCA; Director and Trustee, Rathbone Training Ltd, since 2002; Member, Board of Partners, Deloitte & Touche (formerly Touche Ross & Co.), 1990–2000 (Chairman, 1992–95); *b* 24 April 1942; *s* of late Harry Shaw Stafford and May Alexandra (*née* Moore); *m* 1973, Elspeth Anne, *d* of James Steel Harvey; one *s* one *d. Educ:* Charterhouse. FCA 1976 (ACA 1965). Articled Clerk, Garnett Crewdson & Co., Manchester, 1960–64; Arthur Andersen, 1966–68; Partner, 1968–71, Garnett Crewdson & Co., merged with Spicer & Oppenheim: Partner, 1971–90; Managing Partner, 1990; merged with Touche Ross & Co. Member: Council for Industry and Higher Educn, 1993–97; Professional Standards Dept, ICAEW, 1998–2002. Governor, Terra Nova Sch., 1976–2004. *Recreations:* travel, gardening. *Address:* Holmes Chapel, Cheshire. *T:* (01477) 533339. *Clubs:* Royal Over-Seas League; St James's (Manchester) (Hon. Treas., 2002–04).

STAFFORD-CLARK, Maxwell Robert Guthrie Stewart, (Max); artistic director and founder, Out of Joint Theatre Company, since 1993; *b* 17 March 1941; *s* of late Dr David Stafford-Clark, FRCP, FRCPsych and Dorothy Stewart (*née* Oldfield); *m* 1st, 1971, Carole Hayman; 2nd, 1981, Ann Pennington; one *d. Educ:* Felstead School; Riverdale Country Day School, NY; Trinity College, Dublin. Associate dir, Traverse, 1966, artistic dir, 1968–70; dir, Traverse Workshop Co., 1970–74; founder, Joint Stock Theatre Group, 1974; Artistic Dir, English Stage Company at Royal Court Theatre, 1979–93. Productions include: Cloud 9, 1980; Top Girls, 1982; Falkland Sound, 1983; Tom and Viv, Rat in the Skull, 1984; Serious Money, 1987; Our Country's Good, 1988; King Lear, 1993; The Steward of Christendom, 1995; Shopping and Fucking, 1996; Blue Heart, 1997; Feelgood, 2001; Duck, The Permanent Way, 2003, Macbeth, Talking to Terrorists, 2004; O Go My Man, 2006; The Overwhelming, 2006; The Convict's Opera, 2008. *Publications:* Letters to George, 1989; Taking Stock, 2006. *Address:* 7 Thane Works, Thane Villas, N7 7NU. *Clubs:* Groucho; Front Line.

STAFFORD SMITH, Clive Adrian, OBE 2000; Founder and Counsel, Reprieve; *b* 9 July 1959; *s* of Richard Stafford Smith and Jean Stafford Smith; *m* 1998, Emily MacSween Bolton. *Educ:* Radley Coll., Abingdon; Univ. of North Carolina, Chapel Hill (John Motley Morehead Scholar; BA Pol Sci. 1981); Columbia Law Sch., NY (Harlan Fiske Stone Merit Scholar 1982, 1983, 1984; JD 1984). Staff attorney, Southern Prisoners' Defense Cttee, subseq. Southern Center for Human Rights, Atlanta, Ga, 1984–93; Dir, Louisiana Capital Assistance Center, New Orleans, 1993–2004. Patron, Lifelines. Documentaries: Fourteen Days in May, 1987; The Journey, 1988; Murder in Room 1215, 1997; The Death Belt, 2003; Torture (presenter), 2005. Hon. LLM Wolverhampton, 2001; Hon. DCL City, 2006. Lifetime Achievement Award, Law Soc., 2003; Benjamin Smith Award, ACLU, La, 2004; Gandhi Peace Award, 2005. *Publications:* (contrib.) A Punishment in Search of a Crime, 1989; Bad Men: Guantanamo and the secret prisons, 2007. *Address:* Reprieve, PO Box 52742, EC4P 4WS. *T:* (020) 7353 4640, *Fax:* (020) 7353 4641; *e-mail:* clivess@mac.com. *Club:* Chelsea Arts.

STAGG, Sir (Charles) Richard (Vernon), KCMG 2008 (CMG 2001); HM Diplomatic Service; High Commissioner to India, since 2007; *b* 27 Sept. 1955; *s* of Walter and Elise Patricia Stagg; *m* 1982, Arabella Clare Faber; three *s* two *d. Educ:* Winchester; Oriel Coll., Oxford. Joined Diplomatic Service, 1977; FCO, 1977–79; Sofia, 1979–82; The Hague, 1982–85; FCO, 1985–86; UK Repn to EC, Brussels, 1987–88; FCO, 1988–91; UK Repn to EC, Brussels, 1991–93; Private Sec. to Foreign Sec., 1993–96; Head, EU (Ext.) Dept FCO, 1996–98; Ambassador to Bulgaria, 1998–2001; Dir of Information, 2001–03; Dir Gen. (Corporate Affairs), 2003–07, FCO. *Recreations:* racing, gardening. *Address:* c/o Foreign and Commonwealth Office, King Charles Street, SW1A 2AH. *Clubs:* Turf; Millennium.

STAHEL, Rolf; Chairman: Chesyl Pharma Ltd, since 2003; Newron Pharmaceuticals SPA, since 2004; Cosmo SPA, since 2006 (Deputy Chairman, 2004–06); EUSA Pharma

Inc., since 2007; *b* 21 April 1944; *s* of Hermann Stahel and Bluette Maillard; *m* 1970, Ewa Stachurska; two *s*. *Educ:* Kantonsschule, Lucerne (Dip. Kfm (CH) Business Studies, 1962; Handels Matura, 1963); 97th AMP, Harvard. Sales Administration, Rhône Poulenc, Switzerland, 1963–67; Wellcome: Rep., UK, 1967; Asst Manager, Switzerland, 1968; Gen. Manager, Italy, 1969–74; Man. Dir, Wellcome Thailand, 1974–79; Regl Dir, Wellcome Singapore, 1979–90; Dir of Marketing, Wellcome plc, UK, 1990–94; Chief Exec., Shire Pharmaceuticals Gp plc, 1994–2003. Mem., Adv. Bd, Imperial Coll. Business Sch., 2007–. CEO of Year, Global Pharmaceutical Award, Informa, 2001; Techmark award, 2003. *Recreations:* golf, opera. *Address:* Neatham, Sleepers Hill, Winchester, Hants SO22 4NB. *T:* (01962) 868224; *e-mail:* rstahel@chesyl.com. *Clubs:* Royal Automobile, Harvard Business School; South Winchester Golf.

STAINTON, Sir (John) Ross, Kt 1981; CBE 1971; retired; *b* 27 May 1914; *s* of late George Stainton and Helen Ross; *m* 1939, Doreen Werner (*d* 2001); three *d*. *Educ:* Glengorse, Eastbourne; Malvern Coll., Worcestershire. Joined Imperial Airways as Trainee, 1933; served in Italy, Egypt, Sudan. Served with RAF in England, West Indies and USA, 1940–46. Man. N America, BOAC, 1949–53; General Sales Man. BOAC, and other Head Office posts, 1954–68; Dep. Man. Dir, 1968–71; Man. Dir, 1971–72; Mem., BOAC Bd, 1968, Chm. and Chief Exec., 1972, until merged into British Airways, 1974; Mem., 1971–, Dep. Chm. and Chief Exec., 1977–79, Chairman, 1979–80, British Airways Bd. Vice Pres., Private Patients Plan, 1986– (Dir, 1979–86). Hon. Treasurer, Air League Council, 1986–91. FCILT (Pres., 1970–71); CRAeS 1978. *Clubs:* Royal Air Force; Royal and Ancient Golf (St Andrews); Sunningdale Golf.

STAIR, 14th Earl of, *cr* 1703; **John David James Dalrymple;** Bt 1664 and 1698 (Scot); Viscount Stair, Lord Glenluce and Stranraer, 1690; Viscount Dalrymple, Lord Newliston, 1703; Baron Oxenfoord (UK), 1841; *b* 4 Sept. 1961; *s* of 13th Earl of Stair, KCVO, MBE and of Davina Katharine, *d* of late Hon. Sir David Bowes-Lyon, KCVO; *S* father, 1996; *m* 2006, Hon. Emily Mary Julia Stonor, 2nd *d* of Baron Camoys, *qv*; one *s*. Commnd Scots Guards, 1982. *Heir: s* John James Thomas Dalrymple, Viscount Dalrymple, *b* 3 Jan. 2008.

STAIR, Claire; *see* Wilcox, C.

STAIR, Julian Francis, PhD; potter, since 1981; *b* 9 March 1955; *s* of Derek Anthony Guthrie (*né* Plank) and Christine Marie Stair (*née* Kelly); *m* 1992, Claire Wilcox, *qv*; two *d* (one *s* decd). *Educ:* Camberwell Sch. of Art (BA Hons 1978); Royal Coll. of Art (MA 1981; PhD 2003). Sen. Lectr, Univ. of Surrey, 1983–98. Fellow in Craft and Criticism, Univ. of Newcastle, 1997–99; Vis. Lectr, Brighton Univ., Westminster Univ. and Cardiff Univ., 1998–2006; Vis. Prof. of Ceramics and Theory, Camberwell Coll. of Art, Univ. of London, 2003–; Res. Fellow, RCA, 2004. Crafts Council: Trustee, 2000–06; Interim Chm., 2005–06; Dep. Chm., 2006–. Trustee, Contemporary Applied Arts, 1997–2003. FRSA. *Publications:* (ed) The Body Politic: the role of the body and contemporary craft, 2000; (contrib.) The Persistence of Craft, ed by Paul Greenhalgh, 2002; contribs to The Times, Art in America, Crafts, Ceramic Review and New Art Examiner. *Recreations:* croquet, bird watching, walking, cinema. *Address:* 127 Court Lane, Dulwich, SE21 7EE. *T:* (020) 8693 8012; *e-mail:* studio@julianstair.com.

STALLWORTHY, Prof. Jon Howie, FBA 1990; Professor of English Literature, Oxford University, 1992–2000, now Emeritus; Senior Research Fellow, Wolfson College, Oxford, since 2000 (Fellow, since 1986; Acting President, 2006–08); *b* 18 Jan. 1935; *s* of Sir John (Arthur) Stallworthy; *m* 1960, Gillian Meredith (*née* Waldock); two *s* one *d*. *Educ:* The Dragon Sch., Oxford; Rugby Sch.; Magdalen Coll., Oxford (MA, BLitt). Served RWAFF (pre-Oxford). At Oxford won Newdigate Prize, 1958 (runner-up, 1957). Joined Oxford Univ. Press, 1959, Dep. Head, Academic Div., 1975–77; John Wendell Anderson Prof. of English Lit., Cornell Univ., 1977–86; Reader in English Lit., Oxford Univ., 1986–92. Chatterton Lectr on an English Poet, British Academy, 1970; during a sabbatical year, 1971–72, was a Visiting Fellow at All Souls Coll., Oxford. FRSL, 1971. *Publications: poems* (collections): The Astronomy of Love, 1961; Out of Bounds, 1963; Root and Branch, 1969; Positives, 1969; The Apple Barrel: selected poems, 1955–63, 1974; Hand in Hand, 1974; A Familiar Tree, 1978; The Anzac Sonata: new and selected poems, 1986; The Guest From the Future, 1995; Rounding the Horn: collected poems, 1998; Body Language, 2004; *criticism:* Between the Lines, W. B. Yeats's Poetry in the Making, 1963; Vision and Revision in Yeats's Last Poems, 1969; Survivors' Songs from Maldon to the Somme, 2008; *biography:* Wilfred Owen, 1974 (winner of Duff Cooper Meml Prize, W. H. Smith Literary Award and E. M. Forster Award); Louis MacNeice (Southern Arts Lit. Prize), 1995; *autobiography:* Singing School: the making of a poet, 1998; *translations:* (with Peter France) Alexander Blok: The Twelve and other poems, 1970; (with Jerzy Peterkiewicz) poems for 2nd edn of Five Centuries of Polish Poetry, 1970; (with Peter France) Boris Pasternak: Selected Poems, 1983; *edited:* The Penguin Book of Love Poetry, 1973; Wilfred Owen: Complete Poems and Fragments, 1983; The Oxford Book of War Poetry, 1984; The Poems of Wilfred Owen, 1985; First Lines: poems written in youth, from Herbert to Heaney, 1987; Henry Reed: Collected Poems, 1991; The War Poems of Wilfred Owen, 1994; (jtly) The Norton Anthology of Poetry, 4th edn, 1996; (jtly) The Norton Anthology of English Literature, 7th edn, 2000; Anthem for Doomed Youth: twelve soldier poets of the First World War, 2002. *Address:* Wolfson College, Oxford OX2 6UD; Long Farm, Elsfield Road, Old Marston, Oxford OX3 0PR. *Club:* Vincent's (Oxford).

STAMER, Sir (Lovelace) Anthony, 5th Bt *cr* 1809; MA; AMIMI; *b* 28 Feb. 1917; *s* of Sir Lovelace Stamer, 4th Bt, and Eva Mary (*d* 1974), *e d* of R. C. Otter; *S* father, 1941; *m* 1st, 1948, Stella Huguette (marr. diss. 1953), *d* of late Paul Burnell Binnie, Brussels; one *s* one *d*; 2nd, 1955, Margaret Lucy (marr. diss. 1959), *d* of late Major Belben; 3rd, 1960, Marjorie June (marr. diss. 1968), *d* of late T. C. Noakes, St James, Cape; 4th, 1983, Elizabeth Graham Smith (*d* 1992), *widow* of G. P. H. Smith, Colyton, Devon; 5th, 1997, Pamela Grace (*née* Hawkins), *widow* of P. B. Cheston. *Educ:* Harrow; Trinity Coll., Cambridge; Royal Agricultural Coll., Cirencester. BA 1947; MA 1963; AMIMI 1963. Served RAF 1939–41; Officer in ATA 1941–45. Executive Director: Bentley Drivers Club Ltd, 1969–73; Bugatti & Ferrari Owners Club, 1973–75; Hon. Treasurer, Ferrari Owners' Club, 1975–81. *Heir: s* Peter Tomlinson Stamer, Sqn Leader, RAF, retd [*b* 19 Nov. 1951; *m* 1979, Dinah Louise Berry (marr. diss. 1989); one *s* one *d*; *m* 1999, Věra Řeháková (marr. diss. 2002)]. *Address:* Old Timbers, Church Street, Moreton-in-Marsh, Glos GL56 0LN.

STAMMERS, Michael Kingsley; Keeper of Merseyside Maritime Museum, 1986–2003, Curator Emeritus, 2004; *b* 30 Aug. 1943; *s* of John Kingsley Stammers and late Thelma Marjorie Stammers (*née* Gooch); *m* 1971, Pauline Birch; one *s* one *d*. *Educ:* Norwich Sch.; Univ. of Bristol (BA Hons History). AMA. Curator of Folk Life, Warwick County Museum, 1966–69; Keeper of Shipping, Liverpool City Museum, 1969–74; Curator of Maritime History, Merseyside County Museums, 1974–86. Mem., Nat. Historic Ships Cttee, 1990–2000. Trustee: Internat. Congress of Maritime Museums, 2002–; Nat. Maritime Mus., Cornwall, 2002–. FRHistS 2000; FSA 2002. *Publications:* West Coast Shipping, 1976, 2nd edn 1989; The Passage Makers, 1978; Liverpool: the port and its ships, 1991; (with J. Kearon) The Jhelum: a Victorian merchant ship, 1992; Mersey Flats and Flatmen, 1993; (with J. G. Read) A Guide to the Records of Merseyside Maritime Museum, 1995; A Maritime Fortress, 2001; Norfolk Shipping, 2002; Charles Cooper: the last emigrant ship, 2003; Suffolk Shipping, 2003; End of Voyages, 2004; Figureheads and Ship Carving, 2005; Crosby Curiosities, 2006; The Industrial Archaeology of Docks and Harbours, 2007; contribs to learned jls. *Recreations:* going to sea, gardening, music. *Address:* 55 Kimberley Drive, Great Crosby L23 5TA. *Club:* Royal Mersey Yacht.

STAMP, family name of **Baron Stamp**.

STAMP, 4th Baron *cr* 1938, of Shortlands; **Trevor Charles Bosworth Stamp,** MD; FRCP; Hon. Consultant Physician, Royal National Orthopaedic Hospital, since 1999; Consultant Physician and Director, Department of Bone and Mineral Metabolism, Institute of Orthopaedics, Royal National Orthopaedic Hospital, 1974–99; *b* 18 Sept. 1935; *s* of 3rd Baron Stamp, MD, FRCPath and Frances Hammond (*d* 1998), *d* of late Charles Henry Bosworth, Evanston, Illinois, USA; *S* father, 1987; *m* 1st, 1963, Anne Carolynn Churchill (marr. diss. 1971); two *d*; 2nd, 1975, Carol Anne (marr. diss. 1997), *d* of late Robert Keith Russell; one *s* one *d*. *Educ:* The Leys School; Gonville and Caius Coll., Cambridge; Yale Univ.; St Mary's Hosp. Medical School. MSc (Yale) 1957; MD (Cantab) 1972; FRCP 1978. Qualified in medicine, 1960; Med. Registrar, Professorial Medical Unit, St Mary's Hosp., 1964–66; Hon. Senior Registrar 1968–73, and Hon. Sen. Lecturer 1972–73, Dept of Human Metabolism, University College Hosp. and Medical School; Hon. Consultant Physician and Sen. Lectr, Middlesex Hosp. and UCL School of Medicine, 1974–99, now Emeritus Consultant, UCL Hosps. Mem., Scientific Adv. Bd, Nat. Osteoporosis Soc. Patron, Nat. Assoc. for Relief of Paget's Disease; Vice-Patron, British Sch. of Osteopathy. Hon. Life Member: Bone and Tooth Soc.; Internat. Skeletal Soc. Prix André Lichtwitz, France, 1973. *Publications:* numerous papers on disorders of mineral metabolism. *Recreations:* music, golf, contract bridge. *Heir: s* Hon. Nicholas Charles Trevor Stamp, *b* 27 Feb. 1978. *Address:* 15 Ceylon Road, W14 0PY. *T:* (020) 7603 0487.

STAMP, Gavin Mark, MA, PhD; FSA; architectural historian and writer; *b* 15 March 1948; *s* of Barry Hartnell Stamp and Norah Clare (*née* Rich); *m* 1982, Alexandra Frances Artley (marr. diss. 2007); two *d*. *Educ:* Dulwich Coll.; Gonville and Caius Coll., Cambridge (MA, PhD). Lectr, 1990–99, Sen. Lectr, 1999–2003, Mackintosh Sch. of Architecture, Glasgow Sch. of Art; Mellon Sen. Fellow and Bye-Fellow, Gonville and Caius Coll., Cambridge, 2003–04. Contributor to The Spectator, The Independent, Daily Telegraph, Private Eye, Architects' Jl, etc. Chm., Twentieth Century (formerly Thirties) Soc., 1983–2007; Founder and Chm., Alexander Thomson Soc., 1991–2003. Hon. Prof., Glasgow Univ., 2003. FSA 1998. Hon. FRIAS 1994; Hon. FRIBA 1998. *Publications:* The Architect's Calendar, 1973; Silent Cities, 1977; (text only) Temples of Power, 1979; (jtly) The Victorian Buildings of London 1837–1887, 1980; Robert Weir Schultz and his work for the Marquesses of Bute, 1981; The Great Perspectivists, 1982; The Changing Metropolis, 1984; The English House 1860–1914, 1986; (jtly) The Church in Crisis, 1986; The Telephone Boxes, 1989; (ed jtly) Greek Thomson, 1994; (ed) Recollections of Sir Gilbert Scott, 1995; Alexander 'Greek' Thomson, 1999; Edwin Lutyens Country Houses, 2001; (ed jtly) Lutyens Abroad, 2002; An Architect of Promise: George Gilbert Scott junior and the late Gothic revival, 2002; The Memorial to the Missing of the Somme, 2006; Britain's Lost Cities, 2007; articles in Arch. History, Arch. Design, Jl of RSA, etc. *Address:* 15 Belle Vue Court, Devonshire Road, SE23 3SY; *e-mail:* gavin.stamp@btopenworld.com.

STAMP, Malcolm Frederick, CBE 2002; Chief Executive, Provider Agency, NHS London, since 2007; *b* 29 Dec. 1952; *s* of Frederick and Elizabeth Stamp; *m* Linda (marr. diss.); two *d*. *Educ:* Stand Grammar Sch. Unit Gen. Manager, N Manchester HA, 1985–88; District General Manager: Crewe HA, 1988–90; Liverpool HA, 1990–92; Chief Executive: Royal Liverpool Univ. Hosps NHS Trust, 1992–94; Norfolk and Norwich Univ. Hosp. NHS Trust, 1994–2002; Addenbrooke's NHS Trust, then Cambridge Univ. Hosps NHS Foundn Trust, 2002–06; Chief Exec., Waikato Dist Health Bd, 2006–07. Mem., IMS, 1975; MIHM 1978. Hon. DCL UEA, 2000. *Publication:* Appraisal for Consultants in the NHS, 2000. *Recreations:* football, gardening, family. *Address:* NHS London, Southside, 105 Victoria Street, SW1E 6QT. *Club:* Royal Commonwealth Society.

STAMP, Terence Henry; actor and author; *b* 22 July 1938; *s* of Thomas Stamp and Ethel Esther Perrott. *Educ:* Plaistow County Grammar School; Webber-Douglas Dramatic Acad. (Amehurst Webber Meml Schol., 1958). *Films include:* Billy Budd, 1962; The Collector, 1964; Far from the Madding Crowd, 1966; Blue, 1967; Spirits of the Dead (Fellini sect.), 1967; Theorem, 1968; Superman, 1977; Meetings with Remarkable Men, 1977; Superman 2, 1978; The Hit, 1984; Legal Eagles, 1985; Wall Street, 1987; Young Guns, 1988; The Sicilian, 1988; Prince of Shadows, or Beltenebros, 1993; The Real McCoy, 1994; The Adventures of Priscilla the Queen of the Desert, 1994; Bliss, 1995; Limited Edition, 1995; Kiss the Sky, 1998; Love Walked In, 1998; The Limey, 1999; Red Planet, 2000; My Wife is an Actress, 2002; My Boss's Daughter, 2003; The Haunted Mansion, 2003; These Foolish Things, 2006; *stage:* Alfie, Morosco, NY, 1965; Dracula, Shaftesbury, 1978; Lady from the Sea, Roundhouse, 1979. Launched, with Elizabeth Buxton, Stamp Collection range of organic food, 1994. Hon. DArts East London, 1993. *Publications:* autobiography: Stamp Album, 1987; Coming Attractions, 1988; Double Feature, 1989; The Night (novel), 1992; (with Elizabeth Buxton) The Stamp Collection Cookbook, 1997. *Address:* c/o Markham & Froggatt, 4 Windmill Street, W1P 1HF. *Club:* New York Athletic (New York).

STANAGE, Rt Rev. Thomas Shaun; Warden, Community of St Michael and All Angels, Bloemfontein, since 1998; Bishop of Bloemfontein, 1982–97; *b* 6 April 1932; *s* of late Robert and Edith Clarice Stanage. *Educ:* King James I Grammar Sch., Bishop Auckland; Univ. of Oxford (MA, Hons Theology, 1956). Curate, St Faith, Great Crosby, 1958–61; Minister of Conventional District of St Andrews, Orford, 1961–63; Vicar, St Andrew, Orford, 1963–70; Rector, All Saints, Somerset West, 1970–75; Dean of Kimberley, 1975–78; Bishop Suffragan of Johannesburg, 1978–82. Liaison Bishop to Missions to Seafarers, Southern Africa. Lectr in Systematic Theol., Biblical Studies and Religious Educn, Univ. of Orange Free State, 1998–2001. Hon. DD Nashotah Theol Sem., Wisconsin, 1986. *Recreations:* flying (private pilot), music (organ, violin and piano). *Address:* Walden Lodge, 24 Hippocrene Street, Helicon Heights, Bloemfontein 9301, S Africa. *Clubs:* Bloemfontein; Good Hope Flying, Cape Aero (Cape Town).

STANBRIDGE, Ven. Leslie Cyril; Archdeacon of York, 1972–88, Archdeacon Emeritus since 1988; *b* 19 May 1920. *Educ:* Bromley County Grammar Sch., Kent; St John's Coll., Durham Univ. (MA, DipTheol). Asst Curate of Erith Parish Church, Kent, 1949–51; Tutor and Chaplain, St John's Coll., Durham, 1951–55; Vicar of St Martin's, Hull, 1955–64; Examining Chaplain to the Archbishop of York, 1962–74; Rector of Cottingham, Yorks, 1964–72; Canon of York, 1968–2000, now Emeritus; Succentor Canonicorum, 1988–2000; Rural Dean of Kingston-upon-Hull, 1970–72; Warden, York Diocesan Readers' Assoc., 1988–95. *Recreations:* walking, cycling. *Address:* 39 Lucombe Way, New Earswick, York YO32 4DS. *T:* (01904) 750812.

STANBRIDGE, Roger Andrew; Headteacher, Stratford-upon-Avon Grammar School for Girls, 1991–2005; *b* 22 June 1948; *s* of Bert and Kit Stanbridge; *m* 1972, Sandy Black; three *d. Educ:* Varndean Boys' Grammar Sch., Brighton; Hull Univ. (BSc 1969); Univ. of Newcastle upon Tyne. Hd of Sci., Moulton Sch., Northampton, 1980–87; Dep. Headteacher, Stratford-upon-Avon Grammar Sch. for Girls, 1987–91. Principal Examiner: for Univ. of Cambridge Local Exams Syndicate, 1988–; for Edexcel, 2005–. *Recreations:* overseas travel, supporter of Brighton and Hove Albion FC. *Address: e-mail:* zen79983@zen.co.uk.

STANBROOK, Clive St George Clement, OBE 1987; QC 1989; Partner, McDermott, Will & Emery/Stanbrook (formerly Stanbrook & Hooper), since 1980; *b* 10 April 1948; *s* of late Ivor Robert Stanbrook and Joan Stanbrook (*née* Clement); *m* 1971, Julia Suzanne Hillary; one *s* three *d. Educ:* Dragon Sch.; Westminster; University Coll. London. Called to the Bar, Inner Temple, 1972; called to Turks and Caicos Bar, 1986, New York Bar, 1988. Founded Stanbrook & Hooper, 1980. President: British Chamber of Commerce for Belgium and Luxembourg, 1985–87; Exec. Cttee, Overseas Countries and Territories Assoc., EU. *Publications:* Extradition: the law and practice, 1979, 2nd edn 2000; Dumping: manual of EEC rules, 1980; Dumping and Subsidies, 1982, 3rd edn (with A. P. Bentley) 1996. *Recreations:* tennis, travel. *Address:* McDermott, Will & Emery/Stanbrook, 245 Rue Père Eudore Devroye, Brussels 1150, Belgium.

STANCIOFF, Ivan; Ambassador-at-Large for Bulgaria, since 1994; *b* 1 April 1929; *s* of late Ivan Robert Stancioff and Marion (*née* Mitchell); *m* 1st, 1957, Deirdre O'Donnell (marr. diss.); two *s* two *d*; 2nd, Alexandra Lawrence. *Educ:* Georgetown Univ., Washington (BA); New York Univ. Sch. of Business. Economist, Amer. and Foreign Power Corp., 1957–60; Dir Marketing, IBM World Trade Corp., São Paulo, 1961–63; Rio, 1963–65; Paris, 1965–70; Manager, ITT, Athens, 1970; Vice-Pres., ITEL Corp., London, 1971–74; Dir, Safestore Ltd, London, 1975–77; Vice-Pres., Storage Technol. Corp., London, 1977–81; Dir, Cresta Marketing SA, Geneva, 1981–90; Advr to UDF, Sofia, 1990–91; Ambassador to UK, 1991–94; Minister of Foreign Affairs, Bulgaria, 1994–95; Director: Cresta Marketing, 1995–; Balkan Holdings plc, 2005–. Foreign Policy Advr to Pres. of Bulgaria, 1999–. Dir, Inst. for Intercultural Relations, Sofia, 1992; Chm., Karin Dom Foundn, 1995–. Mem., Sustrans, Bristol, 1989–. FLS; FRGS. Good Conduct Medal, US Army, 1956; Commander, Legion of Honour (France), 1994; Grand Cross, Rio Branco (Brazil), 2002. *Recreations:* history, gardening, travel, painting. *Address:* 28 Cresswell Place, SW10 9RB. *Club:* Annabel's.

STANCLIFFE, Rt Rev. David Staffurth; *see* Salisbury, Bishop of.

STANCLIFFE, Martin John, FSA; RIBA; Surveyor to the Fabric, St Paul's Cathedral, since 1990; *b* 28 Dec. 1944; *s* of Very Rev. Michael Staffurth Stancliffe and Barbara Elizabeth Tatlow; *m* 1979, Sara Judith Sanders; two *d. Educ:* Westminster Sch.; Magdalene Coll., Cambridge (MA, DipArch). AABC. Dir, Martin Stancliffe Architects, 1975–2004; Sen. Principal (formerly Strategy Partner), Purcell Miller Tritton, 2004–. Architect to: Lichfield Cath., 1983–2003; Southwell Minster, 1989–; Christ Church Cath., Oxford, 1990–95. Member: Exec. Cttee, Council for the Care of Churches, 1980–91; Cathedrals' Fabric Commn for England, 1991–2001; Archbishops' Commn on Cathedrals, 1992–94; Historic Bldgs and Areas Adv. Cttee, English Heritage, 1995–2001; Expert Adv. Panel on Bldgs and Land, Heritage Lottery Fund, 1997–99; Cultural Tourism Cttee, ICOMOS UK, 1997–; Fabric Adv. Cttee, York Minster, 2007–. Chairman: Cathedral Architects Assoc., 1999–2005; York Consortium for Conservation and Craftsmanship, 2005–. Trustee, York Civic Trust, 2008–. Marvin Breckinridge Patterson Lectr, Univ. of Maryland, 2000. Hon. Vis. Fellow, Dept of Archaeol., Univ. of York, 2002–. FSA 1995. *Recreations:* the baroque oboe, old buildings, sailing. *Address:* 29 Marygate, York YO30 7WH. *T:* (01904) 644001.

See also Bishop of Salisbury.

STANDAGE, Simon Andrew Thomas; violinist; *b* 8 Nov. 1941; *s* of Thomas Ralph Standage and Henrietta Florence Sugg; *m* 1964, Jennifer Ward; three *s. Educ:* Bryanston Sch.; King's Coll., Cambridge (MA). Harkness Fellow, 1967–69; Sub-leader, English Chamber Orch., 1974–78; leader and soloist, English Concert, 1973–91; Founder and Leader, Salomon String Quartet, 1981–; founded Collegium Musicum 90, 1990; Associate Dir, Acad. of Ancient Music, 1991–95. Professor of Baroque Violin: Royal Acad. of Music, 1983–; Dresdner Akademie für Alte Musik, 1993–2004. Has made numerous recordings. *Recreation:* crosswords. *Address:* 106 Hervey Road, Blackheath, SE3 8BX. *T:* (020) 8319 3372.

STANDING, John; *see* Leon, Sir J. R.

STANDRING, Prof. Susan Margaret, PhD, DSc; Professor of Anatomy, since 2007, and Head, Department of Anatomy and Human Sciences (formerly Division of Anatomy, Cell and Human Biology), since 2000, School of Biomedical and Health Sciences (formerly Guy's, King's and St Thomas' School of Biomedical Sciences), King's College London; *b* 22 Feb. 1947; *d* of William and Margaret Hall; *m* 1970, Guy Lewis Standring; two *d. Educ:* Sch. of St Clare, Penzance; Guy's Hosp. Medical Sch., Univ. of London (BSc, PhD; DSc); King's Coll. London (Postgrad. Dip. in Teacher Educn Medicine and Dentistry; FKC 2008). Reader in Experimental Neurobiology, UMDS of Guy's and St Thomas' Hosps, 1989–98; Admissions Dean for Medicine, UMDS, subseq. GKT, KCL, 1996–2002; Prof of Experimental Neurobiol., Sch. of Biomed. and Health Scis (formerly GKT Sch. of Biomed. Scis), KCL, 1998–2007. President: Peripheral Nerve Soc., 2001–03; Anatomical Soc. of GB and Ireland, 2008–; Mem., Court of Examiners, 2002–, Anatomy Develt Tutor, 2008–, RCS. Trustee, Changing Faces, 2008–. *Publications:* (ed) Gray's Anatomy, 40th edn, 2008; (as Susan Hall) over 150 papers in peer-reviewed scientific jls. *Recreations:* walking, especially in Isles of Scilly, reading. *Address:* School of Biomedical and Health Sciences, King's College London, Hodgkin Building, Guy's Campus, SE1 1UL. *T:* (020) 7848 6083; *e-mail:* susan.standring@kcl.ac.uk.

STANES, Ven. Ian Thomas; Archdeacon of Loughborough, 1992–2005; *b* 29 Jan. 1939; *s* of Sydney Stanes and Iris Stanes (*née* Hulme); *m* 1962, Sylvia Alice (*née* Drew); one *d* (one *s* decd). *Educ:* Sheffield Univ. (BSc 1962); Linacre Coll., Oxford (BA 1965; MA 1969); Wycliffe Hall, Oxford. Ordained: deacon, 1965; priest, 1966; Curate, Holy Apostles, Leicester, 1965–69; Vicar, Broom Leys, Coalville, Leicester, 1969–76; Priest Warden, Marrick Priory, Ripon, 1976–82; Willesden Area Officer for Mission, Ministry and Evangelism, London, 1982–92. Prebendary, St Paul's Cathedral, 1989–92. *Recreations:* walking, photography, theatre, singing, music, art appreciation, model and stamp collecting. *Address:* 192 Bath Road, Bradford on Avon, Wilts BA15 1SP. *T:* (01225) 309036; *e-mail:* ianstanes@surefish.co.uk.

STANESBY, Rev. Canon Derek Malcolm, PhD; Canon of St George's Chapel, Windsor, 1985–97 (Steward, 1987–94; Treasurer, 1994–97); *b* 28 March 1931; *s* of Laurence J. C. Stanesby and late Elsie L. Stanesby (*née* Stean); *m* 1958, Christine A. Payne; three *s* one *d. Educ:* Orange Hill Central School, London; Northampton Polytechnic, London; Leeds Univ. (BA Hons); Manchester Univ. (MEd, PhD); College of the Resurrection, Mirfield. GPO Radio Research Station, Dollis Hill, 1947–51; RAF (Navigator), 1951–53. Ordained, 1958; Curate: Old Lakenham, Norwich, 1958–61; St Mary, Welling, Dio. Southwark, 1961–63; Vicar, St Mark, Bury, Dio. Manchester, 1963–67; Rector, St Chad, Ladybarn, Manchester, 1967–85. Mem., Archbishop's Commn on Christian Doctrine, 1986–91. FRSA 1993. *Publications:* Science, Reason and Religion, 1985; various articles. *Recreations:* hill walking, sailing, woodwork, idling. *Address:* 32 Elizabeth Way, Uppingham, Rutland LE15 9PQ. *T:* (01572) 821298.

STANFORD, Rear Adm. Christopher David, CB 2002; Partner, Odgers Ray and Berndtson, Executive Search, since 2002; *b* 15 Feb. 1950; *s* of late Joseph Gerald Stanford and Elspeth Stanford (*née* Harrison); *m* 1972, Angela Mary, *d* of Commander Derek G. M. Gardner, VRD, RSMA; one *s* three *d. Educ:* St Paul's Sch.; Britannia RN Coll., Dartmouth; Merton Coll., Oxford (MA History and French). Joined RN 1967; served HM Ships Puma, Jupiter, Hubberston, Exmouth, Newcastle, Antrim, Brilliant, Fife; commanded: HMS Boxer, 1988–89; HMS Coventry and First Frigate Sqdn, 1993–94; Asst Dir (Ships), Directorate of Operational Requirements, 1990–93; rcds 1995; Dir, Naval Staff Duties, 1995–97; Dir, Operational Capability, 1997–98; COS to Surgeon Gen., MoD, 1999–2002. FNI (Vice Pres., 1999–2007). Gov., King Edward VII's Hosp., 2008. Freeman: City of London, 2000; Master Mariners' Co., 2000; Younger Brother, Trinity House, 2006. Chm., Combined Services Rugby Union, 2001–02; Vice President: RN Rugby Union, 1996–2002; N Dorset RFC, 1999–; Chairman: Royal Naval Lay Readers Soc., 1999–2002; Somerset and Dorset Sea Cadet Assoc., 2002–. FRSA 2003. DUniv UCE 2002. OStJ 2001. *Publications:* contribs to learned and professional jls on maritime, health and leadership issues. *Recreations:* art, Rugby, travel, maritime affairs. *Address:* Odgers Ray and Berndtson, 11 Hanover Square, W1S 1JJ. *Clubs:* Naval and Military, Woodroffe's, Hon. Society of Anchorites (Pres., 2003).

STANFORD, James Keith Edward, OBE 1999; Director General, Leonard Cheshire Foundation, 1991–98; a Vice President, Leonard Cheshire, since 2000; *b* 12 April 1937; *s* of late Lt-Col J. K. Stanford, OBE, MC, author and naturalist, and Eleanor Stanford; *m* 1964, Carol Susan Harbord; one *s* one *d. Educ:* Rugby Sch.; RMA Sandhurst. 17th/21st Lancers, 1955–64; IBM Corp., 1965–72; Industry and City, 1973–90; Chm., David Brown Corp., 1987–90; Dir, Aerospace Engrg, 1990–94. Vice-Chm., Holiday Care Service, 1991–99. March Dir, Countryside Alliance, 1999–2004. Dir, Dorset NHS Ambulance Trust, 2001–05. Chm. of Govs, Milton Abbey Sch., 2004–. *Recreations:* country activities. *Address:* Nippards Farmhouse, Whitsbury, nr Fordingbridge SP6 3QB.

See also Earl of Radnor.

STANFORD, Peter James; writer and broadcaster; *b* 23 Nov. 1961; *s* of late Reginald James Hughes Stanford and Mary Catherine (*née* Fleming); *m* 1995, Siobhan, *d* of James Cross and late Celine Cross; one *s* one *d. Educ:* St Anselm's Coll., Birkenhead; Merton Coll., Oxford (BA Hons 1983). Reporter, The Tablet, 1983–84; News Editor, 1984–88, Editor, 1988–92, The Catholic Herald. Chm., ASPIRE (Assoc. for Spinal Res., Reintegration and Rehabilitation), 1992–2001 and 2005–. Dir, CandoCo Dance Co., 1994–98 (Patron, 1998–). Dir, Frank Longford Charitable Trust, 2002–. Panellist: FutureWatch, TV, 1996; radio: The Moral Maze, 1996; Vice or Virtue, 1997; Presenter: The Mission, TV, 1997; various Radio 2 and Radio 4 documentaries, 1999–. *Publications:* (ed) Hidden Hands: child workers around the world, 1988; (with Simon Lee) Believing Bishops, 1990; (ed) The Seven Deadly Sins, 1990; (with Kate Saunders) Catholics and Sex, 1992 (televised, 1992; Bronze Medal, NY TV Fest., 1993); Cardinal Hume and the changing face of English Catholicism, 1993; Lord Longford: an authorised life, 1994; revd edn as The Outcasts' Outcast, 2003; (with Gerard Noel) The Anatomy of the Catholic Church, 1994; (with Leanda de Lisle) The Catholics and their Houses, 1995; The Devil: a biography, 1996 (televised 1998); The She-Pope: a quest for the truth behind the mystery of Pope Joan, 1998 (televised 1998); Bronwen Astor: her life and times, 2000; Heaven: a travellers' guide, 2002; Being a Dad, 2004; (ed) Why I'm Still a Catholic, 2005; (ed with Julian Filochowski) Opening Up, 2005; C. Day-Lewis: a biography, 2007; Teach Yourself Catholicism, 2008. *Recreations:* old cars, my children, north Norfolk. *Address:* c/o A. P. Watt, 20 John Street, WC1N 2DR.

STANGER, David Harry, OBE 1987; IEng; FCQI; consultant; Partner, Al Hoty-Stanger Ltd, Saudi Arabia/United Arab Emirates, since 1975; Chairman and Managing Director, David H. Stanger sprl, 1997–2000; *b* 14 Feb. 1939; *s* of Charles Harry Stanger, CBE and Florence Bessie Hepworth Stanger; *m* 1963, Jill Patricia (*née* Barnes); one *s* two *d. Educ:* Oundle Sch.; Millfield Sch. IEng (TEng 1971); FFB 1977; FCQI (FIQA 1982); MSocIS 1982; MInstRE. Served Corps of RE, 1960–66; joined R. H. Harry Stanger, 1966; Chm. and Man. Dir, Harry Stanger Ltd, 1975–90 (Sen. Partner, 1972–90); non-exec. Chm., Stanger Consultants Ltd, 1990–93. Chm., Adv. Cttee, NAMAS, 1985–87. Secretary General: Union Internationale des Laboratoires Indépendants, 1983–93 and 2001–03 (Mem. Governing Bd, 1997–; Hon. Mem., 1993–); Eur. Orgn for Testing and Certification, 1993–97. Member: Steering Cttee, NATLAS, 1981–87; Adv. Council for Calibration and Measurement, 1982–87; Council, EUROLAB, 1990–93; EQI Adv. Council, 2007–; Adv. and Technical Cttee, Dubai Accreditation Centre, 2008–; Chairman: Standards, Quality and Measurement Adv. Cttee, 1988–92; British Measurement and Testing Assoc., 1990–93; Inst. of Quality Assurance, 1990–93 (a Vice-Pres., 1986–); Adv. Bd, Brunel Centre for Manufacturing Metrology, 1991–93; ILAC Lab. Cttee, 1998–2002 (Mem., 1998–). Mem., RSA, 2006, IoD, 2007, Belgium. Pingat Peringatan, Malaysia, 1966. *Recreation:* collecting vintage wines. *Address:* Rue du Tabellion 41, 1050 Brussels, Belgium. *T:* and *Fax:* (2) 3451242; *e-mail:* dhs@dhs.be.

STANHOPE, family name of **Earl of Harrington**.

STANHOPE, Janet Anne, (Lady Stanhope); Director of Resources, Devon County Council, 2000–04; *b* 3 Oct. 1952; *d* of late Thomas Flynn and of Anne Flynn (*née* Atkinson); *m* 1975, Adm. Sir Mark Stanhope, *qv*; one *d. Educ:* Nottingham High Sch. for Girls; Somerville Coll., Oxford (MA Hons Physics). CIPFA 1978. Trainee stockbroker, Montagu, Loebl, Stanley & Co., 1974–75; trainee accountant, W Sussex CC, 1975–77; Devon County Council: various accountancy posts, 1977–93; Dep. Co. Treas., 1993–98; Dep. Dir of Resources, 1998–2000. Mem., Exeter Southernhay Rotary Club, 1994–. Lady Sponsor, RFA Cardigan Bay, 2005–; Trustee, RN and RM Charity, 2008–. *Recreations:* reading, spending time with the family, playing bridge, golf. *Address:* Following Seas, 6 Barton Close, Exton, Exeter, Devon EX3 0PE.

STANHOPE, Adm. Sir Mark, KCB 2004; OBE 1988; FNI; Commander-in-Chief Fleet and Commander Allied Maritime Component Command Northwood, since 2007; Vice-Admiral of the United Kingdom, since 2007; *b* 26 March 1952; *s* of late Frederick William Stanhope and Sheila Mary Hattemore (*née* Cutler); *m* 1975, Janet Anne Flynn (*see* J. A. Stanhope); one *d. Educ:* London Nautical Sch.; Worthing High Sch.; St Peter's Coll., Oxford (MA Hons Physics). FNI 2008. Joined Royal Navy, 1970: Commanding Officer: HMS Orpheus, 1982–84; HMS Splendid, 1987–88; Submarine Comd Course (Teacher), 1989–90; HMS London, 1991–92; Capt., Submarine Sea Trng, 1993–94; Dep. Principal Staff Officer to CDS, MoD, 1994–96; rcds 1997; CO and ADC, HMS Illustrious, 1998–2000; Dir, Operational Mgt, NATO Regl Comd N, 2000–01; on secondment to

Cabinet Office, 2002; Dep. C-in-C Fleet, 2002–04; Dep. Supreme Allied Comdr (Transformation), 2004–07. Member: RNSA; RUSI. Freeman, City of London, 1993; Liveryman, Upholders' Co., 1996. Younger Brother, Trinity House, 2003. *Publications:* contribs to Naval Rev., RUSI. *Recreations:* family life, reading, sailing. *Address:* c/o Fleet and Allied Maritime Component Command HQ Northwood, Sandy Lane, Northwood, Middx HA6 3HP. *Clubs:* Army and Navy, Royal Navy of 1765 and 1785.

STANIER, Sir Beville (Douglas), 3rd Bt *cr* 1917, of Peplow Hall, Hodnet, Salop; farmer, since 1976; *b* 20 April 1934; *o s* of Brig. Sir Alexander Stanier, 2nd Bt, DSO, MC and Dorothy Gladys Miller (*d* 1973); *S* father, 1995; *m* 1963, Shelagh Sinnott (*d* 2007); one *s* two *d*. *Educ:* Eton Coll. Joined Welsh Guards, 1952; commnd 2nd Lieut, 1953; Lieut, 1955; Captain, 1958; ADC to Governor-General of Australia, 1959–60. Stockbroker with Kitcat & Aitken, 1960–76 (Partner, 1968–76). Mem. (C), Aylesbury Vale DC, 1999– (Mem. Cabinet, 2001–). Chairman: Buckingham Constituency Cons. Assoc., 1999–2003; Oxon and Bucks Area Cons. Party, 2003–04. *Recreations:* shooting, cricket. *Heir: s* Alexander James Sinnott Stanier, *b* 10 April 1970. *Address:* Kings Close House, Whaddon, Buckinghamshire MK17 0NG. *T:* (01908) 501738. *Club:* MCC.

STANIFORTH, Martin John; non-executive Director, Local Care Direct, since 2005; *b* 11 Feb. 1953; *s* of late Trevor Staniforth and Doris Nellie Staniforth (*née* Quaife). *Educ:* Kingston Grammar Sch., Kingston upon Thames; Univ. of Newcastle upon Tyne (BA Hons Eng. Lang. and Lit.). Joined DHSS as Admin Trainee, 1975, Principal, 1985–91; Department of Health: Asst Sec., 1991–96; Hd of Corp. Affairs, NHS Exec., 1996–99; Dep. Dir of Human Resources, subseq. Workforce, 1999–2005. Mem., Registration and Conduct Cttees, Gen. Social Care Council, 2007–. Mem. Council, Leeds Civic Trust, 2006–. *Recreations:* hill walking, opera going, cricket watching. *Address:* 2 Ashwood Terrace, Leeds LS6 2EH.

STANIFORTH, Sarah Elizabeth, (Hon. Lady Porritt); Historic Properties Director, National Trust, since 2005; *b* 14 Jan. 1953; *d* of Malcolm Arthur Staniforth and Bridget Christian Salkeld Hall; *m* 1986, Hon. Sir Jonathon Porritt, *qv*; two *d*. *Educ:* St Hilda's Coll., Oxford (BA Hons); Courtauld Inst. of Art, London Univ. (Dip Conservation of Paintings). Higher Scientific Officer, Scientific Dept, Nat. Gall., 1980–85; National Trust: Advr on Paintings Conservation and Envmtl Control, 1985–2004; Head Conservator, 2002–04. Trustee, Hunterian Collection, RCS, 1997–; Westminster Abbey Fabric Comr, 1998–. Vice-Pres., Internat. Inst. for Conservation of Historic and Artistic Works, 1998–2005; Chm., Accreditation Cttee, UKIC, 2002–05; Ind. Museums Councillor, Museums Assoc., 2005–. *Publications:* (ed jtly) Durability and Change, 1994; (ed with C. Sitwell) Studies in the History of Painting Restoration, 1998; (ed jtly) National Trust Manual of Housekeeping, 2005; papers in mus. and conservation jls and conf. proc. *Recreations:* swimming, walking. *Address:* 9 Lypiatt Terrace, Lypiatt Road, Cheltenham, Glos GL50 2SX. *T:* (01242) 518218.

STANISZEWSKI, Stefan; Commander's Cross, Order of Polonia Restituta, and other orders; Ambassador of Poland to Libya, 1990–95; *b* 11 Feb. 1931; *s* of Andrzej and Katarzyna Staniszewski; *m* 1953, Wanda Szuszkiewicz; one *d*. *Educ:* Warsaw Univ. (BA Philosophy); Jagiellonian Univ. (BA Pol. Sciences). Active in students' and social organizations, 1951–58; Head of Editorial Dept, ISKRY state publishing firm, 1958–60; entered foreign service, 1960; Minister's Cabinet, Min. of Foreign Affairs, 1960–63; successively 2nd Sec., 1st Sec. and Counsellor, Polish Embassy, Paris, 1963–69; Head of West European Dept and Mem. of Minister's Council, Min. of Foreign Affairs, 1969–72; Ambassador to Sweden, 1972–77; Head of Press, Cultural and Scientific Co-operation Dept, Min. of Foreign Affairs, 1977–81; Ambassador to UK, 1981–86, and to Ireland, 1984–86; Head of Press and Information Dept, 1986–90, and spokesman, 1988–90, Polish Min. of Foreign Affairs. Commander, Légion d'Honneur, 1972; Order of the Star of the North, Sweden, 1977; Commander, Order of the Aztec Eagle, Mexico, 1979. *Recreation:* swimming. *Address:* ul. Okrąg 1 m. 51, 00415 Warsaw, Poland.

STANLEY, family name of **Earl of Derby** and **Baron Stanley of Alderley**.

STANLEY OF ALDERLEY, 8th Baron *cr* 1839 (UK); **Thomas Henry Oliver Stanley;** DL; Bt 1660; Baron Sheffield (Ire), 1783; Baron Eddisbury, 1848; Captain (retired), Coldstream Guards; Tenant Farmer of New College, Oxford, since 1954; *b* 28 Sept. 1927; *s* of Lt-Col The Hon. Oliver Hugh Stanley, DSO, JP (3rd *s* of 4th Baron) (*d* 1952), and Lady Kathleen Stanley (*d* 1977), *e d* of 5th Marquess of Bath; *S* cousin (known as Baron Sheffield), 1971; *m* 1955, Jane Barrett, *d* of Ernest George Hartley; three *s* one *d*. *Educ:* Wellington College, Berks. Coldstream Guards, 1945–52; Guards Parachute Battalion and Independent Company, 1947–50; Northamptonshire Institute of Agriculture, 1952–53. Mem., Cttee of Management, RNLI, 1981–2003; Chm., Fund Raising Cttee, RNLI, 1985–94. Governor, St Edward's Sch., Oxford, 1979–98. FRAgS 2005. DL Gwynedd, 1985. *Recreations:* sailing, ski-ing, fishing. *Heir: e s* Hon. Richard Oliver Stanley, BSc [*b* 24 April 1956; *m* 1983, Carla, *er d* of Dr K. T. C. McKenzie, Solihull; three *d* (one *s* decd)]. *Address:* Trysglwyn Fawr, Amlwch, Anglesey LL68 9RF. *T:* (01407) 830364; Rectory Farm, Stanton St John, Oxford OX9 1HF. *T:* (01865) 351214. *Clubs:* Farmers', Pratt's.

STANLEY, Lord; Edward John Robin Stanley; *b* 21 April 1998; *s* and *heir* of Earl of Derby, *qv*.

STANLEY, Colin; *see* Stanley, G. C.

STANLEY, Prof. Eric Gerald, MA (Oxford and Yale); PhD (Birmingham); FBA 1985; Rawlinson and Bosworth Professor of Anglo-Saxon in the University of Oxford, and Fellow of Pembroke College, Oxford, 1977–91; Emeritus Professor and Fellow, since 1991; *b* 19 Oct. 1923; *m* 1959, Mary Bateman, MD, FRCP; one *d*. *Educ:* Queen Elizabeth's Grammar Sch., Blackburn; University Coll., Oxford. Lectr in Eng. Lang. and Lit., Birmingham Univ., 1951–62; Reader in Eng. Lang. and Lit., 1962–64, Prof. of English, 1964–75, Univ. of London at QMC; Prof. of English, Yale Univ., 1975–76. Mem., Mediaeval Acad. of America, 1975– (Corresp. Fellow, 2008–); Corresponding Member: Fryske Akad., Netherlands, 1991–; Bavarian Acad. of Scis, 1994–. Sir Israel Gollancz Meml Lectr, British Acad., 1984. Co-Editor, 1963–2002, Adv. Ed., 2003–, Notes and Queries. Hon. DSL Univ. of Trinity Coll., Toronto; Hon. DLaws Toronto. *Publications:* (ed) The Owl and the Nightingale, 1960, 2nd edn 1972; The Search for Anglo-Saxon Paganism, 1975; A Collection of Papers with Emphasis on Old English Literature, 1987; In the Foreground: Beowulf, 1994; Die altenglische Rechtspflege, 1999; Imagining the Anglo-Saxon Past, 2000; academic articles. *Address:* Pembroke College, Oxford OX1 1DW. *Club:* Athenæum.

STANLEY, Prof. Fiona Juliet, AC 1996; MD; Director, Telethon Institute for Child Health Research, since 1990; Professor, School of Paediatrics and Child Health, University of Western Australia, since 1990; Executive Director, Australian Research Alliance for Children and Youth, since 2004 (Chief Executive Officer, 2001–04); *b* 1 Aug. 1946; *d* of Prof. Neville Stanley and Muriel MacDonald Stanley; *m* 1973, Prof. Geoffrey Shellam; two *d*. *Educ:* Univ. of Western Australia (MB BS 1970; MD 1986); LSHTM, Univ. of London (MSc 1976). FFPH (FFPHM 1989); FAFPHM 1991; FRACP 1994; FRANZCOG 1995; FASSA 1996; FAA 2002. Doctor, Princess Margaret Hosp. Aboriginal Clinic, Perth, 1972; Scientific Staff, MRC Social Medicine Unit, 1972–73, NH & MRC Fellow in Clin. Scis, 1974–75, LSHTM; vis. appt, Nat. Inst. Child Health and Human Devélt, NIH, 1976; University of Western Australia: NH & MRC Clin. Scis Res. Fellow, Unit of Clin. Epidemiology, Dept of Medicine, 1977; SMO (Child Health), Community and Child Health Services, Public Health Dept, 1978–79; Dep. Dir, 1980–88, Dir, 1988–90, NH & MRC Res. Unit in Epidemiology and Preventive Medicine. Hon. FRACGP 2004; Hon. FRCPCH 2006. Hon. DSc Murdoch, 1998; DUniv Queensland Univ. of Tech., 2001; Hon. MD Sydney, 2005. Australian of the Year, Nat. Australia Day Council, 2003. *Publications:* (ed jtly) The Epidemiology of Prematurity, 1977; (ed jtly) The Epidemiology of the Cerebral Palsies, 1984; (ed) The Role of Epidemiology and Perinatal Databases for both Research and Care, 1997; (jtly) The Cerebral Palsies: epidemiology and causal pathways, 2000; (jtly) Children of the Lucky Country?: how Australian society has turned its back on children and why children matter, 2005; papers in learned jls, reports, and chapters in books. *Recreations:* bushwalking, swimming. *Address:* Telethon Institute for Child Health Research, PO Box 855, West Perth, WA 6872, Australia. *T:* (8) 9489 7968.

STANLEY, (Geoffrey) Colin; Director General, British Printing Industries Federation, 1988–95; *b* 3 May 1937; *s* of Harold Bertram Smerdon Stanley and Ruth Mary (*née* Dunn); *m* 1962, Lesley Shadrach McWilliam; one *s* one *d*. *Educ:* Wallasey Grammar Sch. Joined Wiggins Teape, 1957: Director and General Manager: Wiggins Teape Toys & Crafts, 1976–78; Wiggins Teape Stationery Ltd, 1979–82; Dir and Manager, Wiggins Teape Paper Ltd, 1982–87; Dir, Wiggins Teape (UK) plc, 1983–85. Dir, John Howitt Gp, 1995–99. Man. Dir, Wessex Childcare Ltd, 1996–98; Chm., Wessex Children's Hospice Trust, 1997–99. Pres., Nat. Assoc. of Paper Merchants, 1986–88. Mem., Council, CBI, 1988–95 (Chm., Industrial Relns, Wages and Conditions Cttee, 1992–95; Mem., Employment Affairs Cttee, 1992–95). FRSA 1991. Freeman, City of London, 1985; Liveryman, Co. of Stationers & Newspaper Makers, 1987–. *Recreations:* golf, gardening, music, reading. *Address:* 2 Abbey Hill Close, Winchester, Hants SO23 7AZ.

STANLEY, Rev. Canon John Alexander, OBE 1999; Vicar of Huyton, since 1974; Chaplain to the Queen, 1993–2001; *b* 20 May 1931; *s* of Edward Alexander Stanley and Lucy Vida Stanley; *m* 1956, (Flora) Elaine Wilkes; three *s* two *d*. *Educ:* Birkenhead Sch.; Tyndale Hall Theol Coll., Bristol. Assistant Curate: All Saints', Preston, 1956; St Mark's, St Helens, 1960; Vicar, St Cuthbert's, Everton, Liverpool, 1963; Priest in Charge, St Saviour, Everton, 1969; Vicar, St Saviour with St Cuthbert, Everton, 1970; Area Dean of Huyton, 1989–2003; Hon. Canon of Liverpool Cathedral, 1987–. Mem., Gen. Synod, and Proctor in Convocation, 1973–2000; Chm., Diocesan House of Clergy, 1979–85; Prolocutor, York Convocation, 1990–2000. A Church Comr, 1983–99 (Mem., Bd of Govs, 1989–99); Member: Crown Appointments Commn, 1992–2000; Archbishops' Council, 1999–2000. Mem., BCC, 1984–87; Trustee, Church Urban Fund, 1987–2003. *Recreations:* golf, bees, photography. *Address:* The Vicarage, Huyton, Merseyside L36 7SA. *T:* (0151) 449 3900, *Fax:* (0151) 480 6002; *e-mail:* John.Stanley@btinternet.com.

STANLEY, John Mallalieu; Director of Legal Services A, Department of Trade and Industry, 1996–2001; *b* 30 Sept. 1941; *s* of William and Rose Margaret Stanley; *m* 1968, Christine Mary Cunningham; two *s* one *d*. *Educ:* Welwyn Garden City Grammar Sch.; Clare College, Cambridge (MA). Solicitor. Church, Adams, Tatham & Co., 1965–68; Jaques & Co., 1968–75; Department of Industry, later of Trade and Industry, 1975–2001: Under Sec. (Legal), 1989–96. *Address:* 12 Westcombe Park Road, SE3 7RB.

STANLEY, Rt Hon. Sir John (Paul), Kt 1988; PC 1984; MP (C) Tonbridge and Malling, since Feb. 1974; *b* 19 Jan. 1942; *s* of late Mr and Mrs H. Stanley; *m* 1968, Susan Elizabeth Giles; one *s* one *d* (and one *s* decd). *Educ:* Repton Sch.; Lincoln Coll., Oxford (MA). Conservative Research Dept with responsibility for Housing, 1967–68; Research Associate, Internat. Inst. for Strategic Studies, 1968–69; Rio Tinto-Zinc Corp. Ltd, 1969–79. PPS to Rt Hon. Margaret Thatcher, 1976–79; Minister of State (Minister for Housing and Construction), DoE, 1979–83; Minister of State: for the Armed Forces, MoD, 1983–87; Northern Ireland Office, 1987–88. Mem., Parly Select Cttee on Nationalised Industries, 1974, on Foreign Affairs, 1992–. Mem., NATO Parly Assembly, 2001–. Director: Fidelity Japanese Values plc, 1994–; Henderson High Income Trust plc, 1997–. Trustee, ActionAid, 1989–99. *Publication:* (jtly) The International Trade in Arms, 1972. *Recreations:* music, sailing. *Address:* House of Commons, SW1A 0AA.

STANLEY, Prof. Margaret Anne, OBE 2004; PhD; Professor of Epithelial Biology, University of Cambridge, since 2001; Fellow, Christ's College, Cambridge, since 1990; *b* 19 July 1939; *d* of Colin Campbell Coutts and Clara Coutts; *m* 1964, Philip Edward Stanley; one *s* one *d*. *Educ:* Bedford Coll., London (BSc); Univ. of Bristol (PhD 1964). Sen. Lectr in Pathol., Univ. of Adelaide, S Australia, 1974–80; Lectr in Pathol., 1980–96, Reader in Epithelial Biol., 1996–2001, Univ. of Cambridge. FMedSci 2005. *Publications:* numerous articles in peer-reviewed jls. *Recreation:* cooking. *Address:* Department of Pathology, University of Cambridge, Tennis Court Road, Cambridge CB2 1QP. *T:* (01223) 333690, *Fax:* (01223) 333346; *e-mail:* mas@mole.bio.cam.ac.uk.

STANLEY, Martin Edward; Chief Executive, Competition Commission, since 2004; *b* 1 Nov. 1948; *s* of Edward Alan and Dorothy Stanley; *m* 1971, Marilyn Joan Lewis (marr. diss. 1992); one *s*; *m* 1996, Janice Margaret Munday, *qv*; one *s* (and one *s* decd). *Educ:* Royal GS, Newcastle upon Tyne; Magdalen Coll., Oxford (BA Hons). Inland Revenue, 1971–80; Department of Trade and Industry, 1980–98: various posts, 1980–87; Head, Industry/Educn Unit, 1987–90; Principal Private Sec., 1990–92; Hd of Vehicles, Metals and Minerals Div., later Engrg Automotive and Metals Div., 1992–96; Chief Exec., Oil and Gas Projects and Supplies Office, then Infrastructure and Energy Projects Directorate, 1996–98; Dir, Better Regulation, then Regulatory Impact, Unit, Cabinet Office, 1998–2000; Chief Exec., Postal Services Commn, 2000–04. Ed., www.civilservant.org.uk, 2000–. *Publication:* How to be a Civil Servant, 2000, 2nd edn 2004. *Recreations:* walking, sailing. *Address:* Competition Commission, Victoria House, Southampton Row, WC1B 4AD. *T:* (020) 7271 0118.

STANLEY, Oliver Duncan; Chairman, 1972–97 and Director, 1972–2000, Rathbone Brothers (formerly Comprehensive Financial Services) PLC; *b* 5 June 1925; *s* of Bernard Stanley and Mabel Best; *m* 1954, Ruth Brenner, JP, BA (*d* 2002); one *s* three *d*. *Educ:* Christ Church, Oxford (MA); Harvard Univ., USA. Called to the Bar, Middle Temple, 1963. Served War, 8 Hussars, 1943–47. HM Inspector of Taxes, 1952–65; Dir, Gray Dawes Bank, 1966–72; founded Comprehensive Financial Services Gp of Cos, 1971. Chief Taxation Adviser, CLA, 1975–83 (Mem., Tax Cttee, 1983–2002). Chairman: Profile Books Ltd, 1996–2005; Esterel Ltd, 2003–; Dir, Axa Equity and Law, 1992–97. Member: Soc. of Authors, 1967–; Council of Legal Educn, 1992–96. Gov., Inns of Court Sch. of Law, 1996–99. Trustee, Age Concern Barnet, 2003–; Trustee and Chm., Barnet Capers, 2007–. *Publications:* A Guide to Taxation, 1967; Taxology, 1971; Creation and Protection of Capital, 1974; Taxation of Farmers and Landowners, 1981, 17th edn 2005; Offshore Tax Planning, 1986; Hotel Victoire (novel), 2007; 1941 (novel), 2008; contrib.

The Times and The Sunday Times, 1966–83; numerous articles in legal and agricultural periodicals. *Recreations:* music, tennis, French civilisation. *Club:* Travellers.

STANNARD, Ven. Colin Percy, TD 1966; Archdeacon of Carlisle and Residentiary Canon of Carlisle Cathedral, 1984–93, now Archdeacon and Canon Emeritus; *b* 8 Feb. 1924; *s* of Percy and Grace Adelaide Stannard; *m* 1950, Joan Callow; one *s* two *d*. *Educ:* Woodbridge School; Selwyn Coll., Cambridge (BA 1947, MA 1949); Lincoln Theological Coll. Deacon 1949, priest 1950; Curate, St James Cathedral, Bury St Edmunds, 1949–52; Priest-in-charge, St Martin's, Grimsby, 1952–55; CF (TA), 1953–67; Vicar: St James's, Barrow-in-Furness, 1955–64; St John the Baptist's, Upperby, 1964–70; Rector of Gosforth, 1970–75; RD of Calder, 1970–75; Hon. Canon of Carlisle, 1975–84; Priest-in-charge of Natland, 1975–76, Vicar, 1976–84; RD of Kendal, 1975–84. *Recreations:* walking, bringing order out of chaos—especially in gardens. *Address:* 51 Longlands Road, Carlisle, Cumbria CA3 9AE. *T:* (01228) 538584.

STANNARD, Prof. (Frank) Russell, OBE 1998; PhD; Professor of Physics, Open University, 1971–98, now Emeritus; *b* 24 Dec. 1931; *s* of Frank and Lillie Stannard; *m* 1984, Glenys Margaret; two *s* two *d*, and two step *s* (and one step *s* decd). *Educ:* University Coll. London (BSc 1953; PhD 1956; Fellow, 2000). FInstP 1973. Res. Asst, UCL, 1956–59; Res. Physicist, Radiation Lab., Berkeley, 1959–60; Lectr, UCL, 1960–69; Open University: Reader, 1968–71; Hd, Physics Dept, 1971–75 and 1977–92; Pro Vice Chancellor, 1975–77. Mem., Center of Theological Inquiry, Princeton, 1988–89. Trustee, John Templeton Foundn, 1993–99 and 2000–06. Bragg Medal, Inst. of Physics, 2000. *Publications: for adults:* Science and the Renewal of Belief, 1982; Grounds for Reasonable Belief, 1989; Doing Away with God?, 1993; Science and Wonders, 1996; The God Experiment, 1999; The New World of Mr Tompkins, 1999; God for the 21st Century, 2000; Why?, 2003; *for children:* The Time and Space of Uncle Albert, 1989; Black Holes and Uncle Albert, 1991; Here I Am!, 1992; World of 1001 Mysteries, 1993; Uncle Albert and the Quantum Quest, 1994; Our Universe, 1995; A Short History of God, Me and the Universe, 1995; Letters to Uncle Albert, 1996; More Letters to Uncle Albert, 1997; Ask Uncle Albert: 100½ tricky science questions answered, 1998; The Curious History of God, 1998; Space, Time, Rhythm and Rhyme, 1999; Lab Cats on the Move, Lab Cats Get up Steam, Lab Cats Switch On, and Lab Cats See the Light, 2001; Dr Dyer's Academy, 2002; Virtutopia, 2003; over 60 articles in jls incl. Physical Rev., Physical Rev. Letters, Nature, Physics Letters, Procs of Physical Soc., etc. *Recreations:* sculpture, attending opera, ballet and concerts, enjoying 15 grandchildren. *Address:* 21 Alwins Field, Leighton Buzzard, Beds LU7 2UF. *T:* (01525) 371106; *e-mail:* russell.stannard@tesco.net.

STANSBY, John; Chairman, UIE (UK) Ltd, 1974–2000 (UK parent company of UIE Scotland Ltd and subsidiary of Bouygues Group); Director, Bouygues UK, 1998–2000; *b* 2 July 1930; *s* of late Dumon Stansby and Vera Margaret Main; *m* 1966, Anna Maria Kruschewsky; one *d* and one step *s* one step *d*. *Educ:* Oundle; Jesus Coll., Cambridge (Schol., MA). FInstPet. Commissioned, Queen's Royal Regt, 1949; Service, 1949–50, Somaliland Scouts. Domestic Fuels Manager, Shell Mex & BP Ltd, 1955–62; Sen. Mktg Consultant, AIC Ltd, 1962–66; Dir, Rank Leisure Services, Rank Organisation, 1966–70; Dir, P&O Energy, P&OSN Co., 1970–74; Chm., Dumon Stansby & Co. Ltd, 1974–2000; Dep. Chm., London Transport Exec., 1978–80; Chairman: SAUR (UK) Ltd, 1986–89; Cementation-SAUR Water Services Ltd, 1986–88; Bouygues (UK) Ltd, 1987–2005; SAUR UK Development PLC, 1989–91; Dep. Chm., Energy Resources Ltd, 1990–92. Mem. Develt Bd, Almeida Th., 1990–2000. European Bobsleigh Champion, 1952. Chevalier de l'Ordre Nat. du Mérite (France), 1997. *Recreations:* theatre, church music, history. *Address:* Apt 5, 17 Cranley Gardens, SW7 3BD. *T:* (020) 7835 1913, *Fax:* (020) 7370 5259. *Club:* Travellers.

STANSFIELD, George Norman, CBE 1985 (OBE 1980); HM Diplomatic Service, retired; *b* 28 Feb. 1926; *s* of George Stansfield and Martha Alice (*née* Leadbetter); *m* 1947, Elizabeth Margaret Williams. *Educ:* Liscard High Sch. Served War, RAF, 1944–47. Ministries of Food and Supply, 1948–58; Private Sec. to Dir-Gen. of Armament Prodn, 1958–61; CRO, 1961; Second Secretary: Calcutta, 1962–66; Port of Spain, 1966–68; First Secretary: FCO, 1968–71; Singapore, 1971–74; Consul, Durban, 1974–78; FCO, 1978; Counsellor, and Head of Overseas Estate Dept, 1980–82; High Comr, Solomon Islands, 1982–86. Training consultant and instructor, FCO, 1986–2002. *Recreations:* sailing, wildlife. *Address:* Deryn's Wood, 80 Westfield Road, Woking, Surrey GU22 9QA. *Club:* Civil Service.

STANSFIELD, Jill; Executive Director for Communities, London Borough of Barnet, since 2006 (Director of Children's Services, 2002–06); *b* 18 Sept. 1951; *d* of Richard and Ivy Stansfield; *m* 1977, Paul Temple. *Educ:* Royal Holloway Coll., London (BA Hons Hist. 1973); Warwick Business Sch. (MPA 2005). Administrative officer, GLC and ILEA, 1973–89; Asst Dir, 1989–95, Actg Dir, 1995–96, of Educn, Lambeth BC; Strategic Dir of Learning and Develt, Milton Keynes Council, 1996–2002. Member: Barnet Coll. Corp., 2003–; Bd, Milton Keynes Gall., 2003–. *Recreations:* gardening, playing the piano, art. *Address:* Barnet Council Building 4, North London Business Park, Oakleigh Road South, N11 1NP. *T:* (020) 8359 7850, *Fax:* 0870 889 7453; *e-mail:* jill.stansfield@barnet.gov.uk.

STANSFIELD SMITH, Sir Colin, Kt 1993; CBE 1988; consultant architect; Professor of Architectural Design, University of Portsmouth (formerly Portsmouth Polytechnic), 1990–2001, now Professor Emeritus; *b* 1 Oct. 1932; *s* of Stansfield Smith and Mary (*née* Simpson); *m* 1961, Angela Jean Earnshaw; one *s* one *d*. *Educ:* William Hulme's Grammar Sch., Manchester; Cambridge Univ. Sch. of Architecture (MA, DipArch). ARIBA. Schools Div., LCC, 1958–60; Sen. Asst then Associate Partner, Emberton Frank & Tardrew, Architects, 1960–65; Partner, Emberton Tardrew & Partners, 1965–71; Dep. County Architect, Cheshire CC, 1971–73; County Architect, Hants CC, 1973–92. Mem., Royal Fine Art Commn, 1997–99. RIBA Royal Gold Medal, 1991. *Publications:* Hampshire Architecture (1974–1984), 1985; Schools of Thought, Hampshire Architecture (1974–1991), 1991; articles in Architects' Jl and Architectural Review. *Recreations:* golf, painting. *Address:* 8 Christchurch Road, Winchester, Hants SO23 9SR. *T:* (01962) 851970. *Club:* Hockley Golf (Twyford, Hants).

STANSGATE, Viscountcy of (*cr* 1942, of Stansgate); title disclaimed by 2nd Viscount (*see* Benn, Rt Hon. Tony).

STANTON, Alan William, RDI 2005; RIBA; Director, Stanton Williams Architects, since 1985; *b* 19 April 1944; *s* of William and Irene Stanton; *m* 1st, 1967, Marilyn Tindall (marr. diss. 1983); one *d*; *m* 2nd, 1985, Wendy Robin; one *d*. *Educ:* Architectural Assoc., London (AA Dip. Hons); Univ. of California, Los Angeles (MArch). RIBA 1979. Architect: with Norman Foster, 1967–68; Centre Pompidou, Paris (Piano & Rogers), 1970–77; in private practice, 1978–85 (projects in Paris, Italy and London); in partnership with Paul Williams, 1985–: award-winning projects in UK, Switzerland and Italy include: Casa Fontana, Lugano, 2000; Wellcome Trust Millennium Seed Bank, Sussex, 2000; Whitby Abbey Mus. and Visitor Centre, 2002; Tower Hill Environs, London, 2004; Compton Verney Art Gall., 2004. Lectr, AA, 1978–81. Mem., Design Rev. Panel, CABE, 2001–05. Mem. Council and Vice Pres., AA, 2000–04. Has lectured in Europe and USA. FRSA 1993. SADG Medal 1967. *Publications:* numerous contribs to architectural books and jls. *Address:* Stanton Williams, Diespeker Wharf, 36 Graham Street, N1 8GJ. *T:* (020) 7880 6400, *Fax:* (020) 7880 6401; *e-mail:* info@stantonwilliams.com.

STANTON, David, CB 2000; Director (Grade 3), Analytical Services Division, Department for Work and Pensions (formerly Department of Social Security), 1992–2002; *b* 5 Nov. 1942; *s* of Frederick Charles Patrick Stanton and Ethel (*née* Cout); *m* 1967, Isobel Joan Blair; one *s* one *d*. *Educ:* Bishops Stortford Coll.; Worcester Coll., Oxford (BA PPE 1965); LSE (MSc(Econ) 1970). ODI/Nuffield Fellow, Govt of Uganda, 1965–67; Lectr, Brunel Univ., 1967–70; Economic Adviser: Min. of Transport, 1970; Min. of Housing, then DoE, 1971–74; HM Treasury, 1974–75; Senior Economic Adviser: seconded to Hong Kong Govt, 1975–77; also Head of Unit for Manpower Studies, Dept of Employment, 1977–81; Econs Br., Dept of Employment, 1981–83; also Dir, Employment Market Res. Unit, 1983–87; Chief Economist (Grade 3), Dept of Employment, 1988–92. *Recreations:* people, dogs and other animals, singing. *Address:* 1 Darell Road, Richmond, Surrey TW9 4LF.

STANTON, David Leslie; Chairman of Trustees, UNICEF UK, since 2004; *b* 29 April 1943; *s* of Leslie Stanton and C. Mary Stanton (*née* Staynes); *m* 1989, Rosemary Jane Brown; one *d*. *Educ:* Bootham Sch., York; Balliol Coll., Oxford (BA Hons). Asst Principal, ODM, 1965–69; SSRC Sen. Scholarship, Oxford Univ., 1969–71; Principal, ODA, 1971–75; First Sec., Office of UK Permanent Rep. to EC, 1975–77; Mem., Bd of Dirs, Asian Develt Bank, 1979–82; Head of Dept, ODA, 1982–92; Advr, Finance and Admin, EBRD, 1990–91 (on secondment); Mem. Bd of Dirs, World Bank Gp, 1992–97; UK Ambassador and Perm. Delegate to UNESCO, 1997–2003. Mem., Exec. Bd, 1997–2003, Chm., Finance and Admin. Commn, 2000–01, UNESCO. Chm., Campaign for Nubia and Cairo Museums, 2002–03. Vice Chair of Govs, Canonbury Sch., 2003–06. *Recreations:* mountaineering, ski-ing, painting. *Address:* UNICEF UK, UNICEF House, Great Sutton Street, EC1V 0DU.

STANTON, Prof. Graham Norman, PhD; Lady Margaret's Professor of Divinity, 1998–2007, now Emeritus, and Chairman, Faculty Board of Divinity, 2001–03, University of Cambridge; Fellow of Fitzwilliam College, Cambridge, 1998–2007; *b* 9 July 1940; *s* of Norman Schofield Stanton and Gladys Jean Stanton (*née* McGregor); *m* 1965, (Valerie) Esther Douglas, MA; two *s* one *d*. *Educ:* Univ. of Otago, NZ (BA 1960; MA 1961; BD 1964); Fitzwilliam Coll., Cambridge (PhD 1969). Temp. Lectr, Princeton Theological Seminary, 1969; Naden Res. Student, St John's Coll., Cambridge, 1969–70; King's College, London: Lectr in New Testament Studies, 1970–77; Prof. of New Testament Studies, 1977–98; Head of Department: Biblical Studies, 1982–88; Theology and Religious Studies, 1996–98. Gresham Prof. of Divinity, 1982–86. Humboldt Stiftung Res. Fellow, Tübingen, 1974; lectures on NT and Early Christianity, in Australia, NZ, Singapore, Ireland, Canada, Finland, Netherlands, Switzerland, Belgium, Israel, US and UK. Chm., British SNTS, 1989–92; Pres., SNTS, 1996–97 (Sec., 1976–82). FKC 1996. Hon. DD Otago, 2000. Burkitt Medal for Biblical Studies, British Acad., 2006. Editor: New Testament Studies, 1982–90; SNTS Monograph Series, 1982–91; Gen. Editor, International Critical Commentaries, 1984–2008. *Publications:* Jesus of Nazareth in New Testament Preaching, 1974, repr. 2004; (ed) The Interpretation of Matthew, 1983, 2nd edn 1994; The Gospels and Jesus, 1989 (trans. Japanese and Korean), 2nd edn 2002; A Gospel for a New People: studies in Matthew, 1992; (ed jtly) Resurrection, 1994; Gospel Truth? new light on Jesus and the Gospels, 1995 (trans. French, Dutch, Italian and Spanish); (ed jtly) Tolerance and Intolerance in Early Judaism and Christianity, 1998; (ed jtly) Reading Texts, Seeking Wisdom: scripture and theology, 2003; (jtly) Lady Margaret Beaufort and her Professors of Divinity at Cambridge, 2003; Jesus and Gospel, 2004 (trans. French, Italian and Spanish); (ed jtly) The Holy Spirit and Christian Origins, 2004; *festschrift:* The Written Gospel, ed M. Bockmuehl and D. A. Hogner, 2008; contrib. learned jls and symposia in UK, Europe and USA. *Recreations:* walking, music, cricket, gardening. *Address:* 11 Dane Drive, Cambridge CB3 9LP. *T:* (01223) 740560; *e-mail:* gns23@cam.ac.uk.

STANTON, Rev. John Maurice, MA; Rector of Chesham Bois, 1973–83; *b* 29 Aug. 1918; *s* of Frederick William Stanton, MInstCE and Maude Lozel (*née* Cole); *m* 1947, Helen Winifred (*née* Bowden); one *s* two *d*. *Educ:* King's School, Rochester; University College, Oxford (Gunsley Exhibnr; 2nd Class Hons, Final Hon. Sch. of Nat. Science, 1947; MA 1947). Commissioned Royal Artillery, 1940, 92nd Field Regt, RA, 1940–43. Inter Services Liaison Detachment, Central Med. Force, 1943–46. Assistant Master, Tonbridge School, 1947–59; Headmaster, Blundell's School, 1959–71; Curate, St Matthew's, Exeter, 1972. Ordained Deacon, 1952; Priest, 1953. Sec., Oxford Diocesan Bd of Patronage, 1984–90. *Recreations:* water colour painting, gardening. *Address:* 16 Emden House, Barton Lane, Headington, Oxford OX3 9JU. *T:* (01865) 765206.

STANTON, Lyndon, PhD; non-executive Director: Environment Agency, since 2002; Nuclear Decommissioning Authority, since 2004; *b* 22 Dec. 1942; *s* of late Joseph Reginald Stanton and of Violet Hazel Stanton (*née* Sears); *m* 1964, Carol Ann Smith; two *d*. *Educ:* Newport High Sch. for Boys; Univ. of Wales (BSc 1st cl. Hons; PhD); Emmanuel Coll., Cambridge (Salters' Res. Fellowship). Various tech. and commercial appts, ICI Ltd, UK and Brussels, 1969–79; Arco Chemical Europe: Gen. Manager, Sales and Mktg, 1979–81; Manager, Mergers and Acquisitions, 1981–83; Business Manager, Urethanes, 1983–88; Dir of Business Develt, 1988–91; Vice Pres., Business Mgt, 1991–94; Pres. and Chief Exec., Arco Chemical Europe, 1994–98, subseq. Lyondell Chemical Europe, 1998–2000. Chm., Industry Cttee, and Southern Reg. Adv. Panel, EA, 2002–. Trustee: Prince of Wales's Phoenix Trust, 1996–2004 (Chm., 2003–04); Earthwatch Europe, 1997–2002; Churches Conservation Trust, 1999–2005 (Dep. Chm., 2001–05); Norden Farm Centre for Arts, 2002–. Liveryman, Horners' Co., 2000– (Mem., Ct of Assts, 2004–). *Publications:* scientific papers on nonlinear optics, scattering and atomic and molecular physics in learned jls, various business pubns and speeches in conf. procs. *Recreations:* water sports (esp. scuba diving), collecting antique furniture and antiquarian scientific books, photography, music. *Address:* Broadley, 11 Woodlands Ride, Ascot, Berks SL5 9HP. *T:* (01344) 626904, *Fax:* (01344) 627045; *e-mail:* lyndon.stanton@btinternet.com. *Club:* Athenæum.

STANTON, Prof. Stuart Lawrence Richard, FRCS, FRCSE, FRCOG; Professor of Pelvic Surgery and Urogynaecology, St George's Hospital Medical School, 1997–2003, now Emeritus Professor; Consultant Gynaecologist and Director of Urogynaecology Unit, St George's Hospital, 1984–2003; *b* 24 Oct. 1938; *s* of Michael Arthur Stanton and Sarah (*née* Joseph); *m* 1965, Anne Frances Goldsmith (marr. diss. 1991); three *d*; *m* 1991, Julia Heller; one *s* one *d*. *Educ:* City of London Sch.; London Hosp. Med. Sch. (MB BS 1961). FRCS 1966; FRCSE 1966; FRCOG 1987. Surgical Registrar, Royal Masonic Hosp., 1964–65; SHO, Queen Charlotte's Hosp., 1967; Res. Registrar, Inst. of Urology, London, 1971–72; Sen. Registrar, Dept of Obstetrics and Gynaecology, St George's Hosp., London, 1972–74; Consultant Obstetrician and Gynaecologist, St Helier Hosp., 1974–84. Lectures: William Blair Bell Meml, 1974, William Meredith Fletcher Shaw, 1996, RCOG; Victor Bonney, RCS, 1984; J. Marion Sims, Amer. Urogynecologic Soc.,

1995. Pres., British Soc. of Urogynaecology, 2003–. FRSocMed 1975. Hon. FRANZCOG 2000. *Publications:* (ed jtly) Surgery of Female Incontinence, 1980, 2nd edn 1986; (ed) The Principles of Gynaecological Surgery, 1992; (ed jtly) Gynaecology, 2nd edn 1997, 3rd edn 2002; (ed jtly) Clinical Urogynaecology, 1999. *Recreations:* family, photography, modern ceramics, biographies, music. *Address:* Flat 10, 43 Wimpole Street, W1G 8EA. *T:* (020) 7486 0677; 1 Church Hill, SW19 7BN.

STAPELY, Sue; solicitor; independent strategic communications counsel, since 2001; *b* 11 July 1946; *d* of Stanley Sly and Kathleen MacIvor; two *s. Educ:* Kingston Univ. (LLB Hons). Production posts, BBC TV, 1966–73; Manager, various CABx, 1973–83; Partner, Heald Nickinson (solicitors), 1985–89; Hd of PR, Law Soc., 1989–96 (Mem., 1989–); Dir, Fishburn Hedges, 1996–2001. Contested (SDP) Chertsey and Walton, 1987. Mem., Nat. Exec. Cttee, SDP, 1986–88; Chm., Women for Social Democracy, 1987–88; Founding Nat. Chm., 300 Group, 1986–88. Member Board: SW Thames RHA, 1993–94; London Ambulance Service, 1993–94; Countryside Agency, 2000–03; LAMDA, 1998–; Spare Tyre Theatre Co., 1999–; Brighton Fest., 2006–; Media Standards Trust, 2007–; Mem. Develt Council, Royal Court Theatre, 1998–2006. Mem. Bd, Dignity in Dying (formerly Voluntary Euthanasia Soc.), 2004–06. Trustee, Solicitors' Pro Bono Gp. FRSA 1994; FCIPR (FIPR 2002). *Publication:* Media Relations for Lawyers, 1994, 2nd edn 2003. *Recreations:* conversation, travel, theatre, fast cars. *Address:* 40 Cumberland Street, SW1V 4LX; Star Cottage, Little Compton, Glos GL56 0RY.

STAPLE, George Warren, CB 1996; Consultant, Clifford Chance, since 2001 (Partner, 1987–92 and 1997–2001); Director, Serious Fraud Office, 1992–97; *b* 13 Sept. 1940; *s* of late Kenneth Harry Staple and Betty Mary Staple; *m* 1968, Olivia Deirdre Lowry; two *s* two *d. Educ:* Haileybury. Solicitor, admitted 1964. Associate with Condon and Forsyth, NY, 1963; Asst Solicitor, 1964–67, Partner, 1967–87, Clifford-Turner & Co. Legal Assessor, Disciplinary Cttee, Stock Exchange, 1978–92; DTI Inspector, Consolidated Gold Fields, 1986, Aldermanbury Trust, 1988; a Chairman, Authorisation and Disciplinary Tribunals: of The Securities Assoc., 1987–91; of Securities and Futures Authy, 1991–92; Member: Commercial Court Cttee, 1977–92; Law Adv. Cttee, British Council, 1998–2001; Sen. Salaries Review Body, 2000–04; Tribunal Panel, Accountancy and Actuarial Discipline Bd, 2005–; Chm., Review Bd for Govt Contracts, 2002–. Mem. Council, Law Soc., 1986–2000 (Treas., 1989–92). Trustee, Royal Humane Soc., 2007–. Gov., City of London Polytechnic, subseq. London Guildhall Univ., 1982–94; Chm. Govs, Haileybury, 2001–. FCIArb 1986. Hon. QC 1997; Hon. Bencher, Inner Temple, 2000. *Recreations:* cricket, walking, gardening. *Address:* Clifford Chance, 10 Upper Bank Street, E14 5JJ. *Clubs:* Brooks's, City of London, MCC.

See also W. P. Staple.

STAPLE, William Philip; Chief Executive, Hanson Westhouse Ltd (formerly Managing Partner, Westhouse Securities LLP), since 2005; *b* 28 Sept. 1947; *s* of late Kenneth Harry Staple and Betty Mary Staple (*née* Lemon); *m* 1977, Jennifer Frances Walker (marr. diss. 1986); one *s* one *d. Educ:* Haileybury; Coll. of Law. Called to the Bar, Inner Temple, 1971; Executive at Cazenove, 1972–81; N. M. Rothschild and Sons Ltd: Asst Dir, 1981–86; Dir, 1986–94 and 1996–99; Dir Gen., Takeover Panel, 1994–96; Man. Dir, Benfield Advisory, 1999–2001; Dir, Corporate Finance, Brown, Shipley & Co. Ltd, 2001–04. *Recreations:* various sports, theatre, reading. *Address:* (office) 1 Angel Court, EC2R 7HJ. *Clubs:* White's, City of London.

See also G. W. Staple.

STAPLEFORD, Sally Anne, OBE 1999; President, National Ice Skating Association of UK Ltd, 1995–2006; *b* 7 July 1945; *d* of Richard Harvey Stapleford and Alice Elizabeth Stapleford. *Educ:* Streatham Hill High Sch.; Clapham High Sch.; private tutor. British Jun. Ice Skating Champion, 1961; Southern Regl Sen. Ice Skating Champion, 1961–63; Gold Medal: Britain, and Canada, 1961; America, 1962; British Sen. Ice Skating Champion, 1963–68; competed in: European Championships, 1963–68 (Silver Medal, 1965); World Championships, 1964–68; Winter Olympics, 1964, 1968; won Edinburgh Internat. Trophy, 1968. Nat. judge and referee, 1968–2006; internat. judge and referee, 1972–2003; National Ice Skating Association (formerly National Skating Association): Mem., Governing Body, 1970–; Chm., Ice Figure Cttee, 1989–94; Vice-Chm., Fedn of Ice Skating, 1990; Technical Orgnr, internat. figure skating events in UK; Mem., 1988–92, Chm., 1992–2002, Figure Skating Technical Cttee, Internat. Skating Union. *Address:* Flat 3, St Valery's, 54 Beulah Hill, Upper Norwood, SE19 3ER. *T:* (020) 8771 0778.

STAPLES, Brian Lynn; Chairman: Pendle (UK) Ltd, since 2003; Effective Solutions Group Ltd, since 2003; Scottish Biopower, since 2004; Scottish Resources Group, since 2005; Director and Chief Executive, Conversion Technologies Ltd, since 2003; *b* 6 April 1945; *s* of Stanley Holt Staples and Catherine Emma Annie Staples (*née* Walding); *m* 1st, 1965; one *d*; 2nd, 1973; one *s* two *d*; 3rd, 1999, Anne-Marie Smith; two *s. Educ:* Sweyne Grammar Sch., Rayleigh. Joined Tarmac Group, 1964; Chief Executive: Tarmac Construction, 1991–94; United Utilities Plc (formerly North West Water Gp), 1994–97; Amey PLC, 1997–2003. Non-exec. Dir, Mining Scotland Gp, 2004–; Dep. Chm., Mining (Scotland) Ltd, 2006–. *Recreations:* Rugby, music, theatre. *Address:* Pendle House, Castle Hill, Prestbury, Cheshire SK10 4AR.

STAPLES, (Hubert Anthony) Justin, CMG 1981; HM Diplomatic Service, retired; Ambassador to Finland, 1986–89; *b* 14 Nov. 1929; *s* of late Francis Hammond Staples, formerly ICS, and Catherine Margaret Mary Pownall; *m* 1962, Susan Angela Collingwood Carter; one *s* one *d. Educ:* Downside; Oriel Coll., Oxford. Served in RAF 1952–54 (Pilot Officer). Entered Foreign (later Diplomatic) Service, 1954; 3rd Sec., Bangkok, 1955; Foreign Office, 1959; 1st Sec., Berlin (Dep. Political Adviser), 1962; Vientiane, 1965 (acted as Chargé d'Affaires in 1966 and 1967); transf. to FO and seconded to Cabinet Office, 1968; Counsellor, UK Delegn to NATO, Brussels, 1971; Counsellor and Consul-General, Bangkok, 1974 (acted as Chargé d'affaires, 1975 and 1977); Counsellor, Dublin, 1978–81; Ambassador to Thailand, 1981–86 and concurrently to Laos, 1985–86. Pres., Anglo-Finnish Soc., 1993–. Order of the Lion (Finland), 2003. *Recreation:* golf. *Address:* 48 Crescent Road, Kingston, Surrey KT2 7RF. *Clubs:* Travellers (Chm., 2003–06); Roehampton; Royal Bangkok Sports (Bangkok).

STAPLES, Sir Richard Molesworth, 17th Bt *cr* 1628, of Lissan, co. Tyrone; *b* 11 June 1914; 3rd *s* of Thomas Staples and Mary Ussher Staples (*née* Greer); *S* brother, 1999; *m* 1954, Marjory Charlotte (*née* Jefcoate) (*d* 1998). *Educ:* St Andrew's Coll., Dublin. RAF, 1940–52 (Burma Star, 1943); RNZAF, 1952–59. Teachers' Trng Coll., Christchurch, NZ, 1959–74. *Publications:* John Cain Mole, Airman, WW2, 1998; A Wild Gosling's Footprints, 2008. *Recreations:* travel, reading, gardening, writing, watching tennis on TV. *Club:* Union Jack.

STAPLETON, Air Vice-Marshal Deryck Cameron, CB 1960; CBE 1948; DFC; AFC; psa; *b* 15 Jan. 1918; *s* of John Rouse Stapleton, OBE, Sarnia, Natal; *m* 1942, Ethleen Joan Clifford, *d* of late Sir Cuthbert William Whiteside. *Educ:* King Edward VI Sch., Totnes. Joined RAF, 1936; served Transjordan and Palestine (AFC), 1937–39; War of 1939–45 (DFC). Middle East, N Africa, Italy. Asst Sec. (Air), War Cabinet Offices, 1945–46; Secretary, Chiefs of Staff Cttee, Ministry of Defence, 1947–49; OC RAF, Odiham, 1949–51; subsequently, Plans, Fighter Comd HQ and Ops at AFCENT Fontainebleau; then OC, RAF, Oldenburg (Germany); Plans, Bomber Comd HQ, 1957–60; Air Ministry, 1960–62; Dir, Defence Plans, Min. of Defence, 1963–64; AOC No 1 Group, RAF Bomber Command, 1964–66; Comdt, RAF Staff Coll., Bracknell, 1966–68. BAC Area Manager, Libya, 1969–70; BAC Rep. CENTO Area, Tehran, later BAe Chief Exec. Iran, and Man. Dir, Irano-British Dynamics Co. Iran, 1970–79; Rep. BAe, Beijing, China, and Chm., British Cos Assoc., Beijing, 1979–83. Associate Fellow, British Interplanetary Soc., 1960. *Publication:* (jtly) Winged Promises, 1996. *Recreations:* most sports.

STAPLETON, Guy, CB 1995; Chief Executive, Intervention Board Executive Agency (formerly Intervention Board for Agricultural Produce), 1986–95; *b* 10 Nov. 1935; *s* of William Algernon Swann Stapleton and Joan Denise Stapleton (*née* Wilson). *Educ:* Malvern Coll. Clerical Officer, Min. of Transport and Civil Aviation, 1954–58; Exec. Officer, 1958; transf. to Min. of Aviation, 1959; Civil Aviation Asst, British Embassy, Rome, 1960–63; Private Sec. to Controller of National Air Traffic Control Services, 1963–65; Asst Principal, MAFF, 1965; Private Sec. to Jt Parly Sec., 1967–68; Principal, 1968; Asst Sec., 1973; Dept of Prices and Consumer Protection, 1974–76; Under Sec., 1981; European Secretariat, Cabinet Office, 1982–85; Dir of Establishments, MAFF, 1985–86. *Publications:* A Walk of Verse, 1961; (compiled) Poet's England: 2, Gloucestershire, 1977, 2nd edn 1982; 4, Avon and Somerset, 1981; 7, Devon, 1986; 9, Hertfordshire, 1988; 12, Leicestershire and Rutland, 1992; 13, Nottinghamshire, 1993; 19, Dorset, 1996; Vale of Moreton Churches, 1989, revd edn 2002; (ed) Memories of Moreton, 1989; Four Shire Memories, 1992; Moreton & Batsford Roll of Honour, 2000; History of Moreton-in-Marsh Hospital, 2001. *Recreations:* local and family history, topographical verse. *Club:* Royal Over-Seas League.

STAPLETON, Very Rev. Henry Edward Champneys; Dean of Carlisle, 1988–98; *b* 17 June 1932; *s* of Edward Parker Stapleton and Frances Mary Champneys; *m* 1964, Mary Deborah Sapwell; two *d. Educ:* Lancing College; Pembroke Coll., Cambridge (BA 1954, MA 1958); Ely Theological Coll. Deacon 1956, priest 1957, York; Assistant Curate: St Olave with St Giles, 1956–59; Pocklington, 1959–61; Vicar of Seaton Ross with Everingham, Harswell and Bielby, 1961–67; RD of Weighton, 1966–67; Rector of Skelton, 1967–75; Vicar of Wroxham with Hoveton, 1975–81; Priest in Charge of Belaugh, 1976–81, with Hoveton St Peter, 1979–81; Canon Residentiary and Precentor of Rochester Cathedral, 1981–88; Warden of Readers, 1981–88. Church Comr, 1993–98; Member: Council for the Care of Churches, 1965–91; Churches Conservation Trust (formerly Redundant Churches Fund), 1976–98; Royal Commn on Historical Manuscripts, 1992–2002. Chm., Incorp. Church Building Soc., 2002–. Trustee, Nat. Churches Trust (formerly Historic Churches Preservation Trust), 1983–. Member: Liby Cttee, Lambeth Palace, 1999–2006; Archbishops' Adv. Panel for Archives and Libraries, 2006–. Fellow, Woodard Corp., 1990–2002. FSA 1974. Editor, Cathedral, 1976–82. Hon. Fellow, Univ. of Northumbria, Newcastle, 1995. *Publications:* Skelton Village, 1971; Heirs without Title, 1974; The Skilful Master Builder, 1975; The Model Working Parson, 1976; (ed and contrib.) Churchyards Handbook, 2nd edn 1976, 3rd edn 1988; articles in Churchscape and other ecclesiastical jls. *Recreations:* the writings of R. H. Benson, genealogy, visiting churches, second-hand bookshops. *Address:* Rockland House, 20 Marsh Gardens, Honley, Holmfirth, W Yorks HD9 6AF. *T:* (01484) 666629.

STAPLETON, Nigel John; Chairman, Postal Services Commission, since 2004; *b* 1 Nov. 1946; *s* of Frederick Ernest John Stapleton and Katie Margaret Stapleton (*née* Tyson); *m* 1982, Johanna Augusta Molhoek; one *s* one *d. Educ:* City of London Sch.; Fitzwilliam Coll., Cambridge (MA; Hon. Fellow 1998). Planning, finance and gen. mgt positions, incl. Vice Pres., Finance, Unilever United States Inc., Unilever plc, 1968–86; Reed International plc: Dir, 1986–99; Finance Dir, 1986–96; Dep. Chm., 1994–97; Chm., 1997–99; Co-Chm., 1996–98, Co-Chief Exec., 1998–99, Reed Elsevier plc; Chairman: Veronis, Suhler Internat. Ltd, 1999–2002; Uniq plc, 2001–06. Non-executive Director: Allied Domecq plc, 1992–99; Marconi plc (formerly GEC), 1997–2002; Axa UK (formerly Sun Life and Provincial Hldgs) plc, 1999–2002; Reliance Security Gp plc, 2002–. Dir, London Stock Exchange, 2001–. Trustee, Royal Opera House Trust, 1999–2001. *Recreations:* theatre, opera, travel, tennis. *Address:* Postal Services Commission, Hercules House, 6 Hercules Road, SE1 7DB. *T:* (020) 7593 2102, *Fax:* (020) 7593 2142; *e-mail:* Nigel.Stapleton@psc.gov.uk. *Club:* Oxford and Cambridge.

STAPLETON, Prof. Richard Christopher, PhD; Professor of Finance (part-time), University of Manchester, since 2003; *b* 11 Oct. 1942; *s* of Leonard Stapleton and Rosamund Kathleen May Stapleton; *m* 1968, Linda Cairns; one *s* one *d. Educ:* Univ. of Sheffield (BAEcon, PhD Business Studies); Open Univ. (BA Maths). Lectr in Business Finance, Sheffield Univ., 1965–73; Asst Prof. of Finance, New York Univ., 1973–76; Sen. Res. Fellow, 1976–77, Nat. West. Bank Prof. of Business Finance, 1977–86, Manchester Business Sch., Univ. of Manchester; Fellow, Churchill Coll., Cambridge, 1986–89; Wolfson Prof. of Finance, Lancaster Univ., 1989–98; Prof. of Finance, Strathclyde Univ., 1998–2003. Hon. MBA Manchester, 1980. *Publications:* The Theory of Corporate Finance, 1970; International Tax Systems and Financing Policy, 1978; Capital Markets and Corporate Financial Decisions, 1980; contrib. Econ. Jl, Jl of Finance, Jl of Financial Econs, Qly Jl of Econs. *Recreations:* running, golf, reading, travel. *Address:* Department of Accounting and Finance, Manchester Business School, University of Manchester, Manchester M13 9PL.

STAPLETON-COTTON, family name of **Viscount Combermere**.

STARK, David; *see* Stark, J. D. S.

STARK, George Robert, PhD; FRS 1990; Distinguished Scientist, Lerner Research Institute, Cleveland Clinic Foundation, since 2002 (Chairman, 1992–2002); *b* 4 July 1933; *s* of Jack and Florence Stark; *m* 1956, Mary Beck; one *s* one *d. Educ:* Columbia College, NY (BA 1955); Columbia Univ., NY (Chemistry; PhD 1959). Asst Prof., Rockefeller Univ., 1961; Stanford University: Asst Prof., 1963; Associate Prof., 1966; Prof. of Biochemistry, 1971; ICRF, 1983–92 (Associate Dir of Res., 1989–92). Member: European Molecular Biol. Orgn, 1985; NAS, USA, 1987; Inst. of Medicine, USA, 2002. *Publications:* contribs to scientific jls. *Recreations:* sports, stamps, books, records. *Address:* Cleveland Clinic Foundation, 9500 Euclid Avenue, Cleveland, OH 44195, USA. *T:* (216) 4443900, *Fax:* (216) 4443279.

STARK, (John) David (Sinclair), CEng; Chairman, Norcros Group (Trustee) Ltd, since 2005 (Director, since 1999); *b* 16 April 1939; *s* of John and Bertha Stark; *m* 1964, Pamela Margaret Reed; one *s* one *d. Educ:* St Bees Sch., Cumberland; Leeds Univ. (BSc). CEng, MIET (MIEE 1966). GEC plc, 1960–62; Morgan Crucible plc, 1962–76; Bestobell plc, 1976–81; Man. Dir, Bestobell Australia Ltd, 1981–84; Divl Chief Exec., Unitech plc, 1984–85; Divl Dir, 1985–86, Dir, 1986–97, Tomkins plc; Chm., Glentay, subseq. Brauer Technologies, Ltd, 1997–2004; Dir, Norcros plc, 1997–99. Non-exec. Dir, Royal Mint,

2000–04 (Chm., 2002–04). Mem., Monopolies and Mergers, subseq. Competition, Commn, 1998–2005. Gov., Esher Church Sch., 1998–2006. *Recreations:* inland waterways, opera, amateur dramatics. *Address:* Tara, 15 Copsem Drive, Esher, Surrey KT10 9HD. *T:* (01372) 466781.

STARK, Jürgen; Member, Executive Board, European Central Bank, since 2006; *b* 31 May 1948. *Educ:* Univ. of Hohenheim (first degree in econs 1973; DEc 1975); Eberhard Karls Univ., Tübingen. Res. Asst, Univ. of Hohenheim, 1973–78; Official, Econ. Policy Dept, Min. of Econs, Germany, 1978–88; First Sec., Perm. Repn of Fed. Rep. of Germany to GATT, Geneva, 1982–83; Hd of Div., For. Trade and Payments, Money and For. Currency, Financial Mkts, Federal Chancellery, 1988–92; Ministry of Finance: Dep. Hd of Dept, Nat. Monetary Policy, Capital Mkt Policy, Germany as Financial Centre, Borrowing, 1992; Hd of Dept, Internat. Monetary and Financial Relns, Financial Relns in EC, 1993–94; State Sec. and Personal Rep. of Federal Chancellor in preps for G7/G8 Econ. Summits, 1995–98; Vice Pres., Deutsche Bundesbank, 1998–2006. Hon. Prof., Faculty of Econs, Eberhard Karls Univ., Tübingen, 2005–. Alternate Gov. and Delegate for Germany to IMF, 1995–2006; Member: Monetary Cttee, 1995–98, Econ. and Financial Cttee, 1999–, EU; G7 and G10 Deputies, 1995–2006, G20 Deputies, 1999–2006; Internat. Relns Cttee, ESCB, 1998–2006; Cttee on Global Financial System, 1998–2006; Financial Stability Forum, 1999–2006. Member Supervisory Board: Deutsche Telekom AG, 1995–98; Deutsche Bahn AG, 1995–98; German Investment and Develt Corp., 1997–98; Dep. Mem., Bd of Dirs, BIS, 1998–2006. Dep. Chm., Ifo Inst., Munich, 1999–; Chm., Univ. of Hildesheim Foundn, 2003–. *Address:* European Central Bank, Kaiserstrasse 29, 60311 Frankfurt, Germany.

STARKER, Janos; concert cellist, recording artist; Distinguished Professor of Cello, Indiana University, since 1958; *b* Budapest, 5 July 1924; *s* of F. Sandor and M. Margit; *m* 1944, Eva Uranyi; one *d*; *m* 1960, Rae D. Busch; one *d*. *Educ:* Franz Liszt Academy of Music, Budapest; Zrinyi Gymnasium, Budapest. Professional solo cellist, 1939–; Budapest Opera and Philh., 1945–46; Dallas Symphony, 1948–49; Metropolitan Opera, 1949–53; Chicago Symphony, 1953–58; concert tours on all continents in recitals and as soloist with orchestras; numerous recordings (Grand Prix du Disque, 1948; Grammy Award, 1998). Member: Amer. Fedn Musicians; Indiana Acad. of Arts and Scis; Amer. Acad. of Arts and Scis, 1999; Hon. RAM, 1981. Invented the Starker Bridge. Hon. DMus: Chicago Conservatory Coll., 1961; Cornell, 1978; East-West Univ., 1982; Williams Coll., 1983; Lawrence Univ., 1990; New England Conservatory of Music, 2006. George Washington Award, 1972; Sanford Fellowship Award, Yale, 1974; Herzl Award, Israel, 1978; Ed Press Award, 1983; Kodály Commemorative Medallion, NY, 1983; Arturo Toscanini Award, Toscanini Foundn, 1986; Tracy Sonneborn Award, Indiana Univ., 1986; Pro Cultura Hungarica, 1992; Indiana Governors Award, 1995; La Médaille de la ville de Paris, 1995; Pres.'s Medal for Excellence, Indiana Univ., 1999; Pres. of Hungary's Gold Medal, 1999; Isaac Stern Award, 2005. Chevalier, l'Ordre des Arts et des Lettres (France), 1997. *Publications:* Cello Method: an organised method of string playing, 1963; Bach Suites, 1971; Concerto Cadenzas, 1976; Beethoven Sonatas, 1978; Beethoven Variations, 1979; Bach Sonatas, 1979; Schubert-Starker Sonatina, 1980; Dvorak Concerto, 1981; Bottermund-Starker Variations, 1982; Encores, 1985; many articles and essays. *Recreations:* writing, swimming, staying alive. *Address:* Indiana University Music Department, Bloomington, IN 47405, USA; *c/o* Colbert Artists, 111 West 57th Street, New York, NY 10019, USA.

STARKEY, Dr David Robert, CBE 2007; FSA; FRHistS; historian and broadcaster; *b* 3 Jan. 1945; *s* of Robert Starkey and Elsie Starkey (*née* Lyon). *Educ:* Kendal GS; Fitzwilliam Coll., Cambridge (Open Schol.; Hon. Fellow, 2006). FRHistS 1984; FSA 1994. Fitzwilliam College, Cambridge: Res. Fellow, 1970–72; Vis. Fellow, 1998–2001; Bye-Fellow, 2001–06; Pres., Fitzwilliam Soc., 2003–04. Lectr in History, Dept of Internat. History, LSE, 1972–98. Vis. Vernon Prof. of Biography, Dartmouth Coll., New Hampshire, 1987, 1989; British Council Specialist Visitor, Australia, 1989; Hon. Vis. Prof. of History, Univ. of Kent, 2007–. Guest Curator: Henry VIII: a European court in England, Nat. Maritime Mus., 1991; Elizabeth, Nat. Maritime Mus., 2003; Lost Faces, Philip Mould Ltd, 2007; Henry VIII: man and monarch, British Library, 2009. Presenter and writer of television series: This Land of England, 1985; Henry VIII, 1998 (Indie Award, 2002); Elizabeth I, 2000; Six Wives of Henry VIII, 2001 (Siver Medal, NY Festivals World, 2004; Cine Golden Eagle, Thirteen/WNET, NY, 2006); The Unknown Tudors, 2002; Monarchy, 2004–07; panellist, Moral Maze, BBC Radio 4, 1992–2001; Presenter, Starkey on Saturday, then Starkey on Sunday, Talk Radio, 1995–98. Mem., Commemorative Plaques Wkg Gp, English Heritage, 1993–2006; Pres., Soc. for Court Studies, 1996–2005. Vice-Pres., Tory Campaign for Homosexual Equality, 1994–. Liveryman, Co. of Barbers, 1999– (Freeman, 1992). Mem. Editl Bd, History Today, 1980–; Hon. Associate: Rationalist Press Assoc., 1995–; Nat. Secular Soc., 1999–. Hon. Commodore, Nat. Maritime Mus., 2005. Hon. DLitt: Lancaster, 2004; Kent, 2006. Norton Medlicott Medal, for services to history, Historical Assoc., 2001. *Publications:* (jtly) This Land of England, 1985; The Reign of Henry VIII: personalities and politics, 1985, 3rd edn 2002; (ed jtly) Revolution Reassessed: revisions in the history of Tudor government and administration, 1986; (ed) The English Court from the Wars of the Roses to the Civil War, 1987; (ed) Rivals in Power: the lives and letters of the great Tudor dynasties, 1990; Henry VIII: a European court in England, 1991; (ed jtly) The Inventory of Henry VIII, vol. I, 1998; Elizabeth: apprenticeship, 2000 (W H Smith Award for Biog./ Autobiog., 2001); Six Wives: the Queens of Henry VIII, 2003; The Monarchy of England, vol. 1: the beginnings, 2004; Monarchy: from the Middle Ages to Modernity, 2006; contribs to newspapers, numerous articles in learned jls. *Recreations:* decorating, gardening, treading on toes. *Address:* Fitzwilliam College, Cambridge CB3 0DG.

STARKEY, Sir John (Philip), 3rd Bt *cr* 1935; DL; *b* 8 May 1938; *s* of Sir William Randle Starkey, 2nd Bt, and Irene Myrtle Starkey (*née* Francklin) (*d* 1965); *S* father, 1977; *m* 1966, Victoria Henrietta Fleetwood, *y d* of Lt-Col Christopher Fuller, TD; one *s* three *d*. *Educ:* Eton College; Christ Church, Oxford. Sloan Fellow, London Business School. A Church Commissioner and Mem. Commissioners' Assets Cttee, 1985–91; Mem., Archbishop's Commn on Rural Areas, 1988–90. Chairman: Notts Br., CLA, 1977–80; E Midlands Regional Cttee, Nat. Trust, 1986–97. UK Vice-Pres., Confedn of European Agriculture, 1989–2000; Pres., Newark Chamber of Commerce, 1980–82. Notts: DL, 1981; High Sheriff, 1987–88; JP Newark, 1981–88. *Recreations:* cricket, painting, golf. *Heir: s* Henry John Starkey [*b* 13 Oct. 1973; *m* 2002, Georgina Gemma, *y d* of Richard Whittington; two *s*]. *Address:* Norwood Park, Southwell, Notts NG25 0PF. *Club:* MCC.

STARKEY, Dr Phyllis Margaret; MP (Lab) Milton Keynes South West, since 1997; *b* 4 Jan. 1947; *d* of Dr John Williams and Catherine Hooson Williams (*née* Owen); *m* 1969, Hugh Walton Starkey; two *d*. *Educ:* Perse Sch. for Girls, Cambridge; Lady Margaret Hall, Oxford (BA Biochem.); Clare Hall, Cambridge (PhD). Research posts: Strangeways Lab., Cambridge, 1970–81; Sir Wm Dunn Sch. of Pathology, Oxford, 1981–84; Lectr in Obstetrics and Gynaecology, 1984–93, and Fellow of Somerville Coll., 1987–93, Univ. of Oxford; Head of Assessment, BBSRC, 1993–97. Mem. (Lab), Oxford City Council, 1983–97 (Leader, 1990–93); Chm., Local Govt Inf. Unit, 1992–97. PPS to FCO

Ministers, 2001–02, to Minister of State (Minister for Europe), FCO, 2002–05. Mem., Foreign Affairs Select Cttee, 1999–2001; Chm., Select Cttee for DCLG (formerly ODPM), 2005–. Chm., POST, 2002–05. *Publications:* numerous scientific articles in learned jls. *Recreations:* gardening, cinema, walking. *Address:* Labour Hall, Newport Road, New Bradwell, Milton Keynes MK13 0AA. *T:* (01908) 225522.

STARLING, Keith Andrew; Headmaster, The Judd School, 1986–2004; *b* 12 June 1944; *s* of Stanley Ernest Starling and Gladys Joyce Starling; *m* 1968, Jacqueline Eagers; two *s*. *Educ:* The Perse Sch.; Fitzwilliam Coll., Cambridge (MA, CertEd). Asst Master, Lancaster Royal Grammar Sch., 1968–71; Head of Geography, Sedbergh Sch., 1971–80; Dep. Headmaster, Portsmouth Grammar Sch., 1980–86. Gov., Stamford Endowed Schs, 2005–. Liveryman, Skinners' Co., 2004–. *Recreations:* music, walking. *Address:* Elderberry Cottage, Orchard Close, Egleton, Rutland LE15 8AG.

STARLING, Nicholas James; Director of General Insurance and Health (formerly Director of General Insurance), Association of British Insurers, since 2005; *b* 16 March 1956; *s* of Richard James Starling and late Helen Mary Starling; *m* 1984, Catherine Susannah Thompson; two *d*. *Educ:* George Watson's Coll., Edinburgh; St John's Coll., Cambridge (BA Archaeol. and Anthropology 1977); St John's Coll., Oxford (DPhil 1983). Theodor Heuss Fellow, Univ. of Cologne, 1981–82; Randall Maciver Student in Archaeol., Queen's Coll., Oxford, 1982–83; Department of Transport: joined, 1984; Pvte Sec. to Minister for Roads and Traffic, 1986–88; Principal, 1988–94; Asst Sec., 1994–98; Dep. Dir, Internat. Aviation, 1994–98; Hd, Nuclear and Hazardous Installations Policy, 1998–2000, Dir, Safety Policy, 2000–03, Policy Dir, 2003–05, HSE. *Publications:* various articles in archaeol. jls. *Recreations:* family, music, especially Schubert, singing, cooking, Guardian crossword. *Address:* Association of British Insurers, 51 Gresham Street, EC2V 7HQ. *T:* (020) 7696 8999; *e-mail:* info@abi.org.uk.

STARMER, Keir; QC 2002; Director of Public Prosecutions, since 2008; *b* 2 Sept. 1962; *s* of Rod and Jo Starmer; *m* Victoria Alexander; one *s*. *Educ:* Leeds Univ. (LLB 1st Cl. Hons 1985); St Edmund Hall, Oxford (BCL 1986). Called to the Bar: Middle Temple, 1987; St Lucia, 1997; St Vincent, 1997; Belize, 2002. Fellow, Human Rights Centre, Essex Univ., 1998–. Human Rights Advr to NI Policing Bd, 2003–08. Mem., Foreign Sec.'s Adv. Panel on the Death Penalty, 2002–. Mem., Governance Adv. Bd, British Council, 2002. Mem. Council, Justice, 1999–. Human Rights Lawyer of the Year Award, Justice/Liberty, 2001. *Publications:* (ed) Justice in Error, 1995; Three Pillars of Liberty: political rights and freedom in the UK, 1996; Signing up for Human Rights: the UK and international standards, 1998; (ed) Miscarriages of Justice, 1999; European Human Rights Law, 1999; Blackstone's Human Rights Digest, 2001; Criminal Justice, Police Powers and Human Rights, 2001; (contrib.) Human Rights Principles, 2001; (contrib.) Mithani's Directors' Disqualification, 2001; (contrib.) Human Rights and Civil Practice, 2001; contribs to Public Law. *Recreations:* football, classical music. *Address:* Crown Prosecution Service, 50 Ludgate Hill, EC4M 7EX.

STARMER-SMITH, Nigel Christopher; International Rugby Board consultant and TV commentator, since 2002; *b* 25 Dec. 1944; *s* of late Harry Starmer-Smith and Joan Mary Starmer-Smith (*née* Keep); *m* 1973, Rosamund Mary Bartlett; one *s* (and one *s* one *d* decd). *Educ:* Magdalen Coll. Sch., Oxford; University Coll., Oxford (MA). Schoolmaster, Epsom Coll., 1967; Producer and Reporter, BBC Radio Outside Broadcasts, 1971; Sports Commentator, BBC TV, 1973–2002; Commentator, ITV Rugby World Cup, 2003; Presenter and Commentator, Rugby Special; commentator, hockey and other sports. Publisher and Editor, Rugby World and Post magazine, 1984–93. Former Rugby Union international: Harlequins, Oxford Univ., Barbarians, England. Gov., Shiplake Coll., 2003–. Trustee, Reading and Dist. Hospitals Charity, 1991–. *Publications:* include: The Barbarians, 1977; Rugby: a way of life, 1986. *Recreations:* family, tennis, piano playing, horse racing, gardening. *Address:* Cobblers Cottage, Skirmett, Henley-on-Thames RG9 6TD. *T:* (01491) 639422. *Clubs:* Vincent's (Oxford); Leander (Henley); Harlequins FC.

STATHATOS, Stephanos; Commander, Order of Phoenix; Officer, Order of George I; *b* 30 Sept. 1922; *s* of Gerassimo and Eugenia Stathatos; *m* 1947, Thalia Mouzina. *Educ:* Law School, Athens Univ.; post graduate studies: Ecole des Sciences Politiques, Paris; LSE. Entered Greek Diplomatic Service, 1953; served Cairo, NATO, Paris, Athens, Washington; Dep. Perm. Rep. to UN, NY, 1968–72; Dir, Middle East Political Affairs, Min. of Foreign Affairs, 1972–74; Ambassador, Perm. Rep. to EEC, 1974–79; Ambassador, Paris, 1979–82; non-resident Ambassador to Holy See, 1981–82; Dep. Political Dir, 1982–84, Political Dir, 1984–85, Min. of Foreign Affairs; Ambassador to UK, 1986–89, and non-resident Ambassador to Iceland; Head of Prime Minister's Diplomatic Office, 1989–90. Pres., EU *ad hoc* Gp on Stability Pact, 1994; Nat. Rep. to Reflexion Gp for revision of Maastricht Treaty, 1995. Mem., Hon. Council, Hellenic Foundn for Eur. and Foreign Policy. Holds numerous foreign orders and decorations. *Publications:* Greece's Stance Towards EU Evolution, 2001; Forty Years in the Diplomatic Arena, 2007. *Address:* 24 Raviné Street, Athens 11521, Greece. *T:* (1) 7222004. *Club:* Athenæum.

STATMAN, Philip Richard; His Honour Judge Statman; a Circuit Judge, since 2002; *b* 28 March 1953; *s* of Martin and Evelyn Statman; *m* 1997, Mary Louise Cameron (*d* 2006); two *s*. *Educ:* Mid Essex Tech. Coll. (LLB Hons London (ext.)); Inns of Court Sch. of Law. Called to the Bar, Middle Temple, 1975; specialised in criminal law; Asst Recorder, 1997–2000; a Recorder, 2000–02. *Recreations:* travel, Association Football, cinema, literature, antiques. *Address:* Maidstone Combined Court Centre, Barker Road, Maidstone ME16 8EQ. *T:* (01622) 202000.

STAUGHTON, Rt Hon. Sir Christopher (Stephen Thomas Jonathan Thayer), Kt 1981; PC 1988; FCIArb; arbitrator; a Lord Justice of Appeal, 1987–97; Judge of the Court of Appeal, Gibraltar, 2000–06 (President, 2005–06); *b* 24 May 1933; *yr s* of late Simon Thomas Samuel Staughton of Melbourne, Australia and Edith Madeline Jones of Halifax, Canada; *m* 1960, Joanna Susan Elizabeth, DL, *er d* of late George Frederick Arthur Burgess; two *d*. *Educ:* Eton Coll. (Scholar); Magdalene Coll., Cambridge (Scholar; George Long Prize for Roman Law, 1955; BA 1956; MA 1961; Hon. Fellow 1988). 2nd Lieut, 11th Hussars PAO, 1952–53. Called to Bar, Inner Temple, 1957, Bencher, 1978, Reader, 1996, Treasurer, 1997; QC 1970; a Recorder of the Crown Court, 1972–81; a Judge of the High Court of Justice, QBD, 1981–87. Appeal Adjudicator, enemy property claims, 2001–08. Mem., Senate of the Inns of Court and the Bar, 1974–81; Chm., Code of Conduct sub-cttee, 1979–80. Member: Adv. Bd, British Library, 1999–2002; Police Surveillance Commn, 1999–2000. Chm., St Peter's Eaton Square Church of England Sch., 1974–83. Hon. LLD Hertfordshire, 1996. *Publications:* (Jt Editor) The Law of General Average (British Shipping Laws vol. 7), 1964, new edn, 1975; (jtly) Profits of Crime and their Recovery, 1984; articles on plain English in the law. *Recreations:* bridge, growing dahlias. *Address:* 20 Essex Street, WC2R 3AL. *T:* (020) 7842 1200, *Fax:* (020) 7583 1341; *e-mail:* clerks@20essexst.com.

STAUNTON, Imelda Mary Philomena Bernadette, OBE 2006; actress, since 1976; *b* 9 Jan. 1956; *d* of Joseph Staunton and Bridie McNicholas; *m* 1983, Jim Carter, actor; one *d*. *Educ:* La Sainte Union Convent, Highgate; RADA. *Theatre* includes: rep., 1976–81; The Corn is Green, Old Vic, 1985; Calico, Duke of York's, 2004; There Came a Gypsy Riding, Almeida, 2007; *National Theatre:* Guys and Dolls, 1982, 1996; Beggar's Opera, Chorus of Disapproval (Olivier Award, best supporting actress), 1985; Life × 3, 2000, transf. Old Vic; *Royal Shakespeare Company:* Fair Maid of the West, Wizard of Oz, 1986; Uncle Vanya, Vaudeville, 1988; Into the Woods, Phoenix, 1990 (Olivier Award, best actress in a musical, 1991); *television* includes: The Singing Detective, 1986; Yellowbacks, 1990; Sleeping Life; Roots; Up the Garden Path, 1990; Antonia & Jane; Is it Legal?; Murder, 2002; Cambridge Spies, 2003; Fingersmith, 2005; Cranford, 2007; *films* include: Peter's Friends, 1992; Much Ado About Nothing, 1993; Deadly Advice, 1994; Sense and Sensibility, Twelfth Night, Remember Me, 1996; Shakespeare in Love, 1999; Rat, 2001; Crush, 2002; Blackball, Virgin of Liverpool, Bright Young Things, 2003; Vera Drake, 2004 (BAFTA Award, best actress, 2005); Nanny McPhee, 2005; Freedom Writers, 2006; Harry Potter and the Order of the Phoenix, 2007; Three and Out, 2008. *Address:* c/o ARG, 4 Great Portland Street, W1W 8PA.

STAUNTON, Prof. James, PhD; FRS 1998; Professor of Chemical Biology, 1999–2002, and Fellow of St John's College, since 1969, University of Cambridge; *b* 18 March 1935; *s* of James and Elizabeth Staunton; *m* 1961, Dr Ruth Mary Berry, MB, ChB. *Educ:* St Edward's Coll., Liverpool; Univ. of Liverpool (BSc 1956; PhD 1959); MA Cantab 1969. Postdoctoral Fellow, Stanford Univ., 1959–60; Fellow, 1960–62, Lectr in Organic Chemistry, 1962–69, Liverpool Univ.; Lectr in Organic Chemistry, 1969–78, Reader, 1978–99, Cambridge Univ. Natural Products Award, 1987, Tilden Medal, 1989, Robert Robinson Award, 2001, RSC. *Publications:* Primary Metabolism: a mechanistic approach, 1978; articles in chemical and biochemical jls. *Recreations:* walking, cycling, gardening, travel, DIY. *Address:* St John's College, Cambridge CB2 1TP.

STAUNTON, Marie; Chief Executive, Plan International UK, since 2000; *b* 28 May 1952; *d* of Ann and Austin Staunton; *m* 1986, James Albert Provan; two *d*. *Educ:* Lancaster Univ.; College of Law (BA). Solicitor. Head of casework for Simon Community Hostels for Addicts, Alcoholics and Homeless Families (England, NI and Eire), 1970–72; Articled Clerk and Solicitor in private practice and Law Centres, 1976–83; Legal Officer, NCCL, 1983–87; Dir, British Section, Amnesty Internat., 1987–90 (Vice-Chm., Internat. Exec. Cttee, 1993–95); Publishing Dir, Longman Law Tax & Finance, then Financial Times Law & Tax, 1990–96; Ed., Solicitors' Jl, 1990–95; Dep. Dir, UK Cttee for UNICEF, 1997–2000. UK Ind. Mem., Mgt Bd, EU Fundamental Rights Agency. *Publications:* Data Protection: putting the record straight, 1987; contribs to NCCL works; chapters in books on allied subjects. *Address:* (office) 5–6 Underhill Street, NW1 7HS. *T:* (020) 7485 6612.

STAVELEY, Maj.-Gen. Robert; *b* 3 June 1928; *s* of Brig. Robin Staveley, DSO, and Ilys (*née* Sutherland); *m* 1958, Airlie, *d* of Maj.-Gen. W. H. Lambert, CB, CBE; one *s* one *d*. *Educ:* Wellington. RMA Sandhurst, 1947; Staff Colls India and Camberley; commissioned RA, 1948; served BAOR, 1949–51; ADC to GOC Malta, 1951–53; Air OP pilot, Malaya, 1954–57 (despatches); ADC to GOC-in-C Northern Command, 1957–58; Indian Staff Coll., 1959; Staff Officer and Missile Battery Comdr, BAOR, 1960–65; Instructor, Staff Coll., 1966–68; commanded 47 Lt Regt RA, UK and Hong Kong, 1969–71; MoD, 1972; CRA 2nd Div., BAOR, 1973–74; RCDS 1975; Director of Operational Requirements, MoD, 1976–79; C of S, Logistic Exec. (Army), 1979–82. Admin. Controller, Norton Rose, solicitors, 1983–91. Col Comdt, RA, 1982–87. Chm., Bd of Govs, Royal Sch., Hampstead, 1993–98. FCMI (FBIM 1983). *Recreations:* good food, sailing, ski-ing, music. *Address:* c/o Lloyds TSB (Cox's & King's Branch), 7 Pall Mall, SW1Y 5NA. *Clubs:* Army and Navy, Royal Ocean Racing; Royal Artillery Yacht (Commodore, 1980–83; Admiral, 1991–97).

STAVERT, Most Rev. Alexander Bruce; *see* Quebec, Archbishop of.

STAVORDALE, Lord; Simon James Fox-Strangways; *b* 25 Aug. 1972; *s* and *heir* of Earl of Ilchester, *qv*.

STEAD, Prof. Christian Karlson, ONZ 2007; CBE 1985; PhD, DLitt; FRSL; writer; Professor of English, University of Auckland, 1968–87, now Emeritus; *b* 17 Oct. 1932; *s* of James Walter Ambrose Stead and Olive Ethel Stead; *m* 1955, Kathleen Elizabeth Roberts; one *s* two *d*. *Educ:* Univ. of NZ (MA 1955); Univ. of Bristol (PhD 1962); Univ. of Auckland (DLitt 1981). Lectr in English, Univ. of New England, NSW, 1956–57; Michael Hiatt Baker Schol., Univ. of Bristol, 1957–59; Lectr, then Sen. Lectr in English, 1960–64, Associate Prof., 1964–68, Univ. of Auckland. Sen. Vis. Fellow, St John's Coll., Oxford, 1996–97. FRSL 1995. Hon. DLitt Bristol, 2001. *Publications: poetry:* Whether the Will is Free, 1964; Crossing the Bar, 1972; Quesada, 1975; Walking Westward, 1978; Geographies, 1981; Paris, 1984; Poems of a Decade, 1985; Between, 1987; Voices, 1990; Straw into Gold: poems new and selected, 1997; The Right Thing, 2000; Dog, 2002; The Red Tram, 2004; The Black River, 2007; *fiction:* Smith's Dream, 1971; Five for the Symbol (stories), 1981; All Visitors Ashore, 1984; The Death of the Body, 1986; Sister Hollywood, 1988; The End of the Century at the End of the World, 1991; The Singing Whakapapa, 1994; Villa Vittoria, 1996; Talking about O'Dwyer, 1999; The Secret History of Modernism, 2002; Mansfield: a novel, 2004; My Name Was Judas, 2006; *literary criticism:* The New Poetic, 1964; In the Glass Case: essays on New Zealand literature, 1981; Pound, Yeats, Eliot and the Modernist Movement, 1986; Answering to the Language, 1989; The Writer at Work, 2000; Kin of Place: essays on twenty New Zealand writers, 2002; Book Self: the reader as writer and the writer as critic, 2008; *edited:* New Zealand Short Stories, 2nd series, 1966; Measure for Measure: a casebook, 1971; Letters and Journals of Katherine Mansfield, 1977; Collected Stories of Maurice Duggan, 1981; Faber Book of Contemporary South Pacific Stories, 1993; Werner Forman's New Zealand (photographs), 1995. *Recreations:* music, walking. *Address:* 37 Tohunga Crescent, Auckland 1052, New Zealand.

STEAD, Ian Mathieson, PhD; FSA; FBA 1991; Deputy Keeper, Department of Prehistoric and Romano-British Antiquities, British Museum, 1977–96 (Assistant Keeper, 1974–77); *b* 9 Jan. 1936; *er s* of Sidney William Stead and Edith Johann (*née* Mathieson); *m* 1962, Sheelagh Mary Johnson; one *s* one *d*. *Educ:* Nunthorpe Grammar Sch., York; Fitzwilliam House, Cambridge Univ. (MA; PhD 1965). FSA 1966. Asst Inspector of Ancient Monuments, 1962, Inspector, 1964–74, Min. of Works. Chairman: Herts Archaeol Council, 1970–75; Humberside Jt Archaeol Cttee, 1974–81; Sec., Prehistoric Soc., 1974–76. Hon. Life Mem., Yorks Philosophical Soc., 1982; Corresp. Mem., Deutsches Archäologisches Institut, 1976. Silver Medal, Yorks Archaeol Soc. 2005. *Publications:* La Tène Cultures of Eastern Yorkshire, 1965; Winterton Roman Villa, 1976; Arras Culture, 1979; (with J.-L. Flouest) Iron Age Cemeteries in Champagne, 1979; Rudston Roman Villa, 1980; The Gauls, 1981; Celtic Art in Britain, 1985, 2nd edn 1996; Battersea Shield, 1985; (with J. B. Bourke and D. Brothwell) Lindow Man, the Body in the Bog, 1986; (with V. Rigby) Baldock, 1986; (with V. Rigby) Verulamium, the King Harry Lane Site, 1989; Iron Age Cemeteries in East Yorkshire, 1991; (with Karen Hughes) Early Celtic Designs, 1997; The Salisbury Hoard, 1998 (British Archaeol Awards Book Award, 2000); (with V. Rigby) The Morel Collection, 1999; British Iron Age Swords and Scabbards, 2006; (with J.-L. Flouest and V. Rigby) Iron Age and Roman Burials in Champagne, 2006; papers in learned jls. *Address:* Ratcliffe House, Ashwell, Herts SG7 5NP. *T:* (01462) 742396.

STEADMAN, Alison, OBE 2000; actress; *b* Liverpool, 26 Aug. 1946; *d* of late George Percival Steadman and Marjorie Steadman; *m* 1973, Mike Leigh, *qv* (marr. diss. 2001); two *s*. *Theatre includes:* Abigail's Party, Hampstead (Best Actress, Evening Standard Awards), 1977; Joking Apart, Globe, 1979; Uncle Vanya, Hampstead, 1979; Cinderella and her Naughty Sisters, Lyric, Hammersmith, 1980; A Handful of Dust, Lyric, Hammersmith, 1982; Tartuffe, Maydays, RSC, 1985; Kafka's Dick, Royal Court, 1986; Cat on a Hot Tin Roof, NT, 1988; The Rise and Fall of Little Voice, Aldwych (Olivier Best Actress Award), 1992; Marvin's Room, Hampstead, transf. Comedy, 1993; When We Are Married, Chichester, transf. Savoy, 1996; The Provok'd Wife, Old Vic, 1997; The Memory of Water, Vaudeville, 1999; Entertaining Mr Sloane, Arts, 2001; The Woman Who Cooked Her Husband, New Ambassadors, 2002; Losing Louis, Hampstead, transf. Trafalgar Studios, Whitehall, 2005, nat. tour, 2006; Enjoy, Th. Royal, Bath, 2008; *television includes:* Nuts in May, 1976; Through the Night, 1976; Abigail's Party, 1977; Our Flesh and Blood, 1978; Pasmore, 1980; P'tang Yang Kipperbang, 1982; The Singing Detective, 1986; Virtuoso, 1989; A Small Mourning, 1989; News Hounds, Gone to the Dogs, 1990; Gone to Seed, 1991; Selling Hitler, 1992; Pride and Prejudice, 1995; Wimbledon Poisoner, 1995; Karaoke, 1996; No Bananas, 1996; The Missing Postman, 1997; Let Them Eat Cake, 1999; Fat Friends, 2000, 2002, 2004, 2005; Adrian Mole: The Cappuccino Years, 2001; The Worst Week of my Life, 2004; The Worst Christmas of My Life, 2006; The Last Detective, 2006; The Dinner Party, 2007; Fanny Hill, 2007; Gavin and Stacey, 2007, 2008; *films include:* Champions, 1983; A Private Function, 1984; Number One, 1985; Clockwise, 1986; The Adventures of Baron Münchhausen, Shirley Valentine, Wilt, 1989; Life is Sweet, Blame it on the Bellboy, 1991; Topsy-Turvy, 1999; DIY Hard, 2002; Chunky Monkey, The Life and Death of Peter Sellers, 2004. Hon. MA Univ. of East London, 1996; DU Essex, 2003. *Address:* c/o United Agents, 12–26 Lexington Street, W1F 0LE.

STEADMAN, Dr John Hubert; consultant in regulatory and environmental toxicology and environmental health, since 1996; *b* 10 Aug. 1938; *s* of late Dr Harry Hubert Steadman and Janet Gilchrist Steadman (*née* MacDonald); *m* 1972, Dr Anthea Howell; one *s* one *d*. *Educ:* Wimbledon Coll.; Guy's Hosp. (MB, BS); University Coll. London (MSc). University College Hospital, London: Beit Meml Fellowship, 1968–72; Sen. Registrar, Dept of Haematology, 1972–78, with secondments to Ahmadu Bello Univ. Hosp., Nigeria, 1973, and Royal Perth Hosp., WA, 1974; Cons. Haematologist, King George Hosp., Ilford, 1978–81; MO 1981, SMO 1982, PMO 1984, DHSS; SPMO, Head of Div. of Toxicology and Envmtl Health, subseq. Health Aspects of Envmt and Food, DoH, 1988–93; Hd of Safety and Envmtl Assce, Unilever, 1993–96. Expert Advr on food safety, WHO, 1988–93. *Publications:* articles in learned jls on regulatory toxicology, haematology and biochemistry. *Recreations:* cooking, languages, political philosophy. *Address:* c/o Messrs C. Hoare & Co., 37 Fleet Street, EC4P 4DQ.

See also J. M. M. Curtis-Raleigh.

STEADMAN, Ralph Idris; freelance cartoonist, artist and writer; *b* 15 May 1936; *s* of Lionel Raphael Steadman (English), and Gwendoline (Welsh); *m* 1st, 1959, Sheila Thwaite (marr. diss. 1971); two *s* two *d*; 2nd, 1972, Anna Deverson; one *d*. *Educ:* Abergele Grammar Sch.; London Coll. of Printing and Graphic Arts. Apprentice, de Havilland Aircraft Co., 1952; Cartoonist, Kemsley (Thomson) Newspapers, 1956–59; freelance for Punch, Private Eye, Telegraph, during 1960s; Political Cartoonist, New Statesman, 1978–80; retired to work on book about Leonardo da Vinci; as a positive political statement, refuses to draw another politician; 15 Save the Children originals auctioned in aid of Ethiopia Fund, 1990. Retrospective exhibitions: Nat. Theatre, 1977; Royal Festival Hall, 1984; exhibitions: Wilhelm Busch Mus., Hannover, 1988; October Gall. (sculptures and silk screen prints), 1990, Gulf war collages, 1991; Peacock Gall., Aberdeen, 1993; Aberdeen City Art Gall., 1994; The Lord is an Animal, One on One Gall., Denver, USA, 1997; Contemporary Satirists, RA, 1997; Les Sixties, Les Invalides, Paris, transf. Brighton, 1997; centenary Lewis Carroll exhibn, Warrington Mus., 1998; Making a Mark, William Havu Gall., Denver, 2000; Who? Me! No!! Why?? (pictures and artefacts from book Doodaaa), NY, 2003. Designed set of stamps of Halley's Comet, 1986; opera libretto and concept, Plague and the Moonflower, Exeter Cathedral and Festival, 1989 (artist-in-residence), St Paul's Cathedral, 1989, Canterbury Cathedral and Festival, 1990, performed as Hearts Betrayed, St Martin-in-the-Fields, 1993, televised 1995, recorded 1999; libretto and concept, Love Underground, Norwich Fest., 1997; artist-in-residence, Cheltenham Fest., 1994; designer, Gulliver's Travels, Theatr Clwyd, 1995; artist-in-residence, Leviathan series of films, BBC2, 1999; designer of set and costumes, The Crucible, Royal Ballet, 2000. Writer, dir and performer, TV film, Hanging Garden Centres of Kent, 1992. Hon. Fellow, Kent Inst. of Art and Design, 1993. Hon. DLitt Kent, 1995. D & AD Gold Award (for outstanding contribution to illustration), 1977, and Silver Award (for outstanding editorial illustration), 1977; Black Humour Award, France, 1986; W. H. Smith Illustration Award for best illustrated book for last five years, 1987; BBC Design Award for postage stamps, 1987; Empire Award (for involvement with film Withnail and I), Empire Magazine, 1996; Milton Caniff Award, Nat. Cartoonists Soc. of America, 2005; Star of Saatchi and Saatchi Clio Creative Hero Show, 2008. *Publications:* Jelly Book, 1968; Still Life with Raspberry: collected drawings, 1969; The Little Red Computer, 1970; Dogs Bodies, 1971; Bumper to Bumper Book, 1973; Two Donkeys and the Bridge, 1974; Flowers for the Moon, 1974; America: drawings, 1975; America: collected drawings, 1977 (rev. edn, Scar Strangled Banger, 1987); Between the Eyes, 1984; Paranoids, 1986; The Grapes of Ralph, 1992; Teddy! Where are you?, 1994; Untrodden Grapes, 2005; The Joke's Over: memories of Hunter S. Thompson, 2006; *written and illustrated:* Sigmund Freud, 1979 (as The Penguin Sigmund Freud, 1982); A Leg in the Wind and other Canine Curses, 1982; I, Leonardo, 1983; That's My Dad, 1986 (Critici in Erba Prize, 1987); The Big I Am, 1988; No Room to Swing a Cat, 1989; Near the Bone, 1990; Tales of the Weirrd, 1990; Still Life with Bottle, Whisky According to Ralph Steadman, 1994; Jones of Colorado, 1995; Gonzo: the art, 1998; little.com, 2000; Garibaldi's Biscuits, 2008; designed and printed, Steam Press Broadsheets; *illustrated:* Frank Dickens, Fly Away Peter, 1961; Mischa Damjan: The Big Squirrel and the Little Rhinoceros, 1962; The False Flamingoes, 1963; The Little Prince and the Tiger Cat, 1964; Two Cats in America, 1968; Richard Ingrams, The Tale of Driver Grope, 1964; Love and Marriage, 1964; Daisy Ashford, Where Love Lies Deepest, 1964; Fiona Saint, The Yellow Flowers, 1965; Alice in Wonderland, 1967; Midnight, 1967; Tariq Ali, The Thoughts of Chairman Harold, 1968; Dr Hunter S. Thompson: Fear and Loathing in Las Vegas, 1972, 25th anniv. edn, 1997; The Curse of Lono, 1984, 2nd (limited) edn 2004; Kurt Baumann, The Watchdog and the Lazy Dog, 1974; Contemporary Poets set to Music series, 1972; Through the Looking Glass, 1972; Night Edge: poems, 1973; The Poor Mouth, 1973; John Letts Limericks, 1974; The Hunting of the Snark, 1975; Dmitri Sidjanski, Cherrywood Cannon, 1978; Bernard Stone: Emergency Mouse, 1978; Inspector Mouse, 1980; Quasimodo Mouse, 1984; Ted Hughes, The Threshold (limited edn), 1979; Adrian

Mitchell, For Beauty Douglas, 1982; Flann O'Brien, More of Myles, 1982; Wolf Mankowitz, The Devil in Texas, 1984; Treasure Island, 1985; The Complete Alice and The Hunting of the Snark, 1986; Friendship (short stories), 1990 (in aid of John McCarthy); Animal Farm, 50th anniv. edn, 1995; Adrian Mitchell, Heart on the Left, Poems 1953–1984, 1997; Roald Dahl, The Mildenhall Treasure, 1999; Doodaaa: the balletic art of Gavin Twinge (novel), 2002; Ambrose Bierce, The Devil's Dictionary, 2003; Fahrenheit 451, 50th anniv. limited edn, 2003; Hunter S. Thompson, Fire in the Nuts, 2004; Will Self, PsychoGeography, 2007. *Recreations:* gardening (planted vineyard), collecting, writing, sheep husbandry, fishing, guitar, trumpet. *Web:* www.ralphsteadman.com. *Club:* Chelsea Arts.

STEAR, Air Chief Marshal Sir Michael (James Douglas), KCB 1990; CBE 1982; QCVSA 1969; DL; FRAeS; Deputy Commander-in-Chief, Allied Forces Central Europe, 1992–96; *b* 11 Oct. 1938; *s* of late Melbourne Douglas Stear and Barbara Jane Stear (*née* Fletcher); *m* 1966, Elizabeth Jane, *d* of late Donald Edward Macrae, FRCS and of Janet Wallace Macpherson Simpson; two *s* one *d*. *Educ:* Monkton Combe Sch.; Emmanuel Coll., Cambridge (MA; CU Air Sqn (RAFVR), 1959–62). Nat. Service, 1957–59. Joined RAF, 1962; served on 1 Sqn, 1964–67, on 208 Sqn, Persian Gulf, 1967–69; exchange tour with USAF, 1969–71; Air Sec.'s Br., MoD, 1972–74; OC 17 Sqn, Germany, 1974–76; OC 56 Sqn, RAF Wattisham, 1976; PSO to CAS, MoD, 1976–79; OC RAF Gutersloh, 1980–82; Asst C of S (Ops), HQ 2 ATAF, 1982; Air Cdre Plans, HQ Strike Command, 1982–85; AOC No 11 Gp, 1985–87; ACDS (Nato/UK), 1987–89; AOC No 18 Gp, and Comdr Maritime Air Eastern Atlantic and Channel, 1989–92. Mem., Commonwealth War Graves Commn, 1998–2003. Member: RUSI, 1989–99; Council, Malcolm Clubs, 1988–2003; RFU Cttee, 1987–98 (Mgt Bd Jt Vice-Chm. (admin), 1997–98); Air League, 1999–; Pres., RAF RU, 1992–97 (Chm., 1983–86). Nat. Pres., RAFA, 1998–2002 (Vice-Pres., 1997–98; Life Vice-Pres., 2002–; Service Vice-Pres., Europe Area, 1992–96); Hon. Pres., Devon & Som Wing, ATC, 2000–. FRAeS 1997. DL Devon, 2000. *Recreations:* Rugby football, keeping sheep, gardening, fishing, shooting. *Club:* Royal Air Force (Vice-Pres., 1990–98).

STEAR, Roderick Morton, (Rory); Founder and Executive Chairman, Freeplay Energy Group, since 1994; *b* 17 March 1959; *s* of Robert and Natalie Stear; *m* 1995, Kristine Joy Pearson. *Educ:* Grey High Sch., Port Elizabeth, SA. Founder and Man. Dir, Seeff Corporate Finance, 1990–94. Member, President Nelson Mandela's business delegation: to UK, 1996; to USA, 1998. Student, Birthing of Grants prog., MIT, 2000. Member: Dean's Council, John F. Kennedy Sch. of Govt, Harvard Univ., 2005–; Adv. Bd, Business Sch., Nelson Mandela Univ., Port Elizabeth, SA, 2005–. Mem., African Business Roundtable, 1995. Mem., Global Agenda Council on Alternative Energies, World Economic Forum. Founder, Freeplay Foundn, 1998. CNN Principal Voice, 2007; Hero of the Envmt, Time, 2007. *Recreations:* golf, gym, music, reading. *Address:* Freeplay Energy plc, 71 Gloucester Place, W1U 8JW. *T:* (020) 7935 5226, *Fax:* (020) 7487 1328; *e-mail:* rstear@freeplayenergy.com. *Clubs:* Royal Automobile; Wentworth Golf; Jockey (S Africa).

STEARNS, Elizabeth Jane Elford, FFFLM; HM Coroner, Eastern District, Greater London, since 1998; *b* 20 Nov. 1946; *d* of Cecil Smith and Audrey Quelch; *m* 1972, Michael Patrick Stearns; three *s*. *Educ:* Wycombe Abbey Sch.; Guy's Hosp. Dental and Med. Schs, London (BDS Hons, LDS RCS 1970; MB BS 1974). FFFLM 2006. Assistant Deputy Coroner: City of London, 1993; N London, 1994–95; Dep. Coroner, N London, 1995–98. Called to the Bar, 1997. Examnr for Dips in Forensic Med. Scis. Pres., SE Coroners' Soc., 2005–06; Vice-Pres., Faculty of Forensic and Legal Medicine, RCP, 2006–. *Address:* Coroner's Court, Queen's Road, Walthamstow, E17 8QP.

STEBBING, Nowell, PhD; Chairman, Pharmagene plc (formerly Pharmagene Laboratories Ltd), 1996–2003; *b* 5 Sept. 1941; *s* of Lionel Charles Stebbing and Margarita (*née* Behrenz); *m* 1st, 1963, Nancy Lynah (marr. diss.); two *d* (one *s* decd); 2nd, 1973, Birgit Griffiths (*née* Evjen); one *s*. *Educ:* Michael Hall Sch., Sussex; Univ. of Edinburgh (BSc Hons 1964; PhD 1968). Demonstrator, Univ. of Edinburgh, 1967–69; Director of Biology: G. D. Searle & Co., 1969–79; Genentech Inc., San Francisco, 1979–82; Vice-Pres., Scientific Affairs, Amgen Inc., Thousand Oaks, Calif, 1982–86; Gen. Manager, Res., ICI Pharmaceuticals, UK, 1986–93; Chief Exec. and Dep. Chm., Chiroscience Gp PLC, 1993–95. Chm., Axis Genetics, 1995–99. *Publications:* numerous papers and articles in scientific and med. jls and books. *Recreations:* theatre, old cars, gardens, wine making in Italy.

STEDMAN JONES, Prof. Gareth, DPhil; Professor of Political Science, University of Cambridge, since 1997; Co Director, Centre for History and Economics, Cambridge, since 1991; Fellow of King's College, Cambridge, since 1974; *b* 17 Dec. 1942; *s* of Lewis and Joan Olive Stedman Jones; one *s* by Prof. Sally Alexander; one *s* by Prof. Miri Rubin. *Educ:* St Paul's Sch.; Lincoln Coll., Oxford (BA 1964); Nuffield Coll., Oxford (DPhil 1970). Res. Fellow, Nuffield Coll., Oxford, 1967–70; Sen. Associate Mem., St Antony's Coll., Oxford, 1971–72; Humboldt Stiftung Fellow, Dept of Philosophy, Goethe Univ., Frankfurt, 1973–74; University of Cambridge: Lectr in History, 1979–86; Reader in History of Social Thought, 1986–97. Mem., CNRS, 2005–. Mem., Editl Bd, New Left Review, 1964–81; Jt Founder and Jt Ed., History Workshop Jl, 1976–. *Publications:* Outcast London, 1971, 2nd edn 1976; Languages of Class, 1983; Klassen, Politik, Sprache, 1988; (ed) Charles Fourier, The Theory of the Four Movements, trans. I. Patterson, 1994; (ed) Karl Marx and Friedrich Engels, The Communist Manifesto, 2002; An End to Poverty?, 2004 (trans. French, 2007); Columbia, 2005. *Recreations:* country walks, collecting old books, cricket. *Address:* King's College, Cambridge CB2 1ST. *T:* (01223) 331197.

STEEDMAN, Prof. Mark, PhD; FRSE; FBA 2002; Professor of Cognitive Science, University of Edinburgh, since 1998; *b* 18 Sept. 1946; *s* of George and Nan Steedman; *m* 1987, Prof. Bonnie Lynn Webber. *Educ:* Univ. of Sussex (BSc); Univ. of Edinburgh (PhD 1973). Res. Fellow, Univ. of Sussex, 1973–76; Lectr in Psychology, Univ. of Warwick, 1976–83; Lectr, 1983–86, Reader, 1986–88, in Computational Linguistics, Univ. of Edinburgh; Associate Prof. of Computer and Inf. Sci., 1988–92, Prof., 1992–98, Adjunct Prof., 1998–, Univ. of Pennsylvania. FAAAI 1993; FRSE 2002; MAE 2006. *Publications:* Surface Structure and Interpretation, 1996; The Syntactic Process, 2000; articles in Linguistics & Philosophy, Cognition, Cognitive Science, Linguistic Inquiry, Computational Linguistics, etc. *Recreations:* jazz, hill-climbing. *Address:* School of Informatics, University of Edinburgh, 2 Buccleuch Place, Edinburgh EH8 9LW. *T:* (0131) 650 4631, *Fax:* (0131) 650 6626.

STEEDMAN, Martha, (Mrs R. R. Steedman); *see* Hamilton, M.

STEEDMAN, Robert Russell, OBE 1997; RSA 1979 (ARSA 1973); RIBA; FRIAS; MLI; Partner, Morris and Steedman, Architects and Landscape Architects, Edinburgh, 1959–2002; *b* 3 Jan. 1929; *s* of late Robert Smith Steedman and Helen Hope Brazier; *m* 1st, 1956, Susan Elizabeth (marr. diss. 1974), *d* of Sir Robert Scott, GCMG, CBE; one *s* two *d*; 2nd, 1977, Martha Hamilton, *qv*. *Educ:* Loretto Sch.; School of Architecture, Edinburgh College of Art (DA); Univ. of Pennsylvania (MLA). RIBA 1955; ALI 1979. Lieut, RWAFF, 1947–48. Worked in office, Alfred Roth, Zürich, 1953. Architectural works include: Principal's House, Univ. of Stirling; Head Offices for Christian Salvesen, Edinburgh; Administration Building for Shell UK Exploration and Production; Moss Morran Fife; Restoration of Old Waterworks, Perth, to form Tourist Information Centre and Offices; Nat. Lighthouse Mus., Fraserburgh. Ten Civic Trust Awards, 1963–88; British Steel Award, 1971; Saltire Award, 1971, 1999; RIBA Award for Scotland, 1974 and 1989; European Architectural Heritage Medal, 1975; Assoc. for Preservation of Rural Scotland Award, 1977 and 1989. Chm., Central Scotland Woodlands Project, 1984–87; Member: Countryside Commn for Scotland, 1980–88; Adv. Panel on Management of Popular Mountain Areas in Scotland, 1989; Royal Fine Art Commn for Scotland, 1984–96 (Dep. Chm., 1994–96); Council, Nat. Trust for Scotland, 1999–2005; Sec., Royal Scottish Acad., 1983–90 (Mem. Council 1981–, Dep. Pres. 1982–83, 2000–01); Mem. Bd, Friends of Royal Scottish Acad., 1984–92; Governor, Edinburgh College of Art, 1974–88; Mem., Edinburgh Festival Soc., 1978–; past Mem. Council, RIAS and Soc. of Scottish Artists. Trustee: House of Falkland, 1999–; St Andrews Preservation Trust, 2002–. Member Panel: Saltire Patrick Geddes Award, 1995–; Assoc. for Protection of Rural Scotland Annual Awards, 1995–99. Hon. Senior, St Leonards Sch., 1987–. FRSA 1995. Hon. DLitt St Andrews, 2006. *Recreations:* hill-walking, photography, redesigning other people's houses. *Address:* Muir of Blebo, Blebocraigs, by Cupar, Fife KY15 5UG. *T:* (01334) 850781. *Clubs:* New (Edinburgh); Royal & Ancient Golf (St Andrews).

STEEDS, Prof. John Wickham, FRS 1988; FInstP; Professor of Physics, since 1985 and Henry Overton Wills Professor, 2002–06, Bristol University; *b* 9 Feb. 1940; *s* of John Henry William Steeds and Ethel Amelia Tyler; *m* 1969, Diana Mary Kettlewell; two *d*. *Educ:* University College London (BSc 1961); PhD Cantab 1965. FInstP 1991. Research Fellow, Selwyn Coll., Cambridge, 1964–67; IBM Res. Fellow, 1966–67; Fellow, Selwyn Coll., Cambridge, 1967; Bristol University: Lectr in Physics, 1967–77; Reader, 1977–85; Hd of Microstructural Gp, 1985–2001; Dir, Interface Analysis Centre, 1990–2001; Hd of Physics Dept, 2001–05. Visiting Professor: Univ. of Santiago, Chile, 1971; Univ. of California, Berkeley, 1981. Chairman: Science Res. Foundn, Emersons Green, 1989–99; Commn on Electron Diffraction, Internat. Union of Crystallography, 1993–99; Emersons Innovations Ltd, 1999–2006; Mem., Council, European Pole Univ., Lille, 1993–97. Pres., W of England Metals and Materials Assoc., 2003–04. Holweck Medal and Prize, French Physical Soc., 1996. *Publications:* Introduction to Anistropic Elasticity Theory of Dislocations, 1973; (with J. F. Mansfield) Electron Diffraction of Phases in Alloys, 1984; (ed jtly) Thin Film Diamond, 1994; papers on electron diffraction, materials science and solid state physics. *Recreations:* tennis, overseas travel. *Address:* 21 Canynge Square, Clifton, Bristol BS8 3LA. *T:* (0117) 973 2183.

STEEL, family name of **Baron Steel of Aikwood**.

STEEL OF AIKWOOD, Baron *cr* 1997 (Life Peer), of Ettrick Forest in the Scottish Borders; **David Martin Scott Steel,** KT 2004; KBE 1990; PC 1977; DL; journalist and broadcaster; Member (Lib Dem) Lothians, and Presiding Officer, Scottish Parliament, 1999–2003; Lord High Commissioner, General Assembly, Church of Scotland, 2003 and 2004; *b* Scotland, 31 March 1938; *s* of late Very Rev. Dr David Steel; *m* 1962, Judith Mary, *d* of W. D. MacGregor, CBE, Dunblane; two *s* one *d*. *Educ:* Prince of Wales School, Nairobi, Kenya; George Watson's Coll.; Edinburgh Univ. (MA 1960; LLB 1962). President: Edinburgh University Liberals, 1959; Students' Representative Council, 1960. Asst Secretary, Scottish Liberal Party, 1962–64. MP (L 1965–88, Lib Dem 1988–97) Roxburgh, Selkirk and Peebles, 1965–83, Tweeddale, Ettrick and Lauderdale, 1983–97; youngest member of 1964–66 Parliament, of Privy Council, 1977. Liberal Chief Whip, 1970–75; Mem. Parly Delegn to UN Gen. Assembly, 1967; Sponsor, Private Member's Bill to reform law on abortion, 1966–67. Leader of Liberal Party, 1976–88; Co-Founder, Social and Liberal Democrats, 1988. Pres., Liberal International, 1994–96. President: Anti-Apartheid Movement of GB, 1966–69; Med. Aid for Palestinians, 1996–2004; Scottish Castles Assoc., 2002–; Chairman: Shelter, Scotland, 1969–73; Countryside Movement, 1995–96; Patron, Scottish Assoc. of Prostate Cancer Support Gps, 2002–. Mem., British Council of Churches, 1971–75; Chubb Fellow, Yale Univ., 1987. BBC television interviewer in Scotland, 1964–65; Presenter of STV weekly religious programme, 1966–67, and for Granada, 1969, and BBC, 1971–76. Rector, Edinburgh Univ., 1982–85. DL Roxburgh, Ettrick and Lauderdale, 1990. Awarded Freedom of Tweeddale, 1988, of Ettrick and Lauderdale, 1990. DUniv: Stirling, 1991; Heriot-Watt, 1996; Open, 2001; Hon. DLitt Buckingham; Hon. LLD: Edinburgh, 1997; Strathclyde, 2000; Aberdeen, 2001; St Andrews, 2003; Glasgow Caledonian, 2004. Commander's Cross, Order of Merit (Germany), 1992; Chevalier, Légion d'Honneur (France), 2003; Order of Brilliant Star (Taiwan), 2004. *Publications:* Boost for the Borders, 1964; Out of Control, 1968; No Entry, 1969; The Liberal Way Forward, 1975; A New Political Agenda, 1976; Militant for the Reasonable Man, 1977; New Majority for a New Parliament, 1978; High Ground of Politics, 1979; A House Divided, 1980; (with Judy Steel) Border Country, 1985; (presenter) Partners in One Nation: a new vision of Britain 2000, 1985; (with Judy Steel) Mary Stuart's Scotland, 1987; Against Goliath: David Steel's autobiography, 1989; contrib. to The Times, The Guardian, The Scotsman, other newspapers and political weeklies. *Recreations:* angling, classic car rallying (bronze medallion in London - Capetown, 1998). *Address:* House of Lords, SW1A 0PW; Aikwood Tower, by Selkirk TD7 5HJ. *Clubs:* National Liberal, Royal Over-Seas League.

See also C. M. Steel.

STEEL, Dame (Anne) Heather, (Dame Heather Beattie), DBE 1993; a Judge of the High Court of Justice, Queen's Bench Division, 1993–2001; Judge of the Courts of Appeal of Jersey and Guernsey, since 2004; *b* 3 July 1940; *d* of late His Honour Edward Steel and Mary Evelyn Griffith Steel; *m* 1967, David Kerr-Muir Beattie; one *s* one *d*. *Educ:* Howell's School, Denbigh; Liverpool University (LLB). Called to the Bar, Gray's Inn, 1963, Bencher, 1993; practice on N Circuit; Prosecuting Counsel to DHSS on N Circuit, 1984–86; a Recorder, 1984–86; a Circuit Judge, 1986–93. Mem., Criminal Cttee, Judicial Studies Bd, 1992–95. President: Merseyside Medico Legal Soc., 1992–94; Law Faculty Assoc., Liverpool Univ., 1994–. Member: Council, Rossall Sch., 1990–2002; Adv. Council, Soc. for Advanced Legal Studies, 2001–. Mem., Guild of Freeman, City of London, 1996–. Freeman, City of London, 1993; Liveryman: Pattenmakers' Co., 1993 (Master, 2003–04); Fan Makers' Co., 2005. *Recreations:* theatre, gardening, art, antiques.

See also Her Honour E. M. Steel.

STEEL, Prof. (Christopher) Michael, PhD, DSc; Professor in Medical Science, University of St Andrews, 1994–2005, now Emeritus; *b* 25 Jan. 1940; *s* of late Very Rev. David Steel; *m* 1962, Dr Judith Margaret Spratt, MBE; two *s* one *d*. *Educ:* Prince of Wales Sch., Nairobi; George Watson's Coll., Edinburgh; Univ. of Edinburgh (Bsc Hons, MB, ChB Hons, PhD, DSc). FRCPE; FRCSE (*ad hominem*) 1994; FRCPath; FRSE. Jun. hosp. posts in Edinburgh teaching hosps, 1965–68; Graduate Res. Fellow, Univ. of Edinburgh Faculty of Medicine, 1968–71; Mem. of Clin. Sci. Staff, MRC Human Genetics Unit, Edinburgh, 1971–93 (Asst Dir, 1979–93); MRC Travelling Res. Fellow, Univ. of Nairobi Med. Sch., 1972–73. Hon. Cons., Lothian Health Bd, 1976–. Member: Adv. Cttee, UK

Gene Therapy, 1995–2000; MRC Adv. Bd, 2000–05. Founder FMedSci 1998. *Publications:* (with D. K. Apps and B. B. Cohen) Biochemistry: a concise text for medical students, 1992; papers on molecular biology of cancer in learned jls. *Recreations:* golf, skiing. *Address:* Breakers, 3a The Scores, St Andrews, Fife KY16 9AR. *T:* (01334) 472877. *Club:* Royal Society of Medicine.
See also Baron Steel of Aikwood.

STEEL, Danielle; *see* Schüelein-Steel, D. F.

STEEL, Hon. Sir David (William), Kt 1998; **Hon. Mr Justice David Steel;** a Judge of the High Court of Justice, Queen's Bench Division, since 1998; a Judge of the Commercial Court, since 1998 (Judge in charge, 2006–07); Presiding Judge, Western Circuit, 2002–06; *b* 7 May 1943; *s* of Sir Lincoln Steel and late Barbara (*née* Goldschmidt); *m* 1970, Charlotte Elizabeth Ramsay; two *s*. *Educ:* Eton Coll.; Keble Coll., Oxford (MA Hons Jurisprudence). Called to the Bar, Inner Temple, 1966, Bencher, 1991; with Coudert Bros (Attorneys), New York, 1967–68; commenced practice in England, 1969; Junior Counsel to the Treasury (Common Law) 1978–81; Junior Counsel to the Treasury (Admiralty), 1978–81; QC 1981; a Recorder, 1991–98; a Dep. High Court Judge, 1993–98; Judge, Admiralty Ct, 1998–. Wreck Commissioner for England and Wales, 1982–98; Mem., panel of Lloyd's Salvage Arbitrators, 1982–98. Chm., Commercial Bar Assoc., 1990–91; Mem., Lord Chancellor's Adv. Cttee on Legal Educn and Conduct, 1994–98. Chm., OUBC Trust Fund Cttee, 1990–93. *Publications:* Editor: Temperley: Merchant Shipping Acts, 1976–98; Forms and Precedents: British Shipping Laws, 1977–98; Kennedy: Salvage, 1981–98. *Recreations:* golf, shooting, fishing. *Address:* Royal Courts of Justice, Strand, WC2A 2LL.

STEEL, Donald MacLennan Arklay; golf correspondent and golf course architect; *b* 23 Aug. 1937; *s* of William Arklay Steel and Catherine Fanny (*née* Jacobs), internat. golfer; *m* 1988, Rachel Ellen. *Educ:* Fettes Coll.; Christ's Coll., Cambridge (MA). Golf correspondent: Sunday Telegraph, 1961–90; Country Life, 1983–93; golf course architect, 1965–: with C. K. Cotton, Pennink, Lawrie and Partners; with C. K. Cotton, Pennink, Steel & Co.; with Donald Steel & Co. President: British Inst. of Golf Course Architects, 1989–91 (Hon. Sec., 1971–83; Chm., 1983–86); Assoc. of Golf Writers, 1993–98 (Treas., 1977–90); English Golf Union, 2006. *Publications:* (ed jtly) Shell World Encyclopaedia of Golf, 1975; (ed) Guinness Book of Golf Facts and Feats, 1980; Bedside Books of Golf, 1965, 1971; The Classic Links, 1992; (ed) 14 edns, The Golf Course Guide of the British Isles (Sunday Telegraph), 1968–96; (jtly) Traditions and Change: the Royal and Ancient Golf Club 1939–2004, 2004. *Recreations:* cricket, wine. *Address:* 1 March Square, Chichester, West Sussex PO19 5AN. *T:* (01243) 528506. *Clubs:* MCC; Hawks (Cambridge); Royal and Ancient Golf.

STEEL, Her Honour Elizabeth Mary, (Mrs Stuart Christie); DL; a Circuit Judge, 1991–2007; *b* 28 Nov. 1936; *d* of His Honour Edward Steel and Mary Evelyn Griffith Steel (*née* Roberts); *m* 1972, Stuart Christie; one *s* one *d*. *Educ:* Howells Sch., Denbigh; Liverpool Univ. (LLB). Admitted solicitor, 1960; Partner, John A. Behn Twyford & Co., 1968–80; Partner, Cuff Roberts, 1980–91; a Recorder, 1989. Member: Cripps Cttee, 1967–69; Race Relations Bd, 1970–78; Council, Radio Merseyside, 1974–78; Gen. Adv. Council, BBC, 1979–82 (Chm., NW Adv. Council). Member: Law Soc., 1960; Liverpool Law Soc., 1960 (Pres., 1989–90); Chm., Steering Cttee, Hillsborough Solicitors' Gp, 1989–91. Member: Royal Liverpool Univ. Hosp. NHS Trust, 1991; Liverpool Playhouse Bd, 1968–95 (Vice-Pres., 1995–99). Nat. Vice-Chm., YCs, 1965–67. Pres., Merseyside Br., ESU, 2006–. Gov., Liverpool John Moores Univ., 2001–. DL Merseyside, 1991. Hon. LLD Liverpool, 2007. *Recreations:* theatre (amateur and professional), music, needlework, cooking. *Address:* 70 Knowsley Road, Cressington Park, Liverpool L19 0PG; *e-mail:* elizabeth_christie@hotmail.com. *Clubs:* University Women's; Athenæum (Pres., 2002–03) (Liverpool).
See also Dame A. H. Steel.

STEEL, Dame Heather; *see* Steel, Dame A. H.

STEEL, Henry, CMG 1976; OBE 1965; Principal Legal Adviser: Government of British Antarctic Territory, 1989–2005; Government of British Indian Ocean Territory, 1991–2005; consultant on international and commonwealth law; *b* 13 Jan. 1926; *yr s* of late Raphael Steel; *m* 1960, Jennifer Isobel Margaret, *d* of late Brig. M. M. Simpson, MBE; two *s* two *d*. *Educ:* Christ's Coll., Finchley; New Coll., Oxford. BA Oxon 1950. Military Service, RASC and Intell. Corps, 1944–47. Called to Bar, Lincoln's Inn, 1951; Legal Asst, Colonial Office, 1955; Senior Legal Asst, CO, 1960; Asst Legal Adviser, CRO, 1965; Legal Counsellor, FCO, 1967–73; Legal Adviser, UK Mission to UN, NY, 1973–76; Legal Counsellor, FCO, 1976–79; Asst Under-Sec. of State (on loan to Law Officers' Dept), 1979; Legal Adviser to Governor of Southern Rhodesia, 1979–80; Asst Legal Secretary (Under-Secretary), Law Officers' Dept, 1980–83, Legal Sec. (Dep. Sec.), 1983–86; Dir, Commonwealth Legal Adv. Service, British Inst. of Internat. and Comparative Law, 1986–87; Leader, UK Delegn to UN Human Rights Commn, 1987–92 and 1994–97; special consultant to FCO on human rights reporting, 1992–2003. *Address:* College Place, Chapel Lane, Bledington, Oxon OX7 6UZ.

STEEL, John Brychan; QC 1993; a Recorder, Midland Circuit, since 2000; *b* 4 June 1954; *s* of late John Exton Steel and Valentine Brychan-Rees; *m* 1981, Susan Rebecca Fraser; two *s* one *d*. *Educ:* Harrow Sch.; Durham Univ. (BSc Hons Chem.). Pres., Durham Univ. Athletic Union, 1975–76. Lieut, Inns of Court and City Yeomanry, 1977–81; called to the Bar, Gray's Inn, 1978 (Gray's Inn Moots Prize, 1979; Bencher, 2006); Attorney-General's Suppl. Panel (Common Law), 1989–93; an Asst Recorder, 1998–2000. Mem. Cttee, Planning and Envmtl Bar Assoc. Hon. Legal Adviser: Air League, 2002–; Mission Aviation Fellowship; Hon. Legal Advr and Trustee, Bentley Priory Battle of Britain Trust; Mem., Air Squadron. Jt Founder, Busoga Trust. Chm., Kandahar Ski Club Racing, 1998–2000. FRGS 2002; FRAeS 2003; FRSA 2006. *Recreations:* ski-ing, flying, walking. *Address:* 4–5 Gray's Inn Square, WC1R 5AY. *T:* (020) 7404 5252. *Clubs:* Boodle's, Travellers'; Kandahar (Chm., 1992–96), Ski of GB (Dep. Chm., 1989–91).

STEEL, Michael; *see* Steel, C. M.

STEEL, Patricia Ann, OBE 1990; Secretary, Institution of Highways and Transportation, 1973–90; *b* 30 Oct. 1941; *d* of Thomas Norman Steel and Winifred Steel. *Educ:* Hunmanby Hall, near Filey, Yorks; Exeter Univ. (BA). Parly Liaison, Chamber of Shipping of UK and British Shipping Fedn, 1968–71; Sec., Highway and Traffic Technicians Assoc., 1972–73. Director: LRT, 1984–91; Docklands Light Railway, 1984–91 (Chm., 1988–89); Victoria Coach Station Ltd, 1988–91. Non-executive Director: TRL, 1992–96; Richmond, Twickenham and Roehampton Healthcare NHS Trust, 1992–99; NHS Litigation Authy, 2002–. Mem., Occupational Pensions Bd, 1979–84; Lay Mem., Transport Tribunal, 1999–. *Recreations:* music, travel, politics.

STEEL, Robert, CBE 1979; Secretary-General, Royal Institution of Chartered Surveyors, 1968–85 (Fellow, 1961; Hon. Member, 1985); *b* 7 April 1920; *e s* of late John Thomas Steel and Jane (*née* Gordon), Wooler, Northumberland; *m* 1943, Averal Frances, *d* of Arthur Pettitt; one *s* one *d*. *Educ:* Duke's Sch., Alnwick, Northumb.; Univ. of London (BSc 1945); Gray's Inn (Barrister, 1956). Surveyor, 1937–46; Asst Sec., Under Sec., RICS, 1946–61; Dir of Town Development, Basingstoke, 1962–67. Hon. Sec.-Gen., Internat. Fedn of Surveyors, 1967–69, Vice-Pres., 1970–72, Hon. Mem., 1983; Hon. Sec., Commonwealth Assoc. of Surveying and Land Economy, 1969–90; Sec., Aubrey Barker Trust, 1970–96; Member: South East Economic Planning Council, 1974–76; Council, British Consultants Bureau, 1977–85. Chm., Geometers Liaison Cttee, EEC, 1972–86. Hon. Editor, Commonwealth Surveying and Land Economy, 1975–90. Founder Mem., 1977, Mem. Ct of Assts, 1977–94, Master, 1988–89, Worshipful Co. of Chartered Surveyors. Organised national networks of beacons for Queen's Silver Jubilee celebrations, 1977, and for the Wedding of Prince Charles and Lady Diana Spencer, 1981. Raised: £71,210 for RICS Benev. Fund by sponsored walk of 1000 miles, John O'Groats to Land's End, 1979; £66,333 for RICS Benev. Fund and The Prince's Trust by walk of 1100 miles, Cape Wrath to Dover and London, 1985; £113,739 for Lord Mayor of London's Charity Appeal for Children, 1988, by walk of 1,200 miles from Strathy Point, Sutherland, to Portland Bill, Dorset, and London; £133,500 for National Trust Enterprise Neptune, 1990, by walk of 2,000 miles around the perimeter of England; £116,820 for Nat. Trust Centenary 1995 by walk of 4,444 miles around the perimeter of mainland Britain; £80,015 for RICS Benev. Fund and Marie Curie Cancer Care, by walk of 2,000 kms, Iona to Canterbury, 2000; £75,000 for RICS Benev. Fund, Macmillan Cancer Support and Treloar Trust, by walk of 650 miles, Balmoral to Snowdon, 2007. Hon. Member: Bulgarian Mountain Rescue Service, 1964; Union Belge des Géomètres Experts, 1976; Hon. Fellow, Inst. of Surveyors, Malaysia, 1983. Hon. LLD Aberdeen, 1985. Distinguished Service Award, Surveyors Inst. of Sri Lanka, 1986; Help the Aged Tunstall Golden Award for Outstanding Achievement, 1995. Silver Jubilee Medal, 1977. *Publications:* The Housing Repairs and Rent Act, 1954; The Rent Act, 1957; Steel Nuggets: a personal chronicle, 2002; contrib. professional jls and internat. conferences. *Recreations:* mountain walking, travel, music, family genealogy.

STEEL, Rupert Oliver; *b* 30 April 1922; *s* of Joseph Steel and Beatrice Elizabeth Courage; *m* 1st, Marigold Katharine, *d* of Percy Lowe; two *s*; 2nd, Lucinda Evelyn Tennant, *d* of Arthur James; one *s* one *d*. *Educ:* Eton. Served War of 1939–45 (despatches), Pilot, RNVR, Fleet Air Arm, 1941–46. Courage & Co. Ltd, 1946–78; Imperial Group Ltd, 1975–78; Chm., Everards Brewery Ltd, 1978–81; Director: Lloyds Bank UK Management, 1970–85; Lloyds Bank Ltd, 1977–79; Umeco plc, 1979–95; South Uist Estates Ltd, 1980–94. High Sheriff, Berks, 1985–86. *Recreation:* country. *Address:* Winterbourne Holt, Newbury, Berks RG20 8AP. *T:* (01635) 248220.

STEELE, Dr Bernard Robert; Development and Property Director (formerly Property Secretary), Methodist Homes for the Aged, 1987–91; *b* 21 July 1929; *s* of late Robert Walter and Phyllis Mabel Steele; *m* 1953, Dorothy Anne Newman; one *s* two *d*. *Educ:* Oakham Sch.; Selwyn Coll., Cambridge (MA, PhD). Scientific Officer, Min. of Supply, 1953–55; Section Leader, UKAEA, Springfields, 1955–66; Building Research Station: Head, Materials Div., 1966–69; Asst Dir, 1969–72; Dep. Dir, Building Res. Estabt, 1972–75; Borough Housing Officer, Haringey, 1975–78; Dir, Science and Research Policy, DoE, 1978–82; Head, Housing Services, GLC, 1982–86. Vis. Prof., Bartlett Sch. of Architecture and Planning, UCL, 1987–89. Chm., Environment Cttee, SRC, later SERC, 1978–81. Pres., RILEM (Internat. Union of Testing and Res. Labs for Materials and Structures), 1974–75. Chm., Watford Churches Housing Assoc., 1975–78. *Publications:* contrib. numerous scientific publications on chemistry, materials science and building. *Recreations:* travelling, photography. *Address:* 1 Broom Grove, Watford WD17 4RY. *T:* (01923) 447584.

STEELE, John Ernest, FCIPS; consultant to shipbuilding and allied industries, 1989–94; Director, Morganite Special Carbons Ltd, 1990–97; *b* 4 June 1935; *s* of William Steele and Amelia Steele (*née* Graham); *m* 1958, Lucy Wilkinson; one *s* three *d*. *Educ:* Rutherford College of Technology, Newcastle upon Tyne. MNECInst. Swan Hunter and Wigham Richardson Ltd: apprentice shipbuilder, 1951–56; Management Progression, 1956–68; Swan Hunter Shipbuilders Ltd: Local Dir, 1968–71; Purchasing Dir, 1971–74; Dep. Chm. and Dep. Chief Exec., 1974–78; Chief Exec., 1977–82; Chm. and Chief Exec., 1978–82; British Shipbuilders: Div. Man. Dir, Composite Yards, 1981–83; part time Bd Mem., 1979–82; Exec. Bd Mem., Offshore, 1982–84; a Corp. Man. Dir, Offshore, 1982–84; Exec. Bd Mem., Procurement, 1984–85; Corporate Man. Dir, Procurement and Special Projects, 1985–89; North East Shipbuilders Ltd: Commercial Dir, 1986–88; Man. Dir, 1988–89. Chairman: Cammell Laird Shipbuilders Ltd, 1981–84; V. O. Offshore Ltd, 1982–84; Scott Lithgow Ltd, 1983–84; Lyon Street Railway Ltd, 1977–84; Vosper Thorneycroft (UK) Ltd, 1984–86; Sunderland Forge Services, 1987–89; Exec. Cttee, Rigby Metal Components Ltd, 1990–91. British Cttee Mem., Det Norske Veritas, 1981–91. Director: Euroroute Construction Ltd, 1985–89; Sunderland Shipbuilders Ltd, 1988–89; non-exec. Dir, Gibraltar Shiprepair Ltd, 1987–90. Freeman, Shipwrights' Co. *Recreations:* Rugby football, golf, reading.

STEELE, John Hamilton; Vice President, Esso Norge AS, 1997; *b* 13 March 1941. *Educ:* North Carolina State Univ. (BS Civil Engr, MS Engr). MInstPet. Exxon Corp., USA: joined 1965; Oil & Gas Production; Calif. Dist Manager, 1976–78; Production Manager, Esso Production Malaysia Inc., Malaysia, 1978–82; Dir, Esso Exploration, Stavanger, 1982–85; Exxon Company, USA: Div. Manager, New Orleans, 1985–92; Production Ops Manager, Houston, 1992–93; Vice-Pres., Production, Houston, 1993–94; Man. Dir, Esso Exploration and Prodn UK, 1995–97. Mem., Soc. of Petroleum Engineers. *Recreations:* golf, ballet, opera.

STEELE, Dr John Hyslop, FRS 1978; FRSE; President, Woods Hole Oceanographic Institution, Mass, 1986–92, now President Emeritus (Director, 1977–89); *b* 15 Nov. 1926; *s* of Adam Steele and Annie Hyslop Steele; *m* 1956, Margaret Evelyn Travis; one *s*. *Educ:* George Watson's Boys' Coll., Edinburgh (Higher Cert. of Educn); University Coll., London Univ. (BSc, DSc). FRSE 1968. Marine Lab., Aberdeen, Scotland: Marine Scientist, 1951–66; Sen. Principal Scientific Officer, 1966–73; Dep. Dir, 1973–77. Dir, Exxon Corp., 1989–97. Mem., Cttee for Res. and Exploration, Nat. Geographic Soc., 1987–2000. Trustee, Robert Wood Johnson Foundn, 1991–2001. Fellow, Amer. Acad. of Arts and Sciences, 1980; FAAAS 1985. Hon. Prof., Aberdeen Univ., 1993–. Agassiz Medal, Nat. Acad. of Sciences, USA, 1973. *Publications:* Structure of Marine Ecosystems, 1974; over 100 pubns in oceanographic and ecological jls. *Recreation:* sailing. *Address:* Woods Hole Oceanographic Institution, Woods Hole, MA 02543, USA. *T:* (508) 2892220; *e-mail:* jsteele@whoi.edu.

STEELE, John Martin, CB 1995; OBE 1986 (MBE 1979); TD 1970; DL; a Civil Service Commissioner for Northern Ireland, 1999–2006; *b* 20 May 1938; *s* of John and Margaret Steele; *m* 1st, 1961, Molly Fulton (*d* 1988); one *s* two *d*; 2nd, 1992, Margaret Norma Armstrong, ISO. *Educ:* Belfast High Sch.; Queen's Univ., Belfast. Various posts, NI Civil Service, 1962–66; staff of NI Parlt, 1966–72; Dept of Community Relations, 1972–73; Second Clerk Asst, NI Assembly, 1973–74; Co-Sec., Gardiner Cttee on measures to deal with terrorism in NI, 1974; Second Clerk Asst, NI Constitutional Convention, 1975–76; DoE, NI, 1976–78; DHSS, NI, 1978–82; Dir, NI Court Service, 1982–87; Northern Ireland Office: Controller of Prisons, 1987–92; Dir, Security, 1992–96; Sen. Dir (Belfast), and Dir, Policing and Security, 1996–98. Mem., TA, 1958–85; formerly Dep. Comd 23 Artillery Bde and CO 102 Air Defence Regt, RA(V); Hon. Colonel: 102 AD Regt, 1987–93; 105 AD Regt, 1998–2004; Pres., NI Area, RAA; Vice-Chm., Council of NI War Meml Bldg. Chm., Bryson Charitable Gp (formerly Bryson House), Belfast, 2001–. DL Belfast, 1992. *Recreations:* gardening, fly-fishing, reading, cooking. *Clubs:* Army and Navy; Ulster Reform (Belfast).

STEELE, John Roderic, CB 1979; Chairman, Prisma Consulting Group (formerly Prisma Transport Consultants), since 1987; *b* 22 Feb. 1929; *s* of late Harold Graham Steele and Doris Steele (*née* Hall); *m* 1956, Margaret Marie, *d* of late Joseph and Alice Stevens; two *s* two *d*. *Educ:* Queen Elizabeth Grammar Sch., Wakefield; Queen's Coll., Oxford (MA). Asst Principal, Min. Civil Aviation, 1951; Private Sec. to Parly Sec., MTCA, 1954; Principal, Road Trans. Div., 1957; Sea Transport, 1960; Shipping Policy, 1962; Asst Sec., Shipping Policy, BoT, 1964; Counsellor (Shipping), British Embassy, Washington, 1967; Asst Sec., Civil Aviation Div., DTI, 1971; Under-Secretary, Department of Trade: Space Div. (Dep. Chm., ESA), 1973, Shipping Policy Div. (Chm., Maritime Gp of Nations for Negotiation of UN Convention on Law of the Sea; Chm., NATO Planning Bd for Ocean Shipping), 1974, Gen. Div., 1975; Dep. Sec., Dept of Trade (Chm., Policy Cttee, European Civil Aviation Conf.), 1976–80, Dept of Industry, 1980–81; Dir-Gen. for Transport, EEC, 1981–86. Chm., P & O European Transport Service, 1989–95; Director: P & O Containers Ltd, 1987–96; P&OSN Co., 1992–99. Mem., Dover Harbour Bd, 1990–92. Dir, Business Aircraft Users Assoc., 1999–2004. *Recreations:* normal. *Address:* 4 Wickham Court, Bristol BS16 1DQ; Square Ambiorix 30, Bte 30, 1000 Bruxelles, Belgium. *Clubs:* Oxford and Cambridge; Philippics.

STEELE, Jonathan Peter; journalist and author; Senior Foreign Correspondent and Assistant Editor, The Guardian, since 1994; *b* Oxford, 15 Feb. 1941; *s* of Paul Herbert Steele and Gabriele Steele (*née* Wiegand); *m* 1967, Ruth Gordin; two *s*. *Educ:* Eton Coll.; King's Coll., Cambridge (BA 1963); Yale Univ. (MA 1965). The Guardian: reporter, 1965–67; leader-writer, 1967–71; E Eur. corresp., 1971–75; Washington corresp., 1975–79; Foreign News Ed., 1979–82; Chief Foreign Corresp., 1982–88; Moscow corresp., 1988–94. Internat. Reporter of Year, British Press Awards, 1981, 1991; James Cameron Award, 1998; Media Award, Amnesty Internat., 1999; Martha Gellhorn Special Award, 2006. *Publications:* (with Ruth First and Christabel Gurney) The South African Connection, 1972; Eastern Europe since Stalin, 1974; Socialism with a German Face, 1977; (with Noam Chomsky and John Gittings) Superpowers in Collision, 1982; (with Eric Abraham) Andropov in Power, 1984; The Limits of Soviet Power, 1985; Eternal Russia, 1994; Defeat: why they lost Iraq, 2008. *Recreations:* tennis, yoga, reading, walking. *Address:* 8 Wren Street, WC1X 0HA. *T:* (020) 7837 9743. *Club:* Athenæum.

STEELE, Maj.-Gen. Michael Chandos Merrett, MBE 1972; DL; Chief of Joint Services Liaison Organization, Bonn, 1983–86; Regimental Comptroller, Royal Artillery, 1989–2001; *b* 1 Dec. 1931; *s* of late William Chandos Steele and Daisy Rhoda Steele (*née* Merrett); *m* 1961, Judith Ann Huxford; two *s* one *d*. *Educ:* Westminster School; RMA Sandhurst. Commissioned RA, 1952; Staff Coll., Camberley, 1962; BM RA, 53rd Welsh Div., 1965–67; BM, 8th Inf. Brigade, 1970–72; CO 22nd Light Air Defence Regt, RA, 1972–74; GSO1, HQ DRA, 1974–76; Comdr, 7th Artillery Brigade, 1976–78; Nat. Defence Coll., Canada, 1978–79; BGS, Defence Sales Organization, 1979–82. Col Comdt, RA, 1988–94. Hon. Col 104 Air Defence Regt, RA(V), 1987–96. Chm., Tree Council, 1994–96. Trustee, Haig Homes, 1998–2003. DL Surrey, 1996. *Recreations:* lawn tennis, gardening. *Address:* Elders, Masons Bridge Road, Redhill, Surrey RH1 5LE. *T:* (01737) 763982.

STEELE, Richard Charles, FIBiol, FICFor; Director General, Nature Conservancy Council, 1980–88; *b* 26 May 1928; *s* of Richard Orson Steele and Helen Curtis Steele (*née* Robertson); *m* 1956, Anne Freda Nelson; two *s* one *d*. *Educ:* Univ. of Wales (BSc Forestry and Botany); Univ. of Oxford. National Service, 1946–48. Assistant Conservator of Forests, Colonial Forest Service (later HMOCS), Tanganyika (later Tanzania), 1951–63; Head: Woodland Management Section, Nature Conservancy, Monks Wood, 1963–73; Terrestrial Life Sciences Section, Natural Environment Research Council, London, 1973–78; Division of Scientific Services, NERC Inst. of Terrestrial Ecology, Cambridge, 1978–80. Past Pres., Inst. of Foresters of Gt Britain. *Publications:* Wildlife Conservation in Woodlands, 1972; ed, Monks Wood: a nature reserve record, 1974; numerous papers on nature conservation, ecology and forestry in professional and scientific jls. *Recreations:* hill-walking, gardening, collecting books on natural history and E African travel. *Address:* 11 Hallgarth Close, Corbridge, Northumberland NE45 5BS. *T:* (01434) 633041.

STEELE, Prof. Robert James Campbell, MD; FRCSE, FRCS, FCSHK; Professor of Surgery (formerly of Surgical Oncology), University of Dundee, since 1996; *b* 5 March 1952; *s* of Robert Steele and Elizabeth (*née* Sheridan); *m* 1981, Susan Cachia; one *s* two *d*. *Educ:* Univ. of Edinburgh (BSc; MB ChB; MD). FRCSE 1984; FRCS 1995; FCSHK 1995. Lecturer in Surgery: Univ. of Edinburgh, 1980–85; Chinese Univ. of Hong Kong, 1985–86; Univ. of Aberdeen, 1986–90; Sen. Lectr and Reader in Surgery, Univ. of Nottingham, 1990–95. *Publications:* Practical Management of Acute Gastrointestinal Bleeding, 1993; Gastrin Receptors in Gastrointestinal Tumours, 1993; Essential Surgical Practice, 2002; many articles in learned jls. *Recreations:* music, Scottish country dancing, country sports. *Address:* Department of Surgery and Molecular Oncology, Ninewells Hospital and Medical School, Dundee DD1 9SY. *T:* (01382) 632174, *Fax:* (01382) 496361; *e-mail:* r.j.c.steele@dundee.ac.uk.

STEELE, Tommy, (Thomas Hicks), OBE 1979; actor; *b* Bermondsey, London, 17 Dec. 1936; *s* of late Thomas Walter Hicks and Elizabeth Ellen (*née* Bennett); *m* 1960, Ann Donoghue; one *d*. *Educ:* Bacon's Sch. for Boys, Bermondsey. First appearance on stage in variety, Empire Theatre, Sunderland, Nov. 1956; first London appearance, variety, Dominion Theatre, 1957; Buttons in Rodgers and Hammerstein's Cinderella, Coliseum, 1958; Tony Lumpkin in She Stoops to Conquer, Old Vic, 1960; Arthur Kipps in Half a Sixpence, Cambridge Theatre, London, 1963–64 and Broadhurst Theatre (first NY appearance), 1965; Truffaldino in The Servant of Two Masters, Queen's, 1969; Dick Whittington, London Palladium, 1969; Meet Me In London, Adelphi, 1971; Jack Point, in The Yeomen of the Guard, City of London Fest., 1978; London Palladium: The Tommy Steele Show, 1973; Hans Andersen, 1974 and 1977; one-man show, Prince of Wales, 1979; Singin' in the Rain (also dir.), 1983; Some Like It Hot, Prince Edward, (also dir.), 1992; What a Show!, Prince of Wales, 1995; Scrooge (title rôle), UK tour, 2003, London Palladium, 2005; Dr Doolittle, UK tour, 2008; *films:* Kill Me Tomorrow, 1956; The Tommy Steele Story; The Duke Wore Jeans; Tommy the Toreador; Touch It Light; It's All Happening; The Happiest Millionaire; Half a Sixpence; Finian's Rainbow; Where's Jack?; *television:* wrote and acted in Quincy's Quest, 1979. Composed and recorded, My Life, My Song, 1974; composed: A Portrait of Pablo, 1985; Rock Suite—an Elderly Person's Guide to Rock, 1987. Hon. DLitt South Bank, 1998. *Publications:* Quincy, 1981; The Final Run, 1983. *Recreations:* squash, sculpture, painting. *Address:* c/o International Artistes, 4th Floor, 193–197 High Holborn, WC1V 7BD.

STEELE-BODGER, Prof. Alasdair, CBE 1980; FRCVS; FRAgS, FRASE; freelance consultant in forensic veterinary medicine; Professor of Veterinary Clinical Studies, University of Cambridge, 1979–90; *b* 1 Jan. 1924; *s* of late Harry Steele-Bodger, MRCVS, and Mrs K. Steele-Bodger (*née* MacDonald); *m* 1948, Anne, 2nd *d* of late Captain A. W. J. Finlayson, RN, and Mrs Nancy Finlayson; three *d*. *Educ:* Shrewsbury Sch.; Caius Coll., Cambridge (BA 1945, MA); Royal 'Dick' Veterinary Coll., Edinburgh Univ. (BSc, MRCVS 1948). Hon. FRCVS 1975; Scientific FZS 1989. Gen. vet. practice, Lichfield, Staffs, 1948–77; consultant practice, Fordingbridge, Hants, 1977–79. Hon. Vet. Consultant to British Agricl Export Council, 1967–88. Vis. Prof., Univ. of Toronto, 1973. Pres., British Small Animal Vet. Assoc., 1962; Member: Horserace Scientific Adv. Cttee (formerly Jockey Club's Horserace Anti-Doping Cttee), 1973–92; UGC's Agricl and Vet. Sub-Cttee, 1973–81; Council: BVA, 1957–85 (Pres., 1966; Hon. Mem., 1985); RCVS, 1960–90 (Pres., 1972); Jt RCVS/BVA Cttee on Eur. Vet. Affairs, 1967–90; Eur. Liaison Gp for Agriculture, 1972–90; Cttee of Inquiry on Experiments on Animals, 1963–65; Council, RASE, 1967–98 (Hon. Fellow, 1993; Hon. Vice-Pres., 1996); Animal Feedingstuffs Industry/BVA/ADAS HQ Liaison Cttee, 1967–85. UK Deleg. to Fedn of Veterinarians of EEC, 1967–90; EEC Official Vet. Expert, 1974–98; Member: EEC Adv. Cttee on Vet. Trng, 1981–90; Home Office Panel of Assessors under Animals (Scientific Procedures) Act, 1986–98. Vice-Pres., Inst. of Animal Technology, 1988–2000. Dir, B & K Universal Ltd (formerly Bantin & Kingman Ltd), 1980–2000. Hon. Vet. Consultant, Nat. Cattle Breeders' Assoc., 1979–99. Mem. Bd of Advisers, Univ. of London, 1984–98. Gov., Cambs Coll. of Agric. and Hortic., 1989–90. Gen. Comr to Bd of Inland Revenue, 1969–81. Chairman: Editorial Bd, Veterinary Times (formerly Veterinary Drug), 1978–88; Adv. Bd, British Veterinary Formulary, 1987–96. Ehrenbürger, Tierärztlich Hochschule, Hannover, 1992. FRASE 1986; ARAgS 1996, FRAgS 1998. Crookes' Prize, 1970; Dalrymple-Champneys Cup and Medal, 1972. Cambridge Triple Blue. *Publications:* Society of Practising Veterinary Surgeons Economics Report, 1961, and papers in vet. jls on clinical subjects and vet. econs. *Recreations:* swimming, travel. *Address:* The Little Rectory, Grosmont, Monmouth, Wales NP7 8LW. *Clubs:* Farmers'; Hawks (Cambridge).

See also M. R. Steele-Bodger.

STEELE-BODGER, Michael Roland, CBE 1990; veterinary surgeon in private practice, retired; *b* 4 Sept. 1925; *s* of late Henry William Steele-Bodger and Kathrine Macdonald; *m* 1955, Violet Mary St Clair Murray; two *s* one *d*. *Educ:* Rugby Sch.; Gonville and Caius Coll., Cambridge. MRCVS. Mem., Sports Council, 1976–82. England Rugby Selector, 1954–70; Pres., RFU, 1973–74; Mem., Internat. Rugby Football Bd, 1974–84; Chm., Four Home Rugby Unions' Tours Cttee, 1976–88; Pres., Barbarians FC, 1987–. Cambridge Univ. Rugby Blue, Captain 1946; England Rugby Internat., 1947–48. *Recreation:* interest in all sport. *Address:* Laxford Lodge, Bonehill, Tamworth, Staffs B78 3HY. *T:* (01827) 251001. *Clubs:* East India, Devonshire, Sports and Public Schools (Life Pres.); Hawks (Cambridge).

See also A. Steele-Bodger.

STEELE-PERKINS, Crispian G.; trumpet soloist; *b* 18 Dec. 1944; *s* of Dr Guy Steele-Perkins and Sylvia de Courcey Steele-Perkins; *m* 1st, 1967, Angela Helen Hall (*d* 1991); one *s* two *d*; 2nd, 1995, Jane Elizabeth Mary (*née* Steele-Perkins). *Educ:* Marlborough Coll.; Guildhall Sch. of Music (LGSM, AGSM; Alumni 1995). Has performed with: Sadlers Wells (later ENO), 1966–73; London Gabrieli Brass Ensemble, 1974–84; RPO, 1976–80; English Baroque Soloists, 1980–91; The King's Consort, 1985–. *Address:* 5 Westfield Gardens, Dorking, Surrey RH4 3DX. *T:* (01306) 885339, (01424) 842401; *e-mail:* crispiansp@trumpet1.co.uk; *web:* www.CrispianSteele-Perkins.co.uk.

STEEMERS, Prof. Koen Alexander, PhD; RIBA; Director, Martin Centre for Architectural and Urban Studies, since 2002, and Professor of Sustainable Design, since 2005, University of Cambridge; Fellow, Wolfson College, Cambridge, since 1998; *b* 21 Nov. 1961; *s* of Theo and Greetje Steemers; *m* 1992, Jeanette Peasey; two *s*. *Educ:* European Sch., Karlsruhe; Springdale First Sch., Dorset; Queen Elizabeth's Sch., Dorset; European Sch., Brussels; Univ. of Bath (BSc, BArch); Darwin Coll., Cambridge (MPhil 1988; PhD 1992). RIBA 1991; ARB. Architect: ECD, London, 1984 and 1988–91; Borchers Metzner Kramar, Darmstadt, 1986–87; Cambridge University: Res. Associate, then Sen. Res. Associate, 1992–95; Lectr, 1995–2000; Sen. Lectr, 2000–03; Reader in Envmtl Design, 2003–05. Dir, Cambridge Architectural Res. Ltd, 1991–. Guest Prof., Chongqing Univ., China, 2002–. Pres., Passive and Low Energy Architecture Internat., 2005–. *Publications:* (jtly) Daylighting in Architecture, 1993; (with N. V. Baker) Energy and Environment in Architecture, 2000; (with N. V. Baker) Daylight Design in Architecture, 2002; (jtly) The Selective Environment, 2002; (with M. A. Steane) Environmental Diversity in Architecture, 2004. *Recreations:* red wine and Roquefort. *Address:* Department of Architecture, University of Cambridge, 1 Scroope Terrace, Cambridge CB2 1PX.

STEEN, Anthony David; MP (C) Totnes, since 1997 (Liverpool Wavertree, Feb. 1974–1983, South Hams, 1983–97); barrister; youth leader; social worker; underwriter; *b* 22 July 1939; *s* of late Stephen Nicholas Steen; *m* 1965, Carolyn Padfield, educational psychologist; one *s* one *d*. *Educ:* Westminster Sch.; occasional student University Coll., London. Called to Bar, Gray's Inn, 1962; practising Barrister, 1962–74; Defence Counsel, MoD (Court Martials), 1964–68. Lectr in Law, Council of Legal Educn, 1964–67; Adv. Tutor, Sch. of Environment, Central London Poly., 1982–83. Youth Club Leader, E London Settlement, 1959–64; Founder, 1964, and First Director, 1964–68, Task Force to help London's old and lonely, with Govt support; Govt Foundn YVFF, tackling urban deprivation, 1968–74; Consultant to Canadian Govt on student and employment matters, 1970–71. PPS to Sec. of State for Nat. Heritage, 1992–94. Member, Select Committee: on Race Relations, 1975–79; on the Envmt, 1991–94; on European Scrutiny, 1997–; on Deregulation, 1997–; on Public Admin, 2001–02. Chairman: Backbench gps on Youth and Young Children, 1976–79; Cons. Cttee on Cities, Urban and New Town Affairs, 1979–83; Parly Urban and Inner City Cttee, 1987–90; All Party Friends of Cycling, 1979–88; All-Party Gp on Trafficking of Women and Children, 2006–; Vice-Chairman: Health and Social Services Cttee, 1979–80; All-Party Fisheries Cttee, 1997–; Mem., All-Party Child Abuse Cttee; Secretary: Parly Caribbean Gp, 1979– (Vice-Chm.); Cons. back bench Trade and Industry Cttee, 1997–99; 1922 Cttee, 2001–. Chm., Chm.'s Unit Marginal Seats, 1982–84, Minority Parties Unit, 1999–2000, Cons. Central Office. Vice-Chm., Envmt Cttee, 1983–85; Chairman: Prime Minister's Cons. Deregulation Cttee, 1993–97; Sane Planning Gp, 1989–96; West Country Mems, 1992–94; Member: Parly Population and Develt Gp; Commons and Lord's Cycle Gp; Services Cttee; Chm., Cons. Friends of English Wine; Jt Nat. Chm., Impact 80's Campaign. Member: Exec. Council, NPFA; Board, Community Transport; Council of Reference, Internat. Christian Relief; Council Mem., Anglo-Jewish Assoc.; Founder Mem., CSA Monitoring Gp; Chm., Outlandos Charitable Trust; Vice-Chm., Task Force Trust; Vice-President: Ecology Bldg Soc.; Internat. Centre for Child Studies; Bentley Operatic Soc.; S Hams Young Farmers; Assoc. of District Councils; Marlborough with S Huish Horticultural Soc.; Devon CPRE;

Dartmoor Preservation Assoc.; Trustee: Educn Extra; Dartington Summer Arts Foundn; Patron: Liverpool's Open Circle for Detached Youth Work; St Luke's Hospice, Plymouth; Kidscape; Sustrans. Pres., Devon Youth Assoc. *Publications:* New Life for Old Cities, 1981; Tested Ideas for Political Success, 1983, 2nd edn 1991; Plums, 1988. *Recreations:* piano, mountain climbing, cycling. *Address:* House of Commons, SW1A 0AA; Totnes Conservative Association, Station Road, Totnes, Devon TQ9 5HW. *T:* (01803) 866069. *Clubs:* Royal Automobile; Churchill (Liverpool); Brixham (Torbay); Totnes Conservative (South Hams).

STEER, Sir Alan (William), Kt 2004; Headmaster, Seven Kings High School, Redbridge, since 1985; *b* 30 Jan. 1948; *s* of Jack and Esther Steer; *m* 1970, Julie Hodgkin. *Educ:* Magdalen Coll. Sch., Oxford; Univ. of Warwick (BA Hons 1970). Teacher: West Leeds Boys' High Sch., Leeds, 1971–76; Weavers Sch., Wellingborough, 1976–82; Dep. Hd, then Actg Hd, Grange Park Sch., Herts, 1982–85. FRSA. *Recreations:* political cartoons, Fulham Football Club, ancient history, gardening. *Address:* Seven Kings High School, Ley Street, Ilford, Essex IG2 7BT. *T:* (020) 8554 8935; *e-mail:* a.steer@skhs.net.

STEER, David; QC 1993; a Recorder, 1991–2005; *b* 15 June 1951; *s* of Alcombe Steer and Nancy Steer; *m* 1974, Elizabeth May Hide; one *s*. *Educ:* Rainford High Sch.; Manchester Poly. (BA Hons Law). Called to the Bar, Middle Temple, 1974, Bencher, 2001. Mem., Bar Council, 1995–97, 2002–04. Leader, Northern Circuit, 2002–04. *Recreations:* Rugby League, gardening. *Address:* 7 Harrington Street, Liverpool L2 9YH. *T:* (0151) 242 0707.

STEER, Deirdre V.; *see* Clancy, D. V.

STEER, James Kelly, CEng, FCILT; transport consultant; Founder, 1978, and Director, since 2002, Steer Davies Gleave (Managing Director, 1978–2002); Director and Founder, Greengauge 21, since 2005; *b* 7 Dec. 1948; *s* of Desmond and Josephine Steer; *m* 1973, Adrianne Jenifer Harris (*d* 1979); two *s*; partner, Mary Anderson Wright; one *d*. *Educ:* Somers Park Primary Sch., Malvern; Worcester Royal Grammar Sch.; University of Wales Swansea (BSc Hons Civil Engrg); Imperial Coll., London (MSc Transport; DIC). CEng 1975; MICE 1975; MIHT 1975; FCILT (MCIT 1976, FCIT 1999). Asst Engr, Freeman Fox Wilbur Smith Associates, 1969–71; Consultant, Alan M. Voorhees Associates, then Associate, MVA, 1972–78; on secondment to Strategic Rail Authy as Mem., Exec. and Man. Dir, Strategic Planning, 2002–05. Columnist, Transport Times, 2005–. Pres., Railway Study Assoc., 2008–09. *Publications:* contrib. jl articles on rail, LRT, economic appraisal, research, finance and planning. *Recreations:* sailing, admiring grand-children, overlong hikes, reflecting on the years 1645–49. *Address:* Steer Davies Gleave, 28–32 Upper Ground, SE1 9PD.

STEER, Prof. John Richardson, FSA 1981; Emeritus Professor of the History of Art, University of London; art-historian and director; *b* 14 Oct. 1928; *s* of Walter Wallis Steer and Elsie Gertrude (*née* Colman). *Educ:* Clayesmore Sch., Dorset; Keble Coll., Oxford (MA); Courtauld Inst. of Art, Univ. of London (BA). Gen. Asst, City Art Gall., Birmingham, 1953–56; Asst Lectr, Dept of Fine Art, Univ. of Glasgow, 1956–59; Lectr in Hist. of European Art, Univ. of Bristol, 1959–67; Prof. of Fine Arts, Univ. of St Andrews, 1967–80; Prof. of Hist. of Art, Birkbeck Coll., Univ. of London, 1980–84. Chm., Adv. Cttee on Validation, Heriot-Watt Univ./Edinburgh Coll. of Art, 1978–91; Chm., Art Historians Assoc. of GB, 1980–83; Vice-Chm., Scottish Theatre Ballet, 1969–71; Mem., Cttee for Art and Design, CNAA, 1977–82 (Chm., Hist. of Art/Design and Complementary Studies Bd, 1977–79); Member: Theatre Museum Adv. Council, 1981–83; Theatre Museum Cttee, V&A Mus., 1984–2001; Exec., Genius of Venice Exhibn, RA, 1983–84; Royal Fine Art Commn, 1992–99. Chm., Theatre Manoeuvres Ltd, 1991–2000. Trustee, V&A Mus., 1991–99. Adjudicator, National Student Drama Festival, 1977. Theatrical prodns include: The Seagull, St Andrews, 1971; And When Love Speaks, Edinburgh, 1975; The Privacy of the Patients, Edinburgh Fringe, 1977, ICA, 1978; Waiting for Godot, St Andrews, 1978; Minna von Barnhelm, plc, Theatre Co., Young Vic Studio, 1987. Hon. FRCA 1996. Hon. DLitt: St Andrews, 1990; Heriot-Watt, 1991. *Publications:* A Concise History of Venetian Painting, 1967; Mr Bacon's Titian (Selwyn Brinton Lecture, RSA), 1977; Alvise Vivarini, 1982; (with A. White) Atlas of Western Art History, 1994; contribs to Burlington Magazine, Apollo, Art History. *Recreation:* travel. *Address:* 1 Cheriton Square, SW17 8AE.

STEER, Wilfred Reed; QC 1972; *b* 23 Aug. 1926; *s* of George William and Dorothy Steer; *m* 1953, Jill Park; one *s* one *d*, and two step *s*. *Educ:* Bede Collegiate Sch., Sunderland, Co. Durham; London Sch. of Economics. LLB (Lond.) 1949. Called to the Bar, Gray's Inn, 1950. *Address:* Park Court Chambers, 16 Park Place, Leeds LS1 1SJ. *T:* (0113) 243 3277.

STEERE; *see* Lee-Steere.

STEFF-LANGSTON, Group Captain John Antony, MBE 1959; Executive Secretary, Royal Astronomical Society, 1980–91; *b* 5 Nov. 1926; *s* of William Austen Paul Steff-Langston, organist and composer, and Ethel Maude (*née* Fletcher); *m* 1959, Joyce Marian Brown. *Educ:* Cathedral Choir Sch., Canterbury; King's Sch., Canterbury; Pembroke Coll., Cambridge. RAF Coll., 1945–46; 45 Sqn, Ceylon, 1948; 61 Gp, Kenley, 1949; 34 Sqn, 1950–51; 80 Sqn, Hong Kong, 1951–54; 540, 58 and 82 Sqns, Wyton and Singapore, 1955–57; HQ 3 Gp, 1957–59; 80 Sqn, Germany, 1959–62; Staff Coll., Andover, 1962–63; Air Sec.'s Dept, 1963–65; OC 114 Sqn, Benson, 1966–68; aws 1968; CO Northolt, 1969–71; Defence Advr to High Comrs to NZ and Fiji, 1971–74; sowc Greenwich, 1974–75; AMPs Dept, 1975–78; retd 1978. FCMI (FBIM 1978); ARAeS 1987; FRAS 1992. Freeman, City of London, 1994; Liveryman, Fletchers' Co., 1994–. *Recreations:* ornithology, photography, travel, music, cricket. *Address:* 6 Beech Wood, Church Hill, Caterham, Surrey CR3 6SB. *T:* (01883) 344348. *Club:* Royal Air Force.

STEGGLE, Terence Harry, CMG 1990; HM Diplomatic Service, retired; Ambassador to Paraguay, 1989–91; *b* 4 March 1932; *s* of Henry Richard Steggle and Jane Steggle; *m* 1st, 1954, Odette Marie (*née* Audisio) (*d* 1988); two *d*; 2nd, 1989, Annemarie Klara Johanne (*née* Wohle). *Educ:* Chislehurst and Sidcup County Grammar School. Crown Agents, 1950–57; Lieut RA (TA), 1951–53; seconded to Govt of E Nigeria, 1957–58, 1960–62; FO 1963; served Laos, 1963, France, 1964, Zaire, 1970, Bolivia, 1978–82; Ambassador to Panama, 1983–86; Consul-Gen., São Paulo, 1986–87; Counsellor, FCO, 1987–89. *Recreations:* swimming, bridge. *Address:* c/o Foreign and Commonwealth Office, SW1A 2AH. *Club:* Rotary (Benahavis, Spain).

STEGMANN, Graham Murray, CBE 2006; Special Adviser to President of African Development Bank, since 2006; International Trustee, British Red Cross, since 2007; *b* 1 Nov. 1948; *s* of Andrew Murray Stegmann and Mary Isobel Stegmann; *m* 1979, Carol Anne Mayle; one *s* two *d*. *Educ:* University Coll., Rhodesia (BA Hons London); Fitzwilliam Coll., Cambridge (Commonwealth Schol.; MLitt 1979). Posts with DFID and FCO in London and abroad, 1975–96: Hd of Div., N, Central and Southern Africa, Malaŵi, 1986–89; Hd of Estabts, 1989–93; Hd, Develt Div., Southern Africa, Pretoria, 1993–95; Department for International Development: Hd, Aid Policy Resources, then Principal Finance Officer, 1996–2000; Africa Dir, 2000–04; Strategic Advr, 2004–06 and Dir, 2005. *Recreations:* tennis, cricket, squash, travel. *Address:* c/o African Development Bank, Tunis, Tunisia. *T:* 71102063; *e-mail:* g.stegmann@afdb.org. *Club:* Mandarins Cricket.

STEICHEN, René; Senior Partner, Arendt & Medernach, Luxembourg and Brussels, since 1995; *b* Luxembourg, 27 Nov. 1942; *s* of Félix Steichen and Hélène Rausch; *m* 1975, Marianne Belche; two *s* one *d*. *Educ:* Lycée Classique, Diekirch; Cours Supérieurs, Luxembourg; Univ. of Aix-en-Provence; Univ. of Paris (LLD); Institut d'Etudes Politiques, Paris (Dip. Econs and Finance 1966). Qualified as notary, then solicitor, 1969; practised in Diekirch, 1969–84. Mem., Diekirch DC, 1969–84, Mayor, 1974–84. MP (Social Christian) North constituency, Luxembourg, 1979–93; Sec. of State for Agric. and Viticulture, 1984–89; Minister for Agric., Viticulture and Rural Develt and Minister for Cultural Affairs and Scientific Res., 1989–93; Mem., Commn of the European Communities, 1993–95. Chm. Bd, SES (formerly Soc. Européene des Satellites), 1996–. *Address:* 36 rue Clairefontaine, 9201 Diekirch, Luxembourg.

STEIN, Christopher Richard, (Rick), OBE 2003; broadcaster; Chef, The Seafood Restaurant, Padstow, since 1975; *b* 4 Jan. 1947; *s* of late Eric and Dorothy Stein; *m* 1975, Jill Newstead (marr. diss. 2007); three *s*. *Educ:* Uppingham; New Coll., Oxford (BA English Lit. 1971). Proprietor: St Petroc's Hotel, Rick Stein's Café, Stein's Gift Shop, Stein's Patisserie, Stein's Deli, Stein's Fish & Chips, Padstow Seafood School (all in Padstow). Presenter, BBC TV series: Rick Stein's Taste of the Sea, 1995; Rick Stein's Fruits of the Sea, 1997; Rick Stein's Seafood Odyssey, 1999; Fresh Food, 1999; Rick Stein's Seafood Lovers' Guide, 2000 (Glenfiddich Food and Drink Award, for best TV prog., 2001; Glenfiddich Trophy, 2001); Rick Stein's Food Heroes, 2002; Rick Stein's Food Heroes: another helping, 2004; Rick Stein's French Odyssey, 2005; Rick Stein in Du Maurier Country, 2006; Rick Stein and the Japanese Ambassador, 2006; Rick Stein's Mediterranean Escapes, 2007. *Publications:* English Seafood Cookery, 1988 (Glenfiddich Cook Book of the Year, 1989); Taste of the Sea, 1995 (André Simon Cook Book of the Year, 1996); Fish, 1996; Fruits of the Sea, 1997; Rick Stein's Seafood Odyssey, 1999; Rick Stein's Seafood Lovers' Guide, 2000; Rick Stein's Seafood, 2001 (James Beard Award, 2005); Rick Stein's Food Heroes, 2002; Rick Stein's Guide to the Food Heroes of Britain, 2003; Rick Stein's Food Heroes: another helping, 2004; Rick Stein's French Odyssey, 2005; Rick Stein's Mediterranean Escapes, 2007; Coast to Coast, 2008. *Address:* The Seafood Restaurant, Riverside, Padstow, Cornwall PL28 8BY. *T:* (01841) 532700. *Club:* Groucho.

STEIN, Colin Norman Ralph; Sheriff of Tayside Central and Fife at Arbroath, since 1991; *b* 14 June 1948; *s* of late Colin Hunter Stein and of Margaret Lindsay Stein; *m* 1979, Dr Linda McNaught; one *s*. *Educ:* Glenalmond Coll.; Durham Univ. (BA Hons Modern History); Edinburgh Univ. (LLB). Admitted Member of Faculty of Advocates, 1975. Standing Jun. Counsel to MoD (RAF), Scotland, 1983–91; Temp. Sheriff, 1987–91. *Recreations:* angling, gardening. *Address:* c/o Sheriff Court, High Street, Arbroath DD11 1HC.

STEIN, Cyril; Chairman, St James's Club Ltd, 1995–2005; Ladbroke Group PLC, 1966–93; *b* 20 Feb. 1928; *s* of late Jack Stein and Rebecca Stein (*née* Selner); *m* 1949, Betty Young; two *s* one *d*.

STEIN, Paul Jonathan, CEng, FREng, FIET; Science and Technology Director, Ministry of Defence, since 2006; *b* London, 26 July 1957; *s* of late Philip Stein and of Greta Stein (now Bennett); *m* 2007, Juliet Esther Goodden; two step *s*; one *s* two *d* from a previous marriage. *Educ:* Beverley Boys' Sch., New Malden; King's Coll., London (BScEng Electronic Engrg). CEng 1995; FIET 2003; FREng 2006. Electronic Engr, Philips Research Labs, 1978–84; Advanced Develt Manager, MEL, 1984–91; Business Sector Manager, Thomson UK, 1991–93; Roke Manor Research: Business Unit Dir, Radio Communications Dept, 1993–96; Man. Dir, 1996–2006. Mem., Siemens UK Exec. Mgt Bd, 2000–06; non-exec. Dir, GCHQ, 2007–. *Recreations:* woodworking, guitar, motorcycling, model helicopters, computer programming, using technology. *Address:* c/o Ministry of Defence, Main Building, Whitehall, SW1A 2HB. *T:* (020) 7218 2848, *Fax:* (020) 7218 6481; *e-mail:* paul.stein894@mod.uk.

STEIN, Prof. Peter Gonville, FBA 1974; JP; Regius Professor of Civil Law in the University of Cambridge, 1968–93, now Emeritus; Fellow of Queens' College, Cambridge, since 1968; *b* 29 May 1926; *o s* of late Walter Stein, MA, Solicitor, and Effie Drummond Stein (*née* Walker); *m* 1st, 1953, Janet Chamberlain (marr. diss. 1978); three *d*; 2nd, 1978, Anne M. Howard (*née* Sayer); one step *s*. *Educ:* Liverpool Coll. (Life Gov., 1976); Gonville and Caius Coll., Camb. (Hon. Fellow, 1999); University of Pavia. Served in RN, Sub-lieut (Sp) RNVR, 1944–47. Admitted a Solicitor, 1951; Asst Lecturer in Law, Nottingham Univ., 1952–53; Lecturer in Jurisprudence, 1953–56, Prof. of Jurisprudence, 1956–68, Dean of Faculty of Law, 1961–64, Aberdeen Univ.; Chm., Faculty Bd of Law, Cambridge, 1973–76; Vice Pres., Queens' Coll., 1974–81 (Acting Pres., 1976 and 1980–81). Visiting Prof. of Law: Univ. of Virginia, 1965–66, 1978–79; Colorado, 1966; Witwatersrand, 1970; Louisiana State, 1974, 1977, 1983, 1985; Chicago, 1985, 1988, 1990, 1992, 1995; Padua and Palermo, 1991; Tulane, New Orleans, 1992, 1996 and 1998; Salerno, 1994; Lateran, Rome, 1997; Lectures: R. M. Jones, QUB, 1978; Irvine, Cornell, 1979; Sherman, Boston, 1979; Tucker, Louisiana State, 1985; David Murray, Glasgow, 1987; Maccabaean, British Acad., 1995. Fellow, Winchester Coll., 1976–91. Member: Council, Max Planck Inst. for European Legal History, Frankfurt, 1966–88; Council, Internat. Assoc. of Legal History, 1970– (Vice-Pres, 1985–); Internat. Acad. of Comparative Law, 1987–; Sec. of State for Scotland's Working Party on Hospital Endowments, 1966–69; Bd of Management, Royal Cornhill and Assoc. (Mental) Hospitals, Aberdeen, 1963–68 (Chm. 1967–68); UGC, 1971–75; US-UK Educnl (Fulbright) Commn, 1985–91; Council, British Acad., 1988–90. Chm., Ely Diocesan Trust Cttee, 1987–94. Pres., Soc. of Public Teachers of Law, 1980–81; Vice-Pres., Selden Soc., 1984–87. Foreign Fellow: Accad. di Scienze morali e politiche, Naples, 1982; Accademia Nazionale dei Lincei, Rome, 1987; Corres. Fellow, Accademia degli Intronati, Siena, 1988; Fellow, Academia Europaea, 1989; Foreign Fellow, Koninklijke Academie voor Wetenschappen, Belgium, 1991. JP Cambridge, 1970 (Supplementary List, 1988). Hon. QC 1993. Hon. Dr jur Göttingen, 1980; Hon. Dott. Giur. Ferrara, 1991; Hon. LLD Aberdeen, 2000; Hon. Dr: Perugia, 2001; Paris II, 2001. *Publications:* Fault in the formation of Contract in Roman Law and Scots Law, 1958; editor, Buckland's Textbook of Roman Law, 3rd edn, 1963; Regulae Iuris: from juristic rules to legal maxims, 1966; Roman Law in Scotland in Ius Romanum Medii Aevi, 1968; Roman Law and English Jurisprudence (inaugural lect.), 1969; (with J. Shand) Legal Values in Western Society, 1974, Italian edn 1981; (ed jtly) Adam Smith's Lectures on Jurisprudence, 1978; Legal Evolution, 1980, Japanese edn 1987; (ed jtly) Studies in Justinian's Institutes, 1983; Legal Institutions: the development of dispute settlement, 1984, Italian edn 1987; The Character and Influence of the Roman Civil Law: historical essays, 1988; (with F. de Zulueta) The Teaching of Roman Law in England around 1200, 1990; (ed and contrib.) Notaries Public in England since the Reformation (English and Italian edns), 1991; Roman Law in European History, 1999 (German trans., 1996, Spanish and Italian trans., 2001, Japanese trans., 2003, French trans., 2004, Hungarian trans., 2005); articles in legal periodicals mainly on Roman Law and legal history. *Address:* 36 Wimpole Road, Great Eversden, Cambridge CB23 1HR. *T:* (01223) 262349.

See also Lord Howard of Effingham.

STEIN, Rick; *see* Stein, C. R.

STEINBERG, Baron *cr* 2004 (Life Peer), of Belfast in the County of Antrim; **Leonard Steinberg;** President (formerly Chairman), Stanley Leisure plc (formerly L. Stanley), since 1958; *b* 1 Aug. 1936. *Educ:* Royal Belfast Academical Inst. Founded L. Stanley, Belfast, 1958; expanded group by acquisition of betting shops and casinos, incl. Mecca chain, 1989; Chairman: Stanley Casinos Ltd; Stanley Racing Ltd. Dep. Treas., Cons. Party, 1994–2002. *Address:* Stanley Leisure plc, Stanley House, 151 Dale Street, Liverpool L2 2JW.

STEINBERG, Gerald Neil, (Gerry); *b* 20 April 1945; *s* of Harry and Esther Steinberg; *m* 1969, Margaret Cruddace Thornton; one *s* one *d. Educ:* St Margaret's Primary Sch.; Whinney Hill Secondary Sch.; Durham Johnston Sch.; Sheffield Coll. of Education; Newcastle Polytechnic. Cert. of Educn for Backward Children. Teacher, Dukeshouse Wood Camp Sch., Hexham, 1966–69; Teacher, Elemore Hall, 1969–75, Dep. Head, 1975–79; Head Teacher, Whitworth House Special Sch., 1979–87. Mem., Durham City Council, 1975–87 (Sec., Labour Gp, 1981–87). MP (Lab) City of Durham, 1987–2005. Member, Select Committee: on Education, 1987–96; on Educn and Employment, 1996–98; on Public Accounts, 1998–2005; on Catering, 1998–2001; Vice Chm., Labour Educn Cttee, 1997–98 (Chm., 1990–96). *Recreations:* Sunderland AFC supporter, loves all sport (Vice Pres., Brandon AFC). *Clubs:* Sherburn Workman's, Brandon Workman's, Nevilles Cross Workman's.

STEINBERG, Prof. Hannah; Professor Emerita of Psychopharmacology, University of London, since 1989; Hon. Research Professor in Psychology, School of Social Science, Middlesex University, 1992–2001; *b* 16 March; *d* of late Michael Steinberg, doctor of law, and Marie (*née* Wein). *Educ:* Schwarzwaldschule, Vienna; Putney High School; Queen Anne's School, Caversham; Univ. of Reading (Cert. Comm.); Denton Secretarial Coll., London; University College London (BA 1st cl. Hons Psychology, PhD; Troughton Schol., 1948–50); DSc Psychopharmacol., London, 2002. FBPsS 1959, CPsychol 1990. Pres., Univ. of London Union, 1947–48; Univ. of London Postgrad. Studentship in Psychol., 1948–50. Sec. to Man. Dir, Omes Ltd, 1943–44. Part-time Lectr, LSE, 1951; University College London: Asst Lectr in Pharmacology, 1954–55; Lectr, 1955–62; Reader in Psychopharmacology, 1962–70; Prof. of Psychopharmacology (first in W Europe and USA), 1970–92; Head of Psychopharmacology Gp, Dept of Psychology, 1979–92; Hon. Res. Fellow, Dept of Psychol., 1992–. Hon. Consulting Clinical Psychologist, Dept of Psychological Medicine, Royal Free Hosp., 1970. Member MRC working parties on: Biochemistry and Pharmacology of Drug Dependence, 1968–73; Biological Aspects of Drug Dependence, 1971–75. Vice-President: Collegium Internationale Neuro-Psychopharmacologicum (CINP), 1968–74 (Emeritus Fellow, 1996; Pioneer Award, 2008); Brit. Assoc. for Psychopharmacology, 1974–76 (Mem., 1st Council, 1974; Hon. Mem., 1989); Mem., Biological Council, 1977–80. Distinguished Affiliate of Amer. Psychol Assoc., Psychopharmacology Div., 1978–; Founder Member: European Coll. of Neuropsychopharmacology; European Behavioural Pharmacol Soc.; British Psychological Society: Mem., 1954; Ed., Bulletin, 1955–62; First Hon. Sec., Psychology of Sport and Exercise Div., 1995–2000; Hon. Fellow, 2007. Member: British Pharmacol Soc. (Mem., Editl Bd, 1965–72); Experimental Psychol. Soc.; Soc. for Study of Addiction; European Health Psychol Soc.; Soc. for Medicines Res., etc. Convener, Academic Women's Achievement Gp, 1979–92. Accredited Sport Psychologist, British Assoc. of Sport and Exercise Scis, 1992. Special Trustee, Middx Hosp., 1989–92. Initiator (with E. A. Sykes), Steinberg Principle, Town and Country Planning Act, Listed Buildings Act 1990, on new develts in conservation areas. British Assoc. for Psychopharmacology/ AstraZeneca Lifetime Achievement Award, 2001. Past ed. of scientific jls. *Publications:* (trans. and ed jtly) Animals and Men, 1951; organiser of symposia, workshops and editor: (jtly) Animal Behaviour and Drug Action, 1963; Scientific Basis of Drug Dependence, 1968; (jtly) Psychopharmacology, Sexual Disorders and Drug Abuse, 1972; Joint Editor, Occasional Publications of British Psychological Society: Exercise Addiction, 1995; Quality and Quantity, 1996; Teams and Teamwork, 1996; Cognitive Enhancement, 1997; What Sport Psychologists Do, 1998; Sport Psychology in Practice: the early stages, 2000; numerous articles and reviews on psychopharmacology, drug addiction, drug combinations, psychological benefits and hazards of physical exercise, exercise addiction, creativity and writer's block. *Address:* c/o Pharmacology Department, University College London, WC1E 6BT. *T:* (020) 7267 4783, *Fax:* (020) 7267 4780.

STEINBERG, Saul Phillip; Founder, 1961, and Chairman, 1961–2001, Reliance Group Holdings Inc. (Chief Executive Officer, 1961–2000); *b* 13 Aug. 1939; *m* 3rd, 1984, Gayfryd McNabb; one *d*, one step *s*, and three *s* one *d* by previous marriages. *Educ:* Wharton School of Univ. of Pennsylvania (BScEcon). Director: Zenith National Insurance Corp.; Symbol Technologies Inc. Dir, Long Island Jewish Medical Center. Mem., Bd of Overseers, Cornell Univ. Medical Coll.; Chm., Wharton Bd of Overseers; Trustee: Univ. of Pennsylvania; NY Public Library.

STEINBERGER, Prof. Jack; Professor of Physics, Scuola Normale Superiore, Pisa, since 1986; *b* 25 May 1921; *s* of Ludwig and Bertha Steinberger; *m* 1st, 1943, Joan Beauregard; two *s*; 2nd, 1962, Cynthia Eve Alff; one *s* one *d. Educ:* New Trier Township High Sch.; Armour Inst. of Technology; Univ. of Chicago (BS Chem 1942; PhD Phys 1948). Mem., Inst. of Advanced Study, Princeton, 1948–49; Asst, Univ. of California, Berkeley, 1949–50; Prof., Columbia Univ., 1950–68 (Higgins Prof., 1965–68); Physicist, CERN, Geneva, 1968–86. Member: Nat. Acad. of Sciences; Amer. Acad. of Arts and Sciences; Heidelberg Acad. of Science; Accad. Nationale dei Lincei. (Jtly) President's Science Award, USA, 1988; (jtly) Nobel Prize for Physics, 1988; Mateuzzi Medal, Soc. Italiana della Scienze, 1991. *Publications:* papers in learned jls on discoveries leading to better understanding of elementary particles. *Recreations:* flute; formerly mountaineering, tennis, yachting. *Address:* CERN, 1211 Geneva 23, Switzerland; 25 Ch. des Merles, 1213 Onex, Switzerland.

STEINBRÜCK, Peer; Minister of Finance, Germany, since 2005; *b* Hamburg, 10 Jan. 1947; *m* 1976, Gertrud Isbary; one *s* two *d. Educ:* Christian-Albrechts Univ., Kiel (degree in econs 1974). Military service, 1968–70; Federal Government of Germany: Construction Ministry (Regl Planning), 1974–76; Planning Gp, Min. of Res. and Technol., 1976–77; Personal Sec. to Ministers Matthöfer and Hauff, 1977–78; div. responsible for Ministry of Res. and Technol., Federal Chancellery, 1978–81; Econs Directorate, Perm. Mission of Federal Rep. of Germany, E Berlin, 1981; Personal Sec. to Minister of Res. and Technol., 1981–82; Co-ordinating Desk Officer, envmtl protection, SPD Parly Gp, Bundestag, 1983–85; North Rhine-Westphalia: Desk Officer for nat. econ. policy, Planning Gp, Min. of Envmt and Agric., 1985–86; Hd, Office of the Premier,

1986–90; Schleswig-Holstein: State Secretary: Min. of Nature, Envmt and Land Develt, 1990–92; Min. of Econs, Technol. and Transportation, 1992–93; Minister of Econs, Technol. and Transportation, 1993–98; North Rhine-Westphalia: Minister of Econs and Small Business, Technol. and Transportation, 1998–2000; Finance Minister, 2000–02; Mem., State Assembly, 2002; Premier, 2002–05. Joined SPD, 1969 (a Dep. Chm., 2005–). *Address:* Ministry of Finance, Wilhelmstrasse 97, 10117 Berlin, Germany.

STEINBY, Prof. Eva Margareta, FSA; Professor of Archaeology of the Roman Empire, and Fellow of All Souls College, University of Oxford, 1994–2004; *b* 21 Nov. 1938; *d* of Kaarlo Erkki Wilén and Doris Margareta Steinby. *Educ:* Univ. of Helsinki (Hum. Kand. 1963; Fil. Kand. 1964; Fil. Lic. 1970; Fil. Dr 1976); MA Oxon 1995. FSA 1997. Institutum Romanum Finlandiae, Rome: Asst, 1973–77; Dir, 1979–82 and 1992–94; Sen. Res. Fellow, Finnish Acad., Helsinki, 1985–92. Docent in History, Univ. of Helsinki, 1977–; Vis. Fellow, All Souls Coll., Oxford, 1990–91. Fellow, Suomen Historiallinen Seura, 1978; Corresp. Fellow, Pontificia Accademia Romana di Archeologia, 1982, Fellow, 1993; Fellow: Societas Scientiarum Fennica, 1983; Academia Scientiarum Fennica, 2000; Corresp. Fellow, Deutsches Archäologisches Institut, 1984; For. Hon. Mem., Archaeol Inst. of America, 1998. Medaglia d'Oro per Benemeriti Culturali (Italy), 1983; Finnish Cultural Foundn Prize, 2003. Officer, 1st Cl., Order of White Rose (Finland), 1991. *Publications:* La cronologia delle figlinae doliari urbane, 1976; Lateres signati Ostienses, Vol. I 1977, Vol. II 1978; Indici complementari ai bolli doliari urbani (CIL, XV, 1), 1987; (ed) Lacus Iuturnae I, 1989; (ed) Lexicon Topographicum Urbis Romae, 6 vols, 1993–2000; (ed) Ianiculum-Gianicolo, 1997; La necropoli della Via Triumphalis: il tratto sotto l'Autoparco vaticano, 2003; articles in Italian, German and Finnish learned jls. *Address:* Kalevank 61 A 13, 00180 Helsinki, Finland. *T:* (9) 6852829.

STEINER, Achim; Executive Director, United Nations Environment Programme, since 2006; *b* Carazinho, Brazil, 17 May 1961; *s* of Roland Steiner and Helga Steiner; *m* 2001, Elizabeth Clare Rihoy; two *s. Educ:* Worcester Coll., Oxford (BA 1983); Sch. of Oriental and African Studies, Univ. of London (MA 1985); German Development Inst.; Harvard Business Sch. Tech. Advr, Masaara Shams Omania, Sultanate of Oman, 1979–80; community develt worker, Anthyodhaya Sangh, 1983–84; GTZ: Tech. Advr, 1986–88; Desk Officer, Asia/Middle East, 1988–89; Policy Advr, 1989–91; International Union for Conservation of Nature: Prog. Coordinator, Regl Office for S Africa, 1991–94; Sen. Policy Advr, Global Policy Unit, 1994–97; Chief Tech. Advr, Mekong River Commn, 1997–98; Sec. Gen., World Commn on Dams, 1998–2001; Dir Gen., IUCN, 2001–05. *Address:* (office) PO Box 47074, 00100 Nairobi, Kenya. *T:* (20) 7624001, (20) 7624002, *Fax:* (20) 7624275, (20) 7624006; *e-mail:* executiveoffice@unep.org.

STEINER, Prof. (Francis) George, MA, DPhil; FBA 1998; FRSL; Fellow, Churchill College, Cambridge, since 1961; Weidenfeld Professor of Comparative Literature, and Fellow of St Anne's College, Oxford, 1994–95; *b* 23 April 1929; *s* of Dr F. G. and Mrs E. Steiner; *m* 1955, Zara Shakow (*see* Z. Steiner); one *s* one *d. Educ:* Paris (BèsL); Univ. of Chicago (BA); Harvard (MA); Oxford (DPhil). Member, staff of the Economist, in London, 1952–56; Inst. for Advanced Study, Princeton, 1956–58; Gauss Lectr, Princeton Univ., 1959–60; Prof. of English and Comparative Literature, Univ. of Geneva, 1974–94, Prof. Emeritus, 1994–. Lectures: Massey, 1974; Leslie Stephen, Cambridge, 1986; W. P. Ker, 1986, Gifford, 1990, Univ. of Glasgow; Page-Barbour, Univ. of Virginia, 1987; Paul Tillich, Harvard, 1999. Fulbright Professorship, 1958–69; Vis. Prof., Collège de France, 1992; Charles Eliot Norton Prof., Harvard, 2001–02. Pres., English Assoc., 1975; Corresp. Mem., (Federal) German Acad. of Literature, 1981; Hon. Mem., Amer. Acad. of Arts and Scis, 1989; Hon. FRA 1999; Hon. RA 2000. FRSL 1964. Hon. Fellow: Balliol Coll., Oxford, 1995; St Anne's Coll., Oxford, 1998. Hon. DLitt: East Anglia, 1976; Louvain, 1980; Mount Holyoke Coll., USA, 1983; Bristol, 1989; Glasgow, 1990; Liège, 1990; Ulster, 1993; Durham, 1995; Kenyan Coll., USA, 1996; Trinity Coll., Dublin, 1996; Rome, 1998; Sorbonne, 1998; Salamanca, 2002; Athens, 2004; Bologna, 2006; London, 2006. O. Henry Short Story Award, 1958; Guggenheim Fellowship, 1971–72; Zabel Award of Nat. Inst. of Arts and Letters of the US, 1970; Faulkner Stipend for Fiction, PEN, 1983; PEN Macmillan Fiction Prize, 1993; Truman Capote Lifetime Award for Lit., 1999; Prince of Asturias Prize, Spain, 2001; Ludwig Börne Prize, Germany, 2003; Mondello Prize, Italy, 2004; Redonda Prize, Spain, 2007. Chevalier de la Légion d'Honneur (France), 1984; Comdr, Ordre des Arts et des Lettres (France), 2001. *Publications:* Tolstoy or Dostoevsky, 1958; The Death of Tragedy, 1960; Anno Domini, 1964; Language and Silence, 1967; Extraterritorial, 1971; In Bluebeard's Castle, 1971; The Sporting Scene: White Knights in Reykjavik, 1973; After Babel, 1975 (adapted for TV as The Tongues of Men, 1977); Heidegger, 1978; On Difficulty and Other Essays, 1978; The Portage to San Cristobal of A. H., 1981; Antigones, 1984; George Steiner: a reader, 1984; Real Presences: is there anything in what we say?, 1989; Proofs and Three Parables, 1992; The Deeps of the Sea (fiction), 1996; No Passion Spent, 1996; Errata: an examined life, 1997; Grammars of Creation, 2001; Lessons of the Masters, 2003; My Unwritten Books, 2008. *Recreations:* music, chess, mountain walking. *Address:* 32 Barrow Road, Cambridge CB2 2AS. *Clubs:* Athenæum; Harvard (New York).

STEINER, Prof. Hillel Isaac, PhD; FBA 1999; Professor of Political Philosophy, University of Manchester, since 1995; *b* 1942; *m* 1966. *Educ:* Univ. of Toronto (BA); Carleton Univ. (MA); Univ. of Manchester (PhD). Lectr in Politics and Public Admin, Univ. of Saskatchewan, 1966–67; Res. Associate, 1967–71, Lectr, then Sen. Lectr, 1971–95, Reader, 1995, in Pol Philosophy, Univ. of Manchester. *Publications:* Essay on Rights, 1994; A Debate Over Rights, 1998; Left-Libertarianism and its Critics, 2000; Freedom: a philosophical anthology, 2007; contrib. to learned jls. *Address:* Manchester Centre for Political Theory, School of Social Sciences, University of Manchester, Oxford Road, Manchester M13 9PL.

STEINER, Prof. Robert Emil, CBE 1979; Professor of Diagnostic Radiology, University of London, Royal Postgraduate Medical School, 1961–83, now Emeritus; *b* 1 Feb. 1918; *s* of Rudolf Steiner and Clary (*née* Nordlinger); *m* 1945, Gertrude Margaret Konirsch; two *d. Educ:* University of Vienna; University College, Dublin. Dep. Director, Dept of Radiology, Hammersmith Hosp.; Lecturer Diagnostic Radiology, Postgraduate Med. School of London, 1950, Sen. Lecturer, 1955, Director, 1955–. Vice-Chm., Nat. Radiological Protection Bd, 1972–83. Past Consultant Adviser in Radiology to DHSS; Past Civil Consultant in Radiology to Med. Dir-Gen., Navy. Warden of Fellowship, Faculty of Radiologists. Former Mem. Council, RCS; Past Pres., British Inst. Radiology; Pres., RCR, 1977–80. Hon. Fellow: Amer. Coll. of Radiology; Australian Coll. of Radiology; Faculty of Radiologists, RCSI. Hon. Mem., Radiological Socs of Finland, N America, Switzerland and Austria; Amer. Roentgen Ray Soc.; Germany Roentgen Soc. Barclay Medal, British Inst. of Radiology; Gold Medal, RCR, 1986; Gold Medal, European Radiology Assoc., 2007. Former Editor, British Jl of Radiology. *Publications:* Clinical Disorders of the Pulmonary Circulation, 1960; Recent Advances of Radiology, vols 4–8, 1979–85; contrib. to British Journal of Radiology, Clinical Radiology, British Heart Jl, Lancet, BMJ, etc. *Address:* 12 Stonehill Road, East Sheen, SW14 8RW. *T:* (020) 8876 4038. *Club:* Hurlingham.

STEINER, Prof. Ullrich; John Humphrey Plummer Professor of Physics of Materials, University of Cambridge, since 2004; *b* 27 March 1963; *s* of Richard Steiner and Elisabeth Steiner (*née* Konrad); *m* 1995, Barbara Gorodecki; one *d*. *Educ:* Dip. Physics; Dr rer. nat.; Habilitation. Prof. of Polymer Science, Univ. of Groningen, 1999–2004. (Jtly) Raymond and Beverley Sackler Prize for Physical Scis, Tel Aviv Univ., 2002. *Publications:* 60 articles in scientific jls; 3 patents. *Recreations:* ski-ing, sailing, cycling. *Address:* Department of Physics, University of Cambridge, Cavendish Laboratory, J. J. Thomson Avenue, Cambridge CB3 0HE. *T:* (01223) 337390, *Fax:* (01223) 337074.

STEINER, Dr Zara, FBA 2007; Fellow, New Hall, Cambridge, 1965–96, Fellow Emeritus, 1997; *b* 6 Nov. 1928; *d* of Joseph and Frances Shakow; *m* 1955, Prof. (Francis) George Steiner, *qv*; one *s* one *d*. *Educ:* Swarthmore Coll. (BA 1948); St Anne's Coll., Oxford (BA 1950); Radcliffe Coll., Harvard Univ. (PhD 1962). Lectr, Center of Internat. Studies, Princeton Univ., 1957–58 and 1960–61. Visiting Professor: Stamford Univ., Calif, 1979–80; Inst. Univ. des Hautes Etudes Internationales, Geneva, 1980–81; Univ. of N Carolina, 1985. Hon. DLitt S Sewanee, Tennessee, 1997. *Publications:* The State Department and the Foreign Service, 1958; Present Problems of the Foreign Service, 1961; The Foreign Office and Foreign Policy 1898–1914, 1969, rev. edn 1986; Britain and the Origins of the First World War, 1977, 2nd edn (with K. Neilson), 2005; (ed) The Times Survey of Foreign Ministries of the World, 1982; The Lights that Failed: European International History 1919–1933, 2005; articles in jls incl. Jl Modern Hist., Historical Jl, Relns Internationales, Diplomacy and Statecraft. *Recreation:* dog walking. *Address:* 32 Barrow Road, Cambridge CB2 8AS. *T:* (01223) 461043; *e-mail:* zs202@hermes.cam.ac.uk. *Club:* Lansdowne.

STEINFELD, Alan Geoffrey; QC 1987; *b* 13 July 1946; *s* of Henry Chaim Steinfeld and Deborah Steinfeld; *m* 1976, Josephine Nicole (*née* Gros); two *s*. *Educ:* City of London Sch.; Downing Coll., Cambridge (BA Hons, LLB). Arnold McNair Schol. in Internat. Law, 1967; Whewell Schol. in Internat. Law, 1968. Called to the Bar, Lincoln's Inn, 1968, Bencher, 1996; commenced pupillage at the Bar, 1968, practice at the Bar, 1969; a Dep. High Court Judge, 1995–. *Recreations:* tennis, ski-ing, sailing, opera. *Address:* (chambers) 24 Old Buildings, Lincoln's Inn, WC2A 3UJ. *T:* (020) 7404 0946. *Club:* Royal Automobile.

STEINMEIER, Frank-Walter; Minister for Foreign Affairs, Germany, since 2005; *b* 5 Jan. 1956; *s* of Walter Steinmeier and Ursula Steinmeier (*née* Broy); *m* 1995, Elke Büdenbender; one *d*. *Educ:* Blomberg Grammar Sch.; Justus Liebig Univ., Giessen (1st State Law Exam 1982, 2nd State Law Exam 1986; Doctorate 1991). State Chancellery of Lower Saxony: Hd, Dept, 1994–96, responsible for policy guidelines and interministerial co-ordination and planning; State Sec. and Head, 1996–98; State Sec., Federal Chancellery and Comr for Federal Intelligence Services, 1998–99; Hd, Federal Chancellery, 1999–2005. Cavaliere di Gran Croce, 2006. *Publications:* Made in Germany; Sicherheit im Wandel (The Changing Face of Security); Bürger ohne Obdach (Citizens without Shelter). *Address:* Deutscher Bundestag, Platz der Republik, 11011 Berlin, Germany.

STELL, Edward Jedidiah; Parliamentary Counsel, since 2005; *b* 8 June 1962; *s* of Christopher Fyson Stell and Dorothy Jean Stell (*née* Mackay); *m* 1991, Jocelyn Helen Whyte; two *s* one *d*. *Educ:* Merchant Taylors' Sch., Northwood; Corpus Christi Coll., Oxford (BA 1985, MA 1988). Articled clerk, 1988–1990, asst solicitor, 1990–93, Ashurst Morris Crisp; Office of the Parly Counsel, 1993–. *Recreations:* cycling, books, trying to understand things. *Address:* Office of the Parliamentary Counsel, 36 Whitehall, SW1A 2AY.

STELLINI, Salv. John, MOM 2005; Ambassador of Malta to Portugal, 2003–08; *b* 19 July 1939; *s* of Joseph and Victoria Stellini; *m* 1969, Lucinda Flannery; one *s* one *d*. *Educ:* Royal Univ. of Malta (BA Hons); Univ. of Alberta (MA); LSE (Dip. Int. Rel.). Teacher, 1959–65; Maltese Diplomatic Service, 1966–80: 2nd Sec., New York, 1968–71; 1st Sec., London, 1974–79; Dir for Internat. Marketing, 1981–87; Ambassador to USA, 1988–91; High Comr for Malta in London, 1991–96; Ministry of Foreign Affairs, Malta: Perm. Sec., 1996–2001; Advr, 2001–05. *Recreations:* reading, visiting historical sites, museums, theatre. *Address:* c/o Ministry of Foreign Affairs, Palazzo Parisio, Merchant's Street, Valletta CMR 02, Malta.

STELMACH, Hon. Edward Michael; MLA (Progressive C) Fort Saskatchewan-Vegreville, Canada, since 2004 (Vegreville-Viking, 1993–2004); Premier of Alberta and Minister for Public Affairs Bureau, since 2006; Leader, Progressive Conservative Party, since 2006; *b* 11 May 1951; *s* of Michael Stelmach and Nancy Stelmach; *m* Marie Warshawski; four *c*. *Educ:* Univ. of Alberta. Mixed farm business, 1973–. Minister: of Agriculture, Food and Rural Develt, 1997–99; of Infrastructure, 1999–2001; of Transportation, 2001–04; of Internat. and Intergovtl Relns, 2004–06. Chm. Bd, Vegreville Health Unit; Member Board: Archer Meml Hosp.; Lamont Auxiliary Hosp. and Nursing Home. Member: Andrew Co-op. Assoc.; Lamont 4-H Dist Council; Andrew 4-H Beef Club. *Recreations:* golf, reading. *Address:* (office) 307 Legislative Building, 10800 97th Avenue, Edmonton, AB T5K 2B6, Canada. *T:* (780) 4272251, *Fax:* (780) 4271349; *e-mail:* premier@gov.ab.ca.

STELZER, Irwin Mark, PhD; Director, Economic Policy Studies, and Senior Fellow, Hudson Institute, since 1998; President, Irwin M. Stelzer Associates, since 1981; Columnist, Sunday Times, since 1985; *b* 22 May 1932; *s* of Abraham Stelzer and Fanny Dolgins Stelzer; *m* 1981, Marian Faris Stuntz; one *s*. *Educ:* New York Univ. (BA 1951; MA 1952); Cornell Univ. (PhD 1954). Researcher and consultant, 1951–61; Lectr, New York Univ., and City Coll., NY, 1951–61; Teaching Asst, Cornell Univ., 1953–54; Instr, Univ. of Connecticut, 1954–55; Pres., Nat. Economic Res. Associates, 1961–81; Dir, Energy and Envmtl Policy Center, Harvard Univ., 1985–88; Resident Schol., American Enterprise Inst., 1990–98. Vis. Fellow, Nuffield Coll., Oxford, 2004–; Sen. Res. Fellow, Smith Inst., 2005–. Mem., Pres., Adv. Cttee to US Trade Rep. Mem. Bd of Dirs, Regulatory Policy Inst., Oxford, 2000–. Mem., Vis. Cttee, Harris Sch., Univ. of Chicago. Mem., Editl Bd, Public Interest. *Publications:* Selected Antitrust Cases: landmark decisions, 1955; The Antitrust Laws: a primer, 1996, 4th edn 2001; Neoconservatism, 2004; contrib. to Public Interest, Commentary and other jls. *Recreation:* photography. *Clubs:* Reform, Royal Automobile; Cosmos, Metropolitan (Washington).

STEMBRIDGE, David Harry; QC 1990; a Recorder of the Crown Court, 1977–97; *b* 23 Dec. 1932; *s* of Percy G. Stembridge and Emily W. Stembridge; *m* 1956, Therese C. Furer; three *s* one *d*. *Educ:* St Chad's Cathedral Choir Sch., Lichfield; Bromsgrove Sch.; Birmingham Univ. (LLB Hons). Called to the Bar, Gray's Inn, 1955; practising barrister, 1956–2003. *Recreations:* music, sailing. *Address:* Omega, 101 Court Road, Newton Ferrers, Plymouth PL8 1DE. *Club:* Bar Yacht.

STEMPLOWSKI, Prof. Ryszard, PhD, DHabil; Professor of History and International Relations, Jagellonian University, Cracow, since 2005; *b* 25 March 1939; *s* of Kazimierz Stemplowski and Eugenia Białecka; *m* 1975, Irena Zasłona; two *d*. *Educ:* Tech. Lycée (Civil Build.), Bydgoszcz; Tech. Univ., Wrocław; Univ. of Wrocław (LLM 1968); Inst. of History, Polish Acad. of Scis (PhD 1973); Dr Habilitatus (Hist.) Warsaw Univ., 1999. Res. Fellow, Inst. of History, 1973–90; Chief of Chancellery of Sejm (Chamber of Deputies), Poland, 1990–93; Polish Ambassador to UK, 1994–99; Dir, Polish Inst. of Internat. Affairs, Warsaw, 1999–2004; Prof. of Political Theory, Warsaw Sch. of Econs, 2001–05. Ed., Polish Diplomatic Rev., 2000–04. Vis. Fellow, St Antony's Coll., Oxford, 1974; Vis. Scholar and Alexander von Humboldt Fellow, Univ. of Cologne, 1981–82. Interfaith Golden Medallion, Peace Through Dialogue, UK, 1999. Kt Cross, Order of Polonia Restituta (Poland), 2000; Grand Cross of Merit, Constantinian Order of St George (House of Bourbon Two Sicilies), 1996. *Publications:* Dependence and Defiance: Argentina and rivalries among USA, UK and Germany 1930–46, 1975; (jtly) History of Latin America 1850–1980, 3 vols, 1978–80; (jtly) Economic Nationalism in East Central Europe and South America 1918–39, 1990; (jtly) The Slavic Settlers in Misiones 1897–1947, 1992; State-Socialism in the Actually Existing Capitalism: Chile 1932, 1996; An Introduction to Polish Foreign Policy Analysis, 2006, 2nd edn 2007; numerous other works and translations in Polish, German, Spanish, English. *Recreations:* music, astrophysics. *Address:* ul. Gubinowska 7m.151, 02–956 Warszawa, Poland; *e-mail:* ryszard@stemplowski.pl.

STEPAN, Prof. Alfred, PhD; FBA 1997; Wallace S. Sayre Professor of Government, Columbia University, New York, since 1999; *b* 22 July 1936; *s* of Alfred C. Stepan, Jr and Mary Louise Quinn; *m* 1964, Nancy Leys; one *s* one *d*. *Educ:* Univ. of Notre Dame (BA 1958); Balliol Coll., Oxford (BA PPE 1960; MA 1963); Columbia Univ. (PhD Comparative Politics 1969). Special Corresp., Economist, 1964; Staff Mem., Social Sci. Dept, Rand Corp., 1966–69; Yale University: Asst Prof., Associate Prof., and Prof. of Political Science, 1970–83; Dir, Concilium on Internat. and Area Studies, 1982–83; Columbia University: Dean, Sch. of Internat. and Public Affairs, 1983–91; Prof. of Political Sci., 1983–87; Burgess Prof. of Political Sci., 1987–93; first Rector and Pres., Central European Univ., Budapest, Prague and Warsaw, 1993–96; Gladstone Prof. of Govt, and Fellow of All Souls Coll., Oxford Univ., 1996–99. Guggenheim Fellow, 1974–75; Vis Prof. and Lectr to numerous acad. bodies and confs, USA, Europe, S America and Asia. Former Member: Bd of Govs, Foreign Policy Assoc.; NEC, Americas Watch. Former Chm., Richard Tucker Music Foundn. Fellow, Amer. Acad. of Arts and Scis. Member, Editorial Board: Jl of Democracy, 1989–; Government and Opposition, 1996–; Jl of Civil Soc. Hon. Fellow, St Antony's Coll., Oxford, 2006. Mem., Order of Rio Branco (Brazil), 2002. *Publications:* The Military in Politics: changing patterns in Brazil, 1971; The State and Society: Peru in comparative perspective, 1978; Rethinking Military Politics: Brazil and the southern cone, 1988; (with Juan J. Linz) Problems of Democratic Transition and Consolidation: Southern Europe, South America and post-Communist Europe, 1996; Arguing Comparative Politics, 2001; editor, jt editor and contrib. to numerous other works and learned jls. *Recreations:* opera, gardening, walking. *Address:* 210 Riverside Drive, New York, NY 10025, USA; 8 Frognal Gardens, NW3 6UX.

STEPHANOPOULOS, Konstantinos; President of Greece, 1995–2005; *b* Patras, 1926; *s* of Demetrius and Vrisiis Stephanopoulos; *m* 1959, Eugenia El Stounopoulou; two *s* one *d*. *Educ:* Univ. of Athens. Private law practice, 1954–74. MP for Achaia: (Nat. Radical Union), 1964; (New Democracy Party), 1974–89; (Party of Democratic Renewal), 1989–93; Under-Sec. of Commerce, 1974; Minister of the Interior, 1974–76; Minister of Social Services, 1976–77; Prime Minister's Office, 1977–81; Parly Rep., New Democracy Party, 1981–85; Leader, Party of Democratic Renewal, 1985–94. *Address:* Valaoritou Street 9B, Athens 10671, Greece.

STEPHEN, Alexander, FCCA; Chief Executive, Dundee City Council, since 1995; *b* 17 Sept. 1948; *m* Joyce Robertson; one *s* one *d*. FCCA 1977. Local govt posts, 1970–; Chief Exec., Dundee City DC, 1991–95. Treas., Revival, 1991–. *Address:* (office) 21 City Square, Dundee DD1 3BY. *T:* (01382) 434201.

STEPHEN, Barrie Michael Lace; *see* Stephen, M.

STEPHEN, David; *see* Stephen, J. D.

STEPHEN, David; Chief Executive, Student Awards Agency for Scotland, since 1999; *b* 21 Nov. 1947; *s* of John and Margaret Stephen; *m* 1970, Rosalyn Slater; one *s* one *d*. *Educ:* Aberdeen Grammar Sch.; Univ. of Aberdeen. Chartered FCIPD 2003. Asst Dir of Manpower, NHS Mgt Exec., 1988–91; Hd, Personnel Policy, Scottish Office, 1991–98; Dir of Ops, Student Awards Agency for Scotland, 1998–99. *Recreations:* golf, swimming, travel. *Address:* Student Awards Agency for Scotland, Gyleview House, 3 Redheughs Rigg, Edinburgh EH12 9HH. *T:* (0131) 244 5867, *Fax:* (0131) 244 5717; *e-mail:* david.stephen@scotland.gsi.gov.uk. *Club:* Glencorse Golf.

STEPHEN, Dr (George) Martin; High Master, St Paul's School, since 2004; *b* 18 July 1949; *s* of Sir Andrew Stephen, MB, ChB and late Lady Stephen (*née* Frances Barker); *m* 1971, Jennifer Elaine Fisher, JP; three *s*. *Educ:* Uppingham Sch.; Univ. of Leeds (BA); Univ. of Sheffield (Dip Ed, Dist., PhD; Hallam Prize for Educn, 1971). Child supervisor, Leeds and Oxford Remand Homes, 1966–67; Teacher of English, Uppingham, 1971–72, Haileybury, 1972–83 (and Housemaster); Second Master, Sedbergh, 1983–87; Headmaster, Perse Sch. for Boys, Cambridge, 1987–94; High Master, Manchester Grammar Sch., 1994–2004. Vis. Lectr, Manchester Univ., 2001–. Member: ESRC, 1990–; Naval Review, 1992–; Community Service Volunteers' Educnl Adv. Council, 1994–; HMC/GSA Univ. Admissions Working Gp, 1994–; British Assoc. for Sport and Law, 1995–; Chm., HMC, 2004 (Chm., Community Service Cttee, 1992–95). Associate Mem., Combination Room, GCCC, 1988–94. Member: Portico Library, Manchester, 1995–2000; Bd, Royal Exchange Theatre, Manchester, 1999–; Bd, LAMDA, 2004–. Trustee, Project Trust, 1994–. Mem. Court, Univ. of Salford, 2000–04; Governor: Withington Sch., Manchester, 1994–2002; Pownall Hall Sch., Wilmslow, 1994–2004; Ducie High Sch., Moss Side, 1995–2004; Orley Farm Sch., 2004–; Manchester City Acad., 2004–; The Hall Sch., Hampstead, 2004–; Durston House Sch., 2005–. FRSA 1996. Hon. DEd De Montfort, 1997. *Publications:* An Introductory Guide to English Literature, 1984; Studying Shakespeare, 1984; British Warship Designs since 1906, 1985; English Literature, 1986, 4th edn 1999; (ed) Never Such Innocence, 1988, 3rd edn 1993; Sea Battles in Close Up, 1988, 2nd edn 1996; The Fighting Admirals, 1991; (ed) The Best of Saki, 1993, 2nd edn 1996; The Price of Pity: poetry, history and myth in the Great War, 1996; (contrib.) Machiavelli, Marketing and Management, 2000; The Desperate Remedy, 2002; The Conscience of the King, 2004; The Galleons' Grave, 2005; The Rebel Heart, 2006; The Diary of a Stroke, 2008; contrib. York Notes series; articles and reviews for various jls. *Recreations:* writing, directing plays, pen and ink drawing, field and water sports, music. *Address:* St Paul's School, Lonsdale Road, Barnes, SW13 9JT. *Clubs:* Athenæum, East India (Hon. Mem.).

STEPHEN, Henrietta Hamilton, (Rita), MBE 1973; National Officer, GMB, 1989–91; *b* 9 Dec. 1925; *d* of late James Pithie Stephen, engine driver, Montrose and late Mary Hamilton Morton, South Queensferry. *Educ:* Wolseley Street and King's Park Elem.

Schs, Glasgow; Queen's Park Sen. Secondary, Glasgow; Glasgow Univ. (extra-mural); LSE (TUC Schol.). McGill Univ. and Canada/US Travel, 1958–59. Law office junior, 1941; Clerk, Labour Exchange (Mem. MLSA), 1941–42; Post Office Telephonist, 1942–60; Officer, Union of Post Office Workers, Glasgow Br., 1942–60; Member: UPW Parly Panel, 1957; London and Home Counties Area Organiser, CAWU, 1960–65; Nat. Sec., CAWU, subseq. APEX, 1965–89. Editor, The Clerk, 1965–71; Union Educn Officer, 1965–72; Delegate: TUC; Labour Party Annual Confs; Member: EDC for Food and Drink Manufacturing, 1976–90; Food Standards Cttee, 1968–80; Mary Macarthur Educnl Trust, 1965–; Distributive Industry Trng Bd, 1968–73; Monopolies and Mergers Commn, 1973–83; British Wool Marketing Bd, 1973–88; Trustee, Mary Macarthur Holiday Trust, 1993–. Mem., TUC Women's Adv. Cttee, 1983; Chair, Nat. Jt Cttee of Working Women's Organisations, 1983–84. Life Mem., Work Foundn (formerly Industrial Soc.), 1992–. Mem., Court of Govs, LSE, 1976–2005 (Gov. Emeritus, 2005). *Publications:* (jtly) Training Shop Stewards, 1968; (with Roy Moore) Statistics for Negotiators, 1973; contrib. Clerk, Industrial Soc. Jl, Target, etc. *Recreations:* food, walking, conversation, travel, theatre, reading. *Address:* 3 Pond Road, SE3 9JL. *T:* and *Fax:* (020) 8852 7797; *e-mail:* rita-stephen@o2.co.uk.

STEPHEN, (John) David; independent writer and consultant on international affairs, since 2006; Associate, Action for a Global Climate Community, since 2006; Partner, European Political Affairs Associates, since 2007; *b* 3 April 1942; *s* of late John Stephen and Anne Eileen Stephen; *m* 1968, Susan Dorothy (*née* Harris); three *s* one *d*. *Educ:* Denbigh Road Primary Sch., Luton; Luton Grammar Sch.; King's Coll., Cambridge (BA Mod. Langs, 1964); Univ. of San Marcos, Lima, Peru; Univ. of Essex (MA Govt, 1968). Educn Officer, CRC, 1969–70; with Runnymede Trust, 1970–75 (Dir, 1973–75); Latin American Regional Rep., Internat. Univ. Exchange Fund, 1975–77; Special Adviser to Sec. of State for Foreign and Commonwealth Affairs, 1977–79; Editor, International Affairs, 1979–83; Dir, UK Immigrants Advisory Service, 1983–84; Commonwealth Development Corporation: Mem., Management Bd, 1984–92; Head of External Relations, 1985–89; Dir of Corporate Relns, 1989–92; Principal Officer, Exec. Office of Sec.-Gen., UN, 1992–96 and March–Sept 1997; Dir, UN Verification Mission, Guatemala, June 1996–Feb. 1997; Rep. of UN Sec.-Gen., and Dir, UN Office for Somalia, 1997–2001; Rep. of UN Sec.-Gen., and Hd, UN Peace-building Support Office for Guinea-Bissau, 2002–04; Dir, European Movement, 2004–06. Trustee, Action Aid, 1981–92. Contested (SDP-Liberal Alliance), N Luton, 1983, 1987. *Address:* Raggot Hill Cottage, North Tamerton, Cornwall EX22 6RJ. *Club:* Royal Automobile.

STEPHEN, Martin; *see* Stephen, G. M.

STEPHEN, Mhairi Margaret; Sheriff of Lothian and Borders at Edinburgh, since 1997 (Floating Sheriff, 1997–2001); *b* 22 Jan. 1954; *d* of William Strachan Stephen and Alexandrina Wood Stephen (*née* Grassam). *Educ:* George Watson's Ladies' Coll.; Univ. of Edinburgh (BA 1974; LLB 1976). With Allan McDougall & Co., SSC, Edinburgh, 1976–97, Partner, 1981–97. *Recreations:* curling, hill-walking, golf, music. *Address:* Edinburgh Sheriff Court, 27 Chambers Street, Edinburgh EH1 1LB. *T:* (0131) 225 2525. *Clubs:* Murrayfield Golf, Murrayfield Curling.

STEPHEN, Michael; company director; *b* 25 Sept. 1942; *s* of late Harry Lace Stephen and of Edna Florence Stephen; *m* 1989, Virginia Mary (*née* de Trensé). *Educ:* Stanford Univ. (LLM 1971); Harvard Univ. Admitted Solicitor, 1964 (DistCompany Law); called to the Bar, Inner Temple, 1966 (Hons); commissioned, The Life Guards, 1966–70; Harkness Fellowship in Internat. Law, 1970–72; Asst Legal Adviser, UK Delegn to UN, 1971; London Bar practice, 1972–87; Internat. Trade and Public Affairs Consultant, 1988–92. Chm., Severnside Internat. Airport Consortium, 2000–05; Gp Dep. Chm., Symphony Envmtl Technologies plc, 2007–. Mem., RIIA, 1984–. County Councillor, Essex, 1985–91; Mem., Nat. Exec., ACC, 1989–91; contested (C) Doncaster North, 1983. MP (C) Shoreham, 1992–97. Member: Select Cttee on the Environment, 1994–97; Trade and Industry Select Cttee, 1996–97; European Standing Cttee, 1994–97. Vice Chm., Cons. Parly Home Affairs and Legal Cttees, 1994–97. Author: S. 36 Criminal Justice Act, 1988; Bail (Amendment) Act, 1993. *Publications:* numerous political pamphlets. *Recreations:* tennis, sailing, history, theatre. *Address:* *e-mail:* kkrkyz@gmail.com.

STEPHEN, Nicol Ross; Member (Lib Dem) Aberdeen South, Scottish Parliament, since 1999; *b* 23 March 1960; *s* of R. A. Nicol Stephen and Sheila G. Stephen; *m* Caris Doig; two *s* two *d*. *Educ:* Robert Gordon's Coll., Aberdeen; Aberdeen Univ. (LLB 1980); Edinburgh Univ. (DipLP 1981). Admitted Solicitor, 1983; C&PH Chalmers, 1981–83; Milne & Mackinnon, 1983–88; Sen. Corporate Finance Manager, Touche Ross & Co., 1988–90. Dir, Glassbox Ltd, 1992–99. Mem. (Lib Dem) Grampian Regl Council, 1982–92 (Chm., Econ. Develt and Planning Cttee, 1986–91). MP (Lib Dem) Kincardine and Deeside, Nov. 1991–1992. Scottish Executive: Dep. Minister for Enterprise and Lifelong Learning, 1999–2000, for Educn, Europe and Ext. Affairs, 2000–01, for Educn and Young People, 2001–03; Minister for Transport, 2003–05; Dep. First Minister, and Minister for Enterprise and Lifelong Learning, 2005–07. Leader, Scottish Lib Dems, 2005–08. Contested: Kincardine and Deeside, (L/All) 1987, (Lib Dem) 1992; (Lib Dem) Aberdeen S, 1997. *Recreations:* golf, swimming. *Address:* Scottish Parliament, Edinburgh EH99 1SP.

STEPHEN, Rt Hon. Sir Ninian (Martin), KG 1994; AK 1982; GCMG 1982; GCVO 1982; KBE 1972; PC 1979; Governor-General of Australia, 1982–89; *b* 15 June 1923; *o s* of late Frederick Stephen and Barbara Stephen (*née* Cruickshank); *m* 1949, Valery Mary, *d* of late A. Q. Sinclair and of Mrs G. M. Sinclair; five *d*. *Educ:* George Watson's Sch., Edinburgh; Edinburgh Acad.; St Paul's Sch., London; Chillon Coll., Switzerland; Scotch Coll., Melbourne; Melbourne Univ. (LLB). Served War, HM Forces (Australian Army), 1941–46. Admitted as Barrister and Solicitor, in State of Victoria, 1949; signed Roll of Victorian Bar, 1951; QC 1966. Appointed Judge of Supreme Court of Victoria, 1970; Justice of High Court of Australia, 1972–82; Australian Ambassador for the Envmt, 1989–92; Chm., Anglo-Irish Talks (2nd strand), 1992; Judge, Internat. War Crimes Tribunal for Yugoslavia, 1993–97; Chm., UN Expert Gp on Cambodia, 1998–99. Mem., Ethics Commn, IOC, 2000–. Hon. Bencher Gray's Inn, 1981. Chm., Nat. Liby of Aust., 1989–94. Hon. Liveryman, Clothworkers' Co., 1991. Hon. LLD: Sydney, 1984; Melbourne, 1985; Griffith, 1988; Hon. DLitt WA, 1993. KStJ 1982. Comdr, Legion of Honour (France), 1993. *Address:* Flat 13/1, 193 Domain Road, South Yarra, Vic 3141, Australia.

STEPHEN, Peter James; Lord Lieutenant and Lord Provost, City of Aberdeen, since 2007; *b* 24 April 1937; *m* 1960, Sandra McDonald; one *s* one *d*. *Educ:* Robert Gordon's Coll., Aberdeen. Nat. Service, RAF, 1955–57. Union Bank of Scotland Ltd, subseq. Bank of Scotland: mgt apprentice, 1953; Accountant, 1969, Asst Manager, 1973, Stirling Br.; Manager, Strathaven, Lanarkshire, 1977; Senior Manager: Fraserburgh, 1982; Kirkcaldy, 1989–91; self-employed business consultant, 1992–96; Inland Revenue Tax Comr, 1999–2007. Mem. (Scottish Lib Dem), Aberdeen CC, 2002–. Mem., Chartered Inst. of Banking in Scotland, 1961. *Recreations:* outdoor mostly. *Address:* 11 Coldstone Avenue, Kingswells, Aberdeen AB15 8TT. *T:* (office) (01224) 522637, *Fax:* (01224) 523747; *e-mail:* lordprovost@aberdeencity.gov.uk. *Club:* Rotary (Aberdeen).

STEPHEN, Rita; *see* Stephen, H. H.

STEPHENS, Anthony William, CB 1989; CMG 1976; Deputy Under Secretary of State, Northern Ireland Office, 1985–90; *b* 9 Jan. 1930; *s* of late Donald Martyn Stephens and Norah Stephens (*née* Smith-Cleburne); *m* 1954, Mytyl Joy, *d* of late William Gay Burdett; four *d*. *Educ:* Bradfield Coll.; Bristol Univ. (LLB); Corpus Christi Coll., Cambridge. RM (commnd), 1948–50. Colonial Administrative Service, 1953; District Officer, Kenya, 1954–63; Home Civil Service, 1964; Principal, MoD, 1964–70; Asst Private Sec. to successive Secretaries of State for Defence, 1970–71; Asst Sec., 1971; Chief Officer, Sovereign Base Areas, Cyprus, 1974–76; Under Sec., NI Office, 1976–79; Asst Under Sec. of State, General Staff, 1979–83, Ordnance, 1983–84, MoD. Trustee, Sherborne House Trust, 1995–2004. *Recreations:* travel and the outdoor life, music, theatre. *Address:* Virginia Cottage, Bradford Abbas, Sherborne, Dorset DT9 6SA. *Club:* Royal Over-Seas League.

STEPHENS, Barbara Marion, (Mrs T. J. Stephens), OBE 2002; Principal, Carbon Leadership, since 2007; *b* 25 Aug. 1951; *d* of late Sydney and of Edna Webb; *m* 1970, Trevor James Stephens. *Educ:* Mid-Essex Technical Coll. (HNC Engrg); NE London Poly. (DMS); City Univ. (MBA Engrg Mgt). IEng; MIET (MIProdE 1976); MIIE (MIET 1992). Mechanical technician apprentice, Marconi Co., 1969–73; various technical and managerial posts, Marconi Communication Systems Ltd, 1973–88; Industrial Advr, Electronic Applications, NEDO, 1988–92; Dir of Ops, then Chief Exec., W Cumbria Develt Agency, 1993–98; Chief Exec., Local Govt Commn for England, 1998–2002; Hd of Public Sector, subseq. Higher Educn, Practice, kmc internat., 2002–07. Member: Engineering Council, 1990–96; HEFCE, 1995–2002; Adv. Forum (formerly Council) for Develt of RN Personnel, 1995–2002 (Chm., 2001–02); a Dir, Assoc. of MBAs, 2001–06 (Chm., 2005–06). Chm., NHSU, 2003–05. Non-executive Director: Cumbria Ambulance Service NHS Trust, 1996–98; EBS Trust, 2001–08. Bd Mem., New Opportunities Fund, 2001–04. Lay Mem., Professional Conduct and Complaints Cttee, Gen. Council of Bar, 2000– (Lay Vice Chm., 2006–). FCMI (FIMgt 1994; MBIM 1978); FRSA 1992. DUniv Bradford, 2005. *Address:* Crook Hall, 28 High Seaton, Workington, Cumbria, CA14 1PD. *T:* (01900) 871095.

STEPHENS, Sir Barrie; *see* Stephens, Sir E. B.

STEPHENS, Sir Benjamin; *see* Stephens, Sir W. B. S.

STEPHENS, Catherine Anne, (Mrs C. P. G. Qadir), OBE 1996; Director, Innovation, and Member of Executive Board, British Council, since 2007; *b* 24 Feb. 1951; *d* of Geoffrey Francis Stephens and Jeannine Christianne Langer Stephens; *m* 1998, Cecil Parvaiz Ghulam Qadir; one *d*, and one step *s*. *Educ:* Univ. of Hull (BA 1st Cl. American Studies 1978). Sec., George G. Harrap, 1970; Personal Asst, Penguin Books, 1970–71; Sec., UNESCO, Paris, 1972–73; Admin. Asst, US Peace Corps, Kabul, 1973–74; joined British Council, 1978: Asst, Educnl Contracts Dept, 1978–81; Zimbabwe, 1981–82; Asst Rep., Cameroon, 1982–85; Regl Officer, Central and E Africa S of Sahara Dept, 1985–88; First Sec., Develt, New Delhi, 1988–93; Deputy Director: Indonesia, 1993–96; India, 1996–2000; Regl Dir, W Africa, 2001–03; Dir, Africa and Asia, 2003–07. *Recreations:* travel, reading. *Address:* The British Council, 10 Spring Gardens, SW1A 2BN.

STEPHENS, Prof. Christopher David, OBE 1999; FDSRCS, FDSRCSE; Professor of Child Dental Health, University of Bristol, 1984–2002, now Emeritus; *b* 29 May 1942; *s* of late Wilfred Ernest Donnington Stephens, OBE, PhD, and of Phyllis Margaret Stephens (*née* Lecroissette); *m* 1966, Marion Kay Prest; two *s*. *Educ:* Dulwich Coll.; Guy's Hosp. Dental Sch. (BDS); MDS Bristol. DOrthRCS 1968, MOrthRCS 1988; FDSRCSE 1970; FDSRCS 1986. Hse Surgeon, 1965, Registrar in Children's Dentistry, 1966–69, Guy's Hosp. Dental Sch.; Registrar in Orthodontics, Royal Dental Hosp., 1969–71; Lectr in Orthodontics, 1971–76, Consultant Sen. Lectr in Orthodontics, 1976–84, Univ. of Bristol. Civil Consultant in Orthodontics to RAF, 1988–2005. Mem., Standing Dental Adv. Cttee, 1992–98. Pres., British Orthodontic Soc., 2001–02. Hon. Life Mem., European Orthodontic Soc., 2003. Fellow, BDA, 2004. Ballard Medal, Consultant Orthodontists Gp, 2003. *Publications:* (jtly) Functional Orthodontic Appliances, 1990; (with K. G. Isaacson) Practical Orthodontic Assessment, 1990; (jtly) A Textbook of Orthodontics, 2nd edn 1992; contrib. numerous papers to refereed jls. *Recreations:* amateur radio, dry stone-walling, woodland management, walking. *Address:* 12 Berkshire Road, Bristol BS7 8EX. *T:* (0117) 942 9944.

STEPHENS, Christopher Wilson Treeve; *see* Stephens, W. T.

STEPHENS, Sir (Edwin) Barrie, Kt 1998; CEng; Chairman, 1990–98, Hon. President, since 1998, Siebe plc. *Educ:* Christ Coll., Brecon; Manchester Univ. CEng 1962. Industrial Engr, General Dynamics, USA, 1954; Production Manager, Barden Corp., Conn, USA, 1962; Dir. of Manufg, Barden Corp. Ltd, UK, 1962–63; Man. Dir, Siebe Gorman and Co. Ltd, 1963–75; Gp Man. Dir and CEO, Siebe Gorman Hldgs Ltd, 1975–86; Vice-Chm., 1987–90, CEO, 1987–93, Siebe plc. Hon. DSc Plymouth, 1993. *Club:* Carlton.

STEPHENS, Prof. Elan Closs, CBE 2001; Professor of Communications and Creative Industries, Aberystwyth University (formerly University of Wales, Aberystwyth), since 2001; Chair, Welsh Fourth Channel Authority, 1998–2006; *b* 16 June 1948; *d* of William Jones and Mair Closs Roberts (*née* Williams); *m* 1972, Roy Stephens (*d* 1989); one *s* one *d*. *Educ:* Ysgol Dyffryn Nantlle, Penygroes; Somerville Coll., Oxford (Open Schol.; BA 1969). University of Wales, Aberystwyth: Lectr, 1976–84; Hd of Dept, 1984–91; Sen. Lectr, 1994–2001. Member: Broadcasting Council for Wales, 1984–89; S4C Authy, 1990–95; Council, Nat. Liby of Wales, 1995–2005; Wales Adv. Cttee, CRE, 2003–; Vice-Chm., Welsh Language Bd, 1994–99; Chairman: Chwarae Teg, 2002–04; Wales Adv. Cttee, British Council, 2005–. Governor: BFI, 2001–; Univ. of Glamorgan, 2002–. FRSA 2002. Hon. Fellow, Trinity Coll., Carmarthen, 2004. *Publications:* chapters and articles on Welsh theatre and media policy. *Recreations:* reading, theatre, television, film, cookery and eating out with friends. *Address:* Fronhyfryd, Ffordd Llanbadarn, Aberystwyth SY23 1EY. *T:* (01970) 625653.

STEPHENS, Jonathan Andrew de Sievrac; Permanent Secretary, Department for Culture, Media and Sport, since 2006; *b* 8 Feb. 1960; *s* of Prescot and Peggy Stephens; *m* 1983, Rev. Penny; one *s* one *d*. *Educ:* Sevenoaks Sch.; Christ Church, Oxford (MA). NI Office, 1983–89; HM Treasury, 1989–92; Northern Ireland Office, 1992–2000: Principal Private Sec., 1993–94; Associate Pol Dir, 1996–2000; Dir, Modernising Public Services, Cabinet Office, 2000–01; Dir, Public Services, 2001–03, Public Spending, 2003–04, Man. Dir, Public Services, 2004–06, HM Treasury. *Address:* Department for Culture, Media and Sport, 2–4 Cockspur Street, SW1Y 5DH.

STEPHENS, Prof. Kenneth Gilbert, CEng, FIET; CPhys, FInstP; Professor of Electronic and Electrical Engineering, 1978–96, now Emeritus, and Dean of the Faculty of Engineering, 1992–96, University of Surrey; *b* 3 May 1931; *s* of George Harry Stephens and Christiana Stephens; *m* 1980, Elizabeth Carolynn (*née* Jones); one *s* one *d*, and two step *s*. *Educ:* Bablake Sch., Coventry; Birmingham Univ. (BSc, PhD). Nuclear Reactor Res. Physicist, AEI Ltd, Aldermaston, 1955–62; Sen. Res. Engr, Pye Ltd, Cambridge, 1963–66; University of Surrey: Lectr 1966; Reader 1967; Head, Dept of Electronic and Electrical Engrg, 1983–91. Chm., Bd of Govs, Royal Grammar Sch., Guildford, 1996–2004. *Publications:* (ed jtly) Low Energy Ion Beams (conf. procs), 1978, 1980; (ed jtly) Ion Implantation Technology (conf. procs), 1991; articles on ion beam effects on semiconductors in learned jls. *Recreations:* reading, music, gardening, watching sport, especially cricket. *Address:* 10 Brockway Close, Merrow, Guildford, Surrey GU1 2LW. *T:* (01483) 575087. *Clubs:* MCC; Blackheath Cricket.

STEPHENS, Malcolm George, CB 1991; Chairman: International Financial Consulting, since 1998; IFC Training, since 2001; *b* 14 July 1937; *s* of Frank Ernest Stephens and Janet (*née* McQueen); *m* 1975, Lynette Marie Caffery, Brisbane, Australia. *Educ:* St Michael's and All Angels; Shooter's Hill Grammar Sch.; St John's Coll., Oxford (Casberd Scholar; BA 1st Cl. Hons PPE; MA 1995). National Service, RAOC, 1956–58. CRO, 1953; British High Commission: Ghana, 1959–62; Kenya, 1963–65; Export Credits Guarantee Dept, 1965–82: Principal, 1970; seconded to Civil Service Coll., 1971–72; Asst Sec., 1974; Estab. Officer, 1977; Under Sec., 1978; Head of Proj. Gp B, 1978–79; Principal Finance Officer, 1979–82; Internat. Finance Dir, Barclays Bank Internat. Ltd, 1982–84; Dir, Barclays Export Services, 1984–87; Export Finance Dir, Barclays Bank PLC, 1985–87; Chief Executive: ECGD, 1987–91; London Chamber of Commerce and Industry, 1991–92; Pres., 1989–91, Sec.-Gen., 1992–98, Internat. Union of Credit and Investment Insurers (Berne Union); Man. Dir and Dep. Chm., Commonwealth Investment Guarantee Agency, 1998–99; Exec. Dir, IPCIS, 1999–2001. Chm., Del Credere Insurance Services Ltd, 1999–2001; Director: European Capital, 1992–2000; Arab-British Chamber of Commerce, 1992–95; Major Projects Assoc., 1995–99; Berry, Palmer & Lyle, 1997–2001; EULER Internat., 1998–2000. Mem. Adv. Council, Zurich Emerging Markets, 2001–; Advr to Sinosure, China, 2000–; Consultant: to EU PHARE Prog., 1997–99; to World Bank, 1997–2001; Eur. Commn, 1999–2000; OECD (Russia), 2001; APEC, 2002, 2003; Asian Develt Bank, 2005; Govt of Chile, 1999, of Bangladesh, 1999, of Iran, 2000, of Sri Lanka, 2000, of S Africa, 2000, 2002, of Australia, 2000, 2001, 2002, 2003, of NZ, 2001, of Turkey, 2001, of Canada, 2001, 2003, 2007, 2008; of Fiji, 2003; of Romania, 2007. Advr, CDR Internat., 1998–2000; Exec. Vice-Pres., SGA Internat., Florida, 1998–2000. Member: Overseas Projects Bd, 1985–87; BOTB, 1987–91. Vis. Schol., IMF, 1998–99. Mem., Cook Soc., 2002–. FCIB (FIB 1984); FIEx 1987; MICM 1990. *Publication:* The Changing Role of Export Credit Agencies, 1999. *Recreations:* gardening, reading, tapestry, watching cricket and football (Charlton Athletic), bush walking. *Address:* 38 Argyle Street, Bong Bong Hill, Moss Vale, NSW 2577, Australia. *Club:* Union (Sydney).

STEPHENS, Martin; *see* Stephens, S. M.

STEPHENS, Rev. Peter; *see* Stephens, Rev. W. P.

STEPHENS, Peter Norman Stuart; Director, News Group Newspapers, 1978–87, Editorial Director, 1981–87; *b* 19 Dec. 1927; *s* of J. G. Stephens; *m* 1950, Constance Mary Ratheram; two *s* one *d*. *Educ:* Mundella Grammar Sch., Nottingham. Newark Advertiser, 1945–48; Northern Echo, 1948–50; Daily Dispatch, 1950–55; Daily Mirror, Manchester, 1955–57; Asst Editor, Newcastle Journal, 1957–60; Asst Editor, Evening Chronicle, Newcastle, 1960–62, Editor 1962–66; Editor, Newcastle Journal, 1966–70; Asst Editor, The Sun, 1970–72, Dep. Editor 1972; Associate Editor, News of the World, 1973, Editor, 1974–75; Associate Editor, The Sun, 1975–81. *Publications:* (ed) Newark: the magic of malt, 1993; Grey Sanctuary: the story of the Newark Friary, 1996; P. S. on a life in newspapers, 2003. *Recreations:* the printed word, Derby County FC. *Address:* 6 Homefield Road, Sevenoaks, Kent TN13 2DU.

STEPHENS, Philip Francis Christopher; Associate Editor and Columnist, Financial Times, since 2003; *b* 2 June 1953; *s* of Haydn Stephens and Theresa (*née* Martin); partner, Patty Hemingway; one *s* one *d*. *Educ:* Wimbledon Coll.; Worcester Coll., Oxford (BA Hons Mod. Hist.). Correspondent London and Brussels, Reuters, 1979–83; Financial Times: Econs Correspondent, 1983–88; Political Ed., 1988–94; Political Commentator, 1994–99; Ed., UK Edn, 1999–2003. Fulbright Fellow, LA Times, 1988. Gov., The Ditchley Foundn, 2006–. David Wait Meml Prize for Outstanding Political Journalism, RTZ, 2002; Political Journalist of the Year, Political Studies Assoc., 2004; Political Journalist of the Year, British Press Awards, 2008. *Publications:* Politics and the Pound, 1996; Tony Blair: the price of leadership, 2004. *Recreation:* chauffeuring Jessica and Benedict. *Address:* c/o Financial Times, 1 Southwark Bridge, SE1 9HL; *e-mail:* stephenspfc@hotmail.com. *Club:* Chelsea Football.

STEPHENS, (Stephen) Martin; QC 1982; **His Honour Judge Stephens;** a Circuit Judge, since 1986; a Judge of the Central Criminal Court, since 1999; *b* 26 June 1939; *s* of late Abraham Stephens and Freda Stephens, Swansea; *m* 1965, Patricia Alison, *d* of late Joseph and Anne Morris, Mapperley, Nottingham; one *s* one *d* (and one *s* decd). *Educ:* Swansea Grammar Sch.; Wadham Coll., Oxford (MA). Called to the Bar, Middle Temple, 1963, Bencher, 2004; Wales and Chester Circuit; a Recorder, 1979–86. Mem., Parole Bd, 1995–2001. Mem., Criminal Cttee, 1995–2000, Main Bd, 1997–2000, Judicial Studies Bd. *Recreations:* cricket, theatre. *Address:* c/o Central Criminal Court, Old Bailey, EC4M 7EH.

STEPHENS, Toby; actor; *b* 21 April 1969; *s* of Sir Robert Graham Stephens and of Dame Maggie Smith, *qv*; *m* 2001, Anna-Louise Plowman; one *s*. *Educ:* Aldro Sch.; Seaford Coll.; LAMDA. Crewed, Chichester Festival Th., 1986 and 1987; *theatre* includes: Tartuffe, Playhouse, 1991; Royal Shakespeare Company: All's Well That Ends Well, Antony and Cleopatra, Tamburlaine, Unfinished Business, Wallenstein, 1992; Coriolanus, A Midsummer Night's Dream, Measure for Measure, 1994; Hamlet, The Pilate Workshop, 2004; A Streetcar Named Desire, Haymarket, 1996; Phèdre, Britannicus, Almeida, 1998, transf. NY, 1999; Ring Round the Moon, NY, 1999; Japes, The Royal Family, Haymarket, 2001; Betrayal, Donmar Warehouse, The Country Wife, Haymarket, 2007; *films* include: Photographing Fairies, 1997; Cousin Bette, 1998; Onegin, 1999; Space Cowboys, 2000; Possession, Die Another Day, 2002; Severance, 2006; *television* includes: The Camomile Lawn, 1992; The Tenant of Wildfell Hall, 1996; The Great Gatsby, 2000; Perfect Strangers, 2001; Cambridge Spies, Poirot – Five Little Pigs, 2003; The Queen's Sister, 2005; The Best Man, Sharpe's Challenge, Jane Eyre, 2006. *Address:* c/o Ms Lindy King, United Agents, 12–26 Lexington Street, W1F 0LE.

STEPHENS, Sir (William) Ben(jamin Synge), Kt 2007; **Hon. Mr Justice Stephens;** a Judge of the High Court of Justice, Northern Ireland, since 2007; *b* 28 Dec. 1954; *s* of Denis Synge Stephens and Gladys Joyce Stephens (*née* Clarke); *m* 1982, Nicola Gladys Skrine; one *s* one *d*. *Educ:* Swanbourne House Sch., Swanbourne, Bucks; Campbell Coll., Belfast; Manchester Univ. (LLB 1st cl. Hons). Called to the Bar: NI, 1977; Lincoln's Inn, 1978; Ireland, 1996; QC (NI) 1996. Vice-Chm., Gen. Council of the Bar of NI, 2006–07. *Address:* Royal Courts of Justice, Belfast BT1 3JF.

STEPHENS, Rev. Prof. (William) Peter; Methodist Minister, since 2006, Superintendent Minister, since 2007, Camborne Circuit; *b* 16 May 1934; *s* of Alfred Cyril William Joseph Stephens and Jennie Eudora Stephens (*née* Trewavas). *Educ:* Lescudjack Sch., Penzance; Truro Sch.; Clare Coll., Cambridge (MA, BD); Wesley House, Cambridge; Univs of Lund, Strasbourg (Docteur ès Sciences Religieuses) and Münster. Asst Tutor, Hartley Victoria Coll., Manchester, 1958–61; ordained, Methodist Ministry, 1960; Minister in Nottingham and Methodist Chaplain to Univ. of Nottingham, 1961–65; Minister, Shirley, Croydon, 1967–71; Ranmoor Prof. of Church History, Hartley Victoria Coll., Manchester, 1971–73; Randles Prof. of Historical and Systematic Theology, Wesley Coll., Bristol, 1973–80; Res. Fellow, 1980–81, Lectr in Church History, 1981–86, Queen's Coll., Birmingham; University of Aberdeen: Prof. of Church History, 1986–99; Dean, 1987–89, Provost 1989–90, Faculty of Divinity. Vis. Prof., 2001–04, Hon. Univ. Fellow, 2004–, Exeter Univ. Pres., Methodist Conf., 1998–99; Superintendent Minister, Plymouth Methodist Mission, 1999–2000; Minister, Mint Church, Exeter, and Methodist Chaplain, Univ. of Exeter, 2000–02; Superintendent Minister, Liskeard and Looe Circuit, 2002–03; Chm. and Gen. Superintendent, Methodist Church in The Gambia, 2003–04; Minister, Uckfield and Lewes, 2004–06. Mem., Bristol City Council, 1976–83. Member: Central Cttee, Conf. of European Churches, 1974–92; Conservative and Churches Standing Cttee, 1998–2006. Sec., Soc. for the Study of Theology, 1963–77; Pres., Soc. for Reformation Studies, 1995–98. Max Geilinger Prize, Switzerland, 1997. *Publications:* (trans. jtly) Luther's Works, Vol. 41, 1966; The Holy Spirit in the Theology of Martin Bucer, 1970; Faith and Love, 1971; The Theology of Huldrych Zwingli, 1986 (French edn, 1999); Zwingli: An Introduction to His Thought, 1992 (German edn, 1997; Korean edn, 2007); Methodism in Europe, 1993; (ed) The Bible, the Reformation and the Church, 1995; contributions to religious works; articles and reviews in learned jls and other pubns. *Recreations:* squash, swimming, tennis, gardening, hill-walking, theatre, opera. *Address:* Trewavas House, 8 Polwithen Road, Penzance, Cornwall TR18 4JS. *T:* (01736) 350016.

STEPHENS, Wilson (Treeve); Editor of The Field, 1950–77, Consultant 1987–90; Consultant, Country Illustrated (formerly Countryweek), since 1991; *b* 2 June 1912; *s* of Rev. Arthur Treeve Stephens, Shepton Beauchamp, Somerset, and Margaret Wilson; *m* 1st, 1934, Nina, *d* of Arthur Frederick Curzon, Derby; two *d*; 2nd, 1960, Marygold Anne, *o d* of Major-General G. O. Crawford, CB, CBE; two *d*. *Educ:* Christ's Hosp. Served War of 1939–45, Royal Artillery. Formerly on editorial staffs of several provincial newspapers, and of The Daily Express. *Publications:* The Guinness Guide to Field Sports, 1979; Gundog Sense and Sensibility, 1982, 4th edn 2004; Pigeon Racing, 1983; A Year Observed, 1984; Rivers of Britain (series) 1985–; contribs to numerous publications. *Recreations:* fly-fishing, shooting. *Address:* c/o Blake, Friedmann, 122 Arlington Road, NW1 7HP.

STEPHENSON, Ashley; *see* Stephenson, R. A. S.

STEPHENSON, Charles Lyon, TD 1972; Vice Lord-Lieutenant of Derbyshire, since 2004; *b* 15 Aug. 1935; *s* of Col C. E. K. Stephenson and Nancy Stephenson; *m* 1st, 1960, Jane Tinker (marr. diss. 1972); two *s* one *d*; 2nd, 1974, Hon. Sarah Norrie. *Educ:* Eton Coll. Employed in family engrg business Stephenson Blake (Holdings) Ltd, 1956–2000, Gp Man. Dir, 1985–2000. Non-exec. Director: Bramber Engrg Co. Ltd, 1980–87; Lyon and Lyon plc, 1982–90; Director: Carlton Main Brickworks Ltd, 1977–; Kestrel Travel Consultancy Ltd, 1998–; Hotel and Catering Staff Supplies Ltd, 1998–. Chairman: Derbys Br., Rural Develt Commn, 1987–93; Wynkin de Worde Soc., 1990; Derbys Br., SSAFA Forces Help, 2001–. High Sheriff, 1984–85, DL, 2004, Derbys. *Recreations:* gardening, shooting, fishing, theatre, travel. *Address:* The Cottage, Great Longstone, Bakewell, Derbyshire DE45 1UA. *T:* (01629) 640213, *Fax:* (01629) 640135; *e-mail:* Charles@kestreltravel.com. *Club:* Cavalry and Guards.

STEPHENSON, Darryl Leslie; DL; Managing Director, Hardmoor Associates Ltd, since 2005; Strategic Adviser, Deloitte, since 2005; *b* 4 Sept. 1950; *s* of late Lawrence Stephenson and of Olga Mary Stephenson; *m* 1984, Susan Marialuisa Lockwood; one *s* one *d*. *Educ:* Warwick Sch.; Trent Poly. (BA Hons); Coll. of Law, Chester; Univ. of Birmingham (Advanced Mgt Develt Prog., 1986). Admitted Solicitor, 1980. Articled Clerk, W Bromwich CBC, 1972–74; Solicitor, Warwick DC, 1974–80; Principal Asst Chief Exec., Leicester CC, 1980–89; Dep. Town Clerk, subseq. Town Clerk and Chief Exec., Hull CC, 1989–95; Chief Exec., ER of Yorks Unitary Council, 1995–2005; Interim Chief Exec., NE Lincs Council, March–Nov., 2004. Vis. Prof., Univ. of Hull, 2005–. Co. Sec., Humber Forum Ltd, 1992–. Clerk to: Humber Bridge Bd, 1993–96; Humberside Police Authy, 1996–97; Lord Lieut, E Riding of Yorks, 1996–2005; Sec., N Eastern Sea Fisheries Cttee, 1996–; Humberside Police Appts Cttee, 2004–. Chm., E Riding Drug Action Team, 1995–2002; Mem. Council, Hull and E Riding Chamber of Commerce, Industry and Shipping, 1995–. Member: Adjudication Panel for England, 2002–; Bd, Hull Pathfinders, 2004–. Mem. of Court, Univ. of Hull, 1993–; Gov., Beverley Coll., 1998–. Trustee: Age Concern E Yorks, 2005–; Beverley Meml Hall, 2006–. DL ER of Yorks, 2005. *Recreations:* motor boating, music, painting, food and wine. *Address:* Hardmoor Grange, Hardmoor Lane, Hotham, ER Yorks YO43 4UJ. *Club:* Portcullis (Warwick).

STEPHENSON, Rev. Canon Eric George; Vicar, St George's Church, East Boldon, 1985–2008; Chaplain to the Queen, since 2002; *b* 26 April 1941; *s* of Albert and Nora Stephenson. *Educ:* Bede Coll., Durham (Teaching Cert., 1963); Birmingham Univ. (DipTh 1965; Dip. Liturgy and Architecture 1966). Ordained deacon, 1966, priest, 1967; Curate: St John the Baptist, Wakefield, 1966–69; Seaham with Seaham Harbour, Durham, 1969–73; Cockerton, Darlington, 1973–75; Licence to officiate, 1975–85; Teacher, Haughton Comp. Sch., Darlington, 1975–85. Area Dean of Jarrow, 1992–2001; Non-residentiary Canon, Durham Cathedral, 1993–. *Recreations:* current affairs, history, archaeology, music appreciation.

STEPHENSON, George Anthony C.; *see* Carter-Stephenson.

STEPHENSON, Sir Henry Upton, 3rd Bt *cr* 1936; TD; Director: Stephenson Blake & Co. Ltd, 1952–75; Stephenson, Blake (Holdings) Ltd, 1972–99; *b* 26 Nov. 1926; *s* of Lt-Col Sir Henry Francis Blake Stephenson, 2nd Bt, OBE, TD, and Joan, *d* of Major John Herbert Upton (formerly Upton Cottrell-Dormer); *S* father, 1982, but his name does not appear on the Official Roll of the Baronetage; *m* 1962, Susan, *o d* of Major J. E. Clowes, Ashbourne, Derbyshire; four *d*. *Educ:* Eton. Formerly Major, QO Yorkshire Dragoons. High Sheriff of Derbyshire, 1975. *Heir: cousin* Timothy Hugh Stephenson [*b* 5 Jan. 1930; *m* 1959, Susan Lesley, *yr d* of late George Arthur Harris; two *s*]. *Address:* Tissington Cottage, Rowland, Bakewell, Derbyshire DE45 1NR.

STEPHENSON, Prof. Hugh; writer and journalist; Professor of Journalism, City University, 1986–2003, now Emeritus; *b* 18 July 1938; *s* of late Sir Hugh Stephenson; *m* 1st, 1962, Auriol Stevens, *qv* (marr. diss. 1987); two *s* one *d*; 2nd, 1990, Diana Eden. *Educ:*

Winchester Coll.; New Coll., Oxford (BA); Univ. of Calif, Berkeley. Pres., Oxford Union, 1962. HM Diplomatic Service, 1964–68; joined The Times, 1968; Editor, The Times Business News, 1972–81; Editor, The New Statesman, 1982–86. Dir, Eur. Journalism Centre, Maastricht, 1993– (Chm., 1995–2002). Mem., Cttee to Review Functioning of Financial Instns, 1977–80. Councillor, London Bor. of Wandsworth, 1971–78. Dir, History Today Ltd, 1981–. FRSA 1987. *Publications:* The Coming Clash, 1972; Mrs Thatcher's First Year, 1980; Claret and Chips, 1982; (jtly) Libel and the Media, 1997; Secrets of the Setters, 2005. *Address:* 7 Clifton Terrace, Brighton, E Sussex BN1 3HA.

STEPHENSON, His Honour Jim; a Circuit Judge, 1983–98; *b* 17 July 1932; *s* of late Alex and Norah Stephenson, Heworth, Co. Durham; *m* 1964, Jill Christine, *d* of late Dr Lindeck, Fairwarp, Sussex; three *s*. *Educ:* Royal Grammar Sch. and Dame Allan's Sch., Newcastle; Exeter Coll., Oxford (Exhibnr, BA). Pres., Oxford Univ. Law Society, Michaelmas, 1955. Called to Bar, Gray's Inn, 1957. Mem., General Council of the Bar, 1961–64; Junior, NE Circuit, 1961; a Recorder of the Crown Court, 1974–83. Pres., NE Br., Magistrates' Assoc., 1988–92. Additional Mem. of Bd, Faculty of Law, Newcastle Univ., 1984–90. Gov., Newcastle Prep. Sch., 1985–92. *Recreations:* music, travel, history. *Address:* Garth House, Wetheral, Carlisle CA4 8JN. *T:* (01228) 560986.

STEPHENSON, Maj.-Gen. John Aubrey, CB 1982; OBE 1971; defence consultant, 1991–93; Managing Director, Weapon Systems Ltd, 1982–91; Deputy Master General of the Ordnance, 1980–81; *b* 15 May 1929; *s* of Reginald Jack Stephenson and Florence Stephenson; *m* 1953, Sheila Colbeck; two *s* one *d*. *Educ:* Dorchester Grammar School. Commnd RA, 1948; served Malaya (despatches, 1951), Libya, Canal Zone and Germany, 1949–58 (student pilot, 1953–54); student, RMCS, 1958–60; 39 Missile Regt, 1960–61; student, RMCS and Staff Coll., 1961–62; served UK and Germany, 1962–67; Staff, RMCS, 1967–69; CO 16 Light Air Defence Regt RA, 1969–71; Project Manager, 155mm Systems, Woolwich, 1971–73; student, RCDS, 1974; Comdr, 1st Artillery Bde, Germany, 1975–77; Sen. Mil. Officer, RARDE, 1977–78; Dir Gen. Weapons (Army), 1978–80. Dir, ATX Ltd, 1984–91. Col Comdt, RA, 1984–89; Hon. Regtl Col, 16 Regt (formerly 16 Light Air Defence Regt), RA, 1989–95. Governor, The Dorchester Thomas Hardye Sch. (formerly Hardye's Sch.), 1984–96. Pres., Houghton and District Br., RBL, 1987–2000, 2002–. Vice Pres., Stockbridge FC, 2002–. FCMI. *Recreations:* fishing, sailing, gardening, bridge, golf, military history. *Address:* Collingwood, 27 Trafalgar Way, Stockbridge, Hants SO20 6ET. *T:* (01264) 810458.

STEPHENSON, Lynne, (Mrs Chaim Stephenson); *see* Banks, L. R.

STEPHENSON, Margaret Maud; *see* Tyzack, M. M.

STEPHENSON, Prof. Patrick Hay, MA, CEng, FIMechE; retired consultant Mechanical Engineer; *b* 31 March 1916; *e s* of late Stanley George Stephenson and Florence (*née* Atkinson); *m* 1947, Pauline Roberts (*d* 2000); two *s* one *d*. *Educ:* Wyggeston Sch., Leicester; Cambridge Univ. (MA). Apprenticeship and Research Engr, Brit. United Shoe Machinery Co., 1932–39. War Service as Ordnance Mechanical Engr and REME, India and Far East, 1939–45; held as POW by Japanese, 1942–45. Chief Mechanical Engr, Pye Ltd, 1949–67; Prof. of Mech. Engrg, Univ. of Strathclyde, 1967–79; Dir, Inst. of Advanced Machine Tool and Control Technology, Min. of Technology, 1967–70; Dir, Birniehill Inst. and Manufacturing Systems Group, DTI, 1970–72; Head of Research Requirements Branch 2, DoI, 1972–77. Research advisor to Institution of Mechanical Engineers; senior industrial advisor to the Design Council. Mem. Council, IMechE, 1960–68; Member: Bd, UKAC, 1964–73; Engrg Bd, SRC, 1973–. *Publications:* papers and articles in technical press. *Recreations:* music, vintage motoring. *Address:* Toft Lane, Great Wilbraham, Cambridge CB1 5JH. *T:* (01223) 880405.

STEPHENSON, Paul; Regional Director, Wales and the West, Focus Consultancy Ltd, 1992–2000; *b* 6 May 1937; *s* of Olive Stephenson; *m* 1965, Joyce Annikie; one *s* one *d*. *Educ:* Westhill Coll. of Educn, Selly Oak, Birmingham. MCIPR (MIPR 1978). Youth Tutor, St Paul's, Bristol, 1962–68; Sen. Community Relations Officer, Coventry, 1968–72; National Youth Trng Officer, Community Relations Commn, 1972–77; Sen. Liaison Officer, CRE, 1980–92. Chm., Muhammad Ali Sports Develt Assoc., Brixton and Lambeth, 1974–; Member: British Sports Council, 1976–82; Press Council, 1984–90. Chm., Bristol Legacy Commn, 2008–. Freeman, City of Bristol, 2007. *Recreations:* travel, cinema, reading, international politics. *Address:* 12 Downs Park East, Westbury Park, Bristol BS6 7QD. *T:* (0117) 962 3638.

STEPHENSON, Sir Paul, Kt 2008; QPM 2000; Deputy Commissioner, Metropolitan Police, since 2005; *b* 26 Sept. 1953; *s* of late Jack Stephenson and of Rose Cathryne (*née* Sullivan); *m* 1974, Lynda, *d* of late James Alexander Parker; three *d*. *Educ:* Bacup and Rawtenstall Grammar Sch. Mgt trainee, E. Sutton & Son, 1973–75; with Lancashire Constabulary, 1975–94: Chief Inspector, 1986; Supt, 1988; Asst Chief Constable, Merseyside, 1994–99; Dep. Chief Constable, 1999–2001, Chief Constable, 2002–05, Lancs Constabulary. *Recreations:* walking, reading. *Address:* New Scotland Yard, Broadway, SW1H 0BG.

STEPHENSON, (Robert) Ashley (Shute), LVO 1990 (MVO 1979); FIHort; Bailiff of the Royal Parks, 1980–90; *b* 1 Sept. 1927; *s* of late James Stephenson and Agnes Maud Stephenson; *m* 1955, Isabel Dunn; one *s* one *d*. *Educ:* Walbottle Secondary Sch. Diploma in Horticulture, RHS, Wisley, 1954; MIHort 1987, FIHort 1998. Apprenticeship, Newcastle upon Tyne Parks Dept, 1942; served RASC, Palestine and Cyprus, 1946; Landscape Gardener, Donald Ireland Ltd, 1949; Student, RHS's gardens, Wisley, 1952; Royal Parks, 1954–: Supt, Regent's Park, 1969; Supt, Central Royal Parks, 1972. Gardening Correspondent, The Times, 1982–87. President: British Pelargonium and Geranium Soc., 1983–95; South East in Bloom, 2001 (Chm., 1990–2001); Member: Cttee, RHS, 1981–; London in Bloom Cttee, English Tourism Council (formerly English Tourist Bd), 1980–91 (Vice-Chm., 1983); Chm., Floral Jersey, 1990–2001; Nat. Chm., Britain in Bloom, 1991–2001; Mem., The Queen's Anniversary Cttee 1952–92, 1992– (Chm., Horticl Cttee, 1992–). Contributor to television and radio programmes; regularly on BBC Radio Sussex gardening programmes; gardening correspondent to professional and amateur papers. *Publications:* The Garden Planner, 1981; contribs to nat. press. *Recreations:* sport, judging horticultural shows, natural history, walking, golf. *Address:* 17 Sandore Road, Seaford, E Sussex BN25 3PZ.

STEPHENSON, Stanley, CMG 1987; HM Diplomatic Service, retired; *b* 30 Sept. 1926; *s* of George Stephenson and Margaret Jane (*née* Nicholson); *m* 1957, Grace Claire Lyons (*d* 1987); one *s* one *d*. *Educ:* Bede Sch., Sunderland. Inland Revenue, 1942; Royal Navy, 1944–48; Foreign (later Diplomatic) Service, 1948–: Cairo, Jedda, Damascus, Curaçao, Ciudad Trujillo (now Santo Domingo), San José, Seoul, Santiago de Cuba, Bogotá (twice), Asunción, San Francisco, FCO; Diplomatic Service Inspector, 1978–80; Ambassador to Panama, 1981–83; Consul-Gen., Vancouver, 1983–86. *Recreations:* watching most sports, theatre, gardening. *Address:* Marymount, Raggleswood, Chislehurst, Kent BR7 5NH. *T:* (020) 8467 6066. *Clubs:* Civil Service; Crescent Lawn Tennis (Sidcup).

STEPHENSON, Prof. Terence John, DM; FRCP, FRCPCH; Professor of Child Health, since 1996, and Dean, Faculty of Medicine and Health Sciences, since 2003, University of Nottingham; *b* 6 Dec. 1957; *s* of James Ewing Stephenson and late Cora Bell Stephenson (*née* Elliott); *m* 1987, Amanda Jane Lilley; one *s* one *d*. *Educ:* Larne Grammar Sch.; Bristol Univ. (BSc 1st Cl. Hons); Imperial Coll. London; New Coll., Oxford (BM BCh); MD Nottingham 1992. MRCP 1986, FRCP 1995; FRCPCH 1997. Jun. hosp. appts at John Radcliffe Hosp., Oxford, Royal United Hosp., Bath, St Thomas' Hosp., London, Nat. Hosp. for Nervous Diseases, Queen Sq. and UCH, London, 1983–86; Lectr in Child Health, 1986–90, Sen. Lectr, 1990–96, Nottingham Univ. Sometime advisor: Official Solicitor to Supreme Court, 1997; DoH, 1999–2006; Eur. Agency for Evaluation of Med. Products, 2001–05. External Examiner: UCL; TCD; UC, Galway; Univs of Leicester, Birmingham and Putra. Treas., Council of Heads of Med. Schs, 2005–. Vice-Pres. for Res. and Sci., 2007–, Pres. elect, 2009–, RCPCH. Pres., Trent Paediatric Soc., 1999–2005; Sec., Neonatal Soc., 2001–03; Treas., Paediatric Res. Soc., 2001–03. Hon. Sec., Assoc. of Clinical Profs of Paediatrics, 2003–05. *Publications:* (with H. Wallace) Clinical Paediatrics for Post Graduate Examinations, 1991, 2nd edn 1995; (with C. O'Callagahan) Pocket Paediatrics, 1992, 2nd edn 2003; (with C. O'Callaghan) Data Interpretation for the MRCP, 1994; (jtly) Pocket Neonatology, 2000; (jtly) Short Cases for the MRCPCH, 2004; (jtly) How to Write a Guideline, 2008; contrib. numerous peer-reviewed papers in various fields of child health and disease. *Recreations:* golf (badly), football and Rugby (former competitor, now spectator), ski-ing, ecclesiastical architecture. *Address:* Dean's Office, Faculty of Medicine and Health Sciences, Medical School, Queen's Medical Centre, Nottingham NG7 2UH. *T:* (0115) 823 0019. *Clubs:* Lansdowne, 1942; Wollaton Park Golf; Nottingham Medical Students Rugby (Vice-Pres.).

STEPHENSON, Air Vice-Marshal Tom Birkett, CB 1982; Assistant Chief of Defence Staff (Signals), 1980–82, retired; *b* 18 Aug. 1926; *s* of Richard and Isabel Stephenson; *m* 1951, Rosemary Patricia (*née* Kaye) (*d* 1984); one *s* three *d*. *Educ:* Workington Secondary Sch.; Manchester Univ.; Southampton Univ. (DipEl). Commissioned in RAF Engrg Branch, 1945; Staff Coll., 1962; Wing Comdr, Station and Staff appointments, until 1967; Command Electrical Engr, HQASC, 1967–69; Dep. Director Op. Requirements, 1969–72; AOEng, HQ NEAF, 1972–74; RCDS 1975; Director of Signals (Air), 1976–79. *Recreations:* sport, walking, reading. *Address:* c/o National Westminster Bank, High Street, Maidenhead SL6 1PY. *Club:* Royal Air Force.

STEPNEY, Area Bishop of, since 2003; **Rt Rev. Stephen John Oliver;** *b* 7 Jan. 1948; *s* of John Oliver and Nora Oliver (*née* Greenhalgh); *m* 1969, Hilary Joan Barkham; two *s*. *Educ:* St Augustine's Coll., Canterbury; King's Coll. London (AKC 1970). Ordained deacon, 1971, priest, 1972; Asst Curate, Clifton, Nottingham, 1970; Vicar, Christ Church, Newark on Trent, 1975; Rector, St Mary Plumtree, Nottingham, 1979; Producer, Religious Programmes, BBC, 1985, Chief Producer, 1987; Rector of Leeds, 1991–97; Canon Residentiary, St Paul's Cathedral, 1997–2003. Mem., Liturgical Commn, Gen. Synod of C of E, 1991–2001. Hon. Canon, Ripon Cathedral, 1996. Chm., Praxis, 1997–2001; Member: Elida Gibbs Ethics Cttee, 1994–96; W Yorks Playhouse Community and Educn Cttee, 1991–96; Leeds Common Purpose Adv. Gp, 1994–96; Unilever Central Ethical Compliance Gp, 1997–2003. Trustee, More Than Gold, 2008. Chairman, Governors: Leeds Girls' High Sch., 1993–96; Agnes Stewart High Sch., 1993–96. Pres., Leeds Church Inst., 1991–96. *Publications:* Why Pray?, 1993; (ed) Pastoral Prayers, 1996; (contrib.) New SCM Dictionary of Liturgy and Worship, 2002; Guiding Stars, 2005. *Recreations:* reading, theatre, flying. *Address:* 63 Coborn Road, Bow, E3 2DB.

STEPTOE, Prof. Andrew Patrick Arthur, DPhil; FBPsS, AcSS; British Heart Foundation Professor of Psychology, University College London, since 2000; *b* 24 April 1951; *s* of Patrick Christopher Steptoe, CBE, FRS, and Sheena Macleod Steptoe; *m* 1st, 1980, Jane Horncastle (marr. diss. 1984); two *s*; 2nd, 1991, Jane Wardle. *Educ:* Gonville and Caius Coll., Cambridge (BA 1972; MA 1976); Magdalen Coll., Oxford (DPhil 1976); DSc London, 1995. FBPsS 1988. Res. Lectr, Christ Church Coll., Oxford, 1975–77; St George's Hospital Medical School: Lectr in Psychology, 1977–81; Sen. Lectr, 1981–87; Reader, 1987–88; Prof. of Psychology, 1988–2000; Chm. Acad. Bd, 1997–99. President: Soc. of Psychosomatic Res., 1983–85; Internat. Soc. of Behavioral Medicine, 1994–96. Editor, British Jl of Health Psychology, 1995–2001; Associate Editor: Psychophysiology, 1982–86; Jl of Psychosomatic Res., 1989–97; British Jl of Clinical Psychology, 1992–95; Annals of Behavioral Medicine, 1992–97. AcSS 2001; MAE 2003. FMedSci 2008. *Publications:* Psychological Factors in Cardiovascular Disorders, 1981; Problems of Pain and Stress, 1982; Health Care and Human Behaviour, 1984; Clinical and Methodological Issues in Cardiovascular Psychophysiology, 1985; The Mozart-Da Ponte Operas, 1988; Behavioural Medicine in Cardiovascular Disorders, 1988; Stress, Personal Control and Health, 1989; Psychosocial Processes and Health, 1994; Mozart, 1996; Genius and the Mind: studies of creativity and temperament, 1998; Depression and Physical Illness, 2006. *Recreations:* music, theatre, reading, family. *Address:* Department of Epidemiology and Public Health, University College London, 1–19 Torrington Place, WC1E 6BT. *T:* (020) 7679 1804, *Fax:* (020) 7916 8542; *e-mail:* a.steptoe@ucl.ac.uk.

STERCKX, Prof. Roel, PhD; Joseph Needham Professor of Chinese History, Science and Civilisation, University of Cambridge, since 2008 (Professor of Chinese, 2007); Fellow of Clare College, Cambridge, since 2006; *b* 13 May 1969; *s* of Herman Sterckx and Angèle Sterckx (*née* Vos); *m* 2003, Dr Ang Cheng Eng. *Educ:* Gemeentelijke Basisschool Retie, Belgium; St Jan Berchmans Coll., Mol; Katholieke Universiteit Leuven (BA, MA Sinology and Hist. 1991; PGCE 1991); National Taiwan Univ., Taipei (studied philosophy 1992); Univ. of Cambridge (MPhil 1993; PhD Oriental Studies 1997). Jun. Res. Fellow, Wolfson Coll., Oxford, 1997–2000; Asst Prof. of E Asian Studies, Univ. of Arizona, 2000–02; Univ. Lectr, then Sen. Lectr, in Chinese Studies, Univ. of Cambridge, 2002–07. Sec.-Gen., Europ. Assoc. for Chinese Studies, 2006–. FRAS 2006; FRHistS 2006. *Publication:* The Animal and the Daemon in Early China, 2002; Of Tripod and Palate: food, politics and religion in traditional China, 2005; Of Self and Spirits: exploring 'shen' in China, 2007. *Recreations:* music, gardening, fishing. *Address:* Clare College, Trinity Lane, Cambridge CB2 1TL.

STERLING, family name of **Baron Sterling of Plaistow**.

STERLING OF PLAISTOW, Baron *cr* 1991 (Life Peer), of Pall Mall in the City of Westminster; **Jeffrey Maurice Sterling,** GCVO 2002; Kt 1985; CBE 1977; Chairman: The Peninsular and Oriental Steam Navigation Company, 1983–2005; Sterling Guarantee Trust, since 2005; P&O Princess Cruises, 2000–03; Chairman, Motability, since 1994 (Chairman of Executive, since 1977); Chairman of Trustees, National Maritime Museum, since 2005; *b* 27 Dec. 1934; *s* of late Harry and of Alice Sterling; *m* 1985, Dorothy Ann Smith; one *d*. *Educ:* Reigate Grammar Sch.; Preston Manor County Sch.; Guildhall School of Music. Paul Schweder & Co. (Stock Exchange), 1955–57; G. Eberstadt & Co., 1957–62; Fin. Dir, General Guarantee Corp., 1962–64; Man. Dir, Gula Investments Ltd,

1964–69; Chm., Sterling Guarantee Trust plc, 1969–85, when it merged with P&O Steam Navigation Co. Mem., British Airways Bd, 1979–82. Special Advr to Sec. of State for Industry, later for Trade and Industry, 1982–90. Mem. Exec., 1966–, Chm. Organisation Cttee, 1969–73, World ORT Union; Chm., ORT Technical Services, 1974–; Vice-Pres., British ORT, 1978–; President: Gen. Council of British Shipping, 1990–91; EC Shipowners' Assocs, 1992–94. Dep. Chm. and Hon. Treasurer, London Celebrations Cttee, Queen's Silver Jubilee, 1975–83; Chm., Queen's Golden Jubilee Weekend Trust, 2002. Chm., Young Vic Co., 1975–83; Chm., of the Governors, Royal Ballet Sch., 1983–99; Gov., Royal Ballet, 1986–99. Freeman, City of London. Hon. Captain, 1991, Hon. Cdre, 2005, RNR. Elder Brother, Trinity House, 1991. Hon. FIMarEST (Hon. FIMarE 1991); Hon. FICS 1992; Hon. MRICS 1993; FSVA 1995; Hon. FRINA 1997. Hon. DBA Nottingham Trent, 1995; Hon. DCL Durham, 1996; Hon. DSc City, 2006. Interfaith Medallion, Internat. CCJ, 2003. KStJ 1998. Grand Officer, Order of May (Argentina), 2002; Officer's Cross, Order of Merit (Germany), 2004; Officier, Légion d'Honneur (France), 2005. *Recreations:* music, swimming, tennis. *Clubs:* Garrick, Hurlingham.

STERLING, David Robert; Deputy Secretary, Department of Enterprise, Trade and Investment, Northern Ireland, since 2008; *b* 7 March 1958; *s* of Ronald and Kathleen Sterling; *m* 1987, Lynda Elaine Robinson; one *s* one *d*. *Educ:* Royal Belfast Academical Instn; Univ. of Ulster (MSc). Northern Ireland Civil Service, 1978–: Police Authority; NI Office; Dept of Finance and Personnel; Dep. Sec., Dept for Regl Develt, 2003–08. *Recreations:* golf, cycling, walking. *Address:* e-mail: david.sterling@detini.gov.uk.

STERLING, Dr (Isobel Jane) Nuala, CBE 1993; FRCP; Consultant Physician in Geriatric Medicine, Southampton University Hospitals NHS Trust (formerly Royal South Hants Hospital), 1979–2002, now Emeritus; *b* 12 Feb. 1937; *d* of Prof. F. Bradbury and Mrs J. Bradbury; *m* 1961, Dr G. M. Sterling; five *s* (one *d* decd). *Educ:* Friends' Sch., Saffron Walden; King's Coll. and St George's Hosp., London (MB BS 1960). MRCS LRCP 1960; MRCP 1971, FRCP 1982. House Officer and Registrar posts, St George's Hosp., 1960–67; in general practice: London, 1963–64; Oxford, 1968; Lectr in Medicine, Univ. of Calif., San Francisco, 1969–70; Sen. House Officer then Registrar, Oxford, 1970–71; Sen. Registrar and Lectr in Geriatric Medicine, Southampton Univ. Hosps, 1972–79. Member: Standing Med. Adv. Cttee to Sec. of State for Health, 1986–96 (Chm., 1990–94); Clinical Standards Adv. Gp, 1990–94; Indep. Review Panel on Advertising of Medicines, 2000–; Vice-Chairman: Wessex Regl Adv. Cttee on Distinction Awards, 1998–99; Southern Regl Adv. Cttee on Distinction Awards, 2000–03. Royal College of Physicians: Chm., Standing Cttee of Mems, 1978–79; Mem., Jt Consultants Cttee, 1986–92; Pres., Medical Women's Fedn, 1989–90. Trustee: Wessex Medical Trust, 1999–2004; King Edward VII Hosp., Midhurst, 2000–06. *Publications:* research publications on immunology and cancer, endocrine and respiratory disorders in the elderly, provision of medical services and training. *Recreations:* music, modern art, growing orchids and lilies, watching cricket. *Address:* Vermont House, East Boldre, Hants SO42 7WX.

STERLING, Michael John Howard, FREng, FIET; FInstMC; Vice-Chancellor and Principal, Birmingham University, since 2001; *b* 9 Feb. 1946; *s* of Richard Howard Sterling and Joan Valeria Sterling (*née* Skinner); *m* 1969, Wendy Karla Anstead; two *s*. *Educ:* Hampton Grammar Sch., Middx; Univ. of Sheffield (BEng 1968; PhD 1971; DEng 1988). CEng 1975. Student apprentice, AEI, 1964–68; research engineer, GEC-Elliott Process Automation, 1968–71; Sheffield University: Lectr in Control Engineering, 1971–78; Industrial Liaison Officer, 1976–80; Sen. Lectr in Control Engineering, 1978–80; Prof. of Engineering, Univ. of Durham, 1980–90 (Dir, Microprocessor Centre, 1980–85); Vice-Chancellor and Princ., Brunel Univ., 1990–2001. Chairman: OCEPS Ltd, 1990–; WASMACS Ltd, 1994–2002; MidMAN, 2001. Director: COBUILD Ltd, 2001–; UCAS, 2001–; Universitas 21, 2001–. Member: UUK (formerly CVCP), 1990– (Mem. Council, 1994–95); Cttee for Internat. Co-op. in Higher Educn, British Council, 1991–96. Chairman: Univs Statistical Record, 1992–95; Higher Educn Stats Agency, 1992–2003; Jt Performance Indicators Wkg Gp, Higher Educn Councils for England, Scotland and Wales, 1992–95; Russell Gp, 2003–06; Member: Quality Assessment Cttee, 1992–95, Additional Student Numbers and Funds Adv. Gp, 1997–99, HEFCE; Mech. Aeronautical and Prodn Engrg Assessment Panel, RAE, 1992, 1996; Bd, W Midlands Higher Educn Authy, 2001–; AWM Broadband Steering Gp, 2002–03; Bd, AWM, 2003–. Member: Electricity Supply Res. Council, 1987–89; ESRC, 1987–89; Engrg Bd, SERC, 1989–92; Engrg Council, 1994–96; Council for Sci. and Technol., 2004–. FREng (FEng 1991; Mem., Standing Cttee for Educn, Trng and Competence to Practise, 1993–97; Mem., Membership Panel, 2000–02; Chm., 2002); FInstMC 1983 (Mem. Cttee, 1975–80, Chm., 1979–80, S Yorks Sect.; Mem. Council, 1983–91; Vice Pres., 1985–88; Nat. Pres., 1988); FIEE 1985 (Mem. Council, 1991–93 and 1997–; Chm., Qualifications Bd, 1997–; Vice-Pres., 1997–2001; Dep. Pres., 2001–02; Pres., 2002–03). FRSA 1984. Dir, W London TEC, 1999–2001 (Dir, Charitable Trust, 1999–). Governor: Hampton Sch., 1991–2001 (Chm., 1997–2001); Burnham Grammar Sch., 1991–2001; Pres., Elmhurst Sch. for Dance, 2002–. Trustee: Hillingdon Partnership Trust, 1993–98; Barber Inst. of Fine Art, 2001–. Freeman, City of London, 1996; Liveryman, Engineers' Co., 1998–. Hon. DEng Sheffield, 1995. *Publications:* Power Systems Control, 1978; contribs to: Large Scale Systems Engineering Applications, 1980; Computer Control of Industrial Processes, 1982; Real Time Computer Control, 1984; Comparative Models for Electrical Load Forecasting, 1985; over 120 papers in learned jls. *Recreations:* gardening, DIY, computers, model engineering. *Address:* Birmingham University, Birmingham B15 2TT.

STERLING, Nuala; *see* Sterling, I. J. N.

STERN, family name of **Baron Stern of Brentford**.

STERN, Baroness *cr* 1999 (Life Peer), of Vauxhall, in the London Borough of Lambeth; **Vivien Helen Stern,** CBE 1992; Secretary-General, Penal Reform International, 1989–2006; Senior Research Fellow, International Centre for Prison Studies, King's College, London, since 1997; *b* 25 Sept. 1941; *d* of Frederick Stern and Renate Mills; *m* Andrew Gerard Coyle, *qv*. *Educ:* Kent Coll., Pembury, Kent; Bristol Univ. (BA, MLitt, CertEd). Lectr in Further Educn until 1970; Community Relations Commn, 1970–77; Dir, NACRO, 1977–96. Vis. Fellow, Nuffield Coll., Oxford, 1984–91. Member: Special Programmes Bd, Manpower Services Commn, 1980–82; Youth Training Bd, 1982–88; Gen. Adv. Council, IBA, 1982–87; Cttee on the Prison Disciplinary System, 1984–85; Adv. Council, PSI, 1993–96; Bd, Assoc. for Prevention of Torture, Geneva, 1993–99; Bd, Eisenhower Foundn, Washington, 1993–; Law Adv. Council, 1995–2001, Governance Adv. Cttee, 2002–06, British Council; Adv. Council, ILANUD (UN Latin Amer. Inst. for Prevention of Crime and Treatment of Offenders), 2001–; Council, Français Incarcérés au Loin, 2001–07. Convener, Scottish Consortium on Crime and Criminal Justice, 2003–. Member: Select Cttee on EU, H of L, 1999–2003; Jt Cttee on Human Rights, 2004–. Pres., New Bridge, 2001–05. Pres., Assoc. of Members of Ind. Monitoring Bds, 2004–. Hon. Fellow, LSE, 1997. Hon. LLD: Bristol, 1990; Oxford Brookes, 1996; DUniv Stirling, 2008. Margaret Mead Award for contribution to social justice, Internat. Assoc. for Residential & Community Alternatives, 1995. *Publications:* Bricks of Shame, 1987; Imprisoned by Our Prisons, 1989; Deprived of their Liberty, a report for Caribbean Rights, 1990; A Sin Against the Future: imprisonment in the world, 1998; Alternatives to Prison in Developing Countries, 1999; (ed) Sentenced to Die?: the problem of TB in prisons in Eastern Europe and Central Asia, 1999; Developing Alternatives to Prison in East and Central Europe and Central Asia: a guidance handbook, 2002; Creating Criminals: prisons and people in a market society, 2006. *Address:* House of Lords, SW1A 0PW.

STERN OF BRENTFORD, Baron *cr* 2007 (Life Peer), of Elsted in the County of West Sussex and of Wimbledon in the London Borough of Merton; **Nicholas Herbert Stern,** Kt 2004; FBA 1993; I. G. Patel Professor of Economics and Government, Chairman, Grantham Institute on Climate Change and the Environment, and Director, India Observatory, London School of Economics, since 2007; *b* 22 April 1946; *s* of Adalbert Stern and Marion Fatima Stern; *m* 1968, Susan Ruth (*née* Chesterton); two *s* one *d*. *Educ:* Peterhouse, Cambridge (BA Mathematics; Hon. Fellow, 2006); Nuffield Coll., Oxford (DPhilEcon). Jun. Res. Fellow, The Queen's Coll., Oxford, 1969–70; Fellow/Tutor in Econs, St Catherine's Coll., and Univ. Lectr, Oxford, 1970–77; Prof. of Econs, Univ. of Warwick, 1978–85; Sir John Hicks Prof. of Econs, LSE, 1986–97; Chief Economist, 1994–99, and Special Counsellor to Pres., 1997–99, EBRD; School Prof. of Econs, LSE, 1999–2003 (on leave of absence); Chief Economist and Sen. Vice-Pres., World Bank, 2000–03; HM Treasury: Second Perm. Sec., Hd of Govt Econ. Service and Hd Review on Econs of Climate Change, 2003–05 (report published 2006); Man. Dir, Budget and Public Finance, 2003–04. Dir of Policy and Res., Prime Minister's Commn for Africa, 2004–05; Govt Advr on econs of climate change and develt, Cabinet Office, 2005–07. Research Associate/Visiting Professor: MIT, 1972; Ecole Polytech., 1977; Indian Statistical Inst. (Overseas Vis. Fellow of British Acad., 1974–75, and Ford Foundn Vis. Prof., 1981–82); People's Univ. of China, Beijing, 1988; Hon. Prof., People's Univ. of China, 2001; Vis. Prof. of Econs, LSE, 2003–07; Vis. Fellow, Nuffield Coll., Oxford, 2004–. For. Hon. Mem., Amer. Acad. of Arts and Scis, 1998. Fellow, Econometric Soc., 1978. Hon. Fellow: St Catherine's Coll., Oxford, 2000; LSE, 2003; Queen's Coll., Oxford, 2007. Hon. DSc Warwick, 2006. Hon. Dr: Cambridge, Nottingham, Exeter, Sussex, Roehampton, 2007; Sheffield, York, E Anglia, 2008. Editor, Journal of Public Economics, 1980–98. *Publications:* An Appraisal of Tea Production on Smallholdings in Kenya, 1972; (ed jtly) Theories of Economic Growth, 1973; (jtly) Crime, the Police and Criminal Statistics, 1979; (jtly) Palanpur: the economy of an Indian village, 1982; (jtly) The Theory of Taxation for Developing Countries, 1987; (jtly) Economic Development in Palanpur over Five Decades, 1998; (jtly) Growth and Empowerment: making development happen, 2005; articles in American Econ. Rev., Econ. Jl, Rev. of Econ. Studies, Jl of Public Econs, Jl of Develt Econs, and others. *Recreations:* reading novels, walking, watching sport, food. *Address:* London School of Economics, Houghton Street, WC2A 2AE.

STERN, Prof. Claudio Daniel, DPhil, DSc; FRS 2008; J. Z. Young Professor and Head, Department of Cell and Developmental Biology (formerly Department of Anatomy and Developmental Biology), University College London, since 2001; *b* 9 Feb. 1954; *s* of Erico and Trude Stern; *m* 2000, Andrea Streit. *Educ:* Univ. of Sussex (BSc Hons Biol Scis 1975; DPhil Develtl Biol. 1978); Christ Church, Oxford (DSc Physiol Scis 1994). Res. Fellow, UCL, 1978–84; Univ. Demonstrator, Univ. of Cambridge, 1984–85; Univ. Lectr, Univ. of Oxford, and Fellow, Christ Church, Oxford, 1985–94; Prof. and Chm. of Genetics and Develt, Columbia Univ., NY, 1994–2001. Member: Ibero-Amer. Molecular Biol. Orgn, 1998; EMBO, 2002. FMedSci 2001. Foreign Fellow, Latin-Amer. Acad. of Scis, 2001. Waddington Medal, British Soc. for Develtl Biol., 2006. *Publications:* (jtly) The Making of the Nervous System, 1988; (with P. W. Ingham) Gastrulation (Development 1992 supplement), 1992; (with P. W. H. Holland) Essential Developmental Biology: a practical approach, 1993 (trans. Japanese); (jtly) Cellular and Molecular Procedures in Developmental Biology, 1998; Gastrulation: from cells to embryo, 2004; more than 150 articles in internat. learned jls inc. Nature, Science, Cell, Neuron, Developmental Cell, Development and others. *Recreations:* playing Baroque and Renaissance woodwind musical instruments, gastronomy. *Address:* Department of Cell and Developmental Biology, University College London, Gower Street, WC1E 6BT.

STERN, Ian Michael; QC 2006; a Recorder, since 2000; *b* 26 Jan. 1957; *s* of Harold and Laura Stern; *m* 1987, Helen Appleton; three *d*. *Educ:* Queen Elizabeth's Grammar Sch. for Boys, Barnet; Univ. of Warwick (BA Hons Pol Sci 1979); City Univ., London (Dip. Law 1982). Called to the Bar, Inner Temple, 1983; in practice as a barrister; Asst Recorder, 1998–2000. *Recreations:* running, travel, family. *Address:* 2 Bedford Row, WC1R 4BU. *T:* (020) 7440 8888, *Fax:* (020) 7242 1738; *e-mail:* istern@2bedfordrow.co.uk.

STERN, John Andrew; Editor, The Wisden Cricketer, since 2003; *b* 12 March 1970; *s* of Peter and Gill Stern; *m* 2004, Clare Alison Henderson; two step *d*. *Educ:* Arnold House; King's Sch., Canterbury; Univ. of Manchester (BA Hons Classics). Hayters Sports Agency, 1992–97; freelance sports writer, 1997–2001 (mostly cricket reporting for The Times and Sunday Times); cricket columnist, Sunday Times, 1998–; Dep. Ed., Wisden Cricket Monthly, 2001–03. *Publication:* (contrib.) Wisden Cricketers' Almanack, annually 1999–. *Recreations:* cricket (Wendover CC), football, American football, travel, wine, eating out. *Address:* Wisden Cricketer, 46 Loman Street, SE1 0EH. *T:* (020) 7471 6950, *Fax:* (020) 7471 6901; *e-mail:* john.stern@wisdencricketer.com.

STERN, Michael Charles, FCA; Proprietor, Michael Stern & Co., since 1998; *b* 3 Aug. 1942; *s* of late Maurice Leonard Stern and Rose Stern; *m* 1976, Jillian Denise Aldridge; one *d*. *Educ:* Christ's College Grammar School, Finchley. Mem. ICA 1964; FCA 1969. Partner, Percy Phillips & Co., Accountants, 1964–80; Partner, Halpern & Woolf, Chartered Accountants, 1980–92; Consultant, Cohen Arnold & Co., 1992–98. Chm., The Bow Group, 1977–78; co-opted Mem., Educn Cttee, Borough of Ealing, 1980–83. Contested (C) Derby S, 1979. MP (C) Bristol NW, 1983–97; contested (C) same seat, 1997. PPS to Minister of State, HM Treasury, 1986–87, to Paymaster General, 1987–89, to Minister for Corporate Affairs, DTI, 1991. Chief Finance Officer, 1988–91, Vice-Chm., 1991–92, Cons. party. *Publications:* papers for The Bow Group. *Recreations:* fell walking, bridge, chess. *Address:* 61 Shalimar Gardens, Acton, W3 9JG. *Clubs:* Royal Automobile, United and Cecil.

STERNBERG, Michael Vivian; QC 2008; barrister; *b* Belsize Park, London, 12 Sept. 1951; *s* of Sir Sigmund Sternberg, *qv* and late Ruth Sternberg; *m* 1975, Dr Janine Levinson; one *s* two *d*. *Educ:* Carmel Coll., Wallingford; Queens' Coll., Cambridge (BA 1973, LLB 1975). Called to the Bar, Gray's Inn, 1975; Mem., Inner Temple, 2006; in practice as barrister, 1975–, specialising in all aspects of family law, esp. allocation of resources on divorce; 4 Paper Buildings, 1994–. Asst Sec., Family Law Bar Assoc., 1986–88. Trustee, Sternberg Charitable Foundn, 1983–; Jt Convenor, Legal Gp, Three Faiths Forum, 2005–. Freeman, City of London, 1983; Liveryman, Horners' Co., 1986–. FRSA 2007. Silver Benemerenza Medal, Sacred Mil. Constantinian Order of St George, 1990. *Publication:*

(contrib.) Pension and Marriage Breakdown, 2005, 2nd edn as Pensions and Family Breakdown, 2008. *Recreations:* walking, Mozart, family law. *Address:* 4 Paper Buildings, EC4Y 7EX. *T:* (020) 7583 0816, *Fax:* (020) 7353 4979; *e-mail:* clerks@4pb.com. *Club:* Reform.

STERNBERG, Sir Sigmund, Kt 1976; JP; Chairman, Martin Slowe Estates Ltd, since 1971; *b* Budapest, 2 June 1921; *s* of late Abraham and Elizabeth Sternberg; *m* 1970, Hazel (*née* Everett Jones); one *s* one *d*, and one *s* one *d* from a previous marriage. Chairman: St Charles Gp, HMC, 1974; Inst. for Archaeo-Metallurgical Studies. Hon. Life Pres., Labour Finance and Industry Gp, 2002– (Dep. Chm., 1972–93); Life Vice Pres., Royal Coll. of Speech and Lang. Therapists, 2002– (Sen. Vice-Pres., 1995–2002). Pres., Reform Synagogues of GB, 1998–; Patron, Internat. Council of Christians and Jews; Mem., Board of Deputies of British Jews (Patron, Charitable Trust, 2005–); Governor, Hebrew Univ. of Jerusalem; Life Pres., Sternberg Centre for Judaism, 1996; Founder, Three Faiths Forum (Christians, Muslims & Jews Dialogue Gp), 1997; Co-ordinator, Religious Component, World Econ. Forum, 2002–. Life Mem., Magistrates' Assoc., 1965. Mem., John Templeton Foundn, 1998– (Templeton Prize for Progress in Religion, 1998). Founding Patron, Anne Frank Trust. Mem., Court, Essex Univ. Vice-Pres., Keston Inst., 2003–. Freeman, City of London, 1970; Liveryman, Co. of Horners. JP Middlesex, 1965. Life Mem., Inst. of Dirs, 2007. FRSA 1979. Life FRSocMed 2002; Hon. FCST 1989; Hon. Fellow, UCL, 2001. DU: Essex, 1996; Hebrew Union Coll., Cincinnati, 2000; DUniv Open, 1998; Hon. LLD Leicester, 2007; Hon. DHLitt Richmond American Internat., 2008. Paul Harris Fellow, Rotary Foundn of Rotary Internat., 1989 (Rotary Internat. Award of Honour, 1998); Medal of Merit, Warsaw Univ., 1995; Wilhelm Leuschner Medal, Wiesbaden, 1998; (jtly) St Robert Bellarmine Medal, Gregorian Univ., 2002; (jtly) Dist. Service Award, Internat. CCJ, 2005. OStJ 1988. KCSG 1985; Order of Merit (Poland), 1989, Comdr's Cross, 1992, Comdr's Cross with Star, 1999; Order of the Gold Star (Hungary), 1990; Commander's Cross, 1st cl. (Austria), 1992; Comdr of the Order of Civil Merit (Spain), 1993; Comdr, Order of Honour (Greece), 1996; Comdr, Royal Order of Polar Star (Sweden), 1997; Order of Commendatore (Italy), 1999; Gran Oficial, Orden de Mayo al Merito (Argentina), 1999; Grand Cross, Order of Bernado O'Higgins (Chile), 2000; Order of Ukraine, 2001; Order of Merit with star (Portugal), 2002; Officier, Légion d'Honneur (France), 2003; Order of Madara Horseman (Bulgaria), 2003; Order of White Two-Armed Cross (Slovakia), 2003; Order of Francisco de Miranda (Venezuela), 2004; Comdr's Cross, Order of Merit (Hungary), 2004; Knight Grand Cross, Royal Order of Francis I, 2005; Knight Comdr's Cross, Order of Merit (Germany), 2006 (Comdr's Cross, 1993); Comdr, Order Pentru Merit (Romania), 2007; St Mellitus Medal, 2008. *Recreations:* reading the religious press, swimming. *Address:* 80 East End Road, N3 2SY. *Fax:* (020) 7485 4512. *Clubs:* Reform, City Livery.

See also M. V. Sternberg.

STEVELY, Prof. William Stewart, CBE 2004; DPhil; FIBiol; Principal and Vice-Chancellor, Robert Gordon University, 1997–2005; Chairman, NHS Ayrshire and Arran, since 2006; *b* 6 April 1943; *s* of Robert Reid Stevely and Catherine Callow Stevely; *m* 1968, Sheila Anne Stalker; three *s* two *d*. *Educ:* Ardrossan Acad.; Glasgow Univ. (BSc 1965; DipEd 1973); St Catherine's Coll., Oxford (DPhil 1968). FIBiol 1988. Asst Lectr, 1968–70, Lectr, 1970–83, Sen. Lectr, 1983–88, in Biochemistry, Univ. of Glasgow; Prof. and Head of Dept of Biology, 1988–92, Vice Principal, 1992–97, Paisley Coll. of Tech., then Univ. of Paisley. Chm., Scottish Council, Inst. of Biology, 1993–95. Chm., UCAS, 2001–05; Member: Nat. Bd for Nursing, Midwifery and Health Visiting for Scotland, 1992–2002; SHEFC, 1993–96; Bd, QAA, 1998–2002; Bd, Scottish Enterprise Grampian (formerly Grampian Enterprise) Ltd, 1998–2006; Bd, Scottish Univs for Industry, 2004–08; Bd, Skills Development Scotland, 2008–. Member: Council, Inst. for Learning and Teaching in Higher Educn, 1998–2000; Bd, Scottish Agricl Coll., 2005–. Convener, Universities Scotland, 2002–04. *Publications:* papers on herpes viruses. *Address:* 10 Evergreen Estate, Coalhall, Ayr KA6 6PQ.

STEVENS, family name of **Barons Stevens of Kirkwhelpington** and **Stevens of Ludgate**.

STEVENS OF KIRKWHELPINGTON, Baron *cr* 2005 (Life Peer), of Kirkwhelpington in the county of Northumberland; **John Arthur Stevens,** Kt 2000; QPM 1992; DL; Commissioner, Metropolitan Police, 2000–05; Senior Adviser to the Prime Minister on International Security Issues, since 2007; *b* 21 Oct. 1942; *s* of C. J. and S. Stevens; *m*; two *s* one *d*. *Educ:* St Lawrence Coll., Ramsgate; Leicester Univ. (LLB Hons; LLD 2000); Southampton Univ. (MPhil). Joined Metropolitan Police, 1963; DS, Police Staff Coll., 1983–84; Asst Chief Constable, Hampshire Constabulary, 1986–89; Dep. Chief Constable, Cambridgeshire Constab., 1989–91; Chief Constable, Northumbria, 1991–96; HM Inspector of Constabulary, 1996–98; Dep. Comr, Metropolitan Police, 1998–99. Chairman: Jt Cttee on Offender Profiling, 1991; ACPO Crime Prevention Sub-Cttee, 1994. Chm., NI Enquiry into alleged collusion between paramil. and security forces (Stevens Enquiry), 1989–92; headed Enquiry into alleged malpractice at Nat. Criminal Intelligence Service, 1994–96; 'Stevens 3' NI Enquiry into Collusion, 1999–2003; inquiry into the deaths of Diana, Princess of Wales and Dodi Al-Fayed, 2003–06. Advr, Forensic Sci. Service; Advr to Govts of S Africa, Jamaica and Romania on police matters and anti corruption, 2002–; Chairman: Strategic Adv. Panel, Interpol, 2005–; Quest Ltd, 2005–; Skills for Security, 2005–. Vis. Prof., City Univ., NY, 1984–85; Vis. Lectr, Internat. Crime Prevention Centre, Canada, 1998–; Sen. Mem., 1996–, Hon. Fellow, 2000, Wolfson Coll., Cambridge. Chancellor, Northumbria Univ., 2005–. Pres., Aircraft Owners and Pilots Assoc., 2005–. Patron of charities, Brixton and Romania. Hon. Col, Northumbria Cadet Force, 2006–. Freeman, City of London, 2002. DL Greater London, 2001. FRSA 2002. Hon. DCL Northumbria, 2001; Hon. LLD Newcastle, 2006. KStJ 2002. *Publication:* Not for the Faint-hearted (autobiog.), 2005. *Recreations:* walking, cricket, squash, Rugby, flying (qualified pilot). *Address:* House of Lords, SW1A 0PW. *Clubs:* East India, Royal Air Force; Northern Counties, Durham County Cricket (Pres., 2004–06; Dir, 2006–).

STEVENS OF LUDGATE, Baron *cr* 1987 (Life Peer), of Ludgate in the City of London; **David Robert Stevens;** Chairman: United News & Media (formerly United Newspapers plc), 1981–99 (Director, 1974–99); Express Newspapers, 1985–99; *b* 26 May 1936; *s* of late (Arthur) Edwin Stevens, CBE; *m* 1st Patricia Rose (marr. diss. 1971); one *s* one *d*; 2nd, 1977, Melissa Milicevich (*d* 1989); 3rd, 1990, Meriza Giori. *Educ:* Stowe Sch.; Sidney Sussex Coll., Cambridge (MA Hons Econ). Management Trainee, Elliott Automation, 1959; Director: Hill Samuel Securities, 1959–68; Drayton Group, 1968–74. Chairman: Alexander Proudfoot Hldgs (formerly City & Foreign), 1976–95; Drayton Far East, 1976–93; English & International, 1976–79; Consolidated Venture (formerly Montagu Boston), 1979–93; Drayton Consolidated, 1980–92; Drayton Japan, 1980–88; Oak Industries, 1989–96; Mid States, 1989–95; Premier Asset Mgt plc, 1997–2001; PNC Tele.Com (formerly Personal Number Co.), 1998–2002; Chief Exec., 1980–87, Chm., 1980–93, Montagu Investment Management, subseq. INVESCO MIM Management; Dep. Chm., 1987–89, Chm., 1989–93, Britannia Arrow Hldgs, subseq. INVESCO MIM. Chm., EDC for Civil Engrg, 1984–86. *Recreations:* golf, gardening. *Address:* House of Lords, SW1A 0PW. *Clubs:* White's; Sunningdale Golf, Swinley Golf.

STEVENS, Prof. Anne Frances, PhD; Professor of European Studies, Aston University, 1998–2008 (Head, School of Languages and European Studies, 1998–2003); *b* 28 Dec. 1942; *d* of late Robert Ross, FLS and of Margaret Helen Ross (*née* Steadman); *m* 1966, Handley Michael Gambrell Stevens, *qv*; three *d*. *Educ:* Blackheath High Sch. for Girls; Newnham Coll., Cambridge (BA 1964; MA 1975); LSE, Univ. of London (MSc Econ (with distinction) 1975; PhD 1980). Asst Principal, Dept of Technical Co-operation, ODM, 1964–66; part-time Lectr, Univ. of Malaya, 1966–68; HEO, British High Commn, Kuala Lumpur, 1968–69; School of European Studies, University of Sussex: Lectr in Politics, 1978–90; Dean, 1988–90; Prof. of European Studies, Univ. of Kent at Canterbury, 1991–98. *Publications:* (jtly) Hostile Brothers: competition and closure in the European electronics industry, 1990; The Government and Politics of France, 1992, 3rd edn 2003; Brussels Bureaucrats: the administration of the European Union, 2000; Women, Power and Politics, 2007; articles on comparative admin. *Recreations:* walking, English dancing, needlework. *Address:* 18A Belsize Lane, NW3 5AB. *T:* (020) 7794 0874.

STEVENS, Anthony John; Post Graduate Veterinary Dean for London and South East England, Royal College of Veterinary Surgeons/British Veterinary Association, 1986–97; engaged in consultancy and literary work; *b* 29 July 1926; *s* of John Walker Stevens and Hilda Stevens; *m* 1954, Patricia Frances, *d* of Robert Gill, Ponteland; one *s* two *d*. *Educ:* Liverpool and Manchester Univs; Magdalene Coll., Cambridge. MA, BVSc, MRCVS, DipBact. Veterinary Investigation Officer, Cambridge, 1956–65; Animal Health Expert for UNO, 1959–63; Suptg Veterinary Investigation Officer, Leeds, 1965–68; Ministry of Agriculture, Fisheries and Food: Dep. Dir, Central Vet. Lab., 1968–71; Asst Chief Vet. Officer, 1971–73; Dep. Chief Vet. Officer, 1973–78; Dir, Vet. Labs, MAFF, 1979–86. External Examr, Dublin, Liverpool and Edinburgh Univs., 1964–70. Past Pres., Veterinary Research Club. Vice Pres., Zoological Soc., 1989–90 and 1995–98 (Mem. Council, 1987–91, 1994–98). Vice Chm., Surrey Industrial History Gp, 1990–2002. FRSA. *Publications:* UN/FAO Manual of Diagnostic Techniques; regular contributor to Veterinary Record, etc. *Recreations:* industrial archaeology particularly canals, all forms of livestock. *Address:* Marigold Cottage, Great Halfpenny Farm, Guildford, Surrey GU4 8PY. *T:* (01483) 565375.

STEVENS, Auriol, (Lady Ashworth); Editor, Times Higher Education Supplement, 1992–2002; *d* of Capt. E. B. K. Stevens and Ruth M. Howard (*née* Pugh); *m* 1st, 1962, Prof. Hugh Stephenson, *qv* (marr. diss. 1987); 2nd, 1988, Dr J. M. Ashworth (*see* Sir J. M. Ashworth). *Educ:* Somerville Coll., Oxford (BA Hons); London Univ. (Dip. (Ext.)). Freelance journalist, 1962–72; TES, 1972–78; educn corresp., Observer, 1978–83; reporter, A Week in Politics, TV, 1983–86; Dir, Univs Inf. Unit, Cttee of Vice-Chancellors, 1986–92. Chm. Govs, Elliot Sch., Putney, 1981–85; Council Member: PSI, 1985–91; RCA, 1998–2006 (Vice-Chm., 2004–06); Essex Univ., 2002– (Pro-Chancellor, 2005–); Gov., UEL, 2002–05. Member: Exec. Cttee, Forum UK, 1999–2003; Inst. of Cancer Res., 2000–; Exec. Cttee, Wivenhoe Soc., 2003–06. Hon. FRCA 2007. Hon. DLitt Nottingham Trent, 2003. *Publication:* Clever Children in Comprehensive Schools, 1978. *Recreations:* textiles, walking, sailing, gardening, domestic arts. *Address:* Garden House, Wivenhoe, Essex CO7 9BD. *T:* (01206) 822256. *Clubs:* Athenæum, Forum UK; Wivenhoe Sailing.

STEVENS, Rt Rev. Douglas; *see* Riverina, Bishop of.

STEVENS, Glenn Robert; Chairman and Governor, Reserve Bank of Australia, since 2006; *b* 23 Jan. 1958; *s* of Robert Frank Hollis Stevens and Audrey Grace Stevens; *m* 1983, Susan Elizabeth Dunbar; two *d*. *Educ:* Univ. of Sydney (BEc Hons 1979); Univ. of Western Ontario (MA Econ 1985). Reserve Bank of Australia: joined, 1980; Head: Econ. Analysis Dept, 1992–95; Internat. Dept, 1995–96; Asst Gov. (Econ.), 1996–2001; Dep. Gov., 2001–06. Vis. Scholar, Fed. Reserve Bank of San Francisco, 1990. *Recreation:* flying. *Address:* Reserve Bank of Australia, 65 Martin Place, Sydney, NSW 2000, Australia. *T:* (2) 95518111, *Fax:* (2) 95518030; *e-mail:* governor@rba.gov.au.

STEVENS, Handley Michael Gambrell, PhD; Visiting Research Associate, European Institute, London School of Economics and Political Science, since 1994; *b* 29 June 1941; *s* of Ernest Norman Stevens and Kathleen Emily Gambrell; *m* 1966, Anne Frances Ross (*see* A. F. Stevens); three *d*. *Educ:* The Leys Sch., Cambridge; Phillips Acad., Andover, Mass (E-SU schol.); King's Coll., Cambridge (BA 1963; MA 1971; PhD 2007). Joined Foreign Office, 1964; Third, later Second, Sec., Kuala Lumpur, 1966; Asst Private Sec. to the Lord Privy Seal, 1970; Principal: CSD, 1971; DTI, 1973; Asst Sec., Dept of Trade, 1976; Under Sec., Dept of Transport, 1983–94. *Publications:* Transport Policy in Britain, 1998; Brussels Bureaucrats?, 2000; Transport Policy in the European Union, 2003. *Recreations:* music, hill walking, travel. *Address:* 18a Belsize Lane, NW3 5AB.

STEVENS, Sir Jocelyn (Edward Greville), Kt 1996; CVO 1993; Chairman: Prince of Wales's Phoenix Trust, 2000–04; The Prince's Regeneration through Heritage Trust, 2002–04; *b* 14 Feb. 1932; *s* of late Major C. G. B. Stewart-Stevens and Mrs Greville Stevens (*née* Hulton); *m* 1956, Jane Armyne Sheffield (marr. diss. 1979); one *s* two *d* (and one *s* decd). *Educ:* Eton; Cambridge. Military service in Rifle Bde, 1950–52; Journalist, Hulton Press Ltd, 1955–56; Chairman and Managing Dir, Stevens Press Ltd, and Editor of Queen Magazine, 1957–68; Personal Asst to Chairman of Beaverbrook Newspapers, May-Dec. 1968; Director, 1971–81; Managing Director: Evening Standard Co. Ltd, 1969–72; Daily Express, 1972–74; Beaverbrook Newspapers, 1974–77; Express Newspapers, 1977–81 (Dep. Chm. and Man. Dir); Editor and Publisher, The Magazine, 1982–84; Dir, Centaur Communications, 1982–84; Rector and Vice Provost, RCA, 1984–92; Dep. Chm., ITC, 1991–96; Dir, TV Corp., 1996–2002. Chairman: English Heritage, 1992–2000; RCHME, 1999–2000. Personal Special Advr on Stonehenge to Sec. of State for Culture, Media and Sport, 2000–. Chm., Silver Trust, 1990–93; Trustee: Mental Health Foundn, 1972–94; Eureka! The Museum for Children, 1986–2000; Butrint Foundn, 2000–; Vice-Chm., Prince's Foundn, 2000–02; Pres., Cheyne Walk Trust, 1989–93. Governor: Imperial Coll. of Science, Technology and Medicine, 1985–92; Winchester Sch. of Art, 1986–89. FRSA 1984; Senior Fellow RCA, 1990. Hon. FCSD 1990. Hon. DLitt: Loughborough, 1989; Buckingham, 1998. *Address:* 136 Oswald Building, Chelsea Bridge Wharf, 374 Queenstown Road, SW8 4PJ. *Clubs:* Buck's, Beefsteak, White's.

STEVENS, John Christopher Courtenay; Adviser, THS Capital Fund, since 1999; Director, Airtrack Railways Ltd, since 2002; *b* 23 May 1955; *s* of Sir John Melior Stevens, KCMG, DSO, OBE and of Anne Hely-Hutchinson. *Educ:* Winchester Coll.; Magdalen Coll., Oxford (BA Jurisprudence). Foreign exchange and Bond trader, Banque Indosuez, Paris, 1976–77; Bayerische Hypotheken und Wechselbank, Munich, 1977–78; Morgan Grenfell, London, 1979–89, Internat. Dir, 1986–89; Advr, St James's Place Capital plc, 1989. MEP (C) Thames Valley, 1989–99. *Recreations:* riding, ski-ing. *Address:* 40 Smith Square, SW1P 3HL. *Club:* National Liberal.

STEVENS, Hon. John Paul; Associate Justice, Supreme Court of the United States, since 1975; *b* 20 April 1920; *s* of Ernest James Stevens and Elizabeth Stevens (*née* Street); *m* 1st, 1942, Elizabeth Jane Sheeren; one *s* three *d*; 2nd, 1979, Maryan Mulholland. *Educ:* Univ. of Chicago (AB 1941); Northwestern Univ. (JD 1947). Served War, USNR, 1942–45 (Bronze Star). Law Clerk to US Supreme Ct Justice Wiley Rutledge, 1947–48; Associate, Poppenhusen, Johnston, Thompson & Raymond, 1948–50; Associate Counsel, sub-cttee on Study Monopoly Power, Cttee on Judiciary, US House of Reps, 1951; Partner, Rothschild, Hart, Stevens & Barry, 1952–70; US Circuit Judge, 1970–75. Lectr, anti-trust law, Northwestern Univ. Sch. of Law, 1953; Univ. of Chicago Law Sch., 1954–55; Mem., Attorney-Gen.'s Nat. Cttee to study Anti-Trust Laws, 1953–55. Mem., Chicago Bar Assoc. (2nd Vice-Pres. 1970). Order of Coif, Phi Beta Kappa, Psi Upsilon, Phi Delta Phi. *Publications:* chap. in book, Mr Justice (ed Dunham and Kurland); contrib. to Antitrust Developments: a supp. to Report of Attorney-Gen.'s Nat. Cttee to Study the Anti-trust Laws, 1955–58; various articles etc, in Ill. Law Rev., Proc. confs, and reports. *Recreations:* flying, tennis, bridge, reading, travel. *Address:* Supreme Court of the United States, Washington, DC 20543, USA.

STEVENS, John Williams, CB 1988; Member, 1989–90, Deputy Chairman, 1991–94, Civil Service Appeal Board; *b* 27 Feb. 1929; *s* of John Williams and Kathleen Stevens; *m* 1949, Grace Stevens; one *s* one *d*. *Educ:* St Ives School. Min. of Supply, 1952; UK Defence Res. and Supply Staff, Australia, 1958–61; HM Treasury, 1966; Civil Service Dept, 1969–73; Price Commn, 1973–74; Head of Personnel, Stock Exchange, 1975–76; Principal Private Sec. to Lord Pres. of the Council and Leader of the House of Commons, 1977–79, to Chancellor of Duchy of Lancaster and Leader of the House, 1979–80; Principal Estabts and Finance Officer, Cabinet Office, 1980–89; Under Sec. 1984. *Recreations:* Cornwall, reading, theatre. *Address:* 14 Highbury Crescent, Portsmouth Road, Camberley, Surrey GU15 1JZ. *Club:* Athenæum.

STEVENS, Kenneth Allen, DCNZM 2007; Chairman, Glidepath Group, since 1997; *b* Christchurch, NZ, 1 Feb. 1944; *s* of Arthur Edward Stevens and Marion Glover Cotter; *m* Glenice Jean McKenzie; one *s* one *d*. *Educ:* Seddon Memorial Tech. Coll., Auckland. Owner and Manager, Glidepath Ltd, 1972–2008. Chm., NZ Aviation Jt Action Gp, 1994–97. Chairman: Export New Zealand, 2008– (Mem. Bd, NZ Export Inst., 1980–83); Howick Ltd, 2008–; Member: Bd of Trustees, Asia NZ Foundn, 2007–; Bd, Icehouse, 2008–. Business Champion, Export Year 2007, 2006–07. Mem., Experimental Aircraft Assoc., Milwaukee, 2003–. *Recreations:* Rugby, boating, DIY, mentoring exporters. *Address:* Glidepath Group, 30 Cartwright Road, Glen Eden, Auckland, New Zealand. *T:* (9) 8183354, *Fax:* (9) 8189994; *e-mail:* ken.stevens@glidepathgroup.com. *Club:* Royal New Zealand Yacht Squadron.

STEVENS, Prof. Kenneth William Harry; Professor of Theoretical Physics, 1958–87, now Emeritus, and Senior Research Fellow, 1987–88, University of Nottingham; *b* 17 Sept. 1922; *s* of Harry and Rose Stevens; *m* 1949, Audrey A. Gawthrop; one *s* one *d*. *Educ:* Magdalen College School, Oxford; Jesus and Merton Colleges, Oxford. MA 1947, DPhil 1949. Pressed Steel Company Ltd Research Fellow, Oxford University, 1949–53; Research Fellow, Harvard University, 1953–54; Reader in Theoretical Physics, University of Nottingham, 1953–58. Leverhulme Emeritus Fellow, 1990. Mem., IUPAP Commn on Magnetism, 1984–87. (Jtly) Maxwell Medal and Prize, 1968. *Publications:* Magnetic Ions in Crystals, 1997; contrib. to learned journals. *Recreations:* music, tennis, walking. *Address:* The University, Nottingham NG7 2RD.

STEVENS, Lewis David, MBE 1982; management and industrial engineering consultant (self-employed), since 1979; *b* 13 April 1936; *s* of Richard and Winnifred Stevens; *m* 1959, Margaret Eileen Gibson; two *s* one *d*. *Educ:* Oldbury Grammar Sch.; Liverpool Univ.; Lanchester Coll. RAF 1956–58. Various engrg cos, mainly in industrial engrg and production management positions, 1958–79. Mem., Nuneaton Borough Council, 1966–72. MP (C) Nuneaton, 1983–92; contested (C) Nuneaton, 1992. *Address:* 151 Sherbourne Avenue, Nuneaton, Warwicks CV10 9JN. *T:* (024) 7674 4541.

STEVENS, Dr Robert Bocking; Of Counsel, Covington & Burling, Washington and London, since 1992; Senior Research Fellow, Constitution Unit, University College London, since 2001; *b* 8 June 1933; *s* of John Skevington Stevens and Enid Dorothy Stevens; *m* 1st, 1961, Rosemary Anne Wallace (marr. diss. 1982); one *s* one *d*; 2nd, 1985, Katherine Booth; one *d*. *Educ:* Oakham Sch.; Keble Coll., Oxford (BA 1956; BCL 1956; MA 1959; DCL 1984; Hon. Fellow, 1983); Yale Univ. (LLM 1958). Called to the Bar, Gray's Inn, 1956, Bencher, 1999. Yale University: Asst Prof. of Law, 1959–61; Associate Prof., 1961–65; Prof., 1965–76; Provost, Tulane Univ., 1976–78; Pres., Haverford Coll., 1978–87; Chancellor, Univ. of Calif., Santa Cruz, 1987–91; Master, Pembroke Coll., Oxford, 1993–2001 (Hon. Fellow, 2001). Mem., Nat. Council of the Humanities, 1982–88. Chairman: Marshall Aid Commemoration Commn, 1995–2000; Sulgrave Manor Trust, 2002–06. Gov., Abingdon Sch., 1993–2000. Hon. LLD: NY Law Sch., 1984; Villanova, 1985; Pennsylvania, 1987; Hon. DLitt Haverford Coll., 1991. *Publications:* (with B. S. Yamey) The Restrictive Practices Court, 1965; (with B. Abel-Smith) Lawyers and the Courts, 1967; (with B. Abel-Smith) In Search of Justice, 1968; Income Security, 1970; (with R. A. Stevens) Welfare Medicine in America, 1974; Law and Politics, 1978; The American Law School, 1983; The Independence of the Judiciary, 1993; The English Judges, 2002, 2nd edn 2005; From University to Uni, 2004, rev. edn 2005. *Recreations:* history, politics, scepticism. *Address:* 19 Burgess Mead, Oxford OX2 6XP. *T:* (01865) 558420; Covington & Burling, 265 Strand, WC2R 1BH. *T:* (020) 7067 2000. *Clubs:* Reform; Elizabethan (New Haven).

STEVENS, Rear Adm. Robert Patrick, CB 2000; Chief Executive Officer, British Marine Federation, since 2006; *b* 14 March 1948; *s* of late Major Philip Joseph Stevens, RMP and Peggy Stevens (*née* Marshall); *m* 1973, Vivien Roberts; one *s* one *d*. *Educ:* Prince Rupert Sch., Wilhelmshaven; BRNC, Dartmouth. Commanding Officer: HMS Odin, 1979–81; comdg officers qualifying course, HMS Dolphin, 1983–85; HMS Torbay, 1985–88; USN War Coll., 1988–89; Asst Dir, Strategic Systems, MoD, 1989–91; Captain: 7th Frigate Sqdn and CO, HMS Argonaut, 1992–93; Navy Presentation team, 1993–94; Dir, Jt Warfare, MoD, 1994–98; FO, Submarines, Comdr Submarines (NATO), Eastern Atlantic and NW, and COS (Ops) to C-in-C Fleet, 1998–2001; COS to Comdr Allied Naval Forces Southern Europe, and Sen. British Officer Southern Reg., 2002–05. Pres., RN Football Assoc., 1998–2005. Mem., RNSA. *Recreations:* hockey, tennis, ski-ing, sailing, cricket (RNCC). *Address:* Dial Cottage, Shepperton Road, Laleham, Middx TW18 1SE. *Clubs:* Royal Navy of 1765 and 1785; South West Shingles Yacht.

STEVENS, Timothy John, OBE 2000; FSA; Director, Gilbert Collection, Somerset House, 2002–08 (Executive Director, Hermitage Rooms, 2001–03); *b* 17 Jan. 1940; *s* of Seymour Stevens and Joan Rudgard; *m* 1969, Caroline Sankey; twin *s*. *Educ:* King's Sch., Canterbury; Hertford Coll., Oxford (MA); Courtauld Inst., Univ. of London (Academic Diploma, History of Art). Walker Art Gallery: Asst Keeper of British Art, 1964–65; Keeper of Foreign Art, 1965–67; Dep. Dir, 1967–70; Dir, 1971–74; Dir, Merseyside CC Art Galls, 1974–86; Dep. Dir, Nat. Museums and Galleries on Merseyside, 1986–87; Keeper of Art, Nat. Mus. of Wales, 1987–94; Asst Dir (Collections), V&A Mus., 1994–2000. Trustee: NACF, 2000–; Leeds Castle Foundn, 2008–. Hon. LittD Liverpool, 1985. Chevalier de l'Ordre des Arts et des Lettres (France), 1988. *Recreation:* gardening. *Address:* Luddenham Court, Faversham, Kent ME13 0TH.

STEVENS, Rt Rev. Timothy John; *see* Leicester, Bishop of.

STEVENS, William David; President and Chief Operating Officer, Mitchell Energy & Development Corp., Houston, 1994–2002; Director, EOG Resources Inc., 2004–08; *b* USA, 18 Sept. 1934; *s* of Walter Gerald and Amy Grace Stevens; *m* 1st, 1954, Barbara Ann Duncan (marr. diss. 1994); one *s* three *d*; 2nd, 1994, Virginia L. Wilkinson. *Educ:* Texas A&I Univ. (BScEng). Joined Humble Oil, 1958: various assignments, US Gulf Coast, 1958–73; Exxon Corporation: Executive Asst to President, 1974; various assignments, New York, 1974–77; Vice Pres., Gas, 1977–78; Man. Dir, Esso UK Ltd, London, and Vice Pres. Upstream, Esso Europe, Inc., 1978–85; Executive Vice President: Esso Europe, 1985–86; Exxon Co., USA, Houston, 1986–87; Pres., Exxon Co., 1988–92, retired. *Recreations:* golf, shooting, hiking.

STEVENSON, family name of **Baron Stevenson of Coddenham**.

STEVENSON OF CODDENHAM, Baron *cr* 1999 (Life Peer), of Coddenham, in the county of Suffolk; **Henry Dennistoun Stevenson, (Dennis),** Kt 1998; CBE 1981; DL; Chairman: Halifax plc, since 1999; HBOS plc, since 2001; Governor, Bank of Scotland, since 2006; *b* 19 July 1945; *s* of Alexander James Stevenson and Sylvia Florence Stevenson (*née* Ingleby); *m* 1972, Charlotte Susan, *d* of Hon. Sir Peter Vanneck, GBE, CB, AFC, AE; four *s*. *Educ:* Glenalmond; King's Coll., Cambridge (MA). Chairman: SRU Gp of cos, 1972–96; GPA, then AerFi, Gp, 1993–2000; Pearson plc, 1997–2005 (Dir, 1986–97); Director: British Technology Gp, 1979–89; Tyne Tees Television, 1982–87; Manpower Inc. (formerly Blue Arrow), 1988–2006; Thames Television plc, 1991–93; J. Rothschild Assurance plc, 1991–97; J. Rothschild Assurance Hldgs plc, 1991–97; English Partnerships, 1993–99; BSkyB Gp plc, 1994–2000; Lazard Bros, 1997–2000; Whitehall Trust Ltd, 1997–2004; St James's Place Capital, 1997–2002 (Hon. Pres., 2002–04); Economist Newspapers, 1998–; Western Union Co., 2006–; Loudwater Investment Partners Ltd, 2007–; Culture and Sport Glasgow, 2007–. Chm., Trustees, Tate Gall., 1988–98. Chairman: Newton Aycliffe and Peterlee New Town Develt Corp., 1971–80; Intermediate Technology Develt Gp, 1983–90; Director: Nat. Building Agency, 1977–81; LDDC, 1981–88. Chairman: govt working party on role of voluntary movements and youth in the envmt, 1971, '50 Million Volunteers' (HMSO); Indep. Adv. Cttee on Pop Fests, 1972–76, 'Pop Festivals, Report and Code of Practice' (HMSO); Advr on Agricl Marketing to Minister of Agric., 1979–83; Special Advr to PM and Sec. of State for Educn on use of IT in Educn, 1997–2000; Chm., H of L Appts Commn, 2000–; Member: Panel on Takeovers and Mergers, 1992–2000; Bd, British Council, 1996–2003. Chairman: NAYC, 1973–81; Sinfonia 21 (formerly Docklands Sinfonietta), 1989–99; Aldeburgh Music, 2000–; Trustee: Tate Gall. Foundn, 1998–; Horse's Mouth, 2006–. Mem. Admin. Council, Royal Jubilee Trusts, 1978–80. Chancellor, Univ. of the Arts London (formerly London Institute), 2000–. Governor: LSE, 1995–2002; London Business Sch., 1999–2002. DL Suffolk, 2008. *Recreation:* home. *Clubs:* Brooks's, Garrick, MCC.

STEVENSON, Anne Katharine, (Mrs Peter Lucas); freelance writer and poet; *b* Cambridge, England, 3 Jan. 1933; *d* of Charles Leslie Stevenson, philosopher, and Louise Destler Stevenson; *m* 1987, Peter David Lucas; two *s* one *d* by previous marriages. *Educ:* Univ. of Michigan, Ann Arbor (BA 1954, Major Hopwood Award 1954; MA 1961; Athena Award for dist. alumni 1990). School teacher, 1955–1961; Advertising Manager (as Mrs A. Hitchcock), A&C Black Publishers Ltd, 1956–57; Fellow: Radcliff Inst., Harvard, 1970–71; in Writing, Univ. of Dundee, 1973–75; Lady Margaret Hall, Oxford, 1975–77; Bulmershe Coll., Reading, 1977–78; Northern Arts Fellow, Newcastle and Durham, 1982–86; Fellow in Writing, Edinburgh Univ., 1987–89. FEA 2002. Hon. DLitt: Loughborough, 1997; Durham, 2005; Hull, 2006. Poetry Award, Scottish Arts Council, 1974; Cholmondeley Award, Soc. of Authors, 1997; Writer's Award, Northern Rock Foundn, 2002; Neglected Masters Award, Poetry Foundn, USA, 2007; Lannan Literary Award for Lifetime Achievement for Poetry, 2007; Aiken-Taylor Award, Sewanee Rev., 2007. *Publications: poetry:* Living in America, 1965; Reversals, 1967; Correspondences, 1974; Travelling Behind Glass, 1974; Enough of Green, 1977; Minute by Glass Minute, 1982; The Fiction Makers, 1985; Winter Time (pamphlet), 1986; Selected Poems, 1987; The Other House, 1990; Four and a Half Dancing Men, 1993; Collected Poems, 1996; Granny Scarecrow, 2000; Hearing with my Fingers (pamphlet), 2001; A Report from the Border, 2003; Poems 1955–2005, 2005; A Lament for the Makers, 2006; Stone Milk, 2007; Selected Poems, 2007; *criticism and biography:* Elizabeth Bishop, 1966; Bitter Fame: a life of Sylvia Plath, 1989; Five Looks at Elizabeth Bishop, 1998, 2nd edn 2006; Between the Iceberg and the Ship (essays in criticism), 1998; contrib. articles and revs to TLS, Poetry Nation Rev., Poetry Rev., Hudson Rev., Michigan Qly Rev., and to many other poetry pubns in UK and USA; *festschrift:* The Way You Say the World, 2003. *Recreations:* good music, good company, laughter. *Address:* 38 Western Hill, Durham DH1 4RJ. *T:* (0191) 386 2115; Pwllymarch, Llanbedr, Gwynedd, N Wales, LL45 2PL. *T:* (01341) 241208; *e-mail:* anne.stevenson@dial.pipex.com.

STEVENSON, (Arthur) William, TD 1980; QC 1996; a Recorder, since 1992; *b* 17 Oct. 1943; *s* of late Arthur John Stevenson, TD, MA and Olivia Diana Stevenson (*née* Serocold); *m* 1969, Bridget Laura York; two *s* one *d*. *Educ:* Marlborough Coll.; Trinity Coll., Oxford (MA). Called to the Bar, Lincoln's Inn, 1968, Bencher, 2001; in practice, 1968–. *Recreations:* country sports, ski-ing, sailing. *Address:* Crown Office Chambers, Temple, EC4Y 7HJ. *T:* (020) 7797 8100, *Fax:* (020) 7797 8101; *e-mail:* awsqc@crownofficechambers.com. *Clubs:* Boodle's, Bar Yacht.

STEVENSON, Christopher Terence S.; *see* Sinclair-Stevenson.

STEVENSON, Prof. David John, PhD; FRS 1993; George Van Osdol Professor of Planetary Science, California Institute of Technology, since 1995; *b* 2 Sept. 1948; *s* of Ian McIvor Stevenson and Gwenyth (*née* Carroll). *Educ:* Rongotai Coll.; Victoria Univ., Wellington, NZ (BSc, BSc Hons, MSc); Cornell Univ., NY (PhD). Res. Fellow, ANU, 1976–78; Asst Prof., UCLA, 1978–80; California Institute of Technology: Associate Prof., 1980–84; Prof. of Planetary Science, 1984–95; Chm., Div. of Geol and Planetary Scis, 1989–94. Fellow, Amer. Geophysical Union, 1986 (Whipple Award, 1994; Hess Medal, 1998). Hon. DSc Victoria Univ. of Wellington, 2002. Urey Prize, Amer. Astronomical Soc., 1984. *Publications:* numerous papers in learned jls, principally in earth and planetary scis. *Recreations:* hiking, biking. *Address:* Division of Geological and Planetary Sciences, California Institute of Technology, Pasadena, CA 91125, USA. *T:* (626) 3956534.

STEVENSON, Prof. Freda Kathryn, DPhil; FRCPath, FMedSci; Professor of Immunology, and Consultant (non-clinical) Immunologist, University of Southampton, since 1997; *b* 27 April 1939; *d* of Richard Pollard Hartley and Joyce Elizabeth Hartley; *m* 1963, George Telford Stevenson, *qv*; three *s*. *Educ:* Univ. of Manchester (BSc 1960, MSc 1961); St Hugh's Coll., Oxford (DPhil 1964). Lectr in Biochem., Univ. of Sydney,

1965–67; Post-doctoral Fellow, Univ. of Oxford, and Lectr in Biochem., Oriel Coll., Oxford, 1967–70; Southampton General Hospital: MRC Staff (external), 1970–73, Tenovus Post-doctoral Fellow, 1973–81, Tenovus Lab.; PSO, Regl Immunology Service, 1981–86; Top Grade SO, 1986–97; Reader in Immunology, Southampton Univ., 1986–97. *Publications:* 190 peer-reviewed articles, mainly in internat. jls, in field of immunology with focus on strategies to vaccinate against cancer using genetic technology. *Recreations:* music, literature, walking. *Address:* University of Southampton, Cancer Sciences Division, Somers Cancer Research Building, Mailpoint 891, Southampton General Hospital, Tremona Road, Southampton SO16 6YD. *T:* (02380) 796923, *Fax:* (02380) 701385; *e-mail:* fs@soton.ac.uk; Sudbury House, Sudbury Lane, Longworth, Abingdon OX13 5EL. *T:* (01865) 820646. *Club:* University Women's.

STEVENSON, Prof. George Telford; Professor of Immunochemistry, Faculty of Medicine, University of Southampton, 1974–97, now Visiting Professor; *b* 18 April 1932; *s* of Ernest George Stevenson and Mary Josephine Madden; *m* 1963, Freda Kathryn Hartley (*see* F. K. Stevenson); three *s*. *Educ:* North Sydney High Sch.; Univ. of Sydney (MB, BS; MD); Univ. of Oxford (DPhil). Resident MO, 1955–56, Resident Pathologist, 1957, Sydney Hosp.; Research Fellow, Dept of Medicine, Univ. of Sydney, 1958–61; Nuffield Dominions Demonstrator, Dept of Biochemistry, Univ. of Oxford, 1962–64; Sen. Research Fellow, Dept of Biochemistry, Univ. of Sydney, 1965–66; Scientific Staff, MRC Immunochemistry Unit, Univ. of Oxford, 1967–70; Dir, Tenovus Research Lab., Southampton Gen. Hosp., 1970–97; Consultant Immunologist, Southampton Univ. Hosps, 1976–97, now Hon. Consultant Immunologist. Hammer Prize for Cancer Research (jtly) (Armand Hammer Foundn, LA), 1982. *Publications:* Immunological Investigation of Lymphoid Neoplasms (with J. L. Smith and T. J. Hamblin), 1983; research papers on immunology and cancer, considered mainly at molecular level. *Address:* Sudbury House, Sudbury Lane, Longworth, Abingdon OX13 5EL. *T:* (01865) 820646.

STEVENSON, George William; *b* 30 Aug. 1938; *s* of Harold and Elsie May Stevenson; *m* 1st, 1958, Doreen June (decd); two *s* one *d*; 2nd, 1991, Pauline Brookes. *Educ:* Uttoxeter Road Primary School; Queensberry Road Secondary School, Stoke-on-Trent. Pottery caster, 1953–57; coal miner, 1957–66; transport driver, 1966–84; shop steward, TGWU 5/24 Branch, 1968–84 (Mem., 1964–; Chm., 1975–81). Deputy Leader: Stoke-on-Trent City Council, 1972–83; Staffs County Council, 1981–85. MEP (Lab) Staffs East, 1984–94; Pres., Eur. Parlt Delegn for Relations with S Asia, 1989–92 (Vice-Pres., 1984–89). MP (Lab) Stoke on Trent South, 1992–2005. Member, Select Committee: on European Legislation, 1995–2005; on Environment, Transport and the Regions, 1997–2005; Mem., Speaker's Panel of Chairmen. Chairman: All-Party Tibet Gp, 1995–2005; PLP Agric. Cttee, 1993–2001. *Recreations:* walking, cinema, travel, reading.

STEVENSON, Hugh Alexander; Chairman, Equitas Ltd, since 1998; *b* 7 Sept. 1942; *s* of William Hugh Stevenson and Elizabeth Margaret (*née* Wallace); *m* 1965, Catherine May Peacock; two *s* two *d*. *Educ:* Harrow Sch.; University Coll., Oxford (BA 1964; Hon. Fellow 1999); Harvard Business School (AMP 103). Admitted as Solicitor, 1967; with Linklaters & Paines, 1964–70; with S. G. Warburg & Co., 1970–92; Dir, S. G. Warburg Gp plc, 1986–95; Chairman: Mercury Asset Management Gp plc, 1992–98 (Dir, 1986–98); The Merchants Trust plc, 2000– (Dir, 1999–); Standard Life Investments, 2004– (Dir, 2000–); Dir, Standard Life plc (formerly Standard Life Assurance), 1999–. Director: British Museum Co., 1984–2006; Securities Inst., 1994–98 (Hon. FSI 1998); IMRO, 1995–2000; FSA, 2004–. Chm., Instnl Fund Managers Assoc., 1998–99. Hon. Treas., Inst. of Child Health, 1991–96 (Hon. Fellow 1996); Chairman: The Sick Children's Trust, 1982–99; Gt Ormond St Hosp. Redevelt Adv. Bd (formerly Gt Ormond St Hosp. Develt Trust), 1999–2006; Special Trustee, Gt Ormond St Hosp., 1996–2007. Hon. Treas., Millennium Bridge Trust, 1998–2002. Chm., Swinley Forest Golf Club, 2007–. Hon. Fellow, UCL, 2000. *Address:* Equitas Ltd, 33 St Mary Axe, EC3A 8LL. *T:* (020) 7342 2000.

See also Dame E. A. Griffiths.

STEVENSON, (James Alexander) Stewart; Member (SNP) Banff and Buchan, Scottish Parliament, since June 2001; Minister for Transport, Infrastructure and Climate Change, since 2007; *b* 15 Oct. 1946; *s* of late James Thomas Middleton Stevenson, MB ChB and Helen Mary Berry MacGregor, MA; *m* 1969, Sandra Isabel Pirie, MA. *Educ:* Bell Baxter Sch., Cupar; Univ. of Aberdeen (MA 1969). Various technology posts, later Dir of Technology Innovation, Bank of Scotland, 1969–99; pt-time Lectr, Sch. of Mgt, Heriot-Watt Univ., 2001–. Scottish Parliament: contested (SNP) Linlithgow, 1999–; Shadow Dep. Minister for Health and Social Justice, 2003–07; Member: Rural Develt Cttee, 2001–03; Justice Cttee, 2001–03. Mem., SNP, 1961–. *Recreations:* private pilot, computing, travel, public speaking. *Address:* Scottish Parliament, Edinburgh EH99 1SP; (constituency) 17 Maiden Street, Peterhead, Aberdeenshire AB42 1EE. *Clubs:* Edinburgh Flying; Moray Flying.

STEVENSON, Prof. Jane Barbara, (Mrs P. R. K. A. Davidson), PhD; Regius Professor of Humanity, University of Aberdeen, since 2007; *b* 12 Feb. 1959; *d* of John Lynn Stevenson and Winifred Mary Stevenson (*née* Temple); *m* 1989, Prof. Peter Robert Keith Andrew Davidson, *qv*. *Educ:* Haberdashers' Aske's Sch. for Girls, Elstree; Newnham Coll., Cambridge (BA 1981; PhD 1986). Drapers' Res. Fellow, Pembroke Coll., Cambridge, 1985–88; Lectr in Late Antique and Early Medieval Hist., Univ. of Sheffield, 1988–95; Sen. Res. Fellow, Univ. of Warwick, 1995–2000; University of Aberdeen: Reader in English, 2000–02; Reader in Postclassical Latin and Renaissance Studies, Sch. of Divinity, Hist. and Philosophy, 2002–05; Prof. of Latin, 2005–07. *Publications:* Women Writers in English Literature, 1992; The Laterculus Malalianus and the School of Archbishop Theodore, 1995; Several Deceptions, 1999; London Bridges, 2000; Astraea, 2001; The Pretender, 2002; The Empress of the Last Days, 2003; Good Women, 2005; Women Latin Poets: language, gender and authority from antiquity to the Eighteenth Century, 2005; Edward Burra: Twentieth Century eye, 2007; edited with Peter Davidson: Walter Scott, Old Mortality, 1993; The Closet of Sir Kenelm Digby, Kt, Opened, 1997; Early Modern Women Poets, 2001. *Recreations:* sleeping, being nice to cats. *Address:* Burnside House, Turriff, Aberdeenshire AB53 5PP. *T:* (01888) 562244; *e-mail:* janebstevenson@yahoo.com.

STEVENSON, Dr John, FRHistS; Reader in History, University of Oxford, since 1995; Visiting Fellow, Oriel College, Oxford, since 2007; *b* 26 Sept. 1946; *s* of John Stevenson and Bridget Stevenson; *m* 1971, Jacqueline Patricia Johns. *Educ:* Boteler GS, Warrington; Worcester Coll., Oxford (MA 1968; DPhil 1975). Lectr in Hist., Oriel Coll., Oxford, 1971–76; Lectr, 1976, Sen. Lectr, 1979, Reader in History, 1986–90, Univ. of Sheffield; Fellow and Tutor, Worcester Coll., Oxford, 1990–2006; Fellow, Greyfriars Hall, Oxford, 2006–08. Editor, English Historical Rev., 1996–2000. *Publications:* (with R. E. Quinault) Popular Protest and Public Order, 1974; Social Conditions in Britain between the Wars, 1977; London in the Age of Reform, 1977; (jtly) Crime and Law in Nineteenth Century Britain, 1978; Popular Disturbances in England, 1700–1870, 1979, 2nd edn 1992; (with M. Bentley) High and Low Politics in Modern Britain, 1983; British Society 1914–45, 1984; (with A. J. Fletcher) Order and Disorder in early modern England, 1985; (with S. Salter), The Working Class and Politics in Europe and America 1929–1945, 1990; The Macmillan Dictionary of British and European History since 1914, 1991; (with A. O'Day) Irish Historical Documents since 1800, 1992; Third Party Politics since 1945, 1993; (with J. C. Binfield) Sport, Culture and Politics, 1993; (with J. Gregory) The Longman Companion to the Eighteenth Century, 1999; (jtly) Advancing with the Army 1790–1850, 2006; with C. P. Cook: The Slump: society and politics during the Depression, 1977, 2nd edn 1993; The Longman Atlas of Modern British History, 1978; British Historical Facts 1760–1830, 1980; The Longman Handbook of Modern British History 1714–1980, 1983, 4th edn 2001; The Longman Handbook to Modern European History 1760–1985, 1987, 2nd edn 1998; British Historical Facts 1688–1760, 1988; The Longman Handbook of World History since 1914, 1991; The Longman Companion to Britain since 1945, 1996, 2nd edn 2000; The Longman Handbook of the Modern World, 1998; The History of Europe, 2002; The Longman Handbook of Twentieth Century Europe, 2003; The Routledge Companion to European History since 1763, 2005; The Routledge Companion to World History since 1914, 2005; Advancing with the Army, 2006. *Recreations:* book-collecting, gardening. *Address:* Merrifield, Down St Mary, Crediton, Devon EX17 6ED.

STEVENSON, Joseph Aidan; non-executive Director, Johnson Matthey plc, 1991–95; Chairman, Young Group plc, 1992–95; *b* 19 April 1931; *s* of Robert and Bridget Stevenson; *m* 1956, Marjorie Skinner; one *s* two *d*. *Educ:* Birmingham Univ. (BSc Hons Metallurgy). Instr Lieut, RN, 1955–58. Joined Johnson Matthey, 1958, as development metallurgist; held a number of sen. management, operating and div. dirships within the Johnson Matthey Gp; Gp Exec. Dir, 1982–91; Chief Exec. Officer, 1989–91. Chm. of Govs, Combe Bank Indep. Girls' Sch., Kent, 1985–91. Royal London Society for the Blind: Mem. Council, 1990–98 (Vice-Chm., 1995–98); Special Advr, Workbridge Scheme for employment of blind people, 1998–2005; Chm. Govs, RLSB Coll. of Further Educn (Dorton House), 1995–98. FIMMM (FIM 1990; Mem. Council, 1991–). Liveryman: Goldsmiths' Co.; Clockmakers' Co. Distinguished Achievement Award, Inst. of Precious Metals, 1989. *Recreations:* golf, sailing. *Club:* Knole Park Golf (Sevenoaks).

STEVENSON, Juliet Anne Virginia, CBE 1999; actress; Associate Artist, Royal Shakespeare Company; *b* 30 Oct. 1956; partner, Hugh Brody; one *s* one *d*. *Educ:* RADA (Bancroft Gold Medal). With Royal Shakespeare Company, 1978–86: Les Liaisons Dangereuses; As You Like It; Troilus and Cressida; Measure for Measure; A Midsummer Night's Dream; The Witch of Edmonton; Money; Henry IV parts I and II; Once in a Lifetime; The White Guard; Hippolytus; Antony and Cleopatra; The Churchill Play; Breaking the Silence; *other plays* include: Yerma, NT, 1987; Hedda Gabler, NT, 1989; Burn This, Hampstead, transf. Lyric, 1990; Death and the Maiden, Royal Court, transf. Duke of York's, 1991; The Duchess of Malfi, Greenwich, transf. Wyndhams, 1995; Caucasian Chalk Circle, RNT, 1997; Not I, and Footfalls, RSC and European tour, 1998; Private Lives, RNT, 1999; The Country, 2000, Alice Trilogy, 2005, Royal Court; The Seagull, NT, 2006; *films* include: Drowning by Numbers, 1988; Ladder of Swords, 1990; Truly, Madly, Deeply, 1991; The Trial, 1993; The Secret Rapture, 1994; Emma, 1996; Bend It Like Beckham, 2002; Food of Love, 2002; Nicholas Nickleby, 2003; Mona Lisa Smile, 2004; Being Julia, 2004; Pierrepoint, 2006; Infamous, 2007; And When Did You Last See Your Father?, 2007; several television rôles. *Publication:* (jtly) Clamorous Voices, 1988.

STEVENSON, Katharine Jane; *see* Marshall, K. J.

STEVENSON, Rt Rev. Kenneth William; *see* Portsmouth, Bishop of.

STEVENSON, Michael Charles; Head of Global Education, CISCO Systems, since 2007; *b* 14 Aug. 1960; *s* of Michael Anthony and Ena Elizabeth Stevenson; *m* 1987, Deborah Frances Taylor; one *s* two *d*. *Educ:* Doncaster Grammar Sch.; Christ Church, Oxford (LitHum). British Broadcasting Corporation, 1983–2003: trainee, 1983; Producer, Talks and Documentaries, Radio, 1984; Producer, News and Current Affairs, TV, 1988; Chief Assistant, Policy and Planning Unit, 1990; Dep. Editor, On The Record, 1991; Secretary, 1992–96; Dep. Dir, Regl Broadcasting, 1996–99; Dir of Educn, 1999–2000; Jt Dir, Factual and Learning, 2000–03; Department for Education and Skills: Dir of Strategy and Communications, 2003–05; Dir of Technology and Chief Information Officer, 2005–06. Non-exec. Dir, Granada Learning, 2007–. Mem. Bd, Re:source, then MLA, 2000–06. Mem. Council, Nat. Coll. for Sch. Leadership, 2000–03. Sir Huw Wheldon Fellow, Univ. of Wales, 1989. *Recreations:* music, tennis. *Address:* 49 Thurleigh Road, SW12 8TZ.

STEVENSON, Prof. Olive, CBE 1994; DLitt; Professor of Social Work Studies, University of Nottingham, 1984–94 (Head, School of Social Studies, 1987–91), now Professor Emeritus; Fellow, St Anne's College, University of Oxford, since 1970; *b* 13 Dec. 1930; *d* of John and Evelyn Stevenson. *Educ:* Purley County Grammar Sch. for Girls; Lady Margaret Hall, Oxford (BA EngLitt, MA 1955); London Sch. of Economics (Dip. in Social Studies, Dip. in Child Care); DLitt Nottingham, 1992. Tavistock Clinic; Child Care Officer, Devon CC, 1954–58; Lecturer in Applied Social Studies: Univ. of Bristol, 1959–61; Univ. of Oxford, 1961–68; Social Work Adviser, Supplementary Benefits Commn, 1968–70; Reader in Applied Social Studies, Univ. of Oxford, 1970–76; Prof. of Social Policy and Social Work: Univ. of Keele, 1976–82; Univ. of Liverpool, 1983–84. Member: Royal Commn on Civil Liability, 1973–78; Social Security Adv. Cttee, 1982–2002; Registered Homes Tribunal, 1985–90; Chairman: Adv. Cttee, Rent Rebates and Rent Allowances, 1977–83; Age Concern England, 1980–83; Councils of Voluntary Service Nat. Assoc., 1985–88; Care and Repair, 1993–97; Peterborough, Cambridge, Leicester City, Leics and Rutland County Area Child Protection Cttees, 1997–2000; Serious Case Review, 1999–2003; Fostering Options Adv. Cttee, 2004–. Research Report on Sexual Abuse of Elderly People, Anne Craft Trust, 2003. Series Ed., Working Together for Children, Young People and Families, 1996–99. Hon. Professor: Kingston Univ., 2003; Hong Kong Poly Univ., 2004. Hon. LittD: East Anglia, 1996; Kingston, 2004. *Publications:* Someone Else's Child, 1965, rev. edn 1977; Claimant or Client?, 1970; Social Service Teams: the practitioner's view, 1978; Child Abuse: interprofessional communication, 1979; Specialisation in Social Service Teams, 1981; (with Fuller) Policies, Programmes and Disadvantage, 1983; Age and Vulnerability, a guide to better care, 1988; (ed) Child Abuse: public policy and professional practice, 1989; (jtly) Community Care and Empowerment, 1993; Neglected Children: issues and dilemmas, 1998, 2nd edn 2007; (jtly) Child Welfare in the UK, 1998. *Recreations:* music, cookery, conversation. *Address:* c/o Centre for Social Work, University of Nottingham, Nottingham NG7 2RD.

STEVENSON, Maj.-Gen. Paul Timothy, OBE 1985 (MBE 1975); Clerk to Carpenters' Co., 1992–2007; *b* 9 March 1940; *s* of Ernest Stevenson and Dorothy Stevenson (*née* Trehearn); *m* 1965, Ann Douglas Drysdale; one *s* one *d*. *Educ:* Bloxham Sch. Commissioned Royal Marines 1958; 41 Commando, 1960; 45 Commando, Aden, 1962; HMS Mohawk, Gulf and W Indies, 1965–68; Army Staff Coll., 1972; 45 Commando, 1973–75; HMS Bulwark, 1975; Instructor, RN Staff Coll., 1978; SO Plans, HQ Land Forces, Falklands Campaign, 1982; CO 42 Commando, 1983; NATO Defence Coll., 1986; Dir, RM Personnel, 1987–88; RCDS 1989; Comdr, British Forces, Falkland

Is, 1989–90. Pres., RMA, 1997–2002. Modern Pentathlon British Team, 1962–69 (Olympic Team Manager, 1964); Biathlon British Team, 1965. *Recreations:* field sports, golf, gardening, ski-ing. *Address:* Lacys, Wortley, Wotton-under-Edge, Glos GL12 7QP. *Club:* Army and Navy.

STEVENSON, Robert Lindsay, (Robert Lindsay); actor; *b* 13 Dec. 1949; *s* of Norman Stevenson and late Joyce Stevenson; one *d* by Diana Weston; *m* 2006, Rosemarie Ford; two *s*. *Educ:* Gladstone Boys' Sch., Ilkeston; Clarendon Coll.; RADA. *Theatre:* The Roses of Eyam, 1970, Guys and Dolls, 1972, Northcott, Exeter; Godspell, Wyndhams, 1973; The Changeling, Riverside Studios, 1978; Trelawny of the Wells, Old Vic, 1980; How I Got That Story, Hampstead, 1981; Me and My Girl, Adelphi, 1985, NY, 1986 (Laurence Olivier Award, 1985; Tony Award, 1987); Becket, 1991, Cyrano de Bergerac, 1992, Th. Royal, Haymarket; Oliver!, Palladium, 1996 (Laurence Olivier Award, 1997); Richard III, RSC, 1998, Savoy, 1999; Power, RNT, 2003; The Entertainer, Old Vic, 2007; Royal Exchange, Manchester: The Cherry Orchard; Lower Depths; Hamlet, 1983 (and UK tour); Beaux Stratagem; Philoctetes; Julius Caesar; Leaping Ginger; Three Musketeers. *Films:* That'll Be the Day, 1973; Three for All, 1974; Strike It Rich, 1990; Fierce Creatures, 1997; Remember Me?, 1997; Divorcing Jack, 1998; Wimbledon, 2004. *Television:* Get Some In, 1975–77; Citizen Smith, 1977; Twelfth Night, 1980; Seconds Out, 1981; All's Well That Ends Well, 1981; A Midsummer Night's Dream, 1981; Cymbeline, 1982; Give Us a Break, 1983; King Lear, 1984; Much Ado About Nothing, 1984; Confessional, 1989; Bert Rigby, You're a Fool, 1989; Nightingales, 1990; GBH, 1991 (BAFTA Award, RTS Award, 1992); Genghis Cohn, 1993; The Wimbledon Poisoner, 1994; Jake's Progress, 1995; The Office, 1996; Brazen Hussies, 1996; Goodbye My Love, 1997; Hornblower, 1998, 1999, 2001, 2003; Oliver Twist, 1999; My Family (9 series), 2000–; Hawk, 2001; Don't Eat the Neighbours, 2001; Friends and Crocodiles, 2005, 2006; A Very Social Secretary, 2005; Jericho, 2005; Gideon's Daughter, 2006; The Trial of Tony Blair, 2007. *Address:* c/o Hamilton Hodell Ltd, 5th Floor, 66–68 Margaret Street, W1W 8SR.

STEVENSON, Robert Wilfrid, (Wilf); Director, Smith Institute, since 1997; *b* 19 April 1947; *s* of James Alexander Stevenson and Elizabeth Anne Stevenson (*née* Macrae); *m* 1st, 1972, Jennifer Grace Antonio (marr. diss. 1979); 2nd, 1991, Elizabeth Ann Minogue; one *s* two *d*. *Educ:* Edinburgh Academy; University College, Oxford (MA Natural Sciences, Chemistry); Napier Polytechnic. FCCA. Research Officer, Edinburgh Univ. Students' Assoc., 1970–74; Sec., Napier Coll., Edinburgh, 1974–87; Dep. Dir, 1987–88, Dir, 1988–97, BFI. Hon. DArts Napier, 2008. *Publications:* (ed) Gordon Brown Speeches, 2006; (ed) Moving Britain Forward, 2006. *Recreations:* cinema, bee keeping, bridge. *Address:* Missenden House, Little Missenden, Amersham, Bucks HP7 0RD. *T:* (01494) 890689, *Fax:* (01494) 868127; *e-mail:* wilfstevenson@msn.com.

STEVENSON, Sir Simpson, Kt 1976; DL; *b* 18 Aug. 1921; *s* of T. H. Stevenson, Greenock; *m* 1945, Jean Holmes Henry, JP, Port Glasgow. *Educ:* Greenock High Sch. Member: Greenock Town Council, 1949–67 and 1971–74 (Provost of Greenock, 1962–65); Inverclyde DC, 1974–99 (Provost, 1984–88); Vice-Chm., Clyde Port Authority, 1966–69; Chm., Greater Glasgow Health Bd, 1973–83; Chm., Scottish Health Services Common Service Agency, 1973–77, 1983–87. Member: Western Regional Hosp. Bd (Scotland), 1959–; Scottish Hosp. Administrative Staffs Cttee, 1965–74 (Chm., 1972–74); Chm., W Regional Hosp. Bd (Scotland), Glasgow, 1967–74; Member: Scottish Hosp. Endowments Commn, 1969–70; Scottish Health Services Planning Council; Royal Commn on the NHS, 1976–79. Chm., Consortium of Local Authorities Special Programme (CLASP), 1974. DL Renfrewshire, 1990. Hon. LLD Glasgow, 1982. *Recreations:* football, reading, choral singing. *Address:* 3F Cragburn Gate, Albert Road West, Gourock PA19 1NZ.

STEVENSON, Stewart; *see* Stevenson, J. A. S.

STEVENSON, Struan John Stirton; farmer; Member (C) Scotland, European Parliament, since 1999; *b* 4 April 1948; *s* of late Robert Harvey Ure Stevenson and Elizabeth Robertson (*née* Stirton); *m* 1974, Patricia Anne Taylor; two *s*. *Educ:* Strathallan Sch.; West of Scotland Agricl Coll. (DipAgr 1970). Member (C): Girvan DC, 1970–74; Kyle and Carrick DC, 1974–92 (Leader, 1986–88); Conservative Gp Leader, COSLA, 1986–88; Scottish agriculture spokesman, 1992–97, Scottish spokesman on envmt, transport, media, arts, heritage and tourism, 1997–98, Conservative Party. European Parliament: UK spokesman on fisheries, and dep. UK spokesman on agric., 1999–2002, 2004–; Chm., Fisheries Cttee, 2002–04; Vice-Pres., EPP-ED Gp, 2005–. Contested (C) Carrick, Cumnock and Doon Valley, 1987; Edinburgh S, 1992; Dumfries, 1997; NE Scotland, EP elecn, Nov. 1998. Chm., Tuesday Club, 1998–2001 (Hon. Pres., 2001–). Hon. Prof., Semey State Shakarim Univ., Kazakhstan, 2007. Hon. DSc State Med. Acad. of Semipalatinsk, Kazakhstan, 2000. Hon. Citizen, Semipalatinsk, Kazakhstan, 2003. Shapagat Medal, Kazakhstan, 2007. *Publication:* Crying Forever, 2006. *Recreations:* contemporary art, music, opera, poetry, theatre, cinema, photography. *Address:* European Parliament, Rue Wiertz, 1047 Brussels, Belgium. *T:* (2) 2847710. *Club:* New (Edinburgh).

STEVENSON, Timothy Edwin Paul, OBE 2004; Lord-Lieutenant of Oxfordshire, since 2008; Chairman: Travis Perkins plc, since 2001; Morgan Crucible Co. plc, since 2006; *b* 14 May 1948; *s* of late Derek Paul Stevenson, CBE; *m* 1973, Marion Emma Lander Johnston; three *d*. *Educ:* Canford Sch., Dorset; Worcester Coll., Oxford (BA Jurisp.). Called to the Bar, Inner Temple, 1971. Burmah Castrol: Asst Gp Legal Advr, 1975–77; Gp Planning Manager, 1977–81; Chief Exec., Castrol España, 1981–85; Marketing Manager, Develt, 1985–86; Manager, Corporate Develt, 1986–88; Chief Exec., Expandite Gp, 1988–90; Chief Exec., Fuels Gp, 1990–93; Dir, Lubricants, 1993–98; Chief Exec., 1998–2000. Non-exec. Director, DfES, 1997–2004; Partnerships UK Ltd, 2000–04; Tribal Gp plc, 2004–; Sen. Ind. Dir, and Chm. Audit Cttee, National Express, 2001–05. Mem. Council, Modern Art Oxford (formerly MOMA, Oxford), 1998–2004. Chm. Govs, Oxford Brookes Univ., 2004– (Gov., 2002–). Sloan Fellow, London Business Sch., 1988. DL Oxon, 2006. *Recreations:* hill walking, reading, music. *Address:* 263 Woodstock Road, Oxford OX2 7AE. *T:* (01865) 515477; Morgan Crucible Co. plc, Quadrant, 55–57 High Street, Windsor, Berks SL4 1LP.

STEVENSON, Wilf; *see* Stevenson, R. W.

STEVENSON, William; *see* Stevenson, A. W.

STEWARD, Rear Adm. Cedric John, CB 1984; Chief of Naval Staff, New Zealand, 1983–86, retired; *b* 31 Jan. 1931; *s* of Ethelbert Harold Steward and Anne Isabelle Steward; *m* 1952, Marie Antoinette Gurr; three *s*. *Educ:* Northcote College, Auckland, NZ; RNC Dartmouth; RNC Greenwich. Served: HMS Devonshire, 1950; HMS Illustrious, 1950; HMS Glory, 1951 (Korean Campaign and UN Medals, 1951); HMAS Australia, HMAS Barcoo, 1952; HM NZ Ships Hawea, 1953, Kaniere, 1954 (NZ GSM Korea 2002), Tamaki, 1955–58, Stawell, 1958–59; HMAS Creswell (RAN College), 1959–62; HM NZ Ships Rotoiti, 1962–63 (Antarctic support), Tamaki, 1963–64, Royalist, 1965–66 (Confrontation; Naval GSM Malaya 2002), Philomel, 1966, Inverell (in Command), 1966–67; JSSC Latimer, 1968; RNZN Liaison Officer Australia and Dep. Head, NZ Defence Liaison Staff, Canberra, 1969–73; in Command, HMNZS Otago, 1973–74; in Command and Captain F11, HMNZS Canterbury, 1974–75; Defence HQ, 1976–77; RCDS, 1978; Dep. Chief of Naval Staff, NZ, 1979–81; Commodore, Auckland, and NZ Maritime Comdr, 1981–83. Life Member: US Naval Inst., 1983; Australian Naval Inst., 1993. NZ Armed Forces Medal and Clasp, 1984; NZ Operational Service Medal, 2002. Pingat Jasa Malaysia, 2006. *Recreation:* philately. *Clubs:* Helensville Golf (Kaukapakapa), Auckland Racing (Ellerslie).

STEWART; *see* Vane-Tempest-Stewart, family name of Marquess of Londonderry.

STEWART, family name of **Earl of Galloway** and **Baron Stewartby**.

STEWART, Sir Alan (d'Arcy), 13th Bt *cr* 1623; yachtbuilder; *b* 29 Nov. 1932; *s* of Sir Jocelyn Harry Stewart, 12th Bt, and Constance Mary (*d* 1940), *d* of D'Arcy Shillaber; *S* father, 1982; *m* 1952, Patricia, *d* of Lawrence Turner; two *s* two *d*. *Educ:* All Saints College, Bathurst, NSW. *Heir:* *s* Nicholas Courtney d'Arcy Stewart, BSc, HDipEd, *b* 4 Aug. 1953. *Address:* One Acre, Ramelton, Co. Donegal, Ireland.

STEWART, Alastair James, OBE 2006; ITV News presenter; *b* 22 June 1952; *s* of Group Captain James F. Stewart and late Joan Mary Stewart (*née* Lord); *m* 1978, Sally Ann Jung; three *s* one *d*. *Educ:* St Augustine's Abbey Sch., Ramsgate; Univ. of Bristol. Dep. Pres., Nat. Union of Students, 1974–76. Reporter and presenter, Southern ITV, 1976–80; industrial corresp., ITN, 1980; presenter, ITN: News at Ten, 1981; Channel 4 News, 1983; News at One, 1985; News at 5.45, 1986; Parliament Programme, 1988; News at Ten, 1989, 1991–92; Washington corresp., 1990–91; London Tonight, 1993–; Live with Alastair Stewart, ITV News Channel, 2003–; ITV News at 10.30, 2006–; ITV Lunchtime News, 2007–; presenter: BBC Radio, 1994; Missing, LWT, 1992–96; The Carlton Debates, 1993–; The Sunday Prog. with Alastair Stewart, GMTV, 1994–2001; Police, Camera, Action, Carlton TV, 1994–2003, ITV, 2007–; Ask Ken, 2001–08; Moral of the Story, ITV, 2006–07. Commentator and presenter, numerous parly programmes and State occasions, UK and overseas, incl. first live transmission from House of Lords, 1985, House of Commons, 1989; ITV General Election, 1987, 1992, 1997, 2005; Gulf War and liberation of Kuwait, 1991; Who Wants to be a London Mayor?, 2000; King of the Castle, 2001; Funeral of Pope John Paul II, 2005; London's Mayor – You Decide, 2008. Trustee, Just a Drop, 2004–. Vice President: Homestart UK, 1997–; NCH Action for Children, 1998–. Patron: Lord Mayor Treloar Coll.; Hope Medical; Kids 4 Kids, 2003–; Samantha Dixon Trust, 2003–; Loomba Trust, 2005–; Scope, 2006–; Vice Patron: Missing Person's Helpline, 1993–; Zito Trust, 1995–; SANE, 1999–. Ambassador: Investors in People, 2002–; Crisis, 2007–. Governor, Ravensbourne Coll., 2006–. Hon. LLD Bristol, 2007. Annual Award, RBL, 1996; Face of London, RTS, 2002; Presenter of the Year, RTS, 2004. *Recreations:* travel, cartography, a catholic taste in music. *Address:* ITN, 200 Gray's Inn Road, WC1X 8XZ. *T:* (020) 7833 3000. *Club:* Reform.

STEWART, Alastair Lindsay; QC (Scot.) 1995; Sheriff of Tayside, Central and Fife at Dundee, 1990–2004; Temporary Judge in Supreme Courts, Scotland, since 1996; *b* 28 Nov. 1938; *s* of Alexander Lindsay Stewart and Anna Stewart; *m* 1st, 1968, Annabel Claire Stewart (marr. diss. 1991), *yr d* of late Prof. W. McC. Stewart; two *s*; 2nd, 1991, Sheila Anne Mackinnon (*née* Flockhart), *o d* of late David H. Flockhart. *Educ:* Edinburgh Academy; St Edmund Hall, Oxford (BA); Univ. of Edinburgh (LLB). Admitted to Faculty of Advocates, 1963; Tutor, Faculty of Law, Univ. of Edinburgh, 1963–73; Standing Junior Counsel to Registrar of Restrictive Trading Agreements, 1968–70; Advocate Depute, 1970–73; Sheriff of South Strathclyde, Dumfries and Galloway, at Airdrie, 1973–79, of Grampian, Highland and Islands, at Aberdeen and Stonehaven, 1979–90; Interim Sheriff Principal, Lothian and Borders, Glasgow and Strathkelvin, 2005. Chairman: Grampian Family Conciliation Service, 1984–87 (Hon. Pres., 1987–90); Scottish Assoc. of Family Conciliation Services, 1986–89. Mem., Judicial Studies Cttee, 2000–04. Governor, Robert Gordon's Inst. of Technology, 1982–90 (Vice-Chm. of Governors, 1985–90). Hon. Prof., Sch. of Law (formerly Faculty of Law and Accountancy), Univ. of Dundee, 2001–. Editor, Scottish Civil Law Reports, 1992–95. *Publications:* (contrib.) Sheriff Court Practice, by I. D. Macphail, 1988, jt gen. editor, 2nd edn, vol. 1 1998, vol. 2 2002; The Scottish Criminal Courts in Action, 1990, 2nd edn 1997; Evidence reissue, Stair Memorial Encyclopædia of the Laws of Scotland, 2006; various articles in legal jls. *Recreations:* reading, music, walking. *Address:* 86 Albany Road, Broughty Ferry, Dundee DD5 1JQ. *T:* (01382) 477580. *Club:* New (Edinburgh).

STEWART, Sir Alastair (Robin), 3rd Bt *cr* 1960, of Strathgarry, Perth; *b* 26 Sept. 1925; 2nd *s* of Sir Kenneth Dugald Stewart, 1st Bt, GBE and Noel (*d* 1946), *yr d* of Kenric Brodribb, Melbourne; *S* brother, 1992; *m* 1953, Patricia Helen, MBE, ARIBA, *d* of late J. A. Merrett; one *s* three *d*. *Educ:* Marlborough Coll. Lieut, 1st Royal Gloucestershire Hussars, 1945–47. Dir, Neale & Wilkinson Ltd, 1947–71; Man. Dir, Stewart & Harvey Ltd, 1971–90. *Recreation:* gardening. *Heir:* *s* John Kenneth Alexander Stewart, *b* 15 Dec. 1961. *Address:* Walters Cottage, North Hill, Little Baddow, Chelmsford, Essex CM3 4TQ. *T:* (01245) 222445.

STEWART, Alec James, OBE 2003 (MBE 1998); cricketer; *b* 8 April 1963; *s* of Michael James, (Micky), Stewart and Sheila Marie Macdonald Stewart; *m* 1991, Lynn Blades; one *s* one *d*. *Educ:* Tiffin Boys' Sch. Joined Surrey County Cricket Club, 1981, capped 1985, Captain, 1992–97, retired from County team, 2003; Test début, 1989; Mem., 1989–2003, Captain, 1998–99, England Test team; played 133 Test Matches, scored 15 centuries, took 263 catches, 14 stumpings; overseas tours with England team: W Indies, 1989–90, 1993–94 (Vice Capt.), 1997–98; Australia and NZ, 1990–91; India and Sri Lanka, 1992–93; Australia, 1994–95, 1998–99, 2002–03; S Africa, 1995–96, 1999–2000; Zimbabwe and NZ, 1996–97. *Publications:* (with Brian Murgatroyd) Alec Stewart: a Captain's Diary, 1999; Playing for Keeps (autobiog.), 2003. *Address:* c/o Surrey County Cricket Club, The Oval, SE11 5SS.

STEWART, Alexandra Joy, (Mrs M. McBride); Recruitment Consultant, since 2003, and Head of Higher Education Practice, since 2004, Saxton Bampfylde Ltd (formerly Saxton Bampfylde Hever Ltd); *b* 11 April 1953; *d* of Charles Stewart and Myrtle Stewart (*née* Sheppard); *m* 1st, 1976, Andrew Smyth (marr. diss. 1990); one *d*; 2nd, 1991, Michael McBride. *Educ:* Bexhill Grammar Sch. for Girls; Durham Univ. (BA Hons). Joined DES, 1975; admin trainee, 1975–79; Private Sec. to Minister for Educn, 1979–81; Principal, 1981–88; Assistant Secretary: Hd of City Technol. Unit, 1988–92; with DNH, subseq. DCMS, 1992–2003; Hd of Sports Div., then Finance Dir, 1992–99; Dir, Museums, Galleries, Libraries and Heritage, subseq. Art and Culture, 1999–2003. *Recreations:* my family, gardening, the South Downs, horses. *Address:* Saxton Bampfylde Ltd, 35 Old Queen Street, SW1Y 9JA.

STEWART, Allan; *see* Stewart, J. A.

STEWART, Andrew Struthers, (Andy); farmer; Chairman, Agricultural Training Board, 1992–98; *b* 27 May 1937; *s* of late James Stewart and of Elizabeth Stewart; *m* 1961, Louise Melvin (*née* Skimming); one *s* one *d*. *Educ:* Strathaven Acad., Scotland; West of Scotland Agricl Coll. Farming Beesthorpe Manor Farm, 1961–. Mem., Caunton Parish Council, 1973–83; Conservative Mem., Notts CC, 1975–83 and 2002–; Cons. spokesman on leisure services, 1981–83. MP (C) Sherwood, 1983–92; contested (C) Sherwood, 1992. PPS to Minister of Agriculture, Fisheries and Food, 1987–89, to Sec. of State for Educn and Science, 1989–90, to Lord Pres. of Council and Leader of H of C, 1990–92. Comr, Rural Develt Commn, 1993–99. Chairman: Strathaven Br., Young Conservatives, 1957 and 1958; Caunton, Maplebeck and Kersall Cons. Br., 1970–73 (Founder Mem.). Chairman: Lantra, NTO for land based industries, 1998–2000; Lantra Trust, 2000–; Member: Newark Br., NFU, 1961– (Mem., County Exec. Cttee, 1966–); Newark and Notts Agricl Soc.; Adv. Mem., Nottingham University Coll. of Agriculture, 1977–82 (formerly Chm., Notts Coll. of Agriculture Brackenhurst); formerly Chm., Governing Bd, Rufford Comprehensive Sch. Youth Club Leader, 1965–76; Life Vice President: Southwell Rugby Club; Caunton Cricket Club; Trustee, Southwell Recreation Centre, 1979–83. Hon. Assoc. Mem., BVA, 1991. *Address:* Beesthorpe Manor Farm, Caunton, Newark, Notts NG23 6AT. *T:* (01636) 636270. *Clubs:* Farmers'; Bentinck Conservative (Hucknall, Notts).

STEWART, Angus; QC (Scot.) 1988; *b* 14 Dec. 1946; *s* of late Archibald Ian Balfour Stewart, CBE, BL, FSAScot and of Ailsa Rosamund Mary Massey; *m* 1975, Jennifer Margaret Stewart; one *d*. *Educ:* Edinburgh Acad.; Balliol Coll., Oxford (BA); Edinburgh Univ. (LLB). Called to the Scottish Bar, 1975. Keeper, Advocates' Liby, 1994–2002. Sen. Advocate Depute, 2005–. Chm., Scottish Council of Law Reporting, 1997–2001. Trustee: Nat. Liby of Scotland, 1994–2005; Stewart Heritage Trust, 1994–2001; Internat. E Boat Class Assoc., 1993–. Chm., Abbotsford Liby Project, 1996–2002. Pres., Stewart Soc., 2001–04. *Address:* 8 Ann Street, Edinburgh EH4 1PJ. *T:* (0131) 332 4083.

See also P. L. McI. Stewart.

STEWART, Annie; Editor, The Voice, 1995–99; *b* 24 Dec. 1959; *d* of Charles Alanzo Stewart and Madge Petrona Stewart; one *d*. *Educ:* Stratford Grammar Sch. Reporter: Walthamstow Express, 1986–87; The Voice, 1987–95; Editor-in-Chief, The Weekly Jl, 1997–99. Dir, M&M Media, 1997–. *Recreations:* stocks and shares, travel. *Address:* 7 Capstan Court, 24 Wapping Wall, E1 9TE. *T:* (020) 7737 7377. *Club:* Royal Commonwealth Society.

STEWART, Brian Edward; HM Diplomatic Service, retired; Ambassador to Algeria, 2004–05; *b* 4 Feb. 1950; *s* of late Edward Stewart and of Carrol Stewart (*née* Medcalf); *m* 1975, Anne Cockerill. *Educ:* Melsetter Sch., Southern Rhodesia; Keith Grammar Sch., Scotland; Keele Univ. (BA Hons). Entered FCO, 1972; MECAS, Lebanon, 1973–75; 3rd, later 2nd Sec., Amman, 1975–78; on loan to Cabinet Office, 1978–80; First Sec., FCO, 1980–82; First Secretary and Head of Chancery: Singapore, 1982–85; Tunis, 1986–89; First Sec., FCO, 1989–93; Dep. Hd of Mission, Damascus, 1993–96; Counsellor, FCO, 1996–98; Dep. Hd of Mission and Counsellor, Kuwait, 1998–2001; FCO, 2002; rcds 2003. *Publication:* (contrib.) The Arabists of Shemlan, 2006. *Recreations:* restoring and maintaining potential classic cars, tackling essential household DIY, playing tennis and cricket with more enthusiasm than skill. *Address:* c/o Foreign and Commonwealth Office, King Charles Street, SW1A 2AH.

STEWART, Sir Brian (John), Kt 2002; CBE 1996; non-executive Chairman, Scottish & Newcastle plc, 2003–08 (Chairman, 2000–03); *b* 9 April 1945; *m* 1971, Seonaid Duncan; two *s* one *d*. *Educ:* Edinburgh Univ. (MSc). Mem., Scottish Inst. of Chartered Accountants. Scottish and Newcastle Breweries, subseq. Scottish and Newcastle plc: joined 1976; Finance Dir, 1988–91; Gp Chief Exec., 1991–2000; Dep. Chm., 1997–2000. Dir, Booker, 1993–99; Chm., Standard Life Assurance Co., 2003–07 (Dir, 1993–2007). *Recreations:* golf, ski-ing.

STEWART, Brian Thomas Webster, CMG 1969; Hon. Lecturer, Hong Kong University, 1986–98; *b* 27 April 1922; *s* of late Redvers Buller Stewart and Mabel Banks Sparks, Broich, Crieff; *m* 1946, Millicent Peggy Pollock (marr. diss. 1970); two *d*; *m* 1972, Sally Nugent; one *s* one *d*. *Educ:* Trinity Coll., Glenalmond; Worcester Coll., Oxford (MA). Commnd The Black Watch (RHR), 1942; served Europe and Far East (Capt.). Joined Malayan Civil Service, 1946; studying Chinese Macau, 1947; Asst Sec., Chinese Affairs, Singapore, 1949; Devonshire Course, Oxford, 1950; Asst Comr for Labour, Kuala Lumpur, 1951; Sec. for Chinese Affairs, Supt of Chinese Schs, Malacca and Penang, 1952–57; joined HM Diplomatic Service, 1957; served Rangoon, Peking, Shanghai, Manila, Kuala Lumpur, Hanoi; Asst Sec., Cabinet Office, 1968–72; Counsellor, Hong Kong, 1972–74; FCO, 1974–78. Special Rep., Rubber Growers Assoc., Malaysia, 1979–82; Dir of Ops (China), Racal Electronics, 1982–96. *Publications:* All Men's Wisdom (anthology of Chinese Proverbs), 1957; Scrapbook of a Roving Highlander (memoirs), 2002; Smashing Terrorism in Malaya, 2003; Fiji Jottings, 2005; Call to Arms, 2006. *Recreations:* walking, chamber music, orientalia particularly chinoiserie. *Address:* c/o Royal Bank of Scotland, Crieff, Perthshire PH7 3RX. *Clubs:* Athenæum, Special Forces; Royal Perth Golf; Hong Kong.

STEWART, Rev. Dr Charles Edward; Chaplain, Royal Hospital School, since 2000; *b* 10 June 1946; *s* of Charles Stewart and Mary Stewart (*née* McDougall); *m* 1970, Margaret Marion Smith; two *s* one *d*. *Educ:* Strathclyde Univ. (BSc; PhD); Glasgow Univ. (BD); Edinburgh Univ. (MTh). Ordained, C of S, 1976; Chaplain: HMS Sea Hawk, RNAS Culdrose, 1976–78; Clyde Submarine Base, 1978–80; Staff of Flag Officer 3rd Flotilla, 1980; Chaplain: HMS Hermes, Falklands Conflict, 1981; HMS Neptune, 1982–85; HMS Drake and Staff of Flag Officer Plymouth, 1985–87; HMS Raleigh, 1987–90; BRNC, Dartmouth, 1990–93; Asst Dir Naval Chaplaincy Service, 1992–94; HMS Invincible, Bosnia, 1994–96; Dir Naval Chaplaincy Service, 1996–97; Dir Gen. Naval Chaplaincy Service, 1997–2000; Chaplain of the Fleet, 1998–2000. QHC 1996–2000. South Atlantic Medal, 1982; NATO Medal, 1995. *Recreations:* gardening, water colours (painting), music, hill walking, model ship construction.

STEWART, Colin MacDonald, CB 1983; FIA; Directing Actuary, Government Actuary's Department, 1974–84; *b* 26 Dec. 1922; *s* of John Stewart and Lillias Cecilia MacDonald Fraser; *m* 1948, Gladys Edith Thwaites (*d* 2003); three *d*. *Educ:* Queen's Park Secondary Sch., Glasgow. Clerical Officer, Rosyth Dockyard, 1939–42. Served War: Fleet Air Arm (Lieut (A) RNVR), 1942–46. Govt Actuary's Dept, London, 1946–84. Head of Actuarial Res., Godwins Ltd, 1985–88. FIA 1953. *Publications:* The Students' Society Log 1960–85, 1985; (contrib.) Life, Death and Money, 1998; numerous articles on actuarial and demographic subjects in British and internat. jls. *Recreations:* genealogical research, foreign travel, grandchilding. *Address:* 8 The Chase, Coulsdon, Surrey CR5 2EG. *T:* (020) 8660 3966.

STEWART, Sir David James H.; *see* Henderson-Stewart.

STEWART, David John; Member (Lab) Highlands and Islands, Scottish Parliament, since 2007; *b* 5 May 1956; *s* of John and Alice Stewart; *m* 1982, Linda MacDonald; one *s* one *d*. *Educ:* Paisley Coll. (BA Hons); Stirling Univ. (Dip. Social Wk, CQSW); Open Univ. (Professional Dip. Mgt). Social work manager, 1980–97; Asst Dir for Rural Affairs, SCVO, 2005–07. Member (Lab): Nithsdale DC, 1984–86; Inverness DC, 1988–96 (Dep. Leader, Labour Gp). Contested (Lab): Inverness, Nairn and Lochaber, 1987 and 1992; Inverness, Nairn, Badenoch and Strathspey, 2005. MP (Lab) Inverness E, Nairn and Lochaber, 1997–2005. A Lab Whip, 2007–, Shadow Envmt Minister, 2007–, Scottish Parlt. *Address:* Scottish Parliament, Edinburgh EH99 1SP.

STEWART, Captain Sir David (John Christopher), 7th Bt *cr* 1803, of Athenree, Tyrone; *b* 19 June 1935; *s* of Sir Hugh Charlie Godfray Stewart, 6th Bt and his 1st wife, Rosemary Elinor Dorothy, *d* of Maj. George Peacocke; *S* father, 1994; *m* 1959, Bridget Anne, *er d* of late Patrick W. Sim; three *d*. *Educ:* Bradfield Coll.; RMA Sandhurst. Commnd Royal Inniskilling Fusiliers, 1956; seconded to Trucial Oman Scouts, 1957–58 (Jebel Akhdar Campaign, 1957); Adjt 1958; served in Trucial States, Oman and Muscat, 1957–58, Germany, 1958–59, Kenya, 1960–62 (Kuwait Operation, 1961), UN Peacekeeping Force, Cyprus, 1964; retd as Captain, 1965. Representative for E. S. & A. Robinson, Bristol, 1965–69; Director: Maurice James Holdings, Coventry, 1969–77; Papropak UK, 1977–79; self-employed, 1979–; owner, George Inn, Middlezoy, Somerset, 1982–85. Hon. Organiser, RBL Poppy Appeal, Wiveliscombe, 1996–2002; Hon. Treas., Friends of Somerset SSAFA-Forces Help, 1998–2006. Medal, Order of Tower of Al Qassimi (UAE), 2003. *Recreations:* golf, cricket. *Heir:* half *b* Hugh Nicholas Stewart [*b* 20 April 1955; *m* 1976, Anna Leeke; one *s* three *d*]. *Address:* 16 Blackdown View, Curry Rivel, Langport, Somerset TA10 0ER. *Clubs:* MCC; XL.

STEWART, George Girdwood, CB 1979; MC 1945; TD 1954; Cairngorm Estate Adviser, Highlands and Islands Enterprise, 1988–98; *b* 12 Dec. 1919; *o s* of late Herbert A. Stewart, BSc, and of Janetta Dunlop Girdwood; *m* 1950, Shelagh Jean Morven Murray (*d* 2004); one *s* one *d*. *Educ:* Kelvinside Academy, Glasgow; Glasgow Univ.; Edinburgh Univ. (BSc). Served RA, 1940–46 (MC, despatches); CO 278 (Lowland) Field Regt RA (TA), 1957–60. Dist Officer, Forestry Commn, 1949–61; Asst Conservator, 1961–67; Conservator, West Scotland, 1967–69; Comr for Forest and Estate Management, 1969–79; National Trust for Scotland: Mem., Council, 1975–79; Rep., Branklyn Garden, Perth, 1980–84; Regional Rep., Central and Tayside, 1984–88; Forestry Consultant, 1989–93. Specialist advr, Select Cttee on EEC Forestry Policy, 1986; Associate Dir, Oakwood Envmtl, 1990–2003. Member: BR Bd Envt Panel, 1980–90; Countryside Commn for Scotland, 1981–88; Chm., Scottish Wildlife Trust, 1981–87; Cairngorm Mountain Trust (formerly Cairngorm Recreation Trust), 1986–. Pres., Scottish Nat. Ski Council, 1988–94 (Hon. Vice-Pres., 1998–). Pres., Scottish Ski Club, 1971–75; Vice-Pres., Nat. Ski Fedn of GB; Chm., Alpine Racing Cttee, 1975–78. Mem., British Team, ITF Veterans World Team Tennis Championships, 1999, 2001, 2002; Winner of Doubles, ITF Super-Seniors World Individual Championships, 2006, 2007. FRSA; FICFor; Hon. FLI. Nat. Service to Sport Award, Scottish Sports Council, 1995. *Recreations:* ski-ing, tennis, studying Scottish painting. *Address:* 11 Mansfield Road, Scone, Perth PH2 6SA. *T:* (01738) 551815. *Club:* Ski Club of Great Britain.

STEWART, (George Robert) Gordon, OBE 1984; Secretary, 1976–83, Legal Adviser 1983–87, Institute of Chartered Accountants of Scotland; *b* 13 Oct. 1924; *s* of David Gordon Stewart and Mary Grant Thompson or Stewart; *m* 1952, Rachel Jean Morrison; two *s* one *d*. *Educ:* George Watson's Coll., Edinburgh; Edinburgh Univ. (MA 1947, LLB 1949). WS. Mem., Law Soc. of Scotland, 1949–92. Served War, 1943–46: Captain, Royal Signals; Burma and SEAC. In practice as WS, Melville & Lindesay, WS, Edinburgh, 1950–59; Asst Sec., subseq. Sec., and Dir, Ideal-Standard Ltd, Hull, 1959–75. *Recreation:* gardening.

STEWART, Prof. George Russell, PhD, DSc; Dean, Faculty of Life and Physical Sciences, University of Western Australia, since 2002 (Executive Dean, Faculty of Science, 1998–2001); *b* 25 Feb. 1944; *s* of George and Isobella Stewart; *m* 1978, Janice Anne Grimes; three *d*. *Educ:* Pinner County Grammar Sch.; Univ. of Bristol (BSc 1965; PhD 1968); DSc London 1991. Lectr in Botany, Univ. of Manchester, 1968–81; London University: Prof. of Botany and Head of Dept, Birkbeck Coll., 1981–85; Quain Prof. of Botany, 1985–91 and Head of Dept of Biology, 1987–91, UCL; Dean of Faculty of Sci., 1990–91; Prof. of Botany, Univ. of Queensland, 1992–98. Vis. Lectr, Dept of Biology, Univ. of Lagos, Nigeria; Visiting Professor: Dept of Botany, Univ. of Queensland, Aust.; Dept of Biology, Univ. of Campinas, Brazil; Dept of Biology, Univ. of WA. Member: Plants and Envmt Cttee, AFRC, 1989–91; Plants and Envmt Res. Bd, AFRC (Chm., 1989–91); Agriculture Cttee, Long Ashton Res. Station, 1990–91; Inter-Agency Cttee on Res. into Global Envmtl Change (Working Gp 2), 1990–91; Zool Parks Authy, WA, 2006–. Mem., Bd of Dirs, SciTech Discovery Centre, 1999–. Dep. Pres., WA Br., Australia-China Business Council, 2005–07. Foreign expert consultant, Beijing Assoc. for Sci. Hon. Mem., Shanghai Assoc. for Sci. and Tech., 2006. *Publications:* (ed jtly) The Genetic Manipulation of Plants and its Application to Agriculture, 1984; numerous scientific papers on plant physiology and metabolism and chapters in books and conf. proc. *Recreations:* cycling, cooking. *Address:* Faculty of Life and Physical Sciences, University of Western Australia, Crawley, WA 6009, Australia. *T:* (8) 93803159; *e-mail:* gstewart@science.uwa.edu.au.

STEWART, Gillian Mary, CB 2003; Head of Children and Young People's Group, Scottish Executive Education Department, 1999–2002; *b* 2 June 1945; *d* of John Knott and Nora Elizabeth Knott; marr. diss.; two *s*. *Educ:* Blyth Grammar Sch.; Univ. of Durham (BA Hons Class 1 German). Joined Scottish Office, 1970; posts in educn and social work; Asst Sec., 1984; posts in historic buildings and local govt; Under-Sec., 1992; Hd of Criminal Justice Gp, 1992–97; Hd of Social Work Services Gp, Home Dept, 1997–99. FSAC (formerly CSSB) Assessor, 2003–. Chair, Waverley Care AIDS Trust, 2003–; Mem., Council and Scottish Cttee, Barnardo's, 2003–; Vice-Chm., Families Outside, 2006–. Mem. Ct, Edinburgh Univ., 2003–. *Recreations:* swimming, walking, music, theatre, gardening.

STEWART, Gordon; *see* Stewart, G. R. G.

STEWART, Prof. Gordon Thallon, MD; FFPH; Mechan Professor of Public Health, University of Glasgow, 1972–84, now Emeritus Professor; Hon. Consultant in Epidemiology and Preventive Medicine, Glasgow Area Health Board; *b* 5 Feb. 1919; *s* of John Stewart and Mary L. Thallon; *m* 1946, Joan Kego; two *s* two *d*; *m* 1975, Neena Walker. *Educ:* Paisley Grammar Sch.; Univs of Glasgow and Liverpool. BSc 1939; MB, ChB 1942; DTM&H 1947; MD (High Commendation) 1949; FRCPath 1964; FFPH (FFCM 1972); MRCPGlas 1972; FRCPGlas 1975. House Phys. and House Surg., 1942–43; Surg. Lieut RNVR, 1943–46; Res. Fellow (MRC), Univ. of Liverpool, 1946–48; Sen. Registrar and Tutor, Wright-Fleming Inst., St Mary's Hosp., London, 1948–52; Cons. Pathologist, SW Metrop. Regional Hosp. Bd, 1954–63; Res. Worker at MRC Labs Carshalton, 1955–63; Prof. of Epidem. and Path., Univ. of N Carolina, 1964–68; Watkins Prof. of Epidem., Tulane Univ. Med. Center, New Orleans, 1968–72.

Vis. Prof., Dow Med. Coll., Karachi, 1952–53 and Cornell Univ. Med. Coll., 1970–71; Cons. to WHO, and to NYC Dept of Health; Vis. Lectr and Examr, various univs in UK and overseas. Sen. Fellow, Nat. Science Foundn, Washington, 1964; Delta omega, 1969. *Publications:* (ed) Trends in Epidemiology, 1972; (ed jtly) Penicillin Allergy, 1970; Penicillin Group of Drugs, 1965; papers on chemotherapy of infectious diseases, drug allergy and epidemiology in various med. and sci. jls. *Recreations:* gardening, drawing, music. *Address:* 29/8 Inverleith Place, Edinburgh EH3 5QD.

STEWART, Hugh Parker, FCA; Chairman: Demaglass Ltd, 1994–99; Image Precision International Ltd, 1997–99; *b* 23 May 1934; *s* of George and Barbara Stewart; *m* 1960, Marion Gordon Cairns; one *s* one *d. Educ:* Sullivan Upper Sch., Holywood, Co. Down; Queen's Univ., Belfast (LLB Hons). Audit Manager, Hill Vellacott & Bailey, Belfast, 1959–62; Financial Comptroller, STC (NI) Ltd, Monkstown, 1962–67; Admin Manager, AMF Beaird, Belfast, 1967–70; Gp Financial Controller, Brightside Engrg Hldgs, Sheffield, 1970–71; SMM Ltd, Greenwich: Financial Dir., 1971–74; Overseas Dir, 1974–78; Man. Dir, SMM Foundries Ltd, Greenwich, 1978–79; Finance Dir, Westland plc, 1979–81; Finance Dir, Westland plc, and Exec. Dir, Westland Technologies Ltd, 1981–84; Man. Dir, Westland Technologies Ltd, 1984–85; Chief Exec., Westland Gp plc, 1985–88. Chm., Scheduling Technology Gp Ltd, 1989–90; Practice Chm., Aaron & Partners, Solicitors, 1989–91; Chairman: Programming Research Ltd, 1990–91; Wootton Jeffreys Consultants Ltd, 1991–94; Aerospace Systems & Technologies, 1993–95; Western Computer Gp, 1993–95; Wellmann plc, 1995–98 (Dir, 1992–98); Director: DSK Systems Ltd, 1989–91; Cityflyer Express Ltd, 1991–99; Chessington Computer Centre, 1995–96 (Mem., Ministerial Adv. Bd, 1995–96). Governor, Sherborne Sch., 1982–2004. *Recreations:* golf, gardening. *Club:* Sloane.

STEWART, Ian; MP (Lab) Eccles, since 1997; *b* 28 Aug. 1950; *s* of John and Helen Stewart; *m* 1968, Merilyn Holding; two *s* one *d. Educ:* David Livingstone Primary Meml Sch., Blantyre; Calder Street Secondary, Blantyre; Alfred Turner Secondary Modern Sch., Salford; Stretford Technical Coll.; Manchester Metropolitan Univ. Regl Officer, TGWU, 1978–97. PPS to Minister of State for Industry and Energy, subseq. for Energy and Construction, 2001–03, to Minister of State (Minister for Energy, the Post Office, E-Govt and Corporate Social Responsibility), 2003–04, DTI; PPS to Financial Sec. to HM Treasury, 2004–05; PPS, DTI, 2005–06. Member: Deregulation Select Cttee, 1997–2001; Information Select Cttee, 1998–2001; Innovation, Sci. and Skills Select Cttee, 2007–; PLP Employment and Trng Cttee, 1997–; PLP Trade and Industry Cttee, 1997–; PLP Foreign Affairs Cttee, 1997–; Exec., PITCOM, 1998–; Chairman: All Party Community Media Gp, 2002–; All Party Parly Gp for Prevention of Bullying and Work Related Violence; Vice Chairman: All Party China Gp, 1997– (Mem., GB China Centre Exec., 1997–); All Party Parly Kazakhstan Gp; Chm., Parly Gp for Vaccine Damaged Children, 1998–2001. Defence Sports Advr to Minister of State (Minister for Sport), DCMS, 2002–; Govt Rep. for Defence Sports. Founder, Eur. Foundn for Social Partnership and Continuing Trng Initiatives, 1993. Member: UK Soc. of Industrial Tutors, 1980–; Manchester Industrial Relations Soc., 1994–; Member: Internat. Soc. of Indust. Relns, 1996–; Council, Eur. Informatics Market, 1998–; Council, Eur. Information Soc. Fellow, Industry and Parlt Trust, 1997; Vis. Fellow, Salford Univ., 1998. *Address:* House of Commons, SW1A 0AA.

STEWART, Prof. Ian George; Professor of Economics, University of Edinburgh, 1967–84; *b* 24 June 1923; *s* of David Tweedie Stewart, MA and Ada Doris Montgomery Haldane; *m* 1949, Mary Katharine Oddie; one *s* two *d. Educ:* Fettes Coll.; Univ. of St Andrews (MA 1st Class Hons); MA Cantab 1954. Pilot, RAF, 1942–46. Commonwealth Fund Fellow, 1948–50. Research Officer, Dept of Applied Economics, Univ. of Cambridge, 1950–57; University of Edinburgh: Lectr in Economics, 1957–58; Sen. Lectr, 1958–61; Reader, 1961–67; Curator of Patronage, 1979–84. Vis. Associate Prof., Univ. of Michigan, 1962; Vis. Prof., Univ. of S Carolina, 1975. Dir, Scottish Provident Instn, 1980–90, Dep. Chm., 1983–85. Mem., British Library Bd, 1980–87. Governor, Fettes Coll., 1976–89. *Publications:* National Income of Nigeria (with A. R. Prest), 1953; (ed) Economic Development and Structural Change, 1969; articles in jls and bank reviews. *Recreations:* golf, fishing, gardening. *Club:* New (Edinburgh).

STEWART, Very Rev. Ian Guild; Priest-in-charge, St David, Inverbervie, since 1992; Rector, St Mary and St Peter, Montrose, since 1992; Dean of Brechin, since 2007; *b* 1943. *Educ:* Edinburgh Theol Coll. Ordained deacon, 1984, priest, 1985; Non-Stipendiary Minister, St Mary Magdalene, Dundee, 1984–87; Non-Stipendiary Minister, 1987–90, Asst Curate, 1990–92, St Martin, Dundee; Non-Stipendiary Minister, 1987–90, Asst Curate, 1990–92, St John the Baptist, Dundee; Canon, St Paul's Cathedral, Dundee, 2001–. *Address:* The Rectory, 17 Panmure Place, Montrose DD10 8ER.

STEWART, Ian James, CB 1997; Chief Executive, Cambridgeshire County Council, 2003–07; *b* 30 Aug. 1946; *m* 1967, Morag Gardiner Duncan; two *d. Educ:* Perth Acad. Area Dir, Newcastle Benefits Directorate, 1990–92; Mem. Bd of Mgt and Dir, Benefits Agency, DSS, 1993–95; Project Dir, Jobseekers' Allowance, DfEE, 1995–97; Dir Gen., Benefit Fraud Inspectorate, DSS, 1997–99; Chief Exec., Bradford CC, 1999–2003.

STEWART, Prof. Ian Nicholas, PhD; FRS 2001; CMath, FIMA, CBiol, FIBiol; Professor of Mathematics, University of Warwick, since 1990; *b* 24 Sept. 1945; *s* of Arthur Reginald Stewart and Marjorie Kathleen Stewart (née Diwell); *m* 1970, Avril Bernice Montgomery; two *s. Educ:* Cambridge Univ. (MA); Warwick Univ. (PhD). FIMA 1993; CMath 1993; CBiol 2004; FIBiol 2004. University of Warwick: Lectr, 1969–84; Reader, 1984–90. Humboldt Fellow, Tübingen, 1974; Vis. Fellow, Auckland, 1976; Associate Prof., Storrs, Conn, 1977–78; Professor: Carbondale, Ill, 1978; Houston, Texas, 1983–84; Gresham Prof. of Geometry, 1994; Adjunct Prof., Houston Univ., 2001–. Hon. DSc: Westminster, 1999; Louvain, 2000; Kingston, 2003. Michael Faraday Medal, Royal Soc., 1995; IMA Gold Medal, 2000; Ferran Sunyer i Balaguer Prize, 2001; Public Understanding of Sci. and Tech. Award, AAAS, 2002. *Publications* include: Galois Theory, 1973; Concepts of Modern Mathematics, 1975; Catastrophe Theory and its Applications, 1978; The Problems of Mathematics, 1987; Does God Play Dice?, 1989; Game Set & Math, 1991; Another Fine Math You've Got Me Into, 1992; Fearful Symmetry, 1992; The Collapse of Chaos, 1994; Nature's Numbers, 1995; From Here to Infinity, 1996; Figments of Reality, 1997; The Magical Maze, 1997; Life's Other Secret, 1998; (jtly) The Science of Discworld, 1999; (jtly) Wheelers, 2000; Flatterland, 2001; What Shape is a Snowflake?, 2001; The Annotated Flatland, 2001; (jtly) The Science of Discworld II: the globe, 2002; (jtly) Evolving the Alien, 2002; (jtly) What Does a Martian Look Like?, 2004; Math Hysteria, 2004; (jtly) Heaven, 2004; (jtly) The Science of Discworld III: Darwin's watch, 2005; The Mayor of Uglyville's Dilemma, 2005; Letters to a Young Mathematician, 2006; How to Cut a Cake, 2006; Why Beauty is Truth: the history of symmetry, 2007; Professor Stewart's Cabinet of Mathematical Curiosities, 2008. *Recreations:* science fiction, painting, guitar, keeping fish, geology, Egyptology, snorkelling. *Address:* Mathematics Institute, University of Warwick, Coventry CV4 7AL. *T:* (024) 7652 3740.

STEWART, Sir Jackie; *see* Stewart, Sir John Young.

STEWART, Sir James (Douglas), Kt 1983; agricultural consultant; Principal, Lincoln University College of Agriculture, 1974–84, retired; *b* 11 Aug. 1925; *s* of Charles Edward Stewart and Edith May Stewart (née Caldwell); *m* 1953, Nancy Elizabeth Dunbar; one *s* three *d. Educ:* Lincoln UC (Dip. Valuation and Farm Management); Canterbury Univ. (MA); Reading Univ. (DPhil). Lectr in Farm Management, Lincoln Coll., NZ, 1951–59; Research Fellow, Reading Univ., 1959–61; Sen. Lectr, Lincoln Coll., 1962–64; Prof. of Farm Management, Lincoln Coll., 1964–74, now Emeritus. Chairman: NZ Vice-Chancellors Cttee, 1981–82; NZ Wheat Bd, 1986–87 (Dep. Chm., 1984–86); NZ Nat. Educn Qualifications Authority, 1989–95. Chm., Pyne Gould Guinness Internat. Ltd, 1987–95; Director: Pyne Gould Corp., 1982–95; Alpine Dairy Products Ltd, 1985–91. Chairman: Canterbury Develt Corp., 1983–89 (Dir, 1983–85); Christchurch Sch. of Medicine, 1987–88; NZ Crown Res. Insts Implementation Cttee, 1991–. Silver Jubilee Medal, 1977. *Publications:* contrib. Jl Agricl Econs, Jl Farm Econs, Econ. Record, etc. *Recreations:* swimming, part-time farming. *Address:* 7 Hilton Drive, Amberley, New Zealand.

STEWART, James Harvey; consultant in healthcare management; Chief Executive (formerly District General Manager), Barking and Havering (formerly Barking, Havering and Brentwood) Health Authority, 1985–95; *b* 15 Aug. 1939; *s* of Harvey Stewart and Annie (née Gray); *m* 1965, Fiona Maria Maclay Reid (*d* 2004); three *s* one *d. Educ:* Peterhead Acad.; Aberdeen Univ. (MA 1962); Manchester Univ. (DSA 1964). Hosp. Sec., Princess Margaret Rose Orthopaedic Hosp., Edinburgh, 1965–67; Principal Admin. Asst, 1967–68, and Dep. Gp Sec. and sometime Acting Gp Sec., 1968–73, York A HMC; Area Administrator, 1973–82, and Dist Administrator, 1982–83, Northumberland AHA; Regional Administrator, East Anglian RHA, 1983–85. Mem., Cambridge CHC, 1999–2002; Bd Mem., S Cambs PCT, 2002–. Hon. Treasurer, Assoc. of Chief Administrators of Health Authorities in England and Wales, 1982–85 (Mem. Council, 1975–82). Member: (LibDem) S Cambs DC, 1998– (Chm., 2007–); Hardwick Parish Council, 1999–. Mem., Cambridge Rotary Club, 1983–. Hon. Pres., Cambs Rehab. Club for Visually Handicapped, 1999–; Trustee, Cambridgeshire Soc. for Blind (Camsight), 2005–. *Recreations:* music, reading, walking, sport. *Address:* White Cottage, Hardwick, Cambridge CB23 7QU. *T:* (01954) 210961.

STEWART, Sir (James) Moray, KCB 1995 (CB 1990); Chairman, Board of Management, North Glasgow College, since 2005 (Member, since 1996); Member, Board, Association of Scotland's Colleges, since 2005; *b* 21 June 1938; third *s* of James and Evelyn Stewart; *m* 1963, Dorothy May Batey, *o d* of Alan and Maud Batey; three *s. Educ:* Marlborough Coll.; Univ. of Keele (BA First Cl. Hons History and Econs). Sec., Univ. of Keele Union, 1960–61. Breakdown and Information Service Operator, AA, 1956–57; Asst Master, Northcliffe Sch., Bognor Regis, 1957–58; Asst Principal, Air Min., 1962–65; Private Sec. to 2nd Permanent Under Sec. of State (RAF), MoD, 1965–66; Principal, MoD, 1966–70; First Sec. (Defence), UK Delegn to NATO, 1970–73; Asst Sec., MoD, 1974–75; Private Sec. to successive Secs of State for NI, 1975–77; Dir, Naval Manpower Requirements, MoD, 1977; Dir, Defence Policy Staff, MoD, 1978–80; Asst Under Sec. of State, MoD, 1980–84; Asst Sec. Gen. for Defence Planning and Policy, NATO, 1984–86; Dep. Under Sec. of State, Personnel and Logistics, 1986–88, Defence Procurement, 1988–90, MoD; Second Permanent Under Sec. of State, MoD, 1990–96. Chm., CS Healthcare, 1993–2000. Commissioner: Royal Hosp. Chelsea, 1986–88; Queen Victoria Sch., Dunblane, 1996–2006; Trustee, Imperial War Museum, 1986–88. Mem. Council, RUSI, 1988–92. Vice Pres., Eurodefense UK, 2002–. Pres., SSAFA-Forces Help, Fife, 2003–. Vice Pres., Civil Service RFU, 1993–. Chairman: Arvon Foundn in Scotland, 1998–2003; Elie Harbour Trust, 1999–2007; Trustee, Pegasus Trust, 1993–. Hon. DLitt Keele, 1995. *Recreations:* reading, listening to music. *Address:* c/o Drummonds, Royal Bank of Scotland, 49 Charing Cross, SW1A 2DX. *Clubs:* Farmers'; New (Edinburgh); Golf House (Elie).

STEWART, James Robertson, CBE 1971 (OBE 1964); Principal, University of London, 1978–83; *b* 25 July 1917; *s* of James and Isabella Stewart; *m* 1941, Grace Margaret Kirsop (*d* 1992); two *s* one *d. Educ:* Perth Acad.; Whitley and Monkseaton High Sch.; Armstrong Coll. (later King's Coll.), Newcastle, Univ. of Durham. BA Dunelm (1st cl. hons Mod. History) 1937; DThPT (1st cl.) 1938; research in Canada (Canada Co.), 1938–39; awarded Holland Rose Studentship, Cambridge, and William Black Noble Fellowship, Durham, 1939; admitted to Christ's Coll., Cambridge, 1939; MA Dunelm 1941. Served Army, 1939–46: Royal Artillery (BEF); Combined Ops HQ; Directorate of Combined Ops, India and SE Asia; Major (Actg Lt–Col); Certif. of Good Service. Dep. Clerk of Court, Univ. of London, 1946–49, Clerk of Court, 1950–82. Dir, Charterhouse Venture Fund Management, 1984–94. Mem., Sec. of State's Adv. Gp on London Health Services, 1980–81. Member, governing bodies: RPMS, 1983–89; Sch. of Pharmacy, London Univ., 1983–99 (Hon. Treas., 1984–99); Wye Coll., 1983–91; Inst. of Educn, 1983–93; RVC, 1983–2001 (Hon. Treas., 1984–96); LSE, 1984–89; Brunel Univ., 1984–89; Inst. of Germanic Studies, 1984–92 (Chm.); Roedean Sch., 1984–99; Sussex Univ., 1985–97; Westfield Coll., London, 1985–89. Hon. Fellow: KCL, 1982; Sch. of Pharmacy, London Univ., 1982; Birkbeck Coll., London, 1982; LSE, 1982; UCL, 1982; Wye Coll., 1987; Queen Mary and Westfield Coll., London, 1989 (Westfield Coll., 1981); Inst. of Germanic Studies, 1993. Hon. LLD: London, 1983; Western Ontario, 1984. Symons Medal, ACU, 1983; Betts Prize, RVC, 1994. *Recreations:* military history, gardening, watching soccer and cricket. *Address:* 2 Hilltop, Dyke Road Avenue, Brighton, Sussex BN1 5LY. *T:* (01273) 551039. *Club:* Athenæum.

See also N. A. Stewart.

STEWART, James Simeon Hamilton; QC 1982; **His Honour Judge James Stewart;** a Circuit Judge, since 2002; *b* 2 May 1943; *s* of late Henry Hamilton Stewart, MD, FRCS and Edna Mary Hamilton Stewart; *m* 1st, 1972, Helen Margaret Whiteley (*d* 1998); one *d* (and one *d* decd); 2nd, 2006, Deborah Marion Rakusen (née Rose). *Educ:* Cheltenham Coll.; Univ. of Leeds (LLB Hons). Called to the Bar, Inner Temple, 1966; Bencher, 1992. A Recorder, 1982–2002; a Dep. High Court Judge, 1993–2002. *Recreations:* cricket, golf, gardening. *Address:* Leeds Combined Court Centre, Oxford Row, Leeds LS1 3BG. *Clubs:* Sloane; Leeds Taverners (Leeds); Royal Suva Yacht (Fiji).

STEWART, (John) Allan; *b* 1 June 1942; *s* of Edward MacPherson Stewart and Eadie Barrie Stewart; *m* 1973, Marjorie Sally (Susie); one *s* one *d. Educ:* Bell Baxter High Sch., Cupar; St Andrews Univ. (1st Cl. Hons MA 1964); Harvard Univ. (Rotary Internat. Foundn Fellow, 1964–65). Lectr in Polit. Economy, St Andrews Univ., 1965–70 (Warden, John Burnet Hall, 1968–70); Confederation of British Industry: Head of Regional Develt Dept, 1971–73; Dep. Dir (Econs), 1973–76; Scottish Sec., 1976–78; Scottish Dir, 1978–79. Councillor, London Bor. of Bromley, 1975–76. Contested (C) Dundee E, 1970. MP (C): E Renfrewshire, 1979–83; Eastwood, 1983–97. PPS to Minister of State for Energy, 1981; Parly Under-Sec. of State, Scottish Office, 1981–86 and 1990–95. Mem., Select Cttee on Scottish Affairs, 1979–81 and 1995–97. Mem., Chairman's Panel, H of C, 1996–97. *Publications:* (with Harry Conroy) The Long March of the Market Men, 1996; articles in academic and gen. pubns on econ. and polit. affairs.

Recreations: bridge, hedgehogs. *Address:* Crofthead House, Neilston, E Renfrewshire G78 3LE.

STEWART, Rt Rev. John Craig; Associate Priest, Parish of Holy Trinity, Bacchus Marsh, Victoria, since 2005; *b* 10 Aug. 1940; *s* of J. J. Stewart; *m* 1967, Janine (*née* Schahinger); two *s*. *Educ:* Newington Coll., Sydney; Wesley Coll., Melbourne; Ridley Theol Coll., Melbourne. Ordained: deacon, 1965; priest, 1966; Curate, S Australia, 1965–68; Associate Priest, St John's, Crawley, 1968–70; Vicar: St Aidan's, Parkdale, 1970–74; St Luke's, Frankston, 1974–79; Gen. Sec., Church Missionary Soc., Victoria, 1979–84; Asst Bishop, Dio. Melbourne, 1984–2001; Rector, Parish of Woodend, Vic, 2001–04. *Publications:* From London to Dartmoor, 1996; From Bolton to Ballarat, 1996. *Recreations:* family history, geology, music. *Address:* PO Box 928, Bacchus Marsh, Vic 3440, Australia.

STEWART, Prof. John David, DPhil; Professor of Local Government and Administration, Birmingham University, 1971–96, Hon. Professor, 1996–99, Emeritus Professor, since 1999; *b* 19 March 1929; *s* of Dr David Stewart and Phyllis Stewart (*née* Crossley); *m* 1953, Theresa Stewart, *qv*; two *s* two *d*. *Educ:* Stockport Grammar Sch.; Balliol Coll., Oxford (MA 1966); Nuffield Coll., Oxford (DPhil 1966). Industrial Relns Dept, NCB, 1954–66; Birmingham University: Sen. Lectr, 1966–71, Dir, 1976–83, Inst. of Local Govt Studies; Hd of Sch. of Public Policy, 1990–93. Member: Layfield Cttee on Local Govt Finance, 1974–76; Acad. Adv. Panel on local govt, DETR, 1997–98. President's Award for Outstanding Contribn to Local Govt, SOLACE, 2007. *Publications:* British Pressure Groups, 1958; Management in Local Government, 1971; The Responsive Local Authority, 1974; (jtly) Corporate Management in English Local Government, 1974; Local Government: the conditions of local choice, 1983; (jtly) The Case for Local Government, 1983; Understanding the Management of Local Government, 1988; (jtly) The Politics of Hung Authorities, 1992; Management for the Public Domain, 1994; (jtly) The Changing Organisation and Management of Local Government, 1994; (ed jtly) Local Government in the 1990s, 1995; The Nature of British Local Government, 2000; Modernising British Local Government, 2003. *Recreations:* gardening, walking. *Address:* 15 Selly Wick Road, Birmingham B29 7JJ. *T:* (0121) 472 1512.

STEWART, John Hall; Sheriff of South Strathclyde, Dumfries and Galloway at Hamilton (formerly at Airdrie), since 1985; *b* 15 March 1944; *s* of Cecil Francis Wilson Stewart and Mary Fyfe Hall or Stewart; *m* 1968, Marion MacCalman; one *s* two *d*. *Educ:* Airdrie Acad.; St Andrews Univ. (LLB). Advocate. Enrolled solicitor, 1970–77; Mem. Faculty of Advocates, 1978–. *Recreations:* scuba diving, spectator sports, his grandchildren. *Address:* 43 Grieve Croft, Bothwell, Glasgow G71 8LU. *T:* (01698) 853854. *Club:* Uddingston Rugby (Past Pres.), Uddingston Cricket and Sports (Past Pres.).

STEWART, John Morrison, FCIB; Group Chief Executive, National Australia Bank, 2004–08 (Executive Director, Principal Board, and Chief Executive of European Operations, 2003–04); *b* 31 May 1949; *s* of Peter and Jane Stewart; *m* 1971, Sylvia Jameson; one *s* one *d*. *Educ:* Boroughmuir Sch., Edinburgh; Open Univ. (BA 1975). ACII 1979; FCIB 1989. Posts with Legal & General; Woolwich Building Society: joined 1977, as Br. Manager; Asst Gen. Manager, Insurance Services, 1988–91; General Manager: Financial Services, 1991–92; Retail Ops, 1992–95; Group Ops Dir, 1995–96; Gp Chief Exec., Woolwich Bldg Soc., subseq. Woolwich plc, 1996–2000; Dep. Gp Chief Exec., Barclays Bank, 2000–03. Chm., Woolwich Indep. Financial Adv. Services (Dir, 1989–95); Director: Banca Woolwich, Italy, 1996–2000; Banque Woolwich, France, 1996–2000. Pres., CIB, 2002–03 (Dep. Pres., 2001–02). CCMI (CIMgt 1996). Hon. DLitt Heriot-Watt, 1997. *Recreation:* sailing. *Address:* c/o National Australia Bank, 500 Bourke Street, Melbourne, Vic 3000, Australia.

STEWART, Sir (John) Simon (Watson), 6th Bt *cr* 1920, of Balgownie; MD, FRCP, FRCR; Consultant in Clinical Oncology at St Mary's Hospital and Imperial College School of Medicine (formerly Royal Postgraduate Medical School), since 1989; *b* 5 July 1955; *s* of Sir John Keith Watson Stewart, 5th Bt and of Mary Elizabeth, *d* of John Francis Moxon; *S* father, 1990; *m* 1978, Dr Catherine Stewart, *d* of H. Gordon Bond; one *s* one *d*. *Educ:* Uppingham Sch.; Charing Cross Hosp. Med. Sch. BSc (1st cl. Hons) 1977; MB BS Lond. 1980; MRCP 1983, FRCP 1994; FRCR 1986; MD 1989. Mem., Cavalhead Soc., 1978–. *Heir: s* John Hamish Watson Stewart, *b* 12 Dec. 1983. *Address:* 8 Chiswick Wharf, Chiswick, W4 2SR. *T:* (020) 8995 2213. *Club:* Oriental.

STEWART, Sir John Young, (Sir Jackie), Kt 2001; OBE 1972; racing driver, retired 1973; developed Gleneagles Jackie Stewart Shooting School; Chairman, Stewart Grand Prix Ltd, 1996–2000; *b* 11 June 1939; *s* of late Robert Paul Stewart and of Jean Clark Young; *m* 1962, Helen McGregor; two *s*. *Educ:* Dumbarton Academy. First raced, 1961; competed in 4 meetings, 1961–62, driving for Barry Filer, Glasgow; drove for Ecurie Ecosse and other private entrants, winning 14 out of 23 starts, 1963; 28 wins out of 53 starts, 1964; drove Formula 1 for BRM, 1965–67 and for Ken Tyrrell, 1968–73; has won Australian, New Zealand, Swedish, Mediterranean, Japanese and many other non-championship major internat. Grands Prix; set up new world record by winning his 26th World Championship Grand Prix (Zandvoort), July 1973, and 27th (Nurburgring), Aug. 1973; 3rd in World Championship, 1965; 2nd in 1968 and 1972; World Champion, 1969, 1971, 1973. Global Ambassador, Royal Bank of Scotland, 2004–. Chm., Motorsport Steering Cttee, Cranfield Univ., 2000–. President: Dyslexia Scotland, 2004–; Springfield Club, 1976–; Vice President: British Dyslexia Assoc., 1998–; Vice-Chm. and Founding Trustee, Scottish Internat. Educn Trust, 1970– (Mem., Internat. Adv. Bd to the Scottish Parlt, 2002–). Founder, Trustee and Chm., Grand Prix Mechanics Charitable Trust, 1987–. Hon. Prof., Stirling, 1998–. Hon. Dr Automotive Engrg, Lawrence Inst. of Technology, Mich, USA, 1973; Hon. DEng: Glasgow Caledonian, 1986; Heriot-Watt, 1996; Glasgow, 2001; Hon. Dr: Cranfield, 1998; Stirling, 2001; Edinburgh, 2006. BARC Gold Medal, 1971, 1973. Daily Express Sportsman of the Year, 1971, 1973; World Sportsman of the Year, 1973; BBC Sports Personality of the Year, 1973; Scottish Sportsman of the Year, 1973; Sports Illustrated American Sportsman of the Year, 1973; ABC Sports Personality of the Year, 1973; Seagrove Trophy, 1973, 1999. *Film:* Weekend of a Champion, 1972. *Publications:* World Champion, 1970 (with Eric Dymock); Faster!, 1972 (with Peter Manso); On the Road, 1983; (with Alan Henry) Jackie Stewart's Principles of Performance Driving, 1986; The Jackie Stewart Book of Shooting, 1991; Winning is Not Enough: the autobiography, 2007. *Recreations:* golf, fishing, tennis, shooting (Mem. Scottish and British Teams for Clay Pigeon shooting; former Scottish, English, Irish, Welsh and British Champion; won Coupe des Nations, 1959 and 1960; reserve for two-man team, 1960 Olympics). *Clubs:* (Hon.) Royal Automobile, British Racing Drivers' (Pres., 2000–06; Vice Pres., 2006–); Scottish Motor Racing (Duns) (Pres., 1968–); Royal and Ancient (St Andrews); Prestwick Golf; (Hon.) Gleneagles; Sunningdale; Loch Lomond Golf; Geneva Golf.

STEWART, Joseph Martin, OBE 1994; JP; Director of Human Resources, Police Service of Northern Ireland, since 2001; *b* 5 Nov. 1955; *s* of late Joseph Aloysius Stewart and of Annie Margaret Mary Stewart (*née* Friel); *m* 1978, Deirdre Ann Ritchie. *Educ:* Queen's Univ., Belfast (LLB Hons 1978); Univ. of Ulster (Post Grad. Dip. in Mgt Studies 1980). Engineering Employers Federation (NI) Association: Asst Indust. Relns Officer, 1978–80; Indust. Relns Officer, 1980–85; Dir, 1985–90; Personnel Dir, Harland & Wolff Shipbuilding and Heavy Industries Ltd, 1990–95; Sec. and Chief Exec., Police Authy for NI, 1995–2001. JP Ards Circuit, 1990. *Recreations:* game shooting, pedigree sheep breeding, motorcycle touring. *Address:* Police Service of Northern Ireland Lisnasharragh, 42 Montgomery Road, Belfast BT6 9LD. *Club:* Ulster Reform (Belfast).

STEWART, Sir Ludovic Houston S.; *see* Shaw Stewart.

STEWART, Mary (Florence Elinor), (Lady Stewart); *b* 17 Sept. 1916; *d* of Rev. Frederick A. Rainbow, Durham Diocese, and Mary Edith (*née* Matthews), NZ; *m* 1945, Sir Frederick Henry Stewart, FRS (*d* 2001); no *c*. *Educ:* Eden Hall, Penrith, Cumberland; Skellfield School, Ripon, Yorks; St Hild's Coll., Durham Univ. BA 1938; MA 1941. Asst Lectr in English, Durham Univ., 1941–45; Part-time Lectr in English, St Hild's Training Coll., Durham, and Durham Univ., 1948–56. Hon. Fellow, Newnham Coll., Cambridge, 1986. *Publications: novels:* Madam, Will You Talk?, 1954; Wildfire at Midnight, 1956; Thunder on the Right, 1957; Nine Coaches Waiting, 1958; My Brother Michael, 1959; The Ivy Tree, 1961; The Moonspinners, 1962; This Rough Magic, 1964; Airs Above the Ground, 1965; The Gabriel Hounds, 1967; The Wind Off The Small Isles, 1968; The Crystal Cave, 1970 (Frederick Niven Award); The Little Broomstick, 1971; The Hollow Hills, 1973; Ludo and the Star Horse, 1974 (Scottish Arts Council Award); Touch Not the Cat, 1976; The Last Enchantment, 1979; A Walk in Wolf Wood, 1980; The Wicked Day, 1983; Thornyhold, 1988; Frost on the Window and Other Poems, 1990; Stormy Petrel, 1991; The Prince and the Pilgrim, 1995; Rose Cottage, 1997; also articles, radio plays. *Recreations:* gardening, music, painting. *Address:* House of Letterawe, Loch Awe, Dalmally, Argyll PA33 1AH.

STEWART, Michael James; Reader in Political Economy, University College, London University, 1969–94, now Emeritus; *b* 6 Feb. 1933; *s* of late John Innes Mackintosh Stewart; *m* 1962, Frances Kaldor, *d* of Baron Kaldor, FBA; one *s* two *d* (and one *d* decd). *Educ:* Campbell Coll., Belfast; St Edward's Sch., Oxford; Magdalen Coll., Oxford. 1st cl. PPE (Oxon), 1955. Asst Res. Officer, Oxford Univ. Inst. of Statistics, 1955–56; Barnett Fellow, Cornell Univ., 1956–57; Econ. Asst, HM Treasury, 1957–60; Sec. to Council on Prices, Productivity and Incomes, 1960–61; Econ. Adviser, HM Treasury, 1961–62, Cabinet Office, 1964–67 (Senior Econ. Advr, 1967), Kenya Treasury, 1967–69; Special Adviser to Sec. of State for Trade, Apr.-Oct. 1974; Economic Adviser to Malta Labour Party, 1970–73; Special Econ. Advr to Foreign Sec., 1977–78. Guest Scholar, Brookings Instn, Washington, DC, 1978–79. Mem., Acad. Adv. Panel, Bank of England, 1977–83. Contested (Lab): Folkestone and Hythe, 1964; Croydon North-West, 1966. Asst Editor, Nat. Inst. Econ. Review, 1962–64. Consultant to various UN agencies, 1971–. *Publications:* Keynes and After, 1967; The Jekyll and Hyde Years: politics and economic policy since 1964, 1977; Controlling the Economic Future: policy dilemmas in a shrinking world, 1983; (with Peter Jay) Apocalypse 2000: economic breakdown and the suicide of democracy 1989–2000, 1987; Keynes in the 1990s: a return to economic sanity, 1993. *Recreations:* looking at paintings, eating at restaurants in France. *Address:* 79 South Hill Park, NW3 2SS. *T:* (020) 7435 3686. *Club:* Oxford and Cambridge.

STEWART, Sir Moray; *see* Stewart, Sir J. M.

STEWART, Neill Alastair; His Honour Judge Stewart; a Circuit Judge, since 1999; *b* 8 June 1947; *yr s* of James Robertson Stewart, *qv*; *m* 2000, Tiffany, *d* of His Honour William Llewellyn Monro Davies, *qv*; one *s* one *d*. *Educ:* Whitgift Sch.; Clare Coll., Cambridge (BA Mech. Scis Tripos). Engr, Sir Alexander Gibb & Partners, 1968–70; called to the Bar, Middle Temple, 1973; in practice at the Bar, 1975–99. *Address:* c/o Guildford Crown Court, Bedford Road, Guildford GU1 4ST.

STEWART, Nicholas John Cameron; QC 1987; *b* 16 April 1947; *s* of John Cameron Stewart and Margaret Mary (*née* Botsford); *m* 1974, Pamela Jean Windham (marr. diss. 2000); one *s* two *d*, one *d* by Dr Tabea Lauktien. *Educ:* Bedford Modern Sch.; Worcester Coll., Oxford (BA). CDipAF. Called to the Bar, Inner Temple, 1971, Bencher, 1999; Dep. High Ct Judge, Chancery Div., 1991–. Chm., Bar Human Rights Cttee, 1994–98. Pres., Union Internationale des Avocats, 2001–02. Narrator, No Further Questions, BBC Radio series, 1993 and 1995. *Recreations:* walking, Spain, photography. *Address:* Ely Place Chambers, 30 Ely Place, EC1N 6TD.

STEWART, Nikola Caroline, (Mrs A. R. Milne); Sheriff of South Strathclyde, Dumfries and Galloway at Lanark, since 2000; *b* 29 July 1956; *d* of James Lumsden Stewart and Joyce Elizabeth Stewart (*née* Urquhart); *m* 1989, Alastair Robert Milne; two *d*. *Educ:* Harris Acad., Dundee; Dundee Univ. (MA, LLB, DipLP). Admitted Advocate, 1987; called to the Scottish Bar, 1987; in practice as advocate, 1987–2000; Temp. Sheriff, 1997–99. Chm., Child Support Appeal Tribunals, 1990–97. *Address:* Medwynbrae, Carlops Road, West Linton EH46 7DS.

STEWART, Norman MacLeod; Senior Partner, 1984–97, Consultant, 1997–99, Allan, Black & McCaskie; President, The Law Society of Scotland, 1985–86; *b* 2 Dec. 1934; *s* of George and Elspeth Stewart; *m* 1959, Mary Slater Campbell; four *d*. *Educ:* Elgin Acad.; Univ. of Edinburgh (BL); SSC. Alex. Morison & Co., WS, Edinburgh, 1954–58; Allan, Black & McCaskie, Solicitors, Elgin, 1959–99, Partner, 1961–97. Law Society of Scotland: Mem. Council, 1976–87; Convener: Public Relations Cttee, 1979–81; Professional Practice Cttee, 1981–84; Vice-Pres., 1984–85. Chm., Elgin and Lossiemouth Harbour Bd, 1993–. Hon. Mem., American Bar Assoc., 1985–. *Recreations:* walking, golf, music, Spanish culture. *Address:* Argyll Lodge, Lossiemouth, Moray IV31 6QT. *T:* (01343) 813150; *e-mail:* norman666@btinternet.com. *Club:* New (Edinburgh).

STEWART, Patricia Ann; Deputy Chief Executive, Food Standards Agency, 2003–07; *b* 22 March 1949; *d* of late Walter William Stewart and Freda Dorothy Stewart (*née* Rolfe); *m* 1st, 1978, Jeremy Gye Colman, *qv* (marr. diss.); 2nd, 1996, Lt Comdr Nicholas Austen Bates, RN. *Educ:* Palmer's Grammar Sch. for Girls, Grays; Univ. of Sussex (BSc (Maths with Electronic Engrg) 1970). FSS 1975. Statistician: Civil Service Dept, 1970–79; Local Govt Finance, DoE, 1979–83, seconded to EC, Luxembourg, 1983; Department of Health: Chief Statistician, 1984–86; Assistant Secretary: NHS Finance, 1986–89; NHS Liaison, London and S England, 1989–91; Hd, Facilities and Corporate Mgt, 1991–95; Public Health Div., 1996–97; Food Standards Agency: Hd of Implementation Div., Jt Food Safety and Standards Gp, 1997–2000; Dir, Corporate Resources and Strategy, 2000–07. *Recreations:* music (voice, viol, keyboard), reading, boating, organising music workshops, contributing to village life. *Address: e-mail:* pas@watermusic.me.uk. *Club:* Chichester Yacht.

STEWART, Patrick, OBE 2001; actor; *b* 13 July 1940; *s* of late Alfred Stewart and Gladys Stewart (*née* Barrowclough); *m* 1st, 1966, Sheila Falconer (marr. diss. 1990); one *s* one *d*; 2nd, 2002, Wendy Neuss (marr. diss.). *Educ:* Mirfield Secondary Modern Sch.; Bristol Old Vic Theatre Sch. Joined RSC, 1966, Associate Artist, 1967–87; CEO, Flying Freehold Prodns, 1998–. *Theatre includes:* Antony and Cleopatra, 1979; Henry IV, RSC, 1984;

Yonadab, NT, 1986; Who's Afraid of Virginia Woolf?, Young Vic, 1987; A Christmas Carol (one-man show), NY, 1991, 1992, Albery, 2005; The Tempest, NY, 1995; Othello, Washington, 1997; The Ride Down Mount Morgan, NY, 1998, 2000; The Master Builder, Albery, 2003; A Life in the Theatre, Apollo, 2005; Antony and Cleopatra, RSC, 2006; The Tempest, RSC, 2006, transf. Novello, 2007; Twelfth Night, Chichester, 2007; Macbeth, Chichester, transf. Gielgud, 2007; Hamlet, RSC, 2008; *television includes:* Hedda, 1975; I Claudius, 1976; Oedipus Rex, 1976; Tinker Tailor Soldier Spy, 1979; Hamlet, Prince of Denmark, 1980; Smiley's People, 1982; Maybury, 1980; The Mozart Inquest, 1985; The Devil's Disciple, 1987; Star Trek: The Next Generation (series), 1987–94; Death Train, 1993; The Canterville Ghost (also co-prod), 1996; Moby Dick, 1998; A Christmas Carol (also prod), 1999; King of Texas (also prod), 2002; The Lion in Winter (also prod), 2003; Eleventh Hour, 2006; *films include:* Excalibur, 1981; Dune, 1984; Lady Jane, 1986; LA Story, 1991; Robin Hood: Men in Tights, 1993; Gunmen, 1994; Star Trek: Generations, 1994; Jeffrey, 1996; Star Trek: First Contact, 1996; Conspiracy Theory, 1997; Masterminds, 1997; Dad Savage, 1998; Star Trek: Insurrection, 1998; X Men, 2000; Star Trek: Nemesis, 2002; X2, 2003; Steamboy, 2005; X-Men: The Last Stand, 2006. Cameron Mackintosh Vis. Prof. of Contemporary Th., Univ. of Oxford, 2007. Chancellor, 2004–, Prof. of Performing Arts, 2008, Univ. of Huddersfield, 2004–. *Address:* c/o Independent Talent Group Ltd, Oxford House, 76 Oxford Street, W1D 1BS.

STEWART, Patrick Loudon McIain, MBE 2000; Consultant, Messrs Stewart Balfour & Sutherland, Solicitors, Campbeltown, Argyll, since 2000; Vice Lord-Lieutenant, Argyll and Bute, since 2003; *b* 25 July 1945; *s* of late Archibald Ian Balfour Stewart, CBE and of Ailsa Rosamund Mary Stewart (*née* Massey); *m* 1969, Mary Anne McLellan; one *s* one *d*. *Educ:* Dalintober Primary Sch.; Edinburgh Acad.; Edinburgh Univ. (LLB). WS 1968; NP 1968. Partner, 1970–82, Sen. Partner, 1982–2000, Stewart Balfour & Sutherland, Solicitors. Asst Sec., 1970–74, Sec., 1974–, Clyde Fishermen's Assoc. Clerk to Comrs of Income Tax, Argyll-Islay, 1972–. DL Argyll and Bute, 1987. Hon. Sheriff at Campbeltown, 1997–. CO, Campbeltown Unit, Sea Cadet Corps, 1972–88; Mem., Sea Cadet Council, 1983–93; Trustee, Sea Cadet Assoc., 2000–04; Life Vice Pres., Marine Soc. and Sea Cadets, 2005. Cadet Forces Medal, 1984. *Recreations:* sailing, field sports. *Address:* PO Box 9261, Campbeltown, Argyll PA28 6YE. *T:* (01586) 551717, *Fax:* (01586) 551746; *e-mail:* plms@clydefish.org.

See also Angus Stewart.

STEWART, Col Robert Alexander, (Bob), DSO 1993; director, writer and broadcaster; *b* 7 July 1949; *s* of late A. A. Stewart, MC and Marguerita Joan Stewart; *m* 1st (marr. diss. 1993); one *s* one *d*; 2nd, 1994, Claire Podbielski; one *s* three *d*. *Educ:* Chigwell Sch.; RMA Sandhurst; Univ. of Wales, Aberystwyth (BSc 1st Cl. Hons Internat. Politics). Commnd, Cheshire Regt, 1969; Instructor, RMA, 1979–80; Army Staff Coll., 1981; Company Comdr, N Ireland, 1982–83; Staff Officer, MoD, 1984–85; 2 i/c 1st Bn Cheshire Regt, 1986–87; JSSC 1988; MA to Chm., NATO Mil. Cttee, HQ NATO, Brussels, 1989–91; CO, 1st Bn Cheshire Regt, 1991–93; Chief of Policy, SHAPE, 1994–95; resigned Regular Army, 1996. Sen. Consultant, Public Affairs, Hill & Knowlton (UK) Ltd, 1996–98; Sen. Vice Pres., WorldSpace UK, 1998–2001; Man. Dir, Action Leadership, 2001–. Chm., Ind. Defence Media Assoc., 2003–. *Publications:* Broken Lives, 1993; Thoughts on Leadership, 2004. *Recreations:* writing, history. *Address:* 35 Crescent Road, Kingston upon Thames, Surrey KT2 7RD. *T:* (020) 8546 5205, 07771 863894. *Clubs:* Army and Navy, Special Forces.

STEWART, Lt-Col Sir Robert (Christie), KCVO 2002; CBE 1983; TD 1962; Lord-Lieutenant of Clackmannan, 1994–2001; *b* 3 Aug. 1926; *m* 1953, Ann Grizel Cochrane; three *s* two *d*. *Educ:* Eton; University College, Oxford. Lt Scots Guards, 1945–49. Oxford Univ., 1949–51 (BA Agric.). TA, 7 Argyll and Sutherland Highlanders, 1948–66; Lt-Col Comdg 7 A & SH, 1963–66. Hon. Col, 1/51 Highland Volunteers, 1972–75. Chm. and Pres., Bd of Governors, E of Scotland Coll. of Agric., 1970–83. Chm., Kinross CC, 1963–73. DL Kinross, 1956, Vice Lieut, 1958; Lord-Lieutenant, Kinross-shire, 1966–74. *Address:* Mains of Arndean, by Dollar, Clackmannanshire FK14 7NT. *T:* (01259) 742527. *Club:* Royal Perth Golfing Society.

See also Earl of Romney.

STEWART, Robin Milton; QC 1978; a Recorder of the Crown Court, 1978–99; *b* 5 Aug. 1938; *s* of late Brig. Guy Milton Stewart and Dr Elaine Oenone Stewart, MD, BS; *m* 1962, Lynda Grace Medhurst; three *s*. *Educ:* Winchester; New Coll., Oxford (MA). Called to the Bar, Middle Temple, 1963, Bencher, 1988; called to the Irish Bar, King's Inns, Dublin, 1975. Prosecuting Counsel to Inland Revenue, NE Circuit, 1976–78. Dir, Bar Mutual Indemnity Fund, 1988–93. Mem., Professional Conduct Cttee, Bar Council, 1991–93; (first) Chm., Professional Negligence Bar Assoc., 1991–93. Contested (C) Newcastle upon Tyne West, Feb. and Oct. 1974. Freeman, City of London, 1966; Liveryman, Co. of Glaziers, 1966–98. Trustee, Parkinson's Disease Soc., 1999–2002. Confrère des Chevaliers du Fromage de Livarot, 2002. *Recreations:* pictures, gardening, Scottish family history. *Address:* Kilburn House, 96 Front Street, Sowerby, Thirsk, N Yorks YO7 1JJ. *T:* (01845) 522922. *Club:* Oriental.

STEWART, Roderick David, CBE 2007; singer and songwriter; *b* 10 Jan. 1945; *s* of Robert Joseph Stewart and Elsie Stewart; *m* 1st, 1979, Alana Collins (marr. diss. 1984); one *s* one *d*; 2nd, 1990, Rachel Hunter (marr. diss.); one *s* one *d*; one *d* by Kelly Emberg; 3rd, 2007, Penny Lancaster; one *s*. *Educ:* William Grimshaw Secondary Modern Sch., Hornsey. Singer with Jeff Beck Group, 1968–69, with The Faces, 1969–75. Albums include: with Jeff Beck Group: Truth, 1968; Cosa Nostra Beck Ola, 1969; with The Faces: First Step, 1970; Long Player, 1971; A Nod's as Good as a Wink…To a Blind Horse, 1971; Ooh La La, 1973; Coast to Coast, 1974; solo: An Old Raincoat Won't Ever Let You Down, 1969; Gasoline Alley, 1970; Every Picture Tells a Story, 1971; Never a Dull Moment, 1972; Smiler, 1974; Atlantic Crossing, 1975; A Night on the Town, 1976; Foot Loose and Fancy Free, 1977; Blondes Have More Fun, 1978; Foolish Behaviour, 1980; Tonight I'm Yours, 1981; Body Wishes, 1983; Camouflage, 1984; Every Beat of My Heart, 1986; Out of Order, 1988; Vagabond Heart, 1991; A Spanner in the Works, 1995; When We Were the New Boys, 1998; Human, 2001; It Had To Be You—The Great American Songbook, 2002; Sweet Little Rock N Roller, 2002; As Time Goes By—The Great American Songbook, Vol. II, 2003; Stardust—The Great American Songbook, Vol. III, 2004. *Address:* c/o Warner Music, 28 Kensington Church Street, W8 4EP.

STEWART, Roger Paul Davidson; QC 2001; a Recorder, since 2002; *b* 17 Aug. 1963; *s* of late Martin Neil Davidson Stewart and of Elizabeth Janet Stewart (*née* Porter); *m* 1988, Georgina Louise Smith; two *s* one *d*. *Educ:* Oundle Sch.; Jesus Coll., Cambridge (MA, LLM). Called to the Bar, Inner Temple, 1986, Bencher, 2002; Barrister, Lincoln's Inn, 2000–; Hd of Chambers, 2006–. *Publication:* (ed) Jackson and Powell on Professional Negligence, 3rd edn 1992, 4th edn 1997, (gen. ed.) 5th edn 2002, 6th edn 2007. *Recreations:* sailing, ski-ing, reading military history. *Address:* 4 New Square, Lincoln's Inn, WC2A 3RJ. *Clubs:* National Liberal; Lost Valley Mountaineering (Glencoe).

STEWART, Rosemary Gordon, (Mrs I. M. James), PhD; author of management books; *d* of William George Stewart and Sylvia Gordon Stewart (*née* Sulley); *m* 1961, Ioan Mackenzie James, *qv*. *Educ:* Univ. of British Columbia (BSc); London School of Economics, Univ. of London (MSc, PhD). Dir, Acton Soc. Trust, 1956–61; Res. Fellow, London Sch. of Economics, 1964–66; Fellow in Organizational Behaviour, Templeton Coll. (formerly Oxford Centre for Mgt Studies), 1967–93; Dir, Centre for Develt and Population Activities, Washington, 1988–2004; Co-Dir, Oxford Health Care Mgt Inst., Templeton Coll., Oxford, 1993–2000. Organiser, NHS Chairs Workshop, 1993–. Mem., Oxfordshire Res. Ethics Cttee, 2001–. Gov., Headington Sch., Oxford, 1991–2003. Hon. Fellow, Templeton Coll., Oxford, 2000. Hon. DPhil Uppsala, 1998. *Publications:* (jtly) The Boss: the life and times of the British businessman, 1958; The Reality of Management, 1963, 3rd edn 1997; Managers and their Jobs, 1967, 2nd edn 1988; The Reality of Organizations, 1970, 3rd edn 1993; How Computers Affect Management, 1971; Contrasts in Management, 1976 (John Player Award for best British mgt book); (contrib.) The District Administrator in the NHS, 1982; Leading in the NHS, 1989, 2nd edn 1995; Managing Today and Tomorrow, 1994; (jtly) The Diversity of Management, 1994; (contrib.) Managing in Britain and Germany, 1994; (ed) Managerial Work, 1998; (ed) Management of Health Care, 1998; Evidence-based Management, 2001. *Recreations:* travel, painting, art history, golf, gardening. *Address:* Green Templeton College, Oxford OX2 6HG. *T:* (01865) 422500.

STEWART, Sir Simon; *see* Stewart, Sir J. S. W.

STEWART, Stephen Paul; QC 1996; **His Honour Judge Stephen Stewart;** a Circuit Judge, since 2003; Senior Circuit Judge and Designated Civil Judge, Liverpool, since 2003; *b* 9 Oct. 1953; *s* of Cyril Stewart and Phyllis Mary Stewart; *m* 1980, Dr (Mary) Felicity Dyer; one *s* one *d*. *Educ:* Stand GS, Whitefield, Manchester; St Peter's Coll., Oxford (MA; half blue for badminton). Called to the Bar, Middle Temple, 1975 (Harmsworth Major Exhibnr, 1973; Harmsworth Schol., 1975); in practice on Northern Circuit; Asst Recorder, 1995–99; a Recorder, 1999–2003; Dep. Judge, Technol. and Construction Court, 2000–03. *Recreations:* running, music, foreign languages. *Address:* Liverpool Civil and Family Court, 35 Vernon Street, Liverpool L2 2BX. *Clubs:* Royal Over-Seas League; Alderley Edge Cricket.

STEWART, Suzanne Freda; *see* Norwood, S. F.

STEWART, Theresa; Member (Lab), Birmingham City Council, 1970–2002 (Leader, 1993–99); Lord Mayor of Birmingham, 2000–01; *b* 24 Aug. 1930; *d* of John Raisman and Ray Raisman (*née* Baker); *m* 1953, John David Stewart, *qv*; two *s* two *d*. *Educ:* Cowper Street Sch., Leeds; Allerton High Sch., Leeds; Somerville Coll., Oxford (MA; Hon. Fellow, 2001). Member: Birmingham Regl Hosp. Bd, 1968–71; W Midland CC, 1974–77; Birmingham City Council: Chair: Birmingham Community Develt Project, 1973–76; Social Services Cttee, 1981–82 and 1984–87; Direct Labour Contract Services Cttee, 1989–93; Policy and Resources Cttee, 1997–; W Midlands Jt Cttee, 1998–. Vice-Chm., AMA Social Services Cttee, 1985–87; Chair, W Midlands LGA, 1999– (Sen. Vice Chair, 1998–99). Chm., Assoc. of Direct Labour Orgns, 1994–95. Hon. LLD Birmingham, 2000. *Recreations:* relaxing in a hot bath with a good book, walking, cooking. *Address:* 15 Selly Wick Road, Birmingham B29 7JJ. *T:* (0121) 472 1512.

STEWART, Sir William (Duncan Paterson), Kt 1994; PhD, DSc; FRS 1977; FRSE; Chairman: Health Protection Agency, since 2003; National Radiological Protection Board, 2003–05; Chief Scientific Adviser, Cabinet Office, 1990–95, and Head of Office of Science and Technology, 1992–95; *b* 7 June 1935; *s* of John Stewart and Margaret (*née* Paterson); *m* 1st, 1958, Catherine MacLeod (*d* 1998); one *s*; 2nd, 2000, Elizabeth Smales. *Educ:* Bowmore Junior Secondary Sch., Isle-of-Islay; Dunoon Grammar Sch.; Glasgow Univ. (BSc, PhD, DSc). FRSE 1973. Asst Lectr, Univ. of Nottingham, 1961–63; Lectr, Westfield Coll., Univ. of London, 1963–68; Boyd Baxter Prof. of Biology, 1968–94, Vice-Principal, 1985–87, Univ. of Dundee; Sec. and Chief Exec., AFRC, 1988–90. Chm., Microbiol Res. Authy, Porton Down, 1999–2002. Chairman: Internat. Cttee on Microbial Ecology, 1983–86; Royal Soc. Biotechnology and Educn Wkg Gp, 1980–81; Independent Adv. Gp on Gruinard Is., 1985–87; President: British Phycological Soc., 1975–77; Council, Scottish Marine Biol. Assoc., 1985–87; Bioindustry Assoc., 1995–99; RSE, 1999–2002; BAAS, 2000–01; Member: Council, Marine Biol. Assoc., 1973–76, 1977–80, 1981–84; British Nat. Cttee for problems of environment, 1979–85; UNESCO Panel on Microbiology, 1975–81; Council, NERC, 1979–85; Internat. Cell Res. Org., 1979–84; Royal Soc. Study Gp on Science Educn, 1981–82; Council, Royal Soc., 1984–86 (Vice-Pres., 1995–97); Royal Commn on Environmental Pollution, 1986–88; DSAC, 1990–95. Chairman: Govt Technol. Foresight Steering Gp, 1993–95; Govt Sci. and Engrg Base Co-ordinating Cttee, 1993–95; Ind. Expert Gp on Mobile Phones and Health, 1999–2000; Mem., DTI Link Steering Gp, 1990–94. Dir (non-exec.), Water Research Centre plc, 1995–2002; Chm., Cyclacel Ltd, 1998–2003. Member, Governing Body: Scottish Hort. Res. Inst., 1971–80; Scottish Crop Res. Inst., 1980–88; Macaulay Land Use Res. Inst., 1987–88; Trustee, Royal Botanic Gardens, Kew, 2006–. Chairman: Dundee Teaching Hosps NHS Trust, 1997–99; Tayside Univ. Hosps NHS Trust, 1999–2000. 25 hon. degrees and fellowships. President's Medal, Royal Acad. Engrg, 1995. *Publications:* Nitrogen Fixation in Plants, 1966; (jtly) The Blue-Green Algae, 1973; Algal Physiology and Biochemistry, 1974; (ed) Nitrogen Fixation by Free-living Organisms, 1975; (ed jtly) Nitrogen Fixation, 1980; (ed jtly) The Nitrogen Cycle of the United Kingdom, 1984; over 250 papers in learned jls of repute. *Recreations:* watching soccer, watching people, playing the bagpipes (occasionally). *Address:* 1 Clarendon Drive, Perth Road, Dundee DD2 1JU. *Clubs:* Farmers; New (Edinburgh); Dundee United.

STEWART, William Ian; *see* Allanbridge, Hon. Lord.

STEWART-CLARK, Sir John, (Sir Jack), 3rd Bt *cr* 1918; Chairman, Dundas Castle Ltd, since 1999; Member (C) European Parliament, East Sussex and Kent South, 1994–99 (Sussex East, 1979–94); a Vice-President, 1992–97; *b* 17 Sept. 1929; *e s* of Sir Stewart Stewart-Clark, 2nd Bt, and Jane Pamela (*d* 1993), *d* of late Major Arundell Clarke; *S* father, 1971; *m* 1958, Lydia Frederike, *d* of J. W. Loudon, Holland; one *s* four *d*. *Educ:* Eton; Balliol College, Oxford; Harvard Business School. Commissioned with HM Coldstream Guards, 1948–49. Oxford, 1949–52. With J. & P. Coats Ltd, 1952–69; Managing Director: J. & P. Coats, Pakistan, Ltd, 1961–67; J. A. Carp's Garenfabrieken, Holland, 1967–69; Philips Industries, 1971–79: Managing Director: Philips Electrical Ltd, London, 1971–75; Pye of Cambridge Ltd, 1975–79. Director: A. T. Kearney Ltd, 1979–92; Low and Bonar plc, 1980–95; Pioneer Concrete plc, 1986–99; TSB Scotland, 1986–89. Pres. Supervisory Bd, Eur. Inst. for Security, 1984–86; Mem. Council, RUSI, 1979–83. Dir and Trustee, Eur. Centre for Work and Society, 1982–2005; Mem., Bd of Govs, Eur. Inst. for Media, 1995–2000; Chairman: Conf. of Regions of North Western Europe, 1986–92; Eur. Parliamentarians and Industrialists Council, 1990–99. European Drugs Monitoring Centre: Mem., Mgt Bd, 1999–2006; Mem., Policy Bureau, 2001–06; Mem., Mentor UK Foundn, 1999–. Chm., EP delegn to Canada, 1979–84; Mem., EP delegn to Japan, 1984–94 (Sen. Vice-Chm., 1992). Treas., Eur. Democratic Group, 1979–92. Member Royal Company of Archers, Queen's Body Guard for Scotland. Contested (U) North Aberdeen, Gen. Election, 1959. *Publications:* Competition Law in the European Community, 1990; It's My Problem As Well: drugs prevention and education, 1993.

Recreations: golf, tennis, photography, vintage cars. *Heir: s* Alexander Dudley Stewart-Clark, *b* 21 Nov. 1960. *Address:* Dundas Castle, South Queensferry, near Edinburgh EH30 9SP. *T:* (0131) 331 1114.

STEWART-JONES, Mrs Richard; *see* Smith, Emma.

STEWART-RICHARDSON, Sir Simon (Alaisdair), 17th Bt *cr* 1630; *b* 9 June 1947; *er s* of Sir Ian Rorie Hay Stewart-Richardson, 16th Bt, and of Audrey Meryl (who *m* 1975, P. A. P. Robertson, *qv*), *e d* of late Claude Odlum; *S* father, 1969; *m* 1990, Marilene Cabal do Nascimento (marr. diss.); one *s* one *d. Educ:* Trinity College, Glenalmond. *Heir: s* Jason Rorie Stewart-Richardson, *b* 5 Oct. 1990. *Address:* Lynedale, Longcross, near Chertsey, Surrey KT16 0DP. *T:* (01932) 872329.

STEWART-ROBERTS, Phyllida Katharine, OBE 1995; Lord-Lieutenant, East Sussex, 2000–08 (Vice Lord-Lieutenant, 1996–2000); Superintendent-in-Chief, St John Ambulance Brigade, 1990–93; *b* 19 Aug. 1933; *d* of Lt-Col Walter Harold Bamfield, Royal Welch Fusiliers and Veronica Grissell; *m* 1955, Andrew Kerr Stewart-Roberts; one *s* one *d. Educ:* Tormead Sch.; Royal Acad. of Music (DipEd). Primary sch. teacher, LCC, 1954–57; Love Walk Hostel for Disabled Workers: Mem., Management Cttee, 1972–94; Vice Chm., 1980–83; Chm., 1983–89; Pres., 1994–. Trustee: Community Service Volunteers, 1984–; Orders of St John Care Trust, 1994–2005; Defence Medical Welfare Service, 2000–; Member: Management Cttee, Habinteg Housing Assoc., 1988–96 (Chm., Southern Cttee, 1994–96); St John Ambulance Brigade, Sussex, 1962–89, 1994–; Jt Pres., Council of Order of St John, Sussex, 2000– (County Pres., 1984–89; Chm., 1995–2000); Chm., Jt Cttee, Order of St John of Jerusalem and BRCS, 1991–2001 (Mem., 1990–2001); Mem., Florence Nightingale Foundn, 1990–; Vice-Pres., VAD Assoc., 1989–95. Mem. Council, Sussex Univ., 1995–2001 (Vice-Chm., 1999–2001). JP Inner London, 1980–95. DL E Sussex, 1991. DStJ 1993. *Recreations:* needlework, the gentler country pursuits. *Address:* Mount Harry Lodge, Offham, Lewes, E Sussex BN7 3QW.

STEWART-SMITH, Christopher Dudley, CBE 1995; DL; Chairman, Cautley Ltd, since 1997; Producer, Stanley Hall Opera, since 2001; *b* 21 Jan. 1941; *s* of late Ean Stewart-Smith and Edmee von Wallerstain und Marnegg; *m* 1964, Olivia Barstow (marr. diss. 1989); one *s* two *d. Educ:* Winchester; King's Coll., Cambridge (MA Mod Langs); MIT (SM Management). Courtaulds, 1962–65; McKinsey & Co. Management Consultants, 1966–71; joined Sterling Guarantee Trust, 1971, Dir, 1973; served on main bd after merger with Town & City Properties and later with P&OSNCo., until 1986; Chairman: Earls Court and Olympia Exhibns Gp, 1974–85; Sutcliffe Catering Gp, 1975–85; Butlers Warehousing & Distribution, 1971–85; Sterling Guards, 1974–85; P&O Cruises, Swan Hellenic, and Princess Cruises, 1985–86; Conder Group plc, 1987–92; Collett Dickenson Pearce Internat., 1990–91; Producer Responsibility Gp and V-Wrag, 1994–96; London & Henley Ltd, 1995–98; Healthcall Gp plc, 1991–98; Leighton & Henley PLC, 2007–. Director: Outer London Reg. Bd, 1984–88, Southern Adv. Bd, 1988–92, Nat. Westminster Bank; Williamson Tea Holdings, 1986–94; Life Sciences Internat., 1987–97; Erith plc, 1992–95; Strategic Partnership, 1997–2000; Gartmore SNT plc, 1998–2005; Brompton Bicycle Ltd, 2000–. Chm., London Chamber of Commerce and Industry, 1988–90; Pres., British Chambers of Commerce, 1992–94; Vice-Pres. and Hd of UK Delegn, Eurochambres SA, Brussels, 1994–2002. Member: Council, Worldaware, 1988–2000 (Trustee, 2000–02); Council of Management, Acad. of St Martin-in-the-Fields, 1990–93; Cttee, Royal Tournament, 1976–85; Vice-Pres., Olympia Internat. Showjumping, 1977–85; Hon. Mem., Royal Smithfield Club, 1985–. Trustee, Personal Support Unit, Royal Courts of Justice, 2001–. Chm. of Govs, Oundle Sch., 2001–04. Mem. Ct of Assts, Grocers' Co., 1990–. High Sheriff, Essex, 2006–07; DL Essex, 2008. *Recreations:* opera, organic farming, design of gardens and buildings, tennis, shooting, skiing. *Address:* 52 Westbourne Terrace, W2 3UJ. *T:* (020) 7262 0514. *Club:* Travellers.

STEWART-SMITH, Kirstie Louise; *see* Hamilton, K. L.

STEWART-WILSON, Lt-Col Sir Blair (Aubyn), KCVO 1994 (CVO 1989 LVO 1983); Deputy Master of the Household and Equerry to Her Majesty, 1976–94, an Extra Equerry, since 1994; *b* 17 July 1929; *s* of late Aubyn Wilson and late Muriel Stewart Stevens; *m* 1962, Helen Mary Fox; three *d. Educ:* Eton; Sandhurst. Commnd Scots Guards, 1949, Atholl Highlanders, 1952 (Major, 1996; Lt-Col Comdg, 2003–); served with Scots Guards in UK, Germany and Far East; Adjutant 2nd Bn, 1955–57; ADC to Viscount Cobham, Governor General and C-in-C, New Zealand, 1957–59; Equerry to late Duke of Gloucester, 1960–62; Regtl Adjutant, 1966–68; GSO1, Foreign Liaison Sect. (Army), MoD, 1970–73; Defence, Military and Air Attaché, British Embassy, Vienna, 1975–76. HM's Rep. Trustee, Bd of Royal Armouries, 1995–2004. Somerset County Patron, Cancer Res. UK (formerly Cancer Res. Campaign), 1999–; Trustee, Wells Cathedral Preservation Trust, 1997–. *Address:* c/o Royal Bank of Scotland, 84 Atholl Road, Pitlochry PH16 5BJ. *T:* (home) (01823) 490111. *Club:* Pratt's.

STEWARTBY, Baron *cr* 1992 (Life Peer), of Portmoak in the District of Perth and Kinross; **Bernard Harold Ian Halley Stewart of Stewartby,** Kt 1991; PC 1989; RD 1972; FBA 1981; FRSE 1986; *b* 10 Aug. 1935; *s* of late Prof. H. C. Stewart of Stewartby, CBE and Dorothy Irene (*née* Lowen); *m* 1966, Hon. Deborah Charlotte Buchan, JP, *d* of 3rd Baron Tweedsmuir; one *s* two *d. Educ:* Haileybury; Jesus Coll., Cambridge (1st cl. hons Class. Tripos; MA; LittD 1978; Hon. Fellow, 1994). Nat. Service, RNVR, 1954–56; subseq. Lt-Comdr RNR. Seccombe, Marshall & Campion Ltd, bill brokers, 1959–60; joined Brown, Shipley & Co. Ltd, 1960, Dir 1971–83; Director: Diploma plc, 1990–; Standard Chartered plc, 1990–2004 (Dep. Chm., 1993–2004); Chm., Throgmorton Trust, 1990–2005; Dep. Chm., Amlin, 1995–2006. Mem., SIB, later FSA, 1993–97. MP (C) Hitchin, Feb. 1974–1983, N Herts, 1983–92. PPS to Chancellor of the Exchequer, 1979–83; Parly Under-Sec. of State for Defence Procurement, MoD, Jan.–Oct. 1983; Economic Sec. to HM Treasury, 1983–87; Minister of State: for the Armed Forces, MoD, 1987–88; NI Office, 1988–89. Jt Sec., Cons. Parly Finance Cttee, 1975–76, 1977–79; Member: Public Expenditure Cttee, 1977–79; Public Accounts Cttee, 1991–92. UK rep., Europ. Budget Council, 1983–85; responsible for: Trustee Savings Banks Act, 1985; Building Socs Act, 1986; Banking Act, 1987. Trustee, Parly Contributory Pension Fund, 2000–05. Mem. British Academy Cttee for Sylloge of Coins of British Isles, 1967– (Chm., 1993–2003); Numismatic advr, NACF, 1988–; Chm., Treasure Valuation Cttee, 1996–2001. Hon. Treas., Westminster Cttee for Protection of Children, 1960–70, Vice-Chm., 1975–92. FSA (Mem. Council 1974–76); FSAScot; Dir, British Numismatic Soc., 1965–75 (Sanford Saltus Gold Medal 1971); FRNS (medallist 1996). Mem. Council, British Museum Soc., 1975–76. Life Governor, 1977, Mem. Council, 1980–95, Haileybury; Trustee, Sir Halley Stewart Trust, 1978– (Pres., 2002–). Hon. Vice-Pres., Stewart Soc. 1989–. County Vice-Pres., 1978–2007, Pres., 2007–, St John Ambulance for Herts; KStJ 1992. *Publications:* The Scottish Coinage, 1955 (2nd edn 1967); Scottish Mints, 1971; (ed with C. N. L. Brooke and others) Studies in Numismatic Method, 1983; (with C. E. Blunt and C. S. S. Lyon) Coinage in Tenth-Century England, 1989; (with C. E. Challis and others) New History of the Royal Mint, 1992; many papers in Proc. Soc. Antiquaries of Scotland, Numismatic Chronicle, British Numismatic Jl, etc. *Recreations:* history; tennis (Captain CU Tennis Club, 1958–59; 1st string v Oxford, 1958 and 1959; winner Coupe de Bordeaux 1959; led 1st Oxford and Cambridge Tennis and Rackets team to USA, 1958); Homer. *Address:* House of Lords, SW1A 0PW. *Clubs:* Beefsteak, MCC; New (Edinburgh); Hawks, Pitt (Cambridge).

STEYN, family name of **Baron Steyn**.

STEYN, Baron *cr* 1995 (Life Peer), of Swafield in the county of Norfolk; **Johan Steyn,** Kt 1985; PC 1992; a Lord of Appeal in Ordinary, 1995–2005; *b* 15 Aug. 1932; *m* Susan Leonore (*née* Lewis); two *s* two *d* by previous *m*, and one step *s* one step *d. Educ:* Jan van Riebeeck Sch., Cape Town, S Africa; Univ. of Stellenbosch, S Africa (BA, LLB); University Coll., Oxford (MA; Hon. Fellow, 1995). Cape Province Rhodes Scholar, 1955; commenced practice at S African Bar, 1958; Sen. Counsel of Supreme Court of SA, 1970; settled in UK; commenced practice at English Bar, 1973 (Bencher, Lincoln's Inn, 1985); QC 1979; a Presiding Judge, Northern Circuit, 1989–91; Judge of the High Court, QBD, 1985–91; a Lord Justice of Appeal, 1992–95. Member: Supreme Court Rule Cttee, 1985–89; Deptl Adv. Cttee on Arbitration Law, 1986–89 (Chm., 1990–94); Chairman: Race Relations Cttee of the Bar, 1987–88; Lord Chancellor's Adv. Cttee on Legal Educn and Conduct, 1994–96; Takeover Appeal Bd, 2006–. Chm., Adv. Council, Centre for Commercial Law Studies, QMW, 1993–94. Pres., British Insce Law Assoc., 1992–94. Hon. Member: Amer. Law Inst., 1999; Soc. of Legal Scholars, 2002; Hon. Fellow, UCL, 2005. Hon. LLD: QMW, 1997; UEA, 1998; Cape Town, 2007. *Address:* House of Lords, SW1A 0PW.

STHEEMAN, Robert Alexander Talma, CB 2008; Chief Executive, United Kingdom Debt Management Office, since 2003; *b* 7 June 1959; *s* of Sape Talma Stheeman and Cécile Talma Stheeman (*née* Mendelssohn Bartholdy); *m* 1989, Elisabeth Haas; four *s. Educ:* Stowe Sch.; Chamber of Commerce, Hamburg (Bank Business Degree 1982). Vereins-und Westbank AG, Hamburg, 1979–85; Deutsche Bank AG, Frankfurt and London, 1986–2002 (Dir, 1991–2002). *Recreations:* family, music, walking. *Address:* United Kingdom Debt Management Office, Eastcheap Court, 11 Philpot Lane, EC3M 8UD. *T:* (020) 7862 6500, *Fax:* (020) 7862 6509; *e-mail:* robert.stheeman@dmo.gsi.gov.uk.

STIBBARD, Peter Jack, CStat; Head, Labour Market Statistics Group, Central Statistical Office, 1995–96; international consultancies, 1996–99; *b* 15 May 1936; *s* of late Frederick Stibbard and Gladys Stibbard (*née* Daines); *m* 1964, Christine Fuller; two *d. Educ:* City of Norwich Grammar School; Hull Univ. (BSc Econ). Served RAF, 1954–56. Kodak Ltd, 1959–64; Thos Potterton Ltd, 1964–66; Greater London Council, 1966–68; Central Statistical Office, 1968–82; HM Treasury, 1982–85; Under Sec., Statistics Div. 2, DTI, 1985–89; Dir of Statistics, Dept of Employment, 1989–95. *Publications:* articles in official and trade jls. *Address:* 62 Allington Drive, Tonbridge, Kent TN10 4HH.

STIBBON, Gen. Sir John (James), KCB 1988; OBE 1979; CEng, FICE; Chief Royal Engineer, 1993–99; *b* 5 Jan. 1935; *s* of Jack Stibbon and Elizabeth Matilda Stibbon (*née* Dixon); *m* 1957, Jean Fergusson Skeggs, *d* of John Robert Skeggs and Florence Skeggs (*née* Hayes); two *d. Educ:* Portsmouth Southern Grammar School; Royal Military Academy; Royal Military College of Science. BSc (Eng). CEng 1989; FICE 1989. Commissioned RE, 1954; CO 28 Amphibious Engineer Regt, 1975–77; Asst Military Secretary, 1977–79; Comd 20 Armoured Brigade, 1979–81; rcds 1982; Comdt, RMCS, 1983–85; ACDS Operational Requirements (Land Systems), 1985–87; Master Gen. of the Ordnance, 1987–91. Dir, Chemring Gp plc, 1993–2005; Chm., ITT Defence, 1993–2004. Colonel Commandant: RAPC, 1985–92; RPC, 1986–91; RE, 1987–99. Vice Pres., Royal Star & Garter Home, 1996–; Chm., Gordon Foundn, 1992–2002; Comr, Duke of York's Royal Mil. Sch., 1993–99. Hon. DSc: Cranfield Inst. of Technology, 1989; Greenwich, 2001. *Recreations:* Association football, athletics, painting, palaeontology. *Club:* Army and Navy.

STIBBS, Prof. Douglas Walter Noble, MSc Sydney, DPhil Oxon; FRAS; FRSE; Visiting Professor, Mathematical Sciences Institute, Centre for Mathematics and its Applications, since 1990, Hon. Librarian to the Institute, since 1996, and Visiting Fellow, since 2005, Australian National University; *b* 17 Feb. 1919; 2nd *s* of Edward John Stibbs, Sydney, NSW; *m* 1949, Margaret Lilian Calvert, BSc, DipEd (Sydney), *er d* of Rev. John Calvert, Sydney, NSW; two *d. Educ:* Sydney High Sch.; Univ. of Sydney; New College, Oxford. Deas Thomson Scholar, Sch. of Physics, Univ. of Sydney, 1940; BSc (Sydney), 1st Class Hons, Univ. Medal in Physics, 1942; MSc (Sydney), 1943; DPhil (Oxon), 1954. Johnson Memorial Prize and Gold Medal for Advancement of Astronomy and Meteorology, Oxford Univ., 1956. Res. Asst, Commonwealth Solar Observatory, Canberra, ACT, 1940–42; Asst Lectr, Dept of Mathematics and Physics, New England University Coll., Armidale, NSW (now the Univ. of New England), 1942–45; Scientific Officer and Sen. Scientific Officer, Commonwealth Observatory, Canberra, ACT, 1945–51; Radcliffe Travelling Fellow in Astronomy, Radcliffe Observatory, Pretoria, S Africa, and Univ. Observatory, Oxford, 1951–54; PSO, UKAEA, 1955–59; University of St Andrews: Napier Prof. of Astronomy, and Dir, Univ. Observatory, 1959–89; Sen. Prof. Senatus Academicus, 1987–89; Napier Prof. Emeritus, 1990–; Vis. Fellow, ANU Res. Sch. of Astronomy and Astrophysics, 1990–2005. Vis. Prof. of Astrophysics, Yale Univ. Observatory, 1966–67; British Council Vis. Prof., Univ. of Utrecht, 1968; Prof., Collège de France, 1975–76 (Médaille du Collège, 1976). University College, London: External Expert (appts and promotions), 1970–74 and 1976–80; External Examr (BSc Astronomy), 1977–81. Member: Internat. Astronomical Union, 1951– (Chm. Finance Cttee, 1964–67, 1973–76, 1976–79); Amer. Astronomical Soc., 1956–73; Adv. Cttee on Meteorology for Scotland, 1960–69, 1972–75, 1978–80; Board of Visitors, Royal Greenwich Observatory, 1963–65; Council RAS, 1964–67, 1970–73 (Vice-Pres., 1972–73), Editorial Board, 1970–73; Council, RSE, 1970–72; National Cttee for Astronomy, 1964–76; SRC Cttees for Royal Greenwich Observatory, 1966–70, and Royal Observatory, Edinburgh, 1966–76, Chm., 1970–76; SRC Astronomy, Space and Radio Bd, 1970–76; SRC, 1972–76; S African Astron. Obs. Adv. Cttee, 1972–76; Chairman: Astronomy Policy and Grants Cttee, 1972–74; Northern Hemisphere Observatory Planning Cttee, 1972–75; Astronomy II Cttee, 1974–75; Mem., Centre National de la Recherche Scientifique Cttee, Obs. de Haute Provence, 1973–82. Life Member: Sydney Univ. Union, 1942; New Coll. Soc., 1953; New England Univ. Union, NSW, 1957. Mem., Western Province Masters Athletics Assoc., Cape Town, 1983–. Marathon Medals: Paris, Caithness, Edinburgh (3hrs 59mins), Flying Fox (British Veterans Championships), Honolulu, 1983; London, Loch Rannoch, Aberdeen (Veterans Trophy Winner), 1984; Stoke-on-Trent (Potteries), Athens, Honolulu, 1985; London, Edinburgh (Commonwealth Games Peoples Marathon), Stoke-on-Trent (Potteries), Berlin, Honolulu, 1986; Boston, 1987; Half-marathons: 13 events incl. Windsor Great Park, Dundee, Dunfermline, Wagga (Australian Veterans Games, 1991, Gold Medallist), Canberra. *Publications:* The Outer Layers of a Star (with Sir Richard Woolley), 1953; contrib. Theoretical Astrophysics and Astronomy in Monthly Notices of RAS and other jls. *Recreations:* music, ornithology, photography, golf, coaching (long-distance running). *Address:* Mathematical Sciences Institute, Australian National University, Canberra, ACT 0200, Australia. *Club:* Royal and Ancient (St Andrews).

STIGLITZ, Prof. Joseph Eugene, PhD; Professor of Economics, Columbia Business School, Columbia University, since 2001; Chairman, Brooks World Poverty Institute, University of Manchester, since 2006; *b* 9 Feb. 1943; *m*; two *s* two *d*. *Educ:* Amherst Coll. (BA 1964); MIT (PhD 1967); Fitzwilliam Coll., Cambridge Univ. (MA 1970; Hon. Fellow, 2006). Professor of Economics: Yale Univ. 1970–74; Stanford Univ., 1974–76; Drummond Prof. of Political Economy, Oxford Univ. and All Souls Coll., 1976–79; Prof. of Economics, Princeton Univ., 1979–88; Prof. of Econs, Stanford Univ., 1992–2001. Mem., 1993–97, Chm., 1995–97, Council of Econ. Advrs to Pres. of USA; Chief Economist, World Bank, 1997–2000. Fellowships: Nat. Sci. Foundn, 1964–65; Fulbright, 1965–66; SSRC Faculty, 1969–70; Guggenheim, 1969–70; Oskar Morgenstern Distinguished Fellowship, Mathematica and Inst. for Advanced Study, Princeton, 1978–79. Consultant: Nat. Sci. Foundn, 1972–75; Ford Foundn Energy Policy Study, 1973; Dept of Labor (Pensions and Labor Turnover), 1974; Dept of Interior (Offshore Oil Leasing Programs), 1975; Federal Energy Admin (Intertemporal Biases in Market Allocation of Natural Resources), 1975–79; World Bank (Cost Benefit Analysis; Urban Rural Migration; Natural Resources), 1975–; Electric Power Res. Inst., 1976–; OECD; Office of Fair Trading; Treasury (Office of Tax Analysis), 1980; US AID (commodity price stabilization), 1977; Inter-American Development Bank; Bell Laboratories; Bell Communications Research; State of Alaska; Seneca Indian Nation. Internat. Prize, Academia Lincei, 1988; Union des Assurances de Paris Scientific Prize, 1989; Rechtenwald Prize, 1999. Gen. Editor, Econometric Soc. Reprint Series; Associate Editor: Jl of Economic Theory, 1968–73; American Economic Rev., 1972–75; Jl of Economic Perspectives, 1988–93; Co-editor, Jl of Public Economics, 1968–83; American Editor, Rev. of Economic Studies, 1968–76; Editorial Bd, World Bank Economic Review, The Geneva Papers, Revista de Econometrica, Assicurazioni. Vice-Pres., American Econ. Assoc. 1985. Fellow: Econometric Soc., 1972 (Sec./Treasurer, 1972–75); Amer. Acad. of Arts and Scis; Inst. for Policy Reform, 1990–; American Philosophical Assoc.; NAS; Senior Fellow: Hoover Instn, 1988–93; Brookings Instn, Washington, 2000–01. Corresp. FBA 1993. Hon. MA Yale, 1970; Hon. DHL Amherst, 1974; Hon. Dr: Pomona Coll.; New Sch.; Northwestern; Bard Coll.; Toronto; Naumur; Leuven; Ben Gurion; Barcelona; Bucharest; Lisbon Tech.; Charles Univ., Prague. John Bates Clark Medal, Amer. Econ. Assoc; (jtly) Nobel Prize for Economics, 2001. *Publications:* (ed) Collected Scientific Papers of P. A. Samuelson, 1965; (ed with H. Uzawa) Readings in Modern Theory of Economic Growth, 1969; (with A. B. Atkinson) Lectures in Public Finance, 1980; (with D. Newbery) The Economic Impact of Price Stabilization, 1980; Economics of the Public Sector, 1986; Globalization and its Discontents, 2002; Making Globalization Work, 2006; (with L. Bilmes) The Three Trillion Dollar War: the true cost of the Iraq conflict, 2008; contribs on economics of growth, development, natural resources, information, uncertainty, imperfect competition, corporate finance and public finance in Amer. Econ. Rev., Qly Jl of Econs, Jl of Pol. Econ., Econometrica, Internat. Econ. Rev., Econ. Jl, Rev. of Econ. Studies, Jl of Public Econs, Jl of Econ. Theory, Oxford Econ. Papers. *Address:* Room 814, Uris Hall, Columbia Business School, New York, NY 10027, USA. *T:* (212) 8540671.

STIHLER, Catherine Dalling; Member (Lab) Scotland, European Parliament, since 1999; *b* 30 July 1973; *d* of Gordon McLeish Taylor and Catherine Doreen Taylor; *m* 2000, David Stihler. *Educ:* Coltness High Sch., Wishaw; Univ. of St Andrews (MA Hons Geography and Internat. Relns 1996; MLitt Internat. Security Studies 1998). Pres., Univ. of St Andrews Students' Assoc., 1994–95. Young Labour Representative: Exec. Cttee, SLP, 1993–95; Lab Party NEC, 1995–97; Women's Rep. and Local Orgns Rep., SLP Exec., 1997–99. Researcher and facilitator to Anne Begg, MP, 1997–99. Contested (Lab) Angus, 1997. *Publication:* (contrib.) Women and the Military, 2000. *Recreations:* going to the gym, watching films, singing, playing backgammon. *Address:* European Parliament, Rue Wiertz, 1047 Brussels, Belgium.

STILGOE, Richard Henry Simpson, OBE 1998; DL; songwriter, lyricist, entertainer and broadcaster, since 1962; *b* 28 March 1943; *s* of late John Henry Tweedie Stilgoe and Joan Lucy Strutt Stilgoe; *m* 1st, 1964, Elizabeth Caroline Gross; one *s* one *d*; 2nd, 1975, Annabel Margaret Hunt; two *s* one *d*. *Educ:* Liverpool Coll.; Monkton Combe Sch.; Clare Coll., Cambridge (choral exhibnr). One-man show worldwide, incl. Windsor Castle, 1982 and British Embassy, Washington, 1986; Two-man show with Peter Skellern, 1985–2002. Author and composer: Bodywork (children's musical), 1987; Brilliant the Dinosaur, 1991. Word-processor for Andrew Lloyd Webber on Cats, Starlight Express and Phantom of the Opera. Stilgoe Saturday Concerts, RFH, 1999–. Founder and Dir, Orpheus Trust (music and disabled people), 1985–; Pres., Surrey Care Trust, 1986–2000; Trustee, Nat. Foundn for Youth Music, 1999– (Chm., 2007–). FRSA 1992. Hon. ARAM 2003. Hon. DLitt: Greenwich, 1999; Southampton, 2005. Monaco Radio Prize, 1984, 1991, 1996; NY Radio Fest. Gold Award, 1989; Prix Italia, 1991. DL, 1996, High Sheriff, 1998, Surrey. *Publications:* The Richard Stilgoe Letters, 1981; Brilliant The Dinosaur, 1994. *Recreations:* sailing, cricket, architecture, building, demolition, children. *Address:* c/o The Orpheus Trust, Trevereux Manor, Limpsfield Chart, Oxted, Surrey RH8 0TL. *Clubs:* MCC, Lord's Taverners (Pres., 2003); Surrey CC (Pres., 2005).

STILLMAN, Dr Bruce William, AO 1999; FRS 1993; Chief Executive Officer, since 2000, President, since 2003, Cold Spring Harbor Laboratory, New York (Director, 1994–2003); *b* Melbourne, Australia, 16 Oct. 1953; *s* of Graham Leslie Stillman and Jessie May (*née* England); *m* 1981, Grace Angela Begley; one *s* one *d*. *Educ:* Glen Waverley High Sch.; Sydney Boys' High Sch.; Univ. of Sydney (BSc Hons); ANU (PhD). Cold Spring Harbor Laboratory, New York: Damon Runyon-Walter Winchell Postdoctoral Res. Fellow, 1979–80; Staff Investigator, 1981–82; Sen. Staff Investigator, 1983–85; Sen. Scientist, 1985–90; Asst Dir, 1990–93; Adjunct Prof. of Microbiology, SUNY, 1982–. Damon Runyon-Walter Winchell Cancer Fund Fellow, 1979–80; Rita Allen Foundn Scholar, 1982–87; Charter Fellow, Molecular Medicine Soc., 1995. Lectures: Harvey Soc., 1993; Nieuwland, Univ. of Notre Dame, 1993; Doty, Harvard Univ., 1998. For. Associate, NAS, USA, 2000; Fellow, Amer. Acad. of Microbiol., 2000. Hon. DHL Hofstra, 2001; Hon. DSc NY Inst. Tech. Commonwealth Postgrad. Award, 1976–80; Merit Award, NIH, 1986. *Publications:* numerous scientific pubns. *Address:* Cold Spring Harbor Laboratory, One Bungtown Road, Cold Spring Harbor, NY 11724, USA. *T:* (516) 3678383.

STIMSON, Prof. Gerald Vivian, PhD; Executive Director, International Harm Reduction Association, since 2004; *b* 10 April 1945; *s* of late Geoffrey Edward Vivian Stimson and Maud Ellen Stimson; *m* 1st, 1971, Carol Anne Fowler (marr. diss. 1992, she *d* 1997); two *s*; 2nd, 1993, Elizabeth Louise Tacey; one *s*. *Educ:* City of London Sch.; London Sch. of Econs (BSc 1966; MSc 1967); Inst. of Psychiatry, Univ. of London (PhD 1971). Res. worker, Addiction Res. Unit, Inst. of Psychiatry, Univ. of London, 1967–71; Res. Fellow, Med. Sociology Res. Centre, UC of Swansea, 1971–75; London University: Lectr, then Sen. Lectr, Addiction Res. Unit, Inst. Psychiatry, 1975–78; Goldsmiths' College: Sen. Lectr in Sociology, 1978–89; Head, Sociology Dept, 1980–83; Dir, Monitoring Res. Gp, Sociology Dept, 1987–89; Imperial College: Dir, Centre for Res. on Drugs and Health Behaviour, 1990–2004; Prof. of Sociology of Health Behaviour, 1991–2004, now Emeritus; Hd, Dept of Social Science and Medicine, 1997–2004. Fulbright Schol., NY Univ., 1983; Vis. Prof., Thames Valley Univ., 1995–; Hon. Prof., LSHTM, 2006–. Advisory Council on Misuse of Drugs: Mem., 1984–99; Mem., Wkg Gp on AIDS and Drug Misuse, 1987–92; Chm., Stats Inf. and Res. Cttee, 1990–99; Member: Council, Inst. for Study of Drug Dependence, 1985–90 (Vice-Chm., 1987); Scientific Cttee, Eur. Monitoring Centre for Drugs and Drug Addiction, 1994–97; Founder Mem., UK Harm Reduction Alliance, 2001 (Chm., 2001–02). Pres., Action on Hepatitis C, 2000–. Member, Editorial Board: Addiction Res., 1991–; AIDS, 1993–96; Ed., Internat. Jl Drug Policy, 2000–. Trustee, AIDS Educnl and Res. Trust, 1995–2003. *Publications:* Heroin and Behaviour: diversity among addicts attending London clinics, 1973; (with B. Webb) Going to See the Doctor: the consultation process in general practice, 1975; (with E. Oppenheimer) Heroin Addiction: treatment and control in Britain, 1982; (ed jtly) AIDS and Drug Misuse: the challenge for policy and practice in the 1990's, 1990; (ed jtly) Drug Injecting and HIV Infection: global issues and local responses, 1998; (ed jtly) Drug Use in London, 1998; (ed jtly) Drugs and the Future: brain science, addiction and society, 2006; (ed) Drinking in Context: patterns, interventions and partnerships, 2006. *Recreations:* walking, the countryside, travel. *Club:* Athenæum.

STIMSON, Robert Frederick, CBE 1992; Governor and Commander-in-Chief of St Helena and its Dependencies, 1988–91; *b* 16 May 1939; *s* of Frederick Henry Stimson and Gladys Alma Stimson (*née* Joel); *m* 1961, Margaret Faith Kerry (*d* 2004); two *s* one *d*. *Educ:* Rendcomb Coll.; Queen Mary Coll., London (BSc First Cl. Hons; MSc (by thesis) mathematical physics). HM Diplomatic Service: FO, 1966–67; Saigon, 1967–68; Singapore, 1968–70; Cabinet Office, 1970–73; Mexico City, 1973–75; FCO, 1975–80; Counsellor, East Berlin, 1980–81; Head of Home Inspectorate, 1982–83; Counsellor and Hd of Chancery, Dublin, 1984–87. Order of Aztec Eagle, Mexico, 1975. *Publications:* contrib. Jl Physics and Chemistry of Solids.

STINCHCOMBE, Paul David; barrister; *b* 25 April 1962; *s* of Lionel Walter Stinchcombe and Pauline Sylvia Ann (*née* Hawkins); *m* 1990, Suzanne Jean Gardiner; two *s* one *d*. *Educ:* Royal Grammar Sch., High Wycombe; Trinity Coll., Cambridge (Sen. Schol.; BA Law double 1st cl. Hons 1983); Harvard Law Sch. (Frank Knox Fellow; LLM 1984). Called to the Bar, Lincoln's Inn, 1985; in practice at the Bar, 1985–. Vis. Fellow, Centre of Public Law, Cambridge Univ., 2005–06. Mem. (Lab), Camden Council, 1990–94 (Chm., Labour Gp, 1992–94). MP (Lab) Wellingborough, 1997–2005; contested (Lab) same seat, 2005. *Recreations:* football, cricket, golf. *Address:* 4/5 Gray's Inn Square, WC1R 5AY.

STING; *see* Sumner, G. M.

STINSON, His Honour David John; a Circuit Judge (formerly County Court Judge), 1969–86; *b* 22 Feb. 1921; *er s* of late Henry John Edwin Stinson, MC, MA, LLB, Beckenham, Kent (sometime Chief Commoner of City of London, solicitor) and Margaret Stinson (*née* Little); *m* 1950, Eleanor Judith (*er d* of K. M. Chance, DSO, Cumberland); two *s* two *d* (and one *s* decd). *Educ:* Eastbourne Coll.; Emmanuel Coll., Cambridge. MA 1946; Jesters Club, 1949 (Rugby Fives). Served War of 1939–45: Essex Yeomanry, Captain, RA, and Air OP, 1941–46 (despatches). Called to Bar, Middle Temple, 1947 (Harmsworth Schol., 1948); Dep. Chm., Herts QS, 1965–71; Suffolk and Essex County Court Circuit, 1973–86. Chancellor, dio. of Carlisle, 1971–90. Chm., Ipswich Family Conciliation Service, 1982–88; Pres., Parents' Conciliation Trust, 1988–99. *Recreations:* bird-watching, gardening. *Address:* Barrack Row, Fishpond Road, Waldringfield, Woodbridge, Suffolk IP12 4QX. *T:* (01473) 736280.

STIRLING, Sir Alexander (John Dickson), KBE 1981; CMG 1976; HM Diplomatic Service, retired; Council Member, SOS Sahel International—UK, since 1987 (Chairman, 1993–97); *b* 20 Oct. 1926; *e s* of late Brig. A. Dickson Stirling, DSO, MB, ChB, DPH, and Isobel Stirling, MA, DipEd, DipPsych, *d* of late Rev. J. C. Matthew (former senior Presidency Chaplain, Bombay); *m* 1955, Alison Mary, *y d* of Gp Capt. A. P. Campbell, CBE; two *s* two *d*. *Educ:* Edinburgh Academy; Lincoln Coll., Oxford (MA). RAFVR, 1945–48 (Egypt, 1945–47). Entered Foreign Office, 1951; Lebanon, 1952; British Embassy, Cairo, 1952–56 (Oriental Sec., 1955–56); FO, 1956–59; First Sec., British Embassy, Baghdad, 1959–62; First Sec. and Consul, Amman, 1962–64; First Sec., British Embassy, Santiago, 1965–67 (led UK Delegn to Fourth Antarctic Treaty Consultative Meeting, 1966); FO, 1967–69; British Political Agent, Bahrain, 1969–71, Ambassador, 1971–72; Counsellor, Beirut, 1972–75; RCDS 1976; Ambassador to Iraq, 1977–80, to the Tunisian Republic, 1981–84, to the Sudan, 1984–86. Chm., 1989–92, Mem. Council, 1994–2000, Soc. for Protection of Animals Abroad (formerly Soc. for Protection of Animals in N Africa).

See also C. J. M. Stirling.

STIRLING, Sir Angus (Duncan Æneas), Kt 1994; Director-General, National Trust, 1983–95 (Deputy Director-General, 1979–83); *b* 10 Dec. 1933; *s* of late Duncan Alexander Stirling and Lady Marjorie Murray, *e d* of 8th Earl of Dunmore, VC, DSO, MVO; *m* 1959, Armyne Morar Helen Schofield, *e d* of late W. G. B. Schofield and Hon. Armyne Astley, *d* of 21st Baron Hastings; one *s* two *d*. *Educ:* Eton Coll.; Trinity Coll., Cambridge; London Univ. (Extra Mural) (Dip. History of Art). Christie, Manson and Woods Ltd, 1954–57; Lazard Bros and Co. Ltd, 1957–66; Asst Dir, Paul Mellon Foundn for British Art, 1966–69 (Jt Dir, 1969–70); Dep. Sec.-General, Arts Council of GB, 1971–79. Sen. Policy Advr, Nat. Heritage Meml Fund, 1996–97; Chairman: Greenwich Foundn for RNC, 1996–2003; JNCC, 1997–2002. Mem., Govt Task Force on Tourism and the Envmt, 1991. Mem. Bd, Royal Opera House, Covent Garden, 1979–96 (Chm., 1991–96); Mem., Council, Friends of Covent Garden, 1981– (Chm., 1981–91); Dep. Chm., Royal Ballet Bd, 1988–91; a Gov., Royal Ballet, 1988–96; Member: Crafts Council, 1980–85; Council of Management, Byam Shaw Sch. of Art, 1965–89; Bd of Trustees, Courtauld Inst. of Art, 1981–83, 2002–; Adv. Council, London Symphony Orchestra, 1979–; Bd of Governors, Live Music Now, 1982–89; Bd of Trustees, The Theatres Trust, 1983–91; Bd of Trustees, Heritage of London Trust, 1983–95; Tourism Cttee, ICOMOS UK, 1993–2003; Council, RSCM, 1996–98; Fabric Adv. Cttee, Wells Cathedral, 2001–. Chm., Adv. Panel for Local Heritage Initiative, Countryside Commn, 1998–99; Chm., Policy Cttee, 1996–2001, Pres., Som Br., 2002–07, CPRE; Mem. Adv. Cttee, Stowe Landscape Gardens, 1996–; Trustee: Stowe House Preservation Trust, 1998–; Samuel Courtauld Trust (formerly Home House (Courtauld Collection)), 1983–; World Monuments Fund in Britain, 1996–2008. President: Friends of Holland Park, 2003–; KADFAS Kensington and Chelsea, 2008. Vice Patron, Almshouses Assoc., 2000– (Chm., Adv. Panel, Patron's Award, 2001–03). Member, Board of Governors: Gresham Sch., 1999–2007; City and Guilds Art Sch., 2003–. CCMI; FRSA. Hon. FTCL 2004. Mem., Court, Fishmongers' Co., 1991– (Prime Warden, 2004–05). Hon. DLitt: Leicester, 1995; Greenwich, 2002. *Recreations:* painting, music, travel, walking. *Address:* 25 Ladbroke Grove, W11 3AY. *Clubs:* Garrick, Brooks's, Beefsteak, Grillions.

STIRLING, Prof. Charles James Matthew, FRS 1986; CChem, FRSC; Professor of Organic Chemistry, University of Sheffield, 1990–98, now Emeritus; *b* 8 Dec. 1930; *s* of Brig. Alexander Dickson Stirling, DSO, MB, ChB, DPH, RAMC, and Isobel Millicent Stirling, MA, DipPsych; *m* 1956, Eileen Gibson Powell, BA, MEd, *yr d* of William Leslie and Elsie May Powell; two *d* (and one *d* decd). *Educ:* Edinburgh Acad.; Univ. of St Andrews (Harkness Exhibn; BSc; Biochem. Medal 1951); Univ. of London (PhD, DSc). FRSC, CChem 1967. Civil Service Jun. Res. Fellowship, Porton, 1955, Sen. Fellowship, 1956; ICI Fellowship, Univ. of Edinburgh, 1957; Lectr, QUB, 1959; Reader in Org. Chem., KCL, 1965; University of Wales, Bangor: Prof. of Organic Chemistry, 1969–81; Dean of Faculty of Science, 1977–79; Hd of Dept of Chemistry, 1981–90; Sheffield University: Hd, Dept of Chemistry, 1991–94; Dir, Engrg and Physical Scis Div., Grad. Sch., 1994–97; Public Orator, 1995–. Vis. Prof., Hebrew Univ. of Jerusalem, 1981; Vis. Fellow, ANU, Canberra, 1999. Royal Instn Christmas Lects, BBC TV, 1992. Mem., IUPAC Commn on Physical Organic Chemistry, 1992–95. Mem., Perkin Council, RSC, 1971–93 (Vice-Pres., 1985–88 and 1991–93, Pres., 1989–91); Pres., Section B (Chemistry), BAAS, 1990; Pres., Yorks and Humberside Sect., ASE, 1993–95. Hon. Mem., Società Chimica Italiana, 2002. Hon. Fellow, Univ. of Wales, Bangor, 2004. Hon. DSc: St Andrews, 1994; Aix-Marseille, 1999; Sheffield, 2007. Award for Organic Reaction Mechanisms, RSC, 1988; Millennium Commn Award, 1999. *Publications:* Radicals in Organic Chemistry, 1965; (ed) Organic Sulphur Chemistry, 1975; (ed) The Chemistry of the Sulphonium Group, 1981; (ed) The Chemistry of Sulphones and Sulphoxides, 1988; numerous res. papers mainly in Jls of RSC. *Recreations:* choral music, the collection of chiral objects, furniture restoration. *Address:* Department of Chemistry, University of Sheffield, Sheffield S3 7HF. *T:* (0114) 222 9453; 114 Westbourne Road, Sheffield S10 2QT.

See also Sir A. J. D. Stirling.

STIRLING, James; *see* Stirling, W. J.

STIRLING of Garden, Col Sir James, KCVO 2006; CBE 1987; TD; FRICS; Lord-Lieutenant of Stirling and Falkirk, 1983–2005; *b* 8 Sept. 1930; *s* of Col Archibald Stirling of Garden, OBE; *m* 1958, Fiona Janetta Sophia Wood Parker; two *s* two *d*. *Educ:* Rugby; Trinity Coll., Cambridge (BA; Dip. Estate Mgt). Commnd Argyll and Sutherland Highlanders, 1950; served in Korea, wounded; transf. 7th Bn TA, comd 1965–67, 3rd Bn, 1967–68. Chartered Surveyor in private practice. Partner, K. Ryden and Partners, Chartered Surveyors, 1962–89. Director: Local Bd, Scotland and N Ireland, Woolwich Building Soc., 1973–97; Scottish Widows and Life Insurance Fund, 1975–96. Hon. Sheriff, Stirling, 1998. DL 1970, Vice-Lieutenant 1979–83, Stirling. Hon. Guild Brother, Stirling Guildry, 1996. Chm., Highland TAVR Assoc., 1982–87 (Pres., 1992). Hon. Col, 3/51st Highland Volunteers, TA, 1979–86. DUniv Stirling, 2004. GCStJ 2005 (KStJ 1987; Prior, Order of St John, Scotland, 1995–). *Address:* Garden, Buchlyvie, Stirlingshire FK8 3NR. *T:* (01360) 850212. *Club:* New (Edinburgh).

STIRLING, John Fullarton; JP; Librarian, University of Exeter, 1972–94; *b* 12 April 1931; *s* of Reginald Stirling and Jeanette Sybil (*née* Fullarton); *m* 1960, Sheila Mary Fane; two *d*. *Educ:* Waterloo Grammar sch.; Univ. of Liverpool (BA 1st Cl. Hons 1953; MA 1962). Asst, Liverpool Public Libraries, 1953–56; Asst Librarian, UCL, 1956–62; Sub-librarian, 1962–64, Dep. Librarian, 1964–66, Univ. of York; Librarian, Univ. of Stirling, 1966–71; Librarian designate, Univ. of Exeter, 1971–72. Member: various cttees, SCONUL, 1977–; UGC Working Gp on Liby Automation, 1986; British Liby Cttee for Bibliographic Services, 1987. JP Exeter, 1976. *Publications:* (ed) University Librarianship, 1981; contrib. various professional jls. *Address:* c/o Devon and Exeter Institution, 7 Cathedral Close, EX1 1EZ. *T:* (01392) 274727. *Club:* Devon and Exeter Institution (Chm., 2001–04) (Exeter).

STIRLING, Prof. (William) James, CBE 2006; PhD; FRS 1999; Jacksonian Professor of Natural Philosophy, University of Cambridge, since 2008; *b* 4 Feb. 1953; *s* of late John Easton Stirling and of Margaret Eleanor Stirling (*née* Norris); *m* 1975, Paula Helene Close; one *s* one *d*. *Educ:* Belfast Royal Acad.; Peterhouse, Cambridge (MA, PhD 1979). CPhys, FInstP 1992. Res. Associate, Univ. of Washington, 1979–81; Res. Fellow, Peterhouse, 1981–83; Fellow and Staff Mem., CERN, Geneva, 1983–86; University of Durham: Lectr, 1986–89, Sen. Lectr, 1989–90, Reader, 1990–92, Prof., 1992–2008, Depts of Math. Scis and Physics; Dir, Inst. for Particle Physics Phenomenology, 2000–05; Pro-Vice-Chancellor (Res.), 2005–08. SERC and PPARC Sen. Fellow, 1993–98. Chm., Sci. Cttee, PPARC, 2001–03. Mem. Council, Royal Soc., 2007–08. Gov., Royal Grammar Sch., Newcastle, 1996–2005. Humboldt Res. Award, 1997. *Publications:* (jtly) QCD and Collider Physics, 1996; numerous articles on elementary particle theory in learned jls. *Recreations:* playing and listening to Irish music, outdoor activities. *Address:* Department of Physics, University of Cambridge, Cavendish Laboratory, J J Thomson Avenue, Cambridge CB3 0HE. *T:* (01223) 337200.

STIRLING-HAMILTON, Sir Malcolm William Bruce, 14th Bt *cr* 1673 (NS), of Preston, Haddingtonshire; *b* 6 Aug. 1979; *s* of Sir Bruce Stirling-Hamilton, 13th Bt and of Stephanie (who *m* 1990, Anthony Tinsley), *d* of Dr William Campbell, LRCP, LRCS; *S* father, 1989. *Educ:* Stowe. *Heir: cousin* Rev. Andrew Robert Hamilton [*b* 5 Sept. 1937; *m* 1972, Josephine Mary, *d* of Reginald Sargant].

STIRRAT, Prof. Gordon Macmillan, MA, MD; FRCOG; Fellow, Institute for Advanced Studies, University of Bristol, since 2003 (Vice-Provost, 1999–2003); Senior Research Fellow, Centre for Ethics in Medicine, since 2000; Professor of Obstetrics and Gynaecology, University of Bristol, 1982–2000, now Emeritus; *b* 12 March 1940; *s* of Alexander and Caroline Mary Stirrat; *m* 1965, Janeen Mary (*née* Brown); three *d*. *Educ:* Hutcheson's Boys' Grammar Sch., Glasgow; Glasgow Univ. (MB, ChB); MA Oxon, MD London. FRCOG 1981. Jun. hosp. doctor appts, Glasgow and environs, and London, 1964–71; Lectr, St Mary's Hosp. Med. Sch., London, 1971–75; Clinical Reader, Univ. of Oxford, 1975–81; Dean, Faculty of Medicine, 1990–93, Pro-Vice-Chancellor, 1993–97, Univ. of Bristol. Dep. Chm., Bristol and Dist HA, 1991–96. Member: Acad. of Experts, 1996–2004 (Fellow, 2004–); Expert Witness Inst., 1997–2006. Chm., House of Laity, Bristol Dio., 2003–. Lay Canon, Bristol Cathedral, 2008–. *Publications:* Legalised Abortion: the continuing dilemma, 1979; Obstetrics Pocket Consultant, 1981, 2nd edn 1986; Aids to Reproductive Biology, 1982; (jtly) You and Your Baby—a Mother's Guide to Health, 1982; Aids to Obstetrics and Gynaecology, 1983, 4th edn 1996; (jtly) The Immune System in Disease, 1992; (jtly) Handbook of Obstetric Management, 1996; (jtly) Notes on Obstetrics and Gynaecology, 2002. *Recreations:* fly-fishing, walking, photography. *Address:* Malpas Lodge, 24 Henbury Road, Westbury-on-Trym, Bristol BS9 3HJ. *T:* (0117) 950 5310.

STIRRUP, Air Chief Marshal Sir Graham Eric, (Sir Jock), GCB 2005 (KCB 2002; CB 2000); AFC 1983; FRAeS; Chief of the Defence Staff, since 2006; Air Aide-de-Camp to the Queen, since 2003; *b* 4 Dec. 1949; *s* of William Hamilton Stirrup and Jacqueline Brenda Stirrup (*née* Coulson); *m* 1976, Mary Alexandra Elliott; one *s*. *Educ:* Merchant Taylors' Sch., Northwood; Royal Air Force Coll., Cranwell. Qualified Flying Instr, 1971–73; Loan Service, Sultan of Oman's Air Force, 1973–75; Fighter Reconnaissance Pilot, 1976–78; Exchange Pilot, USAF, 1978–81; Flt Comdr, 1982–84; OC No II (Army Co-operation) Sqn, 1985–87; PSO to CAS, 1987–90; OC RAF Marham, 1990–92; rcds, 1993; Dir, Air Force Plans and Progs, MoD, 1994–97; AOC No 1 Gp, 1997–98; ACAS, 1998–2000; Dep. C-in-C, Strike Comd, Comdr NATO Combined Air Ops Centre 9, and Dir European Air Gp, 2000–02; Dep. Chief of Defence Staff (Equipment Capability), MoD, 2002–03; Chief of Air Staff, MoD, 2003–06. FCMI (FIMgt 1983); FRAeS 1991. Hon. DSc Cranfield, 2005. *Recreations:* golf, music, theatre, history. *Clubs:* Royal Air Force, Royal Commonwealth Society.

STIRTON, Prof. Charles Howard, PhD; FLS; futurist, writer; *b* 25 Nov. 1946; *s* of Charles Aubrey and Elizabeth Maud Stirton; *m* 1979, Jana Žantovská; one *d*. *Educ:* Univ. of Natal (BSc, BSc Hons, MSc); Univ. of Cape Town (PhD 1989). Botanist, Botanical Res. Inst., Pretoria, 1975–82; S African Liaison Botanist, 1979–82, B. A. Krukoff Botanist for Neotropical Legumes, 1982–87, Royal Botanic Gardens, Kew; Associate Prof., Univ. of Natal, Pietermaritzburg, 1988–90; self-employed, 1990; economic botanist, 1990–92, Dep. Dir, and Dir, Sci. and Horticulture, 1992–96, Royal Botanic Gardens, Kew; Dir, Nat. Botanic Gdn of Wales, 1996–2002. Chm., Contextua, 2002–05. Vis. Prof., Univ. of Reading, 1993–96; Hon. Prof., Univ. of Wales, 1997–; Hon. Res. Associate, Univ. of Cape Town, 2008–. Trustee, Gateway Gardens Trust, 2003–. Mentor, Mellon Foundn, 2008–. Founding Trustee, Ourobos Res. and Educn Trust. FLS 1975. Hon. DSc Glamorgan, 2001. *Publications:* (ed) Plant Invaders: beautiful but dangerous, 1978; (ed with J. Zarucchi) Advances in Legume Biology, 1990; (ed) Advances in Legume Systematics 3, 1987; (ed) The Changing World of Weeds, 1995; contrib. numerous scientific papers. *Recreations:* gardening, reading, postal history, postcards, cinema. *Address:* e-mail: chstirton@tiscali.co.uk.

STITT, (Thomas) Clive Somerville; HM Diplomatic Service; a Director, Strategy and Communications Group, UK Trade & Investment (formerly Director, Export Services Section, Central Services Group, British Trade International), 1999; *b* 1 Jan. 1948; *m* 1977, Margaret Ann Milward; two *d*. FCO, 1970; Kabul, 1972; Third, then Second, Sec., New Delhi, 1974; First Sec., FCO, 1977; UK Mission to UN, Geneva, 1982; First Sec., then Counsellor, FCO, 1986; Counsellor, UK Mission to UN, NY, 1992–95; Overseas Inspector, Mgt Consultancy and Inspection Dept, FCO, 1996–99.

STOATE, Dr Howard Geoffrey Alvan, FRCGP; MP (Lab) Dartford, since 1997; *b* 14 April 1954; *s* of Alvan Stoate and Maisie Stoate (*née* Russell); *m* 1979, Deborah Jane Dunkerley; two *s*. *Educ:* Kingston Grammar Sch.; King's Coll., London (MB BS 1977; MSc 1989). DRCOG 1981; FRCGP 1994. GP training, Joyce Green Hosp., Dartford, 1978–81; gen. med. practice, Albion Surgery, Bexleyheath, 1982–; GP Tutor, Queen Mary's Hosp., Sidcup, 1989–2006; Chm., Local Res. Ethics Cttee, Bexley HA, 1995–97; Vice-Chm., Regl Graduate Educn Bd, South Thames, 1997–99. Mem. (Lab) Dartford BC, 1990–99 (Chm., Finance and Corporate Business Cttee, 1996–99); Vice Pres., Dartford Racial Equality Council. PPS to Minister of State for Crime Reduction, Policy and Community Safety, Home Office, 2001–03; PPS to Minister for the Arts, 2003–05. Mem., Health Select Cttee, 1997–2001 and 2005–; Co-Chairman: All Party Parly Gp on Primary Care and Public Health, 1998–; All Party Parly Gp on Obesity, 2002–; Chairman: All Party Pharmacy Gp, 2000–; All Party Gp on Men's Health, 2001–. Mem. Assembly, Univ. of Greenwich, 1997–. *Recreations:* running, sailing, travelling, reading, car building. *Address:* House of Commons, SW1A 0AA. *Club:* Emsworth Sailing.

STOATE, Isabel Dorothy; HM Diplomatic Service, retired; Counsellor, Foreign and Commonwealth Office, 1980–82; *b* 31 May 1927; *d* of late William Maurice Stoate and Dorothy Evelyn Stoate (*née* French). *Educ:* Talbot Heath Sch., Bournemouth; St Andrews Univ. Athlone Press, London Univ., 1950–52; joined HM Diplomatic Service, 1952; served Cyprus, Vienna, Buenos Aires, Tokyo, Athens, Rio de Janeiro and FCO, 1952–80. *Recreations:* travel, tapestry. *Address:* 177 Gloucester Street, Cirencester, Glos GL7 2DP.

STOATE, Jane Elizabeth; *see* Davidson, J. E.

STOBART, John; a District Judge (Magistrates' Courts), since 2004; *b* 6 May 1948; *s* of Joe and Jean Stobart; *m* 2001, Tracey Kirwin. *Educ:* Birmingham Univ. (LLB Hons 1971); Inns of Court Sch. of Law. Called to the Bar, Gray's Inn, 1974; in practice as barrister, specialising in crime, 1974–2004; a Dep. Dist Judge, 1999–2004. *Recreations:* golf, ski-ing, sailing, drinking and eating. *Address:* c/o Nottingham Magistrates' Court, Carrington Street, Nottingham NG2 1EE. *T:* (0115) 958 8111, ext. 233; *e-mail:* jstobart@lix.co.uk.

STOCK, Francine Elizabeth; writer and broadcaster; *b* 14 March 1958; *d* of John Hubert Stock and Jean Anne Stock (*née* Mallet); *m* 1987, Robert Lance Hughes; two *d*. *Educ:* St Catherine's, Bramley; Jesus Coll., Oxford (BA Hons Modern Langs; Hon. Fellow, 2007). Journalist, Petroleum Economist, 1980–82; joined BBC, 1983: Producer, The World at One, 1983–85; reporter: Money Prog., 1986–87; and Presenter, Newsnight, 1988–93; Presenter: Europe on the Brink series, 1993; Money Prog., 1995–96; Antiques Show, 1997–98; Front Row, 1998–2004; The Film Programme, 2004–. Film Critic, The Tablet, 2008–. Chair, Tate Members' Council, 2005–; a Judge, Man Booker Prize, 2003; Chair of Judges: Nat. Short Story Prize, 2006; Gulbenkian Prize for Mus and Galls, 2007. *Publications:* A Foreign Country, 1999; Man-Made Fibre, 2002. *Address:* c/o Aitken Alexander Associates, 18–21 Cavaye Place, SW10 9PT.

STOCK, Very Rev. Victor Andrew, OAM 2002; Dean of Guildford, since 2002; *b* 24 Dec. 1944; *s* of Arthur and Violet Stock. *Educ:* Christopher Wren Sch.; King's Coll., London (AKC 1968); St Boniface Coll., Warminster. Ordained deacon, 1969, priest, 1970; Curate, Pinner, 1969–73; Resident Chaplain, London Univ. Church of Christ the King, Gordon Sq., 1973–79; Rector: Friern Barnet, 1979–86; St Mary le Bow, City of London, 1986–2002. Chaplain, UK/Europe Gp, Order of Australia Assoc., 1988–. FRSA 1995. *Publication:* Taking Stock: confessions of a city priest (autobiog.), 2001. *Recreations:* gardening, London, travel, politics, broadcasting. *Address:* The Deanery, 1 Cathedral Close, Guildford GU2 7TL. *T:* (01483) 560328. *Clubs:* Reform; Guildford County.

STOCK, Rt Rev. (William) Nigel; *see* St Edmundsbury and Ipswich, Bishop of.

STOCK-NORMAN, Gailene Patricia, AM 1997; Director, Royal Ballet School, since 1999; *b* 28 Jan. 1946; *d* of Roy Keith Stock and Sylvia May Stock; *m* 1976, Gary William Norman; one *d*. *Educ:* Convent of Mercy, Melbourne; RMIT (Grad. DipEd Visual and Performing Arts); Royal Acad. Dancing (Overseas Schol. at Royal Ballet Sch.; ARAD). Soloist and Principal Artist, Australian Ballet, 1962–74; Principal Artist: Nat. Ballet Canada, 1974–76; Royal Winnipeg Ballet, 1976–77; Australian Ballet, 1977–78; Dir, Nat. Ballet Sch., Vic, Australia, 1979–85; Lectr in Classical Dance, Vic Coll. of Arts, 1985–88; Administrator, Nat. Ballet Sch., Vic, 1988–90; Dir, Australian Ballet Sch., 1990–98. *Recreations:* reading, gardening, travelling, welfare of animals. *Address:* Royal Ballet School, 46 Floral Street, Covent Garden, WC2E 9DA. *T:* (020) 7836 8899.

STOCKDALE, David Andrew; QC 1995; a Recorder, since 1993; a Deputy Judge of the High Court, Queen's Bench Division, since 2008; *b* 9 May 1951; 2nd *s* of late John Ramsden Stockdale and Jean Stewart Stockdale (*née* Shelley); *m* 1985, Melanie Jane, *e d* of late Anthony Newis Benson and Barbara Benson; one *s* three *d*. *Educ:* Giggleswick Sch.; Pembroke Coll., Oxford (MA Lit.Hum.). Called to the Bar, Middle Temple, 1975, Bencher, 2003; in practice on Northern Circuit, 1976– (Jun., 1978; Treas., 2008–); Asst Recorder, 1990–93. Governor: Giggleswick Sch., 1982– (Chm. of Govs, 1997–2007);

Terra Nova Sch., 2000–08. *Recreations:* family, the outdoors, motorcycling, remote Scotland. *Address:* Deans Court Chambers, 24 St John Street, Manchester M3 4DF. *T:* (0161) 214 6000. *Club:* Sloane.

STOCKDALE, His Honour Eric; a Circuit Judge, 1972–94; *b* 8 Feb. 1929; *m* 1952, Joan (*née* Berry); two *s*. *Educ:* Collyers Sch., Horsham; London Sch. of Economics; LLB, BSc(Econ.), LLM, PhD (Lond.); MSc (Cranfield). 2nd Lieut, RA, 1947–49. Called to the Bar, Middle Temple, 1950, Bencher, 2004; practised in London and on Midland Circuit until 1972; admitted to State Bar, Calif, 1983. Mem., Supreme Court Procedure Cttee, 1982–94. Tech. Advr, Central Council of Probation Cttees, 1979–84; Vice-Pres., NACRO, 1980–94 (Mem. Council, 1970–80); President: British Soc. of Criminology, 1978–81; Soc. of English and Amer. Lawyers, 1986–89 (Chm., 1984–86). Member: Central Council for Educn and Trng in Social Work, 1984–89; Parole Board, 1985–89; Criminal Injuries Compensation Bd, 1995–2000; Criminal Injuries Compensation Appeals Panel, 1997–2005. Vis. Prof., Queen Mary and Westfield Coll., London Univ., 1989–93. Governor, 1977–89, Vis. Fellow, 1986–94, Vis. Prof., 1994–, Univ. of Hertfordshire (formerly Hatfield Poly.). Consultant Ed., Blackstone's Criminal Practice, first 16 edns, 1991–2006. Hon. LLD Hertfordshire, 1995. *Publications:* The Court and the Offender, 1967; A Study of Bedford Prison 1660–1877, 1977; Law and Order in Georgian Bedfordshire, 1982; The Probation Volunteer, 1985; (with Keith Devlin) Sentencing, 1987; (ed with Silvia Casale) Criminal Justice Under Stress, 1992; 'Tis Treason, My Good Man!, 2005; (with Randy J. Holland) Middle Temple Lawyers and the American Revolution, 2007; From Wig and Pen to Computer, 2008; The Man Who Shot the President – and other lawyers, 2008. *Address:* 20 Lyonsdown Road, New Barnet, Herts EN5 1JE. *T:* (020) 8449 7181. *Club:* Athenæum.

STOCKDALE, Sir Thomas (Minshull), 2nd Bt *cr* 1960, of Hoddington, Co. Southampton; barrister; *b* 7 Jan. 1940; *s* of Sir Edmund Villiers Minshull Stockdale, 1st Bt and Hon. Louise Fermor-Hesketh (*d* 1994), *er d* of 1st Lord Hesketh; *S* father, 1989; *m* 1965, Jacqueline Ha-Van-Vuong; one *s* one *d*. *Educ:* Eton; Worcester Coll., Oxford (MA). Called to Bar, Inner Temple, 1966; Bencher, Lincoln's Inn, 1994. *Recreations:* shooting, travel. *Heir: s* John Minshull Stockdale, *b* 13 Dec. 1967. *Address:* Manor Farm, Weston Patrick, Basingstoke, Hants RG25 2NT; 73 Alderney Street, SW1V 4HH. *Clubs:* Turf, MCC.

STOCKEN, Oliver Henry James; Chairman: Rutland Trust, 1999–2007; Home Retail Group, since 2006; *b* 22 Dec. 1941; *s* of late Henry Edmund West Stocken and Sheila Guiscard Stocken (*née* Steele); *m* 1967, Sally Forbes Dishon; two *s* one *d*. *Educ:* Felsted Sch.; University Coll., Oxford (BA). FCA 1978. Director: N M Rothschild & Sons Limited, 1968–77; Esperanza Trade & Transport, 1977–79; Barclays Merchant Bank, 1979–81; Man. Dir, Barclays Australia, 1982–84; Finance Director: BZW, 1985–93; Barclays plc, 1993–99. Non-executive Director: Steel Burrill Jones Group plc, 1992–96; MEPC plc, 1995–2000; Pilkington plc, 1998–2006; Rank plc, 1998–2006; Bunzl plc, 1998–2000; 3i Group plc, 1999– (Dep. Chm., 2002–); Novar plc, 2000–05; GUS plc, 2000–06; Stanhope plc, 2000– (Chm.); Standard Chartered Bank plc, 2004–. Chairman: Lupus Capital plc, 1999–2002; Oval Insurance Gp, 2006–. Trustee: Natural Hist. Mus., 1999– (Chm., 2006–); Henley River and Rowing Mus., 2002–. Mem. Council, RCA, 1998–2007 (Treas., 2002–07). Chairman, Trustees: Children's Leukaemia Trust, 1993–2002; Devas Club, 1997–2004. Gov., Felsted Sch., 2008–. *Recreations:* running, Rugby, cricket. *Address:* 25c Marryat Road, Wimbledon, SW19 5BB. *Clubs:* Brooks's, Garrick, MCC (Mem. Cttee, 1998–, Treas., 2000–06, Trustee, 2007–); Australian (Sydney).

STOCKER, Diane Louise; *see* Corner, D. L.

STOCKER, John Wilcox, AO 1999; PhD; FRACP; Principal, Foursight Associates Pty Ltd, since 1996; Chairman, Sigma Co. Ltd, since 1999; *b* 23 April 1945; *s* of W. R. Stocker and Gladys Noelle Davies; *m* 1973, Joanne Elizabeth Gross; two *d*. *Educ:* Wesley Coll., Univ. of Melbourne (MB BS BMedSc). FTS. RMO, Royal Melbourne Hosp., 1970–72; Res. Scientist, Walter & Eliza Hall Inst. of Med. Res., 1974–76; Mem., Basel Inst. of Immunology, 1976–78; Central Res. Unit, 1979–84; Dir, Pharm. Res., Hoffman-La Roche & Co., Basel, 1986–87; Dir, Vic. Govt Strategic Res. Foundn, 1988–93; Chief Exec., CSIRO, 1990–95; Govt Chief Scientist, Australia, 1996–99. Founding Man. Dir, AMRAD, 1987–90; Director: Gene Shears Pty, 1992–96; Cambridge Antibody Technology Ltd, 1995–2006; Telstra Corp., 1996–; Circadian Technologies Pty Ltd, 1996–; Rothschild Bioscience Managers Ltd, 1996–98; Nufarm Ltd, 1998–. Chairman: Australian Sci. Technol. and Engrg Council, 1997–98; Grape and Wine R&D Corp., 1997–2004; Mem., numerous Industry and Govt sci. orgns. Centenary Medal, Australia, 2003. *Publications:* scientific papers, contribs to learned jls. *Recreations:* tennis, tiling, viticulture, reading. *Address:* Foursight Associates Pty Ltd, Level 15, 1 Nicholson Street, Melbourne, Vic 3000, Australia. *Club:* Winzergenossenschaft zur Landskron (Switzerland).

STOCKING, Dame Barbara Mary, (Dame Barbara MacInnes), DBE 2008 (CBE 2000); Director, Oxfam, since 2001; *b* 28 July 1951; *d* of Percy Frederick Stocking and Mary Stocking; *m* 1981, Dr R. John MacInnes; two *s*. *Educ:* New Hall, Cambridge (BA); Univ. of Wisconsin (MS). Teaching Asst, Dept of Physiology and Biophysics, Univ. of Illinois, 1972–73; Staff Associate, Nat. Acad. of Scis, Washington, 1974–76; Jt Research Fellow, Nuffield Provincial Hosps Trust and Centre for Med. Res., Univ. of Sussex, 1977–79; Sec., WHO Independent Commn on Long Term Prospects of Onchocerciasis Control Programme, LSHTM, 1979–91; Fellow in Health Policy, Innovation and Evaluation, King's Fund Coll., 1983–86; Dir, King's Fund Centre for Health Services Develt, 1987–93; Chief Executive: Oxford RHA, 1993–94; Anglia and Oxford RHA, 1994–96; Regl Dir, Anglia and Oxford, 1994–98, South East, 1999–2000, NHS Exec., DoH; Dir, NHS Modernisation Agency, 2000–01 (on secondment). Chair: NHS Patient Partnership Steering Gp, 1993–98; NHS Resource Allocation Gp, 1995–97. Member: UK Harkness Fellowships Adv. and Selection Cttee, 1989–95; NHS Central R&D Cttee, 1992–96. Member: UN Inter Agency Standing Cttee for Humanitarian Response, 2006–; Founder Bd High Level Panel on delivering Millennium Develt Goals, FAO, 2006–; Founder Bd Mem., Global Humanitarian Forum, 2007–. Hon. DSc: Luton, 1998; Oxford Brookes, 1999; Loughborough, 2003. *Publications:* (jtly) The Image and the Reality: a case study of the impacts of medical technology, 1978; Initiative and Inertia: case studies in the health services, 1985; (ed) Expensive Medical Technologies, 1988; (Series Editor) A Study of the Diffusion of Medical Technology in Europe, 3 vols, 1991; (jtly) Criteria for Change, 1991; Medical Advances: the future shape of acute services, 1991. *Recreations:* music, family.

STOCKPORT, Bishop Suffragan of, since 2008; **Rt Rev. Robert Ronald Atwell;** *b* Ilford, Essex, 3 Aug. 1954; *s* of Ronald Victor Atwell and Marcia Blanche Atwell (*née* Newton). *Educ:* Wanstead High Sch.; St John's Coll., Durham Univ. (BA 1975; MLitt 1979); Westcott House, Cambridge; Venerable English Coll., Rome. Ordained deacon, 1978, priest, 1979; Asst Curate, John Keble, Mill Hill, 1978–81; Chaplain, Trinity Coll., Cambridge, 1981–87; Benedictine Monk, Burford Priory, 1987–98; Vicar, St Mary-the-Virgin, Primrose Hill, 1998–2008. *Publications:* Celebrating the Saints, 1998, enlarged edn, 2004; Celebrating the Seasons, 1998; Gift: 100 readings – celebration of birth and parenthood, 2005; Love: 100 readings – celebration of marriage and love, 2005; Remember: 100 readings for those in grief and bereavement, 2005. *Recreations:* theatre, gardening, hill-walking. *Address:* Bishop's Lodge, Back Lane, Dunham Town, nr Altrincham, Cheshire WA14 4SG. *T:* (0161) 928 5611; *e-mail:* bpstockport@chester.anglican.org.

STOCKTON, 2nd Earl of, *cr* 1984; **Alexander Daniel Alan Macmillan;** Viscount Macmillan of Ovenden, 1984; *b* Oswestry, Shropshire, 10 Oct. 1943; *s* of Viscount Macmillan of Ovenden, PC, MP (*d* 1984) and of Katharine Viscountess Macmillan of Ovenden, DBE; *S* grandfather, 1986; *m* 1st, 1970, Hélène Birgitte Hamilton (marr. diss. 1991); one *s* two *d*; 2nd, 1995, Miranda Elizabeth Louise, Lady Nuttall, *d* of Richard Quarry and Diana, Lady Mancroft. *Educ:* Eton; Université de Paris, Strathclyde Univ. FRICS 1999. Contested (C) Bristol, EP elecns, 1994; MEP (C) SW Region, England, 1999–2004. FRSA 1987. Liveryman: Worshipful Co. of Merchant Taylors, 1972 (Mem., Ct of Assts, 1987–; Master, 1992–93); Worshipful Co. of Stationers and Newspaper Makers, 1973 (Mem., Ct of Assts, 1996–2008). DUniv Strathclyde, 1993; Hon. DLitt: De Montfort, 1993; Westminster, 1995; London Inst., 2003. *Heir: s* Viscount Macmillan of Ovenden, *qv*. *Address:* Flat M, 9 Warwick Square, SW1V 2AA. *T:* (020) 7834 6004; Avenue Jules César, 1150 Brussels, Belgium. *T:* (786) 0461497. *Clubs:* Beefsteak, Pratt's, White's.

STOCKWIN, Prof. (James) Arthur (Ainscow); Nissan Professor of Modern Japanese Studies, and Director of Nissan Institute of Japanese Studies, University of Oxford, 1982–2003; Fellow, St Antony's College, Oxford, 1982–2003, now Emeritus (Sub-Warden, 1999–2001); *b* 28 Nov. 1935; *s* of Wilfred Arthur Stockwin and Edith Mary Stockwin; *m* 1960, Audrey Lucretia Hobson Stockwin (*née* Wood); one *s* two *d* (and one *s* decd). *Educ:* Exeter Coll., Oxford Univ. (MA); Australian Nat. Univ. (PhD). Australian National University: Lectr, Dept of Political Science, 1964–66; Sen. Lectr, 1966–72; Reader, 1972–81. Pres., British Assoc. of Japanese Studies, 1994–95. Gen. Ed., Nissan Inst.—Routledge Japanese Studies Series, 1984–. *Publications:* The Japanese Socialist Party and Neutralism, 1968; (ed) Japan and Australia in the Seventies, 1972; Japan, Divided Politics in a Growth Economy, 1975, 2nd edn 1982; Why Japan Matters, 1983; (jtly, also ed) Dynamic and Immobilist Politics in Japan, 1988; (trans.) Junji Banno, The Establishment of the Japanese Constitutional System, 1992; The Story of Tim, 1993; (ed jtly) The Vitality of Japan: sources of national strength and weakness, 1997; Governing Japan, 1999, new edn 2007; Dictionary of the Modern Politics of Japan, 2003; Collected Writings of J. A. A. Stockwin, Part I, 2004; Thirty-Odd Feet Below Belgium: an affair of letters in the Great War 1915–1916, 2005; articles, largely on Japanese politics and foreign policy, in Pacific Affairs, Aust. Outlook, Aust. Jl Politics and History, Asian Survey, Asia-Pacific Review, Japan Forum, etc. *Recreations:* languages, exercise. *Address:* Glym Cottage, Glympton Road, Wootton, Woodstock, Oxon OX20 1EL.

STODDART, family name of **Baron Stoddart of Swindon**.

STODDART OF SWINDON, Baron *cr* 1983 (Life Peer), of Reading in the Royal County of Berkshire; **David Leonard Stoddart;** *b* 4 May 1926; *s* of Arthur Leonard Stoddart, coal miner, and Queenie Victoria Stoddart (*née* Price); *m* 1961, Jennifer Percival-Alwyn; two *s* (one *d* by previous marr.). *Educ:* elementary; St Clement Danes and Henley Grammar Schools. Youth in training, PO Telephones, 1942–44; business on own account, 1944–46; Railway Clerk, 1947–49; Hospital Clerk, 1949–51; Power Station Clerical Worker, 1951–70. Joined Labour Party, 1947; Reading County Borough Council: Member, 1954–72; served at various times as Chairman of Housing, Transport and Finance Cttees; Leader, Labour Group of Councillors, 1962–70; Leader of Council, 1967–72. Contested (Lab) Newbury, 1959 and 1964, Swindon, 1969, 1983. MP (Lab) Swindon, 1970–83; PPS to Minister for Housing and Construction, 1974–75; an Asst Govt Whip, 1975; a Lord Comr, HM Treasury, 1976–77; an opposition whip, and opposition spokesman on energy, House of Lords, 1983–88. Chairman: Campaign for an Indep. Britain, 1985–2007; Alliance Against the European Constitution (formerly Anti-Maastricht Alliance), 1992–2007; Global Britain, 1998–. *Recreations:* gardening, music. *Address:* Sintra, 37A Bath Road, Reading, Berks RG1 6HL. *T:* (0118) 957 6726.

STODDART, Anne Elizabeth, CMG 1996; HM Diplomatic Service, retired; Deputy Permanent Representative (Economic Affairs), UK Mission to the United Nations, Geneva, 1991–96; *b* 29 March 1937; *d* of late James Stoddart and Ann Jack Stoddart (*née* Inglis). *Educ:* Kirby Grammar School, Middlesbrough; Somerville College, Oxford. MA. Entered Foreign Office, 1960; British Military Govt, Berlin, 1963–67; FCO, 1967–70; First Secretary (Economic), Ankara, 1970–73; Head of Chancery, Colombo, 1974–76; FCO, 1977–81; Dep. Permanent UK Rep. to Council of Europe, Strasbourg, 1981–87; seconded to External Eur. Policy Div., DTI, 1987–91. *Address:* Flat 1, 63 The Avenue, Richmond, Surrey TW9 2AH.

STODDART, Caroline Ann Tuke; *see* Malone, C. A. T.

STODDART, Charles Norman, PhD; Sheriff of Lothian and Borders at Edinburgh, since 1995; *b* 4 April 1948; *s* of Robert Stoddart and Margaret (*née* Allenby); *m* 1981, Anne Lees; one *d*. *Educ:* Edinburgh Univ. (LLB, PhD); McGill Univ. (LLM). Admitted Solicitor, 1972, practised, 1972–73, 1980–88; Lectr in Scots Law, Edinburgh Univ., 1973–80; Sheriff of N Strathclyde at Paisley, 1988–95. Dir, Judicial Studies in Scotland, 1997–2000. Member: Maclean Cttee on Serious, Violent and Sexual Offenders, 1999–2000; Sentencing Commn for Scotland, 2003–06; Civil Courts Rev. Policy Gp, 2007–. Editor, Green's Criminal Law Bulletin, 1992–. *Publications:* (with H. Neilson) The Law and Practice of Legal Aid in Scotland, 1979, 4th edn 1994; (with C. H. W. Gane and J. Chalmers) A Casebook on Scottish Criminal Law, 1980, 4th edn 2008; Bible John (crime documentary), 1980; (with C. H. W. Gane) Cases and Materials on Scottish Criminal Procedure, 1983, 2nd edn 1994; Criminal Warrants, 1991, 2nd edn 1999; contribs to professional jls. *Recreations:* music, foreign travel. *Address:* Sheriff's Chambers, Sheriff Court House, 27 Chambers Street, Edinburgh EH1 1LB. *T:* (0131) 225 2525.

STODDART, Christopher West; Chief Executive Officer, ATR plc (formerly Go Racing), 2001–03; *b* 10 April 1950; *s* of Dr Ian West Stoddart and Bridget Stoddart (*née* Pilditch); *m* 1st, 1972, Deborah Ounsted (marr. diss. 1984); 2nd, 1985, Dr Hazel Grasmere, *d* of Hon. Robert and Evelyn Grasmere, USA. *Educ:* Winchester Coll.; Churchill Coll., Cambridge (BA Hons 1971). Joined CS, 1971; DoE, 1971–75; Research Sec., Centre for Envmtl Studies, 1976–80; Regl Companies Sec., 1980–81, Sec. 1981–82, ITCA; Tyne Tees Television: Gen. Manager, 1982–83; Dir of Resources, 1983–88; Man. Dir and Chief Exec., Satellite Information Services Ltd, 1988–92; Man. Dir, GMTV, 1992–2001. Non-exec. Dir, Sterling Publishing Gp, 1999–2001. Chm., Trustees, Changing Faces, 1999–2002. *Publication:* The Inner City as Testing Ground for Government-funded Research, 1980. *Recreations:* mountaineering, photography, travel.

STODDART, Sir (James) Fraser, Kt 2007; FRS 1994; CChem, FRSC; FRSE; Board of Trustees Professor of Chemistry, Northwestern University, since 2007; Kavli Professor of NanoSystems Science, University of California at Los Angeles, 2003–07, Emeritus Professor of Chemistry, 2008; *b* 24 May 1942; *s* of Thomas Fraser Stoddart and Jane Spalding Hislop Stoddart; *m* 1968, Norma Agnes Scholan (*d* 2004); two *d*. *Educ:* Melville Coll., Edinburgh; Univ. of Edinburgh (BSc 1964; PhD 1966; DSc 1980). CChem, FRSC 1978. Nat. Res. Council of Canada Post-doctoral Fellow, Queen's Univ., Canada, 1967–69; University of Sheffield: ICI Res. Fellow, subseq. Lectr in Chemistry, 1970–82; seconded to Catalysis Gp, ICI Corporate Lab., Runcorn, 1978–81; Reader in Chemistry, 1982–91; Prof. of Organic Chem., 1990–97, Hd, Sch. of Chem., 1993–97, Univ. of Birmingham; Winstein Prof. of Organic Chemistry, 1997–2003, Dir, California NanoSystems Inst., 2003–07, UCLA. Vis. Lectr, Univ. of Parana, Brazil, 1972; SRC Sen. Vis. Fellow, UCLA, 1978; Visiting Professor: Texas A&M Univ., 1980; Univ. of Messina, Italy, 1986–88; Mulhouse, France, 1987. FRSE 2008. Hon. DSc: Birmingham, 2005; Twente, 2006; Sheffield, 2008. Awards include: Internat. Izatt-Christensen in macrocyclic chem., 1993; Arthur C. Cope Schol. Award, 1999, Arthur C. Cope Award, 2008, ACS; Nagoya Gold Medal in Organic Chemistry, Nagoya Univ., Japan, 2004; Alumnus of the Year Award, Univ. of Edinburgh, 2005; Fusion Award, Univ. of Nevada, 2006; King Faisal Internat. Award in Sci. (Chemistry), King Faisal Foundn, 2007; Davy Medal, Royal Soc., 2008. Mem., various editl bds in Europe and USA. *Publications:* over 800 papers, reviews and monographs in Angewandte Chemie, Chemistry—A Europ. Jl, Jl of the American Chemical Soc. on nanoscale science and self-assembly processes. *Address:* Department of Chemistry, Northwestern University, 2145 Sheridan Road, Evanston, IL 60208–3113, USA.

STODDART, Prof. John Little, CBE 1994; PhD, DSc; FIBiol; FRAgS; Director of Research, Institute of Grassland and Environmental Research, Agricultural and Food Research Council, 1988–93; *b* 1 Oct. 1933; *s* of John Little Stoddart and Margaret Pickering Dye; *m* 1957, Wendy Dalton Leardie; one *d* (one *s* decd). *Educ:* South Shields High Sch. for Boys; University Coll., Durham (BSc Botany 1954); University of Wales, Aberystwyth (PhD 1961); Durham Univ. (DSc 1973). FIBiol 1984; ARPS 1985; FRAgS 1993. Nat. Service, RA, UK, Hong Kong and Malaya, 1954–56. Fulbright-Hays Sen. Fellow, 1966–67; Res. Associate, Mich. State Univ./Atomic Energy Commn Plant Res. Lab., 1966–67; Welsh Plant Breeding Station: Dep. Dir, 1985–87; Dir, 1987–88; Head of Plants and Soils Div., 1985–88. Hon. Prof., Sch. of Agric. and Biol Scis, Univ. of Wales, 1988–. Chm., Plant Sci. Prog. Adv. Cttee, ODA, 1995–98. Mem. Council, NIAB, 1988–93. Non-executive Director: Derwen NHS Trust (W Wales), 1994–97; Pembrokeshire & Derwen NHS Trust, 1997–2008; IGER Technologies, 2000–. Trustee, Stapledon Meml Trust, 1996–2007 (Mem., 1988–). *Publications:* scientific articles, reviews and contribs to scientific books. *Recreations:* photography (pictorial), golf. *Address:* Institute of Biological Sciences, Aberystwyth University, Aberystwyth, Ceredigion SY23 3DA. *Club:* St David's (Aberystwyth).

STODDART, John Maurice, CBE 1995; Principal and Vice-Chancellor, Sheffield Hallam University, 1992–98 (Principal, Sheffield City Polytechnic, 1983–92); *b* 18 Sept. 1938; *s* of Gordon Stoddart and May (*née* Ledder). *Educ:* Wallasey Grammar Sch.; Univ. of Reading (BA Pol Econ.). Teacher, Wallasey GS, 1960–62; Lectr, Mid Cheshire Coll. of Further Educn, 1962–64; Lectr, Enfield Coll., 1964–70; Head, Dept of Econs and Business Studies, Sheffield Polytechnic, 1970–72; Asst Dir, NE London Polytechnic, 1972–76; Dir, Hull Coll. of Higher Educn (now Univ. of Humberside), 1976–83. Dir, Sheffield Science Park Co. Ltd, 1988–96; Deputy Chairman: Northern Gen. Hosp. NHS Trust, 1999–2001; Sheffield Teaching Hosps NHS Trust, 2001–06. Chm., CNAA Cttee for Business and Management, 1985–88 (Chm., Undergrad. Courses Bd, 1976–83); Mem., CNAA, 1982–88, 1991–93; Chm., Cttee of Dirs of Polys, 1990–93 (Vice-Chm., 1988–90). Member: Sea Fisheries Trng Council, 1976–80; Architects Registration Council, UK, 1979–85; Council for Industry and Educn, 1989–94; Council for Educn and Trng in Social Work, 1989–94; BTEC, 1991–95; Chm., Higher Educn Quality Council, 1992–97. Member: Court, Univ. of Hull, 1976–83; Council, Univ. of Sheffield, 1983–92. Companion, British Business Graduates Soc., 1983; Hon. Fellow: Humberside Coll., 1983; Univ. of Bolton, 2005. FRSA 1977. CCMI (FBIM 1977; CBIM 1990). Hon. DEd CNAA, 1992; Hon. DLitt Coventry, 1993; DUniv: Middlesex, 1993; Sheffield Hallam, 1998; Hon. LLD Sheffield, 1998. *Publications:* articles on business and management educn. *Address:* 6 Tapton Park Gardens, Sheffield S10 3FP. *T:* (0114) 230 5467. *Clubs:* Reform; Leander (Henley-on-Thames).

STODDART, Sir Kenneth (Maxwell), KCVO 1989; AE 1942; JP; DL; Lord-Lieutenant, Metropolitan County of Merseyside, 1979–89; *b* 26 May 1914; *s* of late Wilfrid Bowring Stoddart and Mary Hyslop Stoddart (*née* Maxwell); *m* 1940, Jean Roberta Benson Young, DL; two *d*. *Educ:* Sedbergh; Clare Coll., Cambridge. Chairman: Cearns and Brown Ltd, 1973–84; United Mersey Supply Co. Ltd, 1978–81. Commissioned No 611 (West Lancashire) Sqdn, Auxiliary Air Force, 1936; served War, UK and Europe; comd W Lancashire Wing, Air Trng Corps, 1946–54; Vice-Chm. (Air) W Lancashire T&AFA, 1954–64. Pres., Merseyside Wing, ATC, 1991–99. Chairman, Liverpool Child Welfare Assoc., 1965–81. DL Lancashire 1958 (transf. to Metropolitan County of Merseyside, 1974); JP Liverpool 1952; High Sheriff of Merseyside, 1974. Hon. Fellow, Liverpool John Moores Univ. (formerly Liverpool Poly.), 1989. Hon. LLD Liverpool, 1986. KStJ 1979. *Recreation:* gardening. *Address:* Dunlins, 8 Hadlow Lane, Willaston, Neston CH64 2UH. *T:* (0151) 327 5183.

STODDART, Michael Craig, FCA; Chairman, Electra Investment Trust, 1986–2000; Senior Business Advisor, Fleming Family and Partners, since 2001; *b* 27 March 1932; *s* of late Frank Ogle Boyd Stoddart and Barbara (*née* Craig); *m* 1961, (Susan) Brigid (*née* O'Halloran); two *s* two *d*. *Educ:* Abberley Hall, Worcs; Marlborough Coll. Chartered Accountant 1955; joined Singer & Friedlander, 1955: resp. for opening provincial network; retired as Jt Chief Exec., 1973; Dep. Chm. and Chief Exec., Electra Investment Trust, 1974–86; pioneered into substantial unlisted investments, incl. developing venture capital arm; Chm., Electra Kingsway Gp, 1989–95. Non-executive Chairman: Britax (formerly BSC) plc, 1994–2000; Elderstreet Millennium (formerly Gartmore) Venture Capital Trust plc, 1996–2007; non-executive Director: Bullough, 1968–2002; Chesterfield Properties plc, 1997–99; Private Investors Capital Ltd, 1997–2004, and other UK cos. Underwriting Mem. of Lloyd's, 1972–96. Chm., Foundn for Entrepreneurial Mgt, London Business Sch., 1997–2004. (Mem., Develt Bd); Mem. Bd, Britech Foundn Ltd, 1999–2002. *Recreations:* country pursuits, shooting, golf, theatre. *Address:* Fleming Family and Partners, Ely House, 37 Dover Street, W1S 4NJ; Compton House, Kinver, Worcs DY7 5LY; 27 Crown Reach, 145 Grosvenor Road, SW1V 3JU. *Clubs:* Boodle's, Pratt's.

STODDART, Dr Simon Kenneth Fladgate, FSA; Fellow, Magdalene College, Cambridge, since 1998; Senior Lecturer, University of Cambridge, since 2000; *b* 8 Nov. 1958; *s* of Kenneth Bowring Stoddart and Daphne Elizabeth Fladgate (*née* Hughes); *m* 1983, Dr Caroline Ann Tuke Malone, *qv*; two *d*. *Educ:* Winchester Coll.; Magdalene Coll., Cambridge (BA 1980; PhD 1987); Univ. of Michigan (MA 1983). FSA 1994. Rome Schol. in Archaeol., British Sch. at Rome, 1980–81; Power Schol., Univ. of Michigan, 1981–83; Res. Fellow, Magdalene Coll., Cambridge, 1986–89; Lecturer: Univ. of York, 1988–90; Univ. of Bristol, 1990–94 (Sen. Lectr, 1994–96); Univ. of Cambridge, 1996–2000. Ed., Antiquity, 2001–02. Charter Fellow, Wolfson Coll., Oxford, 1992–93; Balsdon Fellow, British Sch. at Rome, 2004; Res. Associate Prof., State Univ. of NY, 2004–06. MIFA 1987. *Publications:* (ed with C. Malone) Papers in Italian Archaeology, Vols 1–4, 1985; (with N. Spivey) Etruscan Italy, 1990; (ed with C. Mathers) Development and Decline in the Mediterranean Bronze Age, 1994; (ed with C. Malone) Territory, Time and State: the archaeological development of the Gubbio Basin, 1994; (ed) Landscapes from Antiquity, 2000; (ed with G. Carr) Celts from Antiquity, 2002; (ed with G. Malone) Mortuary Ritual in Prehistoric Malta, 2008; An Historical Dictionary of the Etruscans, 2008; contrib. acad. articles. *Recreations:* walking, travel, cycling, recycling. *Address:* Magdalene College, Cambridge CB3 0AG. *T:* (01223) 332168.

STODDART, Thomas; photo-journalist; *b* 28 Nov. 1953; *s* of Tommy and Kathleen Stoddart. *Educ:* Seahouses Secondary Sch., Northumberland. Freelance photographer working on humanitarian issues, such as the siege of Sarajevo, 1992–97, Sudan famine, and AIDS catastrophe in Sub-Saharan Africa, for internat. magazines, incl. Time, Newsweek, Stern, and Sunday Times Mag. Member: RPS; RGS. *Publications:* Sarajevo, 1998; A Day in the Life of Africa, 2002. *Recreations:* lifelong fan of Newcastle United, watching sport, photography, enjoying good food, friends and wine. *Address:* 13 Tradewinds Court, Asher Way, E1W 2JB; *e-mail:* tom@tomstoddart.com.

STOICHEFF, Prof. Boris Peter, OC 1982; FRS 1975; FRSC 1965; Professor of Physics, 1964–89, now Emeritus, and University Professor, 1977–89, now Emeritus, University of Toronto; *b* 1 June 1924; *s* of Peter and Vasilka Stoicheff; *m* 1954, Lillian Joan Ambridge; one *s*. *Educ:* Univ. of Toronto, Faculty of Applied Science and Engineering (BASc), Dept of Physics (MA, PhD). McKee-Gilchrist Fellowship, Univ. of Toronto, 1950–51; National Research Council of Canada: Fellowship, Ottawa, 1952–53; Res. Officer in Div. of Pure Physics, 1953–64; Mem. Council, 1978–83. Exec. Dir, Ontario Laser and Lightware Res. Centre, 1988–91. Visiting Scientist, Mass Inst. of Technology, 1963–64. Chm., Engrg Science, Univ. of Toronto, 1972–77. Izaak Walton Killam Meml Scholarship, 1977–79; Senior Fellow, Massey Coll., Univ. of Toronto, 1979–. Dist. Vis. Prof., Univ. of Central Florida, 2000. H. L. Welsh Lecture, Univ. of Toronto, 1984; Elizabeth Laird Meml Lecture, Univ. Western Ontario, 1985; UK/Canada Rutherford Lectr, 1989. Pres., Canadian Assoc. of Physicists, 1983–84; Council Mem., Assoc. of Professional Engrs of Ontario, 1985–91; Vice-Pres., IUPAP, 1994–96. For. Co-Sec., RSC, 1995–2000. Fellow, Optical Soc. of America, 1965 (Pres. 1976); Fellow, Amer. Phys. Soc., 1969; Geoffrey Frew Fellow, Australian Acad. of Science, 1980. Hon. Fellow: Indian Acad. of Scis, 1971; Macedonian Acad. of Sci. and Arts, 1981; Foreign Hon. Fellow, Amer. Acad. of Arts and Scis, 1989. Hon. DSc: York, Canada, 1982; Skopje, Yugoslavia, 1982; Windsor, Canada, 1989; Toronto, 1994; Western Ontario, 2007. Gold Medal for Achievement in Physics of Canadian Assoc. of Physicists, 1974; William F. Meggers Award, Optical Soc. of America, 1981; Frederic Ives Medal, Optical Soc. of America, 1983; Henry Marshall Tory Medal, RSC, 1989; Dist. Service Award, Optical Soc. of America, 2002. Centennial Medal of Canada, 1967; Golden Jubilee Medal, 2002. *Publications:* Gerhard Herzberg: an illustrious life in science, 2002; numerous scientific contribs to phys. and chem. jls. *Address:* Department of Physics, University of Toronto, 60 St George Street, Toronto, ON M5S 1A7, Canada. *T:* (416) 9782948.

STOKE-UPON-TRENT, Archdeacon of; *see* Stone, Ven. G. O.

STOKER, Dr Dennis James, FRCP, FRCS, FRCR; Consultant Radiologist: Royal National Orthopaedic Hospital, 1972–93, and 1997–2002, now Emeritus; St George's Hospital, 1972–87; London Clinic, 1976–93; King Edward VII Hospital for Officers, 1985–98; part-time consultant, Frimley Park Hospital, 1994–2008; *b* 22 March 1928; *yr s* of Dr George Morris Stoker and Elsie Margaret Stoker (*née* Macqueen); *m* 1st, 1951, Anne Sylvia Nelson Forster (*d* 1997); two *s* two *d*; 2nd, 1999, Sheila Mary Mercer. *Educ:* Oundle Sch.; Guy's Hosp. Med. Sch. MB BS; DMRD; FRCR (FFR RCS 1972); FRCP 1976; FRCS 1992. Guy's Hosp. appts, 1951–52; RAF Med. Branch, 1951–68; served Cyprus and Aden; Wing Cdr (retd). Consultant Physician, RAF, 1964–68; Registrar and Sen. Registrar, Diagnostic Radiology, St George's Hosp., London, 1968–72; Sen. Lectr and Dir of Radiological Studies, 1977–93, Dean, 1987–91, Inst. of Orthopaedics. Royal Society of Medicine: Fellow, 1958; Mem. Council, Section of Radiol., 1975–77; Vice-Pres., 1978–80; Royal College of Radiologists: Fellow, 1976; Examr, 1981–84 and 1985–88; George Simon Lectr, 1988; Dean and Vice-Pres., 1989–91; Robert Knox Lectr, 1992. Fellow, British Orth. Assoc.; Founder Mem., Internat. Skeletal Soc., 1974– (Medal, 1993). Special Trustee, Royal Nat. Orthopaedic Hosp., 1984–2000 (Chm., 1992–98). Editor, Skeletal Radiology, 1984–96; Mem., Editl Bd, Clinical Radiology, 1974–84. *Publications:* Knee Arthrography, 1980; (jtly) Self Assessment in Orthopaedic Radiology, 1988; The Radiology of Skeletal Disorders, 1990; chapters in textbooks; papers on metabolic medicine, tropical disease and skeletal radiology. *Recreations:* philology, medical history, genealogy. *Address:* 3 Pearce's Orchard, Henley-on-Thames, Oxon RG9 2LF. *T:* (01491) 575756; *e-mail:* stoker@dj3.demon.co.uk. *Clubs:* Royal Air Force; Phyllis Court (Henley).

STOKER, John Francis; independent consultant; Commissioner for the Compact (between Government and the voluntary/community sector), 2006–07; *b* 11 Sept. 1950; *s* of Francis Charles Stoker and Joyce Stoker (*née* Barnwell); *m* 1982, Julie Puddicombe. *Educ:* King Edward's Sch., Birmingham; Brasenose Coll., Oxford (BA Lit.Hum.). Department of the Environment: Admin Trainee, 1973–78; Principal, 1978; Tenant's Right to Buy, 1979–81; Alternatives to Rates, 1981–83; Cabinet Office, 1983–85; Grade 5, 1985; Envmt White Paper Div., 1990–92; Grade 3, 1992; Regl Dir, Govt Office for Merseyside, 1992–96; Dep. Dir Gen., 1997–98, Dir Gen., 1998–99, Nat. Lottery; Chief Charity Comr, 1999–2004. Chief Exec., London Bombings Relief Charitable Fund, 2005. Mem., SRA (formerly Law Soc. Regulation Bd), 2006–. *Recreations:* books, music, gardening. *Clubs:* Travellers; Middlesex CC.

STOKER, Sir Michael (George Parke), Kt 1980; CBE 1974; FRCP 1979; FRS 1968; FRSE 1960; President of Clare Hall, Cambridge, 1980–87 (Fellow, 1978; Hon. Fellow 1995); *b* 4 July 1918; *e s* of Dr S. P. Stoker, Maypole, Monmouth; *m* 1942, Veronica Mary English (*d* 2004); three *s* two *d*. *Educ:* Oakham Sch.; Sidney Sussex Coll., Cambridge (Hon. Fellow 1981); St Thomas' Hosp., London. MRCS, LRCP 1942; MB, BChir 1943; MD 1947. RAMC, 1942–47; Demonstrator in Pathology, Cambridge Univ., 1947–48; Univ. Lecturer in Pathology, 1948–50; Huddersfield Lecturer in Special Pathology, 1950–58; Asst Tutor and Dir of Medical Studies, Clare Coll., 1949–58; Fellow of Clare College, 1948–58, Hon. Fellow, 1976; Prof. of Virology, Glasgow Univ., and Hon. Dir, MRC Experimental Virus Research Unit, 1959–68; Dir, Imperial Cancer Res. Fund Laboratories, 1968–79. Hon. Consultant, ICRF Cell Interactions Lab., Cambridge Univ. Med. Sch., 1980–90. WHO Travel Fellow, 1951; Rockefeller Foundn Travel Fellow, 1958; Vis. Prof., UCL, 1968–79. Royal Society: For. Sec., 1977–81; a Vice-Pres., 1977–81; Leeuwenhoek Lecture, 1971, Blackett Meml Lecture, 1980; Mendel Gold Medal, 1978. Dir, Celltech Ltd, 1980–86. Member: European Molecular Biology Organisation; Council for Scientific Policy, DES, 1970–73; Gen. Cttee, Internat. Council of Scientific Unions, 1977–81; Eur. Acad. of Arts, Scis and Humanities, 1980; Med. Res. Council, 1982–86; Chairman: UK Co-ordinating Cttee, Cancer Res., 1983–86; Scientific Cttee, Ludwig Inst. Cancer Res., 1985–93. Foreign Hon. Member: Amer. Acad. of Arts and Scis, 1973; Czech Acad. of Scis, 1980. Chm. of Trustees, Strangeways Res. Lab., Cambridge, 1981–93. Hon. DSc Glasgow, 1982. *Publications:* various articles on cell biology and virology. *Recreation:* painting. *Address:* 7 Grange Court, Cambridge CB3 9BD.

STOKES, Dr Adrian Victor, OBE 1983; CChem; CEng; FBCS; Chief Executive, CAT Ltd, since 2000; Managing Director, Elvis Memories (UK) Ltd, since 2001; *b* 25 June 1945; *s* of Alfred Samuel and Edna Stokes; *m* (marr. diss.). *Educ:* Orange Hill Grammar School, Edgware; University College London (BSc (1st cl. Hons) 1966; PhD 1970). CChem 1976; MRSC 1976; FBCS 1978; CEng 1990; CSci 2004; CITP 2004. Research Programmer, GEC-Computers Ltd, 1969–71; Research Asst, Inst. of Computer Science, 1971–73; Research Fellow, UCL, 1973–77; Sen. Research Fellow and Sen. Lectr, Hatfield Polytechnic, 1977–81; Dir of Computing, St Thomas' Hosp., 1981–88 (King's Fund Fellow, 1981–84); Consultant, 1986–88 (on secondment), Principal Consultant, 1989–97, NHS Centre for IT, then Inf. Mgt Centre; Asst Dir, NHS Inf. Mgt Centre, 1997–99; Jt Dir, NHS Inf. Authy (Standards), 1999–2000. Chairman: European Workshop for Open Systems Expert Gp on Healthcare, 1991–97; BSI Inf. Systems Assembly and Exec. Cttee, 2000–. Vis. Prof., Nene Coll., 1994–96 (Hon. Vis. Prof., 1996–99); Hon. Research Fellow, King Alfred's Coll., Winchester, 2001–04. Non-executive Director: Barnet Primary Care Trust, 2001–; Nat. Clinical Assessment Authy, 2001–05; Special Trustee, Royal Nat. Orthopaedic Hosp. NHS Trust, 2003–. Mem., Administrative Justice & Tribunals Council (formerly Council on Tribunals), 2003–. Member: Silver Jubilee Cttee on Improving Access for Disabled People, 1977–78; Cttee on Restrictions Against Disabled People, 1979–81; Social Security Adv. Cttee, 1980–2001; Dept of Transport Panel of Advisers on Disability, 1983–85; Disabled Persons' Transport Adv. Cttee, 1986–89; Disability Appeal Tribunal, 1992–. Chm., Disabled Drivers' Motor Club, 1972–82, 1991–94, 1997–2000, Vice-Pres., 1982–2005; Chm., Exec. Cttee, RADAR, 1985–92 (Vice-Pres., 1999–). Governor, Motability, 1978–; Trustee: PHAB, 1982–90; Independent Living (1993) Fund, 1993–2002; Independent Living (Extension) Fund, 1993–2002; Mobility Choice, 1998–; Mobilise Orgn, 2005– (Vice-Pres., 2005–). Freeman, City of London, 1988; Freeman, Co. of Information Technologists, 1988. Gov., Univ. of Hertfordshire, 2007–. MCMI (MBIM 1986); FInstD 1986; FRSA 1997. Hon. DSc Hertfordshire, 1994. *Publications:* An Introduction to Data Processing Networks, 1978; Viewdata: a public information utility, 1979, 2nd edn 1980; The Concise Encyclopaedia of Computer Terminology, 1981; Networks, 1981; (with C. Saiady) What to Read in Microcomputing, 1982; Concise Encyclopaedia of Information Technology, 1982, 3rd edn 1986, USA edn 1983; Integrated Office Systems, 1982; (with M. D. Bacon and J. M. Bacon) Computer Networks: fundamentals and practice, 1984; Overview of Data Communications, 1985; The A to Z of Business Computing, 1986; Communications Standards, 1986; OSI Standards and Acronyms, 1987, 3rd edn 1991; (with H. de Glanville) The BJHC Abbreviary, 1995; numerous papers and articles, mainly concerned with computer technology. *Recreations:* philately, science fiction, collecting Elvis Presley records, computer programming. *Address:* 97 Millway, Mill Hill, NW7 3JL. *T:* (020) 8959 6665, (mobile) 07785 502766, *Fax:* (020) 8906 4137.

STOKES, Dr Alistair Michael; Chairman: Ipsen Ltd, since 2007; Ipsen Biopharm Ltd, since 2007; *b* 22 July 1948; *s* of Alan Philip and Janet Ross Stokes; *m* 1970, Stephanie Mary Garland; two *d*. *Educ:* University College, Cardiff (BSc, PhD). With Pharmacia AB (Sweden), 1974–76; Monsanto Co., St Louis, USA, 1976–82; Glaxo Pharmaceuticals, 1982–85; Regional Gen. Manager, Yorkshire RHA, 1985–87; Dir, Glaxo Pharmaceuticals, 1987–90; Dir and Chief Operating Officer, Porton Internat., 1990–95; CEO, Speywood Pharmaceuticals, then Ipsen Ltd, 1995–2007. Chairman: Stowic PLC, 1998–99; Quadrant Healthcare PLC, 1999–2000. Director: Octagen Corp., 1999–2008; Spirogen Ltd, 2003–. Chm., E Berks Community Health NHS Trust, 1993–98. Gov., Thames Valley Univ., 2007–. *Publications:* Plasma Proteins, 1977; biochemical and scientific papers. *Recreations:* music, cricket, travel. *Address:* Ipsen Ltd, 190 Bath Road, Slough SL1 3XE. *Club:* Naval and Military.

STOKES, Harry Michael; HM Diplomatic Service, retired; Counsellor, Foreign and Commonwealth Office, 1979–81; *b* 22 July 1926; *s* of late Wing Comdr Henry Alban Stokes, RAF, and Lilian Frances (*née* Ede); *m* 1951, Prudence Mary Watling; two *s* one *d*. *Educ:* Rossall Sch.; Worcester Coll., Oxford (BA, Dip. Slavonic Studies). Served RAF, 1944–47. Joined Foreign Service, 1951; attached Control Commission, Germany, 1952–55; Foreign Office, 1955; Singapore, 1958; FO, 1959; Washington, 1961; Copenhagen, 1963; FO 1965; New Delhi, 1976; FO, 1977. Chm., British Assoc. for Cemeteries in S Asia, 1985–92. Dir, Indo-British Review, 1988–92. *Recreations:* walking, racquet games, photography, music. *Club:* Royal Commonwealth Society.

STOKES, John Fisher, MA, MD, FRCP; Physician, University College Hospital, since 1947; *b* 19 Sept. 1912; *e s* of late Dr Kenneth Stokes and Mary (*née* Fisher); *m* 1940, Elizabeth Joan, *d* of Thomas Rooke and Elizabeth Frances (*née* Pearce); one *s* one *d*. *Educ:* Haileybury (exhibitioner); Gonville and Caius Coll., Cambridge (exhibitioner); University Coll. Hosp. (Fellowes Silver Medal for clinical medicine). MB BChir (Cambridge) 1937; MRCP 1939; MD (Cambridge) 1947 (proxime accessit, Horton Smith prize); FRCP 1947; FRCPE 1975; Thruston Medal, Gonville and Caius Coll., 1948. Appointments on junior staff University Coll. Hosp. and Victoria Hosp. for Children, Tite St, 1937–42; RAMC 1942–46; served in Far East, 1943–46, Lt-Col (despatches). Examiner in Medicine, various Univs, 1949–70. Member of Council, Royal Soc. of Med., 1951–54, 1967–69. Vice-Pres., RCP, 1968–69; Harveian Orator, RCP, 1981. Trustee, Leeds Castle Foundn, 1984–. Amateur Squash Rackets Champion of Surrey, 1935, of East of England, 1936, Runner-up of British Isles, 1937; English International, 1938; Technical Adviser to Squash Rackets Assoc., 1948–52; Chm. Jesters Club, 1953–59. *Publications:* Examinations in Medicine (jtly), 1976; contrib. on liver disease and general medicine in medical journals. *Recreations:* music, tennis, painting. *Address:* 24 Gypsy Lane, Hunton Bridge, Kings Langley, Herts WD4 8PR.

STOKES, Michael George Thomas; QC 1994; **His Honour Judge Michael Stokes;** a Senior Circuit Judge, since 2006 (a Circuit Judge, since 2001); Resident Judge, Nottingham Crown Court, since 2006; Hon. Recorder of Nottingham, since 2007; *b* 30 May 1948; *e s* of late M. P. Stokes, Leyland, Lancs; *m* 1994, Alison Hamilton Pollock; one *s* one *d*. *Educ:* Preston Catholic Coll.; Univ. of Leeds (LLB Hons 1970). Asst Lectr, Univ. of Nottingham, 1970–72; called to the Bar, Gray's Inn, 1971; in practice on Midland and Oxford Circuit, 1973–2001; Asst Recorder, 1986–90, Recorder, 1990–2001; Res. Judge, Leicester Crown Ct, 2002–06. Pres., Mental Health Review Tribunals, 1999–. Circuit Rep., Remuneration and Terms of Work (formerly Fees & Legal Aid) Cttee, Bar Council, 1996–2000; Mem., Northants Criminal Justice Strategy Cttee, 2000–01. *Recreations:* racing, France. *Address:* c/o Nottingham Crown Court, 60 Canal Street, Nottingham NG1 7EJ.

STOKOE, Maj. Gen. John Douglas, CB 1999 CBE 1991 (MBE 1981); Director Defence, BT, since 2006; Chairman, Debut Services Ltd, since 2006; *b* 30 Dec. 1947; *s* of late Major John Alexander Gordon Stokoe and Elsie Mary Stokoe; *m* 1972, Jenny (*née* Beach); one *s* two *d*. *Educ:* Richmond Grammar Sch.; Army Apprentices Coll., Harrogate; RMA, Sandhurst. Commnd Royal Signals, 1968; served Far East, UK and BAOR; Comdr Communications, Germany, 1991–93; Higher Comd and Staff Course, 1992; DCS, Germany, 1993–94; rcds 1994; Dir, Army Staff Duties, 1994–97; DCS, HQ Land Comd, 1997–98; Dep. C-in-C, HQ Land Comd and Insp. Gen., TA, 1998–99. Defence Business Develt Dir, Amey Gp, 1999–2001; Man. Dir, Amey Defence, 2001–03; Director: Defence, Lend Lease, 2003–04; Corporate Affairs, Lend Lease Europe, 2004–06. Col Comdt, RCS, 1998–2004; Hon. Col, 31 (City of London) Signal Regt (Vols), 2002–07; Hon. Col, FANY, 2006–. *Recreations:* fell walking, water colour artist.

STOLLER, Anthony David, CBE 2004; Deputy Chairman, Joseph Rowntree Foundation, since 2005; *b* 14 May 1947; *s* of Louis and Pearl Stoller; *m* 1969, Andrea Lewisohn; one *s* one *d*. *Educ:* Hendon County Grammar Sch.; Gonville and Caius Coll., Cambridge (MA, LLB). Head of Radio Programming, IBA, 1974–79; Dir, Assoc. of Indep. Radio Contractors, 1979–81; Man. Dir, Thames Valley Broadcasting, 1981–85; John Lewis Partnership, 1985–95: Man. Dir, Tyrrell and Green, 1987–95; Chief Exec., Radio Authy, 1995–2003; External Relations Dir, Ofcom, 2003–06. Chm., Cttee of Reference, Friends Provident Stewardship Fund, 2007– (Mem., 1999–). Lay Mem., Information Tribunal, 2007–. Ed., The Friends Quarterly, 2008–. *Publication:* Wrestling with The Angel, 2001. *Recreations:* cricket, sailing, music. *Address:* 6 Porters House, Porters Lane, Southampton SO14 2AR.

STOLLERY, Prof. John Leslie, CBE 1994; DScEng; FREng; FCGI; FAIAA; Professor of Aerodynamics, 1973–95, now Emeritus, and Head, College of Aeronautics, 1976–86, and 1992–95, Cranfield University (formerly Cranfield Institute of Technology); *b* 21 April 1930; *s* of George and Emma Stollery; *m* 1956, Jane Elizabeth, *d* of Walter and Mildred Reynolds; four *s*. *Educ:* East Barnet Grammar Sch.; Imperial Coll. of Science and Technol., London Univ. (BScEng 1951, MScEng 1953, DScEng 1973). DIC; CEng, FREng (FEng 1992); FCGI 1984; FAIAA 1988. Aerodynamics Dept, De Havilland Aircraft Co., 1952–56; Lectr, 1956, Reader, 1962, Aeronautics Dept, Imperial Coll., London; Dean, Faculty of Engrg, 1976–79, Pro Vice-Chancellor, 1982–85, Cranfield Inst. of Technol. Chairman: Aerospace Technology Bd, MoD, 1986–89; Aviation Cttee, DTI, 1986–94; Mem., Airworthiness Requirements Bd, 1990–2000. Pres., RAeS, 1987–88. Visiting Professor: Cornell Aeronautical Labs, Buffalo, USA, 1964; Aeronaut. Res. Lab., Wright Patterson Air Force Base, 1971; Nat. Aeronaut. Lab., Bangalore, India, 1977; Univ. of Queensland, 1983. Hon. FRAeS (FRAeS 1975). *Publications:* (Chief Editor) Shock Tube Research, 1971; papers in Jl of Fluid Mechanics, and various other aeronautical jls. *Recreations:* watching football, travelling. *Address:* 28 The Embankment, Bedford MK40 3PE. *T:* (01234) 406773.

STOLTENBERG, Thorvald; President, Norwegian Red Cross, since 1999; *b* 8 July 1931; *s* of Emil and Ingeborg Stoltenberg; *m* 1957, Karin Heiberg; one *s* two *d*. *Educ:* Oslo Univ. (law degree). Joined Foreign Service, Norway, 1958; served: San Francisco, 1959–61; Belgrade, 1961–64; Personal Secretary, Foreign Min., 1964–65; Executive Officer: Foreign Minister's Secretariat, 1965–70; Lagos, 1970; State Secretary: Foreign Min., 1971–72; MoD, 1973–74; Min. of Commerce and Shipping, 1974–76; Min. of Foreign Affairs, 1976–79; Defence Minister, 1979–81; Minister for Foreign Affairs, Norway, 1987–89; Ambassador to UN, NY, 1989–90; UN High Comr for Refugees, 1989–90; Minister for Foreign Affairs, 1990–93; Special Rep. of UN Sec.-Gen. for Former Yugoslavia, 1993–94; UN peace negotiator, Former Yugoslavia, 1993–96; Ambassador of Norway to Denmark, 1996–99. Internat. Sec., Norwegian Fedn of Trade Unions, 1970–71, 1972–73 and 1981–83; active in local politics in Oslo, 1983–87; Dep. Mayor of Oslo, 1985–87. *Address:* Norwegian Red Cross, PO Box 1 Grønland, 0133 Oslo, Norway. *T:* 22054000, *Fax:* 22054040.

STOMBERG, Dr Rolf Wilhelm Heinrich; non-executive Chairman, Management Consulting Group (formerly Proudfoot Consulting), 2000–08; *b* Emden, Germany, 10 April 1940; *s* of Friedrich Stomberg and Johanna (*née* Meiners). *Educ:* Univ. of Hamburg (Dipl. Kfm. 1966; Dr. rer. pol. 1969). Apprenticeship in shipping; Asst Prof., Univ. of Hamburg, 1966–69; joined BP Group, 1970; Finance Dir and Mem., Bd of Mgt, Deutsche BP, 1981–83; Oilstream Dir, 1983–86; Dep. Chm., Deutsche BP, 1986–89; Chm., Europe-Continental Div., BP Oil Internat., 1988; Chm., Bd of Mgt, Deutsche BP, 1989–91; CEO, BP Oil Europe, 1990; Chm., BP Europe, 1994; Man. Dir, BP plc and CEO, BP Oil Internat., 1995–97. Non-executive Chairman: John Mowlem & Co. PLC, 1999–2001; Unipoly SA, Luxembourg, 1999–2002; non-executive Director: Smith & Nephew, 1998–; Cordiant Communications plc, 1998–2003; Scania AB, 1998–2004; Stinnes AG, 1998–2003; TPG Gp, 1998–; Reed Elsevier plc, 1999–2007. Mem. Adv. Bd, Dresdner Bank AG, 1991–2003; Chm., Supervisory Bd, Lanxess AG. Vis. Prof., Imperial Coll., London, 1997–2004.

STONE, family name of **Baron Stone of Blackheath**.

STONE OF BLACKHEATH, Baron *cr* 1997 (Life Peer), of Blackheath in the London Borough of Greenwich; **Andrew Zelig Stone;** *b* 7 Sept. 1942; *s* of Sydney Stone and Louise Sophia Stone (*née* Gould); *m* 1973, Vivienne Wendy Lee; one *s* two *d*. *Educ:* Cardiff High School. Joined Marks & Spencer, 1966: Dir, 1990–99; Jt Man. Dir, 1994–99. Deputy Chairman: Deal Gp Media plc, 2005–; Sindicatum Carbon Capital Hldgs Ltd, 2007–; non-executive Director: Thorn plc, 1996–98; Design Ville Ltd, 2001–03; N. Brown Gp, 2002–; Ted Baker plc, 2002–05; Mem., Adv. Bd, McDonald's Restaurants, 2005–07. Chm., Dipex, 2004–. Mem., Nat. Adv. Cttee on Culture and Creativity in Educn, 1998–2001. Non-executive Director: Science Media Centre, 2001–07; ODI, 2002–. Governor: Weizmann Inst. of Sci., 1996–07; Tel Aviv Univ., 2000–05; British Univ. of Egypt, 2006–; Mem., European Council, Ben Gurion Univ., 2002–; Mem. Council, Royal Instn. Trustee, The Olive Tree Project, 2003–. Hon. Vice Pres., Reform Synagogues of GB, 2000–. Patron, The Forgiveness Project, 2004–. Risk Comr, RCA. Hon. Dr Law Oxford Brookes, 1998; Hon. DDes Kingston, 1999. *Recreations:* reading, walking, thinking. *Address:* House of Lords, SW1A 0PW.

STONE, Maj.-Gen. Anthony Charles Peter, CB 1994; Defence Adviser, PricewaterhouseCoopers, 2006–08; *b* 25 March 1939; *s* of late Major Charles C. Stone and Kathleen M. Stone (*née* Grogan); *m* 1967, (Elizabeth) Mary, *d* of Rev. Canon Gideon Davies; two *s*. *Educ:* St Joseph's Coll.; RMA, Sandhurst; Staff Coll., Camberley. Commnd RA, 1960; served in light, field, medium, heavy, locating and air defence artillery in BAOR, FE and ME and in various general and weapons staff appts in MoD; commanded 5th Regt, RA, 1980–83; founded Special OP Troop, 1982; Col, Defence Progs Staff, MoD, 1983–84; Mil. Dir of Studies, RMCS, 1985–86; Ministry of Defence: Dir of Operational Requirements (Land), 1986–89; Dir of Light Weapons Projects, 1989–90; Dir Gen. Policy and Special Projects (VMGO), 1990–92; Dir Gen. Land Fighting Systems, MoD (PE), 1992–95. Chm. and Man. Dir, The Nash Partnership Ltd, internat. defence advrs, 1996–2005; Defence Advr, Gracemoor Consultants (UK) Ltd, 1997–2006. Hon.

Col, 5th Regt, RA, 1990–2008; Col Comdt, 1993–2001, Rep. Col Comdt, 1998, Royal Regt of Artillery. Vis. Res. Fellow, Dept of Defence Studies, Univ. of York, 1996. Army Mem., Steering Cttee, UK Defence Forum, 1997–2007; Mem., European-Atlantic Gp, 1999–2007. FRUSI 1997. *Publications:* papers on defence, security, policy and acquisition. *Recreations:* shooting (game), family. *Club:* Army and Navy.

STONE, David Lewis, MD; FRCP, FRCPE; Consultant Cardiologist, since 1988, and Medical Director, since 2002, Papworth Hospital; *b* 31 May 1948; *s* of Sidney David Stone and Dorothy Stone; *m* 1972, Helen Sharman; one *s* one *d. Educ:* Bancroft's Sch.; Charing Cross Hosp. Med. Sch., London (BSc 1968; BBS 1971; MD 1985); MA Cantab 2001. MRCP 1974, FRCP 1992; FRCPE 1997. Associate Lectr, Faculty of Clinical Medicine, Univ. of Cambridge, 1997–. Consultant Cardiologist, W Suffolk Hosps, 1988–2007. *Publications:* (contrib.) The Future of the NHS, 2006; articles in field of cardiac imaging. *Recreations:* music, travel, reading. *Address:* Papworth Hospital, Papworth Everard, Cambridge CB23 8RE. *T:* (01480) 364585, *Fax:* (01480) 364799; *e-mail:* david.stone@papworth.nhs.uk.

STONE, David Radcliffe, OBE 1997; CEng, FIMMM; Chairman, Sheffield Teaching Hospitals NHS Foundation Trust (formerly Sheffield Teaching Hospitals NHS Trust), since 2001; *b* 19 Sept. 1935; *s* of Arthur Thomas Stone and Esther Stone; *m* 1959, Janet Clarke (*d* 1996); two *d. Educ:* Barking Abbey Sch., Essex; Univ. of Manchester (BSc Hons 1957). CEng 1983; FIMMM (FIM 1994). Manager, United Steel Cos Ltd, 1957–68; Consultant, PA Mgt Consultants, 1968–73; Works Dir, Firth Brown Ltd, 1973–78; Managing Director: Doncaster Sheffield Ltd, 1978–85; Stocksbridge Engrg Steels Ltd, 1985–89; UES Steels 1989–94; United Engrg Steels Ltd, 1994–96. Pres., British Iron and Steel Producers Assoc., 1993–94. Chairman: Weston Park Hosp. NHS Trust, 1997–99; Central Sheffield Univ. Hosps NHS Trust, 1999–2001; S Yorks Forum, 1997–2001; Convenor, UK Univ. Hosps Chairs Gp, 2004–08; Trustee: Weston Park Cancer Care Appeal, 1996–; Freshgate Foundn, 1996–; Sheffield Botanical Gardens, 1997–. Guardian, Sheffield Assay Office, 1998–. Freeman, City of London, 1995; Liveryman, Co. of Blacksmiths, 1997–; Master Cutler, Co. of Cutlers in Hallamshire, 1995–96 (Freeman, 1979–). Hon. Consul, Finland, 1996–. *Recreations:* golf, gardening, fishing, music. *Address:* 98 Graham Road, Sheffield S10 3GQ. *T:* (0114) 263 0334; *e-mail:* david.stone@talktalk.net. *Clubs:* Hallamshire and Lindrick Golf; Cressbrook and Litton Flyfishers'.

STONE, Evan David Robert; QC 1979; a Recorder of the Crown Court, 1979–98; *b* 26 Aug. 1928; *s* of Laurence George and Lillian Stone; *m* 1959, Gisela Bridget Mann; one *s. Educ:* Berkhamsted; Worcester Coll., Oxford (MA). National Service (commnd, Army), 1947–49; served Middle East and UK. Called to Bar, Inner Temple, 1954, Bencher, 1985; sometime HM Deputy Coroner: Inner West London; West Middlesex; City of London. Mem. Senate of Inns of Court and the Bar, 1985–86. Formerly Associate Editor, Medico-Legal Journal. Councillor, later Alderman, London Borough of Islington, 1969–74 (Dep. Leader, later Leader of Opposition). Chm., City and Hackney HA, 1984–92. Mem., Criminal Injuries Compensation Bd, 1989–2002. Governor: Moorfields Eye Hosp., 1970–79; Highbury Grove Sch., 1971–86 (Chm. of Governors, 1978–83). Hon. Sec., Harleian Soc., 2008. *Publications:* Forensic Medicine, 1987 (with Prof. H. Johnson); contrib. Social Welfare and the Citizen (paperback), 1957; contribs to Medico-Legal Jl and other professional jls. *Recreations:* reading, writing, sport, listening to music. *Address:* 60 Canonbury Park South, N1 2JG. *T:* (020) 7226 6820; The Mill House, Ridgewell, Halstead, Essex CO9 4SR. *T:* (01440) 785338. *Clubs:* Garrick, MCC.

STONE, Prof. (Francis) Gordon (Albert), CBE 1990; FRS 1976; Head of Department of Inorganic Chemistry, and Professor, Bristol University, 1963–90, now Professor Emeritus; Robert A. Welch and University Distinguished Professor of Chemistry, Baylor University, Texas, since 1990; *b* 19 May 1925; *s* of Sidney Charles and Florence Stone; *m* 1956, Judith M. Hislop, Sydney, Australia; three *s. Educ:* Exeter Sch.; Christ's Coll., Cambridge (BA 1948, MA and PhD 1952, ScD 1963). Fulbright Schol., Univ. of Southern Calif., 1952–54; Instructor and Asst Prof., Harvard Univ., 1954–62; Reader, Queen Mary Coll., London, 1962–63. Vis. Professor: Monash Univ., 1966; Princeton Univ., 1967; Univ. of Arizona, 1970; Carnegie-Mellon Univ., 1972; Texas A&M Univ., 1980; ANU, 1982; Guggenheim Fellow, 1961; Sen. Vis. Fellow, Australian Acad. of Sciences, 1966; A. R. Gordon Distinguished Lectr, Univ. of Toronto, 1977; Misha Strassberg Vis. Lectr, Univ. of WA, 1982. Lectures: Boomer, Univ. of Alberta, 1965; Firestone, Univ. of Wisconsin, 1970; Tilden, Chem. Soc., 1971; Ludwig Mond, RSC, 1982; Reilly, Univ. of Notre Dame, 1983; Waddington, Univ. of Durham, 1984; Sir Edward Frankland Prize, RSC, 1987; G. W. Watt, Univ. of Texas (Austin), 1988. Member: Council, Royal Soc. of Chemistry (formerly Chemical Soc.), 1968–70, 1981–83; Dalton Div. Council, 1971–74, 1981–85 (Vice-Pres. 1973 and 1984–85; Pres., 1981–83); Chemistry Cttee, SERC, 1982–85 (Mem., Chem. Cttee, SRC, 1971–74); Council, Royal Soc., 1986–88 (Vice-Pres., 1987–88). Hon. DSc: Exeter, and Waterloo, Canada, 1992; Durham, Salford, 1993; Zaragoza, 1994. Organometallic Chemistry Medal, 1972, Transition Metal Chemistry Medal, 1979, RSC; Chugaev Medal, Inst. of Inorganic Chem., USSR Acad. of Sciences, 1978; Amer. Chem. Soc. Award in Inorg. Chem., 1985; Davy Medal, Royal Soc., 1989; Longstaff Medal, RSC, 1990. *Publications:* Leaving No Stone Unturned (autobiog.), 1993; (Editor) Advances in Organometallic Chemistry, vols 1–47, 1964–2000; (ed) Comprehensive Organometallic Chemistry, 1985–1995 (14 vols), 1995; numerous papers in Jl Chem. Soc., Jl Amer. Chem. Soc., etc. *Recreation:* world travel. *Address:* St Oswalds Orchard, Oswaldkirk, York YO62 5XT; 88 Hackberry Avenue, Waco, TX 76706, USA. *T:* (254) 7523617.

STONE, Frederick Alistair, CBE 1988; DL; solicitor, now retired; Clerk and Chief Executive, Surrey County Council, 1973–88; *b* 13 Sept. 1927; *s* of Cyril Jackson and Elsie May Stone; *m* 1963, Anne Teresa Connor; one *s* one *d. Educ:* William Hulme's Grammar Sch.; Dulwich Coll.; Brasenose Coll., Oxford (BCL, MA). Asst Solicitor: Norwich City Council, 1954–58; Hampshire CC, 1958–60; Sen. Solicitor, CC of Lincoln (Parts of Lindsey), 1960–63; Asst Clerk, Hampshire CC, 1963–65; Dep. Clerk, Cheshire CC, 1965–73. Chairman: RIPA, 1979–81; Assoc. of County Chief Executives, 1986–87. Chm., Surrey Bd, Prince's Youth Business Trust, 1989–96; Dep. Chm., Anchor Housing Assoc. and Trust, 1990–97. Chm. of Govs, Worth Sch., 1990–99. DL Surrey, 1988. *Recreations:* music, walking, gardening. *Address:* Stables Cottage, Kiln Lane, Brockham, Betchworth RH3 7LZ. *T:* (01737) 842178.

STONE, Gerald Charles, PhD; FBA 1992; University Lecturer in non-Russian Slavonic Languages, Oxford University, and Fellow of Hertford College, Oxford, 1972–99; *b* 22 Aug. 1932; *s* of Albert Leslie Stone and Grace Madeline Stone (*née* Varndell); *m* 1st, 1953, Charlotte Johanna Steinbach (marr. diss. 1973); two *s* one *d*; 2nd, 1974, Vera Fedorovna Konnova; one *d. Educ:* Windsor Grammar Sch.; School of Slavonic Studies, London Univ. (BA 1964; PhD 1969). Nat. service, Army, Trieste, 1951–53. Metropolitan Police, 1953–64; Asst Master, Bexhill Grammar Sch., 1964–65; Asst Lectr, 1966–67, Lectr, 1967–71, Nottingham Univ.; Asst Dir of Res., Cambridge Univ., 1971–72. General Editor, Oxford Slavonic Papers, 1983–94. *Publications:* The Smallest Slavonic Nation: the Sorbs of Lusatia, 1972; (with B. Comrie) The Russian Language since the Revolution, 1978; An Introduction to Polish, 1980, 2nd edn 1992; (ed with D. Worth) The Formation of the Slavonic Literary Languages, 1985; (ed) Kèrluše, 1995; (with B. Comrie and M. Polinsky) The Russian Language in the Twentieth Century, 1996; (ed) Kjarliže, 1996; (ed) A Dictionarie of the Vulgar Russe Tongue Attributed to Mark Ridley, 1996; Upper Sorbian-English Dictionary, 2002; Der erste Beitrag zur sorbischen Sprachgeographie, 2003. *Recreations:* gardening, walking, visiting pubs. *Address:* 6 Lathbury Road, Oxford OX2 7AU. *T:* (01865) 558227.

STONE, Ven. Godfrey Owen; Archdeacon of Stoke-upon-Trent, since 2002; *b* 15 Dec. 1949; *s* of Guy and Shirley Stone; *m* 1977, Dot Caswell; one *s* one *d. Educ:* Exeter Coll., Oxford (BA Geog. 1971, Theol. 1978); W Midlands Coll. of Educn (PGCE 1972); Sheffield Univ. (Dip. Leadership, Renewal and Mission Studies, 1997). Ordained deacon, 1981, priest, 1982; Asst Curate, Rushden-with-Newton Bromswold, 1981–87; Dir, Pastoral Studies, Wycliffe Hall, Oxford, 1987–92; Team Rector, Bucknall Team Ministry, 1992–2002; RD, Stoke-upon-Trent, 1998–2002. *Recreations:* walking, gardening, travel, meteorology, music. *Address:* Archdeacon's House, 39 The Brackens, Clayton, Newcastle-under-Lyme, Staffs ST5 4JL. *T:* (01782) 663066; *e-mail:* archdeacon.stoke@lichfield.anglican.org.

STONE, Gordon; *see* Stone, F. G. A.

STONE, Gregory; QC 1994; **His Honour Judge Stone;** a Circuit Judge, since 2001; a Deputy High Court Judge, since 2008; *b* 12 Dec. 1946; *s* of Frederick Albert Leslie Stone and Marion Gerda Stone (*née* Heller); *m* (separated); three *d. Educ:* Chislehurst and Sidcup Grammar Sch.; St Joseph's Coll., London; Université de Rennes; Queen's Coll., Oxford (MA); Univ. of Manchester (Dip. Econ. Develt (distinction) 1971; MA (Econ.) 1972). Sen. Economist, Morgan Grenfell, 1974–76; called to the Bar, Inner Temple, 1976; Standing Counsel to DTI for Criminal Matters on South Eastern Circuit, 1989–90; a Recorder, 2000–01. *Publications:* The Law of Defective Premises, 1982; The Architect's Legal Handbook, 2nd edn, 1978, to 7th edn 1999. *Recreations:* travel, walking, cinema, theatre, opera, architecture, landscape. *Address:* Southwark Crown Court, 1 English Grounds, Southwark, SE1 2HU. *Club:* Athenæum.

STONE, James Hume Walter Miéville; Member (Lib Dem) Caithness, Sutherland and Easter Ross, Scottish Parliament, since 1999; *b* 16 June 1954; *s* of Edward Reginald Stone and Susannah Gladys Hume (*née* Waddell-Dudley); *m* 1981, Flora Kathleen Margaret Armstrong; one *s* two *d. Educ:* Tain Royal Acad.; Gordonstoun Sch.; St Andrew's Univ. (MA 1977). Cleaner, Loch Kishorn, fish-gutter, Faroe Is, English teacher, Sicily, 1977–79; stores clerk, Wimpey Internat., 1979–81; Asst Site Administrator, then Site Administrator, subseq. Project Co-ordinator, Bechtel GB Ltd, 1981–84; Admin Manager, Odfjell Drilling and Consulting Co. Ltd, 1984–86; Dir, Highland Fine Cheeses Ltd, 1986–94; Mem., Cromarty Firth Port Authy, 1998–2000; freelance newspaper columnist and broadcaster, 1990–. Chm., Tain Community Council, 1984; Member: (Ind, 1986–88, Lib Dem, 1988–96) Ross and Cromarty DC, 1986–96 (Vice Chm., Policy and Resources); (Lib Dem) Highland Council, 1995–99 (Vice-Chm., Finance); Scottish Constitutional Convention, 1988–96; Scottish Lib Dem agriculture spokesman, 1998–99; Scottish Parliament: Lib Dem spokesman on educn and children, 1999–2000, on Highlands and Fisheries, 2000–01, on equal opportunities, 2001–03, on finance, 2002–03, on enterprise, lifelong learning and tourism, 2003–07; Mem., Holyrood Progress Gp, 2000–04; Co-Convener: Cross Pty Gp on tackling debt, 2004–; Cross Pty Gp on Scottish economy, 2005–; Cross Pty Gp on oil and gas, 2007– (Vice-Convener, 2003–07); Convener, Subordinate Legislation Cttee, 2007–; Dep. Convener, Communities Cttee, 2006–07; Chm., Scottish Parlt Business Exchange, 2004–06 (Dir, 2003–). Mem., Exec. Cttee (Scotland), CPA, 2005–. Chm., Dornoch Firth Fest., 1990–92; Director: Highland Fest., 1994–2000; Grey Coast Theatre, 2000–. Trustee: Tain Guildry Trust, 1987–; Tain Mus. Trust, 1992–; Highland Building Preservation Trust, 1995–2002. Gov., Eden Court Th., Inverness, 1995–99. FRSA. *Recreations:* shooting, reading, music, gardening, funghi, steam engines, the identification of butterflies. *Address:* Scottish Parliament, Edinburgh EH99 1SP; Sloibcoyle, Edderton, Tain IV19 1LQ. *T:* (01862) 821500. *Clubs:* New (Edinburgh); Armagh (N Ireland).

STONE, Prof. James McLellan, PhD; Professor, since 2003, and Director, Graduate Studies, Department of Astrophysical Sciences, Princeton University; *b* 29 Nov. 1962; *s* of William and Helen Stone; *m* 1984, Penelope Janet (*née* Rose); two *d. Educ:* Queen's Univ., Kingston, Ont. (BS Hons, MS); Univ. of Illinois, Champaign-Urbana (PhD 1990). Postdoctoral Fellow, Univ. of Illinois, 1990–92; Prof., Dept of Astronomy, Univ. of Maryland, College Park, 1992–2002; Prof. of Mathematical Physics, Cambridge Univ., 2002–03. *Publications:* contrib. numerous papers to refereed jls. *Recreations:* hiking, ski-ing. *Address:* Department of Astrophysical Sciences, Princeton University, Peyton Hall, Ivy Lane, Princeton, NJ 08544–1001, USA.

STONE, Lucille Madeline, (Lucy), (Mrs C. Coleman); QC 2001; *b* 16 Oct. 1959; *d* of late Alexander Stone and of Rene Stone; *m* 1994, Charles Coleman; one *s. Educ:* Newnham Coll., Cambridge (MA 1984); Inns of Court Sch. of Law. Called to the Bar, Middle Temple, 1983; specialist in divorce law. *Recreations:* family, entertaining, reading. *Address:* Queen Elizabeth Building, Temple, EC4Y 9BS. *T:* (020) 7797 7837.

STONE, Marcus; Sheriff of Lothian and Borders, 1984–93; Advocate; *b* 22 March 1921; *s* of Morris and Reva Stone; *m* 1956, Jacqueline Barnoin; three *s* two *d. Educ:* High Sch. of Glasgow; Univ. of Glasgow (MA 1940, LLB 1948). Served War of 1939–45, RASC: overseas service, West Africa, att. RWAFF. Admitted Solicitor, 1949; Post Grad. Dip., Psychology, Univ. of Glasgow, 1953; admitted Faculty of Advocates, 1965; apptd Hon. Sheriff Substitute, 1967, Sheriff, 1971–76, of Stirling, Dunbarton and Clackmannan, later N Strathclyde at Dumbarton; Sheriff of Glasgow and Strathkelvin, 1976–84. Accredited Mediator, Centre for Dispute Resolution, London, 1993; Principal, The Mediation Bureau; practising mediator, 1994–; Hon. Pres., Assoc. of Mediators, 1997–2001. *Publications:* Proof of Fact in Criminal Trials, 1984; Cross-examination in Criminal Trials, 1988, 2nd edn 1995; Fact-finding for Magistrates, 1990; Representing Clients in Mediation, 1998. *Recreations:* swimming, music.

STONE, Prof. Norman; Professor of International Relations, Bilkent University, Ankara, since 1997 (on leave at Koç University, Istanbul, 2005–07); *b* 8 March 1941; *s* of late Norman Stone and Mary Stone (*née* Pettigrew); *m* 1st, 1966, Nicole Aubry (marr. diss. 1977); two *s*; 2nd, 1982, Christine Margaret Booker (*née* Verity); one *s. Educ:* Glasgow Acad.; Gonville and Caius Coll., Cambridge (MA). Research student in Austria and Hungary, 1962–65; University of Cambridge: Research Fellow, Gonville and Caius Coll., 1965–67; Univ. Lectr in Russian History, 1967–84; Fellow and Dir of Studies in History, Jesus Coll., 1971–79; Fellow of Trinity Coll., 1979–84; Prof. of Modern History, and Fellow, Worcester Coll., Univ. of Oxford, 1984–97. Vis. Lectr, Sydney Univ., 1978. Trustee, Margaret Thatcher Foundn, 1991–. Order of Merit (Polish Republic), 1993. *Publications:* The Eastern Front 1914–1917, 1975, 3rd edn 1978 (Wolfson Prize for History, 1976); Hitler, 1980; Europe Transformed 1878–1919 (Fontana History of Europe), 1983; (ed jtly) Czechoslovakia, 1989; (jtly) The Other Russia, 1990; The

Russian Chronicles, 1990; World War One: a short history, 2007. *Recreations:* Eastern Europe, music, languages, Turkey. *Address:* 22 St Margaret's Road, Oxford OX2 6RX. *T:* (01865) 439481; *e-mail:* norman@bilkent.edu.tr. *Clubs:* Beefsteak, Garrick, Polish.

STONE, Oliver William; actor, screenwriter and director; *b* NYC, 15 Sept. 1946; *s* of Louis Stone and Jacqueline Stone (*née* Goddet). *Educ:* Yale Univ.; NY Univ. (BFA). Film Sch. Teacher, Cholon, Vietnam, 1965–66; wiper, US Merchant Marine, 1966; served US Army, Vietnam, 1967–68 (Purple Heart with oak leaf cluster, Bronze Star); taxi driver, NYC, 1971. *Screenwriter:* Seizure, 1974; Midnight Express, 1978 (Acad. Award, Writers' Guild of Amer. Award); The Hand, 1981; (with J. Milius) Conan the Barbarian, 1982; Scarface, 1983; (with M. Cimino) Year of the Dragon, 1985; (with D. L. Henry) 8 Million Ways to Die, 1986; (with R. Boyle) Salvador, 1986; (also Dir) Platoon, 1986 (Acad. Award, Dirs Guild of Amer. Award, BAFTA Award); *co-writer:* Evita, 1996; *co-writer and director:* Wall Street, 1987; Talk Radio, 1988; The Doors, 1991; *screenwriter, producer and director:* Born on the Fourth of July, 1989 (Acad. Award, 1990); JFK, 1991; Heaven & Earth, 1993; Natural Born Killers, 1994; Nixon, 1995; Any Given Sunday, 1999; Commandante, 2003; Persona Non Grata, 2003, Looking for Fidel, 2004; Alexander, 2005; *producer and director:* World Trade Center, 2006; *director:* U-Turn, 1997; *producer:* Reversal of Fortune, 1990; Blue Steel, 1990; South Central, 1992; Zebrahead, 1992; The Joy Luck Club, 1993; New Age, 1994; Wild Palms (TV mini-series), 1993; Freeway, 1996; The People vs Larry Flynt, 1996; Saviour, 1998; *executive producer:* Iron Maze, 1991; Killer: A Journal of Murder, 1996; (HBO) Indictment: The McMartin Preschool, 1995; The Last Day of Kennedy and King, 1998; The Corrupter, 1999; The Day Reagan Was Shot, 2001. Member: Writers' Guild of America; Directors' Guild of America; Acad. of Motion Picture Arts and Scis. *Publication:* A Child's Night Dream, 1997.

STONE, Maj.-Gen. Patrick Philip Dennant, CB 1992; CBE 1984 (OBE 1981 MBE 1975); Director General, Personal Services (Army), 1988–91; *b* 7 Feb. 1939; *s* of Philip Hartley Stone and Elsie Maude Stone (*née* Dennant); *m* 1967, Christine Iredale Trent; two *s* one *d*. *Educ:* Christ's Hospital; psc 1972. Nat. Service, 1959; commissioned East Anglian Regt, 1959; seconded 6 KAR, 1960–62 (Tanganyika); served British Guyana and Aden, 1962–65; ADC to Governor of W Australia, 1965–67; RAF Staff Coll., 1972; Comd 2nd Bn, Royal Anglian Regt, 1977–80 (UK and Berlin); Chief of Staff, 1st Armoured Div., 1981–84; Comdr, Berlin Inf. Bde, 1985–86; Dep. Mil. Sec. (B), 1987. Dep. Col, Royal Anglian Regt, 1986–91, Col, 1991–97; Col Comdt, Mil. Provost Staff Corps, 1988–92; Dep. Col Comdt, AGC, 1992–93. *Recreations:* country interests, travel, conservation. *Address:* c/o Lloyds TSB, 90A Mill Road, Cambridge. *Club:* Army and Navy.

STONE, Richard Frederick; QC 1968; *b* 11 March 1928; *s* of Sir Leonard Stone, OBE, QC, and Madeleine Marie (*née* Scheffler); *m* 1st, 1957, Georgina Maxwell Morris (decd); two *d*; 2nd, 1964, Susan van Heel; two *d*. *Educ:* Lakefield College Sch., Canada; Rugby; Trinity Hall, Cambridge (MA). Lt, Worcs Regt, 1946–48. Called to Bar, Gray's Inn, 1952, Bencher, 1974, Treasurer, 1992; retired, 2006. Member: Panel of Lloyd's Arbitrators in Salvage Cases, 1968–99; Panel of Wreck Comrs, 1968–98. *Recreation:* sea fishing. *Address:* 18 Wittering Road, Hayling Island, Hants PO11 9SP. *T:* (023) 9246 3645; Flat N, Rectory Chambers, Old Church Street, Chelsea, SW3 5DA. *T:* (020) 7351 1719.

STONE, Prof. Richard Thomas Horner; Professor of Law, University of Lincoln, since 2003; *b* 7 March 1951; *s* of late Rev. Ross Stone and of Bettine Stone (*née* Horner); *m* 1973, Margaret Peerman; one *s* three *d*. *Educ:* Reading Sch.; Southampton Univ. (LLB); Hull Univ. (LLM 1978). Called to the Bar, Gray's Inn, 1998. Leicester University: Lectr in Law, 1975–89; Sen. Lectr in Law, 1989–93; Dean, Faculty of Law, 1987–90; Resident Dir, Sunway Coll., Malaysia, 1989; Prof., 1993–97, Dean, 1996–97, Nottingham Law Sch., Nottingham Trent Univ.; Principal, Inns of Court Sch. of Law, 1997–2001. Vis. Lectr, Loughborough Univ., 1978–91; Visiting Professor: City Univ., 1997–2002; UC, Northampton, 2002–04. FRSA 1998; FICPD 1998. *Publications:* Entry, Search and Seizure, 1985, 4th edn 2005; Textbook on Civil Liberties, 1994, 7th edn 2008; Principles of Contract Law, 1994, 7th edn, as Modern Law of Contract, 2007; Law of Agency, 1996; Offences Against the Person, 1999; articles in legal jls. *Recreations:* books, music. *Address:* Lincoln Law School, University of Lincoln, Brayford Pool, Lincoln LN6 7TS. *T:* (01522) 886915; *e-mail:* rstone@lincoln.ac.uk.

STONE, Rt Rev. Ronald Francis, AM 2008; Bishop of Rockhampton, 1996–2003; Ministry Development Officer, 2004–08, and Vicar General, 2008, Diocese of Bendigo; Assistant to Bishop of Bendigo, since 2007; *b* Armadale, Vic, 10 Sept. 1938; *s* of late Allan Francis Stone and Beatrice Rose Stone (*née* Hubber); *m* 1964, Lisbeth Joan Williams; two *s* one *d*. *Educ:* Caulfield South High Sch.; Caulfield Tech. Coll.; Taylors' Coll., Melbourne; St John's Coll., Morpeth, NSW (ThL 1963). Rector of Kerang, 1969–83; Canon, All Saints Cathedral, Bendigo, 1979–82; Archdeacon of Bendigo, 1983–92; VG, Diocese of Bendigo, 1983–92; Provincial Officer, Province of Victoria, 1988–92; Asst Bishop of Tasmania, 1992–96. Convener, Gen. Synod Rural Ministry Task Gp, 1991–98; Mem., Gen. Synod Ministry and Trng Commn, 1991–98. Chairman: Bd of Dirs, Anglican Superannuation Australia, 1999–2003; Nat. Home Mission Fund—Anglican Outback Fund, 2007–. Editor, The Anglican Gazette, 1997–2003. *Publications:* A Kangaroo is Designed to Move Forward...But Which Direction for the Rural and Remote Area Church?, 1998 (Felix Arnott Meml Lect.); paper on rural ministry in Bush Telegraph. *Recreations:* gardening, philately, furniture restoration, golf, music, radio broadcasting. *Address:* 18 Hewitt Avenue, Bendigo, Vic 3550, Australia. *T:* (3) 54436099; *e-mail:* stonebgo@bigpond.net.au. *Club:* Barham.

STONE, Prof. Trevor William, PhD, DSc; Professor of Pharmacology, University of Glasgow, since 1989; *b* 7 Oct. 1947; *s* of late Thomas William Stone and Alice Stone (*née* Reynolds); *m* 1st, 1971, Anne Corina (marr. diss. 2003); 2nd, 2005, Dr Lynda Gail Ramsey (*née* Darlington). *Educ:* Sch. of Pharmacy, London Univ. (BPharm 1969; DSc 1983); Aberdeen Univ. (PhD 1972). Lectr in Physiology, Univ. of Aberdeen, 1970–77; Sen. Lectr, 1977–83, Reader, 1983–86, Prof., 1986–88, in Neurosci., St George's Hosp. Sch. of Medicine, Univ. of London. Res. Fellow, Nat. Inst. of Mental Health, Washington, 1974, 1977; Vis. Prof. of Pharmacology, Univ. of Auckland, 1988. Man. Dir, Imagery, 1984–89; Dir of Res., Shinkanco, 2001–. FRSocMed; Fellow, British Pharmacol Soc., 2005. Hon. Mem., Portuguese Pharmacol Soc., 1989. *Publications:* Microiontophoresis and Pressure Ejection, 1985; Purines: basic and clinical aspects, 1989; Quinolinic Acid and Kynurenines, 1989; Adenosine in the Nervous System, 1991; CNS Transmitters and Neuromodulators, I 1994, II and III 1995, IV 1996; Neuropharmacology, 1995; Pills, Potions & Poisons, 2000; over 400 sci. papers. *Recreations:* piano, photography, snooker, music, work. *Address:* West Medical Building, University of Glasgow, Glasgow G12 8QQ. *T:* (0141) 330 4481.

STONEFROST, Maurice Frank, CBE 1983; DL; Director General and Clerk, Greater London Council, 1984–85; *b* 1 Sept. 1927; *s* of Arthur and Anne Stonefrost, Bristol; *m* 1953, Audrey Jean Fishlock; one *s* one *d*. *Educ:* Merrywood Grammar Sch., Bristol (DPA). IPFA. Nat. Service, RAF, 1948–51; local govt finance: Bristol County Borough, 1951–54; Slough Borough, 1954–56; Coventry County Borough, 1956–61; W Sussex CC, 1961–64; Sec., Inst. of Municipal Treasurers and Accountants, 1964–73; Comptroller of Financial Services, GLC, 1973–84; Chief Exec., BR Pension Fund, 1986–90; Chairman: Municipal Mutual Insce, 1990–93; CLF Municipal Bank, 1993–98. Dep. Pro Chancellor, and Vice-Chm. Council, City Univ., 1992–99. President: Soc. of County Treasurers, 1982–83; CIPFA, 1984–85. Chm., Commn on Citizenship, 1989–90; Member: Layfield Cttee on Local Govt Finance, 1976; Marre Cttee on Future of Legal Profession, 1989–90; Review Cttee of Finances of C of E, 1993; Chm., Cttee on Finance of Liverpool CC, 1985. Member: Architectural Heritage Fund, 1990–96 (Vice Chm., 1996–98); Foundn for Accountancy and Financial Management, Eastern Europe, 1993–2000; London Pensions Fund Authority, 1996–2001. Chm., Dolphin Sq. Trust, 1993–2001. DL Greater London, 1986. Hon. DSc City Univ., 1987. *Recreation:* gardening.

See also W. J. G. Keegan.

STONEHAM, Prof. (Arthur) Marshall, PhD; FRS 1989; Massey Professor of Physics, and Director, Centre for Materials Research, 1995–2005, now Emeritus Professor, University College London (Honorary Fellow, 2006); *b* 18 May 1940; *s* of Garth Rivers Stoneham and Nancy Wooler Stoneham (*née* Leslie); *m* 1962, Doreen Montgomery; two *d*. *Educ:* Univ. of Bristol (BSc 1961; PhD 1964). CPhys, FInstP 1981; FIMMM (FIM 1996). Harwell Laboratory, UKAEA, 1964–95: Group Leader, 1974; Individual Merit promotions to Band level, 1974, and Sen. level, 1979; Hd of Materials Physics and Metallurgy Div., 1989–90; Hd of Technical Area, Core and Fuel Studies, UKAEA, 1988–90; Dir of Res., AEA Industrial Technology, 1990–93; Chief Scientist, UKAEA, 1993–97 (pt-time based at UCL, 1995–97). Wolfson Industrial Fellow, Oxford Univ., 1985–89; Fellow, Wolfson Coll., Oxford, 1989–95; Sen. Fellow, BT Labs, subseq. Corning Res. Centre, 1998–2000. Visiting Professor: Univ. of Illinois, 1969; Univ. of Connecticut, 1973; Univ. of Keele, 1988–; Univ. of Salford, 1992–; visiting scientist: Gen. Electric, Schenectady, 1969; Centre d'Etudes Nucléaires Grenoble, 1970; KFA Julich, 1973; IBM Yorktown Heights, 1982; PTB Braunschweig, 1985, etc. Member, Council: Royal Soc., 1994–96; Inst. of Physics, 1994–2001 (Vice Pres., 1997–2001). Dir, Oxford Authentication, 1997–. Fellow: APS, 1997; World Innovation Foundn, 2001. Guthrie Prize, Inst. of Physics, 2006. Dir, Inst. of Physics Publications, 1987–2001; Editor, Jl of Physics C: Solid State Physics, 1983–88; Divl Associate Ed., Physical Review Letters, 1992–96; Ed. in Chief, Jl Physics of Condensed Matter, 2002–06; mem. editl bds of other learned jls. *Publications:* Theory of Defects in Solids, 1975, new edn 1985, repr. as Oxford Classic, 2001 (Russian edn 1978); (with W. Hayes) Defects and Defect Processes in Non-Metallic Solids, 1985; Current Issues in Semiconductor Science, 1986; Current Issues in Condensed Matter Structure, 1987; (with M. G. Silk and J. A. G. Temple) Reliability of Non-Destructive Inspection, 1987; Ionic Solids at High Temperatures, 1989; Current Issues in Condensed Matter Spectroscopy, 1990; Materials Modelling: from theory to technology, 1992; (with S. C. Jain) GeSi Strained Layers and their Applications, 1995; (with J. A. Gillaspie and D. L. Clark) Wind Ensemble Sourcebook, 1997 (C. B. Oldman Prize, IAML, 1999); (with J. A. Gillaspie and D. L. Clark) The Wind Ensemble Catalog, 1998; (with N. Itoh) Materials Modification by Electronic Excitation, 2000; research papers on defect properties of the solid state, quantum diffusion, and ordered structures in Jl Phys C: Solid State Phys, Phys Rev., Phys Rev. Lett., Procs of Royal Soc., etc. *Recreations:* music, esp. horn playing in orchestral and chamber music, musical scholarship, reading. *Address:* 14 Bridge End, Dorchester-on-Thames, Wallingford, Oxon OX10 7JP. *T:* (01865) 340066; *e-mail:* ucapams@ucl.ac.uk.

STONES, (Elsie) Margaret, AM 1988; MBE 1977; botanical artist; *b* 28 Aug. 1920; *d* of Frederick Stones and Agnes Kirkwood (*née* Fleming). *Educ:* Swinburne Technical Coll., Melbourne; Melbourne National Gall. Art Sch. Came to England, 1951; working independently as botanical artist, 1951–: at Royal Botanic Gardens, Kew; Nat. Hist. Museum; Royal Horticultural Soc., and at other botanical instns; Contrib. Artist to Curtis's Botanical Magazine, 1957–82. Drawings (water-colour): 20, Aust. plants, National Library, Canberra, 1962–63; 250, Tasmanian endemic plants, 1962–77; Basalt Plains flora, Melbourne Univ., 1975–76; Vis. Botanical Artist, Louisiana State Univ., 1977–86 (200 drawings of Louisiana flora, exhibited: Fitzwilliam, Cambridge, Royal Botanic Garden, Edinburgh, Ashmolean Mus., Oxford, 1991). Tapestries commissioned for Govt House, Victoria (Victorian Tapestry Workshop), 2004. Exhibitions: Colnaghi's, London, 1967–; retrospective, Melbourne Univ., 1976; Louisiana Drawings, Smithsonian, USA, 1980, Louisiana State Mus., 1985, Univ. of Virginia, 1993; Baskett & Day, 1984, 1989; Boston Athenæum, 1993; 50 year retrospective, Nat. Gall. of Victoria, Melbourne, 1996. Workshop, Cornell Univ., USA, 1990. Hon. DSc: Louisiana State Univ. Bâton Rouge, 1986; Melbourne Univ., 1989; DUniv Swinburne, 2003. Eloise Payne Luquer Medal, Garden Club of Amer., 1987; Gold Veitch Meml Medal, RHS, 1989. *Publications:* The Endemic Flora of Tasmania (text by W. M. Curtis), 6 Parts, 1967–78; Flora of Louisiana: water-colour drawings, 1991; Beauty in Truth: the botanical art of Margaret Stones (text by Irena Zdanowicz), 1996; illus. various books. *Recreations:* gardening, reading. *Address:* 26 Hunter Street, Hawthorn, Vic 3122, Australia. *T:* (3) 98183320.

STONES, Sir William (Frederick), Kt 1990; OBE 1980; Managing Director, China Light & Power Co., Hong Kong, 1984–92 (Director, 1975–93); Chairman, Hong Kong Nuclear Investment Co., 1985–93; *b* 3 March 1923; *s* of Ralph William Stones and Ada Stones (*née* Armstrong); *m* 1st, 1946, Irene Mary Punter (marr. diss.); one *s* one *d*; 2nd, 1968, Margaret Joy Catton. *Educ:* Rutherford Coll., Newcastle upon Tyne. Chief Chemist, Michie & Davidson, 1948–51; Regional Res. Dir, CEGB NE Region, 1951–63; Supt, Ferrybridge Power Station, 1963–66; CEGB NE Region: Group Manager, 1966–68; Dir, Operational Planning, 1968–71; Dir, Generation, and Dep. Dir-Gen., 1971–75; Gen. Manager, China Light & Power Co., 1975–83. Dep. Chm., Guangdong Nuclear Power Joint Venture Co., 1985–93; Sen. Advr, West Merchant Bank, 1993–2000. Commander, Order of Leopold II (Belgium), 1986. *Recreations:* fishing, country life.

STONHAM, Rt Rev. Dom Paul, OSB; Abbot of Belmont, since 2000; *b* 22 Feb. 1947; *s* of Robert Stonham and Anna Maria (*née* Frezzini). *Educ:* Univ. of Birmingham (BA (Hons) Mod. Langs 1969); Coll. Sant' Anselmo, Rome (STB 1975). Housemaster, Belmont Abbey Sch., 1975–81; Parish Priest, Tambogrande, Peru, 1981–86; Superior, Monasterio de la Encarnación, Peru, 1986–2000; Prof., Seminario Arquidiocesano, Piura, Peru, 1988–2000; Parish Priest, San Lorenzo, Peru, 1994–98. Dean, Herefordshire, 2001–. Mem., Equipe Internat. Alliance Inter Monastères, 2001–. *Recreations:* reading, walking, music, travel, animal life. *Address:* Belmont Abbey, Hereford HR2 9RZ. *T:* (01432) 374718; *e-mail:* abbot@belmontabbey.org.uk.

STONHOUSE, Rev. Sir Michael Philip, 19th Bt *cr* 1628 and 15th Bt *cr* 1670, of Radley, Berkshire; Rector and Incumbent, St James, Saskatoon, Saskatchewan, since 1992; *b* 4 Sept. 1948; *er s* of Sir Philip Allan Stonhouse, 18th Bt and 14th Bt, and Winnifred Emily (*d* 1989), *e d* of J. M. Shield; *S* father, 1993; *m* 1977, Colleen Coucill; three *s*. *Educ:* Medicine Hat Coll., Univ. of Alberta (BA); Wycliffe Coll. (MDiv). Ordained deacon, 1977, priest, 1978, dio. Calgary, Canada. Asst Curate, St Peter's, Calgary, 1977–80; Rector and Incumbent: Parkland Parish, Alberta, 1980–87; St Mark's Innisfail and St

Matthew's Bowden, Alberta, 1987–92. *Heir: s* Allan James Stonhouse, *b* 20 March 1981. *Address:* 3413 Balfour Street, Saskatoon, SK S7H 3Z3, Canada.

STONIER, Prof. Peter David, PhD; consultant in pharmaceutical medicine, since 2000; Director of Education and Training, Faculty of Pharmaceutical Medicine, Royal Colleges of Physicians of the UK, since 2003; *b* 29 April 1945; *s* of Frederick Stonier and Phyllis Maud Stonier; *m* 1989, Elizabeth Margaret Thomas; one *s* one *d. Educ:* Cheadle Hulme Sch.; Univ. of Birmingham (BSc 1st cl. Hons 1966); Univ. of Sheffield (PhD 1969); Univ. of Manchester (MB ChB Hons 1974); Open Univ. (BA 1990). FFPM 1989; FRCPE 1993; MRCPsych 1994; FRCP 1998. House Officer, Manchester Royal Infirmary, 1974–75; Senior House Officer: Univ. Hosp. S Manchester, 1975–76; Leicester Royal Infirmary, 1976–77; Med. Advr, 1977–80, Head of Med. Services, 1980–81, Med. Dir, 1982–2000, and Bd Mem., 1994–2000, Hoechst UK Ltd, later Hoechst Roussel Ltd, then Hoechst Marion Roussel Ltd. Visiting Professor: Univ. of Surrey, 1992– (Course Dir, MSc in Pharmaceutical Medicine, 1993–2001); KCL, 1998–. Member: Pharm. Industry Trng Council, 1998–2002; Appeal Panel, NICE, 2000–. Chm., British Assoc. of Pharmaceut. Physicians, 1988–90; Mem. Council, British Assoc. of Psychopharmacology, 1993–97; Council, RCP, 1997–2001; Faculty of Pharmaceutical Medicine, Royal Colleges of Physicians of UK: Vice Pres., 1992–96, Pres., 1997–2001; Mem., Bd of Examrs, 1994–97; Chm., Fellowship Cttee, 1997–2001; Convenor and Chair, Task Force for Specialist Trng in Pharmaceut. Medicine, 1995–99. Pres., Internat. Fedn of Assocs of Pharmaceut. Physicians, 1996–98. FRSocMed 1982 (Pres., Sect. of Pharmaceut. Medicine and Res., 1994–96); FMS 1999; FRSA 2000; AMInstD 1995. Founder Ed., Pharmaceutical Physician, 1989–98; Associate Editor, Human Psychopharmacology, 1990–2007; Internat. Jl of Pharmaceut. Medicine, 1997–. Lifetime Achievement Award, Acad. of Pharmaceutical Physicians & Investigators, 2006. *Publications:* (ed jtly) Perspectives in Psychiatry, 1988; (ed with I. Hindmarch) Human Psychopharmacology: methods and measures, vol. 1 1988, vol. 2 1989, vol. 3 1991, vol. 4 1993, vol. 5 1996, vol. 6 1997; (ed) Discovering New Medicines: careers in pharmaceutical research and development, 1994, 2nd edn as Careers with the Pharmaceutical Industry, 2003; (ed jtly) Clinical Research Manual, 1994–; (ed jtly) Medical Marketing Manual, 2001; (ed jtly) Principles and Practice of Pharmaceutical Medicine, 2002, 2nd edn 2007; (ed jtly) Paediatric Clinical Research Manual, 2005; articles on psychopharmacology and pharmaceut. medicine. *Recreations:* opera, writing, cooking, collecting prints. *Address:* 5 Branstone Road, Kew, Richmond-on-Thames, Surrey TW9 3LB. *T:* (020) 8948 5069.

STONOR, family name of **Baron Camoys**.

STONOR, Air Marshal Sir Thomas (Henry), KCB 1989; Group Director and Controller, National Air Traffic Services, 1988–91; *b* 5 March 1936; *s* of Alphonsus and Ann Stonor; *m* 1964, Robin Antoinette, *er d* of late Wilfrid and Rita Budd; two *s* one *d. Educ:* St Cuthbert's High Sch., Newcastle upon Tyne; King's Coll., Univ. of Durham (BSc (Mech Eng) 1957). Commissioned, RAF, 1959; served No 3 Sqn, 2ATAF, 1961–64; CFS, 6 FTS and RAF Coll., Cranwell, 1964–67; No 231 Operational Conversion Unit, 1967–69; RAF Staff Coll., Bracknell, 1970; HQ, RAF Germany, 1971–73; OC 31 Sqn, 1974–76; Mil. Asst to VCDS, MoD, 1976–78; OC RAF Coltishall, 1978–80; RCDS, 1981; Inspector of Flight Safety, RAF, 1982–84; Dir of Control (Airspace Policy), NATS, 1985–86; Dep. Controller, NATS, 1986–88. Sen. Consultant, Siemens Plessey Systems, 1991–98; Defence Advr, BT Defence Sales Sector, 1991–2003; non-exec. Dir, Parity PLC (formerly COMAC Gp), 1994–2001. *Recreations:* gardening, music. *Address:* 213 Woodstock Road, Oxford OX2 7AD. *Club:* Royal Air Force.

STOPFORD, family name of **Earl of Courtown**.

STOPFORD, Viscount; James Richard Ian Montagu Stopford; *b* 30 March 1988; *s* and *heir* of Earl of Courtown, *qv. Educ:* Eton; Univ. of Durham. *Recreations:* ski-ing, Rugby.

STOPFORD, Prof. John Morton, DBA; Professor of International Business, London Business School, 1974–2002, now Emeritus; *b* 16 Sept. 1939; *s* of Rt Rev. and Rt Hon. Robert Wright Stopford, KCVO, CBE, DD and Winifred Sophia Stopford (*née* Morton); *m* 1966, Sarah Woodman; two *s. Educ:* Sherborne Sch.; Hertford Coll., Oxford (BA); MIT (SM); Harvard Univ. (DBA). Apprentice fitter, Baker Perkins, 1958; Engineer, Shell Chemicals, 1962–64; Acting Man. Dir, Guyana Stockfeeds, 1965; Sen. Lectr, Manchester Business Sch., 1968–70; Vis. Prof., Harvard Business Sch., 1970–71; Reader, London Business Sch., 1971–74. Non-exec. Dir, Shell UK, 1973–77; Chairman: The Learning Partnership Inc., 1997–; Strategic Partnership, 2000–02 (Dir, 1994–99). Pres., Eur. Internat. Business Assoc., 1978–79; Vice-Pres., Acad. of Internat. Business, 1994–96; Sen. Staff Officer, UN Centre on Transitional Corps, NY, 1977–78. Visiting Professor: MIT, 1993; Stockholm Sch. of Econs, 1994–95; Aoyama Gakuin Univ., Tokyo, 1994–95; Murmann Sch., Kiel, 2008–; Harry Reynolds Vis. Prof., Wharton Sch., Univ. of Penn., 1999–2000. Governor, Goodenough Coll., 2005–. Mem., Steering Cttee, Order of St John, 2004–. US Acad. of Management Book Prize, 1992. *Publications:* (with L. T. Wells) Managing the Multinational Enterprise, 1972; (with B. Garratt) Breaking down Barriers, 1980; Growth and Organisational Change, 1980; The Directory of Multinationals, 1980, 2nd edn, 1992; (with J. H. Dunning) Multinationals, 1983; (with L. Turner) Britain and the Multinationals, 1985; (with S. Strange) Rival States, Rival Firms, 1991; (with C. Baden-Fuller) Rejuvenating the Mature Business, 1992, rev. edn 1994; (ed jtly) Handbook of Organizational Learning, 2000; (ed jtly) The Future of the Multinational Company, 2003; contribs to learned jls. *Recreations:* hill-walking, tennis, reading. *Address:* 6 Chalcot Square, NW1 8YB.

STOPFORD, Maj.-Gen. Stephen Robert Anthony, CB 1988; MBE 1971; Director General Fighting Vehicles and Engineer Equipment, Ministry of Defence (Procurement Executive), 1985–89; *b* 1 April 1934; *s* of Comdr Robert Stopford, RN, and Elsie Stopford; *m* 1963, Vanessa (*née* Baron). *Educ:* Downside; Millfield. MIET. Commissioned Royal Scots Greys, 1954; regimental service and various staff appts until 1977; Project Manager, MBT80, 1977–80; Military Attaché, Washington, 1983–85. Dir, David Brown Vehicle Transmissions Ltd, 1990–99. *Recreations:* sailing, scuba diving, shooting. *Address:* 18 Thornton Avenue, SW2 4HG. *T:* (020) 8674 1416.

STOPPARD, Miriam, (Lady Hogg), MD; FRCP; writer and broadcaster; Founder and Executive Chairman, Miriam Stoppard Lifetime Ltd, since 2001; *b* 12 May 1937; *d* of Sydney and Jenny Stern; *m* 1st, 1972, Sir Tom Stoppard, *qv* (marr. diss. 1992); two *s* and two step *s*; 2nd, 1997, Sir Christopher Hogg, *qv. Educ:* Newcastle upon Tyne Central High Sch. (State Scholar, 1955); Royal Free Hosp. Sch. of Medicine, Univ. of London (Prize for Experimental Physiol., 1958); King's Coll. Med. Sch. (Univ. of Durham), Newcastle upon Tyne (MB, BS Durham, 1961; MD Newcastle, 1966). FRCP 1998 (MRCP 1964). Royal Victoria Infirmary, King's Coll. Hosp., Newcastle upon Tyne: House Surg., 1961; House Phys., 1962; Sen. House Officer in Medicine, 1962–63; Univ. of Bristol: Res. Fellow, Dept of Chem. Pathol., 1963–65 (MRC Scholar in Chem. Pathol.); Registrar in Dermatol., 1965–66 (MRC Scholar in Dermatol.); Sen. Registrar in Dermatol., 1966–68; Syntex Pharmaceuticals Ltd: Associate Med. Dir, 1968; Dep. Med. Dir, 1971; Med. Dir, 1974; Dep. Man. Dir, 1976; Man. Dir, 1977–81. TV series: Where There's Life (5 series), 1981; Baby & Co. (2 series), 1984; Woman to Woman, 1985; Miriam Stoppard's Health and Beauty Show, 1988; Dear Miriam, 1989. MRSocMed (Mem. Dermatol. Sect., Endocrinol. Sect.); Member: Heberden Soc.; Brit. Assoc. of Rheumatology and Rehabilitation. Hon. DSc Durham, 2000; Hon. DCL Newcastle, 2004. *Publications:* Miriam Stoppard's Book of Baby Care, 1977; (contrib.) My Medical School, 1978; Miriam Stoppard's Book of Health Care, 1979; The Face and Body Book, 1980; Everywoman's Lifeguide, 1982; Your Baby, 1982; Fifty Plus Lifeguide, 1982; Your Growing Child, 1983; Baby Care Book, 1983; Pregnancy and Birth Book, 1984; Baby and Child Medical Handbook, 1986; Everygirl's Lifeguide, 1987; Feeding Your Family, 1987; Miriam Stoppard's Health and Beauty Book, 1988; Every Woman's Medical Handbook, 1988; Lose 7 lb in 7 Days, 1990; Test Your Child, 1991; The Magic of Sex, 1991; Conception, Pregnancy and Birth, 1993; The Menopause, 1994; Questions Children Ask and How to Answer Them, 1997; Sex Ed—Growing up, Relationships and Sex, 1997; The New Parent, 1998; Healthcare series (15 titles), 1998–2002; Drugs Info File, 1999; Baby's Play and Learn Pack, 2000; Women's Health Handbook, 2001; Teach Your Child, 2001; Family Health Guide, 2002; Baby First Aid, 2003; Defying Age, 2003; The Grandparent's Book: making the most of a very special relationship, 2006; over 40 pubns in med. jls. *Recreations:* my family, gardening. *Address:* c/o Dorling Kindersley, 80 Strand, WC2R 0RL.

STOPPARD, Sir Tom, OM 2000; Kt 1997; CBE 1978; FRSL; playwright and novelist; *b* 3 July 1937; *yr s* of late Eugene Straussler and of Mrs Martha Stoppard; *m* 1st, 1965, Jose (marr. diss. 1972), *yr d* of John and Alice Ingle; two *s*; 2nd, 1972, Dr Miriam Moore-Robinson (*see* Miriam Stoppard) (marr. diss. 1992); two *s. Educ:* abroad; Dolphin Sch., Notts; Pocklington, Yorks. Journalist: Western Daily Press, Bristol, 1954–58; Bristol Evening World, 1958–60; freelance, 1960–63. Mem. Bd, RNT, 1982–2003. Pres., London Library, 2004–. Hon. degrees: Bristol, 1976; Brunel, 1979; Leeds, 1980; Sussex, 1980; London, 1982; Kenyon Coll., 1984; York, 1984. Shakespeare Prize, 1979. *Plays:* Enter a Free Man, London, 1968 (TV play, A Walk on the Water, 1963); Rosencrantz and Guildenstern are Dead, Nat. Theatre, 1967, subseq. NY, etc (Tony Award, NY, 1968; NY Drama Critics Circle Award, 1968); The Real Inspector Hound, London, 1968; After Magritte, Ambiance Theatre, 1970; Dogg's Our Pet, Ambiance Theatre, 1972; Jumpers, National Theatre, 1972 (Evening Standard Award); Travesties, Aldwych, 1974 (Evening Standard Award; Tony Award, NY, 1976); Dirty Linen, Newfoundland, Ambiance Theatre, 1976; Every Good Boy Deserves Favour (music-theatre), 1977; Night and Day, Phoenix, 1978 (Evening Standard Award); Dogg's Hamlet and Cahoot's Macbeth, Collegiate, 1979; Undiscovered Country (adaptation), NT, 1979; On the Razzle, NT, 1981; The Real Thing, Strand, 1982 (Standard Award), subseq. NY (Tony Award, 1984); Rough Crossing (adaptation), NT, 1984; Dalliance (adaptation), NT, 1986; Hapgood, Aldwych, 1988; Arcadia, NT, 1993 (Evening Standard Award; Olivier Award); Indian Ink, Aldwych, 1995; The Seagull (trans.), Old Vic, 1997; The Invention of Love, NT, 1997 (Evening Standard Award); The Coast of Utopia (trilogy), NT, 2002, NY (Tony Award), 2007; Henry IV (adaptation), Donmar Warehouse, 2004; Heroes (trans.), Wyndham's, 2005; Rock 'n' Roll, Royal Court, transf. Duke of York's (Best Play, London Evening Standard Theatre Awards, and Critics' Circle Theatre Awards), 2006; *radio:* The Dissolution of Dominic Boot, 1964; M is for Moon Among Other Things, 1964; If You're Glad I'll Be Frank, 1965; Albert's Bridge, 1967 (Prix Italia); Where Are They Now?, 1970; Artist Descending a Staircase, 1972; The Dog it was That Died, 1982 (Giles Cooper Award; televised 1988); In the Native State, 1991; *television:* A Separate Peace, 1966; Teeth, 1967; Another Moon Called Earth, 1967; Neutral Ground, 1968; (with Clive Exton) Boundaries, 1975; (adapted) Three Men in a Boat, 1976; Professional Foul, 1977; Squaring the Circle, 1984; *screenplays:* (with T. Wiseman) The Romantic Englishwoman, 1975; Despair, 1978; The Human Factor, 1979; (with Terry Gilliam and Charles McKeown) Brazil, 1985; Empire of the Sun, 1987; Rosencrantz and Guildenstern are Dead, 1990 (also dir); The Russian House, 1991; Billy Bathgate, 1991; (with Marc Norman) Shakespeare in Love (Oscar Award for Best Screenplay), 1999; Enigma, 2001. John Whiting Award, Arts Council, 1967; Evening Standard Award for Most Promising Playwright, 1968. *Publications:* (short stories) Introduction 2, 1964; (novel) Lord Malquist and Mr Moon, 1965; *plays:* Rosencrantz and Guildenstern are Dead, 1967; The Real Inspector Hound, 1968; Albert's Bridge, 1968; Enter a Free Man, 1968; After Magritte, 1971; Jumpers, 1972; Artists Descending a Staircase, and, Where Are They Now?, 1973; Travesties, 1975; Dirty Linen, and New-Found-Land, 1976; Every Good Boy Deserves Favour, 1978; Professional Foul, 1978; Night and Day, 1978; Undiscovered Country, 1980; Dogg's Hamlet, Cahoot's Macbeth, 1980; On the Razzle, 1982; The Real Thing, 1983; The Dog it was that Died, 1983; Squaring the Circle, 1984; Four plays for radio, 1984; Rough Crossing, 1985; Dalliance and Undiscovered Country, 1986; (trans.) Largo Desolato, by Vaclav Havel, 1987; Hapgood, 1988; In the Native State, 1991; Arcadia, 1993; The Television Plays 1965–1984, 1993; The Invention of Love, 1997; The Coast of Utopia, 2002; Henry IV, 2004; Heroes, 2005; Rock 'n' Roll, 2006. *Address:* c/o United Agents, 12–26 Lexington Street, W1F 0LE.

STOPPS, Ian Robert, CBE 2003; FRAeS; Chief Executive, Lockheed Martin UK Ltd, since 1999; *b* 7 Oct. 1946; *s* of late Rowland Arthur Stopps and Megan Maynard Stopps; *m* 1969, Alexandra Margaret Gebbie; two *d. Educ:* Loughborough Univ. of Technol. (BSc 1st cl. Hons (Mech. Engrg) 1969). MIMechE 1969; MASME 1970; FRAeS 2005. Various posts with GE Co. (USA), 1971–87; General Manager: Dynamic Products, BF Goodrich, 1987–90; GE-Aerospace-Europe, 1990–93; Pres., European Region, Martin Marietta, London, 1993–95; merged with Lockheed, 1995 to form Lockheed Martin; Pres., Western Europe Region, Lockheed Martin Corp., 1995–99. Dir, Lockheed Martin Aerospace Systems Integration Corp. (LMASIC), 1999–; Chm., British American Business Inc. (BABi), 2003–05. Member Council: SBAC, 1996–; RUSI, 2002–04; Mem. of Ct, Cranfield Univ., 2002–. *Publications:* contribs to ASME, IMechE and RUSI jls. *Recreations:* county and national squash and tennis, Real tennis, golf, travel. *Address:* (office) Manning House, 22 Carlisle Place, SW1P 1JA. *T:* (020) 7798 2850, *Fax:* (020) 7798 2852; *e-mail:* ian.stopps@lmco.com. *Clubs:* Wentworth; Queen's, Sheen Tennis and Squash, Richmond Squash.

STOPS, Timothy William Ashcroft J.; *see* Jackson-Stops.

STORER, David George; Under Secretary, Department of Social Security (formerly of Health and Social Security), 1984–89; *b* 27 June 1929; *s* of Herbert Edwards Storer; *m* 1960, Jean Mary Isobel Jenkin; one *s* two *d. Educ:* Monmouth School; St John's Coll., Cambridge (MA). Assistant Principal, Min. of Labour, 1952; Principal, 1957; Cabinet Office, 1963–66; Asst Secretary, Dept of Employment, 1966–73; Director, Training Opportunities Scheme, 1973–77; Dir of Corporate Services, MSC, 1977–84. *Recreations:* reading, walking. *Address:* 5a Carlton Road, Redhill, Surrey RH1 2BY.

STORER, James Donald, CEng, MRAeS; author and museum consultant; Keeper, Department of Science, Technology and Working Life, Royal Museum of Scotland, Edinburgh, 1985–88; *b* 11 Jan. 1928; *s* of James Arthur Storer and Elizabeth May Gartshore (*née* Pirie); *m* 1955, Shirley Anne (*née* Kent); one *s* one *d. Educ:* Hemsworth

Grammar Sch., Yorks; Imperial Coll., London (BSc Hons, ACGI). MRAeS (AFRAeS 1958). Design Office, Vickers Armstrongs (Aircraft) Ltd, and British Aircraft Corporation, Weybridge, 1948–66; Dept of Technology, Royal Scottish Museum, 1966–85. Hon. Sec., British Aviation Preservation Council, 1990–95 (Vice-Pres., 1996); Chm., Friends of Ironbridge Gorge Museum, 1994–98. *Publications:* Steel and Engineering, 1959; Behind the Scenes in an Aircraft Factory, 1965; It's Made Like This: Cars, 1967; The World We Are Making: Aviation, 1968; A Simple History of the Steam Engine, 1969; How to Run An Airport, 1971; How We Find Out About Flight, 1973; Flying Feats, 1977; Book of the Air, 1979; Great Inventions, 1980; (jtly) Encyclopedia of Transport, 1983; (jtly) East Fortune: Museum of Flight and history of the airfield, 1983; The Silver Burdett Encyclopedia of Transport: Air, 1984; Ship Models in the Royal Scottish Museum, 1986; The Conservation of Industrial Collections, 1989; (jtly) Fly Past, Fly Present, 1995; (contrib.) Biographical Dictionary of the History of Technology, 1996; (jtly) Industry and Transport in Scottish Museums, 1997; Liverpool on Wheels, 1998. *Recreations:* aircraft preservation, industrial archaeology, gardening. *Address:* 41 Campion Way, Sheringham, Norfolk NR26 8UN. *T:* (01263) 825086.

STORER, Prof. Roy; Professor of Prosthodontics, 1968–92 and Dean of Dentistry, 1977–92 (Clinical Sub-Dean, 1970–77), The Dental School, University of Newcastle upon Tyne, Professor Emeritus, since 1992; *b* 21 Feb. 1928; *s* of late Harry and Jessie Storer; *m* 1953, Kathleen Mary Frances Pitman; one *s* two *d*. *Educ:* Wallasey Grammar Sch.; Univ. of Liverpool. LDS (Liverpool) 1950; FDSRCS 1954; MSc (Liverpool) 1960; DRD RCS Ed, 1978. House Surg., 1950, and Registrar, 1952–54, United Liverpool Hosps; Lieut (later Captain) Royal Army Dental Corps, 1950–52; Lectr in Dental Prosthetics, Univ. of Liverpool, 1954–61; Visiting Associate Prof., Northwestern Univ., Chicago, 1961–62; Sen. Lectr in Dental Prosthetics, Univ. of Liverpool, 1962–67; Hon. Cons. Dental Surgeon: United Liverpool Hosps, 1962–67; United Newcastle Hosps (later Newcastle Health Authority), 1968–92. Chm., Div. of Dentistry, Newcastle Univ. Hosps, 1972–75. Mem. Council and Sec., British Soc. for the Study of Prosthetic Dentistry, 1960–69 (Pres., 1968–69); Member: GDC, 1977–92 (Chm. Educn Cttee, 1986–91); Bd of Faculty, RCS, 1982–90; Dental Sub-Cttee, UGC, 1982–89; EC Dental Cttee for trng of dental practitioners, 1986–93; Med. Cttee, UFC, 1989–92. Pres., Med. Rugby Football Club (Newcastle), 1968–82; Mem. Bd of Dirs, Durham CCC, 1994–98. Mem., Northern Sports Council, 1973–88; External Examiner in Dental Subjects: Univs of Belfast, Birmingham, Bristol, Dublin, Dundee, Leeds, London, Newcastle upon Tyne, RCS, and RCPSGlas. Church Warden, St Mary the Virgin, Ponteland, 2000–04. *Publications:* A Laboratory Course in Dental Materials for Dental Hygienists (with D. C. Smith), 1963; Immediate and Replacement Dentures (with J. N. Anderson), 3rd edn, 1981; papers on sci. and clin. subjects in dental and med. jls. *Recreations:* cricket, Rugby football, gardening, vexillology. *Address:* 164 Eastern Way, Darras Hall, Ponteland, Newcastle upon Tyne NE20 9RH. *T:* (01661) 823286. *Clubs:* MCC, East India.

STOREY, Christopher Thomas; QC 1995; a Recorder, since 2000; *b* 13 Feb. 1945; *s* of Leslie Hall Storey and Joan Storey; *m* 1968, Hilary Johnston; two *s*. *Educ:* Rugby Sch. Chartered Accountant, 1967; Glass & Edwards, Liverpool, 1964–68; Price Waterhouse & Co., 1968–70; A. E. Smith Coggins Group, 1970–72; Stacey's, 1972–74; private practice as Chartered Accountant, 1974–82; called to the Bar, Lincoln's Inn, 1979; practising Barrister, NE Circuit, 1982–2007. *Recreations:* music, cricket, classic cars, flying light aircraft (instructor). *Address:* Park Lane Chambers, 19 Westgate, Leeds LS1 2RD. *T:* (0113) 228 5000.

STOREY, David Malcolm; writer and dramatist; *b* 13 July 1933; *s* of Frank Richmond Storey and Lily (née Cartwright); *m* 1956, Barbara Rudd Hamilton; two *s* two *d*. *Educ:* Queen Elizabeth Grammar Sch., Wakefield, Yorks; Slade School of Fine Art, London. Fellow, UCL, 1974. *Plays:* The Restoration of Arnold Middleton, 1967 (Evening Standard Award); In Celebration, 1969 (Los Angeles Critics' Award); The Contractor, 1969 (Writer of the Year Award, Variety Club of GB, NY Critics' Award) (televised, 1989); Home, 1970 (Evening Standard Award, Critics' Award, NY); The Changing Room, 1971 (Critics' Award, NY); Cromwell, 1973; The Farm, 1973; Life Class, 1974; Mother's Day, 1976; Sisters, 1978; Early Days, 1980; The March on Russia, 1989; Stages, 1992. *Publications:* This Sporting Life, 1960 (Macmillan Fiction Award, US); Flight into Camden, 1960 (John Llewellyn Meml Prize); Radcliffe, 1963 (Somerset Maugham award); Pasmore, 1972 (Geoffrey Faber Meml Prize, 1973); A Temporary Life, 1973; Edward, 1973; Saville, 1976 (Booker Prize, 1976); A Prodigal Child, 1982; Present Times, 1984; Storey's Lives: poems 1951–1991, 1992; A Serious Man, 1998; as it happened, 2002; Thin-Ice Skater, 2004. *Address:* c/o Jonathan Cape, Random House, 20 Vauxhall Bridge Road, SW1V 2SA.

STOREY, Dr Hugo Henry; a Senior Immigration Judge, Asylum and Immigration Tribunal (formerly a Vice-President, Immigration Appeal Tribunal), since 2000; *b* 30 Sept. 1945; *s* of Harry MacIntosh Storey and Barbara Storey; *m* 1983, Sehba Haroon; three *s*. *Educ:* N Sydney Boys' High Sch.; Univ. of Sydney (BA Hons 1967; Medal in Govt); Balliol Coll., Oxford (BPhil Politics); Nuffield Coll., Oxford; Univ. of Leeds (PhD 1988). Adult educn teaching, legal res., and journalism, 1971–76; Organiser, Tribunal Assistance Unit, Chapeltown CAB, 1976–78; Sen. Legal Worker, Chapeltown and Harehills Law Centre, 1978–88; Human Rights Fellow, Council of Europe, 1983–88; legal worker, John Howell & Co., 1989–90; Sen. Lectr, Law Dept, Leeds Poly., 1990–91; Lectr and Dep. Dir for Study of Law in Europe, Law Dept, 1991–95, Hon. Res. Fellow, 1995–98, Univ. of Leeds. Adjudicator, Immigration Appellate Authy, 1995–2000. Mem. Council, Internat. Assoc. Refugee Law Judges, 1998–. *Publications:* (jtly) I Want to Appeal: a guide to Supplementary Benefit Appeal Tribunals, 1978; (jtly) Social Security Appeals: a guide to National Insurance Local Tribunals and Medical Appeal Tribunals, 1980; (with G. Crawford) Sacked? Made Redundant? Your Rights if You Lose Your Job: a guide to Industrial Tribunals and the Employment Appeal Tribunal, 1981; (with W. Collins) Immigrants and the Welfare State, 1985; (ed jtly) Asylum Law, 1995; (ed jtly) Butterworth's Immigration Law Handbook, 2001; contribs to various legal jls in UK, Europe and internat. *Recreations:* family, travel, golf, writing poetry (esp. haiku), music, chess. *Address:* (office) Field House, 15–25 Bream's Buildings, EC4A 1DZ. *T:* (020) 7073 4256.

STOREY, Jeremy Brian; QC 1994; a Recorder, since 1995; Deputy Judge of the Technology and Construction Court (formerly Official Referee), since 1996; Acting Deemster, Isle of Man Courts, since 1999; *b* 21 Oct. 1952; *s* of late Captain James Mackie Storey and Veronica Walmsley; *m* 1981, Carolyn Margaret Ansell; two *d*. *Educ:* Uppingham Sch.; Downing Coll., Cambridge (Scholar; BA Law 1st Class, MA). MCIArb 1999 (ACIArb 1997). Called to the Bar, Inner Temple, 1974, Bencher, 2006; Asst Recorder, 1991–95; Head of Chambers, 2008–. Asst Boundary Comr for Eng. and Wales, 2000–. Member: ADR Chambers (UK) Ltd; Western Circuit; Technology and Construction Bar Assoc.; Commercial Bar Assoc.; Soc. of Construction Law; Professional Negligence Bar Assoc.; Soc. for Computers and Law; Panel, WIPO Arbitration and Mediation Center, Geneva; ACI Panel of Arbitrators; ACI Panel of Mediators; Civil Mediation Council. *Recreations:* travel, cricket, theatre. *Address:* 4 Pump Court, Temple, EC4Y 7AN. *T:* (020) 7842 5555. *Clubs:* MCC; Glamorgan CC.

STOREY, Maurice, CB 2003; CEng, FIMarEST; FRINA; Chief Executive, Maritime and Coastguard Agency, 1998–2003; Hon. Chairman, Evergreen-Marine UK Ltd (formerly Hatsu Marine Ltd), since 2007 (Chairman, 2003–06, Hon. Chairman, 2006–07, Hatsu Marine Ltd); *b* 14 June 1943; *s* of Albert Henry Storey and Violet Esther Storey; *m* 1987, Linda Mears; two *s* one *d*. *Educ:* HNC Naval Architecture 1963. CEng 1969; FRINA 1969; FIMarEST 1972. Apprentice, Swan Hunter Shipbuilders, 1958–62; Ship Repair Manager, Swan Hunter Ship Repairers, 1962–67; Asst to Marine Superintendent, then Tech. Superintendent, Shaw Savill Line, 1967–72; Hd, Tech. Dept, Kuwait Oil Tanker Co., 1972–76; Director: Sea Containers Ltd, 1976–90; Hoverspeed Ltd, 1986–90; Ship and Port Mgt, Stena Line Ltd, 1990–98; non-exec. Dir, James Fisher plc, 2003–. Chm. and Dir, Fishguard and Rosslare Rlys and Harbours Co., 1992–98; Dir, Soc. du Terminal Transmanche de Dieppe, 1992–98. Chamber of Shipping UK: Vice-Chm., Cruise Ship and Ferry Section, 1991–96; Chm., Marine Policy Cttee, 1996–98; Vice-Pres., 2005–06; Pres., 2006–07. Pres., Inst. of Marine Engrg, Sci. and Tech., 2005–06. RNLI: Mem. Council, 2002–; Mem. Technical Commn, 2003–. Hon. MBA Nottingham Trent, 2000. *Recreations:* walking, golf. *Address:* 69 Greenhill, Staplehurst, Tonbridge, Kent TN12 0SU. *T:* and *Fax:* (01580) 890530.

STOREY, Michael John, CBE 2002 (OBE 1994); Headteacher, Plantation County Primary School, Halewood, Knowsley; Member (Lib Dem), Liverpool City Council, since 1973 (Leader, 1998–2005); *b* 25 May 1949. *Educ:* Liverpool Univ. (BEd). Teacher: Prescot C of E Primary Sch.; New Hutte Primary Sch., Halewood; Deputy Headteacher, Halsnead Primary Sch., Whiston; Headteacher, St Gabriel's C of E Primary Sch., Huyton. Liverpool City Council: Chm., Educn Cttee, and Dep. Leader, 1980–83; Leader, Lib Dem Opposition, 1991–98. Member, Board: Mersey Partnership, 1993–; Liverpool Vision (Dep. Chm.); North West Develt Agency; Speke Garston Develt Co. *Address:* Plantation Primary School, Hollies Road, Halewood, Knowsley L26 0TH; Municipal Buildings, Dale Street, Liverpool L69 2DH; 36 Countisbury Drive, Liverpool L16 0JJ.

STOREY, Paul Mark; QC 2001; a Recorder, since 2000; a Deputy High Court Judge, since 2004; *b* 12 March 1957; *s* of George Daniel Storey and late Denise Edna Storey (née Baker); *m* 1st, 1977, Margaret Jane Aucott (marr. diss. 1994); two *d*; 2nd, 1994, Alexa Roseann Rea; three *s* one *d*. *Educ:* Notre Dame Sch., Lingfield; John Fisher Sch., Purley; N London Poly.; Newcastle Poly.; UCL; Inns of Court Law Sch.; BA Hons; CPE. Called to the Bar, Lincoln's Inn, 1982; in practice as barrister, 1983–; Asst Recorder, 1999–2000. *Publications:* contrib. various articles to Family Law. *Recreations:* football (Fulham FC), cycling, Rugby (Harlequins RFC), cricket, my family. *Address:* (chambers) 29 Bedford Row, WC1R 4HE.

STOREY, Hon. Sir Richard, 2nd Bt *cr* 1960; CBE 1996; DL; Chairman of Portsmouth and Sunderland Newspapers plc, 1973–98 (Director, 1962–99); *b* 23 Jan. 1937; *s* of Baron Buckton (Life Peer) and Elisabeth (*d* 1951), *d* of late Brig.-Gen. W. J. Woodcock, DSO; *S* to baronetcy of father, 1978; *m* 1961, Virginia Anne, 3rd *d* of Sir Kenelm Cayley, 10th Bt; one *s* two *d*. *Educ:* Winchester; Trinity Coll., Cambridge (BA, LLB). National service commission, RNVR, 1956. Called to the Bar, Inner Temple, 1962. Administers agricultural land and woodland in Yorkshire. Director: One Stop Community Stores Ltd, 1971–98; Reuters Hldgs PLC, 1986–92; Press Association Ltd, 1986–95 (Chm., 1991–95); Fleming Enterprise Investment Trust PLC, 1989–2002 (Chm., 1996–2002); Foreign & Colonial Smaller Cos PLC, 1993–2002; Sunderland PLC, 1996–2004; eFinancialNews Ltd, 2000–06; Croydon Cable. Chm., York Health Services Trust, 1991–97. Member: Nat. Council and Exec., CLA, 1980–84, Yorks Exec., CLA (Chm., 1974–76); Employment Policy Cttee, CBI, 1984–88, CBI Regl Council, Yorks and Humberside, 1974–76; Press Council, 1980–86; Pres., Newspaper Soc., 1990–91 (Mem. Council, 1980–98). Chm., Sir Harold Hillier Arboretum Management Cttee, 1989–2005; Trustee: Royal Botanic Gardens Kew Foundn, 1990–2004; Castle Howard Arboretum Trust, 1997–. Mem. Council: INCA-FIEJ Res. Assoc., 1983–88; European Newspaper Publishers' Assoc., 1991–96. Contested (C): Don Valley, 1966; Huddersfield W, 1970. High Sheriff, 1992–93, DL 1998, N Yorks. Trustee, Hope and Homes for Children, 2002–. Hon. Fellow, Univ. of Portsmouth, 1989. Hon. DLitt Sunderland Poly., 1992. Veitch Meml Medal, RHS, 2005. *Recreations:* architecture, silviculture, dendrology. *Heir:* *s* Kenelm Storey [*b* 4 Jan. 1963; *m* 2001, Karen, *d* of Keith Prothero; one *s* two *d*]. *Address:* Settrington Grange, Malton, Yorks YO17 8NU. *T:* (01944) 768200; 11 Zetland House, Marloes Road, W8 5LB. *T:* (020) 7937 8823; (office) 18 Lexham Mews, W8 5LB. *T:* (020) 7937 2888; *e-mail:* storey.london@btinternet.com.

STORIE-PUGH, Col Peter David, CBE 1981 (MBE 1945); MC 1940; TD 1945 and 3 clasps; DL; Lecturer, University of Cambridge, 1953–82; Fellow of Wolfson College, Cambridge, 1967–82, now Emeritus; *b* 1 Nov. 1919; *s* of late Prof. Leslie Pugh, CBE, BSc, MA, FRCVS and Paula Storie; *m* 1st, 1946, Alison (marr. diss. 1971), *d* of late Sir Oliver Lyle, OBE; one *s* two *d*; 2nd, 1971, Leslie Helen, *d* of Earl Striegel; three *s* one *d*. *Educ:* Malvern; Queens' Coll., Cambridge (Hon. Foundn Scholar; MA, PhD); Royal Veterinary Coll., Univ. of London. FRCVS; CChem, FRSC. Served War of 1939–45, Queen's Own Royal W Kent Regt (escaped from Spangenberg and Colditz); comd 1st Bn, Cambs Regt, comd 1st Bn Suffolk and Cambs Regt; Col, Dep. Comdr, 161 Inf. Bde, ACF County Comdt. Wellcome Res. Fellow, Cambridge, 1950–52. Mem. Council, RCVS, 1956–84 (Chm. Parly Cttee, 1962–67; Pres., 1977–78); President: Cambridge Soc. for Study of Comparative Medicine, 1966–67; Internat. Pig Vet. Soc., 1967–69 (Life Pres., 1969); British Veterinary Assoc., 1968–69 and 1970–71 (Hon. Life Mem., 1984; Dalrymple-Champneys Cup and Medal, 1986); Mem. Exec. Cttee, Cambridgeshire Farmers Union, 1960–65; UK delegate, EEC Vet. Liaison Cttee, 1962–75 (Pres., 1973–75); UK Rep., Fedn of Veterinarians of EEC, 1975–83 (Pres. of Fedn, 1975–79); Chm., Eurovet, 1971–73; Mem. Jt RCVS/BVA Cttee on European Vet. Affairs, 1971–92; Observer, European Liaison Gp for Agric., 1972–80; Jt Pres., 1st European Vet. Congress, Wiesbaden, 1972; Permanent Mem. EEC Adv. Vet. Cttee, 1976–82; Mem. Council, Secrétariat Européen des Professions Libérales, 1976–80; Mem. Permanent Cttee, World Vet. Assoc., 1964–75. Member: Parly and Sci. Cttee, 1962–67; Home Sec.'s Adv. Cttee (Cruelty to Animals Act, 1876), 1963–80; Nat. Agric. Centre Adv. Bd, 1966–69; Production Cttee, Meat and Livestock Commn, 1967–70; Min. of Agriculture's Farm Animal Adv. Cttee, 1970–73; Econ. and Social Cttee, EEC, 1982–90. Chm., Nat. Sheep Breeders' Assoc., 1964–68; Vice-Pres., Agric. Section, British Assoc., 1970–71. Corresp. Mem., Bund Deutscher Veterinäroffiziere, 1979–. Robert von Ostertag Medal, German Vet. Assoc., 1972. DL Cambs, 1963. *Publications:* (and ed jtly) Eurovet: an Anatomy of Veterinary Europe, 1972; Eurovet-2, 1975. *Address:* Fort Mahon, 81630 Salvagnac, France. *T:* 563335427.

STORKEY, Elaine; President, Tear Fund, since 1997; *b* 1 Oct. 1943; *d* of James and Anne Lively; *m* 1968, Alan James Storkey; three *s*. *Educ:* UCW, Aberystwyth (BA); McMaster Univ., Ontario (MA); York Univ. Tutor, Manchester Coll., Oxford, 1967–68; Res. Fellow, Univ. of Stirling, 1968–69; Tutor, then Lectr, Open Univ., 1976–90; Exec. Dir,

Inst. for Contemporary Christianity, 1990–98. Visiting Professor: Calvin Coll., USA, 1980–81; Covenant Coll., Chattanooga, USA, 1981–82; Vis. Scholar, KCL, 1996–; New Coll. Schol., Univ. of NSW, 1997; Sen. Res. Fellow, Wycliffe Hall, Univ. of Oxford, 2003–07; Micah Lectr, Port au Prince, Haiti, 2008. Associate Ed., Third Way, 1988–. Member: Cathedrals Commn, 1992–96; Crown Nominations (formerly Crown Appts) Commn, 2002–; Gen. Synod of C of E, 1987–; Forum for the Future, 1994–2001. Vice-Pres., Gloucestershire Univ. (formerly Cheltenham & Gloucester Coll.), 1995–. DD Lambeth 1998; Hon. PhD Gloucester, 2000. *Publications:* What's Right with Feminism, 1986; Mary's Story, Mary's Song, 1993; The Search for Intimacy, 1995; Magnify the Lord, 1998; (with Margaret Hebblethwaite) Conversations on Christian Feminism, 1999; Men and Women: created or constructed, 2000; Origins of Difference, 2002; Word on the Street, 2003; contrib. to Scottish Jl Theol., Gospel and Culture, The Independent. *Recreations:* broadcasting, making film documentaries. *Address:* (home) The Old School, Coton, Cambs CB3 7PL. *T:* (01954) 212381.

STORMER, Prof. Horst Ludwig, PhD; physicist; Professor of Physics and Applied Physics, Columbia University, since 1998; Adjunct Physics Director, Lucent Technologies (formerly AT&T Bell Laboratories), since 1997; *b* Frankfurt am Main, 6 April 1949; *s* of Karl Ludwig Stormer and Marie Stormer (*née* Ihrig); *m* 1982, Dominique A. Parchet. *Educ:* Univ. of Stuttgart (PhD 1977). AT&T Bell Laboratories: Mem., Technical Staff, 1978–83; Dept Head, 1983–92; Dir, Physical Res. Lab., 1992–97. Bell Labs Fellow, 1983. Mem., US Nat. Acad. of Scis, 1999. Buckley Prize, 1984; Otto Klung Prize, Free Univ., Berlin, 1985; Benjamin Franklin Medal, 1998; (jtly) Nobel Prize for Physics, 1998; NYC Mayor's Award for Excellence in Sci. and Technol., 2000. Officier de la Légion d'Honneur (France), 1999; Grosse Verdienstkreuz mit Stern (Germany), 1999. *Address:* Department of Physics and Department of Applied Physics, Columbia University, 704 Pupin Hall, New York, NY 10027, USA.

STORMONT, Viscount; Alexander David Mungo Murray; *b* 17 Oct. 1956; *s* and *heir* of 8th Earl of Mansfield and Mansfield, *qv*; *m* 1985, Sophia Mary Veronica, *o d* of Biden Ashbrooke, St John, Jersey; one *s* three *d*. *Educ:* Eton. *Heir:* *s* Master of Stormont, *qv*. *Address:* Scone Palace, Perthshire PH2 6BD.

STORMONT, Master of; Hon. William Philip David Mungo Murray; *b* 1 Nov. 1988; *s* and *heir* of Viscount Stormont, *qv*.

STORMONTH DARLING, Peter; Chairman, Welbeck Land Ltd, since 2001; Consultant, Soditic Limited, since 2007; *b* 29 Sept. 1932; *s* of Patrick Stormonth Darling and Edith Mary Ormston Lamb; *m* 1st, 1958, Candis Hitzig; three *d*; 2nd, 1971, Maureen O'Leary. *Educ:* Winchester; New Coll., Oxford (MA). 2nd Lieut, Black Watch, 1950–53, served Korean War; RAFVR, 1953–56. Dir, 1967–2001, Chm., 1995–2001, Deltec Panamerica, then Deltec Internat., SA. Chairman: Mercury Asset Mgt Gp, 1979–92 (Dir, 1969–98); Mercury International Investment Trust, 1990–98; Mercury European Investment (formerly Mercury Europe Privatisation) Trust, 1994–2004; Atlas Capital Gp (incorporating Deltec Internat. Gp), 2001–06; Alta Advisers Ltd, 2004–07. Director: S. G. Warburg & Co. Ltd, 1967–85 (Vice-Chm., 1977–85); S. G. Warburg Group plc, 1974–94; Europe Fund, 1990–2000; Scottish Equitable plc, 1992–99; Merrill Lynch UK (formerly Mercury Keystone) Investment Co., 1992–2002; Greenwich Associates, 1993–2006; Scottish and Southern Energy (formerly Scottish Hydro-Electric) plc, 1994–2000; Sagitta Asset Mgt Ltd, 1996–2003; Guardian Capital Gp Ltd (Canada), 1998–; Aegon (UK) plc, 1999–2003; Invesco Perpetual Select Trust plc, 2001–08; Howard de Walden Estates Ltd, 2001–; Galahad Gold plc, 2005–08. Director: The UK Fund Inc., 1994–2000; Advent Capital Hldgs, 2006–. Member: UN Pension Fund Investments Cttee, 1990–2005; Exec. (formerly Finance and Investments) Cttee, IISS, 1994–2007; Finance Cttee, World Monuments Fund, 2002–. Chm. Council, Winchester Coll. Soc., 2007–. *Publication:* City Cinderella, 1999. *Address:* Soditic Limited, Wellington House, 125 Strand, WC2R 0AP.

See also R. A. Stormonth Darling.

STORMONTH DARLING, Robin Andrew; Chairman: Capital Opportunities (formerly Voyageur European Smaller Companies) Trust, 1994–2004; Dumyat Investment Trust, 1995–2001; Intrinsic Portfolio Fund PCC Ltd, 2000–03; *b* 1 Oct. 1926; *s* of Patrick Stormonth Darling and Edith Mary Ormston Lamb; *m* 1st, 1956, Susan Marion Clifford-Turner (marr. diss. 1970); three *s* one *d*; 2nd, 1974, Harriet Heathcoat-Amory (*née* Nye) (marr. diss. 1978); 3rd, 1981, Carola Marion Brooke, *er d* of Sir Robert Erskine-Hill, 2nd Bt. *Educ:* Abberley Hall; Winchester Coll. Served Fleet Air Arm (Pilot), 1945; 9th Queen's Royal Lancers, 1946–54: ADC to GOC-in-C Scotland, 1950–52; Officer Cadet Instr, 1952–54. Alexanders Laing & Cruickshank (formerly Laing & Cruickshank), 1954–87, Chm., 1980–87; Director: Austin Motor Co., 1959; British Motor Corp., 1960–68; British Leyland, 1968–75. Chm., Tranwood Gp, subseq. Tranwood, 1987–91. Director: London Scottish Bank (formerly London Scottish Finance Corp.), 1984–92; Mercantile House Holdings, 1984–87 (non-exec. Dep. Chm., 1987); GPI Leisure Corp. (Australia), 1986–90; Ptarmigan Internat. Capital Trust, 1993–2003. Stock Exchange: Mem., 1956–87; Mem. Council, 1978–86; Chairman: Quotations Cttee, 1981–85; Disciplinary Appeals Cttee, 1985–90. Dep. Chm., Panel on Take-Overs and Mergers, 1985–87; Mem., Securities and Investments Bd, 1985–87. Hon. Consul of Mexico at Edinburgh, 1992–. *Recreations:* shooting, ski-ing, flying, swimming. *Address:* Balvarran, Enochdhu, Blairgowrie, Perthshire PH10 7PA. *T:* (01250) 881248. *Clubs:* White's, MCC, Hurlingham; Perth Hunt.

See also P. Stormonth Darling.

STOTHARD, Sir Peter (Michael), Kt 2003; Editor, The Times Literary Supplement, since 2002; *b* 28 Feb. 1951; *s* of late Wilfred Max Stothard and of Patricia J. Stothard (*née* Savage); *m* 1980, Sally Ceris Emerson; one *s* one *d*. *Educ:* Brentwood Sch., Essex; Trinity Coll., Oxford (BA Lit Hum.; MA; Hon. Fellow, 2000). BBC journalist, 1974–77; with Shell Internat. Petroleum, 1977–79; business and political writer, Sunday Times, 1979–80; The Times: Features Ed. and Leader writer, 1980–86; Dep. Ed., 1986–92; US Ed., 1989–92; Editor, 1992–2002. Chairman of Judges: Forward Poetry Prize, 2003; Hessell Tiltman Prize for History, 2004. Dir, Roundhouse Trust, 2004–. *Publication:* Thirty Days: a month at the heart of Blair's war, 2003. *Recreation:* ancient and modern literature. *Address:* The Times Literary Supplement, Times House, 1 Pennington Street, E98 1BS. *Club:* Garrick.

STOTT, Sir Adrian, 4th Bt *cr* 1920; management consultant, since 1989; *b* 7 Oct. 1948; *s* of Sir Philip Sidney Stott, 3rd Bt, and Cicely Florence (*d* 1996), *o d* of Bertram Ellingham; *S* father, 1979. *Educ:* Univ. of British Columbia (BSc (Maths) 1968, MSc (Town Planning) 1974); Univ. of Waterloo, Ont (MMaths (Computer Science) 1971). Dir of Planning for a rural region of BC, 1974; formed own consulting practice, 1977; property develt, gen. management and town planning consultant, 1977–85; Manager: BC Govt Real Estate Portfolio, 1980; Islands Trust (coastal conservation and property develt control agency), 1985; Man. Dir, direct sales marketing company, 1986–88. Member: Cdn Inst. of Planners (MCIP); Assoc. for Computing Machinery. *Recreations:* music, inland waterways, computers, politics. *Heir:* *b* Vyvyan Philip Stott, *b* 5 Aug. 1952. *Address:* The Downs, Little Amwell, Herts SG13 7SA.

STOTT, Andrew Charles; Deputy Government Chief Information Officer, and Director, Service Transformation, Cabinet Office (formerly Head, Service Transformation, e-Government Unit), since 2004; *b* 11 Sept. 1955; *s* of Prof. Peter Frank Stott and Vera Stott (*née* Watkins). *Educ:* Westminster Sch.; Clare Coll., Cambridge (BA 1976). Civil Service Dept, 1976; Prime Minister's Efficiency Unit, 1983–85; HM Prison Service, 1985–87; DSS, 1987–2001; Dir, Digital Infrastructure and e-Champion, DWP, 2001–03; Modernisation Dir, DfT, 2003–04. *Recreation:* walking. *Address:* Cabinet Office, Admiralty Arch, SW1A 2WH.

STOTT, Rev. John Robert Walmsley, CBE 2006; DD; Director, London Institute for Contemporary Christianity, 1982–86, now President; Chaplain to the Queen, 1959–91, Extra Chaplain, since 1991; *b* 27 April 1921; *s* of late Sir Arnold W. Stott, KBE, physician, and late Emily Caroline Holland. *Educ:* Rugby Sch.; Trinity Coll., Cambridge (MA); Ridley Hall, Cambridge. Curate of All Souls, Langham Place, 1945; Rector of All Souls, 1950–75 (with St Peter's, Vere Street, 1952), now Rector Emeritus. DD Lambeth, 1983; Hon. DD: Trinity Evangelical Divinity Sch., Deerfield, USA, 1971; Wycliffe Coll., Toronto, 1993; Brunel, 1997; Trinity Episcopal Sch. for Ministry, 2003. *Publications:* Men with a Message, 1954, revd edn with Stephen Motyer, 1994; What Christ Thinks of the Church, 1958; Basic Christianity, 1958; Your Confirmation, 1958, 2nd edn 1991; Fundamentalism and Evangelism, 1959; The Preacher's Portrait, 1961; Confess Your Sins, 1964; The Epistles of John, 1964; Canticles and Selected Psalms, 1966; Men Made New, 1966; Our Guilty Silence, 1967; The Message of Galatians, 1968; One People, 1969; Christ the Controversialist, 1970; Understanding the Bible, 1972; Guard the Gospel, 1973; Balanced Christianity, 1975; Christian Mission in the Modern World, 1975; Baptism and Fullness, 1975; The Lausanne Covenant, 1975; Christian Counter-Culture, 1978; Focus on Christ, 1979, 2nd edn as Life in Christ, 1991; God's New Society, 1979; I Believe in Preaching, 1982; The Bible Book for Today, 1982; Issues Facing Christians Today, 1984, 4th edn 2006; The Authentic Jesus, 1985; The Cross of Christ, 1986; (with David Edwards) Essentials, 1988; The Message of Acts, 1990; The Message of I and II Thessalonians, 1991; The Contemporary Christian, 1992; The Message of Romans, 1994; The Message of Timothy and Titus, 1996; Evangelical Truth, 1999; The Birds Our Teachers: Biblical lessons from a lifelong bird-watcher, 1999; The Incomparable Christ, 2001; Calling Christian Leaders, 2002; People My Teachers: around the world in 80 years, 2002; Why I am a Christian: this is my story, 2003; Through the Bible Through the Year, 2006; The Living Church: convictions of a lifelong pastor, 2007. *Recreation:* bird watching. *Address:* The College of St Barnabas, Blackberry Lane, Lingfield, Surrey RH7 6NJ.

STOTT, Kathryn Linda; pianist; *b* 10 Dec. 1958; *d* of Desmond Stott and Elsie Stott (*née* Cheetham); *m* 1st, 1979, Michael Ardron (marr. diss. 1983); 2nd, 1983, John Elliott (marr. diss. 1997); one *d*. *Educ:* Yehudi Menuhin Sch.; Royal Coll. of Music, London (ARCM). Regular duo partner of Yo-Yo Ma, Truls Mork, Natalie Clein, Janine Jansen, Christian Poltera, Noriko Ogawa; has worked with all major British orchs; recitals throughout UK; tours of Europe, USA and Far East; world premières of concertos by Graham Fitkin, George Lloyd, Michael Nyman and Sir Peter Maxwell Davies. Artistic Director: Fauré and the French Connection, 1995; Piano 2000, Piano 2003. Prof., RAM, 2004–; Vis. Prof., Chetham's Sch. of Music, 2004–. Numerous recordings. Chevalier de l'Ordre des Arts et des Lettres (France), 1996. *Recreations:* food, travel, Italian language. *Address:* c/o Jane Ward, 60 Shrewsbury Road, Oxton, Wirral CH43 2HY.

STOUGHTON-HARRIS, Anthony Geoffrey, CBE 1989; DL; FCA; Deputy Chairman, Nationwide Building Society, 1990–95; *b* 5 June 1932; *s* of Geoffrey Stoughton-Harris and Kathleen Mary (*née* Baker Brown); *m* 1959, Elizabeth Thackery (*née* White); one *s* two *d*. *Educ:* Sherborne Sch., Dorset. FCA 1956. Partner, Norton Keen & Co., chartered accountants, 1958–74; Maidenhead & Berkshire Building Society, subseq. South of England, London & South of England, Anglia, Nationwide Anglia, then Nationwide Building Society: Dir, 1967–95; Man. Dir, 1975; Chief Gen. Manager, 1983–87; Vice-Chm., 1987–90. Chm., Electronic Funds Transfer Ltd, 1984–89; Director: Southern Electric, 1981–98 (Dep. Chm., 1993–98); Guardian Royal Exchange, 1990–95. Gen. Comr, Inland Revenue, 1982–2000. Part-time Treasurer, W Herts Main Drainage Authority, 1964–70. Chairman: BSA, 1987–89; Northants TEC, 1990–95; Northants Chamber of Commerce, Trng and Enterprise, 1995–96. FCBSI. DL 1994, High Sheriff, 2000, Northants. *Recreations:* sport, gardening, DIY. *Address:* The Beeches, 26 Granville Road, Limpsfield, Oxted, Surrey RH8 0DA. *T:* (01883) 717026.

STOURTON, family name of **Baron Mowbray, Segrave and Stourton**.

STOURTON, Edward John Ivo; Presenter, BBC News and Current Affairs programmes, since 1993; *b* 24 Nov. 1957; *s* of Nigel John Ivo Stourton, CBE, and Rosemary Jennifer Rushworth Stourton (*née* Abbott), JP; *m* 1st, 1980, Margaret (marr. diss. 2001), *e d* of Sir James Napier Finnie McEwen, 2nd Bt; two *s* one *d*; 2nd, 2002, Fiona Murch, *d* of John Edward King, *qv*. *Educ:* Ampleforth; Trinity Coll., Cambridge (MA; Pres., Cambridge Union, Lent, 1979). Joined ITN, 1979; founder mem., Channel 4 News, 1982, Washington Corresp., 1986–88; Paris Corresp., BBC TV, 1988–90; Diplomatic Ed., ITN, 1990–93; BBC Television: Presenter: One O'Clock News, 1993–99; Call Ed Stourton, 1997–98; Reporter: Correspondent, 1996–2001; Panorama, 1998; Presenter, Today, 1999–, Sunday, 2001–, Radio 4; has written and presented series for BBC2 and Radio 4, incl. Asia Gold (Sony Gold Award for Current Affairs, 1997), and Israel Accused (Amnesty Award for best television current affairs prog., 2001). *Publications:* Absolute Truth: the Catholic Church in the world today, 1998; In the Footsteps of St Paul, 2004; John Paul II: man of history, 2006. *Recreations:* conversation, buying books, croquet, racing demon. *Address:* BBC Television Centre, Wood Lane, W12 7RJ. *T:* (020) 8743 8000. *Clubs:* Hurlingham, Travellers.

STOUT, Andrea Mary; *see* Sutcliffe, A. M.

STOUT, David Ker; Director, Centre for Business Strategy, and Professor of Economics, London Business School, 1992–97; Hon. Research Fellow in Economics, University College London, since 2001; *b* Bangor, N Wales, 27 Jan. 1932; *s* of late Prof. Alan Ker Stout, FAHA, FASSA and of Evelyn Roberts; *m* 1956, Margaret Sugden; two *s* two *d*. *Educ:* Sydney High Sch.; Sydney Univ., NSW (BA 1st Cl. English Lit, Econs, and University Medal in Econs, 1953); NSW Rhodes Scholar 1954; Magdalen Coll., Oxford; George Webb Medley Jun. Scholar 1955, Sen. Scholar 1956; PPE 1st Cl. 1956; Nuffield Coll., Oxford (Studentship 1956); Magdalen Prize Fellow by Examination, 1958–59. Fellow and Lectr in Econs, University Coll., Oxford, 1959–76; Economic Dir, NEDO, 1971–72 and 1976–80; Tyler Prof. of Econs, Leicester Univ., 1980–82; Head of Econs, Unilever, 1982–92. Adviser on tax structure to Syrian Govt, 1965, and New Hebrides Condominium, 1966; Sen. Econ. Adviser to Monopolies Commn, 1969; Consultant on VAT, Nat. Bureau of Econ. Res., NY, 1970; Adviser to Australian Govt on Prices Justification, 1973, and on Wage Indexation, 1975–76. Member: Exec. Cttee, NIESR, 1974–82, 1992–98 (Gov., 1974–); EEC Expert Gp on Community Planning, 1976–78, and on Adjustment Policy, 1979–80; ESRC, 1989–92 (Mem., Econ. Affairs Cttee, 1980–86; Chm., Industry, Economics and Envmt Cttee, 1989–92); Manufacturing Foresight Panel, OST, 1994–98; Technology Interaction Bd, BBSRC, 1994–96; Bd of Trustees, Strategic Planning Inst., Cambridge, Mass, 1983–87. Editor, Business Strategy Review, 1994–98. FRSA. *Publications:* papers on taxation policy, VAT, investment, incomes policy, trade performance, indust. policy, de-industrialisation, and European planning. *Recreations:* music, chess, bivalves. *T:* (01732) 780904; *e-mail:* davidkerstout@aol.com.

STOUT, Prof. Robert William, MD, DSc; FRCP, FRCPE, FRCPI, FRCPGlas, FMedSci; Professor of Geriatric Medicine, Queen's University, Belfast, 1976–2007, now Emeritus; Director of Research and Development, Northern Ireland Health and Personal Social Services, 2001–07; *b* 6 March 1942; *s* of William Ferguson Stout, CB and Muriel Stout (*née* Kilner); *m* 1969, Helena Patricia Willis; two *s* one *d*. *Educ:* Campbell Coll., Belfast (schol.); Queen's Univ., Belfast (MD, DSc). FRCP 1979; FRCPE 1988; FRCPI 1989; FRCPGlas 1994. MRC Eli Lilly Foreign Educnl Fellow, Univ. of Washington Sch. of Medicine, Seattle, 1971–73; Queen's University, Belfast: BHF Sen. Res. Fellow, 1974; Sen. Lectr in Medicine, 1975; Dean, Faculty of Medicine, 1991–96; Provost for Medicine and Health Scis., 1993–98; Dean, Faculty of Medicine and Health Scis, 1998–2001. Mem., GMC, 1991–2003 (Member: Standards Cttee, 1993–94; Educn Cttee, 1992–93, 1995–98, 1999–2002). Chairman: Specialty Adv. Cttee on Geriatric Medicine, Jt Cttee on Higher Med. Trng, 1986–92; Benchmark Cttee for Medicine, QAA, 2000–02; Main Panel B (Clinical Medicine), 2008 RAE; Member, Health & Social Services Boards: Southern, 1982–91; Eastern, 1993–2002; Member: Royal Commn on Long-Term Care for the Elderly, 1997–99; Distinction and Meritorious Awards Cttee for NI, 2001–04; Health Res. Bd, Dublin, 2002–07; Dep. Chm. and Med. Dir, NI Clinical Excellence Awards Cttee, 2005–. Vice-Pres., Age Concern Northern Ireland, 1988–2001 (Chm., 1985–88). NI Regl Advr, RCP, 1984–90; British Geriatrics Society: Mem., Council, 1984–90; Chm., NI Reg., 1984–90; Mem., Exec., 1987–90; Chm., Editl Bd, Age and Ageing, 1999–2002; Pres.-elect, 2000–02; Pres., 2002–04. Jt Chm., Centre for Ageing Res. and Develt in Ireland, 2005–. Mem., Bd of Govs, Methodist Coll., Belfast, 1983–2002 (Chm., 1994–97); Chm. Bd of Govs, Edgehill Theol Coll., Belfast, 2005–; Governor, Research in Ageing, 1989–2001 (Mem., Med. Adv. Cttee, 1982–89). Visiting Professor: Univ. of Auckland, NZ, 1990; Hong Kong Geriatric Soc., 1993. Founder FMedSci 1998. *Publications:* Hormones and Atherosclerosis, 1982; Arterial Disease in the Elderly, 1984; Diabetes and Atherosclerosis, 1992; articles in scientific jls on geriatric medicine and related topics. *Recreations:* golf, gardening, reading. *Address:* 3 Larch Hill Drive, Craigavad, Co. Down BT18 0JS. *T:* (028) 9042 2253. *Clubs:* Royal Society of Medicine; Royal Belfast Golf.

STOUTE, Sir Michael (Ronald), Kt 1998; race horse trainer, since 1972; *b* 22 Oct. 1945; *m*; one *s* one *d*. *Educ:* Harrison College, Barbados. Leading flat racing trainer, 1981, 1986, 1989, 1994, 1997, 2000, 2003 and 2005; leading international trainer, 1986, 1996 and 1997; trained: Derby winners, Shergar, 1981, Shahrastani, 1986, Kris Kin, 2003, North Light, 2004; Irish Derby winners, Shergar, 1981, Shareef Dancer, 1983, Shahrastani, 1986; 1000 Guineas winners, Musical Bliss, 1989, Russian Rhythm, 2003; Irish 1000 Guineas winner, Sonic Lady, 1986; 2000 Guineas Winners, Shadeed, 1985, Doyoun, 1988, Entrepreneur, 1997, King's Best, 2000, Golan, 2001; Irish 2000 Guineas winner, Shaadi, 1989; Oaks winners, Fair Salinia, 1978, Unite, 1987; Irish Oaks winners, Fair Salinia, 1978, Colorspin, 1986, Unite, 1987, Melodist, 1988, Pure Grain, 1995, Petrushka, 2000; Breeders Cup Turf winners, Pilsudski, 1996, Kalanisi, 2000; Breeders' Cup Filly and Mare Turf winner, Islington, 2003; Japan Cup winner, Singspiel, 1996, Pilsudski, 1997; Dubai World Cup winner, Singspiel, 1997. *Recreations:* golf, deep sea fishing. *Address:* Freemason Lodge, Bury Road, Newmarket, Suffolk CB8 7BY. *T:* (01638) 663801.

STOW and LINDSEY, Archdeacon of; *see* Sinclair, Ven. J. E. M.

STOW, Graham Harold, CBE 2004; FCIB; Executive Vice Chairman, Britannia Building Society, 2002–03 (Group Chief Executive, 1999–2002); Chairman, Home and Legacy Insurance Services, 2003–06; *b* 29 April 1944; *s* of Joseph Stow and Carrie Stow (*née* Meakin); *m* 1st, 1966, Susan Goldingay (marr. diss. 1983); three *s*; 2nd, 1984, Christine Probert. *Educ:* Liverpool Collegiate Sch. FCIB 2002. Captain, Royal Signals (TA), 1976–82. Retail Ops, then Divl Dir, Personnel, Littlewoods Orgn, 1962–82; Dir, Marlar Internat., 1982–84; ASDA Group plc: Personnel Dir, ASDA Stores, 1984–87; Gp Human Resources Dir, 1987–88; Man. Dir, 1988–89, Chief Exec., 1989–91, ASDA Stores; Director: George Davies Corp., 1991–92; Sandpiper Consultants, 1992; Exec. Vice Pres., Minet Gp, 1992–96; Retail Ops Dir, 1996–98, Dep. Gp Chief Exec., 1998–99, Britannia Building Soc. Non-executive Director: Northern Racing, 2001–07 (Chm., 2004–07); Uttoxeter Leisure & Develt Co., 2003–04; Co-op. Financial Services, 2003–; Co-op. Bank, 2003–; CIS, 2003–; Co-op. Gen. Insce, 2006–; Co-op. Food Div., 2007–; non-exec. Chm., Iprism Underwriting Agency Ltd, 2006–. Chm., Building Socs Assoc., 2002–03 (Dep. Chm., 2001–02). Chm., Staffordshire Moorlands Local Agenda 21 Cttee, 1999–2001; Ind. Bd Mem., DSS, 2000–01; non-executive Director: DWP, 2001–05; Jobcentre Plus, 2003–05. Chm., InStaffs, 2007–. Trustee: Second World War Experience Centre, 2003–07 (Chm. of Trustees, 1998–2002); Staffordshire Yeomanry Mus., 2007– (Chm. of Trustees, 2008–); Lichfield Cathedral, 2007–. Chm. of Trustees, Staffs Community Foundn, 2008–. Mem., Regl Council, Nat. Meml Arboretum, 2008–. Pres., Inst. of Home Econs, 1990–91; Mem., Council and Court, Leeds Univ., 1991–94; Vice Chm. of Govs, Harrogate GS, 1989–91; Governor: Leeds GS, 1989–94; Staffordshire Univ., 1999– (Dep. Chm., 2002–04, Chm., 2004–); Denstone Coll., 1999–2001. Mem., HAC. Hon. Col, Staffs and W Midland Army Cadet Force, 2008. FCIPD (FIPD 1986); FRSA 1990. Freeman, City of London, 1994; Liveryman, Co. of Curriers, 1994–. High Sheriff, Staffs, 2007–08. *Recreations:* horse racing, military history. *Clubs:* Special Forces; British Pottery Manufacturers' Fedn (Stoke-on-Trent); Burton (Burton upon Trent).

STOW, (Julian) Randolph; writer; *b* Geraldton, W Australia, 28 Nov. 1935; *s* of Cedric Ernest Stow, barrister and Mary Stow (*née* Sewell). *Educ:* Guildford Grammar Sch., W Australia; Univ. of Western Australia. Lecturer in English Literature: Univ. of Leeds, 1962; Univ. of Western Australia, 1963–64; Harkness Fellow, United States, 1964–66; Lectr in English and Commonwealth Lit., Univ. of Leeds, 1968–69. Reviewer, TLS, 1976–2002. Miles Franklin Award, 1958; Britannica Australia Award, 1966; Patrick White Award, 1979. *Publications: poems:* Outrider, 1962; A Counterfeit Silence, 1969; *novels:* To The Islands, 1958, rev. edn 1981; Tourmaline, 1963; The Merry-go-round in the Sea, 1965; Visitants, 1979; The Girl Green as Elderflower, 1980; The Suburbs of Hell, 1984; *music theatre* (with Peter Maxwell Davies): Eight Songs for a Mad King, 1969; Miss Donnithorne's Maggot, 1974; *for children:* Midnite, 1967. *Address:* c/o Sheil Land Associates Ltd, 52 Doughty Street, WC1N 2LS.

STOW, Sir Matthew P.; *see* Philipson-Stow.

STOW, Ralph Conyers, CBE 1981; FCIS, FCIB; President and Chairman, Cheltenham & Gloucester Building Society, 1982–87 (Managing Director, 1973–82); *b* 19 Dec. 1916; *s* of Albert Conyers Stow and Mabel Louise Bourlet; *m* 1943, Eleanor Joyce Appleby; one *s* one *d*. *Educ:* Woodhouse Sch., Finchley. FCIS 1959; FBS 1952. Supt of Branches, Temperance Permanent Bldg Soc., 1950, Asst Manager 1958; Gen. Man. and Sec., Cheltenham & Gloucester Bldg Soc., 1962, Dir 1967. Pres., Bldg Socs Inst., 1971–72; Chm., Midland Assoc. of Bldg Socs, 1973–74; Chm., Bldg Socs Assoc., 1977–79. Mem., Glos AHA, 1973–81; Chm., Cheltenham DHA, 1981–88. *Recreations:* photography, oil painting. *Club:* Rotary (Cheltenham).

STOW, Randolph; *see* Stow, J. R.

STOW, Timothy Montague Fenwick; QC 1989; **His Honour Judge Stow;** a Circuit Judge, since 2000; *b* 31 Jan. 1943; *s* of late Geoffrey Montague Fenwick Stow and Joan Fortescue Stow (*née* Flannery); *m* 1965, Alisoun Mary Francis Homberger; one *s* one *d*. *Educ:* Eton Coll. Called to the Bar, Gray's Inn, 1965, Bencher, 1998; became a tenant in common law chambers of David Croom-Johnson, QC (later Lord Justice Croom-Johnson), 1966; Hd of Chambers, 1998; a Recorder, 1989–2000. *Recreations:* swimming, squash, tennis, foreign travel, music, looking after their country property. *Address:* Croydon Crown Court, Altyre Road, Croydon, Surrey CR9 5AB.

STOW, William Llewelyn, CMG 2002; Director General, Strategy and Evidence Group, Department for Environment, Food and Rural Affairs, since 2007; *b* 11 Jan. 1948; *s* of Alfred Frank and Elizabeth Mary Stow; *m* 1976, Rosemary Ellen Burrows; two *s*. *Educ:* Eastbourne Grammar Sch.; Churchill Coll., Cambridge (MA). Joined DTI, 1971; seconded to FCO, 1980–83 (UK Delegn to OECD) and 1985–88 (UK Perm. Repn to EC, Brussels); Internal European Policy, 1988–91; Financial and Resource Management, 1991–94; Hd, EC and Trade Policy Div., 1994–96; Dep. Dir-Gen., Trade Policy and Europe, 1996–98; Dir, Employment Relns, 1998; UK Dep. Perm. Rep. to EU, 1999–2003; Dir Gen., Envmt, DEFRA, 2003–07. *Recreations:* hill and coastal walking, bird-watching, cricket, reading. *Address:* Department for Environment, Food and Rural Affairs, Nobel House, 17 Smith Square, SW1P 3JR.

STOWE, Sir Kenneth (Ronald), GCB 1986 (KCB 1980; CB 1977); CVO 1979; Trustee and Member of Council, Cancer Research UK, 2001–08 (Council Member, Cancer Research Campaign, 1987–2002); *b* 17 July 1927; *er s* of Arthur and Emily Stowe; *m* 1949, Joan Frances Cullen (*d* 1995); two *s* one *d*. *Educ:* County High Sch., Dagenham; Exeter Coll., Oxford (MA; Hon. Fellow, 1989). Asst Principal, Nat. Assistance Board, 1951; Principal, 1956; seconded UN Secretariat, New York, 1958; Asst Sec., 1964; Asst Under-Sec. of State, DHSS, 1970–73; Under Sec., Cabinet Office, 1973–75, Dep. Sec., 1976; Principal Private Sec. to the Prime Minister, 1975–79; Permanent Under Sec. of State, NI Office, 1979–81; Perm. Sec., DHSS, 1981–87. Member: President's Commn to review Public Service, Zimbabwe, 1987–89; Pres. Mandela's Commn on Public Service of SA, 1996–98. Mem., Bd of Dirs, Commonwealth Assoc. for Public Admin and Management, 1994–98, now Emeritus Dir (Chm., Founding Conf., PEI, 1994); Advr on admin. reform to HM Govt, UN Develt Prog., and Commonwealth Secretariat; Chm., wkg gp of voluntary-community sector on compact with Lab. govt, 1997–2002; Chm., HM Treasury reference gp on future builders fund for voluntary sector develt, 2002–03. Chairman: Inst. of Cancer Res., 1987–97; Thrombosis Res. Inst., 1998–2000; Dir, Royal Marsden Hosp. NHS Trust, 1994–97; Trustee: CHASE Children's Hospice, 1999–2004; Carnegie UK Trust, 1988–99; Chairman: Carnegie Inquiry into The Third Age, 1989–93; Carnegie Young People Project, 1996–99. *Recreations:* listening and thinking. *Club:* Athenæum.

STOWELL, Dr Michael James, FRS 1984; Distinguished Research Fellow, Department of Materials Science and Metallurgy, University of Cambridge, since 1999; *b* 10 July 1935; *s* of Albert James Stowell and Kathleen Maud (*née* Poole); *m* 1st, 1962, Rosemary Allen (marr. diss. 1990); one *s* one *d*; 2nd, 1995, Kerry June Brice (*née* Kern) (*d* 1998). *Educ:* St Julian's High Sch., Newport; Bristol Univ. (BSc 1957, PhD 1961). Res. Scientist and Gp Leader, Tube Investments Research Labs, 1960–78; Research Manager, Materials Dept, TI Research, 1978–88; Prin. Consulting Scientist, 1989–90, Res. Dir, 1990–94, Alcan Internat. Ltd. Post-doctoral Res. Fellow, Ohio State Univ., 1962–63; Res. Fellow, Univ. of Minnesota, 1970. L. B. Pfeil Medal, Metals Soc., 1976; Sir Robert Hadfield Medal, Metals Soc., 1981. *Publications:* papers on electron microscopy, epitaxy, nucleation theory, superplasticity and physical metallurgy, in various jls. *Recreation:* music. *Address:* 1 Buckingham Drive, Ely, Cambs CB6 1DR. *T:* and *Fax:* (01353) 661305; *e-mail:* stowell290@btinternet.com.

STRABANE, Viscount; James Alfred Nicholas Hamilton; *b* 30 Oct. 2005; *s* and *heir* of Marquess of Hamilton, *qv*.

STRABOLGI, 11th Baron *cr* 1318, of England; **David Montague de Burgh Kenworthy;** a Deputy Speaker and Deputy Chairman of Committees, House of Lords, 1986–2001; an Extra Lord in Waiting to the Queen, since 1998; *b* 1 Nov. 1914; *e s* of 10th Baron Strabolgi and Doris Whitley (*d* 1988), *o c* of late Sir Frederick Whitley-Thomson, MP; *S* father, 1953; a co-heir to Baronies of Cobham and Burgh; *m* 1961, Doreen Margaret, *e d* of late Alexander Morgan, Ashton-under-Lyne, and Emma Morgan (*née* Mellor). *Educ:* Gresham's School; Chelsea Sch. of Art. Served with HM Forces, BEF, 1939–40; MEF, 1940–45, as Lt-Col RAOC. Mem. Parly Delegations to USSR, 1954, SHAPE, 1955, and France, 1981, 1983 and 1985; PPS to Minister of State, Home Office, 1968–69; PPS to Leader of the House of Lords and Lord Privy Seal, 1969–70; Asst Opposition Whip, and spokesman on the Arts, House of Lords, 1970–74; Captain of the Queen's Bodyguard of the Yeomen of the Guard (Dep. Govt Chief Whip), and Govt spokesman on Energy and Agriculture, 1974–79; Opposition spokesman on arts and libraries, 1979–85. Member: Jt Cttee on Consolidation Bills, 1986–2001; Select Cttee for Privileges, 1987–; Private Bills Cttee, 1987–96; Ecclesiastical Jt Cttee, 1991–2001; Select Cttee on Procedure, 1993–96, 1998–2001; Franco-British Parly Relations Cttee (Hon. Treas., 1991–96); Vice Pres., All-Pty Arts and Amenities Gp; elected Mem., H of L, 1999. Pres., Franco-British Soc.; Member: British Sect., Franco-British Council, 1981–98; Council, Alliance Française in GB, 1972–97. Dir, Bolton Building Soc., 1958–74, 1979–87 (Dep. Chm., 1983, Chm., 1986–87). Hon. Life Mem., RPO, 1977. Freeman, City of London, 1960. Officier de la Légion d'Honneur, 1981. *Heir-pres.: nephew* Andrew David Whitley Kenworthy, *b* 11 Feb. 1967. *Address:* House of Lords, SW1A 0PW. *Club:* Reform.

STRACEY, Sir John (Simon), 9th Bt *cr* 1818; *b* 30 Nov. 1938; *s* of Captain Algernon Augustus Henry Stracey (2nd *s* of 6th Bt) (*d* 1940) and Olive Beryl (*d* 1972), *d* of late Major Charles Robert Eustace Radclyffe; *S* cousin, 1971; *m* 1968, Martha Maria, *d* of late Johann Egger; two *d*. *Heir: cousin* Henry Mounteney Stracey [*b* 24 April 1920; *m* 1st, 1943, Susanna, *d* of Adair Tracey; one *d*; 2nd, 1950, Lysbeth, *o d* of Charles Ashford, NZ; one *s* one *d*; 3rd, 1961, Jeltje, *y d* of Scholte de Boer]. *Address:* Holbeam Wood Cottage, Wallcrouch, Wadhurst, East Sussex TN5 7JT. *T:* and *Fax:* (01580) 201061.

STRACHAN, Alan Lockhart Thomson; theatre director, writer and broadcaster; *b* 3 Sept. 1946; *s* of Roualeyn Robert Scott Strachan and Ellen Strachan (*née* Graham); *m* 1977, Jennifer Piercey-Thompson. *Educ:* Morgan Acad., Dundee; St Andrews Univ.

(MA); Merton Coll., Oxford (B.Litt). Associate Dir, Mermaid Theatre, 1970–75; Artistic Director: Greenwich Th., 1978–88; Theatre of Comedy Co., 1991–97; Churchill Theatre, Bromley, 1995–97. *Productions directed include: Mermaid:* The Watched Pot, 1970; John Bull's Other Island, The Old Boys, 1971; (co-deviser) Cowardy Custard, 1972; Misalliance, 1973; Children, (co-deviser and dir) Cole, 1974; *Greenwich:* An Audience Called Edouard, 1978; The Play's the Thing, I Sent a Letter to my Love, 1979; Private Lives (transf. Duchess), Time and the Conways, 1980; Present Laughter (transf. Vaudeville), The Golden Age, The Doctor's Dilemma, 1981; Design for Living (transf. Globe), The Paranormalist, French Without Tears, 1982; The Dining Room, An Inspector Calls, A Streetcar Named Desire, 1983 (transf. Mermaid, 1984); The Glass Menagerie, Biography, 1985; One of Us, Relatively Speaking, For King and Country, 1986; The Viewing, The Perfect Party, 1987; How the Other Half Loves (transf. Duke of York's), 1988; *freelance:* Family and a Fortune, Apollo, 1975; (deviser and dir) Shakespeare's People, world tours, 1975–78; Confusions, Apollo, 1976; (also jt author) Yahoo, Queen's, 1976; Just Between Ourselves, Queen's, 1977; The Immortal Haydon, Mermaid, 1977 (transf. Greenwich, 1978); Bedroom Farce, Amsterdam, 1978; Noël and Gertie, King's Head, 1983, Comedy, 1989; (replacement cast) Woman in Mind, Vaudeville, 1987; The Deep Blue Sea, Haymarket, 1988; Re: Joyce!, Fortune, 1988 (transf. Vaudeville, 1989; USA, 1990), Vaudeville, 1991; (replacement cast) Henceforward ..., Vaudeville, 1989; June Moon, Scarborough, 1989, Hampstead, transf. Vaudeville, 1992; Toekomstmuziek, Amsterdam, 1989; Alphabetical Order, Scarborough, 1990; (replacement cast) Man of the Moment, Globe, 1990; Other People's Money, Lyric, 1990; Taking Steps, NY, 1991; London Assurance, Dublin, 1993; Make Way for Lucia, Bromley and tour, 1995; Switchback, Bromley and tour, 1996; Høfeber, Copenhagen, 1996; All Things Considered, Scarborough, 1996, Hampstead, 1997; Loot, W Yorks Playhouse, 1996; Live and Kidding, Duchess, 1997; Mrs Warren's Profession, Guildford and tour, 1997; Hooikoorts, Amsterdam, 1997; New Edna—The Spectacle!, Haymarket, 1998; Troilus and Cressida, Regent's Park, 1998; How the Other Half Loves, Oxford Playhouse and tour, 1998; The Merry Wives of Windsor, Regent's Park, 1999; Private Lives, Far East tour, 1999; Hobson's Choice, Scarborough, 1999; Larkin with Women, Scarborough, 1999, Orange Tree Th., Richmond, 2006; A Midsummer Night's Dream, Regent's Park, 2000, 2001; Harvey, Singapore, 2000; The Real Thing, Bristol Old Vic and tour, 2001, Plymouth and tour, 2002; Henry IV, Pt One, Regent's Park, 2004; Going Straight, Windsor and tour, 2004; Glorious!, Birmingham Rep., transf. Duchess, 2005; Entertaining Angels, Chichester, 2006; The Letter, Wyndham's, 2007; How the Other Half Loves, Bath and tour, 2007; Absurd Person Singular, Garrick, 2007; Year of the Rat, W Yorks Playhouse, 2008; Relatively Speaking, Bath and tour, 2008. *Producer/co-Producer:* Out of Order, tour, 1991; The Pocket Dream, Albery, 1992; Six Degrees of Separation, Royal Court, transf. Comedy, 1992; Hay Fever (also dir), Albery, 1992; Happy Families, tour, 1993; Hysteria, Royal Court, 1993; Under Their Hats (also devised), King's Head, 1994; The Prime of Miss Jean Brodie (also dir.), Strand, 1994; (exec. prod.) Love on a Branch Line, BBC1, 1994. *Publications:* Secret Dreams: a biography of Michael Redgrave, 2004; contribs to periodicals and newspapers. *Recreations:* music, tennis, travelling. *Address:* c/o Macnaughton Lord Ltd, Unit 10, Broomhouse Studios, 50 Sulivan Road, SW6 3DX. *T:* (020) 7384 9517. *Club:* Garrick.

STRACHAN, Alexander William Bruce, OBE 1971; HM Diplomatic Service, retired; *b* 2 July 1917; *s* of William Fyfe and Winifred Orchar Strachan; *m* 1940, Rebecca Prince MacFarlane; one *s* one *d. Educ:* Daniel Stewart's Coll., Edinburgh; Allen Glen's High Sch., Glasgow. Served Army, 1939–46 (dispatches). GPO, 1935; Asst Postal Controller, 1949–64; Postal Adviser to Iraq Govt, 1964–66; First Sec., FCO, 1967–68; Jordan, 1968–72; Addis Ababa, 1972–73; Consul General, Lahore, 1973–74; Counsellor (Economic and Commercial) and Consul General, Islamabad, 1975–77. Order of Istiqlal, Hashemite Kingdom of Jordan, 1971.

STRACHAN, Major Benjamin Leckie, CMG 1978; HM Diplomatic Service, retired; Special Adviser (Middle East), Foreign and Commonwealth Office, 1990–91; *b* 4 Jan. 1924; *e s* of late Dr C. G. Strachan, MC FRCPE and Annie Primrose (*née* Leckie); *m* 1958, Lize Lund; three *s*, and one step *s* one step *d. Educ:* Rossall Sch. (Scholar); RMCS; Univ. of Aberdeen (MA 2005). Royal Dragoons, 1944; France and Germany Campaign, 1944–45 (despatches); 4th QO Hussars, Malayan Campaign, 1948–51; Middle East Centre for Arab Studies, 1952–53; GSO2, HQ British Troops Egypt, 1954–55; Technical Staff Course, RMCS, 1956–58; 10th Royal Hussars, 1959–61; GSO2, WO, 1961; retd from Army and joined Foreign (subseq. Diplomatic) Service, 1961; 1st Sec., FO, 1961–62; Information Adviser to Governor of Aden, 1962–63; FO, 1964–66; Commercial Sec., Kuwait, 1966–69; Counsellor, Amman, 1969–71; Trade Comr, Toronto, 1971–74; Consul General, Vancouver, 1974–76; Ambassador to Yemen Arab Republic, 1977–78, and to Republic of Jibuti (non-resident), 1978, to the Lebanon, 1978–81, to Algeria, 1981–84. Principal, Mill of Strachan Language Inst., 1984–89. Vice Chm., Kincardine and Deeside Lib Dems, 1993–95; Chm., W Aberdeenshire and Kincardine Lib Dems, 1995–2000 (Pres., 2000–); Mem. Policy Cttee, Scottish Lib Dems, 1998–. *Publication:* The Skirts of Alpha: an alternative to the Materialist Philosophy. *Recreations:* crofting, writing. *Address:* Mill of Strachan, Strachan, Kincardineshire AB31 6NS. *T:* (01330) 850663. *Club:* Lansdowne.

STRACHAN, Crispian; *see* Strachan, J. C.

STRACHAN, Hon. Sir Curtis (Victor), Kt 1996; CVO 1985; Speaker, House of Representatives, Grenada, West Indies, 1995–2002; *b* 29 May 1926; *s* of Walter and Rosanna Strachan; *m* 1959; one *s. Educ:* Constantine Methodist Sch.; Grenada Boys' Secondary Sch.; Univ. of W Indies. Public Officer, Grenada, 1946, then Perm. Sec.; Clerk of Parlt, Grenada, 1959. *Publications include:* Mainly for Parliamentary Freshmen; Assisting the New Member; The Basic Procedure. *Recreations:* tennis, swimming. *Address:* Bloomsbury, PO Box 681, 5 Tanteen Terrace, Grenada, West Indies. *T:* 4402687.

STRACHAN, (Douglas) Mark (Arthur); QC 1987; a Recorder, 1990–2002; a Deputy High Court Judge, Queen's Bench Division, 1993–2002; *b* 25 Sept. 1946; *s* of late William Arthur Watkin Strachan and Joyce Olive Strachan; *m* 1995, Elizabeth Vickery; one *s. Educ:* Orange Hill Grammar Sch., Edgware, Middx; St Catherine's Coll., Oxford (Open Exhibnr in Eng. Lit.; BCL, MA); Nancy Univ. (French Govt Schol.). Called to the Bar, Inner Temple, 1969 (Major Schol. 1969–71), Hong Kong, 2002; Asst Recorder, 1987–90. *Publications:* contributor to Modern Law Rev. *Recreations:* son Charlie, France, Far East, antiques, paintings, food.

STRACHAN, Prof. Hew Francis Anthony, PhD; DL; FRSE; Chichele Professor of The History of War, and Fellow of All Souls College, Oxford, since 2002; Director, Leverhulme Programme on the Changing Character of War, Oxford University, since 2004; *b* 1 Sept. 1949; *s* of late Michael Francis Strachan, CBE and Iris Strachan; *m* 1st, 1971, Catherine Margaret Blackburn (marr. diss. 1980); two *d*; 2nd, 1982, Pamela Dorothy Tennant (*née* Symes); one *s*, and one step *s* one step *d. Educ:* Rugby; Corpus Christi Coll., Cambridge (MA, PhD 1977). FRSE 2003. Res. Fellow, Corpus Christi Coll., Cambridge, 1975–78; Sen. Lectr in War Studies, RMA, Sandhurst, 1978–79; Corpus Christi College, Cambridge: Fellow, 1979–92, Life Fellow, 1992; Admissions Tutor, 1981–88, Sen. Tutor, 1989–92; Dean of Coll., 1981–86; Prof. of Modern Hist., 1992–2001, and Dir, Scottish Centre for War Studies, 1996–2001, Glasgow Univ. Vis. Prof., Royal Norwegian Air Force Acad., 2000–. Lees Knowles Lectr, Cambridge, 1995; Thank Offering to Britain Fellow, British Acad., 1998–99. Comr, Commonwealth War Graves Commn, 2006–. Member of Council: Lancing Coll., 1982–90; Nat. Army Mus., 1994–2003; Governor: Rugby Sch., 1985–; Stowe Sch., 1990–2002. Mem., Royal Co. of Archers, Queen's Bodyguard for Scotland, 1996– (Mem., Council, 2003–). DUniv Paisley, 2005. DL Tweeddale, 2006. *Publications:* British Military Uniforms 1768–1796, 1975; History of Cambridge University Officers' Training Corps, 1976; European Armies and the Conduct of War, 1983; Wellington's Legacy: the reform of the British Army, 1984; From Waterloo to Balaclava: tactics, technology and the British Army 1815–1854, 1985 (Templer Medal, Soc. for Army Histl Res.); The Politics of the British Army, 1997 (Westminster Medal, RUSI); (ed) Oxford Illustrated History of the First World War, 1998; (ed) The British Army, Manpower and Society, 2000; The First World War: vol. 1, To Arms, 2001; The First World War: a new illustrated history, 2003; (ed) Big Wars and Small Wars, 2006; Clausewitz's On War: a biography, 2007. *Recreations:* shooting, Rugby football (now spectating). *Address:* All Souls College, Oxford OX1 4AL. *Clubs:* Hawks (Cambridge); New (Edinburgh).

STRACHAN, James Murray; Member of Court, Bank of England, since 2006 (Member, Audit Committee, since 2006); *b* 10 Nov. 1953; *s* of Eric Alexander Howieson Strachan and Jacqueline Georgina Strachan. *Educ:* King's Sch., Canterbury; Christ's Coll., Cambridge (exhibnr, BA); London Coll. of Printing; London Business Sch. Chase Manhattan Bank, 1976–77; joined Merrill Lynch, 1977, Exec. Dir, 1982–86, Man. Dir, 1986–89; writer and photographer, 1989–97; Associate Photographer, Getty Images (formerly Tony Stone), 1990–; Chief Exec., 1997–2002, Chm., 2002–07, Vice Pres., 2008–, RNID (Mem., Finance Cttee and Trustee, 1994–96); Chm., Audit Commn, 2002–06. Vis. Fellow, LSE, 2005–. Rotating Chair, Disability Charities Consortium, 1997–2002; Co-Chair: Task Force on Social Services Provision for Deaf and Hard of Hearing People, 1998–2002; NHS Modernising Hearing Aid Services Gp, 1999–2002; Chm., Task Force on Audiology Services, 2000–02; Member: Ministerial Disability Rights Task Force, 1997–99; Ministerial Disability Benefits Forum, 1998–99; Bd and Audit Cttee, Ofgem, 2000–04; Bd, Community Fund, 2001–03; Comr for Communications, Disability Rights Commn, 1999–2002; Audit, Remuneration and Nomination Committees: Bd, Legal and General Gp plc, 2003–; Bd, Welsh Water Ltd, 2007–; Bd, Remuneration Cttee, Sarasin & Partners LLP, 2008–; Chm., Remuneration and Mem. Nominations Cttees, Bd, Care UK plc, 2006–. Non-exec. Dir, Social Finance Ltd, 2008–. Ext. Mem., DTI Transition Gp (Energy), 2001–02; Ind. Mem., DTI Business Bd, 2002–04. Mem., Adv. Gp on Diversity, NCVO, 2001–03; Pres., Midland Regl Assoc. for Deaf, 2001–. Trustee: Save the Children, 1999–2002; Somerset House Trust, 2003–08 (Chm., Audit and Finance Cttee, 2006–08). Leadership Patron, Nat. Coll. of School Leadership, 2003–. Hon. Fellow, Univ. of the Arts, London (formerly London Inst.), 2002. *Publications:* Madrid, 1991; numerous illustrated travel books as photographer; contrib. The Times, Financial Times and Sunday Times. *Recreations:* film, reading, swimming, photography. *Address:* 10B Wedderburn Road, NW3 5QG; *e-mail:* james.strachan@mac.com.

STRACHAN, Jeremy Alan Watkin; Secretary, British Medical Association, 2001–04; *b* 14 Dec. 1944; *s* of William Arthur Watkin Strachan and Joyce Olive Strachan; *m* 1976, Margaret Elizabeth McVay; two step *d. Educ:* Haberdashers' Aske's Sch., Elstree; St Catharine's Coll., Cambridge (MA, LLM). Called to the Bar, Inner Temple, 1969 (Paul Methven Entrance Schol.); Legal Asst, Law Commn, 1967–72; Legal Advr, BSC, 1972–78; Principal Legal Advr and Hd, Legal and Patent Services, ICL, 1978–84; Gp Legal Advr, Standard Telephones and Cables, 1984–85; Dir, Gp Legal Services, and Corporate Affairs, Glaxo Hldgs, 1986–91; Exec. Dir, responsible for legal services, corporate policy and public affairs, and business develt, Glaxo Wellcome, 1992–2000. Non-exec. Dir, NHS Business Services Authy, 2005–. Vice-Chm., Disciplinary Appeals Cttee, CIMA, 2005–. *Recreations:* France, food, controversy.

STRACHAN, John Charles Haggart, FRCS, FRCSE; Orthopaedic Consultant, Chelsea and Westminster Hospital, 1993; *b* 2 Oct. 1936; *s* of late Charles George Strachan, MBE and Elsie Strachan; *m* 1966, Caroline Mary Parks; one *s* three *d. Educ:* St Mary's Hosp., Univ. of London (MB BS 1961). Consultant Orthopaedic Surgeon, Charing Cross Hosp., 1971–95; Consultant Surgeon, Royal Ballet, 1971. *Publications:* contribs to professional jls. *Recreations:* sailing, fishing. *Address:* 28 Chalcot Square, NW1 8YA. *T:* (020) 7586 1278. *Clubs:* Garrick, Flyfishers', Royal Thames Yacht; Royal Southern Yacht.

STRACHAN, (John) Crispian, CBE 2003; QPM 1996; DL; Director, OSL, since 2005; *b* 5 July 1949; *s* of late Dr (Mark) Noel Strachan and Barbara Joan Strachan; *m* 1974, Denise Anne Farmer; one *s* three *d. Educ:* Jesus Coll., Oxford (BA Jurisp 1971; MA 1989); Sheffield Univ. (MA Criminology 1972). Joined Metropolitan Police, 1972; Inspector, 1977–83; Chief Inspector, 1983–87; Superintendent, 1987–90; Chief Superintendent, 1990–93; Asst Chief Constable, Strathclyde Police, 1993–98; Chief Constable, Northumbria Police, 1998–2005. DL Tyne and Wear, 2002. Dep. County Pres., St John Ambulance Northumbria, 2006–. Trustee, Royal Grammar Sch. (Newcastle upon Tyne) Educnl Trust, 2006–. FRSA 2005. OStJ 2005. *Publications:* (with A. Comben) A Short Guide to Policing in the UK, 1992; (contrib.) Clinical Forensic Medicine, 3rd edn 2007. *Recreations:* woodworking, photography, the countryside, family above all. *Address:* Clifton House, Clifton, Morpeth, Northumberland NE61 6DQ; *e-mail:* crispianstrachan@hotmail.co.uk, c.strachan@outsource.us.com.

STRACHAN, Mark; *see* Strachan, D. M. A.

STRACHAN, Dame Valerie (Patricia Marie), DCB 1998 (CB 1991); Vice Chair, Big Lottery Fund, 2004–06; Deputy Chair, Community Fund (formerly National Lottery Charities Board), 2000–04; *b* 10 Jan. 1940; *d* of John Jonas Nicholls and Louise Nicholls; *m* 1965, John Strachan; one *s* one *d. Educ:* Newland High Sch., Hull; Manchester Univ. (BA). Joined HM Customs and Excise, 1961; Dept of Economic Affairs, 1964; Home Office, 1966; Principal, HM Customs and Excise, 1966; Treasury, 1972; Asst Secretary, HM Customs and Excise, 1974, Comr, 1980; Head, Joint Management Unit, HM Treasury/Cabinet Office, 1985–87; a Dep. Chm., 1987–93, Chm., 1993–2000, Bd of Customs and Excise. External Mem., H of L Audit Cttee, 2002–. Chm., Communications and Public Service (formerly CS, PO and BT) Lifeboat Fund, 1998–2004. Pres., British Internat. Freight Assoc., 2002–04. Chairman: Govs, James Allen's Girls' Sch., 2004–; Council, Univ. of Southampton, 2006–. CCMI. Hon. LLD Manchester, 1995.

STRACHEY, family name of **Baron O'Hagan**.

STRACHEY, Charles; local government officer, retired; *b* 20 June 1934; *s* of Rt Hon. Evelyn John St Loe Strachey (*d* 1963) and Celia (*d* 1980), 3rd *d* of late Rev. Arthur Hume Simpson; *S* to baronetcy of cousin, 2nd Baron Strachie, 1973 as 6th Bt *cr* 1801, but does not use the title, and his name does not appear on the Official Roll of the Baronetage; *m*

1973, Janet Megan, *d* of Alexander Miller; one *d*. *Heir: kinsman* Henry Leofric Benvenuto Strachey, *b* 17 April 1947. *Address:* 31 Northchurch Terrace, N1 4EB. *T:* (020) 7684 5479.

STRADBROKE, 6th Earl of, *cr* 1821; **Robert Keith Rous;** Bt 1660; Baron Rous 1796; Viscount Dunwich 1821; grazier, Mount Fyans Station, Darlington, Victoria; *b* 25 March 1937; *s* of 5th Earl of Stradbroke and Pamela Catherine Mabell (*d* 1972), *d* of Captain Hon. Edward James Kay-Shuttleworth; *S* father, 1983, but does not use the title; *m* 1960, Dawn Antoinette (marr. diss. 1977), *d* of Thomas Edward Beverley, Brisbane; two *s* five *d*; 2nd, 1977, Roseanna Mary Blanche, *d* of late Francis Reitman, MD; six *s* two *d*. *Educ:* Harrow. *Recreation:* making babies. *Heir: s* Viscount Dunwich, *qv*. *Address:* Box 383, Richmond, Vic 3121, Australia. *T:* (4) 27901294, *Fax:* (3) 94259957.

STRADLING, Donald George; Group Personnel Director, John Laing & Son Ltd, then John Laing plc, 1969–89; Director, Quantum Care, 2000–04; *b* 7 Sept. 1929; *s* of George Frederic and Olive Emily Stradling; *m* 1st, 1955, Mary Anne Hartridge (*d* 2000); two *d*; 2nd, 2004, Elizabeth Lilian Jane Dennis (*née* Hewitt). *Educ:* Clifton Coll.; Magdalen Coll., Oxford (Open Exhibnr; MA). CIPM. School Master, St Albans Sch., 1954–55; Group Trng and Educn Officer, John Laing & Son Ltd, Building and Civil Engrg Contractors, 1955. Vis. Prof., Univ. of Salford, 1989–94. Comr, Manpower Services Commn, 1980–82; Mem. Council, Inst. of Manpower Studies, 1975–81; Member: Employment Policy Cttee, CBI, 1978–84, 1986–91; Council, CBI, 1982–86; FCEC Wages and Industrial Cttee, 1978–95; Council, FCEC, 1985–95; National Steering Gp, New Technical and Vocational Educn Initiative, 1983–88; NHS Trng Authy, 1985–89. Director: Building and Civil Engrg Benefits Scheme (Trustee, 1984–2004); Building and Civil Engrg Holidays Scheme Management, 1984–2004; Construction ITB, 1985–90. Vice-Pres., Inst. of Personnel Management, 1974–76. Vice-Chm. of Governors, St Albans High Sch., 1977–95; Mem. Council, Tyndale House, 1977–96. Liveryman, Glaziers' and Painters of Glass Co., 1983–95, 2003–. Hon. PhD Internat. Management Centre, Buckingham, 1987; Hon. DSc Salford, 1995. *Publications:* contribs on music and musical instruments, et al. to New Bible Dictionary, 1962. *Recreations:* listening to music (espec. opera), walking. *Address:* Courts Edge, 12 The Warren, Harpenden, Herts AL5 2NH. *Club:* Institute of Directors.

STRAFFORD, 8th Earl of, *cr* 1847; **Thomas Edmund Byng;** Baron Strafford, 1835; Viscount Enfield, 1847; nurseryman, riverkeeper and artist's companion; *b* 26 Sept. 1936; *s* of 7th Earl of Strafford, and Maria Magdalena Elizabeth, *d* of late Henry Cloete, CMG, Alphen, S Africa; *S* father, 1984; *m* 1963, Jennifer Mary (marr. diss. 1981), *er d* of late Rt Hon. W. M. May, FCA, PC, MP, and of Mrs May, Mertoun Hall, Holywood, Co. Down; two *s* two *d*; 2nd, 1981, Mrs Julia Mary Howard, (Judy), *d* of Sir Dennis Pilcher, CBE. *Educ:* Eton; Clare Coll., Cambridge. Lieut, Royal Sussex Regt (National Service). Councillor, Winchester and District, 1983–87. *Recreations:* gardening, travelling. *Heir: s* Viscount Enfield, *qv*. *Address:* Apple Tree Cottage, Easton, Winchester, Hants SO21 1EF. *T:* (01962) 779467.

See also Hon. J. E. Byng.

STRAKER, Anita, CB 2001; OBE 1990; *b* 22 June 1938; *d* of David William Barham and Laura Barham; *m* 1961, Patrick Vincent Straker; four *s*. *Educ:* Weston-super-Mare Grammar Sch. for Girls; University Coll. London (BSc Hons); Royal Holloway Coll., Univ. of London (MSc); Univ. of Cambridge Inst. of Educn (PGCE). Teacher, 1961–62 and 1968–74; Inspector for maths, Surrey LEA, 1974–78; Gen. Advr, Wilts LEA, 1978–83; Dir, Microelectronics Educn Prog. Primary Project, DES, 1983–86; Dist Inspector, ILEA, 1986–89; Principal Advr, Berks LEA, 1989–93; Dep. Dir of Educn, Camden LEA, 1993–96; Dir, Nat. Numeracy Strategy, DFE, then DfEE, 1996–2000; Dir, Key Stage 3 Nat. Strategy, DfEE, then DfES, 2000–02. Hon. LLD UEA, 2002. *Publications:* Mathematics for Gifted Pupils, 1980; Children Using Computers, 1988; Mathematics from China, 1990; Primary Maths Extension Activities, 1991; Talking Points in Mathematics, 1993; Mental Maths (series), 1994; Home Maths (series), 1998; Exploring Maths, 2008. *Recreations:* holidays abroad, cooking, reading, swimming. *Address:* Mundays, St Mary Bourne, Andover, Hants SP11 6AY. *T:* (01264) 738474.

STRAKER, Major Ivan Charles; Chairman, Seagram Distillers plc, 1984–93 (Chief Executive, 1983–90); *b* 17 June 1928; *s* of Arthur Coppin Straker and Cicely Longueville Straker; *m* 1st, 1954, Gillian Elizabeth Grant (marr. diss. 1971); one *s* one *d* (and one *s* decd); 2nd, 1976, Sally Jane Hastings (marr. diss. 1986); one *s*; 3rd, 1998, Rosemary Ann Whitaker. *Educ:* Harrow; RMA, Sandhurst. Commissioned 11th Hussars (PAO), 1948; served Germany, N Ireland, Middle East and Mil. Intell. Staff, War Office; left HM Armed Forces, 1962. Man. Dir, D. Rintoul & Co., 1964; Man. Dir, The Glenlivet and Glen Grant Agencies, 1964–71; apptd Main Board, The Glenlivet and Glen Grant Distillers, 1967; Chief Exec., The Glenlivet Distillers Ltd, 1971. Dir, Lothians Racing Syndicate Ltd, 1986–. Council Mem., Scotch Whisky Assoc., 1978–90 (Chm., Public Affairs Cttee, 1986–90). *Recreations:* fishing, shooting, racing. *Address:* Oaktree Cottage, Acomb, Hexham, Northumberland NE46 4PL. *T:* (01434) 604509. *Clubs:* Jockey, Cavalry and Guards, White's.

STRAKER, Timothy Derrick; QC 1996; a Recorder, since 2000; *b* 25 May 1955; *s* of late Derrick Straker, solicitor, and Dorothy Elizabeth, *o d* of late Brig. T. L. Rogers, CBE; *m* 1982, Ann Horton Baylis (marr. diss. 2007); two *d*. *Educ:* Malvern Coll.; Downing Coll., Cambridge (BA 1st Cl. Hons Law, MA). Called to the Bar: Gray's Inn, 1977 (Holt Schol.), Bencher, 2004; Lincoln's Inn, *ad eundem*, 1979; NI, 2001; Trinidad and Tobago, 2001; in practice at the Bar, 1977–; an Asst Recorder, 1998–2000. Jt Hd of Chambers, 2002–. Member: Admin. Law Bar Assoc., 1986–; Local Govt, Planning and Envmtl Bar Assoc., 1986–; Crown Office Users' Cttee, 1993–2000; Administrative Court Users' Assoc., 2000–. Contrib. Ed., Civil Court Practice, 1999–2008. *Publications:* Annotated Current Law Statutes, 1994; (Consultant Ed.) Registration of Political Parties: a guide to Returning Officers, 1999; (with Iain Goldrein) Human Rights and Judicial Review: case studies in context, 2000; (with Philip Coppel) Information Rights, 2004; Electoral Administration Act, 2006; contrib. Halsbury's Laws of England (Public Health and Environmental Protection, 2000; Local Government, 2001; Markets, 2002); contrib. Rights of Way Law Review, Judicial Review. *Recreations:* cricket, history. *Address:* 4–5 Gray's Inn Square, Gray's Inn, WC1R 5AH. *T:* (020) 7404 5252. *Clubs:* Lansdowne, Royal Over-Seas League.

STRAND, Prof. Kenneth T.; Professor, Department of Economics, Simon Fraser University, 1968–86, now Emeritus; *b* Yakima, Wash, 30 June 1931; Canadian citizen since 1974; *m* 1960, Elna K. Tomaske; no *c*. *Educ:* Washington State Coll. (BA); Univ. of Wisconsin (PhD, MS). Woodrow Wilson Fellow, 1955–56; Ford Foundn Fellow, 1957–58; Herfurth Award, Univ. of Wisconsin, 1961 (for PhD thesis). Asst Exec. Sec., Hanford Contractors Negotiation Cttee, Richland, Wash, 1953–55; Asst Prof., Washington State Univ., 1959–60; Asst Prof., Oberlin Coll., 1960–65 (on leave, 1963–65); Economist, Manpower and Social Affairs Div., OECD, Paris, 1964–66; Assoc. Prof., Dept of Econs, Simon Fraser Univ., 1966–68; Pres., Simon Fraser Univ., 1969–74 (Acting Pres., 1968–69). Mem., Canadian Industrial Relations Assoc. (Pres., 1983). Hon. LLD Simon Fraser Univ., 1983. FRSA 1972. *Publications:* Jurisdictional Disputes in Construction: The Causes, The Joint Board and the NLRB, 1961; contribs to Review of Econs and Statistics, Amer. Econ. Review, Industrial Relations, Sociaal Mannblad Arbeid. *Recreations:* fishing, ski-ing. *Address:* PO Box 5009, Lac Le Jeune, BC V1S 1Y8, Canada.

STRANG, family name of **Baron Strang**.

STRANG, 2nd Baron *cr* 1954, of Stonesfield; **Colin Strang;** Professor of Philosophy, University of Newcastle upon Tyne, 1975–82; Dean of the Faculty of Arts, 1976–79; retired 1982; *b* 12 June 1922; *s* of 1st Baron Strang, GCB, GCMG, MBE, and Elsie Wynne (*d* 1974), *d* of late J. E. Jones; *S* father, 1978; *m* 1st, 1948, Patricia Marie, *d* of Meiert C. Avis, Johannesburg; 2nd, 1955, Barbara Mary Hope Carr (*d* 1982); one *d*; 3rd, 1984, Mary Shewell. *Educ:* Merchant Taylors' School; St John's Coll., Oxford (MA, BPhil). *Heir:* none. *Address:* Broombank, Lochranza, Isle of Arran KA27 8JF.

STRANG, David James Reid, QPM 2002; Chief Constable, Lothian and Borders Police, since 2007; *b* Glasgow, 9 April 1958; *s* of William Guthrie Strang and Morag Langlands Strang; *m* 1981, Alison; one *s* two *d*. *Educ:* Glasgow Acad.; Loretto Sch.; Univ. of Durham (BSc 1980); Birkbeck Coll., London (MSc 1989). Metropolitan Police, 1980–98; Asst Chief Constable, Lothian and Borders Police, 1998–2001; Chief Constable, Dumfries and Galloway Constabulary, 2001–07. *Address:* Lothian and Borders Police Headquarters, Fettes Avenue, Edinburgh EH4 1RB. *T:* (0131) 311 3086; *e-mail:* chief.constable@lbp.pnn.police.uk.

STRANG, Rt Hon. Gavin (Steel); PC 1997; MP (Lab) Edinburgh East, 1970–97 and since 2005 (Edinburgh East and Musselburgh, 1997–2005); *b* 10 July 1943; *s* of James Steel Strang and Marie Strang (*née* Finkle); *m*. *Educ:* Univs of Edinburgh and Cambridge. BSc Hons Edinburgh, 1964; DipAgricSci Cambridge, 1965; PhD Edinburgh, 1968. Mem., Tayside Econ. Planning Consultative Group, 1966–68; Scientist with ARC, 1968–70. Opposition front bench spokesman on Scottish affairs, 1972–73, on energy, 1973–74; Parly Under-Sec. of State, Dept of Energy, March-Oct. 1974; Parly Sec., MAFF, 1974–79; Opposition front bench spokesman on agriculture, 1979–82, on employment, 1987–89, on food, agriculture and rural affairs, 1992–97; Mem., Shadow Cabinet, 1994–97; Minister for Transport, 1997–98. Chm., PLP Defence Group, 1984–87. *Publications:* articles in Animal Production. *Recreations:* golf, swimming, watching football. *Club:* Newcraighall Miners' Welfare (Edinburgh).

STRANG, Prof. John Stanley, MD; FRCPsych; FRCP; Professor of the Addictions, Institute of Psychiatry, London University, and Director, National Addiction Centre, since 1995; *b* 12 May 1950; *s* of late William John Strang, CBE, FRS, and of Margaret Nicholas Strang (*née* Howells); *m* 1984, Jennifer Abbey; two *s* (one *d* decd). *Educ:* Bryanston Sch., Dorset; Guy's Hosp. Med. Sch. (MB BS; MD 1995). FRCPsych 1994; FRCP 2006. Consultant psychiatrist in drug dependence: Manchester, 1982–86; Maudsley Hosp., London, 1986–; Getty Sen. Lectr in the Addictions, Nat. Addiction Centre, Inst. of Psychiatry, 1991–95. Consultant Advr (drugs), DoH, 1986–2003. Mem., Adv. Council on Misuse of Drugs, 1989–2001. Hon. FAChAM 2005. *Publications:* (with G. Stimson) AIDS and Drug Misuse: the challenge for policy and practice in the 1990's, 1990; (jtly) Drugs, Alcohol and Tobacco: making the science and policy connections, 1993; (with M. Gossop) Heroin Addiction and Drug Policy: the British system, 1994; (with J. Sheridan) Drug Misuse and Community Pharmacy, 2002; (with G. Tober) Methadone Matters, 2003; (with M. Gossop) Heroin Addiction and the British System, 2 vols, 2005. *Address:* National Addiction Centre, Addiction Sciences Building, 4 Windsor Walk, SE5 8AF. *T:* (020) 7848 0438. *Club:* Athenæum.

STRANG STEEL, Major Sir (Fiennes) Michael, 3rd Bt *cr* 1938, of Philiphaugh, Selkirk; CBE 1999; DL; Vice Lord-Lieutenant, Borders Region (Roxburgh, Ettrick and Lauderdale), since 2008; *b* 22 Feb. 1943; *s* of Sir (Fiennes) William Strang Steel, 2nd Bt and Joan Strang Steel (*d* 1982), *d* of Brig.-Gen. Sir Brodie Haldane Henderson, KCMG, CB; *S* father, 1992; *m* 1977, Sarah Jane Russell; two *s* one *d*. *Educ:* Eton. Major, 17/21 Lancers, 1962–80, retd. Forestry Comr, 1988–99. Ensign, Royal Co. of Archers, Queen's Body Guard for Scotland, 2007–. DL Borders Region (Districts of Roxburgh, Ettrick & Lauderdale), 1990. *Heir: s* (Fiennes) Edward Strang Steel, *b* 8 Nov. 1978. *Address:* Philiphaugh, Selkirk TD7 5LX. *Club:* Cavalry and Guards.

STRANGE, 17th Baron *cr* 1628; **Adam Humphrey Drummond;** *b* 20 April 1953; *s* of Captain Humphrey ap Evans, MC, who assumed name of Drummond of Megginch by decree of Lord Lyon, 1965, and Baroness Strange (16th in line); *S* mother, 2005; *m* 1988, Hon. Mary Emma Jeronima Dewar, *d* of Baron Forteviot, *qv*; one *s* one *d*. *Educ:* Eton; RMA Sandhurst; Heriot-Watt Univ. (MSc (Housing)). MCIH. Major, Grenadier Guards. *Heir: s* Hon. John Adam Humphrey Drummond, *b* 3 Nov. 1992. *Club:* Royal Perth Golfing Society.

STRANGE, Rt Rev. Mark Jeremy; *see* Moray, Ross and Caithness, Bishop of.

STRANGWAYS; *see* Fox-Strangways, family name of Earl of Ilchester.

STRANRAER-MULL, Very Rev. Gerald; Dean of Aberdeen and Orkney, 1988–2008, now Emeritus; Rector of Ellon and Cruden Bay, 1972–2008; *b* 24 Nov. 1942; *s* of Gerald and Lena Stranraer-Mull; *m* 1967, Glynis Mary Kempe; one *s* one *d* (and one *s* decd). *Educ:* Woodhouse Grove School, Apperley Bridge; King's College, London (AKC 1969); Saint Augustine's College, Canterbury. Journalist, 1960–66. Curate: Hexham Abbey, 1970–72; Corbridge, 1972; Priest-in-Charge of St Peter's, Peterhead, 2001–04. Editor of Aberdeen and Buchan Churchman, 1976–84, 1991–94; Director of Training for Ministry, Diocese of Aberdeen and Orkney, 1982–90; Canon of Saint Andrew's Cathedral, Aberdeen, 1981–2008. Director: Oil Chaplaincy Trust, 1993–2008; Duncraig, Iona (formerly Iona Cornerstone Foundn), 1995–. Warden, Soc. of Our Lady of the Isles, Isle of Fetlar, Shetland, 2006–. *Publications:* A Turbulent House: the Augustinians at Hexham, 1970; View of the Diocese, 1977; A Church for Scotland: the story of the Scottish Episcopal Church, 2000. *Address:* 75 The Cairns, Muir of Ord, Ross-shire IV6 7AT. *T:* (01463) 870986.

STRATFORD, Ian Dodd; Chief Executive, Newcastle City Council, since 2002; *b* 26 June 1954; *s* of John and Elsie Stratford; *m* 1994, Debra Jean Wolstenholme; one *s* one *d*. *Educ:* Univ. of Salford (BSc Hons Geog. 1977). MCIH 1982. Area Housing Manager, Middlesbrough, 1983–88; Dep. Dir, 1987–90, Dir, 1990–97, of Housing, Enfield LBC; Exec. Dir, Personal Services, 1997–2000, Dep. Chief Exec., 2000–02, Thurrock Council. Chm., London Business Innovation Centre, 1995–97; Clerk, Tyne and Wear PTA, 2002–; non-exec. Dir, Nexus Transport Exec., 2002–; Director: NewcastleGateshead Initiative, 2002–; Tyne and Wear Develt Co., 2002–. Company Sec., Newcastle Th. Royal, 2002–; Member of Board: Newcastle Science City, 2005–; NewcastleGateshead City Develt Co., 2008–; Lay Mem., Court, Univ. of Newcastle upon Tyne, 2005–. *Recreations:* live music, sailing, walking in Northumberland. *Address:* Newcastle City Council, Civic Centre, Newcastle upon Tyne NE99 2BN. *T:* (0191) 211 5001, *Fax:* (0191) 211 4908.

STRATFORD, Neil Martin; Keeper of Medieval and Later Antiquities, British Museum, 1975–98, now Keeper Emeritus; *b* 26 April 1938; *s* of late Dr Martin Gould Stratford and Dr Mavis Stratford (*née* Beddall); *m* 1966, Anita Jennifer Lewis; two *d*. *Educ:* Marlborough Coll.; Magdalene Coll., Cambridge (BA Hons English 1961, MA); Courtauld Inst., London Univ. (BA Hons History of Art 1966). 2nd Lieut Coldstream Guards, 1956–58; Trainee Kleinwort, Benson, Lonsdale Ltd, 1961–63; Lecturer, Westfield Coll., London Univ., 1969–75; Prof. of Hist. of Medieval Art, Ecole Nationale des Chartes, Paris, 2000–03. British Academy/Leverhulme Sen. Res. Fellow, 1991; Mem., Inst. for Advanced Study, Princeton, 1998–99; Appleton Vis. Prof., Florida State Univ., 2000; Vis. Sen. Lecturing Fellow, Duke Univ., 2006. Chm., St Albans Cathedral Fabric Cttee, 1995–; Mem., Conseil Scientifique, Société Française d'Archéologie, 1994–; Pres., Comité scientifique pour la restauration et mise en valeur de l'ancienne abbaye de Cluny, 2005–. Liveryman, Haberdashers' Company 1959–. Hon. Mem., Académie de Dijon, 1975; For. Mem., Société Nationale des Antiquaires de France, 1985; For. Corresp. Mem., Acad. des Inscriptions et Belles-Lettres, 2002. FSA 1976. Officier, Ordre des Arts et des Lettres (France), 2006. *Publications:* La Sculpture Oubliée de Vézelay, 1984; Catalogue of Medieval Enamels in the British Museum, vol. II, Northern Romanesque Enamel, 1993; Westminster Kings and the medieval Palace of Westminster, 1995; The Lewis Chessmen and the enigma of the hoard, 1997; Studies in Burgundian Romanesque Sculpture, 1998; La Frise romane monumental de Souvigny, 2002; Chronos et Cosmos: le pilier roman de Souvigny, 2005; articles in French and English periodicals. *Recreations:* opera, food and wine, cricket and football. *Address:* 17 Church Row, NW3 6UP. *T:* (020) 7794 5688. *Clubs:* Beefsteak, Garrick, MCC, I Zingari; University Pitt, Hawks (Cambridge).

STRATHALLAN, Viscount; James David Drummond; Director, Westover (formerly Creswell) Medical Ltd, since 2006; *b* 24 Oct. 1965; *s* and *heir* of Earl of Perth, *qv*. *Address:* Stobhall, Perth PH2 6DR. *T:* (01821) 640332.

STRATHALMOND, 3rd Baron *cr* 1955; **William Roberton Fraser,** CA; Finance Director, Gerling at Lloyd's (formerly Owen & Wilby Underwriting Agency) Ltd, 1995–2000; *b* 22 July 1947; *s* of 2nd Baron Strathalmond, CMG, OBE, TD, and of Letitia, *d* of late Walter Krementz, New Jersey, USA; *S* father, 1976; *m* 1973, Amanda Rose, *yr d* of Rev. Gordon Clifford Taylor; two *s* one *d*. *Educ:* Loretto. Man. Dir, London Wall Members Agency Ltd, 1986–91 (Dir, 1985–91); Dir, London Wall Hldgs plc, 1986–91; Chm., R. W. Sturge Ltd, 1991–94. Dir, N Atlantic Salmon Fund (UK), 2003–08. Pres., RSAS Agecare, 2008– (Chm. Trustees, 1984–2001; Vice-Pres., 2001–08). Liveryman, Girdlers' Co., 1979–. *Heir: s* Hon. William Gordon Fraser, *b* 24 Sept. 1976. *Address:* Holt House, Elstead, Surrey GU8 6LF.

STRATHCARRON, 3rd Baron *cr* 1936; **Ian David Patrick Macpherson;** Bt 1933; *b* 31 March 1949; *er s* of 2nd Baron Strathcarron and Diana Hawtrey Curle (*née* Deane); *S* father, 2006; *m* 1974, Gillian Rosamund Allison; one *s* one *d*. *Educ:* Grenoble Univ. *Heir: s* Hon. Rory David Alasdair Macpherson, *b* 15 April 1982.

STRATHCLYDE, 2nd Baron *cr* 1955, of Barskimming; **Thomas Galloway Dunlop du Roy de Blicquy Galbraith;** PC 1995; Leader of the Opposition, House of Lords, since 1998; *b* 22 Feb. 1960; *s* of Hon. Sir Thomas Galloway Dunlop Galbraith, KBE, MP (*d* 1982) (*e s* of 1st Baron) and Simone Clothilde Fernande Marie Ghislaine (*d* 1991), *e d* of late Jean du Roy de Blicquy; *S* grandfather, 1985; *m* 1992, Jane, *er d* of John Skinner; three *d*. *Educ:* Wellington College; Univ. of East Anglia (BA 1982); Université d'Aix-en-Provence. Insurance Broker, Bain Dawes, subseq. Bain Clarkson Ltd, 1982–88. Contested (C) Merseyside East, European Parly Election, 1984. Spokesman for DTI, Treasury and Scotland, H of L, 1988–89; Govt Whip, 1988–89; Parly Under-Sec. of State, Dept of Employment, 1989–90, DoE, 1990, 1992–93, Scottish Office (Minister for Agric. and Fisheries), 1990–92, DTI, 1993–94; Minister of State, DTI, 1994; Captain of the Hon. Corps of Gentlemen at Arms (Govt Chief Whip in H of L), 1994–97; Opposition Chief Whip, House of Lords, 1997–98; elected Mem., H of L, 1999. *Heir: b* Hon. Charles William du Roy de Blicquy Galbraith [*b* 20 May 1962; *m* 1992, Bridget, *d* of Brian Reeve; three *s* one *d*]. *Address:* House of Lords, SW1A 0AA. *T:* (020) 7219 5353.

STRATHCONA AND MOUNT ROYAL, 4th Baron *cr* 1900; **Donald Euan Palmer Howard;** *b* 26 Nov. 1923; *s* of 3rd Baron Strathcona and Mount Royal and Diana Evelyn (*d* 1985), twin *d* of 1st Baron Wakehurst; *S* father, 1959; *m* 1st, 1954, Lady Jane Mary Waldegrave (marr. diss. 1977), 2nd *d* of 12th Earl Waldegrave, KG, GCVO; two *s* four *d* (incl. twin *s* and *d*); 2nd, 1978, Patricia (*née* Thomas), *widow* of John Middleton. *Educ:* King's Mead, Seaford; Eton; Trinity Coll., Cambridge; McGill University, Montreal (1947–50). Served War of 1939–45: RN, 1942–47: Midshipman, RNVR, 1943; Lieutenant, 1945. With Urwick, Orr and Partners (Industrial Consultants), 1950–56. Lord in Waiting (Govt Whip), 1973–74; Parly Under-Sec. of State for Defence (RAF), MoD, 1974; Jt Dep. Leader of the Opposition, House of Lords, 1976–79; Minister of State, MoD, 1979–81. Dir, Computing Devices, Hastings, 1981–92. Chairman, Bath Festival Society, 1966–70. Dep. Chm., SS Great Britain Project, 1970–73; Founder Chm., Coastal Forces Heritage Trust, 1995–; President: Falkland Is Trust, 1982–; Steamboat Assoc. of GB, 1972–; Mem. Council, RN Mus., 1982–95. *Recreations:* gardening, sailing. *Heir: s* Hon. Donald Alexander Smith Howard [*b* 24 June 1961; *m* 1992, Jane Maree, *d* of Shaun Gibb; one *s*]. *Address:* Townsend Barn, Poulshot, Devizes, Wilts SN10 1SD. *T:* (01380) 828329; Kiloran, Isle of Colonsay, Argyll PA61 7YU. *T:* (01951) 200301. *Clubs:* Brooks's, Pratt's; Royal Yacht Squadron.

STRATHEDEN, 6th Baron *cr* 1836, **AND CAMPBELL,** 6th Baron *cr* 1841; **Donald Campbell;** *b* 4 April 1934; *s* of 5th Baron Stratheden and Campbell and of Evelyn Mary Austen, *d* of late Col Herbert Austen Smith, CIE; *S* father, 1987; *m* 1st, 1957, Hilary Ann Holland (*d* 1991), *d* of Lt-Col William D. Turner; one *s* three *d*; 2nd, 2001, Elaine Margaret Fogarty. *Educ:* Eton. *Heir: s* Hon. David Anthony Campbell [*b* 13 Feb. 1963; *m* 1993, Jennifer Margaret Owens; two *d*]. *Address:* Yalara, 120 Happy Jack Creek Road, Ridgewood, Cooroy, Qld 4563, Australia.

STRATHERN, Prof. Andrew Jamieson, PhD; Andrew Mellon Professor of Anthropology, University of Pittsburgh, since 1987; Emeritus Professor of Anthropology, University of London; Hon. Research Fellow, Institute of Papua New Guinea Studies, Port Moresby, since 1977 (Director, 1981–86); *b* 19 Jan. 1939; *s* of Robert Strathern and Mary Strathern (*née* Sharp); *m* 1963, Ann Marilyn Evans (marr. diss. 1986); two *s* one *d*; *m* 1997, Pamela J. Stewart. *Educ:* Colchester Royal Grammar Sch.; Trinity Coll., Cambridge (BA, PhD). Research Fellow, Trinity Coll., Cambridge, 1965–68; Research Fellow, then Fellow, Australian National Univ., 1969–72; Professor, later Vis. Professor, Dept of Anthropology and Sociology, Univ. of Papua New Guinea, 1973–77; Prof. of Anthropology and Hd of Dept of Anthropology, UCL, 1976–83. Hon. Mem., Phi Beta Kappa, 1993. Rivers Memorial Medal, RAI, 1976. 10th Independence Anniv. Medal (PNG), 1987. *Publications:* The Rope of Moka, 1971; One Father, One Blood, 1972; (with M. Strathern) Self-decoration in Mount Hagen, 1972; Melpa Amb Kenan, 1974; Myths and Legends from Mt Hagen, 1977; Beneath the Andaiya Tree, 1977; Ongka, 1979; (with Malcolm Kirk) Man as Art, 1981; Inequality in New Guinea Highlands Societies, 1982; Wiru Laa, 1983; A line of power, 1984; (ed jtly) Strauss, The Mi Culture of the Mount Hagen People, 1990; (with P. Birnbaum) Faces of Papua New Guinea, 1991; Landmarks: reflections on anthropology, 1993; Voices of Conflict, 1993; Ru, 1993; Body Thoughts, 1996; (ed jtly) Millennial Markers, 1997; (ed jtly) Bodies and Persons, 1998; (ed jtly) Identity Work, 2000; (jtly) Oceania: an introduction to the cultures and identities of Pacific Islanders, 2002; with P. J. Stewart: A Death to Pay For: individual voices, 1998; Curing and Healing, 1999; Collaborations and Conflicts: a leader through time, 1999; Arrow Talk, 2000; The Python's Back: pathways of comparison between Indonesia and Melanesia, 2000; Minorities and Memories: survivals and extinctions in Scotland and western Europe, 2001; Humors and Substances: ideas of the body in New Guinea, 2001; Gender, Song and Sensibility: folktales and folksongs in the Highlands New Guinea, 2002; Remaking the World: myth, mining and ritual change among the Duna of Papua New Guinea, 2002; Violence: theory and ethnography, 2002; (ed) Landscape, Memory and History, 2003; Witchcraft, Sorcery, Rumors and Gossip, 2003; articles in Man, Oceania, Ethnology, Jl Polyn Soc., Amer. Anthropology, Amer. Ethnology, Mankind, Bijdragen, Jl de la Soc. des Océanistes, Oral History, Bikmaus, Pacific Studies, Ethos, Jl of Ethnomusicology, Canberra Anthropology, Historische Anthropologie, Aust. Jl of Anthropology, Ethnohistory. *Address:* Department of Anthropology, University of Pittsburgh, Pittsburgh, PA 15260, USA. *T:* (office) (412) 6487519.

STRATHERN, Dame (Ann) Marilyn, DBE 2001; FBA 1987; Mistress of Girton College, Cambridge, 1998–Sept. 2009; William Wyse Professor of Social Anthropology, University of Cambridge, 1993–2008; *b* 6 March 1941; *d* of Eric Charles Evans and Joyce Florence Evans; *m* 1963, Andrew Jamieson Strathern, *qv* (marr. diss. 1986); twin *s* one *d*. *Educ:* Bromley High Sch (GPDST); Girton Coll., Cambridge (MA, PhD). Asst Curator, Mus. of Ethnology, Cambridge, 1966–68; Res. Fellow, ANU, 1970–72 and 1974–75; Bye-Fellow, Sen. Res. Fellow, then Official Fellow, Girton Coll., 1976–83; Fellow and Lectr, Trinity Coll., Cambridge, 1984–85 (Hon. Fellow, 1999); Prof. and Hd of Dept of Social Anthropology, Manchester Univ., 1985–93; Professorial Fellow, Girton Coll., Cambridge, 1993–98. Sen. Res. Fellow, ANU, 1983–84; Vis. Prof., Univ. of California, Berkeley, 1984. Hon. Foreign Mem., Amer. Acad. Arts and Scis, 1996. Hon. DSc (Soc Sci): Edinburgh, 1993; Copenhagen, 1994; Hon. DLitt Oxford, 2004; Hon. DSc: Helsinki, 2006; Panteion, Athens, 2006; Durham, 2007. Rivers Meml Medal, 1976, Huxley Meml Medal, 2004, RAI; Viking Fund Medal, Wenner-Gren Foundn for Anthropol Res., NY, 2003. *Publications:* Self-Decoration in Mt Hagen (jtly), 1971; Women In Between, 1972; (co-ed) Nature, Culture and Gender, 1980; Kinship at the Core: an anthropology of Elmdon, Essex, 1981; (ed) Dealing With Inequality, 1987; The Gender of the Gift, 1988; Partial Connections, 1991; (ed) Big Men and Great Men in Melanesia, 1991; After Nature, 1992; Reproducing the Future, 1992; (jtly) Technologies of Procreation, 1993; (ed) Shifting Contexts, 1995; Property, Substance and Effect, 1999; (ed) Audit Cultures, 2000; Kinship, Law and the Unexpected, 2005. *Address:* Girton College, Cambridge CB3 0JG.

STRATHMORE AND KINGHORNE, 18th Earl of, *cr* 1677 (Scot.); Earl (UK) *cr* 1937; **Michael Fergus Bowes Lyon;** DL; Lord Glamis, 1445; Earl of Kinghorne, Lord Lyon and Glamis, 1606; Viscount Lyon, Lord Glamis, Tannadyce, Sidlaw and Strathdichtie, 1677; Baron Bowes (UK), 1887; Captain, Scots Guards; *b* 7 June 1957; *s* of 17th Earl of Strathmore and Kinghorne and of Mary Pamela, DL, *d* of Brig. Norman Duncan McCorquodale, MC; *S* father, 1987; *m* 1984, Isobel (marr. diss. 2004), *yr d* of Capt. A. E. Weatherall, Cowhill, Dumfries; three *s*; *m* 2005, Dr Damaris Stuart-William; one *s*. *Educ:* Univ. of Aberdeen (BLE 1979). Page of Honour to HM Queen Elizabeth The Queen Mother, 1971–73; commissioned, Scots Guards, 1980. A Lord in Waiting (Govt Whip), 1989–91; Captain of the Yeomen of the Guard (Dep. Govt Chief Whip), 1991–94. Director: Polypipe PLC, 1994–99; Lancaster PLC, 1994–99. Pres., Boys' Brigade, 1994–99. DL Angus, 1993. *Heir: s* Lord Glamis, *qv*. *Address:* Glamis Castle, Forfar, Angus DD8 1QJ. *Clubs:* Turf, Pratt's, Mark's; Third Guards'; Perth (Perth).

STRATHNAVER, Lord; Alistair Charles St Clair Sutherland; DL; Master of Sutherland; with Sutherland Estates, since 1978; Vice Lord-Lieutenant of Sutherland, since 1993; *b* 7 Jan. 1947; *e s* of Charles Noel Janson, and the Countess of Sutherland, *qv*; *heir* to mother's titles; *m* 1st, 1968, Eileen Elizabeth, *o d* of Richard Wheeler Baker, Jr, Princeton, NJ; two *d*; 2nd, 1980, Gillian, *er d* of Robert Murray, Gourock, Renfrewshire; one *s* one *d*. *Educ:* Eton; Christ Church, Oxford. BA. Metropolitan Police, 1969–74; with IBM UK Ltd, 1975–78. DL Sutherland, 1991. *Heir: s* Hon. Alexander Charles Robert Sutherland, *b* 1 Oct. 1981. *Address:* Sutherland Estates Office, Golspie, Sutherland KW10 6RP. *T:* (01408) 633268.

STRATHSPEY, 6th Baron *cr* 1884; **James Patrick Trevor Grant of Grant;** Bt (NS) 1625; Chief of Clan Grant; *b* 9 Sept. 1943; *s* of 5th Baron and his 1st wife, Alice, *o c* of late Francis Bowe; *S* father, 1992; *m* 1st, 1966, Linda (marr. diss. 1984), *d* of David Piggott; three *d*; 2nd, 1985, Margaret (marr. diss. 1993), *d* of Robert Drummond. *Heir:* half *b* Hon. Michael Patrick Francis Grant of Grant, *b* 22 April 1953.

STRATHTAY AND STRATHARDLE, Earl of; Michael Bruce John Murray; *b* 5 March 1985; *s* and *heir* of Marquess of Tullibardine, *qv*.

STRATTON, Frances; Headteacher, and geology teacher, South Wilts Grammar School, since 2003; *b* 21 Jan. 1952; *d* of Thomas and Mary Clift; *m* 1973, Brian Stratton (marr. diss. 2003); one *s*. *Educ:* St Catherine's Primary Sch.; Hollies Convent Grammar Sch.; University Coll. of Wales, Aberystwyth (BSc Hons Geol.; PGCE). Luton Sixth Form College: Teacher of Geol., 1974–98; Hd of Sci., 1990–92; Dir, then Asst Principal, 1992–98; Dep. Hd, 1998–2002, Actg Hd, 2002–03, Corfe Hills Sch., Dorset. Chief Examr for Geol. A Level, 2000–. *Publications:* Action Science, 1994; OCR AS and A2 Geology, 2008. *Recreations:* gardening, walking the Dorset Jurassic coast, geological holidays. *Address:* South Wilts Grammar School, Stratford Road, Salisbury, Wilts SP1 3JJ.

STRATTON, Prof. Michael Rudolf, PhD; FRCPath, FMedSci; FRS 2008; Deputy Director, since 2006, and Head, Cancer Genome Project, since 2000, Wellcome Trust Sanger Institute (formerly Sanger Centre); Professor of Cancer Genetics, Institute of Cancer Research, since 1997; *b* 22 June 1957; *s* of Henry Stratton and Nita Stratton; *m* 1981, Dr Judith Breuer; one *s* one *d*. *Educ:* Brasenose Coll., Oxford (BA Physiol Scis); Guy's Hosp. Med. Sch., London (MB BS 1982); Inst. Cancer Res., London (PhD 1989). MRCPath 1991, FRCPath 2008. House and res. posts at Guy's Hosp., Beckenham Hosp., Inst. Psychiatry and Westminster Hosp., 1982–84; Registrar in Histopathol., RPMS, Hammersmith Hosp., 1984–86; MRC Trng Fellow, Inst. Cancer Res., 1986–89; Sen. Registrar, Dept Neuropathol., Inst. Psychiatry, 1989–91; Institute of Cancer Research: Team Leader, 1991–; Reader in Molecular Genetics of Cancer, 1996–97. Hon. Consultant, Royal Marsden Hosp., 1992–. FMedSci 1999. *Publications:* contrib. papers on genetic basis of cancer. *Address:* Wellcome Trust Sanger Institute, Genome Campus, Hinxton, Cambridge CB10 1SA.

STRAUSFELD, Prof. Nicholas James, PhD; FRS 2002; Regents Professor of Neurobiology, since 1987, MacArthur Fellow, since 1995, and Director, Center for Insect

Science, since 2005, University of Arizona, Tucson (Guggenheim Fellow, 1994); *b* 22 Oct. 1942. *Educ:* University Coll. London (BSc 1965; PhD 1968). Scientist, Max Planck Inst. for Biol Cybernetics, Tübingen, Germany, 1970–75; Gp Leader, Neurobiol., EMBL, 1975–86. *Publications:* Atlas of an Insect Brain, 1976; (jtly) Neuroanatomical Techniques: insect nervous system, 1981; Functional Neuroanatomy, 1984; contrib. learned jls. *Address:* Division of Neurobiology, University of Arizona, Arizona Research Laboratories, 611 Gould-Simpson Building, Tucson, AZ 85721, USA.

STRAUSS, Claude L.; *see* Levi-Strauss.

STRAUSS, Nicholas Albert; QC 1984; a Recorder, since 2000; *b* 29 July 1942; *s* of late Walter Strauss and Ilse Strauss (*née* Leon); *m* 1972, Christine M. MacColl; two *d. Educ:* Highgate School; Jesus College, Cambridge (BA 1964; LLB 1965). Called to the Bar, Middle Temple, 1965 (Harmsworth Scholar); a Dep. High Court Judge, 1995–. *Address:* 1 Essex Court, Temple, EC4Y 9AR. *T:* (020) 7583 2000.

STRAUSS-KAHN, Dominique Gaston André; Managing Director, International Monetary Fund, since 2007; *b* 25 April 1949; *s* of Gilbert Strauss-Kahn and Jacqueline (*née* Fellus); *m* 1991, Anne Sinclair; four *c* from previous marriages. *Educ:* Lycée de Monaco; Lycée Carnot à Paris; Univ. de Paris X-Nanterre (DEconSc). Lectr, Univ. de Nancy II, 1977–80; Scientific Advr, l'Institut national de la statistique et des études économiques, 1978–80; Dir, Cerepi, CNRS, 1980–; Prof., Univ. de Paris X-Nanterre, 1981; Hd, Dept of Finance, Gen. Commn of the Nat. Plan, 1982–84, Asst Comr, 1984–86. Mem., Exec. Cttee, Socialist Party, 1983– (Nat. Sec., 1984–89). National Assembly, France: Deputy (Soc.) from Haute-Savoie, 1986–88, from Val-d'Oise, 1988–91, 2001–07; Pres., Commn of Finance, 1988–91; Minister: in Dept of Finance, 1991–92; for Industry and Foreign Trade, 1992–93; of the Econ. and of Finance, 1997–99. Mayor, 1995–97, Dep. Mayor, 1997–2001, Sarcelles. *Publications:* Economie de la famille et Accumulation patrimoniale, 1977; (jtly) La Richesse des Français, 1977; (jtly) L'Epargne et la Retraite, 1982. *Address:* International Monetary Fund, 700 19th Street NW, Washington, DC 20431, USA; BP26, 95203 Sarcelles, France.

STRAW, Alice Elizabeth, (Mrs J. W. Straw); *see* Perkins, A. E.

STRAW, Edward; Chairman of Trustees, Demos, since 2007; *b* Buckhurst Hill, Essex, 16 Jan. 1949; *s* of Walter Arthur Whitaker Straw and Joan Sylvia Straw; *m* 2008, Lindsey Colbourne; three *s* two *d* from previous marriages. *Educ:* Staples Rd Prim. Sch., Loughton; Brentwood Sch.; Univ. of Manchester (BSc Engrg 1971); Manchester Business Sch. (MBA 1973). Coopers & Lybrand, subseq. PricewaterhouseCoopers: Local Govt Consultant, 1982–88; Partner, Govt Services, and Dir of Quality, 1988–94; Hd, Entertainment and Media Consulting, EMEA, 1994–2002; Partner, Central Govt, 2002–08; Bd Dir, 1996–98; Global Bd Dir, 1997–2002. Chm., 1994–2000, Vice-Pres., 2000–, Relate. Founder Trustee, Family and Parenting Inst., 1999–2007; Trustee, Stroud Valley Arts, 2003–. Orgnl Architect, New Labour, 1992–95. FCMI. *Publications:* Relative Values, 1998; The Dead Generalist, 2004; numerous articles on morality, engagement, media industries. *Recreations:* anarchy, thinking, camping, entertaining with words, electronic music composition. *Address:* Demos, 136 Tooley Street, SE1 2TU. *T:* 0845 458 5949.

STRAW, Rt Hon. John Whitaker, (Rt Hon. Jack); PC 1997; MP (Lab) Blackburn, since 1979; Lord Chancellor and Secretary of State for Justice, since 2007; *b* 3 Aug. 1946; *s* of Walter Arthur Whitaker Straw and Joan Sylvia Straw; *m* 1st, 1968, Anthea Lilian Weston (marr. diss. 1978); (one *d* decd); 2nd, 1978, Alice Elizabeth Perkins, *qv*; one *s* one *d. Educ:* Brentwood Sch., Essex; Univ. of Leeds (LLB 1967); Inns of Court Sch. of Law. Called to Bar, Inner Temple, 1972, Bencher, 1997. Political Advr to Sec. of State for Social Services, 1974–76; Special Advr to Sec. of State for Environment, 1976–77; on staff of Granada TV (World in Action), 1977–79. Pres., Leeds Univ. Union, 1967–68; Pres., Nat. Union of Students, 1969–71; Mem., Islington Borough Council, 1971–78; Dep. Leader, Inner London Educn Authority, 1973–74; Mem., Labour Party's Nat. Exec. Sub-Cttee on Educn and Science, 1970–82; Chm., Jt Adv. Cttee on Polytechnic of N London, 1973–75. Vice-Pres., Assoc. of District Councils, 1984–. Contested (Lab) Tonbridge and Malling, Feb. 1974. Opposition spokesman on the Treasury, 1980–83, on the environment, 1983–87; Principal Opposition Spokesman on educn, 1987–92, on the envmt (local govt), 1992–94, on home affairs, 1994–97; Sec. of State for the Home Office, 1997–2001; Sec. of State for Foreign and Commonwealth Affairs, 2001–06; Lord Privy Seal and Leader of H of C, 2006–07. Mem., Shadow Cabinet, 1987–97; Mem., NEC, Labour Pty, 1994–95. Vis. Fellow, Nuffield Coll., Oxford, 1990–98. Member Council: Inst. for Fiscal Studies, 1983–96; Lancaster Univ., 1988–91; Governor: Blackburn Coll., 1990–; Pimlico Sch., 1994–2000 (Chm., 1995–98). FSS 1995. Hon. LLD: Leeds, 1999; Brunel, 2007. *Publications:* Granada Guildhall Lecture, 1969; University of Leeds Convocation Lecture, 1978; Policy and Ideology, 1993; contrib. pamphlets, articles. *Recreations:* walking, cycling, cooking puddings, music. *Address:* House of Commons, SW1A 0AA.

STRAWSON, Maj.-Gen. John Michael, CB 1975; OBE 1964; idc, jssc, psc; Senior Military Adviser, Westland Aircraft Ltd, 1978–85 (Head of Cairo Office, 1976–78); *b* 1 Jan. 1921; *s* of late Cyril Walter and Nellie Dora Strawson; *m* 1960, Baroness Wilfried von Schellersheim; two *d. Educ:* Christ's Coll., Finchley. Joined Army, 1940; commnd, 1941; served with 4th QO Hussars in Middle East, Italy, Germany, Malaya, 1942–50, 1953–54, 1956–58; Staff Coll., Camberley, 1950; Bde Major, 1951–53; Instructor, Staff Coll. and Master of Drag Hounds, 1958–60; GSO1 and Col GS in WO and MoD, 1961–62 and 1965–66; comd QR Irish Hussars, Malaysia and BAOR, 1963–65; comd Inf. Bde, 1967–68; idc 1969; COS, Live Oak, SHAPE, 1970–72; COS, HQ UKLF, 1972–76. Col, Queen's Royal Irish Hussars, 1975–85. US Bronze Star, 1945. *Publications:* The Battle for North Africa, 1969; Hitler as Military Commander, 1971; The Battle for the Ardennes, 1972; The Battle for Berlin, 1974; (jtly) The Third World War, 1978; El Alamein, 1981; (jtly) The Third World War: the untold story, 1982; A History of the SAS Regiment, 1984; The Italian Campaign, 1987; Gentlemen in Khaki: the British Army 1890–1990, 1989; Beggars in Red: the British Army 1789–1889, 1991; The Duke and the Emperor, 1994; Churchill and Hitler: in victory and defeat, 1997; On Drag-hunting, 1999; If By Chance, 2002; Hussars, Horses and History, 2007. *Recreations:* equitation, shooting, reading. *Club:* Cavalry and Guards.

STREAMS, Peter John, CMG 1986; HM Diplomatic Service, retired; Ambassador to Sudan, 1991–94; *b* 8 March 1935; *s* of Horace Stanley Streams and Isabel Esther (*née* Ellaway); *m* 1956, Margareta Decker; two *s* one *d. Educ:* Wallington County Grammar Sch. BoT, 1953; Bombay, 1960, Calcutta, 1962, Oslo, 1966; FCO, 1970; Mexico, 1973; FCO, 1977, Counsellor, 1979; Consul-Gen., Karachi, 1982; Counsellor, Stockholm, 1985; Ambassador to Honduras and concurrently to El Salvador, 1989. Head, EU Monitoring Mission to former Yugoslavia, 1998. *Recreations:* walking, golf. *Address:* c/o Foreign and Commonwealth Office, SW1A 2AH.

STREATFEILD, Maj.-Gen. Timothy Stuart Champion, CB 1980; MBE 1960; Director, Royal Artillery, 1978–81; *b* 9 Sept. 1926; *s* of Henry Grey Champion and Edythe Streatfeild; *m* 1951, Annette Catherine, *d* of Sir John Clague, CMG, CIE, and Lady Clague; two *s* one *d. Educ:* Eton; Christ Church, Oxford (MA). Commnd into RA, 1946; Instructor, Staff Coll., Camberley, 1963–65; Chief Instructor, Sudan Armed Forces Staff Coll., 1965–67; Commander, 7th Parachute Regt, RHA, 1967–69; Col Adjt and QMG, 4 Div., 1969–70; Commander, RA 2 Div., 1971–72; RCDS, 1973; Brigadier Adjt and QMG, 1st Corps, 1974–75; COS, Logistic Exec., MoD, 1976–78. Regtl Comptroller, RA, 1986–89. Colonel Commandant: RA, 1980–91; RHA, 1981–91. FCMI. *Recreations:* fishing, sporting, the countryside, music. *Address:* Toatley Farm, Chawleigh, Chulmleigh, N Devon EX18 7HW. *T:* (01363) 83363. *Club:* Army and Navy.

STREATFEILD-JAMES, David Stewart; QC 2001; *b* 22 Oct. 1963; *e s* of Capt. John Jocelyn Streatfeild-James, *qv*; *m* 1991, Alison; two *s* two *d. Educ:* Charterhouse; University Coll., Oxford. Called to the Bar, Inner Temple, 1986. *Recreations:* family, sport, gardening, cookery. *Address:* The Manor, Queen Charlton, Bristol BS32 2SH. *T:* (0117) 986 2025.

STREATFEILD-JAMES, Captain John Jocelyn; RN retired; *b* 14 April 1929; *s* of late Comdr Rev. Eric Cardew Streatfeild-James, OBE, and Elizabeth Ann (*née* Kirby); *m* 1962, Sally Madeline (*née* Stewart); three *s* (one *d* decd). *Educ:* RNC, Dartmouth. Specialist in Undersea Warfare. Naval Cadet, 1943–47; Midshipman, 1947–49; Sub-Lt, 1949–51; Lieutenant: Minesweeping, Diving and Anti-Bandit Ops, Far East Stn, 1951; Officer and Rating Trng, Home Stn, 1952–53; specialised in Undersea Warfare, 1954–55; Ship and Staff Duties, Far East Stn, 1955–57; Exchange Service, RAN, 1957–59; Lieutenant-Commander: instructed Officers specialising in Undersea Warfare, 1960–61; Sea Duty, Staff of Flag Officer Flotillas, Home Stn, 1962–63; Sen. Instr, Jt Anti-Submarine Sch., HMS Sea Eagle, 1964–65; Commander: Staff of C-in-C Western Fleet and C-in-C Eastern Atlantic Area, 1965–67; Jt Services Staff Coll., 1968; Staff of Comdr Allied Naval Forces, Southern Europe, Malta, 1968–71; HMS Dryad, 1971–73; Captain: Sen. Officers' War Course, RNC, Greenwich, 1974; Dir, OPCON Proj., 1974–77; HMS Howard (i/c), Head of British Defence Liaison Staff, Ottawa, and Defence Advr to British High Comr in Canada, 1978–80 (as Cdre); HMS Excellent (i/c), 1981–82; ADC to the Queen, 1982–83. *Recreations:* sailing, carpentry, painting. *Address:* South Lodge, Tower Road, Hindhead, Surrey GU26 6SP. *T:* (01428) 606064.

See also D. S. Streatfeild-James.

STREATOR, Edward (James); consultant; *b* 12 Dec. 1930; *s* of Edward J. and Ella S. Streator; *m* 1957, Priscilla Craig Kenney; one *s* two *d. Educ:* Princeton Univ. (AB). US Naval Reserve, served to Lieut (jg), 1952–56; entered Foreign Service, 1956; Third Sec., US Embassy, Addis Ababa, 1958–60; Second Sec., Lome, 1960–62; Office of Intelligence and Research, Dept of State, 1962–64; Staff Asst to Sec. of State, 1964–66; First Sec., US Mission to NATO, 1966–69; Dep. Director, then Director, Office of NATO Affairs, Dept of State, 1969–75; Dep. US Permanent Representative to NATO, Brussels, 1975–77; Minister, US Embassy, London, 1977–84; US Ambassador to OECD, 1984–87. Mem., South Bank Bd, 1990–99. Member: Council, RUSI, 1988–92; Exec. Cttee, IISS, 1988–99; Bd, British Amer. Arts Assoc., 1989–99; Develt Cttee, Nat. Gallery, 1991–95; Adv. Bd, Fulbright Commn, 1995–2001; Chm., New Atlantic Initiative, 1996–. President: American Chamber of Commerce (UK), 1989–94; European Council, American Chambers of Commerce, 1992–95. Mem. Exec. Cttee, The Pilgrims, 1984–2000; Governor: Ditchley Foundn, 1984–; ESU, 1989–95; President: Northcote Parkinson Fund, 2007–08 (Trustee, 2004–08); Train Foundation, 2008– (Trustee, 2008–). Hon. FRSA 1992. Benjamin Franklin Medal, RSA, 1992. *Recreation:* swimming. *Address:* 535 Park Avenue, New York, NY 10665–8198, USA; *e-mail:* estreator@nyc.rr.com. *Clubs:* White's, Beefsteak; Metropolitan (Washington); Mill Reef (Antigua); Century Association, Knickerbocker (New York).

STREEP, Mary Louise, (Meryl); American actress; *b* 22 June 1949; *d* of Harry and Mary Streep; *m* 1978, Donald Gummer; one *s* three *d. Educ:* Vassar Coll. (BA 1971); Yale (MA 1975). *Stage appearances include:* New York Shakespeare Fest., 1976; Alice in Concert, NY Public Theater, 1981; The Seagull, NY, 2001; *television appearances include:* The Deadliest Season (film), 1977; Holocaust, 1978; Angels in America (film), 2004; *films include:* The Deer Hunter, 1978; Manhattan, 1979; The Seduction of Joe Tynan, 1979; Kramer versus Kramer, 1979 (Academy Award, 1980); The French Lieutenant's Woman (BAFTA Award), 1981; Sophie's Choice (Academy Award), Still of the Night, 1982; Silkwood, 1983; Falling in Love, 1984; Plenty, Out of Africa, 1985; Heartburn, 1986; Ironweed, 1987; A Cry in the Dark, 1989; She-Devil, 1990; Postcards from the Edge, Defending your Life, 1991; Death Becomes Her, 1992; The House of the Spirits, 1994; The River Wild, The Bridges of Madison County, 1995; Before and After, 1996; Marvin's Room, 1997; Dancing at Lughnasa, 1998; One True Thing, 1999; Music of the Heart, 2000; The Hours, Adaptation, 2003; Stuck on You, The Manchurian Candidate, Lemony Snicket's A Series of Unfortunate Events, 2004; Prime, The Devil Wears Prada, 2006; A Prairie Home Companion, Evening, Rendition, Lions for Lambs, 2007; Mamma Mia!, 2008. Hon. DFA: Dartmouth Coll., 1981; Yale, 1983. *Address:* c/o Creative Artists Agency, 2000 Avenue of the Stars, Los Angeles, CA 90067, USA.

STREET, Hon. Anthony Austin; manager and company director; *b* 8 Feb. 1926; *s* of late Brig. the Hon. G. A. Street, MC, MHR; *m* 1951, Valerie Erica, *d* of J. A. Rickard; three *s. Educ:* Melbourne C of E Grammar Sch. RAN, 1945–46. MP (L) Corangamite, Vic, 1966–84 (resigned); Mem., various Govt Mems Cttees, 1967–71; Mem., Fed. Exec. Council, 1971–; Asst Minister for Labour and Nat. Service, 1971–72; Mem., Opposition Exec., 1973–75 (Special Asst to Leader of Opposition and Shadow Minister for Labour and Immigration, March–Nov. 1975); Minister for Labour and Immigration, Caretaker Ministry after dissolution of Parliament, Nov. 1975; Minister for Employment and Industrial Relations and Minister Assisting Prime Minister in Public Service Matters, 1975–78; Minister for: Industrial Relations, 1978–80; Foreign Affairs, 1980–83. Chm., Fed. Rural Cttee, Liberal Party, 1970–74. *Recreations:* cricket, golf, tennis, flying. *Address:* 153 The Terrace, Ocean Grove, Vic 3226, Australia. *Clubs:* MCC; Melbourne; Barwon Heads Golf.

STREET, Hon. Sir Laurence (Whistler), AC 1989; KCMG 1976; QC (NSW) 1963; commercial mediator; Lieutenant-Governor of New South Wales, 1974–89; Chief Justice of New South Wales, 1974–88; *b* Sydney, 3 July 1926; *s* of Hon. Sir Kenneth Street, KCMG; *m* 1st, 1952, Susan Gai, AM, *d* of E. A. S. Watt; two *s* two *d*; 2nd, Penelope Patricia, *d* of G. Ferguson; one *d. Educ:* Cranbrook Sch., Sydney; Univ. of Sydney (LLB Hons). RANVR, incl. war service in Pacific, 1943–47; Comdr, Sen. Officer RANR Legal Br., 1964–65. Admitted to NSW Bar, 1951; Judge, Supreme Court of NSW, 1965–74; Judge of Appeal, 1972–74; Chief Judge in Equity, 1972–74. Director: John Fairfax Holdings Ltd, 1991–97 (Chm., 1994–97); Monte Paschi Aust. Ltd, 1992–97. Lectr in Procedure, Univ. of Sydney, 1962–63, Lectr in Bankruptcy, 1964–65; Member: Public Accountants Regn Bd, 1962–65; Companies Auditors Bd, 1962–65; Pres., Courts-Martial Appeal Tribunal, 1971–74; Chairman: Aust. Commercial Disputes Centre Planning

Cttee, 1985–86; Aust. Govt Internat. Legal Services Adv. Council, 1990–; Aust. Mem., WIPO Arbitration Consultative Commn, Geneva, 1994–2003; Aust. Govt Designated Conciliator, ICSID, Washington, 1995–. Mem. Court, London Court of Internat. Arbitration, 1988–2003 (Pres., Asia-Pacific Council, 1989–2006). Pres., Aust. Br., 1990–94, World Pres., 1990–92, Life Vice-Pres., 1992, Internat. Law Assoc.; Chm., Judiciary Appeals Bd and Drug Tribunal, NSW Rugby League, 1989–. President: Sydney Univ. Law Grads Assoc., 1963–65; Cranbrook Sch. Council, 1966–74; St John Amb. Aust. (NSW), 1974–2006. Hon. Col, 1st/15th Royal NSW Lancers, 1986–96. FCIArb 1992. Hon. FIArbA 1989; Hon. Fellow, Aust. Inst. of Bldg, 2004. Hon. LLD: Sydney, 1984; Macquarie, 1989; Univ. of Technol., Sydney, 1998 (Fellow, 1990); Hon. DEc New England, 1996. KStJ 1976. Grand Officer of Merit, SMO Malta, 1977. *Address:* 233 Macquarie Street, Sydney, NSW 2000, Australia. *T:* (2) 92230888, *Fax:* (2) 92230588. *Clubs:* Union (Sydney); Royal Sydney Golf.

STREET, Prof. Peter Ronald, PhD; Development Director, Genus International Consultancy, since 1999; Director, Produce Studies Ltd, since 1992; *b* 4 May 1944; *s* of Leslie Arthur John and Winifred Marjorie Street; *m* 1969, Christine Hill; two *d*. *Educ:* Univ. of Reading (BScAgr, PhD Management and Econs). Lectr in Management and Econs, Faculty of Agricl Sci., Univ. of Nottingham, 1971–74; Tropical Products Institute: Principal Res. Officer, 1974–82; Sen. Principal Res. Officer and Head, Mkting and Industrial Econs Dept, 1982–85; Mem., Directorate Bd, 1982–85; Dir and Chief Economist, Produce Studies Ltd, 1985–89; Prof. of Agricl Systems and Head, Dept of Agriculture, Univ. of Reading, 1989–92. Visiting Professor: ICSTM, 1998–; Imperial Coll., London, 1998–; RAC, 2000–. Chm., Selskya Zhign Consultants, Moscow, 1994–; Mem. Bd, British Consultants Bureau, 1999–; Man. Dir, GFA-RACE Partners Ltd, 2000–; Vice Pres., Online Global Commodities Exchange, 2000–. Numerous internat. consultancy assignments. MCMI (MBIM 1972). *Publication:* (ed with J. G. W. Jones) Systems Theory Applied to Agriculture and the Food Chain, 1990. *Recreations:* gardening, fly fishing. *Address:* Brooklyn, Crow, Ringwood, Hants BH24 3EA. *T:* (01425) 475222.

STREET, Prof. Robert, AO 1985; DSc; Vice-Chancellor, University of Western Australia, 1978–86, Hon. Research Fellow, since 1986; *b* 16 Dec. 1920; *s* of late J. Street, Allerton Bywater, Yorkshire, UK; *m* 1943, Joan Marjorie Bere; one *s* one *d*. *Educ:* Hanley High Sch.; King's Coll., London. BSc, MSc, PhD, DSc (London). MIET, FInstP, FAIP, FAA. Scientific Officer, Dept of Supply, UK, 1942–45; Lectr, Dept of Physics, Univ. of Nottingham, 1945–54; Sen. Lectr, Dept of Physics, Univ. of Sheffield, 1954–60; Foundn Prof. of Physics, Monash Univ., Melbourne, Vic., 1960–74; Dir, Research Sch. of Physical Sciences, Aust. Nat. Univ., 1974–78. Former President: Aust. Inst. of Nuclear Science and Engrg; Aust. Inst. of Physics; Mem. and Chm., Aust. Research Grants Cttee, 1970–76; Chm., Nat. Standards Commn, 1967–78; Member: State Energy Adv. Council, WA, 1981–86; Australian Science and Technology Council, 1977–80; Council, Univ. of Technology, Lae, Papua New Guinea, 1982–84; Bd of Management, Royal Perth Hosp., 1978–85. Fellow, Aust. Acad. of Science, 1973 (Treas., 1976–77). Hon. DSc: Sheffield, 1986; Western Australia, 1988. Jt Special Award, Insts of Physics, UK and Australia, 2000. *Publications:* research papers in scientific jls. *Recreation:* swimming. *Address:* Department of Physics, University of Western Australia, 35 Stirling Highway, Crawley, WA 6009, Australia. *Club:* Weld (Perth).

STREET, Sarah Elizabeth; *see* Brown, S. E.

STREET, Dame Susan (Ruth), DCB 2005; strategic advisor, Deloitte & Touche, since 2007; *b* 11 Aug. 1949; *d* of late Dr Stefan Galeski and of Anna Galeski; *m* 1972, Richard Street; one *s* one *d*. *Educ:* St Andrews Univ. (MA Philosophy). Home Office, 1974–2001: Course Dir, Top Mgt Prog., Cabinet Office, 1989–91 (on secondment); Supervising Consultant, Price Waterhouse, 1991–94; Director: Central Drugs Co-ordination Unit, Cabinet Office, 1994–96 (on secondment); Fire and Emergency Planning, 1996–99; Sentencing and Correctional Policy, 1999–2000; Criminal Policy, 2000–01; Permanent Sec., DCMS, 2001–06. FRSA 1992. *Recreations:* family, ballet, theatre, remedial tennis. *Address:* 1 Blenheim Road, NW8 0LU.

STREET-PORTER, Janet; journalist and broadcaster, since 1967; Editor-at-large, The Independent on Sunday, since 2001 (Editor, 1999–2001); *b* 27 Dec. 1946; *m* 1st, 1967, Tim Street-Porter (marr. diss. 1975); 2nd, 1976, A. M. M. Elliott, *qv* (marr. diss. 1978); 3rd, 1978, Frank Cvitanovich (marr. diss. 1988; he *d* 1995). *Educ:* Lady Margaret Grammar Sch., Fulham; Architectural Assoc. TV presenter, 1975–; TV producer, 1981–; Exec., BBC TV, 1988–94; Man. Dir, Live TV, 1994–95. Pres., Ramblers Assoc., 1994–97. FRTS 1994. Hon. FRIBA 2001. Award for originality, BAFTA, 1988; Prix Italia, 1993. *Publications:* The British Teapot, 1977; Scandal, 1981; Coast to Coast, 1998; As the Crow Flies, 1999; Baggage: my childhood, 2004; Fallout, 2006; Life's Too F***ing Short, 2008. *Recreations:* walking, talking, modern art. *Address:* c/o Emma Hardy, Princess Productions, Whiteley's Centre, 151 Queensway, W2 4SB. *T:* (020) 7985 1985; *e-mail:* emma.hardy@princesstv.com.

STREETEN, Paul Patrick, DLitt; Professor, Boston University, 1980–93, now Emeritus (Director: Center for Asian Development Studies, 1980–84; World Development Institute, 1984–90); *b* 18 July 1917; *e s* of Wilhelm Hornig, Vienna; changed name to Streeten under Army Council Instruction, 1943; *m* 1951, Ann Hilary Palmer, *d* of Edgar Higgins, Woodstock, Vermont; two *d*, and one step *s*. *Educ:* Vienna; Aberdeen Univ.; Balliol Coll., Oxford (Hon. Schol.); 1st cl. PPE, 1947; Student, Nuffield Coll., Oxford, 1947–48. DLitt Oxon, 1976. Mil. service in Commandos, 1941–43; wounded in Sicily, 1943. Fellow, Balliol Coll., Oxford, 1948–66 (Hon. Fellow, 1986); Associate, Oxford Univ. Inst. of Econs and Statistics, 1960–64; Dep. Dir-Gen., Econ. Planning Staff, Min. of Overseas Develt, 1964–66; Prof. of Econs, Fellow, Acting and Dep. Dir of Inst. of Develt Studies, Sussex Univ., 1966–68; Warden of Queen Elizabeth House, Dir, Inst. of Commonwealth Studies, Univ. of Oxford, and Fellow of Balliol Coll., 1968–78; Special Adviser, World Bank, 1976–79; Dir of Studies, Overseas Develt Council, 1979–80. Rockefeller Fellow, USA, 1950–51; Fellow, Johns Hopkins Univ., Baltimore, 1955–56; Fellow, Center for Advanced Studies, Wesleyan Univ., Conn.; Vis. Prof., Econ. Develt Inst. of World Bank, 1984–86; Jean Monnet Prof., European Univ. Inst., Florence, 1991. Sec., Oxford Econ. Papers, until 1961, Mem. Edit. Bd, 1971–78; Editor, Bulletin of Oxford Univ. Inst. of Econs and Statistics, 1961–64; Chm. Editorial Bd, World Develt, 1972–2003. Member: UK Nat. Commn of Unesco, 1966; Provisional Council of Univ. of Mauritius, 1966–72; Commonwealth Develt Corp., 1967–72; Statutory Commn, Royal Univ. of Malta, 1972–; Royal Commn on Environmental Pollution, 1974–76. Mem., Internat. Adv. Panel, Canadian Univ. Service Overseas. Vice-Chm., Social Sciences Adv. Cttee, 1971; Member, Governing Body: Queen Elizabeth House, Oxford, 1966–68; Inst. of Develt Studies, Univ. of Sussex, 1968–80 (Vice-Chm.); Dominion Students' Hall Trust, London House; Mem. Council, Overseas Develt Institute, until 1979. Pres., UK Chapter, Soc. for Internat. Develt until 1976. Mem., Phi Beta Delta. Hon. Fellow, Inst. of Develt Studies, Sussex, 1980. Raffaele Mattioli Lectr, Milan, 1991. Hon. LLD Aberdeen, 1980; Hon. DLitt Malta, 1992. Development Prize, Justus Liebig Univ., Giessen, 1987; Leontief Prize, Global Develt and Envmt Inst., Tufts Univ., 2001. Silver Sign of Honour (Vienna), 2002. *Publications:* (ed) Value in Social Theory, 1958; Economic Integration, 1961, 2nd edn 1964; (contrib.) Economic Growth in Britain, 1966; The Teaching of Development Economics, 1967; (ed with M. Lipton) Crisis in Indian Planning, 1968; (contrib. to) Gunnar Myrdal, Asian Drama, 1968; (ed) Unfashionable Economics, 1970; (ed, with Hugh Corbet) Commonwealth Policy in a Global Context, 1971; Frontiers of Development Studies, 1972; (ed) Trade Strategies for Development, 1973; The Limits of Development Research, 1975; (with S. Lall) Foreign Investment, Transnationals and Developing Countries, 1977; Development Perspectives, 1981; First Things First, 1981; (ed with Richard Jolly) Recent Issues in World Development, 1981; (ed with H. Maier) Human Resources, Employment and Development, 1983; What Price Food?, 1987; (ed) Beyond Adjustment, 1988; Mobilizing Human Potential, 1989; Paul Streeten in South Africa, 1992; Strategics for Human Development, 1994; (co-ed) The UN and the Bretton Woods Institutions, 1995; Thinking About Development, 1995; Globalisation: threat or opportunity, 2001; contribs to learned journals; *festschrift:* (ed S. Lall and F. Stewart) Theory and Reality in Development, 1986. *Address:* 54 Hamlet Court, Skillman, NJ 08558, USA. *Club:* Oxford and Cambridge.

STREETER, Gary Nicholas; MP (C) Devon South West, since 1997 (Plymouth Sutton, 1992–97); *b* 2 Oct. 1955; *s* of Kenneth Victor Streeter and Shirley Nellie (*née* Keable); *m* 1978, Janet Stevens; one *s* one *d*. *Educ:* Tiverton Grammar Sch.; King's Coll., London (LLB 1st cl. Hons). Articled at Coward Chance, London, 1978–80; admitted solicitor, 1980; joined Foot & Bowden, solicitors, Plymouth, 1980, Partner, 1984–99. Plymouth City Council: Mem., 1986–92; Chm., Housing Cttee, 1989–91. PPS to Solicitor-General, 1993–95, and to Attorney-General, 1994–95; an Asst Govt Whip, 1995–96; Parly Sec., Lord Chancellor's Dept, 1996–97; Opposition front bench spokesman on European affairs, 1997–98; Shadow Sec. of State for Internat. Develt, 1998–2001; Shadow Minister of State for Foreign Affairs, 2003–04. A Vice Chm., Cons. Party, 2001–02; Chm., Cons. Party Internat. Office, 2005–08. *Publication:* (ed) There is Such a Thing as Society, 2002. *Recreations:* lover of cricket and Rugby. *Address:* House of Commons, SW1A 0AA. *T:* (020) 7219 4070.

STREETON, Sir Terence (George), KBE 1989 (MBE 1969); CMG 1981; HM Diplomatic Service, retired; Chairman: Healthco Pvt Ltd, Harare, since 1994; Director, Contact International Ltd, Harare, 1992–2007; *b* 12 Jan. 1930; *er s* of late Alfred Victor Streeton and Edith Streeton (*née* Deiton); *m* 1962, Molly Horsburgh; two *s* two *d*. *Educ:* Wellingborough Grammar School. Inland Revenue, 1946; Prison Commission, 1947; Government Communications Headquarters, 1952; Foreign Office (Diplomatic Wireless Service), 1953; Diplomatic Service, 1965–89: First Secretary, Bonn, 1966; FCO, 1970; First Secretary and Head of Chancery, Bombay, 1972; Counsellor and Head of Joint Admin Office, Brussels, 1975; Head of Finance Dept, FCO, 1979; Asst Under-Sec. of State and Prin. Finance Officer, FCO, 1982–83; High Comr to Bangladesh, 1983–89. Pres., Bangladesh-British Chamber of Commerce, 1993–97. *Recreation:* collecting fountain pens. *Address:* 189 Billing Road, Northampton NN1 5RS. *T:* (01604) 473510. *Club:* Northampton and County (Northampton).

STREISAND, Barbra Joan; singer, actress, director, producer, writer, composer, philanthropist; *b* Brooklyn, NY, 24 April 1942; *d* of Emanuel and Diana Streisand; *m* 1963, Elliott Gould (marr. diss. 1971); one *s*; *m* 1998, James Brolin. *Educ:* Erasmus Hall High Sch. Nightclub début, Bon Soir, Greenwich Village, 1961; NY theatre début, Another Evening with Harry Stoones, 1961; musical comedy, I Can Get It For You Wholesale, 1962 (NY Critics' Best Supporting Actress Award, 1962); musical, Funny Girl, NY, 1964, London, 1966 (Best Foreign Actress, Variety Poll Award, 1966). Special Tony Award, 1970. *Films:* Funny Girl, 1968 (Golden Globe Award, Acad. Award, 1968); Hello Dolly, 1969; On a Clear Day You Can See Forever, 1970; The Owl and the Pussycat, 1971; What's Up Doc?, 1972; Up the Sandbox, 1972; The Way We Were, 1973; For Pete's Sake, 1974; Funny Lady, 1975; A Star is Born (also prod), 1976; The Main Event (also prod), 1979; All Night Long, 1981; Yentl (also co-wrote, dir. and prod), 1984 (Golden Globe Award for Best Picture and Best Dir); Nuts (also prod), 1987; The Prince of Tides (also dir. and prod), 1990; The Mirror Has Two Faces (also dir. and co-prod), 1997; Meet the Fockers, 2005. *Television specials:* My Name is Barbra, 1965 (5 Emmy Awards, Peabody Award); Color Me Barbra, 1966; Belle of 14th Street, 1967; A Happening in Central Park, 1968; Musical Instrument, 1973; One Voice, 1986; Barbra Streisand, the Concert (also prod and co-dir.), 1994 (Peabody Award, 3 Cable Ace Awards, 5 Emmy Awards); Serving in Silence: the Margarethe Cammermeyer story (exec. prod.), 1995. Began recording career, 1962; Grammy Awards for best female pop vocalist, 1963, 1964, 1965, 1977, 1986, for best songwriter (with Paul Williams), 1977; (jtly) Acad. Award for composing best song (Evergreen), 1976; awarded: 37 Gold Albums (exceeded only by Elvis Presley and The Beatles); 22 Platinum Albums; 12 Multi-Platinum Albums (most for any female artist). *Albums include:* People, 1965; My Name is Barbra, 1965; The Way We Were, 1974; Guilty, 1980; The Broadway Album, 1986; Just for the Record (retrospective album), 1991; Back to Broadway, 1993; Barbra Streisand, the Concert (double album and video), 1994; The Mirror Has Two Faces (soundtrack), 1996; Higher Ground, 1997; A Love Like Ours, 1999; Christmas Memories, 2001. *Address:* Barwood Productions, 433 N Camden Drive, Suite 500, Beverley Hills, CA 90210, USA.

STRETTON, James; Chairman, The Wise Group, since 2002; *b* 16 Dec. 1943; *s* of Donald and Muriel Stretton; *m* 1968, Isobel Robertson; two *d*. *Educ:* Laxton Grammar Sch., Oundle; Worcester Coll., Oxford (BA Maths). FFA 1970. Standard Life Assurance Company, 1965–2001: Asst Pensions Manager, 1974–77; Asst Investment Manager, 1977–84; General Manager (Ops), 1984–88; Dep. Man. Dir, 1988–94; Chief Exec., UK Ops, 1994–2001. Dir, Bank of England, 1998–2003; Chm., Bank of England Pension Fund Trustee Co., 2001–05; Member: Franchise Bd, Lloyd's of London, 2003–; Disciplinary Bd of Actuarial profession, 2004–06. Member: Scottish New Deal Adv. Task Force, 1997–99; Scottish Business Forum, 1998–99. Pres., YouthLink Scotland, 1994–2000. Director: PIA, 1992–94; Scottish Community Educn Council, 1996–99. Chm., Foresight Ageing Population Panel, 1999–2000. Dir, Edinburgh Internat. Fest. Ltd, 1997–. Mem. Court, 1996–2002, Rector's Assessor, 2003–06, Univ. of Edinburgh. *Recreations:* music, reading, gardening, golf. *Address:* 15 Letham Mains, Haddington EH41 4NW.

STRETTON, His Honour Peter John; a Circuit Judge, 1986–2002; *b* 14 June 1938; *s* of Frank and Ella Stretton; *m* 1973, Eleanor Anne Wait; three *s* one *d*. *Educ:* Bedford Modern Sch. Called to the Bar, Middle Temple, 1962; Head of Chambers, 1985. A Recorder, 1982–86. *Recreations:* squash, gardening, golf.

STREVENS, Bonnie Jean Holford; *see* Blackburn, B. J.

STRICK, Robert Charles Gordon; Clerk to the Drapers' Company, 1980–93 (Liveryman, Court of Assistants, 1994); *b* 23 March 1931; *m* 1960, Jennifer Mary Hathway; one *s* one *d*. *Educ:* Royal Grammar Sch., Guildford; Sidney Sussex Coll., Cambridge (MA). Served RA, 1949–51; TA, 1951–55. Spicers Ltd, 1954–55; joined HMOCS, 1955; Dist Officer, Fiji, 1955–59; Sec., Burns Commn into Natural Resources and Population Trends, 1959–60; Asst Sec., Suva, 1960–61; Sec. to Govt, Tonga, 1961–63; Develt Officer and Divl Comr, 1963–67, Sec. for Natural Resources, 1967–71, Fiji; retired 1971; Under Sec., ICA, 1971–72; Asst Sec.-Gen., RICS, 1972–80; Clerk, Chartered Surveyors' Co., 1977–80. Hon. Member: CGLI, 1991; Shrewsbury Co. of Drapers, 1992. Hon. Old Student, Aberystwyth, 1993. Hon. Fellow, Queen Mary, London Univ. (formerly QMW), 1993. Hon. DLitt Coll. of William and Mary, Virginia, USA, 1993. *Recreations:* the countryside, walking, golf, gardening. *Address:* Lane End, Sheep Lane, Midhurst GU29 9NT. *T:* (01730) 813151.

STRICKLAND, Benjamin Vincent Michael, FCA; Group Managing Director (Group Strategy, Finances and Operations), and Director, Schroders PLC, 1983–91; *b* 20 Sept. 1939; *s* of Maj.-Gen. Eugene Vincent Michael Strickland, CMG, DSO, OBE, MM, and of Barbara Mary Farquharson Meares Lamb, *d* of Major Benjamin Lamb, RFA; *m* 1965, Tessa Mary Edwina, *d* of Rear-Adm. John Grant, CB, DSO; one *s* one *d*. *Educ:* Mayfield Coll.; University Coll., Oxford, 1960–63 (MA PPE); Harvard Business Sch. (AMPDip 1978). FCA 1967. Lieutenant: 17/21 Lancers, BAOR, 1959–60; Inns of Court and City Yeomanry, 1963–67. Manager, Price Waterhouse & Co., 1963–68; joined J. Henry Schroder Wagg & Co. in Corp. Finance, 1968: Dir, Schroder Wagg, 1974–91; Chm., G. D. Peters Engineering, 1972–74; Dir, Property Hldgs Internat. (USA), 1974–75; Chm. and Chief Exec., Schroders Australia, 1978–82. Adviser: *inter alia,* on strategy to City law firm, and to media gp; on mission and finances, Westminster Cathedral (Chm., Planning and Finance Cttee, 1991–96); mentor to chief execs, 2005–. Mem. steering gp, Vision for London, 1991–2000; voluntary reading help in a state primary sch., 2004–. Mem. Council, St George's Med. Sch., 1984–87. FRSA. *Publications:* Bow Group pamphlet on Resources of the Sea (with Laurance Reed), 1965; (contrib.) Financial Services Handbook, 1986. *Recreations:* travel, military and general history, theatre, film. *Address:* 23 Juer Street, SW11 4RE. *T:* (020) 7585 2970. *Clubs:* Boodle's, Hurlingham.

STRICKLAND, Frank, OBE 1986; Vice-President, The Building Societies Association, since 1992 (Deputy Chairman, 1987–89; Chairman, 1989–91); *b* 4 Feb. 1928; *s* of Robert and Esther Strickland; *m* 1953, Marian Holt; one *d*. *Educ:* Harris Inst., Preston, Lancs. Asst Sec., Chorley and District Building Soc., 1952; Branch Manager, Hastings and Thanet Building Soc., 1955; Asst Sec., later Jt Sec., Corporation and Eligible Building Soc., 1965; Sunderland and Shields Building Society, later North of England Building Society: Gen. Manager, 1969; Chief Exec., 1975–89; Dir, 1982–92; Exec. Dep. Chm., 1989–91. Pres., European Fedn of Bldg Socs, 1989–91. *Recreations:* bowls, cricket. *Address:* 15 Glyne Hall, De La Warr Parade, Bexhill-on-Sea, East Sussex TN40 1LY. *T:* (01424) 734020. *Club:* MCC.

STRICKLAND-CONSTABLE, Sir Frederic, 12th Bt *cr* 1641, of Boynton, Yorkshire; *b* 21 Oct. 1944; *er s* of Sir Robert Frederick Strickland-Constable, 11th Bt and Lettice, *yr d* of Major Frederick Strickland; *S* father, 1994; *m* 1981, Pauline Margaret Harding, one *s* one *d*. *Educ:* Westminster; Corpus Christi Coll., Cambridge (BA); London Business Sch. (MSc). *Heir: s* Charles Strickland-Constable, *b* 10 Oct. 1985. *Address:* Estate Office, Old Maltongate, Malton YO17 7EG.

STRIKER, Prof. Gisela, DPhil; Walter C. Klein Professor of Philosophy and of the Classics, Harvard University, since 2002 (Professor of Classical Philosophy, 2000–02); *b* 26 Nov. 1943. *Educ:* Univ. of Göttingen (DPhil 1969). Asst. Prof., 1970–83, Prof., 1983–86, Univ. of Göttingen; Prof., Dept of Philosophy, Columbia Univ., NY, 1986–89; Prof. of Classical Philosophy, 1989–90, George Martin Lane Prof. of Philosophy and Classics, 1990–97, Harvard Univ.; Laurence Prof. of Ancient Philosophy, Univ. of Cambridge, and Fellow, Trinity Coll., Cambridge, 1997–2000. *Publications:* Essays on Hellenistic Epistemology and Ethics, 1996; articles in learned jls. *Address:* Department of Philosophy, Emerson Hall, Harvard University, Cambridge, MA 02138, USA.

STRINGER, Prof. Christopher Brian, PhD, DSc; FRS 2004; Research Leader in Human Origins, Natural History Museum, London, since 2006 (Head, Human Origins Programme, 1990–93 and 1999–2006); *b* 31 Dec. 1947; *s* of late George Albert Stringer and Evelyn Beatrice Stringer, and foster *s* of late Harry Kennett and Lilian Kennett; *m* 1977, Rosemary Susan Margaret (marr. diss. 2004); two *s* one *d*. *Educ:* UCL (BSc Hons (Anthropol.) 1969); Univ. of Bristol (PhD 1974; DSc 1990). Natural History Museum, London, 1973–: Sen. Res. Fellow, 1973–77; SSO, 1977–87; PSO, 1987–94; Hd, Anthropology, 1989–90; Individual Merit Promotion Band 2, 1994. Vis. Prof., Royal Holloway, London, 1998–; Res. Associate, Centre for Ecology and Evolution, UCL, 1999–; Dir, Ancient Human Occupation of Britain project, 2001–. Vis. Lectr, Dept of Anthropol., Harvard Univ., 1979. Lectures: Lyell, BAAS, 1988; Radcliffe, Green Coll., Oxford, 1996; Dalrymple, Univ. of Glasgow, 2001; Mulvaney, ANU, 2001; Darwin, Centre for Ecology and Evolution, London, 2003; Millennium Distinguished Lectr, Amer. Anthropol Assoc., 2000. Hon. Dr of Laws Bristol, 2000. Osman Hill Medal, Primate Soc. of GB, 1998; Henry Stopes Medal, Geologists' Assoc., 2000; Rivers Meml Medal, RAI, 2004. *Publications:* (ed) Aspects of Human Evolution, 1981; (with A. Gray) Our Fossil Relatives, 1983; (ed with P. Mellars) The Human Revolution: behavioural and biological perspectives in the origins of modern humans, 1989; (with P. Andrews) Human Evolution: an illustrated guide, 1989; (ed jtly) The Origin of Modern Humans and the Impact of Chronometric Dating, 1993; (with C. Gamble) In Search of the Neanderthals: solving the puzzle of human origins, 1993 (Archaeol. Bk of the Year, 1994); (with R. McKie) African Exodus, 1996, 2nd edn 1997; (jtly) Westbury Cave: the Natural History Museum excavations 1976–1984, 1999; (ed jtly) Neanderthals on the Edge: 150th anniversary conference of the Forbes' Quarry discovery, Gibraltar, 2000; (with J. Weiner) The Piltdown Forgery, 2003; (with P. Andrews) The Complete World of Human Evolution, 2005; *Homo britannicus,* 2006 (Kistler Book Award, 2008); articles in learned jls. *Recreations:* music, current affairs, travel, watching soccer, astronomy. *Address:* Department of Palaeontology, Natural History Museum, Cromwell Road, SW7 5BD. *Clubs:* Tetrapods; West Ham United Football.

STRINGER, Sir Donald (Edgar), Kt 1993; CBE 1987; *b* 21 Aug. 1930; *o s* of late Donald Bertram Frederick and Marjorie Stringer, Croydon; *m* 1957, Pamela Irene Totty; three *s*. *Educ:* Whitgift Sch., Croydon. Served Army, RMP, 1951–53. Conservative Party Agent, Fulham, Harrow and Honiton, 1954–65; Conservative Central Office: Dep. Area Agent, W Midlands, 1965–71; Central Office Agent: Northern Area, 1971–73; Greater London Area, 1973–88; Wessex Area, 1988–93. Member: Cons. Agents Exam. Bd, 1987–93; Agents Employment Adv. Cttee, 1988–93. Chm., Salisbury Abbeyfield Soc., 1996–2006. Treas.-Trustee, Fovant Badges Soc., 2001–07. Mem., Guild of Freemen, City of London, 1988. *Recreations:* walking, military history, philately. *Address:* Beech Cottage, Barford St Martin, Salisbury, Wilts SP3 4AS.

STRINGER, Graham Eric; MP (Lab) Manchester Blackley, since 1997; *b* 17 Feb. 1950; *s* of late Albert Stringer and of Brenda Stringer. *Educ:* Moston Brook High Sch.; Sheffield Univ. (BSc Hons Chemistry). Analytical chemist. Mem. (Lab), Manchester City Council, 1979–98 (Leader, 1984–96; Chm., Policy and Resources Cttee); Chm., Manchester Airport, 1996–97. A Lord Comr of HM Treasury (Govt Whip), 2001–02. *Address:* House of Commons, SW1A 0AA.

STRINGER, Sir Howard, Kt 2000; Chairman, Group Chief Executive Officer and Representative Corporate Executive Officer, Sony Corporation, since 2005 (Board Member, since 1999; Vice Chairman, 2003–05); Chairman and Chief Executive Officer, Sony Corporation of America, since 1998; *b* Cardiff, 19 Feb. 1942; naturalised US citizen, 1985 (dual nationality); *s* of Harry and Marjorie Mary Stringer; *m* 1978, Jennifer Kinmond Patterson; one *s* one *d*. *Educ:* Oundle Sch.; Merton Coll., Oxford (BA Modern History 1964; MA; Hon. Fellow, 2000). Served US Army, Vietnam, 1965–67 (Commendation Medal). Joined CBS Inc., 1965; Executive Producer: CBS Reports, 1976–81; CBS Evening News, 1981–84; Exec. Vice Pres., 1984–86, Pres., 1986–88, CBS News; Pres., CBS Broadcast Gp, 1988–95; Chm. and CEO, Tele-TV, 1995–97. Joined Sony Corp. of America, 1997; Corp. Hd, Sony Corp. Entertainment Business Gp, 2003–; Board Member: Sony BMG, 2004–; Sony Ericsson, 2006–. Board Member: Amer. Theater Wing; Amer. Friends of BM; NY Presbyterian Hosp.; Carnegie Hall. Chm., Bd of Trustees, Amer. Film Inst., 1999– (Mem., 1989–); Trustee, Paley Center for Media (Visionary award, 2007). Hon. FRWCMD 2001. Hon. PhD London Inst., 2003; Hon. Dr Glamorgan, 2005. Foundn Award, Internat. Radio and TV Soc., 1994; Steven J. Ross Humanitarian Award, UJA-Fedn of NY, 1999; Internat. Emmy (Founders) Award, 2002; Phoenix House Award for Public Service, 2002; Medal of Honor, St George Soc., 2004; Dist. Service Award, Lincoln Center for the Performing Arts, 2006. *Address:* Sony Corporation of America, 550 Madison Avenue, New York, NY 10022–3211, USA. *T:* (212) 833 6921; Sony Corp., 1–7–1 Konan, Minato-ku, Tokyo 108–0075, Japan.

STRINGER, Prof. Joan Kathleen, CBE 2001; PhD; FRSE; Principal and Vice-Chancellor, Napier University, since 2003; *b* 12 May 1948; *d* of Francis James and Doris Joan Bourne; *m* 1993, Roelof Marinus Mali. *Educ:* Portland House High Sch., Stoke-on-Trent; Stoke-on-Trent Coll. of Art; Keele Univ. (BA, CertEd, PhD Politics 1986). Graphic designer, ICL, 1966–70; Local Govt Officer, Staffs, 1970–74; teacher, Sudbury Open Prison, Derbys, 1978–80; Robert Gordon University: Lectr, 1980–88; Head, Sch. of Public Admin and Law, 1988–91; Asst Principal, 1991–96; Queen Margaret College, subseq. Queen Margaret University College, Edinburgh: Principal and Vice Patron, 1996–2002. Comr (Scotland), EOC, 1995–2001; Chm. Wkg Gp, NI Equality Commn, 1999. Mem., Scottish Parlt Consultative Steering Gp and Financial Issues Adv. Gp, 1998–99; Comr, Scottish Election Commn, 1999–2000; Chm., Scottish Exec. Strategic Gp on Women, 2003. Mem., HFEA, 1996–99. Vice-Convener, Univs Scotland (formerly Cttee of Scottish Higher Educn Prins), 1998–2002; Chair, Education UK Scotland, 2006–. Member: CVCP Commn on Univ. Career Opportunities, 1996–2001; Scottish Cttee, Cttee of Inquiry into Higher Educn (Dearing Cttee), 1996–97; Scottish Council for Postgrad. Med. and Dental Educn, 1999–2002; Scottish Health Minister's Learning Together Strategy Implementation Gp, 2000–01; Exec. Cttee, Scottish Council Develt and Industry, 1998–; Scottish Cttee, British Council, 2000–; Bd, Higher Educn Careers Services Unit, 2000–; DoH Wkg Gp on modernisation of SHO, 2001–02; Adv. Gp, Scottish Nursing and Midwifery Educn Council, 2001–02; UUK Equality Challenge Steering Gp, 2001–03; Judicial Appts Bd for Scotland, 2002–07; Bd, QAA, 2002–06; Bd, Higher Educn Statistics Agency, 2003–. Convener, SCVO, 2001–07. Non-exec. Dir, Grampian Health Bd, 1994–96. Convenor, Product Standards Cttee, Scottish Quality Salmon, 2001–03. Mem., Develt Adv. Bd, Scottish Opera and Ballet, 2000–02. Mem., Bd of Mgt, Aberdeen Coll., 1992–96. Member Council: World Assoc. for Co-op. Educn, 1998–2003; Edinburgh Internat. Festival Soc., 1999–2005. Fellow, 48 Group Club, 2006. CCMI (CIMgt 1999; MIMgt 1990); FRSA 1994; FRSE 2001. Hon. DLitt Keele. *Publications:* contrib. articles in field of politics with particular ref. to British Public Admin and employment and trng policy. *Recreations:* music (especially opera), gardening, cats. *Address:* Napier University, Craighouse Campus, 10 Craighouse Road, Edinburgh EH10 5LG.

STROHM, Prof. Paul Holzworth, PhD; Professor of Medieval Literature, Columbia University, since 2003; Research Fellow, St Anne's College, University of Oxford, 2003; *b* 30 July 1938; *s* of Paul H. Strohm and Catherine Poole Strohm; *m* 1960, Jean Sprowl (marr. diss. 1977); two *s*. *Educ:* Amherst Coll. (BA 1960); Univ. of California, Berkeley (PhD 1965). Indiana University: Asst Prof., 1965–68; Associate Prof., 1968–73; Full Prof. of English, 1973–98; J. R. R. Tolkien Prof. of Medieval Lang. and Lit., and Fellow, St Anne's Coll., Oxford Univ., 1998–2003. Guggenheim Fellow, 1994–95; Vis. Fellow, Clare Hall, Cambridge, 1994–95; Henry R. Luce Fellow, Nat. Humanities Center, 1996–97. First Vice Pres., Amer. Assoc. of Univ. Profs, 1985–86, Ed., Academe: Bull. of AAUP, 1986–92; Pres., New Chaucer Soc., 1998–2000. *Publications:* Social Chaucer, 1989; Hochon's Arrow: the social imagination of medieval texts, 1992; England's Empty Throne: usurpation and the language of legitimation, 1998; Theory and the Premodern Text, 2000; Politique, 2005. *Address:* Department of English and Comparative Literature, Columbia University, New York, NY 10027, USA.

STROHM, Prof. Reinhard, PhD; FBA 1993; Professor of Music, Oxford University, since 2007; Fellow, Wadham College, Oxford, 1996–2007, now Emeritus; *b* 4 Aug. 1942. *Educ:* Tech. Univ., Berlin (PhD 1971). Lectr, then Reader, in Music, KCL, 1975–83; Prof. of Music Hist., Yale Univ., 1983–89; Reader, 1990–91, Prof. of Histl Musicology, 1991–96, KCL; Heather Prof. of Music, Univ. of Oxford, 1996–2007. Edward J. Dent Medal, Royal Musical Assoc., 1977. *Publications:* Italienische Opernarien des frühen Settecento, 1976; Die italienische Oper im 18 Jahrhundert, 1979, 2nd edn 1991; Music in Late Medieval Bruges, 1985, 2nd edn 1990; Essays on Handel and Italian Opera, 1985; The Rise of European Music 1380–1500, 1993; Dramma per Musica: Italian opera seria of the 18th century, 1997; (ed) The Eighteenth-century Diaspora of Italian Music and Musicians, 2001; (ed with B. J. Blackburn) Music as Concept and Practice in the Late Middle Ages, 2001; many contribs to books and learned jls. *Recreations:* travel, mountaineering. *Address:* Faculty of Music, St Aldate's, Oxford OX1 1DB; 19 Hunt Close, Bicester, Oxon OX26 6HX.

STRONACH, David Brian, OBE 1975; FSA; Professor of Near Eastern Studies in the Graduate Division, University of California, Berkeley, since 2004 (Professor of Near Eastern Studies, 1981–2004; Chair of Department, 1994–97); *b* 10 June 1931; *s* of Ian David Stronach, MB, FRCSE, and Marjorie Jessie Duncan (*née* Minto); *m* 1966, Ruth Vaadia; two *d*. *Educ:* Gordonstoun; St John's Coll., Cambridge (MA). Pres., Cambridge Univ. Archaeological Field Club, 1954. British Inst. of Archaeology at Ankara: Scholar, 1955–56; Fellow, 1957–58; Fellow, British Sch. of Archaeology in Iraq, 1957–60; Brit. Acad. Archaeological Attaché in Iran, 1960–61; Dir, British Inst. of Persian Studies, 1961–80, Hon. Vice Pres., 1981–; Curator of Near Eastern Archaeol., Hearst (formerly Lowie) Mus. of Anthropol., Berkeley, 1982–2001. Asst on excavations at: Istanbul, 1954; Tell Rifa'at, 1956; Beycesultan, 1956–57; Hacilar, 1957–59; Nimrud, 1957–60; Charsada, 1958. Director, excavations at: Ras al'Amiya, 1960; Yarim Tepe, 1960–62; Pasargadae, 1961–63; Tepe Nush-i Jan, 1967–77; Nineveh, 1987–90; Co-director, excavations at: Shahr-i Qumis, 1967–78; Horom, 1992–93; Velikent, 1994–97; Erebuni, 2007–. Mem., Internat. Cttee of Internat. Congresses of Iranian Art and Archaeology, 1968–80. Hagop Kevorkian Visiting Lectr in Iranian Art and Archaeology, Univ. of Pennsylvania, 1967; Lectures: Rhind, Edin., 1973; Norton, Amer. Inst. of Archaeology, 1980; Columbia in Iranian Studies, Columbia Univ., 1986; Leventritt, Harvard Univ., 1991; Cohodas,

Hebrew Union Coll., Jerusalem, 1992; McNicoll, Univ. of Sydney, 1994. Vis. Prof. of Archaeology, Hebrew Univ., Jerusalem, 1977; Vis. Prof. of Archaeology and Iranian Studies, Univ. of Arizona, Tucson, 1980–81; Vis. Prof., Collège de France, Paris, 1999; Walker Ames Prof., Univ. of Washington, 2002. Mem., German Archaeological Inst., 1973 (Corr. Mem., 1966); Associate Mem., Royal Belgian Acad., 1988–. Ghirshman Prize, Académie des Inscriptions et Belles-Lettres, Paris, 1979; Sir Percy Sykes Meml Medal, Royal Soc. for Asian Affairs, 1980; Gold Medal, Archaeol Inst. of America, 2004. Adv. Editor: Jl of Mithraic Studies, 1976–79; Iran, 1980–; Iranica Antiqua, 1984–; Bulletin of Asia Inst., 1986–; Amer. Jl of Archaeol., 1989–97. *Publications:* Pasargadae, a Report on the Excavations conducted by the British Institute of Persian Studies, 1978; (with M. Roaf) Nush-i Jan I, The Major Buildings of the Median Settlement, 2007; archaeological articles in: Jl of Near Eastern Studies; Iran; Iraq; Anatolian Studies, etc. *Recreations:* fly fishing, mediaeval architecture, tribal carpets; repr. Cambridge in athletics, 1953. *Address:* Department of Near Eastern Studies, University of California, Berkeley, CA 94720–1940, USA. *Clubs:* Achilles; Hawks (Cambridge); Explorers' (New York).

STRONG, Air Cdre David Malcolm, CB 1964; AFC 1941; *b* 30 Sept. 1913; *s* of Theo Strong; *m* 1941, Daphne Irene Warren-Brown (*d* 2008); two *s* one *d*. *Educ:* Cardiff High School. Pilot, under trng, 1936; Bomber Sqdn, 1937–41; POW, 1941–45. Station Commander, RAF Jurby, RAF Driffield, 1946–48; Staff Coll. (psa), 1949; Staff Officer, Rhodesian Air Trng Gp, 1949–51; Directing Staff, Staff Coll., 1952–55; Air Warfare Coll. (pfc), 1956; Station Comdr, RAF Coningsby, 1957–59; Dir of Personnel, Air Min., 1959–61; Senior Air Staff Officer, RAF Germany, 1962–63; Officer Commanding, RAF Halton, 1964–66. Retired, 1966. Chairman: RAF Rugby Union, 1954–56; RAF Golf Soc., 1964–66. *Recreation:* golf. *Clubs:* Royal Air Force; Ashridge Golf.

STRONG, Hilary Jane Veronica; Director, National Council for Drama Training, since 2007; *b* 3 June 1957; *d* of Robert Hedley Strong and Estelle Flora Strong (*née* Morris). *Educ:* Chichester High Sch. for Girls; Lombard Sch. of Dancing. Freelance stage-manager and actress, 1979–83; Administrator: Merlin Theatre, Frome, 1986–88; Natural Theatre Co., Bath, 1989–94; Dir, Edinburgh Festival Fringe, 1994–99; Exec. Dir, Greenwich Theatre, 1999–2007; estabd Greenwich Musical Theatre Acad., 2003. Member Board: Nat. Campaign for Arts, 1990–92; Dance Base, Edinburgh, 1995–99; Mem., Arts Council of England, 1998–2002. *Recreation:* travelling on buses abroad. *Address:* c/o National Council for Drama Training, 1–7 Woburn Walk, WC1H 0JJ.

STRONG, Jaqueline Ann Mary; education consultant, since 2004; *b* 2 Oct. 1944; *d* of Donald Cameron McKeand and Gwendoline Mary Ann McKeand (*née* Graham); *m* 1966, Roger Francis Strong. *Educ:* Sexey's Grammar Sch.; Chipping Sodbury Grammar Sch.; Univ. of Wales (BSc, DipEd 1st cl.); Univ. of Bristol (MEd). Teacher, St Julian's Jun. High Sch., Newport, 1966–69; Lectr, Rhydyfelin Coll. of FE, 1967–70; teacher: Belfast, 1970–73; St Peter's Comp. Sch., Huntingdon, 1974, Dep. Head Teacher, 1974–81; Warden, The Village Coll., Bassingbourn, 1981–88; Asst Dir of Educn, Cambs CC, 1988–93; Director of Education: Leeds MDC, 1993–95; Leics CC, 1995–2004. Mem., Exec. Bd, Encounter, 1984–. Mem. Council, Univ. of Loughborough, 1995–. Voluntary worker for animal charities, Prodogs, Blue Cross and Pets as Therapy, 2000–. *Publications:* articles in educational magazines. *Recreations:* singing, exotic foreign travel, photography, walking, reading, concert and theatre going, taking in unwanted Great Danes.

STRONG, Dr John Anderson, CBE 1978 (MBE (mil.) 1942); MD; FRCP; FRCPE; FRSE; President, Royal College of Physicians of Edinburgh, 1979–82; *b* 18 Feb. 1915; *s* of Charles James Strong and Mabel Emma Strong (*née* Anderson); *m* 1939, Anne Frances Moira Heaney (*d* 1997); one *s* two *d*. *Educ:* Monkton Combe Sch., Bath; Trinity Coll., Dublin (MB 1937, MA, MD). Served RAMC, UK, India and Burma, 1939–46 (despatches, Burma, 1945); Hon. Lt-Col RAMC, 1946. Senior Lecturer, Dept of Medicine, Univ. of Edinburgh, 1949; Hon. Cons. Phys., Western General Hosp., Edinburgh, 1949; Hon. Physician, MRC Clinical and Population Cytogenetics Unit, 1959–80; Professor of Medicine, Univ. of Edinburgh, 1966–80, Professor Emeritus, 1981. Mem., Medicines Commn, 1976–83; Chm., Scottish Health Educn Co-ordinating Cttee, 1986–88. Hon. FACP 1980; Hon. FRCPI 1980; Hon. Fellow: Coll. of Physicians of Philadelphia, 1981; TCD, 1982; Coll. of Physicians of S Africa, 1982; Fellow *ad eundem*, RCGP, 1982; Mem., Acad. of Medicine, Singapore, 1982. *Publications:* chapter on Endocrinology in Principles and Practice of Medicine, ed L. S. P. Davidson, 1952, 12th edn 1977; articles in general medical and endocrinological jls. *Recreations:* fishing, golf, stalking, natural history. *Club:* Hon. Company of Edinburgh Golfers (Muirfield).

STRONG, Liam; Partner, Cerberus European Capital Advisers LLP, since 2006; Chairman, Virtual IT, since 2002; *b* 6 Jan. 1945; *s* of Gerald Strong and Geraldine Strong (*née* Crozier); *m* 1970, Jacqueline Gray; one *s* one *d*. *Educ:* Trinity Coll., Dublin. Procter & Gamble, 1967–71; Reckitt & Colman, 1971–88; Dir of Mktg and Ops, British Airways, 1988–91; Chief Executive: Sears plc, 1991–97; WorldCom Internat., 1997–2001; Teleglobe Inc., 2003–06. Dir, Aercap Holdings NV, 2006–. Chm., UK Govt Telecoms Adv. Bd, 2002–05. Gov., Ashridge Management Coll., 1996–. *Recreation:* sailing.

STRONG, Hon. Maurice Frederick; PC (Can.) 1993; OC 1976; FRSC 1987; Senior Advisor to the President, World Bank, since 1995; Special Advisor to Secretary-General of the United Nations, since 1998; *b* 29 April 1929; *s* of Frederick Milton Strong and late Mary Fyfe Strong; *m* 1st, 1950 (marr. diss. 1980); two *s* two *d*; 2nd, 1981, Hanne Marstrand; one foster *d*. *Educ:* Public and High Sch., Oak Lake, Manitoba, Canada. Served in UN Secretariat, 1947; worked in industry and Pres. or Dir, various Canadian and internat. corporations, 1948–66; Dir-Gen., External Aid Office (later Canadian Internat. Develt Agency), Canadian Govt, 1966–71; Under-Sec.-Gen. with responsibility for envmtl affairs, and Sec.-Gen. of 1972 Conf. on the Human Environment, Stockholm, 1971–72; Exec. Dir, UN Envmtl Programme, 1972–75; Pres., Chm. of Bd and Chm. of Exec. Cttee, Petro-Canada, 1976–78; Chm. of Bd, AZL Resources Inc., USA, 1978–83; Under-Sec.-Gen., UN, 1985–87 and 1989–92; Exec. Co-ordinator, UN Office for Emergency Ops in Africa, NY, 1985–87; Sec.-Gen., UN 1992 Conf. on Envmt and Develt, 1990–92; Under-Sec. Gen. and Exec. Co-ordinator for UN Reform, 1997. Chm. and CEO, Ontario Hydro, 1992–95; Chairman: Quantum Energy Technols Corp., subseq. Super Critical Combustion; Technology Development Corp.; Strovest Hldgs Inc.; formerly: Dir, Massey Ferguson, Canada; Dir, Mem. Exec. Cttee and Vice Chm., Canada Develt Corp., Toronto; Chm., Canada Develt Investment Corp., Vancouver. Chairman: Centre for Internat. Management Studies, Geneva, 1971–78; American Water Development, Denver, 1986; Internat. Energy Develt Corp., Geneva (also Special Advr); Bd of Govs, Internat. Develt Res. Centre, 1977–78; Co-Chm., Interaction Policy Bd, Vienna; Vice-Chm. and Dir, Soc. Gén. pour l'Energie et les Ressources, Geneva, 1980–86; Foundn Dir, World Economic Forum. Chm., Internat. Adv. Gp, CH2M Hill Cos Ltd; Member: Internat. Adv. Bd, Toyota Motor Corp.; Adv. Bd, Lamont-Doherty Observatory; Bd, Bretton Woods Cttee, Washington; World Commn on Envmt and Develt; Alt. Gov., IBRD, ADB, Caribbean Develt Bank. President: World Fedn of UN Assocs, 1987; Better World Soc., 1988; Chairman: North South Energy Roundtable, Washington; North South Energy Roundtable, Rome; World Resources Inst.; Earth Council; Stockholm Envmt Inst.; Adv. Cttee, UN Univ., Tokyo, Japan; Pres. Council and Rector, UN Univ. for Peace; Mem., and Chm. Exec. Cttee, UN Foundn. Director: Leadership for Envmt and Develt; Lindisfarne Assoc.; Mem., Internat. Asia Soc., NY. Trustee: Rockefeller Foundn, 1971–78; Aspen Inst., 1971–; Internat. Foundn for Develt Alternatives. Hon. Prof., Peking Univ., 2004. FRSA. Holds numerous hon. degrees from univs and colls in Canada, USA and UK. First UN Internat. Envmt Prize. Order of the Star of the North (Sweden); Comdr, Order of the Golden Ark (Netherlands). *Publications:* Where on Earth are We Going?, 2000; articles in various jls, including Foreign Affairs Magazine, Natural History Magazine. *Recreations:* swimming, skin-diving, farming, reading. *Address:* c/o The Earth Council Institute, 255 Consumers Road, Suite 401, Toronto, ON M2J 5B6, Canada. *Clubs:* Yale (New York); University (Toronto).

STRONG, Sir Roy (Colin), Kt 1982; PhD; FSA; FRSL; writer and historian, diarist, lecturer, critic, columnist, contributor to radio and television and organiser of exhibitions; Director, Oman Productions Ltd; *b* 23 Aug. 1935; *s* of G. E. C. Strong; *m* 1971, Julia Trevelyan Oman, CBE, RDI (*d* 2003). *Educ:* Edmonton Co. Grammar Sch.; Queen Mary Coll., London (Fellow, 1976); Warburg Inst., London. Asst Keeper, 1959, Director, Keeper and Secretary 1967–73, Nat. Portrait Gallery; Dir, Victoria and Albert Museum, 1974–87. Ferens Prof. of Fine Art, Univ. of Hull, 1972. Walls Lectures, Pierpont Morgan Library, 1974; Andrew Carnduff Ritchie Lectr, Yale Univ., 1999. Member: Fine Arts Adv. Cttee, British Council, 1974–87; Westminster Abbey Architectl Panel, 1975–89; Council, RCA, 1979–87; Arts Council of GB, 1983–87 (Chm., Arts Panel, 1983–87); Vice-Chm., South Bank Centre (formerly South Bank Bd), 1985–90. High Baliff and Searcher of the Sanctuary, Westminster Abbey, 2000–. Pres., 2001–02, 2004–, Vice-Pres., 2002–04, Garden History Soc.; Vice-Pres., RSPCA, 2000–05. Trustee: Arundel Castle, 1974–86; Chevening, 1974–87; Sutton Place, 1982–84; Patron, Pallant House, Chichester, 1986– (Trustee, 1980–86). Writer and presenter, TV series incl. Royal Gardens 1992; The Diets That Time Forgot, 2008. Sen. Fellow, RCA, 1983; FRSL. Hon. DLitt: Leeds, 1983; Keele, 1984; Hon. MA Worcester, 2005. Shakespeare Prize, FVS Foundn, Hamburg, 1980. *Publications:* Portraits of Queen Elizabeth I, 1963; (with J. A. van Dorsten) Leicester's Triumph, 1964; Holbein and Henry VIII, 1967; Tudor and Jacobean Portraits, 1969; The English Icon: Elizabethan and Jacobean Portraiture, 1969; (with Julia Trevelyan Oman) Elizabeth R, 1971; Van Dyck: Charles I on Horseback, 1972; (with Julia Trevelyan Oman) Mary Queen of Scots, 1972; (with Stephen Orgel) Inigo Jones: the theatre of the Stuart court, 1973; contrib. Burke's Guide to the Royal Family, 1973; Splendour at Court: Renaissance Spectacle and the Theatre of Power, 1973; (with Colin Ford) An Early Victorian Album: the Hill-Adamson collection, 1974; Nicholas Hilliard, 1975; (contrib.) Spirit of the Age, 1975; The Cult of Elizabeth: Elizabethan Portraiture and Pageantry, 1977; And When Did You Last See Your Father?, 1978; The Renaissance Garden in England, 1979; (contrib.) The Garden, 1979; Britannia Triumphans: Inigo Jones, Rubens and Whitehall Palace, 1980; (introd.) Holbein, 1980; (contrib.) Designing for the Dancer, 1981; (jtly) The English Miniature, 1981; (with Julia Trevelyan Oman) The English Year, 1982; (contrib.) Pelican Guide to English Literature vol. 3, 1982; (with J. Murrell) Artists of the Tudor Court, 1983; The English Renaissance Miniature, 1983; (contrib.) Glyndebourne: a celebration, 1984; Art & Power, 1984; Strong Points, 1985; Henry, Prince of Wales and England's Lost Renaissance, 1986; (contrib.) For Veronica Wedgwood These, 1986; Creating Small Gardens, 1986; Gloriana, Portraits of Queen Elizabeth I, 1987; A Small Garden Designer's Handbook, 1987; Cecil Beaton: the Royal Portraits, 1988; Creating Small Formal Gardens, 1989; (contrib.) British Theatre Design, 1989; Lost Treasures of Britain, 1990; (contrib.) Sir Philip Sidney's Achievements, 1990; (contrib.) England and the Continental Renaissance, 1990; (ed) A Celebration of Gardens, 1991; The Garden Trellis, 1991; Small Period Gardens, 1992; Royal Gardens, 1992; A Country Life, 1994; Successful Small Gardens, 1994; William Larkin, 1995; The Tudor and Stuart Monarchy, vol. I, Tudor, 1995, vol. II, Elizabethan, 1996, vol. III, Jacobean and Caroline, 1998; The Story of Britain, 1996; Country Life 1897–1997: the English Arcardia, 1996; The Roy Strong Diaries 1967–1987, 1997; (with Julia Trevelyan Oman) On Happiness, 1998; The Spirit of Britain, 1999, 2nd edn as The Arts in Britain: a history, 2004; Garden Party, 2000; The Artist and the Garden, 2000; Ornament in the Small Garden, 2001; Feast: a history of grand eating, 2002; The Laskett: the story of a garden, 2003; Passions Past and Present, 2005; Coronation: a history of kingship and the British monarchy, 2005; A Little History of the English Country Church, 2007. *Recreations:* gardening, cooking, keeping fit. *Address:* The Laskett, Much Birch, Herefords HR2 8HZ. *Club:* Garrick.

STRONG, Prof. Russell Walker, AC 2001; CMG 1987; RFD 1995; FRCS, FRACS, FACS; FRACDS; Professor of Surgery, University of Queensland, since 1992; Director of Surgery, Princess Alexandra Hospital, Brisbane, since 1981; *b* 4 April 1938; *s* of Aubrey and Anne Strong; *m* 1960, Judith Bardsley; two *d*. *Educ:* Lismore High Sch.; Univ. of Sydney (BDS); Charing Cross Hosp. Med. Sch., Univ. of London (MB BS). LRCP 1965; MRCS 1965; FRCS 1970; FRACDS 1966; FRACS 1974; FACS 1984. Intern, Bromley Hosp., Kent, 1965–66; Tutor in Anatomy, Charing Cross Hosp. Med. Sch., 1966–67; SHO, Birmingham Accident Hosp., 1968; Surgical Registrar: Charing Cross Hosp., 1969; St Helier Hosp., 1970–71; Sen. Surgical Registrar, Whittington Hosp., 1972–73; Surgical Supervisor, Princess Alexandra Hosp., Brisbane, 1973–80. Vis. Prof. and Guest Lectr on numerous occasions worldwide. James IV Surgical Traveller, 1987; Vis. Schol., Pembroke Coll., Cambridge, 2001. Hon. Fellow: Assoc. of Surgeons of GB and Ireland, 1996; Surgical Res. Soc. of SA, 1996; Hon. FRCSE 2001; Distinguished Academician, Acad. of Medicine, Singapore, 1998; Hon. Mem., Internat. Coll. of Surgeons, 1989. Inaugural Award for Excellence in Surgery, RACS, 1993; Prize, Internat. Soc. of Surgeons, 2001. *Publications:* contrib. book chapters and numerous articles in scientific jls. *Recreations:* golf, tennis. *Address:* 7 Wills Court, Mt Ommaney, Brisbane, Qld 4074, Australia. *T:* (7) 33762357.

STRONGE, Christopher James; Partner, Coopers & Lybrand Deloitte, 1967–92; *b* 16 Aug. 1933; *s* of Reginald Herbert James Stronge and Doreen Marjorie Stronge; *m* 1964, Gabrielle; one *s* one *d*. *Educ:* Chigwell Sch.; Magdalene Coll., Cambridge (MA Math.). FCA. Deloitte Haskins & Sells: joined 1957; Partner 1967; Dep. Sen. Partner, 1985. Member: Accounting Standards Cttee, 1980–83; Internat. Accounting Standards Cttee, 1985–90; Treasurer, RIIA, 1981–91. *Recreations:* opera, golf, sailing. *Club:* Little Ship.

STRONGE, Sir James Anselan Maxwell, 10th Bt *cr* 1803; *b* 17 July 1946; *s* of Maxwell Du Pré James Stronge (*d* 1973) (*g g s* of 2nd Bt) and Eileen Mary (*d* 1976), *d* of Rt Hon. Maurice Marcus McCausland, PC, Drenagh, Limavady, Co. Londonderry; *S* cousin, 1981, but his name does not appear on the Official Roll of the Baronetage. *Heir:* none. *Address:* Camphill Community Clanabogan, 15 Drudgeon Road, Clanabogan, Omagh, Co. Tyrone BT78 1TJ.

STROUD, Derek H.; *see* Hammond-Stroud.

STROUD, Ven. Ernest Charles Frederick; Archdeacon of Colchester, 1983–97, now Emeritus; *b* 20 May 1931; *s* of Charles Henry and Irene Doris Stroud; *m* 1959, Jeanne Marguerite Evans; two *d*. *Educ:* Merrywood Grammar School; Merchant Venturers'

Technical College; St Chad's Coll., Univ. of Durham. BA (Hons Theology), Diploma in Theology, Diploma in Rural Ministry and Mission. Esso Petroleum Co. Ltd, 1947–55. Deacon 1960, priest 1961, dio. Wakefield; Asst Curate, All Saints, S Kirkby, Yorks, 1960–63; Priest-in-Charge, St Ninian, Whitby, 1963–66; Minister of Conventional District, and first Vicar, All Saints, Chelmsford, 1966–75; Vicar of St Margaret of Antioch, Leigh on Sea, 1975–83; Asst RD of Southend, 1976–79; RD of Hadleigh, 1979–83; Hon. Canon of Chelmsford, 1982–. Member: General Synod, 1981–96; C of E Pensions Bd, 1984– (Vice-Chm., 1990–94, Chm., 1994–96, Finance and Investment Cttee). Chairman: Additional Curates Soc., 1988–98; Church Union, 1989–96; Dr George Richard's Charity, 1990–97. *Publication*: contrib. on ministry of healing to Christian. *Recreations*: travel, music, theatre. *Address*: St Thérèse, 67 London Road, Hadleigh, Benfleet, Essex SS7 2QL.

STROUD, Dr Michael Adrian, OBE 1993; FRCP, FRCPE; Senior Lecturer and Consultant in Medicine, Gastroenterology and Nutrition, Southampton General Hospital, since 1998 (Research Fellow in Nutrition and Gastroenterology, 1995–98); *b* 17 April 1955; *s* of Victor and Vivienne Stroud; *m* 1987, Thea de Moel; one *s* one *d*. *Educ*: University Coll. London (BSc; Fellow 2005); St George's Hosp. Med. Sch. (MB, BS, MD); FRCP 1994; FRCPE 1994. Med. trng, St George's Hosp., London, 1973–79; postgrad. trng and work in various NHS hosps, 1979–89; govt res. in survival and endurance physiology, 1989–95. Has taken part in many expeditions to Polar regions, incl. the first unassisted crossing of Antarctica on foot, with Sir Ranulph Fiennes, 1992–93; Land Rover 7x7x7 Challenge (7 marathons in 7 days on 7 continents), with Sir Ranulph, 2003. Hon. DSc Robert Gordon, 2006. Polar Medal, 1995. *Publications*: Shadows on the Wasteland: crossing Antarctica with Ranulph Fiennes, 1993; Survival of the Fittest, 1998; articles on thermal and survival physiology, endurance exercise, and nutrition in med. jls. *Recreations*: climbing, multi-sport endurance events. *Address*: Institute of Human Nutrition, Southampton General Hospital, Tremona Road, Southampton SO16 6YD. *T*: (023) 8079 6317.

STROWGER, (Gaston) Jack, CBE 1976; Managing Director, Thorn Electrical Industries, 1970–79; *b* 8 Feb. 1916; *s* of Alfred Henry Strowger, Lowestoft boat-owner, and Lily Ellen Tripp; *m* 1939, Katherine Ellen Gilbert; two *s* one *d*. *Educ*: Lowestoft Grammar School. Joined London Electrical Supply Co., 1934; HM Forces, 1939–43. Joined TEI, as an Accountant, 1943; Group Chief Accountant, 1952; joined Tricity Finance Corp. as Dir, 1959; Exec. Dir, TEI, 1961; full Dir 1966; Financial Dir 1967; Dep. Chm., Tricity Finance Corp., 1968; Chm., Thorn-Ericsson, 1974–81. Dir (non-exec.), Hornby Hobbies (Chm., 1981–93). FCMI. *Recreations*: gardening, bowling. *Address*: 43 Blake Court, 1 Newsholme Drive, Winchmore Hill, N21 1SQ.

STROYAN, Rt Rev. John Ronald Angus; *see* Warwick, Bishop Suffragan of.

STROYAN, His Honour Ronald Angus Ropner; QC 1972; a Circuit Judge, 1975–96; a Senior Circuit Judge, 1993–96; Hon. Recorder of Newcastle upon Tyne, 1993–96; *b* 27 Nov. 1924; *e s* of Ronald S. Stroyan of Boreland, Killin; *m* 1st, 1952, Elisabeth Anna Grant (marr. diss. 1965), *y d* of Col J. P. Grant of Rothiemurchus; one *s* two *d*; 2nd, 1967, Jill Annette Johnston, *d* of late Sir Douglas Marshall; one *s*, and two step *s* two step *d*. *Educ*: Harrow School; Trinity College, Cambridge; BA(Hons). Served 1943–45 with The Black Watch (NW Europe); attd Argyll and Sutherland Highlanders, Palestine, 1945–47 (despatches); Captain; later with Black Watch TA. Barrister-at-Law, 1950, Inner Temple. Dep. Chm., North Riding QS, 1962–70, Chm., 1970–71; a Recorder of the Crown Court, 1972–75. Member: Gen. Council of the Bar, 1963–67, 1969–73 and 1975; Parole Bd, 1996–2002. Chm., West Rannoch Deer Management Gp, 1989–2003. *Recreation*: country sports. *Address*: Boreland, Killin, Perthshire FK21 8TT. *T*: (01567) 820252. *Club*: Caledonian.

See also Bishop Suffragan of Warwick.

STRUDWICK, Air Cdre Arthur Sidney Ronald, CB 1976; DFC 1945; *b* 16 April 1921; *s* of Percival and Mary Strudwick; *m* 1941, Cissily (*d* 1983); two *s* one *d*. *Educ*: Guildford Tech. Coll.; RAF Colls. Joined RAF 1940; War Service as Fighter Pilot, 1941–43; POW Germany, 1944; Test Flying, Canada, 1948–50; CO No 98 Sqdn, 1951–53; Staff Coll., Camberley, 1954; Commanded Jt Services Trials Unit, Woomera, 1956–59; JSSC, 1959–60; MoD Planning Staff, 1960–62; Dir of Plans, Far East, 1962–64; Commanded RAF Leuchars, 1965–67; Air Cdre Plans, Strategic Comd, 1967–69; IDC 1969; Dir of Flying (R&D), MoD PE, 1970–73; AOC Central Tactics and Trials Orgn, 1973–76, retired 1976. Defence Liaison Officer, Singer Co., Link-Miles Div., 1976–86. *Recreations*: golf, gardening. *Club*: Royal Air Force.

STRUDWICK, Maj. Gen. Mark Jeremy, CBE 1990; Chief Executive, The Prince's Scottish Youth Business Trust, since 2000; *b* 19 April 1945; *s* of late Ronald Strudwick and Mary Strudwick (*née* Beresford); *m* 1970, Janet Elizabeth Coleridge Vivers; one *s* one *d*. *Educ*: St Edmund's Sch., Canterbury; RMA Sandhurst. Commnd Royal Scots (The Royal Regt), 1966; served UK, BAOR, Cyprus, Canada, India, NI (despatches twice); Comd, 1st Bn Royal Scots, 1984–87; Instr, Staff Coll., 1987–88; ACOS HQ NI, 1988–90; Higher Comd and Staff Course, 1989; Comd 3 Inf. Bde, 1990–91; NDC New Delhi, 1992; Dep. Mil. Sec., MoD, 1993–95; Dir of Infantry, 1996–97; ADC to the Queen, 1996–97; GOC Scotland and Gov. of Edinburgh Castle, 1997–2000. Col, Royal Scots, 1995–2005; Col Comdt, Scottish Div., 1997–2000. Mem., Queen's Body Guard for Scotland, Royal Company of Archers, 1994 (Brig. 2006). Chm., Scottish Veterans' Residences, 2001–. Trustee, Historic Scotland Foundn, 2001–. Cdre, Infantry Sailing Assoc., 1997–2000. Governor: Royal Sch., Bath, 1993–2000; Gordonstoun Sch., 1999–2007. *Recreations*: golf, shooting, sailing. *Address*: (office) 15 Exchange Place, Glasgow G1 3AN. *T*: (0141) 248 4999, *Fax*: (0141) 248 4836; *e-mail*: team@psybt.org.uk. *Clubs*: Army and Navy, Royal Scots (Trustee, 1995–) (Edinburgh).

STRUNIN, Prof. Leo, MD; FRCA; BOC Professor of Anaesthesia, Bart's and The London School of Medicine and Dentistry, Queen Mary (formerly London Hospital Medical College, then St Bartholomew's and Royal London School of Medicine and Dentistry, Queen Mary and Westfield College), University of London, 1990–2003, now Emeritus Professor; *b* 19 Nov. 1937; *m* 1968, Jane Smith. *Educ*: Univ. of Durham (MB BS 1960); Univ. of Newcastle upon Tyne (MD 1974). FRCA (FFARCS 1964); FRCP(C) 1980. Training posts, Newcastle upon Tyne, Sunderland, Manchester and London, 1960–67; Lectr, 1967–69, Sen. Lectr, 1969–72, Anaesthetics Unit, London Hosp. Med. Coll.; Sen. Lectr, 1972–74, Prof., 1975–79, Anaesthetic Dept, King's Coll. Hosp. and Med. Sch.; Prof. and Head, Dept of Anaesthesia, Univ. of Calgary, Canada, 1980–90. President: RCAnaes, 1997–2000; Assoc. of Anaesthetists of GB and Ire., 2000–02. *Publications*: Anaesthesia and the Liver, 1977; (with S. Thomson) Anaesthesia and the Liver, 1992; (with J. A. Stamford) Neuroprotection, 1996. *Recreation*: whippet and greyhound racing. *Address*: The Grange, Firsby, Spilsby, Lincs PE23 5QL. *T*: (01754) 830585. *Club*: Athenæum.

STRUTHERS, Alastair James, OBE 1995; *b* 25 July 1929; *s* of Alexander Struthers and Elizabeth Struthers (*née* Hutchison); *m* 1967, Elizabeth Henderson; three *d*. *Educ*: Stowe;

Trinity Coll., Cambridge (MA). Chairman: J. & A. Gardner & Co. Ltd, 1962–; Scottish National Trust plc, 1983–98; Caledonian MacBrayne Ltd, 1990–94. Chairman: Steamship Mutual Underwriting Assoc., 1988–95; Steamship Mutual Trustees (Bermuda) Ltd, 2000–. Dir, Hamilton Park Racecourse, 1973–. Chm., Racing and Thoroughbred Breeding Trng Bd, 1992–98. Comr, Northern Lighthouse Bd, 1980–99. Dep. Sen. Steward, Jockey Club, 1990–94. *Recreations*: racing, shooting, golf. *Address*: Garden Cottage, Craigmaddie, Milngavie, by Glasgow G62 8LB. *T*: (0141) 956 1262. *Club*: Western (Glasgow).

STRUTHERS, Prof. Allan David, MD; FRCP, FESC; Professor of Cardiovascular Medicine and Therapeutics, since 1992, and Head, Division of Medicine and Therapeutics, since 2002, University of Dundee; *b* Glasgow, 14 Aug. 1952; *s* of Dr David Struthers and Margaret Struthers; *m* 1979, Julia Elizabeth Anne Diggens; one *s* one *d*. *Educ*: Hutchesons' Boys' Grammar Sch., Glasgow; Univ. of Glasgow (BSc Hons Biochem. 1973; MB ChB Hons 1977; MD 1984); FRCPE 1990; FRCPG 1990; FRCP 1992; FESC 1994. Sen. Med. Registrar, RPMS and Hammersmith Hosp., London, 1982–85; Wellcome Sen. Lectr, Univ. of Dundee, 1985–89. Chairman: SIGN Guidelines on Heart Failure, 2003–07; Nat. Scientific Adv. Cttee, TENOVUS charity, 2004–. SmithKline Beecham Prize, Brit. Pharmacol Soc., 1990. *Publications*: Atrial Natriuretic Peptide, 1993; papers on B-type natriuretic peptide (BNP), aldosterone antagonists and xanthine oxidase inhibitors in cardiovascular jls. *Recreations*: cycling, walking, travel, opera. *Address*: Division of Medicine and Therapeutics, Ninewells Hospital and Medical School, Dundee DD1 9SY. *T*: (01382) 632180, *Fax*: (01382) 644972; *e-mail*: a.d.struthers@dundee.ac.uk.

STRUTT, family name of **Barons Belper** and **Rayleigh**.

STUART; *see* Crichton-Stuart, family name of Marquess of Bute.

STUART, family name of **Earl Castle Stewart**, **Earl of Moray** and **Viscount Stuart of Findhorn**.

STUART, Viscount; Andrew Richard Charles Stuart; lecturer; *b* 7 Oct. 1953; *s* and heir of 8th Earl Castle Stewart, *qv*; *m* 1973, Annie Le Poulain (marr. diss. 2003), St Malo, France; one *d*. *Educ*: Wynstones, Glos; Millfield, Som.; Univ. of Exeter. *Recreations*: running, hiking, bellringing. motorcycling. *Address*: The Old Barn, Stone Lane, E Pennard, Shepton Mallet, Somerset BA4 6RZ.

STUART OF FINDHORN, 3rd Viscount *cr* 1959, of Findhorn co. Moray; **Dominic Stuart**; *b* 25 March 1948; *s* of 2nd Viscount Stuart of Findhorn and his 1st wife, Grizel Mary Wilfreda, *d* of D. T. Fyfe and *widow* of Michael Gillilan; *S* father, 1999; *m* 1979, Yvonne Lucienne (marr. diss. 2002), *d* of Edgar Després. *Educ*: Eton. *Heir*: half-*b* Hon. Andrew Moray Stuart, *b* 20 Oct. 1957. *Address*: Flat 3, 15 Oakhurst Grove, East Dulwich, SE22 9AH.

STUART, Andrew Christopher, CMG 1979; CPM 1961; HM Diplomatic Service, retired; Vice-President, Centre for British Teachers, since 2005 (Chairman, 1991–2005); *b* 30 Nov. 1928; *s* of late Rt Rev. Cyril Edgar Stuart and Mary Summerhayes; *m* 1959, Patricia Kelly; two *s* one *d*. *Educ*: Bryanston; Clare Coll., Cambridge (MA). Royal Navy, 1947–49. Colonial Admin. Service, Uganda, 1953; retd from HMOCS as Judicial Adviser, 1965. Called to Bar, Middle Temple, 1965. Entered HM Diplomatic Service, 1965; 1st Sec. and Head of Chancery, Helsinki, 1968; Asst, S Asian Dept, FCO, 1971; Head of Hong Kong and Indian Ocean Dept, FCO, 1972–75; Counsellor, Jakarta, 1975–78; British Resident Comr, New Hebrides, 1978–80; Ambassador to Finland, 1980–83. Principal, United World Coll. of the Atlantic, 1983–90. Consultant, VSO, 1990–96. Order of the Lion (Finland), 1990. *Publication*: Of Cargoes, Colonies and Kings, 2001. *Recreations*: sailing, gliding. *Address*: Long Hall, North Street, Wareham, Dorset BH20 4AG. *T*: (01929) 551658; *e-mail*: andrew@astuart.eclipse.co.uk. *Clubs*: Oxford and Cambridge, Royal Commonwealth Society, Alpine; Jesters; Royal Naval Sailing Association.

STUART, Antony James Cobham E.; *see* Edwards-Stuart.

STUART, (Charles) Murray, CBE 1995; Chairman, Scottish Power, 1992–2000 (Director, 1990–2000); *b* 28 July 1933; *s* of Charles Maitland Stuart and Grace Forrester Stuart (*née* Kerr); *m* 1963, Netta Caroline; one *s* one *d*. *Educ*: Glasgow Acad.; Glasgow Univ. (MA, LLB). Scottish Chartered Accountant; CA. With P. & W. McLellan, Ford Motor Co., Sheffield Twist Drill & Steel Co., and Unicorn Industries, 1961–73; Finance Dir, Hepworths, 1973–74; Finance Dir and Dep. Man. Dir, ICL, 1974–81; Metal Box, subseq. MB Group: Finance Dir, Dir—Finance, Planning and Admin, 1981–86; Man. Dir, Dec. 1986–Dec. 1987; Gp Chief Exec., 1988–89; Chm., 1989–90; Finance Dir, 1990–91, Chief Exec., 1991, Berisford International. Vice Chm., CMB Packaging SA, 1989–90; Vice-Chm. and Dir, Hill Samuel, 1992–93; Chairman: Hill Samuel Scotland, 1993–94; Intermediate Capital Group PLC, 1993–2001; Hammersmith Hospitals NHS Trust, 1996–2000; non-executive Director: Save & Prosper Insurance, 1987–91; Save & Prosper Securities, 1988–91; Hunter Saphir, 1991–92; Clerical Medical & General Life Assurance Soc., 1993–96; Royal Bank of Scotland Gp, 1996–2002; Royal Bank of Scotland, 1996–2002; Willis Corroon Gp plc, 1996–97; CMG plc, 1998–2002; Old Mutual PLC, 1999–2003; Nat. Westminster Bank, 2000–02; Administrateur, 2000–, and Prés., 2004–, Comité des comptes et de l'audit, Veolia Environnement SA; Mem., European Adv. Bd, Credit Lyonnais, 2000–04. Dep. Chm., Audit Commn, 1991–95 (Mem., 1986–95); Mem., Private Finance Initiative Panel, 1995–97. Mem., W Surrey and NE Hants HA, 1990–93. Mem., Meteorological Office, 1994–98. Non-exec. Dir, Royal Scottish Nat. Orch., 1998–2000. DUniv: Paisley, 1999; Glasgow, 2001. *Recreations*: theatre, gardening, travel. *Address*: Longacre, Guildford Road, Chobham, Woking, Surrey GU24 8EA. *T*: (01276) 857144. *Club*: Caledonian.

STUART, Prof. David Ian, PhD; FRS 1996; Professor, Division of Structural Biology, Wellcome Trust Centre for Human Genetics, University of Oxford; Fellow of Hertford College, Oxford, since 1985. *Educ*: London Univ. (BSc); PhD Bristol; MA Oxon. University of Oxford: Lectr in Structural Molecular Biology, 1985–96; MRC Prof. of Structural Biology, 1996–2004; MRC Prof. of Biochemistry, 2004–05. FMedSci 2006. *Address*: Wellcome Trust Centre for Human Genetics, Roosevelt Drive, Headington, Oxford OX3 7BN.

STUART, Duncan, CMG 1989; HM Diplomatic Service, retired; Special Operations Executive Adviser, Foreign and Commonwealth Office, 1996–2002; *b* 1 July 1934; *s* of late Ian Cameron Stuart and Patricia Forbes; *m* 1961, Leonore Luise Liederwald; one *s* one *d*. *Educ*: Rugby Sch.; Brasenose Coll., Oxford (MA). Served 1st Bn Oxfordshire and Bucks LI, 1955–57 (2nd Lieut). Joined Foreign, later Diplomatic, Service, 1959; Office of Political Advr, Berlin, 1960–61; FO, 1961–64; Helsinki, 1964–66; Head of Chancery, Dar-es-Salaam, 1966–69; FCO, 1969–70; Helsinki, 1970–74; FCO, 1974–80; Counsellor, Bonn, 1980–83; FCO, 1983–86; Counsellor, Washington, 1986–88; FCO, 1988–92; Advr, MoD, 1992–94. Chm. and Chief Exec., Cyrus Internat., 1994–95. Gov.,

St Clare's, Oxford, 1991–2008. *Address:* c/o C. Hoare & Co., 37 Fleet Street, EC4P 4DQ. *Clubs:* Boodle's, Oxford and Cambridge, Special Forces, MCC.

STUART, Gisela Gschaider; MP (Lab) Birmingham Edgbaston, since 1997; *b* 26 Nov. 1955; *d* of late Martin and of Liane Gschaider; *m* 1980, Robert Scott Stuart (marr. diss. 2000); two *s*. *Educ:* Staatliche Realschule, Vilsbiburg; Manchester Poly.; London Univ. (LLB 1991). Dep. Dir, London Book Fair, 1982; Law Lectr, Worcester Coll. of Technol., 1992–97; res. in pension law, Birmingham Univ., 1995–97. PPS to Minister of State, Home Office, 1998–99; Parly Under-Sec. of State, DoH, 1999–2001. Member: Social Security Select Cttee, 1997–98; Foreign Affairs Select Cttee, 2001–. Mem. Presidium, Convention on Future of Europe. Associate Ed., 2001–05, Ed., 2006–, The House mag. Trustee: Westminster Foundn for Democracy; Henry Jackson Soc. *Publication:* The Making of Europe's Constitution, 2003. *Address:* House of Commons, SW1A 0AA. *T:* (020) 7219 3000.

STUART, Graham Charles; MP (C) Beverley and Holderness, since 2005; *b* 12 March 1962; *s* of late Dr Peter Stuart and of Joan Stuart; *m* 1989, Anne Crawshaw; two *d*. *Educ:* Glenalmond Coll.; Selwyn Coll., Cambridge. Dir, CSL Publishing Ltd, 1987–. Mem. (C) Cambridge CC, 1998–2004 (Leader, 2000–04). Chm., Cambridge Univ. Cons. Assoc., 1985. *Recreations:* cricket, rowing, motorcycling. *Address:* House of Commons, SW1A 0AA. *T:* (020) 7219 4340; *e-mail:* graham@grahamstuart.com.

STUART, Ven. Canon Herbert James, CB 1983; Canon Emeritus of Lincoln Cathedral, since 1983 (Canon, 1980–83); *b* 16 Nov. 1926; *s* of Joseph and Jane Stuart; *m* 1955, Adrienne Le Fanu; two *s* one *d*. *Educ:* Mountjoy School, Dublin; Trinity Coll., Dublin (BA Hons, MA). Priest, 1950; served in Church of Ireland, 1950–55; Chaplain, RAF, 1955; Asst Chaplain-in-Chief, RAF, 1973; Chaplain-in-Chief and Archdeacon, RAF, 1980–83; QHC, 1978–83; Rector of Cherbury, 1983–87. *Recreations:* gardening, travel, books. *Club:* Royal Air Force.

STUART, Rt Rev. Ian Campbell; Assistant Bishop, Diocese of Liverpool, since 1999; Pro Vice-Chancellor, Liverpool Hope University, since 2005; *b* 17 Nov. 1942; *s* of Campbell Stuart and Ruth Estelle Stuart (*née* Butcher); *m* 1976, Megan Helen Williams; one *s* two *d*. *Educ:* Univ. of New England (BA, Cert Ed); Univ. of Melbourne (MA, DipEdAdmin). Headmaster, Christchurch Grammar Sch., Melbourne, 1977–84; ordained deacon and priest, 1985; Principal, Trinity Anglican Sch., Queensland, 1984–93; Warden, St Mark's Coll., James Cook Univ., 1993–96; Principal, All Souls' and St Gabriel's Sch., 1993–98; Diocese of North Queensland: Archdeacon, 1989–92; Asst Bishop, and Bishop Administrator, 1992–98; Chaplain, 1999–2001, Provost and Dir, Student Services, 2001–05, Liverpool Hope Univ. *Recreations:* reading, travel. *Address:* Pro Vice-Chancellor's Office, Liverpool Hope University, Hope Park, Liverpool L16 9JD. *T:* (0151) 291 3547.

STUART, Sir (James) Keith, Kt 1986; Chairman, Associated British Ports Holdings PLC, 1983–2002; *b* 4 March 1940; *s* of James and Marjorie Stuart; *m* 1966, Kathleen Anne Pinder (*née* Woodman); three *s* one *d*. *Educ:* King George V School, Southport; Gonville and Caius College, Cambridge (MA). FCILT. District Manager, South Western Electricity Bd, 1970–72; British Transport Docks Board: Sec., 1972–75; Gen. Manager, 1976–77; Man. Dir, 1977–82; Dep. Chm., 1980–82; Chm., 1982–83. Dir, Internat. Assoc. of Ports and Harbors, 1983–2000 (Vice-Pres., 1985–87); Pres., Inst. of Freight Forwarders, 1983–84. Director: Royal Ordnance Factories, 1983–85; BAA Plc, 1986–92; Seeboard plc, 1989–96 (Chm., 1992–96); City of London Investment Trust plc, 1999–; RMC Group plc, 1999–2005; Mallett plc, 2005–06. Consultant, Gas and Electricity Markets Authy, 2007– (Mem., 2000–06). Chm., UK-S Africa Trade Assoc., 1988–93; Vice-Chairman: UK-Southern Africa Business Assoc., 1994–95; Southern Africa Business Assoc., 1995–2002. Chartered Inst. of Transport: Mem. Council, 1979–88; Vice-Pres., 1982–83; Pres., 1985–86. Pres. and Chm. Bd, British Quality Foundn, 1997–2001. Freeman, City of London, 1985; Liveryman, Clockmakers' Co., 1987 (Mem. Ct of Assts, 1998–). Vice-Chm., Mgt Bd, London Mozart Players, 2002–. Gov., NYO of GB, 1997–2004; Chm., Trinity Coll. London, 2009– (Dir, 1992–2009); Trustee, Trinity Coll. of Music, 2001– (Gov., 1991–2003; Chm., 2008–). FRSA; CCMI. Hon. FTCL 1998. *Recreation:* music. *Clubs:* Brooks's, Oxford and Cambridge (Trustee, 1989–94).

STUART, Prof. (John) Trevor, FRS 1974; Professor of Theoretical Fluid Mechanics, Imperial College of Science, Technology and Medicine, University of London, 1966–94, now Emeritus; Dean, Royal College of Science, 1990–93; *b* 28 Jan. 1929; *s* of Horace Stuart and Phyllis Emily Stuart (*née* Potter); *m* 1957, Christine Mary (*née* Tracy); two *s* one *d*. *Educ:* Gateway Sch., Leicester; Imperial Coll., London. BSc 1949, PhD 1951; FIC 1998. Aerodynamics Div., Nat. Physical Lab., Teddington, 1951–66; Sen. Principal Scientific Officer (Special Merit), 1961; Hd, Maths Dept, Imperial Coll., London, 1974–79, 1983–86. Vis. Lectr, Dept of Maths, MIT, 1956–57; Vis. Prof. of Maths, MIT, 1965–66; Vis. Prof. of Theoretical Fluid Mechanics, Brown Univ., 1978–; Hon. Prof., Tianjin Univ., China, 1983–. Member: Council, Royal Soc., 1982–84; SERC, 1989–94 (Chm., Mathematics Cttee, 1985–88). Pres., London Mathematical Soc., 2000–02 (Vice-Pres., 1999–2000). 1st Stewartson Meml Lectr, Long Beach, Calif., 1985; 1st DiPrima Meml Lectr, Troy, NY, 1985; Ludwig Prandtl Meml Lectr, Dortmund, 1986. Hon. ScD: Brown Univ., 1986; East Anglia, 1987. Senior Whitehead Prize, London Mathematical Soc., 1984; Otto Laporte Award, Amer. Physical Soc., 1987. *Publications:* (contrib.) Laminar Boundary Layers, ed L. Rosenhead, 1963; articles in Proc. Royal Soc., Phil. Trans Royal Soc., Jl Fluid Mech., Proc. 10th Int. Cong. Appl. Mech., Jl Lub. Tech. (ASME). *Recreations:* theatre, music, gardening, reading, ornithology. *Address:* Mathematics Department, Imperial College, SW7 2AZ. *T:* (020) 7594 8535; 3 Steeple Close, Wimbledon, SW19 5AD. *T:* (020) 8946 7019; *e-mail:* t.stuart@imperial.ac.uk.

STUART, Joseph B.; *see* Burnett-Stuart.

STUART, Sir Keith; *see* Stuart, Sir J. K.

STUART, Prof. Sir Kenneth (Lamonte), Kt 1977; MD, FRCP, FRCPE, FACP, FFPM, FFPH, DTM&H; Hon. Medical and Scientific Adviser, Barbados High Commission, since 1991; *b* 16 June 1920; *s* of Egbert and Louise Stuart; *m* 1958, Barbara Cecille Ashby; one *s* two *d*. *Educ:* Harrison Coll., Barbados; Queen's Univ., Belfast (MB, BCh, BAO 1948). Consultant Physician, University Coll. Hospital of the West Indies, 1954–76; University of the West Indies: Prof. of Medicine, 1966–76; Dean, Medical Faculty, 1969–71; Head, Dept of Medicine, 1972–76; Mem. Council, 1971–76; Medical Adviser, Commonwealth Secretariat, 1976–84. Rockefeller Foundation Fellow in Cardiology, Massachusetts Gen. Hosp., Boston, 1956–57; Wellcome Foundation Research Fellow, Harvard Univ., Boston, 1960–61; Gresham Prof. of Physic, 1988–92. Consultant to WHO on Cardiovascular Disorders, 1969–89. Chairman: Commonwealth Caribbean MRC, 1989–96; Adv. Council, Centre for Caribbean Medicine, UK, 1998; Commonwealth Health Res. Inter-regional Consultation, 1998–. Chm., Court of Governors, LSHTM, 1982–86; Member: Council, Liverpool Sch. of Tropical Medicine, 1980–97; Council, UMDS Guy's and St Thomas's Hosps, 1994–98; Council, KCL, 1998–2001; Court of Governors, Internat. Develt Res. Centre of Canada, 1985–90; Council, London Lighthouse, 1994–2000; Central Council, Royal Over-Seas League, 1994–2001. Trustee, Schools, subseq. Students, Partnership Worldwide, 1986–; Chm., Errol Barrow Meml Trust, 1989–2000; Dir, Internat. Medical Educn Trust 2000, 2000–. Freeman, City of London, 1994. Hon. DSc QUB, 1986. *Publications:* articles on hepatic and cardiovascular disorders in medical journals. *Recreations:* tennis, music. *Address:* 3 The Garth, Cobham, Surrey, KT11 2DZ. *Clubs:* Athenæum, Royal Commonwealth Society.

STUART, Marian Elizabeth; *b* 17 July 1944; *d* of William and Greta Stuart; one *s* one *d*. *Educ:* Eye Grammar School, Suffolk; Mount Grace Comprehensive School, Potters Bar; Leicester Univ. (MA). Joined Min. of Health as Asst Principal, 1967; Principal, DHSS, 1971; Asst Sec., 1979; Dep. Chief Inspector of Social Services, 1988; Under Sec., Finance Div., DoH, 1989–93; Resident Chm., CSSB, 1993–99 (on secondment); consultant on on social issues, particularly child care projects, DoH, 1993–99. *Publications:* (jtly) Progress on Safeguards for Children Living Away from Home: a review of action since the People Like Us report, 2004; (jtly) Safeguards for Vulnerable Children, 2004. *Recreations:* golf, reading, bridge. *Address:* 15 Connaught Avenue, SW14 7RH. *T:* (020) 8878 1173.

STUART, Sir Mark M.; *see* Moody-Stuart.

STUART, Moira, OBE 2001; Presenter, Breakfast News, BBC, 2000–06; *d* of Harold and Marjorie Stuart. Joined BBC Radio as prodn asst, Talks and Documentaries Dept, 1981; newsreader, Radio 4; presenter of news progs incl. News After Noon, 5.40 News, Nine O'Clock News, Six O'Clock News. Presenter of radio and TV progs incl. The Quincy Jones Story, Best of Jazz, Open Forum, Holiday Programme, Cashing In, Moira Stuart in Search of Wilberforce. Mem., Human Genetics Adv. Commn, 1996–99. Dr hc Edinburgh, 2006.

STUART, Murray; *see* Stuart, C. M.

STUART, Nicholas Willoughby, CB 1990; Director General for Lifelong Learning, Department for Education and Skills (formerly Department for Education and Employment), 2000–01; *b* 2 Oct. 1942; *s* of Douglas Willoughby Stuart and Margaret Eileen Stuart; *m* 1st, 1963, Sarah Mustard (marr. diss. 1974); one *d* (one *s* decd); 2nd, 1975, Susan Jane Fletcher; one *s* one *d*. *Educ:* Harrow Sch.; Christ Church Coll., Oxford (MA). Asst Principal, DES, 1964–68; Private Sec. to Minister for the Arts, 1968–69; Principal, DES, 1969–73; Private Secretary to: Head of the Civil Service, 1973; Prime Minister, 1973–76; Asst Sec., DES, 1976–78; Advr, Cabinet of Pres. of EEC, 1978–80; Under Sec., 1981–87, Dep. Sec., 1987–92, DES; Dir of Resources and Strategy, Dept of Employment, 1992–95; Dir Gen. for Employment and Lifelong Learning, later for Employment, Lifelong Learning and Internat. Directorate, DFEE, 1995–2000. Bd Mem., Investors in People (UK), 1995–2001; Dir, UFI Ltd, 2001–07. Chm., Nat. Inst. of Adult Contg Educn, 2003– (Vice-Pres., 2001–03); Council Member: Univ. of London Inst. of Educn, 2001–; C&G, 2001–02; GDST, 2002–; Member: QCA, 2002–; Bd, CAFCASS, 2003–. Trustee: Harrow Mission, 2001–; PSI, 2002–; Specialist Schs and Acads Trust, 2003–; Chm., Grants Cttee, John Lyon's Charity, 2002– (Mem., 1996–2002). Governor: John Lyon's Sch., 1996–2005; Harrow Sch., 1996–; South Hampstead High Sch., 1997–2002; Edward Wilson Sch., 2001– (Chm.). *Recreations:* collecting Tunbridgeware, cruising the canals.

STUART, Sir Phillip (Luttrell), 9th Bt *cr* 1660; late F/O RCAF; President, Agassiz Industries Ltd; *b* 7 Sept. 1937; *s* of late Luttrell Hamilton Stuart and Irene Ethel Jackman; *S* uncle, Sir Houlton John Stuart, 8th Bt, 1959, but his name does not appear on the Official Roll of the Baronetage; *m* 1st, 1962, Marlene Rose Muth (marr. diss. 1968); one *d*; 2nd, 1969, Beverley Clare Pieri; one *s* one *d*. *Educ:* Vancouver. Enlisted RCAF, Nov. 1955; commnd FO (1957–62). *Heir:* *s* Geoffrey Phillip Stuart, *b* 5 July 1973. *Address:* #50 10980 Westdowne Road, Ladysmith, BC V9G 1X3, Canada.

STUART, Trevor; *see* Stuart, J. T.

STUART-BROWN, Gillian Margaret; Her Honour Judge Stuart-Brown; a Circuit Judge, since 2006; *b* 11 Oct. 1947; *d* of Joseph Moss and Margaret Gladys Moss; *m* 1970, Malcolm Stuart-Brown. *Educ:* Newbury Girls Grammar Sch.; London Univ. (LLB 1969 ext.). Admitted Solicitor, 1974; private practice, Bath, 1974–84; Partner, Stuart-Brown Practice, Calne, 1984–90; a District Judge, 1990–2006. *Recreation:* ski-ing in the afternoon winter sunshine from Scheidegg to Brandegg for apple doughnuts. *Address:* Gee Street County Court, 29–41 Gee Street, EC1V 3RE.

STUART-MENTETH, Sir James; *see* Menteth.

STUART-MOORE, Michael; QC 1990; **Hon. Mr Justice Stuart-Moore;** Vice-President of the Court of Appeal of Hong Kong, since 1999; a Recorder of the Crown Court, since 1985; *b* 7 July 1944; *s* of (Kenneth) Basil Moore and Marjorie (Elizabeth) Moore; *m* 1973, Katherine Ann, *d* of William and Ruth Scott; one *s* one *d*. *Educ:* Cranleigh School. Called to the Bar, Middle Temple, 1966. A Judge of the High Court, later of the Court of First Instance of the High Court, Hong Kong, 1993–98; a Judge of the Court of Appeal of the High Court, Hong Kong, 1998–99. *Recreations:* photography, travel, music, tennis. *Address:* 2 Hare Court, Temple, EC4Y 7BH. *T:* (020) 7353 5324; Court of Appeal, High Court, 38 Queensway, Hong Kong. *Club:* Hong Kong.

STUART-PAUL, Air Marshal Sir Ronald (Ian), KBE 1990 (MBE 1967); RAF, retired; Chief Executive, British Aerospace, Saudi Arabia, 1997–2001; *b* 7 Nov. 1934; *s* of Dr J. G. Stuart-Paul and Mary (*née* McDonald); *m* 1963, Priscilla Frances (*née* Kay); one *s* one *d*. *Educ:* Dollar Acad.; RAF Coll., Cranwell. Served 14, 19, 56 and 92 Sqns and 11 and 12 Groups, 1957–73; Defence Attaché, Saudi Arabia, 1974–75; Stn Comdr, RAF Lossiemouth, 1976–78; RCDS, 1979; Dep. Comdr, NAEW Force, SHAPE, 1980–82; Dir of Ops Air Defence, RAF, 1982–83; AO Training, RAF Support Command, 1984–85; Dir Gen., Saudi Air Force Project, 1985–92. *Recreations:* golf, campanology, rug-making. *Address:* Sycamore House, Gaunts Common, Wimborne, Dorset BH21 4JP. *T:* (01258) 840430. *Club:* Royal Air Force.

STUART-SMITH, James, CB 1986; QC 1988; Judge Advocate General, 1984–91 (Vice Judge Advocate General, 1979–84); a Recorder, 1985–91; *b* 13 Sept. 1919; *s* of James Stuart-Smith and Florence Emma (*née* Armfield); *m* 1957, Jean Marie Therese Young Groundsell, *d* of Hubert Young Groundsell, Newport, IoW; one *s* one *d*. *Educ:* Brighton Coll.; London Hospital. Medical student, 1938. Served War of 1939–45: commnd KRRC, 1940; served ME and Italy, and staff appointments in UK; demobilised 1947. Called to Bar, Middle Temple, 1948; practised in London, 1948–55; Legal Asst, JAG's Office, 1955; Dep. Judge Advocate, 1957; Asst Judge Advocate General, 1968; Dep. Judge Advocate, Middle East Comd (Aden), 1964–65; Dep. Judge Advocate General, British Forces Germany, 1976–79. Hon. Pres., Internat. Soc. for Military Law and the Law of War, 1991– (Vice-Pres., 1979–85; Pres., 1985–91). *Publications:* contribs to Internat. Soc. for Military Law and Law of War Rev. and Law Qly Rev., on history and practice of

British military law. *Recreations:* composing letters, inexpert carpentry. *Address:* 3 Marine Parade, Bognor Regis PO21 2LT. *T:* (01243) 842255. *Club:* Royal Air Force.

STUART-SMITH, Rt Hon. Sir Murray, Kt 1981; PC 1988; a Lord Justice of Appeal, 1988–2000; *b* 18 Nov. 1927; *s* of Edward Stuart-Smith and Doris Mary Laughland; *m* 1953, Joan Elizabeth Mary Motion, BA, JP, DL (High Sheriff of Herts, 1983); three *s* three *d. Educ:* Radley; Corpus Christi Coll., Cambridge (Foundn Scholar; 1st Cl. Hons Law Tripos, Pts I and II; 1st Cl. Hons LLM; MA; Hon. Fellow 1994). 2nd Lieut, 5th Royal Inniskilling Dragoon Guards, 1947. Called to the Bar, Gray's Inn, 1952 (Atkin Scholar), Bencher 1977; Vice-Treas., 1997; Treas., 1998; QC 1970; a Recorder of the Crown Court, 1972–81; a Judge of the High Court of Justice, QBD, 1981–88; Presiding Judge, Western Circuit, 1983–87. Judge of Court of Appeal: Gibraltar, 2001– (Pres., 2008–); Bermuda, 2004–. Jt Inspector into Grays Bldg Soc., 1979. Mem., Criminal Injuries Compensation Bd, 1980–81. Commissioner: for the Security Service, 1989–2000; for the Intelligence Services, 1994–2000. Chairman: Proscribed Orgns Appeal Commn, 2001–02; Pathogens Access Appeal Commn, 2002. Pres., Dacorum SO, 1994–. *Recreations:* playing 'cello, shooting, building, playing bridge. *Address:* Serge Hill, Abbots Langley, Herts WD5 0RY.

STUART TAYLOR, Sir Nicholas (Richard), 4th Bt *cr* 1917; *b* 14 Jan. 1952; *s* of Sir Richard Laurence Stuart Taylor, 3rd Bt, and of Iris Mary, *d* of Rev. Edwin John Gargery; *S* father, 1978; *m* 1984, Malvena Elizabeth Sullivan, (marr. diss. 1999); two *d. Educ:* Bradfield. Admitted Solicitor, 1977. *Recreations:* ski-ing and other sports. *Heir:* none. *Address:* 30 Siskin Close, Bishop's Waltham, Hants SO32 1RQ. *Club:* Ski Club of Great Britain.

STUBBS, Andrew James; QC 2008; a Recorder, since 2003; *b* York, 16 April 1965; *s* of William Charles Stubbs and Janice Pickles; *m* 1998, Jane Louise; two *s. Educ:* Nottingham Univ.; Inns of Court Sch. of Law. Called to the Bar, Lincoln's Inn, 1988. *Recreations:* golf, theatre, wine. *Address:* St Paul's Chambers, 23 Park Square, Leeds LS1 2NP. *T:* (0113) 245 5866, *Fax:* (0113) 245 5807.

STUBBS, Imogen Mary, (Lady Nunn); actress; *b* 20 Feb. 1961; *d* of late Robin Desmond Scrivener Stubbs and Heather Mary Stubbs (*née* McCracken); *m* 1994, Trevor Robert Nunn (*see* Sir T. R. Nunn); one *s* one *d. Educ:* St Paul's Girls' Sch.; Westminster Sch.; Exeter Coll., Oxford (BA 1st cl. Hons); RADA. *Theatre:* Cabaret, Ipswich, 1985; The Rover, 1986, The Two Noble Kinsmen, 1987, Desdemona in Othello, 1989, RSC; Heartbreak House, Theatre Royal, Haymarket, 1992; title rôle, St Joan, Strand, 1994; Uncle Vanya, Chichester Fest., then Albery, 1996; A Streetcar Named Desire, Theatre Royal, Haymarket, 1996; Closer, Lyric, 1998; Betrayal, RNT, 1998; The Relapse, RNT, 2001; Three Sisters, Bath Royal and tour, 2002; Mum's The Word, Albery and tour, 2003; Hamlet, Old Vic, 2004; title rôle, The Duchess of Malfi, W Yorks Playhouse, 2006; *play written:* We Happy Few, Gielgud, 2004; *television:* The Rainbow, 1988; Othello, 1990; After the Dance, 1992; Anna Lee, 1994; Big Kids; *films:* Nanou, 1985; Erik the Viking, 1988; Fellow Traveller, 1990; True Colors, 1990; Sandra, c'est la vie; Lucy in Sense and Sensibility, 1995; Viola in Twelfth Night, 1996; Three Guesses; dir, Snow on Saturday (Kino Best British Short Award). *Publications:* (jtly) Amazonians; regular contribs to Daily Telegraph and Harpers & Queen. *Address:* c/o United Agents, 12–26 Lexington Street, W1F 0LE.

STUBBS, Prof. Michael Wesley, PhD; Professor of English Linguistics, University of Trier, Germany, since 1990; *b* 23 Dec. 1947; *s* of late Leonard Garforth Stubbs and Isabella Wardrop (*née* McGavin). *Educ:* Glasgow High Sch. for Boys; King's Coll., Cambridge (MA); Univ. of Edinburgh (PhD 1975). Res. Associate, Univ. of Birmingham, 1973–74; Lectr in Linguistics, Univ. of Nottingham, 1974–85; Prof. of English in Educn, Inst. of Educn, Univ. of London, 1985–90. Vis. Prof. of Linguistics, Univ. of Tübingen, Germany, 1985; Hon. Sen. Res. Fellow, Univ. of Birmingham, 1994–99. Chm., BAAL, 1988–91. Mem., Nat. Curriculum English Working Gp (Cox Cttee), 1988–89. *Publications:* Language, Schools and Classrooms, 1976, 2nd edn 1983; Language and Literacy, 1980; Discourse Analysis, 1983; Educational Linguistics, 1986; Text and Corpus Analysis, 1996; Words and Phrases, 2001; (jtly) Text, Discourse and Corpora, 2007; articles in Lang. and Educn, Applied Linguistics, Jl of Pragmatics, Functions of Lang., Text, Internat. Jl of Corpus Linguistics, Lang. and Lit. *Recreation:* walking. *Address:* FB2 Anglistik, University of Trier, 54286 Trier, Germany. *T:* (651) 2012278.

STUBBS, Sukhvinder Kaur; Chief Executive, Barrow Cadbury Trust, since 2001; *b* Punjab, India, 25 Oct. 1962; *d* of S. Inderjit Singh Thethy and Charanjit Kaur; *m* 1985, David Brian Stubbs (marr. diss. 2008); one *d. Educ:* Hertford Coll., Oxford (MA Geography; Henry Oliver Becket Meml Prize). MCIM 1992. Lectr, Orpington Coll., 1984–85; Graduate Manager, British Telecom, 1985–86; Mkting Exec., Prisoners Abroad, 1986–87; Appeals Dir, British Dyslexia Assoc., 1987–90; Dir of Corporate Affairs, Community Develt Foundn, 1990–94; Community Develt Manager, English Partnerships, 1994–96; Chief Exec., Runnymede Trust, 1996–2000; Chair: European Network Against Racism, 1998–2002; Young Enterprise (WM), 2002–05. Non-executive Director: W Midlands Regl Develt Agency (Advantage W Midlands), 1998–2003; CPS, 2000–02; Severn Trent Water, 2002–06. Member: Learning and Skills Res. Develt Unit, 2001–03; Cabinet Office Better Regulation Taskforce, 2002–06; National Consumer Council, 2007–. Council Mem., Britain in Europe Trust, 2000–05; Steering Gp Mem., UN Cttee on World Conf. against Racism, 2001. Chm., Birmingham Secondary Educn Commn, 1998; Mem., Birmingham Democracy Commn, 2000–01. Trustee, Demos, 1998–2006. Mem., Lunar Soc., 1999. FRSA 1996. *Publications:* (contrib.) Renewing Citizenship and Democracy, 1997; (contrib.) Mindfields, 1998; Fear and Loathing in the EU, 2000; Islam, Race and Being British, 2005; papers, articles in jls. *Recreations:* adventure travel, mountain hiking, gardening. *Address:* (office) 629 Kings Road, Birmingham B44 9HW.

STUBBS, Thomas, OBE 1980; HM Diplomatic Service, retired; *b* 12 July 1926; *s* of Thomas Stubbs and Lillian Marguerite (*née* Rumball, formerly Bell); *m* 1951, Dorothy Miller (*d* 1997); one *s* one *d. Educ:* Heaton Tech. Sch., Newcastle upon Tyne. Served in Army, 1944–48. Joined Min. of Nat. Insce, later Min. of Pensions and Nat. Insce, 1948; transf. to CRO, 1960; New Delhi, 1962; CRO, 1964; Wellington, NZ, 1965; Vice-Consul, Düsseldorf, 1970; seconded to BOTB, 1974; First Sec. (Commercial) and Consul, Addis Ababa, 1977; Consul, Hannover, 1980; Dep. High Comr, Madras, 1983–86. Mayor, Borough of Spelthorne, 1992–93 (Mem. (C) Council, 1987–2003; Vice-Chairman: Leisure and Amenities Cttee, 1987–89; Planning Cttee, 1999–2002; Chairman: Personnel Cttee, 1989–91; Resources Cttee, 1995–96; Finance Sub-Cttee, 1996–98; Dep. Mayor, 1991–92). Chm., SE Employers, 2000–03. Pres., Spelthorne Cons. Constituency Assoc., 2002–05. Hon. Pres., County of Middlesex Trust, 1992–. *Recreation:* reading. *Address:* 17 Chester Close, Ashford Common, Middx TW15 1PH. *Club:* Sunbury-on-Thames Conservative.

STUBBS, William Frederick; QC 1978; *b* 27 Nov. 1934; *s* of William John Stubbs and Winifred Hilda (*née* Johnson); *m* 1961, Anne Katharine (*d* 1966), *d* of late Prof. W. K. C. Guthrie, FBA; one *s* one *d. Educ:* The High Sch., Newcastle-under-Lyme, Staffs; Gonville and Caius Coll., Cambridge; Harvard Law Sch. Open Minor Scholar in Nat. Sci., Gonville and Caius Coll., 1951; Student, Gray's Inn, 1953; 1st Cl. Hons Law Tripos Pt I, and George Long Prize for Roman Law, Cambridge, 1954; Major Scholar, Gonville and Caius Coll., 1954; 1st Cl. Hons with Distinction Law Tripos Pt II, Cambridge, 1955; LLB 1st Cl. Hons with Dist., and Chancellor's Medal for English Law, Cambridge, 1956; Tapp Post-Grad. Law Scholar, Gonville and Caius Coll., 1956 (also awarded Schuldham Plate); Joseph Hodges Choate Meml Fellow, Harvard Coll., 1957; Bar Final Exam., 2nd Cl. Hons Div. 1, 1957; Holker Sen. Scholar and Macaskie Scholar, Gray's Inn, 1957; called to the Bar, Gray's Inn, 1957, Bencher, 1987. Has practised in Courts of Malaysia, Singapore, Hong Kong, Cayman Is and IOM. *Recreations:* reading, walking, natural history. *Address:* 3 Atherton Drive, SW19 5LB. *T:* (020) 8947 3986. *Club:* MCC.

STUBBS, Sir William (Hamilton), Kt 1994; Chairman, Oxford Radcliffe Hospitals NHS Trust, since 2003; *b* 5 Nov. 1937; *s* of Joseph Stubbs and Mary Stubbs (*née* McNicol); *m* 1963, Marie Margaret Pierce; three *d. Educ:* Workington Grammar Sch.; St Aloysius Coll., Glasgow; Glasgow Univ. (BSc, PhD). Res. Associate, Univ. of Arizona, 1963–64; with Shell Oil Co., San Francisco, 1964–67; teaching, 1967–72; Asst Dir of Educn, Carlisle, 1972–74; Asst Dir of Educn, 1974–76, Second Dep. Dir of Educn, 1976–77, Cumbria; Second Dep. Educn Officer, 1977–79, Dir of Educn (Schools), 1979–82, Educn Officer and Chief Exec., 1982–88, ILEA; Chief Exec., PCFC, 1988–93; Chief Exec., FEFC, 1992–96; Rector, The London Inst., 1996–2001. Member: Council, CRAC, 1993–2004; Nat. Cttee of Inquiry into Higher Educn, 1996–97; Bd, NACETT, 1997–2002; Council, Inst. of Employment Studies, 1997–2005; Design Council, 1999–2004; Chairman: CBI Educn Foundn, 1996–99; Qualifications and Curriculum Authority, 1997–2002. Hon. Prof., Dept of Continuing Educn, Univ. of Warwick, 1993. Trustee, Geffrye Mus., 1999–; Pres., Assoc. of Colls Trust, 2001–2003. Chancellor, Thames Valley Univ., 2001–04. Gov., Birkbeck Coll., London, 1998–2004. CCMI; FRSA. DUniv: Open, 1995; Sheffield Hallam, 1996; Strathclyde, 2004; Hon. DLitt Exeter, 1996; Hon. DSc UWE, 1997; Hon. DEd Greenwich, 2007; Hon. LLD Brighton, 2007. *Address:* Lockes Cottage, Manor Road, West Adderbury, near Banbury, Oxon OX17 3EL.

STUCKEY, Rev. Thomas James; President of the Methodist Conference, 2005–06; Chair, Southampton Methodist District, 1998–2006; Canon, Salisbury Cathedral, 2002–06; *b* 10 May 1940; *s* of Howard and Pat Stuckey; *m* 1966, Christine Plympton; two *s* one *d. Educ:* Yeovil Grammar Sch.; City Univ. (BScEng 1964); Richmond Coll. (BD London Univ. 1967); Edinburgh Univ. (MTh 1972). Engrg appts with Westland Aircraft and Fairey Aviation, 1956–63; theol trng, Richmond Coll., 1964–67; Methodist Circuit appts, Coatbridge, Airdrie and Armadale, Bristol Mission, Exeter, 1967–76; Tutor in Applied Theol., Hartley Victoria Coll., 1982–90; Supt, Reading and Silchester Methodist Circuit, 1990–98. *Publications:* Into the Far Country, 2003; Beyond the Box, 2005; The Edge of Pentecost, 2007; articles in Worship and Preaching, Epworth Review. *Recreations:* music, theology, theatre, films, watercolour painting, MG club, enjoying the company of my wife. *Address:* 11 The Meadway, Christchurch BH23 4NT.

STUCLEY, Sir Hugh (George Coplestone Bampfylde), 6th Bt *cr* 1859; DL; Lieut Royal Horse Guards, retired; *b* 8 Jan. 1945; *s* of Major Sir Dennis Frederic Bankes Stucley, 5th Bt, and Hon. Sheila Bampfylde (*d* 1996), *o d* of 4th Baron Poltimore; *S* father, 1983; *m* 1969, Angela Caroline, *e d* of Richard Charles Robertson Toller, MC, Theale, Berks; two *s* two *d. Educ:* Milton Abbey School; Royal Agricultural College, Cirencester. Chm., Badgworthy Land Co., 1999–2004. Chm., Devon Br., CLA, 1995–97; Pres., Devonshire Assoc., 1997–98. Chm., Wessex Br., Historic Houses Assoc., 2007–. DL 1998, High Sheriff, 2006–07, Devon. *Heir: s* George Dennis Bampfylde Stucley [*b* 26 Dec. 1970; *m* 1997, Amber, *yr d* of Thomas Gage; two *s*]. *Address:* Affeton Castle, Worlington, Crediton, Devon EX17 4TU. *Club:* Sloane.

STUDD, Sir Edward (Fairfax), 4th Bt *cr* 1929; *b* 3 May 1929; *s* of Sir Eric Studd, 2nd Bt, OBE, and Stephana (*d* 1976), *o d* of L. J. Langmead; *S* brother, 1977; *m* 1960, Prudence Janet, *o d* of Alastair Douglas Fyfe, OBE, Riding Mill, Northumberland; two *s* one *d. Educ:* Winchester College. Lieutenant Coldstream Guards, London and Malaya, 1947–49; Macneill & Barry Ltd, Calcutta, 1951–62; Inchcape & Co. Ltd, London, 1962–86 (Dir, 1974–86). Master, Merchant Taylor's Co., 1987–88 and 1993–94. *Recreation:* rural activities. *Heir: s* Philip Alastair Fairfax Studd [*b* 27 Oct. 1961; *m* 1987, Georgina (marr. diss. 1999), *d* of Sir Roger Neville, VRD; one *s* one *d*].

STUDD, Prof. John William Winston, MD, DSc; FRCOG; Professor of Gynaecology, Imperial College London, 1998, now Emeritus; Consultant Gynaecologist, Chelsea and Westminster Hospital, since 1994; *b* 4 March 1940; *s* of late Eric Dacombe Studd and Elsie Elizabeth (*née* Kirby); *m* 1980, Margaret Anne Johnson, *qv*; one *s* two *d. Educ:* Royal Hosp. Sch., Holbrook; Univ. of Birmingham (MB ChB 1962; MD 1969; DSc 1995). MRCOG 1967, FRCOG 1982. Res. Fellow, Queen Elizabeth Hosp., Birmingham, 1967–70; Lectr in Obstetrics and Gynaecol., UC of Rhodesia, 1970–71; Consultant and Sen. Lectr, Univ. of Nottingham, 1974–75; Consultant Obstetrician and Gynaecologist, KCH, 1975–94; Dir, Fertility and Endocrine Centre, Lister Hosp., Chelsea, 1987. Visiting Professor: Yale Univ., 1982; Duke Univ., 1984; Univ. of Singapore, 1989; Harvard Univ., 1995; Cornell Univ., 2008. Mem. Council, 1980–97, and Pres., Sect. of Obstetrics and Gynaecol., 1994–95, RSocMed. Chm., Nat. Osteoporosis Soc., 1992–; Pres., Internat. Soc. Reproductive Medicine. Chm., PMS and Menopause Trust. Ed., Yearbook, 1993–97, Publications Officer, 1994–97, RCOG. Editor: Menopause Digest, 1994–; Obstetric and Gynaecol Reviews, 1994–; The Diplomate, 1995–; Member Editorial Board: Brit. Jl Obstetrics and Gynaecol.; Jl RSocMed; N American Jl of Menopause; Europ. Menopause Jl; Brit. Jl Hosp. Medicine; Osteoporosis Internat. *Publications:* Management of Labour, 1985; Self Assessment in Obstetrics and Gynaecology, 1985; Management of the Menopause, 1988, 4th edn 2003; (ed) Progress in Obstetrics and Gynaecology, Vols 1–18, 1982–2008; Multiple Choice Questions in Obstetrics and Gynaecology, 1993; The Menopause and Osteoporosis, 1993; Annual Progress in Reproductive Medicine, Vols 1 and 2, 1993–94; (with S. S. Sheth) Vaginal Hysterectomy, 2001; contrib. numerous articles on the menopause, osteoporosis, pre-menstrual syndrome, post-natal depression, labour, sickle cell disease and HIV infection in women. *Recreations:* theatre, opera, history of medicine, collecting antiquarian medical books. *Address:* 27 Blomfield Road, W9 1AA. *T:* (020) 7266 0058, *Fax:* (020) 7289 1417; London PMS & Menopause Centre, 46 Wimpole Street, W1G 8SD.

STUDD, Margaret Anne; *see* Johnson, M. A.

STUDER, Cheryl Lynn; opera singer, freelance since 1986; *b* Midland, USA, 24 Oct. 1955; *m* 1992, Ewald Schwarz; two *d. Educ:* Interlochen Arts Acad.; Oberlin Coll. Conservatory, Ohio; Univ. of Tennessee; Hochschule für Musik und Darstellende Kunst, Vienna. First professional recital, Virginia Highlands Fest., 1977; operatic début, Bavarian State Opera, 1980; *débuts:* Royal Opera House, Covent Garden, 1984; Bayreuth Fest., 1985; La Scala, Milan, 1987; NY Met, 1988; Vienna State Opera, 1989; has sung at all major opera houses and festivals in the world; regular appearances at Bayreuth and Salzburg

Fests; extensive concert tours with all major orchestras and conductors; world-wide recitals. Many recordings, incl. La Traviata, Faust, Salomé, Lohengrin, Figaro, Strauss' Four Last Songs. Franz Schubert Inst. Award, 1979; Grammy Award, 1991, 1994; Internat. Classical Music Award for best female singer, 1992; Furtwängler Preis, 1992; Vocalist of the Year Award, Musical America Directory of Performing Arts, 1994.

STUDHOLME, Sir Henry (William), 3rd Bt *cr* 1956, of Perridge, Co. Devon; DL; *b* 31 Jan. 1958; *s* of Sir Paul Henry William Studholme, 2nd Bt and Virginia (*d* 1990), *yr d* of Sir (Herbert) Richmond Palmer, KCMG, CBE; *S* father, 1990; *m* 1988, Sarah Lucy Rosita (*née* Deans-Chrystall); two *s* one *d*. *Educ:* Eton; Trinity Hall, Cambridge (MA). ACA, CTA. Chairman: SW Regl Adv. Cttee on Forestry, 2000–07; SW Cttee Country Land and Business Assoc., 2001–03; SW Chamber of Rural Enterprise, 2003–; SW Food and Drink, 2004–; Member: England Forestry Forum, 2002–07; Bd, SW RDA, 2002– (Chm., Rural Adv. Gp and Audit Cttee, 2003–08). A Forestry Comr, 2007–. DL Devon, 2006. *Heir: s* Joshua Henry Paul Studholme, *b* 2 Feb. 1992. *Club:* Brooks's.

See also J. G. Studholme.

STUDHOLME, Joseph Gilfred; Chairman and Co-founder, Getmapping (formerly Getmapping.com) plc, 1998–2002; *b* 14 Jan. 1936; *s* of Sir Henry Gray Studholme, 1st Bt, CVO and Judith Joan Mary (*née* Whitbread); *m* 1959, Rachel Fellowes, *d* of Sir William Albemarle Fellowes, KCVO; three *s*. *Educ:* Eton; Magdalen Coll., Oxford (MA). Nat. Service, 2nd Lieut, KRRC (60th Rifles), 1954–56. Man. Dir, King & Shaxson Ltd (Billbrokers), 1961–63; Co-founder, Chm. and Man. Dir, Editions Alecto Gp, 1963–2002. Mem. Council, Byam Shaw Sch. of Art, 1963–94 (Chm., 1988–94). Chm., Wessex Regl Cttee, NT, 1996–2006 (Mem., 1993–2006). Sen. Fellow, RCA, 1999. *Address:* The Court House, Lower Woodford, Salisbury, Wilts SP4 6NQ. *T:* (01722) 782237. *Clubs:* Garrick, Double Crown, MCC.

STUDZINSKI, John Joseph Paul, CBE 2008; Senior Managing Director, Blackstone Group International Ltd, since 2006; *b* 19 March 1956; *s* of Alfred Edward Studzinski and Jennie Mary Studzinski (*née* Gaieski). *Educ:* Bowdoin Coll., Maine (AB Biol. and Sociol. 1978); Univ. of Chicago (MBA Finance and Marketing 1980). Morgan Stanley International Ltd: Head: Corporate Finance, Europe, 1989–92; M&A, Europe, 1992–97; Investment Banking, Europe, 1997–2001; Dep. Chm., 2001–03; Chief Exec., Corporate, Investment Banking and Markets, and Mem., Gp Mgt Bd, HSBC, 2003–06. Trustee: Tate Gall., 1998–2007; Sir John Soane Mus., 1999–. Founder and Chm., Genesis Foundn, 2000–. Chm., Business Action on Homeless, 1998–; Member: Bd of Dirs, Human Rights Watch, 1999– (Vice-Chm., 2005–); Trustees, Passage Day Centre for Homeless, 2000–. Prince of Wales's Ambassador's Award, 2000. KSS, KSG 2001. *Recreations:* voluntary work with homeless, human rights, nurturing young artists. *Address:* Blackstone Group International Ltd, 40 Berkeley Square, W1J 5AL.

STUNELL, (Robert) Andrew, OBE 1995; MP (Lib Dem) Hazel Grove, since 1997; *b* 24 Nov. 1942; *s* of late Robert George and Trixie Stunell; *m* 1967, Gillian (*née* Chorley); two *s* three *d*. *Educ:* Surbiton Grammar Sch.; Manchester Univ.; Liverpool Poly. Architectural asst, CWS Manchester, 1965–67, Runcorn New Town, 1967–81, freelance, 1981–85; various posts incl. Political Sec., Assoc. of Liberal Democrat Councillors, 1985–97. Member: Chester City Council, 1979–90; Cheshire CC, 1981–91 (Leader, Lib Dem Gp); Stockport MBC, 1994–2002. Vice-Chm., ACC, 1985–90. Contested: (L) 1979, (Lib/Alliance), 1983 and 1987, City of Chester; (Lib Dem) Hazel Grove, 1992. Lib Dem Chief Whip, 2001–06; Lib Dem front bench spokesman on communities and local govt, 2006–. *Address:* House of Commons, SW1A 0AA; 84 Lyme Grove, Romiley, Stockport SK6 4DJ.

STURDEE, Rear-Adm. (Arthur) Rodney (Barry), CB 1971; DSC 1945; *b* 6 Dec. 1919; *s* of Comdr Barry V. Sturdee, RN, and Barbara (*née* Sturdee); *m* 1st, 1953, Marie-Claire Amstoutz (*d* 1995), Mulhouse, France; one *s* one *d*; 2nd, 2001, Joyce (*née* Jeacock), *widow* of Major James Hunter. *Educ:* Canford Sch. Entered Royal Navy as Special Entry Cadet, 1937. Served War of 1939–45: Midshipman in HMS Exeter at Battle of the River Plate, 1939; Lieut, 1941; specialised in Navigation, 1944; minesweeping in Mediterranean, 1944–45 (DSC). Lt-Comdr, 1949; RN Staff Coll., 1950–51; Staff of Navigation Sch., 1951–52; Comdr, 1952; JSSC, 1953; BJSM, Washington, 1953–55; Fleet Navigating Officer, Medit., 1955–57; Exec. Officer, RNAS, Culdrose, 1958–59; Captain 1960; NATO Defence Coll., 1960–63; Queen's Harbour-Master, Singapore, 1963–65; Staff of Chief of Defence Staff, 1965–67; Chief of Staff to C-in-C, Portsmouth (as Cdre), 1967–69; Rear-Adm. 1969; Flag Officer, Gibraltar, 1969–72; retired 1972. ADC to the Queen, 1969. *Address:* Cider Mill Cottage, Hancocks Lane, Castlemorton Common, Malvern, Worcestershire WR13 6LG. *T:* (01684) 573627.

STURDY, Robert William; Member (C) Eastern Region, England, European Parliament, since 1999 (Cambridgeshire, 1994–99); *b* 22 June 1944; *s* of late Gordon Sturdy and of Kathleen Sturdy (*née* Wells); *m* 1969, Elizabeth Hommes; one *s* one *d*. *Educ:* Ashville Coll., Harrogate. Accountant; Partner, G. E. Sturdy & Son. European Parliament: Cons. spokesman on agriculture, 1994–2001, on rural affairs, 2001–04, on internat. trade, 2004–06; Vice-Pres., Delegn to SE Europe, 1994–99; Dep. Leader, Cons. Delegn in Europe, 1999–2001; Chm., Canadian Interparly Delegn, 1999–2002; Chm., Aust. and NZ Interparly Delegn, 2002–04; ACP-EU Delegn, 2004–; Mem., Agriculture Cttee, 1994–2004; Substitute Mem., Cttee on Envmt, 1999–, on Agriculture, 2004–; EPP-ED Co-ordinator for Internat. Trade, 2004–; Co-Chair, WTO Steering Gp of Parly Assembly. *Recreations:* fishing, tennis, ski-ing, cricket. *Address:* 153 St Neots Road, Hardwick, Cambridge CB23 7QJ. *T:* (01954) 211790.

STURGE, Maj.-Gen. (Henry Arthur) John, CB 1978; *b* 27 April 1925; *s* of Henry George Arthur Sturge and Lilian Beatrice Sturge; *m* 1953, Jean Ailsa Mountain; two *s* one *d*. *Educ:* Wilson's Sch., (formerly) Camberwell, London; Queen Mary Coll., London. Commissioned, Royal Signals, 1946; UK, 1946–50; Egypt, 1950–53; UK, incl. psc, 1953–59; Far East, 1959–62; jssc, 1962; BAOR, 1963–64; RMA, Sandhurst, 1965–66; BAOR, incl. Command, 1966–69; UK Comd 12 Sig. Bde, 1970–71; Min. of Defence, 1972–75; Chief Signal Officer, BAOR, 1975–77; ACDS (Signals), 1977–80. Col Comdt, Royal Corps of Signals, 1977–85. Colonel, Queen's Gurkha Signals, 1980–86. Gen. Manager, 1981–84, Dir, 1983–84, Marconi Space and Defence Systems; Man. Dir, 1984–85, Chm., 1985–86, Marconi Secure Radio Systems; Prin. Consultant, Logica Space and Defence Systems, 1986–90; Chm., Logica Defence and Civil Government Ltd, 1991–94. Vice Chm., Governors, Wilson's Sch., 1979–99. *Recreations:* sailing, (formerly) Rugby.

STURGEON, Nicola; Member (SNP) Glasgow Govan, Scottish Parliament, since 2007 (Glasgow, 1999–2007); Deputy First Minister and Cabinet Secretary for Health and Wellbeing, since 2007; *b* 19 July 1970; *d* of Robert and Joan Sturgeon. *Educ:* Univ. of Glasgow (LLB Hons; Dip. Legal Practice). Trainee Solicitor, McClure Naismith, Glasgow, 1993–95; Asst Solicitor, Bell & Craig, Stirling, 1995–97; Associate Solicitor, Drumchapel Law Centre, Glasgow, 1997–99. Dep. Leader, SNP, 2004–. *Recreations:* theatre, reading. *Address:* Scottish Parliament, Edinburgh EH99 1SP. *T:* (0131) 348 5695.

STURKEY, (Robert) Douglas, CVO 1995; AM 1999; PhD; Official Secretary to the Governor-General of Australia, 1990–98; Secretary of the Order of Australia, 1990–98; *b* 7 Sept. 1935; *s* of late James Robert Sturkey and Jessie Grace (*née* Meares). *Educ:* Wesley Coll., S Perth; Univ. of WA (BA Hons); ANU (MA 2000; PhD 2004). Mem., Australian Diplomatic Service, 1957–90: service abroad at Wellington, Lagos, Suva, Malta, Calcutta; Counsellor, later Dep. Perm. Rep., UN, New York, 1974–77; Ambassador to Saudi Arabia (also concurrently to countries of Arabian peninsula), 1979–84; Head, S Asia, Africa and ME Br., Dept of Foreign Affairs, Canberra, 1984–87; Principal Advr, Asia Div., Dept of Foreign Affairs and Trade, Canberra, 1987–90. CStJ 1992. *Publication:* The Limits of American Power: prosecuting a Middle East peace, 2007. *Recreations:* opera, music, theatre. *Address:* PO Box 5562, Hughes, ACT 2605, Australia. *T:* (2) 62324722.

STURLEY, Air Marshal Philip Oliver, CB 2000; MBE 1985; FRAeS; President, Royal Air Forces Association, since 2005; *b* 9 July 1950; *s* of William Percival Sturley and Delia Agnes Sturley (*née* Grogan); *m* 1972, Micheline Leetch; one *d*. *Educ:* St Ignatius Coll., London; Southampton Univ. (BSc 1971). FRAeS 1993. Pilot trng, RAF Coll., Cranwell, 1971–72; 41 Sqn Coningsby, 1973–76; II (Army Co-operation) Sqn Laarbruch, 1977–80, 1982–84, OC, 1987–89; HQ 1 (British) Corps Bielefeld, 1980–82; jsdc, 1984; Comd Briefing Team, 1984–85, Plans, 1985–86, HQ Strike Comd; Air Plans, 1989–90, Dir of Air Staff Briefing and Co-ordination, 1990–92, MoD; OC RAF Cottesmore, 1992–94; Sec. IMS, HQ NATO, 1994–98; SASO HQ Strike Comd and AOC No 38 Gp, 1998–2000; ACAS, MoD, 2000–03; COS AirNorth Comd, Ramstein, 2003–05. Specialist Advr to H of C Defence Cttee, 2006–. *Recreations:* gliding, golf, ski-ing. *Address:* c/o RAFA Central HQ, 117½ Loughborough Road, Leicester LE4 5ND. *Club:* Royal Air Force.

STURMAN, James Anthony; QC 2002; *b* 19 July 1958; *s* of Gp Capt Roger Sturman, RAF (retd) and Anne Sturman; *m* 1986, Marcella Mineo; three *s*. *Educ:* Bembridge Sch., Isle of Wight; Reading Univ. (LLB). Called to the Bar, Gray's Inn, 1982; criminal defence barrister. *Recreations:* soccer, cricket, punk rock music, my three children. *Address:* 2 Bedford Row, WC1R 4BU. *T:* (020) 7440 8888, *Fax:* (020) 7242 1738; *e-mail:* jsturman@2bedfordrow.co.uk.

STURRIDGE, Charles; writer and director; *b* 24 June 1951; *s* of Jerome Francis Sturridge and Alyson Sturridge (*née* Burke); *m* 1985, Phoebe Nicholls; two *s* one *d*. *Educ:* Beaumont Coll.; Stonyhurst Coll.; University Coll., Oxford (BA). Mem., NYT, 1967–70; film début as actor, If..., 1968; director: *theatre* includes: The Seagull, Queen's, 1985; *films* include: Runners, 1982; (co-writer) A Handful of Dust, 1988; (co-writer) Where Angels Fear to Tread, 1991; (screenplay) Fairytale—A True Story, 1997 (Best Children's Film, British Acad., 1998); Ohio Impromptu, 2001 (Best TV Drama, LWT Awards); (writer and producer) Lassie, 2005; *television* includes: 16 episodes of Coronation Street; 4 documentary films for World in Action, 1976; Brideshead Revisited, 1981 (Best Series, BAFTA); A Foreign Field, 1993; Gulliver's Travels, 1996 (Best Series, Emmy Awards); (also writer) Longitude, 2000 (Best Series, BAFTA); (also writer) Shackleton, 2002. *Address:* c/o United Agents, 12-26 Lexington Street, W1F 0LE. *T:* (020) 3214 0800.

STURROCK, John Garrow; QC (Scot.) 1999; Chief Executive, Core Solutions Group, since 2004; Director, Core Mediation, since 2000; *b* 15 April 1958; *s* of John Chesser Sturrock and Lilian Sturrock; *m* 1984, Fiona Swanson; two *s* one *d*. *Educ:* Univ. of Edinburgh (LLB 1st Cl. Hons 1980); Univ. of Pennsylvania (LLM 1985). MCIArb 2001. Solicitor, 1983–84; Harkness Fellow, 1984–85; admitted Faculty of Advocates, 1986; in practice as advocate, 1986–2002; Dir, Trng and Educn, Faculty of Advocates, 1994–2002. Standing Jun. Counsel to Dept of Transport in Scotland, 1991–94; Accredited Mediator, CEDR, 1996. Man. Dir, Core Consulting, 2000–04. Vis. Prof. of Advocacy Skills and Conflict Resolution, Univ. of Strathclyde, 1999–. Member: Jt Standing Cttee on Legal Educn, Scotland, 1988–2005; Judicial Studies Cttee, Scotland, 1997–2005; Standards Commn, Internat. Mediation Inst., 2007–; Global Adv. Council, Mediators Beyond Borders, 2008–. Assessor, SHEFC, 1995–96. FRSA 2001. *Recreations:* family, church, golf, music. *Address:* Rutland House, 19 Rutland Square, Edinburgh EH1 2BB. *T:* (0131) 221 2520; *e-mail:* John.Sturrock@core-solutions.com.

STURROCK, Philip James; Chairman, Osprey Publishing, since 2007; *b* 5 Oct. 1947; *s* of James Cars Sturrock and Joyce Sturrock (*née* Knowles); *m* 1st, 1972, Susan Haycock (marr. diss. 1995); one *s* two *d*; 2nd, 2000, Madeleine Frances Robinson. *Educ:* Queen Mary's School, Walsall; Trinity College, Oxford (MA); Manchester Business School (MBA). Managing Director: IBIS Information Services, 1972–80; Pitman Books, 1980–83; Group Man. Dir, Routledge & Kegan Paul, 1983–85; Chm. and Man. Dir, Cassell, 1986–99; Chm. and Gp Chief Exec., Continuum Internat. Publishing Gp, 1999–2006. Chm., Soc. of Bookmen, 2001–02. Governor, Pusey House, Oxford, 1975–95. Trustee, St Albans Cathedral Educn Trust, 1988–2003. FRSA 1992. Liveryman, Glaziers' Co., 1983–. *Recreations:* reading, walking, music. *Address:* 62 Benbow House, New Globe Walk, SE1 9DS. *T:* (020) 3267 1136. *Club:* Athenæum.

STUTTAFORD, Dr (Irving) Thomas, OBE 1996; medical columnist, The Times, since 1991; *b* 4 May 1931; 2nd *s* of late Dr W. J. E. Stuttaford, MC, Horning, Norfolk and Mrs Marjorie Stuttaford (*née* Royden); *m* 1957, Pamela, *d* of late Col Richard Ropner, TD, DL, Tain; three *s*. *Educ:* Gresham's Sch.; Brasenose Coll., Oxford; West London Hosp. 2nd Lieut, 10th Royal Hussars (PWO), 1953–55; Lieut, Scottish Horse (TA), 1955–59. Qualif. MRCS, LRCP, 1959; junior hosp. appts, 1959 and 1960. Gen. Med. practice, 1960–70. Mem. Blofield and Flegg RDC, 1964–66; Mem., Norwich City Council, 1969–71. MP (C) Norwich S, 1970–Feb. 1974; Mem. Select Cttee Science and Technology, 1970–74. Contested (C) Isle of Ely, Oct. 1974, 1979. Physician, BUPA Medical Centre, 1971–96; Clinical Assistant to: The London Hosp., 1975–93; Queen Mary's Hosp. for East End, 1974–79; Moorfields Eye Hosp., 1975–79. Member: Council, Research Defence Soc., 1970–79; Birth Control Campaign Cttee, 1970–79; British Cancer Council, 1970–79. Medical Adviser: Rank Organisation, 1980–85; Barclays Bank, Standard Chartered Bank, Hogg Robinson, Rank Hotels and other cos; Medical Corresp. to The Times, 1982–91. Contributor to: Elle, For Him, Oldie, Options, etc. *Publications:* To Your Good Health: the wise drinker's guide, 1997; (jtly) In Your Right Mind, 1999; Understanding Your Common Symptoms, 2003; Stress and How to Avoid It, 2004. *Recreation:* country life. *Address:* 8 Devonshire Place, W1G 6HN. *T:* (020) 7935 5011; 36 Elm Hill, Norwich, Norfolk NR3 1HG. *T:* (01603) 615133. *Clubs:* Athenæum, Reform, Cavalry and Guards, Beefsteak; Norfolk (Norwich).

STUTTARD, Sir John (Boothman), Kt 2008; JP; Adviser, PricewaterhouseCoopers, since 2005 (Vice Chairman, Advisory Panel, since 2008); Lord Mayor of London, 2006–07; *b* 6 Feb. 1945; *s* of Thomas Boothman Stuttard and Helena Stuttard (*née* Teasdale); *m* 1970, Lesley Sylvia Daish; two *s*. *Educ:* Shrewsbury Sch.; Churchill Coll., Cambridge (BA 1966, MA 1970). FCA 1979. Teacher with VSO, SOAS Coll., Brunei, 1966–67; Coopers & Lybrand, then PricewaterhouseCoopers: articled clerk, then Chartered Accountant, 1970–75; Partner, 1975–2005; Chm., Coopers & Lybrand China, subseq. PricewaterhouseCoopers China, 1994–99. Advr, Central Policy Rev. Staff, Cabinet Office, 1981–83. Director: China-Britain Business Council, 2000–06; Finnish-

British Chamber of Commerce, 2001– (Chm., 2002–06). Mem., Fund Raising Adv. Bd, 2000–, Council, 2006–, VSO. University of Cambridge: Mem., Appts Bd, 1977–81; Mem. Adv. Cttee, East Asia Inst., Faculty of Oriental Studies, 2001–; By-Fellow, Møller Centre, Churchill Coll., Cambridge. Chancellor, 2006–07, Pro-Chancellor and Chm. Council, 2008–, City Univ. Mem. Court and Fellow, Bridewell Royal Hosp. and Gov., King Edward VII Sch., Witley, 2002–. Trustee: Lord Mayor of London's Disaster Relief Appeal, 2002–; Charities Aid Foundn, 2003– (Chm., Audit, Risk and Compliance Cttee, 2003–06); Lord Mayor's 800th Anniv. Appeal, 2005–; Morden Coll., 2005–; Advr, St Paul's Cath. Foundn, 2005–. Hon. Treas., New Horizon Youth Centre, 1972–77; Dir, Totteridge Manor Assoc., 1980–2005 (Chm., 2002–05); Hon. Vice-President: Totteridge Residents Assoc., 2006; Cambridge Univ. Land Soc., 2008. Hon. Fellow: Foreign Policy Assoc., USA, 2000; Securities & Investment Inst., 2007; Hon. Mem., GSMD, 2008. Alderman, City of London, Lime Street, 2001–; Sheriff, City of London, 2005–06; Freeman and Ct Asst, Guild of Educators, 2002–; Liveryman: Glaziers' and Painters of Glass Co., 2000– (Ct Asst, 2003–; Upper Warden, 2008–); Chartered Accountants' Co., 2002– (Ct Asst, 2004–); Plumbers' Co., 2005– (Hon. Ct Asst, 2005–). JP City of London, 2001. Hon. DLitt City, 2006. KStJ 2006. Knight 1st Cl., 1995, Comdr, 2004, Order of the Lion (Finland); Companion, League of Mercy, 2007; Silver Medal, City of Helsinki, 2007. *Publication:* The New Silk Road—Secrets of Business Success in China Today, 2000. *Recreations:* travelling, rallying old cars, theatre, opera, tennis. *Address:* PricewaterhouseCoopers LLP, 1 Embankment Place, WC2N 6RH. *T:* (020) 7213 4590; *e-mail:* john.stuttard@uk.pwc.com. *Clubs:* Travellers, East India, Walbrook, Pilgrims; Rolls-Royce Enthusiasts of Great Britain, 20-Ghost; Automobile (Monaco); China (Beijing and Hong Kong).

STUTTLE, Barbara Charmaine, CBE 2004; Director of Quality and Nursing, South West Essex Primary Care Trust, since 2008; National Clinical Lead Nursing, Connecting for Health, NHS, since 2005; *b* 4 May 1952; *d* of Philip George Albert Coote and Edith Marion Coote; two *s*. *Educ:* Hurlingham Sch. for Girls, Fulham; Sweyne Sch., Rayleigh; Southend Hosp.; City Univ., London (MSc Health Mgt 1996). SRN, 1971–73; Staff Nurse, Southend Hosp., 1974–75; Dist Nurse, Southend, 1975–79; Southend Community Care Trust: Dist Nurse, 1981–89; Nursing Officer, 1989–90; Asst Dir of Nursing, 1990–93; Sen. Manager, Thameside Community Care Trust, 1993–99; Dir of Integrated Care and Exec. Nurse, Castle Point and Rochford PCT, 1999–2005; Dir, Primary Care and Modernisation, Thurrock PCT, 2005–06; Exec. Nurse, SW Essex PCT, 2006–08. Nurse Prescribing Proj. Lead, London and SE Reg., DoH, 1998–2002. Fellow, Queen's Nursing Inst., 2007. *Publication:* Independent and Supplementary Prescribing: an essential guide, 2004. *Recreations:* going to the gym - reluctantly, reading, eating out, drinking wine, spending time with grandchildren.

STYBELSKI, Peter Stefan; Chief Executive, Cumbria County Council, since 2004; *b* 26 Oct. 1952; *s* of Czeslaw and Mary Stybelski; *m* 1980, Lorna Bell; one *s*. *Educ:* Plymouth; Wye Coll., Univ. of London (BSc Hons Geog. 1972; MSc Landscape, Ecol., Design and Maintenance 1976). Dist Grounds Superintendent, Bucks AHA, 1976–78; Parks Superintendent, Oxford CC, 1978–80; Asst Dir (Ops), Blackpool BC, 1980–83; Chief Amenities Officer, RBK&C, 1983–89; Dir, Leisure Services, Bolton MBC, 1989–2000; Town Clerk and Chief Exec., Carlisle CC, 2000–04. *Recreations:* being exercised by two chocolate labradors, landscape gardening, restoring property, music. *Address:* Chief Executive's Office, Cumbria County Council, The Courts, Carlisle, Cumbria CA3 8NA. *T:* (01228) 226301, *Fax:* (01228) 606302; *e-mail:* peter.stybelski@cumbriacc.gov.uk.

STYLE, Vice-Adm. Charles Rodney, CBE 2002; Commandant, Royal College of Defence Studies, since 2008; *b* 15 Jan. 1954; *s* of Lt-Comdr Sir Godfrey William Style, CBE, DSC, RN, and Sigrid Elisabeth Julin (*née* Carlberg); *m* 1981, Charlotte Amanda Woodford; three *d*. *Educ:* Eton; St Catharine's Coll., Cambridge (Exhibnr; BA Geog. 1975; MA). Served: HMS Endurance, 1977–78; Navigating Officer, HMS Bacchante, 1978–79; Royal Yacht Britannia, 1980–81; Commanding Officer: HMS Sandpiper, 1981–82; HMS Wotton, 1982–83; Ops Officer, HMS Arethusa, 1984–85; Naval Assistant to C-in-C Fleet, 1985–87; CO, HMS Andromeda, 1988–89; Naval Planner, MoD, 1989–92; COS to Comdr UK Task Gp, 1992–93; CO, HMS Campbeltown, 1993–95 (Task Gp Comd, Gulf, 1993–94); Dep. Flag Officer Sea Trng, 1995–96; hcsc 1997; Prin. SO to CDS, 1997–98; rcds 1999; CO, HMS Illustrious, 2000–01 (Task Gp Comd, Arabian Sea, 2001); Capability Manager (Strategic Deployment and Precision Attack), MoD, 2002–04; Comdr UK Maritime Force, 2004–05; DCDS (Commitments) and Dir of Ops, MoD, 2006–07. Mem., Master Mariners' Co., 2003–. Younger Brother, Trinity House, 1991–. *Recreations:* sailing, fishing, reading, music. *Address:* Royal College of Defence Studies, Seaford House, Belgrave Square, SW1X 8NS. *Clubs:* White's; Royal Yacht Squadron (Cowes).

STYLE, Christopher John David; QC 2006; Solicitor with Linklaters, since 1977: Head: of Litigation and Arbitration, since 1999; of Commercial Division, since 2002; *b* 13 April 1955; *s* of David and Anne Style; *m* 1990, Victoria Miles; three *s* one *d*. *Educ:* St Bees Sch.; Trinity Hall, Cambridge (BA Law 1976). Admitted solicitor, 1979. *Publication:* (with Charles Hollander) Documentary Evidence, 1984, 6th edn 1997. *Recreations:* my family, the country, high mountains. *Address:* Linklaters, One Silk Street, EC2Y 8HQ. *T:* (020) 7456 4286, *Fax:* (020) 7456 2222; *e-mail:* cstyle@linklaters.com.

STYLE, Sir William Frederick, 13th Bt *cr* 1627, of Wateringbury, Kent; *b* 13 May 1945; *s* of Sir William Montague Style, 12th Bt, and of La Verne, *d* of late T. M. Comstock; *S* father, 1981, but his name does not appear on the Official Roll of the Baronetage; *m* 1st, 1968, Wendy Gay (marr. diss. 1971), *d* of Gene Wittenberger, Hartford, Wisconsin, USA; two *d*; 2nd, 1986, Linnea Lorna, *d* of Donn Erickson, Sussex, Wisconsin, USA; one *s* two *d*. *Heir: s* William Colin Style, *b* 1 Sept. 1995.

STYLER, Granville Charles; His Honour Judge Styler; a Circuit Judge, since 1992; *b* 9 Jan. 1947; *s* of Samuel Charles Styler and Frances Joan Styler (*née* Clifford); *m* 1971, Penelope Darbyshire; three *d*. *Educ:* King Edward VI Sch., Stratford-on-Avon. Called to the Bar, Gray's Inn, 1970; a Recorder, 1988–92. *Recreations:* carriage driving, tennis, gardening, horse racing. *Address:* c/o Stoke-on-Trent Crown Court, Bethesda Street, Hanley, Stoke-on-Trent ST1 3BP. *Club:* Outer Hebrides Tennis.

STYLES, Prof. Peter, PhD; CGeol, FGS; FRAS; CSci; FIMMM; geophysicist; Professor of Applied and Environmental Geophysics, since 2000, and Director, Environment, Physical Sciences and Applied Mathematics Research Institute, since 2005, Keele University; *b* 4 Sept. 1950; *s* of Daniel and Alice Styles; *m* 1975, Roslyn Schmeisser; two *s* two *d*. *Educ:* Dukes Grammar Sch., Alnwick; Wadham Coll., Oxford (BA Hons Physics 1972); Univ. of Newcastle upon Tyne (PhD Geophysics 1977). Lectr, 1977–87, Sen. Lectr, 1987–88, in Geophysics, Univ. of Wales, Swansea; Sen. Lectr, 1988–98, Reader, 1998–99, in Geophysics, Univ. of Liverpool; Hd, Sch. of Earth Sci. and Geog., Univ. of Keele, 2001–03. Chair, Criteria Proposals Gp: Managing Radioactive Waste Safely, DEFRA, 2007–. Mem. Bd, British Geol. Survey, 2001–. Professional Sec., 1996–99, Pres., 2004–06, Geol Soc. of London; Pres., BAAS (Geol. Section), 2007. *Recreations:* guitar, singing British folk music, photography, travelling. *Address:* 6 Swan Lane, Bunbury, Cheshire CW6 9RA.

SUÁREZ, Juan L.; *see* Lechín-Suárez.

SUÁREZ, Michael Angel; Executive Director of Finance and Resources (formerly of Finance), London Borough of Lambeth, since 2005; *b* 1 Nov. 1967; *s* of Antonio Suárez and Mary Theresa Suárez; *m* 1996, Jacqueline Elizabeth Bates; two *s* one *d*. *Educ:* Keele Univ. (BSc Jt Hons Biol. and Mgt Sci.). CPFA 1995. Southwark LBC, 1989–98; Asst Dir Finance for Educn, Soc. Services and Housing, Westminster CC, 1998–2002; Strategic Dir of Finance and Property, Slough BC, 2002–05. Non-exec. Dir, London Authorities' Mutual Ltd; Mem., London Finance Adv. Cttee, 2006–. Member: Soc. of London Treasurers, 2005; Soc. of Municipal Treasurers, 2005. Treas., Squirrels Day Nursery, 2003–05. *Recreations:* squash, swimming and when I can, scuba diving. *Address:* Finance and Resources Department, London Borough of Lambeth, 3rd Floor, Olive Morris House, 18 Brixton Hill, SW2 1RL. *T:* (020) 7926 9337; *e-mail:* msuarez@lambeth.gov.uk.

SUBAK-SHARPE, Prof. John Herbert, CBE 1991; FRSE 1970; Professor Emeritus and Hon. Senior Research Fellow, University of Glasgow, since 1994 (Professor of Virology, 1968–94); Hon. Director, Medical Research Council Virology Unit, 1968–94; *b* 14 Feb. 1924; *s* of late Robert Subak and late Nelly (*née* Bruell), Vienna, Austria; *m* 1953, Barbara Naomi Morris; two *s* one *d*. *Educ:* Humanistic Gymnasium, Vienna; Univ. of Birmingham. BSc (Genetics) (1st Cl. Hons) 1952; PhD 1956. Refugee by Kindertransport from Nazi oppression, 1939; farm pupil, 1939–44; HM Forces (Parachute Regt), 1944–47. Asst Lectr in Genetics, Glasgow Univ., 1954–56; Mem. scientific staff, ARC Animal Virus Research Inst., Pirbright, 1956–60; Nat. Foundn Fellow, California Inst. of Technology, 1961; Mem. Scientific staff of MRC, in Experimental Virus Research Unit, Glasgow, 1961–68. Visiting Professor: US Nat. Insts of Health, Bethesda, Md, 1967; US Univ. of Health Services, Bethesda, Md, 1985; Vis. Fellow, Clare Hall, Cambridge, 1986–87. Sec., Genetical Soc., 1966–72, Vice-Pres. 1972–75, Trustee 1971–99. Member: European Molecular Biology Orgn, 1969– (Chm., Course and Workshops Cttee, 1976–78); Genetic Manipulation Adv. Gp, 1976–80; Biomed. Res. Cttee, SHHD Chief Scientist Orgn, 1979–84; British Nat. Cttee of Biophysics, 1970–76; Governing Body, W of Scotland Oncological Orgn, 1974–; Scientific Adv. Body, W German Cancer Res. Centre, 1977–82; Governing Body, Animal Virus Res. Inst., Pirbright, 1986–87; MRC Training Awards Panel, 1985–89 (Chm., 1986–89); Scientific Adv. Gp of Equine Virology Res. Foundn, 1987–98; MRC Cell and Disorders Bd, 1988–92. CIBA Medal, Biochem. Soc., 1993. *Publications:* articles in scientific jls on genetic studies with viruses and cells. *Recreations:* travel, hill walking, bridge. *Address:* 63 Kelvin Court, Glasgow G12 0AG. *T:* (0141) 334 1863. *Club:* Athenæum.

SUBBA ROW, Raman, CBE 1991; Chairman, Test and County Cricket Board, 1985–90; *b* 29 Jan. 1932; *s* of Panguluri Venkata Subba Row and Doris Mildred Subba Row; *m* 1960, Anne Dorothy (*née* Harrison); two *s* one *d*. *Educ:* Whitgift Sch., Croydon; Trinity Hall, Cambridge (MA Hons). Associate Dir, W. S. Crawford Ltd, 1963–69; Man. Dir, Management Public Relations Ltd, 1969–92; internat. cricket match referee, 1993–2002. *Recreations:* sport, bridge. *Address:* Leeward, Manor Way, South Croydon, Surrey CR2 7BT. *T:* (020) 8688 2991. *Clubs:* Royal Air Force, Institute of Directors, MCC, Surrey County Cricket; Bloemfontein (South Africa); Cricket of India (Bombay); Kingston Cricket (Jamaica).

SUCH, Frederick Rudolph Charles; Immigration Adjudicator, London Region, 2000–06 (part-time, 2006–07); *b* 19 June 1936; *s* of Frederick Sidney Such and Anne Marie Louise (*née* Martin); *m* 1961, Elizabeth, *d* of late Judge Norman and Mrs Harper, Cloughton, Yorkshire; one *s* one *d*. *Educ:* Mbeya Sch., Tanganyika Territory, E Africa (Tanzania); Taunton Sch.; Keble Coll., Oxford (MA). Called to the Bar, Gray's Inn, 1960; practised: London, 1960–69, then North Eastern Circuit, 1969–2000; a Recorder, 1979–2001. FCIArb 1995. *Recreations:* theatre, opera, Real tennis. *Clubs:* Jesters, Queen's; Jesmond Dene Real Tennis.

SUCHET, David, OBE 2002; actor; associate artiste, Royal Shakespeare Co. (Governor, since 2005); *b* 2 May 1946; *s* of late Jack Suchet and Joan (*née* Jarché); *m* 1976, Sheila Ferris, actress; one *s* one *d*. *Educ:* Wellington Sch.; LAMDA (Best Drama Student, 1968). *Stage:* repertory theatres, incl. Chester, Birmingham, Exeter, Worthing, Coventry, 1969–73; for Royal Shakespeare Co.: Romeo and Juliet (Mercutio and Tybalt), As You Like It (Orlando), Once in a Lifetime (Glogauer), Measure for Measure (Angelo), The Tempest (Caliban), King Lear (The Fool), King John (Hubert), Merchant of Venice (Shylock), Troilus and Cressida (Achilles), Richard II (Bolingbroke), Every Good Boy Deserves Favour, 1983, Othello (Iago), 1986, Timon of Athens (title rôle), 1991; Separation, Comedy, 1988; Oleanna, Royal Court, 1993 (Variety Club Award for Best Actor, 1994); Who's Afraid of Virginia Woolf?, Aldwych, 1996 (Best Actor Award, Critics' Circle and South Bank Awards); Saturday, Sunday, Monday, Chichester, 1998; Amadeus, Old Vic, 1998 (Variety Club Award for Best Actor, 1999), Los Angeles and NY, 1999–2000 (Drama League Award); Man and Boy, Duchess, 2005; Once in a Lifetime, NT, 2006; The Last Confession, Chichester, transf. Th. Royal, Haymarket, 2007; *films include:* Tale of Two Cities, 1978; The Missionary, 1982; Red Monarch (Best Actor award, Marseilles Film Fest.), 1983; Falcon and the Snowman, 1985; Thirteen at Dinner, 1985; Song for Europe, 1985; Harry and the Hendersons, 1986; When the Whales came, 1990; Deadly Voyage, 1995; Executive Decision, 1996; Sunday, 1996 (winner, Sundance Film Festival); Wing Commander, 1998; A Perfect Murder, 1998; RKO, 2000; Sabotage, 2000; The In-Laws, 2003; Live from Baghdad, 2003; Fool Proof, 2003; The Bank Job, 2007; serials and series for *television:* Oppenheimer, 1978; Reilly, 1981; Saigon, 1982; Freud, 1983; Blott on the Landscape, 1984; Oxbridge Blues, 1984; Playing Shakespeare, 1985; Great Writers, 1988; Agatha Christie's Hercule Poirot, 1989, 1990, 1991, 1992, 1993, 1994, 2000, 2001, 2002, 2003, 2005, 2007–08; The Secret Agent, 1992; Solomon, 1997; Seesaw, 1998; National Crime Squad, 2001; Murder in Mind, 2001; Victoria and Albert, 2001; The Way We Live Now, 2001; Henry VIII, 2003; Get Carman, 2003; The Flood, 2006; Dracula, 2006; Maxwell, 2007; *radio:* one-man show, Kreutzer Sonata (Best Radio Actor, Pye Radio Awards, 1979); The Gorey Details, 2003; Einstein in Cromer, 2004; Dracula, 2006; numerous other parts. Mem. Council, LAMDA, 1985–. Lectr, US univs; Vis. Prof., Univ. of Nebraska, 1975. FRSA 2005. Numerous awards, incl. Best Actor, RTS, 1986. *Publications:* (contrib.) Players of Shakespeare, 2 vols, 1985 and 1988; essays on interpretation of roles. *Recreations:* clarinet, photography, reading, ornithology, theology, narrow boating. *Address:* c/o Gillie Sanguinetti, Ken McReddie Associates Ltd, 36–40 Glasshouse Street, W1B 5DL. *Clubs:* Garrick, St James's.

See also J. A. Suchet.

SUCHET, John Aleck; television journalist and author; *b* 29 March 1944; *s* of late Jack and Joan Suchet; *m* 1st, 1968, Moya Hankinson (marr. diss. 1985); three *s*; 2nd, 1985, Bonnie Simonson. *Educ:* Uppingham; Univ. of St Andrews (MA Hons). Reuters News Agency, 1967–71; BBC TV News, 1971–72; Independent Television News, 1972–2004: reporter, 1976–86; Washington corresp., 1981–83; newscaster, 1986–2004; newscaster,

Channel Five, 2006–07. Gov., RAM, 2003–07; Pres., Friends of RAM, 1998–2006. Hon. FRAM 2001. Hon. LLD Dundee, 2000. TV Journalist of the Year, RTS, 1986; Newscaster of the Year, TRIC, 1996; Lifetime Achievement Award, RTS, 2008. *Publications:* TV News: the inside story, 1989; The Last Master (fictional biography of Ludwig van Beethoven): vol. 1, Passion and Anger, 1996; vol. 2, Passion and Pain, 1997; vol. 3, Passion and Glory, 1998; Classic FM Friendly Guide to Beethoven, 2006; The Treasures of Beethoven, 2008. *Recreations:* classical music, exploring the life, times and music of Beethoven. *Address:* c/o David Foster Management, PO Box 1805, Andover, Hants SP10 3ZN.

See also D. Suchet.

SUCKLING, Dr Charles Walter, CBE 1989; FRS 1978; FRSC; *b* 24 July 1920; *s* of Edward Ernest and Barbara Suckling (*née* Thomson); *m* 1946, (Eleanor) Margaret Watterson; two *s* one *d*. *Educ:* Oldershaw Grammar Sch., Wallasey; Liverpool Univ. (BSc, PhD). ICI: joined Gen. Chemicals Div., 1942; R&D Director, Mond Div., 1967; Dep. Chairman, Mond Div., 1969; Chairman, Paints Div., 1972; Gen. Man., Res. and Technol., 1977–82; Chm., Bradbury, Suckling and Partners, 1982–93; Dir, Albright and Wilson, 1982–89. Hon. Visiting Professor: Univ. of Stirling, 1968–93; UEA, 1977–83. Member: BBC Science Consultative Gp, 1980–85; Royal Commn on Environmental Pollution, 1982–92; Electricity Supply Res. Council, 1983–90; ABRC/NERC Gp into Geol Surveying, 1985–87; Cttee of Inquiry into Teaching of English Language, 1987–88; Nat. Curriculum English Working Gp, 1988–89; Nat. Curriculum Mod. For. Langs Wkg Gp, 1989–90; Council, RCA, 1981–90 (Treasurer, 1984–90); Chm., Roy. Soc. Study Gp on Pollution Control Priorities, 1988–92; Member: Nat. Adv. Gp on Eco-labelling, 1990–92; Adv. Cttee on Dangerous Pathogens Microbiol Risk Assessment Wkg Gp, 1993–95. Bicentennial Lecture, Washington Coll., Maryland, 1981; Robbins Lecture, Stirling Univ., 1990; Joseph Clover Lecture, Royal Coll. of Anaesthetists, 1994. Senior Fellow, RCA, 1986. Hon. DSc Liverpool, 1980; DUniv Stirling, 1985. Liverpool Univ. Chem. Soc. Medal, 1964; John Scott Medal, City of Philadelphia, 1973; Medal, Royal Coll. of Anaesthetists, 1992. *Publications:* (with A. Baines and F. R. Bradbury) Research in the Chemical Industry, 1969; (with C. J. Suckling and K. E. Suckling) Chemistry through Models, 1978; papers on anaesthetics, industrial research and strategy in journals. *Recreations:* music, gardening, languages, writing. *Address:* 1 Desborough Drive, Tewin, Welwyn, Herts AL6 0HQ. *T:* (01438) 798250.

See also Prof. C. J. Suckling.

SUCKLING, Prof. Colin James, OBE 2006; PhD, DSc; FRSC, FRSE; Freeland Professor of Chemistry, University of Strathclyde, since 1989; *b* 24 March 1947; *s* of Dr Charles Walter Suckling, *qv*; *m* 1972, Catherine Mary Faulkner; two *s* one *d*. *Educ:* Univ. of Liverpool (BSc 1967; PhD 1970; DSc 1989). CChem 1977; FRSC 1980. University of Strathclyde: Lectr, 1972–84; Prof. of Organic Chemistry, 1984–89; Dean, Faculty of Sci., 1992–94; Dep. Principal, 1995–98; Vice Principal, 1998–2002. Chairman: West of Scotland Schs Orch. Trust, 1995–; Scottish Adv. Cttee for Distinction Awards, NHS Scotland, 2002–; Mem., Jt Cttee on Higher Surgical Trng and Senate of Surgery, 2002–05. Member: Bd of Govs, Bell Coll. of Technol., 1999–2007; Court, Univ. of Paisley, 2007–. FRSE 1987; FRSA 1991; FRCSGlas 2004. Hon. FRCSEd 2005. Gold Medal, Lord Provost of Glasgow, 2000. *Publications:* (with C. W. Suckling and K. E. Suckling) Chemistry through Models, 1978; Biological Chemistry, 1980; Enzyme Chemistry Impact and Applications, 1984, 3rd edn 1998; approx. 190 papers and patents on biol chemistry. *Recreations:* horn playing, composing and conducting. *Address:* Department of Pure and Applied Chemistry, University of Strathclyde, 295 Cathedral Street, Glasgow G1 1XL. *T:* (0141) 548 2271, *Fax:* (0141) 548 5473; *e-mail:* c.j.suckling@strath.ac.uk.

SUDBOROUGH, Air Vice-Marshal Nigel John, CB 2002; OBE 1989; FCIPD; JP; Director-General, Winston Churchill Memorial Trust, 2002–07; Director, Sudborough Investments Ltd, since 2003; *b* 23 March 1948; *s* of Alexander and Beryl Sudborough; *m* 1971, Anne Brown; one *s* one *d*. *Educ:* Oundle Sch. Commnd as navigator, Royal Air Force, 1967; various flying tours, incl. Vulcan, Phantom and Tornado; PSO to Vice-Chief of Air Staff, MoD, 1983–85; i/c 29 (F) sqdn, 1985–87; RAF Mt Pleasant, Falkland Is, 1987–88; DS, RAF Staff Coll., 1988–90; HQ RAF Germany, 1990–93; i/c RAF Leuchars, 1993–95; rcds 1996; AO Plans, HQ Strike Comd, 1997–2000; DCS Ops, Strike Comd, 2000–02. Non-exec. Dir, Leicester Partnership NHS Trust, 2007–. FCIPD 2000; FRAeS 2001. Freeman, City of London, 1985; Liveryman, Co. of Pattenmakers, 1985. JP Leicester, 2004. *Recreations:* fly-fishing, philately. *Address:* Knoll House, 5 London Road, Uppingham, Rutland LE15 9TJ. *Club:* Royal Air Force.

SUDBURY, Archdeacon of; *see* Brierley, Ven. D. J.

SUDBURY, Dr Wendy Elizabeth, (Mrs A. J. Bates); Director, Cambridge Management Group, since 1994; *b* 14 June 1946; *d* of Clifford Frank Edwards and Betty Edwards (*née* Foster); one *d*; *m* 1st, 1973, R. M. Sudbury (marr. diss. 1980); 2nd, 1993, Alexander John Bates; one step *s* two step *d*. *Educ:* Finchley Co. Grammar Sch.; Lucy Cavendish Coll., Cambridge (MA); Christ Church, Oxford; Cranfield Sch. of Mgt (PhD 1992). Chief Exec., Mus. Documentation Assoc., 1989–97; Dir, Records Centre, C of E, 2001–03. Expert Advr, EC, 1996–. Mem., RCHM, 1997–99. Mem. Adv. Bd, Judge Inst. of Mgt Studies, Cambridge Univ., 1992–94. FRSA 2002. *Publications:* (with A. Fahy) Information: the Hidden Resource, Museums & the Internet, 1995; contrib. to learned jls. *Recreations:* humanities, travel, gardening, hiking, family life.

SUDELEY, 7th Baron *cr* 1838; **Merlin Charles Sainthill Hanbury-Tracy,** FSA; *b* 17 June 1939; *o c* of late Captain Michael David Charles Hanbury-Tracy, Scots Guards, and Colline Ammabel (*d* 1985), *d* of late Lt-Col C. G. H. St Hill and *widow* of Lt-Col Frank King, DSO, OBE; *S* cousin, 1941; *m* 1980, Hon. Mrs Elizabeth Villiers (marr. diss. 1988), *d* of late Viscount Bury (*s* of 9th Earl of Albemarle); *m* 1999, Mrs Margarita Kellett (marr. diss. 2006). *Educ:* at Eton and in the ranks of the Scots Guards. Former Chairman: Monday Club; Constitutional Monarchy Assoc.; Vice-Chancellor, Monarchist League. Patron, Assoc. of Bankrupts; Lay Patron, Prayer Book Soc. *Publications:* (jtly) The Sudeleys—Lords of Toddington, 1987; (contrib.) The House of Lords: a thousand years of British tradition, 1994; contribs to Quarterly Review, Contemporary Review, Family History, Trans of Bristol and Gloucestershire Archaeol. Soc., Montgomeryshire Collections, Bull. of Manorial Soc., Die Waage (Zeitschrift der Chemie Grünenthal), Monday Club Jl, London Miscellany. *Recreations:* ancestor worship; cultivating his sensibility. *Heir: kinsman* Desmond Andrew John Hanbury-Tracy [*b* 30 Nov. 1928; *m* 1st, 1957, Jennifer Lynn (marr. diss. 1966), *d* of Dr R. C. Hodges; one *s*; 2nd, 1967, Lillian, *d* of Nathaniel Laurie; one *s*; 3rd, 1988, Mrs Margaret Cecilia White, *d* of late Alfred Henry Marmaduke Purse]. *Address:* 25 Melcombe Court, Dorset Square, NW1 6EP. *Club:* Brooks's.

SUDJIC, Deyan, OBE 2000; Director, Design Museum, since 2006; *b* 6 Sept. 1952; *s* of Milivoj Jovo Sudjic and Miroslava Pavlovic; *m* 2002, Sarah Isabel Miller; one *d*. *Educ:* Latymer Upper Sch.; Edinburgh Univ. (BSc Soc. Sci.; DipArch). Founding Ed., Blueprint mag., 1983–94; Architecture Critic: Guardian, 1991–97; Observer, 2000–06; Ed., Domus mag., 2000–04; Dean, Faculty of Art and Design, Kingston Univ., 2005–06; Director: Glasgow 1999 UK City of Architecture and Design, 1996–2000; Venice Architecture Biennale, 2002. Visiting Professor: Acad. for Applied Arts, Vienna, 1993–98; RCA, 2002–. Exhibition Curator: *exhibitions:* Royal Acad., 1986; ICA, 1988; Louisiana Mus., Copenhagen, 1996; McLennan Galls, Glasgow, 1999; BM, 2001. Fellow, Glasgow Sch. of Art, 1999. Hon. FRIAS 2000; Hon. FRIBA 2003. Bicentennial Medal, RSA, 2005. *Publications:* Cult Objects, 1983; Foster, Rogers, Stirling: new British architecture, 1986; Rei Kawskubo and Comme des Garçons, 1991; The Hundred Mile City, 1992; The Architecture Pack, 1996; Ron Arad, 1999; John Pawson: Works, 2000; The Edifice Complex, 2005. *Recreation:* looking at buildings. *Address:* Design Museum, Shad Thames, SE1 2YD.

SUE-LING, Henry Michael, MD; FRCS, FRCSGlas; Consultant Gastrointestinal Surgeon and Senior Clinical Lecturer, Leeds General Infirmary, since 1995; *b* 3 Feb. 1956; *s* of James and Sheila Sue-Ling; *m* 1979, Susan Marie Lewis; two *s* one *d*. *Educ:* Univ. of Leeds (MB ChB 1980; MD 1986). FRCSGlas 1986; FRCS 1988. Registrar, University Hosp. Wales, Cardiff, 1985–88; Leeds General Infirmary: Lectr in Surgery and Hon. Sen. Registrar, 1988–92; Sen. Lectr in Surgery and Hon. Consultant Surgeon, 1992–95; Lead Clinician in upper gastrointestinal cancer services. Chm., Yorks Cancer Network, 2000–. Silver Scalpel Award for UK Surgical Trainer of the Year, Smith & Nephew Foundn, 2001. *Publications:* contribs to learned jls incl. Lancet, BMJ, Gut and Jl Nat. Cancer Inst. *Recreations:* walking, swimming, tennis, travel. *Address:* St James' University Hospital, Beckett Street, Leeds LS9 7TF. *T:* (0113) 206 8505; *e-mail:* henry.sueling@btinternet.com.

SUENSON-TAYLOR, family name of **Baron Grantchester**.

SUFFIELD, 11th Baron *cr* 1786; **Anthony Philip Harbord-Hamond,** Bt 1745; MC 1950; Major, retired, 1961; *b* 19 June 1922; *o s* of 10th Baron and Nina Annette Mary Crawfuird (*d* 1955), *e d* of John Hutchison of Laurieston and Edingham, Stewartry of Kirkcudbright; *S* father, 1951; *m* 1952, Elizabeth Eve (*d* 1995), *er d* of late Judge Edgedale; three *s* one *d*. *Educ:* Eton. Commission, Coldstream Guards, 1942; served War of 1939–45, in North African and Italian campaigns, 1942–45; Malaya, 1948–50. One of HM Hon. Corps of Gentlemen-at-Arms, 1973–92 (Harbinger, 1990–92). *Recreation:* artist. *Heir: s* Hon. Charles Anthony Assheton Harbord-Hamond [*b* 3 Dec. 1953; *m* 1st, 1983, Lucy (marr. diss. 1990), *yr d* of Comdr A. S. Hutchinson; 2nd, 1999, Mrs Emma Louise Royds, *er d* of Sir Lawrence Williams, Bt, *qv*; two *d*. Commissioned Coldstream Guards, 1972, RARO 1979]. *Address:* Gardeners Cottage, Gunton Park, Hanworth, Norfolk NR11 7HL. *T:* (01263) 768423. *Club:* Pratt's.

SUFFOLK AND BERKSHIRE, 21st Earl of, *cr* 1603; **Michael John James George Robert Howard;** Viscount Andover and Baron Howard, 1622; Earl of Berkshire, 1626; *b* 27 March 1935; *s* of 20th Earl of Suffolk and Berkshire, GC (killed by enemy action, 1941) and Mimi (*d* 1966), *yr d* of late A. G. Forde Pigott; *S* father, 1941; *m* 1st, 1960, Mme Simone Paulmier (marr. diss. 1967), *d* of late Georges Litman, Paris; (one *d* decd); 2nd, 1973, Anita (marr. diss. 1980), *d* of R. R. Fuglesang, Haywards Heath, Sussex; one *s* one *d*; 3rd, 1983, Linda Viscountess Bridport; two *d*. Owns 5,000 acres. *Heir: s* Viscount Andover, *qv*. *Address:* Charlton Park, Malmesbury, Wilts SN16 9DG.

SUFFOLK, Archdeacon of; *see* Arrand, Ven. G. W.

SUFFOLK, John; Government Chief Information Officer and Head of e-Government Unit, Cabinet Office, since 2006; *b* 25 Feb. 1958; *s* of Thomas and Elspeth Suffolk; *m* 1989, Julie Davies. *Educ:* Wolverhampton Business Sch. (MBA; DMS). Various tech. roles, Freight Computer Services, 1975–79; Sen. Programmer, TRW Valves, 1979–80; Midshires Building Society: Sen. Designer, 1980–81; Chief Programmer/Programming Manager, 1981–85; Systems Develt Manager, 1985–86; Technical Services Manager, 1986–87; Birmingham Midshires: Planning and Develt Manager, 1987–89; Asst Gen. Manager, Business Systems, 1989–91; Inf. Services Dir, 1991–95; Hd, Customer Services, 1995–98; Britannia Building Society: Dir of Ops, 1998–2001; Ops Dir, 2001–02; Man. Dir, 2002–03; Dir Gen., Criminal Justice IT, Home Office, 2004–06. Chm., MutualPlus, 2001. Non-exec. Dir, PITO, 2004–. *Recreations:* farming, raising money for charity through challenges. *Address:* Back Forest Farm, Swythamley, Rushton Spencer, Macclesfield, Cheshire SK11 0RF. *T:* (01260) 227643; *e-mail:* john@johnsuffolk.co.uk.

SUGAR, Sir Alan (Michael), Kt 2000; Executive Chairman: Amstrad (formerly Betacom) Plc, 1997–2008; Viglen, since 1997; Amshold Group; *b* 24 March 1947; *s* of Nathan and Fay Sugar; *m* 1968, Ann Simons; two *s* one *d*. *Educ:* Brooke House School, London. Founder Chm., Amstrad, 1968–97; co. divided into Betacom and Viglen, 1997. Chm., 1991–2001, Chief Exec., 1998–2000, Tottenham Hotspur plc. Presenter, The Apprentice (4 series), BBC TV, 2005–. Hon. DSc City, 1988. *Publication:* The Apprentice: how to get hired not fired, 2005. *Recreation:* tennis. *Address:* Brentwood House, 169 King's Road, Brentwood, Essex CM14 4EF. *T:* (01277) 228888.

SUGAR, Vivienne, FCIH; local government consultant; Chair, Welsh Consumer Council, since 2003; *b* Gorseinon, 23 Feb. 1947; *d* of Jack Hopkins and Phyllis Hopkins (*née* Suter); *m* 1972, Adrian Sugar. *Educ:* Mynydd Cynnfig Comprehensive Sch.; Leeds Univ. (BA). Area Improvement Officer, 1979–88, Dir of Housing, 1988–90, Newport BC; Dir of Housing, Cardiff CC, 1990–95; Chief Exec., City and County of Swansea, 1995–2002. Wales Advr to Joseph Rowntree Foundn, 2005–. Pro Chancellor, Swansea Univ. (formerly Vice Pres., Univ. of Wales, Swansea), 2005–. *Publications:* various articles in Municipal Jl, Local Govt Chronicle and Inside Housing. *Recreations:* politics and current affairs, walking, birdwatching, cooking. *Address:* Welsh Consumer Council, 3rd Floor, Capital Tower, Greyfriars Road, Cardiff CF10 3AG.

SUGDEN, Prof. David Edward, DPhil; FRSE; Professor of Geography, since 1987, and Head, School of Geosciences, 2003–06, University of Edinburgh; *b* 5 March 1941; *s* of late John Cyril Gouldie Sugden and of Patricia Sugden (*née* Backhouse); *m* 1966, Britta Valborg, *d* of Harald Stridsberg, Sweden; two *s* one *d*. *Educ:* Warwick Sch.; Jesus Coll., Oxford (BA; DPhil 1965). Scientific officer, British Antarctic Survey, 1965–66; Lectr, then Reader, Univ. of Aberdeen, 1966–87. Vis. Prof., Arctic and Alpine Inst., Boulder, Colo, 1975–76. Pres., IBG, 1995. Member: RSGS; RGS; FRSE 1990. Hon. Dr Stockholm, 1998; Hon. LLB Dundee, 1999. Polar Medal, RGS, 2003. *Publications:* Glaciers and Landscape, 1976 (with B. S. John); Arctic and Antarctic, 1982; (jtly) Geomorphology, 1986. *Recreations:* hill-walking, gardening, ski-ing. *Address:* Institute of Geography, University of Edinburgh, Drummond Street, Edinburgh EH8 9XP. *T:* (0131) 650 7543; *e-mail:* david.sugden@ed.ac.uk.

SUGDEN, John Goldthorp, MA; ARCM; Headmaster, Wellingborough School, 1965–73; *b* 22 July 1921; *s* of A. G. Sugden, Brighouse, Yorkshire; *m* 1954, Jane Machin; two *s*. *Educ:* Radley; Magdalene College, Cambridge. War Service, Royal Signals, 1941–46. Asst Master, Bilton Grange Prep. School, 1948–52; Asst Master, The King's School, Canterbury, 1952–59; Headmaster, Foster's School, Sherborne, 1959–64. *Publications:* Niccolo Paganini, 1980; Sir Arthur Bliss, 1997. *Recreations:* music, golf.

Address: Woodlands, 2 Linksview Avenue, Parkstone, Poole, Dorset BH14 9QT. *T:* (01202) 707497.

SUGDEN, Prof. Robert, DLitt; FBA 1996; Professor of Economics, University of East Anglia, since 1985; *b* 26 Aug. 1949; *s* of late Frank Gerald Sugden and Kathleen Sugden (*née* Buckley); *m* 1982, Christine Margaret Upton; one *s* one *d*. *Educ:* Eston GS, Cleveland; Univ. of York (BA; DLitt 1988); UC, Cardiff (MSc). Lectr in Econs, Univ. of York, 1971–78; Reader in Econs, Univ. of Newcastle upon Tyne, 1978–85. *Publications:* (with A. Williams) The Principles of Practical Cost-Benefit Analysis, 1978; The Political Economy of Public Choice, 1981; The Economics of Rights, Co-operation and Welfare, 1986; (jtly) The Theory of Choice: a critical guide, 1992; (with D. Gauthier) Rationality, Justice and the Social Contract, 1993. *Recreations:* family, walking, gardening. *Address:* School of Economics, University of East Anglia, Norwich NR4 7TJ. *T:* (01603) 593423.

SUIRDALE, Viscount; John Michael James Hely Hutchinson; company director since 1981; *b* 7 Aug. 1952; *s* and *heir* of 8th Earl of Donoughmore, *qv*; *m* 1976, Marie-Claire Carola Etienne van den Driessche (marr. diss. 2006); one *s* two *d*. *Educ:* Harrow. *Recreations:* golf, fishing, etc. *Heir:* *s* Hon. Richard Gregory Hely Hutchinson, *b* 3 July 1980. *Address:* A504 Gilbert Scott Building, Putney, SW15 3SG.

See also Hon. T. M. Hely Hutchinson.

SULIVAN, Maj.-Gen. Timothy John, CB 2001; CBE 1991; Vice-President, Customer Relations, General Dynamics (formerly CDC Systems) UK Ltd, since 2001; *b* 19 Feb. 1946; *s* of late Col John Anthony Sulivan, OBE and Elizabeth Joyce Sulivan (*née* Stevens); *m* 1977, Jane Annette Ellwood; one *s* one *d*. *Educ:* Wellington Coll.; RMCS (BSc); Higher Command and Staff course. Commnd RA, 1966; transf. Blues and Royals, 1980; CO, Blues and Royals, 1987–89; attached US Special Plans Team, C-in-C US CENTCOM, 1990–91; Comd 7 Armd Bde, 1991–93; PSO to CDS, 1993–94; Dir-Gen., Develt and Doctrine, MoD, 1994–96 (deployed as Jt Force Comd Op. Driver, Kuwait/Saudi Arabia, 1994); COS, HQ ARRC, 1996–98; GOC Fourth Div., 1998–2001; Chief Operating Officer, RICS, 2002–05. Director: Screen plc, 2002–06; Customer Relations, Land Securities Trillium, 2006–07. Bronze Star, USA, 1991. *Recreations:* shooting, ski-ing, squash, cabinet making. *Club:* Army and Navy.

SULLIVAN, David Douglas Hooper; QC 1975; author and historian; *b* 10 April 1926; *s* of Michael and Maude Sullivan; *m* 1st, 1951, Sheila, *d* of Henry and Georgina Bathurst; three *d*; 2nd, 1981, Ann Munro, *d* of Malcolm and Eva Betten. *Educ:* Haileybury (schol.); Christ Church, Oxford (schol.). MA 1949, BCL 1951. Served War, with RNVR (Sub-Lieut), 1944–46. Called to Bar, Inner Temple, 1951, Bencher, 1984, retired 1988. Mem., Central Policy Cttee, Mental Health Act Commn, 1983–86. Chm., Burgh House Trust, 1978–95. Author of various plays and media programmes, including: radio: Shadows are Realities to me; A right-royal Burglary; Straw and Steel; stage: John Constable and Maria. *Publications:* The Westminster Corridor, 1994; The Westminster Circle 1086–1307, 2006. *Recreations:* painting, medieval history. *Address:* 18 Greenhill, Prince Arthur Road, NW3 5UB. *T:* (020) 7431 3433.

SULLIVAN, Prof. (Donovan) Michael; Professor of Oriental Art, 1966–85, Christensen Professor, 1975–85, Stanford University, California; Fellow, St Catherine's College, Oxford, 1979–90, now Emeritus Fellow; *b* 29 Oct. 1916; *s* of Alan Sullivan and Elisabeth Hees; *m* 1943, Khoan, *d* of Ngo Eng-lim, Kulangsu, Amoy, China; no *c*. *Educ:* Rugby School; Corpus Christi College, Cambridge (MA); Univ. of London (BA Hons); Harvard Univ. (PhD); LittD Cambridge, 1966; MA, DLitt Oxon, 1973. Chinese Govt Scholarship, Univ. of London, 1947–50; Rockefeller Foundn Travelling Fellowship in USA, 1950–51; Bollingen Foundn Research Fellowship, 1952–54; Curator of Art Museum and Lectr in the History of Art, Univ. of Malaya (now Univ. of Singapore), Singapore, 1954–60; Lectr in Asian Art, Sch. of Oriental and African Studies, Univ. of London, 1960–66. Vis. Prof. of Far Eastern Art, Univ. of Michigan (Spring Semester), 1964; Slade Prof. of Fine Art, Oxford Univ., 1973–74, Cambridge Univ., 1983–84; Guggenheim Foundn Fellowship, 1974; Vis. Fellow, St Antony's Coll., Oxford, 1976–77; Nat. Endowment for the Humanities Fellowship, 1976–77; Professorial Fellow, Corpus Christi Coll., Cambridge, 1983–84; Vis. Fellow, Humanities Centre, ANU, 1987; Fellow, Ashmolean Museum, 2006–. Mem., Amer. Acad. of Arts and Sciences, 1977. Hon. Fellow, Chinese Australian Arts and Culture Res. Centre, Sun Yat-sen (Zhongshan) Univ., 2007. Hon. DLitt Nottingham, 2005. *Publications:* Chinese Art in the Twentieth Century, 1959; An Introduction to Chinese Art, 1961; The Birth of Landscape Painting in China, 1962; Chinese Ceramics, Bronzes and Jades in the Collection of Sir Alan and Lady Barlow, 1963; Chinese and Japanese Art, 1965; A Short History of Chinese Art, 1967, 3rd edn as The Arts of China, 1973, 5th edn 2008; The Cave Temples of Maichishan, 1969; The Meeting of Eastern and Western Art, 1973, rev. and expanded edn 1989; Chinese Art: recent discoveries, 1973; The Three Perfections, 1975, 2nd edn 1999; Chinese Landscape Painting, vol. II, The Sui and T'ang Dynasties, 1979; Symbols of Eternity: the art of landscape painting in China, 1979; Studies in the Art of China and South-East Asia, vol. 1, 1991, vol. 2, 1992; Art and Artists of Twentieth Century China, 1996; A Biographical Dictionary of Modern Chinese Artists, 2006; The Night Entertainments of Han Xizai, 2008; contrib. to learned journals, Encyclopedia Britannica, Chambers's Encyclopædia, etc. *Address:* St Catherine's College, Oxford OX1 3UJ. *Club:* Athenæum.

SULLIVAN, Edmund Wendell, FRCVS; Chief Veterinary Officer, Department of Agriculture for Northern Ireland, 1983–90; *b* 21 March 1925; *s* of Thomas Llewellyn Sullivan and Letitia Sullivan; *m* 1957, Elinor Wilson Melville; two *s* one *d*. *Educ:* Portadown College; Queen's University, Belfast; Royal (Dick) Veterinary College. MRCVS 1947, FRCVS 1991. General Veterinary Practice, Appleby, Westmoreland, 1947; joined staff of State Veterinary Service, Dept. of Agriculture for N Ireland, 1948; Headquarters staff, 1966–90. *Recreations:* hill walking, wood craft, following rugby and cricket. *Address:* Kinfauns, 26 Dillon's Avenue, Newtownabbey, Co. Antrim BT37 0SX. *T:* (028) 9086 2323.

SULLIVAN, Hon. Sir Jeremy (Mirth), Kt 1997; **Hon. Mr Justice Sullivan;** a Judge of the High Court of Justice, Queen's Bench Division, since 1997; *b* 17 Sept. 1945; *s* of late Arthur Brian and of Pamela Jean Sullivan; *m* 1st, 1970, Ursula Klara Marie Hildenbrock (marr. diss. 1993); two *s*; 2nd, 1993, Dr Sandra Jean Farmer; two step *s*. *Educ:* Framlingham Coll.; King's Coll., London. LLB 1967, LLM 1968; LAMTPI 1970, LMRTPI 1976. 2nd Lieut, Suffolk & Cambs Regt (TA), 1963–65. Called to the Bar, Inner Temple, 1968, Bencher, 1993; Lectr in Law, City of London Polytechnic, 1968–71; in practice, Planning and Local Govt Bar, Parly Bar, 1971–97; QC 1982; a Recorder, 1989–97; a Dep. High Court Judge, 1993–97; Attorney Gen. to the Prince of Wales, 1994–97. Hon. Standing Counsel to CPRE, 1994–97. Chm., Tribunals Cttee, Judicial Studies Bd, 1999–2007; Dep. Chm., Parly Boundary Commn for England, 2004–. Mem. Council, RTPI, 1984–87. Gov., Highgate Sch., 1991–2003. *Recreation:* the Wotton Light Railway. *Address:* Royal Courts of Justice, Strand, WC2A 2LL.

SULLIVAN, Linda Elizabeth, (Mrs J. W. Blake-James); QC 1994; a Recorder, since 1990; *b* 1 Jan. 1948; *d* of Donal Sullivan and Esmé Beryl Sullivan (*née* McKenzie); *m* 1972, Dr Justin Wynne Blake-James (marr. diss. 1994); one *s* twin *d*. *Educ:* St Leonard's-Mayfield Sch.; Univ. of Kent (BA Hons Phil. and English 1969); St Hilda's Coll., Oxford (Cert Ed 1970). Called to the Bar, Middle Temple, 1973, Bencher, 1993; Mem., Western Circuit. *Address:* Goldsmith Chambers, Goldsmith Building, Temple, EC4Y 7BL. *T:* (020) 7353 6802.

SULLIVAN, Prof. Michael; *see* Sullivan, D. M.

SULLIVAN, Michael Frederick, MBE 1981; HM Diplomatic Service, retired; Consul-General, Hamburg, 1994–99; *b* 22 June 1940; *s* of late Frederick Franklin Sullivan and Leonora Mary Sullivan; *m* 1967, Jennifer Enid Saunders. *Educ:* King's Sch., Canterbury; Jesus Coll., Oxford (BA). CRO 1962–66; Moscow, 1967; Ulan Bator, Mongolia, 1967–69; Sydney, 1970–74; FCO, 1975–77; First Sec., W Indian and Atlantic Dept, FCO, 1977–79; Consul (Industrial Develt), British Trade Develt Office, NY, 1979–81; Cultural Attaché, Moscow, 1981–85; Assistant Head: Personnel Services Dept, FCO, 1985–86; Energy, Sci. and Space Dept, FCO, 1986–88; Counsellor (Cultural Affairs), Moscow, 1988–89; Counsellor, Export Promotion Policy Unit, DTI, 1989–90; Hd of Nationality, Treaty and Claims Dept, FCO, 1990–93. Res. analyst, FCO, 2000 and 2003. Mem., Panel of Inquiry Secs, Competition Commn, 2004–. Mem., FCO Assoc., 2007–. *Recreations:* piano playing, music and the arts, tennis, jogging, swimming. *Club:* Übersee.

SULLIVAN, Ven. Nicola Ann; Archdeacon of Wells and Canon Residentiary, Wells Cathedral, since 2007; *b* 15 Aug. 1958; *d* of late Peter John Sullivan and Margaret Irene Sullivan (*née* Hancock). *Educ:* St Bartholomew's Hosp. (SRN 1981); Bristol Maternity Hosp. (RM 1984); Wycliffe Hall, Oxford (BTh 1995). Various NHS nursing and midwifery posts, 1981–92; Tear Fund UK, in Ethiopia and Swaziland, 1984, 1988. Ordained deacon, 1995, priest, 1996; Asst Curate, St Anne's, Earlham, Norwich, 1995–99; Associate Vicar, Bath Abbey with St James, 1999–2002; Chaplain, Royal Nat. Hosp. for Rheumatic Diseases NHS Trust, 1999–2002; Bishop's Chaplain and Pastoral Asst to Bishop of Bath and Wells, 2002–07; Sub-Dean and Preb., Wells Cathedral, 2003–07. *Recreations:* reading, theatre (professional and amateur), current affairs. *Address:* 6 The Liberty, Wells, Som BA5 2SU. *T:* (01749) 685147; *e-mail:* adwells@bathwells.anglican.org.

SULLIVAN, Richard Arthur, (9th Bt *cr* 1804, but does not use the title); retired geotechnical engineer; *b* 9 Aug. 1931; *s* of Sir Richard Benjamin Magniac Sullivan, 8th Bt, and Muriel Mary Paget (*d* 1988), *d* of late Francis Charles Trayler Pineo; *S* father, 1977; *m* 1962, Elenor Mary, *e d* of late K. M. Thorpe; one *s* three *d*. *Educ:* Univ. of Cape Town (BSc); Massachusetts Inst. of Technology (SM). Chartered Engineer, UK; Professional Engineer, Ontario, Texas and Louisiana. *Publications:* papers and articles to international conferences and technical journals. *Recreation:* tennis. *Heir:* *s* Charles Merson Sullivan, MA, VetMB Cantab, MRCVS, *b* 15 Dec. 1962. *Address:* 1 Sea Watch Place, Florence, OR 97439, USA.

SULSTON, Sir John (Edward), Kt 2001; PhD; FRS 1986; Staff Scientist, MRC Laboratory of Molecular Biology, Cambridge, 1969–2003; Director, The Sanger Centre (for genome research), Hinxton, Cambridge, 1992–2000; Chair, Institute for Science, Ethics and Innovation, University of Manchester, since 2007; *b* 27 March 1942; *s* of late Rev. Canon Arthur Edward Aubrey Sulston and Josephine Muriel Frearson (*née* Blocksidge); *m* 1966, Daphne Edith Bate; one *s* one *d*. *Educ:* Merchant Taylors' School; Pembroke College, Cambridge (BA, PhD; Hon. Fellow, 2000). Postdoctoral Fellow, Salk Inst., San Diego, 1966–69. Mem., Human Genetics Commn, 2001–. Mem., EMBO, 1989; MAE 2001. Hon. Member: Biochemical Soc., 2002; RSC, 2003; Acad. of Med. Scis, 2003; Physiol Soc., 2003. Freeman, Merchant Taylors' Co., 2004. Hon. ScD: TCD, 2000; Essex, 2002; Cambridge, London, Exeter, 2003; Newcastle, 2004; Hon. LLD Dundee, 2005. W. Alden Spencer Award (jtly), Coll. of Physicians and Surgeons, Columbia Univ., 1986; (jtly) Gairdner Foundn Award, 1991, 2002; Darwin Medal, Royal Soc., 1996; (jtly) Rosenstiel Award, Brandeis Univ., 1998; Sir Frederick Gowland Hopkins Medal, Biochemical Soc., 2000; (jtly) George W. Beadle Medal, Genetics Soc. of Amer., 2000; Pfizer Prize for Innovative Sci., 2000; Edinburgh Medal, 2001; Fothergillian Medal, Med. Soc. of London, 2002; (jtly) Nobel Prize for Physiology or Medicine, 2002. Officier de la légion d'honneur (France), 2004. *Publications:* (with Georgina Ferry) The Common Thread: a story of science, politics, ethics and the human genome, 2002; articles on organic chemistry, molecular and developmental biology in sci. jls. *Recreations:* gardening, walking. *Address:* 39 Mingle Lane, Stapleford, Cambridge CB2 5SY. *T:* (01223) 842248; *e-mail:* jes@sanger.ac.uk.

SULZBERGER, Arthur Ochs; Chairman and Chief Executive Officer, New York Times Co., 1992–97, now Chairman Emeritus; Publisher of The New York Times, 1963–92; *b* 5 Feb. 1926; *s* of late Arthur Hays Sulzberger; *m* 1st, 1948, Barbara Grant (marr. diss. 1956); one *s* one *d*; 2nd, 1956, Carol Fox Fuhrman (*d* 1995); one *d*, and one adopted *d*; 3rd, 1996, Allison Stacey Cowles. *Educ:* Browning School, New York City; Loomis School, Windsor, Conn; Columbia University, NYC. Reporter, Milwaukee Journal, 1953–54; Foreign Correspondent, New York Times, 1954–55; Asst to the Publisher, New York Times, 1956–57; Asst Treasurer, New York Times, 1957–63. Chm. Emeritus, Metropolitan Mus. of Art; Trustee Emeritus, Columbia Univ. Hon. LLD: Dartmouth, 1964; Bard, 1967; Hon. LHD: Montclair State Coll.; Tufts Univ., 1984. *Recreation:* fishing. *Address:* 229 West 43rd Street, New York, NY 10036, USA. *T:* (212) 5561771. *Clubs:* Overseas Press, Explorers (New York); Metropolitan, Army and Navy (Washington, DC).

SUMBERG, David Anthony Gerald; Member (C) North West Region, England, European Parliament, since 1999; *b* 2 June 1941; *s* of Joshua and Lorna Sumberg; *m* 1972, Carolyn Ann Rae Franks; one *s* one *d*. *Educ:* Tettenhall Coll., Staffs; Coll. of Law, London. Qualified as a Solicitor, 1964. Mem. (C) Manchester City Council, 1982–84. Contested (C) Manchester, Wythenshawe, 1979. MP (C) Bury South, 1983–97; contested (C) same seat, 1997. PPS to: Solicitor-General, 1986–87; Attorney-General, 1987–90. Member: Home Affairs Select Cttee, 1991–92; Foreign Affairs Select Cttee, 1992–97. European Parliament: Member: Cttee on Internat. Trade; Delegn to USA. Mem., Adv. Council on Public Records, 1993–97. *Recreation:* family. *Address:* c/o European Parliament, Rue Wiertz, 1047 Brussels, Belgium.

SUMMERFIELD, Prof. (Arthur) Quentin, PhD; Anniversary Professor of Psychology, University of York, since 2004; *b* 18 Sept. 1949; *s* of Arthur Summerfield and Aline Summerfield (*née* Whalley); *m* 1989, Diana Lyn Field; two *d*. *Educ:* Tetherdown Primary Sch., Muswell Hill; University Coll. Sch., Hampstead (ILEA Schol.); Corpus Christi Coll., Cambridge (BA 1971, MA Natural Scis); Queen's Univ., Belfast (PhD Psychol. 1975). NATO Postdoctoral Res. Fellow, Haskins Labs, Yale Univ., 1975–77; Speech and Hearing Scientist, 1977–2004, Dep. Dir, 1993–2004, MRC Inst. of Hearing Res.; Special Prof. of Speech and Hearing, Univ. of Nottingham, 1991–2004. Chair: Med. Res. Adv. Panel, RNID, 2003–05; NHS Rev. of cochlear implantation in Scotland, 2005–06. Chief Res. Advr, Deafness Res. UK, 2007–. Fellow, Acoustical Soc. of America, 1988. *Publication:* (with Dr D. H. Marshall) Cochlear Implantation in the UK 1990–1994, 1995.

Recreations: cycling, spending time with my family. *Address:* Department of Psychology, University of York, Heslington, York YO10 5DD. *T:* (01904) 432913, 433190, *Fax:* (01904) 433181; *e-mail:* aqs1@york.ac.uk. *Club:* Cyclists Touring.

SUMMERFIELD, Lesley; *see* Regan, L.

SUMMERFIELD, Quentin; *see* Summerfield, A. Q.

SUMMERFIELD, Prof. Rodney John, DSc; JP; Professor of Crop Production, 1995–2001, now Emeritus, and Dean, Faculty of Agriculture and Food, 1998–2001, University of Reading; *b* 15 Nov. 1946; *s* of Ronald John Summerfield and Doris Emily Summerfield (*née* Ellis); *m* 1969, Kathryn Dorothy Olive; one *s* one *d. Educ:* Hinckley GS; Univ. of Nottingham (BSc 1st cl. Hons Botany 1968; PhD Eco-Physiol. 1971); Univ. of Reading (DSc 1987); FIBiol 1982–2001. Univ. Demonstr., Univ. of Nottingham, 1969–71; (part-time) Lectr, Trent Poly., 1970–71; University of Reading: Res. Fellow, 1971–73, Lectr in Crop and Plant Physiology, 1973–83, Dept of Agriculture and Horticulture; Dep. Dir, 1979–94, Dir, 1994–99, Plant Envmt Lab.; Reader in Crop Physiology, 1983–90, Prof. of Crop Physiology, 1990–95, Dept of Agriculture; Hd, Dept of Agric., 1992–98. Pres., Eur. Assoc. for Res. in Grain Legumes, 1995–99. EurBiol 1995. JP Devon and Cornwall, 2004. Dr *hc* Debrecen Univ., Hungary, 1999. *Publications:* (ed jtly) Advances in Legume Science, 1980; (ed jtly) Grain Legume Crops, 1985; (ed) World Crops: cool season food legumes, 1988; articles in learned jls. *Recreations:* walking, angling.

SUMMERHAYES, Dr Colin Peter; Executive Director, Scientific Committee on Antarctic Research, since 2004; *b* 7 March 1942; *s* of late Leonard Percy Summerhayes and Jessica Adelaide (*née* Crump); *m* 1st, 1966 (marr. diss. 1977); one *s* one *d*; 2nd, 1978 (marr. diss. 1979); 3rd, 1981, Diana Ridley (*née* Perry); one step *s* one step *d. Educ:* Slough Grammar Sch.; UCL (BSc 1963); Keble Coll., Oxford; Victoria Univ., Wellington, NZ (MSc 1967; DSc 1986); Imperial Coll., London (DIC; PhD 1970). CMarSci; CGeol; FIMarEST; FGS; FRGS. Scientific Officer, DSIR, NZ Oceanographic Inst., 1964–67; Res. Asst, Geol. Dept, Imperial Coll., London, 1967–70; Sen. Scientific Officer, CSIR, Marine Geosci. Unit, Univ. of Cape Town, 1970–72; Asst Scientist, Geol. and Geophys Dept, Woods Hole Oceanographic Instn, 1972–76; Research Associate/Project Leader: Geochem. Br., Exxon Prodn Res. Centre, Houston, 1976–82; Global Paleoreconstruction Sect., Stratigraphy Br., BP Res. Centre, 1982–85; Manager and Sen. Res. Associate, Stratigraphy Br., BP Res. Centre, 1985–88; Dir, NERC Inst. of Oceanographic Scis Deacon Lab., 1988–95; Dep. Dir, and Hd of Seafloor Processes Div., Southampton Oceanography Centre, 1995–97; Dir, Global Ocean Observing System Project Office, Intergovernmental Oceanographic Commn, Unesco, 1997–2004. Vis. Prof., UCL, 1987–95. Member: Challenger Soc. for Marine Sci.; RSPB. *Publications:* 200 papers in books and abstracts. *Recreations:* birdwatching, jogging, reading, bowls, films and theatre. *Address:* Scott Polar Research Institute, Lensfield Road, Cambridge CB2 1ER.

SUMMERHAYES, David Michael, CMG 1975; HM Diplomatic Service, retired; Disarmament Adviser, Foreign and Commonwealth Office, 1983–92; *b* 29 Sept. 1922; *s* of Sir Christopher Summerhayes, KBE, CMG and Anna (*née* Johnson); *m* 1959, June van der Hardt Aberson; two *s* one *d. Educ:* Marlborough; Emmanuel Coll., Cambridge. Served War of 1939–45 in Royal Artillery (Capt.) N Africa and Italy. 3rd Sec., FO, 1948; Baghdad, 1949; Brussels, 1950–53; 2nd Sec., FO, 1953–56; 1st Sec. (Commercial), The Hague, 1956–59; 1st Sec. and Consul, Reykjavik, 1959–61; FO, 1961–65; Consul-General and Counsellor, Buenos Aires, 1965–70; Head of Arms Control and Disarmament Dept, FCO, 1970–74; Minister, Pretoria/Cape Town, 1974–78; Ambassador and Leader, UK Delegn to Cttee on Disarmament, Geneva, 1979–82. Hon. Officer, Order of Orange Nassau. *Recreations:* golf, walking. *Address:* Ivy House, South Harting, Petersfield, Hants GU31 5QQ. *Clubs:* Oxford and Cambridge; Liphook Golf.

SUMMERHAYES, Gerald Victor, CMG 1979; OBE 1969; *b* 28 Jan. 1928; *s* of Victor Samuel and Florence A. V. Summerhayes. Administrative Service, Nigeria, 1952–81; Permanent Secretary: Local Govt, North Western State, 1975–76, Sokoto State, 1976–77; Cabinet Office (Political and Trng), 1977–79; Dir of Trng, Cabinet Office, Sokoto, 1979–81. *Address:* Bridge Cottage, Bridge Street, Sidbury, Devon EX10 0RU. *T:* (01395) 597311.

SUMMERS, Andrew William Graham, CMG 2001; Chief Executive, Design Council, 1995–2003; Chairman: Design Partners, since 2004; Companies House, since 2007; Creative Connexions, since 2007; *b* 19 June 1946; *s* of Basil Summers and Margaret (*née* Hunt); *m* 1971, Frances Halestrap; one *s* two *d. Educ:* Mill Hill Sch. (Exhibnr); Fitzwilliam Coll., Cambridge (MA Natural Scis and Econs); Harvard Business Sch. (Internat. SMP). Various mgt rôles, Ranks Hovis McDougall plc, 1968–75; J. A. Sharwood & Co.: Mkting Manager, 1975–78; Mkting Dir, 1978–80; Man. Dir, 1980–85; RHM Foods Ltd: Commercial Dir, 1986; Man. Dir, 1987–90; Chief Exec., Management Charter Initiative, 1991–94; non-executive Director: S. Daniels plc, 1991–2002; Whitbybird Ltd, 2005–. Chm., Brandsmiths, 2003–06. Adjunct Prof., Hong Kong Polytechnic Univ., 2004–. Policy Advr, DTI, 2003–. Member: Food from Britain Export Council, 1982–86; DTI European Trade Cttee, 1986–2000 (Chm., 1998–2000); BOTB, 1998–99; British Trade Internat., 1999–2003; Creative Industries Export Promotion Adv. Gp, 1998–2002; Adv. Council, Design Mgt Inst. USA, 1998–2006; Small Business Service Strategy Bd, 2000–07; Bd, QAA, 2005–; Bd, CRAC, 2008–; Chairman: Internat. Adv. Bd, Hong Kong Design Centre, 2004–07; RSA Migration Commn, 2004–06. Mem., VSO Adv. Bd, 2004–06. Gov., Conservatoire for Dance and Drama, 2005–. Chm., Friends of St Mary's, Barnes, 2000–. Stockton Lectr, London Bus. Sch., 2000. Mem., Bd of Companions, Chartered Mgt Inst., 2007–. CCMI (CIMgt 1997). FRSA 1991 (Dep. Pres., 2003–); Sen. Fellow, Design Mgt Inst., 2003. Hon. DLitt Westminster, 2003. *Publications:* (contrib.) Future Present, 2000; contribs on design to Design Mgt Jl and Sunday Times. *Recreations:* tennis, fives (Pres., OM Eton Fives Club, 2004–), theatre, cooking. *Address:* 114 Station Road, SW13 0NB. *T:* (020) 8876 6719.

SUMMERS, Janet Margaret, (Mrs L. J. Summers); *see* Bately, J. M.

SUMMERS, Jonathan; baritone; *b* 2 Oct. 1946; *s* of Andrew James Summers and Joyce Isabel Smith; *m* 1969, Lesley Murphy; three *c. Educ:* Macleod High Sch., Melbourne; Prahran Tech. Coll., Melbourne. Professional début, Rigoletto (title rôle), Kent Opera, 1975; performances include: Royal Opera, Covent Garden: début, Der Freischütz, 1977; Samson et Dalila, Don Pasquale, Werther, 1983; Andrea Chénier, A Midsummer Night's Dream, Der Rosenkavalier, 1984; Die Zauberflöte, Le Nozze di Figaro, 1985; Simon Boccanegra, 1986; Falstaff, 1987; Madama Butterfly, 1988; La Bohème, 1990; Fedora, 1994; Nabucco, 1996; The Tempest, 2007; English National Opera: début, I Pagliacci, 1976; Rigoletto, 1982; Don Carlos, 1985; La Bohème, 1986; Simon Boccanegra, 1987; Eugene Onegin, 1989; Macbeth, 1990; Peter Grimes, 1991; The Force of Destiny, 1992; The Pearl Fishers, 1994; Tristan and Isolde, 1996; Figaro's Wedding, 1997; Parsifal, 1999; Opera Australia, Sydney: début, La Traviata, 1981; Il Trovatore, 1983; Otello, 1991; Un Ballo in Maschera, 1993; Il Tabarro, 1995; Nabucco, Falstaff, 1996; Wozzeck, 1999; Simon Boccanegra, 2000; Peter Grimes, 2001; Tosca, 2002; Otello, 2003; Der Fliegender Holländer, 2004; Rigoletto, 2006; Metropolitan Opera, NY: début, La Bohème, 1988; has also appeared at Glyndebourne, with Opera North, Welsh National Opera, in Toulouse, Chicago, Lausanne, Paris, Hamburg, Munich etc, and as concert soloist. Numerous recordings. *Address:* c/o Patricia Greenan, 7 Whitehorse Close, Royal Mile, Edinburgh EH8 8BU. *T:* (0131) 557 5872.

SUMMERS, Hon. Lawrence H.; Charles W. Eliot University Professor, Harvard University, since 2006; *b* 30 Nov. 1954; *s* of Robert and Anita Summers; *m* (marr. diss.); one *s* twin *d*; *m* 2005, Prof. Elisa New, PhD. *Educ:* MIT (BS 1975); Harvard Univ. (PhD 1982). Economics Prof., MIT, 1979–82; Domestic Policy Economist, President's Council of Economic Advrs, 1982–83; Prof. of Economics, 1983–93, Nathaniel Ropes Prof., 1987, Harvard Univ.; Vice-Pres., Develt Economics and Chief Economist, World Bank, 1991–93; Under Sec. for Internat. Affairs, 1993–95, Dep. Sec., 1995–99, Sec., 1999–2001, US Treasury; Arthur Okun Dist. Fellow, Brookings Instn, 2001; Pres., Harvard Univ., 2001–06. Alan Waterman Award, 1987; John Bates Clark Medal, 1993. *Publications:* Understanding Unemployment, 1990; (jtly) Reform in Eastern Europe, 1991. *Recreations:* tennis, ski-ing. *Address:* c/o Harvard University, Cambridge, MA 02138, USA.

SUMMERS, Nicholas; Under Secretary, Department for Education and Employment (formerly of Education and Science, then for Education), 1981–96; *b* 11 July 1939; *s* of Henry Forbes Summers, CB; *m* 1965, Marian Elizabeth Ottley; four *s. Educ:* Tonbridge Sch.; Corpus Christi Coll., Oxford. Min. of Educn, 1961–64; DES, 1964–74; Private Sec. to Minister for the Arts, 1965–66; Cabinet Office, 1974–76; DES, subseq. Dept for Educn, 1976–96. Mem., Stevenson Commn on Information and Communications Technol. in Schs, 1996–97. Trustee, Inclusion Trust (formerly TheCademy), 2005–. *Recreations:* family, music.

SUMMERSCALE, David Michael, MA; Head Master of Westminster School, 1986–98; *b* 22 April 1937; *s* of late Noel Tynwald Summerscale and Beatrice (*née* Wilson); *m* 1975, Pauline, *d* of late Prof. Michel Fleury, formerly Président de l'Ecole des Hautes Etudes, Paris, and Directeur des Antiquités Historiques de l'Ile-de-France; one *s* one *d. Educ:* Northaw; Sherborne Sch.; Trinity Hall, Cambridge. Lectr in English Literature and Tutor, St Stephen's Coll., Univ. of Delhi, 1959–63; Charterhouse, 1963–75 (Head of English, Housemaster); Master of Haileybury, 1976–86. Director: Namdang Tea Co. (India) Ltd, 1991–95; The Education Group Ltd, 1996–98. Oxford and Cambridge Schs Examination Bd Awarder and Reviser in English. Vice-Chm., E-SU Scholarship Cttee, 1982–93; Member: Managing Cttee of Cambridge Mission to Delhi, 1965; C. F. Andrews Centenary Appeal Cttee, 1970; HMC Academic Policy Sub-Cttee, 1982–86; Council, Charing Cross and Westminster Med. Sch., 1986–97. Governor: The Hall Sch., Hampstead, 1986–98; Arnold House Sch., St John's Wood, 1988–98; King's House Sch., Richmond, 1991–98; Hellenic Coll., London, 1996–2006; Shri Ram Sch., Delhi, 1996–2006; Gayhurst Sch., Gerrards Cross, 1998–2002; Solihull Sch., 1998–2006; Step by Step Sch., Noida. Staff Advr, Governing Body, Westminster Abbey Choir Sch., 1989–98; Member, Governing Body: Merchant Taylors' Sch., 1996–2001 (Nominated Mem., Sch. Cttee, Merchant Taylors' Co., 1988–96): Haberdashers' Aske's Schs, 2001–06; Consultant and Governor: Assam Valley Sch., India, 1989–; Sagar Sch., India, 2001–; Exec. Advr, British Sch., Colombo, Sri Lanka, 1999–; Adviser: Amman Baccalaureate Sch., Jordan, 2002–04; Al Ain English Speaking Sch., 2006–; Scholars Internat. Acad., Dubai, 2006–. Member Council: Queen's Coll., London, 1991–2006 (Vice-Chm., 2000–06); Book Aid Internat. (formerly Ranfurly Library Service), 1992–98. Trustee, Criterion Theatre Trust, 1992–2002. Adviser: Rajiv Gandhi (UK) Foundn, 1999–2002; Pahamane Rehab. Centre, Sri Lanka, 2005–; Ext. Advr, Hong Kong Mgt Assoc. Coll., 1999–2002. Patron, Multi Lang. Acad., Yangon, Myanmar, 1999–2004. FRSA 1984. *Publications:* articles on English and Indian literature; dramatisations of novels and verse. *Recreations:* music, reading, mountaineering, games (squash (Mem. SRA), cricket, tennis, rackets (Mem. Tennis and Rackets Assoc.), golf). *Address:* 4 Ashley Gardens, Ambrosden Avenue, SW1P 1QD. *Clubs:* Athenæum, I Zingari, Free Foresters, Jesters; Club Alpin Suisse.

SUMMERSCALE, Peter Wayne; HM Diplomatic Service, retired; Consultant to Central America Direct (conservation volunteers), since 2005; *b* 22 April 1935; *s* of Sir John Summerscale, KBE; *m* 1st, 1964, Valerie Turner (marr. diss. 1983); one *s* two *d*; 2nd, 1985, Cristina Fournier (marr. diss. 1986); 3rd, 1989, Elizabeth Carro. *Educ:* Rugby Sch.; New Coll., Oxford Univ. (Exhibnr; 1st Cl. Hons Modern History); Russian Res. Centre, Harvard Univ. FO, 1960–62; Polit. Residency, Bahrain, 1962–65; 1st Sec., Tokyo, 1965–68; FCO, 1968–69; Cabinet Office, 1969–71; 1st Sec. and Head of Chancery, Santiago, Chile, 1971–75; Head of CSCE Unit, FCO, 1976–77; Dep. Leader, UK Delegn, Belgrade Rev. Conf., 1977–78; Counsellor and Head of Chancery, Brussels, 1978–79; Vis. FCO Res. Fellow, RIIA, Chatham House, 1979–81; Head of Civilian Faculty, Nat. Defence Coll., 1981–82; Ambassador to Costa Rica, 1982–86, and concurrently (non-resident) to Nicaragua; Dep. Leader, UK Delegn to CSCE, 1986–89; Exec. Sec., London Information Forum, 1989. Hd, EU Monitoring Mission, Zagreb, 1992; Belgrade, 1995; UK expert, EU Programme for Human Rights in Central America, 1992–99. *Publications:* (jtly) Soviet—East European Dilemmas, 1981; The East European Predicament, 1982; articles on E Europe and communism. *Recreations:* tennis, ski-ing, walking. *Address:* 25B Lady Somerset Road, NW5 1TX.

SUMMERSKILL, Ben Jeffrey Peter; Chief Executive, Stonewall, since 2003; *b* 6 Oct. 1961; *s* of late Michael Brynmôr Summerskill and Florence Marion Johnston Summerskill (*née* Elliott). *Educ:* Sevenoaks Sch.; Merton Coll., Oxford (Exhibnr). Dep. Gen. Manager, Mario & Franco Restaurants, 1983–85; Gen. Manager, Lennoxcourt Ltd, 1985–86; Operations Dir, Kennedy Brookes plc, 1986–90; freelance journalist, Time Out, The Face, etc., 1990; Ed., The Pink Paper, 1992; Deputy Editor: Roof, 1993–96; Londoner's Diary, Evening Standard, 1996–98; Media Ed., Daily Express and Sunday Express, 1998–2000; Society and Policy Ed., 2000, Asst Ed., 2001–03, The Observer. Mem., Equality and Human Rights Commn, 2006– (Mem., Govt Steering Cttee, 2004–06). Mem., Westminster CC, 1994–98. Mem., Parkside CHC, 1993–95; Vice Chm., Kensington Chelsea & Westminster CHC, 1995–96. Trustee, Covent Garden Area Trust, 1995–99. Mem. Exec. Cttee, Fabian Soc., 2004–07. *Publication:* (ed) The Way We Are Now: gay and lesbian lives in the 21st century, 2006. *Recreation:* thinking. *Address:* Stonewall, Tower Building, York Road, SE1 7NX. *T:* (020) 7593 1850.

SUMMERSKILL, Dr the Hon. Shirley Catherine Wynne; Medical Practitioner; Medical Officer in Blood Transfusion Service, 1983–91; *b* London, 9 Sept. 1931; *d* of late Dr E. J. Samuel and Baroness Summerskill, CH, PC. *Educ:* St Paul's Girls' Sch.; Somerville Coll., Oxford; St Thomas' Hospital. MA, BM, BCh., 1958. Treas., Oxford Univ. Labour Club, 1952. Resident House Surgeon, later House Physician, St Helier Hosp., Carshalton, 1959; Partner in Gen. Practice, 1960–68. Contested (Lab): Blackpool North by-election, 1962; Halifax, 1983. MP (Lab) Halifax, 1964–83; opposition spokesman on health, 1970–74; Parly Under-Sec. of State, Home Office, 1974–79; opposition spokesman on home affairs, 1979–83. Vice-Chm., PLP Health Gp, 1964–69, Chm., 1969–70; Mem., Labour Party NEC, 1981–83. UK delegate, UN Status of Women Commn, 1968 and 1969; Mem. British delegn, Council of Europe and WEU, 1968, 1969. Mem., BMA.

Publications: A Surgical Affair (novel), 1963; Destined to Love (novel), 1986. *Recreations:* music, reading, attending literature classes.

SUMMERSON, Hugo Hawksley Fitzthomas; Director, Palatine Properties Ltd, since 1983; Director (formerly Principal), Speaker Skills Training, since 1994; *b* 21 July 1950; *s* of late Thomas Hawksley Summerson, OBE and Joan Florence Summerson; *m* 2nd, 1995, Diana, *d* of late Lt-Col T. J. C. Washington, MC; one *s*. *Educ:* Harrow School; Royal Agricultural College. FRICS; MRAC. Land Agent with Knight, Frank and Rutley, 1973–76; travel in S America, 1977; self-employment, 1978–83. Consultant: Amhurst Properties Ltd, 1992–94; Grandfield Public Affairs Ltd, 1996–98; Butler Kelly Ltd, 2001–; Dir, Meridian Clocks Ltd, 1999–2003. Contested (C): Barking, 1983; Walthamstow, 1992. MP (C) Walthamstow, 1987–92. Mem., Select Cttee on Envmt, 1991–92; Treas., British Latin-American Parly Gp, 1990; Vice-Chm., All-Party Parly Gp on Child Abduction, 1991–92; Sec., Cons. Back Bench Agriculture Cttee, 1991–92. Chm., Greater London Area Adopted Parly Candidates Assoc., 1986; Vice-Pres., Greater London Area, Nat. Soc. of Cons. and Unionist Agents, 1989; Mem. Council, British Atlantic Gp of Young Politicians, 1989; Parly Advr to Drinking Fountain Assoc., 1989; Treas., Assoc. of Cons. Parly Candidates (formerly Westminster Candidates' Assoc.), 1998–2001. Fellow, Industry and Parlt Trust, 1991. Member: Professional Speakers Assoc., 2001–05; Assoc. of Former MPs, 2004–. Mem., Internat. Bruckner Soc., 2007–. Trustee: Trinity Chapel Site Charity, 1998–2002; Hyde Park Place Estate Charity, 1998–2002; St George's Hanover Sq. Sch., 1998–2002. Churchwarden, St George's, Hanover Sq., 1998–2002; Rep. for St George's, Westminster (St Margaret) Deanery Synod, 2004–07. Sir Anthony Berry Meml Scholar, 1985. *Recreations:* fishing, music. *Address:* 38 Springfield Avenue, SW20 9JX. *T:* (020) 8543 5550. *Club:* Royal Over-Seas League.

SUMMERTON, Dr Neil William, CB 1997; Chairman, Partnership (UK) Ltd, since 2007 (Chairman and Executive Secretary, 1997–2002, Chairman and Executive Director, 2002–05; Executive Chairman, 2005–07); *b* 5 April 1942; *s* of H. E. W. Summerton and Nancy Summerton; *m* 1965, Pauline Webb; two *s*. *Educ:* Wellington Grammar Sch., Shropshire; King's Coll., London (BA History 1963; PhD War Studies 1970). Min. of Transport, 1966–69; PA to Principal, 1969–71, Asst Sec. (Co-ordination), 1971–74, KCL; DoE, 1974–97; Asst Sec., heading various housing Divs, 1978–85; Under Sec., Planning Land-Use Policy Directorate, 1985–87; Under Sec., Planning and Devel Control Directorate, 1987–88; Under Sec., Local Govt Finance Policy Directorate, 1988–91; Under Sec., Water, 1991–95; Dir, Water and Land, 1996–97; Director: Oxford Centre for the Envmt, Ethics and Society, 1997–2002; Oxford Centre for Water Res., 1998–2002; Supernumerary Fellow, Mansfield Coll., Oxford, 1997–2003, now Emeritus Fellow. Attended HM Treasury Centre for Admin. Studies, 1968–69; Civil Service Top Management Programme, 1985. Non-executive Director: Redland Bricks Ltd, 1988–91; Folkestone and Dover Water Services Ltd, 1998–; North Surrey Water Co. Ltd, 1998–2000; Three Valleys Water, 2000–; Director: Partnership (UK) Ltd, 1994–; Christian Impact Ltd, 1989–98; London Christian Housing plc, 1990–98; Christian Research Assoc., 1992–98; Church Planting Initiative, 2005–. Member: Cttee of Management, Council on Christian Approaches to Defence and Disarmament, 1983– (Hon. Sec., 1984–91); Council, Evangelical Alliance, 1990–96 and 1997–. *Publications:* A Noble Task: eldership and ministry in the local church, 1987, 2nd edn 1994; articles and essays on historical, envmtl, theological and ethical matters. *Address:* Mansfield College, Oxford OX1 3TF.

SUMNER, Sir Christopher (John), Kt 1996; a Judge of the High Court of Justice, Family Division, 1996–2008; *b* 28 Aug. 1939; *s* of His Honour Donald Sumner, OBE, QC and late Muriel Sumner; *m* 1970, Carole Ashley Mann; one *s* two *d*. *Educ:* Charterhouse; Sidney Sussex Coll., Cambridge (MA). Called to the Bar, Inner Temple, 1961, Bencher, 1994; Asst Recorder, 1983; Recorder, 1986; a Circuit Judge, 1987–96. Mem., Judicial Studies Bd, 1991–96, 1999–2005 (Jt Dir of Studies, 1995–96). *Clubs:* Hurlingham; Burnham Overy Staithe Sailing.

SUMNER, Gordon Matthew, (Sting), CBE 2003; musician, songwriter and actor; *b* Northumberland, 2 Oct. 1951; *s* of late Eric and Audrey Sumner; *m* 1st, 1976, Frances Tomelty (marr. diss. 1984); one *s* one *d*; 2nd, 1992, Trudie Styler; two *s* two *d*. *Educ:* St Cuthbert's Grammar Sch., Newcastle; Warwick Coll., Newcastle (BEd 1973). Teacher, St Paul's Primary Sch., Cramlington, Newcastle, 1971–74. Singer, bass-player and songwriter, The Police, 1977–86; tours in UK, Europe and USA; reformed and toured worldwide, 2007. Theatre début in The Threepenny Opera, Washington, 1989. *Records include: with The Police: albums:* Outlandos d'Amour, 1978; Regatta de Blanc, 1979; Zenyatta Mondatta, 1980; Ghost in the Machine, 1981; Synchronicity, 1983; *singles:* Roxanne, 1978; Message in a Bottle, 1979; Walking on the Moon, 1979; Every Breath You Take, 1983; *solo: albums:* Dream of the Blue Turtles, 1985; Bring on the Night, 1986 (Grammy Award for Best Male Pop Vocal Perf., 1988); Nothing Like the Sun, 1987; The Soul Cages, 1991; Ten Summoner's Tales, 1993; Mercury Falling, 1996; Brand New Day, 1999 (Grammy Awards for Best Pop Album and Best Male Pop Vocal Perf., 1999); All This Time, 2001; Sacred Love, 2003; Songs from the Labyrinth, 2006; *singles:* Nothing Like the Sun, 1987; The Soul Cages, 1991 (Grammy Award for Best Rock Song, 1992); Englishman in New York; After the Rain has Gone, 2000. *Film appearances include:* Quadrophenia, 1979; Radio On, 1980; Brimstone and Treacle, 1982; Dune, 1984; The Bride, 1985; Plenty, 1985; Julia and Julia, 1987; Stormy Monday, 1988; The Adventures of Baron von Munchausen, 1989; The Grotesque, 1995; Gentlemen Don't Eat Poets, 1997; Lock, Stock and Two Smoking Barrels, 1998. Co-founder, Rain Forest Foundn, 1989. Hon. DMus Northumbria, 1992. *Publications:* Jungle Stories: the fight for the Amazon, 1989; Broken Music: a memoir, 2003. *Address:* c/o Polydor Records, 72 Black Lion Lane, W6 9BE.

SUMPTION, Jonathan Philip Chadwick, OBE 2003; QC 1986; *b* 9 Dec. 1948; *s* of late Anthony James Chadwick Sumption, DSC; *m* 1971, Teresa Mary (*née* Whelan); one *s* two *d*. *Educ:* Eton; Magdalen College, Oxford (MA). Fellow (in History) of Magdalen College, Oxford, 1971–75; called to the Bar, Inner Temple, 1975, Bencher, 1990. A Recorder, 1993–2001; a Judge of the Courts of Appeal of Jersey and Guernsey, 1995–. Mem., Judicial Appts Commn, 2006–. Trustee, RAM, 2002–. *Publications:* Pilgrimage: an image of medieval religion, 1975; The Albigensian Crusade, 1978; The Hundred Years' War, vol. 1, 1990, vol. 2, 1999. *Recreations:* music, history. *Address:* Brick Court Chambers, 7–8 Essex Street, WC2R 3LD.

SUNDERLAND, Earl of; George Spencer-Churchill; *b* 28 July 1992; *s* and *heir* of Marquess of Blandford, *qv*.

SUNDERLAND, Archdeacon of; *see* Bain, Ven. J. S.

SUNDERLAND, Prof. Eric, CBE 2005 (OBE 1999); PhD; FIBiol; Principal, later Vice-Chancellor, University College of North Wales, Bangor, 1984–95, now Emeritus Professor, University of Wales; Lord-Lieutenant of Gwynedd, 1999–2006; *b* 18 March 1930; *s* of Leonard Sunderland and Mary Agnes (*née* Davies); *m* 1957, Jean Patricia (*née* Watson); two *d*. *Educ:* Amman Valley Grammar Sch.; Univ. of Wales (BA, MA); Univ. of London (PhD). FIBiol 1975. Commnd Officer, RA, 1955–56. Res. Asst, UCL, 1953–54; Res. Scientist, NCB, 1957–58; University of Durham: Lectr, 1958–66; Sen. Lectr, 1966–71; Prof. of Anthropology, 1971–84; Pro Vice-Chancellor and Sub-Warden, 1979–84; Vice-Chancellor, Univ. of Wales, 1989–91. Welsh Supernumerary Fellow, Jesus Coll., Oxford, 1987–88 and 1992–93. Chm., Gypsy-Traveller Accommodation Res. Steering Gp, Welsh Assembly Govt, 2005–06. Sec.-Gen., Internat. Union of Anthropol and Ethnol Sciences, 1978–98 (Pres., 1998–2003); President, Royal Anthropol Inst., 1989–91 (Hon. Sec., 1978–85; Hon. Treasurer, 1985–89); Chm., Biosocial Soc., 1981–85; Pres., N Wales Br., Inst. Biol., 2005–. Member: Welsh Language Bd, 1988–91; Ct of Govs, Nat. Mus. of Wales, 1991–94; Gen. Cttee, ICSU, 1993–99; Bd, British Council, 1996–2001 (Chm., Welsh Cttee, 1996–2001); BBC Broadcasting Council for Wales, 1996–2000; Vice Pres., Internat. Social Sci. Council, 1994; Chairman: Welsh Language Educn Develt Cttee, 1987–94; Local Govt Boundary Commn for Wales, 1994–2001; Adv. Cttee for Wales, Environment Agency, 1996–2001; Wetlands for Wales Project, 2001–; Commn on Local Govt Electoral Arrangements in Wales, 2001–02; CILT Cymru (Centre for Inf. on Language Teaching and Res.), 2002–06; Vice-Pres., Sefydliad (Community Foundn in Wales), 2003–. Vice-Patron, Atlantic Council of UK, 2002–. Chm. Bd, Welsh Chamber Orch., 2003–; Vice-Pres., Welsh Music Guild, 2005–. Pres., Univ. of Wales, Lampeter, 1998–2002. Area Pres., Scouts Assoc., Anglesey, Conwy and Gwynedd, 2002–; Pres., Anglesey Bd, SSAFA, 2005–. Hon. Col, 6th Cadet Bn, RWF (Gwynedd), ACF, 2003–. Mem., Welsh Livery Guild, 2001– (Mem. Court, 2008–). Hon. Mem., The Gorsedd, 1985. High Sheriff, 1998–99, DL 1998, Gwynedd. Hon. Fellow: Univ. of Wales, Lampeter, 1995; Univ. of Wales, Bangor, 1996. Hon. LLD Wales, 1997. CStJ 2000. Golden Jubilee Medal, 2002. *Publications:* Elements of Human and Social Geography: some anthropological perspectives, 1973; (ed jtly) Genetic Variation in Britain, 1973; (ed jtly) The Operation of Intelligence: biological preconditions for the operation of intelligence, 1980; (ed jtly) Genetic and Population Studies in Wales, 1986; contrib. Annals of Human Biol., Human Heredity, Man, Human Biol., Nature, Amer. Jl of Phys. Anthropol., and Trans Royal Soc. *Recreations:* travel, gardening, book collecting, reading. *Address:* Y Bryn, Ffriddoedd Road, Bangor, Gwynedd LL57 2EH. *T:* (01248) 353265. *Club:* Athenæum.

SUNDERLAND, (Godfrey) Russell, CB 1991; FCILT; Deputy Secretary, Aviation, Shipping and International, Department of Transport, 1988–94; *b* 28 July 1936; *s* of Allan and Laura Sunderland; *m* 1965, Greta Jones; one *s* one *d*. *Educ:* Heath Grammar Sch., Halifax; The Queen's College, Oxford (MA). Ministry of Aviation: Asst Principal, 1962; Asst Private Sec. to Minister, 1964; Principal, 1965; HM Diplomatic Service: First Sec. (Civil Air), Beirut, and other Middle East posts, 1969; Principal, Board of Trade, 1971; Asst Sec., DTI, 1973; Under Sec., DTI, 1979; Dir of Shipping Policy and Emergency Planning, Dept of Transport, 1984. Chairman: Consultative Shipping Group, 1984–88; Maritime Transport Cttee, OECD, 1992–94. Non-exec. Dir, Air Miles Travel Promotions Ltd, 1995–2001. Advr, Maersk Co. Ltd, 1994–2001. FCILT (FCIT 1995; Vice Pres., CIT, 1997–2001; Chm., Transport Faculty, CILT(UK), 2004–07). FRSA 1991. *Recreations:* garden, piano, amateur theatre. *Address:* Windrush, Silkmore Lane, West Horsley, Leatherhead, Surrey KT24 6JQ. *T:* (01483) 282660.

SUNDERLAND, Sir John (Michael), Kt 2006; Chairman, Cadbury Schweppes plc, 2003–08 (Chief Executive, 1996–2003); *b* 24 Aug. 1945; *s* of Harry Sunderland and Joyce Eileen Sunderland (*née* Farnish); *m* 1966, Jean Margaret Grieve; three *s* one *d*. *Educ:* St Andrews Univ. (MA Hons). Joined Cadbury, 1968. Non-executive Director: Rank Gp plc, 1998–2006; Barclays plc, 2005–; Member Advisory Board: CVC Capital Partners, 2004–; Ian Jones & Partners, 2002. Dir, Financial Reporting Council, 2004–; Trinsum (formerly Marakon Associates), 2006–. President: ISBA, 2002–05; UK Food and Drink Fedn, 2002–04; CBI, 2004–06 (Dep. Pres., 2003–04, 2007–08). *Address:* Three Barrows, Seale Road, Elstead, Surrey GU8 6LF.

SUNDERLAND, Russell; *see* Sunderland, G. R.

SUNLEY, John Bernard; Chairman, Sunley Holdings plc, since 1979; *b* 31 May 1936; *s* of late Bernard and Mary Sunley; *m* 1st, 1961, Patricia Taylor (marr. diss. 1975); three *s* one *d*; 2nd, 1978, Anne Crosby (marr. diss. 1989); 3rd, 1992, Fiona Bateman; one *s* one *d*. *Educ:* Elstree Sch.; Harrow Sch.; Columbia Univ. Nat. Service, RM, 1954–56. Trainee Accountant, Allan Charlesworth, Chartered Accountants, 1956–57; Trainee Surveyor, Weatherall Green and Smith, Chartered Surveyors, 1957–58; joined family business as jun. exec., 1960; Director: Bernard Sunley Investment Trust Co. Ltd, 1962–; Blackwood Hodge Ltd, 1962–; Chairman: Bernard Sunley and Sons Ltd, 1964– (Dir, 1962–); Sunley Homes Ltd, 1964– (Dir, 1962–). Chm., Bernard Sunley Charitable Foundn, 1964–. High Sheriff, Kent, 1999. *Recreations:* golf, tennis, squash, thoroughbred horse racing, farming, ski-ing. *Address:* Sunley Holdings, 20 Berkeley Square, W1J 6LH. *T:* (020) 7499 8842. *Clubs:* MCC, Royal Thames Yacht; Royal and Ancient Golf; Royal St George's Golf.

SUNNUCKS, Stephen Richard; President, Gap (Europe), since 2005; *b* 30 Sept. 1957; *s* of Richard George Drummond Clitherow Sunnucks and Hilary Mary Sunnucks; *m* 1993, Louise Anita Marston; three *s*. *Educ:* Dr Challoner's Grammar Sch., Amersham; Sheffield Univ. (BA Hons Econs). Various posts with Marks & Spencer plc, 1979–89 (retail mgt, 1979–84; buying depts, 1984–89); J. Sainsbury plc, 1989–94 (Dir, Non-food, Savacentre, 1989–92; Deptl Dir, J. Sainsbury, 1992–94); Burton Gp plc, subsequently Arcadia Gp plc, 1994–98: Man. Dir, Dorothy Perkins Ltd, 1994–97; Man. Dir, Mergers, Acquisitions and New Business Devel, 1997–98; Man. Dir, Retail, New Look plc, 1998–2000; Chief Exec., New Look Gp plc, 2000–04. *Recreations:* golf, tennis, ski-ing. *Address:* e-mail: stephen.sunnucks@btinternet.com.

SUPACHAI PANITCHPAKDI, PhD; Secretary-General, UN Conference on Trade and Development, since 2005; *b* Bangkok, 30 May 1946; *m* Mrs Sasai; one *s* one *d*. *Educ:* Netherlands Sch. of Econs, Rotterdam (Bank of Thailand Schol.; BA, MA; PhD 1973). Vis. Fellow, Dept of Applied Econs, Univ. of Cambridge, 1973; Bank of Thailand, 1974–86, latterly Dir of Financial Instns Supervision Dept; Pres., Thai Military Bank, 1988–92. MP (Democrat Party) Bangkok, 1986–88, 1992–2002; Dep. Minister of Finance, 1986–88; Mem., Nat. Assembly, 1991; Senator, 1992; Dep. Prime Minister, 1992–95; Dep. Prime Minister and Minister of Commerce, Thailand, 1997–2002; Dir Gen., WTO, 2002–05. Kt Grand Cordon (Special Class), Order of White Elephant (Thailand). *Publications include:* Globalization and Trade in the New Millennium, 2001; (with Mark Clifford) China and WTO: changing China changing WTO, 2002. *Address:* UNCTAD, E-9042 Palais des Nations, 8–14 Avenue de la Paix, 1211 Geneva 10, Switzerland.

SUPHAMONGKHON, Dr Konthi, Kt Grand Cordon of the White Elephant, Kt Grand Cordon, Order of the Crown of Thailand; Kt Grand Commander, Order of Chula Chom Klao; Hon. GCVO 1972; *b* 3 Aug. 1916; *m* 1951, Dootsdi Atthakravi; two *s* one *d*. *Educ:* Univ. of Moral and Political Sciences, Bangkok (LLB); Univ. of Paris (Dr-en-Droit). Joined Min. of Foreign Affairs, 1941; Second Sec., Tokyo, 1942–44; Chief of Polit. Div., 1944–48; Dir-Gen., Western Affairs Dept, 1948–50; UN Affairs Dept, 1950–52; Minister to Australia, 1952–56, Ambassador, June 1956–59, and to New Zealand, Oct. 1956–59;

Dir-Gen. of Internat. Organizations, 1959–63; Adviser on Foreign Affairs to the Prime Minister, 1962–64; Sec.-Gen., SEATO, 1964–65; Ambassador to Federal Republic of Germany, 1965–70, and to Finland, 1967–70; Ambassador to Court of St James's, 1970–76. Frequent Lecturer, 1944–; notably at Thammasat Univ., 1944–52, at National Defence Coll., 1960–62, and at Army War Coll., Bangkok, 1960–63. Member: Internat. Law Assoc.; IISS; RIIA. Holds foreign decorations, incl. Grosskreuz des Verdienstordens (Germany), 1970. *Publications:* Thailand and her relations with France, 1940 (in French); Account of a return journey from Marseilles to Singapore, 1965 (in French); Thai Foreign Policy, 1984 (in Thai). *Recreations:* tennis, golf, swimming. *Address:* Kanta Mansion, 73 Soi 26, Sukhumvit Road, Bangkok, Thailand; 60 Kensington Court, Kensington, W8 5DG. *Clubs:* Siam Society, Royal Sport of Bangkok, Royal Turf (Bangkok).

SUPPERSTONE, Michael Alan; QC 1991; a Recorder, since 1996 (Assistant Recorder, 1992–96); a Deputy High Court Judge, since 1998; *b* 30 March 1950; *s* of late Harold Bernard Supperstone and Muriel Supperstone; *m* 1985, Dianne Jaffe; one *s* one *d*. *Educ:* St Paul's School; Lincoln College, Oxford (MA, BCL). Called to the Bar, Middle Temple, 1973, Bencher, 1999; in practice, 1974. Vis. Scholar, Harvard Law Sch., 1979–80; Vis. Lectr, Nat. Univ. of Singapore, 1981, 1982. Chm., Administrative Law Bar Assoc., 1997–99 (Sec., 1986–91; Treas., 1991–94; Vice-Chm., 1995–96). Consulting Ed., Butterworths Local Government Reports, 1999–. *Publications:* Brownlie's Law of Public Order and National Security, 2nd edn 1981; Immigration: the law and practice, 1983, 3rd edn 1994, cons. ed., 4th edn, as Immigration and Asylum, 1996; (contrib.) Halsbury's Laws of England, 4th edn reissue, Administrative Law, 1989, 2001 (Gen. Ed.), Extradition Law, 2000; (ed jtly and contrib.) Judicial Review, 1992, 3rd edn 2005; (contrib.) Butterworths Local Government Law, 1998; (jtly) Local Authorities and the Human Rights Act 1998, 1999; (jtly) The Freedom of Information Act 2000, 2001; (Jt Gen. Ed.) Administrative Court Practice, 2002, 2nd edn 2008; articles on public law. *Recreations:* playing tennis, watching cricket, reading history. *Address:* 11 King's Bench Walk, Temple, EC4Y 7EQ. *T:* (020) 7583 0610. *Clubs:* MCC, Garrick, Royal Automobile.

SUPPLE, Prof. Barry Emanuel, CBE 2000; FRHistS; FBA 1987; Director, Leverhulme Trust, 1993–2001; Professor of Economic History, University of Cambridge, 1981–93, now Professor Emeritus; *b* 27 Oct. 1930; *s* of Solomon and Rose Supple; *m* 1st, 1958, Sonia (*née* Caller) (*d* 2002); two *s* one *d*; 2nd, 2003, Virginia (*née* McNay). *Educ:* Hackney Downs Grammar Sch.; London Sch. of Econs and Polit. Science (BScEcon 1952; Hon. Fellow, 2001); Christ's Coll., Cambridge (PhD 1955); LittD Cantab 1993. FRHistS 1972. Asst Prof. of Business History, Grad. Sch. of Business Admin, Harvard Univ., 1955–60; Associate Prof. of Econ. Hist., McGill Univ., 1960–62; University of Sussex: Lectr, Reader, then Prof. of Econ. and Social Hist., 1962–78; Dean, Sch. of Social Sciences, 1965–68; Pro-Vice-Chancellor (Arts and Social Studies), 1968–72; Pro-Vice-Chancellor, 1978; University of Oxford: Reader in Recent Social and Econ. Hist., 1978–81; Professorial Fellow, Nuffield Coll., 1978–81; Professorial Fellow, 1981–83, Hon. Fellow, 1984, Christ's Coll., Cambridge; Master of St Catharine's Coll., Cambridge, 1984–93 (Hon. Fellow, 1993). Hon. Fellow, Worcester Coll., 1986; Associate Fellow, Trumbull Coll., Yale, 1986. Chm., Consultative Cttee of Assessment of Performance Unit, DES, 1975–80; Member: Council, SSRC, 1972–77; Social Science Fellowship Cttee, Nuffield Foundn, 1974–97. Pres., Econ. Hist. Soc., 1992–95. Foreign Sec., British Acad., 1995–99. Co-editor, Econ. Hist. Rev., 1973–82. Hon. Fellow, Inst. of Historical Res., 2001. Hon. FRAM 2001. Hon. DLitt: London Guildhall, 1993; Sussex, 1998; Leicester, 1999; Warwick, 2000; Bristol, 2001. *Publications:* Commercial Crisis and Change in England, 1600–42, 1959; (ed) The Experience of Economic Growth, 1963; Boston Capitalists and Western Railroads, 1967; The Royal Exchange Assurance: a history of British insurance, 1720–1970, 1970; (ed) Essays in Business History, 1977; History of the British Coal Industry: vol. 4, 1914–46, The Political Economy of Decline, 1987; (ed) The State and Economic Knowledge: the American and British experience, 1990; (ed) The Rise of Big Business, 1992; articles and revs in learned jls. *Recreations:* travel, writing. *Address:* 3 Scotts Gardens, Cambridge CB22 4NR. *T:* (01223) 830606.

See also T. A. Supple.

SUPPLE, Timothy Adam; director of theatre, opera and film; *b* 24 Sept. 1962; *s* of Prof. Barry Emanuel Supple, *qv* and late Sonia Caller; one *s* two *d* by Melly Still. *Educ:* Lewes Priory Comprehensive Sch.; Churchill Coll., Cambridge (BA Hist./English). Assistant Director: York Th. Royal, 1985–87; Royal Court Th., 1987; RNT, 1988–89; Associate Dir, Leicester Haymarket, 1989–90; Artistic Dir, Young Vic Th., 1993–2000; estabd Dash Arts, 2005. *Productions include: theatre:* Accidental Death of an Anarchist, NT, 1990; Grimm Tales, Young Vic, 1994, 1998; Spring Awakening, 1995; Comedy of Errors, RSC, 1996; Haroun and the Sea of Stories, NT, 1998; Tales from Ovid, RSC, 1999; A Servant to Two Masters, RSC, Young Vic, 1999; Midnight's Children, RSC, NY, 2003; Cosmonaut's Last Message, Donmar Warehouse, 2005; A Midsummer Night's Dream, Dash Arts/British Council, India, 2005–06, Verona, 2006, Stratford upon Avon, 2006, 2007, London, 2007, UK Tour, 2007, Australia, USA and Canada, 2008; prodns at Chichester Fest. Th.; Nat. Th. of Norway; Maxim Gorki Th., Berlin; Tel Aviv Opera House; Sheffield Crucible Th.; also tours, British Isles, Europe, USA, Far East, S America, Australia and India; *opera:* Hansel and Gretel, Opera North, 2001; Babette's Feast, Royal Opera, 2002, 2004; The Magic Flute, Opera North, 2003, 2007; *films:* Twelfth Night, 2002; Rockabye, 2004. *Publications:* co-adaptor, theatre adaptations: Dario Fo, Accidental Death of an Anarchist, 1990; Carol Ann Duffy, Grimm Tales, 1994; Salman Rushdie: Haroun and the Sea of Stories, 1998; Midnight's Children, 2003; Ted Hughes, Tales from Ovid, 1999. *Recreations:* reading, walking, music, politics, history, yoga, cooking, travel, children. *Address: e-mail:* timsupple@gmail.com.

SUR, Prof. Mriganka, PhD; FRS 2006; Sherman Fairchild Professor of Neuroscience, since 1998, and Head, Department of Brain and Cognitive Sciences, since 1997, Massachusetts Institute of Technology; *b* Fatehgarh, India, 1953. *Educ:* Indian Inst. of Technol. (BTech 1974); Vanderbilt Univ. (MS 1975; PhD 1978). Postdoctoral res., SUNY Stony Brook; Sch. of Medicine, Yale Univ., 1983–86; joined Dept of Brain and Cognitive Scis, MIT, 1986, Prof., 1993–. *Publications:* articles in jls. *Address:* Department of Brain and Cognitive Sciences, Massachusetts Institute of Technology, 77 Massachusetts Avenue, Cambridge, MA 02139-4307, USA.

SURFACE, Richard Charles; Managing Director, Oliver Wyman (formerly Oliver, Wyman & Co., then Mercer Oliver Wyman), since 2005 (Director, 2000–05); *b* 16 June 1948; *s* of James Richard Surface and Mary Ellen Surface (*née* Shaver); *m* 1977, Stephanie Maria Josefa Ruth Hentschel von Gilgenheimb; two *s* one *d*. *Educ:* Univ. of Minnesota; Univ. of Kansas (BA Maths); Harvard Grad. Sch. of Business Admin (MBA). Actuarial Asst, Nat. Life & Accident Insce Co., Nashville, Tenn, 1970–72; Corporate Treasury Analyst, Mobil Corp., NY, 1974–77; Dir, Corporate Planning, Northwest Industries Inc., Chicago, 1977–81; American Express Co., London and Frankfurt, 1981–89: Regl Vice-Pres. (Card Strategic Planning), 1981–82; Divisional Vice-President: Business Develt, 1982–86; Card Mkting, 1986–87; and Gen. Manager, Personal Financial Services, 1987–89; Gen. Manager, Corporate Develt, Sun Life, 1989–91; Managing Director: Sun Life Internat., 1991–95; Pearl Group PLC, 1995–99; AMP (UK) PLC, 1995–99. *Recreations:* antiquarian books, ski-ing, opera, theatre, tennis. *Clubs:* Royal Automobile, Groucho.

SURREY, Archdeacon of; *see* Beake, Ven. S. A.

SURTEES, John, OBE 2008 (MBE 1961); controls companies in automotive research and development, motorsport and property development; *b* 11 Feb. 1934; *s* of late John Norman and Dorothy Surtees; *m* 1st, 1962, Patricia Phyllis Burke (marr. diss. 1979); 2nd, 1987, Jane A. Sparrow; one *s* two *d*. *Educ:* Ashburton School, Croydon. 5 year engineering apprenticeship, Vincent Engrs, Stevenage, Herts. Motorcycle racing, 1952–60; British Champion, 1954, 1955; World 500 cc Motorcycle Champion, 1956; World 350 and 500 cc Motorcycle Champion, 1958, 1959, 1960. At end of 1960 he retd from motorcycling; motor racing, 1961–72; with Ferrari Co., won World Motor Racing title, 1964; 5th in World Championship, 1965 (following accident in Canada due to suspension failure); in 1966 left Ferrari in mid-season and joined Cooper, finishing 2nd in World Championship; in 1967 with Honda Motor Co. as first driver and develt engr (1967–68); 3rd in World Championship; with BRM as No 1 driver, 1969; designed and built own Formula 1 car, 1970. Team Principal, British A1 Grand Prix Team, 2004–07. Vice-Pres., British Racing Drivers' Club, 1993–2000, 2004– (Dir, 2000–04). Ambassador, Racing Steps Foundn in support of young driver develt prog., 2008. *Publications:* Motorcycle Racing and Preparation, 1958; John Surtees Book of Motorcycling, 1960; Speed, 1963; Six Days in August, 1968; John Surtees—World Champion, 1991; (jtly) The Pirelli Album of Motor Racing Heroes, 1992; Motorcycle Maestro, 2003. *Recreations:* period architecture, mechanical restorations; interested in most sports. *Address:* c/o John Surtees Ltd, Monza House, Fircroft Way, Edenbridge, Kent TN8 6EJ. *T:* (01732) 865496.

SUSMAN, Peter Joseph; QC 1997; a Recorder, since 1993; *b* 20 Feb. 1943; *s* of Albert Leonard Susman and Sybil Rebecca Susman (*née* Joseph); *m* 1st, 1966, Peggy Judith Stone (marr. diss. 1996); one *s* one *d*; 2nd, 2006, Belinda Zoe Schwehr; one *s*. *Educ:* Dulwich Coll.; Lincoln Coll., Oxford (Oldfield Open Law Schol.; BA 1964; MA 1970); Law Sch., Univ. of Chicago (British Commonwealth Fellow; Fulbright Schol.; JD 1965). Called to the Bar, Middle Temple, 1966, Bencher, 2005; in practice as a barrister, 1966–70 and 1972–; Associate, Debevoise, Plimpton, Lyons & Gates, NYC, 1970–71; Asst Recorder, 1989–93. Indep. Standing Counsel to Ofcom, 2003–05. *Recreations:* playing the clarinet, windsurfing, ski-ing. *Address:* Henderson Chambers, 2 Harcourt Buildings, Temple, EC4Y 9DB. *T:* (020) 7583 9020.

SUSSKIND, Janis Elizabeth; Publishing Director, Boosey & Hawkes Music Publishers Ltd, London, since 2005; *b* 27 Nov. 1952; *d* of John H. Tomfohrde, Jr, and Ruth Elizabeth Robbins Tomfohrde; *m* 1st, 1973, Walter Susskind (*d* 1980); 2nd, 1993, Antony Fell. *Educ:* Princeton Univ. (BA *cum laude*). Hd of Promotion, 1984–96, Dir, Composers and Repertoire, 1997–2004, Boosey & Hawkes Music Publishers Ltd. Director: NMC Record Co., 1991–92; Classic Copyright (Hldgs) Ltd, 2004–08. Chm., SPNM, 1983–88. Arts Council of England, subseq. Arts Council England: Mem., Music Panel, 1993–2001; Mem. and Dep. Chm., Stabilization Adv. Panel, 1996–2006. Mem. Council, RCM, 1996–2005. Member Board: Birmingham Contemporary Music Gp, 1991–2000; English National Opera, 2004–. Trustee, Britten-Pears Foundn, 2001–. Hon. RCM 2007. *Recreations:* reading, theatre, contemporary art, ski-ing, tennis, playing chamber music. *Address:* c/o Boosey & Hawkes Music Publishers Ltd, Aldwych House, 71–91 Aldwych, WC2B 4HN.

SUSSKIND, Prof. Richard Eric, OBE 2000; DPhil; FRSE; author and independent consultant, since 1997; Information Technology Adviser to Lord Chief Justice of England, since 1998; *b* 28 March 1961; *s* of Dr Werner and Shirley Susskind; *m* 1985, Michelle Latter; two *s* one *d*. *Educ:* Hutchesons' Grammar Sch., Glasgow; Univ. of Glasgow (LLB Hons 1st class; Dip. Legal Practice); Balliol Coll., Oxford (Snell Exhibnr; DPhil 1986). FRSE 1997. CITP 2004. Tutor in Law, Univ. of Oxford, 1984–86; Head of Expert Systems, Ernst & Young, 1986–89; Special Advr, 1989–94, Mem. of Mgt Bd, 1994–97, Masons. Vis. Prof., 1990–2001, Prof., 2001–, Law Sch., Univ. of Strathclyde; Gresham Prof. of Law, 2000–04; Hon. Prof., 2005, Emeritus Prof. of Law, 2007, Gresham Coll. IT Advr, Lord Woolf's Access to Justice Inquiry, 1995–96. Chm., Soc. for Computers and Law, 1990–92 (Hon. Mem., 1992–). Member: Inf. Technol. and the Courts Cttee, 1990– (Co-Chair, 2006–); Court of Appeal (Civil Div.) Review Team, 1996–97; Modernising Govt Project Bd, 1999–2001; Freedom of Inf. Project Bd, 2003–05; Public Legal Educn Strategy Gp, 2008–; Inf. System Improvement Strategy Prog. Bd, Nat. Policing Improvement Agency, 2008–; Chm., Adv. Panel on Crown Copyright, subseq. Public Sector Inf., 2003–08. IT Advr, Jersey Legal Inf. Bd, 1998–. Mem., Adv. Bd, Lyceum Capital, 2008–. Expert Consultee: Criminal Courts Rev., 2000–01; Tribunals Rev., 2000–01. Gen. Editor, Internat. Jl of Law and Information Technology, 1992–; Law columnist, The Times, 1999–. Trustee, Lokahi Foundn, 2005–. Freeman, City of London, 1992; Freeman, 1992, Liveryman, 1993, Mem. Court, 1994–2003, Co. of Information Technologists. Founder Mem., Adv. Bd, Oxford Internet Inst., 2002–. Member: Council, Gresham Coll., 2002–04; External Adv. Bd, AHRC Res. Centre for Studies in Intellectual Property and Technol. Law, Univ. of Edinburgh, 2002–. Gov., Haberdashers' Aske's Schs, Elstree, 1998–; Mem., Balliol Coll. Campaign Bd, 2000–. FRSA 1992; FBCS 1997. Hon. Fellow, Centre for Law and Computing, Durham Univ., 2001–. George & Thomas Hutcheson Award, 2001. *Publications:* Expert Systems in Law, 1987; (with P. Capper) Latent Damage Law: the expert system, 1988; Essays on Law and Artificial Intelligence, 1993; The Future of Law, 1996; Transforming the Law, 2000; (ed jtly) Essays in Honour of Sir Brian Neill, 2003; (ed) The Susskind Interviews: legal experts in changing times, 2005; The End of Lawyers, 2008. *Recreations:* running, reading, golf, cinema, ski-ing. *Address:* 67 Aldenham Avenue, Radlett, Herts WD7 8JA. *T:* (01923) 469655; *e-mail:* richard@susskind.com.

SUTCH, Rev. Dom Antony; *see* Sutch, C. T.

SUTCH, Ven. Christopher David, TD 1992; Chaplain, St Andrew's, Costa del Sol, since 2007; Archdeacon of Gibraltar, since 2008; *b* Oxford, 27 Aug. 1947; *s* of Christopher Lang Sutch and Gladys Ethelwyn Sutch; *m* 1969, Margaret Anne, (Megan); three *s*. *Educ:* King's Coll., London (AKC 1969); DipHE 2000. Ordained deacon, 1970, priest, 1971; Curate, St Andrew's, Hartcliffe, Bristol, 1970–75; Team Vicar, Dorcan, Swindon, 1975–79; Vicar, St Helen's, Alveston, Bristol, 1979–89; Rector, St Mary's, Yate New Town, 1989–99; Vicar, St Matthew's, Cainscross with Selsey, Glos, 1999–2007. Area Dean: Westbury, 1988–89; Stapleton, 1996–99; Stonehouse, 2005–07. Royal Army Chaplains Dept (Volunteers), 1980–2003; Chaplain, RBL, Glos, 2005–07; Hon. Col, N Somerset Yeomanry Sqdn, 2003–. *Recreations:* digital photography, grandchildren. *Address:* St Andrew's Church, Edificio Jupiter 1, Avenida Nuestro, Padre Jesus Cautivo, 74 Los Boliches, 29640 Fuengirola, Spain. *T:* (952) 580600, *Fax:* (952) 472140; *e-mail:* frdavid@standrews-cofe-spain.com.

SUTCH, Christopher Timothy, (Rev. Dom Antony Sutch); Parish Priest, St Benet, Beccles, since 2003; *b* 19 June 1950; *s* of late Ronald Antony Sutch and of Kathleen Sutch (*née* Roden). *Educ:* Downside Sch.; Exeter Univ.; St Benet's Hall, Oxford. Chartered

Accountant, 1971–75; postulant, 1975, novice, 1977, professed Benedictine monk, 1981; priest, 1981; Housemaster, Caverel House, 1985–95, Headmaster, 1995–2003, Downside Sch. Member: BBC Ind. Assessment Bd on Religious Broadcasting, 1998; Cttee, Catholic Ind. Schs Conf., 2000–03. Mem. (Ind), Beccles Town Council, 2007–. Mem., Governing Body, Bath Univ., 1995–2002; Governor: All Hallows Prep. Sch., 1996–2004; Sacred Heart Primary, Chew Magna, 1996–2004 (Chm., 1997–99); St Mary's Sch., Woldingham, 2001–04; Moor Park Sch., 2002–; St Benet's Primary Sch., Beccles (Vice-Chm.), 2003–; Moreton Hall Prep. Sch., 2004–; St Felix Sch., Southwold, 2006–; Downside Sch., 2006–; Guardian, St Mary's Sch., Shaftesbury, 1999–2003; Trustee, St Edward's Sch., Cheltenham, 2004–. Trustee: Jackdaws Educnl Trust, 2003–06; Theodore Trust, 2006–. Mem. Strategy Bd, Hobsons Guide, 2003–. Dir, Catholic Herald Ltd, 2003–. Presenter and contributor, Thought for the Day, BBC Radio 4, 2003–; TV and radio progs. *Publications:* articles in newspapers, magazines and jls. *Recreations:* gardening, cricket, horse racing. *Address:* The Presbytery, 2 Grange Road, Beccles, Suffolk NR34 9NR. *T:* (01502) 713179. *Clubs:* East India; Emeriti, Ravens Cricket, Stratton Cricket (Pres., 1995–2003).

SUTCH, Ven. David; *see* Sutch, Ven. C. D.

SUTCLIFFE, Allan; a Director, British Gas plc, 1986–91; *b* 30 Jan. 1936; *s* of Bertie and May Sutcliffe; *m* 1983, Pauline, *d* of Mark and Lilian Abrahams; one *s* one *d* by a previous marr. *Educ:* Neath Grammar Sch.; University Coll. London (LLB). FCMA. Graduate trainee, BR, 1957–60; various positions in Finance in Western, Eastern and Southern Regions and at HQ, BR, 1960–70; Wales Gas Board: Chief Accountant, 1970; Dir of Finance, 1972; Deputy Chairman: British Gas W Midlands, 1980; British Gas N Thames, 1983; British Gas plc: Man. Dir, Finance, 1987; Gp Man. Dir, Finance, 1991, retd. Freeman, City of London, 1985. *Publications:* articles on Pepper's Ghost and the Birmingham stage. *Recreations:* music, Dickens (esp. pre-1940 adaptations). *Address:* 106 Kenilworth Road, Knowle, Solihull, W Midlands B93 0JD. *T:* (01564) 771538. *Club:* Royal Automobile.

SUTCLIFFE, Andrea Mary; Chief Executive, Appointments Commission, since 2007; *b* Bradford, 22 March 1964; *d* of David and Rita Sutcliffe; *m* 2008, David Stout. *Educ:* Longfield Sch., Darlington; Queen Elizabeth Sixth Form Coll., Darlington; London Sch. of Econs (BA Hons Medieval and Modern Hist. 1985). Finance Manager, Tower Hamlets HA, 1986–89; Contracting and Policy Manager, Bloomsbury and Islington HA, 1989–92; General Manager: Camden and Islington Community Health Services NHS Trust, 1992–95; St George's Healthcare NHS Trust, 1995–99; Asst Dir, Social Services, London Bor. of Camden, 1999–2000; Planning and Resources Dir, 2000–04, Dep. Chief Exec., 2004–07, NICE. *Recreations:* friends and family, quirky films, reading, hiking, Sunderland FC. *Address:* Appointments Commission, Blenheim House, West One, Duncombe Street, Leeds LS1 4PL. *T:* (0113) 394 2964, *Fax:* (0113) 394 2955; *e-mail:* andrea.sutcliffe@appointments.org.uk.

SUTCLIFFE, Andrew Harold Wentworth; QC 2001; a Recorder, since 2000; a Deputy High Court Judge, since 2004; *b* 7 Sept. 1960; *s* of John Harold Vick Sutcliffe, *qv*; *m* 1988, Emma Elisabeth Stirling; three *d* (one *s* decd). *Educ:* Winchester Coll.; Worcester Coll., Oxford (MA). Pres., Oxford Union Soc., 1981. 2nd Lieut, Royal Scots Dragoon Guards, 1978–79. Called to the Bar, Inner Temple, 1983; in practice as barrister, 1983–, specialising in commercial law, esp. banking and entertainment. Mem., Special Project Gp, Duke of Edinburgh's Award, 1986–96. Mem., Cttee, Moorland Assoc., 1996–; Chm., Kildale Agricl and Horticultural Show Cttee, 1988–; Vice Pres., Black Face Sheep Breeders' Assoc., 1989–. Liveryman, Co. of Fishmongers, 1996–. Gov., Fox Primary Sch., Kensington, 1993–. Trustee, Zebra Housing Assoc., 1988–. *Recreations:* walking, trees, opera. *Address:* Kildale Hall, Whitby, Yorks YO21 2RQ; 3 Verulam Buildings, Gray's Inn, WC1R 5NT. *T:* (020) 7831 8441. *Clubs:* MCC; Cleveland Hunt; Kildale Cricket (Pres.).

SUTCLIFFE, Anne-Marie Christine Elizabeth; Headmistress, Emanuel School, 1998–2004; *b* 24 Jan. 1949; *d* of late Dr Norman Mutton and of Mary Mutton (*née* Dobson); *m* 1970, Victor Herbert Sutcliffe; one *s* one *d*. *Educ:* convent schs; Girton Coll., Cambridge (BA 1st cl. Hons History tripos). Teacher, Stroud Girls' High Sch., 1975–79; Head of History Department: Bishop Thomas Grant Sch., 1979–81; Ursuline Convent High Sch., 1981–86; organising confs, servicing cttees, etc, CAFOD, Council on Christian Approaches to Defence and Disarmament, 1986–88; Teacher, 1988–95, Head of History, 1991–95, St Paul's Girls' Sch.; Dep. Head, Channing Sch., 1995–98. Mem. Cttee, HMC, 2002–03. Ind. Chm., Cranial Forum, 2004–07. Governor: King's Hse Sch., Richmond, 1999–2004; Hampton Sch., Middx, 2004–. *Recreations:* theatre, opera, travel, history. *Address:* Mulberry Coach House, The Green, East Rudham, King's Lynn, Norfolk PE31 8RD. *T:* (01485) 528463.

SUTCLIFFE, Gerard; MP (Lab) Bradford South, since June 1994; Parliamentary Under-Secretary of State, Department for Culture, Media and Sport, since 2007; *b* 13 May 1953; *s* of Henry and Margaret Sutcliffe; *m* 1972, Maria Holgate; three *s*. *Educ:* Cardinal Hinsley Grammar Sch.; Bradford Coll. Salesperson, Brown Muff dept store, 1969–71; display advertising clerk, Bradford Telegraph and Argus, 1971–75; Field Printers, 1975–80; Dep. Sec., SOGAT, subseq. GPMU, 1980–94. Bradford Metropolitan District Council: Councillor, 1982–88 and 1990–94; Leader, 1992–94. PPS to Chief Sec., HM Treasury, 1998, to Sec. of State for Trade and Industry, 1998–99; an Asst Govt Whip, 1999–2001; Vice Chamberlain, HM Household, 2001–03; Parly Under-Sec. of State, DTI, 2003–06, Home Office, 2006–07, Ministry of Justice, 2007. Chm., Parly Football Team. *Recreations:* sport, music, politics. *Address:* House of Commons, SW1A 0AA. *T:* (020) 7219 3247; (office) (01274) 400007.

SUTCLIFFE, James Harry, FIA; Group Chief Executive, Old Mutual plc, 2001–08 (Chief Executive, Life, 2000–01); *b* 20 April 1956; *s* of Robert William Sutcliffe and Margaret Sutcliffe; *m* 1977, Esther Sharon Pincus; two *s* (twins). *Educ:* Univ. of Cape Town (BSc). FIA 1979. Chief Operating Officer, Jackson Nat. Life, 1989–92; Chief Exec., Prudential UK plc, 1995–97; Dep. Chm., Liberty Internat., 1998–99. *Recreations:* golf, bridge. *Address:* *e-mail:* Jim.Sutcliffe1@gmail.com. *Club:* Moor Park Golf.

SUTCLIFFE, James Thomas, (Tom); critic, dramaturg and author; *b* 4 June 1943; *s* of Lt-Comdr James Denis Sutcliffe, OBE, RN and Rosamund Frances Sutcliffe, *d* of Major T. E. G. Swayne; *m* 1973, Meredith Frances Oakes, playwright, librettist, music critic, translator; one *s* one *d*. *Educ:* Prebendal Sch., Chichester; Hurstpierpoint Coll.; Magdalen Coll., Oxford (MA English 1967). English Teacher, Central Tutorial Sch. for Young Musicians, 1964–65; Manager, Musica Reservata, 1965–69; concert perfs with Musica Reservata, Schola Polyphonica, Pro Cantione Antiqua, Concentus Musicus, Vienna, 1965–70; opera début, Ottone in L'incoronazione di Poppea, Landestheater, Darmstadt, 1970; Countertenor Lay Clerk, Westminster Cathedral, 1966–70; Editor, Music and Musicians, 1970–73; Sub-Editor, Features, Dep. Arts Editor, opera & music critic, and feature writer, Dep. Obituaries Editor, The Guardian, 1973–96; opera, theatre and music critic, Vogue, 1975–87; Opera Critic, Evening Standard, 1996–2002; dramaturg on productions: Turn of the Screw, Brussels, 1998; Macbeth, Brussels, 2001; Ernest Bloch's Macbeth, Vienna, 2003; Don Giovanni, Flammen, Vienna, 2006. Chm., music sect., Critics' Circle, 1999–. Mem., Gen. Synod, C of E, 1990–; Member: Exec. Cttee, Affirming Catholicism, 1996–2002; Cathedrals Fabric Commn for England, 2002–. Leverhulme Fellow, 1991, 2005; Fellow, Rose Bruford Coll., 2006. *Publications:* (contrib.) Theatre 71, 1972, Theatre 72, 1973, and Theatre 74, 1975; (ed) Tracts for our Times, 1983; (ed) In Vitro Veritas, 1984; Believing in Opera, 1996; (ed) The Faber Book of Opera, 2000; contrib. San Francisco Opera, Glyndebourne, Brussels and Vienna opera progs, and in Opera News, Musical Times, Opera Now, The Spectator, The Independent. *Address:* 12 Polworth Road, Streatham, SW16 2EU. *T:* (020) 8677 5849.

SUTCLIFFE, John Harold Vick, CBE 1994; DL; company director; Chairman, Great Fosters (1931) Ltd, since 1958; *b* 30 April 1931; *o s* of late Sir Harold Sutcliffe and Emily Theodora Cochrane; *m* 1st, 1959, Cecilia Mary (*d* 1998), *e d* of Ralph Meredyth Turton; three *s* one *d*; 2nd, 2001, Katherine Fox. *Educ:* Winchester Coll.; New Coll., Oxford (MA). 2nd Lieut RA, 1950–51. Called to Bar, Inner Temple, 1956; practised until 1960, Midland Circuit. Chm., North Housing Association Ltd, 1985–94 (Dir, 1977–86); Director: Allied Investors Trusts Ltd, 1958–69; Norton Junction Sand & Gravel Ltd, 1958–64; Tyne Tees Waste Disposal Ltd, 1964–71. Estate management, Kildale, 1965–95. Member: Housing Corp., 1982–88; Bd, Teesside Develt Corp., 1987–98. Mem. Bd, Civic Trust, 1989–93; Chairman: Northern Heritage Trust, 1981–89; NE Civic Trust, 1989–93 (Vice-Chm., 1977–89). Contested (C): Oldham West, 1959; Chorley, Lancs, 1964; Middlesbrough West, 1966. MP (C) Middlesbrough W, 1970–Feb. 1974. Contested (C) Teesside Thornaby, Oct. 1974. Chairman: Country Endeavour, 1983–88; Bow Street Project, Guisborough, 1988–; Pres., N Yorks Youth Clubs, 1984–93 (Chm., 1966–70); Mem., N Yorks Moors Nat. Park Cttee, 1982–88. DL Cleveland, 1983–96, N Yorks, 1996–; High Sheriff, N Yorks, 1987–88. *Recreations:* woodlands, gardening, travel, shooting. *Address:* Warren Farm, Little Kildale, Whitby, N Yorks YO21 2SE. *T:* (01642) 722534; 8 Meadow Road, SW8 1QB. *T:* (020) 7582 9806.

See also A. H. W. Sutcliffe.

SUTCLIFFE, Kevin Anthony; Deputy Head, News and Current Affairs, Channel 4 Television, since 2006; *b* Blackpool, 6 Sept. 1960; *s* of Donald and June Sutcliffe; *m* 2006, Anne Marie Huby; one *s* one *d*. *Educ:* Arnold Sch., Blackpool; Blackpool Technical Coll.; Hornsey Coll. of Art, London (BA Hons Fine Art). Freelance journalist, 1983–86; Researcher then Dir, Watchdog, Asst Prod., Breakfast Time, Prod., Newsnight, BBC TV, 1986–89; Producer: Hard News, Channel 4 TV, 1990; The Late Show, BBC Music and Arts, 1991; Taking Liberties, BBC Documentaries, 1992–94; Public Eye, 1994, Panorama, 1995–99, BBC News and Current Affairs; Exec. Prod., Louis Theroux, MacIntyre Investigates, Anna in Wonderland, BBC Documentaries, 1999–2001; Ed., Dispatches, 2002–04, Commissioning Ed., News and Current Affairs, 2004–06, Channel 4 TV. *Address:* Channel 4 Television, 124 Horseferry Road, SW1P 2TX. *T:* (020) 7306 5359; *e-mail:* ksutcliffe@channel4.co.uk.

SUTCLIFFE, Her Honour Linda, (Mrs P. B. Walker); a Circuit Judge, 1993–2006; *b* 2 Dec. 1946; *d* of James Loftus Woodward and Florence Woodward; *m* 1st, 1968 (marr. diss. 1979); 2nd, 1987, Peter Brian Walker. *Educ:* Eccles Grammar Sch.; LSE (LLB Hons 1968); Open Univ. (Dip. French 2007). Called to the Bar, Gray's Inn, 1975; Lectr in Law, Univ. of Sheffield, 1968–76, part-time 1976–81; in practice at the Bar, 1976–93; a Recorder, 1991–93. Part-time Chm., Industrial Tribunals, 1983–92. *Recreations:* music, gardening, croquet.

SUTCLIFFE, Tom; *see* Sutcliffe, J. T.

SUTER, Helen Anne; *see* Alexander, H. A.

SUTER, Michael; solicitor in private practice, 1992–2002; Chief Executive, Shropshire County Council, 1987–92; *b* 21 Jan. 1944; *s* of Robert and Rose Suter; *m* 1963, Sandra Harrison; two *s*. *Educ:* Liverpool Collegiate Sch.; Liverpool Univ. (LLB). Solicitor. Dep. Chief Exec., Notts CC, 1980–87. *Recreations:* music, gardening, watching old Hollywood films, visiting Spain. *Address:* 1 Creamor Corner, Wem, Shrewsbury, Shropshire SY4 5YB.

SUTHERELL, Maj.-Gen. John Christopher Blake, CB 2002; CBE 1993 (OBE 1990; MBE 1982); DL; General Secretary, Officers' Association, since 2003; *b* 23 Oct. 1947; *s* of Ernest John and Vera Louise Sutherell; *m* 1st, 1979, Stephanie Glover (*d* 1983); 2nd, 1987, Amanda Maxwell-Hudson; one *d*. *Educ:* Christ's Hosp., Horsham; Durham Univ. (BA Hons Geog. 1968); Staff Coll., Camberley. Commnd Royal Anglian Regt, 1968; SO1 DS Staff Coll., 1984–87; CO, 1st Bn, Royal Anglian Regt, 1987–90; Divl Col, Staff Coll., 1990; Comdr, 8th Inf. Bde, 1990–92; Mem., RCDS, 1993; Dep. Mil. Sec. (A), 1994–96; DSF, 1996–99; Comdt, RMCS, 1999–2002. Col Comdt, Queen's Div., 1999–2002; Col, Royal Anglian Regt, 2002–07 (Dep. Col, 1997–2002). Pres., Royal Norfolk Regt Assoc., 2000–. Mem. Council, Army Records Soc., 2001–05 and 2006–. Mem., Exec. Cttee, COBSEO, 2006–. Governor: Heathfield Sch., Ascot, 2004–06; Heathfield St Mary's Sch., Ascot, 2006–. DL Suffolk, 2006. *Recreations:* family, military history.

SUTHERLAND, family name of **Countess of Sutherland** and **Baron Sutherland of Houndwood**.

SUTHERLAND, 7th Duke of, *cr* 1833; **Francis Ronald Egerton;** Bt 1620; Baron Gower 1703; Earl Gower, Viscount Trentham 1746; Marquis of Stafford 1786; Viscount Brackley and Earl of Ellesmere 1846; *b* 18 Feb. 1940; *o s* of Cyril Reginald Egerton and Mary, *d* of Rt Hon. Sir Ronald Hugh Campbell, GCMG; *S* cousin, 2000; *m* 1974, Victoria Mary, twin *d* of Maj.-Gen. Edward Alexander Wilmot Williams, CB, CBE, MC; two *s*. *Educ:* Eton; RAC Cirencester. *Heir:* *s* Marquis of Stafford, *qv*. *Address:* Mertoun, St Boswells, Melrose, Roxburghshire TD6 0EA.

SUTHERLAND, Countess of (24th in line) *cr* (*c*) 1235; **Elizabeth Millicent Sutherland;** Lady Strathnaver (*c*) 1235; Chief of Clan Sutherland; *b* 30 March 1921; *o c* of Lord Alistair St Clair Sutherland-Leveson-Gower, MC (*d* 1921; 2nd *s* of 4th Duke), and Baroness Osten Driesen (*d* 1931); *niece* of 5th Duke of Sutherland, KT, PC; *S* (to uncle's Earldom of Sutherland and Lordship of Strathnaver), 1963; *m* 1946, Charles Noel Janson (DL, 1959–93), late Welsh Guards (*d* 2006); two *s* one *d* (and one *s* decd). *Educ:* Queen's College, Harley Street, W1, and abroad. Land Army, 1939–41; Laboratory Technician: Raigmore Hospital, Inverness, 1941–43; St Thomas' Hospital, SE1, 1943–45. Chm., Dunrobin Castle Ltd. *Recreations:* reading, swimming. *Heir:* *e s* Lord Strathnaver, *qv*. *Address:* Dunrobin Castle, Sutherland; House of Tongue, by Lairg, Sutherland; 39 Edwardes Square, W8 6HH.

SUTHERLAND OF HOUNDWOOD, Baron *cr* 2001 (Life Peer), of Houndwood in the Scottish Borders; **Stewart Ross Sutherland,** KT 2002; Kt 1995; FBA 1992; FRSE; President, Royal Society of Edinburgh, 2002–05; *b* 25 Feb. 1941; *s* of late George A. C. Sutherland and of Ethel (*née* Masson); *m* 1964, Sheena Robertson; one *s* two *d*. *Educ:* Woodside Sch.; Robert Gordon's Coll.; Univ. of Aberdeen (MA); Corpus Christi Coll.,

Cambridge (Hon. Schol.; MA; Hon. Fellow, 1989). FRSE 1995. Asst Lectr in Philosophy, UCNW, 1965; Lectr in Philosophy, 1968, Sen. Lectr, 1972, Reader, 1976, Univ. of Stirling; King's College London: Prof. of Hist. and Philos. of Religion, 1977–85, Titular Prof., 1985–94; Vice-Principal, 1981–85; Principal, 1985–90; FKC 1983; Vice-Chancellor, London Univ., 1990–94; Chief Inspector of Schools, 1992–94; Principal and Vice-Chancellor, Univ. of Edinburgh, 1994–2002; Provost, Gresham Coll., 2002–08; Pro-Chancellor, London Univ., 2006–08. Vis. Fellow, ANU, 1974; Gillespie Vis. Prof., Wooster Ohio, 1975. Lectures: Hope, Stirling, 1979; Ferguson, Manchester, 1982; Wilde, Oxford, 1981–84; Boutwood, Cambridge, 1990; F. D. Maurice, KCL, 1993; Drummond, Stirling, 1993; St George's, Windsor, 1993; Debrabant, Southampton, 1994; Ballard Matthews, Bangor, 1994; Cook, St Andrews and Oxford, 1995; Sir Robert Menzies, Melbourne, 1995. Non-executive Director: NHP, 2001–05; Quarry Products Assoc., 2002–05; Chm., YTL Education (UK), 2003–. Chairman: British Acad. Postgrad. Studentships Cttee, 1987–95; Royal Inst. of Philosophy, 1988–2006; London Conf. on Overseas Students, 1989–94; Cttee on Appeals Criteria and Procedure (Scotland), 1994–96; Associated Bd of Royal Schs of Music, 2006–; Vice-Chm., CVCP, 1989–92. Member: C of E Bd of Educn, 1980–84; Arts Sub-Cttee, UGC, 1983–85; City Parochial Foundn, 1988–90; Council for Sci. and Technology, 1993–2001; Humanities Res. Bd, Brit. Acad., 1994–95; UGC (Hong Kong), 1995–2003; HEFCE, 1996–2002. Chm., Royal Commn on Long Term Care of the Elderly, 1997–99; Member: NW Thames RHA, 1992–94; N Thames RHA, 1994. President: Soc. for the Study of Theology, 1985, 1986; Saltire Soc., 2002–05; Alzheimer Scotland, 2002–; David Hume Inst., 2005–08. Patron, Centre for Dementia, UCL, 2008–. Chm., Ethiopian Gemini Trust, 1987–92. Editor, Religious Studies, 1984–90; Member, Editorial Board: Scottish Jl of Religious Studies, 1980–95; Modern Theology, 1984–91. Associate Fellow, Warwick Univ., 1986–; Hon. Fellow: UCNW, 1990; Birkbeck Coll., London, 2004; Inst. of Educn, London Univ., 2004. FCP 1994. Hon. FRCGP 2004. Hon. LHD: Wooster, Ohio, 1986; Commonwealth Univ. of Virginia, 1992; New York, 1996; Hon. LLD: Aberdeen, 1990; NUI, 1992; St Andrews, 2002; McGill, 2003; Hon. DLitt: Richmond Coll., 1995; Wales, 1996; Glasgow, 1999; Warwick, 2001; Queen Margaret UC, 2004; London, 2004; DUniv Stirling, 1993; Dr hc: Uppsala, 1995; Edinburgh, 2004; Hon. DEd: Robert Gordon, 2005; HK Inst. of Educn, 2005. Publications: Atheism and the Rejection of God, 1977, 2nd edn 1980; (ed with B. L. Hebblethwaite) The Philosophical Frontiers of Christian Theology, 1983; God, Jesus and Belief, 1984; Faith and Ambiguity, 1984; (ed) The World's Religions, 1988; (ed with T. A. Roberts) Religion, Reason and the Self, 1989; articles in books and learned jls. Recreations: Tassie medallions, theatre, jazz. Address: House of Lords, SW1A 0PW; e-mail: sutherlands@parliament.uk. Club: New (Edinburgh).

SUTHERLAND, Rt Hon. Lord; Ranald Iain Sutherland; PC 2000; a Senator of the College of Justice in Scotland, 1985–2001; b 23 Jan. 1932; s of J. W. and A. K. Sutherland, Edinburgh; m 1964, Janice Mary, d of W. S. Miller, Edinburgh; two s. Educ: Edinburgh Academy; Edinburgh University (MA 1951, LLB 1953). Admitted to Faculty of Advocates, 1956; QC (Scot.) 1969. Advocate Depute, 1962–64, 1971–77; Standing Junior Counsel to Min. of Defence (Army Dept), 1964–69. Mem., Criminal Injuries Compensation Bd, 1977–85. Surveillance Comr, 2001–. Justice of Appeal, Botswana, 2002–05. Recreations: sailing, shooting. Address: 38 Lauder Road, Edinburgh EH9 1UE. T: (0131) 667 5280. Clubs: New (Edinburgh); Hon. Company of Edinburgh Golfers.

SUTHERLAND, Alan David Alexander; Chief Executive, Water Industry Commission for Scotland, since 2005 (Water Industry Commissioner for Scotland, 1999–2005); b Glasgow, 8 April 1962; s of George and Kathleen Sutherland; m 1994, Olga Krasnorylkina; one s one d. Educ: Univ. of St Andrews (MA Hons Mod. Russian Studies 1984); Univ. of Pennsylvania (MBA 1993; MA 1993). Mgt trainee, Lloyds Bank, London, 1984; Analyst, Savory Milln & Co., London, 1985; Analyst, 1986–88, Manager, 1988–92, Robert Fleming and Co., London; Consultant, 1992–95, Team Leader, 1995–97, Bain & Co., Moscow, London and Kiev; Man. Dir, Wolverine Russia Ltd, and Gen. Dir, Wolverine CIS, Moscow and Grand Rapids, Mich, 1997–99. Beesley Lect., RA, 2006. Recreations: theatre, fine restaurants, family trips to Walt Disney World in Florida. Address: 2 Northbank Farm Steadings, Strathkinness High Road, St Andrews, Fife KY16 9TZ. T: (01334) 473535, Fax: (office) (01786) 462018; e-mail: alan.sutherland@ watercommission.co.uk, Alan@northbankfarmsteadings.freeserve.co.uk.

SUTHERLAND, Colin John MacLean; see Carloway, Hon. Lord.

SUTHERLAND, Euan Ross, CB 1993; Parliamentary Counsel, 1989–2003; b 24 Nov. 1943; s of Dr Alister Sutherland and Margaret Sutherland; m 1st, 1967, Katharine Mary Jenkins, qv (marr. diss. 1995); one s one d; 2nd, 2002, Mary Anne Kenyon. Educ: Kingswood Sch., Bath; Balliol Coll., Oxford (BA Hist.). Called to the Bar, Inner Temple, 1969; Office of the Parliamentary Counsel, 1974–2003; seconded to: Govt of Solomon Is, 1979–81; Law Commn, 1986–88. Recreations: music, gardening, hill-walking. Address: 57 Sutherland Square, SE17 3EL.

SUTHERLAND, Prof. Grant Robert, AC 1998; FRS 1996; FAA; Emeritus Geneticist, Department of Genetic Medicine (formerly Laboratory Genetics), Women's and Children's Hospital, Adelaide, since 2007 (WCH Foundation Research Fellow, 2002–07); Affiliate Professor, Department of Paediatrics, University of Adelaide, since 1991; b 2 June 1945; s of John Sutherland and Hazel Wilson Mason McClelland; m 1979, Elizabeth Dougan; one s one d. Educ: Numurkah High Sch.; Univ. of Melbourne (BSc 1967; MSc 1971); Univ. of Edinburgh (PhD 1974; DSc 1984). FAA 1997. Cytogeneticist, Mental Health Authy, Melbourne, 1967; Cytogeneticist i/c, Royal Hosp. for Sick Children, Edinburgh, 1971; Dir, Dept of Cytogenetics and Molecular Genetics, Women's and Children's Hosp., Adelaide, 1975–2002. Internat. Res. Scholar, Howard Hughes Med. Inst., Maryland, 1993–97. President: Human Genetics Soc. of Australasia, 1989–91; Human Genome Orgn, 1996–97. Hon. FRCPA 1994. Australia Prize in Molecular Genetics (jtly), 1998. Publications: (with F. Hecht) Fragile Sites on Human Chromosomes, 1985; (with R. J. M. Gardner) Chromosome Abnormalities and Genetic Counselling, 1989, 3rd edn 2003; numerous papers in sci. and med. jls. Recreation: beef cattle farming. Address: Department of Genetic Medicine, Women's and Children's Hospital, Adelaide, SA 5006, Australia. T: (8) 81617284; e-mail: grant.sutherland@adelaide.edu.au; POB 300, Macclesfield, SA 5153, Australia. T: (8) 83889524.

SUTHERLAND, Dr Ian Boyd; Senior Administrative Medical Officer, South Western Regional Hospital Board, 1970–73; Regional Medical Officer, South Western Regional Health Authority, 1973–80; b 19 Oct. 1926; s of William Sutherland and Grace Alexandra Campbell; m 1950, Charlotte Winifred Cordin; two d. Educ: Bradford Grammar Sch.; Edinburgh Univ. MB, ChB; FRCPE, FFCM, DPH. Medical Officer, RAF, 1950–52; Asst MOH, Counties of Roxburgh and Selkirk, 1953–55; Dep. MOH, County and Borough of Inverness, 1955–59; Dep. County MOH, Oxfordshire CC, 1959–60; Asst SMO, Leeds Regional Hosp. Bd, 1960–63; Dep. Sen. Admin. MO, SW Regl Hosp Bd, 1963–70; Community Medicine Specialist, Lothian Health Bd, 1980–86. Research Fellow, Dept of Clin. Surgery, Univ. of Edinburgh, 1986–88. Recreations: reading, art. Address: 8 Chesterfield Road, Eastbourne, E Sussex BN20 7NU.

SUTHERLAND, Dame Joan, OM 1991; AC 1975 DBE 1979 (CBE 1961); soprano; b 7 Nov. 1926; d of McDonald Sutherland, Sydney, NSW, and Muriel Alston Sutherland; m 1954, Richard Bonynge, qv; one s. Educ: St Catherine's, Waverley, Sydney. Début as Dido in Purcell's Dido and Aeneas, Sydney, 1947; subsequently concerts, oratorios and broadcasts throughout Australia. Came to London, 1951; joined Covent Garden, 1952, where she remained resident soprano for 7 years; won international fame with début as Lucia di Lammermoor, Covent Garden, 1959, and by early 1960s had sung throughout the Americas and Europe. Has specialised throughout her career in the popular and lesser-known bel canto operatic repertoire of 18th and 19th centuries, and has made many recordings. Hon. DMus: Sydney, 1984; Oxon, 1992. Publications: The Joan Sutherland Album (autobiog., with Richard Bonynge), 1986; A Prima Donna's Progress: the autobiography of Joan Sutherland, 1997; relevant publications: Joan Sutherland, by R. Braddon, 1962; Joan Sutherland, by E. Greenfield, 1972; La Stupenda, by B. Adams, 1980; Joan Sutherland, by Norma Major, 1987. Recreations: reading, gardening, needlepoint. Address: c/o Ingpen & Williams, 7 St George's Court, 131 Putney Bridge Road, SW15 2PA.

SUTHERLAND, John Alexander Muir; Chief Executive, Celtic Films Ltd, since 1986; b 5 April 1933; m 1970, Mercedes Gonzalez; two s. Educ: India; Trinity Coll., Glenalmond; Hertford Coll., Oxford (MA). 2nd Lieut, HLI, 1952–53. Economist, Fed. Govt of Nigeria, 1957–58; film production, Spain and Portugal, 1958–62; Head of Presentation and Programme Planning, Border TV, 1963–66; Programme Co-Ordinator: ABC TV, 1966–68; Thames TV, 1968–72; Controller of Programme Sales, Thames TV, 1973–74; Man. Dir, 1975–82, Dep. Chm., 1982–86, Thames TV Internat.; Dir of Programmes, Thames TV, 1982–86. Dir, Border TV, 1986–. Productions include: The Saint (TV), 1989; The Monk (film), 1990; Red Fox (TV), 1991; Sharpe (TV films), 1992–96; Kiszko (TV film), 1998; Girl from Rio (film), 2000; Sherpa Challenge (TV film), 2005. Address: Celtic Films Entertainment Ltd, Lodge House, 69 Beaufort Street, SW3 5AH.

SUTHERLAND, Prof. John Andrew, PhD; FRSL; Lord Northcliffe Professor of Modern English Literature, University College London, 1992–2004, now Emeritus; b 9 Oct. 1938; s of Jack Sutherland and Elizabeth (née Salter); m 1st, 1967, Guilland Watt (marr. diss. 2005); one s; 2nd, 2005, Sarah Lee. Educ: Colchester Royal Grammar Sch.; Leicester Univ. (BA 1964; MA 1966); Edinburgh Univ. (PhD 1973). FRSL 1991. Nat. Service, 2nd Lieut, Suffolk Regt, 1958–60. Lectr in English, Univ. of Edinburgh, 1965–72; Lectr, then Reader in English, UCL, 1972–84, Fellow, 2004; Prof. of English, CIT, 1984–92. Hon. DLitt: Leicester, 1998; Surrey, 2002. Publications: Thackeray at Work, 1974; Victorian Novelists and Publishers, 1976; Fiction and the Fiction Industry, 1978; Bestsellers, 1980; Offensive Literature, 1982; The Longman Companion to Victorian Fiction, 1989; Mrs Humphry Ward, 1992; The Life of Walter Scott: a critical biography, 1995; Victorian Fiction: writers, publishers, readers, 1995; (ed) The Oxford Book of English Love Stories, 1996; Is Heathcliff a Murderer?, 1996; Can Jane Eyre Be Happy?, 1997; Who Betrays Elizabeth Bennet?, 1999; Reading the Decades, 2002 (televised, 2002); Stephen Spender, 2004; How to Read a Novel: a user's guide, 2006; The Boy Who Loved Books: a memoir, 2007; Bestsellers: a very short introduction, 2007; Curiosities of Literature: a book-lover's anthology of literary erudition, 2008. Recreation: walking. Address: Department of English, University College London, Gower Street, WC1E 6BT. T: (020) 7679 2000.

SUTHERLAND, John Brewer; (3rd Bt cr 1921, but does not use the title); b 19 Oct. 1931; s of Sir (Benjamin) Ivan Sutherland, 2nd Bt, and Marjorie Constance Daniel (d 1980), yr d of Frederic William Brewer, OBE; S father, 1980; m 1st, 1958, Alice Muireall (d 1984), d of late W. Stamford Henderson, Kelso; three s one d; 2nd, 1988, Heather, d of late David A. Gray, Chester-le-Street. Educ: Sedbergh; St Catharine's Coll., Cambridge. Heir: s Peter William Sutherland [b 18 May 1963; m 1988, Suzanna Mary, d of R. M. Gledson; one s two d].

SUTHERLAND, John Menzies, Eur Ing, CEng, FICE, FIStructE; Secretary, Joint Board of Moderators, Institution of Civil Engineers, 1985–93; b 19 June 1928; s of John Menzies and Margaret Rae Sutherland; m 1962, Margaret Mary (née Collins); one s one d. Educ: Royal Technical Coll., Glasgow. FIStructE 1962; CEng, FICE 1968; Eur Ing 1988. Indentured Civil Engineer, City Engineer, Glasgow, 1945–51; Engineer, Costains Group, 1952–56; Site Agent, Pakistan and Chief Engineer, Middle East, Gammon Group, 1956–61; Engineer Adviser (Colombo Plan), new capital city, Islamabad, Pakistan, 1962–66; Associate Partner, Bullen & Partners, 1966–69; Chief Civil Engineer, overseas plant construction, Union International Co. (Vestey Gp Holding Co.), 1970–74; Board Dir and Dir Engineering Projects, Internat. Military Services Ltd, 1974–83 (2 years Malaysia); Gen. Manager, BTR–Swire Projects, Singapore, 1983–85. Publication: Naval Bases and Infrastructure, 1979. Recreations: music, collecting Victorian ceramics. Address: 6 Fursefield Close, Chislehurst, Kent BR7 5DE. T: (020) 8467 0037. Clubs: Royal Over-Seas League; Chislehurst Golf.

SUTHERLAND, Prof. Kathryn, DPhil; Professor of Bibliography and Textual Criticism, University of Oxford, since 2002; Professorial Fellow, St Anne's College, Oxford, since 1996; b 7 July 1950; d of Ian Donald Sutherland and Joyce Sutherland (née Bartaby). Educ: Bedford Coll., Univ. of London (BA 1971); Somerville Coll., Oxford (DPhil 1978; MA 1996). Lectr in English Literature, Univ. of Manchester, 1975–93; Prof. of modern English Literature, Univ. of Nottingham, 1993–96; Reader in Bibliography and Textual Criticism, 1996–2002. Publications: Adam Smith: interdisciplinary essays, 1995; Electronic Text: method and theory, 1997; Women Prose Writers 1780–1830, 1998; Jane Austen's Textual Lives: from Aeschylus to Bollywood, 2005; Transferred Illusions: digital technology and the forms of print, 2009; critical edns; contrib. books and learned jls. Recreation: gardening. Address: St Anne's College, Oxford OX2 6HS. T: (01865) 274893.

SUTHERLAND, Lorraine; Editor, Official Report (Hansard), since 2005; b 11 Jan. 1958; d of Bunty Sutherland (now Potts); m 1982, Robert Kremer. Educ: Lybster Primary Sch.; Wick High Sch.; Aberdeen Coll. of Commerce. Official Report (Hansard): Principal Asst Editor, 1994–97; Dep. Editor, 1997–2005. Recreations: travelling, planning travel, tennis, cinema, theatre, dreaming on trains. Address: Department of the Official Report, House of Commons, SW1A 0AA. T: (020) 7219 3388; e-mail: sutherlandl@parliament.uk.

SUTHERLAND, Muir; see Sutherland, J. A. M.

SUTHERLAND, Peter Denis, Hon. KCMG 2004; SC; Chairman: Goldman Sachs International, since 1995; BP (formerly BP Amoco), 1998–2009 (Chairman, The British Petroleum Co. plc, 1997–98); London School of Economics, since 2008; b 25 April 1946; s of W. G. Sutherland and Barbara Sutherland (née Nealon); m 1971, Maria Del Pilar Cabria Valcarcel; two s one d. Educ: Gonzaga Coll.; University Coll. Dublin (BCL). Called to Bar: King's Inns, 1968; Middle Temple, 1976, Bencher, 1981 (Hon. Bencher, 2002); Attorney of New York Bar, 1981; Attorney and Counsellor of Supreme Court of USA, 1986. Tutor in Law, University Coll., Dublin, 1968–71; practising member of Irish Bar, 1968–81, and 1981–82; Senior Counsel 1980; Attorney General of Ireland, June

1981–Feb. 1982 and Dec. 1982–Dec. 1984; Mem. Council of State, 1981–82 and 1982–84; Comr for Competition and Comr for Social Affairs and Educn, EEC, 1985–86, for Competition and Relns with European Parliament, 1986–88; Chm., Allied Irish Banks, 1989–93; Dir Gen., GATT, later WTO, 1993–95. Director: GPA, 1989–93; CRH plc, 1989–93; James Crean plc, 1989–93; Delta Air Lines Inc., 1990–93; Investor, 1995–2005; Telefonaktiebolaget LM Ericsson, 1996–2004; Royal Bank of Scotland, 2001–. Chm., Consultative Bd of Dir Gen., WTO; Consultant, Admin of Patrimony of Holy See, 2007–. Chm. (Europe), Trilateral Commn., 2001–. Pres., Federal Trust. Chm., Bd of Govs, Eur. Inst. of Public Admin, 1991–96. Goodwill Ambassador, UNIDO, 2005; Special Rep. of UN Sec.-Gen. for Migration, 2006–. Hon. Bencher, King's Inns, Dublin, 1995. Hon. LLD: St Louis, 1986; NUI, 1990; Dublin City, 1991; Holy Cross, Mass, 1994; Bath, 1995; Suffolk, USA, 1995; TCD, 1996; Reading, 1997; Nottingham, 1999; Exeter, 2000; DUniv Open, 1995. Gold Medal, Eur. Parlt, 1988; NZ Commemorative Medal, 1990; David Rockefeller Internat. Leadership Award, 1996. KCSG 2008. Grand Cross: King Leopold II (Belgium), 1989; Order of Infante Dom Henrique (Portugal), 1998; Grand Cross of Civil Merit (Spain), 1989; Chevalier, Légion d'Honneur (France), 1993; Comdr, Order of Ouissam Alaouite (Morocco), 1994; Order of Rio Branco (Brazil), 1996. *Publications:* Premier Janvier 1993 ce qui va changer en Europe, 1988; contribs to law jls. *Recreations:* sports generally, reading. *Address:* Goldman Sachs International, Peterborough Court, 133 Fleet Street, EC4A 2BB. *Clubs:* Hibernian United Service, Fitzwilliam Lawn Tennis (Dublin); Lansdowne FC.

SUTHERLAND, Ranald Iain; see Sutherland, Rt Hon. Lord.

SUTHERLAND, Prof. Rosamund Jane, PhD; Professor of Education, since 1996, University of Bristol (Head, Graduate School of Education, 2003–06); *b* 19 Jan. 1947; *d* of Percy and Joan Hatfield; *m* 1968, Ian Sutherland; one *s* one *d*. *Educ:* Monmouth Sch. for Girls; Univ. of Bristol (BSc); Hatfield Poly. (Cert Ed); Inst. of Educn, Univ. of London (PhD 1988). Programmer/Analyst, BAC, 1968–69; Res. Asst, Dept of Physiology, Univ. of Bristol, 1969–71; Tutor, Open Univ., 1975–83; Lectr, De Havilland Further Educn Coll., 1979–83; Lectr and Dir of Res. Projects, 1983–93, Sen. Lectr, 1993–96, Inst. of Educn, Univ. of London. Chm., Jt Mathematical Council of the UK, 2006– (Chm., Jt Mathematical Council and Royal Soc. Wkg Gp on Changes to Sch. Algebra, 1997 (report pubd 1997)). *Publications:* (with C. Hoyles) Logo Mathematics in the Classroom, 1989; (with L. Healy) Exploring Mathematics with Spreadsheets, 1990; (ed with J. Mason) Exploiting Mental Imagery with Computers in Mathematics Education, 1995; (with S. Pozzi) The Changing Mathematical Background of Undergraduate Engineers, 1995; (jtly) A Spreadsheet Approach to Maths for GNVQ Engineering, 1996; (ed jtly) Perspectives on School Algebra, 2000; (ed jtly) Learning and Teaching Where Worldviews Meet, 2003; (jtly) Children's Computing in the home (screenplay), 2003; Teaching for Learning Mathematics, 2006. *Recreations:* reading, cycling, dining out, tango. *Address:* 8 Canynge Square, Clifton, Bristol BS8 3LA.

SUTHERLAND, Dame Veronica (Evelyn), DBE 1998; CMG 1988; HM Diplomatic Service, retired; President, Lucy Cavendish College, Cambridge University, 2001–08; *b* 25 April 1939; *d* of late Lt-Col Maurice George Beckett, KOYLI, and of Constance Mary Cavenagh-Mainwaring; *m* 1981, Alex James Sutherland. *Educ:* Royal Sch., Bath; London Univ. (BA); Southampton Univ. (MA); MA Cantab 2001. Joined HM Diplomatic Service, 1965; Second, later First Sec., Copenhagen, 1967–70; FCO, 1970–75; First Sec., New Delhi, 1975–78; FCO, 1978–80; Counsellor, 1981; Perm. UK Deleg. to UNESCO, 1981–84; Counsellor, FCO, 1984–87; Ambassador to Côte d'Ivoire, 1987–90; Asst Under-Sec. of State (Personnel), FCO, 1990–95; Ambassador to Republic of Ireland, 1995–99; Dep. Sec. Gen. (Econ. and Social Affairs), Commonwealth Secretariat, 1999–2001. Chm., Airey Neave Trust, 2000–; Member: Exec. Cttee, British/Irish Assoc., 2002–; Cttee, Elizabeth Nuffield Educnl Fund, 2005–08. Hon. LLD TCD, 1998. *Recreations:* theatre, painting. *Address:* c/o The Athenaeum, SW1Y 5ER.

SUTHERLAND, Sir William (George MacKenzie), Kt 1988; QPM 1981; HM Chief Inspector of Constabulary for Scotland, 1996–98; *b* 12 Nov. 1933; *m* 1957, Jennie Abbott; two *d*. *Educ:* Inverness Technical High Sch. Cheshire Police, 1954–73; Surrey Police, 1973–75; Hertfordshire Police, 1975–79; Chief Constable: Bedfordshire, 1979–83; Lothian and Borders Police, 1983–96. Hon. Sec., ACPO in Scotland, 1985–96; Chm., British Police Athletic Assoc., 1991–96 (Chm., Squash Section, 1984–96; Chm., Ski Section, 1992–96). *Recreations:* golf, ski-ing, hill walking.

SUTHERLAND, Prof. William James, PhD; Miriam Rothschild Professor of Conservation Biology, University of Cambridge, since 2006; *b* 27 April 1956; *s* of late Alasdair Cameron Sutherland and of Gwyneth Audrey Sutherland; *m* 1996, Nicola Jane Crockford; two *d*. *Educ:* Univ. of East Anglia (BSc); Liverpool Poly. (PhD). NERC Postdoctoral Fellow, Wolfson Coll., Oxford, 1980–82; Lectr, Zoology Dept, Liverpool Univ., 1982–83; University of East Anglia: Demonstrator, Sch. of Envmtl Scis, 1983–85; Lectr, 1985–93, Reader, 1993–96, Prof. of Biology, 1996–2006, Sch. of Biol Scis; Nuffield Fellow, 1992–93. Trustee, FFI, 1998–. Scientific Medal, Zool Soc., 1997; Marsh Award for Ecology, British Ecol Soc., 2001; Marsh Award for Conservation Biol., Zool Soc., 2005. *Publications:* (ed with D. A. Hill) Habitat Management, 1995; From Individual Behaviour to Population Ecology, 1996; (ed) Ecological Census Techniques: a handbook, 1996, 2nd edn 2006; (ed) Conservation Science and Action, 1998; The Conservation Handbook: research, management and policy techniques, 2000; (ed with L. M. Gosling) Behaviour and Conservation, 2000; (ed jtly) Bird Ecology and Conservation: a handbook of techniques, 2004; articles on ecology, behaviour and conservation in scientific jls. *Recreations:* natural history, prehistory, photography, painting, cooking. *Address:* Department of Zoology, Cambridge University, Downing Street, Cambridge CB2 3EJ; *e-mail:* w.sutherland@zoo.cam.ac.uk.

SUTHERS, Martin William, OBE 1988; DL; Consultant, Fraser Brown, Solicitors, since 2005; *b* 27 June 1940; *s* of Rev. Canon George Suthers and Susie Mary Suthers (*née* Jobson); *m* 1st, 1970, Daphne Joan Oxland (marr. diss. 1988); 2nd, 1990, Philippa Leah Melville la Borde. *Educ:* Dulwich Coll.; Christ's Coll., Cambridge (MA). Admitted Solicitor, 1965. Asst Solicitor, Wells, Hind, 1965–66; Conveyancing Asst, Clerk's Dept, Notts CC, 1966–69; Asst Solicitor, Fishers, 1969–70; Partner, 1971–92, Sen. Partner, 1992–2000, J. A. Simpson & Coulby, then Hopkins (following merger); Consultant, Hopkins, 2000–05. Pres., Notts Law Soc., 1998–99. Chairman: Queen's Med. Centre Nottingham Univ. Hosp. NHS Trust, 1993–2000; Rushcliffe PCT, 2004–06. Pres., Notts Valuation Tribunal, 1999–. Mem. (C), Nottingham CC, 1967–69, 1976–95, Notts CC, 2000–; Lord Mayor of Nottingham, 1988–89; Hon. Alderman, 1997. DL Notts 1999. Chm., Notts Wildlife Trust, 2004–. *Recreation:* ornithology. *Address:* The Manor House, Main Street, Flintham, Newark, Notts NG23 5LA. *T:* (01636) 525554.

SUTHIWART-NARUEPUT, Dr Owart, Kt Grand Cordon: Order of Crown of Thailand, 1981; Order of White Elephant, 1985; Hon. CMG 1972; Permanent Secretary for Foreign Affairs, Thailand, 1979–80; *b* 19 Sept. 1926; *s* of Luang Suthiwart-Narueput and Mrs Khae; *m* 1959, Angkana (*née* Sthapitanond); one *s* one *d*. *Educ:* Thammasat Univ., Thailand (BA Law); Fletcher Sch. of Law and Diplomacy, Tufts Univ., USA (MA, PhD);

Nat. Defence Coll. Joined Min. of For. Affairs, 1945; Asst Sec. to Minister, 1958; SEATO Res. Officer, 1959; Protocol Dept, 1963; Econ. Dept, 1964; Counsellor, Thai Embassy, Canberra, 1965; Dir-Gen. of Inf. Dept, 1969; Ambassador to India, Nepal, Sri Lanka, and Minister to Afghanistan, 1972; Ambassador to Poland, E Germany and Bulgaria, 1976; Dir-Gen. of Political Dept, 1977; Ambassador to France and Perm. Representative to UNESCO, 1980; Ambassador: to Switzerland and to Holy See, 1983; to UK, 1984–86, concurrently to Ireland, 1985–86. Mem., Civil Service Bd, Min. of Foreign Affairs, 1994–. Commander: Order of Phoenix, Greece, 1963; Order of Orange-Nassau, Netherlands, 1963; Bintang Djasa (1st Cl.), Indonesia, 1970; Order of Merit, Poland, 1979; Grand Officier, l'Ordre Nat. du Mérite, France, 1983. *Publication:* The Evolution of Thailand's Foreign Relations since 1855: from extraterritoriality to equality, 1955. *Recreations:* reading, music. *Address:* 193 Lane 4 Navathanee, Serithai Road, Kannayao, Bangkok 10230, Thailand. *Clubs:* Old England Students' Association, American University Alumni Association (Bangkok).

SUTLIEFF, Barry John; communications consultant; Director, Communications and Learning, Civil Contingencies Secretariat, Cabinet Office, 2001–02; *b* 26 Dec. 1942; *s* of Basil Eric and Ruby Ellen Sutlieff; *m* 1967, Linda Valerie Hook; one *s* one *d*. *Educ:* Brooklands Coll., Weybridge; Coll. for Distributive Trades, London (CAM Dip. PR). Trainee advertising exec., 1961–66; gen. publicity roles, Depts of Trade, Transport and the Envmt, and Price Commn, 1966–75; Chief Press Officer: DoE, 1975–79; Dept of Trade, 1979–83; Dep. Hd of Inf., Home Office, Feb.–July 1985; Dir, Inf. Services, MSC, 1985–87; Director: of Inf., Dept of Employment, 1987–94; of Communication, Cabinet Office, 1994–2000; Fellow, Centre for Management and Policy Studies, Cabinet Office, 2000–01. Non-exec. Dir, Lewis Live Ltd, 2004–06. *Recreations:* travel, reading modern history, lifelong Dickens fanatic, sport, notably football and cricket. *Address:* The Hollies, 26 Hutton Road, Ash Vale, Aldershot, Hants GU12 5HA. *T:* (01252) 654727.

SUTTIE, Sir James (Edward) Grant-, 9th Bt *cr* 1702, of Balgone, Haddingtonshire; farmer; *b* 29 May 1965; *o s* of Sir Philip Grant-Suttie, 8th Bt and of Elspeth Mary Grant-Suttie (*née* Urquhart); *S* father, 1997; *m* 1st, 1989, Emma Jane Craig (marr. diss. 1996); one *s*; 2nd, 1997, Sarah Jane Smale; two *s*. *Educ:* Fettes Coll., Edinburgh; Aberdeen Coll. of Agric. *Recreations:* golf, shooting. *Heir:* *s* Gregor Grant-Suttie, *b* 29 Oct. 1991.

SUTTLE, Stephen John; QC 2003; *b* 28 Sept. 1949; *s* of Ernest Suttle, DMus and Judith Suttle (*née* Gummer); *m* 1984, Rosemary Ann Warren (marr. diss. 2005); two *s* two *d*. *Educ:* Westminster Sch.; Christ Church, Oxford (MA Lit.Hum.). Asst classics master, Stowe Sch., 1973–78; called to the Bar, Gray's Inn, 1980; in practice, specialising in defamation, confidence, privacy and media law. *Recreations:* music, cricket. *Address:* 1 Brick Court, Temple, EC4Y 9BY. *T:* (020) 7353 8845, *Fax:* (020) 7583 9144; *e-mail:* ssuttle@onebrickcourt.com.

SUTTON, Prof. Adrian Peter, PhD; FRS 2003; Professor of Nanotechnology, Department of Physics, Imperial College London, since 2005; *b* 1 July 1955; *s* of Peter Michael Sutton and Beryl Margaret Sutton; partner, 1985, Patricia Joan White. *Educ:* St Catherine's Coll., Oxford (BA 1st cl. (Metallurgy and Sci. of Materials) 1978; MSc by res. 1978); Univ. of Pennsylvania (PhD 1980). CPhys, FInstP 2000; FIMMM 2000; CEng 2001; CChem, FRSC 2003. Oxford University: SRC postdoctoral researcher, 1981–83; Royal Soc. Res. Fellow, 1983–91; Lectr, 1991–97; Prof. of Materials Science, 1997–2004; Fellow, Linacre Coll., Oxford, 1991–2004; Prof. of Computational Engrg, Helsinki Univ. of Technol., 2002–04. *Publications:* Electronic Structure of Materials, 1993 (trans. German, 1996); (with R. W. Balluffi) Interfaces in Crystalline Materials, 1995, reissued 2006; numerous scientific papers in physics, materials science and chemistry jls. *Recreations:* cycling, walking with partner and Border Collie, history, especially of Finland. *Address:* 516 Banbury Road, Oxford OX2 8LG.

SUTTON, Alan John; Founder Chairman and Chief Executive, Anglolink Ltd, since 1985; *b* 16 March 1936; *s* of William Clifford Sutton and Emily Sutton (*née* Batten); *m* 1957, Glenis (*née* Henry); one *s* one *d*. *Educ:* Bristol Univ. BSc (Hons) Elec. Engrg; MIET. Design, Production and Trials Evaluation of Guided Missiles, English Electric Aviation Ltd, 1957–63; Design, Production, Sales and General Management of Scientific Digital, Analogue and Hybrid Computers, Solartron Electronic Group Ltd, 1963–69; International Sales Manager, Sales Director, of A. B. Electronic Components Ltd, 1969–73; Managing Director, A. B. Connectors, 1973–76; Industrial Dir, Welsh Office, 1976–79; Welsh Development Agency: Exec. Dir (Industry and Investment), 1979–83; Exec. Dir (Marketing), 1983–85; Sen. Vice-Pres., USA W Coast Div., WINvest, 1985–88. CEO, DigiTec Direct Ltd, subseq. Chm., A NOVO Digitec Ltd, 1998–2004; Dir, A NOVO UK Ltd, 2001–05; non-exec. Dir, A NOVO SA, 2003–; Chm., Conforto Financial Management Ltd, 2007–. *Recreation:* golf. *Address:* 56 Heol-y-Delyn, Lisvane, Cardiff CF14 0SR. *T:* (029) 2075 3194.

SUTTON, Barry Bridge; JP; MA; Headmaster, Taunton School, 1987–97; *b* 21 Jan. 1937; *s* of Albert and Ethel Sutton; *m* 1961, Margaret Helen (*née* Palmer); one *s* two *d*. *Educ:* Eltham Coll.; Peterhouse, Cambridge (MA Hist. Tripos); Bristol Univ. (PGCE). Asst Master and Housemaster, Wycliffe College, 1961–75; Headmaster, Hereford Cathedral School, 1975–87. Chairman: Cttee, Scout Assoc. Council, 1994–96; Som Co. Scout Council, 1994–; Nat. Scout Awards Bd, 2002–. Sec., Taunton ESU, 2000– (Chm., 1998–2004). Chm., Somerton Anglo-Italian Twinning, 1999–. Churchwarden, 2003–. JP Hereford, 1982, Taunton, 1987–2007 (Chm., Taunton Bench, 2005–06). *Recreations:* hill-walking, scouting. *Address:* Burt's Barn, Peak Lane, Dundon, Somerton, Somerset TA11 6NZ.

SUTTON, David Christopher, PhD; Director, Research Projects, University of Reading Library, since 1982; Leader, Reading Borough Council, 1995–2008; *b* 18 Oct. 1950; *e s* of Derek John Sutton and Sheila Sutton, Stourbridge; *m* 1973, Dr Deborah Jenkins. *Educ:* Leicester Univ. (BA; MA 1973); Sheffield Univ. (MA 1975); Université de Paris VIII; Polytechnic of Central London (PhD 1979). Librarian: Trinity Coll., Dublin, 1973–74; Polytechnic of Central London, 1975–76; BL, 1976–78; Warwick Univ. Library, 1980–82. Mem. (Lab) Reading BC, 1988–2008; Chm., Arts and Leisure Cttee, 1991–95. Chm., Reading Miners' Support Cttee, 1984–85; Trustee, Earley Charity, 1987–. UK Editor, Writers, Artists and Their Copyright Holders, 1994–. FRSA. Archivist of Year, Scone Foundn, 2006. Benson Medal for services to literature, RSL, 2002. *Publications:* Points of View in the Writing of History, 1981; (ed) Location Register of Twentieth-Century English Literary Manuscripts and Letters, 1988; (ed) Location Register of English Literary Manuscripts and Letters: eighteenth and nineteenth centuries, 1995; numerous articles on copyright, literary manuscripts and politics. *Recreations:* football, badminton, walking in Dorset, sitting by the Mediterranean. *Address:* The Coach House, 22 Eldon Place, Reading RG1 4ED; *e-mail:* D.C.Sutton@reading.ac.uk.

SUTTON, Dr (Howard) Michael, CChem, FRSC; Principal Research Fellow, University of Warwick, 1999–2003; *b* 12 Nov. 1942; *s* of Albert Sutton and Constance Olive Sutton (*née* Topham); *m* 1967, Diane Cash; one *s* one *d*. *Educ:* Univ. of Edinburgh (BSc 1965; PhD 1968). Res. Fellow, Univ. of Kent at Canterbury, 1968–70; Warren

Spring Laboratory: Materials Handling Div., 1970–78; Head, Planning and Marketing, 1978–85; Dep. Dir, 1985–88; Department of Trade and Industry: Head, Shipbuilding and Marine Engineering, 1988–91; Head, Single Market Unit, 1991–93; Head, Mech. Engrg Sponsorship, 1993–94; Dir, Trade and Industry, W Midlands, 1994–98; Hd of Secretariat, W Midlands Regl Devel t Agency (in preparation), 1998–99; Advr, Advantage W Midlands—the Develt Agency, 1999–2000. Non-exec. Dir, Manufg Foundn Ltd, 2001–03. *Publications:* contribs to learned jls. *Recreations:* philosophy, music, walking. *Address:* e-mail: sutton07@btinternet.com.

SUTTON, Prof. John, PhD; FBA 1996; Sir John Hicks Professor of Economics, London School of Economics and Political Science, since 1998 (Professor of Economics, 1988–98); *b* 10 Aug. 1948; *s* of John Sutton and Marie (*née* Hammond); *m* 1974, Jean Drechsler; one *s* two *d*. *Educ:* University Coll., Dublin (BSc Physics 1969); Trinity Coll., Dublin (MSc Econ. 1973); PhD Sheffield 1978. Voluntary service, UNA, Turkey, 1969–70; Mgt Services, Herbert-BSA, Coventry, 1970–72; Lectr, Sheffield Univ., 1973–77; Lectr, 1977–84, Reader, 1984–88, LSE. Visiting Professor: Tokyo Univ., 1981; Univ. of Calif, San Diego, 1986; Marvin Bower Fellow, Harvard Business Sch., 1990–91; Gaston Eyskens Prof., Leuven Univ., 1996–97; Vis. Prof. of Econs, Harvard Univ., 1998; William Davidson Vis. Prof., Michigan Univ., 2003; Vis. Prof., Graduate Sch. of Business, Univ. of Chicago, 2006. Member: Adv. Council, Japan External Trade Orgn, Tokyo, 1995–; Council for Econ. Analysis, EU, 2002–04; Enterprise Policy Gp, Ireland, 2003–04. Pres., REconS, 2004–07. Fellow: Econometric Soc., 1991; European Econ. Assoc., 2004. Foreign Hon. Mem., AEA, 2007. Hon. DSc(Econ) NUI, 2003; Hon. DSciEcon Lausanne, 2004; Hon. LLD Dublin, 2004. Medal of Franqui Foundn, Belgium, 1992. *Publications:* (jtly) Protection and Industrial Policy in Europe, 1986; Sunk Costs and Market Structure, 1991; Technology and Market Structure: theory and history, 1998; Marshall's Tendencies: what can economists know?, 2000. *Address:* London School of Economics, Houghton Street, WC2A 2AE. *T:* (020) 7955 7716.

SUTTON, Air Marshal Sir John (Matthias Dobson), KCB 1986 (CB 1981); Chairman, Arrow Group of Companies, 1990–2003; *b* 9 July 1932; *s* of late Harry Rowston Sutton and Gertrude Sutton; *m* 1954 (marr. diss. 1968); one *s* one *d*; *m* 1969, Angela Faith Gray; two *s*. *Educ:* Queen Elizabeth's Grammar Sch., Alford, Lincs. Joined RAF, 1950; pilot trng, commnd, 1951; served on Fighter Sqdns, UK and Germany; Staff Coll., 1963; OC 249 Sqdn, 1964–66; Asst Sec., Chiefs of Staff Cttee, 1966–69; OC 14 Sqdn, 1970–71; Asst Chief of Staff (Policy and Plans), HQ 2 ATAF, 1971–73; Staff, Chief of Def. Staff, 1973–74; RCDS, 1975; Comdt Central Flying Sch., 1976–77; Asst Chief of Air Staff (Policy), 1977–79; Dep. Comdr, RAF Germany, 1980–82; ACDS (Commitments), 1982–84; ACDS (Overseas), 1985; C-in-C, RAF Support Comd, 1986–89; Lt-Gov. and C-in-C, Jersey, 1990–95. Pres., RAFA, 2002–05. Chm., Bd of Governors, UC Northampton (formerly Nene Coll.), 1996–2000. KStJ 1990. *Recreations:* golf, gardening. *Address:* Pantiles, Stretton, Rutland LE15 7QZ. *Clubs:* Royal Air Force; Colonels; Greetham Valley Golf.

SUTTON, John Sydney, CBE 1996; education consultant; Director, International Business Education Co-operation Charitable Trust, 1998–2002; General Secretary, Secondary Heads Association, 1988–98; *b* 9 June 1936; *s* of late Sydney and of Mabel Sutton; *m* 1961, Carmen Grandoso Martinez; three *s*. *Educ:* King Edward VI Sch., Southampton; Univ. of Keele (BA Hons, MA). Asst Teacher, Christopher Wren Sch., London, 1958–60; Asst Master, later Head of History, Bemrose Sch., Derby, 1960–68; Head, Social Studies Dept, Sir Wilfrid Martineau Sch., Birmingham, 1968–73; Headmaster: Corby Grammar Sch., 1973; Southwood Sch., Corby, 1973–82; Queen Elizabeth Sch., Corby, 1982–88. Mem. Council, Hansard Soc. for Parly Govt, 1973–2000. Trustee, Teaching Awards Trust, 1998–. *Publications:* American Government, 1974; Understanding Politics in Modern Britain, 1977; (with L. Robbins and T. Brennan) People and Politics in Britain, 1985; (jtly) School Management in Practice, 1985; (as Archimedes) TES Management Guide for Heads and Senior Staff, 1996. *Recreations:* walking, wine appreciation, Geddington Volunteer Fire Brigade. *Address:* 24 Bright Trees Road, Geddington, Kettering, Northants NN14 1BS. *T:* (01536) 742559. *Club:* Rotary (Kettering Huxloe).

SUTTON, Rt Rev. Keith Norman; Bishop of Lichfield, 1984–2003; *b* 23 June 1934; *s* of Norman and Irene Sutton; *m* 1963, Edith Mary Jean Geldard (*d* 2000); three *s* one *d*. *Educ:* Jesus College, Cambridge (MA 1959). Ordained deacon, 1959, priest, 1960. Curate, St Andrew's, Plymouth, 1959–62; Chaplain, St John's Coll., Cambridge, 1962–67; Tutor and Chaplain, Bishop Tucker Coll., Mukono, Uganda, 1968–73; Principal of Ridley Hall, Cambridge, 1973–78; Bishop Suffragan of Kingston-upon-Thames, 1978–83; Archbp of Canterbury's envoy to Southern Africa, 1986. General Synod: Chairman: Bd for Mission and Unity, 1989–91; Bd of Mission, 1991–94; Member: Standing Cttee, 1989–94; Theol Gp, House of Bishops, 1989–2002. Select Preacher, Univ. of Cambridge, 1987. Pres., Queen's Coll., Birmingham, 1986–94. Entered House of Lords, 1989. Episcopal Visitor, Simon of Cyrene Theol Inst., 1992–. Hon. Vice-Pres., CMS, 1995. Patron: Russian Poets Fund, Keele Univ., 1995–; New Art Gall., Walsall, 1998–. DUniv Keele, 1992; Hon. DLitt Wolverhampton, 1994. *Publication:* The People of God, 1983. *Recreations:* Russian literature, third world issues, music.

SUTTON, Kenneth David, CB 2008; Deputy Chief Executive, Border and Immigration Agency (formerly Deputy Director General, Immigration and Nationality), Home Office, 2006–08; *b* 17 May 1958; *s* of David Vivien Sutton and Audrey Sutton; *m* 1982, Ruth Hopkin; two *s* one *d*. *Educ:* Cefn Hengoed Comprehensive Sch., Swansea; University Coll., Oxford (BA 1st Cl. Hons PPE 1979). Home Office, 1979–: Private Sec. to Parly Under Sec. of State, 1983–85; Private Sec. to Permanent Under Sec. of State, 1991–92; Asst Sec., Immigration and Nationality Dept, 1992–95; Principal Private Sec. to Home Secretary, 1995–99; Dir of Regimes, subseq. of Resettlement, HM Prison Service, 1999–2002; Dir, Street Crime Action Team, 2002, Sen. Dir for Asylum Support, Casework and Appeals, 2003–06, Home Office. *Recreations:* cycling, holidays in France and Wales. *Address:* Home Office, 2 Marsham Street, SW1P 4DF.

SUTTON, Michael; *see* Sutton, H. M.

SUTTON, Rt Rev. Peter (Eves), CBE 1990; Bishop of Nelson, New Zealand, 1965–90; Senior Anglican Bishop, 1979–90; Acting Primate, New Zealand, 1985–86; *b* Wellington, NZ, 7 June 1923; *m* 1956, Pamela Cherrington, *e d* of R. A. Dalley, Patin House, Kidderminster; one *s* one *d*. *Educ:* Wellesley Coll.; Nelson Coll.; University of New Zealand. BA 1945; MA 1947; LTh 1948. Deacon, 1947; Priest, 1948 (Wellington); Curate of Wanganui, New Zealand, 1947–50; St John the Evangelist, Bethnal Green, 1950–51; Bishops Hatfield, Diocese of St Albans (England), 1951–52; Vicar of St Cuthberts, Berhampore (NZ), 1952–58; Whangarei, Diocese of Auckland, New Zealand, 1958–64; Archdeacon of Waimate, 1962–64; Dean of Dunedin and Vicar of St Paul's Cathedral, Dunedin, 1964–65. Mem. Bd, 1965–93, Chm., 1977–90, Cawthron Inst. Founding Mem., Nelson Civic Trust; Founder: Protect our Heritage, Nelson; Friends of Nelson City; Life Mem., Founder's Mus., Nelson; Rep., Nelson Provincial Mus. Cttee, 1989–95; Patrons' Rep., Suter Art Gall. Bd, 1990–93; NZ Co-ordinator, All Religions, Amnesty Internat., 1989–2003; NZ Rep., St Deiniol's Library, Hawarden, 1988–90; Trustee, Nelson Civic Heritage Protection, 1995–2003. Governor, St John's Coll., Auckland, 1965–90. ChStJ 1986; Sub-Prelate, Order of St John, NZ, 1987–. Silver Jubilee Medal, 1977; NZ Commemoration Medal, 1990. *Publication:* Freedom for Convictions, 1971. *Recreation:* golf (Canterbury Univ. Blue). *Address:* 3 Ngatiawa Street, Nelson, New Zealand.

SUTTON, Dr Peter Morgan; Director, Public Health Laboratory Service Centre for Applied Microbiology and Research, Porton Down, 1979–92; *b* 21 June 1932; *s* of Sir Graham Sutton, CBE, FRS and late Lady Sutton (*née* Doris Morgan); *m* 1959, Helen Ersy Economides; two *s* two *d*. *Educ:* Bishop Wordsworth Sch., Salisbury; Wrekin Coll., Wellington; University Coll. (Fellow, 1985) and University Coll. Hosp. Med. Sch., London. House Surgeon and House Physician, UCH, 1956–57; Graham Scholar in Pathology, Univ. of London, 1958–59; on academic staff of UCH Med. Sch., 1960–65; Vis. Asst Prof. of Pathology, Univ. of Pittsburg, USA, 1966–67; Hon. Consultant Pathologist, UCH, 1967–79; Reader in Pathology, Univ. of London, 1971–79; Vice-Dean, UCH Med. Sch., 1973–78. Vis. Prof., Dept of Biochemical Pathology, UCL, 1983–. Sometime Examr in Pathology, Univ. of London and RCS. *Publications:* The Nature of Cancer, 1962; various papers on fibrinolytic enzymes and novel antiviral compounds. *Recreations:* English literature, history of science. *Address:* Manderley, 34 Bower Gardens, Salisbury, Wilts SP1 2RL. *T:* (01722) 323902.

SUTTON, Philip, PhD; FIET, FInstP; FREng; Director General, Research and Technology, Ministry of Defence, since 2004; *b* 28 Nov. 1953; *s* of Percy Ronald and Ivy Nora Sutton; *m* 1974, Kim Cummins; one *s* one *d*. *Educ:* Southampton Univ. (BSc Hons Physics; PhD Electronics 1982). FIET (FIEE 1996); FInstP 1998; FREng 2006. Ministry of Defence: ASWE, Portsdown 1975–83; BAe Dynamics, Bristol, 1983–85; Above Water Sector, ARE, then DRA, Portsdown, 1985–92, Chief Scientist, 1992–94; Hd, Battlefield and Vehicle Systems Dept, DERA, 1994–98; Director: of Corporate Res., 1998–2001; of Technol. Develt, 2001–04. Visiting Professor: Cranfield Univ., 1990–; Loughborough Univ., 1992–; Imperial Coll. London, 2006–. Dir, Cancer Care Soc., 2000–. Gov., Welbeck Coll., 2005–. Mem., Whiteley Ch Council, 1998–. Member: NT; RNLI. *Publications:* numerous tech. reports and papers; named inventor on 17 patents and patent applications. *Recreations:* sailing, sub-aqua diving, snow-boarding, cycling.

SUTTON, Philip John, RA 1989 (ARA 1977); *b* 20 Oct. 1928; *m* 1954; one *s* three *d*. *Educ:* Slade Sch. of Fine Art, UCL. One-man exhibitions: Roland Browse and Delbanco (now Browse and Darby) Gallery, London, 1958–81; Leeds City Art Gallery, 1960; Newcastle-on-Tyne, 1962; Bradford, 1962; Edinburgh, 1962; Sydney, 1963, 1966, 1970, 1973; Perth, 1963, 1972; Royal Acad. (Diploma Gall.), London, 1977; David Jones Gall., Sydney, 1980; Bonython Art Gall., Adelaide, 1981; Norwich, Bath and New York, 1983; Lichfield Fest., 1985; Beaux Arts Gall., Bath, 1985; Galerie Joël Salaün, Paris, 1988; Gallery 27, and Cork St, London, 2004; Richmond Hill Art Gall., 2006; exhibn of ceramics, Oditte Gilbert Gall., London, 1987; Agnews, London, 1992; touring exhibn, Wales, 1993–94; Shakespeare exhibn, RA, Internat. Shakespeare Globe Centre, RSC Stratford, Royal Armouries Mus., Leeds, Berkeley Square Gall., 1997; Piano Nobile, London 2001; Hay-on-Wye Fest., 2001; exhibn of woodcuts 1962–1976, RA, 2005. Designed Post Office 'Greetings' stamps, 1989. *Recreations:* swimming, running. *Address:* 3 Morfa Terrace, Manorbier, Tenby, Pembrokeshire SA70 7TH.

SUTTON, Prof. Richard, DSc (Med); FRCP, FACC, FESC, FAHA; FHRS; Consultant Cardiologist: Imperial College Healthcare NHS Trust (formerly St Mary's Hospital NHS Trust), since 2007; Chelsea and Westminster Hospital (formerly Westminster Hospital), since 1976; Professor of Clinical Cardiology, Imperial College London, since 2003; *b* 1 Sept. 1940; *s* of late Dick Brasnett Sutton and Greta Mary (*née* Leadbeter); *m* 1964, Anna Gunilla (*née* Cassö) (marr. diss. 1998); one *s*. *Educ:* Gresham's Sch.; King's Coll., London; King's Coll. Hosp. (MB, BS 1964); DSc (Med) London 1988. FRCP 1983 (MRCP 1967); FACC 1975; FESC 1990; FAHA 2001; FHRS 2006. Gen. medical trng followed graduation; career in cardiology began at St George's Hosp., London, 1967; Fellow in Cardiol., Univ. of NC, 1968–69; Registrar, Sen. Registrar, then Temp. Consultant, National Heart Hosp., London, 1970–76. Consultant Cardiologist: St Stephen's Hosp., 1976–89; Royal Brompton Nat. Heart and Lung Hosp., subseq. Royal Brompton and Harefield Trust, 1993–2007; Hon. Consultant Cardiologist: Italian Hosp., London, 1977–89; St Luke's Hosp., London, 1980–. Chm., Eur. Wkg Gp on Cardiac Pacing, 1998–2000. Exec. Bd Mem., Eur. Heart Rhythm Assoc., 2004–06. Member: British Medical Assoc.; British Cardiac Soc.; Heart Rhythm Soc.; Heart Rhythm UK (formerly British Pacing and Electrophysiology Gp) (Co-Founder, Past Pres. and Hon. Sec.). Governors' Award, Amer. Coll. of Cardiol., 1979 (Scientific Exhibit, Physiol Cardiac Pacing), and 1982 (1st Prize; Scientific Exhibit, 5 yrs of Physiol Cardiac Pacing). Editor in Chief: European Jl of Cardiac Pacing and Electrophysiology, 1991–97; Europace, 1998–2006. *Publications:* Foundations of Cardiac Pacing, pt 1, 1991, pt 2, 1999; articles on many aspects of cardiology incl. cardiac pacing, coronary artery disease, left ventricular function, and assessment of pharm. agents, in Circulation, Jl of Amer. Coll. of Cardiol., Amer. Jl of Cardiol., Amer. Heart Jl, Brit. Heart Jl, Heart, Pace, Lancet, BMJ, and Oxford Textbook of Medicine, 1967–. *Recreations:* opera, foreign travel. *Address:* 5 Devonshire Place, W1G 6HL. *T:* (020) 7935 4444.

SUTTON, Richard Lewis; Regional Director, Northern Region, Department of Industry, 1974–81; *b* 3 Feb. 1923; *s* of William Richard Sutton and Marina Susan Sutton (*née* Chudleigh); *m* 1944, Jean Muriel (*née* Turner). *Educ:* Ealing County Grammar Sch. Board of Trade, 1939. Served War: HM Forces (Lieut RA), 1942–47. Asst Trade Comr, Port of Spain, 1950–52; BoT, 1953–62; Trade Comr, Kuala Lumpur, 1962–66; Monopolies Commn, 1966; BoT, 1967–68; Dir, British Industrial Develt Office, New York, 1968–71; Regional Dir, West Midland Region, Dept of Trade and Industry, 1971–74. *Recreations:* music, walking, bridge. *Address:* Barton Toft, Dowlish Wake, Ilminster, Somerset TA19 0QG. *T:* (01460) 57127.

SUTTON, Sir Richard (Lexington), 9th Bt *cr* 1772; farmer; *b* 27 April 1937; *s* of Sir Robert Lexington Sutton, 8th Bt, and of Gwynneth Gwladys, *o d* of Major Arnold Charles Gover, MC; *S* father, 1981; *m* 1959, Fiamma, *o d* of G. M. Ferrari, Rome; one *s* one *d*. *Educ:* Stowe. *Recreations:* ski-ing, sailing, swimming, tennis. *Heir:* *s* David Robert Sutton [*b* 26 Feb. 1960; *m* 1992, Annette (marr. diss.), *o d* of B. David; one *d*]. *Address:* Moorhill, Higher Langham, Gillingham, Dorset SP8 5NY. *T:* (01747) 862665.

SUTTON, Richard Patrick; QC 1993; a Recorder, since 1994 (Assistant Recorder, 1991–94); *b* 13 Nov. 1944; *s* of Jack Doherty Sutton and Beryl Clarisse Scholes Sutton (*née* Folkard); *m* 1978, Jean Folley; one *s* one *d*. *Educ:* Culford Sch.; Wadham Coll., Oxford (BA Hons Jurisprudence). Called to the Bar, Middle Temple, 1969, Bencher, 2002. *Recreations:* playing guitar, meeting people.

SUTTON, Robert Hiles; Partner, Macfarlanes, Solicitors, since 1983 (Senior Partner, 1999–2008); *b* 19 Jan. 1954; *s* of late John Ormerod Sutton and of (Margaret) Patricia Sutton; *m* 1981, Carola, (Tiggy), Dewey; one *s* one *d* (and one *s* decd). *Educ:* Winchester

Coll.; Magdalen Coll., Oxford (BA 1st Cl. Hons Modern Hist.). Admitted solicitor, 1979; joined Macfarlanes, 1976. Fellow, Winchester Coll., 2003. *Recreations:* tennis, wine, family. *Address:* Macfarlanes, 10 Norwich Street, EC4A 1BD. *T:* (020) 7849 2340; *e-mail:* rhs@macfarlanes.com. *Clubs:* Boodle's, City.

SUTTON, Prof. Stephen Robert, PhD; Professor of Behavioural Science, University of Cambridge, since 2001; *b* 24 Feb. 1952; *s* of Robert Frank Sutton and Marjorie Sutton (*née* Hook); *m* 1985, Pamela Anne (*née* Stevens). *Educ:* Univ. of Leicester (BA 1973); LSE (MSc 1975); Inst. of Psychiatry, Univ. of London (PhD 1981); City Univ. (MSc 1991). Institute of Psychiatry, University of London: Res. Worker, 1975–90, Lectr, 1980–88, Sen. Lectr, 1988–90, Addiction Res. Unit; Sen. Lectr in Social Psychology, Health Behaviour Unit, 1990–96; Reader in Social/Health Psychology, 1996–2000, Prof. in Social/Health Psychology, 2000–01, Health Behaviour Unit, Dept of Epidemiology and Public Health, UCL. Vis. Prof. of Psychology, Univ. of Bergen, 1996–; Vis. Prof. of Social/Health Psychology, Dept of Psychiatry and Behavioural Scis, UCL, 2000–. *Publications:* numerous papers in learned jls. *Recreations:* squash (occasional), walking, bird-watching. *Address:* University of Cambridge, Institute of Public Health, Forvie Site, Robinson Way, Cambridge CB2 2SR. *T:* (01223) 330594, *Fax:* (01223) 762515; *e-mail:* srs34@medschl.cam.ac.uk.

SUVA, Archbishop of, (RC), since 1976; **Most Rev. Petero Mataca;** *b* 28 April 1933; *s* of Gaberiele Daunivucu and Akeneta Taina. *Educ:* Holy Name Seminary, Dunedin, NZ; Propaganda Fidei, Rome. Priest, Rome, 1959; Vicar-Gen. of Archdiocese of Suva, 1966; Rector of Pacific Regional Seminary, 1973; Auxiliary Bishop of Suva, 1974. Pres., Episcopal Conf. of South Pacific, 1981. *Address:* Archbishop's House, Box 393, Suva, Fiji. *T:* 301955.

SUYIN; *see* Han Suyin.

SUZMAN, Mrs Helen, OM (Gold) South Africa, 1997; Hon. DBE 1989; Member, South African Human Rights Commission, 1996–98; *b* 7 Nov. 1917; *d* of late Samuel Gavronsky; *m* 1937, Dr M. M. Suzman, FRCP (*d* 1994); two *d. Educ:* Parktown Convent, Johannesburg; Univ. of Witwatersrand (BCom). Lectr in Economic History, Univ. of Witwatersrand, 1944–52. Elected MP for Houghton, RSA, 1953 (United Party, 1953–61; Progressive Party (later Progressive Reform Party and Progressive Federal Party), 1961–89); Inaugural Mem. Progressive Party, 1959; sole rep. of Progressive Party in Parlt, 1961–74; returned unopposed as Progressive Federal Party MP, 1977. Mem., Ind. Electoral Commn, 1994. Pres., SA Inst. of Race Relns, 1991–93. Hon. Fellow: St Hugh's Coll., Oxford, 1973; London Sch. of Economics, 1975; New Hall, Cambridge, 1990. Hon. DCL Oxford, 1973; Hon. LLD: Harvard, Witwatersrand, 1976; Columbia, Smith Coll., 1977; Brandeis, 1981; Cape Town, Jewish Theological Seminary, NY, 1986; Ohio, Western Ontario, 1989; Rhodes, S Africa, Cambridge, Glasgow, Nottingham, Warwick, Ulster, 1990; Indiana, Rutgers, 1992; Toronto, 1993; De Montfort, 1994; Wales, 1996; KCL, 2008; Hon. DHL: Denison, 1982; New Sch. for Social Res., NY, Sacred Heart Univ., USA, 1984; DUniv Brunel, 1991; Hon. Dr: Yale, 1999; Stellenbosch, 2006. UN Human Rights Award, 1978; Roger E. Joseph Award, Hebrew Union Coll., NY, 1986; Moses Mendelssohn Prize, Berlin Senate, 1988; B'Nai B'Rith Dor L'Dor Award, 1992; Notre Dame Univ., Indiana, Award, 1995; Liberal Internat. Prize for Freedom, 2002. Freedom of Sandton, 1989. *Publication:* In No Uncertain Terms (autobiog.), 1993. *Recreations:* swimming, fishing, bridge. *Address:* 52 2nd Avenue, Illovo, Sandton, Gauteng 2196, South Africa. *T:* and *Fax:* (11) 7882833; *e-mail:* helen01@icon.co.za. *Clubs:* Lansdowne; Inanda, Wanderers (Johannesburg).
See also Prof. J. L. Jowell.

SUZMAN, Janet; actress and director; *b* 9 Feb. 1939; *d* of Saul Suzman; *m* 1969, Trevor Robert Nunn (*see* Sir T. R. Nunn) (marr. diss. 1986); one *s. Educ:* Kingsmead Coll., Johannesburg; Univ. of the Witwatersrand (BA); London Acad. of Music and Dramatic Art. Hon. Associate Artist, RSC, 1980. Vis. Prof of Drama Studies, Westfield Coll., London, 1983–84. Lectures: Spencer, Harvard Univ., 1988; Tanner, Brasenose Coll., Oxford, 1995; Sixth World Shakespeare Congress, LA, 1996; Judith Wilson, Trinity Coll., Cambridge, 1996; Drapers', QMW, 1997; Morrell Meml Address on Toleration, Univ. of York, 1999. Vice-Pres., LAMDA Council, 2002– (Mem., 1978–2002, Vice-Chm., 1992–2002). Trustee: The Theatres Trust, 1977–83; Rose of Kingston Th. Trust, 2007–. Rôles played for *Royal Shakespeare Co.* incl.: Joan La Pucelle in The Wars of the Roses, 1963–64; Lulu in The Birthday Party, Rosaline, Portia, 1965; Ophelia, 1965–66; Katharina, Celia, and Berinthia in The Relapse, 1967; Beatrice, Rosalind, 1968–69; Cleopatra and Lavinia, 1972–73; Clytemnestra and Helen of Troy in The Greeks, 1980; The Hollow Crown, 2002, tour of Australia, 2003; Volumnia in Coriolanus, 2007; *other rôles* incl.: Kate Hardcastle, and Carmen in The Balcony, Oxford Playhouse, 1966; Hester in Hello and Goodbye, King's Head Theatre, 1973; Masha in Three Sisters, Cambridge, 1976; Good Woman of Setzuan, Newcastle, 1976, Royal Court, 1977; Hedda Gabler, Duke of York's, 1977; Boo-hoo, Open Space, 1978; The Duchess of Malfi, Birmingham, 1979; Cowardice, Ambassadors, 1983; Boesman and Lena, Hampstead, 1984; Vassa, Greenwich, 1985; Andromache, Old Vic, 1988; Another Time, Wyndham's, 1989; Hippolytus, Almeida, 1991; The Sisters Rosenweig, Greenwich, 1994, Old Vic, 1994–95; The Retreat from Moscow, Chichester, 1999; Cherished Disappointments in Love, Soho, 2001; Whose Life is it Anyway?, Comedy, 2005; *director:* Othello, Market Theatre, Johannesburg, 1987 (Best Prodn, Vita Awards, 1988); A Dream of People, The Pit, 1990; The Cruel Grasp, Edinburgh Fest., 1991; No Flies on Mr Hunter, Chelsea Centre, 1992; Death of a Salesman, 1993 (Liverpool Echo and Daily Post Arts Awards, Best Production, 1994), The Deep Blue Sea, 1996, Theatr Clywd; The Good Woman of Sharkville, Market Theatre, Johannesburg, 1996, UK tour, 1998; The Free State, Birmingham, 1997, UK tour, 2000 (Barclays Theatrical Managers' Assoc. Award, Best Dir, 1997); The Snow Palace, tour and Tricycle Theatre, 1998, Warsaw Fest., 1999; The Guardsman, Albery, 2000; Measure For Measure, Guildhall Sch., 2004; Hamlet, Cape Town, 2005, Stratford, 2006. *Films:* A Day in the Death of Joe Egg, 1970; Nicholas and Alexandra, 1971; The Priest of Love, 1980; The Draughtsman's Contract, 1981; E la Nave Va, 1983; A Dry White Season, 1990; Nuns on the Run, 1990; Leon the Pig Farmer, 1993; Max 2001; *television:* plays for BBC and ITV incl.: St Joan, 1968; Three Sisters, 1969; Macbeth, 1970; Hedda Gabler, 1972; Twelfth Night, 1973; Three Men in a Boat, 1973; Antony and Cleopatra, 1974; Miss Nightingale, 1974; Clayhanger, serial, 1975–76; Mountbatten—The Last Viceroy, 1986; The Singing Detective, 1986, The Miser, 1987; dir., Othello, 1988; Cripples, 1989; The Amazon, 1989; master class on Shakespearean comedy, BBC, 1990; White Clouds, 2002. Acad. Award Nomination, Best Actress, 1971; Evening Standard Drama Awards, Best Actress, 1973, 1976; Plays and Players Award, Best Actress, 1976. Hon. MA Open, 1984; Hon. DLitt: Warwick, 1990; Leicester, 1992; London, 1997; Southampton, 2002; Middx, 2003; Kingston, 2006. *Publications:* Acting with Shakespeare, 1996; The Free State: a South African response to Chekhov's Cherry Orchard, 2000; (commentary) Antony and Cleopatra, 2001. *Address:* c/o Steve Kenis & Co., Royalty House, 72–74 Dean Street, W1D 3SG. *T:* (020) 7434 9055.

SVENSON, Dame Beryl; *see* Grey, Dame Beryl.

SVENSSON, Lars; author, since 1989; editor; ornithologist; *b* 30 March 1941; *s* of Georg Svensson and Cecilia Svensson (*née* Lovén); *m* 2003, Lena Rahoult; one *s* one *d. Educ:* Univ. of Graphic Arts, Stockholm. Graphic designer and publishing editor, 1965–; ornithologist; lectr and tour leader; taxonomic res. in mus. collections and in the field. Swedish Ornithological Society: Mem. Bd, 1971–77; Ed., jl, Vår Fågelvärld, 1971–74; Founder, Swedish Rarities Cttee (Chm., 1971–86); Member: Nomenclature Cttee, 1971–84; Taxonomic Cttee, 2000–. Mem., BOU Taxonomic Sub-cttee, 2005–. Hon. Ringer, British Trust for Ornithology, 1985–; Hon. Mem., Spanish Ornithol Soc., 2004–. PhD *hc* Uppsala, 2004. *Publications:* Identification Guide to European Passerines, 1970, 4th edn 1992; (with H. Delin) Birds of Britain and Europe, 1986, 3rd edn 1992; Fågelsång i Sverige (Birdsong in Sweden), 1990; Collins Birdguide, 1999. *Recreations:* wine-tasting, golf, classic music. *Address:* S:ta Toras väg 28, 260 93 Torekov, Sweden. *T:* and *Fax:* 86632655, 431364022; *e-mail:* lars@lullula.se.

SVENSSON, Prof. Lars Eric Oscar, PhD; Deputy Governor, Sveriges Riksbank, since 2007; Professor of Economics, Princeton University, since 2001 (on leave, since 2007); *b* 1947; *m* 2002, Lena Askesjo; one *s* from a former marriage. *Educ:* Royal Inst. of Technol., Stockholm (MS); Stockholm Univ. (BA; PhD 1976). Res. Fellow, 1975–78, Sen. Res. Fellow, 1978–84, Prof. of Internat. Econs, 1984–2003, Inst. for Internat. Econ. Studies, Stockholm Univ. (on leave 2001–03). Vis. Prof. and Scholar at many univs, res. orgns and central banks in several countries. Associate Mem., 1986, Sec., 1988–92, Mem., 1993–2002, Chm., 1999–2001, Prize Cttee, Nobel Prize in Econ. Scis. Mem., Royal Swedish Acad. of Scis, 1989; Foreign Mem., Finnish Acad. of Sci. and Letters, 1998; Foreign Hon. Mem., American Acad. of Arts and Scis, 2000; MAE, 1992. Fellow, Econometric Soc., 1990. *Publications:* articles in jls on monetary econs and monetary policy, exchange-rate theory and policy, and gen. internat. macroecons. *Address:* Department of Economics, Princeton University, Princeton, NJ 08544–1021, USA. *T:* (609) 2580329, *Fax:* (609) 2585398.

SWABY, Peter; County Treasurer, 1991–2006, Strategic Director, 2006–07, Derbyshire County Council; *b* 8 Oct. 1947; *s* of late Arthur Swaby and Mona Swaby; *m* 1974, Yvette Shann; one *s* one *d. Educ:* Longcroft Sch., Beverley. CPFA (CIPFA 1973). E Riding CC, 1967; Humberside CC, 1974, Chief Internal Auditor, 1983; Asst County Treasurer, S Glam CC, 1985. Hon. Sec., 2001–04, Vice Pres., 2004–05, Pres., 2005–06, Soc. of Co. Treas; Pres., Police Authy Treasurers' Soc., 2003–04. *Recreation:* classical guitarist (ALCM, ALCM(TD)).

SWADE, Doron David, PhD; FBCS; Director, Babbage Project and Guest Curator, Computer History Museum, Mountain View, California, since 2006; *b* 14 Oct. 1946; *s* of Max Jack Swade and Ruth Leah Swade (*née* Rosenberg). *Educ:* Univ. of Cape Town (BSc Hons 1969; MSc 1971); UCL (PhD 2003). CEng 1994; FBCS 2001. Consultant to computer industry, 1972–96; consultant electronics design engr, UK and USA, 1975–82; Science Museum: Electronics Design Engr, 1982–83; Section Head, audiovisual, electronics and computer-based displays, 1983–85; Sen. Curator, Computing and IT, 1985–99; Asst Dir and Hd of Collections, 1999–2002. Visiting Professor: (Interaction Design), RCA, 2004–06; Hist. of Computing, Univ. of Portsmouth, 2005–; Hon. Res. Fellow, Dept of Computer Sci., Royal Holloway, Univ. of London, 2006–. Mem., Scientific Cttee, Musée Nat. de la Voiture et du Tourisme, Compiègne, 2002–. *Publications:* Charles Babbage and his Calculating Engines, 1991; (jtly) The Dream Machine: exploring the computer age, 1991; The Cogwheel Brain: Charles Babbage and the quest to build the first computer, 2000; popular and scholarly articles. *Recreations:* writing, restoring woodworking machinery, making things. *Address:* 54 Park Road, Kingston upon Thames, Surrey KT2 6AU. *T:* (020) 8392 0072.

SWAFFIELD, Sir James (Chesebrough), Kt 1976; CBE 1971; RD 1967; Chairman, British Rail Property Board, 1984–91; solicitor, retired; *b* 16 Feb. 1924; *s* of Frederick and Kate Elizabeth Swaffield, Cheltenham; *m* 1950, Elizabeth Margaret Ellen, 2nd *d* of A. V. and K. E. Maunder, Belfast; two *s* two *d. Educ:* Cheltenham Grammar Sch.; Haberdashers' Aske's Hampstead Sch.; London Univ. (LLB); MA Oxon 1974. RNVR, 1942–46. Articled Town Clerk, Lincoln, 1946–49; Asst Solicitor: Norwich Corp., 1949–52; Cheltenham Corp., 1952–53; Southend-on-Sea Corp., 1953–56; Dep. Town Clerk, subseq. Town Clerk and Clerk of Peace, Blackpool, 1956–62; Sec., Assoc. of Municipal Corps, 1962–73; Dir-Gen. and Clerk to GLC, Clerk to ILEA and Clerk of Lieutenancy for Greater London, 1973–84. Chm., London Marathon Charitable Trust, 1980–2006; Vice-Pres., Maritime Volunteer Service; Trustee, Jubilee Walkway Trust. Lt Comdr RNR retd. DL Greater London, 1978–99. OStJ. Dist. Service Award (Internat. City Management Assoc.), 1984. *Address:* 2 Andrew Court, 68 Wickham Road, Beckenham, Kent BR3 6RG. *Club:* Naval.

SWAINE, Sir John (Joseph), Kt 1995; CBE 1987 (OBE 1980); QC (Hong Kong) 1975; JP; President, Legislative Council, Hong Kong, 1993–95; *b* 22 April 1932; *s* of Henry Edward Swaine, MBE and Gladys Elizabeth Luke Swaine; *m* 1959, Fatima Gwendoline Jorge Cotton; four *s* one *d. Educ:* Univ. of Hong Kong (BA). Admin. Officer, Hong Kong Govt, 1952–57; called to the Bar, Lincoln's Inn, 1960, Hong Kong, 1960; in practice, 1960–. Non-exec. Dir, Hong Kong & Shanghai Banking Corp. Ltd, 1986–97. JP Hong Kong, 1975. Hon. LLD: Baptist, HK, 1992; City, HK, 1993; Hon. PhD (Hum) Lingnan Coll., HK, 1994; Hon. DLett Open, HK, 1996. *Recreation:* breeding and racing thoroughbred horses. *Clubs:* Hong Kong Jockey (Chm., 1993–96), Country (Hong Kong).

SWAINSON, Eric, CBE 1981; Vice-Chairman, Fairey Group, 1987–97; Director, Lloyds TSB Group plc, 1996–97; *b* 5 Dec. 1926; *m* 1953, Betty Heywood; two *d. Educ:* Sheffield Univ. (BMet 1st cl. Hons; W. H. A. Robertson medal, 1959). Joined Imperial Chemical Industries Metals Div. (now IMI), 1946; Technical Officer, Res. Dept, 1946–53; Manager, Titanium Melting Plant, 1953–56; Asst Manager, Technical Dept, 1956–59; Gen. Manager and Man. Dir, Lightning Fasteners, 1961–69; Dir, IMI, 1969–86; Asst Man. Dir, 1972–74; Man. Dir, 1974–86; Dep. Chm., Pegler-Hattersley plc, 1986; Lloyds Bank plc: Dir, 1986–95; Vice-Chm., 1992–95. Director: Birmingham Broadcasting, 1973–92; AMEC, 1987–95; Midlands Radio Hldgs, 1988–92; Lloyds Merchant Bank Hldgs, 1989–93; Cheltenham & Gloucester Bldg Soc., 1995–97; Chm., Birmingham and West Midlands Reg. Bd, Lloyds Bank, 1985–91 (Reg. Dir, 1979–91). Chm., W Midlands Industrial Develt Bd, 1985–90; Member: Review Bd for Govt Contracts, 1978–93; NEDC Cttee on Finance for Industry, 1978–86; Council, CBI, 1975–86; W Midlands Reg. Council, CBI, 1973–83 (Chm. 1976–78); Industrial Develt Adv. Bd, 1982–88. Pro-Chancellor, Aston Univ., 1981–86. FRSA 1985. Hon. DSc Aston, 1986. *Address:* Paddox Hollow, Norton Lindsey, Warwick CV35 8JA.

SWAINSON, Roy; Executive Director, Merseyside Special Investment Fund, since 1998; non-executive Director, St Helens and Knowsley Hospitals NHS Trust, since 2006; *b* 15 April 1947; *s* of William Swainson and Florence Swainson (*née* Moss); *m* 1973, Irene Ann Shearson; one *s* one *d. Educ:* Merchant Taylors' Sch., Crosby; Univ. of Manchester (LLB). Southport County Borough Council: Asst Solicitor, 1969–71; Sen. Asst Solicitor, 1971–74; Asst Borough Solicitor and Sec., Sefton MBC, 1974–82; Dep. City Solicitor and

Sec., Liverpool CC, 1982–90; Chief Exec. and Dir Gen., Merseytravel, 1990–98. Non-exec. Chm., Air Safety Support Internat. Ltd, 2003–06. *Recreations:* reading, theatre, travel. *Address:* Merseyside Special Investment Fund, 5th Floor, Cunard Building, Pier Head, Liverpool L3 1DS. *T:* (0151) 236 4040.

SWAINSTON, Michael George; QC 2002; barrister; *b* 30 Jan. 1961; *s* of George and Ruth Swainston; *m* 1993, Carmita Ferreira Guerreiro; two *s*. *Educ:* Sir William Turner's Grammar Sch.; Downing Coll., Cambridge (MA); University Coll., Oxford (BCL). Called to the Bar: Lincoln's Inn, 1985, Bencher, 2008; California (inactive), 1988. *Address:* Brick Court Chambers, 7-8 Essex Street, WC2R 3LD.

SWALES, Prof. Martin William, PhD; FBA 1999; Professor of German, University College London, 1976–2003, now Emeritus; *b* 3 Nov. 1940; *s* of Percy Johns Swales and Doris (*née* Davies); *m* 1966, Erika Marta Meier; one *s* one *d*. *Educ:* King Edward's Sch., Birmingham; Christ's Coll., Cambridge (BA 1961); Univ. of Birmingham (PhD 1963). Lectr in German, Univ. of Birmingham, 1964–70; Associate Prof. of German, Univ. of Toronto, 1970–72; Reader in German, KCL, 1972–75; Prof. of German, Univ. of Toronto, 1975–76. Hon. Fellow, UCL, 1996. Verdienstkreuz (Germany), 1994. Hon. DLitt Birmingham, 2003. *Publications:* Arthur Schnitzler, 1971; The German Novelle, 1977; The German Bildungsroman, 1978; Thomas Mann, 1980; Goethe's Werther, 1987; Thomas Mann's Buddenbrooks, 1991; Epochenbuch Realismus, 1997; Reading Goethe, 2001. *Recreations:* music, theatre (incl. amateur dramatics), incompetent house and car maintenance. *Address:* Department of German, University College London, Gower Street, WC1E 6BT. *T:* (020) 7380 7120.

SWALLOW, Dr Deborah Anne; Director, Courtauld Institute of Art, since 2004; *b* 27 Aug. 1948; *d* of Arnold Birkett Swallow and Denise Vivienne Swallow (*née* Leighton). *Educ:* Perse Sch. for Girls; New Hall, Cambridge (MA); Darwin Coll., Cambridge (PhD). Cambridge University: Asst Curator, Mus. of Archaeology and Anthropology, 1974–83; Lectr, Girton Coll., 1975–80; Fellow, Darwin Coll., 1975–83; Victoria and Albert Museum: Asst Keeper, Indian Dept, 1983–89; Chief Curator, Indian and SE Asian Dept, 1989–2001; Dir of Collections, and Keeper, Asian Dept, 2001–04. *Address:* Courtauld Institute of Art, Somerset House, Strand, WC2R 0RN. *T:* (020) 7848 2687, *Fax:* (020) 7848 2657; *e-mail:* Deborah.Swallow@courtauld.ac.uk.

SWALLOW, Comdt Patricia; *see* Nichol, Comdt D. P.

SWALLOW, Sydney; Senior Director, Procurement, Post Office, 1977–81; Chief Procurement Officer, British Telecommunications, 1981–83; *b* 29 June 1919; *s* of William and Charlotte Lucy Swallow; *m* 1950, Monica Williams (*d* 2007); one *s*. *Educ:* Woking County Sch.; St Catharine's Coll., Cambridge (Scholar; BA 1st cl. Hons 1940, MA). Mines Dept, Board of Trade, 1940–42. Served War: Royal Engineers (Survey), 1942–46. Nat. Coal Bd, 1946–59; Central Electricity Generating Bd, 1959–65; Associated Electrical Industries Ltd, 1965–68; General Electric Co. Ltd, 1968; Dir of Supplies, GLC, 1968–77. Chm., Educn Cttee, Inst. of Purchasing and Supply, 1967–77; Visiting Prof., Univ. of Bradford Management Centre, 1972–75; Vis. Fellow, ASC, 1976–80. FCIPS. *Publications:* various articles on purchasing and supply in professional jls. *Recreation:* watching cricket. *Address:* 17 Garricks House, Wadbrook Street, Charter Quay, Kingston upon Thames, Surrey KT1 1HS. *T:* (020) 8541 3407.

SWAMINATHAN, Dr Monkombu Sambasivan, FRS 1973; Chairman, M. S. Swaminathan Research Foundation, since 1990; Hon. Director, since 1990, and UNESCO Professor in Ecotechnology, since 1996, Centre for Research on Sustainable Agricultural and Rural Development, Madras; Member, Rajya Sabha, India, since 2007; *b* 7 Aug. 1925; *m* Mina Swaminathan; three *d*. *Educ:* Univs of Kerala, Madras and Cambridge. BSc Kerala, 1944; BSc (Agric.) Madras, 1947; Assoc. IARI 1949; PhD Cantab, 1952. Responsible for developing Nat. Demonstration Project, 1964, and for evolving Seed Village concept; actively involved in develt of High Yielding Varieties, Dryland Farming and Multiple Cropping Programmes. Dir, Indian Agricultural Res. Inst., 1961–72; Sec., Dept of Agricultural Res. and Educn, India, 1972–79; Principal Sec., Min. of Agriculture, 1979–80; Acting Dep. Chm. and Mem. (Sci. and Agriculture), Planning Commn, 1980–82; Dir-Gen., Internat. Rice Res. Inst., Manila, 1982–88. Vice-Pres., Internat. Congress of Genetics, The Hague, 1963; Gen. Pres., Indian Science Congress, 1976. President: IUCN, 1984–90; WWF (India), 1989–96; Nat. Acad. of Agricultural Scis, 1991–96, 2005–07; Pugwash Confs on Science and World Affairs, 2002–07. Chairman: UN Science Adv. Cttee, 1980; Nat. Commn on Farmers, 2004–06; Indep. Chm., FAO Council, 1981–85. First Zakir Hussain Meml Lectr, 1970; UGC Nat. Lectr, 1971; lectures at many internat. scientific symposia. Foreign Associate, US Nat. Acad. of Scis; For. Mem., All Union Acad. of Agricl Scis, USSR; Hon. Mem., Swedish Seed Assoc.; Hon. Fellow, Indian Nat. Acad. of Sciences. FNA; Fellow, Italian Nat. Sci. Acad. Hon. DSc from 54 univs. Shanti Swarup Bhatnagar Award for contribs in Biological Scis, 1961; Mendel Centenary Award, Czechoslovak Acad. of Scis, 1965; Birbal Sahni Award, Indian Bot. Soc., 1965; Ramon Magsaysay Award for Community Leadership, 1971; Silver Jubilee Award, 1973, Meghnath Saha Medal, 1981, Indian Nat. Science Acad.; R. B. Bennett Commonwealth Prize, RSA, 1984; Albert Einstein World Science Award, 1986; World Food Prize, 1987; Tyler Prize for Envmtl Achievement, 1991; Honda Prize for Eco-technology, 1991; Jawaharlal Nehru Centenary Award, 1993; Sasakawa Envmt Prize, UN, 1994; Volvo Internat. Envmt Prize, 1999; Indira Gandhi Prize for Peace, Disarmament and Development, 2000; Franklin D. Roosevelt Four Freedoms Medal, 2000; UNESCO Mahatma Gandhi Prize, 2000; Lal Bahadur Sastri Nat. Award, 2007. Padma Shri, 1967; Padma Bhushan, 1972; Padma Vibhushan, 1989. *Publications:* numerous scientific papers. *Address:* 21 Rathna Nagar, Teynampet, Madras 600018, India; M. S. Swaminathan Research Foundation, Third Cross Street, Taramani Institutional Area, Chennai (Madras) 600113, India.

SWAN, Sir Conrad (Marshall John Fisher), KCVO 1994 (CVO 1986 LVO 1978); PhD; Garter Principal King of Arms, 1992–95; Genealogist: Order of the Bath, 1972–95; Grand Priory, OStJ, 1976–95; First Hon. Genealogist, Order of St Michael and St George, 1989–95; *b* 13 May 1924; *yr s* of late Dr Henry Peter Swan, Major RAMC and RCAMC, of BC, Canada and Colchester, Essex, and of Edna Hanson Magdalen (*née* Green), Cross of Honour Pro Ecclesia et Pontifice; *m* 1957, Lady Hilda Susan Mary Northcote (*d* 1995), Dame of Honour and Devotion, SMO Malta, 1979, and of Justice of SMO of Constantine St George, 1975, *yr d* of 3rd Earl of Iddesleigh; one *s* four *d*. *Educ:* St George's Coll., Weybridge; Sch. of Oriental and African Studies, Univ. of London; Univ. of Western Ontario (BA 1949; MA 1951); Peterhouse, Cambridge (PhD 1955). Served Europe and India (Capt. Madras Regt, IA), 1942–47. Assumption Univ. of Windsor, Ont.: Lectr in History, 1955–57; Asst Prof. of Hist., 1957–60; Univ. Beadle, 1957–60. Rouge Dragon Pursuivant of Arms, 1962–68; York Herald of Arms, 1968–92; Registrar and Sen. Herald-in-Waiting, College of Arms, 1982–92. Inspector of Regimental Colours, 1993–95. On Earl Marshal's staff for State Funeral of Sir Winston Churchill, 1965 and Investiture of HRH Prince of Wales, 1969. In attendance: upon HM The Queen at Installation of HRH Prince of Wales as Great Master of Order of the Bath, 1975; during Silver Jubilee Thanksgiving Service, 1977; on Australasian Tour, 1977; at Commonwealth Heads of Govt Conf., 1987; Gentleman Usher-in-Waiting to HH the Pope, GB visit, 1982. Woodward Lectr, Yale, 1964; Centennial Lectr, St Thomas More Coll., Univ. of Saskatchewan, 1967; Inaugural Sir William Scott Meml Lectr, Ulster-Scot Hist. Foundn, 1968; 60th Anniv. Lectr, St Joseph's Coll., Univ. of Alberta, 1987; first Herald to execute duties across Atlantic (Bermuda, 1969) and in S Hemisphere (Brisbane, Qld, 1977) (both in tabard) and in Canada in attendance upon the Sovereign (Vancouver, 1987), to visit Australia, 1970, S America, 1972, Thailand, Japan, 1973, NZ, 1976, Poland, 1991, 1995, Lithuania, 1994. World lecture tours, 1970, 1973, 1976. Adviser to PM of Canada on establishment of Nat. Flag of Canada and Order of Canada, 1964–67; at invitation of Sec. of State of Canada participated in nat. forum on heraldry in Canada, 1987; assisted at the burial of HIM The Emperor Haile Selassie, Addis Ababa, 2000. Co-founder (with Lady Hilda Swan), Heraldic Garden, Boxford, Suffolk, 1983. Hon. Citizen, State of Texas; Freemanships in USA; Freeman: St George's, Bermuda, 1969; City of London, 1974. Fellow, 1976, Hon. Vice-Pres. and a Founder, Heraldry Soc. of Canada; Fellow, Geneal. Soc. of Victoria (Australia), 1970; FSA 1971; FZS 1986. Master, Gunmakers' Co., 1993 (Liveryman and Freeman, 1974; Mem., Ct of Assts, 1983). Hon. LLD Assumption, Ontario, 2006. Heraldic Award, Governor-Gen. of Antigua and Barbuda, 2002. KStJ 1976. Kt of Honour and Devotion, SMO of Malta, 1979 (Kt of Grace and Devotion, 1964) (Genealogist Br. Assoc., 1974–95); Cross of Comdr of Order of Merit, SMO of Malta, 1983; Comdr (with Star), Royal Norwegian Order of Merit, 1995; Cross of Kt Comdr, Order of Merit (Poland), 1995; Knight's Cross, Order of Grand Duke Gediminas (Lithuania), 2002; Kt Grand Cross, Order of the Nation (Antigua and Barbuda), 2003. *Publications:* Heraldry: Ulster and North American Connections, 1972; Canada: Symbols of Sovereignty, 1977; (contrib.) The Royal Encyclopedia, 1991; (jtly) Blood of the Martyrs, 1993; A King from Canada (autobiog.), 2005; many articles in learned jls on heraldic, sigillographic and related subjects. *Recreations:* hunting, driving (horse drawn vehicles), rearing ornamental pheasants and waterfowl, marine biology. *Address:* Boxford House, Suffolk CO10 5JT. *T:* (01787) 210208.

SWAN, Dermot Joseph, MVO 1972; HM Diplomatic Service, retired; HM Consul-General, Marseilles, 1971–77; *b* 24 Oct. 1917; *s* of Dr William Swan and Anne Cosgrave; *m* 1947, Jeanne Labat; one *d*. *Educ:* St George's, Weybridge; University Coll., London Univ. BA (Hons) French and German. Served War, HM Forces, 1939–46. HM Foreign (later Diplomatic) Service: Vice-Consul, Marseilles, 1947; Saigon, 1949; Foreign Office, 1951; Brazzaville, 1951; Budapest, 1953; FO 1955; First Sec., 1958; Head of Chancery, Phnom Penh, 1959, and Budapest, 1961; UK Mission, New York, 1963; FO (later FCO), 1967; Counsellor, Special Asst to Sec.-Gen. of CENTO, Ankara, 1969. *Recreations:* swimming, golf, bridge. *Address:* Las Brisas, San Feliu de Guixols, 17220 Spain.

SWAN, Sir John (William David), KBE 1990; JP; Founder, Chairman, Swan Group of Companies, since 1999; Premier of Bermuda, 1982–95; *b* 3 July 1935; *s* of late John N. Swan and of Margaret E. Swan; *m* 1965, Jacqueline A. D. Roberts; one *s* two *d*. *Educ:* West Virginia Wesleyan Coll. (BA). Salesman, Real Estate, Rego Ltd, 1960–62; Founder, John W. Swan Ltd, 1962 (Chm. and Chief Exec., 1962–2008). MP (United Bermuda Party) Paget E, 1972–95; Minister for: Marine and Air Services; Labour and Immigration, 1977–78; Home Affairs, 1978–82; formerly: Parly Sec. for Finance; Chairman: Bermuda Hosps Bd; Dept of Civil Aviation; Young Presidents' Organization, 1974–86. Member: Chief Execs Orgn; World Business Council, 1986. Mem. and Fellow, Senate, Jun. Chamber Internat., 1992. Hon. Freeman of London, 1985. Hon. LLD: Univ. of Tampa, Fla, 1985; W Virginia Wesleyan Coll., 1987; Atlantic Union Coll., Mass, 1991. Internat. Medal of Excellence (1st recipient), Poor Richard Club of Philadelphia, 1987; Outstanding Learning Disabled Achiever Award, Lab Sch. of Washington, 1992. *Recreations:* sailing, tennis. *Address:* 11 Grape Bay Drive, Paget PG 06, Bermuda. *T:* 361303; Challenger Banks Ltd, PO Box HM 2413, Hamilton HM JX, Bermuda. *T:* 2951785, *Fax:* 2956270; *e-mail:* sirjohn@ibl.bm. *Clubs:* Sandys Rotary, Royal Bermuda Yacht (Bermuda); Bohemian (San Francisco); Chevy Chase (Maryland).

SWAN, Robert Charles, OBE 1995; FRGS; polar explorer, since 1980; *b* 28 July 1956; *s* of late Robert Douglas Swan and of Margaret Swan; *m*; one *s*; *m* 2003, Nicole Beyers. *Educ:* Aysgarth Sch.; Sedbergh Sch.; Durham Univ. (BA). With British Antarctic Survey, 1980–81; planning and fund raising, In the Footsteps of Scott, Antarctic Expedn, 1979–84; arrived at South Pole with R. Mear and G. Wood, 11 Jan. 1986; planning and fund raising, Icewalk, North Pole Expedn, 1988–89; Icewalk Internat. Student Expedn (22 participants from 15 nations), 1989; reached North Pole with 8 walkers from 7 nations (first person to have walked to both Poles), 14 May 1989; One Step Beyond (35 young explorers from 25 nations), 1996–97; started Mission Antarctica, ten year challenge dedicated to preservation of Antarctic wilderness, 1997; Internat. Antarctic Expedns, 1, 2003, 2, 2004, 3, 2005, 4, 2006, 5, 2007. Vis. Prof., Sch. of Envmt, Leeds Metropolitan Univ., 1992–. Former Dir, 2nd Nature Ltd; Dir, Mission Antarctica Ltd. Founded: Robert Swan Foundn (for promotion of youth and scientific endeavour in the envmt), 1993; 2041.com. Keynote speaker at first Earth Summit, Rio de Janeiro, 1992. Mem. Council, WWF (UK), 1987; Vice-Pres., Countryside Mgt Assoc., 1995; Pres., Scott Soc., 2000. UN Goodwill Ambassador with special resp. for youth, 1989; Special Envoy to Dir Gen., UNESCO, 1994; EC Goodwill Ambassador for Envmt, 2003. Liveryman, Wheelwright's Co., 2002. FRGS 1987. Hon. LittD Robert Gordon, 1993. Polar Medal, 1988. Global 500 Award, UN, 1989; Paul Harris Fellow, Rotary Internat., 1991; Smithsonian Award, 1998. *Publications:* In the Footsteps of Scott, 1987; A Walk to the Pole, 1987; Antarctic Survival, 1989; Destination South, 1990; Icewalk, 1990. *Recreations:* yachting, running, tree surgery. *Address:* BCM Box 9090, London WC1N 3XX. *T:* (01768) 341860; *e-mail:* robert@robertswan.org; *web:* www.robertswan.org. *Clubs:* Special Forces; Amstel (Netherlands); Explorers (New York).

SWANN, Benjamin Colin Lewis; Controller, Finance, British Council, 1975–79, retired; *b* 9 May 1922; *s* of Henry Basil Swann and Olivia Ophelia Lewis; *m* 1946, Phyllis Julia Sybil Lewis; three *s* one *d*. *Educ:* Bridgend County School. CA. RAFVR, 1941; Transatlantic Ferry, 1942; Flt Lieut, Transport Command, 1944; Flt Supervisor, BOAC, 1946. Apprentice Chartered Accountant, 1950; Audit Asst, George A. Touche & Co., 1953; Treasury Acct, Malaya, 1954; Financial Adviser, Petaling Jaya, 1956; Partner, Milligan Swann & Co., Chartered Accountants, Exeter, 1957; British Council, 1960; Regional Acct, SE Asia, 1961; Dep. Dir Audit, 1965; Asst Representative, Delhi, 1970; Director, Budget, 1972; Dep. Controller, Finance, 1972. *Recreations:* cuisine, lepidoptery.

SWANN, Julian Dana Nimmo H.; *see* Hartland-Swann.

SWANN, Kathryn, (Kate); Chief Executive Officer, WH Smith, since 2003; *b* 1964; *d* of Ian and Sheila Prior; *m* 1987; two *d*. *Educ:* Bradford Univ. (BSc Hons Business Mgt). Grad. trainee, Tesco, 1986–88; Brand Manager, Homepride Foods, 1988–91; Mktg Controller, Coca Cola Schweppes, 1991; Mktg Dir, Currys, 1992–96; Homebase: Mktg Dir, 1996–99; Man. Dir, 1999; Man. Dir, Argos, 2000–03. *Address:* WH Smith, 180 Wardour Street, W1F 8FY. *T:* (020) 7494 1800; *e-mail:* kate.swann@whsmith.co.uk.

SWANN, Sir Michael (Christopher), 4th Bt *cr* 1906, of Prince's Gardens, Royal Borough of Kensington; TD 1979; Partner, Smith Swann & Co., since 1992; *b* 23 Sept.

1941; *s* of Sir Anthony Swann, 3rd Bt, CMG, OBE and Jean Margaret, *d* of late John Herbert Niblock-Stuart; *S* father, 1991; *m* 1st, 1965, Hon. Lydia Hewitt (marr. diss. 1985), *e d* of 8th Viscount Lifford; two *s* one *d*; 2nd, 1988, Marilyn Ann Morse (*née* Tobitt). *Educ:* Eton Coll. APMI 1978. Lt KRRC (The Royal Green Jackets), 1960–63; T&AVR 4th Bn The Royal Green Jackets, 1964–79 (Brevet Lt-Col 1979). Director: Wright Deen (Life and Estate Duty), 1964–74; Richards Longstaff (Holdings) Ltd, 1974–86; Richards Longstaff Ltd, 1974–88; Gerrard Vivian Gray (Life & Pensions), 1988–92 (Man. Dir). Trustee, Gabbitas Truman and Thring, 1978– (Chm., 1998–). General Comr of Income Tax, 1988–. *Recreations:* bridge, golf, ski-ing, gardening, growing orchids, racing. *Heir: s* Jonathan Christopher Swann [*b* 17 Nov. 1966; *m* 1994, Polly, *d* of Comdr David Baston; twin *s*]. *Address:* 38 Hurlingham Road, SW6 3RQ. *T:* (020) 7731 5601. *Clubs:* Turf, Hurlingham, IZ, MCC; New Zealand Golf.

SWANNELL, John, FRPS; professional photographer specialising in fashion and portraits; *b* 27 Dec. 1946; *s* of Ted and Lily Swannell; *m* 1982, Marianne Lah; one *s* three *d*. *Educ:* Bishopswood Sch., Highgate. FRPS 1993. Left sch. at 16; Vogue Studios, 1966–69; asst to David Bailey, 1969–74; founded own studio, 1975; worked for Vogue, Harpers & Queen, Sunday Times, Tatler. Exhibitions: show, Royal Acad., Edinburgh, 1989; NPG, Edinburgh, 1990; retrospective of fashion work, RPS, 1990; exhibn of nudes, Hamilton Gall., 1991; exhibn of portraits, NPG, 1996–97; photographs in permanent collections: V&A; NPG, London and Scotland; RPS. Royal portraits: the Princess Royal, 40th birthday 1992, 50th birthday 2002; Diana, Princess of Wales with Princes William and Harry, 1994; the Queen, Queen Mother, Prince of Wales and Prince William, 2001; the Queen and Duke of Edinburgh for Golden Jubilee, 2002; Royal Mail stamps: wedding of Duke and Duchess of Wessex, 1999; Queen Mother's 100th birthday; other portraits include: King Hussein of Jordan, King Abdullah and Queen Rania of Jordan, Rowan Atkinson, Helena Bonham Carter, Michael Caine, Joan Collins, Billy Connolly, Dame Judy Dench, Bryan Ferry, Sir Norman Foster, Sir John Gielgud, Gilbert and George, John Hurt, Elton John, Joanna Lumley, Spike Milligan, Roger Moore, Peter O'Toole, Michael Palin, Michael Parkinson, Margaret Thatcher. *Publications:* Fine Lines, 1982; Naked Landscape, 1986; Twenty Years On, 1996; Ten Out of Ten, 2001; I'm Still Standing, 2003; Nudes 1978–2003, 2003. *Recreation:* landscape photography. *Address:* Ivy House, 128 Highgate Hill, N6 5HD. *T:* (020) 8348 5965, *Fax:* (020) 8348 4693; *e-mail:* j.swannell@btconnect.com.

SWANNELL, Nicola Mary, (Mrs Graham Swannell); *see* Pagett, N. M.

SWANNEY, Rajni; Floating Sheriff, North Strathclyde at Greenock, since 1999; *b* 27 Aug. 1954; *d* of Sat Dev Dhir and Swarn Lata Dhir; *m* 1981, Robert Todd Swanney; two *s*. *Educ:* Glasgow Univ. (LLB). Court Assistant: MacRoberts, Glasgow, 1978–80; various Glasgow firms, 1982–88; Chm. (pt-time), Child Support Tribunal, 1993–96; Immigration Adjudicator (pt-time), 1995–99. *Recreations:* gardening, reading, enjoying all things French! *Address:* Greenock Sheriff Court, Nelson Street, Greenock PA15 1TR. *T:* (01475) 787073.

SWANSEA, 5th Baron *cr* 1893, of Singleton, co. Glamorgan; **Richard Anthony Hussey Vivian;** Bt 1882; *b* 24 Jan. 1957; *s* of 4th Baron Swansea and Miriam Antoinette Vivian (*née* Caccia-Birch); *S* father, 2005; *m* 1996, Anna Clementine Brooking (*née* Austin); one *s* one *d*. *Educ:* Eton Coll.; Univ. of Durham (BA Hons); City Univ. Business Sch. (MBA). Financial journalist, 1979–97; res. ed., various investment banks, 1998–, incl. WestLB AG, 2004–. Mem. (C) Wandsworth BC, 1994–2006 (Dep. Mayor, 2000–01; Hon. Alderman, 2006). Mem. Sch. Council, Newton Prep. Sch., Battersea, 2001–. Vice Pres., Morriston RFC Male Choir, 2007–. *Publication:* China's Metals and World Markets, 1992. *Recreations:* racing, Su Doku puzzles, croquet. *Heir: s* Hon. James Henry Hussey Vivian, *b* 25 June 1999. *Address:* 48 Weyside Road, Guildford, Surrey GU1 1HX.

SWANSEA AND BRECON, Bishop of, since 2008; **Rt Rev. John David Edward Davies;** *b* 6 Feb. 1953; *s* of William Howell Davies and Doiran Rallison Davies; *m* 1986, Joanna Lucy Davies (*née* Aulton); one *s* one *d*. *Educ:* Southampton Univ. (LLB 1974); Coll. of Law; St Michael's Coll., Llandaff (DipTh Wales 1984); Univ. of Wales (LLM Canon Law 1995). Admitted Solicitor, 1977; private practice, 1975–82. Ordained deacon, 1984, priest, 1985; Asst Curate, Chepstow, 1984–86; Curate-in-charge, Michaelston-y-Fedw and Rudry, 1986–89; Rector, Bedwas and Rudry, 1989–95; Vicar, St John Evangelist, Newport, 1995–2000; Dean of Brecon, 2000–08. *Recreations:* cooking, golf, music (mainly classical), playing the organ, theatre, opera, reading, current affairs, sport (especially Test Match Special and Peter Alliss), planning walks for the family (and accompanying them when feeling energetic), entertaining my family by trying to convince them of the inestimable benefits of knowing Latin and of appreciating other lost glories of the past. *Address:* Ely Tower, Castle Square, Brecon, Powys LD3 9DB. *T:* (01874) 622008.

SWANSON, John Alexander; His Honour Judge Swanson; a Circuit Judge, since 1996; *b* 31 May 1944; *s* of Sidney Alexander Swanson and Joan Swanson; *m* 1981, Pauline Ann Hearn (*née* Woodmansey) (marr. diss.); two *d*. *Educ:* Giggleswick Sch., Settle; Univ. of Newcastle upon Tyne (LLB 1966). Solicitor, 1970–75; called to the Bar, Inner Temple, 1975; a Recorder, 1994–96. Asst Comr, Boundary Commn for England, 1992–95. *Recreations:* hill-walking, American West, 19th and 20th century music, history of railways, malt whisky. *Address:* Sheffield Combined Court, West Bar, Sheffield S3 8PH. *T:* (0114) 281 2400. *Clubs:* Bridlington Rugby Union Football; Bridlington Yacht.

SWANSON, Dr Kenneth Macgregor; JP; farmer, since 1991; Vice Lord-Lieutenant for Caithness, 1996–2005; *b* 14 Feb. 1930; *s* of Magnus Houston Swanson and Margaret Swanson (*née* Macgregor); *m* 1956, Elspeth Janet Will Paton; two *s* one *d*. *Educ:* Wick High Sch.; St Andrews Univ. (BSc 1st cl. Hons Natural Philosophy 1951; PhD 1959). Nat. service, FO (Pilot), RAF, 1952–54; St Andrews Univ. Air Sqn, RAFVR, 1954–58. Lectr in Physics, UCNW, Bangor, 1955–58; United Kingdom Atomic Energy Authority, Dounreay: SSO, Fast Reactor Fuel Develt, 1958–61; PSO, 1961–71; Res. Manager, Fuels, 1971–86; Asst Dir, 1986–91, retired. Chm., European Cttee on Fast Reactor Fuel Develt, 1987–90; Mem. Bd, NW Reg., 1992–97, Northern Areas, 1997–99, Scottish Natural Heritage; Chm., Caithness Jobs Commn, 1988–98; Dir, Caithness and Sutherland Enterprise, 1990–99 (Vice Chm., 1995–99). JP, 1970, DL, 1977, Caithness. *Publications:* papers and patents on develt of plutonium fuels for electricity production. *Recreations:* enjoying the countryside, sailing. *Address:* Knockglass, Westfield, Thurso, Caithness KW14 7QN. *T:* (01847) 871201.

SWANSON, Prof. Sydney Alan Vasey, FREng; Professor of Biomechanics, Imperial College, University of London, 1974–97; *b* 31 Oct. 1931; *s* of Charles Henry William Swanson and Hannah Elizabeth Swanson (*née* Vasey); *m* 1956, Mary Howarth; one *s* one *d*. *Educ:* Scarborough Boys' High Sch.; Imperial Coll., London. DSc (Eng), PhD, DIC, FCGI, FIMechE; FREng (FEng 1987). Engineering Laboratories, Bristol Aircraft Ltd, 1955–58; Imperial College, London: Lectr, Mechanical Engineering, 1958–69; Reader in Biomechanics, 1969–74; Dean, City and Guilds Coll., 1976–79; Head of Mechanical Engineering Dept, 1978–83; Pro Rector, 1983–86; Pro Rector (Educnl Quality), 1994–97; Dep. Rector, 1997. *Publications:* Engineering Dynamics, 1963; Engineering in Medicine (with B. M. Sayers and B. Watson), 1975; (with M. A. R. Freeman) The Scientific Basis of Joint Replacement, 1977; papers on bone, cartilage and joints in learned jls. *Recreations:* photography, cycling, fell-walking. *Address:* 12 Holmwood Gardens, Wallington, Surrey SM6 0HN. *Club:* Lyke Wake (Northallerton).

SWANSTON, Roderick Brian, FRCM, FRCO; Reader in Historical and Interdisciplinary Studies, Royal College of Music, since 1997; *b* 28 Aug. 1948; *s* of Comdr David Swanston and Sheila Anne Swanston (*née* Lang). *Educ:* Stowe Sch.; Royal Coll. of Music (ARCM 1967; GRSM 1969; FRCM 1994); Pembroke Coll., Cambridge (Organ Schol., 1969; BA 1971, MA 1974; MusB 1975). LRAM 1970; FRCO 1975. Asst Organist, Tower of London, 1967–68; Director of Music: Christ Church, Lancaster Gate, 1972–77; St James, Sussex Gardens, 1977–80; Tutor, Faculty of Contg Educn, Birkbeck Coll., London Univ., 1974–; freelance lectr, 1974–, and broadcaster, 1990–; Prof., RCM, 1976–; Lectr in Humanities, Imperial Coll., London Univ., 1996–; Vis. Prof., Dartmouth Coll., NH, 1995, 1999. Artistic Dir, Austro-Hungarian Music Fest., 1994–. *Publications:* A Dictionary of Biblical Interpretation, 1990; Fairest Isle, 1995; Ultimate Encyclopaedia of Instruments, 1996; Collins Encyclopaedia of Music, 2000; contrib. Musical Times, Gramophone, Early Music, Classic CD. *Recreations:* reading, poetry, theatre, thinking. *Address:* Royal College of Music, Prince Consort Road, SW7 2BS. *T:* (020) 7589 3643. *Club:* Athenæum.

SWANSTON, Roy; Chairman, Shaftesbury Housing Group, 2005–07; *b* 31 Oct. 1940; *s* of Robert Trotter Swanston and Margaret Ann Swanston (*née* Paxton); *m* 1963, Doreen Edmundson; one *s* one *d*. *Educ:* Berwick-upon-Tweed Grammar Sch. FRICS, FCMI. County Borough of Sunderland, 1958–67; Clasp Develt Gp, Nottingham, 1967–71; Notts CC, 1971–74; Durham CC, 1974–75; Dir of Building Economics, 1975–82, of Dept of Architecture, 1982–87, Cheshire CC; Sen. Management Consultant, Peat Marwick McLintock, 1987–88; Dir of Develt, Bucknall Austin, 1988–90; Dir, Properties in Care, 1990–93, Res. and Professional Services, 1993–95, English Heritage; Chm., Local Govt Residuary Bd (England), 1995–99. Chairman: W Herts HA, 1996–2001; E and N Herts NHS Trust, 2001–02. Chairman: Jones Lang Wootton Educn Trust, 1995–2000; Jt Contracts Tribunal for Standard Form of Building Contract, 1995–2002. Mem., E of England Heritage Lottery Cttee, 2006–. Pres., RICS, 1994–95 (Pres., QS Div., 1982–83; Hon. Treas., 1987–90; Chm., Bldg Conservation Diploma Adv. Bd, 2000–); Sec. Gen., Internat. Fedn of Surveyors, 1995–99. Visiting Professor: Liverpool John Moores Univ., 1995–; Luton Univ., 1996– (Mem. Court, 1999–); Salford Univ., 1999– (Vis. Fellow, 1986–99). Mem., Yorks Dales Nat. Park Authy, 2001–04. Trustee, NE Civic Trust, 1998– (Chm., 2006–). Mem., Barnardo's Council, 1989–2005; Chm., Barnardo's Pension Fund, 2003–05 (Trustee, 1998–2002). Governor: Culford Methodist Ind. Sch., 1999– (Chm., 2008–); Springhill Special Sch., 2001–04 (Chm., 2001–04). Methodist Local Preacher. Hon. DSc Salford, 1994. *Recreations:* supporter of Sunderland AFC, fell walking.

SWANTON, Robert Howard, MD; FRCP; Consultant Cardiologist, University College London Hospitals, since 1979, now at The Heart Hospital, W1; *b* 30 Sept. 1944; *s* of Robert Neil and Sue Swanton; *m* 1969, Lindsay Ann (*née* Jepson); one *s* one *d*. *Educ:* Monkton Combe Sch.; Queens' Coll., Cambridge (MB BChir 1969; MA; MD 1980); St Thomas's Hosp. Med. Sch. FRCP 1984. Senior Registrar: St Thomas' Hosp., 1975–77; Nat. Heart Hosp., 1977–79; Consultant Cardiologist: Middlesex Hosp., 1979–2005; King Edward VII Hosp. for Officers, 1984–. Mem. Med. Adv. Panel on Cardiology, CAA, 1998; Chm. Adv. Panel on Cardiology, DVLA, 2002–. Hon. Sec., 1988–90, Pres., 1998–2001, British Cardiac Soc. FESC 1994; FACC 2005. Mem. Editorial Bd, Hospital Medicine, 1986–. *Publications:* Cardiology, 1984, 6th edn 2008; articles in med. literature incl. Heart, American Jl Cardiology, Hospital Medicine, European Heart Jl, etc. *Recreations:* music, photography. *Address:* (home) Kent Lodge, 10 Dover Park Drive, Roehampton, SW15 5BG. *T:* (020) 8788 6920; *e-mail:* howard.swanton@uclh.org; (office) 42 Wimpole Street, W1G 8YF. *T:* (020) 7486 7416, *Fax:* (020) 7487 2569. *Clubs:* Arts; St Albans Medical; Chelsea Clinical.

SWARBRICK, Catherine Marie; Director of Administration, University of London, since 2004; *b* 25 Nov. 1950; *d* of Hubert Joseph Swarbrick and Margaret Swarbrick. *Educ:* Goldsmiths' Coll., Univ. of London (BA Hons, PGCE). Secondary sch. teacher, 1973–79; Sec., Law Dept, LSE, 1980–82; Exams Officer, British Computer Soc., 1982–85; Sen. Manager, RCGP, 1985–95; Dir, Nat. Childbirth Trust, 1995–99; School Sec., St George's Hosp. Med. Sch., 1999–2004. *Recreations:* reading, art history. *Address:* University of London, Senate House, Malet Street, WC1E 7HU.

SWARBRICK, Prof. James, PhD, DSc; FRSC, CChem; FRPharmS; President, PharmaceuTech Inc., since 2001; *b* 8 May 1934; *s* of George Winston Swarbrick and Edith M. C. Cooper; *m* 1960, Pamela Margaret Oliver. *Educ:* Sloane Grammar Sch.; Chelsea Coll., Univ. of London (BPharm Hons 1960; PhD 1964; DSc 1972). FRSC (FRIC 1970); FRPharmS (FPS 1978; MPS 1961). Asst Lectr, 1962, Lectr, 1964, Chelsea Coll.; Vis. Asst Prof., Purdue Univ., 1964; Associate Prof., 1966, Prof. and Chm. of Dept of Pharmaceutics, 1969, Asst Dean, 1970, Univ. of Conn; Dir of Product Develt, Sterling-Winthrop Res. Inst., NY, 1972; first Prof. of Pharmaceutics, Univ. of Sydney, 1975–76; Dean, Sch. of Pharmacy, Univ. of London, 1976–78; Prof. of Pharmacy and Chm., Res. Council, Univ. of S California, Los Angeles, 1978–81; Prof. of Pharmaceutics and Chm., Div. of Pharmaceutics, Univ. of N Carolina, 1981–93; Vice-Pres., R&D, 1993–99, Scientific Affairs, 1999–2006, Applied Analytical Industries Inc., subseq. aaiPharma Inc. Vis. Scientist, Astra Labs, Sweden, 1971; Vis. Prof., Shanghai Med. Univ., 1991–92. Indust. Cons., 1965–72, 1975–; Cons., Aust. Dept. of Health, 1975–76; Mem., Cttee on Specifications, National Formulary, 1970–75; Chm., Jt US Pharmacopoeia-Nat. Formulary Panel on Disintegration and Dissolution Testing, 1971–75. Member: Cttee on Grad. Programs, Amer. Assoc. of Colls of Pharmacy, 1969–71; Practice Trng Cttee, Pharm. Soc. of NSW, 1975–76; Academic Bd, Univ. of Sydney, 1975–76; Collegiate Council, 1976–78; Educn Cttee, Pharmaceutical Soc. of GB, 1976–78; Working Party on Pre-Registration Training, 1977–78. Pharmaceutical Manufacturers Assoc. Foundation: Mem., Basic Pharmacology Adv. Cttee, 1982–91; Chm., Pharmaceutics Adv. Cttee, 1986–2007; Mem., Scientific Adv. Cttee, 1986–2007; Mem., Generic Drugs Adv. Cttee, Food and Drug Admin, 1992–96 (Chm., 1994–96). FAAAS 1966; Fellow: Acad. of Pharm. Sciences, 1973; Amer. Assoc. of Pharmaceutical Scientists, 1987. Kenan Res. Study Award, 1988. Mem. Editorial Board: Jl of Biopharmaceutics and Pharmacokinetics, 1973–79; Drug Development Communications, 1974–82; Pharmaceutical Technology, 1978–; Biopharmaceutics and Drug Disposition, 1979–; series Editor, Current Concepts in the Pharmaceutical Sciences, Drugs and the Pharmaceutical Sciences. *Publications:* (with A. N. Martin and A. Cammarata) Physical Pharmacy, 2nd edn 1969, 3rd edn 1983; (ed) Encyclopedia of Pharmaceutical Technology, 3rd edn 2007; contributed: American Pharmacy, 6th edn 1966 and 7th edn 1974; Remington's Pharmaceutical Sciences, 14th edn 1970 to 21st edn 2005; contrib. Current Concepts in the Pharmaceutical Sciences: Biopharmaceutics, 1970; res. contribs to internat. sci. jls. *Recreations:* woodworking, listening to music, golf. *Address:* PharmaceuTech Inc., 180 Doral Drive, Pinehurst, NC 28374–8682, USA. *T:* (910) 2553015; *e-mail:* pharmaceutech@earthlink.net.

SWARBRICK, William Alfred, CEng; DL; Chief Executive, Cumbria County Council, 1997–2000; *b* 30 Sept. 1940; *s* of William and Agnes Swarbrick; *m* 1963, Catherine Lamey; one *s* one *d. Educ:* Manchester Grammar Sch.; Manchester Univ. (BSc Tech.). CEng, MICE 1968; Dip. in Traffic Engrg, IMunE, 1971; FIHT 1991. Cumberland CC, later Cumbria CC, 1963–2000; Gen. Manager, County Contracting, 1987–92; Dir, Cumbria Contract Services, 1992–97. Chm., PAC Ltd, 2000–. Chairman: Victim Support Cumbria, 2001– (Mem., Nat. Council); Carlisle RFC, 2000–. Pres., Cumbria Youth Orch., 2004–. MCMI (MIMgt 1987). DL Cumbria, 2006. *Recreations:* cooking, gardening, viola and timpani playing. *Address:* 5 St Aidan's Road, Carlisle CA1 1LT.

SWARTZ, Rt Rev. George Alfred; Bishop of Kimberley and Kuruman, 1983–91; *b* 8 Sept. 1928; *s* of Philip and Julia Swartz; *m* 1957, Sylvia Agatha (*née* George); one *s* one *d. Educ:* Umbilo Road High Sch., Durban; Univ. of the Witwatersrand, Johannesburg; Coll. of the Resurrection, Mirfield, Yorks; St Augustine's Coll., Canterbury. BA, Primary Lower Teacher's Cert., Central Coll. Dip. (Canterbury). Asst Teacher, Sydenham Primary Sch., 1951–52; Deacon, 1954; Priest, 1955; Asst Curate, St Paul's Church, Cape Town, 1955–56; Priest in Charge, Parochial Dist of St Helena Bay, Cape, 1957–60; St Augustine's Coll., Canterbury, 1960–61; Dir, Cape Town Dio. Mission to Muslims, 1962–63; Dir, Mission to Muslims and Rector St Philip's Church, Cape Town, 1963–70; Regional Dean of Woodstock Deanery, 1966–70; Priest in Charge, Church of the Resurrection, Bonteheuwel, Cape, 1971–72; a Bishop Suffragan of Cape Town, 1972–83; Canon of St George's Cathedral, Cape Town, 1969–72. Dean of the Province, Church of the Province of Southern Africa, 1986–89. *Recreations:* cinema, music (traditional jazz; instruments played are guitar and saxophone). *Address:* 11 Tanglin, Thomas Road, Kenilworth, Cape Town, 7708, Republic of South Africa. *T:* (21) 7979079.

SWARUP, Prof. Govind, PhD; FRS 1991; Professor of Eminence, Physics and Radio Astronomy, 1990–94, Professor Emeritus, 1994–99, Homi Bhabha Senior Fellow, 1999–2001, Tata Institute of Fundamental Research, Bombay; *b* 29 March 1929; *m* Bina Jain; one *s* one *d. Educ:* Allahabad Univ. (BSc 1948; MSc 1950); Stanford Univ., USA (PhD 1961). Sec., Radio Res. Cttee, CSIR, Nat. Physical Lab., New Delhi, 1950–53; Colombo-Plan Fellowship, CSIRO, Sydney, 1953–55; Res. Associate, Harvard Univ., 1956–57; Grad. Student, Stanford Univ., USA, 1957–60, Asst Prof. 1961–63; Tata Institute of Fundamental Research, Bombay: Reader, 1963–65; Associate Prof., 1965–70; Prof., 1970–79; Sen. Prof., 1979–90; Dir, Giant Metrewave Radio Telescope Project, 1987–96. INSA Hon. Scientist, 2001–05. Visiting Professor: Univ. of Md, USA, 1980; Univ. of Groningen, Netherlands, 1980–81; Univ. of Leiden, Netherlands, 1981. Chm., Indian Nat. Cttee, URSI, 1986–88, 1994–97. Fellow: Indian Nat. Sci. Acad.; Indian Acad. Scis; Nat. Acad. Scis, India; Indian Geophysical Union; Third World Acad. of Scis; Academician, Internat. Acad. of Astronautics. Associate, RAS; Member: Astronomical Soc. India (Pres., 1975–77); IAU (Pres., Radio Astronomy Commn, 1979–82); Indian Physics Assoc.; Indian Physical Soc. Member Editorial Board: Indian Jl Radio and Space Physics; Nat. Acad. of Science, India. Numerous awards, incl. Delinger Award, URSI; S. S. Bhatnager Award, India, 1973; Tsiolkovsky medal, Fedn of Cosmonautics, USSR, 1987; Third World Acad. of Scis Award, Trieste, 1988; R. D. Birla Award, India, 1990; Khwarizmi Award, Iran, 1999; Herschel Medal, RAS, 2006; Grote Reber Medal, Tasmania, 2007. *Publications:* (ed jtly) Quasars, 1986; (ed jtly) History of Oriental Astronomy, 1987. *Address:* 10 Cozy Retreat, Road No 3, Sindh Society, Aundh, Pune 411007, India. *T:* (office) (20) 25697107, (home) (20) 25899030.

SWASH, Prof. Michael, MD; FRCP, FRCPath; Consultant Neurologist: Royal London Hospital, 1972–2006; London Independent Hospital, since 1980; Professor of Neurology, Bart's and the London School of Medicine and Dentistry, Queen Mary (formerly St Bartholomew's and the Royal London School of Medicine and Dentistry, Queen Mary and Westfield College), University of London, 1993–2006, now Emeritus; *b* 29 Jan. 1939; *s* of Edwin Frank Swash and Kathleen Swash; *m* 1966, Caroline Mary Payne; three *s. Educ:* Forest Sch., London; London Hosp. Med. Coll., Univ. of London (MB BS 1962; MD 1973); Univ. of Virginia, USA. FRCP 1977; FRCPath 1991. House appts, London and Bath, 1962–63; GP, Westbury, Wilts and Tottenham, 1965; postgrad. trng in neurol. and neurophysiol., Case-Western Reserve Univ., Cleveland, Ohio and Washington Univ., St Louis, Mo, 1965–68; MRC Res. Fellow in Neuropathol., then Sen. Registrar in Neurol., Royal London Hosp., 1968–72; Consultant Neurologist, Newham HA, 1972–91; Sen. Lectr in Neuropathol., London Hosp. Med. Coll., 1976–90; Med. Dir, Royal London NHS Trust, 1990–93. CMO, Swiss Reinsce Ltd, 1985–. Vis. lectr or vis. prof., various univs in Europe, Asia, Australia and N America; Spinoza Vis. Prof., Univ. of Amsterdam, 1999–2000. Hon. Prof. of Neurology, Univ. of Lisbon, 2007–. Ed., Associate Ed. and mem. editl bds, various neurol and other scientific jls. Mem., Neurosci. Bd, MRC, 1987–91. Hon. Secretary: Sect. Neurol., RSocMed, 1977–79; Assoc. of British Neurologists, 1981–87; Motor Neurone Disease Association: Chm., Annual Symposium Cttee, 1991–99; Chm. Trustees, 1998–2001; Chm., World Fedn of Neurol. Res. Gp on MNDs, 1997–. Medals and prizes incl. Forbes H. Norris Internat. Prize for res. and care in MND/ALS. *Publications:* (jtly) Colour Guide to Neurology, 1972, 3rd edn 2005; (ed) Hutchison's Clinical Methods, 16th edn, 1975 to 22nd edn, 2007; (jtly) Neuromuscular Disorders: a practical approach to diagnosis and management, 1981, 3rd edn 1999; (jtly) Clinical Neuropathology, 1983; (jtly) Biopsy Pathology of Muscle, 1984, 2nd edn 1991; (jtly) Scientific Basis of Neurology, 1985; (jtly) Coloproctology and the Pelvic Floor, 1985, 2nd edn 1992; (jtly) Neurology: a concise clinical text, 1989; (jtly) Hierarchies in Neurology, 1989; (jtly) Clinical Neurology, 2 vols, 1989; (jtly) Motor Neuron Disease, 1994; Outcomes in Neurology and Neurosurgery, 1998; (jtly) Amyotrophic Lateral Sclerosis, 2000, 2nd edn 2006; (jtly) ALSAQ User Manual, 2001; (jtly) The Pelvic Floor, 2002; (jtly) Neurology in Focus, 2009; contrib. numerous papers to med. and scientific jls. *Recreations:* pianoforte, chamber music and opera, hill walking, Morgan Plus 8. *Address:* London Independent Hospital, E1 4NL. *T:* (020) 7780 2400, *Fax:* (020) 7638 4043; *e-mail:* mswash@btinternet.com. *Clubs:* Athenæum; London Rowing; Rowfant (Cleveland, Ohio).

SWAYNE, Desmond Angus, TD 2000; MP (C) New Forest West, since 1997; *b* 20 Aug. 1956; *s* of George Joseph Swayne and Elizabeth McAlister Swayne (*née* Gibson); *m* 1987, Moira Cecily Teek; one *s* two *d. Educ:* Bedford Sch.; Univ. of St Andrews (MTh). Schoolmaster: Charterhouse, 1980–81; Wrekin Coll., 1982–87; Systems Manager, Royal Bank of Scotland, 1988–96. Opposition front bench spokesman on health, Jan.–Sept. 2001, on defence, 2001–02, on NI, 2003–04; Opposition Whip, 2002–03; PPS to Leader of the Opposition, 2004–. TA Officer, 1987–. Prison visitor, 1989–. *Address:* House of Commons, SW1A 0AA. *Clubs:* Cavalry and Guards; Serpentine Swimming.

SWAYNE, Giles Oliver Cairnes; composer; *b* 30 June 1946; *s* of Sir Ronald Oliver Carless Swayne, MC and Charmian (*née* Cairnes); *m* 1st, 1972, Camilla Rumbold (marr. diss. 1983); one *s*; 2nd, 1984, Naa Otua Codjoe (marr. diss. 2001); 3rd, 2002, Malu Lin. *Educ:* Ampleforth; Trinity Coll., Cambridge; Royal Acad. of Music. Dir, Gonzaga Music Ltd, 2002–. Composer in Residence, Clare Coll., Cambridge, 2006–. *Compositions:* Six songs of lust, La rivière, 1966; The kiss, 1967; Sonata for string quartet, 1968; Three Shakespeare songs, 1969; Chamber music for strings, Four lyrical pieces, 1970; The good-

morrow, String quartet no 1, Paraphrase, 1971; Trio, Canto for guitar, 1972; Canto for piano, Canto for violin, 1973; Orlando's music, Synthesis, Scrapbook, 1974; Canto for clarinet, Charades, Duo, 1975; Suite for Guitar, Pentecost-music, Alleluia!, 1976; String quartet no 2, 1977; A world within, 1978; Phoenix variations, CRY, 1979; The three Rs, Freewheeling, 1980; Count-down, Canto for cello, 1981; Rhythm-studies 1 and 2, Magnificat I, 1982; Riff-raff, A song for Haddi, 1983; Symphony for small orchestra, Le nozze di Cherubino, NaaOtwa Lala, 1984; Missa Tiburtina, 1985; Into the light, Solo, godsong, Nunc dimittis I, O magnum mysterium, 1986; PP, Tonos, Veni creator I, Veni creator II, Songlines, The coming of Saskia Hawkins, 1987; The song of Leviathan, Harmonies of Hell, 1988; A memory of sky, 1989; No quiet place, No man's land, 1990; Circle of silence, 1991; Zebra music, The song of the Tortoise, 1992; The Owl and the Pussycat I, String quartet no 3, 1993; Fiddlesticks, Goodnight sweet ladies, Squeezy, 1994; All about Henry, The tiger, Communion service in D, A convocation of worms, 1995; Two romantic songs, The silent land, Ophelia drowning, 1996; Tombeau, Beatus vir, Mr Leary's mechanical maggot, Chinese whispers, Petite messe solitaire, Echo, 1997; Winter Solstice carol, Groundwork, Merlis Lied, 1998; The flight of the Swan, HAVOC, 1999; Perturbèd spirit, Canto for flute, The Akond of Swat, 2000; Mancanza, The murder of Gonzago, 2001; Bits and Bobs, Epitaph and refrain, 2002; The Owl and the Pussycat II, Midwinter, Sangre viva, 2003; Stabat Mater, Four Passiontide motets, Ave verum corpus, Stations of the Cross I, Mr Bach's Bottle-bank, Magnificat II, 2004; Four Christmas Carols, Nunc dimittis II, Lonely hearts, Stations of the Cross II, Bits of Mrs Bach, Epithalamium, Elegy for a wicked world, 2005; Sonata for cello and piano, Sinfonietta concertante, Ten Terrible Tunes, A Clare Eucharist, Creepy-crawlies, Two little motets, There is no rose, 2006; Bagatelles 1–3 for piano, Suite for solo cello, Symphony no 1, Threnody, 2007; Leonardo's Dream, Agnes Wisley's Chillout Fantasy, Magnificat III, Bagatelles 4–10 for piano, 2008. *Recreations:* walking, Racing Demon. *Address:* c/o Sam Wilcock, Chester Novello, 14–15 Berners Street, W1T 3LJ; *e-mail:* gs@gonzagamusic.co.uk.

SWAYTHLING, 5th Baron *cr* 1907, of Swaythling, co. Southampton; **Charles Edgar Samuel Montagu;** Bt 1894; Director, The Health Partnership; *b* 20 Feb. 1954; *o s* of 4th Baron Swaythling and of Christine Françoise (*née* Dreyfus); *S* father, 1998; *m* 1996, Hon. Angela, *d* of Baron Rawlinson of Ewell, PC, QC; one *d.* Member: Amer. Council of Hypnotist Examiners (Mem. Adv. Bd); British Council of Hypnotist Examiners; Scientific and Medical Network; Adv. Bd, British Council for Complementary Medicine. Trustee, Crossroads Foundn, Antigua. *Heir: unde* Hon. Anthony Trevor Samuel Montagu [*b* 3 Aug. 1931; *m* 1962, Deirdre Bridget (*née* Senior); two *s* one *d*]. *Address:* c/o The Health Partnership, 12A Thurloe Street, SW7 2ST.

SWEENEY, Brendan, MBE 2003; FRCGP; Principal in general practice, Govan, since 1975; *b* 11 July 1946; *s* of James and Angela Sweeney; *m* 1973, Dr Rosalie T. Dunn; two *s* three *d. Educ:* Univ. of Glasgow (MA 1965; MB ChB 1971). DObstRCOG 1973; MRCGP 1975, FRCGP 1985. McKenzie Lectr, RCGP, 1997. Hon. Sen. Lectr, Dept of Postgrad. Med. Educn, Univ. of Glasgow. Royal College of General Practitioners: Vice-Chm., Council, 1994–97; Chairman: Cttee of Med. Ethics, 1992–98; W of Scotland Cttee on Postgrad. Med. Educn, 1997–. *Recreations:* squash, golf, opera, theatre, books. *Address:* 25 Stewarton Drive, Cambuslang, Glasgow G72 8DF. *T:* (0141) 583 1513. *Clubs:* Turnberry Golf, Cathkin Braes Golf; Newlands Squash and Tennis.

SWEENEY, Brian Philip, QFSM 2005; Chief Officer/Chief Executive, Strathclyde Fire & Rescue (formerly Strathclyde Fire Brigade), since 2004; *b* 14 July 1961; *s* of Philip and Mary Sweeney; *m* 1995, Pamela Barratt; three *s. Educ:* Holyrood; Coventry Univ. (MA Mgt 2000). Strathclyde Fire Brigade: Firefighter, 1981, Leading Firefighter, 1983; Station Officer, Bde Trng Centre, 1990; Asst Divnl Officer, N Glasgow, 1993; Hd of Ops, E Command HQ, Motherwell, 1996; Hd of Personnel and Trng, Central Command, 1997; Dep. Comdr, Central Command, 1998–2000; Dir of Ops, 2000–03; Dep. Chief Officer, 2003; Temp. Firemaster, 2004. MIFireE 1996; Mem., Chief Fire Officers' Assoc., 2000–. Freeman, City of Glasgow, 2004. DUniv Glasgow Caledonian, 2005. *Recreations:* reading, music, accumulating stress. *Address:* Strathclyde Fire & Rescue, Headquarters, Bothwell Road, Hamilton ML3 0EA. *T:* (01698) 338240, *Fax:* (01698) 338494; *e-mail:* brian.sweeney@strathclydefire.org.

SWEENEY, Edward; Chairman, Advisory, Conciliation and Arbitration Service, since 2007; *b* 6 Aug. 1954; *s* of William Sweeney and Louise Sweeney; *m* 1987, Janet Roydhouse. *Educ:* Warwick Univ. (BA Hons); London Sch. of Economics (MSc Econ.). Banking, Insurance and Finance Union: Research Officer, 1976–79; Negotiating Officer (TSB), 1979–86; National Officer: Scotland, 1986–89; Insurance, 1989–91; Dep. Gen. Sec., 1991–96; Gen. Sec., 1996–99, when BIFU amalgamated with UNIFI; UNIFI: Jt Gen. Sec., 1999–2000; Gen. Sec., 2000–04, when UNIFI merged with Amicus; Dep. Gen. Sec., Amicus, 2004–07. *Recreations:* sport, reading, Egyptology. *Address:* ACAS, Brandon House, 180 Borough High Street, SE1 1LW.

SWEENEY, Sir George, Kt 2000; Principal, Knowsley Community College, since 1990; *b* 26 Jan. 1946; *s* of George Sweeney and Margaret, (Peggy), Sweeney (*née* Carlin); *m* 1968, Susan Anne Wilson; two *d. Educ:* Prescot Boys' GS; Hull Univ. (BA Hons Hist. and Pols 1967; MA 1973). Teacher: Hull Coll. of Technol., 1967–70; Kirby Coll., Teesside, 1970–73; S Trafford Coll., 1973–75 and 1977–83; S Cheshire Coll., 1975–77; Vice Principal, Grimsby Coll. of Technol., 1983–90; Actg Principal, Sheffield Coll., Jan.–Aug. 2000. *Recreations:* painting, drawing, gardening, political biography. *Address:* 12 Red Lane, Appleton, Cheshire WA4 5AD. *T:* (01925) 265113.

SWEENEY, Hon. Sir Nigel Hamilton, Kt 2008; **Hon. Mr Justice Sweeney;** a Judge of the High Court of Justice, Queen's Bench Division, since 2008; *b* 18 March 1954; *s* of Alan Vincent Sweeney and Dorothy Sweeney; *m* 1st, 1985, Joanna Clair Slater (marr. diss.); one *s* one *d*; 2nd, 2002, Dr Sheila Theresa Diamond. *Educ:* Wellington Sch., Som; Nottingham Univ. (LLB 1975). Called to the Bar, Middle Temple, 1976 (Harmsworth Schol. 1976), Bencher, 1997. Central Criminal Court: Jun. Prosecuting Counsel to the Crown, 1987–91; First Jun. Prosecuting Counsel, 1991–92; Sen. Prosecuting Counsel, 1992–97; First Sen. Prosecuting Counsel, 1997–2000; Recorder, 1997–2008; QC 2000. *Recreations:* golf, tennis, the arts. *Address:* Royal Courts of Justice, Strand, WC2A 2LL. *Clubs:* Garrick; Wisley Golf.

SWEENEY, Thomas Kevin; Senior Medical Officer, Department of Health and Social Security, 1983–88, retired; *b* 10 Aug. 1923; *s* of John Francis and Mildred Sweeney; *m* 1950, Eveleen Moira Ryan; two *s* two *d. Educ:* O'Connell Sch., Dublin; University Coll., Dublin (MB, BCh, BAO NUI; DTM&H London; TDD Wales). FFPH (FFCM 1983). Principal Med. Officer, Colonial Medical Service, 1950–65, retd; Asst Sen. Med. Officer, Welsh Hosp. Bd, 1965–68; Department of Health and Social Security: Med. Officer, 1968–72; Sen. Med. Officer, 1972–79; SPMO, 1979–83. QHP 1984–87. *Publication:* contrib. BMJ. *Recreations:* gardening, golf, cathedrals. *Address:* Tresanton, Wych Hill Way, Woking, Surrey GU22 0AE. *T:* (01483) 828199.

SWEENEY, Timothy Patrick; Director: AIB Group UK, since 2001; Waste Resources Action Programme plc, since 2001; Chairman, Amicus Vision, 2001–05; *b* 2 June 1944; *s* of John Sylvester Sweeney and Olive Bridget (*née* Montgomery-Cunningham); *m* 1965, Carol Ann Wardle; one *s* one *d*. *Educ:* Pierrepont School; Sussex Univ. (MA Philosophy); Surrey Univ. (MSc Econs). With Bank of England, 1967–94; Dir Gen., BBA, 1994–2001. Dir, Money Advice Trust, 2000–04. Mem., Better Regulation Commn (formerly Task Force), 2002–06. *Recreations:* music, archery, walking. *Address:* Hollowell Hill House, W Chinnock, Crewkerne, Som TA18 7PS.

SWEENEY, Walter Edward; Solicitor, Yorkshire Law (formerly Walter Sweeney & Co.), since 1997; *b* Dublin, 23 April 1949; *s* of Patrick Anthony Sweeney, veterinary surgeon and Jane Yerbury Sweeney, retired head teacher; *m* 1992, Dr Nuala Maire Kennan; three *d*. *Educ:* Church Lawford Primary Sch.; Lawrence Sheriff Sch., Rugby; Univ. of Aix-Marseille; Univ. of Hull (BA Hons; MA); Darwin Coll., Cambridge (MPhil); Cert. Ed. TEFL. Admitted Solicitor, 1976. Mem., Vale of Glam CHC, 1991–92. Joined Cons. Party, 1964; Chairman: Rugby Div. YCs, 1965; Church Lawford Cons. Br., 1969; Rugby Cons. Political Centre, 1970. Member: Church Lawford Parish Council, 1971–74; Rugby BC, 1974–77; Beds CC, 1981–89 (Vice-Chm. and Gp spokesman on Police Cttee). Contested (C) Stretford, 1983. MP (C) Vale of Glamorgan, 1992–97; contested (C) same seat, 1997. Member, Select Committee: on Welsh Affairs, 1992–97; on Home Affairs, 1995–97; on Channel Tunnel Rail Link, 1995–96; Vice Chairman: All-Party Penal Affairs Cttee, 1993–97 (Sec., 1992–93); Cons. back bench Legal Affairs Cttee, 1995–97 (Sec., 1994–95); Sec., Cons. back bench Home Affairs Cttee, 1994–97. Pres., Hull Incorp. Law Soc., 2004–05 (Vice-Pres., 2003–04). Mem., N Cave Parish Council, 2003–07 (Vice-Chm., 2005–07). Gov., N Cave C of E Primary Sch., 2003–. *Recreations:* walking, swimming, theatre, reading. *Address:* (home) Newbegin House, 10 Newbegin, Beverley HU17 8EG.

SWEET, Andrew Francis; a District Judge (Magistrates' Courts), since 2004; *b* 12 Nov. 1954; *s* of Rev. Mervyn Thomas Sweet and Joan Myra Dorothy Sweet (*née* Reece); *m* 1980, Fiona (*née* McMurdy); two *d*. *Educ:* Cordwallis Prep. Sch., SA; Northbrook Secondary Sch., London; South Bank Polytech. (BA Hons Law); Coll. of Law, Guildford. Admitted solicitor of Supreme Court, 1984; solicitor in private practice: Surrey, 1980–90; London, 1992–2004; Crown Prosecutor, 1990–92. Administrator to Richmond Court Duty Solicitor Scheme and Police Station Duty Solicitor Administrator, 1995–2004. Dep. Dist Judge, 1997–2004. LEA Sch. Gov., Grand Avenue Primary Sch., 1994–2004. *Recreations:* reading, motorcycles, mountain trekking. *Address:* West London Magistrates' Court, 181 Talgarth Road, Hammersmith, W6 8DN. *T:* (020) 8700 9302.

SWEETBAUM, Henry Alan; Chairman, Huntingdon Securities, 1973–2006; Managing Director, PS Capital LLC, since 1997; *b* 22 Nov. 1937; *s* of late Irving and Bertha Sweetbaum; *m* 1st, 1960, Suzanne Milberg (decd); three *s*; 2nd, 1971, Anne Betty Leonie de Vigier; one *s*. *Educ:* Wharton School, Univ. of Pennsylvania (BS Econ 1959). Underwood Corp., 1960; Exec. Vice-Pres. and Dir, Reliance Corp., 1962–70; Exec. Dir, Plessey Corp., 1970; Data Recording Instrument Co.: non-exec. Dir, 1973–76; Chm., 1976–82; Chm. and Chief Exec., Wickes plc, 1982–96. Non-exec. Dir, Mikronite Technologies Gp Inc., 2004–; Mem., Investment Cttee, Accelerator Technology Hldgs, 2005–. University of Pennsylvania Wharton School Board Member: Bd of Overseers, 1994–2005; European Adv. Bd, 1988–2006; SEI Center for Advanced Management Studies, 1989–. CCMI (CIMgt 1993). *Publication:* Restructuring the Management Challenge, 1990. *Recreation:* swimming. *Clubs:* Reform; University (New York).

SWEETING, Col John William Frederick, CBE 2004; Chief Executive, Treloar Trust, 1997–2005; *b* 16 Feb. 1946; *s* of late Quilter William Victor Sweeting and Mary Edith Violet Sweeting (*née* Dewey); *m* 1976, Mary Clark (*née* Millington); two *s* one *d*. *Educ:* Tonbridge Sch.; Univ. of Bristol (LLB 1967). Commnd RE 1967; Staff Coll., Camberley, 1978; SO1 Defence Commitments (Rest of World), 1985–86; CO 28 Amph. Engr Regt, 1987–89; COS Engr in Chief (Army), 1990–91. Bursar, Lord Mayor Treloar Coll., 1991–97. Founder Mem. and Treas., Nat. Assoc. of Ind. and Non-maintained Special Schs (NASS), 1998–2001; Chm., Assoc. of Nat. Specialist Colls (NATSPEC), 1999–2004; Founder Trustee and Chm., RECOM (nat. org. for recycling computers to disabled), 2000–04; Trustee, Fortune Centre of Riding Therapy, 2005–. Reader, C of E, 1968–; Chaplain to High Sheriff of Hampshire, 2008–April 2009. *Recreations:* choral singing, travel, gardening, golf. *Address:* 17 Lynn Way, Kings Worthy, Winchester, Hants SO23 7TG. *T:* (01962) 884325; *e-mail:* john.sweeting@talktalk.net. *Club:* Rotary (Winchester).

SWEETING, Prof. Sir Martin (Nicholas), Kt 2002; OBE 1996; FRS 2000; FREng, FIET, FRAeS, FInstP; Professor of Satellite Engineering, since 1990, and Director, Surrey Space Centre (formerly Centre for Satellite Engineering Research), since 1996, University of Surrey; Executive Chairman (formerly Managing Director and Chief Executive Officer), Surrey Satellite Technology Ltd, since 1994; *b* 12 March 1951; *s* of Frank Morris Sweeting and Dorothy May Sweeting; *m* 1975, Christine Ruth Taplin. *Educ:* Aldenham School, Elstree; University of Surrey (BSc Hons 1974; PhD 1979). Marconi Space & Defence Systems, 1972–73; University of Surrey: Research Fellow, 1978–81; Lectr, 1981–86; Univ. Research Fellow in Satellite Engrg, 1984–87; Dir, Satellite Engrg, 1986–90; Dep. Dir, Centre for Satellite Engrg Res., 1990–96. Res. Dir, Satellites Internat., 1983–84; Surrey Satellite Technology: Technical Dir, 1985–94; Acting Man. Dir, 1989–94. Member: Internat. Acad. of Astronautics, 1999–; Defence and Aerospace Panel, UK Technology Foresight Cttee, 2003–05; EU Framework Prog. 6 Space Adv. Panel, 2003–06; ESA Aurora Adv. Cttee, 2003–; a Vice-Pres., Internat. Astronautics Fedn, 2000–05. FREng (FEng 1996); FInstP 2001. Silver Medal, Royal Acad. Engrg, 1995; Gold Medal, UK Engrg Council, 1998; Space Achievement Medal, British Interplanetary Soc., 1998; Mullard Prize, Royal Soc., 2000; Frank Malina Medal, Int. Acad. of Astronautics, 2003; Gold Medal, Royal Inst. Navigation, 2006. *Publications:* papers in professional jls. *Recreations:* travelling in China, photography, languages, music, amateur radio.

SWEETMAN, Jennifer Joan, (Mrs Ronald Andrew); *see* Dickson, J. J.

SWEETMAN, John Francis, CB 1991; TD 1964; Clerk Assistant, 1987–90 and Clerk of Committees, 1990–95 of the House of Commons; *b* 31 Oct. 1930; *s* of late Thomas Nelson Sweetman and Mary Monica (*née* D'Arcy-Reddy); *m* 1st, 1959, Susan Margaret Manley; one *s* one *d*; 2nd, 1983, Celia Elizabeth, *yr d* of Sir William Nield, GCMG, KCB; two *s*. *Educ:* Cardinal Vaughan Sch.; St Catharine's Coll., Cambridge (MA Law). 2nd Lieut, RA, Gibraltar, 1949–51; TA (City of London RA) and AER, 1951–65. A Clerk of the House of Commons, 1954–95: Clerk of Select Cttees on Nationalised Industries and on Sci. and Technol., 1962–65, 1970–73; Second Clerk of Select Cttees, 1979–83; Clerk of the Overseas Office, 1983–87; Clerk of Select Cttee on Sittings of the House, 1991–92. Parly Advr, BBC, 1996–98. Parly missions to Armenia, Croatia, Fiji, Gambia, Kazakhstan, Kyrgyzstan, Moldova, Nigeria, Sierra Leone, Sri Lanka, Uganda, Ukraine and Yemen, 1996–2004. Member: Assoc. of Secs-Gen. of Parliaments, IPU, 1987–; Assoc. of Clerks-at-the-Table, Canada, 1996–. Mem., Oxford and Cambridge Catholic Educn Bd, 1964–84. *Publications:* contrib. to: Erskine May's Parliamentary Practice; Halsbury's Laws of England; parly jls; (ed) Council of Europe, Procedure and Practice of the Parliamentary Assembly. *Address:* 41 Creffield Road, W5 3RR. *T:* (020) 8992 2456. *Clubs:* Garrick, MCC.

SWEETMAN, Stuart John, FCA; Group Managing Director, Royal Mail Group plc (formerly Post Office, then Consignia plc), 1999–2002; mature student, Surrey University, since 2004; *b* 6 Aug. 1948; *s* of Arthur John Sweetman and Joan Sweetman; *m* 1977, Patricia Dean; two *s* one *d*. *Educ:* University Coll. London (BSc Geog.). FCA 1979. Joined Touche Ross & Co., Chartered Accountants, 1969; held various posts from Articled Clerk to Sen. Manager; Dir, Financial Accounts, PO, 1982–86; Royal Mail: Finance Dir, 1986–92; Business Centres Dir, 1992–94; Service Delivery Dir, 1994–95; Asst Man. Dir, 1995–96; Man. Dir, PO Counters Ltd, 1996–99. Chm. and Dir, Consignia (Customer Mgt) Ltd (formerly Subscription Services Ltd), 1999–2001. Dir, British Quality Foundn, 1998–2002; Member: Bd, Inst. of Customer Services, 1998–2001; Customer Panel, Assoc. of Energy Supplies, 2003–. Mem. Adv. Cttee for Business in the Envmt, DTI/DETR, 1997–2001. *Recreations:* family, walking, archaeology, golf, bowls, watercolour painting, cooking and eating. *Address:* 1 Chalmers Road, Banstead, Surrey SM7 3HF.

SWEETNAM, Sir (David) Rodney, KCVO 1992; CBE 1990; MA; FRCS; Orthopaedic Surgeon to the Queen, 1982–92; President: Royal College of Surgeons of England, 1995–98 (Vice-President, 1992–94); Royal Medical Benevolent Fund, 1998–2002; *b* 5 Feb. 1927; second *s* of late Dr William Sweetnam and Irene (*née* Black); *m* 1959, Patricia Ann, *er d* of late A. Staveley Gough, OBE, FRCS; one *s* one *d*. *Educ:* Clayesmore; Peterhouse, Cambridge (Titular Scholar; BA 1947, MA 1951; Hon. Fellow, 2003); Middlesex Hosp. Med. Sch. (MB, BChir 1950). FRCS 1955. Surg. Lieut RNVR, 1950–52. Jun. appts, Middx Hosp., London Hosp. and Royal National Orthopaedic Hosp.; Consultant Surgeon to: The Middlesex Hospital, 1960–92; King Edward VII Hospital for Officers, London, 1964–97. Hon. Civil Consultant in Orth. Surgery to the Army, 1974–92; Hon. Consultant Orthopaedic Surgeon, Royal Hosp., Chelsea, 1974–92. Consultant Advisor in Orth. Surgery to DHSS, 1981–90; Hon. Consultant Surgeon, Royal Nat. Orthopaedic Hosp., 1983–92. Dir, Medical Sickness Annuity and Life Assce Soc. Ltd, 1982–97; Dir and Vice-Chm., Permanent Insurance Co., 1989–95. Chairman: DHSS Adv. Gp on Orthopaedic Implants, 1973–81; MRC's Working Party on Bone Sarcoma, 1980–85. Royal College of Surgeons: Mem. Council, 1985–98; Jacksonian Prize, 1966; Hunterian Prof., 1967; Gordon Taylor Meml Lectr, 1982; Stanford Cade Meml Lectr, 1986; Bradshaw Lectr, 1992; Robert Jones Lectr, 1993. President: Combined Services Orthopaedic Soc., 1983–86; British Orthopaedic Assoc., 1984–85 (Hon. Fellow, 1998); Vice-Pres., Age Care, 1999–. Trustee: Frances and Augustus Newman Foundn, 1989– (Chm., 2000–); Hunterian Collection, 1998– (Chm., 2005–08). Fellow, UCL, 1993. Chm., British Editorial Soc. of Bone and Joint Surgery, 1992–95 (Sec. and Treas., 1975–92). Hon. FRCSGlas 1997; Hon. FRCSI 1997; Hon. FCSSA 1998; Hon. FACS 1998; Hon. FDS RCS 1998; Hon. FRCSE 1999. *Publications:* (jtly) Essentials of Orthopaedics, 1965; (ed jtly) The Basis and Practice of Orthopaedics, 1980; contrib. med. books and jls in field of gen. orth. surgery, trauma and bone tumours. *Recreation:* gardening. *Address:* 25 Woodlands Road, Bushey, Herts WD23 2LS. *T:* (01923) 223161.

SWIFT, Anita; *see* Klein, A.

SWIFT, Hon. Dame Caroline Jane, (Lady Openshaw), DBE 2005; **Hon. Mrs Justice Swift;** a Judge of the High Court of Justice, Queen's Bench Division, since 2005; *b* 30 May 1955; *d* of late Vincent Seymour Swift and of Amy Ruth Swift; *m* 1979, Charles Peter Lawford Openshaw (*see* Hon. Sir C. P. L. Openshaw); one *s* one *d*. *Educ:* Lancaster Girls' Grammar Sch.; Univ. of Durham (BA Hons Law). Pres., Durham Union Soc., 1975. Called to the Bar, Inner Temple, 1977, Bencher, 1997; practised on Northern Circuit, 1978–2005; Asst Recorder, 1992–95; QC 1993; a Recorder, 1995–2005; a Dep. High Court Judge, 2000–05. Leading counsel, Shipman Inquiry, 2001–05. *Publications:* (jtly) Ribchester: 100 years in photographs, 1994; Ribchester: a millennium record, 2001. *Recreations:* home and family, cooking, theatre, walking. *Address:* Royal Courts of Justice, Strand, WC2A 2LL.

SWIFT, Clive Walter; actor, author, teacher; initiator, 1980, now Adviser to the Board, Actor's Centre; *b* 9 Feb. 1936; *s* of Abram Swift and Lillie (*née* Greenman); *m* 1960, Margaret Drabble (*see* Dame Margaret Drabble) (marr. diss. 1975); two *s* one *d*. *Educ:* Clifton Coll., Bristol; Caius Coll., Cambridge (MA Hons Eng. Lit.). Teaching at LAMDA and RADA, 1967–79; teaching verse-speaking at Actor's Centre, 1980–. *Theatre:* début, Nottingham Playhouse, 1959; RSC, 1960–68; Man and Superman, Arts, Vaudeville, and Garrick, 1965; The Young Churchill, Duchess, 1969; Dirty Linen, Arts, 1976; Inadmissible Evidence, Royal Court, 1978; The Potsdam Quartet, Lyric, Hammersmith, 1980; Messiah, Hampstead, Aldwych, 1982; The Genius, Royal Court, 1983; King Lear, New Vic, 1986; The Sisterhood, New End, 1987; An Enemy of the People, Young Vic, Playhouse, 1988; Othello, Other Place, Young Vic, 1990; Pooter, in Mr and Mrs Nobody, nat. tour, 1993–94; Whittlestaff, in An Old Man's Love, Royal, Northampton, and tour, 1996; Doña Rosita, Almeida, 1997; Higher than Babel, Bridewell, 1999; Hysteria, Minerva Theatre, Chichester, 2000; Richard Bucket Overflows!, Theatre Clwyd, Edinburgh Fringe, 2007; Chichester Festival theatre seasons, 1965 and 1971; *director:* at LAMDA: The Wild Goose Chase, 1969; The Cherry Orchard, 1973; The Lower Depths, 1969; *television:* Love Story, 1961; Dombey & Son, 1968; Waugh on Crime, 1970; The Exorcism, 1972; South Riding, 1974; Clayhanger, 1974; Gibbon, 1975; Barchester Chronicles, 1982; Pickwick Papers, 1984; First Among Equals, 1985; Keeping up Appearances, 5 series, 1990–95; Peak Practice, 1997; Aristocrats, 1998; Born and Bred, 2001–04; *radio:* Radio Rep, 1973; Sword of Honour, 1974; narrator, Babar, 1986; Getting Stratford (monologue), 1987; Heavy Roller, 1988; From the depths of Waters, 1990 (Sony Award Winner); Madame Bovary, 1992; Black Box, 1993; The Double Dealer, 1995; Happy Days, 1995; Everybody Comes to Schicklgruber's, 1996; Altaban the Magnificent, 1999; The Right Time, 2000–04; Poor Pen, 2001; The Go-Between, 2002; Oblomov, 2005; Insane Object of Desire, 2005; Fridays when it Rains, Betjeman's Women, 2006; The Loved One, Dickens Confidential, 2007; *films:* Catch us if You Can, 1963; Frenzy, 1971; The National Health, 1972; Excalibur, 1980; A Passage to India, 1984; Sir Horace Jones, in Tower Bridge Permanent Exhibn film, 1994; Gaston's War, 1996; Vacuums, 2001. Mem., BAFTA, 2000–. Hon. Fellow, Liverpool John Moores Univ., 1999. Cyprus Medal, 1956. *Publications:* The Job of Acting, 1976, 2nd edn 1985; The Performing World of the Actor, 1981. *Recreations:* playing and listening to music, watching Lancashire CCC and Arsenal. *Address:* c/o Roxane Vacca, Vacca Management, 73 Beak Street, W1F 9SR. *T:* (020) 7734 8085.

SWIFT, David Rowland; His Honour Judge Swift; a Circuit Judge, since 1997; *b* 21 April 1946; *s* of James Rowland Swift and Iris Julia Swift; *m* 1974, Josephine Elizabeth Williamson; two *s* two *d*. *Educ:* Kingsmead Sch., Hoylake; Ruthin Sch.; Liverpool Coll. of Commerce. Admitted Solicitor, 1970; Partner, Percy Hughes and Roberts, Birkenhead, 1971–97; a Recorder, 1993–97. Pres., Liverpool Law Soc., 1995–96. Chairman: Wirral Adult Literacy Project, 1978–84; Liverpool Bd of Legal Studies, 1985–88. Gov., Ruthin Sch., 1988–2005 (Chm. Govs, 1993–99). FRSA. *Publications:* Proceedings Before the

Solicitors Disciplinary Tribunal, 1996; articles in legal jls. *Recreations:* sailing, walking, history. *Clubs:* Athenæum; North West Venturers Yacht.

SWIFT, Graham Colin, FRSL; author; *b* 4 May 1949; *s* of Sheila Irene Swift and Lionel Allan Stanley Swift. *Educ:* Dulwich Coll.; Queens' Coll., Cambridge (MA; Hon. Fellow, 2005); Univ. of York. Hon. LittD: UEA, 1998; London, 2003; DUniv York, 1998. *Publications:* novels: The Sweet Shop Owner, 1980; Shuttlecock, 1981 (Geoffrey Faber Meml Prize, 1983); Waterland, 1983 (Winifred Holtby Award, RSL, 1983); Guardian Fiction Prize, 1983; Premio Grinzane Cavour, 1987); Out of This World, 1988; Ever After, 1992 (Prix du Meilleur Livre Etranger, 1994); Last Orders (Booker Prize, James Tait Black Meml Prize), 1996; The Light of Day, 2003; Tomorrow, 2007; short stories: Learning to swim and other stories, 1982; *non-fiction:* (ed with David Profumo) The Magic Wheel (anthology), 1985; Making an Elephant, 2009. *Recreation:* fishing. *Address:* c/o A. P. Watt, 20 John Street, WC1N 2DR.

SWIFT, John Anthony; QC 1981; Head of Monckton Chambers, 1999–2001; *b* 11 July 1940; *s* of late Jack Swift and Clare Medcalf; *m* 1972, Jane Carol Sharples; one *s* one *d*. *Educ:* Birkenhead Sch.; University Coll., Oxford (MA); Johns Hopkins Univ.; Bologna. Called to the Bar, Inner Temple, 1965, Bencher, 1992. Rail Regulator, 1993–98. FCILT (FCIT 1994). *Recreations:* theatre, walking, gardening, golf. *Address:* Monckton Chambers, Gray's Inn, WC1R 5NR. *Clubs:* Reform; Huntercombe Golf.

SWIFT, Lionel; QC 1975; JD; Barrister, since 1961; a Recorder of the Crown Court, and Deputy High Court Judge, 1979–96; *b* Bristol, 3 Oct. 1931; *s* of late Harris and Bessie Swift, Hampstead; *m* 1966, Elizabeth (*née* Herzig) (Liz E, London fashion writer); one *d*. *Educ:* Whittingehame Coll., Brighton; University Coll., London (LLB 1951); Brasenose Coll., Oxford (BCL 1959); Univ. of Chicago (Juris Doc, 1960). Solicitor, Natal, S Africa, 1954; called to the Bar, Inner Temple, 1959, Bencher, 1984. British Commonwealth Fellow, Univ. of Chicago Law Sch., 1960; Amer. Social Science Res. Council Grant for work on admin of criminal justice, 1960. Jun. Counsel to Treasury in Probate Matters, 1974. Chm., Inst. of Laryngology and Otology, 1985–86. *Publication:* The South African Law of Criminal Procedure (Gen. Editor, A. B. Harcourt, QC), 1957. *Address:* (chambers) 4 Paper Buildings, Temple, EC4Y 7EX.

SWIFT, Malcolm Robin Farquhar; QC 1988; a Recorder, since 1987; *b* 19 Jan. 1948; *s* of late Willie Swift and Heather May Farquhar Swift, OBE (*née* Nield); *m* 1st, 1969, Anne Rachael (marr. diss. 1993), *d* of Ernest Rothery Ayre; one *s* two *d*; 2nd, 2003, Angela, *d* of Reuben Walters. *Educ:* Colne Valley High Sch., Yorks; King's Coll. London (LLB, AKC). Called to the Bar, Gray's Inn, 1970, Bencher, 1998. Co-opted Mem., Remuneration Cttee of Bar Council, 1978–89 (rep. NE Circuit); Mem., Bar Council, 1995–2001; Leader, NE Circuit, 1998–2001. *Recreations:* cycling, re-cycling. *Address:* Park Court Chambers, 16 Park Place, Leeds LS1 2SJ. *T:* (0113) 243 3277; 9 Lincoln's Inn Fields, WC2A 3BP. *T:* (020) 7831 4344.

SWINBURN, Lt-Gen. Sir Richard (Hull), KCB 1991; farmer; *b* 30 Oct. 1937; *s* of late Maj.-Gen. H. R. Swinburn, CB, OBE, MC and Naomi Barbara Swinburn, *d* of late Maj.-Gen. Sir Amyatt Hull, KCB, and *sister* of late Field Marshal Sir Richard Hull, KG, GCB, DSO; *m* 1964, Jane Elise Brodie (*d* 2001), *d* of late Antony Douglas Brodie and of Juliane (*née* Falk). *Educ:* Wellington Coll.; RMA Sandhurst. Commnd 17th/21st Lancers, 1957; Adjt, Sherwood Rangers Yeomanry and 17th/21st Lancers, 1963–65; sc 1968–69; MA to VCGS, 1971–72; Instructor, Staff Coll., 1975–76; MA to COS AFCENT, 1976–78; CO 17th/21st Lancers, UK and BAOR, 1979–81; Col ASD 2, MoD, Falklands Campaign, 1982; Comdr, 7th Armoured Bde, BAOR, 1983–84; rcds 1985; Dir Army Plans, 1986–87; GOC 1st Armoured Div., BAOR, 1987–89; ACGS, MoD, 1989–90; Lt-Gen., 1990; GOC SE Dist, 1990–92; GOC Southern Dist, 1992–94; Dep. C-in-C, UKLF, Comdr, UK Field Army, and Inspector Gen., TA, 1994–95, retd. Chm., Cavalry Cols, 1997–2001; Col, Queen's Royal Lancers, 1995–2001; Hon. Col, Exeter Univ. OTC, 1994–2003. Dir, Glancal Property Co., 1990–96. President: Somerset Army Benevolent Fund, 1999–; Combined Cavalry Old Comrades Assoc., 2003–. Vice-Pres., St Margaret's Hospice, Somerset, 2004–. Mem. Council, RUSI, 1991–95. Comr, Duke of York's Royal Mil. Sch., 1990–94. Huntsman: RMA Sandhurst Beagles, 1956–57; Dhekelia Draghounds, Cyprus, 1971; (and Master) Staff Coll. Draghounds, 1975–76; Chm., Army Beagling Assoc., 1988–94. Hon. Fellow, Exeter Univ., 2003. *Recreations:* agricultural and country pursuits. *Address:* Stone, Exford, Somerset TA24 7NX. *Club:* Cavalry and Guards.

SWINBURN, Walter Robert John; racehorse trainer, since 1994; jockey, 1977–2000; *b* 7 Aug. 1961; *s* of Walter Swinburn; *m* 2002, Alison Palmer, *d* of Peter Harris; two *d*, and one step *s* one step *d*. Joined Frenchie Nicholson, 1977; rode 1st winner, Kempton, 1978; first jockey for Michael Stoute, 1981, for Sheikh Maktoum Al Maktoum, 1993. Won on Shergar, 1981, Chester Vase, Derby and King George VI and Queen Elizabeth Diamond Stakes; Irish Derby, 1983, on Shareef Dancer; Derby and Irish Derby, 1986, on Sharastani; Derby, 1995, on Lammtarra; Irish 1,000 Guineas, 1986, on Sonic Lady, 1992, on Marling; Oaks, 1987, on Unite; 2,000 Guineas, 1988, on Doyoun; 1,000 Guineas, 1989, on Musical Bliss, 1992, on Hatoof, 1993, on Sayyedati; Irish 2,000 Guineas, 1989, on Shaadi; Prix de l'Arc de Triomphe, 1983, on All Along.

SWINBURNE, John; Member (Scottish Senior Citizens Unity) Scotland Central, Scottish Parliament, 2003–07; *b* 4 July 1930; *s* of Ben and Janet Swinburne; *m* 1953, Mary Hunter Baird; three *s* one *d* (and one *s* decd). *Educ:* Dalziel High Sch., Motherwell. Mechanical engr, 1947–80; apprentice marine engr, Barclay, Curle & Co., Whiteinch, Glasgow and PC&W, Motherwell, 1947–52; freelance journalist, 1980–81; Commercial Manager, 1981–2000, Dir, 2000–, Motherwell Football and Athletic Club. Contested (Scottish Sen. Citizens Unity) Motherwell and Wishaw, Scottish Parlt, 2007. Founder and Leader, Scottish Sen. Citizens Unity Party. *Publications:* A History of the Steelmen: Motherwell Football Club 1886–1986, 1986; Well Worth the Wait, 1991; Images of Sport: Motherwell Football Club 1886–1999, 1999. *Recreation:* Association Football. *Address:* Meiklecourse Hill House, Stewarton, E Ayrshire KA3 5JH.

SWINBURNE, Prof. Richard Granville, FBA 1992; Nolloth Professor of Philosophy of Christian Religion, University of Oxford, 1985–2002, now Emeritus; Fellow, Oriel College, Oxford, 1985–2002, now Emeritus; *b* 26 Dec. 1934; *s* of William Henry Swinburne and Gladys Edith Swinburne (*née* Parker); *m* 1960, Monica Holmstrom (separated 1985); two *d*. *Educ:* Exeter College, Oxford (Scholar). BPhil 1959, MA 1961, DipTheol 1960. Fereday Fellow, St John's Coll., Oxford, 1958–61; Leverhulme Res. Fellow in Hist. and Phil. of Science, Univ. of Leeds, 1961–63; Lectr in Philosophy, then Sen. Lectr, Univ. of Hull, 1963–72; Prof. of Philosophy, Univ. of Keele, 1972–84. Vis. Associate Prof. of Philosophy, Univ. of Maryland, 1969–70; Dist. Vis. Schol., Univ. of Adelaide, 1982; Vis. Prof. of Philosophy, Syracuse Univ., 1987; Vis. Lectr, Indian Council for Philosophical Res., 1992; Visiting Professor: Univ. of Rome, 2002; Catholic Univ. of Lublin, 2002; Yale Univ., 2003; St Louis Univ., 2003; Lectures: Wilde, Oxford Univ., 1975–78; Forwood, Liverpool Univ., 1977; Marrett Meml, Exeter Coll., Oxford, 1980; Gifford, Univ. of Aberdeen, 1982–84; Edward Cadbury, Univ. of Birmingham, 1987; Wade, St Louis Univ., 1990; Dotterer, Pennsylvania State Univ., 1992; Aquinas,

Marquette Univ., 1997; Paul Holmer, Univ. of Minnesota, 2006. *Publications:* Space and Time, 1968, 2nd edn 1981; The Concept of Miracle, 1971; An Introduction to Confirmation Theory, 1973; The Coherence of Theism, 1977, rev. edn 1993; The Existence of God, 1979, 2nd edn 2004; Faith and Reason, 1981, 2nd edn 2005; (with S. Shoemaker) Personal Identity, 1984; The Evolution of the Soul, 1986, rev. edn 1997; Responsibility and Atonement, 1989; Revelation, 1992, 2nd edn 2007; The Christian God, 1994; Is There a God?, 1996; Providence and the Problem of Evil, 1998; Epistemic Justification, 2001; The Resurrection of God Incarnate, 2003; articles and reviews in learned jls. *Address:* 50 Butler Close, Oxford OX2 6JG. *T:* (01865) 514406.

See also D. R. Cope.

SWINBURNE, Prof. Terence Reginald; Professor of Horticultural Development, Wye College, London University, 1994–98, now Emeritus; *b* 17 July 1936; *s* of Reginald and Gladys Swinburne; *m* 1958, Valerie Parkes; two *s*. *Educ:* Imperial Coll., Univ. of London (DSc, ARCS, DIC, PhD); FIHort. Plant Pathology Res. Div., Min., later Dept, of Agriculture for NI, 1960–80; Scientific Officer, 1960–62; Sen. Scientific Officer, 1962–71; PSO, 1971–79; SPSO, 1979–80; Queen's University, Belfast: Asst Lectr, Faculty of Agriculture, 1961–64; Lectr, 1965–77; Reader, 1977–80; Head of Crop Protection Div., E Malling Res. Stn, 1980–85; Dir, Inst. of Hortl Res., AFRC, 1985–90; Sen. Res. Fellow, Wye Coll., London Univ., 1990–94. Kellogg Fellow, Oregon State Univ., 1964–65; Vis. Prof., Dept of Pure and Applied Biology, Imperial Coll., London, 1986–91. Gov., Hadlow Coll., 2000– (Chm., 2003–). *Publication:* Iron Siderophores and Plant Diseases, 1986. *Recreation:* sailing. *Address:* Tan House, 15 Frog Lane, West Malling, Kent ME19 6LN. *T:* (01732) 846090. *Club:* Farmers'.

SWINDELLS, Maj.-Gen. (George) Michael (Geoffrey), CB 1985; Controller, Army Benevolent Fund, 1987–97; *b* 15 Jan. 1930; *s* of late George Martyn Swindells and Marjorie Swindells; *m* 1955, Prudence Bridget Barbara Tully; two *d* (and one *s* decd). *Educ:* Rugby School. Nat. Service Commission, 5th Royal Inniskilling Dragoon Guards, 1949; served in Germany, Korea and Canal Zone; Adjutant, Cheshire Yeomanry, 1955–56; Staff Coll., 1960; transfer to 9th/12th Royal Lancers, to command, 1969–71; Comdr 11th Armd Brigade, 1975–76; RCDS course, 1977; Dir of Op. Requirements (3), MoD, 1978–79; Chief of Jt Services Liaison Organisation, Bonn, 1980–83; Dir of Management and Support of Intelligence, 1983–85. Col, 9th/12th Royal Lancers, 1990–95. Chairman: Royal Soldiers' Daughters Sch., 1985–89; BLESMA, 1991–96; Pres., British Korean Veterans Assoc., 2006–. Mem. Council, Wilts Wildlife Trust, 1998–2004; Trustee, Royal Soc. for Asian Affairs, 1999–2005. *Recreations:* country life, gardening.

SWINDELLS, Heather Hughson, (Mrs R. Inglis); QC 1995; **Her Honour Judge Swindells;** a Circuit Judge, since 2005; a Deputy High Court Judge, since 2000; *d* of late Mrs Debra Hughson Swindells; *m* 1976, Richard Inglis, *qv*; one *s*. *Educ:* Nottingham High Sch. for Girls; St Anne's Coll., Oxford (MA Lit.Hum.). Called to the Bar, Middle Temple, 1974, Bencher, 2005; a Recorder, 1994–2005. *Publications:* Family Law and the Human Rights Act 1998, 1999; (contrib.) Family Law: essays for the new millennium, 2000; Adoption: the modern law, 2003; (jtly) Adoption: the modern procedure, 2006. *Recreations:* books, music, art, archaeology. *Address:* Lincoln Combined Court Centre, 360 High Street, Lincoln LN5 7PS.

SWINDELLS, Matthew James; Managing Director for Health, Tribal Group, since 2008; *b* Brighton, 31 Dec. 1964; *s* of Derek and Jacqueline Swindells; *m* 1995, Victoria Rae; two *d*. *Educ:* Blatchington Mill Comp. Sch.; Brighton Hove and Sussex 6th Form Coll.; Univ. of Hull (BSc Hons Econs); Brunel Univ. (MBA). NHS graduate supplies trainee, NW RHA, 1987–89; IT Purchasing Manager, SE Thames RHA, 1989–91; IT Strategy Prog. Manager, St Thomas' Hosp., London, 1991–93; IT Manager, 1993–94, Clin. Ops Manager, 1994–99, Guy's and St Thomas' Hosp., London; Dir of Clin. Services, Heatherwood and Wexham Park Hosp., Slough, 1999–2002; Principal Advr, Prime Minister's Office of Public Service Reform, 2002–03; Chief Exec., Royal Surrey County Hosp., Guildford, 2003–05; Policy Advr to Sec. of State for Health, 2005–07; Dir Gen. for Inf. and Prog. Integration and Chief Inf. Officer, 2007–08, DoH. Vis. Prof., Sch. of Mgt, Univ. of Surrey, 2005–. Chm., Charity Trustees, Imperial Coll. Healthcare NHS Trust, 2008–. *Recreations:* playing football and cricket, listening to the poetry of Bob Dylan, supporting Everton, travel, spending time with my wife, enjoying the company of my children. *Address:* Tribal Group plc, 87–91 Newman Street, W1T 3EY. *T:* (020) 7323 7217, *Fax:* (020) 7323 7210; *e-mail:* matthew.swindells@tribalgroup.co.uk. *Club:* Commonwealth.

SWINDELLS, Robert Edward; children's author, since 1973, full-time author, since 1980; *b* 20 March 1939; *s* of Albert Henry Hugh and Alice Alberta Swindells; *m* 1st, 1962, Catherine Hough (marr. diss. 1976); two *d*; 2nd, 1982, Brenda Blamires. *Educ:* Huddersfield Poly. (Teacher's Cert.); Univ. of Bradford (MA Peace Studies). Copyholder, local newspaper, 1954–57; RAF, 1957–60; clerk, local newspaper, 1960–66; engineering inspector, 1966–69; student teacher, 1969–72; teacher, 1972–80. *Publications:* When Darkness Comes, 1973; The Very Special Baby, 1977; Dragons Live Forever, 1978; Moonpath and other stories, 1979; Norah's Ark, 1979; Norah's Shark, 1979; Ghostship to Ganymede, 1980; Norah to the Rescue, 1981; Norah and the Whale, 1981; Science Fiction Stories, 1982; Candle in the Dark, 1983; Weather Clerk, 1983; World Eater, 1983; Brother in the Land, 1984 (Children's Book Award, 1985); Ghost Messengers, 1988; Mavis Davis, 1988; Night School, 1989; A Serpent's Tooth, 1989; Room 13 (Children's Book Award), 1990; Staying Up, 1990; Tim Kipper, 1990; Daz 4 Zoe, 1991; Dracula's Castle, 1991; Follow a Shadow, 1991; Hydra, 1991; Postbox Mystery, 1991; Go-Ahead Gang, 1992; Ice Palace, 1992; Rolf and Rosie, 1992; You Can't Say I'm Crazy, 1992; Inside the Worm, 1993; Sam and Sue and Lavatory Lou, 1993; Secret of Weeping Wood, 1993; Siege of Frimly Prim, 1993; Stone Cold (Carnegie Medal), 1993; Thousand Eyes of Night, 1993; We Didn't Mean To, Honest, 1993; Kidnap at Denton Farm, 1994; Timesnatch, 1994; Voyage to Valhalla, 1994; Ghosts of Givenham Keep, 1995; The Muckitups, 1995; Unbeliever, 1995; Jacqueline Hyde, 1996; Last Bus, 1996; Hurricane Summer, 1997; Nightmare Stairs, 1997; Smash, 1997; Abomination, 1998; Peril in the Mist, 1998; Strange Tale of Ragger Bill, 1998; Invisible, 1999; Orchard Book of Vikings, 1999; Roger's War, 1999; Doodlebug Alley, 2000; Orchard Book of Egyptian Gods and Pharaohs, 2000; A Wish For Wings, 2001; Wrecked!, 2001; Blitzed, 2002; No Angels, 2003; Ruby Tanya, 2004; Branded, 2005; Snapshot, 2005; Snakebite, 2006; In the Nick of Time, 2007; Burnout, 2007; The Shade of Hettie Daynes, 2008; Knife Edge, 2008. *Recreations:* walking, cruising, theatre, painting, travel. *Address:* Reservoir Cats, 4 Spring Row, Denholme Road, Oxenhope, Keighley, W Yorks, BD22 9NR.

SWINDON, Bishop Suffragan of, since 2005; **Rt Rev. Lee Stephen Rayfield,** PhD; *b* 30 Sept. 1955; *s* of Ronald Reginald Rayfield and Doris Lilian Rayfield; *m* 1978, Elizabeth Vivienne Rundle; two *s* one *d*. *Educ:* Univ. of Southampton (BSc Hons Biology) 1978); St Mary's Hosp. Med. Sch., Univ. of London (PhD 1981); Ridley Hall, Cambridge. Post-doctoral Res. Fellow, St Mary's Hosp. Med. Sch., Univ. of London, 1981–84; Lectr in Immunology, UMDS, Guy's and St Thomas' Hosps, Univ. of London, 1984–91. Ordained deacon, 1993; priest, 1994; Asst Curate, Woodford Wells, dio.

Chelmsford, 1993–97; Priest-in-charge, 1997–2004, Vicar, 2004–05, Furze Platt, dio. Oxford; part-time Chaplain, St Mark's Hosp., Maidenhead, 1997–2005; Area Dean: Maidenhead, 2000–03; Maidenhead and Windsor, 2003–05. Mem., UK Gene Therapy Adv. Cttee, 2000–. Mem., SOSc, 1995–. *Publications:* contrib. chapters in med. and dental textbks; many scientific papers in immunol jls, incl. Nature, Transplantation, European Jl of Immunology; two papers in theol jls. *Recreations:* athletics (400m, 800m), cross country running, watching Rugby Union, making cider. *Address:* Mark House, Field Rise, Swindon, Wilts SN1 4HP. *T:* (01793) 538654; *e-mail:* bishop.swindon@bristoldiocese.org. *Clubs:* Swindon Harriers Athletics, Swindon Striders.

SWINFEN, 3rd Baron *cr* 1919; **Roger Mynors Swinfen Eady;** *b* 14 Dec. 1938; *s* of 2nd Baron Swinfen and Mary Aline (*née* Farmar, later Siepmann; writer, as Mary Wesley, CBE) (*d* 2002); *S* father, 1977; *m* 1962, Patricia Anne (MBE 2006), *o d* of late F. D. Blackmore, Dundrum, Dublin; one *s* three *d*. *Educ:* Westminster; RMA, Sandhurst. ARICS 1970–99. Mem., Direct Mail Services Standards Bd, 1983–97. Mem., Select Cttee on EC Sub-Cttee C (Envmtl and Social Affairs), 1991–94; elected Mem., H of L, 1999; Member: Select Cttee on Draft Disability Bill, 2004–; Select Cttee on EU Sub-Cttee B, 2004–06; Select Cttee on EU Sub-Cttee C, 2006–. Chm., Parly Gp, Video Enquiry Working Party, 1983–85. Pres. SE Reg., British Sports Assoc. for the Disabled, 1986–; Patron: Disablement Income Gp, 1995–; 1 in 8 Gp, 1996–2004; Labrador Rescue SE, 1996–; World Orthopaedic Concern, 2002–; KunDe Foundn, 2007–; Hon. Pres., Britain Bangladesh Friendship Soc., 1996–2004. Fellow, Industry and Parlt Trust. Liveryman, Drapers' Co. JP Kent, 1983–85. *Publications:* reports in med. jls. *Heir:* *s* Hon. Charles Roger Peregrine Swinfen Eady, *b* 8 March 1971. *Address:* House of Lords, SW1A 0PW.

SWINGLAND, Prof. Ian Richard, OBE 2007; Founder and Director, Durrell Institute of Conservation and Ecology, 1989–99 and Founder Professor of Conservation Biology, University of Kent, 1994–99, now Emeritus; *b* 2 Nov. 1946; *s* of late Hugh Maurice Webb Swingland and of Flora Mary Swingland (*née* Fernie); *m* 1985, Fiona Mairi Lawson; one *s* one *d*. *Educ:* Haberdashers' Aske's Sch.; QMC, Univ. of London (BSc 1969); Univ. of Edinburgh (Throgmorton Trotman Sen. Exhibn; FCO Schol.; PhD 1974). FZS 1974; FIBiol 1993. Res. Scientist, Shell Research, 1969; Wildlife Mgt Biologist, Kafue Nat. Park, Zambia, 1973–74; Vis. Scientist, Royal Soc. Res. Station, Aldabra Atoll, Seychelles, 1974–79; Post-doctoral Fellow and Tutor, St Peter's Hall, St Catherine's Coll., Magdalen Coll., Lady Margaret Hall, Oxford, 1974–79; Lectr, then Sen. Lectr in Natural Scis, Univ. of Kent, 1979–94. Res. Associate, Smithsonian Instn, 1987–; Visiting Professor: of Biology, Univ. of Michigan, 1986–87 (Sen. Res. Fellow, Mus. of Zoology, 1986–87); of Conservation, Univ. of Florence, 1996–2000; of Conservation Biology, Univ. of Auckland, 1996–2001; of Conservation Biology, Manchester Metropolitan Univ., 1998–2001; Ext. Examiner in Biodiversity and Conservation, Univ. of Leeds, 1998–2002. Founding Editor, Biodiversity and Conservation, 1989–99. Member: IUCN Species Survival Commn, 1979–; Council, RURAL, 1980– (Founding Mem.); Council, Fauna and Flora Preservation Soc., 1985–91; Council, RSPCA, 1990–96 (150th Anniv. Lecture, 1990); Darwin Initiative, 2000–; IUCN Nat. Parks Commn, 2000–03; Director: First World Congress of Herpetology, 1984–89; Sustainable Forestry Mgt LLC, 1998–; Conservation Research and Development Ltd, 2008–; Ultra Green Fuels Ltd, 2008–. Founder and Vice Pres., Herpetological Conservation Trust, 1989–; Pres., British Chelonia Gp, 1989–2005 (Hon. Life Member, 1989–); Chairman: Apple and Pear Res. Council, 1997–2003; Durrell Trust for Conservation Biology, 1998–; Internat. Bd of Trustees, Iwokrama Internat. Centre for Rain Forest Conservation and Develt, 2002–03; Governor, Powell Cotton Mus., 1984–2006; Trustee: Biodiversity Foundn for Africa, 1992–; Earthwatch, 1999–; Operation Wallacea, 1999–; Director: Derwent Forest, 2004–07; Durrell Wildlife, 2005–07. Staff Consultant, Asian Develt Bank, 1996–2007; Chief Policy Advr, Countryside Alliance, 1999–2003; Scientific Advr, FCO, 1999–2002; Panel of Experts, World Bank, 1999–2002; Mem. Adv. Bd, Centre for Biodiversity and Restoration Ecology, Victoria Univ. of Wellington. Bioscience Fellow, Commonwealth Agricl Bureau Internat., 2002. FRGS 1992; FRSA 1992. Hon. Life Mem., Durrell Wildlife Conservation Trust, 2000. Freedom of the City of London, 2001. DSc Kent 2005. *Publications: edited jointly:* The Ecology of Animal Movement, 1983; Living in a Patchy Environment, 1990; New Techniques in Integrated Protected Area Management, 1998; Carbon, biodiversity, conservation and income: an analysis of a free-market approach to land-use changes and forestry in developing and developed countries, 2002; Capturing Biodiversity and Conserving Biodiversity: a market approach, 2003; contrib. books and jls incl. Nature, Phil Trans Royal Soc., Jl Theor. Biology, Jl Zoology, London Jl Animal Ecology, Biodiversity and Conservation, Proc. Biol. Soc. Washington, Applied Animal Behaviour Sci., Animal Behaviour, Can. Jl Zool., Proc. Royal Soc. of London, etc. *Recreations:* growing trees, cooking, being alone in remote wild places, being iconoclastic, losing things. *Address:* Herons Hall, Nash, Kent CT3 2JX. *T:* 07971 669915, *Fax:* (office) (01304) 812099. *Club:* Athenæum.

SWINGLER, Raymond John Peter; editorial and information technology consultant, since 1992; *b* 8 Oct. 1933; *s* of Raymond Joseph and Mary Swingler; *m* 1960, Shirley (*d* 1980), *e d* of Frederick and Dorothy Wilkinson, Plymouth; two *d*. *Educ:* St Bede's Coll., Christchurch, NZ; Canterbury Univ. Journalist, The Press, Christchurch, NZ, 1956–57; Marlborough Express, 1957–59; Nelson Mail, 1959–61; freelance Middle East, 1961–62; Cambridge Evening News, 1962–79. Press Council: Mem., 1975–78; Mem., Complaints Cttee, 1976–78; Sec. and conciliator, 1980–91; Asst Dir, 1989–91; Asst Dir, Press Complaints Commn, 1991. Member: Nat. Exec. Council, Nat. Union of Journalists, 1973–75, 1978–79; Provincial Newspapers Industrial Council, 1976–79; Chm., General Purposes Cttee (when journalists' Code of Professional Conduct (revised) introduced), 1974–75. Partner: Haringey Telematics Project, 1995–98; Lee Valley Univ. for Industry, 1997–99; Hon. Sec./Treas., Connexions Project (teaching IT to the disabled), 1994–97. Mem., Metropolitan Police Authy Stop and Search Rev. Bd. 2005–. Pres., Walthamstow Village Residents' Assoc., 1997–. *Recreation:* horses and horsewomen. *Address:* 11A Church Path, E17 9RQ.

SWINLEY, Margaret Albinia Joanna, OBE 1980; British Council Service, retired; *b* 30 Sept. 1935; *er* twin *d* of late Captain Casper Silas Balfour Swinley, DSO, DSC, RN and Sylvia Jocosa Swinley, 4th *d* of late Canon W. H. Carnegie. *Educ:* Southover Manor Sch., Lewes; Edinburgh Univ. (MA Hons Hist.). English Teacher/Sec., United Paper Mills, Jämsänkoski, Finland, 1958–60; joined British Council, 1960; Birmingham Area Office, 1960–63; Tel Aviv, 1963; Lagos, 1963–66; seconded to London HQ of VSO, 1966–67; New Delhi, 1967–70; Dep. Rep., Lagos, 1970–73; Dir, Tech. Assistance Trng Dept, 1973–76; Rep., Israel, 1976–80; Asst, then Dep., Controller, Educn, Medicine and Science Div., 1980–82; Controller, Africa and Middle East Div., 1982–86; Controller, Home Div., 1986–89. Trustee, Lloyd Foundn. Mem., S Wales Shire Horse Soc., 1993– (Pres., 1998, 2005). Pres., Flaxley WI, 2002–05. Lay Mem., Local Ministry Team, benefice of Westbury-on-Severn with Flaxley and Blaisdon, 1998–. *Recreations:* theatre-going, country life, keeping dogs and Shire horses. *Club:* Royal Commonwealth Society.

SWINNERTON-DYER, Prof. Sir (Henry) Peter (Francis), 16th Bt *cr* 1678; KBE 1987; FRS 1967; Chief Executive, Universities Funding Council, 1989–91; *b* 2 Aug. 1927; *s* of Sir Leonard Schroeder Swinnerton Dyer, 15th Bt, and Barbara (*d* 1990), *d* of Hereward Brackenbury, CBE; *S* father, 1975; *m* 1983, Dr Harriet Crawford, *er d* of Rt Hon. Sir Patrick Browne, OBE, TD, PC. *Educ:* Eton; Trinity College, Cambridge (Hon. Fellow 1981). University of Cambridge: Research Fellow, 1950–54, Fellow, 1955–73, Dean, 1963–73, Trinity Coll.; Master, St Catharine's Coll., 1973–83 (Hon. Fellow, 1983); Univ. Lectr, 1960–71 (at Mathematical Lab., 1960–67); Prof. of Maths, 1971–88; Vice-Chancellor, 1979–81. Commonwealth Fund Fellow, Univ. of Chicago, 1954–55. Vis. Prof., Harvard Univ., 1971. Hon. Fellow, Worcester Coll., Oxford, 1980. Chairman: Cttee on Academic Organisation, Univ. of London, 1980–82; Meteorological Cttee, 1983–94; UGC, 1983–89; CODEST, 1986–91; European Sci. and Technol. Assembly, 1994–97. Chm., Sec. of State for Nat. Heritage's Adv. Cttee, Liby and Inf. Services Council, 1992–95; Mem., Library and Information Commn, 1995–98. Hon. DSc: Bath, 1981; Ulster, Wales, 1991; Birmingham, Nottingham, 1992; Warwick, 1993; Hon. LLD Aberdeen, 1991. *Publications:* numerous papers in mathematical journals. *Recreation:* gardening. *Heir:* kinsman David Dyer-Bennet [*b* 1954; *m* 1982, Pamela Collins Dean]. *Address:* The Dower House, Thriplow, Royston, Herts SG8 7RJ. *T:* (01763) 208220.

SWINNEY, John Ramsay; Member (SNP) North Tayside, Scottish Parliament, since 1999; Cabinet Secretary for Finance and Sustainable Growth, since 2007; *b* 13 April 1964; *s* of Kenneth Swinney and Nancy Swinney (*née* Hunter); *m* 1st, 1991, Lorna Ann King (marr. diss. 2000); one *s* one *d*; 2nd, 2003, Elizabeth Quigley. *Educ:* Univ. of Edinburgh (MA Hons Politics). Sen. Managing Consultant, Developments Options Ltd, 1988–92; Strategic Planning Principal, Scottish Amicable, 1992–97. MP (SNP) North Tayside, 1997–2001. Scottish Parliament: Dep. Leader of the Opposition, 1999–2000, Leader, 2000–04; SNP spokesman for finance and public service reform, 2005–07; Convener: Enterprise and Lifelong Learning Cttee, 1999–2000; European Cttee, 2004–05. Scottish National Party: Nat. Sec., 1986–92; Vice Convener for Publicity, 1992–97; Treasury Spokesman, 1995–2000; Dep. Leader, 1998–2000; Leader, 2000–04. *Recreations:* cycling, hill walking. *Address:* 35 Perth Street, Blairgowrie PH10 6DL. *T:* (01250) 876576.

SWINSON, Christopher, OBE 2006; FCA; Comptroller and Auditor General, Jersey, since 2005; Senior Partner, BDO Stoy Hayward, 1997–2004 (Partner, 1993–97); *b* 27 Jan. 1948; *s* of Arthur Montagu Swinson and Jean Swinson; *m* 1972, Christine Margaret Hallam; one *s*. *Educ:* Wadham Coll., Oxford (MA). FCA 1979 (ACA 1974). Price Waterhouse, 1970–77; Hacker Young, 1977–79; with Binder Hamlyn, 1979–92 (Nat. Man. Partner, 1989–92). Institute of Chartered Accountants in England and Wales: Mem. Council, 1985–2001; Vice-Pres., 1996–97; Dep. Pres., 1997–98; Pres., 1998–99; Chm., Regulation Review Working Party, 1995–2001. Mem., Audit Commn, 2000–03; Chm., Audit Cttee, HM Treasury, 2001–05; Bd Mem., Pensions Regulator, 2005–. Vis. Prof., Bournemouth Univ., 2006–. Treasurer: Navy Records Soc., 1987–94; Soc. for Nautical Res., 1991–95; NCVO, 1993–97. Trustee, Greenwich Foundn, RNC, 1997–2002. FRSA 1992. *Publications:* Companies Act 1989, 1990; Regulation of Auditors, 1990; Delivering a Quality Service, 1992; Group Accounts, 1993. *Recreation:* model railway construction. *Address:* Roseheath Wood, Bullbeggars Lane, Berkhamsted, Herts HP4 2RS. *T:* (01442) 877564; *e-mail:* chris@swinson.co.uk. *Clubs:* Athenæum; Victoria (St Helier).

SWINSON, Jo; MP (Lib Dem) Dunbartonshire East, since 2005; *b* 5 Feb. 1980; *d* of Peter and Annette Swinson. *Educ:* London Sch. of Econs (BSc 1st Cl. Hons Mgt 2000). Mktg Exec. then Manager, Viking FM, 2000–02; Mktg Manager, SpaceandPeople Ltd, 2003–04; Scottish Develt Officer, UK Public Health Assoc., 2004–05. Vice Chm., Lib Dem Youth and Students, 1999–2001; Chm., Lib Dem Campaign for Gender Balance (formerly Gender Balance Task Force), 2006–08 (Vice Chm., 2003–06). Contested (Lib Dem): Hull East, 2001; Strathkelvin and Bearsden, Scottish Parlt, 2003. Lib Dem Shadow posts: Arts Minister, 2005–06; Sec. of State for Scotland, 2006–07; Minister for Women and Equality, 2007; Minister for Foreign Affairs, 2008–. *Recreations:* reading, running. *Address:* House of Commons, SW1A 0AA. *T:* (020) 7219 8088; *e-mail:* swinsonj@parliament.uk.

SWINTON, Susan, Countess of; *see* Masham of Ilton, Baroness.

SWINTON, 3rd Earl of, *cr* 1955; **Nicholas John Cunliffe-Lister;** Viscount Swinton, 1935; Baron Masham, 1955; *b* 4 Sept. 1939; *s* of Major Hon. John Yarburgh Cunliffe-Lister (*d* of wounds received in action, 1943) and Anne Irvine (*m* 2nd, 1944, Donald Chapple-Gill; she *d* 1961), *yr d* of late Rev. Canon R. S. Medlicott; *S* brother, 2006; *m* 1st, 1966, Hon. Elizabeth Susan (marr. diss. 1996), *e d* of 1st Viscount Whitelaw, KT, CH, MC, PC; two *s* one *d*; 2nd, 1996, Pamela June Sykes (*née* Wood). *Educ:* Winchester; Worcester Coll., Oxford. *Heir:* *s* Lord Masham, *qv*.

SWINTON, Maj.-Gen. Sir John, KCVO 1979; OBE 1969; Lord-Lieutenant of Berwickshire, 1989–2000; *b* 21 April 1925; *s* of late Brig. A. H. C. Swinton, MC, Scots Guards; *m* 1954, Judith, *d* of late Harold Killen, Merribee, NSW; three *s* one *d*. *Educ:* Harrow. Enlisted, Scots Guards, 1943, commissioned, 1944; served NW Europe, 1945 (twice wounded); Malaya, 1948–51 (despatches); ADC to Field Marshal Sir William Slim, Governor-General of Australia, 1953–54; Staff College, 1957; DAA&QMG 1st Guards Brigade, 1958–59; Regimental Adjutant Scots Guards, 1960–62; Adjutant, RMA Sandhurst, 1962–64; comd 2nd Bn Scots Guards, 1966–68; AAG PS12 MoD, 1968–70; Lt Col Comdg Scots Guards, 1970–71; Comdr, 4th Guards Armoured Brigade, BAOR, 1972–73; RCDS 1974; Brigadier Lowlands and Comdr Edinburgh and Glasgow Garrisons, 1975–76; GOC London Dist and Maj.-Gen. Comdg Household Div., 1976–79; retired 1979. Mem., Queen's Body Guard for Scotland (Royal Co. of Archers), 1954– (Capt., 2003–07); Hon. Col 2nd Bn 52nd Lowland Volunteers, 1983–90. Pres., Lowland TA & VRA, 1992–96; Nat. Chm., Royal British Legion Scotland, 1986–89 (Nat. Vice-Chm., 1984–86); Mem. Council, British Commonwealth Ex-Services League, 1984–98. Mem., Central Adv. Cttee on War Pensions, 1986–89. Pres., Borders Area SSAFA, 1993–2006. Trustee: Army Museums Ogilby Trust, 1978–90; Scottish Nat. War Meml, 1984– (Vice-Chm., 1987–96; Chm., 1996–); Scots at War Trust, 1996–; Berwick Mil. Tattoo, 1996–2007; Chm., Thirlestane Castle Trust, 1984–90. Patron, Prosthetic and Orthotic Worldwide Educn and Relief, 1995–. Borders Liaison Officer, Duke of Edinburgh's Award Scheme, 1982–84. Chairman: Berwicks Civic Soc., 1982–98 (Pres., 1998–2005); Roxburgh and Berwickshire Cons. Assoc., 1983–85; Jt Management Cttee, St Abb's Head Nat. Nature Reserve, 1991–98; Berwicks Recreation Sports Trust, 1997–2005; Scottish Nat. Motorsport Collection, 1998–2001; Pres., Berwickshire Naturalists Club, 1996–97. Pres., RHAS, 1993–94. DL, 1980–89, JP, 1989–2008, Berwickshire. *Address:* Kimmerghame, Duns, Berwickshire TD11 3LU. *T:* (01361) 883277; *e-mail:* kimmerghame@amserve.com.

SWIRE, Sir Adrian (Christopher), Kt 1982; Hon. President and Adviser, John Swire & Sons Ltd, since 2005 (Chairman, 1987–97 and 2002–04); Director: Cathay Pacific Airways, 1965–2005; Swire Pacific Ltd, since 1978; *b* 15 Feb. 1932; *yr s* of late John Kidston Swire and Juliet Richenda, *d* of Theodore Barclay; *m* 1970, Lady Judith Compton, *e d* of 6th Marquess of Northampton, DSO; two *s* one *d*. *Educ:* Eton; University Coll., Oxford (MA). Served Coldstream Guards, 1950–52; RAFVR and RAux AF (AE

1961; Hon. Air Cdre, 1987–2000). Joined Butterfield & Swire in Far East, 1956; John Swire & Sons Ltd: Dir, 1961; Dep. Chm., 1966–87; Hon. Pres. and Exec. Dir, 1998–2002. Director: Brooke Bond Gp, 1972–82; NAAFI, 1972–87; HSBC Hldgs plc, 1995–2002; Mem., Internat. Adv. Council, CITIC, Beijing, 1995–2004. Mem., Gen. Cttee, Lloyd's Register, 1967–99. Pres., General Council of British Shipping, 1980–81; Chm., Internat. Chamber of Shipping, 1982–87. Elder Brother, Trinity House, 1990. Vis. Fellow, Nuffield Coll., Oxford, 1981–89 (Hon. Fellow, 1998). Chm., RAF Benevolent Fund, 1996–2000. Trustee, RAF Mus., 1983–91. Pres., Spitfire Soc., 1996–. Pro-Chancellor, Southampton Univ., 1995–2004. Mem. Council, Wycombe Abbey Sch., 1988–95. Hon. CRAeS 1991. Liveryman: Fishmongers' Co., 1962; GAPAN, 1986. DL Oxon, 1989–2007. Hon. DSc Cranfield, 1995; DUniv Southampton, 2002. Air League Founders' Medal, 2006. *Address:* Swire House, 59 Buckingham Gate, SW1E 6AJ. *Clubs:* White's, Brooks's, Pratt's; Hong Kong (Hong Kong).

See also Sir J. A. Swire.

SWIRE, Hugo George William; MP (C) Devon East, since 2001; *b* 30 Nov. 1959; *s* of late Humphrey Roger Swire and of Philippa Sophia Montgomerie (she *m* 2004, Marquess Townshend, *qv*); *m* 1996, Alexandra, (Sasha), Petruška Mina, *d* of Rt Hon. Sir John William Frederic Nott, *qv*; two *d*. *Educ:* Eton; Univ. of St Andrews; RMA Sandhurst. Lieut, 1 Bn Grenadier Guards, 1980–83; Head, Devlt Office, Nat. Gall., 1988–92; Sotheby's, 1992–2001: Dep. Dir, 1996–97; Dir, 1997–2001. Contested (Scottish C and Unionist) Greenock and Inverclyde, 1997. Shadow Minister for the Arts, 2004–05, for Culture, 2005; Shadow Sec. of State for Culture, Media and Sport, 2005–07. FRSA 1993. *Recreation:* showing my pig. *Address:* House of Commons, SW1A 0AA. *Club:* Exmouth Conservative (Pres., 2005–).

SWIRE, Sir John (Anthony), Kt 1990; CBE 1977; DL; Life President, John Swire & Sons Ltd, since 1997 (Chairman, 1966–87, Executive Director, 1955–92; Hon. President and Director, 1987–97); *b* 28 Feb. 1927; *er s* of late John Kidston Swire and Juliet Richenda, *d* of Theodore Barclay; *m* 1961, Moira Cecilia Ducharne; two *s* one *d*. *Educ:* Eton; University Coll., Oxford (MA). Served Irish Guards, UK and Palestine, 1945–48. Joined Butterfield & Swire, Hong Kong, 1950; Director: Swire Pacific Ltd, 1965–92; Royal Insurance plc, 1975–80; British Bank of the Middle East, 1975–79; James Finlay plc, 1976–92; Ocean Transport & Trading plc, 1977–83; Shell Transport and Trading Co., 1990–95. Chairman: Hong Kong Assoc., 1975–87; Cook Soc., 1984. Member: London Adv. Cttee, Hongkong and Shanghai Banking Corp., 1969–89; Euro-Asia Centre Adv. Bd, 1980–91; Adv. Council, Sch. of Business, Stanford Univ., 1981–90; Council, Univ. of Kent at Canterbury, 1989–99 (Dep. Pro-Chancellor, 1993–99). Hon. Fellow: St Antony's Coll., Oxford, 1987; University Coll., Oxford, 1989. Hon. LLD Hong Kong, 1989; Hon. DCL Kent, 1995. DL Kent, 1996. *Address:* Swire House, 59 Buckingham Gate, SW1E 6AJ. *T:* (020) 7834 7717. *Clubs:* Brooks's, Pratt's, Cavalry and Guards, Flyfishers' (Pres., 1988–89); Hong Kong (Hong Kong).

See also Sir A. C. Swire.

SWITZER, Barbara; Assistant General Secretary, Manufacturing Science Finance, 1988–97; *b* 26 Nov. 1940; *d* of Albert and Edith McMinn; *m* 1973, John Michael Switzer. *Educ:* Chorlton Central Sch., Manchester; Stretford Technical Coll. City & Guilds Final Cert. for Electrical Technician. Engrg apprentice, Metropolitan Vickers, 1957–62; Draughtswoman: GEC, Trafford Park, 1962–70; Cableform, Romiley, 1970–71; Mather & Platt, 1972–76; Divisional Organiser 1976–79, National Organiser 1979–83, AUEW (TASS); Dep. Gen. Sec., TASS—The Manufacturing Union, 1983–87. President: CSEU, 1995–97; Nat. Assembly of Women, 1999–; Mem., TUC Gen. Council, 1993–97. Mem., Employment Appeal Tribunal, 1996–. Mem. Council, Women of the Year Lunch and Assembly, 1996–. TUC Women's Gold Badge for services to Trade Unionism, 1976. *Address:* 16 Follett Drive, Abbots Langley, Herts WD5 0LP.

SWORD, Dr Ian Pollock, CBE 2002; FRCPE; CChem, FRSC; FRSE; Chairman, Inveresk Research Group Inc. (formerly Inveresk Research International Ltd), 1989–2004; *b* 6 March 1942; *s* of John Pollock Sword and Agnes McGowan (*née* Fyfe); *m* 1967, Flora Collins; two *s* one *d*. *Educ:* Univ. of Glasgow (BSc; PhD). CChem 1975; FRSC 1975; FRSE 1996; FRCPE 1997. Univ. of Princeton, 1967–69; Res. Associate, Univ. of Oxford, 1969–70; Hd of Metabolism, then Chemistry Dept, Huntingdon Res. Centre, 1970–73; Inveresk Research International Ltd: Dep. Man. Dir, 1973–78; Man. Dir, 1978–89. Sen. Exec. Vice-Pres., Société Générale de Surveillance, 1993–2002. Mem., MRC, 1995–98. Chm., Scottish Stem Cell Network, 2006–08. Dir, Archangel Informal Investment Ltd, 2003–. Trustee: Carnegie Trust for Univs of Scotland, 2005–; Royal Botanic Garden Edinburgh, 2007–. Hon. Prof., Univ. of Dundee, 2007–. Hon. DSc Glasgow, 2008. *Publications:* (ed) Standard Operating Procedures, vol. 3, 1980, vol. 4, 1981. *Recreations:* music, golf. *Club:* New (Edinburgh).

SYAL, Meera, MBE 1998; actress and writer; *b* 27 June 1964; *d* of Surendra Kumar Syal and Surrinder Syal; *m* 2005, Sanjeev Bhaskar, *qv*; one *s*; one *d* from previous marriage. *Educ:* Manchester Univ. (BA Hons English and Drama, double 1st). Various regular appearances on national television and theatre, 1992–; *actress:* television: Goodness Gracious Me, 1998–2001; The Kumars at No. 42, 2001–; All About Me, 2002; Life Isn't All Ha Ha Hee Hee (also co-writer), 2005; Murder Investigation Team, 2005; theatre: Rafta, Rafta, Nat. Th., 2007; *writer:* My Sister Wife (film), 1992; Bhaji on the Beach (film), 1993; Anita and Me (film), 2002; co-writer, Bombay Dreams (musical), Apollo, 2002, transf. Broadway Th., NY, 2004. Hon. PhD: Wolverhampton, 2000; Leeds, 2002; Birmingham, 2003. *Publications: novels:* Anita and Me, 1997; Life Isn't All Ha Ha Hee Hee, 1999. *Recreations:* netball, jazz singer. *Address:* c/o Rochelle Stevens, 2 Terretts Place, Islington, N1 1QZ.

SYCAMORE, Phillip; His Honour Judge Sycamore; a Circuit Judge, since 2001; a President, First Tier Tribunal, since 2008; *b* 9 March 1951; *s* of Frank and Evelyn Martin Sycamore; *m* 1974, Sandra, JP, *d* of late Peter Frederick Cooper and of Marjorie Cooper; two *s* one *d*. *Educ:* Lancaster Royal Grammar Sch.; Holborn Coll. of Law (LLB London (ext.) 1972). Admitted Solicitor, 1975; Partner, Lonsdales, solicitors, 1980–2001; Asst Recorder, 1994–99; a Recorder, 1999–2001; Liaison Judge, Mental Health Review Tribunal, 2002–. Law Society: Mem. Council, 1991–99; Vice-Pres., 1996–97; Pres., 1997–98. Member: Woolf Civil Justice Review (Access to Justice), 1994–96; Criminal Injuries Compensation Panel, 2000–01. Gov., Lancaster Royal Grammar Sch., 2001–. Hon. Recorder of Lancaster, 2008–. Hon. LLD: Westminster, 1998; Lancaster, 1999. *Recreations:* family, golf, theatre, travel, ski-ing. *Address:* Preston Law Courts, Ringway, Preston PR1 2LL. *Clubs:* Athenæum; Royal Lytham and St Anne's Golf.

SYDNEY, Archbishop of, and Metropolitan of the Province of New South Wales, since 2001; **Most Rev. Peter Jensen;** *b* 11 July 1943; *s* of Arthur Henry Jensen and Dorothy Lake Jensen (*née* Wilins); *m* 1968, Christine Willis Jensen (*née* O'Donell); three *s* two *d*. *Educ:* Univ. of London (BD 1970); Sydney Univ. (MA 1976); Magdalen Coll., Oxford (DPhil 1980). Ordained deacon, 1969, priest, 1970, Anglican Ch of Australia; Curate, Broadway, 1969–76; Asst Minister, St Andrew, N Oxford, 1976–79; Moore College: Lectr, 1973–76 and 1980–84; Principal, 1985–2001. *Publications:* The Quest for Power, 1973; At the Heart of the Universe, 1991; The Revelation of God, 2002; The Future of Jesus, 2005. *Recreations:* golf, reading. *Address:* Anglican Church Diocese of Sydney, PO Box Q190, Sydney, NSW 1230, Australia. *T:* (2) 92651521.

SYDNEY, Archbishop of, (RC), since 2001; **His Eminence Cardinal George Pell,** AC 2005; DD, DPhil; *b* 8 June 1941; *s* of G. A. and M. L. Pell. *Educ:* St Patrick's Coll., Vic; Corpus Christi Coll., Vic; Urban Univ., Rome (STB, STL); Campion Hall, Oxford Univ. (DPhil); Monash Univ. (MEd). FACE. Episcopal Vicar for Educn, dio. Ballarat, 1973–84; Principal, Inst. for Catholic Educn, 1981–84; Rector, Corpus Christi Coll., Clayton, 1985–87; Auxiliary Bishop, archdio. of Melbourne, 1987–96; Archbishop of Melbourne, 1996–2001. Cardinal, 2003. Nat. Chaplain, Order of St Lazarus, 2001–07; Grand Prior, NSW Lieutenancy of the Equestrian Order of the Holy Sepulchre of Jerusalem, 2001–; Conventual Chaplain ad honorem, SMO Malta, 2007. Member: Vatican Council for Justice and Peace, 1990–95, 2002–; Vatican Congregation for the Doctrine of the Faith, 1990–2000; Vatican Council, Synod of Bishops, 2001–; Presidential Cttee, Vatican Council for the Family, 2003–; Vatican Congregation for Divine Worship, 2005–; Vatican Supreme Cttee, Pontifical Missions Socs, 2005–; Vatican Council of Cardinals on Orgnl and Econ. Problems of the Holy See, 2007–; Pres., Vatican *Vox Clara* Cttee, 2001–. Chm., Australian Catholic Relief, 1989–97. Foundn Pres., John Paul II Institute for Marriage and the Family, Melbourne, 2000–01. Foundn Pro-Chancellor, Australian Catholic Univ., 1990–95 (Pres., 1996–). Apostolic Visitor, Seminaries of NZ, 1994, PNG, and Solomon Is, 1995, Pacific, 1996, Irian Jaya, and Sulawesi, 1998. Hon. Fellow, St Edmund's Coll., Cambridge, 2003. LHD *hc* Christendom Coll., Va, 2006. Honour of the Pallium, Rome, 1997, 2001; GCLJ 1998; KGCHS 2002; Bailiff Grand Cross of Honour and Devotion, SMO Malta, 2008. *Publications:* The Sisters of St Joseph in Swan Hill 1922–72, 1972; Catholicism in Australia, 1988; Rerum Novarum: one hundred years later, 1992; Issues of Faith and Morals, 1996; Catholicism and the Architecture of Freedom, 1999; Be Not Afraid, 2004; God and Caesar, 2007. *Address:* St Mary's Cathedral, Sydney, NSW 2000, Australia. *Clubs:* Melbourne, Australian (Sydney); Richmond Football (Vic).

SYDNEY, NORTH, Bishop of; *see* Davies, Rt Rev. G. N.

SYDNEY, SOUTH, Bishop of; *see* Forsyth, Rt Rev. R. C.

SYDNEY, Assistant Bishops of; *see* Davies, Rt Rev. G. N.; Forsyth, Rt Rev. R. C.

SYED, Matthew Philip; table tennis player; Managing Director, MPS Consulting Ltd, since 2002; *b* 2 Nov. 1970; *s* of Abbas Syed and Dilys Syed. *Educ:* Maiden Erleigh Comprehensive Sch.; Balliol Coll., Oxford (MA). Represented GB, Olympic Games, Barcelona, 1992 and Sydney, 2000; British No. 1, 1995–2004; English Men's Singles Champion, 1997, 1998, 2000, 2001; Commonwealth Men's Singles Champion, 1997, 1999, 2001. Sports columnist, The Times, 1999–. Co-founder and Dir, TTK Greenhouse (sports charity), 2002–. Feature Writer of the Year, Sports Journalists' Assoc., 2007. *Recreations:* walking in Richmond Park, looking at London architecture. *Address:* Flat 5, 38 Montague Road, Richmond, Surrey TW10 6QJ. *T:* (020) 8948 6050; *e-mail:* matthew@msyed.freeserve.co.uk.

SYFRET, Nicholas; QC 2008; a Recorder, since 2001; *b* Windlesham, Surrey, 25 Oct. 1954; *s* of Edward Herbert Vyvyan Syfret and Anne Syfret; *m* 1980, Katharine Frances Allinson; two *s* one *d*. *Educ:* Winchester Coll.; Emmanuel Coll., Cambridge (BA 1976). Called to the Bar, Middle Temple, 1979; in practice as barrister specialising in criminal law; 6 King's Bench Walk, 1980–93, 13 King's Bench Walk, 1993–. *Recreations:* countryside, messing about in boats, painting, chess. *Address:* St Margaret's Cottage, 15 The Moors, Pangbourne, Reading RG8 7LP. *T:* (01189) 843690; *e-mail:* NSyfret@aol.com.

SYKES, Alastair; Chairman and Chief Executive, Nestlé UK, since 2001; *b* 25 Jan. 1953; *s* of John and Jackie Sykes; *m* 1982, Kate Rutter; one *s*. *Educ:* UMIST (BSc Hons Mgt Sci. 1978). Joined Gillette, 1978; held various commercial roles, 1978–89; Eur. Sales and Mktg Dir, 1989–91; Managing Director: McCormick Foods, 1991–95; Spillers UK, 1995–98; Nestlé Rowntree, 1998–2001. Pres., Inst. of Grocery Distribution, 2007–. *Recreations:* golf, Rugby. *Address:* Nestlé UK Ltd, St George's House, Park Lane, Croydon CR9 1NR. *T:* (020) 8667 5115.

SYKES, Prof. Brian Douglas, PhD; FRS 2000; FRSC 1986; University Professor since 1997, and Chair, Department of Biochemistry, since 1999, University of Alberta; *b* Montreal, 30 Aug. 1943; *s* of Douglas Lehman Sykes and Mary Anber Sykes; *m* 1968, Nancy Sengelaub; two *s*. *Educ:* Univ. of Alberta (BSc 1965); Stanford Univ. (PhD 1969). Asst Prof. of Chemistry, 1969–74, Associate Prof., 1974–75, Harvard Univ.; University of Alberta: Associate Prof., 1975–80, Prof., 1980–97; Mem., 1975–, Dir, 1995–, MRC Gp in Protein Structure and Function; Leader, Alberta Node, 1990–, Dep. Scientific Leader, 1995–98, Protein Engrg Network of Centres of Excellence; Actg Chair, Dept of Biochem., 1998–99; Canada Res. Chair, 2001–08. Pres., Canadian Biochem. Soc., 1989–90. *Publications:* over 400 scientific papers. *Address:* Department of Biochemistry, University of Alberta, Edmonton, AB T6G 2H7, Canada; 11312–37 Avenue, Edmonton, AB T6J 0HS, Canada.

SYKES, Sir David Michael, 4th Bt *cr* 1921, of Kingsknowes, Galashiels, co. Selkirk; Chairman, Bennett Sykes Group (formerly Libra Office Equipment) Ltd, since 2000; *b* 10 June 1954; *s* of Michael le Gallais Sykes and Joan Sykes (*née* Groome); *S* uncle, 2001; *m* 1st, 1974, Susan Elizabeth Hall (marr. diss. 1987); one *s*; 2nd, 1987, Margaret Lynne McGreavy; one *d*. *Educ:* Purbrook Park Grammar Sch. Sales Dir, Frank Groome (Nottingham) Ltd, 1974–85; Sen. Partner, Sykes Office Supplies, 1985. Mem., LTA. *Recreations:* travel, food and wine, tennis. *Heir: s* Stephen David Sykes, *b* 14 Dec. 1978.

SYKES, Dr Donald Armstrong; Principal of Mansfield College, Oxford, 1977–86, now Hon. Fellow; *b* 13 Feb. 1930; *s* of late Rev. Leonard Sykes and Edith Mary Sykes (*née* Armstrong); *m* 1st, 1962, Marta Sproul Whitehouse (*d* 2000); two *s*; 2nd, 2002, Sarah Yates. *Educ:* The High Sch. of Dundee; Univ. of St Andrews (MA 2nd cl. Classics 1952; Guthrie Scholar); RAEC, 1952–54; Mansfield Coll., Oxford (BA 1st cl. Theol. 1958; MA 1961; DPhil 1967); Univ. of Glasgow (DipEd). Fellow in Theology, 1959–77, Senior Tutor, 1970–77, and Sen. Res. Fellow, 1986–89, Mansfield Coll., Oxford; retired from tutoring, 2000. Vis. Prof. in Classics and Religion, St Olaf Coll., Northfield, Minn, 1969–70, 1987. Hon. DD St Olaf, 1979. *Publications:* (contrib.) Studies of the Church in History: essays honoring Robert S. Paul, ed Horton Davies, 1983; (introd., trans. and commentary) Gregory of Nazianzus, *Poemata Arcana*, 1997; articles and reviews in Jl Theological Studies, Studia Patristica, Byzantinische Zeitschrift. *Recreations:* miscellaneous reading, recorded music, walking, gardening. *Address:* 52 Pond Bank, Blisworth, Northampton NN7 3EL. *T:* (01604) 859373. *Club:* Oxford and Cambridge.

SYKES, Eric, CBE 2005 (OBE 1986); actor, writer, director, producer; *b* 4 May 1923; *s* of Vernon and Harriet Sykes; *m* 1952, Edith Eleanore Milbrandt; one *s* three *d*. Wireless Operator, Mobile Signals Unit, RAF, 1941–49. *Films include:* actor: Orders are Orders;

Watch Your Stern; Very Important Person; Heavens Above; Shalako; Those Magnificent Men in their Flying Machines, 1964; Monte Carlo or Bust!, 1969; The Boys in Blue, 1982; Absolute Beginners, 1986; The Others, 2001; Son of Rambow, 2008; *radio* includes: writer: Educating Archie; Variety Bandbox; *television* includes: actor: Sykes and A…, 1960–80 (also writer); Charley's Aunt, 1977; If You Go Down to the Woods Today (also prod. and dir), 1980; The 19th Hole, 1989; *silent films:* (actor, writer and dir): The Plank, 1980 (Press Award, Montreux Fest.); Mr H is Late; It's Your Move, 1984; The Big Freeze; Rhubarb, Rhubarb; *theatre* includes: actor: Big Bad Mouse, tour of Australia, 1977–78; A Hatful of Sykes, tour of Australia, Canada, Rhodesia, UK, 1977–78; Run For Your Wife, Shaftesbury, Criterion, and tour of Canada; The 19th Hole, nat. tour, 1992; Two of a Kind, nat. tour, 1995; Fools Rush In, nat. tour, 1996; The School for Wives, Kafka's Dick, 1998, Piccadilly; Charley's Aunt, nat. tour, 2001; Caught in the Net, Vaudeville, 2001; The Three Sisters, Playhouse, 2003; As You Like It, Th. Royal, Bath, 2003. Freeman, City of London, 1988. Hon. Fellow, Univ. of Lancashire, 1999. Lifetime Achievement Award, Writers' Guild, 1992. *Publications:* Sykes of Sebastopol Terrace, 1981, 2nd edn 2000; The Great Crime of Grapplemick (novel), 1985; UFOs are coming Wednesday, 1995; Smelling of Roses, 1997; Eric Sykes' Comedy Heroes, 2003; If I Don't Write It, Nobody Else Will, 2005. *Address:* c/o Eric Sykes Ltd, 9 Orme Court, W2 4RL. *T:* (020) 7727 1544. *Club:* Royal and Ancient Golf.

SYKES, Sir (Francis) John (Badcock), 10th Bt *cr* 1781, of Basildon, Berkshire; Partner, Thring Townsend (formerly Townsends), solicitors, Bath, Swindon and Newbury, 1972–2002, Consultant, 2002–05; *b* 7 June 1942; *s* of Sir Francis Godfrey Sykes, 9th Bt and Lady Eira Betty Sykes (*née* Badcock) (*d* 1970); *S* father, 1990; *m* 1966, Susan Alexandra, *er d* of Adm. of the Fleet Sir E. B. Ashmore, *qv*; three *s*. *Educ:* Shrewsbury; Worcester Coll., Oxford (MA). Admitted solicitor, 1968; Assistant Solicitor: Gamlens, Lincoln's Inn, 1968–69; Townsends, 1969–71. Hon. Solicitor, 1973–98, Pres., 1981, Swindon Chamber of Commerce. Governor: Swindon Coll., 1982–90; Swindon Enterprise Trust, 1982–89. Trustee: Roman Research Trust, 1990–2002; Merchant's House (Marlborough) Trust, 1991–; Wilts Community Foundn, 1993–2000; Duchess of Somerset's Hosp., 2003–. Member: HAC; City Barge Club, Oxford. *Recreations:* local and Anglo-Indian history, venetian rowing. *Heir:* *s* Lt Col Francis Charles Sykes, *b* 18 June 1968. *Address:* Kingsbury Croft, Kingsbury Street, Marlborough, Wilts SN8 1HU.

SYKES, Sir Hugh (Ridley), Kt 1997; DL; Chairman, Mid Yorkshire NHS Trust, 2005–08; *b* 12 Sept. 1932; *m* 1st, 1957, Norah Rosemary Dougan; two *s*; 2nd, 1978, Ruby Anderson; two *s*. *Educ:* Bristol Grammar Sch.; Clare Coll., Cambridge (MA, LLB). CA 1960. Articled with Thomson McLintock, Chartered Accountants, 1956–61; Treas., 1961–69, Asst Man. Dir, 1969–72, Man. Dir (Finance), 1972–73, Steetley & Co.; Chm. and Chief Exec., Thermal Scientific plc, 1977–88. Chm., BHH (Brookfield) Ltd (formerly Bamford Hall Hldgs Ltd), 1972–; non-exec. Dep. Chm., Harris Queensway plc, 1978–83; non-executive Chairman: Harveys Furnishings, 1988–94; Yorkshire Bank plc, 1999–2004 (Dir, 1990–2004); Nat. Australia Gp (Europe) Ltd, 2002–04 (Dir, 1997–2004); non-exec. Dir, Clydesdale Bank plc, 1999–2004. Consultant, Bd, Nat. Australia Bank, 2002–04. Chairman: Sheffield Develt Corp., 1988–97; Renaissance S Yorks, 2004–; non-exec. Chm., 2000–05, Dir, 2005–07, Sheffield One; Dir, Creative Sheffield 2007–; Mem. Bd, Sheffield TEC, 1990–95. Director: Inst. of Dirs, 2003–; A4E, 2005–. Chairman: Hugh and Ruby Sykes Charitable Trust, 1988–; Sheffield Galleries and Museums Trust, 1998–2008; Industrial Trust, 2001– (Trustee, 1998–). Mem. Council, Univ. of Sheffield, 1997–2002 (Treas., 1998–2002). DL S Yorks, 1996. Freeman, City of London, 1990. FCIB 2001. Hon. Fellow, Sheffield Hallam Univ., 1991. Hon. LLD Sheffield, 1996. *Publications:* Working for Benefit, 1997; Welfare to Work: the new deal—maximising the benefits, 1998. *Recreations:* walking, travel, golf, Victorian paintings, shooting, helping to find a solution to the problem of unemployment. *Address:* Brookfield Manor, Hathersage, Hope Valley S32 1BR. *T:* (01433) 651190. *Clubs:* Carlton, Mark's; Lindrick Golf, Sickleholme Golf.

SYKES, Jean Margaret; Librarian and Director of IT Services, London School of Economics and Political Science, since 1998; *b* 11 April 1947; *d* of David Thomson and Doreen Thomson (*née* Rose). *Educ:* Univ. of Glasgow (MA Hons, MLitt); Liverpool Poly. (DipLib). Actg Hd, Library Services, Middlesex Poly., 1985–87; Dep. Dir, Information Resource Services, Poly. of Central London, subseq. Univ. of Westminster, 1987–97. Chairman: M25 Consortium of Higher Educn Libraries, 1994–96; Soc. of College, Univ. and Nat. Libraries, 2000–02. FRSA 2002. *Publications:* contrib. librarianship and IT jls. *Recreations:* theatre, travel, French language and literature, wine. *Address:* British Library of Political and Economic Science, London School of Economics and Political Science, 10 Portugal Street, WC2A 2HD.

SYKES, Sir John; *see* Sykes, Sir F. J. B.

SYKES, Rev. Canon John; Vicar, St Mary with St Peter, Oldham and Team Rector, Parish of Oldham, 1987–2004; Chaplain to the Queen, since 1995; *b* 20 March 1939; *s* of George Reginald Sykes and Doris Sykes (*née* Briggs); *m* 1967, Anne Shufflebotham; one *s* one *d*. *Educ:* St James C of E Sch., Slaithwaite; Royds Hall Grammar Sch., Huddersfield; W Bridgford Grammar Sch., Nottingham; Manchester Univ. (BA); Ripon Hall, Oxford. Ordained deacon, 1963, priest, 1964; Curate: St Luke's, Heywood, 1963–67; i/c Holy Trinity, Bolton, 1967–71; Lectr, Bolton Inst. of Technol., 1967–71; Chaplain to Bolton Colls of Further Educn, 1967–71; Rector, St Elisabeth, Reddish, 1971–78; Vicar, Saddleworth, 1978–87. Proctor in Convocation and Mem., Gen. Synod of C of E, 1980–90. Council for the Care of Churches: Mem., 1986–90; Vice-Chm., Art and Design Sub-cttee, 1988–90. Mem., various Manchester Diocesan Cttees and Councils, 1968–93. Chaplain to: Coliseum Theatre, Oldham, 1987–2006; four Mayors of Oldham, 1989–99; High Sheriff of Gtr Manchester, 1993–94, 1996–97; Gtr Manchester Police, Q Div., 1995–99. Hon. Canon, Manchester Cathedral, 1991–2004, now Canon Emeritus. *Recreations:* architecture, fine arts, music, walking. *Address:* 53 Ivy Green Drive, Springhead, Oldham OL4 4PR. *T:* and *Fax:* (0161) 678 6767; *e-mail:* john.sykes@mypostoffice.co.uk. *Club:* Manchester Pedestrians.

SYKES, John David; Director: Group Petroleum Retail Division, Shaws Fuels Ltd, since 1981; Shawspetroleum Ltd, since 1986; Farnley Tyas Estates Ltd, since 1986; *b* 24 Aug. 1956; *m* 1st, 1981, Jane Aspinall (marr. diss. 2003); one *s* two *d*; 2nd, 2007, Vivien Broadbent. *Educ:* St David's Prep. Sch., Huddersfield; Giggleswick Sch., N Riding. Joined Shaws Fuels Ltd (family company), 1974: graduated through every company dept, specialising in sales and transport; Dir, 1978–2000; also Dir, subsid. cos. MP (C) Scarborough, 1992–97; contested (C) Scarborough and Whitby, 1997, 2001. PPS to Lord Privy Seal and Leader of H of L, 1995–97. Mem., Select Cttee on Deregulation, 1995–97; Vice Chm., Backbench Deregulation Cttee, 1995–97 (Sec., 1993–95). *Recreations:* walking, reading, Rugby Union, playing piano. *Address:* Farnley House, Manor Road, Farnley Tyas, Huddersfield, W Yorks HD4 6UL.

SYKES, Prof. Katharine Ellen, PhD; CPhys, FInstP; Professor of Sciences and Society, University of Bristol, since 2006 (Collier Professor of Public Engagement in Science and Engineering, 2002–06); *b* 20 Dec. 1966; *d* of Dr John Sykes and Pauline Sykes. *Educ:* Univ. of Bristol (BSc Hons (Physics) 1989; PhD (Physics) 1996). VSO as Hd, Maths Dept and physics teacher, Zhombe High Sch., Zimbabwe, 1989–92; researcher; Hd of Sci., Explore@Bristol, 1996–2001. Dir, Cheltenham Fest. of Sci., 2001–. Mem., Council for Science and Technology, 2004–; Trustee, NESTA, 2007–. Presenter, BBC and OU series, incl. Alternative Therapies, Rough Science, Ever Wondered and Mindgames. *Publications:* papers in scientific jls on biodegradable plastic poly hyroxybutyrate; numerous conf. procs on science engagement; contrib. Science. *Recreations:* scuba-diving, mountain-climbing, dancing, singing, good food. *Address:* Royal Fort House, University of Bristol, Bristol BS8 1UJ; *e-mail:* kathy.sykes@bristol.ac.uk.

SYKES, Sir Keith; *see* Sykes, Sir M. K.

SYKES, Sir (Malcolm) Keith, Kt 1991; Nuffield Professor of Anaesthetics, University of Oxford, 1980–91, Emeritus Professor since 1991; Hon. Fellow of Pembroke College, Oxford, since 1996 (Fellow, 1980–91, Supernumary Fellow, 1991–96); *b* 13 Sept. 1925; *s* of Joseph and Phyllis Mary Sykes; *m* 1956, Michelle June (*née* Ratcliffe); one *s* three *d*. *Educ:* Magdalene Coll., Cambridge (MA, MB, BChir); University Coll. Hosp., London (DA; FFARCS). RAMC, 1950–52. House appointments, University Coll. and Norfolk and Norwich Hosps, 1949–50; Sen. House Officer, Registrar and Sen. Registrar in anaesthetics, UCH, 1952–54 and 1955–58; Rickman Godlee Travelling Scholar and Fellow in Anesthesia, Mass. General Hosp., Boston, USA, 1954–55; RPMS and Hammersmith Hosp., 1958–80: Lectr and Sen. Lectr, 1958–67; Reader, 1967–70; Prof. of Clinical Anaesthesia, 1970–80. Vis. Prof., univs in Canada, USA, Australia, NZ, Malaysia, Europe. Eponymous lectures: Holme, 1970; Clover, 1976; Weinbren, 1976; Rowbottom, 1978; Gillespie, 1979; Gillies, 1985; Wesley Bourne, 1986; Husfeldt, 1986; Della Briggs, 1988; E. M. Papper, 1991; BOC Healthcare, 1992; Harold Griffith, 1992; Sir Robert Macintosh, 1992. Mem. Bd, Fac. of Anaesthetists, 1969–85; Pres., Section of Anaesthetics, RSM, 1989–90; Vice Pres., Assoc. of Anaesthetists, 1990–92 (Mem. Council, 1967–70); Senator and Vice Pres., European Acad. of Anaesthesiology, 1978–85. Hon. FANZCA (Hon. FFARACS 1979); Hon. FCA(SA) (Hon. FFA(SA) 1989). Dudley Buxton Prize, Fac. of Anaesthetists, 1980; Fac. of Anaesthetists Medal, 1987; John Snow Medal, Assoc. of Anaesthetists, 1992; Hickman Medal, RSocMed, 2008. *Publications:* Respiratory Failure, 1969, 2nd edn 1976; Principles of Measurement for Anaesthetists, 1970; Principles of Clinical Measurement, 1980; Principles of Measurement and Monitoring in Anaesthesia and Intensive Care, 1991; Respiratory Support, 1995; Respiratory Support in Intensive Care, 1999; Anaesthesia and the Practice of Medicine: historical perspectives, 2007; chapters and papers on respiratory failure, intensive care, respiratory and cardiovascular physiology applied to anaesthesia, etc. *Recreations:* sailing, walking, birdwatching, gardening, music. *Address:* Treyarnon, Cricket Field Lane, Budleigh Salterton, Devon EX9 6PB. *T:* (01395) 445884.

SYKES, Sir Richard (Brook), Kt 1994; FRS 1997; Rector, Imperial College of Science, Technology and Medicine, University of London, 2001–08; *b* 7 Aug. 1942; *s* of late Eric Sykes and of Muriel Mary Sykes; *m* 1969, Janet Mary Norman; one *s* one *d*. *Educ:* Queen Elizabeth Coll., London (1st Cl. Hons Microbiol.); Bristol Univ. (PhD Microbial Biochem.); DSc London, 1993. Glaxo Res. UK (Head of Antibiotic Res. Unit), 1972–77; Squibb Inst. for Med. Res., USA, 1977–86 (Vice-Pres., Infectious and Metabolic Diseases, 1983–86); Glaxo Group Research: Dep. Chief Exec., 1986; Chm. and Chief Exec., 1987–93; Glaxo plc: Group R&D Dir, 1987–93; Dep. Chm. and Chief Exec., 1993–97; Dep. Chm. and Chief Exec., 1993–97, Chm., 1997–2000, Glaxo Wellcome; Chm., GlaxoSmithKline, 2000–02. Dir, British Pharma Gp, 1998–2001. Non-executive Chairman: Merlion Pharmaceuticals Pte Ltd, 2005–; Circassia Ltd, 2007–; non-executive Director: Rio Tinto plc, 1997–2008; Rio Tinto Ltd, 1997–2008; Lonza, 2003–; Eurasian Nat. Resources Corpn, 2007–. Chairman: Adv. Council, Life Scis Exec. Cttee, EDB, Singapore, 2000–; Healthcare Adv. Gp (Apax Partners Ltd), 2002–; Bioscience Leadership Council, 2004–07; WHO Internat. Adv. Bd overseeing Internat. Clinical Trials Registry Platform, 2005–; CATALYST, 2005–08. Member: Council for Sci. and Technol., 1993–2003; Adv. Council, Save British Science, subseq. Campaign for Sci. and Engrg, 1993–; Foundn for Sci. and Technol. Council, 1994–2000; Trade Policy Forum, 1995–2000; Internat. Adv. Council, Economic Develt Bd, 1995–; Council for Industry and Higher Educn, 1995–2008; Bd, Eur. Fedn of Pharm. Industries and Assocs, 1997–2000; Council, Internat. Fedn of Pharm. Manufrs Assocs, 1998–2001; HEFCE, 2002–; Engrg & Tech. Bd, 2002–05; DTI Strategy Bd, 2002–04; Temasek Internat. Adv. Panel, Singapore, 2004–. President: BAAS, 1998–99; Res. and Develt Soc., 2002–; Hon. Vice-Pres., Res. Defence Soc., 2004–; Hon. Mem., British Soc. for Antimicrobial Chemotherapy, 2006. Chairman: Business Leader Gp, British Lung Foundn, 1993–; Global Business Council on HIV/AIDS, 1997–2000; UK Stem Cell Foundn, 2005–. Vice-Pres., Nat. Soc. for Epilepsy, 1995–. Mem. Council, St George's House, Windsor Castle, 2004–. Patron, Huddersfield Enterprise Foundn, 2005–. Mem. Bd Trustees, Natural Hist. Mus., 1996–2005; Trustee, Royal Botanic Gardens Kew, 2003–05. Member: Bd of Mgt, LSHTM, 1994–2003; Council, RCM, 2001–; Internat. Adv. Council, King Abdullah Univ. of Sci. and Technol., 2007–; Bd of Trustees, Masdar Inst. of Sci. and Technol., 2008–, Nanyang Technol Univ., Singapore, 2008–. MInstD 1995. Fleming Fellow, Lincoln Coll., Oxford, 1992; FKC 1997; FIC 1999. Founder FMedSci 1998. Hon. FRCP 1995; Hon. FRSC 1999; Hon. FRPharmS 2001; Hon. FRCPath 2003; Hon. FREng 2004. Hon. Fellow, Univ. of Wales, 1997; Hon. FCGI 2002. Hon. DPharm Madrid, 1993; Hon. DSc: Brunel, Hull, Hertfordshire, 1994; Bristol, Newcastle, 1995; Huddersfield, Westminster, 1996; Leeds, 1997; Edinburgh, Strathclyde, 1998; London, Cranfield, Leicester, Sheffield, Warwick, 1999; Hon. MD Birmingham, 1995; Hon. LLD Nottingham, 1997. *Recreations:* opera, tennis, swimming. *Address:* Flat 11, Hale House, 34 De Vere Gardens, W8 5AQ. *T:* (020) 7937 0742. *Club:* Athenæum.

SYKES, Robert Hedley, OBE 2008; Chief Executive, Worcestershire County Council, 1997–2007; *b* 21 Aug. 1952; *s* of Hedley Sykes and Edith (*née* Oliver); *m* 1987, Jill Frances Brice; two *d*. *Educ:* Danum Grammar Sch.; Leeds Univ. (BSc, CQSW); Sheffield Poly. (DMS). Social worker, later Principal Officer (Children's Services), Doncaster MBC, 1975–86; Dep. Divl Dir, Social Services, N Yorks CC, 1986–89; Dep. Dir, Social Services, Oxfordshire CC, 1989–92; Dir, Social Services, Hereford and Worcester CC, 1992–97; non-exec. Dir, Crown Prosecution Service, 2007–. CInstLM 2007. FRSA 1999. *Recreations:* family, badminton, theatre.

SYKES, Roger Michael Spencer, OBE 2002; HM Diplomatic Service; High Commissioner to Fiji, and concurrently to Tonga, Vanuatu, Tuvalu, Kiribati and Nauru, since 2006; *b* 22 Oct. 1948; *s* of Kenneth and Joan Sykes; *m* 1976, Anne Lesley Groves Gidney; three *s*. *Educ:* Wintringham Grammar Sch.; John Wilmott Grammar Sch.; Newport Grammar Sch. Entered FCO, 1969; served: Caracas, 1971–72; Freetown, 1972–75; Karachi, 1976–78; Cultural Attaché, Valetta, 1978–81; Press Officer, FCO, 1981–82; Attaché, Lagos, 1982–86; Dep. High Comr, Vila, 1986–90; S Asia Dept, FCO, 1990–93; Political and Econ. Sec., Amman, 1993–97; Hd of Post, Alkhobar, 1997–2001; Dep. Hd of Mission, Karachi, 2002–05. Dir, St John's Hall Mgt Co., 2006–. *Recreations:* golf, game fishing, cricket, social history, comparing the different attributes of old and new world red wines. *Address:* c/o Foreign and Commonwealth Office, King Charles Street,

SW1A 2AH; *e-mail:* roger.sykes@fco.gov.uk; c/o British High Commission, Victoria House, PO Box 1355, Suva, Republic of Fiji Islands. *T:* 3229100, *Fax:* 3229140. *Clubs:* Sheringham Golf; Suva Golf.

SYKES, Rt Rev. Prof. Stephen Whitefield; Principal, St John's College, and Professor of Theology, University of Durham, 1999–2006; Assistant Bishop, diocese of Durham, since 1999; *b* 1 Aug. 1939; *m* 1962, Marianne Joy Hinton; one *s* two *d*. *Educ:* St John's Coll., Cambridge (BA 1961; MA 1964). Univ. Asst Lectr in Divinity, Cambridge Univ., 1964–68, Lectr, 1968–74; Fellow and Dean, St John's Coll., Cambridge, 1964–74; Van Mildert Canon Prof. of Divinity, Durham Univ., 1974–85; Regius Prof. of Divinity, and Fellow, St John's College, Cambridge, 1985–90; Bishop of Ely, 1990–99. Mem., Archbishop's Cttee on Religious Educn, 1967. Chairman: Doctrine Commn of C of E, 1997–2005; InterAnglican Theol and Doctrinal Commn, 1999–. Hon. Canon of Ely Cathedral, 1985–90. Examining Chaplain to Bishop of Chelmsford, 1970–75. Edward Cadbury Lectr, Univ. of Birmingham, 1978; Hensley Henson Lectr, Univ. of Oxford, 1982–83. Chm., North of England Inst. for Christian Educn, 1980–85. Pres., Council of St John's Coll., Durham, 1984–94. *Publications:* Friedrich Schleiermacher, 1971; Christian Theology Today, 1971; (ed) Christ, Faith and History, 1972; The Integrity of Anglicanism, 1978; (ed) Karl Barth: studies in his theological method, 1980; (ed) New Studies in Theology, 1980; (ed) England and Germany, Studies in Theological Diplomacy, 1982; The Identity of Christianity, 1984; (ed) Authority in the Anglican Communion, 1987; (ed) The Study of Anglicanism, 1988; (ed) Karl Barth: Centenary Essays, 1989; (ed) Sacrifice and Redemption, 1991; Unashamed Anglicanism, 1995; The Story of Atonement, 1997; Power and Christian Theology, 2006. *Recreations:* walking (especially relearning how to walk), retirement cookery. *Address:* Ingleside, Whinney Hill, Durham DH1 3BE. *T:* (0191) 384 6465.

SYKES, Sir Tatton (Christopher Mark), 8th Bt *cr* 1783; landowner; *b* 24 Dec. 1943; *s* of Sir (Mark Tatton) Richard Tatton-Sykes, 7th Bt and Virginia (*d* 1970), *d* of late John Francis Grey Gilliat; *S* father, 1978; granted use of additional arms of Tatton, 1980. *Educ:* Eton; Univ. d'Aix-Marseille; Royal Agric. Coll., Cirencester. *Heir: b* Jeremy John Sykes [*b* 8 March 1946; *m* 1982, Pamela June (marr. diss. 1995; she *m* 2nd, Earl of Swinton, *qv*), *o d* of Thomas Wood]. *Address:* Sledmere, Driffield, East Yorkshire YO25 3XG.

SYLVA, Prof. Kathleen Danaher, Hon. OBE 2007; PhD; Professor of Educational Psychology, University of Oxford, since 1998; Fellow of Jesus College, Oxford, since 1997. *Educ:* Harvard Univ. (BA 1964; MA 1972; PhD 1974). Lectr in Applied Social Studies, Univ. of Oxford, 1977–88; Fellow of Jesus Coll., Oxford, 1977–88; Prof. of Primary Educn, Univ. of Warwick, 1988–90; Prof. of Child Develt and Primary Educn, Inst. of Educn, Univ. of London, 1990–97; Reader in Educnl Studies, Univ. of Oxford, 1997–98. *Publications:* (ed jtly) Play: its role in development and evolution, 1976; (jtly) Childwatching at Playgroup and Nursery School, 1980; (with I. Lunt) Child Development: a first course, 1982; (ed jtly) Assessing Children's Social Behaviour and Competence, 1997; (jtly) Assessing Quality in the Early Years, 2003; articles in learned jls. *Address:* Department of Educational Studies, University of Oxford, 15 Norham Gardens, Oxford OX2 6PY.

SYMES, Dr Robert Frederick, OBE 1996; FGS; Keeper of Mineralogy, Natural History Museum, 1995–96; *b* 10 Feb. 1939; *s* of Alfred Charles Symes and Mary Emily Symes; *m* 1965, Carol Ann Hobbs; two *d*. *Educ:* Birkbeck Coll., London Univ. (BSc Hons); Queen Mary Coll., London Univ. (PhD 1981). FGS 1991. Nat. service, RAF, 1959–61. Natural History Museum, 1957–96: Asst Scientific Officer, 1957–59 and 1961–72; SSO, 1972–81; PSO, 1981–92; Dep. Keeper, 1992–95. Pres., GA, 1996–98. Lay Mem., Exeter Univ. Council, 2002–06. Hon. Curator, Sidmouth Mus., Devon, 2001–. *Publications:* (jtly) Minerals of Cornwall and Devon, 1987; Rock and Mineral, 1988; (jtly) Crystal and Gem, 1991. *Recreations:* countryside, industrial archaeology, local history, tennis, Association Football. *Address:* Violet House, Salcombe Road, Sidmouth, Devon EX10 8PU. *T:* (01395) 578114.

SYMES, Susie; economist; Chairman, Museum of Immigration and Diversity, since 1998; *b* 24 April 1954; *d* of late Oliver Symes and Judith Symes (*née* Blumberg); *m* 1972, Ian Paul Abson (marr. diss. 1977); partner, Philip Jonathan Black; (one *d* decd). *Educ:* Withington Girls' Sch.; Anglo-American Coll.; City Univ., London (Adam Smith Prize 1974); St Antony's Coll., Oxford (Pres., JCR); London Sch. of Econs. Vis. Lectr, Univ. of Buckingham, 1975–77; Lectr and Sen. Res. Officer, Civil Service Coll., 1977–84; Econ. Advr, HM Treasury, 1985–90; Sen. Official, EC, 1990–92; Dir, European Prog., RIIA, 1992–95. Vis. Prof., Nat. Inst. of Defence Studies, Tokyo, 1994. Dir, Charter for Europe, 1997. Fellow, British American Proj., 1993–; Conseiller, Federal Trust, 1996–97; Trustee: Foundn for English Coll. in Prague, 1996–; Alzheimer's Soc., 2000–03; Mem. Adv. Council, London East Res. Inst., 2004–. Founding Pres., La Légion des Femmes Efficaces, 1998–; Co-Founder, Probo, 2006–. Mem. Adv. Bd, Prospect magazine, 1995–; exec. co-producer, Voices (audio anthol.), 1998 (prize for special achievement, Talking Newspaper Assoc. of UK). *Publications:* (jtly) Economics Workbook, 1989; (jtly) European Futures: alternative scenarios, 1998; occasional articles in learned and light jls. *Recreations:* making connections, marmalade and papier mâché. *Address:* The Museum of Immigration and Diversity, c/o 19 Princelet Street, E1 6QH. *T:* (020) 7247 5352; *e-mail:* office@19princeletstreet.org.uk. *Clubs:* Reform, Serpentine.

SYMMONDS, Algernon Washington, GCM 1980; QC (Barbados) 1995; solicitor and attorney-at-law; *b* 19 Nov. 1926; *s* of late Algernon French Symmonds and Olga Ianthe (*née* Harper); *m* 1954, Gladwyn Ward; one *s* one *d*. *Educ:* Combermere Sch.; Harrison Coll.; Codrington Coll., Barbados. Solicitor, Barbados, 1953, enrolled in UK, 1958; in practice as Solicitor, Barbados, 1953–55; Dep. Registrar, Barbados, 1955–59; Crown Solicitor, Barbados, 1959–66; Permanent Secretary: Min. of Home Affairs, 1966–72; Min. of Educn, 1972–76; Min. of External Affairs and Head of Foreign Service, 1976–79; appointed to rank of Ambassador, 1977; High Comr in UK, 1979–83 and non-resident Ambassador to Denmark, Finland, Iceland, Norway and Sweden, 1981–83, and to the Holy See, 1982–83; Perm. Sec., Prime Minister's Office, Barbados, 1983–86; Head of CS, 1986. President: Barbados CS Assoc., 1958–65; Fedn of British CS Assocs in Caribbean, 1960–64; Dep. Mem. Exec., Public Services Internat., 1964–66. Pres., Barbados Bar Assoc., 2001, 2002, 2003 (Chm. Disciplinary Cttee, 1991–97); Vice-Pres., Orgn of Commonwealth Caribbean Bar Assoc., 2001–03; Chm., Barbados Br., WI Cttee, 1992–95; Dep. Chm., Caribbean Examinations Council, 1973–76. Past Pres., Barbados Lawn Tennis Assoc. *Recreations:* tennis, cricket broadcasting (represented Barbados in football, lawn tennis, basketball). *Address:* Melksham, 12 Margaret Terrace, Pine Gardens, St Michael, Barbados, WI; Symmonds, Greene, Reifer, Pinfold Street, Bridgetown, Barbados, WI. *Clubs:* Empire (Cricket and Football) (Life Mem. and Past Vice-Pres.), Summerhayes Tennis (Past Pres.) (Barbados).

See also Dame O. P. Symmonds.

SYMMONDS, Dame (Olga) Patricia, DBE 2000; GCM 1985; Senator, Parliament of Barbados, 1994–2007; Deputy President of the Senate, 2003–07; *b* 18 Oct. 1925; *d* of late Algernon French Symmonds and Olga Ianthe Symmonds (*née* Harper). *Educ:* Queen's Coll., Barbados; Univ. of Reading (BA 2nd Cl. Hons); Inst. of Educn, Univ. of London (PGCE). Teacher, 1945–85, Dep. Principal, 1963–76, Principal, 1976–85, St Michael Sch., Barbados; pt-time Lectr and Tutor, Cave Hill Campus, Univ. of WI, 1963–65. PC (Barbados), 1997–2000. *Publications:* On Language and Life Styles, 1989; (jtly) Caribbean Basic English, 1993; Longer Lasting than Bronze, 1993; contrib. to educnl jls. *Recreations:* reading, music. *Address:* Bank Hall, Main Road, St Michael 11078, Barbados. *T:* 4266470. *Clubs:* Barbados Cricket, Barbados Tennis Association Inc.

See also A. W. Symmonds.

SYMON, Prof. Lindsay, CBE 1994; TD 1967; FRCS, FRCSE; Professor of Neurological Surgery, Institute of Neurology, London University and the National Hospital, Queen Square, 1978–95, now Emeritus; *b* 4 Nov. 1929; *s* of William Lindsay Symon and Isabel Symon; *m* 1954, Pauline Barbara Rowland; one *s* two *d*. *Educ:* Aberdeen Grammar Sch.; Aberdeen Univ. (MB, ChB Hons). FRCSE 1957; FRCS 1959. House Physician and Surgeon, Aberdeen Royal Infirmary, 1952–53; Jun. Specialist in Surgery, RAMC, 1953–55; Surgical Registrar, Aberdeen Royal Infirmary, 1956–58; Neurosurgical Registrar, Middlesex and Maida Vale Hosps, 1958–61, Sen. Neurosurgical Registrar, 1962–65; Mem., External Scientific Staff, MRC, 1965–78; Consultant Neurosurgeon: Nat. Hosp. for Nervous Diseases, Queen Square and Maida Vale, 1965–78; St Thomas' Hosp., 1970–78. Hon. Consultant Neurological Surgeon, St Thomas' Hosp., Hammersmith Hosp., Royal Nose, Throat and Ear Hosp., 1978–95; Hon. Consultant Neurosurgeon, Nat. Hosp. for Neurology and Neurosurgery, 1978–95; Civilian Advr in Neurological Surgery to RN, 1979–95. Adjunct Prof., Dept of Surgery, Southwestern Med. Sch., Dallas, 1982–95. Rockefeller Travelling Fellow in Medicine, Wayne State Univ., Detroit, 1961–62. Pres., Harveian Soc., of London, 1998. Hon. Pres., World Fedn Neurosurgical Socs, 1993– (Pres., 1989–93). Freeman, City of London, 1982. Hon. FACS 1994; Hon. FRSocMed 1997. Jamieson Medal, Australasian Neurosurgical Soc., 1982; John Hunter Medal, RCS, 1985; K. J. Zulch Medal, Max Planck Ges., 1993; Otfrid Förster Medal, Deutsche Ges. für Neurochirurgie, 1998; Medal of Honour, Soc. of British Neurol Surgeons, 2008. *Publications:* Operative Surgery/Neurosurgery, 1976, 2nd edn 1986; Advances and Technical Standards in Neurosurgery, 1972, 18th edn 1991; numerous papers on cerebral circulation and metabolism, brain tumours, general neurosurgical topics, etc. *Recreation:* golf. *Address:* Maple Lodge, Rivar Road, Shalbourne, near Marlborough, Wilts SN8 3QE. *T:* and *Fax:* (01672) 870501. *Clubs:* Caledonian; Royal & Ancient (St Andrews).

SYMON, Rev. Canon Roger Hugh Crispin; Canon Residentiary, Canterbury Cathedral, 1994–2002, now Canon Emeritus; *b* 25 Oct. 1934; *s* of Rev. Alan Symon and Margaret Sarah Symon (*née* Sharp); *m* 1963, Daphne Mary Roberts; two *d*. *Educ:* King's Sch., Canterbury; St John's Coll., Cambridge (MA); Coll. of the Resurrection, Mirfield. Curate, St Stephen's, Westminster, 1961–66; Priest-in-Charge, St Peter's, Hascombe, 1966–68; Chaplain, Univ. of Surrey, Guildford, 1966–74; Vicar, Christ Church, Lancaster Gate, 1974–79, with St James, Sussex Gardens, 1977–79; Home Staff, USPG, 1980–86; Actg Sec. for Anglican Communion Affairs to Archbp of Canterbury, 1987–91, Sec., 1991–94. *Address:* 5 Bath Parade, Cheltenham, Glos GL53 7HL.

SYMONDS, Ann Hazel S.; *see* Spokes Symonds.

SYMONDS, Jane Ursula; *see* Kellock, J. U.

SYMONDS, Matthew John; Industry Editor, The Economist, since 2007; *b* 20 Dec. 1953; *s* of Lord Ardwick and Anne Symonds; *m* 1981, Alison Mary Brown; one *s* two *d*. *Educ:* Holland Park, London; Balliol College, Oxford (MA). Graduate trainee, Daily Mirror, 1976–78; Financial Times, 1978–81; economics and defence leader writer, economics columnist, Daily Telegraph, 1981–86; Founding Director, Newspaper Publishing plc, 1986–94; The Independent: Dep. Editor, 1986–94; Exec. Editor, 1989–94; columnist, Sunday Express, 1995; Dir of Strategy, BBC Worldwide Television, 1995–97; The Economist: Technol. and Communications Ed., 1997–2000; Associate Ed., 2001; Political Ed., 2002–07. Sen. Financial Journalist, Wincott Awards, 1999. *Publication:* Softwar, 2003. *Recreations:* history, churches, novels, theatre, boating, tennis, Chelsea FC. *Address:* 16 St Peter's Road, St Margarets, Twickenham, Middx TW1 1QX.

SYMONS OF VERNHAM DEAN, Baroness *cr* 1996 (Life Peer), of Vernham Dean in the county of Hampshire; **Elizabeth Conway Symons;** PC 2001; *b* 14 April 1951; *d* of Ernest Vize Symons, CB and Elizabeth Megan Symons (*née* Jenkins); *m* 2001, Philip Alan Bassett; one *s*. *Educ:* Putney High Sch. for Girls; Girton Coll., Cambridge (MA; Hon. Fellow, 2001). Research, Girton Coll., Cambridge, 1972–74; Administration Trainee, DoE, 1974–77; Asst Sec. 1977–88, Dep. Gen. Sec., 1988–89, Inland Revenue Staff Fedn; Gen. Sec., Assoc. of First Div. Civil Servants, 1989–96. Parly Under-Sec. of State, FCO, 1997–99; Minister of State, MoD, 1999–2001; Minister of State (Minister for Trade), FCO and DTI, 2001–03; Minister of State (Minister for ME), FCO, 2003–05. Mem., Employment Appeal Tribunal, 1995. Mem., EOC, 1995–97. Member: Gen. Council, TUC, 1989–96; Council, RIPA, 1989–97; Exec. Council, Campaign for Freedom of Information, 1989–97; Hansard Soc. Council, 1992–97; Council, Industrial Soc., 1994–97; Trustee, IPPR, 1993; Exec. Mem., Involvement and Participation Assoc., 1992. Member: Council, Open Univ., 1994–97; Adv. Council, Civil Service Coll., 1992–97; Governor: Polytechnic of North London, 1989–94; London Business Sch., 1993–97. FRSA. Hon. Associate, Nat. Council of Women, 1989. *Recreations:* reading, gardening, friends.

SYMONS, Christopher John Maurice; QC 1989; a Deputy High Court Judge, since 1998; *b* 5 Feb. 1949; *s* of late Clifford Louis Symons and Pamela Constance Symons; *m* 1974, Susan Mary Teichmann; one *s* one *d*. *Educ:* Sherborne Prep. Sch.; Clifton Coll.; Kent Univ. (BA Hons (Law)). Called to the Bar, Middle Temple, 1972, Bencher, 1998; called to the Bar of Gibraltar, 1985, to the Irish Bar, 1988, to the NI Bar, 1990, to the Brunei Bar, 1999. Jun. Crown Counsel (Common Law), 1985–89; an Asst Recorder, 1990–93; a Recorder, 1993–2004. *Recreation:* hitting balls. *Address:* 3 Verulam Buildings, Gray's Inn, WC1R 5NT. *T:* (020) 7831 8441. *Clubs:* Boodle's; All England Lawn Tennis, Hurlingham; Berkshire Golf, Royal Tennis Court (Hampton Court), Jesters; Royal Sotogrande Golf, Valderrama Golf (Spain).

SYMONS, Sir Patrick (Jeremy), KBE 1986; Chairman, Sussex Weald and Downs (formerly Chichester Priority Care Services) NHS Trust, 1994–98; *b* 9 June 1933; *s* of Ronald and Joanne Symons; *m* 1961, Elizabeth Lawrence; one *s* one *d*. *Educ:* Dartmouth Royal Naval College. Commissioned 1951; in command, HMS Torquay, 1968–70, HMS Birmingham, 1976–77, HMS Bulwark, 1980–81; Naval Attaché, Washington, 1982–84; C of S to Comdr, Allied Naval Forces Southern Europe, 1985–88; SACLANT's Rep. in Europe, 1988–92; retired in rank of Vice-Adm. *Recreation:* swimming.

SYMS, Robert Andrew Raymond; MP (C) Poole, since 1997; *b* 15 Aug. 1956; *s* of Raymond Syms and Mary Syms (*née* Brain); *m* 2000, Fiona Mellersh (separated 2007), *d* of Air Vice-Marshal F. R. L. Mellersh, CB, DFC and bar; one *s* one *d*. *Educ:* Colston's Sch., Bristol. Dir, C. Syms & Sons Ltd, family building and plant hire gp, 1975–. Mem.,

Wessex RHA, 1988–90. Member (C): N Wilts DC, 1983–87 (Vice Chm., 1984–87; Leader, Cons. Gp, 1984–87); Wilts CC, 1985–97. Contested (C) Walsall N, 1992. PPS to Chm., Conservative Party, 1999; opposition front bench spokesman on the envmt, 1999–2001; an Opposition Whip, 2003; opposition spokesman, DCLG (formerly ODPM), 2003–07. Member: Health Select Cttee, 1997–2000 and 2007–; Procedure Select Cttee, 1998–99; Transport Select Cttee, 2001–03; Vice-Chm., Cons. back bench Constitutional Cttee, 1997–2001. A Vice-Chm., Cons. Party, 2001–03. N Wiltshire Conservative Association: Treas., 1982–83; Dep. Chm., 1983–84; Chm., 1984–96; Vice Pres., 1986–88. FCIOB 1999. *Recreations:* reading, travel, cycling. *Address:* House of Commons, SW1A 0AA; c/o Poole Conservative Association, 38 Sandbanks Road, Poole BH14 8BX. *T:* (01202) 739922.

SYNGE, Sir Robert Carson, 8th Bt *cr* 1801; Manager and Owner, Rob's Furniture; *b* 4 May 1922; *s* of late Neale Hutchinson Synge (2nd *s* of 6th Bt) and Edith Elizabeth Thurlow (*d* 1933), Great Parndon, Essex; *S* uncle, 1942; *m* 1944, Dorothy Jean Johnson, *d* of T. Johnson, Cloverdale; two *d. Heir: cousin* Allen James Edward Synge, *b* 15 Jan. 1942.

SYNNOTT, Sir Hilary (Nicholas Hugh), KCMG 2002 (CMG 1997); HM Diplomatic Service, retired; Consulting Fellow, International Institute of Strategic Studies, since 2004; *b* 20 March 1945; *s* of late Commander Jasper Nicholas Netterville Synnott, DSC, RN and Florence England Synnott (*née* Hillary); *m* 1973, Anne Penelope Clarke; one *s* decd. *Educ:* Beaumont College; Dartmouth Naval College (scholar); Peterhouse, Cambridge (MA); RN Engineering College. CEng; MIEE. RN 1962–73 (HM Submarines, 1968–73). Joined HM Diplomatic Service, FCO, 1973; UK Delegn to OECD, Paris, 1975; Bonn, 1978; FCO, 1981; Head of Chancery, Amman, 1985; Head of Western European Dept, FCO, 1989; Head of Security Co-ordination Dept, FCO, 1991; Minister and Dep. High Comr, New Delhi, 1993–96; Dir (S and SE Asia), FCO, 1996–98; Vis. Fellow, Inst. of Developing Studies, Univ. of Sussex, and IISS, 1999–2000; High Comr to Pakistan, 2000–03; Coalition Provisional Administrator, Southern Iraq, 2003–04. Patron, Asian Studies Gp, Islamabad, 2001–03; Trustee, Impact Foundn, 2004–07. Chm., Peterhouse Soc., 2007–. Eric Lane Fellow, Clare Coll., Cambridge, 2007. *Publications:* The Causes and Consequences of South Asia's Nuclear Tests, 1999; State Building in Southern Iraq, 2005; Bad Days in Basra: my turbulent time as Britain's man in southern Iraq, 2008. *Address:* Long Barrow, Barrow Hill, Goodworth Clatford, Hants SP11 7SE. *Club:* Oxford and Cambridge.

SYSONBY, 3rd Baron *cr* 1935, of Wonersh; **John Frederick Ponsonby;** *b* 5 Aug. 1945; *s* of 2nd Baron Sysonby, DSO and Sallie Monkland, *d* of Dr Leonard Sanford, New York; *S* father, 1956. *Address:* c/o Friars, White Friars, Chester CH1 1XS.

SZÉLL, Patrick John, CMG 2001; Head, International and EC Environmental Law Division, 1985–2002, and Director (Legal), Department for Environment, Food and Rural Affairs (formerly Department of the Environment, then Department of the Environment, Transport and the Regions), 1992–2002; *b* Budapest, Hungary, 10 Feb. 1942; *s* of Dr János Széll and Vera Széll (*née* Beckett); *m* 1967, Olivia (*née* Brain), JP; two *s* one *d. Educ:* Reading Sch.; Trinity Coll., Dublin (MA, LLB; Julian Prize 1964). Called to the Bar, Inner Temple, 1966. Joined Min. of Housing and Local Govt as Legal Asst, 1969; Department of the Environment: Sen. Legal Asst, 1973–85; Asst Solicitor, 1985–92. Legal Advr to UK Delegns at internat. envmtl negotiations, 1974–2002, including: UN/ECE Convention on Long-Range Transboundary Air Pollution and its protocols, 1979–2002 (Chm., Implementation Cttee, 1999–2005); Vienna Convention for Protection of Ozone Layer and Montreal Protocol, 1982–2002; Basle Convention on Transboundary Movements of Hazardous Wastes, 1988–93; Climate Change Convention and Kyoto Protocol, 1990–2002; Biodiversity Convention and Biosafety Protocol, 1990–2000. Member: Internat. Council of Envmtl Law, Bonn, 1982–; IUCN Commn on Envmtl Law, 1994–2005. Global Ozone Award, UNEP, 1995; Elizabeth Haub Prize, Free Univ. of Brussels, 1995; Stratospheric Ozone Protection Award, US Envmtl Protection Agency, 2002; Montreal Protocol Visionaries Award, UNEP, 2007. *Recreations:* travel, hockey, ancient churches. *Address:* Croft's Folly, Windfallwood Common, Haslemere, Surrey, GU27 3BX.

SZENTIVÁNYI, Gábor, Hon. GCVO 1999; State Secretary and Political Director, Ministry of Foreign Affairs, Hungary, since 2007; *b* 9 Oct. 1952; *s* of Jozsef Szentiványi and Ilona Fejes; *m* 1976, Gabriella Gönczi; one *s* one *d. Educ:* Budapest Univ. of Econmic Scis. Min. of Foreign Affairs, Hungary, 1975; Sec. for Press, Cultural and Educnl Affairs, Baghdad, 1976–81; Protocol Dept, Min. of Foreign Affairs, 1981–86; Counsellor for Press and Media Relations, Washington, 1986–91; Man. Dir, Burson-Marsteller Budapest, 1991–94; Spokesman and Dir Gen., Press and Internat. Information Dept, Min. of Foreign Affairs, 1994–97; Ambassador to UK, 1997–2002; Dep. State Sec., Min. of Foreign Affairs, 2002–04; Ambassador to the Netherlands and to OPCW, 2004–07. Member: Foreign Affairs Soc., Hungary, 1993–; Atlantic Council, Hungary, 1997–. Officer, Order of Prince Henry the Navigator (Portugal), 1983; Grand Cross of Merit (Chile), 2002; Middle Cross, Order of Merit (Hungary), 2004; Knight Grand Cross, Order of Orange-Nassau (Netherlands), 2007. *Recreation:* boating. *Address:* Ministry of Foreign Affairs, Bem rakpart 47, 1027 Budapest, Hungary. *T:* (1) 4582213.

SZIRTES, George Gábor Nicholas, PhD; FRSL; freelance writer; Co-ordinator of Creative Writing, Norwich School of Art and Design, since 1994; *b* Budapest, 29 Nov. 1948; *s* of László Szirtes and Magdalena Szirtes (*née* Nussbacher); *m* 1970, Clarissa Upchurch; one *s* one *d. Educ:* Leeds Coll. of Art (BA 1st cl. Hons (Fine Art) 1972); Goldsmiths Coll., London (ATC 1973); Anglia Polytechnic Univ. (PhD by published work 2002). Teacher, Art, Hist. of Art and English, various schs and colls, 1973–91; Dir, Art, St Christopher Sch., Letchworth, 1982–89; Norwich School of Art and Design: Vis. Lectr, 1989–91; estd Creative Writing course, 1991–94. FRSL 1982. Gold Star, Hungarian Republic, 1991. *Publications: poetry:* Poetry Introduction 4, 1978 (jtly); The Slant Door, 1979 (Faber Meml Prize, 1980); November and May, 1981; Short Wave, 1984; The Photographer in Winter, 1986; Metro, 1988; Bridge Passages, 1991; Blind Field, 1994; Selected Poems, 1996; The Red-All-Over Riddle Book (for children), 1997; Portrait of my Father in an English Landscape, 1998; The Budapest File, 2000; An English Apocalypse, 2001; (with Ana Maria Pacheco) A Modern Bestiary, 2004; Reel, 2004 (T. S. Eliot Prize, 2005); Collected and New Poems, 2008; *translations:* Madách, The Tragedy of Man, 1989 (Déry Prize for Translation, 1990); (pt translator) Csoóri, Barbarian Prayer, 1989; (ed and pt translator) Vas, Through the Smoke, 1989; Kosztolányi, Anna Édes, 1991; (ed and translator) Orbán, The Blood of the Walsungs, 1993; (ed and translator) Rakovszky, New Life, 1994 (European Poetry Translation Prize, 1995); (ed jtly and translator) The Colonnade of Teeth: twentieth century Hungarian poetry, 1996; (ed and translator) The Lost Rider: Hungarian poetry 16th–20th century, 1998; Krúdy, The Adventures of Sindbad, 1999; Krasznahorkai, The Melancholy of Resistance, 1999; (ed and translator) The Night of Akhenaton: selected poems of Ágnes Nemes Nagy, 2004; Márai, Casanova in Bolzano, 2004; Krasznahorkai, War and War, 2005; Márai, The Rebels, 2007; *other works:* (ed) Birdsuit (nine anthologies), 1991–99; (ed) The Collected Poems of Freda Downie, 1995; (ed with Penelope Lively) New Writing 10, 2001; Exercise of Power: the art of Ana Maria Pacheco, 2001; (ed jtly) An Island of Sound: Hungarian fiction and poetry at the point of change, 2004. *Recreations:* music, art, some sports. *Address:* 16 Damgate Street, Wymondham, Norfolk NR18 0BQ. *T:* and *Fax:* (01953) 603533; *e-mail:* george@georgeszirtes.co.uk.

SZMUKLER, Prof. George Isaac, MD; FRCPsych, FRANZCP; Professor of Psychiatry and Society, Institute of Psychiatry, and Chairman, King's Health and Society Network, King's College, London, since 2007; Consultant Psychiatrist, Maudsley Hospital, South London and Maudsley NHS Trust, since 1993; *b* 23 April 1947; *s* of Judel Szmukler and Leja Soyka; *m* 1983, Linnet Michele Lee; one *d. Educ:* Univ. of Melbourne (MB BS 1970; MD 1984); DPM 1974. MRCPsych 1977, FRCPsych 1989; FRANZCP 1985. Jun. RMO, Royal Melbourne Hosp., 1971–72; SHO, then Registrar in Psychiatry, Royal Free Hosp., 1972–75; Lectr in Psychiatry, Royal Free Hosp. Sch. of Medicine, Univ. of London, 1975–79; Lectr in Psychiatry, Inst. of Psychiatry, Univ. of London, 1980–82; Sen. Lectr, Inst. of Psychiatry, and Hon. Consultant Psychiatrist, Maudsley and Bethlem Royal Hosp., 1982–85; Consultant Psychiatrist, Royal Melbourne Hosp., and Sen. Associate, Univ. of Melbourne, 1985–92; Med. Dir, Bethlem and Maudsley NHS Trust, 1997–99; Jt Med. Dir, S London and Maudsley NHS Trust, 1999–2001; Dean and Hd of Sch., Inst. of Psychiatry, KCL, 2001–06. FKC 2007. *Publications:* (jtly) Making Sense of Psychiatric Cases, 1986; (jtly) The Family in the Practice of Psychiatry, 1994; (ed) Eating Disorders: a handbook of theory, practice and research, 1994; (ed) A handbook on Mental Illness for Carers, 2001; (ed with G. Thornicroft) Textbook of Community Psychiatry, 2001; papers on eating disorders, families, health services res., mental health law and ethics. *Recreations:* music (especially Baroque), art, cinema, wine. *Address:* Institute of Psychiatry, De Crespigny Park, Denmark Hill, SE5 8AF. *T:* (020) 7848 0154, *Fax:* (020) 7848 0117; *e-mail:* g.szmukler@iop.kcl.ac.uk.

SZOMBATI, Béla; Head of Department for Strategic Planning and Information Management, Ministry of Foreign Affairs, Hungary, since 2006; *b* 16 July 1955; *s* of Béla Szombati and Éva Szombati (*née* Herbály); *m* 1978, Zsuzsa Mihályi; two *s. Educ:* Eötvös Loránd Univ., Budapest (MA Hist. and French Lang. and Lit.). Joined Hungarian Diplomatic Service, 1980; Dept of Internat. Security, Min. of Foreign Affairs, 1980–82; Third Sec., Hanoi, 1982–85; Dept of W Europe and N America, Min. of Foreign Affairs, 1986–88; Second Sec., Washington, 1988–91; Foreign Policy Advr, Office of Pres. of the Republic, 1991–94; Ambassador, Paris, 1994–99; Dep. Hd, State Secretariat for European Integration, Min. of Foreign Affairs, 1999–2002; Ambassador to UK, 2002–06. Commander's Cross, Order of Merit (Poland), 2001; Officier, Légion d'Honneur (France), 2002. *Recreations:* music, walking, football. *Address:* Ministry of Foreign Affairs, Bem rakpart 47, Budapest 1027, Hungary. *Clubs:* Athenæum, Travellers.

SZYMBORSKA, Wisława; Polish poet, translator, literary critic; *b* 2 July 1923; *d* of Wincenty Szymborski and Anna Rottermund; *m* Adam Włodek. *Educ:* Jagiellonian Univ., Cracow. Editorial Staff, Zycie Literackie, 1953–67. Mem., 1952–83, Mem. Gen. Bd, 1978–83, Polish Writers' Assoc. Nobel Prize for Literature, 1996. Gold Cross of Merit (Poland), 1955; Kt Cross, Order of Polonia Restituta (Poland), 1974. *Publications:* Dlatego żyjemy, 1952; Pytania zadawanie sobie, 1954; Wołanie do Yeti, 1957; Sól, 1962; Wiersze wybrane, 1964; Poezje wybrane, 1967; Sto pociech, 1967; Poezje, 1970; Wszelki wypadek, 1972; Wybór wierszy, 1973; Tarsjusz i inne wiersze, 1976; Wielka liczba, 1976; Poezje wybrane II, 1983; Ludzie na moście, 1986; People on a Bridge, 1990; Koniec i początek, 1993; View with a Grain of Sand, 1995; Widok z ziarnkiem piasku, 1996; Poems New and Collected 1957–1997, 1998; Wiersze wybrane, 2000; Chwila, 2002. *Address:* (office) ul. Kanonicza 7, 31–002 Kraków, Poland. *Fax:* (12) 4224773; c/o Forest Books, 20 Forest View, Chingford, E4 7AY.

T

TABACHNIK, Eldred; QC 1982; a Recorder, since 2000; *b* 5 Nov. 1943; *s* of Solomon Joseph Tabachnik and Esther Tabachnik; *m* 1966, Jennifer Kay Lawson; two *s* one *d*. *Educ:* Univ. of Cape Town (BA, LLB); Univ. of London (LLM). Called to the Bar, Inner Temple, 1970, Bencher, 1988. Lectr, UCL, 1969–72. Pres., Bd of Deputies of British Jews, 1994–2000. *Recreation:* reading. *Address:* 11 King's Bench Walk, Temple, EC4Y 7EQ. *T:* (020) 7632 8500. *Club:* Reform.

TABAKSBLAT, Morris; Chairman, Reed Elsevier plc, 1999–2005; *b* Rotterdam; *m*; two *s* one *d*. *Educ:* Leiden Univ. (law degree). Joined Unilever, 1964; positions in Spain, Brazil, Holland; Dir, 1984; Personal Products Co-ordinator, 1984; Regl Dir for N America, NY, 1987–90; Chm., Foods Exec., 1990–92; Mem., Unilever Special Cttee, 1992–99; Chm. and CEO, Unilever NV, 1994–99. Former Chm., Mauritshuis Mus.; Chm., War Trauma Foundn.

TABBARA, Hani Bahjat, Hon. GCVO 1984; *b* 10 Feb. 1939; *s* of Bahjat and Nimat Tabbara; *m* 1980, Wafa; three *s*. *Educ:* University of Alexandria. Entered Jordanian Govt service, 1963; Jordan Embassy, London, 1971–73; Counsellor, Foreign Ministry, Amman, 1973; Minister Plenipotentiary, Jordan Embassy, London, 1973–76; Private Sec. to Prime Minister, Amman, 1976–77; Ambassador: Morocco, 1977–80; Romania, 1980–82; Saudi Arabia, 1982–84; UK, 1984–85; Turkey, 1985–87; Yugoslavia, 1987–92; Australia, 1993–99; Inspector Gen., 2000–02, Sec. Gen., 2003–04, Foreign Ministry. Mem. of Senate, Jordan, 2004. First Order of El Istiqlal (Jordan), 1988. *Address:* c/o Ministry of Foreign Affairs, PO Box 35217, Amman, Jordan.

TABBERER, Ralph; Director General, Schools, Department for Children, Schools and Families (formerly Department for Education and Skills), since 2006; *b* 5 Aug. 1954; *s* of James William Waring Tabberer and Joyce (*née* Eldered); *m* 1996, Helen Margaret White; one *s* one *d* (and one *d* decd), and three step *s* two step *d*. *Educ:* Gonville and Caius Coll., Cambridge (BA 1976; MA); Brunel Univ. (PGCE 1977). Sen. Advr, W Sussex LEA, 1989–94; Asst Dir, NFER, 1994–97; Department for Education and Employment: Sen. Educn Advr, Standards and Effectiveness Unit, 1997–99; Hd, Nat. Grid for Learning, 1999–2000; Chief Exec., TTA, subseq. TDA, 2000–06. FRSA 2001. *Address:* Department for Children, Schools and Families, Sanctuary Buildings, Great Smith Street, SW1P 3BT. *T:* (020) 7925 6504; *e-mail:* ralph.tabberer@dcsf.gsi.gov.uk.

TABONE, Dr Vincent, (Censu), FRCSE; President of Malta, 1989–94; *b* 30 March 1913; *s* of Elisa Calleja and Nicolo Tabone; *m* 1948, Maria Wirth; three *s* five *d* (and one *s* decd). *Educ:* St Aloysius Coll.; Univ. of Malta. Dip. Ophth. Oxford 1946; FRCSE 1948; Dip. RCP; Dip. RCS; Dip. in Med. Jurisp., Soc. of Apothecaries of London, 1963. Surgeon Captain, Royal Malta Artillery (campaign medals), 1939–45 War. WHO Consultant on Trachoma in Taiwan, Indonesia, Iraq; Dep., Internat. Panel of Trachoma Experts, WHO, 1956; Lectr in Clinical Ophthalmology, Dept of Surgery, Univ. of Malta, 1960. MP, 1966–89; Minister of Labour, Employment and Welfare, 1966–71; Minister of Foreign Affairs, 1987–89. Mem., Council of Europe Cttees; Chm., Council of Ministers, 1988. Founded Medical Officers Union of Malta, 1954. Vis. Prof., Univ. of Malta, 1995–. Hon. LLD Univ. of Malta, 1989. Awarded UN Testimonial for service to UN Programme on Aging, 1989. *Recreations:* reading, watch repairing, travel. *Address:* 33 Carmel Street, St Julian's, Malta. *Clubs:* Casino Maltese (1852), Sliema Band.

TACKABERRY, John Antony; QC 1982; FCIArb, FFB; a Recorder, 1988–2005; *b* 13 Nov. 1939; *s* of late Thomas Raphael Tackaberry and Mary Catherine (*née* Geoghegan); *m* 1st, 1966, Penelope Holt (*d* 1994); two *s*; 2nd, 1996, Kate Jones (*d* 2008); one *d*. *Educ:* Downside; Trinity Coll., Dublin; Downing Coll., Cambridge (MA, LLM). Called to the Bar, Gray's Inn, 1967, Ireland, 1987, California, 1988. FCIArb 1973; FFB 1979. Teacher in China, 1964–65; Lectr, Poly. of Central London, 1965–67. Adjunct Prof. of Law, Qld Univ. of Technology, 1989. Comr, UN Compensation Commn, 1998–2003. Chm., CIArb, 1990–91 (Mem. Council, 1985–94; Vice-Pres., 1988); President: Soc. of Construction Law, 1983–85; Eur. Soc. of Construction Law, 1985–87; Soc. of Construction Arbitrators, 2007–. Registered Arbitrator, 1993; Mem., many panels of internat. arbitrators. Chm., Street UK, 2004–. *Publications:* (contrib.) Bernstein's Handbook of Arbitration and Dispute Resolution, 1st edn 1987, 2nd edn 1993, (Principal Ed.) 3rd edn, 1998, 4th edn 2003; (ed jtly) International Dispute Resolution, vol. I, Materials, 2004, (ed) vol. II, Cases, 2004; contrib. numerous articles. *Recreations:* good food, good wine, good company, photography. *Address:* Arbitration Chambers, 22 Willes Road, NW5 3DS. *T:* (020) 7267 2137, *Fax:* (020) 7482 1018; *e-mail:* john.tackaberry@arbitration-chambers.com. *Club:* Athenæum.

TADIÉ, Prof. Jean-Yves; Chevalier de la Légion d'honneur, 2002; Chevalier de l'Ordre National du Mérite, 1974; Officier des Palmes académiques, 1988; Professor of French Literature, Université de Paris-Sorbonne, 1991–2005, now Emeritus; Editor, Gallimard, since 1991; *b* 7 Sept. 1936; *s* of Henri Tadié and Marie (*née* Férester); *m* 1962, Arlette Khoury; three *s*. *Educ:* St Louis de Gonzague, Paris; Lycée Louis-le-Grand; Ecole Normale Supérieure (Agrégé de lettres); DèsL Sorbonne 1970; MA Oxford 1988. Lectr, Univ. of Alexandria, 1960–62; Asst Prof., Faculté des Lettres de Paris, 1964; Professor: Univ. de Caen, 1968–69; Univ. de Tours, 1969–70; Univ. de la Sorbonne nouvelle, Paris III, 1970; Hd of French Dept, Cairo Univ., 1972–76; Dir, French Inst., London, 1976–81; Marshal Foch Prof. of French Literature, and Fellow, All Souls Coll., Oxford Univ., 1988–91. Corresp. FBA, 1991. Grand Prix de l'Acad. française, 1988. Officier de l'Ordre de la Couronne de Belgique, 1979. *Publications:* Introduction à la vie littéraire du XIXe Siècle, 1970; Lectures de Proust, 1971; Proust et le Roman, 1971; Le Récit poétique, 1978; Le Roman d'aventures, 1982; Proust, 1983; La Critique littéraire au XXe Siècle, 1987; (ed) M. Proust, A la Recherche du Temps perdu, 1987–89; Portrait de l'Artiste, 1990; Le Roman au XXe Siècle, 1990; Marcel Proust (biography), 1996, Eng. edn 2000; (ed) N. Sarraute, Oeuvres Complètes, 1996; Le Sens de la Mémoire, 1999; (ed) W. Scott, Romans, 2003; (ed) A. Malraux, Ecrits sur l'art, 2004; Regarde de tous tes yeux - regarde!: Jules Verne, 2005; De Proust à Dumas, 2006; (ed) W. Scott, Romans II, 2007; Debussy, 2008. *Recreations:* tennis, opera, cinema. *Address:* 112 rue Saint-Dominique, 75007 Paris, France.

TAEL, Dr Kaja; Under Secretary of European Union Affairs, Ministry of Foreign Affairs, Estonia, since 2006; *b* 24 July 1960. *Educ:* Tartu Univ., Estonia; Estonian Acad. Scis (PhD 1985). Researcher, 1984–90, Dir, 1991–95, Estonian Inst. for Lang. and Lit.; foreign policy advr to Pres. of Estonia, 1995–98; Ministry of Foreign Affairs, Estonia: Exec. Sec., Estonian-Russian Inter-govtl Commn, 1998–99; Dir Gen., Dept of Policy Planning, 1995–2001; Estonian Ambassador to UK, 2001–05. Order of White Star (Estonia), 2000. Order of: Polar Star (Sweden), 1995; Lion (Finland), 1995; Aztec Eagle (Mexico), 1996. *Publications:* translated into Estonian: John Stuart Mills, On Liberty, 1996; Henry Kissinger, Diplomacy, 2002; Eric Hobsbawm, The Age of Extremes, 2002; articles and abstracts for internat. confs. *Address:* Ministry of Foreign Affairs, Islandi Väljak 1, Tallinn 15049, Estonia.

TAFFIN de GIVENCHY, Olivier Jean; Managing Director, United Kingdom, JP Morgan Private Bank, since 2005; Director, JP Morgan International Bank Ltd; *b* Beauvais, France, 27 Aug. 1963; *s* of Jean-Claude Taffin de Givenchy and Patricia Taffin de Givenchy (*née* Myrick); *m* (marr. diss.); one *s* one *d*. *Educ:* Manhattanville Coll., Purchase, NY (BA Internat. Studies 1985). Citibank, 1985–89; Bankers Trust, 1989–93; JP Morgan, 1993–. Trustee, JP Morgan UK Foundn, 2005–; Supervisory Cttee, JP Morgan Chase Foundn, 2006–. Chm., Children in Crisis, 2006–. *Recreations:* tennis, fishing, shooting. *Address:* JP Morgan International Bank Ltd, 125 London Wall, EC2Y 9AQ. *T:* (020) 7742 7512, *Fax:* (020) 7742 2990. *Club:* Racquet and Tennis (NY).

TAFIDA, Dr Dalhatu Sarki, OFR 1983; FNMCP, FWACP; High Commissioner of Nigeria in the United Kingdom, since 2007; *b* Zaria, Kaduna State, 24 Nov. 1940; *s* of Garba Tafida and Badariyyatu Tafida; *m* Salamatu Ndana Mohammed; six *s* three *d*. *Educ:* Coll. of Medicine, Univ. of Lagos (MB BS 1967); Univ. of Liverpool (Postgrad. Dip. Public Health 1972). MRCP 1971; FNMCP 1975; FWACP 1975. Ahmadu Bello University: House Officer, 1967–68; Sen. House Officer, 1968–69; Registrar, 1969–70; Clin. Asst in Medicine, Royal Victoria Infirmary, Newcastle upon Tyne, 1970–71; Sen. Registrar in Medicine, Katsina Specialist Hosp., 1972–73; Consultant Physician, 1973–76, Perm. Sec., 1976–80, Min. of Health, Kaduna; Chief Physician to Pres. of Nigeria, 1980–83; Comr for Health, Agric. and Educn, Kaduna State, 1984–87; Mem., Constitutent Assembly to review Nigerian Constitution, 1988–89; Chm. and Pro Chancellor, Univ. of Agric., Malcurdi; Federal Minister of Health, 1993–95. Mem. Kaduna North, Senate, 2003–07 (Senate Majority Leader, 2003–07). Tafidan Zazzau, 1995. *Publication:* Purple Parliament, 2007. *Recreations:* Scrabble, table tennis. *Address:* Nigeria High Commission, 9 Northumberland Avenue, WC2N 5BX. *T:* (020) 7839 2037, *Fax:* (020) 7839 7872; *e-mail:* tafida@nigeriahc.org.uk. *Club:* Royal Commonwealth Society.

TAFROV, Stefan Lubomirov; Permanent Representative of Bulgaria to the United Nations, 2001–06; *b* Sofia, 11 Feb. 1958; *s* of Lubomir Tafrov and Nadezhda Tafrova. *Educ:* Sofia Univ. (MA in Journalism). Foreign News Editor, Democratzia, newspaper, Jan. 1990; Chief, Foreign Affairs Dept, Union of Democratic Forces, Feb.–Aug. 1990; Foreign Affairs Advr to Pres. of Bulgaria, 1990–92; First Dep. Minister of Foreign Affairs, 1992–93; Ambassador to Italy, 1993–95, to UK, 1995–98; Ambassador to France, and Perm. Deleg. to UNESCO, 1998–2001. *Recreation:* music. *Address:* c/o Ministry of Foreign Affairs, ul. Al. Zhendov 2, 1040 Sofia, Bulgaria.

TAFT, William Howard, IV; Of Counsel, Fried, Frank, Harris, Shriver & Jacobson, since 2005 (Partner, 1992–2001); *b* 13 Sept. 1945; *s* of William Howard Taft, III and Barbara Bradfield Taft; *m* 1974, Julia Ann Vadala; one *s* two *d*. *Educ:* St Paul's Sch., Concord, NH; Yale Coll. (BA 1966); Harvard Univ. (JD 1969). Attorney, Winthrop, Stimson, Putnam & Roberts, NY, 1969–70; Attorney Advr to Chm., Federal Trade Commn, 1970; Principal Asst to Dep. Dir, Office of Management and Budget, 1970–72, Exec. Asst to Dir, 1972–73; Exec. Asst to Sec., Health, Educn and Welfare, 1973–76; Gen. Counsel, Dept of Health, Educn and Welfare, 1976–77; Partner, Leva, Hawes, Symington, Martin & Oppenheimer, 1977–81; General Counsel 1981–84, Dep. Sec. of Defense 1984–89, US Dept of Defense; US Perm. Rep. on N Atlantic Council, 1989–92; Legal Advr, US Dept of State, 2001–05. Mem., DC Bar Assoc., Washington. Bd Mem., Washington Opera, 1977–81, 1992–2001. Woodrow Wilson Vis. Teaching Fellow, Woodrow Wilson Foundn, 1977–81. Dir, Atlantic Council, 1993–2001. *Publication:* contrib. Indiana Law Jl. *Recreation:* tennis. *Address:* Fried, Frank, Harris, Shriver & Jacobson, #800, 1001 Pennsylvania Avenue NW, Washington, DC 20004, USA. *Clubs:* Cosmos, Leo, Literary Society (Washington, DC).

TAGER, Romie; QC 1995; *b* 19 July 1947; *s* of Osias Tager and Minnie Tager (*née* Mett); *m* 1971, Esther Marianne Sichel; twin *s*. *Educ:* Hasmonean Grammar Sch., Hendon; University Coll. London (Hurst prize; LLB 1st Cl. Hons 1969). Called to the Bar, Middle Temple, 1970; Head of Chambers, Selborne Chambers, 2002–. Chm., Greenquest Gp, 1998–. Hon. Sec., Jewish Book Council, 1990–. Chm. Trustees, Hampstead Dyslexia Charitable Trust. 1999–. *Recreations:* opera, theatre, travel. *Address:* Selborne Chambers, 10 Essex Street, WC2R 3AA. *T:* (020) 7420 9500.

TAIN, Paul Christopher; His Honour Judge Tain; a Circuit Judge, since 2005; *b* 18 Feb. 1950; *s* of Reginald Tain and Kathleen (*née* Hoffland); *m* 1971, Angela Margaret Kirkup; four *s*. *Educ:* London Univ. (BA Hist.); Inst. of Judicial Admin, Birmingham

Univ. (MJur). Admitted solicitor, 1975; solicitor, Wolverhampton MBC and N Yorks County Council, 1976–80; private practitioner, 1980–92; Dep. Stipendiary Magistrate, 1989–92; Stipendiary Magistrate, subseq. District Judge (Magistrates' Courts), 1992–2005; Asst Recorder, 1996–2000, Recorder, 2000–05. Columnist, Solicitors' Jl, 1998. *Publications:* Local Authority Lawyers and Childcare, 1980; Childcare Law, 1993; Criminal Justice Act, 1994; Public Order Law, 1996; Public Order: the criminal law, 2001. *Recreations:* sailing, sailing and sailing. *Address:* Lewes Crown Court, Lewes, East Sussex BN7 1YB.

TAIT, Dr Alan Anderson; Director, International Monetary Fund in Geneva, 1995–98; *b* 1 July 1934; *s* of Stanley Tait and Margaret Ruth (*née* Anderson); *m* 1963, Susan Valerie Somers; one *s*. *Educ:* Heriot's Sch., Edinburgh; Univ. of Edinburgh (MA); Trinity Coll., Dublin (PhD; Hon. Fellow, 1996). Lectr, Trinity Coll., Dublin, 1959–71 (Fellow, 1968, Sen. Tutor, 1970); Visiting Prof., Univ. of Illinois, 1965–66. Economic adviser to Irish Govt on industrial develt and taxation and chief economic adviser to Confedn of Irish Industry, 1967–71; Prof. of Money and Finance, Univ. of Strathclyde, 1971–77; economic consultant to Sec. of State for Scotland, 1972–77; International Monetary Fund: Visiting Scholar, 1972; Consultant, 1973, 1974, 1999, 2001; Chief, Fiscal Analysis Div., 1976–79; Asst Dir, 1979–82; Dep. Dir, Fiscal Affairs Dept, 1982–94. Hon. Prof., Univ. of Kent at Canterbury, 2000–. Co-Chm., Wkg Gp on Financing Health, Commn on Macroeconomics and Health, 2000–02. *Publications:* The Taxation of Personal Wealth, 1967; (with J. Bristow) Economic Policy in Ireland, 1968; (with J. Bristow) Ireland: some problems of a developing economy, 1971; The Value Added Tax, 1972; The Value Added Tax: international practice and problems, 1988; (ed) Value Added Tax: administrative and policy issues, 1991; articles on public finance in Rev. of Economic Studies, Finanzarchiv, Public Finance, Staff Papers, etc. *Recreations:* painting and gardening. *Address:* Cramond House, Harnet Street, Sandwich, Kent CT13 9ES. *T:* (01304) 621038. *Club:* Cosmos (Washington DC).

TAIT, Andrew Charles Gordon; QC 2003; *b* 18 May 1957; *s* of Adm. Sir (Allan) Gordon Tait, KCB, DSC and of Philippa, *d* of Sir Bryan Todd; *m* 1990, Francesca Sulivan; one *s* three *d*. *Educ:* Eton; Hertford Coll., Oxford (Open Exhibnr; MA). Called to the Bar, Inner Temple, 1981; in practice as barrister, 1982–. Asst Parly Boundary Comr, 2000–. *Address:* Francis Taylor Building, Temple, EC4Y 7BY. *T:* (020) 7353 8415. *Clubs:* White's, Hurlingham.

TAIT, Andrew Wilson, OBE 1967; Deputy Chairman, Barratt plc, 1991–96 (Director, 1988–96); Chairman, National House-Building Council, 1984–87 (Director-General, 1964–84); *b* 25 Sept. 1922; *s* of late Dr Adam and Jenny Tait; *m* 1954, Elizabeth Isobel Maclennan; three *d*. *Educ:* George Watson's Coll., Edinburgh; Edinburgh Univ. (MA 1st Class Hons History). Served Army, 1942–45. Leader writer, The Scotsman, 1947–48; Scottish Office, 1948–64. Chairman: Housing Res. Foundn, 1969–85; Internat. Housing and Home Warranty Assoc., 1984–87; Jt Land Requirements Cttee, 1981–87; Home Buyers Adv. Service, 1985–; Bridging the Gap, 1986–; New Homes Mktg Bd, 1988–89; Johnson Fry Property, 1988–95; New Homes Envmtl Gp, 1988–91; Cost Reduction Partnership, 1995–2000. Mem., Lloyd's, 1985–98. *Recreations:* golf, tennis, chess. *Address:* Orchard Croft, Grimmshill, Great Missenden, Bucks HP16 9BA. *T:* (01494) 862061. *Club:* Caledonian.

TAIT, Arthur Gordon; Secretary-General, Institute of Actuaries, 1991–97; *b* 28 July 1934; *s* of George Aidan Drury Tait and Margaret Evelyn Tait (*née* Gray); *m* 1958, Ann Sutcliffe Gilbert; two *s* two *d* (and one *s* decd). *Educ:* Eton Coll.; St John's Coll., Cambridge (BA Hist., MA). FCIPD. Commnd KRRC, 1953–54. Imperial Chemical Industries, 1957–91: Personnel Dir, Mond Div., 1976–82; Internat. Personnel Manager, 1983–91. Chairman: Friends of Brompton Cemetery, 1998–; Nat. Fedn of Cemetery Friends, 2003–. FRSA. *Publications:* A Story of Staple Inn on Holborn Hill, 2001; St Mary, The Boltons: the country church in Kensington and Chelsea, 2004. *Recreations:* family, swimming, travel, friends who visit, following most sports. *Address:* 65 Cheyne Court, SW3 5TT. *T:* (020) 7352 5127.

TAIT, Blyth; *see* Tait, R. B.

TAIT, Eric, MBE 1980; Director of European Operations, since 1989 and International Executive Director, since 1992, PKF International Ltd (formerly Pannell Kerr Forster, Chartered Accountants); *b* 10 Jan. 1945; *s* of William Johnston Tait and Sarah Tait (*née* Jones); *m* 1st, 1967, Agnes Jean Boag (*née* Anderson) (marr. diss. 1998); one *s* one *d*; 2nd, 1998, Stacey Jane (*née* Todd). *Educ:* George Heriot's Sch., Edinburgh; RMA Sandhurst; Univ. of London (BSc Eng); Churchill Coll., Cambridge (MPhil). 2nd Lieut, Royal Engineers, 1965; despatches 1976; 68 advanced staff course, RAF Staff Coll., Bracknell, 1977; OC 7 Field Sqn, RE, 1979–81; Lt-Col 1982; Directing Staff, Staff Coll., Camberley, 1982–83, retired, at own request, 1983; Sec., Inst. of Chartered Accountants of Scotland, 1984–89. Mem. of Exec., Scottish Council (Develt and Industry), 1984–89. Editor in Chief, The Accountant's Magazine, 1984–89. Chm., European Forum, Nottingham Trent Univ., 1993–98. FRSA 1997. *Recreations:* swimming, hill walking, reading. *Address:* PKF International Ltd, Farringdon Place, 20 Farringdon Road, EC1M 3AP. *T:* (020) 7065 0000.

TAIT, Prof. James Francis, PhD; FRS 1959; engaged in making photographic guide to North Yorkshire and writing scientific history; Emeritus Professor, University of London, since 1982; *b* 1 Dec. 1925; *s* of Herbert Tait and Constance Levinia Brotherton; *m* 1956, Sylvia Agnes Simpson (*née* Wardropper), FRS (*d* 2003). *Educ:* Darlington Grammar Sch.; Leeds Univ. Lectr in Medical Physics, Middlesex Hospital Medical School, 1948–55; External Scientific Staff, Medical Research Council, Middlesex Hospital Medical School, 1955–58; Senior Scientist, Worcester Foundation for Experimental Biology, USA, 1958–70; Joel Prof. of Physics as Applied to Medicine, Univ. of London, 1970–82; Co-Dir, Biophysical Endocrinology Unit, Physics Dept, Middlesex Hosp. Med. Sch., 1970–85. (With S. A. S. Tait) R. Douglas Wright Lectr and Medallion, Univ. of Melbourne, 1989. Hon. DSc Hull, 1979. Society for Endocrinology: Medal, 1969 and Sir Henry Dale Medal, 1979; Tadeus Reichstein Award, Internat. Soc. of Endocrinology, 1976; CIBA Award, Amer. Heart Assoc. for Hypertension Research, 1977. *Publications:* papers on medical physics, biophysics and endocrinology. *Recreations:* photography, seeing Yorkshire. *Address:* Granby Court, Granby Road, Harrogate, N Yorkshire HG1 4SR. *T:* (01423) 524284; *e-mail:* jftait@globalnet.co.uk.

TAIT, Michael Logan, CMG 1987; LVO 1972; HM Diplomatic Service, retired; Chairman, Oxford and Edinburgh Consultants, since 1995; *b* 27 Sept. 1936; *s* of William and Dorothea Tait; *m* 1st, 1968, Margaret Kirsteen Stewart (marr. diss. 1990); two *s* one *d*; *m* 2nd, 1999, Amel Boureghda; one *d*. *Educ:* Calday Grange Grammar Sch.; New College, Oxford. Nat. service, 2nd Lieut Royal Signals, 1955–57. Foreign Office, 1961; served MECAS, 1961; Bahrain, 1963; Asst Political Agent, Dubai, Trucial States, 1963; FO, 1966; Private Sec. to Minister of State, FO, later FCO, 1968; First Sec. and Hd of Chancery, Belgrade, 1970; First Sec. (Political), Hd of Chancery and Consul, Amman, 1972; FCO, 1975; Counsellor and Hd of Chancery, Baghdad, 1977; Counsellor, FCO, 1978; Dep. Hd of Delegn, CSCE, Madrid, 1980; Dep. Hd of Delegn and Counsellor (Econ. and Finance), OECD, Paris, 1982; Hd of Economic Relns Dept, FCO, 1984; Ambassador to UAE, 1986–89; Asst Under-Sec. of State with responsibility for Soviet Union and Eastern Europe, 1990–92; Ambassador to Tunisia, 1992–95. *Recreations:* languages, mountains, sailing. *Address:* c/o Oxford and Edinburgh Consultants, 8 Chalcot Crescent, NW1 8YD. *Club:* Garrick.

TAIT, Prof. Richard Graham, CBE 2003; DPhil; Professor, School of Journalism, Media and Cultural Studies, and Director, Centre for Journalism Studies, Cardiff University, since 2003; *b* 22 May 1947; *s* of Dr William Graham Tait and Isabella Dempster Tait (*née* Cumiskey); *m* 1st, 1980, Sandra Janine McKenzie McIntosh (marr. diss. 1984); 2nd, 1995, Kathryn Jane Ellison; one *d*. *Educ:* Bradfield Coll.; New Coll., Oxford (BA Mod. Hist.; MA; DPhil 1978). St Edmund Jun. Res. Fellow, St Edmund Hall, Oxford, 1972–74; BBC Television: Researcher, Money Prog., 1974–75; Producer, Nationwide, 1976–82; Editor: People and Power, 1982; Money Prog., 1983–85; Newsnight, 1985–87; General Election Results Prog., 1987; Independent Television News: Editor: Channel Four News, 1987–90; Channel Four progs, 1990–95; Editor-in-Chief, 1995–2002. A Governor, BBC, 2004–06; a Trustee, BBC Trust, 2007–. Member: Internat. Bd, IPI, 1998–2004 (Vice-Chm., 2000–06); Adv. Bd, Internat. News Safety Inst., 2003–. FRTS 1996; Fellow, Soc. of Editors, 2002. *Recreations:* history, ballet, opera, tennis, ski-ing. *Address:* Bute Building, Cardiff University, Cardiff CF10 3NB.

TAIT, (Robert) Blyth, MBE 1992; three-day event rider; *b* 10 May 1961; *s* of Robert and Glenise Tait. *Educ:* Whangarei Boys' High Sch., NZ. Individual World Champion: Stockholm, 1990, Rome, 1998; Olympic Games: Individual Bronze, Barcelona, 1992; Individual Gold, Atlanta, 1996; ranked World No 1, 1992, 1994, 1995, 1996, 1998; winner: Burghley Horse Trials, 1998, 2001; Kentucky Horse Trials, 2000. Hon. Dr Essex. *Publications:* Eventing Insights, 1991; Blyth Tait's Cross Country Clinic, 1998; Six of the Best, 1999. *Recreations:* water ski-ing, snow ski-ing, tennis. *Address:* Chesterfields, 52 McKenzie Road, RD 4 Pukekohe, New Zealand; *e-mail:* blythtait@hotmail.com.

TAK; *see* Drummond, T. A. K.

TALBOT; *see* Chetwynd-Talbot, family name of Earl of Shrewsbury and Waterford.

TALBOT OF MALAHIDE, 10th Baron *cr* 1831 (Ire.); **Reginald John Richard Arundell;** Hereditary Lord Admiral Malahide and Adjacent Seas; Vice Lord-Lieutenant of Wiltshire, 1996–2006; *b* 9 Jan. 1931; *s* of Reginald John Arthur Arundell (*g g g s* of 1st Baroness) (who assumed by Royal Licence, 1945, names and arms of Arundell in lieu of Talbot, and *d* 1953), and Winifred (*d* 1954), *d* of R. B. S. Castle; *S* cousin, 1987; *m* 1st, 1955, Laura Duff (*d* 1989), *d* of late Group Captain Edward John Tennant, DSO, MC; one *s* four *d*; 2nd, 1992, Patricia Mary Blundell-Brown, *d* of late J. Riddell, OBE. *Educ:* Stonyhurst. DL Wilts. KStJ 1988 (CStJ 1983; OStJ 1978); Chm., St John Council for Wilts, 1976–97. Knight of Malta, 1977. Hon. Citizen, State of Maryland, USA, 1984. *Heir:* *s* Hon. Richard John Tennant Arundell [*b* 28 March 1957; *m* 1984, Jane Catherine, *d* of Timothy Heathcote Unwin; one *s* four *d*]. *Address:* Park Gate, Donhead, Shaftesbury, Dorset SP7 9EU. *Clubs:* Pratt's, Farmers'.

TALBOT, John Andrew, FCA; Chief Executive, Johnson Service Group plc, since 2007; *b* 2 Aug. 1949; *s* of Robert Talbot and Lucy E. Talbot (*née* Jarvis); *m* 1st, 1969, Susan Hollingbery (marr. diss.); one *s* one *d*; 2nd, 1983, Jennifer Anne Houghton; one *s* two *d*. CA 1971; accountant in manufacturing, 1972–73; Bernard Phillips & Co., Accountants, 1973–75; Spicer & Pegler, 1975–83, Partner, 1979; Partner, Arthur Andersen, 1983–99: Hd, UK Insolvency Practice, 1988; Man. Partner, Worldwide Global Corporate Finance Practice, 1995–99; Administrator, Maxwell Private Cos, 1991; Receiver: Leyland DAF, 1993; Transtec plc, 2000; Sen. Partner, Talbot Hughes, then Talbot Hughes McKillop, LLP, 2001–05; European Chm., Kroll Talbot Hughes, 2005–08; Chief restructuring officer, Marconi PLC, 2002–03. Chm., ENB, 2004–; Member: Bd, Conservatoire for Dance and Drama, 2001–07; Cttee, Kettles Yard Art Gall., Cambridge, 2003–. *Recreations:* contemporary art, iron age history, modern and classical dance. *Address:* Johnson Service Group plc, Johnson House, Abbots Park, Monks Way, Preston Brook, Cheshire WA7 3GH. *T:* (01928) 704600, *Fax:* (01928) 704620.

TALBOT, Commandant Mary (Irene), CB; Director, Women's Royal Naval Service, 1973–76; *b* 17 Feb. 1922. *Educ:* Bristol Univ. BA Hons, Philosophy and Economics. Joined WRNS as a Naval recruiting asst, Nov. 1943; Officer training course, 1944, and apptd to HMS Eaglet, in Liverpool, as an Educn and Resettlement Officer; served on staffs of C-in-Cs: Mediterranean; the Nore; Portsmouth, 1945–61; First Officer, and apptd to staff of Dir Naval Educn Service, 1952; subseq. served HMS Condor, Dauntless and Raleigh; Chief Officer, and apptd Sen. WRNS Officer, the Nore, 1960; on staff of Dir Naval Manning, 1963–66, and then became Asst Dir, WRNS; Superintendent, and served on staff of C-in-C Naval Home Command, 1969; Supt in charge, WRNS training estabt, HMS Dauntless, near Reading, 1972–73. Hon. ADC, 1973–76. Hon. LLD Bristol, 1993. *Recreations:* bridge, gardening, racing. *Address:* Sonning Cottage, Pound Lane, Sonning-on-Thames RG4 6XE. *T:* (0118) 969 4309.

TALBOT, Prof. Michael Owen, FBA 1990; James and Constance Alsop Professor of Music, University of Liverpool, 1986–2003, Emeritus Professor, 2004; *b* 4 Jan. 1943; *s* of Alan and Annelise Talbot; *m* 1970, Shirley Ellen Mashiane; one *s* one *d*. *Educ:* Welwyn Garden City Grammar Sch.; Royal Coll. of Music (ARCM); Clare Coll., Cambridge (Open, later Meml Scholar; MusB Hons 1963; MA; PhD 1968). Lectr in Music, 1968, Sen. Lectr, 1979, Reader, 1983–86, Univ. of Liverpool. Corresp. Mem., Ateneo Veneto, Venice, 1986. Order of Merit (Italy), 1980. *Publications:* Vivaldi, 1978 (Italian, German and Polish edns); Vivaldi, 1979 (Japanese, Brazilian and Spanish edns); Albinoni: Leben und Werk, 1980; Antonio Vivaldi: a guide to research, 1988 (Italian edn); Tomaso Albinoni: the Venetian composer and his world, 1990; Benedetto Vinaccesi: a musician in Brescia and Venice in the age of Corelli, 1994; The sacred vocal music of Antonio Vivaldi, 1995; Venetian Music in the Age of Vivaldi, 1999; The Finale in Western Instrumental Music, 2001; The Chamber Cantatas of Antonio Vivaldi, 2006. *Recreations:* chess, reading novels, travel. *Address:* 36 Montclair Drive, Liverpool L18 0HA. *T:* (0151) 722 3328.

TALBOT, Patrick John; QC 1990; a Recorder, since 1997; *b* 28 July 1946; *s* of John Bentley Talbot, MC, and late Marguerite Maxwell Talbot (*née* Townley); *m* 1st, 1976, Judith Anne Urwin (marr. diss. 1999); one *s* two *d*; 2nd, 2000, Elizabeth, (Beth), Evans; two *s*. *Educ:* Charterhouse (Foundn Schol.); University Coll., Oxford (MA). Called to Bar, Lincoln's Inn, 1969, Bencher, 1996; in practice at Chancery Bar, 1970–. Member: Senate of Inns of Court and the Bar, 1976–78; Council of Legal Educn, 1977–95 (Vice-Chm., 1992–95). A Judicial Chm., City Disputes Panel, 1997–2000; CEDR Accredited Mediator, 2005–. A Lieut Bailiff of Guernsey, 2000–. Affiliate British Trustee, British Amer. Educnl Foundn, 1984–. Chm., Ripieno Choir, 2003–07. Hon. Life Mem., Nat. Union of Students, 1982. *Recreations:* cricket, singing. *Address:* Serle Court, 6 New Square, Lincoln's Inn, WC2A 3QS. *T:* (020) 7242 6105; 9 Grove Road, East Molesey, Surrey KT8 9JS. *Clubs:* MCC, Wimbledon Wanderers CC.

TALBOT, Sarah Patricia; *see* Connolly, S. P.

TALBOT RICE, (Alice) Elspeth (Middleton); QC 2008; barrister; *b* Newcastle upon Tyne, 5 May 1967; *d* of David Middleton Lindsley and Elizabeth Anne Dickinson Lindsley; *m* 1991, Robert Harry Talbot Rice; three *d. Educ:* Queen Mary's Sch., Duncombe Park; Roedean Sch.; Univ. of Durham (BA Hons Law). Called to the Bar, Lincoln's Inn, 1990; in practice as barrister specialising in commercial chancery litigation. *Recreations:* playing polo enthusiastically but badly, playing lacrosse increasingly slowly, playing the French horn occasionally, cooking and eating. *Address:* 24 Old Buildings, Lincoln's Inn, WC2A 3UP. *T:* (020) 7691 2424; *e-mail:* etr@xxiv.co.uk.

TALBOYS, Rt Hon. Sir Brian (Edward), Hon. AC 1982; CH 1981; KCB 1991; PC 1977; *b* Wanganui, 7 June 1921; *s* of Francis Powell Talboys and Katherine Janet (*née* Balfour); *m* 1950, Patricia Floyd Adamson, *d* of Adam Laurence Adamson and Alice Floyd Harrington; two *s. Educ:* Wanganui Collegiate Sch.; Univ. of Manitoba; Victoria Univ., Wellington (BA). Served war of 1939–45, RNZAF. MP for Wallace, NZ, 1957–81; Dep. Leader, National Party, 1974–81; Parly Under-Sec. to Minister of Trade and Industry, 1960; Minister of Agriculture, 1962–69; Minister of Science, 1964–72; Minister of Education, 1969–72; Minister of Overseas Trade and Trade and Industry, 1972; Minister of Nat. Develt, 1975–77; Dep. Prime Minister and Minister of For. Affairs and Overseas Trade, 1975–81. Leader of a number of NZ delegns to overseas confs; NZ Rep., Standing Cttee of Pacific Economic Co-operation Conf., 1983–90. Grand Cross 1st Class, Order of Merit, Fed. Republic of Germany, 1978. Hon. DSc Massey Univ., 1981; Hon. DLitt Chung-Ang Univ., Seoul, 1981. *Address:* Winton, New Zealand.

TALINTYRE, Douglas George; Director, Office of Manpower Economics, 1989–92; *b* 26 July 1932; *o s* of late Henry Matthew Talintyre and Gladys Talintyre; *m* 1956, Maureen Diana Lyons (*d* 2004); one *s* one *d. Educ:* Harrow County Grammar School; London School of Economics. BSc (Econ.) 1956; MSc (Industrial Relns and Personnel Management) 1983. Joined National Coal Board, 1956: Administrative Assistant, 1956–59; Marketing Officer, Durham Div., 1959–61; Head of Manpower Planning and Intelligence, HQ, 1961–62; Dep. Head of Manpower, HQ, 1962–64; Head of Wages and Control, NW Div., 1964–66. Entered Civil Service, 1966: Principal, Naval Personnel (Pay) Div., MoD, 1966–69; Senior Industrial Relations Officer, CIR, 1969–71; Director of Industrial Relations, CIR, 1971–74; Asst Secretary, Training Services Agency, 1974–75; Counsellor (Labour), HM Embassy, Washington DC, 1975–77; Head of Policy and Planning, Manpower Services Commn, 1977–80; Department of Employment: Hd of Health and Safety Liaison, 1980–83; Asst Sec., Industrial Relations Div., 1983–86; Under Sec., 1986; Dir of Finance and Resource Management, and Principal Finance Officer, 1986–89. Freeman, Co. of Cordwainers, Newcastle upon Tyne, 1952. *Recreations:* travel, wine, gardening, short tennis. *Address:* Woodwards, School Lane, Cookham Dean, Berks SL6 9PQ. *Club:* Reform.
See also P. A. Rowan.

TALLBOYS, Richard Gilbert, CMG 1981; OBE 1974; FCA; FCIS; FCPA; cruise ship lecturer on international affairs, since 1996; *b* 25 April 1931; *s* of late Harry Tallboys; *m* 1954, Margaret Evelyn, *d* of late Brig. H. W. Strutt, DSO, ED, Hobart; two *s* two *d. Educ:* Palmer's Sch.; LLB (London); BCom (Tasmania). Merchant Navy apprentice, 1947–51; Third/Second Mate, Australian coast, 1952–55; Lt-Comdr, RANR (ASM (FESR) 1945–75, AASM (Malaysia)), retd 1991. Accounting profession in Australia, 1955–62; Alderman, Hobart City Council, 1958–62; Australian Govt Trade Commissioner, Johannesburg, Singapore, Jakarta, 1962–68. HM Diplomatic Service, 1968–88: First Secretary i/c Brasilia, 1969; Head of Chancery, Phnom Penh, 1972 (Chargé d'Affaires *ai* 1972, 1973); FO, 1973; Counsellor Commercial, Seoul, 1976–80 (Chargé d'Affaires *ai* 1977, 1978, 1979); Consul-General, Houston, 1980–85; Ambassador to Vietnam, 1985–87; Chief Exec., World Coal Inst., London, 1988–93. Mem., Internat. Trade Cttee, and Mem. Council, London Chamber of Commerce and Industry, 1990–93, 1995–98. Mem. Council, RIIA, 1995–2001. Councillor (C), City of Westminster, 1998–2002. Freeman, City of London, 1985; Mem., Chartered Secretaries and Administrators' Co., 1999–. FRAS 2001. *Publications:* (ed) Developing Vietnam, 1995; (jtly) 50 Years of Business in Indonesia 1945–1995, 1995; (contrib.) Travellers' Tales & More Travellers' Tales, 2005. *Recreations:* sailing, cautious adventuring. *Address:* PO Box 1060, Sandy Bay, Tas 7006, Australia. *Clubs:* Tasmanian, Royal Yacht of Tasmania (Hobart).

TALLING, John Francis, DSc; FRS 1978; *b* 23 March 1929; *s* of Frank and Miriam Talling; *m* 1959, Ida Björnsson; one *s* one *d. Educ:* Sir William Turner's Sch., Coatham; Univ. of Leeds. BSc, PhD, DSc. Lecturer in Botany, Univ. of Khartoum, 1953–56; Visiting Research Fellow, Univ. of California, 1957; Plant Physiologist (SPSO), Freshwater Biological Assoc., 1958–89; Hon. Reader, 1979–84, Vis. Prof., 1992–2001, Univ. of Lancaster. *Publications:* (jtly) Water Analysis: some revised methods for limnologists, 1978; (jtly) Ecological Dynamics of Tropical Inland Waters, 1998; papers in various learned jls. *Recreation:* country walking. *Address:* Hawthorn View, The Pines, Bongate, Cumbria CA16 6HR. *T:* (017683) 53380.

TALLIS, Prof. Raymond Courteney, FRCP; Professor of Geriatric Medicine, University of Manchester, 1987–2006; Hon. Consultant Physician in Health Care of the Elderly, Salford Royal Hospitals NHS Trust, 1987–2006; *b* 10 Oct. 1946; *s* of Edward Ernest Tallis and Mary Tallis (*née* Burke); *m* 1972, Theresa Bonneywell; two *s. Educ:* Liverpool Coll.; Keble Coll., Oxford (Open schol., 1964; BA 1967; BM BCh 1970); St Thomas' Hosp. Med. Sch. FRCP 1989. Clinical Res. Fellow, Wessex Neurological Centre, 1977–80; Sen. Lectr in Geriatric Medicine, Univ. of Liverpool, 1982–87. Chm., Cttee on Ethical Issues in Medicine, RCP, 2003–05. Numerous vis. professorships, named lectures, etc. Mem., various med. socs. FMedSci 2000. Hon. DLitt: Hull, 1997; Manchester, 2002. *Publications:* Not Saussure, 1988, 2nd edn 1995; In Defence of Realism, 1988, 2nd edn 1998; Clinical Neurology of Old Age, 1988; The Explicit Animal, 1991, 2nd edn 1999; (ed jtly) Brocklehurst's Textbook of Geriatric Medicine and Gerontology, 4th edn 1992, 6th edn 2003; Newton's Sleep, 1995; Epilepsy in Elderly People, 1996; Enemies of Hope, 1997, 2nd edn 1999; Theorrhoea and After, 1998; Increasing Longevity: medical, social and political implications, 1998; On the Edge of Certainty: philosophical explorations, 1999; A Raymond Tallis Reader, 2000; A Conversation with Martin Heidegger, 2002; The Hand: a philosophical inquiry into human being, 2003; I Am: a philosophical inquiry into first-person being, 2004; Hippocratic Oaths: medicine and its discontents, 2004; Why the Mind is Not a Computer: a pocket lexicon of neuromythology, 2004; The Knowing Animal: a philosophical inquiry into knowledge and truth, 2005; The Enduring Significance of Parmenides: unthinkable thought, 2008; The Kingdom of Infinite Space: a fantastical journey around your head, 2008; Hunger: the art of living, 2008; *fiction:* Absence (novel), 1999; short stories; *poetry:* Between the Zones, 1985; Glints of Darkness, 1989; Fathers and Sons, 1993; over 200 scientific papers and articles mainly in the fields of neurology and neurological rehabilitation of older people; numerous pubns in literary criticism, theory and philosophy, especially philosophy of the mind. *Recreations:* thinking, my family, Stella Artois, music. *Address:* 5 Valley Road, Bramhall, Stockport, Cheshire SK7 2NH. *T:* (0161) 439 2548. *Club:* Athenæum.

TALLON, John Mark; QC 2000; FCA; *b* 19 March 1948; *s* of late Claude Reginald Tallon and Blanche Mary Tallon; *m* 1st, 1974, Josephine Rowntree (marr. diss.); one *s* one *d*; 2nd, 1988, Patricia Steel. *Educ:* Rugby Sch. FCA 1970. Called to the Bar, Middle Temple, 1975; Mem., Pump Court Tax Chambers, 1976–. *Recreations:* golf, tennis, reading. *Address:* 16 Bedford Row, WC1R 4EB. *T:* (020) 7414 8080. *Club:* Huntercombe Golf (Oxfordshire).

TALWAR, Rana Gurvirendra Singh; Chairman, Sabre Capital Worldwide, since 2003; *b* 22 March 1948; *s* of R. S. and Veera Talwar; *m* 1st, 1970, Roop Som Dutt (marr. diss.); one *s* one *d*; 2nd, 1995, Renuka Singh; one *s. Educ:* Lawrence Sch., Sanawar, India; St Stephen's Coll., Delhi (BA Hons Econs). Citibank, 1969–97: exec. trainee for internat. banking, 1969–70; various operational, corporate and institutional banking assignments, India, 1970–76; Gp Hd for Treasury and Financial Instns, 1976; Regl Manager for Eastern India, 1977; Gp Hd, Treasury and Financial Instns Gp, Saudi American Bank (Citibank affiliate), Jeddah, 1978–80; COS, Asia Pacific Div., 1981; Regl Consumer Business Manager, Singapore, Malaysia, Indonesia, Thailand and India, 1982–88; Div. Exec., Asia Pacific, 1988–91; Exec. Vice Pres. and Gp Exec. responsible for Consumer Bank in Asia Pacific, ME and Eastern Europe, 1991–95; Exec. Vice Pres., Citicorp and principal subsid., Citibank, resp. for US and Europe, 1996–97; Standard Chartered Plc: Gp Exec. Dir, 1997–98; CEO, 1997–2001. Non-exec. Dir, Pearson plc, 2000–. Governor: Indian Business Sch., 1998–; London Business Sch., 1999–. *Recreations:* golf, tennis, bridge, travel. *Address:* Sabre Capital Worldwide, 2/F Berkeley Square House, Berkeley Square, W1J 6BD. *Clubs:* Tanglin (Singapore); Bengal (Calcutta); Delhi Golf (New Delhi).

TAM, Robin Bing-Kuen; QC 2006; *b* 1 June 1964; *s* of Sheung Wai Tam and Arleta Yau Ling Tam (*née* Chang); *m* 2007, Rosemary Jane Anger. *Educ:* Leys Sch., Cambridge; St John's Coll., Cambridge (BA 1985); Inns of Court Sch. of Law. Called to the Bar, Middle Temple, 1986; in practice as barrister, 1987–, specialising in admin. and public law, immigration and asylum work; Standing Prosecuting Jun. Counsel to Inland Revenue, 1993; Jun. Counsel to the Crown, 1994–2006 (A Panel, 1999–2006). *Publication:* (jtly) Asylum and Human Rights Appeals Handbook, 2008. *Address:* 1 Temple Gardens, Temple, EC4Y 9BB. *T:* (020) 7583 1315.

TAMARÓN, 9th Marqués de; **Santiago de Mora-Figueroa;** Spanish Ambassador to the Court of St James's, 1999–2004; *b* 18 Oct. 1941; *s* of José de Mora-Figueroa, 8th Marqués de Tamarón, and Dagmar Williams; *m* 1966, Isabelle de Yturbe; one *s* one *d. Educ:* Univ. of Madrid; Escuela Diplomática. Lieut, Spanish Marine Corps, 1967; joined Spanish Diplomatic Service, 1968; Secretary: Mauritania, 1968–70; Paris, 1970–73; Banco del Noroeste (on voluntary leave), 1974; Counsellor, Denmark, 1975–80; Minister Counsellor, Ottawa, 1980–81; Private Sec. to Minister of Foreign Affairs, 1981–82; Head of Studies and Dep. Dir, Escuela Diplomática, 1982–88; Dir, Inst. de Cuestiones Internacionales y Política Exterior, 1988–96; Dir, Inst. Cervantes, 1996–99. Comdr, Orden de Carlos III (Spain), 1982; Gran Cruz, Orden del Mérito Naval (Spain), 1999; Commander: Order of Dannebrog (Denmark), 1980; Order of Merit (Germany), 1981; Officier, Ordre Nat. du Mérite (France), 1974. *Publications:* Pólvora con Aguardiente, 1983; El Guirigay Nacional, 1988; Trampantojos, 1990; El Siglo XX y otras Calamidades, 1993; (jtly) El Peso de la Lengua Española en el Mundo, 1995; El Rompimiento de Gloria, 2003. *Recreations:* mountain walking, gardening, philology. *Address:* Castillo de Arcos, 11630 Arcos de la Frontera, Spain.

TAMBLIN, Air Cdre Pamela Joy, CB 1980; retired; Director, Women's Royal Air Force, 1976–80; *b* 11 Jan. 1926; *d* of late Albert Laing and Olga Victoria Laing; *m* 1970, Douglas Victor Tamblin (*d* 2006); one step *s* one step *d. Educ:* James Gillespie's High Sch., Edinburgh; Heaton High Sch., Newcastle upon Tyne; Durham Univ. (BA Hons). ATS, 1943–45. Essex County Council Planning Officer, 1949–51. Joined Royal Air Force, 1951; served Education Branch, 1951–55: RAF Locking; RAF Stanmore Park; RAF Wahn, Germany; Secretarial subseq. Administrative, Branch, 1955–76; Schools Liaison Recruiting, 1955–59; Accountant Officer, RAF St Mawgan and RAF Steamer Point, Aden, 1959–61; Staff College, 1962–63; MoD, Air Secretary's Dept, 1963–66; Sen. Trng Officer, RAF Spitalgate, 1966–68; Admin. Plans Officer, HQ Maintenance Comd, 1968–69; Command WRAF Admin. Officer, HQ Strike Comd, 1969–71; Station Comdr, RAF Spitalgate, 1971–74; Command Accountant, HQ Strike Comd, 1974–76. Chm., Cttee on Women in NATO Forces, 1977–79. Pres., E Cornwall Branch, RAFA, 1984–; Chm., S Western Area Council, RAFA, 1991–93 (Mem., 1986–93; Vice-Chm., 1988–91). FCMI (FBIM 1977, CBIM 1979); FRSA 1979. *Recreations:* various charitable works, tapestry work, church choir. *Address:* Trecairne, 3 Plaidy Park Road, Looe, Cornwall PL13 1LG. *Club:* Royal Air Force.

TAMBLING, Pauline Ann; Executive Director, Programmes and Industry, Creative and Cultural Skills, since 2008; *b* 23 April 1955; *d* of James William and Anne Dorling; *m* 1976, Jeremy Tambling; one *s* one *d. Educ:* Ely High Sch. for Girls; Stockwell Coll., Bromley (Cert Ed London); Univ. of Leeds (MA). Teacher, 1976–83; Head of Educn, Royal Opera House, 1983–97; Arts Council of England, subseq. Arts Council England: Dir, Educn and Trng, 1997–99; Exec. Dir, Res. and Develt, 1999–2001; Change Prog. Dir, 2001–03; Exec. Dir, Develt, 2003–07; arts consultant, 2007. Chair, Shape, 2007–. Strategy Cttee, Clore Leadership Prog., 2003–. Trustee, Shakespeare Schs Fest., 2007–. Mem. Bd, Univ. (formerly UC) of the Creative Arts, 2007–. Deviser/writer, Top Score, TV series, 1996–97; co-dir/researcher, orchestral educn programmes, NFER, 1997–98. FRSA 1990. *Publications:* Performing Arts in the Primary School, 1990; Lessons in Partnership, 1996; articles in Cultural Trends, British Jl Music Educn. *Recreations:* arts, cinema, travel, current affairs. *Address:* (office) Lafone House, The Leathermarket, Weston Street, SE1 3HN; 9 Sumburgh Road, SW12 8AJ. *T:* (020) 7228 8089.

TAMBUNTING, Jesus Paraiso; Chairman, since 1975, and Chief Executive Officer, Planters Development Bank, Philippines; *b* 21 Dec. 1937; *s* of Antonio Tambunting and Aurora Paraiso Tambunting; *m* 1967, Margarita Ansaldo; two *s* two *d. Educ:* Univ. of Maryland (BS, BA Econs). Chm., Planters DB Leasing Corp., 1992–. Perm. Rep. of Philippines to IMO, 1993; Ambassador to UK and concurrently to Ireland, 1993–98. Hon. Pres., British-Philippine Soc., 1993. *Recreations:* tennis, golf. *Address:* Planters Development Bank, 314 Sen. Gil J. Puyat Avenue, Makati City, Metro Manila, Philippines. *Clubs:* Queen's; Roehampton Golf.

TAMI, Mark Richard; MP (Lab) Alyn and Deeside, since 2001; an Assistant Government Whip, since 2007; *b* 3 Oct. 1962; *s* of Michael John Tami and Patricia Tami; *m* 1992, Sally Daniels; two *s. Educ:* Enfield Grammar Sch.; UCW, Swansea (BA Hons). Head of Res. and Communications, 1992–99, Head of Policy, 1999–2001, AEEU. Chm., Welsh PLP, 2006–. *Publication:* Votes for All: compulsory voting in elections, 2000. *Recreations:* football, cricket, antiques. *Address:* House of Commons, SW1A 0AA.

TAMMADGE, Alan Richard; Headmaster, Sevenoaks School, 1971–81; *b* 9 July 1921; *m* 1950, Rosemary Anne Broadribb; two *s* one *d. Educ:* Bromley County Sch.; Dulwich Coll.; Emmanuel Coll., Cambridge. BA (Maths) 1950; MA 1957. Royal Navy Special Entry, 1940; resigned, 1947 (Lt); Cambridge, 1947–50; Lectr, RMA Sandhurst, 1950–55;

Asst Master, Dulwich College, 1956–58; Head of Mathematics Dept, Abingdon School, 1958–67; Master, Magdalen College School, Oxford, 1967–71. Royal Instn Mathematics Master Classes, 1982–94. Pres., Mathematical Assoc., 1978–79. FIMA 1965. *Publications:* Complex Numbers, 1965; (jtly) School Mathematics Project Books 1–5, 1965–69; (jtly) General Education, 1969; Parents' Guide to School Mathematics, 1976; articles in Mathemat. Gazette, Mathematics Teacher (USA), Aspects of Education (Hull Univ.). *Recreations:* music, gardens.

TAMUNO, Prof. Tekena Nitonye, CON 2003; OFR 2002; DLit; Emeritus Professor, University of Ibadan, since 1994; Distinguished Fellow, National Institute for Policy and Strategic Studies, Kuru, Nigeria, 1992–94 (Research Professor in History, 1990–92); *b* 28 Jan. 1932; *s* of late Chief Mark Tamuno Igbiri and Mrs Ransoline I. Tamuno; *m* 1963, Olu Grace Tamuno (*née* Esho); two *s* two *d. Educ:* University Coll. Ibadan; Birkbeck Coll., Univ. of London; Columbia Univ., New York City. BA (Hons) History, PhD History, DLit (London). University of Ibadan: Professor of History, 1971; Head, Dept of History, 1972–75; Dean of Arts, 1973–75; Chairman, Cttee of Deans, 1974–75; Vice-Chancellor, 1975–79; Res. Prof. in History, Inst. of African Studies, 1979–90. Principal, University Coll., Ilorin, Oct.–Nov. 1975; Pro-Chancellor and Chm. Council, Rivers State Univ. of Sci. and Technol., Port-Harcourt, 1981–88; Vis. Prof. in History, Nigerian Defence Acad., Kaduna, 1989–90. Mem., Nat. Univs Commn Bd, 2002–05. Chairman: Presidential Panel on Nigeria Since Independence History Project, 1980–2000; Panel on Policing Nigeria Project, 1992–93; Presidential Panel on Nat. Security, 2001–02; Okrika Community Peace Cttee, Port Harcourt, Rivers State, Nigeria, 2005–07. Chm. Bd of Dirs, New Nigerian Newspapers Ltd, 1984–89. Pres. and Chm., Bd of Trustees, Bells Univ. of Technol., Ota, Nigeria, 2005–. Nat. Vice-Pres., Historical Soc. of Nigeria, 1974–78 (Fellow, 1992). Nigerian Academy of Letters: Fellow, 2000; Vice-Pres., 2000–02; Pres., 2002–04. Gen. Ed., African Leadership Forum Biographical Series, 1991. JP Ibadan, 1976. *Publications:* Nigeria and Elective Representation, 1923–1947, 1966; The Police in Modern Nigeria, 1961–1965, 1970; The Evolution of the Nigerian State: The Southern Phase, 1898–1914, 1972; (ed with Prof. J. F. A. Ajayi) The University of Ibadan, 1948–1973: A History of the First Twenty-Five Years, 1973; History and History-makers in Modern Nigeria, 1973; Herbert Macaulay, Nigerian Patriot, 1975; (ed with E. J. Alagoa) Eminent Nigerians of the Rivers State, 1980; (ed) Ibadan Voices: Ibadan University in Transition, 1981; Songs of an Egg-Head (poems), 1982; (ed) National Conference on Nigeria since Independence: addresses at the formal opening, 1983; (ed) Proceedings of the National Conference on Nigeria since Independence, Zaria, March 1983, Vol. III: The Civil War Years, 1984; Nigeria Since Independence: The First Twenty-Five Years (ed with J. A. Atanda) Vol. III, Education, 1989; (ed with J. A. Atanda) Vol. IV, Government and Public Policy, 1989; (ed with S. C. Ukpabi) Vol. VI, The Civil War Years, 1989; (ed with E. J. Alagoa) Land and People of Nigeria: Rivers State, 1989; Peace and Violence in Nigeria, 1991; (ed jtly) Policing Nigeria: past, present and future, 1993; Festival of Songs & Drums (poems), 1999; The Niger Delta Question, 2000; Lamentations of Yeske: poems in honour of HRH Professor Egbe Ifie, 2005. *Recreations:* music, photography, swimming, horse-riding, gardening, domestic pets. *Address:* Institute of African Studies, University of Ibadan, Ibadan, Nigeria.

TAMWORTH, Viscount; Robert William Saswalo Shirley, FCA; Managing Director: Ruffer Investment Management Ltd, since 1999 (Director, since 1994); Ruffer LLP, since 2004; *b* 29 Dec. 1952; *s* and *heir* of 13th Earl Ferrers, *qv*; *m* 1980, Susannah, *y d* of late C. E. W. Sheepshanks, Arthington Hall, Yorks; two *s* one *d. Educ:* Ampleforth. Teaching in Kenya, under CMS's Youth Service Abroad Scheme, 1971–72. Articled to Whinney Murray & Co., CA, 1972–76; employed at Ernst & Whinney, 1976–82, Asst Manager, 1981–82; Gp Auditor, 1982–85, Sen. Treasury Analyst, 1986, BICC plc; Director: Viking Property Gp Ltd, 1987–88 (Financial Controller and Company Sec., 1986–87); Ashby Securities, subseq. Norseman Hldgs, 1987–92; Derbyshire Student Residences Ltd, 1996–2003. Dir, Assoc. of Private Client Investment Managers. Admitted to ICAEW, 1976. Kt SMO Malta, 2005. *Recreations:* the British countryside and related activities, the garden. *Heir: s* Hon. William Robert Charles Shirley, *b* 10 Dec. 1984. *Address:* Ditchingham Hall, Ditchingham, Norfolk NR35 2JX. *Club:* Boodle's.

TAN, Melvyn, FRCM; pianist; *b* 13 Oct. 1956; *s* of Keng Hian Tan and Sov Yuen Wong. *Educ:* Anglo-Chinese Sch.; Yehudi Menuhin Sch.; Royal Coll. of Music. FRCM 2000. Performer of classical piano repertoire on period instruments, 1983–; solo career, 1985–; extended repertoire to include modern piano, 1996–; performs in internat. music festivals, incl. Austria, Germany, Holland, France, Scandinavia, UK, USA, Japan, Australia, in major venues and with leading orchestras worldwide; pioneered interest in keyboard music of 18/19th centuries, incl. tour with Beethoven's own Broadwood piano, 1992; cycle of complete Beethoven sonatas, Japan, 1994–97. Numerous recordings incl. piano sonatas and complete piano concertos of Beethoven, Debussy Preludes Books 1 and 2. *Recreations:* swimming, wine, travelling to places where free of performing. *Address:* Valerie Barber PR & UK Personal Management, Suite 2, 9a St John's Wood High Street, NW8 7NG.

TANAKA, Koichi; General Manager, Mass Spectrometry Laboratory, Shimadzu Corporation, Japan, since 2003 (Assistant Manager, Life Science Laboratory, 2002); *b* 3 Aug. 1959; *m* 1995, Yuko Ikegami. *Educ:* Toyama Chubu High Sch.; Tohoku Univ. (BEng). Shimadzu Corporation: joined Central Res. Lab., 1983; Kratos Analytical Ltd, UK, 1992; R&D Dept, Analytical Instruments Div., Japan, 1992–97; Shimadzu Res. Lab. (Europe) Ltd, 1997–99; Kratos Analytical Ltd, UK, 1999–2002. (Jtly) Nobel Prize in Chemistry, 2002. *Address:* Shimadzu Corporation, 1 Nishinokyo-Kuwabara-cho, Nakagyo-ku, Kyoto 604–8511, Japan.

TANBURN, Jennifer Jephcott; research consultant, 1984–94; *b* 6 Oct. 1929; *d* of late Harold Jephcott Tanburn and Elise Noel Tanburn (*née* Armour). *Educ:* St Joseph's Priory, Dorking; Settrington Sch., Hampstead; University Coll. of the South West, Exeter (BSc (Econ)). Market Research Dept, Unilever Ltd, 1951–52; Research and Information, Lintas Ltd, 1952–66, Head of Div., 1962–66, Head of Special Projects, 1966–74; British Airways Board, 1974–76; Head of Res. and Consumer Affairs, 1975–76, a Dir, 1976–83, Booker McConnell Food Distbn Div. Member: Marketing Policy Cttee, 1977–80, and Potato Product Gp, 1980–82, Central Council for Agricl and Hortl Co-operation; Packaging Council, 1978–82; Chm., Consumers' Cttees for GB and England and Wales under Agricl Marketing Act of 1958, 1982–91; Hon. Mem., Marketing Gp of GB, 2000–. Hon. Vis. Academic, Middlesex Univ., 1997–2003. Hon. Fellow, Durham Univ. (Business Sch.), 1991–94. *Publications:* Food, Women and Shops, 1968; People, Shops and the '70s, 1970; Superstores in the '70s, 1972; Retailing and the Competitive Challenge: a study of retail trends in the Common Market, Sweden and the USA, 1974; Food Distribution: its impact on marketing in the '80s, 1981; (with Judy Slinn) The Booker Story, 2004; articles on retailing and marketing subjects. *Recreations:* television viewing, reading. *Address:* 5 Finch Green, Cedars Village, Dog Kennel Lane, Chorleywood, Herts WD3 5GE. *T:* (01923) 497422.

TANCRED, Sir Henry L.; *see* Lawson-Tancred.

TANDY, Virginia Ann; Director, Manchester City Galleries, since 1998; *b* 29 Feb. 1956; *d* of William Arthur Francis Tandy and Lucy Tandy (*née* Saunders); *m* 1984, Brian Stephen Fell; one *s. Educ:* Newcastle upon Tyne Poly. (BA Hons); Manchester Univ. (Post-grad. Dip. Mus. Studies). Museums Officer, Tameside MBC, 1980–84; Exhibns Officer, Cornerhouse Arts Centre, 1985–87; Visual Arts Officer and Hd, Visual Arts, NW Arts Bd, 1988–94; Dir, Cornerhouse Arts Centre, 1994–98. Member: Arts Council Capital Services Adv. Panel, 1998–2001; Creative Industries Develt Service, 2001–; Commns in the Envmt, 2002–04; Bd, Museums, Libraries and Archives Council, 2004–06 (Mem., Bd of Mgt, NW, 2003–). Museums Association: Mem. Council and Public Affairs Cttee, 2001–; Professional Vice Pres., 2004–06; Pres., 2006–08. FRSA 2006. Trustee, Campaign for Museums, 2005–06. *Recreations:* family, gardening. *Address:* Manchester Art Gallery, Mosley Street, Manchester M2 3JL.

TANFIELD, Jennifer Bridget, (Mrs J. B. Bannenberg); Librarian, House of Commons, 1993–99; *b* 19 July 1941; *d* of Doylah and Phyllis Tanfield; *m* 2002, Nick Bannenberg, Australia. *Educ:* Abbots Bromley; LSE (BSc Econ 1962). House of Commons: Library Clerk, 1963–72; Head, Econ. Affairs Section, later Statistical Section, 1972–87; Head, Parly Div., 1987–91; Dep. Librarian, 1991–93. Mem., IFLA Sect. on Liby and Res. Services for Parlts (Chm., 1997–99). *Publications:* In Parliament 1939–1951, 1991; (ed) Parliamentary Library, Research and Information Services of Western Europe, 2000. *Recreations:* opera, theatre, travel.

TANG, Sir David (Wing-cheung), KBE 2008 (OBE 1997); Chairman, D.W.C. Tang Development Ltd, since 1990; *b* Hong Kong, 2 Aug. 1954; *s* of late Pak Kan Tang and of Chiu Sim Chan; *m* 1st, 1983, Susanna Cheung Suk-yee (marr. diss. 1994); one *s* one *d*; 2nd, 2003, Lucy Wastnage. *Educ:* La Salle, Hong Kong; The Perse, Cambridge; Bedford Coll., Univ. of London (BA Hons Philos. 1975). Lectr, Peking Univ., 1983–84. Founder: China Club Hong Kong, 1991; Pacific Cigar Co. Ltd, 1992 (Dir); Shanghai Tang Hong Kong, 1994; Havana House, Canada, 1994; China Club Peking, 1996; China Club Singapore, 2000 (Dir); Cipriani Hong Kong, 2002 (Dir); China Tang London, 2005. Director: Lai Sun Develt Co. Ltd, Hong Kong, 1988–; First Pacific Co. Ltd, Hong Kong, 1989–; China Club Ltd, 1990–; China Club Beijing Ltd, 1994–; Tommy Hilfiger Inc., USA, 2003–; China Tang Restaurant, 2005–; Advisor: Asprey and Garrard, London; Blackstone Gp, NY; Savoy Gp of Hotels, London; BA Travel Adv. Bd. Chairman: Asia-Pacific Acquisitions Cttee, Tate Modern; (and Founder) Community English Lang. Lab.; (and Founder) Hong Kong Cancer Fund; Special Fundraising Cttee, Youth Outreach; Vice Chm., EORTC Foundn; President: London Bach Soc.; Pro Musicis (Hong Kong) Foundn; Royal Commonwealth Soc., Hong Kong; China Mental Handicap; Hong Kong Down Syndrome Assoc.; Trustee: Royal Acad. of Arts Trust; (and Founder) Anglo-Hong Kong Trust; Mem., Chm.'s Develt Circle, South Bank; Adviser: LSO; St Martin's-in-the-Field Develt Trust; Member, Advisory Council: Orbis; Befrienders Internat.; Chances for Children; Dir, Asia Art Achieve; Patron: Save China's Tigers; Royal Overseas League, Hong Kong; Hong Kong Youth Arts Fest. Chevalier de l'Ordre des Arts et des Lettres (France), 1995. *Publications:* trans. Chinese, Roald Dahl's Charlie and the Chocolate Factory, 1984; An Apple a Week (anthol.), 2006. *Recreations:* reading, collecting art, the roulette. *Address:* 1112 Jardine House, Central, Hong Kong. *T:* 25255320, *Fax:* 28101804; *e-mail:* patriciali@dwctang.com. *Clubs:* Beefsteak, Brooks's, Chelsea Arts, Pratt's, White's; Foreign Correspondents', Hong Kong, Hong Kong Jockey (Hong Kong); Brook (NY).

TANGAROA, Hon. Sir Tangaroa, Kt 1987; MBE 1984; Queen's Representative, Cook Islands, 1984–90; *b* 6 May 1921; *s* of Tangaroa and Mihiau; *m* 1941; two *s* seven *d. Educ:* Avarua Primary School, Rarotonga. Radio operator, 1939–54; Shipping Clerk, A. B. Donald Ltd and J. & P. Ingram Ltd, 1955–63; MP for Penrhyn, 1958–84; Minister of Educn, Works, Survey, Printing and Electric Power Supply; Minister of Internal Affairs, 1978–80; retired from politics, 1984. Pres., Cook Is Crippled Children's Soc., 1966–; Deacon, Cook Is Christian Church (served 15 years in Penrhyn, 28 years in Avarua); former community positions: Mem., Tereora Coll. Sch. Cttee for 20 years and 10 as Sec./Treasurer; Pres., Cook Is Boys Brigade for 15 years; delegate to Cook Is Sports Assoc. *Address:* PO Box 870, Avarua, Rarotonga, Cook Islands.

TANKERVILLE, 10th Earl of, *cr* 1714; **Peter Grey Bennet;** Baron Ossulston, 1682; *b* 18 Oct. 1956; *s* of 9th Earl of Tankerville, and Georgiana Lilian Maude (*d* 1998), *d* of late Gilbert Wilson, MA, DD, PhD; *S* father, 1980. *Educ:* Oberlin Conservatory, Ohio (Bachelor of Music); San Francisco State Univ. (Master of Music). Working as musician, San Francisco. *Heir: cousin* Adrian George Bennet [*b* 5 July 1958; *m* 1st, 1984, Lucinda Mary Bell (marr. diss. 1991); 2nd, 1991, Karel Ingrid Juliet Wensby-Scott]. *Address:* 139 Olympia Way, San Francisco, CA 94131, USA.

TANLAW, Baron *cr* 1971 (Life Peer), of Tanlawhill, Dumfries; **Simon Brooke Mackay;** Chairman, Fandstan Electric Group Ltd (formerly Fandstan Ltd), since 1973; *b* 30 March 1934; *s* of 2nd Earl of Inchcape; *m* 1st, 1959, Joanna Susan, *d* of Major J. S. Hirsch; one *s* two *d* (and one *s* decd); 2nd, 1976, Rina Siew Yong Tan, *d* of late Tiong Cha Tan and Mrs Tan; one *s* one *d. Educ:* Eton College; Trinity College, Cambridge (MA 1966). Served as 2nd Lt XII Royal Lancers, Malaya. Inchcape Group of Companies, India and Far East, 1960–66; Managing Director, Inchcape & Co., 1967–71, Dir 1971–92; Chm., Thwaites & Reed Ltd, 1971–74; Chm. and Man. Dir, Fandstan Electric Group of private cos, 1973–. Chm., Building Cttee, Univ. of Buckingham (formerly UC at Buckingham), 1973–78, Mem. Council of Management 1973–2000, Hon. Fellow, 1981, DUniv 1983; Mem. Ct of Governors, LSE, 1980–96. Mem., Lord Chancellor's Inner London Adv. Cttee on Justices of the Peace, 1972–83. Contested (L) Galloway, by-election and gen. election, 1959, and gen. election, 1964. Mem., EC Cttee Sub-Cttee F (Energy, Transport Technology and Research), H of L, 1980–83; Chairman: Parly Liaison Gp for Alternative Energy Strategies, 1981–83; Parly Astronomy and Space Envmt Gp, 1999–2007 (Pres., 2007); Lighter Evenings All-Party Gp, 2007–08. Joint Treasurer, 1971–72, Dep. Chm., 1972, Scottish Liberal Party. Pres., Sarawak Assoc., 1973–75, 1999–2001. Chm., Tanlaw Foundn, 1996–. FBHI 1996; FRAS 2003. *Publications:* articles and papers on horology in learned jls. *Recreations:* horology, astronomy. *Address:* Tanlawhill, By Langholm, Dumfriesshire DG13 0PQ; 101 Centurion Building, Chelsea Bridge Wharf, Queenstown Road, SW8 4NZ. *Clubs:* White's, Oriental; Puffin's (Edinburgh).

TANNER, Brian Michael, CBE 1997; DL; Chairman, Taunton and Somerset NHS Trust, 1998–2006; *b* 15 Feb. 1941; *s* of Gerald Evelyn Tanner and Mary Tanner; *m* 1963, June Ann Walker; one *s* one *d. Educ:* Acklam Hall Grammar Sch., Middlesbrough; Bishop Vesey Grammar Sch., Sutton Coldfield; Bristol Univ. (BA 1st class Hons). CIPFA. Trainee Accountant, Birmingham CBC, 1962–66; Economist, Coventry CBC, 1966–69; Chief Accountant, Teesside CBC, 1969–71; Warwickshire County Council: Asst County Treasurer, 1971–73; Asst Chief Exec., 1973–75; Somerset County Council: County Treasurer, 1975–90; Chief Exec., 1990–97; Treasurer, Avon and Somerset Police Authy, 1975–91. Advr, ACC Cttees on agric., educn, nat. parks, finance, policy, police, 1976–92; Mem., Accounting Standards Cttee, 1982–85; Chief Negotiator with Central Govt on Rate Support Grant, 1985–88; Mem., Investment Cttee, Nat. Assoc. of Pension Funds,

1988–91. Director: Avon Enterprise Fund, 1988–97; Somerset TEC, 1990–97; Jupiter Internat. Green Investment Trust, 1997–2001; Somerset Community Foundn, 2002–07; Redstone Trust, 2007–. Chairman: SW Reg., Nat. Lottery Charities Bd, 1997–2002; Taunton Town Centre Partnership, 1998–2002; Taunton Vision Commn, 2002; Council, Wells Cath., 2007–; a Comr, Public Works Loan Bd, 1997–; Member: SW Regl FEFC, 1997–99; Wessex Ofwat, 1998–99. Trustee: Central Bureau for Educnl Visits and Exchanges, 1981–92; Avon and Somerset Police Trust, 1999–; Somerset Crimebeat, 2000–06; St Margaret's Hospice, Somerset, 2005–. Governor: Millfield Sch., 1989–99; Bridgwater Coll., 1994–2002; Somerset Coll. of Arts and Technol., 2004–. Freeman, City of London, 1990. DL 1998, High Sheriff, 2003–04, Somerset. *Publication:* Financial Management in the 1990's, 1989. *Recreations:* gardening, golf, philately, antiques. *Address:* 8 Broadlands Road, Taunton, Somerset TA1 4HQ. *T:* (01823) 337826. *Club:* Sloane.

TANNER, Lt-Col Cecil Eustace; Vice Lord-Lieutenant of Bedfordshire, 1998–2005; *b* 14 Oct. 1934. Commnd 2nd Lieut, RASC, 1955; GSO 2, MoD, 1969–71; DAQMG (Logistics), HQ Land SE, 1973–75; Lt-Col 1976; CO 156 Regt, RCT(V), 1977; retd 1987. Formerly Cadet EO for Beds, ACF, TA. *Address:* c/o Lieutenancy Office, County Hall, Cauldwell Street, Bedford MK42 9AP.

TANNER, David Whitlock, OBE 2003; Performance Director and International Manager, Amateur Rowing Association, since 1996; *b* 29 Dec. 1947; *s* of Douglas and Connie Tanner. *Educ:* Univ. of Bristol (BA Hons Hist.); Univ. of London (PGCE). Dep. Head, Greenford High Sch., 1985–87; Headmaster, Longford Community Sch., 1987–96. Olympic Rowing Coach, GB Team, Olympic Games: Moscow, 1980; Seoul, 1988; Team Manager, Rowing, GB Team, Olympic Games: Barcelona, 1992; Atlanta, 1996; Sydney, 2000; Athens, 2004; Beijing, 2008. FRSA 1992. *Recreations:* theatre, classical music, sport, travel, history. *Address:* Amateur Rowing Association, 6 Lower Mall, W6 9DJ. *T:* and *Fax:* (020) 8892 7852; *e-mail:* david.tanner@gbrowing.org.uk. *Clubs:* Leander, Remenham, London Rowing, Molesey Boat.

TANNER, David Williamson, DPhil; Under Secretary, Head of Science Branch, Department of Education and Science, 1981–89; *b* 28 Dec. 1930; *s* of late Arthur Bertram Tanner, MBE and of Susan (*née* Williamson); *m* 1960, Glenis Mary (*née* Stringer); one *s* two *d*. *Educ:* Raynes Park County Grammar Sch.; University Coll., Oxford (MA, DPhil); UEA (BA Hons Phil. 1st cl., 1997). Univ. of Minnesota (post-doctoral research), USA, 1954–56; Dept of Scientific and Industrial Research (Fuel Research Station and Warren Spring Lab.), 1957–64; Dept of Educn and Science, 1964–89. *Publications:* papers on physical chem. in Trans Faraday Soc., Jl Applied Chem., Jl Heat and Mass Transfer, etc. *Recreations:* family, philosophy. *Address:* 72 Highfields Road, Highfields Caldecote, Cambs CB23 7NX. *T:* (01954) 211546.

TANNER, Elizabeth; *see* Tanner, K. E.

TANNER, John W., CBE 1983; FRIBA, FRTPI; Director, United Nations Relief and Works Agency for Palestine Refugees, Jordan, 1971–83 (accorded rank of Ambassador to Hashemite Kingdom of Jordan, 1973); *b* 15 Nov. 1923; *s* of Walter George Tanner and Elizabeth Wilkes Tanner (*née* Humphreys); *m* 1st, 1948, Hazel Harford Harford-Jones (*d* 1996); one *s* two *d*; 2nd, 1999, Jacqueline Mary Richards (*née* Hands). *Educ:* Clifton Coll.; Liverpool Univ. Sch. of Architecture and Dept of Civic Design. MCD, BArch (Hons). Sen. Planning Officer, Nairobi, 1951; Architect, Nairobi, 1953; Hon. Sec., Kenya Chapter of Architects, 1954; UN Relief and Works Agency: Architect and Planning Officer, Beirut, 1955; Chief Techn. Div., 1957. Past Mem. Cttee, Fedn of Internat. Civil Servants Assoc., 1968–70. *Buildings:* vocational and teacher training centres (Damascus, Syria; Siblin, Lebanon; Ramallah; Wadi Seer; Amman, Jordan); schools; low cost housing and health centres; E African Rugby Union HQ, Nairobi. *Publications:* The Colour Problem in Liverpool: accommodation or assimilation, 1951; Building for the UNRWA/UNESCO Education and Training Programme, 1968. *Recreations:* formerly: Rugby football (Waterloo, Lancs, 1950; Kenya Harlequins, Kenya and E Africa); ski-ing, squash, board sailing. *Address:* 69B La Pleta, Ordino, Andorra.

TANNER, Prof. (Kathleen) Elizabeth, DPhil; CEng, FREng; FIMechE, FIMMM; Professor of the Mechanics of Materials and Structures, University of Glasgow, since 2007; *b* 20 March 1957; *d* of John Darley Tanner and Elizabeth Gordon Tanner (*née* Holmes). *Educ:* Wycombe Abbey Sch.; Lady Margaret Hall, Oxford (MA; DPhil 1985). CEng 1989; FIMechE 1994; FIMMM (FIM 1997); FBSE 2004; CSci 2004; FREng 2006. Queen Mary and Westfield College, subsequently Queen Mary, University of London: Res. Asst, 1983–88; EPSRC Advanced Res. Fellow, 1988–93; Lectr, 1993–95; Reader, 1995–98; Prof. of Biomedical Materials, 1998–2007; Associate Dir of IRC in Biomed. Materials, 1998–2001; Dean of Engrg, 1999–2000. Adjunct Prof., Dept of Orthopaedics, Lund Univ., Sweden, 1998–. Pres., UK Soc. for Biomaterials, 2000. Sec., Eur. Soc. for Biomaterials, 2005–. Gisela Sturm Prize, Eur. Fedn of Nat. Assocs in Orthopaedics and Traumatol., 1996; Göran Selvik Prize, Eur. Orthopaedics Res. Soc., 1999. *Publications:* (ed jtly) Bioceramics 4, 1991; (ed jtly) Strain Measurement in Biomechanics, 1992; res. papers on biomaterials and biomechanics in learned jls. *Recreations:* riding, tennis, cookery, dress-making. *Address:* Departments of Civil and Mechanical Engineering, James Watt South Building, University of Glasgow, Glasgow G12 8QQ. *T:* (0141) 330 3733, *Fax:* (0141) 330 4343.

TANNER, Dame Mary (Elizabeth), DBE 2008 (OBE 1999); European President, World Council of Churches, since 2006; *b* 23 July 1938; *d* of Harold Fussell and Marjorie (*née* Teucher); *m* 1961, John Bryan Tanner; one *s* one *d*. *Educ:* Colston's Girls' Sch., Bristol; Birmingham Univ. (BA Hons). Lecturer in: OT and Hebrew, Hull Univ., 1960–67; OT and Hebrew, Bristol Univ., 1972–75; OT, Westcott House, Cambridge, 1978–82; Theol Sec., Bd for Mission and Unity, C of E, 1982–91; Sec., Council for Christian Unity, General Synod of C of E, 1991–98. Lay Canon, Guildford Cathedral, 2002. DD Lambeth, 1988; Hon. DD: General Seminary, NY, 1991; Birmingham, 1997; Virginia Seminary, 1999. Plaque of St Erik, Ch of Sweden, 1997. Officer's Cross, Order of Merit (Germany), 1991; Comdr, Royal Order of the Polar Star (Sweden), 2000. *Publications:* essays in: Feminine in the Church, 1984; The Study of Anglicanism, 1988; Runcie by His Friends, 1989; Women and Church, 1991; Encounters for Living, 1995; Living Evangelism, 1996; Festschrift for Jean Tillard, 1996; The Vision of Christian Unity, 1997; A Church for the 21st Century, 1998; Ecumenical Theology in Worship, Doctrine and Life, 1999; Runcie on Reflection, 2002; The Unity we have and the Unity we seek, 2003; Apostolicity and Unity, 2003; Seeking the Truth of Change in the Church, 2004; Cracks in the Wall, 2005; The Holy Spirit, the Church and Christian Unity, 2005; A Theology for Europe, 2005; One Lord, One Faith, One Baptism, 2006; Who is That Man?: Christ in the renewal of the Church, 2006; articles in Theology, Ecumenical Rev., One in Christ, Ecclesiology, etc. *Recreations:* music, gardening. *Address:* Bainton Farmhouse, Bainton, Stamford, Lincs PE9 3AF. *T:* (01780) 740216.

TANNER, Matthew Richard, MBE 2007; Director, SS Great Britain Trust, since 2000; *b* Tynemouth, 3 April 1966; *s* of John and Valerie Tanner; *m* 2000, Rebecca Stevens; one *s* two *d*. *Educ:* Sevenoaks Sch., Kent; St Andrews Univ. (MA Hons Classics; MPhil Maritime Archaeol.). Curator, Scottish Fisheries Mus., 1990–93; Maritime Curator, Merseyside Maritime Mus., 1993–97; Curator, SS Great Britain Project, 1997–2000. Mem., Adv. Cttee on Historic Ships, DCMS, 2006–. Vice Chm., Assoc. of Ind. Museums, 2008–. Trustee: Bristol Cultural Develt Partnership, 2005–; Underfall Restoration Trust, 2007–. FRSA. *Publications:* Scottish Fishing Boats, 1995; The Ship and Boat Collection of Merseyside Maritime Museum, 1995; (ed) Manual of Maritime Curatorship, 2003; The Mystery of the Mary, 2008. *Recreations:* classical music (listening and playing), sailing, scuba diving, popular science writings. *Address:* c/o SS Great Britain Trust, Great Western Dock, Bristol BS1 6TY. *T:* (0117) 926 0680, *Fax:* (0117) 925 5788; *e-mail:* matthewt@ssgreatbritain.org.

TANNER, Meg; *see* Beresford, M.

TANNER, Prof. Roger Ian, PhD; FRS 2001; FAA, FTSE; P. N. Russell Professor of Mechanical Engineering, University of Sydney, since 1975; *b* 25 July 1933; *s* of Reginald Jack Tanner and Ena Maud Tanner (*née* Horsington); *m* 1957, Elizabeth Bogen; two *s*, three *d*. *Educ:* Univ. of Bristol (BSc 1956); Univ. of California (MS 1958); Manchester Univ. (PhD 1961). FAA 1979; FTSE 1977. Lectr, Manchester Univ., 1958–61; Reader, Univ. of Sydney, 1961–66; Prof. Brown Univ., Providence, USA, 1966–75. *Publications:* Engineering Rheology, 1985, 2nd edn 2000; (with K. Walters) Rheology: an historical perspective, 1998; several hundred jl papers. *Recreations:* tennis, golf. *Address:* School of Aerospace, Mechanical and Mechatronic Engineering, University of Sydney, Sydney, NSW 2006, Australia. *T:* (2) 9351 7153.

TANNER, Simon John, FFPH; Regional Director of Public Health for London (formerly Director of Public Health, Strategic Health Authority for London), and Health Adviser to Greater London Authority, since 2007; *b* 2 Sept. 1957; *s* of John George Tanner and Marianne Tanner; *m* 1982, Katrina Anne Morris; two *d*. *Educ:* St Olave's and St Saviour's Grammar Sch., Orpington; Univ. of Southampton (BM 1981); London Univ. (MSc 1993); DCH 1983; DRCOG 1984; MRCGP 1985; MFPHM 1997, FFPH 2003. Principal in gen. practice, Alresford, 1986–93; Specialist Registrar in Public Health, 1993–97; Consultant in Public Health Medicine, 1997–99; Director of Public Health: N and Mid Hampshire HA, 1999–2002; Hampshire and IoW Strategic HA, 2002–06; Regl Dir of Public Health, NHS S Central, 2006–07. *Recreations:* choral singing, piano playing, my family.

TANNOCK, Dr (Timothy) Charles Ayrton; Member (C) London, European Parliament, since 1999; *b* 25 Sept. 1957; *s* of Robert Cochrane William Tannock and Anne (*née* England); *m* 1st, 1984, Rosa Maria Vega Pizarro (marr. diss. 1988); one *s*; 2nd, 2007, Dr Silvia Janicinova; two *d*. *Educ:* St George's Sch., Rome; St Julian's Sch., Lisbon; Bradfield Coll.; Balliol Coll., Oxford (BA Hons Natural Scis; MA); Middlesex Hosp. Med. Sch. (MB BS). MRCPsych 1988. House surgeon, Middx Hosp., and house physician, Harefield Hosp., 1984–85; W London Psychiatric Registrar Rotation, Charing Cross and Westminster Hosps, 1985–90; Res. Fellow, Charing Cross and Westminster Hosp. Med. Sch., 1988–90; N London Psychiatric Sen. Registrar Rotation, UCH and Middx Hosp., 1990–95; Consultant Psychiatrist and Hon. Sen. Lectr, Camden and Islington NHS Community Trust at UCH and UCL Med. Sch., 1995–99. European Parliament: Member: Economic and Monetary Affairs Cttee, 1999–2001; Foreign Affairs, Human Rights, Common Security and Defence Policy Cttee, 2002– (Vice-Pres., EP-Human Rights Sub-Cttee, 2004–07); substitute Member: Envmt, Public Health and Consumer Affairs Cttee, 1999–2004; Develt Cttee, 2000–01; Economic and Monetary Affairs, 2002–; Conservative delegation: financial services spokesman, 1999–2001, Asst Whip, 2000–03, Dep. Chief Whip, 2003–05; foreign affairs spokesman, 2002–; Member: EP-Slovakia Jt Parly Cttee, 1999–2004; EP-Ukraine, Belarus and Moldova Delgn, 2002–04 (Vice-Pres., Ukraine Delgn, 2004–). Mem. (C), RBK&C, 1998–2000. Freeman: City of London, 2000; City of Cartagena, Columbia, 2006. Commendatore, Order of St Maurice and St Lazarus, 2000; Order of Merit (Ukraine), 2006. *Publications: political:* Community Care: the need for action, 1989; A Marriage of Convenience - or reform of the Community Charge, 1991; *medical:* numerous contribs to med. jls in areas of mood disorders and chronic fatigue syndrome. *Recreations:* travel, surfing the internet. *Address:* (office) 1A Chelsea Manor Street, SW3 5RP. *T:* (020) 7349 6946, *Fax:* (020) 7351 5885; *e-mail:* charles.tannock@europarl.europa.eu, MT@charlestannock.com; *web:* www.charlestannock.com.

TANNOUDJI, Claude C.; *see* Cohen-Tannoudji, C.

TANSEY, Geoffrey William; freelance writer and consultant, since 1981; *b* 3 June 1950; *s* of William Tansey and Lucy Tansey (*née* Dando); *m* 1973, Kathleen Allan Christie; two *d*. *Educ:* Prescot Grammar Sch.; Univ. of Aberdeen (BSc Hons Soil Sci); Sussex Univ. (MSc Hist. and Social Studies of Sci.); Case Western Reserve Univ. (Rotary Foundn Grad. Fellow in Hist. of Sci. and Technol.). Editl asst, Energy Policy, 1974–75; Asst Ed., Food Policy, 1975–77; freelance writer, 1977–78; Tech. Co-operation Officer, Ege Univ., Izmir, ODA, 1978–81. Consultant on develt work in Turkey, Albania, Kazakstan, Mongolia; contributor to BBC, Financial Times and specialist media; advisor on food biodiversity and intellectual property: to Quaker UN Office, Geneva, 2000–07; Quaker Internat. Affairs Prog., Ottawa, 2003–07. Hon. Vis. Prof. in Food Policy, Leeds Metropolitan Univ., 1996–99; Hon. Visiting Fellow: Food Policy Res. Unit, Univ. of Bradford, 1990–97; Centre for Rural Econ., Univ. of Newcastle upon Tyne, 2005–; Hon. Vis. Res. Fellow, Dept of Peace Studies, Univ. of Bradford, 2000–. Joseph Rowntree Charitable Trust funded Visionary, working for a fair and sustainable food system, 2006–. Hon. Campaigns Consultant, World Develt Movt, 1989–94. *Publications:* (ed jtly) A World Divided: militarism and development after the Cold War, 1994; (with A. Worsley) The Food System: a guide, 1995; (ed with J. D'Silva) The Meat Business: devouring a hungry planet, 1999; (ed jtly) Negotiating Health: intellectual property and access to medicines, 2006; (ed with T. Rajotte) The Future Control of Food: a guide to international negotiations and rules on intellectual property, biodiversity and food security, 2008; contrib. various monographs, book chapters and jl articles on food, agriculture, develt and intellectual property. *Recreations:* reading, cinema. *Address:* c/o Joseph Rowntree Charitable Trust, The Garden House, Water End, York YO30 6WQ. *T:* (01904) 627810, *Fax:* (01904) 651990; *e-mail:* geoff.tansey@jrct.org.uk. *Club:* Penn.

TANSEY, Rock Benedict; QC 1990; a Recorder, since 1995; *m* 1964, Wendy Carver; one *s* two *d*. *Educ:* Bristol Univ. (LLB Hons; Dip. Social Studies). Called to the Bar, Lincoln's Inn, 1966, Bencher, 2004. Chm., European Criminal Bar Assoc. of Defence Advocates, 1996–2003. *Recreations:* politics, theatre, opera, football, tennis, golf. *Address:* 25 Bedford Row, WC1R 4HD.

TANSLEY, (Anthony) James (Nicholas); HM Diplomatic Service; Deputy High Commissioner, Nigeria, since 2006; *b* 19 July 1962; *er s* of late Thomas Anthony Tansley and Marian Tansley; *m* 1998, Bláithín Mary Curran; two *s* one *d* (of whom one *s* one *d* are twins). *Educ:* Tonbridge Sch.; St John's Coll., Oxford (MA); Sch. of Oriental and African Studies, Univ. of London (MSc); London Business Sch. (MSc). Joined FCO, 1984: lang. trng, 1986; Second Secretary (Chancery): Riyadh, 1988–89; Baghdad,

1989–91; First Secretary: FCO, 1991–94; Dublin, 1994–98; Counsellor and Dep. Hd of Mission, Muscat, 1998–2001; Sloan Masters Prog., London Business Sch., 2002–03; Hd, Strategic Planning Team, FCO, 2003–05; Hd, British Office, and Consul-Gen., Basra, 2005–06. *Recreations:* Islamic architecture, history, cricket, wine. *Address:* c/o Foreign and Commonwealth Office, King Charles Street, SW1A 2AH.

TANTUM, Geoffrey Alan, CMG 1995; OBE 1981; Middle East consultant; HM Diplomatic Service, retired; *b* 12 Nov. 1940; *s* of George Frederick Tantum and Margaret Amelia Tantum (*née* Goozée); *m* 1st, 1977, Caroline Kent (marr. diss. 2005); three *d*; 2nd, 2007, Carin Lake (*née* Wood); two step *d*. *Educ:* Hampton Grammar Sch.; RMA Sandhurst; St John's Coll., Oxford (MA 1st Class Hons Oriental Studies (Arabic)). MCIL. HM Forces, 1959–66; joined Diplomatic Service, 1969; Kuwait, 1970–72; Aden, 1972–73; FCO, 1973–76; Amman, 1977–80; FCO, 1980–85; Counsellor, Rome, 1985–88; FCO, 1988–95. Mem. Adv. Bd, Good Governance Gp. Order of the Star of Jordan, 2nd cl., 1995. *Publication:* Muslim Warfare: Islamic arms and armour, 1979. *Recreations:* sailing, oriental studies. *Club:* Travellers.

TANZER, John Brian Camille; His Honour Judge Tanzer; a Circuit Judge, since 2001; *b* 27 Dec. 1949; *s* of William and Edith Tanzer; *m* 1980, Suzanne Coates, *qv*; two *s*. *Educ:* Town Sch., NY; St Faith's Sch., Cambridge; The Leys, Cambridge; Keble Coll., Oxford; Sussex Univ. (BA); Inns of Court Sch. of Law. Teacher, Japan, 1968; engr, Southampton, 1973; called to the Bar, Gray's Inn, 1975; in practice, specialising in criminal and common law, Brighton, 1975–91, London, 1991–2001. *Recreations:* sailing, ski-ing, photography, computing, motor-cycling. *Address:* Law Courts, Altyre Road, Croydon CR9 5AB; Woodfield House, Isaacs Lane, Burgess Hill, W Sussex RH15 8RA; *e-mail:* john@tanzer.co.uk. *Clubs:* Travellers, Bar Yacht; Royal Gibraltar Yacht.

TAPLIN, Prof. Oliver Paul, DPhil; FBA 1995; Professor of Classical Languages and Literature, University of Oxford, 1996–2008; Tutorial Fellow in Classics, Magdalen College, Oxford, 1973–2008; *b* 2 Aug. 1943; *s* of Walter Taplin and Susan (*née* Rosenberg); *m* 1st, 1964, Kim Stampfer (marr. diss. 1996); one *s* one *d*; 2nd, 1998, Beaty Rubens; one *d*. *Educ:* Sevenoaks Sch.; Corpus Christi Coll., Oxford (MA; DPhil 1974). Fellow by Examination, Magdalen Coll., Oxford, 1968–72; Fellow, Center for Hellenic Studies, Washington, 1970–71; Lectr, Bristol Univ., 1972–73; Reader in Greek Lit., Oxford Univ., 1994–96. Visiting Professor: Dartmouth Coll., 1981; UCLA, 1987, 1990. Pres., Classical Assoc., 1999. *Publications:* The Stagecraft of Aeschylus, 1977; Greek Tragedy in Action, 1978; Greek Fire, 1989; (jtly) An Odyssey Round Odysseus, 1990; Homeric Soundings, 1992; Comic Angels, 1993; (ed) Literature in the Greek and Roman Worlds, 2000; Pots and Plays, 2007. *Recreations:* theatre, swimming in the Aegean. *Address:* Magdalen College, Oxford OX1 4AU. *T:* (01865) 276069.

TAPP, David Robert George; District Judge (Magistrates' Courts) (formerly Provincial Stipendiary Magistrate): County of Merseyside, 1992–2002; Greater Manchester Magistrates' Court, 2002; *b* 13 Oct. 1948; *s* of Victor George Tapp and May Allen Tapp. *Educ:* Stockport Sch.; Manchester Univ. (LLB Hons). Solicitor. Articled Clerk, Wigan Magistrates' Court, 1971–73; Principal Asst, Eccles Magistrates' Court, 1973–80; Dep. Justices' Clerk, 1980–83, Justices' Clerk, 1983–92, Stoke-on-Trent Magistrates' Court. Mem., British Pottery Manufrs' Fedn Club. *Recreations:* watching sport, waterfowl, music, Manchester City FC, Lancashire CCC.

TAPPER, Prof. Colin Frederick Herbert; Professor of Law, Oxford University, 1992–2002; Fellow, Magdalen College, Oxford, 1965–2002, now Emeritus; *b* 13 Oct. 1934; *s* of Herbert Frederick Tapper and Florence Gertrude Tapper; *m* 1961, Margaret White; one *d*. *Educ:* Bishopshalt Grammar Sch.; Magdalen Coll., Oxford. Lectr, LSE, 1959–65; All Souls Reader in Law, Oxford Univ., 1979–92. Special Consultant on Computer Law to Masons (Solicitors), 1990–2002. Visiting Professor, Universities of: Alabama, 1970; NY, 1970; Stanford, 1975; Monash, 1984; Northern Kentucky, 1986; Sydney, 1989; Western Australia, 1991. *Publications:* Computers and the Law, 1973; Computer Law, 1978, 4th edn 1990; (ed) Crime Proof and Punishment, 1981; (ed) Cross on Evidence, 6th edn 1985, to 11th edn 2007; (ed) Cross and Wilkins Introduction to Evidence, 6th edn 1986; (ed) Handbook of European Software Law, 1993. *Recreations:* reading, computing, writing. *Address:* Corner Cottage, Stonesfield, Oxon OX29 8QA. *T:* (01993) 891284.

TAPPIN, Michael; Lecturer in Politics, School of Politics and the Environment (formerly Department of American Studies), University of Keele, since 1974; *b* 22 Dec. 1946; *s* of Thomas and Eileen Tappin; *m* 1971, Angela Florence (*née* Reed); one *s* one *d*. *Educ:* Univ. of Essex; LSE; Strathclyde Univ. Mem. (Lab), Newcastle-under-Lyme BC, 1980–84; Staffordshire County Council: Mem. (Lab), 1981–97; Chairman: Planning Cttee, 1985–89; Enterprise and Econ. Develt Cttee, 1989–94; European Cttee, 1990–94; Mem. (Lab), Stoke-on-Trent CC, 2004–08 (Cabinet Mem. for Resources, 2006–08; Leader, Labour Gp, 2007–08). MEP (Lab) Staffordshire West and Congleton, 1994–99; contested (Lab) W Midlands Reg., 1999. European Parliament: Member: Budget Cttee, 1994–99; Budget Control Cttee, 1994–99; Substitute Mem., Econ. and Monetary Affairs Cttee, 1994–99; Mem., Delegn for relations with USA, 1994–99. Dep. Chm., Staffs Develt Assoc., 1985–94; Chm., N Staffs Steel Partnership Trng, 2000–04; Member: Stoke-on-Trent Local Strategic Partnership, 2000– (Chair: Health & Social Care Cttee, 2002–04; Econ. Develt and Enterprise Cttee, 2004–07); Bd, N Staffs Regeneration, 2006–08 (Chm., Employment and Enterprise Sub-Cttee, 2006–08). Chm., W Midlands Regl Forum of Local Authorities, 1993–94. Chm., S Stoke Primary Care Trust, 2001–06. Pres., Staffs Ramblers' Assoc., 1998–2000. *Publication:* (jtly) American Politics Today, 1980, 3rd edn 1993. *Recreations:* squash, reading, cinema, theatre. *Address:* 7 Albert Road, Trentham, Stoke-on-Trent, Staffs ST4 8HE. *T:* and *Fax:* (01782) 659554; *e-mail:* michaeltappin@yahoo.com. *Club:* British Pottery Manufacturers Federation (Stoke-on-Trent).

TAPPING, Susan Amanda Mary; Her Honour Judge Tapping; a Circuit Judge, since 2001; *b* 3 Nov. 1953; *d* of Tony and Frankie Tapping; *m* 1988, Michael; one *s* one *d*. *Educ:* Bristol Univ. (LLB). Called to the Bar, Middle Temple, 1975; specialised in criminal law; Asst Recorder, 1995–99; Recorder, 1999–2001. *Address:* Harrow Crown Court, Hailsham Drive, Harrow, Middx HA1 4TU.

TAPPS GERVIS MEYRICK; *see* Meyrick.

TAPSELL, Sir Peter (Hannay Bailey), Kt 1985; MP (C) Louth and Horncastle, since 1997 (Nottingham West, 1959–64; Horncastle, Lincs, 1966–83; East Lindsey (Lincs), 1983–97); *b* Hove, Sussex, 1 Feb. 1930; *s* of late Eustace Bailey Tapsell (39th Central India Horse) and Jessie Maxwell (*née* Hannay); *m* 1st, 1963, Hon. Cecilia Hawke (marr. diss. 1971), 3rd *d* of 9th Baron Hawke; (one *s* decd); 2nd, 1974, Mlle Gabrielle Mahieu, *e d* of late Jean and Bathelde Mahieu, Normandy, France. *Educ:* Tonbridge Sch.; Merton Coll., Oxford (1st Cl. Hons Mod. Hist., 1953; Hon. Postmaster, 1953; MA 1957; Hon. Fellow, 1989). Nat. Service, Subaltern, Royal Sussex Regt, 1948–50 (Middle East). Librarian of Oxford Union, 1953; Rep. Oxford Union on debating tour of United States, 1954 (Trustee, Oxford Union, 1985–93). Conservative Research Department, 1954–57 (Social Services and Agriculture). Personal Asst to Prime Minister (Anthony Eden) during 1955 General Election Campaign. Contested (C) Wednesbury, bye-election, Feb. 1957. Opposition front bench spokesman on Foreign and Commonwealth affairs, 1976–77, on Treasury and economic affairs, 1977–78. Mem., Trilateral Commn, 1979–98. London Stock Exchange, 1957–90; Partner, James Capel & Co., 1960–90. Internat. investment advr to several central banks, foreign banks and trading cos; Hon. Member: Brunei Govt Investment Adv. Bd, 1976–83; Business Adv. Council, UN, 2001–; Hon. Dep. Chm., Mitsubishi Trust Oxford Foundn, 1988–; Member: Court, Univ. of Nottingham, 1959–64; Court, Univ. of Hull, 1966–92; Council, Inst. for Fiscal Studies, 1983–2005. Chm., Coningsby Club, 1957–58. Jt Chm., British-Caribbean Assoc., 1963–64. Mem. Organising Cttee, Zaire River Expedn, 1974–75. Vice Pres., Tennyson Soc., 1966–. Hon. Life Mem., 6th Sqdn RAF, 1971. Brunei Dato, 1971. *Recreations:* travel in Third World, walking in mountains, reading history. *Address:* c/o House of Commons, SW1A 0AA. *T:* (020) 7219 3000. *Clubs:* Athenæum, Carlton, Hurlingham.

TAPSELL, Hon. Sir Peter (Wilfred), KNZM 1997; MBE 1968; FRCSE, FRCS; *b* Rotorua, 21 Jan. 1930; *s* of Peter and May Tapsell; *m* 1956, Margaret Diane Bourke; two *s* two *d*. *Educ:* Rotorua High Sch.; Otago Univ. Med. Sch. (MB ChB 1954). FRCSE 1959; FRCS 1961. Hse surgeon, Waikato Hosp., 1955; demonstrator in anatomy, Sch. of Medicine, Dunedin, 1956; Resident Surgical Officer, Dunedin Public Hosp., 1957–58; post-grad. trng, Royal Infirmary, Edinburgh and London, 1958–61; Resident Surgeon, Woolwich, 1959; Orthopaedics Specialist, Orthopaedic Hosp., Oswestry, 1960–61; Orthopaedic Surgeon, Rotorua and Queen Elizabeth Hosps, 1961–81. MP (Lab) Eastern Maori, NZ, 1981–96; Minister of Internal Affairs, Civil Defence, Minister for the Arts and Associate Minister for Local Govt and Tourism, 1984–87; Minister: of Police, 1987–89; of Forestry and Recreation and Sport, 1987–90; of Lands, Survey and Land Inf. and in charge of Valuation Dept, 1987–90; of Science and DSIR, 1989; of Defence, 1990; Speaker, House of Reps, 1994–96. Dep. Mayor, Rotorua City, 1979–83. Chm., NZ Maori Arts and Crafts Inst., 1973–82. Member Council: Univ. of Waikato, 1975; Waikato Teachers' Trng Coll., 1976. Hon. Fellow, Inst. Architects of NZ, 1986. Played Rugby for Otago and NZ Univs; Vice-Capt., Maori All Blacks tour to Fiji, 1954. Hon. LLD Otago, 1996; Hon. Dr Waikato, 1997. *Recreations:* hunting, shooting, fishing. *Address:* 2 Ngahu Street, Rotorua, New Zealand.

TAPSTER, Caroline Marion; Chief Executive, Hertfordshire County Council, since 2003; *b* 9 April 1957. *Educ:* Weymouth Grammar Sch.; Goldsmiths' Coll., London. Social work services: Dorset, 1978–82; E Sussex, 1982–89; NHS, 1989–90; Kent CC, 1990–95; Hertfordshire County Council, 1995–: Asst Dir (Commng) for Social Services, 1995–2000; Dir, Social Services, 2000–01; Dir, Adult Care Services, 2001–03. *Address:* Hertfordshire County Council, County Hall, Hertford, Herts SG13 8DE. *T:* (01992) 555600, *Fax:* (01992) 555505; *e-mail:* caroline.tapster@hertscc.gov.uk.

TARAR, Muhammad Rafiq; President of Pakistan, 1998–2001; *b* 2 Nov. 1929; *s* of Chaudhry Sardar Tarar; *m* Razia Tarar; three *s* one *d*. *Educ:* Univ. of the Punjab, Lahore (BA, LLB). Pleader, 1951–53; Advocate of the High Court, 1953–66; Additional Dist and Sessions Judge, 1966; Dist and Sessions Judge, 1967–74; Judge, High Court Bench, 1974–89; Chief Justice, Lahore High Court, 1989–91; Judge, Supreme Court of Pakistan, 1991–94. Mem., Senate, 1997–98. *Recreations:* reading, walking. *Club:* Islamabad (Islamabad).

TARASSENKO, Prof. Lionel, DPhil; FREng; FIET; Professor of Electrical and Electronic Engineering, and Fellow of St John's College, since 1997, and Director, Institute of Biomedical Engineering, since 2008, University of Oxford; *b* 17 April 1957; *s* of Sergei and Rachel Tarassenko; *m* 1st, 1978, Lady Ann Mary Elizabeth (marr. diss. 2001), *d* of 6th Earl of Craven; two *s* one *d*; 2nd, 2001, Anne Elizabeth Le Grice (*née* Moss); two step *s* one step *d*. *Educ:* Keble Coll., Oxford (BA 1978; Edgell Shepee Prize, 1978; MA; DPhil 1985). FIET (FIEE 1996). Electronics Engr, Racal Research Ltd, 1978–81; Lectr in Engrg Science, and Fellow of St Hugh's Coll., Oxford Univ., 1988–97. Founder Director: Third Phase Ltd, 2000–02; Oxford BioSignals Ltd, 2000–; t+ Medical (formerly e-San) Ltd, 2002–. Scientific co-ordinator, Foresight Project on Cognitive Systems, OST, DTI, 2002–04. Chm., Oxford Pastorate Trust, 2006–. FREng 2000. BCS Medal, 1996; Rolls-Royce Chairman's Award, 2001; Silver Medal, Royal Acad. of Engrg, 2006; Innovation in Engrg IT Award, IET, 2006; Sir Henry Royce Award for High Valve Patent, IET, 2008. *Publications:* (with A. F. Murray) Analogue Neural VLSI, 1994; A Guide to Neural Computing Applications, 1998; (ed jtly) Cognitive Systems: information processing meets brain science, 2005; contribs to jls on electronics, signal processing and artificial intelligence. *Recreations:* family life, football. *Address:* Department of Engineering Science, University of Oxford, Parks Road, Oxford OX1 3PJ. *T:* (01865) 617674.

TARBAT, Viscount; Colin Ruaridh Mackenzie; *b* 7 Sept. 1987; *s* and *heir* of Earl of Cromartie, *qv*.

TARGETT, Prof. Geoffrey Arthur Trevor, PhD, DSc; Professor of Immunology of Protozoal Diseases, London School of Hygiene and Tropical Medicine, 1983–2006, now Emeritus; *b* 10 Dec. 1935; *s* of Trevor and Phyllis Targett; *m* 1st, 1958, Sheila Margaret Gibson (*d* 1988); two *s* three *d*; 2nd, 1997, Julie Ann Thompson. *Educ:* Nottingham Univ. (BSc Hons Zool. 1957); London Univ. (PhD 1961; DSc 1982). Research Scientist: MRC Bilharzia Res. Gp, 1957–62; Nat. Inst. for Med. Res., 1962–64; Lectr, Dept of Natural History, St Andrews Univ., 1964–70; London School of Hygiene and Tropical Medicine: Sen. Lectr, 1970–76; Reader, 1976–83; Hd of Dept of Med. Parasitology, 1988–97; Acting Dean, 2000. Develt Ambassador, Gates Malaria Partnership, 2007– (Dep. Dir, 2000–05). *Publications:* Malaria: waiting for the vaccine, 1991; numerous papers in internat. med. and scientific jls. *Recreations:* golf, music, travel. *Address:* London School of Hygiene and Tropical Medicine, Keppel Street, WC1E 7HT. *T:* (020) 7299 4708.

TARJANNE, Pekka; Chairman, Futurice Ltd, Finland, since 2002; *b* 19 Sept. 1937; *s* of P. K. Tarjanne and Annu Tarjanne; *m* 1962, Aino Kairamo; two *s* one *d* (and one *d* decd). *Educ:* Helsinki Univ. of Technology (Dr Tech. 1962). Prof. of Theoretical Physics, Univ. of Oulu, 1965–66, Univ. of Helsinki, 1967–77. MP, Finland, 1970–77; Minister of Communications, 1972–75; Dir Gen., Posts and Telecommunications, 1977–89; Sec. Gen., ITU, UN, 1989–99; Vice-Chm., Project Oxygen, 1999–2000; Exec. Co-ordinator, ICT Task Force, UN, 2001–03. Chm., Internat. Selection Bd, Millennium Technology Prize, Finland, 2003–. Commander, Order of White Rose of Finland, 1977; Grand Cross, Order of Finnish Lion, 1998; Comdr, Legion of Honour (France), 1999.

TARLO, Christine; *see* McCafferty, C.

TARN, Prof. John Nelson, OBE 1992; DL; Professor of Architecture, 1995–99 (Roscoe Professor, 1974–95), and Pro-Vice-Chancellor, 1988–91 and 1994–99, University of Liverpool; *b* 23 Nov. 1934; *s* of Percival Nelson Tarn and Mary I. Tarn (*née* Purvis); unmarried. *Educ:* Royal Grammar Sch., Newcastle upon Tyne; Univ. of Durham (1st cl. hons BArch); Univ. of Cambridge (PhD). FRIBA, FRSA, FRHistS, FSA. Lectr in Architecture, Univ. of Sheffield, 1963–70; Prof. of Architecture, Univ. of Nottingham,

1970–73; Actg Vice-Chancellor, 1991–92, Public Orator, 1994–2002, Liverpool Univ. Member: Professional Literature Cttee, RIBA, 1968–77; RIBA Educn Cttee, 1978–97 (Vice-Chm., 1983–95; Chm., Moderators and Examiners Cttee, 1975–97); Council, RIBA, 1987–93; Council, ARCUK, 1980–90 (Vice-Chm., 1986–87; Chm., 1987–90; Vice-Chm., Bd of Educn, 1981–83, Chm., 1983–86); Technology Sub-Cttee, UGC, 1974–84; Adv. Cttee on Architectural Educn to EEC, Brussels, 1987–90; CNAA Built Environment Bd, 1987–90; Ministerial nominee, Peak Park Jt Planning Bd, 1973–82, a rep. of Greater Manchester Council, PPJPB, 1982–86 (Vice-Chm. of Bd, 1981–86; co-opted Mem., Planning Control Cttee and Park Management Cttee, 1986–97; Chm., Planning Control Cttee, 1979–97); Mem., National Parks Review Cttee, 1990. Trustee, Museums and Art Galls in Merseyside, 1996–2006 (Chm., Building and Design Cttee, 1996–2006). Chm., Art and Architecture Dept, Liturgy Commn, Archdio. of Liverpool, 1978–; Member: Design and Planning Cttee, Central Council for Care of Churches, 1981–86; DAC for Derby, 1979–93; Liverpool Cathedral Adv. Cttee, 1992–; Sub-cttee for Patrimony, Catholic Bishops' Conf. for England and Wales, 1995–2001. Chm., Riverside Gp (formerly Riverside Housing Assoc.), 1998– (Dep. Chm., 1997–98). Pres., Wirral Soc., 2001–; Vice-President: Peak Dist and S Yorks CPRE, 2002–; Merseyside Civic Soc., 2007–. DL Merseyside, 1999. Hon. Fellow, Chinese Univ. of HK, 2004. DUniv Sheffield Hallam, 1997; Hon. LLD Liverpool, 1999. *Publications:* Working Class Housing in Nineteenth Century Britain, 1971; The Peak District National Park: its architecture, 1971; Five Per Cent Philanthropy, 1974; (adv. ed.) Sir Banister Fletcher's History of Architecture, 19th edn, 1987. *Recreations:* music, cooking. *Address:* 2 Ashmore Close, Barton Hey Drive, Caldy, Wirral CH48 2JX. *Club:* Athenæum.

TARR, Robert James; Principal, The OakVine Consultancy, since 1997; Director, OakVine.net, since 1999; *b* 8 June 1944; *s* of Jack William Tarr; *m* 1966, Linda Andrews. *Educ:* Whytemead and Downsbrook Schools, Worthing; Worthing High Sch. for Boys; BSc(Econ) Hons London, 1977; BA Open Univ., 1979. CPFA (IPFA 1967); FCILT (FCIT 1989). W Sussex CC, Worthing BC, Denbighshire CC, Sunderland Met. BC to 1975; Corporate Planning Co-ordinator and Head of Policy Unit, Bradford Met. Council, 1975–81; Chief Exec., Royal Borough of Kingston upon Thames, 1981–83; Chief Exec. and Town Clerk, Coventry City Council, 1983–87; Dir Gen., Centro (W Midlands PTE), 1987–95; Sec. Gen., Light Rail Transit Assoc., 1997–99. *Publications:* contribs to jls and conf. papers. *Recreations:* viticulture and wine-making, soaking up sun and scenery, the Pre-Raphaelites and Victorian architecture, mountains and alpine flowers, canal-boating, photography, computing, amateur radio (call sign G3PUR), keeping fit.

TARRANT, Christopher John, OBE 2004; radio and television presenter, producer and writer; *b* 10 Oct. 1946; *s* of late Major Basil Tarrant, MC, and of Joan Ellen Tarrant (*née* Cox); *m* 1st, 1977, Sheila Roberton (marr. diss.); two *d*; 2nd, 1991, Ingrid Dupré (marr. diss. 2008); one *s* one *d*. *Educ:* King's Sch., Worcester; Univ. of Birmingham (BA Hons). *Television* includes: presenter and writer, ATV Today, 1972–74; presenter, writer and producer: Tiswas, 1974–82; OTT, 1981–83; presenter: Everybody's Equal, 1989–91; Tarrant on Television, 1989–; Lose a Million, 1993; Pop Quiz, 1994–95; Man o Man, 1996–98; Who Wants to be a Millionaire?, 1998–; *radio:* presenter, Breakfast Show, Capital Radio, 1987–2004. Sony Radio Awards: Radio Personality of the Year, 1990; Best Use of Comedy, 1990; Silver Medal, 1992, 1993; Best Breakfast Show, 1995; Gold Award, 2001; Best On-Air Personality, Internat. Radio Fest. of NY, 1987; Radio Personality of the Year, TRIC, 1989; Ind. Radio Personality, Variety Club of GB, 1991; Best Breakfast Show, NY World Awards, 1997; ITV Personality of the Year, Variety Club of GB, 1998; GQ Radio Man of the Year, 1999; Best TV Performer in non-acting role, BPG TV Awards, 1999; Nat. TV Awards Special Recognition, 2000; Lifetime Achievement Award, ITV, 2000; Lifetime Achievement Award, Radio Acad., 2002; Lifetime Achievement Award, British Comedy Awards, 2006. Pres., Anglers' Conservation Assoc., 2002–04. *Publications:* Ken's Furry Friends, 1986; Fishfriar's Hall Revisited, 1987; Ready Steady Go, 1990; Rebel Rebel, 1991; Tarrant off the Record, 1997; The Ultimate Book of Netty Nutters, 1998; Tarrant on Millionaires, 1999; Millionaire Moments, 2002; Tarrant on Top of the World: in search of the polar bear, 2005. *Recreations:* fishing, cricket. *Address:* c/o Paul Vaughan, PVA Management Ltd, Hallow Park, Worcester WR2 6PG. *T:* (01905) 640663, *Fax:* (01905) 641842; *e-mail:* md@pva.co.uk. *Clubs:* Lord's Taverners, White Swan Piscatorials, Red Spinners Fishing, Variety Club of Great Britain.

TARRANT, Prof. John Rex, PhD; DL; Secretary General, Association of Commonwealth Universities, since 2007; *b* 12 Nov. 1941; *s* of Arthur Rex Tarrant and Joan Mary (*née* Brookes); *m* 1991, Biddy Fisher. *Educ:* Marling Grammar Sch., Stroud; Univ. of Hull (BSc; PhD 1966). Asst Lectr, UC, Dublin, 1966–68; University of East Anglia: Sen. Lectr, 1974–82; Dean, Sch. of Envmtl Scis, 1974–77 and 1981–84; Reader, 1982–94; Pro Vice-Chancellor, 1985–88; Dep. Vice-Chancellor, 1989–95; Prof., 1994–95; Hon. Fellow, 1996; Vice-Chancellor and Principal, Univ. of Huddersfield, 1995–2006. Vis. Prof., Dept of Geog., Univ. of Nebraska, 1970; Vis. Lectr, Dept of Geog., Univ. of Canterbury, NZ, 1973; Vis. Res. Associate, Internat. Food Policy Res. Inst., Washington, 1977–78; Vis. Schol., Food Res. Inst., Stanford Univ., USA, 1978; Harris Vis. Prof., Coll. of Geoscis, Texas A&M Univ., 1989. Chm., MLA Yorkshire, 2007–. DL W Yorks, 2007. Hon. DSc: Hull, 2000; Huddersfield, 2007. *Publications:* Agricultural Geography, 1974; Food Policies, 1980; Food and Farming, 1991; contrib. chapters in books; numerous articles in professional jls. *Recreations:* gliding, motor-cycling. *Address:* Association of Commonwealth Universities, Woburn House, 20–24 Tavistock Square, WC1H 9HF. *T:* (020) 7380 6700.

TARTAGLIA, Rt Rev. Philip; *see* Paisley, Bishop of, (RC).

TARUA, Ilinome Frank, CBE 1988 (OBE 1980); Consultant specialising on Papua New Guinea and South Pacific, since 1993; *b* 23 Sept. 1941; *s* of Peni Frank Tarua and Anaiele Tarua; *m* 1970, Susan Christine (*née* Reeves); two *d*. *Educ:* Sydney University; University of Papua New Guinea (BL 1971). Legal Officer, Dept of Law, 1971–72; Legal Constitutional Advisor to Prime Minister, 1972–76; Dep. Perm. Head, Prime Minister's Dept, 1977–78; Secretary to Cabinet, 1978–79; High Commissioner to NZ, 1980; Ambassador to UN, 1980–81; Perm. Head, Dept of Public Service, 1982; Perm. Head, Prime Minister's Dept, 1982–83; High Comr in London, 1983–89, concurrently Ambassador to Greece, Israel and Italy; Consul Gen., Sydney, 1989–91; Consultant Lawyer with Gadens Ridgeway Lawyers, Australia and PNG, 1991–93. *Recreations:* cricket, squash, golf.

TARUSCHIO, Franco Vittorio, Hon. OBE 2003; consultant, chef; chef and restaurateur, Walnut Tree Inn, Abergavenny, 1963–2001; *b* 29 March 1938; *s* of Giuseppe Taruschio and Apina (*née* Cecati); *m* 1963, Ann Forester; one adopted *d* (and one *d* decd). *Educ:* Hotel Sch., Bellagio, Italy. Trainee Chef: Hotel Splendide, Lugano, 1958; Restaurant La Belle Meunière, Clermont-Ferrand, 1959–60; Head Waiter, Three Horseshoes Hotel, Rugby, 1961–63. Cookery sch. teacher, Coleg Gwent, Abergavenny, 2002–. Pres., St Anne's Hospice, Malpas, Gwent, 2001–. *Publications:* Leaves from the Walnut Tree: recipes of a lifetime, 1993; Bruschetta, Crostoni and Crostini, 1995; Franco and Friends: Food from the Walnut Tree, 1997; Ice Creams and Semi Freddi, 1997; 100 Great Pasta Dishes, 2002. *Recreations:* funghi and wild food foraging, swimming, walking. *Address:* The Willows, 26 Pen y Pound Road, Abergavenny, Monmouthshire NP7 7RN. *T:* (01873) 859026.

TASKER, Prof. Philip Westerby, PhD; FRSC, FInstP; Vice Chancellor, De Montfort University, since 1999; *b* 6 July 1950; *s* of John Westerby Tasker and Alianore Doris Tasker (*née* Whytlaw-Gray); *m* 1974, Alison Helen Davis; one *s* one *d*. *Educ:* King Alfred's Grammar Sch., Wantage; Univ. of Birmingham (BSc Chem. 1971; PhD 1974). FInstP 1989; FRSC 1990. Research Fellow: Univ. of Bristol, 1974–75; Theoretical Physics Div., Harwell Lab., UKAEA, 1975–90; Divl Manager, AEA Technol., 1990–93; Chief Exec., Safeguard Internat. 1993–96; Pro-Vice Chancellor, De Montfort Univ., 1996–99. FRSA. *Publications:* contribs to Philosophical Mag., Jl Physics, Faraday Trans, Physical Rev., etc. *Address:* De Montfort University, The Gateway, Leicester LE1 9BH.

TASMANIA, Bishop of, since 2000; **Rt Rev. John Douglas Harrower,** OAM 2000; *b* 16 Oct. 1947; *s* of John Lawrence Harrower and Enid Dorothy Harrower (*née* Thomas); *m* 1970, Gayelene Melva Harrower (*née* Robin); two *s*. *Educ:* Melbourne Univ. (BE 1970, BA 1973); Ridley Coll., ACT (ThL 1992); Bible Col. of Vict., ACT (MA (Theol.) 1996, Adv. Dip. Missiol Studies 1996). CEng 1976; MIChemE 1976. Process Engr, Petroleum Refineries (Aust.) P/L, Melbourne, 1970–72; Project Officer, Tariff Bd, Melbourne, 1972–74; Director: Industry Studies Br., Industries Assistance Commn, 1975; IMPACT Project, Melbourne, 1975–78; Univ. Chaplain, Buenos Aires, 1979–81; Missionary, CMS, Argentina, 1979–88; Exec Chm., CERTEZA-ABUA, Buenos Aires, 1981–87; Gen. Sec., Argentine Univs Bible Assoc., 1981–86; ordained deacon, 1984, priest, 1986, Buenos Aires; Asst Minister, Iglesia Anglicana de San Salvador, Buenos Aires, 1984–88; Vicar: St Paul's, Glen Waverley, Vic, Aust., 1989–95; St Barnabas Anglican Ch, Glen Waverley, 1995–2000; Area Dean, Waverley-Knox, 1992–94; Archdeacon of Kew, Dio. Melbourne, 1994–2000. Dir, World Vision, Australia, 2006–. MAICD 2007. Centenary Medal, Australia, 2003. *Publications:* all in Spanish: Personal Evangelism, 1985, new edn 1996; (with Silvia Chaves) Spiritual Gifts: a body in mission, 1985, new edn 1989; 30 Days with Jeremiah, 1989, new edn 1998; (in English) Cry of Hope, 2001. *Recreations:* reading, pottering in the garden. *Address:* Diocese of Tasmania, GPO Box 748, Hobart, Tas 7001, Australia. *T:* (3) 62202020, *Fax:* (3) 62238968; *e-mail:* bishop@anglicantas.org.au. *Clubs:* Athenæum, Tasmanian (Hobart).

TATA, Dr Jamshed Rustom, FRS 1973; Head, Division of Developmental Biochemistry, National Institute for Medical Research, 1973–96; *b* 13 April 1930; *s* of Rustom and Gool Tata; *m* 1954, Renée Suzanne Zanetto; two *s* one *d*. *Educ:* Univ. of Bombay (BSc); Univ. of Paris, Sorbonne (DèsSc). Post-doctoral Fellow, Sloan-Kettering Inst., New York, 1954–56; Beit Memorial Fellow, Nat. Inst. for Med. Research, 1956–60; Vis. Scientist, Wenner-Gren Inst., Stockholm, 1960–62; Mem., Scientific Staff, MRC, Nat. Inst. for Med. Research, 1962–96. Visiting Professor: King's Coll., London, 1968–69, and 1970–77; Univ. of California, Berkeley, 1969–70; Vis. Senior Scientist, Nat. Institutes of Health, USA, 1977, 1997; Fogarty Scholar, NIH, USA, 1983, 1986, 1989. The Wellcome Trust: Chm., Cell and Molecular Panel, 1990–92; Mem., Basic Sci. Gp, 1992–93; Mem., Internat. Interest Gp, 1997–2002. Chm., Bd of Trustees, Oxford Internat. Biomed. Centre, 1999–2007 (Trustee, 1996–). Non-exec. Dir, Biotech Analytics, 2000–05. Chm., Elections and Awards, Third World Acad. of Sci., 2000–; Mem., Grants Cttee, Royal Soc., 2005–08. Sci. Advr, EU NR Consortium, 2006–. Fellow: Indian Nat. Science Acad., 1978; Third World Acad. of Sci., 1986. Van Meter Award, 1954; Colworth Medal, 1966; Medal of Soc. for Endocrinology, 1973; Jubilee Medal, Indian Inst. of Sci., 1985. *Publications:* (jtly): The Thyroid Hormones, 1959; The Chemistry of Thyroid Diseases, 1960; Metamorphosis, 1996; Hormonal Signalling and Postembryonic Development, 1998; papers in jls of: Biochemistry; Developmental Biology. *Address:* 15 Bittacy Park Avenue, Mill Hill, NW7 2HA. *T:* (020) 8346 6291.

TATCHELL, Peter Gary; gay rights and human rights campaigner; journalist and author; *b* Melbourne, 25 Jan. 1952; *s* of Gordon Basil Tatchell and Mardi Aileen Tatchell (*née* Rhodes, now Nitscke). *Educ:* Mount Waverley High Sch., Melbourne; Polytech. of N London (BSc Hons (Sociol.) 1977). Sec., Christians for Peace, 1970–71; Exec., Vietnam Moratorium Campaign, 1971; Chm., Rockingham Estate Tenants' Assoc., 1980–81; Sec., Southwark and Bermondsey, Labour Party, 1980–85; activist/organiser: Gay Liberation Front London, 1971–73; UK AIDS Vigil Orgn, 1987–89; Green and Socialist Confs, 1987–89; ACT UP London, 1989–91; OutRage!, 1990–. Contested (Lab) Bermondsey by-election, 1983; candidate (ind. green left) London Assembly, 2000; Prospective Parly Cand. (Green), Oxford East, 2007–. Member: NUJ, 1986–; Republic, 2002–; Green Party, 2004–. *Publications:* The Battle for Bermondsey, 1983; Democratic Defence: a non-nuclear alternative, 1985; AIDS: a guide to survival, 1986, 3rd edn 1990; Europe in the Pink: lesbian and gay equality in the New Europe, 1992; Safer Sexy: the guide to gay sex safely, 1994; We Don't Want to March Straight: masculinity, queers and the military, 1995; *contributor:* Nuclear-Free Defence, 1983; Into the Twenty-First Century, 1988; Getting There: steps to a green society, 1990; Anti-Gay, 1996; The Penguin Book of Twentieth Century Protest, 1998; Teenage Sex: what should schools teach children?, 2002; The Hate Debate: should hate be punished as a crime?, 2002; Sex and Politics in South Africa, 2005. *Recreations:* mountain hiking, surfing, art and design, ambushing tyrants and torturers. *Address:* c/o OutRage!, PO Box 17816, London SW14 8WT; *e-mail:* peter@petertatchell.net. *Clubs:* G.A.Y., Heaven.

TATE, Ann; Vice Chancellor, University of Northampton, since 2005; *b* 27 May 1949; *d* of Norman Cooper and Sybil (*née* Judson); *m* 1975, Rodney Tate; one *d*. *Educ:* Queen Elizabeth's Grammar Sch., Middleton; Univ. of London ext. (BSc Hons Sociol. 1970); Bedford Coll., Univ. of London (MSc Sociol. Applied to Medicine 1984). Asst Teacher, Lancs LEA, 1970–71; Lecturer: Belfast Coll. of Business Studies, 1972–74; Ulster Poly., 1974–84; University of Ulster: Sen. Lectr, 1984–95; Pro-Vice-Chancellor, 1995–2002; Rector, UC Northampton, 2002–05. Board Member: HEFCE, 2003–; W Northants Develt Corp., 2005–; Mem., Northants LSC, 2003–. FRSA 1999. DUniv Ulster, 2007. *Recreations:* golf, cooking, walking. *Address:* University of Northampton, Boughton Green Road, Northampton NN2 7AL. *T:* (01604) 892001; *e-mail:* ann.tate@northampton.ac.uk. *Club:* Reform.

TATE, Brian; *see* Tate, R. B.

TATE, Dr (Edward) Nicholas, CBE 2001; Director-General, International School of Geneva, since 2003; *b* 18 Dec. 1943; *s* of Joseph Edwin Tate and Eva Elsie Tate; *m* 1973, Nadya Grove; one *s* two *d*. *Educ:* Huddersfield New Coll.; Balliol Coll., Oxford (Scholar; MA); Univ. of Bristol (PGCE); Univ. of Liverpool (MA; PhD 1985). Teacher, De La Salle Coll., Sheffield, 1966–71; Lectr, City of Birmingham Coll. of Educn, 1972–74; Lectr, then Sen. Lectr, Moray House Coll. of Educn, Edinburgh, 1974–88; Professional Officer, Nat. Curriculum Council, 1989–91; Asst Chief Exec., Sch. Exams and Assessment Council, 1991–93; Asst Chief Exec., 1993–94, Chief Exec., 1994–97, SCAA; Chief Exec., QCA, 1997–2000; Headmaster, Winchester Coll., 2000–03. Trustee, Nat. Trust, 1996–99. Hon. DCL Huddersfield, 1998. *Publications:* various history books for schools;

articles on history and education. *Recreations:* reading, music. *Address:* Ecole Internationale de Genève, 62 route de Chêne, 1208 Geneva, Switzerland. *Club:* Reform.

TATE, Sir (Henry) Saxon, 5th Bt *cr* 1898, of Park Hill, Streatham; CBE 1991; Chairman, London Futures and Options Exchange (formerly London Commodity Exchange Co. Ltd), 1985–91; Director, Tate & Lyle Ltd, 1956–99; *b* 28 Nov. 1931; *er s* of Lt-Col Sir Henry Tate, 4th Bt, TD and his 1st wife, Nairne (*d* 1984), *d* of Saxon Gregson-Ellis, JP; *S* father, 1994; *m* 1st, 1953, Sheila Ann (marr. diss. 1975; she *d* 1987), *e d* of Duncan Robertson; four *s* (incl. twin *s*); 2nd, 1975, Virginia Sturm. *Educ:* Eton; Christ Church, Oxford. National Service, Life Guards (Lieut), 1949–50. Joined Tate & Lyle Ltd, 1952, Director, 1956; Pres. and Chief Executive Officer, Redpath Industries Ltd, Canada, 1965–72; Tate & Lyle Ltd: Chm., Executive Cttee, 1973–78; Man. Dir, 1978–80; Vice Chm., 1980–82. Chief Executive, Industrial Development Bd of NI, 1982–85. Fellow, Amer. Management Assoc., 1972; FCMI (FBIM 1975). *Recreations:* various. *Heir: s* Edward Nicholas Tate, *b* 2 July 1966. *Address:* 26 Cleaver Square, SE11 4EA.

TATE, Dr Jeffrey Philip, CBE 1990; Musical Director, Teatro San Carlo, Naples, since 2005; Chief Conductor, Hamburg Symphoniker, from autumn 2009; *b* 28 April 1943; *s* of Cyril Henry Tate and Ivy Ellen Naylor (*née* Evans). *Educ:* Farnham Grammar Sch.; Christ's Coll., Cambridge (MA; MB, BChir; Hon. Fellow, 1989); St Thomas' Hosp., London. Trained as doctor of medicine, 1961–67; left medicine for London Opera Centre, 1969; joined Covent Garden Staff, 1970; assisted conductors who included Kempe, Krips, Solti, Davies, Kleiber, for performances and recordings; records made as harpsichordist, 1973–77; Assistant to Boulez for Bayreuth Ring, 1976–81; joined Cologne Opera as assistant to Sir John Pritchard, 1977; conducted Gothenberg Opera, Sweden, 1978–80; NY Metropolitan Opera début, USA, 1979; Covent Garden début, 1982; Salzburg Fest. début (world première Henze/Monteverdi), 1985; Principal Conductor, English Chamber Orch., 1985–95; Principal Conductor, 1986–91, Principal Guest Conductor, 1991–94, Royal Opera House, Covent Garden; Chief Conductor and Artistic Dir, Rotterdam Phil. Orch., 1991–94; Chief Guest Conductor, Geneva Opera, 1983–95; Principal Guest Conductor: Orchestre National de France, 1989–98; RAI Nazionale Orch., Turin, 1998–2002 (Hon. Dir, 2002; Hon. Conductor, 2004–); Artistic Dir, Minnesota Orch. Summer Fest., 1997–2000. Appearances with major symph. orchs in Europe and Amer.; numerous recordings with English Chamber Orch. President: ASBAH, 1989–; Music Space Trust, 1991–. Hon. DMus Leicester, 1993. Comdr, Ordre des Arts et des Lettres (France); Chevalier, Légion d'Honneur (France), 1999. *Recreation:* church-crawling, with gastronomic interludes.

TATE, Nicholas; *see* Tate, E. N.

TATE, Prof. (Robert) Brian, FBA 1980; FRHistS; Professor and Head of Department of Hispanic Studies, Nottingham University, 1958–83, retired; *b* 27 Dec. 1921; *s* of Robert and Jane Grantie Tate; *m* 1951, Beth Ida Lewis; one *s* one *d*. *Educ:* Royal Belfast Academical Instn; Queen's Univ. Belfast (MA, PhD). FRHistS 1990. Asst Lectr, Manchester Univ., 1949–52; Lectr, QUB, 1952–56; Reader in Hispanic Studies, Nottingham Univ., 1956–58. Vis. Prof., Univs of Harvard, Cornell, SUNY at Buffalo, Texas and Virginia. Corresponding Fellow: Institut d'Estudis Catalans, Barcelona, 1964; Real Academia de Historia, Madrid, 1974; Real Academia de Buenas Letras de Barcelona, 1980. Hon. DArts Girona, 2004. *Publications:* Joan Margarit i Pau, Cardinal Bishop of Gerona: a biographical study, 1954; Ensayos sobre la historiografía peninsular del siglo XV, 1970; The Medieval Kingdoms of the Iberian Peninsula, in P. E. Russell, Spain: a companion to Spanish studies, 1973; El Cardenal Joan Margarit, vida i obra, 1976; (trans.) Pierre Vilar, A Brief History of Spain, 1978; (with Marcus Tate) The Pilgrim Route to Santiago, 1987; Pilgrimages to St James of Compostella from the British Isles during the Middle Ages, 1990; *edited:* (with A. Yates) Actes del Colloqui internacional de llengua i literatura catalanes, 1976; Essays on Narrative Fiction in the Iberian Peninsula, 1982; (with T. Turville Petre) Two Pilgrim Itineraries of the Later Middle Ages, 1995; *edited with introduction and notes:* Fernán Pérez de Guzmán, Generaciones y Semblanzas, 1965; Fernando del Pulgar, Claros varones de Castilla, 1971, rev. edn 1985; (with I. R. Macpherson) Don Juan Manuel, Libro de los estados, 1974, rev. edn 1991; Anon, Directorio de príncipes, 1977; Alfonso de Palencia, Epistolario, 1983; (with J. H. N. Lawrance) Alfonso de Palencia, Gesta Hispaniensia, vols 1 and 2, 1998, vol. 3, 2008; contrib. articles in numerous learned jls. *Recreations:* architecture and the history of art, jazz. *Address:* 11 Hope Street, Beeston, Nottingham NG9 1DJ. *T:* (0115) 925 1243.

TATE, Sir Saxon; *see* Tate, Sir H. S.

TATE, William John; Director of Legal Services, Independent Police Complaints Commission, since 2004; *b* 12 June 1951; *s* of William Kenneth Tate and Dorothy Tate; *m* 1976, Helen Elizabeth Quick; one *s* one *d*. *Educ:* Eastcliffe Grammar Sch., Newcastle upon Tyne; King's Coll., London (LLB 1973). Called to the Bar, Gray's Inn, 1974; Flt Lieut, RAF Directorate of Legal Services, 1976–78; Solicitor's Office, HM Customs and Excise: Legal Asst, 1978–80; Sen. Legal Asst, 1980–86; Sen. Prin. Legal Officer, 1986–88; Asst Dir, Serious Fraud Office, 1988–96; Dep. Parly Comr for Admin, 1996–99; Solicitor to Bloody Sunday Inquiry, 1999–2003. Non-exec. Dir, Kingston NHS PCT, 2007–. *Publication:* (Delegated Legislation Ed.) Current Law, annually 1975–95. *Recreations:* rowing, reading, music, gardening. *Address:* Independent Police Complaints Commission, 90 High Holborn, WC1V 6BH. *T:* (020) 7166 3038. *Clubs:* Royal Air Force; Kingston Grammar School Veterans Rowing.

TATHAM, David Everard, CMG 1991; HM Diplomatic Service, retired; consultant; *b* 28 June 1939; *s* of late Lt-Col Francis Everard Tatham and of Eileen Mary Wilson; *m* 1963, Valerie Ann Mylechreest; three *s*. *Educ:* St Lawrence Coll., Ramsgate; Wadham Coll., Oxford (BA History). Entered HM Diplomatic Service, 1960; New York, 1962–63; Milan, 1963–67; ME Centre for Arabic Studies, 1967–69; Jeddah, 1969–70; FCO, 1971–74; Muscat, 1974–77; Asst Head of ME Dept, FCO, 1977–80; Counsellor, Dublin, 1981–84; Ambassador to Yemen Arab Republic, also accredited to Republic of Djibouti, 1984–87; Hd of Falkland Is Dept, FCO, 1987–90; Ambassador to Lebanese Republic, 1990–92; Governor, Falkland Is, and Comr for S Georgia and S Sandwich Is, 1992–96; High Comr, Sri Lanka, also accred to Republic of Maldives, 1996–99. Adviser to Palestinian Authy on Diplomatic Trng, 2000; Census Dist Manager, Ledbury/Ross, 2000–01. Chairman: Shackleton Scholarship Fund, 1999–; Falkland Islands Assoc., 2004–. Ed., Dictionary of Falklands Biography Project, 2002–08. *Publication:* The Dictionary of Falklands Biography, 2008. *Recreations:* walking uphill, fishing, historical research. *Address:* c/o Foreign and Commonwealth Office, SW1A 2AH. *T:* (home) (01531) 634085. *Clubs:* Athenæum, Geographical.

See also M. H. Tatham.

TATHAM, Michael Harry; HM Diplomatic Service; Ambassador to Bosnia and Herzegovina, since 2008; *b* 2 July 1965; *s* of David Everard Tatham, *qv*; *m* 1998, Belinda Cherrington. *Educ:* Oundle Sch.; Merton Coll., Oxford (BA Hons). Entered FCO, 1987; Third, later Second, Sec., Prague, 1989–93; FCO, 1993–95; Private Sec. to Minister of State, 1995–96; Dep. Hd of Mission, Sofia, 1997–99; on secondment as Private Sec. to Prime Minister, 1999–2002; Dep. Hd of Mission, Prague, 2002–05; Balkans Co-ordinator and Hd, Western Balkans Gp, 2006–08. *Recreations:* mountain hiking, the music of Bob Dylan, cookery. *Address:* c/o Foreign and Commonwealth Office, SW1A 2AH.

TATTEN, Jonathan Altenburger; Consultant, Denton Wilde Sapte (formerly Denton Hall), Solicitors, since 2008 (Partner, 1983–2008; Managing Partner, 1993–99; Head of European and Competition Law Department, 2003–07); *b* 17 March 1952; *s* of John Stephenson Tatten and Anna Tatten. *Educ:* Duke of York Sch., Nairobi; Exeter Univ. (LLB); Harvard Business Sch. (AMP). Trainee solicitor, Trower Still & Keeling, 1973–76; solicitor, Holman Fenwick & Willan, Solicitors, 1976–83. *Recreations:* opera, pugs, eating. *Address:* The Ferns, St James Street, Dunwich, Suffolk IP17 3DT. *T:* (01728) 0648504.

TATTERSALL, Geoffrey Frank; QC 1992; a Recorder, since 1989; a Deputy High Court Judge, since 2003; *b* 22 Sept. 1947; *s* of late Frank Tattersall and of Margaret (*née* Hassall); *m* 1971, Hazel Shaw; one *s* two *d*. *Educ:* Manchester Grammar Sch.; Christ Church, Oxford (MA Jurisprudence). Called to the Bar, Lincoln's Inn, 1970 (Tancred Studentship in Common Law), Bencher, 1997; in practice, Northern Circuit, 1970–; called to the Bar, NSW, 1992; SC 1995; Judge of Appeal, IOM, 1997–. External Reviewer of Decisions of Dir of Fair Access, 2005–. Lay Chm., Bolton Deanery Synod, 1993–2002; Chm., House of Laity and Vice Pres., Manchester Diocesan Synod, 1994–2003; Mem., Gen. Synod, 1995– (Chm., Standing Orders Cttee, 1999–); Diocesan Chancellor: Carlisle, 2003–; Manchester, 2004–; Dep. Diocesan Chancellor, Durham, 2003–05; Dep. Vicar-Gen., Dio. of Sodor and Man, 2004–08; Chairman: Disciplinary Tribunals under Clergy Discipline Measure, 2006–; Revision Cttees for draft C of E Marriage Measure, 2006–07 and draft Ecclesiastical Offices Measure, 2007–08. Hon. Lay Canon, Manchester Cathedral, 2003–; Parish Clerk, St George-in-the-East. *Recreations:* family, music, travel. *Address:* 12 Byrom Street, Manchester M3 4PP. *T:* (0161) 829 2100.

TATTERSALL, Jane Patricia; *see* Griffiths, J. P.

TATTERSFIELD, Prof. Anne Elizabeth, OBE 2005; MD; Professor of Respiratory Medicine, University of Nottingham, 1984–2005, now Emeritus; Hon. Consultant Physician, City Hospital, Nottingham, 1984–2005; *b* 13 June 1940; *d* of Charles Percival Tattersfield and Bessie Wharton Tattersfield (*née* Walker). *Educ:* Fairfield High Sch., Manchester; Durham Univ. (MB BS 1963); MD Newcastle 1970. MRCP 1966, FRCP 1979. Jun. hosp. posts, Royal Victoria Infirmary, Newcastle, Leicester Royal Infirmary, Central Middx Hosp. and Brompton Hosp., 1963–66; Medical and Research Registrar posts: Central Middx Hosp., 1966–69; Hammersmith Hosp., 1969–71; Sen. Registrar, London Hosp., 1971–74; Sen. Lectr and Reader in Medicine, Southampton Univ., 1974–83. Sir James Wattie Meml Vis. Prof., NZ, 1987. Altounyan Lectr, British Thoracic Soc., 1995; Philip Ellman Lectr, RCP, 1999. Pres., British Thoracic Soc., 2000 (Gold Medal, 2004). *Publications:* (with M. W. McNicol) Respiratory Disease, 1987; contribs to scientific pubns on asthma, airway pharmacol. and lymphangioleiomyomatosis. *Recreations:* travel, opera, gardening. *Address:* Priory Barn, The Hollows, Thurgarton, Notts NG14 7GY. *Club:* Lansdowne.

TATTON-BROWN, Timothy William Trelawny; architectural historian; freelance archaeologist; *b* 3 Feb. 1947; *s* of Robert and Daphne Tatton-Brown; *m* 1979, Veronica Wilson; two *s* two *d*. *Educ:* Tonbridge Sch., Kent; Inst. of Archaeol., University Coll. London (BA Hons Roman Archaeol.). Dir, Canterbury Archaeological Trust, 1975–85; consultant archaeologist: to Canterbury Cathedral, 1976–87; Rochester Cathedral, 1987–2006; Chichester Cathedral, 1988–93; Salisbury Cathedral, 1990–; St George's Chapel, Windsor Castle, 1991–; Westminster Abbey, 1998–2004; Lambeth Palace, 1998–2001; Westminster Sch., 2002–. Chairman: British Brick Soc., 1981–86; Rescue - British Archaeol Trust, 1983–86. Vice Pres., Royal Archaeol Inst., 2008. *Publications:* Great Cathedrals of Britain, 1989; (ed jtly) St Dunstan: his life, times and cult, 1992; Canterbury: history and guide, 1994; Lambeth Palace: a history of the Archbishops of Canterbury and their houses, 2000; The English Cathedral, 2002; (ed with R. Mortimer) Westminster Abbey: the Lady Chapel of Henry VII, 2003; The English Church, 2005; The Abbeys and Priories of England, 2006; (ed with T. Ayers) Medieval Art, Architecture and Archaeology at Rochester, 2006. *Recreations:* choral singing, canal boating, book collecting, walking and landscape study, church crawling. *Address:* Fisherton Mill House, Mill Road, Salisbury, Wilts SP2 7RZ.

TAUBE, Prof. (Hirsch) David, FRCP; Professor of Transplant Medicine, Imperial College London, since 2006; Consultant Nephrologist, St Mary's Hospital, London, Northwick Park Hospital, Harrow, and Royal Brompton Hospital, London, since 1990, and Hammersmith Hospital, London, since 2004; Clinical Director, West London Renal and Transplant Centre, since 2004, and Medical Director, since 2007, Imperial College Healthcare NHS Trust (formerly Hammersmith Hospitals NHS Trust); *b* 4 Oct. 1948; *s* of Ernest and Hilary Taube; *m* 1990, Dr Clare Allen; one *s* one *d*. *Educ:* St Catharine's Coll., Cambridge (BA 1970); Magdalen Coll., Oxford (BM BCh 1970). FRCP 1987. Consultant Nephrologist, King's Coll. Hosp., 1985–90. Chief of Service, W London Renal and Transplant Medicine, St Mary's NHS Trust and Hammersmith Hosps NHS Trust, 2000–04. *Publications:* over 120 articles in learned jls, mainly on transplantation and renal medicine. *Recreations:* swimming, digital photography, work. *Address:* West London Renal and Transplant Centre, Hammersmith Hospital, Du Cane Road, W12 0HJ. *T:* (020) 8383 5183, *Fax:* (020) 7886 6901; 66 Harley Street, W1G 7HD. *T:* (020) 7636 6628, *Fax:* (020) 7631 5341; *e-mail:* davidtaube@msn.com.

TAUBE, Simon Axel Robin; QC 2000; *b* 16 June 1957; *s* of late Nils Taube and of Idonea Taube; *m* 1984, Karen Pilkington; three *d*. *Educ:* Merton Coll., Oxford (BA Hist.). Called to the Bar, Middle Temple, 1980, Bencher, 2008; in practice at Chancery Bar, 1980–. *Recreations:* singing, tennis, hill-walking. *Address:* 10 Old Square, Lincoln's Inn, WC2A 3SU. *T:* (020) 7405 0758.

TAUNTON, Bishop Suffragan of, since 2006; **Rt Rev. Peter David Maurice;** *b* 16 April 1951; *s* of Eric and Pamela Maurice; *m* 1977, Elizabeth Maun; two *s* one *d*. *Educ:* Durham Univ. (BA 1972); Coll. of the Resurrection, Mirfield. Ordained deacon, 1975, priest, 1976; Curate, St Paul, Wandsworth, 1975–79; Team Vicar, Mortlake with E Sheen, 1979–85; Vicar, Holy Trinity, Rotherhithe, 1985–96; RD, Bermondsey, 1991–96; Vicar, All Saints, Tooting, 1996–2003; Archdeacon of Wells, 2003–06. *Recreations:* avid sports fan, enjoying holidays, birdwatching. *Address:* Bishop's Lodge, 72 Bath Road, Wells, Som BA5 3LJ. *T:* (01749) 683146.

TAUNTON, Archdeacon of; *see* Reed, Ven. J. P. C.

TAUSSIG, Andrew John, PhD; Research Associate (Media Programme), Centre for Socio-Legal Studies, University of Oxford, since 2001; *b* 30 March 1944; *s* of Leo Charles Taussig and Magdalene Taussig (*née* Szücs); *m* 1971, Margaret Celia Whines; one *s* two *d*. *Educ:* Bramcote Sch., Scarborough; Winchester Coll. (Schol.); Magdalen Coll., Oxford (MA Hons Modern History 1962); Harvard Univ. (PhD Pol Sci. 1970). British Broadcasting Corporation, 1971–2000: Gen. Trainee, World Service Talks Dept, BBC

North Leeds, and Radio Current Affairs, 1971–72; TV Current Affairs, 1973–80; Special Asst to Dir, News and Current Affairs, 1979–80; Dep. Editor, Nationwide, 1980–81; Chief Asst, TV Current Affairs, 1982–86; Head of Central European Service, 1986–88; Controller, European Services, 1988–94; Regl Head, Europe, 1994–96; Dir, World Service Regions (all foreign lang. services), 1996–2000. Consultant, British Council, World Summit on Inf. Soc., Geneva, 2003; Moderator, Asia-Europe Foundn Colloquium, Larnaca, 2006, Nanjing, 2007. Lectr, Cardiff Univ. Sch. of Journalism, Media and Cultural Studies, 2002–03. Member: Commonwealth Partners for Technol. Management, 2001–; Council, RIIA (Chatham Hse), 2002–05; Internat. Adv. Council, Asia Media Inf. and Communication Centre, 2004–; Trustee, Steering Cttee, Internat. Inst. of Communications, 2005–. Trustee, Voice of the Listener & Viewer, 2004–. MInstD 2002. *Recreations:* photography, travelling. *Address:* 115 Rosebery Road, Langley Vale, Epsom Downs, Surrey KT18 6AB. *T:* (01372) 276257. *Club:* Le Beaujolais.

TAUWHARE, Richard David, MVO 1983; HM Diplomatic Service; Governor, Turks and Caicos Islands, 2005–08; *b* 1 Nov. 1959; *s* of Albert and Ann Tauwhare; *m* 1985, Amanda; one *s* two *d. Educ:* Abingdon Sch.; Jesus Coll., Cambridge (BA Hist. 1980); Sch. of Oriental and African Studies, London. Joined FCO, 1980; Swahili lang. trng, 1982; Third, then Second Sec., Nairobi, 1982–86; Second, then First Sec., UK Delegn to OECD, 1986–89; FCO, 1989–94; First Sec., then Dep. Perm. Rep., UK Disarmament Delegn, Geneva, 1994–99; FCO, 1999–2005. *Recreations:* tennis, golf, reading, travel. *Address:* c/o Foreign and Commonwealth Office, King Charles Street, SW1A 2AH; *e-mail:* Richard.Tauwhare@fco.gov.uk.

TAVARÉ, Sir John, Kt 1989; CBE 1983; CEng; Chairman, Luxonic Lighting plc, 1986–2000; *b* 12 July 1920; *s* of Leon Alfred Tavaré and Grace Tavaré; *m* 1949, Margaret Daphne Wray; three *s* (and one *s* decd). *Educ:* Chatham House, Ramsgate; Bromley Grammar Sch.; King's Coll., London (BScEng 1946). FInstD 1983; FIWEM 1991; FIMechE 1996. Trainee, Thames Board Mills Ltd, 1938–43; Works Manager, Wm C. Jones Ltd, 1946–48; Personnel Administration Ltd, UK, Australia and NZ, 1949–58; Thames Board Mills Ltd (Unilever), 1958–68: Sales and Marketing Dir, 1960–65; Vice-Chm., 1966–68; Paper, Plastics and Packaging Bd, Unilever, 1968–70; Whitecroft plc, 1970–85: Gp Man. Dir, 1973–76; Chm. and Gp Man. Dir, 1976–85. Chm., Mersey Basin Campaign, DoE, 1985–92. Member: Nat. Council, CBI, 1978–85 (Chm., NW Reg., 1980–82); Nat. Rivers Authy Adv. Bd, NW Region, 1989–92. *Recreations:* golf, garden, environment, business. *Address:* The Gables, 4 Macclesfield Road, Prestbury, Macclesfield, Cheshire SK10 4BN. *T:* (01625) 829778.

See also S. Tavaré.

TAVARÉ, Prof. Simon, PhD; Professor of Cancer Research (Bioinformatics), Department of Oncology, and Professor, Department of Applied Mathematics and Theoretical Physics, University of Cambridge, since 2003; Fellow, Christ's College, Cambridge, since 2004; *b* 13 May 1952; *s* of Sir John Tavaré, *qv*; *m* 1973, Caroline Jane Page; one *s* one *d. Educ:* Oundle Sch.; Univ. of Sheffield (BSc 1974, MSc 1975; PhD 1979). CStat 1993. Lectr, Univ. of Sheffield, 1977–78; Res. Fellow, 1978–79, Instructor, 1978–81, Univ. of Utah; Asst and Associate Prof., Colorado State Univ., 1981–85; Associate Prof., Univ. of Utah, 1985–89; Prof., 1989–, George and Louise Kawamoto Chair of Biol Scis, 1998–, USC. Vis. posts at univs in USA, Australia, England, Switzerland and France. Medallion Lectr, Inst. Mathematical Stats, 1993, 2001. FIMS 1992; FAAAS 1998; FASA 2004. *Publications:* (ed with P. J. Donnelly) Progress in Population Genetics and Human Evolution, 1997; (jtly) Logarithmic Combinatorial Structures: a probabilistic approach, 2003; (with O. Zeitouni) Lectures on Probability and Statistics, Ecole d'Etés de Probabilité de Saint-Flour XXXI, 2004; (jtly) Computational Genome Analysis: an introduction, 2005; numerous articles in learned jls. *Address:* Department of Oncology, University of Cambridge, Cancer Research UK Cambridge Research Institute, Li Ka Shing Centre, Robinson Way, Cambridge CB2 0RE. *T:* (01223) 404290, *Fax:* (01223) 404128; *e-mail:* s.tavare@damtp.cam.ac.uk.

TAVENER, Sir John (Kenneth), Kt 2000; composer; *b* 28 Jan. 1944; *m* 1991, Maryanna (*née* Schaefer); one *s* two *d. Educ:* Highgate Sch.; Royal Academy of Music (LRAM). Prof. of Composition, Trinity Coll. of Music, London, 1968–. Hon. FRAM, Hon. FTCL, Hon. FRSCM. Russian Orthodox religion. Apollo Award, Friends of Greek Nat. Opera, 1993. *Compositions include: orchestral:* Grandma's Footsteps; Theophany; Towards the Son: Ritual Procession; *solo instrument/voice and orchestra:* Eternal Memory; Ikon of Eros; Palintropos; Piano Concerto; The Protecting Veil; The Repentant Thief; Tears of the Angels; *choral and orchestra:* Akhmatova Requiem; Eternity's Sunrise; Agraphon; In Alium; The Immurement of Antigone; Lament for Jerusalem; Sappho; Lyrical Fragments; 16 Haiku of Seferis; Three Holy Sonnets; Akathist of Thanksgiving; The Apocalypse; Celtic Requiem; Ikon of St Seraphim; Introit for March 27th, the Feast of St John Damascene; Kyklike Kinesis; The Last Discourse; Resurrection; Ultimos Ritos; The Veil of the Temple; We Shall See Him As He Is; The Whale; Risen!; Agraphon; Let's Begin Again; Total Eclipse; Fall and Resurrection; *choral:* Annunciation; Canticle of the Mother of God; A Christmas Round; Eonia; The Great Canon of St Andrew of Crete; Ikon of Light; Ikon of St Cuthbert of Lindisfarne; Ikon of the Trinity; The Lamb; Lament of the Mother of God; Let Not the Prince be Silent; Liturgy of St John Chrysostom; O, Do Not Move; Orthodox Vigil Service; Panikhida; Prayer for the World; Psalm 121, I Will Lift Up Mine Eyes Unto The Hills; Song for Athene; Thunder Entered Her; Today the Virgin; Two Hymns to the Mother of God; The Tyger; The Uncreated Eros; A Village Wedding; The World is Burning; Three Antiphons; Innocence; Svyati (O Holy One); Amen; As One Who Has Slept; Hymn of the Unwaning Light; Notre Père; Prayer to the Holy Trinity; Wedding Prayer; *choral and instruments:* The Myrrh-Bearer; Hymns of Paradise; Responsorium in Memory of Annon Lee; Akhmatova Songs; The Child Lived; Lamentation, Last Prayer and Exaltation; Let's Begin Again; Meditation on the Light; Six Abbasid Songs; Three Sections from T. S. Eliot's 'The Four Quartets'; Three Surrealist Songs; Feast of Feasts; Schuon Lieder, 2004; *chamber:* Greek Interlude; The Hidden Treasure; In Memoriam Igor Stravinsky; The Last Sleep of the Virgin; Trisagion; Mandelion; Mandoodles; Palin; Thrinos; Lament for Phaedra; Chant for Solo Cello; Akhmatova Songs; Diodia; Vlepondas; Samaveda; Kaleidoscopes; *opera:* Cain and Abel (1st Prize, Monaco); The Cappemakers; Eis Thanaton; A Gentle Spirit; Mary of Egypt; Thérèse. *Publications:* (jtly) Ikons: meditations in words and music, 1994; (ed Brian Keeble) The Music of Silence: a composer's testament, 1999. *Address:* c/o Chester Music, 14–15 Berners Street, W1T 3LJ.

TAVERNE, family name of **Baron Taverne**.

TAVERNE, Baron, *cr* 1996 (Life Peer), of Pimlico in the City of Westminster; **Dick Taverne;** QC 1965; Chairman, Monitoring Board, AXA Sun Life plc, since 2001 (Director, 1972–97, Chairman, 1997–2001, AXA Equity & Law Life Assurance Society plc); *b* 18 Oct. 1928; *s* of Dr N. J. M. and Mrs L. V. Taverne; *m* 1955, Janice Hennessey; two *d. Educ:* Charterhouse School; Balliol College, Oxford (First in Greats). Oxford Union Debating tour of USA, 1951. Called to Bar, 1954. MP (Lab) Lincoln, March 1962–Oct. 1972, resigned; MP (Democratic Lab) Lincoln, March 1973–Sept. 1974; Parliamentary Under-Secretary of State, Home Office, 1966–68; Minister of State, Treasury, 1968–69; Financial Secretary to the Treasury, 1969–70. Chm., Public Expenditure (General) Sub-Cttee, 1971–72. Institute for Fiscal Studies: First Dir, 1970; Dir-Gen., 1979–81; Chm., 1981–82; Chm., Public Policy Centre, 1984–87. Non-exec. Dir, BOC Gp, 1975–95; Dir, PRIMA Europe Ltd, 1987–98 (Chm., 1991–93; Pres., 1993–98). Mem., Internat. Ind. Review Body to review workings of European Commn, 1979. Chairman: Alcohol and Drug Prevention and Treatment Ltd, 1996–; Sense About Science, 2002–. Member: Nat. Cttee, SDP, 1981–87; Federal Policy Cttee, Liberal Democrats, 1989–90. Contested (SDP): Southwark, Peckham, Oct. 1982; Dulwich, 1983. *Publications:* The Future of the Left: Lincoln and after, 1973; The March of Unreason - Science, Democracy and the New Fundamentalism, 2005. *Recreation:* sailing. *Address:* 60 Cambridge Street, SW1V 4QQ.

See also S. Taverne.

TAVERNE, Suzanna; Chairman, National Council for One Parent Families, since 2002 (Trustee, since 1996); non-executive Director, Nationwide Building Society, since 2005; *b* 3 Feb. 1960; *d* of Baron Taverne, *qv* and Janice Taverne (*née* Hennessey); *m* 1993, Marc Vlessing; one *s* one *d. Educ:* Balliol Coll., Oxford (BA Hons 1982). S. G. Warburg and Co. Ltd, 1982–90; Head, Strategic Planning, 1990–92, Finance Dir, 1992–94, Newspaper Publishing plc; Consultant, Saatchi and Saatchi, 1994–95; Dir, Strategy and Develt, then Man. Dir FT Finance, Pearson plc, 1995–98; Man. Dir, British Museum, 1999–2002; Dir of Ops, Imperial Coll. London, 2003–05. *Address:* 35 Camden Square, NW1 9XA.

TAVERNER, Marcus Louis; QC 2000; *b* 24 April 1958; *s* of Geoffrey Clifford Taverner, DFC and Mildred Taverner (née Thomas); *m* 1983, Dr Deborah Mary Hall; one *s* three *d. Educ:* Monmouth Sch.; Leicester Univ. (LLB Hons); King's Coll. London (LLM). Called to the Bar, Gray's Inn, 1981, Bencher, 2007. *Recreations:* my 4 children, poetry, trees, guitar, theatre, dramatics, Robin Trower, Stevenage Borough FC. *Address:* Benington Park, Benington, Stevenage, Herts SG2 7BU. *T:* (01438) 869007.

TAVERNOR, Prof. Robert William, PhD; RIBA; Professor of Architecture and Urban Design, and Director, Cities Programme, London School of Economics, since 2005; *b* 19 Dec. 1954; *s* of Michael Frederic Tavernor and Elisabeth Veronica Tavernor (*née* Hooker); *m* 1976, Denise Alexandra Mackie; one *s* two *d. Educ:* Poly. of Central London (BA 1976; DipArch with Dist. 1979); British Sch. at Rome (Scholar in Arch. 1980); St John's Coll., Cambridge (PhD 1985). RIBA 1985. Lectr in Arch., Univ. of Bath, 1987–92; Forbes Prof. of Arch., Univ. of Edinburgh, 1992–95; University of Bath: Prof. of Arch., 1995–2005; Hd, Dept of Arch. and Civil Engrg, 2003–05. Dir, Professor Robert Tavernor Consultancy Ltd, 2000–. Visiting Professor: UCLA, 1998; Univ. of São Paulo, 2004; EU Vis. Scholar, Texas A&M Univ., 2002. *Publications:* Palladio and Palladianism, 1991; (ed) Edinburgh, 1996; On Alberti and the Art of Building, 1998; (ed jtly) Body and Building: essays on the changing relation of body and architecture, 2002; Smoot's Ear: the measure of humanity, 2007; *translations:* (jtly) Alberti, On the Art of Building in Ten Books, 1988; (jtly) Palladio, The Four Books on Architecture, 1997. *Recreations:* writing, running with Archie, watching Bath Rugby. *Address:* 6 Springfield Place, Lansdown, Bath BA1 5RA; *e-mail:* r.tavernor@lse.ac.uk.

TAVINOR, Very Rev. Michael Edward; Dean of Hereford, since 2002; *b* 11 Sept. 1953; *s* of Harold and Elsie Tavinor. *Educ:* Durham Univ. (BA Music 1975); Emmanuel Coll., Cambridge (PGCE 1976); King's Coll., London (AKC, MMus 1977); Ripon Coll., Cuddesdon (BA 1981, MA 1986, Oxon). ARCO 1977. Ordained deacon, 1982, priest, 1983; Curate, St Peter, Ealing, 1982–85; Precentor, Sacrist and Minor Canon, Ely Cathedral, 1985–90; Priest i/c, Stuntney, 1987–90; Vicar, Tewkesbury Abbey with Walton Cardiff, 1990–2002, also Twyning, 1999–2002. Hon. Canon, Gloucester Cathedral, 1997–2002. Pres., Ch Music Soc., 2003–. Hon. FGCM, 2006. *Publications:* Pilgrim Guide to Tewkesbury Abbey, 1998; Pilgrim Guide to Hereford Cathedral, 2003; (contrib.) Sacred Space: House of God, Gate of Heaven, 2007. *Recreations:* walking, music, gardening, coin collecting. *Address:* The Deanery, College Cloisters, Cathedral Close, Hereford HR1 2NG. *T:* (01432) 374203; *e-mail:* Dean@herefordcathedral.org.

TAVISTOCK, Marquess of; Henry Robin Charles Russell; *b* 7 June 2005; *s* and *heir* of Duke of Bedford, *qv*.

TAVNER, Teresa, (Terry); Consultant Editor, since 2005; Editor, She Magazine, 2003–05; *b* 18 Jan. 1952; *d* of Bernard Joseph Hayes and Hanorah Hayes; *m* 1972, Barry Tavner; one *s* one *d. Educ:* Notre Dame Grammar Sch., Battersea. Sub Ed. and Fiction Ed., Honey mag., 1981–84; Dep. Chief Sub-Ed., then Chief Sub-Ed., then Asst Ed., She mag., 1984–88; Editor: Chat mag., 1988–96; Eva mag., 1997–98; Woman's Own, 1998–2002. Editors' Editor, BSME, 1990. *Recreations:* ski-ing, travelling, cinema, reading, socialising. *Address: e-mail:* ttavner@aol.com.

TAYLER, His Honour (Harold) Clive; QC 1979; a Circuit Judge, 1984–99; *b* 4 Nov. 1932; *m* 1959, Catherine Jane (*née* Thomas); two *s* one *d. Educ:* Solihull Sch.; Balliol Coll., Oxford (Eldon Schol.); BCL and BA (Jurisprudence); Inner Temple Entrance Schol. Called to the Bar, Inner Temple, 1956; in practice, Birmingham, 1958–84, and London, 1979–84; a Recorder of the Crown Court, 1974–84; Midland and Oxford Circuit.

TAYLOR; *see* Suenson-Taylor, family name of Baron Grantchester.

TAYLOR, family name of **Barons Kilclooney**, **Taylor of Blackburn**, **Taylor of Holbeach**, **Taylor of Warwick** and **Baroness Taylor of Bolton**.

TAYLOR OF BLACKBURN, Baron *cr* 1978 (Life Peer), of Blackburn in the County of Lancashire; **Thomas Taylor,** CBE 1974 (OBE 1969); JP; DL; *b* 10 June 1929; *s* of James and Edith Gladys Taylor; *m* 1950, Kathleen Nurton; one *s. Educ:* Mill Hill Primary Sch.; Blakey Moor Elementary Sch. Mem., Blackburn Town Council, 1954–76 (Leader, 1972–76; Chm., Policy and Resources Cttee, 1972–76). Chm., Electricity Cons. Council for NW and Mem. Norweb Bd, 1977–80; Former Member: NW Econ. Planning Council; NW AHA (Chm. Brockhall HMC, 1972–74, Vice-Chm. Blackburn HMC, 1964–74); Council for Educational Technology in UK; Nat. Foundn for Educn Research in Eng. and Wales; Schools Council; Regional Rent Tribunal; Nat. Foundn for Visual Aids. Chm., Govt Cttee of Enquiry into Management and Govt of Schools, 1977. Former Mem., Public Schools Commn; past Pres., Assoc. of Educn Cttees. Former Dir, Councils and Education Press. University of Lancaster: Founder Mem. and Mem. Council; author of Taylor Report on problems in univs; Dep. Pro-Chancellor, 1972–95. Former Dep. Dir, Central Lancs Family and Community Project. Non-executive Director: Drax Ltd; A Division Hldgs; Consultant: BAE Systems plc; Initial Electronic Security Systems Ltd; Adviser: Electronic Data Systems Ltd; AES Electric Ltd; United Utilities plc; Experian; Capgemini UK plc; Pres., Wrens Hotel Gp. Pres., Friends of Blackburn Mus. and Art Gall.; Vice-Pres., Assoc. of Lancastrians in London; Patron: Holidays for Carers; Lancs Wildlife Trust; Friends of Real Lancs; Outreach Schs. Elder, URC; Pres., Free Church Council, 1962–63. Hon. LLD Lancaster, 1996. JP Blackburn, 1960, DL Lancs, 1994; former Chm., Juvenile Bench. Freeman: Blackburn, 1992; City of London. *Address:*

Mabelle, Promenade, Knott End-on-Sea, Poulton-le-Fylde, Lancs FY6 0AN. *T:* (01253) 812736.

TAYLOR OF BOLTON, Baroness *cr* 2005 (Life Peer), of Bolton in the county of Greater Manchester; **Winifred Ann Taylor;** PC 1997; Parliamentary Under-Secretary of State, Ministry of Defence, since 2007; *b* Motherwell, 2 July 1947; *m* 1966, David Taylor; one *s* one *d.* *Educ:* Bolton Sch.; Bradford Univ.; Sheffield Univ. Formerly teaching. Past part-time Tutor, Open Univ.; interested in intelligence and security matters, and education. Monitoring Officer, Housing Corp., 1985–87. Member: Association of Univ. Teachers; APEX; Holmfirth Urban District Council, 1972–74. Contested (Lab): Bolton W, Feb. 1974; Bolton NE, 1983. MP (Lab): Bolton W, Oct. 1974–1983; Dewsbury, 1987–2005. PPS to Sec. of State for Educn and Science, 1975–76; PPS to Sec. of State for Defence, 1976–77; an Asst Govt Whip, 1977–79; Opposition front bench spokesman on education, 1979–81, on housing, 1981–83, on home affairs, 1987–90 (Shadow Water Minister, 1988), on environment, 1990–92, on education, 1992–94; Shadow Chancellor of Duchy of Lancaster, 1994–95; Shadow Leader of H of C, 1994–97; Pres. of Council and Leader of H of C, 1997–98; Parly Sec. to HM Treasury (Govt Chief Whip), 1998–2001. Mem., Select Cttee on Standards and Privileges, 1995–97; Chairman, Select Committee: on modernisation, 1997–98; on intelligence and security, 2001–05. Hon. Fellow: Birkbeck Coll., 1995; St Anthony's Coll., Oxford, 2004. *Address:* House of Lords, SW1A 0PW.

TAYLOR OF HOLBEACH, Baron *cr* 2006 (Life Peer), of South Holland in the County of Lincolnshire; **John Derek Taylor,** CBE 1992; Chairman, Conservatives Abroad, since 2001; Deputy Chairman, Conservative Party, and Chairman, National Conservative Convention, 2000–03; *b* 12 Nov. 1943; *s* of late Percy Otto Taylor and of Ethel Taylor (*née* Brocklehurst); *m* 1968, Julia Aileen Cunnington, *d* of late Leslie and Evelyn Cunnington, Bedford; two *s.* *Educ:* Holbeach Primary Sch.; St Felix Sch., Felixstowe; Bedford Sch. Dir, family horticultural and farming businesses, 1968–. Dir, 1990–, Chm., 2000–, Springfields Horticl Soc. Ltd, and associated cos. Chairman: EC Working Party on European Bulb Industry, 1982; NFU Bulb Sub-cttee, 1982–87. Governor: Glasshouse Crops Res. Inst., 1984–88; Inst. of Horticl Res., 1987–90; Mem., Horticl Develt Council, 1986–91. Member, Minister of Agriculture's Regional Panel: Eastern Reg., 1990–92; E Midlands Reg., 1992–96. Chm., Holbeach and E Elloe Hosp. Charitable Trust, 1989–2006, now Patron; Trustee, Brogdale Horticl Trust, 1998–2005. Mem., Lincoln Diocesan Bd of Finance, 1995–2001 (Mem., Assets Cttee, 1995–2001, 2003–). East Midlands Conservative Council: Mem., Exec. Cttee, 1966–98; Hon. Treas., 1984–89; Chm., 1989–94; Mem., Cons. Bd of Finance, 1985–89; Mem., Cons. Bd of Mgt, 1996–98; National Union of Conservative Associations: Member: Exec. Cttee, 1966–68 and 1984–98; Gen. Purposes Cttee, 1988–98; Standing Rev. Cttee, 1988–98; Agents Employment Adv. Cttee, 1988–94; Agents Exam Bd, 1994–98; Vice Pres., 1994–97; Pres. and Cons. Conf. Chm., 1997–98; Chairman: Candidates Cttee, Cons. Party, 1997–98, 2002–05; Cons. Party Constitutional Review, 1998–2000; Cons. Agents' Superannuation Fund, 2006–. House of Lords: Opposition Whip, 2006–; Opposition Spokesman: on Envmt, and on Wales, 2006–07; on Work and Pensions, 2006–; Shadow Minister, Environment, Food and Rural Affairs, 2007–. Founder Chm., local Young Cons. Br., 1964; Mem., Holland with Boston Cons. Assoc., 1964–95 (formerly Treas., Vice Chm., Chm. and Pres.); Pres., S Holland and The Deepings Cons. Assoc., 1995–2001, now Patron. Contested (C): Chesterfield, Feb. and Oct. 1974; Nottingham, EP elections, 1979. FRSA 1994. *Publication:* (ed) Taylor's Bulb Book, 1994. *Recreations:* English landscape and vernacular buildings, France, literature, arts, music. *Address:* House of Lords, SW1A 0PW. *Club:* Farmers'.

TAYLOR OF WARWICK, Baron *cr* 1996 (Life Peer), of Warwick in the county of Warwickshire; **John David Beckett Taylor;** barrister-at-law; writer; radio and television presenter; *b* 21 Sept. 1952; *s* of late Derief David Samuel Taylor and of Enid Maud Taylor; *m* 1981, Dr Jean Katherine Taylor (*née* Binysh); one *s* two *d.* *Educ:* Univ. of Keele (BA Hons Law). Called to the Bar, Gray's Inn, 1978; practised on Midland and Oxford Circuit, 1978–90. Special Advr to Home Sec. and Home Office Ministers, 1990–91. Consultant, Lowe Bell Communications Ltd, 1991–92; Producer/Presenter, BBC Radio and Television, 1994–; Chairman: Warwick Consulting Internat. Ltd, 1997–; Warwick Leadership Foundn, 1999–. Member: Solihull FPC, 1986–90; Greater London FEFC Cttee, 1994–96. Non-exec. Dir, NW Thames RHA, 1992–93. Vice-President: Small Business Bureau, 1997–; BBFC, 1998–. Dir, City Technology Colls Trust, 1994–95. Mem. (C), Solihull DC, 1986–90. Contested (C): Birmingham, Perry Barr, 1987; Cheltenham, 1992. MInstD 1997. Barker, Variety Club Children's Charity; Patron: Parents for Children, adoption charity; Kidscape, 1997–; Mem. Exec. Cttee, Sickle Cell Anaemia Relief. Pres., Ilford Town FC, 1998–; Mem., Aston Villa FC. Freeman: City of London, 1999; Lexington, Ky, USA, 2004. Hon. LLD: Warwick, 1999; Asbury Coll., Ky, USA, 2004. *Recreations:* soccer, cricket, singing, spending time with my lovely family. *Address:* House of Lords, SW1A 0PW. *T:* (020) 7219 3000, *Fax:* (020) 7219 5979; *e-mail:* taylorjdb@parliament.uk; *web:* www.lordtaylor.org.

TAYLOR, Alan; *see* Taylor, Robert A.

TAYLOR, His Honour Alan Broughton; a Circuit Judge, 1991–2005; *b* 23 Jan. 1939; *yr s* of Valentine James Broughton Taylor and Gladys Maud Taylor; *m* 1964, Diana Hindmarsh; two *s.* *Educ:* Malvern Coll.; Geneva Univ.; Birmingham Univ. (LLB); Brasenose Coll., Oxford (BLitt, re-designated MLitt 1979). Called to the Bar, Gray's Inn, 1961; barrister on Oxford Circuit, subseq. Midland and Oxford Circuit, 1963–91; a Recorder, 1979–91. A Pres., Mental Health Rev. Tribunal, 2001–. Gov., St Matthew's Sch., Sandwell, 1988–92. FCIArb 1994; Chartered Arbitrator, 2005–. *Publications:* (contrib.) A Practical Guide to the Care of the Injured, ed P. S. London, 1967; (contrib.) Crime and Civil Society, ed Green, Grove and Martin, 2005. *Recreations:* philately, fell walking. *Address:* Wetherlam, Wood Close, Grasmere, Cumbria LA22 9SG.

TAYLOR, Andrew David; Partner, Reed Smith Richards Butler (formerly Richards Butler), Solicitors, since 1983; *b* 6 March 1952; *s* of Vernon Stephen Taylor and Elizabeth Taylor; *m* 1977, Alison Jane Wright; one *s* two *d.* *Educ:* Magdalen Coll. Sch., Oxford; Lincoln Coll., Oxford (MA). Joined Richards Butler, Solicitors, 1977, Chm., 2000–05; specialises in shipping law. Treas./Sec., British Maritime Law Assoc., 2005–. *Publication:* Voyage Charters, 1993, 3rd edn 2007. *Recreations:* ski-ing, walking, opera, wine. *Address:* Reed Smith Richards Butler, Beaufort House, 15 St Botolph Street, EC3A 7EE. *Clubs:* Travellers, City University, City Law; Vincent's (Oxford).

TAYLOR, Andrew Dawson, OBE 1999; DPhil; FRSE; FInstP; Director, Facility Operations and Development, Science and Technology Facilities Council, since 2007; Director, ISIS Facility, since 1993, and Head, since 2007, Rutherford Appleton Laboratory; *b* Falkirk, 1 March 1950; *s* of Millar Taylor and Jean Taylor (*née* Dawson); *m* 1973, Elizabeth Slimming; two *s* two *d.* *Educ:* Denny High Sch., Stirlingshire; Univ. of Glasgow (Joseph Black Medal 1969; BSc 1st Cl. Hons 1972); St John's Coll., Oxford (DPhil 1976). FRSE 2006; FInstP 2007. SSO, Rutherford Lab., 1975–80; Vis. Scientist, Los Alamos Nat. Lab., New Mexico, 1980–83; SSO, 1983–85, Excitations Gp Leader, 1985–93, ISIS Facility, Rutherford Appleton Lab. Dep. Chief Exec., 2000–04, Exec. Dir, CCLRC Facilities, 2005–07, Mem., 2007–, CCLRC. Sec., Eur. Spallation Source Council, 1992–2000; Member: Steering Cttee, Institut Laue Langevin, 1993–; Adv. Bd, Los Alamos Neutron Sci. Center, 1994–2004; Neutron Rev. Panel, Univ. of Chicago, 1996–2004; Spallation Neutron Source Adv. Bd, USA, 1998–; Internat. Adv. Cttee, Japan Proton Accererator Res. Complex, 2002–; Bd, Humphrey Davy Lab., Royal Instn, 2006–; Eur. Spallation Source Scandinavia Round Table, Sweden, 2007–; Internat. Adv. Cttee, ESS Bilbao, 2008–; Chairman: Canadian Foundn for Innovation Spallation Neutron Source Review, 2004; RIKEN Muon Review, 2007. Glazebrook Medal, Inst. of Physics, 2006. *Publications:* articles on develt and exploitation of pulsed neutron sources for condensed matter research. *Recreations:* family, hill walking, ski-ing, gastronomy. *Address:* Rutherford Appleton Laboratory, Harwell Science and Innovation Campus, Chilton, Oxon OX11 0QX. *T:* (01235) 446681; *e-mail:* andrew.taylor@stfc.ac.uk.

TAYLOR, Andrew John, FCA; Chairman and Chief Executive, Sanctuary Group plc, 2002–06; *b* 23 Feb. 1950; *s* of Thomas Sowler Taylor and Sarah Taylor; *m* 1985, Elizabeth (*née* Robertson); two *d.* *Educ:* Trinity Coll., Cambridge (MA). FCA 1982. Sanctuary Group: Founder, 1976; CEO and Chm., 1976–98; CEO, 1998–2002. FRSA. *Recreations:* wine, cinema, books, fell walking, horse racing. *Address:* Bridle House, 36 Bridle Lane, W1F 9BZ; *e-mail:* andy.taylor@phantom-music.com.

TAYLOR, Sir Anthony John N.; *see* Newman Taylor.

TAYLOR, Sir (Arthur) Godfrey, Kt 1980; DL; Chairman, The Shrievalty Association, 1995–98; *b* 3 Aug. 1925; *s* of Fred and Lucy Taylor; *m* 1945, Eileen Dorothy Daniel; one *s* two *d* (and one *d* decd). *Educ:* Stockport Secondary School. Sutton and Cheam Borough Council: Councillor, 1951–62; Alderman, 1962–65; London Bor. of Sutton: Alderman, 1964–78; Councillor, 1978–82; Hon. Freeman, 1978. Managing Trustee, Municipal Mutual Insurance Ltd, 1979–86; Chairman: Southern Water Authority, 1981–85; London Residuary Body, 1985–96. Chm., Assoc. of Metropolitan Authorities, 1978–80. Chm., London Bor. Assoc., 1968–71. High Sheriff, 1984, DL, 1988, Greater London. *Recreation:* golf. *Address:* 23 Somerhill Lodge, Somerhill Road, Hove, E Sussex BN3 1RU. *T:* (01273) 776161.

TAYLOR, Arthur Robert; President, Muhlenberg College, Pennsylvania, 1992–2002; *b* 6 July 1935; *s* of Arthur Earl Taylor and Marian Hilda Scott; *m* Kathryn Pelgrift; three *d* by previous marriage. *Educ:* Brown Univ., USA (AB, MA). Asst Dir, Admissions, Brown Univ., June 1957–Dec. 1960; Vice-Pres./Dir, The First Boston Co., Jan. 1961–May 1970; Exec. Vice-Pres./Director, Internat. Paper Co., 1970–72; Pres., CBS Inc., 1972–76; Chm., Arthur Taylor & Co. Inc., 1977–. Dean, Grad. Sch. of Business, Fordham Univ., 1985–92. Director: Louisiana Land & Exploration Co.; Pitney Bowes; Nomura Pacific Basin Fund, Inc.; Trustee, Drucker Foundn; Trustee Emeritus, Brown Univ. Hon. degrees: Dr Humane Letters: Simmons Coll., 1975; Rensselaer Polytechnic Inst., 1975; Dr of Humanities, Bucknell Univ., 1975. *Publications:* contrib. chapter to The Other Side of Profit, 1975; articles on US competitiveness and corporate responsibility in jls. *Recreations:* sailing, tennis, riding. *Address:* c/o Muhlenberg College, 2400 Chew Street, Allentown, PA 18104–5586, USA. *Clubs:* Century (New York); Metropolitan (Washington); California (Los Angeles).

TAYLOR, Arthur Ronald, MBE (mil.) 1945; DL; Chairman, Willis Faber plc, 1978–81; Vice-Chairman, Legal and General Group plc, 1984–86 (Director, 1982–86); *b* 13 June 1921; *yr s* of late Arthur Taylor and Kathleen Frances (*née* Constable Curtis); *m* 1949, Elizabeth Josephine Kiek; three *s.* *Educ:* Winchester Coll.; Trinity Coll., Oxford. Served Grenadier Guards, 1940–53 (despatches); sc; Bde Major 32nd Guards Bde. Laurence Philipps & Co. (Insurance) Ltd, 1953–58; Member of Lloyd's, 1955; Director, Willis, Faber and Dumas Ltd, 1959; Dep. Chm., Willis Faber Ltd, 1974. Vice-President: Corporation of Insurance Brokers, 1967–78; British Insurance Brokers Assoc., 1978–81. DL Hants, 1994. *Recreations:* golf, shooting. *Address:* Coutts & Co., 440 Strand, WC2R 0QS.

TAYLOR, Bernard David, CBE 1993; Director, Cambridge Laboratories Ltd, since 2006 (Chairman, 1997–2006); *b* 17 Oct. 1935; *s* of Thomas Taylor and Winifred (*née* Smith); *m* 1959, Nadine Barbara; two *s* two *d.* *Educ:* Univ. of Wales, Bangor (BSc Zoology). Science Teacher, Coventry Educn Authority, 1958; Sales and Marketing, SK&F, 1960; Sales and Marketing Manager, Glaxo NZ, 1964; New Products Manager, Glaxo UK, 1967; Man. Dir, Glaxo Australia, 1972; Dir, Glaxo Holdings plc, and Man. Dir, Glaxo Pharmaceuticals UK, 1984; Chief Exec., Glaxo Holdings, 1986–89; Chm., Medeva plc, 1990–96. Councillor and Vice-Pres., Aust. Pharm. Manufrs' Assoc., 1974–79; Councillor, Victorian Coll. of Pharmacy, 1976–82. Member: CBI Europe Cttee, 1987–89; BOTB, 1987–96. Trustee, WWF (UK), 1990–96. CCMI (CBIM 1986). Fellow, London Business Sch., 1988.

TAYLOR, Bernard John, CChem, FRSC; CSci; Chairman and Chief Executive, Evercore Partners Ltd (formerly Braveheart Financial Services Ltd), since 2006; Vice-Chairman, Evercore Partners Inc., since 2007; *b* 2 Nov. 1956; *s* of late John Taylor and Evelyn Frances Taylor; *m* 1984, Sarah Jane, *d* of John Paskin Taylor, Paris; one *s.* *Educ:* Cheltenham Coll.; St John's Coll., Oxford (Schol.; BA; Hon. Fellow 2008). LRPS 1974; CChem, FRSC 1991; CSci 2004. Business Planning and Acquisitions, 1979–82, Dir, Med. Div., 1983–85, Smiths Industries plc; Exec. Dir, Baring Bros & Co. Ltd, 1985–94; Chm. and Chief Exec., Robert Fleming & Co. Ltd, 1994–2001; Dir, Robert Fleming Hldgs Ltd, 1995–2001 (Jt Chief Exec., Investment Banking, 1998–2000); Vice Chm., EMEA, Chase Manhattan, 2000; Vice-Chm., JP Morgan, 2001–06. Non-executive Director: New Focus Healthcare Ltd, 1986–89; Isis Innovation Ltd, 1997– (Chm., 2001–); Ti Automotive Ltd, 2001–07 (Dep. Chm.); Oxford Instruments plc, 2002–. Mem., Royal Commn for the Exhibn of 1851, 2005– (Chm., Finance Cttee, 2006–). Mem. Council, Univ. of Oxford, 2003– (Chm., Audit and Scrutiny Cttee and Chm., Remuneration Cttee). *Publications:* Photosensitive Film Formation on Copper, I, 1974, II, 1976; Synthesis and Mesomorphic Properties of a Liquid Crystal, 1977; Oxidation of Alcohols to Carbonyl Compounds, Synthesis, 1979; Selective Organic Reactions, 1979. *Recreations:* gardening, photography, wine, opera. *Address:* Evercore Partners Ltd, 10 Hill Street, W1J 5NQ. *T:* (020) 7268 2700, *Fax:* (020) 7268 2710. *Clubs:* Brooks's, Oxford and Cambridge, Mark's.

TAYLOR, Sir Bill; *see* Taylor, Sir W. G.

TAYLOR, Prof. Brent William, PhD; FRACP, FRCPCH; Professor of Community Child Health, University College London Institute of Child Health (formerly at Royal Free Hospital School of Medicine, then Royal Free and University College Medical School), since 1988; *b* 21 Nov. 1941; *s* of Robert Ernest Taylor and Norma Gertrude Taylor; *m* 1970, Moira Elizabeth Hall; one *s* one *d.* *Educ:* Christchurch Boys' High Sch.; Otago Univ. (MB ChB 1966); Bristol Univ. (PhD 1986). FRACP 1977; FRCPCH 1997. Jun. hosp. posts, Christchurch, NZ, 1967–71; Res. Fellow and Sen. Registrar, Great Ormond Street Hosp. for Sick Children and Inst. of Child Health, 1971–74; Senior Lecturer: in Paediatrics, Christchurch Clin. Sch. of Medicine, 1975–81; in Social

Paediatrics and Epidemiology, Bristol Univ., 1981–84; in Child Health, St Mary's Hosp. Med. Sch., 1985–88. Hon. Prof., Inst. of Child Health, 1994–; Vis. Prof., Tongji Med. Univ., Wuhan, China, 1995–. Chm., Nat. Child Health Informatics Consortium, 1995–. *Publications:* chapters and papers on child health, social influences, vaccine safety, respiratory problems and informatics. *Recreations:* family, music (Handel), walking. *Address:* General and Adolescent Paediatric Unit, University College London Institute of Child Health, 30 Guilford Street, WC1N 3EH; *e-mail:* b.taylor@ich.ucl.ac.uk.

TAYLOR, Brian Arthur Edward, CB 2002; Director General, Civilian Personnel (formerly Assistant Under-Secretary of State, Civilian Management), Ministry of Defence, 1996–2001; *b* 10 Jan. 1942; *s* of Arthur Frederick Taylor and Gertrude Maclean Taylor (*née* Campbell); *m* 1967, Carole Ann Smith; three *s* one *d*. *Educ:* St Benedict's Sch., Ealing; Corpus Christi Coll., Oxford (MA Lit.Hum.). Ministry of Defence, 1965–2001: Asst Private Sec. to Sec. of State, 1969–70; Private Sec. to Chief of Air Staff, 1973–75; Head, Management Services Div., 1977–79; Head, Naval Personnel Div., 1979–81; RCDS 1982; Central Policy Review Staff, Cabinet Office, 1983; Head, Civilian Management Div., MoD, 1984–86; Asst Under-Sec. of State (Quartermaster), 1986–88, Air (PE), 1988–91; Head of Personnel Policy Gp (Under Sec.), HM Treasury, 1992–94; Asst Under-Sec. of State (Civilian Mgt (Policy)), MoD, 1994–96. Assessor, Fast Stream Assessment Centre, 2005–. *Recreations:* sport, music, reading, family. *Club:* Richmond Rugby.

TAYLOR, Brian William; Under Secretary, Civil Service Commission, retired; Resident Chairman, Recruitment and Assessment Services, Office of Minister for Civil Service, 1990–93; *b* 29 April 1933; *s* of late Alan Taylor and Betty Taylor; *m* 1959, Mary Evelyn Buckley; two *s* two *d*. *Educ:* Emanuel School. Entered Ministry of Nat. Insurance (subseq. DHSS, then DSS) as Exec. Officer, 1952; Higher Exec. Officer, 1963; Principal, 1968; Asst Sec., 1976; Under Sec., 1982; on loan from DSS, 1990–93. *Recreations:* music, theatre, literature, walking, grandchildren, trying to keep fit.

TAYLOR, (Bryan) Hugo M.; *see* Mascie-Taylor.

TAYLOR, Catherine Dalling; *see* Stihler, C. D.

TAYLOR, Cavan; Senior Partner, Lovell White Durrant, 1991–96; *b* 23 Feb. 1935; *s* of late Albert William Taylor and Constance Muriel (*née* Horncastle); *m* 1962, Helen Tinling; one *s* two *d*. *Educ:* King's Coll. Sch., Wimbledon; Emmanuel Coll., Cambridge (BA 1958; LLM 1959). 2nd Lieut, RASC, 1953–55. Articled with Herbert Smith & Co., 1958–61; qualified as solicitor, 1961; Legal Dept, Distillers' Co. Ltd, 1962–65; Asst Solicitor, Piesse & Sons, 1965–66, Partner, 1966; by amalgamation, Partner, Durrant Piesse and Lovell White Durrant; Dep. Sen. Partner, Lovell White Durrant, 1990–91. Director: Hampton Gold Mining Areas plc, 1979–86; Ludorum Management Ltd, 1996–2000; Link Plus Corp., 1999–2003. Adjudicator for Investment Ombudsman, 1996–2001. Gov., King's Coll. Sch., Wimbledon, 1970–2004 (Chm., 1973–90, 2000–04; Hon. Fellow, 2004). Vice-Pres., Surrey Co. RFU, 2006–. Trustee, School Fees Charitable Trust, 2000–. Pres., Old Boys RFC, King's Coll. Sch., Wimbledon, 1997–2002. Liveryman, Solicitors' Co., 1983–. *Publications:* articles in legal jls. *Recreations:* reading, gardening, conversation with my children, Rugby football. *Address:* Covenham House, 10 Broad Highway, Cobham, Surrey KT11 2RP. *T:* (01932) 864258, *Fax:* (01932) 865705. *Club:* Travellers.

TAYLOR, (Charles) Jeremy (Bingham); Chief Executive, Cheshire County Council, 2002–March 2009; *b* 28 Oct. 1947; *s* of Dr Charles Bingham Taylor and Sydna Mary Taylor (*née* Howell); *m* 1972, Rachel Suzanne Hampson; one *d*. *Educ:* Selwyn Coll., Cambridge (BA, MA 1968). FCIPD 1987. Personnel Manager, ICI Ltd, 1968–72; Sen. Lectr, Univ. of Huddersfield, 1972–79; Cheshire County Council: Director: of Personnel, 1987–91; of Policy, 1991–97; of Community Develt, 1997–2002; Clerk, Cheshire Lieutenancy, 2002–. Sen. Vice Chm., ACCE, 2008– (Hon. Sec., 2006–08). Gov. and Trustee, Brathay Hall Trust, 1987–91. FCMI 1989; FRSA 1990. *Recreations:* gardening, film, theatre, the Greek Islands, opera, cats. *Address:* (until March 2009) Cheshire County Council, County Hall, Chester CH1 1SF. *T:* (01244) 972101, *Fax:* (01244) 972100; *e-mail:* jeremy.taylor@cheshire.gov.uk. *Club:* Royal Over-Seas League.

TAYLOR, Prof. Charles Margrave, CC 1996; GOQ 2000; DPhil; FBA 1979; Professor of Political Science, McGill University, since 1982; *b* 5 Nov. 1931; *s* of Walter Margrave Taylor and Simone Beaubien; *m* 1st, 1956, Alba Romer (*d* 1990); five *d*; 2nd, 1995, Aube Billard. *Educ:* McGill Univ. (BA History); Oxford Univ. (BA PPE, MA, DPhil). Fellow, All Souls Coll., Oxford, 1956–61; McGill University: Asst Prof., later Associate Prof., later Prof. of Polit. Science, Dept of Polit. Science, 1961–76; Prof. of Philosophy, Dept. of Philos., 1973–76; Chichele Prof. of Social and Political Theory, and Fellow of All Souls Coll., Oxford Univ., 1976–81; Mem., Sch. of Social Science, Inst. for Advanced Study, Princeton, 1981–82. Prof. asst, later Prof. agrégé, later Prof. titulaire, Ecole Normale Supérieure, 1962–64, Dept de Philos., 1963–71, Univ. de Montréal. Vis. Prof. in Philos., Princeton Univ., 1965; Mills Vis. Prof. in Philos., Univ. of Calif, Berkeley, 1974. For. Hon. Mem., Amer. Acad. of Arts and Scis, 1986. *Publications:* The Explanation of Behavior, 1964; Pattern of Politics, 1970; Hegel, 1975; Erklarung und Interpretation in den Wissenschaften vom Menschen, 1975; Social Theory as Practice, 1983; Philosophical Papers, 1985; Negative Freiheit, 1988; Sources of the Self, 1989; The Ethics of Authenticity, 1992; Philosophical Arguments, 1995; Varieties of Religion Today, 2002; Modern Social Imaginaries, 2004; A Secular Age, 2007. *Recreations:* ski-ing, swimming. *Address:* 6603 Jeanne Mance, Montréal, QC H2V 4L1, Canada.

TAYLOR, Very Rev. Charles William; Dean of Peterborough, since 2007; *b* 16 March 1953; *s* of Rev. Preb. Richard John Taylor and Marjorie Taylor; *m* 1983, Catherine Margaret, *d* of Very Rev. Trevor Randall Beeson, *qv*; one *s* one *d*. *Educ:* Chorister, St Paul's Cathedral Choir Sch.; Marlborough Coll.; Selwyn Coll., Cambridge (BA Hons Theology; MA 1977); Cuddesdon Coll., Oxford; Church Divinity Sch. of the Pacific, Berkeley, Calif, USA. Ordained deacon, 1976, priest, 1977; Curate, Collegiate Church of St Peter, Wolverhampton, 1976–79; Chaplain, Westminster Abbey, 1979–84; Vicar, Stanmore with Oliver's Battery, Winchester, 1984–90; Rector, N Stoneham and Bassett, Southampton, 1990–95; Tutor in Liturgy, Salisbury and Wells Theol Coll., 1992–94; Canon Residentiary and Precentor, Lichfield Cathedral, 1995–2007. Hon. FGCM 2007. *Publications:* numerous papers for Cathedrals' Liturgy and Music Gp. *Recreations:* music, food and wine, hospitality, Black Country humour, classic cars, following sport from a sedentary position, family holidays. *Address:* The Deanery, Minster Precincts, Peterborough PE1 1XS. *T:* (01733) 355311; *e-mail:* charles.taylor@peterborough-cathedral.org.uk.

TAYLOR, Christopher Charles, FSA; FBA 1995; Head, Archaeological Survey, Royal Commission on Historical Monuments, 1985–93, retired; *b* 7 Nov. 1935; *s* of Richard Hugh Taylor and Alice Mary Taylor (*née* Davies); *m* 1st, 1961, Angela Ballard (*d* 1983); one *s* one *d*; 2nd, 1985, Stephanie, *d* of Wing Comdr R. J. S. Spooner; one step *d*. *Educ:* King Edward VI Sch., Lichfield; Univ. of Keele (BA 1958); Inst. of Archaeol., Univ. of London (Dip. Archaeol. 1960). FSA 1966; MIFA 1987. Investigator, Sen. Investigator and Principal Investigator, RCHM, 1960–93. Member: Historic Parks and Gardens Adv. Cttee, 1987–2001, Historic Settlement and Landscape Adv. Cttee, 2001–03, English Heritage. Pres., Cambridge Antiquarian Soc., 1994–96. Hon. DLitt Keele, 1997. *Publications:* Dorset, 1970, 2nd edn 2004; The Making of the Cambridgeshire Landscape, 1973; Fieldwork in Medieval Archaeology, 1974; Fields in the English Landscape, 1975, 3rd edn 1987; Roads and Tracks in Britain, 1979, 2nd edn 1982; The Archaeology of Gardens, 1983; Village and Farmstead, 1983; (ed) W. G. Hoskins, The Making of the English Landscape, rev. edn 1988; Parks and Gardens of Britain, 1998; contrib. to various pubns of RCHM; papers in learned jls on archaeol. and landscape hist. *Recreations:* gardening, garden history. *Address:* 11 High Street, Pampisford, Cambridge CB22 3ES.
See also D. H. C. Taylor.

TAYLOR, Prof. Christopher Malcolm, FREng, FIMechE; Vice-Chancellor and Principal, University of Bradford, 2001–07; *b* 15 Jan. 1943; *s* of William Taylor and Esther Hopkinson; *m* 1st, 1968, Gillian Walton (marr. diss. 1986); one *d*; 2nd, 1994, Diane Shorrocks. *Educ:* King's College London (BScEng); Univ. of Leeds (MSc, PhD, DEng). FIMechE 1986. Research Engineer, English Electric Co.; Sen. Engr, Industrial Unit of Tribology, Leeds, 1968–71; University of Leeds: Lectr, 1971–80; Sen. Lectr, 1980–86; Reader, 1986–90; Prof. of Tribology, 1990–2001; Head of Dept of Mechanical Engrg, 1992–96; Dean of Faculty of Engrg, 1996–97; Pro-Vice-Chancellor, 1997–2001. Vice-Pres., 1997–2001, Dep. Pres., 2001–03, Pres., 2003–04, IMechE. Editor, Part J, Procs IMechE, 1993–2001. FREng (FEng 1995); FCGI 1999. Tribology Trust Silver Medal, 1992; Donald Julius Groen Prize, IMechE, 1993; Jacob Wallenberg Foundn Prize, 1994. *Publications:* numerous contribs to learned jls. *Recreations:* walking, cycling. *Address:* Sunnybank, Crag Lane, Huby, Leeds LS17 0BW. *T:* (01423) 734285; *e-mail:* cmtdt@btinternet.com.

TAYLOR, Claire Mavis, RRC 1994 (ARRC 1977); Matron-in-Chief, 1994–97, and Captain (formerly Principal Nursing Officer), Queen Alexandra's Royal Naval Nursing Service, 1990–97; *b* 26 May 1943; *d* of late William Taylor and Sybil (*née* Matthews). *Educ:* George Dixon Grammar Sch., Edgbaston. SRN 1964; SCM 1967; RNT 1977. Served QARNNS, 1967–73; Nursing Sister, Papua New Guinea, 1973–74; rejoined QARNNS 1975; QHNS, 1994–97. OStJ. *Recreations:* travel, reading. *Address:* c/o Lloyds TSB, 20–24 High Street, Gosport, Hants PO12 1DE. *Club:* Army and Navy.

TAYLOR, Clifford; Director, Resources Television, BBC, 1988–93 (Deputy Director, 1987–88); *b* 6 March 1941; *s* of Fred Taylor and Annie Elisabeth (*née* Hudson); *m* 1962, Catherine Helen (*née* Green); two *d*. *Educ:* Barnsley and District Holgate Grammar Sch.; Barnsley College of Mining and Technology. ACMA. NCB, 1957–65; Midlands Counties Dairies, 1965–68; BBC: Radio Cost Accountant, 1968–71; Television Hd of Costing, 1971–76; Chief Accountant, Corporate Finance, 1976–77 and 1982–84; Chief Acct, Engineering, 1977–82; Dep. Dir, Finance, 1984–86. *Recreations:* sport - plays golf, enjoys horse racing. *Address:* 35 Hare Hill Close, Pyrford, near Woking, Surrey GU22 8UH. *T:* (01932) 348301. *Clubs:* MCC, BBC.

TAYLOR, Sir Cyril (Julian Hebden), GBE 2004; Kt 1989; Trustee, Specialist Schools and Academies Trust (formerly Technology Colleges Trust, then Specialist Schools Trust), since 2007 (Chairman, 1987–2007); Chairman, American Institute for Foreign Study, since 1964; *b* 14 May 1935; *s* of Cyril Eustace Taylor and Margaret Victoria (*née* Hebden); *m* 1965, June Judith Denman; one *d*. *Educ:* St Marylebone Grammar Sch.; Trinity Hall, Cambridge (MA); Harvard Business Sch. (MBA). National Service, Officer with KAR in Kenya during Mau Mau Emergency, 1954–56 (seconded from E Surrey Regt). Brand Manager in Advertising Dept, Procter & Gamble, Cincinnati, Ohio, 1961–64; Founder Chm., American Institute for Foreign Study, 1964–: group cos include: Amer. Inst. for Foreign Study; Amer. Council for Internat. Studies; Camp America; Au Pair in America. Advr to ten successive Secs of State for Educn on specialist schs and academies initiative, 1987–. Mem. for Ruislip Northwood, GLC, 1977–86: Chm., Professional and Gen. Services Cttee, 1979–81; Opposition spokesperson for employment, 1981–82, transport, 1982–85, policy and resources, 1985–86; Dep. Leader of the Opposition, 1983–86; Mem., Wkg Party reviewing legislation to abolish GLC and MCCs, 1983–86. Pres., Ruislip Northwood Cons. Assoc., 1986–97; contested (C): Huddersfield E, Feb. 1974; Keighley, Oct. 1974. Member: Bd of Dirs, Centre for Policy Studies, 1984–98; Council, Westfield Coll., Univ. of London, 1983–89; Council, RCM, 1988–95; Bd of Governors, Holland Park Comprehensive Sch., 1971–74; Chm., Bd of Trustees, Richmond, The American Internat. Univ. in London, 1977–2005 (Chancellor, 2005–). Chm., Lexham Gdns Residents' Assoc., 1986–. Pres., Harvard Business Sch. Club, London, 1990–93; Chm., British Friends of Harvard Business Sch., 1991–97, 2001–; Vice Pres., Alumni Council, Harvard Business Sch., 1994–96 (Mem., 1993–96). FRSA 1990. High Sheriff, Greater London, 1996. Hon. LLD: New England, 1991; Richmond, The American Internat. Univ. in London, 1998; DUniv: Open, 2000; Brunel, 2005. *Publications:* (jtly) The New Guide to Study Abroad, USA 1969, 4th edn 1976; Peace has its Price, 1972; No More Tick, 1974; The Elected Member's Guide to Reducing Public Expenditure, 1980; A Realistic Plan for London Transport, 1982; Reforming London's Government, 1984; Quangoes Just Grow, 1985; London Preserv'd, 1985; Bringing Accountability Back to Local Government, 1985; Employment Examined: the right approach to more jobs, 1986; Raising Educational Standards, 1990; The Future of Higher Education, 1996; (jtly) Excellence in Education: the making of great schools, 2004; Education, Education, Education: 10 years on with Tony Blair, 2007. *Recreations:* keen tennis player, swimmer, gardener, theatre-goer. *Address:* 1 Lexham Walk, W8 5JD. *T:* (020) 7370 2081; American Institute for Foreign Study, 37 Queen's Gate, SW7 5HR. *T:* (020) 7581 7391, *Fax:* (020) 7581 7388; *e-mail:* ctaylor@aifs.co.uk. *Clubs:* Carlton, Hurlingham, Chelsea Arts; Harvard, Racquet (New York).

TAYLOR, Daria Jean, (Dari); MP (Lab) Stockton South, since 1997; *b* 13 Dec. 1944; *d* of Daniel and Phyllis Jones; *m* 1970, David Taylor; one *d*. *Educ:* Nottingham Univ. (BA Hons 1970); Durham Univ. (MA 1990). Lectr in Further Educn, Nottingham, 1970–80; part-time Lectr in Sociology and Social Policy, N Tyneside, 1986–90; Regl Educn Officer, GMB, 1990–97. Mem. (Lab) Sunderland CC, 1986–97. PPS to Parly Under Sec. of State, MoD, 2001–03, to Minister of State, Home Office, 2003–05. Member: Defence Select Cttee, 1997–99; Intelligence and Security Select Cttee, 2005–. Mem., All Party Cancer Gp, 1998–; Chm., All Party Gp on Adoption, 2001–; Treasurer: All Party Chemical Industries Gp, 1997–; All Party Opera Gp, 1998–. Vice Chm., Westbridgford Br., NATFHE, 1970–80. *Recreations:* opera, walking, classical music, travelling. *Address:* House of Commons, SW1A 0AA. *T:* (020) 7219 4608; (office) 109 Lanehouse Road, Thornaby on Tees TS17 8AB. *T:* (01642) 604546.

TAYLOR, David Leslie; MP (Lab and Co-op) Leicestershire North West, since 1997; *b* 22 Aug. 1946; *s* of late Leslie Taylor and of Eileen Mary Taylor; *m* 1969, Pamela (*née* Caunt); four *d* (one *s* decd). *Educ:* Ashby-de-la-Zouch Boys' Grammar Sch.; Leicester Poly.; Lanchester Poly. (CPFA); Open Univ. (BA Maths and Computing). Accountant and computer manager, Leics CC, 1977–97. Mem. (Lab) NW Leics DC, 1981–87,

1992–95. Contested (Lab) Leics NW, 1992. JP Ashby-de-la-Zouch, 1985. *Address:* House of Commons, SW1A 0AA.

TAYLOR, Prof. David Samuel Irving, FRCP, FRCS, FRCOphth, FRCPCH; Consultant Ophthalmologist, Great Ormond Street Hospital, London, since 1976; Professor, Institute of Child Health, London, since 2003 (Senior Lecturer, 1976–2003); *b* 6 June 1942; *s* of Samuel Donald Taylor and Winifred Alice May Marker; *m* 1976, Anna (*née* Rhys Jones); two *s*. *Educ:* Dauntsey's Sch.; Liverpool Univ. (MB ChB 1967); DSc (Med) London 2001. FRCS 1973; FRCP 1984; FRCOphth 1990; FRCPCH 1998. House Surgeon and Physician, Liverpool Royal Infirmary, 1967–68; Registrar, then Sen. Registrar, Moorfields Eye Hosp., 1972–75; Research Fellow: Great Ormond Street Hosp., London, 1975–76; Neuro-ophthalmology Dept, Univ. of California, San Francisco, 1976–77; Consultant Neuro-ophthalmologist, National Hosps, London, 1976–89. Hon. Mem. Council, Royal London Soc. for the Blind, 1988. Hon. FRSocMed 2005; Hon. FRCOphth 2006. Member, Editorial Board: Brit. Jl of Ophthalmology, 1977–90, 2000–07; European Jl of Ophthalmology, 1998–2007. *Publications:* (ed) Paediatric Ophthalmology, 1990, 3rd edn (ed with C. S. Hoyt) 2004; (with C. S. Hoyt) Practical Paediatric Ophthalmology, 1997 (trans. Japanese, Portuguese, Spanish, Russian); 220 other publications as book chapters or in learned jls. *Recreations:* tennis, sailing, forestry, gardening. *Address:* (home) 23 Church Road, Barnes, SW13 9HB. *T:* (020) 8878 0305, (office) (020) 7935 7916, *Fax:* (020) 7323 5430; *e-mail:* dsit@btinternet.com.

TAYLOR, David William; educational consultant, since 2004; Director of Inspection, Office for Standards in Education, 1999–2004; *b* 10 July 1945; *s* of Harry William Taylor and Eva Wade Taylor (*née* Day); *m* 1972, Pamela Linda (*née* Taylor); one *s* one *d*. *Educ:* Bancroft's Sch.; Worcester Coll., Oxford (BA Hons 1967; MA 1972); Inst. of Education, Univ. of London (PGCE, Distinction; Story-Miller Prize, 1968). Watford Grammar School: Classics Teacher, 1968–73; Head of Classics, 1973–78; HM Inspector of Schools, 1978–86; Staff Inspector, 1986–92; seconded to Touche Ross Management Consultants, 1991; Office for Standards in Education: Manager, Work Prog., 1992–93; Head, Strategic Planning, 1993–96; Head, Teacher Educn and Training, 1996–99. Exec. Sec., JACT, 1976–78. Schoolteacher Fellowship, Merton Coll., Oxford, 1978. FRSA. *Publications:* Cicero and Rome, 1973; Work in Ancient Greece and Rome, 1975; Acting and the Stage, 1978; Roman Society, 1980; The Greek and Roman Stage, 1999; numerous articles in professional jls. *Recreations:* chess, classical (esp. choral) music, cricket, classical literature, theatre, poetry, travel, gardening, rookie golf. *Address:* Firgrove, Seal Hollow Road, Sevenoaks, Kent TN13 3SF. *T:* (01732) 455410; *e-mail:* firgrove@fairadsl.co.uk. *Clubs:* Athenæum; Nizels Golf.

TAYLOR, David Wilson, CBE 2007; Chairman, David Taylor Partnerships Ltd, since 2000; *b* 9 May 1950; *s* of Eric and Sybil Taylor; *m* 1980, Brenda Elizabeth Birchall; two *s*. *Educ:* Galashiels Acad.; Dundee Univ. Sch. of Architecture; Architectural Assoc. (DipArch, Dip. Urban and Regl Planning). Research and journalism, 1979–81; Advisor on regl policy to John Prescott, MP, 1981–83; Lancashire Enterprises Ltd: Dep. Man. Dir, 1983–85; Man. Dir, 1985–89; AMEC plc: Man. Dir, AMEC Regeneration, 1989–92; Man. Dir, AMEC Develts, 1992–93; Chief Exec., English Partnerships, 1993–96; Gp Chief Exec., Lancs Enterprises, subseq. Enterprise plc, 1996–2000. Director: INWARD, 1996–99; Preston North End plc, 1996– (Dep. Chm.); non-executive Chairman: Vektor Ltd, 1996–2004; Angela Campbell Gp, 1996–98; Era Ltd, 1997–2005; Hull Citybuild Ltd, 2003–; Elevate East Lancs, 2003–; Silvertown Quays Ltd, 2003–; BL-Canada Quays Ltd, 2005–; Parking Eye Ltd, 2005–; Professional Development TV Ltd, 2005–; non-executive Director: John Maunders Gp plc, 1996–98; Central Lancs Develt Agency, 1997–2001; United Waste Services, 1997–2000; Manchester Commonwealth Games Ltd, 1999–2003; London and Southern Ltd, 2000–05; UK Regeneration Ltd, 2004–06. Special Advr to Dep. Prime Minister, 1997–98. Chm., NW Film Commn, 1996–2001; Dir, Olympic Delivery Authy, 2006–. Chm., Phoenix Trust, 1997–2001; Trustee, Prince's Foundn, 2000–03. FRSA 2006. Hon. Fellow, Univ. of Central Lancashire, 1996. *Recreations:* football (British and American), Rugby (Union and League). *Address:* (office) 88 Fishergate Hill, Preston PR1 8JD. *T:* (01772) 883888. *Clubs:* Royal Automobile, Royal Commonwealth Society.

TAYLOR, Desmond Philip S.; *see* Shawe-Taylor.

TAYLOR, Douglas Hugh Charles, PhD; FREng; independent consultant on internal combustion engines, since 1992; *b* 4 April 1938; *s* of Richard Hugh Taylor and Alice Mary Davies; *m* 1970, Janet Elizabeth Scott (marr. diss.); two *d*; *m* 2001, Thea Caroline Lilian Vinter. *Educ:* King Edward VI Grammar Sch., Lichfield; Loughborough University of Technology. PhD, BTech. FREng (FEng 1987); FIMechE. Ruston & Hornsby/GEC Ruston Diesels, 1962–72, Chief Research Engineer, 1968; Ricardo Consulting Engineers, 1972–90: Head of Large Engines, 1973; Dir, 1977; Man. Dir, 1984–90; Chm., 1987–90; Gp Man. Dir, Ricardo Internat., 1990–91. Vis. Prof., Loughborough Univ., 1994–. Hon. DTech 2007. *Recreations:* campanology, flying.
See also C. C. Taylor.

TAYLOR, Duncan John Rushworth, CBE 2002; HM Diplomatic Service; High Commissioner to Barbados and (non-resident) to Antigua and Barbuda, Commonwealth of Dominica, Grenada, St Kitts and Nevis, St Lucia, and St Vincent and Grenadines, since 2005; *b* 17 Oct. 1958; *s* of Sir John Lang, (Jock), Taylor, KCMG and Molly Taylor; *m* 1981, Marie-Beatrice Terpougoff; two *s* three *d*. *Educ:* Trinity Coll., Cambridge (MA Hons Modern Langs 1980). Retail analyst, Gulf Oil GB, 1980–82; entered FCO, 1982; Third Sec., FCO, 1982–83; Third, later Second, Sec., Havana, 1983–87; First Sec., FCO, 1987–92; Hd, Commercial Section, Budapest, 1992–96; on secondment to Rolls Royce plc as Dir, Latin American Affairs, 1996–97; Counsellor, FCO, 1997–2000; Dep. Consul Gen. and Dep. Hd of Mission, New York, 2000–05. *Recreations:* sports, travel, theatre, films, books, food. *Address:* BFPO 5560, HA4 6EP; *e-mail:* duncan.taylor@fco.gov.uk; British High Commission, Lower Collymore Rock, Bridgetown 11000, Barbados. *T:* 4307800.

TAYLOR, Sir Edward Macmillan, (Sir Teddy), Kt 1991; journalist, consultant and company director; *b* 18 April 1937; *s* of late Edward Taylor and Minnie Hamilton Taylor; *m* 1970, Sheila Duncan; two *s* one *d*. *Educ:* Glasgow High School and University (MA (Hons) Econ. and Politics). Commercial Editorial Staff of Glasgow Herald, 1958–59; Industrial Relations Officer on Staff of Clyde Shipbuilders' Assoc., 1959–64. Director: Shepherds Foods, 1968–; Ansvar (Temperance) Insurance, 1970–98. Advr, Port of Tilbury Police Fedn (formerly Port of London Police Fedn), 1972–2004. MP (C): Glasgow, Cathcart, 1964–79; Southend East, March 1980–1997; Rochford and Southend East, 1997–2005. Parly Under-Sec. of State, Scottish Office, 1970–71, resigned; Parly Under-Sec. of State, Scottish Office, 1974; Opposition spokesman on Trade, 1977, on Scotland affairs, 1977–79. Vice-Chm., Cons. Parly Party Home Affairs Cttee, 1992–94 (Sec., 1983–92). *Publications:* (novel) Hearts of Stone, 1968; contributions to the press. *Address:* 12 Lynton Road, Thorpe Bay, Southend-on-Sea, Essex SS1 3BE. *T:* (01702) 586282.

TAYLOR, Prof. Edwin William, FRS 1978; Louis Block Professor of Molecular Genetics and Cell Biology, University of Chicago, 1984–99, half-time, 1999, now Emeritus (Professor, Department of Biophysics, 1975–99); part-time Research Professor, Department of Cell and Molecular Biology, Northwestern University Medical School, since 2000; *b* Toronto, 8 June 1929; *s* of William Taylor and Jean Taylor (*née* Christie); *m* 1956, Jean Heather Logan; two *s* one *d*. *Educ:* Univ. of Toronto (BA 1952); McMaster Univ. (MSc 1955); Univ. of Chicago (PhD 1957). Asst Prof., 1959–63, Associate Prof., 1963–67, Prof., 1967–72, Univ. of Chicago; Prof. of Biology, King's College and MRC Unit, London, 1972–74; Associate Dean, Div. of Biol Sci and Medicine, 1977–79, Prof. and Chm., Dept of Biology, 1979–84, Univ. of Chicago. Rockefeller Foundn Fellow, 1957–58; Nat. Insts of Health Fellow, 1958–59, cons. to NIH, 1970–72, 1976–80. Instructor in Physiology, Marine Biol Lab. summer program, Woods Hole, Ma, 1991–98. Member: Amer. Biochem. Soc.; Biophysical Soc.; Fellow, Amer. Acad. of Arts and Scis, 1991; NAS, USA, 2001. E. B. Wilson Medal, Amer. Soc. for Cell Biology, 1999. *Address:* Cummings Life Sciences Center, University of Chicago, 920 East 58th Street, Chicago, IL 60637, USA. *T:* (773) 7021660; 5805 South Dorchester Avenue, Apt 11C, Chicago, IL 60637, USA. *T:* (773) 9552441.

TAYLOR, Dame Elizabeth (Rosemond), DBE 2000; film actress; *b* London, 27 Feb. 1932; *d* of late Francis Taylor and Sara (*née* Sothern); *m* 1st, 1950, Conrad Nicholas Hilton, Jr (marr. diss.; he *d* 1969); 2nd, 1952, Michael Wilding (marr. diss.; he *d* 1979); two *s*; 3rd, 1957, Mike Todd (*d* 1958); one *d*; 4th, 1959, Eddie Fisher (marr. diss. 1964); 5th, 1964, Richard Burton, CBE (marr. diss.; remarried 1975; marr. diss. 1976; he *d* 1984); 7th, 1976, Senator John Warner (marr. diss. 1982); 8th, 1991, Larry Fortensky (marr. diss.). *Educ:* Byron House, Hampstead; Hawthorne School, Beverly Hills; Metro-Goldwyn-Mayer School; University High School, Hollywood. First film, There's One Born Every Minute, 1942. *Films include:* Lassie Come Home, The White Cliffs of Dover, 1943; Jane Eyre, National Velvet, 1944; Courage of Lassie, Life with Father, 1946; Cynthia, 1947; A Date With Judy, 1948; Julia Misbehaves, 1948; The Big Hangover, 1949; Father's Little Dividend, Little Women, The Conspirator, Father of the Bride, 1950; A Place in the Sun, Love is Better than Ever, 1951; Ivanhoe, 1952; Beau Brummel, Elephant Walk, Rhapsody, 1954; Last Time I Saw Paris, 1955; Giant, 1956; Raintree County, 1957; Cat on a Hot Tin Roof, 1958; Suddenly Last Summer, 1959; Holiday in Spain, Butterfield 8 (Academy Award for Best Actress), 1960; Cleopatra, The VIPs, 1963; The Sandpiper, 1965; Who's Afraid of Virginia Woolf? (Academy Award for Best Actress), 1966; The Taming of the Shrew, Doctor Faustus, 1967; Boom!, The Comedians, Reflections in a Golden Eye, Secret Ceremony, 1968; The Only Game in Town, 1970; Under Milk Wood, Zee and Co., Hammersmith is Out, 1972; Night Watch, 1973; Ash Wednesday, 1974; The Driver's Seat, Blue Bird, 1975; A Little Night Music, 1977; Winter Kills, 1979; The Mirror Crack'd, 1980; Between Friends, 1983; Young Toscanini, 1988; The Flintstones, 1994. Stage debut as Regina in The Little Foxes, NY, 1981, London stage debut, Victoria Palace, 1982; Private Lives, NY, 1983. Fellow, BAFTA, 1999. Initiated Elizabeth Taylor-Ben Gurion Univ. Fund for Children of the Negev, 1982; founded American Foundn for AIDS Res., 1985, Internat. Fund, 1985, Elizabeth Taylor AIDS Foundn, 1991. Aristotle S. Onassis Foundn Award, 1988; Humanitarian Award, American Academy, 1993. Comdr of Arts and Letters (France), 1985; Legion of Honour (France), 1987. *Publications:* (with Richard Burton) World Enough and Time, 1964; Elizabeth Taylor, 1966; Elizabeth Takes Off, 1988; Elizabeth Taylor: my love affair with jewellery, 2002. *Address:* PO Box 55995, Sherman Oaks, CA 91413, USA.

TAYLOR, Enid, FRCS, FRCOphth; Consultant Ophthalmic Surgeon, North Middlesex Hospital, 1974–98; *b* 18 June 1933; *d* of Joseph William Wheldon and Jane Wheldon; *m* 1959, Thomas Henry Taylor; two *s*. *Educ:* Girton Coll., Cambridge (MA); London Hosp. Med. Coll. (MB BChir; DO 1963). FRCS 1965; FRCOphth 1988. Consultant Ophthalmic Surgeon, Elizabeth Garrett Anderson Hosp., 1966–73. Chm., NE Thames Ophthalmic Adv. Cttee, DHSS, 1979–86. Member Council: Faculty of Ophthalmologists, 1980–88; Coll. of Ophthalmologists, 1988–90; Sect. Ophthalmol, RSocMed, 1981–85 (Vice-Pres., 1985–88); Mem., Ophthalmic Cttees, BMA, 1982–2000. Liveryman, 1973, Asst, 1989–, Master, 2002–03, Soc. of Apothecaries. *Publications:* contrib. papers and presentations on diabetic retinal disease. *Recreations:* cooking, needlework. *Address:* 60 Wood Vale, N10 3DN. *T:* (020) 8883 6146.
See also S. W. Taylor.

TAYLOR, Eric; a Recorder of the Crown Court, 1978–98; *b* 22 Jan. 1931; *s* of Sydney Taylor and Sarah Helen (*née* Lea); *m* 1958, Margaret Jessie Taylor, *qv*. *Educ:* Wigan Grammar Sch.; Manchester Univ. (LLB 1952; Dauntesey Sen. Legal Scholar; LLM 1954). Admitted solicitor, 1955. Partner, Temperley Taylor (formerly Temperley Taylor Chadwick), Middleton, Manchester, 1957–2001, Consultant (full-time), 2001–05. Part-time Lectr in Law, Manchester Univ., 1958–80, Hon. Special Lectr in Law, 1980–2005. Examr, (Old) Law Soc. Final Exams, 1968–81, Chief Examr, (New) Law Soc. Final Exams, 1978–83; External Examiner, Qualified Lawyers' Transfer Test, 1990–2002; Chief Examr for solicitors qualifying to appear as advocates, 1993–97. President: Oldham Law Assoc., 1970–72; Rochdale Law Assoc., 1998–99. Chairman: Manchester Young Solicitors' Gp, 1963; Manchester Nat. Insurance Appeal Tribunal, 1967–73; Disciplinary Cttee, Architects Registration Council, 1989–95. Member: Council, Law Soc., 1972–91 (Chm., Educn and Trng Cttee, 1980–83; Chm., Criminal Law Cttee, 1984–87); CNAA Legal Studies Bd, 1975–84; Lord Chancellor's Adv. Cttee on Trng of Magistrates, 1974–79. Governor: Coll. of Law, 1984–2000; Bd, Common Professional Examn, 1990–2002. *Publications:* Modern Conveyancing Precedents, 1964, 2nd edn 1989; Modern Wills Precedents, 1969, 3rd edn 1997; contrib. legal jls. *Recreations:* equestrian sports. *Address:* 10 Mercers Road, Heywood, Lancs OL10 2NP. *T:* (01706) 366630.

TAYLOR, Prof. Eric Andrew, FRCP, FRCPsych, FMedSci; Professor of Child and Adolescent Psychiatry, Institute of Psychiatry, King's College London, since 1999; Hon. Consultant, Maudsley Hospital, since 1978; *b* 22 Dec. 1944; *s* of Dr Jack Andrew Taylor and Grace Taylor; *m* 1969, Anne Patricia Roberts (*d* 2000); two *s*. *Educ:* Trinity Hall, Cambridge (MA); Harvard Univ.; Middx Hosp. Med. Sch. (MB). FRCP 1986; FRCPsych 1988. SHO, Middx Hosp., 1969–71; Res. Fellow, Harvard Univ., 1971; Registrar, then Sen. Registrar, Maudsley Hosp., 1973–76; Institute of Psychiatry: Lectr, then Sen. Lectr, 1976–86; Reader, 1986–93; Prof. of Developmental Neuropsychiatry, 1993–99; Clinical Scientist, MRC, 1990–99. Cantwell Lectr, UCLA, 2004; Emanuel Miller Lectr, Assoc. for Child Psychol. and Psychiatry, 2004. Editor: Jl Child Psychol. and Psychiatry, 1984–95; Eur. Child and Adolescent Psychiatry, 2003–. FMedSci 2000. Hon. Mem., child psychiatry assocs in Germany, Chile and UK. *Publications:* The Hyperactive Child: a parents' guide, 1985, 3rd edn 1997; The Overactive Child, 1986 (Spanish and Japanese edns 1991); The Epidemiology of Childhood Hyperactivity, 1991; (ed jtly) Child and Adolescent Psychiatry: modern approaches, 3rd edn 1994, 4th edn 2001; contrib. numerous papers to scientific jls on child neuropsychiatry. *Address:* Department of Child and Adolescent Psychiatry, Institute of Psychiatry, King's College London, De Crespigny Park, SE5 8AF. *T:* (020) 7848 0488. *Club:* Royal Society of Medicine.

TAYLOR, Floella; *see* Benjamin, F.

TAYLOR, Dr Frank Henry, CBE 2003; Secretary, Charles Wallace India Trust, 1992–2004; *b* 20 Jan. 1932; *s* of Frank Taylor and Norah (*née* Dunn). *Educ:* Frimley and Camberley Co. Grammar Sch.; King's Coll., London (BSc 1953; PhD 1957). Beit Meml Fellow for Med. Res., Imperial Coll., London and Pasteur Inst., Paris, 1957–60; British Council, 1960–92: Science Officer, 1960–61; Asst Cultural Attaché, Cairo, 1961–64; Asst Regl Rep., Calcutta, 1965–69; Science Officer, Rio de Janeiro, 1970–74; Dir, Science and Technology Dept, 1974–78; Rep., Saudi Arabia, 1978–81; Head Operations, Technical Educn and Trng in Overseas Countries, and Dep. Controller, Science, Technology and Education Div., 1981–84; Counsellor, British Council and Cultural Affairs, Ankara, 1984–87; Dep. Controller, Asia and Pacific Div., then S and W Asia Div., 1987–88; Controller, Africa and ME Div., 1989–90; Dir, Libraries, Books and Inf. Div., 1990–92. *Publications:* articles on surface chemistry and reviews in Proc. Royal Soc., etc. *Recreations:* music, bridge, bookbinding, Middle East. *Address:* 9 Shaftesbury Road, Richmond, Surrey TW9 2TD.

TAYLOR, Prof. Fredric William, DPhil; Halley Professor of Physics, Oxford University, since 2000 (Head of Department of Atmospheric, Oceanic and Planetary Physics, 1979–2000); Fellow, Jesus College, Oxford, since 1979; *b* 24 Sept. 1944; *s* of William Taylor and Ena Lloyd (*née* Burns); *m* 1969, Doris Jean Buer. *Educ:* Duke of Northumberland's Sch.; Univ. of Liverpool (BSc 1966); Univ. of Oxford (DPhil 1970; MA 1983). Resident Res. Associate, US Nat. Res. Council, 1970–72; Sen. Scientist, 1972–79, Dist. Vis. Scientist, 1996–, Jet Propulsion Lab., CIT; Oxford University: Reader in Atmospheric Physics, 1983–89; Prof. of Atmospheric Physics, 1990–99. *Publications:* Cambridge Atlas of the Planets, 1982, 2nd edn 1986 (trans. German 1984, Italian 1988); Remote Sounding of Atmospheres, 1984, 2nd edn 1987; (with A. Coustenis) Titan, 1999; (with M. Lopez-Puertas) Non-LTE Radiative Transfer in the Atmosphere, 2001; The Cambridge Guide to the Planets, 2002; Elementary Climate Physics, 2005; (with I. Vardavas) Radiation and Climate, 2007; contrib. to learned jls. *Recreations:* walking, motoring, poker, literature, history, railways. *Address:* Clarendon Laboratory, Oxford OX1 3PU. *T:* (01865) 272903; Jesus College, Oxford OX1 3DW.

TAYLOR, Geoffrey Keith, CB 2007; PhD; Director (part-time), External Relations, Government Communications Headquarters, since 2001; *b* 1 March 1948; *s* of Wilfred Taylor and Irene Isobel Taylor (*née* Smith); *m* 1969, Patricia Anne Angell; two *s*. *Educ:* Nottingham High Sch.; Queens' Coll., Cambridge (BA 1970); Univ. of Leicester (PhD 1973). Res. Demonstrator, Univ. of Leicester, 1970; Government Communications Headquarters: joined, 1973, Asst Deptl Specialist; Principal, 1978; Sen. Civil Service, 1987; Dir, Special Progs, 1999–2001. Mem., Croquet Assoc. *Publications:* papers on quantum molecular dynamics in Physical Rev., etc. *Recreations:* croquet, buying, selling and mending anything, foreign travel, playing 1930s popular piano music poorly, mooching. *Address:* c/o Government Communications Headquarters, Hubble Road, Cheltenham GL51 0EX. *Clubs:* Nottingham Croquet, Cheltenham Croquet.

TAYLOR, Sir Godfrey; *see* Taylor, Sir A. G.

TAYLOR, Gordon, OBE 2008; Chief Executive, Professional Footballers' Association, since 1981; *b* 28 Dec. 1944; *s* of Alec and Mary Taylor; *m* 1968, Catharine Margaret Johnston; two *s*. *Educ:* Ashton-under-Lyne Grammar Sch.; Bolton Technical Coll.; Univ. of London (BScEcon Hons (ext.)). Professional footballer with: Bolton Wanderers, 1960–70; Birmingham City, 1970–76; Blackburn Rovers, 1976–78; Vancouver Whitecaps (N American Soccer League), 1977; Bury, 1978–80, retd. Professional Footballers Association: Mem., Management Cttee, 1971; Chm., 1978–80; (full-time) Asst Sec., 1980; Sec./Treasurer, 1981; Pres., Internat. Assoc. of Professional Footballers Unions, 1994–2005 (Hon. Pres., 2005–). Hon. MA Loughborough Univ. of Technol., 1986 (for services to football); Hon. DArts De Montfort, 1998. *Recreations:* theatre, dining-out, watching football, reading. *Address:* (office) 20 Oxford Court, Bishopsgate, Manchester M2 3WQ. *T:* (0161) 236 0575.

TAYLOR, Dr Gordon William; Managing Director, Firemarket Ltd, since 1988; *b* 26 June 1928; *s* of William and Elizabeth Taylor; *m* 1954, Audrey Catherine Bull; three *s* two *d*. *Educ:* J. H. Burrows Sch., Grays, Essex; Army Apprentice Sch.; London Univ. (BScEng Hons, PhDEng). MICE, MIMechE, MIET. Kellogg Internat. Corp., 1954–59; W. R. Grace, 1960–62; Gen. Man., Nalco Ltd, 1962–66; BTR Industries, 1966–68; Managing Director: Kestrel Chemicals, 1968–69; Astral Marketing, 1969–70; Robson Refractories, 1970–87. Greater London Council: Alderman, 1972–77; Mem. for Croydon Central, 1977–80; Chairman: Public Services Cttee, 1977–78; London Transp. Cttee, 1978–79. Chm., W London Residents' Assoc., 2003–. *Recreations:* theatre, reading, tennis, croquet. *Club:* Holland Park Lawn Tennis.

TAYLOR, Graham, OBE 2002; football summarizer, Radio Five Live, since 2003; football media correspondent, since 2003; *b* Worksop, Notts, 15 Sept. 1944; *s* of Tommy Taylor; *m* 1965, Rita Cowling; two *d*. *Educ:* Scunthorpe Grammar Sch. Professional football player: Grimsby Town, 1962–68; Lincoln City, 1968–72; Manager: Lincoln City, 1972–77; Watford, 1977–87 and 1996–2001; Aston Villa, 1987–90 and 2002–03; England Football Team, 1990–93; Wolverhampton Wanderers, 1994–95.

TAYLOR, Hamish Wilson; Chief Executive, Hamish Taylor Skills Exchange Network, since 2004; *b* Kitwe, N Rhodesia, 18 June 1960; *s* of late Dr Douglas James Wilson Taylor and of Mairi Helen Taylor (*née* Pitt); *m* 1984, Fiona Marion Darroch; three *s*. *Educ:* Skinners' Sch., Tunbridge Wells; Univ. of St Andrews (Pres., Athletic Union, 1981–82; MA Hons Econs 1982); Emory Univ., Atlanta (Robert T. Jones Schol., 1983; Business Sch. Fellow; St Andrews Soc of Washington Schol., 1983–84; MBA 1984). FCILT (FCIT 1999); FCIB 2001. Brand Manager, Procter and Gamble Ltd, 1984–90; Mgt Consultant, Price Waterhouse, 1990–93; Gen. Manager, Brands, British Airways, 1993–97; Man. Dir, Eurostar (UK) Ltd, 1997–99; Chief Exec., Eurostar Gp, 1999; Chief Executive: Sainsbury's Bank, 2000–02; Vision UK, 2002–04. Non-exec. Dir, Chartered Brands, 2003–; Mem., Adv. Panel, Bright Grey, 2003–. Chm., Europe, Middle East and Africa Adv. Bd, Emory Univ., 2006–. Trustee, Robert T. Jones Meml Trust, 2005–. FRSA 1999. Freeman, City of Glasgow, 1979. Rail Professional Business Manager of the Year, Rail Professional Magazine, 1998; Sheth Dist. Internat. Alumni Award, Emory Univ., 2004. *Recreations:* athletics (Scottish Junior international, 1979), football, piano. *Address:* e-mail: hamish@hamishtaylor.com.

TAYLOR, Hugh Henderson, CB 2000; Permanent Secretary, Department of Health, since 2006; *b* 22 March 1950; *s* of late Leslie Henderson Taylor and of Alison Taylor; *m* 1989, Diane Bacon; two *d*. *Educ:* Brentwood Sch.; Emmanuel Coll., Cambridge (BA). Joined Home Office, 1972; Private Sec. to Minister of State, 1976–77; Principal Private Sec. to Home Sec., 1983–85; Asst Sec., 1984; Prison Service, 1985–88 and 1992–93; seconded to Cabinet Office, 1988–91; Under Sec., 1993–96, and Dir, Top Mgt Prog., 1994–96, Cabinet Office; Dir of Services, Prison Service, 1996–97; Dir of Human Resources, NHS Exec., 1998–2001; Dir Gen. of Ext. and Corporate Affairs, then Corporate Affairs, subseq. of Deptl Mgt, DoH, 2001–06. *Recreations:* arts, sport. *Address:* Department of Health, Richmond House, 79 Whitehall, SW1A 2NS. *Club:* MCC.

TAYLOR, Hugo M.; *see* Mascie-Taylor.

TAYLOR, Rt Rev. Humphrey Vincent; Bishop Suffragan of Selby, 1991–2003; Hon. Assistant Bishop, dioceses of Gloucester and Worcester, since 2004; *b* 5 March 1938; *s* of late Maurice Humphrey Taylor and Mary Patricia Stuart Taylor (*née* Wood, later Pearson); *m* 1965, Anne Katharine Dart; two *d*. *Educ:* Harrow School; Pembroke College, Cambridge (MA); London University (MA). Nat. Service Officer, RAF, 1956–58; Cambridge 1958–61; College of the Resurrection, Mirfield, 1961–63; Curate in London, 1963–66; Rector of Lilongwe, Malaŵi, 1967–71; Chaplain, Bishop Grosseteste Coll., Lincoln, 1971–74; Sec. for Chaplaincies in Higher Education, Gen. Synod Bd of Education, 1974–80; Mission Programmes Sec., USPG, 1980–84; Sec., USPG, 1984–91. Hon. Canon of Bristol Cathedral, 1986–91; Provincial Canon of Southern Africa, 1989. Moderator, Conf. for World Mission, BCC, 1987–90; Chairman: Internat. and Develt Affairs Cttee, Archbps' Council, 1996–2003; Northern and Yorkshire Adv. Cttee on Spiritual Care and Chaplaincy, 1997–2003. *Recreations:* music, gardening. *Address:* 10 High Street, Honeybourne, Worcs WR11 7PQ.

See also R. M. Thornely-Taylor.

TAYLOR, Ian Colin, MBE 1974; MP (C) Esher and Walton, since 1997 (Esher, 1987–97); *b* 18 April 1945; *s* of late Horace Stanley Taylor and Beryl Taylor (*née* Harper); *m* 1974, Hon. Carole Alport, *d* of Baron Alport, PC, TD; two *s*. *Educ:* Whitley Abbey Sch., Coventry; Keele Univ. (BA); London School of Economics (Res. Schol.). Corporate financial adviser; Director: Mathercourt Securities Ltd, 1980–90; Petards Gp (formerly Screen plc), 1999– (Dep. Chm., 2003–); Next Fifteen Group plc, 1999–; Speed-Trap Ltd, 1999–. Nat. Chm., Fedn of Cons. Students, 1968–69; Chm., Europ. Union of Christian Democratic and Cons. Students, 1969–70; Hon. Sec., Brit. Cons. Assoc. in France, 1976–78; Chairman: Commonwealth Youth Exchange Council, 1980–84; Cons. Foreign and Commonwealth Council, 1990–96; Nat. Chm., Cons. Gp for Europe, 1985–88 and 2007–. Contested (C) Coventry SE, Feb. 1974. Parliamentary Private Secretary: FCO, 1990; to Sec. of State for Health, 1990–92; to Chancellor of Duchy of Lancaster, 1992–94; Parly Under-Sec. of State, DTI (Minister for Sci. and Technol.), 1994–97; opposition front bench spokesman on NI, 1997. Member, Select Committee on: Foreign Affairs, 1987–90; Science and Technol., 1998–2001. Chairman: Cons. Parly European Affairs Cttee, 1988–89; Cons. Policy Taskforce on Sci., 2006–. Chairman: European Movement, 2000–04; Cuba Initiative, 2008–. Chm., Tory Europe Network, 2002–. Vice-Chm., Assoc. of Cons. Clubs, 1988–92. Gov., Research into Ageing, 1997–2001; Centre of Cell, 2004–. Liveryman, Co. of Information Technologists, 1998–. *Publications:* various pamphlets; contrib. to various jls, etc, on politics and business. *Recreations:* opera, cigars, shooting. *Address:* House of Commons, SW1A 0AA. *T:* (020) 7219 5221; *e-mail:* taylori@parliament.uk. *Club:* Buck's.

TAYLOR, Prof. Ian Galbraith, CBE 1987; MD; FRCP, FRCPCH; Ellis Llwyd Jones Professor of Audiology and Education of the Deaf, University of Manchester, 1964–88, now Emeritus; *b* 24 April 1924; *s* of David Oswald Taylor, MD, and Margaret Ballantine Taylor; *m* 1954, Audrey Wolstenholme; two *d*. *Educ:* Manchester Grammar Sch.; Univ. of Manchester (MB, ChB, DPH; MD (Gold Medal) 1963). MRCP 1973, FRCP 1977; FRCPCH 1997. Ho. Surg., Manchester Royal Infirm., 1948; DAD, Army Health of N Regional Canal Zone, and OC Army Sch. of Hygiene, ME, 1949–51; Asst MO, City of Manchester, 1951–54. Univ. of Manchester: Hon. Special Lectr and Ewing Foundn Fellow, Dept of Education of the Deaf, 1956–60; Lectr in Clinical Audiology, 1963–64. Consultant in Audiological Medicine, United Manchester Hosps, 1968. Pres., Hearing Concern (formerly British Assoc. of the Hard of Hearing), 1981. *Publication:* Neurological Mechanisms of Hearing and Speech in Children, 1964. *Recreations:* gardening, fishing. *Address:* Croft Cottage, Cinderhill, Whitegate, Northwich, Cheshire CW8 2BH.

TAYLOR, Prof. Irving, MD; FRCS; Professor of Surgery, University College London, since 1993; Vice Dean and Director, Clinical Studies, Royal Free and University College Medical School (formerly University College London Medical School), since 2002 (Chairman, Academic Division of Surgical Specialties and Head of Department, 1993–2004); *b* 7 Jan. 1945; *s* of Sam and Fay Taylor; *m* 1969, Berenice Penelope Brunner; three *d*. *Educ:* Roundhay Sch., Leeds; Sheffield Univ. Med. Sch. (MB ChB 1968; MD 1973; ChM 1978). FRCS 1972. Royal Infirmary, then Royal Hospital, Sheffield: House Officer, 1968; SHO, 1969–70; Surg. Registrar, 1971–73; Sen. Registrar in Surgery, 1973–77; Sen. Lectr and Consultant Surgeon, Liverpool Univ., 1977–81; Prof. of Surgery, Univ. of Southampton, 1981–93. Hunterian Prof., RCS, 1981 (Jacksonian Award, 1996; Stanford Cade Medal, 2000); Bennett Lectr, TCD, 1990; Gordon Bell Lectr, RACS, 1996. Mem. Council, RCS, 2004– (Examnr, 2000–01); Chm., MRC Colorectal Cancer Cttee, 1990–95; President: British Assoc. of Surgical Oncology, 1995–98; Soc. of Academic and Res. Surgeons, 2005–; Eur. Soc. of Surgical Oncology, 2006–08 (Vice-Pres., 2004–06); Sec., Surgical Res. Soc., 1988–90; Editorial Sec., Assoc. of Surgeons, 1988–91. Case Examiner, Fitness to Practise Directorate, GMC, 2003–. Editor-in-Chief: Eur. Jl of Surgical Oncology, 1995–2003; Annals of RCS, 2004–. FRSocMed 1983; FMedSci 2000; FRCPSGlas 2001. *Publications:* Progress in Surgery, 1985, 3rd edn 1989; Complications of Surgery of the Gastrointestinal Tract, 1985; Benign Breast Disease, 1990; Essential General Surgical Oncology, 1995; Surgical Principles, 1996; Recent Advances in Surgery, annually, 1991–; Fast Facts: colorectal cancer, 1999, 2nd edn 2002; articles and papers on gen. surgery, surgical educn, surgical oncology, breast, colorectal and liver cancer in med. jls. *Recreations:* bridge, swimming, rambling, watching cricket, travel, supporting Leeds United. *Address:* 43 Francklyn Gardens, Edgware HA8 8RU. *T:* (020) 7263 8086.

TAYLOR, Dr James; Geographical Director, Africa, Middle East and South Asia, British Council, 2000–03; *b* 22 April 1951; *s* of George Thomson Taylor and Elizabeth Gibson Taylor (*née* Dunsmore); *m* 1986, Dianne Carol Cawthorne; one *s*. *Educ:* Cumnock Acad.; Strathclyde Univ. (BSc 1973; PhD 1977). ACS Petroleum Res. Fellow, Bristol Univ., 1977–78; von Humboldt Fellow, Univ. des Saarlandes, Germany, 1978–79; Res. Chemist, Procter & Gamble, 1979–80; SSO, Scottish Marine Biol Assoc., 1980–84; British Council: Asst Dir, Kuwait, 1984–86; First Sec. (Sci. and Develt), British High Commn, Calcutta, 1986–88; Head, Tech. Adv. Service, Sci. and Technol. Dept, 1988–90; Asst Registrar, Res. Support Unit, Leeds Univ., 1990–92; Development and Training Services, British Council: Contract Dir, Central and Eastern Europe, 1992–93; Head, Europe Gp, 1993–95; Head, Africa and ME Gp, 1995–97; Dir, Zimbabwe and Head, Africa Gp, 1997–2000. *Publications:* contribs on marine sediment chem. to sci. jls. *Recreations:* gardening, TV soaps, walking. *T:* (01730) 231287.

TAYLOR, James Alastair; Sheriff Principal of Glasgow and Strathkelvin, since 2005; *b* 21 Feb. 1951; *s* of Alastair and Margaret Taylor; *m* 1980, Lesley Doig Macleod; two *s*. *Educ:* Nairn Acad.; Univ. of Aberdeen (BSc; LLB). Partner, A. C. Morrison & Richards, Solicitors, Aberdeen, 1980–87; Partner, 1988–98, Hd of Litigation Dept, 1992–98, McGrigor Donald, Solicitors, Glasgow; Sheriff: of Lothian and Borders, 1998–99; of Glasgow and Strathkelvin, 1999–2005. Chm., Disciplinary Tribunal, ICAS, 2000–. Mem. Bd, Civil Justice Review. *Publications:* (contrib.) International Intellectual Property

Litigation, 1998; (contrib.) Sentencing Practice, 2000; (contrib.) Macphail Sheriff Court Practice, 3rd edn, 2006. *Recreations:* golf, wine, good food, jazz. *Address:* Sheriff Principal's Chambers, 1 Carlton Place, Glasgow G5 9DA. *T:* (0141) 429 8888, *Fax:* (0141) 418 5869; *e-mail:* sheriffp.jtaylor@scotcourts.gov.uk. *Clubs:* Nairn Golf; Royal Aberdeen Golf; Pollok Golf.

TAYLOR, Jeremy; *see* Taylor, C. J. B.

TAYLOR, Jessie; *see* Taylor, M. J.

TAYLOR, John Ashley; His Honour Judge John Taylor; a Circuit Judge, since 2006; *b* 11 July 1946; *s* of late Cyril Ernest Taylor and of Mary Taylor; *m* 1968, Anne C. M. Walker; one *s* two *d*. *Educ:* Leeds City High Sch. Admitted solicitor, 1980; in private practice, 1974–98; Dist Judge, 1998–2006. *Recreations:* sailing, cycling, travel, listening to music. *Address:* Leeds Combined Court Centre, 1 Oxford Row, Leeds LS1 3BG.

TAYLOR, Rt Rev. John Bernard, KCVO 1997; Bishop of St Albans, 1980–95; Lord High Almoner to HM the Queen, 1988–97; Hon. Assistant Bishop: diocese of Ely, since 1995; diocese of Europe, since 1998; *b* 6 May 1929; *s* of George Ernest and Gwendoline Irene Taylor; *m* 1956, Linda Courtenay Barnes; one *s* two *d*. *Educ:* Watford Grammar Sch.; Christ's Coll., Cambridge; Jesus Coll., Cambridge. MA Cantab. Vicar of Henham and Elsenham, Essex, 1959–64; Vice-Principal, Oak Hill Theological Coll., 1964–72; Vicar of All Saints', Woodford Wells, 1972–75; Archdeacon of West Ham, 1975–80. Examining Chaplain to Bishop of Chelmsford, 1962–80. Hon. Chaplain, Jesus Coll., Cambridge, 1997–. Chm., Gen. Synod's Cttee for Communications, 1986–93. Member: Churches' Council for Covenanting, 1978–82; Liturgical Commn, 1981–86; Doctrine Commn, 1989–95. Chairman Council: Haileybury Coll., 1980–95; Wycliffe Hall, Oxford, 1985–99; Tyndale House, Cambridge, 1997–2004. President: Hildenborough Evangelistic Trust, 1985–99; Garden Tomb Assoc., Jerusalem, 1986–; Church's Ministry among Jewish People, 1996–; Bible Soc., 1997–2004. Took his seat in House of Lords, 1985. Hon. LLD Hertfordshire, 1995. *Publications:* A Christian's Guide to the Old Testament, 1966; Evangelism among Children and Young People, 1967; Tyndale Commentary on Ezekiel, 1969; Preaching through the Prophets, 1983; Preaching on God's Justice, 1994. *Address:* 22 Conduit Head Road, Cambridge CB3 0EY. *T:* (01223) 313783. *Club:* National.

TAYLOR, Rev. John Brian, PhD; President, Methodist Conference, 1997–98; Chairman, Liverpool District, Methodist Church, 1995–2003; *b* 3 July 1937; *s* of Frank and Alice Taylor; *m* 1959, Patricia Margaret Lord; two *s*. *Educ:* Buxton Coll.; Durham Univ. (BA, DipEd); Hartley Victoria Coll. and Manchester Univ. (BD); PhD Open Univ. 1992. Headmaster, Cours Secondaire Protestant de Dabou, Côte d'Ivoire, 1961–64; Methodist Minister, 1964–; Chaplain, Univ. of Sheffield, 1976–79; Tutor, Queen's Coll., Birmingham, 1979–88 (Hon. Fellow, 2001); Gen. Sec., Methodist Church Div. of Ministries, 1988–95. Commandeur: l'Ordre National (Côte d'Ivoire), 1997; l'Ordre du Mono (Togo), 2000. *Publications:* Preaching as Doctrine, 2001; various articles in learned jls. *Recreations:* genealogy, gardening, music. *Address:* 7 Mordaunt Drive, Four Oaks, Sutton Coldfield B75 5PT.

TAYLOR, Prof. John Bryan, FRS 1970; Fondren Professor of Plasma Theory, University of Texas at Austin, 1989–94; *b* 26 Dec. 1928; *s* of Frank and Ada Taylor, Birmingham; *m* 1951, Joan M. Hargest; one *s* one *d*. *Educ:* Oldbury Grammar Sch.; Birmingham Univ., 1947–50 and 1952–55. RAF, 1950–52. Atomic Weapons Research Establishment, Aldermaston, 1955–59 and 1960–62; Harkness Fellow, Commonwealth Fund, Univ. of California (Berkeley), 1959–60; Culham Laboratory (UKAEA), 1962–69 and 1970–89 (Head of Theoretical Physics Div., 1963–81; Chief Physicist, 1981–89); Inst. for Advanced Study, Princeton, 1969. FInstP 1969. Fellow, Amer. Phys. Soc., 1984. Maxwell Medal, IPPS, 1971; Max Born Medal, German Phys. Soc., 1979; Award for Excellence in Plasma Physics Res., 1986, James Clerk Maxwell Prize, 1999, Amer. Phys. Soc.; Dist. Career Award, Fusion Power Associates, 1999; Hannes Alfven Prize, Eur. Phys. Soc., 2004. *Publications:* contribs to scientific learned jls. *Recreations:* gliding, model engineering. *Address:* Radwinter, Winterbrook Lane, Wallingford OX10 9EJ. *T:* (01491) 837269.

TAYLOR, John Charles; QC 1983; *b* 22 April 1931; *s* of late Sidney Herbert and Gertrude Florence Taylor, St Ives, Cambs; *m* 1964, Jean Aimée Monteith; one *d*. *Educ:* Palmers Sch., Grays, Essex; Queens' Coll., Cambridge (MA, LLB); Harvard Law School (LLM). Called to the Bar, Middle Temple, 1958. Mem., Stephens Cttee on Minerals Planning Control, 1972–74; Chm., Examn in Public Panel, Leics and Rutland Structure Plan, 1985; Inspr, County Hall (London) Inquiries, 1990, 1991. Contested: (C) Kettering, 1970; (Referendum) NE Beds, 1997. *Recreations:* country pursuits, art. *Address:* Clifton Grange, Clifton, Shefford, Beds SG17 5EW. *Clubs:* Travellers, Royal Ocean Racing.

TAYLOR, John Clayton, PhD; FRS 1981; FInstP; Professor of Mathematical Physics, Cambridge University, and Fellow of Robinson College, Cambridge, 1980–95, now Professor and Fellow Emeritus; *b* 4 Aug. 1930; *s* of Leonard Taylor and Edith (*née* Tytherleigh); *m* 1959, Gillian Mary (*née* Schofield); two *s*. *Educ:* Selhurst Grammar Sch., Croydon; Peterhouse, Cambridge (MA). Lectr, Imperial Coll., London, 1956–60; Lectr, Cambridge Univ., and Fellow of Peterhouse, 1960–64; Reader in Theoretical Physics, Oxford Univ., and Fellow of University Coll., Oxford, 1964–80 (Hon. Fellow, 1989). *Publications:* Gauge Theories of Weak Interactions, 1976; Hidden Unity in Nature's Laws, 2001; Gauge Theories in the Twentieth Century, 2001. *Address:* 9 Bowers Croft, Cambridge CB1 8RP.

TAYLOR, John D.; *see* Debenham Taylor.

TAYLOR, John Edward; Chief Executive, Advisory, Conciliation and Arbitration Service, since 2001; *b* 14 Nov. 1949; *s* of Thomas Taylor and Margaret Jane Taylor (*née* Renwick); *m* 1977, Valerie Joan Ticehurst (marr. diss. 1982). *Educ:* Chester-le-Street Grammar Sch.; Durham Univ. (BA Gen. Arts). Grad. Trainee, Littlewoods Orgn, 1971–72; Department of Employment: various posts as Exec. Officer, 1972–79; Private Sec. to Minister of State, 1979–80; Head: of Personnel, 1980–83; of Res. Br., 1983–84; Regl Employment Manager, Midlands, 1984–86; Hd, Overseas Labour Div., 1986–88; Dep. Chief Exec., Rural Develt Commn, 1988–95; Chief Executive: Develt Bd for Rural Wales, 1995–98; SE Wales TEC, 1998–2001. German Marshall Fellowship Schol., USA, 1986. Vis. Prof. for Employment Relns, Glamorgan Univ., 2001–. Public Sector examiner, Inst. of Dirs, 2006–. Member: UK Delegn to USSR on SME Develt, 1991; NHS Partnership Bd, 2001–; Employment Tribunal System Taskforce, 2003–06; Learning and Skills Develt Agency, 2004–06; Central Govt Sector Skills Council, 2005–; Employment Tribunal System Steering Bd, 2006–; Quality Improvement Agency, 2006–; Adv. Bd, unionlearn, 2006–. Governor: Thames Valley Univ., 2005–; Reading Further Educn Coll., 2007–. CCMI 2003. *Recreations:* Sunderland AFC, all sport, CAMRA, travel. *Address:* ACAS, Brandon House, 180 Borough High Street, SE1 1LW. *Club:* Durham County Cricket.

TAYLOR, Prof. John Gerald; Professor of Mathematics, King's College, University of London, 1971–96, now Emeritus; *b* 18 Aug. 1931; *s* of William and Elsie Taylor; *m* Pamela Nancy (*née* Cutmore); two *s* three *d*. *Educ:* King Edward VI Grammar Sch., Chelmsford; Mid-Essex Polytechnic, Chelmsford; Christ's Coll., Cambridge. Fellow, Inst. for Advanced Study, Princeton, NJ, USA, 1956–58 (Mem., 1961–63); Fellow, Christ's Coll., Cambridge, 1958–60; Asst Lectr, Faculty of Mathematics, Univ. of Cambridge, 1959–60; Member: Inst. des Hautes Etudes Scient., Paris, 1960; Res. Inst. Advanced Study, Baltimore, Md, USA, 1960. Sen. Res. Fellow, Churchill Coll., Cambridge, 1963–64; Prof. of Physics, Rutgers Univ., New Brunswick, NJ, 1964–66; Fellow, Hertford Coll., Oxford, and Lectr. Math. Inst., Oxford, 1966–67; Reader in Particles and Fields, Queen Mary Coll., London, 1967–69; Prof. of Physics, Univ. of Southampton, 1969–71. Guest Scientist, Inst. of Medicine, Res. Centre, Juelich, Germany, 1996–99. Dir, Centre for Neural Networks, KCL, 1990–; Consultant Dir of Res., ECONOSTAT Ltd, 1998–. Chm., 1982–87, Vice-Chm., 1988–91, Mathematical Physics Gp, Inst. of Physics. Chm., Jt European Neural Net Initiative, 1990–91; Convener, British Neural Networks Soc., 1989–94; President: European Neural Network Soc., 1993–94 (Vice-Pres., 1991–93); Internat. Neural Network Soc., 1995–96 (Past Pres., 1996–97); Dir, NEURONET, 1994–95; Co-ordinator, EC GNOSYS Cognitive Robot Proj., 2004–07. Institute of Physical and Chemical Research, Tokyo: Mem. Adv. Council, Human Sci. Frontiers Program, 1995–97; Mem. Adv. Bd, Brain Scis Inst., 1998–. European Editor-in-Chief, Neural Networks, 1991–. *Publications:* Quantum Mechanics, an Introduction, 1969; The Shape of Minds to Come, 1970; The New Physics, 1972; Black Holes: the end of the Universe?, 1973; Superminds, 1975; Special Relativity, 1975; Science and the Supernatural, 1980; The Horizons of Knowledge, 1982; Finite Superstrings, 1992; The Promise of Neural Networks, 1993; When the Clock Struck Zero, 1994; The Race for Consciousness, 1999; The Mind: a user's manual, 2006; *edited:* Supergravity, 1981; Supersymmetry and Supergravity, 1982; Tributes to Paul Dirac, 1987; Recent Developments in Neural Computation, 1990; Coupled Oscillating Neurons, 1992; Theory and Applications of Neural Networks, 1992; Mathematical Approaches to Neural Networks, 1993; Neural Networks, 1995; Concepts for Neural Networks, 1997; also scientific papers in Proc. Royal Soc., Phys. Rev., Proc. Camb. Phil. Soc., Jl Math. Phys., Neural Networks, Neural Computation, etc. *Recreations:* listening to music, theatre, walking. *Address:* 33 Meredyth Road, Barnes, SW13 0DS. *T:* (020) 8876 3391.

TAYLOR, John H.; *see* Hermon-Taylor.

TAYLOR, John Jeffrey, FIChemE; Chief Executive, Borealis A/S, 2001–07; *b* 26 Nov. 1947; *s* of F. John Taylor and M. Joan Taylor; *m* 1971, Julie Anne Oldman; three *d*. *Educ:* Hurstpierpoint Coll., Sussex; Univ. of Wales Coll. of Swansea (BSc Hons ChemEng 1969). FIChemE 1998. Exxon Chemical: London and Belgium, 1969; Product Exec. for Olefins, Connecticut, USA, 1983; European HQ Manager, Elastomers, 1985; Vice-Pres., Polymers Marketing, 1986; European Vice-Pres., Polyolefins, 1990; Chief Exec., British Nuclear Fuels plc, 1996–2000. Pres., PlasticsEurope, 2004–08. *Recreations:* Rugby, squash, sailing, ski-ing, travel, theatre. *Address:* Overy Manor, Dorchester-on-Thames, Oxon OX10 7JU. *T:* (01865) 343069. *Club:* Royal Automobile.

TAYLOR, John Mark; *b* 19 Aug. 1941; *s* of Wilfred and Eileen Martha Taylor. *Educ:* Eversfield Prep. School; Bromsgrove School and College of Law. Admitted Solicitor, 1966; Senior Partner, John Taylor & Co., 1983–88. Member: Solihull County Borough Council, 1971–74; W Midlands Metropolitan County Council, 1973–86 (Opposition (Conservative) Leader, 1975–77; Leader, 1977–79). Mem., W Midlands Economic Planning Council, 1978–79. Mem. (C) Midlands E, European Parlt, 1979–84; EDG spokesman on Community Budget, 1979–81, Group Dep. Chm., 1981–82. Contested (C): Dudley East, Feb. and Oct. 1974; Solihull, 2005. MP (C) Solihull, 1983–2005. PPS to Chancellor of Duchy of Lancaster and Minister for Trade and Industry, 1987–88; an Asst Govt Whip, 1988–89; a Lord Comr of HM Treasury (Govt Whip), 1989–90; Vice Chamberlain of HM Household, 1990–92; Parly Sec., Lord Chancellor's Dept, 1992–95; Parly Under-Sec. of State for Competition and Consumer Affairs, DTI, 1995–97; an Opposition Whip, 1997–99; Opposition spokesman on NI, 1999–2003. Mem., Select Cttee on the Environment, 1983–87, on modernisation, 2001–02; Sec., Cons. Back bench Cttee on Eur. Affairs, 1983–86 (Vice-Chm., 1986–87); Vice-Chm., Cons. Back bench Cttee on Sport, 1986–87; on Trade and Industry, 1997, on Legal Affairs, 1997. Mem., Parly Assembly, Council of Europe and WEU, 1997. Vice-Pres., AMA, 1979–86 (Dep. Chm., 1978–79). Governor, Univ. of Birmingham, 1977–81. *Publication:* Please Stay to the Adjournment, 2003. *Recreations:* fellowship, cricket, golf, reading. *Address:* Apartment 8, Blossomfield Gardens, 34 Blossomfield Road, Solihull, West Midlands B91 1NZ. *T:* (0121) 705 5467. *Club:* MCC.

TAYLOR, (John) Martin; Chairman, Syngenta AG, since 2005 (Director, since 2000); Vice-Chairman, 2004–05); Vice-Chairman, RTL Group SA, since 2004 (Director, since 2000); *b* 8 June 1952; *m* 1976, Janet Davey (marr. diss. 2002); two *d*; partner, Pippa Wicks; one *s*. *Educ:* Eton; Balliol Coll., Oxford. Reuters, 1974–78; Financial Times, 1978–82; Courtaulds plc, 1982–90 (Dir, 1987–90); Courtaulds Textiles plc, 1990–93 (Chief Exec., 1990–93; Chm., 1993); Chief Exec., Barclays plc, 1994–98; Chm., W. H. Smith Gp plc, 1999–2003. Dir, Antigenics Inc., 1999–2003; advr, Goldman Sachs Internat., 1999–2005. Govt advr on tax and welfare issues. Sec.-gen., Bilderberg Gp, 1999–2005. *Address:* Syngenta AG, PO Box, 4002 Basel, Switzerland.

TAYLOR, (John) Maxwell (Percy); Chairman, Mitsui Sumitomo (London) Ltd, since 2008 (non-executive Director, since 2006); *b* 17 March 1948; *s* of Harold Guy Percy Taylor and Anne Katherine Taylor (*née* Stafford); *m* 1970, Dawn Susan Harling; one *s* one *d*. *Educ:* Haileybury; ISC. Joined Willis Faber & Dumas, 1970; Dir, Willis Faber, then Willis Corroon Gp plc, 1990–97; Chm., Lloyd's, 1998–2000. Chm., Lloyd's Insce Brokers Cttee, 1997. Dep. Chm., Aon Ltd, 2001–08; Dir, Henderson Smaller Companies Investment Trust plc, 1997–2008. Dir, Financial Services Compensation Scheme, 2007–. Chairman: BIIBA, 2004–07; BIPAR, 2004. Pres., Insurance Inst. of London, 2001. Chm. Council, Univ. of Surrey, 2007–. *Recreations:* music, travel. *Clubs:* Royal Automobile, City.

TAYLOR, Sir John (Michael), Kt 2004; OBE 1994; PhD; FRS 1998; FREng; Chairman, Roke Manor Research Ltd, since 2004; *b* 15 Feb. 1943; *s* of Eric and Dorothy Taylor; *m* 1965, Judith Moyle; two *s* two *d*. *Educ:* Emmanuel Coll., Cambridge (MA; PhD 1969; Hon. Fellow, 2000). FIET (FIEE 1985); FBCS 1986; FREng (FEng 1986). Supt, Communication Systems Div., 1977–79, Computer Applications Div., 1979–81; RSRE; Head, Command, Control and Communications Dept, ARE, 1981–84; Dir, Hewlett-Packard Labs, Europe, 1984–98. Non-exec. Dir, Rolls Royce, 2004–07. Dir Gen. of Res. Councils, OST, DTI, 1999–2004. Pres., IEE, 1998–99; Mem. Council, Royal Acad. Engrg, 2004–07. Vis. Prof., Univ. of Oxford, 2003–. FInstP. Hon. Fellow, Cardiff Univ., 2002. Hon. DEng: Bristol, 1998; UWE, 1999; Surrey, 1999; Exeter, 2000; Brunel, 2000; Birmingham, 2002. *Recreations:* family, photography, sailing, music. *Address:* Roke Manor Research Ltd, Roke Manor, Romsey, Hants SO51 0ZN.

TAYLOR, Rt Rev. John Mitchell; Bishop of Glasgow and Galloway, 1991–98; Assistant Bishop of Glasgow and Galloway, since 2000; *b* 23 May 1932; *m* 1959, Edna Elizabeth (*née* Maitland); one *s* one *d*. *Educ:* Banff Acad.; Aberdeen Univ. (MA 1954); Edinburgh Theol Coll. Ordained deacon, 1956, priest, 1957; Asst Curate, St Margaret, Aberdeen, 1956–58; Rector: Holy Cross, Glasgow, 1958–64; St Ninian, Glasgow, 1964–73; St John the Evangelist, Dumfries, 1973–91; Chaplain: Crichton Royal Hospital; Dumfries and Galloway Royal Infirmary, 1973–91; Canon, St Mary's Cathedral, 1979–91, Hon. Canon, 1999–. *Recreations:* angling, hill walking, music, ornithology. *Address:* 10 St George's, Castle Douglas DG7 1LN. *T:* and *Fax:* (01556) 502593.

TAYLOR, John Russell; Art Critic, The Times, since 1978; *b* 19 June 1935; *s* of Arthur Russell and Kathleen Mary Taylor (*née* Picker); civil partnership 2006, Ying Yeung Li. *Educ:* Dover Grammar Sch.; Jesus Coll., Cambridge (MA); Courtauld Inst. of Art, London. Sub-Editor, Times Educational Supplement, 1959; Editorial Asst, Times Literary Supplement, 1960; Film Critic, The Times, 1962–73. Lectr on Film, Tufts Univ. in London, 1970–71; Prof., Div. of Cinema, Univ. of Southern California, 1972–78. Editor, Films and Filming, 1983–90. *Publications:* Anger and After, 1962; Anatomy of a Television Play, 1962; Cinema Eye, Cinema Ear, 1964; Penguin Dictionary of the Theatre, 1966; The Art Nouveau Book in Britain, 1966; The Rise and Fall of the Well-Made Play, 1967; The Art Dealers, 1969; Harold Pinter, 1969; The Hollywood Musical, 1971; The Second Wave, 1971; David Storey, 1974; Directors and Directions, 1975; Peter Shaffer, 1975; Hitch, 1978; The Revels History of Drama in English, vol. VII, 1978; Impressionism, 1981; Strangers in Paradise, 1983; Ingrid Bergman, 1983; Alec Guinness, 1984; Vivien Leigh, 1984; Portraits of the British Cinema, 1985; Hollywood 1940s, 1985; Orson Welles, 1986; Edward Wolfe, 1986; Great Movie Moments, 1987; Post-war Friends, 1987; Robin Tanner, 1989; Bernard Meninsky, 1990; Impressionist Dreams, 1990; Liz Taylor, 1991; Ricardo Cinalli, 1993; Igor Mitoraj, 1993; Muriel Pemberton, 1993; Claude Monet, 1995; Michael Parkes: the stone lithographs, 1996; Bill Jacklin, 1997; Antonio Saliola, 1998; The Sun is God, 1999; Roberto Bernardi, 2001; Peter Coker, 2002; Philip Sutton Printmaker, 2005; Roboz, 2005; Adrian George, 2005; Donald McGill, 2006; The Art of Michael Parkes, 2006; Carl Laubin, 2007; The Art of Jeremy Ramsay, 2007; Exactitude, 2008. *Address:* c/o The Times, 1 Pennington Street, E98 1TT.

TAYLOR, Jonathan Francis, CBE 2005; Chairman: Booker Prize Foundation, since 2001; Booker plc, 1993–98 (Chief Executive, 1984–93); *b* 12 Aug. 1935; *s* of Sir Reginald Taylor, CMG and Lady Taylor; *m* 1965, Anthea Gail Proctor; three *s*. *Educ:* Winchester College; Corpus Christi College, Oxford (Schol.; BA Mod. Hist.; MA; Hon. Fellow 1996). Joined Booker, 1959; Chm., Agricultural Div., 1976–80; Dir, Booker plc, 1980; Pres., Ibec Inc. (USA), 1980–84; Dir, Arbor Acres Farm Inc., 1980–98 (Dep. Chm., 1985–90; Chm., 1990–95). Director: Sifida Investment Bank, Geneva, 1978–90; Tate & Lyle, 1988–99; MEPC, 1992–2000; Equitable Life Assurance Soc., 1995–2001; Chm., Ellis & Everard, 1993–99. Mem., Adv. Council, UNIDO, 1986–93; Director: Foundn for Develt of Polish Agric., 1991–99 (Chm., 1992–99); Internat. Agribusiness Management Assoc., 1991– (Pres., 1993–94); Winrock Internat. Inst. for Agricl Develt (US), 1991–2001. Chm., Marshall Aid Commemoration Commn, 2000–07. Chm., Governing Body, SOAS, London Univ., 1999–2005 (Gov., 1988–2005); Governor: RAC, Cirencester, 1995–; Commonwealth Inst., 1998–2005. Co-opted Curator, Bodleian Library, 1989–97; Chairman: Bodleian Liby Develt Bd, 1989–2000; Paintings in Hosps, 1996–2006. *Recreations:* collecting water colours, travel. *Address:* 48 Edwardes Square, W8 6HH. *Club:* Brooks's.

TAYLOR, Jonathan McLeod Grigor; Director General, London Investment Banking Association, since 2005; *b* 5 March 1955; *s* of John Grigor Taylor and Dorothy Jean Taylor (*née* McLeod); *m* 1984, Stella Schimmel; one *s* one *d*. *Educ:* Bedales Sch.; New Coll., Oxford (BA PPE). HM Treasury, 1977–2002: Admin. trainee, 1977–79; Private Sec. to Perm. Sec., 1979–81; Principal, 1981; First Sec. (Budget), UK Perm. Rep., Brussels, 1982–84 (on secondment); Private Sec. to Chancellor of Exchequer, 1987–89; Asst Sec., 1990; Counsellor (Econ. and Financial), UK Perm. Rep., Brussels, 1994–98 (on secondment); Dir, Macroeconomic Policy and Internat. Finance Directorate, 1998–2002; Man. Dir and Hd of Public Policy, Internat., UBS AG, 2002–05. *Address:* London Investment Banking Association, 6 Frederick's Place, EC2R 8BT.

TAYLOR, Jonathan Peter; Partner, Bird & Bird Solicitors, since 2007; *b* Bristol, 6 Nov. 1967; *s* of Gavin and Louise Taylor; *m* 2004, Kate Thefaut; two *d*. *Educ:* University Coll., Oxford (BA 1st Cl. Hons Juris. 1989); Univ. of Virginia (LLM 1990). Called to the Bar, NY, 1991; admitted solicitor, England and Wales, 1997; Associate, Schulte Roth & Zabel, NYC, 1990–97; Solicitor, Townleys, 1997–2001; Partner, Hammonds, 2001–07. Tutor, University Coll., Oxford, 1992–93; Dir of Studies in Sports Law, KCL, 2000–08. Member: Anti-Doping Appeal Panel, Under 19 World Cup, ICC, 2007; Anti-Doping Panel, Internat. Baseball Fedn, 2008–. *Publication:* (ed jtly) Sport: law & practice, 2003, 2nd edn 2008. *Recreations:* family, Fulham FC. *Address:* c/o Bird & Bird, 15 Fetter Lane, EC4A 1JP; *e-mail:* jonathan.taylor@twobirds.com.

TAYLOR, Prof. Joseph Hooton, Jr, PhD; James McDonnell Distinguished University Professor of Physics, Princeton University, 1986–2006, now Emeritus (Professor of Physics, 1980–86; Dean of the Faculty, 1997–2003); *b* 29 March 1941; *s* of Joseph Taylor and Sylvia Taylor (*née* Evans); *m* 1st, 1963, Alexandra Utgoff (marr. diss. 1975); one *s* one *d*; 2nd, 1976, Marietta Bisson; one *d*. *Educ:* Haverford Coll. (BA Physics 1963); Harvard Univ. (PhD Astronomy 1968). Res. Fellow and Lectr, Harvard Univ., 1968–69; University of Massachusetts, Amherst: Asst Prof. of Astronomy, 1969–72; Associate Prof., 1973–77; Prof., 1977–81. Wolf Prize in Physics, Wolf Foundn, 1982; Einstein Prize, Albert Einstein Soc., 1991; (jtly) Nobel Prize in Physics, 1993. *Publications:* (with R. N. Manchester) Pulsars, 1977; over 150 articles in jls. *Recreations:* sailing, ham radio, golf. *Address:* Department of Physics, Princeton University, PO Box 708, Princeton, NJ 08544, USA.

TAYLOR, Judy, (Julia Marie), (Judy Hough), MBE 1971; writer and publisher; *b* 12 Aug. 1932; adopted *d* of Gladys Spicer Taylor; *m* 1980, Richard Hough, writer (*d* 1999). *Educ:* St Paul's Girls' Sch. Joined The Bodley Head, 1951, specialising in children's books; Director: The Bodley Head Ltd, 1967–84 (Dep. Man. Dir, 1971–80); Chatto, Bodley Head & Jonathan Cape Ltd, 1973–80; Chatto, Bodley Head & Jonathan Cape Australia Pty Ltd, 1977–80. Publishers Association: Chm., Children's Book Gp, 1969–72; Mem. Council, 1972–78; Member: Book Develt Council, 1973–76; Unicef Internat. Art Cttee, 1968–70, 1976, 1982–83; UK Unicef Greeting Card Cttee, 1982–85. Consultant to Penguin (formerly to Frederick Warne) on Beatrix Potter, 1981–87, 1989–92; Associate Dir, Weston Woods Inst., USA, 1984–2003; Consulting Ed., Reinhardt Books, 1988–93. Chm., Beatrix Potter Soc., 1990–97, 2000–03, 2006–; Volunteer Reading Help: Mem., 1993–99, Chm., 1989–99, London, subseq. Inner London, Cttee; Trustee, 2000–05. FRSA. *Publications: children's:* Sophie and Jack, 1982; Sophie and Jack Help Out, 1983; Sophie and Jack in the Snow, 1984; Dudley and the Monster, 1986; Dudley Goes Flying, 1986; Dudley in a Jam, 1986; Dudley and the Strawberry Shake, 1986; My Dog, 1987; My Cat, 1987; Dudley Bakes a Cake, 1988; Sophie and Jack in the Rain, 1989; *non-fiction:* My First Year: a Beatrix Potter baby book, 1983; Beatrix Potter: artist, storyteller and countrywoman, 1986, 3rd edn 2002; That Naughty Rabbit: Beatrix Potter and Peter Rabbit, 1987, 2nd edn 2002; Beatrix Potter and Hawkshead, 1988; Beatrix Potter and Hill Top, 1989; (ed) Beatrix Potter's Letters: a selection, 1989; (ed) Letters to Children from Beatrix Potter, 1992; (ed) So I Shall Tell You a Story: encounters with Beatrix Potter, 1993; (ed) The Choyce Letters: Beatrix Potter to Louie Choyce 1916–1943, 1994; (ed) Beatrix Potter: a holiday diary, 1996; (ed) Beatrix Potter's Farming Friendship, 1998; (ed) Sketches for Friends, by Edward Ardizzone, 2000; *play:* (with Patrick Garland) Beatrix, 1996; numerous professional articles. *Recreations:* collecting early children's books, growing things. *Address:* 31 Meadowbank, Primrose Hill Road, NW3 3AY. *T:* (020) 7722 5663; *e-mail:* taylor.hough@talk21.com.

TAYLOR, Kenneth, OBE 1981; FREng, FIMechE, FIET; consultant on railway mechanical and electrical engineering; Director of Mechanical and Electrical Engineering, British Railways Board, 1977–82; *b* 29 Sept. 1921; *s* of Charles Taylor and Amy (*née* Booth); *m* 1945, Elsie Armitt; one *d*. *Educ:* Manchester Coll. of Technol. FIMechE; FIET (FIEE 1971); FREng (FEng 1981). Principal appts with British Railways: Electric Traction Engr, Manchester, 1956; Electrical Engr, LMR, 1963; Chief Mech. and Elec. Engr, LMR, 1970; Traction Engr, BR Bd HQ, 1971. *Recreations:* golf, gardening. *Address:* 137 Burley Lane, Quarndon, Derby DE22 5JS. *T:* (01332) 550123.

TAYLOR, Prof. Kenneth MacDonald, MD; FRCSE, FRCSGlas; FSAScot; Professor and Chief of Cardiac Surgery, Imperial College School of Medicine (formerly Royal Postgraduate Medical School), Hammersmith Hospital, 1983–2007, now Emeritus; British Heart Foundation Professor of Cardiac Surgery, University of London, 1983–2007; Deputy Head, National Heart & Lung Institute (formerly Division of Heart, Lung and Circulation), Imperial College Faculty of Medicine, 1997–2007; Clinical Director of Cardiac Sciences, Imperial College Healthcare NHS Trust (formerly Hammersmith Hospitals NHS Trust), 2003–07; *b* 20 Oct. 1947; *s* of late Hugh Baird Taylor and Mary Taylor; *m* 1971, Christine Elizabeth (*née* Buchanan); one *s* one *d*. *Educ:* Jordanhill College School; Univ. of Glasgow (MB ChB, MD; Cullen Medal, 1968; Gairdner Medal, 1969; Allan Hird Prize, 1969). Univ. of Glasgow: Hall Fellow in Surgery, 1971–72, Lectr and Sen. Lectr in Cardiac Surgery, 1975–83; Consultant Cardiac Surgeon, Royal Infirmary and Western Infirmaries, Glasgow, 1979–83. Vis. Prof., Dept of Bio-engineering, Univ. of Strathclyde, 1997–2007. Chm., Specialist Adv. Cttee in Cardiothoracic Surgery, 1992–95 (Mem., 1986–92); Dir, UK Heart Valve Registry, 1986–2007; Clin. Dir, UK Sch. of Perfusion Science, 1987–97. Member: Exec. Cttee, Soc. of Cardiothoracic Surgeons of GB and Ire., 1992–95; Wkg Gp on Cardiac Waiting Times, DoH, 1994–95; Central R & D Cttee, Acute Sector Panel, DoH, 1996–2007; Reference Gp, Nat. Service Framework, Coronary Heart Disease, DoH, 1999–2002; Chairman: Database Cttee, European Assoc. for Cardiothoracic Surgery, 1994–2000; UK Cardiac Audit Steering Gp, 1994–2001. FESC 1995; FECTS 1998 (Mem., 1988); Member: British Cardiac Soc., 1983–; Amer. Soc. of Thoracic Surgeons, 1984–; Council and Exec. Cttee, BHF, 2001– (Trustee, 2006–); Hon. Member: Amer. Acad. of Cardiovascular Perfusion, 1993; Amer. Assoc. for Thoracic Surgery, 1998 (Mem., 1988–98; Honoured Guest, 1998); Soc. of Perfusionists of GB and Ire., 1998 (Pres., 1989–93; Hon. Life Mem., 1999). Trustee: Garfield Weston Trust, 1998–; European Soc. of Perfusion, 2002–. Hon. Alumnus, Cleveland Clinic, USA, 2000. Governor, Drayton Manor High Sch., London, 1989–96. Pres., Friends of Hammersmith Hosp., 2007–. Editor, Perfusion, 1986–2008; Member, Advisory Editorial Board: Annals of Thoracic Surgery, 1990–2000; Jl of Cardiovascular Anaesthesia, 1993–2000; Jl of Heart Valve Disease, 1993–2000. Peter Allen Prize, Soc. of Thoracic and Cardiovascular Surgeons, 1975; Patey Prize, Surgical Res. Soc., 1977; Fletcher Prize, RCSG, 1977; Watson Prize, RCSG, 1982. *Publications:* Pulsatile Perfusion, 1979, 2nd edn 1982; Handbook of Intensive Care, 1984; Cardiopulmonary Bypass, 1986; Cardiac Surgery, 1987; Principles of Surgical Research, 1989, 2nd edn 1995; The Brain and Cardiac Surgery, 1992; numerous articles on cardiac surgery. *Recreations:* family, church, music. *Address:* 129 Argyle Road, Ealing, W13 0DB.

TAYLOR, Kim; *see* Taylor, L. C.

TAYLOR, Prof. Laurence John, (Laurie); Professor of Sociology, University of York, 1974–93; *s* of Stanley Douglas Taylor and Winifred Agnes (*née* Cooper); marr. diss.; one *s*. *Educ:* St Mary's Coll., Liverpool; Rose Bruford College of Drama, Kent; Birkbeck Coll., Univ. of London (BA); Univ. of Leicester (MA). Librarian, 1952–54; Sales Asst, 1954–56; Professional Actor, 1960–61; English Teacher, 1961–64; Lectr in Sociology, 1965–73, Reader in Sociology, 1973–74, Univ. of York. Vis. Prof., 1994–, Fellow, 1996–, Birkbeck Coll., Univ. of London. *Publications:* Deviance and Society, 1971; (jtly) Psychological Survival, 1972; (jtly) Crime, Deviance and Socio-Legal Control, 1972; (ed jtly) Politics and Deviance, 1973; Man's Experience of the World, 1976; (jtly) Escape Attempts, 1976, 2nd edn 1992; (jtly) Prison Secrets, 1978; (jtly) In Whose Best Interests?, 1980; In the Underworld, 1984; (jtly) Uninvited Guests, 1986; Professor Lapping Sends His Apologies, 1987; The Tuesday Afternoon Time Immemorial Committee, 1989; Laurie Taylor's Guide to Higher Education, 1994; (jtly) What Are Children For?, 2003; articles, reviews, broadcasts, TV series. *Address: e-mail:* lolsoc@dircon.co.uk.
See also Matthew Taylor.

TAYLOR, Len Clive, (Kim); Director, Calouste Gulbenkian Foundation (UK Branch), 1982–88, retired; *b* 4 Aug. 1922; *s* of late S. R. Taylor, Calcutta, India; *m* 1951, Suzanne Dufault, Spencer, Massachusetts, USA; one *s* two *d*. *Educ:* Sevenoaks School; New College, Oxford; Chicago University. New College, Oxford; 1st Cl. Hons Mod. Hist.; Commonwealth Fund Fellowship. Assistant Master, St Paul's School, Darjeeling, India, 1940–42 and 1945–46; Indian Army Intelligence Corps, 1942–45; New College, Oxford, 1946–49; Chicago University, 1949–50; Senior History Master, Repton School, 1950–54; Headmaster, Sevenoaks School, 1954–68; Dir, Nuffield Foundn 'Resources for Learning' Project, 1966–72; Principal Administrator, Centre for Educnl Res. and Innovation, OECD, Paris, 1972–77; Head of Educnl Prog. Services, IBA, 1977–82. Comdr, Order of Henry the Navigator (Portugal), 1989. *Publications:* Experiments in Education at Sevenoaks, 1965; Resources for Learning, 1971; (ed) Camões, Epic and Lyric, 1990; (ed) They Went to Portugal Too, 1990; (ed) A Centenary Pessoa, 1995; (ed) A Companion History of Portugal, 1997. *Address:* 8 Litten Terrace, Chichester, W Sussex PO19 7SA. *T:* (01243) 528091.

TAYLOR, Louise Méarie; Director, Crafts Council, 2002–05; *b* 8 Sept. 1967; *d* of Prof. A. Taylor and J. M. Taylor; *m* 2000, Jason Brooks; one *d*. *Educ:* Univ. of Warwick (BA Hons (Hist. of Art) 1988); Staffordshire Univ. (PhD (Design Hist.) 1995). Craftspace Touring: Exhibns Dir, 1991–95; Actg Dir, 1995–96; Crafts Council: Hd, Exhibns and Collection, 1996–99; Dir, Artistic Programming and Information, 1999–2002. Hon. FRCA 2004. *Publications:* editor and joint author: Recycling: forms for the next century, 1996; Handmade in India, 1998; Satellites of Fashion, 1998; No Picnic 1997–1998, 1998; Contemporary International Basketmaking, 1999; Contemporary Japanese Jewellery, 2000. *Recreations:* tennis, dance, fashion. *Address:* 201 Alaska Buildings, 61 Grange Road, SE1 3BB; *e-mail:* louisembtaylor@yahoo.co.uk.

TAYLOR, Malcolm; *see* McDowell, M.

TAYLOR, (Margaret) Jessie, OBE 1989; piano teacher, since 2001; Headmistress, Whalley Range High School for Girls, 1976–88; *b* 30 Nov. 1924; *d* of Thomas Brown Gowland and Ann Goldie Gowland; *m* 1958, Eric Taylor, *qv*. *Educ:* Queen Elizabeth's Grammar Sch., Middleton; Manchester Univ. (BA Hons, DipEd). Jun. Classics Teacher, Cheadle Hulme Sch., 1946–49; North Manchester Grammar School for Girls: Sen. Classics Teacher, 1950; Sen. Mistress, 1963; Actg Headmistress, Jan.–July 1967; Dep. Head Teacher, Wright Robinson Comprehensive High Sch., 1967–75. Voluntary worker, UNICEF, 1988–97. Dir, Piccadilly Radio, 1979–2000. Chm., Manchester High Sch. Heads Gp, 1984–88; Member: Council and Exams Cttee, Associated Lancs Schs Examining Bd, 1976–91 (Mem. Classics Panel, 1968–72); Exams Cttee, Northern Exams Assoc., 1988–92; Nursing Educn Cttee, S Manchester Area, 1976–84; Home Office Cttee on Obscenity and Film Censorship, 1977–79; Consultant Course Tutor, NW Educnl Management Centre, Padgate, 1980–82. Mem. Court, Salford Univ., 1982–88; Gov., William Hulme's Grammar Sch., 1989–. FRSA 1980. *Recreations:* music, riding. *Address:* 10 Mercers Road, Hopwood, Heywood, Lancs OL10 2NP. *T:* (01706) 366630.

TAYLOR, Mark Christopher; Director, Museums Association, since 1989; *b* 24 Nov. 1958; *s* of Norman and June Taylor; *m*; two *s* one *d*. *Educ:* Loughborough Grammar Sch.; Birmingham Univ. (BA Medieval and Modern Hist.); Leeds Poly. (postgrad. Hotel Management qualification). Hotel Management, Norfolk Capital Hotels, 1981–84; Conf. Manager, Museums Assoc., 1984–89. Chairman: Network of Eur. Museum Orgns, 1998–2001; Campaign for Learning through Museums, 1998–2003; Cultural Tourism and Heritage Export Cttee, 2003–05; Board Member: Nat. Campaign for Arts, 1999–; Bedfordshire Music, 2003–; Creative and Cultural Industries Sector Skills Council, 2004–05. Trustee: Museum Prize Trust, 2002–; Campaign for Museums, 2004–; Culture Unlimited, 2008–. *Recreations:* sport, films, food. *Address:* Museums Association, 24 Calvin Street, E1 6NW. *T:* (020) 7426 6950; *e-mail:* mark@museumsassociation.org.

TAYLOR, Prof. Mark Peter, PhD; Managing Director, Barclays Global Investors Ltd, since 2006; Professor of International Finance and Macroeconomics (formerly of Macroeconomics), University of Warwick, since 1999; *b* 17 May 1958; *s* of Arthur Leslie Taylor and Lorna Kathleen Taylor; *m* 1980, Anita Margaret Phillips; two *s* one *d*. *Educ:* St John's Coll., Oxford (BA (PPE) 1980; MA 1984); Birkbeck Coll., London (MSc (Econs) 1982; PhD (Econs) 1984); Liverpool Univ. (MA (Eng. Lit.) 2001). Foreign exchange dealer, Citibank, London, 1980–82; Lectr in Econs, Univ. of Newcastle upon Tyne, 1984–86; Res. Economist, Bank of England, 1986–87; Professor of Economics: Dundee Univ., 1987–88; City Univ. Business Sch., 1988–90; Sen. Econ. Advr, IMF, Washington, 1990–94; Prof. of Econs, Univ. of Liverpool, 1994–97; Fellow in Econs, University Coll., Oxford, 1997–99. Sen. Econ. Advr to Labour Party, 1994–97; Consultant, IMF, 1999–2005. Res. Fellow, Centre for Econ. Policy Res., 1987–. Councillor, REconS, 2002–. *Publications:* Macroeconomic Systems, 1987; The Balance of Payments: new perspectives on open economy macroeconomics, 1990; Money and Financial Markets, 1991; Applied Econometric Techniques, 1992; Policy Issues in the Operation of Currency Unions, 1993; Modern Perspectives on the Gold Standard, 1996; Speculation and Financial Markets, 2001; The Economics of Exchange Rates, 2002; Economics, 2006; numerous articles in learned jls. *Recreations:* languages, literature, beekeeping, antiques, horology, wine, trying to keep fit, living beyond my means. *Address:* Department of Economics, University of Warwick, Coventry CV4 7AL. *T:* (024) 7652 3055, *Fax:* (024)7652 3032; *e-mail:* mark.taylor@warwick.ac.uk. *Club:* Reform.

TAYLOR, Martin; *see* Taylor, J. M.

TAYLOR, Martin Gibbeson, CBE 1993; FCA; Vice Chairman, Hanson plc, 1988–95; *b* 30 Jan. 1935; *s* of late Roy G. Taylor and Vera Constance (*née* Farmer); *m* 1960, Gunilla Chatarina Bryner; two *s*. *Educ:* Haileybury; St Catharine's Coll., Cambridge (MA 1962). Company Sec., Dow Chemical (UK), 1963–69; joined Hanson plc, 1969, Dir 1976–95. Chm., National Westminster Life, 1992–2000; Dep. Chm., Charter plc, 1995–2002. Non-executive Director: Vickers plc, 1986–99; National Westminster Bank plc, 1990–2000; Securities Assoc., 1987–90; UGI plc, 1979–82; Millennium Chemicals Inc., 1996–2003. Confederation of British Industry: Mem. Council, 1981–96; Member: Companies Cttee, 1981–94 (Chm., 1990–94); City/Industry Task Force, 1987; President's Cttee, 1990–94; Steering Gp on Long Termism & Corporate Governance, 1990–92; Takeover Panel 1989–95. Mem., Industrial Develt Adv. Bd, 1993–97. Hon. Treas., Snapshot Appeal, Nat. Assoc. for Epilepsy, 1992–95. Governor, Mall Sch. Trust, 1987–2000. *Recreations:* art, books, sport, theatre. *Clubs:* MCC, Oxford and Cambridge.

TAYLOR, Prof. Martin John, PhD; FRS 1996; Professor of Pure Mathematics, University of Manchester (formerly University of Manchester Institute of Science and Technology), since 1986; *b* 18 Feb. 1952; *s* of John Maurice Taylor and Sheila Mary Barbara Taylor (*née* Camacho); *m* 1973, Sharon Lynn Marlow; two *s* two *d*. *Educ:* St Clare's Prep. Sch., Leicester; Wyggeston Boys' Sch., Leicester; Pembroke Coll., Oxford (BA 1st Class); King's College, London (PhD). Res. Assistant, KCL, 1976–77; Jun. Lectr, Oxford Univ., 1977–78; Lectr, QMC, 1978–81; Fellow, Trinity Coll., Cambridge, 1981–85; Univ. Asst Lectr, Cambridge, 1984–85. Associate Researcher, CNRS, Besançon, 1979–80; NSF Researcher, Univ. of Illinois, Urbana, 1981; Royal Soc. Leverhulme Sen. Res. Fellowship, 1991–92; CNRS Poste Rouge, Bordeaux, 1996; EPSRC Sen. Res. Fellow, 1999–2004; Royal Soc. Wolfson Res. Fellow, 2002–. Pres., London Mathematical Soc., 1998–2000; Mem. Council, 2000–01, Vice-Pres. and Physical Sec., 2004–, Royal Soc.; Mem. Council, EPSRC, 2004–. Hon. DSc Leicester, 2006. *Publications:* Class Groups of Group Rings, 1984; (with Ph. Cassou-Noguès) Elliptic Functions and Rings of Integers, 1987; (with J. Coates) L-functions and Arithmetic, 1991; (with A. Fröhlich) Algebraic Number Theory, 1991; (with K. Roggenkamp) Group Rings and Class Groups, 1992. *Recreations:* fly fishing, hill walking. *Address:* Department of Mathematics, University of Manchester, PO Box 88, Manchester M60 1QD. *T:* (0161) 200 3640.

TAYLOR, Matthew; Chief Executive, Royal Society for the Encouragement of Arts, Manufactures and Commerce, since 2006; *b* 5 Dec. 1960; *s* of Prof. Laurence John Taylor, *qv* and Jennifer Howells; partner, Claire Holland; two *s*. *Educ:* Southampton Univ. (BA Sociol.); Warwick Univ. (MA Industrial Relns). Set up Res. Unit, NAS/UWT, 1985–88; Dir, W Midlands Health Service Monitoring Unit, 1988–90; Sen. Res. Fellow, Univ. of Warwick, 1990–93; Asst Gen. Sec., Labour Party, 1994–98; Dir, IPPR, 1998–2003; Chief Advr on Political Strategy to Prime Minister, 2003–06. Regular contributor on public service reform, political strategy and communities to newspapers and jls. *Publication:* (with L. J. Taylor) What Are Children For?, 2003. *Recreations:* running, watching sons play football, West Bromwich Albion. *Address:* Royal Society for the Encouragement of Arts, Manufactures and Commerce, 8 John Adam Street, WC2N 6EZ. *T:* (020) 7451 6883.

TAYLOR, Matthew Owen John; MP (Lib Dem) Truro and St Austell, since 1997 (MP Truro, March 1987–1997, L, 1987–88, Lib Dem, 1988–97); *b* 3 Jan. 1963; *s* of Ken Taylor and Jill Taylor (*née* Black); *m* 2007, Victoria Sophie Garner; two *s*. *Educ:* Treliske School, Truro; University College School; Lady Margaret Hall, Oxford (Scholar; BA Hons). Pres., Oxford Univ. Student Union, 1985–86. Economic policy researcher to Parly Liberal Party (attached to David Penhaligon, MP), 1986–87. Parly spokesman on energy, 1987–88, on local govt, 1988–89, on trade and industry, 1989–90, on educn, 1990–92, on citizen's charter, 1992–94, on environment, 1994–99, and transport, 1997–99, on the economy, 1999–2003, on social exclusion, 2006–; Special Advr to Govt on sustainable rural communities, 2007–. Liberal Democrats: Communications Chm., 1989–92; Chm. of Campaigns and Communications, 1992–94; Chm., Parly Party, 2003–05. *Address:* House of Commons, SW1A 0AA. *T:* (020) 7219 6686.

See also V. M. T. Heywood.

TAYLOR, Rt Rev. Maurice, DD; Bishop of Galloway, (RC), 1981–2004, now Emeritus; *b* 5 May 1926; *s* of Maurice Taylor and Lucy Taylor (*née* McLaughlin). *Educ:* St Aloysius Coll., Glasgow; Our Lady's High School, Motherwell; Pontifical Gregorian Univ., Rome (DD). Served RAMC in UK, India, Egypt, 1944–47. Ordained to priesthood, Rome, 1950; lectured in Philosophy, 1955–60, in Theology 1960–65, St Peter's Coll., Cardross; Rector, Royal Scots Coll., Valladolid, Spain, 1965–74; Parish Priest, Our Lady of Lourdes, East Kilbride, 1974–81. Vice-Pres., Progressio (formerly Catholic Inst. for Internat. Relations), 1985–; Episcopal Sec., Bishops' Conf. of Scotland, 1987–2004; Chm., Internat. Commn on English in the Liturgy, 1997–2002. *Publications:* The Scots College in Spain, 1971; Guatemala: a bishop's journey, 1991; El Salvador: portrait of a parish, 1992; (with Ellen Hawkes) Opening Our Lives to the Saviour, 1995; (with Ellen Hawkes) Listening at the Foot of the Cross, 1996; (compiled) Surveying Today's World, 2003; Being a Bishop in Scotland, 2006. *Address:* 41 Overmills Road, Ayr KA7 3LH. *T:* (01292) 285865.

TAYLOR, Maxwell; *see* Taylor, J. M. P.

TAYLOR, Rev. Prof. Michael Hugh, OBE 1998; Professor of Social Theology, University of Birmingham, 1999–2004, now Emeritus; Director, World Faiths Development Dialogue, 2002–04; *b* 8 Sept. 1936; *s* of Albert Ernest and Gwendoline Louisa Taylor; *m* 1960, Adèle May Dixon; two *s* one *d*. *Educ:* Northampton Grammar School; Univ. of Manchester (BA, BD, MA); Union Theological Seminary, NY (STM). Baptist Minister, N Shields, 1961–66, Birmingham Hall Green, 1966–69; Principal, Northern Baptist Coll., Manchester, 1970–85; Lectr, Univ. of Manchester, 1970–85; Dir, Christian Aid, 1985–97; Pres. and Chief Exec., Selly Oak Colls, 1998–99. Mem. Council, ODI, 1989–2000; Chairman: Assoc. of Protestant Develt Agencies in Europe, 1991–94; The Burma Campaign UK, 2000–; Health Unlimited, 2002–; Mem., WCC Commn on Sharing and Service, 1991–. Trustee: Mines Adv. Gp, 1998– (Chm., 2000–); Responding to Conflict, 2004– (Chm., 2007–); St Philip's Centre, Leicester, 2006–. Gov., Fircroft Coll., Birmingham, 1998– (Chm., 2006–). Hon. Canon, Worcester Cathedral, 2002–07. JP Manchester, 1980–85. DLitt Lambeth, 1997. *Publications:* Variations on a Theme, 1973; Sermon on the Mount, 1982; (ed) Christians and the Future of Social Democracy, 1982; Learning to Care, 1983; Good for the Poor, 1990; Christianity and the Persistence of Poverty, 1991; Not Angels But Agencies, 1996; NGOs and their Future in Development, 1997; Poverty and Christianity, 2000; Christianity, Poverty and Wealth, 2003; Eat, Drink and Be Merry for Tomorrow We Live, 2005; Border Crossings: social theology in Christianity and Islam, 2006; contribs to books and jls. *Recreations:* walking, cooking, music, cinema, theatre. *Address:* University of Birmingham, Selly Oak, Bristol Road, Birmingham B29 6LQ.

TAYLOR, Michael John; His Honour Judge Michael Taylor; a Circuit Judge, since 1996; *b* 28 Feb. 1951; *m* 1973, Pamela Ann Taylor. *Educ:* Hull Univ. (LLB). Called to the Bar, Inner Temple, 1974; in practice, 1974–96. *Address:* Teesside Combined Court Centre, Russell Street, Middlesbrough TS1 2AE.

TAYLOR, Michael John Ellerington, CBE 1992; TD 1972; DL; North West and West Midlands Regional Commissioner, Appointments (formerly NHS Appointments) Commission, since 2001; *b* 15 Sept. 1937; *s* of Leonard George Taylor and Marjorie Ellerington Taylor. *Educ:* Harrow Sch.; Emmanuel Coll., Cambridge (BA Hons 1962; LLB Hons 1963; MA 1967). Shell UK and Shell Internat., 1969–91; Chief Exec., Mgt Charter Initiative, 1990–91; Investors in People: Nat. Assessor, 1991–96; Chief External Verifier, 1996–2001. Chairman: Council, RFCA, 2000–04; Nat. Artillery Assoc., 1988–2003 (Vice Pres., 2004–); W Chester Regeneration Bd, 2000–05; Chester Aid to the Homeless, 2001–; Pres., Nat. Home Service Force Assoc., 2004–. Vice-Chm., W. Cheshire Coll., 2001–04. Col, TA, 1982–93; ADC to the Queen, 1988–92; Hon. Col Comdt, RA, 1994–2005. DL Cheshire, 1998. *Recreations:* Territorial Army, inland waterways. *Address:* 36 King Street, Chester CH1 2AH. *T:* (01244) 314588, *Fax:* (01244) 340241. *Club:* Army and Navy.

TAYLOR, Miranda; *see* Haines, M.

TAYLOR, Neil; *see* Taylor, R. N.

TAYLOR, Neville, CB 1989; Director-General, Central Office of Information and Head of Government Information Service, 1985–88; *b* 17 Nov. 1930; *y s* of late Frederick Taylor and of Lottie Taylor; *m* 1954, Margaret Ann, *y d* of late Thomas Bainbridge Vickers and Gladys Vickers; two *s*. *Educ:* Sir Joseph Williamson's Mathematical Sch., Rochester; Coll. of Commerce, Gillingham, Kent. Junior Reporter, Chatham News Group, 1947; Royal Signals, 1948–50; Journalism, 1950–58; Asst Information Officer, Admiralty, 1958; Information Officer (Press), Admiralty, 1960; Fleet Information Officer, Singapore, 1963; Chief Press Officer, MoD, 1966; Information Adviser to Nat. Economic Develt Office, 1968; Dep. Dir, Public Relns (Royal Navy), 1970; Head of Information, Min. of Agriculture, Fisheries and Food, 1971; Dep. Dir of Information, DoE, 1973–74, Dir of Information, 1974–79; Dir of Information, DHSS, 1979–82; Chief of Public Relations, MOD, 1982–85. *Recreation:* fishing. *Address:* Crow Lane House, Crow Lane, Rochester, Kent ME1 1RF. *T:* (01634) 842990.

TAYLOR, Sir Nicholas Richard S.; *see* Stuart Taylor.

TAYLOR, Prof. Pamela Jane, (Mrs J. C. Gunn), FRCPsych; FMedSci; Professor of Forensic Psychiatry, Cardiff University (formerly University of Wales College of Medicine), since 2004; Hon. Consultant Psychiatrist, Bro Morgannwg NHS Trust, since 2004; *b* 23 April 1948; *d* of Philip Geoffrey Taylor and Joan Taylor (*née* Alport); *m* 1989, John Charles Gunn, *qv*. *Educ:* Merchant Taylors' Girls' Sch., Liverpool; Guy's Hosp. Med. Sch. and King's Coll. Hosp. Med. Sch. (MB BS 1971). MRCP 1974; MRCPsych 1976, FRCPsych 1989. Gen. prof. trng in psychiatry, Guy's Hosp., 1972–74; Teaching Fellow in Psychiatry, Univ. of Vermont, 1975; clin. res., Guy's Hosp. Trustees, 1976–79; MRC res. scientist, Inst. of Psychiatry, 1979–81; Sen. Lectr in Forensic Psychiatry, and Hon. Cons. Psychiatrist, 1982–89, Dir of Medium Secure Service, 1988–89, Inst. of Psychiatry and Bethlem Royal and Maudsley Hosp.; Hd of Med. Services, Special Hosps' Service Authy, 1990–95; Prof. of Special Hosp. Psychiatry, Inst. of Psychiatry, KCL, 1995–2004; Hon. Consultant Psychiatrist: Broadmoor Hosp., 1995–2005; Bethlem Royal and

Maudsley Hosp., 1995–2005. Vis. Prof., Inst. of Psychiatry, KCL, 2004–. Advr on Forensic Psychiatry to CMO, Welsh Assembly Govt. Member: Inner London Probation Bd, 1990–2001; DoH and Home Office Steering Gp, Review of Health and Social Services for Mentally Disordered Offenders and other requiring similar services, 1990–94 (Chm., Res. Sub Gp, 1990–91); Wkg Party on Genetics of Mental Disorders, Nuffield Council on Bio-Ethics, 1996–98. Member: RSocMed, 1972–; British Soc. of Criminology, 1980–; Mental Health Foundn, 1990–94; Howard League for Penal Reform, 1990–; Council, RCPsych, 2003– (Mem., various cttees and wkg parties, 1982–). Jt Founder and Jt Editor, Criminal Behaviour and Mental Health, 1991–; Internat. Ed., Behavioral Scis and the Law, 2003–. FMedSci 2004. Gaskell Gold Medal and Prize, RCPsych, 1978. *Publications:* (ed jtly) Forensic Psychiatry: clinical, legal and ethical issues, 1993; (ed) Violence in Society, 1993; Couples in Care and Custody, 1999; Personality Disorder and Serious Offending, 2006; numerous sci. papers, editorials, reviews and contribs to books. *Recreations:* family, friends, an acre of previously neglected garden and, in every spare moment, a book. *Address:* Department of Psychological Medicine, Cardiff University, Cardiff CF14 4XN. *T:* (029) 2074 3090, *Fax:* (029) 2024 7839.

TAYLOR, Pamela Margaret, OBE 2004; Chief Executive, Water UK, since 1998; *b* 25 March 1949; *d* of late Geoffrey Higgins and of Elena Higgins; *m* 1972, John Marc Taylor. Hd of Public Affairs, BMA, 1977–92; Dir, Corporate Affairs, BBC, 1992–94; mgt consultant, 1994–95; Chief Exec., Water Companies Assoc., 1995–98. President: IPR, 1993; Eur. Union of Nat. Assocs of Water Suppliers and Waste Water Services, 2002. Member Board: PHLS, 1998–2003; Health Protection Agency, 2002–. Trustee, Wateraid, 2003– (Vice Chm., 2008–). Trustee and Treas., RSA, 2000–; Trustee, RIPH. MInstD. *Publications:* (ed) Smoking Out the Barons, 1986; articles in BMJ and Jl of American Med. Assoc. *Recreations:* running, working out, wines, ballet, football, cricket. *Address:* Water UK, 1 Queen Anne's Gate, SW1H 9BT. *T:* (020) 7344 1800, *Fax:* (020) 7344 1853; *e-mail:* ptaylor@water.org.uk. *Clubs:* Mosimann's, Annabel's.

TAYLOR, Paul B.; choreographer; Artistic Director, Paul Taylor Dance Company, since 1954; Board Chairman, Paul Taylor Dance Foundation, since 1966; *b* 29 July 1930; *s* of Paul B. Taylor and Elizabeth P. Rust. *Educ:* Virginia Episcopal Sch.; Syracuse Univ.; Juilliard Sch.; Metropolitan Sch. of Ballet; Martha Graham Sch. of Contemporary Dance. Former dancer with companies of Martha Graham, George Balanchine, Charles Weidman, Anna Sokolow, Merce Cunningham, Katherine Litz, James Waring and Pearl Lang; Paul Taylor Dance Company, 1954–: dancer, 1954–75, choreographer and dir; co. has performed in over 500 cities in more than 62 countries; formed Taylor 2, 1993; choreographed 127 dances including: Three Epitaphs, 1956; Junction, 1961; Aureole, 1962; From Sea to Shining Sea, 1965; Big Bertha, 1970; Esplanade, 1975; Runes, 1975; Cloven Kingdom, 1976; Images, 1976; Dust, 1977; Airs, 1978; Profiles, 1979; Le Sacré du Printemps (The Rehearsal), 1980; Arden Court, 1981; Lost, Found and Lost, 1982; Mercuric Tidings, 1982; Sunset, 1983; Last Look, 1985; Musical Offering, 1986; Speaking in Tongues, 1988 (Emmy Award, 1991); Company B, 1991; Fact and Fancy, 1991; Piazzolla Caldera, 1997; Black Tuesday, 2001; Promethean Fire, 2002. Guggenheim Fellow, 1961, 1965, 1983. Hon. Mem. American Acad. and Inst. of Arts and Letters, 1989. Hon. DFA: Connecticut Coll.; Duke Univ., 1983; Syracuse, 1986; Juilliard Sch.; Skidmore Coll.; State Univ. of NY, Purchase; Calif. Inst. of Arts. Centennial Achievement Award, Ohio State Univ., 1970; Creative Arts Award Gold Medal, Brandeis Univ., 1978; Dance Magazine Award, 1980; American Dance Fest. Award, Samuel H. Scripps, 1983; MacArthur Foundn Fellow, 1985; NY State Governor's Award, 1987; NY City Mayor's Award of Honor for Arts and Culture, 1989; Kennedy Center Honor, 1992; Nat. Medal of Arts, 1993; Award, Chicago Internat. Film Fest., 1993; Award for Excellence in the Arts, Algur H. Meadows, 1995. Chevalier, 1969, Officier, 1984, Commandeur, 1990, de l'Ordre des Arts et des Lettres (France); Légion d'Honneur (France), 2000. *Publication:* Private Domain (autobiog.), 1987. *Recreations:* gardening, snorkelling. *Address:* Paul Taylor Dance Company, 552 Broadway, New York, NY 10012, USA.

TAYLOR, Paul David; Director-General, Equipment, Ministry of Defence; *b* 30 Aug. 1962; *s* of Keith Taylor and Ann Taylor; *m* 1989, Jacqueline Green; one *s* one *d*. *Educ:* St Bartholomew's Sch., Newbury; Teesside Poly. (BSc Hons Chem. Engrg). Science fast stream trainee, MoD, 1988; Pvte Sec. to Chief Scientific Advr, MoD, 1993–95; Dir, Chemical and Biological Defence, CBD Porton Down, 1997–2000; Chief Technol. Officer, Bespak plc, 2000–02 (Chm., Scientific Adv. Cttee, 2002–); Dir of Strategic Technologies, MoD, 2002–05. MInstD 1997. *Recreations:* walking, rough and game shooting, reading, pub quiz team. *Club:* Civil Service.

TAYLOR, Ven. Paul Stanley; Archdeacon of Sherborne, since 2004; *b* 28 March 1953; *s* of Stanley and Beryl Taylor; *m* 1984, Janet Wendy Taylor (*née* Harris); three *s*. *Educ:* Westminster Coll., Oxford (BEd 1975; MTh 1998); Westcott House, Cambridge. Ordained deacon, 1984, priest, 1985; Curate, St Stephen, Bush Hill Park, 1984–88; Asst Dir, 1987–94, Dir, 1994–2000 and 2002–04, Post Ordination Trng, Dio. London; Vicar: St Andrew, Southgate, 1988–97; St Mary, Hendon, 1997–2001; Priest-in-charge, Christ Ch, Hendon, 1997–2001; Vicar, St Mary and Christ Ch, Hendon, 2001–04; Area Dean, W Barnet, 2000–04. *Recreations:* golf, fell walking, running, Rugby Union, sailing. *Address:* Aldhelm House, West Stafford, Dorchester DT2 8AB. *T:* and *Fax:* (01305) 269074; *e-mail:* adsherborne@salisbury.anglican.org. *Clubs:* Dorset Golf and Country (Bere Regis); Castle Cove Sailing (Weymouth).

TAYLOR, Ven. Peter Flint; Archdeacon of Harlow, since 1996; *b* 7 March 1944; *s* of late Alan Flint Taylor and Josephine Overbury Taylor (*née* Dix); *m* 1971, Joy M. Sampson; one *d*. *Educ:* Clifton Coll., Bristol; Queens' Coll., Cambridge (MA); London Coll. of Divinity (BD ext. London Univ.). Ordained deacon, 1970, priest, 1971; Assistant Curate: St Augustine's, Highbury, 1970–73; St Andrew's, Plymouth, 1973–77; Vicar, Christ Church, Ironville, Derbys, 1977–83; Priest-in-charge, St James, Riddings, 1982–83; Rector, Holy Trinity, Rayleigh, Chelmsford, 1983–96. Part-time Chaplain, Bullwood Hall Prison and Youth Custody Centre, 1986–90; Rural Dean of Rochford, 1989–96. *Recreations:* walking, electronics and computing, astronomy, archaeology of Jerusalem. *Address:* Glebe House, Church Lane, Sheering, Bishops Stortford CM22 7NR. *T:* (01279) 734524, *Fax:* (01279) 734426; *e-mail:* a.harlow@chelmsford.anglican.org.

TAYLOR, Prof. Peter James, PhD; FBA 2004; Professor of Geography, Loughborough University, since 2005; *b* 21 Nov. 1944; *s* of Peter Taylor and Margaret Alice Taylor; *m* 1965, Enid; one *s* one *d*. *Educ:* Univ. of Liverpool (BA Hons; PhD). Lectr, Sen. Lectr, Reader, then Prof., Univ. of Newcastle upon Tyne, 1971–95. Visiting positions: Univ. of Iowa, 1970–71; Univ. of Alberta, 1976; Clark Univ., 1978–79; Univ. of Illinois, 1985; Binghamton Univ., 1990; Univ. of Amsterdam, 1991; Virginia Tech, 1992–93, 2002, 2003; Univ. of Paris, 1995; Ghent Univ., 2004–05. Francqui Medal, Francqui Foundn, Brussels, 2005; Ghent Univ. Medal, 2005. *Publications:* (with Colin Flint) Political Geography: world-economy, nation-state, locality, 1985, 4th edn 1999; Britain and the Cold War: 1945 as geopolitical transition, 1990; The Way the Modern World Works, 1996; Modernities: a geohistorical introduction, 1999; World City Network, 2004. *Recreations:* watching sport, collecting postcards, playing with grandchildren. *Address:* 33 Percy Park, Tynemouth NE30 4JZ. *T:* (0191) 259 1113, *Fax:* (01509) 223930; *e-mail:* p.j.taylor@lborough.ac.uk.

TAYLOR, Peter John Whittaker, OBE 1990; Director, Spain, British Council, 1995–99; *b* 22 April 1939; *s* of late Claud Whittaker Taylor and of Mary Elizabeth Taylor (*née* Garlick); *m* 1987, Carolina Haro; one *d* by previous marriage. *Educ:* Solihull Sch.; St Catharine's Coll., Cambridge (MA Hons English); Reading Univ. (MA Applied Linguistics). Dir, Internat Lang. Centre, Paris, 1970–78; British Council, 1978–99: Eng. Lang. Officer, Mexico, 1979–81; Regl Dir, Valencia, Spain, 1981–85; Dep. Dir, Saudi Arabia, 1985–87; Dir, Morocco, 1987–90; Dep. Dir, Africa and ME Div., 1990–93; Regl Dir, ME and N Africa, 1993–94. *Recreations:* books, classical music.

TAYLOR, Peter William Edward; QC 1981; *b* 27 July 1917; *s* of late Peter and Julia A. Taylor; *m* 1948, Julia Mary Brown (*d* 1997), *d* of Air Cdre Sir Vernon Brown, CB, OBE; two *s*. *Educ:* Peter Symonds' Sch., Winchester; Christ's Coll., Cambridge (MA; Wrangler, Math. Tripos, Part II; 1st Class, Law Tripos, Part II). Served RA, 1939–46: France and Belgium, 1939–40; N Africa, 1942–43; NW Europe, 1944–45 (mentioned in dispatches); Actg Lt-Col 1945; transferred to TARO as Hon. Major, 1946. Called to the Bar, Inner Temple, 1946; Lincoln's Inn, *ad eundem*, 1953 (Bencher, 1976); practice at the Bar, 1947–94; Occasional Lectr, LSE, 1946–56; Lectr in Construction of Documents, Council of Legal Educn, 1952–70; Conveyancing Counsel of the Court, 1974–81. Member: General Council of the Bar, 1971–74; Senate of Inns of Court and the Bar, 1974–75; Inter-Professional Cttee on Retirement Provision, 1974–92; Land Registration Rule Cttee, 1976–81; Standing Cttee on Conveyancing, 1985–87; Incorporated Council of Law Reporting, 1977–91 (Vice-Chm., 1987–91); Council, Selden Soc., 1977–. Bar Musical Society: Hon. Sec., 1952–61; Treas. and External Sec., 1961–80; Chm., 1980–86; Vice-Pres., 1986–. *Recreations:* sailing, shooting, music. *Address:* 46 Onslow Square, SW7 3NX. *T:* (020) 7589 1301.

TAYLOR, Philippe Arthur; Managing Director, Seatrain Sailing, since 1993; *b* 9 Feb. 1937; *s* of Arthur Peach Taylor and Simone Vacquin; *m* 1973, Margaret Nancy Wilkins; two *s*. *Educ:* Trinity College, Glenalmond; St Andrews University. Procter & Gamble, 1963; Masius International, 1967; British Tourist Authority, 1970; Chief Executive, Scottish Tourist Board, 1975–80; Man. Dir, Taylor and Partners, 1980–82; Chief Exec., Birmingham Convention and Visitor Bureau Ltd, 1982–94. Vice-Chm., Ikon Gall., 1982–92; Chm., British Assoc. of Conf. Towns, 1987–90. *Publications:* childrens' books; various papers and articles on tourism. *Recreations:* sailing, making things, tourism, reading. *Address:* The Granary, Theberton, Suffolk IP16 4RR. *Clubs:* Royal Northumberland Yacht (Blyth); Orford Sailing.

TAYLOR, Phyllis Mary Constance, MA; Honorary Associate, Institute of Education, London, 1983–85; *b* 29 Sept. 1926; *d* of Cecil and Constance Tedder; *m* 1949, Peter Royston Taylor; one *s*. *Educ:* Woodford High Sch.; Sudbury High Sch., Suffolk; Girton Coll., Cambridge (State Scholar; BA Hons History, 1948; MA 1951). Asst Hist. Mistress, Loughton High Sch., 1948–51, Head of Hist., 1951–58; Teacher of Hist. and Religious Educn, Lancaster Royal Grammar Sch. for Boys, 1959; Head of Hist., Casterton Sch. (private boarding), Kirby Lonsdale, 1960; Teacher of Gen. Subjects, Lancaster Girls' Grammar Sch., 1960–61, Head of Hist., 1961–62; Dep. Headmistress, Carlisle Sch., Chelsea, 1962–64; Headmistress: Walthamstow High Sch. for Girls, 1964–68; Walthamstow Sen. High Sch., 1968–75; Wanstead High Sch., London Borough of Redbridge, 1976–82. Consultant Head to NE London Polytechnic (Counselling/Careers sect.), 1974–78; Moderator, Part-time Diploma, Pastoral Care and Counselling, 1979–85. Pres., Essex Sector, Secondary Heads' Assoc., 1978–79. Member: UGC, 1978–83 (Mem., Educn Sub-Cttee, 1978–85, and Wkg Party on Continuing Educn, 1983); Teacher Trng Sub-Cttee, Adv. Cttee on Supply and Educn of Teachers, 1980–85; former Mem., Nat. Exec., Assoc. of Head Mistresses. Mem., RAM Foundn Appeals Cttee, 1985–86. Parish Councillor, High Roding, 1995–. Chm., Dunmow Liberals, 1986–88. Governor, Rodings Primary Sch., 1988–90. *Publications:* (as Julianne Royston) The Penhale Saga: The Penhale Heiress, 1988; The Penhale Fortune, 1989. *Recreations:* music, theatre, bridge, horses, country life, ecology. *Address:* White Horses, High Roding, Great Dunmow, Essex CM6 1NS. *T:* (01371) 873161.

TAYLOR, Prof. Richard Edward, CC (Can.) 2005; FRS 1997; Professor, Stanford Linear Accelerator Center, Stanford University, 1968–2003, now Emeritus; *b* 2 Nov. 1929; *s* of Clarence Richard Taylor and Delia Alena Taylor (*née* Brunsdale); *m* 1951, Rita Jean Bonneau; one *s*. *Educ:* Univ. of Alberta (BS 1950; MS 1952); Stanford Univ. (PhD 1962). Boursier, Lab. de l'Accelerateur Linéaire, France, 1958–61; physicist, Lawrence Berkeley Lab., Berkeley, Calif., 1961–62; staff mem., 1962–68, Associate Dir, 1982–86, Stanford Linear Accelerator Center. Distinguished Prof., Univ. of Alberta, 1992–2003, now Emeritus. Fellow: Guggenheim Foundn, 1971–72; Amer. Phys. Soc (W. K. H. Panofsky Prize, Div. of Particles and Fields, 1989); FRSC; Fellow, Amer. Acad. of Arts and Scis, 1992. Foreign Associate, NAS, USA. Hon. DSc: Paris-Sud, 1980; Alberta, 1991; Lethbridge, 1993; Victoria, 1994; Blaise Pascal, 1997; Carleton, Ottawa, 1999; Liverpool, 1999; Queen's, Kingston, Ont., 2000; Hon. LLD Calgary, 1993. Von Humboldt Award, 1982; Nobel Prize in Physics, 1990. *Address:* Stanford Linear Accelerator Center, 2575 Sand Hill Road, M/S 43, Menlo Park, CA 94025, USA. *T:* (650) 9262417.

TAYLOR, Prof. Richard Kenneth Stanley, PhD; Professor and Director of Continuing Education and Lifelong Learning, University of Cambridge, since 2004; *b* 18 Nov. 1945; *s* of Jeanne Ann Taylor and Kenneth Charles Taylor; *m* 1967, Jennifer Teresa Frost (marr. diss. 2004); one *s* two *d*. *Educ:* Merchant Taylors' Sch., Northwood; Exeter Coll., Oxford (MA 1967); PhD Leeds 1983. Admin. Asst, Univ. of Lancaster, 1967–70; University of Leeds: Admin. Asst, Dept of Adult and Continuing Educn, 1970–73; Warden, Non-Residential Centre for Adult Educn, Bradford, 1973–83; Dir of Extramural Studies, 1985–88; Head, Dept of Adult and Continuing Educn, 1988–91; Prof. and Dir of Continuing Educn, 1991–2004. Sec., Univs Assoc. for Continuing Educn, 1994–98, 2002–03; Chairman: Nat. Inst. for Adult Continuing Educn, 1999–2006 (Vice Chm., 1996–99); Trustees, WEA, 2006–. *Publications:* (with Colin Pritchard) Social Work: reform or revolution?, 1978; (with Colin Pritchard) The Protest Makers, 1980; (jtly) Adult Education in England and the USA, 1985; (with Kevin Ward) Adult Education and the Working Class, 1986; Against the Bomb: the British peace movement 1958–65, 1988; (with Nigel Young) Campaigns for Peace, 1988; (with Tom Steele) Learning Independence, 1995; Beyond the Walls, 1996; (with David Watson) Lifelong Learning and the University: a post-Dearing agenda, 1998; (with Tom Steele and Jean Barr) For a Radical Higher Education: after postmodernism, 2002. *Recreations:* mountain walking and climbing, cricket, politics, pubs. *Address:* Institute of Continuing Education, University of Cambridge, Madingley Hall, Madingley, Cambridge CB23 8AQ. *T:* (01954) 280213, *Fax:* (01954) 280201; *e-mail:* rkst2@cam.ac.uk. *Clubs:* Royal Commonwealth Society; Yorkshire County Cricket.

TAYLOR, Prof. Richard Lawrence, PhD; FRS 1995; Professor of Mathematics, Harvard University, since 1996; *b* 19 May 1962; *s* of John Clayton Taylor and Gillian Mary

Taylor (*née* Schofield); *m* 1995, Christine Jiayou Chang; one *s* one *d*. *Educ:* Magdalen Coll. Sch., Oxford; Clare Coll., Cambridge (BA); Princeton Univ. (PhD). Fellow, Clare Coll., Cambridge, 1988–95; Asst Lectr, 1989–92, Lectr, 1992–94, Reader, 1994–95, Cambridge Univ.; Savilian Prof. of Geometry, and Fellow of New Coll., Oxford Univ., 1995–96. *Recreation:* hill walking. *Address:* Department of Mathematics, Harvard University, 1 Oxford Street, Cambridge, MA 02138, USA. *T:* (617) 4955487.

TAYLOR, Prof. R(ichard) Neil, PhD; Professor of Geotechnical Engineering, City University, since 1996; *b* 14 May 1955; *s* of Charles L. Taylor and Mary Taylor; *m* 1995, Chrysanthi Savvidou; one *d*. *Educ:* Emmanuel Coll., Cambridge (BA 1976; MPhil 1979; MA 1980; PhD 1984). MICE 1990. Lectr in Geotechnical Engrg, 1984–91, Sen. Lectr, 1991–96, City Univ. Associate, Geotechnical Consulting Gp, 1990–. Sec. Gen., Internat. Soc. for Soil Mechanics and Geotechnical Engrg, 1999–. *Publications:* (ed) Geotechnical Centrifuge Technology, 1995; contrib. papers to jls and confs mainly associated with ground movements caused by tunnels and excavations incl. geotechnical centrifuge modelling and analysis. *Recreation:* walking. *Address:* Geotechnical Engineering Research Centre, City University, Northampton Square, EC1V 0HB. *T:* (020) 7040 8157.

TAYLOR, Richard Thomas, FRCP; MP (Ind) Wyre Forest, since 2001; *b* 7 July 1934; *s* of Thomas Taylor and Mabel (*née* Hickley); *m* 1st, 1962, Ann Brett (marr. diss.); one *s* two *d*; 2nd, 1990, Christine Miller; one *d*. *Educ:* Leys Sch.; Clare Coll., Cambridge (BA); Westminster Med. Sch. (MB, BChir). FRCP 1979. Jun. hosp. doctor trng posts, Westminster Hosp. and other London hosps, 1959–72; MO, RAF, 1961–64; Consultant Physician, Kidderminster Gen. Hosp., 1972–95 (Chm., Hosp. Med. Staff Cttee, 1975–77 and 1986–90). Consultant Rep., Kidderminster DHA, 1982–86. Mem., Select Cttee on Health, 2001–. Chairman: Kidderminster Hosp. League of Friends, 1996–2001; Save Kidderminster Hosp. Campaign Cttee, 1997–2001. Pres., Kidderminster Med. Soc., 1993. *Publications:* articles on drug treatment and rheumatic diseases in med. jls. *Recreations:* family, ornithology, gardening, classic cars. *Address:* House of Commons, SW1A 0AA. *T:* (020) 7219 4598; 11 Church Walk, Kidderminster, Worcs DY11 6XY. *Club:* Royal Society of Medicine.

TAYLOR, (Robert) Alan; Chief Executive and Town Clerk, Royal Borough of Kensington and Chelsea, 1990–2000; *b* 13 Sept. 1944; *s* of Alfred Taylor and Hilda Mary (*née* Weekley); *m* 1st, 1965, Dorothy Joan Walker (*d* 1986); two *s*; 2nd, 1987, Margaret Susanne Barnes. *Educ:* Thornbury Grammar Sch., Thornbury, Glos.; King's Coll., Univ. of London (LLB). Solicitor. Asst Solicitor, Plymouth CBC, 1970–74; Plymouth City Council: Dep. City Solicitor and Sec., 1974–76; Asst Town Clerk, 1976–81; Chief Exec., London Borough of Sutton, 1981–90. Lay Mem., Investigation Cttee, CIMA, 2002–05. Pres., SOLACE, 1998–99 (Hon. Sec., 1992–95; Sen. Vice-Pres., 1997–98); Trustee, Voluntary Reading Help, 2001–07. Chm., Dartmoor Local Access Forum, 2003–06; Mem., Devon and Cornwall Regl Cttee, NT, 2004–. *Recreations:* theatre, books, walking, choral singing. *Address:* Old Venn, Bridford, Exeter, Devon EX6 7LF. *T:* (01647) 252611.

TAYLOR, His Honour Robert Carruthers; a Circuit Judge, 1984–2004; *b* 6 Jan. 1939; *o s* of late John Taylor, CBE and Barbara Taylor; *m* 1968, Jacqueline Marjorie, *er d* of Nigel and Marjorie Chambers; one *s* one *d*. *Educ:* Wycliffe Coll.; St John's Coll., Oxford. MA 1967. Called to Bar, Middle Temple, 1961; practised NE Circuit, 1961–84; a Recorder, 1976–84. Chm., Agricl Land Tribunal, Yorks and Humberside Areas, 1979–; Mem., Mental Health Tribunal, 2001–. *Recreations:* reading, music, gardening, walking, family. *Address:* Abbotsview, 59 King's Road, Ilkley, W Yorks LS29 9BZ. *T:* (01943) 607672. *Club:* Royal Commonwealth Society.

TAYLOR, Prof. Robert Henry, PhD; Vice-Chancellor, University of Buckingham, 1997–2001; *b* 15 March 1943; *s* of Robert E. Taylor and Mabelle L. Taylor (*née* Warren), Greenville, Ohio; *m* 1st (marr. diss.); one *s* one *d*; 2nd, 2000, Ingrid Porteous. *Educ:* Ohio Univ. (BA 1965); Antioch Coll. (MA 1967); Cornell Univ. (PhD 1974). Social Studies Teacher, Cardozo High Sch., Washington DC, 1965–67; Instructor in Pol. Sci., Wilberforce Univ., Ohio, 1967–69; Lectr in Govt, Univ. of Sydney, 1974–79; School of Oriental and African Studies, University of London: Lectr, 1980–88, Sen. Lectr, 1988–89, in Politics (with ref. to SE Asia); Prof. of Politics, 1989–96; Pro-Dir, 1991–96; Professorial Res. Associate, 2003–. Associate Sen. Fellow, Inst. of Southeast Asian Studies, Singapore, 2003–; Vis. Prof., Univ. of Buckingham. Lay Mem., Asylum and Immigration Tribunal, 2004–. *Publications:* Marxism and Resistance in Burma, 1985; The State in Burma, 1987; (contrib.) In Search of Southeast Asia: a modern history, 1987; (ed) Handbooks of the Modern World: Asia and the Pacific, 2 vols, 1991; (ed) The Politics of Elections in Southeast Asia, 1996; (ed) Burma: political economy under military rule, 2001; (ed) The Idea of Freedom in Asia and Africa, 2002; (ed jtly) The Emergence of Southeast Asia, 2005; (ed) Myanmar: beyond politics to societal imperatives, 2005; (ed) Dr Maung Maung: gentleman, scholar and patriot, 2008; The State in Myanmar, 2008; numerous articles in books and learned jls. *T:* (020) 8361 4002; *e-mail:* r_h_taylor@btopenworld.com. *Clubs:* Travellers; North Middlesex Golf.

TAYLOR, Dr Robert Thomas, CBE 1990; Chairman, Management Interviewing and Research Institute, 1993–2004; *b* 21 March 1933; *s* of George Taylor and Marie Louise Fidler; *m* 1965, Rosemary Janet Boileau; three *s* one *d*. *Educ:* Boteler Grammar Sch., Warrington; University Coll., Oxford (Open Exhbnr; BA 1954, MA 1957; DPhil 1957). Fulbright Scholar. Research Associate, Randall Lab. of Physics, Univ. of Michigan, USA, 1957–58; ICI Research Fellow, 1958–59, Lectr, Physics Dept, 1959–61, Univ. of Liverpool; Chief Examr for NUJMB, GCE Physics (Scholarship Level), 1961; British Council: Asst Regional Rep., Madras, 1961–64; Science Officer, Madrid, 1964–69; Dir, Staff Recruitment Dept, 1969–73; Regional Educn Advr, Bombay, 1973–77; Rep., Mexico, 1977–81; Controller, Personnel, 1981–86; Rep., Greece, 1986–90; Asst Dir-Gen., British Council, 1990–93. Mem. (C), Weald Central Ward, Ashford BC, 2003–. Vis. Sen. Fellow, Manchester Business Sch., 1993–99. *Publications:* contrib. to Chambers Encyclopaedia, 1967 edn; papers in scientific jls. *Recreations:* computers, war and war gaming. *Address:* Mark Haven, Ashford Road, High Halden, Kent TN26 3LY. *T:* (01233) 850994.

TAYLOR, Roger Miles Whitworth; Managing Director, Pinnacle Consulting, since 2000; *b* 18 May 1944; *s* of Richard and Joan Taylor; *m* 1969, Georgina Lucy Tonks (marr. diss. 2003); two *s* two *d*; *m* 2003, Gabriele Eva Bock. *Educ:* Repton School; Birmingham University (LLB). Solicitor, admitted 1968; Asst Sol., Cheshire CC, 1969–71; Asst County Clerk, Lincs parts of Lindsey, 1971–73; Dep. County Secretary, Northants CC, 1973–79; Dep. Town Clerk, 1979–85, Town Clerk and Chief Exec., 1985–88, City of Manchester; Chief Exec., Birmingham CC, 1988–94; Dir, 1994–2000, Chm., 1997–2000, Newchurch and Co. Mem., Farrand Cttee on Conveyancing, 1983–84; Clerk, Greater Manchester Passenger Transport Authy, 1986–88. Sec., W Midlands Jt Cttee, 1988–94. Chairman: Birmingham Marketing Partnership, 1993–94; Birmingham Common Purpose, 1994; Local Govt Television Adv. Bd, 1994–95; Dir, Birmingham TEC, 1990–93. Mem., Standards Bd for England, 2001–. Dir, Ex Cathedra Chamber Choir, 1996–98. Mancunian of the Year, Manchester Jun. Chamber of Commerce, 1988. *Publications:* contribs to Local Govt Chronicle, Municipal Review, Municipal Jl. *Recreations:* sailing, walking. *Address:* Pinnacle Consulting, Caxton House, Floor 4, 2 Farringdon Road, EC1M 3HN; *e-mail:* roger.taylor@pinnacle-psg.com.

TAYLOR, Ronald George, CBE 1988; Director-General, British Chambers of Commerce (formerly Association of British Chambers of Commerce), 1984–98; *b* 12 Dec. 1935; *s* of Ernest and May Taylor; *m* 1960, Patricia Stoker; one *s* two *d*. *Educ:* Jesus College, Oxford (BA Modern Langs). Commnd Royal Signals, 1957–59. Leeds Chamber of Commerce and Industry: joined, 1959; Asst Sec., 1964–74; Director, 1974–84. *Recreations:* family history, Rugby Union, bridge. *Address:* 2 Holly Bush Lane, Harpenden, Herts AL5 4AP. *T:* (01582) 712139.

TAYLOR, Prof. Ronald Wentworth, MD; FRCOG; Professor Emeritus of Obstetrics and Gynaecology, United Medical and Dental Schools of Guy's and St Thomas' Hospitals, since 1989; *b* 28 Oct. 1932; *s* of George Richard and Winifred Taylor; *m* 1962, Mary Patricia O'Neill; three *s* one *d*. *Educ:* St Mary's Coll., Crosby; Liverpool Univ. (MB ChB 1958; MD 1972). MRCOG 1965, FRCOG 1975. Jun. House Officer posts, Liverpool, 1958–59; Sen. House Officer posts, Preston, 1960, Manchester, 1962; GP, Ormskirk, Lancs, 1962–63; Registrar, Whittington Hosp., London, 1963–64; St Thomas' Hospital: Lectr, 1965–67; Sen. Lectr, 1968–76; Prof., 1977–89, subseq. at UMDS of Guy's and St Thomas' Hosps. Founder Mem., Expert Witness Inst., 1995– (Fellow, 2000). *Publications:* Gynaecological Cancer, 1975; "Ten Teachers" Obstetrics and Gynaecology, 14th edn 1985; (ed) Confidential Enquiry into Perinatal Deaths, 1988; Endometrial Cancer, 1988. *Recreations:* sailing, silversmithing, restoration of furniture, photography. *Address:* Keld Head, Keld Shap, Penrith, Cumbria CA10 3QF. *T:* (01931) 716553. *Club:* Royal Society of Medicine.

TAYLOR, Rupert Maurice T.; *see* Thornely-Taylor.

TAYLOR, Russell Philip, MBE 2003; writer and cartoonist; *b* 8 July 1960; *s* of Captain Hal Taylor and Iona Taylor (*née* Mackenzie); *m* 1990, Anne-Frederique Dujon (marr. diss. 2007). *Educ:* St Anne's Coll., Oxford (BA Russian and Philosophy). Freelance writer and journalist, 1984–87; writer of Alex cartoon (with Charles Peattie) in: London Daily News, 1987; The Independent, 1987–91; Daily Telegraph, 1992–; writer of Celeb cartoon (with Charles Peattie and Mark Warren), Private Eye, 1987–; Alex (stage play), Arts Th., 2007; composer of film and TV music, 1991–. *Publications:* The Looniness of the Long Distance Runner, 2001; (with Marc Polonsky) USSR from an original idea by Karl Marx, 1986; with Charles Peattie: Alex, 1987; The Unabashed Alex, 1988; Alex II: Magnum Force, 1989; Alex III: Son of Alex, 1990; Alex IV: The Man with the Golden Handshake, 1991; Celeb, 1991; Alex V: For the Love of Alex, 1992; Alex Calls the Shots, 1993; Alex Plays the Game, 1994; Alex Knows the Score, 1995; Alex Sweeps the Board, 1996; Alex Feels the Pinch, 1997; The Full Alex, 1998; The Alex Technique, 1999; The Best of Alex, 1998–2001, 2001; The Best of Alex, annually 2002–08. *Recreations:* playing piano, running, perudo, time-wasting. *Address:* PO Box 39447, London N10 3WA. *T:* (020) 8374 1225; *e-mail:* alex@alexcartoon.com. *Clubs:* Groucho, Soho House.

TAYLOR, Sandra Anne; specialist management consultant, since 2002; Chief Executive, Barnsley NHS Foundation Trust, since 2007; *b* 5 Sept. 1953; *d* of Harold E. Taylor and May Taylor (*née* Draper). *Educ:* Portsmouth Poly. (BA Hons); Essex Univ. (MA). Lectr and Tutor, Hull Univ., 1977–80; Res. Fellow and Lectr, UCL, 1981–82; Nottinghamshire County Council: Community Develt Officer, 1982–86; Principal Officer, 1986–88, Principal Asst, 1988–89, Asst Dir, 1990–96, Social Services Dept; Dir, Social Services, Leics City Council, 1996–99; Dir of Social Services, Birmingham CC, 1999–2002. Social Services expert consultant, Capita Business Services, 2003; Advr, Vertex Customer Services, 2003; interim Dir of Policy, 2003–04, interim Exec. Dir of Develt, 2004–05, Surrey and Sussex Strategic HA; Project Dir, Health Reconfiguration, E Berks Health Economy/Slough BC, 2006. *Publications:* (ed) Nottinghamshire Labour Movement, 1986; (jtly) Housing Futures: housing policy, management and practice, 1992; (ed) Managing Housing in a larger authority, 1993. *Recreations:* swimming, gardening, walking. *Address:* (office) 118 Gawber Road, Barnsley S75 2EP.

TAYLOR, Simon Wheldon; QC 2003; a Recorder, since 2002; *b* 4 July 1962; *s* of Thomas Henry Taylor and Enid Taylor, *qv*; *m* 1990, Elizabeth Lawes Paine; one *s* two *d*. *Educ:* Trinity Coll., Cambridge (BA Hons); London Hosp. Med. Coll. (MB BChir); Inns of Court Sch. of Law. Called to the Bar, Middle Temple, 1984; qualified doctor, 1987; pupillage, 1988; tenancy, 1989; in practice as barrister, 1989–. *Address:* Cloisters, 1 Pump Court, Temple, EC4Y 7AA. *T:* (020) 7827 4000; *e-mail:* st@cloisters.com.

TAYLOR, Sir Teddy; *see* Taylor, Sir E. M.

TAYLOR, Victoria Mary; *see* Edwards, V. M.

TAYLOR, Wendy Ann, CBE 1988; FRBS 1995; sculptor; Member, Royal Fine Art Commission, 1981–99; *b* 29 July 1945; *d* of Edward Philip Taylor and late Lilian Maude Wright; *m* 1982, Bruce Robertson; one *s*. *Educ:* St Martin's School of Art. LDAD (Hons). One-man exhibitions: Axiom Gall., London, 1970; Angela Flowers Gall., London, 1972; 24th King's Lynn Fest., Norfolk, and World Trade Centre, London, 1974; Annely Juda Fine Art, London, 1975; Oxford Gall., Oxford, 1976; Oliver Dowling Gall., Dublin, 1976 and 1979; Building Art—the process, Building Centre Gall., 1986; Austin, Desmond and Phipps, 1992; Nature and Engineering, Osborne Gp, London, 1998; Cass Gall., London, 2005. Shown in over 100 group exhibitions, 1964–82. Represented in collections around the world. Major commissions: The Travellers 1970, London; Gazebo (edn of 4) 1970–71, London, New York, Suffolk, Oxford; Triad 1971, Oxford; Timepiece 1973, London (Grade II listed, 2004); Calthae 1978, Leicestershire; Octo 1980, Milton Keynes; Counterpoise 1980, Birmingham; Compass Bowl 1980, Basildon; Sentinel 1981, Reigate; Bronze Relief 1981, Canterbury; Equatorial Sundial 1982, Bletchley; Essence 1982, Milton Keynes; Opus 1983, Morley Coll., London; Gazebo 1983, Golder's Hill Park, London; Network, 1985, London; Roundacre Improvement Scheme Phase I, 1985–88, Phase II, 1989–90, Basildon; Geo I & Geo II 1986, Stratford-Upon-Avon; Landscape, and Tree of the Wood 1986, Fernhurst, Surrey; Pharos 1986, Peel Park, E Kilbride; Ceres 1986, Fernhurst, Surrey; Nexus 1986, Corby, Northants; Globe Sundial 1987, Swansea Maritime Quarter; Spirit of Enterprise 1987, Isle of Dogs, London; Silver Fountain 1988, Continuum 1990, Guildford, Surrey; The Whirlies 1988, Pharos II 1989, Phoenix 1989–90, E Kilbride; Pilot Kites 1988, Norwich Airport; Fireflow 1988, Strathclyde Fire Brigade HQ, Hamilton; Armillary Sundial 1989, The New Towns, Essex; Globe Sundial II 1990, London Zool Gdns; Butterfly Mosaic 1990, Barking and Dagenham Council; Square Piece 1991, Plano, Ill; Sundial Meml 1991, Sheffield; Anchorage 1991, Salford Quays, Manchester; Wyvern 1992, Leics; stained glass window, St George's Church, Sheffield Univ., 1994; The Jester, Emmanuel Coll., Cambridge, 1994; Challenge, Stockley Park, Middx, 1995; Equilibrium, Coopers & Lybrand, London, 1995; Spirit, Vann, Guildford, 1996; Rope Circle, Hermitage Waterside, London, 1997; Waves, Berners Mews, London, 1998; Dancer, Chelsea and Westminster Hosp., 1998; Dung Beetles, Millennium Conservation Bldg, Zool Soc., Regent's Park, 1999; Mariner's Astrolabe, Virginia Settlers Meml, Brunswick Quay, 1999; Globe View, Blackfriars, 2000;

Millennium Fountain, Chase Gardens, Enfield, 2000 (Civic Trust Award, 2002); Voyager, Cinnibar Wharf, London, 2001; Three Reclining Rope Figures, and Conqueror, GlaxoSmithKline, Middx, 2001; Through the Loop, and Around the Square, Pacific Place, HK, 2002; Hunters Square, Chain Piece, Warren, Ohio, 2002; Knowledge, Library Sq., Queen Mary, Univ. of London, 2003; Acorn Wall Relief, Switch House, Brunswick Wharf, London, 2003; Anchor Iron, Anchor Iron Wharf, Greenwich, 2004; Feather Piece, Capital East, Royal Victoria Docks, 2005; Gravesend Heritage, Gravesham, 2005; Silver Fountain II, Bryn Mawr, Penn, 2006; Square Chain Piece, Bartlesville, Oklahoma, 2007; WW II Meml to civilians of E London, Hermitage Meml Gdn, Wapping, 2007; Spirit I, Royal Docks, London, 2008. Mem., CNAA, 1980–85 (Specialist Advr, 1985–93; Mem., Cttee for Art and Design, 1987–91); Consultant, New Town Commn (Basildon) (formerly Basildon Develt Corp.), 1985–; Design Consultant, London Borough of Barking and Dagenham, 1989–93 and 1997–2003; LDDC Mem., Design Adv. Panel, 1989–98; Mem., Design Panel, Thames Gateway Area. Mem., Adv. Gp, PCFC, 1989–90. Examiner, Univ. of London, 1982–83; Mem. Court, RCA, 1982–; Mem. Council, Morley Coll., 1984–88. Trustee, Leicestershire's Appeal for Music and the Arts, 1993–. FZS 1989; Fellow, QMW, 1993; FRSA 2004. Awards: Walter Neurath, 1964; Pratt, 1965; Sainsbury, 1966; Arts Council, 1977; Duais na Riochta (Kingdom Prize), 1977; Gold Medal, Eire, 1977; 1st Prize Silk Screen, Barcham Green Print Comp., 1978. *Recreation:* gardening. *Address:* 73 Bow Road, Bow E3 2AN. *T:* (020) 8981 2037, *Fax:* (020) 8980 3153.

TAYLOR, Sir William, Kt 1990; CBE 1982; *b* 31 May 1930; *s* of Herbert and Maud E. Taylor, Crayford, Kent; *m* 1954, Rita, *d* of Ronald and Marjorie Hague, Sheffield; one *s* two *d*. *Educ:* Erith Grammar Sch.; London Sch. of Economics (BSc Econ 1952); Westminster Coll., Oxford (Hon. Fellow, 1990); Univ. of London Inst. of Educn (PhD 1960). Teaching in Kent, 1953–56; Deputy Head, Slade Green Secondary Sch., 1956–59; Sen. Lectr, St Luke's Coll., Exeter, 1959–61; Head of Educn Dept, Bede Coll., Durham, 1961–64; Tutor and Lectr in Educn, Univ. of Oxford, 1964–66; Prof. of Educn and Dir of Sch. of Educn, Univ. of Bristol, 1966–73; Dir, Univ. of London Inst. of Educn, 1973–83; Principal, Univ. of London, 1983–85; Vice-Chancellor: Univ. of Hull, 1985–91; Univ. of Huddersfield, 1994–95; Thames Valley Univ., 1998–99. Hd, Winchester Sch. of Art, Univ. of Southampton, 2004. Visiting Professor of Education: Oxford Univ., 1991–97; Southampton Univ., 1998–; Commonwealth Vis. Fellow, Australian States, 1975; NZ UGC Prestige Fellowship, 1977; Hon. Vis. Fellow, Green Coll., Oxford, 1991–97. Academic Adviser: States of Jersey Educn Cttee, 2000–05; SE Essex Coll., 2001–03; Special Advr, H of C Cttee on Educn and Skills, 2000–07. Research Consultant, Dept of Educn and Science (part-time), 1968–73; Chairman: European Cttee for Educnl Research, 1969–71; UK Nat. Commn for UNESCO, 1975–83 (Mem., 1973–83); Educnl Adv. Council, IBA, 1974–82; UCET, 1976–79; Cttee on Training of Univ. Teachers, 1981–88; NFER, 1983–88; CATE, 1984–93; Univs Council for Adult and Continuing Educn, 1986–90; N of England Univs Management and Leadership Prog., 1987–91; Studies in Education, 1991–95; Convocation of Univ. of London, 1994–97; UUK Higher Educn Funding Review Gp, 2000–01; IoW Tertiary Strategy Gp, 2002–03; Southampton Travel-to-learn Review, 2002–04; Strategic Area Rev. of 16+ educn and trng, Hants and IoW, 2002–05. Member: UGC Educn Cttee, 1971–80; British Library Res. and Develt Cttee, 1975–79; Open Univ. Academic Adv. Cttee, 1975–82; SSRC Educnl Research Board, 1976–80 (Vice-Chm., 1978–80); Adv. Cttee on Supply and Training of Teachers, 1976–79; Working Gp on Management of Higher Educn, 1977–78; Steering Cttee on Future of Examinations at 16+, 1977–78; Cttee of Vice-Chancellors and Principals, 1980–91; Adv. Cttee on Supply and Educn of Teachers (Sec. of State's nominee), 1980–83. UK Rep., Permanent Educn Steering Cttee, Council of Europe, 1971–73; Rapporteur, OECD Review of Educn in NZ, 1982–83. Member: Senate, Univ. of London, 1977–85; Cttee of Management, Inst. of Advanced Legal Studies, 1980–83; Council, Open Univ., 1984–88; Council, Coll of Preceptors, 1987–89; Editl Adv. Bd, World Book Internat., 1989–2007; CBI Educn Foundn, 1993–98. President: Council for Educn in World Citizenship, 1979–90; English New Educn Fellowship, 1979–86; Comparative Educn Soc. of GB, 1981–84; Assoc. of Colls of Further and Higher Educn, 1984–88; European Assoc. for Institnl Res., 1990–92; Univs of N of England Consortium for Internat. Develt, 1991–94; N of England Educn Conference, 1992; Inst. of Educn Soc., 1990–93; Soc. for Res. in HE, 1996–2001; Vice President: British Educnl Admin, and Management Soc., 1985–; Council for Internat. Educn, 1992–; Soc. for Res. in Higher Educn, 2002–. Chm., NFER/Nelson Publishing Co., 1985–86, 1987–99; Dir, Fenner plc, 1988–93. Trustee, Forbes Trust, 1987–88. Governor: Wye Coll., 1981–83; Hymers Coll., Hull, 1985–91; Westminster Coll., Oxford, 1991–96; Univ. of Glamorgan (formerly Poly. of Wales), 1991–2002; Sevenoaks Sch., 1994–97; Christ Church UC, Canterbury, 1996–2004; Mem. Council, Hong Kong Inst. of Educn, 1998–2004. Freeman, City of London, 1985. Yeoman, 1982–87, Liveryman, 1988–, Worshipful Soc. of Apothecaries of London. Hon. FCP 1977; Hon. FCCEA 1980. Hon. Fellow: Thames Polytechnic, 1991; Inst. of Educn, Univ. of London, 1995; Christ Church Canterbury UC, 2005. Hon. DSc Aston (Birmingham), 1977; Hon. LittD Leeds, 1979; Hon. DCL Kent, 1981; DUniv: Open, 1983; Ulster, 2000; Glamorgan, 2004; Hon. DLitt: Loughborough, 1984; Southampton, 1998; London, 1999; Leicester, 2004; Essex, 2004; Hon. LLD: Hull, 1992; Huddersfield, 1996; Bristol, 2001; Hon. DEd: Kingston, 1993; Oxford Brookes, 1993; Plymouth, 1993; UWE, 1994; Hong Kong Inst. of Educn, 2004; Hon. DSc (Educ) QUB, 1997. *Publications:* The Secondary Modern School, 1963; Society and the Education of Teachers, 1969; (ed with G. Baron) Educational Administration and the Social Sciences, 1969; Heading for Change, 1969; Planning and Policy in Post Secondary Education, 1972; Theory into Practice, 1972; Research Perspectives in Education, 1973; (ed with R. Farquhar and R. Thomas) Educational Administration in Australia and Abroad, 1975; Research and Reform in Teacher Education, 1978; (ed with B. Simon) Education in the Eighties: the central issues, 1981; (ed) Metaphors of Education, 1984; Universities Under Scrutiny, 1987; Policy and Strategy for Higher Education: collaboration between business and higher eduction, 1989; articles and papers in professional jls. *Recreations:* writing, walking. *Address:* Centre for Higher Education Management and Policy, University of Southampton, Highfield, Southampton SO17 1BJ. *T:* (01962) 883485; *e-mail:* william.taylor@btinternet.com.

TAYLOR, William, CBE 2001; QPM 1991; HM Chief Inspector of Constabulary for Scotland, 1999–2001; *b* 25 March 1947; *s* of late William Taylor and Margaret Taylor; *m* 1978, Denise Lloyd; two step *s*. *Educ:* Blairgowrie High Sch.; Nat. Police Coll. (8th Special Course and 16th Sen. Command Course). Joined Metropolitan Police Service, 1966; served Central London locations as Det. Constable, Sergeant and Inspector, and Chief Inspector, 1966–76; New Scotland Yard: Community Relations Branch, 1976–78; Det. Supt, Central Drugs Squad, 1978–79; Staff Officer to Comr of Police, 1980–82 (Det. Chief Supt); Comdr CID NE London, then Uniform Comdr, Hackney; Comdr Robbery Squad (Flying Squad) and Regional Crime Squad, 1982–85; Asst Comr, City of London Police, 1985–89; Dep. Chief Constable, Thames Valley Police, 1989–90; Asst Comr, Specialist Ops, Metropolitan Police, 1990–94; Comr, City of London Police, 1994–98; HM Inspector of Constabulary, 1998. Chm., Crime Cttee, ACPO, 1994–98; Mem. Exec. Cttee, Interpol, 1995–98; Dir, Police Extended Interviews, 1996–98. Police Long Service and Good Conduct Medal, 1988. *Recreations:* reading (travel, management and historical), hill walking, horse riding, collecting some Dalton ware.

TAYLOR, His Honour William Edward Michael; a Circuit Judge, Western Circuit, 1989–2006; Resident Judge for Plymouth, 1990–2006; *b* 27 July 1944; *s* of William Henry Taylor and Winifred Mary (*née* Day); *m* 1969, Caroline Joyce Gillies; two *d*. *Educ:* Denstone Coll., Uttoxeter, Staffs; Council of Legal Educn. Called to the Bar, Inner Temple, 1968; practised from 2 Harcourt Bldgs, Temple; a Recorder, 1987–89; Liaison Judge for Devon and Cornwall, 1999–2006; Hon. Recorder of Plymouth, 2004–. Lectr, Council of Legal Educn, 1976–89. Chairman: Criminal Justice Strategy Cttee for Devon and Cornwall, 2000–06; Area Judicial Forum, 2004–06. Mem., Probation Cttees for Devon and Cornwall, 1995–2006. Hon. Pres., Univ. of Plymouth Law Soc., 1994–. Governor: Blundell's Sch., Tiverton, 2001–; Plymouth Univ., 2006–; Chm., Blundell's Prep. Sch. Cttee, 2001–. Chm., River Yealm and Dist Assoc.; Pres., Devon Safer Communities Trust. Patron, Twelve's Co. charity, Plymouth. Hon. LLD Plymouth, 2005. *Recreations:* music, opera, fishing, vintage cars, wine. *Address:* c/o Area Director for Devon and Cornwall, HM Courts Service, Trevecca, Culverland Road, Liskeard, Cornwall PL14 6RF. *Clubs:* Royal Western Yacht (Plymouth); English XX.

TAYLOR, Sir William George, (Sir Bill), Kt 2003; Managing Director, Improve Your Council consultancy, since 2006; *b* 10 April 1952; *s* of Colin Frey Taylor and Isobel Lauder Yule Taylor (now Allsopp); *m* 1978, Anne Charles; one *s* one *d*. *Educ:* Church Road (Yardley) Primary Sch., Birmingham; Sheldon Heath Comprehensive Sch., Birmingham; Univ. of Lancaster (BA Hons 1973, MA 1985); Manchester Poly. (Advanced Cert Ed 1976). Various professional roles in youth and community work, 1973–2006. Member: Bd, City Challenge, 1994–98; Bd, Elevate E Lancs Housing Mkt Restructuring Pathfinder, 2002–04; Chairman: Strategic Partnership Bd with Capita, 2001–04; Blackburn and Darwen Strategic Partnership Exec. (Local Strategic Partnership), 2002–04; E Lancs Partnership Forum, 2003–04. Associate Consultant: IDeA; Solace Enterprises; Nat. Youth Agency; Warwick Business Sch. Local Govt Centre. Member: NW Unitary Councils and Assoc. of Gtr Manchester Authorities, 2001–04; NW Regl Assembly and NW Constitutional Convention, 2001–04. Blackburn with Darwen Borough Council: Mem. (Lab), 1980–2004; Mayor, 1989–90, Dep. Mayor, 1990–91, of Blackburn; Dep. Leader 1994–2001; Leader, 2001–04; Exec. Mem. for Educn and Lifelong Learning, 2000–01; Chairman of Committees: Recreation, 1984–86; Community and Leisure Services, 1986–89; Urban Prog., 1990–93; Urban Regeneration, 1993–94; Mgt and Finance, 1994–97; City Challenge, 1994; Educn and Trng, 1997–2000; Chairman: Early Years Sub-cttee, 1997–98; Ethnic Minorities Consultative Panel, 1990–91 and 1992–96; Vice-Chm., Exec. and Forum, Educn Action Zone, 1999–2001. Non-executive Director: Vision Twenty One, 2006–; Blackburn Community Business Partnership, 2006–. Assoc. Lectr, Univ. of Cumbria (formerly St Martin's Coll.), 2006–. Mem., 1995–2001, Chm., 1996–2001, Prince's Trust Volunteers Bd, Lancs; Vice-Chm., Prince's Trust Strategic Forum, Lancs, 2000–01. Governor, Blackburn Coll., 1981–93 and 2002– (Chm., 2008). *Publications:* various in youth and community work, education, regeneration, leadership and local govt jls. *Recreations:* golf (off 20), sampling good wines and food, trying to engage with the world of digital technology, photography. *Address:* Arden House, Eden Park, Blackburn, Lancs BB2 7HJ. *T:* (01254) 668404; *e-mail:* sirbilltaylor@btinternet.com, sirbill@improveyourcouncil.co.uk. *Club:* Blackburn Golf.

TAYLOR, Rev. William Henry; Vicar, St John, Notting Hill, since 2002; *b* 23 Dec. 1956; *s* of Thomas Mather Taylor and Barbara Taylor (*née* Pitt). *Educ:* Westcott House, Cambridge. BA, MTh, MPhil. Ordained deacon, 1983, priest, 1984; Asst Curate, All Saints and St Philip with Tovil, Canterbury, 1983–86; Archbp's Advisor on Orthodox Affairs, Lambeth Palace, 1986–88; Sen. Curate, All Saints, Margaret St, London, 1986–88; Chaplain, Guy's Hosp., 1988; CMS 1988–91; Chaplain, Jordan Chaplaincy, 1988–91; Vicar, St Peter, Ealing, 1991–2000; Area Dean, Ealing, 1993–98; Provost, subseq. Dean, of Portsmouth, 2000–02. Chm., Anglican and Eastern Churches Assoc., 2001–; Mem., Internat. Commn of Anglican-Oriental Orthodox Dialogue, 2001–. FRAS 1982. Freeman, City of London, 1997. *Publications:* (ed) Christians in the Holy Land, 1994; Antioch and Canterbury, 2005. *Recreations:* good wine, challenging travel. *Address:* 25 Ladbroke Road, W11 3PD. *T:* (020) 7727 3439, *T:* and *Fax:* (office) (020) 7727 4262. *Club:* Nikaean.

TAYLOR, William James; QC (Scot.) 1986; QC 1998; *b* 13 Sept. 1944; *s* of Cecil Taylor and Ellen Taylor (*née* Daubney). *Educ:* Robert Gordon's College, Aberdeen; Aberdeen Univ. (MA Hons 1966; LLB 1969); Glasgow Univ. (Cert. in European Law (French) 1990). Admitted Faculty of Advocates, 1971; called to the Bar, Inner Temple, 1990. Standing Junior Counsel to DHSS, 1978–79, to FCO, 1979–86; Temp. Sheriff, 1997–99; part-time Sheriff, 2003–. Member: Criminal Injuries Compensation Bd, 1997–; Scottish Criminal Cases Review Commn, 1999–. Former Chairman: Traverse Th., Edinburgh; Fedn of Scottish Theatres; former Mem., TMA; former Member, Board: Scottish Ballet; Scottish Opera (Chm., 2004–07). Trustee, Univ. of Highlands and Islands Develt Trust, 2008–. Contested (Lab) Edinburgh W, Feb. and Oct. 1974; Regional Councillor (Lab), 1973–82. FRSA. *Recreations:* the arts, ski-ing, sailing, Scottish mountains, swimming, travel, restoring a garden, cooking. *Address:* 3A Northumberland Street, Edinburgh EH3 6LL. *T:* (0131) 556 0101; (office) Parliament House, Parliament Square, Edinburgh EH1 1RF. *T:* (0131) 226 2881, *Fax:* (0131) 225 3642; Carmelite Chambers, 9 Carmelite Street, EC4Y 0DR. *T:* (020) 7797 7111; *e-mail:* william.taylor@wanadoo.fr. *Clubs:* Scottish Arts, Traverse Theatre (Edinburgh); Royal Highland Yacht (Oban).

TAYLOR, William McCaughey; Chief Executive, Northern Ireland Police Authority, 1979–86; *b* 10 May 1926; *s* of William and Georgina Lindsay Taylor; *m* 1955, June Louise Macartney; two *s* two *d*. *Educ:* Campbell College, Belfast; Trinity College, Oxford (MA 1950). Lieut, Royal Inniskilling Fusiliers, 1944–47. International Computers Ltd, 1950–58; Lobitos Oilfields Ltd, 1958–60; HM Vice Consul, New York, 1960–63, HM Consul, 1963–65; NI Dept of Commerce, 1965–79. Chm., NI Coal Importers Assoc., 1986–91. *Recreations:* golf, bridge, gardening, piano. *Address:* 1 Knocktern Gardens, Belfast BT4 3LZ. *Club:* Royal Belfast Golf.

TAYLOR, William Rodney E.; *see* Eatock Taylor.

TAYLOR BRADFORD, Barbara; *see* Bradford.

TAYLOR THOMPSON, (John) Derek, CB 1985; Commissioner of Inland Revenue, 1973–87; Secretary, Churches' Main Committee, 1990–2007; *b* 6 Aug. 1927; *o s* of late John Taylor Thompson and Marjorie (*née* Westcott); *m* 1954, Helen Laurie Walker; two *d*. *Educ:* St Peter's Sch., York; Balliol Coll., Oxford. MA. Inland Revenue: Asst Principal, 1951; Private Sec. to Chm., 1954; Private Sec. to Minister without Portfolio (Rt Hon. William Deedes), 1962–64; Asst Sec., 1965; Dir of Manpower & Organisation, 1973–75; Dir, Personal Tax, 1975–81; Dir, Internat. Div., 1981–87. Chm., Fiscal Affairs Cttee, OECD, 1984–89. Chm., Legislation-Monitoring Service for Charities, 1991–2007. *Recreations:* rural pursuits, reading, historical writing. *Address:* Jessops, Bell Lane, Nutley, Sussex TN22 3PD. *Club:* Oxford and Cambridge.

TAYLOR-WOOD, Samantha; artist; *b* 4 March 1967; *m* 1997, Jeremy Michael Neal, (Jay), Jopling, *qv*; two *d*. *Educ:* Goldsmiths' Coll., London (BA Hons Fine Art 1990). *Solo exhibitions include:* Sam Taylor-Wood: Killing Time, Showroom, London, 1994; Travesty of a Mockery, White Cube, London, 1995; Pent-Up, Chisenhale Gall., London, and Sunderland City Art Gall., 1996; 16mm, Ridinghouse Editions, London, 1996; Sam Taylor-Wood: Five Revolutionary Seconds, Barcelona, 1997; Sustaining the Crisis, LA, 1997; Milan, Seattle, 1998, Stuttgart, 1999, Warsaw, Madrid and NY, 2000; Directions, Washington, 1999; Mute, White Cube, London, 2001; Sam Taylor-Wood: Films and Photographs, Paris, 2001, Amsterdam, 2002; Hayward Gall., Montreal and Tokyo, 2002, Vienna, 2003, St Petersburg and Moscow, 2004; The Passion, NY, 2002; David, Nat. Portrait Gall., 2004; Strings, Edinburgh, 2004; Sorrow, Suspension, Ascension, NY, 2004; New Work, White Cube, 2004; Ascension, Chicago, 2004; Sex and Death and a Few Trees, Rome, 2005; Still Lives, Baltic, Gateshead, 2006; *group exhibitions include:* General Release, Venice Biennale, 1995; Brilliant! New Art from London, Walker Art Centre, Minneapolis, and Contemporary Art Mus., Houston, 1995; Sensation, RA, Hamburger Bahnhof, Berlin, and Brooklyn Mus., NY, 1997; work in public collections including: British Council, Contemp. Art Soc., Nat. Portrait Gall., Saatchi Collection, Tate Gall., London; Stedelijk Mus., Amsterdam; Bangkok Mus. of Contemp. Art; Fundacio "la Caixa", Barcelona; Royal Mus. of Fine Arts, Copenhagen; Collection Lambert, Geneva; Israel Mus., Jerusalem; Inst. d'Arte Contemporanea, Lisbon; Walker Art Centre, Minneapolis; New Orleans Mus.; Guggenheim, NY; Robert Shiffler Collection, Ohio; Astrup Fearnley Mus., Oslo; Caldic Collection, Rotterdam; San Francisco Mus. of Mod. Art; Samsung Mus., Seoul. Illy Cafe Prize for most promising young artist, Venice Biennale, 1997. *Publications:* Unhinged, 1996; Sam Taylor-Wood: third party, 1999; Contact, 2001; Sam Taylor-Wood, 2001; Sam Taylor-Wood: crying men, 2004. *Address:* White Cube, 48 Hoxton Square, N1 6PB.

TAYLORSON, John Brown, OBE 2007; Managing Director: John Taylorson Associates, 1990–2001; Inflight Marketing Services, 1990–2001; *b* 5 March 1931; *s* of John Brown Taylorson and Edith Maria Taylorson; *m* 1st, 1960, Barbara June (*née* Hagg) (marr. diss.); one *s* one *d*; 2nd, 1985, Helen Anne (*née* Parkinson); one *s*. *Educ:* Forest School, Snaresbrook; Hotel School, Westminster. Sales Director, Gardner Merchant Food Services Ltd, 1970–73; Managing Director: International Division, Gardner Merchant Food Services, 1973–77; Fedics Food Services, 1977–80; Chief Executive, Civil Service Catering Organisation, 1980–81; Hd of Catering Servs, British Airways, 1981–89; Chief Exec., Inflight Catering Services, 1990–96. Dir, Internat. Service Industry Search, 1990–97. Corporate Appeals Dir, 1993–2007, Dir, Internat. Res. Appeal, 2007–, DEBRA. Pres., Internat. Flight Catering Assoc., 1983–85; Chm., Inflight Services Gp, Assoc. of European Airlines, 1983–85. *Recreations:* golf, theatre, crossword puzzles. *Address:* Deer Pond Cottage, Highfields, East Horsley, Surrey KT24 5AA. *Clubs:* Old Foresters; Burhill Golf.

TAYLOUR, family name of **Marquess of Headfort**.

TAYTON, Lynn Margaret; QC 2006; barrister, since 1981; *b* 5 Feb. 1959; *d* of Gerald and Margaret Tayton; *m* 2006, Rupert Webb; one *s*. *Educ:* Barrs Hill Sch., Coventry; University Coll. London (LLB Hons 1980); Council of Legal Educn. Called to the Bar, Gray's Inn, 1981; barrister, Nottingham, 1982–89; Sen. Lectr in Law, Nottingham Trent Poly., 1990–91; barrister, London, 1995–. Chair, Herts and Beds Bar Mess, 2007–. Associate Lectr, OU, 2006; Mem., OU Law Prog. Cttee, 2007–. *Recreations:* going to the theatre, cookery, variety of not too energetic physical pursuits, spending time with my family and other people who make me laugh. *Address:* 36 Bedford Row, WC1R 4JH; *e-mail:* ltayton@36bedfordrow.co.uk.

TCHALENKO, Janice Anne, FRCA; potter, since 1964; Chief Designer, Dartington Pottery, 1984–2006; *b* 5 April 1942; *d* of late Eric Cooper and Marjorie Cooper (*née* Dodd); *m* 1964, Dr John Stephen Tchalenko; one *s*. *Educ:* Barr's Hill Grammar Sch., Coventry. FRCA 1987. Clerical Officer, PO Telephones, Coventry and FO, London, 1958–60; Art Therapist, The Priory, Roehampton, 1965–69; studio pottery course, Harrow Sch. of Art, 1969–71; travelled extensively in Soviet Union and Middle East, 1965–77; set up workshop, London, 1971; pt-time Tutor, Camberwell Sch. of Art and Crafts, 1972–86; Tutor, RCA, 1981–96; Curator: Colours of the Earth exhibn, British Council, 1989–92 (toured India, 1991–92); British Ceramics for Brazil, British Council, 2000 (touring). Mem., Crafts Council, 1994–2000. Consultant: Goa You Porcelain Factory, China, 1991; Blue Factory, China, 1991–92. *Works* include: (with Spitting Image Workshop) Seven Deadly Sins, 1993, Modern Antiques, 1996; pottery designs for Dartington range, 1984–2006, Designers Guild, 1985, Next Interiors, 1986, and Poole Pottery, 1994–2000; exhibits in major public collections, including: Helsinki Mus. of Decorative Art; Los Angeles County Mus. of Art; Mus. für Kunst und Gewerbe, Hamburg; Nat. Mus. of Modern Art, Kyoto; Stockholm Nat. Mus.; V&A Mus.; *solo exhibitions* include: Sideshow, ICA, 1980; Craftshop, V&A Mus., 1981; Scottish Gall., Edinburgh, 1989, 2001; Stockholm Nat. Mus., 1990; retrospective, Ruskin Gall., Sheffield, and tour, 1992; Beaux Arts, Bath, 1997. Laura Ashley Fellowship, Laura Ashley Foundn, 2001. *Recreations:* gardening, reading. *Address:* 30 Therapia Road, East Dulwich, SE22 0SE.

TCHURUK, Serge; Chairman, Alcatel-Lucent (formerly Alcatel Alsthom, then Alcatel), since 2006 (Chairman and Chief Executive Officer, 1995–2006); *b* 13 Nov. 1937; *s* of Georges Tchuruk and Mathilde (*née* Dondikian); *m* 1960, Héléna Kalfus; one *d*. *Educ:* Ecole Nationale Supérieure de l'Armement; Ecole Polytechnique. With Mobil Oil in France, USA and Netherlands, 1968–80; Head, Mobil Oil BV, Rotterdam, 1979–80; with Rhône-Poulenc, 1980–86: Gen. Manager, Fertilizer Div., 1980–82; Mem., Exec. Cttee, 1981; Dep. Man. Dir, 1982–83; Man. Dir, 1983–86; Chm. Mgt Bd, 1986–87, Chm. and CEO, 1987–90, CDF Chimie, later ORKEM; Chm. and CEO, Total SA, Paris, 1990–95. Officier de la Légion d'Honneur, 1998. *Recreations:* music, ski-ing, tennis. *Address:* Alcatel-Lucent, 54 rue La Boétie, 75008 Paris, France. *T:* 40761010, *Fax:* 40761400.

TEACHER, Michael John, FCA; Chief Executive, Ontex, since 2006; Chairman: Unipoly, since 2001; Peek Traffic, since 2004; *b* 2 June 1947; *s* of Charles and Ida Teacher; *m* 1972, Sandra Posner; three *s*. *Educ:* City Univ. (MSc Financial Mgt 1972). FCA 1969. Articled Clerk, Abey, Lish & Co., 1964–69; Audit Senior, Deloitte & Co., 1969–71; Corporate Finance Exec., Corinthian Holdings, then Welbeck Investment, 1973–76; Man. Dir, Holding Co. Ltd, Welbeck Investment Plc, 1976–82; Exec. Dir, Sir Joseph Causton Plc, 1983–84; Man. Dir, Pointon York Ltd, Venture Capital Co., 1984–87; Hillsdown Holdings PLC: Man. Dir, HIT Plc (Venture Capital subsid.), 1987–93; Exec. Dir, 1993–98; Chief Exec., 1998–99. Non-executive Chairman: Networks by Wireless Ltd (formerly Wireless Lans Hldgs), 2000–; eTechnology VCT plc, 2000–. *Recreations:* tennis, soccer, running, charitable work.

TEAGLE, Vice-Adm. Sir Somerford (Francis), KBE 1994; Chief of Defence Force, New Zealand, 1991–95; *b* 9 June 1938; *s* of Leonard Herbert Teagle and Muriel Frances Teagle; *m* 1961, Leonie Marie Maire; one *s* one *d*. *Educ:* Christ's Coll., Christchurch, NZ; Royal Naval Coll., Dartmouth. Royal New Zealand Navy: Sea and Staff appts, 1958–85: Commanding Officer HMNZS: Manga, 1962–64; Taranaki, 1977; jssc, Canberra, 1977; CO HMNZS Canterbury, 1978–79; Captain, Naval Trng, 1981–84; ndc, Canada, 1983; Cdre, Auckland, 1986–87; Dep. Chief of Naval Staff, 1988–89; Chief of Naval Staff, 1989–91. *Recreation:* wine growing. *Address:* Omarere, Ponatahi Road, PO Box 84, Martinborough, New Zealand. *Club:* Wellington (Wellington).

TEAGUE, (Edward) Thomas (Henry); QC 2000; **His Honour Judge Teague;** a Circuit Judge, since 2006; *b* Weymouth, 21 May 1954; *s* of Harry John Teague and Anne Elizabeth Teague (*née* Hunt); *m* 1980, Helen Mary Howard; two *s*. *Educ:* St Francis Xavier's Coll., Liverpool; Christ's Coll., Cambridge (MA). Called to the Bar, Inner Temple, 1977; Mem., Wales and Chester Circuit, 1978–2006, Western Circuit, 2002–06; Asst Recorder, 1993–97; a Recorder, 1997–2006. Legal Assessor, GMC, 2002–06. FRAS 1991. *Recreations:* music, fly-fishing, astronomy. *Address:* The Law Courts, Legh Street, Warrington WA1 1UR. *T:* (01925) 256700. *Club:* Lansdowne.

TEAR, Robert, CBE 1984; concert and operatic tenor; first Professor of International Singing, Royal Academy of Music, since 1985; *b* 8 March 1939; *s* of Thomas Arthur and Edith Tear; *m* 1961, Hilary Thomas; two *d*. *Educ:* Barry Grammar Sch.; King's Coll., Cambridge (MA; Hon. Fellow 1989). Hon. RCM, RAM. Mem., King's Coll. Choir, 1957–60; subseq. St Paul's Cathedral and solo career; joined English Opera Group, 1964. By 1968 worked with world's leading conductors, notably Karajan, Giulini, Bernstein and Solti; during this period created many rôles in operas by Benjamin Britten. Has appeared in all major festivals; close association with compositions of Sir Michael Tippett, 1970–; Covent Garden: début, The Knot Garden, 1970, closely followed by Lensky in Eugène Onégin; Fledermaus, 1977; Peter Grimes, 1978; Rake's Progress, 1979; Thérèse, 1979; Loge in Rheingold, 1980; Admetus in Alceste, 1981; David in Die Meistersinger, 1982; Captain Vere in Billy Budd, 1982; appears regularly with Royal Opera. Glyndebourne: début, Aschenbach in Death in Venice, 1989; Marriage of Figaro, and Rake's Progress, 1994; The Makropoulos Case, 1997. Started relationship with Scottish Opera (singing in La Traviata, Alceste, Don Giovanni), 1974. Paris Opera: début, 1976; Lulu 1979. Début as conductor with Thames Chamber Orchestra, QEH, 1980. Has conducted Minneapolis Orch., ECO, LSO, Philharmonia, London Mozart Players. Has worked with every major recording co. and made numerous recordings (incl. solo recital discs). Sermon, King's Coll. Chapel, Cambridge Univ., 1990. *Publications:* Victorian Songs and Duets, 1980; Tear Here (autobiog.), 1990; Singer Beware, 1995. *Recreations:* any sport; interested in 18th and 19th century English water colours. *Club:* Arts.

TEARE, Andrew Hubert; Chief Executive, Rank Group (formerly Rank Organisation) plc, 1996–98; *b* 8 Sept. 1942; *s* of Arthur Hubert Teare and Rosalind Margaret Baker; *m* 1964, Janet Nina Skidmore; three *s*. *Educ:* Kingswood School, Bath; University College London (BA Hons Classics 1964). Turner & Newall, 1964–72; CRH, 1972–83 (Gen. Manager Europe, 1978–83); Rugby Group, 1983–90 (Asst Man. Dir, 1983–84; Man. Dir, 1984–90); Gp Chief Exec., English China Clays plc, 1990–95. Non-executive Director: Heiton Holdings, 1984–90; NFC, 1989–96; Prudential Corp., 1992–98. Pres., Nat. Council of Building Material Producers, 1990–92. CCMI. *Publication:* The Chairman (novel), 2005. *Recreations:* ski-ing, mountain walking, reading. *Address:* Flat 56, The Little Adelphi, 10–14 John Adam Street, WC2N 6HA. *Club:* Hibernian United Service (Dublin).

TEARE, Jonathan James; His Honour Judge Teare; a Circuit Judge, since 1998; Presiding Senior Judge, Sovereign Base Areas, Cyprus, since 2007 (Deputy Senior Judge, 2001–07); *b* 13 Dec. 1946; *y s* of Prof. Donald Teare, MD, FRCP, FRCPath, DMJ and Kathleen Teare; *m* 1972, Nicola Jill, 2nd *d* of Lt-Col Peter Spittall, RM, CP and Peggy Spittall; two *d*. *Educ:* Pinewood Sch.; Rugby Sch. Called to the Bar, Middle Temple, 1970; practised, Midland and Oxford Circuit, 1971–98; Asst Recorder, 1985–90; Recorder, 1990–98. Member: Mental Health Review Tribunal, 2002–; Notts Probation Bd, 2004–. Served TA, HAC, 1965–69, RRF, 1970–72. Trustee, Hollygirt Sch., 2002–. Freeman, City of London, 1981; Liveryman, Soc. of Apothecaries, 1980–. *Recreations:* gardening, shooting, travel, wine. *Address:* Nottingham Crown Court, Canal Street, Nottingham NG1 7EL. *T:* (0115) 910 3551.

TEARE, Hon. Sir Nigel (John Martin), Kt 2006; **Hon. Mr Justice Teare;** a Judge of the High Court of Justice, Queen's Bench Division, since 2006; *b* 8 Jan. 1952; *s* of Eric John Teare and Mary Rackham Teare; *m* 1975, Elizabeth Jane Pentecost; two *s* one *d*. *Educ:* King William's Coll., Isle of Man; St Peter's Coll., Oxford (BA 1973; MA 1975). Called to the Bar, Lincoln's Inn, 1974, Bencher, 2004; practising barrister, 1975–2006; Jun. Counsel to Treasury in Admiralty matters, 1989–91; QC 1991; Asst Recorder, 1993–97; a Recorder, 1997–2006; a Dep. High Court Judge, 2002–06. Acting Deemster, IOM, 2000–06. Lloyd's Salvage Arbitrator, 1994–2000, Lloyd's Salvage Appeal Arbitrator, 2000–06. *Recreations:* collecting Manx paintings, squash, tennis, golf. *Address:* Royal Courts of Justice, Strand, WC2A 2LL. *Club:* Royal Automobile.

TEASDALE, Sir Graham Michael, Kt 2006; FRCP, FRCSE, FRCSGlas; Professor and Head of Department of Neurosurgery, University of Glasgow, 1981–2003; President, Royal College of Physicians and Surgeons of Glasgow, 2003–06; *b* 20 Sept. 1940; *s* of Thomas Teasdale and Eva Teasdale (*née* Elgey); *m* 1971, Dr Evelyn Muriel Arnott; three *s* one *d*. *Educ:* Johnston Grammar Sch., Durham; Durham Univ. Med. Sch. (MB BS 1963). MRCP 1966, FRCP 1988; FRCSE 1970; FRCSGlas 1981. Trng in medicine, surgery and specialisation in neurosurgery, 1963–75; University of Glasgow: Sen. Lectr in Neurosurgery, 1975–79; Reader in Neurosurgery, 1979–81; Associate Dean for Med. Res., 1999–2003. President: Internat. Neurotrauma Soc., 1994–98; Eur. Brain Injury Consortium, 1993–2003; Soc. of British Neurological Surgeons, 2000–02. FMedSci 1999; FRSE 2001. Hon. FACS 2002. Hon. DM Athens 2002. *Publications:* (jtly) Management of Head Injuries, 1982; (jtly) Current Neurosurgery, 1992; articles and papers on med. res., particularly on head injuries, in med. jls. *Recreations:* water sports, hill walking and midge dodging in the West of Scotland. *Address:* c/o Royal College of Physicians and Surgeons, 242 St Vincent Street, Glasgow G2 5RJ.

TEASDALE, John Douglas, PhD; FBA 2000; Special Scientific Appointment, MRC Cognition and Brain Sciences (formerly Applied Psychology) Unit, 1991–2004; *b* 1 Sept. 1944; *s* of George Eric Teasdale and Vera Joan Teasdale; *m* 1969, Jacqueline Blackburn; two *s*. *Educ:* Emmanuel Coll., Cambridge (BA 1965, MA); Inst. of Psychiatry, Univ. of London (Dip. Psych. 1966; PhD 1971). Lectr, Psychology Dept, Inst. of Psychiatry, Univ. of London, 1967–71; Principal Clin. Psychologist, University Hosp. of Wales, Cardiff, 1971–74; Sen. Res. Worker, Dept of Psychiatry, Univ. of Oxford, 1974–85; Sen. Scientist, MRC Applied Psychol. Unit, 1985–91. Vis. Prof., Inst. of Psychiatry, Univ. of London, 1995–2004. FMedSci 2000. *Publications:* (with P. J. Barnard) Affect, Cognition and Change, 1993; (with Z. V. Segal and J. M. G. Williams) Mindfulness-Based Cognitive Therapy for Depression, 2002; (jtly) The Mindful Way through Depression, 2007; approx. 100 articles in books and learned jls. *Recreation:* sitting quietly, doing nothing. *Address:* 15 Chesterford House, Southacre Drive, Cambridge CB2 7TZ.

TEATHER, Sarah Louise; MP (Lib Dem) Brent East, since Sept. 2003; *b* 1 June 1974. *Educ:* Leicester Grammar Sch.; St John's Coll., Cambridge (BA 1996). Policy analyst, Macmillan Cancer Relief, until 2003. Mem. (Lib Dem), Islington LBC, 2002–03. Contested (Lib Dem) Finchley & Golders Green, 2001. Lib Dem spokesman: on mental health, 2003–04; on London, 2004–05; on communities and local govt, 2005–06; on educn and skills, 2006–07; on innovation, univs and skills, 2007–08; on business, enterprise and regulatory reform, 2008–. Chair, All Party Parly Gp on Guantanamo Bay, 2006–. FRSA 2007. *Address:* House of Commons, SW1A 0AA.

TEBBIT, family name of **Baron Tebbit**.

TEBBIT, Baron *cr* 1992 (Life Peer), of Chingford, in the London Borough of Waltham Forest; **Norman Beresford Tebbit,** CH 1987; PC 1981; Director: Sears (Holdings) PLC, 1987–99; British Telecommunications plc, 1987–96; BET, 1987–96; Spectator (1828) Ltd, 1989–2004; *b* 29 March 1931; 2nd *s* of Leonard and Edith Tebbit, Enfield; *m* 1956, Margaret Elizabeth Daines; two *s* one *d*. *Educ:* Edmonton County Grammar Sch. Embarked on career in journalism, 1947. Served RAF: commissioned GD Branch; qualif. Pilot, 1949–51; Reserve service RAuxAF, No 604 City of Middx Sqdn, 1952–55. Entered and left publishing and advertising, 1951–53. Civil Airline Pilot, 1953–70 (Mem. BALPA; former holder various offices in that Assoc.). Active mem. and holder various offices, Conservative Party, 1946–. MP (C) Epping, 1970–74, Chingford, 1974–92; PPS to Minister of State, Dept of Employment, 1972–73; Parly Under Sec. of State, Dept of Trade, 1979–81; Minister of State, Dept of Industry, 1981; Secretary of State for: Employment, 1981–83; Trade and Industry, 1983–85; Chancellor of the Duchy of Lancaster, 1985–87; Chm., Conservative Party, 1985–87. Former Chm., Cons. Members Aviation Cttee; former Vice-Chm. and Sec., Cons. Members Housing and Construction Cttee; Sec. House of Commons New Town Members Cttee. Dir, J. C. Bamford Excavators, 1987–91. Co-presenter, Target, Sky TV, 1989–98; columnist: The Sun, 1995–97; The Mail on Sunday, 1997–2001. *Publications:* Upwardly Mobile (autobiog.), 1988; Unfinished Business, 1991. *Address:* c/o House of Lords, SW1A 0PW.

TEBBIT, Sir Donald (Claude), GCMG 1980 (KCMG 1975; CMG 1965); HM Diplomatic Service, retired; *b* 4 May 1920; *m* 1947, Barbara Margaret Olson Matheson; one *s* two *d* (and one *d* decd). *Educ:* Perse School; Trinity Hall, Cambridge (MA). Served War of 1939–45, RNVR. Joined Foreign (now Diplomatic) Service, 1946; Second Secretary, Washington, 1948; transferred to Foreign Office, 1951; First Secretary, 1952; transferred to Bonn, 1954; Private Secretary to Minister of State, Foreign Office, 1958; Counsellor, 1962; transferred to Copenhagen, 1964; Commonwealth Office, 1967; Asst Under-Sec. of State, FCO, 1968–70; Minister, British Embassy, Washington, 1970–72; Chief Clerk, FCO, 1972–76; High Comr in Australia, 1976–80. Chairman: Diplomatic Service Appeals Bd, 1980–87; E-SU, 1983–87; Mem., Appeals Bd, Council of Europe, 1981–90. Dir, RTZ Corp., 1980–90. Dir Gen., British Property Fedn, 1980–85. Pres. (UK), Australian-British Chamber of Commerce, 1980–90; Chairman: Zimbabwe Tech. Management Training Trust, 1983–91; Marshall Aid Commemoration Commn, 1985–95; Jt Commonwealth Socs Council, 1987–93. Governor, Nuffield Hospitals, 1980–90, Dep. Chm., 1985–90. President: Old Persean Soc., 1981–82; Trinity Hall Assoc., 1984–85. *Address:* Morningside, 38 Chapel Street, Ely, Cambs CB6 1AD.

TEBBIT, Sir Kevin (Reginald), KCB 2002; CMG 1997; Chairman, Finmeccanica UK; Permanent Secretary, Ministry of Defence, 1998–2005; *b* 18 Oct. 1946; *s* of R. F. J. Tebbit and N. M. Tebbit (*née* Nichols); *m* 1969, Elizabeth Alison, *d* of John and Elizabeth Tinley; one *s* one *d*. *Educ:* Cambridgeshire High Sch.; St John's Coll., Cambridge (Schol.; BA Hons 1969). Asst Principal, MoD, 1969–72; Asst Private Sec. to Sec. of State for Defence, 1973–74; Principal, MoD, 1974–79; First Sec., UK Delegn to NATO, 1979–82; transferred to FCO, 1982; E European and Soviet Dept, 1982–84; Hd of Chancery, Ankara, 1984–87; Dir, Cabinet of Sec. Gen. of NATO, 1987–88; Counsellor (Politico-Mil.), Washington, 1988–91; Hd, Econ. Relns Dept, FCO, 1992–94; Dir (Resources) and Chief Inspector, FCO, 1994–97; Dep. Under-Sec. of State, FCO, 1997; Dir, GCHQ, 1998. Non-exec. Dir, Smiths Gp plc, 2006–. Vis. Prof., QMUL, 2006–. Chm., Lifeboat Fund, 2004–. Gov., Ditchley Foundn, 2004–. Trustee, British Friends of Aphrodisias, 1997–. *Recreations:* music, countryside, archaeology, West Ham Utd. *Club:* Savile.

TECKMAN, Jonathan Simon Paul; Director, Fletcher Teckman Consulting Ltd; Public Sector Tutor, Ashridge; *b* 27 May 1963; *s* of Sidney Teckman and Stephanie Audrey Teckman (*née* Tresman); *m* 1997, Anne Caroline Fletcher; two *s*. *Educ:* Weston Favell Upper Sch., Northampton; Univ. of Warwick (BSc Hons Mgt Scis). Admin trainee, 1984–86, HEO (Develt), 1986–90, DoE; Gp Finance Manager, Historic Royal Palaces Agency, 1990–93; Department of National Heritage, subsequently Department for Culture, Media and Sport: Principal, Nat. Lottery Div., 1993–95; Films Div., 1995–98 (Sec. to Adv. Cttee on Film Finance); Dep. Dir, 1998, Dir, 1999–2002, BFI. Mem., BAFTA. *Recreations:* cinema, reading, cricket, golf. *Club:* Bold Dragoon Cricket (Northampton).

TEDDER, family name of **Baron Tedder**.

TEDDER, 3rd Baron *cr* 1946, of Glenguin, Co. Stirling; **Robin John Tedder;** investor and vigneron; Director, Glenguin Wine Co., since 1996; *b* 6 April 1955; *er s* of 2nd Baron Tedder and of Peggy Eileen Growcott; *S* father, 1994; *m* 1st, 1977, Jennifer Peggy (*d* 1978), *d* of John Mangan, NZ; 2nd, 1980, Rita Aristeia, *yr d* of John Frangidis, Sydney, NSW; two *s* one *d*. MW; Associate, Securities Inst. of Australia, 1981. *Heir: s* Hon. Benjamin John Tedder, *b* 23 April 1985. *Address:* 11 Kardinia Road, Clifton Gardens, Sydney, NSW 2088, Australia.

TEELOCK, Dr Boodhun, GOSK 1997; High Commissioner for Mauritius in London, 1989–92; *b* 20 July 1922; *s* of Ramessur Teelock and Sadny Teelock; *m* 1956, Riziya; three *d*. *Educ:* Edinburgh Univ. (MB ChB 1950); Liverpool Univ. (DTM&H 1951). DPH. Ministry of Health, Mauritius: School MO, 1952–58; Senior School MO, 1958–59; Principal MO, 1960–68; World Health Organisation: Regional Adviser, Public Health Administration, Brazzaville, 1968–71; Chief of Mission, Tanzania, 1971–74, Kenya and Seychelles, 1974–79; Immunisation MO, Air Mauritius, 1980–88. *Recreation:* reading. *Address:* 12 Labourdonnais Avenue, Quatre Bornes, Mauritius.

TEGNER, Ian Nicol, CA; *b* 11 July 1933; *s* of Sven Stuart Tegner, OBE, and Edith Margaret Tegner (*née* Nicol); *m* 1961, Meriel Helen, *d* of Brig. M. S. Lush, CB, CBE, MC; one *s* one *d*. *Educ:* Rugby School. CA. Clarkson Gordon & Co., Toronto, 1958–59; Manager 1959–65, Partner 1965–71, Barton Mayhew & Co., Chartered Accts; Finance Dir, Bowater Industries, 1971–86; Chm., Cayzer Steel Bowater, 1981–86; Dir, Gp Finance, Midland Bank, 1987–89. Chairman: Control Risks Gp, 1992–2000; Crest Packaging, 1993–99; Director: Wiggins Teape Appleton, subseq. Arjo Wiggins Appleton, 1990–2000; Opera 80, subseq. English Touring Opera, 1991–99; TIP Europe plc, 1992–93; Teesside Power Ltd, 1993–2001; Coutts & Co., 1996–98. Institute of Chartered Accountants of Scotland: Mem. Council 1981–86; Pres., 1991–92; Mem., Accounting Standards Cttee of CCAB, 1984–86; Chm., Hundred Gp of Finance Dirs, 1988–90. Chm., Children of the Andes, 2001–03. *Publications:* articles on accountancy in various jls and pubns. *Recreations:* book collecting, travel, hill-walking, choral singing, family life. *Address:* 44 Norland Square, W11 4PZ.

TEHRANI, Joanna Elizabeth; *see* Glynn, J. E.

TEJAN-JALLOH, Sulaiman; Ambassador for Sierra Leone to United States of America, 2006–08; *b* 21 July 1949; *s* of late Alihaj A. B. Tejan-Jalloh and Hajja Isatu Tejan-Jalloh; *m* 1989, Marima Tejan-Jalloh (*née* Jabbie); two *s* two *d*. *Educ:* American Univ., Washington (BSc Admin of Justice); SOAS, London (LLB Hons). Called to the Bar, Gray's Inn, 1980; enrolled Sierra Leone Bar, 1981, in practice as barrister and solicitor, 1981–96. MP (People's Party) Sierra Leone, 1996–98; Minister of Transport, Communications and Envmt, 1996–98; Dep. High Comr to UK, 1999–2000; High Comr to UK, and Ambassador to Scandinavia, Spain, Greece, Portugal and Ireland, 2000–06. *Recreations:* music, walking, gardening.

TE KANAWA, Dame Kiri (Jeanette Claire), ONZ 1995; DBE 1982 (OBE 1973); opera singer; *b* Gisborne, New Zealand, 6 March 1944; *m* 1967, Desmond Stephen Park (marr. diss. 1997); one *s* one *d*. *Educ:* St Mary's Coll., Auckland, NZ; London Opera Centre. Major rôles at Royal Opera House, Covent Garden, include: the Countess, in Marriage of Figaro; Elvira, in Don Giovanni; Mimi, in La Bohème; Desdemona, in Otello; Marguerite, in Faust; Amelia, in Simon Boccanegra; Fiordiligi, in Così Fan Tutte; Tatiana, in Eugene Onegin; title rôle in Arabella; Rosalinde, in Die Fledermaus; Violetta, in La Traviata; Manon, in Manon Lescaut. Has sung leading rôles at Metropolitan Opera, New York, notably, Desdemona, Elvira, and Countess; also at the Paris Opera, Elvira, Fiordiligi, and Pamina in Magic Flute, title rôle in Tosca; at San Francisco Opera, Amelia and Pamina; at Sydney Opera House, Mimi, Amelia, and Violetta in La Traviata; Elvira, with Cologne Opera; Amelia at La Scala, Milan; Countess in Le Nozze di Figaro at Salzburg Fest. Many recordings, incl. Maori songs. Estabd Kiri Te Kanawa Foundn, 2004. Hon. DMus: Oxford, 1983; Cambridge, 1997. Hon. AC 1990. *Publications:* Land of the Long White Cloud, 1989; Opera for Lovers, 1997. *Recreations:* golf, swimming, tennis. *Address:* c/o Michael Storrs Music Ltd, 11 Maiden Lane, WC2E 7NA.

TELFER, Robert Gilmour Jamieson, (Rab), CBE 1985; PhD; Executive Chairman, BSI Standards, 1989–92; Director, Manchester Business School, 1984–88; *b* 22 April 1928; *s* of late James Telfer and Helen Lambie Jamieson; *m* 1953, Joan Audrey Gunning; three *s*. *Educ:* Bathgate Academy (Dawson Trust Bursary); Univ. of Edinburgh (Mackay-Smith Prize; Blandfield Prize; BSc (Hons 1st cl.) 1950, PhD 1953). Shift Chemist, AEA, 1953–54; Imperial Chemical Industries Ltd: Res. Chemist, Billingham Div., 1954–58; Heavy Organic Chemicals Div., 1958–71; Fibre Intermediates Dir and R & D Dir, 1971–75; Div. Dep. Chm., 1975–76, Div. Chm., 1976–81, Petrochemicals Div.; Chm. and Man. Dir, 1981–84, Dir, 1984, Mather & Platt Ltd; Chm., European Industrial Services Ltd, 1988–89. Mem. Bd, Philips-Imperial Petroleum Ltd, 1975–81; Director: Renold PLC, 1984–98 (Chm., Audit Cttee, 1993–98); Volex PLC, 1986–98 (Chm., Audit Cttee, 1993–98); Teesside Hldgs Ltd, 1993–95. Sen. Vis. Fellow, Manchester Business Sch., 1988–. Group Chm., Duke of Edinburgh's Study Conf., 1974; Mem., ACORD for Fuel and Power, 1981–87; Chm., Adv. Council on Energy Conservation, 1982–84. Personal Adviser to Sec. of State for Energy, 1984–87. British Standards Institution: Mem. Main Bd, and Mem. Finance Cttee, 1988–92; non-exec. Chm., Standards Bd and Testing Bd, 1988–89. Member: Civil Service Coll. Adv. Council, 1986–89; HEFCE, 1992–97 (Chairman: Audit Cttee, 1993–97; Quality Assessment Cttee, 1996–98); Dir, Quality Assurance Agency for Higher Educn, 1997–98. Governor, Univ. of Teesside (formerly Teesside Polytechnic), 1989–97 (Chm., Govs, 1992–97; Chm., Resources Cttee, 1989–92). CCMI. Hon. MBA Manchester, 1989; Hon. LLD Teesside, 1998. *Publications:* papers in Jl Chem. Soc. and Chemistry and Industry. *Recreations:* walking, swimming, fossil hunting, decorative egg collecting, supporting Middlesbrough FC. *Address:* Downings, Upleatham Village, Redcar, Cleveland TS11 8AG.

TELIČKA, Pavel; Partner, BXL Consulting Ltd; *b* 24 Aug. 1965; *s* of František Telička and Marie Teličková; *m* 1990, Eva Pašková; one *s* one *d*. *Educ:* Charles Univ., Prague (Dr of Law). Dir Gen. for Integration (EU, NATO and UN), 1996–98; Dep. Minister of Foreign Affairs, 1998–2000; State Sec. for European Affairs and 1st Dep. Minister of Foreign Affairs, 2000–03; Ambassador of Czech Republic to the EU, 2003–04; Mem., EC, 2004. President's Medal for contribn to integration process of Czech Republic into EU, 2003. *Publication:* How We Entered the EU, 2003. *Address:* BXL Consulting Ltd, Rond-Point Schuman 11, 1040 Brussels, Belgium.

TELITO, Rev. Sir Filoimea, GCMG 2007; MBE 1997; Governor-General of Tuvalu, since 2005; *b* 19 March 1945; *s* of Telogo Telito and Moti Silaati; *m* 1978, Pepapeti Tilafolau; one *s* two *d*. *Educ:* Vaitupu Primary Sch., Tuvalu; King George V Secondary Sch., Kiribati; Ardmore Teachers' Coll., NZ; Trinity Theol Coll., NZ (Dip. Christian Educn); Univ. of S Pacific, Fiji (DipEd (Secondary)); Pacific Theol Coll., Fiji (BD). Principal, 1968–70, 1974–76 and 2002–05, Chaplain, 1983–87, Motufoua Secondary Sch.; Parson, Funafuti Parish, Tuvalu, 1989–91; Principal, Fituvalu Secondary Sch., Tuvalu, 1991–94; Gen. Sec., Christian Ch of Tuvalu, 1995–98; Tuvalu Chaplaincy, Suva, Fiji Is, 1999–2002. Mem., Boys' Bde. *Recreations:* reading, table-tennis, gardening. *Address:* c/o Government House, PO Box 30, Funafuti, Tuvalu. *T:* 20715, *Fax:* 20709; *e-mail:* telito@tuvalu.tv.

TELLO, Manuel, Hon. CMG 1975; Permanent Representative of Mexico to the United Nations, 1993–94 and 1995–2000; *b* 15 March 1935; *s* of late Manuel Tello and Guadalupe M. de Tello; *m* 1983, Rhonda M. de Tello. *Educ:* schools in Mexico City; Georgetown Univ.; Sch. for Foreign Service, Washington, DC; Escuela Libre de Derecho; Institut de Hautes Etudes Internationales, Geneva. Equivalent of BA in Foreign Service Studies; post-grad. studies in Internat. Law. Joined Mexican Foreign Service, 1957; Asst Dir Gen. for Internat. Organizations, 1967–70, Dir Gen., 1970–72; Dir for Multilateral Affairs, 1972–74; Dir for Political Affairs, 1975–76; Ambassador to UK, 1977–79; Under Sec., Dept of Foreign Affairs, Mexico, 1979–82; Perm. Rep. of Mexico to Internat. Orgns, Geneva, 1983–89; Ambassador to France, 1989–92; Minister of Foreign Affairs, 1994–95. Alternate Rep. of Mexico to: OAS, 1959–63; Internat. Orgs, Geneva, 1963–65; Conf. of Cttee on Disarmament, Geneva, 1963–66; Rep. of Mexico to: Org. for Proscription of Nuclear Weapons in Latin America, 1970–73; 3rd UN Conf. on Law of the Sea, 1971–76 and 1982. Has attended several Sessions of UN Gen. Assembly. Pres., Matías Romeros Inst. of Diplomatic Studies, 2002–04. Holds decorations from Chile, Ecuador, Egypt, France, Italy, Jordan, Panama, Senegal, Sweden, Venezuela, Yugoslavia. *Publications:* contribs to learned jls in the field of international relations. *Recreations:* reading, theatre, music.

TEMIRKANOV, Yuri; Music Director and Principal Conductor, St Petersburg (formerly Leningrad) Philharmonic Orchestra, since 1988; Principal Guest Conductor, Danish National Symphony Orchestra, since 2004; *b* 10 Dec. 1938. *Educ:* Leningrad Conservatory (graduated violinist, 1962, conductor, 1965). Musical Dir, Leningrad Symphony Orch., 1969–77; Artistic Dir and Chief Conductor, Kirov Opera, Leningrad, 1977–88; Principal

Conductor, Royal Philharmonic Orch., 1978–98, now Conductor Laureate; Music Dir, Baltimore SO, 2000–06. Principal Guest Conductor, Dresden Philharmonic Orch., 1994–98. Has conducted: Boston Symphony; Dresden Philharmonic; Danish Nat. Radio Symphony; Orch. of Santa Cecilia, Rome; Orch. Nat. de France; La Scala, Milan; Philadelphia Orch.; San Francisco Symphony; New York Philharmonic, etc. Recordings of major orchestral works of Tchaikovsky, Stravinsky, Prokofiev, Mussorgsky and Shostakovich. Abbiati Prize for best conductor, Italian Critics' Assoc., 2002. *Address:* c/o IMG Artists Europe,The Light Box, 111 Power Road, Chiswick, W4 5PY. *T:* (020) 7957 5800.

TEMKIN, Prof. Jennifer, (Mrs G. J. Zellick); Professor of Law, University of Sussex, since 1992; *b* 6 June 1948; *d* of late Michael Temkin and Minnie Temkin (*née* Levy); *m* 1975, Prof. Graham Zellick, *qv*; one *s* one *d. Educ:* S Hampstead High Sch. for Girls; LSE (LLB, LLM (Dist.), LLD); Inns of Court Sch. of Law. Called to the Bar, Middle Temple, 1971; Lectr in Law, LSE, 1971–89; Prof. of Law and Dean, Sch. of Law, Univ. of Buckingham, 1989–92; Dir, Centre for Legal Studies, Univ. of Sussex, 1994–96. Vis. Prof., Univ. of Toronto, 1978–79. Mem., Cttee of Heads of Univ. Law Schs, 1989–92, 1994–96. Member: Scrutiny Cttee on Draft Criminal Code, CCC, 1985–86; Home Sec's Adv. Gp on Use of Video Recordings in Criminal Proceedings, 1988–89; NCH Cttee on Children Who Abuse Other Children, 1990–92; External Reference Gp, Home Office Sex Offences Review, 1999–2000; Cttee of Experts on Treatment of Sex Offenders, Council of Europe, 2003–05; Expert Gp on Rape and Sexual Assault, Victims of Violence and Abuse Prevention Prog., DoH and Nat. Inst. for Mental Health in England, 2005–07. Patron, Standing Cttee on Sexually Abused Children, 1993–96. Gov., S Hampstead High Sch. for Girls, 1991–99. FRSA 1989. Member: Editl Adv. Gp, Howard Jl of Criminal Justice, 1984–; Editl Bd, Jl of Criminal Law, 1986–2005. *Publications:* Rape and the Legal Process, 1987, 2nd edn 2002; Rape and Criminal Justice, 1995; (with Barbara Krahe) Sexual Assault and the Justice Gap: a question of attitude, 2008; articles in Mod. Law Rev., Criminal Law Rev., Cambridge Law Jl, Law Qly Rev., Internat. and Comparative Law Qly and other learned and professional jls. *Address:* School of Law, University of Sussex, Falmer, Brighton, Sussex BN1 9QN. *T:* (01273) 678580; *e-mail:* j.temkin@sussex.ac.uk.

TEMKO, Edward James, (Ned); Chief Political Correspondent, The Observer, since 2005; *b* 5 Nov. 1952; *s* of Stanley L. Temko and Francine (*née* Salzman); *m* 1st, 1980, Noa Weiss (marr. diss. 1984); 2nd, 1986, Astra Bergson Kook; one *s. Educ:* Williams Coll., USA (BA Hons Pol Sci. and Econs). Reporter, Associated Press, Lisbon, 1976; United Press International: Europe, ME and Africa Editl Desk, Brussels, 1977; Correspondent, ME Office, Beirut, 1977–78; Christian Science Monitor: Chief ME Correspondent, Beirut, 1978–80; Moscow Correspondent, 1981–83; ME Correspondent, Jerusalem, 1984–85; SA Correspondent, Johannesburg, 1986–87; Sen. TV Correspondent for Europe, ME and Africa in London, World Monitor TV, 1989–90; Editor, Jewish Chronicle, 1990–2005. *Publications:* To Win or To Die: a biography of Menachem Begin, 1987. *Recreations:* tennis, reading, computers, travel. *Address:* The Observer, 3–7 Herbal Hill, EC1R 5EJ.

TEMPEST, Annie; cartoonist; *b* 22 Aug. 1959; *d* of Henry and Janet Tempest; *m* 1991, James McConnel, composer (marr. diss. 2006); one *s* one *d. Educ:* Rye St Anthony Sch., Oxford; St Mary's Sch., Ascot. Cartoonist: The Yuppies, Daily Mail, 1985–93; Tottering-by-Gently, Country Life Magazine, 1994–; Senior Moments, WI Home & Country, 2005–06. Strip Cartoonist of the Year, Cartoonists' Club of GB, 1989. *Publications:* Turbocharge Your Granny!, 1985; How Green are your Wellies?, 1985; Hooray Henry, 1986; Henry on Hols, 1987; Westenders, 1988; Tottering-by-Gently, vol. I, 1996, vol. II, 1998, vol. III, 2003; Tottering Hall, 2001; Lady Tottering's Journal, 2002; At Home with the Totterings, 2007; *illustrator/contributor:* Publish and Be Damned!, 1988; Best Cartoons of the Year, 1988; Anneka Rice, The Recycled Joke Book, 1989; Mary Killen, Best Behaviour, 1991; Michael Seed, I Will See You in Heaven Where Animals Don't Bite..., 1991; Crime-check!, 1992; R. Rushbrooke, Where Did I Go Wrong?, 1992; Jonathan Ray, Berry's Best Cellar Secrets, 1998; Michael Seed, Will I See You in Heaven?, 1999; Alistair Sampson, The Guest from Hell, 2000; Robin Page, Why the Reindeer has a Velvet Nose, 2002. *Recreations:* inventing labour-saving devices, carving in hard woods, sculpting in all media, music, people watching, good wine, gory medical documentaries. *Address:* Tylers Barn, Wood Norton Road, Stibbard, Norfolk NR20 4RF; The O'Shea Gallery, No 4 St James's Street, SW1A 1EF; *e-mail:* daffy@tottering.com. *Clubs:* British Cartoonists' Association; Muthaiga (Nairobi).

TEMPLE OF STOWE, 8th Earl *cr* 1822; **Walter Grenville Algernon Temple-Gore-Langton;** *b* 2 Oct. 1924; *s* of Comdr Hon. Evelyn Arthur Temple-Gore-Langton, DSO, RN (*d* 1972) (*y s* of 4th Earl) and Irene (*d* 1967), *d* of Brig.-Gen. Cavendish Walter Gartside-Spaight; *S* cousin, 1988; *m* 1st, 1954, Zillah Ray (*d* 1966), *d* of James Boxall; two *s* one *d*; 2nd, 1968, Margaret Elizabeth Graham, *o d* of late Col H. W. Scarth of Breckness. *Heir: s* Lord Langton, *qv*.

TEMPLE, Anthony Dominic Afamado; QC 1986; a Recorder, since 1989; *b* 21 Sept. 1945; *s* of Sir Rawden John Afamado Temple, CBE, QC and late Margaret Jessie Temple; *m* 1st, 1975 (marr. diss.); 2nd, 1983, Suzie Bodansky; two *d. Educ:* Haileybury and ISC; Worcester College, Oxford (Hon. Sec., OU Modern Pentathlon Assoc.). Called to the Bar, Inner Temple, 1968, Bencher, 1995; Crown Law Office, Western Australia, 1969; Assistant Recorder, 1982; a Dep. High Ct Judge, 1994–. Chm., Modern Pentathlon Assoc. of GB, 2004–. *Recreations:* modern pentathlon, travel, history. *Address:* 4 Pump Court, EC4Y 7AN.

See also V. B. A. Temple.

TEMPLE, Jane Rosemary; *see* Ray, J. R.

TEMPLE, Jill; *see* Stansfield, J.

TEMPLE, Prof. Sir John (Graham), Kt 2003; FRCSE, FRCS, FRCPE, FRCP; Professor of Surgery, University of Birmingham, 1995, now Emeritus; President, Royal College of Surgeons of Edinburgh, 2000–03; *b* 14 March 1942; *s* of Joseph Henry Temple and Norah Temple; *m* 1966, Margaret Jillian Leighton Hartley; two *s* one *d. Educ:* William Hulme's Grammar Sch., Manchester; Liverpool Univ. Med. Sch. (MB ChB Hons; ChM). FRCSE 1969; FRCS 1970 (Hon. FRCS 2004); FRCP, FRCPE 1999; FRCPSGlas (*ad eundem*) 2003; FRCA 2005. Consultant Surgeon, Queen Elizabeth Hosp., Birmingham, 1979–98; Regl Postgrad. Dean, W Midlands, 1991–2000. Chm., Conf. Postgrad. Med. Deans UK, 1995–2000. Mem. Council, RCSE, 1997–2003. Mem., Specialist Trng Authy, 1996– (Chm., 2001–08); Hon. Col, 202 Field Hospital (V), 2004–. FMedSci 1998; Fellow, Polish Soc. Surgeons, 1997. Hon. FHKCS 2001; Hon. FRACS 2002; Hon. FRCSI 2004. *Publications:* papers on postgraduate education and training. *Recreations:* off-shore sailing and racing, ski-ing. *Address:* Wharncliffe, 24 Westfield Road, Edgbaston, Birmingham B15 3QG.

TEMPLE, Martin John, CBE 2005; Chairman, Engineering Employers Federation, since 2008 (Director General, 1999–2008); *b* 30 Aug. 1949; *s* of John Douglas Temple and Kathleen Temple; *m* 1972, Lesley Imeson; one *s* one *d. Educ:* Bridlington Sch.; Univ. of Hull (BSc Hons 1970); Newcastle Poly. (Dip Mktg 1972); INSEAD (AMP 1991). Gen. Manager, British Steel Corp. Refractories Gp, 1979–85; Works Dir, GR-Stein Refractories, 1985–87; Dir, Sales and Mktg, British Steel Stainless, 1987–92; Avesta Sheffield: Dir, Mktg and Sales, 1992–95; Vice Pres., 1995–98. Bd Mem., Namtec Ltd, 2004–; Dir, Vestry Court Ltd, 2000–; Chm., 600 Gp plc, 2007–. Chm., Transition Mgt Bd, Business Support Simplification Prog., BERR, 2008–. Board Member: Council of Eur. Employers of Metal, Engrg and Technology-based Industries, 1999– (Chm., 2005–); Women in Sci. and Engrg, 2001–08 (former Chm.); Engrg Develt Trust, 2000–07; Sci. Engrg Manufacturing Technol. Alliance, 2000–; Engrg and Technol. Bd, 2002–08; Mem. Supervisory Bd, Sci., Engrg, Technol. and Maths Network, 2001–07. Hon. FFOM. Freeman, Co. of Cutlers, 1998. *Recreations:* Rugby, music, countryside, current affairs. *Address:* 63 Vestry Court, Monck Street, Westminster, SW1P 2BW. *T:* (020) 7233 3898; *e-mail:* mtemple@eef-fed.org.uk. *Clubs:* Oriental, St Stephen's.

TEMPLE, Nicholas John; Chairman: Fox IT Ltd, since 2003; Capula Ltd, since 2007; Hotelscene, since 2008; *b* 2 Oct. 1947; *s* of late Leonard Temple and of Lilly Irene Temple (*née* Thornton); *m* 1st; one *s* two *d*; 2nd, 2004, Lucinda (*née* Westmacott). *Educ:* King's Sch., Glos. Joined IBM, 1965; Chief Exec., 1992–94, Chm., 1994–96, IBM UK; Vice Pres., Industries, IBM Europe, 1995–96; mgt consultant, N. M. Rothschild & Sons, 1996. Non-executive Director: Electrocomponents PLC, 1997–; Datacash, 2000–; Datatech, 2003–. Council Mem., Foundn for Mfg and Ind., 1993–96. Chm., Action: Employees in the Community, 1993–96. Mem., President's Adv. Gp, Spastics' Soc., 1993–95. *Recreations:* rowing, ski-ing, opera. *Address:* 10 Markham Square, SW3 4UY. *T:* (020) 7581 2181.

TEMPLE, Reginald Robert, CMG 1979; HM Diplomatic Service, retired; *b* 12 Feb. 1922; *s* of Lt-Gen. R. C. Temple, CB, OBE, RM, and Z. E. Temple (*née* Hunt); *m* 1st, 1952, Julia Jasmine Anthony (marr. diss. 1979); one *s* one *d*; 2nd, 1979, Susan McCorquodale (*née* Pick); one *d* (one step *s* one step *d*). *Educ:* Wellington College; Peterhouse, Cambridge. HM Forces, 1940–46, RE and Para Regt; Stockbroking, 1947–51; entered HM Foreign Service, 1951; Office of HM Comr Gen. for SE Asia, 1952–56; 2nd Sec., Beirut, 1958–62; 1st Sec., Algiers, 1964–66, Paris, 1967–69; FCO, 1969–79; Counsellor 1975; Sultanate of Oman Govt Service, 1979–85. Dir, Shearwater Securities Ltd, I of M, 1989–92; Consultant, Capital International Securities Ltd, I of M, 1996–. American Silver Star, 1944; Order of Oman, 3rd Class, 1985. *Recreations:* sailing, fishing. *Address:* Scarlett House, near Castletown, Isle of Man IM9 1TB. *Clubs:* Army and Navy, Royal Cruising.

TEMPLE, Sir Richard (Carnac Chartier), 5th Bt *cr* 1876, of The Nash, Kempsey, co. Worcester; Founder and Director, The Temple Gallery, since 1959; *b* 17 Aug. 1937; *er s* of Sir Richard Temple, 4th Bt, MC and Lucy Geils de Lotbinière; *S* father, 2007; *m* 1964, Emma Rose, 2nd *d* of Maj.-Gen. Sir Robert Laycock, KCMG, CB, DSO; three *d. Educ:* Stowe. PhD. Lieut, Royal Horse Guards (The Blues), 1958 (Gen. Service Medal, 1958). Lectr, Sch. of Traditional Arts, The Prince's Foundation, 1997–. *Publications:* Icons and the Mystical Origins of Christianity, 1991, 2nd edn 2001; Icons: divine beauty, 2004; numerous scholarly articles and catalogues. *Recreations:* music, travel, philosophy. *Heir: b* Anthony St George Temple [*b* 23 Feb. 1941; *m* 1986, Angelika Reda; one *s*]. *Address: e-mail:* richard@templegallery.com. *T:* (020) 7727 3809.

TEMPLE, Victor Bevis Afoumado; QC 1993; a Recorder of the Crown Court, since 1989; *b* 23 Feb. 1941; *s* of Sir Rawden John Afamado Temple, CBE, QC and Margaret Jessie Temple; *m* 1974, Richenda Penn-Bull; two *s. Educ:* Shrewsbury Sch.; Inns of Court Sch. of Law. TA, Westminster Dragoons, 1960–61. Marketing Exec., 1960–68. Called to the Bar, Inner Temple, 1971, Bencher, 1996; Jun. Prosecuting Counsel to the Crown, 1985–91, Sen. Treasury Counsel, 1991–93, CCC. DTI Inspector into Nat. Westminster Bank Ltd, 1992. Mem. Panel of Chairmen, Police Discipline Tribunals, 1993–. *Recreations:* rowing, carpentry. *Address:* 6 King's Bench Walk, Temple, EC4Y 7DR. *T:* (020) 7583 0410. *Club:* Thames Rowing.

See also A. D. A. Temple.

TEMPLE COX, Richard, CBE 2002; Chairman: Birmingham and Solihull NHS Local Improvement Finance Trust, 2004–07; Community Regeneration Partnership, since 2005; *b* 25 Dec. 1937; *s* of Richard G. Cox and Marianne A. Cox (*née* Ladbrook); *m* 1990, Caroline Mary Fauset Jefferson (*née* Welsh); one *s* two *d* from previous marriage. *Educ:* King Edward's Sch., Birmingham; Birmingham Sch. of Architecture (DipArch 1963). RIBA 1964. Secretary: Birmingham Civic Soc., 1964–71; Victorian Soc. W Midlands, 1969–71; Chm., Temple Cox Nicholls Architects, 1970–2000. Pres., Birmingham Architectural Assoc., 1983–84; Royal Institute of British Architects: Council Mem., 1987–93; Sen. Vice Pres., 1989–91; Chm., Educn Cttee, 1989–91. Mem., Construction Industry Council, 1991–94. Chm., Castle Vale HAT, 1992–2005. Mem., Community, Voluntary and Local Services Honours Selection Cttee, 2005–. Trustee: Birmingham Pub Bombing Lord Mayor's Appeal, 1974; Sense in Midlands, 1988–92; Nat. Council, Deaf Blind Rubella Assoc., 1991–93; Chm., Birmingham Inst. for Deaf, 1976–94; Founder Chm., Access for Disabled, Birmingham, 1986. *Publications:* occasional contribs to RIBA Jl and Regeneration and Renewal. *Recreations:* travel, music, golf, gardening, after-dinner speaking, philately, military history. *Clubs:* Aberdovey Golf; Ombersley Golf.

TEMPLE-GORE-LANGTON, family name of **Earl Temple of Stowe**.

TEMPLE-MORRIS, family name of **Baron Temple-Morris**.

TEMPLE-MORRIS, Baron *cr* 2001 (Life Peer), of Llandaff in the County of South Glamorgan and of Leominster in the County of Herefordshire; **Peter Temple-Morris;** Consultant Solicitor, Moon Beever, Solicitors, since 2001; *b* 12 Feb. 1938; *o s* of His Honour Sir Owen Temple-Morris, QC and Lady (Vera) Temple-Morris (*née* Thompson); *m* 1964, Taheré, *e d* of late HE Senator Khozeimé Alam, Teheran; two *s* two *d. Educ:* Hillstone Sch., Malvern; Malvern Coll.; St Catharine's Coll., Cambridge (MA). Chm., Cambridge Univ. Conservative Assoc., 1961; Mem. Cambridge Afro-Asian Expedn, 1961. Called to Bar, Inner Temple, 1962. Judge's Marshal, Midland Circuit, 1958; Mem., Young Barristers' Cttee, Bar Council, 1962–63; in practice on Wales and Chester Circuit, 1963–66; London and SE Circuit, 1966–76; 2nd Prosecuting Counsel to Inland Revenue, SE Circuit, 1971–74; admitted a solicitor, 1989. Contested (C): Newport (Mon), 1964 and 1966; Norwood (Lambeth), 1970; MP Leominster, Feb. 1974–2001 (C, Feb. 1974–1997, Ind., 1997–98, Lab, 1998–2001). PPS to Minister of Transport, 1979. Member: Select Cttee on Agriculture, 1982–83; Select Cttee on Foreign Affairs, 1987–90. Chairman: British-Lebanese Parly Gp, 1983–94 (Vice-Chm., 1994–97); British-Netherlands Parly Gp, 1988–2001 (Sec., 2001–); British-Iranian Parly Gp, 1989–2005 (Sec., 1974–89); British-South Africa (formerly British-Southern Africa) All-Party Gp, 1992–95 (Vice-Chm., 1995–2001); British-Russian All-Party Gp, 1992–94; British-Spanish All-Party Gp, 1994–2001 (Treas., 2001–05); House of Lords and Commons Solicitors Gp, 1992–97; H of L Cttee on Delegated Legislation and Regulatory Powers, 2002–06; Co-Chm., Working Party to establish British-Irish Inter-Parly Body, 1988–90, first British Co-Chm., 1990–97, Mem., 1997–05; Secretary: Conservative Parly Transport Cttee, 1976–79; Cons. Parly Legal Cttee, 1977–78; Vice-Chairman: Cons. Parly Foreign and Commonwealth Affairs Cttee, 1982–90 (Sec., 1979–82); Cons. Parly NI Cttee, 1989–92; British-Argentina Parly Gp, 1990–94; European-Atlantic Gp, 1991–97. Member: Exec. British Branch, IPU, 1977–97 (Chm., 1982–85; British delegate, fact-finding mission on Namibia, 1977); Exec. Cttee, UK Br., CPA, 1993–98; Mem., 1980, Leader, 1984, Parly Delegation to UN Gen. Assembly; Mem., Argentine-British Conf., 1991. Chm., Hampstead Conservative Political Centre, 1971–73; Society of Conservative Lawyers: Mem. Exec., 1968–71, 1990–97 (Chm., 1995–97); Vice-Chm., Standing Cttee on Criminal Law, 1976–79; Chm., F&GP Cttee, 1992–95. Chm., Bow Gp Standing Cttee on Home Affairs, 1975–79. Chm., Afghanistan Support Cttee, 1981–82; Vice-Chm., GB-USSR Centre (formerly GB-USSR Assoc.), 1993–98 (Mem. Council, 1982–92); Pres., Iran Soc., 1995– (Mem. Council, 1968–80); Chm. Bd, British Iranian Chamber of Commerce, 2002–04; Mem. Adv. Council, British Inst. of Persian Studies., 1997–. Mem., RIIA. Nat. Treas., UNA, 1987–97 (Hon. Vice Pres., 1997–). Mem., Lord Chancellor's Adv. Cttee, Nat. Records Office and Archives, Kew, 2008–. Freeman, City of London. Gov., Malvern Coll., 1975– (Council Mem., 1978–2002); Mem. Council, Wilton Park Conf. Centre, (FCO), 1990–97. Pres., St Catharine's Coll., Cambridge Soc., 2003–04. Fellow, Industry and Parlt Trust, Barclays Bank, 1988. Hon. Associate, BVA, 1976. Hon Citizen: New Orleans; Havana, Cuba. Chevalier du Tastevin, 1991; Jurade de St Emilion, 1999. Knight, Order of Orange-Nassau (Netherlands), 2007. *Recreations:* travel, wine and food, family relaxation. *Address:* House of Lords, SW1A 0PW. *Clubs:* Reform; Cardiff and County.

TEMPLEMAN, family name of **Baron Templeman**.

TEMPLEMAN, Baron *cr* 1982 (Life Peer), of White Lackington in the County of Somerset; **Sydney William Templeman,** Kt 1972; MBE 1946; PC 1978; a Lord of Appeal in Ordinary, 1982–94; *b* 3 March 1920; *s* of late Herbert William and Lilian Templeman; *m* 1st, 1946, Margaret Joan (*née* Rowles) (*d* 1988); two *s*; 2nd, 1996, Mrs Sheila Barton Edworthy (*d* 2008). *Educ:* Southall Grammar School; St John's College, Cambridge (Schol.; MA 1944; Hon. Fellow 1982). Served War of 1939–45: commnd 4/1st Gurkha Rifles, 1941; NW Frontier, 1942; Arakan, 1943; Imphal, 1944; Burma with 7 Ind. and 17 Ind. Divisions, 1945 (despatches; Hon. Major). Called to the Bar, 1947; Harmsworth and MacMahon schols; Mem., Middle Temple and Lincoln's Inn; Mem., Bar Council, 1961–65, 1970–72; QC 1964; Bencher, Middle Temple, 1969 (Treasurer, 1987). Attorney Gen. of the Duchy of Lancaster, 1970–72; a Judge of the High Court of Justice, Chancery Div., 1972–78; a Lord Justice of Appeal, 1978–82. Member: Tribunal to inquire into matters relating to the Vehicle and General Insurance Co., 1971; Adv. Cttee on Legal Education, 1972–74; Royal Commn on Legal Services, 1976–79; Chm., Bishop of London's Commn on City Churches, 1992–94. Treasurer, Senate of the Four Inns, 1972–74; Pres., Senate of the Inns of Court and the Bar, 1974–76. President: Bar Assoc. for Commerce, Finance and Industry, 1982–85; Bar European Gp, 1987–95; Assoc. of Law Teachers, 1997–2000. Pres., Holdsworth Club, 1983–84. Hon. Member: Canadian Bar Assoc., 1976; Amer. Bar Assoc., 1976; Newfoundland Law Soc., 1984. Hon. DLitt Reading, 1980; Hon. LLD: Birmingham, 1986; CNAA, 1990; Exeter, 1991; W of England, 1993; Nat. Law Sch. of India, 1994. *Address:* Mellowstone, 1 Rosebank Crescent, Exeter EX4 6EJ. *T:* (01392) 275428.

TEMPLEMAN, Michael; Group Tax Director, Schroders PLC; Head of Taxation, Institute of Directors, since 2004; *b* 6 May 1943; *s* of late Dr Geoffrey Templeman, CBE, founding Vice-Chancellor, Univ. of Kent at Canterbury, and Dorothy May Templeman (*née* Heathcote); *m* 1970, Jane Margaret Willmer Lee; four *d*. *Educ:* King Edward's Sch., Birmingham; Selwyn Coll., Cambridge (MA). Inland Revenue, 1965–93: Inspector of Taxes, 1965; Dist Inspector, Cannock, 1971–72; Head Office Specialist, Oil Taxation, 1972–78; Dist. Inspector, Luton, 1978–81; Head Office Specialist, Financial Concerns, 1981–89; Controller, Oil Taxation Office, 1989–92; Dir, Financial Institutions Div., 1992–93; J. Henry Schroder Wagg, then J. Henry Schroder, & Co., now Schroders PLC: Gp Tax Dir, 1994–. *Recreations:* cricket, classical music, cooking, cliff walking. *Address:* (office) 31 Gresham Street, EC2V 7QA. *T:* (020) 7658 6450.

TEMPLEMAN, Miles Howard; Director General, Institute of Directors, since 2004; *b* 4 Oct. 1947; *s* of Robert James and Margot Elizabeth Templeman; *m* 1970, Janet Elizabeth Strang; two *s* one *d*. *Educ:* Haberdashers' Aske's Boys' Sch.; Jesus Coll., Cambridge (BA 1969, MA). Young & Rubicam, 1970–73; Beecham Foods, 1973–79; Levi Strauss, 1979–85; Whitbread, 1985–2000; Chief Exec., Bulmers, 2002–03; Eldridge Pope, 2002–04. Non-executive Director: Ben Sherman, 2000–03; Royal Mail, 2001–03; Shepherd Neame, 2002– (Chm., 2005–); Portman Gp, 2003; non-exec. Chm., YO! Sushi, 2003–. *Recreations:* tennis, golf, reading, opera. *Address:* Institute of Directors, 116 Pall Mall, SW1Y 5ED. *Club:* Queen's.

TEMPLER, Maj.-Gen. James Robert, CB 1989; OBE 1978 (MBE 1973); Managing Director, Templers Gardening (formerly Templers Flowers), since 1990; *b* 8 Jan. 1936; *s* of Brig. Cecil Robert Templer, DSO and Angela Mary Templer (*née* Henderson); *m* 1963 (marr. diss. 1979); two *s* one *d*; 2nd, 1981, Sarah Ann Evans (*née* Rogers). *Educ:* Charterhouse; RMA Sandhurst. RCDS, psc. Commissioned Royal Artillery, 1955; Instructor, Staff Coll., 1974–75; Comd 42nd Regt, 1975–77; Comd 5th Regt, 1977–78; CRA 2nd Armd Div., 1978–82; RCDS 1983; ACOS Training, HQ UKLF, 1983–86; ACDS (Concepts), MoD, 1986–89. Mem., British Cross Country Ski Team, 1958; European 3 Day Event Champion, 1962; Mem., British Olympic 3 Day Event Team, 1964. FCMI (FBIM 1988). *Recreations:* sailing, ski-ing, gardening, fishing, DIY. *Address:* c/o Lloyds TSB, Crediton, Devon EX17 3AH.

TEMPLETON, Prof. Allan, FRCOG, FRCP, FRCPE, FMedSci; Professor of Obstetrics and Gynaecology, University of Aberdeen, since 1985 (Regius Professor of Obstetrics and Gynaecology, 1985–2007); President, Royal College of Obstetricians and Gynaecologists, 2004–07; *b* 28 June 1946; *s* of Richard and Minnie Templeton; *m* 1980, Gillian Constance Penney; three *s* one *d*. *Educ:* Aberdeen Grammar School; Univ. of Aberdeen (MB ChB 1969; MD Hons 1982). MRCOG 1974, FRCOG 1987; FRCPE 2005; FRCP 2006. Resident and Registrar, Aberdeen Hosps, 1969–75; Lectr and Sen. Lectr, Dept of Obst. and Gyn., Univ. of Edinburgh, 1976–85; Hd, Dept of Obst. and Gyn., Univ. of Aberdeen, 1985–2007. Chm., Soc. for the Study of Fertility, 1996–99; Mem., HFEA, 1995–2000. Hon. Sec., RCOG, 1998–2004. FMedSci 2002. *Publications:* The Early Days of Pregnancy, 1988; Reproductive Medicine and the Law, 1990; (ed jtly) Infertility, 1992; The Prevention of Pelvic Infection, 1996; Evidence-based Fertility Treatment, 1998; Management of Infertility, 2000; clinical and sci. articles on human infertility and *in vitro* fertilisation. *Recreation:* mountaineering. *Address:* Knapperna House, Udny, Aberdeenshire AB41 6SA. *T:* (01651) 842481.

TEMPLETON, Darwin Herbert, CBE 1975; Senior Partner, Price Waterhouse Northern Ireland (formerly Ashworth Rowan Craig Gardner), 1967–82; *b* 14 July 1922; *s* of Malcolm and Mary Templeton; *m* 1950; two *s* one *d*. *Educ:* Rocavan Sch.; Ballymena Academy. FICAI. Qualified as Chartered Accountant, 1945. Partner, Ashworth Rowan, 1947. Chm., Ulster Soc. of Chartered Accountants, 1961–62; Pres., ICAI, 1970–71. Mem., Royal Commn on Legal Services, 1976–79. Chm. and Dir, several cos. *Recreations:* music, golf, motor racing. *Address:* 4 Cashel Road, Broughshane, Ballymena, Co. Antrim, Northern Ireland BT42 4PL. *T:* (028) 2586 1017.

TEMPLETON, Mrs Edith; author, since 1950; *b* 7 April 1916; *m* Edmund Ronald, MD (*d* 1984); one *s*. *Educ:* Prague and Paris; Prague Medical University. During War of 1939–45 worked in American War Office, in office of Chief Surgeon. Conference Interpreter for British Forces in Germany, 1945–46, rank of Capt. *Publications:* Summer in the Country, 1950 (USA 1951), repr. 1985; Living on Yesterday, 1951, repr. 1986; The Island of Desire, 1952, repr. 1985; The Surprise of Cremona, 1954 (USA 1957), repr. 1988; This Charming Pastime, 1955; (as Louise Walbrook) Gordon, 1966 (US edn as The Demon's Feast, 1968), repr. 2003; Three (USA 1971); Murder in Estoril, 1992; The Darts of Cupid and Other Stories, 2003; contributor to The New Yorker, Holiday, Atlantic Monthly, Vogue, Harper's Magazine, Abroad, The Gourmet's Companion, The Compleat Imbiber, Italian Pleasures. *Recreation:* travel, with the greatest comfort possible. *Address:* 76 Corso Europa, 18012 Bordighera, Italy.

TEMPLETON, Ian Godfrey; Warden, Glenalmond College, Perth, 1992–2003; *b* 1 Feb. 1944; *s* of late Anthony Godard Templeton and Mary Gibson Templeton (*née* Carrick Anderson); *m* 1970, Elisabeth Aline Robin; one *s* one *d*. *Educ:* Gordonstoun Sch.; Edinburgh Univ. (MA); Bedford Coll., London Univ. (BA 1st cl. Hons Philosophy). Asst Master, 1969–71, Housemaster, 1971–73, Melville Coll.; Housemaster, Daniel Stewart's and Melville Coll., 1973–78; Asst Headmaster, Robert Gordon's Coll., Aberdeen, 1978–85; Headmaster, Oswestry Sch., 1985–92. FRSA. *Recreations:* golf, choral singing, travel. *Address:* 18 Craigleith Crescent, Edinburgh EH4 3JL. *T:* (0131) 332 2449. *Clubs:* Royal & Ancient; Bruntsfield Links Golfing Society.

TEMPLETON, John Marks, Jr; MD; FACS; President, since 1987, and Chairman, since 2006, John Templeton Foundation; *b* 19 Feb. 1940; *s* of Sir John Marks Templeton; *m* 1970, Josephine Gargiulo; two *d*. *Educ:* Yale Univ. (BA 1962); Harvard Med. Sch. (MD 1968). FACS 1980. Intern in Surgery, 1968–69, Surgical Resident, 1969–73, Med. Coll. of Virginia; Pediatric Surgical Resident, Children's Hosp. of Philadelphia, 1973–75; Instructor in Pediatric Surgery, Univ. of Pennsylvania, 1973–75; Asst Prof., Dept of Surgery, Eastern Virginia Med. Sch., 1975–77; Asst Prof., 1978–86, Associate Prof., 1986–95, Prof. of Pediatric Surgery, 1995, Adjunct Prof., 1995–, Univ. of Pennsylvania; Barclay Fellow, Templeton Coll., Oxford, 1995. Hd of Pediatric Surgery, Naval Regl Med. Center, Portsmouth, Va, 1975–77; Children's Hospital of Philadelphia: Asst Surgeon, 1977–83; Associate Surgeon, 1983–95; Co-Chm., Emergency Services Cttee, 1978–85; Chm., Trauma Cttee, 1985–95; Co-Dir, Trauma Service, 1986–88; Trauma Prog. Dir, 1988–95; Pediatric Surgical Cons., Pennsylvania Hosp., 1980–95. Member: Amer. Med. Assoc.; Amer. Pediatric Surgical Assoc.; Eastern Assoc. for Surgery of Trauma; Amer. Assoc. for Surgery of Trauma; Bd, Amer. Trauma Soc.; Assoc. for Advancement of Automotive Med.; Internat. Assoc. for Surgery of Trauma and Surgical Intensive Care. Mem., Health and Safety Cttee, Univ. of Penn, 1984–90. Mem., Editl Adv. Bd, Trauma Quarterly, 1990–93. Member: Bd, Eastern Univ.; Foreign Policy Res. Inst.; Cradle of Liberty Council, Boy Scouts of Amer.; Melmark Foundn; Nat. Recreation Foundn; Nat. Bible Assoc. Hon. LLD Beaver Coll., Glenside, Penn, 1989; Hon. DHumLit: Buena Vista Univ., 1998; Commonwealth Univ., Richmond, Va, 2000; Alvernia Coll., Reading, Penn, 2001; Hon. Dr Sacred Theol., Florida Center for Theol Studies, 2001. I. A. Bigger Award, Med. Coll. of Va, 1973; Silver Beaver Award, Philadelphia Council, Boy Scouts of Amer., 1987; Curtis Artz Award, Amer. Trauma Soc., 1995; Heroes of Liberty Award, Nat. Liberty Mus., 2006; Three Faiths Forum Interfaith Gold Medallion, 2006; Canterbury Medal, Becket Fund for Religious Liberty, 2006. *Publications:* (ed jtly) Textbook of Pediatric Emergency Medicine, 1983, 2nd edn 1993; (contrib.) Textbook of Penetrating Trauma, 1996; A Searcher's Life, 1999; Thrift and Generosity: the joy of giving, 2004. *Address:* c/o Barbara McGraw, 601 Pembroke Road, Bryn Mawr, PA 19010, USA. *T:* (610) 5251961, *Fax:* (610) 5254943; *e-mail:* bmcgraw@templeton.org. *Clubs:* Athenæum, Royal Over-Seas League, Oxford and Cambridge, White's; Lyford Cay (Bahamas); Merion Cricket (Haverford, Penn); Union League (Philadelphia, Penn).

TEMPLETON-COTILL, Rear-Adm. John Atrill, CB 1972; retired; *b* 4 June 1920; *s* of late Captain Jack Lionel Cottle, Tank Corps. *Educ:* Canford Sch.; New Coll., Oxford (MA 1946). Joined RNVR, 1939; served war 1939–45; HMS Crocus, 1940–41; British Naval Liaison Officer, French warship Chevreuil, 1941–42; staff, GOC New Caledonia (US), 1942; US Embassy, London, 1943; Flag Lieutenant to Vice-Adm., Malta, 1943–44; 1st Lieut, MTB 421, 1944–45; ADC to Governor of Victoria, 1945–46; served in HMS London, Loch Quoich, Whirlwind, Jutland, Barrosa and Sparrow, 1946–55; Comdr 1955; comd HMS Sefton and 108th Minesweeping Sqdn, 1955–56; jssc 1956; Comdr-in-Charge, RN School of Work Study, 1957–59; HMS Tiger, 1959–61; Captain 1961; British Naval Attaché, Moscow, 1962–64; comd HMS Rhyl and Captain (D), 23rd Escort Sqdn, 1964–66; Senior Naval Mem., Defence Operational Analysis Establt, 1966–68; comd HMS Bulwark, 1968–69; Rear-Adm. Jan. 1970; Chief of Staff to Comdr Far East Fleet, 1970–71; Flag Officer, Malta, and NATO Comdr, SE Area Mediterranean, 1971–73; Comdr, British Forces Malta, 1972–73. Director: Sotheby Parke Bernet (France), 1974–81; Sotheby Parke Bernet (Monaco), 1975–81. *Recreations:* gardening, riding, shooting, travel, ski-ing. *Address:* Moulin de Fontvive, Ribas, par 30290 Laudun, France. *T:* 66794737.

TENBY, 3rd Viscount *cr* 1957, of Bulford; **William Lloyd-George;** *b* 7 Nov. 1927; 2nd *s* of 1st Viscount Tenby, TD, PC, and Edna Gwenfron (*d* 1971), *d* of David Jones, Gwynfa, Denbigh; *S* brother, 1983; *m* 1955, Ursula Diana Ethel, *y d* of late Lt-Col Henry Edward Medlicott, DSO; one *s* two *d*. *Educ:* Eastbourne College; St Catharine's Coll., Cambridge (Exhibnr; BA 1949). Captain, Royal Welch Fusiliers, TA. Consultant, Williams Lea & Co., 1988–93; Chm., St James Public Relations, 1990–93; non-exec. Dir, Ugland Internat. plc, 1993–96. House of Lords: Member: Cttee on Procedure, 1995–98; Cttee of Selection, 1998–; Sub-Cttee on Admin and Works, 1992–95; All Party Media Gp; elected Mem., H of L, 1999. Pres., Hants Br., CPRE. JP Hants (Chm., NE Hants (formerly Odiham) Bench, 1990–94). *Heir:* *s* Hon. Timothy Henry Gwilym Lloyd-George, *b* 19 Oct. 1962. *Address:* The White House, Dippenhall Street, Crondall, Farnham, Surrey GU10 5PE.

TENCH, David Edward, OBE 1987; Head of Legal Department, 1988–94, Director of Legal Affairs, 1991–94, Consumers' Association (publishers of Which?); consultant on public policy and consumer law, since 1994; *b* 14 June 1929; *s* of late Henry George Tench and Emma Rose (*née* Orsborn); *m* 1st, 1957, Judith April Seaton Gurney (*d* 1986); two *s* one *d*; 2nd, 1988, Elizabeth Ann Irvine Macdonald. *Educ:* Merchant Taylors' Sch., Northwood, Middx. Solicitor, 1952. Private practice, 1954–58; Office of Solicitor of Inland Revenue, 1958–69. Chm., Domestic Coal Consumers' Council, 1976–87; Energy Comr, 1977–79. Broadcaster on consumer affairs, 1964–. *Publications:* The Law for Consumers, 1962; The Legal Side of Buying a House, 1965 (2nd edn 1974); Wills and

Probate, 1967 (6th edn 1977); How to Sue in the County Court, 1973; Towards a Middle System of Law, 1981. *Recreations:* music, bland gardening. *Address:* Crown Meadow, The Platt, Amersham, Bucks HP7 0HX. *T:* (01494) 724974.

TENCH, Leslie Owen; Chairman, SIG plc, since 2004 (Deputy Chairman, 2003–04). *Educ:* Univ. of Nottingham (BSc Metallurgy). Steetley plc; Twyfords Bathrooms; Reed International; Procter & Gamble; Managing Director: CRH UK, 1992–98; CRH Europe - Building Products, 1998–2002. Non-exec. Dir, Shepherd Bldg Gp, 1994–2004. *Recreations:* walking, theatre, music, travelling to unusual places. *Address:* SIG plc, Hillsborough Works, Langsett Road, Sheffield S6 2LW.

TENDULKAR, Sachin Ramesh, Padma Vibhushan 2008 (Padma Shri 1999); cricketer; *b* Mumbai, 24 April 1973. Youngest cricketer (aged 14) to play in Mumbai team in Ranji Trophy 1st cl. cricket tournament; youngest player (aged 15) to score a century in Ranji Trophy; only player to have scored a century on début in all of India's 1st cl. cricket tournaments - Ranji Trophy, Duleep Trophy and Irani Trophy; Test Cricket debut for India against Pakistan, 1989 (aged 16); 2nd youngest player to captain India in Test Cricket (aged 23); captained India in 17 Test matches and 54 limited overs Internats, 1996–97, 1999–2000; second youngest cricketer to have scored a century against England, 1990; first overseas player to play for Yorkshire CCC, 1992; highest aggregate run scorer (1796 runs) in World Cup cricket tournaments; leading run scorer in limited over internat. cricket (16,361 runs by Aug. 2008); highest century scorer in Test Cricket (39 centuries in 150 Tests by Aug. 2008). Chatrapati Shivaji Award, 1990–91, Maharashtra Bhushan, 2001, Maharashtra State. Arjuna Award (India), 1994; Rajiv Gandhi Khel Ratna Award (India), 1998. *Address:* 10th Floor, La Mer, Mistry Park, Kadeshwari Road, Bandra Reclamation, Mumbai 400 050, India.

TENENBAUM, Jane Elaine; *see* Lush, J. E.

TENET, George John; Managing Director, Allen & Company LLC, since 2007; *b* 5 Jan. 1953; *m* A. Stephanie Glakas; one *s. Educ:* Georgetown Univ., Washington; Columbia Univ., NY (MIA 1978). Legislative Asst specialising in nat. security and energy issues, then Legislative Dir to Senator H. John Heinz, III; Designee to Vice Chm., Senator Patrick J. Leahy, 1985–86; Dir, Oversight of Arms Control Negotiations between Soviet Union and US, then Staff Dir, Senate Select Cttee on Intelligence, 1986–93; National Security Council: Mem., Presidential Transition Team, 1993; Special Asst to Pres. and Sen. Dir for Intelligence Programs, 1993–95; Dep. Dir, CIA, 1995–97; Dir, CIA, 1997–2004; Prof. of Diplomacy, Georgetown Univ., Washington, DC, 2004–07. Non-executive Director: Guidance Software; L-1 Identity Solutions; QinetiQ, 2006–08; QinetiQ North America, 2008–. *Publications:* The Ability of US Intelligence to Monitor the Intermediate Nuclear Force Treaty; At the Center of the Storm: my years at the CIA (memoirs), 2007.

TENISON; *see* Hanbury-Tenison.

TENISON; *see* King-Tenison.

TENNANT, family name of **Baron Glenconner**.

TENNANT, Sir Anthony (John), Kt 1992; Senior Adviser, Morgan Stanley UK Group, 1993–2000; Deputy Chairman, Arjo Wiggins Appleton plc, 1996–2000; *b* 5 Nov. 1930; *s* of late Major John Tennant, TD and Hon. Antonia, *d* of 1st Baron Charnwood and later Viscountess Radcliffe; *m* 1954, Rosemary Violet Stockdale; two *s. Educ:* Eton; Trinity College, Cambridge (BA). National Service, Scots Guards (Malaya). Mather & Crowther, 1953–66 (Dir, 1959); Marketing Consultancy, 1966–70; Dir, 1970, then Dep. Man. Dir, Truman Ltd; Dir, Watney Mann & Truman Brewers, 1972–76; Man. Dir, 1976–82, Chm., 1983–87, International Distillers & Vintners Ltd; Gp Chief Exec., 1987–89, Chm., 1989–92, Guinness plc; Deputy Chairman: Forte plc, 1992–96; Wellcome plc, 1994–95; Chm., Christie's Internat. plc, 1993–96 (Dir, 1993–98); Director: Exploration Co. plc, 1967–89; El Oro Mining and Exploration Co. plc, 1967–89; Grand Metropolitan PLC, 1977–87; Close Brothers Group plc, 1980–90; Guardian Royal Exchange, 1989–99; Guardian Assurance, 1989–94; BNP UK Hldgs, subseq. BNP Paribas UK Hldgs Ltd, 1990–2002; Savoy Hotel, 1995–96; Mem., Supervisory Bd, LVMH Moet Hennessy Louis Vuitton, Paris, 1988–92. Dir (non-exec.), Internat. Stock Exchange of UK and Republic of Ireland Ltd, 1991–94. Chm., Priorities Bd for R & D in Agric. and Food, 1992–93; Mem. Council, Food From Britain, 1983–86. Chairman: RA Trust, 1996–2002 (Trustee, 1994–2002); Southampton Univ. Develt Trust, 1996–2002 (Trustee, 1992–2002); Trustee, Cambridge Foundn, 1992–2000. Hon. DBA Nottingham Trent, 1996; DUniv Southampton, 2000. Médaille, Ville de Paris, 1989. Chevalier, Légion d'Honneur (France), 1991. *Address:* 18 Hamilton House, Vicarage Gate, W8 4HL. *T:* (020) 7937 6203. *Club:* Boodle's.

See also M. I. Tennant of Balfluig.

TENNANT, Bernard; Director of Retail, British Chambers of Commerce, 1993–95; *b* 14 Oct. 1930; *s* of Richard and Phyllis Tennant; *m* 1956, Marie (*née* Tonge); two *s* one *d. Educ:* Farnworth Grammar Sch.; Open Univ. (BA Hons Govt and Modern European Hist.). Nat. Service, RAF, 1949. Local authority admin, Worsley and Bolton, 1950; Secretary: Bolton Chamber of Trade, 1960–74; Bolton Chamber of Commerce and Industry, and numerous trade associations, 1968–74; National Chamber of Trade, 1975–92, Dir Gen., 1987–92. Member: British Retail Consortium Council, 1986–95; Home Office Standing Cttee on Crime Prevention, 1986–92; Dept of Employment Retail Price Index Adv. Cttee, 1988–92. Magistrate, Bolton, 1968–75; Reading, 1975–78. Founder Sec., Moorside Housing Gp of charitable housing assocs, 1964–75. Editor, NCT News, 1986–92. *Publications:* articles in professional and trade jls, historical and lifestyle magazines. *Recreations:* music, photography, collating historical chronology.

TENNANT, David; *see* McDonald, D. J.

TENNANT, Lady Emma; Chairman, National Trust Gardens Advisory Panel, 1984–2001; Member, Council, National Trust, 1990–2002; *b* 26 March 1943; *d* of 11th Duke of Devonshire, KG, MC, PC and of Dowager Duchess of Devonshire, *qv*; *m* 1963, Hon. Tobias William Tennant, *y s* of 2nd Baron Glenconner; one *s* two *d. Educ:* St Elphins' Sch., Darley Dale; St Anne's Coll., Oxford (BA History 1963). *Publication:* Rag Rugs, 1992. *Recreations:* gardening, painting. *Address:* Shaws, Newcastleton, Roxburghshire TD9 0SH. *T:* (01387) 376241.

TENNANT, Emma Christina, FRSL 1982; writer; *b* 20 Oct. 1937; *d* of 2nd Baron Glenconner and Elizabeth Lady Glenconner; one *s* two *d. Educ:* St Paul's Girls' School. Freelance journalist to 1973; became full time novelist, 1973; founder Editor, Bananas, 1975–78; general editor: In Verse, 1982–; Lives of Modern Women, 1985–. TV film script, Frankenstein's Baby, 1990. Hon. DLitt Aberdeen, 1996. *Publications:* The Colour of Rain (pseud. Catherine Aydy), 1963; The Time of the Crack, 1973; The Last of the Country House Murders, 1975; Hotel de Dream, 1976; (ed) Bananas Anthology, 1977; (ed) Saturday Night Reader, 1978; The Bad Sister, 1978; Wild Nights, 1979; Alice Fell, 1980; Queen of Stones, 1982; Woman Beware Woman, 1983; Black Marina, 1985; Adventures of Robina by Herself, ed Emma Tennant, 1986; Cycle of the Sun: The House of Hospitalities, 1987, A Wedding of Cousins, 1988; The Magic Drum, 1989; Two Women of London, 1989; Sisters and Strangers, 1990; Faustine, 1991; Tess, 1993; Pemberley, 1993; An Unequal Marriage, 1994; Elinor and Marianne, 1996; Emma in Love, 1996; Strangers: a family romance, 1998; Girlitude: a memoir of the 50s and 60s, 1999; Burnt Diaries, 1999; The Ballad of Sylvia and Ted, 2001; A House in Corfu, 2001; Felony: the private history of the Aspern Papers, 2002; Corfu Banquet, 2004; Heathcliff's Tale, 2005; The Harp Lesson, 2005; The French Dancer's Bastard, 2006; Confessions of a Sugar Mummy, 2007; The Autobiography of the Queen, 2007; Seized, 2008; (as Isabel Vane, jtly) Balmoral, 2004; (contrib.) Novelists in Interview (ed John Haffenden), 1985; (contrib.) Women's Writing: a challenge to theory (ed Maria Monteith), 1986; *for children:* The Boggart (with Mary Rayner), 1979; The Search for Treasure Island, 1981; The Ghost Child, 1984. *Recreation:* walking about. *Address:* c/o Jonathan Cape, Random House, 20 Vauxhall Bridge Road, SW1V 2SA.

TENNANT, Helen Anne, (Lena); Lecturer, Faculty of Education, University of Glasgow (formerly St Andrew's College, Glasgow), 1989–2004; *b* 15 Dec. 1943; *d* of late Joseph Dawson and Anna Dawson (*née* Giavarini); *m* 1975, Gerard E. Tennant; three *s* one *d. Educ:* St Mary's Acad., Bathgate; Notre Dame Coll. of Education, Glasgow (DipCE); RSAMD (Dip. Speech and Drama). Lectr in Speech and Drama, Notre Dame Coll. of Educn, Glasgow, 1969–75; extra-mural Lectr, St Peter's Seminary, Cardross, subseq. Glasgow, 1972–92; part-time Lectr, Coatbridge Coll., 1983–89. Member: Viewer's Consultative Council (Scotland), 1989–94; Radio Authy, 1995–2000. *Recreations:* theatre-going, playing church organ.

TENNANT of Balfluig, Mark Iain; Master of the Supreme Court, Queen's Bench Division, 1988–2005; Baron of Balfluig; *b* 4 Dec. 1932; *s* of late Major John Tennant, TD, KStJ and Hon. Antonia Mary Roby Benson, *d* of 1st Baron Charnwood and later Viscountess Radcliffe; *m* 1965, Lady Harriot Pleydell-Bouverie, *y d* of 7th Earl of Radnor, KG, KCVO; one *s* one *d. Educ:* Eton College; New College, Oxford (MA 1959). Lieut, The Rifle Brigade (SRO). Called to the Bar, Inner Temple, 1958, Bencher, 1984; Recorder, 1987–96. Restored Balfluig Castle (barony of Balfluig *cr* of Charles II, 1650), dated 1556 in 1967 (the first to obtain a grant from Historic Bldgs Council for Scotland for bldg not inhabited or inhabitable). Chm., Royal Orchestral Soc. for Amateur Musicians, 1989–. *Recreations:* music, architecture, books, shooting. *Address:* Balfluig Castle, Aberdeenshire AB33 8EJ; 30 Abbey Gardens, NW8 9AT. *T:* (020) 7624 3200. *Club:* Brooks's.

See also Sir A. J. Tennant.

TENNANT, Michael Humphrey; a District Judge, 1992–2008; President, Association of District Judges, 2007–08; *b* 11 Sept. 1942; *s* of Norman Humphrey Tennant and Marjorie Lillian Tennant (*née* Coles); *m* 1st, 1965, Kathleen Nicolette Chapman (marr. diss. 1998); two *d*; 2nd, 1998, June Mary Dixon. *Educ:* Bedford Modern Sch.; University College London (LLB Hons 1963). Admitted solicitor, 1966; Partner, Damant & Sons, 1969–84; High Court District Registrar and County Court Registrar, 1984; Asst Recorder, 1989; a Recorder, 1992. *Recreations:* music—listening to classical (mostly instrumental) and jazz and playing piano (classical), sailing—racing own National Sonata nationally and internationally, defending occasional hard-won sailing trophies, cruising wherever possible when time permits. *Address:* Chazey House, Salisbury Road, Sherfield English, Hants SO51 6FQ. *T:* (01794) 323344. *Clubs:* Sloane; Island Sailing (Cdre, 1989–92).

TENNANT, Maj.-Gen. Michael Trenchard, CB 1994; Army Adviser, British Aerospace, 1998–2001; *b* 3 Sept. 1941; *s* of Lt-Col Hugh Trenchard Tennant, MC and Mary Isobel Tennant (*née* Wilkie); *m* 1st, 1964, Susan Daphne (*d* 1993), *d* of Lt-Col Frank Beale, LVO; three *s*; 2nd, 1996, Jacqueline Mary Parish (*née* ap Ellis), *widow* of David Parish; two step *d. Educ:* Wellington College. psc†. Commissioned RA 1961; served Bahrain, Aden, BAOR, Hong Kong, UK, 1962–71; Staff College, 1972–73; MoD, 1974–75; Bty Comdr, 127 (Dragon) Bty, BAOR, 1976–78; Directing Staff, Staff Coll., 1978–80; CO, 1 RHA, UK and BAOR, 1980–83; Comdr British Training Team, Nigeria, 1983–85; CRA 3 Armd Div., BAOR, 1985–87; CRA UKLF, 1988–91; Dir, RA, 1991–94. Hd of External Commns, Royal Ordnance Div., BAe, 1994–98. Col Comdt, RA, 1994–2005; Hon. Col, 1 RHA, 1994–99. Chm., CCF Assoc., 1996–2003. President: Army Cricket, 1992–93; RA Golf Soc., 1998–. *Recreations:* bridge, golf, tennis. *Clubs:* Army and Navy; Fadeaways; Denham Golf, Rye Golf, Senior Golfers.

TENNANT, Veronica, CC 2003 (OC 1975); ballet dancer, broadcaster and writer; *b* London, 15 Jan. 1947; *d* of Harry Tennant and Doris Tennant (Bassous); *m* 1969, Dr John Robert Wright; one *d. Educ:* Bishop Strachan Sch., Toronto; National Ballet Sch., Toronto. Prima Ballerina, Nat. Ballet of Canada, 1965–89; major performances include: début, Juliet in Romeo and Juliet, with Earl Kraul, 1965; Pulcinella, Triptych; Les Rendezvous; Solitaire; Swan Lake; The Lesson; Cinderella; Kraanerg (created leading rôle); Le Loup; La Sylphide; première perf. as Princess Aurora with Rudolf Nureyev in his Sleeping Beauty, 1972; La Sylphide, with Mikhail Baryshnikov, 1974; Giselle, with Rudolf Nureyev, 1974; Swanhilda in Coppelia, 1975; Washington Square, with Peter Schaufuss, 1978; La Fille Mal Gardée, 1979, and Le Corsaire Pas de Deux, 1980, with Peter Schaufuss; Napoli; The Dream, with Anthony Dowell, 1981; début, Tatiana in Onegin, with Raymond Smith, 1985; farewell perfs, Romeo and Juliet, with Raymond Smith and A Passion for Dance: Celebrating the Tennant Magic (gala tribute), 1989; film maker and writer, 1989–; host and consultant/writer, Sunday Arts Entertainment CBC TV, 1989–92; producer and dir for CBC Television and Bravo!FACT; founded Veronica Tennant Prodns, 1998; television producer: Salute to Dancers for Life, 1994; Margie Gillis: Wild Hearts in Strange Times, 1996; Governor General's Performing Arts Awards Gala, 2000; The Four Seasons, 2000; television producer and director: Mavis Staines—"Courage...", 1998; Karen Kain: Dancing in the Moment, 1999 (Internat. Emmy Award for Perf. Arts); Song of Songs, 1999; The Dancers' Story: the National Ballet of Canada, 2002; Northern Light: Visions and Dreams, 2003; A Pairing of SwanS, 2004; Shadow Pleasures, 2004; A Pair of RED Shorts, 2005. Dancers' Rep., Bd of Dirs, Nat. Ballet Co., 1972, 1984; Director: Ontario Arts Council, 1975–78; Toronto Arts Awards Foundn, 1988–90; Glenn Gould Foundn, 1989–92; Dancer Transition Centre, 1992–95; Governor General's Performing Arts Awards, 1992–95; Mem. Bd of Dirs, City of Toronto Olympic Bid 2008, 1998– (Chm., Arts and Culture Cttee, 1998–2000). Adjunct Prof., Fine Arts, 1989–2004, Fellow, Winters Coll., 1991–99, York Univ. Hon. DLitt: Brock, 1985; McGill, 2005; Hon. LLD: York, 1987; Simon Fraser, 1992; Toronto, 1992. Walter Carsen Prize for Excellence in the Performing Arts, 2004. *Publications:* On Stage, Please, 1977; The Nutcracker, 1986; articles in Toronto Star, Dance International, Saturday Night Mag. and The Globe and Mail.

TENNET, Michael John; QC 2006; barrister; *b* 18 Jan. 1963; *s* of Brian and Margaret Tennet; *m* 1998, Jessica; two *s. Educ:* Solihull Sixth Form Coll.; New Coll., Oxford (MA 1st cl. Law 1984). Called to the Bar, Inner Temple, 1985; barrister, 1986–. *Publications:* (contrib.) Professional Negligence and Liability; (contrib.) International Trust Laws. *Recreations:* golf, tennis, National Hunt horseracing. *Address:* Wilberforce Chambers, 8

New Square, Lincoln's Inn, WC2A 3QP. *T:* (020) 7306 0802; *e-mail:* mtennet@ wilberforce.co.uk.

TENNYSON, family name of **Baron Tennyson**.

TENNYSON, 6th Baron *cr* 1884; **David Harold Alexander Tennyson;** *b* 4 June 1960; *s* of James Alfred Tennyson, *g g s* of 1st Baron Tennyson, and of Beatrice Aventon (*née* Young); *S* cousin, 2006. *Educ:* Univ. of Canterbury, NZ (ME). *Heir: b* Alan James Drummond Tennyson [*b* 28 Jan. 1965; *m* 1998, Susanna Ruth Brow; one *s*].

TENNYSON-d'EYNCOURT, Sir Mark (Gervais), 5th Bt *cr* 1930, of Carter's Corner Farm, Herstmonceux; *b* 12 March 1967; *o s* of Sir Giles Gervais Tennyson-d'Eyncourt, 4th Bt and of Juanita, *d* of late Fortunato Borromeo; *S* father, 1989. *Educ:* Charterhouse; Kingston Polytechnic (BA Hons Fashion). Freeman, City of London, 1989. *Heir:* none.

TENZIN GYATSO; The Dalai Lama XIV; spiritual and temporal leader of Tibet, since 1940; *b* 6 July 1935; named Lhamo Thondup; *s* of Chokyong Tsering and Diki Tsering. *Educ:* Monasteries of Sera, Drepung and Gaden, Lhasa; traditional Tibetan degree equivalent to Dr in Buddhist philosophy, 1959. Enthroned Dalai Lama, Lhasa, 1940; given name Jetsun Jampel Ngawang Losang Yeshi Tenzin Gyatso Sisum Wang-gyur Tsungpa Mepai De Pel Sangpo. Fled to Chumbi, South Tibet, on Chinese invasion, 1950; negotiated with China, 1951; fled to India after abortive revolt of Tibetan people against Communist Chinese, 1959, and established govt-in-exile in Dharamsala. Awards include: Magsaysay, Philippines, 1959; Lincoln, USA, 1960; Albert Schweitzer Humanitarian, USA, 1987; Congressional Gold Medal, USA, 2007; numerous other awards, hon. doctorates, hon. citizenships from France, Germany, India, Mongolia, Norway, USA; Nobel Peace Prize, 1989. *Publications:* My Land and My People (autobiog.), 1962; The Opening of the Wisdom Eye, 1963; An Introduction to Buddhism, 1965; Key to the Middle Way, 1971; Universal Responsibility and Good Heart, 1977; Four Essential Buddhist Commentaries, 1982; A Human Approach to World Peace, 1984; Kindness, Clarity and Insight, 1987; Freedom in Exile (autobiog.), 1990; The Good Heart, 1996; Ethics for the New Millennium, 1998; Ancient Wisdom, Modern World, 1999; A Simple Path, 2000; Advice on Dying, 2002; (jtly) The Art of Happiness at Work, 2003; (jtly) The Wisdom of Forgiveness, 2005. *Address:* Thekchen Choeling, Mcleod Ganj 176219, Dharamsala, HP, India.

TEO Eng Cheng, Michael; High Commissioner of Singapore in the United Kingdom, and concurrently Ambassador to Ireland, since 2001; *b* 19 Sept. 1947; *m* Joyce; one *s* one *d*. *Educ:* Auburn Univ., USA (BSc Business Admin); Fletcher Sch. of Law and Diplomacy, Tufts Univ., USA (MA). Joined Republic of Singapore Air Force, 1968: Comdr, 1985; Dist. Grad., USAF War Coll., 1985; Brig.-Gen., 1987; Chief of Air Force, 1990; High Comr to NZ, 1994–96; Ambassador, Republic of Korea, 1996–2001. Gold Public Admin Medal (Mil.) (Singapore), 1989; Most Noble Order of Crown (Thailand), 1981; Outstanding Achievement Award (Philippines), 1989; Bintang Swa Bhuana Paksa Utama (Indonesia), 1991; Comdr, Legion of Merit (USA), 1991; Gwanghwa Medal (Korea), 2002. *Recreations:* golf, hiking, reading. *Address:* Singapore High Commission, 9 Wilton Crescent, Belgravia, SW1X 8SP. *T:* (020) 7201 5850, *Fax:* (020) 7245 6583; *e-mail:* info@ singaporehc.org.uk.

TERESHKOVA, Valentina Vladimirovna; Russian cosmonaut; Chairman, Russian Association of International Co-operation, since 1992; Head, Russian Centre for International Scientific and Cultural Co-operation, Russian Federation, since 1994; *b* Maslennikovo, 6 March 1937; *d* of late Vladimir Aksyonovich Tereshkov and of Elena Fyodorovna Tereshkova; *m*; one *d*. Formerly textile worker, Krasny Perekop mill, Yaroslavl; served on cttees; Sec. of local branch, Young Communist league, 1960; Member: CPSU, 1962–91; Central Cttee, CPSU, 1971–90; Deputy, 1966–90, Mem. of Presidium, 1970–90, USSR Supreme Soviet; Chairperson: Soviet Women's Cttee, 1968–87; Union of Soviet Societies for Friendship and Cultural Relns with Foreign Countries, 1987–92. Joined Yaroslavl Air Sports Club, 1959, and started parachute jumping; joined Cosmonaut Training Unit, 1962; became first woman in the world to enter space when she made 48 orbital flights of the earth in spaceship Vostok VI, 16–19 June 1963. Hero of the Soviet Union; Order of Lenin; Gold Star Medal; Order of October Revolution; Joliot-Curie Peace Medal; Nile Collar (Egypt), 1971; holds honours and citations from other countries. *Address:* 14 Vozdvizhenka Street, 103885 Moscow, Russia.

TERFEL, Bryn; see Jones, B. T.

ter HAAR, Rev. Roger Eduard Lound; QC 1992; a Recorder, and Deputy High Court Judge, since 2003; *b* 14 June 1952; *s* of late Dirk ter Haar and Christine Janet ter Haar; *m* 1977, Sarah Anne Martyn; two *s* one *d*. *Educ:* Felsted Sch.; Magdalen Coll., Oxford (BA 1973). Called to the Bar, Inner Temple, 1974, Bencher, 1992. Ordained deacon, 2006, priest, 2007; OLM, Bramley and Graffham, 2006–07; Asst Priest, Hascombe and Dunsford, 2007–. *Recreations:* gardening, reading. *Address:* Crown Office Chambers, 2 Crown Office Row, Temple, EC4Y 7HJ. *T:* (020) 7797 8100. *Clubs:* Brooks's, Garrick.

TERRELL, Prof. (Richard) Deane, AO 2002; PhD; Vice-Chancellor, 1994–2000, now Emeritus Professor and Visiting Fellow, National Graduate School of Management, Australian National University; *b* 22 April 1936; *s* of Norman Walter Terrell and Dorothy Ismay Terrell; *m* 1961, Jennifer Anne Kathleen, *d* of Leonard Spencer and Margaret Rose Doman; two *s* one *d*. *Educ:* St Peter's Coll., Adelaide; Adelaide Univ. (Joseph Fisher Medal, 1958; Rhodes Scholar, 1959; BEc Hons); Oxford Univ.; ANU (PhD). Teaching appts, Univ. of Adelaide and MIT, 1959–64; Australian National University: Lectr, 1964–70; Sen. Lectr, Stats, 1970; Prof. of Econometrics, 1971–89; Dean, Faculty of Econs and Commerce, 1975–77, 1982–89; Head, Dept of Stats, 1979–82, 1989–91; Chm., Bd of Faculties, 1989–92; Acting Dep. Vice-Chancellor, and Dep. Vice-Chancellor, 1991–93. Visiting Professor: Pennsylvania, 1969; Princeton and LSE, 1972–73. Chm., Bd of Mgt, AARNet; Vice-Pres., IDP Educn Australia, 1995–2004. Chm. Bd, IELTS (Aust.) Pty Ltd, 2002–; Bd Dir, Gen. Sir John Monash Foundn, 2003–. Dep. Chm., Canberra Symphony Orch., 2006–. *Publications:* numerous articles in professional jls. *Recreations:* farming and grape growing, football, cricket. *Address:* c/o National Graduate School of Management, Sir Roland Wilson Building No 120, Australian National University, Canberra, ACT 0200, Australia. *Club:* Commonwealth (Canberra).

TERRINGTON, 6th Baron *cr* 1918, of Huddersfield, co. York; **Christopher Richard James Woodhouse,** FRCS; Professor of Adolescent Urology, University College London, since 2005; Consultant Urologist, Royal Marsden Hospital, since 1981; *b* 20 Sept. 1946; *s* of 5th Baron Terrington, DSO, OBE and Lady Davina Woodhouse (*née* Lytton), *widow* of 5th Earl of Erne; *S* father, 2001; *m* 1975, Hon. Anna Philipps, *d* of 3rd Baron Milford; one *s* one *d*. *Educ:* Winchester; Guy's Hosp. Med. Sch. (MB, BS 1970). FRCS 1975. Sen. Registrar in Urology, Inst. of Urology and St Peter's Hosps, 1977–81; Sen. Lectr in Urology, Inst. of Urology, 1981–97; Reader in Adolescent Urology, UCL, 1997–2005. Consultant Urologist, St George's Hosp., 1985–95; Clin. Dir of Urology, UCL Hosps, 2001–03. Hon. Consultant Urologist: Inst. of Urology, University Coll.

London Hosps (formerly St Peter's Hosps), 1981–; Hosp. for Children, Great Ormond Street, 1981–. Vis. Professorships in Europe, USA and Australasia. Fellow, European Bd of Urology, 1993. Pres., Soc. of Genito-Urinary Reconstructive Surgeons, USA, 2002–03. Corresp. Member: Amer. Urological Assoc., 1985; German Assoc. of Urology, 2004; American Assoc. of Genito-Urinary Surgeons, 2005; Hon. Mem.: Australasian Urological Assoc., 1999. *Publications:* (with F. D. Thompson) Physiological Basis of Medicine: disorders of the kidney and urinary tract, 1987; Long Term Paediatric Urology, 1991; (jtly) Management of Urological Emergencies, 2004; contrib. to learned jls. *Recreations:* gardening, walking. *Heir: s* Hon. Jack Henry Lehmann Woodhouse, *b* 7 Dec. 1978. *Address:* Apartment 31, Eustace Building, 329 Queenstown Road, SW8 4NT. *T:* (020) 7498 9402; *e-mail:* cwoodhouse2@compuserve.com. *Club:* Leander (Henley-on-Thames).

See also Hon. N. M. J. Woodhouse.

TERRY, Air Marshal Sir Colin George, KBE 1998 (OBE 1983); CB 1995; DL; CEng, FREng; FRAeS; aerospace consultant; Chairman, Meggitt plc, since 2004; *b* 8 Aug. 1943; *e s* of George Albert Terry and Edna Joan Terry (*née* Purslow); *m* 1966, Gillian, *d* of late Conrad Glendor Grindley and Muriel Grace Grindley (*née* Duffield); two *s* one *d*. *Educ:* Bridgnorth Grammar Sch.; RAF Coll.; Imperial Coll., London (BScEng (Hons) 1965; FIC). CEng; FRAeS 1986; FCGI 1997; FREng 2001. Commnd, Engr Br., RAF, 1962; served Abingdon, RAF Coll., Church Fenton, Leeming, Oakington, Finningley, RNAY Belfast, Laarbruch, Wildenrath, HQ Strike Comd; Student, RAF Coll., 1979; OC Eng Wing, RAF Coltishall, 1979–82; Eng Authy Staff, HQ Strike Comd, 1982–84; OC Eng Wing, RAF Stanley, 1982–83; Dep. Comd Engr, HQ Strike Comd, 1985–86; Station Comdr, RAF Abingdon, 1986–88; RCDS 1989; Dir, Support Management and Sen. Dir, MoD Harrogate, 1990–92; Dir Gen., Support Management, RAF, 1993–95; COS and Dep. C-in-C, Logistics Comd, RAF, 1995–97; AOC-in-C, Logistics Comd and Air Mem. for Logistics, RAF, 1997–99; Chief Engr (RAF), 1996–99. Gp Man. Dir, Inflite Engrg Services Ltd, 1999–2001; Adv. Bd, Kingfisher Airlines, Mumbai, 2006–. Chm., Engineering Council, 2002–06 (Mem. of Senate, 1999–2002); President: RAeS, 2005–06 (Mem. Council, 1999–; Chm., Learned Soc. Bd, 2003–06); Council of European Aerospace Socs, 2006–; Member: ETB, 2002–06; Queen's Awards for Enterprise Cttee, 2002–06. FRSA; FILog. Commodore, RAF Sailing Assoc., 1994–99; Pres., Assoc. of Service Yacht Clubs, 1997–99; Flying Officer, RAFVR(T), 1999. Mem. Council, CGLI, 2004–; Pres., C & G Coll. Assoc., 2003–04. DL Bucks, 2005. *Recreations:* sailing, flying, ski-ing, modern languages, music. *Address:* 6 AEF, RAF Benson, Wallingford, Oxon OX10 6AA. *Club:* Royal Air Force.

TERRY, Ian Keith; Partner, Freshfields Bruckhaus Deringer (formerly Freshfields), since 1986; *b* 26 July 1955; *s* of late Keith Harold Terry and Shirley Margaret Terry; *m* 1993, Dr Elizabeth Ann Fischl; one *d*. *Educ:* Leeds Grammar Sch.; Keble Coll., Oxford (BA, BCL). Freshfields: trainee solicitor, 1978–80; admitted solicitor, 1980; Partner (Commercial Litigation), 1986–96; Managing Partner, worldwide, 1996–2001; Practice Gp Leader, Dispute Resolution, 2006–. *Recreations:* tennis, golf, horses, ski-ing, opera, family. *Address:* (office) 65 Fleet Street, EC4Y 1HS. *T:* (020) 7936 4000.

TERRY, (John) Quinlan, FRIBA 1962; architect in private practice, since 1967; *b* 24 July 1937; *s* of Philip and Phyllis Terry; *m* 1961, Christine de Ruttié; one *s* four *d*. *Educ:* Bryanston School; Architectural Association; Rome Scholar. Assistant to Raymond Erith, RA, FRIBA, 1962, Partner 1967–, Erith & Terry, subseq. Quinlan & Francis Terry; work includes: new Infirmary, Royal Hospital Chelsea; offices, shops and flats at Richmond Riverside; 20–32 Baker Street; 264–7 Tottenham Court Road; new retail bldgs in historic centre of Colonial Williamsburg, Va; six classical Villas in Regent's Park for Crown Estate Comrs; new Library, Lecture Theatre, and Residential Bldg, Downing Coll., Cambridge; new Brentwood Cathedral; restoration of the three State Drawing Rooms, 10 Downing Street; restoration of St Helen's, Bishopsgate, and Castletown Cox, Co. Kilkenny. Mem., Royal Fine Art Commn, 1994–97. *Publications:* Architects Anonymous, 1994; Radical Classicism, 2006. *Recreation:* the Pauline epistles. *Address:* Old Exchange, High Street, Dedham, Colchester, Essex CO7 6HA. *T:* (01206) 323186.

TERRY, Sir Michael Edward Stanley I.; see Imbert-Terry.

TERRY, Nicholas John, RIBA; Chairman, BDP South, since 2006; *b* 12 Nov. 1947; *s* of John Edmund Terry and Winifred Nina Terry (*née* White); *m* 1970, Dorothy Atkins; one *d*. *Educ:* Peveril Sch., Nottingham; Bilborough Grammar Sch., Nottingham; Univ. of Bath Sch. of Architecture (BSc Hons; BArch Hons). RIBA 1973; MAIBC, MRAIC 1976. Architect: Terry Associates, Bath, 1970–72; Building Design Partnership, Manchester, 1972–75; Arthur Erickson Architects, Canada, 1975–77; J. S. Bonnington Partnership, St Albans, 1978–81; Man. Dir, Heery Architects & Engrs, 1981–89; joined Building Design Partnership, London, 1990: Equity Partner, 1995–97, Dir, 1997–; Chm., 2002–06; Chairman: Dixon Jones BDP, 1996–; BDP Design Ltd, 1996–. *Projects include:* Durham Millburngate, 1972–75 (RIBA award, 1977, Europa Nostra medal and Civic Trust award, 1978); Citibank HQ, London, 1981, Frankfurt, 1983; Cribbs Causeway Regional Shopping Centre, 1997 (BCSC and ICSC (USA) awards, 2000); Niketown, London, 1998; Royal Opera House, 1999 (RIBA and RICS awards, 2000; Europa Nostra dip., 2001); Jubilee Place, Canary Wharf, 2003; Royal Albert Hall, 2004 (Civic Trust and Europa Nostra awards). *Exhibitions:* Royal Acad. Summer Exhibns, 1974 (Durham Millburngate), 1975 (Albert Dock); MOMA, NY, 1979; RIBA, 1982 (Kuwait Stock Exchange). Member: IoD, 1988; British Council of Offices, 1990–; British Council of Shopping Centres, 1995–; Internat. Council of Shopping Centres, 1995–. Chairman: Internat. Alliance for Interoperability, 2001– (Chm., UK Chapter, 2001–; Vice Chm., Internat. Council, 2005–); European Enterprise Interoperability Centre, 2006–; Bldg and Civil Engrg Sector Policy 4 Strategy Cttee, BSI, 2007–. FRSA 2005. *Publications:* numerous articles in architecture/design press and jls. *Recreations:* walking, gardening, reading, architecture and design. *Address:* Building Design Partnership, 16 Brewhouse Yard, Clerkenwell, EC1V 4LJ. *T:* (020) 7812 8071; *e-mail:* nj-terry@bdp.co.uk; Lansdown, 26A Middle Street, Thriplow, Royston, Herts SG8 7RD.

TERRY, Air Chief Marshal Sir Peter (David George), GCB 1983 (KCB 1978; CB 1975); AFC 1968; QCVSA 1959 and 1962; *b* 18 Oct. 1926; *s* of James George Terry and Laura Chilton Terry (*née* Powell); *m* 1946, Betty Martha Louisa Thompson; one *s* one *d* (and one *s* decd). *Educ:* Chatham House Sch., Ramsgate. Joined RAF, 1945; commnd in RAF Regt, 1946; Pilot, 1953. Staff Coll., 1962; OC, No 51 Sqdn, 1966–68; OC, RAF El Adem, 1968–70; Dir, Air Staff Briefing, MoD, 1970–71; Dir of Forward Policy for RAF, 1971–74; ACOS (Policy and Plans), SHAPE, 1975–77; VCAS, 1977–79; C-in-C RAF Germany and Comdr Second Allied Tactical Air Force, 1979–81; Dep. C-in-C, Allied Forces Central Europe, Feb.–April 1981; Dep. Supreme Allied Commander, Europe, 1981–84; Governor and C-in-C, Gibraltar, 1985–89. Vice-Pres., Re-Solv, 1985–. KStJ 1986. *Recreation:* golf. *Club:* Royal Air Force.

TERRY, Quinlan; see Terry, J. Q.

TESLER, Brian, CBE 1986; Deputy Chairman, LWT (Holdings) plc, 1990–94; Chairman: London Weekend Television Ltd, 1984–92 (Managing Director, 1976–90; Deputy Chairman, 1982–84; Deputy Chief Executive, 1974–76); The London Studios Ltd (formerly LWT Production Facilities Ltd), 1989–92; LWT International Ltd, 1990–92; LWT Programmes Ltd, 1990–92; *b* 19 Feb. 1929; *s* of late David Tesler and of Stella Tesler; *m* 1959, Audrey Mary Maclean; one *s. Educ:* Chiswick County School for Boys; Exeter Coll., Oxford (State Schol.; MA). Theatre Editor, The Isis, 1950–51; Pres., Oxford Univ. Experimental Theatre Club, 1951–52. British Forces Broadcasting Service, 1947–49; Producer/Director: BBC Television, 1952; ATV, 1957; ABC Television: Head of Features and Light Entertainment, 1960; Programme Controller, 1961; Dir of Programmes, 1962; Dir of Programmes, Thames Television, 1968. Chairman: ITV Superchannel Ltd, 1986–88; ITCA, 1980–82; Indep. TV Network Prog. Cttee, 1976–78, 1986–88; LWT Programme Adv. Bd, 1990–92; ITCA Cable and Satellite Television Wkg Party, 1981–88; ITV Film Purchase Cttee, 1989–90; The Magazine Business Ltd, 1992–96. Director: ITN Ltd, 1979–90; Channel Four Television Ltd, 1980–85; Oracle Teletext Ltd, 1980–92; Services Sound and Vision Corp. (formerly Services Kinema Corp.), 1981–2004. Chm., Lord Chancellor's Adv. Cttee on JPs, 1993–96 (Mem., 1991–96); Lay Interviewer for Judicial Appts, 1994–99; Ind. Assessor, OCPA, 2001–. Member: British Screen Adv. Council, 1985–94 (Wkg Party on Future of British Film Industry, 1975–77; Interim Action Cttee on Film Industry, 1977–85); TRIC, 1979– (Pres., 1979–80; Companion, 1986); Vice-Pres., RTS, 1984–94 (FRTS 1992). Governor: Nat. Film and TV Sch. (formerly Nat. Film Sch.), 1977–95; BFI, 1986–95 (Dep. Chm., 1993–95). Daily Mail Nat. TV Award, 1954; Guild of Television Producers and Directors Award, 1957; Lord Willis Trophy for Outstanding Services to Television, Pye Television Award, 1986; Presidential Award, TRIC, 1991. *Recreations:* books, theatre, cinema, music.

TESORIÈRE, (Harcourt) Andrew (Pretorius), FRGS; HM Diplomatic Service; OSCE Ambassador to Kyrgystan, since 2008; *b* 2 Nov. 1950; *s* of Pieter Ivan Tesorière and Joyce Margaret Tesorière (*née* Baxter); *m* 1987, Dr Alma Gloria Vasquez. *Educ:* Nautical Coll., Pangbourne; Britannia Royal Naval Coll., Dartmouth; University Coll. of Wales, Aberystwyth (BScEcon Hons); Ecole Nat. d'Admin, Paris. RNR, 1964–68; RN Officer, 1969–73; joined FCO, 1974; Persian lang. student, SOAS and Iran, 1975–76; Oriental Sec., Kabul, 1976–79; Third Sec., Nairobi, 1980–81; Second Sec., Abidjan (also accredited to Ouagadougou and Niamey), 1981–84; First Sec. and Hd of Chancery, later Chargé d'Affaires, Damascus, 1987–91; Hd, Field Ops, UN Office for Co-ordination of Humanitarian Assistance to Afghanistan, Afghanistan, 1994–95; Ambassador to Albania, 1996–98; Actg Hd of Mission and Sen. Pol Advr, UN Special Mission to Afghanistan, 1998–2000 (on secondment); Chargé d'Affaires *ai*, Kabul, 2001–02; Ambassador to Latvia, 2002–05; Ambassador to Algeria, 2005–07; Sen. Policy Advr to Internat. Security Assistance Force Comdr S, Afghanistan, 2007–08. FRGS 1993. NATO Medal, ISAF. *Recreations:* travel, sport, foreign languages, art, countryside. *Address:* c/o Foreign and Commonwealth Office, King Charles Street, SW1A 2AH.

TESSIER-LAVIGNE, Prof. Marc, PhD; FMedSci; FRS 2001; FRSC 1999; Executive Vice-President, Research Drug Discovery, Genentech Inc., since 2008 (Senior Vice-President, 2003–08); Professor of Biological Sciences, Stanford University, since 2001, on leave of absence (Susan B. Ford Professor, School of Humanities and Sciences, 2001–03); *b* 18 Dec. 1959; *s* of Sheila and Jacques Tessier-Lavigne; *m* 1989, Mary Alanna Hynes; two *s* one *d. Educ:* McGill Univ., Montreal (BSc 1st Cl. Hons Physics 1980); New Coll., Oxford (BA 1st Cl. Hons Phil. and Physiol., 1982); University Coll. London (PhD 1987; Schaffer Prize). University of California, San Francisco: Asst Prof., Dept of Anatomy, 1991–95; Associate Prof., 1995–97; Prof., Depts of Anatomy and Biochem. and Biophysics, 1997–2001; Asst Investigator, 1994–97, Investigator, 1997–2003, Howard Hughes Med. Inst. Mem., Nat. Acad. of Scis, USA, 2005. FAAAS 2001; FMedSci 2004. McKnight Investigator Award, 1994; Charles Judson Herrick Award in Comparative Neurol., Amer. Assoc. Anatomists, 1995; Ameritec Foundn Prize, 1995; (jtly) Fondation IPSEN Prize for Neuronal Plasticity, 1996; Viktor Hamburger Award, Internat. Soc. for Develtl Neurosci., 1997; Young Investigator Award, Soc. for Neurosci., USA, 1997; (jtly) Wakeman Foundn Award for contribs in field of neuronal regeneration, 1998; Robert Dow Neurosci. Award, Oregon Health Sci. Univ., 2003. *Publications:* contribs in physiol. and develtl neurobiol. to scientific jls. *Recreations:* family, history. *Address:* Research Division, Genentech Inc., South San Francisco, CA 94080, USA.

TESTINO, Mario; fashion photographer; *b* Lima, 1954. *Educ:* American Sch. of Lima; Univ. del Pacifico; Pontificia Univ. Católica del Perú; Univ. of San Diego, Calif. Photograph subjects include Naomi Campbell, Diana, Princess of Wales, Cameron Diaz, Elizabeth Hurley, Janet Jackson, Keira Knightley, Madonna, Kate Moss, Gwyneth Paltrow, Julia Roberts, Catherine Zeta-Jones, Prince Harry, Prince Charles and Duchess of Cornwall. Exhibitions include: NPG, 2002; Kensington Palace, 2005. *Publications:* Any Objections?, 1998; Front Row/Backstage, 1999; Alive, 2001; Portraits, 2002; Kids, 2003; Let Me In, 2007; (ed) Lima Peru, 2007. *Address:* c/o Art Partner, 155 Sixth Avenue, 15th Floor, New York, NY 10013, USA.

TETLEY, Air Vice-Marshal John Francis Humphrey, CB 1987; CVO 1978; *b* 5 Feb. 1932; *s* of Humphrey and Evelyn Tetley; *m* 1960, Elizabeth, *d* of Wing Comdr Arthur Stevens; two *s. Educ:* Malvern College. RAF Coll., Cranwell, 1950–53; served No 249 Sqn, No 204 Sqn and HQ Coastal Command, 1955–64; RAF Staff Coll., 1964; HQ Middle East Command, 1965–67; OC No 24 Sqn, 1968–70; JSSC 1970; MoD (Air), 1971–72; RAF Germany, 1973–75; Dir Air Staff Briefing, MoD (Air), 1975–76; Silver Jubilee Project Officer, 1977; RCDS, 1978; SASO HQ 38 Group, 1979–82; Dir of Ops (Air Support), RAF, 1982–83; AO Scotland and NI, 1983–86; Sen. Directing Staff (Air), RCDS, 1986–87; retired 1987. Mem. Exec. Cttee, RNLI, 1993– (Vice-Pres., 1996; Dep. Chm., 2000–02). *Recreations:* gardening, photography, boating. *Club:* Royal Air Force.

TETLEY, Ven. Joy Dawn, PhD; Archdeacon of Worcester and Canon Residentiary of Worcester Cathedral, 1999–2008; *b* 9 Nov. 1946; *d* of Frederick and Mary Payne; *m* 1980, Rev. Brian Tetley, BA, FCA. *Educ:* Durham Univ. (BA 1968; PhD 1988); Leeds Univ. (CertEd 1969); St Hugh's Coll., Oxford (BA 1975; MA 1980); NW Ordination Course. Ordained deaconess 1977, deacon 1987, priest 1994; Deaconess: Bentley, 1977–79; St Aidan, Buttershaw, 1979–80; Durham Cathedral, 1980–83; Lectr, Trinity Coll., Bristol, and Deaconess, Chipping Sodbury and Old Sodbury, 1983–86; Deacon, 1987–89, Hon. Canon, 1990–93 (Canon Emeritus, 1993–), Rochester Cathedral, and Dio. Dir, Post-Ordination Trng, 1988–93; Principal, E Anglian Ministerial Trng Course, 1993–99. Columnist, Church Times, 1993–95. FRSA 2006. *Publications:* Encounter with God in Hebrews, 1995; Sunday by Sunday, 1995; A Way into Hebrews, 1998; Jonah, 2003. *Address:* 23 Cripley Road, Oxford OX2 0AH. *T:* (01865) 250209; *e-mail:* briantetley@btinternet.com.

TETLOW, His Honour Christopher Bruce; a Circuit Judge, 1992–2007; *b* 27 Feb. 1943; *s* of George Wilfred Tetlow and Betty Tetlow; *m* 1981, Rosalind Jane Cope; two *s* one *d. Educ:* Stowe Sch.; Magdalene Coll., Cambridge (MA). Called to the Bar, Middle Temple, 1969. *Club:* St James's (Manchester).

TETTAMANZI, His Eminence Cardinal Dionigi; *see* Milan, Archbishop of, (RC).

TETTENBORN, Richard Garstin, OBE 1993; Treasurer: Staffordshire County Council, 1992–2003; Staffordshire Police Authority, 1995–2008; Stoke on Trent and Staffordshire Combined Fire Authority, 1997–2003; *b* 23 Sept. 1940; *s* of Philip Arthur de Gleichen Tettenborn and Helena Louise Tettenborn (*née* Sharpe); *m* 1983, Susan Margaret Wrigley (*née* Crew); one *s. Educ:* Herbert Strutt Sch., Belper; Brasenose Coll., Oxford (MA). IPFA 1967. Trainee accountant, Derbyshire CC, 1963–67; Sen. Accountant, London Borough of Sutton, 1967–70; Asst Treas., W Sussex CC, 1970–76; Dep. Treas., Mid Glamorgan CC, 1976–79; Treas., S Glamorgan CC, 1980–92. Financial Advr, Welsh Counties Cttee, 1984–91; Comr, Public Works Loan Bd, 1991–95. Mem. Bd, Police IT Orgn, 1998–2000. President: Soc. of Co. Treasurers, 1992–93; CIPFA, 1994–95; Police Authy Treasurers Soc., 2006–07. *Recreations:* family, golf, watching sport, theatre. *Address:* Sweetbriar, 68 Weeping Cross, Stafford ST17 0DL. *T:* (01785) 604613. *Club:* Oxford and Cambridge.

TEVERSON, family name of **Baron Teverson**.

TEVERSON, Baron *cr* 2006 (Life Peer), of Tregony, in the County of Cornwall; **Robin Teverson;** *b* 31 March 1952; *s* of Dr Crofton Teverson and Joan Teverson; *m* 1st, 1975, Rosemary Anne Young (marr. diss. 2005); two *d*; *m* 2nd, 2006, Terrye Lynn Jones. *Educ:* Exeter Univ. (BA Hons Econs). Managing Director: SPD Ltd and Dir, Exel Logistics, 1987–89; Supply Chain Consultancy (Rationale Ltd), 1989–94; Chm., Finance SW Ltd, 1999–2002; Chief Exec., Finance Cornwall, 2002–06. MEP (Lib Dem) Cornwall and West Plymouth, 1994–99; contested (Lib Dem) SW Reg., 1999. *Recreations:* history, riding, astronomy, travel, music. *Address:* House of Lords, SW1A 0PW.

TEVERSON, Paul Richard; Master of the Supreme Court, Chancery Division, since 2005; *b* 1 May 1953; *s* of late George Eric Teverson and Ailsa Betty Teverson (*née* Moor); *m* 1978, Hon. Joanna Rosamund Georgina, *d* of Baron Gore-Booth, GCMG, KCVO; two *s* one *d. Educ:* St Paul's Sch., London (Sen. Schol.); Corpus Christi Coll., Cambridge (Exhibnr; BA 1975). Called to the Bar, Inner Temple, 1976; in practice at Chancery Bar, 1978–2005. Dep. Chancery Master, 2000–05. *Publication:* (contrib.) The White Book, 2007. *Recreations:* reading, cycling (Mem., Barnes Bikers), theatre, opera. *Address:* Royal Courts of Justice, WC2A 2LL. *Club:* Hurlingham.

TEVIOT, 2nd Baron *cr* 1940, of Burghclere; **Charles John Kerr;** genealogist; *b* 16 Dec. 1934; *s* of 1st Baron Teviot, DSO, MC, and Florence Angela (*d* 1979), *d* of late Lt-Col Charles Walter Villiers, CBE, DSO; *S* father, 1968; *m* 1965, Patricia Mary Harris; one *s* one *d. Educ:* Eton. Bus Conductor and Driver; genealogical and historical record agent. Director: Debrett's Peerage Ltd, 1977–83; Burke's Peerage Research, 1983–85; Burke's Peerage Ltd, 1984–85. Mem., Adv. Council on Public Records, 1974–83. Pres., Assoc. of Genealogists and Record Agents, 1997–. Fellow, Soc. of Genealogists, 1975. *Recreations:* reading, walking. *Heir: s* Hon. Charles Robert Kerr [*b* 19 Sept. 1971; *m* 2000, Yamaleth Molina Guillen; one *d* (and one *d* decd)]. *Address:* 28 Hazel Grove, Burgess Hill, West Sussex RH15 0BY. *T:* (01444) 242605.

TEW, Prof. John Hedley Brian, OBE 1988; PhD; Midland Bank Professor of Money and Banking, University of Nottingham, 1967–82; *b* 1 Feb. 1917; *s* of Herbert and Catherine Mary Tew; *m* 1944, Marjorie Hoey Craigie; one *s* one *d. Educ:* Mill Hill School, Leicester; University College, Leicester; Peterhouse, Cambridge. BSc (Econ.) London; PhD Cantab. Iron and Steel Control, 1940–42; Ministry of Aircraft Production, 1942–45; Industrial and Commercial Finance Corp., 1946; Professor of Economics, Univ. of Adelaide (Australia), 1947–49; Professor of Economics, University of Nottingham, 1950–67. External Prof., Dept of Econs, Univ. of Loughborough, 1982–99. Part-time Member: Iron and Steel Board, 1964–67; East Midlands Electricity Board, 1965–76; Tubes Div., BSC, 1969–73; Mem., Cttee of Enquiry on Small Firms, Dept of Trade and Industry, 1969–71. *Publications:* Wealth and Income, 1950; International Monetary Co-operation 1952; (jt editor) Studies in Company Finance, 1959; Monetary Theory, 1969; The Evolution of the International Monetary System, 1977. *Address:* 121 Bramcote Lane, Wollaton, Notts NG8 2NJ.

TEWKESBURY, Bishop Suffragan of, since 1996; **Rt Rev. John Stewart Went;** *b* 11 March 1944; *s* of Douglas and Barbara Went; *m* 1968, Rosemary Evelyn Amy (*née* Dunn); three *s. Educ:* Corpus Christi Coll., Cambridge (1st Cl Classics Pt I, starred 1st Theology Pt II; MA). Curate, Emmanuel, Northwood, Middx, 1969–75; Vicar, Holy Trinity, Margate, 1975–83; Vice-Principal, Wycliffe Hall, Oxford, 1983–89; Archdeacon of Surrey, 1989–95. Warden of Readers, Gloucester dio., 1996–2000. Chairman: Diocesan Council for Unity and Mission, Guildford, 1990–95; Vocation, Recruitment and Selection Cttee, C of E Ministry Div., 2002–. Member Council: Bible Reading Fellowship, 1989–; World Vision, 1996–2006. *Publications:* (contrib.) Changing Rural Life: a Christian response to key rural issues (ed J. Martineau, L. J. Francis and P. Francis), 2004; contrib. to One in Christ. *Recreations:* music, photography, crosswords. *Address:* The Bishop's House, Church Road, Staverton, Cheltenham GL51 0TW. *T:* (01242) 680188, *Fax:* (01242) 680233; *e-mail:* bshptewk@star.co.uk.

TEWSON, Jane, (Mrs C. Lane), CBE 1999; Founder and Director, Pilotlight Australia, since 2000; *b* 9 Jan. 1958; *d* of Dr Tim Tewson, Oxford, and Dr Blue Tewson (*née* Johnston); *m* 1992, Dr Charles Lane; two *s. Educ:* Headington Sch., Oxford; Lord William's Sch., Thame. Project Co-ordinator, MENCAP, 1979–83; Founder: and Chief Exec., Charity Projects and Comic Relief, 1984–96; Pilotlight UK, 1996–99; TimeBank, 1999. Trustee: Media Trust, 1996–99; Oxfam, 1996–99; Camelot Foundn, 1997–2000; Diana, Princess of Wales Meml Cttee, 1997–2000; St James Ethics Centre, 2000–; Reichstein Foundn, 2000–; Virgin Unite, 2005–. *Recreations:* travel, walking, gardening, reading. *Address:* 35 Cressy Street, Malvern, Melbourne, Vic 3144, Australia.

TEYNHAM, 20th Baron *cr* 1616; **John Christopher Ingham Roper-Curzon;** *b* 25 Dec. 1928; *s* of 19th Baron Teynham, DSO, DSC, and Elspeth Grace (who *m* 2nd, 1958, 6th Marquess of Northampton, DSO, and *d* 1976), *e d* of late William Ingham Whitaker; *S* father, 1972; *m* 1964, Elizabeth, *yr d* of Lt-Col the Hon. David Scrymgeour-Wedderburn, DSO, Scots Guards (killed on active service 1944), and of Patricia, Countess of Dundee; five *s* five *d* (of whom one *s* one *d* are twins). *Educ:* Eton. A Land Agent. Late Captain, The Buffs (TA), formerly Coldstream Guards; active service in Palestine, 1948. ADC to Governor of Bermuda, 1953 and 1955; ADC to Governor of Leeward Islands, 1955; Private Secretary and ADC, 1956; ADC to Governor of Jamaica, 1962. Pres., Inst. of Commerce, 1972–; Vice Pres., Inst. of Export. Member of Council, Sail Training Association, 1964–69. OStJ. Lord of the Manors of South Baddesley and Sharpricks. *Recreations:* shooting and fishing. *Heir: s* Hon. David John Henry Ingham Roper-Curzon [*b* 5 Oct. 1965; *m* 1st, 1985, Lydia Lucinda (marr. diss. 2003), *d* of Maj.-Gen. Sir Christopher Airy, *qv*; two *s* one *d*; 2nd, 2003, Melanie Hayward; one *s* one *d* (twins)]. *Address:* Pylewell Park, Lymington, Hants SO41 5SJ. *Clubs:* Turf; House of Lords Yacht; Ocean Cruising; Puffin's (Edinburgh).

THACKER, David Thomas; theatre, film and television director; *b* 21 Dec. 1950; *s* of Thomas Richard Thacker and Alice May (*née* Beaumont); *m* 1983, Margot Elizabeth Leicester; three *s* one *d. Educ:* Wellingborough Grammar Sch.; Univ. of York (BA English and Related Lit.; MA Shakespeare). Theatre Royal, York: Asst Stage Manager, Dep. Stage Manager and Stage Manager, 1974–75; Asst Dir, 1975–76; Gateway Theatre, Chester: Arts Council Asst Dir, 1975–76; Associate Dir, 1977–78; Duke's Playhouse, Lancaster: Arts Council Associate Dir, 1978–79; Dir, 1980–84; Dir, Young Vic Theatre, 1984–93; Dir-in-Residence, RSC, 1993–95. *Theatre productions:* over 100 including: Young Vic: Ghosts, 1987; Who's Afraid of Virginia Woolf?, 1987; A Touch of the Poet, An Enemy of the People, 1989; The Winter's Tale, 1991; The Last Yankee, 1993; RSC: Pericles, The Two Gentlemen of Verona, 1991; As You Like It, 1992; The Merchant of Venice, 1993; Julius Caesar, Coriolanus, 1995; Bingo, The Tempest, 1995; Broken Glass, RNT, 1994, transf. Duke of York's, 1995; A View from the Bridge, Bristol Old Vic, 1994, transf. Strand, 1995; Death of a Salesman, RNT, 1996. *Television:* over 30 productions including: A Doll's House, 1992; Measure for Measure, 1994; Death of a Salesman, 1996; Broken Glass; The Scold's Bridle, 1998; Grafters; Kavanagh QC; The Vice; Waking the Dead; Murder in Mind; Blue Dove; The Mayor of Casterbridge, 2003; Faith, 2005. Trustee: Hoghton Tower Shakespeare Centre; Shakespeare North Trust; Haringey Shed Trust. Gov., Tetherdown Sch. Dir of the Year, Laurence Olivier Awards, 1991. *Recreations:* sport, family, film and television, reading, politics. *Address:* 55 Onslow Gardens, Muswell Hill, N10 3JY. *T:* and *Fax:* (020) 8444 8436; *e-mail:* davidthacker@blueyonder.co.uk.

THAKKER, Prof. Rajesh Vasantlal, MD; FRCP, FRCPE, FRCPath, FMedSci; May Professor of Medicine, and Fellow of Somerville College, University of Oxford, since 1999; *b* 27 Aug. 1954; *s* of late Vasantlal Gordhandas Thakker and of Indira Vasantlal Thakker; *m* 1980, Julie Clare Magee; one *d. Educ:* Pembroke Coll., Cambridge (MA, MB BChir, MD); Middlesex Hosp. Med. Sch. MRCP 1983, FRCP 1993; FRCPE 1997; FRCPath 1998. Middlesex Hospital: House Physician, 1980–81; Registrar, 1983–85; MRC Trng Fellow and Hon. Sen. Registrar, 1985–88; Sen. House Physician, Northwick Park Hosp. and Hammersmith Hosp., 1981–83; MRC Clin. Scientist and Consultant Physician, Northwick Park Hosp., 1988–92; Sen. Lectr and Consultant Physician, 1988–94, Reader of Medicine, 1994–95, RPMS; Hd of MRC Molecular Endocrinology Gp, 1994–99, and Prof. of Medicine, 1995–99, RPMS, then ICSM, Univ. of London. FMedSci 1999. *Publications:* (ed) Genetic and Molecular Biological Aspects of Endocrine Disease, 1995; (ed) Molecular Genetics of Endocrine Disorders, 1997; articles in jls. *Recreations:* running, rambling, reading. *Address:* Somerville College, Oxford OX2 6HD.

THAKSIN SHINAWATRA, PhD; Prime Minister of Thailand, 2001–06; *b* 26 July 1949; *m* Khunying Potjaman Shinawatra. *Educ:* Police Cadet Acad., Thailand; Eastern Kentucky Univ., USA (MA Criminal Justice 1975); Sam Houston State Univ., Texas (PhD Criminal Justice 1978). Royal Thai Police Department, 1973–87: Dep. Supt, Policy and Planning Subdiv.; Police Lt Col, 1987. Founder and Chm., Shinawatra Computer and Communications Gp, 1987–94. Minister of Foreign Affairs, Thailand, 1994–95; Leader, Palang Dharma Party, 1995–96; Dep. Prime Minister i/c of traffic and transportation, Bangkok, 1995–96; Dep. Prime Minister, 1997; MP (party list), 1998–2001; Founder and Leader, Thai Rak Thai Party, 1998–2006. Founder and Vice Chm., Thaicom Foundn, 1993–; Chm. Adv. Cttee, Pre-Cadet Class 10 and Police Cadet Class 26, 1994–; Honorary Member: Council, Police Cadet Acad.; Assoc. of Ex-Military Officers; President: Northerners' Assoc. of Thailand, 1998; Professional Golf Assoc. of Thailand; Honorary Advisor: Bangkok Club; Thai Northerners' Assoc. of Illinois, 1999; Northerners Club of Nontaburi. ASEAN Businessman of the Year Award, Asian Inst., Indonesia, 1992; Kiattiyod Jakdao Award in Economical Develt, Cttee of Armed Forces Prep. Sch. Foundn, 1992; 1993 Outstanding Telecom Man of Year Award, 1994; Outstanding Criminal Justice Alumnus Award, Sam Houston State Univ., 1996; Hon. Award, Mass Media Photographer Assoc. of Thailand, 1997. Kt Grand Cordon (Special Cl.), Order of Crown (Thailand), 1995, Order of White Elephant (Thailand), 1996; Kt Grand Cross (First Cl.), Order of Direkgunabhorn (Thailand), 2001; Grand Cross, Order of Sahametrei (Cambodia), 2001.

THANE, Prof. Patricia Mary, PhD; FBA 2006; FRHistS; Leverhulme Professor of Contemporary British History, Institute of Historical Research, University of London, since 2001; *b* 17 Aug. 1942; *d* of John Lawrence Williams, RAF (killed in action, 1944) and of Violet (*née* Beckett); *m* 1966, John Sutherland Thane (separated 1982); one *d. Educ:* Convent of the Holy Family, Birkenhead; St Anne's Coll., Oxford (BA, MA Mod. Hist. 1964); LSE (DSA 1965; PhD 1970). FRHistS 1985. Asst Lectr, Lectr, Sen. Lectr, then Reader in Social Hist., Dept of Social Sci. and Admin, Goldsmiths' Coll., Univ. of London, 1967–94; Prof. of Contemp. Hist., Univ. of Sussex, 1994–2001. Hon. Treas., 1992–96, Vice-Pres., 2006–, RHistS; Vice-Pres., Internat. Econ. Hist. Assoc., 1998–2001; Chm., Social Hist. Soc., UK, 2001–08. Mem., Fawcett Soc., 2000–. *Publications:* (ed and contrib.) The Origins of British Social Policy, 1978; The Foundations of the Welfare State, 1982 (trans. Japanese), 2nd edn 1996 (trans. Japanese); (ed jtly and contrib.) The Power of the Past: essays for Eric Hobsbawm, 1984; (ed jtly) Essays in Social History, vol. 2, 1986; (ed with Gisela Book) Maternity and Gender Policies: women and the rise of the European welfare states 1880s–1950s, 1991; (ed with Paul Johnson) Old Age from Antiquity to Post-Modernity, 1998; (ed jtly) Labour's First Century: the Labour Party 1900–2000, 2000; Old Age in English History: past experiences, present issues, 2000; (ed with Lynne Bothelho) Women and Ageing in British Society since 1500, 2001; Companion to Twentieth Century British History, 2001; (ed) The Long History of Old Age, 2005; numerous articles in learned jls and contribs to edited vols. *Recreation:* cooking. *Address:* 5 Twisden Road, NW5 1DL. *T:* (office) (020) 7862 8797, *Fax:* (020) 7862 8812.

THANE, Sarah Ann, (Mrs S. A. Wenban), CBE 2003; JP; FRTS; Member, National Lottery Commission, since 2005; *b* 21 Sept. 1951; *d* of John and Winifred Thane; *m* 1996, Peter Wenban; three step *s* two step *d. Educ:* Sutton Coldfield Grammar Sch. for Girls; Co. High Sch., Stourbridge; City of Birmingham Poly. (Dip. Communication Studies). Independent Television Commission: Dir of Public Affairs, 1990–96; Dir of Progs and Cable, 1996–2001; Dir of Progs and Advertising, 2001–03; Advisor: Content and Standards, Ofcom, 2004–05; (pt-time) to BBC Governors, 2005–06, to BBC Trust, 2007–. Non-exec. Dir, Films of Record, 2005–. Vice-Chm., 1998–2000, Chm., 2000–02, RTS. FRTS 1994. JP W Suffolk, 2005. *Recreations:* music, visual arts, cooking, gardening, time with friends and family. *Address: e-mail:* sarahwenban@hotmail.com, S.Thane@natlotcomm.gov.uk. *Club:* Reform.

THANKI, Bankim; QC 2003; *b* 19 April 1964; *s* of late B. D. Thanki and of Vijayalaxmi Thanki (*née* Modha); *m* 1988, Catherine Jane Margaret Spotswood; three *s* one *d. Educ:* Owen's Sch., Herts; Balliol Coll., Oxford (BA 1st cl. Hons Ancient and Modern History, 1986; MA 1989). Called to the Bar, Middle Temple, 1988 (Harmsworth Schol.), Bencher, 2008; in practice as barrister, specialising in commercial law, 1989–. Mem., Commercial Bar Assoc., 1989–. *Publications:* (jtly) Carriage by Air, 2000; (ed jtly) Commercial Court Procedure, 2001; (contrib.) Brindle & Cox, Law of Bank Payments, 2004; (ed) Law of Privilege, 2006. *Recreation:* Manchester United FC. *Address:* (chambers) Fountain Court, Temple, EC4Y 9DH. *T:* (020) 7583 3335, *Fax:* (020) 7353 0329. *Club:* Royal Automobile.

THANKI, (Frances) Jane; *see* McIvor, F. J.

THAPAR, Prof. Romila, PhD; Professor of History, Jawaharlal Nehru University, New Delhi, 1970–91, now Professor Emeritus; *b* 30 Nov. 1931; *d* of Daya Ram Thapar and Kaushalya Khosla. *Educ:* Punjab Univ. (BA Hons Lit. 1952); Sch. of Oriental and African Studies, Univ. of London (BA Hons Hist. 1955; PhD Hist. 1958). Reader in Ancient Indian Hist., Delhi Univ., 1963–70. Kluge Vis. Prof., Library of Congress, 2003–04. Corresp. FBA 1999; Corresp. Fellow, RSE, 2006. Hon. Fellow: Lady Margaret Hall, Oxford, 1986; SOAS, 1991. Hon. DLitt: Chicago, 1992; Oxford, 2002; Hon. DSc Edinburgh, 2004. *Publications:* Aśoka and the Decline of the Mauryas, 1961, 2nd edn 1997; History of India, Vol. 1, 1966; Ancient Indian Social History: some interpretations, 1978; From Lineage to State, 1984; Cultural Pasts, 2000; Śakuntalā, 2001; Early India, 2002; Somanatha, 2004; (ed) India: historical beginnings and the concept of the Aryan, 2006; for children: Indian Tales, 1961, 2nd edn 1993. *Recreations:* music, poetry, searching for unusual finger rings. *Address:* 23 B Road, Maharani Bagh, New Delhi 110065, India.

THAROOR, Shashi, PhD; Chairman, Afras Ventures, since 2007; *b* 9 March 1956; *s* of Chandran Tharoor and Lily Tharoor; *m* 1st, 1977, Tilottama Mukheji (marr. diss. 2000); two *s* (twins); 2nd, 2007, Christa Giles. *Educ:* St Stephen's Coll.; Delhi Univ. (BA Hons); Fletcher Sch. of Law and Diplomacy, Tufts Univ. (MA 1976; MALD 1977; PhD 1978). United Nations High Commissioner for Refugees: Asst to Dir for External Affairs, 1978–81; Rep., Singapore, 1981–84; Dep. Chief of Secretariat, 1984–87; Exec. Asst to Dep. High Comr, 1987–89; United Nations Headquarters: Special Asst to Under-Sec.-Gen. for Peacekeeping, 1989–96; Exec. Asst to Sec.-Gen., 1997–98; Dir, Communications and Special Projs, 1998–2001; Under Sec.-Gen. for Commns and Public Inf., 2001–07. Member Advisory Board: Indo-American Arts Council; Virtue Foundn; Breakthrough: the Vijay Amritraj Foundn. Fellow, NY Inst. of the Humanities. Bd of Overseers, Fletcher Sch. of Law and Diplomacy. Columnist: The Times of India; The Hindu; former Contrib. Editor, Newsweek Internat. Pravasi Bharatiya Samman, 2004. *Publications:* Reasons of State, 1982; The Great Indian Novel (novel), 1989; The Five-Dollar Smile and Other Stories, 1990; Show Business (novel), 1992; India: from midnight to the millennium, 1997, rev. edn as India: from midnight to the millennium and beyond, 2006; Nehru: the invention of India, 2003; Riot (novel), 2001; Bookless in Baghdad and Other Reflections on Literature, 2005; The Elephant, the Tiger and the Cellphone: reflections on India in the 21st century, 2007. *Recreations:* cricket, theatre, reading. *Address:* 230 Park Avenue, Suite 2525, New York, NY 10169, USA. *T:* (646) 2928456, *Fax:* (212) 6612153; *e-mail:* tharoor@afras.ae. *Club:* India International Centre (New Delhi).

THARP, Twyla; American dancer and choreographer; *b* 1 July 1941; *m* Peter Young (marr. diss.); *m* Robert Huot (marr. diss.); one *s. Educ:* Pomona Coll.; American Ballet Theatre Sch.; Barnard Coll. (BA Art History 1963). With Paul Taylor Dance Co., 1963–65; Founder, 1965, choreographer, 1965–87, Twyla Tharp Dance Foundn; Artistic Associate Choreographer, American Ballet Theatre, 1988–91; regrouped Twyla Tharp Dance, 1991; *modern dances/ballets* choreographed include: Tank Dive, 1965; Re-Moves, 1966; Generation, 1968; Medley, 1969; Shout, The One Hundreds, 1970; Eight Jelly Rolls, 1971; Deuce Coupe, Joffrey Ballet, 1973; As Time Goes By, Joffrey Ballet, 1973; Sue's Leg, 1975; Push Comes to Shove, American Ballet Theatre, 1976; Mud, 1977; Baker's Dozen, 1979; The Catherine Wheel, 1981; The Little Ballet, American Ballet Theatre, 1984; In the Upper Room, 1987 (Olivier Award, 1991); Everlast, 1989; The Rules of the Game, 1990; (with Mikhail Baryshnikov) Cutting Up, 1993; Demeter and Persephone, 1994; Mr Wordly Wise, Royal Ballet, Covent Garden, 1995; Heroes, Sweet Fields, 66, 1997; Known By Heart, 1998; The Beethoven Seventh, 2000; also dir., Movin' Out (Tony Award for best choreography), 2002; *films* choreographed: Hair, 1979; Ragtime, 1980; Amadeus, 1984; White Nights, 1985; I'll Do Anything, 1994; *television* includes directing: Making Television Dance; The Catherine Wheel; Baryshnikov by Tharp. Hon. Mem., Amer. Acad. Arts and Letters, 1997. Creative Arts Award, Brandeis Univ., 1972; Astaire Award, 2003; Drama League Award for Sustained Achievement in Musical Theater, 2003. *Publications:* Push Comes to Shove (autobiog.), 1992; The Creative Habit: learn it and use it for life, 2003.

THATCHER, family name of **Baroness Thatcher**.

THATCHER, Baroness *cr* 1992 (Life Peer), of Kesteven in the County of Lincolnshire; **Margaret Hilda Thatcher,** LG 1995; OM 1990; PC 1970; FRS 1983; *b* 13 Oct. 1925; *d* of late Alfred Roberts, Grantham, Lincs; *m* 1951, Denis Thatcher, later Sir Denis Thatcher, 1st Bt (*d* 2003); one *s* one *d* (twins). *Educ:* Kesteven and Grantham Girls' School; Somerville College, Oxford (MA, BSc). Research Chemist, 1947–51; called to the Bar, Lincoln's Inn, 1954, Hon. Bencher, 1975. MP (C) Finchley, 1959–92; Joint Parly Sec., Min. of Pensions and National Insurance, Oct. 1961–64; Sec. of State for Educn and Sci., 1970–74; Leader of the Opposition, 1975–79; Prime Minister and First Lord of the Treasury, 1979–90. Co-Chm., Women's Nat. Commn, 1970–74. Chancellor: Univ. of Buckingham, 1992–98; William and Mary Coll., Virginia, 1993–2000. Chm. Bd, Inst. of US Studies, London Univ., 1994–2002. Hon. Fellow, Somerville Coll., Oxford, 1970. Freedom of Borough of Barnet, 1980, of City of London, 1989. Donovan Award, USA, 1981. *Publications:* In Defence of Freedom, 1986; The Collected Speeches of Margaret Thatcher, 1997; Statecraft: strategies for a changing world, 2002; *memoirs:* The Downing Street Years 1979–90, 1993; The Path to Power, 1995. *Recreations:* music, reading. *Address:* House of Lords, SW1A 0PW. *Club:* Carlton.

See also Hon. Sir M. Thatcher, Bt.

THATCHER, Anthony Neville, CEng, FIMechE; Vice Chairman, Thyssen-Bornemisza SAM, since 1993 (President and Chief Executive Officer, Thyssen-Bornemisza Group, 1991–92); *b* 10 Sept. 1939; *s* of Edwin Neville Thatcher and Elsie May Webster; *m* 1968, Sally Margaret Clark. *Educ:* Sir John Lawes Sch., Harpenden; Luton Tech. Coll.; Manchester Univ. (MSc). Student apprentice, Haywards Tyler & Co., Luton, 1956–64; Project Engineer, Smiths Industries, 1964–67; Ultra Electronics: Operations Res. Asst, Acton, 1967–69; Vice-Pres., Sales, USA, 1970–73; Marketing Dir, Acton, 1973–77; Managing Dir, Ultra Electronic Controls, 1977; Managing Director: Dowty Electronic Controls, 1978–82; Electronics Div., Dowty Gp, 1982; Dir, 1983–91, Chief Exec., 1986–91, Dowty Gp. Member: Avionics Cttee, Electronics and Avionics Requirements Bd, DTI, 1981–85; Council, Electronics Engineering Assoc., 1983–91 (Pres., 1986–87); RARDE Management Bd (Indust.), 1986–91; Council, SBAC, 1986–91; Innovation Adv. Bd, DTI, 1988–91; Engrg Markets Adv. Bd, DTI, 1988–90; Engrg Council, 1989–91. Council Mem., Cheltenham Ladies' Coll., 1988–91. Freeman, City of London; Liveryman and Trustee, Glass Sellers' Co. *Recreations:* art, jazz piano, opera, fishing, gardening, bird watching. *Address:* 12 Gayfere Street, SW1P 3HP. *Clubs:* Athenæum, Carlton; Georgetown (Washington).

THATCHER, Arthur Roger, CB 1974; Director, Office of Population Censuses and Surveys, and Registrar General for England and Wales, 1978–86; *b* 22 Oct. 1926; *s* of

Arthur Thatcher and Edith Mary Ruth (*née* Dobson); *m* 1950, Mary Audrey Betty (*née* Street); two *d*. *Educ:* The Leys Sch.; St John's Coll., Cambridge (MA). Instr Lieut, Royal Navy, 1947–49. North Western Gas Board, 1949–52; Admiralty, 1952–61; Cabinet Office, 1961–63; Ministry of Labour, 1963–68; Director of Statistics, Dept of Employment, 1968–78, Dep. Sec., 1972–78. *Publications:* (jtly) The Force of Mortality at Ages 80 to 120, 1998; official publications; articles in jls. *Address:* 35 Thetford Road, New Malden, Surrey KT3 5DP. *Club:* Army and Navy.

THATCHER, Hon. Sir Mark, 2nd Bt *cr* 1991, of Scotney in the County of Kent; *b* 15 Aug. 1953; *s* of Sir Denis Thatcher, 1st Bt, MBE, TD and of Baroness Thatcher, *qv*; *S* father, 2003; *m* 1st, 1987, Diane Bergdorf (marr. diss. 2007), Dallas, Texas; one *s* one *d*; 2nd, 2008, Sarah-Jane Russell (*née* Clemence). *Educ:* Harrow. *Heir:* *s* Michael Thatcher, *b* 28 Feb. 1989.

THAW, Sheila, (Mrs John Thaw); *see* Hancock, S.

THEAKSTON, John Andrew; Director, Black Sheep Brewery, since 1992; *b* 23 May 1952; *s* of Robert Francis Theakston and Jane Hawley (*née* Boyle); *m* 1977, Elizabeth Jane Morgan; one *s* one *d*. *Educ:* Sedbergh Sch., Yorks; Worcester Coll., Oxford (MA Mod. History); Durham Univ. (MSc). Trainee, T. & R. Theakston, Brewers, 1975–77; Donald Macpherson Group: Corporate Planning Manager, 1977–81; Overseas Div. Manager, 1981–84; Higgs & Hill, subseq. Swan Hill Group, plc: Business Develt Manager, 1985–87; Gp Finance Dir, 1987–89; Jt Gp Man. Dir. 1989–90; Chief Exec., 1991–2004. Non-executive Director: ARCO Ltd, 2005– (non-exec. Chm., 2006–); Halcrow Ltd, 2006–. *Recreations:* sailing, walking, trout fishing.

THEIS, Lucy Morgan; QC 2003; a Recorder, since 2000; *b* 6 Nov. 1960; *d* of Michael and Jill Theis; *m* 1991, Andrew Firrell; one *s* one *d*. *Educ:* Birmingham Univ. (LLB 1981). Called to the Bar, Gray's Inn, 1982, Bencher, 2007; Asst Recorder, 1998–2000. *Recreations:* gardening, riding, farming. *Address:* 2 and 5 Field Court, Gray's Inn, WC1R 5BB. *T:* (020) 7405 6114.

THELLUSSON, family name of **Baron Rendlesham**.

THE MURRAY, Bishop of; *see* Murray.

THEOBALD, George Peter; JP; company director, since 1958; *b* 5 Aug. 1931; *s* of late George Oswald Theobald and Helen (*née* Moore); *m* 1955, Josephine Mary (*née* Boodle); two *s* three *d*. *Educ:* Betteshanger Sch.; Harrow. National Service commission, 5 Regt RHA, 1950–52; 290 (City of London) RA (TA), 1953–59. Robert Warner Ltd, 1953–74: Director, 1958; Man. Dir, Chm. Gp subsidiaries, 1965; private company director, 1974–2008; Tea Clearing House, 1959–72 (Chm., 1970–72); Moran Holdings (formerly Moran Tea Holdings) plc, 1980–2005 (Chm., 1992–2005); Moran Tea Co. (India) plc, 1981–2005 (Chm., 1992–2005). City of London (Queenhithe Ward): Chm., Ward Club, 1966–68; Common Councilman, 1968–74; Alderman, 1974–79. Member: Transport Users' Consultative Cttee for London, 1969–84 (Dep. Chm. 1978); London Regional Passengers Cttee, 1984–90. Governor: Bridewell Royal Hosp., 1974–93; King Edward's Sch., Witley, 1974–93 (Trustee, Educational Trust, 1977–95); Donation Governor, Christ's Hosp., 1976–91; Governor, St Leonards-Mayfield Sch., 1982–88; Chm., St John's Sch., Northwood, 1989–97; Mem. Cttee, Langford Cross Children's Home, 1976–90; Trustee: National Flood and Tempest Distress Fund, 1977–; Harrow Mission, 1978–2001. Church Commissioner for England, 1978–79. Master, Merchant Taylors' Co., 1989–90, 1991–92. JP City of London, 1974. *Recreations:* gardening, transport, walking. *Clubs:* Oriental, City Livery, Guildhall, MCC.

THEOCHAROUS, Archbishop Gregorios; His Eminence The Most Rev. Gregorios; Greek Orthodox Archbishop of Thyateira and Great Britain, since 1988; *b* 2 Jan. 1929. *Educ:* High Sch., Lefkoniko, Famagusta; Pan Cyprian Gymnasium, Nicosia; Theol Faculty, Univ. of Athens. Monk in the Sacred Monastery, Stavrovouni, Cyprus; ordained: deacon, 1953; presbyter, 1959; asst parish priest and later parish priest, All Saints, Camden Town, 1959–69; Archdiocese of Thyateira: Chancellor, 1965–79; Asst Bishop of Tropaeou, 1970–88; locum tenens on death of Archbishop Athenagoras, 1979; spiritual oversight of Community of St Barnabas, Wood Green, 1970–88. Dr *hc* North London, 1993. *Address:* Thyateira House, 5 Craven Hill, W2 3EN. *T:* (020) 7723 4787, *Fax:* (020) 7224 9301; *e-mail:* mail@thyateira.org.uk.

THÉODORE, Jean-François; Deputy Chief Executive Officer and Director, NYSE Euronext, since 2007 (Chief Executive, Euronext, 2000–07); *b* 5 Dec. 1946; *m* 1976, Claudine Lefebvre; one *s* two *d*. *Educ:* Univ. of Paris (Licencé); Institut d'Etudes Politiques; Ecole Nationale d'Administration. Asst Hd, State Holdings Bureau, French Treasury, 1974–78; seconded to Credit National, as Mem., Exec. Bd, 1978–80; Treasury: Hd, African States-Franc Zone Bureau, 1980–82; Hd, Foreign Investment Bureau, 1982–84; Dep. Dir i/c, Banking Dept, 1984–86; Dep. Dir, Investments, State Participations and Public Corps Dept, 1986–90; CEO, 1990–99, Chm., 1991–99, SBF-Paris Bourse; Chm., MATIF, 1998–99; CEO and Chm., Paris Bourse, 1999–2000. Chm., SICOVAM, 1993–2000. President: Internat. Fedn of Stock Exchanges, 1993–94; Fedn European Stock Exchanges, 1998–2000. Chm. Steering Cttee, Paris Europlace. Chevalier, Légion d'Honneur, 1994. *Address:* NYSE Euronext, 39 rue Cambon, 75039 Paris Cedex 01, France. *T:* 49271102. *Clubs:* Paris-Europlace, Bourse (Paris).

THERBORN, Prof. Göran, PhD; Professor of Sociology, University of Cambridge, since 2006; *b* 23 Sept. 1941; *s* of Ragnar and Karin Therborn; *m* 1982, Sonia Piña; one *s* one *d*. *Educ:* Lund Univ. (PhD 1974). Reader in Sociol., Lund Univ., 1975–81; Professor: of Political Sci., Catholic Univ., Nijmegen, Netherlands, 1981–87; of Sociol., Gothenburg Univ., Sweden, 1987–2003; Dir, Swedish Collegium for Advanced Social Scis, Uppsala, 1996–2006. Eur. Prof. of Social Policy, Budapest, 1996; Visiting Professor: FLACSO Mexico, and ANU, 1978; Sorbonne, 1980; UCLA, 1991; Buenos Aires, 1992; L'Institut des scis politiques, Paris, 2004. Dr *hc* Roskilde, 2007. *Publications:* European Modernity and Beyond, 1995, French edn 2008; Between Sex and Power: family in the world 1900–2000, 2004, Brazilian edn 2006; Asia and Europe in Globalization, 2006; Inequalities of the World, 2006; From Marxism to Post-Marxism?, 2008. *Recreations:* travelling, arts, country house. *Address:* Byvägen 4, 38892 Ljungbyholm, Sweden. *T:* (480) 30613; *e-mail:* goran.therborn@scasss.uu.se; Faculty of Social and Political Science, Free School Lane, Cambridge CB2 3RQ; *e-mail:* gt274@cam.ac.uk.

THÉRIAULT, Hon. Camille Henri; President and Chief Executive Officer, Mouvement des Caisses Populaires Acadiennes, since 2004; *b* 25 Feb. 1955; *m* Gisèle; two *s*. *Educ:* Baie-Sainte-Anne High Sch.; Université de Moncton (BSocSc Political Sci.). Formerly: Vice-Pres., Corporate Affairs, United Maritime Fisherman's Co-operative; Manager, Kent Industrial Commn. Government of New Brunswick: MLA (L) Kent South, 1987–March 2001; Minister of: Fisheries and Aquaculture, 1991–94; Advanced Educn and Labour, 1994–95; Economic Develt and Tourism, 1995–98; Premier, 1998–99; Leader of the Opposition, 1999–2001. Chair: Public Accounts Cttee, 1987; Select Cttee on Representation and Electoral Boundaries; Jt Chair, Ministerial Cttee on Creating New Options; Member: Standing Cttee on Estimates, 1987; Cabinet Cttee on Policy and Priorities, 1994. Leader, NB Liberal Party, 1998–2001. Mem., 2001–, Chm., 2002–, Transportation Safety Bd. *Address:* (office) Place de l'Acadie, 295 Boulevard St-Pierre Ouest, CP 5554, Caraquet, NB E1W 1B7, Canada.

THEROUX, Paul Edward, FRSL; FRGS; writer; *b* 10 April 1941; *s* of Albert Eugene Theroux and Anne Dittami Theroux; *m* 1st, 1967, Anne Castle (marr. diss. 1993); two *s*; 2nd, 1995, Sheila M. L. Donnelly. *Educ:* Univ. of Massachusetts (BA). Lecturer: Univ. of Urbino, 1963; Soche Hill Coll., Malawi, 1963–65; Makerere Univ., Kampala, Uganda, 1965–68; Univ. of Singapore, 1968–71; Writer-in-Residence, Univ. of Virginia, 1972. Mem., AAAL (formerly AAIL), 1984. Hon. DLitt: Trinity Coll., Washington DC, 1980; Tufts Univ., Mass, 1980; Univ. of Mass, 1988. *Publications: novels:* Waldo, 1967; Fong and the Indians, 1968; Girls at Play, 1969; Murder in Mount Holly, 1969; Jungle Lovers, 1971; Sinning with Annie, 1972; Saint Jack, 1973 (filmed, 1979); The Black House, 1974; The Family Arsenal, 1976; Picture Palace, 1978 (Whitbread Award, 1978); A Christmas Card, 1978; London Snow, 1980; The Mosquito Coast, 1981 (James Tait Black Prize, 1982; filmed, 1987); Doctor Slaughter, 1984 (filmed as Half Moon Street, 1987); O-Zone, 1986; My Secret History, 1989; Chicago Loop, 1990; Doctor de Marr, 1990; Millroy the Magician, 1993; My Other Life, 1996; Kowloon Tong, 1997; The Collected Short Novels, 1998; Hotel Honolulu, 2001; Blinding Light, 2005; The Elephanta Suite, 2007; *short stories:* The Consul's File, 1977; World's End, 1980; The London Embassy, 1982 (televised, 1987); The Collected Stories, 1997; The Stranger at the Palazzo d'Oro and Other Stories, 2003; *play:* The White Man's Burden, 1987; *criticism:* V. S. Naipaul, 1972; *memoir:* Sir Vidia's Shadow, 1998; *travel:* The Great Railway Bazaar, 1975; The Old Patagonian Express, 1979; The Kingdom by the Sea, 1983; Sailing through China, illus. Patrick Procktor, 1983; Sunrise with Seamonsters: travels and discoveries 1964–84, 1985; The Imperial Way, 1985; Riding the Iron Rooster, 1988; Travelling The World, 1990; The Happy Isles of Oceania, 1992; The Pillars of Hercules, 1995; Fresh-Air Fiend, 2000; Dark Star Safari, 2002; Ghost Train to the Eastern Star: on the tracks of The Great Railway Bazaar, 2008; *screenplay:* Saint Jack, 1979; reviews in New York Times, etc. *Recreation:* paddling. *Address:* c/o Hamish Hamilton Ltd, 80 Strand, WC2R 0RC.

THESIGER, family name of **Viscount Chelmsford**.

THETFORD, Bishop Suffragan of, since 2001; **Rt Rev. David John Atkinson;** *b* 5 Sept. 1943; *s* of Thomas John Collins and Adèle Mary Atkinson; *m* 1969, Suzan Elizabeth; one *s* one *d*. *Educ:* King's Coll., London (BSc, PhD, AKC); Bristol Univ. (MLitt); Oxford Univ. (MA). Ordained deacon, 1972, priest, 1973; Assistant Curate: St Peter Halliwell, Bolton, 1972–74; Harborne Heath, Birmingham, 1974–77; Librarian, Latimer House, Oxford, 1977–80; Chaplain, 1980–93, Fellow, 1984–93, Corpus Christi Coll., Oxford; Canon Chancellor and Missioner, Southwark Cathedral, 1993–96; Archdeacon of Lewisham, 1996–2001. Co-Founder, Oxford Christian Inst. for Counselling, 1985. Mem., SOSc, 1987. *Publications:* To Have and To Hold, 1979; The Bible Speaks Today (series): Ruth, 1983; Genesis 1–11, 1990; Job, 1991; Proverbs, 1996; Peace in Our Time?, 1985; Pastoral Ethics, 1989, 2nd edn 1994; (jtly) Counselling in Context, 1994, 2nd edn 1998; (ed jtly) New Dictionary of Christian Ethics and Pastoral Theology, 1995; Jesus, Lamb of God, 1996; God So Loved the World, 1999; Renewing the Face of the Earth, 2008; articles and reviews in jls. *Recreations:* music, walking, painting. *Address:* The Red House, 53 Norwich Road, Stoke Holy Cross, Norwich NR14 8AB. *T:* (01508) 491014.

THEW, Rosemary Constance Evelyn; Chief Executive, Driving Standards Agency, since 2005; *b* 3 Nov. 1949; *d* of John Henry Thew and Enid Thew. *Educ:* Preston Manor County Grammar Sch. Civil Service: County Court Clerk, Lord Chancellor's Dept, 1967–70; Exec. Officer, IR, 1970–79; Manpower Services Commn, 1979–86; Regl Employment Manager, W Midlands, Dept of Employment, 1986–89; Implementation and Policy Manager, 1989–96, W Midlands Regl Dir, 1996–2001, Employment Service, Employment Dept Gp, then DfEE; Field Dir, W Midlands Jobcentre Plus, 2001–05. *Recreations:* gardening, walking, golf. *Address:* Driving Standards Agency, The Axis Building, 112 Upper Parliament Street, Nottingham NG1 6LP. *T:* (0115) 936 6010; *e-mail:* rosemary.thew@dsa.gsi.gov.uk.

THEWLES, Col (Francis) Edmund, OBE 1989; Vice Lord-Lieutenant of Shropshire, since 2007; *b* 11 Nov. 1942; *s* of Wing Comdr H. J. A. Thewles, OBE and Rhoda Frances Thewles (*née* Hulme); *m* 1969, Caroline, *y d* of Col R. W. B. Simonds, CBE and Laetitia (*née* Melsome); one *s* two *d*. *Educ:* Berkhamstead Sch.; RMA, Sandhurst. Commnd Worcestershire Regt, later Worcs and Sherwood Foresters Regt, 1964–93. Chm., Shropshire AFC Trust, 2000–. *Recreations:* clocking, mountain walking, theatre, travel. *Address:* 18 Crescent Place, Town Walls, Shrewsbury SY1 1TQ. *T:* (01743) 353424, 07817 757835.

THEWLIS, Sarah Anne; Chief Executive and Registrar, Nursing and Midwifery Council, since 2002; *b* 12 May 1958; *d* of Geoffrey Frank Bennett and Mollie Bennett (*née* Bates); *m* 1983, Rev. Dr John Charles Thewlis. *Educ:* Dartford Grammar Sch. for Girls; Univ. of Hull (BA Hist. 1979); Relate Cert. in Marital and Couple Counselling. MIPD 1991, FCIPD 1998. Marks and Spencer, 1979–91, Divl Personnel Controller for Distribution Centres; Dep. Sec., RCP, 1991–94; Chief Exec., RCGP, 1994–2002. Lay Mem., Employment Tribunal Panel, 1999–. Member: Bishop's Equal Opportunities Cttee, 2001–; Deployment, Remuneration and Conditions of Service Cttee, Archbishops' Council, 2006–. Governor: Deansfield Sch., Eltham; Horne Park Sch., Eltham. FRSA 2001. Hon. FRCGP. *Recreations:* horses, cats, people, current affairs. *Address:* The Rectory, 2 Talbot Road, Carshalton, Surrey SM5 3BS. *T:* (020) 8647 2366; *e-mail:* sat@pavoicellus.demon.co.uk; Nursing and Midwifery Council, 23 Portland Place, W1B 1PZ. *T:* (020) 7333 6528; *e-mail:* sarah.thewlis@nmc-uk.org. *Club:* Royal Society of Medicine.

THIAN, Robert Peter; Chairman, Equiniti Limited (formerly Lloyds TSB Registrars), since 2007; *b* 1 Aug. 1943; *s* of Clifford Peter Thian and Frances Elizabeth (*née* Stafford-Bird); *m* 1964, Liselotte von Borges; two *d*. *Educ:* Geneva Univ. (Lic. en Droit 1967). Called to the Bar, Gray's Inn, 1971. Glaxo Group plc: Legal Advr, 1967–71; Man. Dir, Portugal, 1972–80; Abbott Laboratories (USA): European Business Develt Dir, 1981–84; Regional Dir, Europe, 1985–87; Vice Pres., Internat. Operations, Novo Industri A/S (Denmark), 1987–89; Gp Chief Exec., North West Water Group, 1990–93; Founder and Chief Exec., Renex Ltd, 1993–; Chief Exec., The Stationery Office Gp, 1996–99; Chairman: IMO Gp, 1999–2000; Tactica Solutions Ltd, 1999–2001; Astron Gp, 2001–05; Orion Gp, 2001–04; Whatman Plc, 2002–07; Southern Water Gp (formerly Southern Water Services Ltd), 2003–07; Cardpoint plc, 2006–08. Non-executive Director: Celltech Gp, 1992–99; Medeval Ltd, 1995–98. *Recreations:* horses, golf, reading. *Address:* 16 Princes Gate Mews, SW7 2PS; *e-mail:* bob.thian@renex.net. *Clubs:* Lansdowne; Chantilly Golf.

THIESSEN, Gordon, OC 2002; PhD; Chair, Canadian Public Accountability Board, 2002–07; *b* 14 Aug. 1938; *m* 1964, Annette Hillyar; two *d*. *Educ:* Univ. of Saskatchewan (BA 1960; MA 1961); London School of Economics (PhD 1972). Lectr in Economics, Univ. of Saskatchewan, 1962; joined Bank of Canada, 1963; Res., and Monetary and Financial Analysis Depts, 1963–79; Advr to Gov., 1979–84; Dep. Gov. (Econ. Res. and

Financial Analysis), 1984–87; Sen. Dep. Gov., 1987–94; Gov., 1994–2001; Mem., Exec. Cttee, 1987–2001; Mem., 1987–2001, Chm., 1994–2001, Bd of Dirs. Vis. Economist, Reserve Bank of Australia, 1973–75.

THIN, Andrew; Chairman, Scottish Natural Heritage, since 2006; *b* Edinburgh, 21 Jan. 1959; *s* of James and Marjorie Thin; *m* 1985, Frances Elizabeth Clark; one *s* one *d*. *Educ:* Edinburgh University (BSc Hons 1982; MBA 1988; DipM 1991). Team leader, Highlands and Is Develt Bd, 1989–91; Chief Exec., Caithness and Sutherland Enterprise, 1991–95; Chm., John Muir Trust, 1997–2003; Convener, Cairngorms Nat. Park Authy, 2003–06. Mem. Bd, Crofters Commn, 2001–06. *Recreations:* long-distance running, canoeing, hill walking, climbing. *Address:* Wester Auchterflow Cottage, Munlochy, Ross-shire IV8 8PQ. *T:* (01463) 811632; *e-mail:* andrew.thin@snh.gov.uk.

THIRD, Rt Rev. Richard Henry McPhail; Assistant Bishop, Diocese of Bath and Wells, since 1992; *b* 29 Sept. 1927; *s* of Henry McPhail and Marjorie Caroline Third; *m* 1966, Helen Illingworth; two *d*. *Educ:* Alleyn's Sch.; Reigate Grammar Sch.; Emmanuel Coll., Cambridge (BA 1950, MA 1955); Lincoln Theological Coll. Ordained deacon 1952, priest 1953, Southwark; Curate: St Andrew, Mottingham, 1952–55; Sanderstead (in charge of St Edmund, Riddlesdown), 1955–59; Vicar of Sheerness, 1959–67; Vicar of Orpington, 1967–76; RD of Orpington, 1973–76; Hon. Canon of Rochester, 1974–76; Proctor in Convocation, 1975–76 and 1980–85; Bishop Suffragan: of Maidstone, 1976–80; of Dover, 1980–92. Hon. DCL Kent, 1990. *Recreations:* music, walking, reading, gardening. *Address:* 25 Church Close, Martock, Somerset TA12 6DS. *T:* (01935) 825519.

THIRLWALL, Prof. Anthony Philip, PhD; Professor of Applied Economics, University of Kent, 1976–2004, now Emeritus; *b* 21 April 1941; *s* of Isaac Thirlwall and Ivy Florence Ticehurst; *m* 1966, Gianna Paoletti (separated 1986); one *s* one *d* (and one *s* decd); partner, Dr Penélope Pacheco-López. *Educ:* Harrow Weald County Grammar Sch.; Univ. of Leeds (BA 1962; PhD 1967); Clark Univ. (MA 1963). Teaching Fellow, Clark Univ., 1962–63; Tutor, Cambridge Univ., 1963–64; Asst Lectr, Univ. of Leeds, 1964–66; Lectr and Reader, Univ. of Kent, 1966–76. Economic Adviser: ODM, 1966; Dept of Employment, 1968–70. Res. Associate, Princeton Univ., 1971–72; Visiting Professor: West Virginia Univ., 1967; Melbourne Univ., 1981, 1988; Vis. Scholar, King's Coll., Cambridge, 1979; Bye-Fellow, Robinson Coll., Cambridge, 1985–86; Dist. Vis. Fellow, La Trobe Univ., 1994. Consultant: Pacific Islands Develt Program, 1989–90, 1996; African Develt Bank, 1993–94 and 1999; Asian Develt Bank, 2003; UNCTAD, 2004–. Member: Council and Exec. Cttee, Royal Econ. Soc., 1979–89; Council, Business for Sterling, 1999–; Governor, NIESR, 1979–. Trustee, New Europe Res. Trust, 1999–. Member, Editorial Board: Jl of Develt Studies, 1979–; Jl of Post Keynesian Econs, 1998–; African Develt Review, 1999–. *Publications:* Growth and Development, 1972, 8th edn 2006 (trans. Chinese and Greek 2002); Inflation, Saving and Growth in Developing Economies, 1974 (trans. Spanish 1978); (with R. Dixon) Regional Growth and Unemployment in the UK, 1975; Financing Economic Development, 1976 (trans. Greek 1977, Spanish 1978, Turkish 1980); (with H. Gibson) Balance of Payments Theory and the UK Experience, 1980, 4th edn 1992; Nicholas Kaldor, 1987; (with S. Bazen) Deindustrialisation, 1989, 3rd edn 1997; Performance and Prospects of the Pacific Island Economies in the World Economy, 1991; (with J. McCombie) Economic Growth and the Balance of Payments Constraint, 1994; Economics of Growth and Development: selected essays, vol. 1, 1995; Macroeconomic Issues from a Keynesian Perspective: selected essays, vol. 2, 1997; The Euro and Regional Divergence in Europe, 2000; The Nature of Economic Growth: an alternative framework for understanding the performance of nations, 2002 (trans. Spanish and Japanese, 2003, Portuguese, 2005); Trade, the Balance of Payments and Exchange Rate Policy in Developing Countries, 2003; (with J. McCombie) Essays on Balance-of-Payments Constrained Growth: theory and evidence, 2004; (with P. Pacheco-López) Trade Liberalisation and The Poverty of Nations, 2008; numerous edited books, esp. on Lord Keynes and Lord Kaldor; articles in professional jls; *festschrift* Growth and Economic Development: essays in honour of A. P. Thirlwall, 2006. *Recreations:* athletics (rep. GB, European Veterans Athletics Champs (400m, 800m), 1982), tennis, gardening, travel. *Address:* 14 Moorfield, Canterbury, Kent CT2 7AN. *T:* (01227) 769904; *e-mail:* at4@kent.ac.uk. *Club:* Royal Over-Seas League.

THIRLWALL, Kathryn Mary; QC 1999; a Recorder, since 2000; *b* 21 Nov. 1957; *d* of Brian Edward Thirlwall and Margaret Thirlwall (*née* Earl); *m* 1984, Prof. Charles Kelly; one *s* one *d*. *Educ:* St Anthony's Sch., Sunderland; Bristol Univ. (BA Hons 1980); Newcastle Poly. (CPE 1981). Called to the Bar, Middle Temple, 1982. *Address:* (chambers) 7 Bedford Row, WC1R 4BU.

THIRSK, Dr (Irene) Joan, CBE 1994; FBA 1974; Reader in Economic History in the University of Oxford, and Professorial Fellow of St Hilda's College, Oxford, 1965–83 (Hon. Fellow, 1983); *b* 19 June 1922; *d* of William Henry Watkins and Daisy (*née* Frayer); *m* 1945, James Wood Thirsk; one *s* one *d*. *Educ:* Camden School for Girls, NW5; Westfield Coll., Univ. of London (BA; Hon. Fellow, QMW, 1996); PhD London; MA Oxford. Subaltern, ATS, Intelligence Corps (Bletchley Park), 1942–45. Asst Lectr in Sociology, LSE, 1950–51; Sen. Res. Fellow in Agrarian History, Dept of English Local History, Leicester Univ., 1951–65. Ford Lectr in English History, Oxford, 1975. Sen. Mellon Fellow, Nat. Humanities Centre, 1986–87. Member: Royal Commn on Historical Monuments (England), 1977–86; Econ. and Social Hist. Cttee, SSRC, 1978–82; Royal Commn on Historical Manuscripts, 1989–96. Mem. Council, Economic Hist. Soc., 1955–83; Vice-Chm., Standing Conf. for Local Hist., 1965–82; President: British Agricl Hist. Soc., 1983–86, 1995–98 (Mem. Exec. Cttee, 1953–83, Chm. Exec. Cttee, 1974–77); Edmonton Hundred Historical Soc., 1978–96; Oxfordshire Local Hist. Assoc., 1981–86 (Vice-Pres., 1980–81); Conf. of Teachers of Regional and Local Hist. in Tertiary Educn, 1981–82; British Assoc. for Local Hist., 1986–92; Kent Hist. Fedn, 1990–99; Vice-President: Soc. for Lincs Hist. and Archaeol., 1979–; Past and Present Soc., 2003–. Foreign Mem., Amer. Philos. Soc., 1982–. Editor, Agricultural History Review, 1964–72; Gen. Editor, The Agrarian History of England and Wales, 1974–2000 (Dep. Gen. Ed., 1966–74); Mem. Editorial Bd, Past and Present, 1956–92. FRHistS 1954. Hon. Fellow, Kellogg Coll., Oxford, 1998. Hon. DLitt: Leicester, 1985; East Anglia, 1990; Kent, 1993; Sussex, 1994; Southampton, 1999; Greenwich, 2001; DUniv Open, 1991; Hon. DAgric Wageningen Agricl Univ., Netherlands, 1993. *Publications:* English Peasant Farming, 1957; Suffolk Farming in the Nineteenth Century, 1958; Tudor Enclosures, 1959; The Agrarian History of England and Wales: vol. IV, 1500–1640, 1967; vol. V, 1640–1750, 1984; (with J. P. Cooper) Seventeenth-Century Economic Documents, 1972; The Restoration, 1976; Economic Policy and Projects, 1978; The Rural Economy of England (collected essays), 1985; England's Agricultural Regions and Agrarian History 1500–1750, 1987; Alternative Agriculture: a history from the Black Death to the present day, 1997; The English Rural Landscape, 2000; Food in Early Modern England, 2007; Hadlow: life, land and people in a Wealden parish 1460–1600, 2007; articles in Economic History Rev., Agric. History Rev., Past and Present, History, Jl Modern History, etc. *Recreations:* gardening, sewing, machine-knitting. *Address:* 1 Hadlow Castle, Hadlow, Tonbridge, Kent TN11 0EG; *e-mail:* jthirsk@onetel.com.

THISELTON, Prof. Rev. Canon Anthony Charles, PhD, DD; Professor of Christian Theology, University of Nottingham, 1992–2001 and since 2006 (Head, Department of Theology, 1992–2001; Professor Emeritus in Residence, 2001–06); Canon Theologian: Leicester Cathedral, since 1994; Southwell Minster, since 2000; *b* 13 July 1937; *s* of Eric Charles Thiselton and Hilda Winifred (*née* Kevan); *m* 1963, Rosemary Stella Harman; two *s* one *d*. *Educ:* City of London School; King's Coll., London. BD 1959; MTh 1964 (London); PhD (Sheffield) 1977; DD (Durham) 1993. Curate, Holy Trinity, Sydenham, 1960–63; Lectr and Chaplain, Tyndale Hall, Bristol, 1963–67, Sen. Tutor, 1967–70; Recognised Teacher in Theology, Univ. of Bristol, 1965–71; University of Sheffield: Sir Henry Stephenson Fellow, 1970–71; Lectr in Biblical Studies, 1971–79; Sen. Lectr, 1979–86; Principal, St John's Coll., Nottingham and Special Lectr in Theology, Univ. of Nottingham, 1986–88; Principal, St John's Coll. with Cranmer Hall, Univ. of Durham, 1988–92; Public Orator, Nottingham Univ., 1999–2001. British Acad. Res. Leave Award, 1995–96. Visiting Professor: Calvin Coll., Grand Rapids, USA, 1982–83; Regent Coll., Vancouver, 1983; Fuller Theolog. Seminary, Pasadena, Calif, 1984 and 2002; North Park Coll. and Seminary, Chicago, 1984; Res. Prof. of Christian Theology, Univ. of Chester (formerly Chester UC), 2003–; Scottish Jl of Theol. Lectures, 1994. Exam. Chaplain to Bishop of Sheffield, 1977–80, to Bishop of Leicester, 1979–89 and 1993–. Member: C of E Faith and Order Adv. Group, 1971–81, 1987–90; Doctrine Commn, 1977–90, 1996–2005 (Vice-Chm., 1987–90); Wkg Pty on Revised Catechism, 1988–89; Steering Gp, Revised Weekday Lectionary, 2004–05; Gen. Synod of C of E, 1995– (Mem., Theol. Educn and Trng Cttee, 1999–2005; Chm., Evangelical Gp, 1999–2004; Mem., Appts Cttee, 2005–); Crown Nominations (formerly Appts) Commn, 2000–; Wkg Pty on Women in the Episcopate, 2001–; C of E Evangelical Council, 2001–04; C of E Bd of Educn, 2005–. Consultant, Clergy Discipline (Doctrine) Gp, 2000–04; Mem., Task Gp for Theol Educn in the Anglican Communion, 2003–06. Mem., HFEA, 1995–99. Council for National Academic Awards: Vice-Chm., Bd of Theol and Religious Studies, 1984–87; Mem., Cttee for Humanities, 1987–89. Pres., Soc. for the Study of Theology, 1998–2000. Adv. Editor, Jl for Study of NT, 1981–91; Editl Consultant, Ex Auditu (Princeton and Chicago), 1985–; Mem. Editl Bd, Biblical Interpretation (Brill, Leiden), 1992–2003, Internat. Jl Systematic Theol., 1999–. DD Lambeth, 2002. *Publications:* The Two Horizons: New Testament Hermeneutics and Philosophical Description, 1980; (with C. Walhout and R. Lundin) The Responsibility of Hermeneutics, 1985; New Horizons in Hermeneutics: theory and practice of transforming biblical reading, 1992; Interpreting God and the Postmodern Self, 1995; (with C. Walhout and R. Lundin) The Promise of Hermeneutics, 1999; First Corinthians: a commentary on the Greek text, 2000; Concise Encyclopedia of Philosophy of Religion, 2002; (ed jtly) Reading Luke: interpretation, reflection, formation, 2005; Thiselton on Hermeneutics: collected works, 2006; Shorter Exegetical and Pastoral Commentary on 1 Corinthians, 2006; The Hermeneutics of Doctrine, 2007; Hermeneutics, 2009; contribs to learned jls and other books on New Testament, doctrine, and philosophical hermeneutics. *Recreation:* choral and organ music. *Address:* Department of Theology, University of Nottingham, University Park, Nottingham NG7 2RD. *T:* (0115) 917 6391, *Fax:* (0115) 917 6392; South View Lodge, 390 High Road, Chilwell, Nottingham NG9 5EG; *e-mail:* thiselton@ntlworld.com. *Club:* National.

THOBURN, Prof. June, CBE 2002; LittD; Professor of Social Work, University of East Anglia, Norwich, 1994–2004, now Emeritus; *b* 17 May 1939; *d* of late William Shuttleworth Bailey and Elizabeth Anne Bailey; *m* 1965, John Thomas Thoburn; two *s*. *Educ:* Univ. of Reading (BA Hons French); Oxford Univ. (Dip. Public and Soc. Admin); Univ. of East Anglia (MSW; LittD). Social worker, Social Services Depts of Leicester CC, RBK&C and Norfolk CC, 1964–79; University of East Anglia: Lectr in Social Work, 1979–94; Dean, Sch. of Social Work, 1998–2001. Non-exec. Dir, E Norfolk HA, 1994–98; Member: Pres. of Family Division's Adv. Gp, 1998–2004; Gen. Social Care Council, 2001–; Advr on child protection and adoption to DoH, 1995–2004. FRSA 2001; AcSS 2002. Editor, Child and Family Social Work, 2002–04. *Publications:* Permanence in Child Care, 1986; Child Placement: principles and practice, 1988, 2nd edn 1994; Safeguarding Children with the Children Act 1989, 1999; Permanent Family Placement for Children of Minority Ethnic Origin, 2000; Family Support in Cases of Emotional Maltreatment and Neglect, 2000; Child Welfare Services for Minority Ethnic Families, 2004. *Recreations:* dinghy sailing, films, travel. *Address:* School of Social Work, University of East Anglia, Norwich NR4 7TJ. *T:* (01603) 593566, *Fax:* (01603) 573552; *e-mail:* j.thoburn@uea.ac.uk.

THOM, Dr Gordon; International Managing Director, Dyson Ltd, 2001; *b* 18 May 1953; *m* 1977, Margaret Pringle; one *s* one *d*. *Educ:* Univ. of Aberdeen (PhD). DoE, 1978; joined FCO, 1979; Second, subseq. First Sec., Tokyo, 1981; FCO, 1985–89; First Sec., New Delhi, 1989–93; Economic Counsellor, Tokyo, 1994–98; Man. Dir, Dyson Japan, 1998–2001.

THOM, James Alexander Francis; QC 2003; a Recorder, since 2002; *b* 19 Oct. 1951; *s* of James Flockhart Thom and Elspeth Margaret Thom (*née* Macnaughton); *m* 1st, 1974, Theresa Lindsie Hawkins (marr. diss. 1997); two *s* one *d*; 2nd, 1999, Elisabeth Jane Campbell Mardall. *Educ:* Corpus Christi Coll., Oxford (MA, BCL). Called to the Bar, Middle Temple, 1974; admitted to Bar: of St Vincent and Grenadines, 1997; of British Virgin Islands, 2005. *Recreations:* walking, reading, cooking, wine. *Address:* New Square Chambers, 12 New Square, Lincoln's Inn, WC2A 3SW. *T:* (020) 7419 8000, *Fax:* (020) 7419 8050; *e-mail:* james.thom@newsquarechambers.co.uk.

THOM, Kenneth Cadwallader; HM Diplomatic Service, retired; *b* 4 Dec. 1922; *m* 1948, Patience Myra (*née* Collingridge); three *s* one *d*. *Educ:* University College School, London; St Andrews Univ. (MA (Hons)). Army Service, 1942–47; Assistant District Officer, then District Officer, Northern Nigerian Administration, 1950–59; 1st Secretary: FO, 1959; UK Mission to UN, NY, 1960–63; FO, 1963–66; Budapest, 1966–68; FCO, 1968–72; Counsellor, Dublin, 1972–74; Counsellor, FCO, 1974–78; Consul-General: Hanover, 1978–79; Hamburg, 1979–81; retired, and re-employed, FCO, 1981–85. *Address:* Heybrook, Lower Backway, Bruton, Somerset BA10 0EA.

THOMAS; see Elis-Thomas.

THOMAS, family name of **Barons Thomas of Gresford**, **Thomas of Macclesfield**, **Thomas of Swynnerton** and **Baroness Thomas of Walliswood**.

THOMAS OF GRESFORD, Baron *cr* 1996 (Life Peer), of Gresford in the co. borough of Wrexham; **Donald Martin Thomas,** OBE 1982; QC 1979; a Recorder of the Crown Court, since 1976; *b* 13 March 1937; *s* of Hywel and Olwen Thomas; *m* 1st, 1961, Nan Thomas (*née* Kerr) (*d* 2000); three *s* one *d*; 2nd, 2005, Baroness Walmsley, qv. *Educ:* Grove Park Grammar Sch., Wrexham; Peterhouse, Cambridge (MA, LLB). Solicitor at Wrexham, 1961–66; Lectr in Law, 1966–68; called to the Bar, Gray's Inn, 1967, Bencher, 1989; Barrister, Wales and Chester Circuit, 1968–; Dep. Circuit Judge, 1974–76; Dep. High Court Judge, 1985–. Mem., Criminal Injury Compensation Bd, 1985–93. Contested (L): W Flints, 1964, 1966, 1970; Wrexham, Feb. and Oct. 1974, 1979, 1983, 1987; Vice Chm., Welsh Liberal Party, 1967–69, Chm. 1969–74; President: Welsh Liberal Party,

1977, 1978, 1979; Welsh Liberal Democrats, 1993–97 (Vice-Pres., 1991–93). Chairman: Marcher Sound, 1991–2000 (ind. local radio for NE Wales and Cheshire) (Vice Chm., 1983–91); Southbank Sinfonia Develt Council, 2003–. President: London Welsh Choral, 2002–; Sirenian Singers, 2003–; Friends of Gresford Church, 1998–. *Recreations:* Rugby football, rowing, golf, music-making, fishing, cooking. *Address:* Glasfryn, Gresford, Wrexham, Clwyd LL12 8RG. *T:* (01978) 852205. *Clubs:* Reform; Western (Glasgow).

THOMAS OF MACCLESFIELD, Baron *cr* 1997 (Life Peer), of Prestbury in the co. of Cheshire; **Terence James Thomas**, CBE 1997; Managing Director, The Co-operative Bank, 1988–97; Chairman, Internexus, 2002–04; *b* 19 Oct. 1937; *s* of late William Emrys Thomas and Mildred Evelyn Thomas; *m* 1963, Lynda, *d* of late William John Stevens; three *s*. *Educ:* Queen Elizabeth Grammar Sch., Carmarthen; Univ. of Bath (Postgrad. Dip. Business Admin); INSEAD (AMP). FCIB. Nat. Provincial, later Nat. Westminster Bank, 1962–71; Joint Credit Card Co., 1971–73; The Co-operative Bank: Mkting Manager, 1973–77; Asst Gen. Manager, then Jt Gen. Manager, 1977–83; Dir, 1984; Exec. Dir, Gp Develt, 1987. Director: Stanley Leisure Organisation plc, 1994–98; Capita Gp, 1998–99; Rathbone CI, 1998–99. Chm., Venture Technic (Cheshire) Ltd, 1984–97. Director: English Partnerships (Central), 1998–99; Commn for the New Towns, 1998–99; CDA; Chairman: NW Partnership, 1994–97; Northwest Develt Agency, 1998–2002. Mem., Regl Economic Develt Commn. Mem., Gen. Council, CIB, until 1997; Pres., Internat. Co-operative Banking Assoc., 1988–95. Chm., NW Media Charitable Trust, 1998–99. Vis. Prof., Univ. of Stirling, 1988–91. Mem., Ct of Governors, UMIST, 1996–2004. Mem. Bd Trustees, UNICEF, 1998–99. FRSA; CCMI. Hon. Fellow, Univ. of Central Lancs, 2000. Hon. DLitt Salford, 1996; Hon. DBA Manchester Metropolitan, 1998; DUniv: Manchester, 1999; UMIST, 1999. Mancunian of the Year, 1998. *Publication:* An Inclusive Community with Integrity, 2008. *Address:* 51 Willowmead Drive, Prestbury, Cheshire SK10 4DD.

THOMAS OF SWYNNERTON, Baron *cr* 1981 (Life Peer), of Notting Hill in Greater London; **Hugh Swynnerton Thomas**, FRSL, FRHistS; historian; *b* 21 Oct. 1931; *s* of Hugh Whitelegge Thomas, CMG, sometime Sec. for Native Affairs, Gold Coast (Ghana) and late Margery Swynnerton, sometime Colonial Nursing Service; *m* 1962, Vanessa Jebb, *d* of 1st Baron Gladwyn, GCMG, GCVO, CB; two *s* one *d*. *Educ:* Sherborne; Queens' Coll., Cambridge (Scholar; Hon. Fellow 2008); Sorbonne, Paris. Pres. Cambridge Union, 1953. Foreign Office, 1954–57; Sec. to UK delegn to UN Disarmament Sub-Cttee, 1955–56; Lectr at RMA Sandhurst, 1957; Prof. of History, 1966–76, and Chm., Grad. Sch. of Contemp. European Studies, 1973–76, Univ. of Reading. Anshen Lectr, Frick Mus., NY, 1991; Yaseen Lectr, Met. Mus. of Art, NY, 1995. King Juan Carlos I (Vis.) Prof., New York Univ., 1995; Vis. Prof. of History, Univ. of Boston, 1996; Univ. Prof., Boston Univ., 1997–. Chm., Centre for Policy Studies, 1979–90. Trustee, Fundación Medinaceli, 1996–. Corresp. Mem., Real Acad. de la Historia, Madrid, 1994. Somerset Maugham Prize, 1962; Arts Council prize for History (1st Nat. Book Awards), 1980; Calvo Serer Prize, Diario Madrid Foundn, 2008. Order of Aztec Eagle (Mexico), 1994; Knight Grand Cross, Order of Isabel la Católica (Spain), 2001; Commandeur, Ordre des Arts et des Lettres (France), 2008. *Publications:* (as Hugh Thomas) The World's Game, 1957; The Spanish Civil War, 1961, rev. edn 1977, rev. illustrated edn, Spain, 1979; The Suez Affair, 1967; Cuba, or the Pursuit of Freedom, 1971; (ed) The selected writings of José Antonio Primo de Rivera, 1972; Goya and The Third of May 1808, 1972; Europe, the Radical Challenge, 1973; John Strachey, 1973; The Cuban Revolution, 1977; An Unfinished History of the World, 1979, rev. edn 1982 (US 1979, A History of the World); The Case for the Round Reading Room, 1983; Havannah (novel), 1984; Armed Truce, 1986; A Traveller's Companion to Madrid, 1988; Klara (novel), 1988; Ever Closer Union: Britain's destiny in Europe, 1991; The Conquest of Mexico, 1993; The Slave Trade: the history of the Atlantic slave trade 1440–1870, 1997; The Future of Europe, 1997; Who's Who of the Conquistadors, 2000; Rivers of Gold, 2003; Letter from Asturias, 2006; Beaumarchais in Seville, 2006; Don Eduardo, 2008. *Address:* 29 Ladbroke Grove, W11 3BB.

THOMAS OF WALLISWOOD, Baroness *cr* 1994 (Life Peer), of Dorking in the County of Surrey; **Susan Petronella Thomas**, OBE 1989; DL; a Deputy Speaker, House of Lords, 2002–07; Chairman, Surrey County Council, 1996–97 (Member (Lib Dem), 1985–97; Vice Chairman, 1993–96); *b* 20 Dec. 1935; *m* 1958, David Churchill Thomas, *qv*; one *s* two *d*. *Educ:* Cranborne Chase Sch.; Lady Margaret Hall, Oxford. NEDO, 1971–74; Chief Exec., British Clothing Industries Council for Europe, 1974–78. Chm. and Treas., Richmond Liberal Assoc., 1974–77; former Pres., Women Lib Dems. Chm., Highways and Transport Cttee, Surrey CC, 1993–96; Member: Surrey Probation Cttee, 1997–2001; Surrey Area Probation Bd, 2001–04. Contested: (Lib Alliance) Mole Valley, 1983 and 1987; (Lib Dem) Surrey, Eur. Parly elecns, 1994. Lib Dem spokesman, H of L, on transport, 1994–2001, on women, 2001–06, on Equality, 2007–. Chm., Associate (formerly All-Party) Parly Gp on Sex Equality, 1998–2001; Mem., H of L European Select Cttee on EU, 2005–07 (Mem., Law and Instns Sub-Cttee, 2003–05; Chm., Social and Consumer Affairs Sub-Cttee, 2005–07). DL Surrey, 1996. *Address:* House of Lords, SW1A 0PW. *T:* (020) 7219 3599, *Fax:* (020) 7219 2082.
See also Hon. D. W. P. Thomas.

THOMAS OF WINCHESTER, Baroness *cr* 2006 (Life Peer), of Winchester in the County of Hampshire; **Celia Marjorie Thomas**, MBE 1985; Head, Liberal Democrat (formerly Liberal) Whips' Office, House of Lords, 1977–2006; *b* 14 Oct. 1945; *d* of David and Marjorie Thomas. *Educ:* St Swithun's Sch., Winchester. Winchester Diocesan Bd of Finance, 1963–65; Winchester Cathedral Appeal, 1965–66; The Pilgrims' Sch., Winchester, 1967–72; Christ Church Cathedral Sch., Oxford, 1972–74; Asst in office of Rt Hon. Jeremy Thorpe, MP, 1975–76. Party Agent: (Lib) Winchester, Oct. 1974; (Lib/ SDP Alliance, later LibDem) Brecon and Radnor, 1987 and 1992. House of Lords: Member: Merits of Statutory Instruments Select Cttee, 2006–; Procedure Select Cttee, 2007–; Liaison Select Cttee, 2007–; Refreshment Select Cttee, 2007–. Chm., Keynes Forum (formerly Lib Summer Sch.), 2001–; Mem., Mgt Bd, CentreForum, 2006–. Vice-Pres., Lloyd George Soc., 2005–. Pres., Winchester Lib Dems, 2007–. *Recreations:* music, theatre, gardening, butterfly conservation, watching cricket. *Address:* House of Lords, SW1A 0PW. *T:* (020) 7219 3586; *e-mail:* thomascm@parliament.uk. *Club:* Two Brydges.

THOMAS, Prof. Adrian Tregerthen; Professor of Music, University of Wales, Cardiff, since 1996; *b* 11 June 1947; *s* of Owen George Thomas and Jean Tregerthen. *Educ:* Univ. of Nottingham (BMus 1969); University Coll., Cardiff (MA 1971). Lectr in Music, 1973–82, Sen. Lectr, 1982–85, Hamilton Harty Prof. of Music, 1985–96, QUB. Gresham Prof. of Music, 2003–06. Hd of Music, BBC Radio 3, 1990–93. Medal of Polish Composers' Union, for Distinguished Service to Contemporary Polish Music, 1989; Order of Merit for Polish Culture, 1996; Lutosławski Medal, Lutosławski Soc., 2005. *Publications:* Grazyna Bacewicz: chamber and orchestral music, USA 1985; (contrib.) Cambridge Companion to Chopin, 1992; (contrib.) New Grove Dictionary of Opera, 1993; (contrib.) New Grove Dictionary of Women Composers, 1994; Górecki, 1997; (contrib.) New Grove Dictionary of Music and Musicians, 2nd edn 2000; Polish Music since Szymanowski, 2005; contrib. Music Rev., THES, Contemp. Music Rev., Music and

Letters. *Recreations:* poetry, oriental arts, hill-walking. *Address:* School of Music, Cardiff University, Cardiff CF10 3EB.

THOMAS, Sir Alan; *see* Thomas, Sir J. A.

THOMAS, Andrew Martin; QC 2008; *b* Wrexham, 18 Oct. 1965; *s* of Martin and Nan Thomas; *m* 1995, Jodie Swallow; one *s* one *d*. *Educ:* Darland Comp. Sch., Rossett; Yale Sixth Form Coll., Wrexham; Peterhouse, Cambridge (BA 1987). Called to the Bar, Gray's Inn, 1989; barrister, 1990–. *Recreations:* family, running, ski-ing, holidaying in Scotland. *Address:* c/o 1 Stanley Place, Chester CH1 2LU. *T:* (01244) 348282; *e-mail:* clerks@ 1stanleyplace.co.uk. *Club:* Tattenhall Runners.

THOMAS, Aneurin Morgan; Director, Welsh Arts Council, 1967–84; *b* 3 April 1921; *s* of Philip Thomas and Olwen Amy Thomas (*née* Davies); *m* 1947, Mary Dineen (*d* 2005); one *s* one *d*. *Educ:* Ystalyfera Intermediate Sch., Glamorgan; Swansea School of Art and Crafts. British and Indian Armies, 1941–46 (Major). Lecturer, later Vice-Principal, Somerset College of Art, 1947–60; Vice-Principal, Hornsey College of Art, 1960–67. Member, Board of Governors: Loughborough Coll. of Art and Design, 1980–89; S Glamorgan Inst. of Higher Educn, 1985–89 (Chm., Faculty of Art and Design Adv. Cttee, 1985–90); Carmarthenshire Coll. of Tech. and Art, 1985– (Chm., Faculty of Art and Design Adv. Cttee, 1985–); Vice-President: Nat. Soc. for Art Educn, 1967–68; Llangollen Internat. Music Eisteddfod, 1970–. Chm., Assoc. of Art Instns, 1977–78. *Publications:* periodic contribs to books and professional jls. *Recreation:* observing with interest and humour, but with increasing bewilderment. *Address:* Netherwood, 8 Lower Cwrt-y-vil Road, Penarth, Vale of Glamorgan CF64 3HQ. *T:* (029) 2070 2239.

THOMAS, (Anthony) Richard, CMG 1995; HM Diplomatic Service, retired; High Commissioner, Jamaica, and non-resident Ambassador to Haiti, 1995–99; *b* 11 July 1939; *s* of Frederick James Thomas and Winifred Kate Apthorpe Webb; *m* 1976, Ricky Parks Prado, London and Lima; one *s* one *d*. *Educ:* Ampleforth; Peterhouse, Cambridge (MA). FO 1962; served Caracas, Budapest, Washington, Madrid and FCO; Counsellor, Dep. Consul-Gen., Johannesburg, 1981; Minister Counsellor and Consul-Gen., Brasilia, 1985; FCO 1989; Ambassador to Angola, São Tomé and Principe, 1993. *Recreations:* listening to music, reading, theatre, visual arts, cooking. *Address:* c/o 83 Broxash Road, SW11 6AD.

THOMAS, Prof. (Antony) Charles, CBE 1991; DL; DLitt; FSA; FRHistS; FBA 1989; Professor of Cornish Studies, University of Exeter, 1971–91, Professor Emeritus, 1993; Director, Institute of Cornish Studies, 1971–91; *b* 24 April 1928; *s* of late Donald Woodroffe Thomas and Viva Warrington Thomas; *m* 1959, Jessica Dorothea Esther, *d* of late F. A. Mann, CBE, FBA, Hon. QC; two *s* two *d*. *Educ:* Winchester; Corpus Christi Coll., Oxon (BA Hons Jurisp.); Univ. of London (Dipl. Prehist. Archaeol.; Fellow, UCL, 1993); DLitt Oxon, 1983. FSA 1960; FRHistS 1983. Lectr in Archaeology, Univ. of Edinburgh, 1957–67; Prof. of Archaeology, Univ. of Leicester, 1967–71. Leverhulme Fellowship, 1965–67; Sir John Rhys Fellow, Univ. of Oxford, and Vis. Sen. Res. Fellow, Jesus Coll., 1985–86; Emeritus Leverhulme Fellowship, 1993–95. Lectures: Dalrymple, Univ. of Glasgow, 1991; (first) Whithorn Trust, 1992; (first) John Jamieson, Scottish Church History Soc., 1997; Rhind, Edinburgh, 1999. President: Council for British Archaeology, 1970–73; Royal Instn of Cornwall, 1970–72; Cornwall Archaeol. Soc., 1984–88; Soc. for Medieval Archaeology, 1986–89; Soc. for Landscape Studies, 1993–; Cornwall Methodist History Soc., 2003–. Chairman: BBC SW Reg. Adv. Council, 1975–80; DoE Area Archaeol Cttee, Cornwall and Devon, 1975–79; Cornwall Cttee Rescue Archaeol., 1976–88; Soc. for Church Archaeol., 1995–98; Mem., Royal Commn on Historical Monuments (England), 1983–97 (Acting Chm., 1988–89; Vice Chm., 1991–97). DL Cornwall, 1988. Hon. MRIA 1973; Hon. Fellow: RSAI, 1975; St David's UC Lampeter, 1992; Hon. FSAScot 2000. Hon. DLitt NUI, 1996. William Frend Medal, Soc. of Antiquaries, 1982. *Publications:* Christian Antiquities of Camborne, 1967; The Early Christian Archaeology of North Britain, 1971; Britain and Ireland in Early Christian Times, 1971; (with A. Small and D. Wilson) St Ninian's Isle and its Treasure, 1973; (with D. Ivall) Military Insignia of Cornwall, 1974; Christianity in Roman Britain to AD 500, 1981; Exploration of a Drowned Landscape, 1985; Celtic Britain, 1986; Views and Likenesses: photographers in Cornwall and Scilly 1839–70, 1988; Tintagel, Arthur and Archaeology, 1993; And Shall These Mute Stones Speak?: post-Roman inscriptions in Western Britain, 1994; Christian Celts, Messages and Images, 1998; Silent in the Shroud, 1999; The Penzance Market Cross, 1999; Whispering Reeds, 2002; (with D. R. Howlett) Vita Sancti Paterni, 2003. *Recreations:* military history, archaeological fieldwork. *Address:* Lambessow, St Clement, Truro, Cornwall TR1 1TB.

THOMAS, Hon. Barbara; *see* Thomas Judge, Hon. Barbara Singer.

THOMAS, Catherine; Member (Lab) Llanelli, National Assembly for Wales, 2003–07; *b* 1963. *Educ:* Llanelli Girls' Grammar Sch.; Univ. of Glamorgan; Univ. of Wales, Cardiff (MSc). Formerly press and PR officer, Wales gp, Tidy Britain. Mem., Children in Wales. Contested (Lab) Llanelli, Nat. Assembly for Wales, 2007. *Address:* c/o National Assembly for Wales, Cardiff CF99 1NA.

THOMAS, Charles; *see* Thomas, A. C.

THOMAS, Ven. Charles Edward; Archdeacon of Wells, 1983–93; *b* 30 Dec. 1927. *Educ:* St David's Coll., Lampeter (BA 1951); College of the Resurrection, Mirfield. Deacon 1953, priest 1954; Curate of Ilminster, 1953–56; Chaplain and Asst Master, St Michael's Coll., Tenbury, 1956–57; Curate of St Stephen's, St Albans, 1957–58; Vicar, St Michael and All Angels, Boreham Wood, 1958–66; Rector, Monksilver with Elworthy, 1966–74, with Brompton Ralph and Nettlecombe, 1969–74 (Curate-in-charge of Nettlecombe, 1968–69); Vicar of South Petherton with the Seavingtons, 1974–83. RD of Crewkerne, 1977–82. *Address:* Geryfelin, Pentre, Tregaron, Ceredigion SY25 6ND. *T:* (01974) 298102.

THOMAS, (Christopher) Paul; consultant; *b* 9 Feb. 1951; *s* of Donald Thomas and Rita Thomas (*née* Kershaw); *m* 1981, Colleen Doey. *Educ:* Hutton Grammar Sch.; Bridlington Sch.; Keble Coll., Oxford (MA PPE). Civil Service, 1973–97: Customs & Excise, HM Treasury, Cabinet Office, Dept of Employment, and DfEE; Regl Policy Advr, Yorks and Humberside TECs, 1997–98; Dep. Chief Exec., Manchester TEC, subseq. Manchester Enterprises, 1998–2006. *Recreations:* cricket, golf, walking, sailing, jazz. *Address:* Croft Head, Aston Lane, Hope, Hope Valley, Derbys S33 6RA. *T:* (01433) 621764.

THOMAS, Christopher Sydney; QC 1989; PhD; FCIArb; a Recorder, since 2000; *b* 17 March 1950; *s* of late John Raymond Thomas and of Daphne May Thomas; *m* 1979, Patricia Jane Heath; one *s* one *d*. *Educ:* King's Sch., Worcester; Univ. of Kent at Canterbury (BA Hons, 1st Cl.); Faculté International de Droit Comparé, Paris (Diplôme de Droit Comparé (avec mérite), 1972); King's Coll., London (PhD 1994). FCIArb 1994. Hardwick Scholar and Jenkins Scholar, Lincoln's Inn; called to the Bar, Lincoln's Inn, 1973; Asst Recorder, 1994–2000. Called to Gibraltar Bar, 1989. CEDR accredited Mediator, 1999. *Recreations:* farming, sailing. *Address:* Keating Chambers, 15 Essex Street, WC2R 3AA. *T:* (020) 7544 2600.

THOMAS, Claire C.; *see* Curtis-Thomas.

THOMAS, Clarence; Associate Justice of the Supreme Court of the United States, since 1991; *b* 23 June 1948. *Educ:* Yale Univ. (JD). Asst to Attorney Gen., State of Missouri, 1974–77; attorney in private practice, 1977–79; Legislative Asst, US Senate, 1979–81; Asst Sec. for Civil Rights, Dept of Educn, Washington, 1981–82; Chm., Equal Employment Opportunity Commn, Washington, 1982–90; Judge, US Court of Appeals, 1990–91. *Publication:* My Grandfather's Son: a memoir, 2007. *Address:* United States Supreme Court, 1 First Street NE, Washington, DC 20543, USA.

THOMAS, David; *see* Thomas, W. D.

THOMAS, Rt Rev. David; Provincial Assistant Bishop, Church in Wales, 1996–2008; *b* 22 July 1942; *s* of late Rt Rev. John James Absalom Thomas; *m* 1967, Rosemary Christine Calton; one *s* one *d*. *Educ:* Christ College, Brecon; Keble College, Oxford; St Stephen's House, Oxford. MA Oxon. Curate of Hawarden, 1967–69; Tutor, St Michael's College, Llandaff, Cardiff, 1969–70, Chaplain 1970–75; Secretary, Church in Wales Liturgical Commn, 1970–75; Vice-Principal, St Stephen's House, Oxford, 1975–79; Vicar of Chepstow, 1979–82; Principal, St Stephen's House, Oxford, 1982–87; Vicar of St Peter's, Newton, Swansea, 1987–96; Residentiary Canon, Brecon Cathedral, 1994–96. Mem., Standing Doctrinal Commn, 1975–93, Standing Liturgical Adv. Commn, 1987–2008, Church in Wales. *Publication:* (contrib.) The Ministry of the Word (ed G. J. Cuming), 1979. *Recreations:* music, walking. *Address:* 65 Westland Avenue, West Cross, Swansea SA3 5NR.

THOMAS, Prof. David; Professor of Geography, University of Birmingham, 1978–95, now Professor Emeritus; *b* 16 Feb. 1931; *s* of William and Florence Grace Thomas; *m* 1955, Daphne Elizabeth Berry; one *s* one *d*. *Educ:* Bridgend Grammar School; University College of Wales, Aberystwyth (BA, MA); PhD London. Asst Lectr, Lectr, Reader, University College London, 1957–70; Prof. and Head of Dept, St David's University College, Lampeter, 1970–78; Birmingham University: Head of Dept of Geography, 1978–86; Head of Sch. of Geog., 1991–93; Pro Vice-Chancellor, 1984–89. Pres., IBG, 1988 (Hon. Sec., 1976–78); Mem., Council, RGS, 1988–91. *Publications:* Agriculture in Wales during the Napoleonic Wars, 1963; London's Green Belt, 1970; (ed) An Advanced Geography of the British Isles, 1974; (with J. A. Dawson) Man and his world, 1975; (ed) Wales: a new study, 1977; (with P. T. J. Morgan) Wales: the shaping of a nation, 1984; articles in learned jls. *Recreations:* music, wine, spectating. *Address:* 3 Is-y-Coed, Wenvoe, Cardiff CF5 6DL. *T:* (029) 2059 2861.

THOMAS, David; Principal Ombudsman, Financial Ombudsman Service, since 2000; *b* 7 Nov. 1945; *s* of late Harold Bushell Thomas and Margaret Thomas; *m* (marr. diss.); three *s* one *d*; partner, Jane Bibby. *Educ:* St Anselm's Coll., Birkenhead; Liverpool Univ. (LLB Hons 1966). Admitted Solicitor, England and Wales, 1969, Ireland, 1991; with F. S. Moore & Price, subseq. Lees Moore & Price, Birkenhead, then Lees Lloyd Whitley, Liverpool and London: Solicitor, 1969–71; Partner, 1971–84; Managing Partner, 1984–93; Chm., 1993–96; Banking Ombudsman, 1997–2000. Member: Accountancy and Actuarial Discipline (formerly Accountancy Investigation and Discipline) Bd, 2001–; Audit Adv. Cttee, Scottish Public Services Ombudsman, 2007–. Mem., Steering Cttee, FIN-NET, 2006–. Sec., 1981–86, Vice-Pres., 1986–87, Pres., 1987–88, Liverpool Law Soc.; Member: Council, Law Soc., 1987–96; Cttee, City of London Law Soc., 2005–. Mem., Council, Queen Mary, Univ. of London, 2006–. *Recreations:* modern history, theatre, naval aviation, walking. *Address:* Financial Ombudsman Service, South Quay Plaza, 183 Marsh Wall, E14 9SR. *T:* (020) 7964 1000.

THOMAS, David Bowen, PhD; Keeper, Department of Physical Sciences, Science Museum, 1984–87 (Keeper, Department of Physics, 1978–84); *b* 28 Dec. 1931; *s* of Evan Thomas and Florence Annie Bowen. *Educ:* Tredegar Grammar Sch.; Manchester Univ. (BSc). Research Fellow, Wayne Univ., Detroit, USA, 1955–57; Research Scientist, Min. of Agriculture, Fisheries and Food, Aberdeen, 1957–61; Asst Keeper, Science Museum, Dept of Chemistry, 1961–73; Keeper, Dept of Museum Services, 1973–78. Hon. FRPS 1985. *Publications:* The First Negatives, 1964; The Science Museum Photography Collection, 1969; The First Colour Motion Pictures, 1969. *Recreation:* country walking. *Address:* Tanglewood, Moushill Lane, Milford, Godalming, Surrey GU8 5BQ.

THOMAS, David Churchill, CMG 1982; HM Diplomatic Service, retired; Assistant Under Secretary of State, Foreign and Commonwealth Office, 1984–86; *b* 21 Oct. 1933; *o s* of late David Bernard Thomas and Violet Churchill Thomas (*née* Quicke); *m* 1958, Susan Petronella Arrow (*see* Baroness Thomas of Walliswood); one *s* two *d*. *Educ:* Eton Coll.; New Coll., Oxford (Exhibnr). Mod. Hist. 1st Cl., 1957. Army, 2nd Lieut, Rifle Brigade, 1952–54. Foreign Office, 1958; 3rd Sec., Moscow, 1959–61; 2nd Sec., Lisbon, 1961–64; FCO, 1964–68; 1st Sec. (Commercial), Lima, 1968–70; FCO, 1970–73; Head of South West European Dept, 1974; Asst Sec., Cabinet Office, 1973–78; Counsellor (Internal Affairs), Washington, 1978–81; Ambassador to Cuba, 1981–84. Advr on Overseas Scholarships Funding, FCO, 1989–2000. Mem., Marshall Aid Commemoration Commn, 1999–2005. Mem. Council, RIIA, 1988–94. Mem. Bd, Inst. of Latin American Studies, Univ. of London, 1988–93. Associate Fellow, Centre for Caribbean Studies, Warwick Univ., 1990–96. *Publications:* essays and review articles on Latin American affairs. *Recreations:* photography, listening to music. *Address:* 11 Crookham Road, SW6 4EG. *T:* (020) 7736 9096.

See also Hon. D. W. P. Thomas.

THOMAS, David (Edward); *b* 12 Jan. 1955; *m* 1975, Janet Elizabeth Whatrup; one *s* one *d*. *Educ:* Univ. of East Anglia (BA). Served RN, 1972–80; Suffolk Constabulary, 1980–88. Mem. (Lab), Suffolk CC, 1993–95, 2000–; Mem., Police Authy. MEP (Lab) Suffolk and SW Norfolk, 1994–99; contested (Lab) Eastern Reg., 1999.

THOMAS, David Emrys, OBE 1998; management and personnel consultant, 1991–2001; Member, Local Government Commission for England, 1992–98; *b* Ewell, 9 July 1935; *s* of Emrys and Elsie Florence Thomas; *m* 1957, Rosemary, *d* of Alexander and Kathleen De'Ath of Hampton, Middx; two *s* one *d*. *Educ:* Tiffin Grammar Sch., Kingston upon Thames. Dip. Mun. Admin; FCIPD. Local Govt Administrator, 1951–63; Indust. Relations Officer, LACSAB, 1963–68; Chief Admin. Officer, LGTB, 1968–69; Dep. Estab. Officer, Surrey CC, 1969–70; County Personnel Officer, Surrey, 1970–77; Under-Sec. (Manpower), AMA, 1977–81; Dep. Sec., 1981–87, Sec., 1987–91, LACSAB; Employers' Sec. to nat. jt negotiating councils in local govt, 1987–91; Official Side Sec., Police Negotiating Bd, 1987–91; Sec., UK Steering Cttee on Local Govt Superannuation, 1987–91. Founder Pres., Soc. of Chief Personnel Officers in Local Govt, 1975. *Recreations:* unskilled gardening, the musical theatre (Mem., Olivier Awards panel, 1998; Sec., Stage Musical Appreciation Soc., 1996–2006). *Address:* The White House, Three Pears Road, Merrow, Guildford, Surrey GU1 2XU. *T:* (01483) 569588; *e-mail:* DEThomas41@aol.com.

THOMAS, Prof. David Glyndor Treharne, FRCSE, FRCP, FRCPG, FRCS; Professor of Neurological Surgery and Head of Division of Neurological Surgery, Institute of Neurology, National Hospital, Queen Square, 1995–2006, now Emeritus Professor; *b* 14 May 1941; *s* of Dr John Glyndor Treharne Thomas, MC and Ellen Thomas (*née* Geldart); *m* 1970, Dr Hazel Agnes Christina Cockburn, FFARCS; one *s*. *Educ:* Perse Sch., Cambridge; Gonville and Caius Coll., Cambridge (BA, MA); St Mary's Hosp. Med. Sch.; MB BChir Cantab. Hosp. appts at St Mary's to 1969 and Asst Lectr in Anatomy, 1967–68; Sen. House Officer in Surgery, 1970, Registrar in Cardio-Thoracic Surgery, 1970–71, RPMS; Registrar, Sen. Registrar and Lectr in Neurosurgery, Inst. of Neur. Scis, Glasgow, 1972–76; Sen. Lectr, 1976–92, Prof. of Neurosurgery, 1992–95, Inst. of Neurology; Consultant Neurosurgeon: Nat. Hosp. for Neurology and Neurosurgery and Northwick Park Hosp., Harrow, 1976–2006; St Mary's Hosp., 1994–2006. Vice-President: Eur. Assoc. of Neurosurgical Socs, 1991–95; Eur. Soc. for Stereotactic and Functional Neurosurgery, 1994–. *Publications:* (ed with D. I. Graham) Brain Tumours, 1980; (ed with M. D. Walker) Biology of Brain Tumour, 1986; (ed) Neuro-oncology: primary brain tumours, 1989; (ed) Stereotactic and Image Directed Surgery of Brain Tumours, 1993; (ed with D. I. Graham) Malignant Brain Tumours, 1995. *Recreation:* military and naval history. *Address:* The National Hospital, Queen Square, WC1N 3BG. *T:* (020) 7391 8993; 1 Bryanston Square, W1H 2DH. *T:* (020) 7724 2614. *Clubs:* Athenæum, Royal Society of Medicine.

THOMAS, David Hugh; Chairman (non-executive), Altima Partners LLP, since 2004; *b* 6 Dec. 1951; *s* of late John William Hugh Thomas and Joyce Thomas (*née* Fox); *m* 1978, Frances Mary Brown; one *s* one *d*. *Educ:* Hertford GS; Corpus Christi Coll., Oxford (BA 1st cl. Hons Lit. Hum. 1974; Sec., then Librarian, Oxford Union Soc., 1973); St John's Coll., Oxford (MA; DPhil 1978). Joined Morgan Grenfell & Co. Ltd, 1978: Italian Export Credits, 1978–83; Eurobonds, 1983–84; Interest Rate and Currency Swaps, 1984–87; Dir, 1988–March 2002, Nov. 2002–2004; Market and Credit Risk Mgt, 1988–97; Global Head of Risk, Investment Banking Activities, Deutsche Bank Gp, 1995–98; Chief Executive: Morgan Grenfell & Co. Ltd, 1997–2002; Bankers Trust Internat. PLC, 1999–2002 (non-exec. Chm., 2002–04); non-exec. Chm., Morgan Grenfell & Co. Ltd, subseq. DB UK Bank Ltd, 2002–04; non-exec. Dir, Schroder & Co. Ltd, 2005–. Trustee, Oxford Lit. and Debating Union Trust, 2003–08. Gov., 1999–, Vice-Chm., 2002–, Abbot's Hill Sch. *Recreations:* classical studies, especially Greek history, playing the piano (very badly). *Address:* c/o Altima Partners LLP, Stirling Square, 7 Carlton Gardens, SW1Y 5AD. *T:* (020) 7968 6427.

THOMAS, Prof. David (John), MD; FRCP; Professor Emeritus of Clinical Neurosciences, Imperial College London, 2007 (Professor of Stroke Medicine, 2005); Chairman, St Mary's Therapy & Imaging Ltd, since 2006; *b* 7 Dec. 1943; *s* of Jack and Rachel Lloyd Thomas, Cwmgorse; *m* 1966, Celia Margaret Barratt, *d* of Sir Charles and Lady Barratt; two *s* three *d*. *Educ:* Alleyn's Sch.; Clare Coll., Cambridge (BA Nat. Sci. 1966; BChir 1969; MA, MB 1970); Univ. of Birmingham Med. Sch. (MD 1977). MRCP 1972, FRCP 1985. Consultant Neurologist: King Edward VII Hosp., Windsor, Heatherwood Hosp., Ascot, Wexham Park Hosp., Slough and St Mark's Hosp., Maidenhead, 1978–2000; Sen. Consultant Neurologist, St Mary's Hosp., London, 1978–2006; Sen. Lectr in Neurology, Inst. of Neurology and Hon. Consultant Neurologist, Nat. Hosp. for Neurology and Neurosurgery, 1979–2006, and Chalfont Centre for Epilepsy, 1995–2006. Sec. and Chm., Special Adv. Cttee on Neurology to RCP, 1985–91. Member: Council, Stroke Assoc., 1992–2008; Stroke Council, Amer. Heart Assoc., 1992–; European Stroke Council, 1993–. Chm., Charitable Assoc. Supplying Hosps, 1984–99 (Life Pres., 1999–). Governor, Nat. Soc. for Epilepsy, 2001–04; Trustee, Assoc. of British Neurologists, 2005–. *Publications:* Strokes and their Prevention, 1988; The Eye and Systemic Disease, 1989; Neurology: what shall I do?, 1990, 2nd edn 1997; papers on cerebrovascular disease and other neurological subjects. *Recreation:* photography. *Address:* Woolletts, Fulmer, Bucks SL3 6JE. *T:* (01753) 663698. *Club:* Royal Society of Medicine.

THOMAS, Sir David (John Godfrey), 12th Bt *cr* 1694, of Wenvoe, Glamorganshire; *b* 11 June 1961; *o s* of Sir Michael Thomas, 11th Bt and of Margaret Greta Thomas (*née* Cleland); *S* father, 2003; *m* 2004, Nicola Jane Lusty. *Educ:* Harrow; Ealing Coll. Health club owner. *Recreations:* squash, tennis. *Heir:* none. *Address:* 1 Waters Edge, Eternit Walk, SW6 6QU. *T:* and *Fax:* (020) 7381 4078. *Clubs:* Hurlingham, MCC, Escorts, Jesters.

THOMAS, David Malcolm, CBE 2000; LVO 2007; Chairman, In Kind Direct, 2004–07; *b* 20 Feb. 1944; *s* of Edward Reginald Thomas and Edna Thomas (*née* Lowcock); *m* 1969, Ursula Maria Brinkbaumer; one *s* one *d*. *Educ:* Burnage Grammar Sch.; Univ. of Manchester (BA Hons 1965); Manchester Business Sch. (Dip. Advanced Studies in Business Mgt); Harvard Business Sch. (AMP 1988). Mktg Controller, CWS, 1965–71; Regl Gen. Manager, Finefare, 1971–73; Regl Dir, Linfood, 1973–82; Regl Man. Dir, Grand Metropolitan, 1982–84; Whitbread: Regl Dir, 1984–89; Man. Dir, Whitbread Inns, 1989–91; Man. Dir, Restaurants and Leisure, 1991–97; Chief Exec., 1997–2004. Non-executive Director: Xansa, 2000–07; Sandown Park, 2004–. Mem., Honours Selection Cttee (Economy), 2005–. *Recreations:* opera, ballet, gardening, horse racing, golf, wine, foreign travel. *Address:* *e-mail:* dm.thomas@btconnect.com. *Club:* Woking Golf.

THOMAS, (David) Roger, CMG 2000; HM Diplomatic Service, retired; Senior Consultant, MEC International Ltd, since 2003; Partner, Cley Energy Consultants, since 2003; Director, Eurasia Energy Ltd, since 2006; *b* 1 Jan. 1945; *s* of late Alun Beynon Thomas, FRCS, and Doreen Thomas; *m* 1st, 1968 (marr. diss. 1977); two *d*; 2nd, 1978, Fiona Tyndall. *Educ:* Leys Sch., Cambridge; Sch. of Oriental and African Studies, London Univ. (BA Hons Turkish). Entered Foreign Office, 1968: FO, 1968–71; Third Sec. (Chancery), Cairo, 1971–74; Second Sec. (Envmt), UK Repn to EEC, Brussels, 1974–78; Consul, Ankara, 1979–82; UN and EC Dept, FCO, 1982–86; Consul (Commercial), Frankfurt, 1986–90; Consul-Gen., Stuttgart, 1990–93; Non-Proliferation, FCO, 1993–97; Ambassador to Azerbaijan, 1997–2000; Consul-Gen., San Francisco, 2001–03. *Recreations:* gardening, ski-ing, sailing, photography. *Address:* *e-mail:* roger@drthomas.f2s.com.

THOMAS, Prof. David Stephen Garfield, DPhil; Professor of Geography, since 2004, and Head, School of Geography and Environment, since 2008, University of Oxford; Fellow of Hertford College, Oxford, since 2004; *b* Dover, 2 Oct. 1958; *s* of Frederick Garfield Thomas and Ruth Muriel Thomas; *m* 1st, 1987, (Helen) Elizabeth Martin (*d* 1990); 2nd, 1992, Lucy Marie Heath; two *d*. *Educ:* Dover Grammar Sch. for Boys; Hertford Coll., Oxford (BA Hons 1980; PGCE 1981; DPhil 1984). Department of Geography, University of Sheffield: Lectr, 1984–93; Sen. Lectr, 1993–94; Prof., 1994–2004; Chm., 1997–2000; Dir, Sheffield Centre of Internat. Drylands Res., 1994–2004. Occasional Consultant, UNEP, 1990–. Mem. Council, RGS, 2001– (Hon. Sec., 2001–02; Vice Pres., 2002–05); Chm., British Geomorphological Res. Gp, 2002–03. Res. into long and short term envmtl change in drylands, dry land geomorphology, human-envmt interactions in drylands, esp. in Southern Africa. Editor, Jl of Arid Envmt,

1990–. *Publications:* Arid Zone Geomorphology, 1989, 2nd edn 1997; (with P. Shaw) The Kalahari Environment, 1991; (with N. Middleton) World Atlas of Desertification, 1992, 2nd edn 1997; (ed with R. Allison) Landscape Sensitivity, 1993; (with N. Middleton) Desertification: exploding the myth, 1995; (ed with A. Goudie) Dictionary of Physical Geography, 3rd edn 2000; (with D. Sporton) Sustainable Livelihoods in Kalahari Environments, 2002. *Recreations:* Africa, Dover Athletic FC, Cabernet Sauvignon, gardening. *Address:* School of Geography and Environment, Oxford University Centre for the Environment, Dyson-Perrins Building, South Parks Road, Oxford OX1 3QY.

THOMAS, David W.; *see* Wynford-Thomas.

THOMAS, Hon. David (William Penrose); author, journalist; *b* 17 Jan. 1959; *s* of David Churchill Thomas, *qv* and Baroness Thomas of Walliswood, *qv*; *m* 1986, Clare Jeremy; one *s* two *d. Educ:* Eton; King's College, Cambridge (BA History of Art). Freelance journalist, 1980–84; Editor, The Magazine, 1984–85; Editor, Extra Magazine, Sunday Today, 1986; Asst Editor and Chief Feature Writer, You Magazine, Mail on Sunday, 1986–89; Ed., Punch, 1989–92; TV Critic, Sunday Express, 1991–96. Young Journalist of the Year (British Press Awards), 1983; Columnist of the Year (Magazine Publishing Awards), 1989. *Publications:* Not Guilty: in defence of the modern man, 1993; Great Sporting Moments, 1990; Girl (novel), 1995; Show Me The Money, 2000; Foul Play, 2003; (as Tom Cain) The Accident Man, 2007; The Survivor, 2008; with Ian Irvine: Bilko: the Fort Baxter Story, 1985; Fame and Fortune, 1988; Sex and Shopping, 1988. *Recreations:* if only …. *Address:* c/o LAW Ltd, 14 Vernon Street, W14 0RJ. *T:* (020) 7471 7900. *Clubs:* Groucho, West Ham United.

THOMAS, Derek John, CBE 1996; DL; CPFA; Chief Executive, Surrey County Council, 1988–95; *b* 3 Dec. 1934; *s* of late James Llewellyn Thomas and Winifred Mary Thomas; *m* 1st (marr. diss.); three *d*; 2nd, 1978, Christine (*née* Brewer); one *s. Educ:* Hele's Sch., Exeter. Formerly: Treasurer's Depts: Devon CC; Corby Development Corporation; Bath CC; Taunton Bor. Council; Sen. Asst Bor. Treasurer, Poole Bor. Council; Asst County Treasurer, Gloucestershire CC; Principal Asst County Treasurer, Avon CC; County Treasurer, Surrey CC. Mem. Council, CIPFA, 1977–78, 1985–87; Mem. Cttee of Mgt, Schroder Exempt Property Unit Trust, 1981–2001. Chm., Local Management in Schools Initiative, 1988–93. Mem. Bd, Surrey TEC, 1990–95; Chm., Surrey First, 1996–2002. Chm., Disability Initiative, 1996–; Trustee, Nat. Centre for Young People with Epilepsy, 2001–08. Surrey University: Mem. Council, 1994–2004; Chm., F and GP Cttee, 1995–2004; Treas., 1997–2004. CCMI. DL Surrey, 1996. *Publication:* (ed jtly) A Fresh Start for Local Government, 1997. *Address:* Squirrels Leap, 14 Lime Avenue, Camberley, Surrey GU15 2BS. *T:* (01276) 684433.

THOMAS, Sir Derek (Morison David), KCMG 1987 (CMG 1977); HM Diplomatic Service, retired; *b* 31 Oct. 1929; *s* of K. P. D. Thomas and Mali McL. Thomas; *m* 1956, Lineke van der Mast; two *c. Educ:* Radley Coll., Abingdon; Trinity Hall, Cambridge (Mod. Langs Tripos; MA; Hon. Fellow, 1997). Articled apprentice, Dolphin Industrial Developments Ltd, 1947. Entered HM Foreign Service, 1953; Midshipman 1953, Sub-Lt 1955, RNVR; FO, 1955; 3rd, later 2nd, Sec., Moscow, 1956–59; 2nd Sec., Manila, 1959–61; UK Delegn to Brussels Conf., 1961–62; 1st Sec., FO, 1962; Sofia, 1964–67; Ottawa, 1967–69; seconded to Treasury, 1969–70; Financial Counsellor, Paris, 1971–75; Head of N American Dept, FCO, 1975–76; Asst Under Sec. of State, FCO, 1976–79; Minister Commercial and later Minister, Washington, 1979–84; Dep. Under Sec. of State for Europe and Political Dir, FCO, 1984–87; Amb. to Italy, 1987–89. European Advr to N. M. Rothschild & Sons, 1990–2004; Director: Rothschild Italia, 1990–97; Christow Consultants, 1990–99; N. M. Rothschild & Sons, 1991–99; Nexus Marketing Consultancy, 1991–92; Associate, CDP Nexus, 1990–92. Chm., Liberalisation of Trade in Services Cttee, BI, 1992–96; Mem., Export Guarantees Adv. Cttee, 1992–97. Member, Council: RIIA, 1994–97; Reading Univ., 1991–99. Chm., British Inst. of Florence, 1987–89 and 1997–2002. Hon. LLD Leicester, 2003. *Recreations:* listening to people and music; being by, in or on water; grandfathering, gardening. *Address:* Flat 1, 12 Lower Sloane Street, SW1W 8BJ; Ferme l'Epine, 14490 Planquery, France. *Clubs:* Oxford and Cambridge; Leander.

See also Sir E. W. Gladstone, Bt.

THOMAS, Donald Michael; poet and novelist; *b* Redruth, Cornwall, 27 Jan. 1935; *s* of Harold Redvers Thomas and Amy (*née* Moyle); two *s* one *d. Educ:* Redruth Grammar Sch.; Univ. High Sch., Melbourne; New Coll., Oxford (BA 1st cl. Hons in English; MA). School teacher, Teignmouth Grammar Sch., 1959–63; Lectr, Hereford Coll. of Educn, 1964–78; full-time author, 1978–. *Publications: poetry:* Penguin Modern Poets 11, 1968; Two Voices, 1968; Logan Stone, 1971; Love and Other Deaths, 1975; The Honeymoon Voyage, 1978; Dreaming in Bronze, 1981; Selected Poems, 1983; Dear Shadows, 2004; *novels:* The Flute-Player, 1979; Birthstone, 1980; The White Hotel, 1981; Russian Nights, a quintet (Ararat, 1983; Swallow, 1984; Sphinx, 1986; Summit, 1987; Lying Together, 1990); Flying in to Love, 1992; Pictures at an Exhibition, 1993; Eating Pavlova, 1994; Lady with a Laptop, 1996; Charlotte, 2000; *play:* Hell Fire Corner, 2004; *translations:* Requiem and Poem without a Hero, Akhmatova, 1976; Way of All the Earth, Akhmatova, 1979; Bronze Horseman, Pushkin, 1982; *memoirs:* Memories and Hallucinations, 1988; *biography:* Alexander Solzhenitsyn: a century in his life, 1998. *Recreations:* travel, Russia and other myths, the culture and history of Cornwall, the life of the imagination. *Address:* The Coach House, Rashleigh Vale, Truro, Cornwall TR1 1TJ.

THOMAS, Donnall; *see* Thomas, Edward D.

THOMAS, Dudley Lloyd; a District Judge (Magistrates' Courts) (formerly Stipendiary Magistrate), Somerset and Avon, 1999–2008, and Gloucestershire, 2004–08; Member: Family Proceedings Court Panel, 1991–2008; Youth Court Panel, 1994–2008; *b* 11 Jan. 1946; *s* of late Myrddin Lloyd Thomas and Marjorie Emily (*née* Morgan); *m* 1970, Dr Margaret Susan Early; two *s* (and one *s* decd). *Educ:* King Edward's Sch., Bath; Coll. of Law, London. Justices Clerk's Asst, 1966–71; admitted as solicitor, 1971; Partner, Trump & Partners, Bristol, 1973–88; called to the Bar, Gray's Inn, 1988; Metropolitan Stipendiary Magistrate, 1990–99. Mem., Western Circuit. Member: Bristol Medico-Legal Soc.; Heritage in Wales. Friend: Royal Acad. of Arts; V&A. *Recreations:* Rugby football, cricket, music, theatre, travel, walking. *Club:* Royal Over-Seas League.

THOMAS, Prof. (Edward) Donnall, MD; Member, Fred Hutchinson Cancer Research Center, Seattle, since 1974 (Director, Medical Oncology, 1974–89; Associate Director, Clinical Research Programs, 1982–89); Professor Emeritus of Medicine, University of Washington School of Medicine, Seattle, since 1990; *b* Mart, Texas, 15 March 1920; *m* 1942, Dorothy Martin; two *s* one *d. Educ:* Univ. of Texas, Austin (BA 1941; MA 1943); Harvard Medical Sch. (MD 1946). Assignments in internal medicine, US Army, 1948–50; Nat. Res. Council Postdoctoral Fellow in Medicine, Dept of Biol., MIT, 1950–51; Chief Med. Resident and Sen. Asst Resident, Peter Bent Brigham Hosp., Boston, 1951–53; Hematologist, 1953–55; Instructor in Medicine, Harvard Med. Sch. and Res. Associate, Cancer Res. Foundn, Children's Med. Center, Boston, 1953–55; Physician-in-Chief, Mary Imogene Bassett Hosp., Cooperstown, NY and Associate Clinical Prof. of Medicine,

Coll. of Physicians and Surgeons, Columbia Univ., NY, 1955–63; Prof. of Medicine, Univ. of Washington Sch. of Medicine, Seattle, 1963–90, Hd, Div. of Oncology, 1963–85. Consulting Physician, Children's Orthopedic Hosp. and Med. Center, Seattle, 1963–90; Attending Physician, Seattle: Univ. of Washington Hosp., 1963–90; Harborview Med. Center, 1963–90; Veterans Admin Hosp., 1963–90; Providence Med. Center, 1973–90; Swedish Hosp., 1975–90. Member Editorial Board: Blood, 1962–75, 1977–82; Transplantation, 1970–76; Procs Soc. Exptl Biol. and Medicine, 1974–81; Leukemia Res., 1977–87; Hematological Oncology, 1982–87; Jl Clinical Immunology, 1982–87; Amer. Jl Hematology, 1985–; Bone Marrow Transplantation, 1986–. Member: Amer. Assoc. Cancer Res.; Amer. Assoc. Physicians; Amer. Fedn Clinical Res.; Amer. Soc. Clinical Oncology; Amer. Soc. Clinical Investigation; Amer. Soc. Hematology (Pres., 1987–88); Nat. Acad. Scis and other foreign socs on related subjects. Lectures in US and UK on hematology and cancer res. Numerous awards from instns in N America and abroad incl. Nobel Prize for Physiology or Medicine, 1990; Presidential Medal of Science, 1990. *Recreations:* hunting, fishing, hiking. *Address:* c/o Fred Hutchinson Cancer Research Center, 1100 Fairview Avenue N, D5–100, PO Box 19024, Seattle, WA 98109–1024, USA.

THOMAS, Edward Stanley, FIA; Pension Director, Law Debenture Corporation plc, 2002–08; *s* of Stanley Frederick Thomas and Kate Dickason Thomas; *m* 1974, Elizabeth Mary Helen Casson; three *s* one *d. Educ:* King Edward VI Grammar Sch., Stourbridge; Slough Grammar Sch.; Clare Coll., Cambridge (MA). FIA 1974; ACII. Teacher, Sherwood Coll., Naini Tal, India, 1965; Actuarial trainee, Prudential, 1968–70; joined Bacon & Woodrow, 1970, Partner, 1978–98; Nat. Sec., Nat. Council of YMCAs, 1998–2002. Treas., Scripture Union. Liveryman, Actuaries' Co. *Club:* Royal Automobile.

THOMAS, Elizabeth; *see* Thomas, M. E.

THOMAS, Elizabeth Marjorie; Secretary General, 1979–83, Literary Consultant, 1984–85, The Authors' Lending and Copyright Society; *b* 10 Aug. 1919; *d* of Frank Porter and Marjorie Porter (*née* Pascall); *m* 1941, George Thomas; one *s* one *d. Educ:* St George's Sch., Harpenden; Girton Coll., Cambridge (BA 1st Cl.; MA 1998). Journalist, 1951–59 and Literary Editor, 1959–71, Tribune; Asst Literary Editor, New Statesman, 1971–76; Political Adviser to Rt Hon. Michael Foot, MP, Lord Pres. of the Council and Leader of the House of Commons, 1976–79. Mem., Arts Council, 1974–77 (Mem., Literature Panel, 1971–77); Chm., Literature Panel, Eastern Arts Assoc., 1978–84; Mem., British Council Bd, 1982–88. *Publication:* (ed) Tribune 21, 1959. *Address:* 27 Delavale Road, Winchcombe, Glos GL54 5YL. *T:* (01242) 602788.

THOMAS, Emyr, CBE 1980; DL; LLB, LMRTPI; General Manager, Telford New Town Development Corporation, 1969–80; Chairman, Telford Community Council, 1980–84; *b* 25 April 1920; *s* of late Brinley Thomas, MA, Aldershot; *m* 1947, Barbara J. May; one *d. Educ:* Aldershot County High School. Served War of 1939–45, RASC. Admitted Solicitor, 1947. Asst Solicitor, Exeter City Council, 1947–50; Sen. Asst Solicitor, Reading County Borough Council, 1950–53; Dep. Town Clerk, West Bromwich County Borough Council, 1953–64; Sec. and Solicitor, Dawley (later Telford) Development Corp., 1964–69. First Hon. Sec., 1968–89, Hon. Curator and Vice-Pres., 1989–, Ironbridge Gorge Museum Trust. DL Salop, 1979. *Publications:* Coalbrookdale and the Darby Family, 1999; Coalbrookdale in the 18th Century, 2001; (ed) Private Journal of Adelaide Darby of Coalbrookdale, 2004. *Recreation:* industrial archaeology. *Address:* 8 Vixen Walk, New Milton, Hampshire BH25 5RU. *T:* (01425) 628826.

THOMAS, Prof. Eric Jackson, DL; MD; Vice-Chancellor, University of Bristol, since 2001; *b* 24 March 1953; *s* of late Eric Jackson Thomas and Margaret Mary Thomas (*née* Murray); *m* 1976, Narell Marie Rennard; one *s* one *d. Educ:* Ampleforth Coll.; Univ. of Newcastle upon Tyne (MB BS 1976; MD 1987). MRCOG 1983, FRCOG 2001; FRCP 2004. Jun. hosp. posts, 1976–84; Res. Fellow, and Lectr, Univ. of Sheffield, 1984–87; Sen. Lectr, Univ. of Newcastle upon Tyne, 1987–90; Consultant Obstetrician and Gynaecologist: Newcastle Gen. Hosp., 1987–90; Princess Anne Hosp., Southampton, 1991–2001; Southampton University: Prof. of Obstetrics and Gynaecol., 1991–2001; Hd of Sch. of Medicine, 1995–98; Dean, Faculty of Medicine, Health and Biol Scis, 1998–2000. Mem., Medicines Commn, 2002–03. Chm., 7th World Congress of Endometriosis, 2000. Mem. Council, RCOG, 1995–2001 (Chm. Scientific Adv. Cttee, 1998–2000). Non-executive Director: Southampton Univ. Hosps NHS Trust, 1998–2000; Southampton and SW Hampshire HA, 2000–01. Dir, 2000–, Chm., 2003–07, Worldwide Univs Network Ltd; Member: Bd, SW RDA, 2003–08; Regl Sports Bd, 2003–06; Bd, UUK, 2006– (Chm., Res. Policy Strategy Cttee, 2006–); Chairman: HERDA-SW, 2002–04; DfES Taskforce on Increasing Voluntary Giving in Higher Educn, 2003–04. Trustee, Nat. Endometriosis Soc., 1998–2000. William Blair Bell Meml Lectr, RCOG, 1987. Founder FMedSci 1998. FRSA 1998. DL Bristol, 2005. Hon. LLD Bristol, 2004; Hon. DSc Southampton, 2006. *Publications:* (ed jtly) Modern Approaches to Endometriosis, 1991; articles on endometriosis and reproductive biology. *Recreations:* Newcastle United, golf. *Address:* University of Bristol, Senate House, Tyndall Avenue, Bristol BS8 1TH. *Club:* Athenæum.

THOMAS, Franklin Augustine; lawyer, consultant; *b* 27 May 1934; *s* of James Thomas and Viola Thomas (*née* Atherley); *m* (marr. diss.); two *s* two *d. Educ:* Columbia College, New York (BA 1956); Columbia Univ. (LLB 1963). Admitted to NY State Bar, 1964; Attorney, Fed. Housing and Home Finance Agency, NYC, 1963–64; Asst US Attorney for Southern District, NY, 1964–65; Dep. Police Comr, charge legal matters, NYC, 1965–67; Pres., Chief Exec. Officer, Bedford Stuyvesant Restoration Corp., Brooklyn, 1967–77; Pres., Ford Foundn, 1979–96. Hon. LLD: Yale, 1970; Fordham, 1972; Pratt Institute, 1974; Pace, 1977; Columbia, 1979. *Address:* 380 Lexington Avenue, New York, NY 10168, USA.

THOMAS, Gareth; barrister; *b* 25 Sept. 1954; *s* of William and Megan Thomas; *m*; one *s* one *d. Educ:* Rockferry High Sch., Birkenhead; UCW, Aberystwyth (LLB). ACII. Worked in insurance industry. Called to the Bar, Gray's Inn, 1977. Member (Lab), Flints CC, 1995–97. MP (Lab) Clwyd West, 1997–2005. Contested (Lab) Clwyd West, 2005. PPS to Sec. of State for Wales, 2001–02; to Sec. of State for NI, 2002–05. Member: Social Security Select Cttee, 1999–2001; Jt Human Rights Cttee, 2000–01. Bd Mem., N Wales Housing Assoc., 2006–. *Recreations:* walking, theatre, music. *Address:* Pine Lodge, Llanfwrog, Rhuthun, Denbighshire LL15 2LN; Atlantic Chambers, 4–6 Cook Street, Liverpool L2 9QU.

THOMAS, Gareth Richard; MP (Lab) Harrow West, since 1997; Minister of State, Department for Business, Enterprise and Regulatory Reform and Department for International Development, since 2008; *b* 15 July 1967; *s* of Howard and Susan Thomas. *Educ:* UCW, Aberystwyth (BScEcons Hons Politics 1988); Univ. of Greenwich (PGCE 1991); KCL (MA Imperial and Commonwealth Hist. 1997). Teacher, 1992–97. Mem. (Lab) Harrow BC, 1990–97. PPS to Minister Without Portfolio and Party Chairman, 2001–02, to Sec. of State for Educn and Skills, 2002–03; Parly Under-Sec. of State, DFID, 2003–08, BERR, 2007–08. Chm., Parly Renewable and Sustainable Energy Gp,

1998–2003. Chm., Co-op Party, 2000–. *Publications:* At the Energy Crossroads (pamphlet), 2001; From Margins to Mainstream: making social responsibility part of corporate culture (pamphlet), 2002. *Recreations:* theatre, road running, supporting Arsenal, Swansea City FC and Harrow Borough FC, watching London Welsh RFC. *Address:* House of Commons, SW1A 0AA.

THOMAS, Dr Geoffrey Price; Director, University of Oxford Department for Continuing Education, 1986–2007; President, Kellogg College (formerly Rewley House), 1990–2007, now President Emeritus (Honorary Fellow, 2008); *b* 3 July 1941; *s* of Richard Lewis Thomas and Aerona (*née* Price); *m* 1965, Judith Vaughan, *d* of Arsul John Williams; two *d*. *Educ:* Maesteg Grammar Sch.; UC of Swansea (BSc 1st Cl. Hons Physics); Churchill Coll., Cambridge (PhD 1966); Univ. of Oxford (MA). Post-doctoral res., Cavendish Lab., Univ. of Cambridge, 1966–67; Staff Tutor, UC of Swansea, 1967–78; Dep. Dir, Dept of Ext. Studies, Univ. of Oxford, 1978–86; Fellow, Linacre Coll., Oxford, 1978–90, Hon. Fellow, 1990. Co-Chm., Council on Scientific Literacy, Chicago Acad. of Sci., 1993–. Mem., HEFCW, 2000–. Visiting Scholar: Smithsonian Instn, 1986; Northern Illinois Univ., 1986; Univ. of Calif, Berkeley, 1993; Univ. of Washington, 1993; Harvard Univ., 1993; Univ. of Georgia, 1999. Hon. Fellow, Trinity Coll., Carmarthen, 2007. *Publications:* (ed jtly) The Nuclear Arms Race, 1982; (ed jtly) Science and Sporting Performance, 1982; numerous articles on public understanding of science, and on continuing educn policy. *Address:* c/o Kellogg College, 62 Banbury Road, Oxford OX2 6PN. *Club:* Oxford and Cambridge.

THOMAS, Prof. Geraint Wynn, DPhil; Professor of Equity and Property Law, Queen Mary School of Law, University of London, since 1999; *b* 10 Aug. 1948; *s* of David and Mair Thomas; *m* 1972, Janice Lilian Tilden; one *s* one *d* (and one *d* decd). *Educ:* Ardudwy Sch., Harlech; University Coll. of Swansea (BA 1969); Balliol Coll., Oxford (DPhil 1974). Called to the Bar, Inner Temple, 1976; in practice as barrister, specialising in trusts, estate, planning and pensions, 1981–2002; Lectr in Law, Univ. of Kent, 1976–91; Sen. Lectr in Law, QMW, 1995–99. *Publications:* Taxation and Trusts, 1981; Powers, 1998; (with A. Hudson) The Law of Trusts, 2004; (contrib.) International Trust Laws, ed J. Glasson, 2002. *Address:* School of Law, Queen Mary and Westfield College, University of London, E1 4NS. *T:* (020) 7882 3603; *e-mail:* G.W.Thomas@qmul.ac.uk.

THOMAS, Sir (Gilbert) Stanley, Kt 2006; OBE 1994; Co-Founder and Chairman, TBI, airport owner and operator, 1993–2005; *b* 20 Sept. 1941; *s* of Thomas Stanley Thomas, MBE and Connie Thomas; *m* 1962, Shirley Mary Powell; two *s* one *d*. Food manufacturer; founder and Jt Man. Dir, Peter's Savoury Products Ltd, 1970–88, when co. sold. Pres., Boys' and Girls' Clubs of Wales, 1991–; Chairman: Noah's Ark Appeal, 1999–; NSPCC Full Stop Campaign, Wales, 2005–. Freeman of Merthyr Tydfil, 2000. OStJ 1996. *Recreations:* Rugby, golf, sailing. *Address:* The Paddocks, Druidstone Road, St Mellons, Cardiff CF3 6XD. *T:* (029) 2079 5840. *Clubs:* Cardiff Rugby; La Moye Golf (Jersey); Aloha Golf (Marbella).

THOMAS, Gwenda; Member (Lab) Neath, National Assembly for Wales, since 1999; *b* 22 Jan. 1942; *d* of Hermas and Menai Evans (*née* Parry); *m* 1963, Morgan Thomas; one *s*. *Educ:* Pontardawe Grammar Sch. Clerical Officer, County Courts Br., LCD; Exec. Officer, Benefits Agency. Member: Gwaun Cae Gurwen Community Council, 1986–99 (Chm., 1988–89); Llanguicke Community Council, 1981–86; W Glamorgan CC, 1989–96 (Chm., Social Services Cttee); Neath Port Talbot CBC, 1996–99 (Chm., Social Services Cttee). Chm., review into services for vulnerable children, 2003–06 (report, Keeping Us Safe, 2006). Dep. Minister for Social Services, Nat. Assembly for Wales, 2007–. Mem., CPSA (Br. Chm., 1974–84). *Address:* National Assembly for Wales, Cardiff Bay, Cardiff CF99 1NA.

THOMAS, Gwyn Edward Ward, CBE 1973; DFC; Chairman and Chief Executive, Yorkshire-Tyne Tees Television Holdings plc; Chairman, Irving International, since 2005; *b* 1 Aug. 1923; *o s* of William J. and Constance Thomas; *m* 1st, 1945, Patricia Cornelius (marr. diss. 1989); one *d*; 2nd, 1991, Janice Thomas; one *s*. *Educ:* Bloxham Sch.; The Lycée, Rouen. Served RAF, 1 Group Bomber Command and 229 Group Transport Command, 1941–46. Swissair, 1947–53; Granada Television, 1955–61; Man. Dir, Grampian Television, 1961–67; Man. Dir, 1967–73, Dep. Chm., 1973–81, Yorkshire Television; Man. Dir, 1970–84, Chm., 1976–84, Trident Television. Chairman: Castlewood Investments Ltd, 1969–83; Don Robinson Holdings Ltd, 1969–83; Watts & Corry Ltd, 1969–83; Trident Casinos, 1982–84. British Bureau of Television Advertising: Dir, 1966; Chm., 1968–70; Mem. Council, Independent Television Companies Assoc., 1961–76 (Chairman: Labour Relations Cttee, 1967; Network Programme Cttee, 1971). Croix de Guerre, 1945. *Recreations:* ski-ing, boats, photography. *Address:* Pipers Lodge, Pipers End, Wentworth, Surrey GU25 4AW. *Club:* British Racing Drivers'.

THOMAS, Harvey, CBE 1990; international public relations consultant, since 1976; Consultant Director of Presentation, Conservative Party, 1986–91; *b* 10 April 1939; *s* of John Humphrey Kenneth Thomas and Olga Rosina Thomas (*née* Noake); *m* 1978, Marlies (*née* Kram); two *d*. *Educ:* Westminster School; Northwestern Bible College, Minneapolis; Univs of Minnesota and Hawaii. Billy Graham Evangelistic Assoc., 1960–75; Dir of Press and Communications, Conservative Party, 1985–86; Producer, Jeddah Economic Forum, 2006–07. Mem., Bd of Dirs, London Cremation Co., 1984–. FCIPR, FCIJ, FRSA. *Publications:* In the Face of Fear, 1985; Making an Impact, 1989; If they haven't heard it—you haven't said it, 1995, 2000. *Recreations:* travel, family, trains. *Address:* 23 The Service Road, Potters Bar, Herts EN6 1QA. *T:* (01707) 649910, *Fax:* (01707) 662653; *e-mail:* harvey@hthomas.net. *Club:* Institute of Directors.

THOMAS, Helen Frances Octavia; Head, Strategic Policy (formerly Strategy and Equality) Division, Welsh Assembly Government, since 2006; *b* 21 Sept. 1950; *d* of George Longmate Proctor and Anne Innes Louie Angus; marr. diss.; two *d*. *Educ:* Red Maids' Sch., Bristol; Newnham Coll., Cambridge (BA 1973; MA); UWCC (MSc Econ 1992); Univ. of Glamorgan (MA 2006). Joined Welsh Office as Admin. Trainee, 1975; Principal, Schs Curriculum Div., 1987–90; Asst Sec., Central Mgt Services, 1991–97; Grade 5, Social Services and Children, 1997–99; National Assembly for Wales, later Welsh Assembly Government: Dir, Social Policy Gp, 1999–2004; Dir, Regulation and Inspection Review, 2004–06. *Recreation:* women's history. *Address:* c/o Welsh Assembly Government, Cathays Park, Cardiff CF10 3NQ. *T:* (029) 2081 1292.

THOMAS, Prof. Howard, DSc; Dean, Warwick Business School, University of Warwick, since 2000; *b* 31 Jan. 1943; *m* 1978. *Educ:* LSE (BSc 1964, MSc 1965); Univ. of Chicago (MBA 1966); Edinburgh Univ. (PhD 1970; DSc 2007). First Internat. Business Prog. Fellow, Grad. Sch. of Business, Univ. of Chicago, 1965–66; Lectr in Stats and Operational Res., Univ. of Edinburgh, 1966–69; Lectr, Sen. Lectr, then Adjunct Prof., London Business Sch., 1969–77; Foundn Prof. of Mgt, Australian Grad. Sch. of Mgt, Sydney, 1977–80; University of Illinois, Urbana-Champaign: James F. Towey Prof. of Strategic Mgt, Coll. of Business Admin, 1980–2000; Dean, Coll. of Business Admin, 1991–2000; Prof. Emer. and Dean Emer., 2000. Visiting Professor: Harvard Business Sch., 1970; USC, 1975; UBC, 1979; Sloan Sch. of Mgt, MIT, 1987; Kellogg Sch. of Mgt, Northwestern Univ., 1990. *Publications:* (with H. Behrend) Incomes Policy and the Individual, 1967; Decision Theory and the Manager, 1972; (with P. G. Moore) Case Studies in Decision Analysis, 1976; (with P. G. Moore) Anatomy of Decisions, 1976, 2nd edn 1988; (with G. M. Kaufman) Modern Decision Analysis, 1977; (with D. W. Bunn) Formal Methods in Policy Formulation, 1978; (with D. B. Hertz) Risk Analysis and its Applications, 1983; (with D. B. Hertz) Practical Risk Analysis, 1984; (with J. McGee) Strategic Management Research: an European perspective, 1986; (jtly) Managing Ambiguity and Change, 1988; (with R. Bettis) Risk and Strategy, 1990; (with H. Daems) Strategic Groups, Strategic Moves and Performance, 1994; (jtly) Building the Strategically–Responsive Organization, 1995; (jtly) Strategic Renaissance and Business Transformation, 1995; (jtly) Entrepreneurship: perspectives on theory building, 1995; (with W. C. Bogner) Drugs to Market, 1996; (with D. O'Neal) Strategic Integration, 1996; (jtly) Dynamics of Competence–Based Competition: theory and practice of competence–based competition, 1996; (jtly) Strategy, Structure and Style, 1997; (jtly) Strategic Discovery: competing in new arenas, 1997; (jtly) Auditing Organizations Through a Strategic Systems Lens, 1997; (jtly) Strategic Flexibility: managing in a turbulent environment, 1998; (jtly) Handbook of Strategy and Management, 2001; (jtly) Strategy: analysis and practice, 2005; numerous articles in Jl Business Venturing, Jl Mgt Studies, Strategic Mgt Jl, Acad. of Mgt Jl, Acad. of Mgt Rev, Admin. Sci. Qly. *Recreations:* golf, Rugby (spectating), reading, swimming. *Address:* Warwick Business School, University of Warwick, Coventry CV4 7AL. *T:* (024) 7652 4534, *Fax:* (024) 7657 4170; *e-mail:* Howard.Thomas@wbs.ac.uk.

THOMAS, Prof. Howard Christopher, PhD; FRCP, FRCPath, FMedSci; Professor of Medicine, since 1987, Head of Department of Hepatology and Gastroenterology, since 2004, Vice Chairman, Division of Medicine, 1997–2004, and Clinical Dean, 2001–04, Imperial College Faculty of Medicine (formerly St Mary's Hospital Medical School), London University; *b* 31 July 1945; *s* of Harold Thomas and Hilda Thomas; *m* 1975, Dilys Ferguson; two *s* one *d*. *Educ:* Univ. of Newcastle (BSc Physiol; MB, BS); PhD Glasgow. MRCPath 1983, FRCPath 1992; MRCP 1969, FRCP 1983; FRCPGlas 1984. Lectr in Immunology, Glasgow Univ., 1971–74; Royal Free Hospital Medical School, London: Lectr in Medicine, 1974–78; Sen. Wellcome Fellow in Clin. Sci., 1978–83; Reader in Medicine, 1983–84; Titular Prof. of Medicine, 1984–87; Chm., Dept of Medicine, St Mary's Hosp. Med. Sch., London Univ., 1987–97; Consultant Physician and Hepatologist, St Mary's Hosp., 1987–. Non-exec. Dir, Riotech Pharmaceuticals, 2004–. Member: Scientific Cttee, European Assoc. for Study of Liver, 1983–86; DoH Adv. Gp on Infected Health Care Personnel, 1994–2000; Australian Cttee to Review Nat. Hepatitis C Strategy, 2002–03; Nat. Expert Panel on New and Emerging Infections, 2003–; Adv. Bd, German Network of Competence in Medicine (viral hepatitis) (Hep-Net), 2003–; British Liver Disease Clinical Interest Gp, 2007–; Comprehensive CRN (hepatology gp), 2007; DoH Ad Hoc Hepatology Expert Gp, 2007; Chairman: DoH Adv. Gp on Hepatitis, 1999–; DoH Strategy Cttee on Hepatitis C, 2001–02; NW Thames Hepatology Network, 2004–; Pan-London Hepatitis Commissioning Gp, 2004–06. Vice Pres., British Liver Trust, 2000–; Pres., British and Eur. Assocs for Study of the Liver, 1996–97; Mem., Assoc. of Physicians of GB and Ireland, 1983–; Member Council: RCP, 2002–04; British Soc. of Gastroenterol., 2002–05. Chm. of Trustees, Liver Res. Trust, 1987–; Trustee, Hepatitis B Foundn, 2007–. Editor, Jl of Viral Hepatitis, 1993–. Lectures: Humphry Davy Rolleston, 1986; Cohen, Israel, 1988; Bushell, Australia, 1990; Ralph Wright, Southampton, 1999; Sheila Sherlock, British Soc. of Gastroenterol., 2005. FMedSci 1999. British Soc. of Gastroenterol. Res. Medal, 1984; Hans Popper Internat. Prize for Distinction in Hepatology, 1989; Ivanovsky Medal of Russian Acad. of Med. Scis, 1997. *Publications:* Clinical Gastrointestinal Immunology, 1979; (ed jtly) Recent Advances in Hepatology, vol. 1, 1983, vol. 2, 1986; (ed jtly) Viral Hepatitis, 1996, 3rd edn 2005; pubns in Hepatology. *Recreations:* fishing, golf. *Address:* Department of Medicine, Imperial College Faculty of Medicine, St Mary's Hospital, Praed Street, W2 1PG. *T:* (020) 7725 6454. *Club:* Athenæum.

THOMAS, Hugh; *see* Thomas of Swynnerton, Baron.

THOMAS, Rev. (Hywel) Rhodri Glyn; Member (Plaid Cymru) Carmarthen East and Dinefwr, National Assembly for Wales, since 1999; Minister for Heritage, since 2007; *b* 11 April 1953; *s* of late Thomas Glyn Thomas and Eleanor Glyn Thomas; *m* 1975, Marian Gwenfair Davies; two *s* one *d*. *Educ:* Ysgol Morgan Llwyd, Wrexham; UCW, Aberystwyth, Bangor and Lampeter. Minister of Religion, St Clears Area, 1978–89 and 1992–; Man. Dir, Cwmni'r Gannwyll Cyf, 1989–95; Welsh Spokesman, Forum of Private Business, 1992–99; Dir, "Sgript" Cyf, 1992–. National Assembly for Wales: Shadow Minister for Agricl and Rural Affairs, 2002–03, for Envmt, Planning and the Countryside, 2003; for Health and Social Services, 2004–05; Chairman: Agricl and Rural Affairs Cttee, 1999–2000; Culture Cttee, 2000–03; SW Wales Regl Cttee, 2001–02; HSS Cttee, 2006–; Dep. Ldr, Plaid Cymru Assembly Gp, 2003–. *Address:* National Assembly for Wales, Cardiff Bay, Cardiff CF99 1NA; Llanddwyn, Llangynin, St Clears, Carmarthenshire SA33 4JY; (office) 37 Wind Street, Ammanford, Carmarthenshire SA18 3DN.

THOMAS, Prof. Hywel Rhys, PhD, DSc; CEng, FREng; FICE; FGS; Professor of Civil Engineering, since 1995, and Head, since 2002, Cardiff School of Engineering, Cardiff University (formerly University of Wales College of Cardiff); *b* 20 April 1951; *s* of Howard Lionel Thomas and Elizabeth Sybil Thomas; *m*; one *s* two *d*. *Educ:* UC, Swansea (BSc 1st cl. Hons (Civil Engrg); PhD 1980); Imperial Coll., London (MSc (Soil Mechanics) 1973; DIC); Univ. of Wales (DSc 1994). CEng 1977; FICE 2000. Grad. engr, 1973–76, then Asst Resident Engr, 1976–78, Scott Wilson Kirkpatrick and Partners; Sen. Res. Asst, UC, Swansea, 1978–80; University College Cardiff, later University of Wales College of Cardiff: Lectr in Civil Engrg, 1980–90; Sen. Lectr, Sch. of Engrg, 1990–92; Reader, 1992–95; Cardiff School of Engineering: Dir, Geoenvmtl Res. Centre, 1996–; Sen. Dep. Hd, 1999–2002; Hd, Div. of Civil Engrg, 2002. FREng 2003. *Publications:* The Finite Element Method in Heat Transfer Analysis, 1996; numerous contribs to learned jls. *Address:* Cardiff School of Engineering, Cardiff University, Queen's Building, Newport Road, Cardiff CF24 3AA. *T:* (029) 2087 4965, *Fax:* (029) 2087 4004; *e-mail:* thomashr@cardiff.ac.uk.

THOMAS, Prof. Hywel Rhys, PhD; Professor of the Economics of Education, University of Birmingham, since 1993; *b* 11 Jan. 1947; *s* of John Howard Thomas and Eva Beryl Thomas (*née* James); *m* 1st, 1968, Patricia Anne Beard (marr. diss.); 2nd, 1980, Christine MacArthur; one *s* two *d*. *Educ:* Llanelli Boys' Grammar Sch.; Univ. of Manchester (BA, MEd, PGCE); Univ. of Birmingham (PhD 1988). Parkinson Cowan Ltd, 1968–69; teacher: New Mills Sch., Derbys, 1970–73; Kersal High Sch., Salford, 1974–79; University of Birmingham: Lectr, 1979–89; Sen. Lectr, 1989–91; Reader, 1991–93; Hd, Sch. of Educn, 1993–2003; Dir of Lifelong Learning, 2000–02; Dir, Centre for Res. in Med. and Dental Educn, 2001–. Sen. Educn Advr, British Council, 1997–2000. Hon. FRCGP 2006. *Publications:* Managing Education: the system and the institution, 1985; Economics and Education Management, 1986; Education Costs and Performance, 1990; Financial Delegation and Local Management of Schools, 1990; Managing Resources for School Improvement, 1996; Schools at the Centre?, 1997.

Address: School of Education, University of Birmingham, Edgbaston, Birmingham B15 2TT. *T:* (0121) 415 8288; 30 Linden Road, Bournville, Birmingham B30 1JU.

THOMAS, James Bowen, CMG 1989; Senior Director, Global Security, Pfizer Inc., New York, 1999–2009; *b* 3 July 1942; *s* of William George Thomas and Rose Thomas (*née* Bowen); *m* 1966, Gaynor Margaret Wilkins (*d* 2005); one *s* one *d*. *Educ:* Queen Elizabeth I Grammar Sch., Carmarthen; University Coll. of Wales, Aberystwyth (BA Hons; MSc Econ. Internat. Politics). Lectr in Modern Chinese Hist., Oxford Poly., 1968–71; MoD, 1971–99; attached to FCO as First Sec., Washington, 1979–81. Trustee, Surrey Care Trust, 2008–. *Recreations:* Rugby (Welsh), travel, the visual arts, giving TLC to old properties. *Address: e-mail:* jamesbowenthomascmg@hotmail.com.

THOMAS, Dame Jean Olwen, DBE 2005 (CBE 1993); ScD; FMedSci; FRS 1986; Master of St Catharine's College, Cambridge, since 2007; Professor of Macromolecular Biochemistry, University of Cambridge, since 1991; *b* 1 Oct. 1942; *o c* of John Robert Thomas and Lorna Prunella Thomas (*née* Harris). *Educ:* Llwyn-y-Bryn High School for Girls, Swansea; University Coll., Swansea, Univ. of Wales (BSc and Ayling Prize, 1964; PhD and Hinkel Research Prize, 1967 (Chem.)); MA Cantab 1969; ScD Cantab 1985. Beit Meml Fellow, MRC Lab. of Molecular Biology, Cambridge, 1967–69; Cambridge University: Demonstrator in Biochemistry, 1969–73; Lectr, 1973–87; Reader in the Biochemistry of Macromolecules, 1987–91; New Hall, Cambridge: Fellow, 1969–2006; Coll. Lectr, 1969–91; Tutor, 1970–76; Vice-Pres., 1983–87; Hon. Fellow, 2007. Chm., Cambridge Centre for Molecular Recognition, 1993–2002. Member: SERC, 1990–94; Council, Royal Soc., 1990–92, 2007–; EPSRC, 1994–97; Council and Scientific Adv. Cttee, ICRF, 1994–2001; Scientific Adv. Cttee, Lister Inst., 1994–2000. Pres., Biochemical Soc., 2001–05. Trustee, BM, 1994–2004. Gov., Wellcome Trust, 2000–07; Pres., Techniquest, 2005–. Mem., EMBO, 1982; MAE 1991; FMedSci 2002. Hon. Fellow: UCW, Swansea, 1987; Univ. of Wales, Cardiff, 1998; Darwin Coll., Cambridge, 2007. Hon. DSc: Wales, 1992; UEA, 2003; London, 2007. K. M. Stott Research Prize, Newnham Coll., Cambridge, 1976. *Publications:* Companion to Biochemistry: selected topics for further study, vol. 1, 1974, vol. 2, 1979 (ed jtly and contrib.); papers in sci. jls, esp. on chromatin structure and DNA-binding proteins. *Recreations:* reading, music, walking. *Address:* Department of Biochemistry, 80 Tennis Court Road, Cambridge CB2 1GA. *T:* (01223) 333670; St Catharine's College, Cambridge CB2 1RL. *T:* (01223) 338349.

THOMAS, Jenkin; HM Diplomatic Service, retired; Deputy UK Permanent Representative and Counsellor (Economic and Financial), OECD, Paris, 1990–94; *b* 2 Jan. 1938; *s* of late William John Thomas and of Annie Muriel (*née* Thomas). *Educ:* Maesydderwen Sch.; University Coll. London (BA Hons); Univ. of Michigan, Ann Arbor (MA). Joined HM Foreign (subseq. Diplomatic) Service, 1960; Foreign Office, 1960–63; Pretoria/Cape Town, 1963–66; Saigon, 1966–68; FCO, 1968–73; Washington, 1973–77; FCO, 1977–79; Cabinet Office, 1979–80; Tokyo, 1980–82; Athens, 1982–87; FCO, 1987–90. Mem., Council, Cymmrodorion Soc. *Recreations:* reading, music, amateur musical comedies. *Address:* 43 Charleville Mansions, Charleville Road, W14 9JA.

THOMAS, Sir Jeremy (Cashel), KCMG 1987 (CMG 1980); HM Diplomatic Service, retired; *b* 1 June 1931; *s* of Rev. H. C. Thomas and Margaret Betty (*née* Humby); *m* 1957, Diana Mary Summerhayes; three *s*. *Educ:* Eton; Merton Coll., Oxford. 16th/5th Lancers, 1949–51. Entered FO, 1954; served Singapore, Rome and Belgrade; Dep. Head, Personnel Ops Dept, FCO, 1970–74; Counsellor and Head of Chancery, UK Mission to UN, NY, 1974–76; Head of Perm. Under-Sec.'s Dept, FCO, 1977–79; Ambassador to Luxembourg, 1979–82; Asst Under-Sec. of State, FCO, 1982–85; Ambassador to Greece, 1985–89. Chm., Chichester Harbour Trust, 2002–. *Publication:* The Rhythm of the Tide: tales through the ages of Chichester Harbour, 1999. *Recreations:* sailing, fishing. *Address:* East Manor Farm, Pook Lane, East Lavant, near Chichester, West Sussex PO18 0AH. *T:* (01243) 531661. *Clubs:* Oxford and Cambridge; Itchenor Sailing, Bosham Sailing.

THOMAS, Maj. Gen. Jeremy Hywel, DSO 2007; Senior British Military Advisor to Headquarters United States Central Command, Tampa, since 2007; *b* 12 April 1957; *s* of Brian and Eslie Thomas; *m* 1978, Oenone French; one *s* one *d*. *Educ:* Worthing High Sch. for Boys; Worthing Sixth Form Coll. Royal Marines: joined, 1975; Army Staff Coll., Camberley, 1989; Comdr L Company, 42 Commando, 1993–95; COS 3 Commando Bde, 1995–97; Comdr 45 Commando Gp, 1997–99; COS Jt Force HQ, 1999–2001; HCSC 2000; Dir Intelligence Ops, Defence Intelligence Staff, 2003–05; Commanded: 3 Commando Bde, 2006–07; UK Task Force in Afghanistan, Oct. 2006–April 2007. *Recreations:* gardening, reading, running, spending time with my wife and children on bikes, boards and skis. *Address:* UK SBMA, BFPO 651. *T:* (813) 8271043.

THOMAS, Jeremy Jack; film producer; Chairman, Recorded Picture Co., since 1973; *b* 26 July 1949; *s* of late Ralph Philip Thomas, MC and Joy Thomas; *m* 1st, 1977, Claudia Frolich (marr. diss. 1981); one *d*; 2nd, 1982, Vivien Coughman; two *s*. *Educ:* Millfield. Has worked in most aspects of film prodn, esp. in editing dept before becoming a producer. Chm., BFI, 1993–97. Producer: Mad Dog Morgan, 1974; The Shout, 1977; The Great Rock 'n Roll Swindle, 1979; Bad Timing, 1980; Merry Christmas, Mr Lawrence, 1982; Eureka, 1982; The Hit, 1984; Insignificance, 1985; The Last Emperor, 1987 (9 Acad. Awards incl. Best Film); Everybody Wins, 1990; The Sheltering Sky, 1990; The Naked Lunch, 1991; Let Him Have It, 1991; Little Buddha, 1992; Stealing Beauty, 1996; The Brave, 1996; Blood and Wine, 1997; Brother, 1999; Sexy Beast, 2001; Young Adam, 2003; The Dreamers, 2003; Tideland, 2006; Fast Food Nation, 2007; Franklyn, 2008; Executive Producer: Crash, 1995; The Cup, 1999; Gohatto, 1999; Triumph of Love, 2001; Rabbit Proof Fence, 2002; Promised Land Hotel, 2004; Dreaming Lhasa, 2004; Don't Come Knocking, 2004; Glastonbury, 2005; Joe Strummer: the future is unwritten, 2007; Palermo Shooting, 2008; Prod./Dir, All The Little Animals, 1998. Special Award for Outstanding Contribn to Cinema, Evening Standard, 1990; Michael Balcon Award for Outstanding Contribn to Cinema, BAFTA, 1991; European Achievement in World Cinema, European Film Awards, 2006; Life Fellow, BFI, 1998. *Clubs:* Garrick, Royal Automobile.

THOMAS, Sir (John) Alan, Kt 1993; Chairman: Three Valleys Water plc, since 2000; Hyder Consulting plc, since 2002; Global Design Technologies LLC, since 2005; *b* 4 Jan. 1943; *s* of late Idris Thomas and of Ellen Constance Thomas (*née* Noakes); *m* 1966, Angela Taylor; two *s*. *Educ:* Dynevor Sch.; Nottingham Univ. (Richard Thomas & Baldwin's Industrial Schol.; BSc Mech. Engrg). FCMA (First Prizewinner); CEng; FIET. Chief Exec., Data Logic, 1973–85; Vice Pres., Raytheon Co. (US), 1985–89; Pres. and Chief Exec. Officer, Raytheon Europe, 1985–89; Chm., Tag Semi-Conductors (US), 1985–89; Dir, Eur. subsids, 1978–89; seconded to MoD as Head of Defence Export Services Orgn, 1989–94. Chairman: Micro Quoted Growth Trust plc, 1997–2001; Chelverton Asset Mgt, 1997–2005; Director: Powergen plc, 1996–99; Radstone Technology plc, 2004–06; Sen. Industrial Advr, OFWAT, 1997–2000. Member: Defence Industries Council, 1990–94; Engrg Council, 1994–96. Dir, Centre for Policy Studies, 1996–2003. University of Westminster (formerly Polytechnic of Central London): Vis. Prof., 1981–; Gov., 1989–2005, Chm., Ct of Govs, 1999–2005. Dir, London Welsh RFC, 1997–. Pres., Computing Services Assoc., 1980–81. Liveryman, Co. of Information Technologists, 1988–. Hon. DSc Westminster, 2005. *Recreations:* music, sport. *Address:* (office) Three Valleys Water plc, Bishops Rise, Hatfield, Herts AL10 9HL. *T:* (01707) 277306; *e-mail:* siralanthomas@aol.com. *Club:* Athenæum.

THOMAS, Dr John Anthony Griffiths; Director and Trustee: Relate Avon, since 2004; Bath Festivals, since 2007; publishing consultant; *b* 28 Aug. 1943; *s* of late William and Bernice Thomas; *m* 1965, Sylvia Jean Norman; two *d*. *Educ:* Leeds Univ. (BSc Chem. 1965); Univ. of Keele (PhD 1968). Teacher of Chemistry, Leeds Grammar Sch., 1968–69; Reed Business Publishing Ltd: Editor, 1969–75; Editorial Dir, 1975–77; Publishing Dir, 1977–84; Divisional Man. Dir, Med. Div., 1984–86; BBC Enterprises Ltd: Dir, BBC Magazines and Electronic Publishing Gp, 1986–93; Man. Dir, 1993–94; Managing Director: BBC Worldwide Television Ltd, 1994–95; BBC Worldwide Learning, 1995–97; Dep. Chm., BBC Worldwide Publishing, 1994–97; Dir, BBC Worldwide Ltd, 1994–97. Chairman: Redwood Publishing Ltd, 1988–93; Frontline Ltd, 1990–94; BBC Haymarket Exhibns Ltd, 1992–94; Galleon Ltd, 1993–94; Dir, Periodicals Publishing Assoc., 1989–94. Stanford Univ. Alumni, 1991. Mem., BPsS, 2004. *Publications:* (ed) Energy Modelling, 1974; Energy Today, 1977; (ed) Energy Analysis, 1977; The Quest for Fuel, 1978. *Recreations:* psychology, reading, music, walking.

THOMAS, Prof. John David, PhD; FBA 1989; Professorial Fellow in Papyrology, University of Durham, 1990–92, now Emeritus Professor; *b* 23 June 1931; *s* of Henry Thomas and Elsie Thomas (*née* Bruin); *m* 1956, Marion Amy Peach; two *s*. *Educ:* Wyggeston Grammar Sch., Leicester; Worcester Coll., Oxford (MA); PhD Wales. Lectr in Classics, UCW, Aberystwyth, 1955–66; University of Durham: Lectr, then Sen. Lectr in Palaeography, 1966–77; Reader in Papyrology, 1977–90. Vis. Fellow, Wolfson Coll., Oxford, 1981. Member: Inst. for Advanced Study, Princeton, 1972; Comité Internat. de Papyrologie, 1983–95. *Publications:* Greek Papyri in the Collection of W. Merton III, 1967; The Epistrategos in Ptolemaic and Roman Egypt, Pt I 1975, Pt II 1982; (with A. K. Bowman) Vindolanda: the Latin writing tablets, 1983; (with A. K. Bowman) The Vindolanda writing-tablets: Tabulae Vindolandenses II, 1994, III, 2003; contribs to the Oxyrhynchus Papyri XXXVIII, XLIV, XLVII, L, LVII, LXV–LXVII, LXX, LXXII; articles and reviews in learned jls. *Recreations:* music, bird watching, walking. *Address:* 39 Wearside Drive, Durham DH1 1LE. *T:* (0191) 3861723.

THOMAS, Sir John Meurig, Kt 1991; MA, PhD, DSc, ScD; FRS 1977; Distinguished Research Fellow, Department of Materials Science and Metallurgy, University of Cambridge, 1993–2002, now Hon. Professor in Solid State Chemistry; Master of Peterhouse, Cambridge, 1993–2002, Hon. Fellow, 2002; *b* Llanelli, Wales, 15 Dec. 1932; *s* of David John and Edyth Thomas; *m* 1959, Margaret (*née* Edwards) (*d* 2002); two *d*. *Educ:* Gwendraeth Grammar Sch. (State Scholar); University College of Swansea (Hon. Fellow, 1985); Queen Mary Coll., London; DSc Wales, 1964; ScD Cantab, 1994. Scientific Officer, UKAEA, 1957–58; Asst Lectr 1958–59, Lectr 1959–65, Reader 1965–69, in Chemistry, UCNW, Bangor; Prof. and Head of Dept of Chemistry, UCW, Aberystwyth, 1969–78 (Hon. Fellow, 1996); Prof. and Head of Dept of Physical Chemistry, and Fellow of King's Coll., Univ. of Cambridge, 1978–86; Dir, Royal Instn of GB, and Davy Faraday Res. Lab., 1986–91; Resident Prof. of Chemistry, 1986–88, Fullerian Prof. of Chemistry, 1988–94, Prof. of Chemistry, 1994–2002, Emeritus Prof., 2002, Royal Instn of GB; Dep. Pro-Chancellor, Univ. of Wales, 1991–94. Visiting appointments: Tech. Univ. Eindhoven, Holland, 1962; Penna State Univ., USA, 1963, 1967; Tech. Univ. Karlsruhe, Germany, 1966; Weizmann Inst., Israel, 1969; Univ. of Florence, Italy, 1972; Amer. Univ. in Cairo, Egypt, 1973; IBM Res. Center, San José, 1977; Harvard, 1983; Ecole Nat. Sup. de Chimie de Paris, 1991; Scuola Normale Superiore, Pisa, 2003; USC, 2005–; Cardiff, 2005–; Southampton, 2006–Dec. 2009; York, 2008–. Ind. Mem., Radioactive Waste Management Cttee, 1978–80; Member: Chem. SRC, 1976–78; SERC, 1986–90; Adv. Cttee, Davy-Faraday Labs, Royal Instn, 1978–80; Scientific Adv. Cttee, Sci. Center, Alexandria, 1979–; ACARD (Cabinet Office), 1982–85; COPUS, 1986–92; Bd of Governors, Weizmann Inst., 1982–; Academia Europaea, 1989. Mem., Royal Commn for Exhibn of 1851, 1995– (Chm., Scientific Res. Cttee, 1996–2006). Chm., Chemrawn (Chem. Res. Applied to World Needs), IUPAC, 1987–93; Member, International Advisory Board: NSF Lab. of Molecular Scis, CIT, 1999–; Nat. Inst. of Informatics, Tokyo, 2000–; President: Chem. Section, BAAS, 1988–89; London Internat. Youth Sci. Fortnight, 1989–93. Trustee: BM (Natural Hist.), 1987–92; Science Mus., 1990–95. Vice-President: Cambridge Univ. Musical Soc., 1994–; Cambridge Philosophical Soc., 1994–2000. Hon. Visiting Professor: in Physical Chem., QMC, 1986–; of Chem., Imperial Coll., London, 1986–91; Academia Sinica, Beijing; Inst. of Ceramic Sci., Shanghai, 1986–. New mineral, meurigite, named in his honour, 1995. Lectures: BBC Welsh Radio Annual, 1978; Gerhardt Schmidt Meml, Weizmann Inst., 1979; Baker, Cornell Univ., 1982–83; Hund-Klemm, Max Planck Ges., Stuttgart, 1987; Christmas Lectures, Royal Instn, 1987 (televised, 1988); First Kenneth Pitzer, Coll. of Chem., Univ. of Calif, Berkeley, 1988; Van't Hoff, Royal Dutch Acad. of Arts and Scis, 1988; Bakerian, Royal Soc., 1990; Bruce Preller Prize, RSE, 1990; Sir Krishnan Meml, Delhi, 1991; Watson Centennial, CIT, 1991; Birch, ANU Canberra, 1992; Liversidge, Univ. of Sydney, 1992; Sir Joseph Larmor, Cambridge Philos. Soc., 1992; Patten, Indiana Univ., 1993; François Gault, Eur. Fedn of Catalyst Socs, 1995; Prettre, Lyons, 1996; Rutherford Meml (presented at seven locations in NZ), Royal Soc., 1997; Tetelman, Yale Univ., 1997; Pollack, Technion Haifa, 1998; Ziegler Centenary, Max Planck Inst., Mülheim, 1998; Linus Pauling, CIT, 1999; Taylor, Penn State, 1999; Major, Univ. of Connecticut, 2000; Miller, Univ. of Calif., Berkeley, 2000; Linus Pauling, Oregon State, 2000; John C. Polanyi Nobel Laureate Series Speaker, Univ. Toronto, 2000; Griffiths Meml (250th anniv.), Hon. Soc. of Cymmrodorion, London, 2001; Debye, Univ. of Utrecht, 2001; Plenary Speaker, World Congress of Chemistry, Brisbane, 2001; Annual Public, Univ. of Surrey, 2002; Inst. of Appl. Catalysis Annual, UK, 2002; Linus Pauling (and Gold Medallist), Stanford Univ., 2003; Eyring, Arizona State Univ., 2003; Guggenheim, Reading Univ., 2003; Giulio Natta Centenary (and Centenary Gold Medallist), Italian Chem. Soc., 2003; Barrer, Penn State Univ., 2004; Ipatieff, Northwestern Univ., 2004; Discours Éminents, Geneva, 2005; David Lloyd George Meml, Criccieth Fest., 2005; Woodward, Yale, 2006; Golden Jubilee Dist., Hong Kong Baptist Univ., 2006; Max T. Rogers Dist., Michigan State Univ., 2007; Pirkey, Texas A & M Univ., 2007; A. S. Williams Dist., Univ. of S Carolina, 2007; Oersted, Danish Tech. Univ., 2007. Hon. FRSE 1993; Hon. FInstP 1999; Hon. FREng 1999. Hon. Fellow: Indian Acad. of Science, 1980; UMIST, 1984; UCNW, Bangor, 1988; RMS, 1989; Queen Mary and Westfield Coll., London, 1990; Foreign Fellow, INA, 1985; Hon. Foreign Member: Amer. Acad. of Arts and Scis, 1990; Venezuelan Acad. of Scis, 1994; Hon. For. Assoc., Engrg Acad. of Japan, 1991; For. Mem., Amer. Philosophical Soc., 1993; Hon. Foreign Fellow: Russian Acad. of Scis, 1994; Hungarian Acad. of Sci., 1998; Polish Acad. of Arts and Scis, 1999; Amer. Carbon Soc., 1999; Göttingen Acad. of Natural Scis, 2003; Russian Chem. Soc., 2004; Accademia Nazionale dei Lincei, Rome, 2004. Hon. Bencher, Gray's Inn, 1987. Hon. LLD Wales, 1984; Hon. DLitt CNAA, 1987; Hon. DSc: Heriot-Watt, 1989; Birmingham, 1991; Complutense, Madrid, 1994; Western Ontario, Glamorgan, 1995; Hull, 1996; Aberdeen, 1997; Hong Kong Baptist, 2008; DUniv: Open, 1991;

Surrey, 1997; Dr *hc*: Lyon, 1994; Eindhoven, 1996; American Univ., Cairo, 2002; Turin, 2004; Clarkson, NY, 2005; Sydney, 2005; Osaka Univ., 2006. Corday Morgan Silver Medal, Chem. Soc., 1967; first Pettinos Prize, American Carbon Soc., 1969; Tilden Medal and Lectr, Chem. Soc., 1973; Chem. Soc. Prizewinner in Solid State Chem., 1978; Hugo Müller Medal, RSC, 1983; Faraday Medal and Lectr, RSC, 1989; Messel Medal, SCI, 1992; Davy Medal, Royal Soc., 1994; Gibbs Gold Medal, ACS, 1995; Longstaff Medal, RSC, 1996; Hon. Medal, Polish Acad. of Scis, Warsaw, 1996; Semenov Centenary Medal, Russian Acad. of Sci., 1996 (first recipient) ACS Award for creative res. in homogeneous or heterogeneous catalysis, 1999; Hon. Soc. of Cymmrodorion Medal, 2003; Sir George Stokes Gold Medal for innovation in analytical chem., RSC, 2005; Silver Medal for services to sci., Univ. of Siena, 2005; Dist. Achievement Award, Internat. Precious Metal Inst., 2007. Crystals and Lasers, TV series, 1987; Dylanwadau, radio series, 1990. Founding Editor: (jtly), Catalysis Letters, 1988; (jtly) Topics in Catalysis, 1992; (jtly) Current Opinion in Solid State and Materials Sci., 1996. *Publications:* (with W. J. Thomas) Introduction to the Principles of Heterogeneous Catalysis, 1967 (trans. Russian 1970); Pan edrychwyf ar y nefoedd, 1978; Michael Faraday and the Royal Institution: the genius of man and place, 1991 (trans. Japanese 1994, Italian 2007); (with K. I. Zamaraev) Perspectives in Catalysis, 1992; Heterogeneous Catalysis: theory and practice, 1997; numerous articles on solid state materials and surface chemistry, catalysis and influence of crystalline imperfections, in Proc. Royal Soc., Jl Chem. Soc., etc. *Recreations:* ancient civilizations, bird watching, hill walking, Welsh literature, music, reading other people's recreations in Who's Who. *Address:* Department of Materials Science and Metallurgy, University of Cambridge, New Museums Site, Cambridge CB2 3QZ. *T:* (01223) 34300, *Fax:* (01223) 34567.

THOMAS, Prof. Jonathan Paul, DPhil; FBA 2002; Professor of Economics, University of Edinburgh, since 2002; *b* 28 May 1957; *s* of Berwyn Harold Thomas and Christine Erica Thomas (*née* Foden); *m* 1992, Ruth McFadyen; one *s*. *Educ:* Llanishen High Sch., Cardiff; St John's Coll., Cambridge (BA); MPhil 1981, DPhil 1989, Oxon. Res. Officer, Dept of Applied Econs, Univ. of Cambridge, 1982–84; temp. Lectr in Econs, Univ. of Bristol, 1984–85; Lectr, 1985–93, Sen. Lectr, 1993–96, Prof. of Econs, 1996–99, Univ. of Warwick; Prof. of Econs, Univ. of St Andrews, 1999–2002. Professorial Fellow, Univ. of Edinburgh, 2001–02. Hon. Prof., Univ. of Warwick, 1999–. *Publications:* contribs to Econometrica, Rev. of Econ. Studies, Jl of Econ. Theory, American Econ. Review, etc. *Recreations:* tennis, golf, ski-ing. *Address:* Department of Economics, University of Edinburgh, William Robertson Building, 50 George Square, Edinburgh EH8 9JY; *e-mail:* Jonathan.Thomas@ed.ac.uk.

THOMAS, Kathrin Elizabeth, (Mrs E. V. Thomas), CVO 2002; JP; Lord-Lieutenant of Mid Glamorgan, since 2003 (Vice Lord-Lieutenant, 1994–2002); *b* 20 May 1944; *d* of Dillwyn Evans and Dorothy Nelle (*née* Bullock); *m* 1967, Edward Vaughan Thomas (*d* 2006); two *s*. *Educ:* Cheltenham Ladies' Coll. Chairman: Mid Glamorgan FHSA, 1990–94; Mid Glamorgan HA, 1994–96; Bro Taf HA, 1996–99; Prince's Trust, Cymru, 1999–2001; Mem., Prince's Trust Council, 1996–2001; Pres., Royal Welsh Agricl Show, 2009. Hon. Col 203 (Welsh) Field Hosp. (V), 1998–2006 (Hon. Patron, 2008). Mid Glamorgan: JP 1983; High Sheriff 1986–87; DL 1989. *Recreations:* family, travel, reading. *Address:* Gelli Hir, Nelson, Treharris, Mid Glamorgan CF46 6PL. *Club:* Army and Navy.

THOMAS, Keith Garfield; His Honour Judge Keith Thomas; a Circuit Judge, since 2004; *b* 10 Aug. 1955; *s* of Howard and Shirley Thomas; *m* 2003, Melinda Jane (*née* Vaughan). *Educ:* Mill Hill Sch.; Bristol Polytech. (LLB). Called to the Bar, Gray's Inn, 1977; Asst Provincial Stipendiary Magistrate, 1995; Asst Recorder, 1996–2000; Recorder, 2000–04. *Recreations:* Rugby Union, cricket. *Address:* c/o Crown Court, St Helens Road, Swansea SA1 4PF. *Club:* Glamorgan Wanderers Rugby Football (Vice Chm., 1999–).

THOMAS, Keith Henry Westcott, CB 1982; OBE 1962; FREng, FRINA; RCNC; Chief Executive, Royal Dockyards, and Head of Royal Corps of Naval Constructors, 1979–83; *b* 20 May 1923; *s* of Henry and Norah Thomas; *m* 1946, Brenda Jeanette Crofton; two *s*. *Educ:* Portsmouth Southern Secondary Sch.; HM Dockyard Sch., Portsmouth; RNC, Greenwich. Asst Constructor, Admiralty Experiment Works, Haslar, 1947–49; Constructor: Admty, London, 1949–56; Large Carrier Design Section, Admty, Bath, 1956–60; Submarines and New Construction, HM Dockyard, Portsmouth, 1960–63; Project Leader, Special Refit HMS Hermes, Devonport, 1963–66; Dep. Planning Manager, HM Dockyard, Devonport, 1966–68; Project Man., Ikara Leanders, MoD(N), 1968–70; Dir-Gen. of Naval Design, Dept of Navy, Canberra, Aust. (on secondment), 1970–73; Planning Man., 1973–75, Gen. Man., 1975–77, HM Dockyard, Rosyth; Gen. Manager, HM Dockyard, Devonport, 1977–79. Member: Portsmouth Royal Dockyard Historical Trust, 1995–2006 (Pres., Portsmouth Royal Dockyard Historical Soc., 1988–95); Nat. Historic Ships Cttee, 1996–2000. FCMI. *Recreations:* music, lapidary, painting. *Address:* 6 Wyborn Close, Hayling Island, Hants PO11 9HY. *T:* (023) 9246 3435.

THOMAS, Sir Keith (Vivian), Kt 1988; FBA 1979; Fellow of All Souls College, Oxford, 1955–57 and since 2001; President of Corpus Christi College, Oxford, 1986–2000 (Hon. Fellow, 2000); *b* 2 Jan. 1933; *s* of late Vivian Jones Thomas and Hilda Janet Eirene Thomas (*née* Davies); *m* 1961, Valerie Little; one *s* one *d*. *Educ:* Barry County Grammar Sch.; Balliol Coll., Oxford (Brackenbury Schol.; 1st Cl. Hons Mod. History, 1955; Hon. Fellow 1984). Oxford University: Senior Scholar, St Antony's Coll., 1955; Fellow of St John's Coll., 1957–86 (Tutor, 1957–85; Hon. Fellow, 1986); Reader in Modern Hist., 1978–85; Prof. of Modern Hist., Jan.–Sept. 1986; Pro-Vice-Chancellor, 1988–2000; Mem., Hebdomadal Council, 1988–2000. Vis. Professor, Louisiana State Univ., 1970; Vis. Fellow, 1978, Lawrence Stone Vis. Prof., 2001, Princeton Univ.; Kratter Univ. Prof., Stanford Univ., 2004. Joint Literary Director, Royal Historical Soc., 1970–74, Mem. Council, 1975–78, Vice-Pres., 1980–84, Hon. Vice-Pres., 2001; Pres., British Acad., 1993–97. Member: ESRC, 1985–90; Reviewing Cttee on Export of Works of Art, 1989–92; Royal Commn on Historical Manuscripts, 1992–2002; Trustee: Nat. Gall., 1991–98; British Museum, 1999–2008; Chairman: British Liby Adv. Cttee for Arts, Humanities and Social Scis, 1997–2002; Adv. Council, Warburg Inst., Univ. of London, 2000–08; Supervisory Cttee, Oxford DNB, 1992–2004. Delegate, OUP, 1980–2000 (Chm., Finance Cttee, 1988–2000). Lectures: Stenton, Univ. of Reading, 1975; Raleigh, British Acad., 1976; Neale, University Coll. London, 1976; G. M. Trevelyan, Univ. of Cambridge, 1978–79; Sir D. Owen Evans, University Coll. of Wales, Aberystwyth, 1980; Kaplan, Univ. of Pennsylvania, 1983; Creighton, Univ. of London, 1983; Ena H. Thompson, Pomona Coll., 1986; Prothero, RHistS, 1986; Merle Curti, Univ. of Wisconsin-Madison, 1989; Spinoza, Univ. of Amsterdam, 1992; Ford's in British History, Univ. of Oxford, 2000; British Acad., 2001; Menahem Stern, Jerusalem, 2003; Leslie Stephen, Univ. of Cambridge, 2004. MAE 1993 (Trustee, 1997–2001); For. Hon. Mem., Amer. Acad. of Arts and Scis, 1983. Hon. Fellow, Univ. of Wales Coll. of Cardiff, 1995. Hon. DLitt: Kent, 1983; Wales, 1987; Hull, 1995; Leicester, 1996; Sussex, 1996; Warwick, 1998; London, 2006; Hon. LLD: Williams Coll., Mass, 1988; Oglethorpe Univ., Ga, 1996; Hon. LittD: Sheffield, 1992; Cambridge, 1995. Norton Medlicott Medal, Histl Assoc., 2003. Cavaliere Ufficiale, Ordine al Merito della Repubblica Italiana, 1991. Gen. Editor, Past Masters Series, OUP, 1979–2000. *Publications:* Religion and the Decline of Magic, 1971 (Wolfson Lit. Award for History, 1972); Rule and Misrule in the Schools of Early Modern England, 1976; Age and Authority in Early Modern England, 1977; (ed with Donald Pennington), Puritans and Revolutionaries, 1978; Man and the Natural World, 1983; (ed) The Oxford Book of Work, 1999; (ed with Andrew Adonis) Roy Jenkins: a retrospective, 2004; Changing Conceptions of National Biography, 2005; The Ends of Life, 2009; contribs to historical books and jls. *Recreation:* looking for secondhand bookshops. *Address:* All Souls College, Oxford OX1 4AL; The Broad Gate, Broad Street, Ludlow, Shropshire SY8 1NJ.

THOMAS, Kristin S.; *see* Scott Thomas.

THOMAS, Prof. Lancelot, FInstP; Professor of Physics, University of Wales, Aberystwyth, 1981–95, Research Professor, 1995–97, now Emeritus Professor (Head of Department, 1981–94); *b* 4 Aug. 1930; *s* of Evan Lancelot Redvers Thomas and Olive Margaretta Thomas; *m* 1955, Helen McGraith Reilly; two *s* one *d*. *Educ:* Port Talbot Secondary Grammar Sch.; University College of Swansea (BSc, PhD, DSc). Nat. Service Trng, Flying Officer, RAF, 1954–56; Royal Soc. post-doctoral appt, UC of Swansea, 1956–58; SSO, PSO, then Individual Merit SPSO, SERC Appleton Lab., 1959–65, 1966–81; Guest Worker, Envmtl Res. Labs, Nat. Oceanic and Atmospheric Admin, Boulder, Colorado, 1965–66; Principal Investigator, SERC/NERC VHF Radar Facility, 1981–97. Chm., British Nat. Cttee for Solar Terrestrial Physics, Royal Soc., 1982–87; Member: Adv. Cttee on Solar Systems, ESA, 1973–76; Royal Soc. Study Gp on Pollution in the Atmosphere, 1975–77; Wkg Gp for Scientific Definition of Spacelab Missions, NASA, 1975–77; Solar System Cttee, Astronomy, Space and Radio Bd, SERC, 1975–79; Scientific Adv. Cttee, British Antarctic Survey, 1983–86; Earth Observation Prog. Bd, BNSC, 1987–88; Astronomy and Planetary Sci. Bd, SERC, 1989–93; Royal Soc. Interdisciplinary Sci. Cttee on Space Res., 1990–93; Astronomy Cttee, PPARC, 1994–97; Council, Inst. of Physics, 1994–98. Hon. Fellow, Univ. of Wales, Swansea, 1998. Charles Chree Medal and Prize, Inst. of Physics, 1991. *Publications:* (ed with T. M. Donahue and P. A. Smith) COSPAR: Space Research X, 1970; papers in learned journals on theoretical studies of the upper atmosphere and ionosphere with related experimental work using laser radar techniques, VHF radar facility and rocket soundings. *Recreations:* music, modern history, golf. *Address:* 4 Celia Court, Holmesdale Road, Kew, Richmond, Surrey TW9 3LA. *T:* (020) 8948 5838.

THOMAS, Leslie John, OBE 2005; author; *b* 22 March 1931; *s* of late David James Thomas and late Dorothy Hilda Court Thomas, Newport (Mon); *m* 1st, 1956, Maureen Crane (marr. diss.); two *s* one *d*; 2nd, 1970, Diana Miles; one *s*. *Educ:* Dr Barnardo's, Kingston-upon-Thames; Kingston Technical Sch.; SW Essex Technical Coll., Walthamstow. Local Newspapers, London area, 1948–49 and 1951–53; Army, 1949–51 (rose to Lance-Corporal); Exchange Telegraph News Agency, 1953–55; Special Writer, London Evening News, 1955–66; subseq. author. Vice Pres., Barnardo's, 1998–. Hon. MA Wales, 1995; Hon. DLitt Nottingham, 1998. *Publications: autobiography:* This Time Next Week, 1964; In My Wildest Dreams, 1984; *novels:* The Virgin Soldiers, 1966; Orange Wednesday, 1967; The Love Beach, 1968; Come to the War, 1969; His Lordship, 1970; Onward Virgin Soldiers, 1971; Arthur McCann and All His Women, 1972; The Man with Power, 1973; Tropic of Ruislip, 1974; Stand up Virgin Soldiers, 1975; Dangerous Davies, 1976; Bare Nell, 1977; Ormerod's Landing, 1978; That Old Gang of Mine, 1979; The Magic Army, 1981; The Dearest and the Best, 1984; The Adventures of Goodnight and Loving, 1986; Dangerous in Love, 1987; Orders For New York, 1989; The Loves and Journeys of Revolving Jones, 1991; Arrivals and Departures, 1992; Dangerous by Moonlight, 1993; Running Away, 1994; Kensington Heights, 1996; Chloë's Song, 1997; Dangerous Davies and the Lonely Heart, 1998; Other Times, 1999; Waiting for the Day, 2003; Dover Beach, 2005; Soldiers and Lovers, 2007; *non-fiction:* Some Lovely Islands, 1968; The Hidden Places of Britain, 1981; A World of Islands, 1983; Short Singles, 1986; TV plays and documentaries, etc, incl. Channel Four series, Great British Isles (also presented), 1989; The Last Detective (series, adaptation of Dangerous Davies novels), 2003, 2004, 2005; also short stories. *Recreations:* islands, antiques, cricket. *Address:* De Vaux House, De Vaux Place, Salisbury, Wilts SP1 2SN. *Clubs:* MCC, Saints and Sinners, Lord's Taverners.

THOMAS, Margaret, Women's International Art Club, 1940; RBA 1947; NEAC 1950; Contemporary Portrait Society, 1970; RWA 1971; practising artist (painter); *b* 26 Sept. 1916; *d* of late Francis Stewart Thomas and Grace Whetherly. *Educ:* privately; Slade Sch.; RA Schools. Slade Scholar, 1936. Hon. Sec. Artists International Assoc., 1944–45; FRSA 1971. Group exhibitions, Wildensteins, 1946, 1949 and 1962; First one-man show at Leicester Galls, 1949, and subsequently at same gallery, 1950; one-man shows in Edinburgh (Aitken Dotts), 1952, 1955, 1966, and at Outlook Tower, Edinburgh, during Internat. Fest., 1961; RBA Galleries, London, 1953; at Canaletto Gall. (a barge, at Little Venice), 1961; Exhibition of Women Artists, Wakefield Art Gall., 1961; Howard Roberts Gallery Cardiff, 1963, The Minories, Colchester, 1964, QUB, 1967, Mall Galls, London, 1972; Octagon Gall., Belfast, 1973; Court Lodge Gallery, Kent, 1974; Gallery Paton, Edinburgh, 1977; Scottish Gall., Edinburgh (major retrospective), 1982; Sally Hunter, London, 1988, 1991, 1995 and 1998; RWA, 1992; Messum Gall., London, 2001, 2003; Strand Gall., Aldeburgh, 2006, 2007, 2008; regular exhibitor Royal Academy and Royal Scottish Academy. Official purchases: Prince Philip, Duke of Edinburgh; Chantrey Bequest; Arts Council; Exeter College, Oxford; Min. of Education; Min. of Works; Wakefield, Hull, Paisley and Carlisle Art Galleries; Edinburgh City Corporation; Nuffield Foundation Trust; Steel Co. of Wales; Financial Times; Mitsukoshi Ltd, Tokyo; Scottish Nat. Orchestra; Robert Flemming collection; Lloyd's of London; Sock Shop Internat.; Mercury Asset Mgt; Nat. Library of Wales; GLC and county education authorities in Yorks, Bucks, Monmouth, Derbyshire, Hampshire and Wales. Coronation painting purchased by Min. of Works for British Embassy in Santiago. Winner, Hunting Gp Award for best oil painting of the year, 1981 and 1996. *Publications:* work reproduced in: Daily Telegraph, News Chronicle, Listener, Studio, Scottish Field, Music and Musicians, The Lady, Arts Review, Western Mail, Illustrated London News, The Artist, The Spectator, Eastern Daily Press, Country Life. *Recreations:* antique collecting, gardening, vintage cars. *Address:* Ellingham Mill, Mill Pool Lane, near Bungay, Suffolk NR35 2EP. *T:* (01508) 518656.

THOMAS, Mark David; Editor, The People, 2003–07; *b* 1 March 1967; *s* of Rick and Jennie Thomas; *m* ; two *s* two *d*. *Educ:* Rutlish Sch., London. News reporter, The People, 1988–94; News reporter, then Chief Reporter, News of the World, 1994–97; Features Ed., then Asst Ed., Daily Mirror, 1997–2001; Dep. Ed., Sunday Mirror, 2001–03. *Address:* *e-mail:* mark@tm-media.co.uk. *T:* 07710 740468.

THOMAS, Martyn Charles, CBE 2007; FREng, FIET; FBCS; Director and Principal Consultant, Martyn Thomas Associates Ltd, since 1998; *b* 13 Aug. 1948; *s* of Leslie and Ruth Thomas; *m* 1980, Anne Rogers; one *s* one *d*. *Educ:* University Coll. London (BSc Biochem. 1969). FBCS 1980; CEng 1993; FIET (FIEE 1994); FREng 2007. Researcher, 1969–70, Systems Programmer, 1970–73, UCL; Designer, Standard Telephones &

Cables, 1973–75; South West Universities Regional Computer Centre: Team Ldr, 1975–79; Systems Manager, 1979–83; Dep. Dir, 1980–83; Founder and Chm., Praxis plc, 1983–92; Partner, Deloitte & Touche, 1992–98. Visiting Professor: Univ. of Wales, Aberystwyth, 1993–; Bristol Univ., 1994–; Oxford Univ., 1999–. Ind. Mem., EPSRC, 2002–05. Assce and Innovation Dir, Aspect Assce Ltd, 2001–03. Chm., First Earth Ltd, 2001–03. FRSA 1987. Hon. DSc: Hull, 1994; Edinburgh, 2004; City, 2005. Achievement Medal in Computing and Control, IEE, 1993. *Publications:* (with M. Ould) The Fell Revival, 2000; (jtly) Harry Carter – Typographer, 2005; (with A. Rogers) Three Pieces, 2005; numerous papers, lectures and broadcasts. *Recreations:* pretending to be a printer and typographer, backgammon. *Address:* Holly Lawn, Prospect Place, Bath BA2 4QP. *T:* (01225) 469441; *e-mail:* martyn@thomas-associates.co.uk.

THOMAS, (Mary) Elizabeth; with Shropshire Music Service (part-time), 1993–98; Director, West Midlands Board, Central Television plc, 1982–92 (Member, Regional Advisory Council, 1993); *b* 22 March 1935; *d* of Kathleen Mary Thomas (*née* Dodd) and David John Thomas; *m* 1962, Brian Haydn Thomas; two *d*. *Educ:* Dr Williams' School, Dolgellau; Talbot Heath School, Bournemouth; Royal Acad. of Music. ARCM, GRSM. Head of Music, High Sch., Totnes, 1958–61; Music Lectr, Ingestre Hall, Stafford, 1962; Berkshire Music Schs, 1964–66; Adult Educn Lectr, Bridgnorth Coll. of Further Educn, 1966–69. Chm., Pentabus Arts Ltd, 1983–87. Arts Council of Great Britain: Member, 1984–88; Chm., Regl Adv. Cttee, 1984–86; Chm., Planning and Develt Bd, 1986–88. Chairman: W Midlands Arts, 1980–84; Council, Regional Arts Assocs, 1982–85; Nat. Assoc. of Local Arts Councils, 1980–82 (Vice-Pres., 1982); City of Birmingham Touring Opera, 1987–92. Chairman: Shropshire Schs Forum, 2003–06; Standards Cttee, Bridgnorth DC, 2004–07 (Vice-Chm., 2003–04). Mem., Much Wenlock Town Council, 1995–2007 (Mayor, 2000–01, 2004–05). *Recreation:* gardening.

THOMAS, Rt Rev. Maxwell McNee, ThD; Warden of St Paul's College, University of Sydney, 1985–94; Lecturer in History and Thought of Christianity, University of Sydney, 1986–94; *b* 23 Aug. 1926; *s* of Rev. Charles Elliot Thomas, ThL, and Elsie Frances Thomas (*née* McNee); *m* 1952, Elaine Joy Walker; two *s* one *d*. *Educ:* St Paul's Coll., Univ. of Sydney (MA, BD); General Theological Seminary, New York (ThD). Lectr in Theology and Greek, St John's Coll., Morpeth, NSW, 1950; deacon, 1950; priest, 1952; Curate: St Peter's, E. Maitland, 1951–52; St Mary Magdalene, Richmond, Surrey, 1952–54; All Saints', Singleton, NSW, 1955. Priest-in-Charge and Rector, The Entrance, NSW, 1955–59; Fellow and Tutor, General Theol. Seminary, NY, 1959–63; Hon. Chaplain to Bishop of New York, 1959–63; Chaplain, 1963–64; Chaplain, Univ. of Melbourne and of Canterbury Fellowship, 1964–68; Consultant Theologian to Archbishop of Melbourne, Stewart Lectr in Divinity, Trinity Coll. and Chaplain of Canterbury Fellowship, 1968–75; Bishop of Wangaratta, 1975–85. Member: Gen. Synod's Commn on Doctrine, 1970–92 (Chm., 1976–92); Faith and Order Commn, WCC, 1977–79; Internat. Commn for Anglican-Orthodox Theol Dialogue (formerly Anglican-Orthodox Jt Doctrinal Discussion Gp), 1978–2007. *Address:* Martha's Point, 27/165 Osborne Drive, Mount Martha, Vic 3934, Australia. *Fax:* (3) 59754060.

THOMAS, Mervyn; Director, Human Resources, Department for Transport, since 2007; *b* Cardiff, 8 May 1965; *s* of Richard Thomas and Hazel Thomas; civil partnership 2006, Malcolm Collingwood (*d* 2006). *Educ:* Open Univ. (MBA). Hd, Human Resources, European Investment Banking, Citigroup, 1998–2002; Hd, Human Resources, Corporate Banking Div., Royal Bank of Scotland, 2002–07. *Recreations:* running, gym, writing, feeding the ducks in Richmond. *Address:* Richmond upon Thames, Surrey.

THOMAS, Prof. (Meurig) Wynn, OBE 2007; FBA 1996; Professor of English, since 1994, and Director, Centre for Research into the English Literature and Language of Wales, since 1998, Swansea University (formerly University College of Swansea, then University of Wales, Swansea); *b* 12 Sept. 1944; *s* of William John Thomas and Tydfil Thomas (*née* Rees); *m* 1975, Karen Elizabeth Manahan; one *d*. *Educ:* Gowerton Boys' Grammar Sch.; UCW, Swansea (BA 1965). University College of Swansea: Asst Lectr, 1966–69; Lectr in English, 1969–88; Sen. Lectr, 1988–94. Mem., British Library Adv. Cttee, Arts, Humanities and Social Scis, 2000–. Visiting Professor: Harvard, 1991–92; Univ. of Tübingen, 1994–95; Obermann Fellow, Univ. of Iowa, 1992. Mem., Welsh Arts Council and Chm., Literature Cttee, 1985–91; Vice-Chm., Welsh Language Section, Welsh Acad., 1996–97; Chm., Welsh Books Council, 2005–; Mem., Wales Arts Review Panel, 2006. Sec., Univ. of Wales Assoc. for Study of Welsh Writing in English, 1983–96; Adjudicator, David Cohen Prize, 1996–97. Hon. Mem., Nat. Eisteddfod Gorsedd of Bards, 2000. Literary Executor, R. S. Thomas (unpublished work), 2000–. FEA 2005. *Publications:* Morgan Llwyd, 1984; The Lunar Light of Whitman's Poetry, 1987; (ed) Morgan Llwyd, Llyfr y Tri Aderyn, 1988; Emyr Humphreys, 1989; (ed) Emyr Humphreys, A Toy Epic, 1989; (ed) R. S. Thomas: y cawr awenydd, 1990; (ed) Wrenching Times: Whitman's Civil War poetry, 1991; Morgan Llwyd: ei gyfeillion a'i gyfnod, 1991 (Welsh Arts Council Prize, Vernam Hull Meml Prize, Ellis Griffith Meml Prize); Internal Difference: literature in twentieth-century Wales, 1992; (ed) The Page's Drift: R. S. Thomas at eighty, 1993; (ed) DiFfinio Dwy Lenyddiaeth Cymru (essays), 1995; (trans.) Dail Glaswellt, 1995; John Ormond, 1997; Corresponding Cultures: the two literatures of Wales, 1999; (ed) Gweld Sêr: Cymru a chanrif America, 2001; (ed) Emyr Humphreys: conversations and reflections, 2002; Kitchener Davies, 2002; (ed jtly) James Kitchener Davies: detholion o'i waith, 2002; (ed) R. S. Thomas, Residues, 2002; (ed) Welsh Writing in English, 2003; Transatlantic Connection: Whitman US-UK, 2005; contrib. to jls and books. *Recreations:* reading, music, televiewing sport. *Address:* Department of English, Swansea University, Singleton Park, Swansea SA2 8PP. *T:* (01792) 295926.

THOMAS, Meyric Leslie, OBE 1987; Vice Lord-Lieutenant of West Glamorgan, 1997–2001; Consultant, Hutchinson Thomas (formerly L. C. Thomas and Son, later Hutchinson Thomas), Solicitors, since 1990 (Partner, 1956–90); *b* 17 Nov. 1928; *s* of Charles Leslie Thomas and Edith Annie Thomas; *m* 1956, Jillian Hamilton Armstrong; two *s* one *d*. *Educ:* Beaudesert Park; Clifton Coll.; Jesus Coll., Oxford (Mem., Univ. Boat Race crew, 1952, 1953; Pres., OUBC, 1953; MA Jurisprudence). Admitted Solicitor, 1956. Nat. Service, Glos Regt, 1947–49 (Belt of Honour, Eaton Hall, 1948). Mem. (Ind.), Neath BC, 1957–74 (Mayor, 1967). Pres., Neath RFC, 1973–78. DL W Glamorgan, 1993. *Recreations:* Rugby Union (spectator), bowls. *Address:* Braye Lea, Val Reuters, Alderney, Channel Islands GY9 3XE. *T:* (01481) 823465. *Club:* Alderney Bowls.

THOMAS, Sir Michael; *see* Thomas, Sir W. M. M.

THOMAS, Michael Christopher Pryce; Legal Advisor to the European Union Committee, House of Lords, since 2008; *b* 31 Oct. 1949; *s* of late David Hamilton Pryce Thomas, CBE and of Eluned Mair Thomas (*née* Morgan); *m* 1978, Pauline Marie Buckman. *Educ:* St John's Coll., Oxford (BA); Univ. of Sussex (MA). Admitted solicitor, 1976; in private practice as asst solicitor, 1976–79; Legal Dept, MAFF, 1980–86; Law Officers' Dept, 1986–88; Grade 5, Legal Dept, MAFF, 1988–92; Legal Adviser: Dept of Transport, later DETR, 1993–97; European Secretariat, Cabinet Office, 1997–2004; Dir,

Legal Services A, DTI, 2004–06; Legal Counsellor, FCO, 2006–07. *Recreations:* music, theatre. *Address:* House of Lords, SW1A 0PW. *T:* (020) 7219 3043.

THOMAS, Michael David, CMG 1985; QC 1973; barrister in private practice; Attorney-General of Hong Kong, 1983–88; Member, Executive and Legislative Councils, Hong Kong, 1983–88; Chairman, Law Reform Commission, Hong Kong, 1983–88; *b* 8 Sept. 1933; *s* of late D. Cardigan Thomas and Kathleen Thomas; *m* 1st, 1958, Jane Lena Mary (marr. diss. 1978), *e d* of late Francis Neate; two *s* two *d*; 2nd, 1981, Mrs Gabrielle Blakemore (marr. diss. 1986); 3rd, 1988, Hon. Lydia Dunn (*see* Baroness Dunn). *Educ:* Chigwell Sch., Essex; London Sch. of Economics. LLB (Hons) 1954. Called to Bar, Middle Temple, 1955 (Blackstone Entrance Schol., 1952; Harmsworth Schol., 1957); Bencher, 1981. Nat. Service with RN, Sub-Lt RNVR, 1955–57. In practice at Bar from 1958. Junior Counsel to Minister of Defence (RN) and to Treasury in Admty matters, 1966–73. Wreck Commissioner under Merchant Shipping Act 1970; one of Lloyd's salvage arbitrators, 1974. Governor: Chigwell Sch., 1971–83; LSE, 2001–. *Publications:* (ed jtly) Temperley: Merchant Shipping Acts, 6th edn 1963 and 7th edn 1974. *Recreations:* music, travel. *Address:* Essex Court Chambers, 24 Lincoln's Inn Fields, WC2A 3ED; Temple Chambers, 16F One Pacific Place, 88 Queensway, Hong Kong. *Clubs:* Garrick, Queen's; Hong Kong (Hong Kong).

THOMAS, Col Michael John Glyn; private consultant in transfusion medicine, since 1995; Clinical Director, Blood Care Foundation, since 1995; Director, MG & SJ Enterprises, since 1995; *b* 14 Feb. 1938; *s* of Glyn Pritchard Thomas and Mary Thomas (*née* Moseley); *m* 1969, Sheelagh Thorpe; one *d*. *Educ:* Haileybury and ISC; Trinity College, Cambridge; St Bartholomew's Hosp. MA, MB, BChir, LMSSA, DTM&H. FRCPE 1997. Qualified 1962; House Surgeon, Essex County Hosp. and House Physician, St James, Balham, 1963; Regtl MO, 2nd Bn The Parachute Regt, 1965; Trainee Pathologist, BMH Singapore, 1968; Specialist in Pathology, Colchester Mil. Hosp., 1971; Senior Specialist in Pathology, Army Blood Supply Depot, 1977; Exchange Pathologist, Walter Reed Army Inst. of Research, 1982–84; Officer in Charge of Leishman Lab., Cambridge Mil. Hosp., 1985–87; CO, Army Blood Supply Depot, 1987–95. Hon. Consultant Haematologist, UCH/Middlesex Hosp., 1987. Member: Council, BMA, 1974–82 (Chm., Junior Mems Forum, 1974–75; Chm., Central Ethical Cttee, 1978–82; Mem., expert panel on AIDS, 1986–; Mem., Bd of Sci. and Educn, 1987–93; Fellow, 1995); Cttee on Transfusion Equipment, BSI; Economic and Social Cttee, EEC, 1989–; Council, British Blood Transfusion Soc., 1998–2001 (Founder Chm., 1992–98; Sec., 1998–2004, Autologous Transfusion Special Interest Gp). Congress Pres., XXVIIIth Congress of Internat. Soc. of Blood Transfusion, 2004. *Publications:* contribs to ref. books, reports and jls on Medical Ethics, Haematology and Blood Banking, Malariology and subjects of general medical interest. *Recreations:* sailing, travel, photography, philately. *Address:* 3 Cholseley Drive, Fleet, Hants GU51 1HG. *Club:* Tanglin (Singapore).

THOMAS, Rear-Adm. Michael Richard, BSc (Eng); CEng, FIET. RN, 1960–96: served HMS Lincoln, Dido, and Andromeda; subseq. HM Dockyards Devonport and Portsmouth; Naval Sec's Dept, MoD; Naval Asst to Chief of Fleet Support; Supt Ships, Devonport; comd HMS Drake, 1992; Pres., Ordnance Bd, and DG Technical Services, 1994–96. Comdr 1977; Capt. 1985; Cdre 1993. Dir, Electrical Contractors' Assoc., 1996; Man. Dir, Penzance Drydock Co. Ltd, 1997–2008; Chm., Fleet Club Ltd, 2002–. President: Plymouth Scouts; Sea Cadet Corps. Gov., Plymouth Univ., 2000–05. FCMI; MInstD. *Recreation:* Rugby administration. *Address:* Millstone, Links Lane, Yelverton, Devon PL20 6BZ.

THOMAS, Michael Stuart, (Mike); Chairman: Corporate Communications Strategy, since 1988; SMF International Ltd, since 2000; non-executive Director, Finance South East, since 2008; *b* 24 May 1944; *s* of Arthur Edward Thomas. *Educ:* Latymer Upper Sch.; King's Sch., Macclesfield; Liverpool Univ. (BA). Pres., Liverpool Univ. Guild of Undergraduates, 1965–66; Past Mem. Nat. Exec., NUS. Head of Research Dept, Co-operative Party, 1966–68; Sen. Res. Officer, Political and Economic Planning (now PSI), 1968–73; Dir, Volunteer Centre, 1973–74; Dir of Public Relations and Public Affairs, Dewe Rogerson, 1984–88; Mem., BR Western Reg. Bd, 1985–92; Chairman: Media Audits, 1990–2001; Fotorama (Holdings) Ltd, 1995–2000; Atalink Ltd, 1998–2001; Music Choice Europe, 2000–05; 422 Ltd, 2001–02; WWA Ltd, 2003–08; H. K. Wentworth Ltd, 2005–08; Utarget plc, 2007–08; Director: Lopex plc, 1998–2000; Metal Bulletin plc, 2000–02. MP (Lab and Co-op 1974–81, SDP 1981–83) Newcastle upon Tyne E, Oct. 1974–1983. Mem., Select Cttee on Nationalised Industries, 1975–79; Chm., PLP Trade Gp, 1979–81; SDP spokesman on health and social services, 1981–83; Member: SDP Nat. Cttee, 1981–90; SDP Policy Cttee, 1981–90; Chairman: Organisation Cttee of SDP, 1981–88; By-election Cttee, SDP, 1984–88; SDP Finance Working Gp, 1988–90; a Vice-Pres., SDP, 1988–90; Mem., Alliance Strategy Cttee, 1983–87. Contested: (SDP) Newcastle upon Tyne East, 1983; (SDP/Alliance) Exeter, 1987. Founder of parly jl The House Magazine. *Publications:* Participation and the Redcliffe Maud Report, 1970; (ed) The BBC Guide to Parliament, 1979, 1983; various PEP pamphlets, contribs, etc, 1971–; various articles, reviews, etc. *Recreations:* collecting pottery and medals relating to elections, architectural and garden history, gardening, garden design, theatre, opera, music, cooking. *Address:* Milton Lodge, Iver, Bucks SL0 0AA. *T:* (01753) 772572. *Club:* Reform.

THOMAS, Michael T.; *see* Tilson Thomas.

THOMAS, Neville; *see* Thomas, R. N.

THOMAS, Prof. Nicholas Jeremy, PhD; FBA 2005; Professor of Historical Anthropology, and Director, Museum of Archaeology and Anthropology, University of Cambridge, since 2006; Fellow of Trinity College, Cambridge, since 2007; *b* 21 April 1960; *s* of Keith James Thomas and Sylvia Lawson; *m* Prof. Annie Coombes. *Educ:* Australian National Univ. (BA 1982; PhD 1986). Res. Fellow, King's Coll., Cambridge, 1986–89; Australian National University: Queen Elizabeth II Res. Fellow, 1990–92; Sen. Res. Fellow, 1993–96; Dir, Centre for Cross-Cultural Res., 1997–99; Prof. of Anthropology, Goldsmiths Coll., London, 1999–2006. *Publications:* Out of Time: history and evolution in anthropological discourse, 1989; Marquesan Societies: inequality and political transformation in eastern Polynesia, 1990; Entangled Objects: exchange, material culture and colonialism in the Pacific, 1991; Colonialism's Culture: anthropology, travel, and government, 1994; Oceanic Art, 1995; In Oceania: visions, artefacts, histories, 1997; Possessions: indigenous art/colonial culture, 1999; Discoveries: the voyages of Captain James Cook, 2003; many articles in jls. *Address:* Museum of Archaeology and Anthropology, University of Cambridge, Downing Street, Cambridge CB2 3DZ. *T:* (01223) 333316.

THOMAS, Norman, CBE 1980; HM Chief Inspector of Schools (Primary Education), 1973–81; Specialist Professor in Primary Education, University of Nottingham, 1987–88; *b* 1 June 1921; *s* of Bowen Thomas and Ada Thomas (*née* Redding); *m* 1942, Rose Henshaw (*d* 2005); two *d*. *Educ:* Latymer's Sch., Edmonton; Camden Coll. Qual. Teacher, 1948. Commerce and Industry, 1937–47. Teacher, primary schs in London and Herts,

1948–56; Head, Longmeadow Jun. Mixed Sch., Stevenage, 1956–61; HM Inspector of Schools, Lincs and SE England, 1962–68; HMI, Staff Inspector for Primary (Junior and Middle) Schs, 1969–73. Chm., Cttee of Enquiry on Primary Educn in ILEA, 1983–84. Adviser to Parly Cttee on Educn, Science and Art, 1984–86, on Educn, 1994–97. Visiting Professor: NE London Polytechnic, 1984–86; Univ. of Herts (formerly Hatfield Poly.), 1991–; Hon. Prof., Univ. of Warwick, 1986–94. Hon. FCP 1988. Hon. DLitt Hertfordshire, 1998. *Publications:* Primary Education from Plowden to the 1990s, 1990; chapters in books and articles in professional jls. *Recreations:* photography, reading. *Address:* Kingsbury Manor, St Michael's, St Albans, Herts AL3 4SE.

THOMAS, Owen John; Member (Plaid Cymru) Central South Wales, National Assembly for Wales, 1999–2007; *b* 3 Oct. 1939; *s* of late John Owen Thomas and Evelyn Jane Thomas; *m* 1985, Siân Wyn Evans; twin *s*; three *s* one *d* by a previous marriage. *Educ:* Glamorgan Coll. of Educn (Cert Ed 1971); UC, Cardiff (MA 1990). Tax Officer, Inland Revenue, 1956–61; Chemical Analyst, 1961–68; Primary Sch. Teacher, 1971–78; Dep. Headteacher, 1979–99. Shadow Minister for Culture, Sport and Welsh Lang., Nat. Assembly for Wales, 2001–07. *Recreations:* reading, socialising. *Address:* 4 Llwyn y Grant Place, Penylan, Cardiff CF23 9EX. *T:* (029) 2049 9868. *Club:* Ifor Bach (Cardiff).

THOMAS, Patricia Anne, CBE 2006; Commissioner for Local Administration in England, 1985–2005; Vice-Chairman, Commission for Local Administration in England, 1994–2005; *b* 3 April 1940; *d* of Frederick S. Lofts and Ann Elizabeth Lofts; *m* 1968, Joseph Glyn Thomas; one *s* two *d*. *Educ:* King's College London. LLB, LLM. Lectr in Law, Univ. of Leeds, 1962–63, 1964–68; Teaching Fellow, Univ. of Illinois, 1963–64; Sen. Lectr, then Principal Lectr, Head of Sch. of Law and Prof., Lancashire Polytechnic, 1973–85. Mem., Administrative Justice & Tribunals Council (formerly Council on Tribunals), 2005–. Mem., 1976–84, Vice-Pres., 1984, Pres., 1985, Greater Manchester and Lancashire Rent Assessment Panel; Chm., Blackpool Supplementary Benefit Appeal Tribunal, 1980–85. Hon. Fellow, Lancashire Polytech., 1991. *Publication:* Law of Evidence, 1972. *Recreations:* farming, family.

THOMAS, Patrick Anthony; QC 1999; **His Honour Judge Thomas;** a Circuit Judge, since 2008; *b* 30 Oct. 1948; *s* of Basil and Marjorie Thomas; *m* 1978, Sheila Jones; two *d*. *Educ:* Rugby Sch.; Lincoln Coll., Oxford (BA). Called to the Bar, Gray's Inn, 1973, Bencher, 2005; Recorder, 1992–2008. *Recreations:* reading, theatre, walking. *Address:* Birmingham Crown Court, Queen Elizabeth II Law Courts, 1 Newton Street, Birmingham B4 7NA.

THOMAS, Paul; *see* Thomas, C. P.

THOMAS, Paul; Vice-President of Marketing, Ford of Europe, since 2006; *m* Karen; two *c*. *Educ:* City Univ. (BSc). Joined Ford as trainee, 1974; sales and mktg posts with Ford of Britain, Ford Credit and Ford of Europe; Manager of Business Planning, Ford Credit, 1987–89; Gen. Field Manager, 1989–90, Mktg and Product Plans Manager, 1990–93, Ford of Britain; Vehicle and Derivative Progs Manager, Ford of Europe, 1993–95; Dist Manager, Midlands, Ford of Britain, 1995–99; Mktg Plans and Brand Develt Manager, Ford Product Develt Europe, 1999; European c-car Brand Manager, Ford Focus, 1999–2001; Dir of Sales, 2001–02, Man. Dir, 2002–06, Ford of Britain. *Address:* Ford Motor Company, Eagle Way, Brentwood, Essex CM13 3BW.

THOMAS, Rear Adm. Paul Anthony Moseley, CB 1998; FREng, FIMechE; Director, Environment, Health, Safety and Quality, British Nuclear Fuels plc, since 2001; *b* 27 Oct. 1944; *s* of Glyn Pritchard Thomas and Mary (*née* Moseley); *m* 1972, Rosalyn Patricia Lee; one *s* two *d*. *Educ:* Haileybury; London Univ. (BSc(Eng) 1969); MSc CNAA 1971. CEng 1985, FREng (FEng 1998); FIMechE 1993; MCGI 1995. Joined RN, 1963; Asst Marine Engr Officer, HMS Renown, 1971–77; Sen. Engr Officer, HMS Revenge, 1977–82 (mentioned in despatches, 1979); Asst Dir, Reactor Safety, 1982–84; Naval Superintendent, Vulcan Naval Reactor Test Estabt, Dounreay, 1984–87; Chm., Naval Nuclear Technical Safety Panel, 1987–90; Dir, Nuclear Propulsion, 1990–94; Captain, RNEC Manadon, 1994–95; Chief Strategic Systems Exec., MoD (PE), 1995–98; AEA Technology Nuclear Engineering: Dir, Engrg Projects, 1999–2000; Dir, Strategic Develt, 2000–01. Non-exec. Dir, Rail Safety and Standards Bd, 2005–. Hon. FINucE 2005. *Recreations:* cycling, sailing, ballooning, railways. *Address:* Byway, Chapel Lane, Box, Corsham, Wilts SN13 8NU.

THOMAS, Paul Huw; QC 2003; a Recorder, since 2000; *b* 25 June 1957; *s* of Hubert and Joan Thomas; *m* 1984, Mayda Elisabeth Jones; one *s* one *d*. *Educ:* Gowerton Sch.; Fitzwilliam Coll., Cambridge (MA). Called to the Bar, Gray's Inn, 1979, Bencher, 2008; Barrister, Iscoed Chambers, Swansea, 1980–; Jt Hd of Chambers, 2006–; Asst Recorder, 1996–2000. Asst Boundary Comr for Wales, 2003–. Mem., Dermatology Council for Wales, 2005–; Chm., Skin Care Cymru, 2006–. Trustee: Swansea Rugby Foundn, 1996–; Assoc. of Friends of Glynn Vivian Art Gall., 2006–; Changing Faces, 2008–. *Recreations:* sport, especially Rugby, history, the arts, Rhossili. *Address:* Iscoed Chambers, 86 St Helens Road, Swansea SA1 4BQ. *T:* (01792) 652988, *Fax:* (01792) 458089; *e-mail:* PThomas393@aol.com. *Clubs:* Swansea Rugby Football; Gowerton Cricket.

THOMAS, Sir Philip (Lloyd), KCVO 2003; CMG 2001; HM Diplomatic Service, retired; Senior Advisor, Shell International Ltd, since 2006; *b* 10 June 1948; *s* of Gwyn Thomas and Eileen Thomas (*née* Jenkins); one *s*. *Educ:* Dulwich Coll.; St John's Coll., Cambridge (MA). Joined HM Diplomatic Service, 1972; Third Sec., FCO, 1972–74; Second Sec., Belgrade, 1974–77, FCO, 1977–80; First Secretary: (Commercial), Madrid, 1981–87; UK Perm. Representation to EU, Brussels, 1987–89; Cabinet Office, 1989–91; Counsellor (Politico-Military), Washington, 1991–96; Head, Eastern Dept, FCO, 1996–98; Consul Gen., Düsseldorf, and Dir-Gen. for Trade and Investment Promotion in Germany, 1999–2000; High Comr, Nigeria, 2001–04; Consul-Gen., New York, and Dir Gen., Trade and Investment in US, 2004–06.

THOMAS, Prof. Phillip Charles, FRSE; FIBiol; FRAgS; Managing Director, Artilus Ltd, since 1999; Chairman, Animal Medicines Training Regulatory Authority, since 1999; Principal, 1990–99, now Emeritus Professor of Agriculture, Scottish Agricultural College; *b* 17 June 1942; *s* of William Charles Thomas and Gwendolen (*née* Emery); *m* 1967, Pamela Mary Hirst; one *s* one *d*. *Educ:* University College of North Wales, Bangor (BSc, PhD). FIBiol 1983; FRSE 1993; FRAgS 1997. Lectr in animal nutrition and physiology, Univ. of Leeds, 1966–71; progressively, SSO to SPSO, Hannah Research Inst., 1971–87; Principal, West of Scotland Coll., 1987–90; Prof. of Agriculture, Univ. of Glasgow, 1987–99. Hon. Prof., Edinburgh Univ., 1990–; Vis. Prof., Univ. of Glasgow, 1999–2001. Chairman: Govt Adv. Cttee on Animal Feedingstuffs, 1999–2001; Cumbria Foot and Mouth Disease Inquiry, 2002; Member: Scottish Food Adv. Cttee, 2000–05; Scottish Natural Heritage Bd, 2005–. Chm., Central Scotland Forest Trust, 2001–. *Publications:* (with J. A. F. Rook) Silage for Milk Production, 1982; (with J. A. F. Rook) Nutritional Physiology of Farm Animals, 1983. *Address:* 33 Cherry Tree Park, Balerno, Midlothian EH14 5AJ. *Club:* Farmers'.

THOMAS, Sir Quentin (Jeremy), Kt 1999; CB 1994; President, British Board of Film Classification, since 2002; Head of Constitution Secretariat, Cabinet Office, 1998–99; *b* 1 Aug. 1944; *s* of late Arthur Albert Thomas and Edith Kathleen Thomas (*née* Bigg); *m* 1969, Anabel Jane, *d* of late J. H. Humphreys; one *s* two *d*. *Educ:* Perse School, Cambridge; Gonville and Caius College, Cambridge. Home Office, 1966; Private Sec. to Perm. Under-Sec. of State, 1970; Crime Policy Planning Unit, 1974–76; Sec. to Royal Commn on Gambling, 1976–78; Civil Service (Nuffield and Leverhulme) Travelling Fellowship, 1980–81; Head, Broadcasting Dept, Home Office, 1984–88; Under Sec., 1988–91, Dep. Sec., then Political Dir, 1991–98, NI Office. Led Cabinet Office Review of BBC Monitoring, 2004–05; Chm., BBC Governors' Impartiality Review of BBC coverage of Israeli-Palestinian Conflict, 2005–06.

See also R. C. Thomas.

THOMAS, Rachel Mary S.; *see* Sandby-Thomas.

THOMAS, Dr Raymond Tudor, OBE 1994; Director, Brussels, British Council, 2003–06; *b* 19 May 1946; *s* of Edgar William Thomas and Lilian Phylis Thomas; *m* 1973, Gloria Forsyth; two *s*. *Educ:* King's Sch., Macclesfield; Jesus Coll., Oxford (BA Modern Hist. 1968); Inst. of Internat. Relns, Univ. of WI (Dip. 1970); Univ. of Sussex (DPhil 1976). Tutor, Davies's Ltd, 1969–70; Lectr, Inst. of Internat. Relns, Trinidad, 1970–71; British Council: Assistant Representative: Morocco, 1974–77; Pakistan, 1977–80; Malaysia, 1980–82; Regl Rep., Sabah, Malaysia, 1982–84; Projects Officer, London, 1984–85; Dep. Dir 1985–88, Dir 1988–90, Educnl Contracts Dept; Dir, EC Relns, Brussels, 1990–95; Regl Dir, subseq. Policy Dir, Middle East and N Africa, 1995–2000; Dir, Turkey, 2000–03. *Publication:* Britain and Vichy: the dilemma of Anglo-French relations 1940–42, 1979. *Recreations:* family life, travel, reading, fly-fishing. *Address:* 52 St Anne's Crescent, Lewes, East Sussex BN7 1SD.

THOMAS, Rev. Rhodri Glyn; *see* Thomas, Rev. H. R. G.

THOMAS, Richard; *see* Thomas, A. R.

THOMAS, Richard, CMG 1990; HM Diplomatic Service, retired; Vice-President, Leonard Cheshire, since 2006 (Trustee, 1999–2005; International Chairman, 2000–05); *b* 18 Feb. 1938; *s* of late Anthony Hugh Thomas, JP and Molly Thomas, MBE; *m* 1966, Catherine Jane Hayes, Sydney, NSW; one *s* two *d*. *Educ:* Leighton Park; Merton Coll., Oxford (MA). Nat. Service, 2nd Lt, RASC, 1959–61. Entered CRO, later FCO, 1961; Accra, 1963–65; Lomé, 1965–66; UK Delegn NATO, Paris and Brussels, 1966–69; FCO, 1969–72; New Delhi, 1972–75; FCO, 1976–78; FCO Visiting Res. Fellow, RIIA, 1978–79; Counsellor, Prague, 1979–83; Ambassador, Iceland, 1983–86; Overseas Inspector, 1986–89; Ambassador to Bulgaria, 1989–94; High Comr, Eastern Caribbean, 1994–98. Trustee, Rye Arts Fest., 2003– (Chm., 2006–). *Publication:* India's Emergence as an Industrial Power: Middle Eastern Contracts, 1982. *Recreations:* foreign parts, gardening, sketching. *Address:* Whole Farm Cottage, Stone-in-Oxney, Tenterden, Kent TN30 7JG. *Club:* Oxford and Cambridge.

THOMAS, Richard James, LLB; Information Commissioner, since 2002; *b* 18 June 1949; *s* of Daniel Lewis Thomas, JP, and Norah Mary Thomas; *m* 1974, Julia Delicia, *d* of Dr E. G. W. Clarke; two *s* one *d*. *Educ:* Bishop's Stortford Coll.; Univ. of Southampton (LLB Hons); College of Law. Admitted Solicitor, 1973. Articled clerk and Asst Solicitor, Freshfields, 1971–74; Solicitor, CAB Legal Service, 1974–79; Legal Officer and Hd of Resources Gp, Nat. Consumer Council, 1979–86; Under Sec. and Dir of Consumer Affairs, OFT, 1986–92; Dir, Public Policy, Clifford Chance, 1992–2002. Vis. Prof., Northumbria Univ., 2007. Chm., British Univs N America Club, 1970–71; Member: Management Cttee, Royal Courts of Justice CAB, 1992–98; London Electricity Cons. Council, 1979–84; European Consumer Law Gp, 1981–86; European Commn Working Party on Access to Justice, 1981–82; Lord Chancellor's Adv. Cttee on Civil Justice Rev., 1985–88; Council, Office of Banking Ombudsman, 1992–2001; Adv. Cttee, Oftel, 1995–98; Advertising Adv. Cttee, ITC, 1996–2002; Bd, Financial Ombudsman Service, 1999–2002; Bd, NCC, 2001–02; Bd, Consumers Assoc. 2008–; Bd, Whitehall and Industry Gp, 2008–. FRSA 1992. Hon. LLD Southampton, 2007. Internat. Privacy Leadership Award, 2008. *Publications:* reports, articles and broadcasts on range of legal, consumer privacy, data protection and freedom of information issues. *Recreations:* family, maintenance of home and garden, travel. *Address:* Information Commissioner, Wycliffe House, Water Lane, Wilmslow, Cheshire SK9 5AF.

THOMAS, Rita Margaret Easen-; *see* Donaghy, R. M.

THOMAS, Dr Robert Kemeys, FRS 1998; Aldrichian Praelector and Reader in Physical Chemistry, University of Oxford, since 2002; Fellow, University College, Oxford, since 1978; *b* 25 Sept. 1941; *s* of Preb. H. S. G. Thomas and Dr A. P. Thomas; *m* 1968, Pamela Woods; one *s* two *d*. *Educ:* Radley Coll., Abingdon; St John's Coll., Oxford (MA, DPhil 1968). Royal Soc. Pickering Fellow, 1970–75; Fellow, Merton Coll., Oxford, 1975–78; Lectr in Physical Chemistry, Univ. of Oxford, 1978–2002. Hon. Prof., Inst. of Chemistry, Chinese Acad. of Scis, Beijing, 1999–. *Publications:* contribs to chemical jls. *Recreations:* flora, funghi, music, Chinese language. *Address:* Physical and Theoretical Chemistry Laboratory, South Parks Road, Oxford OX1 3QZ.

THOMAS, (Robert) Neville; QC 1975; barrister-at-law; a Recorder of the Crown Court, 1975–82; *b* 31 March 1936; *s* of Robert Derfel Thomas and Enid Anne Thomas; *m* 1970, Jennifer Anne Brownrigg; one *s* one *d*. *Educ:* Ruthin Sch.; University Coll., Oxford (MA, BCL). Called to Bar, Inner Temple, 1962, Bencher, 1985. *Recreations:* fishing, walking, gardening, reading. *Address:* Glansevern, Berriew, Welshpool, Powys SY21 8AH. *Club:* Garrick.

THOMAS, Roger; *see* Thomas, D. R.

THOMAS, Roger, CBiol; Chief Executive, Countryside Council for Wales, since 2002; *b* 26 Jan. 1953; *s* of Gerwyn and Daphne Thomas; *m* 1988, Jan Tyrer; one *s* twin *d*. *Educ:* NE London Poly. (BSc Hons); Henley Coll. of Mgt (MBA). MIBiol, CBiol 1978. Various posts, incl. Lab. Manager, Welsh Water Scientific Directorate, 1976–92; Area Manager, NRA, 1992–95; Regl Gen. Manager, NRA Wales, 1995–96; Area Manager, 1996–98, Dir, 1998–2002, Envmt Agency Wales. *Recreations:* cycling, walking, junior Rugby coach, music, reading. *Address:* Countryside Council for Wales, Maes y Ffynnon, Ffordd Penrhos, Bangor, Gwynedd LL57 2DW. *Club:* Bangor Rugby.

THOMAS, Prof. Roger Christopher, FRS 1989; Professor of Physiology, University of Cambridge, 1996–2006, now Emeritus (Head of Department, 1996–2005); Fellow, Downing College, Cambridge, 1996–2006; *b* 2 June 1939; *e s* of late Arthur Albert Thomas and Edith Kathleen (*née* Bigg); *m* 1964, Monica Mary, *d* of late Lt-Comdr William Peter Querstret, RN; two *s*. *Educ:* Perse Sch., Cambridge; Univ. of Southampton (BSc, PhD). Res. Associate, Rockefeller Univ., NY, 1964–66; Hon. Res. Asst, Biophysics, UCL, 1966–69; Bristol University: Lectr, 1969–77; Reader in Physiology, 1977–86; Prof. of Physiol., 1986–96; Hd of Dept of Physiol., 1985–90; Dean, Faculty of

Science, 1990–93. Visiting Professor: Yale Univ., 1979–80; SISSA, Trieste, 2002–03. *Publications:* Ion-Sensitive Intracellular Microelectrodes, 1978; many papers on ion transport in learned jls. *Recreation:* cooking. *Address:* Physiological Laboratory, Downing Street, Cambridge CB2 3EG. *T:* (01223) 333869, *Fax:* (01223) 333840; *e-mail:* rct26@cam.ac.uk.

See also Sir Q. J. Thomas.

THOMAS, Roger Humphrey; strategy consultant; Chairman, Raymarine plc (formerly Raymarine Group Ltd), 2001–05; Chairman and Managing Director, Black & Decker, 1983–96; *b* 12 April 1942; *s* of Cyril Lewis Thomas and Phyllis Amy Thomas; *m* 1962, Myfanwy Ruth, (Nikki), Nicholas; three *s. Educ:* Slough Grammar School. FCCA. Black & Decker, 1970–96. *Recreations:* theatre, DIY, golf. *Address:* Stayes Wood, Northend, nr Henley-on-Thames, Oxon RG9 6LH. *T:* (01491) 638676.

THOMAS, Rt Hon. Sir (Roger) John Laugharne, Kt 1996; PC 2003; **Rt Hon. Lord Justice Thomas;** a Lord Justice of Appeal, since 2003; Senior Presiding Judge for England and Wales, 2003–06; *b* 22 Oct. 1947; *s* of Roger Edward Laugharne Thomas and Dinah Agnes Thomas, Cwmgiedd; *m* 1973, Elizabeth Ann, *d* of S. J. Buchanan, Ohio, USA; one *s* one *d. Educ:* Rugby School; Trinity Hall, Cambridge (BA; Hon. Fellow, 2004); Univ. of Chicago (Commonwealth Fellow; JD). Called to Bar, Gray's Inn, 1969, Bencher, 1992; QC 1984; a Recorder, 1987–96; a Judge of the High Court of Justice, QBD, 1996–2003; Judge of the Commercial Court, 1996–2003; Judge i/c Commercial Court List, 2002–03. Presiding Judge, Wales and Chester Circuit, 1998–2001. Asst Teacher, Mayo College, Ajmer, India, 1965–66; Lord Morris of Borth-y-Gest Lectr, Univ. of Wales, 2000. Faculty Fellow, Law Sch., Univ. of Southampton, 1990. DTI Inspector, Mirror Gp Newspapers plc, 1992. Vice Pres., British Maritime Law Assoc., 1996–; President: British Insurance Law Assoc., 2004–06; Eur. Network of the Councils of the Judiciary, 2008–. Hon. Fellow: Univ. of Wales, Aberystwyth, 2002; Univ. of Wales, Swansea, 2003; Cardiff, 2005; Bangor, 2008. Hon. LLD: Glamorgan, 2003; UWE, 2008. *Publications:* papers and articles on commercial, maritime and insurance law, the Welsh courts and devolution, constitutional law. *Recreations:* gardens, walking, travel. *Address:* Royal Courts of Justice, Strand, WC2A 2LL. *T:* (020) 7947 6399; *e-mail:* Lordjustice.Thomas@judiciary.gsi.gov.uk.

THOMAS, Roger Lloyd; Senior Clerk (Acting), Committee Office, House of Commons, 1979–84 and Clerk, Select Committee on Welsh Affairs, 1982–84, retired; *b* 7 Feb. 1919; *er s* of Trevor John Thomas and Eleanor Maud (*née* Jones), Abercarn, Mon; *m* 1945, Stella Mary, *d* of Reginald Ernest Willmett, Newport, Mon; three *s* one *d. Educ:* Barry County Sch.; Magdalen Coll., Oxford (Doncaster Schol.; Heath Harrison Trav. Schol.). BA 2nd Mod. Langs, 1939; MA 1946. Pres., OU Italian Soc., 1938–39. Served 1939–46, RA and Gen. Staff (Major GSO2) in India, Middle East, N Africa, Italy and Germany. Civil Servant, 1948–70: Min. of Fuel and Power, Home Office, Treasury, Welsh Office and Min. of Housing and Local Govt; Private Sec. to Perm. Under-Sec. of State, Home Office, 1950 and to successive Parly Under-Secs of State, 1951–53; Sec., Interdeptl Cttee on powers of Subpoena, 1960; Asst Sec., 1963; Sec., Aberfan Inquiry Tribunal, 1966–67; Chm., Working Party on Building by Direct Labour Organisations, 1968–69; Gen. Manager, The Housing Corporation, 1970–73; Asst Sec., DoE, 1974–79. *Publications:* sundry reports. *Recreation:* growing flowers. *Address:* 5 Park Avenue, Caterham, Surrey CR3 6AH. *T:* (01883) 342080. *Club:* Union (Oxford).

THOMAS, Roger Lloyd; QC 1994; a Recorder, since 1987; *b* 7 Feb. 1947; *s* of David Eyron Thomas, CBE and Marie Lloyd Thomas; *m* 1974, Susan Nicola Orchard; one *s* one *d. Educ:* Cathays High Sch., Cardiff; University Coll. of Wales Aberystwyth (LLB). Called to the Bar, Gray's Inn, 1969. *Recreations:* tennis, music, reading. *Address:* 9 Park Place, Cardiff CF1 3DP. *T:* (029) 2038 2731. *Club:* Cardiff Lawn Tennis.

THOMAS, Roger Martin; QC 2000; **His Honour Judge Thomas;** a Circuit Judge, since 2004; *b* 18 Aug. 1954; *s* of Donald Thomas and Jessie Thomas (*née* Attwood); *m* 1981, Vanessa Julia Valentine Stirum; one *s* two *d. Educ:* Worksop Coll., Notts; Univ. of Hull (LLB). Called to the Bar, Inner Temple, 1976. *Recreation:* sport. *Address:* Manchester Crown Court, Minshull Street, Manchester M1 3FS.

THOMAS, Roger R.; *see* Ridley-Thomas.

THOMAS, Ronald Richard; *b* 16 March 1929; *m* Lilian Audrey Jones; two *s. Educ:* Ruskin Coll. and Balliol Coll., Oxford (MA). Sen. Lectr, Econ. and Indust. Studies, Univ. of Bristol. Contested (Lab): Bristol North-West, Feb. 1974; Bristol East, 1987; MP (Lab) Bristol NW, Oct. 1974–1979. Former Mem., Bristol DC. Mem. ASTMS. *Address:* 64 Morris Road, Lockleaze, Bristol BS7 9TA.

THOMAS, Prof. Sandra Mary, PhD; Deputy Director, Government Office for Science, and Head (formerly Director) of Foresight, Department for Innovation, Universities and Skills (formerly Department of Trade and Industry), since 2006; Professor of Science Policy, University of Sussex, 2005–06, Hon. Professor, since 2006; *b* 1 June 1951; *d* of late Alan Wallace Thomas and Josette Charlotte Jeanne Thomas (*née* Costa); *m* 1983, Alan Smith (marr. diss. 1993); one *s* one *d. Educ:* Dunsmore Sch. for Girls, Rugby; Westfield Coll., London (BSc 1971; PhD 1980); Brunel Univ. (MSc 1975). Tutor, Open Univ., 1978–90; Lectr, Goldsmiths' Coll., London, 1979–82, 1985–87; Prog. Dir, Schiller Internat. Univ., London, 1982–85; Res. Fellow, 1987–94, Sen. Res. Fellow, 1994–97, Univ. of Sussex; Dir, Nuffield Council on Bioethics, 1997–2006. Member: Econ. and Social Cttee of EU, 1998–2002; Expert Adv. Gp on Genomes, DTI, 1999–2000; DFID Commn on IP Rights, 2000–02; UK Intellectual Adv. Cttee, 2000–05; Foresight Adv. Gp, 2000–02; Expert Adv. Gp on Clinical Res., Acad. Med. Scis, 2002–03; Expert Adv. Gp, MHRA, 2003–04; Ethics and Governance Council, UK Biobank, 2004–06; Sci. and Soc. Cttee, Royal Soc., 2004–06; Human Remains Adv. Gp, 2006–; Vice Chm., Cttee on IP, Human Genome Orgn, 2003–. Trustee: Centre for Mgt of IP in Health R&D, 2003–07; SciDev.Net, 2008–. *Address:* Government Office for Science, Department for Innovation, Universities and Skills, Kingsgate House, 66–74 Victoria Street, SW1E 6SW. *Club:* Cape Town (SA).

THOMAS, Sarah Joan; Head of Bryanston School, since 2005; *b* 5 Sept. 1961; *d* of Raymond John Peter Thomas and Joan Mary Thomas (*née* Day); *m* 1985, Adrian Boote; two *d. Educ:* Birkenhead High Sch. GDST; Hertford Coll., Oxford (BA Lit.Hum. 1984); King's Coll. London (PGCE 1986). Classics Teacher, Sevenoaks Sch., 1986–99; Dep. Hd, Uppingham Sch., 1999–2005. *Recreations:* family, food, friends. *Address:* Bryanston School, Blandford, Dorset DT11 0PX. *T:* (01258) 452411.

THOMAS, Simon; special adviser on economic development and rural affairs, Plaid Cymru, since 2007; *b* Aberdare, 28 Dec. 1963; *m* 1997, Gwen Lloyd Davies; one *s* one *d. Educ:* UCW, Aberystwyth (BA Hons Welsh 1985); Coll. of Librarianship, Aberystwyth (Post-grad. DipLib 1988). Asst Curator, Nat. Liby of Wales, Aberystwyth, 1986–92; Policy and Res. Officer, Taff-Ely BC, 1992–94; Develt Officer, 1994–97, Manager, Jigso, 1997–2000, Wales Council for Voluntary Action. Mem. (Plaid Cymru) Ceredigion CC, 1999–2000. MP (Plaid Cymru) Ceredigion, Feb. 2000–2005. Contested (Plaid Cymru) Ceredigion, 2005. Mem., Standards and Privileges Cttee, H of C, 2003–05; Vice Chairman: Parly Envmt Gp, 2000–05; PRASEG, 2002–05; Mem., Envmtl Audit Cttee, 2000–05. Plaid Cymru: Member: Nat. Exec., 1995–98; Nat. Assembly Policy Gp, 1997–99; Policy Forum, 1999– (Policy Co-ordinator for the Envmt). Vice-Chm., Global Legislators for a Better Environment, 2003–. *Publications:* As Good as Our Words: guidelines for the use of Welsh by voluntary organisations, 1996; Plaid Cymru election manifestos, 1997, 1999; contrib. numerous articles in Welsh and English lang. jls. *Recreations:* culture and literature, cycling, family life. *Address:* c/o Plaid Cymru, Tŷ Gwynfor, 18 Park Grove, Cardiff CF10 3BN.

THOMAS, Sir Stanley; *see* Thomas, Sir G. S.

THOMAS, Susan Kanter; Partner, ST Partnership Ltd; *b* NYC, 29 Feb. 1952; *d* of Capt. Marvin W. Kanter and Miriam Graboys Kanter; *m* 1974, Stewart Thomas. *Educ:* Nasson Coll., Maine (BA Pol Sci.). FCIPD 1994. Personnel Director posts, London Borough of Hackney, 1976–82; Hd of Personnel, S Bank Poly., 1982–86; Asst Chief Personnel Officer, 1986–93, Dir, Personnel and Admin, 1993–99, London Borough of Lewisham; Interim Dir, Corporate Services, GLA, 1999–2000; Dir-Gen., Corporate Services and Develt, and Bd Mem., DfES, 2000–06. Mem., Warner Cttee, DoH. Pres., Soc. of Chief Personnel Officers, 1997–98. FRSA. *Address:* ST Partnership Ltd, 3rd Floor, 167 Fleet Street, EC4A 2EA; *e-mail:* susan@st-partners.co.uk.

THOMAS, Rt Hon. Sir Swinton (Barclay), Kt 1985; PC 1994; a Lord Justice of Appeal, 1994–2000; *b* 12 Jan. 1931; *s* of late Brig. William Bain Thomas, CBE, DSO, and Mary Georgina Thomas; *m* 1967, Angela, Lady Cope; one *s* one *d. Educ:* Ampleforth Coll.; Lincoln Coll., Oxford (Scholar; MA; Hon. Fellow, 1995). Served with Cameronians (Scottish Rifles), 1950–51, Lieut. Called to Bar, Inner Temple, 1955 (Bencher, 1983; Reader, 2000; Treas., 2001); QC 1975; a Recorder of the Crown Court, 1975–85; a Judge of the High Court of Justice, Family Div., 1985–90, QBD, 1990–94. A Presiding Judge, Western Circuit, 1987–90. Member: General Council of the Bar, 1970–74; Criminal Injuries Compensation Bd, 1984–85; Vice-Chairman: Parole Bd, 1994 (Mem., 1992–95); Review on Child Protection in Catholic Church in England and Wales, 2000–01; Comr for the Interception of Communications, 2000–06. Chm., Assoc. of Papal Orders in GB, 2005–. KCSG 2002. *Recreations:* reading, travel. *Club:* Garrick.

THOMAS, Sybil Milwyn; Her Honour Judge Thomas; a Circuit Judge, since 2005; *d* of late Terence Barrington Thomas and Ann Veronica Thomas. *Educ:* Edgbaston High Sch. for Girls, Birmingham; Univ. of Bristol (LLB Hons 1995). Called to the Bar, Gray's Inn, 1976; in practice, Midland and Oxford Circuit, 1977–2005; Asst Recorder, 1993–97; a Recorder, 1997–2005. Dep. Chancellor, Dio. of Lichfield, 2006–. *Address:* c/o The Priory Courts, 33 Bull Street, Birmingham B4 6DS.

THOMAS, Trevor Anthony, FRCA; Emeritus Consultant Anaesthetist, United Bristol Healthcare NHS Trust (formerly United Bristol Hospitals), since 2002 (Consultant Anaesthetist, 1972–2002); *b* 16 March 1939; *s* of Arthur William Thomas and Gladys Mary Gwendoline Thomas (*née* Hulin); *m* 1965, Yvonne Louise Mary Branch; one *s. Educ:* Bristol Grammar Sch.; Univ. of St Andrews (MB ChB 1964). FRCA (FFARCS 1969). Chm., Dept of Anaesthesia, United Bristol Hosps, 1977–80; Hon. Clin. Sen. Lectr, Bristol Univ., 1980–2002. SW Regl Assessor in Anaesthesia, 1978–2000, Central Assessor, 1999–2003, Confidential Enquiries into Maternal Deaths in UK (formerly Confidential Enquiry into Maternal Deaths in England and Wales). Chm., Med. Cttee, Bristol and Weston DHA, 1988–90. Mem. Council, 1989–96, Hon. Sec., 1994, Sect. of Anaesthetists, RSocMed; Obstetric Anaesthetists Association: Mem. Cttee, 1978–85; Minute Sec., 1980–81; Hon. Sec., 1981–85; Mem. Cttee and Pres. Elect, 1994–95; Pres., 1995–99; Society of Anaesthetists, SW Region: Mem. Cttee, 1975–85; Hon. Sec., 1985–88; Pres., 1997–98. Examr, Fellowship Exams, RCAnaes, 1985–96. Trustee and Mem. Council, St Peter's Hospice, 1996–. Asst Ed., 1975–76, Ed., 1976–80, Anaesthesia Points West. *Publications:* (with A. Holdcroft) Principles and Practice of Obstetric Anaesthesia and Analgesia, 2000; contrib. chapters to textbooks; contribs to learned jls, mainly on matters related to obstetric anaesthesia. *Recreations:* music, theatre, scuba diving, Tai Chi, genealogy. *Address:* 14 Cleeve Lawns, Downend, Bristol BS16 6HJ. *Club:* Royal Society of Medicine.

THOMAS, Victor Gerald B.; *see* Bulmer-Thomas.

THOMAS, Vivian Elliott Sgrifan, CBE 1998 (OBE 1992); Chairman, British Standards Institution, 1992–2002; *b* 13 March 1932; *s* of William Edward Thomas and Cicely (*née* Elliott); *m* 1962, Valerie Slade Thomas; one *s* one *d. Educ:* Swindon High Sch.; Southampton Univ. (1st Class Marine Engrg). Engr Officer, Union Castle Line, 1953–58; with British Petroleum plc, 1959–92; Chief Exec. Officer, BP Oil UK Ltd, 1989–92. Director: Southern Water plc, 1992–96; Jaguar Ltd, 1993–2006; Gowrings Plc, 1992–2002. *Recreations:* golf, music, theatre. *Address:* Camelot, Bennett Way, West Clandon, Guildford, Surrey GU4 7TN. *T:* (01483) 222665. *Club:* Royal Automobile.

THOMAS, Maj.-Gen. Walter Babington, CB 1971; DSO 1943; MC and Bar, 1942; Commander, HQ Far East Land Forces, Nov. 1970–Nov. 1971 (Chief of Staff, April–Oct. 1970); retired Jan. 1972; *b* Nelson, NZ, 29 June 1919; *s* of Walter Harington Thomas, Farmer; *m* 1947, Iredale Edith Lauchlan (*née* Trent); three *d. Educ:* Motueka Dist High Sch., Nelson, NZ. Clerk, Bank of New Zealand, 1936–39. Served War of 1939–45 (despatches, MC and Bar, DSO): 2nd NZEF, 1940–46, in Greece, Crete, Western Desert, Tunis and Italy; Comd 23 (NZ) Bn, 1944–45; Comd 22 (NZ) Bn, in Japan, 1946; transf. to Brit. Army, Royal Hampshire Regt, 1947; Bde Major, 39 Inf. Bde Gp, 1953–55 (despatches); GSO2, UK JSLS, Aust., 1958–60; AA&QMG, HQ 1 Div. BAOR, 1962–64; Comd 12 Inf. Bde Gp, 1964–66; IDC, 1967; GOC 5th Div., 1968–70. Silver Star, Medal, 1945 (USA). *Publications:* Dare to be Free, 1951; Touch of Pitch, 1956; (with Denis McLean) Pathways to Adventure, 2004. *Recreation:* riding. *Address:* Kerry Road, M/S 413, Beaudesert, Qld 4285, Australia.

THOMAS, (William) David; a District Judge (Magistrates' Courts) (formerly Stipendiary Magistrate), South Yorkshire, since 1989; *b* 10 Oct. 1941; *s* of Arnold and Ada Thomas; *m* 1st, 1966, Cynthia Janice Jackson (marr. diss. 2000); one *s* two *d*; 2nd, 2000, Mrs Muriel Hainsworth. *Educ:* Whitcliffe Mount Grammar Sch., Cleckheaton; LSE (LLB Hons 1963); Part II, Law Society Finals, 1964. Admitted Solicitor, 1966. Asst Solicitor 1966, Partner, 1967–89, Finn Gledhill & Co., Halifax. *Publications:* contribs to Yorkshire Ridings Magazine and Pennine Radio, Bradford. *Recreations:* Rugby, theatre, ballet, gardening. *Address:* Bradford Magistrates' Court, PO Box 187, The Tyrls, Bradford BD1 1JL. *T:* (01274) 390111. *Club:* Halifax Rugby Union Football.

THOMAS, (William) David; QC 2002; *b* 20 Dec. 1958; *s* of John Lloyd Thomas and Kathleen Thomas; *m* 1987, Victoria Susan Cochrane; one *s* one *d. Educ:* The Heights; Midhurst Grammar Sch.; Wadham Coll., Oxford (MA). Called to the Bar, Middle Temple, 1982; in practice as barrister, 1983–. *Publication:* (contrib.) Keating on

Construction Contracts, 8th edn 2006. *Recreations:* gardening, cricket, wine, tennis. *Address:* Keating Chambers, 15 Essex Street, WC2R 3AA; *e-mail:* dthomas@keatingchambers.com. *Clubs:* MCC; Kirdford Cricket.

THOMAS, William Ernest Ghinn, FRCS; Consultant Surgeon, Sheffield Teaching Hospitals NHS Foundation Trust, since 1986 (Clinical Director of Surgery, 1989–2008); Joint Vice President, Royal College of Surgeons of England, since 2008; *b* London, 13 Feb. 1948; *s* of late Kenneth Dawson Thomas and of Monica Isobel Thomas; *m* 1973, Grace Violet Samways; two *s* three *d.* *Educ:* Dulwich Coll.; King's Coll. London (BSc 1969); St George's Hosp. Med. Sch., London (MB BS 1972); MS London 1980. MRCS 1972, FRCS 1976; LRCP 1972; ECFMG 1972. Consultant Surgeon, Royal Hallamshire Hosp., Sheffield, 1986–; Hon. Sen. Lectr in Surgery, Univ. of Sheffield, 1986–. Phase 2 Assessor, GMC, 1999–2003. Royal College of Surgeons of England: Bernard Sunley Fellow, 1977; Arris and Gale Lect., 1981–82; Hunterian Prof., 1986–87; Mem., Court of Examrs, 1992–2000; Surgical Skills Tutor, 1994–2004; Mem., Council, 2002–; Internat. Dir, 2002–; Chm., Educn, 2003–08; Zachary Cope Meml Lect., 2005. Member: Surgical Cttee, British Soc. of Gastroenterology, 1991–95; Intercollegiate Panel of Examrs, Gen. Surgery, 1995–2002; Internat. Bd of Dirs, Gastrointestinal Workshop, 2000–; Pres., Surgical Section, RSocMed, 2000–01. Hon. Sec., E Midlands Surgical Soc., 1994–99. Hon. FSACS 2006. Editl Bd, Hospital Doctor, 1987–2001; Chm. and Exec. Ed., Current Practice in Surgery, 1988–97; Series Ed. and Chm., Editl Bd, Surgery, 2000–; Ed., Bulletin, RCS, 2002–. Lectures: State of the Art, British Soc. of Gastroenterology, 1986; Martin Allgöwer, Internat. Soc. of Surgery, 2005; Heyendael Prize, Nijmegen, 2006. Award for bravery, Royal Humane Soc., 1974; Eur. Soc. for Surgical Res. Prize, 1981; Dr of the Yr Award, BUPA Med. Foundn, 1985. *Publications:* Preparation and Revision for the FRCS, 1986; Self-Assessment Exercises in Surgery, 1986; (with E. Rhys Davies) Nuclear Medicine: applications in surgery, 1988; (with J. H. F. Smith) Colour Guide to Surgical Pathology, 1992; Basic Surgical Skills, 1996, 2nd edn 1999; Preparation and Revision for MRCS, 1999, 2nd edn 2004; Specialist Registrar Skills in General Surgery, 1999; (with A. Aluwihare) Introduction to Surgical Skills, 2001; (with A. Wyman) The Abdomen, STEP Course Module VII, 2001; MCQs and Extended Matching Questions for the MRCS, 2002; (jtly) An Introduction to the Symptoms and Signs of Surgical Disease, 4th edn 2005 (1st Prize, BMA Med. Book Competition, 2006); (ed jtly) Anastomosis Techniques in the Gastro-Intestinal Tract, 2007; Short Stay Surgery, 2008; over 200 articles in learned jls. *Recreations:* ski-ing, oil painting, photography. *Address:* Ash Lodge, 65 Whirlow Park Road, Whirlow, Sheffield S11 9NN. *T:* (0114) 262 0852, *Fax:* (0114) 236 3695; *e-mail:* wegthomas@btinternet.com; *web:* www.wegthomas.com.

THOMAS, His Honour William Fremlyn Cotter; a Circuit Judge, 1990–2005; *b* 18 March 1935; *s* of Stephen Kerr Thomas and Nâdine Dieudonnée Thomas (*née* March); *m* 1st, 1960, Mary Alanna Mudie (decd); one *d*; 2nd, 1968, Thalia Mary Edith Myers (marr. diss. 1975); 3rd, 1978, Hon. Ursula Nancy Eden, *d* of 7th Baron Henley and of Nancy, Lady Henley; one *s* one *d.* *Educ:* Bryanston Sch.; University Coll., Oxford. National Service, 2nd Lieut, 1954–56. Called to the Bar, Inner Temple, 1961; SE Circuit; a Recorder, 1986. *Recreations:* music, architecture. *Address:* c/o Kingston-upon-Thames Crown Court, 6–8 Penrhyn Road, Kingston-upon-Thames, Surrey KT1 2BB. *Club:* Reform.

THOMAS, Ven. William Jordison; Archdeacon of Northumberland, 1983–92, Archdeacon Emeritus 1993; *b* 16 Dec. 1927; *s* of Henry William and Dorothy Newton Thomas; *m* 1954, Kathleen Jeffrey Robson, *d* of William Robson, Reaveley, Powburn, Alnwick. *Educ:* Holmwood Prep. School, Middlesbrough; Acklam Hall Grammar School, Middlesbrough; Giggleswick School; King's Coll., Cambridge (BA 1951, MA 1955); Cuddesdon College. National Service, RN, 1946–48. Assistant Curate: St Anthony of Egypt, Newcastle upon Tyne, 1953–56; Berwick Parish Church, 1956–59; Vicar: Alwinton with Holystone and Alnham and the Lordship of Kidland, 1959–70; Alston with Garrigill, Nenthead and Kirkhaugh, 1970–80, i/c Knaresdale, 1973–80; Industrial Chaplain, 1972–80; Team Rector of Glendale, 1980–82; RD of Bamburgh and Glendale, 1980–82. Travel leader, chaplain and lectr with leading pilgrimage, tour and cruise cos, 1992–. Hon. Chaplain: Actors' Church Union, 1953–56; Northumberland County NFU, 1978–2000. Harbour Comr, N Sunderland, 1990–92. *Recreations:* sailing own dinghy and other people's yachts, making pictures, travelling and making magic. *Clubs:* Victory Services; Northern Constitutional (Newcastle upon Tyne).

THOMAS, Sir William Michael, 3rd Bt *cr* 1919, of Ynyshir, co. Glamorgan; *b* 5 Dec. 1948; *er s* of Sir William James Cooper Thomas, 2nd Bt, TD, and Freida Dunbar Thomas (*née* Whyte); *S* father, 2005, but his name does not appear on the Official Roll of the Baronetage. *Educ:* Harrow; Christ Church, Oxford. *Heir: brother* Stephen Francis Thomas [*b* 13 April 1951; *m* 1986, Hon. Jane Ridley, *e d* of Baron Ridley of Liddesdale, PC; two *s*].

THOMAS, Sir (William) Michael (Marsh), 3rd Bt *cr* 1918; *b* 4 Dec. 1930; *s* of Sir William Eustace Rhyddlad Thomas, 2nd Bt, and Enid Helena Marsh; *S* father 1957; *m* 1957, Geraldine Mary (*d* 2002), *d* of Robert Drysdale, Anglesey; three *d.* *Educ:* Oundle School, Northants. Formerly Man. Dir, Gors Nurseries Ltd.

THOMAS, Wyndham, CBE 1982; Chairman, Cambridge New Town Corporation PLC, 1999–2008; *b* 1 Feb. 1924; *s* of Robert John Thomas and Hannah Mary; *m* 1947, Elizabeth Terry Hopkin; one *s* three *d.* *Educ:* Maesteg Grammar School. Served Army (Lieut, Royal Welch Fusiliers), 1943–47. Schoolmaster, 1950–53; Director, Town and Country Planning Association, 1955–67; Gen. Manager, Peterborough New Town Develt Corp., 1968–83; Chm., Inner City Enterprises, 1983–92. Member: Land Commission, 1967–68; Commission for the New Towns, 1964–68; Property Adv. Gp, DoE, 1978–90; London Docklands Develt Corp., 1981–88. Chm., House Builders' Fedn Commn of Inquiry into Housebuilding and the Inner Cities, 1986–87 (report published 1987). A Vice-Pres., TCPA, 1992–. Mayor of Hemel Hempstead, 1958–59. Contested (Lab) SW Herts, 1955. Hon. MRTPI 1979 (Mem. Council, 1989–98). Officer of the Order of Orange-Nassau (Netherlands), 1982. *Publications:* many articles on town planning, housing, etc, in learned jls. *Recreations:* collecting/restoring old furniture, writing. *Address:* 8 Westwood Park Road, Peterborough PE3 6JL. *T:* (01733) 564399.

THOMAS, Wynn; *see* Thomas, M. W.

THOMAS JUDGE, Hon. Barbara Singer, (Lady Judge); Chairman: United Kingdom Atomic Energy Authority, since 2004; LIFE, since 2007; Deputy Chairman: Friends Provident plc, since 2001; Financial Reporting Council, since 2003; *b* 28 Dec. 1946; *d* of Jules Singer and Marcia Bosniak; *m* 1978, Allen Lloyd Thomas (marr. diss. 2002); one *s*; *m* 2003, Sir Paul Rupert Judge, *qv.* *Educ:* Univ. of Pennsylvania (BA 1966); New York Univ. Sch. of Law (JD with Hons 1969). Partner, Kaye Scholer, Fierman, Hays & Handler, 1973–80; Comr, US Securities and Exchange Commn, 1980–83; Exec. Dir, Samuel Montagu & Co. Ltd, 1984–86; Sen. Vice Pres. and Gp Hd, Bankers Trust Co., 1986–90; Dir, News International plc, 1993–94; Chairman: Whitworths Gp Ltd, 1996–2000; Private Equity Investor plc, 2000–04 (Dir, 2004–). Non-exec. Dir, DCA, 2004–06. Mem. Bd of Dirs, Lauder Inst. of Internat. Mgt, Wharton Sch., Univ. of Pennsylvania; Institute of Directors: Mem., Policy and Exec. Cttee; Chm., Professional Standards Cttee. Chm. Benjamin West Gp and Mem. Corporate Develt Bd, RA; Trustee, Wallace Collection, 2004–07. Governor, SOAS, 1997–2005 (Chm., 2006–). *Recreations:* collections of antiques and oriental porcelain. *Address:* c/o Eversheds, 85 Queen Victoria Street, EC4V 4JL. *T:* (020) 7919 0623. *Clubs:* Reform; River (New York); Cosmopolitan (New York).

THOMASON, Prof. George Frederick, CBE 1983; Montague Burton Professor of Industrial Relations, University College, Cardiff, 1969–85, now Emeritus; *b* 27 Nov. 1927; *s* of George Frederick Thomason and Eva Elizabeth (*née* Walker); *m* 1953, Jean Elizabeth Horsley; one *s* one *d.* *Educ:* Kelsick Grammar Sch.; Univ. of Sheffield (BA); Univ. of Toronto (MA); PhD (Wales). University College, Cardiff: Research Asst, 1953; Asst Lectr, 1954; Research Associate, 1956; Lectr, 1959; Asst Man. Dir, Flex Fasteners Ltd, Rhondda, 1960; University College, Cardiff: Lectr, 1962; Sen. Lectr, 1963; Reader, 1969; Dean, Faculty of Economics, 1971–73; Dep. Principal (Humanities), 1974–77. Member: Doctors' and Dentists' Pay Review Body, 1979–95; Pay Rev. Body for Nurses, Midwives, Health Service Visitors and Professions allied to Medicine, 1983–95. Chm., Prosthetic and Orthotic Worldwide Educn and Relief, 1995–2002. *Publications:* Welsh Society in Transition, 1963; Personnel Manager's Guide to Job Evaluation, 1968; Professional Approach to Community Work, 1969; The Management of Research and Development, 1970; Improving the Quality of Organization, 1973; Textbook of Personnel Management, 1975, 5th edn as Textbook of Human Resource Management, 1988; Job Evaluation: Objectives and Methods, 1980; Textbook of Industrial Relations Management, 1984. *Recreation:* gardening. *Address:* Ty Gwyn, 149 Lake Road West, Cardiff CF23 5PJ. *T:* (029) 2075 4236.

THOMASON, (Kenneth) Roy, OBE 1986; Chairman, Charminster Estates Ltd, since 1998; director of other property companies; solicitor; *b* 14 Dec. 1944; *s* of Thomas Roger and Constance Dora Thomason; *m* 1969, Christine Ann (*née* Parsons); two *s* two *d.* *Educ:* Cheney Sch., Oxford; London Univ. (LLB). Admitted Solicitor, 1969; Partner, 1970–91, Sen. Partner, 1979–91, Horden & George, Bournemouth. Chm., London Strategic Housing, 2002–06. Mem., Bournemouth Council, 1970–92 (Leader, 1974–82; past Chm. Policy, Ways and Means, and Finance Cttees). Association of District Councils: Mem. Council, 1979–91; Leader, 1981–87; Chm., 1987–91; Chm., Housing and Environmental Health Cttee, 1983–87. Mem., Cons. Nat. Local Govt Adv. Cttee, 1981–97; various Cons. Party positions at constituency and area level, 1966–97 (Constituency Chm., 1981–82); contested (C) Newport E, 1983. MP (C) Bromsgrove, 1992–97. Member: Envmt Select Cttee, 1992–97; Jt Statutory Instrument Cttee, 1992–97; Chm., All-Party Export Gp, 1996–97 (Sec., 1993–96); Vice Chm., Cons. Parly Envmt Cttee, 1993–97. Fellow, Industry and Parlt Trust, 1996. Mem. Bd, London Strategic Housing, 2001–06 (Chm., 2002–06). Office holder, Dodford PCC, 2000–. FRSA. Hon. Alderman, Bournemouth BC, 1993. *Recreations:* walking, reading, architectural history, local activities. *Address:* Fockbury House, Fockbury, Dodford, Bromsgrove, Worcs B61 9AP.

THOMÉ, David Geoffrey C.; *see* Colin-Thomé.

THOMLINSON, Nicholas Howard, FRICS; Chairman, Knight Frank Group, since 2004; *b* 9 Jan. 1953; *s* of John and Lorna Thomlinson; *m* 2001, Lucy Joly de Lotbinière; two *s*, and three step *s.* *Educ:* Stowe Sch.; Keble Coll., Oxford (MA). FRICS 1978. With Knight Frank & Rutley, subseq. Knight Frank, 1974–. *Recreations:* making marmalade and chutney, bee-keeping, tennis. *Address:* Knight Frank, 55 Baker Street, W1V 8AN. *T:* (020) 7629 8171; *e-mail:* nick.thomlinson@knightfrank.com. *Clubs:* Hurlingham; Wimbledon.

THOMPSON; *see* Pullein-Thompson.

THOMPSON, Alan, CB 1978; Chairman, Review Group on the Youth Service, 1981–82; *b* 16 July 1920; *s* of Herbert and Esther Thompson; *m* 1944, Joyce Nora Banks (*d* 2000); two *s* one *d.* *Educ:* Carlisle Grammar Sch.; Queen's Coll., Oxford. Joined Min. of Education, 1946; Private Sec. to Minister of Education, 1954–56; Asst Sec., Further Education Br., 1956–64; Under Sec., UGC, 1964–71; Under Sec., Science Br., DES, 1971–75; Dep. Sec., DES, 1975–80. *Address:* 1 Haven Close, Wimbledon, SW19 5JW.

THOMPSON, Prof. Alan Eric; A. J. Balfour Professor of the Economics of Government, 1972–87, Professor Emeritus, since 1987, Heriot-Watt University; *b* 16 Sept. 1924; *o c* of late Eric Joseph Thompson and Florence Thompson; *m* 1960, Mary Heather Long; three *s* one *d.* *Educ:* Kingston-upon-Hull GS; University of Edinburgh (MA 1949, MA (Hons Class I, Economic Science), 1951, PhD 1953, Carnegie Research Scholar, 1951–52). FSAScot 1995. Served army (including service with Central Mediterranean Forces), World War II. Asst in Political Economy, 1952–53, Lectr in Economics (formerly Political Economy), 1953–59, and 1964–71, Univ. of Edinburgh. Parly Adviser to Scottish Television, 1966–76; Scottish Governor, BBC, 1976–79. Visiting Professor: Graduate School of Business, Stanford Univ., USA, 1966, 1968; Marmara Univ., Istanbul, 1982. Contested (Lab) Galloway, 1950 and 1951; MP (Lab) Dunfermline, 1959–64. Mem., Speaker's Parly Delegn to USA, 1962. Chm., Adv. Bd on Economics Educn (Esmée Fairbairn Research Project), 1970–76; Jt Chm., Scottish-USSR Co-ordinating Cttee for Trade and Industry, 1985–90; Member: Scottish Cttee, Public Schools Commn, 1969–70; Cttee enquiring into conditions of service life for young servicemen, 1969; Scottish Council for Adult Educn in HM Forces, 1973–98; Jt Mil. Educn Cttee, Edinburgh and Heriot-Watt Univs, 1975–; Local Govt Boundary Commn for Scotland, 1975–82; Royal Fine Art Commn for Scotland, 1975–80; Adv. Bd, Defence Finance Unit, Heriot-Watt Univ., 1987–90; Chm., Northern Offshore (Maritime) Resources Study, 1974–77; Chm., Edinburgh Cttee, Peace Through NATO, 1984–95. Parly Adviser, Pharmaceutical Gen. Council (Scotland), 1984–2000. Hon. Vice-Pres., Assoc. of Nazi War Camp Survivors, 1960–; Pres., Edinburgh Amenity and Transport Assoc., 1970–75; Dir, Scottish AIDS Res. Foundn, 1988–97. Chm. of Governors, Newbattle Abbey Coll., 1980–82 (Governor, 1975–82); Governor, Leith Nautical Coll., 1981–85; Trustee, Bell's Nautical Trust, 1981–85. Has broadcast and appeared on TV (economic and political talks and discussions) in Britain and USA. FRSA 1972. *Publications:* Development of Economic Doctrine (jtly), 1980; contribs to learned journals. *Address:* 11 Upper Gray Street, Edinburgh EH9 1SN. *T:* (0131) 667 2140. *Club:* New (Edinburgh).

THOMPSON, Amanda; Managing Director, Blackpool Pleasure Beach, since 2004 (Director, since 1988); President, Stageworks Worldwide Productions, since 1982; *b* 2 Sept. 1962; *d* of William Geoffrey Thompson, OBE, DL and Barbara Thompson; *m* 2003, Stephen Thompson. *Educ:* Badminton Sch., Bristol; Dover Brooks, Oxford. Ran dance studio; worked for Disney, Florida; produced first ice shows in Myrtle Beach, USA, 1982; Dep. Man. Dir, Blackpool Pleasure Beach, 2000–04. Mem., Bd of Dirs, Internat. Assoc. of Amusement Parks and Attractions. *Recreations:* shows, cinema, ski-ing, travel, fashion and interior design. *Address:* Blackpool Pleasure Beach, Ocean Boulevard, Blackpool FY4 1EZ. *T:* (0870) 444 5588, *Fax:* (01253) 343958.

THOMPSON, His Honour Anthony Arthur Richard; QC 1980; a Circuit Judge, 1992–2003; Designated Civil Judge for Hampshire and Dorset, 1999–2003; *b* 4 July 1932; *s* of late William Frank McGregor Thompson and Doris Louise Thompson (*née* Hill); *m* 1958, Françoise Alix Marie Reynier; two *s* one *d* (and one *s* decd). *Educ:* Latymer Upper Sch.; University Coll., Oxford; La Sorbonne. FCIArb 1991. Called to the Bar, Inner Temple, 1957, Bencher, 1986; admitted to Paris Bar, 1988; a Recorder, 1985–92; Liaison Judge for Cornwall, 1993–99; Resident Judge for Cornwall, 1995–99. Chm., Bar European Gp, 1984–86 (Vice-Chm., 1982–84); Mem., Internat. Relations Cttee, Bar Council, 1984–86. QC: Singapore, 1985; Hong Kong, 1986; St Vincent and the Grenadines, 1986. Vice Pres., Cornwall Magistrates' Assoc., 1995–2005. Contested (Lab) Arundel and Shoreham, Oct. 1964. *Recreations:* food and wine, lawn tennis, theatre, cinema, 19th century music, 20th century painting. *Club:* Roehampton.

See also R. P. R. Thompson.

THOMPSON, Aubrey Gordon D.; *see* Denton-Thompson.

THOMPSON, Bruce Kevin, MA; Head, Strathallan School, since 2000; *b* 14 Nov. 1959; *s* of Keith Bruce Thompson, *qv*; *m* 1993, Fabienne Goddet; two *d*. *Educ:* Newcastle High Sch., Newcastle-under-Lyme; New Coll., Oxford (MA Lit.Hum.). Asst Master, 1983–86, Head of Classics, 1986–94, Cheltenham Coll.; Dep. Rector, Dollar Acad., 1994–2000. *Recreations:* coaching Rugby, weight training, rowing, literature, music. *Address:* c/o Strathallan School, Forgandenny, Perth PH2 9EG. *T:* (01738) 815000. *Club:* Leander (Henley-on-Thames).

THOMPSON, Catriona Helen Moncrieff; *see* Kelly, C. H. M.

THOMPSON, Charles Norman, CBE 1978; CChem; FRSC; Head of Research and Development Liaison, and Health, Safety and Environment Administration, Shell UK Ltd, 1978–82, retired; Consultant to Shell UK Ltd, since 1982; *b* 23 Oct. 1922; *s* of Robert Norman Thompson and Evelyn Tivendale Thompson (*née* Wood); *m* 1946, Pamela Margaret Wicks; one *d*. *Educ:* Birkenhead Institute; Liverpool Univ. (BSc Hons 1943). Research Chemist, Thornton Research Centre (Shell Refining & Marketing Co. Ltd), 1943; Lectr, Petroleum Chemistry and Technology, Liverpool Coll. of Technology, 1947–51; Personnel Supt and Dep. Associate Manager, Thornton Research Centre, Shell Research Ltd, 1959–61; Dir (Res. Admin), Shell Research Ltd, 1961–78. Mem. Council, 1976–82, Vice Pres., 1977–80, 1981–82, Inst. of Petroleum (Chm., Res. Adv. Cttee, 1973–82). Pres., RIC, 1976–78. Chairman: Professional Affairs Bd, 1980–84, Water Chemistry Forum, 1987–90, RSC; Council of Science and Technology Insts, 1981–83 (Chm., Health Care Scientific Adv. Cttee, 1986–94); Bd Mem., Thames Water Authority, 1980–87; Member: Technician Educn Council, 1980–83; Ct, Univ. of Surrey, 1980–; Parly and Scientific Cttee, 1976–. *Publications:* Reviews of Petroleum Technology, vol. 13: insulating and hydraulic oils, 1953; numerous papers in Jl Inst. Petroleum, Chem. and Ind., Chem. in Brit., on hydrocarbon dielectrics, insulating oils, diffusion as rate-limiting factor in oxidation, antioxidants in the oil industry, mechanism of copper catalysis in insulating oil oxidation, scientific manpower, etc. *Recreations:* golf, bowls. *Address:* Delamere, Horsell Park, Woking, Surrey GU21 4LW. *T:* (01483) 714939.

THOMPSON, Prof. Christopher, MD; FRCP, FRCPsych; Chief Medical Officer (formerly Director of Healthcare), Priory Group, since 2004; *b* 23 Sept. 1952; *s* of Derek and Margaret Thompson; *m* 1976, Celia Robertson; three *d*. *Educ:* Lincoln Grammar Sch.; Strode's Sch., Egham; University Coll. London (BSc 1974; MB BS 1977; MD 1987). FRCPsych 1991; FRCP 1995; MRCGP 2000. Registrar in Psychiatry, Maudsley Hosp., 1978–81; Res. Fellow and Lectr, Inst. of Psychiatry, 1981–84; Sen. Lectr, Charing Cross Hosp. Med. Sch., 1984–88; University of Southampton: Prof. of Psychiatry, 1988–2003; Hd, Sch. of Medicine, 2000–03. Royal College of Psychiatrists: Registrar, 1993–97; Vice Pres., 1997–99; Pres., Internat. Soc. for Affective Disorders, 2000–06. Mem. Bd, Depression Alliance. Mem. Council, UCL. FRSA. *Publications:* (ed and contrib.) Research Instruments in Psychiatry, 1989; (jtly) Caring for a Community, 1995; edited jointly and contributed: Psychological Applications in Psychiatry, 1985; The Origins of Modern Psychiatry, 1987; Learning Psychiatry through MCQ, 1988; Melatonin: clinical perspectives, 1988; Seasonal Affective Disorders, 1989; Violence: basic and clinical science, 1993; 3 official govt reports; over 100 scientific articles in learned jls. *Recreations:* enthusiastic amateur of the classical guitar, tyro private pilot. *Address:* Priory House, Randalls Way, Leatherhead, Surrey KT22 7TP. *T:* (01372) 860427; *e-mail:* christhompson@priorygroup.com.

THOMPSON, Lt-Col Sir Christopher (Peile), 6th Bt *cr* 1890; non-executive Chairman, Nuclear Decommissioning Ltd, 1995–2000 (Director, 1994–2000); *b* 21 Dec. 1944; *s* of Lt-Col Sir Peile Thompson, 5th Bt, OBE, and Barbara Johnson (*d* 1993), *d* of late H. J. Rampling; *S* father, 1985; *m* 1st, 1969, Anna Elizabeth (marr. diss. 1997), *d* of Major Arthur Callander; one *s* one *d*; 2nd, 2001, Penelope (*née* Allin), *widow* of 9th Viscount Portman. *Educ:* Marlborough; RMA Sandhurst. Commnd 11th Hussars (PAO), 1965; Tank Troop Leader and Reconnaissance Troop Leader, 11th Hussars, 1965–69; Gunnery Instructor, RAC Gunnery Sch., 1970–72; Sqdn Second i/c, A Sqdn, Royal Hussars, 1972–75; GSO 3 Intelligence, Allied Staff, Berlin, 1975–76; RMCS Shrivenham, 1977; Staff Coll., Camberley, 1978; DAAG (a) M2 (A) (Officer Manning), MoD, 1978–81; C Sqdn Ldr, Royal Hussars, 1981–83; GSO 2 (Operational Requirements), HQ DRAC, 1983–85; CO, Royal Hussars (PWO), 1985–87; SO1, Sen. Officers Tactics Div., 1987–90, retd. Equerry to HRH Prince Michael of Kent, 1989– (Private Sec., 1990–92). Director: Logical Security Ltd, 1996–98; Falcon Security Control (Overseas) Ltd, 2000–04; Nuclear Decommissioning Services Ltd, 2007–. Dir, Hyde Park Appeal, 1990–96; Trustee: Bike Aid, 1990–94; Queen Elizabeth Gate Appeal, 1990–96; Tusk, 1994–2002 (Patron, 2002–); Antigua Heritage Trust (UK), 1997–2000. Mem., Standing Council of the Baronetage, 2001–. Patron, Earth 2000, 1997–2002. *Recreations:* fishing, shooting, reading, golf, tennis. *Heir: s* Peile Richard Thompson, *b* 3 March 1975. *Clubs:* White's, Cavalry and Guards, Woodroffe's; Mill Reef (Antigua).

THOMPSON, Christopher Ronald; Senior Partner, Aldenham Business Services Ltd, since 1984; *b* 14 Dec. 1927; *s* of late Col S. J. Thompson, DSO, DL and Margaret Thompson (*née* Green); *m* 1st, 1949, Rachael Meynell (*d* 2003); one *s* one *d* (and one *s* decd); 2nd, 2006, Lucy Carolyn (*née* Fisher), *widow* of Charles Shakerley. *Educ:* Shrewsbury School; Trinity College, Cambridge. 1st Bn KSLI (Lieut), 1946–48. Dir, John Thompson Ltd, 1954–68, Chm., 1969; Dir, Rockwell-Thompson Ltd, 1973–74; Vice-Pres., Rockwell Europe, 1974–78. Chairman: NEI Internat., 1979–84; Wynn Electronics, 1983–87; Filtermist Internat. plc, 1985–97; John Sutcliffe Shipping Ltd, 1986–89; Director: Saraswati Syndicate pte India, 1954–; Barclays Bank Birmingham Bd, 1974–87; G. T. Japan Investment Trust, 1983–; Isotron plc, 1984–2003; Craven Grain Storage Ltd, 1984–95; Plessey Co. plc, 1988–89. Member: Overseas Projects Bd, BOTB, 1981–84; Sino-British Trade Council, 1983–85.; Indo-British Industrial Forum, 1987–93. Pres., BEAMA, 1984–85. Chm., CLA Cttee for Shropshire, 1996–. Mem. Council, HHA, 1992–2004. Chm., Anglo-Venezuelan Soc., 1981–85. Trustee: Hereford Cathedral Trust, 1984–98; Mappa Mundi Trust, 1990–98. High Sheriff, Shropshire, 1984–85. *Recreations:* flyfishing, shooting, forestry. *Address:* Aldenham Park, near Bridgnorth, Shropshire WV16 4RN. *T:* (01746) 714218. *Club:* Boodle's.

THOMPSON, Clive Hepworth, CBE 1998; *b* 7 July 1937; *s* of late Sidney Hepworth Thompson and Vera Wynne; *m* 1962, Joan Mary Kershaw; two *s*. *Educ:* Holywell Grammar Sch.; Manchester Univ. (BTech, MSc); Harvard Business Sch. BP Chemicals: Technical and Management appts; Works Gen. Manager, Barry Plant, 1975–78, Baglan Bay Plant, 1978–82; Gen. Manager, later Dir, Worldwide Petrochemicals, Production and Human Resources, 1982–90; Vice-Pres., Ops and Supply, Arco Chemical Europe, 1990–95. Mem., Audit Commn, 1990–97 (Dep. Chm., 1995–97). Member: Welsh Water Authy, 1980–82; Chem. Industries Assoc. Cttees, 1985–; Chm., Inter-Company Productivity Group, 1987–90 (Mem., 1983–90). Non-exec. Dir, Frimley Park Hosp. NHS Trust, 1999–2002; Chm., Ashford and St Peter's Hosps NHS Trust, 2002–. Liveryman, Horners' Co. (Mem., Ct of Assts, 1995–). *Publications:* contribs to newspapers and learned jls on petrochemicals, environment policy and costs, quality management. *Recreations:* hill walking, opera, music, golf, reading history. *Address:* Dwr Golau, 13 Heronscourt, Lightwater, Surrey GU18 5SW. *T:* (01276) 476410. *Clubs:* Harvard Business School; Windlesham Golf.

THOMPSON, Sir Clive (Malcolm), Kt 1996; Deputy Chairman, Strategic Equity Capital plc, since 2005; *b* 4 April 1943; *s* of Harry Louis Thompson and Phyllis Dora Thompson; *m* 1968, Judith Howard; two *s*. *Educ:* Clifton Coll.; Univ. of Birmingham (BSc). Marketing Executive: Royal Dutch Shell Gp, 1964–67; Boots Co. plc, 1967–70; Gen. Manager, Jeyes Gp Ltd, 1970–73; Managing Director: Aerosols Internat. Ltd, 1973–75; Jeyes Ltd, 1975–78; Health and Hygiene Div., Cadbury Schweppes, 1978–82; Gp Chief Exec. Designate, 1982, Gp Chief Exec., 1983–2003, Chm., 2002–04, Rentokil Initial (formerly Rentokil Gp) plc. Chm., Farepak, then Kleeneze, subseq. European Home Retail plc, 2001–06 (Dir, 1988–); Director: Caradon plc, 1986–96; Wellcome plc, 1993–95; Sainsbury plc, 1995–2001; BAT Industries plc, 1995–98; Seeboard plc, 1995–96. Member: BOTB, 1997–99; Cttee on Corporate Governance, 1996–98; Dep. Chm., Financial Reporting Council, 1999–2001. Vice Pres., Chartered Inst. of Marketing, 1996–; Pres., CBI, 1998–2000 (Dep. Pres., 1997–98 and 2000–01). Hon. DSc Birmingham, 1999. *Recreations:* current affairs, stockmarket, golf, walking. *Address:* Strategic Equity Capital plc, 111 Strand, WC2R 0AS. *Club:* Wildernesse (Sevenoaks).

THOMPSON, Collingwood Forster James; QC 1998; a Recorder, since 1997; *b* 19 Dec. 1952; *s* of Collingwood Forster James Thompson and Lillian Thompson; *m* 1985, Valerie Joyce Britchford. *Educ:* Merchiston Castle Sch., Edinburgh; University Coll. London (LLB Hons 1974). Called to the Bar, Gray's Inn, 1975; in practice at the Bar, 1977–. *Recreations:* fly-fishing (badly), hill walking (slowly), wine tasting (frequently), music, reading. *Address:* 7 Bedford Row, WC1R 4BU. *T:* (020) 7242 3555.

THOMPSON, Damian Mark, PhD; Editor-in-Chief, and Director, The Catholic Herald, since 2004; *b* 24 Jan. 1962; *s* of late Leonard Gilbert Thompson and of Pamela Mary Thompson. *Educ:* Presentation Coll., Reading; Mansfield Coll., Oxford (MA); London Sch. of Econs (PhD). Religious Affairs Corresp., Daily Telegraph, 1990–94; freelance feature writer and television critic, 1994–; leader writer, Daily Telegraph, 2003–. Gov., INFORM, 2003–. *Publications:* The End of Time: faith and fear in the shadow of the millennium, 1996; (ed) Loose Canon: a portrait of Brian Brindley, 2004; Waiting for Antichrist: charisma and apocalypse in a Pentecostal Church, 2005; Counterknowledge: how we surrendered to conspiracy theories, quack medicine, bogus science and fake history, 2008. *Recreation:* listening to Beethoven and murdering him on the piano. *Address:* 19 Moorhouse Road, W2 5DH. *T:* 07968 119540; *e-mail:* damianmt@yahoo.com. *Club:* Brooks's.

THOMPSON, Sir David (Albert), KCMG 2002; Vice-President, Royal Commonwealth Society for the Blind, since 2002 (Chairman, 1991–2001); *b* 28 Jan. 1932; *s* of Frederick Thompson and Mildred (*née* Dennis); *m* 1956, Doreen Jo Pryce; one *s* one *d*. *Educ:* various UK schs. Nat. Service, Military Police, Germany, 1950–52. Served Northern Rhodesia Colonial Police, then with copper mining gp, Southern Rhodesia, 1953–58; sales and mktg posts with IBM UK, 1959–63; new product planning, IBM World Trade Corp., Ky, 1963–65; Rank Xerox, 1965–93: Sen. Mktg posts, London, 1965–67; Man. Dir, Rank Xerox Holland, Amsterdam, 1967–69; Sen. Mktg Exec., UK, 1969–72; Regl Dir for Australia, NZ, Hong Kong and Singapore, Sydney, 1972–74; Main Bd Dir, 1975–79; Pres., Xerox Latin America, 1979–83; Main Bd Dir, Rank Xerox Ltd, 1984–90; Chairman: Rank Xerox Pensions Ltd, 1989–93; Rank Xerox (UK) Ltd, 1990–93; Xerox Engrg Systems (Inc.), USA, 1990–93; Dir, Lyell Hldgs (Inc.) USA, 1990–93; non-exec. Chm., Gestetner Hldgs Plc, 1993–95. Mem., Internat. Adv. Bd, Bank Austria Vienna, 1993–95. London Transport: Mem. (pt-time), London Transport Property Bd, 1991–95 (Vice Chm., 1993–95); Chm., London Buses, 1992–93; Mem., Audit, Safety, Remuneration and Design Cttees, 1992–95. Vice Chm., 1989–94, Chm., 1994–2001, Bd of Govs, Commonwealth Inst. Pres., Inst. Trng and Develt, 1992–94. Mem., President's Council, 1990–93, Overseas Trade Cttee, 1990–93, CBI. *Recreations:* dog walking, reading, voluntary work. *Address:* 26 Water Lane, Cobham, Surrey KT11 2PB. *Club:* Carlton.

THOMPSON, David Anthony Roland, FCA; Deputy Chief Executive, Boots Co. plc, 2000–02; *b* 4 Sept. 1942; *s* of Harold Alfred Thompson and Olive Edna (*née* Marlow); *m* 1966, Stella Eunice Durow; two *s*. *Educ:* Burton Grammar Sch. FCA 1964. Joined Boots Co. plc, 1966: Gp Mgt Accountant, 1973–77; Vice-Pres. Finance, Boots Drug Stores, Canada, 1977–80; Finance Dir, Retail Div., 1980–89; Gp Financial Controller, 1989–90; Gp Finance Dir, 1990–2002; Jt Gp Man. Dir, 1997–2000. Non-executive Director: E Midlands Electricity, 1996–97; Cadbury Schweppes, 1998–2008; Nottingham Building Soc., 2002– (Chm., 2004–). Chairman: Southwell Care Project, 2002–; Nottingham Positive Futures Healthy Living Centre, 2003–05. *Recreations:* all sports (especially football), music, cinema, theatre.

THOMPSON, David Brian; Director, Cheveley Park Stud Ltd, since 1975; Chairman, Union Square plc, 1987–91; *b* 3 April 1936; *s* of Bernard Thompson and Rosamund Dee; *m* 1962, Patricia Henchley; one *s* two *d*. *Educ:* Haileybury and ISC. Jt Man. Dir, B. Thompson Ltd, 1960–70; Chm. and co-founder, 1974–84, Jt Chm., 1984–87, Dir, 1987–89, Hillsdown Holdings plc. *Recreations:* family, business, breeding and racing of bloodstock, swimming.

THOMPSON, David George; Member (SNP) Highlands and Islands, Scottish Parliament, since 2007; *b* 20 Sept. 1949; *s* of John Thompson and Doreen Thompson; *m* 1969, Veronica Macleod; one *s* three *d*. *Educ:* Lossiemouth High Sch.; Cert. in Legal Metrol., Dept of Trade, 1971; Dip. in Consumer Affairs, Trading Standards Inst., 1976; Inverness Coll. (HNC Gaelic 2004). Apprentice mechanic, Avery Scales, 1965–67; Trainee, then Trading Standards Officer, Banff, Moray and Nairn CC, 1967–73; Asst Chief Trading Standards Officer, Ross and Cromarty CC, 1973–75; Chief Trading Standards Officer, Comhairle Nan Eilean Siar, 1975–83; Dep. Dir of Trading Standards, 1983–86, Dir of Trading Standards, 1986–95, Highland Regl Council; Dir of Protective

Services, Highland Council, 1995–2001. Contested (SNP): Inverness, Nairn, Badenoch and Strathspey, 2005; Ross, Skye and Inverness W, Scottish Parlt, 2003. *Recreations:* DIY, golf, bridge, football, hill walking. *Address:* Regional Office, Thorfin House, Bridgend Business Park, Dingwall IV15 9SL. *T:* (01349) 864701, *Fax:* (01349) 866327; *e-mail:* dave.thompson.msp@scottish.parliament.uk.

THOMPSON, David George Fossett; Chairman, Marston's (formerly Wolverhampton & Dudley Breweries) plc, since 2001 (Managing Director, 1986–2001); *b* 4 July 1954; *s* of late Edwin John and Helen Wilson Thompson; *m* 1980, Marika Ann Moran Davies; one *s* three *d. Educ:* Winchester Coll.; Magdalene Coll., Cambridge (Exhibnr; Schol.; BA 1975). Cons. Research Dept, 1975–76; Whitbread plc, 1976–77; various posts with Wolverhampton & Dudley Breweries, subseq. Marston's plc, 1977–. Chief Exec., Anglia Maltings (Hldgs) Ltd, 2005–; Chm., Smiths Flour Mills, 2007–; non-executive Director: Income & Growth Trust plc, 1994–2006 (Chm., 2005–06); Persimmon plc, 1999–; Warburtons Ltd, 2002–05; Caledonia Investments plc, 2003–; Tribal Gp plc, 2004–. Chm., Wolverhampton TEC, 1990–95; Dir, W Midlands Regl Develt Agency, 1998–2001. *Address:* Marston's plc, Park Brewery, Wolverhampton WV1 4NY. *T:* (01902) 329508.

THOMPSON, David John; Director, Analysis and Economics (formerly Analysis and Strategy), Department for Transport, since 2005; *b* 22 Nov. 1951; *s* of Cyril Thompson and Doris (*née* Savage). *Educ:* Beverley Grammar Sch.; Manchester Univ. (BA Econs 1973); London Sch. of Economics (MSc Econs 1977). Economist: DoE and Dept of Transport, 1973–83; Monopolies and Mergers Commn, 1984; Dept of Transport, 1987–88; HM Treasury, 1989–91; Dir of Res. on Regulation, Inst. for Fiscal Studies, 1985–86; Sen. Economic Advr, DfEE, 1992–98; Hd of Econs and Stats, MAFF, 1998–2001, DEFRA, 2001–04; Dir, Central Analytical Directorate, DEFRA, 2004–05. Sen. Res. Fellow, London Business Sch., 1989–91. Dir, Economics Plus, 1996–98. *Publications:* contribs to books, articles in learned jls. *Recreations:* watching soccer, Rugby League and the Tour de France, rock and roll. *Address:* Department for Transport, Great Minster House, 76 Marsham Street, SW1P 4DR.

THOMPSON, David Marcus; Head of Films and Single Drama, BBC, 1997–2007; *b* London, 18 July 1950; *s* of Louis and Cynthia Thompson. *Educ:* St Catharine's Coll., Cambridge (BA Hons English). English and Gen. Studies teacher, Bedales Sch.; joined BBC, 1975: Documentary Producer, Open Univ. Prodns, 1975–79; Producer, Everyman, 1979–85 (incl. first drama, Shadowlands (BAFTA and Emmy Awards)); BBC Drama, 1985–94 (created Screenplay series focusing on new talent); Exec. Producer, Single Drama, 1994–97. Exec. producer of films for cinema and TV incl. Shadowlands, 1985; Road, 1987; The Firm, 1988; Safe, 1993; Captives, 1994; Face, Woman in White, 1997; A Rather English Marriage, 1998; Wonderland, Mansfield Park, Ratcatcher, 1999; Nice Girl, Maybe Baby, Born Romantic, Last Resort, Liam, Billy Elliot, Madame Bovary, 2000; When I Was 12, Perfect Strangers, Iris, 2001; Conspiracy, The Gathering Storm, Dirty Pretty Things, In this World, Morvern Callar, Out of Control, Tomorrow La Scala!, 2002; Heart of Me, The Lost Prince, I Capture the Castle, 2003; Mrs Henderson Presents, 2005; The History Boys, 2006; Miss Potter, Notes on a Scandal, 2007. *Recreations:* family life, tennis.

THOMPSON, (David) Robin (Bibby), CBE 1997; TD 1987; DL; Director, Bibby Line Ltd, 1974–87; Deputy Chairman, Rural Development Commission, 1992–96 (Member, 1986–96); *b* 23 July 1946; *s* of Noel Denis Thompson and Cynthia Joan (*née* Bibby); *m* 1971, Caroline Ann Foster (marr. diss. 1998); one *s* one *d*; *m* 1999, Jane Craddock; one *d*. *Educ:* Uppingham Sch.; Mons Officer Cadet Sch. Short service commn, QRIH, 1965; comd Queen's Own Yeomanry (TA), 1984–87; Hon. ADC to the Queen, 1987–90. Member: Council, Royal Agricl Soc. of England, 1985–91; Bd, Housing Corp., 1989–98; Chm., S Shropshire Housing Assoc., 1991–2000. Vice Chm., Pony Club, 2008. Shropshire: High Sheriff, 1989; DL, 2004. *Recreations:* ski-ing, horses, conservation. *Address:* Alderton House, Harmer Hill, Shrewsbury, Shropshire SY4 3EL. *Club:* Cavalry and Guards.

THOMPSON, Dianne; see Thompson, I. D.

THOMPSON, Dr Dorothy Joan, FBA 1996; Fellow, since 1968 and Lecturer in Classics and History, 1968–2006, Girton College, Cambridge; Isaac Newton Trust Lecturer in Classics, University of Cambridge, 1992–2005; *b* 31 May 1939; *d* of Frank William Walbank, *qv* and late Mary (*née* Woodward); *m* 1st, 1966, Michael Hewson Crawford, *qv* (marr. diss. 1979); 2nd, 1982, John Alexander Thompson. *Educ:* Birkenhead High Sch.; Girton Coll., Cambridge (BA 1961; MA 1965; PhD 1966); Bristol Univ. (CertEd 1962). Girton College, Cambridge: Research Fellow, 1965–68; Grad. Tutor (Arts), 1971–81 and 1995–96; Sen. Tutor, 1981–92; Dir of Studies in Classics, 1983–; Clare College, Cambridge: Lectr in Classics, 1973–; Bye-Fellow, 2006–. Vis. Mem., IAS, Princeton, 1982–83; Vis. Prof., Princeton Univ., 1986; Fellow, Nat. Humanities Center, N Carolina, 1993–94; Leverhulme Trust Major Res. Fellowship, 2002–04. President: Assoc. Internationale de Papyrologues, 2002; Cambridge Philological Soc., 2002–04. James H. Breasted Prize, American Historical Assoc., 1989. *Publications:* Kerkeosiris: an Egyptian village in the Ptolemaic period, 1971; (jtly) Studies on Ptolemaic Memphis, 1980; Memphis under the Ptolemies, 1988; (with W. Clarysse) Counting the People in Hellenistic Egypt, 2 vols, 2006; numerous articles and reviews in learned jls. *Recreations:* reading, walking. *Address:* Girton College, Cambridge CB3 0JG. *T:* (01223) 338999.

THOMPSON, Emma; actor; *b* 15 April 1959; *d* of late Eric Norman Thompson and of Phyllida Ann Law; *m* 2003, Greg Wise; one *d. Educ:* Newnham College, Cambridge (MA; Hon. Fellow, 1996). *Stage:* Footlights, Australia, 1982; Me and My Girl, Adelphi, 1984; Look Back in Anger, Lyric, 1989; King Lear, and A Midsummer Night's Dream, Renaissance Th. Co. world tour, 1989; *films:* Henry V, 1988; The Tall Guy, 1988; Impromptu, 1989; Dead Again, 1990; Howards End, 1992 (BAFTA Best Actress, Academy Award, Golden Globe Award, 1993); Peter's Friends, 1992; Much Ado About Nothing, 1993; The Remains of the Day, 1993; In the Name of the Father, 1993; Junior, 1994; Carrington, 1995; Sense and Sensibility (also wrote screenplay; BAFTA Best Actress; awards for screenplay incl. Academy Award), 1996; The Winter Guest, 1997; Judas Kiss, 1997; Primary Colors, 1998; Wit, 2001; Imagining Argentina, 2003; Love Actually, 2003; Harry Potter and the Prisoner of Azkaban, 2004; Nanny McPhee (also wrote screenplay), 2005; Stranger than Fiction, 2006; Harry Potter and the Order of the Phoenix, 2007; *television:* Alfresco, 1983; Tutti Frutti, 1986 (BAFTA Best Actress); Fortunes of War, 1986 (BAFTA Best Actress); Thompson, 1987; Angels in America, 2004. *Recreations:* reading, walking, cooking, acting. *Address:* c/o Hamilton Hodell Ltd, 5th Floor, 66–68 Margaret Street, W1W 8SR.

THOMPSON, Prof. Francis Michael Longstreth, CBE 1992; FBA 1979; Director, Institute of Historical Research, and Professor of History in the University of London, 1977–90, now Emeritus Professor; *b* 13 Aug. 1925; *s* of late Francis Longstreth-Thompson, OBE; *m* 1951, Anne Challoner; two *s* one *d. Educ:* Bootham Sch., York; Queen's Coll., Oxford (Hastings Schol.; MA, DPhil). MRICS (ARICS 1968). War

service, with Indian Artillery, 1943–47; James Bryce Sen. Schol., Oxford, 1949–50; Harmsworth Sen. Schol., Merton Coll., Oxford, 1949–51; Lectr in History, UCL, 1951–63; Reader in Economic History, UCL, 1963–68; Prof. of Modern Hist., Univ. of London, and Head of Dept of Hist., Bedford Coll., London, 1968–77. Joint Editor, Economic History Review, 1968–80. Sec., British Nat. Cttee of Historical Scis, 1978–94; British Mem., Standing Cttee for Humanities, European Sci. Foundn, 1983–93; President: Economic Hist. Soc., 1983–86; RHistS, 1988–92 (Fellow, 1964); British Agricl Hist. Soc., 1989–92; Hon. Treas., Internat. Econ. History Assoc., 1986–94. Member: Senate and Academic Council, Univ. of London, 1970–78; Senate and Collegiate Council, 1981–89. Ford's Lectr, Oxford Univ., 1994. Fellow, RHBNC, 1992. DUniv York, 1995; Hon. DLitt Hertfordshire, 2006. *Publications:* English Landed Society in the Nineteenth Century, 1963; Chartered Surveyors: the growth of a profession, 1968; Victorian England: the horse-drawn society, 1970; Countrysides, in The Nineteenth Century, ed Asa Briggs, 1970; Hampstead: building a borough, 1650–1964, 1974; introd. to General Report on Gosford Estates in County Armagh 1821, by William Greig, 1976; Britain, in European Landed Elites in the Nineteenth Century, ed David Spring, 1977; Landowners and Farmers, in The Faces of Europe, ed Alan Bullock, 1980; 2 chapters in The Victorian Countryside, ed G. E. Mingay, 1981; (ed) The Rise of Suburbia, 1982; (ed) Horses in European Economic History, 1983; Towns, Industry and the Victorian Landscape, in The English Landscape, ed S. R. J. Woodell, 1985; Private Property and Public Policy, in Salisbury: The Man and his Policies, ed Lord Blake and Hugh Cecil, 1987; Rise of Respectable Society: a social history of Victorian Britain, 1988; (ed) The Cambridge Social History of Britain 1750–1950, vol. 1 Regions and Communities, vol. 2 People and their Environment, vol. 3 Social Agencies and Social Institutions, 1990; (ed) The University of London and the World of Learning 1836–1986, 1990; (ed) Landowners, Capitalists, and Entrepreneurs: essays for Sir John Habakkuk, 1994; Gentrification and the Enterprise Culture: Britain 1780–1980, 2001; numerous articles in Economic History Review, History, English Historical Review, etc. *Recreations:* gardening, walking, carpentry. *Address:* Holly Cottage, Sheepcote Lane, Wheathampstead, Herts AL4 8NJ. *T:* (01582) 833129.

THOMPSON, Geoffrey Austin; Head, Mill Hill County High School, since 2004; *b* Belfast, 23 July 1952; *s* of Herbert, (Tommy), and Patricia Thompson; *m* 2000, Sally Mary (*née* Pulford); two step *s* one step *d. Educ:* Campbell Coll., Belfast; St Catharine's Coll., Cambridge (BA 1974); Stockwell Coll. (PGCE London 1978); South Bank Univ. (MBA Educn 1994). Teacher of English and Hist., Cannock Sch., 1974–77; Asst Dir of Music, Dir of Music, then Hd of Yr, Langley Park Boys' Sch., Beckenham, 1978–93; Dep. Hd, Downham Market High Sch., 1993–97; Hd, The Duchess's Community High Sch., Alnwick, 1997–2003. FCMI. *Recreations:* pianist, classical music, theatre, mountain sports, modern history. *Address:* Mill Hill County High School, Worcester Crescent, Mill Hill, NW7 4LL. *T:* (020) 8238 8184; *e-mail:* geoffreyandsally@btinternet.com.

THOMPSON, Rt Rev. (Geoffrey) Hewlett; Hon. Assistant Bishop, diocese of Carlisle, since 1999; *b* 14 Aug. 1929; *o s* of late Lt-Col R. R. Thompson, MC, RAMC; *m* 1954, Elisabeth Joy Fausitt, MA (Oxon), *d* of late Col G. F. Taylor, MBE and Dr Frances Taylor; two *s* two *d. Educ:* Aldenham Sch.; Trinity Hall, Cambridge (MA); Cuddesdon Theol College. 2nd Lieut, Queen's Own Royal West Kent Regt, 1948–49 (Nat. Service). Ordained deacon, 1954, priest, 1955; Curate, St Matthew, Northampton, 1954–59; Vicar: St Augustine, Wisbech, 1959–66; St Saviour, Folkestone, 1966–74; Bishop Suffragan of Willesden, 1974–79, Area Bishop of Willesden, 1979–85; Bishop of Exeter, 1985–99. Chairman: Community and Race Relations Unit, BCC, 1980–84 (Vice-Chm., 1976–80); Hospital Chaplaincies Council, 1991–97. Introduced into House of Lords, 1990. *Recreations:* fell walking, reading, gardening, music. *Address:* Low Broomrigg, Warcop, Appleby, Cumbria CA16 6PT. *T:* (017683) 41281. *Club:* Oxford and Cambridge.

THOMPSON, Rev. George H.; Parish Priest, St Peter's, Dalbeattie, 1995–2004; *b* 11 Sept. 1928. *Educ:* Dalry Sch.; Kirkcudbright Acad.; Edinburgh Univ. Teacher, modern languages, Kirkcudbright Academy; Principal Teacher of French, 1979–85, Principal Teacher of Modern Languages, 1985–86, Annan Acad., Dumfriesshire. Contested (SNP): Galloway, Feb. 1974, 1979; Galloway and Upper Nithsdale, 1983. Former SNP Asst Nat. Sec.; MP (SNP) Galloway, Oct. 1974–1979; SNP Spokesman: on health, Oct. 1974–1979; on forestry, 1975. Deacon, RC dio. of Galloway, 1989, priest 1989; Asst Priest, St Teresa's, Dumfries, 1989–93; Administrator, St Margaret of Scotland's, Irvine, 1993–95. *Address:* 53 Kirkland Street, Dalry, Castle Douglas DG7 3UX. *T:* (01644) 430254.

THOMPSON, Sir Gilbert (Williamson), Kt 1993; OBE 1985; Chairman: British Airports Group, 1995–2001; Alltram, 1997–2001; Chief Executive, 1981–93, and Board Member, 1986–93, Manchester Airport plc; *b* 1 March 1930; *s* of Henry Gordon Thompson and Isabella Thompson; *m* 1954, Dorothy Millar; two *d. Educ:* London Business Sch.; Manchester Business Sch. British European Airways, later British Airways: mgt trainee, Belfast, 1950; Regl Manager, Los Angeles, 1965–67; Manager, Irish Republic, 1967–69; General Manager: USA, 1969–72; Scotland, 1972–74; N of England, 1974–81. Dep. Chm., Campbell & Armstrong, 1996–2001. Pres., British Amer. Business Gp, 1995–2001; Member: British Amer. Business Council, 1995–2001; Bd, Nimtech, 1996–2001; BOTB, 1997–2001. Hon. DLitt Salford, 1993. *Recreations:* golf, bridge, soccer, jogging, keep fit. *Address:* Arncliffe, The Penthouse, Apartment 5, 66 South Downs Road, Bowdon, Cheshire WA14 3DR.

THOMPSON, Glenn; see Thompson, J. McM. S. H. G.

THOMPSON, Sir Godfrey James M.; see Milton-Thompson.

THOMPSON, (Henry) Antony Cardew W.; see Worrall Thompson.

THOMPSON, Rt Rev. Hewlett; see Thompson, Rt Rev. G. H.

THOMPSON, Howard; see Thompson, James H.

THOMPSON, (Hugh) Patrick; *b* 21 Oct. 1935; *s* of late Gerald Leopold Thompson and Kathleen Mary Lansdown Thompson; *m* 1962, Kathleen Howson. *Educ:* Felsted Sch., Essex; Emmanuel Coll., Cambridge (MA). Nat. Service, 2nd Lieut, KOYLI, 1957–59; TA, Manchester, 1960–65; Gresham's Sch., CCF, 1965–82 (CFM 1980); Major, retd. Engr, English Electric Valve Co., Chelmsford, 1959–60; Sixth Form Physics Master: Manchester Grammar Sch., 1960–65; Gresham's Sch., Holt, 1965–83. MP (C) Norwich North, 1983–97. Parliamentary Private Secretary: to Minister of State for Transport, 1987–88; to Minister of State, Dept of Social Security, 1988–89; to Minister for Health, 1992–94. Member: Parly and Scientific Cttee, 1983–97; Select Cttee, Educn, Science and the Arts, 1991–92; Select Cttee, Sci. and Technol., 1995–97; Speaker's Panel of Chairmen, 1994–97; Founder Mem., All Party Gp for Engrg Develt, 1985–97; Secretary: Cons. Back Bench Energy Cttee, 1986–87; Cons. Back Bench European Cttee, 1991–92. *Publication:* Elementary Calculations in Physics, 1963. *Recreations:* travel, music, gardening. *Club:* Norfolk (Norwich).

THOMPSON, Ian; Director, IKT Consulting Ltd, since 2003; *b* 20 May 1951; *s* of Eber Edward Thompson and Edith (*née* Gilchrist); *m* 1st, 1972, Anne Rosalind Clouston (marr. diss. 1995); one *d*; 2nd, 1998, Karin Bell. *Educ:* Workington Grammar Sch.; Univ. of Hull (BSc). IPFA. With Humberside CC, 1974–80; Northamptonshire County Council, 1980–89: Chief Acctnt, 1986–88; Sen. Asst Educn Officer, 1988–89; Berkshire County Council: Sen. Asst Co. Treas., 1989–93; Co. Treas., 1993–96; Chief Finance and Property Officer, subseq. Dir of Finance and Property, then Dir of Resources, Swindon BC, 1997–2003. *Recreations:* playing guitar, playing squash, playing trains. *Address:* Snowberry House, Hinton Parva, Swindon SN4 0DW. *T:* (01793) 790970.

THOMPSON, Dr (Ian) McKim; Vice President, British Medical Association, since 1998; *b* 19 Aug. 1938; *s* of late J. W. Thompson and Dr E. M. Thompson; *m* 1962, Dr Veronica Jane Richards (marr. diss. 1988); two *s* one *d*. *Educ:* Epsom Coll.; Birmingham Univ. (MB, ChB 1961). Lectr in Pathology, Univ. of Birmingham, 1964–67; Sen. Registrar, Birmingham RHB, 1967–69; Sen. Under Sec., 1969–85, Dep. Sec., 1985–96, BMA. Consulting Forensic Pathologist to HM Coroner, City of Birmingham, 1966–97. Part time Tutor, Dept of Adult and Continuing Educn, Keele Univ., 1985–; Tutor, Wedgwood Meml Coll., Barlaston, 1990–. Member: GMC, 1979–94; Royal Medical Foundn, 1998–; Pres., Birmingham Med. Inst., 2003–; Dep. Chm., Retired Members Forum, BMA, 2007–09. Hon. MO, Inland Waterways Assoc., 1976–. Pres., Sands Cox Soc., Univ. of Birmingham, 2006–07 (Vice-Pres., 2005–06). FRSocMed 1987. Hon. Collegian, Med. Colls of Spain, 1975. *Publications:* (ed) The Hospital Gazeteer, 1972; (ed) BMA Handbook for Hospital Junior Doctors, 1977, 5th edn 1990; (ed) BMA Handbook for Trainee Doctors in General Practice, 1982, 3rd edn 1985; various medical scientific papers. *Recreations:* inland waterways, rambling. *Address:* Canal Cottage, Hinksford Lane, Kingswinford DY6 0BH. *T:* (01384) 294131.

THOMPSON, Rev. Ian Malcolm; Dean, King's College, Cambridge, since 2005; *b* 24 June 1959; *s* of Ernest Henry Thompson and Kathleen Joyce (*née* Cavanagh); *m* 1980, Ann Perry. *Educ:* Harris Acad., Dundee; William Booth Meml Coll., London (CertEd 1979); Univ. of Aberdeen (BTh 1998). Officer, Salvation Army, 1979–93; ordained deacon, 1994, priest, 1995; Curate in charge, Central Buchan, 1994–96; Rector, St Mary's Aberdeen, 1996–99; Chaplain and Dean of Chapel, Selwyn Coll., Cambridge, 1999–2005; Hon. Asst Priest, Little St Mary's, Cambridge, 2004–06. *Recreations:* swimming, rowing. *Address:* King's College, Cambridge CB2 1ST. *T:* (01223) 331419, *Fax:* (01223) 331315; *e-mail:* dean@kings.cam.ac.uk.

THOMPSON, (Ila) Dianne, CBE 2006; Chief Executive, Camelot Group plc, since 2000 (Commercial Director, 1997–2000); *b* 31 Dec. 1950; *d* of Ronald Wood and Joan Wood (*née* Pinder); *m* 1972, Roger Thompson (marr. diss. 1992); one *d*. *Educ:* Batley Girls' Grammar Sch.; Manchester Poly. (BA Hons ext. London). Product Manager, CWS, 1972–74; Mktg Manager, ICI, 1974–79; Lectr, Manchester Poly., 1979–86; Mktg Dir, Sterling Roncraft, 1986–88; Man. Dir, Sandvik Saws & Tools, 1988–92; Marketing Director: Woolworths plc, 1992–94; Signet Gp, 1994–97. Mem., Mktg Gp of GB, 1993. Mem., Press Complaints Commn, 2003–. FCIM 1988; Fellow, Mktg Soc., 1998; FRSA 2000; CCMI 2001. Veuve Cliquot Businesswoman of the Year, 2000; Marketer of the Year, Mktg Soc., 2001; Gold Medal, Chartered Mgt Inst., 2006. *Recreations:* theatre, cinema, entertaining, travel. *Address:* Camelot Group plc, Tolpits Lane, Watford WD18 9RN.

THOMPSON, James, FCLIP; University Librarian, University of Birmingham, 1987–95; *b* 11 Jan. 1932; *s* of James Thompson and Mary Margaret Thompson (*née* Harland); *m* 1st, 1958, Mary Josephine McAndrew (marr. diss. 1987); one *s* one *d*; 2nd, 1988, Susan Lesley Challans. *Educ:* St Cuthbert's Grammar Sch.; Univ. of Durham (BA 1st Cl. Hons English). FCLIP (FLA 1963). Newcastle City Libraries, 1948–59; Nottingham Univ. Liby, 1959–63; Sen. Asst Librarian, UEA, 1963–65; Dep. Librarian, Univ. of Glasgow, 1965–67; Univ. Librarian, Univ. of Reading, 1967–87. Member: Council, LA, 1972–74; Berks Co. Liby Sub-cttee, 1973–87; SCONUL Council, 1983–86. Pres., Reading AUT, 1981–83. Project Hd, Location Register of Twentieth Century English Literary MSS and Letters, 1982–87. *Publications:* The Librarian and English Literature, 1968, 2nd edn as English Studies, 1971; Books: an anthology, 1968; An Introduction to University Library Administration, 1970, 4th edn 1987 (Spanish edn 1989); Library Power, 1974; A History of the Principles of Librarianship, 1977; (ed) University Library History, 1980; The End of Libraries, 1982; Redirection in Academic Library Management, 1991; A Centennial History of the Library of the University of Birmingham, 2000; contribs to books, conf. proceedings and jls. *Recreation:* gardening. *Address:* 35 Meadow Rise, Bournville, Birmingham B30 1UZ. *T:* (0121) 472 1735.
See also R. Coe.

THOMPSON, James Craig; Chairman, MD Presscom Ltd, 1997–2007; *b* 27 Oct. 1933; *s* of Alfred Thompson and Eleanor (*née* Craig); *m* 1957, Catherine (*née* Warburton); one *s* one *d*. *Educ:* Heaton Grammar Sch., Newcastle upon Tyne; Rutherford Coll., Newcastle upon Tyne. Commercial Exec., Belfast Telegraph, Newcastle Chronicle and Journal, Scotsman Publications, Liverpool Post and Echo, 1960–76; Advertising and Marketing Manager, Kent Messenger Gp, 1976–79, Dir, 1972–79; Man. Dir, South Eastern Newspapers, 1975–79; Chm. and Man. Dir, 1973–89, Consultant Dir, 1989–92, Adverkit Internat. Ltd; Chm. and Man. Dir, Harvest Publications Ltd, 1983–95; Director of Policy: Maidstone and Mid Kent Chamber of Commerce and Industry Ltd, 1994–2003; Kent Gateway Chamber of Commerce, 2001–03. Dir, Weekly Newspaper Advtg Bureau, 1977. Director: Ad Builder Ltd, 1971–89; MLO Ltd, 2000–; Business Point Maidstone Ltd, 1996–2002; Maidstone Enterprise Agency Ltd, 1998–2002; Associated Kent Chambers, 2001–03. Chm., Otham Parish Council, Kent, 2005–. Life Governor, Kent County Agricl Soc., 1974. Hon. Life Mem., Kent CCC, 1978; Mem., Catenian Assoc. (Pres., Maidstone Circle, 1974–75). Chm., Maidstone United Football Club, 1970–92; Chm., Southern Football League, 1977–79 (Life Mem., 1985); Pres., The Football Conf. Ltd, 1989–2008; Mem. Council, Football Assoc., 1982–92. FInstD; MInstM; MCMI. Freeman, City of London; Liveryman, Co. of Stationers and Newspaper Makers. Distinguished Service Award, Internat. Classified Advertising Assoc., Baltimore, 1968. *Publications:* numerous articles on commercial aspects of newspaper publishing and Association football. *Recreations:* walking, Northumbrian history. *Address:* Greenlands, Honey Lane, Otham, Maidstone, Kent ME15 8RJ. *T:* (01622) 861606. *Clubs:* MCC; Maidstone (Maidstone) (Life Mem., Pres., 1997).

THOMPSON, (James) Howard, OBE 1984; Programme Manager, Schistosomiasis Control Initiative, Imperial College London, 2002–08; *b* 26 March 1942; *s* of James Alan Thompson and Edna (*née* Perkins); *m* 1965, Claire Marguerite Dockrell; one *s* one *d*. *Educ:* Northampton Grammar Sch.; Magdalene Coll., Cambridge (BA); Stanford Univ. (MA). English Language Officer, British Council, Yugoslavia, 1966–69; Associate Prof., Punjab Univ., 1970–73; Dep. Representative, British Council, Kenya, 1974–78; Advr, Schs and Further Educn Dept, 1978–80; Educn Attaché, British Embassy, Washington, 1980–84; Dep. Controller, 1984–87, Controller, 1987–89, Science, Technology and Educn Div., British Council; Chm., Educn and Trng Export Cttee, 1988–89; British Council Director: Indonesia, 1989–92; Egypt, 1993–96; Brazil, 1997–2002. Vice Chm., Govs, Bentworth Prim. Sch., Hammersmith, 2008–. *Publication:* Teaching English, 1972. *Recreations:* photography, travel, golf. *Address:* 1 Homefield Road, W4 2LN.

THOMPSON, Janet, CB 2000; DPhil; CPhys, FInstP; Chief Executive, Forensic Science Service, 1988–2001; *b* 23 Oct. 1941; *d* of late Arthur Hugh Denison Fairbarns and Eleanor Mary Fairbarns (*née* Cattel); *m* 1999, Elliot Grant; one *s* one *d*, and one *s* from a former marriage. *Educ:* North London Collegiate Sch.; Brighton Coll. of Technol. (BSc 1963); Univ. of Oxford (DPhil 1968). CPhys, FInstP 1999. Chm., Science, Technol. and Mathematics Council, 1999–2001. Chm., European Network of Forensic Insts, 1997–99.

THOMPSON, Jeff; *see* Thompson, John J.

THOMPSON, Jeremy Gordon; Presenter, Live at Five, Sky News, since 1999; *b* 23 Sept. 1947; *s* of Gordon and Betty Thompson; *m* 1st, Nicky Wood (marr. diss. 1979); two *s*; 2nd, 1986, Lynn Bowland. *Educ:* Sevenoaks Prep. Sch.; Sevenoaks Sch.; King's Sch., Worcester. Reporter: Cambridge Evening News, 1967–71; BBC Radio Sheffield, 1971–74; BBC TV Look North, Leeds, 1974–77; N of England corresp., BBC TV News, 1977–82; Chief Sports Corresp., 1982–86, Asia Corresp., 1987–90, Africa Corresp., 1991–93, ITN; Sky News: Africa Corresp., 1993–95; USA Corresp., 1995–98; presenter, 1998–. Emmy Award for Internat. News Reporting; Presenter of the Yr, RTS, 2005; Gold Award for Best Internat. Reporter, NY Fest. *Recreations:* travelling, safaris, walking, golf, watching sport. *Address:* c/o Sky News, British Sky Broadcasting, Grant Way, Isleworth, Middx TW7 5QD. *T:* 0870 240 3000; *e-mail:* jeremy.thompson@bskyb.com. *Clubs:* Cricket Writers', Rugby Writers'; Hampton Court Palace Golf.

THOMPSON, John; DL; *b* 27 Aug. 1928; *s* of Nicholas and Lilian Thompson; *m* 1952, Margaret Clarke; one *s* one *d*. *Educ:* Bothal Sch.; Ashington Mining Coll. Electrical Engr, 1966–83. Councillor: Wansbeck DC, 1974–79; Northumberland CC, 1974–85 (Leader, and Chm., Policy and Resources, and Employment Cttees, 1981–83). MP (Lab) Wansbeck, 1983–97. An Opposition Whip, 1990–97. Mem., Select Cttee on Educn, Science and Arts, 1985–87; Chm., Northern Labour MPs, 1991–92 (Sec., 1985–90). Member: Council of Europe (Chm., Fisheries Sub Cttee, 1995–97); WEU (Chm., Rules and Privileges Cttee, 1992–97). Chm., Ashington Educn Achievement Zone, 1999–2002. DL Northumberland, 1996. *Address:* 20 Falstone Crescent, Ashington, Northumberland NE63 0TY. *T:* (01670) 817830.

THOMPSON, John, MBE 1975; consultant; HM Diplomatic Service, retired; Ambassador to Angola, and St Thomas and Prince, 2002–05; *b* 28 May 1945; *s* of late Arthur Thompson and Josephine (*née* Brooke); *m* 1966, Barbara Hopper; one *d*. *Educ:* Whiteheath County Primary Sch., Ruislip, Middx; St Nicholas Grammar Sch., Northwood, Middx; Polytechnic of Central London (DMS). Joined FO, 1964; Vice-Consul, Düsseldorf, 1966–69; Consular Officer, later Vice-Consul, Abu Dhabi, 1969–72; Vice-Consul, Phnom Penh, 1972–74; seconded to DTI, 1975–77; First Sec., FCO, 1977–79; First Sec., Hd of Chancery and Consul, Luanda, 1979–81; Consul (Commercial), São Paulo, 1981–85; Assistant Head: S Pacific Dept, FCO, 1985–87; Aid Policy Dept, FCO, 1987–88; High Comr to Vanuatu, 1988–92; Dep. Consul-Gen. and Dir of Trade, NY, 1992–97; Hd of Inf. Systems Dept and Library and Records Dept, FCO, 1997–99; Hd of Inf. Mgt Gp, FCO Services, FCO, 1999–2001. *Recreations:* philately, walking, reading, bridge.

THOMPSON, Sir John; *see* Thompson, Sir T. d'E. J.

THOMPSON, John Brian, CBE 1980; Director of Radio, Independent Broadcasting Authority, 1973–87; *b* 8 June 1928; *y s* of late John and Lilian Thompson; *m* 1957, Sylvia, *d* of late Thomas Waterhouse, CBE, and of Doris Waterhouse (*née* Gough); two *s* one *d*. *Educ:* St Paul's; Pembroke College, Oxford (BA; MA). Eileen Power Studentship, LSE, 1950; Glaxo Laboratories Ltd, 1950–54; Masius & Fergusson Ltd, 1955; Asst Editor, Truth, 1956–57; Daily Express, 1957–59 (New York Correspondent; Drama Critic); ITN, 1959–60 (Newscaster/Reporter); Editor, Time and Tide, 1960–62; News Editor, The Observer, 1962–66; Editor, Observer Colour Magazine, 1966–70; Publisher and Editorial Dir, BPC Publishing Ltd, 1971; Editor, The Viewer, 1988–90. Vis. Prof., Sch. of Media, Lancashire Poly., 1987–90. Sen. Advr on Radio to Minister of Posts and Telecommunications, 1972; Mem., MoD Study Group on Censorship, 1983. Director: Worlds End Productions Ltd, 1987–91; The Observer, 1989–93; Dep. Chm., Zabaxe Gp, 1988–90. Vice-Chm. (radio), EBU, 1986–88. Mem. Delegacy, Goldsmiths' Coll., London, 1986–96. Associate Mem., Nuffield Coll., Oxford, 1988–90. Judge, Booker Fiction Prize, 1987; Panel of Selection Bd Chairmen, CS Commn/RAS, 1988–93. Sony Radio special award, 1983. *Address:* 1 Bedwyn Common, Great Bedwyn, Marlborough, Wilts SN8 3HZ. *T:* (01672) 870641. *Clubs:* Garrick, Groucho.
See also Sir R. G. Waterhouse.

THOMPSON, (John) Derek T.; *see* Taylor Thompson.

THOMPSON, Prof. John Griggs, PhD; FRS 1979; Rouse Ball Professor of Mathematics, University of Cambridge, 1971–93, now Professor Emeritus; Fellow of Churchill College, Cambridge, since 1968; *b* Kansas, 13 Oct. 1932; *s* of John and Eleanor Thompson; *m* 1960, Diane Oenning; one *s* one *d*. *Educ:* Yale (BA 1955); Chicago (PhD 1959); MA Cantab 1972. Prof. of Mathematics, Chicago Univ., 1962–68; Vis. Prof. of Mathematics, Cambridge Univ., 1968–70. Hon. DSc Oxon, 1987. Cole Prize, 1966; Field Medal, 1970; Berwick Prize, London Math. Soc., 1982; Sylvester Medal, Royal Soc., 1985; Wolf Prize, 1992; Poincaré Medal, 1992; (jtly) Abel Prize, Norwegian Acad. of Sci. and Letters, 2008. *Address:* 16 Millington Road, Cambridge CB3 9HP.

THOMPSON, John Handby, CB 1988; CVO 1994; Ceremonial Officer, Cabinet Office, and Secretary, Political Honours Scrutiny Committee, 1988–94; *b* 21 Feb. 1929; *s* of late Rev. John Thomas Thompson and Clara Handby. *Educ:* Silcoates Sch., Wakefield; St John's Coll., Oxford (MA); Sheffield Univ. (PhD 1991). Served Intell. Corps, 1947–49. HM Inspector of Taxes, 1953–63; Dept of Educn and Science, 1964–88: Schs Council, 1971–73; Asst Sec., 1973; Mem., Prep. Cttee of European Univ. Inst., 1973–75; Dep. Accountant-Gen., 1976–78; Under Sec., 1978; Head of Schs Br. 1, 1978–80; Head of Further and Higher Educn Br. 1, 1980–84; Dir of Estabts and Orgn, 1985–88. Gov., Univ. (formerly Poly.) of N London, 1989–98 (Hon. Fellow, 1999). Pres., Chapels Soc., 1998–2001. Chm., Friends of the Congregational Library, 2001–06; Trustee: Congregational Meml Hall Trust, 2003–; Lord Wharton's Charity, 2005–. *Publications:* A History of the Coward Trust 1738–1988, 1998; Highgate Dissenters: their history since 1660, 2001; (contrib.) Modern Christianity and Cultural Aspirations, 2003; (contrib.) Who They Were in the Reformed Churches of England and Wales 1901–2000, 2007. *Recreations:* reading about Albania, Nonconformist history. *Address:* 2 Alwyne Villas, N1 2HQ. *Club:* Reform.

THOMPSON, Air Marshal John Hugh, CB 2000; FRAeS; Director General, Saudi Armed Forces Project, 2002–06; *b* 18 Sept. 1947; *m* 1969, Mary Elizabeth Emerson; two *s* one *d*. *Educ:* Fielding High Sch., NZ; RAF Coll., Cranwell. Hunter pilot, Bahrain,

1970–71; Harrier pilot, weapons instructor and Sqdn Comdr; Army Staff Coll., 1982; Station Comdr, Wittering, 1988–90; RCDS, 1991; Higher Comd and Staff Course, 1992; SASO, Rheindahlen, 1993–96; Office of the High Rep., Sarajevo, 1996; AOC and Comdt, RAF Coll., Cranwell, 1997–98; AOC No 1 Gp, 1998–2000; Defence Attaché and Head of British Defence Staff, Washington, 2000–02. FRAeS 2007. *Recreations:* golf, reading. *Club:* Royal Air Force.

THOMPSON, Prof. John Jeffrey, (Jeff), CBE 1989; PhD; CChem, FRSC; Professor of Education, 1979–2005, and Director, Centre for the Study of Education in an International Context, 1992–2005, University of Bath, now Professor Emeritus; *b* 13 July 1938; *s* of late John Thompson and Elsie May Thompson (*née* Wright); *m* 1963, Kathleen Audrey Gough; three *d. Educ:* King George V Sch., Southport; St John's Coll., Cambridge (MA); Balliol Coll., Oxford (MA); PhD (CNAA); DipEd (Oxon). Asst Master, Blundell's Sch., 1961–65; Head of Chemistry, Watford Grammar Sch., 1965–69; Lectr in Educn, KCL, 1968–69; Shell Fellow, UCL, 1969–70; Lectr and Tutor, Dept of Educnl Studies, Oxford Univ., 1970–79; Lectr in Chemistry, Keble Coll., Oxford, 1970–76; Pro-Vice-Chancellor, Univ. of Bath, 1986–89. Chief Examnr, Internat. Baccalaureate, 1970–89 (Chm., Bd of Chief Examnrs, 1985–89); International Baccalaureate Organisation: Chm. Res. Cttee, 1998–2004; Dir for Internat. Educn, 2000–02; Academic Dir, 2003–04; Hd of Res. Unit, 2000–05; Chm., Examination Appeals Bd, 2003– (Dep. Chm., 1999–2003). Chairman: Assoc. for Science Educn, 1981; Nat. Curriculum Science Working Gp, 1987–88; Adv. Bd, Total Science Solutions, 2003–05. Mem., Council, 1988–92, Dep. Chm., 1989–92, School Exams and Assessment Council; Member: Nat. Commn on Educn, 1991–93; English Nat. Bd for Nursing, Midwifery and Health Visiting, 1993–2002. Pres., Educn Div., Royal Soc. of Chemistry, 1983–85; Dep. Chm., Educn Cttee, Royal Soc., 1995–98; British Association for the Advancement of Science: Vice Pres., 1996–2001; Vice Pres. and Gen. Sec., 1985–91; Chm. Council, 1991–96. Governor and Mem. Council, United World Coll. of the Atlantic, 1992– (Dir, Internat. Bd, 2005–; Gov., UWC Mostar, 2005–). Hon. Mem., ASE, 1994; Hon. Fellow, BAAS, 2006. Mem. Council, Wildfowl Trust, 1981–91. FRSA 1983. Freeman, 1992, Liveryman, 1995, Goldsmiths' Co., 1992; Freeman, City of London, 1992. Gen. Editor, Bath Science series, age gps 16–19 (12 titles), and 5–16 (78 titles), 1990–2000; Ed.-in-Chief, Jl for Res. in Internat. Educn, 2002–06. Hon DLitt Hertfordshire, 2000. Distinguished Service Award: Internat. Schs Assoc., 2005; Eur. Council for Internat. Schs, 2005. *Publications:* Introduction to Chemical Energetics, 1967; European Curriculum Studies; Chemistry, 1972; (ed) Practical Work in Sixthform Science, 1976; Foundation Course in Chemistry, 1982; Modern Physical Chemistry, 1982; (ed) Dimensions of Science (9 titles), 1986; The Chemistry Dimension, 1987; International Education: Principles and Practice, 1998; (ed) International Schools and International Education, 2000; (ed) International Education in Practice, 2002; (ed) A Handbook of Research in International Education, 2006; (jtly) International Schools: growth and influence, 2008. *Recreations:* music (brass bands and blue grass), North Country art, collecting sugar wrappers. *Address:* University of Bath, Claverton Down, Bath BA2 7AY.

THOMPSON, John Keith Lumley, CMG 1982; MBE (mil.) 1965; TD 1961; President, Lumley Associates, since 1983; *b* 31 March 1923; *s* of late John V. V. and Gertrude Thompson; *m* 1950, Audrey Olley; one *s. Educ:* Wallsend Grammar Sch.; King's Coll., Durham Univ. (BSc). MSAE 1983. Served War of 1939–45: Officer in REME, 1942–47, NW Europe; BEME 44 Para Bde (V), 1948–70. Dep. Inspector, REME (V) Southern Comd, 1970–72 (Lt-Col); Dep. Comdr, 44 Para Bde (V), 1972–75 (Col). Road Research Lab., DSIR, 1948–55; AWRE, Aldermaston, 1955–64; Staff of Chief Scientific Adviser, MoD, 1964–65; Head of E Midlands Regional Office, Min. Tech., 1965–70; Head, Internat. Affairs, Atomic Energy Div., Dept of Energy, 1972–74; Regional Dir, W Midlands and Northern Regional Offices, DoI, 1970–72 and 1974–78; Counseller (Sci. and Tech.), Washington, 1978–83. ADC to the Queen (TAVR), 1974–78. FCMI (FBIM; MBIM 1975). *Publications:* papers on vehicle behaviour, crash helmets and implosion systems; numerous articles on American science and technology. *Recreations:* outdoor activities, reading. *Address:* c/o Lumley Associates, 7 School Lane, Baston, Peterborough PE6 9PD. *T:* (01778) 560374.

THOMPSON, John Leonard C.; *see* Cloudsley-Thompson.

THOMPSON, (John McMaster Samuel Hugh) Glenn, CB 2001; business consultant, since 2001; *b* 11 Nov. 1949; *s* of Hugh Glenn Thompson and Sarah (*née* McMaster); *m* 1971, Elizabeth McClements; two *d. Educ:* Regent House Grammar Sch., Newtownards. Clerk to Principal, NICS, 1967–86; Asst Sec., Industrial Develt Bd for NI, 1986–89; Regl Manager, 1989–92, Exec. Dir, 1992–96, Crestacare plc; Under-Sec., Civil Service, 1996–2001. *Recreations:* travel, Rugby Union.

THOMPSON, John Michael Anthony, FMA; museums and heritage consultant, since 1991; Senior Consultant, Prince Research Consultants Ltd, 1995–2007; *b* 3 Feb. 1941; *s* of George Thompson and Joan Smith; *m* 1965, Alison Sara Bowers; two *d. Educ:* William Hulme's Grammar Sch., Manchester; Univ. of Manchester. BA, MA; FMA 1980. Research Asst, Whitworth Art Gall., 1964–66; Keeper, Rutherston Collection, City Art Gall., Manchester, 1966–68; Director: North Western Museum and Art Gall. Service, 1968–70; Arts and Museums, Bradford City Council, 1970–74; Chief Arts and Museums Officer, Bradford Metropolitan Council, 1974–75; Dir, Art Galls and Museums, Tyne and Wear County Museums, 1975–91. Councillor, Museums Assoc., 1977–80, 1984–87 (Chm., Accreditation Cttee, 1978–80); Advisor to Arts and Recreation Cttee, AMA, 1981–91; Pres., Museums North, 1977, and 1991–92; Chm., Soc. of County Museum Dirs, 1982–86; Founder Mem. and Hon. Sec., Gp of Dirs of Museums in the British Isles, 1985–91. Dir, Museums and Galleries Consultancy Ltd, 1992–95; Mem. Bd, Jarrow 700 AD Ltd, 1992–2006. External Verifier: Museum Trng Inst., 1996–99; Qualifications for Industry, 1999–. Advr to UNESCO, 2001–; Educn and Access Advr to Heritage Lottery Fund, 2005–. Chm., Gosforth Adult Educn Assoc., 1994–. Vice Chm. Governors, Gosforth High Sch., 1997–99. Mem. Council, Tyne and Wear Building Preservation Trust, 2008–. *Publications:* (ed) The Manual of Curatorship: a guide to museum practice, 1984, 2nd edn 1993; Contracting Culture: museums and local government, 1994; articles in Museums Jl, Penrose Annual, Connoisseur. *Recreations:* classical guitar, running, walking. *Address:* 21 Linden Road, Gosforth, Newcastle upon Tyne NE3 4EY. *T:* and *Fax:* (0191) 284 7304.

THOMPSON, Prof. John Michael Tutill, FRS 1985; Professor of Nonlinear Dynamics, Department of Civil and Environmental Engineering, and Director, Centre for Nonlinear Dynamics and Its Applications, University College London, 1991–2002, now Emeritus Professor; a Sixth Century Professor in Theoretical and Applied Dynamics (part-time), University of Aberdeen, since 2006; Chairman, ES-Consult (Consulting Engineers), Copenhagen, since 1995; *b* 7 June 1937; *s* of John Hornsey Thompson and Kathleen Rita Thompson (*née* Tutill); *m* 1959, Margaret Cecilia Chapman; one *s* one *d. Educ:* Hull Grammar Sch.; Clare Coll., Cambridge (MA, PhD, ScD). FIMA; CMath. Research Fellow, Peterhouse, 1961–64; Vis. Res. Associate, Stanford (Fulbright grant), 1962–63; Lectr, 1964–68, Reader, 1968–77, Prof. of Structural Mechanics, 1977–91, UCL; Chm., Bd of Studies in Civil and Mech. Eng., Univ. of London, 1984–86. Vis. Prof., Faculté des Sciences, Univ. Libre de Bruxelles, 1976–78; Vis. Mathematician, Brookhaven Nat. Lab., 1984; Vis. Res. Fellow, Centre for Nonlinear Studies, Univ. of Leeds, 1987–97; Sen. Fellow, SERC, 1988–93; Hon. Fellow, Dept of Applied Maths and Theoretical Physics, Univ. of Cambridge, 2003–. Hon. Prof., Aberdeen Univ., 2004. Member Council: IMA, 1989–92 (Organizer, Conf. on Chaos, UCL, 1990); Royal Soc., 2002–03. Hon. DSc Aberdeen, 2004. Cambridge University Prizes: Rex Moir, 1957; Archibald Denny, 1958; John Winbolt, 1960; OMAE Award, ASME, 1985; James Alfred Ewing Medal, ICE, 1992; Gold Medal for Mathematics, IMA, 2004. Organizer and Editor, IUTAM Symposium: on Collapse: the buckling of structures in theory and practice, 1982; on non-linearity and chaos in engrg dynamics, 1993; Ed., Phil. Trans Roy. Soc., Series A, 1998–2007 (Actg Ed., 1990; Ed. and Organizer, first Theme Issue, 1990 and three Millennium Issues, 2000; Mem. Editl Bd, 2008–); sci. contribs to radio and TV, 1975–. *Publications:* (with G. W. Hunt) A general theory of elastic stability, 1973; Instabilities and catastrophes in science and engineering, 1982; (with G. W. Hunt) Elastic instability phenomena, 1984; (with H. B. Stewart) Nonlinear dynamics and chaos, 1986, 2nd edn 2002; (ed) Localisation and solitary waves in solid mechanics, 1999; Visions of the Future, vol. I, Astronomy and Earth Science, vol. II, Physics and Electronics, vol. III, Chemistry and Life Science, 2001; (ed) Advances in Astronomy: from big bang to the solar system, 2005; (ed) Advances in Earth Science: from earthquakes to global warming, 2007; Advances in Nanoengineering: electronics, materials and assembly, 2007; 200 articles in learned jls (and mem., editl bds). *Recreations:* walking, wildlife photography, badminton, tennis, astronomy with grandchildren. *Address:* 33 West Hill Road, Foxton, Cambs CB22 6SZ. *T:* (01223) 704354.

THOMPSON, John William McWean, CBE 1986; Editor, Sunday Telegraph, 1976–86; *b* 12 June 1920; *s* of Charles and Charlotte Thompson; *m* 1947, Cynthia Ledsham; one *s* one *d. Educ:* Roundhay Sch., Leeds. Previously on staffs of Yorkshire Evening News, Evening Standard, London, and The Spectator (Dep. Editor); joined Sunday Telegraph, 1970; Asst Editor, 1975. *Publications:* (as Peter Quince) Country Life, 1975; articles and reviews in many jls. *Address:* Corner Cottage, Burnham Norton, Norfolk PE31 8DS. *T:* (01328) 738396. *Club:* Travellers.

See also D. B. Johnson.

THOMPSON, Jonathan Michael; Director General, Corporate Services, Department for Children, Schools and Families (formerly for Education and Skills), since 2006; Head, Government Finance Profession, HM Treasury, since 2008; *b* 29 Dec. 1964; *s* of John and Jenny Thompson; *m* 1987, Dawn Warnes; three *s. Educ:* Earlham High Sch.; Norwich City Coll.; Suffolk Coll.; Anglia Poly. CIPFA 1989. Audit and accountancy posts, Norfolk CC, 1983–91; Superintendent, Eagle Star Gp, 1991–93; Manager, 1993–95, Sen. Manager, 1995–97, Ernst & Young; North Somerset Council: Finance Strategy Advr, 1997–2001; Hd, Corporate Finance, 2001–02; Dir, Finance and Resources, 2002–04; Dir of Finance, Ofsted, 2004–06; Dir Gen., Finance, DfES, May–July 2006. *Recreations:* Church, community activities, movies, reading, cooking, wood-turning. *Address:* Department for Children, Schools and Families, Sanctuary Buildings, Great Smith Street, SW1P 3BT. *T:* (020) 7925 7402; *e-mail:* jon.thompson@dcsf.gsi.gov.uk.

THOMPSON, Julian; *see* Thompson, R. J. de la M.

THOMPSON, Maj.-Gen. Julian Howard Atherden, CB 1982; OBE 1978; Visiting Professor, Department of War Studies, King's College London, since 1997; *b* 7 Oct. 1934; *s* of late Major A. J. Thompson, DSO, MC and Mary Stearns Thompson (*née* Krause); *m* 1960, Janet Avery, *d* of late Richard Robinson Rodd; one *s* one *d. Educ:* Sherborne School. 2nd Lieut RM, 1952; served 40, 42, 43, 45 Commandos RM, 1954–69; Asst Sec., Chiefs of Staff Cttee, 1970–71; BM, 3 Cdo Brigade, 1972–73; Directing Staff, Staff Coll., Camberley, 1974–75; CO 40 Cdo RM, 1975–78; Comdr 3 Cdo Brigade, 1981–83, incl. Falklands campaign (CB); Maj.-Gen. Comdg Trng Reserve Forces and Special Forces RM, 1983–86, retired. Sen. Res. Fellow in Logistics and Armed Conflict in the Modern Age, KCL, 1987–97. Life Vice-Pres., British Assoc. for Physical Training, 1998 (Pres., 1988–98). *Publications:* No Picnic: 3 Commando Brigade in the South Atlantic 1982, 1985; Ready for Anything: The Parachute Regiment at War 1940–1982, 1989; (contrib.) Military Strategy in a Changing Europe, 1991; (contrib.) Fallen Stars, 1991; The Lifeblood of War, 1991; (contrib.) The Observer at 200, 1992; The Imperial War Museum Book of Victory in Europe: North West Europe 1944–45, 1994; The Imperial War Museum Book of the War at Sea: the Royal Navy in the Second World War, 1996; (contrib.) Leadership and Command, 1997; The Imperial War Museum Book of War Behind Enemy Lines, 1998; (contrib.) Dimensions of Sea Power, 1998; The Royal Marines: from Sea Soldiers to a Special Force, 2000; (contrib.) Lightning Strikes Twice: the Great World War 1914–1945, 2000; (ed) The Imperial War Museum Book of Modern Warfare, 2002; The Imperial War Museum Book of the War in Burma 1942–1945, 2002; The Imperial War Museum Book of the War at Sea: 1914–1918, 2004; The Victory in Europe Experience, 2004; The 1916 Experience: Verdun and the Somme, 2006; (contrib.) Amphibious Assault: manoeuvre from the sea, 2007; Masters of the Battlefield, 2007; Dunkirk: retreat to victory, 2008. *Recreations:* sailing, shooting, history, cross-country ski-ing, ballet, opera, jazz. *Address:* c/o Lloyds TSB, Royal Parade, Plymouth, Devon PL1 1HB. *Clubs:* Army and Navy; Royal Marines Sailing.

THOMPSON, Julian O.; *see* Ogilvie Thompson.

THOMPSON, Keith Bruce; Vice-Chancellor, Staffordshire University, 1992–95, now Emeritus; *b* 13 Sept. 1932; *m* 1956, Kathleen Reeves; one *s* one *d. Educ:* Bishopshalt School, Hillingdon; New College, Oxford (Sec./Librarian, Oxford Union). PPE 1955, Dip Educn (distn), 1956, MA 1959; MEd Bristol, 1968. Schoolmaster, City of Bath Boys' School, 1956–62; Lectr, Newton Park Coll., Bath, 1962–67; Head of Dept, Philippa Fawcett Coll., Streatham, 1967–72; Principal, Madeley Coll. of Educn, 1972–78; Dep. Dir, 1978–86, Dir, 1987–92, N Staffs, later Staffs Poly. Chairman: Standing Conf. on Studies in Educn, 1980–82; Undergraduate Initial Training Bd (Educn), CNAA, 1981–85; Polytechnics Central Admissions System, 1989–93; Dep. Chm., UCAS, 1993–95; Mem. Bd, Nat. Adv. Body for Public Sector Higher Educn, 1983–88 (Chm., Teacher Educn Gp, 1983–85). Sec., British Philos. of Sport Assoc., 2002–05. Editor, Educn for Teaching, 1968–74. *Publications:* Education and Philosophy, 1972; (jtly) Curriculum Development, 1974; articles on educn, philosophy, physical educn, sport. *Recreations:* sport, music, books. *Address:* 3 Swindon Manor, Swindon Village, Cheltenham GL51 9TP. *T:* (01242) 698554.

See also B. K. Thompson.

THOMPSON, McKim; *see* Thompson, I. McK.

THOMPSON, Marjorie Ellis; Consultant, C_3I (Campaigns, Communications, Cause-related marketing and Imagination), since 2002; *b* St Louis, Mo, 8 June 1957; *d* of John William Thompson, III and Janet Ann (*née* Neubeiser); *m* 1982, Kevin Mark Williams (marr. diss. 2000); partner 1984–92, Dafydd Elis Thomas (now Baron Elis-Thomas). *Educ:* Woodrow Wilson High Sch., Long Beach, California; Colorado Coll., Colorado Springs (BSc Hons 1978); LSE (MSc Econ 1979). Campaign for Nuclear Disarmament: Parly

Officer, 1983–86; Hd of Press and Public Relns, 1986–87; Vice-Chair, 1987–90; Chair, 1990–93; Researcher for Ann Clwyd, MP, 1987; Royal College of Nursing: Parly Officer, 1988–91; Advr, Dept of Nursing Policy and Practice, 1991–93; Head of Communications, CRE, 1993–97; Dir, Cause Connection, Saatchi & Saatchi, 1997–2001; Dir, Cause Related Marketing, Octagon Marketing, 2001–02. Co-Chair, Cttee to Stop War in the Gulf, 1990–91. Member: IISS, 1992–94; IPR, 1993–97; IPRA, 2004–05. Fellow: British-American Project, 1990–; Davos World Econ. Forum, 2000; Chair, Bd Dirs, Catalyst, 1997–2000. Trustee: Foster Art, 2006; S London Maudsley Charitable Trust, 2006–07; Stand to Reason, 2007–. Mem. Editl Bd and contrib., Jl of Nonprofit and Voluntary Sector Marketing, 1998–2001. *Publications:* (contrib.) Nursing: the hidden agenda, 1993; (with Hamish Pringle) Brand Spirit: how cause-related marketing builds brands, 1999; with Peter Whales) Managing CSR, 2008; contrib. New Statesman & Society, Tribune, AdMap, Harpers & Queen, Market Leader. *Recreations:* watching Wales play Rugby, African safaris, entertaining, Jack Russell Ria de Janeira. *Address: e-mail:* marjoriet@freeuk.com.

THOMPSON, Mark; *see* Thompson, O. M.

THOMPSON, Mark John Thompson; Director General, BBC, since 2004; *b* 31 July 1957; *s* of late Duncan John Thompson and Sydney Columba Corduff; *m* 1987, Jane Emilie Blumberg; two *s* one *d. Educ:* Stonyhurst Coll.; Merton Coll., Oxford (BA; Violet Vaughan Morgan English Prize; MA; Hon. Fellow, 2006). BBC Television: Research Asst Trainee, 1979–80; Asst Producer, Nationwide, 1980–82; Producer, Breakfast Time, 1982–84; Output Editor: London Plus, 1984–85; Newsnight, 1985–87; Editor: Nine O'Clock News, 1988–90; Panorama, 1990–92; Head of Features, 1992–94; Head of Factual Progs, 1994–96; Controller, BBC2, 1996–98; Dir of Nat. and Regl Broadcasting, 1998–2000; Dir of Television, 2000–01; Chief Exec., Channel Four, 2002–04. Chm., Edinburgh Internat. TV Fest., 1996. Vis. Fellow, Nuffield Coll., Oxford, 2005. FRTS 1998; FRSA 2000. *Recreations:* walking, cooking. *Address:* c/o BBC, Media Centre, 201 Wood Lane, W12 7TQ. *Club:* Reform.

THOMPSON, Michael, FRAM; Professor of Horn, Royal Academy of Music, since 1985; Principal Horn, London Sinfonietta, since 1986; *b* 4 Jan. 1954; *s* of Ronald and Joan Thompson; *m* 1975, Valerie Botwright; two *s* one *d. Educ:* Royal Acad. of Music. FRAM 1988. Principal Horn: BBC Scottish SO, 1972–75; Philharmonia Orch., 1975–85; internat. soloist and recording artist, 1985–. *Publications:* Warm-up Exercises, 1986; Schumann, Konzertstuck: performing edition, 1988; Cadenzas for Haydn and Mozart Horn Concerti, 1990. *Recreations:* reading, walking, cooking. *Address:* 26 Presburg Road, New Malden, Surrey KT3 5AH. *T:* (020) 8942 0768.

THOMPSON, Michael Harry Rex, OBE 1992; FCIB; Director: Wellington Underwriting plc, 1996–2001; Wellington Underwriting Agencies Ltd, 1995–2001; Deputy Chairman, Lloyds Bank Plc, 1991–95 (Director, 1986–95); *b* 14 Jan. 1931; *s* of late William Henry Thompson and Beatrice Hylda Thompson (*née* Heard); *m* 1958, Joyce (*née* Redpath); one *s* one *d. Educ:* St John's Sch., Leatherhead, Surrey. Joined Lloyds Bank, 1948; Dep. Chief Exec., 1987–91; Director: National Bank of New Zealand, 1978–82, 1991–95; Lloyds Abbey Life 1991–95; Chm., German Investment Trust, 1990–95. Financial Advr to Dean and Chapter, 1995–2001, Lay Canon, 1996–2001, Salisbury Cathedral. Trustee, Bankers Club, 1995–2001. *Recreation:* Rugby football.

THOMPSON, Michael Jacques, CMG 1989; OBE 1977; HM Diplomatic Service, retired; *b* 31 Jan. 1936; *s* of late Christopher Thompson and of Colette Jeanne-Marie Thompson; *m* 1967, Mary Susan (*née* Everard); one *s* one *d. Educ:* Uppingham; Christ's Coll., Cambridge (Law Tripos, 1956–60; MA). National Service, Kenya, Aden and Cyprus, 1954–56. HMOCS, Kenya, 1960–63; FCO, 1964; served Kuala Lumpur, Saigon, Lusaka and FCO, 1965–79; Counsellor, Kuala Lumpur, 1979–82; seconded to Comdr, British Land Forces, Hong Kong, 1982–85; Counsellor, FCO, 1985. Mem., Royal Asia Soc. Mem., Co. of Barbers. *Recreations:* tennis, golf, gardening. *Clubs:* Oxford and Cambridge; Huntercombe Golf.

THOMPSON, Sir Michael (Warwick), Kt 1991; DSc; FInstP; Deputy Chairman, Alliance & Leicester PLC, 1997–2000; Vice-Chancellor and Principal, University of Birmingham, 1987–96, Emeritus Professor, since 1996; *b* 1 June 1931; *s* of Kelvin Warwick Thompson and Madeleine Thompson; *m* 1st, Sybil (*née* Spooner) (*d* 1999); two *s*; 2nd, 2000, Jennifer (*née* Mitchell). *Educ:* Rydal Sch.; Univ. of Liverpool (BSc, DSc). Research scientist, AERE, Harwell, 1953–65; Sussex University: Prof. of Experimental Physics, 1965–80; Pro-Vice-Chancellor, 1973–77, actg Vice-Chancellor, 1976; Vis. Prof., 1980–86; Vice-Chancellor, UEA, 1980–86. Chairman: Physics Cttee, SRC, 1975–79; British Council Cttee for Academic Res. Collaboration with Germany, 1989–2000; Review of ISIS Neutron Source for Central Lab. of Res. Councils, 1997–98. Member: E Sussex Educn Cttee, 1973–78; E Sussex AHA, 1974–79; non-exec. Dir, W Midlands RHA, 1987–96; Chm., Review of London SHAs, 1993. Member: Council, Birmingham Chamber of Industry and Commerce, 1987–96; Council, CNAA, 1989–91; Council for Internat. Co-operation in Higher Educn, 1989–91; Council, CVCP, 1990–93, 1994–96 (Chm. Med. Cttee, 1994–96); Council for Industry and Higher Educn, 1991–96; Council, ACU, 1991–95; Standing Gp of Depts of Health and Educn on Undergrad. Med. and Dental Educn and Res., 1994–96. Director: Alliance & Leicester PLC (formerly Alliance Bldg Soc., then Alliance & Leicester Bldg Soc.), 1979–2000; Cobuild Ltd, 1987–96. Member Council: Eastbourne Coll., 1977–2000; QMW, 1996–2000 (Chm., Med. Sub-Cttee, 1996–2000). Trustee: Barber Inst. of Fine Arts, 1987–2007; St Bartholomew's Hosp. Med. Coll., 1998–2000. Mem., Birmingham Lunar Soc., 1991–96. President: Bodmin DFAS, 2000–; Fowey River Assoc., 2001–07. Hon. LLD Birmingham, 1997; Hon. DSc Sussex, 1998. Oliver Lodge Prizewinner, Univ. of Liverpool, 1953; Prizewinner, Materials Science Club, 1970; C. V. Boys Prizewinner, Inst. of Physics, 1972. Officer's Cross, Order of Merit (Germany), 1997. *Publications:* Defects and Radiation Damage in Metals, 1969; (jtly) Channelling, 1973; over 100 papers in sci. jls. *Recreations:* the arts, walking, navigation in small ships, fly fishing. *Address:* Readymoney Cottage, 3 Tower Park, Fowey, Cornwall PL23 1JD. *Clubs:* Athenæum; Royal Fowey Yacht.

See also P. Warwick Thompson.

THOMPSON, Nicholas, RIBA; theatre architect in private practice; Director, 1974–2005, Leader, Arts Team, 1998–2005, Consultant, 2005–07, Renton Howard Wood Levin LLP; *b* 25 Feb. 1936; *s* of Eric Thompson and Dorothy (*née* Lake); *m* 1966, Clare Ferraby; two *s. Educ:* Christ's Hosp., Horsham; Oxford Sch. of Architecture (DipArch). RIBA 1961. Specialist in building design for performing arts, including: Crucible Th., Sheffield, 1971; Univ. of Warwick Arts Centre, 1973; Th. Royal and Royal Concert Hall, Nottingham, 1978–82; Old Vic, 1984; Alhambra, Bradford, 1986; Th. Royal, Newcastle, 1988; Lyceum Th., Sheffield, 1990; New Victoria Th., Woking, 1992; Donmar Warehouse, 1992; Anvil Concert Hall, Basingstoke, 1994; Bridgewater Concert Hall, Manchester, 1996; Sadler's Wells Th., 1998; masterplan and boarding houses for Christ's Hosp. Sch., 1998–2001; renovation of London Coliseum for ENO, 1999–2004; Dome Concert Hall and Mus., Brighton, 2002; theatre renovations for Sir Cameron Mackintosh, incl. Prince Edward Th., 1993 and 2004, Prince of Wales Th., 2004; refurbishment of Wigmore Hall, 2004; Wells Cathedral Sch., 2006–; *overseas projects* include: Concert Hall and Acad. of Music for Sultan of Oman, 1992; National Th., Damascus, 1993; Musik Th., Stuttgart, 1995; Musik Th., Duisburg, 1996; design consultant, Lazaristes Th. and Art Gall., Thessalonika, 1996; consultant: Athens Opera House, 1997–2004; Gennadius Lecture Th., American Sch. of Classical Studies, Athens, 2000; Fine Arts Bldg, Chicago, 2003–; Montecasino Th., Johannesburg, 2005–07. Dir, Paxos Fest. Trust, 1998–. FRSA 1999. Goodwin & Wimperis Silver Medal, RIBA, 1964. *Publications:* articles in architectural press and lectures. *Recreations:* outdoors and active by day (travel, sailing, painting, making gardens), watching performances by night, collecting modern art. *Address:* 22 Lichfield Road, Richmond, Surrey TW9 3JR. *T:* and *Fax:* (020) 8948 0645; *e-mail:* thompsonferraby@btinternet.com. *Club:* Garrick.

THOMPSON, Sir Nicholas (Annesley Marler), 2nd Bt *cr* 1963, of Reculver, co. Kent; solicitor with CMS Cameron McKenna LLP (formerly Cameron McKenna), since 1997; *b* 19 March 1947; *s* of Sir Richard Hilton Marler Thompson, 1st Bt and of Anne Christabel de Vere Marler Thompson (*née* Annesley); *S* father, 1999; *m* 1982, Venetia Catherine, *yr d* of Mr and Mrs John Heathcote; three *s* one *d. Educ:* King's Sch., Canterbury; Univ. of Kent at Canterbury (BA Law 1969). Admitted a solicitor, 1973. Mem. (C) Westminster City Council, 1978–86; Dep. Lord Mayor of Westminster, 1983–84. Contested (C) Newham South, 1983. Mem. Exec. Cttee, Standing Council of the Baronetage, 2003–. *Recreations:* foreign travel, cycling, walking, theatre, reading. *Heir: s* Simon William Thompson, *b* 10 June 1985. *Address:* Maxgate, George Road, Kingston upon Thames, Surrey KT2 7NR. *T:* (020) 8942 7251. *Club:* Carlton.

THOMPSON, Nicolas de la Mare; Chairman, Heinemann Educational Books, 1985–91; *b* 4 June 1928; *s* of Rupert Spens Thompson and Florence Elizabeth Thompson (*née* de la Mare); *m* 1st, 1956, Erica Pennell (*d* 1993); two *s* one *d*; 2nd, 1997, Caroline Graham (*née* Middleton). *Educ:* Eton; Christ Church, Oxford (MA). Managing Director, George Weidenfeld and Nicolson, 1956–70; Publishing Dir, Pitman, 1970–85; Managing Dir, Heinemann Gp of Publishers, 1985–87; Director: Octopus Publishing Gp, 1985–92; Reed Internat. Books, 1990–93; Internat. Book Develt Ltd, 1991–2004; Chairman: Ginn & Co., 1985–91; Heinemann Professional Publishing, 1986–90; George Philip & Son, 1988–90; Mitchell Beazley, 1988–90; Copyright Licensing Agency Ltd, 1994–96. Chairman: Book Development Council, 1984–86; Publishers Licensing Soc., 1992–96; Treas., Publishers Assoc., 1986–88. Dir, Almeida Theatre Co. Ltd, 1993–2001. *Address:* 5 Walham Grove, SW6 1QP.

THOMPSON, Sir Nigel (Cooper), KCMG 2002; CBE 1996; CEng, FICE, FIStructE; Chairman, Campaign to Protect Rural England, 2003–08; Director, Trevor Estate, since 1985; *b* 18 June 1939; *s* of Henry Cooper Thompson and Beatrix Mary Cooper Thompson; *m* 1965, Nicola Jane Bonnett; one *s* two *d. Educ:* St Paul's Sch. CEng 1967; FIStructE 1985; FICE 2000. Joined Ove Arup and Partners, Consulting Engrs, 1960: Main Bd Dir, 1986; Dep. Chm., 1998–2005. Chm., St Helena Leisure Co., 2002–. Chm., British Consulting Bureau, 1993–94. Chm., Construction Procurement Gp, DoE, 1993–96; Dep. Chm., British Airports Gp, DTI, 1996–98. Chairman: Govt/Private Sector Task Force for Kosovo, 1999–2000; Govt Task Force for Serbia and Montenegro, 2000–02. Mem., Business Adv. Council for Stability Pact for SE Europe, 2001. Founder Mem. Council, British Council of Offices, 1994; Mem. Council, CBI, 1993–96. Chm., BUILD - Building Understanding through Internat. Links for Develt, 2003–. Major, Logistics Staff Corps, RE, 2001. Mem. Cttee, Kennet Gp, CPRE; Chm., Action for the River Kennet, 2003–. Chm., Parish Council, Mildenhall, Wilts., 2004– (Vice-Chm., 2000–04). Liveryman, Engrs' Co., 2002–. Hon. Vice-Pres., Cambridge Univ. Land Soc., 2005. Gov., St Paul's Sch., 2007–. Internat. Medal, ICE, 2000; Outstanding Contribn Award, ACE, 2001. *Recreations:* cricket, Rugby, landscape/estate gardening. *Address:* Grove House, Stitchcombe, Marlborough, Wilts SN8 2NG. *Clubs:* Boodle's, D-Group.

THOMPSON, Nimble; *see* Thompson, P. J. S.

THOMPSON, Dr Noel Brentnall Watson, CEng; education and training consultant; Councillor (Lab), London Borough of Brent, 1999–2006; *b* 11 Dec. 1932; *s* of George Watson Thompson and Mary Henrietta Gibson; *m* 1957, Margaret Angela Elizabeth Baston; one *s. Educ:* Manchester Grammar School; Cambridge Univ. (MA); Imperial College, London (MSc Eng, PhD). National Service, RN (Sub-Lieut), 1951–53. Research, Imperial Coll., 1958–61; Lectr in Physical Metallurgy, Univ. of Birmingham, 1961–65; Dept of Education and Science, 1966–67, 1969–77 and 1979–88 (Under Sec., 1980–88; Head of Higher and Further Educn III Br., 1980–86; Head of Schools 2 Br. and Internat. Relations, 1986–88); Secretary, National Libraries Cttee, 1967–69; Cabinet Office, 1977–79; Chief Exec., Nat. Council for Educnl Technol., 1988–92. Consultant and Vis. Prof. of Educnl Develt, Luton Univ., 1993–98. Chief Exec., English Folk Dance and Song Soc., 1995–97. *Publications:* papers in professional journals. *Recreations:* railways of all sizes, mechanics, music, traditional dance, modern history, photography, walking. *Address:* 101 Woodcock Hill, Kenton, Harrow HA3 0JJ. *T:* (020) 8907 1716; *e-mail:* nbwt@waitrose.com.

THOMPSON, (Owen) Mark; theatre designer; *b* 12 April 1957; *s* of late Owen Edgar Thompson and of Barbara Adele (*née* Lister). *Educ:* Radley Coll.; Birmingham Univ. (BA Hons Drama and Theatre Arts). Worked in rep. at Worcester, Exeter, Sheffield and Leeds; designs for: The Scarlet Pimpernel, Chichester, 1985 (transf. Her Majesty's); Cabaret, Strand, 1986; The Sneeze, Aldwych, 1988; Ivanov, and Much Ado About Nothing, Strand, 1989; A Little Night Music, Piccadilly, 1989; Shadowlands, Queen's, 1989 (transf. NY); Joseph and the Amazing Technicolor Dreamcoat, Palladium and Canadian, Australian and American tours, 1991 (Set Design Olivier Award, 1992); Company, Albery, 1996; Art, Wyndhams and NY, 1997; The Blue Room, Donmar Warehouse and NY, Dr Dolittle, Apollo Labbatts, 1998; Mamma Mia!, Prince Edward, 1999, Toronto, 2000, US tour, Australia, NY 2001; Blast!, Apollo, 1999, NY, 2001; Lady in the Van, Queen's, 1999; Follies, NY, 2001; Bombay Dreams, Apollo Victoria, 2002, NY 2004; And Then There Were None, Gielgud, 2005; God of Carnage, Gielgud, 2008; The Female of the Species, Vaudeville, 2008; Funny Girl, Chichester Festival Th.; *for Royal Exchange Manchester:* Jumpers, 1984; The Country Wife, Mumbo Jumbo, 1986; The School for Scandal, 1990; *for RSC:* Measure for Measure, 1987; The Wizard of Oz, Much Ado About Nothing, 1988; The Comedy of Errors, 1990 (Set Design and Costume Design Olivier Awards, 1992); The Unexpected Man, 1998, NY 2001; *for Almeida:* Volpone, 1990; Betrayal, Party Time, 1991; Butterfly Kiss, 1992; *for Royal National Theatre:* The Wind in the Willows, 1990 (Olivier Award, Plays and Players Award, Critics Circle Award, 1991); The Madness of George III, 1991 (costume design for film, 1994); Arcadia, 1993; Pericles, 1994; What the Butler Saw, 1997; The Day I Stood Still, 1998; Life x 3, 2000, also NY 2003; The Duchess of Malfi, 2003; The Alchemist, 2006; The Rose Tattoo, 2007; *for Royal Court:* Six Degrees of Separation, 1992 (transf. Comedy); Hysteria, 1994 (Olivier Award for Set Design); The Kitchen, 1995 (Critics' Circle Award); Mouth to Mouth, 2001; The Woman Before, 2005; Piano/Forte, 2006; *opera:* Montag aus Licht, La Scala, 1989 (costume design only); Falstaff, Scottish Opera, 1991; Peter Grimes,

Opera North, 1989; Ariadne auf Naxos, Saltzburg, 1991; Il Viaggio a Reims, Royal Opera, 1992; Hansel and Gretel, Sydney, 1992; The Two Widows, ENO, 1993; Queen of Spades, 1995, Macbeth, 2007, Metropolitan Opera, NY; *ballet:* Don Quixote, Royal Ballet, 1993. *Recreations:* cooking, gardening. *Address:* c/o Simpson Fox Associates, 52 Shaftesbury Avenue, W1V 7DE. *T:* (020) 7434 9167.

THOMPSON, Patrick; *see* Thompson, H. P.

THOMPSON, Sir Paul (Anthony), 2nd Bt *cr* 1963; company director; *b* 6 Oct. 1939; *s* of Sir Kenneth Pugh Thompson, 1st Bt, and Nanne (*d* 1994), *yr d* of Charles Broome, Walton, Liverpool; *S* father, 1984; *m* 1971, Pauline Dorothy, *d* of Robert O. Spencer, Bolton, Lancs; two *s* two *d*. *Educ:* Aldenham School, Herts. *Heir: s* Richard Kenneth Spencer Thompson, *b* 27 Jan. 1976. *Address:* Woodlands Farmhouse, Ruff Lane, Ormskirk, Lancs L39 4UL.

THOMPSON, Prof. Paul Richard, DPhil; social historian; Research Professor in Social History, University of Essex, 1988–2008, now Emeritus Professor; Founder, National Life Story Collection, 1987; *b* 1935; *m* 1st, Thea Vigne; one *s* one *d*; 2nd, Natasha Burchardt; one *d*; 3rd, Elaine Bauer. *Educ:* Bishop's Stortford Coll.; Corpus Christi Coll., Oxford (MA); The Queen's Coll., Oxford (Junior Research Fellow, 1961–64); DPhil Oxon 1964. University of Essex: Lectr in Sociology, 1964–69; Sen. Lectr, 1969–71; Reader, 1971–88; Sen. Res. Fellow, Nuffield Coll., Oxford, 1968–69; Vis. Prof. of Art History, Johns Hopkins Univ., 1972; Hoffman Wood Prof. of Architecture, Univ. of Leeds, 1977–78; Benjamin Meaker Prof., Univ. of Bristol, 1987. Dir, Qualidara, 1994–2001. Editor: Victorian Soc. Conf. Reports, 1965–67; Oral History, 1970–; Life Stories, 1985–89; International Yearbook of Oral History and Life Stories, 1992–96; Memory and Narrative, 1996–2002. Hon. DLitt Aberdeen, 2007. *Publications:* History of English Architecture (with Peter Kidson and Peter Murray), 1965, 2nd edn 1979; The Work of William Morris, 1967, 3rd edn 1991; Socialists, Liberals and Labour: the struggle for London 1880–1914, 1967; The Edwardians: the remaking of British Society, 1975, 2nd edn 1992; The Voice of the Past: Oral History, 1978, 3rd edn 2000; Living the Fishing, 1983; I Don't Feel Old: the experience of later life, 1990; (with Raphael Samuel) The Myths We Live By, 1990; (with Gloria Wood) The Nineties, 1993; (with Hugo Slim) Listening for a Change, 1993; (with Cathy Courtney) City Lives, 1996; (with Daniel Bertaux) Pathways to Social Class, 1997; (jtly) Growing Up in Stepfamilies, 1997; (with Mary Chamberlain) Narrative and Genre, 1998; (with Daniel Bertaux) On Living Through Soviet Russia, 2004; (with Elaine Bauer) Jamaican Hands Across the Atlantic, 2006. *Recreations:* cycling, drawing, music, friendship, travel. *Address:* 5 West Street, Wivenhoe, Essex CO7 9DE. *T:* (01206) 824644; *e-mail:* paulth@youngfoundation.org.

THOMPSON, Paul W.; *see* Warwick Thompson.

THOMPSON, Sir Peter (Anthony), Kt 1984; FCILT; Chairman: Douglas Stewart Ltd, since 1992; Goldcrest Homes plc, since 1998; Green Energy plc, since 2001; Goodnights Entertainments, since 2003; Milton Keynes Theatre Production Company Ltd, since 2004; *b* 14 April 1928; *s* of late Herbert Thompson and Sarah Jane Thompson; *m* 1st, 1958, Patricia Anne Norcott (*d* 1983); one *s* two *d*; 2nd, 1986, Lydia Mary Kite (*née* Hodding); two *d*. *Educ:* Royal Drapers Sch.; Bradford Grammar Sch.; Leeds Univ. (BA Econ). Unilever, 1952–62; GKN, 1962–64; Transport Controller, Rank Organisation, 1964–67; Head of Transport, BSC, 1967–72; Group Co-ordinator, BRS Ltd, 1972–75; Exec. Vice-Chm. (Operations), Nat. Freight Corp., 1975–77; Chief Exec., Nat. Freight Corp., later Nat. Freight Co., 1977–80; Dep. Chm. and Chief Exec., 1980–82, Chm. and Chief Exec., 1982–84, Exec. Chm., 1984–90, Pres., 1991–93, NFC. Dir, 1989–90, Dep. Chm., 1989–90, Chm., March–July 1990, British & Commonwealth Hldgs; Chairman: Community Hospitals plc, 1981–96; Child Base Ltd, 1989–2005 (Pres., 2006–); FI Group plc, 1990–99; Phoenix Asset Mgt Ltd, 1998–2003, 2005–; Goldcrest Land PLC, 1999–; Stocktrade, 2000–01; Durabuild, 2001–02; OMG Ltd, 2001–02; Dep. Chm., Wembley plc, 1991–95; Director: Granville & Co. Ltd, 1984–90; Pilkington plc, 1985–93; Kenning Motor Group, 1985–86; Smiths Industries PLC, 1986–98; Meyer International, 1988–92; Aegis plc, 1993–99; Brewin Dolphin Gp, 1994–2000; Legal Document Co., 2001–07; Ecorider Ltd, 2006–07; Pres., ProShare, 1994–99 (Chm., 1992–94). Mem., Nat. Trng Task Force, 1989–93. President: Inst. of Freight Forwarders, 1982–83; Inst. of Logistics and Distribn Management (formerly Inst. of Physical Distribn Management), 1988–93 (Chm., 1985–88); Vice-Pres., CIT, 1982–85; Chm., CBI Wider Share Ownership Task Force, 1990. Chm., Milton Keynes Theatre Gall. Trust, 1995–2003. CCMI. Hon. LLD: Leeds, 1991; Nottingham, 1991; Hon. DTech Bradford, 1991; Hon. DSc Cranfield Inst. of Technol., 1992. Hambro Businessman of the Year, 1983; BIM Gold Medal, 1991. *Publication:* Sharing the Success: the story of the NFC, 1990. *Recreations:* golf, walking, shooting, theatre, music. *Address:* The Mill House, Mill Street, Newport Pagnell, Bucks MK16 8ER. *Club:* Royal Automobile.

THOMPSON, Peter James; Owner, Peter Thompson Associates, since 1970; *b* Sheffield, 23 Feb. 1945; *s* of Andrew and Janet Thompson. *Educ:* Hurstpierpoint Coll.; Sussex Univ. (BA Hons). Founder, Peter Thompson Associates, PR agency, 1970. *Recreations:* food, drink, travel. *Address:* Flat 1, 12 Bourchier Street, W1D 4HZ. *T:* (020) 7439 1210, *Fax:* (020) 7439 1202.

THOMPSON, Peter John; education and training consultant; *b* 17 April 1937; *s* of late George Kenneth Thompson and Gladys Pamela (*née* Partington), W Midlands; *m* 1961, Dorothy Ann Smith; one *s* three *d*. *Educ:* Aston Univ. (BSc 1st Cl. Hons MechEngrg; MSc); CNAA (DTech). Whitworth Soc. Prize. CEng, FIET; FIPD. With Tube Investments, 1952–61; Lectr 1961, Sen. Lectr 1968–70, Harris Coll., Preston; Sen. Sci. Officer, UKAEA, Preston, 1965–68; Prin. Lectr, Sheffield City Poly., 1970–77; Hd of Dept and Dean of Engrg, Trent Poly., Nottingham, 1977–83; Pro Rector, then Dep. Rector, Poly. of Central London, 1983–86; Professor: Trent Poly., 1980–83; Poly. of Central London, 1983–86; Chief Exec., NCVQ, 1986–91; Vis. Prof., Sch. of Mgt, Open Univ., 1991–94. School Inspector, OFSTED, 1984–. Partner, P & D Medallions, 1986–; Consultant, HR Services, 1997–. Mem., then Chm., Manufacturing Bd, CNAA, 1978–86; Mem., Cttee for Sci. and Technology, CNAA, 1982–86; Mem. then Chm., Cttee for Engrg in Polytechnics, 1981–86; Member: Engrg Adv. Cttee, NAB, 1980–84; Engrg Scis Divl Bd of IMechE, 1984–86; Chm., Materials Tech. Activities Cttee, IMechE, 1984–86; Mem., Council, Open Coll., 1987–90. Sen. Awards Consultant, C&G, 1992–95. Hon. Mem., C&G, 1991. FRSA. *Publications:* numerous papers on engrg manufacture and vocational educn and trng, 1968–, incl. papers on hydrostatic extension, lubrication, cutting tool wear and mechanics and metal forming; patents. *Recreations:* genealogy, numismatics, golf. *Address:* Berkhamsted, Herts HP4 3JJ. *T:* (01442) 865127.

THOMPSON, Peter John; His Honour Judge Peter Thompson; a Circuit Judge, since 1998; *b* 30 Dec. 1943; *s* of late Eric Thompson and Olive Ethel Thompson (*née* Miskin); *m* 1969, Elizabeth Anne Granger Rees; one *s* two *d*. *Educ:* Glyn Grammar Sch., Epsom; St Catherine's Coll., Oxford (MA Jurisp.). Admitted Solicitor, 1970; Solicitor and Barrister, Supreme Court of Vic., Australia, 1972; Partner: Turner Martin & Symes, Solicitors, Ipswich, 1976–91; Eversheds, Solicitors, Ipswich, 1991–98. *Recreations:* jazz, playing and listening, soccer, playing and watching, jogging and walking in English and French countryside, family, literature, travel. *Address:* The Court House, 1 Russell Road, Ipswich, Suffolk IP1 2AG. *T:* (01473) 228585.

THOMPSON, Peter John Stuart, (Nimble); Chairman, N. G. Bailey Ltd, since 2001; *b* 28 Sept. 1946; *s* of Douglas Thompson and Rene Thompson, OBE; *m* 1970, Morven Mary Hanscomb; one *s* one *d* (and one *s* decd). *Educ:* Rossall Sch.; Univ. of Leeds (LLB). MCIArb. Admitted solicitor, 1971; Managing Partner, Hepworth & Chadwick, 1989–94; Eversheds: Sen. Partner, Leeds and Manchester, 1994–99; Dep. Chm., 1995–98. Non-executive Director: TEP Electrical Distributors, 1975–; S. Lyles plc, 1994–99; Denney O'Hara Ltd, 1999–; Judicium plc, 2000–; Rushbond plc, 2002–; Scarborough Building Soc., 2005–; Institute of Dirs, 2008– (Regl Chm., Yorks, 2005–). Chairman: Bd, Leeds Metropolitan Univ., 2000–06; Eureka!, the Mus. for Children, Halifax, 2003–07; Gov., Giggleswick Sch., 1998– (Vice Chm., 2002–07). Hon. DLaws Leeds Metropolitan, 2006. *Recreations:* fishing, wine, family, friends. *Address:* The Grange, Kirkby Malzeard, Ripon, N Yorks HG4 3RY. *T:* (01765) 658398; *e-mail:* nimble@nimble.entadsl.com.

THOMPSON, Peter Kenneth James; Solicitor to Departments of Health and of Social Security, 1989–97; *b* 30 July 1937; *s* of Kenneth George Thompson and Doreen May Thompson; *m* 1970, Sandy Lynne Harper; two *d*. *Educ:* Worksop Coll.; Christ's Coll., Cambridge (MA, LLB). Called to the Bar, Lincoln's Inn, 1961; practised at Common Law Bar, 1961–73; Lawyer in Govt Service: Law Commission, 1973–78; Lord Chancellor's Dept, 1978–83; Under Sec., DHSS, 1983. General Editor: The County Court Practice, 1991–98; The Civil Court Practice, 1999–. Hon. QC 1997. *Publications:* The Unfair Contract Terms Act 1977, 1978; The Recovery of Interest, 1985; *radio plays:* A Matter of Form, 1977; Dormer and Grand-Daughter, 1978. *Recreation:* writing.

THOMPSON, Raymond, CBE 1988; PhD; FRSC; FREng; Deputy Chairman, Borax Research Ltd, 1986–90 (Managing Director, 1980–86); Director: RTZ Chemicals (formerly Borax Consolidated) (Borides) Ltd, 1986–89; Boride Ceramics and Composites Ltd, 1990–92; Azmat Ltd, since 1993; *b* 4 April 1925; *s* of late William Edward Thompson and Hilda Thompson (*née* Rowley). *Educ:* Longton High Sch.; Univ. of Nottingham (MSc 1950, PhD 1952); Imperial Coll., Univ. of London (DIC 1953). Research Manager, Borax Consolidated, 1961; Res. Dir, 1969–86, Business Develt Dir, 1986–87, Scientific Advr, 1987–95, Borax Hldgs Ltd, later RTZ Borax and Minerals Ltd. Consultant: RTZ Chemicals Ltd, 1988–89; CRA Ltd, 1988–91; Rhône-Poulenc, 1989–92. Special Professor of Inorganic Chemistry, Univ. of Nottingham, 1975–96; Hon. Prof., Molecular Sciences, Univ. of Warwick, 1975–94. Member Council: Royal Inst. of Chemistry, 1969–72; Chemical Soc., 1977–80 (Chm., Inorganic Chemicals Gp, 1972–83); RSC, 1983–88 (Vice-Pres., Industrial Div., 1981–83, Pres., 1983–85 and 1988–89). Governor, Kingston-upon-Thames Polytechnic, 1978–88. Hon. Associate, RHC, London Univ., 1984. Freeman, City of London. FREng (FEng 1985). Industrial Chemistry Award, Chem. Soc., 1976. *Publications:* (ed) The Modern Inorganic Chemicals Industry, 1977; (ed) Mellors Comprehensive Treatise, Boron Supplement, Part A, 1979, Part BI, 1981; (ed) Speciality Inorganic Chemicals, 1981; (ed) Energy and Chemistry, 1981; (ed) Trace Metal Removal From Aqueous Solution, 1986; (ed) The Chemistry of Wood Preservation, 1991; Industrial Inorganic Chemicals: production and uses, 1995; various papers on inorganic boron and nitrogen chemistry. *Address:* 10 Waldorf Heights, Hawley Hill, Camberley, Surrey GU17 9JH. *T:* (01276) 32900.

THOMPSON, Rhodri William Ralph; QC 2002; *b* 5 May 1960; *s* of Ralph Kenneth Thompson and Dilys Grace Thompson (*née* Hughes); *m* 1989, Paula Mary Donaghy; one *s* two *d*. *Educ:* Eastbourne Coll.; University Coll., Oxford (BPhil, MA); City Univ. (Dip. Law). Called to the Bar, Middle Temple, 1989; in practice as barrister, 1989–; Monckton Chambers, 1990–2000 (Brussels, 1990–92, London, 1993–2000); Founder Mem., Matrix Chambers, 2000– (Chm., Mgt Cttee, 2004–06). *Publications:* (contrib.) Bellamy & Child, EC Law of Competition, 4th edn 1993 to 6th edn 2008; Single Market for Pharmaceuticals, 1994; Montgomery and Ormerod, Fraud, Criminal Law and Procedure (looseleaf), 2008. *Recreations:* walking, golf, tennis, philosophy. *Address:* Matrix Chambers, Griffin Building, Gray's Inn, WC1R 5LN. *T:* (020) 7611 9316; Westgate House, 93 High Street, Lewes, E Sussex BN7 1XH; *e-mail:* rhodrithompson@matrixlaw.co.uk.

THOMPSON, Sir Richard (Paul Hepworth), KCVO 2003; DM; FRCP; Physician to the Queen and Head of HM Medical Household, 1993–2005 (Physician to the Royal Household, 1982–93); Consultant Physician, St Thomas' Hospital, 1972–2005, Emeritus Consultant, Guy's and St Thomas' NHS Trust, since 2005; Physician, King Edward VII Hospital for Officers, 1982–2005; *b* 14 April 1940; *s* of Stanley Henry and Winifred Lilian Thompson; *m* 1974, Eleanor Mary Hughes. *Educ:* Epsom Coll.; Worcester Coll., Oxford (MA, DM); St Thomas's Hosp. Med. Sch. MRC Clinical Res. Fellow, Liver Unit, KCH, 1967–69; Fellow, Gastroenterology Unit, Mayo Clinic, USA, 1969–71; Lectr, Liver Unit, KCH, 1971–72. Mem., Lambeth, Southwark and Lewisham AHA, 1979–82. Examiner in Medicine: Soc. of Apothecaries, 1976–80; Faculty of Dental Surgery, RCS, 1980–86; Examr, 1991–2003, Censor, 1998–2000, Treas., 2003–, RCP. Governor, Guy's Hosp. Med. Sch., 1980–82; Member Cttee of Management: Inst. of Psychiatry, 1981–95; King Edward VII Hosp. Fund, 1985–89, 1992–96 (Mem., Gen. Council, 1985–); Mem. Council, Royal Med. Foundn of Epsom Coll., 2003–. Mem., Council, BHF, 2001– (Vice-Chm., 2001); Trustee, Thrive, 2001–. Hon. Associate Nightingale Fellow, 2004. *Publications:* Physical Signs in Medicine, 1980; Lecture Notes on the Liver, 1986; papers and reviews in med. jls. *Address:* 36 Dealtry Road, SW15 6NL. *T:* (020) 8789 3839.

THOMPSON, Richard Paul Reynier, OBE 2001; Chief Constable, Civil Nuclear Constabulary, since 2007; *b* 17 Aug. 1960; *s* of His Honour Anthony Arthur Richard Thompson, *qv*; two *s* one *d* with Louisa (*née* Yeates). *Educ:* St Paul's Sch.; Exeter Univ. (LLB); Harvard Business Sch. Served Army, RGJ, 1978–88. Entered FCO, 1989; Second, later First Sec., Stockholm, 1991–93; First Secretary: FCO, 1993–96; UK Mission to UN, Geneva, 1996–99; Counsellor: Pristina, 1999–2000; FCO, 2000–04; Baghdad, 2004–05; FCO, 2006–07. *Recreations:* keeping fit, reading (politics and history). *Address:* Civil Nuclear Constabulary, Culham Science Centre, Abingdon, Oxon OX14 3DB.

THOMPSON, Robert; *see* Thompson, W. R.

THOMPSON, Robin; *see* Thompson, D. R. B.

THOMPSON, (Rupert) Julian (de la Mare); Chinese art consultant; *b* 23 July 1941; *s* of Rupert Spens Thompson and Florence Elizabeth (*née* de la Mare); *m* 1965, Jacqueline Mary Ivimy; three *d*. *Educ:* Eton Coll.; King's Coll., Cambridge (MA). Joined Sotheby's, 1963: appointed a Director, 1969; Chm., 1982–86; Dep. Chm., 1987–92; Chm., Sotheby's International, 1982–85, 1987–88; non-exec. Chm., Sotheby's Asia, 1992–2003. *Address:* Crossington Farm, Upton Bishop, Ross-on-Wye, Herefordshire HR9 7UE. *T:* (01989) 780471.

See also N. de la M. Thompson.

THOMPSON, Ruth; Director General, Higher Education, Department for Innovation, Universities and Skills (formerly Department for Education and Skills), since 2007 (Acting Director, 2006–07); *b* 4 July 1953; *d* of Arthur Frederick (Pat) Thompson and late Mary Thompson (*née* Barritt); *m* 2004, Hon. Sir David Michael Bean, *qv*. *Educ:* Somerville Coll., Oxford (MA Modern Hist.); St Antony's Coll., Oxford and Instituto di Tella, Buenos Aires (DPhil Econ. Hist. 1978). Depts of Industry, Trade and Prices and Consumer Protection, 1978–90; Private Sec. to Parly Under-Sec., Dept of Trade and successive Secs of State for Trade and Industry, 1982–84; Cabinet Office (on secondment), 1987; Asst Sec., DTI, 1990–92; HM Treasury, 1992–98; DSS, 1999–2000; Dir of Finance, DfEE, then DfES, 2000–03; Dir, Higher Educn Strategy and Implementation Gp, DfES, 2003–06. *Recreations:* walking, swimming. *Address:* Department for Innovation, Universities and Skills, Kingsgate House, Victoria Street, SW1E 6SW. *T:* (020) 3300 8351.

THOMPSON, Dame Tanni Carys Davina G.; *see* Grey-Thompson.

THOMPSON, Sir (Thomas d'Eyncourt) John, 6th Bt *cr* 1806, of Hartsbourne Manor, Hertfordshire; Director, Rockspring Iberia, Madrid, since 2006; *b* 22 Dec. 1956; *o s* of Sir (Thomas) Lionel Tennyson Thompson, 5th Bt and of Margaret Thompson (*née* Brown); *S* father, 1999; *m* 2002, Tanya, *d* of Michael Willcocks; one *s* one *d*. *Educ:* Eton; King's Coll., London (BA; MSc). MRICS (ARICS 1993). Associate Partner, Folkard & Hayward, London, 1984–90; Investment Surveyor, King Sturge, London, 1991–93, Brussels, 1994; Dir, Weatherall Green & Smith, Madrid, 1995–97; Partner, King Sturge, Madrid, 1997–2006. *Heir: s* Thomas Boulden Cameron Thompson, *b* 31 Jan. 2006.

THOMPSON, William John; *b* 26 Oct. 1939; *s* of William H. Thompson and Catherine Thompson; *m* 1962, Violet Joyce Armstrong; one *s* two *d*. *Educ:* Edenderry Primary Sch.; Deverney Primary Sch.; Omagh Acad. With Tyrone CC, 1957–66; radio and TV retailer, 1966–97. Member: NI Assembly, 1973–74 and 1982–85; NI Convention, 1975–76; Omagh DC, 1981–93. MP (UU) Tyrone West, 1997–2001; contested same seat, 2001. Methodist local preacher, 1962–. *Recreations:* reading, occasional round of golf. *Address:* 129 Donaghanie Road, Beragh, Co. Tyrone, N Ireland BT79 0XE.

THOMPSON, (William) Robert; freelance cartoonist, since 1992; *b* 21 July 1960; *s* of Wildon and Eileen Thompson; *m* 1993, Siobhán Maria Doyle; one *s* one *d*. *Educ:* Leeds Polytechnic (BA Hons Graphic Design). Art Dir, Camden Graphics, 1985–92. Contrib. cartoons/illustrations to Guardian, Observer, Spectator, Private Eye, Times, Daily Telegraph, Radio Times, New Statesman, Prospect. *Publications:* Pointless Things to Do, 1995; illustrator: Private Eye's Cutting Humour, 1993; Can They Do That?, 2003; The Origins of Words and Phrases, 2007. *Recreations:* walking my Jack Russell, growing vegetables, eating dark chocolate, drinking red wine, having heart palpitations. *Address:* e-mail: rtcartoonist@btinternet.com; *web:* www.robertthompsoncartoons.com.

THOMPSON, Willoughby Harry, CMG 1974; CBE 1968 (MBE 1954); *b* 3 Dec. 1919; *m* 1963, Sheelah O'Grady; no *c*. Served War: RA, and E African Artillery, 1939–47. Kenya Govt Service, 1947–48; Colonial Administrative Service, Kenya, 1948–63; Colonial Sec., Falkland Islands, 1963–69 (Actg Governor, 1964 and 1967); Actg Judge, Falkland Islands and Dependencies Supreme Court, 1965–69; Actg Administrator, British Virgin Islands, May–July 1969; HM Comr in Anguilla, July 1969–1971; Governor of Montserrat, 1971–74.

THOMPSON, Yvonne, CBE 2003; Managing Director, ASAP Communications Ltd, since 1995; *b* 1957; one *d*. Founder, Positive Publicity, 1983–89. Dir, Choice FM Radio. Member: Bd, Britain in Europe, 1999–; Bd, London Develt Agency, 2000–; Small Business Council, DTI, 2000–; Comr, Local Govt Inf. Unit; Chairman: London Central LSC, 2000–; Ethnic Minority Business Forum, DTI, 2000–. Founder and Pres., Eur. Fedn of Black Women Business Owners, 1997–. *Address:* ASAP Communications Ltd, Suite 1, 2 Tunstall Road, SW9 8DA.

THOMPSON-McCAUSLAND, Benedict Maurice Perronet; Partner, Temax Associates, since 1991; Group Managing Director, National & Provincial Building Society, 1987–90; *b* 5 Feb. 1938; *s* of late Lucius P. Thompson-McCausland, CMG and Helen Laura McCausland; *m* 1964, Frances Catherine Fothergill Smith; three *d*. *Educ:* Eton Coll.; Trinity Coll., Cambridge (MA; Rowing Blue). FCA 1974–2003. Articled to Coopers & Lybrand, Chartered Accountants, 1961–64; Arbuthnot Latham & Co. Ltd, 1964–80: Asst to Dirs, 1964; Banking Manager, 1967; Dir, 1968; Dep. Chm., 1978; London Life Association Ltd: Dir, 1976–81; Vice-Pres., 1979–87; Chief Exec., 1981–87. Dir, Advanced Personnel Technology, 1993–2001; formerly Director: Western Trust & Savings Ltd; Concord Internat.; First National Finance Corp. plc. Chm., Lombard Assoc., 1979–81. Director: British Sch. of Osteopathy, 1991–2000 (Chm., 1996–2000); Harefield Hosp. NHS Trust, 1992–98. Mem. Council, 1987–2000, and Mem. Exec. Cttee, 1988–91, Industrial Soc. Mem., Council of Management, Arnolfini Gall., 1983–86. John Loxham Lectr, Inst. of Quality Assurance, 1997. *Publications:* (with Derek Biddle) Change, Business Performance and Values, 1985; (with J. Bergwerk) Leading to Success: how leaders unlock energy, 1994; articles in business jls. *Recreations:* windsurfing, rough gardening. *Address:* 91 Blenheim Crescent, W11 2EQ. *T:* (020) 7727 1266. *Clubs:* Leander (Henley-on-Thames); Hawks (Cambridge).

THOMS, Jennifer Linda; *see* Simpson, J. L.

THOMSEN, Kim Stuart L.; *see* Lerche-Thomsen.

THOMSON, family name of **Barons Thomson of Fleet** and **Thomson of Monifieth**.

THOMSON OF FLEET, 3rd Baron *cr* 1964; **David Kenneth Roy Thomson;** Chairman, The Thomson Corporation, since 2002; *b* 12 June 1957; *s* of 2nd Baron Thomson of Fleet and of Nora Marilyn (*née* Lavis); *S* father, 2006; *m* 1st, 1988, Mary Lou La Prairie (marr. diss. 1997); two *d*; 2nd, 2000, Laurie Ludwick; one *s*. *Educ:* Upper Canada Coll.; Selwyn Coll., Cambridge (MA). *Heir: s* Hon. Benjamin James Ludwick Thomson, *b* 10 March 2006. *Address:* The Thomson Corporation, 65 Queen Street West, Toronto, ON M5H 2M8, Canada.

THOMSON OF MONIFIETH, Baron *cr* 1977 (Life Peer), of Monifieth, Dundee; **George Morgan Thomson,** KT 1981; PC 1966; Chairman, Independent Broadcasting Authority, 1981–88 (Deputy Chairman, 1980); Chancellor, Heriot Watt University, 1977–91; *b* 16 Jan. 1921; *s* of late James Thomson, Monifieth; *m* 1948, Grace Jenkins; two *d*. *Educ:* Grove Academy, Dundee. Served War of 1939–45, in Royal Air Force, 1940–46. Assistant Editor, Forward, 1946, Editor, 1948–53. Contested (Lab) Glasgow, Hillhead, 1950; MP (Lab) Dundee East, July 1952–72. Joint Chm., Council for Education in the Commonwealth, 1959–64; Adviser to Educational Institute of Scotland, 1960–64. Minister of State, Foreign Office, 1964–66; Chancellor of the Duchy of Lancaster, 1966–67; Joint Minister of State, Foreign Office, 1967; Secretary of State for Commonwealth Affairs, Aug. 1967–Oct. 1968; Minister Without Portfolio, 1968–69; Chancellor of the Duchy of Lancaster, 1969–70; Shadow Defence Minister, 1970–72. Chm., Labour Cttee for Europe, 1972–73; Commissioner, EEC, 1973–Jan. 1977. Mem., Lib Dems, 1989– (spokesman on foreign affairs and broadcasting, H of L, 1990–98). Chairman: European Movement in Britain, 1977–80; Advertising Standards Authority, 1977–80; European TV and Film Forum, 1989–91. First Crown Estate Comr, 1978–80. Director: Royal Bank of Scotland Gp, 1977–90; ICI plc, 1977–89; Woolwich Equitable Building Soc., 1979–91 (Dep. Chm., 1988–91); Chairman: Value and Income Trust, 1988–2000; Grant Leisure, 1990–94; Woolwich Europe, 1990–92. President: Hist. of Advertising Trust, 1985–99; Prix Italia, 1989–91; Dir, ENO, 1987–93. Chm., Suzy Lamplugh Trust, 1990–93; Dep. Chm., Ditchley Foundn, 1983–87; Pilgrims Trustee, 1977–97; Trustee: Thomson Foundn, 1977–; Leeds Castle Foundn, 1978–2001 (Chm., 1994–2001). FRSE 1985; FRTS 1990 (Vice-Pres., 1982–89). Hon. LLD Dundee, 1967; Hon. DLitt: Heriot-Watt, 1973; New Univ. of Ulster, 1984; Hon. DSc Aston, 1976. *Address:* House of Lords, SW1A 0PW.

See also C. Thomson.

THOMSON, Adam McClure; HM Diplomatic Service; Director, South Asia and Afghanistan, Foreign and Commonwealth Office, since 2006; *b* 1 July 1955; *e s* of Sir John Thomson, *qv*; *m* 1984, Fariba Shirazi; one *s* two *d*. *Educ:* Westminster Sch.; Trinity Coll., Cambridge (MA); Harvard Univ. (MPP). Joined FCO, 1978; Third, later Second Sec., Moscow, 1981–83; Second, later First Sec., UK delegn to NATO, Brussels, 1983–86; First Sec., FCO, 1986–89; Cabinet Office, 1989–91; First Sec. (Politico-Military), Washington, 1991–95; Counsellor (Political), New Delhi, 1995–98: Counsellor, Security Policy Dept, FCO, 1998–2002; Ambassador and Dep. Perm. Rep., UK Mission to UN, NY, 2002–06. *Address:* c/o Foreign and Commonwealth Office, King Charles Street, SW1A 2AH. *Club:* Athenæum.

THOMSON, Prof. Andrew James, OBE 2008; DPhil; FRS 1993; CChem, FRSC; Professor of Chemistry, University of East Anglia, since 1985; *b* 31 July 1940; *s* of late Andrew Henderson Thomson and Eva Frances Annie (*née* Moss); *m* 1966, Anne Marsden; two *s*. *Educ:* Steyning Grammar Sch.; Wadham Coll., Oxford (MA, DPhil). FRSC 1990. Res. Asst Prof., Dept of Biophysics, Michigan State Univ., 1967; School of Chemical Sciences, University of East Anglia: Demonstrator, 1967–68; Lectr, 1968–77; Sen. Lectr, 1977–83; Reader, 1983–85; Hd of Inorganic Chem. Sector, 1984–97; Norwich Res. Park Prof., 1995–2007; Dean, Sch. of Chemical Scis and Pharmacy, 1999–2004; Dean, Faculty of Sci., 2004–07. Royal Society of Chemistry: Silver Medal for analytical chemistry, 1991; Hugo Muller Lectureship, 1997; Interdisciplinary Award, 2000; Chatt Lectureship, 2004. *Publications:* papers in scientific jls. *Recreation:* walking. *Address:* 12 Armitage Close, Cringleford, Norwich NR4 6XZ. *T:* (01603) 504623; *e-mail:* a.thomson@uea.ac.uk.

THOMSON, Prof. Andrew William John, PhD; OBE 1993; Professor, School of Management, Open University, 1988–2001, Professor Emeritus, 2006; *b* 26 Jan. 1936; *s* of Andrew Edward Thomson and Helen Thomson; *m* 1st, 1966, Joan Marjorie Hughes (marr. diss. 1980); two *s*; 2nd, 1992, Rosemary Joy Hetherington Smith (*d* 1998); 3rd, 2001, Prof. Angela Marilyn Bowey, *qv*. *Educ:* St Bees Sch.; St Edmund Hall, Oxford (BA Hons PPE 1959); Cornell Univ. (MS 1961; PhD 1968). 2nd Lieut, RA, 1954–56; Lieut, Parachute Regt TA, 1958–63; Brand Manager, Lever Brothers, 1961–65; University of Glasgow: Lectr, Sen. Lectr and Reader, 1968–78; Prof. of Business Policy, 1978–87; Dean: Scottish Business Sch., 1983–87; Sch. of Management, Open Univ., 1988–93. Prof., Univ. of Chicago, 1973, 1977. Dir, Scottish Transport Gp, 1977–84; Mem., Scottish Agricl Wages Bd, 1985–99; Vice-Chairman: Mgt and Industrial Relations Cttee, SSRC, 1982–85; Industry and Employment Cttee, ESRC, 1985–88; Chm., Jt Cttee, ESRC–SERC, 1987–90. Chairman: Council of Univ. Mgt Schs, 1985–87; British Acad. of Mgt, 1990–93. *Publications:* (with L. C. Hunter) The Nationalised Transport Industries, 1973; (with S. R. Engleman) The Industrial Relations Act, 1975; (with V. V. Murray) Grievance Procedures, 1976; (with P. B. Beaumont) Collective Bargaining in the Public Sector, 1978; (ed with M. Warner) The Behavioural Sciences and Industrial Relations, 1981; (ed with M. B. Gregory) A Portrait of Pay, 1990; (jtly) Changing Patterns of Management Development, 2001; (with J. Wilson) The Making of Modern Management: British management in historical perspective, 2006. *Recreations:* golf, walking. *Address:* PO Box 113, Paihia, New Zealand. *T:* (9) 4028416. *Clubs:* Waitangi Golf; Bay of Islands Rotary.

THOMSON, Caroline, (Mrs R. Liddle); Chief Operating Officer, BBC, since 2007; *b* 15 May 1954; *d* of Lord Thomson of Monifieth, *qv*; *m* 1st, 1977, Ian Bradley (marr. diss. 1980); 2nd, 1983, Roger John Liddle, *qv*; one *s*. *Educ:* Mary Datchelor Grammar Sch.; Univ. of York (BA Hons). BBC trainee, 1975–77; producer: Analysis, BBC Radio, 1978–81; Panorama, 1982; Political Advr to Rt Hon. Roy Jenkins, 1983; Commng Ed., Business and Sci., 1984–90, Hd, Corporate Affairs, 1991–95, Channel 4; Dep. Chief Exec., BBC World Service, 1995–2000; Dir, Public Policy, 2000–04, Strategy, 2004–06, BBC. Non-executive Director: Pensions Regulator, 2005–; Digital UK, 2006–. Pres., Prix Italia, 2005–08. FRTS, 2007. *Recreation:* domesticity. *Address:* BBC, Room 5127, White City, 201 Wood Lane, W12 7TS. *T:* (020) 8008 1801.

THOMSON, Sir David; *see* Thomson, Sir F. D. D.

THOMSON, Rt Rev. David; *see* Huntingdon, Bishop Suffragan of.

THOMSON, David; writer and film critic; *b* London, 1941; *m* Lucy Gray; two *s*. *Educ:* Dulwich Coll.; London Sch. of Film Technique. Various posts with Penguin. Contribs to Independent on Sunday, New York Times, New Republic, Sight and Sound, Film Comment, Movieline, Salon. *Publications:* Wild Excursions: the life and fiction of Laurence Sterne, 1972; A Biographical Dictionary of the Cinema, 1975, 4th edn, as The New Biographical Dictionary of Film, 2002; Suspects (novel), 1985; Warren Beatty and Desert Eyes: a life and a story, 1987; Silver Light (novel), 1990; Showman: life of David O. Selznick, 1993; Rosebud: the story of Orson Welles, 1996; 4–2, 1996; Big Sleep, 1997; Alien Quartet, 1998; Beneath Mulholland: thoughts on Hollywood and its ghosts, 1998; (with Lucy Gray) In Nevada: the land, the people, God and chance, 2000; Hollywood: a celebration!, 2001; The Whole Equation: a history of Hollywood, 2005; Nicole Kidman, 2006. *Address:* c/o Time Warner Books UK, Brettenham House, Lancaster Place, WC2E 7EN.

THOMSON, David Paget, RD 1969; *b* 19 March 1931; *s* of Sir George Paget Thomson, FRS, Nobel Laureate, and Kathleen Buchanan Smith; *m* 1959, Patience Mary, *d* of Sir William Lawrence Bragg, CH, OBE, MC, FRS, Nobel Laureate; two *s* two *d*. *Educ:* Rugby Sch.; Grenoble Univ.; Trinity Coll., Cambridge (MA). Nat. Service, RN (Sub-Lieut), 1953–55; subseq. Lieut-Comdr RNR. Lazard Bros & Co., 1956, Director, 1965–86; seconded to HM Diplomatic Service, 1971–73, as Counsellor (Economic), Bonn. Dir Gen., BIEC, 1987–90. Chairman: Kleinwort, subseq. Dresdner RCM, Emerging Markets Trust, 1993–2002; Medical Sickness Annuity and Life Assce Soc. Ltd, 1995–97; Dep. Chm., Permanent Insce Co., 1995–97; Director: Finance Co. Viking, Zurich, 1969–87; Richard Daus & Co., bankers, Frankfurt, 1974–81; Applied Photophysics, 1976–87; Wesleyan Assce Soc. Ltd, 1997–2000; Foreign & Colonial European Investment Trust, 1998–2002. Mem., Monopolies and Mergers Commn,

1984–94. Member: Council, Brunel Univ., 1974–85; Court of Governors, Henley Management Coll., 1979–94. Hon. Treasurer, British Dyslexia Assoc., 1984–86. Chairman: Fitzwilliam Mus. Trust, 1988–93; Portsmouth Naval Base Property Trust, 1992–98; Royal Institution: Treasurer, 1976–81; Chm. Council, 1985. CC Oxon 1985–89. Master, Plumbers' Co., 1980–81. *Recreations:* hill-walking, gardening, real tennis. *Address:* Little Stoke House, Wallingford, Oxon OX10 6AX. *T:* (01491) 837161. *Club:* Athenæum (Chm., 1995–98).

See also S. L. Bragg, Sir J. A. Thomson.

THOMSON, Maj.-Gen. David Phillips, CB 1993; CBE 1989; MC 1965; Senior Army Member, Royal College of Defence Studies, 1992–95; *b* 30 Jan. 1942; *s* of Cyril Robert William Thomson and Louise Mary Thomson (*née* Phillips). *Educ:* Eastbourne Coll.; RMA Sandhurst. Commnd, Argyll and Sutherland Highlanders, 1962; despatches, 1968; Bde Major, 6th Armd Bde, 1975; Instr, Staff Coll., 1980; CO, 1st Bn, A and SH, 1982; Chief of Staff: RMCS, 1985; 1st Armd Div., 1986; Comdr, 1st Inf. Bde/UK Mobile Force, 1987; despatches, 1992. Col, Argyll and Sutherland Highlanders, 1992–2000. Captain, Royal Castle of Tarbert, 1992–2000. Chm., Sussex Combined Services Museum Trust, 1995–2007. FRGS 1993. *Recreations:* golf, historical research. *Address:* Home HQ, Argyll and Sutherland Highlanders, The Castle, Stirling FK8 1EH. *T:* (01786) 475165.

THOMSON, Prof. Derick Smith, FBA 1992; FRSE; Professor of Celtic, University of Glasgow, 1963–91, now Emeritus; *b* 5 Aug. 1921; *s* of James and Christina Thomson; *m* 1952, Carol Mac Michael Galbraith; five *s* one *d*. *Educ:* Nicolson Inst., Stornoway; Univ. of Aberdeen (MA); University College of North Wales, Bangor; Emmanuel Coll., Cambridge (BA 1948). Asst in Celtic, Univ. of Edinburgh, 1948–49; Lectr in Welsh, Univ. of Glasgow, 1949–56; Reader in Celtic, Univ. of Aberdeen, 1956–63. Chm., Gaelic Books Council, 1968–91; Pres., Scottish Gaelic Texts Soc., 1964–96. Editor: Scottish Gaelic Studies, 1962–76; Gairm, 1952–2002. Hon. DLitt: Wales, 1987; Aberdeen, 1994. First recipient, Ossian Prize, FVS Foundn, Hamburg, 1974. *Publications:* The Gaelic Sources of Macpherson's Ossian, 1952; Branwen Verch Lyr, 1961, 2nd edn 1968; An Introduction to Gaelic Poetry, 1974, 2nd edn 1990; The Companion to Gaelic Scotland, 1983, 3rd edn 1994; The MacDiarmid MS Anthology, 1992; Gaelic Poetry in the Eighteenth Century, 1993; Alasdair Mac Mhaighstir Alasdair, Selected Poems, 1996; *poetry:* Creachadh Na Clàrsaich (Plundering the Harp), Collected Poems, 1982; Smeur an Dòchais (Bramble of Hope), 1992; Meall Garbh (The Rugged Mountain), 1995; Suil air Fàire (Surveying the Horizon), 2007. *Recreations:* writing, travel, politics, gardening. *Address:* 15 Struan Road, Cathcart, Glasgow G44 3AT. *T:* (0141) 637 3704. *Clubs:* Glasgow Art, Town and Gown (Glasgow).

THOMSON, Dick; HM Diplomatic Service, retired; Consul General, Barcelona, 1999–2002; *b* 18 Dec. 1942; *s* of Adam and Janet Alexander Thomson; *m* 1972, Jacqueline Margaret Dunn (*d* 2003); one *s* one *d*. *Educ:* Port Glasgow High Sch.; Greenock High Sch. With Ministry of Transport, 1961–66; entered FCO, 1966; served: Havana, 1969–70; Athens, 1970–71; Rome, 1971–72; Warsaw, 1972–73; Personnel Dept, FCO, 1973–76; San Francisco, 1976–80; Consul, Algiers, 1980–83; Near East and N Africa Dept, FCO, 1984–87; First Sec., Copenhagen, 1988–92; Head of Parly Relns Unit, FCO, 1992–95; Ambassador to Dominican Republic, 1995–98. *Recreations:* mainly sport—soccer, tennis, swimming. *Address:* 202 Chesterfield Drive, Sevenoaks, Kent TN13 2EH.

THOMSON, Duncan, PhD; Keeper, Scottish National Portrait Gallery, 1982–97; *b* 2 Oct. 1934; *s* of Duncan Murdoch Thomson and Jane McFarlane Wilson; *m* 1964, Julia Jane Macphail; one *d*. *Educ:* Airdrie Acad.; Univ. of Edinburgh (MA 1956, PhD 1970); Edinburgh Coll. of Art (Cert. of Coll.; Post-Dip. Scholarship); Moray House Coll. of Educn. Teacher of Art, 1959–67; Asst Keeper, Scottish National Portrait Gall., 1967–82. Scottish Arts Council: Mem., Art Cttee, 1983–89; Chm., Exhibn Panel, 1985–89. Chm., Mansfield Traquair Trust, 1996–. Vice-Pres., Art in Healthcare, 2007–. Mem., Editl Bd, Scottish Cultural Resources Access Network, 1998–. Hon. Fellow, Sch. of Arts, Culture and Envmt, Univ. of Edinburgh, 1998–. *Publications:* The Life and Art of George Jamesone, 1974; Sir Henry Raeburn, 1994; Arikha, 1994; (jtly) The Skating Minister, 2004; *exhibition catalogues:* A Virtuous and Noble Education, 1971; Painting in Scotland 1570–1650, 1975; Eye to Eye, 1980; (jtly) John Michael Wright, 1982; (jtly) The Queen's Image, 1987; Raeburn: the art of Sir Henry Raeburn 1756–1823, 1997; (jtly) Avigdor Arikha From Life, 2006. *Recreation:* reading poetry (and thinking about writing it). *Address:* 3 Eglinton Crescent, Edinburgh EH12 5DH. *T:* (0131) 225 6430. *Club:* Scottish Arts (Edinburgh).

THOMSON, Elaine Margaret; Support Centre Manager, Absoft Ltd (Information Technology Consultant, 1995–99 and 2003); *b* 10 Aug. 1957; *d* of Dr Charles Thomson and Moira Thomson; partner, Archie Flockhart. *Educ:* Aberdeen Univ. (BSc Pure Sci.); Robert Gordon Univ. (Postgraduate Cert. in Corporate Communications and Public Affairs). Analyst/Programmer, ABB Vetco Gray UK Ltd, 1982–94. MSP (Lab) Aberdeen N, 1999–2003; contested same seat, 2003, 2007. Chair, Cornerstone Community Care, 2005– (Dir, 2003–). *Recreations:* ski-ing, walking, reading. *Address:* *e-mail:* elaine.thomson@talk21.com.

THOMSON, Sir (Frederick Douglas) David, 3rd Bt *cr* 1929; Chairman: Britannia Steam Ship Insurance Association Ltd, since 1986 (Director, since 1965); Through Transport Mutual Insurance Ltd, since 1983 (Director, since 1973); *b* 14 Feb. 1940; *s* of Sir James Douglas Wishart Thomson, 2nd Bt, and of Evelyn Margaret Isabel, (Bettina), *d* of Lt-Comdr D. W. S. Douglas, RN; *S* father, 1972; *m* 1st, 1967, Caroline Anne (marr. diss. 1994), *d* of Major Timothy Stuart Lewis; two *s* one *d*; 2nd, 2003, Hilary Claire, *d* of Sidney Paul Youldon, MC. *Educ:* Eton; University College, Oxford (BA Agric). Worked for Ben Line, 1961–89. Director: S. A. Meacock, 1996–; The Investment Co., 2005–. Member: Queen's Body Guard for Scotland, Royal Company of Archers. *Recreations:* shooting, ski-ing, music. *Heir:* *s* Simon Douglas Charles Thomson, *b* 16 June 1969. *Address:* Holylee, Walkerburn, Peeblesshire EH43 6BD. *T:* (01896) 870673. *Club:* Boodle's.

THOMSON, James Phillips Spalding; Consultant Surgeon, St Mark's Hospital, 1974–99, now Emeritus (Clinical Director, 1990–97); Administrator, Priory Church of St Bartholomew the Great, 2000–02; Master, Sutton's Hospital in Charterhouse, since 2001; *b* 2 Oct. 1939; *s* of late Peggy Marion Thomson (*née* Phillips) and James Laing Spalding Thomson, MB ChB, MRCGP; *m* 1968, Dr Anne Katharine (*née* Richards), MB BS, MRCP, DCH; one *s* three *d*. *Educ:* Haileybury and Imperial Service Coll.; Middlesex Hosp. Med. Sch., Univ. of London (MB BS 1962; MS 1974). LRCP, MRCS, 1962, FRCS 1969; DObst RCOG 1964. Jun. med. and surgical appts, 1962–71; Demonstrator, Dept of Anatomy, Middlesex Hosp. Med. Sch., 1964–66; Consultant Surgeon: Royal Northern Hosp., 1975–77; Hackney Hosp., 1977–86; Homerton Hosp., 1986–90. Hon. Consultant Surgeon: St John's Hosp. for Diseases of the Skin, 1973–75; St Mary's Hosp., 1982–99; St Luke's Hosp. for the Clergy, 1976–99; Civil Cons. in Surgery, RAF, 1984–99, now Hon. Civil Cons.; Civilian Cons. in Colorectal Surgery, RN, 1986–99, now Emeritus Cons. in Surgery; Hon. Lectr in Surgery, Bart's Hosp. Med. Coll., 1977–94; Hon. Clin. Sen. Lectr in Surgery, Imperial Coll. Sch. of Medicine at St Mary's (formerly St Mary's Hosp. Med. Sch., Imperial Coll.), London, 1994–99. Hon. Cons. Advr in Surgery, Ileostomy Assoc., 1986–99. Examr in Surgery, Univs of Cambridge, Liverpool and London; Mem., Court of Examrs, RCS, 1986–92. President: Section of Coloproctology, RSocMed, 1994–95; Travelling Surgical Soc., 1998–2001; St Mark's Assoc., 1999; Hunterian Soc., 2001–02; Friends of St Mark's Hosp., 2006–; Haileybury Soc., 2006–07; Patron and Fellow, Burgon Soc., 2002–. Vice-Chm. of Council and Trustee, St Luke's Hosp. for the Clergy, 1992–2004; Trustee: Med. Coll. of St Bartholomew's Hosp. Trust, 2002–; St Andrew Holborn Church Foundn, 2003–. Governor, Corp. of Sons of the Clergy, 1988–. Liveryman: Apothecaries' Soc., 1980–; Barbers' Co., 1992–. Hon. Fellow, Queen Mary, Univ. of London, 2007. Frederick Salmon Medal, RSocMed, 1996. DM Lambeth, 1987. *Publications:* (jtly) Colorectal Disease, 1981; (jtly) Frontiers in Colorectal Disease, 1986; (jtly) Updates in Coloproctology, 1992; contribs to books and learned jls. *Recreations:* church music, railways, canals. *Address:* Master's Lodge, Charterhouse, Charterhouse Square, EC1M 6AN. *T:* (020) 7253 0272; St Martin's House, The Street, Hindringham, Norfolk NR21 0PR. *T:* (01328) 822093, 07801 648802; *e-mail:* JamesPSThomson@aol.com. *Clubs:* Athenæum, Royal Society of Medicine.

THOMSON, Sir John (Adam), GCMG 1985 (KCMG 1978; CMG 1972); MA; HM Diplomatic Service, retired; *b* 27 April 1927; *s* of late Sir George Thomson, FRS, Master of Corpus Christi Coll., Cambridge, 1952–62 (*s* of Sir J. J. Thomson, OM, FRS, Master of Trinity Coll., Cambridge, 1919–40), and late Kathleen, *d* of Very Rev. Sir George Adam Smith, DD, LLD, Principal of Aberdeen Univ., 1909–35; *m* 1st, 1953, Elizabeth Anne McClure (*d* 1988), *d* of late Norman McClure, Pres. of Ursinus Coll., Penn, USA; three *s* one *d*; 2nd, 1992, Judith Ogden Bullitt, *d* of late John Stanley Ogden, NY, and Olga Geddes Bradshaw, Melbourne. *Educ:* Phillips Exeter Acad., USA; Univ. of Aberdeen; Trinity Coll., Cambridge. Foreign Office, 1950; Third Sec., Jedda, 1951; Damascus, 1954; FO, 1955; Private Sec. to Permanent Under-Secretary, 1958–60; First Sec., Washington, 1960–64; FO, 1964; Acting Head of Planning Staff, 1966; Counsellor, 1967; Head of Planning Staff, FO, 1967; seconded to Cabinet Office as Chief of Assessments Staff, 1968–71; Minister and Dep. Permanent Rep. to N Atlantic Council, 1972–73; Head of UK Delegn to MBFR Exploratory Talks, Vienna, 1973; Asst Under-Sec. of State, FCO, 1973–76; High Comr to India, 1977–82; UK Perm. Rep. to UN, 1982–87. Chm., Fleming Emerging Markets Investment Trust, 1991–98; Internat. Advr, ANZ Grindlays Bank, 1996–97 (Dir, 1987–96). Mem., Howie Cttee on Scottish Secondary Educn, 1990–93. Trustee, Nat. Museums of Scotland, 1991–99. Principal Dir, 21st Century Trust, 1987–90; Dir, Minority Rights Gp, USA, 1993–99; Chm., Minority Rights Gp Internat., 1991–99. Member: Council, IISS, 1987–96; Council, ODI, 1987–96; Governing Body, IDS, 1987–96. Director's Visitor, IAS, Princeton, 1995–96. Trustee, Indian Nat. Trust, 1989–. Associate Mem., Nuffield Coll., Oxford, 1987–91. Hon. LLD: Ursinus Coll., Penn, 1984; Aberdeen, 1986; Hon. DHL Allegheny Coll., Penn, 1985. *Publication:* Crusader Castles (with R. Fedden), 1956. *Recreations:* carpets, castles, walking. *Clubs:* Athenæum; Century (New York).

See also A. McC. Thomson, D. P. Thomson.

THOMSON, Prof. Joseph McGeachy, FRSE; Commissioner, Scottish Law Commission, since 2000; *b* 6 May 1948; *s* of James Thomson and Catherine (*née* McGeachy); *m* 1999, Marilyn Ann Iverson. *Educ:* Keil Sch., Dumbarton; Univ. of Edinburgh (LLB 1970). FRSE 1996. Lectr in Law, Univ. of Birmingham, 1970–74; Lectr in Laws, King's Coll., London, 1974–84; Prof. of Law, Univ. of Strathclyde, 1984–90; Regius Prof. of Law, Glasgow Univ., 1991–2005. Vis. Prof., Glasgow Caledonian Univ., 2005. Dep. General Editor, Stair Meml Encyclopaedia of Laws of Scotland, 1984–96. Dir, Scottish Universities Law Inst., 2000–. Pres., SPTL, 2000–01; Hon. Vice-Pres., Assoc. of Law Teachers, 2003–. Hon. Fellow, Soc. for Advanced Legal Studies, 2001. *Publications:* Family Law in Scotland, 1987, 5th edn 2006; Delictual Liability, 1994, 3rd edn 2004; (with H. MacQueen) Contract Law in Scotland, 2000, 2nd edn 2007; Scots Private Law, 2006; contribs to Law Qly Review, Modern Law Review, Juridical Review, Scots Law Times, etc. *Recreations:* opera, ballet, wine and food. *Address:* Scottish Law Commission, 140 Causewayside, Edinburgh EH9 1PR. *T:* (0131) 668 2131; 27 Howe Street, Edinburgh EH3 6TF. *Club:* Scottish Arts (Edinburgh).

THOMSON, Kenneth Andrew Lyons; Director, Constitution, Law and Courts, Scottish Government, since 2007; *b* 18 Oct. 1962; *s* of Andrew Leslie Thomson and Jennifer Thomson (*née* Lyons); *m* 1986, Ursula Schlapp; one *s* one *d*. *Educ:* Inch and Cramond Prim. Schs; Royal High Sch., Edinburgh; Univ. of St Andrews (MA Hons Music); Open Univ. (MBA). Admin Trainee, Civil Service, 1988; Higher Exec. Officer (Develt) 1988–90; Pvte Sec. to Minister of State, Scottish Office, 1990–91; Principal Officer, 1991; Asst Dir, Scottish Financial Enterprise, 1991–93; project team, Setting Forth, 1993–96; Bill Manager, Crime and Punishment (Scotland) Act, 1996–97; work on 'Scotland's Parliament', 1997; Asst Sec., 1997; Principal Pvte Sec. to Sec. of State for Scotland, 1997–99, to First Minister of Scotland, 1999; Dir, Corporate Develt, Scottish Exec., 1999–2000; Hd, Health Policy Gp, 2000–02; Dir, Corporate Services, Scottish Prison Service, 2002–05; Dir, Constitutional and Parly Secretariat, Scottish Exec., 2005–07. Trustee, Dunedin Concerts Trust, 2007–. *Recreations:* cycling, cooking, crosswords, consort music. *Address:* c/o Scottish Government, St Andrew's House, Edinburgh EH1 3DG.

THOMSON, Malcolm George; QC (Scot.) 1987; *b* 6 April 1950; *s* of late George Robert Thomson, OBE, and of Daphne Ethel Thomson; *m* 1st, 1978, Susan Gordon Aitken (marr. diss. 2001); two *d*; 2nd, 2008, Maybel Hutton. *Educ:* Edinburgh Acad.; Edinburgh Univ. (LLB). Advocate 1974; called to the Bar, Lincoln's Inn, 1991. Standing Junior Counsel to Dept of Agriculture and Fisheries for Scotland and Forestry Commn in Scotland, 1982–87. Chm., NHS Tribunal (Scotland), 1995–2005; Mem., Scottish Legal Aid Bd, 1998–2006; Temp. Judge, Court of Session, 2002–. Trustee, Nat. Liby of Scotland, 1995–. *Recreations:* sailing, ski-ing. *Address:* 12 Succoth Avenue, Edinburgh EH12 6BT. *T:* (0131) 337 4911. *Club:* New (Edinburgh).

THOMSON, Sir Mark (Wilfrid Home), 3rd Bt *cr* 1925, of Old Nunthorpe, Co. York; *b* 29 Dec. 1939; *s* of Sir Ivo Wilfrid Home Thomson, 2nd Bt and Sybil Marguerite, *yr d* of C. W. Thompson; *S* father, 1991; *m* 1976, Lady Jacqueline Rufus Isaacs (marr. diss. 1997), *o d* of 3rd Marquess of Reading, MBE, MC; three *s* one *d* (incl. twin *s*). *Heir:* *s* Albert Mark Home Thomson, *b* 3 Aug. 1979.

THOMSON, Nigel Ernest Drummond, CBE 1993; Sheriff of Lothian and Borders, at Edinburgh and Peebles, 1976–96; *b* 19 June 1926; *y s* of late Rev. James Kyd Thomson and Joan Drummond; *m* 1964, Snjólaug Magnússon, *yr d* of late Consul-General Sigursteinn Magnússon; one *s* one *d*. *Educ:* George Watson's College, Edinburgh; Univs of St Andrews and Edinburgh. Served with Scots Guards and Indian Grenadiers, 1944–47. MA (St Andrews) 1950; LLB (Edin.) 1953. Called to Scottish Bar, 1953. Standing Counsel to Scottish Educn Dept, 1961–66; Sheriff of Lanarkshire, later S Strathclyde, Dumfries and Galloway, at Hamilton, 1966–76. Chm., Music Cttee, Scottish Arts Council, 1978–83; Chm., Edinburgh Youth Orchestra, 1986–92. Convenor, Council for Music in Hosps in

Scotland, 1992–2001. Pres., Speculative Soc., Edinburgh, 1960; Vice President: Tenovus-Scotland, 1985–2001; British Assoc. for Counselling, 1992–2002. Hon. Texas Ranger, 1994. *Recreations:* music, woodwork, golf. *Address:* 50 Grange Road, Edinburgh. *T:* (0131) 667 2166. *Clubs:* New (Edinburgh); Bruntsfield Golf (Edinburgh).

THOMSON, Peter Alexander Bremner, CVO 1986; HM Diplomatic Service, retired; *b* 16 Jan. 1938; *s* of Alexander Thomson, financial journalist, and Dorothy (*née* Scurr); *m* 1965, Lucinda Sellar; three *s. Educ:* Canford School; RN College, Dartmouth; Sch. of Oriental and African Studies, London (BA 1970; MPhil 1975; MA 1991). Sub Lieut and Lieut RN in HM Ships Albion, Plover, Tiger, Ark Royal, Eagle; Lt Comdr ashore in Taiwan and Hong Kong; joined Diplomatic Service, 1975; First Sec., FCO, Lagos, Hong Kong, 1975–84; Counsellor, Peking, 1984–87; High Comr, Belize, 1987–90; Counsellor, FCO, 1991–95; High Comr, Seychelles, 1995–97. *Publication:* Belize: a concise history, 2005. *Recreations:* sailing, walking. *Address:* The Red House, Charlton Horethorne, near Sherborne DT9 4NL.

THOMSON, Prof. Richard Geoffrey, FRCP, FFPH; Professor of Epidemiology and Public Health, Institute of Health and Society, Medical School, University of Newcastle upon Tyne, since 1999; *b* 2 May 1958; *s* of Lesley Bambridge and Honor Thomson (*neé* Gooding); *m* 1989, Tracy Robson; two *d. Educ:* Stamford Sch., Stamford; St Edmund Hall, Oxford (BA Physiol. 1979; BM BCh 1982); Univ. of Newcastle upon Tyne (MD 1990). FRCP 1996; FFPH 1996. Sen. House Officer, Medicine, Freeman Hosp., Newcastle upon Tyne, 1983–85; Res. Fellow, Newcastle upon Tyne Univ., 1985–88; Registrar, then Sen. Registrar in Public Health, 1988–89, Dir, Service Quality and Standards, 1989–92, Northern RHA; Sen. Lectr and Consultant in Public Health, Medical Sch., Newcastle upon Tyne Univ., 1992–99. Director: UK Quality Indicator Proj., 1997–2007; Epidemiology and Res., Nat. Patient Safety Agency, 2004–07. Mem., Steering Gp on Internat. Patient Safety Classification, WHO, 2005–07. Mem., 13th Club. Associate Editor, Quality and Safety in Health Care, 1991–. *Publications:* numerous articles in professional jls on stroke epidemiology, health care quality and safety and health services research. *Recreations:* tennis, literature, theatre, good food, fine wine, sitting with a fishing rod contemplating. *Address:* Institute of Health and Society, Medical School, Framlington Place, Newcastle upon Tyne NE2 4HH. *T:* (0191) 222 8760, *Fax:* (0191) 222 8422; *e-mail:* richard.thomson@newcastle.ac.uk.

THOMSON, Prof. Richard Ian, PhD; FRSE; Watson Gordon Professor of Fine Art, University of Edinburgh, since 1996; *b* 1 March 1953; *s* of late Rev. George Ian Falconer Thomson and Mary Josephine Lambart Thomson (*née* Dixon); *m* 1978, Belinda Jane Greaves; two *s. Educ:* Shrewsbury Sch.; St Catherine's Coll., Oxford (Exhibnr; BA); Univ. of Oxford (Dip. Hist. of Art); Courtauld Inst. of Art, Univ. of London (MA; PhD 1989). FRSE 1998. Lectr, 1977–88, Sen. Lectr, 1988–95, Reader, 1995–96, in History of Art, Univ. of Manchester. Guest Scholar, J. Paul Getty Mus., Malibu, 1993; Van Gogh Vis. Fellow, Univ. of Amsterdam, 2007; Slade Prof. of Fine Art, Univ. of Oxford, 2008–09. Trustee, Nat. Galls of Scotland, 2002–; Comité Scientifique, Institut National d'Histoire de l'Art, Paris, 2008–. Exhibitions curated or co-curated: Harold Gilman, 1981–82; Impressionist Drawings, 1986; The Private Degas, 1987; Camille Pissarro: impressionism, landscape and rural labour, 1990; Toulouse-Lautrec, 1991–92; Monet to Matisse: landscape painting in France 1874–1914, 1994; Seurat and the Bathers, 1997; Theo van Gogh, 1999; Monet 1878–1883: the Seine and the Sea, 2003; Toulouse-Lautrec and Montmartre, 2005; Degas, Sickert and Toulouse-Lautrec: London and Paris 1870–1910, 2005. *Publications:* Toulouse-Lautrec, 1977; French Nineteenth Century Drawings in the Whitworth Art Gallery, 1981; Seurat, 1985; Degas, the Nudes, 1988; Edgar Degas, Waiting, 1995; (ed) Framing France, 1998; (ed jtly) Soil and Stone: impressionism, urbanism, environment, 2003; The Troubled Republic: visual culture and social debate in France 1889–1900, 2004; Vincent van Gogh: Starry Night, 2008. *Recreations:* gardening, jazz, hill walking. *Address:* School of Arts, Culture and the Environment, University of Edinburgh, Minto House, 20 Chambers Street, Edinburgh EH1 1JZ. *T:* (0131) 650 4124, *Fax:* (0131) 650 6638; *e-mail:* R.Thomson@ed.ac.uk.

THOMSON, Robert James; Publisher, Dow Jones & Company, since 2007; *b* 11 March 1961; *s* of Jim and Gen Thomson; *m* 1992, Wang Ping; two *s. Educ:* Royal Melbourne Inst. of Technol. (BA Journalism). Finance and gen. affairs reporter, The Herald, Melbourne, then Sydney, 1979–83; Sen. Feature Writer, Sydney Morning Herald, 1983–85; Financial Times: Beijing corresp., 1985–89; Tokyo corresp., 1989–94; Foreign News Ed., 1994–96; Asst Ed., and Ed., Weekend FT, 1996–98; Man. Ed., based in NY, 1998–2002; Ed., The Times, 2002–07. Chm., Arts Internat., 2001–02. Dir, Soc. of Amer. Business Editors and Writers, 2001–02. *Publications:* The Judges: a portrait of the Australian judiciary, 1986; (jtly) The Chinese Army, 1990; (ed) True Fiction, 1998. *Recreations:* reading, tennis, cinema. *Address:* Dow Jones & Company, 1 World Financial Center, 200 Liberty Street, New York, NY 10281, USA.

THOMSON, Prof. Robert William, PhD; FBA 1995; Calouste Gulbenkian Professor of Armenian Studies, University of Oxford, 1992–2001, now Professor Emeritus; Fellow of Pembroke College, Oxford, 1992–2001, now Supernumerary Fellow; *b* 24 March 1934; *s* of late David William Thomson and Lilian (*née* Cramphorn); *m* 1963, Judith Ailsa Cawdry; two *s. Educ:* George Watson's Boys' Coll., Edinburgh; Sidney Sussex Coll., Cambridge (BA 1955); Trinity Coll., Cambridge (PhD 1962). Halki Theol Coll., Istanbul, 1955–56; Jun. Fellow, Dumbarton Oaks, Washington, 1960–61; Louvain Univ., 1961–62; Harvard University: Instructor, then Asst Prof. of Classical Armenian, Dept of Near Eastern Langs, 1963–69; Mashtots Prof. of Armenian Studies, 1969–92; Chm., Dept of Near Eastern Langs, 1973–78, 1980–81. Dir, Dumbarton Oaks, Washington DC, 1984–89. Hon. PhD Tübingen, 2003. *Publications:* (ed with J. N. Birdsall) Biblical and Patristic Studies in Memory of Robert Pierce Casey, 1963; Athanasiana Syriaca, 4 parts, 1965–77; Athanasius: Contra Gentes and De Incarnatione, 1971; The Teaching of Saint Gregory, 1971, 2nd edn 2001; Introduction to Classical Armenian, 1975; Agathangelos: history of the Armenians, 1977; (with K. B. Bardakjian) Textbook of Modern Western Armenian, 1977; Moses Khorenatsi: history of the Armenians, 1978, 2nd edn 2006; Elishe: history of Vardan, 1982; (ed with N. G. Garsoian and T. J. Mathews) East of Byzantium, 1982; (with B. Kendall) David the Invincible Philosopher, 1983; Thomas Artsruni: history of the Artsruni House, 1985; The Armenian Version of Dionysius the Areopagite, 2 vols, 1987; Lazar Parpetsi: history of the Armenians, 1991; Studies in Armenian Literature and Christianity, 1994; The Syriac Version of the Hexaemeron by Basil of Caesarea, 1995; A Bibliography of Classical Armenian Literature, 1995; Rewriting Caucasian History: the Armenian version of the Georgian Chronicles, 1996; (ed with J.-P. Mahé) From Byzantium to Iran: Armenian studies in honour of Nina G. Garsoian, 1997; (with J. Howard-Johnston) The Armenian History of Sebeos, 1999; The Lawcode of Mxit'ar Gosh, 2000; The Armenian Adaptation of the Ecclesiastical History of Socrates Scholasticus, 2001; Hamam: commentary on Proverbs, 2005; Nerses of Lambron: commentary on Revelation, 2007; contribs to Jl Theol Studies, Le Muséon, Revue des études arméniennes, Dumbarton Oaks Papers, Oxford Dictionary of Byzantium, Encyclopedia Iranica. *Address:* Oriental Institute, Pusey Lane, Oxford OX1 2LE.

THOMSON, Sir Thomas (James), Kt 1991; CBE 1984 (OBE 1978); FRCPGlas, FRCP, FRCPEd, FRCPI; retired; Chairman, Greater Glasgow Health Board, 1987–93; Consultant Physician and Gastroenterologist, Stobhill General Hospital, Glasgow, 1961–87; Hon. Lecturer, Department of Materia Medica, University of Glasgow, 1961–87; *b* 8 April 1923; *s* of Thomas Thomson and Annie Jane Grant; *m* 1948, Jessie Smith Shotbolt; two *s* one *d. Educ:* Airdrie Acad.; Univ. of Glasgow (MB, ChB 1945). FRCPGlas 1964 (FRFPSG 1949); FRCP 1969 (MRCP 1950); FRCPEd 1982; FRCPI 1983. Lectr, Dept of Materia Medica, Univ. of Glasgow, 1953–61; Postgrad. Adviser to Glasgow Northern Hosps, 1961–80. Sec., Specialist Adv. Cttee for Gen. Internal Medicine for UK, 1970–74; Chairman: Medico-Pharmaceutical Forum, 1978–80 (Chm., Educn Adv. Bd, 1979–84); National Med. Consultative Cttee for Scotland, 1982–87; Conf. of Royal Colls and Faculties in Scotland, 1982–84; Hon. Sec., 1965–73, Pres., 1982–84, RCPSGlas. Active participation in postgrad. med. educnl cttees, locally, nationally, in EEC and in Libya, Kuwait, Jordan and Oman. Mem. Ct, Strathclyde Univ., 1993–97. Hon. FACP 1983. Hon. LLD Glasgow, 1988; DUniv Strathclyde, 1997. *Publications:* (ed jtly) Dilling's Pharmacology, 1969; Gastroenterology—an integrated course, 1972, 3rd edn 1983; pubns related to gen. medicine, gastroent. and therapeutics. *Recreations:* swimming, golfing. *Address:* 1 Varna Road, Glasgow G14 9NE. *T:* (0141) 959 5930. *Club:* Royal Air Force.

THOMSON, Prof. Wendy, CBE 2005; PhD; Professor and Director, School of Social Work, McGill University, Montreal, since 2005; *b* Montreal, 28 Oct. 1953; *d* of Shirley and Grace Thomson; *m* 1995, David Dorne (*d* 1999); two step *s*; one *d. Educ:* McGill Univ. (BSW; Masters of Social Work); Univ. of Bristol (PhD 1989). Asst Chief Exec., Islington BC, 1987–93; Chief Executive: Turning Point, 1993–96; Newham BC, 1996–99; Dir of Inspection, Audit Commn, 1999–2001; Prime Minister's Advr on Public Services Reform, Cabinet Office, 2001–05. Non-executive Director: Montreal Health and Social Services Agency, 2006– (Mem. Planning Cttee, 2006–); René Cassin Health and Social Services Centre, 2006–; McGill Univ. Health Centre, 2007–. Consultant: Office of Pres., Republic of Ghana, 2006–; UNDP, 2006–; Internat. Advr, Global Forum on Re-inventing Govt, 2007. *Recreations:* yoga, gardening, theatre, travel, shopping. *Address:* School of Social Work, McGill University, 3506 University Street, Montreal, QC H3A 2A7, Canada.

THOMSON, William Oliver, MD, DPH, DIH; Chief Administrative Medical Officer, Lanarkshire Health Board, 1973–88; *b* 23 March 1925; *s* of William Crosbie Thomson and Mary Jolie Johnston; *m* 1956, Isobel Lauder Glendinning Brady; two *s. Educ:* Allan Glen's Sch., Glasgow; Univ. of Glasgow (MB ChB, MD). DPA; FFCM; FRCPGlas 1988 (MRCPGlas 1986). Chronic student of Gray's Inn, London. Captain, RAMC, 1948–50. Hospital appointments, 1951–53; appointments in Public Health, Glasgow, 1953–60; Admin. MO, Western Regional Hospital Bd, 1960–70; Group Medical Superintendent, Glasgow Maternity and Women's Hospitals, 1970–73; Mem., Health Services Ind. Adv. Cttee, 1980–86. Visiting Lecturer: Univ. of Michigan, Ann Arbor; Ministry of Health, Ontario; Hon. Lectr, Univ. of Glasgow. Med. Advr, Scottish TV, 1992–98. Diploma of Scottish Council for Health Educn (for services to health educn), 1979. *Publications:* (jtly) In England Now, 1989; articles on clinical medicine, community medicine, general practice, occupational health and health education, in various medical jls; humorous pieces in The Lancet, BMJ, etc. *Recreations:* walking, talking, writing. *Address:* Flat 7, Silverwells Court, Bothwell, Glasgow G71 8LT. *T:* (01698) 852586.

THONEMANN, Peter Clive, MSc, DPhil; Professor Emeritus, University of Wales, Swansea; *b* 3 June 1917; *m*; one *s* one *d. Educ:* Melbourne Church of England Grammar Sch., Melbourne; Sydney and Oxford Univs. BSc Melbourne, 1940; MSc Sydney, 1945; DPhil Oxford, 1949. Munition Supply Laboratories, Victoria, Australia, 1940; Amalgamated Wireless, Australia, 1942; University of Sydney, Commonwealth Research Fellow, 1944; Trinity Coll. and Clarendon Laboratory, Oxford, ICI Research Fellow, 1946; initiated research for controlled fusion power, 1947–49; United Kingdom Atomic Energy Authority: Head of Controlled Fusion Res., 1949–60; designed and built prototype fusion reactor, ZETA, 1954–57; with Res. Unit, 1960–64, Head of B Div., 1964–67, Dep. Dir, 1967–68, Culham Laboratory; Prof. and Hd of Dept of Physics, UC, Swansea, 1968–84. *Publications:* many contributions to learned journals. *Address:* Department of Physics, Swansea University, Singleton Park, Swansea, Wales SA2 8PP; 130 Bishopston Road, Swansea SA3 3EU. *T:* (01792) 232669.

't HOOFT, Prof. Gerardus; Professor of Theoretical Physics, Utrecht University, since 1977; *b* 5 July 1946; *s* of H. 't Hooft and M. A. van Kampen; *m* 1972, Albertha A. Schik, MD; two *d. Educ:* Dalton Lyceum Gymnasium beta, The Hague; Utrecht Univ. Fellow, Theoretical Physics Div., CERN, Geneva, 1972–74; Asst Prof., Univ. of Utrecht, 1974–77. Heineman Prize, APS, 1979; Wolf Prize, Wolf Foundn, Israel, 1982; Franklin Medal, Franklin Inst., Philadelphia, 1995; (jtly) Nobel Prize for Physics, 1999; several decorations and 10 hon. doctorates. Commandeur de Orde van de Nederlandse Leeuw, 1999. *Publications:* De bouwstenen van de Schepping, 1992 (In Search of the Ultimate Building Blocks, 1996); Under the Spell of the Gauge Principle, 1994; over 200 scientific pubns. *Address:* Spinoza Institute, Leuvenlaan 4, PO Box 80.195, 3508 TD Utrecht, Netherlands. *T:* 302531863; *web:* http://www.phys.uu.nl/~thooft.

THORBURN, Andrew, BSc; FRTPI; FTS; Principal, Thorburns, since 1990; Chairman, Bow Street Partners, 1999–2005; *b* 20 March 1934; *s* of James Beresford Thorburn and Marjorie Clara Burford; *m* Margaret Anne Crack; one *s* two *d. Educ:* Bridport Grammar Sch.; Univ. of Southampton (BSc). MRTPI 1959, FRTPI 1969. National Service, RN, 1954–56. Planning Asst, Kent CC, 1957–59; Planning Officer, Devon CC, 1959–63; Asst County Planning Officer, Hampshire CC, 1963–68; Dir, Notts and Derbyshire Sub-Region Study, 1968–70; Dep. County Planning Dir, Cheshire CC, 1970–73; County Planning Officer, E Sussex CC, 1973–83; Chief Exec., English Tourist Bd, 1983–85; Head of Tourism and Leisure Div., Grant Thornton, 1986–90. Pres., RTPI, 1982; Mem. Exec., Town and Country Planning Assoc., 1969–81; Founder Trustee, Sussex Heritage Trust, 1978–99. Fellow, Tourism Soc., 1983–. *Publications:* Planning Villages, 1971; The Missing Museum, 2006. *Recreations:* sailing, countryside appreciation. *Address:* 1 Mill House, Lower Quay, Fareham, Hants PO16 0RH. *Club:* Fareham Sailing and Motor Boat.

THORLEY, Giles Alexander; Chief Executive, Punch Taverns plc, since 2003 (Executive Chairman, 2001–03); *b* 29 June 1967; *s* of Hugh A. Thorley and Jillian E. Thorley; *m* 1993, Michelle Britt; three *s. Educ:* Hereford Cathedral Sch.; QMC, Univ. of London (LLB); Inns of Court Sch. of Law. Called to the Bar, Inner Temple, 1990. Director: Nomura Internat. plc, 1990–98; Inntrepreneur Pub Co., 1998–99; Chief Exec., Unique Pub Co. plc, 1999–2001. Dir and Supervisory Bd Mem., Brewers and Licenced Retailers Assoc., subseq. British Beer and Pub Assoc., 1998–. *Recreations:* ski-ing, water sports, the family. *Address:* Punch Taverns plc, Jubilee House, Second Avenue, Burton on Trent, Staffs DE14 2WF.

THORLEY, Simon Joe; QC 1989; *b* 22 May 1950; *s* of Sir Gerald Bowers Thorley, TD and of Beryl, *d* of G. Preston Rhodes; *m* 1983, Jane Elizabeth Cockcroft (*d* 2007); two *s* one *d.* *Educ:* Rugby Sch.; Keble Coll., Oxford (MA Jurisprudence). Called to the Bar, Inner Temple, 1972, Bencher, 1999; pupilled to William Aldous; in practice at Patent Bar; apptd by Lord Chancellor to hear Trade Mark Appeals, 1996–2003; Dep. High Court Judge, 1998–. Dep. Chm., Copyright Tribunal, 1998–2006. Chm., IP Bar (formerly Patent Bar) Assoc., 1995–99; Member: Gen. Council of the Bar, 1995–99; Council, British Gp, Internat. Assoc. for Protection of Industrial Property, 1993–95. *Publication:* (co-ed) Terrell on The Law of Patents, 13th edn 1982 to 16th edn 2005. *Recreations:* family, shooting, opera. *Address:* 3 New Square, Lincoln's Inn, WC2A 3RS. *T:* (020) 7405 1111.

THORN, John Leonard, MA; writer and educational consultant; Headmaster of Winchester College, 1968–85; *b* 28 April 1925; *s* of late Stanley and Winifred Thorn; *m* 1955, Veronica Laura (*d* 1999), *d* of late Sir Robert Maconochie, OBE, QC; one *s* one *d.* *Educ:* St Paul's School; Corpus Christi College, Cambridge. Served War of 1939–45, Sub-Lieutenant, RNVR, 1943–46. Asst Master, Clifton Coll., 1949–61; Headmaster, Repton School, 1961–68. Dir, Winchester Cathedral Trust, 1986–89. Dir, Royal Opera House, Covent Garden, 1971–76. Chm., Headmasters' Conference, 1981. Member: Bd, Securities Assoc., 1987–91; Exec. Cttee, Cancer Res. Campaign, 1987–90; Chm., Hants Bldgs Preservation Trust, 1992–96 (Vice-Chm., 1989–92); Trustee: British Museum, 1980–85; Oakham Sch., 1985–89. Governor, Stowe Sch., 1985–90; Chm. of Governors, Abingdon Sch., 1991–94. *Publications:* (joint) A History of England, 1961; The Road to Winchester (autobiog.), 1989; various articles. *Address:* 6 Chilbolton Avenue, Winchester SO22 5HD. *T:* (01962) 855990. *Club:* Garrick.

THORN, Sir John (Samuel), Kt 1984; OBE 1977; Mayor, Port Chalmers Borough Council, 1956–89 (Member, 1938–41, 1947–50 and 1950–53); *b* 19 March 1911; *s* of J. S. Thorn; *m* 1936, Constance Maud (*d* 1997), *d* of W. T. Haines; one *s.* *Educ:* Port Chalmers School; King Edward Technical College. Served 1939–45 war, 3rd Div. Apprentice plumber, later plumbing contractor and land agent; Manager, Thorn's Bookshop, 1950–80. Chairman: Municipal Insce Co.; Coastal N Otago United Council. Pres., Municipal Assoc., 1974–; Dep. Chm., Nat. Roads Board, 1974–83. *Address:* 94C Stevenson Avenue, Sawyers Bay, Dunedin, New Zealand.

THORN, Roger Eric; QC 1990; **His Honour Judge Thorn;** a Circuit Judge, since 2004; *b* 23 March 1948; twin *s* of late James Douglas 'Pat' Thorn and of Daphne Elizabeth (*née* Robinson); *m* 2005, Clare, *d* of late George Lillywhite, OBE and of Maureen Lillywhite. *Educ:* Mill Hill Sch.; Newcastle Univ. (LLB Hons). Called to the Bar, Middle Temple, 1970 (Harmsworth Schol. and Major Exhibn; Bencher, 1999); NE Circuit, 1970–; Asst Recorder, 1995–99; a Recorder, and Dep. High Ct Judge, 1999–2004. Member: Bd of Faculty of Law, Newcastle Univ., 1990–94; Advocacy Studies Bd, Bar Council, 1996–2002; Panel of Arbitrators, Bar Council, 1999–2004; Restricted Patients Panel, Mental Health Rev. Tribunal, 2000–; Faculty, Middle Temple Advocacy, 2004–06. Hd of Mission to Kosovo, Bar Human Rights Cttee, 2000. Liaison Judge to Law Sch., 2004–, Mem. Ct, 2006–, Univ. of Hull. Life Gov., Mill Hill Sch., 1994. *Publications:* A Practical Guide to Road Traffic Accident Claims, 1987, 2nd edn 1991; legal contributor to Negotiating Better Deals, by J. G. Thorn (twin *b*), 1988; (jtly) Kosovo 2000: justice not revenge, 2000. *Recreations:* theatre, music, walking, local Amenity Society (Chairman, 1986–99). *Address:* Hull Combined Court Centre, Lowgate, Hull HU1 2EZ; Holly House, Main Street, Corbridge, Northumberland NE45 5LE. *Clubs:* National Liberal; Old Mill Hillians; Durham County.

THORNBERRY, Emily; MP (Lab) Islington South and Finsbury, since 2005; *b* 27 July 1960; *d* of Sallie Thornberry; *m* 1991, Christopher George Nugee, *qv*; two *s* one *d.* *Educ:* Univ. of Kent (BA 1982). Called to the Bar, Gray's Inn, 1983; in practice, specialising in criminal law, 1985–. *Address:* (office) 65 Barnsbury Street, N1 1EK; House of Commons, SW1A 0AA.

THORNBURGH, Richard Lewis; Counsel, Kirkpatrick & Lockhart Preston Gates Ellis (formerly Kirkpatrick & Lockhart Nicholson Graham) LLP, since 1994; *b* 16 July 1932; *s* of Charles G. and Alice S. Thornburgh; *m* 1955, Virginia Hooton (decd); *m* 1963, Virginia Judson; four *s.* *Educ:* Yale Univ. (BEng 1954); Univ. of Pittsburgh Sch. of Law (LLB 1957). Staff Counsel, Aluminum Co. of America, 1957–59; Associate, Kirkpatrick, Pomeroy, Lockhart & Johnson, 1959–69; US Attorney, Western District, Pennsylvania, 1969–75; Asst Attorney General, Criminal Div., US Dept of Justice, 1975–77; Partner: Kirkpatrick Lockhart, Johnson & Hutchison, 1977–79; Kirkpatrick & Lockhart LLP, 1987–88 and 1991–92; Governor, Commonwealth of Pennsylvania, 1979–87; Attorney Gen. of the USA, 1988–91; Under-Sec.-Gen. for Admin and Management, UN, 1992–93. Dir, Inst. of Politics, John F. Kennedy Sch. of Govt, 1987–88. Numerous hon. degrees. *Publications:* articles in professional jls. *Address:* 2540 Massachusetts Avenue NW, Washington, DC 20008, USA; Kirkpatrick & Lockhart Preston Gates Ellis LLP, 1601 K Street, Washington, DC 20006–1600, USA.

THORNE, Benjamin, CMG 1979; MBE 1966; *b* 19 June 1922; *m* 1949, Sylvia Una (*née* Graves); one *s* two *d.* *Educ:* St Marylebone Grammar Sch.; Regent Street Polytechnic. Served War, RAF, 1940–46. Joined Civil Service, 1946; British Trade Commission: India, 1950–54; Ghana, 1954–58; Nigeria, 1958–61; Hong Kong, 1964–68; Dir, British Week in Tokyo, 1968–69; Commercial Counsellor, Tokyo, 1973–79, retd. Life Vice Pres., Japan Soc., 1998. Japanese Order of the Sacred Treasure, 3rd cl., 1975. *Recreations:* cricket, travel, gardening, reading. *Address:* 34 Quarry Hill Road, Borough Green, Sevenoaks, Kent TN15 8RH. *T:* (01732) 882547. *Clubs:* Civil Service; Hong Kong (Hong Kong); Foreign Correspondents' (Tokyo); Yokohama Country and Athletic.

THORNE, Rear-Adm. (retd) Edward Courtney, CB 1975; CBE 1971; Chairman, New Zealand Fire Service Commission, 1976–86; Chief of Naval Staff, New Zealand, 1972–75; *b* 29 Oct. 1923; *s* of Ernest Alexander Thorne and Ethel Violet Thorne; *m* 1949, Fay Bradburn (*née* Kerr) (*d* 2006); three *s.* *Educ:* Rongotai Coll.; Nelson Coll., NZ. IDC 1966. Chm., Nat. Council, United World Colls, 1982–94; Mem., Nat. Council, Duke of Edinburgh Award Scheme, 1976–89; Pres., Sea Cadet Assoc. of NZ, 1990–98. Hon. FIFireE 1983. *Recreations:* gardening, walking. *Address:* Apt 28, 36 James Cook Crescent, Remuera, Auckland, New Zealand.

THORNE, Prof. Michael Philip, PhD; Vice Chancellor, Anglia Ruskin University, since 2007; *b* 19 Oct. 1951; *m* 1975, Val Swift; three *s.* *Educ:* Queen Mary Coll., Univ. of London (BSc Hons); Univ. of Birmingham (PhD 1979). Lecturer: SE Derbyshire Coll., 1973–75; UCL, 1978–79; UC Cardiff, 1979–88; Hd, Sch. of Computing, 1989–93, Pro Vice Chancellor, 1993–97, Univ. of Sunderland; Vice Principal, Napier Univ., 1998–2001; Vice Chancellor, Univ. of E London, 2001–06. Member: Foresight Panel (Leisure and Learning), OST, 1998–2001; Scottish Further Educn Funding Council, 1999–2003; Bd, Learning and Skills Network, 2006–; Bd, Office of the Ind. Adjudicator, 2007–. Mem. Bd, London Thames Gateway Develt Corp., 2004–07. Non-exec. Dir, Scottish Univ. for Industry, 1998–2004. Formerly Chair: Open Learning Foundn; Lead Scotland; Chm., Adv. Cttee on Libraries, 2007–. Formerly Member Board: Northern Sinfonia; Northern Jun. Philharmonic; Learning World; Northern Informatics Applications Agency; Council of Administrators, Eur. Lifelong Learning Initiative. Radio and TV progs. FIMA; FBCS. FRSA. *Publications:* contrib. acad. papers and articles. *Recreations:* music (bassoon and conducting), theatre, hill-walking, reading Funding Council circulars. *Address:* Anglia Ruskin University, Bishop Hall Lane, Chelmsford, Essex CM1 1SQ. *T:* 0845 196 4221, *Fax:* (01245) 495419; *e-mail:* michael.thorne@anglia.ac.uk. *Club:* Reform.

THORNE, Sir Neil (Gordon), Kt 1992; OBE 1980; TD 1969; DL; *b* 8 Aug. 1932; *s* of late Henry Frederick Thorne and Ivy Gladys Thorne. *Educ:* City of London Sch.; Coll. of Estate Mgt (BSc London Univ.). FCGI; FRICS. Asst Adjt, 58 Med. Regt, RA, BAOR, 1957–59. Sen. Partner, Hull & Co., Chartered Surveyors, 1962–76. Councillor, London Borough of Redbridge, 1965–68, Alderman, 1975–78; Mem., GLC and Chm., Central Area Bd, 1967–73. MP (C) Ilford South, 1979–92; contested (C) same seat, 1992, 1997. Founder and first Chm., Unpaired Members Gp, 1982–85; Chairman: British Nepalese Parly Gp, 1983–92; British Korean Parly Gp, 1988–92; Vice Chm., UK Br., IPU, 1987–90; Member: Defence Select Cttee, 1983–92; Court of Referees, 1987–92. Chm., H of C Motor Club, 1985–91; Founder and Chairman: Armed Forces Parly Scheme, 1988–; Police Service Parly Scheme, 1996–. Chm., Britain-Nepal Soc., 1992–98 (Vice Pres., 1998–). Fellow, Industry and Parliament Trust, 1980 and 1990; Pres., Inst. of Civil Defence and Disaster Studies, 1996–2008; Chairman: Nat. Council for Civil Defence, 1982–86; St Edward's Housing Assoc., 1986–93; Ilford Age Concern, 1984–87, 1990–93; President: Redbridge Parkinson's Disease Soc., 1982–2001; Ilford Arthritis Care, 1986–2001; Gtr London Dist, St John Ambulance, 1992–2003; Redbridge Age Concern, 1993–; N and E London REME Assoc., 2000–; Vice Pres., Ilford Tuberculosis and Chest Care Assoc., 1987–2000; Patron: Jubilee Club for Visually Handicapped, 1986–2000; Benevolent Fund for W Essex Hospices, 2001–; Trustee: Children In Distress, 1986–; Meml Gates Trust, 1999–2007 (Dir of Develt for Constitution Hill Commonwealth War Meml); Amb., Girl Guiding, 2002–. Chm., Lord Mayor's £5 million Appeal for St Paul's Cathedral, 1993–94. Founder Mem., Royal Artillery Firepower Mus., 2001–. Mem., Mil. Educn Cttee, 1994–, and Court, 1995–2001, Univ. of Leeds. Prime Warden, Blacksmiths' Co., 2000–01. Member: TA, 1952–82; Metropolitan Special Constab. (HAC), 1983–92 (Hon. Vice Comdt, 2007); CO, London Univ. OTC, 1976–80; Hon. Col, Leeds Univ. OTC, 1997–2007. DL Greater London, 1991; Rep. DL London Bor. of Brent, 2001–07. KStJ 1995 (Mem., Chapter Gen., 1989–97; Almoner, 1995–97). HQA (Pakistan), 1991; GDB (Nepal), 1991. *Publications:* Pedestrianised Streets: a study of Europe and America, 1973; Highway Robbery in the Twentieth Century: policy reform for compulsory purchase, 1990. *Address:* 13 Cowley Street, Westminster, SW1P 3LZ. *T:* (020) 7222 0480. *Club:* Honourable Artillery Company.

THORNE, Nicholas Alan, CMG 2002; HM Diplomatic Service; UK Permanent Representative to the Office of the United Nations and other international organisations, Geneva, 2003–08; *b* 31 March 1948; *s* of late James Leslie Thorne and Grace Agnes Thorne; *m* 2003, Kristna Tronningsdal; one *s* one *d* by previous marriage. *Educ:* Chatham House Grammar Sch.; Westminster Univ. Joined HM Diplomatic Service, 1965; Yaounde, 1971; UK Repn to EC, Brussels, 1974–80; UKMIS, UN, NY, 1980–83; Hd of Chancery, Manila, 1983–87; Dep. Hd, UN Dept and Hd, Human Rights, FCO, 1987–89; on secondment to Thorn/EMI, 1989–91; Dep. Hd of Mission, Helsinki, 1991–95; UKMIS, UN, NY, 1995–2003. Mem., UN Adv. Cttee on finance and mgt issues, 1998–2003. *Recreations:* travel, flying light aircraft, cooking. *Address:* c/o Foreign and Commonwealth Office, King Charles Street, SW1A 2AH; *e-mail:* nick.thorne@fco.gov.uk. *Club:* Royal Over-Seas League.

THORNELY, Gervase Michael Cobham; Headmaster of Sedbergh School, 1954–75; *b* 21 Oct. 1918; *er s* of late Major J. E. B. Thornely, OBE, and late Hon. Mrs M. H. Thornely; *m* 1954, Jennifer Margery, *d* of late Sir Hilary Scott, Knowle House, Addington, Surrey; two *s* two *d.* *Educ:* Rugby Sch.; Trinity Hall, Cambridge (Organ Scholar; 2nd Cl. Hons, Modern and Mediæval Languages Tripos; BA 1940; MA 1944). Assistant Master, Sedbergh School, 1940. FRSA 1968. *Recreations:* music, fly-fishing. *Address:* High Stangerthwaite, Killington, Sedbergh, Cumbria LA10 5EP. *T:* (01539) 620444.

THORNELY-TAYLOR, Rupert Maurice; Consultant in Noise, Vibration and Acoustics, since 1968; Director, Rupert Taylor Ltd, since 1993; farmer; *b* Whalton, Northumberland, 21 May 1946; *s* of late Maurice Humphrey Taylor and Mary Patricia Stuart Taylor (*née* Wood); surname changed to Thornely-Taylor by Deed Poll, 1988; *m* 1st, 1964, Alison Grant, *d* of late Alistair Grant Saunders (marr. diss. 1987, she *d* 1999); 2nd, 1988, Frances Marion, *d* of late William John Lindberg. *Educ:* Harrow Sch. Acoustical engr, Burgess Products Co. Ltd, 1964–68; Dir, Rupert Taylor and Partners Ltd, 1970–81; Consultant to: London Underground, 1984–2001; LDDC, 1984–98; Railtrack, 1999–2003; Associated British Ports, 2000–06; Network Rail, 2003–05; Transport for London, 2004–; BAA plc, 2007–; res. contract, DoE, 1996. Consultant, New Victoria Th., N Staffs, 1984–. Breeder, Rumsden Herd of Pedigree Charolais Cattle (King's Trophy, Royal Smithfield Show, 2002). Conservator, Ashdown Forest, 1997–2003 and 2006– (Chm., Finance and Gen. Purposes Cttee, 2007–). Member: Noise Adv. Council, 1970–80 (Chm., Wkg Gp on Noise Monitoring); Project Bd, DEFRA, 2004–. Mem. Council, British Acoustical Soc., 1968–71; Founder Member and Hon. Treasurer: Assoc. Noise Consultants, 1970–74 (Vice Chm., 2001–03; Chm., 2003–05; Pres., 2006–); Inst. Acoustics, 1971–74 (Fellow, 1981). Dir, Internat. Inst. Acoustics and Vibration, 2007–. Mem. (C) Wealden DC, 1995–2003 (Leader, 1999–2003). Member: E Sussex Econ. Partnership, 1999–2003; Inter-reg. Jt Monitoring Cttee, 1999–2001; SE England Regl Assembly, 1999–2003; Mem., Exec. Cttee, Wealden Constituency Cons. Assoc., 1993–2003. Churchill Fellow, USA, 1972. Hon. Treas., Nat. Pony Soc., 1991–97. *Publications:* Noise, 1970, 4th edn 2001; Le Bruit et ses Méfaits, 1972; (ed) Noise Control Data, 1976; (jtly) Handbook of Noise Assessment, 1978; Electricity, 1979; (jtly) Measurement and Assessment of Groundborne Noise and Vibration, 2002; contrib. papers to Proc. Inst. Acoustics, Internat. Inst. Acoustics and Vibration, Internat. Inst. Noise Control Engrg. *Recreations:* painting, music, gardening, Tibetan Spaniels. *Address:* Spring Garden, Fairwarp, Uckfield, E Sussex TN22 3BG. *T:* (01825) 712435.

See also Rt Rev. H. V. Taylor.

THORNEYCROFT, Rev. Prebendary Pippa Hazel Jeanetta; Priest-in-Charge, Shareshill, 1996–Feb. 2009, and Essington, 2006–Feb. 2009; Prebendary of Lichfield Cathedral, 2000–Feb. 2009; Chaplain to the Queen, since 2001; *b* 18 Feb. 1944; *d* of Philip Fitzgerald Mander and Priscilla Patricia (*née* Waller); *m* 1965, John Patrick Thorneycroft; two *s* two *d.* *Educ:* Cheltenham Ladies' Coll.; Exeter Univ. (BA Hons French 1965); W Midlands Ministerial Trng Course, Queen's Coll., Birmingham (GOE 1988). Ordained deacon, 1988, priest, 1994; Curate (non-stipendiary), St Mary Magdalene, Albrighton, 1988–90; asst deacon/priest (non-stipendiary), Badger, Beckbury, Kemberton, Ryton, Stockton and Sutton Maddock, 1990–96; Advr for Women in Ministry, Lichfield Dio., 1993–99; Rural Dean of Penkridge, 2001–05. Mem., Skinners' Co., 1966–. *Recreations:* walking, cycling, bee-keeping. *Address:* (until Feb. 2009) The Vicarage, 11 Brookhouse Lane, Featherstone, Wolverhampton WV10 7AW. *T:* (01902) 727579; Poole's Yard, Kemberton, Shifnal, Shropshire TF11 9LL.

THORNHILL, Andrew Robert; QC 1985; a Recorder, 1997–2004; *b* 4 Aug. 1943; *s* of Edward Percy Thornhill and Amelia Joy Thornhill; *m* 1971, Helen Mary Livingston; two *s* two *d*. *Educ:* Clifton Coll. Prep. Sch.; Clifton Coll.; Corpus Christi Coll., Oxford. Called to the Bar, Middle Temple, 1969, Bencher, 1995; entered chambers of H. H. Monroe, QC, 1969. Chm. Council, Clifton Coll., 1994–. *Publications:* (ed) Potter & Monroe: Tax Planning with Precedents, 7th edn 1974, to 9th edn 1982; (jtly) Tax Planning Through Wills, 1981, 1984; (jtly) Passing Down the Family Farm, 1982; (jtly) Passing Down the Family Business, 1984. *Recreations:* wooden boats, dinghy sailing, squash, Real tennis, rackets, walking. *Address:* 37 Canynge Road, Clifton, Bristol BS8 3LD. *T:* (0117) 974 4015. *Clubs:* Oxford and Cambridge, Bar Yacht, Royal Thames Yacht; Tamesis (Teddington).

THORNICROFT, Prof. Graham John, PhD; FRCPsych, FMedSci; Professor of Community Psychiatry, since 1996, and Head, Health Services and Population Research Department, since 1999, Institute of Psychiatry, King's College London; Consultant Psychiatrist, since 1991, and Director, Research and Development, since 1999, South London and Maudsley NHS Foundation Trust. *Educ:* Queens' Coll., Cambridge (BA 1st cl. Hons Soc. and Pol Sci. 1977); Guy's Hosp. Med. Sch., London (MB BS 1984); London Sch. of Hygiene and Tropical Medicine (MSc Epidemiol. 1989); Univ. of London (PhD 1995). MRCPsych 1988, FRCPsych 2000; MFPHM 1999. Sen. Investigator, NIHR, 2007–. Vis. Scientist, Dept of Psychiatry, Univ. of Verona, 2000–; Vis. Prof., Dep. of Epidemiol., Columbia Univ., NY, 2002–. FMedSci 2005. *Publications:* (ed jtly) Measuring Mental Health Needs, 1992, 2nd edn 2001; (jtly) Emergency Mental Health Services in the Community, 1995; (with H. Knudsen) Mental Health Service Evaluation, 1996 (trans. Italian); (with G. Strathdee) Commissioning Mental Health Services, 1996; (jtly) London's Mental Health, 1997; (with D. Goldberg) Mental Health in Our Future Cities, 1998; (jtly) Camberwell Assessment of Need (CAN), 1999; (with M. Tansella) Common Mental Disorders in Primary Care: essay in honour of Professor Sir David Goldberg, 1999; (with M. Tansella) The Mental Health Matrix: a manual to improve services, 1999 (trans. Italian, Romanian, Russian, Spanish); (with A. Reynolds) Managing Mental Health Services, 1999 (trans. Italian, Portuguese); (with G. Szmukler) Textbook of Community Psychiatry, 2001; (with M. Tansella) Mental Health Outcome Measures, 1996, 2nd edn 2001; (jtly) Camberwell Assessment of Need for Adults with Developmental and Intellectual Disabilities (CANDID), 2003; (ed jtly) The Forensic CAN: a needs assessment for forensic mental health service users, 2006; (jtly) International Outcome Measures in Mental Health, 2006; Shunned: discrimination against people with mental illness, 2006 (Book of the Yr Award, Mental Health, BMA, 2007); Actions Speak Louder: tackling discrimination against people with mental illness, 2006; (ed jtly) Mental Health Policy and Practice Across Europe (Baxter Award, Eur. Health Mgt Assoc.), 2007; (ed jtly) Home Treatment Teams, 2008; (with M. Tansella) Better Mental Health Care, 2008; (jtly) Camberwell Assessment of Need: mother's version (CAN-M), 2008; over 190 scientific papers on stigma and discrimination, mental health needs assessment, the development of outcome scales, cost-effectiveness evaluation of mental health treatments, and mental health services in less economically developed countries. *Address:* Health Service and Population Research Department P029, Institute of Psychiatry, King's College London, De Crespigny Park, SE5 8AF. *T:* (020) 7848 0735, *Fax:* (020) 7277 1462; *e-mail:* g.thornicroft@iop.kcl.ac.uk.

THORNING-PETERSEN, Rudolph; Knight Commander, Order of the Dannebrog, 1994; Ambassador; Chamberlain to the Queen of Denmark, since 1998; *b* 17 July 1927; *s* of Erik Thorning-Petersen, FRDanAA, architect, and Helga (*née* Westergaard); *m* 1949, Britta Leyssac; one *d* (one *s* decd). *Educ:* Copenhagen Univ. (LLM 1952). Entered Royal Danish Foreign Service, 1952; alternating service, Min. of Foreign Affairs and at Danish Embassies in Cairo, Moscow and Stockholm, 1952–75; Ambassador: to Lebanon, Syria, Jordan, Iraq and Cyprus (resident Beirut), 1975; to People's Republic of China, 1980; to USSR, 1983–89; to UK, 1989–96; Ambassador at large, 1996–97 (missions on behalf of Chm., OSCE, to Minsk and Belgrade; Hd, OSCE Assistance Gp to Chechnya, May–Dec. 1997). Comdr, Order of Polar Star (Sweden), 1971; Knight Grand Cross: Order of Cedar (Lebanon), 1980; Order of Independence (Jordan), 1980; Kt Comdr, Order of White Rose (Finland), 2001. *Recreations:* modern history, genealogy, history of art. *Address:* Jaegersborg Alle 23,2, 2920 Charlottenlund, Denmark.

THORNTON, Baroness *cr* 1998 (Life Peer), of Manningham in the co. of West Yorkshire; **Dorothea Glenys Thornton;** a Baroness in Waiting (Government Whip), since 2008; *b* 16 Oct. 1952; *e c* of Peter and Jean Thornton; *m* 1977, John Carr; one *s* one *d*. *Educ:* Thornton Secondary Sch., Bradford; LSE (BSc Econ 1976). Nat. Organiser, Gingerbread, 1976–78; N London Area Officer, Greater London CABx, 1978–79; Projects Dir, Inst. of Community Studies, 1979–81; Political Sec., Royal Arsenal Co-op. Soc., 1981–86; Public and Political Affairs Advr, CWS, 1986–92. Chm., Pall Mall Consult, 2001–07. Chm., Social Enterprise Coalition, 2003–07. Fabian Society: Gen. Sec., 1993–94; Develt Dir, 1994–96; Mem., Nat. Exec. Cttee, 1997–2000. Chm., Greater London Labour Party, 1986–91. Director: Labour Women's Network, 1990–; EMILY's List UK, 1993–; Improvement and Develt Agency, 1999–2007; Training for Life, 2003–07. Trustee, Fifteen Foundn. Gov., LSE, 2000–. FRSA 1999. *Recreations:* canoeing, hill-walking, Star Trek. *Address:* House of Lords, SW1A 0PW.

THORNTON, Allan Charles, OBE 2004; Chairman, Environmental Investigation Agency, since 1988 (Co-Founder and Director, 1984–86); *b* 17 Nov. 1949; *s* of Robert Charles Antoine Thornton and Jessie (Waldram) Thornton; *m* 1995, Polly Ghazi, journalist and author; two *d*. *Educ:* Banff Centre of Fine Art, Banff, Canada. Co-ordinator of Banff Centre Creative Writing Programme, 1976, 1977; established Greenpeace UK, 1977; Exec. Dir, 1977–81 and 1986–88; co-founder of Greenpeace vessel, Rainbow Warrior, 1978; co-founder, Greenpeace International, 1980; Internat. Project Co-ordinator with Greenpeace International, 1981. Albert Schweitzer Award, 1991; BBC TV Lifetime Achievement Award, 2000. *Publication:* To Save an Elephant, 1990. *Recreation:* viewing elephants and other wildlife in their natural habitat. *Address:* c/o Environmental Investigation Agency, 62–63 Upper Street, N1 0NY. *T:* (020) 7354 7960.

THORNTON, Anthony Christopher Lawrence; QC 1988; **His Honour Judge Thornton;** a Circuit Judge, since 1994; a Judge of the Technology and Construction Court of the High Court, since 1998; *b* 18 Aug. 1947; *s* of Richard Thornton and Margery Alice (*née* Clerk); *m* 1st, 1983, Lyn Christine Thurlby (marr. diss. 1998); one *s*; 2nd, 2006, Dawn Elisabeth Collins. *Educ:* Eton Coll.; Keble Coll., Oxford (BCL, MA). Called to the Bar, Middle Temple, 1970, Bencher, 1992. A Recorder, 1992–94. Mem. (pt-time), Parole Bd, 2002–. Chairman: Fulham Legal Advice Centre, 1973–78; Hammersmith and Fulham Law Centre, 1975–78. External Moderator, Centre of Construction and Project Management, KCL, 1987–; Hon. Sen. Vis. Fellow, Centre for Commercial Law Studies, QMC, 1987–92. Mem., Gen. Council of the Bar, 1988–94 (Treas., 1990–92; Chm., Professional Standards Cttee, 1992–93). Dir, Apex Trust, 1991–94. Liveryman, Leathersellers' Co., 1976– (Mem. Ct, 2002–). Jt Editor, Construction Law Jl, 1984–94. *Publications:* (ed jtly) Building Contracts, in Halsbury's Laws of England, vol. 4, 1972; (contrib.) Construction Disputes: liability and the expert witness, 1989; contribs to Construction Law Jl. *Recreations:* football, opera, legal history. *Address:* Technology and Construction Court, St Dunstan's House, 133–137 Fetter Lane, EC4A 1HD. *T:* (020) 7947 6022. *Club:* Royal Automobile.

THORNTON, Air Marshal Sir Barry (Michael), KCB 2007 (CB 2004); CEng, FIMechE; FRAeS; Air Member for Materiel and Chief of Materiel (Air), Defence Equipment and Support, since 2007; *b* 19 Nov. 1952; *s* of Ronald Thornton and Enid Margaret Thornton (*née* Baxendale); *m* 1977, Delia Brown, barrister; two *s*. *Educ:* Baines Grammar Sch.; Nottingham Univ. (BSc); RMCS, Cranfield Univ. (MSc). CEng 1981; FIMechE 1994; FRAeS 2002. Joined RAF, 1971; initial and professional trng, 1974–75; aircraft and weapon systems appts at RAF Waddington, RAF Lyneham, RAF Abingdon and HQ RAF Germany, 1975–87; Advanced Staff Trng, 1988; OC Engrg and Supply Wing, RAF Honington, 1988–90; OC Engrg Wing, RAF Detachment Tabuk, Gulf War; Weapons Support Authy and Standardization, MoD, 1991–93; Combat Aircraft Test and Evaluation, DERA, MoD, 1994–96; rcds 1997; Dir Maritime Projects, MoD PE, 1998; Nimrod MRA4 Integrated Project Team Leader, Defence Procurement Agency, MoD, 1998–2000; Controller Aircraft RAF, and Exec. Dir, Defence Procurement Agency, MoD, 2000–03; Dir-Gen. Equipment Support (Air), 2003–04, Air Mem. for Logistics and Dir Gen. Logistics (Strike), 2004–06, Defence Logistics Orgn, MoD; Air Mem. for Personnel and C-in-C PTC, 2006–07. FCMI (FIMgt 1995). *Recreations:* golf, gardening, ski-ing. *Address:* Defence Equipment and Support, Ministry of Defence, Abbey Wood, Bristol BS34 8JH. *Club:* Royal Air Force.

THORNTON, Clive Edward Ian, CBE 1983; FInstLEx, FCIB; corporate consultancy services, since 2003; Chairman: Melton Mowbray Building Society, 1991–2003 (Director, 1988–2003; Hon. President, since 2003); Armstrong Capital Holdings Ltd, 1988–98; *b* 12 Dec. 1929; *s* of Albert and Margaret Thornton; *m* 1956, Maureen Carmine (*née* Crane); one *s* one *d*. *Educ:* St Anthony's Sch., Newcastle upon Tyne; Coll. of Commerce, Newcastle upon Tyne; College of Law, London; LLB 1977, BA Hons 1996, MA 1999, DipTh 2001, LLM 2005, London Univ. (ext.); BSc Hons 1998, Dip. Geog. 1998, Open Univ. FInstLEx 1958; FCIB (FCBSI 1970). Solicitor. Associate, Pensions Management Inst., 1978. Articled to Kenneth Hudson, solicitor, London, 1959; admitted solicitor of Supreme Court, 1963. Asst Solicitor, Nationwide Building Soc., 1963; Solicitor, Cassel Arenz Ltd, Merchant Bankers, 1964–67; Abbey National Building Society: Chief Solicitor, 1967; Dep. Chief Gen. Man., 1978; Chief Gen. Manager, 1979–83; Dir, 1980–83; Partner, Stoneham Langton and Passmore, Solicitors, 1985–88. Chm., Metropolitan Assoc. of Building Socs, 1981–82. Chairman: Mirror Group Newspapers, 1984; Financial Weekly, 1985–87; Thamesmead Town Ltd, 1986–90; Gabriel Communications (formerly Universe Publications) Ltd, 1986–96; Dir, Investment Data Services Ltd, 1986–90. Proprietor, Thorndale Devon Cattle, 1983–2007; Pres., Devon Cattle Breeders Soc., 1997–98. Member: Law Soc. (Chm., Commerce and Industry Gp, 1974); Council, Chartered Bldg Socs Inst., 1973–81; Council, Building Socs Assoc., 1979–83; Bd, Housing Corp., 1980–86. Chairman: SHAC, 1983–86; Belford Hall Management Co. Ltd, 1990–93. Member: Council, St Mary's Hosp. Med. Sch., 1984–96; St Mary's Develt Trust, 1984–98. Freeman, City of London; Liveryman, Worshipful Co. of Bakers. *Publications:* Building Society Law, Cases and Materials, 1969 (3rd edn 1988); History of Devon Cattle, 1994. *Recreations:* antique collecting, music, reading, greyhounds, Modena pigeons. *Address:* The Manor, The Green, Woughton on the Green, Milton Keynes MK6 3BE.

THORNTON, Sir (George) Malcolm, Kt 1992; Chairman: Keene Public Affairs Consultants Ltd, since 1997; Value Based Solutions, since 2006; *b* 3 April 1939; *s* of George Edmund and Ethel Thornton; *m* 1st, 1962; (one *s* decd); 2nd, 1972, Shirley Ann, (Sue) (*née* Banton) (*d* 1989); 3rd, 1990, Rosemary (*née* Hewitt). *Educ:* Wallasey Grammar Sch.; Liverpool Nautical Coll. Liverpool Pilot Service, 1955–79 (Sen. 1st cl. Licence holder). Chm., Broadskill Ltd (formerly Intuition Gp Ltd), 2002–08; non-exec. Dir, Stack Computer Solutions, 2000–. Member: Wallasey County Borough Council, 1965–74 (Chm., Transport Cttee, 1968–69); Wirral Metropolitan Council, 1973–79 (Council Leader, 1974–77); Chairman: Merseyside Metropolitan Districts Liaison Cttee, 1975–77; Educn Cttee, AMA, 1978–79 (Mem., 1974–79); Council of Local Educn Authorities, 1978. Mem., Burnham (Primary and Secondary) Cttee, 1975–79. MP (C) Liverpool, Garston, 1979–83, Crosby, 1983–97; contested Crosby, 1997. PPS to Sec. of State for Industry, 1981–83, for the Environment, 1983–84. Chairman: Select Cttee on Educn, Sci. and the Arts, 1989–96 (Mem., 1985–96); Select Cttee on Educn and Employment, 1996–97. Pro Chancellor and Chm., Liverpool John Moores Univ., 2007– (Mem. Bd, 2000–; Chm., Audit Cttee, 2003–07). Trustee, Mersey Mission to Seafarers, 1999– (Chm., 2002–). Hon. Col 156 (NW) Transport Regt, RLC (V), 2000–05. FRSA. Hon. DEd De Montfort, 1994. *Recreations:* fishing, walking, golf, cooking. *Address:* Meadow Brook, 79 Barnston Road, Heswall, Wirral CH60 1UE. *Club:* Heswall Golf.

THORNTON, Helen Ann Elizabeth, (Mrs J. E. C. Thornton); *see* Meixner, H. A. E.

THORNTON, Prof. Janet M., CBE 2000; PhD; FRS 1999; Director, European Bioinformatics Institute, European Molecular Biology Laboratory, since 2001 (on secondment from University College London and Birkbeck College, London); *b* 23 May 1949; *d* of Stanley James McLoughlin and Kathleen McLoughlin (*née* Barlow); *m* 1970, Alan D. Thornton; one *s* one *d*. *Educ:* Nottingham Univ. (BSc 1st Cl. Hons Physics); King's Coll. London and NIMR (PhD 1973). Research Assistant: Lab. of Molecular Biophysics, Oxford, 1973–78; Molecular Pharmacol., NIMR, 1978; Crystallography Department, Birkbeck College, London: SERC Advanced Fellow, 1979–83; Lectr, 1983–89; Sen. Lectr, 1989–90; Tutor, Open Univ., 1976–83; Prof. of Biomolecular Structure, and Dir, Biomolecular Structure and Modelling Unit, UCL, 1990–2001; Bernal Prof. of Crystallography, Birkbeck Coll., London, 1996–2001; Hd, Jt Res. Sch. in Molecular Scis, UCL and Birkbeck Coll., 1996–2001. Extraordinary Fellow, Churchill Coll., Cambridge, 2002–. For. Associate, NAS, USA, 2003. *Publications:* contrib. numerous articles to jls incl. Jl Molecular Biol., Structure, Nature, Trends in Biochemical Scis, Proc. Nat. Acad. Sci., Protein Science. *Recreations:* reading, music, gardens, home. *Address:* European Bioinformatics Institute, Wellcome Trust Genome Campus, Hinxton, Cambridge CB10 1SD. *T:* (01223) 494648.

THORNTON, John Henry, OBE 1987; QPM 1980; Deputy Assistant Commissioner, Metropolitan Police, 1981–86; *b* 24 Dec. 1930; *s* of late Sidney Thornton and Ethel Thornton (*née* Grinnell); *m* 1st, 1952, Norma Lucille (marr. diss. 1972; she *d* 1999), *d* of late Alfred and Kate Scrivenor; two *s*; 2nd, 1972, Hazel Ann (marr. diss. 1996), *d* of late William and Edna Butler; one *s* one *d* (and one *s* decd); 3rd, 1996, Mary Elizabeth, *d* of John Patrick and late Elizabeth Unity Jackson. *Educ:* Prince Henry's Grammar Sch., Evesham. RN 1949–50. Metropolitan Police, 1950; Comdr, 1976; Head of Community Relations, 1977–80; RCDS, 1981; Dep. Asst Commissioner, 1981; Dir of Information, 1982–83; Hd of Training, 1983–85; NW Area, 1985–86. Vice-Pres., British Section, Internat. Police Assoc., 1969–79. Chm., Breakaway Theatre Co., St Albans, 1987–94; Chm., St Albans Internat. Organ Fest., 1988–91. Chm. of Govs, Townsend C of E Sch., St Albans, 1990–96. Lay Canon and Cathedral Warden, St Albans, 1988–94;

Churchwarden, St Leonard's, Bretforton, Worcs, 2002–. CStJ 1984. *Recreations:* music, gardening, horses. *Address:* c/o Barclays Bank, PO Box 300, St Albans, Herts AL1 3EQ.

THORNTON, Prof. John Lawson; Professor and Director of Global Leadership, Tsinghua University, China, since 2003; Senior Adviser, Goldman Sachs Group, Inc., since 2003; *b* 2 Jan. 1954; *s* of John and Edna Thornton; *m* 1990, Margaret Bradham; two *s* one *d*. *Educ:* Hotchkiss Sch.; Harvard Coll. (AB); Oxford Univ. (MA); Yale Sch. of Mgt. Joined Goldman Sachs, 1980: Gen. Partner, 1988; Co-CEO, Goldman Sachs Internat. (Europe, ME and Africa), 1995–96; Chm., Goldman Sachs-Asia, 1996–98; Pres., and co-Chief Operating Officer, 1999–2003; Dir, Mem. Mgt Cttee, and Co-Chm., Partnership Cttee until 2003. Director: Laura Ashley plc, 1995–2003 (Chm., 1996–99); Ford Motor Co., 1996–; BSkyB Gp plc; Pacific Century Gp, Inc., 2003–; Intel, 2003–; News Corp., 2004–. Mem., Council on Foreign Relns. Dir, Goldman Sachs Foundn. Member, Board of Trustees: Brookings Instn, 2000– (Chm., 2003–); Hotchkiss Sch.; Asia Soc.; Morehouse Coll.; Member: Investment Cttee, Yale Univ.; Adv. Bd, Yale Sch. of Mgt. *Address:* Tsinghua University, 1 Qinghuayuan, Beijing 100084, China.

THORNTON, Sir Malcolm; *see* Thornton, Sir G. M.

THORNTON, Neil Ross; Director, Sustainable Consumption and Production and Waste (formerly Environment Quality and Waste), Department for Environment, Food and Rural Affairs, since 2003; *b* 11 Feb. 1950; *s* of late George and Kay Thornton; *m* 1977, Christine Anne Boyes; two *d*. *Educ:* Sedbergh Sch.; Pembroke Coll., Cambridge (BA Eng. 1971). Private Sec. to Perm. Sec., DoI, 1975; HM Treasury, 1979; Asst Sec., DTI, 1984; Principal Private Sec. to Sec. of State for Trade and Industry, 1988–90; Under Sec., 1990, Head, Europe Div., 1990–93, Exports to Europe and the Americas Div., 1993–96, DTI; Hd of Food, Drink and Marketing Policy Gp, 1996–99, Hd of Food Industry Competitiveness and Consumers, 1999–2000, MAFF; Hd of Animal Health Gp, MAFF, then Dir, Animal Health, DEFRA, 2000–03. *Recreations:* literature, choral singing, golf. *Address:* Department for Environment, Food and Rural Affairs, Nobel House, 17 Smith Square, SW1P 3JR.

THORNTON, Peter Anthony, FRICS; FICE; Chief Executive, Greycoat Estates Ltd (formerly Greycoat Plc), since 1994; *b* 8 May 1944; *s* of Robert and Freda Thornton; *m* 1st, 1969, Patricia Greenwood (marr. diss. 1987); one *s* two *d*; 2nd, 1997, Susan Harris. *Educ:* Bradford Grammar Sch.; Manchester Univ. (BSc). FRICS 1984; FICE 1990. Engineer, Binnie & Partners (Consulting Engrs), 1967–71; self-employed, 1972–75; Commercial Manager, Sears Hldgs plc, 1975–79; Greycoat Plc, 1979–99: Dir, 1981–99; Jt Man. Dir, 1986–94. *Recreations:* cars, tennis, water ski-ing. *Address:* Van Buren Cottage, Queen's Ride, Barnes Common, SW13 0JF. *T:* (020) 8788 1969. *Club:* Harbour.

THORNTON, Sir Peter (Eustace), KCB 1974 (CB 1971); Permanent Secretary, Department of Trade, 1974–77; *b* 28 Aug. 1917; *s* of Douglas Oscar Thornton and Dorothy (*née* Shepherd); *m* 1946, Rosamond Hobart Myers, US Medal of Freedom, Sewanee, Tennessee; two *s* one *d*. *Educ:* Charterhouse; Gonville and Caius Coll., Cambridge. Served with RA, mainly in Middle East and Italy, 1940–46. Joined Board of Trade, 1946. Secretary, Company Law Cttee (Jenkins Cttee), 1959–62; Assistant Under-Secretary of State, Department of Economic Affairs, 1964–67; Under-Sec., 1967–70, Dep. Sec., 1970–72, Cabinet Office, with central co-ordinating role during British negotiations for membership of EEC; Dep. Sec., DTI, March–July 1972; Sec. (Aerospace and Shipping), DTI, 1972–74; Second Permanent Sec., Dept of Trade, 1974. Director: Hill Samuel Gp, 1977–83; Rolls Royce, 1977–85; Courtaulds, 1977–87; Laird Gp, 1978–92; Superior Oil, 1980–84. Mem., Megaw Cttee of Inquiry into Civil Service Pay, 1981–82. Pro-Chancellor, Open Univ., 1979–83 (DUniv 1984). Governor, Sutton's Hosp., Charterhouse, 1980–89.

THORNTON, Peter Ribblesdale; QC 1992; **His Honour Judge Peter Thornton;** a Specialist Circuit Judge, since 2007; *b* 17 Oct. 1946; *s* of Robert Ribblesdale Thornton, CBE; *m* 1981, Susan Margaret Dalal; one *s* one *d*. *Educ:* Clifton Coll.; St John's Coll., Cambridge (BA). Called to the Bar, Middle Temple, 1969, Bencher, 2001; Asst Recorder, 1994–97; Recorder, 1997–2007; Dep. High Ct Judge, 2003–; Co-Hd, Doughty St Chambers, 2005–07. Chair, Fitness to Practise Appeals Panel, Royal Free and UC Med. Sch., 2003–; Chairperson Arbitrator, Sports Dispute Resolution Panel, 2004–. Mem., Editl Bd, Criminal Law Review, 1997–. Chairman: NCCL, 1981–83; Civil Liberties Trust, 1991–95. Trustee, Howard League for Penal Reform, 2004–. *Publications:* (contrib.) Civil Liberties 1984, 1984; We Protest: Public Order Debate, 1985; The Civil Liberties of the Zircon Affair, 1987; Public Order Law, 1987; (contrib.) The Polygraph Test, 1988; Decade of Decline: Civil Liberties in the Thatcher Years, 1989; (ed jtly) Penguin Civil Liberty Guide, 1989; (jtly) Justice on Trial, 1992; (ed jtly) Archbold's Criminal Pleadings, Evidence and Practice, 1992–; (contrib.) Analysing Witness Testimony, 1999. *Address:* Central Criminal Court, Old Bailey, EC4M 7EH.

THORNTON, Sir Richard (Eustace), KCVO 1997; OBE 1980; JP; HM Lord Lieutenant of Surrey, 1986–97; *b* 10 Oct. 1922; *m* 1954, Gabrielle Elizabeth Sharpe; four *d*. *Educ:* Eton Coll.; Trinity Coll., Cambridge (MA). Member: Thames Conservancy, 1968–74; TWA, 1974–80; Royal Commission on Environmental Pollution, 1977–84. Chm., Mount Alvernia Management Trust, 1992–2002. Chm. Govs, Bishop Reindorp Sch., 1985–98; Mem. Governing Body, Charterhouse Sch. (Chm., 1981–89). Surrey: DL; High Sheriff 1978–79; JP. KStJ 1986. *Address:* Hampton, Seale, near Farnham, Surrey GU10 1JE. *T:* (01483) 810208.

THORNTON, Robert John, CB 1980; Assistant Under Secretary of State and Director General of Supplies and Transport (Naval), Ministry of Defence, 1977–81; *b* 23 Dec. 1919; *s* of Herbert John Thornton and Ethel Mary Thornton (*née* Dunning); *m* 1944, Joan Elizabeth Roberts; three *s*. *Educ:* Queen Elizabeth Grammar School, Atherstone. MBIM 1970. Joined Naval Store Dept, Admiralty, as Asst Naval Store Officer, 1938; Singapore, 1941; Dep. Naval Store Officer, Colombo, 1942; Support Ship Hong Siang, 1943; Naval Store Officer, Admiralty, 1945; Gibraltar, 1951; Asst Dir of Stores, 1955; Superintending Naval Store Officer, Portsmouth, 1960; Dep. Dir of Stores, 1964; Dir of Victualling, 1971; Dir of Supplies and Transport (General Stores and Victualling), 1971. *Recreations:* bowls, fly fishing, gardening.

THORNTON, Sally; *see* Burgess, Sally.

THORNTON, Sara Joanne, QPM 2006; Chief Constable, Thames Valley Police, since 2007; *b* Poole, 27 Dec. 1962; *d* of Kenneth and Margreta Thornton; *m* 1st, 1986, Ewan McPhie (marr. diss. 1995); one *s*; 2nd, 1996, Daniel Haigh (marr. diss. 2004); one *s*. *Educ:* Durham Univ. (BA Philos. and Pols); Univ. of Cambridge (Dip. Applied Criminol.). Metropolitan Police Service, 1986–2000; Thames Valley Police: Asst Chief Constable, 2000–03; Dep. Chief Constable, 2003–07. *Publications:* articles in Policing jl. *Recreations:* reading, walking, travelling. *Address:* Thames Valley Police Headquarters, Oxford Road, Kidlington, Oxford OX5 2NX. *T:* (01865) 846002; *e-mail:* sara.thornton@thamesvalley.pnn.police.uk.

THORNTON, Stephen, CBE 2002; Chief Executive, The Health Foundation (formerly PPP Foundation), since 2002; *b* 23 Jan. 1954; *s* of Harry Thornton and Alice Thornton (*née* Ainsworth); *m* 1976, Lorraine Anne Cassells; one *s* one *d*. *Educ:* Paston Sch., N Walsham, Norfolk; Manchester Univ. (BA Hons Politics and Mod. Hist.). MHSM, DipHSM. NHS Nat. Mgt Trng scheme, 1979; Administrator: Prestwich Hosp., Manchester, 1980–82; Salford Royal Hosp., 1982–83; Fulbourn Hosp., Cambridge, 1983–85; Gen. Manager, Community Health Services, Cambs, 1985–89; Dir of Planning, E Anglia RHA, 1989–93; Chief Exec., Cambridge and Huntingdon HA, 1993–97; Cabinet Office Top Mgt Programme, 1996; Chief Exec., NHS Confedn, 1997–2002. Member: NHS Modernisation Bd, 2000–01; Healthcare Commn (formerly Commn for Healthcare Audit and Inspection), 2002–06. Non-exec. Dir, Monitor, 2006–. Mem. Council, Open Univ., 2003–06. Dir, Christian Blind Mission (UK), 2002–04. Trustee, Aquaid Lifeline Fund, 2001–. FRSocMed 1998. Deacon, Girton Baptist Church, 1996–2006. *Publications:* articles in Health Service Jl. *Address:* 100 High Street, Girton, Cambridge CB3 0QL. *T:* (01223) 506306.

THORNTON, Rt Rev. Timothy Martin; *see* Truro, Bishop of.

THORNTON, Dr William Dickson, CB 1990; Deputy Chief Medical Officer, Department of Health and Social Services, Northern Ireland, 1978–90, retired; *b* 9 July 1930; *s* of late William J. Thornton and Elfreda Thornton (*née* Dickson); *m* 1957, Dr Maureen Gilpin; one *s* three *d*. *Educ:* Portora Royal School; Trinity College Dublin (BA, MD). FFPH. General medical practitioner, 1955–65; NI Hospitals Authy, 1966–72; Dept of Health and Social Services (NI), 1973–90. Civil QHP, 1990–92. Chm., 1993–97, Vice-Pres., 2001–, Age Concern (NI). *Recreations:* boating, reading, gardening. *Address:* 54 Deramore Park South, Belfast BT9 5JY. *T:* (028) 9066 0186.

THOROGOOD, Alfreda, (Mrs D. R. Wall), ARAD (PDTC); Artistic Director of Dance, Elmhurst Ballet School, 1994–2004 (Senior Teacher, 1992–94); Artistic Advisor, Royal Academy of Dancing, 1989–92; *b* 17 Aug. 1942; *d* of Alfreda and Edward Thorogood; *m* 1967, David Wall, *qv*; one *s* one *d*. *Educ:* Lady Eden's Sch.; Royal Ballet Sch., Jun. and Sen. Royal Ballet Company, 1960–80: Soloist, Aug. 1965; Principal Dancer, 1968; Bush Davies School: Sen. Teacher, 1982–84; Dep. Ballet Principal, 1984–89; Dir, 1988–89. *Recreations:* listening to music, cooking, interior design, art, painting. *Address:* 34 Croham Manor Road, S Croydon CR2 7BE.

THOROGOOD, Rev. Bernard George, OBE 1992; General Secretary, United Reformed Church, 1980–92; *b* 21 July 1927; *s* of Frederick and Winifred Thorogood; *m* 1952, Jannett Lindsay Paton (*née* Cameron) (*d* 1988); two *s*; *m* 1991, Joan Tierney. *Educ:* Glasgow Univ. (MA); Scottish Congregational College. Ordained in Congregational Church, 1952; missionary appointment under London Missionary Society in South Pacific Islands, 1953–70; Gen. Sec., Council for World Mission, 1971–80. Moderator, Exec. Cttee, BCC, 1984–90; Mem., Central Cttee, WCC, 1984–91. DD Lambeth 1992. *Publications:* Not Quite Paradise, 1960; Guide to the Book of Amos, 1971; Our Father's House, 1983; Risen Today, 1987; The Flag and The Cross, 1988; No Abiding City, 1989; On Judging Caesar, 1990; One Wind Many Flames, 1991; Looking at Leisure: a European view, 1991; (ed) Gales of Change, 1994; Letters to Paul, 1999. *Recreation:* sketching. *Address:* 2 Ashmore Avenue, Pymble, NSW 2073, Australia. *T:* (2) 91441822.

THOROLD, Sir (Anthony) Oliver, 16th Bt *cr* 1642, of Marston, Lincolnshire; *b* 15 April 1945; *o s* of Captain Sir Anthony Thorold, 15th Bt, OBE, DSC and Jocelyn Elaine Laura Thorold (*née* Heathcote-Smith); *S* father, 1999, but his name does not appear on the Official Roll of the Baronetage; *m* 1977, Genevra Mercy Richardson, *qv*; one *s* one *d*. *Educ:* Winchester; Lincoln Coll., Oxford. Called to the Bar, Inner Temple, 1971. *Heir: s* Henry Lowry Thorold, *b* 6 Aug. 1981. *Address:* (chambers) 11 Doughty Street, WC1N 2PG; 8 Richmond Crescent, N1 0LZ.

THORP, David; Partner, ISIS EP LLP (formerly ISIS Capital plc), since 2005 (Director, since 1995; Chairman, 2001–04; Managing Director, Friends Ivory & Sime Private Equity (formerly Ivory & Sime Baronsmead) plc, 1997–2001); Chairman, Sussex Place Ventures Ltd, since 2004; *b* 22 July 1945; *s* of late John and Kathleen Mary Thorp; *m* 1969, Christine Janice Kenyon; three *s*. *Educ:* Portsmouth Grammar Sch.; Queens' College, Cambridge (MA Natural Scis); London Business School (MBA). Alcan (UK), 1967–69; ICFC, then FFI, subseq. 3i plc, 1971–91, Dir, 1985–91; Dir-Gen., ESU, 1991–94. Chairman: Unipalm Ltd, 1992–94; Unipalm Gp plc, 1994–95; non-executive Director: Baronsmead VCT plc, 1995–2005; Patientline plc (formerly Patientline Ltd), 1998–2001 (Chm., Patientline Ltd, 1994–98); Job Opportunities Ltd, 2000–04; Assoc. of Investment Cos, 2007–. Mem. Council, 1997–2002, Chm., 2000–01, BVCA (formerly British Venture Capital Assoc.); Chm., AIC VCT Forum, 2006–. Non-exec. Dir, Royal Surrey County Hosp., 1990–97. *Recreations:* tennis, walking. *Address:* Larks Hill, 16 Longdown, Guildford, Surrey GU4 8PP. *T:* (01483) 561016.

THORP, Jeremy Walter, CMG 2001; HM Diplomatic Service, retired; a Director, British Bankers' Association, and Secretary, Joint Money Laundering Steering Group, 2002–06; *b* 12 Dec. 1941; *s* of Walter and Dorothy Bliss Thorp; *m* 1973, Estela Lessa Guyer. *Educ:* King Edward VII Sch., Sheffield; Corpus Christi Coll., Oxford (MA). HM Treasury, 1963–67; DEA, 1967–69; HM Treasury, 1969–71; First Sec. (Financial), HM Embassy, Washington, 1971–73; HM Treasury, 1973–78; FCO, 1978–82; Head of Chancery, Lima, 1982–86; FCO, 1986–88; Dep. Hd of Mission, Dublin, 1988–92; Head of Resource and Finance, then Resource Planning, Dept, FCO, 1993–97; with Unilever PLC, 1997–98; Ambassador to Colombia, 1998–2001. Dir, British and Colombian Chamber of Commerce, 2003–; Chm., Anglo-Colombian Soc., 2006– (Dep. Chm., 2004–06). Mem. Adv. Council, Farnham Castle Briefing and Conf. Centre, 2002–06. Trustee, Children of the Andes, 2002–. *Recreations:* music, travel, modern Irish history, walking. *Address:* 9 Coutts Crescent, St Albans Road, NW5 1RF.

THORPE, Adrian Charles, CMG 1994; MA; HM Diplomatic Service, retired; Managing Director, Traviata Books Ltd, since 2004; *b* 29 July 1942; *o s* of late Prof. Lewis Thorpe and of Dr Barbara Reynolds, *qv*; *m* 1968, Miyoko Kosugi. *Educ:* The Leys Sch., Cambridge; Christ's Coll., Cambridge (MA). HM Diplomatic Service, 1965–2002: Tokyo, 1965–70; FCO, 1970–73; Beirut, 1973–76 (Head of Chancery, 1975–76); FCO, 1976; Tokyo, 1976–81; FCO, 1981–85, Hd of IT Dept, 1982–85; Counsellor (Econ.), Bonn, 1985–89; Dep. High Comr, Kuala Lumpur, 1989–91; Minister, Tokyo, 1991–95; Ambassador: to the Philippines, 1995–98; to Mexico, 1999–2002. FRSA. *Publications:* articles in journals. *Recreations:* opera, travel, bookshops, comfort. *Address:* The Cider House, Compton Park, Sherborne, Dorset DT9 4QU. *Club:* Oxford and Cambridge.

THORPE, Prof. Alan John, PhD; Chief Executive, Natural Environment Research Council, since 2005; Visiting Professor of Meteorology, University of Reading, since 2006; *b* 15 July 1952; *s* of Jack Fielding Thorpe and Dorothy Kathleen Thorpe (*née* Davey); *m* 1979, Helen Elizabeth Edgar; one *s* one *d*. *Educ:* Univ. of Warwick (BSc Physics); Imperial Coll., London (PhD). Res. Asst, Imperial Coll., London, 1976–81; Scientist, Met. Office, 1981–82; University of Reading: Lectr, 1982–88, Reader,

1988–92, Prof., 1992–2006, Dept of Meteorol; on leave of absence as Dir, Hadley Centre, Met. Office, 1999–2001; Dir, NERC Centres for Atmospheric Sci., 2001–05. *Publications:* over 100 papers in atmospheric sci. jls. *Recreation:* art appreciation. *Address:* Natural Environment Research Council, Polaris House, North Star Avenue, Swindon SN2 1EU. *T:* (01793) 411653, *Fax:* (01793) 411780; *e-mail:* HQPO@nerc.ac.uk.

THORPE, Anthony Geoffrey Younghusband; His Honour Judge Thorpe; a Circuit Judge, since 1990; *b* 21 Aug. 1941; *s* of G. J. Y. Thorpe, MBE; *m* 1966, Janet Patricia; one *s* one *d*. *Educ:* Highgate School; Britannia Royal Naval College (scholarship); King's College London. Royal Navy: served HM Ships Hermes, Ark Royal, Vidal, Blake; Captain 1983; Chief Naval Judge Advocate, 1983–86; retired from RN 1990. Called to the Bar, Inner Temple, 1972 (Treasurer's Prize); Asst Recorder, 1984–89, Recorder, 1989–90; Resident Judge, Chichester Crown Ct, 2000–08. Pres., Ind. Tribunal Service, 1992–94 (Social Security, Medical, Disability, and Vaccine Damage Appeals, Child Support Appeals). *Publications:* articles in learned jls. *Recreation:* sailing. *Address:* The Crown Court, Southgate, Chichester, W Sussex PO19 1SX; c/o Lloyds TSB, Cox's and King's, 6 Pall Mall, SW1Y 5NH. *Club:* Naval.

THORPE, Brian Russell, CBE 1987; Deputy Chairman, Southern Water PLC (formerly Southern Water Authority), 1983–93 (Chief Executive, 1973–88); *b* 12 July 1929; *s* of late Robert and Florrie Thorpe; *m* 1955, Ann Sinclair Raby; three *d*. *Educ:* Rastrick Grammar Sch.; LLB London, LLM Leeds. Solicitor, 1952. Asst Prosecuting Solicitor, Bradford CC, 1954–55; Asst Solicitor, later Asst Town Clerk, Southampton CC, 1955–61; Dep. Town Clerk, Blackpool, 1961–65; Gen. Manager, Sussex River Authority, 1965–73. Churchill Fellow, 1972. *Recreations:* golf, gardening, foreign travel. *Club:* Worthing Golf.

THORPE, Ian James, OAM 2001; swimmer; *b* Sydney, 13 Oct. 1982; *s* of Kenneth William and Margaret Grace Thorpe. *Educ:* East Hills Boys High Sch. Estab. Ian Thorpe's Fountain for Youth, charity, 2000. World Championships: Perth, 1998: Gold Medal: 400m freestyle; 4 x 200m freestyle relay; Fukuoka, 2001: Gold Medal: 200m freestyle; 400m freestyle; 800m freestyle; 4 x 100m freestyle relay; 4 x 200m freestyle relay; 4 x 100m medley relay; Barcelona, 2003: Gold Medal: 200m freestyle; 400m freestyle; 4 x 200m freestyle relay; Silver Medal, 200m individual medley; Bronze Medal, 100m freestyle; Commonwealth Games: Kuala Lumpur, 1998: Gold Medal: 200m freestyle; 400m freestyle; 4 x 100m freestyle relay; 4 x 200m freestyle relay; Manchester, 2002: Gold Medal: 100m freestyle; 200m freestyle; 400m freestyle; 4 x 100m freestyle relay; 4 x 200m freestyle relay; 4 x 100m medley relay; Silver Medal, 100m backstroke; Pan Pacific Championships: Sydney, 1999: Gold Medal: 200m freestyle; 400m freestyle; 4 x 100m freestyle relay; 4 x 200m freestyle relay; Yokohama, 2002: Gold Medal: 100m freestyle; 200m freestyle; 400m freestyle; 4 x 100m freestyle relay; 4 x 200m freestyle relay; Silver Medal, 4 x 100m medley relay; Olympic Games: Sydney, 2000: Gold Medal: 400m freestyle; 4 x 100m freestyle relay; 4 x 200m freestyle relay; Silver Medal: 200m freestyle; 4 x 100m medley relay; Athens, 2004: Gold Medal: 200m freestyle; 400m freestyle; Silver Medal, 4 x 200m freestyle relay; Bronze Medal, 100m freestyle. Aust. Male Athlete of the Year, 1999, 2000, 2001, 2004; Young Australian of the Year, 2000; American Internat. Athlete Trophy, 2001; Telstra People's Choice Award, 2001, 2002; Centenary Medal, 2003. *Publications:* The Journey, 2000; Live Your Dreams, 2002. *Recreations:* surfing, movies, going out with friends, charity work. *Address:* c/o Grand Slam International Pty Ltd, PO Box 402, Manly, NSW 1655, Australia. *Club:* SLC Aquadot (Sydney).

THORPE, Rt Hon. (John) Jeremy; PC 1967; Chairman, Jeremy Thorpe Associates (Development Consultants in the Third World), since 1984; *b* 29 April 1929; *s* of late J. H. Thorpe, OBE, KC, MP (C) Rusholme, and Ursula, *d* of Sir John Norton-Griffiths, 1st Bt, KCB, DSO, sometime MP (C); *m* 1st, 1968, Caroline (*d* 1970), *d* of late Warwick Allpass, Kingswood, Surrey; one *s*; 2nd, 1973, Marion (CBE 2008), *d* of late Erwin Stein. *Educ:* Rectory Sch., Connecticut, USA; Eton Coll.; Trinity Coll., Oxford, Hon. Fellow, 1972. President, Oxford Union Society, Hilary, 1951; Barrister, Inner Temple, 1954. Member Devon Sessions. Contested (L) N Devon, 1955; MP (L) Devon N, 1959–79. Hon. Treasurer, Liberal Party Organisation, 1965–67; Leader, Liberal Party, 1967–76; Pres., N Devon Liberal Democrats (formerly N Devon Liberal Assoc.), 1987–. United Nations Association: Chm., Exec., 1976–80; Chm., Political Cttee, 1977–85. FRSA. Hon. LLD Exeter, 1974. *Publications:* (jtly) To all who are interested in Democracy, 1951; Europe: the case for going in, 1971; In My Own Time, 1999; contrib. to newspapers and periodicals. *Recreations:* music; collecting Chinese ceramics. *Address:* 2 Orme Square, W2 4RS. *Clubs:* National Liberal (Hon. Mem.); N Devon Liberal.

THORPE, Rt Hon. Sir Mathew Alexander, Kt 1988; PC 1995; **Rt Hon. Lord Justice Thorpe;** a Lord Justice of Appeal, since 1995; Deputy Head, Family Justice, and Head of International Family Justice, since 2005; *b* 30 July 1938; *s* of late Michael Alexander Thorpe and Dorothea Margaret Lambert; *m* 1st, 1966, Lavinia Hermione Buxton (marr. diss. 1989); two *s* (and one *s* decd); 2nd, 1989, Mrs Carola Millar. *Educ:* Stowe; Balliol Coll., Oxford. Called to the Bar, Inner Temple, 1961, Bencher, 1985; QC 1980; a Recorder, 1982–88; a Judge of the High Court, Family Div., 1988–95. *Address:* Royal Courts of Justice, Strand, WC2A 2LL.

THORPE, Nigel James, CVO 1991; HM Diplomatic Service, retired; *b* 3 Oct. 1945; *s* of Ronald Thorpe and Glenys (*née* Robilliard); *m* 1969 (marr. diss. 1976); two *s*; *m* 1978 (marr. diss. 2001); three *d*. *Educ:* East Grinstead Grammar Sch.; University Coll. of S Wales and Monmouthshire (BA Hons). Joined HM Diplomatic Service, 1969; Warsaw, 1970–72; Dacca, 1973–74; FCO, 1975–79; Ottawa, 1979–81; seconded to Dept of Energy, 1981–82; Asst Hd of Southern Africa Dept, FCO, 1982–85; Counsellor, Warsaw, 1985–88; Dep. High Comr, Harare, 1989–92; Head, Central European Dept, FCO, 1992–96; Sen. Directing Staff, RCDS (on secondment), 1996–97; Ambassador to Hungary, 1998–2003. Founder, Adam Clark Foundn, 1999; Chm., Vodafone Hungary Foundn, 2003; acting Dir, Vodafone Gp Foundn, 2005–06; Dir, Corporate Affairs, Vodafone Hungary, 2006–07. Pres., Friends of Hungarian Fine Arts Mus., 2007–08. Trustee, Liszt Acad. Network, 2001–. *Publications:* Harmincad Utca 6, a 20th Century History of Budapest, 1999. *Recreations:* my children, reading, history.

THORPE, Phillip Andrew; Chairman and Chief Executive Officer, Qatar Financial Centre Regulatory Authority, since 2005; *b* 26 Aug. 1954; *s* of late Reginald Thorpe, OBE and of Fay Eglantine Thorpe; *m* 1st, 1976, Isabell Hanna Henkel (marr. diss. 1989); one *s* two *d*; 2nd, 1990, Melinda Kilgour Lowis (marr. diss. 1997); one *s* one *d*; 3rd, 1998, Jane Chunhae Kang. *Educ:* Victoria Univ., Wellington, NZ (BA Pol Sci., LLB); Univ. of Hong Kong (MSocSc Dist.). Admitted Barrister and Solicitor of Supreme Court of NZ and as Solicitor and Notary Public, Republic of Nauru. Solicitor, Beyer Christie O'Regan & Partners, Wellington, NZ, 1976–79; Legal Officer and Public Prosecutor, Govt of Republic of Nauru, 1979–81; Solicitor, Registrar-General's Dept, Hong Kong Govt, 1981–83; Hong Kong Securities Commission: Sen. Legal Advr, 1983–86; Asst Comr, 1986–88; Dep. Comr, 1988–89; Exec. Vice-Chm. and Chief Exec., Hong Kong Futures Exchange, 1987–89; Chief Exec., Assoc. of Futures Brokers and Dealers Ltd, 1989–91; Exec. Dir and Dep. Chief Exec., SFA Ltd, 1991–93; Exec. Dir and Chief Exec., London Commodity Exchange (1986) Ltd, 1991–92; Chief Exec., IMRO, 1993–98; Man. Dir, Authorisations, Enforcement, and Consumer Relns, FSA, 1998–2001; Pres., Futures Industry Inst., Washington, 2001–02; Chief Comr, Regulatory Agency, Dubai, then Chief Exec., Dubai Financial Services Authy, 2002–04. *Publication:* (Country Editor for Hong Kong) International Securities Regulation, 1986. *Recreations:* fishing, flying. *Address:* PO Box 22989, Doha, Qatar; *e-mail:* p.thorpe@qfcra.com.

THORPE, Prof. Stephen Austen, PhD; FRS 1991; Professor of Oceanography, University of Southampton, 1986–2003, now Emeritus. *Educ:* Rutherford Coll., Newcastle (BSc 1958); Trinity Coll., Cambridge (BA 1961; PhD 1966). SPSO, Inst. of Oceanographic Scis, NERC, until 1986. Mem., NERC, 1991–94 (Mem., Marine Scis Cttee). Hon. Prof., Sch. of Ocean Scis, Univ. of Wales, Bangor, 2001–06. Pres., RMetS, 1990–92; Vice-Pres., Scottish Assoc. for Marine Sci., 1993–. Walter Munk Medal, US Office of Naval Res. and Oceanography Soc., 1998; Fridtjof Nansen Medal, Eur. Geophysical Soc., 2000. *Publications:* (ed) Oceanography, 1996; (ed jtly) Encyclopedia of Oceanography, 2001; The Turbulent Ocean, 2005; An Introduction to Ocean Turbulence, 2007; contribs to learned jls. *Address:* Bodfryn, Llangoed, Beaumaris, Anglesey LL58 8PH. *T:* (01248) 490210.

THORPE-TRACEY, Stephen Frederick; Controller, Newcastle Central Office, Department of Social Security (formerly of Health and Social Security), 1986–89, retired; *b* 27 Dec. 1929; *s* of Rev. and Mrs J. S. V. Thorpe-Tracey; *m* 1955, Shirley Byles; one *s* two *d*. *Educ:* Plymouth Coll. Emergency Commn, 1948; Short Service Commn, 1950; Regular Commn, DLI, 1952; Staff Coll., Camberley, 1960 (psc); GS02, Defence Operational Res. Estabt, 1961–64; Training Major, 8 DLI (TA), 1964–65; Major, 1 DLI, 1965–66; GSO2, MoD, 1966–70; direct entry, Home Civil Service, 1970; Principal, DHSS, 1970; Asst Sec., 1977; Under Sec., 1986. Chm., Northern Gp, RIPA, 1988–90. Mem., Prescription Pricing Authy, 1990–93. Vice Chm., Carr-Gomm (Tyneside) Housing Assoc. Ltd, 1990–91. Chm., Mid Devon Assoc. of Local Councils, 2001–03. Hon. Secretary: Mid Devon Div., SSAFA Forces Help (formerly SSAFA and FHS), 1992–99; Uffculme Br., RBL, 1995–. Mem., Uffculme Parish Council, 1995–2003. Chm., Uffculme Soc., 1994–2002. Chairman: Trustees, Coldharbour Mill, 1996–2006 (Hon. Sec., 1994–96); Coldharbour Mill Ltd, 1998–2006. Hon. Sec., Civil Service Chess Assoc., 1974–77; Chm., Tiverton Chess Club, 1994–; Pres., Devon County Chess Assoc., 2003–05, 2007–. Cdre, Goring Thames Sailing Club, 1981–82. *Publications:* T^2 series of articles in military jls. *Recreations:* chess, golf. *Address:* 9 Grantlands, Uffculme, Cullompton, Devon EX15 3ED. *T:* (01884) 841864.

THOULD, Anthony Julian, MA; Head Master, King Edward VI School, Southampton, since 2002; *b* 16 June 1958; *s* of late Dr Anthony Keith Thould and of Bernine Thould; *m* 1984, Susan Jane Isabelle Rentoul; three *s* one *d*. *Educ:* King's Coll., Taunton; Pembroke Coll., Oxford (MA Hist.). Distribn Manager, H. P. Bulmer Plc, 1981–84; asst teacher, Westminster Sch., 1984–88; Hd of Hist., 1988–91, Dir of Studies, 1991–97, Cranleigh Sch.; Dir of Studies, King's Sch., Worcester, 1997–2002. *Recreations:* classical guitar, fencing. *Address:* King Edward VI School, Southampton SO15 7UQ; *e-mail:* headmaster@kes.hants.sch.uk.

THOULESS, Prof. David James, FRS 1979; Professor of Physics, University of Washington, 1980–2003, now Emeritus; *b* 21 Sept. 1934; *s* of late Robert Henry Thouless; *m* 1958, Margaret Elizabeth Scrase; two *s* one *d*. *Educ:* Winchester Coll.; Trinity Hall, Cambridge (BA); Cornell Univ. (PhD). Physicist, Lawrence Radiation Laboratory, Berkeley, Calif, 1958–59; ICI Research Fellow, Birmingham Univ., 1959–61; Lecturer, Cambridge Univ., and Fellow of Churchill Coll., 1961–65; Prof. of Mathematical Physics, Birmingham Univ., 1965–78; Prof. of Applied Science, Yale Univ., 1979–80; Royal Soc. Res. Prof., and Fellow of Clare Hall, Cambridge Univ., 1983–86. Mem., US Nat. Acad. Scis, 1995. Wolf Prize for Physics, Wolf Foundn, Israel, 1990; Dirac Prize, Inst. of Physics, 1993. *Publications:* Quantum Mechanics of Many-Body Systems, 1961, 2nd edn 1972; Topological Quantum Numbers in Non-Relativistic Physics, 1998. *Address:* Department of Physics, Box 351560, University of Washington, Seattle, WA 98195, USA.

THRELFALL, David; actor; *b* 12 Oct. 1953. *Educ:* Wilbraham Comprehensive Sch.; Sheffield Art Coll.; Manchester Polytechnic Sch. of Theatre. Associate Artistic Dir, Royal Exchange Theatre, Manchester, 1998–2001. *Stage:* Bed of Roses, Royal Court; 3 years with RSC, incl. Savage Amusement, Nicholas Nickleby, 1980 (Clarence Derwent Award, British Theatre Assoc., SWET Award); Not Quite Jerusalem, Royal Court, 1982; Hamlet, Edinburgh Fest., 1986; Bussy D'Ambois, Old Vic, 1988; Wild Duck, Phoenix, 1990; Count of Monte Cristo, Royal Exchange, 1994; Richard II, Cottesloe, RNT, 1995; Hedda Gabler, Chichester, 1996; Present Laughter, Royal Exchange, 1997; The Rehearsal, NY, 1997; Peer Gynt, Royal Exchange, 1999; Tartuffe, RNT, 2002; The Entertainer, Derby Playhouse, 2003; Skellig, Young Vic, 2003; Someone Who'll Watch Over Me, New Ambassadors, 2005; *television:* The Kiss of Death, 1976; Jumping the Queue, 1989; Clothes in the Wardrobe, 1993; Mary and Jesus, 1999; In the Beginning, 2000; series: Nicholas Nickleby, 1984; Paradise Postponed, 1985; The Marksman, 1988; Nightingales, 1990; Titmuss Regained, 1991; Statement of Affairs, Diana: Her True Story, 1993; Men of the World, 1994; Sex & Chips & Rock-'n'-Roll, 1999; Dinner of Herbs, 2000; Shameless (5 series; also dir 7 episodes), 2004–08 (RTS Award, 2005); The Queen's Sister, 2005 (RTS Award); Constantine, Housewife 49 (BAFTA Award, 2007), 2006; Whistleblower, 2007; *radio:* three series of Baldi; *films:* When the Whales Came, 1989; The Russia House, 1990; Patriot Games, 1992; Master and Commander, 2003; The Golden Age, Hot Fuzz, 2007. Plays and Players Promising Newcomer, 1978. *Recreations:* motor bike, friends. *Address:* c/o Independent Talent Group Ltd, Oxford House, 76 Oxford Street, W1D 1BS.

THRIFT, Prof. Nigel John, PhD, DSc; FBA 2003; Vice-Chancellor, University of Warwick, since 2006; *b* 12 Oct. 1949; *s* of Leonard John Thrift and Joyce Mary Wakeley; *m* 1978, Lynda Jean Sharples; two *d*. *Educ:* UCW, Aberystwyth (BA Hons); Univ. of Bristol (PhD 1979; DSc 1992); MA Oxon 2004. Research Fellow: Dept of Architecture, Univ. of Cambridge, 1975–76; Dept of Geog., Univ. of Leeds, 1976–78; Dept of Human Geog., ANU, 1979–81 (Sen. Res. Fellow, 1981–83); Lectr, 1984–86, Reader, 1986–87, St David's UC, Lampeter; Bristol University: Lectr, 1987–88; Reader, 1988–90; Prof. of Geography, 1990–2003, now Emeritus; Head, Dept of Geog., 1995–99; University of Oxford: Prof. of Geography, 2003–06; Hd, Div. of Life and Envmtl Scis, 2003–05; Student of Christ Church, 2004–06; Pro-Vice-Chancellor (Res.), 2005–06; Vis. Prof. of Geog., 2006–. Visiting Professor: Macquarie Univ., 1989; UCLA, 1992; Univ. of Vienna, 1998; Nat. Univ. of Singapore, 2002. Mem., Geography Res. Assessment Panel, HEFCE RAE, 1997–2003; Chair, Main Panel H, 2008 RAE, 2004–06. Fellow: Netherlands Inst. Advanced Study, 1993; Swedish Collegium for Advanced Study in Social Scis, 1999. AcSS 2001. Heath Award, 1988, Victoria Medal, 2003, RGS; Medal, Univ. of Helsinki, 1999; Dist. Scholarship Honors, Assoc. of Amer. Geographers, 2007. *Publications:* (with D. N. Parkes) Times, Spaces, Places, 1980; (with D. K. Forbes) The Price of War, 1986; Spatial Formations, 1996; (with A. Leyshon) Money/Space, 1997; (jtly) Shopping, Place and Identity, 1998; (with A. Amin) Cities, 2002; Knowing Capitalism, 2005; Non-Representational Theory, 2007; (with P. Glennie) The Measured Heart, 2008; numerous ed volumes; contrib. chapters in ed vols, and papers in learned jls. *Recreations:* reading, writing. *Address:* University of Warwick, Kirby Corner Road, Coventry CV4 8UW.

THROCKMORTON, Clare McLaren, (Mrs Andrew McLaren); *see* Tritton, E. C.

THRUSH, Prof. Brian Arthur, FRS 1976; Professor of Physical Chemistry, University of Cambridge, 1978–95, now Emeritus; Fellow, Emmanuel College, Cambridge, since 1960; *b* Hampstead Garden Suburb, 23 July 1928; *s* of late Arthur Albert Thrush and late Dorothy Charlotte Thrush (*née* Money); *m* 1958, Rosemary Catherine Terry, *d* of late George and Gertrude Terry, Ottawa; one *s* one *d. Educ:* Haberdashers' Aske's Sch.; Emmanuel Coll., Cambridge (Schol. 1946–50). BA 1949, MA, PhD 1953, ScD 1965. University of Cambridge: Demonstrator in Physical Chemistry, 1953; Asst Dir of Research, 1959; Lectr in Physical Chemistry, 1964, Reader, 1969; Hd of Dept of Physical Chemistry, 1986–88; Head of Dept of Chemistry, 1988–93; Tutor, 1963–67, Dir of Studies in Chemistry, 1963–78, Vice-Master, 1986–90 and Acting Master, 1986–87, Emmanuel Coll. Consultant Physicist, US Nat. Bureau of Standards, Washington, 1957–58; Sen. Vis. Scientist, Nat. Res. Council, Ottawa, 1961, 1971, 1980. Tilden Lectr, Chem. Soc., 1965; Vis. Prof., Chinese Acad. of Science, 1980–; Member: Faraday Council, Chem. Soc., 1976–79; US Nat. Acad. of Scis Panel on Atmospheric Chemistry, 1975–80; Lawes Agric. Trust Cttee, 1979–89; NERC, 1985–90; Council, Royal Soc., 1989–91; NATO Panel on Global Change, 1989–92. Pres., Chemistry Sect., BAAS, 1986. Mem., Academia Europaea, 1990 (Mem., Council, 1992–98). M. Polanyi Medal, RSC, 1980; Rank Prize for Opto-Electronics, 1992. *Publications:* papers on gas kinetics and spectroscopy in Proc. Royal Soc., Trans Faraday Soc., etc. *Recreations:* wine, gardening. *Address:* Brook Cottage, Pemberton Terrace, Cambridge CB2 1JA. *T:* (01223) 357637.

THUBRON, Colin Gerald Dryden, CBE 2007; travel writer and novelist, since 1966; *b* 14 June 1939; *s* of late Brig. Gerald Ernest Thubron, DSO, OBE, and of Evelyn (*née* Dryden). *Educ:* Eton Coll. Editorial staff, Hutchinson & Co., 1959–62; freelance television film maker, Turkey, Japan, Morocco, 1962–64; Editorial staff, Macmillan Co., New York, 1964–65. FRSL 1969 (Vice-Pres., 2003–). Hon. DLitt Warwick, 2002. Mungo Park Medal, RSGS, 2000; Lawrence of Arabia Meml Medal, RSAA, 2001. *Publications:* non-fiction: Mirror to Damascus, 1967; The Hills of Adonis, 1968, 2nd edn 1987; Jerusalem, 1969; Journey into Cyprus, 1975; The Royal Opera House, 1982; Among the Russians, 1983; Behind the Wall, 1987 (Thomas Cook Award, Hawthorden Prize, 1988); The Lost Heart of Asia, 1994; In Siberia, 1999; Shadow of the Silk Road, 2006; *novels:* The God in the Mountain, 1977; Emperor, 1978; A Cruel Madness, 1984 (Silver Pen Award, 1985); Falling, 1989; Turning Back the Sun, 1991; Distance, 1996; To The Last City, 2002; contribs The Times, TLS, Sunday Telegraph. *Address:* 28 Upper Addison Gardens, W14 8AJ. *T:* (020) 7602 2522.

THURLEY, Dr Simon John, FSA; Chief Executive, English Heritage, since 2002; *b* 29 Aug. 1962; *s* of late Thomas Manley Thurley and of Rachel Thurley (*née* House); *m* 1998, Katharine (*née* Goodison) (marr. diss. 2007); *m* 2008, Anna (*née* Keay). *Educ:* Kimbolton Sch., Cambs; Bedford Coll., London (BA Hist.; Hon. Fellow, RHBNC, 2003); Courtauld Inst., London (MA, PhD Art Hist.). Inspector of Ancient Monuments, Crown Buildings and Monuments Gp, English Heritage, 1988–90; Curator, Historic Royal Palaces, 1990–97; Dir, Mus. of London, 1997–2002. Vis. Prof. of Medieval London History, Royal Holloway, Univ. of London, 2000–. Member: Cttee, Soc. for Court Studies, 1996–(Chm., 2005–); Council, St Paul's Cathedral, 2001–. President: City of London Archaeol Soc., 1997–2002; Huntingdonshire Local Hist. Soc., 2004–; London and Middlesex Archæol Soc., 2006–08; Vice-Pres., NADFAS, 2000. Trustee, Dickens House Museum, 1998–2002; Patron, London Parks and Gardens Trust, 2001. FSA 2004; MIFA 1998; FRHistS 2006. Hon. RIBA 2006. Writer and Presenter, TV series: The Lost Buildings of Britain, 2004; Buildings that Shaped Britain, 2006. *Publications:* (jtly) Henry VIII: images of a Tudor King, 1989; The Royal Palaces of Tudor England, 1993; Whitehall Palace, 1999; Hampton Court Palace: a social and architectural history, 2003; The Lost Buildings of Britain, 2004; Whitehall Palace, 2008; Somerset House, 2009; contribs to books and jls. *Recreation:* ruins. *Address:* English Heritage, 1 Waterhouse Square, 138–142 Holborn, EC1N 2ST. *T:* (020) 7973 3222; *e-mail:* chief.executive@english-heritage.org.uk.

THURLOW, 8th Baron *cr* 1792; **Francis Edward Hovell-Thurlow-Cumming-Bruce,** KCMG 1961 (CMG 1957); Governor and C-in-C of the Bahamas, 1968–72; *b* 9 March 1912; *s* of 6th Baron Thurlow and Grace Catherine, *d* of Rev. Henry Trotter; *S* brother, 1971; *m* 1949, Yvonne Diana Aubyn Wilson, CStJ 1969 (*d* 1990); one *s* two *d* (and one *s* decd). *Educ:* Shrewsbury Sch.; Trinity Coll., Cambridge. Asst Principal, Dept of Agriculture for Scotland, 1935; transferred to Dominions Office, 1937; Asst Private Sec. to Sec. of State, 1939; Asst Sec., Office of UK High Comr in NZ, 1939; Asst Sec., Office of UK High Comr in Canada, 1944; Secretariat, Meeting of Commonwealth Prime Ministers in London, 1946; served with UK Delegn at Paris Peace Conf., 1946, and at UN Gen. Assemblies, 1946 and 1948; Principal Private Sec. to Sec. of State, 1946; Asst Sec., CRO, 1948; Head of Political Div., Office of UK High Comr in New Delhi, 1949; Establishment Officer, CRO, 1952; Head of Commodities Dept, CRO, 1954; Adviser on External Affairs to Governor of Gold Coast, 1955; Deputy High Comr for the UK in Ghana, 1957; Asst Under-Sec. of State, CRO, April 1958; Deputy High Comr for the UK in Canada, 1958; High Comr for UK: in New Zealand, 1959–63; in Nigeria, 1964–67; Dep. Under-Sec. of State, FCO, 1964. KStJ 1969. *Heir: s* Hon. Roualeyn Robert Hovell-Thurlow-Cumming-Bruce [*b* 13 April 1952; *m* 1980, Bridget Anne, *o d* of H. B. Ismay Cheape, Fossoway Lodge, Kinross; two *s* two *d*.] *Address:* 102 Leith Mansions, Grantully Road, W9 1LJ. *T:* (020) 7289 9664. *Club:* Travellers.

THURLOW, Alan John, FRCO; Organist and Master of the Choristers, Chichester Cathedral, 1980–2008; *b* 18 May 1947; *s* of John Edward Thurlow and Mary Bruce Thurlow (*née* Bennallack); *m* 1974, Christina Mary Perren. *Educ:* Bancroft's Sch., Woodford; Sheffield Univ. (BA 1st cl. Hons 1968); Emmanuel Coll., Cambridge. FRCO 1972. Sub Organist, Durham Cathedral, 1973–80. Chairman: Friends of Cathedral Music, 1990–2002; Organs Adv. Cttee, Council for the Care of Churches, 1997–2006; Pres., Cathedral Organists Assoc., 1995–96. Hon. FRSCM 2007. DMus Lambeth, 2005. *Recreations:* walking, cycling. *Address:* 8 Old Bakery Gardens, Chichester, W Sussex PO19 8AJ. *T:* (01243) 533092. *Club:* Chichester City (Pres., 2004–).

THURSBY, Peter Lionel, FRBS; sculptor; President, Royal West of England Academy, 1995–2000; *b* 23 Dec. 1930; *s* of Lionel Albert Thursby and Florence Bessie Thursby (*née* Macey); *m* 1956, Maureen Suzanne Aspden. *Educ:* Bishop Wordsworth Sch., Salisbury; Mons Officer Cadet Sch.; St Paul's Coll., Cheltenham; West of England Coll. of Art, Bristol; Exeter Coll. of Art (NDD Sculpture); Bristol Univ. (ATD). FRBS 1983 (ARBS 1973); RWA 1971. Nat. Service, 1949–51, RARO, 1951–57. Head of Art, Heles Grammar Sch., Exeter, 1960–71; Head of Sch. of Art and Design, Exeter Coll., 1971–89. Invited Sculptor, Chichester Fest., 1994–96. *Solo exhibitions* include: Arnolfini, Bristol, 1963; AIA Gall., London, 1963; Marjorie Parr Gall., London, 1964, 1965, 1971; Sheviock Gall., Cornwall, 1969; Royal Albert Mus. and Art Gall., Exeter, 1969, Millennium Retrospective, 2000; Univ. of Exeter, 1974; Alwin Gall., London, 1976; RWA, 1981; Bruton Street Gall., London 1994, 1995, 1998; (retrospective) Salisbury Mus., 2003;

Guernsey Mus. and Art Gall., 2005; Dorset County Mus., 2008; *public commissions:* Plymstock School, 1965; Raeburn House, Harrow, 1966; Randolph House, Croydon, 1966; Guildhall Square, Exeter, 1977 (to commemorate Silver Jubilee of HM Queen Elizabeth II); Bronze Fountain, Dallas, 1980; Bronze fountain and relief, Mazda head office, 1982; External bronze relief, City of Westminster, 1986 (Silver Medal, RBS); Bronze fountain, McDonald's Restaurants head office, 1988; Uxbridge, Coca-Cola Schweppes Beverages Ltd, 1988; Bath, NY State, 1996. Hon. DArt UWE, 1995. *Publication:* (illustrated) Roger Iredale, Turning Bronzes: an anthology of poetry, 1974. *Recreations:* genealogy, music, cinema, ornithology, swimming. *Address:* Oakley House, 28 Oakley Close, Pinhoe, Exeter, Devon EX1 3SB. *T:* and *Fax:* (01392) 467931; *e-mail:* mo.thursby@btinternet.com. *Clubs:* Chelsea Arts; Exeter Golf and Country.

THURSO, 3rd Viscount *cr* 1952, of Ulbster; **John Archibald Sinclair;** Bt 1786; MP (Lib Dem) Caithness, Sutherland and Easter Ross, since 2001; *b* 10 Sept. 1953; *er s* of 2nd Viscount Thurso and of Margaret Beaumont Sinclair (*née* Robertson); *S* father, 1995; *m* 1976, Marion Ticknor (*née* Sage); two *s* one *d. Educ:* Summerfields; Eton Coll. FIH (FHCIMA 1991); Master Innholder 1991. Savoy Hotel plc: Trainee, 1972; Gen. Manager and Dir, Lancaster Hotel, Paris, 1981–85; Gen. Manager and Dir, Cliveden, 1985–92; Chief Executive Officer: Granfel Hldgs, 1992–95; Champneys Gp Ltd, 1995–2001; Chm., Scrabster Harbour, 1997–2001; non-executive Director: Savoy Hotel plc, 1993–98; Lochdhu Hotels Ltd, 1975– (Chm., 1995–); Sinclair Family Trust Ltd, 1976– (Chm., 1995–); Thurso Fisheries Ltd, 1979– (Chm., 1995–); Ulbster Hldgs Ltd, 1994– (Chm., 1994–); Profile Selection and Recruitment Ltd, 1995–2002; Walker Greenbank PLC, 1997–2002 (Chm., 1999–2002); Royal Olympic Cruise Lines Inc. (USA), 1997–99; Mossimanns Ltd, 1998–2002. President: Licensed Victuallers Schs, 1997–98; Acad. of Food and Wine Service, 1998–. Patron: HCIMA, 1998–2003; IMS, 1998–. Lib Dem Spokesman: on Tourism, 1997–99, on Food, 1998–99, H of L; on Scottish matters, 2001–06, on transport, 2003–05, H of C. FInstD 1997. *Recreations:* shooting, fishing, food and wine. *Heir: s* Hon. James Alexander Robin Sinclair, *b* 14 Jan. 1984. *Address:* Thurso East Mains, Thurso, Caithness KW14 8HW. *Clubs:* Brooks's; New (Edinburgh).

THUYSBAERT, Jonkheer Prosper; Ambassador of Belgium to the Court of St James's, 1994–97; *b* 7 Dec. 1931; *s* of Prosper Thuysbaert and Marguerite Levie; *m* 1957, Marie-Claire Vuylsteke; two *s. Educ:* Leuven Univ. (grad. in Law and Notarial Scis; BA Thomistic Philosophy). Entered Belgian Diplomatic Service, 1957: Attaché, Luxembourg, 1960–61; Economic Attaché, Paris, 1961–62; 1st Sec., Tel Aviv, 1963–64; Advr to Minister for Foreign Trade, 1964–65; Counsellor, Perm. Repn to EC, 1965–70; European Adviser to: Minister for Foreign Affairs, 1970–77; Prime Minister, 1977–80; Dir, European Orgns, Ministry for Foreign Affairs, 1980–81; Chef de Cabinet to Minister for External Relns, 1981–83; Political Dir, Ministry for Foreign Affairs, 1983–85; Ambassador: Perm. Repn to UN, Geneva, 1985–87; Perm. Repn to NATO, Brussels, 1987–93; EC Consultant for European Stability Pact, 1993–94. Guest Prof., Univ. of Leuven, Belgium, 1992–. Pres., Euro-Atlantic Assoc. of Belgium, 2002. Officer 1978, Comdr 1987, Order of Leopold (Belgium); Comdr 1987, Grand Officer, 1995, Order of Crown (Belgium). Grand Officer, Order of Leopold II (Belgium), 1991. *Publications:* La Diplomatie Multilatérale, 1991; Multilateraal Kunst en Vliegwerk, 1991; Het Belgisch Buitenlandse Beleid, 1995. *Recreations:* art, tennis, ski-ing, swimming, golf. *Address:* Clos d'Orleans 12, 1150 Brussels, Belgium. *Club:* Anglo-Belgian.

THWAITE, Ann Barbara, DLitt; FRSL; writer; *b* London, 4 Oct. 1932; *d* of A. J. Harrop, LittD, PhD and H. M. Valentine of New Zealand; *m* 1955, Anthony Simon Thwaite, *qv*; four *d. Educ:* Marsden School, Wellington, NZ; Queen Elizabeth's Girls' Grammar Sch., Barnet; St Hilda's Coll., Oxford (MA 1959). DLitt Oxford 1998. FRSL 1987. Vis. Prof., Tokyo Women's Univ., 1985–86; Helen Stubbs Meml Lectr, Toronto Public Library, 1990; Ezra Jack Keats Meml Lectr, Univ. of Southern Mississippi, 1992. Churchill Travelling Fellowship, 1993; Gladys Krieble Delmas Fellowship, British Library, 1998–99. Hon. Fellow, Univ. of Surrey Roehampton (Nat. Centre for Res. in Children's Literature), 2001. Regular reviewer of children's books: TLS, 1963–85; Guardian; TES. Vice-Pres., Tennyson Soc., 1997–. Governor: St Mary's Middle Sch., Long Stratton, Norfolk, 1990–2002; Hapton VC Primary Sch., Norfolk, 1995–2006. Hon. DLitt UEA, 2007. *Publications:* Waiting for the Party: the life of Frances Hodgson Burnett, 1974, reissued as Frances Hodgson Burnett: beyond the secret garden, 2007; (ed) My Oxford, 1977; Edmund Gosse: a literary landscape, 1984 (Duff Cooper Meml Prize, 1985); A. A. Milne: his life, 1990 (Whitbread Biography Award); (ed) Portraits from Life: essays by Edmund Gosse, 1991; The Brilliant Career of Winnie-the-Pooh, 1992; Emily Tennyson: the poet's wife, 1996; Glimpses of the Wonderful: the life of Philip Henry Gosse, 2002; *children's books include:* The Camelthorn Papers, 1969; Tracks, 1978; (ed) Allsorts 1–7, 1968–75; (ed) Allsorts of Poems, 1978; The Ashton Affair, 1995; The Horse at Hilly Fields, 1996. *Recreations:* other people's lives, messing about on the river. *Address:* The Mill House, Low Tharston, Norfolk NR15 2YN. *T:* (01508) 489569. *Clubs:* Society of Authors, Royal Over-Seas League.

THWAITE, Anthony Simon, OBE 1990; FRSL; FSA; poet; Editorial Consultant, André Deutsch Ltd, 1992–95 (Director, 1986–92); *b* 23 June 1930; *s* of late Hartley Thwaite, JP, FSA, and Alice Evelyn Mallinson; *m* 1955, Ann Barbara Harrop (*see* A. B. Thwaite); four *d. Educ:* Kingswood Sch.; Christ Church, Oxford (MA). Vis. Lectr in English, Tokyo Univ., 1955–57; Producer, BBC, 1957–62; Literary Editor, The Listener, 1962–65; Asst Prof. of English, Univ. of Libya, 1965–67; Literary Editor, New Statesman, 1968–72; co-editor, Encounter, 1973–85. Henfield Writing Fellow, Univ. of East Anglia, 1972; Vis. Prof., Kuwait Univ., 1974; Japan Foundn Fellow, Tokyo Univ., 1985–86; Poet-in-Residence, Vanderbilt Univ., 1992. Member: Literature Adv. Cttee (formerly English Teaching Adv. Cttee), British Council, 1978–2002; Cttee, Royal Literary Fund, 1993–; Council, RSL, 2003–08. Chm. of Judges, Booker Prize, 1986. Pres., Philip Larkin Soc., 1995–. FRSL 1978; FSA 2000. Hon. Lay Canon, Norwich Cathedral, 2005–. Hon. Fellow, Westminster Coll., Oxford, 1990. Hon. DLitt: Hull, 1989; UEA 2007. Cholmondeley Poetry Award, 1983. *Publications: poetry:* Home Truths, 1957; The Owl in the Tree, 1963; The Stones of Emptiness, 1967 (Richard Hillary Memorial Prize, 1968); Penguin Modern Poets 18, 1970; Inscriptions, 1973; New Confessions, 1974; A Portion for Foxes, 1977; Victorian Voices, 1980; Poems 1953–1983, 1984; Letter from Tokyo, 1987; Poems 1953–1988, 1989; The Dust of the World, 1994; Selected Poems 1956–1996, 1997; A Different Country, 2000; A Move in the Weather, 2003; Collected Poems, 2007; *criticism:* Contemporary English Poetry, 1959; Poetry Today, 1973, rev. and expanded, 1985, 1996; Twentieth Century English Poetry, 1978; Six Centuries of Verse, 1984 (companion to Thames TV/Channel 4 series); Anthony Thwaite in Conversation with Peter Dale and Ian Hamilton, 1999; *travel:* (with Roloff Beny) Japan, 1968; The Deserts of Hesperides, 1969; (with Roloff Beny and Peter Porter) In Italy, 1974; (with Roloff Beny) Odyssey: Mirror of the Mediterranean, 1981; *editor:* (with Geoffrey Bownas) Penguin Book of Japanese Verse, 1964, rev. and expanded, 1998; (with Peter Porter) The English Poets, 1974; (with Fleur Adcock) New Poetry 4, 1978; Larkin at Sixty, 1982; (with John Mole) Poetry 1945 to 1980, 1983; Collected Poems of Philip Larkin, 1988, rev. 2003; Selected Letters of Philip Larkin, 1992; Further Requirements: Philip Larkin, 2001; The Ruins of Time, 2006; Poet-to-Poet: John Skelton, 2008; *for children:* Beyond the Inhabited World, 1976. *Recreations:* archaeology, antiquarian beachcombing, pottery. *Address:* The Mill House, Low Tharston, Norfolk NR15 2YN. *T:* (01508) 489569.

THWAITES, Prof. Sir Bryan, Kt 1986; MA, PhD; CMath, FIMA; Hon. Professor, Southampton University, since 1983; *b* London, 6 Dec. 1923; *e s* of late Ernest James and Dorothy Marguerite Thwaites; *m* 1948, Katharine Mary (*d* 1991), 4th *c* of late H. R. Harries and late Mrs L. Harries, Longhope, Glos; four *s* two *d*. *Educ:* Dulwich College (Fellow, 2006); Winchester College; Clare College, Cambridge (Wrangler, 1944). Scientific Officer, National Physical Laboratory, 1944–47; Lecturer, Imperial College, London, 1947–51; Assistant Master, Winchester College, 1951–59; Professor of Theoretical Mechanics, Southampton Univ., 1959–66; Principal, Westfield Coll., London, 1966–83 (Hon. Fellow, 1983; Hon. Fellow, QMW, 1990). Gresham Prof. in Geometry, City Univ., 1969–72. Co-founder and Co-Chm., Education 2000, 1982–86. Hon. Sec. and Treas., Dulwich College Mission, 1946–57; inventor of the Thwaites Flap, 1947. Chm. and Mem. ARC Cttees, 1948–69. Mem. Exec. Cttee, Internat. Commn on Math. Instruction, 1967–70. Special Lecturer, Imperial College, 1951–58. Chm., Southampton Mathematical Conf., 1961. Founding Director of the School Mathematics Project, 1961–75, Chm. of Trustees, 1966–83, Life Pres., 1984; Chm. of Internat. Mathematical Olympiad, first in UK, 1979; Chm. Adv. Council, ICL/CES, 1968–84. Member: Approved Sch. Cttee, Hampshire CC, 1954–58, 1961–66; US/UK (Fulbright) Commn, 1966–76; Davies Cttee on CSSB, 1969–70; Council, Kennedy Inst. of Rheumatology, 1969–71; Ct of London Univ., 1975–81; Council, Middlesex Hosp. Med. Sch., 1975–83; Court, Southampton Univ., 1981–94; Council, European Atlantic Gp, 2004–. Chm., Collegiate Council, London Univ., 1973–76; Chm., Delegacy, Goldsmiths' Coll., 1975–80. Mem. Acad. Advisory Committee: Univ. of Bath, 1964–71; Open Univ., 1969–75. Chairman of: Council of C of E Colleges of Education, 1969–71; Church of England Higher Educn Cttee, 1974–76; Northwick Park Hosp. Management Cttee, 1970–74; Brent and Harrow AHA, 1973–82; Wessex RHA, 1982–88; King's Fund Enquiry into Sen. Management Trng in NHS, 1975–76; Nat. Staff Cttee for Admin. and Clerical Staff, NHS, 1983–86; Enquiry into Radiotherapy Incident, Exeter Hosp., 1988. Founding Chm., British False Memory Soc., 1993. Chairman: Govs, Heythrop Coll., 1978–82; Friends of Winchester Coll., 1989–91; Govs, More House, 1993–96; Trustee: Westfield Coll. Develt Trust, 1979–83; Southampton Med. Sch. Trust, 1982–88; Richmond Coll., 1987–93 (Academic Gov., 1992–2000); City Tech. Colls Trust, 1987–97; Forbes Trust, 1987–; Patron, Winchester Detached Youth Project, 1990–96. Mercier Lectr, Whitelands Coll., 1973; Foundn Lectr, Inst. of Health Policy Studies, Southampton Univ., 1987; 25th Anniv. Lectr, Nuffield Inst., Leeds Univ., 1988. Shadow Vice-Chancellor, Independent Univ., July–Nov. 1971. Hon. Life Mem., Math. Assoc., 1962. JP, Winchester City Bench, 1963–66. A Vice-Pres., Friends of GPDST, 1975–95. Mem. Council, 1964–94, Pres., 1966–67, Hon. Fellow, 2004, Institute of Mathematics and its Applications. Sponsor, Family and Youth Concern (formerly The Responsible Society), 1979–98 (Trustee, 1992–98). Founding Chm., 2001–04, Life Pres., 2004, Soc. of Our Lady at Winton. *Publications:* (ed) Incompressible Aerodynamics, 1960; (ed) On Teaching Mathematics, 1961; The SMP: the first ten years, 1973; (ed) Hypotheses for Education in AD 2000, 1983; (ed) A Contemporary Catholic Commentary, 1998; numerous contributions to Proc. Royal Soc., Reports and Memoranda of Aeronautical Research Council, Quart. Jl of Applied Mech., Jl of Royal Aeronautical Soc., etc. *Recreations:* music, sailing, writing letters to The Times. *Address:* The Byre, Salthill Park, Fishbourne, W Sussex PO19 3PS. *T:* and *Fax:* (01243) 790142; *e-mail:* bryan.thwaites@btopenworld.com. *Clubs:* Athenæum, Royal Over-Seas League.

THWAITES, Jacqueline Ann; *see* Duncan, J. A.

THWAITES, Ronald; QC 1987; *b* 21 Jan. 1946; *e s* of Stanley Thwaites and Aviva Thwaites; *m* 1972, Judith Myers; three *s* one *d*. *Educ:* Richard Hind Secondary Tech. Sch.; Grangefield Grammar Sch., Stockton-on-Tees; Kingston Coll. of Technol. (subseq. Polytechnic, now Univ.); LLB London (external) 1968. Called to the Bar, Gray's Inn, 1970. *Recreations:* swimming, lighting bonfires. *Address:* (chambers) Ely Place Chambers, 30 Ely Place, EC1N 6TD. *T:* (020) 7400 9600.

THWAITES, Roy; Deputy Director, South Yorkshire Branch, British Red Cross Society, 1990–96; *b* 13 Aug. 1931; *s* of Walter and Emily Alice Thwaites; *m* 1st, 1954, Margaret Anne (*née* Noble) (marr. diss.); one *s*; 2nd, 1991, Mary (*née* Appleby). *Educ:* Southey Green Secondary Sch.; Sheffield Central Technical Sch. City Councillor, Sheffield, 1965–74, Chief Whip and Chm. of Transport Cttee, 1969–74; South Yorkshire County Council: Councillor, 1973–86; Chief Whip and Chm. Passenger Transport Authority, 1973–78; Dep. Leader, 1978–79; Leader, and Chm. of Policy Cttee, 1979–86. Dep. Chm. and Dir, SYT Ltd, 1986–93. Member: E Midlands Airport Consultative Gp, 1982–86; Industrial Tribunals, 1987–2001. Vice-Chm., 1979–84, Dep. Chm., 1984–86, AMA; Member: Local Authorities' Conditions of Service Adv. Bd, 1979–86; Yorks and Humberside County Councils Assoc., 1983–86; Vice-Chm., 1982–85, Chm., 1985–86, NJC Local Govt Manual Workers Employers. Mem., Special Employment Measures Adv. Gp, MSC, 1983–86. Dep. Chm., Nat. Mining Mus. Trust (formerly Yorks Mining Mus. Trust), 1984–93 (Dir, 1986–92). Dep. Pres., Northern Racing Coll. (formerly Northern Racing Sch. Trust), 2004– (Dep. Chm., 1986–2004). Hon. Fellow, Sheffield City Poly., 1982. *Recreations:* walking, reading, photography. *Address:* 2 Borough Road, Sheffield S6 2AY.

THYATEIRA AND GREAT BRITAIN, Archbishop of; *see* Theocharous, Archbishop Gregorios.

THYNE, Malcolm Tod, MA; FRSE; Trustee, Cumbria Cerebral Palsy, since 2003; *b* 6 Nov. 1942; *s* of late Andrew Tod and Margaret Melrose Thyne; *m* 1969, Eleanor Christine Scott; two *s*. *Educ:* The Leys Sch., Cambridge; Clare Coll., Cambridge (MA Nat. Scis with Pt II in Chem.; Cert. of Educn). FRSE 1994. Asst Master, Edinburgh Acad., 1965–69; Asst Master, Oundle Sch., 1969–72, Housemaster, 1972–80; Headmaster: St Bees School, 1980–88; Fettes Coll., Edinburgh, 1988–98. Develt Dir, Arkwright Scholarship Trust, 1999–2000. Gov., St Bees Sch., Cumbria, 2000–05; Dir, Edinburgh Acad., 2000–07. Trustee, CLIC, 2000–03. *Publication:* Periodicity, Atomic Structure and Bonding (Revised Nuffield Chemistry), 1976. *Recreations:* hillwalking, organic gardening. *Address:* Howbeck House, Hesket Newmarket, Wigton, Cumbria CA7 8JN. *T:* (01697) 478216.

THYNN, family name of **Marquess of Bath.**

THYNN, Alexander; *see* Bath, Marquess of.

THYNNE, John Corelli James, CB 1990; PhD, DSc; Adviser to the Chairman, Wesley Clover Corporation, since 2006; *b* 27 Nov. 1931; *s* of Corelli James Thynne and Isabel Ann (*née* Griffiths). *Educ:* Milford Haven Grammar Sch.; Nottingham Univ. (BSc, PhD); Edinburgh Univ. (DSc). Res. Chemist, English Electric Co. (Guided Missile Div.), 1956–58; Fellow: Nat. Res. Council, Ottawa, 1958–59; UCLA, 1959–60; Univ. of Leeds, 1960–63; Lectr in Chemistry and Dir of Studies, Univ. of Edinburgh, 1963–70; Principal, DTI, 1970–73; Counsellor (Scientific), British Embassy, Moscow, 1974–78; Asst Sec., IT Div., DoI, 1978–83; Department of Trade and Industry: Under Sec., 1983; Regl Dir, NW Reg., 1983–86; Electronic Applications Div., 1986–87; IT Div., 1987–89; Dir, Information Engrg Directorate, 1989–90. Dir Gen., Electronic Components Industry Fedn, 1991–94. Chm., ComCare Systems Ltd, 1992–94; Deputy Chairman: nCipher Corp. Ltd, 1996–99; Newport Networks Corp. Ltd, 2000–03; Dir, Camrose Consultancy Services, 1991–99; Sen. Advr, InterMatrix Gp, 1991–98; Director: Newbridge Networks Corp., 1992–2000; LTW Ltd, 1993–95; Celtic House Investment Partners Ltd, 1993–2002; Nolton Consultancy Services Ltd, 1995–2002; Spikes Cavell Ltd, 1996–99; UWS Ventures, 1998–2000; Enfis Ltd, 2001–; Wesley Clover Corp. Ltd, 2002–; InUK Ltd, 2005–08. Member: Exec. Cttee, Nat. Electronics Council, 1986–90; NEDO Electronics Industries Sector Gp, 1986–90; Welsh Funding Councils Res. Gp, 1992–94; Radiocommunications Agency Bd, 1994–99. Mem. Council, Salford Univ., 1984–87; Gov., Univ. of Glamorgan (formerly Poly. of Wales), 1991–95. Vice Chm. Trustees, Mus. of Sci. and Industry, 1991–97. Hon. Fellow, Univ. of Wales Swansea, 1998. Hon. DSc Glamorgan, 1996. *Publications:* contribs on physical chemistry to scientific journals. *Recreation:* cricket. *Address:* 1021 Laguna Street, #3, Santa Barbara, CA 93101, USA; *e-mail:* jthynne@wesleyclover.com. *Clubs:* Athenæum, MCC.

TIBBER, His Honour Anthony Harris; a Circuit Judge, 1977–99; *b* 23 June 1926; *s* of Maurice and Priscilla Tibber; *m* 1954, Rhona Ann Salter; three *s*. *Educ:* University College School, London; Magdelen College School, Brackley. Served in Royal Signals, 1945–48; called to the Bar, Gray's Inn, 1950; a Recorder of the Crown Court, 1976. Member: Matrimonial Causes Rule Cttee, 1980–84; Matrimonial Causes Procedure Cttee (Booth Cttee), 1983–85. Arbitrator and mediator, 2002–. *Recreations:* cultivating, idling, pottering. *Address:* 22 Holmwood Gardens, N3 3NS. *T:* (020) 8349 1287.
See also P. H. Tibber.

TIBBER, Peter Harris, DPhil; HM Diplomatic Service; Consul-General, Dusseldorf, and Director General, Trade and Investment, Germany, since 2005; *b* 7 Sept. 1956; *s* of His Honour Anthony Harris Tibber, *qv*; *m* 1983, Eve Levy-Huet, MSc (Oxon); three *s*. *Educ:* Haberdashers' Aske's Sch.; University Coll., Oxford (MA; DPhil 1983). FCO, 1984–86; Paris, 1986–88; First Sec., FCO, 1988–90; Private Sec. to Minister of State, FCO, 1990–92; Ankara, 1993–96; Dep. Hd of Mission, Mexico City, 1996–2000; Trade Partners UK, subsequently UK Trade & Investment: Dir, Africa and ME, 2000–01; Internat. Mgt Directorate, 2001–02; Dir, Internat. Sectors (formerly Business) Gp, 2002–04. *Recreations:* choral singing, piano, tennis, swimming, fiction. *Address:* BCG Dusseldorf, Box 2002, BFPO 105.

TIBBITT, Rear Adm. Ian Peter Gordon, CBE 2007; FRAeS; Director General Safety and Engineering, Defence Equipment and Support, Ministry of Defence, since 2007; *b* 22 Oct. 1954; *s* of Peter Tibbitt and Daphne Tibbitt; *m* 1980, Marion Diane Lyons; two *d*. *Educ:* Arnold Sch.; Sidney Sussex Coll., Cambridge (BA 1976). MIET, CEng 1984; FRAeS 2003. Joined RN as Air Engr Officer, 1973; Commando Helicopter and Sea Harrier Sqdns; acquisition, logistics and change mgt specialist, Merlin Mk 1 Project Manager, 1996–99; on staff of C-in-C Fleet, 2000–02; Dir Logistic Support (Air), 2002–03; Defence Logistics Orgn Restructuring Team Leader, 2003–04; Dir Logistics Rotary Wing, 2004–07. *Recreation:* hockey (Pres., RN Hockey Assoc.; qualified hockey umpire). *Address:* Maple 2 #2219, Ministry of Defence Abbey Wood, Bristol BS34 8JH. *T:* (0117) 913 2616; *e-mail:* Ian.Tibbitt355@mod.uk.

TIBBS, Craigie John, FRICS; Head of Estates and Planning Department, BBC, 1980; *b* 17 Feb. 1935; *s* of Arthur and Gladys Tibbs; *m* 1959, Carol Ann (*née* Linsell); two *d*. *Educ:* King George V School, Southport; Heaton Grammar School, Newcastle upon Tyne; RMA Sandhurst; London Univ. (BSc). Trainee Estates Officer, London Transport, 1959–62; Valuer and Senior Valuer, Luton Corp., 1962–67; Chief Valuer and Surveyor, London Borough of Newham, 1967–71; Development Officer, City of Birmingham, 1971–73; County Estates Officer, Hants County Council, 1973–76; Under Sec. (Dir of Land Economy), Depts of the Environment and Transport, 1976–80. *Recreations:* music, reading, writing, walking, swimming, golf, the Well Game.

TIBBS, (Geoffrey) Michael (Graydon), OBE 1987; Secretary of the Royal College of Physicians, 1968–86 (Secretary of Joint Faculty of Community Medicine, 1971–72, of Joint Committee in Higher Medical Training, 1972–86, and of Faculty of Occupational Medicine, 1978–86); *b* 21 Nov. 1921; *s* of Rev. Geoffrey Wilberforce Tibbs, sometime Chaplain RN and Vicar of Lynchmere, Sussex, and Margaret Florence Tibbs (*née* Skinner); *m* 1951, Anne Rosemary Wortley; two *s*. *Educ:* Berkhamsted Sch.; St Peter's Hall, Oxford. BA Hons Geography, 1948; MA 1952. FInstAM; MCIPD; FRGS. Served RNVR, Ordinary Seaman/Lieut, 1940–46 (despatches), HMS Cottesmore, HMS Sheffield, HM S/M Tantalus, HM S/M Varne. Sudan Political Service, Kordofan Province, 1949–55: seconded to MECAS, 1950; Dist Comr, Dar Messeria District, 1953. Various appointments in personnel, organisation and overseas services depts, Automobile Assoc., 1955–68. Hon. Mem., Soc. of Occupational Medicine, 1983; Hon. FRCP 1986; Hon. FFOM 1986; Hon. FFCM 1987. Freeman, City of London, 1986. *Publications:* (with Anne Tibbs): A Look at Lynchmere, 1990; A Sudan Sunset, 2000; Another Look at Lynchmere, 2004. *Recreations:* producing pantomimes, parish affairs, preserving lowland heath, making bonfires. *Address:* Welkin, Lynchmere Ridge, Haslemere, Surrey GU27 3PP. *T:* (01428) 643120, 642176. *Club:* Naval.

TICEHURST, David Keith; His Honour Judge Ticehurst; a Circuit Judge, since 1998; *b* 1 May 1950; *s* of Frederick John and Barbara Elisabeth Ticehurst; *m* 1972, Gillian Shepherd; two *s* one *d*. *Educ:* Taunton's Grammar Sch., Southampton; Keynsham Grammar Sch., Bristol; Kingston Poly. (BA). Admitted solicitor, 1975; articled clerk, 1971–73, Solicitor, 1975–78, Lawrence & Co., Bristol; Solicitor, Osborne Clarke, Bristol, 1978–98 (Partner, 1980–98); Asst Recorder, 1991–94; Recorder, 1994–98. Founder Mem., Employment Lawyers' Assoc., 1992. Mem., Equal Treatment Adv. Cttee, Judicial Studies Bd, 2002–06. Gov., Sidcot Sch., 2002–07. *Recreations:* cricket, watching Rugby, painting, reading. *Address:* The Law Courts, Small Street, Bristol BS1 1DA. *Clubs:* Winscombe Rugby Football (Vice-Pres.); Gloucestershire County Cricket (Life Mem.), Old Herpesians Cricket (Pres.).

TICKELL, Clare, (Mrs E. Andres); Chief Executive, Action for Children (formerly National Children's Homes, later NCH, the children's charity), since 2004; *b* 25 May 1958; *d* of Patrick and Diana Tickell; *m* 1997, Edward Andres; two *s*. *Educ:* Bristol Univ. (CQSW 1986). Dep. Chief Exec., Centrepoint, 1986–89; Dir, Riverpoint, 1989–92; Chief Executive: Phoenix House, 1992–97; Stonham Housing Assoc., 1997–2004. Non-exec. Dir, Information Commn, 2003–. FRSA. *Recreations:* swimming, art, literature, photography, walking. *Address:* Action for Children, 85 Highbury Park, N5 1UD. *T:* (020) 7704 7058; *e-mail:* clare.tickell@actionforchildren.org.uk, clare.andres@btopenworld.com.

TICKELL, Sir Crispin (Charles Cervantes), GCMG 1989 KCVO 1983 (MVO 1958); HM Diplomatic Service, retired; Warden, Green College, Oxford, 1990–97 (Hon. Fellow, 1997); Director, Policy Foresight Programme, James Martin Institute for Science and Civilisation, University of Oxford, since 2006; *b* 25 Aug. 1930; *s* of late Jerrard Tickell and Renée (*née* Haynes); *m* 1st, 1954, Chloë (marr. diss. 1976), *d* of late Sir James Gunn, RA, PRP; two *s* one *d*; 2nd, 1977, Penelope, *d* of late Dr Vernon Thorne Thorne. *Educ:* Westminster (King's Schol.; Hon. Fellow, 1993); Christ Church, Oxford (Hinchliffe and Hon. Schol.; 1st Cl. Hons Mod. Hist. 1952). Served with Coldstream Guards, 1952–54; entered HM Diplomatic Service, 1954. Served at: Foreign Office, 1954–55; The Hague, 1955–58; Mexico, 1958–61; FO (Planning Staff), 1961–64; Paris, 1964–70; Private Sec. to successive Ministers responsible for British entry into the European Community, 1970–72; FCO, 1972–75; Fellow, Center for Internat. Affairs, Harvard Univ., 1975–76; Chef de Cabinet to Pres. of Commn of European Community, 1977–81; Vis. Fellow, All Souls Coll., Oxford, 1981; Ambassador to Mexico, 1981–83; Dep. Under-Sec. of State, FCO, 1983–84; Perm. Sec., ODA, 1984–87; British Perm. Rep. to UN, 1987–90. Director: IBM (UK), 1990–95 (Mem. IBM Adv. Bd, 1995–2000); BOC Envmtl Foundn, 1990–2003; Govett Mexican Horizons, 1991–96; Govett American Smaller Cos Trust, 1996–98; Govett Enhanced Income Investment Trust, 1999–2004. Member, Environment Committee: Friends Provident, 1995–99; F&C Asset Mgt, 1999–2007. Chairman: Internat. Inst. for Envmt and Develt, 1990–94; Climate Inst. of Washington, 1990–2002, now Chm. Emeritus; Earthwatch (Europe), 1990–97; Adv. Cttee on the Darwin Initiative for the Survival of Species, 1992–99. Dir, Green Coll. Centre for Envmtl Policy & Understanding, Oxford, 1992–2006. Sen. Vis. Fellow, Center for Envmt, Harvard Univ., 2002–03. Advr-at-Large to Pres., Arizona State Univ., 2004–. Trustee: Baring Foundn, 1992–2002; Natural Hist. Mus., 1992–2001; WWF (UK), 1993–99; Royal Botanic Garden, Edinburgh, 1997–2001; Reuters Foundn, 2000–; Foundn for the Future, 2007–. President: Marine Biol. Assoc., 1990–2001; RGS, 1990–93; Nat. Soc. for Clean Air and Envmtl Protection, 1997–99; Gaia Soc., 1998–2001; Tree Aid, 2007–. Convenor, Govt Panel on Sustainable Develt, 1994–2000; Member, Government Task Force: on Urban Regeneration, 1998–99; on Near Earth Objects, 2000. Chancellor, Univ. of Kent, 1996–2006. Mem., Global 500 (UN Roll of Honour for Envmtl Achievement), 1991. Hon. Fellow, St Edmund's Coll., Cambridge, 1995. Hon. FRIBA 2000; Hon. Fellow, Royal Instn, 2002. Mem. (Dr *hc*), Mexican Acad. of Internat. Law, 1983 (Orden Academico del Derecho, de la Cultura y de la Paz, 1989). Hon. LLD: Massachusetts, 1990; Bristol, Birmingham, 1991; Kent, 1996; Nottingham, 2003; Hon. DSc: UEA, 1990; Sussex, 1991; Cranfield, 1992; Loughborough, 1995; Exeter, 1999; Hull, Plymouth, 2001; St Andrews, Southampton, Oxford Brookes, Univ. du Littoral, 2002; Brighton, 2006; Dr *hc*: Central London Poly., Stirling, 1990; Sheffield Hallam, 1996; E London, 1998; Amer. Univ. of Paris, 2003; DUniv Open, 2006. Global Envmtl Leadership Award, Climate Inst., 1996; Patron's Medal, RGS, 2000. Officer, Order of Orange Nassau (Netherlands), 1958; Order of Aztec Eagle with sash (Mexico), 1994; Friendship Award (China), 2004. *Publications:* Climatic Change and World Affairs, 1977, 2nd edn 1986; Mary Anning of Lyme Regis, 1996; *contributed to:* The Evacuees, 1968; Life After Death, 1976; The United Kingdom/The United Nations, 1990; Sustaining Earth, 1990; Sir Francis Galton, 1991; Monitoring the Environment, 1992; Threats Without Enemies, 1993; Science for the Earth, 1995; The Changing World, 1996; Managing the Earth, 2002; Remaking the Landscape, 2002; Johannesburg Summit, 2002; A Parliament of Sciences, 2003; Roy Jenkins: a retrospective, 2004; Environmental Stewardship, 2005; China and Britain, 2005. *Recreations:* climatology; palæohistory; art, especially pre-Columbian and African; mountains. *Address:* Ablington Old Barn, Ablington, Cirencester, Glos GL7 5NU. *Clubs:* Brooks's, Garrick.

TICKELL, Kenneth Hugh, FRCO; Owner and Director, Kenneth Tickell & Co. Ltd, Organ Designers and Builders, since 1982; *b* 25 Aug. 1956; *s* of Gordon Hugh Tickell and Barbara Tickell (*née* Holmes); *m* 1977, Philippa Louise James; one *d*. *Educ:* Coventry Sch. of Music; Univ. of Hull (Organ Schol.; BA Hons Music 1978). FRCO 1977. Organbuilder, Grant Degens & Bradbeer Ltd, 1978–82. Major commissions include new organs designed and built for: Douai Abbey, 1993; St Barnabas, Dulwich, 1997; Nesbyen, Norway, 1998; Eton Coll., Lower Chapel, 2000; Cheltenham Ladies' Coll., 2006; Worcester Cathedral, 2008; Lincoln's Inn Chapel, 2009; chamber organs for: St Paul's Cathedral, Westminster Abbey, and cathedrals of Blackburn, Exeter, Hereford, Liverpool Metropolitan, Peterborough, Portsmouth, St David's, Truro and Worcester. Organist and Choirmaster, St Mary the Virgin, Northampton, 1980–94. Pres., Inst. of British Organbuilding, 1996–2001. *Publications:* various technical contribs to Organbuilder, Organbuilding, ISO News (Jl of Internat. Soc. of Organbuilders). *Recreations:* photography, gardening. *Address:* (office) 16 Rothersthorpe Crescent, Northampton NN4 8JD. *T:* (01604) 768188, *Fax:* (01604) 706882; *e-mail:* kht@tickell-organs.co.uk.

TICKELL, Maj.-Gen. Marston Eustace, CBE 1973 (MBE 1955); MC 1945; CEng, FICE; Commandant Royal Military College of Science, 1975–78, retired; *b* 18 Nov. 1923; *er s* of late Maj.-Gen. Sir Eustace Tickell, KBE, CB, MC; *m* 1961, Pamela Vere, *d* of Vice-Adm. A. D. Read, CB; no *c*. *Educ:* Wellington Coll.; Peterhouse, Cambridge (MA). Commnd in RE, 1944; NW Europe Campaign and Middle East, 1944–45; psc 1954; Mil. Ops, MoD, 1955–57; served in Libya, Cyprus and Jordan, 1958–59; US Armed Forces Staff Coll. and Instructor RMCS and Staff Coll., 1959–62; Defence Planning Staff, MoD, 1962–64; CRE 4th Div., 1964–66; comd 12 Engr Bde, 1967–69; Indian Nat. Defence Coll., 1970; COS Northern Ireland, 1971–72; E-in-C, MoD, 1972–75. Col Comdt, RE, 1978–83. Hon. Col, Engr and Transport Staff Corps, 1983–88. Lord Chancellor's Panel of Independent Inspectors, 1979–93. Pres., Instn of Royal Engrs, 1979–82. FICE 1974. *Recreation:* sailing. *Address:* The Old Vicarage, Branscombe, Seaton, Devon EX12 3DW. *Clubs:* Army and Navy; Royal Ocean Racing.

TICKLE, Prof. Cheryll Anne, CBE 2005; PhD; FRS 1998; FRSE; Royal Society Foulerton Research Professor, University of Bath, since 2007 (University of Dundee, 2001–07); *b* 18 Jan. 1945; *d* of Lewis Sidney Tickle and Gwendoline Muriel Tickle; *m* 1979, John Gray. *Educ:* Girton Coll., Cambridge (MA); Glasgow Univ. (PhD 1970). NATO Fellowship, Yale Univ., 1970–72; Middlesex Hospital Medical School, subseq. University College London Medical School: Research Fellow, Lectr, Sen. Lectr, 1972–87; Reader, 1987–91; Prof. of Developmental Biology, 1991–98; Prof. of Developmental Biology, Univ. of Dundee, 1998–2001. Mem. Council, BBSRC, 2001–07. FRSE 2000. *Address:* Department of Biology and Biochemistry, University of Bath, Bath BA2 7AY.

TIDMARSH, Christopher Ralph Francis, QC 2002; *b* 11 Dec. 1961; *s* of Peter Francis Charles Tidmarsh and Mary Elizabeth Tidmarsh; *m* 1992, Lorna Clare Johnson; three *s* one *d*. *Educ:* Merton Coll., Oxford (BA Hons Physics); Poly. of Central London (Dip. Law). Called to the Bar, Lincoln's Inn, 1985; Jun. Counsel to Inland Revenue, 1993. *Publications:* contrib. to various jls. *Recreations:* family, garden, surfing. *Address:* 5 Stone Buildings, Lincoln's Inn, WC2A 3XT. *T:* (020) 7242 6201.

TIDMARSH, Prof. David H., PhD; CEng, FIMechE; Vice-Chancellor, Birmingham City University (formerly University of Central England), since 2007. *Educ:* Lanchester Poly. (BSc, PhD). Joined Chrysler as grad. engr; British Leyland Technology; Head of Mech. Engrg, 1988, then Dir, Sch. of Engrg, Sheffield City Poly.; Dean of Engrg, 1993, Pro-Vice-Chancellor, 1998, Univ. of Central England; Vice-Chancellor, Anglia Poly. Univ., subseq. Anglia Ruskin Univ., 2004–07. FCMI. *Address:* Birmingham City University, Perry Barr, Birmingham B42 2SU.

TIDMARSH, Sir James (Napier), KCVO 2008; MBE 1989; Pro Chancellor, University of Bristol, since 2007; Lord-Lieutenant, County and City of Bristol, 1996–2007; *b* 15 Sept. 1932; *yr s* of late Edward and Madeline Tidmarsh; *m* 1967, Virginia, *y d* of late Robin Warren; two *s*. *Educ:* Taunton Sch. National Service: 1st Bn Duke of Cornwall's LI, 1952–54; TA 4/5 Bn Somerset LI, 1955–60. Factory manager, Dir, and Man. Dir, footwear industry, UK and Australasia, 1955–72; Man. Dir, Dycem Ltd, 1972–96; Founder Dir, GWR Radio plc, 1985–89. Director: Bristol Chamber of Commerce and Initiative, 1992–; Learning Partnership West (formerly Western Educn and Trng Partnership), 1995–99. Vice-Chm., Nat. Assoc. Prison Visitors, 1966–69. Patron and Pres. of several regl and local charities and socs. Mem. Council, Bristol Univ., 1994–2000. Governor, Colston's Collegiate Sch., 1986–94. Hon. Col, RM Reserve, Bristol, 1998–2005. Mem., Soc. of Merchant Venturers, 1979– (Master, 1994–95). JP Bristol, 1977; High Sheriff, Avon, 1995–96. FRSA 2000. Hon. LLD: Bristol, 2002; UWE, 2003. KStJ 1997. *Address:* 8 Prince's Buildings, Clifton, Bristol BS8 4LB. *T:* (0117) 973 0462. *Clubs:* Army and Navy, Royal Commonwealth Society, Saintsbury; Clifton (Bristol).

TIDY, Morley David; Assistant Under-Secretary of State (Personnel) (Air), Ministry of Defence, 1990–92; *b* 23 April 1933; *s* of James Morley and Winnie Tidy; *m* 1957, Wendy Ann Bennett; one *s* two *d*. *Educ:* Hove County Grammar School; Magdalene College, Cambridge (MA). National Service, RAF, 1951–53. Dept of Employment, 1956–57; HM Inspector of Taxes, Inland Revenue, 1957–66; MoD, 1966; Manchester Business School, 1967; First Sec. (Defence), UK Delegn to NATO, 1969–72; MoD, 1973; RCDS, 1977; Chief Officer, SBAA, Cyprus, 1980–83; Asst Under-Sec., Air Staff, MoD, 1984; Asst Under-Sec. (Ordnance), MoD, 1985; Asst Under-Sec., Defence Export Services, Administration, MoD, 1988. *Recreations:* cricket, golf, jigsaws.

TIDY, William Edward, (Bill), MBE 2001; freelance cartoonist, since 1958; writer, playwright, television and radio presenter; *b* 9 Oct. 1933; *s* of William Edward Tidy and Catherine Price; *m* 1960, Rosa Colotti; one *s* one *d* (and one *s* decd). *Educ:* Anfield Road Jun. Sch., Liverpool; St Margaret's Sen. Sch., Anfield, Liverpool. Shipping office boy, R. P. Houston, Liverpool, 1950–51. Served RE, 1952–55. Layout artist, Pagan Smith Advertising Agency, 1956–58. Presented for BBC TV: Tidy Up Walsall; Tidy Up Naples; My City; Draw Me; radio broadcasting includes: The News Quiz (also Guest Presenter); Midweek (also Guest Presenter); I'm Sorry I Haven't a Clue; Back to Square One; The Law Game; Trivia Test Match; Down Your Way; radio adaptation, The Fosdyke Saga (with John Junkin). Man. Dir, Tidy Pots, 2002–. After dinner speaker for many major cos. Contrib., Gen. Practitioner, 1965–2001. *Publications: (written and illustrated):* Sporting Chance, 1961; O Cleo, 1962; Laugh with Bill Tidy, 1966; Up the Reds, Up the Blues, 1968; Tidy's World, 1969; The Cloggies, 1969; Tidy Again, 1970; The Fosdyke Saga (14 vols), 1972–85; The Cloggies Dance Back, 1973; The Great Eric Ackroyd Disaster, 1976; The Cloggies Are Back, 1977; Mine's a Pint, What's Yours (The Kegbuster Story), 1981; Robbie and the Blobbies, 1982; Bill Tidy's Little Rude Book, 1984; A Day at Cringemound School, 1985; Bill Tidy's Book of Classic Cockups, 1985; The World's Worst Golf Club, 1987; The Incredible Bed, 1990; Draw me 387 Baked Beans in 10 seconds, 1991; Save Daring Waring with a pencil, 1993; Is there any news of the Iceberg? (autobiog.), 1995; (with P. Bahn) Disgraceful Archaeology, 1999; Bill Tidy's Book of Quotations, 1999; has also illustrated over seventy other books; contrib. to What's Brewing?, Classic FM Magazine, British Archaeology, Archaeology (USA). *Recreation:* cricket (Lord's Taverners, Pres., 2007–). *Address:* Terry Meadow Farm, Boylestone, Derbyshire DE6 5AB. *T:* (01335) 330858; *e-mail:* bill@billtidy.com. *Clubs:* Cartoonist of Great Britain; Nottinghamshire County Cricket.

TIECH, Andrew C.; *see* Campbell-Tiech.

TIERNEY, James Kevin; Sheriff of Grampian, Highland and Islands at Aberdeen; *b* 5 Oct. 1947; *s* of Edward Bird Tierney, schoolmaster, and Catherine Scanlan or Tierney; *m* 1971, Susan Mary Hubb; one *s* two *d*. *Educ:* St Aloysius' Coll., Glasgow; Edinburgh Univ. (LLB 1969). Admitted Law Soc. of Scotland, 1971; Partner: Littlejohns, Solicitors, Stirling, 1976–82; Paull & Williamsons, Advocates, Aberdeen, 1982–2000; Temp. Sheriff, 1987–92 and 1998–99; Sheriff of Tayside, Central and Fife at Perth, 2000. *Recreations:* golf, walking, gardening, European history, spectator sports. *Address:* Sheriff Court House, Castle Street, Aberdeen AB10 1WP; Ardbeck, Banchory, Aberdeenshire AB31 4FE; *e-mail:* sheriff.jktierney@scotcourts.gov.uk.

TIERNEY, John; caseworker, SDLP constituency office, Foyle, since 2003; *b* 9 Dec. 1951; *s* of Paddy and Catherine Tierney; *m* 1972, Bernie Harkin; two *s* one *d*. *Educ:* St Joseph's, Derry. Mem. (SDLP), Derry City Council, 1981–2003, 2007–; Mayor of Derry, 1984–85. Member: NI Forum, 1996–98; (SDLP) Foyle, NI Assembly, 1998–2003; SDLP Dep. Whip, 1999–2002, Whip, 2002–03. *Address:* 2nd Floor, 23 Bishop Street, Derry BT48 6PR. *T:* (028) 7136 0700, *Fax:* (028) 7136 0808.

TIERNEY, Sydney; JP; President, 1977–81, and 1983–91, and National Officer, 1979–91, Union of Shop, Distributive and Allied Workers; Chairman, Labour Party, 1986–87 (Vice-Chairman, 1985–86); *b* 16 Sept. 1923; *m* 1985, Margaret Olive (*née* Hannah); two *d*. *Educ:* Secondary Modern Sch., Dearne; Plater Coll., Oxford. Mem., Co-operative Party; an Official and Member, USDAW. Vice-Chm., W Midlands Labour Gp of MPs, 1974–79; Mem., Labour Party NEC, to 1990. MP (Lab) Birmingham, Yardley, Feb. 1974–1979; PPS to Min. of State for Agriculture, 1976–79. JP Leicester, 1966. *Address:* Rocklands, 56 Priory Lane, Kents Bank, Grange Over Sands, Cumbria LA11 7BJ.

TIETJEN, Tina, (Mrs G. R. Robertson); Chairman: Air Transport Users Council, since 2003; The Willow Foundation, since 2008; *b* 10 June 1947; *d* of Arthur Tietjen and Mary Alice (*née* Storey); *m* 1972, Gordon R. Robertson. *Educ:* Coloma Convent Grammar Sch. Jt Man. Dir, Video Arts Gp Ltd; Dir, MediaKey Gp, 1996–98; Chm., WRVS, 1999–2005. Non-executive Director: Phoenix Business Consultants; Michael Davey Financial Management. Mem. Bd, BITC, 1992–97. Gov., Thames Valley Univ. *Recreations:* travel, theatre, opera, gardening.

TIETMEYER, Dr Hans; President, Deutsche Bundesbank, 1993–99 (Vice-Governor, 1991–93); *b* 18 Aug. 1931; *s* of Bernhard and Helene Tietmeyer; *m* 1st, Marie-Luise Floßdorf (*d* 1978); one *s* one *d*; 2nd, 1980, Maria-Therese Kalff. *Educ:* Univs of Münster, Bonn and Cologne (Dr Rer Pol). Sec., Bischöfliche Studienförderung Cusanuswerk, 1959–62; Fed. Min. of Economics, 1962–82, Head of Div. of Gen. Economic Policy, 1973–82; Mem. and Chm., Econ. Policy Cttees of EC and OECD, 1972–82; Sec. of State, Min. of Finance, 1982–89; Mem., Bd of Dirs, Deutsche Bundesbank, 1990–99. Vice-Chm., BJS, Basel, 2003–. Chm. Bd, German Fed. Foundn for the Envmt, 1990–2003; Chm. of Govs, G–10 Central Bank, 1994–99. Hon. Prof., Faculty of Econ. Scis, Martin Luther Univ., Halle-Wittenberg, 1996–. Pres., European Business Sch., Oestrich Winkel, 2000–. *Publications:* numerous articles on economics. *Recreation:* sport. *Address:* c/o Deutsche Bundesbank, Wilhelm Epstein Strasse 14, 60431 Frankfurt, Germany.

TIKARAM, Hon. Sir Moti, KBE 1980; CF 1996; Justice of the Court of Appeal, Fiji, 1988–2000; Judge of Supreme Court, Fiji, 2000–02; *b* 18 March 1925; *s* of Tikaram and

Singari; *m* 1944, Satyawati (*d* 1981); two *s* one *d*. *Educ:* Marist Brothers High Sch., Suva; Victoria Univ., Wellington, NZ (LLB 1954). Started law practice, 1954; Stipendiary Magistrate, 1960; Puisne Judge, 1968; acted as Chief Justice, 1971 and thereafter on several occasions; Pres., Fiji Court of Appeal, 1994–2000. Ombudsman, Fiji, 1972–87. Patron, Fiji Lawn Tennis Assoc. Scouting Medal of Merit, 1986. *Publications:* articles in The Pacific Way and in Recent Law 131. *Recreation:* tennis. *Address:* Flat No 1, 65 Knolly Street, PO Box 514, Suva, Fiji. *T:* 3308415, *Fax:* 3308615. *Club:* Fiji (Suva).

TIKOISUVA, Pio Bosco; High Commissioner of Fiji in the United Kingdom, also accredited to the Republic of Ireland, Denmark, Germany, Israel, Egypt and the Holy See, since 2008; *b* 13 March 1947; *m* 1973, Seniana Coalala; two *s* two *d*. *Educ:* St John's Coll., Fiji; Twickenham Coll. of Technol. (Dip. Printing 1976); Western Sydney Univ. (Postgrad. Cert. Mgt 2001). Government Printing Office, Fiji: apprentice, 1967–73; Tech. Asst, 1973–76; Sen. Tech. Asst, 1976–77; Fiji Institute of Technology: Hd, Sch. of Printing, 1977–82; Vice Principal, 1982–87; Dir, Min. of Youth and Sports, 1987–95; Regl Youth Develt Advr for S Pacific Commn, Noumea, New Caledonia, 1989–95; Govt Printer, Govt Printing Office, 1996–2001; Comr E Div., Min. of Regl Develt, 2001–05; CEO, Fiji Rugby Union, 2002–05. Rugby: Vice Capt., Fiji Sec. Schs XV against NZ Vikings, 1966; Capt., St John's Coll. 1st XV team, 1966; Mem. Fiji Nat. rep. team, 1968–79; played for Harlequins Rugby Club, Surrey Dist Side, and British Barbarians Team, UK, 1973–76; Capt., Fiji Nat. Team, 1977; Manager/Coach, Fiji Rugby 7s Team to Hong Kong, 1978–79; Coach, Nat. Juniors and Colts Team, 1983–84; Chm., Nat. Rugby Selectors, Fiji, 1989; Manager: Fiji XV Rugby Team, World Cup, France, 2007; Flying Fijians, Pacific Nations Cup, Fiji, 2007. *Address:* Fiji High Commission, 34 Hyde Park Gate, SW7 5DN.

TILBY, Rev. Angela Clare Wyatt; Vicar, St Benedict's, Cambridge, since 2007; Lecturer in Spirituality and Early Church History in the Cambridge Theological Federation, since 1997; *b* 6 March 1950; *d* of Julian George Wyatt Tilby and Constance Mary (*née* Collier). *Educ:* North London Collegiate Sch.; Girton Coll., Cambridge (MA). Producer, Religious Programmes, BBC Radio, 1973–79, BBC TV 1979–94; Sen. Producer, Religious Programmes, BBC North, 1994–97. Ordained deacon, 1997, priest, 1998; NSM, St John the Evangelist, Cherry Hinton, 1997–2006. Tutor, 1997–2007, and Vice Principal, 2001–06, Westcott House, Cambridge. Consultant, C of E Liturgical Commn, 2006– (Mem., 1998–2005). *Publications:* Teaching God, 1978; Won't You Join the Dance, 1984; Let There be Light, 1989; Science and the Soul, 1992; The Little Office Book, 1997; Son of God, 2001; God Before Breakfast, 2005. *Recreations:* science and crime fiction, history, psychology, cooking, wine. *Address:* 47 New Square, Cambridge CB1 1EZ. *T:* (01223) 355146.

TILEY, Prof. John, CBE 2003; LLD; FBA 2008; Professor of the Law of Taxation, University of Cambridge, since 1990; Fellow, Queens' College, Cambridge, since 1967 (Vice-President, 1988–96); *b* 25 Feb. 1941; *s* of William Arthur Tiley, OBE and Audrey Ellen (*née* Burton); *m* 1964, Jillinda Millicent Draper; two *s* one *d*. *Educ:* Winchester Coll.; Lincoln Coll., Oxford (BA 1962; BCL 1963; MA 1967); LLD Cantab 1995. Called to the Bar, Inner Temple, 1964, Hon. Bencher, 1993; a Recorder, 1989–99. Lecturer: Lincoln Coll., Oxford, 1963–64; Univ. of Birmingham, 1964–67; University of Cambridge: Asst Lectr, 1967–72; Lectr, 1972–87; Reader in Law of Taxation, 1987–90. Visiting Professor: Dalhousie Univ., 1972–73; Univ. of W Ontario, 1978–79; Univ. of Melbourne, 1979; Case Western Reserve Univ., 1985–86, 1996, 2002. Gen. Editor, Butterworth's Tax Guide, subseq. Tiley and Collison's UK Tax Guide, 1982–. *Publications:* A Casebook on Equity and Succession, 1968; Revenue Law, 1976, 6th edn 2008; contrib. to legal jls. *Recreations:* walking, cricket, music. *Address:* Queens' College, Cambridge CB3 9ET. *T:* (01223) 335511.

TILGHMAN, Prof. Shirley Marie, PhD; FRS 1995; President, Princeton University, since 2001; *b* 17 Sept. 1946; *d* of Henry W. Caldwell and Shirley P. Carre; *m* (marr. diss.); one *s* one *d*. *Educ:* Queen's Univ., Kingston, Canada (BSc Hons 1968); Temple Univ., Philadelphia (PhD Biochem. 1975). Fogarty Internat. Fellow, NIH, Bethesda, 1975–77; Asst Prof., Temple Univ., 1978–79; Mem., Inst. for Cancer Res., Pa, 1979–86; Princeton University: Howard A. Prior Prof. of Life Scis, 1986–2001; Investigator, Howard Hughes Med. Inst., 1988–2001; Trustee, Jackson Lab., 1994–. Adjunct Associate Prof. of Human Genetics, Biochem. and Biophysics, Univ. of Pa, 1980–86; Adjunct Prof., Dept of Biochem., Univ. of Medicine and Dentistry of New Jersey-Robert Wood Johnson Med. Sch., NJ, 1988–2001. Ed. and Mem., Editl Bd, Molecular and Cell Biol., 1985–94; Member, Editorial Board: Jl Cell Biol., 1988–91; Genes and Develt, 1990–2001. Fellow, Inst. of Medicine, USA, 1995; Foreign Associate, Nat. Acad. of Scis, USA, 1996; Amer. Acad. of Arts and Scis, 1990; Amer. Phil Soc., 2000. Hon. DSc: Mt Sinai Coll. of Med., City Coll. of NY, 1994; Oxford, 2002; British Columbia, 2002; Dickenson Coll., 2002; Bard Coll., 2002; Queen's Univ., Kingston, Ont, 2002; Yale, 2002; Toronto, 2003; Western Ont, 2003; New York, 2005; Columbia, 2005; Univ. of Medicine and Dentistry of NJ, 2005; Rutgers, 2006; Rockefeller, 2006; Washington, 2007; Hon. DLaws: Westminster Choir Coll., Rider Univ., 2002; Simon Fraser, 2002; Harvard, 2004; Hon. DHL Drew Univ., 2004. *Publications:* (ed with K. E. Davies) Genome Analysis: Vol. I 1990, Vols II and III 1991, Vol. IV 1992, Vols V and VI 1993; contrib. chapters in books; contrib. numerous articles and papers in Proc. Nat. Acad. Scis, USA, Jl Biol. Chem., Science, Nature, Genes Develt, Jl Cell Biol., Molecular Cell Biol. and others. *Recreations:* ski-ing, tennis, gardening, reading. *Address:* Office of the President, One Nassau Hall, Princeton University, Princeton, NJ 08544, USA. *T:* (609) 2586100.

TILL, Barry Dorn; Principal of Morley College, London, 1965–86; Adviser, 1973–86, Director, 1986–92, Baring Foundation; *b* 1 June 1923; *s* of John Johnson and Hilda Lucy Till; *m* 1st, 1954, Shirley Philipson (marr. diss. 1965); two *s*; 2nd, 1966, Antonia, *d* of Sir Michael John Sinclair Clapham, KBE; two *d*. *Educ:* Harrow; Jesus College and Westcott House, Cambridge. 1st Class Theology Pt III, 1949; Lightfoot Scholar, 1949. Served War, Coldstream Guards, 1942–46; Italian campaign. Deacon, 1950; Priest, 1951; Asst Curate, Bury Parish Church, Lancs, 1950–53; Fellow of Jesus Coll., Cambridge, 1953–60, Chaplain, 1953–56, Dean, 1956–60, Tutor, 1957–60; Univ. Preacher, Cambridge, 1955; Examining Chaplain to Bishop of Lichfield, 1957–60; Dean of Hong Kong, 1960–64. Chm., Asia Christian Colleges Assoc., 1968–76, Vice-Pres., 1976–2002. Governor, British Inst. of Recorded Sound, 1967–72; Mem., Adv. Council, V&A Museum, 1977–83. Chairman: Greater London AACE, 1976–82; Work-Out, 1986–89; Mary Ward Settlement, 1987–98. Founder Mem., Exec. Cttee, Assoc. of Charitable Foundns, 1989–91. Governor, St Olaf's Grammar Sch., 1973–82 (Chm., 1980–82); Member: Cultural Cttee, European Culture Foundn, 1976–78; Council, London Sinfonietta, 1992–2002. Trustee: Thomas Cubitt Trust, 1978–99; LentA Educnl Trust, 1987–92 (Chm., 1990–92); Open Coll. of the Arts, 1992–2002; Charity House, 1992–98; Transport 2000, 1992–2002; London Educn Business Partnership, 1992–99; Fitzwilliam Mus. Trust, 1993–2003. DD Lambeth, 2008. *Publications:* contrib. to The Historic Episcopate, 1954; Change and Exchange, 1964; Changing Frontiers in the Mission of the Church, 1965; contrib. to A Holy Week Manual, 1967; The Churches Search for Unity, 1972; contrib. Oxford DNB. *Recreations:* travel, gardening, opera. *Address:* 44 Canonbury Square, N1 2AW. *T:* (020) 7359 0708. *Club:* Brooks's.

See also J. W. Till.

TILL, Prof. Geoffrey, PhD; Professor of Maritime Studies, King's College, London, since 1990; *b* 14 Jan. 1945; *s* of Arthur Till and Violet Dorothy Till (*née* Beech); *m* 1968, Cherry (*née* Austin); two *s* one *d*. *Educ:* King's Coll. London (BA Hons Mod. Hist. 1966; PGCE 1967; MA War Studies 1968; PhD 1976; FKC 2006). Lectr, then Sen. Lectr, Britannia RNC, 1968–72; Royal Naval College, Greenwich: Sen., then Prin., Lectr, 1972–89; Prof. of Hist. and Internat. Affairs, 1989–97; Dean of Academic Studies, JSCSC, Shrivenham, 1997–2006. Vis. Lectr, City Univ., 1973–85. *Publications:* Airpower and the Royal Navy, 1979; Maritime Strategy and the Nuclear Age, 1982; The Sea in Soviet Strategy, 1983; Naval Warfare and Policy, 1984; The Future of British Seapower, 1984; Modern Seapower, 1987; East-West Relations in the 1990s, 1990; Seapower: theory and practice, 1994; Seapower in the Millennium, 2001; Seapower: a guide for the 21st century, 2004; The Development of British Naval Thinking, 2006. *Recreations:* visiting country churches, bird watching, travel, extreme gardening. *Address:* Wansdyke Cottage, Allington, Devizes, Wilts SN10 3NL. *T:* (01380) 860176; *e-mail:* gmtill@tiscali.co.uk.

TILL, Prof. James Edgar, OC 1994; PhD; FRS 2000; FRSC; University Professor, University of Toronto, 1984–97, now Professor Emeritus; Senior Scientist, Ontario Cancer Institute, 1957–96, Emeritus, since 1997; Senior Fellow, Massey College, Toronto, since 1990; *b* 25 Aug. 1931; *s* of William Till and Gertrude Ruth Till (*née* Isaac); *m* 1959, Marion Joyce Sinclair; one *s* two *d*. *Educ:* Univ. of Saskatchewan (BA Arts and Sci. 1952; MA Physics 1954); Yale Univ. (PhD Biophysics 1957). Postdoctoral Fellow, Connaught Med. Res. Labs, 1956–57; University of Toronto: Asst Prof., 1958–62, Associate Prof., 1962–65, Dept of Med. Biophysics; Prof., 1965–97; Associate Dean, Life Scis, Sch. of Grad. Studies, 1981–84; Hd, Div. of Biol Res., Ont. Cancer Inst., 1969–82. FRSC 1969. Internat. Award, Gairdner Foundn, 1969; Thomas W. Eadie Medal, RSC, 1991; Robert L. Noble Prize, 1993, R. M. Taylor Medal, 2001, Nat. Cancer Inst. of Canada; Canadian Medical Hall of Fame, 2004; Centenary Medal, RSC, 2005; (jtly) Albert Lasker Award, Lasker Foundn, 2005. *Publications:* contrib. chapters in books and conf. proceedings; numerous contribs to refereed jls. *Address:* Ontario Cancer Institute, University Health Network, 610 University Avenue, Room 9–416, Toronto, ON M5G 2M9, Canada. *T:* (416) 9462948.

TILL, Prof. Jeremy William, RIBA; Professor of Architecture and Head of School, University of Sheffield, since 1999; *b* 5 April 1957; *s* of Barry Dorn Till, *qv*; partner, Prof. Sarah Heath Wigglesworth. *Educ:* Peterhouse, Cambridge (BA 1979); Poly. of Central London (DipArch 1983); Middlesex Univ. (MA 1999). RIBA 1995. Sen. Lectr and Sub-Dean, Bartlett Sch. of Architecture, UCL, 1991–99; Partner, Sarah Wigglesworth Architects, 1996–. Vis. Prof., Technical Univ., Vienna, 1995. *Publications:* The Everyday and Architecture, 1998; Architecture and Participation, 2005; numerous articles on archtl theory of educn. *Recreations:* growing, cooking and eating food. *Address:* School of Architecture, University of Sheffield, Western Bank, Sheffield S10 2TN. *T:* (0114) 222 0347; *e-mail:* j.till@sheffield.ac.uk.

TILL, Very Rev. Michael Stanley; Dean of Winchester, 1996–2005; *b* 19 Nov. 1935; *s* of Stanley Brierley Till and Mary Till; *m* 1965, Tessa, *d* of Capt. Stephen Roskill; one *s* one *d*. *Educ:* Brighton, Hove and Sussex Grammar School; Lincoln Coll., Oxford (BA, History 1960, Theology 1962; MA 1967); Westcott House, Cambridge. Curate, St John's, St John's Wood, NW8, 1964–67; Chaplain 1967–70, Dean and Fellow 1970–81, King's College, Cambridge; Vicar of All Saints', Fulham, 1981–86; Area Dean, Hammersmith and Fulham, 1984–86; Archdeacon of Canterbury, 1986–96. *Address:* Ryde House, Angel Street, Petworth, W Sussex GU28 0BG.

TILL, Stewart Myles, CBE 2000; President and Chief Executive, Stadium Films, since 2007; *b* 24 April 1951; *s* of Ronald Leslie and Olive Till; *m* 1986, Lynda Helen Jones; one *s* one *d*. *Educ:* Dulwich Coll.; Univ. of Bath (BSc Hons Business Studies); Essex Univ. (MA American Politics). Account Exec., Saatchi & Saatchi, 1976–78; Marketing Dir, WEA Records, 1978–83; Vice-Pres., N Europe CBS/Fox Video, 1983–88; Dep. Managing Dir, Sky TV, 1988–92; President: International Polygram Filmed Entertainment, 1992–99; Universal Pictures Internat., 1999–2000; Pres. and Chief Exec., Signpost Films, 2001–02; Chm. and Chief Exec., United Internat. Pictures, 2002–06. Chm., UK Film Council, 2004– (Dep. Chm., 1999–2004). Dep. Chm., Skillset, 2002–; Chm., Skills Action Gp, 2003–04. Trustee, Nat. Film and TV Sch., 1998. Chm., Campaign Television, 2008–. Chm., Fife, 1997–. Mem., Develt Bd, Henley River and Rowing Mus., 2000–05. Mem., Adv. Bd, Sch. of Mgt, Univ. of Bath, 2002–06. Chm., 2006–08, Vice Chm., 2008–, Millwall FC. Gov., Dulwich Coll., 2005–. Hon. Mem., Women in Film and TV, 2004–; Hon. Fellow, Goldsmiths, Univ. of London, 2006. FRSA 2001. DU Essex, 2006. *Recreations:* most sports, family. *Address:* Remenham Place, Remenham Hill, Henley-on-Thames, Oxon RG9 3EU.

TILLER, Ven. John; Archdeacon of Hereford, 2002–04, now Emeritus; *b* 22 June 1938; *s* of Harry Maurice Tiller and Lucille Maisie Tiller; *m* 1961, Ruth Alison (*née* Watson); two *s* one *d*. *Educ:* St Albans Sch.; Christ Church, Oxford (MA, 2nd Cl. Mod. Hist.); Bristol Univ. (MLitt). Ordained deacon 1962, priest 1963, St Albans; Assistant Curate: St Cuthbert, Bedford, 1962–65; Widcombe, Bath, 1965–67; Chaplain and Tutor, Tyndale Hall, Bristol, 1967–71; Lectr in Church History and Worship, Trinity Coll., Bristol, 1971–73; Priest-in-Charge, Christ Church, Bedford, 1973–78; Chief Sec., ACCM, 1978–84; Chancellor and Canon Residentiary, Hereford Cathedral, 1984–2002; Diocesan Dir of Trng, Hereford, 1991–2000. Non-stipendiary Local Ministry Advr, Shrewsbury Episcopal Area, dio. Lichfield, 2005–. Hon. Canon of St Albans Cathedral, 1979–84. *Publications:* The Service of Holy Communion and its Revision (with R. T. Beckwith), 1972; A Modern Liturgical Bibliography, 1974; The Great Acquittal, 1980; Puritan, Pietist, Pentecostalist, 1982; A Strategy for the Church's Ministry, 1983; The Gospel Community, 1987; contribs to: The New International Dictionary of the Christian Church, 1974; Anglican Worship Today, 1980; New Dictionary of Christian Theology, 1988; The Parish Church?, 1988; (ed with G. E. Aylmer) Hereford Cathedral: a history, 2000. *Recreations:* walking, bird-watching, spuddling. *Address:* 2 Pulley Lane, Bayston Hill, Shrewsbury SY3 0JH. *T:* (01743) 873595; *e-mail:* canjtiller@aol.com.

TILLETT, Michael Burn; QC 1996; a Recorder, since 1989; *b* 3 Sept. 1942; *s* of late Cyril Vernon Tillett and Norah Phyllis Tillett; *m* 1977, Kathryn Ann Samuel; two *d*. *Educ:* Marlborough Coll.; Queens' Coll., Cambridge (MA (Hons) Law). Called to the Bar, Inner Temple, 1965; in practice, 1966–; Asst Recorder, 1984–89. Legal Mem., Mental Health Rev. Tribunal, 2000–. *Recreations:* mountaineering, ski-ing, riding, sailing. *Address:* 39 Essex Street, WC2R 3AT. *T:* (020) 7832 1142. *Clubs:* Royal Automobile, Hurlingham; Downhill Only; Seaview Yacht.

TILLEY, Charles Basil; Chief Executive, Chartered Institute of Management Accountants, since 2001; *b* 22 Dec. 1950; *s* of Basil and Irene Tilley; *m* 1983, Sarah Anne Morgan; one *s* one *d*. CA 1973. KPMG, 1974–88, Partner, 1986–88; Gp Finance Dir, Hambros plc, 1989–96; Hd of Finance and Ops, Granville Baird, 1997–2001. Member

Board: Internat. Fedn of Accountants, 2004–07; Gt Ormond St Hosp., 2007–. CCMI; Mem., RSA. *Recreations:* sailing, tennis, cycling, ski-ing. *Address:* The Chartered Institute of Management Accountants, 26 Chapter Street, SW1P 4NP. *T:* (020) 7663 5441, *Fax:* (020) 7663 5442; *e-mail:* charles.tilley@cimaglobal.com. *Clubs:* Sea View Yacht; Telford Park Tennis.

TILLEY, Olwen Mary, (Mrs A. Tilley); *see* Rice, O. M.

TILLING, George Henry Garfield; Chairman, Scottish Postal Board, 1977–84, retired; *b* 24 Jan. 1924; *s* of late Thomas and Anne Tilling; *m* 1956, Margaret Meriel, MStJ, *d* of late Rear-Adm. Sir Alexander McGlashan, KBE, CB, DSO; two *s* two *d. Educ:* Hardye's Sch., Dorchester; University Coll., Oxford (Open Exhibnr, Kitchener Schol., Farquharson Prizeman, MA). Served War of 1939–45, NW Europe: Captain, Dorset Regt, 1943–46. Post Office: Asst Principal, 1948; Principal, 1953; Private Sec. to Postmaster General, 1964; Dep. Dir of Finance, 1965; Dir, Eastern Postal Region, 1967; Sec. of the Post Office, 1973–75; Dir of Postal Ops, 1975–77. Mem. Council, Lord Kitchener Nat. Meml Fund, 1979–90. Order of St John: Mem. Council, London, 1975–77; Mem. Cttee of the Order for Edinburgh, 1978–87; Mem., Scottish Priory Chapter, 1993–99. Trustee, Bield Retirement Housing Trust, 1988–98. Hon. Mem., St Andrew's Ambulance Assoc., 1980. KStJ. FSAScot. *Recreations:* orders and medals, heraldry, uniforms. *Address:* 4 Fountain Place, Loanhead, Midlothian EH20 9EA. *T:* (0131) 440 1433.

TILLMANN, Prof. Ulrike Luise, PhD; FRS 2008; Professor of Mathematics, University of Oxford, since 2000; Fellow of Merton College, Oxford, since 1992; *b* Rhede, FRG, 12 Dec. 1962; *d* of Ewald and Marie-Luise Tillmann; *m* 1995, Jonathan Morris; three *d. Educ:* Gymnasium Georgianum, Vreden; Brandeis Univ. (BA 1985); Stanford Univ. (MA 1987; PhD 1990); Bonn Univ. (Habilitation 1996). SERC Res. Asst, Univ. of Cambridge; 1990–92; Jun. Res. Fellow, Clare Hall, Cambridge, 1990–92; CUF Lectr, Univ. of Oxford, 1992–2000; Tutor, Merton Coll., Oxford, 1992–. *Recreation:* singing. *Address:* Mathematical Institute, University of Oxford, 24–29 St Giles, Oxford OX1 3LB.

TILLMANS, Wolfgang; artist and photographer; Professor of Fine Art, Städelschule, Frankfurt, since 2003; *b* 16 Aug. 1968; *s* of Karl A. and Elisabeth Tillmans. *Educ:* Bournemouth & Poole Coll. of Art & Design. Guest Prof., Sch. of Fine Arts, Hamburg, 1998–99. Hon. Fellow, Arts Inst., Bournemouth, 2001. *Solo exhibitions* include: Kunsthalle, Zurich, 1995; Galerie Daniel Buchholz, Cologne, Andrea Rosen Gall., NY, Deichtorhallen Hamburg, and touring, Mus. Ludwig, Cologne, 2001; Regen Projects, LA, Maureen Paley Interim Art, London, 2002; Tate Britain, 2003; P.S.1 Contemp. Art Center, NY, 2006; Mus. of Contemp. Art, Chicago, 2006; *retrospective exhibition:* Tate Britain, 2003; *group exhibitions* include: MOMA, NY, 1996; Berlin Biennale, 1998; Castello di Rivoli, Turin, Royal Acad. of Art, Tate Britain, 2000; Tate Modern, 2001; Tate Liverpool, 2002. Ars viva Prize, Bundesverband der Deutschen Industrie, 1995; Böttcherstrasse Prize, Bremen, 1995; Turner Prize, 2000. *Publications: monographs:* Concorde, 1995; Burg, 1997; View from Above, 2001; Wolfgang Tillmans, 2002; (jtly) truth study center, 2005; Manual, 2007; exhibn catalogues. *Address:* c/o Maureen Paley, 21 Herald Street, E2 6JT. *T:* (020) 7729 4112, *Fax:* (020) 7729 4113.

TILLOTSON, Maj.-Gen. (Henry) Michael, CB 1983; CBE 1976 (OBE 1970, MBE 1956); writer; *b* 12 May 1928; *er s* of late Henry and May Elizabeth Tillotson; *m* 1st, 1956, Angela Wadsworth Shaw (marr. diss.); two *s* one *d*; 2nd, 2006, Sybil Osborne. *Educ:* Chesterfield Sch.; RMA Sandhurst. Professional soldier, 1948–83: commnd E Yorks Regt, 1948; served: Austria, 1948–50; Germany and Berlin, 1951–52; Indo-China (attached French Union Forces), 1953 (Croix de Guerre with Palm); Malayan Emergency, 1953–55; Indonesian Confrontation, 1964–65; S Arabia, 1965–67 (despatches); MoD Intelligence, 1967–69; Inf. Bn Comdr, Cyprus, 1969–71; Col GS, Hong Kong, 1974–76; Chief of Staff UN Force, Cyprus, and Comdr British Contingent, 1976–78; research mission for UN Sec.-Gen. to UN Forces, Israel, Lebanon, Syria and Sinai, 1978; Dep. Dir, Army Staff Duties, and MoD rep., Cabinet Civil Contingencies Cttee, 1978–79; Chief of Staff (Maj.-Gen.) to C-in-C UKLF, 1980–83. Regl Dir SE Asia, Internat. Mil. Services Ltd, 1983–86. Col, PWO Regt of Yorks, 1979–86. Hon. Life Fellow, RSPB, 1993. *Publications:* Finland at Peace and War 1918–1993, 1993, 2nd edn 1996 (Finnish Gold Medal of Merit, 1996); With the Prince of Wales's Own, 1995; Dwin Bramall: the authorised biography of Field Marshal the Lord Bramall, 2005, rev. and reissued as The Fifth Pillar, 2006; (ed with Ian Brunskill and Guy Liardet) Great Military Lives in Obituaries, 2008; occasional columnist in The Times, 2000–. *Recreations:* abroad, birds, listening to music. *Address:* West End House, Wylye, Wilts BA12 0QT. *Club:* Army and Navy.

TILLSLEY, Gen. Bramwell Harold; General of the Salvation Army, 1993–94; *b* 18 Aug. 1931; *s* of Harold Tillsley and Doris Tillsley (*née* Lawrence); *m* 1953, Maude Pitcher; two *s* one *d. Educ:* Kitchener-Waterloo Collegiate; Univ. of Western Ontario (BA); Wycliffe Coll., Toronto; Salvation Army Trng Coll., Toronto. Social worker, Children's Aid Soc., Kitchener, Ont., 1952–55; Salvation Army: Windsor, Nova Scotia, 1956–58; Oakville, Ont., 1958–59; on staff, Salvation Army Coll., Toronto, 1959–65; Divl Youth Sec., Saskatchewan, 1965–66; N Toronto Congregation, 1966–71; Training Principal: Newfoundland, 1971–74; NY, 1974–77; Provincial Comdr, Newfoundland, 1977–79; Divl Comdr, Metro-Toronto, 1979–81; Trng Principal, London, 1981–85; Chief Sec., USA, South, 1985–89; Territorial Comdr, Australian Southern Territory, 1989–91; COS, Internat. HQ, London, 1991–93. Mem., Rotary Club, Toronto, Melbourne and London. Queen's Medal (Canada), 1978. *Publications:* Life in the Spirit, 1966; Life More Abundant, 1968; Manpower for the Master, 1970; This Mind in You, 1989. *Recreations:* music, golf, sports (ice hockey in youth). *Address:* 65 Spring Garden Avenue, Unit 604, North York, ON M2N 6H9, Canada.

TILLYARD, James Henry Hugh, QC 2002; a Recorder, since 1998; *b* 7 March 1955; *s* of William Stephen Tillyard and Margaret Diana Tillyard; *m* 2000, Helen Patricia Scott; two *d*, and one *s* one *d* by a previous marriage. *Educ:* Sherborne Sch., Dorset; Leeds Univ. (BSc Chem. Eng). Called to the Bar, Middle Temple, 1978; Wales and Chester Circuit; specialises in family law. *Recreations:* boating, spending time with my wife and children. *Address:* 30 Park Place Chambers, Cardiff CF10 3BS. *T:* (029) 2039 8421; *e-mail:* clerks@parkplace.co.uk. *Club:* Cardiff and County.

TILSON, Joseph Charles, (Joe), RA 1991 (ARA 1985); painter, sculptor and printmaker; *b* 24 Aug. 1928; *s* of Frederick Albert Edward Tilson and Ethel Stapley Louise Saunders; *m* 1956, Joslyn Morton; one *s* two *d. Educ:* St Martin's School of Art; Royal Coll. of Art (ARCA); British School at Rome (Rome Scholar). RAF, 1946–49. Worked in Italy and Spain, 1955–59; Vis. Lectr, Slade Sch., Univ. of London and King's Coll., Univ. of Durham, 1962–63; taught at Sch. of Visual Arts, NY, 1966; Vis. Lectr, Staatliche Hochschule für Bildende Kunste, Hamburg, 1971–72. Mem., Arts Panel, Arts Council, 1966–71. Exhib. Venice Biennale, 1964; work at Marlborough Gall., 1961–77, later at Waddington Galls; retrospective exhibitions: Boymans Van Beuningen Mus., Rotterdam, 1973; Vancouver Art Gall., 1979; Volterra, 1983; Castelbasso, 2001; RA, 2002. Biennale Prizes: Krakow, 1974; Ljubljana, 1985, 1995. Subject of TV films, 1963, 1968, 1974. *Recreation:* planting trees.

TILSON THOMAS, Michael; Music Director, San Francisco Symphony Orchestra, since 1995; Principal Guest Conductor, London Symphony Orchestra, since 1995 (Principal Conductor, 1988–95); Artistic Director (formerly Artistic Adviser), New World Symphony, since 1988; concert pianist; *b* 21 Dec. 1944; *s* of Theodor and Roberta Thomas; *g s* of Boris and Bessie Thomashefsky, founders of Yiddish Theater, United States. *Educ:* Univ. of Southern California (Master of Music). Conductor, Young Musicians' Foundn Orchestra, LA, and conductor and pianist, Monday Evening Concerts, 1963–68; musical asst, Bayreuth, 1966–67; Koussevitzky Prize, Tanglewood, 1968; Asst then Principal Guest Conductor, Boston Symphony, 1969–74; NY début, 1969; London début, with LSO, 1970; Music Director: Buffalo Philharmonic, 1971–79; televised NY Philharmonic Young Peoples' Concerts, 1971–77; Principal Guest Conductor, LA Philharmonic, 1981–85; Music Dir, Great Woods Festival, 1985; Co-Artistic Dir, Pacific Music Fest., Sapporo, Japan, 1990–; guest conductor with orchestras and opera houses in US and Europe; numerous recordings. Grammy Award: best orchestral recording, 1997, for Prokofiev's Romeo and Juliet with San Francisco SO; best classical album of the year, 1999, for Stravinsky's Firebird and Rite of Spring with San Francisco SO. *Address:* MTT Inc., 888 7th Avenue, 35th Floor, New York, NY 10106, USA. *Club:* St Botolph (Boston).

TILT, Sir (Robin) Richard, Kt 1999; Social Fund Commissioner for UK, since 2000; Director General, HM Prison Service, 1995–99; *b* 11 March 1944; *s* of Francis Arthur Tilt and Mary Elizabeth (*née* Ashworth); *m* 1966, Kate Busby; two *s* one *d. Educ:* King's Sch., Worcester; Univ. of Nottingham (BA Hons); Open Univ. (Dip). HM Prison Service: Asst Governor, HM Borstal, Wellingborough, 1968–71; Tutor, Prison Service Staff Coll., 1971–74; Governor, HM Borstal, Pollington, 1974–75; Deputy Governor: Ranby, 1975–78; Gartree, 1978–80; Governor, Bedford, 1980–82; Hd, Manpower Section, HQ, 1982–84; Governor, Gartree, 1984–88; Dep. Regl Dir, Midlands, 1988–89; Hd, Industrial Relns, HQ, 1989–92; Hd of Finance, Police Dept, 1992–94; Dir of Services, 1994; Dir of Security and Progs, 1995. Chairman: Kettering Gen. Hosp. NHS Trust, 1999–2000; Northants HA, 2000–02; Leics, Northants and Rutland Strategic HA, 2002–06. Mem., Sentencing Adv. Panel, 1999–2002; Chairman: Social Security Adv. Cttee, 2005–; Indep. Complaints Panel, Portman Gp, 2007–. Churchill Fellow, 1991. Friend of RA. *Recreations:* walking, reading, theatre, art. *Address:* 4th Floor, Centre City Podium, 5 Hill Street, Birmingham B5 4UB.

TILTMAN, Sir John H.; *see* Hessell Tiltman.

TIMBURY, Morag Crichton, MD, PhD; FRSE; FRCP, FRCPGlas, FRCPath; Director, Central Public Health Laboratory, Public Health Laboratory Service, 1988–95; *b* 29 Sept. 1930; *d* of William McCulloch and Dr Esther Sinclair McCulloch (*née* Hood); *m* 1954, Dr Gerald Charles Timbury, FRCPE, FRCPGlas, FRCPsych (decd); one *d. Educ:* St Bride's Sch.; Univ. of Glasgow (MB ChB; MD; PhD). MRCPath 1964, FRCPath 1976; MRCPGlas 1972, FRCPGlas 1974; FRCP 1994; FRSE 1979. University of Glasgow: Maurice Bloch Res. Fellow in Virology, 1960–63; Lectr in Bacteriology, 1963–65; Sen. Lectr in Virology, 1966–76; Reader, 1976–78; Prof. of Bacteriology and William Teacher Lectr, 1978–88. Hon. Cons. in Bacteriology and Virology, 1966–88. Member Council: RCPSG, 1985–88; RCPath, 1987–90. External examiner in med. microbiol., at various univs, 1973–88. Vis. Associate Prof. in Virology, Baylor College of Medicine, Houston, Texas, 1975; Vis. Mayne Guest Prof., Univ. of Queensland, Brisbane, 1990; Hon. Vis. Prof. of Virology, ICSM, 1997–99. Chm., Ind. Rev. Gp, Rev. of Food-Related Scientific Services in Scotland, 1998. Mem., RSM, 1986–. *Publications:* Notes on Medical Virology, 1967, 11th edn 1997; (with J. D. Sleigh) Notes on Medical Bacteriology, 1981, 5th edn 1998; (co-ed) vol. 4, Virology, Topley and Wilson's Principles of Bacteriology, Virology and Immunity, 8th edn 1990; (jtly) Notes on Medical Microbiology, 2002; sci. papers on bacterial and viral infections, genetics of herpes simplex virus type 2. *Recreations:* military history, theatre. *Address:* 1/9 St Vincent Place, Edinburgh EH3 5BX.

TIMMINS, Col Sir John (Bradford), KCVO 2002; OBE (mil.) 1973; TD 1968 (1st Clasp 1974); JP; Lord Lieutenant of Greater Manchester, 1987–2007; Chairman, Warburton Properties Ltd, since 1973; *b* 23 June 1932; *s* of John James Timmins and Janet Gwendoline (*née* Legg); *m* 1956, Jean Edwards; five *s* one *d. Educ:* Dudley Grammar Sch.; Wolverhampton Technical Coll.; Univ. of Aston-in-Birmingham (MSc). Building and Civil Engrg Industry, 1949–80; NW Regional Pres., Nat. Fedn of Building Trade Employers, 1974–75. Commnd RE, 1954; National Service, 1954–56; TA, 1956–80; comd 75 Eng. Regt(V), 1971–73, Hon. Col of the Regt, 1980–90; Hon. Colonel: Manchester and Salford Univ. OTC, 1990–98; Gtr Manchester ACF, 1991–2007. Pres., TA&VRA for NW England, 1994–99 (Vice-Chm., 1983–87; Vice-Pres., 1987–94, 1999–2007). ADC to the Queen, 1975–80. High Sheriff of Gtr Manchester, 1986–87. JP Trafford, 1987. President, Greater Manchester: Order of St John, 1987–2007; Royal Soc. of St George, 1988–. FRSA 1996. Hon. RNCM 1994. Hon. DSc Salford, 1990; Hon. LLD Manchester, 2001. KStJ 1988; KLJ 1990. *Recreations:* sailing, gardening. *Address:* 7 Little Heath Lane, Dunham Massey, Cheshire WA14 4TS. *Club:* Army and Navy.

TIMMINS, Nicholas James Maxwell-; journalist and author; Public Policy Editor, Financial Times, since 1996; *b* 7 Sept. 1949; *s* of Rev. Leslie James and Audrey Maxwell-Timmins; *m* 1981, Elaine Barbara Brown; two *s* (twins) one *d. Educ:* Galleywall Road Prim. Sch., Bermondsey; Priors Court, Newbury; Kingswood Sch., Bath; Regent's Park Coll., Oxford (BA English Lang. and Lit. 1971). Reporter, Nature, 1971–74; Sci. and Medicine Corresp., 1974–78, Chief Labour and Industrial Corresp., 1978–79, Press Assoc.; gen. reporter, 1980, Health and Social Services Corresp., 1983–86, The Times; Health and Social Services Corresp., 1986–90, Political Corresp., 1990–95, The Independent; Public Policy Ed., 1995–96. Dist. Vis. Fellow, 1993, Mem. Adv. Council, 2001–03, Policy Studies Inst. Advr, Work, Income and Social Protection Cttee, Joseph Rowntree Foundn, 1994–98; Member Advisory Board: ESRC Centre for Analysis of Social Exclusion, 1997–2008; ESRC Centre for Market and Public Orgn, 2005–; Mem. Council, Pensions Policy Inst., 2001–; Mem., Phillis Cttee on Govt Communications, 2003–04. Vis. Prof. of Public Mgt, KCL, 2006–. Sen. Associate, Nuffield Trust, 2008–. Pres., Social Policy Assoc., 2008–. Mem. Adv. Bd, Social Dimensions of Health Inst., Dundee and St Andrews Univs, 2005–. *Publications:* The Five Giants: a biography of the welfare state, 1995, 2nd edn 2001; NHS 50th Anniversary: a history of the NHS, 1998; Rejuvenate or Retire?: views of the NHS at 60, 2008. *Recreation:* kitchen talks. *Address:* Financial Times, One Southwark Bridge, SE1 9HL; *e-mail:* nick.timmins@ft.com.

TIMMIS, Prof. Kenneth Nigel, PhD; FRS 2008; Professor, Institute of Microbiology, Technical University of Braunschweig, since 1988; Head, Environmental Microbiology Laboratory, Helmholtz Centre for Infection Research, Braunschweig, since 2006; *b* Blackpool, 16 Feb. 1946; *s* of Ernest Charles Timmis and Edith Primrose Timmis (*née* Holland); *m* 1964, Joan Kathleen Chalkley; one *s. Educ:* Kings Norton Grammar Sch., Birmingham; Univ. of Bristol (BSc Hons Microbiol.; PhD Microbiol. 1971); Free Univ.

of Berlin (Habilitation in Microbiol. and Molecular Biol.). Postdoctoral posts, Yale Univ., 1972–73, Stanford Univ., 1973–76; Hd, Res. Gp, Max-Planck Inst. for Molecular Genetics, Berlin, 1976–81; Prof., Univ. of Geneva Med. Sch., 1981–88; Hd, Div. of Microbiol., Nat. Res. Centre for Biotechnol., Braunschweig, 1988–2006. Founding Editor: Envmtl Microbiol., 1999–; Microbial Biotechnol., 2008–. Mem., EMBO. Mem., Amer. Acad. Microbiol. Erwin Schrödinger Prize, German Assoc. for Promotion of Scis and Humanities, 2001. *Publications:* Handbook of Hydrocarbon and Lipid Microbiology, 2009; contrib. res. papers to learned jls. *Recreations:* family, literature, music, gardening, wine, cinema, cooking. *Address:* Environmental Microbiology Laboratory, Helmholtz Centre for Infection Research, Inhoffenstrasse 7, 38124 Braunschweig, Germany. *T:* (531) 61814000, *Fax:* (531) 61814199; *e-mail:* kti@gbf.de.

TIMMS, Prof. Edward Francis, OBE 2005; PhD; FBA 2006; Research Professor in History, University of Sussex, since 2003; *b* 3 June 1937; *s* of Rev. John Timms and Joan Timms; *m* 1966, Saime Göksu; two *s* one *d. Educ:* Christ's Hosp.; Gonville and Caius Coll., Cambridge (MA 1963; PhD 1967). Asst Lectr in German, Univ. of Sussex, 1963–65; Cambridge University: Lectr in German, 1965–91; Fellow, Gonville and Caius Coll., 1965–91, Life Fellow, 1992–; University of Sussex: Prof. of German, 1992–99; Founder and Dir, Centre for German-Jewish Studies, 1994–2003. Lectr, Middle East Technical Univ., Ankara, 1970. Austrian State Prize for History of the Soc. Scis, 2002. *Publications:* Karl Kraus—Apocalyptic Satirist, Part 1: Culture and Catastrophe in Habsburg Vienna, 1986, Part 2: The Post-War Crisis and the Rise of the Swastika, 2005; (ed with Ritchie Robertson) Vienna 1900: from Altenberg to Wittgenstein (Austrian Studies 1), 1990; (with Saime Göksu) Romantic Communist: the life and work of Nazim Hikmet, 1999, 2nd edn 2006; Freud and the Child Woman: the memoirs of Fritz Wittels, 1995. *Recreations:* exploring archives, compiling memoirs. *Address:* Arts Building, University of Sussex, Brighton BN1 9QN. *T:* and *Fax:* (01273) 678495; *e-mail:* e.timms@sussex.ac.uk.

TIMMS, Kate; *see* Gordon, V. K.

TIMMS, Prof. Noel Walter; Professor of Social Work and Director, School of Social Work, University of Leicester, 1984–89, now Emeritus Professor; *b* 25 Dec. 1927; *s* of Harold John Timms and Josephine Mary Cecilia Timms; *m* 1956, Rita Caldwell; three *s* three *d. Educ:* Cardinal Vaughan School; Univ. of London (BA Hons History; MA Sociology); Heythrop Coll., Univ. of London (MA Theology). Social Worker, Family Service Units, 1952–54; Psychiatric social worker, 1955–57; Lectr, Dept of Social Science, Cardiff University Coll., 1957–61; Lectr, LSE, 1963–69; Prof. of Applied Social Studies, Bradford Univ., 1969–75; Prof. of Social Work Studies, Newcastle upon Tyne Univ., 1975–84. *Publications:* Social Casework, Principles and Practice, 1964; Language of Social Casework, 1968; (with John Mayer) The Client Speaks, 1970; (with Rita Timms) Dictionary of Social Welfare, 1982; Social Work Values: an enquiry, 1983; Family and Citizenship, 1992; (jtly) Secure Accommodation in Child Care, 1993; (jtly) Mediation: the making and remaking of co-operative relationships, 1994; In Pursuit of Quality, 1995; Authority in the Catholic Priesthood, 2001; (jtly) Diocesan Dispositions and Parish Voices in the Roman Catholic Church, 2001. *Recreations:* Evensong, looking at old furniture and at performances of Don Giovanni. *Address:* 157 Kingsway, Orpington, Kent, BR5 1PP. *T:* (01689) 877982.

TIMMS, Rt Hon. Stephen (Creswell); PC 2006; MP (Lab) East Ham, since 1997 (Newham North East, June 1994–1997); Financial Secretary, HM Treasury, since 2008; *b* 29 July 1955; *s* of late Ronald James Timms and of Margaret Joyce Timms (*née* Johnson); *m* 1986, Hui-Leng Lim. *Educ:* Farnborough Grammar Sch.; Emmanuel Coll., Cambridge (MA, MPhil). Consultant, Logica, 1978–86; Ovum: Principal Consultant, 1986–94; Manager, Telecommunications Reports, 1994. Sec., Newham NE Labour Party, 1981–84. Newham Borough Council: Councillor (Lab), 1984–97; Chm., Planning Cttee, 1987–90; Leader, 1990–94. PPS to Minister of State, DFEE, 1997–98, to Sec. of State for NI, 1998; Parly Under-Sec. of State, DSS, 1998–99; Minister of State (Minister for Pensions), DSS, 1999; Financial Sec., HM Treasury, 1999–2001 and 2004–05; Minister of State: (Minister for School Standards), DFES, 2001–02; (Minister for e-commerce and Competitiveness, then for Energy, e-Commerce and Postal Services), DTI, 2002–04; (Minister for Pensions), DWP, 2005–06; Chief Sec. to HM Treasury, 2006–07; Minister of State: BERR, 2007–08; DWP, 2008. Mem., H of C Treasury Select Cttee, 1996–97; Mem. Council, 1996–98, Hon. Treas., 1997–98, Parly IT Cttee. Mem., Plaistow Christian Fellowship; Vice-Chm., Christian Socialist Movement, 1996–99. Mem., Ramblers' Assoc. Hon. Pres., Telecommunications Users' Assoc., 1995–99. Hon. DEd E London, 2002. *Publications:* Broadband Communications: the commercial impact, 1986; ISDN: customer premises equipment, 1988; Broadband Communications: market strategies, 1992. *Address:* House of Commons, SW1A 0AA. *T:* (020) 7219 4000.

TIMMS, Stephen John, OBE 1997; CEng; Chief Operating Officer, Engineering and Technology Board, since 2006; Member Board, Engineering Council, since 2007; *b* Bristol, 25 March 1951; *s* of Raymond John Timms and Jean Vera Timms; *m* 1973, Rosemary Josephine Kennedy; two *s. Educ:* Ashford Boys' Grammar Sch.; BRNC Dartmouth; RNEC Manadon (BSc Hons Mech. Engrg; MSc Marine Engrg); RNC Greenwich (Postgrad. Dip. Nuclear Reactor Technol.); Open Univ. (MBA). CEng 1982; MIMechE 1989; CMarEng 2007; FIMarEST 2007. Engineer Officer: HM Submarines Renown, Resolution, Repulse, 1976–79; HM Submarine Turbulent, 1984–88; Proj. Manager, Sub-surface Ballistic Nuclear reactor instrumentation and future Sub-surface Nuclear propulsion plant, 1988–91; Principal Lectr, Dept of Nuclear Sci. and Technol., 1991–93; JSDC, 1993–94; Dep. Captain Fleet Maintenance, Faslane, 1994–96; UK Mil. Rep. NATO HQ, Brussels, SO for Partnership for Peace, Mediterranean Dialogue, NATO-Russia, NATO-Ukraine, NATO enlargement, Arms Control and Peacekeeping, 1996–99; CSO (Support), British Forces Gibraltar and CO RN Gibraltar, 1999–2000; Naval Attaché, Brasília, 2001–04; Dir, RNR and RN Youth Orgns, 2004–06. UK Rep. on wkg gp of Internat. Arctic Seas Assessment Proj., IAEA, Vienna, 1993–97. Mem. Cttee, Benelux Br., IMechE, 1997–99. Mem Bd., Women in Sci and Engrg, 2008–. Mem., RN Sailing Assoc. *Publications:* co-author of tech. papers for Internat. Arctic Seas Assessment Proj., IAEA, Vienna. *Recreations:* house renovation (of necessity), golf (for the walk), sailing. *Address:* Engineering and Technology Board, 2nd Floor, Weston House, 246 High Holborn, WC1V 7EX. *T:* (020) 3206 0412, *Fax:* (020) 3206 0401; *e-mail:* stimms@etechb.co.uk.

TIMMS, (Vera) Kate; *see* Gordon, V. K.

TIMNEY, Jacqueline Jill; *see* Smith, J. J.

TIMPERLEY, Prof. Stuart Read; Chairman, Stuart Timperley Associates, since 2002; Partner, Stuart Slatter and Co., since 2002; Professor, Istituto Studi Direzionali, University of Milan, since 1998; *b* 30 July 1943; *s* of late Kenneth Read Timperley and of Florence Timperley (*née* Burgess); *m* 1967, Veronica Parke; two *d. Educ:* Birkenhead Sch.; Univ. of Strathclyde (BA 1967; MBA 1968); Univ. of London (BSc 1967); Univ. of Liverpool (Shell Mex Res. Fellow, 1968; PhD 1971). Lectr, Univ. of Liverpool, 1970–72; London Business School: Lectr, 1972–80; Sen. Lectr, 1980–89; Dir, Sloan Fellows Prog., 1976–80; Dir, Centre for Mgt Develt, 1984–91; Associate Prof., 1989–95; Sen. Associate, Judge Inst., Univ. of Cambridge, 1998–2002. Chm., Slatter Timperley Associates, 1990–2002. Vis. Prof., European Inst. for Advanced Studies in Mgt, Brussels, 1973–85. Chm., Freightliner Ltd, 1988–91 (Dir, 1979); Director: Jermyn Hldgs Ltd, 1978–80; Intasun Ltd, 1983–87; ILG Ltd, 1986–89; Communisis plc, 2000–03; Pres., Consulteque.com S.p.A., 2000–03. Mem., Arts Council England, 2002–; Chairman: Arts Council England, East (formerly Eastern Arts Bd), 1998–; English Regl Arts Bds, 2000–01. Chm., Watford FC, 1993–97 (Dir, 1990). Gov., London Business Sch., 1991–94. *Publications:* Personnel Planning and Occupational Choice, 1974; Humanisation of Work, 1982. *Recreations:* performing arts, football. *Address:* Stuart Timperley Associates, 3 Dorset Street, W1U 4EF. *T:* (020) 7486 1585.

TIMPSON, (Anthony) Edward; MP (C) Crewe and Nantwich, since May 2008; *b* Knutsford, Cheshire, 26 Dec. 1973; *s* of John Timpson, CBE and Alex Timpson, MBE; *m* 2002, Julia Helen Still; one *s* two *d. Educ:* Pownall Hall Sch.; Alderley Edge Co. Prim. Sch.; Stockport Grammar Jun. Sch.; Terra Nova Sch.; Uppingham Sch.; Durham Univ. (BA Hons Politics); Coll. of Law, London (LLB). Called to the Bar, Inner Temple, 1998; in practice, specialising in family law, Nicholas Street Chambers, Chester, 1999–. *Recreations:* football (watching and playing), cricket, marathon running, travel, playing with my children. *Address:* House of Commons, SW1A 0AA.

TIMS, Sir Michael (David), KCVO 1992 (CVO 1984; LVO 1973 MVO 1963); Serjeant-at-Arms to HM The Queen, 1987–92, retired; *b* 14 Sept. 1931; *s* of late William Edward Tims and Eva Ida Tims; *m* 1959, Jacqueline Lily Clark; one *s. Educ:* Christ's Hosp. Nat. Service Commn, Army Catering Corps, 1950–52. The Queen's Household: Dep. Comptroller of Supply, 1953–68; Asst to the Master of the Household, 1968–92. Mem., Bd of Green Cloth, 1988–. FRSA 1992. JP Inner London, 1984–91. Freeman, City of London, 1986; Liveryman, Co. of Cooks, 1993–. Various hon. foreign awards. *Publications:* articles on fishing in national magazines. *Recreations:* battling with and painting big game fish. *Address:* Clock Tower House, The Royal Paddocks, Hampton Court Road, E Molesey, Surrey KT8 9DA.

TIMSON, Penelope Anne Constance; *see* Keith, P. A. C.

TINDALE, Gordon Anthony, OBE 1983; Director of Government and Public Affairs, WH Smith (USA) Inc., 1995–99; *b* 17 March 1938; *s* of George Augustus Tindale and Olive Sarah Collier; *m* 1960, Sonia Mary Soper; one *s* one *d. Educ:* Highgate Sch.; Trinity Coll., Oxford (BA (Mod. Hist)); Birkbeck Coll., London (MA (Internat. Relations)). Nat. Service, 1956–58. Joined British Council, 1961; postings in Iraq, Jordan, London and Egypt; Representative: Lesotho, Botswana and Swaziland, 1975–78; Zambia, 1979–83; Controller, Management Div., 1984–87; Representative, Egypt, 1987–89; Cultural Counsellor (formerly Cultural Attaché), Washington, 1989–94. *Recreations:* music, golf. *Address:* 26 Oppidans Road, Primrose Hill, NW3 3AG. *T:* (020) 7722 9343. *Club:* Hendon Golf.

TINDALE, Patricia Randall; architect; Chief Architect, Department of the Environment, 1982–86; *b* 11 March 1926; *d* of Thomas John Tindale and May Tindale (*née* Uttin). *Educ:* Blatchington Court, Seaford, Sussex; Architectural Assoc. Sch. of Architecture (AADip.). ARIBA. Architect, Welsh Dept, Min. of Educn, 1949–50; Min. of Educn Develt Gp, 1951–60; Min. of Housing and Local Govt R&D Gp, 1960–70; DoE Housing Develt Gp, 1970–72; Head, Building Regulations Professional Div., DoE, 1972–74; Dir, Housing Develt Directorate, DoE, 1974–81; Dir, Central Unit of Built Environment, DoE, 1981–82. Member: Building Regulations Adv. Cttee, 1993; British Bd of Agrement, 1993–99; Anchor Housing Assoc., 1993–98. Mem., AA Council, 1965–68. *Publication:* Housebuilding in the USA, 1966. *Recreations:* weaving, travelling. *Club:* Reform.

TINDALE, Stephen Christopher; Visiting Research Fellow, Policy Studies Institute, since 2008; *b* 29 March 1963; *s* of Gordon Anthony Tindale and Sonia Mary Tindale; *m* 1995, Katharine Quarmby; one *s* one *d. Educ:* St Anne's Coll., Oxford (BA Politics, Philosophy, Econs); Birkbeck Coll., Univ. of London (MSc Politics and Admin). FCO, 1986–89; Friends of the Earth, 1989–90; Fabian Soc., 1990–92; Advr to Rt Hon. Christopher Smith, MP, 1992–94; IPPR, 1994–96; Dir, Green Alliance, 1996–97; Advr to Minister for the Environment, 1997–2000; Chief Policy Advr, Greenpeace UK, 2000–01; Exec. Dir, Greenpeace UK, 2001–06. Lectr in Politics, Birkbeck Coll., Univ. of London, 1994–2000. *Publications:* Green Tax Reform, 1996; (ed) The State and the Nations, 1996. *Recreations:* walking, hockey, football. *Address:* Policy Studies Institute, 50 Hanson Street, W1W 6UP.

TINDALL, Gillian Elizabeth, FRSL; novelist, biographer, historian; *b* 4 May 1938; *d* of D. H. Tindall and U. M. D. Orange; *m* 1963, Richard G. Lansdown; one *s. Educ:* Univ. of Oxford (BA 1st cl., MA). Freelance journalism: occasional articles and reviews for Observer, Guardian, London Evening Standard, The Times, Independent, Daily Telegraph and New York Times. Occasional broadcasts, BBC. JP (as Gillian Lansdown), Inner London, 1980–98. Chevalier de l'Ordre des Arts et des Lettres (France), 2001. *Publications: novels:* No Name in the Street, 1959; The Water and the Sound, 1961; The Edge of the Paper, 1963; The Youngest, 1967; Someone Else, 1969, 2nd edn 1975; Fly Away Home, 1971 (Somerset Maugham Award, 1972); The Traveller and His Child, 1975; The Intruder, 1979; Looking Forward, 1983; To the City, 1987; Give Them All My Love, 1989; Spirit Weddings, 1992; *short stories:* Dances of Death, 1973; The China Egg and Other Stories, 1981; Journey of a Lifetime and Other Stories, 1990; *biography:* The Born Exile (George Gissing), 1974; *other non-fiction:* A Handbook on Witchcraft, 1965; The Fields Beneath, 1977, 2nd edn 2002; City of Gold: the biography of Bombay, 1981, 2nd edn 1992; Rosamond Lehmann: an Appreciation, 1985; (contrib.) Architecture of the British Empire, 1986; Countries of the Mind: the meaning of place to writers, 1991; Célestine: voices from a French village, 1995 (Franco-British Soc. Award, 1996); The Journey of Martin Nadaud, 1999; The Man Who Drew London: Wenceslaus Hollar in reality and imagination, 2002; The House by the Thames and the People Who Lived There, 2006. *Recreations:* keeping house, foreign travel. *Address:* c/o Curtis Brown Ltd, 28/29 Haymarket, SW1Y 4SP.

TINDALL, Prof. Victor Ronald, CBE 1992; MD; FRCS, FRCOG; Professor of Obstetrics and Gynaecology, University of Manchester at St Mary's Hospital, 1972–93, now Emeritus; *b* 1 Aug. 1928; *m* 1955, Brenda Fay; one *s* one *d. Educ:* Wallasey Grammar Sch.; Liverpool Univ. (MB ChB; MD); Manchester Univ. (MSc). Sen. Lectr and Consultant, Welsh Nat. Sch. of Medicine, Cardiff, 1965–70; Consultant Obstetrician and Gynaecologist, Univ. Hosp. of Wales, 1970–72. Sen. Vice-Pres., RCOG, 1990–93. FRCS by election, 1991. *Publications:* MCQ Tutor, MRCOG Part I, 1977, 2nd edn 1985, combined edn 1987; (jtly) Practical Student Obstetrics, 1980; Colour Atlas of Clinical Gynaecology, 1981; Essential Sciences for Clinicians, 1981; Clinical Gynaecology, 1986; (ed) Jeffcoates' Principles of Gynaecology, 5th edn 1987; Diagnostic Picture Tests in Obstetrics and Gynaecology, 1986; (ed jtly) Current Approaches to Endometrial Carcinoma, 1988; (jtly) Preparations and Advice for the Members of the Royal College of

Obstetricians and Gynaecologists, 1989; Illustrated Textbook of Gynaecology, 1991; (ed jtly) Self Assessment Picture Tests: obstetrics and gynaecology, 1996; reports for DHSS on maternal deaths in the UK. *Recreations:* ex-England Rugby international, international sporting activities. *Address:* 4 Planetree Road, Hale, Altrincham, Cheshire WA15 9JJ. *T:* (0161) 980 2680, (office) (0161) 904 8222.

TINDEMANS, Leo; Member (Christian Democratic Party), House of Representatives, Belgium, 1961–89; *b* Zwijndrecht, 16 April 1922; *m* 1960, Rosa Naesens; two *s* two *d.* *Educ:* State Univ., Ghent; Catholic Univ., Louvain. Minister: for Community Relations, 1968–71; of Agriculture and Middle Class Affairs, 1972–73; Dep. Prime Minister and Minister for the Budget, 1973–74; Prime Minister of Belgium, 1974–78; Minister of Foreign Relations, 1981–89. MEP (EPP), 1979–81 and 1989–99. Mayor of Edegem, 1965–76. President: Christian Democratic Party, 1979–81; European People's Party, 1976–85; Gp of Eur. People's Party, EP, 1992–94. Prof., Faculty of Social Scis, Catholic Univ., Louvain, 1975–87, now Emeritus; first holder, Jacques Delors Chair, Maastricht, 1993. Pres., Internat. Commn on the Balkans, 1996–. Hon. DLitt: City Univ., 1976; Heriot-Watt Univ., 1978; Georgetown Univ., Washington, 1984; Univ. de Deusto, Bilbao, 1991. Charlemagne Prize, 1976; St Liborius Medaille für Einheit und Frieden, 1977; Stresemann Medaille, 1979; Schuman Prize, 1980; Médaille d'Or du Cercle Chateaubriand, 1992; Heinrich Brauns Prize, 1994. *Publications:* L'autonomie culturelle, 1971; Een handvest voor woelig België, 1972; Dagboek van de werkgroep Eyskens, 1973; European Union, 1975; Europe, Ideal of our Generation, 1976; Atlantisch Europa, 1981; Europa zonder Kompas, 1987; L'Europe de l'Est vue de Bruxelles, 1989; Duel met de Minister, 1991; De toekomst van een idee, 1993; Kaïn in de Balkan, 1996; Memoires, 2002. *Recreations:* reading, writing, walking. *Address:* Jan Verbertlei 24, 2650 Edegem, Belgium.

TINDLE, David, RA 1979 (ARA 1973); painter; *b* 29 April 1932. *Educ:* Coventry Sch. of Art. MA Oxon 1985. Worked as scene painter and commercial artist, 1946–51; subseq. taught at Hornsey Coll. of Art; Vis. Tutor, Royal Coll. of Art, 1972–83, Fellow, 1981, Hon. FRCA, 1984; Ruskin Master of Drawing, Oxford Univ., and Professorial Fellow, St Edmund Hall, Oxford, 1985–87 (Hon. Fellow, 1988). RE, 1988–91. Hon. RBSA 1989. First showed work, Archer Gall., 1952 and 1953; regular one-man exhibns, Piccadilly Gall., from 1954; one-man exhibns at many public and private galleries in Gt Britain incl. Fischer Fine Art, 1985, 1989, 1992; Redfern Gall., London, 1994, 1996, 1998, 2000, 2001, 2003, 2004, 2005, 2007; Galerie du Tours, San Francisco and Los Angeles, 1964; Galleria Vinciana, Milan, 1968; Galleria Carbonesi, Bologna, 1968; Gallery XX, Hamburg, 1974, 1977, 1980; rep. in exhibns at: Piccadilly Gall., 1954–; Royal Acad.; Internat. Biennale of Realist Art, Bruges, 1958 and Bologna, 1967; British Exhibn Art, Basel, 1958; John Moores, 1959 and 1961; Arts Council Shows: British Self-Portraits; Painters in East Anglia; Thames in Art; The British Art Show, 1979–80; Salon de la Jeune Peinture, Paris, 1967; Mostra Mercato d'Arte Contemporanea, Florence, 1967; British Painting 1974, Hayward Gall.; British Painting 1952–77, RA; Six English Painters—Eros in Albion, Arezzo, Italy, 1989; Portrait of the Artist, Tate Gall., 1989. Set of 3 Mural decorations for Open Univ., Milton Keynes, 1977–78. Designed sets for Iolanta, Aldeburgh Fest., 1988. Work rep. in numerous public and private collections, incl. Nat. Portrait Gall.; Chantrey Bequest purchases, 1974 and 1975, now in Tate Gall. Critic Prize, 1962; Europe Prize for Painting, 1969; Critics' Choice, Tooths, 1974; Waddington Prize, Chichester Nat. Art Exhibn, 1975; Johnson Wax Award, RA, 1983. *Address:* Redfern Gallery, 20 Cork Street, W1X 2HL.

TINDLE, Sir Ray (Stanley), Kt 1994; CBE 1987 (OBE 1973); DL; Chairman: Tindle Newspapers Ltd, since 1972; Tindle Radio Ltd, since 1998; *b* 8 Oct. 1926; *s* of late John Robert Tindle and Maud Tindle; *m* 1949, Beryl Julia (*née* Ellis), MBE 2008, MA, DipEd; one *s.* *Educ:* Torquay Grammar Sch.; Strand Sch. FCIS; FCIArb. War service, Devonshire Regt (Captain), 1944–47. Asst to Dir, Newspaper Soc., 1952–58; Managing Director: Surrey Mirror Newspapers, 1959–63; Surrey Advertiser Newspapers, 1963–78 (Chm., 1978–97). Pres., Newspaper Soc., 1971–72; Vice Pres. and Chm. of Appeal, Newspaper Press Fund, 1990; Member: Newspaper Panel, Monopolies and Mergers Commn, 1987–93; Council, CPU, 1987–; Press Bd of Finance, 1990–. Founder, Tindle Enterprise Centres for the Unemployed, 1984–. Master, Stationers' and Newspaper Makers' Co., 1985–86. DL Surrey, 1989. Hon. DLitt Buckingham, 1999. *Publication:* The Press Today and Tomorrow, 1975. *Recreations:* veteran cars, newspapers, boating. *Address:* Tindle Newspapers Ltd, Old Court House, Union Road, Farnham, Surrey GU9 7PT. *Clubs:* Royal Automobile, Veteran Car, City Livery Yacht.

TINER, John Ivan, CBE 2008; Chief Executive, Financial Services Authority, 2003–07; *b* 25 Feb. 1957; *s* of Kenneth Tiner and late Joan Tiner; *m* 1978, Geraldine Kassell; two *s* one *d.* *Educ:* St Peter's Sch., Guildford; Kingston Poly. ACA 1980. Joined Arthur Andersen, 1976: Partner, 1988–2001; Managing Partner, Global Financial Services, 1997–2001; Man. Dir, Consumer, Insce and Investment Directorate, FSA, 2001–03. Director: New Star Asset Management Gp plc, 2008–; Lucida plc, 2008–. Dir, Financial Services Skills Council. *Publication:* Accounting for Treasury Products, 1987, 2nd edn 1990. *Recreations:* family, tennis, sailing, golf, watching football and Rugby.

TING, Prof. Samuel Chao Chung; Thomas D. Cabot Institute Professor, Massachusetts Institute of Technology, since 1977; *b* 27 Jan. 1936; *s* of K. H. Ting and late T. S. Wang; *m*; two *d*; *m* 1985, Susan Carol Marks; one *s.* *Educ:* Univ. of Michigan (PhD). Ford Fellow, CERN, Geneva, 1963; Asst Prof. of Physics, Columbia Univ., 1965; Prof. of Physics, MIT, 1969–. Assoc. Editor, Nuclear Physics B, 1970; Mem. Editorial Board: Nuclear Instruments and Methods, 1977; Mathematical Modeling, 1980. Hon. Professor: Beijing Normal Coll., 1984; Jiatong Univ., Shanghai, 1987. Member: US Nat. Acad. of Science, 1976; European Physical Soc.; Italian Physical Soc.; Foreign Member: Pakistan Acad. of Science, 1984; Academia Sinica (Republic of China), 1975; Soviet Acad. of Science, 1988; Russian Acad. of Sci.; Hungarian Acad. of Sci.; Deutsche Akad. Naturforscher Leopoldina; For. Corresp. Mem., Royal Spanish Acad. of Sci., 2003. Fellow, Amer. Acad. of Arts and Science, 1975. Hon. Fellow, Tata Inst. of Fundamental Res., Mumbai, 2004. Hon. ScD: Michigan, 1978; Chinese Univ. of Hong Kong, 1987; Bologna, 1988; Columbia, 1990; Univ. of Sci. and Technol. of China, 1990; Moscow State Univ., 1991; Bucharest, 1993; Nat. Tsinghua Univ., Taiwan, 2002; Nat. Jiatong Univ., Taiwan, 2003; Hon. Dr: HK Baptist, 2003; Rheinisch Westfälische Technische Hochschule, 2004; Dr *hc* Nat. Central Univ., Taiwan, 2005; Hong Kong Univ. of Sci. and Technol., 2005. Nobel Prize for Physics (jt), 1976; Ernest Orlando Lawrence Award, US Govt, 1976; A. E. Eringen Medal, Soc. of Engineering Science, USA, 1977; Gold Medal in Science, City of Brescia, Italy, 1988; De Gasperi Prize, Italian Republic, 1988; Forum Engelberg Prize, 1996; Public Service Medal, NASA, 2001. *Publications:* articles in Physical Review and Physical Review Letters. *Address:* Department of Physics, Massachusetts Institute of Technology, 77 Massachusetts Avenue, Cambridge, MA 02139–4307, USA. *Club:* Explorers' (NY).

TINKER, Prof. Andrew, PhD; FRCP, FMedSci; Professor of Molecular Medicine, since 2004, and Hon. Consultant, Department of Medicine, since 2001, University College London; *b* 12 June 1963; *s* of Dr Jack Tinker, *qv*; *m* 1987, Janet Elizabeth Sweetnham (*née* Fricker); three *s* one *d.* *Educ:* Queen's Coll., Oxford (BA 1984); Royal Free Hosp., Univ. of London (MB BS Dist. 1987; PhD 1993). MRCP 1990, FRCP 2004. MRC Trng Fellow, Nat. Heart and Lung Inst., 1990–93; Postdoctoral Res. Fellow, UCSF, 1994–96; Wellcome Trust Sen. Res. Fellow, 1996–2001, Reader, 2001–04, UCL. FMedSci 2006. *Publications:* articles on ion channels, in particular in relation to their function in the heart and blood vessels. *Recreations:* running, chess, bridge. *Address:* Department of Medicine, University College London, 5 University Street, WC1E 6JJ. *T:* (020) 7679 6391, *Fax:* (020) 7697 6250; *e-mail:* a.tinker@ucl.ac.uk.

TINKER, Prof. Anthea Margaret, CBE 2000; PhD; AcSS; Professor of Social Gerontology, since 1988, Director, Age Concern Institute of Gerontology, 1988–98, King's College London; *b* 24 Oct. 1932; *d* of Lt-Comdr James Collins and Margaret Collins (*née* Herring); *m* 1956, Rev. Preb. Dr Eric Tinker, OBE; two *s* one *d.* *Educ:* Univ. of Birmingham (BCom Econs, Pol., Sociol. 1953); City Univ. (PhD 1976). Asst Buyer, then Buyer, Boxfoldia Ltd, 1953–54; Res. Officer, BoT, 1954; HM Insp. of Factories, Min. of Labour, 1954–58; (pt-time) Res. Asst to Dir, Inst. of Local Govt Studies, and Lectr in Public Admin, Univ. of Birmingham, 1958–65; (pt-time) Lectr in Public Admin, Birmingham Sch. of Planning, 1958–65; (pt-time) Lectr in Social Policy, Extra-Mural Dept, Univ. of London, 1965–75; engaged in res., Royal Commn on Local Govt, 1967; Res. Fellow, City Univ., 1975–77; Sen., then Principal Res. Officer, DoE, 1977–88. Consultant: OECD, 1989–90; EU, 1991–2001; WHO, 2003–04. Exec. Mem., British Soc. of Gerontology, 1987–93; Member: Cttee on Ageing, C of E Bd of Social Responsibility, 1988–89; Cttee on Long Term Care, Joseph Rowntree Foundn, 1995–96; Chm., Res. Ethics Cttee, KCL, 2002–. Gov., Centre for Policy on Ageing, 1988–94. FRSocMed 1995 (Pres., Sect. of Geriatrics and Gerontology, 1998–2000); FKC 1998; Founder AcSS 1999. *Publications:* The Elderly in Modern Society, 1981, 4th edn as Older People in Modern Society, 1997; Staying at Home: helping elderly people, 1984; The Telecommunication Needs of Disabled and Elderly People, 1989; An Evaluation of Very Sheltered Housing, 1989; *jointly:* Women in Housing: access and influence, 1980; Families in Flats, 1981; A Review of Research on Falls among Elderly People, 1990; Falls and Elderly People: a study of current professional practice in England and innovations abroad, 1991; Life After Sixty: a profile of Britain's older population, 1992; Caring: the importance of third age carers, 1992; Homes and Travel: local life in the third age, 1992; The Information Needs of Elderly People, 1993; The Care of Frail Elderly People in the UK, 1994; Difficult to Let Sheltered Housing, 1995; Alternative Models of Care for Older People, Research Vol. 2, Royal Commn on Long Term Care, 1999; Home Ownership in Old Age, 1999; To Have and to Hold: the bond between older people and the homes they own, 1999; Eighty-five Not Out, 2001; University Research Ethics Committees: their role, remit and conduct, 2004; Facts and Misunderstandings about Pension and Retirement Ages, 2004; Improving the Provision of Information about Assistive Technology, 2005; pamphlets and booklets; numerous papers in learned and other jls. *Recreations:* family, France, houses. *Address:* 35 Theberton Street, N1 0QY. *T:* (020) 7359 4750.

TINKER, Dr Jack, FRCP, FRCSGlas; Emeritus Consultant, University College Hospitals, since 1996; Dean, Royal Society of Medicine, 1998–2002, now Emeritus; *b* 20 Jan. 1936; *s* of Lawrence and Jessie Tinker; *m* 1961, Maureen Ann Crawford; two *s.* *Educ:* Manchester Univ. (BSc (Hons), MB ChB); DIC. Dir, Intensive Therapy Unit, Middlesex Hosp., 1974–88; Hon. Cons. Physician, Middlesex Hosp., 1988–96; Hon. Sen. Clin. Lectr, UCL Med. Sch. (formerly UCMSM), 1988–96; Hon. Sen. Lectr, St Bartholomew's Hosp. Med. Coll., 1991–96; Dean of Postgrad. Medicine, Univ. of London and N Thames RHA, 1988–96. Sen. Med. Consultant, Sun Life of Canada, 1983–2000; Med. Advr, Rio Tinto plc (formerly RTZ Gp), 1986–2006; Med. Dir, Health Screening Unit, London Clinic, 1994–2006. Chm., Dr Foster Ethics Cttee, 2001–. Gov., Expert Witness Inst., 2003–07. FRSocMed 1989 (Hon. Sub-Dean, 1996–98). FRSA 1997. Editor in Chief, British Jl of Hospital Medicine, 1985–; Man. Editor, Intensive Care Medicine, 1973–88. *Publications:* A Course in Intensive Therapy Nursing, 1980; Care of the Critically Ill Patient, 1982, 2nd edn 1991; A Pocket Book for Intensive Care, 1986, 2nd edn 1990; Critical Care, Standards, Audit and Ethics, 1996; contribs to intensive care and cardiological jls. *Recreation:* watching soccer and cricket. *Address:* 1 Rectory Road, Barnes, SW13 0DU. *T:* (020) 8878 0159. *Clubs:* Royal Automobile, MCC; Scarborough.
See also A. Tinker.

TINKER, Prof. Philip Bernard Hague, OBE 2000; PhD, DSc; FIBiol, FRSC; Director of Terrestrial and Freshwater Science, Natural Environment Research Council, 1985–92; *b* 1 Feb. 1930; *s* of Philip and Gertrude Tinker; *m* 1955, Maureen Ellis (*d* 2005); one *s* one *d.* *Educ:* Rochdale High Sch.; Sheffield Univ. (BSc); PhD 1955; MA, DSc 1984, Oxon. FIBiol 1974; FRSC 1985. Overseas Res. Service, 1955–62; Sen. Scientific Officer, Rothamsted Experimental Stn, 1962–65; Lectr, Oxford Univ., 1965–71; Prof. of Agricultural Botany, Leeds Univ., 1971–77; Head of Soils Div., 1977–85, and Dep. Dir, 1981–85, Rothamsted Experimental Stn; Fellow, 1969–72, Sen. Res. Fellow, 1988–96, St Cross Coll., Oxford. Hon. Vis. Prof., Imperial Coll., 1992–95; Sen. Vis. Fellow, Plant Scis Dept, Oxford Univ., 1995–. Lectures: Regents, Univ. of California, 1979; Hannaford Meml, Adelaide, 1990; Francis New Meml and Medal, Fertilizer Soc., 1991. Chairman: UK Man and Biosphere Cttee, 1990–93; UK Cttee for Internat. Geosphere-Biosphere Prog., 1992–98; Biology Cttee, Palm Oil Res. Inst., Malaysia, 1995–98 (Mem., 1987–98). Member: UNESCO Adv. Cttee for Biosphere Reserves, 1992–96; IGBP Scientific Cttee, 1992–98. Pres., British Soil Sci. Soc., 1983–84; Gov., Macaulay Land Use Res. Inst., Aberdeen, 1990–2001. Fellow, Norwegian Acad. of Science and Letters, 1987; Hon. FRASE 1990; Hon. Mem., Internat. Union of Soil Scis, 2002. Busk Medal, RGS, 1994. *Publications:* (with F. E. Sanders and B. Mosse) Endomycorrhizas, 1975; (with P. H. Nye) Solute Movement in the Soil-root System, 1977; Soil and Agriculture—Critical Reviews, 1980; (with L. Fowden and R. M. Barrer) Clay Minerals, 1984; (with A. Läuchli) Advances in Plant Nutrition, vol. I, 1984, vol. II, 1986, vol. III, 1988; (with P. H. Nye) Solute Movement in the Rhizosphere, 2000; Shades of Green: a review of UK farming systems, 2000; (with R. H. V. Corley) The Oil Palm, 2003; *c* 175 papers. *Recreations:* reading, gardening, map collecting. *Address:* The Glebe House, Broadwell, Lechlade, Glos GL7 3QS. *T:* (01367) 860436. *Club:* Farmers'.

TINNISWOOD, Maurice Owen; *b* 26 March 1919; *y s* of late Robert Tinniswood, OBE; *m* 1946, Anne Katharine, *yr d* of late Rev. J. Trevor Matchett; one *s* one *d.* *Educ:* Merchant Taylors' School. Served with Royal Hampshire Regt, 1939–46 (Major). Joined PO, 1938 as Executive Officer, Principal, 1949; Asst Secretary, 1958; Imperial Defence College, 1963; Director of Establishments and Organisation, 1965; Director of Reorganization, 1966; Secretary to the Post Office, 1969–70; Dir of Personnel, BBC, 1970–77. Chm., Kingston, Richmond and Esher Community Health Council, 1980–81; Mem., Kingston and Esher HA, 1982–85. CCMI. *Address:* 66 The Cloisters, Pegasus Grange, Whitehouse Road, Oxford OX1 4QQ. *T:* (01865) 721191.
See also P. M. Tinniswood.

TINNISWOOD, Peter Maurice; Head Master, Lancing College, 1998–2005; *b* 30 May 1951; *s* of Maurice Owen Tinniswood, *qv*; *m* 1975, Catharina Elizabeth Oeschger. *Educ:* Charterhouse; Magdalen Coll., Oxford (MA); INSEAD (MBA 1981). Assistant Master: Repton Sch., 1974–76; Marlborough Coll., 1976–80; Sec. Gen., Franco-British Chamber of Commerce and Industry, Paris, 1981–83; Marlborough College: Asst Master, 1983–91; Head of Dept, 1983–86; Housemaster, 1985–91; Master, Magdalen Coll. Sch., Oxford, 1991–98. Governor: Dorset House Sch., 2000–06; Mowden Sch., 2002–05; St Paul's Sch., Sao Paulo, 2007–. *Publications:* Marketing Decisions, 1981; Marketing and Production Decisions, 1991. *Address:* Samvara, Les Girvaysses, 81170 Noailles, France.

TINSON, Dame Susan (Myfanwy), DBE 1990; media consultant; Director, External Relations, Independent Television News, 2001–03; *b* 15 Jan. 1943; *d* of John and Kathleen Thomas; *m* 1968, Trevor James Tinson (marr. diss. 1979). *Educ:* South Hampstead High Sch.; Hull Univ. (BA Hons Social Studies). Independent Television News: Senior Editor, News at Ten and Asst Editor, ITN, 1982; Associate Editor, 1989–2001; consultant, ITN and ITV, 2003–. Non-executive Director: Yorkshire Building Soc., 1999–2006; Chime Communications plc, 2001–06; St Ives plc, 2004–07; Bd, ITV London, 2004–06. Comr, Commonwealth War Graves Commn, 1999–2004. FRTS 1996. *Address:* 170 Ebury Street, SW1W 8UP.

TINSTON, Robert Sydney, CBE 2001; Regional Director, NHS Executive North West, 1996–2002; *b* 29 March 1951; *s* of Sydney Tinston and Rita (*née* Jardine); *m* 1975, Catherine Mary Somers; one *s* one *d*. *Educ:* Stockport Sch.; Edinburgh Univ. (BSc). DipHSM 1979; MHSM 1979. Assistant Sector Administrator: Withington Hosp., Manchester, 1976–78; King's Coll. Hosp., London, 1978–79; Hosp. Sec., Cookridge Hosp., Leeds, 1979–83; Commissioning Officer, Clarendon Wing, Leeds, 1983–86; Gen. Manager, Leeds General Infirmary, 1986–89; Chief Exec., Royal Liverpool Hosp., 1989–91; Dep. Chief Exec., then Chief Exec., Mersey RHA, 1991–94; Chief Exec., NW RHA, 1994–96. FRSA 1994; CCMI (CIMgt 1997). Hon. Vis. Prof., Univ. of Manchester, 1996–. *Recreations:* astronomy, genealogy, Stockport County Football Club. *Address:* The Thatched Cottage, Utkinton, Tarporley, Cheshire CW6 0LL.

TIPLER, Laura; *see* Drysdale, L.

TIPPER, Prof. Steven Paul, DPhil; FBA 2007; Professor of Cognitive Science, Bangor University (formerly University of Wales, Bangor), since 1993; *b* 12 Sept. 1956; *s* of Malcolm Tipper and June Tipper; *m* 1987, Alison Warner; two *s* one *d*. *Educ:* Wolfson Coll., Oxford (BSc 1980; MSc 1981; DPhil 1985). Asst Prof., Mount Allison Univ., Canada, 1985–89; Associate Prof., McMaster Univ., Canada, 1989–93; Dir, Wolfson Centre of Clinical and Cognitive Neurosci., Univ. of Wales, Bangor, 2004–07. *Publications:* over 100 articles in learned jls, incl. Qly Jl of Exptl Psychology. *Recreations:* spending time with my family, appreciating the beauty of North Wales. *Address:* School of Psychology, Bangor University, Bangor, Gwynedd LL57 2AS. *T:* (01248) 382095, *Fax:* (01248) 382599; *e-mail:* s.tipper@bangor.ac.uk.

TIPPING, Rt Hon. Andrew (Patrick Charles), DCNZM 2006; PC 1998; **Rt Hon. Justice Tipping;** a Judge of the Supreme Court of New Zealand, since 2004; *b* 22 Aug. 1942; *s* of Wing Comdr Patrick Alexander Tipping, RAF retd and Elizabeth Ayliffe Tipping; *m* 1967, Judith Ann Oliver; two *s* one *d*. *Educ:* Christ's Coll., Christchurch; Univ. of Canterbury (BA, LLB 1965; LLM 1st Cl. Hons 1966). Canterbury Dist Law Soc. Gold Medal, 1966; Sir Timothy Cleary Meml Prize, NZ Law Soc., 1967. Partner, Wynn Williams & Co., Barristers and Solicitors, 1967–86; Judge, High Court of NZ, 1986–97; Judge, Ct of Appeal of NZ, 1997–2004. Member of Council: Canterbury Dist Law Soc., 1976–84 (Pres., 1984); NZ Law Soc., 1982–84 (Mem., 1979–86, Chm., 1985–86, Courts and Tribunals Cttee). *Recreations:* gardening, fishing, tramping. *Address:* 14 Cluny Avenue, Kelburn, Wellington 5, New Zealand. *T:* (4) 4753755. *Clubs:* Christchurch (Christchurch); Wellington (Wellington).

TIPPING, Sir David Gwynne E.; *see* Evans-Tipping.

TIPPING, Simon Patrick, (Paddy); MP (Lab) Sherwood, since 1992; *b* 24 Oct. 1949; *m* 1970, Irene Margaret Quinn; two *d*. *Educ:* Hipperholme Grammar Sch.; Nottingham Univ. (BA 1972; MA 1978). Social Worker, Notts, 1972–79; Project Leader, C of E Children's Soc., Nottingham, 1979–83. Mem. (Lab) Notts CC, 1981–93 (Chm., Economic Develt and Finance Cttees); Director: Notts Co-op. Develt Agency, 1983–92; Nottingham Develt Enterprise, 1987–93. Dep. Leader, H of C, 2007. Contested (Lab) Rushcliffe, 1987. Vice Pres., Ramblers Assoc., 1995–. *Recreations:* running, walking, gardening. *Address:* House of Commons, SW1A 0AA.

TIPPLER, John; Director, Network, British Telecom, UK Communications Division, 1986–89, retired; *b* 9 Aug. 1929; *s* of George Herbert and Sarah Tippler, Spalding, Lincs; *m* 1st, 1952, Pauline Taylor (marr. diss. 1983); two *s*; 2nd, 1992, Martha Elisabet Berg, psychoanalyst, Stockholm. *Educ:* Spalding Grammar School. Architect's Dept, Spalding RDC, 1945; Post Office Telephone Service, 1947; Royal Signals, 1949–50; Staff Mem., PO Central Engineering Sch., 1954–59; PO Engineering Develt, 1960–80; Dir, Exchange and Data Systems Op. and Develt, 1980; Dir of Engrg, BT, 1982–86. Dir, IT Inst., 1986–88. Mem., Youth Offending Community Panel, 2002–06. Mem., Exec. Cttee, 1997–2004, Trustee, 2004–, Friends of Birzeit Univ. *Recreations:* music, country walking, travel, cinema, theatre.

TIRAMANI, Jennifer Jane; theatre designer and dress historian; director and designer, Phoebus Cart Theatre Co., since 2005; *b* 16 Aug. 1954; *d* of Fredo Paulo Tiramani and Barbara Doreen Tiramani (*née* King); one *s* with Alastair Brotchie. *Educ:* Dartford Grammar Sch. for Girls; Central Sch. of Art and Design, London (Foundn course); Trent Poly., Nottingham (1st Cl. Dip. Theatre Design 1976). Designer, 7:84 England and 7:84 Scotland Th. Cos, 1978–84; Associate Designer, Theatre Royal, Stratford East, 1980–97; Designer, Renaissance Th. Co., 1988–90; Shakespeare's Globe: Associate Designer, 1997–2002; designs include: Henry V, 1997; Hamlet, 2000; Dir, Th. Design, 2003–05; designs include: Twelfth Night, 2003 (Olivier Award for Best Costume Design); Measure for Measure, The Tempest, 2005; West End prodns include: Steaming, Comedy, 1981; Much Ado About Nothing, Phoenix, 1988. Advr and contrib., Searching for Shakespeare exhibn, NPG, 2006. Vis. Prof., Sch. of Art and Design, Nottingham Trent Univ., 2008–. Sam Wanamaker Award (jtly), Shakespeare's Globe, 2007. *Publications:* contribs to Costume. *Address:* 47 Charles Square, N1 6HT. *T:* and *Fax:* (020) 7490 0987; *e-mail:* jennyt@ruff.co.uk.

TIRVENGADUM, Sir Harry (Krishnan), Kt 1987; Chevalier, Ordre National de la Légion d'Honneur 1986; Chairman and Managing Director, Air Mauritius, 1981–97, 2000–01; Managing Director, Air Afrique, 1997–99; *b* 2 Sept. 1933; *s* of late Govinden Tirvengadum and Meenatchee Sangeelee; *m* 1970, Elahe Amin Amin; three *d*. *Educ:* Royal College, Mauritius; Oxford Univ. Asst Sec., Min. of Works, 1952–67; Principal Assistant Secretary: Min. of Communications, in charge of Depts of Civil Aviation, Telecommunications, Marine Services, Posts & Telegraphs and Meteorological Services, 1968–72; Min. of Commerce and Industry, 1970; Air Mauritius: Gen. Manager, 1972–78; Dep. Chm. and Dep. Man. Dir, 1978–81. Chairman: Rodrigues Hotel, 1981–; New Airport Catering Services, 1988–; Mauritius Shopping Paradise Ltd, 1984–93; Director: Mauritius Hotels Gp, 1973–81; Plaisance Airlift Catering Unit, 1980–92; Mauritius Telecom, 1984–; Mauritius Estate Development & Co., 1986–; Mauritius Commercial Bank, 1989–; State Bank Internat., 1990–. Chm., Municipal Commn, Quatre-Bornes, 1974–77. Chief delegate of Mauritius, Triennial Assemblies, ICAO, 1971–; Rep. of Employers on Employment of Disabled Persons Bd, 1988–. Member: Exec. Cttee, IATA, 1988–91 (Chm., 1992–93); Nat. Educn Award Panel, 1988; Pres., African Airlines Assoc., 1995–96; Chm., Indian Ocean Regl Fund, 1999–2001. FCIT; FInstD. Citoyen d'Honneur, Town of Beau Bassin/Rose Hill, Mauritius, 1986. *Recreations:* bridge, swimming, walking. *Address:* Dr Arthur De Chazal Lane, Floréal, Mauritius. *T:* 6964455. *Club:* Mauritius Gymkhana.

TISHLER, Gillian, (Mrs Richard Wood); Chief Executive, Young Women's Christian Association of Great Britain, 1993–2007; *b* 27 March 1958; *d* of Harry and Joyce Tishler; *m* 1991, Richard Wood. *Educ:* King Edward VI Sch., Morpeth; St Anne's Coll., Oxford (BA Hons Mod. Langs). Ministry of Agriculture, Fisheries and Food: fast stream trainee, 1979; Private Office (Private Sec. to Parly Sec.), 1986–87; Royal National Institute for the Blind: Parly Officer, 1987–89; Head of Public Affairs, 1989–93. *Recreations:* theatre, singing, walking.

TITCHENER, Alan Ronald, CB 1993; Managing Director, Resource (Science and Technology Expertise) Ltd, 1993–96; *b* 18 June 1934; *s* of Edmund Hickman Ronald Titchener and Minnie Ellen Titchener; *m* 1959, Joyce Blakesley; two *s*. *Educ:* Harrow County Grammar Sch.; London School of Economics (BSc(Econ) 1962). RAF, 1952. Colonial Office, 1954; Min. of Transport, 1962; Board of Trade, 1964; HM Consul New York, 1969; Dept of Trade, 1973; HM Consul-Gen., Johannesburg, 1978; Under Secretary, Department of Trade and Industry, 1982–93: Overseas Trade Div., 1982; Enterprise Initiative Div., 1987; Head of Personnel, 1991. FRSA 1993. *Club:* Royal Air Force.

TITCHMARSH, Alan Fred, MBE 2000; VMH; DL; writer and broadcaster; *b* 2 May 1949; *s* of Alan Titchmarsh and Bessie Titchmarsh (*née* Hardisty); *m* 1975, Alison Margaret Needs; two *d*. *Educ:* Ilkley County Secondary Sch.; Shipley Art and Tech. Inst.; Herts Coll. of Agric. and Hortic. (Nat. Cert. Hort.); Royal Botanic Gardens, Kew (DipHort). FIHort 1998. Apprentice gardener, Parks Dept, Ilkley UDC, 1964–68; Supervisor, Staff Trng, Royal Botanic Gardens, 1972–74; Asst Editor, gardening books, Hamlyn Publishing, 1974–76; Asst Editor and Dep. Editor, Amateur Gardening, 1976–79; freelance writer and broadcaster, 1979–; gardening correspondent: Woman's Own, 1980–85; Daily Mail, 1985–99; Daily Express, and Sunday Express, 1999–; Radio Times, 1996–2001, 2004–; gardening editor, Homes & Gardens, 1985–89; contrib. to BBC Gardeners' World Magazine, 1992–, Gardenlife, 2004–06. *BBC radio series include:* You and Yours, Down to Earth, A House in a Garden, Alan Titchmarsh Show; numerous other progs; *BBC TV:* Nationwide, Breakfast Time, Open Air, Daytime Live; Chelsea Flower Show, 1983–97, 2001–; Songs of Praise, 1989–94; Pebble Mill, 1991–96; Sweet Inspiration, 1993–94; Gardeners' World, 1995–2002; Ground Force, 1997–2003; How to be a Gardener, 2002–03; The Royal Gardeners, 2003; British Isles: a natural history, 2004; BBC Proms, 2004–; 20th Century Roadshow, 2005; The Gardener's Year, 2006; The Great British Village Show, 2007; The Nature of Britain, 2007; Saving Planet Earth, 2007; *other TV series include:* Britain's Best, 2007; The Alan Titchmarsh Show, 2007–. Founder, Alan Titchmarsh's Gardens for Schools, 2001–. Vice-President: Wessex Cancer Trust, 1988–; Butterfly Conservation, 2000–; Arboricultural Assoc., 2000–; Patron: Rainbow Trust, 1993–; Kaleidoscope Theatre, 1995–; Seeds for Africa, 1999–; Treloar Trust, 1999–; Henry Spink Foundn, 2000–; Country Holidays for Inner City Kids, 2000–; Cowes Inshore Lifeboat, 2000–; Writtle Coll., 2001–; Horticap, 2002–; Hampshire and Wight Trust for Maritime Archaeology, 2005–; Royal Gardeners' Orphan Fund, 2006–; Hon. Patron, Friends of the Castle of Mey, 2005–; Vice Patron, Jubilee Sailing Trust, 2000–; Trustee, Nat. Maritime Mus., 2004–; President: Gardening for Disabled Trust, 1989–; Telephones for the Blind, 1993–; London Children's Flower Soc., 2001–; Perennial (Gardeners' Royal Benevolent Soc.), 2005–; Ambassador, Prince's Trust, 2003–. Mem., Consultative Cttee, Nat. Pinetum, 1996–2004. Freeman, City of London; Liveryman, Gardeners' Co. DL Hants, 2001; High Sheriff, IoW, 2008. Hon. FCGI 2000. Hon. DSc Bradford, 1999; DUniv: Essex, 1999; Leeds Metropolitan, 2003; Winchester, 2007. Gardening Writer of the Year, 1980, 1983; RHS Gold Medal, Chelsea Flower Show, 1985; Television Broadcaster of the Year, Garden Writer's Guild, 1997, 1998, 1999, 2000; Yorks Man of the Year, 1997, 2007; Lifetime Achievement Award, Garden Writers' Guild, 2004; Special Award, TRIC, 2004. VMH 2004. *Publications:* Starting With House Plants, 1976; Gardening Under Cover, 1979, 2nd edn 1985; Guide to Greenhouse Gardening, 1980; Climbers and Wall Plants, 1980; Everyone's Book of House Plants, 1981; (with R. C. M. Wright) Complete Book of Plant Propagation, 1981; Gardening Techniques, 1981; Pocket Indoor Gardener, 1982; Hamlyn Guide to House Plants, 1982; Pest-Free Plants, 1982; The Allotment Gardener's Handbook, 1982, 2nd edn 1993; The Rock Gardener's Handbook, 1983; How to be a Supergardener, 1983, 3rd edn 1999; (ed) 1,000 Handy Gardening Hints, 1983; Alan Titchmarsh's Avant Gardening, 1984, 2nd edn 1994; Alan Titchmarsh's Gardening Guides, 1984; The Gardener's Logbook, 1985; (ed) A–Z of Popular Garden Plants, 1985; Pocket Guide to Gardening, 1987; (cons. ed.) All Your Gardening Questions Answered, 1988; Daytime Live Gardening Book, 1990; The English River, 1993; Alan Titchmarsh's Favourite Gardens, 1995; (cons. ed) Ground Force Weekend Workbook, 1999; Gardeners' World Complete Book of Gardening, 1999; How to be a Gardener, 2001; Trowel and Error (memoirs), 2002; How to be a Gardener, Book 2, 2003; The Royal Gardeners, 2003; British Isles: a natural history, 2004; (ed and contrib.) Fill My Stocking (anthology), 2005; The Gardener's Year, 2005; Nobbut A Lad (memoir), 2006; The Nature of Britain, 2007; England, Our England (anthology), 2007; The Kitchen Gardener, 2008; *novels:* Mr MacGregor, 1998; The Last Lighthouse Keeper, 1999; Animal Instincts, 2000; Only Dad, 2001; Rosie, 2004; Love and Dr Devon, 2006; Folly, 2008. *Recreations:* art, music, boating. *Address:* c/o Caroline Mitchell, Colt Hill House, Odiham, Hook, Hants RG29 1AL. *T:* (01256) 702839. *Clubs:* Annabel's; Lord's Taverners; Royal London Yacht (Cowes).

TITCHMARSH, Prof. John Michael, DPhil; Royal Academy of Engineering Research Professor in Microanalytical Techniques for Structural Integrity Problems, University of Oxford, 1998–2005; Fellow, St Anne's College, Oxford, 1998–2005, now Emeritus; *b* 4 Sept. 1944; *s* of late Harold Titchmarsh and of Ada Titchmarsh; *m* 1967, Elaine Joy Knightley; two *d*. *Educ:* Christ's Coll., Cambridge (BA Nat. Sci. 1966; MA 1970); Wadham Coll., Oxford (DPhil 1969). Res. Asst, Univ. of Oxford, 1969–74; UKAEA, 1974–94; Philips Prof. in Materials Analysis, Sheffield Hallam Univ., 1994–98. Member of Committee: Inst. of Physics; RMS. Birks Award, Microbeam Analysis Soc., USA, 1995. *Publications:* papers in learned jls on electron microscopy. *Address:* Department of Materials, University of Oxford, Parks Road, Oxford OX1 3PH; St Anne's College, Oxford OX2 6JF.

TITE, Prof. Michael Stanley, DPhil; FSA; Edward Hall Professor of Archaeological Science and Director of Research Laboratory for Archaeology and History of Art, University of Oxford, 1989–2004, now Emeritus; Fellow of Linacre College, Oxford, 1989–2004, now Emeritus; *b* 9 Nov. 1938; *s* of late Arthur Robert Tite and Evelyn Frances Violet Tite (*née* Endersby); *m* 1967, Virginia Byng Noel; two *d*. *Educ:* Trinity Sch. of John Whitgift, Croydon; Christ Church, Oxford (MA, DPhil). FSA 1977. Research Fellow in Ceramics, Univ. of Leeds, 1964–67; Lectr in Physics, Univ. of Essex, 1967–75; Keeper, Dept of Scientific Res. (formerly Res. Lab.), British Museum, 1975–89. Pomerance Award for Sci. Contribs to Archaeol., Archaeol Inst. of America, 2008. *Publications:* Methods of Physical Examination in Archaeology, 1972; papers on scientific methods applied to archaeology in various jls. *Recreations:* travelling with "The Buildings of England", gardening. *Address:* 7 Kings Cross Road, Oxford OX2 7EU. *T:* (01865) 558422.

TITFORD, Jeffrey William; Member (UK Ind) Eastern Region, England, European Parliament, since 1999; *b* 24 Oct. 1933; *s* of Guy Frederick Titford and Queta Mehalah (*née* D'Wit); *m* 1956, Margaret Cheeld; one *s* three *d*. Dip. Funeral Directing. Titford Funeral Service Ltd, 1954–89, Man. Dir, 1970–89. Pres., Nat. Assoc. Funeral Dirs, 1975–76. Ldr, UK Independence Party, 2000–02. Contested: (Referendum) Harwich, 1997; (UKIP) Harwich, 2005. *Recreations:* fishing, walking, golf. *Address:* Bratton House, Charlton Gardens, Ditchling, E Sussex BN6 8WA.

TITHERIDGE, Roger Noel; QC 1973; a Recorder of the Crown Court 1972–99; Barrister-at-Law, retired; *b* 21 Dec. 1928; *s* of Jack George Ralph Titheridge and Mabel Titheridge (*née* Steains); *m* 1963, Annabel Maureen (*née* Scott-Fisher); two *d*. *Educ:* Midhurst Grammar Sch.; Merton Coll., Oxford (Exhibnr; MA (History and Jurisprudence)). Called to the Bar, Gray's Inn, 1954; Holker Sen. Scholar, Gray's Inn, 1954; Bencher, Gray's Inn, 1985; Dep. High Court Judge, QBD, 1984–98; Leader, Western Circuit, 1989–92. *Recreations:* tennis, sailing. *Address:* 1 Paper Buildings, Temple, EC4Y 7EP. *T:* (020) 7353 3728; 13 The Moat, Traps Lane, New Malden, Surrey KT3 4SB. *T:* (020) 8942 2747.

TITLEY, Gary; Member (Lab) North West Region, England, European Parliament, since 1999 (Greater Manchester West, 1989–99); Leader, European Parliamentary Labour Party, since 2002; *b* 19 Jan. 1950; *s* of Wilfred James and Joyce Lillian Titley; *m* 1975, Maria, (Charo), Rosario; one *s* one *d*. *Educ:* York Univ. (BA Hons Hist./Educn, 1973; PGCE 1974). TEFL, Bilbao, 1973–75; taught History, Earls High Sch., Halesowen, 1976–84; Personal Assistant to MEP, 1984–89. Mem., W Midlands CC, 1981–86 (Vice-Chair: EDC, 1981–84; Consumer Services Cttee, 1984–86). Dir, W Midlands Enterprise Bd, 1982–89; Chairman: W Midlands Co-op Finance Co., 1982–89; Black Country Co-op Develt Agency, 1982–88. Contested (Lab): Bromsgrove, 1983; Dudley W, 1987. Pres., Eur. Parlt delegn for relations with Finland, 1992–94; rapporteur, accession of Finland to EU. President: European Economic Area Jt Parly Assembly, 1994–95; Jt Parly Cttee for relns with Lithuania, 1999–2001; Cttee of Jt Parly Assembly and delegn presidents, 2001–02. Commander, White Rose (Finland), 1995; Golden Cross (Austria), 1996; Order of Grand Duke Gediminas (Lithuania), 2003. *Recreations:* family, reading, sport. *Address:* (office) 16 Spring Lane, Radcliffe, Manchester M26 2TQ. *T:* (0161) 724 4008.

TITLEY, Commandant Nursing Officer Jane, CBE 1995; RRC 1990 (ARRC 1986); Director of Defence Nursing Services, 1992–95; *b* 22 April 1940; *d* of Louis and Phyllis Myra (Josephine) Titley. *Educ:* St Catherine's Convent, Nottingham; St Bartholomew's Hosp.; Sussex Maternity Hosp. SRN 1962; SCM 1963. Joined QARNNS, 1965; served in Naval hosps and estabts in UK, Malta, Singapore, Naples and Gibraltar; Matron, 1986; Dep. Matron-in-Chief, 1988; Matron-in-Chief, 1990–94; QHNS, 1990–94. OStJ 1990. *Recreations:* 'to stand and stare', narrow-boating, genealogy. *Address:* Flat 10, 28 Pembridge Square, W2 4DS.

TITTERINGTON, Prof. David Michael; Professor of Organ, since 1991, and Head, Organ Studies, since 1996, Royal Academy of Music, University of London; concert organist, since 1986; *b* 10 Jan. 1958; *s* of Geoffrey Bridge Titterington and Claire Elizabeth Titterington (*née* Parsons). *Educ:* Pembroke Coll., Oxford (Organ Schol.; BA Hons 1980, MA 1984); Conservatoire de Rueil-Malmaison, Paris (1st Prize 1984, Prix d'Excellence 1985). Dir of Music, Dutch Ch, London, 1992–; Organ Consultant: Pembroke Coll., Oxford, 1993–95; Chapel Royal, HM Tower of London, 1997–2000; St Catharine's Coll., Cambridge, 2000–01; Sidney Sussex Coll., Cambridge, 2007–; Canterbury Cathedral, 2007–. Vis. Prof. of Organ, Liszt Ferenc Acad. of Music, Budapest, 1997–; Hon. Prof., Liszt Ferenc State Univ., 1999. Gen. Ed., Organ Repertoire Series, 1987–97. Artistic Director: European Organ Fest. and Comp. (for FCO), 1992; Internat. Organ Fest., St Albans, 2007–. Solo recital début, RFH, 1986; *festival performances* include: Bicentennial Fest., Sydney, 1988; Hong Kong, Adelaide, NZ, Israel, Guelph, Prague Spring, Schleswig Holstein, Lahti, Granada, León, Brezice, BBC Proms, Cheltenham, City of London, Dartington, Belfast; *concerto performances* include: Berlin SO; BBC SO; Lahti SO; BBC Scottish SO; City of London Sinfonia; Britten Sinfonia; Guildhall String Ensemble; Allegri String Quartet. Hon. Fellow, Bolton Inst. of Higher Educn, 1992; Hon. FRCO 1999. Hon. RAM 2008. Hon. DMus Liszt Ferenc State, Budapest, 1999. Arts Council of GB Award, 1984. *Publications:* (with J. Wainright) History of Pembroke College, Organs, 1995; (contrib.) Organs of Britain 1990–1995, 1996; (contrib.) New Grove Dictionary of Music and Musicians, 2000; article in RCO Jl. *Recreations:* silence, the sea, reading, friends. *Address:* Royal Academy of Music, Marylebone Road, NW1 5HT. *T:* (020) 7873 7339, *Fax:* (020) 7873 7439; *e-mail:* d.titterington@ram.ac.uk. *Club:* Athenæum.

TIWARI, Narayan Datt; Governor, Andhra Pradesh, since 2007; Chief Minister, Uttaranchal, 2002–07 (Chief Minister, Uttar Pradesh, 1976–77, 1984–85, March–Sept. 1985 and 1988–89); *b* Balyuti, UP, 18 Oct. 1925; *s* of Poorna Nand Tiwari and Chandrawati Devi Tiwari; *m* 1954, Dr Sushila Tiwari (*d* 1993). *Educ:* Allahabad Univ., UP (Golden Jubilee Schol. 1948; MA Diplomacy and Internat. Affairs; LLB; Pres., Students' Union). Studied Scandinavian Econ. and Budgetary Systems in Sweden, 1959; Congressional Practices and Procedures in USA, 1964; Whitley Council System, UK, and Co-op. Banking System in Germany, Dairy Develt in Denmark. Joined Freedom Movement, 1938, and Quit India Movement, 1942, resulting in 15 months in jail, 1942. MLA (Socialist) UP, 1952, re-elected nine times. State Govt appts, 1969–77: Chm., Public Accts Cttee; Minister for Finance, Heavy Industry, Sugar Cane Develt; Dep. Chm., State Planning Commn, 1980. Leader of Opposition in UP, 1977–79, 1991. MP: Nainital, Lok Sabha, 1980–84, 1995–98 and 1999–2002; Rajya Sabha, 1985–88; Union Minister for Planning and Labour and Dep. Chm., Planning Commn, India, 1980; Union Minister: for Industry and Steel and Mines, 1981–84; of Industry, Petroleum and Natural Gas, Ext. Affairs, Finance and Commerce, 1985–87; of Finance and Commerce, India, 1987–88; Leader of House, Rajya Sabha, 1986–88. Mem., Nat. Working Cttee, Indian Nat. Congress, 1993. Editor, Prabhat (a Hindi Monthly magazine). *Publications:* European Miscellany, 1964; hundreds of articles as a journalist. *Recreations:* playing cricket, hockey, chess; reading. *Address:* Village Padampuri, PO Padampuri, Dist Nainital, UP, India; B 315, Sector B, Dr Sushila Tiwari Marg, Mahanagar, Lucknow, UP, India. *T:* (522) 384859, (522) 239398, (11) 3382259, (11) 3382218.

TIZARD, Prof. Barbara, PhD; FBA 1997; FBPsS; Professor of Education, Institute of Education, University of London, 1982–90, now Emeritus; Director, Thomas Coram Research Unit, Institute of Education, 1980–90; *b* 16 April 1926; *d* of late Herbert Parker and Elsie Parker (*née* Kirk); *m* 1947, Jack Tizard (*d* 1979); one *s* two *d* (and two *s* decd). *Educ:* St Paul's Girls' School; Somerville College, Oxford. BA Oxon, PhD London. Lectr, Dept of Experimental Neurology, Inst. of Psychiatry, 1963–67; Res. Officer then Senior Res. Fellow, Inst. of Education, 1967–77, Reader in Education, 1978–80. Chm., Assoc. of Child Psychology and Psychiatry, 1976–77. Co-editor, British Jl of Psychology, 1975–79; Member Editorial Board: Jl of Child Psychology and Psychiatry, 1979–90; Social Development, 1992–. *Publications:* Early Childhood Education, 1975; Adoption: a second chance, 1977; (with J. Mortimore and B. Burchell) Involving Parents in Nursery and Infant Schools, 1981; (with M. Hughes) Young Children Learning, 1984, 2nd edn 2002; (jtly) Young Children at School in the Inner City, 1988; (with A. Phoenix) Black, White or Mixed Race? Race and racism in the lives of young people of mixed parentage, 1993, revised edn 2002; articles on transracial and intercountry adoption, children in care, child development and early education. *Address:* Thomas Coram Research Unit, 27 Woburn Square, WC1H 0AA.

TIZARD, Dame Catherine (Anne), ONZ 2002; GCMG 1990; GCVO 1995; DBE 1985; QSO 1996; Governor-General of New Zealand, 1990–96; *b* 4 April 1931; *d* of Neil Maclean and Helen Montgomery Maclean; *m* 1951, Rt Hon. Robert James Tizard, *qv* (marr. diss. 1983); one *s* three *d*. *Educ:* Matamata College; Auckland University (BA). Tutor in Zoology, Univ. of Auckland, 1967–84. Member: Auckland City Council, 1971–83 (Mayor of Auckland, 1983–90); Auckland Regional Authy, 1980–83. Chair, NZ Historic Places Trust, 1996–2002; Trustee, NZ SO Foundn, 1996–. *Recreations:* music, reading, drama, cryptic crosswords. *Address:* 12A Wallace Street, Herne Bay, Auckland 1002, New Zealand.

TIZARD, Rt Hon. Robert James, CNZM 2000; PC (NZ) 1985; MP for Tamaki, Otahuhu, Pakuranga, and Panmure, New Zealand, 1957–90; Minister of Defence, Science and Technology, 1987–90; retired; *b* 7 June 1924; *s* of Henry James and Jessie May Tizard; *m* 1951, Catherine Anne Maclean (*see* Dame Catherine Tizard) (marr. diss. 1983); one *s* three *d*; *m* 1983, Mary Christina Nacey; one *s*. *Educ:* Auckland Grammar Sch.; Auckland Univ. MA, Hons Hist., 1949. Served War: RNZAF, 1943–46, incl. service in Canada and Britain; (commnd as a Navigator, 1944). Pres., Students' Assoc., Auckland Univ., 1948; Lectr in History, Auckland Univ., 1949–53; teaching, 1954–57 and 1961–62. MP 1957–60 and 1963–90; Minister of Health and State Services, 1972–74; Dep. Prime Minister and Minister of Finance, 1974–75; Dep. Leader of the Opposition, 1975–79; Minister of Energy, Science and Technol., and Statistics, and Minister i/c Audit Dept, 1984–87. Mem. Auckland District Health Bd, 2007–. *Recreation:* golf. *Address:* 3/131 Grafton Road, Auckland 1010, New Zealand.

TJANDRA, Sir Soekandar, KBE 2001 (MBE 1994); Owner and Managing Director, Papindo Group of Companies, since 1974; *b* Pontianak, Indonesia, 14 Nov. 1947; *s* of Kusuma Tjandra and late Ho Youw Hiang; *m* 1975, Tjan Soe Lan; one *d*. *Educ:* Dip. Electrical Engrg. Arrived in PNG, 1974; established: Papindo Trading Co., 1974; Amalgamated Knitwear Industries, 1976; established or acquired nineteen other cos, 1976–; Papindo branches throughout PNG, 1985–. Mem., Prime Minister's Business Delegn to Qld, 1994, to China, 2001. Member: Food Mktg Inst., USA; Chamber of Commerce and Industries, PNG. Member: Bd of Govs, Lae Provincial High Sch., 1995–; Lae Tech. Coll., 1995–; Adv. Bd, Business Studies Dept, PNG Univ. of Technol., 1999–; Governing Council, Angau Meml Hosp., 1997. Mem., PNG Nat. Shooting Team to NZ, 1989. Hon. Consul-Gen. for Romania in PNG, 1997–. *Recreations:* listening to music, travelling, swimming, recreation fishing, competition pistol and rifle shooting. *Address:* PO Box 1, Lae, Morobe Province, Papua New Guinea 411. *Clubs:* Lae Pistol (Vice-Pres.), Lae Rifle (Vice-Pres.).

TJOENG, Sir James Nang Eng, KBE 2007 (CBE 2002); Chairman, Air Nuigini Ltd, since 2003; *b* Sarmi Irian Jaya, Indonesia; *s* of Sick Jong Tjoeng and Man Moi Leo; *m* 1980, Judith Ann; two *s* two *d*. *Educ:* St Peter's Lutheran Coll., Brisbane. Man. Dir, Garamut Enterprises Pty Ltd, 1974; Director: Mineral Resources Develt Corp., 2003; Central Bank PNG, 2008. *Recreations:* Rugby Union fan, swimming. *Address:* PO Box 88, Gordons, NCD, Papua New Guinea. *T:* 3250729, *Fax:* 3257096; *e-mail:* jtjoeng@hotmail.com. *Clubs:* Tattersalls (Brisbane); Port Moresby Yacht.

TOAL, Patrick Thomas, CB 2007; Permanent Secretary, Department of Agriculture and Rural Development, Northern Ireland, 2003–07; *b* 8 March 1944; *s* of late Edward and Brigid Toal; *m* 1969, Bridget Macklin; one *s*. *Educ:* Abbey Grammar Sch., Newry; QUB. Appointed NI Civil Service, 1968; Department of Agriculture: admin trainee, 1976; various posts in Animal Health, Fisheries, Agricl Mktg and Co-opn, Horticulture, and Milk and Eggs Divs, 1976–83; Princ. Officer, Milk and Eggs Div., 1983–86; Head of Finance, 1986–89; Asst Sec., Hd of Animal Health and Welfare and Agric. Policy Divs, 1989–98; Dep. Sec., Agric. Policy, 1998–2003. Mem. Bd, Intervention Agency for Agricl Produce, 1998–2002. Mem. Council, Royal Ulster Agricl Soc., 2003–. *Recreations:* golf (playing and admin), theatre, reading, amateur dramatics, gardening, Gaelic football, Rugby Union. *Clubs:* Farmers; Fortwilliam Golf (Belfast), Rosapenna Golf (Co. Donegal).

TOASE, Philip Cursley, CBE 2004; Chief Fire Officer and Chief Executive, West Yorkshire Fire & Rescue Service, 2000–08; *b* 26 Sept. 1953; *s* of Gordon and Ray Toase; *m* 2003, Lorraine Robertson; one *s* one *d*, and one step *s*. *Educ:* Queen Elizabeth Grammar Sch., Wakefield; South Bank Univ. (BSc 1996). MCGI 1996. Joined W Yorks Fire Service as Fire fighter, Dewsbury, 1974; Station Officer, 1981; Asst Divl Officer, 1985; Divl Officer, 1987; Sen. Divl Officer, 1990; Asst Chief Fire Officer, 1995–99; Dep. Chief Fire Officer, 1999–2000. Long Service and Good Conduct Medal, 1994. *Recreations:* Manchester United season ticket holder, cricket, Rugby, keeping fit. *Address:* Huddersfield, W Yorks.

TOBIAS, Prof. Jeffrey Stewart, MD; FRCP, FRCR; Consultant in Radiotherapy and Oncology, University College and Middlesex Hospitals, since 1981; Professor of Cancer Medicine, University College London, since 2002; *b* 4 Dec. 1946; *s* of late Gerald Joseph Tobias and of Sylvia Tobias (*née* Pearlberg); *m* 1973, Dr Gabriela Jill Jaecker; two *s* one *d*. *Educ:* Hendon Grammar Sch.; Gonville and Caius Coll., Cambridge (MA, MD, BChir); St Bartholomew's Hosp. Med. Sch. Junior hosp. posts, St Bartholomew's, Whittington, UCH and Hammersmith Hosps, 1971–74; Research Fellow in Oncology, Harvard Med. Sch., 1975–76; Fellow in Oncology, St Bartholomew's and Royal Marsden Hosps, 1976–80; Clinical Dir, Meyerstein Inst. of Oncology, Middlesex Hosp., 1992–97. Chairman: CRC New Studies Breast Cancer Working Party, 1990–2000; UK Co-ordinating Cttee for Cancer Research Head and Neck Working Party, 1990–2000; CRC Educn Cttee, 2000–02; Cancer Res. UK Tobacco Adv. Gp, 2003–06; Member: Nat. Adv. Gp for Screening in Oral Cancer, 1994–97; various MRC Adv. Gps. Advr, Audit

Commn for Nat. Cancer Services, 2000. Founder Sec., British Oncological Assoc., 1986; Member Council: RCR, 1992–94; Cancer Res. UK (formerly CRC UK), 2000– (Trustee, 2002–); Pres., British Assoc. of Head and Neck Oncologists, 1996–98; Chm., Annual British Cancer Res. Meeting, 2004. Lectures include: BAAS, 1997, 2006; Natalie Shipman, RCP, 2006. *Publications:* (with M. J. Peckham) Primary Management of Breast Cancer, 1985; (with R. L. Souhami) Cancer and its Management, 1986, 5th edn 2005; (with C. J. Williams) Cancer, a Colour Atlas, 1993; (with P. R. Thomas) Current Radiation Oncology, 3 vols, 1994, 1995, 1997; Cancer: what every patient needs to know, 1995, rev. edn 1999; (with A. C. Silverstone) Gynecologic Oncology, 1997; (with J. Houghton) Breast Cancer—New Horizons in Research and Treatment, 2000; (with L. Doyal) Informed Consent in Medical Research, 2001; (with K. Eaton) Living with Cancer, 2001; Clinical Governance and Revalidation: a practical guide, 2003; many contribs to newspapers and learned jls about cancer management and medical ethics. *Recreations:* nothing too strenuous: music, cycling, ski-ing, reading, writing. *Address:* Department of Oncology, University College Hospital, NW1 2BU. *T:* (020) 7380 9214, *Fax:* (020) 7380 6999; 48 Northchurch Road, N1 4EJ; *e-mail:* j.tobias@uclh.org. *Clubs:* Garrick, Royal Society of Medicine, Les Six; Albatross Wind and Water.

See also R. D. Tobias.

TOBIAS, Prof. Phillip Vallentine, PhD, DSc; FRCP; FRS 1996; Professor Emeritus and Hon. Professorial Research Fellow, University of the Witwatersrand, since 1993 (Director, Palaeo-anthropology Research Unit, 1966–96); Director, Sterkfontein Research Unit, 1999–2007; *b* 14 Oct. 1925; *s* of Joseph Newman Tobias and Fanny Rosendorff. *Educ:* Univ. of the Witwatersrand, Johannesburg (BSc 1946; BSc Hons 1947; PhD 1953; MB BCh 1950; DSc 1967). FRCP 1992. University of the Witwatersrand Medical School: Lectr in Anatomy, 1951–52; Sen. Lectr, 1953–58; Prof., 1959–93; Hd, Dept of Anatomy, 1959–90; Dean, Faculty of Medicine, 1980–82. Visiting Professor: Univ. of Penn, 1992–94; Univ. of Florence, 1996; Andrew White Prof.-at-Large, Cornell Univ., 1996–2002; Hon. Professor: Univ. of Balearic Isles, 1996–; Univ. of Vienna, 1997–; Nanjing Normal Univ., 2002–; Inst. of Vertebrate Paleontology and Paleoanthropology, Chinese Acad. of Sci., Beijing, 2002–. For. Associate, NAS of USA, 1987; Mem., Amer. Philosophical Soc., 1996. Hon. FRSSAf 1987; Hon. Fellow, Coll. of Medicine, S Africa, 1998; Hon. Member: Amer. Assoc. of Anatomists, 1987; Canadian Assoc. of Anatomists, 1989; Anatomical Soc. of GB and Ireland, 1994; Geol Soc. of S Africa, 1999. Hon. DSc: Natal, 1980; Western Ont, 1986; Alberta, 1987; Cape Town, 1988; Guelph, 1990; S Africa, 1990; Durban-Westville, 1993; Witwatersrand, 1994; Musée Nat. d'Histoire Naturelle, Paris, 1996; Barcelona, 1997; Charles Univ., Prague, 1999; Stellenbosch, 1999; Transkei, 2003; Fribourg, 2003; Hon. ScD: Cambridge, 1988; Penn, 1994; Hon. DMedChir Turin, 1998. Anisfield-Wolf Award in Race Relns, Cleveland Foundn, USA, 1978; Cert. of Honour, Univ. of Calif, Berkeley, 1983; Balzan Internat. Prize for Physical Anthropology, 1987; First L. S. B. Leakey Prize, 1991; Huxley Meml Medal, RAI, 1996; Charles R. Darwin Lifetime Achievement Award, Amer. Assoc. of Physical Anthropologists, 1997; Wood Jones Medal, RCS, 1997. CStJ 2003. Order of Meritorious Service, Gold Class (S Africa), 1992; Order of Southern Cross, Silver Class (S Africa), 1999; Hon. Cross for Sci. and Arts, 1st cl. (Austria), 2002; Commander: Nat. Order of Merit (France), 1998; Order of Merit (Italy), 1998. *Publications:* Chromosomes, Sex-cells and Evolution in a Mammal, 1956; (jtly) Man's Anatomy, 1963, 4th edn 1988; Olduvai Gorge, Vol. 2, 1967, Vols 4A and 4B, 1991; The Brain in Hominid Evolution, 1971; (ed) The Bushmen, 1978; Dart, Taung and the Missing Link, 1984; (ed) Hominid Evolution, Past, Present and Future, 1985; Images of Humanity, 1991; (ed) The Origins and Past of Modern Humans—towards Reconciliation, 1998; (ed) Humanity from African Naissance to Coming Millennia, 2001; Into the Past: a memoir, 2005. *Recreations:* people, music, books, philately, art, writing. *Address:* School of Anatomical Sciences, University of the Witwatersrand Medical School, 7 York Road, Parktown, Johannesburg 2193, South Africa. *T:* (2711) 7172516. *Club:* Explorers (New York).

TOBIAS, Richard David, OBE 1998; Chairman, Best Loved Hotels, since 2004; *b* 6 March 1945; *s* of late Gerald Joseph Tobias and of Sylvia Tobias (*née* Pearlberg); *m* 1971, Brenda Margaret Anderson; two *s*. *Educ:* Clarkes Coll., London. Dir, subseq. Man. Dir, Kids International, 1966–79; Dir, Ardmore Adventure, 1979–88; British Incoming Tour Operators Association: Treas., 1988–90; Vice-Chm., 1990–91; Chm., 1992–93; Chief Exec., 1993–2003; Dir-Gen., Tourism Alliance, 2003–04. Chairman: World Media Publishing, 1999–; Right Connections Associates, 2003–; Yoga For Life, 2008–. Director: Here Is The City, 2007–; Wells Tobias Recruitment, 2008–. Founder Trustee, Just A Drop, 1998–. Frequent speaker, overseas travel and tourism orgns; occasional coll. lectr on tourism industry. FInstD 1994; FTS 1997; FInstTT 2004. *Publications:* contrib. to numerous tourism pubns. *Recreations:* reading, writing, music, golf, good food, Chelsea Football Club. *Address:* 11 Rodmell Slope, N12 7BX. *T:* (020) 8446 7791; *e-mail:* richard@tobias.ftech.co.uk. *Club:* Century.

See also J. S. Tobias.

TOBIN, Hon. Brian Vincent; PC (Can.) 1993; Senior Business Advisor, Fraser Milner Casgrain LLP, Toronto, since 2004; *b* 21 Oct. 1954; *s* of Patrick Vincent Tobin and Florence Mary Tobin (*née* Frye); *m* 1977, Jodean Smith; two *s* one *d*. *Educ:* Meml Univ. of Newfoundland. MP (L): Humber-St Barbe-Baie Verte, 1980–96; Bonavista-Trinity-Conception, 2000–02; Parly Sec. to Minister of Fisheries and Oceans, 1981; Minister: of Fisheries and Oceans, 1993–96; of Industry, 2000–02; MHA (L) Bay of Islands, 1996–99; Straits and White Bay North, 1999–2000; Premier of Newfoundland and Labrador, 1996–2000. Leader, Liberal Party of NF, 1996–2000; Chair, Nat. Liberal Caucus, 1989. Vice Chm., Kruger Inc., 2002. *Publication:* (jtly) All in Good Time (memoirs), 2002. *Recreations:* reading, music, sports.

TOBIN, Patrick Francis John; Administrator, Headmasters' and Headmistresses' Conference Projects in Central and Eastern Europe, since 2003; *b* 4 Oct. 1941; *s* of Denis George and Una Eileen Tobin; *m* 1970, Margery Ann Sluce; one *s* three *d*. *Educ:* St Benedict's Sch., Ealing; Christ Church, Oxford (MA in Modern Hist.); London Univ. (PGCE). Head: of Econs, St Benedict's Sch., Ealing, 1963–71; of History, Christ Coll., Brecon, 1971–75; of History, Tonbridge Sch., 1975–81; Headmaster, Prior Park Coll., Bath, 1981–89; Principal, Mary Erskine Sch. and Daniel Stewart's and Melville Coll., Edinburgh, 1989–2000. Member: HMC, 1981– (Chm., 1998; Vice-Chm., 1999; Chm., Professional Develt Cttee, 1991–95); Governing Council, Scottish Council of Ind. Schs, 1990–94; Scottish Consultative Council for the Curriculum, 1991–95; Assessor, SHA Educnl Assessment Centres, 1991–95. Governor: Bryanston Sch., 2000–06; Portsmouth Grammar Sch., 2001–; Ryde Sch., 2001–; Magdalen Coll. Sch., Oxford, 2001–05; Our Lady's Convent Sen. Sch., Abingdon, 2004– (Chm., 2004–); Advisory Governor: Ampleforth Coll., 2000–; St Benedict's Ealing, 2000–06 (Chm., 2001–06); Downside Sch., 2001–03. *Publications:* Sweet Wells, 1998; Making Good Teachers Better, 1994; Portrait of a Putney Pud: an unpredictable career in teaching (memoir), 2004. *Recreations:* reading, travelling, canal boats. *Address:* Glentruim, Ashlake Copse Lane, Kite Hill, Wootton, Ryde, Isle of Wight PO33 4LG. *Club:* East India.

TOD, John Mackenzie, OBE 1987; Director, France, British Council, and Cultural Counsellor, British Embassy, Paris, 1998–2004; *b* 24 Oct. 1944; *s* of John Alexander Tod and Eleanor May Tod (*née* Darrah); *m* 1970, Christiane Teytaud; two *s* one *d*. *Educ:* Calday Grange GS; King's Coll., Cambridge (BA); Leeds Univ. (postgrad. Dip. TESL 1969); Inst. of Educn, London Univ. (MA Ed 1983). VSO, Malaita, Solomon Is, 1963–64; teacher, Ruffwood Comp. Sch., Kirby, 1965; joined British Council, 1968: Ghana, 1969–72; Brazil, 1972–74; Asst Dir (Educn), Kano, Nigeria, 1975–78; Asst Dir, Overseas Educnl Appts Dept, 1978–82; Rep., Senegal, 1983–88; Regl Dir and Supt Gen., Sociedade Brasileira de Cultura Inglesa, São Paulo, 1988–93; Dir of Arts, 1993–98. *Recreations:* choral music, literature, theatre, travel. *Address:* 35 rue du Tabellion, 1050 Brussels, Belgium. *T:* (2) 5340715.

TOD, Vice-Adm. Sir Jonathan (James Richard), KCB 1996; CBE 1982; Deputy Commander Fleet, 1994–97; *b* 26 March 1939; *e s* of late Col Richard Logan Tod and Elizabeth Allan Tod; *m* 1962, Claire Elizabeth Russell Dixon; two *s*. *Educ:* Gordonstoun Sch. BRNC, Dartmouth, 1957–59; Flying trng, 1961; Hal Far (Malta), 1963; HM Ships: Ark Royal, Hermes, Eagle, RNAS, Lossiemouth, 1962–70; BRNC, Dartmouth, 1970–72; Exec. Officer, HMS Devonshire, 1972–74; Naval Staff, 1975–77; Comd HMS Brighton, 1978–80; Cabinet Office, 1980–82; RCDS 1983; Comd HMS Fife, 1984–85; Dir, Defence Programme, 1986–88; Comd HMS Illustrious, 1988–89; Flag Officer Portsmouth and Naval Base Comdr Portsmouth, 1989–90; ACDS (Policy and Nuclear), MoD, 1990–94. Chm., Sea Cadet Assoc., 1998–2005; Vice Chm., Marine Soc. and Sea Cadets, 2004–05 (Vice Pres., 2005); Mem. Council, RNLI, 2005–July 2009. *Recreations:* sailing, gardening. *Address:* c/o Naval Secretary, Fleet Headquarters, Whale Island, Portsmouth PO2 8BY.

TODD, Rev. Alastair, CMG 1971; *b* 21 Dec. 1920; *s* of late Prof. James Eadie Todd, MA, FRHistS (formerly Prof. of History, Queen's University, Belfast) and Margaret Simpson Johnstone Maybin; *m* 1952, Nancy Hazel Buyers; two *s* two *d*. *Educ:* Royal Belfast Academical Institution; Fettes Coll., Edinburgh; Corpus Christi Coll., Oxford; London Univ. (External); Salisbury and Wells Theological Coll. BA (Oxon), DipTheol (London). Served War, Army, 1940–46, Capt. RHA. Apptd Colonial Administrative Service, Hong Kong, 1946; Joint Services Staff Coll., 1950; Defence Sec., Hong Kong, 1957–60; Dep. Colonial Sec., Hong Kong, 1963–64; Dir of Social Welfare, also MLC, 1966–68; and, again, Defence Sec., 1968–71, retd. Ordained Deacon by Bishop of Chichester, 1973 and Priest, 1974; Asst Curate, Willingdon, 1973–77; Vicar, St Augustine's, Brighton, 1978–86. *Recreations:* reading, embroidery, gardening. *Address:* 59 Park Avenue, Eastbourne BN21 2XH. *T:* (01323) 505843.

TODD, Rev. Andrew Stewart; Minister of St Machar's Cathedral, Old Aberdeen, 1967–93; Extra Chaplain to the Queen in Scotland, since 1996 (Chaplain, 1991–96); *b* 26 May 1926; *s* of late William Stewart Todd and Robina Victoria Fraser; *m* 1953, Janet Agnes Brown Smith, *d* of late John Smith, JP, DL, Glasgow and Symington; two *s* two *d*. *Educ:* High Sch. of Stirling; Edinburgh Univ. (MA Hons, Classics 1947); New Coll., Edinburgh (BD 1950); Basel Univ. Asst Minister, St Cuthbert's, Edinburgh, 1951–52; ordained, 1952; Minister: Symington, Lanarkshire, 1952–60; North Leith, 1960–67. Convener, Gen. Assembly's Cttee on Public Worship and Aids to Devotion, 1974–78; Moderator, Aberdeen Presbytery, 1980–81; Convener, Panel on Doctrine, 1990–95; Member: Church Hymnary Cttee, 1963–73; Church Hymnary Trust, 1965–2008. Hon. President: Church Service Soc.; Scottish Church Soc. Hon. DD Aberdeen, 1982. *Publications:* jt translator, Oscar Cullmann, Early Christian Worship, 1953; translator: Ludwig Koehler, Old Testament Theology, 1957; Ernst Lohmeyer, Lord of the Temple, 1961; contributions to liturgical jls. *Recreations:* music, gardening. *Address:* Fentoun House, 11 Bedford Place, Alloa, Clackmannanshire FK10 1LJ. *Club:* Royal Over-Seas League.

TODD, Prof. Christopher James, PhD; Professor of Primary Care and Community Health, since 2001, and Director of Research, School of Nursing, Midwifery and Social Work, since 2003, University of Manchester; *b* Bournemouth, 1 Dec. 1956; *s* of Ernest James Todd and Pamela Mary Todd (*née* Bramley); *m* 2001, Victoria Jane Brandon. *Educ:* Epsom Coll.; Univ. of Durham (BA Hons Psychol. 1978; MA 1980; PhD 1987). CPsychol 1989, AFBPsS 1990, Chartered Health Psychologist 1998. Temp. Lectr in Psychol., Dept of Soc. Scis, Sunderland Poly., 1980; Interviewer, Study of Doctors' Careers, PSI, London, 1986; Res. Officer, Centre for Applied Health Studies, Univ. of Ulster, Coleraine, 1987–90; University of Cambridge: Res. Associate, 1990–92, Sen. Res. Associate, 1992–93, Dir, 1993–2001, Health Services Res. Gp, Dept of Public Health and Primary Care; Affiliate Lectr, Fac. of Soc. and Pol Scis, 1994–2000; Co-Dir, Cambridge Res. Develt Support Gp, Inst. of Public Health, 1997–2001; Wolfson College, Cambridge: Fellow, 1995–2001; Members' Steward, 1996–2000; Dir of Studies in Soc. and Pol Scis, 1999–2000. Dir, EC Prevention of Falls Network Europe, 2003–. *Publications:* contrib. to papers on palliative care, epidemiology of osteoporosis, falls prevention and health psychol. in jls. *Recreations:* sculling, walking, wine tasting. *Address:* School of Nursing, Midwifery and Social Work, University Place, University of Manchester, Oxford Road, Manchester M13 9PL. *T:* (0161) 306 7865, *Fax:* (0161) 306 7894; *e-mail:* chris.todd@manchester.ac.uk.

TODD, Damian Roderic, (Ric); HM Diplomatic Service; Ambassador to Poland, since 2007; *b* 29 Aug. 1959; *s* of George Todd and Annette Todd (*née* Goodchild); *m* 1987, Alison Digby; one *s* two *d*. *Educ:* Lawrence Sheriff Grammar Sch., Rugby; Worcester Coll., Oxford (BA Hons History). Joined HM Diplomatic Service, 1980; Third Sec., then Second Sec., Pretoria and Cape Town, 1981–84; FCO, 1984–87; HM Consul and First Sec., Prague, 1987–89; FCO, 1989–91; First Sec. (Econ.), Bonn, 1991–95; on secondment to HM Treasury, 1995–97, Hd of Agric. Team, 1996–97; FCO, 1997–98; on loan to HM Treasury as Hd of EU Co-ordination and Strategy Team, 1998–2001; Amb. to the Slovak Republic, 2001–04; Finance Dir, FCO, 2004–07. *Recreations:* history, family life, looking at buildings. *Address:* c/o Foreign and Commonwealth Office, King Charles Street, SW1A 2AH.

TODD, Daphne Jane, (Mrs P. R. T. Driscoll), OBE 2002; RP 1985; NEAC; artist; President, Royal Society of Portrait Painters, 1994–2000; *b* 27 March 1947; *d* of Frank Todd and Annie Mary Todd (*née* Lord); *m* 1984, Lt-Col (Patrick Robert) Terence Driscoll; one *d*. *Educ:* Simon Langton Grammar Sch. for Girls, Canterbury; Slade Sch. of Fine Art, UCL (DFA 1969; HDFA 1971). Vis. Lectr, Byam Shaw Sch. of Art, 1971–75 and 1978–80; Dir of Studies, Heatherley Sch. of Fine Art, 1980–86. NEAC 1984; Royal Society of Portrait Painters: Mem. Council, 1986–90; Hon. Sec., 1990–91. Hon. Mem., Soc. of Women Artists, 1995. Work in exhibitions, including: Royal Acad. Summer Exhibns, 1969–; Critic's Choice, Tooth's, 1972; Slade Centenary, 1972; Slade Ladies, Mall Gall., 1991; President's Exhibn, Birmingham, 1995; solo retrospective exhibn, Morley Gall., London, 1989; solo exhibn, Messum's Gall., 2001, 2004. Work in private and public collections including: Royal Acad. (Chantrey Bequest); Lady Margaret Hall, UC and St Anne's Coll., Oxford; Pembroke, St Catharine's, Girton and Clare Colls, Cambridge; UCL; St David's Univ., Lampeter; De Montfort Univ.; Royal Holloway Mus. and Art Gall.; Bishop's Palace, Hereford; Wellington Barracks; BMA; ICE;

NUMAST; Science Mus.; Nat. Portrait Gall.; Windsor Castle. Portrait commissions include: Grand Duke of Luxembourg; Lord Adrian; Dame Janet Baker; Spike Milligan; Sir Neil Cossons; Baron Klingspor; Sir Kirby and Lady Laing; Christopher Ondaatje; Dame Anne Mueller; Lord Sainsbury of Preston Candover; Lord Sharman; Prof. Marilyn Strathern; Lord Morris of Castle Morris, Sir Tom Stoppard; Lord Tugendhat; Lord Ashburton; Lord Armstrong of Ilminster. Governor: Thomas Heatherley Educnl Trust, 1987–; FBA, 1994–2000. Freeman, Painter-Stainers' Co., 1997 (Hon. Liveryman, 2004). FRSA 1996. Ambassador for E Sussex, 2004–. Hon. DArts De Montfort, 1998. 2nd Prize, John Player Award, Nat. Portrait Gall., 1983 (Special Commendation, 1984); First Prize, Oil Painting of Year, Hunting Gp Nat. Art Prize, 1984; GLC Prize, Spirit of London, RFH, 1985; Ondaatje Prize for Portraiture, and RP Gold Medal, 2001. *Publications:* contribs to The Artist. *Recreation:* gardening. *Address:* Salters Green Farm, Mayfield, E Sussex TN20 6NP. *T:* and *Fax:* (01892) 852472; *e-mail:* daphne.todd@freenet.co.uk. *Clubs:* Arts, Chelsea Arts.

TODD, Prof. Sir David, Kt 1995; CBE 1990 (OBE 1982); FRCP, FRCPE, FRCPGlas, FRACP, FRCPath; Professor of Medicine, University of Hong Kong, 1972–96; *b* 17 Nov. 1928; *s* of Paul J. Todd and Margaret S. Todd. *Educ:* Univ. of Hong Kong (MB BS, MD). FRCPE 1966; FRACP 1974; FRCP 1976; FRCPGlas 1979; FRCPath 1992. University of Hong Kong: Lectr, Sen. Lectr and Reader, 1958–72; Head of Dept, 1974–89; Sub-Dean of Medicine, 1976–78; Pro-Vice-Chancellor, 1978–80. Hong Kong Government: Consultant in Medicine, 1974–89; Chm., Research Grants Council, Hong Kong, 1991–93. President: Hong Kong Coll. of Physicians, 1986–92; Hong Kong Acad. of Medicine, 1992–96; Chm., Council for Aids Trust Fund, Hong Kong, 1993–96. Hon. FAMS Singapore, 1986. Hon. DSc Chinese Univ. of Hong Kong, 1990; Hon. DSc Univ. of Hong Kong, 1992. *Publications:* articles on: haematological disorders in liver disease and splenomegaly; thalassaemia; G6PD deficiency; lymphoma; leukaemia; med. educn and physician training. *Recreations:* swimming, travelling, classical music. *Address:* D12 Breezy Court, 2A Park Road, Mid-levels, Hong Kong. *Clubs:* Hong Kong Golf, Hong Kong Country.

TODD, Sir Ian (Pelham), KBE 1989; FRCS; Consulting Surgeon: King Edward VII Hospital for Officers, since 1989 (Consultant Surgeon, 1972–89); St Bartholomew's Hospital, since 1981 (Consultant Surgeon, 1958–81); St Mark's Hospital, since 1986 (Consultant Surgeon, 1954–86); *b* 23 March 1921; *s* of Alan Herepath and Constance Todd; *m* 1946, Jean Audrey Ann Noble; two *s* three *d. Educ:* Sherborne Sch.; St Bartholomew's Hosp. Med. Coll.; Toronto Univ. (Rockefeller studentship, 1941–43; MD 1945; MS 1956). MRCS, LRCP 1944; DCH 1947; FRCS 1949. Served RAMC, Captain (AER Major). Wellcome Res. Fellow, 1955–56. Lectures: Wilson-Hay Meml, Perth, 1978; Howard H. Frykman Meml, Minneapolis, 1979; Patrick Hanley Meml, New Orleans, 1982; Gordon Watson, St Bart's Hosp., 1982; Purdue Frederick, New Orleans, 1984; Zachary Cope Meml, RCS, 1985; Henry Floyd Meml, Stoke Mandeville, 1986; John Clive Meml, Calif., 1986; Pybus Meml, Durham, 1988; Chesledon, St Thomas' Hosp., 1988; Cutait Oration, São Paulo, 1991. Visiting Professorships incl.: Montevideo; Ribeirao Preto; La Paz; Vellore; New Orleans; Minneapolis; Madras; Detroit. Examiner in Surgery: Univ. of London, 1958–64; Cambridge Univ., 1988; Dhaka, 1990; Ex-civilian Cons. (Proctology), RN, 1970–86. President: Sect. Colo-proctology, RSM, 1970–71; Med. Soc. of London, 1984–85; RCS, 1986–89 (Mem. Council, 1975–89); Hunterian Prof., 1953; Arris and Gale Lectr, 1957–58); British Colostomy Assoc., 1991–95; Vice-President: Imperial Cancer Res. Fund, 1986–89; Internat. Fedn of Surgical Colls, 1990–93. Founder, Leeds Castle Polyposis Gp, 1983. Fellow, Assoc. of Surgeons of GB and Ire., 1960; Founder Mem., Surgical Sixty Club; Hon. Member: Amer. Soc. of Colon and Rectal Surgs, 1974; RACS, 1974; Soc. Gastroent. Belge, 1964; Ileostomy Soc. of GB and Ire.; Surgical Res. Soc. of SA; Hellenic Surgical Assoc.; Assoc. of Surgs of India; Acad. of Medicine of Malaysia; NY State Surgical Soc., and S Amer. socs. Hon. FCSSA 1987; Hon. FRACS 1988; Hon. FACS 1988; Hon. FRCSCan 1989; Hon. FRCPSGlas 1989; FCPS (Bangladesh) 1990; Hon. Fellow, Colo-rectal Soc. of Sydney. Lister Prize in Surgery, Toronto, 1956. Star of Jordan, 1973. *Publications:* Intestinal Stomas, 1978; (ed) Rob and Smith, Operative Surgery, vol. 3, 1982; many articles on surgery of colon and rectum in Brit. and Amer. jls. *Recreations:* travel, music. *Address:* 4 Longmead Close, Farleigh Road, Norton St Philip, Bath BA2 7NS.

TODD, Jane Clare; Consultant Chief Executive, Nottingham City Council, since 2008 (on secondment from Department for Communities and Local Government); *b* 26 March 1951; *d* of Norman Henry Todd and Joyce Mary Todd; *m* (marr. diss.); two *s* one *d. Educ:* Nottingham Univ. (BA Social Policy). Nottingham City Council: Asst Chief Exec., Policy, 1992–97; Dir, Develt, 1997–2000; Dir, Develt and Envmtl Services, 2000–02; Regional Dir, Govt Office for the E Midlands, 2002–07. *Recreations:* motorbiking, walking, reading. *Address:* Nottingham City Council, The Guildhall, Burton Street, Nottingham NG1 4BT. *T:* (0115) 915 4500, *Fax:* (0115) 915 4580; *e-mail:* jane.todd@nottinghamcity.gov.uk.

TODD, Prof. Janet Margaret, PhD; Herbert J. C. Grierson Professor of English Literature, University of Aberdeen, since 2004; President, Lucy Cavendish College, Cambridge, since 2008; *b* 10 Sept. 1942; *d* of George and Elizabeth Dakin; *m* 1966 (marr. diss.); one *s* one *d. Educ:* Newnham Coll., Cambridge (BA 1964); Univ. of Leeds; Univ. of Florida (PhD). Lectr, Univ. of Cape Coast, Ghana, 1966–67; Asst Prof. of English, Univ. of Puerto Rico, 1972–74; Asst, Associate, Full Prof. of English, Rutgers Univ., NJ, 1974–83; Fellow in English, Sidney Sussex Coll., Cambridge, 1983–89; Prof. of English Lit., UEA, 1990–2000; Francis Hutcheson Prof. of English Lit., Univ. of Glasgow, 2000–04. Vis. Prof. Univ. of Southampton, 1982–83. Bye-Fellow, Newnham Coll., Cambridge, 1998; Hon. Fellow, Lucy Cavendish Coll., Cambridge, 2000. General Editor: Complete Works of Jane Austen, 9 vols, 2005–06; Cambridge edn of Jane Austen, 2005–08. Numerous awards. *Publications:* In Adam's Garden: a study of John Clare, 1973; Mary Wollstonecraft: an annotated bibliography, 1976; Women's Friendship in Literature, 1980; (jtly) English Congregational Hymns in the 18th Century, 1983; Sensibility, 1986; Feminist Literary History, 1988; The Sign of Angellica: women writing and fiction 1660–1800, 1989; (ed jtly) The Complete Works of Mary Wollstonecraft, 1989; (ed) A Dictionary of British Women Writers, 1989; (ed) The Works of Aphra Behn, 7 vols, 1992–96; (ed) Aphra Behn's Oroonoko, The Rover and Other Works, 1993; Gender, Art and Death, 1993; (ed) Aphra Behn Studies, 1996; The Secret Life of Aphra Behn, 1996; (ed) Female Education, 6 vols, 1996; The Critical Fortunes of Aphra Behn, 1998; Mary Wollstonecraft: a revolutionary life, 2000; Rebel Daughters: Ireland in conflict 1798, 2003; (ed) Collected Letters of Mary Wollstonecraft, 2003; (ed) Oroonoko, 2003; (ed jtly) Cambridge Companion to Aphra Behn, 2004; (ed) Jane Austen in Context, 2005; Cambridge Introduction to Jane Austen, 2006; Death and the Maidens: Fanny Wollstonecraft and the Shelley Circle, 2007. *Address:* 38 Victoria Park, Cambridge CB4 3EL.

TODD, Prof. John Andrew, PhD; Professor of Medical Genetics, and Fellow of Gonville and Caius College, University of Cambridge, since 1998; *b* 23 June 1958; *s* of William and Elizabeth Todd; *m* 1988, Anne Nicola Roberts; two *s* one *d. Educ:* Coleraine Academical Instn; Edinburgh Univ. (BSc 1st cl. Hons 1980); Gonville and Caius Coll., Cambridge (PhD Biochemistry 1983). Research Fellow: Dept of Biochemistry, Cambridge Univ., 1983–85; MRC Molecular Biology Lab., Cambridge, 1984; SERC/NATO Res. Fellow, Dept of Microbiology and Immunology, Stanford Univ., Calif, 1985–88; Career Develt Award Fellow, Juvenile Diabetes Foundn Internat., 1988–90 (Grodsky Prize, 1998); University of Oxford: Sen. Scientist, Nuffield Dept of Surgery, 1988–98; Mem., Faculty of Medicine, 1989–98; Wellcome Trust Sen. Fellow in Basic Biomed. Sci., 1990–93; Univ. Res. Lectr, 1992–98; Wellcome Trust Prin. Res. Fellow, 1993–98; Prof. of Human Genetics, 1996–98. Wellcome Vis. Prof., Louisiana State Univ., 1997. Lectures: Balfour, Genetical Soc., 1994; Lilly, QUB, 1995; Dorothy Hodgkin, Diabetes UK, 2001. FMedSci 1998. Hon. MRCP 2000. Minkowski Prize, Eur. Assoc. for Study of Diabetes, 1995; Res. Prize, Boehringer Mannheim and Juvenile Diabetes Res. Foundn Internat., 1995; Biennial Biochem. Soc. Medal, Wellcome Trust, 1998; R. and B. Sackler Res. Award, 1998; Carter Medal and Lecture, Clin. Genetics Soc., 1999. *Publications:* articles in learned jls. *Recreations:* lateral thinking, study of natural selection and evolution, fishing, ski-ing, swimming, child minding. *Address:* JDRF/WT Diabetes and Inflammation Laboratory, Cambridge Institute for Medical Research, Wellcome Trust/MRC Building, Hills Road, Cambridge CB2 0XY. *T:* (01223) 762101.

TODD, Prof. John Francis James, PhD; CEng, FInstMC; CChem, FRSC; Professor of Mass Spectroscopy, University of Kent at Canterbury, 1991–2000, now Emeritus; *b* 20 May 1937; *o s* of late Eric Todd and Annie Lewin Todd (*née* Tinkler); *m* 1963, Mavis Georgina Lee; three *s. Educ:* Leeds Grammar Sch.; Leeds Univ. (BSc, Cl. I Hons Chem.). Research Fellow: Leeds Univ., 1962–63; Yale Univ., USA, 1963–65; University of Kent at Canterbury: Asst Lectr in Chemistry, 1965–66; Lectr in Chemistry, 1966–73; Sen. Lectr, 1973–89; Reader in Physical Chemistry, Faculty of Natural Scis, 1990; Dir, Univ. Chemical Lab., 1991–94; Dep. Head, Chemistry Dept (Finance), 1996–97; Master of Rutherford Coll., 1975–85. CIL Distinguished Vis. Lectr, Trent Univ., Canada, 1988. J. B. Cohen Prizeman, Leeds Univ., 1963; Fulbright Research Scholar, 1963–65. Chm., Canterbury and Thanet HA, 1982–86. Chairman: Kent Section of Chem. Soc., 1975; British Mass Spectroscopy Soc., 1980–81 (Treas., 1990–93); Titular Mem., IUPAC Commn on Molecular Structures and Spectroscopy, 1979–91; Nat. Mem. Council, RSC, 1993–95. Mem., Kent Educn Cttee, 1983–88. Member: Clergy Orphan Corp., 1985–96; Council, Strode Park Foundn for the Disabled, 1986–90. Governor: S Kent Coll. of Technology, 1977–89; Canterbury Christ Church Univ. (formerly Canterbury Christ Church Coll., later UC), 1994–2007; Chm. of Govs, St Edmund's Sch., Canterbury, 1996–2006. Mem., Amer. Soc. of Sigma Xi, Yale Chapter. Jt Editor, Internat. Jl of Mass Spectrometry and Ion Processes, 1985–98. Hon. Life Mem., RSC, 2009. Hon. Fellow, Canterbury Christ Church Univ., 2008. Thomson Gold Medal, Internat. Mass Spectrometry Soc., 1997; Aston Medal, British Mass Spectrometry Soc., 2006. *Publications:* Dynamic Mass Spectrometry, vol. 4, 1975, vol. 5, 1978, vol. 6, 1981; Advances in Mass Spectrometry 1985, 1986; Practical Aspects of Ion Trap Mass Spectrometry, vols 1–3, 1995; Quadruple Ion Trap Mass Spectrometry, 2005; Practical Aspects of Trapped Ion Mass Spectrometry, 2009; reviews and papers, mainly on mass spectrometry, in Jl of Chem. Soc. and Jl of Physics, etc. *Recreations:* music, travel, genealogy. *Address:* Ingram Building, School of Physical Sciences, University of Kent, Canterbury, Kent CT2 7NH; West Bank, 122 Whitstable Road, Canterbury, Kent CT2 8EG. *T:* (01227) 769552.

TODD, Keith; *see* Todd, T. K.

TODD, Prof. Malcolm; Principal, Trevelyan College, Durham, 1996–2000; *b* 27 Nov. 1939; *s* of Wilfrid and Rose Evelyn Todd; *m* 1964, Molly Tanner; one *s* one *d. Educ:* Univ. of Wales (BA, DLitt); Brasenose Coll., Oxford (Dip. Class. Archaeol (Dist.)). Res. Assistant, Rheinisches Landesmus., Bonn, 1963–65; Lectr 1965–74, Sen. Lectr 1974–77, Reader in Archaeology 1977–79, Univ. of Nottingham; Prof. of Archaeology, Univ. of Exeter, 1979–96. Vis. Prof., New York Univ., 1979; Visiting Fellow: All Souls Coll., Oxford, 1984; Brasenose Coll., Oxford, 1990–91; Sen. Res. Fellow, British Acad./ Leverhulme Trust, 1990–91. Vice-Pres., Roman Soc., 1985–; Member: RCHM, 1986–92; Council, National Trust, 1987–91. Trustee: Roman Res. Trust, 1994–99; Trevelyan Trust, 1996–2000. Archaeological Consultant, Durham Cathedral, 1996–2000. Pres., Devon History Soc., 2006–. Corr. Mem., German Arch. Inst., 1977–. Editor, Britannia, 1984–89. *Publications:* The Northern Barbarians, 1975, 2nd edn 1987; The Walls of Rome, 1978; Roman Britain, 1981, 3rd edn 1999; The South-West to AD 1000, 1987; (ed) Research on Roman Britain 1960–89, 1989; Les Germains: aux frontières romaines, 1990 (trans. Italian and German); The Early Germans, 1992 (trans. German, Italian, Czech and Turkish); Migrants and Invaders, 2001; (ed) A Companion to Roman Britain, 2004; Charterhouse-on-Mendip (Somerset), 2006; Die Zeit der Völkerwanderung, 2007; papers in Germania, Britannia, Antiquaries Jl, Antiquity, Amer. Jl of Arch. *Recreations:* reading, writing.

TODD, Mark James, CBE 1995 (MBE 1984); equestrian rider; *b* 1 March 1956; *s* of Norman Edward Todd and Lenore Adele Todd; *m* 1986, Carolyn Faye Berry; one *s* one *d. Educ:* Cambridge High Sch., NZ; Hamilton Tech. Inst. (Dip. Agric.). Three-day event wins: Badminton, 1980 (Southern Comfort), 1994 (Horton Point), 1996 (Bertie Blunt); Burghley, 1987 (Wilton Fair, also runner up, on Charisma), 1990 (Welton Greylag), 1991 (Face the Music), 1997 (Broadcast News), 1999 (Diamond Hall Red); Olympic Games: Individual Gold Medal, 1984 (Charisma), 1988 (Charisma); Individual Bronze Medal, 2000 (Eye Spy II); World Championships: NZ Team Gold Medal, 1990; Individual Silver Medal, 1998 (Broadcast News). New Zealand Sportsman of the Year, 1988; Event Rider of the Century, Internat. Equestrian Fedn, 1999; Equestrian Personality of the Century, Horse & Hound, 2000; Sportsman of the Century, Waikato, NZ, 2000; New Zealander of the Year, NZ Soc., 2000. *Publications:* Charisma; Mark Todd's Cross-Country Handbook, 1991; One Day Eventing, 1996; So Far, So Good, 1998. *Recreations:* ski-ing, swimming, tennis, squash, horse racing, music. *Address:* Rivermonte Farms Ltd, Hillcrest, 481 Mount Thomas Road, Fernside, RD1, Rangiora, New Zealand.

TODD, Mark Wainwright; MP (Lab) Derbyshire South, since 1997; *b* 29 Dec. 1954; *s* of Matthew and Viv Todd; *m* 1979, Sarah Margaret (*née* Dawson); one *s. Educ:* Sherborne Sch.; Emmanuel Coll., Cambridge (BA History 1976; MA). Longman Group, later Addison Wesley Longman, 1977–96: Man. Dir, Longman Industry and Public Service Mgt, 1988–92, Longman Cartermill, 1990–92; Dir, IT, 1992–94, Ops, 1994–96. *Address:* House of Commons, SW1A 0AA.

TODD, Michael Alan; QC 1997; *b* 16 Feb. 1953; *y s* of Charles Edward Alan Todd and late Betty Todd (*née* Bromwich); *m* 1976, Deborah Collett. *Educ:* Kenilworth Grammar Sch.; Keele Univ. (BA 1976). Called to the Bar, Lincoln's Inn, 1977, Bencher, 2006; Jun. Counsel to the Crown, Chancery Div., 1992–97. *Recreation:* equestrianism. *Address:* Erskine Chambers, 33 Chancery Lane, WC2A 1EN. *T:* (020) 7242 5532.

TODD, Ric; *see* Todd, D. R.

TODD, Richard, (Richard Andrew Palethorpe-Todd), OBE 1993; actor; *b* 11 June 1919; *s* of Major A. W. Palethorpe-Todd, MC, Castlederg, Co. Tyrone, and Marvil Agar-

Daly, Ballymalis Castle, Kerry; *m* 1st, 1949, Catherine Stewart Crawford Grant-Bogle (marr. diss. 1970); one *d* (one *s* decd); 2nd, 1970, Virginia Anne Rollo Mailer (marr. diss. 1992); one *s* (and one *s* decd). *Educ:* Shrewsbury; privately; RMC Sandhurst, 1940–41. Entered the theatre in 1937. Served in King's Own Yorkshire Light Infantry and The Parachute Regt, 1940–46; GSO iii (Ops), 6 Airborne Div., 1944–45. *Films* since War of 1939–45 include: The Hasty Heart, 1949; Stage Fright, 1950; Robin Hood, 1952; Rob Roy, 1953; A Man Called Peter, 1954; The Dambusters, 1954; The Virgin Queen, 1955; Yangtse Incident, 1957; Chase a Crooked Shadow, 1957; The Long and the Short and the Tall, 1960; The Hellions, 1961; The Longest Day, 1962; Operation Crossbow, 1964; Coast of Skeletons, 1964; The Love-Ins (USA), 1967; Subterfuge, 1968; Dorian Grey, 1969; Asylum, 1972; Secret Agent 008, 1976; The House of the Long Shadows, 1982; The Olympus Force, 1988. *Stage* appearances include: An Ideal Husband, Strand, 1965–66; Dear Octopus, Haymarket, 1967; USA tour, The Marquise, 1972; Australia tour, Sleuth, 1973; led RSC N American tour, 1974; Equus, Australian Nat. Theatre Co., 1975; On Approval (S Africa), 1976; nat. tour of Quadrille, and The Heat of the Moment, 1977; Nightfall (S Africa), 1979; This Happy Breed (nat. tour), 1980; The Business of Murder, Duchess, 1981, Mayfair, 1982–88; The Woman in Black, Sydney Opera House, Liverpool Playhouse, 1991; nat. tour of Sweet Revenge, 1993; nat. tour of Brideshead Revisited, 1995; An Ideal Husband, Old Vic and tour, 1997, Gielgud and Albery, 1998, Theatre Royal, Haymarket and Lyric, 1999. *Television:* Heathcliffe, in Wuthering Heights, 1960; Carrington VC, 1964; H. G. Wells, in Beautiful Lies, 1991; series, Virtual Murder, 1992; Dr Newman, in Silent Witness, 2000; Midsomer Murders, 2002; The Royal, 2002; Heartbeat, 2007. Formed Triumph Theatre Productions, 1970. Pres., Age Concern, Birmingham, 1990–. Past Grand Steward, Past Master, Lodge of Emulation No 21. *Publications:* Caught in the Act (autobiog.), 1986; In Camera (autobiog.), 1989. *Recreations:* fishing, gardening. *Address:* Chinham Farm, Faringdon, Oxon SN7 8EZ; Sandal Cottage, Little Humby, Grantham, Lincs NG33 4HW. *Club:* Army and Navy.

TODD, (Thomas) Keith, CBE 2004; FCMA; Chairman: Knotty Green Consultants Ltd, since 2000; FFastFill plc, since 2002; Amino Technologies, since 2007; Magic Lantern Productions Ltd, since 2006; *b* 22 June 1953; *s* of Thomas William Todd and Cecilie Olive Todd; *m* 1979, Anne Elizabeth Hendrie; two *s* two *d*. FCMA 1985. Chief Accountant, Marconi Co. Ltd, 1978–81; Chief Financial Officer, Cincinnati Electronics, USA, 1981–86; Financial Dir, Marconi Co. Ltd, 1986–87; Dir, Finance and Business Strategy, 1987–96, Chief Exec., 1996–2000, ICL plc; Chm. and CEO, Dexterus Ltd, 2001; Chairman: Ecsoft, plc, 2002–03; Broad Band Stakeholder Gp, 2002–05; Easynet plc, 2002–06. Mem. Board, Camelot Gp plc, 1994–2000. Mem. Council, Open Univ., 1992–2000 (Hon. Treas., 1992–97). Life Mem., BAFTA, 2000. FRSA 1996. DUniv Open, 1999. *Recreation:* sports. *Address:* The Hill, Penn Road, Knotty Green, Bucks HP9 2TS. *Clubs:* Royal Automobile; Beaconsfield Golf.

TODHUNTER, Michael John Benjamin; DL; Director, since 1977, Chairman, since 2002, James Finlay Ltd; Director, 1989–2005, Chairman, 1999–2005, Kleinwort Capital Trust plc; *b* 25 March 1935; *s* of late Brig. Edward Joseph Todhunter and Agnes Mary (*née* Swire); *m* 1959, Caroline Francesca (MVO 2003), *d* of Maj. William Walter Dowding; one *s* two *d*. *Educ:* Eton Coll.; Magdalen Coll., Oxford (MA). 2nd Lieutenant, 11 Hussars, PAO, 1953–55. Banker; with Jessel Toynbee & Co. Ltd, 1958–84 (Dir, 1962, Dep. Chm., 1977); Chief Exec., Alexanders Discount plc, 1984–86; Dir, Mercantile House Hldgs plc, 1984–86; Man. Dir, PK English Trust Co. Ltd, 1986–89; London Advr, Yasuda Trust Banking Co. Ltd, 1989–98. Chm., Clyde Shipping Co. Ltd, 1978–2000. Dir, Newbury Racecourse plc, 1983–2004. Trustee: Gt Ormond St Hosp., 1979–96; Missions to Seamen, 1980–96; Gift of Thomas Pocklington, 1990–99. High Sheriff, 1999, DL, 2005, Berks. Hon. Fellow, Inst. of Child Health, 1994. *Recreations:* travel, shooting. *Address:* The Old Rectory, Farnborough, Wantage OX12 8NX. *T:* (01488) 638298, *Fax:* (01488) 638091; (office) Swire House, 59 Buckingham Gate, SW1E 6AJ. *T:* (020) 7834 7717, *Fax:* (020) 7630 5534. *Clubs:* White's, Pratt's.

TODOLÍ, Vicente; Director, Tate Modern, since 2002; *b* 31 May 1958; *s* of Vicente and Julia Todolí; *m* 1998, Cristina Gimenez. *Educ:* Univ. of Valencia (Master of Geog. and Hist. 1980); Yale Univ. and CUNY (Fulbright Schol.; grad. studies in art). ISP Fellow, Whitney Mus. of American Art, NY, 1985; Chief Curator, 1986–88, Artistic Dir, 1988–96, Inst. Valenciano de Arte Moderno; Dir, Museu Serralves, Porto, Portugal, 1996–2002. Member, Advisory Boards: Museu d'Art Contemporani de Barcelona, 1998–; Manifesta Internat. Foundn, 2002–07; Serralves Foundn, 2003–; Botin Foundn, 2003–; Contemp. Art Soc., 2003–07; La Caixa Foundn, 2003–. Member: Adv. Cttee for Reina Sofia Nat. Mus. of Art, Madrid, 1993–96; Jury and Adv. Cttee, Carnegie Internat., 1995; Advr, for Future, Past, Present, Venice Biennale, 1997. Comendador, Orden de Santiago (Portugal), 2002. *Address:* Tate Modern, Director's Office, Bankside, SE1 9TG.

TOFFOLO, Rt Rev. Mgr Adrian Titian; Episcopal Vicar for Formation, diocese of Plymouth, since 1999; Parish Priest, St Mary's, Barnstaple, since 2003; *b* 22 Sept. 1944; *s* of Sante Battista Toffolo and Ethel Elizabeth (*née* Hannaford-Hill). *Educ:* St Boniface's Coll., Plymouth; Gregorian Univ., Rome (PhL, STL). Asst Priest, Penzance, 1969–72; Prof. of Theology, Oscott Coll., 1972–76; Assistant Priest: Torquay, 1976–80; Plymouth, 1980–84; Parish Priest: St Austell, 1984–85; Truro, 1985–91; Rector, Venerable English College, Rome, 1991–99; Parish Priest, Bovey Tracey and Chudleigh, 1999–2003. Prelate of Honour, 1992. *Recreations:* mountain walking, music, DIY. *Address:* The Presbytery, Higher Church Street, Barnstaple, Devon EX32 8JE. *T:* (01271) 343312.

TOFT, Dr Anthony Douglas, CBE 1995; FRCPE; Consultant Physician, Royal Infirmary, Edinburgh, since 1978; Physician to the Queen in Scotland, since 1996; *b* 29 Oct. 1944; *s* of William Vincent Toft and Anne Laing; *m* 1968, Maureen Margaret Darling; one *s* one *d*. *Educ:* Perth Academy; Univ. of Edinburgh (BSc Hons, MD). FRCPE 1980; FRCP 1992; FRCPI 1993; FRCPGlas 1993; FRCSE (*ad hominem*), 1994. House Physician and House Surgeon, 1969–70, jun. med. posts, 1970–78, Royal Infirmary, Edinburgh. Chief Medical Adviser, Scottish Equitable Life Assurance Soc., 1989–. Mem., Health Appointments Adv. Cttee, 1994–2000. Royal Coll. of Physicians of Edinburgh: Chm., Collegiate Members' Cttee, 1977; Mem. Council, 1986–88; Vice-Pres., 1990–91; Pres., 1991–94; Chm. Trustees, 1999–. Chairman: Scottish Royal Colls, 1993–94; Jt Cttee on Higher Med. Trng, 1994–96; Vice-Chm., UK Conf. of Med. Royal Colls, 1993–94. General Medical Council: Mem., 1999–2003; Occasional Chm., Professional Conduct Cttee, 1999–2004; Chm., Prof. and Linguistic Assessments Bd, 1999–2006. Pres., British Thyroid Assoc., 1997–99; Mem., Assoc. of Physicians of GB and Ireland, 1983–; Sec., Harveian Soc., 1980–94. Hon. Mem., Acad. of Medicine of Malaysia, 1993. Hon. FCPS (Pak) 1990; Hon. FACP 1993; Hon. FRACP 1993; Hon. FRCPC 1994; Hon. FRCGP 1994; Hon. FFPM 1994; Hon. Fellow, Acad. of Medicine of Singapore, 1994; Hon. FCPS (Bangladesh) 1995; Hon. FCEM (Hon. FFAEM 1997). *Publications:* Diagnosis and Management of Endocrine Diseases, 1982; papers on thyroid disease. *Recreations:* golf, gardening, hill-walking. *Address:* 41 Hermitage Gardens, Edinburgh EH10 6AZ. *T:* (0131) 447 2221.

TOH CHIN CHYE; Nila Utama, 1st class, 1990; BSc, PhD, DipSc; *b* 10 Dec. 1921; *m*. *Educ:* Raffles Coll., Singapore; University College, London; Nat. Inst. for Medical Research, London. Reader in Physiology, 1958–64, Research Associate 1964, Vice-Chancellor, 1968–75, Univ. of Singapore. Chm., People's Action Party, 1954–81 (a Founder Mem.); MP, Singapore, 1959–88; Dep. Prime Minister of Singapore, 1959–68; Minister for Science and Technology, 1968–75; Minister for Health, 1975–81. Chm., Applied Res. Corp., 1973–75. Chairman, Board of Governors: Singapore Polytechnic, 1959–75; Regional Inst. of Higher Educn and Develt, 1970–75; Mem. Admin. Bd, Assoc. of SE Asian Insts of Higher Learning, 1968–75. DLitt (*hc*) Singapore, 1976. *Publications:* papers in Jl of Physiology and other relevant jls. *Address:* 23 Greenview Crescent, Singapore 1128.

TÓIBÍN, Colm; writer; *b* 30 May 1955; *s* of Micheál Tóibín and Bríd O'Rourke. *Educ:* University Coll., Dublin (BA). Features Ed., In Dublin mag., 1981–82; Ed., Magill mag., 1982–85. *Publications: novels:* The South, 1990; The Heather Blazing, 1992; The Story of the Night, 1996; The Blackwater Lightship, 1999; The Master, 2004; *short stories:* Mothers and Sons, 2006; *non-fiction:* Walking Along the Border, 1987, reissued as Bad Blood, 1994; Homage to Barcelona, 1990; The Trial of the Generals: selected journalism 1980–90, 1990; The Sign of the Cross: travels in Catholic Europe, 1994; Love in a Dark Time: gay lives from Wilde to Almodovar, 2001; (jtly) The Irish Famine: a documentary, 2001; Lady Gregory's Toothbrush, 2002; (ed) Synge: a celebration, 2005. *T:* (1) 6768383; *e-mail:* ctoibin@eircom.net.

TOKSVIG, Sandra Birgitte, (Sandi); writer and comedian; *b* 3 May 1958; *d* of late Claus Bertel Toksvig and of Julie Anne Toksvig; one *s* two *d*. *Educ:* Mamaroneck High Sch., NY; Tormead, Guildford; Girton Coll., Cambridge (MA Hons). *Television* includes: No 73, 1980–86; Whose Line Is It Anyway?; Behind the Headlines, 1993; Great Journeys, 1993; The Big One, 1993; Island Race, 1995; Call My Bluff, 1996–; *stage* includes: (performer) Nottingham Playhouse Rep., 1980; Open Air Theatre, Regent's Park, 1980; (jt writer) The Pocket Dream, 1993; (performer and writer) Big Night Out at the Little Sands Picture Palace, 1995; *radio* includes: Loose Ends, 1994–; I'm Sorry I Haven't a Clue, 1998–; Presenter: Midweek, 1996; Excess Baggage; Chair, The News Quiz. *Publications: for children:* Tales from the Norse's Mouth, 1994; Unusual Day, 1997; If I Didn't Have Elbows, 1998; Super-saver Mouse, 1999; Super-saver Mouse to the Rescue, 2000; The Troublesome Tooth Fairy, 2001; Hitler's Canary, 2005; *play:* The Pocket Dream, 1994; *travel books:* Great Journeys of the World, 1994; (with John McCarthy) Island Race, 1995; *novels:* Whistling for the Elephants, 1999; Flying Under Bridges, 2001. *Recreations:* golf, ski-ing, scuba diving, sewing. *Club:* Two Brydges.

TOLAND, Prof. John Francis, FRS 1999; FRSE; Professor of Mathematics, University of Bath, since 1982; *b* 28 April 1949; *s* of late Joseph Toland and Catherine Toland (*née* McGarvey); *m* 1977, Susan Frances Beck, *d* of late (James Henry) John Beck. *Educ:* St Columb's Coll., Derry (Alumnus Illustrissimus 2007); Queen's Univ., Belfast (BSc 1970, DSc 1993); Univ. of Sussex (MSc 1971, DPhil 1973). Batelle Advanced Studies Centre, Geneva, 1973; Lectr in Maths and Fellow of Fluid Mechanics Res. Inst., Univ. of Essex, 1973–79; Lectr in Maths, UCL, 1979–82; EPSRC Sen. Res. Fellow, 1997–2002. Scientific Dir, Internat. Centre for Math. Scis, Edinburgh, 2002–; Hon. Professor of Mathematics: Univ. of Edinburgh, 2003–; Heriot-Watt Univ., 2003–. Vis. lectr, Europe, Australia, USA. Pres., LMS, 2005–07. FRSE 2003. Hon. Fellow, UCL, 2008. Hon. DSc: QUB, 2000; Edinburgh, 2007; Heriot-Watt, 2007. Sen. Berwick Prize, LMS, 2000; Wolfson Res. Merit Award, Royal Soc., 2008. *Publications:* mathematical research papers, mainly in nonlinear analysis. *Recreations:* horses, walking the dog. *Address:* Department of Mathematical Sciences, University of Bath, Claverton Down, Bath BA2 7AY. *T:* (01225) 386188; *e-mail:* jft@maths.bath.ac.uk.

TOLER; *see* Graham-Toler, family name of Earl of Norbury.

TOLER, Maj.-Gen. David Arthur Hodges, OBE 1963; MC 1945; DL; *b* 13 Sept. 1920; *s* of Major Thomas Clayton Toler, DL, JP, Swettenham Hall, Congleton; *m* 1951, Judith Mary (*d* 2000), *d* of James William Garden, DSO, Aberdeen; one *s* one *d*. *Educ:* Stowe; Christ Church, Oxford (MA). 2nd Lieut Coldstream Guards, 1940; served War of 1939–45, N Africa and Italy; Regimental Adjt, Coldstream Guards, 1952–54; Bde Major, 4th Gds Bde, 1956–57; Adjt, RMA Sandhurst, 1958–60; Bt Lt-Col 1959; Br Liaison Officer, US Continental Army Comd (Col), 1960–62; comd 2nd Bn Coldstream Guards, 1962–64; comd Coldstream Guards, 1964–65; comd 4th Guards Bde, 1965–68; Dep. Comdt, Staff Coll., Camberley, 1968–69; Dep. Comdr Army, NI, 1969–70; GOC E Midland Dist, 1970–73; retired 1973. Dep. Hon. Col, Royal Anglian Regt (Lincolnshire) TAVR, 1979–84. Emergency Planning Officer, Lincolnshire CC, 1974–77. Chm., Lincoln Dio. Adv. Cttee, 1981–86. Pres., SSAFA, Lincs, 1978–98. DL Lincs, 1982. *Recreation:* gardening. *Address:* Rutland Farm, Fulbeck, Grantham, Lincs NG32 3LG. *Club:* Army and Navy.

TOLHURST, Rear Adm. John Gordon, CB 1995; FRAeS; defence consultant; *b* 22 April 1943; *s* of Cdre Virgil George Tolhurst, VRD, RNR, and Elizabeth Mary Tolhurst. *Educ:* Sevenoaks Sch. Joined RN 1961; Commanding Officer: HMS Berwick, 1977; HMS Exeter, 1984; Asst Dir, Naval Warfare, 1986; Commodore, HMS Nelson, 1988; CO HMS Invincible, 1990; ADC to the Queen, 1990; Flag Officer: Sea Trng, 1992–96; Scotland, Northern England and NI, 1996–97; Mil. Dep. to Head of Defence Export Services, MoD, 1997–2002. Man. Dir, JGT Associates Ltd, 2006–. Chm., Aerospace & Defence Bd, Reed Exhibns, 2005–08. Trustee, RNLI, 2002– (Chm., Ops Cttee, 2002–). Younger Brother, Trinity House. FRAeS 2004. *Recreations:* sailing, classic cars, shooting, gardening. *Address: e-mail:* john.tolhurst@ntlworld.com.

TOLLEMACHE, family name of **Baron Tollemache**.

TOLLEMACHE, 5th Baron *cr* 1876; **Timothy John Edward Tollemache;** Lord-Lieutenant of Suffolk, since 2003 (Vice Lord-Lieutenant, 1994–2003); Director, Fortis (UK), and other companies; farmer and landowner; *b* 13 Dec. 1939; *s* of 4th Baron Tollemache, MC, DL, and Dinah Susan (*d* 1998), *d* of late Sir Archibald Auldjo Jamieson, KBE, MC; *S* father, 1975; *m* 1970, Alexandra Dorothy Jean, *d* of late Col Hugo Meynell, MC; two *s* one *d*. *Educ:* Eton. Commissioned into Coldstream Guards, 1959; served Kenya, Persian Gulf and Zanzibar, 1960–62; Course of Estate Management at Sandringham, Norfolk, 1962–64. President: NW Agronomy, 1983–; E Anglian Productivity Assoc., 1984–88; Suffolk Agricl Assoc., 1988; The Milk Gp, 1994–2002; Chm., CLA, Suffolk, 1990–93; Vice Pres., Suffolk Assoc. of Local Councils, 1996–2003 (Pres., 1978–96). Mem., Firearms Consultative Cttee, 1995–98. Chairman, Lord Chancellor's Advisory Committee: on JPs, 2003–; on Gen. Comrs for Income Tax, 2003–. Vice Pres., Cheshire Red Cross, 1980–; President: Friends of Ipswich Museums, 1980–96; CAB, Ipswich & dist, 1998–2005; Suffolk Historic Churches Trust, 2003– (Chm., 1996–2003); Music for Country Churches, Suffolk, 2003–; Army Benevolent Fund, Suffolk, 2003–; Suffolk Co. Scout Council, 2003–; RLSS, Suffolk, 2003–; Friends of Suffolk Record Office, 2003–; Britain Australia Soc., Suffolk, 2003–; Suffolk Reserve Forces and Cadets Assoc., 2006–; E Anglia Reserve Forces and Cadets Assoc., 2008–.

Chairman: HHA (E Anglia), 1979–83; Bury St Edmunds Cathedral Appeal, 1986–90; Suffolk Family History Soc., 1988–2003. Patron: Suffolk Accident Rescue Service, 1983–; E Suffolk Assoc. for the Blind, 1992–2006; Suffolk, BRCS, 2003–; NSPCC, Suffolk, 2003–; ACRE, Suffolk, 2003–; Magistrates' Assoc., Suffolk, 2003–; Suffolk Wildlife Trust, 2003–; Disability Care Enterprise, 2003–; Help the Aged, Suffolk, 2003–; Gainsborough House Mus., 2003–; Friends of St Edmundsbury Cathedral, 2003–; Suffolk Preservation Soc., 2003– (Vice Patron, 1992–2003); SSAFA/Forces Help, 2003– (Pres., 1996–2003); E Anglia Children's Hospices, 2005–; St Matthew's Housing, 2005–; Friends of Royal Hosp. Sch., 2006–; St Nicholas Hospice, Bury St Edmunds, 2006–; Suffolk Community Foundn, 2006–; E Anglian Air Ambulance, 2006–; Royal Watercolour Soc., 2006–. Gov., Framlingham Coll., 2003–. Mem., 1996–, Trustee, 2000–, SAS Regtl Assoc. DL Suffolk, 1984. KStJ 2004 (CStJ 1988) (Chm., 1982–89, Pres., 2003–, St John's Council for Suffolk). *Recreations:* shooting, fishing, natural history. *Heir: s* Hon. Edward John Hugo Tollemache [*b* 12 May 1976; *m* 2007, Sophie, *d* of Iain Johnstone, *qv*]. *Address:* Helmingham Hall, Stowmarket, Suffolk IP14 6EF. *Clubs:* White's, Pratt's, Special Forces.

TOLLEMACHE, Sir Lyonel (Humphry John), 7th Bt *cr* 1793, of Hanby Hall; JP; DL; *b* 10 July 1931; *s* of Maj.-Gen. Sir Humphry Tollemache, 6th Bt, CB, CBE, DL and Nora Priscilla (*d* 1990), *d* of John Taylor; *S* father, 1990; *m* 1960, Mary Joscelyne, *d* of late Col William Henry Whitbread, TD; one *s* two *d* (and one *s* decd). *Educ:* Uppingham Sch.; RMA Sandhurst; RAC Cirencester. FRICS. Major, Coldstream Guards, retd 1963. Member: Melton and Belvoir RDC, 1969–74, Melton BC, 1974–87 (Mayor, 1981–82); Leics CC, 1985–97. Gov., Royal Star and Garter Home, Richmond, 1985–2001. High Sheriff 1978–79, JP 1978, DL 1980, Leics. *Heir: s* Richard John Tollemache, JP [*b* 4 May 1966; *m* 1992, Amanda, *er d* of Gordon Phillips; one *s* two *d*]. *Address:* The Old Vicarage, Buckminster, Grantham NG33 5RT.

TOLLERVEY, Prof. David, PhD; FRS 2004; FRSE; Wellcome Trust Principal Research Fellow, University of Edinburgh, since 1997; *b* 19 Sept. 1955; *s* of Robert Muirhead Tollervey and Isabella Stewart Tollervey (*née* Davidson); partner, Dr Hildegard Tekotte; three *s* one *d*. *Educ:* George Heriot's Sch., Edinburgh; Univ. of Edinburgh (BSc Hons 1977); Darwin Coll., Cambridge (PhD 1981). Postdoctoral Fellow, Univ. of Calif, San Francisco, 1980–83; Charge de Recherche, Institut Pasteur, Paris, 1984–88; Gp Leader, EMBL, Heidelberg, 1988–97. FRSE 2004. *Publications:* over 130 papers and reviews in scientific jls. *Recreations:* sailing, hill-walking. *Address:* Wellcome Trust Centre for Cell Biology, University of Edinburgh, King's Buildings, Edinburgh EH9 3JR. *T:* (0131) 650 7092, *Fax:* (0131) 650 7040; *e-mail:* d.tollervey@ed.ac.uk. *Club:* Fisherrow Yacht.

TOLLETT, Lorna Ann; *see* Casselton, L. A.

TOLLEY, Carole Anne Bennett; Director General, Scrutiny, Ministry of Defence, since 2007; *b* 4 May 1955; *d* of Sidney and Monica Cox; *m* 1982, Graeme Neil Tolley; two *s*. *Educ:* Lady Margaret Hall, Oxford (BA Hons PPE 1977); University Coll. London (MSc Econs of Public Policy 1978). ACCA 1998. Joined MoD as admin trainee, 1978; Private Secretary: to Chief Scientific Advr, 1983; to Under-Sec. of State for Armed Forces, 1984–85; Assistant Director: Finance and Admin (Nuclear), 1985–86; Naval Pay and Conditions, 1987–88; Financial Mgt Develt Unit, 1988–89; Secretariat (Air Staff), 1989–92; Civilian Mgt, 1992–95; Dir, Intelligence Progs and Resources, 1995–97; rcds 1998; Director: Defence Mgt Trng, 1999–2001; Resources and Plans (Centre), 2001–04; Dir Gen., Financial Mgt, 2004–07. *Recreations:* music, hiking, wind-surfing, gardening, su doku. *Address:* 35 Cavendish Drive, Claygate, Surrey KT10 0QE. *T:* (01372) 465812; *e-mail:* gntolley1@tiscali.co.uk.

TOLLEY, Rev. Canon George, SOSc; Hon. Canon, 1976–98, Hon. Assistant, 1990–2007, now Canon Emeritus and Dean's Chaplain, since 2007, Sheffield Cathedral; *b* 24 May 1925; *s* of George and Elsie Tolley, Old Hill, Staffordshire; *m* 1947, Joan Amelia Grosvenor; two *s* one *d*. *Educ:* Halesowen Grammar Sch.; Birmingham Central Tech. Coll. (part-time); Princeton Univ., USA; Lincoln Theol Coll., 1965–67; Sheffield Univ. (MA). BSc, MSc, PhD (London); FRSC; FIMMM. Rotary Foundation Fellow, Princeton Univ., 1949–50. Head, Department of Chemistry, College of Advanced Technology, Birmingham, 1954–58; Head of Research and Experimental Dept, Allied Ironfounders Ltd, 1958–61; Principal, Worcester Tech. College, 1961–65; Senior Director of Studies, Royal Air Force Coll., Cranwell, 1965–66; Principal, Sheffield Coll. of Technology, 1966–69, Sheffield City Polytechnic, 1969–82; Manpower Services Commission: Dir, Open Tech Unit, 1983–84; Head, Quality Branch, 1984–85; Chief Officer, Review of Vocational Qualifications, 1985–86; Advr, NCVQ, 1986–88; Advr, Trng Commn, then Trng Agency, 1988–90. Ordained deacon, 1967, priest, 1968; Curate, St Andrew's, Sharrow, 1967–90. Chairman: Council, Plastics Inst., 1959–61; Further Educn Adv. Cttee, Food, Drink and Tobacco Ind. Trng Bd, 1974–78; Bd, Further Educn Curriculum Unit, 1978–82; BTec Continuing Educn Cttee, 1983–85; Council of the Selly Oak Colls, Birmingham, 1984–92; Adv. Bd, Pitman Exams Inst., 1987–92; Central Sheffield Univ. Hosps NHS Trust, 1992–95; Pres., Inst. of Home Economics, 1987–90; Vice-Pres., Educn 2000, 1990–92; Hon. Sec., Assoc. of Colleges of Further and Higher Educn, 1975–82; Member: CNAA (Chm., Cttee for Business and Management Studies, 1972–83); Yorks and Humberside Economic Planning Council, 1976–79; RAF Trng and Educn Cttee, 1975–80; Governing Body, Derbyshire Coll. of Higher Educn, 1984–87. Member Council: PSI, 1981–89; RSA, 1983–92. Dep. Chm., S Yorks Foundn, 1986–90. Hon. Treas., SOSc, 1995–. Sheffield Church Burgess. CCMI. Hon. FCP; Hon. Fellow: Sheffield City Polytechnic, 1982; CGLI, 1984; Inst. of Trng and Develt, 1989. Hon. DSc: Sheffield, 1984; CNAA, 1986; DUniv Open, 1984. *Publications:* Meaning and Purpose in Higher Education, 1976; A History of the Sheffield Church Burgesses, 1998; Bringing Prayer to Life, 2001; many papers relating to plastics and education in British and foreign journals. *Recreation:* savouring remembered sounds. *Address:* 74 Furniss Avenue, Dore, Sheffield S17 3QP.

TOLPUTT, John Nigel, MA; Head, The Purcell School, 1999–2007; *b* 1 May 1947; *s* of Basil Tolputt and Betty Durrant; *m* 1971, Patta Davis; one *s* one *d*. *Educ:* St John's Coll., Cambridge (MA); Bristol Univ. (Cert Ed 1969). Teacher, Bromsgrove Sch., 1969–74; Head of English and Drama, Cranleigh Sch., 1974–87; Head, Rendcomb Coll., 1987–99. FRSA 1994. Hon. ARAM 2005. *Recreation:* theatre. *Address:* Mill End, Sir George's Place, Steyning, Sussex BN44 3LS.

TOLSON, James; Member (Lib Dem) Dunfermline West, Scottish Parliament, since 2007; *b* 26 May 1965; *s* of Robert Archibald Tolson and Jane Wallace Tolson; *m* 1996, Alison Patricia Lord. *Educ:* Napier Univ., Edinburgh (BSc Hons Network Computing). Fitter/turner, Babcock Rosyth Defence Ltd, 1981–2000; Sales Advr, British Sky Broadcasting, 2003–07. Scottish Parliament: Lib Dem Shadow Minister for Communities and Sport; Mem., Local Govt and Communities Cttee. *Recreations:* gardening, travel, walking. *Address:* (constituency office) c/o 2nd Floor, 1 High Street, Dunfermline KY12 7DL. *T:* (01383) 841700, *Fax:* (01383) 841793; *e-mail:* jim.tolson.msp@scottish.parliament.uk.

TOLSON, Robin Stewart; QC 2001; a Recorder, since 2000; a Deputy High Court Judge, since 2004; *b* 21 June 1958; *s* of Trevor and Vivian Tolson; *m* 1987, Carol Atkinson; two *d*. *Educ:* Hull Grammar Sch.; Jesus Coll., Cambridge (MA). Called to the Bar, Inner Temple, 1980; in practice as barrister, 1980–, specialising in family law and local govt admin. law; Asst Recorder, 1998–2000. *Publications:* Care Plans and the Human Rights Act, 1998; Family Law, 2002; (contrib.) Encyclopedia of Financial Provision in Family Matters. *Recreations:* triathlon, tennis. *Address:* (chambers) Outer Temple Chambers, 222 Strand, WC2R 1BA. *T:* (020) 7353 6381.

TOM, Peter William Gregory, CBE 2006; non-executive Chairman, Aggregate Industries plc, since 2006 (Chief Executive, 1997–2005); *b* 26 July 1940; *s* of late John Gregory Tom and Barbara Tom (*née* Lambden); one *s* two *d* (and one *s* decd). *Educ:* Hinckley Grammar Sch. Joined Bardon Hill Quarries Ltd, 1956: Man. Dir, 1977; Chm. and Chief Exec., 1985; merged with: Evered plc, 1991, to form Evered Bardon; CAMAS, 1997, to form Aggregate Industries plc. Director: Leicester FC plc, 1997–; Leicester Rugby Club Ltd, 1997–; Leicester Tigers Ltd, 1997–; Bardon Mill House Co., 2003–; Tigers Events Ltd, 2003–; Aga Foodservice Gp plc, 2004–; Rise Rocks Ltd, 2005–; Global Botanical Research Ltd, 2006–; Nature's Defence (UK) Ltd, 2006–; Nature's Defence Investments Ltd, 2006–; Macquarie Growth Income Group, 2006–; Mayven UK plc, 2006–; Mayven International Ltd, 2006–. Chm., Quarry Products Assoc., 1997. *Address:* Aggregate Industries plc, Bardon Hall, Copt Oak Road, Markfield, Leics LE67 9PJ. *T:* (01530) 816600.

TOMALIN, Claire; writer; *b* 20 June 1933; *d* of late Emile Delavenay and of Muriel Herbert; *m* 1st, 1955, Nicholas Osborne Tomalin (*d* 1973); one *s* two *d* (and one *s* one *d* decd); 2nd, 1993, Michael Frayn, *qv*. *Educ:* Hitchin Girls' Grammar Sch.; Dartington Hall Sch.; Newnham Coll., Cambridge (MA). Publishers' reader and editor, Messrs Heinemann, Hutchinson, Cape, 1955–67; Evening Standard, 1967–68; New Statesman: Asst Literary Editor, 1968–70; Literary Editor, 1974–77; Literary Editor, Sunday Times, 1979–86. Stage play, The Winter Wife, Nuffield, Southampton, 1991. Trustee, Nat. Portrait Gallery, 1992–2002. Registrar, Royal Literary Fund, 1984– (Mem. Cttee, 1974–99; Life Vice-Pres., 2000). Vice-Pres., English PEN, 1997–. Trustee, Wordsworth Trust, 2001–03 (Fellow, 2003–). FRSL 1974 (Mem. Council, 1993–2000; Vice-Pres., 2003–). Hon., Mem., Magdalene Coll., Cambridge, 2003; Hon. Fellow: Lucy Cavendish Coll., Cambridge, 2003; Newnham Coll., Cambridge, 2004. Hon. LittD: UEA, 2005; Birmingham, 2005; Greenwich, 2006; Cambridge, 2007; Open, 2008. *Publications:* The Life and Death of Mary Wollstonecraft, 1974; Shelley and his World, 1980; Parents and Children, 1981; Katherine Mansfield: a secret life, 1987; The Invisible Woman: the story of Nelly Ternan and Charles Dickens, 1990 (NCR, Hawthornden, and James Tait Black Prizes, 1991); Mrs Jordan's Profession, 1994; Jane Austen: a life, 1997; (ed) Mary Shelley, Maurice, 1998; Several Strangers: writing from three decades, 1999; Samuel Pepys: the unequalled self, 2002 (Whitbread Prize, 2002; Samuel Pepys Award, 2003; Rose Mary Crawshay Prize, 2003); Thomas Hardy: the time-torn man, 2006; (ed) Selected Poems of Thomas Hardy, 2006; (ed) Selected Poems of John Milton, 2008; literary journalism. *Recreations:* walking, gardening. *Address:* c/o David Godwin, 55 Monmouth Street, WC2H 9DG.

TOMBS, family name of **Baron Tombs**.

TOMBS, Baron *cr* 1990 (Life Peer), of Brailes in the county of Warwickshire; **Francis Leonard Tombs,** Kt 1978; FREng; Chairman: Rolls-Royce, 1985–92 (Director, 1982–92); Old Mutual South Africa Trust, 1994–98; *b* 17 May 1924; *s* of Joseph and Jane Tombs; *m* 1949, Marjorie Evans (*d* 2008); three *d*. *Educ:* Elmore Green Sch., Walsall; Birmingham Coll. of Technology; BSc (Econ) Hons, London. GEC, 1939–45; Birmingham Corp., 1946–47; British Electricity Authority, Midlands, then Central Electricity Authority, Merseyside and N Wales, 1948–57; Gen. Manager, GEC, Erith, 1958–67; Dir and Gen. Man., James Howden & Co., Glasgow, 1967–68; successively Dir of Engrg, Dep. Chm., Chm., South of Scotland Electricity Bd, 1969–77; Chm., Electricity Council, 1977–80. Chairman: Weir Group, 1981–83; Turner & Newall, subseq. T & N, 1982–89; Director: N. M. Rothschild & Sons, 1981–94; Shell-UK, 1983–94. Pres., Molecule Theatre Ltd, 1993–96 (Chm., 1985–92). Member: Nature Conservancy Council, 1978–82; Standing Commn on Energy and the Environment, 1978–; SERC, 1982–85; Chairman: Engrg Council, 1985–88; ACARD, 1985–87 (Mem., 1984–87); ACOST, 1987–90. Chm., H of L Select Cttee on Sustainable Develt, 1994–95; Mem., H of L Select Cttee on Sci. and Technol., 1997–. Pres., IEE, 1981–82; formerly Vice-Pres., Fellowship of Engrg; Vice-Pres., Engineers for Disaster Relief, 1985–94. Chm., Assoc. of British Orchestras, 1982–86. FREng (FEng 1977); FRAeS 1994, Hon. FRAeS 1995; Hon. FIChemE 1985; Hon. FICE 1986; Hon. FIProdE 1986; Hon. FIMechE 1989; Hon. FIET (Hon. FIEE 1991); Hon. FRSE 1996; Hon. Mem., British Nuclear Energy Soc. Pro-Chancellor and Chm. Council, Cranfield Inst. of Technol., 1985–91; Chancellor, Strathclyde Univ., 1991–97 (Hon. LLD 1976; DUniv 1991). Freeman, City of London, 1980; Liveryman, 1981–, and Prime Warden, 1994–95, Goldsmiths' Co. Hon. DTech Loughborough, 1979; Hon. DSc: Aston, 1979; Lodz, Poland, 1980; Cranfield, 1985; Bradford, 1986; City, 1986; Surrey, 1988; Nottingham, 1989; Warwick, 1990; Cambridge, 1990; DSc(Eng) QUB, 1986; DEd CNAA, 1989. KSG 2002. *Recreation:* music. *Address:* Honington Lodge, Honington, Shipston-upon-Stour, Warwickshire CV36 5AA.

TOMBS, Sebastian Martineau, FRIAS; Chief Executive, Architecture and Design Scotland, since 2005; *b* 11 Oct. 1949; *s* of late Dr David M. Tombs and Joan (*née* Parley); *m* 1988, Eva Heirman; four *s* two *d*. *Educ:* Bryanston; Corpus Christi Coll., Cambridge (BArch, DipArch). ACIArb 1977, MCIArb 2002; FRIAS 1992. RMJM, Edinburgh, 1975–76; Roland Wedgwood, Edinburgh, 1976–77; Fountainbridge Housing Assoc., Edinburgh, 1977–78; Housing Corp., 1978–81; Housing Dept, Edinburgh DC, 1982–86; Depute Sec., 1986–94, Sec., 1995–2005, RIAS. Founder and first Sec., Scottish Ecological Design Assoc., 1991–94 (Chm., 1994–97); Founder and first Chm., Assoc. Planning Supervisors, 1995–97. Contested (Lib Dem): Edinburgh N and Leith, Scottish Parlt, 1999, 2003; Edinburgh N and Leith, 2001. *Recreations:* designing cartograms, choral music, doggerel, sketching, reverse cycling. *Address:* Architecture and Design Scotland, Bakehouse Close, 146 Canongate, Edinburgh EH8 8DD. *T:* (0131) 556 6699, *Fax:* (0131) 556 6633; *e-mail:* sebastian.tombs@ads.org.uk.

TOMEI, Anthony Laurence; Director, Nuffield Foundation, since 1995; *b* 1 June 1949; *s* of late Laurence Stephen Tomei and Dora Tomei (*née* Myring); *m* 1977, Nicola Bourn; one *s* two *d*. *Educ:* St Joseph's Coll., London; Univ. of Sussex (BSc); Univ. of Manchester (MSc). Physics teacher, VSO, Johore, Malaysia, 1970–72; teacher, William Ellis Sch., London, 1972–74; Nuffield Foundation: Research Grants Officer, 1977–82; Asst Dir, 1982–95; on secondment to DCSF, 2007. Trustee: Bristol Exploratory, 1983–86; Rutherford Trust, 1992–96; Integrated Educn Fund (NI), 1992–97. Gov., Nuffield Chelsea Curriculum Trust, 1980–98. Gov., Parliament Hill Sch., London, 1992–2000. *Recreations:* tennis, family life, watching Arsenal. *Address:* c/o Nuffield Foundation, 28 Bedford Square, WC1B 3JS. *T:* (020) 7631 0566. *Club:* MCC.

TOMES, Susan Mary; musician (pianist) and writer; *b* 26 May 1954; *d* of Albert Henry Tomes and Catherine Mary Tomes (*née* Brodie); one *d*; *m* 2004, Dr Robert Philip. *Educ:* RSAMD; King's Coll., Cambridge (BA 1975 (first woman to read Music), MA 1978). ARCM 1970. Solo recitalist and concerto soloist, 1979–; Founder Member: Domus Piano Quartet, 1979–95 (Gramophone Awards, 1985, 1995); Florestan Trio, 1995– (Gramophone Award, Classic CD Award, 1999; Royal Philharmonic Soc. Award, 2000). Prof., GSMD, 1995–. Contributor: The Guardian, 2000–; Financial Times, 2002–; book reviewer: The Independent, 2006–; The Guardian, 2008–. Mem., Acad. Adv. Bd, Centre for Hist. and Analysis of Recorded Music, 2005–. *Publications:* Beyond the Notes: journeys with chamber music, 2004; A Musician's Alphabet, 2006. *Recreations:* reading, letter-writing. *Address: e-mail:* suet@gmx.net.

TOMKINS, Patrick Lindsay, QPM 2006; HM Chief Inspector of Constabulary for Scotland, since 2007; *b* 20 Aug. 1960; *m* Susan; one *s* one *d*. *Educ:* Hastings Grammar Sch.; King's Coll., London (BA Hons); Royal Coll. of Defence Studies. With Sussex Police, 1979–93; Chief Superintendent, 1993–97, Comdr, 1997–99, Metropolitan Police; Asst Inspector of Constabulary, 1999–2002; Chief Constable, Lothian and Borders Police, 2002–07. *Recreations:* fly fishing, cycling, reading. *Address:* HM Inspectorate of Constabulary, St Andrew's House, Regent Road, Edinburgh EH1 3DG.

TOMKYS, Sir (William) Roger, KCMG 1991 (CMG 1984); DL; HM Diplomatic Service, retired; Master of Pembroke College, Cambridge, 1992–2004; *b* 15 March 1937; *s* of late William Arthur and Edith Tomkys; *m* 1963, Margaret Jean Abbey; one *s* one *d*. *Educ:* Bradford Grammar Sch.; Balliol Coll., Oxford (Domus Scholar; 1st cl. Hons Lit.Hum.). Entered Foreign Service, 1960; MECAS, 1960; 3rd Sec., Amman, 1962; 2nd Sec., FCO, 1964; 1st Sec., Head of Chancery, Benghazi, 1967; Planning Staff, FCO, 1969; Head of Chancery, Athens, 1972; Counsellor, seconded to Cabinet Office, 1975; Head of Near East and North Africa Dept, FCO, 1977–80; Counsellor, Rome, 1980–81; Ambassador: to Bahrain, 1981–84; to Syria, 1984–86; Asst Under Sec. of State and Principal Finance Officer, FCO, 1987–89; Dep. Under Sec. of State, FCO, 1989–90; High Comr, Kenya, 1990–92. Chm., Arab-British Chamber of Commerce, 2004–. DL Cambridgeshire, 1996. Liveryman: Drapers' Co., 2003–; Merchant Taylors' Co., 2004–. Commendatore dell'Ordine al Merito, 1980; Order of Bahrain, 1st cl., 1984. *Address:* Croydon House Farm, Lower Road, Croydon, Royston, Herts SG8 0EF. *Club:* Royal & Ancient Golf (St Andrews).

TOMLINSON, Baron *cr* 1998 (Life Peer), of Walsall in the co. of West Midlands; **John Edward Tomlinson;** *b* 1 Aug. 1939; *s* of Frederick Edwin Tomlinson, headmaster, and Doris Mary Tomlinson. *Educ:* Westminster City Sch.; Co-operative Coll., Loughborough; Nottingham Univ. (Dip. Polit. Econ. Social Studies); MA (Industrial Relations) Warwick, 1982. Sec., Sheffield Co-operative Party, 1961–68; Head of Research Dept, AUEW, 1968–70; Lectr in Industrial Relations, 1970–74. MP (Lab) Meriden, Feb. 1974–1979; PPS to Prime Minister, 1975–76; Parly Under-Sec. of State, FCO, 1976–79, and ODM, 1977–79. Sen. Lectr in Industrial Relations and Management, later Hd of Social Studies, Solihull Coll. of Tech., 1979–84. MEP (Lab) Birmingham W, 1984–99; Eur. PLP spokesman on budgetary control, 1989–99. Mem., EU Select Cttee, H of L, 1999–2002 and 2005–; H of L Rep., Convention on the Future of Europe, 2002–03; Mem., Jt Cttee on Conventions, 2006–. Mem., Council of Europe and WEU, 2004–. Trustee, Industry and Parlt Trust, 1988– (Pres., 2002–07). Pres., British Fluoridation Soc., 1998–. Contested (Lab) Warwicks N, 1983. *Publication:* Left, Right: the march of political extremism in Britain, 1981. *Address:* House of Lords, SW1A 0PW. *Club:* West Bromwich Labour.

TOMLINSON, Prof. (Alfred) Charles, CBE 2001; Professor of English, University of Bristol, 1982–92, now Emeritus, Senior Research Fellow, since 1996; *b* 8 Jan. 1927; *s* of Alfred Tomlinson and May Lucas; *m* 1948, Brenda Raybould; two *d*. *Educ:* Longton High School; Queens' Coll., Cambridge (MA; Hon. Fellow, 1974); Royal Holloway and Bedford Colls, Univ. of London (MA; Hon. Fellow RHBNC, 1991). Lecturer, 1957–68, Reader in English poetry, 1968–82, Bristol Univ. Visiting Prof., Univ. of New Mexico, 1962–63; O'Connor Prof., Colgate Univ., NY, 1967–68 and 1989; Vis. Fellow, Princeton Univ., 1981; Lamont Prof., Union Coll., NY, 1987; Vis. Prof., McMaster Univ., Canada, 1987; Hon. Prof. of English, Keele Univ., 1989. Arts Council Poetry Panel, 1964–66. Lectures: Witter Bynner, Univ. of New Mexico, 1976; Clark, Cambridge, 1982; Edmund Blunden, Hong Kong, 1987; Stubbs, Toronto, 1992; St Jerome, London, 1995. Exhibition of Graphics: Ely House, OUP, London, 1972; Clare Coll., Cambridge, 1975; Arts Council touring exhibn, 1978–80; Poetry Soc., 1983; Regent's Coll. Gall., 1986; in Surrealism in English Art, touring exhibn, 1986–87; Colby Coll., Maine, USA, 1987; McMaster Univ. Gall., Canada, 1987. FRSL 1974. Hon. Foreign Fellow, Amer. Acad. of Arts and Scis, 1998; Hon. Fellow, MLA, 2003. Hon. DLitt: Keele, 1981; Colgate, 1981; New Mexico, 1986; Bristol, 2004. Cholmondeley Award, 1979; Wilbur Award, 1982; Cittadella Premio Europeo, 1991; Bennett Award, NY, 1993; Il Premio Internazionale di Poesia Ennio Flaiano, 2001; New Criterion Poetry Prize, NY, 2002; Premio Internazionale di Poesia Attilio Bertolucci, 2004. *Publications: poetry:* Relations and Contraries, 1951; The Necklace, 1955, repr. 1966; Seeing is Believing, 1960 (US 1958); A Peopled Landscape, 1963; Poems, 1964; American Scenes, 1966; The Poem as Initiation, 1968; The Way of a World, 1969; Poems, in Penguin Modern Poets, 1969; Renga, 1970, 1972, 1979; Written on Water, 1972; The Way In, 1974; Selected Poems, 1978; The Shaft, 1978; (with Octavio Paz) Air Born, 1981 (Mexico 1979); The Flood, 1981; Notes from New York and other Poems, 1984; Collected Poems, 1985, expanded repr., 1987; The Return, 1987; Nella pienezza del tempo, 1987; Annunciations, 1989; Selected Poems, 1989; The Door in the Wall, 1992; Poemas, 1992; Charles Tomlinson: sette poesie, 1993; Gedichte, 1994; La insistencia de las cosas, 1994; La huella del cievo, 1994; En la plenitud del tiempo, 1994; Jubilation, 1995; In Italia, 1996; Portuguese Pieces, 1996; The Fox Gallery, 1996; Selected Poems 1955–97, 1997; The Vineyard Above the Sea, 1999; Luoghi Italiani, 2000; Skywriting, 2003; En la Plenitud del Tiempo: poemas 1955–2004, 2005; Cracks in the Universe, 2006; Collected Poems, 2009; *prose:* Some Americans: a personal record, 1980 (US); Poetry and Metamorphosis, 1983; The Letters of William Carlos Williams and Charles Tomlinson, 1992, expanded edn, 1999; American Essays: making it new, 2001; Metamorphoses: poetry and translation, 2003; *graphics:* Words and Images, 1972; In Black and White, 1975; Eden, 1985; *translations:* (with Henry Gifford): Versions from Fyodor Tyutchev, 1960; Castilian Ilexes: Versions from Antonio Machado, 1963; Ten Versions from Trilce by César Vallejo, (US) 1970; Translations, 1983; Attilio Bertolucci: selected poems, 1993; *edited:* Marianne Moore: A Collection of Critical Essays, (US) 1969; William Carlos Williams: A Collection of Critical Essays, 1972; William Carlos Williams: Selected Poems, 1976, rev. edn (US) 1985; Octavio Paz: Selected Poems, 1979; The Oxford Book of Verse in English Translation, 1980; George Oppen: selected poems, 1990; Eros Englished: erotic poems from the Greek and Latin, 1992; John Dryden: poems selected by Charles Tomlinson, 2003; contribs to: Agenda, Essays in Criticism, Hudson Review, Modern Painters, New Criterion, Poetry (Chicago), Poetry Nation Review, Sewanee Review, Times Lit. Supp., Vuelta. *Recreations:* music, walking. *Address:* English Department, Bristol University, 3–5 Woodland Road, Bristol BS8 1TB.

TOMLINSON, Sir Bernard (Evans), Kt 1988; CBE 1981; DL; MD; FRCP, FRCPath; Chairman, Northern Regional Health Authority, 1982–90; Emeritus Professor of Pathology, University of Newcastle upon Tyne, since 1985; Consultant Neuropathologist, Newcastle upon Tyne Hospitals NHS Trust (formerly Newcastle Area Health Authority, then Newcastle Health Authority), since 1976; *b* 13 July 1920; *s* of James Arthur Tomlinson and Doris Mary (*née* Evans); *m* 1944, Betty Oxley; one *s* one *d*. *Educ:* Brunts Sch., Mansfield; University Coll. and University Coll. Hosp., London (MB BS 1943, MD 1962). FRCP 1965; FRCPath 1964. Trainee Pathologist, EMS, 1943–47; served RAMC as Specialist Pathologist, 1947–49 (Major). Newcastle upon Tyne General Hospital: Sen. Registrar, Pathology, 1949–50; Consultant Pathologist, 1950–53; Sen. Consultant Pathologist, 1953–82; Hon. Lectr in Path., Univ. of Newcastle upon Tyne, 1960–71, Hon. Prof., 1972–85. Hon. Mem. Scientific Staff, MRC Neurochemical Pathology Unit, 1987–; Founding Chm., Res. Gp on Dementia, World Fedn of Neurology, 1984–87. Chm., Jt Planning Appts Cttee, DHSS, 1986–90; Mem., Disablement Services Authority, 1987–91. Leader of indep. enquiry into London's health services, 1991–92; non-exec. Dir, Newcastle City Health Trust, 1994–95. Mem. Council, Assoc. of Clinical Pathologists, 1965–68; Privy Council Mem., RPharmS, 1990–95 (Hon. Mem., 1997). President: British Neuropathological Soc., 1979–81; NE Alzheimer Disease Soc., 1985–. Hon. Mem., Amer. Neurol Assoc., 1997. Hon. MD Newcastle upon Tyne, 1993. Chm., Friends of Durham Cathedral, 1991–94. DL Tyne and Wear 1988. Dorothy Russell Lectr and Medallist, British Neuropath. Soc., 1989; Gold Medal Sci. Award, 3rd Internat. Conf. on Alzheimer's Disease, Padua, 1992. *Publications:* articles and book chapters on neuropath., partic. on path. of brain injury, brain changes in old age and on dementia. *Recreations:* gardening, golf, music, walking. *Address:* Greyholme, Wynbury Road, Low Fell, Gateshead, Tyne and Wear NE9 6TS.

TOMLINSON, Charles; *see* Tomlinson, A. C.

TOMLINSON, Heather Ann; Director of Children and Young People's Services, Bristol City Council, since 2005 (Director of Education and Lifelong Learning, 2004–05); *b* 23 June 1953; *d* of Kenneth and Joan Veneear; two *d*; *m* Charles George Sisum. *Educ:* Cheshunt Grammar Sch.; Univ. of Sheffield (BEd Hons; MEd; DPSE). Teacher, Rotherham LEA, 1976–80; Teacher, 1981–88, Educn Advr, 1988–98, Sheffield LEA; Regl Advisory Teacher, S Yorks and Humberside LEAs, 1988–90; Asst Dir of Educn, Nottingham City LEA, 1998–2001; Corporate Dir of Educn, Nottingham CC, 2001–04. *Recreations:* sailing, coastal walks, wines. *Address:* PO Box 57, The Council House, College Green, Bristol BS99 7EB. *Club:* St Mawes Sailing (Cornwall).

TOMLINSON, Sir John (Rowland), Kt 2005; CBE 1997; operatic bass; *b* 22 Sept. 1946; *s* of Rowland and Ellen Tomlinson; *m* 1969, Moya (*née* Joel); one *s* two *d*. *Educ:* Accrington GS; Manchester Univ. (BSc Civil Engrg); Royal Manchester Coll. of Music. Since beginning career with Glyndebourne in 1970, has sung over 150 operatic bass roles with ENO, Royal Opera, Covent Garden, Opera North, Scottish Opera, and in Geneva, Lisbon, Bologna, Florence, Milan, Copenhagen, Amsterdam, Stuttgart, Bayreuth, Berlin, Dresden, Madrid, Santiago, Tokyo, Vienna, Paris, Bordeaux, Avignon, Aix-en-Provence, Orange, San Diego, San Francisco, Pittsburgh, Vancouver, NY, Munich, Chicago, Salzburg, Hamburg and Boston; also broadcasts and recordings; best known for interpretations of Wagner bass and bass-baritone rôles, incl. Hans Sachs, Wotan (Bayreuth, 1988–98), Wanderer, Hagen, Gurnemanz and The Flying Dutchman (Bayreuth, 2003, 2004, 2006), König Marke, König Heinrich; other rôles include: Boris Godunov, Figaro, Leporello, Sarastro, Fiesco, Arkel, Balstrode, Kingfisher, Dosifey, four villains in Hoffman, Méphistophélès, Zaccharia, Claggart, Bluebeard, Baron Ochs, Rocco, Golaud, Moses, Philip II, Attila, Oberto, Green Knight, The Minotaur and Borromeo. Hon. FRNCM 1996. Hon. Dr: Sussex, 1997; Manchester, 1998; Hon. DMus: Nottingham, 2004; Birmingham, 2004. Singer of the Year, Royal Philharmonic Soc., 1991, 1998; Grammy Award (for Bartok, Cantata Profana), 1993; Reginald Goodall Award, Wagner Soc., 1996; Evening Standard Opera Award, 1998; Southbank Show Opera Award, 1999; Society's Special Award, Laurence Olivier Awards, 2007. *Address:* c/o Music International, 13 Ardilaun Road, Highbury, N5 2QR. *T:* (020) 7359 5183; *web:* www.johntomlinson.org.

TOMLINSON, Lindsay Peter, OBE 2005; Vice Chairman, Barclays Global Investors, since 2005; *b* Derby, 7 Oct. 1951; *s* of Dr Peter and Dr Jean Tomlinson; *m* 1973, Sarah Caroline Anne Martin; four *s* one *d*. *Educ:* Clifton Coll.; St John's Coll., Cambridge (BA 1972). FIA 1975. Asst Actuary, Commercial Union, 1973–77; Sen. Consultant, Metropolitan Pensions Assoc., 1977–81; Sen. Investment Manager, Provident Mutual, 1981–87; Dir, BZW Investment Mgt, 1987–94; Chief Exec., BZW Asset Mgt, 1994–95; Barclays Global Investors: Jt Chief Exec., 1995–97; Chief Exec., Europe, 1997–2005. Chairman: FTSE Policy Gp, 1997–; Investment Mgt Assoc., 2003–05; Code Cttee, Takeover Panel, 2006–; Director: Nat. Assoc. of Pension Funds, 2007–; Financial Reporting Council, 2007–. *Recreations:* football (Arsenal), Rugby, ballet, cricket, labradors. *Address:* Barclays Global Investors, Murray House, 1 Royal Mint Court, EC3N 4HH. *T:* (020) 7668 8866, *Fax:* (020) 7668 6866; *e-mail:* lindsay.tomlinson@barclaysglobal.com.

TOMLINSON, Sir Michael (John), Kt 2005; CBE 1997; Chief Adviser for London Schools, Department for Children, Schools and Families, since 2008; *b* 17 Oct. 1942; *s* of Edith Cresswell and Jack Tomlinson; *m* 1965, Maureen Janet; one *s* one *d*. *Educ:* Oakwood Technical High Sch., Rotherham; Bournemouth Boys' Sch.; Durham Univ. (BSc Hons Chem.); Nottingham Univ. (post-grad. Cert Ed (First Div.)). Chemistry teacher, Henry Mellish GS, Nottingham, 1965–69; Head of Chemistry, Ashby-de-la-Zouch GS, 1969–77; on secondment to ICI, 1977; Chief Inspector (Schools), HM Inspectorate of Schs, 1989–92; Dep. Dir, 1992–95, Dir of Inspection, 1995–2000, Office for Standards in Education; HM Chief Inspector of Schs, 2000–02; Chm., Hackney Educn Trust, 2002–07. Non-executive Director: RM plc, 2004–; Piscari Ltd, 2008–. Chair, 14–19 Govt Working Gp, 2003–04. Director: Sci. Yr 2002; Planet Science, 2003. Pres., ASE, 2005. Trustee: Comino Foundn, 2002–; Industrial Trust, 2003–07; Business Dynamics, 2004–07; Farming and Countryside Educn, 2008–. Gov., Univ. of Herts, 2004–. FRSA. Hon. DEd: Wolverhampton, 2004; De Montfort, Nottingham Trent, 2005; Durham, 2007; Manchester Metropolitan, 2008; Hon. DCL: UEA, Northumbria, 2005; Leicester, 2006; Hon. Dr Middlesex, 2005. Chem. Soc. Award in Chem. Educn (Bronze Medal), 1975. Silver Jubilee Medal, 1977. *Publications:* New Movements in the Study and Teaching of Chemistry, 1975; Organic Chemistry: a problem-solving approach, 1977; Mechanisms in Organic Chemistry: case studies, 1978; BP educn service contribs, 1974–78; articles in professional jls. *Recreations:* gardening, fishing, food and wine, reading. *Address:* Brooksby, Mayhall Lane, Chesham Bois, Amersham, Bucks HP6 5NR. *T:* (01494) 726967.

TOMLINSON, Prof. Richard Allan, FSA; Director, British School at Athens, 1995–96; *b* 25 April 1932; *s* of James Edward Tomlinson and Dorothea Mary (*née* Grellier); *m* 1957, Heather Margaret Murphy; three *s* one *d*. *Educ:* King Edward's Sch., Birmingham; St John's Coll., Cambridge (BA, MA). FSA 1970. Asst, Dept of Greek, Univ. of Edinburgh, 1957; University of Birmingham: Asst Lectr 1958, Lectr 1961, Sen. Lectr 1969, Prof.,

1971–95, now Emeritus, Dept of Ancient History and Archaeology; Head of Sch. of Antiquity, 1988–91. British School at Athens: Editor, Annual, 1978–91; Chm. Managing Cttee, 1991–95; Vice-Pres., 2001–. *Publications:* Argos and the Argolid, 1972; Greek Sanctuaries, 1976; Epidaurus, 1983; (ed) Greek Architecture, by A. W. Lawrence, 5th edn 1996; (contrib.) Sir Banister Fletcher, A History of Architecture, 20th edn, 1996; Greek Architecture, 1989; The Athens of Alma-Tadema, 1991; From Mycenae to Constantinople, 1992; Greek and Roman Architecture, 1995; articles in Annual of British Sch. at Athens, Jl of Hellenic Studies, Amer. Jl of Archaeology, etc. *Recreations:* architecture, walking. *Address:* 15 Eymore Close, Birmingham B29 4LB.

TOMLINSON, Prof. Sally, PhD; Goldsmiths Professor of Policy and Management in Education, Goldsmiths College, London University, 1992–98, now Emeritus; Senior Research Fellow, Department of Education, University of Oxford, since 1998; *b* 22 Aug. 1936; *d* of Clifford Gilmore Entwistle and Alice Nora Stubbs; *m* 1957, Brian Joseph Tomlinson, Sqdn Ldr, RAF (retd); one *s* two *d*. *Educ:* Macclesfield Grammar Sch.; Liverpool Univ. (BA Hons); Birmingham Univ. (MSocSci); Warwick Univ. (PhD); Manchester Univ. (PGCE). Lectr and Sen. Lectr, West Midlands Coll. of Educn, 1970–74; Sen. Res. Fellow, Warwick Univ., 1974–78; Lectr, then Sen. Lectr, later Prof. of Educn, Lancaster Univ., 1978–91; Prof. of Educn, UC Swansea, 1991–92; Dean, Faculty of Educn, 1992–95, Pro Warden, 1994–97, Goldsmiths' Coll., London Univ. Sen. Associate Mem., St Antony's Coll., Oxford, 1984–85; Res. Associate, Centre for Res. in Ethnic Relns, Univ. of Warwick, 2002–. Vis. Prof., Univ. of Wolverhampton, 2008–. Member: Court, Univ. of Bradford, 2001–04; Council, Univ. of Glos, 2001–. Mem., Commn on Future of Multi-ethnic Britain, 1998–2000. Trustee: Africa Educational Trust, 1992– (Vice-Chair, 2003–04; Chair, 2005–); Learning from Experience Trust, 1992–99; Educn Extra, 1992–2000. FRSA 1996. *Publications:* (with John Rex) Colonial Immigrants in a British City, 1979; Educational Subnormality, 1981; A Sociology of Special Education, 1982; Ethnic Minorities in British Schools, 1983; Home and School in Multicultural Britain, 1984; (ed with Len Barton) Special Education and Social Interests, 1984; (with David Smith) The School Effect, 1989; Multicultural Education in White Schools, 1990; Educational Reform and its consequences, 1994; (jtly) The Assessment of Special Educational Needs: whose problem?, 1994; (ed with Maurice Craft) Ethnic Relations and Schooling, 1995; Education 14–19: critical perspectives, 1997; (ed jtly) School Effectiveness for Whom?, 1998; (jtly) Hackney Downs: the school that dared to fight, 1999; Education in a Post-Welfare Society, 2001, 2nd edn 2005; (with Tony Edwards) Selection isn't Working, 2002; Race and Education: policy and politics in Britain, 2008; many contribs to books and learned jls. *Recreations:* walking, politics. *Address:* Department of Education, University of Oxford, 15 Norham Gardens, Oxford OX2 9PY.

TOMLINSON, Prof. Stephen, CBE 2007; MD; FRCP; FMedSci; Provost, Cardiff University, since 2006; Hon. Consultant Physician, Cardiff and Vale NHS Trust, since 2001; *b* 20 Dec. 1944; *s* of Frank Tomlinson and Elsie Tomlinson (*née* Towler); *m* 1970, Christine Margaret Hope; two *d*. *Educ:* Hayward GS, Bolton; Univ. of Sheffield (MB ChB 1968; MD 1976). FRCP 1982. SHO and Registrar, Sheffield Royal Infirmary, 1969–72; Registrar, Middlesex Hosp., 1972–73; MRC Clin. Res. Fellow, 1973–75, Hon. Lectr, 1974–76, Middlesex Hosp. Med. Sch.; Sen. Registrar, Middlesex Hosp., 1975–76; Sir Henry Wellcome Travelling Fellow, MIT, 1976–77; Sheffield University: Wellcome Trust Sen. Res. Fellow in Clin. Sci., 1977–80; Wellcome Sen. Lectr, 1980–85; Hon. Reader in Medicine, 1982–85; Hon. Cons. Physician, Sheffield HA, 1977–85; Manchester University: Prof. of Medicine, 1985–2001; Dean of Med. Sch. and Faculty of Medicine, 1993–97, of Faculty of Medicine, Dentistry and Nursing, 1997–99; Hon. Consultant Physician, Manchester Royal Infirmary, 1985–2001; Vice-Chancellor, UWCM, 2001–04; Provost, Wales Coll. of Medicine, Biol., Life and Health Scis and Dep. Vice-Chancellor, Cardiff Univ., 2004–06. Chairman: Assoc. of Clin. Profs of Med., 1996–99; Fedn of Assocs of Clin. Profs, 1997–2000; Tropical Health and Educn Trust, 2007–; ASH Wales, 2007–; Pres., Assoc. of Physicians, 2002–03 (Hon. Sec. and Treas., 1988–98); Exec. Sec., Council of Heads of Med. Schs, 1997–99; Mem., GMC, 2001–03 (Mem., Educn Cttee, 1999). Founder FMedSci, 1998. *Publications:* papers on stimulus-response coupling and intracellular signalling in endocrine tissues; the orgn of health services for people with diabetes. *Recreations:* arts and health, history of medicine, good food and wine (mine and others!). *Address:* Office of the Provost, Cardiff University, 2nd Floor, Cardigan House, Heath Park, Cardiff CF14 4XN. *T:* (029) 2074 2075. *Clubs:* Cardiff and County; Medical Pilgrims (Hon. Sec.).

TOMLINSON, Hon. Sir Stephen (Miles), Kt 2000; **Hon. Mr Justice Tomlinson;** a Judge of the High Court of Justice, Queen's Bench Division, since 2000; *b* 29 March 1952; *s* of Enoch Tomlinson and Mary Marjorie Cecilia Tomlinson (*née* Miles); *m* 1980, Joanna Kathleen Greig; one *s* one *d*. *Educ:* King's Sch., Worcester (schol.); Worcester Coll., Oxford (schol.; Eldon Law Schol.; MA). Called to the Bar, Inner Temple, 1974, Bencher, 1990. Lectr in Law, Worcester Coll., Oxford, 1974–76. QC 1988; a Recorder, 1995–2000; a Dep. High Court Judge, 1996–2000; Judge in Charge of Commercial Court, 2003–04. Gov., Shrewsbury Sch., 2003–. *Recreations:* gardening, family, cricket. *Address:* Royal Courts of Justice, Strand, WC2A 2LL. *Clubs:* Garrick, MCC.

TOMPKINS, Hon. Sir David (Lance), KNZM 1999; Judge of the High Court of New Zealand, 1983–97, Acting Judge, 1998–2003; Judge, Court of Appeal of Vanuatu, since 2002; *b* 26 July 1929; *s* of Arthur Lance Tompkins, Judge, Supreme Court of NZ, and Marjorie Rees Tompkins (*née* Manning); *m* 1956, Erica Lya Felicity Ann Faris; two *s* one *d*. *Educ:* Whitiora Primary Sch.; Southwell Sch., Hamilton; King's Coll., Auckland; Auckland University Coll. (LLB 1951). Served 1st Field Regt, RNZA, TA, 1949–59 (Capt. 1958). Partner, Tompkins & Wake, Hamilton, 1953–71; Barrister, 1971; QC (NZ) 1974; Courts Martial Appeal Court Judge, 1982–83; Exec. Judge, Auckland High Court, 1989–92; Judge of the Privy Council and Court of Appeal of Tonga, 1995–; Judge, Criminal Appeal Div., Court of Appeal of NZ, 1996–97; Justice of Appeal, Court of Appeal of Fiji, 1997–2005; Judge, Supreme Court of Vanuatu, 1998–. Chairman: Council of Legal Educn, 1992–97; Nat. Case Mgt Cttee, 1994–97; Electricity Mkt Appeal, 1998–. Pres., Hamilton Dist Law Soc., 1969–71; Mem. Council, 1969–71, Vice Pres., 1979–81, NZ Law Soc.; Mem. Council, 1976–83, Life Mem., 1987, Law Asia; Pres., Auckland Medico-Legal Soc., 1994–95. Associate, Arbitrators' and Mediators' Inst., 1997; Mem., LEADR, 1997–. Pro-Chancellor, 1979–80, Chancellor, 1980–85, Waikato Univ. Outward Bound Trust: Vice-Pres., 1981–83; Pres., 1983–84; Guardian, 1992–. Chm., Chelsea Park Trust. Hon. Dr Waikato Univ., 1986. Silver Jubilee Medal, 1977; Commemoration Medal (NZ), 1990. *Recreations:* sailing, croquet, ski-ing, computers, trout fishing, cooking. *Address:* PO Box 25 153, St Heliers, Auckland, New Zealand. *Clubs:* Hamilton (Life Mem.), Northern (Auckland).

TOMPKINS, Steven Charles, RIBA; Director, Haworth Tompkins Architects Ltd, since 1990; *b* 5 Oct. 1959; *s* of Keith and Patricia Tompkins; *m* 1986, Katherine Claire Tyndall; two *s*. *Educ:* Wellingborough Grammar Sch.; Univ. of Bath (BSc 1st cl., BArch 1st cl.). RIBA 1992. Arup Associates, London, 1984–86; Bennetts Associates, London, 1986–90. Major commissioned projects include: Royal Court Th., 1996–2000; Coin St Housing, London, 1997–2001; Regent's Park Open Air Th., 1998–2000; Almeida Th. at Gainsborough Studios, 2000, at King's Cross, 2001; Young Vic Th., 2003–06; Egg Th., Bath, 2003–06; Hayward Gall., 2003–05; Nat. Theatre Studio, 2004–; Snape Maltings, 2004; London Liby, 2004. *Recreations:* painting, theatre, mountain walking. *Address:* Haworth Tompkins Ltd, 19/20 Great Sutton Street, EC1V 0DR. *T:* (020) 7250 3225, *Fax:* (020) 7250 3226; *e-mail:* steve.tompkins@haworthtompkins.com.

TOMPKINSON, Stephen Philip Patrick; actor; *b* 15 Oct. 1965; *s* of Brian and Josephine Tompkinson; one *d*. *Educ:* St Bede's RC High Sch., Lytham St Anne's; Central Sch. of Speech and Drama. *Theatre* includes: No One Sees the Video, Royal Court, 1990; Across the Ferry, Bush, 1991; Love's Labours Lost, Women Laughing, Manchester Royal Exchange, 1992; Tartuffe, nat. tour, 1997; Art, Wyndham's, 2000; Arsenic and Old Lace, Strand, 2003; Rattle of a Simple Man, Comedy Th., 2004; Cloaca, Old Vic, 2004; Charley's Aunt, nat. tour, 2007; The Revenger's Tragedy, Manchester Royal Exchange, 2008; *films* include: Treacle, 1987; Brassed Off, 1996; Hotel Splendide, 2000; Tabloid TV, 2001; *television* includes: And a Nightingale Sang, 1989; The Deep Blue Sea, 1994; A Very Open Prison, 1995; First Signs of Madness; Flint Street Nativity, 1999; Lucky Jim, In Denial of Murder, 2003; Murder at the Vicarage, 2004; The Last Detective; New Tricks; Taming of the Shrew; Marian Again; *series:* Drop the Dead Donkey, 1990; All Quiet on the Preston Front, 1994 and 1995; Ballykissangel, 1996–98; Grafters, 1998; In Deep, 2001 and 2003; Bedtime, 2001; Ted and Alice; Wild at Heart, 2005, 2006, 2007. Hon. Fellow, Univ. of Central Lancashire, 1998. *Recreations:* cricket, snooker. *Address:* c/o Brown & Simcocks, 1 Bridgehouse Court, 109 Blackfriars Road, SE1 8HW. *T:* (020) 7928 1229, *Fax:* (020) 7928 1909; *e-mail:* mail@brownandsimcocks.co.uk. *Club:* Gerry's.

TOMS, Edward Ernest; Director, Studio Gallery, London, since 2002; *b* 10 Dec. 1920; *s* of Alfred William and Julia Harrington Toms; *m* 1946, Veronica Rose (*d* 2003), Dovercourt, Essex; three *s* one *d*. *Educ:* St Boniface's Coll.; Staff Coll., Camberley (psc), Nat. Defence Coll. (jssc). War service 1939–45; Captain Seaforth Highlanders; Special Forces, W Desert, Italy, Balkans, NW Europe; Regular Army, 1946, Seaforth Highlanders and QO Highlanders; Brigade Major, Berlin, 1959–61; Col GS (UK Cs-in-C Cttee), 1967–69. Principal, Home Civil Service, 1969; Asst Sec., Dept of Employment, 1973; seconded to Diplomatic Service as Counsellor, Bonn and Vienna, 1977–81; Internat. Labour Advr, FCO, 1981–83. Dir, Porcelain & Pictures Ltd, 1983–2002. *Recreation:* hill-walking (founder Mem., Aberdeen Mountain Rescue Assoc., 1964). *Address:* 25 Spanton Crescent, Hythe, Kent CT21 4SF. *Clubs:* Special Forces, Chelsea Arts.

TOMSETT, Alan Jeffrey, OBE 1974; Director, Associated British Ports Holdings PLC, 1983–92 (Finance Director, 1983–87); chartered accountant; *b* 3 May 1922; *s* of Maurice Jeffrey Tomsett and Edith Sarah (*née* Mackelworth); *m* 1948, Joyce May Hill; one *s* one *d*. *Educ:* Trinity School of John Whitgift, Croydon; Univ. of London (BCom). JDipMA. Hodgson Harris & Co., Chartered Accountants, London, 1938. Served War, with RAF, 1941–46 (Middle East, 1942–45). Smallfield Rawlins & Co., Chartered Accountants, London, 1951; Northern Mercantile & Investment Corp. Ltd, 1955; William Baird & Co. Ltd, 1962–63. British Transport Docks Board, later Associated British Ports: Dep. Chief Accountant, 1963; Chief Accountant, 1964; Financial Controller, 1970; Bd Mem., 1974–87 (Finance Dir, 1974–85). Churchwarden, St John's, Shirley, 1988–92. FCA, FCMA, CPFA, FCIS, FCILT (Vice-Pres., 1981–82, Hon. Treasurer, 1982–88, CIT); FRSA 1969. *Address:* 14 Colts Bay, Craigwell on Sea, Bognor Regis, W Sussex PO21 4EH. *T:* (01243) 267211.

TONBRIDGE, Bishop Suffragan of, since 2002; **Rt Rev. Dr Brian Colin Castle;** *b* 7 Sept. 1949; *s* of Ernest and Sarah Castle; *m* 1979, Jane Richmond; one *s* two *d*. *Educ:* UCL (BA (Hons) Classics 1972); Cuddesdon Theol Coll. (MA Theol. Oxford 1980); Birmingham Univ. (PhD Theol. 1989). Social worker, 1972–74; teacher, Lesotho, Southern Africa, 1974. Ordained deacon, 1977, priest, 1978; Assistant Curate: St Nicholas, Sutton, 1977; Limpsfield, Surrey, 1977–81; Priest i/c, Chingola, Chililabombwe and Solwezi, Zambia, 1981–84; Vis Lectr, Ecumenical Inst., Geneva, 1984–85; Vicar, N Petherton and Northmoor Green, Somerset, 1985–92; Vice-Principal and Dir of Pastoral Studies, Ripon Coll. Cuddesdon, Oxford, 1992–2001. Archbps' Advr in alternative spiritualities and new religious movements, 2005–. *Publications:* Hymns: the making and shaping of a theology for the whole people of God, 1990; Sing a New Song to the Lord, 1994; Unofficial God: voices from beyond the walls, 2004; articles in various theol jls. *Recreations:* fly fishing, cross country ski-ing. *Address:* Bishop's Lodge, 48 St Botolph's Road, Sevenoaks, Kent TN13 3AG. *T:* (01732) 456070; *e-mail:* bishop.tonbridge@rochester.anglican.org.

TONBRIDGE, Archdeacon of; *see* Mansell, Ven. C. N. R.

TONEGAWA, Prof. Susumu, PhD; Picower Professor of Biology and Neuroscience, Department of Biology, Massachusetts Institute of Technology; *b* Nagoya, 5 Sept. 1939; *s* of Tsutomo and Miyoko Tonegawa; *m* 1985, Mayumi Yoshinari; two *s* one *d*. *Educ:* Kyoto Univ. (BS); Univ. of San Diego (PhD 1968). Postgraduate work: Univ. of California, San Diego, 1968–69; Salk Inst., San Diego, 1969–70; Mem., Basel Inst. of Immunology, 1971–81; Prof. of Biology and Neurosci., Center for Cancer Res., Dept of Biol., MIT, 1981–; Investigator, Howard Hughes Med. Inst., 1988–; Dir, Picower Center for Learning and Memory, MIT, 1994–2006. Avery Landsteiner Prize, Ges. für Immunologie, 1981; Gairdner Foundn Internat. Award, 1983; Nobel Prize for Physiology or Medicine, 1987. *Address:* Department of Biology, Massachusetts Institute of Technology, 77 Massachusetts Avenue, 46–5285, Cambridge, MA 02139–4307, USA.

TONER, Charles Gerard; Group Chairman, Barratt Developments PLC, 2002–08; *b* 20 Jan. 1942; *s* of Hugh and Sally Toner; *m* 1967, Valerie Anne Metcalfe; one *s* one *d*. *Educ:* Holy Cross Acad., Edinburgh. Mgt trainee in industry, 1959–64; Abbey National Plc, 1964–99: various mgt posts in branch network, 1969–86; Gen. Manager, branches and agencies, 1986–88; Ops Dir, 1988–92; Dir, Plc Bd and Man. Dir, New Business Div., 1992–93; Man. Dir, Retail Bank Div., 1993–96; Dep. Gp CEO, 1996–99, retd. Non-executive Director: NHBC, 1996–2002 (Dep. Chm., 1999–2002); MSB Internat. (Sen. non-exec. Dir), 1999–2002; FCE Bank Plc (Ford), 1999–2007. *Recreations:* golf, tennis, travel. *Address:* Trundles, Crossfield Close, Shootersway, Berkhamsted, Herts HP4 3NT. *T:* (01442) 862985, *Fax:* (01442) 877929; *e-mail:* toner@macace.net. *Clubs:* Rotary (Berkhamsted Bulbourne); Berkhamsted Golf.

TONEY, Terence; Regional Director, South East Europe, British Council, since 2006; *b* 23 Aug. 1952; *s* of Norman Toney and Margaret Toney (*née* Taglione); *m* 1977, Young Hae Kim; one *s*. *Educ:* Cardinal Hinsley Grammar Sch.; King's Coll. London (BA Hons German and Philosophy); Inst. of Educn, Univ. of London (PGCE); Univ. of Lancaster (MA). Lectr in English, British Centre, Sweden, 1975–76; English teacher, Dortmund, 1976–78; Lectr in English, Hokkaido Univ., Japan, 1980–82; British Council, 1983–: Asst Consultant, English Lang., London, 1983–85; Asst English Lang. Officer, Tokyo, 1985–87; English Lang. Officer, Colombia, 1987–90; Acad. Dir, Cultura Inglesa, São Paulo, 1990–94; Director: Korea, 1994–99; Japan, 1999–2002; Educnl Enterprises,

2002–04; Customer Services, 2004–06. *Recreations:* travelling, reading, foreign languages, walking. *Address:* British Council, 10 Spring Gardens, SW1A 2BN.

TONGE, family name of **Baroness Tonge**.

TONGE, Baroness *cr* 2005 (Life Peer), of Kew in the London Borough of Richmond upon Thames; **Jennifer Louise Tonge,** FRIPH; *b* 19 Feb. 1941; *d* of late Sidney Smith and Violet Smith (*née* Williams); *m* 1964, Dr Keith Angus Tonge; two *s* (one *d* decd). *Educ:* Dudley Girls' High Sch.; University Coll. London (MB BS 1964). FRIPH (FRIPHH 1997). GP and family planning doctor, Ealing, 1964–96; Hd, Women's Services, Ealing HA, 1983–89. Mem. (Lib Dem), Richmond on Thames LBC, 1981–90 (Chm., Social Services, 1983–89). Contested (Lib Dem) Richmond and Barnes, 1992. MP (Lib Dem) Richmond Park, 1997–2005. Lib Dem spokesman on internat. develt, 1999–2003, for children, 2003–04. Hon. FFFP 2002. *Address:* House of Lords, SW1A 0PW; 5 Bush Road, Kew Green, Richmond, Surrey TW9 3AN. *T:* (020) 8948 1649. *Club:* National Liberal.

TONGE, Dr Gary James, FREng, FIET; consultant in electronic communications, since 2004; *b* 5 Sept. 1957; *s* of Dennis and Dorothy Tonge; *m* 1978, Fiona Margaret Mackintosh; two *s* two *d*. *Educ:* Univ. of Southampton (BSc 1st Cl. Hons Electronics; PhD Maths 1981). FREng 2001; FIET (FIEE 1993). Independent Broadcasting Authority: jun. engr, rising to Principal Engr, 1980–87; Hd, Engrg Secretariat, 1987–90; Independent Television Commission: Controller of Engrg, 1990–95; Dir, Engrg, 1995–2000; Dir, Technology, 2000–03. FRTS 1995. *Publications:* contrib. to IEEE Trans, RTS Jl, SMPTE Jl, Physics Rev. *Recreations:* Christian work, travel. *Address:* 17 Orion Point, 7 Crews Street, E14 3TU; *e-mail:* garytonge@yahoo.co.uk.

TONGUE, Carole; adviser and lecturer on the media, broadcasting, culture and European affairs, since 1999; artistic producer; *b* 14 Oct. 1955; *d* of Muriel Esther Lambert and Walter Archer Tongue; *m* 1990, Chris Pond, *qv* (marr. diss. 1999); one *d*. *Educ:* Brentwood County High School; Loughborough University of Technology (BA Govt (Hons) and French). Asst Editor, Laboratory Practice, 1977–78; courier/guide in France with Sunsites Ltd, 1978–79; Robert Schuman scholarship for research in social affairs with European Parlt, Dec. 1979–March 1980; sec./admin. asst, Socialist Group of European Parlt, 1980–84. Consultant, Citigate Public Affairs, 2001–03; Associate Dir, Sovereign Strategy, 2003–. MEP (Lab) London E, 1984–99; contested (Lab) London Reg., 1999. Dep. Leader, Eur. PLP, 1989–91. Bd Mem., Westminster Foundn for Democracy, 1990–93. Sen. Vis. Lectr, Dept European Studies, Loughborough Univ., 1995; Vis. Prof., Media Sch., Univ. of the Arts, London (formerly London Inst.), 2000–. Hon. Vice Pres., Professional Land Reform Gp, 2005–. Member: Adv. Bd, Eur. Media Forum, 1996–; Bd, London Film and Video Develt Agency, 1999–2003; Chair, UK Ind. Film Parlt, 2003–. Mem., Professional Conduct Cttee, GMC, 2000–06. Pres., Cities and Cinemas Europe, 1997–; Founder and Coordinator, UK Coalition for Cultural Diversity, 2005–. Patron: Couper Art Collection, 1999–; Federal Trust, 1997–. Member: Fabian Soc.; GMB; MSF. Trustee, CSV, 1995–. FRSA 2000. Hon. Dr Lincoln, 2005. *Publications:* chapters in books on European media; EP reports; articles on culture, film, citizenship, European affairs. *Recreations:* piano, cello, tennis, squash, horse riding, cinema, theatre, opera. *Address:* 246 Caledonian Road, N1 0NG. *T:* (020) 7278 1344; *e-mail:* carole.tongue@sovereignstrategy.com.

TONKIN, Boyd Miles; Literary Editor, The Independent, since 1996; *b* 7 April 1955; *s* of Douglas George Marcus Tonkin and Joan Yvonne Tonkin (*née* Collis). *Educ:* Haberdashers' Aske's Sch., Elstree; Trinity Coll., Cambridge (MA English). Res. Student and pt-time Tutor, Univ. of Cambridge, 1978–81; Adult Educn Lectr, City Univ., 1981–83; Lecturer in English: Manchester Poly., 1983–84; West Sussex Inst., 1984–85; Staff Writer and Features Editor, Community Care mag., 1986–89; Social Affairs Editor, 1989–91, Literary Editor, 1991–96, New Statesman. Broadcaster, BBC Radio arts progs, 1995–. Judge: Whitbread Biography award, 1997; Booker Prize, 1999; Foreign Fiction Award, Independent, 2000– (also Convenor); David Cohen Prize for Literature, 2007. *Publications:* (contrib.) Oxford Readers' Guide to Fiction, 2000; contribs to lit. guides and ref. works; essays in lit. jls in UK, US, France and Germany; articles in jls. *Recreations:* music, cinema, cricket, walking. *Address:* 104 Islington High Street, N1 8EG. *T:* (020) 7005 2656.

TONKIN, Derek, CMG 1982; HM Diplomatic Service, retired; *b* 30 Dec. 1929; *s* of Henry James Tonkin and Norah Wearing; *m* 1953, Doreen Rooke; one *s* two *d* (and one *s* decd). *Educ:* High Pavement Grammar Sch., Nottingham; St Catherine's Society, Oxford (MA). HM Forces, 1948–49; FO, 1952; Warsaw, 1955; Bangkok, 1957; Phnom Penh, 1961; FO, 1963; Warsaw, 1966; Wellington, 1968; FCO, 1972; East Berlin, 1976; Ambassador to Vietnam, 1980–82; Minister, Pretoria, 1983–86; Ambassador to Thailand, and concurrently to Laos, 1986–89. Chairman: Beta Viet Nam Fund Ltd, 1993–99; Beta Mekong Fund Ltd, 1994–2000. Director: Palais Angkor SA, 1998–2006; Euro-Thai Investments Ltd, 1999–2007. Chairman: Adv. Bd, Centre for SE Asia Studies, SOAS, 1990–93; Thai-British Business Assoc., 1991–93; Vietnam-Britain Business Assoc., 1993–94. Dir, Ockenden Internat. Bd of Trustees, 1990–2003. *Recreations:* tennis, music. *Address:* Heathfields, Berry Lane, Worplesdon, Guildford, Surrey GU3 3PU. *Club:* Royal Over-Seas League.

TONKING, (Russel) Simon (William Ferguson); His Honour Judge Tonking; DL; a Circuit Judge, since 1997; *b* 25 March 1952; *s* of John Wilson Tonking and Mary Oldham Tonking (*née* Ferguson); *m* 1976, (Sylvia) Mithra McIntyre; one *s* one *d*. *Educ:* King's Sch., Canterbury; Emmanuel Coll., Cambridge (MA). Called to the Bar, Inner Temple, 1975; barrister, Midland and Oxford Circuit, 1976–97; Asst Recorder, 1991–94; Recorder, 1994–97; Resident Judge at Stafford, 2006–; Hon. Recorder of Stafford, 2008–. Mem., Criminal Cttee, Judicial Studies Bd, 2005–. Lichfield Cathedral: Steward, 1978– (Head Steward, 1985–87, Pres. of Stewards, 2003–04); Mem. Council, 2000– (Mem. Transitional Council, 1998–2000); Dep. Chancellor, Diocese of Southwell, 1997–2005. DL Staffs, 2006. *Recreations:* many! *Address:* c/o Stafford Combined Court Centre, Victoria Square, Stafford ST16 2QQ. *T:* (01785) 610730. *Club:* Vintage Sports Car.

TONKS, Julian Matthew John; Partner, Pinsent Masons (formerly Pinsent Curtis Biddle, later Pinsents) Solicitors (Senior Partner, 2001–05); *b* 19 April 1953; *s* of John and Irene Tonks, Comhampton, Worcs; *m* 1980, Ann Miles Henderson; one *s*. *Educ:* Dudley GS; Trinity Coll., Oxford (Open Scholar; MA, MLitt). Admitted solicitor, 1982; Asst Solicitor, Freshfields, 1982–86; Tax Partner, 1987–94, Sen. Partner, 1994–95, Pinsent & Co.; Sen. Partner, Pinsent Curtis, 1995–2001. Mem. Regl Council, W Midlands, CBI, 1998–. Chairman: Common Purpose, Birmingham, 1994–2001; W Midlands NSPCC Full Stop Appeal, 1999–2001. Trustee, Birmingham Royal Ballet Trust, 1996–2001. *Recreations:* visiting castles, swimming, country sports, wine, reading modern novels and medieval history.

TONRY, Prof. Michael; Sonosky Professor of Law and Public Policy, University of Minnesota, since 1990; Senior Fellow, Netherlands Institute for the Study of Crime and Law Enforcement, Leiden, since 2003; *b* 9 June 1945; *s* of J. Richard Tonry and Frances Zimmerman Tonry (*née* Keedy); *m* 1966, Penelope Tyson; two *s* two *d*. *Educ:* Univ. of N Carolina (AB Hist. 1966); Yale Univ. (LLB). Admitted to legal practice: Illinois, 1970; Pennsylvania, 1975; Maine, 1982. Lecturer in Law: Univ. of Chicago, 1971–73; Univ. of Birmingham, 1973–74; Dechert Price & Rhodes, Esqs, 1974–76; Prof. of Law, Univ. of Md, 1976–83; Pres., Castine Res. Corp., 1983–; Prof. of Law and Public Policy, and Dir, Inst. of Criminology, Univ. of Cambridge, 1999–2004. Ed. and Publisher, The Castine Patriot, 1987–90. *Publications:* Sentencing Reform Impacts, 1987; Malign Neglect: race, crime and punishment in America, 1994; Sentencing Matters, 1996; Confronting Crime, 2003; Punishment and Politics: evidence and emulation in the making of English crime control policy, 2004; Thinking About Crime, 2004; *jointly:* Hypnotically Refreshed Testimony, 1985; Human Development and Criminal Behavior, 1991; *edited:* Ethnicity, Crime and Immigration, 1997; Intermediate Sanctions in Sentencing Guidelines, 1997; Handbook of Crime and Punishment, 1998; Penal Reform in Overcrowded Times, 2001; *edited jointly:* Reform and Punishment: essays on criminal sentencing, 1983; Communities and Crime, 1986; The Sentencing Commission: guidelines for criminal sanctions, 1987; Prediction and Classification, 1987; Managing Appeals in Federal Courts, 1988; Family Violence, 1990; Between Prison and Probation, 1990; Drugs and Crime, 1990; Modern Policing, 1992; Beyond the Law: crime in complex organisations, 1993; Intermediate Sanctions in Overcrowded Times, 1995; Building a Safer Society, 1995; Sentencing Reform in Overcrowded Times, 1997; Youth Violence, 1998; Prisons, 1999; Sentencing and Sanctions in Western Countries, 2001; Ideology, Crime and Criminal Justice, 2002; Reform and Punishment, 2002; Cross-national Studies in Crime and Justice, 2003. *Address:* University of Minnesota, Law School, 312 Mondale Hall, 229–19th Avenue South, Minneapolis, MN 55455, USA.

TOOBY, Michael Bowen; Director, National Museum & Gallery, Cardiff, since 2000; *b* 20 Dec. 1956; *s* of Leslie and Jill Tooby; *m* 1980, Jane Pare; one *s* one *d*. *Educ:* King Henry VIII Sch., Coventry; Magdalene Coll., Cambridge. Asst Curator, Kettle's Yard, Cambridge, 1978–80; Exhibns Orgnr, Third Eye Centre, Glasgow, 1980–84; Keeper, Mappin Art Gall., Sheffield, 1984–92; Founding Curator, Tate Gall. St Ives, and Curator, Barbara Hepworth Mus. and Sculpture Gdn, 1992–99. Chm., engage, (nat. assoc. for visual arts educn), 1999–2004. Vis. Prof. in Contemp. Curatorial Practice, Univ. of Glamorgan, 2007–. Macready Lectr in Canadian Art, Art Gall. of Ontario, 1997. *Publications:* The True North: Canadian painting 1896–1939, 1988; monograph studies of: Lois Williams, 1996; Iwan Bala, 1999; David Nash, 2000; Trevor Bell, 2003. *Address:* c/o National Museum & Gallery, Cathays Park, Cardiff CF10 3NP.

TOOHEY, Hon. John Leslie, AC 1988 (AO 1986); Member, Bloody Sunday Inquiry Tribunal, since 2000; *b* 4 March 1930; *s* of Albert Leslie and Sylvia Josephine Toohey; *m* 1953, Loma Jean Buckenara; two *s* five *d*. *Educ:* Univ. of WA (BA, LLB 1st Cl. Hons). Admitted as Legal Practitioner, WA, 1952; QC (Aust.) 1968; Judge: Federal Court of Australia, 1977–87; Supreme Court of NT, 1977–87; Justice of High Court of Australia, 1987–98. Comr, Aboriginal Land, NT, 1977–87. Hon. LLD Murdoch, 1998; Hon. DLitt Western Australia, 2004. *Recreations:* music, tennis. *Address:* 13A Rosser Street, Cottesloe, WA 6011, Australia. *T:* (8) 93851783.

TOOHEY, Mrs Joyce, CB 1977; Under-Secretary, Department of the Environment, 1970–76; *b* 20 Sept. 1917; *o d* of Louis Zinkin and Lena Zinkin (*née* Daiches); *m* 1947, Monty I. Toohey, MD, MRCP, DCH (*d* 1960); two *d*. *Educ:* Brondesbury and Kilburn High Sch.; Girton Coll., Cambridge (BA 1938, MA 1945); London Sch. of Economics. Asst Principal, Min. of Supply, 1941; transferred to Min. of Works, 1946; Principal, 1948; Asst Secretary, MPBW, 1956; Under-Secretary, 1964. Harvard Business Sch., 1970. *Recreations:* reading, walking. *Address:* 11 Kensington Court Gardens, W8 5QE.

TOOK, John Michael Exton, MBE 1964; Controller, Europe and North Asia Division, British Council, 1983–86, retired; *b* 15 Sept. 1926; *s* of late George Took, Dover, and Ailsa Clowes (*née* Turner); *m* 1964, Judith Margaret, *d* of late Brig. and Mrs W. J. Birkle; two *d*. *Educ:* Dover Coll.; Jesus Coll., Cambridge. Served Indian Army, 1944–47. HM Colonial Admin. Service (later HMOCS), N Rhodesia, 1950–57; Min. of External Affairs, Fedn of Rhodesia & Nyasaland, 1957–63; Min. of External Affairs, Republic of Zambia, 1964–65; joined British Council, 1965; Asst Reg. Dir, Frankfurt, 1965–67; Reg. Dir, Cape Coast, 1967–69; Rep., Cyprus, 1971–74; Cultural Attaché, British Embassy, Budapest, 1974–77; Dep. Controller, European Div., 1977–80; Rep., Greece, 1980–83. Dir, UK Cttee, Eur. Cultural Foundn, 1992–94. Chm., Romney Marsh Historic Churches Trust, 2001–05. *Publications:* Common Birds of Cyprus, 1973, 4th edn 1986; Birds of Cyprus, 1992; contribs to ornithological jls. *Recreations:* ornithology, fishing, natural history. *Address:* Downgate Lodge, Silverden Lane, Sandhurst, Cranbrook, Kent TN18 5NU. *T:* (01580) 851050. *Club:* Oxford and Cambridge.

TOOKE, Sir John (Edward), Kt 2007; DM, DSc; FRCP, FMedSci; Professor of Vascular Medicine, University of Exeter, since 1992; Dean, Peninsula Medical School, since 2000, Executive Dean, Peninsula College of Medicine and Dentistry, Universities of Exeter and Plymouth; Chairman, Medical Schools Council (formerly Council of Heads of Medical Schools), since 2006; *b* 4 March 1949; *s* of Thomas Edward Tooke and Edna (*née* Wilgose); *m* 1972, Elizabeth Moore; one *s* one *d*. *Educ:* St John's Coll., Oxford (MA 1970; MSc 1972; BM BCh 1974; DM 1982; DSc 1998); King's Coll. Hosp. Med. Sch. FRCP 1993. Lectr in Medicine, Leeds Univ., 1979–82; BHF Res. Fellow, Karolinska Inst. Dept of Medicine, Sweden, 1982–83; Wellcome Trust Sen. Lectr in Medicine and Physiol., Charing Cross and Westminster Med. Sch., 1984–87; Sen. Lectr, Univ. of Exeter, 1987–92. Hon. Consultant Physician in diabetes and vascular medicine, Royal Devon and Exeter Healthcare NHS Trust, 2000–. Chm., Ind. Inquiry into Modernising Med. Careers. FMedSci 2000. Camillo Golgi Award, Eur. Assoc. for Study of Diabetes, 1994. *Publications:* (ed with G. D. Lowe) A Textbook of Vascular Medicine, 1996; (ed) Diabetic Angiopathy, 1999. *Recreations:* angling, golf, sailing, le bricolage. *Address:* Peninsula Medical School, The John Bull Building, Tamar Science Park, Research Way, Plymouth PL6 8BU.

TOOKEY, Richard William, CBE 1984; Director and Group Public Affairs Co-ordinator, Shell International Petroleum Co. Ltd, 1984–93; *b* 11 July 1934; *s* of Geoffrey William Tookey, QC and Rosemary Sherwell Tookey (*née* Clogg); *m* 1st, 1956, Jill (*née* Ransford) (marr. diss. 1994); one *s* one *d* (and one *s* decd); 2nd, 1994, Colleen (*née* Channon) (*d* 2002); 3rd, 2006, Zoë (*née* Lambiris). *Educ:* Charterhouse. National Service, 2nd Lieut, 1st King's Dragoon Guards, 1952–54; Lanarkshire Yeomanry (TA), 1954–56; Inns of Court Regt/Inns of Court and City Yeomanry (TA), 1957–64. Joined Royal Dutch/Shell Group, 1954; posts in internat. oil supply and trading, 1954–73; Head of Supply Operations, 1973–75; Vice-Pres., Shell Internat. Trading Co., 1975–77; Man. Dir, Shell Tankers (UK) Ltd, 1978–79, Chm., 1980–84; Man. Dir, Shell Internat. Marine Ltd, 1980–84; Marine Co-ordinator, Shell Internat. Petroleum Co. Ltd, 1980–84. Part-time Mem., BRB, 1985–90; Mem., Gen. Cttee, Lloyd's Register of Shipping, 1978–85; Pres., Gen. Council of British Shipping, 1983–84. Liveryman, Shipwrights' Co., 1983–, Mem.

Ct of Assts, 1987–96. *Recreation:* home. *Address:* 12 Wares Road, Mill Park, Port Elizabeth, 6001, South Africa. *T:* (41) 3745025, *Fax:* (41) 3730100; *e-mail:* rwtookey@iafrica.com.

TOOLEY, Prof. James Nicholas, PhD; Professor of Education Policy, University of Newcastle upon Tyne, since 1998 (on leave of absence); President, Education Fund, Orient Global, since 2007; *b* 21 July 1959; *s* of Arthur Henry Tooley and Barbara May Tooley (*née* Tubby). *Educ:* Kingsfield Sch., Bristol; Univ. of Sussex (BSc 1983; MSc 1986); PhD London 1994. Mathematics Teacher, Zimbabwe, 1983–86; Sen. Res. Officer, NFER, 1988–91; Res. Fellow, Univ. of Oxford, 1994–95; Sen. Res. Fellow, Univ. of Manchester, 1995–98. Dir, Educn Prog., IEA, 1995–2002. *Publications:* Disestablishing the School, 1995; Education without the State, 1996; Educational Research: a critique, 1998; The Global Education Industry, 1999; The Seven Habits of Highly Effective Schools, 1999; Reclaiming Education, 2000; The Miseducation of Women, 2001; The Enterprise of Education, 2001; (ed) Buckingham at 25, 2002; (jtly) HIV and AIDS in Schools, 2002; (jtly) Private Schools for the Poor: a case study from India, 2003; (jtly) Delivering Better Education, 2003; (jtly) Government Failure: E. G. West on education, 2004; Could the Globalisation of Education Benefit the Poor?, 2004; (jtly) What Americans Can Learn from School Choice in Other Countries, 2005; (jtly) Private Education is Good for the Poor: a study of private schools serving the poor in low-income countries, 2005; E. G. West: economic liberalism and the role of government in education, 2008. *Recreation:* walking in the foothills of Simonside. *Address:* Orient Global, Level 46, UOB Plaza 1, 80 Raffles Place, Singapore 048624. *T:* 62105555, *Fax:* 62105556; *e-mail:* jnt@orientglobal.com. *Club:* Athenæum.

TOOLEY, Sir John, Kt 1979; Arts consultant, since 1988; General Director, Royal Opera House, Covent Garden, 1980–88; *b* 1 June 1924; *yr s* of late H. R. Tooley; *m* 1st, 1951, Judith Craig Morris (marr. diss., 1965); three *d*; 2nd, 1968, Patricia Janet Norah Bagshawe (marr. diss. 1990), 2nd *d* of late G. W. S. Bagshawe; one *s*; 3rd, 1995, Jennifer-Anne Shannon (marr. diss. 2003). *Educ:* Repton; Magdalene Coll., Cambridge (Hon. Fellow, 2005). Served The Rifle Brigade, 1943–47. Sec., Guildhall School of Music and Drama, 1952–55; Royal Opera House, Covent Garden: Asst to Gen. Administrator, 1955–60; Asst Gen. Administrator, 1960–70; Gen. Administrator, 1970–80. Chairman: Nat. Music Council Executive, 1970–72; HEFCE Music Conservatories Adv. Gp, 1993–97. Director: Britten Estate Ltd, 1989–97; South Bank Bd, 1991–97; Compton Verney Opera Project, 1991–97; WNO, 1992–2000; David Gyngell & Co. Ltd, 1995–97; Almeida Th., 1997–2002 (Chm., 1990–97); LPO, 1998–; Chm., Monument Insurance Brokers Ltd, 1997–2002; Consultant: Internat. Management Gp, 1988–97; Ballet Opera House, Toronto, 1989–90; Trustee: Wigmore Hall; SPNM; Walton Trust, 1988–2000; Britten Pears Foundn, 1989–99; Dartington Summer Sch., 1989–2000; Purcell Tercentenary Trust, 1991–97; Performing Arts Labs, 1993–97; Sidney Nolan Trust, 1996– (Chm., 2005–). Pres., Salisbury Festival, 1988–2005; Chairman: Salisbury Cathedral Fabric Cttee, 1990–2005; Salisbury Cathedral Girl Choristers' Trust, 1995–2005; Chm., Rudolf Nureyev Foundn, 1995–2008. Gen. Advr, Istanbul Foundn for Culture and Arts, 1993–; Advr, Borusa Chamber Orch., Istanbul, 2005–08. Governor, Repton Sch., 1984–94. Hon. FRAM; Hon. GSM; Hon. RNCM. DUniv UCE, 1996. Queen Elizabeth II Coronation Award, RAD. Commendatore, Italian Republic, 1976. *Publication:* In House, 1999. *Recreations:* walking, theatre. *Address:* 18 Grange Court, Pinehurst, Grange Road, Cambridge CB3 9BD. *T:* (01223) 358737; *e-mail:* tooley@btinternet.com.

TOOTH, Sir (Hugh) John L.; *see* Lucas-Tooth.

TOOZE, Dr John, FRS 1994; Vice President, Scientific and Facility Operations, Rockefeller University, since 2005; *b* 16 May 1938; *s* of Reginald John Tooze and Doris Edith Tooze (*née* Bull); *m* 1st, 1962, Sarah Margaret Wynn (marr. diss.); two *s* one *d*; 2nd, 1983, Sharon Ann Queally; one *s* one *d*. *Educ:* Handsworth Grammar Sch., Birmingham; Jesus Coll., Cambridge (BA 1961); King's Coll. London (PhD 1965); Harvard Univ. Served Army, 1956–58. King's College London: Asst Lectr in Biophysics, 1961–65; Lectr, 1965–68; Wellcome Res. Fellow, Harvard Univ., 1965–67; Dep. Editor, Nature, 1968–70; Res. Administrator, ICRF, 1970–73; Exec. Sec., EMBO, Heidelberg, 1973–94; Associate Dir, EMBL, 1993–94; Dir, Support Services, ICRF, subseq. Res. Services, CRUK, 1994–2005. Editor: Trends in Biochemistry, 1979–85; EMBO Jl, 1982–2003. Trustee, Darwin Trust of Edinburgh, 1991–. EMBO Medal, 1986. *Publications:* Molecular Biology of Tumor Viruses, 1973; DNA Tumor Viruses, 1980; (with J. D. Watson) The DNA Story, 1982; (with C. I. Branden) Introduction to Protein Structure, 1991, 2nd edn 1999. *Recreations:* numismatics, English history, gardening. *Address:* Rockefeller University, 1230 York Avenue, New York, NY 10021, USA. *Club:* Athenæum.

TOPE, family name of **Baron Tope**.

TOPE, Baron *cr* 1994 (Life Peer), of Sutton in the London Borough of Sutton; **Graham Norman Tope,** CBE 1991; Member (Lib Dem) London Assembly, 2000–08; *b* 30 Nov. 1943; *s* of late Leslie Tope, Plymouth and Winifred Tope (*née* Merrick), Bermuda; *m* 1972, Margaret East; two *s*. *Educ:* Whitgift Sch., S Croydon. Company Sec., 1965–72; Insce Manager, 1970–72; Dep. Gen. Sec., Voluntary Action Camden, 1975–90. Pres., Nat. League of Young Liberals, 1973–75 (Vice-Chm., 1971–73); Mem., Liberal Party Nat. Council, 1970–76; Exec. Cttee, London Liberal Party, 1981–84. Sutton Council: Councillor 1974–; Leader, Lib Dem (formerly Soc & Lib Dem) Group, 1974–99 (Liberal Gp, 1974–83, Liberal/SDP Alliance Gp, 1983–88); Leader of Opposition, 1984–86; Leader of Council, 1986–99; spokesperson on libraries, heritage, economic develt and community safety, arts and culture, 1999–2006, on community safety and cultural services, 2006–; Greater London Authority: Member: Metropolitan Police Authy, 2000–08; Mayor's Adv. Cabinet, 2000–04; Chm., Finance Cttee, 2000–08; Leader, Lib Dem Gp, 2000–06. MP (L) Sutton and Cheam, 1972–Feb. 1974; Liberal Party spokesman on environment, Dec. 1972–1974; contested (L) Sutton and Cheam, Oct. 1974. Lib Dem spokesman on educn, H of L, 1994–2000. Vice-Chm., All Party Parly Gp on Libraries, 1998–. Pres., London Lib Dems, 1991–2000; Vice Pres. and Lib Dem European and Internat. spokesperson, Local Govt Assoc., 1997–2005. Mem., Policy Cttee, AMA, 1989–97; Chm., Policy and Finance Cttee, London Boroughs Assoc., 1994–95. EU Committee of the Regions: UK Rep., 1994–; Mem. Bureau, 1996–; Vice Chm., UK Delegn, 1996–; Pres., European Lib Dem Reform Gp, 1998–2002; Chm., Constitutional Affairs Cttee, 2002–04 (First Vice Chm., 2004–06); Mem. Council of Europe, CLRAE, 1996–2004. Vice Chm., 1997–2000, Mem. Leaders' Cttee, 1995–2000, Chm., Local Govt Gp for Europe, 2005–, Assoc. of London Govt. Freeman, City of London, 1998; Liveryman, Needlemakers' Co., 1999–. *Publication:* (jtly) Liberals and the Community, 1974. *Address:* 88 The Gallop, Sutton, Surrey SM2 5SA. *T:* (020) 8770 7269.

TÖPFER, Dr Klaus; Member, Advisory Board, Holcim Foundation for Sustainable Construction, since 2006; *b* Waldenburg, Silesia, 29 July 1938; *m* Mechthildis; three *c*. *Educ:* König-Wilhelm-Gymnasium, Höxter, Weser; Univ. of Münster (DipEcon 1964; PhD 1968). Lectr, Econ. Acad., Hagen and Univ. of Bielefeld, 1965–71; Asst to Dir of Econ. Res., 1965–71, Hd, Econs Dept, 1970–71, Central Inst. for Regl Planning, Univ. of Münster; Lectr, Coll. of Admin. Scis, Speyer, 1971–78; Consultant in field of develt policy, Egypt, Malaŵi, Brazil and Jordan, 1971–78; Prof. and Dir, Inst. for Regl R&D, Univ. of Hanover, 1978–79; Associate Lectr in Envmtl and Resource Econs, Univ. of Mainz, 1985–86. Hd, Dept for Planning and Inf., State Chancellery of Saarland, 1971–78; State Sec., Min. for Social Affairs, Health and Envmt, 1978–85, Minister for Envmt and Health, 1985–87, Rhineland-Palatinate; Federal Minister for Envmt, Nature Conservation and Nuclear Safety, 1987–94; Mem. (CDU) Bundestag, 1990–98; Federal Minister for Regl Planning, Building and Urban Develt, and Co-ordinator for Transfer of Parlt and Federal Govt to Berlin and Compensation for Bonn Reg., 1994–98. Chm., UN Commn on Sustainable Develt, 1994–95; Under-Sec.-Gen., UN, 1998–2006; Dir-Gen., UN Office, Nairobi, 1998; Actg Exec. Dir, UN Centre for Human Settlements (Habitat), 1998–2000; Exec. Dir, UNEP, 1998–2006. Joined Christian Democratic Union, 1972: Dist Chm., Saarbrücken and Mem., State Exec. Cttee, Saarland, 1977–79; Vice-Chm., Fed. Exec. Cttee on Envmtl Questions, 1983–87; Dist Chm., Rhine-Hunsrück, 1987–89; State Chm., Saarland, 1990–95; Mem., Presiding Cttee, 1992. Hon. Prof., Tongji Univ., Shanghai, 1997. Hon Dr: Free Univ., Berlin, 2002; Essen, 2002; Hannover, 2003. TÜV Rheinland Pfalz Envmt Award, 2000; Bruno H. Schubert Envmt Prize, 2002; German Envmt Prize, 2002; Wilhelm Weber Prize, 2003; Golden Steering Wheel Internat. Prize (Russia), 2003. OM (FRG), 1986; Comdr's Cross, 1989, Grand Cross, 1997, OM (FRG); Order of Southern Cross (Brazil), 2002; Danaker Order (Kyrgyz Republic), 2003. *Publications:* Die Beeinflussbarkeit privater Pläne dargestellt unternehmerischen Standortentscheidung, 1968; Regionalpolitik und Standort-entscheidung, 1969; Standortentscheidung und Wohnortwahl, 1974; Die europäische Dimension der Umweltpolitik, 1989; Internationaler Umweltschutz, 1989; numerous contribs to books and to learned jls. *Recreations:* avid fan of card games, including Skat, football, fine wine. *Address:* Holcim Foundation for Sustainable Construction, Hagenholzstrasse 85, 8050 Zurich, Switzerland.

TOPLEY, (William) Keith, MA; Senior Master of the Supreme Court (Queen's Bench Division) and Queen's Remembrancer, 1990–96; Admiralty Registrar of the Supreme Court, 1986–92; *b* 19 Jan. 1936; *s* of late Bryan Topley and Grizel Hester (*née* Stirling); *m* 1980, Clare Mary Pennington; one *s* by former marriage. *Educ:* Bryanston School; Trinity Coll., Oxford (MA). Called to Bar, Inner Temple, 1959, Bencher, 1990; Master of Supreme Court, QBD, 1980–90. Mem., Bar Council, 1967–68. Mem. Adv. Bd, Coll. of Law, 1992–96. Freeman, City of London, 1993; Mem., Watermen and Lightermen's Co., 1993–. *Publication:* (ed jtly) Supreme Court Practice, 1988, 1991. *Recreations:* reading, writing, sailing. *Address:* 22 Queens Road, Cowes, Isle of Wight PO31 8BJ. *T:* (01983) 299742. *Clubs:* Garrick; Royal Yacht Squadron, Royal London Yacht (Cdre, 1996–98) (Cowes); Bar Yacht (Cdre, 1992–95); New Zealand Golf.

TOPOLSKI, Daniel; freelance writer, motivational speaker and broadcaster; photo-journalist; Oxford Boat-Race coach, 1973–87, consultant since 1995; *b* 4 June 1945; *s* of late Feliks Topolski and Marion Everall; *m* 1998, Susan Gilmore; one *s* two *d*. *Educ:* Lycée Français, London; Westminster Sch.; New Coll., Oxford (BA, Geography 1967; DipSoc Anthropology 1968, MA 1970). Writer and TV broadcaster on travel and sport; BBC TV Researcher and Producer, 1969–73; TV and Radio presenter and commentator, 1982–; expedition leader: Brazil, 1963; Iran (Marco Polo), 1973–74; travel in Africa, North and South America, India, Himalayas, China, Middle East, SE Asia, Australia. Rowing Competitor: Boat Race, Oxford, 1967, 1968; World Championships, 1969–78 (Gold medal 1977); Henley Regatta (4 victories); Rowing Coach: Oxford Boat Race Crew, 1973–87 (12 victories, record 10 in a row); Nat. Women's Squad, 1979–80, Olympics, 1980; Nat. Men's Pair and Women's Pair, 1982; Nat. Men's Pair, Olympics, 1984. Churchill Fellow, 1980. FRGS 1993. Radio Travel Prog. of the Year award for Topolski's Travels, 1993. *Publications:* Muzungu: one man's Africa, 1976; (with Feliks Topolski) Travels with my Father: journey through South America, 1983; Boat Race, 1985; (with Patrick Robinson) True Blue, 1989 (Sports Book of the Year, 1990), 2nd edn 1996 (filmed, 1998); Henley: the Regatta, 1989. *Recreations:* theatre, cinema, rowing (Steward, Henley Regatta), ski-ing, travel, family. *Address:* 69 Randolph Avenue, W9 1DW. *T:* (020) 7289 8939. *Clubs:* London Rowing (Putney); Leander (Henley).

TOPP, Air Commodore Roger Leslie; AFC 1950 (Bar 1955, 2nd Bar 1957); independent consultant, aviation and defence, 1988–99; *b* 14 May 1923; *s* of William Horace Topp and Kathleen (*née* Peters); *m* 1945, Audrey Jane Jeffery (*d* 1999); one *s* one *d*. *Educ:* North Mundham Sch.; RAF, Cranwell. Served War: Pilot trg, Canada, 1943–44, commissioned 1944; 'E' Sqdn Glider Pilot Regt, Rhine Crossing, 1945. Nos 107 and 98 Mosquito Sqdns, Germany, 1947–50; Empire Test Pilots' Sch. and RAE Farnborough, 1951–54; Commanded No 111 Fighter Sqdn (Black Arrows) Aerobatic Team, 1955–58; Allied Air Forces Central Europe, Fontainebleau, 1959; Sector Operational Centre, Brockzetel, Germany, 1959–61; jssc, Latimer, 1961–62; commanded Fighter Test Sqdn, Boscombe Down, 1962–64; Station Cmdr, RAF Coltishall, 1964–66; Nat. Def. Coll., Canada, 1966–67; Opl Requirements, MoD (Air), London, 1967–69; Multi-role Combat Aircraft Project, Munich, 1969–70; HQ No 38 Gp, Odiham, 1970; Commandant, Aeroplane and Armament Experimental Estabt, Boscombe Down, 1970–72; Dep. Gen. Man., Multi-role Combat Aircraft Develt and Production Agency, Munich, 1972–78; retd from RAF, 1978. Consultant to Ferranti Defence Systems Ltd, Scotland (Aviation and Defence, FRG), 1978–88. *Recreations:* golf, sailing. *Club:* Royal Air Force.

TOPPIN, Gilbert Anthony Lester; Chief Executive Officer, EEF, since 2008; *b* Barbados, 6 Nov. 1952; *s* of Herbert Lester Toppin and Betty Joan Toppin (*née* Mayers); *m* 2008, Donna Louise Reed; two *s* by a previous marriage. *Educ:* Univ. of Edinburgh (BSc Hons Civil Engrg 1975); Univ. of Southampton (MSc Irrigation Engrg 1976). MICE 1980; CEng 1981; MIStructE 1986; MCIWEM 1987; ACMA 1990; MAPM 1994. Researcher, Hydraulics Res. Station, 1976–77; Engineer: Binnie Black & Veatch, 1977–84; Stewart Lyons Partnership, 1984–86; Consultant, then Partner, Deloitte Consulting, 1986–2003; independent consultant, 2004–07. *Publication:* (with Fiona Czerniawska) Business Consulting, 2005. *Recreations:* diving, family interests. *Address:* EEF, Broadway House, Tothill Street, SW1H 9NQ. *T:* (020) 7654 1514; *e-mail:* gtoppin@eef.org.uk.

TOPPING, Rev. Frank; actor, author, broadcaster and Methodist minister; Warden, John Wesley's Chapel (The New Room), Bristol, 2000–07; *b* 30 March 1937; *s* of late Frank and Dorothy Topping; *m* 1958, June Berry; two *s* one *d*. *Educ:* St Anne's Convent Sch., Birkenhead; St Anselm's Christian Brothers' Coll., Birkenhead; North West School of Speech and Drama. Served RAF, Cyprus, 1955–57. Leatherhead Rep. Th., 1957–59; Royal Court, Chelsea, 1959; Wolverhampton Rep. Th., 1959; Granada TV, 1960–64; read Theology at Didsbury Coll., Bristol, 1964–67; asst minister at Dome Methodist Mission, Brighton, and Methodist univ. chaplain at Sussex, 1967–70; also freelance broadcaster, BBC Radio Brighton, 1967–70; ordained 1970; staff producer, BBC, 1970–80; Supt Methodist Minister, Barnet Circuit, 1997–2001. Song-writing partnership with Donald Swann, 1973–81; two-man show, Swann with Topping, played in Jersey, London fringe theatre, then at Ambassadors; presented three one-man plays, Edinburgh Fest. Fringe, 1986. TV series: Sunday Best, 1981; Topping on Sunday, 1982–84; The 5 Minute Show, TVS, 1989–90. Author of radio plays: On the Hill, 1974 (Grace Wyndham Goldie UNDA Dove award, 1975); A Particular Star, 1977. Formed Emmaus, later

Topping Theatre Prodns with wife, 1985. *Publications:* Lord of the Morning, 1977; Lord of the Evening, 1979; Lord of my Days, 1980; Working at Prayer, 1981; Pause for Thought with Frank Topping, 1981; Lord of Life, 1982; The Words of Christ: forty meditations, 1983; God Bless You—Spoonbill, 1984; Lord of Time, 1985; An Impossible God, 1985; Wings of the Morning, 1986; Act Your Age, 1989; Laughing in my Sleep (autobiog.), 1993; All the Days of my Life, 1994; Here I Stand…, 1997; Grappling with God on the M25, 1998; (ed) Daily Prayer, 2nd edn, 2003; Splinters of Light, 2008. *Recreations:* sailing, travel, photography, late night conversation. *Address:* Lamb Cottage, The Cross, Clearwell, Coleford, Glos GL16 8JU. *T:* and *Fax:* (01594) 834278.

TORDOFF, family name of **Baron Tordoff**.

TORDOFF, Baron *cr* 1981 (Life Peer), of Knutsford in the County of Cheshire; **Geoffrey Johnson Tordoff;** Lib Dem Chief Whip, House of Lords, 1988–94 (Liberal Chief Whip, 1984–88; Deputy Chief Whip, 1983–84); an Extra Lord in Waiting to the Queen, since 2004; *b* 11 Oct. 1928; *s* of Stanley Acomb Tordoff and Annie Tordoff (*née* Johnson); *m* 1953, (Mary) Patricia (*née* Swarbrick); two *s* three *d*. *Educ:* North Manchester School; Manchester Grammar School; Univ. of Manchester. Contested (L), Northwich 1964, Knutsford 1966, 1970. Chairman: Liberal Party Assembly Cttee, 1974–76; Liberal Party, 1976–79 (and its Campaigns and Elections Cttee, 1980, 1981); Member, Liberal Party Nat. Executive, 1975–84; Pres., Liberal Party, 1983–84. Chm. of Cttees, H of L, 2001–02 (Principal Dep. Chm. of Cttees, 1994–2001); Chm., H of L Select Cttee on the EC, 1994–2001. Chm., ME Cttee, Refugee Council, 1990–95. Mem., Press Complaints Commn, 1995–2002. *Address:* House of Lords, SW1A 0PW.

TORO-HARDY, Alfredo; Ambassador of Venezuela to Spain, since 2007; *b* Caracas, 22 May 1950; *s* of Fernando Toro and Ofelia Toro (*née* Hardy); *m* 1st, 1972, Dinorah Carnevali (marr. diss. 1998); two *s* one *d*; 2nd, 2001, Gabriela Gaxiola. *Educ:* Central Univ. of Venezuela (LLB 1973; LLM Internat. Trade Law 1977); Univ. of Paris II (Comparative Law 1974); Internat. Inst. of Public Admin, Paris (Diplomatic Studies 1974); Univ. of Pennsylvania (LLM Corporative Law 1979). Simón Bolívar University, Caracas: Associate Prof., 1989–93; Co-ordinator, Latin American Studies Inst., and Dir, N American Studies Centre, 1989–91; Dir, Diplomatic Acad., with rank of Ambassador, Foreign Affairs Ministry, 1992–94; Ambassador: to Brazil, 1994–97; to Chile, 1997–99; to USA, 1999–2001; to the Court of St James's and concurrently to Republic of Ireland, 2001–07. Advr to Minister of Foreign Affairs, 1992–94; Mem., Consultative Bd, Nat. Security and Defence Council, 1988–2000. Mem., Academic Bd on Social Responsibility, Univ. of Barcelona, 2003–; External Adviser, Univ. of Westminster Review Panel, 2004–. Vis. Schol. and Sen. Fulbright Schol., Princeton Univ., 1986–87; Hon. Prof., Univ. of Brasilia, 1996–97; prof. and guest speaker in several univs and acad. instns in Venezuela, USA, Chile, Brazil, UK and others. Member: Inter-American Peace and Justice Commn, Santiago, 1997–; Windsor Energy Gp, London, 2002–; Global Dimensions, London, 2002–; RIIA, 2003–. Mem., Chairmans Club, 2003–. Weekly columnist and collaborator in numerous media publications, in Venezuela, Mexico, Brazil and Chile, including: El Universal, Caracas, 1994–; El Globo, Caracas, 1989–97. Host, weekly TV prog., Radio Caracas TV, 1992–94. Holds several Venezuelan and foreign decorations. *Publications:* include: Los Libertadores de Venezuela, 1982; Rafael Caldera, 1982; Para qué una Política Exterior?, 1984; Venezuela, Democracia y Política Exterior, 1986; El Desafío Venezolano: Como Influir las Decisiones Políticas Estadounidenses, 1988; La Maldicion de Sísifo: quince años de política exterior Venezolana, 1991; Bajo el Signo de la Incertidumbre, 1992; Las Falacias del Libre Comercio, 1993; De Yalta a Sarajevo: de la guerra fría a la paz caliente, 1993; Del Descalabro Mexicano a la Crisis Venezolana, 1995; El Desorden Global, 1996; The Age of Villages: the small village *vs* the global village, 2002; Irak y la Reconfiguración del Orden Mundiaz, 2003; Tiene Futuro América Latina?, 2004; Los Estadounidenses, 2005; Hegemoniá e Imperio, 2007. *Address:* Venezuelan Embassy, Calle Capitán Haya 1, 13, 28020 Madrid, Spain. *T:* 5550881.

ToROBERT, Sir Henry Thomas, KBE 1981; Governor and Chairman of the Board of the Bank of Papua New Guinea since its formation, 1973–93; Partner, Deloitte Touche Tohmatsu, PNG, since 1993; Chairman, Credit Corporation (PNG) Ltd, 1993–2007; *b* Kokopo, 1942. *Educ:* primary educn in East New Britain; secondary educn in Qld, Australia; Univ. of Sydney, Aust. (BEcon. 1965). Asst Research Officer, Reserve Bank of Australia, Port Moresby, 1965 (one of first local officers to join the bank); Dep. Manager, Port Moresby Branch, 1971; Manager of the Reserve Bank, 1972 (the first Papua New Guinean to hold such a position at a time when all banks were branches of the Aust. commercial banks). Member of the cttee responsible for working out a PNG banking system which came into effect by an act of parliament in 1973; Chairman: Management Bd, PNG Bankers' Coll., 1973–; PNG Currency Working Group advising the Govt on arrangements leading to the introduction of PNG currency, the Kina; ToRobert Cttee to look into problems of administration in PNG Public Service, 1979 (ToRobert Report, 1979); Council, PNG Inst. of Applied Social and Econ. Res., 1975–82; Govt Super Task Force on project implementation, 1994–. Pres., PNG Amateur Sports Fedn and PNG Olympic and Commonwealth Games Cttee, 1980–. *Address:* PO Box 898, Port Moresby, Papua New Guinea.

TORONTO, Archbishop of, (RC), since 2007; **Most Rev. Thomas Collins,** STD; *b* 16 Jan. 1947. *Educ:* St Jerome's Coll., Waterloo, Ont. (BA 1969); St Peter's Seminary, London, Ont. (BTh 1973); Univ. of Western Ontario (MA 1973); Pontifical Biblical Inst., Rome (SSL 1978); Gregorian Univ., Rome (STD 1986). Ordained deacon, 1972, priest, 1973; Associate Pastor, Holy Rosary Parish, Burlington, Ont., and Christ the King Cath., Hamilton, Ont., and teacher and Chaplain, Cathedral Boys' High Sch., Hamilton, Ont., 1973–75; Lectr, Dept of English, King's Coll., Univ. of Western Ontario, 1978–84; St Peter's Seminary: Lectr in Scripture, 1978–84; Gp Leader and Spiritual Dir, 1981–95; Associate Prof. of Scripture, 1985–97; Dean of Theol. and Vice-Rector, 1992–95; Rector, 1995–97; Bishop of St Paul, Alberta, 1997–99; Archbishop of Edmonton (Alberta), (RC), 1999–2007. President: Alberta Conf. of Catholic Bishops, 1999–2007; Ontario Conf. of Catholic Bishops, 2008–; Mem., Permt Council, Canadian Conf. of Catholic Bishops, 1999–2003, 2007– (Chm., Nat. Commn of Theol., 1999–2001; Chm., 2001–03, Mem., 2003–05, Nat. Commn on Christian Unity). Member, Board of Directors: Caritas Health Gp, Edmonton, 1999–2007; Alberta Catholic Health Corp., 1999–2007; Chm., Bd of Dirs, Catholic Charities, Archdiocese of Toronto, 2007–; Trustee, Adv. Bd, Sharelife, 2007–. Chairman, Board of Governors: Newman Theol Coll., Edmonton, 1999–2007; St Joseph's Coll., Edmonton, 1999–2007; St Augustine's Seminary, Toronto, 2007–; Chancellor: Univ. of St Michael's Coll., Univ. of Toronto, 2007–; Pontifical Inst. of Mediaeval Studies, Toronto, 2007–; Chair, Bd of Dirs, Redemptoris Mater Missionary Seminary, Toronto, 2007–. Associate Ed., Discover the Bible, 1989–94; columnist, Bread of Life mag., 1987–89. *Publications:* The Eucharist: It is the Lord!, 2000; Reconciliation: Go in Peace, 2003; contrib. to Journey, Emmanuel, and Canadian Catholic Review. *Address:* 1155 Yonge Street, Toronto, ON M4T 1W2, Canada.

TORONTO, Bishop of, since 2004; **Rt Rev. Colin Robert Johnson;** *b* 6 Nov. 1952; *s* of John McLellan Johnson and Marie Lynn (*née* Johnston); *m* 1976, (Margaret) Ellen Johnson (*née* Smith); one *s* two *d*. *Educ:* Univ. of Western Ont (BA 1974); Trinity Coll., Toronto (MDiv 1977; DD 2005). Ordained deacon, 1977, priest, 1978; Asst Curate, Ch of St Simon-the-Apostle, Toronto, 1977–78; Incumbent, Parish of Georgina, 1978–83; Regional Dean, Deanery of the Holland, 1980–83; Incumbent, Ch of the Holy Trinity, Ajax, 1983–92; Exec. Asst to Archbishop of Toronto, and Hon. Asst, St Martin's Bay Ridges, Pickering, and Assisting Priest, St James' Cathedral, Toronto, 1992–2003; Archdeacon of York, 1994–2003; Acting Dir of Communications, Dio. Toronto, 1994–97 and 2001–03; a Bp Suffragan of Toronto, and Area Bp of Trent Durham, 2003–04. *Recreations:* music, mystery novels, movies, cooking, computers, windsurfing, Jeopardy. *Address:* (office) 135 Adelaide Street East, Toronto, ON M5C 1L8, Canada. *T:* (416) 3636021; *e-mail:* cjohnson@toronto.anglican.ca.

TORONTO, Area Bishops of; *see* Elliott, Rt Rev. M. G. H; Yu, Rt Rev. P. T-S.

TORPHICHEN, 15th Lord *cr* 1564; **James Andrew Douglas Sandilands;** *b* 27 Aug. 1946; *s* of 14th Lord Torphichen, and Mary Thurstan, *d* of late Randle Henry Neville Vaudrey; *S* father, 1975; *m* 1976, Margaret Elizabeth, *o d* of late William A. Beale and of Mrs Margaret Patten Beale, Peterborough, New Hampshire, USA; four *d*. *Heir: cousin* Robert Powell Sandilands, Master of Torphichen [*b* 10 Dec. 1950; *m* 1974, Cheryl Lynn Watson; one *s* one *d*]. *Address:* Calder House, Mid-Calder, West Lothian EH53 0HN.

TORPY, Air Chief Marshal Sir Glenn (Lester), GCB 2008 (KCB 2005); CBE 2000; DSO 1991; Chief of the Air Staff, Ministry of Defence, since 2006; Air Aide de Camp to the Queen, since 2006; *b* 27 July 1953; *s* of Gordon Torpy and Susan Torpy (*née* Lindsey); *m* 1977, Christine Jackson. *Educ:* Imperial Coll., London (BSc Eng). OC No 13 Sqn, 1989–92; PSO to AOC-in-C STC, 1992–94; Stn Comdr, RAF Bruggen, 1994–96; rcds 1997; ACOS Ops, Permanent Jt HQ, 1998–99; Dir Air Ops, MoD, 1999–2000; ACDS (Ops), 2000–01; AOC No 1 Gp, 2001–03; Dep. C-in-C Strike Command, 2003–04; Chief of Jt Ops, MoD, 2004–06. Liveryman, Haberdashers' Co., 2006. FRAeS 2003; FCGI 2007. Officer, Legion of Merit (USA), 2003. *Recreations:* golf, hill walking, military history, cabinet making. *T:* (20) 2187220; *e-mail:* glenn.torpy@virgin.net.

TORRANCE, Very Rev. Prof. Iain Richard, TD 1995; DPhil; President, and Professor of Patristics, Princeton Theological Seminary, New Jersey, since 2004; Trustee, Center for Theological Inquiry, Princeton, since 2004; a Chaplain to the Queen in Scotland, since 2001; *b* 13 Jan. 1949; *yr s* of Very Rev. Prof. Thomas Forsyth Torrance, MBE, FBA and of Margaret Edith Spear; *m* 1975, Morag Ann MacHugh, *er d* of Francis John MacHugh and Wendy Anne Lang; one *s* one *d*. *Educ:* Edinburgh Acad.; Monkton Combe Sch., Bath; Edinburgh Univ. (MA Mental Philosophy, 1971); St Andrews Univ. (BD New Testament Langs and Lit., 1974); Oriel Coll., Oxford (DPhil 1980). Chaplain to the Moderator, Gen. Assembly of Church of Scotland, 1976–77; ordained, 1982; Minister, Northmavine, Shetland, 1982–85; Lecturer: in NT and Christian Ethics, Queen's Coll., Birmingham, 1985–89; in NT and Patristics, Birmingham Univ., 1989–93; Aberdeen University: Lectr in Divinity, 1993–97; Sen. Lectr, 1997–99; Prof. in Patristics and Christian Ethics, 1999–2004; Prof. Emeritus, 2004; Senate Assessor to Univ. Court, 1999–2003; Head, Dept of Divinity and Religious Studies, 2000–01; Dean, Faculty of Arts and Divinity, 2001–03; Master, Christ's Coll., Aberdeen, 2001–04. Moderator, Gen. Assembly of Church of Scotland, 2003–04 (Mem., Bd of Social Responsibility, 2002–04). TA Chaplain, 1982–97; ACF Chaplain, 1996–2000; Convener, Cttee on Chaplains to HM Forces, Gen. Assembly of C of S, 1998–2002. Select Preacher: Univ. of Oxford, 2004; Princeton Univ., 2005; Willard Lect., Charlotte, 2005; W. G. A. Wright Lect., Sandhurst, 2005; Berger Lectr, Potomac, 2006. Member: Dialogue between World Alliance of Reformed Churches and the Orthodox Church, 1992– (Co-Chm., 2005–); Acad. Internat. des Sciences Religieuses, 1997–; Benchmarking Panel for Degrees in Theology and Religious Studies, QAA, 1999–2000. Sec., Soc. for Study of Christian Ethics, 1995–98; Hon. Sec., 1995–98, Hon. Pres., 1998–99, Aberdeen AUT. Judge, Templeton (UK) Award, 1994–99; Mem. Adv. Bd, Templeton Foundn, 2008–. Co-ed., Scottish Jl of Theol., 1982–. Burgess of Guild, City of Aberdeen, 2004. Corresp. FRSE 2007. Hon. DD: Aberdeen, 2005; St Andrews, 2005; Hon. DTheol Reformed Theol Univ., Debrecen, Hungary, 2006; Hon. LHD King Coll., Tennessee, 2007. Friend for Life Award, Equality Network, 2004. *Publications:* Christology after Chalcedon, 1989; (jtly) Human Genetics: a Christian perspective, 1995; Ethics and the Military Community, 1998; (ed jtly) To Glorify God: essays on modern reformed liturgy, 1999; (ed) Bioethics for the New Millennium, 2000; (ed jtly) The Oxford Handbook of Systematic Theology, 2007. *Recreation:* historical Scottish culture (buildings, literature, art). *Address:* (home) Springdale, 86 Mercer Street, Princeton, NJ 08540–6819, USA; (office) Princeton Theological Seminary, PO Box 552, 64 Mercer Street, Princeton, NJ 08542–0803, USA. *T:* (609) 4977800, *Fax:* (609) 9240378; *e-mail:* president@ptsem.edu. *Clubs:* New (Edinburgh); Nassau (Princeton).

TORRANCE, Madeline Mary; *see* Drake, M. M.

TORRANCE, Monica; *see* Ali, M.

TORRANCE, Samuel Robert, OBE 2003 (MBE 1995); professional golfer; *b* Largs, 24 Aug. 1953; *s* of Robert and June Torrance; *m* 1995, Suzanne Danielle; one *s* two *d*. Winner: Under-25 Match Play tournament Radici Open, 1972; Zambian Open, 1975; Martini Internat., Wales, 1976; Scottish PGA Championship, 1978, 1980, 1985, 1991, 1993, 1995; Colombian Open, 1979; Australian PGA Championship, 1980; Irish Open, 1981, 1995; Spanish Open, 1982; Portuguese Open, 1982, 1983; Scandinavian Open, 1983; Tunisian Open, 1984; Benson & Hedges Internat., England, 1984; Sanyo Open, Spain, 1984; Monte Carlo Open, 1985; Italian Open, 1987, 1995; German Masters, 1990; Jersey Open, 1991; Catalan Open, 1993; Kronenbourg Open, Italy, 1993; Honda Open, Germany, 1993; British Masters, 1995; French Open, 1998; Travis Perkins Senior Masters, 2004; European Senior Tour Order of Merit, 2005. Member: Dunhill Cup team, 1985–95 (winners, 1995); World Cup team, 1976–95; Mem., 1981–95, Captain, 2001–02, Ryder Cup team (winners, 1985, 1995, 2002). *Publication:* Sam (autobiog.), 2003. *Recreations:* snooker, tennis, all sport.

TORRAVILLE, Rt Rev. David; *see* Newfoundland, Central, Bishop of.

TORRENTS, Deborah Jane; *see* Bronnert, D. J.

TORRINGTON, 11th Viscount *cr* 1721; **Timothy Howard St George Byng;** Bt 1715; Baron Byng of Southill, 1721; *b* 13 July 1943; *o s* of Hon. George Byng, RN (*d* on active service, 1944; *o s* of 10th Viscount) and Anne Yvonne Wood (she *m* 2nd, 1951, Howard Henry Masterton Carpenter; 3rd, 1990, Michael Ingram Bostock); *S* grandfather, 1961; *m* 1973, Susan, *d* of M. G. T. Webster, *qv*; three *d*. *Educ:* Harrow; St Edmund Hall, Oxford. Mem., Select Cttee on EEC, H of L, 1984–87 (Chm., Sub-Cttee B (Energy, Transport and Broadcasting), 1985–87). Chm., Baltic Mills Ltd, 1995–. *Recreation:* travel. *Heir: kinsman* Colin Hugh Cranmer-Byng [*b* 10 Sept. 1960; *m* 1984, Lisa Anne Dallimore; two *s* four *d*]. *Address:* Belbins House, Whitehill, Mere, Wilts BA12 6BL. *Clubs:* White's, Pratt's; Muthaiga (Nairobi).

TORRY, Sir Peter (James), GCVO 2004; KCMG 2003; HM Diplomatic Service, retired; consultant; *b* 2 Aug. 1948; *m* 1979, Angela Wakeling Wood, *d* of J. N. Wood, *qv*; three *d. Educ:* Dover Coll.; New Coll., Oxford (Open Schol.; BA 1970; Irvine Award, 1968; Rugby Blue, 1968, 1969). Joined FCO, 1970; Third Sec., Havana, 1971; Second Sec., Jakarta, 1974; First Sec., FCO, 1977; Bonn, 1981; First Sec., subseq. Counsellor, FCO, 1985; Washington, 1989; FCO, 1993–98, Dir (Personnel and Security), 1995–98; Ambassador: to Spain, 1998–2003; to the FRG, 2003–07. *Recreations:* golf, walking, ski-ing, books, antique furniture. *Address:* c/o Peter Torry Consultancy, 192 Emery Hill Street, SW1P 1PN. *Clubs:* Oxford and Cambridge; Vincent's (Oxford).

TORTELIER, Yan Pascal; Principal Conductor, BBC Philharmonic, 1992–2002, now Conductor Laureate; *b* 19 April 1947; *s* of late Paul Tortelier and of Maud (*née* Martin); *m* 1970, Sylvie Brunet-Moret; two *s. Educ:* Paris Conservatoire; general musical studies with Nadia Boulanger; studied conducting with Franco Ferrara in Sienna. Leader and Associate Conductor, Orchestre du Capitole de Toulouse, 1974–82; Principal Conductor and Artistic Dir, Ulster Orchestra, 1989–92. Principal Guest Conductor: NYO, 2000–; Pittsburgh SO, 2005–. Has conducted all major British orchestras and toured extensively in USA, Canada, Japan, Australia, Scandinavia, E and W Europe. Numerous recordings incl. complete symphonic works of Debussy and Ravel with Ulster Orch., and Hindemith and Dutilleux series with BBC Philharmonic. Hon. DLitt Ulster, 1992. *Publication:* Première orchestration of Ravel's Piano Trio, 1992. *Recreations:* ski-ing, windsurfing, scuba diving, nature. *Address:* c/o IMG Artists Europe, The Light Box, 111 Power Road, Chiswick, W4 5PY.

TORVILL, Jayne, (Mrs P. L. Christensen), OBE 2000 (MBE 1981); professional ice skater; *b* 7 Oct. 1957; *d* of George Henry Torvill and Betty (*née* Smart); *m* 1990, Philip Lee Christensen; one adopted *s* one adopted *d. Educ:* Clifton Hall Grammar Sch. for Girls, Nottingham. Ice dancer, with Christopher Dean, *qv*; British Champions, 1978, 1979, 1980, 1981, 1982, 1983 and 1994; European Champions, 1981, 1982, 1984 and 1994; World Champions, 1981, 1982, 1983 and 1984; World Professional Champions, 1984, 1985, 1990, 1995 and 1996; Olympic Champions, 1984; Olympic Bronze Medallists, 1994. Trainer, choreographer and performer: Stars on Ice, USA, 1998–99, 1999–2000; Dancing on Ice, ITV, 2006, 2007, 2008. Hon. MA Nottingham Trent, 1994. *Publication:* (with Christopher Dean) Facing the Music, 1995. *Recreations:* dance, theatre, caring for Freddy and Louis, my dogs. *Address:* PO Box 32, Heathfield, E Sussex TN21 0BW. *T:* (01435) 867825.

TORY, Sir Geofroy (William), KCMG 1958 (CMG 1956); HM Diplomatic Service, retired; *b* 31 July 1912; *s* of William Frank Tory and Edith Wreghitt; *m* 1st, 1938, Emilia Strickland; two *s* one *d*; 2nd, 1950, Hazel Winfield (*d* 1985). *Educ:* King Edward VII Sch., Sheffield; Queens' Coll., Cambridge. Apptd Dominions Office, 1935; Private Sec. to Perm. Under-Sec. of State, 1938–39; served War, 1939–43, in Royal Artillery; Prin. Private Sec. to Sec. of State, 1945–46; Senior Sec., Office of UK High Comr, Ottawa, 1946–49; Prin. Sec., Office of UK Rep. to Republic of Ireland, 1949–50; Counsellor, UK Embassy, Dublin, 1950–51; idc 1952; Dep. High Comr for UK in Pakistan (Peshawar), 1953–54, in Australia, 1954–57; Asst Under-Sec. of State, CRO, 1957; High Comr for UK in Fedn of Malaya, 1957–63; Ambassador to Ireland, 1964–66; High Commissioner to Malta, 1967–70. PMN (Malaysia) 1963. *Recreations:* painting, music. *Address:* Cliff Top, Harbour View, Kilbrittain, Co. Cork, Ireland.

TOSELAND, Ronald James, OBE 1991; Deputy Controller, National Air Traffic Services, 1988–91, retired; *b* 7 March 1933; *s* of W. M. and E. Toseland; *m* 1954, Joan Mary (*d* 2002), *d* of A. R. and D. M. Pickett; two *s. Educ:* Kettering Central School. RAF Navigator, 1951–61; Air Traffic Control Officer, 1961–91; i/c Heathrow ATC, 1981–83; Dir, Civil Air Traffic Ops, 1983–87; Joint Field Commander, NATS, 1987–88. *Recreations:* music, walking. *Address:* 1 Marshall Place, Oakley Green, Windsor SL4 4QD. *T:* (01753) 863313.

TOSH, (Neil) Murray, MBE 1987; Member (C) Scotland West, Scottish Parliament, 2003–07 (Scotland South, 1999–2003); *b* 1 Sept. 1950; *s* of late Neil Ferguson Tosh and of Mary Drummond Tosh (*née* Murray); *m* 1970, Christine Hind (*d* 2007); two *s* one *d. Educ:* Kilmarnock Acad.; Univ. of Glasgow (MA 2nd Cl. Hons); Jordanhill Coll. of Educn (Secondary Teaching Qualif.). Teacher of history, Ravenspark Acad., Irvine, 1975–77; principal teacher of history: Kilwinning Acad., 1977–84; Belmont Acad., Ayr, 1984–99. Mem. (C) Kyle and Carrick DC, 1987–96 (Convener, Housing Cttee and Vice Convener, Planning and Develt Cttee, 1992–96). Contested (C) Dumfries, Scottish Parlt, 2007. Scottish Parliament: Convener, Procedures Cttee, 1999–2003; Member: Transport and Envmt Cttee, 1999–2001; Subordinate Legislation Cttee, 2003–07; Dep. Presiding Officer, 2001–07. *Recreations:* hill-walking, reading (historical, political), historic buildings, touring holidays. *Address:* 24/4 Lochend Close, Edinburgh EH8 8BL. *T:* (0131) 557 3420.

TOTARO, Prof. Burt James, PhD; Lowndean Professor of Astronomy and Geometry, University of Cambridge, since 2000; *b* 8 Aug. 1967. *Educ:* Princeton Univ. (AB 1984); Univ. of Calif at Berkeley (PhD 1989). Mathematical Scis Res. Inst., Berkeley, 1989–90; Dickson Instructor, 1990–93, Asst Prof., 1993–99, Dept of Maths, Univ. of Chicago; Mem., Inst. for Advanced Study, Princeton, 1994–95; Lectr, Dept of Pure Mathematics and Mathematical Statistics, Univ. of Cambridge, 1999. Eisenbud Prof., Mathematical Scis Res. Inst., Berkeley, Jan.–May 2009. Ed., Proc. of LMS, 2003–08; Mem., Man. Cttee, Jl of K-Theory, 2007–; Man. Ed., Compositio Mathematica, 2008–. Whitehead Prize, LMS, 2000; Prix Franco-Britannique, Acad. des Scis, 2001. *Recreation:* cats. *Address:* Department of Pure Mathematics and Mathematical Statistics, University of Cambridge, Wilberforce Road, Cambridge CB3 0WB.

TOTNES, Archdeacon of; *see* Rawlings, Ven. J. E. F.

TOTTEN, William John; Sheriff of Glasgow and Strathkelvin at Glasgow, since 1999; *b* 11 Sept. 1954; *s* of David and Sarah Totten; *m* 1985, Shirley Ann Morrison; one *s. Educ:* John Neilson Inst., Paisley; Univ. of Glasgow (LLB Hons 1977). Apprentice, Tindal, Oatts & Rodger, 1977–79; admitted solicitor, 1979; Procurator Fiscal Service, 1979–83; Asst, then Partner, Beltrami & Co., 1983–88; admitted to Faculty of Advocates, 1989; Advocate-Depute, 1993–96; Temp. Sheriff, 1998–99. *Recreations:* cycling, ski-ing, walking, reading, foreign travel. *Address:* Sheriff's Chambers, Sheriff Court House, 1 Carlton Place, Glasgow G5 9DA. *T:* (0141) 429 8888.

TOTTENHAM, family name of **Marquess of Ely**.

TÖTTERMAN, Richard Evert Björnson, Kt Comdr, Order of the White Rose of Finland; Hon. GCVO 1976 (Hon. KCVO 1969); Hon. OBE 1961; DPhil; Finnish Ambassador, retired; *b* 10 Oct. 1926; *s* of Björn B. Tötterman and Katharine C. (*née* Wimpenny); *m* 1953, Camilla Susanna Veronica Huber; one *s* one *d. Educ:* Univ. of Helsinki (Jur. lic.); Brasenose Coll., Oxford (DPhil; Hon. Fellow, 1982). Entered Finnish Foreign Service, 1952: served Stockholm, 1954–56; Moscow, 1956–58; Ministry for Foreign Affairs, Finland, 1958–62; Berne, 1962–63; Paris, 1963–66; Dep. Dir, Min. for For. Affairs, Helsinki, 1966; Sec.-Gen., Office of the President of Finland, 1966–70; Sec. of State, Min. for For. Aff., 1970–75; Ambassador: UK, 1975–83; Switzerland, 1983–90, and (concurrently) to the Holy See, 1988–90. Chm. or Mem. of a number of Finnish Govt Cttees, 1959–75, and participated as Finnish rep. in various internat. negotiations; Chm., Multilateral Consultations preparing Conf. on Security and Co-operation in Europe, 1972–73. Holds numerous foreign orders (Grand Cross, Kt Comdr, etc). *Recreations:* music, outdoor life. *Address:* Parkgatan 9 A 11, 00140 Helsinki, Finland.

TOUCHE, Sir Anthony (George), 3rd Bt *cr* 1920; Deputy Chairman, Friends' Provident Life Office, 1983–96; *b* 31 Jan. 1927; *s* of Donovan Meredith Touche (*d* 1952) (2nd *s* of 1st Bt) and of Muriel Amy Frances (*d* 1983), *e d* of Rev. Charles R. Thorold Winckley; *S* uncle, 1977; *m* 1961, Hester Christina, *er d* of Dr Werner Pleuger; two *s* one *d* (and one *s* decd). *Educ:* Eton College. FCA. Partner in George A. Touche & Co. (later Touche Ross & Co.), 1951; Director of investment trust companies, 1952–90; retired from Touche Ross & Co., 1968; Touche, Remnant Holdings Ltd, 1965–89. Dir, 1968–90, Dep. Chm., 1977–87, National Westminster Bank. Chairman, Assoc. of Investment Trust Companies, 1971–73. Prime Warden, Goldsmiths' Co., 1987. *Recreations:* music, reading, walking. *Heir: s* William George Touche [*b* 26 June 1962; *m* 1987, Elizabeth Louise, *y d* of Allen Bridges; three *s* one *d*]. *Address:* Stane House, Ockley, Dorking, Surrey RH5 5TQ. *T:* (01306) 627397.

TOUCHE, Sir Rodney (Gordon), 2nd Bt *cr* 1962; *b* 5 Dec. 1928; *s* of Rt Hon. Sir Gordon Touche, 1st Bt, and of Ruby, Lady Touche (formerly Ruby Ann Macpherson) (*d* 1989); *S* father, 1972; *m* 1955, Ouida Ann, *d* of F. G. MacLellan, Moncton, NB, Canada; one *s* two *d* (and one *d* decd). *Educ:* Marlborough; University Coll., Oxford. *Heir: s* Eric MacLellan Touche [*b* 22 Feb. 1960; *m* 1990, Leeanne Marie Stringer (marr. diss. 1998); one *s* one *d*]. *Address:* 2403 Westmount Place, 1100 8th Avenue SW, Calgary, AB T2P 3T9, Canada. *T:* (403) 2338800.

TOUHIG, Rt Hon. James Donnelly, (Don); PC 2006; MP (Lab and Co-op) Islwyn, since 1995; *b* 5 Dec. 1947; *s* of Michael Touhig and Catherine Touhig (*née* Corten); *m* 1968, Jennifer Hughes; two *s* two *d. Educ:* St Francis Sch., Aberyschan; E Monmouth Coll., Pontypool. Journalist, 1968–95; Editor, Free Press of Monmouthshire, 1976–90; General Manager: Free Press Gp, 1988–92; (Business Develt) Bailey Gp, 1992–93; Bailey Print, 1993–95. PPS to Chancellor of the Exchequer, 1997–99; an Asst Govt Whip, 1999–2001; Parly Under-Sec. of State, Wales Office, 2001–05, MoD, 2005–06. Member: Welsh Select Cttee, 1996–97; Public Accounts Cttee, 2006–; Chm., All-Party Alcohol Abuse Gp, 1996–99; Jt Sec., All-Party Police Gp, 1996–97; Hon. Sec., Welsh Gp, 1995–99, Mem., Backbench Cttee, 2007, PLP. Lab. Party Parly Advr to Police Fedn of Eng. and Wales, 1996–98. KSS 1991. *Recreations:* reading, cooking for family and friends, walking. *Address:* House of Commons, SW1A 0AA. *T:* (020) 7219 6435.

TOULMIN, John Kelvin, CMG 1994; QC 1980; **His Honour Judge Toulmin;** a Judge of the Technology and Construction Court of the High Court, since 1998; *b* 14 Feb. 1941; *s* of late Arthur Heaton Toulmin and B. Toulmin (*née* Fraser); *m* 1967, Carolyn Merton (*née* Gullick), barrister-at-law; one *s* two *d. Educ:* Winchester Coll.; Trinity Hall, Cambridge (Patterson Law Scholar, 1959; BA 1963, MA 1966); Univ. of Michigan (Ford Foundn Fellow and Fulbright Scholar, 1964; LLM 1965). Called to the Bar, Middle Temple, 1965 (Harmsworth Exhibnr, 1960; Astbury Scholar, 1965; Bencher, 1986; Lent Reader, 2008); Western Circuit; a Recorder, 1984–97; a Dep. High Court Judge, 1994–97; an Official Referee and a Sen. Circuit Judge, 1997–98; called to Bar of NI, 1989, to Irish Bar, 1991. Commissary for Notarial Appeals, 2001–. Cambridge Univ. Debating Tour, USA, 1963. Chm., Young Barristers, 1973–75; Member: Bar Council, 1971–77, 1978–81 and 1987–90 (Chm., Internat. Practice Cttee, 1987); Supreme Court Rules Cttee, 1976–80; Council of Legal Educn, 1981–83; DHSS Enquiry into Unnecessary Dental Treatment in NHS (Report, 1986). Mem., Internat. Panel of Dist. Mediators, CPR Inst. for Dispute Resolution, NY, 1993; Panelist, WTO Disputes Settlement Body, 1996–; William W. Bishop Jr Fellow, Univ. of Michigan Law Sch., 1993. Council of Bars and Law Societies of Europe (CCBE): Mem. UK delegn, 1983–90, Leader, 1987–90; Mem. then Chm. of the cttee at European Courts of Justice, 1984–93; Vice-Pres., 1991–92; Pres., 1993. Senator, European Bar President's Conf., Vienna, 1994–. Member: Bd of Governors, Maudsley and Bethlem Royal Hosps, 1979–82; SHA, 1982–87; Cttee of Management, Inst. of Psychiatry, 1982–2002 (Chm., 1999–2002; Mem. Adv. Cttee, 2002–); Bd of Visitors, Univ. of Michigan Law Sch., 1996–2006; Council, KCL, 1997–. Trustee: Pro Corda, 1992–97; Temple Music Trust, 1993– (Chm., 2002–); Europäische Rechtsakademie, Trier, 1993– (Vice-Chm., 1994–97; Chm., 1997–). Hon. Mem., Law Soc., 1994. FKC 2006. Grand Decoration for Merit (Austria), 1995. *Publications:* (contrib.) The Influence of Litigation in Medical Practice, 1977; European Ed., Encyclopaedia of Banking Law, 1990; Consulting Ed., European Legal Systems, 1992; EFTA Legal Systems, 1993; (contrib.) Practitioners' Handbook of EC Law, 1998. *Recreations:* cricket, music, theatre, Burgundy. *Address:* c/o The High Court of Justice, Technology and Construction Court, St Dunstan's House, 133–137 Fetter Lane, EC4A 1HD. *Clubs:* Pilgrims, MCC.

TOULMIN, Stephen Edelston, MA, PhD; University Professor, since 2002, Professor of Anthropology and International Relations, University of Southern California, since 1993; Avalon Foundation Professor in the Humanities, Northwestern University, 1986–92, now Emeritus; *b* 25 March 1922; *s* of late G. E. Toulmin and Mrs E. D. Toulmin; *m*; two *s* two *d. Educ:* Oundle School; King's College, Cambridge. BA 1943; MA 1946; PhD 1948; MA (Oxon) 1948. Junior Scientific Officer, Ministry of Aircraft Production, 1942–45; Fellow of King's College, Cambridge, 1947–51; University Lecturer in the Philosophy of Science, Oxford, 1949–55; Acting Head of Department of History and Methods of Science, University of Melbourne, Australia, 1954–55; Professor of Philosophy, University of Leeds, 1955–59; Visiting Prof. of Philosophy, NY Univ. and Stanford Univ. (California) and Columbia Univ. (NY), 1959–60; Director, Nuffield Foundation Unit for History of Ideas, 1960–64; Prof. of Philosophy, Brandeis Univ., 1965–69, Michigan State Univ., 1969–72; Provost, Crown College, Univ. of California, Santa Cruz, 1972–73; Prof. in Cttee on Social Thought, Univ. of Chicago, 1973–86; Henry R. Luce Foundn Prof., Center for Multiethnic and Transnat. Studies, USC, 1993–2001. Counsellor, Smithsonian Institution, 1966–75. Thomas Jefferson Lectr, Nat. Endowment for the Humanities, Washington, 1997; Tanner Lectr, Clare Hall, Cambridge, 1998. Hon. DTech Royal Inst. of Technol., Stockholm, 1991. *Publications:* The Place of Reason in Ethics, 1950; The Philosophy of Science: an Introduction, 1953; Metaphysical Beliefs (3 essays: author of one of them), 1957; The Uses of Argument, 1958; Foresight and Understanding, 1961; The Ancestry of Science, Vol. I (The Fabric of the Heavens) 1961, Vol. II (The Architecture of Matter), 1962, Vol. III (The Discovery of Time), 1965; Night Sky at Rhodes, 1963; Human Understanding, vol. 1, 1972; Wittgenstein's Vienna, 1973; Knowing and Acting, 1976; An Introduction to Reasoning, 1979; The Return to Cosmology, 1982; The Abuse of Casuistry, 1987; Cosmopolis, 1989; Beyond Theory, 1996; Return to Reason, 2001; also films, broadcast talks and contribs to learned jls and weeklies. *Address:* School of International Relations, University of Southern California, Los Angeles, CA 90089, USA.

See also M. E. P. Jones.

TOULMIN, Timothy James; Director, Press Complaints Commission, since 2004; *b* 19 Jan. 1975; *s* of Michael Toulmin and Sandy Toulmin (*née* Rawkins). *Educ:* Repton Sch.; Peterhouse, Cambridge (MA (Hist.)). Press Complaints Commission: Dep. Dir, 2000–03; Acting Dir, 2004. Mem. Council, Friends of Peterhouse, 2005–. *Recreations:* popular music, watching cricket, tennis. *Address:* c/o Press Complaints Commission, Halton House, 20–23 Holborn, EC1N 2JD. *T:* (020) 7831 0022, *Fax:* (020) 7831 0070; *e-mail:* tim.toulmin@pcc.org.uk.

TOULSON, Elizabeth, (Lady Toulson), CBE 1999; Chairman, Music for Life Foundation, since 2004; *b* 10 Nov. 1948; *d* of late Henry Bertram Chrimes and of Suzanne Isabel Chrimes (*née* Corbett-Lowe); *m* 1973, Roger Grenfell Toulson (*see* Rt Hon. Sir Roger Toulson); two *s* two *d*. *Educ:* Liverpool Univ.; Clare Hall, Cambridge (LLB). Called to the Bar, Inner Temple, 1974. Women's Royal Voluntary Service: Trustee, 1981–; Vice-Chm., 1989–93; Nat. Chm., 1993–99. Director: Queen Elizabeth Foundn for Disabled People, 1999–; Surrey Voluntary Service Council, 1999–2002; Chm., Children's Soc., 2001–04. Trustee, Elizabeth Finn Trust, 2002–05. Vice-Patron: Guildford Choral Soc., 2001–; Vocaleyes, 2004–. Advr, CAB, 2002–. Chairman: Nyika Vwaza Trust, 2003–08; Music of Life Foundn, 2003–; Time for Families, 2006–; Trustee, Guildford Community Family Trust, 2004–06. Governor: Charterhouse Sch., 1998–; Suttons Hosp., 2004–08. FRSA 2006. *Recreations:* reading, music, walking, tennis, swimming, ski-ing. *Address:* Billhurst Farm, White Hart Lane, Wood Street Village, Guildford, Surrey GU3 3DZ; 201 Rowan House, 9 Greycoat Street, SW1P 2QD.

TOULSON, Rt Hon. Sir Roger Grenfell, Kt 1996; PC 2007; **Rt Hon. Lord Justice Toulson;** a Lord Justice of Appeal, since 2007; *b* 23 Sept. 1946; *s* of late Stanley Kilsha Toulson and Lilian Mary Toulson; *m* 1973, Elizabeth Chrimes (*see* E. Toulson); two *s* two *d*. *Educ:* Mill Hill School; Jesus College, Cambridge (MA, LLB; Hon. Fellow 2007). Called to the Bar, Inner Temple, 1969, Bencher, 1995; QC 1986; a Recorder, 1986–96; a Judge of the High Court of Justice, QBD, 1996–2007; Presiding Judge, Western Circuit, 1997–2002. Chm., Law Commn, 2002–06; Mem., Judicial Appts Commn, 2007–. Hon. LLD UWE, 2002. *Publication:* (with C. M. Phipps) Confidentiality, 1996, 2nd edn 2006. *Recreations:* ski-ing, tennis, gardening. *Address:* Royal Courts of Justice, Strand, WC2A 2LL. *Club:* Old Millhillians.

TOUMAZOU, Prof. Christofer, PhD; FRS 2008; FREng; Professor of Circuit Design, since 1992, Chief Scientist and Director, Institute of Biomedical Engineering, since 2003, and Winston Wong Professor of Biomedical Circuits, since 2005, Imperial College London; *b* Cheltenham, 5 July 1961; *s* of Markos and Andriana Toumazou; *m* 2003, Melanie Anne Joyce; three *s* one *d*. *Educ:* Oxford Brookes Univ. (BSc Hons 1st Cl. 1983; PhD). FIEEE 2002; FIET 2005; FREng 2008. Imperial College London: Lectr, 1986–92; Hd, Bioengrg Dept, 1999–2004. Chairman and Chief Technology Officer: Toumaz Technology, 2000–; Future Waves Ltd, 2003–; Chm. and CEO, DNA Electronics Ltd, 2004–. MAE 2007. *Publications:* Analogue IC Design: the current-mode approach, 1990; (ed jtly) Switched-Currents: an analogue technique for digital technology, 1993; (ed jtly) Trade-Offs in Analog Circuit Design, 2004. *Recreations:* travelling, kendo, classical music. *Address:* 23 Emlyn Road, W12 9TF. *T:* (020) 8743 2037; *e-mail:* c.toumazou@ic.ac.uk.

TOUT, Paul Edward H.; *see* Hill-Tout.

TOVEY, Sir Brian (John Maynard), KCMG 1980; independent art history scholar; Visiting Research Fellow, British Institute of Florence, since 2003; *b* 15 April 1926; *s* of Rev. Collett John Tovey (Canon, Bermuda Cathedral, 1935–38) and Kathleen Edith Maud Tovey (*née* Maynard); *m* 1989, Mary Helen (*née* Lane); one *s* three *d* by previous marriage. *Educ:* St Edward's Sch., Oxford; St Edmund Hall, Oxford, 1944–45; School of Oriental and African Studies, London, 1948–50. BA Hons London. Service with Royal Navy and subseq. Army (Intelligence Corps and RAEC), 1945–48. Joined Government Communications Headquarters as Jun. Asst, 1950; Principal, 1957; Asst Sec., 1967; Under Sec., 1975; Dep. Sec., 1978; Dir, 1978–83, retired. Defence Systems Consultant, 1983–85, and Defence and Political Adviser, 1985–88, Plessey Electronic Systems Ltd; Dir, Plessey Defence Systems Ltd, 1983–85. Chairman: IES Gp PLC, 1993–98; Cresswell Associates Ltd, 1988–2001; Fujitsu Europe Telecoms R & D Centre Ltd, 1990–2001. Vice-Pres. (Information and Communications Technology), Fedn of Electronics Industry, 1995–97. *Publications:* The Pouncey Index of Baldinucci's Notizie, 2005; contrib. Gazette des Beaux-Arts, Art Newspaper, Jl of Soc. for Renaissance Studies, Bull. of Soc. for Renaissance Studies. *Recreations:* music, history of art (espec. 16th and 17th Century Italian, and historical methodology of Filippo Baldinucci). *Address:* 32 Complins Close, Oxford OX2 6PZ. *Club:* Naval and Military (Vice-Pres., 1995–2005).

TOVUE, Sir Ronald, Kt 1987; OBE 1981; Commissioner, Constitution Review Commission, Papua New Guinea, 1995–97; Premier, Provincial Government of East New Britain Province, Papua New Guinea, 1981–87; Member of Provincial Assembly, 1979–87; *b* 14 Feb. 1933; *s* of Apmeledi ToPalanga and Rachael Waruruai; *m* 1971, Suluet Tinvil; two *s* one *d*. *Educ:* Pilapila Community Sch.; Kerevat High Sch. Teacher, 1957–65; Magistrate, 1965–74; Commissioner, 1974–76; businessman, 1977–. *Recreations:* golf, reading, gardening, fishing, church activities. *Address:* Ratavul, PO Box 354, Rabaul, Papua New Guinea. *Club:* Rabaul Golf (Rabaul).

TOWERS, John, CBE 1995; FREng, FIMechE; Chairman, Phoenix Venture Holdings Ltd; Chairman, Rover Group Ltd, 2000–05; *b* 30 March 1948; *s* of Jack Towers and Florence Towers (*née* Abley); *m* 1990, Bethanie Williams; one *s* one *d*. *Educ:* Durham Johnston Sch.; Univ. of Bradford (BSc Hons Mech. Engrg). CEng 1974; FREng (FEng 1992); FIMechE 1992; FIIM 1989. Joined Perkins Engines as student apprentice, 1966: Quality Engr, later Mfg Dir and Gen. Manager, 1983–86; Vice-Pres., Internat. Services, Varity Corp. (Canada), 1986–87; Man. Dir, Massey Ferguson Tractors, 1987–88; Rover Group, 1988–96: Mfg Dir, Land Rover, 1988–89; Product Develt Dir, 1989–90; Dir, 1990–91, Man. Dir, Jan.–Dec. 1991, Product Supply; Gp Man. Dir, 1991–94; Gp Chief Exec., 1994–96; Chief Exec., Concentric Gp, 1996–2000. Director: Midland Bank, 1995–96; B. Elliott, 1996–2000; HatWel Ltd, 1996–. Vis. Prof., Warwick Univ., 1993. Mem., Council for Sci. and Technol., 1993–97. DUniv Central England in Birmingham, 1994. *Recreations:* golf, music, shooting.

TOWLE, Bridget Ellen, CBE 2001; Vice-President, Girlguiding UK, since 2003; *b* 19 April 1942; *d* of late William Henry Towle and Marjorie Louisa (*née* Hardstaff). *Educ:* Westonbirt Sch.; Univ. of Exeter (BA Gen. Hons, BA Hons); Leicester Poly. (Post Grad. Courses in Textile Technol. and Business Mgt). Teacher, VSO, Uganda, 1965–66; Towles plc: marketing mgt roles, 1966–94; Dir, 1972–94; Jt Man. Dir, 1980–94. Guide Association, later Girlguiding UK: various appts, incl. County Comr, Leics, 1985–92; Chief Guide, UK, and Chief Comr, Commonwealth Girl Guide Assocs, 1996–2001. Mem. Council, Univ. of Leicester, 2000–. Trustee: Coll. of Optometrists, 2004– (Chm., Lay Adv. Panel, 2007–); Friends of Nyakasura Sch., Uganda, 2005–; RAF Benevolent Fund, 2005–. FRSA 1999. Hon. LLD Exeter, 2000; Hon. DLitt Loughborough, 2002. Charity Trustee of the Year, Charity Times, 2000. *Recreations:* decorative arts, walking. *Address:* c/o Girlguiding UK, 17–19 Buckingham Palace Road, SW1W 0PT. *Club:* Royal Air Force.

TOWNELEY, Sir Simon (Peter Edmund Cosmo William), KCVO 1994; Lord-Lieutenant and Custos Rotulorum of Lancashire, 1976–96; *b* 14 Dec. 1921; *e s* of late Col A. Koch de Gooreynd, OBE and Baroness Norman, CBE; assumed surname and arms of Towneley by royal licence, 1955, by reason of descent from *e d* and senior co-heiress of Col Charles Towneley of Towneley; *m* 1955, Mary, MBE (*d* 2001), 2nd *d* of Cuthbert Fitzherbert; one *s* six *d*. *Educ:* Stowe; Worcester Coll., Oxford (MA, DPhil; Ruffini Scholar). Served War of 1939–45, KRRC. Lectr in History of Music, Worcester Coll., Oxford, 1949–55. Mem., Agricultural Lands Tribunal, 1960–92. Dir, Granada Television, 1981–92. CC Lancs, 1961–64; JP 1956; DL 1970; High Sheriff of Lancashire, 1971. Mem. Council, Duchy of Lancaster, 1986–96. Patron, Nat. Assoc. for Mental Health (North-West). Pres., NW of England and IoM TA&VRA, 1987–92; Chm., Northern Ballet Theatre, 1969–86; Member: Bd of Governors, Royal Northern Coll. of Music, 1961–98; Council, 1971–97, Court, 1971–98, Univ. of Manchester; Trustee: Historic Churches Preservation Trust, 1984–93; British Museum, 1988–93. Hon. Col, Duke of Lancaster's Own Yeomanry, 1979–88. CRNCM 1990; Hon. Fellow, Lancashire Polytechnic, 1987. Hon. DMus Lancaster, 1994. KStJ; KCSG. *Publications:* Venetian Opera in the Seventeenth Century, 1954 (repr. 1968); contribs to New Oxford History of Music. *Address:* Dyneley, Burnley, Lancs BB11 3RE. *T:* (01282) 423322. *Clubs:* Boodle's, Pratt's, Beefsteak.

See also Sir P. G. Worsthorne.

TOWNEND, James Barrie Stanley, QC 1978; an Assistant Boundary Commissioner, since 2000; *b* 21 Feb. 1938; *s* of late Frederick Stanley Townend and Marjorie Elizabeth Townend (*née* Arnold); *m* 1970, Airelle Claire (*née* Nies) (marr. diss. 2005); one step *d*; *m* 2008, Marleen Marie Lucie (*née* Deknudt). *Educ:* Tonbridge Sch.; Lincoln Coll., Oxford (MA). National Service in BAOR and UK, 1955–57: 2nd Lieut, 18th Medium Regt, RA. Called to Bar, Middle Temple, 1962, Bencher, 1987; Head of Chambers, 1982–99; a Recorder, 1979–2003. Chairman: Sussex Crown Court Liaison Cttee, 1978–89; Family Law Bar Assoc., 1986–88; Member: Kingston and Esher DHA, 1983–86; Bar Council, 1984–88; Supreme Court Procedure Cttee, 1986–88. *Recreations:* sailing, fishing, writing verse. *Address:* 1 King's Bench Walk, Temple, EC4Y 7DB. *T:* (020) 7936 1500.

TOWNEND, John Coupe; Director for Europe, Bank of England, 1999–2002; non-executive Director, LCH.Clearnet Group (formerly LCH.Clearnet) Ltd, since 2004; *b* 24 Aug. 1947; *s* of Harry Norman Townend and Joyce Dentith (*née* Coupe); *m* 1969, Dorothy Allister; three *s*. *Educ:* Liverpool Inst. High Sch. for Boys; London Sch. of Economics (BSc Econ; MSc). With Bank of England, 1968–2002: First Head, Wholesale Markets Supervision Div., 1986–90; Head, Gilt-Edged and Money Markets Div., 1990–94; Dep. Dir, 1994–98. *Publications:* articles in econ. jls. *Recreations:* running, trekking, opera, birds. *Address:* LCH.Clearnet Group Ltd, Aldgate House, 33 Aldgate High Street, EC3N 1EA.

TOWNEND, John Ernest; *b* 12 June 1934; *s* of Charles Hope Townend and Dorothy Townend; *m* 1963, Jennifer Ann; two *s* two *d*. *Educ:* Hymers Coll., Hull. FCA (Plender Prize). Articled Clerk, Chartered Accountants, 1951–56; National Service: Pilot Officer, RAF, 1957–59; J. Townend & Sons Ltd (Hull) Ltd: Co. Sec./Dir, 1959–67; Man. Dir, 1967–77; Chm., 1977–; Vice-Chm., Surrey Building Soc., 1984–93; Dir, AAH Hldgs, 1989–94. Mem., Hull City Council, 1966–74 (Chm., Finance Cttee, 1968–70); Chm., Humber Bridge Bd, 1969–71; Member, Humberside County Council, 1973–79: Cons. Leader of Opposition, 1973–77; Leader, 1977–79; Chm., Policy Cttee, 1977–79. Mem., Policy Cttee, Assoc. of County Councils, 1977–79. MP (C) Bridlington, 1979–97, E Yorks, 1997–2001. PPS to Minister of State for Social Security, 1981–83. Mem., Treasury and Civil Service Select Cttee, 1983–92; Chm., Cons. Small Business Cttee, 1988–92; Vice Chm., Cons. back bench Finance Cttee, 1983–91, 1997–2001 (Chm., 1993–97). Member: Council of Europe, 1992–2001; WEU, 1992–2001. Life Gov., Hymers Coll., Hull, 1965. Chm., Merchant Vintners Co., 1964–2000; Liveryman, Distillers' Co., 1998–; Master, Woolmen's Co., 2004–05. *Recreations:* swimming, tennis. *Address:* Sigglesthorne Hall, Sigglesthorne, E Yorks HU11 5QH. *Club:* Carlton.

TOWNEND, His Honour John Philip; a Circuit Judge, 1987–2001; *b* 20 June 1935; *o s* of Luke and Ethel Townend; *m* 1st, 1959; two *s* one *d*; 2nd, 1981, Anne Glover; one step *s* one step *d*. *Educ:* St Joseph's Coll., Blackpool; Manchester Univ. (LLB). National Service, 1957–58. Called to the Bar, Gray's Inn, 1959; Lectr in Law, Gibson and Weldon College of Law, 1960–65; Asst Legal Advr, Pilkington Bros, 1966–68; Legal Advr, Honeywell Ltd and G. Dew Ltd, 1968–70; joined chambers of Mr Stewart Oakes, Manchester, 1970. *Publications:* articles in various jls on legal topics. *Recreations:* classical music, jazz, food and wine, a decreasing number of active games, mountain walking. *Address:* c/o Preston Crown Court, Openshaw Place, Preston PR1 2LL. *Club:* Silverdale Golf.

TOWNEND, Warren Dennis; HM Diplomatic Service, retired; *b* 15 Nov. 1945; *s* of Dennis Jennings Townend and Mary Elizabeth Townend (*née* Knowles); *m* 1978, Ann Mary Riddle; three *s* one *d*. *Educ:* Netheredge Grammar Sch.; Abbeydale Grammar Sch. Joined Diplomatic Service, 1964; FO 1964–69; Vice Consul, Hanoi, 1969–70; Vice Consul (Commercial), Hamburg, 1970–73; Second Sec. (Commercial), Dacca, 1973–75; FCO, 1976–79; Second, later First, Sec., Bonn, 1979–84; First Sec. (Commercial), Bangkok, 1984–87; FCO, 1987–91; Dep. Consul-Gen. and Dep. Dir-Gen. for Trade and Investment Promotion in Germany, Düsseldorf, 1991–96; Consul-General: Shanghai, 1996–2000; Washington, 2001–04. *Recreations:* DIY, travel. *Address:* 27 Heathside Road, Woking, Surrey GU22 7EY.

TOWNER, Neena; *see* Gill, N.

TOWNES, Charles Hard; University Professor of Physics, 1967–86, Professor in the Graduate School, since 1994, University of California, USA; *b* Greenville, South Carolina, 28 July 1915; *s* of Henry Keith Townes and Ellen Sumter (*née* Hard); *m* 1941, Frances H. Brown; four *d*. *Educ:* Furman Univ. (BA, BS); Duke Univ. (MA); California Institute of Technology (PhD). Assistant in Physics, California Inst. of Technology, 1937–39; Member Techn Staff, Bell Telephone Labs, 1939–47; Associate Prof. of Physics, Columbia Univ., 1948–50; Prof. of Physics, Columbia Univ., 1950–61; Exec. Director, Columbia Radiation Lab., 1950–52; Chairman, Dept of Physics, Columbia Univ., 1952–55; Vice-President and Director of Research, Inst. for Defense Analyses, 1959–61; Provost and Professor of Physics, MIT, 1961–66; Institute Professor, MIT, 1966–67. Guggenheim Fellow, 1955–56; Fulbright Lecturer, University of Paris, 1955–56, University of Tokyo, 1956; Lecturer, 1955, 1960, Dir, 1963, Enrico Fermi Internat. Sch. of Physics; Lectures: Scott, Univ. of Cambridge, 1963; Centennial, Univ. of Toronto, 1967; Rajiv Gandhi, India, 1997; Weinberg, Oak Ridge Nat. Lab., 1997; Henry Norris Russell, AAS, 1998; Sackler Leiden, 1999; Loeb, Harvard, 2000; Hamilton, Princeton, 2000; Bunyan, Stanford, 2000. Dir, Bulletin of Atomic Scientists, 1964–69. Board of Editors: Review of Scientific Instruments, 1950–52; Physical Review, 1951–53; Journal of Molecular

Spectroscopy, 1957–60; Columbia University Forum, 1957–59. Fellow: American Phys. Society (Richtmyer Lecturer, 1959; Member Council, 1959–62, 1965–71; President, 1967); Inst. of Electrical and Electronics Engrs; Chairman, Sci. and Technology Adv. Commn for Manned Space Flight, NASA, 1964–69; Member: President's Science Adv. Cttee, 1966–69 (Vice-Chm., 1967–69); Scientific Adv. Bd, US Air Force, 1958–61; Soc. Française de Physique (Member Council, 1956–58); Nat. Acad. Scis (Mem. Council, 1969–72); American Acad. Arts and Sciences; American Philos. Society; American Astron. Society; American Assoc. of Physics Teachers; Société Royale des Sciences de Liège; Pontifical Acad., 1983; Nat. Acad. of Engrg, 1999; Foreign Member: Royal Society, 1976; Russian Acad. of Scis, 1994; Hon. Mem., Optical Soc. of America. Trustee: Salk Inst. for Biological Studies, 1963–68; Rand Corp., 1965–70; Carnegie Instn of Washington, 1965–; Calif Inst. of Technol., 1979–; California Acad. of Scis, 1987–96. Chairman: Space Science Bd, Nat. Acad. of Sciences, 1970–73; Science Adv. Cttee, General Motors Corp., 1971–73; Bd of Dirs, General Motors, 1973–86; Perkin-Elmer Corp., 1966–85. Trustee: Pacific Sch. of Religion, 1983–93; Center for Theol. and Natural Sci., 1989–; Grad. Theol Union, 1993–; California Vocations, 1994–; Enshrinee, Engrg and Sci. Hall of Fame, Ohio, 1983. Holds numerous honorary degrees. Research Corp. Annual Award, 1958; Comstock Prize, Nat. Acad. of Sciences, 1959; Stuart Ballantine Medal, Franklin Inst., 1959, 1962; Rumford Premium, Amer. Acad. of Arts and Sciences, 1961; Thomas Young Medal and Prize, Inst. of Physics and Physical Soc., England, 1963; Nobel Prize for Physics (jointly), 1964; Medal of Honor, Inst. of Electrical and Electronics Engineers, 1967; C. E. K. Mees Medal, Optical Soc. of America, 1968; Churchman of the Year Award, Southern Baptist Theological Seminary, 1967; Distinguished Public Service Medal, NASA, 1969; Michelson-Morley Award, 1970; Wilhelm-Exner Award (Austria), 1970; Medal of Honor, Univ. of Liège, 1971; Earle K. Plyler Prize, 1977; Niels Bohr Internat. Gold Medal, 1979; Nat. Medal of Sci., 1983; Commonwealth Award, 1993; Frederic Ives/James Quinn Medal, Optical Soc. of America, 1996; Frank Annunzio Award, Columbus Fellowship Foundn, 1999; Rabindranath Tagore Birth Centenary Plaque, Asiatic Soc., 1999; Best Book on Sci., American Inst. of Physics, 2000; Founders Award, NAE, 2000; Lomonosov Gold Medal, Russian Acad. of Scis, 2001; Karl Schwarzschild Medal, Astronomische Ges., 2002; Drake Award, SETI Inst., 2003; Templeton Prize, John Templeton Foundn, 2005; Vannevar Bush Award, Nat. Sci. Foundn, 2006. National Inventors Hall of Fame, 1976; S Carolina Hall of Fame, 1977. Hon. Citizen: Kwangju, Korea, 1996; Pusan, Korea, 1997. Officier, Légion d'Honneur (France), 1990. *Publications:* (with A. L. Schawlow) Microwave Spectroscopy, 1955; (ed) Quantum Electronics, 1960; (ed with P. A. Miles) Quantum Electronics and Coherent Light, 1964; Making Waves, 1995; How the Laser Happened: adventures of a scientist, 1999 (Best Book on Science, Amer. Inst. of Physics, 2000); many scientific articles on microwave spectroscopy, molecular and nuclear structure, quantum electronics, radio and infra-red astrophysics; fundamental patents on masers and (with A. L. Schawlow) lasers. *Address:* Department of Physics, University of California, Berkeley, CA 94720, USA. *T:* (510) 6421128. *Clubs:* Cosmos (Washington); Bohemian (San Francisco).

TOWNLEY, Ven. Peter Kenneth; Archdeacon of Pontefract, since 2008; *b* Manchester, 16 Nov. 1955; *s* of David Townley and Elsie Townley; *m* 1981, Moira Margaret Whitehorn; three *s*. *Educ:* Moston Brook High Sch., Manchester; Univ. of Sheffield (BA 1978); Ridley Hall, Cambridge; Univ. of Manchester (Dip. Social and Pastoral Theol. 1986). Ordained deacon, 1980, priest, 1981; Asst Curate, Christ Church, Ashton-under-Lyne, 1980–83; Priest-in-charge, St Hugh's, Holts, Oldham, 1983–88; Rector, All Saints', Stretford, 1988–96; Vicar, St Mary-le-Tower, Ipswich, 1996–2008; Rural Dean, Ipswich, 2001–08. Member: Meissen Commn, 1991–2001; Gen. Synod, C of E, 1992–95, 2000–08; Porvoo Panel, 2003–. Hon. Canon, Dio. of St Edmundsbury and Ipswich, 2003–08. *Publications:* various newspaper articles and obituaries. *Recreations:* the arts, travel, fun. *Address:* The Vicarage, Kirkthorpe, Wakefield, W Yorks WF1 5SZ. *T:* and *Fax:* (01924) 896327; *e-mail:* archdeacon.pontefract@wakefield.anglican.org. *Club:* Lansdowne.

TOWNSEND, Prof. Alain Robert Michael, PhD; FRS 1992; Professor of Molecular Immunology, since 1992, and Fellow of New College, since 1998, University of Oxford. *Educ:* St Mary's Hosp. Med. Sch., London Univ. (MB BS 1977); PhD London 1984; MA Oxon. MRCP 1979. Oxford University: Lectr in Clin. Immunology, 1985–92; Fellow, Linacre Coll., 1985–98. *Address:* Institute of Molecular Medicine, John Radcliffe Hospital, Headington, Oxford OX3 9DU. *T:* (01865) 222328; New College, Oxford OX1 3BN.

TOWNSEND, Albert Alan, FRS 1960; PhD; Reader (Experimental Fluid Mechanics), Cavendish Laboratory, University of Cambridge, 1961–85 (Assistant Director of Research, 1950–61); Fellow of Emmanuel College, Cambridge, since 1947; *b* 22 Jan. 1917; *s* of A. R. Townsend and D. Gay; *m* 1950, V. Dees; one *s* two *d*. *Educ:* Telopea Park IHS; Melbourne and Cambridge Universities. PhD 1947. *Publications:* The Structure of Turbulent Shear Flow, 1956; papers in technical journals. *Address:* Emmanuel College, Cambridge CB2 3AP.

TOWNSEND, Bryan Sydney, CBE 1994; Chairman, Midlands Electricity plc (formerly Midlands Electricity Board), 1986–96 (Chief Executive, 1990–92); *b* 2 April 1930; *s* of Sydney and Gladys Townsend; *m* 1951, Betty Eileen Underwood; one *s* two *d*. *Educ:* Wolverton Technical Coll. CEng, FIET; FIMgt. Trainee, Northampton Electric Light & Power Co., 1946–50; successive appts, E Midlands, Eastern and Southern Electricity Bds, 1952–66; Southern Electricity Board: Swindon Dist Manager, 1966–68; Newbury Area Engr, 1968–70; Asst Chief Engr, 1970–73; Dep. Chief Engr, SE Electricity Bd, 1973–76; Chief Engr, S Wales Electricity Bd, 1976–78; Dep. Chm., SW Electricity Bd, 1978–86. Chm., Applecourt Develt. *Recreation:* golf.

TOWNSEND, Dr Christina, CPsychol; JP; Chief Executive, Valuation Tribunal Service, since 2007; *b* 10 Jan. 1947; *d* of Sidney Townsend and Vera (*née* Wallis). *Educ:* Dursley Grammar Sch., Glos; Leeds Univ. (BSc Psychol.); Birmingham Univ. (MSc); UWIST (PhD). CPsychol 1969; FCIPD (FIPM 1991). Lectr, UWIST, 1973–75; Sen. Res. Officer, MSC, 1976–78; Asst Dir, Ashridge Mgt Coll., 1978–80; Hd of Div., Inst. of Manpower Studies, 1981–84; NHS Training Authority, subseq. Directorate: Dir, Res. Educn and Trng, 1984–88; Chief Exec., 1988–91; Nat. Trng Dir and Chief Exec., 1991–93; Chief Executive: Business & Technol. Educn Council, subseq. Edexcel Foundn, 1994–2002; Soc. of Chiropodists and Podiatrists, 2002–03; Appeals Service, 2003–06; Efficiency Dir, Tribunals Service, 2006–07. Dep. Chm., Personnel Standards Lead Body, 1991–94; Director: City Technol. Colls Trust, 1994–95; Mgt Charter Initiative, 1994–95; Further Educn Develt Agency, 1994–97; Member Council: Nat. Forum for Mgt Educn and Develt, 1994–99; Inst. for Employment Studies, 1998–; Mem. Bd, British Trng Internat., 1999–2001. Mem., Southwark PCT, 2007. Gov., Corp. of Cambridge Regl Coll., 1997–2003. Chm., Housing for Women, 2007–. Trustee, Volunteer Reading Help, 2002–. MInstD 1991 (Mem., Nat. Employment Cttee, 1991–97); CCMI (CIMgt 1994). JP City of Westminster, 2006. *Recreations:* travelling, hill-walking, theatre, circuit training. *Address:* Valuation Tribunal Service, Block 1, Angel Square, 1 Torrens Street, EC1V 1NY.

TOWNSEND, Sir Cyril (David), Kt 1997; Director, Council for the Advancement of Arab-British Understanding, 1995–2002 (Joint Chairman, 1982–92); *b* 21 Dec. 1937; *s* of late Lt-Col Cyril M. Townsend and Lois (*née* Henderson); *m* 1976, Anita, MA, *d* of late Lt-Col F. G. W. Walshe and Mrs Walshe; two *s*. *Educ:* Bradfield Coll.; RMA Sandhurst. Commnd into Durham LI; served in Berlin and Hong Kong; active service in Cyprus, 1958 and Borneo, 1966; ADC to Governor and C-in-C Hong Kong, 1964–66; Adjt 1DLI, 1966–68. A Personal Assistant: to Edward Heath, 1968–70; to Sir Desmond Plummer, Ldr of GLC, 1970–73; Mem. Conservative Research Dept, 1970–74. MP (C) Bexleyheath, Feb. 1974–1997. PPS to Minister of State, DHSS, 1979; Member: Select Cttee on Violence in the Family, 1975; Select Cttee on Foreign Affairs, 1982–83; Vice-Chairman: Cons. Parly Defence Cttee, 1985–93 (Jt Sec., 1982–85); Cons. Parly Foreign Affairs Cttee, 1991–96; Chairman: Select Cttee on Armed Forces Bill, 1981; British-Cyprus Parly Gp, 1983–92; All-Party Freedom for Rudolf Hess Campaign, 1977–87; Bow Gp Standing Cttee on Foreign Affairs, 1977–84; (and Co-Founder) South Atlantic Council, 1983–95; Organizing Cttee, Argentine-British Conference, 1988–90; UN Parly Gp, 1992–96; Chm., Cons. ME Council, 1992–95 (Jt Vice-Chm., 1988–92); Vice-Chairman: Friends of Cyprus, 1980–92 (Mem., Exec. Cttee); Hansard Soc., 1988–97; Member: Exec. Cttee, UK Branch, CPA, 1992–93; Exec. Bd, UK Cttee, UNICEF, 1995–2000; Vice-Pres., UNA, 1996–2002; Pres., SW Reg., UNA, 1999–2002; Jt Hon. Pres., Islamic Res. Acad., 2000–08; Gov., Centre for World Dialogue, Nicosia, 1998–. Member: South Atlantic Council, 1983–2004; Nat. Cttee, British-Arab Univ. Assoc., 1995–2004. Mem., SE London Industrial Consultative Gp, 1975–83. Pres., Bexley Arthritis Care, 1990–96. Chm., Lord Caradon Lectures Trust, 2002–08. Patron, Forum Against Islamophobia and Racism, 2000–. Trustee, Sir Heinz Koeppler Trust, Wilton Park, 2006–. Fellow, Industry and Parliament Trust, 1982. Introduced Protection of Children Act, 1978. Parly Observer, Presidential Election, Lebanon, 1982; Ldr, Parly Delegn to Iran, 1988; Mem., British Delegn, CSCE, Moscow, 1991; EU Election Observer for elections in Palestine, 1996. Columnist: Al-Hayat, 1990–; Al-Ittihad, 2004–; Arab News, 2005–. *Publications:* Helping Others to Help Themselves: voluntary action in the eighties, 1981; Cyprus and NATO's Southern Flank, 1986; contribs to Western Morning News, Contemporary Review and political jls. *Recreations:* books, music, exercise, exploring Cornwall. *Address:* Chillaton House, Chillaton, Lifton, Devon PL16 0JD.

TOWNSEND, Brig. Ian Glen, CBE 2006; Director (formerly Secretary) General, Royal British Legion, 1996–2006; *b* 7 Feb. 1941; *s* of Kenneth Townsend and Irene (*née* Singleton); *m* 1st, 1964, Loraine Jean (marr. diss. 1988), *d* of late William A. H. Birnie, USA; twin *d*; 2nd, 1989, Susan Natalie, *d* of late Comdr Frank A. L. Heron-Watson, Dalbeattie; two step *s*. *Educ:* Dulwich Coll.; RMA, Sandhurst (psc †). Commnd RA, 1961; served UK, Norway, Singapore, Brussels and Germany, 1961–71; RMCS, 1971–72; Staff Coll., Camberley, 1972–73; MoD, BAOR and NATO, 1973–85; Comdr Artillery, 1st Armd Div., BAOR, 1986–88; ACOS, Trng, HQ UKLF, 1988–91. Hon. Col, 27 Field Regt, 1988–92. Dir, Sales and Marketing, Land Systems, 1991–93, Mil. Advr, 1993–96, VSEL; Director: Townsend Associates, 1993–96; Legion Enterprise Ltd, 1999; RBL Training Coll., 2000–; NMA Enterprise, 2004–08; Nat. Meml Arboretum, 2004–08. Mem., Nat. Meml Cttee for NI, 2004–08. Trustee: Officers' Assoc., 1996–2006; Mil. Mus. of the Pacific, 1997–; Desert Rats 7th Armd Div. Commemoration Fund, 1998–; Armed Forces Meml Trust, 2003–; Chm., Confedn of Service and Ex-Service Orgns, 2002–03; Vice-Pres., World Veterans' Fedn, 2006– (Chm., World Veterans' Fedn, Europe, 2002–). Freeman, City of London, 1999. CCMI 2004 (FCMI) (FInstM 1988); FRSA 2006. Mem., ACEVO (formerly ACENVO), 1997–2006. Gov., Salisbury Coll., 2001–03. *Publications:* articles in professional jls. *Recreations:* walking, painting, music, theatre. *Clubs:* Army and Navy, Royal Over-Seas League.

TOWNSEND, Mrs Joan, MA, MSc; Headmistress, Oxford High School, GPDST, 1981–96; *b* 7 Dec. 1936; *d* of Emlyn Davies and Amelia Mary Davies (*née* Tyrer); *m* 1960, William Godfrey Townsend, Prof. Emeritus, Cranfield Univ.; two *d*. *Educ:* Somerville Coll., Oxford (Beilby Schol.; BA (Cl.I), MA); University College of Swansea, Univ. of Wales (MSc). School teaching and lecturing of various kinds, including: Tutor, Open University, 1971–75; Lectr, Oxford Polytechnic, 1975–76; Head of Mathematics, School of S Helen and S Katharine, Abingdon, 1976–81. FRSA 1986. *Publication:* paper in Qly Jl Maths and Applied Mech., 1965. *Address:* Silver Howe, 62 Iffley Turn, Oxford OX4 4HN. *T:* (01865) 715807.

TOWNSEND, Lady Juliet Margaret, LVO 1981; Lord-Lieutenant of Northamptonshire, since 1998; *b* 9 Sept. 1941; *d* of 2nd Earl of Birkenhead, TD; *m* 1970, John Richard Townsend; three *d*. *Educ:* Westonbirt Sch.; Somerville Coll., Oxford. Lady in Waiting to Princess Margaret, 1965–71, Extra Lady in Waiting, 1971–2002. High Sheriff of Northamptonshire, 1991–92. *Publications:* The Shell Guide to Northamptonshire, 1968; Escape from Meerut, 1971. *Address:* Newbottle Manor, Banbury, Oxon OX17 3DD. *T:* (01295) 811295.

TOWNSEND, Martin; Editor, Sunday Express, since 2001; *b* 11 July 1960; *s* of Ronald Norman Townsend and Margaret Annie Townsend (*née* Pattrick); *m* 1989, Jane O'Gorman; two *s* one *d*. *Educ:* Harrow Co. Grammar Sch.; London Coll. of Printing. Staff writer: Do It Yourself, 1979–81; Caravan, 1981–82; Sen. Writer, No 1, 1983–85; Co-creator, The Hit, 1985; Pop Ed., Today newspaper, 1986–87; freelance journalist, 1987–94; Showbusiness Ed., You mag., 1994–96; Ed., OK! mag., 1998–2001. *Publication:* The Father I Had, 2007. *Recreations:* listening to music, cycling, architecture, football, conversation. *Address:* Sunday Express, The Northern and Shell Building, Number 10, Lower Thames Street, EC3R 6EN; *e-mail:* martin.townsend@express.co.uk.

TOWNSEND, Michael John, OBE 2003; Special Adviser, Environmental Policy, Woodland Trust (Chief Executive, 1997–2004); *b* 12 July 1957; *s* of John and Kathleen Townsend; *m* 1991, Amanda Adkins; two *s*. *Educ:* University Coll. of N Wales (BSc Hons Forestry 1986); Open Univ. (MA Envmt, Policy and Society 2007). MICFor 1990, FICFor 2002. Project leader, VSO, Kenya, 1980–83; Regl Manager, EFG plc, 1986–92; Michael Townsend Forestry & Landscapes, 1992–95; Woodland Ops Dir, Woodland Trust, 1995–97. Trustee, Tree Aid, 2003–05. *Recreations:* hill-walking, gardening. *Address:* The Woodland Trust, Autumn Park, Dysart Road, Grantham, Lincs NG31 6LL.

TOWNSEND, Prof. Paul Kingsley, PhD; FRS 2000; Professor of Theoretical Physics, University of Cambridge, since 1998; *b* 3 March 1951; *m* Fátima Azpiroz; one *d*. *Educ:* Queens' Coll., Cambridge (BA 1972; MA); Brandeis Univ., Mass (PhD 1976). Postdoctoral Fellow, SUNY, 1976–79; UK Fellow, CERN, Geneva, 1980–81; Curie-Joliot Fellow, subseq. CNRS Vis. Fellow, Lab. de Physique Théorique, Ecole Normale Supérieure, Paris, 1982–83; Lectr, 1984–96, Reader, 1996–98, Dept of Applied Maths and Theoretical Physics, Univ. of Cambridge. *Address:* Department of Applied Mathematics and Theoretical Physics, Centre for Mathematical Sciences, Wilberforce Road, Cambridge CB3 0WA.

TOWNSEND, Prof. Peter Brereton, FBA 2004; Professor of International Social Policy, London School of Economics and Political Science, since 1999; Professor of Social

Policy, University of Bristol, 1982–93, now Emeritus; *b* 6 April 1928; *s* of late Philip Brereton Townsend and Alice Mary Townsend (*née* Southcote); *m* 1st, 1949, Ruth (*née* Pearce); four *s*; 2nd, 1977, Joy (*née* Skegg); one *d*; 3rd, 1985, Jean Ann Corston (*see* Baroness Corston); one step *s* one step *d*. *Educ:* Fleet Road Elementary Sch., London; University Coll. Sch., London; St John's Coll., Cambridge Univ.; Free Univ., Berlin. Research Sec., Political and Economic Planning, 1952–54; Research Officer, Inst. of Community Studies, 1954–57; Research Fellow and then Lectr in Social Administration, London Sch. of Economics, 1957–63; Prof. of Sociology, 1963–81, Pro-Vice-Chancellor (Social Policy), 1975–78, Univ. of Essex; Dir, Sch. of Applied Social Studies, Bristol Univ., 1983–85 and 1988–93. Vis. Prof. of Sociology, Essex Univ., 1982–86; Michael Harrington Distinguished Vis. Prof. of Social Sci., CUNY, 1991–92; Vis. Prof. of Social Policy, 1998–99, Acting Dir, Centre for Study of Human Rights, 2002, LSE; Vis. Prof. of Internat. Social Policy, Univ. of Wales, Swansea, 1998–2003 (Hon. Prof., 2008–). Vice Pres., 1989–, and Trustee, 2005–, Fabian Society (Chm., 1965–66; Chairman: Social Policy Cttee, 1970–82; Res. and Pubns Cttee, 1983–86). President: Psychiatric Rehabilitation Assoc., 1968–83; Child Poverty Action Gp, 1989– (Chm., 1969–89); SW Region, MENCAP, 1989–93; Disability Alliance, 1999– (Chm., 1974–99). Member: Chief Scientist's Cttee, DHSS, 1976–78; Govt Working Gp on Inequalities and Health, 1977–80; MSC Working Gp on Quota Scheme for Disabled, 1983–85; Chm., Steering Gp, 2000–02, Standing Cttee, 2002–05, on Allocation of NHS Resources, Nat. Assembly for Wales. UNESCO consultant on poverty and development, 1978–80; Consultant: to GLC on poverty and the labour market in London, 1985–86; to Northern RHA on Inequalities of Health, 1985–86; to a consortium of 7 metropolitan boroughs on deprivation and shopping centres in Greater Manchester, 1987–88; to Islington Borough Council on deprivation and living standards, 1987–88; to UN for world summit on social develt, 1994–95; to UNDP on social safety net in Georgia, 1994; to UNDP and IILS on patterns and causes of social exclusion, 1994; to Ministry of Foreign Affairs, Denmark, 1997–2000; to EC on Eur. Social Policy Forum, 1998; to DFID, 2005–06; to ILO, 2006–07. Chm., C4 Commn on Poverty, 1996. AcSS 1999. DU Essex, 1990; Hon. DLitt: Teesside, 1994; NUI, 2006; DUniv: Open, 1995; York, 2000; Stirling, 2002; Hon. DSc Edinburgh, 1996; Hon. DArts Lincolnshire and Humberside, 1997; Hon. DSSc Baptist Univ. of HK, 2005. Lifetime Achievement Award, Social Policy Assoc., 2008. *Publications:* The Family Life of Old People, 1957; National Superannuation (co-author), 1957; Nursing Homes in England and Wales (co-author), 1961; The Last Refuge: a survey of residential institutions and homes for the aged in England and Wales, 1962; The Aged in the Welfare State (co-author), 1965; The Poor and the Poorest (co-author), 1965; Old People in Three Industrial Societies (co-author), 1968; (ed) The Concept of Poverty, 1970; (ed) Labour and Inequality, 1972; The Social Minority, 1973; Sociology and Social Policy, 1975; Poverty in the United Kingdom: a survey of household resources and standards of living, 1979; (ed) Labour and Equality, 1980; Inequalities in Health (co-author), 1980; Manifesto (co-author), 1981; (ed jtly) Disability in Britain, 1981; The Family and Later Life, 1981; (ed jtly) Responses to Poverty: lessons from Europe, 1984; (jtly) Inequalities of Health in the Northern Region, 1986; Poverty and Labour in London, 1987; (jtly) Health and Deprivation: inequalities and the North, 1987; (jtly) Service Provision and Living Standards in Islington, 1988; (jtly) Inequalities in Health: the Black report and the health divide, 1988, 3rd edn 1993; The International Analysis of Poverty, 1993; A Poor Future, 1996; (jtly) Poverty and Social Exclusion in Britain, 2000; (ed jtly) Breadline Europe: the measurement of poverty, 2001; Targeting Poor Health, 2001; (ed jtly) World Poverty: new policies to defeat an old enemy, 2002; (jtly) Child Poverty in the Developing World, 2003; Inequalities of Health: the Welsh dimension, 2005; The Right to Social Security and National Development: lessons of OECD experience for low-income countries, 2007; (ed) Building Decent Societies: re-thinking the role of social security, 2008. *Recreations:* writing, gardening.

TOWNSEND, Dr Ralph Douglas; Headmaster, Winchester College, since 2005; *b* 13 Dec. 1951; *s* of Harry Douglas Townsend and Neila Margaret McPherson; *m* 1973, Cathryn Julie Arnold; one *s* one *d*. *Educ:* Scotch Coll., WA; Univ. of Western Australia (BA 1973); Univ. of Kent at Canterbury (MA 1975); Keble Coll., Oxford (MA 1983; DPhil 1981). Assistant Master: Dover Coll., 1975–77; Abingdon Sch., 1977–78; Sen. Scholar, Keble Coll., Oxford, 1978–81; Jun. Res. Fellow and Dean of Degrees, Lincoln Coll., Oxford, 1983–85; Asst Master, then Head of English, Eton Coll., 1985–89; Head Master, Sydney Grammar Sch., Australia, 1989–99; Headmaster, Oundle Sch., 1999–2005. Governor: Mowden Hall Sch., Northumberland, 1999–2007; Old Buckenham Hall Sch., Suffolk, 1999–2006; Ardvreck Sch., Perthshire, 2001–06; Bramcote Lorne Sch., Notts, 2003–06; Ampleforth Coll., Yorks, 2003–06; Worth Sch., Sussex, 2004–; St Swithin's Sch., Winchester, 2005–; The Pilgrim's Sch., Winchester, 2005–; Church Schs Co., 2005–; Ct, Univ. of Southampton, 2005–. Adviser: United Learning Trust, 2005–; African Leadership Acad., 2005–; Nat. Coll. of Music, London, 2005–. Trustee, Cothill Educn Trust, 2007–. Hon. Liveryman, Grocers' Co., 2005. *Recreations:* music, reading, walking. *Address:* Winchester College, Winchester, Hants SO23 9NA. *Clubs:* Athenæum; Australian (Sydney).

TOWNSEND, Susan, (Sue); writer; *b* 2 April 1946. *Educ:* South Wigston Girls' High Sch. FRSL 1994. Writer and Presenter, Think of England, BBC TV, 1991. *Publications:* The Secret Diary of Adrian Mole Aged 13¾, 1982; The Growing Pains of Adrian Mole, 1984; Bazaar and Rummage, Groping for Words, and Womberang (plays), 1984; The Great Celestial Cow (play), 1985; The Secret Diary of Adrian Mole (play), 1985; Rebuilding Coventry, 1988; Mr Bevans Dream, 1989; Ten Tiny Fingers, Nine Tiny Toes (play), 1989; Adrian Mole From Minor to Major, 1991; The Queen and I, 1992 (adapted for stage, 1994); Adrian Mole—the Wilderness Years, 1993; Ghost Children, 1997; The Cappuccino Years, 1999; The Public Confessions of a Middle-Aged Woman Aged 55¾, 2001; Number Ten, 2002; Adrian Mole and the Weapons of Mass Destruction, 2004; Queen Camilla, 2006. *Recreation:* listening. *Club:* Groucho.

TOWNSHEND, family name of **Marquess Townshend**.

TOWNSHEND, 7th Marquess *cr* 1787; **George John Patrick Dominic Townshend;** Bt 1617; Baron Townshend of Lynn Regis, 1661; Viscount Townshend of Raynham, 1682; *b* 13 May 1916; *s* of 6th Marquess Townshend and Gladys Ethel Gwendolen Eugenie (*d* 1959), *e d* of late Thomas Sutherst, barrister; *S* father, 1921; *m* 1st, 1939, Elizabeth (marr. diss. 1960; she *m* 1960, Brig. Sir James Gault, KCMG, MVO, OBE; she *d* 1989), *o d* of Thomas Luby, ICS; one *s* two *d*; 2nd, 1960, Ann Frances (*d* 1988), *d* of Arthur Pellew Darlow; one *s* one *d*; 3rd, 2004, Philippa Sophia Swire, *d* of Col George Jardine Kidston-Montgomerie of Southannan, DSO, MC. Norfolk Yeomanry TA, 1936–40; Scots Guards, 1940–45. Chairman: Anglia Television Gp plc, 1971–86; Anglia Television Ltd, 1958–86; Survival Anglia, 1971–86; Anchor Enterprises Ltd, 1967–88; AP Bank Ltd, 1975–87; East Coast Grain Ltd, 1982–90; D. E. Longe & Co. Ltd, 1982–90; Norfolk Agricultural Station, 1973–87; Raynham Farm Co. Ltd, 1957–; Vice-Chairman: Norwich Union Life Insurance Society Ltd, 1973–86; Norwich Union Fire Insurance Society Ltd, 1975–86; Director: London Merchant Securities plc, 1964–95; Napak Ltd, 1982–90; Riggs Nat. Corp., Washington, 1987–89. Chairman, Royal Norfolk Agricultural Association, 1978–85. Hon. DCL East Anglia, 1989. DL Norfolk, 1951–61. *Heir:* *s* Viscount Raynham, *qv*. *Address:* Raynham Hall, Fakenham, Norfolk NR21 7EP. *T:* (01328) 862133. *Clubs:* White's, MCC; Norfolk (Norwich).

See also H. G. W. Swire.

TOWNSHEND, Prof. Charles Jeremy Nigel, DPhil; FBA 2008; Professor of International History, University of Keele, since 1987; *b* Nottingham, 27 July 1945; *s* of John Walter Henwood Townshend and Helen Betty Townshend; *m* 1978, Katherine Jane Lawley; two *s*. *Educ:* Oriel Coll., Oxford (BA 1967; DPhil 1973). Lectr in Hist., 1973–81, Sen. Lectr, 1981–87, Keele Univ. Olin Fellow, Nat. Humanities Center, N Carolina, 1987–88; Fellow, Woodrow Wilson Internat. Center for Scholars, Washington, 1991–92. *Publications:* The British Campaign in Ireland, 1975; Political Violence in Ireland: government and resistance since 1848, 1983; Britain's Civil Wars: counter insurgency in the twentieth century, 1986; Consensus in Ireland: approaches and recessions, 1988; Making the Peace: public order and public security in modern Britain, 1993; The Oxford Illustrated History of Modern War, 1997; Ireland: the 20th century, 1998; The State: historical and political dimensions, 1999; Terrorism: a very short introduction, 2002; Easter 1916: the Irish Rebellion, 2005. *Recreation:* mountain biking. *Address:* 5 Church Plantation, Keele, Staffs ST5 5AY; *e-mail:* hia18@keele.ac.uk.

TOWNSHEND, Peter Dennis Blandford; composer, performer, publisher, author; *b* London, 19 May 1945; *s* of Clifford and Betty Townshend; *m* 1968, Karen Astley; one *s* two *d*. *Educ:* Acton County Grammar Sch.; Ealing Art Coll. Mem., The Who, rock group 1963–; Editor, Faber & Faber, 1983–; *recordings* include: with The Who: Tommy, 1969 (musical, filmed 1975, Grammy Award 1993, staged NY (Tony Award for best score), 1993, Toronto (Dora Mavor Moore Award), 1994, London, 1996 (Olivier Award, 1997)); Quadrophenia, 1973; Endless Wire, 2006; singles: My Generation; I Can See For Miles; Can't Explain; Substitute; Pinball Wizard; solo: Empty Glass, 1980; Iron Man, 1989; Psychoderelict, 1993. Ivor Novello Award, 1981; British Phonographic Industry Lifetime Achievement Award, 1983. BRIT Award for contribn to British Music, 1988; Living Legend Award, Internat. Rock Awards, 1991; Q Lifetime Achievement Award, 1997; Ivor Novello Lifetime Achievement Award, 2001. *Publication:* Horse's Neck, 1986. *Recreation:* sailing.

TOY, Rev. Canon John, PhD; Chancellor of York Minster, 1983–99 (also Librarian and Guestmaster); Residentiary Canon, York Minster, 1983–99, now Emeritus; Prebendary of Laughton-en-le-Morthen, 1994–99; *b* 25 Nov. 1930; *e s* of late Sidney Toy, FSA and late Violet Mary (*née* Doudney); *m* 1963, Mollie, *d* of Eric and Elsie Tilbury; one *s* one *d*. *Educ:* Epsom County Grammar Sch.; Hatfield Coll., Durham (BA 1st cl. Hons Theol. 1953, MA 1962); PhD Leeds 1982. Ordained deacon, 1955, priest, 1956; Curate, St Paul's, Lorrimore Sq., Southwark, 1955–58; Student Christian Movement Sec. for S of England, 1958–60; Chaplain: Ely Theol Coll., 1960–64; St Andrew's Church, Gothenburg, Sweden, 1965–69; St John's College, York: Lectr in Theology, 1969; Sen. Lectr, 1972; Principal Lectr, 1979–83; Prebendary of Tockerington, 1983–94. Kt, Royal Order of Polar Star (Sweden), 2002. *Publications:* Jesus, Man for God, 1988; (jtly) A Pilgrim Guide to York, 1997; English Saints in the Medieval Liturgies of the Scandinavian Churches, 2009; contrib. to learned jls and cathedral booklets. *Recreations:* Scandinavia, history, architecture. *Address:* 11 Westhorpe, Southwell, Notts NG25 0ND. *T:* (01636) 812609.

TOYE, Bryan Edward; JP; Chairman, Toye & Co. and associated companies, since 1969; *b* 17 March 1938; *s* of Herbert Graham Donovan Toye and late Marion Alberta Toye (*née* Montignani); *m* 1982, Fiona Ann, *d* of G. H. J. Hogg, Wellington, NZ; three *s* one *d*. *Educ:* St Andrew's Prep. Sch., Eastbourne; Stowe Sch. Joined Toye & Co., 1956; Dir, Toye Kenning & Spencer, 1962–; Dir, Toye & Co., 1966; Dep. Chm., Futurama Sign Gp Ltd, 1992–96; Mem. Adv. Bd, The House of Windsor Collection Ltd, 1994–95; non-executive Director: Trehaven Trust Ltd, 1990–97; DG HR (Navy) (formerly Naval Manning Agency), 1999–2005. Mem., Lloyd's, 1985–91. Mem., Defence Manufacturers Assoc., 2005– (Chm., Clothing Interest Gp; Dep. Chm., Commercial Gp). Alderman, Ward of Lime Street, City of London, 1983–96; Master, Gold and Silver Wyre Drawers' Co., 1984; Liveryman, Goldsmiths' Co., 1985– (Prime Warden, 2004–05); Member, Court of Assistants: Broderers' Co. (Master, 1996–97); Guild of Freemen of City of London, 1986–97 (Mem., 1983–). Pres., Royal Warrant Holders' Assoc., 1991–92 (Mem. Council, 1983–; Hon. Auditor, 1998–). Mem. Council, NSPCC, London, 1966–69; Chm., Greater London Playing Fields Assoc., 1988–90; Mem. Council, London Playing Fields Soc., 1990–92; Policy and Resources Cttee, King George's Fund for Sailors, 1990–92. Trustee: (founder Mem.) Queen Elizabeth Scholarship Trust, 1990–96; Britain-Australia Bicentennial Trust; Black Country Museum (London Gp), 1991–97; British Red Cross, 1993– (Vice Pres. London Br., 1993–). Governor: City of London Sch., 1985–88; King Edward's Sch., Witley, 1988–93; Bridewell Royal Hosp., 1989–96; Christ's Hosp., 1989–96; City of London Freemen's Sch., 1993–96. Mem. Ct, RCA, 1983–86. Hon. Mem., Ct of Assts, HAC, 1983–96; Hon. Col 55 Ordnance Co. RAOC (V), 1988–93; Hon. Col, 124 Havering Petroleum Sqdn RLC (V), 1994–2000; Hon. Ordnance Officer, Tower of London, 1994–2008. Member: TA&VRA for Gtr London, 1992–99; City of London TA&VRA, 1992–99. Member: Royal Soc. of St George, London Br., 1981–; Huguenot Soc., 1985–; Cttee, Old Stoic Soc., 1985–92; Stewards' Enc., Henley Royal Regatta, 1980–. FInstD 1966; FCMI (FIMgt 1983); FRSA 1985; MCIPS 1991. JP: City of London, 1983–96 (Chm. Bench, 1990–96); Hereford & Worcs, Supplemental list, 1996. OStJ 1980. *Recreations:* cricket, squash, shooting, sailing, swimming, tennis, gardening, classical music, Rugby, entertaining. *Address:* Toye & Co., 19/21 Great Queen Street, WC2B 5BE. *T:* (020) 7242 0471, *Fax:* (020) 7831 8692. *Clubs:* Royal Automobile, City Livery (Pres., 1988–89), MCC; Middlesex Co. RFC; Wasps FC (Trustee and Vice-Pres.); Leander (Henley).

TOYE, Prof. John Francis Joseph; Senior Research Associate, Queen Elizabeth House, Oxford, since 2003; *b* 7 Oct. 1942; *s* of late John Redmond Toye and Adele Toye (*née* Francis); *m* 1967, Janet Reason; one *s* one *d*. *Educ:* Christ's Coll., Finchley; Jesus Coll., Cambridge (schol.; MA); Harvard Univ. (Frank Knox Vis. Fellow); Sch. of Oriental and African Studies, Univ. of London (MScEcon; PhD). Asst Principal, HM Treasury, 1965–68; Res. Fellow, SOAS, Univ. of London, 1970–72; Fellow (later Tutor), Wolfson Coll., Cambridge, 1972–80, and Asst Dir of Develt Studies, Cambridge Univ., 1977–80; Dir, Commodities Res. Unit Ltd, 1980–85; Prof. of Develt Policy and Planning and Dir, Centre for Develt Studies, University Coll. of Swansea, 1982–87; Dir, 1987–97, Fellow, 1987–98, Inst. of Develt Studies, Univ. of Sussex; Dir, Globalisation and Develt Strategies Div., UN Conf. on Trade and Develt, Geneva, 1998–2000; Dir, Centre for Study of African Economies, Oxford, 2000–03. Hon. Fellow, Univ. of Birmingham, Inst. of Local Govt Studies, 1986. Member: Council, ODI, 1988–96; Adv. Cttee on Econ. and Social Res., ODA, 1989–95. *Publications:* (ed) Taxation and Economic Development, 1978; (ed) Trade and Poor Economies, 1979; Public Expenditure and Indian Development Policy 1960–70, 1981; Dilemmas of Development, 1987; (jtly) Does Aid Work in India?, 1990; (jtly) Aid and Power, 1991; Structural Adjustment and Employment Policy, 1995; Keynes on Population, 2000; (jtly) The UN and Global Political Economy, 2004; numerous articles in acad. jls. *Recreations:* walking, music. *Address:* Queen Elizabeth House, 3 Mansfield Road Oxford OX1 3TB.

TOYE, Wendy, CBE 1992; theatrical and film director; choreographer, actress, dancer; *b* 1 May 1917. First professional appearance as Peasblossom in A Midsummer Night's Dream, Old Vic, 1929; principal dancer in Hiawatha, Royal Albert Hall, 1931; Marigold, Phœbe in Toad of Toad Hall and produced dances, Royalty, Christmas, 1931–32; in early 1930s performed and choreographed for the very distinguished Carmargo Society of Ballet; guest artist with Sadler's Wells Ballet and Mme Rambert's Ballet Club; went to Denmark as principal dancer with British Ballet, organized by Adeline Genée, 1932; danced in C. B. Cochran's The Miracle, Lyceum, 1932; masked dancer in Ballerina, Gaiety, 1933; member of Ninette de Valois' original Vic Wells Ballet, principal dancer for Ninette de Valois in The Golden Toy, Coliseum, 1934; toured with Anton Dolin's ballet (choreog. for divertissements and short ballets), 1934–35; in Tulip Time, Alhambra, then Markova-Dolin Ballet as principal dancer and choreog., 1935; in Love and How to Cure It, Globe, 1937. Arranged dances and ballets for many shows and films including most of George Black's productions for next 7 years, notably Black Velvet in which also principal dancer, 1939. Shakespearean season, Open Air Theatre, 1939. *Theatre productions:* Big Ben, Bless the Bride, Tough at the Top (for C. B. Cochran), Adelphi; The Shephard Show, Prince's; Co-Director and Choreographer, Peter Pan, New York; And So To Bed, New Theatre; Co-Director and Choreographer, Feu d'Artifice, Paris; Night of Masquerade, Q; Second Threshold, Vaudeville; Choreography for Three's Company in Joyce Grenfell Requests the Pleasure, Fortune; Wild Thyme, Duke of York's; Lady at the Wheel, Lyric, Hammersmith; Majority of One, Phœnix; Magic Lantern, Saville; As You Like It, Old Vic; Virtue in Danger, Mermaid and Strand; Robert and Elizabeth, Lyric; On the Level, Saville; Midsummer Night's Dream, Shakespeare quatercentenary Latin American tour, 1964; Soldier's Tale, Edinburgh Festival, 1967; Boots with Strawberry Jam, Nottingham Playhouse, 1968; The Great Waltz, Drury Lane, 1970; Showboat, Adelphi, 1971; She Stoops to Conquer, Young Vic, 1972; Cowardy Custard, Mermaid, 1972; Stand and Deliver, Roundhouse, 1972; R loves J, Chichester, 1973; The Confederacy, Chichester, 1974; The Englishman Amused, Young Vic, 1974; Follow The Star, Chichester, 1974, Westminster Theatre, 1976; Made in Heaven, Chichester, 1975; Make Me a World, Chichester, 1976; Once More with Music (with Cicely Courtneidge and Jack Hulbert), 1976; Oh, Mr Porter, Mermaid, 1977; Dance for Gods, Conversations, 1979; Colette, Comedy, 1980; Gingerbread Man, Watermill, 1981; This Thing Called Love, Ambassadors, 1983; (Associate Prod.) Singin' in the Rain, Palladium, 1983; (dir and narr.) Noel and Gertie, Monte Carlo and Canada; (Associate Prod.) Barnum, Manchester, 1984, Victoria Palace, 1985; Birds of a Feather, 1984, and Mad Woman of Chaillot, 1985, Niagara-on-the-Lake; Gala for Joyce Grenfell Tribute, 1985; (Associate Prod.) Torvill and Dean World Tour, 1985; Once Upon a Mattress, Watermill, 1985; Kiss Me Kate, Aarhus and Copenhagen, 1986; Unholy Trinity, Stephenville Fest., 1986; Laburnam Grove, Palace Th. Watford, 1987; Miranda, Chichester Fest., 1987; Get the Message, Molecule, 1987; Songbook, Watermill, 1988; Mrs Dot, Watford, 1988; When That I Was, Manitoba, 1988; Oh! Coward, Hong Kong, 1989; Cinderella, Palace Th., Watford, 1989; Penny Black, Wavendon, 1990; Moll Flanders, Watermill, 1990; Heaven's Up, Playhouse, 1990; Mrs Pat's Profession (workshop with Cleo Laine), Wavendon, 1991; The Drummer, Watermill, 1991; Sound of Music, Sadler's Wells, 1992; See How They Run, Watermill, 1992; Vienna, 1993; Under their Hats, King's Head, 1994, Vienna, 1995; The Anastasia File, 1994, Lloyd George Knew My Father, 1995, Warts and All, Rogues to Riches, 1996, Watermill; Finale Gala, Sadler's Wells, 1996; *opera productions:* Bluebeard's Castle (Bartok), Sadler's Wells and Brussels; The Telephone (Menotti), Sadler's Wells; Rusalka (Dvořák), Sadler's Wells; Fledermaus, Coliseum and Sadler's Wells; Orpheus in the Underworld, Sadler's Wells and Australia; La Vie Parisienne, Sadler's Wells; Seraglio, Bath Festival, 1967; The Impresario, Don Pasquale (for Phoenix Opera Group), 1968; The Italian Girl in Algiers, Coliseum, 1968; La Cenerentola; Merry Widow, 1979, Orpheus in the Underworld, 1981, ENO North; The Mikado, Nat. Opera Co., Ankara, 1982; Italian Girl in Algiers, ENO, 1982; La Serva Padrona and Der Apotoker, Aix-en-Provence Fest., 1991. *Films directed:* The Stranger Left No Card; The Teckman Mystery; Raising a Riot; The Twelfth Day of Christmas; Three Cases of Murder; All for Mary; True as a Turtle; We Joined the Navy; The King's Breakfast; Cliff in Scotland; A Goodly Manor for a Song; Girls Wanted—Istanbul; Trial by Jury (TV). Retrospectives of films directed: Festival de Films des Femmes International, Créteil, Paris, 1990; Tokyo Film Fest., 1991. Productions for TV, etc, inc. Golden Gala, ATV, 1978; Follow the Star, BBC2, 1979; Stranger in Town, Anglia, 1981. Dir concert, Till We Meet Again, RFH, 1989. Advisor, Arts Council Trng Scheme, for many years; Member: Council, LAMDA; (original) Accreditation Bd instig. by Nat. Council of Drama Training for acting courses, 1981–84; Grand Council, Royal Acad. of Dancing. Committee Member: Wavendon Allmusic Scheme; Vivian Ellis Award Scheme; Richard Stilgoe Award Scheme. Trained with Euphen MacLaren, Karsavina, Dolin, Morosoff, Legat, Rambert. Hon. DLitt City, 1996. Silver Jubilee Medal, 1977. *Address:* c/o Jean Diamond, London Management, Noel House, 2–4 Noel Street, W1V 3RB.

TOYN, His Honour Richard John; a Circuit Judge 1972–92; *b* 24 Jan. 1927; *s* of Richard Thomas Millington Toyn and Ethel Toyn; *m* 1955, Joyce Evelyn Goodwin; two *s* two *d*. *Educ:* Solihull Sch.; Bristol Grammar Sch.; Bristol Univ. (LLB). Royal Army Service Corps, 1948–50. Called to the Bar, Gray's Inn, 1950. Mem., Parole Bd, 1978–80. Contributing Ed., Butterworths County Court Precedents and Pleadings, 1985. *Recreations:* music, drama, photography.

TOYNBEE, Polly; columnist, The Guardian, 1977–88 and since 1998; writer; *b* 27 Dec. 1946; *d* of late Philip Toynbee, and of Anne Powell; *m* 1970, Peter Jenkins (*d* 1992); one *s* two *d*, and one step *d*. *Educ:* Badminton Sch.; Holland Park Comprehensive; St Anne's Coll., Oxford. Reporter, The Observer, 1968–71; Editor, The Washington Monthly, USA, 1972–73; Feature Writer, The Observer, 1974–76; Social Affairs Editor, News and Current Affairs, BBC, 1988–95; Associate Editor and columnist, The Independent, 1995–97. Vis. Fellow, Nuffield Coll., Oxford, 2004–. Contested (SDP) Lewisham E, 1983. Gov., LSE, 1988–99. Member: Home Office Cttee on Obscenity and Censorship, 1980; DoH Adv. Cttee on the Ethics of Xenotransplantation, 1996; DoH Nat. Screening Cttee, 1996–2003. Mem. Bd, Political Qly, 2003–. Pres., Social Policy Assoc., 2005–. Chm. of Judges, Orange Prize, 2002; Chair, Brighton Dome and Fest., 2005–. Dir, Wise Gp, 2005–. Hon. LLD: Essex, 2001; South Bank, 2002; Hon. DLitt Loughborough, 2004; DUniv: Stafford, 2004; Open, 2005; Kent, 2007. Catherine Pakenham Award for Journalism, 1975; British Press Award, 1977, 1982, 1986, Columnist of the Year, 2007; BBC What the Papers Say Award, 1996 (Commentator of the Year); Magazine Writer of the Year, PPA, 1996; George Orwell Prize, 1997. *Publications:* Leftovers, 1966; A Working Life, 1970 (paperback 1972); Hospital, 1977 (paperback 1979); The Way We Live Now, 1981; Lost Children, 1985; (with David Walker) Did Things Get Better? an audit of Labour's successes and failures, 2001; Hard Work: life in low-pay Britain, 2003; (with David Walker) Better or Worse? Has Labour Delivered?, 2005; (with David Walker) Unjust Rewards, 2008. *Address:* The Guardian, Kings Place, 90 York Way, N1 9LG.

TOYNE, Prof. Peter; DL; Chairman: Friends of Cathedral Music, since 2002; Liverpool Cathedral Development Trust, since 2002; *b* 3 Dec. 1939; *s* of Harold and Doris Toyne; *m* 1969, Angela Wedderburn; one *s*. *Educ:* Ripon Grammar Sch.; Bristol Univ. (BA); The Sorbonne. Res. Asst, Univ. of Lille, 1964; Univ. of Exeter: Lectr in Geography, 1965–76; Sen. Lectr in Geography and Sub Dean of Social Studies, 1976–78; Dir, DES Credit Transfer Feasibility Study, 1978–80; Hd of Bishop Otter Coll., Chichester, and Dep. Dir (Academic), W Sussex Inst. of Higher Educn, 1980–83; Dep. Rector, NE London Polytechnic, 1983–86; Rector, Liverpool Poly., 1986–92, then Vice-Chancellor and Chief Exec., Liverpool John Moores Univ., 1992–2000 (Hon. Fellow, 2000). Sen. Inspector, Theol Colls, 1980–. Chm., Guidance Accreditation Bd, 1999–2002; Member: Council, Industrial Soc., 1997–2000; C of E Archbishops' Council, 1999–; Merseyside Bd, Nat. Probation Service, 2004–. Chairman: Trustees, Rodolfus Choir, 1995–2001; Trustees, Liverpool St George's Hall, 1996–2000; Groundwork St Helens, Knowsley, Sefton & Liverpool, 1997–2001; Royal Liverpool Philharmonic Soc., 2000–03; Liverpool Culture Co., 2000–03. Chm., Woodlands Hospice, 2005–. Pres., Liverpool YMCA, 1997–. Hon. Life Pres., Liverpool Organists' Assoc., 2000–. DL 1990, High Sheriff 2001, Merseyside. Hon. Col, 33 Signal Regt (V), 1999–2006. FRSA; CCMI; FICPD; Fellow, Eton Coll., 1996–2001. Hon. DEd CNAA, 1992. *Publications:* World Problems, 1970; Techniques in Human Geography, 1971; Organisation, Location and Behaviour, 1974; Recreation and Environment, 1974; Toyne Report: Credit Transfer, 1979; Toyne Report: Environmental Education, 1993; numerous articles in geographical, educnl jls, festschriften and popular press. *Recreations:* railways (model and real), liturgy, music (especially sacred). *Address:* Cloudeslee, Croft Drive, Caldy, Wirral CH48 2JW; *e-mail:* p.toyne@btinternet.com.

TOYNE SEWELL, Maj.-Gen. Timothy Patrick; DL; Director, Goodenough College (formerly The London Goodenough Trust for Overseas Graduates), 1995–2006; *b* 7 July 1941; *s* of late Brig. E. P. Sewell, CBE and of E. C. M. Sewell, MBE (*née* Toyne); *m* 1965, Jennifer Lesley Lunt; one *s* one *d*. *Educ:* Bedford Sch.; RMA, Sandhurst. psc 1973; jsdc 1985; rcds 1988. Commnd KOSB, 1961; ADC to Governor of Aden, 1962–63; helicopter pilot, 2 RGJ and 2 Para, 1966–69; Staff College, 1973; GSO 1, staff of CDS, 1979–81; CO, 1 KOSB, 1981–83; CoS, British Forces Falkland Is, 1983–84; Sen. Directing Staff (Army), JSDC, 1984–85; Comdr, 19 Infantry Bde, 1985–87; RCDS, 1988; Comdr, British Mil. and Adv. Team, Zimbabwe, 1989–91; Comdt, RMA, 1991–94, retired. Team Ldr, Tri Service Study into Services Recruiting Orgns, 1994–95. Col, KOSB, 1995–2001. Chairman: Exec. Cttee, Disability Sport England, 1998–99; Internat. Bd, United World Colls, 2006–. Chm., Benjamin Britten Internat. Violin Competition, 2002–. Gov., Haileybury, 1993–; Chm. of Govs, Lambrook Haileybury Sch., 2003–; Mem. Council, QMW, 1996–2005; Trustee: Med. Coll. of St Bartholomew's Hosp. Trust, 2000–05; Bedford Sch. Foundn, 2006–; North-West Univ. (SA) Trust UK. Non-exec. Dir, Catalyst Investment Gp Ltd, 2007–. DL Greater London, 1999. Freeman, City of London, 2006. *Recreations:* racquet sports, golf, fishing, music. *Club:* Royal Over-Seas League (Mem. Council, 2002–).

TOZZI, Keith, CEng, FICE; Chairman, Concateno plc, since 2006 (Chief Executive, 2005–06); *b* 23 Feb. 1949; *s* of late Edward Thomas Tozzi and Winifred Tozzi (*née* Killick); *m* 1986, Maria Cecilia Buckley; two *s* one *d*. *Educ:* Dartford Grammar Sch.; City Univ. (BSc Hons); Univ. of Kent (MA); Harvard Business Sch. (Internat. SMP). Civil Engr, Thames Water, 1973–75; Southern Water plc: Water Manager, 1975–81; Ops Manager, 1981–86; Engrg Manager, 1986–88; Divl Dir, 1988–92; Gp Technical Dir, 1992–96; Chm., Nat. Jt Utilities Gp, 1993–96; Chief Exec., BSI, 1997–2000; Gp Chief Exec., Mid-Kent Hldgs, subseq. Swan Gp plc, 2000–03; Chief Exec., Clifton Capital Investments, 2003–06. Chairman: RSVP.i (formerly IPID.com), 2000–; Inspicio plc, 2005–08; non-executive Director: Legal & General UK Select Investment Trust, 2000–03; Seal Analytical Ltd, 2004–. Mem., CBI Southern Regl Council, 2000–04. *Publications:* articles in newspapers and technical jls. *Recreations:* gardening, reading, classic cars. *Address:* Littleworth House, Littleworth, W Sussex RH13 8JF. *T:* (01403) 710488.

TOZZI, Nigel Kenneth; QC 2001; *b* 31 Aug. 1957; *s* of Ronald Kenneth Tozzi and Doreen Elsie Florence Tozzi; *m* 1983, Sara Louise Clare Cornish; two *s* one *d*. *Educ:* Hitchin Boys' Grammar Sch.; Exeter Univ. (LLB 1st Cl. Hons); Inns of Court Sch. of Law (1st Cl.). Called to the Bar, Gray's Inn, 1980; in practice as Barrister, specialising in commercial, insce and professional negligence litigation, 1980–. *Recreations:* playing hockey, watching cricket, theatre, cinema. *Address:* 4 Pump Court, Temple, EC4Y 7AN. *T:* (020) 7842 5555. *Clubs:* MCC; Sevenoaks Hockey.

TRACE, Anthony John; QC 1998; *b* 23 Oct. 1958; *s* of Comdr Peter Trace, RD and bar, RNR, and Anne Trace (*née* Allison-Beer); *m* 1986, Caroline Tessa Durrant, *e d* of His Honour A. H. Durrant, *qv*; three *s* one *d*. *Educ:* Vinehall Prep. Sch.; Uppingham Sch.; Magdalene Coll., Cambridge (MA 1st Cl. Hons). Called to the Bar, Lincoln's Inn, 1981, Bencher, 2006. Dep. Managing Ed., Receivers, Administrators and Liquidators' Qly, 1993–2002. Vice-Chm., Chancery Bar Assoc., 2001–04 (Hon. Sec., 1997–2001). Mem., Internat. Editl Bd, Briefings in Real Estate Finance, 2000–02. Freeman, City of London, 1981; Liveryman, Musicians' Co., 1982. Trustee, Uppingham Sch., 1999–. Founder Member: Campaign for Real Gin, 1978; Plodda Falls Swimming Club, 2004; Friends of Turkey, 2006. Jt Winner, Observer Mace Debating Championship, 1981. *Publications:* (contrib.) Butterworths European Law Service (Company Law), 1992; (contrib.) Butterworths Practical Insolvency, 1999. *Recreations:* stalking, shooting, fishing, the Turf, music, messing about in boats. *Address:* Maitland Chambers, 7 Stone Buildings, Lincoln's Inn, WC2A 3SZ. *T:* (020) 7406 1200. *Clubs:* Athenæum, Garrick; Pitt (Cambridge).

TRACEY, Prof. Ian, FRSCM; Organist and Master of the Choristers, 1980–2007, Organist Titulaire, since 2008, Liverpool Cathedral; Professor, Fellow and Organist, Liverpool John Moores University (formerly Liverpool Polytechnic), since 1988; *b* 27 May 1955; *s* of William Tracey and Helene Mignon Tracey (*née* Harris). *Educ:* Trinity Coll. of Music, London (FTCL); St Katharine's Coll., Liverpool (PGCE). FRSCM 2008. Chorus Master, Royal Liverpool Philharmonic Soc., 1985–; Liverpool City Organist (formerly Consultant Organist, City of Liverpool), 1986–; Dir of music, BBC Daily Service, 1998–. Pres., Incorp. Assoc. of Organists of GB, 2001–03. Gov., Liverpool Coll., 1993–. FRSA 1988. Hon. FRCO 2004. Hon. DMus Liverpool, 2006. NW Arts Award for Classical Music, 1994. *Address:* Mornington House, Mornington Terrace, Upper Duke Street, Liverpool L1 9DY. *T:* and *Fax:* (0151) 708 8471. *Club:* Artists' (Liverpool).

TRACEY, Richard Patrick; JP; Member (C) Merton and Wandsworth, London Assembly, Greater London Authority, since 2008; strategic marketing and public affairs consultant, since 1997; *b* 8 Feb. 1943; *o s* of late P. H. (Dick) Tracey and Hilda Tracey; *m* Katharine Gardner; one *s* three *d*. *Educ:* King Edward VI Sch., Stratford-upon-Avon; Birmingham Univ. (LLB Hons). Leader Writer, Daily Express, 1964–66; Presenter/Reporter, BBC Television and Radio, 1966–78: internat. news and current affairs (The World at One, PM, Today, Newsdesk, 24 Hours, The Money Prog.); feature programmes (Wheelbase, Waterline, Motoring and the Motorist, You and Yours, Checkpoint); also documentaries (Colossus, Me and My Migraine); Public Affairs Consultant/Advisor, 1978–83. Non-executive Director: Tallack Golf Course Construction Ltd, 1987–91; Ranelagh Ltd, 1992–96. Member: Econ. Res. Council, 1981–2000; ISIS Assoc., 1981–92. Various Conservative Party Offices, 1974–81; Dep. Chm., Greater London Cons. Party,

1981–83; Mem., Cons. National Union Exec. Cttee, 1981–83. Contested (C) Northampton N, Oct. 1974. MP (C) Surbiton, 1983–97; contested (C) Kingston and Surbiton, 1997. PPS to Min. of State for Trade and Industry (IT), 1984–85; Parly Under Sec. of State, DoE (with special responsibility for sport), 1985–87. Member: Select Cttee on Televising H of C, 1988–92; Selection Cttee, 1992–94; Public Accounts Cttee, 1994–97. Chm., Cons. Parly Greater London MPs' Cttee, 1990–97 (Jt Sec., 1983–84); Sec., Cons. Parly Media Cttee, 1983–84. Community Relns Advr, Battersea Power Station Proj., 2004–08; Chm., Pro-Active S London, Sport England, 2006–08. Fellow, Industry and Parlt Trust, 1984. JP SW London (Wimbledon PSD), 1977. Freeman, City of London, 1984. Mem., Inst. of Advanced Motorists, 1993. *Publications:* (with Richard Hudson-Evans) The World of Motor Sport, 1971; (with Michael Clayton) Hickstead—the first twelve years, 1972; articles, pamphlets. *Recreations:* riding, boating, debating. *Address:* 1 Wycombe Place, SW18 2LU; Greater London Authority, City Hall, The Queen's Walk, SE1 2AA. *e-mail:* richard.tracey@london.gov.uk.

TRACEY, Stanley William, CBE 2008 (OBE 1986); professional pianist, composer and arranger, since 1943; *b* 30 Dec. 1926; *s* of Stanley Clark Tracey and Florence Louise Tracey; *m* 1st, 1946, Joan; 2nd, 1954, Jean; 3rd, 1960, Florence Mary, (Jackie); one *s* one *d*. *Educ:* Tooting, Graveney and Ensham Schools. Leading own small group, 1965–, orchestra, 1969–. Hon. RAM 1984. Fellow, City of Leeds Coll. of Music, 1993. Numerous records of own compositions and arrangements; compositions include: Under Milk Wood suite, 1965; Genesis, 1986; 500 other titles. Subject of BBC TV documentary, Stan Tracey: Godfather of British Jazz, 2003. Hon. DLitt Herts, 1997. Awards include: BASCA Award, 1984; voted best jazz composer, Wire/Guardian, 1989; voted best album of year, Big Band, 1989; pianist of the year, British Jazz Awards, 1992; best album of year, British Jazz Awards, 1993; best arranger/composer, British Jazz Awards, 1995, 1997, BT Jazz Awards, 1999; Jazz Medal, Co. of Musicians, 1997; Lifetime Achievement Award, BBC Jazz Awards, 2002. *Address:* 19 St Augusta Court, Batchwood View, St Albans, Herts AL3 5SS. *T:* (01727) 852595.

TRACEY, Stephen Frederick T.; *see* Thorpe-Tracey.

TRACY; *see* Hanbury-Tracy, family name of Baron Sudeley.

TRACY, Rear-Adm. Hugh Gordon Henry, CB 1965; DSC 1945; *b* 15 Nov. 1912; *e s* of Comdr A. F. G. Tracy, RN; *m* 1938, Muriel (*d* 2005), *d* of Maj.-Gen. Sir R. B. Ainsworth, CB, DSO, OBE; two *s* one *d*. *Educ:* Nautical Coll., Pangbourne. Joined RN, 1929; Lieut, 1934; served in HMS Shropshire, Hawkins and Furious, in Admiralty and attended Advanced Engineering course before promotion to Lt-Comdr, 1942; Sen. Engineer, HMS Illustrious, 1942–44; Asst to Manager, Engineering Dept, HM Dockyard Chatham, 1944–46; Comdr 1946; served in HMS Manxman, Admiralty, RN Engineering Coll. and HM Dockyard Malta; Captain, 1955; Asst Director of Marine Engineering, Admiralty, 1956–58; CO HMS Sultan, 1959–60; Imperial Defence Coll., 1961; CSO (Tech.) to Flag Officer, Sea Training, 1962–63; Rear-Admiral, 1963; Director of Marine Engineering, Ministry of Defence (Navy), 1963–66; retired, 1966. Pres., Wilts Gardens Trust, 1992–97 (Chm., 1985–89). *Recreations:* gardening, plant ecology, assorted collections. *Address:* 21a Sion Hill, Bath BA1 2UL; *e-mail:* hughtracy@googlemail.com.

TRAEGER, Tessa; photographer of still life portraiture and landscape; *b* 30 April 1938; *d* of Thomas Cecil Grimshaw and Hannah Joan (*née* Dearsley); *m* 1965, Ronald S. Traeger (*d* 1968); *m* 2006, Patrick C. Kinmonth. *Educ:* Guildford High Sch. for Girls; Guildford Sch. of Art. Freelance photographer of private and commissioned work, 1960–, incl. Vogue UK, 1975–91; 50 portraits of leading horticulturists commnd by NPG for main collection, 2000. *Exhibitions:* Photographers' Gall., 1978; Gall. Ratié, Paris, 1979; Neal St Gall., 1980; John Hansard Gall., Southampton, 1983; Sheffield Fine Art, 1988; M Gall., Hamburg, 1993; Ardeche Fest. des Arts, France, annually 1994–98, 2003; Michael Hoppen Gall., London, 1997; Witkin Gall., NY, 1997; James Danziger Gall., NY, 1999; Association Gall., London, 2000; Seeing Things, V&A, 2002; Credit Suisse Gall., Zürich, 2005; *solo exhibitions:* Foto Fest., Naarden, Holland, 2001; A Gardener's Labyrinth, NPG, 2003, Bradford, Hove and Scarborough, 2004, Bowes Mus., 2005; *collections:* V&A Mus.; Bibliothèque National, Paris; Metropolitan Mus. of Art, NY; Citibank Private Bank, London; NPG, London; Buhl Collection, USA; New Hall, Cambridge; RHS, London, and many private collections. Contrib. to Oral Hist. of British Photography for Nat. Sound Archive, British Liby, 1996. Silver Award, 1979, Gold Award, 1982, DAAD; Lion d'Or, Cannes Advertising Fest., 1994; Silver Award, Assoc. of Fashion, Advertising and Editorial Photographers, 1997 and 1998. *Publications:* (with A. Boxer) Summer Winter Cookbook, 1978; (with A. Boxer) A Visual Feast, 1991 (Andre Simon Award); (with M. Harrison) Ronald Traeger New Angles: a memoir (to accompany exhibn at V&A Mus.), 1999; (with P. Kinmonth) A Gardener's Labyrinth (to accompany exhibn at NPG), 2003; (with Lora Zarubin) I'm almost always hungry, 2003 (Gourmand World Cookbook Award; Best Cookbook Photography and Internat. Assoc. of Culinary Professionals awards, USA; Julia Child Award); France Profonde (text and photographs), 2009. *Recreations:* gardening, walking in N Devon, restoring 16th century manor house. *Address:* 7 Rossetti Studios, 72 Flood Street, SW3 5TF.

See also Sir N. T. Grimshaw.

TRAFFORD; *see* de Trafford.

TRAFFORD, Dr Bernard St John; Headmaster, Newcastle upon Tyne Royal Grammar School, since 2008; *b* 23 May 1956; *s* of Peter and Josephine Trafford; *m* 1981, Katherine Potts; two *d*. *Educ:* All Hallows Prep. Sch.; Downside Sch.; St Edmund Hall, Oxford (BA Music, MA); Westminster Coll., Oxford (PGCE); Univ. of Birmingham (MEd; PhD; George Cadbury Prize). Teacher, Royal GS, High Wycombe, 1978–81; Wolverhampton Grammar School: Dir of Music, 1981–90; Hd of Sixth Form, 1987–90; Head, 1990–2008. Chair of Trustees, Sch. Councils UK, 2006–; Equal Opportunities Officer, 2001–03, Pubns Officer, 2003–05, Assoc. of Sch. and Coll. Leaders. Chm., HMC, 2007–08. Trustee, youngchoirs, 1984–2006 (Chm., 1998–2006); Trustee and Dir, Nat. Schs SO, 1998–2006. FRSA. *Publications:* Sharing Power in Schools: raising standards, 1993; Participation, Power-sharing and School Improvement, 1997; (ed) Diversity, Inclusivity and Equal Opportunities, 2002; (ed) Making the Most of It: management in schools and colleges, 2002; (jtly) What's It All About?, 2002; (ed) Two Sectors, One Purpose: independent schools in the system, 2002; School Councils, School Democracy, School Improvement: why, what, how, 2003; Raising the Student Voice, 2006; (jtly) The Personal Touch, 2006; (ed) i[2]=Independent and Innovative: examples of innovation in HMC schools, 2006; (jtly) Democratic Governance of Schools, 2007; contribs to educn books and jls. *Recreations:* playing jazz, writing music, walking in Northumberland, running and cycling, trying to get thinner and fitter. *Address:* Royal Grammar School, Eskdale Terrace, Newcastle upon Tyne NE2 4DX. *T:* (01912) 815711, *Fax:* (01912) 120392; *e-mail:* b.trafford@rgs.newcastle.sch.uk.

TRAFFORD, Ian Colton, OBE 1967; Publisher, The Times Supplements, 1981–88, retired; *b* 8 July 1928; *s* of late Dr Harold Trafford and Laura Dorothy Trafford; *m* 1st, 1949, Nella Georgara (marr. diss. 1964); one *d*; 2nd, 1972, Jacqueline Carole Trenque. *Educ:* Charterhouse; St John's Coll., Oxford. Feature writer and industrial correspondent, The Financial Times, 1951–58; UK Correspondent, Barrons Weekly, New York, 1954–60; Director, Industrial and Trade Fairs Holdings Ltd, 1958–71, Managing Director, 1966–71; Director-General British Trade Fairs in: Peking, 1964; Moscow, 1966; Bucharest, 1968; Sao Paulo, 1969; Buenos Aires, 1970; Man. Dir, Economist Newspaper, 1971–81; Chm., Economist Intelligence Unit, 1971–79; Dep. Chm., Times Books Ltd, 1981–86. Local Dir, W London Board, Commercial Union Assce, 1974–83. OBE awarded for services to exports. *Address:* Grafton House, 128 Westhall Road, Warlingham, Surrey CR6 9HF. *T:* (01883) 622048.

TRAHAIR, John Rosewarne, CBE 1990; DL; Chairman, Plymouth District Health Authority, 1981–90; *b* 29 March 1921; *s* of late Percy Edward Trahair and Edith Irene Trahair; *m* 1948, Patricia Elizabeth (*née* Godrich); one *s* one *d*. *Educ:* Leys Sch.; Christ's Coll., Cambridge (MA). FCIS. Served with Royal Artillery, 1941–46 (Captain). Finance Dir, Farleys Infant Food Ltd, 1948–73; Dir 1950–74, Dep. Chm. 1956–74, Western Credit Holdings Ltd. Chairman: Moorhaven HMC, 1959–66; Plymouth and District HMC, 1966–74; Member: SW Regional Hosp. Bd, 1965–74 (Vice-Chm. 1971–73, Chm. 1973–74); South Western RHA, 1974–81. Mem., Devon CC, 1977–81. Pres., Devon County Agricl Assoc., 1993–. High Sheriff, Devon, 1987–88; DL Devon, 1989. *Recreations:* sailing, walking. *Address:* West Park, Ivybridge, South Devon PL21 9JP. *T:* (01752) 892466. *Club:* Royal Western Yacht.

TRAHAR, Anthony John; Chairman, Bartlett Resources LLP, since 2007; *b* 1 June 1949; *s* of Thomas Walter Trahar and Thelma Trahar (*née* Ashmead-Bartlett); *m* 1977, Patricia Jane; one *s* one *d*. *Educ:* St John's Coll., Johannesburg; Witwatersrand Univ. (BComm). Chartered Accountant (South Africa) 1973. Anglo American: joined as mgt trainee, Anglo American Corp. of S Africa Ltd, 1974; PA to Chm., 1976–77; Financial Dir, Anglo American Industrial Corp., 1982–86; Man. Dir, 1986–89, Exec. Chm., 1989–2000, Mondi Paper Co.; Exec. Dir, Anglo American Corp., 1991; Dep. Chm., Anglo American Industrial Corp., 1992–99; Exec. Dir, 1999–2007, CEO, 2000–07, Anglo American plc; Chm., Mondi Europe, 1993–2003. Chairman: S African Motor Corp., 1996–2000; AECI Ltd, 1999–2001. Chm., Paleo-Anthropological Scientific Trust, 1999–2007. MInstD. Hon. PhD 2007. Gold Cross with Star, 1st cl. (Austria), 2004. *Recreations:* trout fishing, shooting, classic cars, music. *Clubs:* Royal Automobile; Rand, River (Johannesburg).

TRAILL, Sir Alan Towers, GBE 1984; QSO 1990; Member of Committee, ARIAS (Insurance Arbitration Society), since 1997; *b* 7 May 1935; *s* of George Traill and Margaret Eleanor (*née* Matthews); *m* 1964, Sarah Jane (*née* Hutt); one *s*. *Educ:* St Andrew's Sch., Eastbourne; Charterhouse; Jesus Coll., Cambridge (MA). ACIArb 1991. Underwriting Member of Lloyd's, 1963–89; Man. Dir, Colburn Traill Ltd, 1989–96; Divl Dir, First City Insurance Brokers Ltd, 1996–2000. Dir, Cayman Is Monetary Authy, 2003–06. British Insurance Brokers Association: Mem. Council, 1978–79; Chairman: Reinsurance Brokers Cttee, 1978–79; UK/NZ 1990 Cttee, 1989–90. Member, Court of Common Council, City of London, 1970–2005; Alderman for Langbourn Ward, 1975–2005; Sheriff, 1982–83; Lord Mayor of London, 1984–85. Master: Cutlers' Co., 1979–80; Musicians' Co., 1999–2000. Dir, City Arts Trust, 1980–. Trustee, Morden Coll., 1995–. Mem. Adv. Cttee, 1995–, Educn Cttee, 1998–, LSO. Patron, Treloar Coll. (Gov., 1986–2002); Governor: Christ's Hosp. Foundn, 1980–; Menuhin Sch., 2000– (Chm., 2006–). KStJ 1985. *Recreations:* DIY, travel, opera, assisting education. *Address:* Wheelers Farm, Thursley, Godalming, Surrey GU8 6QE.

TRAINOR, Prof. Richard Hughes, DPhil; FRHistS; AcSS; Principal, Professor of Social History, and Fellow, King's College London, since 2004; *b* 31 Dec. 1948; *s* of late William Richard Trainor and Sarah Frances (*née* Hughes); *m* 1980, Prof. Marguerite Wright Dupree; one *s* one *d*. *Educ:* Brown Univ. (BA); Princeton Univ. (MA); Merton Coll., Oxford (Rhodes Scholar; MA; Hon. Fellow, 2004); Nuffield Coll., Oxford (DPhil 1982). FRHistS 1990. Jun. Res. Fellow, Wolfson Coll., Oxford, 1977–79; Lectr, Balliol Coll., Oxford, 1978–79; University of Glasgow: Lectr in Econ. Hist., 1979–89; Sen. Lectr in Econ. and Social Hist., 1989–95; Prof. of Social Hist., 1995–2000; Dir, Design and Implementation of Software in Hist. Project, 1985–89; Co-Dir, Computers in Teaching Initiative Centre for Hist., Archaeol. and Art Hist., 1989–99; Dean and Hd of Planning Unit, Faculty of Social Sci., 1992–96; Vice-Principal, 1996–2000; Vice-Chancellor and Prof. of Social Hist., Greenwich Univ., 2000–04. Member: Jt Inf. Systems Cttee, 2001–05; HEFCE Cttee on Quality Assessment, Learning and Teaching, 2003–06; HEFCE Cttee on Leadership, Governance and Mgt, 2006–07; AHRC, 2006–; Universities UK: Mem. UK Bd, 2000–05; Treas., 2005–06; Pres., 2007–; Chm., Steering Gp, UUK/DfES Review of Student Services, 2002; Convenor, Steering Gp, Learning and Teaching Support Network, 2000–04. Chairman: London Metropolitan Network, 2002–06; Adv. Council, Inst. of Histl Res., 2004–; Member: US-UK Fulbright Commn, 2003–; Bd, Higher Educn Acad., 2004–07. Gov., Henley Mgt Coll., 2003–05. Mem., Exec. Cttee, Pilgrims Soc. of GB, 2004–. Pres., Glasgow and W of Scotland Br., HA, 1991–93; Hon. Sec., Econ. Hist. Soc., 1998–2004. AcSS 2001. FRSA 1995. Hon. FTCL 2003. *Publications:* (ed jtly) Historians, Computers and Data: applications in research and teaching, 1991; (ed jtly) Towards an International Curriculum for History and Computing, 1992; (ed jtly) The Teaching of Historical Computing: an international framework, 1993; Black Country Elites: the exercise of authority in an industrialised area 1830–1900, 1993; (ed with R. Morris) Urban Governance: Britain and beyond since 1750, 2000; (jtly) University, City and State: the University of Glasgow since 1870, 2000; contrib. numerous articles to books and jls. *Recreations:* parenting, observing politics, tennis. *Address:* King's College London, James Clerk Maxwell Building, 57 Waterloo Road, SE1 8WA. *T:* (020) 7848 3434. *Club:* Athenæum.

TRAINOR, Roy; Senior Partner (formerly Chairman), ATM Consulting Ltd, since 1990; Chairman, Geneshall Ltd, since 1994; *b* 25 Jan. 1948; *s* of Thomas and Miriam Joyce Trainor; *m* 1972, Elizabeth Ann Evans; two *s*. *Educ:* Kingston Sch., Stafford; Staffordshire Poly. (DMS 1975); Univ. of Warwick (MA 1982). Mgt Trainee, Lotus Ltd, 1965–67; Personnel, Stoke-on-Trent City Council, 1967–68; Personnel Mgt, then Opnl Mgt, then Dir, NHS, 1968–89. Chm., Medistaff Health Gp, 1999–2003. Chm., Foundn NHS Trust, 1996–2001; non-exec. Dir, Corinth Healthcare Ltd, 2003–05. Pres., Stafford Chamber of Commerce and Industry, 1995–96. MIPD, MMS. *Recreations:* walking, reading, travel. *Address:* ATM Consulting Ltd, The Hayes, 19 Newport Road, Stafford ST16 1BA. *T:* (01785) 224854, *Fax:* (01785) 229155; *e-mail:* roy_trainor@atmconsulting.com; Vine Cottage, Coton Wood, Radmore Lane, Gnosall, Stafford ST20 0EG. *T:* (01785) 822097. *Club:* Naval and Military.

TRAPIDO, Barbara Louise; freelance writer, since 1982; novelist; *b* Cape Town, 5 Nov. 1941; *d* of Frits Johan Schuddeboom and Anneliese Schuddebom (*née* Jacobsen); *m* 1963, Stanley Trapido (*d* 2008); one *s* one *d*. *Educ:* Natal Univ., Durban (BA Hons English); London Univ. Inst. of Educn (PGCE). Teacher: schs, London, 1964–67; Coll. of Further Educn, Sunderland, and Remand Centre for Young Offenders, Co. Durham, 1967–70; Supervisor, Jericho Pre-School Playgroup, Oxford, 1970–82. *Publications:* Brother of the More Famous Jack, 1982; Noah's Ark, 1985; Temples of Delight, 1990; Juggling, 1994;

The Travelling Hornplayer, 1999; Frankie & Stankie, 2003. *Recreations:* concerts, opera, ballet, theatre, trawling fine art galleries (all spectator activities), cycling, dogs, family and friends. *Address:* c/o Victoria Hobbs, A. M. Heath & Co., 6 Warwick Court, WC1R5DJ.

TRAPNELL, Barry Maurice Waller, CBE 1982; DL; MA, PhD Cantab; Headmaster of Oundle School, 1968–84; Chairman, Cambridge Occupational Analysts, 1986–2003; *b* 18 May 1924; *s* of Waller Bertram and late Rachel Trapnell; *m* 1951, Dorothy Joan (*d* 2005), *d* of late P. J. Kerr, ICS; two *d. Educ:* University College Sch., Hampstead; St John's Coll., Cambridge (Scholar). Research in physical chemistry in Department of Colloid Science, Cambridge, 1945–46, and Royal Institution, London, 1946–50; Commonwealth Fund Fellow, Northwestern Univ., Ill., 1950–51; Lecturer in chemistry: Worcester Coll., Oxford, 1951–54; Liverpool Univ., 1954–57; Headmaster, Denstone Coll., 1957–68. Visiting Lecturer, American Association for Advancement of Science, 1961. Pres., Independent Schools Assoc. Inc., 1984–97; Member: Adv. Cttee on Supply and Training of Teachers; C of E Commn on Religious Education. E Anglian Regl Dir, Index, 1985–92. Mem. Governing Body, Roedean Sch., 1987–92. Director: Southend Estates Gp plc, 1984–86; Thomas Wall Trust, 1984–92. Hon. FCP, 1995. DL: Staffs, 1967; Northants, 1974–84. Hon. Liveryman, Worshipful Co. of Grocers, 1984. *Publications:* Chemisorption, 1955 (Russian edition, 1958; 2nd English edition, 1964); Learning and Discerning, 1966; papers in British and American scientific journals. *Recreations:* several games (represented Cambridge *v* Oxford at cricket and squash rackets, and Gentlemen *v* Players at cricket; won Amateur Championships at Rugby Fives), English furniture and silver. *Address:* 6 Corfe Close, Cambridge CB2 2QA. *T:* (01223) 249278. *Clubs:* Oxford and Cambridge; Hawks (Cambridge); Vincent's (Oxford).

TRAVERSE-HEALY, Prof. Thomas Hector, (Tim), OBE 1989; FCIPR, FPA; Director, Centre for Public Affairs Studies, since 1969; Senior Partner, Traverse-Healy Ltd, 1947–93; *b* 25 March 1923; *s* of John Healy, MBE, and Gladys Traverse; *m* 1946, Joan Thompson; two *s* three *d. Educ:* Stonyhurst Coll.; St Mary's Hosp., London Univ. DipCAM. Served War, Royal Marines Commandos and Special Forces, 1941–46. Chairman: Traverse-Healy & Regester Ltd, 1985–87; Charles Barker Traverse-Healy, 1987–89; non-exec. Dir, Charles Barker Hldgs, 1990–92. Mem., Public and Social Policy Cttee, National Westminster Bank, 1974–92; Professional Advr, Corporate Communications, 1990–92; Specialist Advr, CNAA, 1990–92. Prof. of Public Relns, Univ. of Stirling, 1988–97; Visiting Professor: Baylor Univ., Texas, 1988–97; Univ. of Wales, 1990–97; Advisor: Ball State Univ., USA; Westminster Univ. President: Internat. PR Res. and Educn Foundn, 1983–86; Internat. Foundn for PR Studies, 1987–89; Chm., (UK) PR Educn Trust, 1990–92; Mem., Professional Practices Cttee, PR Consultants Assoc., 1987–91; Sec., PR Res. Network, 1994–97. Institute of Public Relations: Mem. 1948, Fellow 1956; Pres. 1967–68; Tallents Gold Medal, 1985; Hon. Fellow 1988; Campbell-Johnson Medal, 2005; European PR Federation: Vice-Pres. 1965–69; International PR Association: Sec. 1950–61, Pres. 1968–73, Mem. Emeritus, 1982; Presidential Gold Medal, 1985; Chm., Coll. Emeriti, 2006–07. FRSA 1953; FIPA 1957. Member, US Public Affairs Council, 1975–91; Pres., World PR Congress: Tel Aviv, 1970; Geneva, 1973. Congress Foundn Lecture: Boston, 1976; Bombay, 1982; Melbourne, 1988; Istanbul, 2006. PR News Award, 1983; PR Week Award, 1987; Page Soc. Award, 1990. *Publications:* numerous published lectures and articles in professional jls. *Recreations:* French politics, Irish Society. *Address:* 2 Henman Close, Devizes, Wilts SN10 1HD. *T:* (01380) 725459. *Clubs:* Athenæum; Philippics.

TREACHER, Adm. Sir John (Devereux), KCB 1975; Chairman, CMI Guard (formerly Hatchguard) Ltd, since 2005; Member, Advisory Board, London Technology Fund, since 2007; *b* Chile, 23 Sept. 1924; *s* of late Frank Charles Treacher, Bentley, Suffolk; *m* 1st, 1953, Patcie Jane (marr. diss. 1968), *d* of late Dr F. L. McGrath, Evanston, Ill; one *s* one *d*; 2nd, 1969, Kirsteen Forbes, *d* of late D. F. Landale; one *s* one *d. Educ:* St Paul's School. Joined RN, 1942; war service in HM Ships Nelson, Glasgow, Keppel and Mermaid in Mediterranean, Normandy, Russian convoys; qual. Fleet Air Arm pilot, 1947; Korean War, 800 Sqdn HMS Triumph; CO, 778 Sqdn 1951, 849 Sqdn 1952–53; CO, HMS Lowestoft, 1964–66; CO, HMS Eagle, 1968–70; Flag Officer Carriers and Amphibious Ships and Comdr Carrier Striking Gp 2, 1970–72; Flag Officer, Naval Air Comd, 1972–73; Vice-Chief of Naval Staff, 1973–75; C-in-C Fleet, and Allied C-in-C Channel and Eastern Atlantic, 1975–77. Chief Exec., 1977–81, and Dir, 1977–85, Nat. Car Parks; Chairman: Playboy Clubs Internat., 1981–82; R. L. Glover Ltd, 1985–87; Westland Inc., 1983–89; Dep. Chm., Westland Gp, 1986–89 (Dir, 1978–89); Director: Contipark GmbH, 1978–2001; Meggitt PLC, 1989–95; Chairman: Interparking Hispania SA, 1995–2005; Interoute Telecommunications plc, 1996–98. Non-press Mem., Press Council, 1978–81; Dir, SBAC, 1983–89. Pres., Fly Navy (formerly Swordfish) Heritage Trust, 1994–. FRAeS 1973. *Publication:* Life at Full Throttle, 2004. *Recreations:* family, travel, boating. *Address:* 59 St Mary Abbot's Court, W14 8RB. *Club:* Boodle's.

TREACY, Hon. Sir Colman Maurice, Kt 2002; **Hon. Mr Justice Treacy;** a Judge of the High Court, Queen's Bench Division, since 2002; a Presiding Judge, Midland Circuit, since 2006; *b* 28 July 1949; *s* of Dr Maurice Treacy and Mary Treacy; *m* (marr. diss.); one *s* one *d*; *m* 2002, Jane Ann, *d* of Edwin and Maureen Hooper; one step *d. Educ:* Stonyhurst Coll.; Jesus Coll., Cambridge (Open Scholar in Classics; MA). Called to the Bar, Middle Temple, 1971, Bencher, 1999; QC 1990; an Asst Recorder, 1988–91; a Recorder, 1991–2002; Head of Chambers, 1994–2000. Mem., Mental Health Rev. Tribunal, 1999–2002; Asst Boundary Comr, 2000–02. *Address:* Royal Courts of Justice, Strand, WC2A 2LL.

TREACY, Philip Anthony, Hon. OBE 2007; milliner; *b* Ballinasloe, Co. Galway, Ireland, 26 May 1967; *s* of late James Vincent Treacy and Katie Agnes Treacy. *Educ:* Nat. Coll. of Art and Design, Dublin (BA); Royal Coll. of Art (MDes). Worked for designers incl. Rifat Ozbek, John Galliano and Victor Edelstein; former House Milliner to Marc Bohan and Victor Edelstein. Founder, Philip Treacy Ltd, 1990; first show in London, 1993, in New York, 1997; hat manufacturer to designers incl. Karl Lagerfeld, Gianni Versace, Valentino, Rifat Ozbek, Givenchy, Alexander McQueen; designer for Debenhams, 1997–2001; launched accessory range, 1997; Design Dir, interiors, The G, Monogram Hotels, 2005. Hon. DFA NUI, 2006. Accessory Designer of the Year, British Fashion Awards, 1991, 1992, 1993, 1996, 1997; Irish Fashion Oscar, 1992. *Address:* (office) 1 Havelock Terrace, SW8 4AS; (store) 69 Elizabeth Street, SW1W 9PJ.

TREACY, Hon. Sir Séamus, Kt 2007; **Hon. Mr Justice Treacy;** a Judge of the High Court of Justice of Northern Ireland, since 2007; *b* 22 March 1956; *s* of late Joseph Treacy and Rose Veronica Treacy; *m* 1976, Viviane Jones; one *s* two *d. Educ:* St Malachy's Coll., Belfast; Queen's Univ., Belfast (LLB Hons). Called to the Bar: NI, 1979; Ireland (King's Inns), 1990; Inner Bar of Ireland, 2000; QC (NI) 1999. Mem., Panel of Arbitrators, Motor Insurers Bureau, 2005–07. *Recreations:* cycling, running, the arts. *Address:* Royal Courts of Justice, Belfast BT1 3JF.

TREADGOLD, Hazel Rhona; Central President of the Mothers' Union, 1983–88; *b* 29 May 1936; *m* 1959, Very Rev. John David Treadgold, *qv*; two *s* one *d*. Mothers' Union: has held office, Dioceses of Southwell, Durham and Chichester, and at HQ; Chm., Central Young Families Cttee, 1971–76; a Central Vice-Pres., 1978–83; Life Vice-Pres., Chichester Dio., 2003. Archbishop of Canterbury's Co-ordinator, Bishops' Wives Conf., Lambeth, 1988; Member: Women's Nat. Commn, 1980–83; Exec., Women's Council, 1989–91. Gov., Bishop Luffa C of E Comprehensive Sch., 1990–2006. JP Chichester, 1991–2006. *Recreations:* travel, reading, flower arranging, swimming, theatre. *Address:* 43 Prior's Acre, Boxgrove, W Sussex PO18 0ER. *T:* (01243) 782385.

TREADGOLD, Very Rev. John David, LVO 1990; Dean of Chichester, 1989–2001; Chaplain to the Queen, 1983–89; *b* 30 Dec. 1931; *s* of Oscar and Sybil Treadgold; *m* 1959, Hazel Rhona Bailey (*see* H. R. Treadgold); two *s* one *d. Educ:* Nottingham Univ. (BA); Wells Theological College. Deacon 1959, priest 1960; Vicar Choral, Southwell Minster, 1959–64; Rector of Wollaton, Nottingham, 1964–74; Vicar of Darlington, 1974–81; Canon of Windsor and Chaplain to Windsor Great Park, 1981–89. Chaplain, TA, 1962–67; TAVR, 1974–78; Chaplain to High Sheriff: of Nottinghamshire, 1963–64 and 1975–76; of Durham, 1978–79; of W Sussex, 2002–03. Chairman: Chichester DAC for the Care of Churches, 1990–99; Trustees, Hosp. of St Mary, 1989–2001; Morse-Boycott Trust, 1995–2001. Trustee, Chichester Festival Theatre, 1989–2001 (Patron, 2001–); Vice Pres., Chichester Festivities, 1989–2001. Patron, Pallant Hse Gall., 1998. OStJ 2005 (Mem., Council, Order of St John, Sussex, 1994–2008). Chm. of Govs, Prebendal Sch., Chichester, 1989–2001; Governor: Slindon Coll., 1995–96; Wycombe Abbey Sch., 1995–2000; St Mary's Hall, Brighton, 2002–03. FRSA 1991. *Recreations:* sculpting, musical appreciation, church architecture. *Address:* 43 Prior's Acre, Boxgrove, Chichester, W Sussex PO18 0ER. *T:* (01243) 782385; *e-mail:* treadgold@connectfree.co.uk. *Club:* Sussex.

TREADGOLD, Sydney William, CBE 1999; FCA; Secretary: Financial Reporting Council, 1990–98; Financial Reporting Review Panel, 1991–98; Accountancy Foundation, 2000–01; *b* 10 May 1933; *s* of Harold and Gladys Treadgold; *m* 1961, Elizabeth Ann White; two *s. Educ:* Larkmead Sch., Abingdon. Chartered accountant (ACA 1960, FCA 1970). Served RAF, 1951–53 (Navigator). Wenn Townsend, Chartered Accountants, 1954–62; Asst Finance Officer, Univ. of Liverpool, 1963–65; Principal: Min. of Aviation, 1965–67; Min. of Technol., 1967–71; Asst Sec., DTI, 1972–78; Under Secretary: Price Commn, 1978–79; Depts of Industry and Trade, 1979–83; DTI, 1983–89; Mem., Accounting Standards Task Gp, 1989–90; Secretary: Accounting Standards Bd, 1990–93; Ind. Regulation of Accountancy Profession Implementation Gp, 1999–2001. Certified Accountants' Disciplinary Panel, 1999–2003, Appointments Cttee, 2004–08. FRSA 1988. *Recreations:* Shakespeare, theatre, film, bridge. *Address:* 23 Sturges Road, Wokingham, Berks RG40 2HG.

TREADWELL, Charles James, CMG 1972; CVO 1979; HM Diplomatic Service, retired; *b* 10 Feb. 1920; *s* of late C. A. L. Treadwell, OBE, Barrister and Solicitor, Wellington, NZ. *Educ:* Wellington Coll., NZ; University of New Zealand (LLB). Served with HM Forces, 1939–45. Sudan Political Service and Sudan Judiciary, 1945–55; FO, 1955–57; British High Commn, Lahore, 1957–60; HM Embassy, Ankara, 1960–62; HM Embassy, Jedda, 1963–64; British Dep. High Comr for Eastern Nigeria, 1965–66; Head of Joint Information Services Department, Foreign Office/Commonwealth Office, 1966–68; British Political Agent, Abu Dhabi, 1968–71; Ambassador, United Arab Emirates, 1971–73; High Comr to Bahamas, 1973–75; Ambassador to Oman, 1975–79. *Address:* Cherry Orchard Cottage, Buddington Lane, Midhurst, W Sussex GU29 0QP.

TREDINNICK, David Arthur Stephen; MP (C) Bosworth, since 1987; *b* 19 Jan. 1950; *m* 1983, Rebecca Jane Shott; one *s* one *d. Educ:* Ludgrove Sch., Wokingham; Eton; Mons Officer Cadet Sch.; Graduate Business Sch., Capetown Univ. (MBA); St John's Coll., Oxford (MLitt 1987). Trainee, E. B. Savoury Milln & Co., Stockbrokers, 1972; Account Exec., Quadrant International, 1974; Salesman, Kalle Infotec UK, 1976; Sales Manager, Word Processing, 1977–78; Consultant, Baird Communications, NY, 1978–79; Marketing Manager, Q1 Europe Ltd, 1979–81; Res. asst to Kenneth Warren, MP, and Angela Rumbold, CBE, MP, 1981–87; Dir, Malden Mitcham Properties (family business), 1985–. Contested (C) Cardiff S and Penarth, 1983. PPS to Minister of State, Welsh Office, 1991–94. Chairman: Select Cttee on Statutory Instruments, 1997–2005; Jt Cttee on Statutory Instruments, 1997–2005; All-Party Parly Gp for Complementary and Integrated Healthcare (formerly for Alternative and Complementary Medicine), 2006– (Treas., 1991–2002; Jt Chm., 2002–06); Treas., Parly Gp for World Govt, 1991–95; Secretary: Cons. backbench Defence Cttee, 1990–91; Cons. backbench Foreign Affairs Cttee, 1990–91. Chm., British Atlantic Gp of Young Politicians, 1989–91; Co-Chm., Future of Europe Trust, 1991–94; Chairman: Anglo East European Trade Co., 1990–97; Ukraine Business Agency, 1992–97. *Address:* House of Commons, SW1A 0AA. *T:* (020) 7219 4514.

TREES, Prof. Alexander John, PhD; Professor of Veterinary Parasitology, since 1994, Dean, Faculty of Veterinary Science, 2001–08, University of Liverpool; *b* 12 June 1946; *s* of John Trees and Margaret Trees (*née* Bell); *m* 1970, Frances Ann McAnally; one *d. Educ:* Univ. of Edinburgh (BVM&S 1969; PhD 1976). MRCVS 1969. Asst in gen. veterinary practice, Derby, 1970–71; Res. Asst, Univ. of Edinburgh, 1971–76; Elanco Products Ltd: Veterinary Advr for ME in Rome, 1977–80; Hd, Animal Sci., Rome (ME/N Africa), 1980; Liverpool School of Tropical Medicine, University of Liverpool: Lectr, Dept of Veterinary Parasitol., 1980–91; Sen. Lectr, 1991–94; Head: Veterinary Parasitol., 1992–2001; Parasite and Vector Biol. Div., 1994–97; Mem. Council, 1995–2004. Member, Editorial Board: Res. in Vet. Sci., 1991–2001; Trends in Parasitol. (formerly Parasitol. Today), 1992–. Member Council: RCVS, 2000– (Jun. Vice-Pres., 2008–July 2009; Pres., July 2009–); RSTM&H, 1997–2000. Pres., Assoc. Veterinary Teachers and Res. Workers, 1996–97. Founding DipEVPC, 2003 (Vice-Pres., EVPC, 2006–). Selborne Medal for vet. res., Assoc. of Vet. Teachers and Res. Workers, 2005. *Publications:* numerous peer-reviewed scientific papers and book chapters. *Recreations:* mountaineering, natural history, living life while I'm alive. *Address:* Faculty of Veterinary Science, University of Liverpool, PO Box 147, Liverpool L69 3BX. *T:* (0151) 794 5977, *Fax:* (0151) 705 3373; *e-mail:* trees@liverpool.ac.uk. *Club:* Farmers.

TREFETHEN, Prof. Lloyd Nicholas, PhD; FRS 2005; Professor of Numerical Analysis, Oxford University, since 1997; Fellow, Balliol College, Oxford, since 1997; *b* 30 Aug. 1955; *s* of Lloyd McGregor Trefethen and Florence Newman Trefethen; *m* 1988, Anne Elizabeth Daman; one *s* one *d. Educ:* Harvard Coll. (AB 1977); Stanford Univ. (MS Computer Sci./Numerical Analysis 1980; PhD 1982). NSF Post-doctoral Fellow and Adjunct Asst Prof., Courant Inst. of Mathematical Scis, New York Univ., 1982–84; Massachusetts Institute of Technology: Asst Prof. of Applied Maths, 1984–87; Associate Prof., 1987–91; Cornell University: Associate Prof., 1991–93; Prof. of Computer Sci., 1994–97. Mem., NAE (US), 2007. *Publications:* Numerical Conformal Mapping, 1986; Numerical Linear Algebra, 1997; Spectral Methods in MATLAB, 2000; Schwarz-Christoffel Mapping, 2002; Spectra and Pseudospectra, 2005; numerous technical articles. *Address:* Oxford University Computing Laboratory, Wolfson Building, Parks Road, Oxford OX1 3QD. *T:* (01865) 273886.

TREFGARNE, family name of **Baron Trefgarne**.

TREFGARNE, 2nd Baron *cr* 1947, of Cleddau; **David Garro Trefgarne;** PC 1989; *b* 31 March 1941; *s* of 1st Baron Trefgarne and Elizabeth, *d* of Charles Edward Churchill (she *m* 2nd, 1962, Comdr A. T. Courtney, from whom she obt. a divorce, 1966; 3rd, 1971, H. C. H. Ker (*d* 1987), Dundee); *S* father, 1960; *m* 1968, Rosalie, *d* of Baron Lane of Horsell, *qv*; two *s* one *d*. *Educ:* Haileybury; Princeton University, USA. Opposition Whip, House of Lords, 1977–79; a Lord in Waiting (Govt Whip), 1979–81; Parly Under Sec. of State, DoT, 1981, FCO, 1981–82, DHSS, 1982–83, (Armed Forces) MoD, 1983–85; Minister of State: for Defence Support, 1985–86; for Defence Procurement, 1986–89; DTI, 1989–90; elected Mem., H of L, 1999. Chm., Assoc. of Cons. Peers, 2000–04. Dir of various companies. Chm., Sci., Engrg, Manufacturing Technologies Alliance (formerly Engrg Trng Authority), 1994–2006. Dir, UK Skills, 1999–2005. Chm., Libyan British Business Council, 2003–; Dep. Chm., Arab British Chamber of Commerce, 2006–. Pres., Popular Flying Assoc., 1992–97, 2000–03; Hon. President: British Assoc. of Aviation Consultants, 1994–; IEE, 2003–06; Welding Inst., 2006–08; Mem. Council, Air League, 1996–. Vice Chm., ACF Assoc., 1992–2000. Gov., Guildford Sch. of Acting, 1992–2000; Life Gov., Haileybury, 1992. Trustee, Mary Rose Trust, 1994–2001; Chm., Brooklands Mus. Trust, 2001–. Patron, Catering Equipment Suppliers Assoc., 2005–. Hon. Fellow, Univ. of Central Lancs, 2004. DUniv Staffs, 2004. Awarded Royal Aero Club Bronze Medal (jointly) for flight from England to Australia and back in light aircraft, 1963. *Recreation:* photography. *Heir: s* Hon. George Garro Trefgarne, *b* 4 Jan. 1970. *Address:* House of Lords, SW1A 0PW.

TREFUSIS; *see* Fane Trefusis, family name of Baron Clinton.

TREGEAR, Francis Benedict William; QC 2003; a Recorder, since 2004; *b* 18 May 1957; *s* of late (George Herbert) Benjamin Tregear and of (Elisabeth) Bridget Tregear; *m* 1984, Elizabeth Anne Burke; one *s* one *d*. *Educ:* Lycée Français de Londres; Colet Court; St Paul's Sch.; St John's Coll., Cambridge (BA); Inns of Court Sch. of Law. Called to the Bar, Middle Temple, 1980; Mem., Lincoln's Inn, 1993; called to the Bar, Eastern Caribbean Supreme Ct, 2004; Commercial Chancery practice. *Recreations:* running, music, London. *Address:* 24 Old Buildings, Lincoln's Inn, WC2A 3UP. *T:* (020) 7404 0946, *Fax:* (020) 7405 1360; *e-mail:* francis.tregear@xxiv.co.uk.

TREGEAR, Mary, FBA 1985; Keeper of Eastern Art, Ashmolean Museum, Oxford, 1987–91; *b* 11 Feb. 1924; *d* of late Thomas R. and Norah Tregear. *Educ:* Sidcot Sch., Somerset; West of England Coll. of Art (ATD 1946); London Univ. (BA); MA Oxon. Taught Art, Wuhan, China, 1947–50; Curator/Lectr, Hong Kong Univ., 1956–61; Sen. Asst Keeper, Chinese, Ashmolean Museum, 1961–87. *Publications:* Arts of China, vol. 1 (co-ordinating ed.), 1968; Catalogue of Chinese Greenwares in the Ashmolean Museum, 1976; Chinese Art, 1980 (trans. French and Spanish), 2nd edn 1997; Song Ceramics, 1982; Tesori d'Arte in Cina, 1994 (trans. English, French and Spanish).

TREGLOWN, Prof. Jeremy Dickinson; Professor of English, University of Warwick, since 1993 (Chairman, Department of English and Comparative Literary Studies, 1995–98); *b* 24 May 1946; *s* of late Rev. Geoffrey and Beryl Treglown; *m* 1st, 1970, Rona Bower (marr. diss. 1982); one *s* two *d*; 2nd, 1984, Holly Eley (*née* Urquhart). *Educ:* Bristol Grammar Sch.; St Peter's Coll. and Hertford Coll., Oxford (MA, BLitt); PhD London. Lecturer: Lincoln Coll., Oxford, 1974–77; University College London, 1977–80; Times Literary Supplement: Asst Editor, 1980–82; Editor, 1982–90. Vis. Fellow: All Souls Coll., Oxford, 1986; Huntington Library, San Marino, Calif, 1988; Mellon Vis. Associate, Calif Inst. of Technol., 1988; Hon. Res. Fellow, UCL, 1991–; Ferris Vis. Prof., Princeton Univ., 1991–92; Jackson Brothers Fellow, Beinecke Liby, Yale, 1999; Leverhulme Res. Fellow, 2001–03; Mellon Fellow, Harry Ransom Humanities Res. Center, Univ. of Texas at Austin, 2002; Sokol Fellow, Cullman Center for Scholars and Writers, NY Public Liby, 2002–03. Mem. Council, RSL, 1989–96; FRSL 1991; FRSA 1990; FEA 2001. Chairman of Judges: Booker Prize, 1991; Whitbread Book of the Year Award, 1998. Contributing Editor, Grand Street, NY, 1991–98. *Publications:* Roald Dahl, 1994; Romancing: the life and work of Henry Green, 2000; V. S. Pritchett: a working life, 2004; edited: The Letters of John Wilmot, Earl of Rochester, 1980; Spirit of Wit: reconsiderations of Rochester, 1982; The Lantern Bearers, Essays by Robert Louis Stevenson, 1988; (with B. Bennett) Grub Street and the Ivory Tower: literary journalism and literary scholarship from Fielding to the Internet, 1998; (with D. McVea) Contributors to The Times Literary Supplement 1902–74: a biographical index, 2000; V. S. Pritchett: essential stories, 2005; Roald Dahl: collected stories, 2006; various articles and book introductions. *Address:* Gardens Cottage, Ditchley Park, Enstone, Chipping Norton, Oxon OX7 4EP.

TREISMAN, Prof. Anne Marie, DPhil; FRS 1989; Professor of Psychology, since 1993, James S. McDonnell Distinguished Professor of Psychology, since 1995, Princeton University; *b* 27 Feb. 1935; *d* of Percy Strawson Taylor and Suzanne (*née* Touren); *m* 1st, 1960, Michael Treisman (marr. diss.); two *s* two *d*; 2nd, 1978, Prof. Daniel Kahneman, *qv*. *Educ:* Newnham Coll., Cambridge (BA 1956); DPhil Oxon 1962. University of Oxford: Res. Asst, 1961–63, Mem., MRC Psycholinguistics Res. Unit., 1963–66, Dept of Experimental Psychol.; Lectr in Psychol., 1968–78; Fellow, St Anne's Coll., Oxford, 1967–78; Professor of Psychology: Univ. of BC, 1978–86; Univ. of Calif, Berkeley, 1986–94. Member: US Nat. Acad. of Scis, 1994; Amer. Acad. Arts and Scis, 1995; Amer. Philosophical Soc., 2005. Hon. DSc British Columbia, 2004. Dist. Scientific Contribn Award, Amer. Psychological Assoc., 1990. *Publications:* contrib. chapters in books and articles in learned jls. *Address:* Department of Psychology, Princeton University, Princeton, NJ 08544–1010, USA; 41 Adams Drive, Princeton, NJ 08540–5401, USA.

TREISMAN, Dr Richard Henry, FRS 1994; Director, CRUK London Research Institute (formerly ICRF Laboratories), since 1999, and Head, Transcription Laboratory, (Principal Scientist), since 1988, Cancer Research UK (formerly Imperial Cancer Research Fund); *b* 7 Oct. 1954; *s* of Woolf Benjamin Treisman and Marjorie Elizabeth (*née* Grounsell); *m* 1993, Kathleen Mary Weston; one *s* one *d*. *Educ:* Haberdashers' Aske's Sch.; Christ's Coll., Cambridge (BA 1977); ICRF/UCL (PhD 1981). Postdoctoral Fellow, Harvard Univ., 1981–84; Mem., Scientific Staff, Lab. of Molecular Biol., Cambridge, 1984–88. Mem., EMBO, 1987. Mem., Festiniog Railway Soc., Porthmadog, 1967–. EMBO Medal, 1995; Louis Jeantet Prize for Medicine, 2002. *Publications:* papers in scientific jls. *Recreations:* piano playing, fell-walking. *Address:* Transcription Laboratory, Room 401, Cancer Research UK, London Research Institute, 44 Lincoln's Inn Fields, WC2A 3PX. *T:* (020) 7269 3271.

TREITEL, Sir Guenter (Heinz), Kt 1997; QC 1983; DCL; FBA 1977; Vinerian Professor of English Law, Oxford University, 1979–96, now Emeritus; Fellow of All Souls College, Oxford, 1979–96, now Emeritus; *b* 26 Oct. 1928; *s* of Theodor Treitel and Hanna Lilly Treitel (*née* Levy); *m* 1957, Phyllis Margaret Cook; two *s*. *Educ:* Kilburn Grammar School; Magdalen College, Oxford. BA 1949, BCL 1951, MA 1953, DCL 1976. Called to the Bar, Gray's Inn, 1952, Hon. Bencher, 1982. Asst Lectr, LSE, 1951–53; Lectr, University Coll., Oxford, 1953–54; Fellow, Magdalen Coll., Oxford, 1954–79, Fellow Emeritus, 1979; All Souls Reader in English Law, Univ. of Oxford, 1964–79. Vis. Lectr, Univ. of Chicago, 1963–64; Visiting Professor: Chicago, 1968–69 and 1971–72; W Australia, 1976; Houston, 1977; Southern Methodist, 1978, 1988–89, 1994 (Dist. Vis. Prof., 2000, 2003); Virginia, 1978–79 and 1983–84; Santa Clara, 1981; Vis. Scholar, Ernst von Caemmerer Gedächtnisstiftung, 1990; Clarendon Lectr in Law, Oxford Univ., 2001. Trustee, British Museum, 1983–98; Mem. Council, National Trust, 1984–93. *Publications:* The Law of Contract, 1962, 11th edn 2003; An Outline of the Law of Contract, 1975, 6th edn 2004; Remedies for Breach of Contract: a comparative account, 1988; Unmöglichkeit, "Impracticability" und "Frustration" im anglo-amerikanischen Recht, 1991; Frustration and Force Majeure, 1994, 2nd edn 2004; (jtly) English Private Law, 2000, 2nd edn 2007; (jtly) Carver on Bills of Lading, 2001, 2nd edn 2005; Some Landmarks of Twentieth Century Contract Law, 2002; edited jointly: Dicey's Conflict of Laws, 7th edn 1958; Dicey and Morris, Conflict of Laws, 8th edn 1967; Chitty on Contracts, 23rd edn 1968 to 29th edn 2004; Benjamin's Sale of Goods, 1974, 7th edn 2006. *Recreations:* music, reading.

TRELAWNY, Sir John Barry Salusbury-, 13th Bt *cr* 1628; Director, Goddard Kay Rogers and Associates Ltd, 1984–95; Chairman, GKR Group Ltd, 1993–95; *b* 4 Sept. 1934; *s* of Sir John William Robin Maurice Salusbury-Trelawny, 12th Bt and of his 1st wife, Glenys Mary (*d* 1985), *d* of John Cameron Kynoch; *S* father, 1956; *m* 1958, Carol Knox, *yr d* of late C. F. K. Watson, The Field, Saltwood, Kent; one *s* three *d*. *Educ:* HMS Worcester. Subseq. Sub-Lt RNVR (National Service). Dir, The Martin Walter Group Ltd, 1971–74; various directorships, 1974–83; Dir, 1978–83, Jt Dep. Man. Dir 1981–83, Korn/Ferry Internat. Inc. Pres., London Cornish Assoc., 1997–2005. Pres., Folkestone & Hythe Dist Scout Council, 1980–. FInstM 1974. JP 1973–78. MA Kent, 2007. *Heir: s* John William Richard Salusbury-Trelawny [*b* 30 March 1960; *m* 1st, 1980, Anita (marr. diss. 1986), *d* of Kenneth Snelgrove; one *s* one *d*; 2nd, 1987, Sandra (marr. diss. 1993), *d* of Joseph Thompson; one *s*; 3rd, 2001, Laurian, *d* of Rev. Peter Adams]. *Address:* Beavers Hill, Rectory Lane, Saltwood, Kent CT21 4QA. *T:* (01303) 266476. *Club:* Royal Cinque Ports Yacht.

TRELEAVEN, Prof. Philip Colin, PhD; Professor of Computing, University College London, since 1985 (Pro-Provost, 1994–2008); *b* 15 March 1950; *s* of Frederick Colin and Evelyn Treleaven; *m* 1981, Isabel Gouveia-Lima. *Educ:* Brunel Univ. (BTech); Manchester Univ. (MSc, PhD). Research Fellow, Univ. of Newcastle upon Tyne, 1979–83; Sen. Res. Fellow, Reading Univ., 1983–85. Contested (C): Ealing Southall, 1992; SW London, Eur. Parly elecns, 1994. *Recreation:* politics. *Address:* Department of Computer Science, University College London, Gower Street, WC1E 6BT. *T:* (020) 7679 7288.

TRELFORD, Prof. Donald Gilchrist; journalist and broadcaster; Emeritus Professor in Journalism Studies, Sheffield University, since 2007; Editor, The Observer, 1975–93; *b* 9 Nov. 1937; *s* of late Thomas and Doris Trelford (*née* Gilchrist); *m* 1st, 1963, Janice Ingram; two *s* one *d*; 2nd, 1978, Kate Mark; one *d*; 3rd, 2001, Claire Bishop. *Educ:* Bablake Sch., Coventry (School Captain, 1956); Selwyn Coll., Cambridge (Open exhibnr in English, MA; University Rugby and cricket). Pilot Officer, RAF, 1956–58. Reporter and Sub-Editor, Coventry Standard and Sheffield Telegraph, 1960–63; Editor, Times of Malawi, 1963–66; Correspondent in Africa for The Observer, The Times, and BBC, 1963–66; The Observer: Dep. News Editor, 1966; Asst Man. Editor, 1968; Dep. Editor, 1969; Chief Exec., The Observer Ltd, 1992–93; Prof. and Hd of Dept of Journalism Studies, 1994–2000, Vis. Prof., 2000–04, Sheffield Univ. Acting Editor, The Oldie, 1994; Sports columnist, Daily Telegraph, 1993–. Chm., The Baby Channel, 2000–01; Director: Optomen Television, 1988–97; Observer Films, 1989–93; Central Observer TV, 1990–93; Nat. Acad. of Writing, 2000–03; London Press Club, 2001– (Chm., 2002–07, Pres., 2007–). Ind. Assessor, BBC TV Regl News, 1997. Member: British Executive Cttee, IPI, 1976–2000; Soc. of Editors, 1984–93; Guild of British Newspaper Editors, 1985–2000 (Mem., Parly and Legal Cttee, 1987–91); Council, Media Soc., 1981–2003 (Pres., 1999–2002); Defence, Press and Broadcasting Cttee, 1986–93; Competition Commn (newspaper panel), 1999–2006; Council, ASA, 2002–08; Vice-Pres., Newspaper Press Fund, 1992– (Appeals Chm., 1991). Chm., Eur. Fedn of Press Clubs, 2005–06; Pres., Internat. Assoc. of Press Clubs, 2006–07. Member: judging panel, British Press Awards, 1981– (Chm., 2002–); judging panel, Scottish Press Awards, 1985; Olivier Awards Cttee, SWET, 1984–93; Judge: Whitbread Prize, 1992; Sony Radio Awards, 1994; George Orwell Prize, 1998. Mem. Adv. Bd, London Choral Soc., 1991–98; Chm., Soc. of Gentlemen, Lovers of Musick, 1996–2001. Vice-Pres., British Sports Trust, 1988–2002; Hon. Advr, NPFA, 1996–2004. Mem., Jurade de St Emilion, 1997–2003. Liveryman, Worshipful Co. of Stationers and Newspaper Makers, 1986; Freeman, City of London, 1986. FRSA 1988. Hon. DLitt Sheffield, 1990. Granada Newspaper of the Year Award, 1983, 1993; commended, Internat. Editor of the Year, World Press Rev., NY, 1984. Frequent broadcasts (writer, interviewer and panellist) on TV and radio; presenter: Running Late (C4); LBC Morning Report; TV interviews include: Rajiv Gandhi, Lord Goodman, Sir Leonard Hutton, Gromyko; speaker at internat. media confs in Spain, Egypt, W Germany, Italy, USA, India, Turkey, S Africa, Argentina, Kenya, Trinidad, Lebanon, Canada, Russia, Korea, Peru, Belgium, Singapore, Ethiopia and Dubai. *Publications:* Siege, 1980; (ed) Sunday Best, 1981, 1982, 1983; (contrib.) County Champions, 1982; Snookered, 1986; (contrib.) The Queen Observed, 1986; (with Garry Kasparov) Child of Change, 1987; (contrib.) Saturday's Boys, 1990; (contrib.) Fine Glances, 1991; Len Hutton Remembered, 1992; (contrib.) One Over Par, 1992; (ed) The Observer at 200, 1992; (with Daniel King) World Chess Championship, 1993; (contrib.) Animal Passions, 1994; W. G. Grace, 1998. *Recreations:* snooker, tennis, gardening. *Address:* Flat 3, 6 River Terrace, Henley-on-Thames RG9 1BG; *T:* (01491) 637562, 07850 131742; *e-mail:* donaldtrelford@yahoo.co.uk; Apartado 146, 07460 Pollenca, Mallorca, Spain. *T:* (971) 530277. *Clubs:* Garrick, London Press, MCC (Mem., Cttee, 1988–91).

TREMAIN, Rose, CBE 2007; FRSL; novelist and playright; *b* 2 Aug. 1943; *d* of late Viola Mabel Thomson and Keith Nicholas Home Thomson, MBE; *m* 1st, 1971, Jon Tremain (marr. diss.); one *d*; 2nd, 1982, Jonathan Dudley (marr. diss.); partner, Richard Gordon Heath Holmes, *qv*. *Educ:* Sorbonne, Paris; Univ. of East Anglia (BA Hons Eng. Lit.). Part-time Lectr, UEA, 1988–94. FRSL 1983. Dylan Thomas Prize, 1984; Giles Cooper Award, Best Radio Play, 1984. *Publications: novels:* Sadler's Birthday, 1976; Letter to Sister Benedicta, 1978; The Cupboard, 1981; The Swimming Pool Season, 1984; Restoration, 1989 (Sunday Express Book of the Year Award; filmed, 1996); Sacred Country, 1992 (James Tait Black Meml Prize, 1993; Prix Femina Etranger (France), 1994); The Way I Found Her, 1997; Music and Silence, 1999 (Whitbread Novel Award); The Colour, 2003; The Road Home, 2007 (Orange Broadband Prize for Fiction, Good Housekeeping Fiction of the Year Award, 2008); *short stories:* The Colonel's Daughter, 1982; The Garden of the Villa Mollini, 1986; Evangelista's Fan, 1994; The Darkness of Wallis Simpson, 2005; *for children:* Journey to the Volcano, 1985. *Recreations:* gardening, swimming, yoga. *Address:* 2 High House, South Avenue, Thorpe St Andrew, Norwich NR7 0EZ. *T:* (01603) 439682.

TREMAINE, Prof. Scott Duncan, PhD; FRS 1994; FRSC 1994; Professor and Chairman, Department of Astrophysical Sciences, Princeton University, since 1998; *b* 25 May 1950; *s* of Vincent Joseph Tremaine and Beatrice Delphine (*née* Sharp). *Educ:*

McMaster Univ. (BSc); Princeton Univ. (MA, PhD). Postdoctoral Fellow, CIT, 1975–77; Res. Associate, Inst. of Astronomy, Cambridge, 1977–78; Long-term Mem., Inst. for Advanced Study, Princeton, 1978–81; Associate Prof., MIT, 1981–85; University of Toronto: Prof. of Physics and Astronomy, 1985–97; Dir, Canadian Inst. for Theoretical Astrophysics, 1985–96. Dir, Prog. in Cosmology and Gravity, Canadian Inst. for Advanced Res., 1996–2002. Foreign Hon. Mem., Amer. Acad. of Arts and Scis, 1992; Mem., US NAS, 2003. *Publications:* (with J. J. Binney) Galactic Dynamics, 1987; papers in jls of physics and astronomy. *Address:* Princeton University Observatory, Peyton Hall, Princeton NJ 08544–1001, USA. *T:* (609) 258 3800.

TREMBATH, Graham Robert; QC 2003; *b* 18 May 1952; *s* of late Robert Edward George Trembath, MBE and Gladys Booth Trembath; *m* 1981, Ulrika Lillie Maria; one *s* one *d*. *Educ:* Cambusdoon Prep. Sch.; Fettes Coll.; Southampton Univ. (LLB Hons). Called to the Bar, Middle Temple, 1978; in practice specialising in serious crime defence. *Recreations:* golf, lifelong supporter of Chelsea Football Club, general sports fan. *Address:* 5 Paper Buildings, Temple, EC4Y 7HB. *T:* (020) 7583 6117, *Fax:* (020) 7353 0075; *e-mail:* clerks@5pb.co.uk.

TREMBERG, David; His Honour Judge Tremberg; a Circuit Judge, since 2007; *b* London, 7 July 1961; *s* of late Philip Tremberg and of Sally Tremberg (now Firth); *m* 1987, Alison Jones; one *s*. *Educ:* Craven Park Prim. Sch.; JFS Sch.; Univ. of Hull (LLB Hons); Coll. of Europe, Bruges (Dip. Adv. Eur. Studies); Inns of Court Sch. of Law. Called to the Bar, Lincoln's Inn, 1985; Recorder, 2001–07. *Recreations:* watching and playing sport, spending time with family and friends, reading, cars, caravanning (Mem., Caravan Club). *Address:* Great Grimsby Combined Court Centre, Town Hall Square, Grimsby, Lincs DN31 1HX.

TREMBLAY, Dr Marc-Adélard, OC 1980; GOQ 1995; Professor of Anthropology, Université Laval, Québec, 1956–94, now Emeritus; *b* Les Eboulements, Qué., 24 April 1922; *s* of Willie Tremblay and Lauretta (*née* Tremblay); *m* 1949, Jacqueline Cyr; one *s* five *d*. *Educ:* Montréal Univ. (AB, LSA (Agricl Sci.)); Laval (MA Sociol.); Cornell Univ. (PhD Anthropol.). Research Associate, Cornell Univ., 1953–56; Université Laval: Vice-Dean, Faculty Social Scis, 1969–71; Head, Anthropology Dept, 1970; Dean, Graduate Sch., 1971–79. Pres., RSC, 1982–85. Comr, Nunavik Commn, 1999–2000. Pres. Council, Order of Quebec, 1998–2000. Hon. LLD: Ottawa, 1982; Guelph, 1984; Univ. of Northern BC, 1994; Carleton Univ., 1995; Univ. Ste Anne, 1997; McGill, 1998. Innis-Gerin Medal, RSC, 1979; Centennial Medal, RSC, 1982; Molson Prize, Canada Council, 1987; Marcel Vincent Medal, French Canadian Assoc. for Advancement of Science, 1988; Internat. Order of Merit, Internat. Biog. Inst., 1990; Esdras Minville Prize in Soc. Scis, Soc. St Jean-Baptiste, 1991. *Publications:* The Acadians of Portsmouth, 1954; (jtly) People of Cove and Woodlot, 1960; (jtly) Les Comportements économiques de la famille salariée, 1964; Les Fondements Sociaux de la Maturation chez l'enfant, 1965; (jtly) Rural Canada in Transition, 1966; (jtly) A Survey of Contemporary Indians of Canada, 1967; Initiation à la recherche dans les sciences humaines, 1968; (jtly) Etude sur les Indiens contemporains du Canada, 1969; (jtly) Les Changements socio-culturels à Saint-Augustin, 1969; (jtly) Famille et parenté en Acadie, 1971; (jtly) Communautés et Culture, 1973 (Eng. trans. 1973); (jtly) Patterns of Amerindian Identity, 1976; (jtly) The Individual, Language and Society in Canada, 1977; L'Identité Québécoise en péril, 1983; (jtly) Conscience et Enquête, 1983; L'Anthropologie à l'Université Laval: fondements historiques, pratiques académiques, dynamismes d'évolution, 1989; Les fondements historiques et théoriques de la practique professionnelle en anthropologie, 1990; over one hundred and seventy-five scientific articles. *Recreations:* gardening, cross-country ski-ing. *Address:* 835 Nouvelle-Orléans, Sainte Foy, QC G1X 3J4, Canada. *T:* (418) 6535411.

TREMLETT, Ven. Anthony Frank; Archdeacon of Exeter, 1994–2002; *b* 25 Aug. 1937; *s* of Frank and Sally Tremlett; *m* 1958, Patricia Lapthorn; two *s* one *d*. *Educ:* Plymouth College. Clerk, Management Trainee (Traffic Apprentice), Area Manager, 1953–68, British Rail; Traffic Manager, District Manager, Operations Director, 1968–80, National Carriers (Nat. Freight Corporation). Asst Curate, 1981–82, Priest-in-Charge, 1982–84, Vicar, 1984–88, Southway, Plymouth; RD of Moorside, Plymouth, 1986–88; Archdeacon of Totnes, 1988–94. *Recreations:* music, painting, travel, political and economic affairs. *Address:* 57 Great Berry Road, Crownhill, Plymouth, Devon PL6 5AY. *T:* (01752) 240052.

TREMLETT, George William, OBE 1981; author, journalist and bookseller; Director, Corran Books Ltd, since 1981; Founder Chairman, George Tremlett Ltd, since 1965; *b* 5 Sept. 1939; *s* of late Wilfred George and of Elizabeth Tremlett; *m* 1971, Jane, *o c* of late Benjamin James Mitchell and Mrs P. A. Mitchell; three *s*. *Educ:* Taunton School; King Edward VI School, Stratford upon Avon. Member of Richmond upon Thames Borough Council, 1963–74; Chairman: Further Education Cttee, 1966–68; Barnes School Governors, 1967–73; Schools Cttee, 1972–73; Shene VIth Form Coll. Governors, 1973–74; Housing Cttee, 1972–74; Thames Water Authority, 1973–74. Greater London Council: Mem. (C) for Hillingdon, 1970–73, for Twickenham, 1973–86; Opposition Housing Spokesman, 1974–77; Leader of Housing Policy Cttee, 1977–81. Consultant: Nat. Assoc. of Voluntary Hostels, 1980–84; Local Govt Inf. Unit, 1985–86; Appeal Dir, SHAC and Help the Homeless National Appeal, 1985–87. Member: Housing Minister's Adv. Cttee on Co-operatives, 1977–79; Housing Consultative Council for England, 1977–81; Northampton Develt Corp., 1979–83; Stonham Housing Assoc., 1978–92; Chiswick Family Rescue Appeal Fund, 1979–80; Bd, Empty Property Unit, 1985–86; Adv. Panel, BBC Community Prog. Unit, 1985–87. Founder Chm., Dylan Thomas Meml Trust, 1985–90. Governor, Kingston Polytechnic and Twickenham Coll. of Technology, 1967–70; Court of City Univ., 1968–74. *Publications:* 17 biographies of rock musicians, 1974–77—on John Lennon, David Bowie, 10cc, Paul McCartney, The Osmonds, Alvin Stardust, Cat Stevens, Cliff Richard, Slade, The Who, David Essex, Slik, Gary Glitter, Marc Bolan, Rod Stewart, Queen and the Rolling Stones (published in many different countries); Living Cities, 1979; (with Caitlin Thomas) Life with Dylan Thomas, 1986; Clubmen, 1987; Homeless but for St Mungo's, 1989; Little Legs, 1989; Rock Gold, 1990; Dylan Thomas: in the mercy of his means, 1991; Gadaffi: the desert mystic, 1993; David Bowie, 1995; (with James Nashold) The Death of Dylan Thomas, 1997. *Recreations:* ornithology, exploring old churches, local history, rock 'n' roll music. *Address:* The Ship and Castle, King Street, Laugharne, Carmarthenshire SA33 4RY. *T:* (01994) 427444. *Club:* Laugharne RFC.

TRENCH; *see* Le Poer Trench, family name of Earl of Clancarty.

TRENCH, family name of **Baron Ashtown**.

TRENCH, John; Master of the Supreme Court, Queen's Bench Division, 1986–2002; *b* 15 Sept. 1932; *s* of late Prince Constantine Lobanow-Rostovsky and Princess Violette Lobanow-Rostovsky (*née* Le Poer Trench); *m* 1st, 1955, Roxane Bibica-Rosetti (marr. diss.); two *s* (one *d* decd); 2nd, 1980, Patricia Margaret Skitmore. *Educ:* Oundle; Christ's College, Cambridge (MA). Nat. Service, 1950–52; commissioned The Duke of Wellington's Regt. Called to the Bar, Lincoln's Inn, 1956, practised at the Bar, in London and on the Oxford Circuit, 1956–86. *Recreations:* painting, collecting antique handwriting equipment. *Address:* c/o Royal Courts of Justice, Strand, WC2A 2LL.

TRENCH, Jonathan Charles Stewart C.; *see* Chenevix-Trench.

TRENCHARD, family name of **Viscount Trenchard**.

TRENCHARD, 3rd Viscount *cr* 1936, of Wolfeton; **Hugh Trenchard;** DL; Bt 1919; Baron 1930; Managing Director, Mizuho International plc, since 2007; *b* 12 March 1951; *s* of 2nd Viscount Trenchard, MC and of Patricia, *d* of Admiral Sir Sidney Bailey, KBE, CB, DSO; *S* father, 1987; *m* 1975, Fiona Elizabeth Morrison, *d* of 2nd Baron Margadale, TD, DL; two *s* two *d*. *Educ:* Eton; Trinity Coll., Cambridge (BA 1973). Captain, 4th Royal Green Jackets, TA, 1973–80. Entered Kleinwort Benson Ltd, 1973; Chief Rep. in Japan, 1980–85; Gen. Man., Kleinwort Benson Internat. Inc., Tokyo Br., 1985–88; Dir, Kleinwort Benson Ltd, 1986–96; Pres., 1988–95, Rep. in Japan, 1993–95, Dep. Chm., 1995–96, Kleinwort Benson Internat. Incorporated; Director: Robert Fleming & Co. Ltd, 1996–98; Robert Fleming Internat. Ltd, 1998–2000. Chm., Dejima Fund Ltd, 2001–; Director: KB Berkeley Japan Development Capital Ltd, 1987–97; Dover Japan Inc., 1985–87; ACP Hldgs Ltd, 1990–94; Berkeley Technology (formerly London Pacific Gp) Ltd, 1999–; AC European Finance Ltd, subseq. Westhall Capital Ltd, 2001–03; Dryden Wealth Mgt Ltd, 2004–05; Stratton Street PCC Ltd, 2006–; Senior Advisor: Prudential Financial Inc., 2002–; Bache Global Series, 2008–. Dir Gen., European Fund and Asset Mgt Assoc., 2006. Chm., Securities Cttee, 1993–95, Vice Chm. Council, 1995, European Business Community (Japan); Director: Japan Securities Dealers' Assoc., 1994–95; Bond Underwriters' Assoc. of Japan, 1994–95; Member: Japan Assoc. of Corporate Executives, 1987–95; Council, Japan Soc., 1992–93 and 1995–2004 (Vice-Chm., 1996–2000; Jt Chm., 2000–04). Vice-Chm., British-Japanese Parly Gp, 1997–99 and 2004–; Hon. Treas., H of L All-Party Defence Study Gp, 1992–93; elected Mem., H of L, 2004–. Mem. Council, RAF Benevolent Fund, 1991–2003, 2006– (Chm., 2006–). Hon. Air Cdre, 600 (City of London) Sqn, RAuxAF, 2006–. DL Herts, 2008. *Heir:* *s* Hon. Alexander Thomas Trenchard [*b* 26 July 1978; *m* 2007, Mira, *d* of late Rainer Ostendorf]. *Address:* Standon Lordship, Ware, Herts SG11 1PR. *T:* (01920) 823785. *Clubs:* Brooks's, Pratt's, Cavalry and Guards; Tokyo (Tokyo).

TREND, Hon. Michael (St John), CBE 1997; *b* 19 April 1952; *e s* of Baron Trend, PC, GCB, CVO and Patricia Charlotte, *o d* of Rev. Gilbert Shaw; *m* 1987, Jill Elizabeth Kershaw; one *s* two *d*. *Educ:* Tormore Sch., Upper Deal, Kent; Westminster; Oriel Coll., Oxford; Greek Govt Scholar. Toynbee Hall, 1975–76; Sub-Editor, then Managing Editor, TLS, 1976–81; Editor: History Today, 1981–82; Parliamentary House Magazine, 1984–87; Home Editor, Spectator, 1987–90; Chief Leader Writer, Daily Telegraph, 1990–92. MP (C): Windsor and Maidenhead, 1992–97; Windsor, 1997–2005. PPS to Minister of State, DoH, 1993–94, to Sec. of State for Transport, 1994–95; Dep. Chm. and Dir Gen., Conservative Party, 1995–98; Chm., Cons. Party Internat. Office, 2000–05; Opposition frontbench spokesman on European affairs, 1998–99, on pensions, 1999–2000. Member: Select Cttee on Health, 1992–93, on Public Admin, 2000–05; Speaker's Adv. Cttee on Works of Art, 1993–2005. Asst Chm., Internat. Democrat Union, 1999–2005; Gov. and Vice-Chm., Westminster Foundn for Democracy, 1999–2005. Mem. Bd, Victoria County History, 1992–98. *Publication:* The Music Makers, 1985. *Recreations:* music, hill walking.

TRENTHAM, Dr David Rostron, FRS 1982; Hon. Professor, Randall Division (formerly Centre) of Cell and Molecular Biophysics, King's College London, since 2003; *b* 22 Sept. 1938; *s* of John Austin and Julia Agnes Mary Trentham; *m* 1966, Kamalini; two *s*. *Educ:* Univ. of Cambridge (BA Chemistry, PhD Organic Chemistry). Biochemistry Dept, University of Bristol: Jun. Research Fellow (Medical Research Council), 1966–69; Research Associate, 1969–72; Lectr in Biochemistry, 1972–75; Reader in Biochemistry, 1975–77; Edwin M. Chance Prof., Biochemistry and Biophysics Dept, Univ. of Pennsylvania, 1977–84; Hd of Physical Biochem. Div., NIMR, Mill Hill, 1984–2003. Colworth Medal (an annual award), Biochemical Soc., UK, 1974; Wilhelm Feldberg Prize, Feldberg Foundn Bd for Anglo-German Scientific Exchange, 1990. *Publications:* numerous research papers in scientific jls. *Address:* Randall Division of Cell and Molecular Biophysics, New Hunt's House, King's College London, Guy's Campus, SE1 1UL. *T:* (020) 7848 6434.

TREPTE, Paul, FRCO; Organist and Master of the Choristers, Ely Cathedral, since 1990; *b* 24 April 1954; *s* of Harry and Ruth Trepte; *m* 1981, Sally Lampard; one *d*. *Educ:* New College, Oxford (MA). Asst Organist, Worcester Cathedral, 1976; Dir of Music, St Mary's, Warwick, 1981; Organist and Master of the Choristers, St Edmundsbury Cathedral, 1985. *Publications:* choral works. *Address:* The Old Sacristy, The College, Ely CB7 4JU. *T:* (01353) 660336.

TRESCOWTHICK, Sir Donald (Henry), AC 1991; KBE 1979; Chairman, Signet Group Holdings Pty Ltd, 1978–2005; Executive Director, Australian Olympic Committee, 1992–2001; *b* 4 Dec. 1930; *s* of Thomas Patrick and Elsie May Trescowthick; *m* 1952, Norma Margaret Callaghan; two *s* two *d*. FCPA. Chairman: Charles Davis Ltd, later Harris Scarfe Holdings Ltd, 1972–98; Harris Scarfe, 1976–93. Founder Chm., Victorian Div., Aust. Olympic Team Fund; Emeritus Chm., Sport Australia Hall of Fame, 1996–99; Chairman: Minus Children's Fund, 1975–98; Sir Donald and Lady Trescowthick Foundn; Inaugural Chm., 1972–88, Patron, 1972–, Melbourne to Hobart Yacht Race Cttee; Dir, Aust. Ballet Develt, 1978–93. Pres., Peter MacCallum Cancer Inst. Appeal, 1991–94; Patron: DOXA Youth Welfare Foundn; Special Olympics Australia, 1992–98; Team Equestrian Australia, 1993–2001. Olympic OM, 1981; CLJ 1982; Knight of Magistral Grace, SMO, Malta, 1984; KCSHS 1995. *Recreations:* golf, travel, reading, painting. *Address:* PO Box 93, Toorak, Vic 3142, Australia. *T:* (3) 98266933. *Clubs:* Athenæum, Victoria Racing (Melbourne); Geelong Football.

TRETHEWEY, Ven. Frederick Martyn; Archdeacon of Dudley, since 2001; *b* 24 Jan. 1949; *s* of Kendall and Winifred Trethewey; *m* 1971, Margaret (*née* Davidson); one *s* three *d*. *Educ:* Bedford Coll., London Univ. (BA (Hons) English, 1970); Inst. of Educn, London Univ. (PGCE 1971); Oak Hill Theol Coll. (DipTh 1977). Ordained deacon, 1978, priest 1979; Curate: St Mark with St Anne, Tollington Park, London, 1978–82; St Andrew, Whitehall Park, London, 1982–87; Team Vicar, Hornsey Rise, Whitehall Park Team, 1987–88; Vicar, Brockmoor, W Midlands, 1988–2001; Chaplain, Dudley Gp of Hosps, 1988–2000; RD, Himley, 1996–2001. *Recreations:* sport, walking. *Address:* 15 Worcester Road, Droitwich, Worcs WR9 8AA. *T:* (01905) 773301.

TREUHERZ, Julian Benjamin; art historian and curator; Keeper of Art Galleries, National Museums Liverpool (formerly National Museums and Galleries on Merseyside) (Walker Art Gallery, Lady Lever Art Gallery and Sudley), 1989–2007; *b* 12 March 1947; *s* of late Werner Treuherz and Irmgard (*née* Amberg). *Educ:* Manchester Grammar Sch.; Christ Church, Oxford (MA); Univ. of East Anglia (MA). Dip. Museums Assoc. 1974. Manchester City Art Gallery: Trainee, 1971; Asst Keeper, 1972–74, Keeper, 1974–89, of Fine Art. Member: Victorian Soc. (Hon. Sec., Manchester Gp, 1972–79, Chm.,

1980–83); Cttee, Whitworth Art Gall., 1993–2004; Cttee, Lakeland Arts (formerly Lake District Art Gall. and Mus.) Trust, 1997–; Burlington Mag. Consultative Cttee, 2003–. *Publications:* Pre-Raphaelite Paintings from the Manchester City Art Gallery, 1981; Hard Times: social realism in Victorian art, 1987; (with Peter de Figueiredo) Country Houses of Cheshire, 1988; Victorian Painting, 1993; (jtly) Dante Gabriel Rossetti, 2003; (jtly) The Railway: art in the age of steam, 2008; articles in art-historical jls. *Recreations:* playing the piano, cooking, opera, Sicily. *Address:* 1 Ingestre Road, Oxton, Wirral CH43 5TZ.

TREVELYAN, (Adye) Mary; *see* Fedden, A. M.

TREVELYAN, Dennis John, CB 1981; FCIPD; Principal, Mansfield College, Oxford, 1989–96, Hon. Fellow, 1997; *b* 21 July 1929; *s* of John Henry Trevelyan; *m* 1959, Carol Coombes; one *s* one *d*. *Educ:* Enfield Grammar Sch.; University Coll., Oxford (Scholar; MA). Entered Home Office, 1950; Treasury, 1953–54; Sec. to Parly Under-Sec. of State, Home Office, 1954–55; Principal Private Sec. to Lord President of Council and Leader of House, 1964–67; Asst Sec., 1966; Asst Under-Sec. of State, NI Office, 1972–76; Home Office: Asst Under-Sec. of State, Broadcasting Dept, 1976–77; Dep. Under-Sec. of State and Dir-Gen., Prison Service, 1978–83; First CS Comr and Dep. Sec., Cabinet Office, 1983–89, retd. Secretary: Peppiatt Cttee on a Levy on Betting on Horse Races, 1960; Lord Radcliffe's Cttee of Privy Counsellors to inquire into D Notice Matters, 1967. Vice-Chm., CS Sports Council, 1980–; Vice-Pres., Industrial Participation Assoc., 1987–98; Member: Bd of Management, Eur. Inst. of Public Admin, Maastricht, 1984–89; Council, City Univ. Business Sch., 1986–89; ECCTIS Adv. Group, 1990–98; Governor: Ashridge Management Coll., 1985–89; Contemporary Dance Trust, 1986–89; Oxford Centre for Hebrew and Jewish (formerly for Postgraduate Hebrew) Studies, 1992–2008 (Emeritus Gov., 2008); Mem., Philharmonia Chorus Adv. Develt Bd, 2004–; Trustee, Dancers Resettlement Fund, 1987–91. FRSA 1986. *Recreation:* music. *Address:* Lindfield, 1 Begbroke Lane, Begbroke, Oxon OX5 1RN. *Clubs:* Athenæum, MCC; Vincent's (Oxford).

TREVELYAN, Edward Norman; Statistician - Demography, Population Division, Demographic Directorate, US Bureau of the Census, since 2006; *b* 14 Aug. 1955; *er s* of Norman Irving Trevelyan, and of Jennifer Mary Trevelyan, *d* of Arthur E. Riddett; *m* 1993, Debbie Mullin-Trevelyan; one *s* one *d*. *Educ:* Univ. of Calif, San Diego (BA History 1981); Univ. of Calif, Santa Barbara (MA Political Sci. 1986; PhD Political Sci. 1998). Survey Statistician, Governments Div., Economic Directorate, US Census Bureau, 1999–2006. *Recreation:* yachting (Gold Medal, Soling Class, Olympic Games, 1984). *Address:* 25028 Maplewood Drive, St Michaels, MD 21663, USA. *T:* (410) 7452975; *e-mail:* edward.norman.trevelyan@census.gov.

TREVELYAN, Sir Geoffrey (Washington), 5th Bt *cr* 1874, of Wallington, Northumberland; *b* 4 July 1920; *s* of Rt Hon. Sir Charles Philips Trevelyan, 3rd Bt, PC and Mary Katharine Trevelyan (*d* 1966); *S* brother, 1996; found in 1999 to be rightful claimant to Trevelyan Baronetcy of Nettlecombe, Somerset, *cr* 1662, in abeyance since 1976, but chose not to prove claim nor be entered on the Official Roll of the Baronetage as 11th Bt; *m* 1947, Gillian Isabel Wood (MBE 1999) (*d* 2000); one *s* one *d*. *Educ:* Oundle; Trinity Coll., Cambridge (MA). De Havilland Aircraft Co. Ltd, 1941–61; Dir, Chatto and Windus Ltd, 1962–77; Manager, Seatoller House, Keswick, 1978–81; Chm., The Lake Hunts Ltd, 1979–96; freelance technical writer, 1982–92. *Recreations:* hill-walking, gardening, cabinet-making. *Heir: s* Peter John Trevelyan [*b* 11 Sept. 1948; *m* 1996, Diane Terry; one *s*]. *Address:* Silkstead, 3 Abbey Mill End, St Albans, Herts AL3 4HN. *T:* (01727) 864866.

TREVELYAN, George Macaulay, CB 2005; Finance and Performance Manager, New Forest National Park Authority, since 2006; *b* 1 April 1944; *s* of late (Charles) Humphry Trevelyan and Molly Trevelyan (*née* Bennett); *m* 1st, 1966, Susan Pearson; one *s* two *d*; 2nd, 1980, Valerie Preston; one *s*; 3rd, 2002, Julia Barker (*née* McDonald). *Educ:* Queen's Coll., Oxford (BA Mod. Hist.). Joined MAFF, 1967: Principal, 1971; UK spokesman on numerous agricl mgt cttees under Common Agricl Policy, 1973–81; Mem. of Cabinet, EC Commn for Social Affairs, Brussels, 1981–84; Head, Pesticides Safety, Plant Health, and Cereals/Set Aside Divs, 1984–95; Regl Dir (SE), 1989–91; Chief Exec., Intervention Bd, 1995–2001; Dir of Ops, Foot and Mouth Disease, MAFF, subseq. DEFRA, 2001–02; Dir, Delivery Strategy Team, DEFRA, 2002–04; Managing Consultant, Hedra plc, 2005–06. Councillor (Lab), London Borough of Camden, 1971–74 (Alderman; Chm., Planning and Communications, 1975–76). *Recreations:* sailing, rowing, running. *Address:* 35 New Forest Drive, Brockenhurst, Hants SO42 7QT.

See also L. K. Trevelyan.

TREVELYAN, Laura Kate; BBC Correspondent, United Nations, since 2006; *b* 21 Aug. 1968; *d* of George Macaulay Trevelyan, *qv* and Susan (*née* Pearson); *m* 1998, James Goldston; three *s*. *Educ:* Parliament Hill Sch., London; Bristol Univ. (BA); Univ. of Wales Coll. of Cardiff (dip. newspaper journalism). Reporter, London Newspaper Gp, 1991; Researcher, A Week in Politics, Channel 4, 1991–92; BBC: Researcher, Breakfast News, 1993; Asst Producer, Newsnight, 1994; Reporter: On the Record, 1994–98; Today Prog., Radio 4, 1998–99; Political Corresp., 1999–2004; Political Corresp., Newsnight, 2000–01; Corresp., N America, 2004–06. *Publication:* A Very British Family: the Trevelyans and their world, 2006. *Recreations:* swimming, singing, walking. *Address:* United Nations, Room S475, New York, NY 10017, USA.

TREVERTON-JONES, Gregory Dennis; QC 2002; *b* 23 Nov. 1954; *s* of Paul and Margaret Treverton-Jones; *m* 1990, Tamsin Thomas; one *s* two *d*. *Educ:* Malvern Coll.; New Coll., Oxford (MA). Called to the Bar, Inner Temple, 1977. *Publication:* Imprisonment: the legal status of prisoners, 1989. *Recreations:* most sports including cricket, golf and tennis. *Address:* 39 Essex Street, WC2R 3AT. *T:* (020) 7832 1111, *Fax:* (020) 7353 3978; *e-mail:* gregtj@39essex.com. *Club:* MCC.

TREVES, Vanni Emanuele; Chairman: Equitable Life Assurance Society, since 2001; Intertek Group plc, since 2001; Senior Advisor, Oliver Wyman, since 2007; *b* 3 Nov. 1940; *s* of Giuliano Treves (partisan, killed in action, 1944), and of Marianna Treves (*née* Baer); *m* 1971, Angela Veronica Fyffe; two *s* one *d*. *Educ:* St Paul's Sch. (Foundn Scholar); University Coll. Oxford (MA); Univ. of Illinois (LLM; Fulbright Scholar). Macfarlanes: articled clerk and Solicitor, 1963–68; Partner, 1970–2002; Sen. Partner, 1987–99. Vis. Attorney, White & Case, New York, 1968–69. Director: Oceonics Group, 1984–96; Saatchi & Saatchi, 1987–90; Chairman: BBA Gp plc, 1989–2000; McKechnie plc, 1991–2000; Fledgeling Equity and Bond Funds, 1992–2000; Dennis Gp (formerly Trinity Holdings) PLC, 1996–99; Channel 4 Television, 1998–2004; Korn/Ferry Internat. UK, 2004–; Dir, Amplifon SpA, 2000–. Mem., Council for Industry and Higher Educn, 2003–06. Solicitor to Royal Acad., 1992–. Chm., Develt Cttee, Nat. Portrait Gall., 1991–99. Chairman: NSPCC Justice for Children Appeal, 1997–2000; NSPCC Organised Abuse Appeal, 2004–08. Trustee: J. Paul Getty Jr Charitable Trust, 1985–; 29th May 1961 Charitable Trust, 1970–. Vice-Pres., London Fedn of Clubs for Young People (formerly of Boys' Clubs), 1991– (Hon. Treas., 1976–95). Gov., Sadler's Wells Foundn, 1999–2008. Chairman: Governors, London Business Sch., 1998–2006 (Gov., 1996–2006); Nat. Coll. of Sch. Leadership, 2004–; Governor: Coll. of Law, 1999–2006; Hall Sch., Hampstead, 1983–94. Hon. Fellow, London Business Sch., 2006. *Recreation:* epicurean pursuits. *Address:* First Floor, 123 Buckingham Palace Road, SW1W 9DZ. *Club:* Boodle's.

TREVETHIN, 4th Baron **AND OAKSEY,** 2nd Baron; *see under* Oaksey, 2nd Baron.

TREVETT, Peter George; QC 1992; *b* 25 Nov. 1947; *s* of late George Albert Trevett and Janet Trevett; *m* 1972, Vera Lucia dos Santos Ferreira; two *s* one *d*. *Educ:* Kingston Grammar Sch.; Queens' Coll., Cambridge (MA, LLM). Called to the Bar, Lincoln's Inn, 1971 (Mansfield Schol.), Bencher, 2000; in practice at Revenue Bar, 1973–. *Publications:* contribs to legal pubns. *Recreations:* golf, reading, collecting succulent plants, gardening. *Address:* 11 New Square, Lincoln's Inn, WC2A 3QB. *T:* (020) 7242 4017.

TREVIS, Diane Ellen; theatre director; *b* 8 Nov. 1947; *d* of late Joseph Trevis and of Marjorie Trevis; *m* 1986, Dominic John Muldowney, *qv*; one *d*. *Educ:* Waverley Grammar Sch., Birmingham; Sussex Univ. Actress and dir, Glasgow Citizens' Theatre, 1972–80; Arts Council Associate Dir, Palace Theatre, Westcliff, 1982; Founder, The Workshop, Jerwood Studios, 2001, Dir, Jerwood Workshop, 2001–; Head of Directing, Drama Centre, Univ. of the Arts London, 2003–07; Artistic Dir, Rough Classics Th. Co., 2005–. Director: Royal Shakespeare Company: Taming of the Shrew, Happy End, 1985–86; The Revenger's Tragedy, 1987; Much Ado About Nothing, 1988; Elgar's Rondo, 1993; Royal National Theatre: Irish-Hebrew Lesson, 1981; The Mother, Yerma, School for Wives, A Matter of Life and Death, 1985–86; The Resistible Rise of Arturo Ui, 1991; Inadmissible Evidence, 1993; Happy Birthday Brecht, 1998; Remembrance of Things Past (adapted with Harold Pinter), 2000; Gawain, Royal Opera House, 1991; The Daughter in Law, 1996, The House of Bernarda Alba, 1997, Theatr Clwyd; Human Cannon, Ballad of California, 1997, Awake and Sing, Happy Birthday Brecht, 1998, Univ. of California; Masterclass, Th. Royal, Bath, 1999; Death of a Salesman, Birmingham Rep., 2000; The Voluptuous Tango, Pirate Jenny, Almeida Fest., 2000; Duchess of Malfi, 2005, Fears and Miseries of the Third Reich, 2006, Cochrane Th.; The Voluptuous Tango, As You Like It, 2006, Le Grand Meaulnes, 2007, Pittsburgh; Silverland, NY, 2007; An English Tragedy, The Dresser, Palace Th., Watford, 2008. *Publication:* Remembrance of Things Proust, 2001. *Recreations:* Morocco, movies, mountain walks. *Address:* c/o National Theatre, South Bank, SE1 9PX.

TREVOR, 5th Baron *cr* 1880, of Brynkinalt, co. Denbigh; **Marke Charles Hill-Trevor;** *b* 8 Jan. 1970; *s* of 4th Baron Trevor and of Susan Janet Elizabeth, *o d* of Dr Ronald Bence; *S* father, 1997. *Educ:* Rannoch Sch., Perthshire. *Heir: b* Hon. Iain Robert Hill-Trevor [*b* 12 June 1971; *m* 1998, Kate, *yr d* of David Lord; one *d*]. *Address:* Bryn Kinalt, Chirk, Clwyd LL14 5NS. *T:* (01691) 773510.

TREVOR, Thomas Henry Llewellyn; Director, Arnolfini, Bristol, since 2005; *b* 22 Nov. 1962; *s* of Tudor and Jean Trevor; *m* 1996, Zoë Shearman. *Educ:* Exeter Sch.; Exeter Coll.; Exeter Coll. of Art (Foundn); Pembroke Coll., Oxford (Ruskin Sch. Prize for Painting 1983); Goldsmiths' Coll., London (BA 1st cl. Hons Fine Art 1986). Artist, musician and music producer for TV, 1986–94; independent curator, 1994–99, incl. projs at Inst. of Internat. Visual Arts, Wellcome Trust, UCL, Camden Arts Centre and Freud Mus.; Dir, Spacex Gall., Exeter, 1999–2005, incl. two projs as part of Liverpool Biennial. Chm., Bristol Visual Arts Consortium, 2006–. Trustee: Bristol Cultural Develt Partnership, 2005–; Studio Upstairs, 2006–; Jago Eliot Foundn, 2007–. Mem., Bristol Inst. for Res. in the Humanities and Arts, Univ. of Bristol, 2006–. *Recreations:* philosophy, walking, surfing. *Address:* Arnolfini, 16 Narrow Quay, Bristol BS1 4QA. *T:* (0117) 917 2300, *Fax:* (0117) 917 2303; *e-mail:* tom.trevor@arnolfini.org.uk.

TREVOR, William, (William Trevor Cox), Hon. KBE 2002 (Hon. CBE 1977); CLit 1994; writer; *b* 24 May 1928; *er s* of J. W. Cox; *m* 1952, Jane, *yr d* of C. N. Ryan; two *s*. *Educ:* St Columba's College, Co. Dublin; Trinity College, Dublin. Mem., Irish Acad. Letters. Television plays include: The Mark-2 Wife; O Fat White Woman; The Grass Widows; The General's Day; Love Affair; Last Wishes; Matilda's England; Secret Orchards; Autumn Sunshine. Radio plays include: The Penthouse Apartment; Beyond the Pale (Giles Cooper award, 1980); Travellers; Autumn Sunshine (Giles Cooper award, 1982); Events at Drimaghleen. Hon. Mem., Amer. Acad. of Arts and Letters, 2004. Hon. DLitt: Exeter, 1984; TCD, 1986; Cork, 1990; Hon. DLit Belfast, 1989. Allied Irish Banks Award for Literature, 1976; Bennett Award, Hudson Review, USA, 1990; David Cohen British Literature Prize, 1999; Ireland Funds' Literary Prize, 2005; Nonino Internat. Prize, 2008. *Publications:* A Standard of Behaviour, 1956; The Old Boys, 1964 (Hawthornden Prize; as play, produced Mermaid, 1971); The Boarding-House, 1965; The Love Department, 1966; The Day We Got Drunk on Cake, 1967; Mrs Eckdorf in O'Neill's Hotel, 1969; Miss Gomez and the Brethren, 1971; The Ballroom of Romance, 1972 (adapted for BBC TV, 1982); Going Home (play), 1972; A Night with Mrs da Tanka (play), 1972; Marriages (play), 1973; Elizabeth Alone, 1973; Angels at the Ritz, 1975 (RSL award); The Children of Dynmouth, 1976 (Whitbread Novel Award; televised, 1987); Lovers of Their Time, 1978; Other People's Worlds, 1980; Beyond the Pale, 1981 (televised, 1989); Scenes from an Album (play), 1981; Fools of Fortune, 1983 (Whitbread Novel Award); A Writer's Ireland, 1984; The News from Ireland and other stories, 1986; Nights at the Alexandra, 1987; The Silence in the Garden, 1988; (ed) The Oxford Book of Irish Short Stories, 1989; Family Sins and other stories, 1989; Two Lives, 1991; Juliet's Story (for children), 1992; Excursions in the Real World, 1993; Felicia's Journey, 1994 (Whitbread Book of the Year Award; Sunday Express Book of the Year Award; filmed 1999); After Rain and other stories, 1996; Death in Summer, 1998; The Hill Bachelors, 2000 (PEN/Macmillan award for short stories, Irish Times Irish Lit. award); The Story of Lucy Gault, 2002 (Listowel Prize for Irish fiction, 2003); A Bit on the Side, 2004; Cheating at Canasta, 2007.

TREW, Peter John Edward, MICE; Director, Rush & Tompkins Group plc, 1973–90 (Chairman of Executive Committee, 1986–87); *b* 30 April 1932; *s* of late Antony Trew, DSC and Nora Trew (*née* Houthakker); *m* 1st, 1955, Angela (marr. diss. 1985; she *d* 1991), *d* of Kenneth Rush, CBE; two *s* one *d*; 2nd, 1985, Joan (*d* 2005), *d* of Allan Haworth. *Educ:* Diocesan Coll., Rondebosch, Cape. Royal Navy, 1950–54; served HMS Devonshire, Unicorn and Charity. Chartered Inst. of Secretaries Sir Ernest Clarke Prize, 1955. Contested (C) Dartford, 1966; MP (C) Dartford, 1970–Feb. 1974; Jt Sec., Cons. Parly Finance Cttee, 1972–74; Mem., Select Cttee on Tax Credits, 1972–73. Chm., Kent West Cons. European Constituency Council, 1978–80. Mem. Council, CBI, 1975–83 (Mem., Econ. and Fin. Policy Cttee, 1980–86). *Publications:* The Boer War Generals, 1999; Rodney and the Breaking of the Line, 2006. *Address:* 1 Painshill House, Cobham, Surrey KT11 1DL. *T:* (01932) 863315.

TREWAVAS, Prof. Anthony James, PhD; FRS 1999; FRSE; Professor of Plant Biochemistry, Edinburgh University, since 1990; *b* 17 June 1939; *s* of Clifford John Trewavas and Phyllis (*née* Timms); *m* 1963, Valerie Leng; one *s* two *d*. *Educ:* Roan Grammar Sch.; University Coll. London (BSc 1961; PhD 1964). Sen. Res. Fellow, Univ. of East Anglia, 1964–70; University of Edinburgh: Lectr, 1970–84; Reader, 1984–90.

Visiting Professor: Michigan State Univ., 1973; Univ. of Illinois, 1980; Univ. of Alberta, 1983; Univ. of Calif, Davis, 1985; Univ. of Mexico City, 1987; Univ. of Bonn, 1989; Univ. of Milan, 1996. Mem., Scottish Cttee, LEAF. Mem., Most Highly Cited Researcher gp, Inst. of Scientific Inf.; MAE 2001; Life Mem., Amer. Soc. of Plant Physiologists, 1999; Fellow, World Innovation Foundn, 2001; FRSE 1993; FRSA 1995. *Publications:* Molecular and Cellular Aspects of Calcium in Plant Development, 1985; (with David Jennings) Plasticity in Plants, 1986; 200 res. papers. *Recreations:* music, reading, thinking, good wine. *Address:* Old Schoolhouse, Croft Street, Penicuik, Midlothian EH26 9DH. *T:* (01968) 673372.

TREWEEK, Ven. Rachel; Archdeacon of Northolt, since 2006; *b* 4 Feb. 1963; *d* of Robert Steven Montgomery and Marian Montgomery; *m* 2006, Guy Matthew Treweek. *Educ:* Univ. of Reading (BA Linguistics and Lang. Pathol. (Speech Therapy) 1985); Wycliffe Hall, Oxford (BTh 1994). Paediatric Speech and Language Therapist, Hampstead Health Authority, 1985–91: Hampstead Child Develt Team, 1987–89; Manager for Therapists in Health Centres, Bloomsbury, Hampstead and Islington, 1989–91. Ordained deacon, 1994, priest, 1995; Curate, 1994–97, Associate Vicar, 1997–99, St George's, Tufnell Park; Vicar, St James-the-Less, Bethnal Green, 1999–2006. *Address:* 16 Baldwyn Gardens, W3 6HL.

TREWIN, Ion Courtenay Gill; Literary Director (formerly Administrator), Man Booker annual and International prizes, since 2006; *b* 13 July 1943; *s* of late John Courtenay Trewin, OBE and Wendy Elizabeth Trewin (*née* Monk); *m* 1965, Susan Harriet Merry; one *s* one *d*. *Educ:* Highgate Sch., London. Journalist and editorial staff: The Independent & S Devon Times, 1960–63; Sunday Telegraph, 1963–67; The Times, 1967–79: Ed., The Times Diary, 1969–72; Literary Ed., 1972–79; Ed., Drama Magazine, 1979–81; Publisher: Hodder & Stoughton, 1979–92: Sen. Ed., 1979–85; Editl Dir, 1985–91; Publishing Dir, 1991–92; Orion Publishing Group, 1992–2006: Dir, 1994–2006; Man. Dir, 1996–2001; Ed. in Chief, 2001–06; Publishing Dir, Weidenfeld & Nicolson imprint, 1992–96. Man Booker (formerly Booker) Prize for Fiction: Chm. Judges, 1974; Mem. Mgt Cttee, 1989–; Dep. Administrator, 2004–06. Special Prof., Univ. of Nottingham, 2007–. Chairman: Library Cttee, Highgate Literary and Scientific Instn, 1974–90; Soc. of Bookmen, 1986–88; Cheltenham Fest. of Literature, 1997–2006; Member: Literature Panel, Arts Council of GB, 1975–78; Arts and Library Cttee, MCC, 1988–96. Ronald Politzer Award for Innovation in Publishing, 1976. *Publications:* Journalism, 1975; Norfolk Cottage, 1977; (ed) Alan Clark's Diaries: into politics, 2000, the last diaries, 2002. *Recreations:* indulging grandchildren, gardening, watching cricket, gossip. *Address:* Beck House, 88 Chapel Road, Dersingham, Norfolk PE31 6PL; 44 Cholmeley Lodge, Cholmeley Park, N6 5EN; *e-mail:* itrewin@aol.com. *Clubs:* MCC, Garrick.

TREWSDALE, Janet Margaret, OBE 2000; CStat, FSS; Senior Lecturer in Economics, Queen's University of Belfast, 1995–2004; *b* 8 May 1944; *d* of Keith and Joan Crush; *m* 1970, Dr John M. Trewsdale (*d* 1990). *Educ:* Univ. of York (BA Econs and Stats 1967). FSS 1969; CStat 1993. Lecturer in Economic Statistics: Univ. of Kent, 1969–70; Trent Poly., 1970–71; Lectr in Econs, QUB, 1972–95. Chm., NI Econ. Council, 1998–2006; Mem., Statistics Commn, 2000–08. Vice-Pres., Royal Statistical Soc., 1983–84. *Publications:* numerous contribs to books and learned jls. *Address:* School of Management and Economics, Queen's University of Belfast, Belfast BT7 1NN. *T:* (028) 9097 3296; *e-mail:* j.trewsdale@qub.ac.uk.

TRIBE, Geoffrey Reuben, OBE 1968; Controller, Higher Education Division, British Council, 1981–83, retired; *b* 20 Feb. 1924; *s* of late Harry and Olive Tribe; *m* 1st, 1946, Sheila Mackenzie (marr. diss. 1977); 2nd, 1978, Malvina Anne Butt. *Educ:* Southern Grammar Sch., Portsmouth; University Coll. London (BA). Served War, Royal Hampshire Regt (Lieut), 1942–45. Teaching, 1948–58. Appointed to British Council, 1958; Asst Regional Rep., Madras, 1958–63; Regional Dir, Mwanza, 1963–65; Regional Rep., E Nigeria, 1965–67; Asst Controller, Personnel and Staff Recruitment, 1968–73; Controller, Arts Div., 1973–79; Representative, Nigeria, 1979–81. *Recreations:* walking, writing. *Address:* Holly Cottage, St Andrews View, Fontmell Magna, Shaftesbury, Dorset SP7 0QY. *T:* (01747) 812036.

TRICHET, Jean-Claude Anne Marie Louis; President, European Central Bank, since 2003; *b* 20 Dec. 1942; *s* of Jean Trichet and Georgette (*née* Vincent-Carrefour); *m* 1965, Aline Rybalka; two *s*. *Educ:* Ecole Nat. des Mines, Nancy; Inst. d'Etudes Politiques, Paris; Ecole Nat. d'Admin; Univ. de Paris (LèsSc Econ). Inspector of Finances, 1971–76; Sec.-Gen., Business Restructuring Interministerial Cttee, 1976–78; Advisor: Ministry of Finance, 1978; on industry, energy and res. to the President (Valéry Giscard d'Estaing), 1978–81; Dep. Asst Sec., later Asst Sec., Treasury, 1981–86; Chief of Staff to Minister of Finance (Edouard Balladur), 1986–87; Under-Sec., Treasury, 1987–93; Governor, Bank of France, 1993–2003. Chairman: Paris Club (sovereign debt rescheduling), 1985–93; EC Monetary Cttee, 1992–93; Member, Board of Directors: BIS, 1993–2003, 2006–; Eur. Central Bank (formerly Eur. Monetary Inst.), 1994–; Gov., IBRD, 1993–95; Pres., Gp of 10 Govs, 2003–. Hon. doctorates from Liège, Tel Aviv and Stirling Univs. Policy-maker of the Year, Internat. Economy, 1991, 2007; Zerilli Marimo Prize, Acad. des Scis Morales et Politiques, 1999; Pico della Mirandola Prize, 2002; Franco-German Cultural Prize, 2006; Person of the Year, FT, 2007. Commandeur, Légion d'honneur (France); Officier, Ordre National du Mérite (France); many foreign decorations, including Commander in the Orders of Austria, Belgium, Brazil, Argentina, Germany. *Publications:* articles on monetary policy, finance and economy. *Recreation:* poetry. *Address:* European Central Bank, Kaiserstrasse 29, 60311 Frankfurt-am-Main, Germany.

TRICKER, Prof. Robert Ian, DLitt; FCMA; Hon. Professor: Hong Kong Open University, since 2006; Hong Kong Baptist University, since 2007; Director, International Corporate Policy Group (formerly Corporate Policy Group, Oxford), since 1979; *b* 14 Dec. 1933; *m* 1st, 1958, Doreen Murray (marr. diss. 1982); two *d*; 2nd, 1982, Gretchen Elizabeth Bigelow. *Educ:* King Henry VIII Sch., Coventry; Harvard Business Sch., USA; DLitt CNAA, 1983. FCA 1955–2002. Articled Clerk, Daffern & Co., 1950–55; Sub-Lt, RNVR, 1956–58; Controller, Unbrako Ltd, 1959–64; Directing Staff, Iron & Steel Fedn Management Coll., 1965; Barclays Bank Prof. of Management Information Systems, Univ. of Warwick, 1968–70; Director, Oxford Centre for Management Studies, 1970–79, Professorial Fellow, 1979–84 (P. D. Leake Res. Fellow, 1966–67); Res. Fellow, Nuffield Coll., Oxford, 1979–84 (Vis. Fellow, 1971–79); Dir, Management Develt Centre of Hong Kong, 1984–86; Prof. of Finance and Accounting, Univ. of Hong Kong, 1986–96. Hon. Professor: Univ. of Hong Kong, 1996–2006; Warwick Univ., 1996–2000. Institute of Chartered Accountants in England and Wales: Mem. Council, 1979–84; Mem. Educn and Trng Directorate, 1979–82; Chairman: Examination Cttee, 1980–82; Tech. and Res. Cttee, 1982–84. Member: Council, ICMA, 1969–72; Management and Industrial Relations Cttee, SSRC, 1973–75; Chm., Independent Inquiry into Prescription Pricing Authority for Minister for Health, 1976. Member: Nuffield Hosp. Management Cttee, 1972–74; Adv. Panel on Company Law, Dept of Trade, 1980–83; Company Affairs Cttee, Inst. of Directors, 1980–84; Standing Commn on CS Salaries and Conditions of Service, Hong Kong, 1989–96. Dep. Launching Authy, Torbay Lifeboat, 2001–05. Editor, Corporate Governance—an international review, 1992–2000. *Publications:* The Accountant in Management, 1967; Strategy for Accounting Research, 1975; Management Information and Control Systems, 1976, 2nd edn 1982; The Independent Director, 1978; Effective Information Management, 1982; Governing the Institute, 1983; Corporate Governance, 1984; The Effective Director, 1986; The Director's Manual, 1990; International Corporate Governance, 1993; Harnessing Information Power, 1994; The Economist Pocket Director, 1996, 3rd edn 1999; Corporate Governance, 2000; The Economist Essential Director, 2003 (trans. Chinese and Russian, 2003). *Address:* The Hill House, 22/23 St Peter's Hill, Brixham, Devon TQ5 9TE; *e-mail:* BobTricker@aol.com. *Club:* Naval.

TRICKETT, Anthony Robert, MBE 1998; General Medical Practitioner, Island of Hoy, Orkney, since 1973; Lord-Lieutenant of Orkney, since 2007 (Vice Lord-Lieutenant, 2005–07); *b* 16 Feb. 1940; *s* of late Robert Edward Trickett and Phyllis Trickett (*née* Grocott); *m* 1996, Elizabeth Jean Sadler; three *s* one *d*. *Educ:* Willaston Primary Sch.; Nantwich and Acton Grammar Sch.; Manchester Univ. Med. Sch. MRCS, LRCP 1964. Resident hosp. appts in Manchester, 1964–66; Demonstrator in Anatomy, Manchester Univ., 1966–67; GP, Pembroke, Dyfed, 1967–73. Director: Orkney Enterprise, 2001–06; Hoy & Walls Develt Assoc., 2004–. Hon. Med. Advr, 1973–, Hon. Sec., subseq. Lifeboat Ops Manager, 1995–, Longhope Lifeboat Stn; Med. Referee, 2003–05, Area Med. Advr, 2005–, RNLI (Scotland); Mem., Med. and Survival Cttee, RNLI, 2003–. Chairman: Longhope Lifeboat Mus. Trust, 2001–; Soc. of Friends of St Magnus Cath., 2007–; Orkney Children's Trust, 2007–; Orkney Heritage Property Trust, 2007–; Trustee: Hoy Trust, 1984– (Chm., 1992–); Pickaquay Centre, Kirkwall, 2004–07; Orkney Archaeol Trust, 2007–. Founder and Chm., Hoy Half-Marathon, 1985–. Dir, Gable End Th., Hoy, 2005–. DL Orkney, 1999. Silver Badge, 1994, Gold Badge, 2004, RNLI. *Recreations:* growing trees, hill walking, traditional dancing, ecology, almost all music, especially live, fitness promotion, running - ever more slowly, striving to ward off geriatric decrepitude. *Address:* Glebelands, Longhope, Hoy, Orkney KW16 3PA. *T:* (01856) 701460, *Fax:* (01856) 701294; *e-mail:* tony@hoyorkney.co.uk.

TRICKETT, Jon Hedley; MP (Lab) Hemsworth, since Feb. 1996; *b* 2 July 1950; *s* of Lawrence and Rose Trickett; *m* 1969 (marr. diss.); one *s* one *d*; *m* 1994, Sarah Balfour. *Educ:* Hull Univ. (BA Politics); Leeds Univ. (MA Pol Sociol). Builder/plumber, to 1985. Joined Labour Party, 1971; Leeds City Council: Councillor, Beeston Ward, 1985–96; Chair: Finance Cttee, 1986–89; Housing Cttee, 1988–89; Leader, 1989–96. Chm., Leeds City Development Co., 1989–96; Member of Board: Leeds Development Corp., 1992–96; Leeds Health Care, 1992–96; Director: Leeds/Bradford Airport, 1988–96; Leeds Playhouse, 1988–96; Leeds Theatre Co., 1988–96. PPS to Minister Without Portfolio, 1997–98, to Sec. of State for Trade and Industry, 1998, to the Prime Minister, 2008–. Mem., Public Accounts Select Cttee, 2001–. Mem., GMBATU. *Recreations:* cycling, sailboarding. *Address:* 1a Highfield Road, Hemsworth, West Yorkshire WF9 4DT. *T:* (01977) 722290; House of Commons, SW1A 0AA. *Club:* Cyclists Touring.

TRICKEY, Very Rev. (Frederick) Marc; Dean of Guernsey, 1995–2003; Rector of St Martin de la Bellouse, Guernsey, 1977–2002; Priest-in-charge of Sark, 1996–2003; *b* 16 Aug. 1935; *s* of Alan Paul Trickey and Isabella Livingston (*née* Gunn); *m* 1963, Elisabeth Marriette Plummer; one *s* one *d*. *Educ:* Bristol Grammar Sch.; St John's Coll., Univ. of Durham (BA (Hons) Psychol. 1962; DipTh 1964). Commercial trainee, Nat. Smelting Co. Ltd, Avonmouth, Bristol, 1954–59. Ordained deacon, 1964, priest, 1965; Asst Curate, St Lawrence, Alton, Hants, 1964–68; Rector of St John with Winnall, Winchester, 1968–77. Mem., General Synod of C of E, 1995–2000. Hon. Canon of Winchester Cathedral, 1995–2003, Canon Emeritus, 2003. States of Guernsey: Pres., Ecclesiastical Cttee, 1995–2003; Chairman: Panel of Appeal, Public Assistance Authy, 1985–96; RPI Steering Gp, 1996–; Member: Broadcasting Cttee, 1977–2004; Bd of Industry, 1982–95; Housing Appeal Tribunal, 2005–. Chairman: Guernsey Hard of Hearing Assoc., 1983–95 (Pres., 1995–); MIND, Guernsey, 1985–2002 (Pres., 2002–). Chaplain: Guernsey Assoc. RN and RM, 1977–; St John Ambulance, Guernsey, 2004–. *Publication:* Your Marriage, 1987. *Recreations:* singing, embroidery, walking, photography. *Address:* L'Espérance, La Route des Camps, St Martin's, Guernsey GY4 6AD. *T:* (01481) 238441, *Fax:* (01481) 231018; *e-mail:* fmt@cwgsy.net.

TRICKEY, Jane Elizabeth; *see* Hutt, J. E.

TRIESMAN, Baron *cr* 2004 (Life Peer), of Tottenham in the London Borough of Haringey; **David Maxim Triesman;** Chairman, Football Association, since 2008; *b* 30 Oct. 1943; *s* of Michael Triesman and Rita (*née* Lubran); *m* 2004, Lucy Hooberman. *Educ:* Stationers' Co. Sch., London; Univ. of Essex (BA Hons, MA Philosophy); King's Coll., Cambridge. FSS 1984. Res. Officer in Addiction, Inst. of Psychiatry, 1970–74; ASTMS secondment, 1974–75; Sen. Lectr and co-ord. postgrad. res., Poly. of S Bank, 1975–84; Dep. Sec. Gen. (Nat. Negotiating Sec.), NATFHE, 1984–93; General Secretary: AUT, 1993–2001; Lab. Party, 2001–03. A Lord in Waiting (Govt Whip), 2004–05; Parliamentary Under-Secretary of State: FCO, 2005–07; DIUS, 2007–08. Vis. Prof. in Social Econ., S Lawrence Univ., 1977; Vis. Fellow, Univ. of London Inst. of Educn, 1993–96; Visiting Fellow: in Econs, Wolfson Coll., Cambridge, 2000–; in Govt, LSE, 2005–; Sen. Associate Fellow, Sch. of Engrg, Warwick Univ., 2004–. Member: Greater London Manpower Bd, 1981–86; Home Office Consultative Cttee on Prison Educn, 1980–83; Burnham Further and Higher Educn Cttee, 1980–84; Univ. Entrance and Schs Exams Bd for Soc. Sci., 1980–84; Standing Cttee on Business and the Community, HEFCE, 1999–2002. Mem., Kensington, Chelsea and Westminster AHA, 1976–82. Member: Industrial Relns Public Appointments Panel, DTI, 1996–2001; Indep. Review of Higher Educn Pay and Conditions, 1998–99; Cabinet Office Better Regulation Task Force, 2000–01; Treasury Public Services Productivity Panel, 2000–02; British N American Cttee, 1999–. Non-executive Chairman: Mortgage Credit Corp., 1978–2001; Victoria Mgt Ltd, 2000–01. Chm., Usecolor Foundn, 2001. Member: Fabian Soc., 1974–; Charles Rennie Mackintosh Soc., Glasgow, 1986–; Highgate Literary and Scientific Inst., 1990–. Treas., Public Sector Reform Gp, 2007–. Mem. Council, Ruskin Coll., Oxford, 2000–02; Mem. Governing Council and Hon. Fellow, Univ. of Northampton (formerly Nene Coll. of Higher Educn, then UC Northampton), 1996–. Patron, Tottenham Hotspur Foundn, 2007–; Trustee, Football Foundn, 2008–. Mem. Bd, Wembley Nat. Stadium Ltd, 2008–. FRSA 1990. *Publications:* The Medical and Non-Medical Use of Drugs, 1969; (with G. Viani) Football Mania, 1972; Football in London, 1985; (jtly) College Administration, 1988; Managing Change, 1991; Can Unions Survive (Staniewski Meml Lect.), 1999; Higher Education for the New Century, 2000. *Recreations:* football, art, reading, walking. *Address:* House of Lords, SW1A 0PW; Football Association, 25 Soho Square, W1D 4FA. *Clubs:* Middlesex CC; Tottenham Hotspurs' Supporters.

TRIFFITT, Jayne; Head, Woldingham School, since 2007; *b* Newquay, 14 June 1957; *d* of Kenneth and Margaret Woolcock; *m* 1982, Dr John Triffitt; one *s* one *d*. *Educ:* Truro High Sch.; St Hilda's Coll., Oxford (BA Chem. 1980; PGCE 1981). Teacher of Chemistry and Science: King Alfred's Sch., Wantage, 1981–85; St Michael's Grammar Sch., Finchley, 1985–86; Hd of Chem., St Angela's Sch., Palmer's Green, 1986–88; Hd of Sci., La Sainte Union Sch., London, 1988–98; Head of Sixth Form, St Mary's Sch., Ascot, 1998–2001; Headmistress, St Mary's Sch., Cambridge, 2001–07. *Recreations:* family, swimming, Cornwall. *Address:* Woldingham School, Marden Park, Woldingham, Surrey CR3 7YA. *T:* (01883) 654205, *Fax:* (01883) 348653; *e-mail:* triffittj@woldingham.surrey.sch.uk.

TRIGGER, Ian James Campbell; His Honour Judge Trigger; a Circuit Judge, since 1993; *b* 16 Nov. 1943; *s* of late Walter James Trigger and Mary Elizabeth Trigger; *m* 1971, Jennifer Ann Downs; two *s. Educ:* Ruthin Sch.; UCW, Aberystwyth (LLB); Downing Coll., Cambridge (MA, LLM). Called to the Bar, Inner Temple, 1970 (major scholarship, 1967); Lectr in Law, UWIST, 1967–70; practice on Northern Circuit, 1970–93. Pt-time Pres., Mental Health Review Tribunal, 1995–; pt-time Chm., Immigration Appeal Tribunal, 1999–2005; pt-time Immigration Judge, 2005–. Church in Wales: Lay Reader, 2005–; Judge, Provincial Council, 2006–. *Recreations:* gardening, walking, spending time with family. *Address:* Queen Elizabeth II Law Courts, Derby Square, Liverpool L2 1XA. *T:* (0151) 473 7373.

TRIMBLE, family name of **Baron Trimble**.

TRIMBLE, Baron *cr* 2006 (Life Peer), of Lisnagarvey in the County of Antrim; **William David Trimble;** PC 1998; Member (UU) Upper Bann, 1998–2007, and First Minister, 1998–2002, Northern Ireland Assembly; *b* 15 Oct. 1944; *s* of William and Ivy Trimble; *m* 1978, Daphne Orr; two *s* two *d. Educ:* Bangor Grammar Sch.; Queen's University Belfast (LLB). Called to the Bar of Northern Ireland, 1969; Lectr, 1968, Sen. Lectr, 1977, Faculty of Law, QUB. Mem., Constitutional Convention, 1975–76. MP (UU) Upper Bann, May 1990–2005; contested (UU) same seat, 2005. Leader, Ulster Unionist Party, 1995–2005. (Jtly) Nobel Peace Prize, 1998. *Publications:* Northern Ireland Housing Law, 1986; NI Law Reports, 1975–90. *Recreations:* music, reading. *Address:* (office) 11 Rathfriland Street, Banbridge, Co. Down BT32 3LA.

TRIMBLE, Dame Jenifer; *see* Wilson-Barnett, Dame J.

TRIMLESTOWN, 21st Baron *cr* 1461 (Ire.), of Trimlestown, co. Meath; **Raymond Charles Barnewall;** *b* 29 Dec. 1930; *yr s* of 19th Baron Trimlestown and Muriel (*d* 1937), *d* of Edward Oskar Schneider; *S* brother, 1997. *Educ:* Ampleforth.

TRIMMER, Sir Jon (Charles), KNZM 1999; MBE 1974; Senior Artiste, Royal New Zealand Ballet, since 1993; *b* 18 Sept. 1939; *s* of Charles Trimmer and Lily Pamela (*née* Arrowsmith); *m* 1963, Jacqui de Joux Oswald. *Educ:* Wellington Tech. Coll. Art Sch., NZ. Joined Royal NZ Ballet, 1958; with Sadler's Wells, London, 1960–61; Australian Ballet, 1965–66; Royal Danish Ballet, 1969–71; has performed in 5 Royal Command Performances in NZ and overseas; rôles in dramatic plays on stage and TV. Patron, several arts and dance socs in NZ. Fulbright Scholar, NY, 1981. Turnovsky Award, NZ, 1986. Commemoration Medal (NZ), 1990. *Recreations:* pottery, gardening, writing short stories, painting. *Address:* 29 Ocean Road, Paekakariki, Kapiti Coast, New Zealand.

TRIMMER, Stuart Alan; QC 2006; *b* 5 Oct. 1954; *s* of Alan and Vera Trimmer; *m* 1982, Fiona Hester; two *s* one *d. Educ:* Yeovil Sch.; Poly. of North London (LLB London 1976). Called to the Bar, Gray's Inn, 1977; Jt Head, Valios & Boardman Chambers, 2007–. *Recreations:* active church member, youth camp organiser. *Address:* Valios & Boardman Chambers, 4 Breams Buildings, Chancery Lane, EC4A 1HP. *T:* (020) 7092 1900, *Fax:* (020) 7092 1999; *e-mail:* stuart.trimmer@virgin.net.

TRINDER, Frederick William; Charity Commissioner, 1984–85; *b* 18 Nov. 1930; *s* of Charles Elliott Trinder and Grace Johanna Trinder (*née* Hoadly); *m* 1964, Christiane Friederike Brigitte Dorothea (*née* Hase) (*d* 1994); one *s. Educ:* Ruskin Coll., Oxford (Dip. Pols and Econs); LSE, Univ. of London (BSc). Admitted Solicitor, 1966; Legal Asst/Sen. Legal Asst, Charity Commn, 1966–74; Dep. Charity Comr, 1974–84. Mem., BBC and IBA Central Appeals Adv. Cttees, 1986–92. Trustee, Charities Official Investment Fund, 1988–2002. Mem. (Lab), Wandsworth BC, 1953–56, 1959–62. *Recreations:* travel, gardening, music. *Address:* 37 The Common, West Wratting, Cambridge CB21 5LR. *T:* (01223) 290469.

TRINICK, Christopher John; DL; Chief Executive, Lancashire County Council, 2002–08; *b* 26 Dec. 1948; *s* of George Herbert Trinick and Mary Elizabeth Trinick (*née* Burton); *m* 1976, Pamela May Hall; three *d. Educ:* Northumberland Coll. of Educn (Teacher's Cert. 1971); Univ. of Newcastle (BPhil 1980); Brunel Univ. (MA 1984). Teacher, Kelvin Hall, Hull, 1971–75; Head of House, Seaton Burn High Sch., N Tyneside, 1975–79; Professional Asst, Ealing LBC, 1979–82; Special Educnl Needs Prin. Officer, Bradford MBC, 1982–87; Dep. Chief Educn Officer, Salford City Council, 1987–91; Dir of Educn, Solihull MBC, 1991–96; Chief Educn Officer, then Dir of Educn and Cultural Services, 1996–2001, Exec. Dir for Change, 2001–02, Lancs CC. Clerk, Lancs Lieutenancy, 2002–08; Sec., Lancs Adv. Cttee, 2002–08. Director: E Lancs TEC, 1996–99; Adult Learning Inspectorate, 2001–07 (Vice Chm., 2005); Excellence NW, 2001–05. Mem. Bd, OFSTED, 2007– (Chm., Audit Cttee, 2007–). Mem., All Souls Gp, 2002–04. Treasurer: Soc. of Educn Officers, 1997–2002; Schs Curriculum Award, 1997–2002; Sec., Primary Educn Study Gp, 1997–2002. Mem. Bd, Foundn for IT in Local Govt, 1992–2004; Chm., ACCE, 2007–08 (Vice Chm., 2006–07). Sec., Lord Chancellor's Adv. Cttee on Gen. Comrs of Income Tax, 2002–08. Pro-Chancellor, Edge Hill Univ., 2008–. DL Lancs, 2008. *Recreations:* gardening, outdoors, fly fishing. *Address:* Beech Cottage, Borwick, Carnforth, Lancs LA6 1JT.

TRIPP, Rt Rev. Howard George; an Auxiliary Bishop in Southwark, (RC), 1980–2004, now Emeritus; Titular Bishop of Newport, since 1980; *b* 3 July 1927; *s* of late Basil Howard Tripp and Alice Emily Tripp (*née* Haslett). *Educ:* John Fisher School, Purley; St John's Seminary, Wonersh. Priest, 1953; Assistant Priest: Blackheath SE3, 1953–56; East Sheen, 1956–62; Asst Diocesan Financial Sec., 1962–68; Parish Priest, East Sheen, 1965–71; Dir, Southwark Catholic Children's Soc., 1971–80; VG, 1980–2006. Chm., London Churches Gp, 1993–98. *Recreation:* vegetable gardening. *Address:* 67 Haynt Walk, SW20 9NY. *T:* (020) 8543 4864; *e-mail:* htripp@tiscali.co.uk.

TRIPP, (John) Peter, CMG 1971; Consultant, Al-Tajir Bank, since 1986; *b* 27 March 1921; *s* of Charles Howard and Constance Tripp; *m* 1948, Rosemary Rees Jones; one *s* one *d. Educ:* Bedford Sch.; Sutton Valence Sch.; L'Institut de Touraine. Served War of 1939–45, Royal Marines, 1941–46. Sudan Political Service, 1946–54; Foreign (subsequently Diplomatic) Service, 1954–81; Political Agent, Trucial States, 1955–58; Head of Chancery, Vienna, 1958–61; Economic Secretary, Residency Bahrain, 1961–63; Counsellor 1963; Political Agent, Bahrain, 1963–65; sabbatical year at Durham Univ., 1965; Amman, 1966–68; Head of Near Eastern Dept, FCO, 1969–70; Ambassador to Libya, 1970–74; High Comr in Singapore, 1974–78; Ambassador to Thailand, 1978–81. Political Adviser, Inchcape Gp, 1981–86; Chm., Private Investment Co. for Asia (UK), 1981–84. County Councillor (Ind.), Powys, 1985–87. Chairman: Anglo-Thai Soc., 1983–88; Montgomeryshire Br., CPRW, 1990–94. *Recreations:* theatre, gardening. *Address:* Tanyffridd, Llanfechain, Powys SY22 6UE.

TRIPPIER, Sir David (Austin), Kt 1992; RD 1983; JP; DL; Chairman, W. H. Ireland PLC, Stockbrokers, 1994–2008; *b* 15 May 1946; *s* of late Austin Wilkinson Trippier, MC and Mary Trippier; *m* 1975, Ruth Worthington, Barrister; three *s. Educ:* Bury Grammar School. Commnd Officer, Royal Marines Reserve, 1968 (qualif. parachutist, 1970; sc 1982). Member of Stock Exchange, 1968–; Chairman: Murray VCT, 1995–2005; Cambridgeshire Horizons Ltd, 2004–. Mem., Rochdale Council, 1969–78, Leader Cons. Gp, 1974–76. MP (C) Rossendale, 1979–83, Rossendale and Darwen, 1983–92; contested (C) Rossendale and Darwen, 1992. Sec., Cons. Parly Defence Cttee, 1980–82; PPS to Minister for Health, 1982–83; Parliamentary Under-Secretary of State: (Minister for Small Firms and Enterprise) DTI, 1983–85; Dept of Employment, 1985–87; DoE, 1987–89; Minister of State (Minister for the Envmt and Countryside), DoE, 1989–92. Dep. Chm., Cons. Party, 1990–91. Nat. Vice Chm., Assoc. of Cons. Clubs, 1980–84. Chairman: Tepnel Diagnostics PLC, 1992–94; Envirosystems Ltd, 1992–99; Davenham Gp, 1994–96; Marketing Manchester Ltd, 1996–99; Vector Investments Ltd, 1996–2000; Director: Dunlop Heywood & Co., 1992–99; St Modwen Properties, 1992–2004; Sir David Trippier & Associates, 1992–; Murray Income plc, 1996–2005; Nord Anglia Educn PLC, 1996–2007; Camfil Air Filters Ltd, 1998–2000; UCG Ltd, 2001–03; ITV Granada (formerly Granada) Television Ltd, 2002–07; Consultant: Halliwell Landau, 1992–; Waste Management, 1992–97; Halliday Meecham, 1992–99. President: Manchester Chamber of Commerce and Industry, 1999–2000; Royal Lancs Agricl Soc., 1999–2000. Chm., Tidy Britain Gp, 1996–98. Governor, Manchester Grammar Sch., 1992–2005. President: Northern Reg., RM Assoc., 1988–93; Lancs, RBL, 2004–07; Chm., NW of England Reserve Forces and Cadets Assoc., 2000–08; Vice-Chm., RFCA (RM), 1999–2008. Hon. Col, RM Reserve, Merseyside, 1996–. FRSA 2006. JP Rochdale, 1975; DL Lancs, 1994, High Sheriff, Lancs, 1997–98. OStJ 2000. *Publications:* Defending the Peace, 1982; New Life for Inner Cities, 1989; Lend Me Your Ears (autobiog.), 1999. *Recreation:* gardening. *Address:* Dowry Head, Helmshore, Rossendale, Lancs BB4 4AE. *Club:* Army and Navy.

TRITTON, Alan George, CBE 1999; DL; Director, Barclays Bank Ltd, 1974–91; *b* 2 Oct. 1931; *s* of George Henton Tritton, Lyons Hall, Essex, and Iris Mary Baillie, Lochloy; *m* 1st, 1958, Elizabeth Clare d'Abreu (marr. diss.); two *s* one *d*; 2nd, 1972, Diana Marion Spencer. *Educ:* Eton. Member of British Schools Exploring Soc. Expedn, Arctic Norway, 1949. Lt, 1st Batt. Seaforth Highlanders, active service Pahang, Malaya, 1950–52. Leader, S Orkneys Survey Station, 1952–54, and Antarctic Relief Voyage, 1954, Falkland Islands Dependencies Survey; entered Barclays Bank Ltd, 1954; local Dir, 54 Lombard Street, 1964; Dir, Barclays Bank UK Management Ltd, 1972; India Adv., Barclays Bank, 1992–95. Dir, 1976–99, a Vice-Pres., 1983–99, Equitable Life Assce Soc.; Chairman: Plantation and Gen. Investments, 1994–96; University Life Assce Soc., 1994–99; Permanent Insurance Co. Ltd, 1995–99. A Vice-Pres., Royal Geographical Soc., 1983–86 (Mem. Council, 1975–96, Hon. Treas., 1984–96). Member: Cttee, British Trans-Arctic Expedn, 1966–69; Cttee, British Everest SW Face Expedn, 1974–75; Cttee of Management, Mount Everest Foundn, 1976–80; Friends' Cttee, Scott Polar Research Inst., 1976–80. Chairman: Westminster Abbey Investment Cttee, 1976–94; Calcutta Tercentenary Trust, 1989–2004; Member: Council, Internat. Chamber of Commerce, 1975–90 (Hon. Treas. 1985); Council, Foundn for Aviation and Sustainable Tourism, New Delhi, 1994–; Finance Cttee, 1997–, Council, 1999–2004, 2006–, Royal Asiatic Soc.; Court, Essex Univ., 1995–. Trustee: Brentwood Cathedral Trust, 1996–; Falkland Is Conservation Trust, 1998–2003. High Sheriff, 1992, DL 1993, Essex. *Recreations:* travelling, shooting. *Clubs:* Boodle's, Antarctic, Geographical, Essex; Tollygunge (Calcutta).

TRITTON, Major Sir Anthony (John Ernest), 4th Bt *cr* 1905; *b* 4 March 1927; *s* of Sir Geoffrey Ernest Tritton, 3rd Bt, CBE, and Mary Patience Winifred (*d* 1960), *d* of John Kenneth Foster; *S* father, 1976; *m* 1957, Diana, *d* of Rear-Adm. St J. A. Micklethwait, CB, DSO, and of Clemence Penelope Olga Welby-Everard; one *s* one *d. Educ:* Eton. Commissioned 3rd Hussars, Oct. 1945; retired as Major, 1964, The Queen's Own Hussars. *Recreations:* shooting, fishing. *Heir: s* Jeremy Ernest Tritton, *b* 6 Oct. 1961. *Address:* River House, Heytesbury, Wilts BA12 0EE. *Club:* Cavalry and Guards.

TRITTON, (Elizabeth) Clare, (Clare McLaren-Throckmorton; Mrs Andrew McLaren); QC 1988; Chief Executive, Throckmorton Estates; *b* 18 Aug. 1935; *d* of Prof. Alfonsus d'Abreu and Elizabeth d'Abreu (*née* Throckmorton); *m* 1st, 1958, Alan Tritton, *qv* (marr. diss. 1971); two *s* one *d*; 2nd, 1973, Andrew McLaren (*d* 2007); name changed to McLaren-Throckmorton by deed poll, 1991, following death of uncle, Sir Robert Throckmorton, 11th Bt. *Educ:* Convent of the Holy Child Jesus, Mayfield, St Leonards; Univ. of Birmingham (BA Hons English). Called to the Bar, Inner Temple, 1968. Lived and worked in USA, France, Germany and Italy, intermittently, 1952–86; Centre Organiser, WVS, 1963–64; Charlemagne Chambers, Brussels, 1985–87; founded European Law Chambers, 1987. Chm., Bar European Group, 1982–84; Vice Chm., Internat. Practice Cttee, Gen. Council of the Bar, 1988–91; Chm., Sub Cttee on Eur. Legislation, Hansard Commn on Legislative Reform, 1991–93. Member: Council, Bow Gp, 1963–65; Eur. Cttee, British Invisible Exports Council, 1989–93; Monopolies and Mergers Commn, 1993–97. Dir, Severn Trent plc, 1991–2003. Indep. Mem., Council, FIMBRA, 1991–98. Mem. Cttee, Warwicks CLA, 2004–. Trustee Dir, Birmingham Royal Ballet Trust Co. Ltd, 1996–99. Chm., Primary Immunodeficiency Assoc., 2002–05. Founder, Bar European News, 1983. *Publications:* articles in law magazines on EEC and private internat. law. *Recreations:* reading, gardening, children, travel. *Address:* Coughton Court, Alcester, Warwicks B49 5JA. *T:* (01789) 400777; *e-mail:* secretary@throckmortons.co.uk; Estate Office, Molland, South Molton, North Devon EX36 3ND. *T:* (01769) 550325.

TROLLOPE, Andrew David Hedderwick; QC 1991; a Recorder of the Crown Court, since 1989; *b* 6 Nov. 1948; *s* of late Arthur George Cecil Trollope and of Rosemary (*née* Hodson); *m* 1978, Anne Forbes; two *s. Educ:* Charterhouse; Univ. of Nancy. Called to the Bar, Inner Temple, 1971, Bencher, 2002; Asst Recorder, 1985–89. Chm., N London Bar Mess, 1998–2001. Member: South Eastern Circuit Cttee, 1990–93, 1994–97; Cttee, Criminal Bar Assoc., 1991–2001; Internat. Relns Cttee, Bar Council, 2001–; Mem. Council of Mgt, 2001–06, Mem. Adv. Council, 2006–, British Inst. of Internat. and Comparative Law. Fellow, Soc. of Advanced Legal Studies, 1998. *Recreations:* opera, jazz, swimming, tennis, sailing, travel. *Address:* 187 Fleet Street, EC4A 2AT. *T:* (020) 7430 7430, *Fax:* (020) 7430 7431. *Clubs:* Garrick, Hurlingham.

See also J. Trollope.

TROLLOPE, Sir Anthony (Simon), 17th Bt *cr* 1642, of Casewick, Lincolnshire; schoolteacher; *b* 31 Aug. 1945; *s* of Sir Anthony Owen Clavering Trollope, 16th Bt and of Joan Mary Alexis, *d* of Alexis Robert Gibbs; *S* father, 1987; *m* 1969, Denise, *d* of Trevern and Vida Thompson; two *d. Educ:* Univ. of Sydney (BA 1969); Univ. of New England (MBA 1998); Univ. of Western Sydney (BTeaching 2002). Breeder, in partnership with his wife, of Anglo-Arabian horses and Rhodesian Ridgeback dogs. Mem., Australian Marketing Inst., 1988–. *Heir: b* Hugh Irwin Trollope [*b* 31 March 1947; *m* 1971, Barbara Anne, *d* of William Ian Jamieson; one *s* two *d*]. *Address:* 28 Midson Road,

Oakville, NSW 2765, Australia. *Clubs:* Gordon Rugby, Rhodesian Ridgeback, Arab Horse Society of Australia (Sydney); PH Town Sporting.

TROLLOPE, Joanna, OBE 1996; writer; *b* 9 Dec. 1943; *er d* of late Arthur George Cecil Trollope and of Rosemary Trollope (*née* Hodson); *m* 1st, 1966, David Roger William Potter, *qv* (marr. diss. 1983); two *d*; 2nd, 1985, Ian Bayley Curteis, *qv* (marr. diss. 2001); two step *s*. *Educ:* Reigate County Sch. for Girls; St Hugh's Coll., Oxford (Gamble Scholar; MA 1972). Inf. and Research Dept, Foreign Office, 1965–67; teaching posts, 1967–79, incl. Farnham Girls' Grammar Sch., adult educn, English for foreigners and at Daneshill Sch. Writer in Residence, Victoria Magazine, USA, 1999. Chm., DNH Adv. Cttee on Nat. Reading Initiative, 1996–97; Mem. Govt Adv. Body, Nat. Year of Reading, 1998. Vice President: Trollope Soc., 1995–; West Country Writers' Assoc., 1998–; Mem. Council, Soc. of Authors, 1997–. Trustee, Joanna Trollope Charitable Trust, 1995–. Patron, Mulberry Bush Sch., Witney, 2006–. *Publications:* Eliza Stanhope, 1978; Parson Harding's Daughter, 1979 (reissued under pseudonym Caroline Harvey, 1995); Leaves from the Valley, 1980; The City of Gems, 1981; The Steps of the Sun, 1983 (reissued under pseudonym Caroline Harvey, 1996); Britannia's Daughters: a study of women in the British Empire, 1983; The Taverners' Place, 1986 (reissued under pseudonym Caroline Harvey, 2000); The Choir, 1988 (televised, 1995); A Village Affair, 1989 (televised, 1994); A Passionate Man, 1990; The Rector's Wife, 1991 (televised, 1994); The Men and the Girls, 1992; A Spanish Lover, 1993; (ed) The Country Habit: an anthology, 1993; The Best of Friends, 1995; Next of Kin, 1996; Other People's Children, 1998 (televised, 2000); Marrying the Mistress, 2000 (dramatised for stage, 2005); Girl from the South, 2002; Brother and Sister, 2004; The Book Boy, 2006; Second Honeymoon, 2006; Friday Nights, 2008; *as Caroline Harvey:* Legacy of Love, 1992; A Second Legacy, 1993; A Castle in Italy, 1993; The Brass Dolphin, 1997; contribs to newspapers and magazines. *Recreations:* reading, conversation, very long baths. *Address:* c/o United Agents, 12–26 Lexington Street, W1F 0LE; *web:* www.joannatrollope.com.
See also A. D. H. Trollope.

TRONCHETTI PROVERA, Marco; Chairman: Pirelli & Co. Real Estate SpA, Milan, since 1991; Pirelli & Co. SpA, Milan, since 2003; *b* Milan, 1948; *m*; three *c*. *Educ:* Bocconi Univ., Milan (grad. 1971). Founder, holding co. in field of maritime transportation, 1973–86; joined Pirelli Gp, 1986; Partner, Pirelli & Co., 1986–; Man. Dir and Gen. Manager, Société Internationale Pirelli SA, Basle, 1988–92; Pirelli SpA: Man. Dir and Gen. Manager, Finance and Admin and Gen. Affairs, 1991–92; Exec. Dep. Chm. and Man. Dir, 1992–96; Dep. Chm., 1995–99, Chm., 1999–2003, Pirelli & Co.; Chm. and CEO, Pirelli SpA, 1996–2003; Chairman: Olimpia SpA, 2001–; Telecom Italia SpA, 2001–06; Dep. Chm. and Man. Dir, Olivetti SpA, 2001–. Chm., CAMFIN SpA, Milan. Member: Internat. Adv. Bd, Allianz; Internat. Council, JP Morgan; European Adv. Cttee, NY Stock Exchange. Dep. Chm., Confindustria (Confedn of Italian Industries), 2000–. Board Member: Teatro alla Scala Foundn; Univ. Commerciale Luigi Bocconi; FC Internazionale SpA. Italian Chm., Council for US and Italy. Member: Assonime Steering Cttee; European Round Table of Industrialists; Italian Gp, Trilateral Commn. *Address:* Pirelli & Co. SpA, Via Gaetano Negri 10, 20123 Milan, Italy.

TROOP, Patricia Ann, (Mrs P. A. Dittner), CBE 2001; FRCP, FFPH; Chief Executive, Health Protection Agency, 2003–08; *b* 5 April 1948; *d* of John Ronald Troop and Phoebe Margaret Troop; *m* 1979, Michael Dittner; one *s* one *d*. *Educ:* Manchester Univ. Med. Sch. (MB ChB 1971; MSc Community Medicine 1979); MA Cantab 1988. MFCM 1980, FFPHM (FFCM 1986); FRCP 2001. Dir of Public Health, Cambridge HA, 1988–91; Associate Lectr, Faculty of Medicine, Cambridge Univ., 1988–; Chief Executive: Cambridge HA, 1990–93; Cambs Family Health Services, 1992–93; Director of Public Health: East Anglia RHA, 1993–95; Anglia and Oxford, then Eastern, Regl Office, NHS Exec., DoH, 1995–99; Dep. CMO, DoH, 1999–2003. Mem. and Vice-Chm., Cambs TEC, 1992–93. Vis. Prof., LSHTM, 2000–; Hon. Prof., City Univ., 2003–. Mem., Lucy Cavendish Coll., Cambridge, 1990–99. Hon. DSc: East Anglia, 2005; Cranfield, 2006. *Publications:* articles in various med. jls. *Recreations:* sailing, painting. *Address:* 47a Lode Way, Haddenham, Ely, Cambs CB6 3UL. *T:* (01353) 741087.

TROSS, Jonathan Edward Simon, CB 2004; consultant; non-executive Director, National Institute for Health and Clinical Excellence, since 2007; Member, Trustee Board, and Treasurer, Citizens Advice, since 2005; *b* 21 Jan. 1949; *s* of late Francis Tross and Audrey (*née* Payne); *m* 1972, Ann Humphries; one *s* one *d*. *Educ:* Chislehurst and Sidcup Grammar Sch.; University Coll., Oxford (BA Hons Modern Hist., 1970). Teacher in Kenya, 1971; Department of Health and Social Security: grad. trainee, 1972; Principal, 1977–84; Asst Sec., Supplementary Benefits Review, 1984–87; Asst Dir, Corporate Div., Barclays Bank, on secondment, 1987–90; Pharmaceutical Industry Br., DoH, 1990–91; G3, Head of Planning and Finance Div., 1991–94, G2, Dir of Corporate Mgt, 1994–99, DSS; G2, Head of Constitution Secretariat, Cabinet Office, 1999–2001; Chief Exec., CAFCASS, 2001–04; Collaboration Proj. Dir, LGA, 2004–06. *Recreations:* football, reading, theatre, walking, allotment. *Club:* Fulham Football.

TROTMAN, Andrew Frederick; MA; Warden, St Edward's School, Oxford, since 2004; *b* 9 Dec. 1954; *s* of Campbell Grant Trotman and late Audrey Trotman; *m* 1980, Mary Rosalind Spencer; one *s* one *d*. *Educ:* Alleyne's Grammar Sch., Stevenage; Balliol Coll., Oxford (MA English Language and Lit. 1977); Cert Ed Oxon 1978. Asst Master, Radley Coll., 1978–84; Housemaster, Abingdon Sch., 1984–90; Dep. Rector, Edinburgh Acad., 1991–95; Head Master, St Peter's School, York, 1995–2004. Gov., Cheam Sch., 2005–. MInstD 1997. JP City of York, 1998–2004. *Recreations:* walking, rowing, music, bagpiping. *Address:* St Edward's School, Oxford OX2 7NN. *T:* (01865) 319323. *Clubs:* East India, Lansdowne.

TROTMAN-DICKENSON, Sir Aubrey (Fiennes), Kt 1989; Principal, University of Wales College of Cardiff, 1988–93; Vice-Chancellor, University of Wales, 1975–77, 1983–85 and 1991–93; *b* 12 Feb. 1926; *s* of late Edward Newton Trotman-Dickenson and Violet Murray Nicoll; *m* 1953, Danusia Irena Hewell; two *s* one *d*. *Educ:* Winchester Coll.; Balliol Coll., Oxford (MA, BSc); PhD Manchester; DSc Edinburgh. Fellow, National Research Council, Ottawa, 1948–50; Asst Lecturer, ICI Fellow, Manchester Univ., 1950–53; E. I. du Pont de Nemours, Wilmington, USA, 1953–54; Lecturer, Edinburgh Univ., 1954–60; Professor, University College of Wales, Aberystwyth, 1960–68; Principal; UWIST, Cardiff, 1968–88; UC Cardiff, 1987–88. Chm., Job Creation Programme, Wales, 1975–78. Member: Welsh Council, 1971–79; Planning and Transport Res. Adv. Council, DoE, 1975–79. Tilden Lectr, Chem. Soc., 1963. Hon. LLD Wales, 1995. *Publications:* Gas Kinetics, 1955; Free Radicals, 1959; Tables of Bimolecular Gas Reactions, 1967; (ed) Comprehensive Inorganic Chemistry, 1973; contrib. to learned journals. *Address:* Syston Court, Bristol BS16 9LU. *T:* (0117) 937 2109.

TROTT, Andrew James, FRICS; Surveyor Member, Lands Tribunal, since 2006; *b* 24 Dec. 1953; *s* of John and Lydia Trott; *m* 1981, Fiona Jane Maynard; three *s*. *Educ:* Sir Antony Browne's Sch., Brentwood; Poly. of South Bank (BSc Hons Estate Mgt); Open Univ. (BA, MBA). ARICS 1977, FRICS 1992. RICS Res. Fellow, Poly. of South Bank, 1979–80; Partner, John Trott and Son, 1980–82; Hd of Property Consultancy, London Transport, subseq. Transport for London, 1982–2005. *Recreations:* flying (private pilot's licence), football, Rugby, golf, collecting modern first editions. *Address:* Lands Tribunal, 3rd Floor, Procession House, 55 Ludgate Hill, EC4M 7JW. *T:* (020) 7029 9892; *e-mail:* andrew.trott@dca.gsi.gov.uk.

TROTT, Christopher John; HM Diplomatic Service; Ambassador to Senegal and concurrently to Mali, Guinea-Bissau and Cape Verde, since 2007; *b* 14 Feb. 1966; *s* of John and Averil Trott; *m* 1992, Sunna Park; one *s* one *d*. *Educ:* Hawthorns Sch., Blechingley; Whitgift Sch., S Croydon; Bristol Univ. (BA Hons Hist. 1988); Sch. of Oriental and African Studies, Univ. of London (MA SE Asian Area Studies 1991). Entered FCO, 1991; Dep. Hd of Mission, Rangoon, 1993–96; First Secretary: (Commercial), 1996–99, (Political), 1999–2002, Tokyo; FCO, 2003–07. *Recreations:* travel, reading, skiing, scuba-diving, season ticket holder at Crystal Palace FC. *Address:* British Embassy, 20 rue du Dr Guillet, BP 6025, Dakar, Senegal. *T:* (33) 8237392, *Fax:* (33) 8216115; c/o Foreign and Commonwealth Office, King Charles Street, SW1A 2AH; *e-mail:* Chris.Trott@fco.gov.uk.

TROTTER, Major Alexander Richard; JP; Lord-Lieutenant of Berwickshire, since 2000; Chairman, Meadowhead Ltd (formerly Mortonhall Park Ltd), since 1974; *b* 20 Feb. 1939; *s* of late Major H. R. Trotter, TD, and of Rona Trotter (*née* Murray); *m* 1970, Julia Henrietta, *d* of Capt. Sir Peter McClintock Greenwell, 3rd Bt, TD; three *s*. *Educ:* Eton Coll.; City of London Tech. Coll. Served Royal Scots Greys, 1958–68; Manager, Charterhall Estate and Farm, 1969–; Vice Chm., Border Grain, Ltd, 1984–2003. Dir, Timber Growers GB Ltd, 1977–82. Scottish Landowners' Federation: Mem. Council, 1975–2004; Convener, 1982–85; Vice Pres., 1986–96; Pres., 1996–2001; Mem., NCC and Chm., Scottish Cttee, 1985–90; Mem., UK Cttee, Euro Year of the Envmt, 1986–88. Gen. Comr for Income Tax, Berwickshire, 1973–. Mem. (Ind.), Berwickshire CC, 1969–75 (Chm., Roads Cttee, 1974–75). Chm., Thirlstane Castle Trust, 1996–2007. Officer, Royal Co. of Archers. DL 1987, JP 2000, Berwickshire. OStJ 2005. *Recreations:* golf, bridge, country sports. *Address:* Charterhall, Duns, Berwickshire TD11 3RE. *T:* (home) (01890) 840210, (office) (01890) 840301, *Fax:* (01890) 840651; *e-mail:* alex@charterhall.net. *Clubs:* Turf, Pratt's; New (Edinburgh).

TROTTER, David; *see* Trotter, W. D.

TROTTER, Dame Janet (Olive), DBE 2001 (OBE 1991); DL; Chairman, Gloucestershire Hospitals NHS Foundation Trust (formerly NHS Trust), since 2002; Vice-Chancellor, 2002–06 and Principal, 1990–2006, University of Gloucestershire (formerly Director, Cheltenham and Gloucester College of Higher Education); *b* 29 Oct. 1943; *d* of Anthony George Trotter and Joyce Edith Trotter (*née* Patrick). *Educ:* Derby Lonsdale Coll. of Educn (Cert Ed); BD (ext.) London Univ.; Inst. of Educn, London Univ. (MA); Henley Mgt Coll. (MSc Brunel Univ.). Teacher: St Leonards Secondary Sch., 1965–67; Chartham Secondary Sch., 1967–69; Rochester Grammar Sch. for Girls, 1969–73; Lectr, King Alfred's Coll., Winchester, 1973–84; Vice Principal, St Martin's Coll., Lancaster, 1985–86; Principal, St Paul and St Mary's Coll., Cheltenham, 1986–90. Mem. and Chm., Glos HA, 1991–96; Chair, S and W Reg., NHS Exec., DoH, 1996–2001. Member: HEFCE, 1992–97; TTA, 1994–99. DL Glos, 2006. Hon. Freeman, Cheltenham, 2002. Hon. DTech Pecs, Hungary, 1996; Hon. DEd: UWE, 2001; Brunel, 2004; Hon. DHum Elizabethtown Coll., Pa, 2002; Hon. DLaws Bristol, 2002. *Publications:* various articles. *Recreations:* cycling, music. *Address:* Gloucestershire Hospitals NHS Foundation Trust, 1 College Lawn, Cheltenham, Glos GL53 7AG.

TROTTER, Sir Neville (Guthrie), Kt 1997; JP; DL; FCA; FRAeS, FCIT; Consultant, Thornton Baker, 1974–83, Grant Thornton, Chartered Accountants, 1983–2005; *b* 27 Jan. 1932; *s* of Captain Alexander Trotter and Elizabeth Winifred Trotter (*née* Guthrie); *m* 1983, Caroline, *d* of late Captain John Farrow, OBE, RN and Oona Farrow (*née* Hall); one *d*. *Educ:* Shrewsbury; King's Coll., Durham (BCom). Short service commn in RAF, 1955–58. Partner, Thornton Baker & Co., Chartered Accountants, 1962–74. Former Director: MidAmerican Energy Hldgs Co.; Wm Baird plc; Darchem Ltd; Romag plc. Member Council: NE Chamber of Commerce; Northern Business Forum; Founder Chm., British-American Chamber of Commerce, NE of England, 1999–; Pres., Northern Defence Industries, 2000–; Vice Pres., Soc. of Maritime Industries, 1996–. Member: National Express East Coast Main Line (formerly Great North Eastern Railway) Business Forum; Council, European Atlantic Gp. Mem., Newcastle City Council, 1963–74 (Alderman, 1970–74; Chm., Finance Cttee, Traffic Highways and Transport Cttee, Theatre Cttee). Mem., CAA Airline Users Cttee, 1973–79. Mem., Tyne and Wear Metropolitan Council, 1973–74; Vice-Chm., Northumberland Police Authority, 1970–74. MP (C) Tynemouth, Feb. 1974–1997. Chm., Cons. Party Shipping and Shipbuilding Cttee, 1979–85, 1994–97 (Vice-Chm., 1976–79); Secretary: Cons. Party Industry Cttee, 1981–83; Cons. Party Transport Cttee, 1983–84; Mil. Sec., Cons. Party Aviation Cttee, 1976–79; Member: Industry Sub-Cttee, Select Cttee on Expenditure, 1976–79; Select Cttee on Transport, 1983–92; Select Cttee on Defence, 1993–97; Parly Defence Study Group, 1980–97; Armed Forces Parly Scheme (RAF), 1990–91; formerly Chm., All-Party Gp for Prevention of Solvent Abuse. Private Member's Bills: Consumer Safety, 1978; Licensing Amendment, 1980; Intoxicating Substances Supply (Glue Sniffing), 1985. Pres., North Area Cons. Party, 1996–2003. Vice Pres., Soc. for Prevention of Solvent and Volatile Substance Abuse, 1989–. Former Member: Northern Economic Planning Council; Tyne Improvement Commn; Tyneside Passenger Transport Authority; Industrial Relations Tribunal; Council, RUSI. Member: UK Defence Forum, 1997–; Steering Cttee, Parly Maritime Gp, 1997–; Defence and Security Forum, 2005–; Atlantic Council; Air League; NE RFCA (formerly TAVRA), 1997–; US Naval Inst.; USAF Assoc.; Council, US Navy League in UK; Railway Studies Assoc. Pres., Tyneside Br., RM Assoc., 2001–. Hon. Colonel: Royal Marine Reserve, 1998–2003; Durham ACF, 2003–05. Pres., TS Rodney Gosforth Sea Cadets, 2006–. Pres., Whitley Bay and Dist Scout Council, 2004–. Council Member: Northumbria, Order of St John, 2005–; High Sheriff's Assoc. of England and Wales, 2005–. FRAeS 1998; FCIT 1998. Freeman, City of London, 1978; Member: Co. of Chartered Accountants, 1978; GAPAN, 2006–. JP Newcastle upon Tyne, 1973; DL 1997, High Sheriff, 2004–05, Tyne and Wear. *Recreations:* aviation, gardening, fell-walking, study of foreign affairs, defence and industry. *Clubs:* Royal Air Force; Northern Counties (Newcastle upon Tyne).

TROTTER, Sir Ronald (Ramsay), Kt 1985; FCA; New Zealand business executive; Chairman, Fletcher Challenge Ltd, 1981–95 (Chief Executive, 1981–87); *b* Hawera, 9 Oct. 1927; *s* of Clement George Trotter, CBE and Annie Euphemia Trotter (*née* Young); *m* 1955, Margaret Patricia, *d* of James Rainey; three *s* one *d*. *Educ:* Collegiate School, Wanganui; Victoria Univ. of Wellington; Lincoln Coll., Canterbury (BCom, Cert. in Agric.). FCA 1976. Wright Stephenson & Co., 1958–72: Dir, 1962–68; Man. Dir, 1968–70; Chm. and Man. Dir, 1970–72; Chm. and Man. Dir, Challenge Corp., 1972–81. Chairman: Telecom Corp. of New Zealand Ltd, 1987–90; Post Office Bank, 1989; Ciba-Geigy New Zealand Ltd, 1990–96; Wrightson Ltd, 1993–98; Toyota New Zealand Ltd, 1994–2001 (Dir, 1990–94); Director: Reserve Bank of NZ, 1986–88; Australia and New Zealand Banking Gp, 1988–97 (Inaugural Mem., Internat. Bd of Advice, 1986–93); Air

New Zealand Ltd, 1989–98; Ciba-Geigy Australia Ltd, 1991–96; Wrightson Farmers Finance Ltd, 1993–98; Mem., Internat. Adv. Bd, Proudfoot plc, 1992–95. Trustee and Chm., NZ Inst. of Economic Research, 1973–86; Chairman: Overseas Investment Commn, 1974–77; NZ Business Roundtable, 1985–90; Pacific Basin Econ. Council, 1985–90 (Internat. Pres., 1986–88); Museum of NZ, 1995–2001 (Mem., Project Develt Bd, 1988–92). Pres., NZ Equestrian Fedn, 2001–04. Hon. LLD Victoria Univ. of Wellington, 1984; Hon. DCom Lincoln, 1999. Bledisloe Medal, Lincoln Coll., 1988. NZ Business Hall of Fame, 1999. Silver Jubilee Medal, 1977; NZ Commemoration Medal, 1990. *Address:* Te Kowhai Road, RDI Otaki, New Zealand. *T:* (4) 2933947, *Fax:* (4) 2937339. *Club:* Wellington (Wellington, NZ).

TROTTER, Thomas Andrew, FRCO; Organist, St Margaret's Church, Westminster Abbey, since 1982; Organist to the City of Birmingham, since 1983; *b* 4 April 1957; *s* of late His Honour Richard Stanley Trotter and Ruth Elizabeth Trotter. *Educ:* Malvern Coll.; Royal Coll. of Music, 1974–76 (schol.; ARCM) (organ schol., St George's Chapel, Windsor, 1975–76); King's Coll., Cambridge (organ schol., 1976–79; MA). John Stewart of Rannock Schol. in Sacred Music, Cambridge Univ., 1979; Countess of Munster schol. for further organ studies with Marie-Claire Alain in Paris. Début at Royal Fest. Hall, 1980; Prom. début, 1986; regular broadcasts for Radio 2 and Radio 3; has performed at fests throughout UK and in Europe; concert tours to Australia, USA and Far East; organ recordings. DUniv UCE, 2003; Hon. DMus Birmingham, 2006. Walford Davies Prize, RCM, 1976; First prize and Bach prize, St Albans Internat. Organ Competition, 1979; Prix de Virtuosité, Conservatoire Rueil-Malmaison, 1981; Instrumental Award, Royal Philharmonic Soc., 2001. *Address:* c/o The Town Hall, Birmingham B3 3DQ.

TROTTER, Prof. (Wilfred) David, PhD; FBA 2004; King Edward VII Professor of English Literature, University of Cambridge, since 2002; Fellow, Gonville and Caius College, Cambridge, since 2002; *b* 25 July 1951; *s* of late Wilfred Robert Trotter and Enid Beatrice Trotter (*née* Roulston). *Educ:* Gonville and Caius Coll., Cambridge (BA, PhD). Res. Fellow, Magdalene Coll., Cambridge, 1975–77; University College London: Lectr in English, 1977–87; Reader, 1987–90; Prof. of English, 1990–91; Quain Prof. of English Lang. and Lit., 1991–2002. Vis. Prof., CIT, 1988–89. *Publications:* The Poetry of Abraham Cowley, 1979; The Making of the Reader, 1984; Circulation: Defoe, Dickens and the economies of the novel, 1988; The English Novel in History 1895–1920, 1993; (jtly) A Companion to Edwardian Fiction, 1997; Cooking with Mud: the idea of mess in nineteenth century art and fiction, 2000; Paranoid Modernism, 2001; Cinema and Modernism, 2007. *Address:* Gonville and Caius College, Cambridge CB2 1TA.

TROUBRIDGE, Sir Thomas (Richard), 7th Bt *cr* 1799, of Plymouth; FCA; Partner, PricewaterhouseCoopers (formerly Price Waterhouse), since 1989; *b* 23 Jan. 1955; *s* of Sir Peter Troubridge, 6th Bt and of Hon. Venetia Daphne (who *m* 2nd, Captain W. F. E. Forbes, *qv*), *d* of 1st Baron Weeks; *S* father, 1988; *m* 1984, Hon. Rosemary Douglas-Pennant, *yr d* of 6th Baron Penrhyn, DSO, MBE; two *s* one *d*. *Educ:* Eton College; Durham Univ. (BSc Eng). ACA 1980, FCA 1991. Joined Price Waterhouse, 1977. *Recreations:* sailing, ski-ing. *Heir: s* Edward Peter Troubridge, *b* 10 Aug. 1989. *Address:* The Manor House, Elsted, Midhurst, W Sussex GU29 0JY. *T:* (01730) 825286. *Clubs:* White's, Hurlingham; Itchenor Sailing.

TROUGHTON, Peter, PhD; Chairman, 4RF Ltd, since 1999; *b* 26 Aug. 1943; *s* of late Frank Sydney Troughton and of Joan Vera Troughton (*née* Root); *m* 1967, Joyce Uncles; two *s*. *Educ:* City Univ. (BSc Eng); University College London (PhD). Technical apprentice, Plessey Co., then Post Office apprentice, 1959; PO scholarship, 1964; research for PhD, 1967; develt of microprocessor techniques for control of telephone switching systems, 1970; Dep. Gen. Manager, South Central Telephone Area, 1977; Head of Ops, Prestel, 1979; Gen. Manager, City Telephone Area, 1980; Regional Dir, British Telecom London, 1983; Man. Dir, British Telecom Enterprises, 1984–86; Dir and Partner, Alan Patricof Associates, 1986–88, non-exec. Dir, 1988–90; Man. Dir and Chief Exec. Officer, Telecom Corp. of NZ, 1988–92; Chairman: Trans Power (NZ National Power Grid) Estabt Bd, 1990–92; Marine Air Systems, then MAS Technology Ltd, 1993–98; Troughton, Swier and Associates, 1996–99. Director: Crown Health Enterprise Develt Unit, NZ, 1992–93; Electricity Supply Industry Reform Unit, Vic, Australia, 1993–95. Advr to NZ govt, 1993–94; Special Advr to Vic. Govt on reform and privatisation of electricity, gas and aluminium industries, 1995–99; Advr to Australian Davos Connection, World Econ. Forum, for conf. on energy in 21st century, 1998–2000. Mem., State Owned Enterprises Steering Cttee, 1992–93. Mem., NZ Business Round Table, 1988–92; Chm., Twyford and Dist Round Table, 1981–82. NZ Chief Exec. of the Year Award, 1991. NZ Commemoration Medal, 1990. *Publications:* articles and papers on microwave systems, computers, communications, and on restructuring, regulation and privatisation of utility industries. *Recreations:* travel, archaeology, bridge. *Club:* Wellington (NZ).

TROUGHTON, Peter John Charles; Director, J. Rothschild Services Ltd, since 2005; Director, since 1991, Vice-Chairman, since 2006, Archant Ltd (formerly Eastern Counties Newspaper Group); *b* 18 June 1948; *s* of Sir Charles (Hugh Willis) Troughton, CBE, MC, TD and (Constance) Gillean (*née* Mitford), DL; *m* 1977, Sarah Rose, DL, *d* of Sir Timothy Colman, *qv*; one *s* two *d*. *Educ:* Radley Coll.; Trinity Coll., Cambridge (MA Hons); Harvard Business Sch. (AMP 1987). Joined HM Diplomatic Service 1970; FCO, 1970–72; Jakarta, 1972–75; First Sec., FCO, 1975–79; W. H. Smith Gp plc, 1979–95: Managing Director: News, 1988–91; Retail, 1991–95; Dir, 1991–95; Chief Executive: Rothschild Asset Mgt Internat. Ltd, 1995–99; First Arrow Investment Mgt Ltd, 2000–04. Non-executive Director: East Anglian Daily Times, 1984–89; Community Media Ltd, 1989–91; Lowland Investment Trust plc, 1990–. Trustee: Nat. Gall., 1988–96 (Mem., Publications Cttee, 1982–88); Nat. Gall. Trust, 1996–2007 (Hon. Treas., 2001–07); Royal Opera House Endowment Fund, 2005–; Royal Collection Trust, 2007– (Chm., Audit Cttee, 2007–); Chm., National Gallery Publications Ltd, 1988–96. Mem., Council, Univ. of Bath, 2005– (Chm., 2006–). Gov., St Mary's Sch., Calne, 1992–2002. *Recreations:* reading, walking. *Address:* The Lynch House, Upper Wanborough, near Swindon, Wilts SN4 0BZ. *T:* (01793) 790385. *Clubs:* Brooks's, Pratt's.

TROUNSON, Rev. Ronald Charles, MA; Rector (non-stipendiary), Easton-on-the-Hill, 1994–99 (Rector, Easton-on-the-Hill and Collyweston with Duddington and Tixover, 1989–94); Rural Dean of Barnack, 1991–94; *b* 7 Dec. 1926; *s* of Edwin Trounson and Elsie Mary Trounson (*née* Bolitho); *m* 1952, Leonora Anne Keate (*d* 2008); two *s* three *d*. *Educ:* Plymouth Coll.; Emmanuel Coll., Cambridge (Schol.); Ripon Hall, Oxford (MA). Deacon, 1956; Priest, 1957. National Service, RAF, 1948–50. Asst Master, Scaitcliffe Sch., Englefield Green, Surrey, 1950–52; Sixth Form Classics Master, Plymouth Coll., 1953–58; Asst Curate, St Gabriel's, Plymouth, 1956–58; Chaplain, Denstone Coll., 1958–76; Second Master, 1968–76, Bursar, 1976–78; Principal of St Chad's College and Lectr in Classics, Univ. of Durham, 1978–88. Chm. of Governors, Durham High Sch., 1990–94. Fellow, Woodard Corporation, 1983. FRSA 1984. *Address:* Belmont Grange, Broomside Lane, Belmont, Durham DH1 2QW.

TROUP, Edward; *see* Troup, J. E. A.

TROUP, (John) Edward (Astley); Director, Business and Indirect Tax, HM Treasury, since 2004; *b* 26 Jan. 1955; *s* of Vice-Adm. Sir (John) Anthony (Rose) Troup, KCB, DSC, and of Cordelia Mary Troup; *m* 1978, Siriol Jane Martin; three *s* one *d*. *Educ:* Oundle Sch.; Corpus Christi Coll., Oxford (BA Maths 1976, MA; MSc Applied Maths 1977). ATII 1983. Admitted solicitor, 1981; joined Simmons & Simmons, 1979, Partner, 1985–95, 1997–2004; Special Advr on Tax, HM Treasury, 1995–97. *Recreations:* cinema, cycling, Beethoven, birdwatching, art, astronomy, the Anglo-Saxons and the landscape, buildings and history of the British Isles. *Address:* HM Treasury, One Horse Guards Road, SW1A 2HQ. *T:* (020) 7270 6006; *e-mail:* edward.troup@hm-treasury.gov.uk.

TROUSDELL, Lt Gen. Sir Philip (Charles Cornwallis), KBE 2004; CB 2000; General Officer Commanding Northern Ireland, 2003–05; *b* 13 Aug. 1948; *s* of late Col Philip James Cornwallis Trousdell, OBE and Doreen Mary Trousdell (*née* Durdle); *m* 1986, Sally Caroline Slade Parker; one *s* two *d*. *Educ:* Berkhamstead; RMA, Sandhurst. Commnd Royal Irish Rangers, 1968: CO, 1st Bn, 1989–91; commanded 48 Gurkha Bde, 1992–93; Dir, Public Relns (Army), 1994–97; COS, HQ Land Comd, 1997–2000; Dep. Comdr (Ops) Stabilisation Force, Bosnia Herzegovina, 2000; Comdt, RMA Sandhurst, 2001–03. Col, Queen's Own Gurkha Transport Regt, 1993–2003; Dep. Col, 1996–2001, Col, 2001–, Royal Irish Regt; Colonel Commandant: Media Ops Gp (Vol.), 2001–06; Bde of Gurkhas, 2003–07. Chm., Gurkha Welfare Trust, 2003–07. *Recreations:* reading, bicycling, wine. *Address:* Riverside House, Fordingbridge SP6 2JS. *Club:* Army and Navy.

TROWELL, Prof. Brian Lewis, PhD; Heather Professor of Music and Fellow of Wadham College, University of Oxford, 1988–96, now Emeritus; *b* 21 Feb. 1931; *s* of Richard Lewis and Edith J. R. Trowell; *m* 1958, Rhianon James; two *d*. *Educ:* Christ's Hospital; Gonville and Caius Coll., Cambridge. MA 1959; PhD 1960. Asst Lectr, later Lectr, in Music, Birmingham Univ., 1957–62; freelance scholar, conductor, opera producer, lecturer and editor, 1962–67; Head of BBC Radio opera, 1967–70; Reader in Music, 1970, Professor of Music, 1973, King Edward Prof. of Music, 1974–88, KCL. Regents' Prof., Univ. of California at Berkeley, 1970; Vis. Gresham Prof. of Music, City Univ., 1971–74. Pres., Royal Musical Assoc., 1983–88. Hon. RAM, 1972; Hon. FGSM, 1972; FRCM 1977; FTCL 1978; Fellow: Curwen Inst., 1987; KCL, 1997. Chm., Editorial Cttee, Musica Britannica, 1983–93. *Publications:* The Early Renaissance, Pelican History of Music vol. ii, 1963; Four Motets by John Plummer, 1968; (ed jtly) John Dunstable: Complete Works, ed M. F. Bukofzer, 2nd edn, 1970; (ed) Invitation to Medieval Music, vol. 3 1976, vol. 4 1978; opera translations; contrib. dictionaries of music and articles in learned journals. *Recreations:* theatre, reading, gardening. *Address:* 5 Tree Lane, Iffley Village, Oxford OX4 4EY.

TROWER, William Spencer Philip; QC 2001; *b* 28 Dec. 1959; *s* of late Anthony Gosselin Trower and of Catherine Joan Trower (*née* Kellett); *m* 1986, Mary Louise Chastel de Boinville; four *d*. *Educ:* Eton Coll.; Christ Church, Oxford (MA); City Univ. (Dip. Law). Called to the Bar, Lincoln's Inn, 1983. *Publication:* (ed jtly) The Law and Practice of Corporate Administrations, 1994, 2nd edn as Corporate Administrations and Rescue Procedures, 2004. *Recreations:* family, gardening, countryside, country sports. *Address:* 3–4 South Square, Gray's Inn, WC1R 5HP. *T:* (020) 7696 9900. *Club:* Garrick.

TROWSDALE, Prof. John, PhD; Professor of Immunology, and Head of Division of Immunology, Department of Pathology, University of Cambridge, since 1997; *b* 8 Feb. 1949; *s* of Roy R. Trowsdale and Doris Trowsdale (*née* Graham); *m* 1971, Susan Price; two *s* one *d*. *Educ:* Beverley Grammar Sch.; Univ. of Birmingham (BSc 1970; PhD 1973). European Fellow, Biochemical Soc., Gif-sur-Yvette, France, 1973–75; Res. Fellow, Scripps Clinic and Res. Foundn, Calif, 1975–78; SRC Res. Fellow, Genetics Lab., Univ. of Oxford, 1978–79; Imperial Cancer Research Fund: ICRF Fellow, 1979–82; Res. Scientist, 1982–85; Sen. Scientist, 1986–90; Prin. Scientist, 1990–97. Member: Council, European Fedn of Immunogenetics, 1995–98; Sci. Adv. Bd, Onyvax, 1997–; Chm., Histocompatibility and Immunogenetics Affinity Gp, British Soc. of Histocompatibility and Immunogenetics, 1996–99. FMedSci 2000. *Publications:* (jtly) Advanced Immunology, 1996; res. papers in science jls. *Recreations:* playing rock, jazz and classical music, painting. *Address:* Department of Pathology, Tennis Court Road, Cambridge CB2 1QP. *T:* (01223) 333711.

TRUDGILL, Prof. Peter John, FBA 1989; Professor of English Linguistics, University of Fribourg, 1998–2005, now Emeritus; Hon. Professor of Sociolinguistics, University of East Anglia, since 2005; *b* 7 Nov. 1943; *s* of John Trudgill and Hettie Jean Trudgill (*née* Gooch); *m* 1980, Jean Marie Hannah. *Educ:* City of Norwich Sch.; King's Coll., Cambridge (BA; MA 1966); Edinburgh Univ. (Dip Gen Linguistics 1967; PhD 1971). Asst Lectr, Lectr, Reader, Prof., Dept of Linguistic Sci., Univ. of Reading, 1970–86; Reader, 1986–87, Prof. of Sociolinguistics, 1987–92, Essex Univ.; Prof. of English Linguistics, Univ. of Lausanne, 1993–98. Vis. Prof. at Univs of Hong Kong, Bergen, Aarhus, Illinois, Stanford, Osmania, Tokyo International Christian, ANU, Texas Austin, Toronto, Canterbury (NZ). Fellow: Norwegian Acad. of Sci and Letters, 1995; Royal Norwegian Acad. of Scis, 1996. Hon. PhD: Uppsala, 1995; UEA, 2002. *Publications:* The Social Differentiation of English in Norwich, 1974; Sociolinguistics: an introduction, 1974, 4th edn 2000; Accent, Dialect and the School, 1975; Sociolinguistic Patterns in British English, 1978; (with A. Hughes) English Accents and Dialects, 1979; (with J. K. Chambers) Dialectology, 1980; (with J. M. Hannah) International English, 1982, 3rd edn 1994; On Dialect, 1983; Coping with America, 1983, 2nd edn 1985; Language in the British Isles, 1984; Applied Sociolinguistics, 1984; Dialects in Contact, 1986; The Dialects of England, 1990; (with J. K. Chambers) English Dialects: studies in grammatical variation, 1991; (with L. Andersson) Bad Language, 1991; Introducing Language and Society, 1992; Dialects, 1994; (with L. Bauer) Language Myths, 1998; Sociolinguistic Variation and Change, 2002; New Dialect Formation, 2004. *Recreations:* Norwich City FC, playing the 'cello. *Address:* School of Language, Linguistics and Translation Studies, University of East Anglia, Norwich NR4 7TJ.

TRUDINGER, Prof. Neil Sidney, PhD; FRS 1997; FAA; Professor of Mathematics, Australian National University, since 1973; *b* 20 June 1942; *s* of Laurence Robert Trudinger and Dorothy Winifred Trudinger; *m* 1st, 1964, Patricia Robyn Saunders; one *s* one *d*; 2nd, 1991, Tess Rosario Valdez. *Educ:* Univ. of New England, Australia (BSc Hons 1962); Stanford Univ., USA (MS 1965; PhD 1966). FAA 1978. Courant Instructor, New York Univ., 1966–67; Lectr, then Sen. Lectr, Macquarie Univ., Australia, 1967–70; Reader, then Prof., Univ. of Qld, 1970–73; Australian National University: Head, Dept of Pure Maths, 1973–78; Director: Commonwealth Special Res. Centre for Mathematical Analysis, 1982–96; Centre for Maths and its Applications, 1991–93; Dean, Sch. of Math. Scis, 1992–2000; Prof., Northwestern Univ., 1989–93. *Publications:* Elliptic Partial Differential Equations of the Second Order, 1977, 2nd edn 1983. *Address:* Mathematical Sciences Institute, Australian National University, Canberra, ACT 0200, Australia. *T:* (2) 62492957.

TRUE, Nicholas Edward, CBE 1993; Private Secretary to Leader of the Opposition, and Director, Opposition Whips' Office, House of Lords, since 1997; *b* 31 July 1951; *s* of Edward Thomas True and Kathleen Louise True (*née* Mather); *m* 1979, Anne-Marie Elena

Kathleen Blanco Hood; two *s* one *d*. *Educ:* Nottingham High Sch.; Peterhouse, Cambridge (BA Hons 1973; MA 1978). Mem., Cons. Res. Dept, 1975–82; Asst to Cons. Party Dep. Leader, 1978–82; Special Advr to Sec. of State for Health and Social Security, 1982–86; Dir, Public Policy Unit, 1986–90; Dep. Head, Prime Minister's Policy Unit, 1991–95; Special Advr, Prime Minister's Office, 1997. Councillor (C), Richmond-upon-Thames, 1986–90, 1998– (Dep. Leader, 2002–06; Leader of Opposition, 2006–). Trustee: Olga Havel Foundn, 1990–94; Sir Harold Hood's Charitable Trust, 1996–; Richmond Civic Trust, 2006–. *Publications:* articles in newspapers, jls etc; pamphlets and papers on policy matters. *Recreations:* Byzantium, Italy, gardens, books. *Address:* 114 Palewell Park, East Sheen, SW14 8JH. *T:* (020) 8876 9628; Contrada Salino 15, San Ginesio, Macerata, Italy. *Clubs:* Beefsteak, Brooks's, Travellers.

TRULUCK, Maj. Gen. Ashley Ernest George, CB 2001; CBE 1997; Managing Director, ATA (formerly Ashley Truluck Associates) Ltd, since 2003; National Project Manager, Fire and Rescue Services Communications, since 2005; *b* 7 Dec. 1947; *s* of Maj. George William Truluck, RA and Elizabeth Truluck (*née* Kitchener); *m* 1976, Jennifer Bell; one *s* one *d*. *Educ:* Harvey's Sch.; RMA Sandhurst; BA. Regtl duty, Bde of Gurkhas, Malaysia, Hong Kong, Nepal, 1969–74; ADC to Maj. Gen., Bde of Gurkhas, and Comdr FARELF, 1974–75; Commns Officer, Guards Armoured Bde, 1976–77; sc, 1978–79; GSO2, MoD, 1980–81; Sqn Comdr, BAOR, UK, 1982–84; Dir, Staff RMCS, 1984–86; Regt Comdr, BAOR, 1986–88; Col Army Staff Duties, 1989–90; HCSC, 1990; Comdt, Royal Sch. of Signals, 1991–92; RCDS, 1993; Brig. Gen. Staff, UK Land Comd, 1994–96; Dir, Attack Helicopter, 1997–98; ACOS, SHAPE, 1998–2000. Chief Exec., Gtr London Magistrates' Courts Authy, 2001–03. Col Comdt, RCS, 2001–07; Adm., Royal Signals Yacht Club, 2003–. Chairman: Defence Housing Review, 2001; London Criminal Justice Bd, 2001–03. Chm., Royal Signals Benevolent Fund, 2002–. FCMI (FIMgt 1992); FInstD 2002; MRUSI 2004. *Recreations:* offshore sailing, country pursuits, sketching. *Address:* Firelink National Offices, Victory House, Trafalgar Place, Brighton BN1 4FY. *T:* (01273) 365225. *Clubs:* Army and Navy, Ocean Cruising; Internat. Cape Horners.

TRUMP, Donald John; Chairman and President, Trump Organization; *b* New York, 14 June 1946; *s* of Fred C. Trump and Mary Trump; *m* 1st, 1977, Ivana Zelnicek (marr. diss. 1991); two *s* one *d*; 2nd, 1993, Marla Maples (marr. diss. 1999); one *d*; 3rd, 2005, Melania Knauss; one *s*. *Educ:* New York Military Acad.; Wharton Sch. of Finance, Univ. of Pennsylvania (BS 1968). Joined father's co., Trump Organization; Chm. and CEO, Trump Hotels & Casino Resorts, 1995–2004; Chm., Trump Entertainment Resorts Inc., 2005–; holdings include: Trump Tower, Trump Palace, Trump Plaza, Trump World Tower, Trump International Hotel and Tower, New York; Trump Plaza, Mar-A-Lago, Florida; Trump Plaza Hotel Casino, Trump Castle Casino, Trump Taj Mahal Casino Resort, Atlantic City; acquired 50% stake in Empire State Bldg, 1994. Co-Exec. Prod., TV series, The Apprentice, 2004–. Launched Trump World Magazine, 2004. *Publications:* Trump: the way to the top, 2004; *jointly:* Trump: the art of the deal, 1988; Trump: surviving at the top, 1990; The Art of Survival, 1991; The Art of the Comeback, 1997; The America We Deserve, 2000; Trump: how to get rich, 2004; Trump: think like a billionaire, 2004; Trump Strategies for Real Estate, 2005; Why We Want You to Be Rich: two men - one message, 2006; Take Command, 2006; Trump University Real Estate 101, 2006; Trump University Marketing 101, 2006; Trump 101: the way to success, 2006; Trump University Entrepreneurship 101, 2007. *Address:* Trump Organization, 725 Fifth Avenue, New York, NY 10022, USA.

TRUMPINGTON, Baroness *cr* 1980 (Life Peer), of Sandwich in the County of Kent; **Jean Alys Barker,** DCVO 2005; PC 1992; an Extra Baroness in Waiting to the Queen, since 1998; *d* of late Arthur Edward Campbell-Harris, MC and late Doris Marie Robson; *m* 1954, William Alan Barker (*d* 1988); one *s*. *Educ:* privately in England and France. Land Girl to Rt Hon. David Lloyd George, MP, 1940–41; Foreign Office, Bletchley Park, 1941–45; European Central Inland Transport Orgn, 1945–49; Sec. to Viscount Hinchingbrooke, MP, 1950–52. Conservative Councillor, Cambridge City Council, Trumpington Ward, 1963–73; Mayor of Cambridge, 1971–72; Deputy Mayor, 1972–73; Conservative County Councillor, Cambridgeshire, Trumpington Ward, 1973–75; Hon. Councillor of the City of Cambridge, 1975–. A Baroness in Waiting (Government Whip), 1983–85 and 1992–97; Parly Under-Sec. of State, DHSS, 1985–87, MAFF, 1987–89; Minister of State, MAFF, 1989–92. UK Delegate to UN Status of Women Commn, 1979–82. Member: Air Transport Users' Cttee, 1972–80 (Dep. Chairman 1978–79, Chm. 1979–80); Bd of Visitors to HM Prison, Pentonville, 1975–81; Mental Health Review Tribunal, 1975–81. Gen. Commissioner of Taxes, 1976–83. Pres., Assoc. of Heads of Independent Schs, 1980–89. Steward, Folkestone Racecourse, 1980–92. Hon. Fellow, Lucy Cavendish Coll., Cambridge, 1980. Hon. FRCPath 1992; Hon. ARCVS 1994; Hon. Mem., BVA, 1995. JP Cambridge, 1972–75, South Westminster, 1976–82. Officier, Ordre de la Mérite (France), 2005. *Recreations:* bridge, racing, collecting antiques, needlepoint. *Address:* House of Lords, SW1A 0PW. *Clubs:* Farmers', Grillions.

TRUNDLE, Shirley Jean, CBE 2004 (OBE 1999); Director, Families, Department for Children, Schools and Families, since 2008; *b* 28 Feb. 1958; *d* of Derek and Jean Hayles; *m* 1979, John Malcolm Trundle; one *s* two *d*. *Educ:* Guildford High Sch.; Newnham Coll., Cambridge (MA); St Catharine's Coll., Cambridge (MPhil). Entered DES, 1981, subseq. DFE, then DFEE; Private Sec. to Sec. of State for Educn and Sci., 1986–87; Principal, 1987–93; Divl Manager, Higher Educn Policy and Funding, 1993–96; Sec. to Nat. Cttee of Inquiry into Higher Educn (Dearing Cttee), 1996–97; Head, Childcare Unit, 1998–99; Dir, Opportunity and Diversity Gp, 1999–2001; Department for Work and Pensions: Dir, Universal Banking Prog., 2001–03; Dir, Welfare Strategy and Performance, 2003–06; Dir, Benefit Strategy, 2006–08. *Recreations:* family, music, food. *Address:* Department for Children, Schools and Families, Great Smith Street, SW1P 3BT.

TRURO, Bishop of, from 2009; **Rt Rev. Timothy Martin Thornton;** DL; *b* 14 April 1957; *s* of John and Mary Thornton; *m* 1978, Siân Evans; one *s* one *d*. *Educ:* Southampton Univ. (BA Theol. 1978); St Stephen's House, Oxford (Cert. Theol.); KCL (MA Ecclesl Hist. 1997). Ordained deacon, 1980, priest, 1981; Asst Curate, Todmorden, Dio. Wakefield, 1980–83; Priest i/c, Walsden, 1983–85; Chaplain, UC Cardiff, 1985–87; Bishop's Chaplain: Wakefield, 1987–91; London, 1991–94; Principal, N Thames Ministerial Trng Course, 1994–98; Vicar of Kensington, 1998–2001; Area Bishop of Sherborne, 2001–08. DL Dorset, 2007. *Address:* Lis Escop, Truro, Cornwall TR3 6QQ.

TRURO, Dean of; *see* Hardwick, Very Rev. C. G.

TRUSCOTT, Baron *cr* 2004 (Life Peer), of St James's in the City of Westminster; **Peter Derek Truscott;** parliamentarian, author and political analyst; *b* 20 March 1959; *s* of late Derek Truscott and of Dorothy Truscott; *m* 1991, Svetlana, *d* of late Col Prof. Nicolai Chernicov and Svetlana Chernicova. *Educ:* Newton Abbot Grammar Sch.; Exeter Coll., Oxford (History Prize; BA 1981, MA 1985, DPhil 1986, Modern History). Labour Party Organiser, 1986–89; NACRO, 1989–94. Councillor, Colchester Borough Council, 1988–92; contested (Lab) Torbay, 1992. Member: TGWU, 1986–; Co-op Party, 1987–; posts in Trade Union and Labour movements. MEP (Lab) Hertfordshire, 1994–99; contested (Lab) Eastern Reg., 1999. European Parliament: Labour spokesman on foreign affairs and defence, 1997–99; Vice-Pres., Cttee on Security and Disarmament, 1994–99; Mem., Foreign Affairs Cttee, 1994–99; Substitute Member: Regl Policy Cttee, 1994–97; Economic, Monetary and Industrial Policy Cttee, 1997–99. Deptl liaison peer, MoD, 2004–05; Mem., Select European Sub-Cttee C, H of L, 2005–06, 2007–; Parly Under-Sec. of State for Energy, DTI, and DTI spokesman in H of L, 2006–07. Associate Res. Fellow, IPPR, 2000–06; Associate Fellow, RUSI, 2005–06, 2008–. Mem., Internat. and Domestic Sub-Cttee, Labour Party NEC, 1996–97. Sch. governor, 1988–92. *Publications:* Russia First, 1997; European Defence, 2000; Kursk, 2002; Putin's Progress, 2004; The Ascendancy of Political Risk Management, 2006; numerous articles. *Recreations:* walking, music, theatre, swimming, travel. *Address:* House of Lords, SW1A 0PW.

TRUSCOTT, Ian Derek, PhD; QC (Scot.) 1997; *b* 7 Nov. 1949; *s* of Derek and Jessie Truscott; *m* 1972, Julia Elizabeth Bland; four *s*. *Educ:* Edinburgh Univ. (LLB Hons 1971); Leeds Univ. (LLM 1974); Strathclyde Univ. (PhD 2004). Solicitor, 1973–87; admitted to Faculty of Advocates, 1988; called to the Bar, Gray's Inn, 1995. Pt-time Judge (formerly Chm.), Employment Tribunals, England and Wales, 2002–. Vis. Prof. of Law, Strathclyde Univ., 1999–. *Recreations:* walking, snow dome collecting. *Address:* Advocates' Library, Parliament Square, Edinburgh EH1 1RF. *T:* (0131) 226 5071; Old Square Chambers, 10–11 Bedford Row, WC1R 4BU. *T:* (020) 7269 0300. *Club:* Royal Northern and University (Aberdeen).

TRUSCOTT, Sir Ralph (Eric Nicholson), 4th Bt *cr* 1909, of Oakleigh, East Grinstead, Sussex; *b* 21 Feb. 1966; *o s* of Sir George James Irving Truscott, 3rd Bt and of Yvonne Dora Truscott (*née* Nicholson); *S* father, 2001. *Educ:* Sherborne Sch. *Heir:* none. *Address:* BM QUILL, London WC1N 3XX.

TRUSS, Lynne; writer; *b* 31 May 1955; *d* of Ernest Edward Truss and Joan Dorothy Truss. *Educ:* UCL (BA 1st cl. Hons (English Lang. and Lit.) 1977; Fellow 2004). Literary Ed., The Listener, 1986–90; columnist, TV Critic and Sports Columnist, The Times, 1990–2000. Writer, BBC drama series: Acropolis Now, 2000, 2002; A Certain Age, 2002, 2005; Inspector Steine, 2007, 2008. FRSL 2004. Hon. DLitt Brighton, 2005; DUniv Open, 2006; Hon. DFA, New York Sch. of Visual Arts, 2006. *Publications: novels:* With One Lousy Free Packet of Seed, 1994; Making the Cat Laugh, 1995; Tennyson's Gift, 1996; Going Loco, 1999; *non-fiction:* Tennyson and his Circle, 1999; Eats, Shoots & Leaves, 2003 (Book of the Year, British Book Awards, and USA Today, 2004); Talk to the Hand, 2005; *drama scripts:* A Certain Age, 2007. *Address:* c/o David Higham Associates, 5–8 Lower John Street, Golden Square, W1F 9HA. *T:* (020) 7434 5900, *Fax:* (020) 7437 1072; *e-mail:* dha@davidhigham.co.uk; *web:* www.lynnetruss.com.

TRUSTRAM EVE; *see* Eve, family name of Baron Silsoe.

TRUSWELL, Prof. (Arthur) Stewart, AO 2001; MD, DSc, FRCP, FFPH, FRACP; Professor of Human Nutrition, University of Sydney, since 1978; *b* 18 Aug. 1928; *s* of George Truswell and Molly Truswell (*née* Stewart-Hess); *m* 1st, 1956, Sheila McGregor (marr. diss. 1983); four *s*; 2nd, 1986, Catherine Hull; two *d*. *Educ:* Ruthin Sch., Clwyd; Liverpool Univ.; Cape Town Univ. (MB, ChB 1952, MD 1959); DSc Sydney 1998. FRCP 1975; FFCM 1979; FRACP 1980. Registrar in Pathology, Cape Town Univ., 1954; Registrar in Med., Groote Schuur Hosp., 1955–57; Research Bursar, Clin. Nutrition Unit, Dept. of Med., Cape Town Univ., 1958 and 1959; Adams Meml Trav. Fellowship to London, 1960; Sen. Fellow, Clin. Nutrition, Tulane Univ., USA, 1961; Res. Officer, Clin. Nutrition Unit, Cape Town Univ., 1962; Sen. Mem., Scientific Staff, MRC Atheroma Research Unit, Western Infirmary, Glasgow, 1963 and 1964; full-time Lectr, then Sen. Lectr in Med. and Consultant Gen. Physician, Cape Town Univ. and Groote Schuur Hosp., 1965–71; Warden of Med. Students' Residence, Cape Town Univ., 1967–69; Prof. of Nutrition and Dietetics, Queen Elizabeth Coll., London Univ., 1971–78. Vice-Pres., Internat. Union of Nutritional Sciences, 1985–93; Member, numerous cttees, working parties, editorial bds and socs related to nutrition. *Publications:* Human Nutrition and Dietetics, 7th edn (with S. Davidson, R. Passmore, J. F. Brock), 1979; ABC of Nutrition, 1986, 4th edn 2003; (with J. I. Mann) Essentials of Human Nutrition, 1998, 3rd edn 2007; numerous research papers in sci. jls on various topics in human nutrition. *Recreations:* gardening, walking. *Address:* 23 Woonona Road, Northbridge, NSW 2063, Australia; Human Nutrition Unit, Department of Biochemistry, Sydney University, Sydney, NSW 2006, Australia. *T:* (2) 93513726, *Fax:* (2) 93516022.

TRUSWELL, Paul Anthony; MP (Lab) Pudsey, since 1997; *b* 17 Nov. 1955; *s* of John and Olive Truswell; *m* 1981, Suzanne Clare Evans; two *s*. *Educ:* Firth Park Comprehensive Sch., Sheffield; Leeds Univ. (BA Hons 1977). Journalist, Yorkshire Post newspapers, 1977–88; Local Govt Officer, Wakefield MDC, 1988–97. Member: Leeds HA, 1982–90; Leeds FHSA, 1992–96. Mem. (Lab) Leeds CC, 1982–97. Mem., Envmtl Audit Select Cttee, 1997–99. *Recreations:* playing any sport demanded by my children, photography, cinema. *Address:* House of Commons, SW1A 0AA. *T:* (020) 7219 3504; (constituency office) 10A Greenside, Pudsey, W Yorks LS28 8PU. *T:* (0113) 2293553. *Club:* Civil Service.

TRYON, family name of **Baron Tryon**.

TRYON, 3rd Baron *cr* 1940, of Durnford; **Anthony George Merrik Tryon,** OBE 2001; DL; *b* 26 May 1940; *s* of 2nd Baron Tryon, PC, GCVO, KCB, DSO, and Etheldreda Josephine, *d* of Sir Merrik Burrell, 7th Bt, CBE; *S* father, 1976; *m* 1973, Dale Elizabeth (*d* 1997), *d* of Barry Harper; two *s* two *d* (of whom one *s* one *d* are twins). *Educ:* Eton. Page of Honour to the Queen, 1954–56. Captain Wessex Yeomanry, 1972. Dir, Lazard Bros & Co. Ltd, 1976–83; Chairman: English & Scottish Investors Ltd, 1977–88; Swaine Adeney Brigg, 1991–93. Chm., Salisbury Cathedral Spire Trust, 1985–2000. Pres., Anglers Conservation Assoc., 1985–2000. DL Wilts, 1992. *Recreations:* fishing and shooting. *Heir: s* Hon. Charles George Barrington Tryon, *b* 15 May 1976. *Address:* Fordie Lodge, Comrie, Crieff, Perth PH6 2LT. *T:* (01764) 679060. *Clubs:* White's, Pratt's.

TSANG, Sir Donald Yam-kuen, KBE 1997 (OBE 1993); GBM 2002; Chief Executive, Hong Kong Special Administrative Region, since 2005; *b* 7 Oct. 1944; *m* 1969, Selina Pou; two *s*. *Educ:* Harvard Univ. (MPA). Joined Govt of Hong Kong, 1967: Dep. Dir of Trade, responsible for trade with N America, 1984; Dep. Sec., Gen. Duties, responsible for Sino-British Jt Declaration, 1985; Dir of Admin, Office of Chief Sec., 1989–91; Dir-Gen. of Trade, 1991–93; Sec. for Treasury, 1993–95; Financial Sec., Hong Kong, 1995–2001; Chief Sec. for Admin, HKSAR, 2001–05. *Recreations:* golf, music. *Address:* Office of the Chief Executive, Central Government Offices, Lower Albert Road, Hong Kong; *e-mail:* ceo@ceo.gov.hk.

TSELENTIS, Michael; QC 2003; *b* 4 Nov. 1948; *s* of Anastasios and Helen Tselentis; *m* 1975, Jacqueline de Mowbray Niehaus; two *s*. *Educ:* Univ. of Cape Town (BA 1969; LLB 1971); Magdalen Coll., Oxford (Rhodes Schol. 1972; BCL 1975). Advocate, Supreme Court of South Africa, 1978; SC South Africa, 1989; Acting Judge, Supreme Court of South Africa, 1992; called to the Bar, Gray's Inn, 1995; in practice at the Bar, specialising in commercial law, 1996–. Chm., Johannesburg Bar Council, 1993–94. *Recreations:* squash, swimming, running, golf, reading, music, travelling. *Address:* 20 Essex Street, WC2R 3AL. *T:* (020) 7583 9294, *Fax:* (020) 7583 1341; *e-mail:* mtselentis@20essexst.com. *Clubs:* Oxford and Cambridge; Rand (Johannesburg).

TS'ONG, Fou; *see* Fou Ts'ong.

TSUI, Prof. Daniel C., PhD; Arthur LeGrand Doty Professor, Department of Electrical Engineering, Princeton University, since 1982; *b* Henan, China, 1939; US citizen; *m* Linda Varland. *Educ:* Pui Ching Middle Sch., Hong Kong; Augustana Coll., Rock Island, Ill; Univ. of Chicago (PhD 1967). Res. Associate, Univ. of Chicago, 1967–68; Mem. Technical Staff, Bell Labs, Murray Hill, NJ, 1968–82. Fellow, AAAS; Mem., US NAS, 1987. Nobel Prize for Physics (jtly), 1998; Benjamin Franklin Award in Physics, 1998. *Publications:* contribs to jls. *Address:* Department of Electrical Engineering, Princeton University, Princeton, NJ 08544, USA.

TSUI, Prof. Lap-Chee, OC 1991; OOnt 2000; PhD; FRS 1991; FRSC 1989; Vice-Chancellor, University of Hong Kong, since 2002; Emeritus University Professor, since 2006; *b* 21 Dec. 1950; *s* of Jing-Lue Hsue and Hui-Ching Wang; *m* 1977, Lan Fong (Ellen); two *s. Educ:* Chinese Univ. of Hong Kong (BSc Biol. 1972; MPhil 1974); Univ. of Pittsburgh (PhD Biol Scis 1979). University of Toronto: Asst Prof. 1983–88, Associate Prof. 1988–90, Depts of Med. Genetics and Med. Biophysics; Prof., Dept of Molecular and Med. Genetics, 1990–2002, Univ. Prof., 1994–2006; Hospital for Sick Children, Toronto: Sen. Res. Scientist, 1983–2002; Sellers Chair in Cystic Fibrosis Res., 1989–2002; Dir, Cystic Fibrosis Res. Prog., 1995–99; Geneticist-in-Chief, 1996–2002; Dir, Centre for Applied Genomics, 1998–2002. Mem. of team which identified first DNA marker linked to cystic fibrosis on chromosome 7, 1985; led team which isolated the gene responsible for cystic fibrosis and defined the principal mutation, 1989. Chairman: Gordon Res. Conf. on Human Molecular Genetics, 1995; Genome Canada Task Force, 1998–99; Internat. Sci. Prog. Cttee, Human Genome Meeting 2000, 1999–2000. Trustee, Educn Foundn, Fedn of Chinese Canadian Professionals, Ontario. Eminent Scientist, Inst. of Physical and Chemical Res., Japan, 2000; Vis. Prof., Shantou Univ. Med. Sch., China, 2000. Fellow, World Innovation Foundn, 2001. For. Associate, NAS, USA, 2004. Hon. FRCP 2005. Hon. DCL: Univ. of King's Coll., Halifax, 1991; St Francis Xavier, Antigonish, NS, 1994; Hon. DSc: New Brunswick, Fredericton, 1991; Chinese Univ. of Hong Kong, 1992; York Univ., Toronto, 2001; Tel Aviv, 2005; Toronto, 2007; Aberdeen, 2007. Paul di Sant'Agnese Distinguished Scientific Achievement Award, Cystic Fibrosis Foundn, USA, 1989; Gold Medal of Honor, Pharmaceutical Manufacturers' Assoc., Canada, 1989; Centennial Award, RSCan, 1989; Maclean's Honor Roll, 1989; Award of Excellence, Genetic Soc. Canada, 1990; Courvoisier Leadership Award, 1990; Gairdner Internat. Award, 1990; Cresson Medal, Franklin Inst., 1992; Mead Johnson Award, 1992; Sarsdedt Res. Prize, 1993; Sanremo Internat. Award, 1993; Lecocq Prize, Acad. des Scis, Inst de France, 1994; Henry Friesen Award, 1995; Medal of Honour, Canadian Med. Assoc., 1996; Community Service Award, Toronto Biotechnol. Initiative, 1998; Distinguished Scientist Award, MRC (Canada), 2000; Zellers Sen. Scientist Award, 2001; Killam Prize Award, Canada Council, 2002. *Publications:* numerous papers in learned jls and invited papers and reviews. *Recreations:* cooking, travel, sightseeing. *Address:* University of Hong Kong, Pokfulam Road, Hong Kong. *T:* 28592100, *Fax:* 28589435.

TUAM, Archbishop of, (RC), since 1995; **Most Rev. Michael Neary;** *b* 15 April 1946. Ordained priest, 1971; Titular Bishop of Quaestoriana and Auxiliary Bishop of Tuam, 1992–95. *Address:* Archbishop's House, Tuam, Co. Galway, Ireland. *T:* (93) 24166, *Fax:* (93) 28070; *e-mail:* archdiocesetuam@eircom.net.

TUAM, KILLALA AND ACHONRY, Bishop of, since 1998; **Rt Rev. Richard Crosbie Aitken Henderson,** DPhil; *b* 27 March 1957; *s* of Baron Henderson of Brompton, KBE; *m* 1985, Anita Julia Whiting; one *s* two *d. Educ:* Westminster Sch.; Magdalen Coll., Oxford (MA, DPhil 1984); St John's Coll., Nottingham (DipTh Univ. of Nottingham 1984; Dip Pastoral Studies 1986). Ordained deacon, 1986, priest, 1987; Curate, Chinnor with Emmington and Sydenham, Dio. Oxford, 1986–89; Diocese of Cork, Cloyne and Ross: Incumbent, Abbeystrewry Union, 1989–95; Ross Union, 1995–98; Canon, Cork and Ross Cathedrals, 1993–95; Prebendary of Cork, 1995–98; Dean of Ross, 1995–98. *Publication:* The Jealousy of Jonah, 2006. *Recreation:* woodwork. *Address:* Bishop's House, Knockglass, Crossmolina, Co. Mayo, Ireland. *T:* (96) 31317.

See also Hon. Sir L. D. J. Henderson.

TUCK, Anne Victoria, (Vicky); Principal, Cheltenham Ladies' College, since 1996; *b* 9 Jan. 1953; *m* 1977, Peter John Tuck; two *s. Educ:* Univ. of Kent (BA Hons French and Italian); Univ. of London Inst. of Educn (PGCE); Univ. de Lille et de Paris (Dip. Supérieur de Droit et de français des Affaires); Univ. of South Bank (MA). French and Italian teacher, Putney High Sch., 1976–81; Hd of Mod. Langs, Bromley High Sch., 1981–86; Lectr, Inst. of Educn, London Univ., 1991–94; Dep. Hd, City of London Sch. for Girls, 1994–96. Pres., GSA, 2008. *Address:* Cheltenham Ladies' College, Bayshill Road, Cheltenham, Glos GL50 3EP.

TUCK, Anthony; *see* Tuck, J. A.

TUCK, Sir Bruce (Adolph Reginald), 3rd Bt *cr* 1910; *b* 29 June 1926; *o s* of Major Sir (William) Reginald Tuck, 2nd Bt, and Gladys Emily Kettle (*d* 1966), *d* of late N. Alfred Nathan, Wickford, Auckland, New Zealand, and *widow* of Desmond Fosberry Kettle, Auckland Mounted Rifles; *S* father, 1954; *m* 1st, 1949, Luise (marr. diss. in Jamaica, 1964), *d* of John C. Renfro, San Angelo, Texas, USA; two *s;* 2nd, 1968, Pamela Dorothy Nicholson, *d* of Alfred Nicholson, London; one *d. Educ:* Canford School, Dorset. Lieutenant, Scots Guards, 1945–47. *Heir: s* Richard Bruce Tuck, *b* 7 Oct. 1952. *Address:* Clopton House, 39 Mill Road, Ashley, Newmarket, Cambs CB8 9EE.

TUCK, Clarence Edward Henry; Civil Service Commissioner, 1977–83; *b* 18 April 1925; *s* of Frederick and May Tuck; *m* 1950, Daphne Robinson; one *s* one *d. Educ:* Rendcomb Coll., Cirencester; Merton Coll., Oxford. BA 1949. Served in Royal Signals, 1943–47. Inland Revenue, 1950; Min. of Supply, 1950–55; seconded to Nigerian Federal Govt, Lagos, 1955–57; Ministry of: Supply, 1957–59; Aviation, 1959–60; Defence, 1960–62; Aviation, 1962–66; IDC, 1967; Min. of Technology, 1968–70; Trade and Industry, 1970; CSD, 1971; Trade and Industry, 1973; Dept of Energy, 1974; Civil Service Dept, 1976; Management and Personnel Office, 1981; Dir, Civil Service Selection Board, 1977–81. Asst Principal, 1950; Principal, 1953; Asst Sec., 1962; Under-Sec., 1970.

TUCK, Prof. (John) Anthony, MA, PhD; FRHistS; Professor of Medieval History, University of Bristol, 1990–93, now Emeritus; *b* 14 Nov. 1940; *s* of late Prof. John Philip Tuck and Jane Adelaide Tuck; *m* 1976, Amanda (marr. diss. 2003), *d* of late Dr L. J. Cawley, Carlton Husthwaite, near Thirsk, Yorks; two *s. Educ:* Newcastle upon Tyne Royal Grammar Sch.; Jesus Coll., Cambridge (BA, MA, PhD). FRHistS 1987. Lecturer in History, 1965–75, Sen. Lectr, 1975–78, Univ. of Lancaster; Master of Collingwood Coll., and Hon. Lectr in History, Univ. of Durham, 1978–87; Reader in Medieval History, Univ. of Bristol, 1987–90. Res. Associate, Oxford DNB, 1998–. Hon. Life Fellow, Collingwood Coll., Durham Univ., 1998. Clerk, Stapleford Parish Council, 2000–03. *Publications:* Richard II and the English Nobility, 1973; Crown and Nobility 1272–1461, 1985, 2nd edn 1999; (contrib.) Oxford DNB, 2004; contribs to various acad. jls and vols of essays. *Recreations:* walking, gardening, local history. *Address:* 8 Cherry Garden Lane, Newport, Saffron Walden, Essex CB11 3PZ.

See also R. F. Tuck.

TUCK, Jonathan Philip; Director of Library Services, Royal Holloway, University of London, since 2008; *b* 6 Sept. 1952; *s* of Philip Charles Tuck and Janetta Margaret Tuck; *m* 1982, Ann Lambert; one *s. Educ:* Portsmouth Grammar Sch.; Univ. of Manchester (MA); MA Oxon 1998. MCLIP (ALA 1981). John Rylands University Library of Manchester: Asst Librarian, 1978–90; Sub-Librarian, 1990–94; Asst Dir and Head of Admin, 1994–96; Asst Dir and Dep. Univ. Librarian, 1996–97; Dep. to Dir, Univ. Liby Services, and to Bodley's Librarian, Oxford Univ., 1998–2002; Fellow, Wolfson Coll., Oxford, 1998–2002; Hd, British Collections, BL, 2002–08. *Publications:* contrib. articles on aspects of librarianship, library collections and web archiving. *Recreations:* book collecting, sport, especially cricket, football, Portsmouth Football Club. *Address:* Royal Holloway, University of London, Bedford Library, Egham, Surrey TW20 0EX. *T:* (01784) 443330.

TUCK, Prof. Richard Francis, PhD; FBA 1994; Professor of Government, Harvard University, since 1995; *b* 9 Jan. 1949; *s* of late Prof. John Philip Tuck and Jane Adelaide Tuck; *m* 1st, 1970, Mary Polwarth (marr. diss. 1993); two *s;* 2nd, 1993, Anne Malcolm; one *d. Educ:* Royal Grammar Sch., Newcastle upon Tyne; Jesus Coll., Cambridge (BA 1970; PhD 1976; Hon. Fellow 1997). Cambridge University: Research Fellow, 1970, Fellow, 1971–97, Jesus Coll.; Univ. Asst Lectr in History, 1973–77; Lectr in History, 1977–95; Reader in Political Theory, 1995. Vis. Fellow, Princeton Univ., 1989; Carlyle Lectr, Oxford, 1991. Foreign Hon. Mem., Amer. Acad. of Arts and Scis, 1992. *Publications:* Natural Rights Theories, 1979; Hobbes, 1989; Hobbes' Leviathan, 1991; Philosophy and Government 1572–1651, 1993; The Rights of War and Peace, 2001. *Recreations:* repairing houses, looking after children. *Address:* Department of Government, Littauer Center, Harvard University, Cambridge, MA 02138–3001, USA; 9 Park Terrace, Cambridge CB1 1JH.

See also J. A. Tuck.

TUCK, Vicky; *see* Tuck, A. V.

TUCKER, Andrew Victor Gunn; HM Diplomatic Service; on interchange, since 2005; *b* 20 Dec. 1955; *s* of Kenneth Gunn Tucker and Megan Tucker; *m* 1986, Judith Anne Gibson. *Educ:* Calday Grange Grammar Sch., Wirral; University Coll., Oxford (BA Hons 1978; MA 1986). MCIL (MIL 1988). Jt Tech. Lang. Service, 1978–81; joined HM Diplomatic Service, 1981; lang. trng, SOAS, 1982; Second Sec., Dar es Salaam, 1982–85; First Secretary: on loan to Cabinet Office, 1985–87; and Press Attaché, Moscow, 1987–90; Dep. Hd, CSCE Unit, FCO, 1991–93; on loan to Auswärtiges Amt, 1993–94; Bonn, 1994–97; Dep. High Comr, Nairobi, and concurrently Alternate Perm. Rep. to UNEP and UN Centre for Human Settlements (Habitat), 1997–2000; Ambassador to Azerbaijan, 2000–03; Manager, Prism Prog., FCO, 2003–05. *Recreations:* theatre, long walks, music, crosswords, cooking. *Address:* c/o Foreign and Commonwealth Office, King Charles Street, SW1A 2AH. *Clubs:* Royal Commonwealth Society, Royal Over-Seas League.

TUCKER, Clive Fenemore, CB 1996; Associate Director, Specialist Schools and Academies Trust, since 2008; Director, International Affairs, Department for Education and Skills (formerly Department for Education and Employment), 1995–2006, and Department for Work and Pensions, 2001–06; *b* 13 July 1944; *s* of William Frederick Tucker and Joan Tucker; *m* 1978, Caroline Elisabeth Macready; two *d. Educ:* Cheltenham Grammar Sch.; Balliol Coll., Oxford (BA). Entered Ministry of Labour, 1965; Private Sec. to Perm. Sec., 1968–70; Department of Employment, later Department for Education and Employment: Principal, 1970; Asst Sec., 1978; Grade 4, 1986; Under Sec., 1987. Chm., EU Employment Cttee, 2001–03. Non-exec. Dir, RTZ Chemicals, 1987–90. Mem., Fulbright Commn, 1998–2006. *Recreations:* opera, looking at pictures, tennis.

TUCKER, Elizabeth Mary; Head Mistress, Headington School, Oxford, 1982–96; *b* 20 July 1936; *d* of late Harold and Doris Tucker. *Educ:* Cheltenham Ladies' College; Newnham College, Cambridge (BA Classical Tripos 1958); King's College London (PGCE). Assistant Mistress, Queen Anne's School, Caversham, 1959–64; Head of Classics, Notting Hill and Ealing High School, GPDST, 1964–72; Head Mistress, Christ's Hospital, Hertford, 1972–82. Associate, Newnham Coll., Cambridge, 1986–99. Corporate Mem., Cheltenham Ladies' Coll., 1994. Trustee: Bloxham Project, 1982–2005; Channing Sch., Highgate, 2001– (Mem. Council, 1995–2000); Donation Gov., Christ's Hosp., 2002–. *Recreations:* music (piano), friends and family. *Address:* 78 Manor Drive, N20 0DU. *Club:* University Women's.

TUCKER, His Honour (Henry John) Martin; QC 1975; DL; a Circuit Judge, 1981–99; Resident Judge, Winchester Combined Court Centre, 1994–99; *b* 8 April 1930; *s* of late P. A. Tucker, LDS, RCS and Mrs Dorothy Tucker (*née* Hobbs); *m* 1957, Sheila Helen Wateridge, LRAM; one *s* four *d. Educ:* St Peter's Sch., Southbourne; Downside Sch.; Christ Church, Oxford (MA). Called to Bar, Inner Temple, 1954; Dep. Chm., Somerset QS, 1971; a Recorder of the Crown Court, 1972–81. Pres., Council of HM Circuit Judges, 1993. DL Hampshire, 1996. *Publication:* The Chingri Khal Chronicles, 2006. *Recreations:* walking occasionally; gardening gently; listening to music. *Address:* Chingri Khal, Sleepers Hill, Winchester, Hants SO22 4NB. *T:* (01962) 853927.

TUCKER, Jon(athan Leslie Tucker); Director, Corporate Services, National Museum of Science and Industry, since 2007; *b* 13 Oct. 1961; *s* of Leslie Harold Tucker and Marilyn Alice Tucker; *m* 1991, Janette Roe; one *s* one *d. Educ:* Fitzwilliam Coll., Cambridge (MA Sci. Tripos 1984). ACIB 1987. Lloyds Bank, subseq. Lloyds TSB: various managerial appts, Retail and Commercial Banking, 1984–96; Sen. Manager, Exec. Develt, 1997–98; Asst Dir, 1999–2002, Head, 2002–07, Science Mus. *Recreations:* science, museums and heritage, gardening, wildlife, military history. *Address:* Science Museum, Exhibition Road, SW7 2DD. *T:* (020) 7942 4660; *e-mail:* jon.tucker@nmsi.ac.uk.

TUCKER, Martin; *see* Tucker, H. J. M.

TUCKER, Prof. Maurice Edwin, PhD; FGS; Professor of Geological Sciences, Durham University, since 1993; Master, University College, Durham, since 1998; *b* 6 Nov. 1946; *s* of Edwin Herlin and Winifred Tucker; *m* 1970, Vivienne; one *s* one *d. Educ:* Wanstead High Sch., Redbridge; Durham Univ. (BSc 1st cl. Hons Geol. 1968); Reading Univ. (PhD Sedimentol. 1971). CGeol; FGS 1973. Lecturer: Univ. of Sierra Leone, 1971–72; UC Cardiff, Univ. of Wales, 1973–74; Univ. of Newcastle, 1975–82; Lindemann Trust Fellow, Univ. of Calif, Berkeley, 1980–81; Lectr, 1983–86, Sen. Lectr, 1986–88, Reader, 1988–93, Durham Univ. Pres., Internat. Assoc. of Sedimentologists, 1998–2002. Geological Society: Moiety of Lyell Fund, 1983; Coke Medal, 1994. *Publications:*

Sedimentary Petrology, 1981, 3rd edn 2001; Field Description of Sedimentary Rocks, 1982; Carbonate Sedimentology, 1990; Sedimentary Rocks in the Field, 1996, 3rd edn 2003; edited: Modern and Ancient Lake Sediments, 1978; Techniques in Sedimentology, 1988; Carbonate Platforms, 1990; Carbonate Diagenesis, 1990; Calcretes, 1991; Dolomites, 1994; res. papers in carbonate sedimentol. and limestones. Recreations: tennis, ski-ing, sailing, scuba diving, modern art, North American auto licence plates. Address: Department of Earth Sciences, Durham University, Durham DH1 3LE. T: (0191) 334 2284; University College, The Castle, Durham DH1 3RW. T: (0191) 334 4141.

TUCKER, Paul Michael William; Executive Director, Markets, and Member, Monetary Policy Committee, Bank of England, since 2002; b 24 March 1958; s of Brian William Tucker and late Helen May Tucker (née Lloyd). Educ: Trinity Coll., Cambridge (BA Maths, and Philosophy). Joined Bank of England, 1980; Bank Supervisor, 1980–84, and 1987; seconded to merchant bank as corporate financier, 1985–86; seconded to Hong Kong Govt as Advr to Hong Kong Securities Review Cttee, 1987–88; Mkts Area, 1988–89; Private Sec. to Gov., 1989–92; Gilt-Edged and Money Mkts Div., 1993–96 (Hd of Div., 1994–96); Hd of Monetary Assessment and Strategy Div., 1997–98; Dep. Dir, Financial Stability, 1999–2002. Mem., Monetary Policy Cttee Secretariat, 1997–2002. Address: Bank of England, Threadneedle Street, EC2R 8AH. T: (020) 7601 4444. Club: Athenæum.

TUCKER, Peter Louis; Chairman, Sierra Leone Law Reform Commission, since 2003; b 11 Dec. 1927; s of Peter Louis Tucker and Marion Tucker; m 1st, 1955, Clarissa Mary Harleston; three s one d (and one d decd); 2nd, 1972, Teresa Josephine Ganda; one s. Educ: Fourah Bay Coll., Sierra Leone (MA Latin, Dunelm); Jesus Coll., Oxford (MA Jurisp.); DipEd. Called to Bar, Gray's Inn, 1970; practised as barrister, Sierra Leone, 1983–84. Teacher, 1952–57; Education Officer, 1957–61; Secretary, Training and Recruitment, Sierra Leone Civil Service, 1961–63; Establishment Sec., 1963–66; Sec. to the Prime Minister and Head of Sierra Leone Civil Service, 1966–67; Asst Director, UK Immigrants Advisory Service, 1970–72; Principal Admin. Officer, Community Relations Commn, 1972–74; Dir of Fieldwork and Admin., 1974–77; Dir of Legal and Gen. Services, and Sec., 1977, Chief Exec., 1977–82, CRE; Comr and Chm., Sierra Leone Population Census, 1984; Special Envoy on Foreign Aid to Sierra Leone and Chm., Nat. Aid Co-ordinating Cttee, 1986–90; Chairman: National Constitutional Review Commn, 1990–91; Nat. Policy Adv. Cttee, 1998–99; Advr to Pres., Sierra Leone, 1998–99. DCL (hc) Sierra Leone. Papal Medal Pro Ecclesia et Pontifice, 1966. Publications: The Tuckers of Sierra Leone 1665–1914, 1997; Origin and Philosophy of the Sierra Leone People's Party, 2001; miscellaneous booklets, articles and reports for Community Relations Commission and Govt of Sierra Leone. Recreations: photography, listening to music, the internet. Address: Flat 5, Merewood Court, 60 Carew Road, Eastbourne, E Sussex BN21 2JR. T: and Fax: (01323) 727998.

TUCKER, Sir Richard (Howard), Kt 1985; a Judge of the High Court of Justice, Queen's Bench Division, 1985–2000; b 9 July 1930; s of Howard Archibald Tucker (His Honour Judge Tucker), and Margaret Minton Tucker; m 1st, 1958, Paula Mary Bennett Frost (marr. diss. 1974); one s two d; 2nd, 1975, Wendy Kate Standbrook (d 1988); 3rd, 1989, Jacqueline Suzanne Rossvell Thomson, widow of William Thomson, artist. Educ: Shrewsbury Sch.; The Queen's Coll., Oxford (MA; Hon. Fellow, 1992). 2nd Lieut, RAOC, 1948–50. Called to Bar, Lincoln's Inn, 1954; Bencher, 1979; Treasurer, 2002. QC 1972; a Recorder, 1972–85; Mem. Senate, Inns of Court and the Bar, 1984–86; Dep. Leader, 1984–85, and Presiding Judge, 1986–90, Midland and Oxford Circuit. Member: Employment Appeal Tribunal, 1986–2000; Parole Bd, 1996–2003 (Vice-Chm., 1998–2000); Comr, Royal Ct of Jersey, 2003–. Mediator, 2004–. Commn of Enquiry, Grand Cayman, 2008. Recreations: sailing, shooting, gardening, model railways. Address: Treasury Office, Lincoln's Inn, WC2A 3TL. Clubs: Garrick; Leander (Henley-on-Thames); Bar Yacht.

TUCKETT, William Jonathan; Principal Guest Artist, Royal Ballet; freelance choreographer and director, since 2005; b 3 Feb. 1969; s of John Tuckett and Gillian Gould; partner, Caro Howell. Educ: Bristol Cathedral Sch.; Royal Ballet Upper Sch. Dancer and Choreographer: Sadler's Wells Royal Ballet, 1988–90; Royal Ballet, Covent Garden, 1990–2005; freelance, 2005–, working for Royal Ballet, Royal Opera House (ROH2), English Nat. Ballet, Channel Four, Almeida Th. Recreations: playing with my cats, compulsively buying DVDs, fighting addiction to Bendicks' Bittermints (unsuccessfully). Address: c/o Royal Opera House, Covent Garden, WC2E 9DD.

TUCKEY, Andrew Marmaduke Lane; Vice Chairman, Corporate Finance, Landsbanki Securities (UK) Ltd, since 2007; b 28 Aug. 1943; s of late Henry Lane Tuckey and of Aileen Rosemary Newsom Tuckey; m 1st, 1967, Margaret Louise (née Barnes) (marr. diss. 1998); one s two d; 2nd, 1998, Tracy Elisabeth (née Long); two d. Educ: Plumtree Sch., Zimbabwe. Chartered Accountant, 1966. Dixon Wilson, Chartered Accountants, 1962–66; British American Tobacco, 1966–68; Baring Brothers & Co., Ltd, 1968–95: Dir, 1973–81; Man. Dir, 1981–89; Chm., 1989–95; Dep. Chm., Barings plc, 1989–95; Adviser: Baring Brothers Ltd, 1995–96; Phoenix Securities Ltd, 1996–97; Senior Adviser: Donaldson, Lufkin & Jenrette, 1997–2000; Credit Suisse First Boston, 2000–01; Bridgewell, 2001–07 (Dir, 2003–05; Man. Dir, 2005–07). Dir, Dillon, Read Holding Inc., 1991–95. Member: Federal Reserve Bank of New York Internat. Capital Markets Adv. Cttee, 1992–95; Financial Law Panel, 1993–97; Council, Baring Foundn, 1994–96. Director: Friends of Covent Garden, 1981–98 (Treas., 1981–96); Royal Opera House, 1992–95; City of London Fest., 2004–; Watermill Th., 2005–. Gov., 2005–, Chm., 2007–, Central Sch. of Ballet (Chm., Develt Bd, 2002–05). Trustee: Esmée Fairbairn Charitable Trust, 1986–99; Classic FM Charitable Trust, 1992–99. Recreations: music, tennis. Address: Landsbanki, Bow Bells House, 1 Bread Street, EC4M 9BF. Club: White's. See also Rt Hon. Sir S. L. Tuckey.

TUCKEY, Rt Hon. Sir Simon (Lane), Kt 1992; PC 1998; **Rt Hon. Lord Justice Tuckey;** a Lord Justice of Appeal, since 1998; b 17 Oct. 1941; s of late Henry Lane Tuckey and of Aileen Rosemary Newsom Tuckey; m 1964, Jennifer Rosemary (née Hardie); one s two d. Educ: Plumtree School, Zimbabwe. Called to Bar, Lincoln's Inn, 1964, Bencher, 1989; QC 1981; a Recorder, 1984–92; a Judge of the High Court of Justice, QBD, 1992–98; a Judge, Employment Appeal Tribunal, 1993–98; Presiding Judge, Western Circuit, 1995–97; Judge in Charge, Commercial List, 1997–98. Chm., Review Panel, Financial Reporting Council, 1990–92. Mem., Judicial Studies Bd, 1993–95 (Chm., Civil and Family Cttee, 1993–95). Recreations: sailing, tennis. Address: Royal Courts of Justice, Strand, WC2A 2LL. See also A. M. L. Tuckey.

TUCKMAN, Frederick Augustus, (Fred), OBE 1990; FCIS, FCIPD; b 9 June 1922; s of Otto and Amy Tina Tuchmann (née Adler); m 1966, Patricia Caroline Myers; two s one d. Educ: English and German schools; London School of Economics, 1946–49 (BScEcon). Served RAF, 1942–46. Commercial posts, 1950–65; Management Consultant and Partner, HAY Gp, 1965–85; Managing Director, HAY GmbH, Frankfurt, 1970–80; Partner, HAY Associates, 1975–85; Chm., Suomen HAY, OY, Helsinki, 1973–81;

consultant assignments in Europe, Africa and N America. Hon. Sec., Bow Gp, 1958–59; Councillor, London Borough of Camden, 1965–71 (Chm., Library and Arts, 1968–71). Mem. (C) Leicester, European Parliament, 1979–89; contested (C) Leicester, Eur. Parly elecn, 1989. Mem. Council, Inst. of Personnel Management, 1963–70. Chm., Greater London Area, CPC, 1968–70. European Parliament: Budget Cttee, 1979–81; Social and Employment Cttee, 1981–89 (Cons. spokesman, 1984–89); substitute Mem., Economic and Monetary Cttee, 1979–87; substitute Mem., Budgetary Control Cttee, 1984–87; First Vice Pres., Latin American Delegn, 1982–85; Mem., Israel Delegn, 1987–89; Chm., Internat. Gp on Small Business, 1985–86. UK Chm., European Year of Small Business, 1983; Vice Chm., Small Business Bureau, London, 1985–89. Pres., Anglo-Jewish Assoc., 1989–95 (Vice-Pres., 1995–2003); Vice Pres., Eur. Medium and Small Units, 1985–90. Cross, Order of Merit (FRG), 1989. Recreations: reading, arguing, travel, swimming; priority—family. Address: 6 Cumberland Road, Barnes, SW13 9LY. T: (020) 8748 2392. Club: Athenæum.

TUCKNOTT, John Anthony, MBE 1990; HM Diplomatic Service; Deputy Head of Mission, Baghdad, since 2007; b 2 Jan. 1958; s of late Eric Tucknott and of Ethel Tucknott (née Holland); m 2000, Riitta-Leena Irmeli Lehtinen; one s. Educ: Bournemouth Sch.; King's Coll. London (MA). Dept of Employment, 1975–77; joined HM Diplomatic Service, 1977; Communications Ops Dept, FCO, 1977–78; Lord Privy Seal's Office, 1978–80; Archivist, Rome, 1980–82; Cairo, 1982–85; N American Dept, 1985–87, W African Dept, 1987–88, FCO; Dep. Hd of Mission, Beirut, 1988–93; Hd of Section, Security Policy Dept, FCO, 1993–95; First Sec., UKMIS to UN, NY, 1995–98; Dep. Hd, Non-proliferation Dept, 1998–2000, UK Co-ordinator for War Crimes Issues, 2000–01, FCO; Counsellor (Trade and Investment Develt), Stockholm, 2002–05; Sen. Directing Staff (Civilian), RCDS, 2005–07. Recreations: walking, reading, music, travel. Address: c/o Foreign and Commonwealth Office, King Charles Street, SW1A 2AH.

TUCKWELL, Anthony David, MA; National Director, National Educational Assessment Centre, since 2000; Headmaster, King Edward VI Grammar School, Chelmsford, 1984–99; b 4 July 1943; s of Alec William Tuckwell and Muriel Florence Tuckwell (née Green); m 1967, Kathleen Olivia Hatton. Educ: St Peter's Coll., Oxford (MA); Oxford Univ. Dept of Educn (DipEd); MBA Leeds Metropolitan 1995. History Master, Southern Grammar Sch. for Boys, Portsmouth, 1966–69; St John's College, Southsea: Hd of Hist., 1970–73; Sen. Teacher (Curriculum Co-ordinator), 1973–78; Dep. Headmaster, Sale Co. Grammar Sch. for Boys, 1979–83. Headship Appt Consultant, ASCL, 1999–2008. Mem. Bd of Dirs, Chelmsford Cathedral Fest. Ltd, 1999–2008. Gov., Cobham Hall Sch., 2003–. Publications: (contrib.) School Leadership in the 21st Century, 1996; (contrib.) Living Headship: voices, value, vision, 1999; That Honourable and Gentlemanlike House: a history of King Edward VI Grammar School, Chelmsford 1551–2001, 2000, 2008; New Hall and its School: 'a true school of virtuous demeanour', 2006. Recreations: music, literature, gardening, travel. Address: 28 Oaklands Crescent, Chelmsford, Essex CM2 9PP.

TUCKWELL, Barry Emmanuel, AC 1992; OBE 1965; horn soloist, retired; conductor; Conductor and Music Director, Maryland Symphony Orchestra, 1982–98; b 5 March 1931; s of late Charles and Elizabeth Tuckwell, Australia; m 1st, 1958, Sally Eelin Newton; one s one d; 2nd, 1971, Hilary Jane Warburton; one s; 3rd, 1992, Susan Terry Levitan. Educ: various schs, Australia; Sydney Conservatorium. FRCM 1993. Melbourne Symph. Orch., 1947; Sydney Symph. Orch., 1947–50; Hallé Orch., 1951–53; Scottish Nat. Orch., 1953–54; Bournemouth Symphony Orch., 1954–55; London Symph. Orch., 1955–68; founded Tuckwell Wind Quintet, 1968; Conductor, Tasmanian Symphony Orch., 1979–83; Guest Conductor, Northern Sinfonia, 1993–97. Mem. Chamber Music Soc. of Lincoln Center, 1974–81; Horn Prof., Royal Academy of Music, 1963–74; Pres., Internat. Horn Soc., 1969–77, 1992–94. Has played and conducted annually throughout Europe, GB, USA and Canada; has appeared at many internat. festivals, incl. Salzburg and Edinburgh; took part in 1st Anglo-Soviet Music Exchange, Leningrad and Moscow, 1963; toured: Far East, 1964 and 1975; Australia, 1970–95; S America, 1976; USSR, 1977; People's Republic of China, 1984. Many works dedicated to him; has made numerous recordings. Editor, complete horn literature for G. Schirmer Inc. Professorial Fellow, Univ. of Melbourne, 2005. Hon. RAM, 1966; Hon. GSM, 1967. Hon. DMus Sydney. Harriet Cohen Internat. Award for Solo Instruments, 1968; George Peabody Medal, 1997; Andrew White Medal, Loyola Coll., 1998. Publications: Playing the Horn, 1978; The Horn, 1981. Club: Athenæum.

TUDGE, Colin Hiram, FLS; author; b 22 April 1943; s of late Cyril Tudge and Maisie Tudge; m 1st, 1966, Rosemary Shewan (marr. diss. 2001); one s two d; 2nd, 2001, Ruth West. Educ: Dulwich Coll.; Peterhouse, Cambridge (MA 1966). Writer on various magazines, 1965–80; Features Ed., New Scientist, 1980–85; presenter, BBC Radio 3, 1985–90; freelance author and broadcaster, 1990–. Res. Fellow, Centre for the Philosophy of Social and Natural Scis, LSE, 1995–2005. FLS 1995. Publications: The Famine Business, 1977; (with M. Allaby) Home Farm, 1977; Future Cook, 1980; The Food Connection, 1985; Food Crops for the Future, 1988; Global Ecology, 1991; The Engineer in the Garden, 1993; The Day Before Yesterday, 1995; Neanderthals, Bandits and Farmers, 1998; The Second Creation, 2000; The Variety of Life, 2000; In Mendel's Footnotes, 2001; So Shall We Reap, 2003; The Secret Life of Trees, 2005; Feeding People is Easy, 2007. Recreation: working with farmers and restaurateurs to bring about a people's takeover of the world's food supply chain. Address: 20 Dove House Close, Wolvercote, Oxon OX2 8BQ; e-mail: colintudge@supanet.com; web: www.colintudge.com

TUDHOPE, James Mackenzie, CB 1987; part-time Chairman of Social Security Appeal Tribunals, 1987–91; b 11 Feb. 1927; m Margaret Willock Kirkwood, MA Glasgow; two s. Educ: Dunoon Grammar School; Univ. of Glasgow (BL 1951). Served Army, 1945–48. Admitted Solicitor, 1951. Private legal practice, 1951–55; Procurator Fiscal Depute, 1955, Senior PF Depute, 1962, Asst PF, 1968–70, Glasgow; PF, Kilmarnock, 1970–73; Dumbarton, 1973–76; Regional Procurator Fiscal: S Strathclyde, Dumfries and Galloway at Hamilton, 1976–80; for Glasgow and Strathkelvin, 1980–87. Hon. Sheriff, N Strathclyde, 1989–. Mem. Council, Law Soc. of Scotland, 1983–86. Recreations: serendipity, worrying. Address: Point House, Dundonald Road, Kilmarnock, Ayrshire KA1 1TY.

TUDOR, Rev. Dr (Richard) John, BA; Chaplain to the Regents, Harris Manchester College, Oxford, since 2000; b 8 Feb. 1930; s of Charles Leonard and Ellen Tudor; m 1956, Cynthia Campbell Anderson; one s one d. Educ: Clee Grammar Sch., Grimsby; Queen Elizabeth's, Barnet; Univ. of Manchester, 1951–54 (BA Theology). Served RAF, 1948–51. Junior Methodist Minister, East Ham, London, 1954–57; Ordained, Newark, 1957; Minister, Thornton Cleveleys, Blackpool, 1957–60; Superintendent Minister: Derby Methodist Mission, 1960–71 (Chaplain to Mayor of Derby, Factories and Association with Derby Football Club); Coventry Methodist Mission, 1971–75 (Chaplain to Lord Mayor); Brighton Dome Mission, 1975–81; Westminster Central Hall, London, 1981–95; Free Church Chaplain, Westminster Hosp., 1982–93; Chaplain to Ancient Order of Foresters, 1989–, to Lord Mayor of Westminster, 1993–94. Hon. DD Texas

Wesleyan Univ., Fort Worth, USA, 1981; Hon. Texan, 1965; Freeman of Fort Worth, 1970. *Publication:* Word for all Seasons, 1992. *Recreations:* motoring, cooking, photography, the delights of family life. *Address:* Harris Manchester College, Oxford OX1 3TD. *T:* (01865) 271007.

TUDOR-CRAIG, Pamela; *see* Wedgwood, Pamela Lady.

TUDOR EVANS, Sir Haydn, Kt 1974; a Judge of the High Court of Justice, Queen's Bench Division, 1978–94 (Family Division, 1974–78); *b* 20 June 1920; 4th *s* of John Edgar Evans and Ellen (*née* Stringer); *m* 1947, Sheilagh Isabella Pilkington; one *s. Educ:* Cardiff High Sch.; West Monmouth School; Lincoln College, Oxford. RNVR, 1940–41. Open Scholar, Lincoln Coll., Oxford (Mod. History), 1940; Stewart Exhibitioner, 1942; Final Hons Sch., Mod. History, 1944; Final Hons Sch., Jurisprudence, 1945. Cholmeley Scholar, Lincoln's Inn, 1946; called to the Bar, Lincoln's Inn, 1947, Bencher 1970. QC 1962; Dep. Chm., Kent QS, 1968–72; Recorder of Crown Court, 1972–74; a Judge, Employment Appeal Tribunal, 1982–88. *Recreation:* watching Rugby, racing and cricket. *Address:* 50 James Street, Louth, Lincs LN11 0JW. *Clubs:* Garrick, MCC.

TUDOR JOHN, William; DL; Deputy Chairman, Nationwide Building Society, since 2007; *b* 26 April 1944; *s* of Tudor and Gwen John; *m* 1967, Jane Clark (*d* 2007); three *d. Educ:* Cowbridge Sch., S Wales; Downing Coll., Cambridge (MA). Asst Solicitor, Allen & Overy, 1969–71; Banker, Orion Bank Ltd, 1971–72; Allen & Overy: Partner, 1972–2001; Head of Banking Dept, 1972–92; Man. Partner, 1992–94; Sen. Partner, 1994–2000; Chm. and Man. Dir, European Commitment Cttee, Lehman Brothers, 2000–08; Director: Lehman Brothers Europe Ltd, 2000–08; Lehman Brothers Internat. (Europe), 2000–08; Lehman Brothers European Mezzanine; SICAV, 2004–. Non-executive Chairman: Sutton Seeds (Hldgs) Ltd, 1978–93; Horticultural & Botanical Hldgs Ltd, 1985–93; non-executive Director: Woolwich plc, 2000; Portman Bldg Soc., 2001–07 (Dep. Chm., 2004–06; Chm., 2006–07); Sun Bank plc, 2001–04; Grainger Trust plc, 2005–. Associate Fellow, Downing Coll., Cambridge, 1985–92, 1997–. Member: Law Soc., 1969–; City of London Solicitors' Co., 1974–; IBA, 1978–; Financial Law Panel, 1996–2002; Financial Mkts Law Cttee, 2002– (Vice-Chm., 2002–); Chm., Wales in London, 2002–06. Chm., Law Foundn Adv. Council, Oxford Univ., 1998–2003; Mem., Adv. Bd, Oxford Univ. Develt Prog., 1999–. Non-exec. Dir, Nat. Film and Television Sch., 2000–. Steward of Appeal, BBB of C, 1978–. Freeman, City of London, 1994; Liveryman, Co. of Gunmakers, 1994–. High Sheriff, Herts, 2006–07; DL Herts, 2007. *Recreations:* Rugby football as an observer, music as a listener, shooting and reading as a participant, daughters' banker. *Address:* Willian Bury, Willian, Herts SG6 2AF. *T:* (01462) 683532; *e-mail:* tjwillian@btinternet.com. *Club:* Cardiff and County (Cardiff).

TUFFIN, Alan David, CBE 1993; General Secretary, Union of Communication Workers, 1982–93; *b* 2 Aug. 1933; *s* of Oliver Francis and Gertrude Elizabeth Tuffin; *m* 1957, Jean Elizabeth Tuffin; one *s* one *d. Educ:* Eltham Secondary Sch., SE9. Post Office employment, London, 1949–69; London Union Regional Official for UCW, 1957–69; National Official, 1969; Deputy General Secretary, 1979. Member: TUC Gen. Council, 1982–93 (Pres., 1992–93); HSC, 1986–96; Employment Appeal Tribunal, 1995–2000. Dir, Trade Union Fund Managers Ltd (formerly Trade Union Unit Trust), 1985–; non-exec. Dir, Remploy Ltd, 1999–2006. FRSA 1990. *Recreations:* reading, squash, West Ham United FC. *Address:* c/o TUFM Ltd, Congress House, Great Russell Street, WC1B 3LQ.

TUFFIN, David William, FRICS; FBEng; Managing Partner, Tuffin Ferraby Taylor, since 2004; President, Royal Institution of Chartered Surveyors, 2007–08; *b* 11 June 1948; *s* of Reginald and Dorothy Tuffin; *m* 1968, Brenda King; one *s* one *d. Educ:* Portsmouth Northern Grammar Sch.; Raynes Park Co. Grammar Sch. FRICS 1979; FBEng 1998; MCIArb 1999. Founding Partner, Tuffin Ferraby Taylor, 1973–2004. Chm., RICS Council of England, 2004–06. *Recreations:* shooting, socialising, unsuccessful angling, concocting out of office autoreply messages for my e-mail. *Address:* Tuffin Ferraby Taylor, Strand House, 169 Richmond Road, Kingston upon Thames, Surrey KT2 5DA. *T:* (020) 8549 8763; *e-mail:* dtuffin@tftconsultants.com.

TUFFREY, Michael William; Member (Lib Dem), since Feb. 2002, and Leader, Liberal Democrat Group, since 2006, London Assembly, Greater London Authority; *b* 30 Sept. 1959; *m*; one *s* two *d. Educ:* Douai Sch., Woolhampton; Durham Univ. (BA Hons Econ. Hist. and Econs 1981). ACA 1984. Accountant, Peat Marwick Mitchell & Co., London, 1981–84; Res. and Parly Officer, Lib/SDP whips office, H of L, 1984–87; Dir, Finance and Admin, Action Resource Centre, London, 1987–90; Community Affairs Consultant, Prima Europe, London, 1990–97; Dir, Corporate Citizenship Co., London, 1997–. Mem. for Vauxhall: GLC, 1985–86 (Mem., Industry and Employment, Housing and Planning Cttees); ILEA, 1985–86; Mem. (Lib Dem), Lambeth LBC, 1990–2002 (Gp Leader, Lib Dem, 1990–98; de facto Jt Leader, Council, 1994–98). Contested: (L) Streatham, 1987; (Lib Dem) Vauxhall, June 1989, 1992. London Assembly: Member: London Fire and Emergency Planning Authy, 2002–08 (Leader, Lib Dem Gp, 2006–08); Budget Cttee, 2002–; Envmt Cttee, 2004–. Mem., Assoc. of London Govt Leaders Cttee, 1994–2000 (Dep. Lib Dem Leader, 1994–2000); Lambeth Representative: AMA; LGA; Board Member: Business Link London, 1994–2000; London Develt Partnership, 1998–2000; 1994–98: Brixton City Challenge; Cross River Partnership; Central London Partnership; South Bank Partnership. Chm., Parly Lib Party Staff Assoc., 1986–87. Formerly: Nat. Treas., Gingerbread; Treas., then Chm., L'Arche Lambeth (former Nat. Bd Mem., L'Arche); founding Bd Mem., Vauxhall St Peter's Heritage Centre; Bd Mem., Vauxhall Cross Amenity Trust. Editor, Corporate Citizen Briefing, 1991–. *Recreation:* licensed radio amateur. *Address:* Greater London Authority, City Hall, Queen's Walk, SE1 2AA. *T:* (020) 7983 4362, *Fax:* (020) 7983 4417; *e-mail:* mike.tuffrey@london.gov.uk.

TUFNELL, Col Greville Wyndham, CVO 2002; DL; Development Officer, National Star Centre for Disabled Youth, 1982–95; Lieutenant, Queen's Body Guard of the Yeomen of the Guard, 1993–2002; *b* 7 April 1932; *s* of K. E. M. Tufnell, MC and E. H. Tufnell (*née* Dufaur); *m* 1st, 1962, Hon. Anne Rosemary Trench (*d* 1992), *d* of 5th Baron Ashtown, OBE and *widow* of Capt. Timothy Patrick Arnold Gosselin; three *d*, and one step *d*; 2nd, 1994, Susan Arnot Burrows. *Educ:* Eton; RMA, Sandhurst. Commnd Grenadier Guards, 1952; Adjt, 2nd Bn, 1959–61; GSO 3, War Office, 1962–63; Staff Coll., 1964; Maj. 1965; DAQMG, London Dist, 1966–67; GSO 2, HQ 2 Div., 1969–71; Lt Col 1971; comdg 1st Bn, 1971–73 (despatches, 1972); Bde Maj., Household Div., 1974–76; Col 1976; Lt Col comdg Grenadier Guards, 1976–78; retd 1979. Queen's Body Guard of Yeomen of the Guard: Exon, 1979; Ensign, 1985; Clerk of the Cheque and Adjutant, 1987. Freeman, City of London, 1961; Liveryman, Grocers' Co., 1965–. DL Glos, 1994. *Recreations:* shooting, fishing, gardening. *Address:* Cleeve House, Ampney St Peter, Cirencester, Glos GL7 5SH. *Clubs:* Cavalry and Guards, Sloane, Pitt, MCC.

TUFTON, family name of **Baron Hothfield**.

TUGE-ERECIŃSKA, Barbara; Ambassador of Poland to the Court of St James's, since 2006; *b* 24 March 1956; *d* of Janusz Tuge and Jadwiga Duchnowska; one *s* by Andrej Ereciński. *Educ:* Gdańsk Univ. (MA Scandinavian Studies). Staff mem., Foreign Dept, Nat. Bureau of Solidarity, 1981; Mem., Primate's Cttee for Assistance to Repressed Persons, 1982–87; Hon. Sec., Consular Agency of Sweden, Denmark and Norway, Gdynia, 1987–90; Plenipotentiary of City Bd for foreign contacts, Municipal Office to Gdańsk, 1990–91; Ambassador of Poland to Sweden, 1991–97; Ministry of Foreign Afffairs: Dir, Europe-West Dept, 1997–98; Dir, Eur. Policy Dept, 1998–99; Under-Sec. of State, 1999–2001; Ambassador of Poland to Denmark, 2001–05; Sec. of State, Min. of Foreign Affairs, 2005–06. Golden Cross, Order of Merit (Poland), 1997; Commander's Cross: Order of Merit (Italy), 2000; Order of Merit (Hungary), 2001; Order of the Dannebrog (Denmark), 2005. *Recreations:* reading books, walking (especially along the seashore). *Address:* Embassy of the Republic of Poland, 47 Portland Place, W1B 1JH. *T:* 0870 774 2702, *Fax:* (020) 7291 3576; *e-mail:* polishembassy@polishembassy.org.uk. *Club:* Athenæum.

TUGENDHAT, family name of **Baron Tugendhat**.

TUGENDHAT, Baron *cr* 1993 (Life Peer), of Widdington in the County of Essex; **Christopher Samuel Tugendhat,** Kt 1990; Chairman, Imperial College Healthcare NHS Trust, since 2007; *b* 23 Feb. 1937; *er s* of late Dr Georg Tugendhat; *m* 1967, Julia Lissant Dobson; two *s. Educ:* Ampleforth Coll.; Gonville and Caius Coll., Cambridge (Pres. of Union; Hon. Fellow 1998). Financial Times leader and feature writer, 1960–70. MP (C) City of London and Westminster South, 1974–76 (Cities of London and Westminster, 1970–74); Mem., 1977–85, a Vice-Pres., 1981–85, EEC Commn. Director: Sunningdale Oils, 1971–76; Phillips Petroleum International (UK) Ltd, 1972–76; National Westminster Bank, 1985–91 (Dep. Chm., 1990–91); The BOC Group, 1985–96; Commercial Union Assce, 1988–91; LWT (Hldgs), 1991–94; Eurotunnel plc, 1991–2003; Rio Tinto plc, 1997–2004; Chairman: Abbey National plc, 1991–2002; Blue Circle Industries PLC, 1996–2001; Eur. Adv. Bd, Lehman Brothers, 2002–07. Chm., CAA, 1986–91. Chairman: RIIA (Chatham House), 1986–95; Adv. Council, European Policy Forum, 1998–; Governor, Council of Ditchley Foundn, 1986–; Vice-Pres., British Lung Foundn, 1986–. Chancellor, Univ. of Bath, 1998–. Hon. LLD Bath, 1998; Hon. DLitt UMIST, 2002. *Publications:* Oil: the biggest business, 1968; The Multinationals, 1971 (McKinsey Foundn Book Award, 1971); Making Sense of Europe, 1986; (with William Wallace) Options for British Foreign Policy in the 1990s, 1988; various pamphlets and numerous articles. *Recreations:* being with his family, reading, conversation. *Address:* 35 Westbourne Park Road, W2 5QD. *Clubs:* Athenæum, Royal Anglo-Belgian.

See also Hon. Sir M. G. Tugendhat.

TUGENDHAT, Hon. Sir Michael (George), Kt 2003; **Hon. Mr Justice Tugendhat;** a Judge of the High Court of Justice, Queen's Bench Division, since 2003; *b* 21 Oct. 1944; *s* of late Georg Tugendhat and Maire Littledale; *m* 1970, Blandine de Loisne; four *s. Educ:* Ampleforth Coll.; Gonville and Caius Coll., Cambridge (Scholar; MA); Yale Univ. Henry Fellowship. Called to the Bar, Inner Temple, 1969, Bencher, 1988; QC 1986; a Recorder, 1994–2003; a Dep. High Court Judge, 1995–2003; a Judge of the Courts of Appeal in Jersey and Guernsey, 2000–03. Mem., Bar Council, 1992–94. Chm., Civil Law Working Party on Corruption, 1999. Member, Mgt Cttee, Advice on Individual Rights in Europe Centre, 2000–03. Fellow, Inst. Advanced Legal Studies, 1999–. *Publications:* (contrib.) Restitution and Banking Law, 1998; (contrib.) Yearbook of Copyright and Media Law, 2000; (ed jtly) The Law of Privacy and the Media, 2002; (contrib.) Halsbury's Laws of England, 4th edn; occasional contribs to legal jls. *Address:* Royal Courts of Justice, Strand, WC2A 2LL. *Club:* Brooks's.

See also Baron Tugendhat.

TUGWELL, Very Rev. Simon Charles ffoster, DD, STD; OP; Fellow, Dominican Historical Institute, Rome, since 1987 (President, 1992–97); *b* 4 May 1943; *s* of Major Herbert Frederick Lewen Tugwell and Mary Brigit (*née* Hutchinson). *Educ:* Lancing Coll.; Corpus Christi Coll., Oxford (DD 1993); STD (Angelicum, Rome) 1987, STM (Dominican Order) 1993. Entered English Province of Dominican Order, 1965, ordained priest, 1971; Lectr and Tutor, Blackfriars, Oxford, 1972–92; Regent of Studies, English Dominicans, 1976–90; Mem., Faculty of Theol., Univ. of Oxford, 1982–92. Vis. Lectr, Angelicum, Rome, 1977–92; Flannery Prof. of Theol., Gonzaga Univ., Spokane, WA, 1982–83; Read-Tuckwell Lectr on human immortality, Bristol Univ., 1988. Has lectured and preached in many parts of the world. Founding Ed., Dominican Hist. Newsletter, 1992–97. *Publications:* The Way of the Preacher, 1979; Early Dominicans, 1982; Ways of Imperfection, 1984; Albert and Thomas, 1988; The Apostolic Fathers, 1989; (ed) Letters of Bede Jarrett, 1989; Human Immortality and the Redemption of Death, 1990; (ed) Miraculi sancti Dominici mandato magistri Berengarii collecta, Petri Calo legendae sancti Dominici, 1997; (ed) Bernardi Guidonis scripta de sancto Dominico, 1998; (ed) Humberti de Romanis legendae sancti Dominici, 2008; contribs to books and dictionaries; articles and reviews in learned jls. *Recreations:* teddy bears, writing silly verses. *Address:* Istituto Storico Domenicano, Largo Angelicum 1, 00184 Roma, Italy. *Fax:* 066702270.

TUITA, Sir Mariano (Kelesimalefo), KBE 1992 (OBE 1975); Cross of Solomon Islands, 1985; Managing Director, L. K. P. Hardware Ltd, since 1985; *b* Solomon Is, 12 Nov. 1932; *s* of late Joachim Alick and Ann Maria Tangoia Hagota; *m* 1957, Luisa Mae; three *s* six *d. Educ:* St Joseph's Sch., Tenaru on Guadacanal. Mem. for Lau, Malaita Local Govt Council, 1958–60; Pres., Malaita Council, 1960–68; Member: first Solomon Is Legislative Council, 1960–65; for N Malaita Constituency, 1965–67; for NE Malaita Constituency, 1967–69; Governing Council for Lau and Baelelea, 1970–73; for Lau and Baelelea, Legislative Assembly, Solomon Is Nat. Parlt, 1976–80. *Address:* L. K. P. Hardware Ltd, PO Box 317, Honiara, Solomon Islands. *T:* 22594 and 23848.

TUITE, Sir Christopher (Hugh), 14th Bt *cr* 1622; Director, USA, Green Belt Movement International, since 2005; *b* 3 Nov. 1949; *s* of Sir Dennis George Harmsworth Tuite, 13th Bt, MBE, and Margaret Essie, *d* of late Col Walter Leslie Dundas, DSO; *S* father, 1981; *m* 1976, Deborah Ann, *d* of A. E. Martz, Punxsutawney, Pa; two *s. Educ:* Univ. of Liverpool (BSc Hons); Univ. of Bristol (PhD). Research Officer, The Wildfowl Trust, 1978–81; Controller, The Nature Conservancy, Washington, DC, 1987–99; Dir, Wildlife and Habitat Prog., IFAW, 1999–2004. *Publications:* contribs to Jl of Animal Ecology, Jl of Applied Ecology, Freshwater Biology, Wildfowl. *Heir: s* Thomas Livingstone Tuite, *b* 24 July 1977. *Address:* c/o HSBC, 33 The Borough, Farnham, Surrey GU9 7NJ.

TUIVAGA, Sir Timoci (Uluiburotu), Kt 1981; CF 1995; Chief Justice of Fiji, 1980–87, and 1988–2002; *b* 21 Oct. 1931; *s* of Isimeli Siga Tuivaga and Jessie Hill; *m* 1st, 1958, Vilimaina Leba Parrott Tuivaga (*d* 2000); three *s* one *d*; 2nd, 2002, Raijeli Vasakula. *Educ:* Univ. of Auckland (BA). Called to Bar, Gray's Inn, 1964, and NSW, 1968. Native Magistrate, 1958–61; Crown Counsel, 1965–68; Principal Legal Officer, 1968–70; Acting Director of Public Prosecutions, 1970; Crown Solicitor, 1971; Puisne Judge, 1972; Acting Chief Justice, 1974; sometime Acting Gov.-Gen., 1983–87. *Recreations:* golf, gardening. *Address:* 1 Newboult Place, Suva, Fiji. *T:* 3316619. *Club:* Fiji Golf (Suva).

TULETT, Louise Wendy, (Mrs J. L. W. Lee-Emery); Group Director of Finance, Procurement and Operations, HM Treasury, since 2007; *b* Dorking, 12 March 1960; *d* of

Anthony and Valerie Linfield; *m* 2005, Jason L. W. Lee-Emery; two *s*. *Educ:* Raleigh Primary Sch.; Howard of Effingham Co. Secondary Sch.; Southampton Inst. Higher Educn. CIPFA 1989. Clerical asst, Surrey CC, 1976–78; finance trainee, Waverley DC, 1978–87; trainee accountant, Woking BC, 1987–90; Asst Dir, Finance, NW Surrey HA, 1990–94; Dep. Dir, Finance, Frimley Park Hosp., 1994–2000; Accountant, 2000–04, Team Leader, 2004–07, HM Treasury. *Recreations:* relaxing with family and friends, walking the dogs, reading. *Address:* HM Treasury, 1 Horse Guards Road, SW1A 2HQ. *T:* (020) 7270 5367; *e-mail:* louise.tulett@hm-treasury.x.gsi.gov.uk.

TULLIBARDINE, Marquess of; Bruce George Ronald Murray; *b* 6 April 1960; *s* and *heir* of Duke of Atholl, *qv*; *m* 1984, Lynne Elizabeth (marr. diss. 2003), *e d* of Nicholas Andrew; two *s* one *d*. *Heir: s* Earl of Strathtay and Strathardle, *qv*. *Address:* PO Box 1522, Louis Trichardt, 0920, South Africa.

TULLO, Carol Anne; Director: The National Archives, since 2006; Office of Public Sector Information, since 2005; Controller of HM Stationery Office, Queen's Printer of Acts of Parliament and Government Printer for Northern Ireland, since 1997; Queen's Printer for Scotland, since 1999; *b* 9 Jan. 1956; *d* of Edward Alan Dodgson and late Patricia Dodgson; *m* 1979, Robin Brownrigg Tullo; one *s* one *d*. *Educ:* Hull Univ. (LLB Hons 1976). Called to the Bar, Inner Temple, 1977; Publishing Dir, Sweet & Maxwell Ltd, 1990–96; Consultant, Thomson Legal and Professional Gp, 1996–97. Chair, Law Publishers' Exec., 1995–2004, Bd Mem., Council of Acad. and Professional Publishers, 1996–2005, Publishers Assoc. Vis. Prof., City Univ., 2000–. *Address:* Office of Public Sector Information, Admiralty Arch, The Mall, SW1A 2WH. *T:* (020) 7276 2660.

TULLY, Sir (William) Mark, KBE 2002 (OBE 1985); freelance journalist and broadcaster, since 1994; *b* 24 Oct. 1935; *s* of late William Scarth Carlisle Tully, CBE and Patience Treby Tully; *m* 1960, Frances Margaret (*née* Butler); two *s* two *d*. *Educ:* Twyford School, Winchester; Marlborough College; Trinity Hall, Cambridge (MA; Hon. Fellow, 1994). Regional Dir, Abbeyfield Soc., 1960–64; BBC, 1964–94: Asst, Appointments Dept, 1964–65; Asst, then Actg Rep., New Delhi, 1965–69; Prog. Organiser and Talks Writer, Eastern Service, 1969–71; Chief of Bureau, Delhi, 1972–93; South Asia Correspondent, 1993–94. Padma Shri (India), 1992. Presenter, The Lives of Jesus, BBC TV series, 1996. *Publications:* (with Satish Jacob) Amritsar: Mrs Gandhi's last battle, 1985; (with Z. Masani) From Raj to Rajiv, 1988; No Full Stops in India, 1991; The Heart of India (short stories), 1995; The Lives of Jesus, 1996; (with Gillian Wright) India in Slow Motion, 2002; India's Unending Journey, 2007. *Recreations:* fishing, bird watching, reading. *Address:* 1 Nizamuddin (East), New Delhi 110 013, India. *T:* (11) 4629687/4602878. *Clubs:* Oriental, Travellers; India International Centre, Gymkhana (Delhi), Bengal (Calcutta).

TULVING, Prof. Endel, OC 2006; PhD; FRS 1992; FRSC; Tanenbaum Chair in Cognitive Neuroscience, Rotman Research Institute, Baycrest Centre, Toronto, since 1992; University Professor Emeritus in Psychology, University of Toronto, since 1992; *b* 26 May 1927; *s* of Juhan Tulving and Linda (*née* Soome); *m* 1950, Ruth Mikkelsaar; two *d*. *Educ:* Hugo Treffner Gymnasium; Univ. of Heidelberg; Univ. of Toronto (BA, MA); Harvard Univ. (Foundn Fellow, 1954–55; PhD). FRSC 1979. Teaching Fellow, Harvard Univ., 1955–56; University of Toronto: Lectr, 1956–59; Asst Prof. of Psychol., 1959–62; Associate Prof., 1962–65; Prof., 1965–70; Prof. of Psychol., Yale Univ., 1970–75; University of Toronto: Prof. of Psychol., 1972–92; Chm., Dept of Psychol., 1974–80; Univ. Prof., 1985–92. Vis. Scholar, Univ. of Calif., Berkeley, 1964–65; Fellow, Center for Advanced Study in Behavioural Scis, Stanford, Calif., 1972–73; Commonwealth Vis. Prof., Univ. of Oxford, 1977–78; Distinguished Res. Prof. of Neurosci., Univ. of Calif., Davis, 1993–98; Clark Way Harrison Dist. Vis. Prof. of Psychology and Cognitive Neurosci., Washington Univ., 1996–2007. Izaak Walton Killam Meml Scholarship, 1976; Guggenheim Fellow, 1987–88; William James Fellow, Amer. Psychol Soc., 1990; Montgomery Fellow, Dartmouth Coll., 1999. For. Hon. Mem., Amer. Acad. Arts and Scis, 1986; For. Associate, Nat. Acad. Scis, USA, 1988; Foreign Member: Royal Swedish Acad. Scis, 1991; Academia Europaea, 1996; Estonian Acad. of Scis, 2002. Hon. MA Yale, 1969; Hon. PhD: Umeå, Sweden, 1982; Haifa, Israel, 2003; Hon. DLitt: Waterloo, Canada, 1987; Laurentian, Canada, 1988; Hon. DPsych Tartu, Estonia, 1989; Hon. ScD: Queen's Univ., Ontario, 1996; Univ. of Toronto, 2002; Columbia Univ., NY, 2005. Warren Medal, Soc. of Exptl Psychologists, 1982; Dist. Scientific Contrib. Award, Amer. Psychol Assoc., 1983; Award for Dist. Contribs to Psychol. as a Science, Canadian Psychol Assoc., 1983; Izaak Walton Killam Prize in Health Scis, Canada Council, 1994; Gold Medal Award, Amer. Psychol Foundn, 1994; McGovern Award in the behavioral scis, AAAS, 1996; Wilhelm Wundt-William James Prize, Eur. Fedn of Psychologists' Assocs, 2003; Gairdner Internat. Award, Gairdner Foundn, 2005; Canadian Medical Hall of Fame, 2007. *Publications:* Elements of Episodic Memory, 1983; (ed jtly) Organization of Memory, 1972; Memory Systems 1994, 1994; Oxford Handbook of Memory, 2000; articles in scientific jls. *Recreations:* golf, walking, chess, bridge. *Address:* 45 Baby Point Crescent, Toronto, ON M6S 2B7, Canada. *T:* (416) 7623736.

TUMIM, Winifred Letitia, (Lady Tumim), CBE 2003 (OBE 1992); Chair, National Council for Voluntary Organisations, 1996–2001; *b* 3 June 1936; *d* of Algernon Malcolm Borthwick and Edith Wylde Borthwick (*née* Addison); *m* 1962, Sir Stephen Tumim (*d* 2003); three *d*. *Educ:* Lady Margaret Hall, Oxford (PPE Hons 1958; MA); SOAS, London Univ. (Dip. Linguistics 1979). Non-exec. Dir, Parkside Health NHS Trust, 1992–98. Chairman: Sec. of State's Youth Treatment Service Gp, 1991–95; Ind. Adv. Gp on Teenage Pregnancy, 2000–; Mem., Warnock Cttee of Enquiry on Educn of Handicapped Children, 1974–78. Member: Council, Vol. Council for Handicapped Children, 1981–87; GMC, 1996–2003 (Associate Mem., 2003–); Council for Charitable Support, 1996–; Vice-Chm., Family Housing Assoc., 1983–88; Chairman: RNID, 1985–92; NCVO/Charity Commn On Trust Wkg Party, 1992; Council for Advancement of Communication with Deaf People, 1994–97. Gov., Mary Hare Grammar Sch. for The Deaf, 1974–90; Trustee, United Westminster Schs, 2003–. Trustee: Nat. Portrait Gall., 1992–99; City Parochial Foundn, 1989–2001; Charities Aid Foundn, 1996–2001; Adapt, 2007–; Chm., Foyer Fedn, 2001–04. FRSA 1989. *Recreations:* painting watercolours, gardening, classical music, modern ceramics, tribal rugs. *Club:* Athenæum.

TUMPEL-GUGERELL, Gertrude; Member, Executive Board, European Central Bank, since 2003; *b* Kapelln, Austria, 11 Nov. 1952. *Educ:* grammar sch.; Univ. of Vienna (MSc Hons Econs and Soc. Scis 1975; Doctorate in Econs and Soc. Scis 1981). Economist, Econs Div., Oesterreichische Nationalbank, 1975–81; Econ. Policy Advr to Minister of Finance, and Mem. Supervisory Bd, Oesterreichische Laenderbank AG, 1981–84; Oesterreichische Nationalbank: Dep. Hd, Econs Div., 1985–86; Comptroller Gen. in charge of developing strategic planning and auditing, 1986–92; Dir, Area Corporate Planning and Mgt, 1992–97; Exec. Dir, Econs and Financial Markets Dept, 1997–2003; Vice-Gov., 1998–2003. Alternate Gov. of Austria to IMF, 1997–2003; European Union: Mem., Econ. and Finance Cttee, 1997–2003; Chm., Banking Adv. Cttee, 2002–03; European Central Bank: Member: Internat. Relns Cttee, 1999–2003; Banking Supervision Cttee, 1999–2003; Mem., Supervisory Bd, Financial Market Authy, Austria, 2002–03. Mem. Univ. Council, Univ. of Vienna, 2003–. *Publications:* numerous articles and essays. *Address:* European Central Bank, Kaiserstrasse 29, 60311 Frankfurt am Main, Germany.

TUNBRIDGE, William Michael Gregg, MD; FRCP; Director of Postgraduate Medical Education and Training, Oxford University, 1994–2003; Professorial Fellow of Wadham College, Oxford, 1994–2003, now Fellow Emeritus; *b* 13 June 1940; *s* of Sir Ronald Ernest Tunbridge, OBE and of Dorothy (*née* Gregg); *m* 1965, Felicity Katherine Edith Parrish; two *d*. *Educ:* Kingswood Sch., Bath; Queens' Coll., Cambridge (MA, MD); University Coll. Hosp. House appointments: UCH, 1964–65; Mpilo Hosp., Bulawayo, 1965–66; Manchester Royal Infirmary, 1967–68; Tutor in Medicine, Univ. of Manchester, 1969–70; Registrar, Hammersmith Hosp., 1970–72; Sen. Res. Associate, Univ. of Newcastle, 1972–75; Sen. Registrar in Medicine, Durham, 1975–76; MRC Travelling Fellow, Liège, 1976–77; Consultant Physician, Newcastle Gen. Hosp. and Sen. Lectr in Medicine, Univ. of Newcastle upon Tyne, 1977–94; Consultant Physician, Radcliffe Infirmary, then Oxford Radcliffe Hosps, 1994–2005; Physician Emeritus, Nuffield Dept of Medicine, Oxford Univ., 2005–. President: Thyroid Club, 1994–96; Endocrine Section, Union of European Med. Specialists, 1994–98. *Publications:* (with P. D. Home) Diabetes and Endocrinology in Clinical Practice, 1991; Thyroid Disease: the facts, 3rd edn (with R. I. S. Bayliss) 1998, 4th edn (with M. P. J. Vanderpump) 2008; (ed) Rationing of Health Care in Medicine, 1993. *Recreations:* walking, golf. *Address:* Coppermill, Church Lane, Weston on the Green, Bicester, Oxon OX25 3QS. *T:* (01869) 350691. *Club:* Athenæum.

TUNG Chee Hwa; Chief Executive, Hong Kong Special Administrative Region, 1997–2005; Vice-Chairman, Chinese People's Political Consultative Conference; *b* 29 May 1937; *er s* of Tung Chao Yung and Koo Lee Ching; *m* 1961, Betty Tung Chiu Hung Ping; two *s* one *d*. *Educ:* Liverpool Univ. (BSc Marine Engrg 1960). Chm. and CEO, Orient Overseas (International) Ltd, 1986–96. Advr, Hong Kong Affairs, 1992–96; Member: Basic Law Consultative Cttee, 1985–90; Exec. Council, Hong Kong Govt, 1992–96; Eighth Cttee, Chinese People's Political Consultative Conf., 1993–96, Tenth Cttee, 2005– (Vice Chm., 2005–); Vice-Chm., Prep. Cttee, HKSAR, 1995–96. Member: Hong Kong/Japan Business Co-operation Cttee, 1991–96; Chm., Hong Kong/US Economic Co-operation Cttee, 1993–96. Hon. LLD Liverpool, 1997. *Recreations:* hiking, Tai Chi, swimming, reading.

TUNNELL, Hugh James Oliver Redvers; HM Diplomatic Service, retired; Ambassador to Bahrain, 1992–95; *b* 31 Dec. 1935; *s* of late Heather and Oliver Tunnell; *m* 1st, 1958, Helen Miller (marr. diss.); three *d*; 2nd, 1979, Margaret, *d* of Sir Richard John Randall; two *d*. *Educ:* Chatham House Grammar School, Ramsgate. Royal Artillery, 1954–56. FO, 1956–59; Amman, 1959–62; Middle East Centre for Arab Studies, 1962–63; served FO, Aden, CRO, Damascus and FO, 1964–67; UK Delegn to European Communities, 1968–70; FCO, 1970–72; Kuwait, 1972–76; FCO, 1976–79; Head of Chancery, Muscat, 1979–83; Consul Gen., Brisbane, 1983–88; Comr-Gen., British Section, EXPO 88, 1987–88; Consul Gen., Jedda, 1989–92. Mem. Cttee, Bahrain Soc., 1996–2000. *Recreations:* water sports, tennis. *Address:* 44 Fernberg Road, Paddington, Qld 4064, Australia. *T:* (7) 33697892; *e-mail:* tunnell@optushome.com.au. *Club:* Brisbane (Brisbane).

TUNNICLIFFE, family name of **Baron Tunnicliffe**.

TUNNICLIFFE, Baron *cr* 2004 (Life Peer), of Bracknell in the County of Berkshire; **Denis Tunnicliffe,** CBE 1993; a Lord in Waiting (Government Whip), since 2008; *b* 17 Jan. 1943; *s* of Arthur Harold and Ellen Tunnicliffe; *m* 1968, Susan Dale; two *s*. *Educ:* Henry Cavendish Sch., Derby; University Coll. London (State Schol.; BSc (Special)); College of Air Training, Hamble. Pilot, BOAC, 1966–72; British Airways, 1972–86; Chief Exec., International Leisure Group, Aviation Div., 1986–88; Man. Dir, London Underground Ltd, 1988–98; Mem. of Bd, 1993–2000, Chief Exec., 1998–2000, London Transport. Chairman: UKAEA, 2002–04; Rail Safety and Standards Bd, 2003–08. Councillor, Royal Bor. of New Windsor, 1971–75; Councillor, Royal County of Berkshire, 1974–77; Dist Councillor, Bracknell, 1979–83. FCILT (FCIT 1990); CCMI (CBIM 1991). *Recreations:* flying, boating, church, travelling. *Address:* House of Lords, SW1A 0PW. *Clubs:* Royal Air Force, Royal Automobile.

TUNSTALL, Dr David Prestwich, FInstP; FRSE; Reader in Physics, University of St Andrews, since 1978; *b* 15 July 1939; *s* of Henry Brian Tunstall and Emmeline Grace Tunstall (*née* Denman); *m* 1963, Rosemarie Bebbington; two *s* one *d*. *Educ:* Sir John Talbots Sch., Whitchurch; UCNW, Bangor (BSc *summa cum laude*; PhD). FInstP 1985; FRSE 1990. Post-doctoral Fellow: Zurich, 1963–64; Grenoble, 1964–66; Lectr, 1966–75, Sen. Lectr, 1975–78, Univ. of St Andrews. Visiting Fellow: Cornell Univ., 1973–74; UCLA, 1979. *Publications:* (jtly) Nuclear Magnetic Resonance, 1973; The Metal Non-Metal Transition in Disordered Systems, 1978; (ed jtly) High Temperature Superconductivity, 1991; contrib. to learned jls. *Recreations:* hill walking, ski-ing, tennis. *Address:* 10 The Circus, Bath BA1 2EW. *T:* (01225) 465064; *e-mail:* d.p.tunstall@st-and.ac.uk.

TUNSTALL, Kathryn; Strategic Director for Services to Children and Young People, Bradford Metropolitan District Council, since 2007; *b* St Helens, Merseyside, 26 Nov. 1953; *d* of Eric Thomas Tunstall and Majorie Naomi Tunstall (*née* Guest); *m* 1992, Keith McKay Watson; one *s* one *d*, and two step *d*. *Educ:* Rivington Road Prim. Sch., St Helens; Cowley Girls' Grammar Sch., St Helens (Hd Girl); Univ. of Leeds (BA Hons Psychol./Sociol. 1975); Univ. of Hull (DipASS 1978; CQSW 1978). Qualified Social Worker, 1978, specialising in child protection; Sen. Manager, responsible for Community Social Work Services, Leeds CC, 1998–2002; Bradford Metropolitan District Council: Asst Dir for Children's Services, Social Services, 2002–05; Dir, Social Services, 2005–07. Chairman: Bradford Area Child Protection Cttee, 2002–06; Bradford Safeguarding Children Bd, 2006–; Bradford Youth Offenders Services Bd, 2007–; Bradford Children and Young People's Strategic Partnership, 2007–. *Recreations:* spending time with my own family, worldwide travel, understanding how families tick, indulging in quality food and wine, gardening, bird watching, Coronation Street, supporting St Helens Rugby League Football Club. *Address:* Bradford Metropolitan District Council, City Hall, Bradford BD1 1HY. *T:* (01274) 431266, *Fax:* (01274) 431784; *e-mail:* kath.tunstall@bradford.gov.uk.

TUOHY, Denis John; broadcaster, writer and actor; *b* 2 April 1937; *s* of late John Vincent Tuohy and Anne Mary, (Nan), Tuohy (*née* Doody); *m* 1st, 1960, Moya McCann (marr. diss. 1988); two *s* two *d*; 2nd, 1998, Elizabeth Moran (marr. diss. 2007). *Educ:* Clongowes Wood Coll., Co. Kildare; Queen's Univ., Belfast (BA Hons Classics). Eisenhower Fellow, USA, 1967. BBC: Newscaster and Reporter, NI, 1960–64; Presenter, Late Night Line Up, 1964–67; Reporter and Presenter: 24 Hours, 1967–71; Panorama, 1974–75; Reporter, Man Alive, 1971–72; Presenter, Tonight, 1975–79; Thames Television: Reporter, This Week, 1972–74; Presenter, People and Politics, 1973–74; Presenter and Reporter: TV Eye, 1979–86; This Week, 1986–92; Newscaster, ITN, 1994–2001; Presenter: Something Understood, BBC Radio 4, 1995–99; Cards of Identity, RTE,

2002; A Living Word, RTE, 2003; (and Producer) The Troubles I've Seen, UTV, 2008; panellist, The Sunday Show, RTE, 2003; reporter on numerous documentaries for BBC and ITV, incl. A Life of O'Reilly, 1974; Mr Truman, why did you drop the second bomb?, 1975; Do You Know Where Jimmy Carter Lives?, 1977; To Us a Child (prod jtly by Thames TV and UNICEF), 1986; The Blitz, 1991; The Real Dad's Army, 1998; The Law and the "Lunatic", 1999. Actor: Fair City, and The Clinic, RTE TV series, 2003; Fallout, RTE, 2006; The Tempest, Cork Midsummer Fest., 2006; Strength and Honour (film), 2007; Killinaskully, RTE TV, 2007–08. *Publications:* Wide-eyed in Medialand (memoirs), 2005; articles in Irish Times, Sunday Independent, Belfast Telegraph, Irish News, Scotsman, Independent, New Statesman, The Tablet, etc. *Recreations:* theatre, cinema, Rugby, cricket. *Address:* 16 Aurora na Mara, Shore Road, Rostrevor, Co. Down BT34 3UP.

TUPMAN, William Ivan, DPhil; Director General of Internal Audit, Ministry of Defence, 1974–81; *b* 22 July 1921; *s* of Leonard and Elsie Tupman; *m* 1945, Barbara (*née* Capel); two *s* one *d*. *Educ:* Queen Elizabeth's Hosp., Bristol; New Coll., Oxford (Exhibnr; MA, DPhil). Served War, 1942–45, RN (Lieut RNVR). Entered Admiralty as Asst Principal, 1948; Private Sec. to Parly Sec., 1950–52; Principal, 1952; Civil Affairs Adviser to C-in-C, Far East Station, 1958–61; Private Sec. to First Lord of the Admiralty, 1963; Asst Sec., 1964; IDC, 1967.

TUPPER, Sir Charles Hibbert, 5th Bt *cr* 1888, of Armdale, Halifax, Nova Scotia; retired; *b* 4 July 1930; *o s* of Sir James Macdonald Tupper, 4th Bt, formerly Assistant Commissioner, Royal Canadian Mounted Police, and of Mary Agnes Jean Collins; *S* father, 1967; *m* (marr. diss. 1976); one *s*. *Heir: s* Charles Hibbert Tupper [*b* 10 July 1964; *m* 1987, Elizabeth Ann Heaslip; one *d*]. *Address:* 955 Marine Drive, Apt 1101, West Vancouver, BC V7T 1A9, Canada.

TURBOTT, Sir Ian (Graham), Kt 1968; AO 1997; CMG 1962; CVO 1966; Foundation Chancellor, University of Western Sydney, 1989–2001, Emeritus Chancellor, since 2001; *b* Whangarei, New Zealand, 9 March 1922; *s* of late Thomas Turbott and late E. A. Turbott, both of New Zealand; *m* 1952, Nancy Hall Lantz (*d* 1999), California, USA; three *d*. *Educ:* Takapuna Grammar School, Auckland, NZ; Auckland University; Jesus College, Cambridge; London University. NZ Forces (Army), 1940–46: Solomon Is area and 2 NZEF, Italy. Colonial Service (Overseas Civil Service): Western Pacific, Gilbert and Ellice Is, 1948–56; Colonial Office, 1956–58; Administrator of Antigua, The West Indies, 1958–64; also Queen's Representative under new constitution, 1960–64; Administrator of Grenada and Queen's Representative, 1964–67; Governor of Associated State of Grenada, 1966–68. Partner, Spencer Stuart and Associates Worldwide, 1973–84; Chairman: Spencer Stuart and Associates Pty Ltd, 1970–84; Chloride Batteries Australia Ltd, 1978–85; I. T. Graham Investments plc, 1982–; TNT Security Pty Ltd; Stuart Brooke Consultants Pty Ltd, Sydney, 1974–82; 2MMM Broadcasting Co. Pty Ltd; Melbourne F/M Radio Pty Ltd, 1986–93; Penrith Lakes Develt Corp., 1980–2007; Essington Ltd, 1984–89; New World Pictures (Aust.) Ltd, 1986–89; Triple M FM Radio Group, 1986–93; Cape York Space Agency Ltd, 1987–89; Hoyts Media Ltd, 1991–93; Dir, Hoyts Entertainment Ltd, 1990–93; Dep. Chm., Adv. Bd, Amer. Internat. Underwriting (Aust.) Ltd; Director: Standard Chartered Bank Australia Ltd, 1980–91; Capita Financial Gp, 1979–91; Newcastle F/M P/L, 1983–94. Chairman: Internat. Piano Competition Ltd, Sydney, 1977–84; Duke of Edinburgh's Award Scheme, NSW, 1984–95; Australia Youth Trust, 2001–; Dir, Ted Noffs Foundn, 2000–. Chm., Japan Entrepreneurs and Presidents Assoc., Australia, 1996–2005. Dir, Commonwealth Council, 2001–. Governor, NSW Conservatorium of Music, 1974–89. FRSA; FAIM; FAICD. Hon Consul for Cook Is in Australia, 1995. JP 1972. Hon. DLitt Western Sydney, 1993. CStJ 1964. Silver Jubilee Medal, 1977; Guadalcanal Medal (Solomon Is), 1998. Holds 1939–45 Star, Pacific Star, Italy Star, Defence Medal, War Medal, New Zealand Service Medal. *Publications:* Lands of Sun and Spice, 1996; Nancy - my beloved, 2000; For My Children and Grandchildren - a war record, 2002; Masters of Survival, 2006; various technical and scientific, 1948–51, in Jl of Polynesian Society (on Pacific area). *Recreations:* watching cricket, fishing. *Address:* 8/8 Lauderdale Avenue, Fairlight, NSW 2094, Australia; 38 MacMasters Parade, MacMasters Beach, NSW 2251, Australia. *Clubs:* Australian (Sydney); Royal Sydney Yacht.

TURCAN, Henry Watson; a Recorder of the Crown Court, since 1985; *b* 22 Aug. 1941; *s* of late Henry Hutchison Turcan and Lilias Cheyne; *m* 1969, Jane Fairrie Blair; one *s* one *d*. *Educ:* Rugby School; Trinity College, Oxford (BA, MA). Called to the Bar, Inner Temple, 1965, Bencher, 1992. Legal Assessor to General Optical Council, 1983–2003. Special Adjudicator, Immigration Appeals, 1998–2005; an Immigration Judge, 2005–. *Recreations:* shooting, fishing, golf. *Address:* 4 Paper Buildings, Temple, EC4Y 7EX. *T:* (020) 7583 0816. *Clubs:* New (Edinburgh); Royal and Ancient Golf (St Andrews); Hon. Company of Edinburgh Golfers (Muirfield).

TURCAN, William James; Chief Executive, Elementis (formerly Harrisons & Crosfield plc), 1994–98; *b* 4 Jan. 1943; *m* 1967, Elisabeth Margaret Stewart; three *s* one *d*. *Educ:* Rugby Sch.; Trinity Coll., Oxford (MA). Binder Hamlyn, 1965–70; Pauls Malt, 1970–86; Finance Dir, Pauls plc, 1986–88; Finance Dir, Harrisons & Crosfield, 1988–94. Bd Mem., Glenrothes New Town Develt Corp., 1983–86.

TURCOTTE, His Eminence Cardinal Jean-Claude; *see* Montreal, Archbishop of, (RC).

TUREI, Most Rev. William Brown; Primate of Aotearoa, New Zealand and Polynesia, 2006–08; Archbishop of Aotearoa, 2006–08; *b* 12 Dec. 1924; *s* of Honehiki and Heneriata Waititi; adopted by Nehe and Hariata Turei; *m* 1957, Mary Jane King; one *s* two *d*. *Educ:* Te Auta Coll. Secondary; St John's Theol Coll., Auckland (LTh). Ordained priest, 1950; served in parishes: Tauranga, Whangara, Te Puke, Whakatane, Manutuke, Christchurch and Waipatu, 1949–82; Archdeacon of Tairawhiti, 1982–92; Bishop of Tairawhiti, 1992–2008; Bishop of Aotearoa, 2005–08. *Recreation:* couch participant. *Address:* 33 Emily Street, Gisborne, New Zealand; *e-mail:* browntmihi@xtra.co.nz.

TURING, Sir John Dermot, 12th Bt *cr* 1638 (NS), of Foveran, Aberdeenshire; solicitor; *b* 26 Feb. 1961; *s* of John Ferrier Turing (*d* 1983) and of Beryl Mary Ada, *d* of late Herbert Vaughan Hann; *S* kinsman, Sir John Leslie Turing, 11th Bt, 1987; *m* 1986, Nicola J., *er d* of M. D. Simmonds; two *s*. *Educ:* Sherborne School, Dorset; King's College, Cambridge; New College, Oxford. *Heir: s* John Malcolm Ferrier Turing, *b* 5 Sept. 1988. *Address:* 68 Marshalswick Lane, St Albans AL1 4XF.

TURMEAU, Prof. William Arthur, CBE 1989; PhD; FRSE; CEng, FIMechE; Chairman, Scottish Environment Protection Agency, 1995–99; Principal and Vice-Chancellor, Napier University, 1992–94 (Principal, Napier College, subseq. Napier Polytechnic of Edinburgh, 1982–92); *b* 19 Sept. 1929; *s* of Frank Richard Turmeau and Catherine Lyon Linklater; *m* 1957, Margaret Moar Burnett, MA, BCom; one *d*. *Educ:* Stromness Acad., Orkney; Univ. of Edinburgh (BSc); Moray House Coll. of Educn; Heriot-Watt Univ. (PhD). FIMechE, CEng, 1971; FRSE 1990. Royal Signals, 1947–49. Research Engr, Northern Electric Co. Ltd, Montreal, 1952–54; Mechanical Engr, USAF, Goose Bay, Labrador, 1954–56; Contracts Manager, Godfrey Engrg Co. Ltd, Montreal, 1956–61; Lectr, Bristo Technical Inst., 1962–64; Napier College: Lectr and Sen. Lectr, 1964–68; Head, Dept of Mechanical Engrg, 1968–75; Asst Principal and Dean, Faculty of Technology, 1975–82. Member: CICHE, British Council, 1982–92; CVCP, 1992–94 (Mem., Cttee of Dirs of Polytechnics, 1982–92); Standing Conf. of Rectors and Vice-Chancellors of European Univs, 1990–94; Cttee of Scottish Univ. Principals, 1992–94; Scottish Div. Cttee, Inst. of Dirs, 1992–94; Acad. Standards Cttee, IMechE, 1994–2004. Dir, ASH Scotland, 1996–. Trustee, Dynamic Earth Charitable Trust, 1994–2000. Mem. Court, Edinburgh Acad., 1993–99. Dr *hc* Edinburgh, 1992; DEd *hc* Napier, 1995. *Publications:* various papers relating to higher educn. *Recreations:* modern jazz, Leonardo da Vinci. *Address:* 132 Victoria Street, Stromness, Orkney KW16 3BU. *T:* (01856) 850500; *e-mail:* profwaturmeau@aol.com.

TURNAGE, Mark-Anthony; composer; Mead Composer in Residence, Chicago Symphony Orchestra, since 2006; Composer in Residence, London Philharmonic Orchestra, since 2006; *b* 1960; *m* Gabriella Swallow; two *s* from former marriage. *Educ:* Royal College of Music. Mendelssohn Scholar, Tanglewood, USA, 1983. Composer in Association: City of Birmingham Symphony Orchestra, 1989–93; ENO, 1995–2000; Associate Composer, BBC SO, 2000–03. *Compositions include: stage:* Greek, 1988 (BMW prizes for best opera and best libretto, Munich Biennale, 1988); The Silver Tassie (opera), 2000 (Outstanding Achievement in Opera (jtly), Laurence Olivier Awards, and South Bank Show Award for opera, 2001); *vocal:* Lament for a Hanging Man, 1983; Greek Suite, 1989; Some Days, 1989; Twice Through The Heart, 1997; A Relic of Memory, 2003; The Torn Fields, 2004; Two Baudelaire Songs, 2004; About Water, 2007; *orchestral:* Night Dances, 1981; Three Screaming Popes, 1989; Momentum, 1991; Drowned Out, 1993; Your Rockaby (saxophone concerto), 1994; Dispelling the Fears, 1995; Silent Cities, 1998; Evening Songs, 1999; Another Set To, 2000; Dark Crossing, 2001; Etudes and Elegies, 2002; On Opened Ground (viola concerto), 2002; Scherzoid, 2005; Yet Another Set To (trombone concerto), 2005; From All Sides, 2006; Chicago Remains, 2007; Mambo, Blues and Tarantella (violin concerto), 2008; *ensemble:* On All Fours, 1985; Kai, 1990; Three Farewells, 1990; Blood on the Floor, 1996; About Time, 1999; Bass inventionS, 2000; Slide Stride, 2002; Eulogy, 2003; No Let Up, 2004; Crying Out Loud, 2004; A Prayer Before Stillness, 2007; *instrumental:* Sleep on, 1992; Two Elegies framing a Shout, 1994; True Life Stories, 1995–99; Two Memorials, 1995–2000; Riffs and Refrains (solo clarinet), 2003; A Few Serenades, 2004; A Slow Pavane, A Fast Stomp, A Short Procession (piano trios), 2005. *Relevant publication:* Mark-Anthony Turnage, by Andrew Clements, 2000. *Address:* c/o Cathy Nelson Artists and Projects, The Court House, Dorstone, Herefordshire HR3 6AW. *T:* (01981) 551903.

TURNBERG, family name of **Baron Turnberg**.

TURNBERG, Baron *cr* 2000 (Life Peer), of Cheadle in the county of Cheshire; **Leslie Arnold Turnberg,** Kt 1994; MD; FRCP, FMedSci; Chairman: National Centre for Replacement, Refinement and Reduction of Animals in Research, 2004–07; Medical Advisory Board, Nations Health Care, 2004–07; *b* 22 March 1934; *s* of Hyman and Dora Turnberg; *m* 1968, Edna Barme; one *s* one *d*. *Educ:* Stand Grammar Sch., Whitefield; Univ. of Manchester (MB, ChB 1957, MD 1966). MRCP 1961, FRCP 1973; FRCPE 1993; FRCP(I) 1993; FRCPSGlas 1994; FRCS 1996; FCPS(Pak). Junior medical posts: Manchester Jewish Hosp.; Northern Hosp.; Ancoats Hosp.; Manchester Royal Infirmary, 1957–61 and 1964–66; Registrar, UCH, 1961–64; Lectr, Royal Free Hosp., 1967; Res. Fellow, Univ. of Texas South-Western Med. Sch., Dallas, Texas, 1968; University of Manchester: Lectr, then Sen. Lectr, 1968–73; Dean, Fac. of Medicine, 1986–89; Prof. of Medicine, 1973–97. Chm., Specialist Training Authy, 1996–98. Hon. Consultant Physician, Salford HA, 1973–97. Member: Salford HA, 1974–81 and 1990–92; NW RHA, 1986–89. Chairman: PHLS Bd, 1997–2002; Health Quality Service, 2000–04; Mem. Bd, Renovo Gp, 2005–. Mem., Select Cttee on sci. and technol., H of L, 2001–05. Scientific Advr, Assoc. Med. Res. Charities, 1997–. Royal College of Physicians: Mem. Council, 1989–92; Pres., 1992–97; Chairman: Educn Cttee, 1990–92; Wking Gp on Communication, 1991–92; British Society of Gastroenterology: Mem. Council, 1989–92; Chm., Res. Cttee, 1991–92; Pres., 1999–2000; President: Med. Section, Manchester Med. Soc., 1992–93; Medical Protection Soc., 1997–2007. Trustee, Wolfson Foundn, 1997–. Founder FMedSci 1998 (Vice Pres., 1998–2004). Hon. FFOM 1993; Hon. FRACP 1994; Hon. FRCOphth 1996; Hon. FRCOG 1996; Hon. FFPM 1997; Hon. Fellow: Acad. of Medicine, Singapore, 1994; Coll. of Medicine, S Africa, 1994. Hon. DSc: Salford, 1996; Manchester, 1998; London, 2000. *Publications:* Electrolyte and Water Transport Across Gastro-intestinal Epithelia, 1982; Clinical Gastroenterology, 1989; pubns on mechanisms of intestinal absorption and secretion in health and disease and on clinical gastroenterology. *Recreations:* reading, antiquarian books, painting, walking, talking. *Address:* House of Lords, SW1A 0AA.

TURNBULL, family name of **Baron Turnbull**.

TURNBULL, Baron *cr* 2005 (Life Peer), of Enfield in the London Borough of Enfield; **Andrew Turnbull,** KCB 1998 (CB 1990); CVO 1992; Secretary of the Cabinet and Head of the Home Civil Service, 2002–05; *b* 21 Jan. 1945; *s* of Anthony and Mary Turnbull; *m* 1967, Diane Clarke; two *s*. *Educ:* Enfield Grammar Sch.; Christ's Coll., Cambridge (BA). ODI Fellow working as economist, Govt of Republic of Zambia, Lusaka, 1968–70; Asst Principal, HM Treasury, 1970; Principal, 1972; on secondment to staff of IMF, 1976–78; Asst Sec., HM Treasury, 1978; Private Sec. to the Prime Minister, 1983–85; Under Sec., 1985; Hd of Gen. Expenditure Policy Gp, HM Treasury, 1985–88; Principal Private Sec. to Prime Minister, 1988–92; Dep. Sec. (Public Finance), 1992, Second Permanent Sec. (Public Expenditure), 1993–94, HM Treasury; Permanent Secretary: DoE, later DETR, 1994–98; HM Treasury, 1998–2002. Non-executive Director: Prudential plc, 2006–; British Land Co. plc, 2006–; Arup Gp, 2006–; Frontier Economics, 2006–. Advr, Booz Allen and Hamilton UK, 2006–. Gov., Dulwich Coll. *Recreations:* walking, sailing, opera, golf. *Address:* House of Lords, SW1A 0PW. *Clubs:* Garrick; Tottenham Hotspur.

TURNBULL, Rt Rev. (Anthony) Michael (Arnold); *see* Turnbull, Rt Rev. M.

TURNBULL, David Knight Thomas, FCA; Director: Worldbeater Solutions Ltd, since 2000; XXX Building Ltd, since 1999; *b* 13 Dec. 1948; *s* of Stanley Thomas Turnbull and Lalla Turnbull (*née* Knight); *m* 1972, Monica Belton; one *s* one *d*. *Educ:* Stationers' Co. Sch.; Westfield Coll., London Univ. (BSc). FCA 1975. With Coopers & Lybrand, Sheffield and Iran, 1972–79; Amalgamated Metal Corporation plc: Gp Chief Acct, 1980–84; Corporate Controller, 1984–86; Gen. Manager, Business Develt, 1986–89; Finance Director: PO Counters Ltd, 1989–94; British Council, 1994–2000; Army Benevolent Fund, 2001–06. Sec., Interstate Programmes Ltd, 2000–. *Recreations:* anything old, watching Rugby. *Address:* Halfway Grange, Chantry View Road, Guildford, Surrey GU1 3XR. *T:* (01483) 569285.

TURNBULL, Jeffrey Alan, CBE 1991; FREng; FICE, FIHT; Consultant, Mott MacDonald Group Ltd, 1994–96 (Chairman and Director, 1989–94); *b* 14 Aug. 1934; *s* of Alan Edward Turnbull and Alice May (*née* Slee); *m* 1957, Beryl (*née* Griffith); two *s* one *d. Educ:* Newcastle upon Tyne Royal Grammar Sch.; Liverpool Coll. of Technology. DipTE 1964; CEng; FIHT 1966; FICE 1973; FREng (FEng 1992). National Service, RE, 1956–58. Jun. Engr, Cheshire CC, 1951–55; Engr, Herefordshire CC, 1955–59; Resident Engr, Berks CC, 1959–66; Mott Hay & Anderson, 1966–88: Chief Designer (Roads), 1968; Associate, 1973; Dir, Mott Hay & Anderson International Ltd, 1975–88; Dir, Mott Hay & Anderson, 1978–88; Dir, 1983–88, Chief Exec., 1987–88, Mott Hay & Anderson Holdings Ltd. *Publication:* (contrib.) Civil Engineer's Reference Book, 4th edn 1988. *Recreations:* walking, France. *Address:* 63 Higher Drive, Banstead, Surrey SM1 1PW. *T:* (020) 8393 1054. *Club:* Royal Automobile.

TURNBULL, John William; Chief Executive, Hereford and Worcester County Council, 1993–97; *b* 12 May 1934; *s* of Henry W. Turnbull and Janet Turnbull; *m* 1956, Sheila Batey; two *d. Educ:* Westminster Coll.; LSE (BScEcon); London Inst. of Educn (MA, DipEd). Teacher, 1957–68; Lectr, 1968–70; Educn Officer, 1970–76; Dep. County Educn Officer, Leics, 1977–83; County Educn Officer, Hereford and Worcester, 1984–93. Advr, ACC, 1985 (Advr, Soc. Services Cttee, 1995–97); Mem. Bd, Midlands Examining Gp, 1989–93; Chm., W Midlands Exam. Bd, 1991–93; Mem., Nat. Youth Bureau, 1990–93. Clerk to Lord Lieutenancy, 1993–97. Governor, Further Educn Staff Coll., 1990–93. JP S Worcs, 1998. *Publications:* articles on educn and administration. *Recreations:* reading, playing piano, bowls.

TURNBULL, Hon. Malcolm Bligh; MHR (L) Wentworth, New South Wales, since 2004; *b* 24 Oct. 1954; *s* of late Bruce Bligh Turnbull and Coral (*née* Lansbury); *m* 1980, Lucinda Mary Forrest Hughes, *d* of Hon. Thomas Hughes, AO, QC; one *s* one *d. Educ:* Sydney Grammar Sch.; Sydney Univ. (BA, LLB); Brasenose Coll., Oxford (Rhodes Schol. (NSW) 1978, BCL 1980). Journalist, Nation Review, 1975; Political Correspondent, TCN–9, Sydney, 1976; The Bulletin, 1977–78; Journalist, Sunday Times, London, 1979; admitted to NSW Bar, 1980; Barrister, Sydney, 1980–83; Gen. Counsel and Secretary, Consolidated Press Holdings Ltd, 1983–86; Partner: Turnbull McWilliam, Solicitors, Sydney, 1986–87; Turnbull & Co., Solicitors, 1987–90; Jt Man. Dir, Whitlam Turnbull & Co. Ltd, Investment Bankers, Sydney, 1987–90; Man. Dir, Turnbull & Partners Pty Ltd, Investment Bankers, 1987–97; Man. Dir and Chm., Goldman Sachs Australia, 1997–2001. Chm., Australian Republican Movement, 1993–2000 (Dir, 1991–2002); Deleg., Constitutional Convention, 1998; Hon. Federal Treas., Liberal Party of Australia, 2002–03. Parly Sec. to PM of Australia, 2006–07; Minister for the Envmt and Water Resources, 2007. Chairman: Axiom Forest Resources Ltd, 1991–92; FTR Holdings, then WebCentral Gp, Ltd, 1995–97, 2001–04 (Dir, 1995–2004); OzEmail Ltd, 1995–99 (Dir, 1995–99); Dir, Reach Ltd, 2001–04. Chm., Menzies Res. Centre, 2002–04. Centenary Medal, Australia, 2003. *Publications:* The Spycatcher Trial, 1988; The Reluctant Republic, 1993; Fighting for the Republic, 1999. *Recreations:* riding, swimming. *Address:* Level 1, 5a Bronte Road, Bondi Junction, NSW 2022, Australia. *T:* (2) 93695221, *Fax:* (2) 93695225; (office) PO Box 1840, Bondi Junction, NSW 1355, Australia. *Clubs:* Australian (Sydney); Athenæum (Philadelphia).

TURNBULL, Mark; *see* Turnbull, W. M.

TURNBULL, Rt Rev. Michael, CBE 2003; DL; Bishop of Durham, 1994–2003; Assistant Bishop: diocese of Canterbury, since 2003; diocese of Europe, since 2003; *b* 27 Dec. 1935; *s* of George Ernest Turnbull and Adeline Turnbull (*née* Awty); *m* 1963, Brenda Susan Merchant; one *s* two *d. Educ:* Ilkley Grammar Sch.; Keble Coll., Oxford (MA); St John's Coll., Durham (DipTh). Deacon, 1960; priest, 1961; Curate: Middleton, 1960–61; Luton, 1961–65; Domestic Chaplain to Archbishop of York, 1965–69; Rector of Heslington and Chaplain, York Univ., 1969–76; Chief Secretary, Church Army, 1976–84; Archdeacon of Rochester, also Canon Residentiary of Rochester Cathedral and Chm., Dio. Bd for Mission and Unity, 1984–88; Bishop of Rochester, 1988–94. Entered H of L, 1994. Mem., General Synod, C of E, 1970–75, 1987–2003; Vice-Chm., Central Bd of Finance, C of E, 1990–98; Member: Bd, Church Commissioners, 1989–98; Archbishops' Council, 1998–2000 (Chm., Ministry Div., 1999–2000); Archbps' Commn on Cathedrals, 1992–93; Chairman: Archbps' Commn on orgn of C of E, 1994–96; Foundn for Church Leadership, 2003–07. Chairman: NE Constitutional Convention, 1999–2003; Campaign for English Regs, 2000–03. Chairman: Bible Reading Fellowship, 1985–94; Coll. of Preachers, 1990–98. DL Kent, 2005. Hon. Fellow, St Chad's Coll., Durham, 2002. Hon. DLitt Greenwich, 1994; Hon. DD Dunelm, 2003. *Publications:* (contrib.) Unity: the next step?, 1972; God's Front Line, 1979; Parish Evangelism, 1980; Learning to Pray, 1981; 100 Minute Bible Reflections, 2007. *Recreations:* cricket, family life. *Address:* 67 Strand Street, Sandwich, Kent CT13 9HN. *T:* (01304) 611389; *e-mail:* bstmt@btopenworld.com. *Club:* MCC.

TURNBULL, Rev. Dr Richard Duncan, PhD; Principal, Wycliffe Hall, Oxford, since 2005; *b* 17 Oct. 1960; *s* of Alan Allgood Turnbull and late Kathleen Turnbull; *m* 1986, Caroline Andrew; one *s* three *d. Educ:* Moseley Grammar Sch.; Normanton High Sch.; Univ. of Reading (BA 1982); Univ. of Durham (BA 1992; PhD 1997); Univ. of Oxford (MA 2005). CA 1985. Supervisory and trng posts, 1982–87, Manager, 1987–90, Ernst and Young, chartered accountants; ordination trng, Cranmer Hall, Durham, 1990–94; ordained deacon, 1994, priest, 1995; Curate, Christ Church, Portswood, Southampton, 1994–98; Vicar, Christ Church, Chineham, Basingstoke, 1998–2005. Member: Gen. Synod, 1995–2005 (Chm., Business Cttee, 2004–05); Archbishops' Council, 2003–05. *Publications:* Anglican and Evangelical?, 2007; articles on Evangelicalism in Churchman and Anvil; contrib. dictionary entry on 7th Earl of Shaftesbury to Theologishe Realenzyklopädie, 1999. *Recreations:* walking, reading, visiting historic houses. *Address:* Wycliffe Hall, 54 Banbury Road, Oxford OX2 6PW. *T:* (01865) 274209, *Fax:* (01865) 274215; *e-mail:* richard.turnbull@wycliffe.ox.ac.uk, richard.turnbull@theology.ox.ac.uk. *Club:* Oxford and Cambridge.

TURNBULL, (Wilson) Mark, RIBA; FRIAS, FLI; Principal, Mark Turnbull Landscape Architect, since 1999; Chairman, Envision (formerly TJP Envision), since 1999; *b* 1 April 1943; *s* of Wilson and Margaret Turnbull. *Educ:* Edinburgh Coll. of Art (Andrew Grant scholar, 1964, 1965, 1967, 1968; DipArch (distinction in Design) 1968); Univ. of Pennsylvania (Fulbright scholar, 1968–74; Faculty Medal, Dept of Landscape Arch. and Regl Planning, 1970; MLA 1970). RIBA 1977; MBCS 1984; FLI 1989; FRIAS 1991. Chartered Architect, Landscape Architect and IT Professional, Wallace, McHarg, Roberts and Todd, Landscape Architects and Regl Planners, Philadelphia, 1968–70; Asst Prof., Dept of Architecture, Univ. of S Calif, LA, 1970–74; Envmtl Consultant: Union Carbide; US Atomic Energy Commn, 1971, 1974; Kamnitzer, Marks, Lappin and Vreeland, Architects and Regl Planners, LA, 1973–74; Associate, 1974–77, Partner, 1977–82, W. J. Cairns and Partners, Envmtl Consultants, Edinburgh; Partner, Design Innovations Res., 1978–82; Principal, 1982–99, Chm., 1999–2001, Turnbull Jeffrey Partnership, Landscape Architects. Comr, Royal Fine Art Commn for Scotland, 1996–2005. Member: Council, Cockburn Assoc., Edinburgh Civic Trust, 1984–95; Countryside Commn for Scotland, 1988–92; Envmt and Technical Cttee, Landscape Inst., 1996–; Chm., Edinburgh Green Belt Initiative, 1988–92; Vice-Chm., 1991–2002, Dir, 2002–, Edinburgh Green Belt Trust. Edinburgh Corp. Medal, 1970. *Publications:* numerous articles on landscape architecture, computer visualisation and design methods in jls. *Recreation:* sailing. *Address:* Mark Turnbull Landscape Architect, Creag an Tuirc House, Balquhidder, Lochearnhead, Perthshire FK19 8NY. *T:* (01877) 384728.

TURNER, family name of **Barons Bilston**, **Netherthorpe** and **Turner of Ecchinswell** and **Baroness Turner of Camden**.

TURNER OF CAMDEN, Baroness *cr* 1985 (Life Peer), of Camden in Greater London; **Muriel Winifred Turner;** *b* 18 Sept. 1927; *m* 1955, Reginald Thomas Frederick Turner (*d* 1995), MC, DFC. Asst Gen. Sec., ASTMS, 1970–87. Member: Occupational Pensions Board, 1978–93; Central Arbitration Cttee, 1980–90; TUC General Council, 1981–87; Equal Opportunities Commission, 1982–88. Junior Spokesperson on Social Security, 1986–96, Principal Opposition Spokesperson on Employment, 1988–96, H of L. Chm., Ombudsman Council, PIA, 1994–97. Hon. LLD Leicester, 1991. *Address:* House of Lords, SW1A 0PW.

TURNER OF ECCHINSWELL, Baron *cr* 2005 (Life Peer), of Ecchinswell in the County of Hampshire; **(Jonathan) Adair Turner;** Chairman: Economic and Social Research Council, since 2007 (Member, since 2003); Financial Services Authority, since 2008; *b* 5 Oct. 1955; *s* of Geoffrey Vincent Turner and Kathleen Margaret (*née* Broadhurst); *m* 1985, Orna Ni Chionna; two *d. Educ:* Gonville and Caius Coll., Cambridge (MA Hist. and Econs 1978). Chm., Cambridge Univ. Cons. Assoc., 1976; Pres., Cambridge Union Soc., 1977. BP, 1979; with Chase Manhattan Bank, 1979–82; McKinsey & Co., 1982–95; Principal, 1988; Dir, 1994–95; Dir Gen., CBI, 1995–99; Vice Chm., Merrill Lynch Europe, 2000–06. Non-executive Director: United Business Media, 2000–08; Siemens plc, 2006–; Paternoster UK Ltd, 2006–; Standard Chartered plc, 2006–. Chairman: Low Pay Commn, 2002–06; Pension Commn, 2003–06; Climate Change Cttee, 2008–09. Vis. Prof., 1999–, and Chair, Policy Cttee, Centre for Economic Performance, 1999–2007, LSE; Vis. Prof., Cass Business Sch., 2004–. Trustee: Cambridge Foundn, 2002–; WWF, 2001–07; Save the Children, 2006–. Hon. DSc City, 2002. *Publication:* Just Capital: the liberal economy, 2001. *Recreations:* ski-ing, opera, children. *Address:* House of Lords, SW1A 0PW.

TURNER, Alan B.; *see* Brooke Turner.

TURNER, Amédée Edward; QC 1976; *b* 26 March 1929; *s* of Frederick William Turner and Ruth Hempson; *m* 1960, Deborah Dudley Owen; one *s* one *d. Educ:* Temple Grove, Heron's Ghyll, Sussex; Dauntsey Sch., Wilts; Christ Church, Oxford (MA). Called to Bar, Inner Temple, 1954; practised patent bar, 1954–57; Associate, Kenyon & Kenyon, patent attorneys, NY, 1957–60; London practice, 1960–; Senior Counsel: APCO Europe, Brussels, 1995–98; WorldSpace Ltd, 1999–2001; of Counsel, Oppenheimer Wolff and Donnelly, Brussels, 1994–2003. Dir, CJA Consultants Ltd, 1999– (Chm., 2004–). Contested (C) Norwich N, gen. elections, 1964, 1966, 1970. European Parliament: MEP (C) Suffolk, 1979–94; contested (C) Suffolk and SW Norfolk, 1994; Hon. MEP, 1994; EDG spokesman on energy res. and technol., 1984–89; Chief Whip, EDG, 1989–92; joined EPP Gp, 1992; Mem., EPP Gp Bureau, 1992–94; Chm., Civil Liberties and Internal Affairs Cttee, 1992–94; Vice Chm., Legal Cttee, 1979–84; Member: Economic and Monetary Cttee, 1979–84; ACP Jt Assembly, 1980–94; Transport Cttee, 1981–84; Energy Cttee, 1984–94; Legal Affairs Cttee, 1984–89. PHARE Advr to Macedonian Parlt on improving legislature and democratic effectiveness, 2001–02 (manual, The Approximation of EU Law, 2002). Mem., Exec. Cttee, European League for Econ. Co-operation, 1996–. Mem., Adv. Council to Anglican Observer, UN, 2002–06; organised and prepared report on Anglican, Episcopalian and Muslim discussions on attitudes of lay Muslims to democracy, human rights and rule of law throughout USA and GB, 2005–06; campaign of speaking engagements on report (Muslim Grass-roots in the West Discuss Democracy, 2007), USA, UK and Brussels, 2007–08. *Publications:* The Law of Trade Secrets, 1962, supplement, 1968; The Law of the New European Patent, 1979; many Conservative Party study papers, 1950–70, on defence, oil and Middle East; reports on patent litigation insce for EC, 2003, 2006. *Recreations:* garden design, art deco collection, fish keeping, oil painting. *Address:* Penthouse 7, Bickenhall Mansions, 63–104 Bickenhall Street, W1U 6BS. *T:* (020) 7935 2949, *Fax:* (020) 7935 2950; 5 New Square, Lincoln's Inn, WC2A 3RJ. *T:* (020) 7404 0404; The Barn, Westleton, Saxmundham, Suffolk IP17 3AN. *T:* (01728) 648235; La Combe de la Boissière, St Maximin, Uzès 30700, France. *T:* 466220869; *e-mail:* amedee.turner@btinternet.com. *Clubs:* Coningsby, United & Cecil.

TURNER, Andrew John; MP (C) Isle of Wight, since 2001; *b* Coventry, 24 Oct. 1953; *s* of late Eustace Albert Turner and Joyce Mary Turner (*née* Lowe). *Educ:* Rugby Sch.; Keble Coll., Oxford (BA 1976, MA 1981); Birmingham Univ. (PGCE 1977); Henley Mgt Centre. Teacher of Econs and Geog., Rushden Boys' Comp. Sch., 1977, Lord Williams's Sch., Thame, 1978–84; Res. Officer, Cons. Central Office, 1984–86; Special Advr to Sec. of State for Social Services, 1986–88; Dir, Grant-maintained Schools Foundn, 1988–97; Dep. Dir, Educn Unit, IEA, 1998–2000; Head of Policy and Resources, Educn Dept, Southwark BC, 2000–01. Educn Consultant, 1997–2001, Dir, 2000–02, Empire Packet Co. A Vice-Chm., Conservative Party, 2003–05; Opposition front bench spokesman on charities, 2005–06. FRSA. *Recreations:* walking, the countryside, old movies, avoiding gardening. *Address:* House of Commons, SW1A 0AA; (home) Seal House, Sea Street, Newport, Isle of Wight PO30 5BW; (constituency office) 24 The Mall, Carisbrooke Road, Newport, Isle of Wight PO30 1BW. *T:* (01983) 530808.

TURNER, Prof. (Andrew) Neil, PhD; FRCP, FRCPE; Professor of Nephrology, University of Edinburgh, since 1998; Hon. Consultant Nephrologist, Edinburgh Royal Infirmary, since 1998; *b* 28 April 1956; *s* of Rodney Turner and Eileen (*née* Wade); *m* 1984, Helen Cameron; three *s. Educ:* Downing Coll., Cambridge (MA 1977); Lincoln Coll., Oxford (BM BCh 1980); PhD London 1992. FRCP 1996; FRCPE 1997. Med. trng in Oxford, Croydon, Northampton, Liverpool, Norwich and York, 1980–85; renal trng, Oxford, 1983, and Hammersmith, 1985–92; NKRF Sen. Res. Fellow, 1990; Hon. Consultant, Hammersmith Hosp. and Sen. Lectr, RPMS, 1993; Sen. Lectr in Medicine and Nephrology, Univ. of Aberdeen and Aberdeen Royal Hosp., 1994–98. ILTM 2000. *Publications:* (contrib.) Oxford Textbook of Medicine, 4th edn 2005; (contrib.) Oxford Textbook of Clinical Nephrology, 3rd edn 2005; (contrib.) Davidson's Principles and Practice of Medicine, 20th edn 2006; papers in learned jls on autoimmunity, antigen processing, renal disease, teaching, information technology and health. *Recreations:* art, the outdoors, music. *Address:* Renal Medicine, Royal Infirmary, Little France, Edinburgh EH16 4SA. *T:* (0131) 242 9167, *Fax:* (0131) 242 1233; *e-mail:* neil.turner@ed.ac.uk.

TURNER, Ven. Antony Hubert Michael; Archdeacon of the Isle of Wight, 1986–96, now Archdeacon Emeritus; *b* 17 June 1930; *s* of Frederick George and Winifred Frances Turner; *m* 1956, Margaret Kathleen (*née* Phillips); one *s* two *d. Educ:* Royal Liberty Grammar School, Romford, Essex; Tyndale Hall, Bristol. FCA 1963 (ACA 1952); DipTh (Univ. of London), 1956. Deacon, 1956; Priest, 1957; Curate, St Ann's, Nottingham,

1956–59; Curate in Charge, St Cuthbert's, Cheadle, Dio. Chester, 1959–62; Vicar, Christ Church, Macclesfield, 1962–68; Home Sec., Bible Churchmen's Missionary Soc., 1968–74; Vicar of St Jude's, Southsea, 1974–86; RD of Portsmouth, 1979–84; Priest i/c, St Mary, Rotterdam, 1999–2000. Church Commissioner, 1983–93. Vice Chm., C of E Pensions Bd, 1988–97. *Recreations:* photography, caravanning. *Address:* 15 Avenue Road, Hayling Island, Hants, PO11 0LX. *T:* (023) 9246 5881.

TURNER, Barry Horace Page, PhD; writer and editor; *b* 4 Oct. 1937; *o s* of Laurence and Esther Turner; *m* 1st, 1965, Sandra Hogben (marr. diss. 1972); 2nd, 1974, Gunilla Nordquist (marr. diss. 1986); one *s* one *d*; 3rd, 1997, Mary Elizabeth Fulton. *Educ:* King Edward VII Grammar Sch., Bury St Edmunds; London School of Economics (BSc Econs 1961; PhD 1966); Inst. of Educn, London Univ. (DipEd 1962). Dep. Editor, New Education, 1966–68; Educn Corresp., Observer, 1969–71; Reporter and Presenter, BBC Current Affairs, Thames TV, Yorkshire TV, Granada TV, 1969–77; Mktg Dir, Macmillan Press, 1977–81. Chm., Nat. Acad. of Writing, 2003–. Vis. Prof., UCE, 2006–. Editor: The Writer's Handbook, annually 1988–; The Statesman's Yearbook, annually 1997–. *Plays:* (jtly) Henry Irving, 1995; Agate, 1997. *Publications:* (jtly) Adventures in Education, 1969; Free Trade and Protection, 1971; Equality for Some, 1974; A Place in the Country, 1974; Sweden, 1976; The Other European Community, 1982; (jtly) The Playgoer's Companion, 1983; A Jobbing Actor, 1984; Richard Burton, 1987; East End, West End, 1990; Marks of Distinction, 1988; … And the Policeman Smiled, 1991; The Long Horizon, 1993; Quest for Love, 1994; (jtly) When Daddy Came Home, 1995; The Writer's Companion, 1996; One Small Suitcase (for children), 2003; Countdown to Victory, 2004; Suez 1956: the inside story of the first oil war, 2006; contribs to The Times, Sunday Times. *Recreations:* theatre, old movies, lunch. *Address:* 34 Ufton Road, N1 5BX. *T:* (020) 7241 0116; Le Bernet, 32480 La Romieu, France. *T:* 562288841. *Clubs:* Garrick, Chelsea Arts.

TURNER, Brian James, CBE 2002; Chef/Patron, Brian Turner Mayfair, 2003–08; *b* 7 May 1946; *s* of Lawrence and Lily Turner; *m* 1973, Denise Parker; two *s*. *Educ:* Morley Grammar Sch.; Leeds Coll. of Food Technol. Chef: Simpson's, Strand, 1963–65; Savoy Grill, 1965–68; Beau Rivage Palace, Lausanne, 1969; Claridge's, London, 1970–71; Capital Hotel/Restaurant, London, 1971–86; Turner's Restaurant, London, 1986–2001; Brian Turner's Restaurant, Crowne Plaza Hotel, NEC Birmingham, 2001–05; Turner's Grill, Slough, 2006–08; Turner's Grill, Birmingham, 2006–08; Dir, Foxtrot Oscar, 2001–03. *Television* includes: This Morning, 1992–2000 and 2003–04; Food and Drink, 1992–2000; Ready Steady Cook, 1992–; Great Food Live, 2003–; Saturday Kitchen, 2005–; Saturday Cooks, 2006–; Daily Cooks, 2007–. Member: Acad. of Culinary Arts, 1987– (Chm., 1993–2004; Pres., 2004–); Hospitality Skills, 2001–; UK Skills, 2002–; Prince's Trust, 2002–. Hon. Prof., Thames Valley Univ., 2001. FCGI 2005. Chef of Year Award, 1997, Special Award, 2004, Caterer and Hotelkeeper; Special Award, Craft Guild of Chefs, 1997; Wedgwood Award, 1997; Nestlé Toque d'Or, 2003. *Publications:* Campaign for Great British Food, 1990; Sunday Best, 1995; Out to Lunch, 2 vols, 1996 and 1997; (with A. Worrall Thompson) Ready Steady Cook, Book 1, 1997; The Big Ready Steady Cookbook, 1997; Grills and Barbecues, 1997; A Yorkshire Lad: my life with recipes, 2000; Brian Turner's Favourite British Recipes, 2003; Ready Steady Cook: the top 100 recipes, 2003. *Recreations:* sport, brass band music, opera, travel. *Address:* c/o Millennium Hotel, Grosvenor Square, W1K 2HP. *T:* (020) 7495 0220, *Fax:* (020) 7495 0440; *e-mail:* turnerrest@aol.com.

TURNER, Prof. Bryan Stanley, PhD, DLitt; Professor of Sociology and Research Leader, Asia Research Institute, National University of Singapore, since 2005; *b* 14 Jan. 1945; *s* of Stanley W. Turner and Sophie (*née* Brooks). *Educ:* Univ. of Leeds (BA 1966; PhD 1970; MA 2002); Flinders Univ. (DLitt 1976). Lecturer: Univ. of Aberdeen, 1969–74; Univ. of Lancaster, 1974–78; Sen. Lectr, 1979–80, Reader, 1980–82, Univ. of Aberdeen; Prof. of Sociology, Univ. of Flinders, 1982–88; Prof. of Gen. Social Sci., Univ. of Utrecht, 1988–90; Professor of Sociology: Univ. of Essex, 1990–92; Deakin Univ., 1992–98; Cambridge Univ., 1998–2005; Fellow of Fitzwilliam Coll., Cambridge, 2002–05. FASSA 1988. Editor: (jtly) Body & Society, 1994–; Citizenship Studies, 1997–; (jtly) Jl of Classical Sociology, 2001–. *Publications include:* Weber and Islam, 1974; For Weber, 1981; Religion and Social Theory, 1983; The Body and Society, 1984; Citizenship and Capitalism, 1986; Medical Power and Social Knowledge, 1987; Regulating Bodies, 1992; Orientalism, Postmodernism and Globalism, 1994; (ed) The Blackwell Companion to Social Theory, 1996; Classical Sociology, 1999; Islam: critical concepts in sociology, 2003; The New Medical Sociology, 2004; (ed jtly) International Handbook of Sociology, 2005; The Cambridge Dictionary of Sociology, 2006; Vulnerability and Human Rights, 2006; (ed with Patrick Baert) Pragmatism and European Social Theory, 2007; Rights and Virtues: political essays on citizenship and social justice. *Recreations:* gardening, tourism, walking, collecting books. *Address:* Asia Research Institute, Tower Block, Bukit Timah Road, National University of Singapore, Singapore 117570; 19 Taman Serasi, # 01–25, Botanic Garden View, Singapore 257723.

TURNER, Prof. Cedric Edward, CBE 1987; FREng; Emeritus Professor and Senior Research Fellow, Imperial College, London, since 1991; *b* 5 Aug. 1926; *s* of Charles Turner and Mabel Evelyn (*née* Berry); *m* 1953, Margaret Dorothy (*née* Davies); one *s* two *d*. *Educ:* Brockenhurst Grammar Sch.; University Coll., Southampton (now Univ. of Southampton) (BScEng); DScEng, PhD London. CEng, FIMechE, FREng (FEng 1989). Res. Asst, Imperial Coll., 1948–52; Academic Staff, Imperial Coll., 1952–76 and 1979–: Prof. of Materials in Mech. Engrg, 1975–91; seconded NPL and Brit. Aerospace, 1976–78. Hon. Prof., Shenyang Inst. of Aeronautical Engrg, Shenyang, China, 1987; Leverhulme Emeritus Fellow, 1990–92. Silver Medal, Plastics Inst., 1963; James Clayton Prize, IMechE, 1981. *Publications:* Introduction to Plate and Shell Theory, 1965; (jtly) Post Yield Fracture Mechanics, 1979, 2nd edn 1984; contribs to Proc. Royal Soc., Proc. IMechE, Jl Strain Anal., Amer. Soc. Test & Mat., etc. *Recreations:* Meccano modelling of old machines, reading, friend of Kirkaldy Testing Museum, London. *Address:* The Corner House, 17 Meadway, Epsom, Surrey KT19 8JZ. *T:* (01372) 722989.

TURNER, Rev. Christopher Gilbert; Hon. Assistant Curate, Hook Norton with Great Rollright, Swerford and Wigginton, since 1992; Headmaster, Stowe School, 1979–89; *b* 23 Dec. 1929; *s* of late Theodore F. Turner, QC; *m* 1961, Lucia, *d* of late Prof. S. R. K. Glanville (Provost of King's Coll., Cambridge); one *s* one *d* (and one *d* decd). *Educ:* Winchester Coll. (Schol.); New Coll., Oxford (Exhibnr, MA); Oxford Ministry Course. Asst Master, Radley Coll., 1952–61; Senior Classics Master, Charterhouse, 1961–68; Headmaster, Dean Close Sch., 1968–79. Schoolmaster Student at Christ Church, Oxford, 1967. Foundation Member of Council, Cheltenham Colleges of Educn, 1968. Mem., HMC Cttee, 1974–75, 1987–88; Chm., Common Entrance Cttee, 1976–80; Gov., Chipping Norton Sch., 1996–2006. Ordained deacon, 1992, priest, 1993. *Publications:* chapter on History, in Comparative Study of Greek and Latin Literature, 1969; chapter on Dean Close in the Seventies, in The First Hundred Years, 1986; (contrib.) Encounters, 2007. *Recreations:* music (violin-playing), reading, walking, different forms of manual labour; OUBC 1951. *Address:* Rosemullion, High Street, Great Rollright, near Chipping Norton, Oxon OX7 5RQ. *T:* (01608) 737359.

See also Hon. Sir M. J. Turner.

TURNER, Christopher John, CBE 1990 (OBE 1977); Partner, DCGlobal, since 1998; consultant, EBRD TurnAround Management programme (Balkans); *b* 17 Aug. 1933; *s* of Arthur Basil Turner and Joan Meddows (*née* Taylor); *m* 1961, Irene Philomena de Souza; two *d* (one *s* decd). *Educ:* Truro Cathedral Sch.; Jesus Coll., Cambridge (MA). Served RAF, Pilot Officer (Navigator), 1951–53. Tanganyika/Tanzania: Dist Officer, 1958–61; Dist Comr, 1961–62; Magistrate and Regional Local Courts Officer, 1962–64; Sec., Sch. Admin, 1964–69; Anglo-French Condominium of New Hebrides: Dist Agent, 1970–73; Develt Sec., 1973; Financial Sec., 1975; Chief Sec., 1977–80; Admin. Officer (Staff Planning), Hong Kong, 1980–82; Governor: Turks and Caicos Islands, 1982–87; Montserrat, WI, 1987–90. Manager, Internat. Business Develt, 1990–92, consultant on regl business develt, Santa Domingo, 1990–91, McLane (Wal Mart), Texas; Man. Dir, McLane (UK), 1993; Vice Pres. Develt, McLane Internat., 1994–96; Dir of Mkting, Cambridge Myers (Strasburger Enterprises Inc.), Texas, 1996–98. Vanuatu Independence Medal, 1981. *Recreations:* ornithology, photography, diving, tropical gardening. *Address:* 98 Christchurch Road, Winchester SO23 9TE. *T:* (01962) 870775; (office) 22 Shirlock Road, NW3 2HS. *T:* (020) 7284 4154.

TURNER, Colin Francis; Senior District Judge (formerly Senior Registrar), Family Division of High Court, 1988–91, retired (Registrar, 1971–88); *b* 11 April 1930; *s* of Sidney F. and Charlotte C. Turner; *m* 1951, Josephine Alma Jones; two *s* one *d*. *Educ:* Beckenham Grammar Sch.; King's Coll., London. LLB 1955. Entered Principal Probate Registry, 1949; District Probate Registrar, York, 1965–68. MBOU. Hon. Mem., London Nat. History Soc., 1998. *Publications:* (ed jtly) Rayden on Divorce, 9th, 11th, 12th and 13th edns, consulting editor to 14th edn; an editor of Supreme Court Practice, 1972–90; (jtly) Precedents in Matrimonial Causes and Ancillary Matters, 1985. *Recreations:* birding, fishing. *Address:* Lakers, Church Road, St Johns, Redhill, Surrey RH1 6QA. *T:* (01737) 761807.

TURNER, Colin William; Rector, Glasgow Academy, 1983–94; *b* 10 Dec. 1933; *s* of William and Joyce Turner; *m* 1958, Priscilla Mary Trickett; two *s* two *d*. *Educ:* Torquay Grammar Sch.; King's Coll., London (BSc; AKC). Edinburgh Academy: Asst Master, 1958–82; OC CCF, 1960–74; Head, Maths Dept, 1973–75; Housemaster, 1975–82. *Recreations:* mountaineering, gardening, local history. *Address:* Leat, Lowerdown, Bovey Tracey, Devon TQ13 9LF. *T:* (01626) 832266.

TURNER, Sir Colin (William Carstairs), Kt 1993; CBE 1985; DFC 1944; President, The Colin Turner Group, International Media Representatives and Marketing Consultants, 1988–97 (Chairman, 1985–88); *b* 4 Jan. 1922; *s* of late Colin C. W. Turner, Enfield; *m* 1949, Evelyn Mary, *d* of late Claude H. Buckard, Enfield; three *s* one *d*. *Educ:* Highgate Sch. Served War of 1939–45 with RAF, 1940–45, Air observer; S. Africa and E Africa, 223 Squadron; Desert Air Force, N. Africa, 1942–44; commissioned, 1943; invalided out as Flying Officer, 1945, after air crash; Chm., 223 Squadron Assoc., 1975–93; Pres., Enfield Br., 1979–93, Chm., 1994–99, Pres., 2000–, Sheringham and Dist Br., RAFA. Mem., Enfield Borough Council, 1956–58. Pres., Overseas Press and Media Association, 1965–67, Life Pres., 1982 (Hon. Secretary, 1967; Hon. Treasurer, 1974–82; Editor, Overseas Media Guide, 1968, 1969, 1970, 1971, 1972, 1973, 1974); Chm., PR Cttee, Commonwealth Press Union, 1970–87; Chm., Cons. Commonwealth and Overseas Council, 1976–82 (Dep. Chm. 1975); Vice-Pres., Cons. Foreign and Commonwealth Council, 1985–2008; Mem., Nat. Exec., Cons. Party, 1946–53, 1968–73, 1976–82; President: Enfield North Cons. Assoc., 1984–93 (Chm., 1979–84); North Norfolk Cons. Assoc., 1996–99; Chm., Cons. Europ. Constituency Council, London N, 1984–89. Contested (C) Enfield (East), 1950 and 1951; MP (C) Woolwich West, 1959–64. Editor, The Cholmeleian, 1982–95 (Pres., Old Cholmeleian Soc., 1985–86). *Recreations:* gardening, do-it-yourself, fishing. *Address:* The Thatched House, Balfour Road, West Runton, Norfolk NR27 9QJ. *T:* (01263) 837229.

TURNER, David Andrew; QC 1991; a Recorder of the Crown Court, since 1990; *b* 6 March 1947; *s* of late James and Phyllis Turner; *m* 1978, Mary Christine Moffatt; two *s* one *d*. *Educ:* King George V Sch., Southport; Queens' Coll., Cambridge (MA, LLM). Called to the Bar, Gray's Inn, 1971, Bencher, 2001; Asst Recorder, 1987–90. *Recreations:* squash, music. *Address:* Pearl Assurance House, Derby Square, Liverpool L2 9XX. *T:* (0151) 236 7747.

TURNER, David George Patrick; QC 2000; **His Honour Judge Turner;** a Circuit Judge, since 2004; Deputy Designated Family Judge for London, since 2005; *b* 11 July 1954; *s* of George P. Turner and Elsie B. Turner (*née* McClure); *m* 1978, Jean Patricia Hewett; two *s*. *Educ:* Foyle Coll., Londonderry; King's Coll. London (LLB, AKC 1975). Called to the Bar, Gray's Inn, 1976; in practice at the Bar, 1976–2004; Asst Recorder, 1997–2000; a Recorder, 2000–04; Head of Chambers, 2003–04. Judicial Member: Essex Courts Bd, 2004–07; Beds, Essex, Herts Courts Bd, 2007–; Magistrates' Area Trng Cttee for London, 2006–. Chancellor, dio. of Chester, 1998–; Dep. Chancellor, dio. of Liverpool, 2001–02, and of London, 2002–; Mem., Legal Adv. Commn, C of E, 2007–. Reader, 1981–, Churchwarden, 1983–2006, All Souls, Langham Place. Trustee: Langham Partnership; London Lectures Trust. *Address:* c/o Crown Court, New Street, Chelmsford, Essex CM1 1EL.

TURNER, David John; Chairman, Cobham plc, since 2008 (Deputy Chairman, 2007–08); *b* 7 Feb. 1945; *s* of late Frederick and Sheila Margaret Turner; *m* 1991, Julia Anne Thompson; two *s* three *d*. FCA 1969. Cook & Co., Liverpool, 1963–67; Touche Ross & Co., London, 1967–69; Mgt Auditor, Mobil Oil Corp., 1969–71; Chief Accountant, Mobil Servs Ltd, 1971–73; Special Projects Co-ordinator, Mobil Europe Inc., 1973–74; Finance Director: Booker Agriculture, 1975–84; Booker McConnell Ltd, subseq. Booker plc, 1984–93; GKN plc, 1993–2001; Chief Financial Officer, 2001–03, CEO, 2003–07, Brambles Industries plc. Non-exec. Dir, Whitbread plc, 2001–06; Dir, Commonwealth Bank of Australia, 2006–08. *Recreations:* tennis, fishing, ski-ing, opera. *Address:* Cobham plc, Brook Road, Wimborne, Dorset BH21 2BJ. *Club:* Boodle's.

TURNER, Prof. David Warren, FRS 1973; Fellow of Balliol College, Oxford, 1967–94, now Emeritus Fellow; Professor of Electron Spectroscopy, Oxford, 1985–94, now Emeritus Professor; *b* 16 July 1927; *s* of Robert Cecil Turner and Constance Margaret (*née* Bonner); *m* 1954, Barbara Marion Fisher; one *s* one *d*. *Educ:* Westcliff High Sch.; Univ. of Exeter. MA, BSc, PhD, DIC. Lectr, Imperial Coll., 1958; Reader in Organic Chemistry, Imperial Coll., 1965; Oxford University: Lectr in Physical Chem., 1968; Reader in Physical Chemistry, 1978; Reader in Electron Spectroscopy, 1984. Lectures: Kahlbaum, Univ. of Basle, 1971; Van Geuns, Univ. of Amsterdam, 1974; Harkins, Chicago Univ., 1974; Kistiakowsky, Harvard, 1979; Liversidge, RSC, 1981–82. Tilden Medal, Chemical Soc., 1967; Harrison Howe Award, Amer. Chem. Soc., 1973. Hon. DTech, Royal Inst., Stockholm, 1971; Hon. DPhil Basle, 1980; Hon. DSc Exeter, 1999. *Publications:* Molecular Photoelectron Spectroscopy, 1970; contrib. Phil. Trans Royal

Soc., Proc. Royal Soc., Jl Chem. Soc., etc. *Recreations:* music, gardening, tinkering with gadgets. *Address:* Balliol College, Oxford OX1 3BJ.

TURNER, Prof. Denys Alan, DPhil; Horace Tracy Pitkin Professor of Historical Theology, Yale University, since 2005; *b* 5 Aug. 1942; *s* of Alan Turner and Barbara Turner (*née* Mason); *m* 1969, Marie Lambe; two *s* one *d. Educ:* Nat. Univ. of Ireland (BA 1962; MA 1965); St Edmund Hall, Oxford (DPhil 1975). Asst Lectr, 1967–74, Coll. Lectr, 1974–76, in Philosophy, UC, Dublin; Lectr, 1976–89, Sen. Lectr, 1989–95, in Philosophy of Religion, Dept of Theology and Religious Studies, Univ. of Bristol; H. G. Wood Prof. of Theology, Univ. of Birmingham, 1995–99; Norris Hulse Prof. of Divinity, Cambridge Univ., and Fellow of Peterhouse, Cambridge, 1999–2005 (Emeritus Fellow, 2005–). *Publications:* Marxism and Christianity, 1983; Eros and Allegory: medieval exegesis of the Song of Songs, 1995; The Darkness of God: negativity in Christian mysticism, 1995; Faith Seeking, 2002; Faith, Reason and the Existence of God, 2004. *Recreations:* mediaeval church architecture, classical music from Ockeghem to Mahler, gardens. *Address:* Yale Divinity School, 409 Prospect Avenue, New Haven, CT 06511, USA. *T:* (203) 4325339.

TURNER, Derek, CBE 2003; FREng, CEng; FICE, FCILT; Network (formerly Traffic) Operations Director, Highways Agency, since 2005; *b* 8 May 1953; *s* of Edgar and Maud Turner; *m* 1977, Maggy Sporne (marr. diss. 2005); one *d*, and one step *s. Educ:* Hinchley Wood Co. Secondary Sch.; Sheffield Univ. (BEng Hons). CEng 1979; FICE 1991; FIHT 1991; FCILT (FILT 1995); FREng 2005. Asst Engr, Herts CC, 1974–80; Professional Officer, GLC, 1980–82; Principal Engr, Hackney, 1982–85; Gp Planner, Islington, 1985–86; Dep. Asst Bor. Engr, Wandsworth, 1986–90; Bor. Engr and Surveyor, Haringay, 1990–91; Traffic Dir for London, 1991–2000; Man. Dir, Street Mgt, Transport for London, 2000–03; Principal, Derek Turner Consultancy, 2003–05. Vis. Prof. of Civil and Envmtl Engrg, UCL, 2003–. Non-executive Director: Infocell Hldgs Ltd, 2003–05; EGS Ltd, 2007–; Bd Dir, Colin Buchanan and Partners, 2004–05. MCIM 1985; FRSA 1993. AA Award for Red Route 2000, 2001; European Transport Planner of Year, European Transport Cttee (ETC), 2003; Transport Planner of Year, Transportation Planning Soc., 2003. *Publications:* contribs to Jl ICE (Webb Prize 1997), Traffic Engrg and Control, Amer. Soc. of Civil Engrs. *Recreations:* classical music, walking, countryside, travel. *Address:* Highways Agency, No 5 Broadway, Broad Street, Birmingham B15 1BL. *T:* (0121) 678 8403, *Fax:* (0121) 678 8558; *e-mail:* derek.turner@highways.gsi.gov.uk.

TURNER, Dr Desmond Stanley; MP (Lab) Brighton Kemptown, since 1997; *b* 17 July 1939; *s* of Stanley and Elsie Turner; *m* 1st, 1966, Lynette Gwyn-Jones (marr. diss. 1987); one *d*; 2nd, 1997, Lynn Rogers. *Educ:* Luton Grammar Sch.; Imperial Coll., London (BSc); University Coll. London (MSc); PhD London; Brighton Univ. (PGCE). ARCS. Junior posts, Royal Free and St Mary's Hosps Schs of Medicine, 1963–67; Research Associate and Hon. Lectr, Guy's Hosp. Med. Sch., 1967–71; Research Fellow and Hon. Lecturer: Univ. of Surrey, 1971–76; Univ. of Sussex, 1974–78; Chm. and Man. Dir, Martlet Brewery, 1979–83; science teacher, 1984–95. R. D. Lawrence Meml Fellowship, British Diabetes Assoc., 1970–72. *Publications:* research papers and reviews. *Recreations:* sailing, fencing. *Address:* 49 Queen's Park Terrace, Brighton BN2 2YZ. *T:* (01273) 687732.

TURNER, Donald William, CEng, FICE; *b* 17 Aug. 1925; *s* of William John Turner and Agnes Elizabeth Jane (*née* Bristow); *m* 1947, Patricia (*née* Stuteley); one *s* one *d. Educ:* Wanstead County High Sch.; Birmingham Univ. Served War, Army, 1943–45. Subseq. completed engrg trng in Britain; then took up post in Australia with Qld Railways, 1949. Left Qld, 1954; joined firm of UK consulting engrs and then worked in W Africa on rly and highway construction until 1960. Returned to UK, but remained with consultants until 1966, when joined BAA; Chief Engr, Heathrow Airport, 1970; Dir of Planning and Bd Mem., 1973; Dir of Privatisation, 1985–86; Chm., British Airports International, 1984–87. Dir, London Underground, 1985–93. *Address:* 27 Kingsway Court, Hove, Sussex BN3 2LP.

TURNER, Geoffrey Howard; Chief Executive, Securities Institute, 1997–2003; *b* 23 July 1945; *s* of Charles William Turner and Evelyn Doris (*née* Harris); *m* 1975, Margaret Linda Donaldson; two *d. Educ:* King's Sch., Chester; St Edmund Hall, Oxford (BA, MA; Special Dip. Social Studies). With Simon & Coates, stockbrokers, 1968–70; British India Steam Navigation Co., 1970–73; Stock Exchange, 1973–90: Asst Manager, 1973–75, Manager, 1975–78, Membership Dept; Secretary: Wilson Evidence Cttee, 1978; Planning Cttee, 1977–78; Restrictive Practices Case Cttee, 1978–83; Head of Membership, 1983–86; Dir of Membership, 1986–90; Dir of Authorisation, Securities Assoc., 1986–92; Dir of Public Affairs, SFA, 1993–94; Chief Exec., Assoc. of Private Client Investment Managers and Stockbrokers, 1994–97. External Examr, London Guildhall Univ., 1996–2000. Mem. (C), St Albans DC, 2006–. Mem., Harpenden Village Rotary Club. *Recreations:* visiting country churches, collecting books and prints. *Clubs:* Vincent's (Oxford); Leander (Henley).

TURNER, Rt Rev. Geoffrey Martin; Bishop Suffragan of Stockport, 1994–2000; Hon. Assistant Bishop, diocese of Chester, since 2002; *b* 16 March 1934; *s* of Ernest Hugh Turner and Winifred Rose Turner (*née* Martin); *m* 1959, Gillian Chope; two *s* one *d. Educ:* Bideford Grammar Sch.; Sandhurst; Oak Hill Theol Coll. Ordained deacon, 1963, priest, 1964; Assistant Curate: St Stephen, Tonbridge, 1963–66; St John, Heatherlands, dio. of Salisbury, 1966–69; Vicar: St Peter, Derby, 1969–73; Christ Church, Chadderton, dio. of Manchester, 1973–79; Rector of Bebington, 1979–93; Rural Dean, Wirral North, 1989–93; Hon. Canon, Chester Cathedral, 1989–93; Archdeacon of Chester, 1993–94. *Recreations:* sport, literature. *Address:* 23 Lang Lane, West Kirby, Wirral CH48 5HG. *T:* (0151) 625 8504.

See also M. Turner.

TURNER, George, PhD; *b* 9 Aug. 1940; *s* of late George and Jane Turner; *m* Lesley Duggan; two *d*, and one step *s* one step *d. Educ:* Laxton Grammar Sch.; Imperial Coll., London (BSc Hons); Gonville and Caius Coll., Cambridge (PhD Physics 1967). Formerly Lectr in electronic engrg, Univ. of E Anglia. Mem. (Lab) Norfolk CC, 1977–97. Contested (Lab) Norfolk NW, 1992; MP (Lab) Norfolk NW, 1997–2001; contested same seat, 2001. *Address:* 47 Gayton Road, King's Lynn PE30 4EF.

TURNER, Prof. Grenville, FRS 1980; Professor of Isotope Geochemistry, 1988–2002, Research Professor, since 2002, Manchester University; *b* 1 Nov. 1936; *o s* of Arnold and Florence Turner, Todmorden, Yorks; *m* 1961, Kathleen, *d* of William and Joan Morris, Rochdale, Lancs; one *s* one *d. Educ:* Todmorden Grammar Sch.; St John's Coll., Cambridge (MA); Balliol Coll., Oxford (DPhil). Asst Prof., Univ. of Calif at Berkeley, 1962–64; Lectr, Sheffield Univ., 1964–74, Sen. Lectr, 1974–79, Reader, 1979–80, Prof. of Physics, 1980–88. Vis. Associate in Nuclear Geophysics, Calif Inst. of Technol., 1970–71. Mem. Council, Royal Soc., 1990–92. Fellow: Meteoritical Soc., 1980 (Leonard Medal, 1999); American Geophysical Union, 1998; Geochemistry Fellow, Geochemical Soc. and European Assoc. of Geochemistry, 1996. Rumford Medal, Royal Soc. 1996; Urey Medal, Eur. Assoc. of Geochemistry, 2002; Gold Medal for Geophysics, RAS, 2004. *Publications:* scientific papers. *Recreations:* photography, walking, theatre. *Address:* 42 Edgehill Road, Sheffield S7 1SP. *T:* (office) (0161) 275 0401; *e-mail:* grenville.turner@manchester.ac.uk.

TURNER, Harry Edward; Chairman, Amcom Resources plc, 1995–2000; *b* 28 Feb. 1935; *s* of Harry Turner and Bessie Elizabeth Jay; *m* 1956, Carolyn Bird; one *s* one *d. Educ:* Sloane Grammar Sch., Chelsea. Served Middlesex Regt, Austria, 2nd Lieut, 1953–55. Sales Representative, Crosse & Blackwell Foods, 1955–56; Advertising Executive: Daily Herald, 1956–58; Kemsley Newspapers, 1958–60; Feature Writer and Advtsg Manager, TV International Magazine, 1960–62; Sales Dir, Westward Television, 1962–80; Dir of Marketing, 1980–85, Man. Dir, 1985–92, Television South West; Dir, ITN, 1987–92. Dir, Prince of Wales Trust, 1988–. FRSA 1986. Mem., Middx Regtl Assoc., 1955–. Mem., Solus Club, 1986–. *Publications:* The Man Who Could Hear Fishes Scream (short stories), 1978; The Gentle Art of Salesmanship, 1985; So You Want To Be a Sales Manager, 1987; Innocents in the Boardroom, 1991; The Venetian Chair, 1998; Poems of the Peninsular, 2001; Poems of Nelson's Navy, 2002; Wrapped in Whirlwinds, 2005; Growing Up in Fulham, 2005; Urban Legends, 2006. *Recreations:* tennis, riding, ski-ing, literature, travel. *Address:* Old Boathouse View, Admiral Stirling Court, Weybridge, Surrey KT13 8XX. *T:* (01932) 821465. *Club:* Garrick.

TURNER, Hugh Wason, CMG 1980; Director, National Gas Turbine Establishment, 1980–83, retired; *b* 2 April 1923; *s* of Thomas W. Turner and Elizabeth P. Turner (*née* Pooley); *m* 1950, Rosemary Borley; two *s* two *d. Educ:* Dollar Academy; Glasgow University. BSc Hons (Mech. Eng); CEng; FRAeS. Aeroplane and Armament Experimental Establishment, 1943–52; Chief Tech. Instructor, Empire Test Pilots School, 1953; A&AEE (Prin. Scientific Officer), 1954–64; Asst Director, RAF Aircraft, Min. of Technology, 1965–68; Superintendent, Trials Management, A&AEE, 1968–69; Division Leader, Systems Engineering, NATO MRCA Management Agency (NAMMA), Munich, 1969–74; Chief Superintendent, A&AEE, 1974–75; DGA1 (Dir Gen., Tornado), MoD (PE), 1976–80. *Recreations:* ski-ing, model building, photography, DIY. *Address:* Lavender Cottage, 1 Highcliff Road, Lyme Regis, Dorset DT7 3EW. *T:* (01297) 442310.

TURNER, James; QC 1998; *b* 23 Nov. 1952; *s* of late James Gordon Melville Turner, GC and of Peggy Pamela Hare (*née* Masters); *m* 1979, Sheila Green (separated); three *s* two *d. Educ:* Robertsbridge Co. Secondary Modern Sch.; Bexhill Grammar Sch.; Univ. of Hull (LLB Hons). Called to the Bar, Inner Temple, 1976, Bencher, 2006. *Publication:* (contrib. editor) Archbold: Criminal Pleading, Evidence and Practice, annually, 1992–. *Recreations:* eating, reading, cinema, soul music. *Address:* 1 King's Bench Walk, Temple, EC4Y 7DB. *T:* (020) 7936 1500, *Fax:* (020) 7936 1590; *e-mail:* jturner@1kbw.co.uk.

TURNER, Prof. James Johnson, FRS 1992; Research Professor in Chemistry, University of Nottingham, 1995–97, now Emeritus (Professor of Inorganic Chemistry, 1979–95); *b* 24 Dec. 1935; *s* of Harry Turner and Evelyn Turner (*née* Johnson); *m* 1961, Joanna Margaret Gargett; two *d. Educ:* Darwen Grammar Sch.; King's Coll., Cambridge (MA, PhD 1960; ScD 1985). CChem; FRSC. Research Fellow, King's Coll., Cambridge, 1960; Harkness Fellow, Univ. of Calif, Berkeley, 1961–63; University of Cambridge: Univ. Demonstrator, 1963–68; Univ. Lectr, 1968–71; College Lectr, 1963–71, Admissions Tutor, 1967–71, King's Coll.; Prof. and Head of Dept of Inorganic Chemistry, Univ. of Newcastle upon Tyne, 1972–78; Nottingham University: Hd of Chem. Dept, 1982–85, 1991–93; Pro-Vice-Chancellor, 1986–90. Science and Engineering Research Council (formerly SRC): Mem., 1974–77, Chm., 1979–82, Chemistry Cttee; Mem., Science Bd, 1979–86; Mem. Council, 1982–86. Royal Society of Chemistry: Mem., 1974–77, Vice-Pres., 1982–84 and 1991–93, Pres., 1993–95, Dalton Council; Tilden Lectr, 1978; Liversidge Lectr, 1991; Mem. Council, Royal Soc., 1997–99. *Publications:* papers mainly in jls of Chem. Soc. and Amer. Chem. Soc. *Recreations:* walking, cycling. *Address:* 7 Hallams Lane, Chilwell, Nottingham NG9 5FH. *T:* (0115) 917 0353.

TURNER, Janet Mary, (Mrs Paul Griffin); QC 1996; barrister; *b* 16 Nov. 1957; *d* of Cecil Sidney Turner and Gwendoline Joyce Turner (*née* Loseby); *m* 1983, Paul Griffin; one *s* one *d. Educ:* Wycombe Abbey Sch.; Bristol Univ. (LLB 1st cl. Hons). Called to the Bar, Middle Temple, 1979 (Harmsworth Schol.); practising in field of commercial litigation, 1979–2000; legal consultant, 2000–07; partner, Taylor Vinters, 2007–. Member: London Common Law and Commercial Bar Assoc., 1986–99 (Sec., 1990–97); Commercial Bar Assoc., 1989–99; Charity Law Assoc., 2007–. Non-exec. Dir, Norwich and Peterborough Building Soc., 2007–. *Recreations:* heritage conservation, food and wine, collecting ephemera, gardening. *Address: e-mail:* jmtqc@aol.com.

TURNER, Jean McGiven; Member (Ind) Strathkelvin and Bearsden, Scottish Parliament, 2003–07; *b* Glasgow, 1939. *Educ:* Hillhead High Sch., Glasgow; Aberdeen Univ. (MB ChB 1965; DA 1970). Anaesthetist: Aberdeen Royal Infirmary; Southern Gen. Hosp., Glasgow; GP, Springburn, Glasgow, 1975–2000. Vocational Studies Tutor (pt-time) on gen. practice, Glasgow Univ., 1999–2003. Mem., Health Cttee, Scottish Parlt, 2003–07. Contested (Ind) Strathkelvin and Bearsden, Scottish Parlt, 2007. *Address:* c/o Scottish Parliament, Edinburgh EH99 1SP.

TURNER, John, CB 1999; Under Secretary, Department for Education and Employment (formerly Department of Employment), 1988–99; Member, Civil Service Appeal Board, since 2000; *b* 22 April 1946; *s* of late William Cecil Turner and Hilda Margaret Turner; *m* 1971, Susan Georgina Kennedy; two *s* one *d. Educ:* Ramsey Abbey Grammar Sch.; Northwood Hills Grammar Sch. Entered Civil Service, 1967; Principal, DoI, 1979; MSC, 1981–84; Asst Sec., Dept of Employment, 1985; Prin. Pvte Sec. to Rt Hon. Lord Young of Graffham and Rt Hon. Norman Fowler, 1986–87; Small Firms and Tourism Div., Dept of Employment, 1989; Dep. Chief Exec., Employment Service, 1989–94; Govt Regl Dir for Eastern Reg., 1994–96; Dir of Jobcentre Services, Employment Service, 1997–99. Trustee, Rathbone Trng. Non-exec. Dir, Sheffield Children's NHS Trust, 2002–. *Recreations:* music, reading, the outdoors. *Address:* Thurne Cottage, 110 Mona Road, Sheffield S10 1NH. *T:* (0114) 268 0787.

TURNER, Prof. John Derfel; Sarah Fielden Professor of Education, University of Manchester, 1985–94, now Professor Emeritus; *b* 27 Feb. 1928; *s* of Joseph Turner and Dorothy Winifred Turner; *m* 1951, Susan Broady Hovey; two *s. Educ:* Manchester Grammar Sch.; Univ. of Manchester (BA 1948; MA 1951; Teacher's Diploma 1951). Education Officer, RAF, 1948–50; teacher, Prince Henry's Grammar Sch., Evesham, 1951–53; Lectr in English, 1953–56, Sen. Lectr in Educn, 1956–61, Nigerian Coll. of Arts, Science and Technology; Lectr in Educn, Univ. of Exeter Inst. of Education, 1961–64; Prof. of Educn and Dir, Sch. of Educn, 1964–70, and Pro-Vice-Chancellor, 1966–70, Univ. of Botswana, Lesotho and Swaziland, Emeritus Prof., 1970; University of Manchester: Prof. of Educn and Dir of Sch. of Educn, 1970–76; Dean, Faculty of Educn, 1972–74 and 1986–91; Prof. of Adult and Higher Educn, 1976–85; Pro Vice-Chancellor, 1991–94. Rector, University Coll. of Botswana, Univ. of Botswana and Swaziland, 1981–82 and Vice-Chancellor, Univ. of Botswana, 1982–84. Chairman: Univs Council for Educn of Teachers, 1979–81 and 1988–91 (Vice-Chm., 1976–79); Council of Validating Univs, 1990–94; Presidential Commn on Higher Educn in Namibia, 1991–92, on Education, Culture and Training in Namibia, 1999; Member: UK Nat. Commn for UNESCO, 1975–81; IUC Working Parties on East and Central Africa and on Rural Development, 1975–81; Educn Sub-Cttee, UGC, 1980–81; Educn Cttee and Further Educn Bd, CNAA, 1979–81; Chm., European Develt Fund/IUC Working Party on Academic Develt of Univ. of Juba, 1977–78; Chm. and Mem. Council, Social Studies Adv. Cttee, Selly Oak Colleges, 1975–81. Pres., 1994–2004, Patron, 2004–, Coll. of Teachers (formerly Coll. of Preceptors) (Hon. FCP 1985). Chm., Bd of Governors, Abbotsholme Sch., 1980–98. Chm. Editl Bd, Internat. Jl of Educn and Develt, 1978–81; Ed., Jl of Practice in Educn for Develt, 1994–99. FRSA 2000. Hon. Fellow, Bolton Inst. of Higher Educn, 1988. Hon. LLD Ohio Univ., 1982; Hon. DLitt Botswana, 1995. *Publications:* Introducing the Language Laboratory, 1963; (ed with A. P. Hunter) Educational Development in Predominantly Rural Countries, 1968; (ed with J. Rushton) The Teacher in a Changing Society, 1974; (ed with J. Rushton) Education and Deprivation, 1975; (ed with J. Rushton) Education and Professions, 1976; (ed) The Reform of Educational Systems to Meet Local and National Needs, 1994; (ed) The State and the School, 1996; school text books and contribs to edited works and to jls. *Recreations:* reading, music, theatre, walking; Methodist local preacher. *Address:* 13 Firswood Mount, Gatley, Cheadle, Cheshire SK8 4JY. *T:* (0161) 283 8429, *Fax:* (0161) 282 1022; *e-mail:* johndturner@ntlworld.com.

TURNER, Rt Hon. John Napier; PC (Can.) 1965; CC (Can.) 1995; QC (Can.); Leader of the Liberal Party of Canada, and Leader of the Opposition, 1984–90; Partner, Miller Thomson, Toronto, since 1990; *b* 7 June 1929; *s* of Leonard Turner and Phyllis Turner (*née* Gregory); *m* 1963, Geills McCrae Kilgour; three *s* one *d. Educ:* Normal Model Public Sch., Ottawa, Ont.; Ashbury Coll., 1939–42; St Patrick's Coll., 1942–45; Univ. of BC (BA Hons Pol Sci. 1949); Oxford Univ. (Rhodes Scholar; BA Juris. 1951; BCL 1952; MA 1957). Joined Stikeman, Elliott, Tamaki, Mercier & Turner, Montreal, Quebec; practised with them after being called to English Bar, 1953, Bar of Quebec, 1954 and Bar of Ont., 1968; QC (Ont and Que) 1968; with McMillan Binch, Toronto, 1976–84. MP for Montreal-St Lawrence-St Georges, 1962–68, Ottawa-Carleton, 1968–76, Vancouver Quadra, 1984–93; Parly Sec. to Minister of Northern Affairs and Nat. Resources, 1963–65; Minister without Portfolio, Dec. 1965–April 1967; Registrar-Gen. of Canada, April 1967–Jan. 1968; Minister of Consumer and Corporate Affairs, Dec. 1967–July 1968; Solicitor-Gen., April–July 1968; Minister of Justice and Attorney-Gen. of Canada, July 1968–Jan. 1972; Minister of Finance, Jan. 1972–Sept. 1975; resigned as MP, Feb. 1976; Prime Minister of Canada, June–Sept. 1984. Barbados Bar, 1969; Yukon and Northwest Territories, 1969; Trinidad Bar, 1969; British Columbia, 1969. Hon. LLD: Univ. of New Brunswick, 1968; York Univ., Toronto, 1969; Univ. of Toronto, 1996; Hon. DCL Mt Allison Univ., NB, 1980. *Publications:* Senate of Canada, 1961; Politics of Purpose, 1968. *Recreations:* tennis, canoeing, ski-ing; Canadian Track Field Champion 1948, Mem. English Track and Field Team. *Address:* (office) 40 King Street West, Suite 5800, Toronto, ON M5H 3S1, Canada; (home) 59 Oriole Road, Toronto, ON M4V 2E9, Canada.

TURNER, Prof. (John) Stewart, FAA 1979; FRS 1982; Foundation Professor of Geophysical Fluid Dynamics, Australian National University, 1975–95, now Emeritus; *b* Sydney, Aust., 11 Jan. 1930; *s* of Ivan Stewart Turner and Enid Florence (*née* Payne); *m* 1959, Sheila Lloyd Jones; two *s* one *d. Educ:* North Sydney Boys' High Sch.; Wesley Coll., Univ. of Sydney (BSc, MSc); Trinity Coll., Univ. of Cambridge (PhD). FInstP 1969. Research Officer, CSIRO cloud physics group, 1953–54 and 1960–61; 1851 Exhibition Overseas Schol., 1954–57; postdoctoral research post, Univ. of Manchester, 1958–59; Rossby Fellow, then Associate Scientist, Woods Hole Oceanographic Instn, 1962–66; Asst Director of Research, then Reader, Dept of Applied Mathematics and Theoretical Physics, Univ. of Cambridge, 1966–75; Fellow of Darwin Coll., Cambridge, 1974; Overseas Fellow, Churchill Coll., Cambridge, 1985; Fairchild Scholar, CIT, 1993. Matthew Flinders Lectr, Aust. Acad. of Science, 1990. Member, Australian Marine Sciences and Technologies Adv. Cttee (AMSTAC), 1979–84. Associate Editor, Journal of Fluid Mechanics, 1975–95; Mem. Editorial Adv. Board, Deep-Sea Research, 1974–84. *Publications:* Buoyancy Effects in Fluids, 1973, paperback 1979; papers in various scientific jls. *Recreations:* bushwalking, photography, home handyman. *Address:* Research School of Earth Sciences, Australian National University, Canberra, ACT 0200, Australia.

TURNER, Jonathan Chadwick; QC 2003; a Recorder, 2000–06; *b* 10 Feb. 1951; *s* of David and Joyce Turner; partner, Anna de Vere. *Educ:* Hindley and Abram Grammar Sch.; University Coll. London (LLB Hons). Called to the Bar, Gray's Inn, 1974; in practice, specialising in criminal law, prosecuting and defending; Asst Recorder, 1997–2000. *Recreations:* golf, cricket, football, Rugby League. *Address:* 6 King's Bench Walk, Temple, EC4Y 7DR. *T:* (020) 7583 0410, *Fax:* (020) 7353 8791; *e-mail:* jonathan.turner@6kbw.com, jctqc@aol.com. *Clubs:* Reform; Denham Golf; Wigan Golf; Lancashire County Cricket.

TURNER, Jonathan Richard; QC 2006; *b* 13 Sept. 1963; *s* of Norman Asher Turner and Annette Suzanne Turner; *m* 1991, Manuela Grayson; three *d. Educ:* Trinity Coll., Cambridge (BA 1986); Harvard Law Sch. (LLM 1987); Inns of Court Sch. of Law. Called to the Bar, Middle Temple, 1988; Mem., NY Bar, 1988; in practice, 1988–, specialising in competition, European, public and admin., environmental, and commercial law. *Publication:* (contrib.) Bellamy & Child Common Market Law of Competition, 3rd edn 1987, 4th edn 1993. *Recreations:* squash, literature, social and political theory, family. *Address:* Monckton Chambers, 1 Raymond Buildings, Gray's Inn, WC1R 5NR. *T:* (020) 7405 7211, *Fax:* (020) 7405 2084; *e-mail:* jturner@monckton.com.

TURNER, Kerry; *see* Turner, R. K.

TURNER, Leigh; *see* Turner, R. L.

TURNER, Mark; Headmaster, Abingdon School, since 2002; *b* Hampstead, 19 Sept. 1961; *s* of Rt Rev. Geoffrey Martin Turner, *qv*; *m* 1987, Elizabeth Jane Gugan; two *s. Educ:* Rossall Sch.; Mansfield Coll., Oxford (BA 1984); RMA Sandhurst; Hughes Hall, Cambridge (PGCE 1987). Short service commn RA, 1984–87. Asst Master, 1988–89, Hd of Dept, 1989–90, Housemaster, Laxton House, 1990–95, Oundle Sch.; Headmaster, Kelly Coll., Tavistock, 1995–2001. Inspector, ISI, 1997–. Governor: St Andrew's Sch., Pangbourne, 2004–; Lord Wandsworth Coll., 2006–. *Recreations:* deer stalking, fly fishing. *Address:* Abingdon School, Park Road, Abingdon, Oxon OX14 1DE. *T:* (01235) 521563, *Fax:* (01235) 849077; *e-mail:* hm@abingdon.org.uk. *Club:* East India.

TURNER, Mark George; QC 1998; a Recorder, since 2000; a Deputy High Court Judge, since 2007; *b* 27 Aug. 1959; *s* of Jeffrey Turner and Joyce Turner; *m* 1988, Caroline Sophia Bullock; three *d. Educ:* Sedbergh Sch.; Queen's Coll., Oxford (BA). Called to the Bar, Gray's Inn, 1981, Bencher, 2004; in practice as barrister, Northern Circuit, 1982–; Asst Recorder, 1997–2000. Patron, New Beginnings charity for homeless children, 1999–. *Publications:* Occupational Rhinitis, 1998; Occupational Asthma, 1998; Occupational Stress, 2007. *Recreations:* quizzes, computers, classical music, history. *Address:* Deans Court Chambers, 24 St John Street, Manchester M3 4DF. *T:* (0161) 214 6000.

TURNER, Rev. Martin Hugh; Superintendent Minister and Team Leader, Methodist Central Hall, Westminster, since 2001; *b* Loughton, Essex, 13 July 1948; *s* of Percy and Dorothy Turner; *m* 1976, Biddy Bazlinton; one *s* two *d. Educ:* Brentwood Coll. of Educn (Cert Ed); Wesley Coll., Bristol; West Hill, Birmingham (Postgrad. Cert. Youth and Community Work). Ordained Methodist Minister, 1978; Methodist Chaplain, Bradford Univ., and Asst Minister, Bradford Mission, 1977–80; Minister: St Andrew's Church and Community Centre, Halifax, 1980–86; St Albans Circuit, and Regl Chaplain, NCH, 1986–97; Superintendent Minister, Hemel Hempstead Circuit, and Methodist Chaplain, HM Prison Bovington (Mount Prison), 1997–2001. Member: Methodist Conference, 1982–2008; Methodist Council, 2000–06; Methodist Strategy and Resources Cttee, 2000–06. *Publications:* contrib. to Scripture Union Bible notes. *Recreations:* antiques, fishing, gardening, West Ham Utd, friends and family. *Address:* 4 Cotton Row, SW11 3UG. *T:* (020) 7738 2952; *e-mail:* mhturner@talk21.com.

TURNER, Prof. Martin John Leslie, CBE 2004; FRAS; Principal Research Fellow, since 1995, and Professor, since 2004, Department of Physics and Astronomy, University of Leicester; *b* 7 Oct. 1942; *s* of late Edward Charles Turner and Betsy Turner (*née* Richardson); *m* 1966, Josephine Anne Ward; two *s* one *d. Educ:* Harwich Co. High Sch.; Univ. of Durham (BSc 1965; PhD 1969; DSc 1992). FRAS 1990. Foreign Res. Fellow, Inst. of Physics, Univ. degli Studi di Milano, 1969–72; Department of Physics and Astronomy, University of Leicester: Res. Associate, 1973–80; Res. Fellow, 1980–88; Sen. Res. Fellow, 1988–95. Vis. Fellow, Inst. of Space and Astronautical Sci., Japan, 1987; Vis. Prof., Dept of Physics, Univ. of Tokyo (To Dai), 1988. European Space Agency: Chm., Xeus Sci. Adv. Gp, 1997–; Member: Astronomy Wkg Gp, 1992–94; Astro-E Sci. Wkg Gp, Inst. of Space and Astronautical Sci., Japan, 1995–; European Photon Imaging Camera Internat. Mgt Gp, 1996–; Space Sci. Cttee, ESF, 1999–2003; Particle Physics and Astronomy Research Council: Member: Space Sci. Adv. Cttee, 1996–98; Project Peer Review Panel, 2001–04. *Publications:* Rocket and Spacecraft Propulsion, 2000, 2nd edn 2004; Expedition Mars, 2004; numerous papers in learned jls on instrumentation for space astronomy and x-ray astronomy. *Recreations:* singing English choral music, walking, fishing, old books. *Address:* 63 Elms Road, Leicester LE2 3JD. *T:* (0116) 270 7070; *e-mail:* mjlt@star.le.ac.uk.

TURNER, Hon. Sir Michael (John), Kt 1985; a Judge of the High Court of Justice, Queen's Bench Division, 1985–2002; *b* 31 May 1931; *s* of late Theodore F. Turner, QC; *m* 1st, 1956, Hon. Susan Money-Coutts (marr. diss. 1965); one *s* one *d*; 2nd, 1965, Frances Deborah (marr. diss.), *d* of Rt Hon. Sir David Croom-Johnson, DSC, VRD, PC; two *s*; 3rd, 1995, Ingrid Maria Fear (*née* Ortner). *Educ:* Winchester; Magdalene Coll., Cambridge (BA). Called to Bar, Inner Temple, 1954 (Bencher 1981); a Recorder, 1972–85; QC 1973–85. Chm., E Mids Agricultural Tribunal, 1979–82. Mem., Judicial Studies Bd, 1988–93 (Co-Chm., Civil and Family Cttee, 1988–93). FRGS 2002. *Recreations:* horses, walking, listening to music. *Address:* c/o Royal Courts of Justice, Strand, WC2A 2LL.
See also C. G. Turner.

TURNER, Michael John, CBE 1999; FRAeS; Chairman, Babcock International Group plc, since 2008 (non-executive Director, 2008); *b* 5 Aug. 1948; *s* of Thomas Turner and Hilda Turner (*née* Pendlebury); *m* 1st, 1972, Rosalind Thomas (marr. diss.); two *s*; 2nd, 1985, Jean (*née* Crotty); two step *d. Educ:* Didsbury Tech. High Sch.; Manchester Poly. (BA). ACIS 1973; FRAeS 1991. With British Aerospace, subsequently BAE SYSTEMS, 1966–2008: undergrad. apprentice, Hawker Siddeley Aviation, Manchester, 1966; Contracts Manager (Mil.), 1978–80; Exec. Dir, Admin, 1981–84, Manchester Div.; Division Director and General Manager: Kingston and Dunsfold, 1984–86; Weybridge, Kingston and Dunsfold, 1986–87; Exec. Vice-Pres., Defence Mktg, 1988–92; Chm. and Man. Dir, Regl Aircraft, 1992–99; Main Bd Dir, 1994; Gp Man. Dir, 1997–98; Exec. Dir, 1998–99; Chief Operating Officer, 1999–2002; Chief Exec., 2002–08; Mem., Supervisory Bd, Airbus, 1998–2006. Chm., Aerospace Innovation and Growth Team, DTI, 2005–. President: SBAC, 1996–97; AeroSpace and Defence Industries Assoc. of Europe, 2003–04. Hon. DAdmin Manchester Metropolitan, 2006; Hon. DSc: Cranfield, 2007; Loughborough, 2007. *Recreations:* golf, cricket, Rugby, Manchester United. *Address:* Babcock International Group plc, 2 Cavendish Square, W1G 0PX.

TURNER, Michael Ralph, FRSA; Group Managing Director, 1976–88, Chief Executive, 1982–88, Associated Book Publishers PLC; Chairman, Associated Book Publishers (UK) Ltd, 1977–90; *b* 26 Jan. 1929; *s* of Ralph Victor Turner and May Turner; *m* 1955, Ruth Baylis (*d* 1997); two *s* two *d. Educ:* Newport Sch., Essex; Trinity Coll., Cambridge (BA Hons). Served RAF, Transport Comd, 1947–49. Jun. Editor, J. M. Dent & Sons, 1949–50; Methuen & Co.: Jun. Editor, 1953; subseq. Publicity and Promotion Manager, and Dir; Associated Publishers Ltd: Marketing Dir, 1973; Asst Gp Man. Dir, 1975; Gp Man. Dir, 1976. Chm., Methuen Inc., New York, 1981–88; Pres., Carswell Co. Ltd, Toronto, 1982–84; Dir, ABP Investments (Aust.) Pty Ltd, 1976–88; Sen. Vice-Pres., Publishing Information Gp, Internat. Thomson Orgn Ltd, 1987–89. Chairman: Book Marketing Council, 1981–84; Book Trust, 1990–92; Member: Book Trade Working Party, 1973–74; Council, Publishers Assoc., 1981–90 (Vice-Pres., 1985–87 and 1989–90; Pres., 1987–89; Chm., Home Trade and Services Council, 1989–90); National Council and Exec., NBL, 1980–87; British Library Adv. Council, 1989–94; Centre for the Book Adv. Cttee, 1990–95; Publishing Bd, Design Council, 1991–94. Mem. Adv. Cttee, Book Trade Lives, Nat. Life Story Collection at BL Sound Archive, 1988–2007. Chm., Soc. of Bookmen, 1992–94. FRSA 1984. *Publications:* The Bluffer's Guide to the Theatre, 1967; Parlour Poetry, 1967; (with Antony Miall) The Parlour Song Book, 1972; (with Antony Miall) Just a Song at Twilight, 1975; (with Antony Miall) The Edwardian Song Book, 1982; (with Michael Geare) Gluttony, Pride and Lust and Other Sins from the World of Books, 1984; Do You Scratch Your Bottom in the Bath?, 1998; (with Leslie Lonsdale-Cooper) translations of Hergé's Tintin books, 1958–2005. *Recreations:* reading, music, theatre, maritime painting and models. *Address:* c/o 5 Grove Road, Alton, Hants GU34 1NP. *T:* (01420) 88701. *Club:* Garrick.

TURNER, Neil; MP (Lab) Wigan, since Sept. 1999; *b* 16 Sept. 1945; *m* 1971, Susan Beatrice; one *s*. Quantity surveyor, AMEC Construction, 1963–92. Member (Lab): Wigan CBC, 1972–74; Wigan MBC, 1975–2000 (Chairman: Highways and Works Cttee, 1980–97; Best Value Rev. Panel, 1998–2000). Chairman: Public Services Cttee, AMA, 1995–97; Quality Panel, LGA, 1997–99. *Address:* House of Commons, SW1A 0AA; Gerrard Winstanley House, Crawford Street, Wigan WN1 1NG. *T:* (01942) 242047. *Club:* Marsh Green Labour (Marsh Green, Wigan).

TURNER, Neil; *see* Turner, A. N.

TURNER, Pamela Ann; *see* Major, P. A.

TURNER, Peter; *see* Turner, T. P.

TURNER, Air Vice-Marshal Peter, CB 1979; MA; Bursar and Steward, Wolfson College, Cambridge, 1979–89; *b* 29 Dec. 1924; *s* of late George Allen and of Emma Turner; *m* 1949, Doreen Newbon; one *s. Educ:* Tapton House Sch., Chesterfield. Served

War of 1939–45; 640 Sqdn, 1943–45; Nos 51, 242 and 246 Sqdns, 1945–48; psa 1961; NATO staff, 1963–67; jssc 1967; Chief Equipment and Secretarial Instructor, RAF Coll., Cranwell, 1967–68; Comd Accountant, HQ Air Support Comd, 1968–69; Station Comdr, RAF Uxbridge, 1969–71; RCDS, 1972; Dir of Personnel (Ground) (RAF), MoD, 1973–75; AOA, HQ RAF Support Command, 1975–79, and Head of RAF Admin. Branch, 1976–79. MA Cantab 1979. *Recreation:* retrospective contemplation. *Address:* Hedge End, Potton Road, Hilton, Huntingdon PE28 9NG. *Club:* Royal Air Force.

TURNER, Ven. (Peter) Robin, CB 1999; DL; Hon. Canon of Southwell Minster, since 2002; Chaplain to Sector Ministries, Diocese of Southwell and Nottingham, since 2004; *b* 8 March 1942; *s* of late Ronald James Turner and Irene Bertha (*née* Stocker); *m* 1967, Elizabeth Mary Kennen; two *s. Educ:* Dulwich Coll.; King's Coll. London (AKC); St Luke's Coll., Exeter (PGCE); Open Univ. (BA); Westminster Coll., Oxford (MTh). Ordained deacon, 1966, priest, 1967; Asst Curate, Crediton, 1966–69; Chaplain, RAF: Locking, 1970; Waddington, 1971–72; Nicosia, 1972–74; Little Rissington, 1975–76; Coltishall, 1976–78; Chaplains' Sch., 1978–81; Religious Progs Advr, British Forces Broadcasting Service, Germany, 1981–84; Chaplain, RAF: Odiham, 1984–85; Gutersloh, 1985–88; RAF Coll., Cranwell, 1988–89; Assistant Chaplain-in-Chief: RAF, Germany, 1989–91; RAF Strike Command, 1991–93; QHC, 1991–98; Principal, RAF Chaplains' Sch., 1993–95; Chaplain-in-Chief and Archdeacon, RAF, 1995–98, now Archdeacon Emeritus; non-residentiary Canon, Lincoln, 1995–98; Chaplain: Dulwich Coll., 1998–2002; to Bp of Southwell, subseq. Bp of Southwell and Nottingham, 2002–07. Freeman, City of London, 2001; Liveryman, Musicians' Co., 2003–. President: Friends of St Clement Danes Ch (Central Ch of RAF), 2005–; Notts, RBL, 2007–; Alleyn Club, 2007–08. Trustee, Dulwich Estate, 2005–; Chm., St Boniface Trust, 2005–. FRSA 2000. DL Notts, 2007. *Recreations:* choral singing, classical music, reading history and biography, armchair cricket, wine and its enjoyment. *Address:* 12 Chimes Meadow, Southwell, Notts NG25 0GB. *T:* (01636) 812250; *e-mail:* pr.turner@lineone.net. *Club:* Royal Air Force.

TURNER, Peter William; District Secretary, Hereford and Worcester, Transport and General Workers' Union, 1969–91, retired; *m* Maureen Ann Turner (*née* Hill), Councillor, JP. *Educ:* Bordesley Green Infant and Junior Sch.; Saltley Grammar Sch. (until 1940); various Trade Union weekend courses. Appointed District Officer, TGWU, 1969; District Sec., CSEU, 1974–76; seconded as Industrial Advr to DoI, 1976–78. Member of various cttees including: Chemical Industry Area Productivity Cttee, 1969–76 (Vice-Chm., 1970–72, Chm., 1972–74); TUC Regional Educn Adv. Cttee, 1970–76; Birmingham Crime Prevention Panel, 1973–76; W Midlands Conciliation Cttee on Race Relations, 1974–76; DoE Working Party on Race Relations, 1974–76; Teaching Co. Management Cttee, 1977–82. Member: Birmingham Trades Council, 1956–76; Local Appeals Tribunal, 1969–74. *Recreations:* do-it-yourself, reading, electronics, amateur radio (M0CHY). *Address:* 2 Oakleigh Road, Droitwich, Worcs WR9 0RP.

TURNER, Phil; Member, 1971–2006, and Executive Member, Culture, 2005–06, Camden Borough Council; *b* 7 June 1939; *s* of William Morris Turner and Eileen Lascelles Turner; *m* 1st, 1963, Gillian Sharp (*d* 1988); one *s* two *d* (and one *s* decd); 2nd, 2007, Maureen Alcock; two *s* (and one *s* decd). *Educ:* Beckenham and Penge Grammar School for Boys; University Coll. London (BScEcon). National Coal Board, later British Coal: Management Trainee, 1961–63; Hd of Information, Purchasing and Stores, 1963–65; O & M Officer, 1965–66; Hd of Admin, R & D Dept, 1966–68; Hd of Manpower Planning, 1968–73; Staff Manager, Opencast Exec., 1973–78; Hd of Conditions of Service, 1978–80; Dep. Dir of Staff Pay and Conditions, 1980–86; Head of Employment Policy, 1986–89. Joined Labour Party, 1963; Chair, Hampstead Labour Party, 1968–70; Camden Borough Council, 1971–2006: Chair: Building Works and Services Cttee, 1978–80 and 1986–89; Staff and Management Services Cttee, 1990–93; Leisure Services Cttee, 1993–97, 1998–2001; Corporate Services Cttee, 1997–98; Exec. Mem., Leisure and Community Services, 2001–05; Leader of Council, 1982–86, Dep. Leader, 1992–93, 1994–95 and 2003–06. Member: Assoc. of London Authorities, 1983–86; Policy Cttee, AMA, 1984–86; Vice Chair, Assoc. of London Govt Arts and Leisure Cttee, 1995–2000; Chair: London Steering Gp, Euro '96, 1995–96; London Sport Bd, 1996–2000. Contested (Lab): Cities of London and Westminster South, Feb. and Oct. 1974; (Lab) Hampstead and Highgate, 1987. Board Member: Kingsgate Community Assoc., 2006–; Winchester Project, 2006–. *Recreations:* family, travelling, book collecting. *Address:* 33 Minster Road, NW2 3SH. *T:* (020) 7692 0439.

TURNER, Richard Keith, OBE 2007; CEng, FIHT, FCILT; Chief Executive, Freight Transport Association, 2001–07; *b* 2 Oct. 1944; *s* of Richard Louis Turner and Queenie Kate Turner; *m* 1968, Jenny Georgina Whitehead; two *s* one *d. Educ:* E Barnet Grammar Sch.; Leeds Univ. (BSc Civil Engrg 1965); Bradford Univ. (MSc Traffic Engrg Planning 1972). CEng 1972. Grad. Engr, Herts CC, 1965–67; Sen. Engr, Leeds CC, 1967–73; Freight Transport Association: Highways and Traffic Advr, 1973–83; Dir of Planning, 1983–95; Dep. Dir Gen., 1995–2000. Mem., Commn for Integrated Transport, 2004–; Planning Cttee, London Thames Gateway Develt Corp., 2007–. FIHT 1980; FCILT (FILT 1993); MICE 1972. *Publications:* numerous papers on transport planning and freight. *Recreations:* big DIY, cycling, swimming.

TURNER, Richard Timmis, CMG 2002; OBE 1978; FRAeS; Group Marketing Director, 1991–2002, Director, 1992–2002, Rolls-Royce plc; *b* 17 Aug. 1942; *s* of late Dr John Richard Timmis Turner and of Alison Elizabeth Turner; *m* 1982, Margaret Corbett; two *d. Educ:* Shrewsbury Sch.; Univ. of Manchester (BA Politics and Mod. Hist.). FRAeS 1993. Joined Rolls-Royce Ltd, 1965; Commercial Manager, NY, 1971–74; Mktg Exec., Civil Engines, 1977–88; Commercial Dir, Civil Engines, Rolls-Royce plc, 1988–89; Gp Mktg Dir, 1988–91, Dir, 1989–91, STC plc; rejoinrd Rolls-Royce plc, 1991. Non-executive Director: British Steel, 1994–99; Corus Gp plc, 1999–2004; Senior plc, 1996–2004. Member: BOTB, 1997–99; Bd, British Trade Internat., 1999–2003 (Chm., Business Adv. Panel, 1999–2003). Mem. Council, SBAC, 1992–2002 (Pres., 1994–95). Dep. UK Chm., Singapore British Business Council, 1996–2002; Mem., Indonesian British Business Council, 1997–2002. Mem. Adv. Council, British Expertise (formerly British Consultants and Contractors Bureau), 2001–. Bd Mem., Nat. Campaign for Arts, 2006–. Trustee, Swordfish Heritage Trust (RN), 1998–2002. *Recreations:* music, opera, Rugby football. *Address:* 6 Widcombe Terrace, Bath BA2 6AJ. *T:* 07770 442333; *e-mail:* Richardturner45@yahoo.co.uk. *Club:* Athenæum.

TURNER, Robert Edward, (Ted); American broadcasting company executive; Chairman and President, Turner Broadcasting System Inc., 1970–96; Founder and Chairman, Turner Foundation Inc., since 1991; *b* 19 Nov. 1938; *s* of Robert Edward Turner and Florence Turner (*née* Rooney); *m* 1st, Judy Nye (marr. diss.); one *s* one *d*; 2nd, 1965, Jane Shirley Smith (marr. diss. 1988); one *s* two *d*; 3rd, 1991, Jane Fonda (marr. diss. 2001). *Educ:* Brown Univ. Gen. Manager, Turner Advertising, 1960–63; Pres. and Chief Exec. Officer, various Turner cos, 1963–70; founded Turner Enterprises, 1976; Dir, 1996–2006, Vice Chm., 1996–2003, Time Warner Inc., then AOL Time Warner, subseq. Time Warner; launched Ted's Montana Grill, 2002. Pres., Atlanta Braves, 1976–96; Chm.

of Bd, Atlanta Hawks, 1977–96. Won America's Cup in yacht Courageous, 1977. Pres.'s Award, 1979, 1989, Ace Special Recognition Award, 1980, Nat. Cable TV Assoc.; Special Award, Edinburgh Internat. TV Fest., 1982; Lifetime Achievement Award, NY Internat. Film and TV Fest., 1984; Tree of Life Award, Jewish Nat. Fund, 1985. *Publication:* (jtly) The Racing Edge, 1979.

TURNER, Prof. (Robert) Kerry, CBE 2000; Professor of Environmental Sciences, University of East Anglia, since 1991; *b* 10 Aug. 1948; *s* of Ben Rees Turner and Eunice Ann Turner; *m* 1971, Merryl Noreen Eborne; one *s. Educ:* UC, Swansea (BSc Econs 1970); UC, Cardiff (Cert Ed 1971); Leicester Univ. (MA (Dist) 1972). Lectr in Econs, Coventry Poly., 1974–76; Sen. Res. Fellow, Dept of Econs, Leicester Univ., 1976; Lectr, 1977–88, Sen. Lectr, 1989–91, Sch. of Envmtl Scis, UEA. Chair, Foresight Panel on Natural Resources and the Envmt, OST/DTI, 1995–99; Member: Bd, NRA, 1991–96; Regl Envmtl Protection Agency Cttee (Anglian Reg.), Envmt Agency, 1996–2002; Chair, Broads Authy, 2003– (Mem., 1996–), Vice Chair, 1996–2000, Chair, 2000–02, Envmt Cttee; Chm., Standards Cttee, 2002–03). Ed.-in-Chief, Envmtl and Resource Econs Jl, 1999–; Jt Ed., Regl Envmtl Change Jl, 1999–2002. FRSA 1991. Hon. FCIWEM. *Publications:* Household Waste: separate collection recycling, 1983; *jointly:* Economics of Planning, 1977; Environmental Planning and Management, 1983; Economics of Natural Resources and the Environment, 1990 (trans. Italian, 1992, Spanish, 1995); Elementary Environmental Economics, 1994; Blueprint III, 1993; *edited:* Sustainable Environmental Management: principles and practice, 1988, 2nd edn 1993; *edited jointly:* Bibliography of Environmental Economics, vols 1 and 2, 1976; Progress in Resource Management and Environmental Planning, vol. 2, 1980, vol. 3, 1981, vol. 4, 1983; Wetlands: market and intervention failure, 1991; Economic Incentives and Environmental Policy, 1994; Ecosystems and Nature, 1999; Perspectives on Integrated Coastal Zone Management, 1999; Economics of Coastal and Water Resources, 2000; Managing a Sea: the ecological economics of the Baltic Sea, 2000; Managing Wetlands: an ecological economics approach, 2003; Managing European Coasts: past, present and future, 2005; Valuing Ecosystem Services: the case of multifunctional wetlands, 2008; over 300 contribs to books, articles in jls and reports. *Recreations:* outdoor environment, tennis. *Address:* School of Environmental Sciences, University of East Anglia, Norwich NR4 7TJ. *T:* (01603) 593176.

TURNER, (Robert) Leigh; HM Diplomatic Service; Ambassador to Ukraine, since 2008; *b* 13 March 1958; *s* of John and Susan Turner; *m* 1992, Pamela Ann Major, *qv;* one *s* one *d. Educ:* Downing Coll., Cambridge (BA Geog. 1979). Admin. Trainee, Freight Central Div., Dept of Transport, 1979; Asst to Regl Dir, Germany, PSA, 1980; HEO (Develt), Housing Policy, Pvte Rented Sector, DoE, 1981; IC2/IA3 Div., Supply Side Policy, HM Treasury, 1982; entered FCO, 1983; Second Sec., Vienna, 1984–87; FCO, 1987–92; First Sec., Moscow, 1992–95; FCO, 1995–98; Counsellor, EU and Econ., Bonn and Berlin, 1998–2002; special unpaid leave, 2002–06: writer, 2002–06; freelance journalist, FT, Guardian, Boston Globe, Die Welt, Berliner Morgenpost, Philadelphia Inquirer, 2003–06; Dir, Overseas Territories, FCO, 2006–08. *Recreations:* writing, travel journalism, Lundy Island. *Address:* c/o Foreign and Commonwealth Office, King Charles Street, SW1A 2AH.

TURNER, Robert Lockley; Senior Master of the Supreme Court, Queen's Bench Division, and Queen's Remembrancer, 1996–2007; *b* 2 Sept. 1935; *s* of James Lockley Turner and Maud Beatrice Turner; *m* 1963, Jennifer Mary Leather; one *s* one *d. Educ:* Clifton Coll.; St Catharine's Coll., Cambridge (BA 1957, MA 1973). Called to the Bar, Gray's Inn, 1958, Bencher, 2000. Commnd Gloucestershire Regt (28th/61st), 1959 (2nd Lieut); transf. to Army Legal Services, 1960 (Captain); Major 1962; retd from Army, 1966 (GSM with clasp South Arabia, 1966). Practised at Common Law Bar in London and on Midland and Oxford Circuit, 1967–84; a Recorder of the Crown Court, 1981–84; Master of Supreme Court, QBD, 1984–96. Prescribed Officer for Election Petitions, 1996–2007. Advisor to Law Reform Commn, Malta, 1993–99. Assessor, Access to Justice Inquiry, 1994–96. Mem., Notarial Bd, 1999–. President: Inst. of Credit Mgt, 2003– (Hon. FICM 1997); High Court Enforcement Officers Assoc., 2007–. Chm., Sherbert Foundn. Vis. Fellow, Inst. of Internat. Maritime Law, Malta, 1998–99; Vis. Prof., Univ. of Glos, 2007–. Hon. Sen. Steward, Westminster Abbey, 2003–07 (Hon. Steward, 1985–2007); Churchwarden, St Matthew's, Midgham, 1990–92. Freeman, City of London, 1997; Liveryman: Scriveners' Co., 1999–; Goldsmiths' Co., 2007–. Mem. Court, Hon. Co. of Glos. Trustee, Soldiers of Gloster Mus., 2005–. Chief Advisory Ed., Atkin's Court Forms, 1997–; Sen. Ed., Civil Procedure, 1999–2005. Hon. LLD West of England, 2006. *Publications:* (ed jtly) Supreme Court Practice, 1988–99; The Office of the Queen's Bench Master, 1990; (ed jtly) Chitty and Jacob, Queen's Bench Forms, 1992; (ed jtly) High Court Litigation Manual, 1992; Annual Practice, 1995; (jtly) Awards to Children and Protected Parties, 2007. *Recreations:* Anglo Saxons, grand children. *Address: e-mail:* rturner@meig.demon.co.uk. *Club:* Army and Navy.

TURNER, Ven. Robin; see Turner, Ven. P. R.

TURNER, Stephen Edward; HM Diplomatic Service, retired; Consul General, Auckland, and Director, Trade Development, New Zealand, 2002–05; *b* 25 March 1946; *s* of Leslie and Kathleen Turner; *m* 1966, Maureen Ann Dick; two *s* two *d. Educ:* John Ruskin Grammar Sch., Croydon. Entered FCO, 1963; served: Jakarta, 1968–72; Kuala Lumpur, 1972–75; FCO 1975–78; Malta, 1978–83; Jakarta, 1983–87; FCO, 1987–90; Consul, Seattle, 1990–95; Dep. Hd of Mission and Consul Gen., Hanoi, 1995–98; Dep. High Comr, Dhaka, 1998–2002. *Recreations:* entomology, ornithology, gardening, travel, the study of the life of Alfred Russel Wallace. *Address:* PO Box 1319, Mossman, Qld 4873, Australia.

TURNER, Stephen Gordon; General Secretary, British Association of Journalists, since 1992; *b* 27 July 1935; *s* of John Turner and Lillian Turner (*née* Wiseman); *m* 1st, 1955, Jean Florence Watts (marr. diss. 1978); two *s* one *d*; 2nd, 1979, Deborah Diana Thomas; one *d. Educ:* Triptons Secondary Modern Sch., Dagenham; Royal Liberty Grammar Sch., Romford. Royal Signals radio mechanic, 1953–55. Reporter: Romford Times, 1955–56; Ilford Recorder, 1956; Bristol Evening World, 1957; freelance journalist, 1958–68; News sub-editor: Ipswich Evening Star, 1969; Daily Mail, 1969–71; Features sub-editor, 1971–73, Public Opinion Editor, 1973–90, Daily Mirror; Gen. Sec., NUJ, 1990–92. Independent Councillor, Colchester BC, 1967–68. Mem., NUJ, 1955–92; Father of the Chapel, Daily Mirror, 1976–78, 1986–90. *Address:* 3 Stanley Road, Deal, Kent CT14 7BT.

TURNER, Stewart; see Turner, J. S.

TURNER, Ted; see Turner, R. E.

TURNER, (Thomas) Peter; Evaluation Consultant, since 1985; *b* 8 May 1928; *s* of Thomas Turner and Laura Crawley; *m* 1952, Jean Rosalie Weston; one *s* one *d. Educ:* Ilford County High Sch.; London University. BSc (1st Class Hons), Maths and Physics. GEC, North Wembley, 1947–50; Armament Design Establishment, 1950–54; Air

Ministry (Science 3), 1954–58 and 1962–63; Chief Research Officer, RAF Maintenance Command, 1958–62; Police Research and Development Branch, Home Office, 1963–68; Civil Service Dept (OR), 1968–73; Head of Treasury/CSD Joint Operational Research Unit, 1973–76; Head of Operational Res., CSD, 1977–81, HM Treasury, 1981–84. *Address:* 8 Waring Drive, Green St Green, Orpington, Kent BR6 6DW. *T:* (01689) 851189.

TURNER, Wilfred, CMG 1977; CVO 1979; HM Diplomatic Service, retired; Director, Transportation Systems and Market Research Ltd (Transmark), 1987–90; *b* 10 Oct. 1921; *s* of late Allen Turner and Eliza (*née* Leach); *m* 1947, June Gladys Tite; two *s* one *d. Educ:* Heywood Grammar Sch., Lancs; London Univ. BSc 1942. Min. of Labour, 1938–42. Served War, Capt., REME, 1942–47, Staff 13th Infantry Bde, 1945–47. Min. of Labour, 1947–55; British High Commn, New Delhi (Asst Lab. Adviser), 1955–59; Senior Wages Inspector, Min. of Labour, 1959–60; Min. of Health, 1960–66 (Sec., Cttee on Safety of Drugs, 1963–66; designed and introd Yellow Card for reporting adverse reactions to medicines; initiated drafting of Medicines Bill); joined HM Diplomatic Service, 1966; Commonwealth Office, 1966; First Sec.: Kaduna, Nigeria, 1966–69; Kuala Lumpur, 1969–73; Dep. High Comr, and Commercial/Economic Counsellor, Accra, 1973–77; High Comr to Botswana, 1977–81. Dir and Chief Exec., Southern Africa Assoc., 1983–88. Member: Cttee, Zambia Soc., 1983–91; Central Council, Royal Commonwealth Soc., 1987–94; RIIA, 1987–; Royal African Soc., 1987–. *Recreation:* hill walking. *Address:* 44 Tower Road, Twickenham TW1 4PE. *T:* (020) 8892 1593.

TURNER, Dr William; Regional Medical Officer, Yorkshire Regional Health Authority, 1976–86, retired; *b* 23 Feb. 1927; *s* of Clarence and Mabel Turner; *m* 1950, Patricia Bramham Wilkinson; one *s* two *d. Educ:* Prince Henry's Grammar Sch., Otley, Yorks; Leeds Univ. MB, ChB; DPH, FFCM; LLB. House Officer, Leeds Gen. Infirmary, 1950–51; RAMC, 1951–53; Gen. Practitioner, 1953–55; Public Health Trng, 1955–60; Medical Officer of Health: Hyde, 1960–63; Huddersfield, 1963–67; Bradford, 1967–74; Area MO, Bradford, 1974–76. Member: Standing Med. Adv. Cttee, 1978–82; NHS Steering Gp on Health Services Inf., 1979–84. *Publications:* contrib. BMJ, Medical Officer. *Address:* Bentcliffe, 1 Premiere Park, Ilkley, West Yorks LS29 9RQ. *T:* (01943) 600114.

TURNER LAING, Sophie Henrietta, (Mrs C. Comninos); Managing Director, Entertainment, British Sky Broadcasting Ltd, since 2007; *b* 7 Sept. 1960; *d* of late Graham Turner Laing and of Gillian Vera Turner Laing (*see* G. V. Drummond); *m* 1987, Carlo Comninos; one *s* one *d. Educ:* Oakdene Sch., Bucks. Variety Club of GB, 1979–80; KM Campbell Pty Ltd, Australia, 1980–82; Sales Exec., 1982–85, Sales Dir, 1986–89, Henson Internat. TV; Jt Founder and Dep. Man. Dir, Hit Entertainment, 1989–95; Vice Pres., Broadcasting, Flextech TV, 1995–98; BBC: Controller, Programme Acquisition, 1998–2003; Acting Dir, Marketing and Communications, 2001; Acting Dir, BBC TV, 2002; Dir, Film Channels and Acquisitions, 2003–04, Dep. Man. Dir, Sky Networks, 2004–07, BSkyB. Dir, Portland Media, 2007–. Gov., Nat. Film and TV Sch., 2004–. Member: BAFTA, 2000 (Trustee, 2006–); Variety Club of GB, 2001. *Recreations:* film, theatre, ski-ing. *Address:* (office) Grant Way, Isleworth, Middx TW7 5QD.

TURNER-SAMUELS, David Jessel; QC 1972; barrister; *b* 5 April 1918; *s* of late Moss Turner-Samuels, QC, MP, and Gladys Deborah Turner-Samuels (*née* Belcher); *m* 1939, Norma Turner-Samuels (*née* Verstone) (marr. diss. 1975); one *s* one *d*; *m* 1976, Norma Florence Negus, *qv. Educ:* Westminster Sch. Called to Bar, Middle Temple, 1939 (Bencher 1980); admitted to Trinidad Bar, 1976, Antigua Bar, 1997, St Lucia Bar, 1998. Served War of 1939–45, in Army, 1939–46. *Publication:* (jointly) Industrial Negotiation and Arbitration, 1951. *Recreation:* getting away from it all. *Address:* 4E Oak Lodge, Lythe Hill Park, Haslemere, Surrey GU27 3TF. *T:* (01428) 651970.

TURNER-SAMUELS, Norma Florence, (Mrs D. J. Turner-Samuels); *see* Negus, N. F.

TURNER-WARWICK, Prof. Dame Margaret (Elizabeth Harvey), DBE 1991; MA, DM, PhD; FRCP; Chairman, Royal Devon and Exeter Health Care NHS Trust, 1992–95; President, Royal College of Physicians, 1989–92; Consultant Physician, Brompton Hospital, since 1965 (Professor of Medicine (Thoracic Medicine), 1972–87, Dean, 1984–87, Cardiothoracic Institute, now Emeritus Professor); *b* 19 Nov. 1924; *d* of William Harvey Moore, QC, and Maud Baden-Powell; *m* 1950, Richard Trevor Turner-Warwick, *qv*; two *d. Educ:* Maynard Sch., Exeter; St Paul's Girls' Sch.; Lady Margaret Hall, Oxford (Open Schol. 1943; Hon. Fellow, 1990). DM Oxon, 1956; PhD London, 1961; FRCP 1969; FFOM 1983; FRACP 1983; FRCPE 1990; FFPH (FFPHM 1990); FRCPGlas 1991; FRCGP 1991; FRCPI 1992. University Coll. Hosp., 1947–50: Tuke silver medal, Filliter exhibn in Pathology, Magrath Schol. in Medicine, Atchison Schol.; Postgrad. trng at UCH and Brompton Hosp., 1950–61; Cons. Physician: (Gen. Med.), Elizabeth Garrett Anderson Hosp., 1961–67; Brompton and London Chest Hosps, 1967–72. Sen. Lectr, Inst. of Diseases of the Chest, 1961–72. Lectures: Marc Daniels, 1974, Phillip Ellman, 1980, Tudor Edwards, 1985, Harveian, 1994, RCP; Lettsomian, Med. Soc. of London, 1982. Pres., British Thoracic Soc., 1982–85; Chairman: Central Academic Council, BPMF, 1982–85; Asthma Res. Council (Chm., Med. Res. Cttee, 1982–87); Conf. of Colleges and their Faculties in UK, 1990–92; UKCCCR, 1991–97; Member: MRC Systems Bd (DHSS nomination), 1982–85; Council, British Lung Foundn, 1984–90; Gen. Council, King's Fund, 1991; Council, BHF, 1994–; Mem. Council and Vice-Pres., ASH, 1990–. University of London: Mem. Senate, 1983–87; Mem., Academic Council, 1983–87; Mem., Scholarships Cttee, 1984–87; Mem., Cttee of Extramural Studies, 1984–87. Member: Nuffield Bioethics Council, 1993–; Round Table on Sustainable Develt, 1995–98. Fellow, UCL, 1991; FIC 1996. Founder FMedSci 1998. Hon. Fellow: Girton Coll., Cambridge, 1993; Green Coll., Oxford, 1993; Imperial Coll., London, 1996. Hon. FACP 1988; Hon. FRCP&S (Canada) 1990; Hon. FRCAnaes 1991; Hon. FCMSA 1991; Hon FRCPath 1992; Hon. FRCS 1993; Hon. FRCR 1994. Hon. Bencher, Middle Temple, 1990. Hon. Member: Assoc. of Physicians of GB and Ireland, 1991; S German and Australasian Thoracic Socs; Member; Alpha Omega Alpha, USA, 1987; Acad. of Malaysia, 1991. Hon. DSc: New York, 1985; Exeter, 1990; London, 1990; Hull, 1991; Sussex, 1992; Oxford, 1992; Cambridge, 1993; Leicester, 1998. Osler Meml Medal, Univ. of Oxford, 1995; President's Award, Eur. Respiratory Soc., 1997; President's Medal, British Thoracic Soc., 1999. *Publications:* Immunology of the Lung, 1978; (jtly) Occupational Lung Diseases: research approaches and methods, 1981; Living Medicine: recollections and reflections, 2005; chapters in various textbooks on immunology and thoracic medicine, particularly fibrosing lung disorders and asthma; contrib. original articles: Lancet, BMJ, Quarterly Jl Med., Thorax, Tubercle, Jl Clin. Experimental Immunology, etc. *Recreations:* her family and their hobbies, gardening, country life, watercolour painting, violin playing. *Address:* Pynes House, Thorverton, Exeter EX5 5LT.

TURNER-WARWICK, Richard Trevor, CBE 1991; MA, MSc, DM Oxon, MCh; Hon. DSc; FRCP, FRCS, FRCOG, Hon. FACS; Hon. FRACS; specialist in reconstruction and functional restoration of the urinary tract; Emeritus Surgeon and Urologist to the Middlesex Hospital (Senior Surgeon, 1969–90); Hon. Senior Lecturer, London University Institute of Urology, since 1962; Hon. Consultant Urologist, Royal Prince Alfred Hospital, Sydney, since 1980; Robert Luff Foundation Fellow in Reconstrucive Surgery, since 1990; *b* 21 Feb. 1925; *s* of W. Turner Warwick, FRCS; *m* 1950, Margaret Elizabeth Harvey Moore (*see* Dame Margaret Turner-Warwick); two *d. Educ:* Bedales School; Oriel Coll., Oxford; Middlesex Hosp. Medical School. Pres. OUBC, 1946; Mem. Univ. Boat Race Crew, Isis Head of River crew and Univ. Fours, 1946; Winner OU Silver Sculls, 1946; BSc thesis in neuroanatomy, 1946. Sen. Broderip Schol., Lyell Gold Medallist and Freeman Schol., Middx Hosp., 1949; surgical trng at Middx Hosp. and St Paul's Hosp., London, and Columbia Presbyterian Med. Centre, NY, 1959. Hunterian Prof. of RCS, 1957, 1976; Comyns Berkeley Travelling Fellowship to USA, 1959. British Assoc. of Urological Surgeons: Mem. Council, 1975–78 and 1982–92; Pres., 1988–90; Fellow, 1961; St Peter's Medal, 1978; Member: Council, Royal Coll. of Surgeons, 1980–92; RCOG, 1990–92; Internat. Soc. of Urology, 1966–; European Soc. of Urology; Soc. of Pelvic Surgeons, 1963; Founder Mem., 1969, Pres., 1985, Internat. Continence Soc.; Corresp. Member: Amer. Assoc. of Genito Urinary Surgeons, 1972 (Harry Spence Medal, 1998); American and Australasian Urological Assocs. Fellow UCL, 1992. Fellow: Assoc. of Surgeons of GB and Ireland, 1960; Australasian Soc. Urology, 1989; Hon. FRACS 1981; Hon. FACS 1997; Hon. FRSocMed 2003. Hon. DSc New York, 1985. Moynihan Prize of Assoc. of Surgeons, 1957; Victor Bonney Prize, RCOG, 1987; Valentine Medal, NY Acad. of Medicine, 1992. *Publications:* various articles in scientific jls, contributing to surgery, to develt of operative procedures for the reconstruction and restoration of function of the urinary tract, and to design of surgical instruments. *Recreations:* water, family, fishing, gardening. *Address:* Pynes House, 9 Silver Street, Thorverton, Exeter EX5 5LT. *T:* (01392) 861173, *Fax:* (01392) 860940. *Clubs:* Vincent's (Oxford); The Houghton (Stockbridge); Leander (Henley); Ottery St Mary Fly Fishers.

TURNEY, Alan Harry, CB 1991; Assistant Under Secretary of State, Fire and Emergency Planning Department, Home Office, 1986–92; *b* 20 Aug. 1932; *s* of late Harry Landry Turney and Alice Theresa Turney (*née* Bailey); *m* 1957, Ann Mary Dollimore. *Educ:* St Albans Grammar Sch.; London School of Economics (BScEcon). Asst Principal, Home Office, 1961; Asst Private Sec. to Home Sec., 1962–65; Principal, 1965; Asst Sec., Broadcasting Dept, 1976; Rayner Review of Forensic Science Service, 1981; Criminal Dept, 1981–82; Prison Dept, 1982–86. *Recreations:* Rugby Union football, touring provincial France, enjoying the garden. *Address:* Brookfield Cottage, Bury End, Nuthampstead, Royston, Herts SG8 8NG. *T:* (01763) 848935.

TURNOUR, family name of **Earl Winterton**.

TURNQUEST, Sir Orville (Alton), GCMG 1995; QC (Bahamas) 1992; Governor-General of the Bahamas, 1995–2001; *b* 19 July 1929; *y s* of late Robert Turnquest and Gwendolyn Turnquest; *m* 1955, Edith Louise Thompson; one *s* two *d. Educ:* Govt High Sch.; Univ. of London (LLB). Articled 1947–53; called to Bahamas Bar, 1953; called to the Bar, Lincoln's Inn, 1960 (Hon. Bencher); Counsel and Attorney of Supreme Ct; Notary Public; private practice, 1953–92; stipendiary and circuit magistrate and coroner, 1959; law tutor and Mem., Exam. Bd, Bahamas Bar, 1965–92. Chancellor, Dio. of Nassau and Bahamas. Sec.-Gen., Progressive Liberal Party, 1960–62; MP South Central, Nassau, 1962–67, Montagu, 1982–94; Opposition Leader in Senate, 1972–79; Dep. Leader, Free Nat. Movement, 1987–94; Attorney-Gen., 1992–94; Minister of Justice, 1992–93, of Foreign Affairs, 1992–94; Dep. Prime Minister, 1993–94. Pres., Bahamas Bar Assoc.; Chm., Bahamas Bar Council, 1970–72. Pres., CPA, 1992–93. Member: Anglican Central Educnl Authy; Nat. Cttee of United World Colls; Bd of Govs, St John's Coll. and St Anne's High Sch. Trustee, Governor-General's Youth Award (Bahamas). Patron, Bahamas Games. *Recreations:* swimming, music, reading. *Address:* Kalamalka, Skyline Drive, PO Box N–8181, Nassau, Bahamas.

TUROK, Prof. Neil Geoffrey, PhD; Executive Director, Perimeter Institute of Theoretical Physics, Canada, since 2008; *b* 16 Nov. 1958; *s* of Benjamin and Mary Turok; *m* 1992, Corinne Francesca Squire; one *d. Educ:* Churchill Coll., Cambridge (BA); Imperial Coll., London (PhD). Postdoctoral Fellow, Univ. of California, Santa Barbara, 1983–85; Advanced Res. Fellow, 1985–87, Reader in Theoretical Physics, 1991–92, Imperial Coll.; Associate Scientist, Fermilab, Ill, 1987–88; Asst Prof., 1988–91, Associate Prof., 1992–95, David and Lucile Packard Fellow, 1992–97, Prof., 1995, Princeton Univ.; Prof. of Math. Physics, Univ. of Cambridge, 1996–2008. Founder, African Inst. for Mathematical Scis, 2003. James Clerk Maxwell Prize, Inst. of Physics, 1992. *Publications:* over 100 articles in Nuclear Physics B, Phys. Review, Phys. Review Letters, New Scientist, Scientific American. *Recreations:* jazz, nature, playing with Ruby. *Address:* Perimeter Institute for Theoretical Physics, 31 Caroline Street North, Waterloo, ON N2L 2Y5, Canada.

TURTON, Eugenie Christine, (Genie), CB 1996; non-executive Director, Wates Group, since 2004; *b* 19 Feb. 1946; *d* of late Arthur Turton and Georgina (*née* Fairhurst). *Educ:* Nottingham Girls' High Sch. (GPDST); Girton Coll., Cambridge (schol.; MA). Research student (G. C. Winter Warr Studentship), Univ. of Cambridge, 1967–70; joined CS as Asst Principal, MoT, later DoE, 1970; Private Sec. to Parly Under Sec. of State, 1973–74; Principal, 1974–80; Prin. Private Sec. to successive Secretaries of State for Transport, 1978–80; Asst Sec., 1980–86; seconded to Midland Bank International, 1981–82, and to Cabinet Office/MPO (Machinery of Govt Div.), 1982–85; Under Sec., DoE, 1986–91; Director: Heritage and Royal Estate (formerly Ancient Monuments and Historic Bldgs), 1987–90; Inner Cities, 1990–91; Dep. Sec., DoE, 1991–94; Dir, Citizen's Charter Unit, Cabinet Office, 1994–97; Dir, Govt Office for London, 1997–2000; a Director General: DETR, then DTLR, 2000–02; ODPM, 2002–04. Non-executive Director: Woolwich Building Soc., 1987–91; Rockpools Ltd, 2005–. Trustee: Pilgrim Trust, 1991–; Horniman Mus., 2002–; Dulwich Picture Gall., 2004–; AA Motoring Trust, 2005–07; Sir Edward Heath Charitable Foundn, 2007–. Mem. Council, City Univ., 2000–04. Mem. Chapter, Salisbury Cath., 2007–. *Recreations:* books, music, shopping, gardening. *Address:* 16 Rouse Gardens, Alleyn Park, SE21 8AF.

TURVEY, Garry, CBE 1991; Director-General, Freight Transport Association, 1984–93; *b* 11 Oct. 1934; *s* of Henry Oxley Turvey and Annie Maud Braley; *m* 1960, Hilary Margaret Saines; three *s. Educ:* Morecambe Grammar School. FCIS; FCILT. Metropolitan Vickers Ltd, Manchester, 1956–58; AEI Manchester Ltd, 1958–60; Asst Sec., 1960–67, Sec., 1967–69, Traders' Road Transport Assoc.; Sec., 1969–84 and Dep. Dir-Gen., 1974–84, Freight Transport Assoc. Freeman, City of London, 1994; Liveryman, Carmen's Co., 1994. *Recreations:* cricket, fly-fishing, gardening. *Address:* 139 Imberhorne Lane, East Grinstead, West Sussex RH19 1RP. *T:* (01342) 325829. *Club:* MCC.

TURVEY, Ralph, DSc (Econ); economist; Visiting Professor of Economics, London School of Economics, 1973–75 and since 1990; *b* 1 May 1927; *s* of John and Margaret Turvey; *m* 1st, 1957, Sheila Bucher (*d* 1987); one *s* one *d*; 2nd, 2006, Barbara Williams. *Educ:* Sidcot School; London School of Economics; Uppsala University. Lectr, then Reader, in Economics, at London School of Economics, 1948–64, with interruptions. Vis. Lectr, Johns Hopkins Univ., 1953; Ford Foundation Vis. Res. Prof., Univ. of Chicago,

1958–59; Economic Section, HM Treasury, 1960–62; Center of Economic Research, Athens, 1963. Chief Economist, The Electricity Council, 1964–67. Member, NBPI, 1967–71, Jt Dep. Chm. 1968–71; Economic Advr, Scientific Control Systems Ltd, 1971–75; Economic Advr, then Chief Statistician, ILO, 1975–89; Dir, Dept of Labour Information and Statistics, ILO, until 1989; Res. Fellow, Statistics Canada, 1989–90. Member: Nat. Water Council, 1974–75; Inflation Accounting Cttee, 1974–75; NZ Adv. Cttee on price indices, 1991; RPI Adv. Cttee, 1992–94; Canadian and Swedish adv. cttees on consumer price indices, 1992–2006. Chm., Centre for the Study of Regulated Industries, 1993–. Associate, Frontier Economics, 2003–07. Governor, Kingston Poly., 1972–75. Hon. Fellow, Weimer Sch. of Advanced Studies in Real Estate and Land Econs, 2008. *Publications:* The Economics of Real Property, 1957; Interest Rates and Asset Prices, 1960; (joint author) Studies in Greek Taxation, 1964; Optimal Pricing and Investment in Electricity Supply, 1968; Economic Analysis and Public Enterprises, 1971; Demand and Supply, 1971; (joint author) Electricity Economics, 1977; Consumer Price Indices, 1989; (ed and joint author) Developments in International Labour Statistics, 1989; Consumer Price Indexes, 1999; papers on economic hist. of Victorian London and on electricity pricing. *Recreation:* walking. *Address:* 20 The Croft, Bishopstone, Salisbury SP5 4DF. *Club:* Reform.

TUSA, Sir John, Kt 2003; Managing Director, Barbican Centre, 1995–2007; Chairman of the Governors, University of the Arts, London, since 2007; *b* 2 March 1936; *s* of late John Tusa, OBE and Lydia Sklenarova; *m* 1960, Ann Hilary Dowson; two *s*. *Educ:* Trinity Coll., Cambridge (BA 1st Cl. Hons History). BBC general trainee, 1960; Producer, BBC External Services, 1962; freelance radio journalist, 1965; Presenter: BBC Radio 4 The World Tonight, 1968; BBC2 Newsnight, 1979–86; Man. Dir, World Service, BBC, 1986–92; Presenter, One O'Clock News, BBC TV, 1993–95. Chm., London News Radio, 1993–94. Pres., Wolfson Coll., Cambridge, 1993. Chairman: Adv. Cttee, Govt Art Collection, 1993–2003; BBC Marshall Plan of the Mind Trust, 1992–99; Wigmore Hall Trust, 1999– (Trustee, 1993–95); Dep. Chm. Trustees, BM, 2004– (Trustee, 2000–04); Member: Council, RIIA, 1984–90, 1991–95; Board, Public Radio Internat. (formerly American Public Radio), 1990–99; Adv. Cttee, London Internat. String Quartet Competition, 1991– (Vice-Chm. of Board, 1995–); Board, ENO, 1996–2003; Trustee: Nat. Portrait Gall., 1988–2000; Thomson Foundn, 1992–95; Design Mus. Trust, 1999–2000; Somerset House Trust, 2004–; Turquoise Mountain Trust, 2006–. Hon. FRIBA 2001; Hon. RAM 1999; Hon. GSMD 1999; Hon. Mem., ISM, 2001. Hon. LLD London, 1993; DUniv Heriot-Watt, 1993; Hon. DLitt City, 1997; DU: Essex, 2006; Kingston, 2007; Kent, 2008. TV Journalist of the Year, RTS 1983; Richard Dimbleby Award, BAFTA, 1984; BPG Award for outstanding contribn to radio, 1991; Presenter of the Year, RTS, 1995. Knight First Class, Order of the White Rose (Finland), 1998. *Publications:* Conversations with the World, 1990; A World in Your Ear, 1992; (with Ann Tusa): The Nuremberg Trial, 1983; The Berlin Blockade, 1988; Art Matters: reflecting on culture, 1999; On Creativity, 2003; The Janus Aspect: artists in the twenty first century, 2005; Engaged with the Arts: writings from the front line, 2007. *Recreations:* tennis, chamber music, listening. *Address:* 16 Canonbury Place, N1 2NN. *T:* (020) 7704 2451.

TUSHINGHAM, Rita; actress; *b* 14 March 1942; *d* of John Tushingham; *m* 1962, Terence William Bicknell (marr. diss. 1976); two *d*; *m* 1981, Ousama Rawi (marr. diss. 1996). *Educ:* La Sagesse Convent, Liverpool. Student, Liverpool Playhouse, 1958–60. BBC Personality of the Year, Variety Club of GB, 1988. *Stage appearances:* Royal Court Theatre: The Changeling, 1960; The Kitchen, 1961; A Midsummer Night's Dream, 1962; Twelfth Night, 1962; The Knack, 1962; other London theatres: The Giveaway, 1969; Lorna and Ted, 1970; Mistress of Novices, 1973; My Fat Friend, 1981; Children, Children, 1984; Vagina Monologues, 2003. *Films:* A Taste of Honey, 1961 (Brit. Film Acad. and Variety Club awards for Most Promising Newcomer, 1961; NY Critics, Cannes Film Festival and Hollywood Foreign Press Assoc. awards); The Leather Boys, 1962; A Place to Go, Girl with Green Eyes (Variety Club award), 1963; The Knack, 1964 (Silver Goddess award, Mexican Assoc. of Film Corresps); Dr Zhivago, 1965; The Trap, 1966; Smashing Time, Diamonds For Breakfast, 1967; The Guru, 1968; The Bed-Sitting Room, 1970; Straight on till Morning, 1972; Situation, 1972; Instant Coffee, 1973; Rachel's Man, 1974; The Human Factor, 1976; Pot Luck, State of Shock, 1977; Mysteries, 1978; Incredible Mrs Chadwick, 1979; The Spaghetti House Siege, 1982; Flying, 1984; A Judgement in Stone, Single Room, 1986; Resurrected, Dante and Beatrice in Liverpool, 1989; Hard Days' Hard Nights, 1990; Paper Marriage, Rapture of Deceit, 1991; Desert Lunch, 1992; An Awfully Big Adventure, 1994; The Boy from Mercury, 1995; Under The Skin, 1996; Swing, Out of Depth, 1998; Home Ground, 2000; Being Julia, 2003; Loneliness and the Modern Pentathlon, 2004; Puffball, The Hideout, 2006; Telstar, Come Here Today, 2008. *TV appearances include:* Red Riding Hood (play), 1973; No Strings (own series), 1974; Don't Let Them Kill Me on Wednesday, 1980; Confessions of Felix Krull, 1980; Seeing Red, 1983; Pippi Longstocking, 1984; The White Whale—The Life of Ernest Hemingway (film), 1987; cameo appearance in Bread, 1988; Sunday Pursuit; Gütt, Ein Journalist, 1991; Hamburg Poison, 1992; Family Secrets (film), 1995; I Was Eddie Mostyn, 1995; Shadow Play, 2001; Margo beyond the Box, 2003; New Tricks, 2005; Miss Marple: The Sittaford Mystery, 2005; Angel Cake, 2006; Patty and Chips with Scraps (BBC radio play), 1997. *Recreations:* interior decorating, cooking, watercolour painting. *Address:* c/o Michele Milburn, International Artistes, 4th Floor, Holborn Hall, 193–197 High Holborn, WC1V 7BD.

TUSTIN, Rt Rev. David; Hon. Assistant Bishop of Lincoln, since 2001; Bishop Suffragan of Grimsby, 1979–2000; *b* 12 Jan. 1935; *s* of John Trevelyan Tustin and Janet Reynolds; *m* 1964, Mary Elizabeth (*née* Glover); one *s* one *d*. *Educ:* Solihull School; Magdalene Coll., Cambridge (MA Hons); Geneva Univ. (Cert. in Ecumenical Studies); Cuddesdon Coll., Oxford. Philip Usher Memorial Scholar (in Greece), 1957–58; deacon 1960, priest 1961; Curate of Stafford, 1960–63; Asst Gen. Sec., C of E Council on Foreign Relations and Curate of St Dunstan-in-the-West, Fleet St, 1963–67; Vicar of S Paul's, Wednesbury, 1967–71; Vicar of Tettenhall Regis, 1971–79; RD of Trysull, 1977–79. Canon and Prebendary of Lincoln Cathedral, 1979–2000. Co-Chm., Anglican/Lutheran Internat. Commn, 1986–98; Pres., Anglican/Lutheran Soc., 1986–99; Mem., Gen. Synod of C of E, 1990–2000 (Chm., Council for Christian Unity, 1993–98). DD Lambeth 1998. Comdr, Royal Order of Polar Star (Sweden), 2000. *Recreations:* music, family life, languages, travel, horology. *Address:* The Ashes, Tunnel Road, Wrawby, Brigg, N Lincs DN20 8SF.

TUTT, Prof. Norman Sydney, OBE 2002; Executive Director of Housing and Social Services, London Borough of Ealing, 2001–03 (Director of Social Services, 1999–2001); *b* 8 June 1944; *s* of Sydney Robert Tutt and Stella May Tutt; *m* 1966, Diana Patricia Hewitt; two *s*. *Educ:* Chislehurst and Sidcup Grammar Sch.; Univ. of Keele (BA); Univ. of Leeds (MSc); Univ. of Nottingham (PhD). Clin. Psychologist, Nottingham, 1966–69; Resident Psychologist, St Gilbert's Approved Sch., 1969–73; Professional Advr, Northampton Social Services, 1973–74; Sen. Develt Officer, London Boroughs Children Reg. Planning Cttee, 1974–75; Principal Social Work Services Officer, DHSS, 1975–79; Prof. of Applied Social Studies, 1979–92 (on leave of absence, 1989–92), and Hon. Prof., 1992–95, Lancaster Univ.; Dir of Social Services, Leeds CC, 1989–93; Exec. Dir, Social Information Systems, 1993–98. Man., Gulbenkian Commn on Violence to Children, 1995–96. Vis. Prof., Faculty of Community Health Scis, Univ. of Wales Inst. at Cardiff (formerly Cardiff Inst.), 1994–2000. Mem. Council, ASA, 1996–2002. Mem. Bd, Hanover Housing Assoc., 1996–99. *Publications:* Care or Custody, 1975; (ed) Violence, 1975; (ed) Alternative Strategies for Coping with Crime, 1978; (ed) A Way of Life for the Handicapped, 1983; Children in Custody, 1987; (ed) Children and Homicide, 1996; contributor to other pubns. *Recreations:* work, wine, walks, cracking jokes. *Address:* Chateau Milhau, 34620 Puisserguier, France. *T:* (4) 67893275. *Clubs:* as with Groucho Marx he would not join a club which would have him as a member.

TUTT, Roger Clive, CMG 1994; MBE 1966; HM Diplomatic Service, retired; *b* 22 March 1939; *s* of Clive Pritchard Tutt and Ada (*née* Kyle); *m* 1963, Gwen Leeke; two *s* one *d*. *Educ:* Bristol GS; Ledbury GS; Bristol Univ. (BA Econ). Bristol Univ. expedn to India and S America, 1960–61; Asst Administrator, Turks and Caicos Is, 1963–66; joined HM Diplomatic Service, 1966; Second Secretary: Copenhagen, 1967–69; Lusaka, 1969–71; First Secretary: FCO, 1971–74; Regl Inf. Officer, Barbados, 1974–79; FCO, 1979–87; Counsellor: UKMIS NY, 1987–89; FCO, 1989–94, 1995–2005. *Recreations:* stewardship of a small piece of rural Gloucestershire, fishing, sailing, travel. *Clubs:* Reform, Royal Commonwealth Society.

TUTTLE, Hon. Robert Holmes; Ambassador of the United States of America to the Court of St James's, since 2005; *b* 1944; *s* of Holmes Tuttle; *m* Maria Denise Hummer; two *d* from former marr. *Educ:* Stanford Univ. (BA 1965); Univ. of Southern Calif (MBA 1968). Jt Man. Partner, Tuttle-Click Automotive Gp, until 2005. Special Asst to President of USA, 1982–85; Dir, Presidential Personnel, 1985–89. *Address:* Embassy of the United States of America, 24 Grosvenor Square, W1A 1AE.

TUTU, Most Rev. Desmond Mpilo; Archbishop of Cape Town and Metropolitan of Southern Africa, 1986–96, now Archbishop Emeritus; Chair, Truth and Reconciliation Commission, 1995–99; *b* Klerksdorp, Transvaal, 7 Oct. 1931; *s* of Zachariah and Aletta Tutu; *m* 1955, Leah Nomalizo Shenxane; one *s* three *d*. *Educ:* Johannesburg Bantu High Sch.; Bantu Normal Coll., Pretoria (Higher Teachers' Dip. 1953); Univ. of S Africa (BA 1954); St Peter's Theol Coll., Johannesburg (LTh 1960); King's Coll. London (BD 1965, MTh 1966; FKC 1978). Schoolmaster: Madibane High Sch., Johannesburg, 1954; Munsieville High Sch., Krugersdorp, 1955–57. Theological coll. student, 1958–60; deacon 1960, priest 1961, St Mary's Cathedral, Johannesburg. Curate: St Alban's Church, Benoni, 1960–61; St Philip's Church, Alberton, 1961–62; St Alban's, Golders Green, London, 1962–65; St Mary's, Bletchingley, Surrey, 1965–66; Lecturer: Federal Theol Seminary, Alice, CP, 1967–69; Univ. of Botswana, Lesotho and Swaziland, Roma, Lesotho, 1970–72; Associate Dir, Theol Education Fund (WCC) based in Bromley, Kent, and Hon. Curate, St Augustine's, Grove Park, 1972–75; Dean of Johannesburg, 1975–76; Bishop of Lesotho, 1976–78; Gen. Sec., South African Council of Churches, 1978–85; Rector, St Augustine's Parish, Soweto, 1981–85; Bishop of Johannesburg, 1985–86. Woodruff Vis. Prof., Emory Univ., 1998–2000. Chancellor, Univ. of Western Cape, Cape Town, 1988–. Pres., All Africa Conference of Churches, 1987–97. Trustee, Phelps Stoke Fund, New York. Holds over fifty hon. degrees from academic institutions in UK, Europe and USA. Athena Prize, Onassis Foundation, 1980; Nobel Peace Prize, 1984; Albert Schweitzer Humanitarian Award, Emmanuel Coll., Boston, 1988. Order of Meritorious Service, Gold (S Africa), 1996; Order of Southern Cross (Brazil), 1987; Order of Merit of Brasilia (Brazil), 1987; Grand Cross of Merit (Germany), 1996. *Publications:* Crying in the Wilderness, 1982; Hope and Suffering, 1983; The Words of Desmond Tutu, 1989; The Rainbow People of God, 1994; No Future Without Forgiveness, 1999; God Has a Dream: a vision of hope for our time, 2004; articles and reviews. *Recreations:* music, reading, jogging.

TUYMANS, Luc; artist; *b* Belgium, 14 July 1958. Solo exhibitions worldwide, 1985–, including: Zeno X Gall., Antwerp; White Cube, London, 1999, 2001; Tokyo Opera Art Gall., 2000; Venice Biennale, 2001; Helsinki Kunsthalle, 2003; Tate Modern, 2004. *Address:* c/o Zeno X Gallery, Leopold de Waelplaats 16, 2000 Antwerp, Belgium; *e-mail:* info@zeno-x.com.

TWEEDDALE, 14th Marquis of, *cr* 1694; **Charles David Montagu Hay;** Lord Hay of Yester, 1488; Earl of Tweeddale, 1646; Viscount Walden, Earl of Gifford, 1694; Baron Tweeddale (UK), 1881; Hereditary Chamberlain of Dunfermline; *b* 6 Aug. 1947; *yr* twin *s* of 12th Marquis of Tweeddale, GC and of Hon. Sonia Mary, *d* of 1st Viscount Ingleby, PC; *S* brother, 2005. *Educ:* Milton Abbey, Blandford, Dorset; Trinity Coll., Oxford. *Heir:* *b* (Lord) Alistair James Montagu Hay, DPhil, *b* 4 Nov. 1955; does not use courtesy title.

TWEEDIE, Prof. Sir David (Philip), Kt 1994; Chairman, International Accounting Standards Board, since 2000; *b* 7 July 1944; *s* of Aidrian Ian Tweedie and Marie Patricia Tweedie (*née* Phillips); *m* 1970, Janice Christine Brown; two *s*. *Educ:* Grangemouth High Sch.; Edinburgh Univ. (BCom, PhD). CA 1972. Accountancy trng, Mann, Judd, Gordon (Glasgow), 1969–72; Edinburgh University: Lectr in Accounting, 1973–78; Associate Dean, Fac. of Social Scis, 1975–78; Technical Dir, Inst. of Chartered Accountants, Scotland, 1978–81; Nat. Res. Partner, KMG Thomson McLintock, 1982–87; Nat. Tech. Partner, KPMG Peat Marwick McLintock, 1987–90; Chm., Accounting Standards Bd, 1990–2000. Visiting Professor of Accounting: Univ. of Lancaster, 1978–88; Univ. of Bristol, 1988–2000; Edinburgh Univ., 1999–. UK and Irish Representative: Internat. Auditing Practices Cttee, 1983–88; Internat. Accounting Standards Cttee, 1995–2000; Auditing Practices Committee, Consultative Committee of Accountancy Bodies: Mem., 1985–90; Vice-Chm., 1986–88; Chm., 1989–90. Institute of Chartered Accountants in England and Wales: Mem. Council, 1989–91; Mem., Financial Reporting Council, 1990–2000; Chm., Urgent Issues Task Force, 1990–2000. FRSE 2001. Hon. FIA 1999; Hon. FSIP 2004; Hon. FCCA 2005. Hon. DSc (Econ) Hull, 1993; Hon. LLD: Lancaster, 1993; Exeter, 1997; Dundee, 1998; Hon. DLitt Heriot-Watt, 1996; Hon. DBA: Napier, 1999; Oxford Brookes, 2004; Hon. DSc (Soc.Sci.) Edinburgh, 2001. Centenary Award, Chartered Accountants Founding Socs, 1997; CIMA Award, 1998. *Publications:* (with T. A. Lee) The Private Shareholder and the Corporate Report, 1977; Financial Reporting, Inflation and the Capital Maintenance Concept, 1979; (with T. A. Lee) The Institutional Investor and Financial Information, 1981; (with G. Whittington) The Debate on Inflation Accounting, 1984; contribs to professional and acad. accounting jls and books. *Recreations:* athletics and Rugby (watching, not participating, sadly), walking, gardening. *Address:* c/o International Accounting Standards Board, 30 Cannon Street, EC4M 6XH. *T:* (020) 7246 6410.

TWEEDSMUIR, 4th Baron *cr* 1935, of Elsfield, Oxford; **John William Howard de l'Aigle, (Toby), Buchan;** *b* 25 May 1950; *s* of 3rd Baron Tweedsmuir and Barbara, 2nd *d* of Ernest Nash Ensor; *S* father, 2008; *m* 1st, 1977, Amanda Jocelyn, *d* of Sir Gawain Westray Bell, KCMG, CBE; two *s*; 2nd, 2001, Dominique, *d* of late Dennis Joseph Enright, OBE; one *s* two *d*. *Educ:* Magdalen Coll. Sch., Oxford. *Heir:* *s* Hon. John Alasdair Gawain Buchan, *b* 20 Nov. 1986.

TWEEDY, Colin David, LVO 2003; OBE 2000; Chief Executive, Arts & Business (formerly Director General, Association for Business Sponsorship of the Arts), since 1983; *b* 26 Oct. 1953; *s* of Clifford Harry Tweedy, of Abbotsbury, Dorset and Kitty Audrey (*née* Matthews). *Educ:* City of Bath Boys' Sch.; St Catherine's Coll., Oxford (MA). Manager, Thorndike Theatre, Leatherhead, 1976–78; Corporate Finance Officer, Guinness Mahon, 1978–80; Asst Dir, Streets Financial PR, 1980–83. Chm., Comité Européen pour le Rapprochement de l'Economie et de la Culture; Mem. Council, Japan Festival, 1991; Director: Covent Garden International Festival, 1995–2001; Oxford Stage Co., 1985–; Crusaid, 1987–2004; Mariinsky Theatre Trust, 1999–; Mem. Council, Nat. Musicians' Symphony Orch., 2001–; Member: UK Nat. Cttee, European Cinema and TV Year, 1988–89; Council for Charitable Support, 1998–. Founder, Prince of Wales Arts & Kids Foundn, 2002; Trustee: Serpentine Gall., 1990–; The Ideas Foundn, 2003–; Next Generation Foundn, 2003–. Selector, Discerning Eye 2000 exhibn; a Judge: PR Week Awards, 2000; Art & Work Awards, 2002; Mem. Adv. Panel, Whitbread Bk Awards, 1998–. Freeman, City of London, 1978. CCMI 2002; FRSA. Hollis Sponsorship Personality of the Year, 2003. *Publication:* A Celebration of Ten Years' Business Sponsorship of the Arts, 1987. *Recreations:* the arts in general, opera, theatre and contemporary art in particular, Italy, food, travel. *Address:* Arts & Business, Nutmeg House, 60 Gainsford Street, Butlers Wharf, SE1 2NY. *T:* (020) 7378 8143, *Fax:* (020) 7407 7527; *e-mail:* head.office@AandB.org.uk. *Clubs:* Home House, Groucho.

TWELVETREE, Eric Alan; County Treasurer, Essex County Council, 1974–87; *b* 26 Dec. 1928; *m* 1953, Patricia Mary Starkings; two *d*. *Educ:* Stamford Sch., Lincs; qualif. IPFA and ACCA. Served with Borough Councils: Gt Yarmouth, Ipswich, Stockport, Southampton; County Councils: Gloucestershire, Kent. Pres., Soc. of County Treasurers, 1986–87. Dir, Chelmsford Hospice, then Farleigh Hospice, Chelmsford, 1991–99. Mem., Exec. Cttee, Field Studies Council, 1978–2001. *Recreations:* silversmithing, bookbinding, watercolours. *Address:* 12 Cherry Orchard Road, Tetbury, Glos GL8 8HX.

TWIGG, (John) Derek; MP (Lab) Halton, since 1997; *b* 9 July 1959; *s* of Kenneth and Irene Twigg; *m* 1988, Mary Cassidy; one *s* one *d*. *Educ:* Bankfield High Sch., Widnes; Halton Coll. of Further Educn. Civil service posts, Department of Employment, and DFE, then DFEE, 1975–96; political consultant, 1996–97. Member (Lab): Cheshire CC, 1981–85; Halton DC, 1983–97. PPS to Minister of State, DTI, 1999–2001, to Sec. of State, DTLR, 2001–02; an Asst Govt Whip, 2002–03; a Lord Comr of HM Treasury (Govt Whip), 2003–04; Parliamentary Under-Secretary of State: DFES, 2004–05; DfT, 2005–06; MoD, 2006–08. Mem., Public Accounts Cttee, 1998–99. *Recreations:* various sporting activities, hill walking, reading military history. *Address:* House of Commons, SW1A 0AA. *T:* (020) 7219 3000.

TWIGG, Stephen; Director, Foreign Policy Centre, since 2005 (Board Member, 1998–2005); *b* 25 Dec. 1966; *s* of Ian David Twigg and late Jean Barbara Twigg. *Educ:* Southgate Comprehensive Sch.; Balliol Coll., Oxford (BA Hons). Pres., NUS, 1990–92; Parliamentary Officer: British Sect., Amnesty Internat., 1992–93; NCVO, 1993–94; researcher, office of Margaret Hodge, MP, 1994–96. Mem. (Lab), Islington LBC, 1992–97. Gen. Sec., Fabian Soc., 1996–97 (Mem. Exec., 1997–). MP (Lab) Enfield, Southgate, 1997–2005; contested (Lab) same seat, 2005; prospective Parly candidate (Lab), Liverpool West Derby, 2007–. Parly Sec., Privy Council Office, 2001–02; Parly Under-Sec. of State, DfEE, 2002–04, Minister of State, DfES, 2004–05. Member: Select Cttee on Modernisation of H of C, 1998–2000; Select Cttee on Educn and Employment, 2000–01. Chairman: Labour Campaign for Electoral Reform, 1998–2001; Lab. Friends of Israel, 1998–2001. Dir, Crime Concern, 1997–2000. Dir, Special Projects, AEGIS Charitable Trust, 2005–; Chm., Young People Now Foundn, 2006–. Trustee, WEA, 2006–. Gov., Jubilee Primary Sch., 2006–. *Address:* Liverpool Labour Party, 108 Prescot Road, Liverpool L7 0JA; *web:* www.twigg4westderby.com.

TWIGGER, Terence; Chief Executive, Meggitt plc, since 2001 (Finance Director, 1993–2000); *b* 21 Nov. 1949; *s* of Gilbert and Elizabeth Twigger; *m* 1973, Elizabeth Kimberley; two *d*. *Educ:* King Edward VI Grammar, Nuneaton; Bristol Univ. (BSc). FCA; FRAeS. Touche Ross & Co., 1971–76; various appts, 1977–90, Finance Dir, 1990–93, Lucas Aerospace. *Recreations:* reading, shooting, fishing. *Address:* Meggitt plc, Atlantic House, Aviation Park West, Bournemouth International Airport, Dorset BH23 6EW. *T:* (01202) 597597; The Walled Garden, Holly Hill Lane, Sarisbury Green, Southampton, SO31 7AH.

TWIGGY; *see* Lawson, Lesley.

TWIN, Prof. Peter John, OBE 1991; FRS 1993; Professor of Experimental Physics, University of Liverpool, 1987–2001, Emeritus Professor and Senior Fellow, since 2001; *b* 26 July 1939; *s* of Arthur James and Hilda Ethel Twin; *m* 1963, Jean Esther Leatherland; one *s* one *d*. *Educ:* Sir George Monoux Grammar Sch., Walthamstow; Univ. of Liverpool (BSc Hons, PhD). University of Liverpool: Lectr, 1964–73; Sen. Lectr, 1973–79; Reader, 1979–85; Head, Nuclear Structure Facility, Daresbury Lab., SERC, 1983–87. Vis. Prof., Univ. of Alberta, 1968–69. Reader, dio. of Chester, 1991–. Tom Bonner Prize, APS, 1991; John Price Wetherill Medal, Benjamin Franklin Inst., USA, 1991; Lisa Meitner Prize, Eur. Physical Soc., 2004. *Publications:* numerous papers in learned jls. *Address:* Oliver Lodge Laboratory, University of Liverpool, Liverpool L69 3BX. *T:* (0151) 794 3378.

TWINE, Derek Milton, CBE 2007; FCIPD; Chief Executive, Scout Association, since 1996; *b* 1 May 1951; *s* of late Edward Montague Twine and Winifred May Twine (*née* Milton); *m* 1974, Rhoda, *d* of Very Rev. R. J. N. Lockhart; one *s* one *d*. *Educ:* Reigate GS; UCNW, Bangor (BA Hons Educn 1st cl.). FCIPD (FITD 1987). Researcher, 1973–75, Lectr in Education, 1975–76, Univ. of Wales; Scout Association: Dir, Venture Scout Trng, 1976–79; Dir of Programme, 1979–85; Exec. Comr (Programme and Trng), 1985–96. Member: Youth Panel, Nat. Trust, 1978–85; Voluntary Sector Panel, RSA, 1990–96; Mgt Cttee, Educn and Standards, Nat. Youth Agency, 1991–95 (Chm., 1993–95); National Society for Voluntary Youth Service: Mem., Exec. Cttee, 1979–82; Chm., Develt Project, 1979–82; Chm., Trng Managers' Gp, 1990–96. Trustee: Whitechapel Foundn, 1996–; Croatia Sunrise City Support, 1996–99. Gov., Davenant Foundn Sch., 1994–. FRSA 2002. *Publications:* various articles in youthwork and educnl jls. *Recreations:* church activities, theatre, cooking, cross-country running. *Address:* Scout Association, Gilwell Park, Chingford, E4 7QW. *T:* (020) 8433 7100, *Fax:* (020) 8433 7108.

TWINING, Alexandra Mary; *see* Hall Hall, A. M.

TWINING, Prof. William Lawrence, FBA 1997; Quain Professor of Jurisprudence Emeritus, University College London, since 2004 (Quain Professor of Jurisprudence, 1983–96; Research Professor of Law, 1996–2004); *b* 22 Sept. 1934; *s* of Edward Francis Twining and Helen Mary Twining (*née* Dubuisson); *m* 1957, Penelope Elizabeth Wall Morris; one *s* one *d*. *Educ:* Charterhouse School; Brasenose College, Oxford (BA 1955; MA 1960; DCL 1990); Univ. of Chicago (JD 1958). Lectr in Private Law, Univ. of Khartoum, 1958–61; Sen. Lectr in Law, University Coll., Dar-es-Salaam, 1961–65; Prof. of Jurisprudence, The Queen's Univ., Belfast, 1965–72; Prof. of Law, Univ. of Warwick, 1972–82. Mem., Cttee on Legal Educn in N Ireland, 1972–74; President: Soc. of Public Law Teachers of Law, 1978–79; UK Assoc. for Legal and Social Philosophy, 1980–83; Chairman: Bentham Cttee, 1982–2000; Commonwealth Legal Educn Assoc., 1983–93; vis. appts in several Univs. Foreign Mem., Amer. Acad. of Arts and Scis, 2007. Hon. QC 2002. Hon. LLD: Univ. of Victoria, BC, 1980; Edinburgh, 1994; QUB, 1999; Southampton Inst., 2000; York Univ., Toronto, 2002. General Editor: Law in Context series, 1966–; Jurists series, 1979–. *Publications:* The Karl Llewellyn Papers, 1968; Karl Llewellyn and the Realist Movement, 1973; (with David Miers) How to Do Things with Rules, 1976, 4th edn 1999; (with J. Uglow) Law Publishing and Legal Information, 1981; (ed) Facts in Law, 1983; Theories of Evidence, 1985; (ed) Legal Theory and Common Law, 1986; (ed with R. Tur) Essays on Kelsen, 1986; (ed jtly) Learning Lawyers' Skills, 1989; (ed jtly) Access to Legal Education and the Legal Profession, 1989; Rethinking Evidence, 1990, 2nd edn 2006; (ed) Issues of Self-determination, 1991; (with T. Anderson) Analysis of Evidence, 1991, 2nd edn (with T. Anderson and D. Schum) 2005; (with E. Quick) Legal Records in the Commonwealth, 1994; Blackstone's Tower: the English Law School, 1994; Law in Context: enlarging a discipline, 1997; Globalisation and Legal Theory, 2000; The Great Juristic Bazaar, 2002; (ed jtly) Evidence and Inference in History and Law, 2003. *Address:* 10 Mill Lane, Iffley, Oxford OX4 4EJ.

TWINN, Ian David, PhD; Director of Public Affairs, Incorporated Society of British Advertisers, since 1998; *b* 26 April 1950; *s* of late David Twinn and of Gwynneth Irene Twinn; *m* 1973, Frances Elizabeth Holtby; two *s*. *Educ:* Netherhall Secondary Modern School, Cambridge; Cambridge Grammar School; University College of Wales, Aberystwyth (BA hons); University of Reading (PhD). Senior Lecturer in Planning, Polytechnic of the South Bank, 1975–83. MP (C) Edmonton, 1983–97; contested (C) same seat, 1997. PPS to Minister of State for Industry, 1985–86, to Dep. Chm. of Cons. Party, 1986–88, to Minister of State for Energy, 1987–90, to Minister of State for the Environment, 1990–92, to Paymaster Gen., 1992–94. MEP (C) London Reg., Oct. 2003–2004; contested (C) London Reg., EP elecns, 1999, 2004. Vice Chm., British Caribbean Assoc., 1986–. FRSA 1989; FRGS (MIBG 1972). Comdr, Order of Honour (Greece), 2000. *Recreations:* collecting secondhand books, renovating antique furniture. *Address:* 85 Calton Avenue, SE21 7DF. *T:* (020) 8299 4210.

TWINN, John Ernest; Director General Guided Weapons and Electronics, Ministry of Defence, 1978–81, retired; *b* 11 July 1921; *s* of late Col Frank Charles George Twinn, CMG and Lilian May Twinn (*née* Tomlinson); *m* 1950, Mary Constance Smallwood; three *d*. *Educ:* Manchester Grammar Sch.; Christ's Coll., Cambridge (MA). FIET (FIEE 1981). Air Min., 1941; Telecommunications Research Estabt (later Royal Radar Estabt), 1943; Head of Guided Weapons Gp, RRE, 1965; Head of Space Dept, RAE, 1968; Head of Weapons Dept, RAE, 1972; Asst Chief Scientific Advr (Projects), MoD, 1973; Dir Underwater Weapons Projects (Naval), 1976. *Recreations:* sailing, music, genealogy. *Address:* Timbers, 9 Woodway, Merrow, Guildford, Surrey GU1 2TF. *T:* (01483) 568993.

TWISK, Russell Godfrey; writer; Editor-at-Large, British Reader's Digest, 2002–06 (Editor-in-Chief, 1988–2002); *b* 24 Aug. 1941; *s* of late K. Y. Twisk and of Joyce Brunning; *m* 1965, Ellen Elizabeth Banbury; two *d*. *Educ:* Salesian Coll., Farnborough. Harmsworth Press, Dep. Editor, Golf Illustrated, 1960; Sub Editor, Sphere; freelance journalist, 1962; joined BBC, editorial staff Radio Times, 1966; Deputy Editor, Radio Times, 1971; Development Manager, BBC, 1975; Editor, The Listener, 1981–87. Director: Reader's Digest, 1988–2002; Berkeley Magazines, 1990–2002. Has edited numerous BBC publications; Publisher, BBC Adult Literacy Project; radio critic for The Observer, 1989–94; writer, daily Birthday column, The Times, 2003–. Mem., Press Complaints Commn, 1999–2002. Governor, London College of Printing, 1967–87 (Chm., 1974, 1978). Chm., Reader's Digest Trust, 1988–99. Chm., National Campaign Cttee, Charities Aid Foundn, 1991–94. Chm., BSME, 1990; Pres., Media Soc., 1993–95. Trustee, Christian Responsibility in Public Affairs, 1997–. *Recreations:* golf, walking, watching horses race. *Address:* The Old Barn, East Harting, near Petersfield, Hants GU31 5LZ. *T:* (01730) 825769, *Fax:* (01730) 825725; *e-mail:* rtwisk@aol.com. *Club:* Garrick.

TWISLETON-WYKEHAM-FIENNES; *see* Fiennes.

TWISS, (Lionel) Peter, OBE 1957; DSC 1942 and Bar 1943; marine consultant; Director and General Manager, Hamble Point Marina Ltd, 1978–88; formerly Chief Test Pilot of Fairey Aviation Ltd; *b* 23 July 1921; *m* 1944, Constance Tomkinson (marr. diss.; she *d* 1996); *m* 1950, Mrs Vera Maguire (marr. diss.); one *d* (and one *d* decd), one step *s* one step *d*; *m* 1960, Cherry (marr. diss.), *d* of late Sir John Huggins, GCMG, MC; one *d*; *m* 1964, Mrs Heather Danby (*d* 1988), Titchfield; one step *s* one step *d*; *m* 2002, Jane Mary de Lucey. *Educ:* Sherborne Sch. Joined Fleet Air Arm, 1939; served on catapult ships, aircraft-carriers, 1941–43; night fighter development, 1943–44; served in British Air Commn, America, 1944. Empire Test Pilots School, Boscombe Down, 1945; Test Pilot, Fairey Aviation Co. Ltd, 1946, Chief Test Pilot, 1957–60. Dir, Fairey Marine Ltd, 1968–78. Mem., Lasham Gliding Soc. Holder of World's Absolute Speed Record, 10 March 1956. *Publication:* Faster than the Sun, 1963, 2nd edn 2000. *Address:* Nettleworth, 33 South Street, Titchfield, Hants PO14 4DL. *T:* (01329) 843146. *Club:* Royal Southern Yacht.

TWIST, Kenneth Lyndon; HM Chief Inspector of Mines, 1992–96; *b* 13 Jan. 1938; *s* of Joseph and Sarah Ellen Twist; *m* 1959, Emily Owens; three *s*. *Educ:* Wigan and Dist Mining & Technical Coll. (Dip. Mining Engrg). Colliery Manager's Cert., 1963. FIMinE 1979. Dep. General Manager, Agecroft, 1969–76; Health and Safety Executive: Inspector of Mines, 1976–87; Principal Dist Inspector of Mines, 1987–91; Dep. Chief Inspector of Mines, 1991–92. Chm., Safety in Mines Res. Adv. Bd, HSC, 1992–96. *Publications:* papers in Mining Engineer, Jl of Instn of Mining Engrs. *Recreations:* gardening, reading, photography, computing, golf. *Address:* Ridgeway, Sunnyridge Avenue, Marford, Wrexham LL12 8TE. *T:* (01978) 855638.

TWITE, Robin, OBE 1982; Director, Environmental Program, Israel-Palestine Center for Research and Information, Jerusalem, since 1997; *b* 2 May 1932; *s* of Reginald John Twite and May Elizabeth Walker; *m* 1st, 1958, Sally Randall (marr. diss.); 2nd, 1980, Sonia Yaari; one *s* three step *d*. *Educ:* Lawrence Sheriff School, Rugby; Balliol College, Oxford (BA History 1955). Asst Editor, Schoolmaster, weekly jl of NUT, 1956–58; British Council, 1958–73: served in Israel and London as Sec., Overseas Students Fees Awards Scheme; Sec., Open Univ. of Israel, 1973–76; British Council, 1976–88: adviser on adult and further educn, 1977–79; regional rep., Calcutta, 1980–84; Controller, Books, Libraries and Inf. Div., 1984–88. Hebrew University, Jerusalem: Advr to Chm., Res. Authy, 1988–91; Develt Advr, Truman Res. Inst. for Peace, 1991–93; Dir, Conflict Resolution Project, Leonard Davis Inst. for Internat. Relns, 1994–97. *Publications:* (ed) The Future of Jerusalem, 1993; (ed) Israeli-Arab Negotiations, 1993; (ed) Our Shared Environment: environmental problems of Israel, the West Bank and Gaza, 1994. *Recreations:* travel, music making, local history. *Address:* 10 Noah Emmanuel Street, Jerusalem 93105, Israel. *T:* (2) 5665378.

TWYCROSS, Dr Robert Geoffrey, FRCP, FRCR; Macmillan Clinical Reader in Palliative Medicine, Oxford University, 1988–2001, now Emeritus; Director, palliativedrugs.com, since 2000; *b* 29 Jan. 1941; *s* of Jervis and Irene Twycross; *m* 1964, Deirdre Maeve, *d* of John Richard Campbell; two *s* three *d*. *Educ:* St John's Sch., Leatherhead; St Peter's Coll., Oxford (BA 1962; BM BCh 1965; MA 1965; DM 1977). MRCP 1969, FRCP 1980; FRCR 1996. Hosp. appts, Oxford, Lancaster, Epsom and Manchester, 1966–71; Res. Fellow, St Christopher's Hospice, London, 1971–76; Vis. MO, St Joseph's Hospice, London, 1971–76; Consultant Physician, Sir Michael Sobell House, Churchill Hosp., Oxford, 1976–2001; Fellow of St Peter's Coll., Oxford, 1987–2001, now Emeritus; Hd, WHO Collaborating Centre for Palliative Care, 1988–2005; Academic Dir, Oxford Internat. Centre for Palliative Cancer Care, 1992–2005. Visiting Professor: RSocMed of USA Foundation, 1979; Sir Ernest Finch, Sheffield, 1994; Univ. del Salvador, Buenos Aires, 1999–2005; Amrita Inst. of Med. Scis, Kochi, India, 2003–06. Mem., WHO Expert Adv. Panel on Cancer, 1985–2005. Aid and Co-operation Medal, Poland, 1993; Founder's Award, Nat. Hospice Orgn, USA, 1994; Serturner Prize, Serturner Soc., 1995; Vittorio Ventafridda Award, Internat. Assoc. for Hospice and Palliative Care, 2006; Lifetime Achievement Award: Amer. Acad. of Hospice and Palliative Medicine, 2008; Indian Assoc. for Palliative Care, 2008. *Publications:* The Dying Patient, 1975; (ed) Pain Relief in Cancer, vol. 3 No 1, 1984; A Time to Die, 1984; (ed) Edinburgh Symposium on Pain Control and Medical Education, 1989; Pain Relief in Advanced Cancer, 1994; Introducing Palliative Care, 1995, 4th edn 2003; Symptom Management in Advanced Cancer, 1995, 3rd edn (with A. Wilcock) 2001; (jtly) Palliative Care Formulary, 1998, 3rd edn 2007 (ed jtly, Italian edn 2004, German edn 2005, USA edn, as Hospice and Palliative Care Formulary, 2006, 2nd edn 2008); (ed jtly) Lymphoedema, 2000; with S. A. Lack: Symptom Control in Far-Advanced Cancer: pain relief, 1983; Therapeutics in Terminal Cancer, 1984; Oral Morphine in Advanced Cancer, 1984, (sole author) 4th edn 2007; Control of Alimentary Symptoms in Far-Advanced Cancer, 1986; Oral Morphine: information for patients, families and friends, 1987, (sole author) 2nd edn, as Morphine and the relief of cancer pain, 1999; (ed jtly) Pruritus in advanced disease, 2004; (jtly) Palliative Medicine (Chinese edn), 2005; contribs to learned jls. *Recreations:* gardening, walking, reading, theatre. *Address:* Tewsfield, Netherwoods Road, Oxford OX3 8HF; *e-mail:* robtwy@yahoo.com.

TWYFORD, Donald Henry, CB 1990; Under Secretary, Export Credits Guarantee Department, 1981–89, Director and Chairman of Project Group Board, 1986–89; *b* 4 Feb. 1931; *s* of Henry John Twyford and Lily Hilda (*née* Ridler); *m* 2006, Maria Dolores Quintero Hernández. *Educ:* Wembley County School. Joined Export Credits Guarantee Dept, 1949; Principal, 1965; seconded to Dept of Trade: Principal (Commercial Relations with East Europe), 1972–75; Asst Secretary (Country Policy), 1976; Establishment Officer, 1979–81; Under Secretary, Head of Services Group (internat. and country policy), ECGD, 1981–85; Hd of Project Underwriting Gp, 1985–89. Chairman, European Policy Co-ordination Group, 1981. President: Jávea Fest. Cttee, 2000; Jávea Internat. Civic Soc., 2001–02. Mem. Founding Cttee, Nueva Jávea party, 2006. *Recreations:* gardening, music, travel. *Address:* Cami de la Sabatera 33, Jávea 03739, Alicante, Spain.

TWYMAN, Paul Hadleigh; management consultant; Chairman, Political Strategy Ltd, since 1988; Director: Nationwide (formerly Nationwide Anglia) Building Society, 1987–2002 (Anglia Building Society, 1983–87); Connex Transport UK Ltd, 1999–2002; *s* of late Lawrence Alfred Twyman and Gladys Mary (*née* Williams). *Educ:* Leyton County High Sch.; Chatham House Sch., Ramsgate; Univ. of Sheffield (BAEcon); London Sch. of Econs and Pol Science (MScEcon). Schoolteacher, 1964; Asst Principal, BoT, 1967; Secretariat, Commn on Third London Airport, 1969; Private Sec. to Sec. of State for Trade and Industry, 1971; Dept of Industry, 1975; Anti-Dumping Unit, Dept of Trade, 1976; Asst Sec., and Head of Overseas Projects Group, Dept of Trade, 1978; Dept of Transport, 1983; Cabinet Office, 1984; Under Sec., and Dir, Enterprise and Deregulation Unit, Dept of Employment, 1985. Econ. Adviser to Chm. of Conservative Party, and Head of Econ. Section, Cons. Res. Dept, 1987. Contested (C) Greater Manchester W, European Parly elecn, 1989. Dir, D'Arcy Masius Benton & Bowles, 1990–96; Corporate Strategy Dir, Bates Dorland Ltd, later Bates UK, 1996–99. Mem., Central London LSC, 2001–. Member: Thanet Dist Police Adv. Cttee, 1989–99; Thanet DC, 1991–95. Mem., Lambeth Community Police Consultative Gp, 2003– (Hon. Comptroller, 1998–99; Vice-Chm., 1999–2001). Associate Mem., Kensington, Chelsea and Westminster HA, 1996–2002. Trustee, Opportunity Internat. (UK), 1995–2002. Gov., City of Westminster Coll., 1999–2002. Member: RIIA; Public Mgt and Policy Assoc.; FCMI; MCIT; FRSA. Member: British Pteridological Soc.; Royal African Soc. *Recreations:* family and friends, gardening, hill walking, observing gorillas. *Address:* Political Strategy Ltd, SE5 9AX.

TYACKE, Maj.-Gen. David Noel Hugh, CB 1970; OBE 1957; Controller, Army Benevolent Fund, 1971–80; *b* 18 Nov. 1915; *s* of Capt. Charles Noel Walker Tyacke (killed in action, March 1918) and late Phoebe Mary Cicely (*née* Coulthard), Cornwall; *m* 1940, Diana (*d* 2004), *d* of Aubrey Hare Duke; one *s*. *Educ:* Malvern Coll.; RMC Sandhurst. Commissioned DCLI, 1935; India, 1936–39; France and Belgium, 1939–40; India and Burma, 1943–46; Instructor, Staff Coll., Camberley, 1950–52; CO 1st Bn DCLI, 1957–59; Comdr 130 Inf. Bde (TA), 1961–63; Dir of Administrative Planning (Army), 1963–64; Brig. Gen. Staff (Ops), Min. of Defence, 1965–66; GOC Singapore Dist., 1966–70, retired. Col, The Light Infantry, 1972–77. Mem., Malvern Coll. Council, 1978–88. *Recreations:* walking, motoring, bird-watching. *Address:* c/o Lloyds TSB, Cox's & King's Branch, 7 Pall Mall, SW1Y 5NA.

See also S. J. Tyacke.

TYACKE, Sarah Jacqueline, (Mrs Nicholas Tyacke), CB 1998; FSA; FRHistS; Chief Executive, National Archives (formerly Chief Executive and Keeper of Public Records, Public Record Office), 1992–2005 and Historical Manuscripts Commissioner, 2003–05; *b* 29 Sept. 1945; *d* of late Colin Walton Jeacock and Elsie Marguerite Stanton; *m* 1971, Nicholas, *s* of Maj.-Gen. D. N. H. Tyacke, *qv*; one *d*. *Educ:* Chelmsford County High Sch.; Bedford Coll., London (BA Hons History). FSA 1985; FRHistS 1994. Asst Keeper, Map Room, BM, 1968; Dep. Map Librarian, British Liby, 1973–85; undertook govt scrutiny of BL preservation (under Efficiency Unit, Cabinet Office), 1985–86; Director of Special Collections, British Library, 1986–91. Chm., European Co-ordinating Bd, 1992–96, a Vice-Pres., 1996–2000, Internat. Council on Archives; Vice-Chm., Professional Bd, IFLA, 1987–89. Vice Pres., 1995–97 and 2002–, Trustee, 2004–, Hakluyt Soc. (Jt Hon. Sec., 1984–95; Pres., 1997–2002); a Vice-Pres., RHistS, 2000–03. Dir, Imago Mundi, 1987–; Trustee, Mappa Mundi, 1989–96; Chm. Trustees, Internat. Records Mgt Trust, 2004–. Mem. Council, RHBNC, 2003– (Hon. Fellow, 1999); Gov., London Metropolitan Univ., 2004–. Sandars Lectures, Cambridge, 2007; Leverhulme Emeritus Fellowship, 2005–07. Sen. Res. Fellow, Sch. of Advanced Study, Univ. of London, 2005–. Hon. DPhil: Guildhall, 1996; Essex, 2005; Hon. DLitt London, 2006. *Publications:* Copernicus and the New Astronomy (with H. Swiderska), 1973; (ed jtly with H. M. Wallis) My Head is a Map: essay and memoirs in honour of R. V. Tooley, 1973; London Map-Sellers 1660–1720, 1978; (with John Huddy) Christopher Saxton and Tudor map-making, 1980; (ed) English map-making 1500–1650: historical essays, 1983; Catalogue of maps, charts and plans in the Pepys Library, Magdalene College, Cambridge, 1989; contribs to archival, library and cartographic jls, incl. The Library, Imago Mundi, Cartographic Jl. *Recreations:* the sea, travel, hill-walking, painting. *Address:* 1a Spencer Rise, NW5 1AR. *Club:* Reform.

TYBULEWICZ, Albin, CPhys, FInstP; Scientific Editor, Quantum Electronics, 1994–2000; *b* Poland, 1 March 1929; *s* of Julian and Elżbieta Tybulewicz (*née* Świgost); *m* 1959, Tuliola Sylwina Bryl; one *s* one *d*. *Educ:* schools in Poland, Russia, Iran, India; St Mary's High Sch., Bombay. BSc London 1952. CPhys 1985; FInstP 1967. Research Officer, BICC, 1953–56; Asst Editor, 1956–63, Editor, 1963–67, Physics Abstracts and Current Papers in Physics; Editor: Soviet Physics—Semiconductors, 1967–92; Soviet Jl of Quantum Electronics, 1970–92; Soviet Physics—Solid State (jtly with Prof. L. Azaroff), 1982–92. Founder and Chm., Food for Poland Fund, 1980–84. Mem. Prog. Adv. Bd, Polish Satellite TV (Polonia), 1997–, Vice-Chm., 2002–. Fellow, Amer. Phys. Soc.; Hon. Fellow, Inst. of Translation and Interpreting (Mem. Council, 1986–94, 1995–2001; Vice-Chm., 1999–2001). Natthorst Non-Literary Prize, Fedn Internat. des Traducteurs, 1990; John Sykes Prize for Excellence, Inst. of Translation and Interpreting, 2007. Officer's Cross, Order of Polonia Restituta (Poland), 2006. *Publications:* American Institute of Physics Translation Manual, 1983; trans of numerous Russian physics monographs; contribs to physics and professional jls on language and translation. *Recreations:* theatre, reading, Polish community affairs in England, politics in Poland. *Address:* 2 Oak Dene, West Ealing, W13 8AW. *T:* (020) 8997 8822.

TYDEMAN, John Peter, OBE 2003; Head of BBC Radio Drama, 1986–94; *b* 30 March 1936; *s* of George Alfred Tydeman and Gladys (*née* Johnson). *Educ:* Feltonfleet; Hertford GS; Trinity Coll., Cambridge (MA). Nat. Service, 2 Lieut RA, 1954–56. Joined BBC, 1959; producer, 1962–80; Asst Head, Radio Drama, 1980–86. Dir of stage, radio and television plays. Prix Italia, 1970; Prix Futura, 1979 and 1983; Broadcasting Press Guild Award, 1983; Sony Award, 1994. *Recreations:* theatre, travel, reading, the company of friends. *Address:* Flat 7, 88 Great Titchfield Street, W1W 6SE. *T:* (020) 7636 3886. *Club:* Garrick.

TYE, Alan Peter, RDI 1986; Partner, Tye Design (formerly Alan Tye Design (Industrial & Product Designers)), since 1962; *b* 18 Sept. 1933; *s* of Chang Qing Tai and Emily Tai (*née* Thompson); *m* 1966, Anita Birgitta Göethe Tye; three *s* two *d*. *Educ:* Regent Street Polytechnic Sch. of Architecture. RIBA 1959; FCSD (FSIAD 1979). Qualified as architect, 1958; with Prof. Arne Jacobsen, Copenhagen, 1960–62; formed Alan Tye Design, 1962; incorporated HID Ltd, 1977; launched Healthy Individual Design Practice Method (HID), 1992. Mem., Selection Cttee, Council of Industrial Design, 1967; Civic Trust Award Assessor, 1968, 1969; Vis. Tutor, RCA, 1978–83, External Examr, 1987–90; Specialist Adviser on Industrial Design, CNAA, 1980; London Region Assessor, RIBA, 1981 and 1988; RSA Bursary Judge, 1983–; External Examr, Design Res. for Disability, London Guildhall Univ., 1998–2002. Convenor, Faculty of RDI, RSA, 1991–. Guest Prof., Royal Danish Acad. of Fine Arts, 1996. Internat. Design Prize, Rome, 1962; Council of Industrial Design Award, 1965, 1966, 1981; British Aluminium Design Award, 1966; 1st Prize, GAI Award, 1969; Observer (London) Design Award, 1969; Ringling Mus. of Art (Fla) Award, 1969; Gold Medal, Graphic Design, 1970; 1st Prize, GAI Award, Internat. Bldg Exhibn, 1971; British Aluminium Eros Trophy, 1973; 4 Awards for Design Excellence, Aust., 1973; Commendation for Arch., 1977; Internat. Award, Inst. of Business Designers (NY), 1982; Internat. Bldg Exhibits Top Design Award, 1983, 1985; Resources Council of America Design Award, 1987; Prince Philip Duke of Edinburgh Designer of the Year Finalist, 1993, 1999; RIBA Regl Design Award, 1995; other design awards. *Publication:* (with Dermot O'Flynn) Healthy Industrial Design, 1995. *Recreations:* tai chi, aikido. *Address:* Great West Plantation, Tring, Herts HP23 6DA. *T:* (01442) 825353.

TYLER, family name of **Baron Tyler**.

TYLER, Baron *cr* 2005 (Life Peer), of Linkinhorne in the county of Cornwall; **Paul Archer Tyler,** CBE 1985; DL; public affairs consultant; *b* 29 Oct. 1941; *s* of Oliver Walter Tyler and Ursula Grace Gibbons Tyler (*née* May); *m* 1970, Nicola Mary Ingram; one *s* one *d*. *Educ:* Mount House Sch., Tavistock; Sherborne Sch.; Exeter Coll., Oxford (MA). Pres., Oxford Univ. Liberal Club, 1962. Royal Inst. of British Architects: Admin. Asst, 1966; Asst Sec., 1967; Dep. Dir Public Affairs, 1971; Dir Public Affairs, 1972. Man. Dir, Cornwall Courier newspaper gp, 1976–81; Exec. Dir, Public Affairs Div., 1982–84, Dir, 1985–88, Good Relations plc; Chief Exec., 1984–86, Chm., 1986–87, Good Relations Public Affairs Ltd; Sen. Consultant, Good Relations Ltd, 1987–92; Dir, 1987–95, Man. Dir, 1987–92, Western Approaches Public Relns Ltd, Launceston, Cornwall. County Councillor, Devon, 1964–70; Mem., Devon and Cornwall Police Authority, 1965–70; Vice-Chm., Dartmoor Nat. Park Cttee, 1965–70; Chm., CPRE Working Party on the Future of the Village, 1974–81; Vice-President: YHA, 2000–; British Resorts & Destinations Assoc., 1998–; Mem. Bd of Shelter (Nat. Campaign for the Homeless), and rep. in Devon and Cornwall, 1975–76. Chm., Faiths and Civil Soc. Unit, Anglia Ruskin Univ., 2006–. Sec., L/SDP Jt Commn on Employment and Industrial Recovery, 1981–82. Chm., Devon and Cornwall Region Liberal Party, 1981–82; Chm., Liberal Party NEC, 1983–86. Campaign Adviser to Rt Hon. David Steel, and Mem., Alliance Campaign Planning Gp, 1986–87. Contested (L): Totnes, 1966; Bodmin, 1970, 1979; Beaconsfield, 1982; contested (Soc & Lib Dem) Cornwall and Plymouth, European Parly Election, 1989. MP: (L) Bodmin, Feb.–Sept. 1974; (Lib Dem) North Cornwall, 1992–2005. Parly Liberal spokesman on housing and transport, 1974; Parly adviser to RIBA, 1974; Lib Dem spokesman on agriculture and rural affairs, 1992–97, on transport, 1994–95, on food, 1997–99, on constitutional affairs, 2001–05; Lib Dem Chief Whip, 1997–2001; Shadow Leader of House, 1997–2005. Member: Select Cttee on Modernisation of H of C, 1997–2005; Jt Select Cttee on Parly Privilege, 1997–99, on H of L Reform, 2002–05. Lib Dem Spokesman on constitutional affairs, H of L, 2006–. Mem., Jt Select Cttee on Conventions, 2006–, on Draft Constitutional Renewal Bill, 2008. Dir, Make Votes Count, 2006–; Vice Chm., Hansard Soc., 2008–. DL Cornwall, 2005. *Publications:* A New Deal for Rural Britain (jtly), 1978; Country Lives, Country Landscapes, 1996; Parliament's Last Chance, 2003; Britain's Democratic Deficit: constitutional reform - unfinished business, 2003; (jtly) Reforming the House of Lords: breaking the deadlock, 2005. *Recreations:* sailing, gardening, walking. *Address:* House of Lords, SW1A 0PW.

TYLER, Andrew Oliver, PhD; FIMarEST, RCNC; Director General Ships, Defence Equipment and Support, Ministry of Defence, since 2007; *b* 22 June 1967; *s* of Thomas Tyler and Patricia Tyler; *m* 1995, Emma Tyler (separated); two *s* two *d*; partner, Dr Sarah Cornell. *Educ:* Univ. of Plymouth (BSc 1st cl. Hons Nautical Studies 1989; PhD Marine Sci. 1999); London Business Sch. (MBA Distn 2001). MRICS 1991; FIMarEST 2002; RCNC 2007. British Maritime Technology Group: oceanographer and marine scientist,

1989–96; Man. Dir, BMT Marine Information Systems, 1996–2001; Man. Dir, BMT Defence Services, 2001–05; Chief Exec., BMT Defence, 2005–06; Dir Land and Maritime, Defence Procurement Agency, 2006–07. *Publications:* several papers in field of marine pollution sci. *Recreations:* skating, windsurfing, running (for waist control), progressive/heavy rock and ecclesiastical choral music, bass guitar, hill walking, supporting England's great test cricket team. *Address:* c/o Defence Equipment and Support, Ministry of Defence, Abbeywood, Bristol BS34 8JH.

TYLER, Anne; writer; *b* 25 Oct. 1941; *d* of Lloyd Parry Tyler and Phyllis Mahon Tyler (*née* Mahon); *m* 1963, Taghi M. Modarressi, MD (*d* 1997); two *d. Educ:* Duke Univ. (BA). Mem., AAIL. AAIL Award for Literature, 1977; Nat. Book Critics Circle Award for fiction, 1985. *Publications:* If Morning Ever Comes, 1964; The Tin Can Tree, 1965; A Slipping Down Life, 1970; The Clock Winder, 1972; Celestial Navigation, 1974; Searching for Caleb, 1976; Earthly Possessions, 1977; Morgan's Passing, 1980; Dinner at the Homesick Restaurant, 1982; The Accidental Tourist, 1985; Breathing Lessons, 1988 (Pulitzer Prize for fiction, 1989); Saint Maybe, 1991; Tumble Tower (for children), 1993; Ladder of Years, 1995; A Patchwork Planet, 1998; Back When We Were Grownups, 2001; The Amateur Marriage, 2004; Timothy Tugbottom Says No (for children), 2005; Digging to America, 2006. *Address:* 8 Roland Green, Baltimore, MD 21210, USA.

TYLER, Maj.-Gen. Christopher, CB 1989; Secretary, Royal Humane Society, 1995–2004; *b* 9 July 1934; *s* of Maj.-Gen. Sir Leslie Tyler, KBE, CB, and late Louie Teresa Tyler (*née* Franklin); *m* 1958, Suzanne, *d* of late Eileen Whitcomb and Patrick Whitcomb; one *s* three *d. Educ:* Beaumont College; RMA Sandhurst; Trinity Coll., Cambridge (MA). Commissioned REME, 1954; served UK and BAOR, 1959–65; Army Staff Course, 1966–67; Weapons Staff, 1968–70 and 1972–74; CO 1st Parachute Logistic Regt, 1974–76; MoD, 1976–80; Chief Aircraft Engineer, Army Air Corps, 1980–82; DEME (Management Services), Logistic Exec., 1982–83; Comd Maint., HQ 1 (BR) Corps, 1983–85; Dep. Comdt, RMCS, 1985–87; DCOS (Support), HQ Allied Forces N Europe, 1987–89. Resident Gov. and Keeper of the Jewel House, HM Tower of London, 1989–94. Col Comdt, REME, 1989–94; Hon. Col, REME (V), 1994–2000. External Mem. of Council, Parachute Regt, 1993–98; Trustee: Tower Hill Trust (formerly Tower Hill Improvement Trust), 1990–; Ulysses Trust, 1992–94. Governor: St Mary's Sch., Ascot, 1995–2003; St John's, Beaumont, 1996–2007. Liveryman, Turners' Co., 1979– (Master, 2000–01). *Recreation:* Rugby football (RFU Panel Referee, 1957–59 and 1967–73 and Chm., Army and Combined Services, 1985–86). *Address:* Oak Cottage, Stratfield Saye, Reading, Berks RG7 2EB. *T:* (0118) 933 2562. *Club:* Hawks (Cambridge).
See also Maj.-Gen. T. N. Tyler.

TYLER, David Alan; Chairman, Logica plc, since 2007; *b* Woking, 23 Jan. 1953; *s* of Alan and Jill Tyler; *m* 1977, Sharon Lantin; one *s* one *d. Educ:* Trinity Hall, Cambridge (BA Econs 1974). FCMA 1983; MCT 1991. Unilever plc, 1974–86; County NatWest Ltd, 1986–89; Finance Director: Christie's International plc, 1989–96; GUS plc, 1997–2007. Chm., 3i Quoted Private Equity Ltd, 2007–; non-executive Director: Burberry Gp plc, 2002–; Experian plc, 2006–; Reckitt Benckiser Gp plc, 2007–. *Recreations:* enjoying barn in Sussex, family, friends, current affairs, theatre, jogging, listening to music, washing up. *Address:* Logica plc, Stephenson House, 75 Hampstead Road, NW1 2PL.

TYLER, Ian Paul; Chief Executive, Balfour Beatty plc, since 2005; *b* 7 July 1960; *s* of Ray and Peggy Tyler; *m* Janet; two *d. Educ:* Univ. of Birmingham (BCom). ACA. Arthur Andersen & Co., 1982–88; Gp Treas./Financial Controller, Storehouse Plc, 1988–91; Financial Comptroller, Hanson Plc, 1991–93; Finance Dir, ARC Ltd, 1993–96; Finance Dir, 1996–2002, Chief Operating Officer, 2002–05, Balfour Beatty plc. *Recreations:* private pilot, keeping fit. *Address:* Balfour Beatty plc, 130 Wilton Road, SW1V 1LQ. *T:* (020) 7216 6815; *e-mail:* ian.tyler@balfourbeatty.com.

TYLER, Ven. Leonard George; Rector of St Michael and St Mary Magdalene, Easthampstead, 1973–85, retired; *b* 15 April 1920; *s* of Hugh Horstead Tyler and Mabel Adam Stewart Tyler; *m* 1946, Sylvia May Wilson; one *s* two *d. Educ:* Darwen Grammar School; Liverpool University; Christ's College, Cambridge; Westcott House. Chaplain, Trinity College, Kandy, Ceylon, 1946–48; Principal, Diocesan Divinity School, Colombo, Ceylon, 1948–50; Rector, Christ Church, Bradford, Manchester, 1950–55; Vicar of Leigh, Lancs, 1955–66 (Rural Dean, 1955–62); Chaplain, Leigh Infirmary, 1955–66; Archdeacon of Rochdale, 1962–66; Principal, William Temple College, Manchester, 1966–73. Anglican Adviser to ABC Television, 1958–68. *Publications:* contributor to Theology. *Address:* 11 Ashton Place, Kintbury, Hungerford, Berks RG17 9XS. *T:* (01488) 658510.

TYLER, Prof. Lorraine Komisarjevsky, PhD; FBA 1995; MRC Professor of Cognitive Neuroscience, University of Cambridge, since 1998, and Director (formerly Co-Director), Centre for Speech, Language and the Brain, since 1990; Fellow, Clare College, Cambridge, since 2000; *b* 11 Jan. 1945; *d* of James and Anne Komisarjevsky; *m* 1982, William D. Marslen-Wilson, *qv*; one *s* one *d. Educ:* Leicester Univ. (BA); Chicago Univ. (PhD 1977). Sen. Res. Fellow, Max Planck Inst. for Psycholinguistics, 1977–85; Lectr, Dept of Psychology, Cambridge Univ., 1985–90; Prof. of Psychology, Birkbeck Coll., Univ. of London, 1990–98. *Publications:* Spoken Language Comprehension, 1992; contrib. Brain and Lang., Jl of Memory and Lang., Psychological Rev., Cognition, etc. *Address:* Department of Experimental Psychology, University of Cambridge, Downing Street, Cambridge CB2 3EB. *T:* (01223) 766457.

TYLER, Maj.-Gen. Timothy Nicholas, CB 2008; Director General Land Equipment, 2007–08; *b* 15 Dec. 1953; *s* of Maj.-Gen. Sir Leslie Norman Tyler, KBE, CB and late Sheila Tyler; *m* 1976, Johanna Lee Weston; three *s* six *d. Educ:* Worth Sch.; Christ's Coll., Cambridge (MA 1979). Commnd REME, 1972; Commander: Equipment Support, 1st Armoured Div., 1992–93; REME Trng Gp, 1997–99; Director: Army Staff Duties, 1999–2001; Army Resources and Plans, 2001–02; rcds 2002; COS HQ Adjt Gen., 2003; Dep. Adjt Gen., 2004–05; Quartermaster Gen., 2006–07; Dir Gen. Logistics (Land), 2006–07. Asst Col Comdt, AGC, 2004–05; Colonel Commandant: REME, 2005–; Corps of Army Music, 2005–. *Recreations:* singing, sailing, ponies. *Club:* Army and Navy.
See also Maj.-Gen. C. Tyler.

TYMKEWYCZ, Stefan; Member (SNP) Edinburgh City Council, since 2007; *b* 18 Sept. 1959; *s* of Bohdan and Jean Tymkewycz. *Educ:* St David's Primary and Secondary Schs, Dalkeith; Esk Valley Coll., Dalkeith. Apprentice engr, 1976–80; traveller, 1980–84; Metropolitan Police Officer, 1984–2001; property landlord, 2001–07. MSP (SNP) Lothians, May–Aug. 2007. *Recreations:* travelling, keeping fit, cycling, theatre and cinema, hill walking, football (season ticket holder at Hibernian FC), Scrabble. *Address:* City of Edinburgh Council, City Chambers, High Street, Edinburgh EH1 1YJ; *e-mail:* stef.tymkewycz@snp.org.

TYNAN, Prof. Michael John, MD, FRCP; Professor of Paediatric Cardiology, Guy's Hospital, 1982–99; *b* 18 April 1934; *s* of late Jerry Joseph Tynan and Florence Ann Tynan; *m* 1958, Eirlys Pugh Williams. *Educ:* Bedford Modern School; London Hospital. MD, BS. Senior Asst Resident, Children's Hosp., Boston, Mass, 1962; Registrar, Westminster Hosp., 1964; Registrar, later Lectr, Hosp. for Sick Children, Great Ormond St, 1966; consultant paediatric cardiologist, Newcastle Univ. Hospitals, 1971, Guy's Hosp., 1977. *Publications:* (jtly) Paediatric Cardiology, a textbook, vol. 5, 1983; articles on nomenclature and classification of congenital heart disease and on heart disease in children. *Recreations:* singing, watching cricket, playing snooker. *Address:* 5 Ravensdon Street, SE11 4AQ. *T:* (020) 7735 7119. *Clubs:* Athenæum; Borth and Ynyslas Golf.

TYNAN, William; part-time researcher for John Robertson, MP; *b* 18 Aug. 1940; *s* of late James and Mary Tynan; *m* 1964, Elizabeth Mathieson; three *d. Educ:* St Joseph's Sch.; St Mungo's Acad.; Stow Coll. Press toolmaker, 1961–88. Joined AEU (subseq. AEEU), 1966: shop steward and convener, 1966; Member: Mid Lanark Dist Cttee, 1969; Divl Cttee, 1976; Nat. Cttee, 1977–88; full-time Union Official, 1988–99: Dist Sec., 1988–96; Regl Officer, 1996–99; Political Officer, 1991; Scottish Political Sec., 1993. MP (Lab) Hamilton South, Sept. 1999–2005. Member: Parly Select Cttee on NI, 2001–05; European Scrutiny Cttee, 2001–05; Convenor, Scottish Gp of MPs, 2001–02; Special Advr, All Party Parly Gp on Nuclear Energy (Chm., 2001–05). Joined Labour Party, 1969: Mem. Exec. and Gen. Mgt Cttee, Hamilton N and Hamilton S Constituency Parties, 1979–2005; Chm., Hamilton S CLP, 1987; Member: Scottish Labour Policy Forum, 1998; Scottish Exec., 1982–88. Nat. Coordinator, Trade Unions for Safe Nuclear Energy. Bd Mem., SoLVE, S Lanarkshire. *Recreations:* golf, swimming, gardening, DIY. *Address:* 6 East Scott Terrace, Hamilton, ML3 6SF. *T:* (01698) 421660.

TYNDALL, Rev. Canon Timothy; Chief Secretary, Advisory Council for the Church's Ministry, 1985–90; *b* 24 April 1925; *s* of Rev. Denis Tyndall and Nora Tyndall; *m* 1953, Dr Ruth Mary Turner (*d* 1998); two *s* twin *d. Educ:* Jesus Coll., Cambridge (BA). Parish Incumbent: Newark, 1955; Nottingham, 1960; Sunderland, 1975. *Address:* 29 Kingswood Road, Chiswick, W4 5EU. *T:* (020) 8994 4516.

TYRE, Colin Jack; QC (Scot.) 1998; Commissioner (part-time), Scottish Law Commission, since 2003; *b* 17 April 1956; *s* of James Harrison Tyre and Lilias Carmichael Tyre (*née* Kincaid); *m* 1982, Elaine Patricia Carlin; one *s* two *d. Educ:* Dunoon Grammar Sch.; Univ. of Edinburgh (LLB Hons); Université d'Aix-Marseille (DESU). Admitted Solicitor, 1980; admitted to Faculty of Advocates, 1987. Lectr in Law, Univ. of Edinburgh, 1980–83; Tax Editor, CCH Editions Ltd, 1983–86; Standing Junior Counsel: MoD (PE), 1991–95; Scottish Office Envmt Dept (in planning matters), 1995–98. Pres., CCBE, 2007 (Co-Chm., Deontology Cttee, 2003–04; Hd, UK Delegn, 2004). *Publications:* CCH Inheritance Tax Reporter, 1986; (jtly) Tax for Litigation Lawyers, 2000; contrib. Stair Memorial Encyclopaedia, learned jls. *Recreations:* mountain walking, golf, orienteering, music (especially popular). *Address:* Advocates' Library, Parliament House, Edinburgh EH1 1RF. *T:* (0131) 226 5071.

TYREE, Sir (Alfred) William, Kt 1975; OBE 1971; electrical engineer, chief executive and chairman; *b* Auckland, NZ, 4 Nov. 1921; *s* of J. V. Tyree and A. Hezeltine (who migrated to Australia, 1938); *m* 1946, Joyce (decd), *d* of F. Lyndon; two *s* one *d. Educ:* Auckland Grammar School; Sydney Technical Coll. (Dip. in Elec. Engrg). FIE (Aust) 1968 (Peter Nicol Russell Mem. Award 1985); FIEE 1983. Founded Tyree Industries Ltd and Westralian Transformers and subsids, 1956; Founder, Tyree Hldgs gp of companies incl.: Tytronics Pty Ltd (formerly Technical Components Pty Ltd); Tycan Australia Pty Ltd; Tyree Holdings Pty Ltd; A. W. Tyree Transformers Pty Ltd, subseq. Tyree Transformers (Aust.) Pty Ltd; Wirex Pty Ltd; A. W. Tyree Foundation. Mem., Aust. Inst. of Co. Dirs; Emeritus Councillor, Australian Industry Gp, 2001. Founder and Dir, Sir William Tyree Foundn of the Australian Industry Gp. Hon. Fellow, Univ. of Sydney, 1985; Hon. Life Governor, Aust. Postgrad. Fedn in Medicine, 1985. Hon. DSc Univ. of NSW, 1986; Hon. DEng Sydney, 2008. James N. Kirby Medal, IProdE, Australia, 1980; IEEE USA Centennial Medal, 1984; Award of Merit, Aust. Nat. Cttee, CIGRE, 2000; Centenary Medal, Australia, 2003. *Recreations:* ski-ing, photography, yachting, tennis, music, computers. *Address:* (home) 3 Lindsay Avenue, Darling Point, NSW. *Clubs:* American National (NSW); Royal Prince Alfred Yacht, Royal Motor Yacht, Cruising Yacht, Kosciusko Alpine, Australian Golf.

TYRELL-KENYON; *see* Kenyon.

TYRER, Christopher John Meese; His Honour Judge Tyrer; a Circuit Judge, since 1989; Resident Judge, Aylesbury Crown Court, since 2005; *b* 22 May 1944; *s* of late Jack Meese Tyrer and of Margaret Joan Tyrer (*née* Wyatt); *m* 1974, Jane Beckett, JP, LLB, MA, barrister; one *s* one *d. Educ:* Wellington College; Bristol University. LLB hons. Called to the Bar, Inner Temple, 1968. Asst Recorder, 1979–83; a Recorder, 1983–89; Designated Family Judge, 1991–97, 1998–2005. Governor: St John's Sch., Lacey Green, 1984–92; Speen Sch., 1984–96 (Chm., 1989–91 and 1995–96); Misbourne Sch., 1993–2007 (Vice Chm., 1995–2000, Chm., 2000–07). Mem., Bucks Assoc. of Govs of Primary Schs, 1989–90. Patron, Law Soc., Buckinghamshire Univ. (formerly Buckinghamshire Chilterns University Coll.), 2002–. *Publication:* (ed) Clarke Hall and Morrison on Children, 2003–. *Recreations:* music, boating, following Wycombe Wanderers Football Club. *Address:* Randalls Cottage, Loosley Row, Princes Risborough, Bucks HP27 0NU. *T:* (01844) 344650; Aylesbury Crown Court, County Hall, Market Square, Aylesbury, Bucks HP20 1XD. *T:* (01296) 434401.

TYRER, Prof. Peter Julian, MD; Professor of Community Psychiatry, Imperial College of Science, Technology and Medicine, since 1991; *b* 13 Aug. 1940; *s* (identical twin) of Frank Herbert Tyrer and Mary (May) Jane Tyrer; *m* 1967, Ann Anderson (marr. diss. 2003); one *s* two *d. Educ:* King Edward Sch., Birmingham; Gonville and Caius Coll., Cambridge (BA 1962; MB, BChir 1966; MD 1975); St Thomas's Hosp. Med. Sch., London. FRCPsych 1979; FRCP 1993; FFPH (FFPHM 1999). House Officer in Psychological Medicine, St Thomas' Hosp., 1966–67; Sen. House Officer in Medicine, Burton-on-Trent Gen. Hosp., 1967–68; Registrar in Psychiatry: St John's Hosp., Aylesbury, 1968–69; Maudsley Hosp., 1969–70; MRC Clin. Res. Fellow, 1970–73; Sen. Lectr in Psychiatry, Univ. of Southampton, 1973–79; Cons. Psychiatrist, Mapperley Hosp., Nottingham, 1979–88; Sen. Lectr in Community Psychiatry, St Mary's Hosp. Med. Sch., 1988–91; Hd, Dept of Public Mental Health, 1997–2002, Dept of Psychol Medicine, 2002–05, ICSTM. Andrew Woods Prof., Univ. of Iowa, 1986. Milroy Lectr, RCP, 2007. Ed., British Jl of Psychiatry, 2003–. European Pres., Internat. Soc. for Study of Personality Disorders, 1995–98; Co-Chm., Sect. on Personality Disorders, World Psychiatric Assoc., 2002–. FMedSci 1999. Gaskell Bronze Medal and Res. Prize, RCPsych, 1973. *Publications:* The Role of Bodily Feelings in Anxiety, 1976; Insomnia, 1978; Stress, 1980, 2nd edn 2003; (ed) Drugs in Psychiatric Practice, 1982, 2nd edn 1997; How to Stop Taking Tranquillisers, 1986; (with D. Steinberg) Models for Mental Disorder, 1987, 4th edn 2005; Personality Disorders: diagnosis, management and course,

1988, 2nd edn 2000; (ed) Psychopharmacology of Anxiety, 1989; Classification of Neurosis, 1989; (with C. Freeman) Research Methodology in Psychiatry: a beginner's guide, 1989, 3rd edn 2006; (with B. Puri) Sciences Basic to Psychiatry, 1992, 2nd edn 1998; (with P. Casey) Social Function in Psychiatry: the hidden axis of classification exposed, 1993; Anxiety: a multidisciplinary review, 1999; (with K. Silk) Cambridge Textbook of Effective Treatments in Psychiatry, 2008. *Recreations:* jousting with social workers, anthropophytomorphy, doggerel. *Address:* 52 West Park Avenue, Kew Gardens, Surrey TW9 4AL. *T:* (020) 8876 7996.

TYRIE, Andrew Guy; MP (C) Chichester, since 1997; *b* 15 Jan. 1957; *s* of late Derek and of Patricia Tyrie. *Educ:* Felsted Sch.; Trinity Coll., Oxford (MA); Coll. of Europe, Bruges; Wolfson Coll., Cambridge (MPhil). BP, 1981–83; Cons. Res. Dept, 1983–84; Special Adviser: to Sec. of State for the Envmt, 1985; to Minister for Arts, 1985–86; to Chancellor of the Exchequer, 1986–90; Fellow, Nuffield Coll., Oxford, 1990–91; Woodrow Wilson Scholar, Washington, 1991; Sen. Economist, EBRD, 1992–97. Contested (C) Houghton and Washington, 1992. Opposition front bench spokesman, economic affairs, 2003–05. Member: Select Cttee on Public Admin, 1997–2001; Treasury Select Cttee, 2001–03; Constitutional Affairs Select Cttee, 2005–; Public Accounts Commn, 1997–; Exec. Cttee, 1922 Cttee, 2005–06. *Publications:* The Prospects for Public Spending, 1996; Sense on EMU, 1998; Reforming the Lords, 1998; Leviathan at Large, 2000; Mr Blair's Poodle, 2000; (jtly) Statism by Stealth, 2002; Mr Blair's Poodle Goes to War, 2004; many pamphlets. *Recreation:* golf. *Address:* House of Commons, SW1A 0AA. *Clubs:* Garrick, MCC, Royal Automobile.

TYRIE, Peter Robert; Managing Director, Eton Group, since 1999; *b* 3 April 1946; *m* 1972, Christine Mary Tyrie; three *s* (and one *d* decd). *Educ:* Westminster College Hotel Sch. (BSc Hotel Admin). Manager, Inverurie Hotel, Bermuda, 1969–71; Resident Man., Portman Hotel, London, 1971–73; Project Dir, Pannell Kerr Forster, 1973–77; Operations Dir, Penta Hotels, 1977–80; Managing Director: Gleneagles Hotels plc, 1980–86; Mandarin Oriental Hotel Gp, 1986–89; Balmoral Internat. Hotels, 1989–98. Director: Bell's Whisky, 1983; Dragon Trust, Edinburgh Fund Managers, 1989–. FIH (FHCIMA 1977). *Recreations:* squash, shooting, fishing, Rugby, classic cars. *Address:* Eton Group, 5 Threadneedle Street, EC2R 8AY. *T:* (020) 7657 8160.

TYRONE, Earl of; Henry Nicholas de la Poer Beresford; *b* 23 March 1958; *s* and heir of 8th Marquess of Waterford, *qv*; *m* 1986, Amanda, *d* of Norman Thompson; two *s* one *d*. *Educ:* Harrow School. *Heir:* *s* Baron Le Poer, *qv*. *Address:* Church Farm House, Hawkesbury, Badminton, Glos GL9 1BN.

TYROR, John George, OBE 1999; JP; Director of Safety, United Kingdom Atomic Energy Authority, 1990–92, retired; *b* 5 Nov. 1930; *s* of John Thomas Tyror and Nora Tyror (*née* Tennant); *m* 1956, Sheila Wylie; one *s* one *d*. *Educ:* Manchester Univ. (BSc 1st cl. Hons Maths, MSc); Trinity Hall, Cambridge. FInstP. Asst Lectr, Univ. of Leeds, 1955–56; AEA Harwell, 1956–59; Atomic Energy Estabt, Winfrith, 1959–63; Reactor Develt Lab., Windscale, 1963–66; Winfrith, 1966–87 (Asst Dir, 1979–87); Dir, Safety and Reliability Directorate, Culcheth, 1987–90. Member: Eur./Amer. Cttee on Reactor Physics, 1960–72; Adv. Cttee for Transport of Radioactive Materials, 1981–84; Adv. Cttee on Safety of Nuclear Installations, HSC, 1992–95; Nuclear Safety Adv. Cttee, HSC, 1995–98. Chm., Compensation Scheme for Radiation-Linked Diseases, 2001–07. Mem., Manchester Literary and Philos. Soc., 2001–. JP Poole, 1976, Macclesfield, 1988. *Publication:* An Introduction to the Neutron Kinetics of Nuclear Power Reactors, 1970. *Recreations:* bridge, food and wine, antique map collecting, grandfather. *Clubs:* Lancashire CC, Knutsford Golf.

TYRRELL, Alan Rupert; QC 1976; a Recorder of the Crown Court, 1972–98; a Deputy High Court Judge, 1990–98; Barrister-at-Law; *b* 27 June 1933; *s* of Rev. T. G. R. Tyrrell, and Mrs W. A. Tyrrell, MSc; *m* 1960, Elaine Eleanor Ware, LLB; one *s* one *d*. *Educ:* Bridport Grammar Sch.; London Univ. (LLB). Called to the Bar, Gray's Inn, 1956, Bencher, 1986. Mem., Criminal Injuries Compensation Bd, 1999–2000 (Mem., Appeal Panel, 2000–08). Chm. of the Bar Eur. Gp, 1986–88; Chm. of the Internat. Practice Cttee, Bar Council (co-opted to Bar Council), 1988. Lord Chancellor's Legal Visitor, 1990–; Arbitrator, Internat. Chamber of Commerce, Paris, 1999–2006. Dir, Papworth Hosp. NHS Trust, 1993–2000. Council Mem., Med. Protection Soc., 1990–98. Chm. London Reg., and Mem. Nat. Exec., Nat. Fedn of Self-Employed, 1978–79 (Chm., Employment Law Policy Unit, 2002–). Mem. (C) London E, European Parlt, 1979–84; contested same seat, 1984, 1989. FCIArb 1993–2006. *Publications:* (ed) Moore's Practical Agreements, 10th edn 1965; Students' Guide to Europe, 1984; The Legal Professions in the New Europe, 1992, 2nd edn 1996; Public Procurement in Europe: enforcement and remedies, 1997. *Recreation:* bridge. *Address:* 15 Willifield Way, Hampstead Garden Suburb, NW11 7XU. *T:* (020) 8455 5798; Tanfield Chambers, 2–5 Warwick Court, WC1R 5DJ. *T:* (020) 7421 5300; *e-mail:* alantyrrell@ntlworld.com. *Club:* Athenæum.

TYRRELL, Prof. (Henry John) Valentine, FRSC; Vice-Principal, King's College London (KQC), 1985–87, retired; *b* 14 Feb. 1920; *s* of John Rice Tyrrell and Josephine (*née* McGuinness); *m* 1st, 1947, Sheila Mabel (*née* Straw) (*d* 1985); two *s* three *d* (and one *s* decd); 2nd, 1986, Dr Bethan Davies. *Educ:* state schools; Jesus Coll., Oxford. DSc. Chemical Industry, 1942–47; Sheffield Univ., 1947–65; Chelsea College: Professor of Physical and Inorganic Chemistry, 1965–84; Head of Dept, 1972–82; Vice-Principal, 1976–84; Principal, 1984–85. Royal Institution of Great Britain: Sec., 1978–84; Vice-Pres., 1978–84, 1987–89, 1991–94; Chm. Council, 1987–89. *Publications:* Diffusion and Heat Flow in Liquids, 1961; Thermometric Titrimetry, 1968; Diffusion in Liquids, 1984; papers in chemical and physical jls. *Recreations:* foreign travel, gardening. *Address:* 5 Chapel Lane, Wilmslow, Cheshire SK9 5HZ. *Clubs:* Athenæum, Royal Institution.

TYRRELL, Prof. John, DPhil; Professor, School of Music, Cardiff University, 2003–08 (Professorial Research Fellow in Music, 2000–03); *b* Salisbury, Southern Rhodesia, 17 Aug. 1942; *s* of Henry John Ranger Tyrrell and Florence Ellen Tyrrell (*née* Wright). *Educ:* St John's Coll., Johannesburg; Univ. of Cape Town (BMus); Lincoln Coll., Oxford (DPhil 1969). Associate Ed., Musical Times, 1972–76; Desk Ed., Grove's Dictionary of Music, 1973–76; University of Nottingham: Lectr in Music, 1976–89; Reader in Opera Studies, 1989–96; Prof., 1996–97; Exec. Ed., The New Grove Dictionary of Music and Musicians, 1997–2000 (Dep. Ed., 1996–97). British Acad. Res. Reader in the Humanities, 1992–94. Chm., Music Libraries Trust, 1999–2005. Dr *hc* Masaryk Univ., 2002. *Publications:* (with R. Wise) A Guide to International Congress Reports in Music 1900–1975, 1979; Leoš Janáček: Kát'a Kabanová, 1982; Czech Opera, 1988 (Czech trans. 1992); Janáček's Operas: a documentary account, 1992; (ed and trans.) Intimate Letters: Leoš Janáček to Kamila Stösslová, 1994; (ed with Charles Mackerras) Janáček's Jenůfa, 1996; (jtly) Janáček's Works: a catalogue of the music and writings of Leoš Janáček, 1997; (ed and trans.) Zdenka Janáčková: my life with Janáček, 1998; Janáček: years of a life: Vol.

1, The Lonely Blackbird, 2006, Vol. 2, Tsar of the Forests, 2007. *Recreations:* gardening, walking.

TYRRELL, Robert James; Principal, Bob Tyrrell and Co., since 2000; Chairman, Demos, 2002–06 (Member, Advisory Council, since 1992); *b* 6 June 1951; *s* of Peter John Tyrrell and Mair (*née* Harries); *m* 1983, Jean Linda McKerrow; two *d*. *Educ:* St Peter's Coll., Oxford (MA, PPE), LSE (MSc Phil with dist.). Academic research, Sussex and Glasgow Univs, 1972–74; joined James Morrell & Associates, 1974; Perkins Engines, 1977; Futures Group, USA, 1980; Man. Dir, 1986–92, Chief Exec., 1992–95, Exec. Chm., 1995–96, Henley Centre for Forecasting. Develt Partner, Cognosis Strategy Consultants, 1999–2003. Chairman: Internat. Res. Inst. on Social Change, Paris, 1999–2000; Global Future Forum Europe, 2001–03. Vis. Prof., City Univ. Business Sch., 1994–2001. Director: New Solutions, 1997–2000; La Table du Pain, Luxembourg, 1999–; Sociovision, Paris, 2000–03; SMC Gp plc, 2005–; Chm., Sociovision, UK, 2001–03. Member: Steering Cttee, Econ. Beliefs and Behaviour Prog., ESRC, 1994–99; Council, Conservative Party Policy Forum, 1999–2002. Assoc. Mem., BUPA, 2004–. Trustee and Dir, Golden Oldies, 2007–. Presenter: Opinions, C4, 1994; Analysis, BBC Radio, 1997–. FRSA. *Publications:* (ed jtly) Britain in the 1980s, 1974; (ed jtly) Britain 2001, 1977; (ed jtly) Planning for Social Change, 1991; Things Can Only Get... Different, 2001. *Recreations:* fishing, ski-ing, guitar, theatre, tennis, reading, family, holistic thinking. *Address:* Warberry Lodge, Lansdown Road, Bath BA1 5RB.

TYRRELL, Valentine; *see* Tyrrell, H. J. V.

TYRWHITT, Sir Reginald (Thomas Newman), 3rd Bt *cr* 1919; *b* 21 Feb. 1947; *er s* of Admiral Sir St John Tyrwhitt, 2nd Bt, KCB, DSO, DSC and Bar (*d* 1961), and of Nancy (Veronica) Gilbey (who *m* 1965, Sir Godfrey Agnew, KCVO, CB); S father, 1961; *m* 1972, Sheila Gail (marr. diss. 1980 and annulled 1984), *d* of William Alistair Crawford Nicoll, Liphook, Hants; *m* 1984, Charlotte, *o d* of late Captain and the Hon. Mrs Angus Hildyard, Goxhill Hall, Goxhill, N Lincs; one *s* one *d*. *Educ:* Downside. Served in RA 1966–69. Career spent subseq. in UK paper industry. *Recreations:* shooting, fishing, drawing. *Heir:* *s* Robert St John Hildyard Tyrwhitt, *b* 15 Feb. 1987.

TYSOE, John Sidney; Chairman, Yorkshire Electricity Group, 1992–94; *b* 14 March 1932; *s* of Florence Alice Tysoe (*née* Gypps) and late Sidney George Tysoe; *m* 1953, Ann Dunham; two *s* one *d*. *Educ:* Harrow Weald County Grammar Sch.; City of London Coll. FCCA, CPFA, FIET. Nat. Service Commn, RN, 1950–52. Exchequer and Audit Dept, 1953–65; Southern Electricity Bd, 1966–67; Head, Special Investigations and Asst Management Accountant, BR, 1967–68; Asst and Dep. Financial Advr, Electricity Council, 1969–77; Chief Accountant and Financial Dir, Southern Electricity Bd, 1978–85; Dep. Chm., Yorkshire Electricity Bd, 1985–89; Gp Man. Dir, Yorkshire Electricity Gp, 1989–92. Mem. Council, CBI, 1993–94. *Recreations:* walking, woodcarving, theatre.

TYSON, Prof. Laura D'Andrea, PhD; Dean of London Business School, 2002–06; Professor of Economics and Business Administration, Haas School of Business, University of California at Berkeley; *b* 28 June 1947; *m* Erik Tarloff; one *s*. *Educ:* Smith Coll. (BA 1969); MIT (PhD 1974). Asst Prof., Dept of Econs, Princeton Univ., 1974–77; University of California, Berkeley: Prof. of Econs, 1977–2002; Prof., 1990–2002, Dean, 1998–2002, Haas Sch. of Business; Dir, Inst. of Internat. Studies, 1990–92; Dir of Res., Berkeley Roundtable on Internat. Economy, 1988–92; Dist. Teaching Award, 1982. Chairman: US President's Council of Econ. Advrs, 1993–95; Nat. Econ. Council, 1995–96; Principal, Law and Econs Consulting Gp, 1997–2000; Mem., Council on Foreign Relations, 1997–. Member Board: Eastman Kodak Co., 1997–; Morgan Stanley Co., 1998–; SBC Communications, 1999–; Bruegel, 2005–. Columnist, Business Week. Fellow, Nat. Fellows Prog., Hoover Inst., 1978–79. *Publications:* The Yugoslav Economic System and its Performance in the 1970s, 1980; (ed with Egon Neuberger) The Impact of External Economic Disturbances on the Soviet Union and Eastern Europe, 1980; (ed with John Zysman) American Industry in International Competition: political and economic perspectives, 1983; Economic Adjustment in Eastern Europe, 1984; (ed with Ellen Comisso) Power, Purpose and Collective Choice: economic strategy in socialist states, 1986; (ed with William T. Dickens and John Zysman) The Politics of Productivity: the real story of why Japan works, 1989; Who's Bashing Whom? trade conflict in high technology industries, 1992; articles in professional jls. *Address:* Haas School of Business, 545 Student Services #1900, University of California at Berkeley, Berkeley, CA 94720–1900, USA.

TYSON, Monica Elizabeth; Editor, A La Carte, 1986–87, retired; *b* 7 June 1927; *d* of F. S. Hill and E. Hill; *m* 1st, 1950, P. M. Lyon (marr. diss. 1958); one *d*; 2nd, 1960, R. E. D. Tyson. *Educ:* George Watson's Ladies Coll.; Edinburgh Coll. of Domestic Science. Asst Home Editor, Modern Woman, 1958–60; Ideal Home: Domestic Planning Editor, 1960–64; Asst Editor, 1964–68; Editor, 1968–77; Editor: Woman's Realm, 1977–82; Special Assignments, IPC Magazines, 1982–84; Mother, 1984–86. *Recreations:* travelling, reading. *Address:* Ramsgate, Kent.

TYSZKIEWICZ, Zygmunt Jan Ansgary, CMG 1998; President, Lanckoronski Foundation, since 1996; *b* 4 Feb. 1934; *s* of Count Jan Michal Tyszkiewicz and Anna Maria Tyszkiewicz (*née* Princess Radziwill); *m* 1958, Kerstin Barbro Ekman; two *s* two *d*. *Educ:* Downside Sch.; Sidney Sussex Coll., Cambridge (BA Hons Mod. and Medieval Langs). Officer, XII Royal Lancers, 1956–57. Joined Shell International Petroleum, 1957: Man. Dir, Shell-BP Tanzania, 1970–73; Gen. Manager, Shell Hellas, 1979–85; Sec. Gen., UNICE, Brussels, 1985–98. Member: Bd, Eur. Foundn for Mgt Develt, Brussels, 1985–98; Adv. Council, Involvement and Participation Assoc., London, 1998–. Gov., Eur. Policy Forum, London, 1998–. Hon. DBA Robert Gordon Univ., 2000. KM 1994; Grand Cross ad Merito Melitensi, SMO Malta, 2002; Kt, Order of Dannebrog (Denmark), 1997; Comdr, Order of Leopold (Belgium), 1998. *Publications:* contrib. numerous articles on European and business issues in UK and European jls. *Recreations:* family holidays in Corfu, Greece, politics of European integration. *Address:* 5 Champneys Walk, Cambridge CB3 9AW. *T:* (01223) 302816, *Fax:* (01223) 368596; *e-mail:* zygtysz@zen.co.uk; (May–Sept.) Kouloura, 49083 Corfu, Greece. *T:* (26630) 91662, *Fax:* (26630) 91663. *Clubs:* Cavalry and Guards; Cercle Royal Gaulois Artistique et Littéraire (Brussels).

TYTE, David Christopher, CB 1997; PhD; Director Rationalisation, Defence Evaluation and Research Agency, Ministry of Defence, 1991–97; *b* 19 Aug. 1937. *Educ:* Dulwich Coll.; Imperial Coll., London (PhD, BSc). CEng, FInstP, MIET. NRC Post Doctoral Fellow, Univ. of Western Ontario, 1962–65; Asst Prof., York Univ., Toronto, 1965–67; joined MoD, 1967; Dep. Dir (Underwater), Admiralty Res. Estabt, 1987–89; Technical Dir, DRA, 1989–91.

TYZACK, David Ian Heslop; QC 1999; **His Honour Judge Tyzack;** a Circuit Judge, since 2000; *b* 21 March 1946; *s* of late Ernest Rudolf Tyzack and Joan Mary Tyzack (*née* Palmer); *m* 1973, Elizabeth Anne Cubitt; one *s* one *d*. *Educ:* Allhallows Sch., Rousdon; St

Catharine's Coll., Cambridge (MA 1969). Called to the Bar, Inner Temple, 1970, Bencher, 2007; in practice at the Bar, Western Circuit, 1971–2000; Asst Recorder, 1996–2000; Recorder, 2000; a Dep. High Ct Judge, 2000–; Designated Family Judge: Plymouth, 2003–; Exeter, 2005–. Chm., Devon and Cornwall Br., Family Law Bar Assoc., 1992–2000. Mem., Devonshire Assoc. Churchwarden, Farringdon Ch, Devon, 1992–. *Publication:* (contrib.) Essential Family Practice, 2001. *Recreations:* gardening, house in France, ski-ing, church. *Address:* Southernhay Chambers, 33 Southernhay East, Exeter EX1 1NX. *T:* (01392) 255777, *Fax:* (01392) 412021.

TYZACK, Margaret Maud, OBE 1970; actress; *b* 9 Sept. 1931; *d* of Thomas Edward Tyzack and Doris Moseley; *m* 1958, Alan Stephenson; one *s. Educ:* St Angela's Ursuline Convent; Royal Academy of Dramatic Art. Trained at RADA (Gilbert Prize for Comedy). First engagement, Civic Theatre, Chesterfield. Vassilissa in The Lower Depths, Royal Shakespeare Co., Arts Theatre, 1962; Lady MacBeth, Nottingham, 1962; Miss Frost in The Ginger Man, Royal Court, London, 1964; Madame Ranevsky in The Cherry Orchard, Exeter and Tour, 1969; Jacqui in Find Your Way Home, Open Space Theatre, London, 1970; Queen Elizabeth in Vivat! Vivat Regina!, Piccadilly, 1971; Tamora in Titus Andronicus, Portia in Julius Caesar and Volumnia in Coriolanus, Royal Shakespeare Co., Stratford-on-Avon, 1972; Portia in Julius Caesar, and Volumnia in Coriolanus, RSC, Aldwych, 1973; Maria Lvovna in Summerfolk, RSC, Aldwych, and NY, 1974–75;

Richard III, All's Well That Ends Well, Ghosts, Stratford, Ont., 1977; People Are Living There, Manchester Royal Exchange, 1979; Martha, in Who's Afraid of Virginia Woolf?, Nat. Theatre, 1981 (Best Actress, Olivier Award); Countess of Rousillon, in All's Well That Ends Well, RSC Barbican and NY, 1983; An Inspector Calls, Greenwich, 1983; Tom and Viv, Royal Court, 1984, also New York, 1985; Mornings at Seven, Westminster, 1984; Night Must Fall, Greenwich, 1986; Lettice and Lovage, Globe, 1987 (Variety Club of GB Award for Best Stage Actress), and New York, 1990 (Tony award); The Importance of Being Earnest, Aldwych, 1993; An Inspector Calls, Aldwych, 1994; Indian Ink, Aldwych, 1995; Talking Heads, Chichester, 1996, Comedy, 1996–97, Australian tour, 2004; The Family Reunion, RSC, 1999; Tartuffe, NT, 2002; Auntie and Me, Wyndham's, 2003; His Girl Friday, NT, 2003; As You Desire Me, Playhouse, 2005; Southwark Fair, NT, 2006; The Boy Friend, The Park, 2007; The Chalk Garden, Donmar, 2008. *Films:* Ring of Spies, 2001: A Space Odyssey, The Whisperers, A Clockwork Orange, The Legacy, The King's Whore, Match Point. *Television series include:* The Forsyte Saga; The First Churchills; Cousin Bette, 1970–71; I, Claudius, 1976; Quatermass, 1979; The Winter's Tale; Young Indiana Jones, 1992. Actress of the Year Award (BAFTA) for Queen Anne in The First Churchills, 1969. *Address:* c/o Markham & Froggatt, 4 Windmill Street, W1T 2HZ. *T:* (020) 7636 4412, *Fax:* (020) 7637 5233.

U

UCHIDA, Mitsuko, CBE 2001; pianist; *b* 20 Dec. 1948; *d* of Fujio and Yasuko Uchida. *Educ:* Hochschule für Musik, Vienna. First recital at age of 14 in Vienna; performs regularly with orchestras worldwide incl. Berlin Philharmonic, Vienna Philharmonic, Cleveland, etc.; performed complete Mozart piano sonatas in London, 1982, Tokyo, 1983, and NY, 1991; Schubert and Schoenberg recitals in Salzburg, London, Vienna, NY, Tokyo, etc, 1994–96; repertoire ranges from J. S. Bach to Messiaen. Co-Dir, Marlboro Music Fest., Vermont, USA, 2000–; Founder Mem., Borletti-Buitoni Trust, 2003–. Mem., American Philosophical Soc. Recordings include: complete piano sonatas and concertos of Mozart; Beethoven's piano concertos; Debussy's Etudes; Schumann's Carnaval; Schoenberg piano concerto; Beethoven's last five piano sonatas. Has won many prizes for recordings. *Recreations:* sleeping, listening to music. *Address:* c/o Victoria Rowsell Artist Management, 34 Addington Square, SE5 7LB. *T:* (020) 7701 3219; *e-mail:* management@victoriarowsell.co.uk.

UDALL, Jan; *see* Beaney, J.

UDDIN, family name of **Baroness Uddin**.

UDDIN, Baroness *cr* 1998 (Life Peer), of Bethnal Green in the London Borough of Tower Hamlets; **Pola Manzila Uddin;** *b* Bangladesh, 17 July 1959; *m* 1976, Komar Uddin; four *s* one *d*. Youth and Community Worker, YWCA, 1980–82; Liaison Officer, Tower Hamlets Social Services, 1982–84; Manager: Women's Health Project, 1984–88; Asian Family Counselling Service, 1989–90; Social Worker, Manager and subseq. Mgt Consultant, London Borough of Newham Social Services, 1993–98. Mem. (Lab), Tower Hamlets LBC, 1990–98 (Dep. Leader, Lab Gp, 1993–94; Dep. Leader, Council, 1994–96). House of Lords: former Chairman: Home Office Wkg Gp; Wkg Gp on Pol and Community Leadership; European Select Cttee; former Mem., Community Cohesion Panel. Non-exec. Dir, Carlton TV (Chm., London Licensing Bd). Member: CPA; IPU; former Mem., CETSW. Patron: Bethnal Green and Victoria Park Housing Assoc.; Orbis International; Tower Hamlets Women's Aid; Royal Coll. of Speech and Language Therapy; Disability Trust; Attlee Foundn; Social Action for Health. *Address:* House of Lords, SW1A 0PW. *T:* (020) 7219 8506; *e-mail:* Khanmw@parliament.uk; *web:* www.baronessuddin.com.

UDEN, Martin David; HM Diplomatic Service; Ambassador to South Korea, since 2008; *b* 28 Feb. 1955; *s* of late Rodney Frederick Uden and Margaret Irene Uden (*née* Brunt); *m* 1982, Fiona Jane Smith; two *s*. *Educ:* Ravensbourne Sch. for Boys; Queen Mary Coll., London Univ. (LLB). Called to the Bar, Inner Temple, 1977; joined FCO, 1977; Second Sec., Seoul, 1978–81; Second, later First Sec., FCO, 1981–86; First Sec., Bonn, 1986–90; FCO, 1990–93; Dep. Head, CSCE Unit, FCO, 1993–94; Pol Counsellor and Consul-Gen., Seoul, 1994–97; Econ., then Trade/Econ., Counsellor, Ottawa, 1997–2001; Internat. Dir, Invest-UK, 2001–03; Consul-Gen., San Francisco, 2003–07. *Publications:* (with T. Bennett) Korea: caught in time, 1997; Times Past in Korea, 2003. *Address:* c/o Foreign and Commonwealth Office, King Charles Street, SW1A 2AH.

UDRE, Ingrida; former Speaker of the Saeima, Latvia; *b* 14 Nov. 1958; *m* Gordon Latimir; two *s*. *Educ:* Univ. of Latvia (BEc 1984; MEc 1996). Chartered Acct, 1993. Sen. Audit Manager, Coopers & Lybrand, subseq. PricewaterhouseCoopers, Latvia, 1993–98. MP (Union of Greens and Farmers), Latvia, 1998–2004; Minister of Economy, 1999; Mem., EC, 2004.

UFF, Prof. John Francis, CBE 2002; QC; PhD; FREng, FICE; FCIArb; international arbitrator, advocate and engineer; Nash Professor of Engineering Law, University of London, 1991–2003, now Emeritus Professor; a Recorder, 1998–2005; *b* 30 Jan. 1942; *s* of Frederick and Eva Uff; *m* 1967, Diana Muriel Graveson; two *s* one *d*. *Educ:* Stratton Sch.; King's College London (BSc (Eng), PhD; FKC 1997). Asst engineer, Rendel Palmer & Tritton, 1966–70; Vis. Lectr in civil engineering, 1963–68; called to the Bar, Gray's Inn, 1970, Bencher, 1993; practice at Bar, Keating Chambers, 1970–, Head of Chambers, 1992–97; Asst Recorder, 1993–98; a Dep. Judge, Technology and Construction Court, 1999–2005. Dir, Centre of Construction Law and Management, KCL, 1987–99; arbitrator in construction disputes; lectr to professional bodies in engineering law and arbitration. Vice-Pres., London Court of Internat. Arbitration, 2003–08. Member: Standing Cttee on Structural Safety, 1984–90; Bldg Users Insurance against Latent Defects Cttee, DoE, 1986–88; Adv. Cttee on arbitration law, DTI, 1993–95. Chairman: Indep. Commn of Inquiry into Yorks Water, 1996; Public Inquiry into Southall Rail Accident, 1997–99; Jt Chm., Public Inquiry into Rail Safety Systems, 1999–2000. Mem. Council, ICE, 1982–85; President: Engrg Section, BAAS, 2003–04; Soc. of Construction Arbitrators, 2004–07; Bar Music Soc., 2008–. Vice-Pres., KCL Assoc., 1993–95. FREng (FEng 1995). Prin. Ed., book series of Centre of Construction Law and Mgt, KCL, on construction law, management, environment law and dispute resolution, 1988–. President's Medal, Soc. Construction Law, 2000; Gold Medal, ICE, 2002. *Publications:* Construction Law, 1974, 9th edn 2005; (contrib.) Keating on Building Contracts, 4th edn 1978 to 8th edn 2006; (jtly) ICE Arbitration Practice, 1986; (jtly) Methods of Procurement in Ground Investigation, 1986; (principal draftsman) Construction Industry Model Arbitration Rules, 1998; (contrib.) Chitty on Contracts, 28th edn 1999, 29th edn 2005; technical papers in civil engineering; papers and articles in engineering law and procedure. *Recreations:* playing with violins, painting, farming. *Address:* 15 Essex Street, WC2R 3AU. *T:* (020) 7544 2600; Pale Farm, Chipperfield, Herts WD4 9BH. *Clubs:* Athenæum, Ronnie Scott's.

UFFEN, Kenneth James, CMG 1977; HM Diplomatic Service, retired; Ambassador and UK Permanent Representative to OECD, Paris, 1982–85; *b* 29 Sept. 1925; *s* of late Percival James Uffen, MBE, former Civil Servant, and late Gladys Ethel James; *m* 1954, Nancy Elizabeth Winbolt; one *s* two *d*. *Educ:* Latymer Upper Sch.; St Catharine's Coll., Cambridge. HM Forces (Flt-Lt, RAFVR), 1943–48; St Catharine's Coll., 1948–50; 3rd Sec., FO, 1950–52; Paris, 1952–55; 2nd Sec., Buenos Aires, 1955–58; 1st Sec., FO, 1958–61; 1st Sec. (Commercial), Moscow, 1961–63; seconded to HM Treasury, 1963–65; FCO, 1965–68; Counsellor, Mexico City, 1968–70; Economic Counsellor, Washington, 1970–72; Commercial Counsellor, Moscow, 1972–76; Res. Associate, IISS, 1976–77; Ambassador to Colombia, 1977–82. *Recreations:* music, gardens. *Address:* 40 Winchester Road, Walton-on-Thames, Surrey KT12 2RH.

UGANDA, Archbishop of, since 2003; **Most Rev. Henry Luke Orombi;** Bishop of Kampala, since 2003; *b* 11 Oct. 1949; *s* of Luka Jalobo and Susan Jalobo; *m* 1972, Phoebe Orombi; two *s* one *d* (and one *d* decd). *Educ:* St John's Coll., Nottingham (BTh 1983). Ordained 1979; Diocesan Youth Pastor, Madi/W Nile, 1979–86; Archdeacon, Goli, 1987–93; Bishop of Nebbi, 1993–2003. *Recreations:* music, walking. *Address:* PO Box 14123, Kampala, Uganda. *T:* (41) 270218, *Fax:* (41) 251925; *e-mail:* Orombih@Yahoo.com.

UIST, Hon. Lord; Roderick Francis Macdonald; a Senator of the College of Justice in Scotland, since 2006; *b* 1 Feb. 1951; *s* of late Finlay Macdonald and Catherine Maclean. *Educ:* St Mungo's Acad., Glasgow; Glasgow Univ. (LLB Hons). Admitted advocate, 1975; Advocate-Depute (Crown Counsel), 1987–93; QC (Scot.) 1988; Home Advocate-Depute (Sen. Crown Counsel), 1990–93; called to the Bar, Inner Temple, 1997. Legal Chm., Pension Appeal Tribunals for Scotland, 1995–2001; Member: Criminal Injuries Compensation Bd, 1995–2000; Criminal Injuries Compensation Appeals Panel, 1997–99. *Recreations:* walking, France. *Address:* Court of Session, Parliament House, Edinburgh EH1 1RQ. *T:* (0131) 225 2595.

ULLENDORFF, Prof. Edward, MA Jerusalem, DPhil Oxford; FBA 1965; Professor of Semitic Languages, School of Oriental and African Studies, University of London, 1979–82, now Professor Emeritus (Professor of Ethiopian Studies, 1964–79; Head of Africa Department, 1972–77); *b* 25 Jan. 1920; *s* of late Frederic and Cilli Ullendorff; *m* 1943, Dina Noack. *Educ:* Gymnasium Graues Kloster; Universities of Jerusalem and Oxford. Chief Examiner, British Censorship, Eritrea, 1942–43; Editor, African Publ., British Ministry of Information, Eritrea-Ethiopia, 1943–45; Assistant Political Secretary, British Military Admin, Eritrea, 1945–46; Asst Secretary, Palestine Government, 1947–48; Research Officer and Librarian, Oxford Univ. Inst. of Colonial Studies, 1948–49; Scarbrough Senior Research Studentship in Oriental Languages, 1949–50; Reader (Lectr, 1950–56) in Semitic Languages, St Andrews Univ., 1956–59; Professor of Semitic Languages and Literatures, University of Manchester, 1959–64. Carnegie Travelling Fellow to Ethiopia, 1958; Research Journeys to Ethiopia, 1964, 1966, 1969, etc. Catalogued Ethiopian Manuscripts in Royal Library, Windsor Castle. Chairman: Assoc. of British Orientalists, 1963–64; Anglo-Ethiopian Soc., 1965–68 (Vice-Pres. 1969–77); Pres., Soc. for Old Testament Study, 1971; Vice-Pres., RAS, 1975–79, 1981–85. Joint Organizer, 2nd Internat. Congress of Ethiopian Studies, Manchester, 1963. Chm., Editorial Bd, Bulletin of SOAS, 1968–78; Mem., Adv. Bd, British Library, 1975–83. Vice-Pres., British Acad., 1980–82; Schweich Lectr, British Acad., 1967. FRAS; Hon. Fellow: SOAS, 1985–; Oxford Centre for Hebrew Studies, 1998–; Foreign Fellow, Accademia Lincei, Rome, 1998–. MA Manchester, 1962; Hon. DLitt St Andrews, 1972; Hon. Dr Phil Hamburg, 1990. Imperial Ethiopian Gold Medallion, 1960; Haile Sellassie Internat. Prize for Ethiopian studies, 1972; Festschriften to EU 1989, 2005. *Publications:* The definite article in the Semitic languages, 1941; Exploration and Study of Abyssinia, 1945; Catalogue of Ethiopian Manuscripts in the Bodleian Library, Oxford, 1951; The Semitic Languages of Ethiopia, 1955; The Ethiopians, 1959, 3rd edn 1973; (with Stephen Wright) Catalogue of Ethiopian MSS in Cambridge University Library, 1961; Comparative Semitics in Linguistica Semitica, 1961; (with S. Moscati and others) Introduction to Comparative Grammar of Semitic Languages, 1964; An Amharic Chrestomathy, 1965, 2nd edn 1978; The Challenge of Amharic, 1965; Ethiopia and the Bible, 1968; (with J. B. Pritchard and others) Solomon and Sheba, 1974; trans. and annotated, Emperor Haile Sellassie, My Life and Ethiopia's Progress (autobiog.), 1976; Studies in Semitic Languages and Civilizations, 1977; (with M. A. Knibb) Book of Enoch, 1978; The Bawdy Bible, 1979; (jtly) The Amharic Letters of Emperor Theodore of Ethiopia to Queen Victoria, 1979; (with C. F. Beckingham) The Hebrew Letters of Prester John, 1982; A Tigrinya Chrestomathy, 1985; Studia Aethiopica et Semitica, 1987; The Two Zions, 1988; From the Bible to Enrico Cerulli, 1990; H. J. Polotsky (1905–1991), 1992; From Emperor Haile Sellassie to H. J. Polotsky, 1995; Joint Editor of Studies in honour of G. R. Driver, 1962; Joint Editor of Ethiopian Studies, 1964; articles and reviews in journals of learned societies; contribs to Encyclopaedia Britannica, Encyclopaedia of Islam, DNB, etc; Joint Editor, Journal of Semitic Studies, 1961–64. *Recreation:* music. *Address:* 4 Bladon Close, Oxford OX2 8AD.

ULLMANN, (Frederick) Ralph, MA; JP; Headmaster, Wellingborough School, 1993–2004; *b* 29 July 1945; *s* of late Prof. Walter Ullmann, FBA and Elizabeth Ullmann (*née* Knapp); *m* 1980, Alison Kemp; two *s* one *d*. *Educ:* Trinity Coll., Cambridge (schol.; MA; PGCE). FCollP (ACP). History Teacher, and Head of Gen. Studies, Bishop's Stortford Coll., 1968–72; Head of History and Sen. Housemaster, Bloxham Sch., 1972–85; Headmaster, Ruthin Sch., 1986–93. Member: ASCL (formerly SHA), 1986– (Mem. Council, 1997–); HMC, 1993–2004 (Member: Community Service Cttee, 1995–2001; Professional Develt Cttee, 1997–2004; Cttee, 1998–99; Sec., 1998, Chm., 1999, Midland Div.); Gen. Teaching Council, 2001– (Initial Teacher Trng Cttee, 2001–03; Audit Monitoring and Review Cttee, 2001–07; Professional Develt Adv. Cttee, 2003–04; Co-ordinating Cttee, 2006–07; Exec. Cttee, 2007–; Chm., Policy Services Gp, 2004–07). Founding Dir, Bd, Castle Theatre and Arts Centre, Wellingborough, 1994–98.

Mem. Adv. Bd, 2000–04, Chm., 2004–, Rudolf Kempe Soc. JP Leics. *Recreations:* photography, music, wine. *Address:* 7 School Lane, Braybrooke, Market Harborough LE16 8LS. *Club:* East India.

ULLMANN, Liv (Johanne); actress; *b* Tokyo, 16 Dec. 1938; *d* of late Viggo Ullmann and of Janna (*née* Lund), Norway; *m* 1st, 1960, Dr Gappe Stang (marr. diss. 1965); 2nd, 1985, Donald Saunders. *Educ:* Norway; London (dramatic trng). Stage début, The Diary of Anne Frank (title role), Stavanger, 1956; major roles, National Theatre and Norwegian State Theatre, Oslo; Amer. stage début, A Doll's House, New York Shakespeare Festival, 1974–75; Anna Christie, USA, 1977; The Bear, La Voix humaine, Australia, 1978; I Remember Mama, USA, and Ghosts (Ibsen), Broadway, 1979; British theatre début, Old Times, Guildford, 1985. Wrote and dir. short film, Parting, 1981. Twelve hon. doctorates, including Brown, Smith Coll., Tufts and Haifa. *Films:* Pan, 1965; The Night Visitor, 1971; Pope Joan, 1972; The Emigrants, 1972 (Golden Globe Award); The New Land, 1973 (Best Actress, Nat. Soc. of Film Critics, USA); Lost Horizon, 1973; 40 Carats, 1973 (Golden Globe Award); Zandy's Bride, 1973; The Abdication, 1974; The Wild Duck, 1983; The Bay Boy, 1985; Let's Hope it's a Girl, 1987; Mosca Addio, 1987; Time of Indifference, 1987; La Amiga, 1987; The Ox, 1993; *director:* Sophie, 1993; Kristin Lavrandsdatter (also wrote screenplay), 1995; Private Confessions, 1996; Faithless, 2000; (*dir. by Ingmar Bergman*): Persona, 1966; The Hour of the Wolf, 1968 (Best Actress, Nat. Soc. of Film Critics, USA); Shame, 1968 (Best Actress, Nat. Soc. of Film Critics, USA); The Passion of Anna, 1969; Cries and Whispers, 1972; Scenes from a Marriage, 1974; Face to Face, 1976; The Serpent's Egg, 1977; The Autumn Sonata, 1978 (5 NY Film Critics awards); Saraband, 2005. Goodwill Ambassador, UNICEF, 1980–; Vice Pres., Internat. Rescue Cttee. Peer Gynt Award, Norway (1st female recipient). Commander, Order of St Olav (Norway), 1994. *Publications:* (autobiog.) Changing, 1977; Choices, 1984.

ULLMANN, Ralph; *see* Ullmann, F. R.

ULLRICH, Kay Morrison; Member (SNP) West of Scotland, Scottish Parliament, 1999–2003; *b* 5 May 1943; *d* of John Dallas Morrison and Charlotte McMillan Morrison (*née* Neil); *m* 1st, 1964, Andrew Jofre (marr. diss.); one *s* one *d*; 2nd, 1976, Grady Ullrich. *Educ:* Ayr Acad.; Queen's Coll., Glasgow (CQSW). Schools swimming instructor, N Ayrshire, 1973–81; sch. social worker, 1984–86, hosp. social worker, 1986–92, Strathclyde; sen. court social worker, E Ayrshire, 1992–97. Scottish Parliament: Spokesperson on health and community care, 1999–2000; SNP Chief Whip, 2000–03; Mem., Standards and Equal Opportunities Cttees, 2000–03. Vice-Pres., SNP, 1997–99. Contested (SNP): Cunninghame S, 1983 and 1987; Motherwell S, 1992; Monklands E, June 1994. *Recreations:* swimming, travel, meeting friends. *Address:* Tulsa, Montgomeryfield, Dreghorn, Irvine KA11 4HB. *T:* (01294) 213331.

ULLSTEIN, Augustus Rupert Patrick Anthony; QC 1992; a Recorder, since 1999; *b* 21 March 1947; *s* of late Frederick Charles Leopold Ullstein and Patricia (*née* Guinness); *m* 1970, Pamela Margaret Wells; two *s* two *d*. *Educ:* Bradfield Coll., Berks; LSE (LLB Hons). Called to the Bar, Inner Temple, 1970, Bencher, 2006; in practice as barrister, 1970–; an Asst Recorder, 1993–99. Liveryman, Bowyers' Co., 1980– (Mem. Court, 2004–). *Publications:* (Supervising Editor) Pelling and Purdie, Matrimonial Injunctions, 1982; Compensation for Personal Injury in England, Germany and Italy, 2005. *Recreations:* my children, after dinner speaking. *Address:* 39 Essex Street, WC2R 3AT. *T:* (020) 7832 1111.

ULLSWATER, 2nd Viscount *cr* 1921, of Campsea Ashe, Suffolk; **Nicholas James Christopher Lowther,** LVO 2002; PC 1994; Private Secretary, Comptroller and Equerry to Princess Margaret, Countess of Snowdon, 1998–2002; *b* 9 Jan. 1942; *s* of Lieut John Arthur Lowther, MVO, RNVR (*d* 1942), and Priscilla Violet (*d* 1945), *yr d* of Reginald Everitt Lambert; *S* great-grandfather, 1949; *m* 1967, Susan, *d* of James Howard Weatherby; two *s* two *d*. *Educ:* Eton; Trinity Coll., Cambridge. Captain, Royal Wessex Yeomanry, T&AVR, 1973–78. A Lord in Waiting (Govt Whip), H of L, 1989–90; Parly Under-Sec. of State, Dept of Employment, 1990–93; Capt. of Corps of Gentlemen at Arms (Govt Chief Whip), H of L, 1993–94; Minister of State (Minister for Construction and Planning), DoE, 1994–95; elected Mem., H of L, 2003. *Heir: s* Hon. Benjamin James Lowther, *b* 26 Nov. 1975. *Address:* The Old Rectory, Docking, King's Lynn, Norfolk PE31 8LJ. *T:* (01485) 518822.

ULPH, Prof. David Tregear; Professor of Economics and Head, School of Economics and Finance, University of St Andrews, since 2006; *b* 26 Oct. 1946; *s* of Cyril Ulph and late Myra Ulph; *m* 1971, Elizabeth Mackie; two *d*. *Educ:* Univ. of Glasgow (MA); Balliol Coll., Oxford (BLitt). Lectr in Econs, Univ. of Stirling, 1971–78; Lectr, then Reader in Econs, UCL, 1978–84; Professor of Economics: Univ. of Bristol, 1984–92; UCL, 1992–2001; Chief Economist and Dir, Analysis and Res., subseq. Analysis, HM Inland Revenue, then HMRC, 2001–06. FRSA 2001. *Publications:* over 60 articles in refereed jls and books. *Recreations:* bridge, cinema, travel. *Address:* School of Economics and Finance, The Scores, University of St Andrews, St Andrews, Fife KY16 9AL. *T:* (01334) 462420.

ULRICH, Walter Otto; Deputy Secretary, Department of Education and Science, 1977–87; *b* 1 April 1927. Ministry of Works: Asst Principal, 1951; Principal, 1955; Treasury 1958–60; Principal Private Sec. to Minister of Public Building and Works, 1963–65; Asst Sec., 1965; Min. of Housing and Local Govt, 1966; DoE, 1970; Under-Sec., 1972; Cabinet Office, 1974–76. *Address:* 46 Grinstead Lane, Lancing, W Sussex BN15 9DZ. *T:* (01903) 762169.

ULSTER, Earl of; Alexander Patrick Gregers Richard Windsor; *b* 24 Oct. 1974; *s* of HRH The Duke of Gloucester and HRH The Duchess of Gloucester; *m* 2002, Dr Claire Alexandra, *d* of Mr and Mrs Robert Booth; one *s*. *Educ:* Eton Coll.; King's Coll., London Univ. (BA War Studies 1996); RMA, Sandhurst. Commnd King's Royal Hussars, 1998. *Heir: s* Xan Richard Anders Windsor, Lord Culloden, *b* 12 March 2007.

See under Royal Family.

UNDERHILL, Prof. Allan Edward, PhD, DSc; CChem, FRSC; Professor of Inorganic Chemistry, University College of North Wales, then University of Wales, Bangor, 1983–99, now Emeritus; *b* 13 Dec. 1935; *s* of Albert Edward Underhill and Winifred Underhill (*née* Bailey); *m* 1960, Audrey Jean Foster; one *s* one *d*. *Educ:* Univ. of Hull (BSc 1958; PhD 1962); DSc Wales 1983. Res. Chemist, ICI Ltd, 1961–62; Lectr, Loughborough CAT, 1962–65; University College of North Wales (Bangor): Lectr, 1965–74; Sen. Lectr, 1974–83; Dean, Faculty of Sci., 1985–87, 1994–95; Pro-Vice-Chancellor, 1995–99. *Publications:* over 250 res. papers in RSC jls, Nature, etc. *Recreations:* theatre, bridge, walking, photography.

UNDERHILL, Prof. Michael James, PhD; FREng; Professor of Electronics, University of Surrey, 1992; *b* 22 March 1939; *s* of Gp Capt. (retd) Rev. Wilfrid Underhill, DSC and Barbara Nowell Underhill (*née* James); *m* 1977, Gillian Brown; two *s*. *Educ:* St John's Sch., Leatherhead; Oriel Coll., Oxford (Schol.; Bible Schol.; Capt. of Boats, 1959–60; BA Physics 1960; MA); Univ. of Surrey (PhD Electronics 1972). FIET (FIEE 1982); FREng (FEng 1982). Philips Res. Labs (formerly Mullard Res. Labs), 1960–84 (Head of Systems Div., 1982–84); Tech. Dir, MEL (Philips), 1984–90; Engrg Dir, Thorn EMI Sensors Div., 1990–91; Head of Dept, Electronic and Electrical Engrg, 1992–96, Dean of Engrg, 1996–97, Univ. of Surrey (Vis. Lectr on Systems Engrg, 1968–82; Vis. Prof., 1984–90). Chm., European Frequency and Time Forum, 1996. Member: NATS Res. Adv. Council, 1996–99; Defence Science Adv. Council, 1982–96 (Chm., various bds and cttees). Institution of Electrical Engineers, subseq. of Engineering and Technology: Mem. Council, 1992–2007; Chm., Electronics Div., 1993–94; Chm., Surrey Centre, 1996–97; P. Perring Thoms Award, 1981; J. J. Thomson Award, 1993. Parish Councillor, Rusper, 1977–83. FRSA 1992. *Publications:* 48 patents; 60 papers on frequency control, phase noise, radio and other electronic systems. *Recreations:* licensed radio amateur since 1956, amateur dramatics (Trustee and Pres., Ifield Barn Theatre Club), jazz piano, hack and bash gardening. *Address:* Department of Electronic Engineering, University of Surrey, Guildford, Surrey GU2 7XH. *T:* (01483) 879134.

UNDERHILL, Hon. Sir Nicholas Edward, Kt 2006; **Hon. Mr Justice Underhill;** a Judge of the High Court of Justice, Queen's Bench Division, since 2006; *b* 12 May 1952; *s* of late Judge Underhill, QC and Rosalie Jean Underhill (who *m* 1989, William Anderson Beaumont, *qv*); *m* 1987, Nina Grunfeld; two *s* two *d*. *Educ:* Winchester Coll.; New Coll., Oxford (MA Hons). Called to the Bar, Gray's Inn, 1976, Bencher, 2000. QC 1992; a Recorder, 1994–2006; Attorney Gen. to the Prince of Wales, 1998–2006; a Dep. High Court Judge, 1998–2006; a Judge of the Employment Appeal Tribunal, 2000–03. Chm., Bar Pro Bono Unit, 2002–05. *Publication:* The Lord Chancellor, 1978. *Address:* Royal Courts of Justice, Strand, WC2A 2LL.

UNDERWOOD, Ashley Grenville; QC 2001; *b* 28 Dec. 1953; *s* of Dennis William Underwood and Brenda Margarita Underwood; *m* 1982, Heather Kay Leggett; one *d*. *Educ:* London Sch. of Econs (LLB Hons). Called to the Bar, Gray's Inn, 1976; Hd of Chambers, 1999–2006. *Recreations:* motorcycling, classic cars, conversation. *Address:* Landmark Chambers, 180 Fleet Street, EC4A 2HG.

UNDERWOOD, Sir James (Cresseé Elphinstone), Kt 2005; MD; FRCP, FRCPath, FMedSci; Joseph Hunter Professor of Pathology, University of Sheffield, 1984–2006, now Emeritus Professor (Dean, Faculty of Medicine, 2006); *b* 11 April 1942; *s* of John and Mary Underwood; *m* 1st, 1966 (marr. diss. 1986); one *s* one *d*; 2nd, 1989, Alice Cameron Underwood; one *s*. *Educ:* Downside Sch.; St Bartholomew's Hosp. Med. Coll. (MB BS 1965; MD 1973). MRCS, LRCP 1965; MRCPath 1972, FRCPath 1984; FRCP 2004; FRCPI 2004. SHO, then Registrar in Pathology, St Bartholomew's Hosp., London, 1966–69; University of Sheffield: Lectr in Pathology, 1969–73; Sen. Lectr, 1974–82; Reader, 1983. MRC Clinical Res. Fellow, Chester Beatty Res. Inst., London, 1973–74; Wellcome-Ramaciotti Res. Fellow, Univ. of Melbourne, 1981. Consultant Histopathologist, Sheffield AHA(T), subseq. Central Sheffield Univ. Hosps NHS Trust, later Sheffield Teaching Hosps NHS Foundn Trust, 1974–2006; Hon. Civilian Consultant Histopathologist, RAF, 2002–. President: RCPath, 2002–05 (Vice-Pres., 1999–2002); British Div., Internat. Acad. Pathology, 2000–02. Ed., Histopathology, 1995–2002. FMedSci 2005. Hon. Member: Japanese Soc. Pathology, 1996; Hungarian Soc. Pathologists, 1996. Hon. FCPath: Hong Kong, 2001; S Africa, 2006. Cunningham Medal, British Div., Internat. Acad. of Pathology, 2005. *Publications:* Introduction to Biopsy Interpretation and Surgical Pathology, 1981, 2nd edn 1987; General and Systematic Pathology, 1992, 5th edn 2009; papers on tumour pathology, chronic liver disease and the autopsy. *Recreations:* music, art, photography, walking. *Address:* 258 Fulwood Road, Sheffield S10 3BL. *Club:* Athenæum.

UNDERWOOD, John Morris; Director, Freshwater Group, since 2006; *b* 8 Nov. 1953; *s* of John Edward Underwood and Ella Lillian Morris Underwood; *m* 1987, Susan Clare Inglish; two *s*. *Educ:* Univ. of Sheffield (BSc Hons); University Coll., Cardiff (Graduate Dip. in Journalism). BBC trainee journalist, 1976–78; regional TV reporter, 1978–80; TV reporter, ITN, 1980–82; home affairs corresp., ITN, 1982–83; freelance TV producer and presenter, 1983–89; Exec. Producer, House of Commons Cttee TV, 1989–90; Dir of Campaigns and Communications, Labour Party, 1990–91; Partner, subseq. Dir, Clear Communication, 1991–2006. Mem., Mgt Bd, Catalyst think tank, 1998–2005 (Chm., 2001–05). Hon. Prof., Univ. of Glasgow, 2006–. Editor, New Century, 1993–95. *Publication:* The Will to Win: John Egan and Jaguar, 1989. *Recreations:* theatre, walking. *Address:* 10 Percival Road, SW14 7QE. *T:* (020) 8876 8884.

UNDERWOOD, Hon. Peter George, AO 2002; Governor of Tasmania, since 2008; *b* 10 Oct. 1937; *s* of George Underwood; *m* 1st, 1965 (marr. diss. 1980); one *s* two *d*; 2nd, 1981, Frances, *d* of Col V. P. Northam; one *s*. *Educ:* Launceston High Sch.; Univ. of Tasmania (LLB 1960). Admitted to Bar, Supreme Ct of Tasmania, 1960; legal practitioner, 1960 and 1962–63; Partner, Murdoch Clarke Cosgrove & Drake, 1963–84; Supreme Court of Tasmania: Judge, 1984–2004; Chief Justice, 2004–08; Lieut Gov., Tasmania, 2005–08. Member: Tasmania Law Reform Commn, 1977–84; Supreme Ct Rules Cttee, 1981–84; Tasmania Racing Appeal Bd, 1983–84; Chm., Council of Law Reporting Tasmania, 1988–2005; Mem., 1996–98, Dep. Chm., 1998–, Defence Force Discipline Appeal Tribunal. Member: Bar Assoc. of Tasmania, 1964–74; Legal Assistance Cttee, 1964–67; Tasmanian Law Council, 1969–73; Law Soc. Disciplinary Cttee, 1980–84. Pres., Aust. Inst. of Judicial Admin, 2002–04; Chm., Nat. Judicial Coll. of Australia, 2007–. Dir, Nat. Heart Foundn, 1970–83; Mem., Tasmanian Arts Adv. Bd, 1981–84; Chairman: Bd, Tasmanian Theatre Trust, 1984; Tasmanian Symphony Orch., 1997–2006. Mem., Bd of Govs, Friends Sch., Hobart, 1984–86 (Chm., 1989–94). Hon. LLD Tasmania, 2001. *Recreations:* swimming, music, theatre. *Address:* Government House, Lower Domain Road, Hobart, Tasmania 7000, Australia.

UNDERWOOD, Susan Lois, OBE 2006; FMA; Adviser for Museums to Ruler of Sharjah, United Arab Emirates, since 2008 (Director, Sharjah Museums, 2005–06); *b* 6 Aug. 1956; *d* of John and Lois Underwood; two *s* one *d*. *Educ:* Univ. of St Andrews (MA Hons); Univ. of Leicester (Mus. Studies Grad. Cert.). FMA 1994. Curator, Nat. Railway Mus., York, 1983–85; Keeper of Local Hist., Scunthorpe Mus. and Art Gall., 1985–88; Dep. Dir, N of England Museums Service, 1989–90; Dir, N of England Museums Service, subseq. NE Museums, then Chief Exec., NE MLA, 1990–2005. Comr, English Heritage, 1997–2003. Mem. Bd, One NorthEast, 2005. *Recreations:* the arts, travelling, my children. *Address:* PO Box 39939, Sharjah, United Arab Emirates. *T:* (6) 5566002; *e-mail:* sueunderwood@rulerofficeshj.gov.ae.

UNERMAN, Sandra Diane, CBE 2002; Solicitor and Legal Adviser, Department for Communities and Local Government (formerly Office of the Deputy Prime Minister), since 2004; *b* 23 Aug. 1950; *d* of Cecil Unerman and Renee Unerman (*née* Goldberg). *Educ:* Gartlett Sch.; Orange Hill Grammar Sch.; Bristol Univ. (BA Hons History). Called to the Bar, Inner Temple, 1973; Legal Dept, DoE, later DETR, then DTLR, subseq. ODPM, now DCLG, 1974–; Dep. Solicitor, 1992–2004. UK Civil Service Fellow, Humphrey Inst., Univ. of Minnesota, 1989–90. *Publication:* Trial of Three (novel), 1979. *Recreations:* writing, reading, listening to music, theatre going, folklore, conversation.

Address: Department for Communities and Local Government, Eland House, Bressenden Place, SW1E 5DU.

UNGER, Michael Ronald; Chief Executive, Roy Castle Lung Cancer Foundation, since 2002; Chairman, Piccadilly Radio Ltd, since 2006; *b* 8 Dec. 1943; *s* of Ronald and Joan Maureen Unger; *m* 1st, 1966, Eunice Dickens (marr. diss. 1992); one *s* (one *d* decd); 2nd, 1993, Noorah Ahmed (marr. diss. 2005). *Educ:* Wirral Grammar School. Trainee journalist, Thomson Regional Newspapers, Stockport, 1963; Reading Evening Post, 1965–67; Perth Daily News, W Australia, 1967–71; Daily Post, Liverpool, 1971, Editor, 1977–82; Editor: Liverpool Echo, 1982–83; Manchester Evening News, 1983–97; Gen. Manager, Jazz FM (NW), 2000–02. Dir, Guardian and Manchester Evening News plc, 1983–97. Chm., NW Arts Bd, 1991–93; Mem., Broadcasting Standards Commn, 1999–2000. Chm., Eternal Forest Trust, 2005–; Trustee: Scott Trust, 1986–97; The Lowry, 1994–; Youth Charter for Sport, 1994–2000; NW Film Archives, 1998–2004. *Publication:* (ed) The Memoirs of Bridget Hitler, 1979. *Recreations:* art, reading, walking, gardening.

UNGERER, Jean Thomas, (Tomi); writer and graphic artist; Ambassador for Childhood and Education, Council of Europe, since 2000; *b* Strasbourg, 28 Nov. 1931; *s* of Theo Ungerer and Alice (*née* Essler); *m* 1970, Yvonne Wright; two *s* one *d*. *Educ:* Strasbourg; Ecole Municipale des Arts Décoratifs, Strasbourg. Moved to USA, 1956; joined Harper's, 1957; worked for Amer. magazines and in advertising; moved to Nova Scotia, 1971, to Ireland, 1976; exhibitions: (first) Berlin, 1962; Strasbourg, 1975; Louvre, Paris, 1981; RFH, London, 1985. Chargé de Mission, Jack Lang, Ministre de la Culture, commission inter-ministérielle Franco-Allemande, 1987–94; Pres. and Founder, Culture Bank, Strasbourg, 1990; Founder, European Centre of Yiddish Cultures, 1999. Hon. Dr Karlsruhe. Burckhardt Prize, Goethe Foundn, 1983; Andersen Prize, Denmark, 1998; French culture prize, 1998, European culture prize, 1999. Commandeur des Arts et des Lettres (France), 1985; Officier, Légion d'Honneur (France), 2001 (Chevalier, 1990); Cross of Merit (Germany), 1992; numerous other prizes and awards. Films include: The Three Robbers, 1972; The Beast of Monsieur Racine, 1975. *Publications:* over 130 books in English, French and German, including: Horrible, 1958; Inside Marriage, 1960; The Underground Sketchbook, 1964; The Party, 1966; Fornicon, 1970; Compromises, 1970; The Poster Art of Tomi Ungerer, 1971; Testament, 1985; Once in a Lifetime, 1985; Far Out is not Far Enough, 1985; Joy of Frogs, 1985; Testament, 1985; Cats As Cats Can, 1997; Tomi: a Nazi childhood, 1998; Tortoni Tremolo, 1998; Otto, 1999; Europolitan, 1998; S & M, 2000; Vracs, 2000; Erotoscope: the art of Tomi Ungerer, 2001; Tomi Ungerer et New York, 2001; From Father to Son, 2003; *for children:* The Mellops series: The Mellops go Diving for Treasure; Crictor, 1958; Adelaide, 1959; Christmas Eve at the Mellops', 1960; Emile, 1960; Rufus, 1961; The Three Robbers, 1962; Snail, Where Are You?, 1962; One, Two, Where's My Shoe?, 1964; The Brave Vulture Orlando, 1966; Moon Man, 1967; Zeralda's Ogre, 1967; Ask Me a Question, 1968; The Hat, 1970; The Beast of Monsieur Racine, 1971; I am Papa Snap and These are My Favourite No Such Stories, 1971; No Kiss for Mother, 1973; Allumette, 1974; Flix, 1997; The Blue Cloud, 2000. *Address:* Diogenes Verlag AG, Sprecherstrasse 8, 8032 Zürich, Switzerland; Centre Tomi Ungerer, Musées de Strasbourg, 5 place du Château, 67076 Strasbourg Cedex, France.

UNGLEY, John Guilford Gordon; Master of the Supreme Court, Queen's Bench Division, 1997–2008; Master assigned to clinical negligence cases, 1999–2008; *b* 30 Jan. 1939; *s* of Harold Gordon Ungley and Ella Gwyneth Reay Ungley (*née* Heslop); *m* 1976, Elizabeth Metcalfe (*née* Mayall); one *d*, and two step *d*. *Educ:* Charterhouse. Queen's Royal Irish Hussars, 1960–61. Called to the Bar, Gray's Inn, 1965; in practice at the Bar, Western Circuit, 1966–97; Asst Recorder, 1986–89, Recorder, 1989–2004. *Recreation:* sailing. *Clubs:* Cavalry; Bar Yacht, Royal Solent Yacht.

UNRUH, Prof. William George, PhD; FRS 2001; FRSC 1984; Professor of Physics, University of British Columbia, since 1984; Fellow, Canadian Institute for Advanced Research, since 1987; *b* 28 Aug. 1945; *s* of Benjamin Unruh and Anne Unruh (*née* Janzen); *m* 1974, Patricia Truman; one *s*. *Educ:* Univ. of Manitoba (BSc Hons 1967); Princeton Univ. (MA 1969; PhD 1971). FAPS 2000. NSERC (Rutherford) Post Doctoral Fellow, Birkbeck Coll., 1971–72; Miller Fellow, Univ. of Calif, Berkeley, 1973–74; Asst Prof., McMaster Univ., 1974–76; Asst Prof., Univ. of BC, 1976–81; Dir, Cosmology Prog., Canadian Inst. for Advanced Res., 1987–97. Hon. Foreign Mem., American Assoc. of Arts and Scis, 2003. Sloan Medal, Sloan Foundn, 1978; Rutherford Medal, RSC, 1982; Herzberg Medal, 1983, Medal of Achievement, 1996, Canadian Assoc. of Physicists; Steacie Prize, Steacie Foundn, 1984; Sci. and Engrg Gold Medal, Sci. Council of BC, 1990; Killam Prize in Natural Scis, Canadian Council, 1995; Mathematical Physics Prize, Canadian Assoc. of Physicists and Centre Recherche du Mathématique, 1996. *Publications:* (ed with G. Semenoff) The Early Universe, 1987; contrib. numerous papers to scientific jls. *Address:* Department of Physics and Astronomy, University of British Columbia, Vancouver, BC V6T 1Z1, Canada. *T:* (604) 8223273. *Club:* X (Univ. of BC, Vancouver).

UNSWORTH, Prof. Anthony, PhD, DEng; CEng, FREng, FIMechE, FICE; Professor of Engineering, since 1989, Director, Centre for Biomedical Engineering, since 1989, and Director of Research, Faculty of Science, since 2006, University of Durham; *b* 7 Feb. 1945; *s* of late James Unsworth and Annie Unsworth (*née* Halliwell); *m* 1967, Jill Chetwood. *Educ:* Salford Univ. (BSc 1967); Leeds Univ. (MSc 1968; PhD 1972; DEng 1990). CEng 1972; FIMechE 1984; FREng 1996; FICE 2003. Res. Engr, David Brown Industries, 1967–69; University of Leeds: Res. Fellow, 1969–71; Lectr, 1971–76; University of Durham: Lectr, 1976–79; Sen. Lectr, 1979–84; Reader, 1984–89; Hd, Sch. of Engrg and Applied Sci., then Sch. of Engrg and Computer Sci., 1990–94; Dep. Dean of Sci., 1994–97; Dean of Sci., 1997–2000; Hd, Sch. of Engrg, 2000–06. Vis. Scientist, Cornell Univ., 1981. Dir, Action Research, 1992–95; non-exec. Dir, S Durham HA, 1993–96. Chairman: Engrg in Medicine Gp, IMechE, 1989–92; NHS Res. Ethics Cttee, 1995–96; Mem. Panel 30, 2001 RAE. Editor: Pt H, Proc. IMechE; Jl Engrg in Medicine. Silver Medal in Tribology, 1972; Donald Julius Groen Prize in Tribology, 1991, James Clayton Prize, 1999, IMechE; James Alfred Ewing Medal, ICE, 2005. *Publications:* (contrib.) Tribology of Natural and Artificial Joints, 1981; (contrib.) Introduction to Biomechanics, 1981; (contrib.) Mechanics of Joints, 1993; (contrib.) Oxford Textbook of Rheumatology, 2001; over 270 papers in internat. jls in tribology and biomed. engrg; numerous presentations at internat. confs. *Recreation:* singing sacred music and light opera. *Address:* School of Engineering, University of Durham, Science Laboratories, South Road, Durham DH1 3LE. *T:* (0191) 334 2521, *Fax:* (0191) 334 2512; *e-mail:* tony.unsworth@durham.ac.uk.

UNSWORTH, Barry Forster; author; *b* 10 Aug. 1930; *s* of Michael Unsworth and Elsie (*née* Forster); *m* 1st, 1959, Valerie Irene Moor (marr. diss. 1991); three *d*; 2nd, 1992, Aira Pohjanvaara-Buffa. *Educ:* Stockton Grammar Sch.; Manchester Univ. (BA Hons English). FRSL 1973. Hon. LittD Manchester, 1998. *Publications:* The Partnership, 1966; The Greeks Have a Word for It, 1967; The Hide, 1970; Mooncranker's Gift (Heinemann Award), 1973; The Big Day, 1976; Pascali's Island, 1980; The Rage of the Vulture, 1982;

Stone Virgin, 1985; Sugar and Rum, 1990; Sacred Hunger (jtly, Booker Prize), 1992; Morality Play, 1995; After Hannibal, 1996; Losing Nelson, 1999; The Songs of the Kings, 2002; The Ruby in Her Navel, 2006. *Recreations:* gardening, viticulture, bird-watching. *Address:* c/o Vivien Green, Sheil Land Associates, 52 Doughty Street, WC1N 2LF.

UNWIN, Sir Brian; see Unwin, Sir J. B.

UNWIN, David Charles; QC 1995; *b* 12 May 1947; *s* of Peter Unwin and Rosemary (*née* Locket); *m* 1969, Lorna Bullivant; one *s* one *d*. *Educ:* Clifton Coll.; Trinity Coll., Oxford. Called to the Bar, Middle Temple, 1971; Jun. Counsel to Attorney Gen. in charity matters, 1987–95. Charity Comr, 2002–07. *Recreations:* music, mountaineering, windsurfing. *Club:* Climbers'.

UNWIN, David Storr; author; *b* 3 Dec. 1918; *e s* of Sir Stanley Unwin, KCMG, and Alice Mary Storr; *m* 1945, Periwinkle, *yr d* of late Captain Sidney Herbert, RN; twin *s* and *d*. *Educ:* Abbotsholme. League of Nations Secretariat, Geneva, 1938–39; George Allen & Unwin Ltd, Publishers, 1940–44. *Publications:* The Governor's Wife, 1954 (Authors' Club First Novel Award, 1955); A View of the Heath, 1956; Fifty Years with Father: a Relationship (autobiog.), 1982; *for children:* (under pen name David Severn) Rick Afire!, 1942; A Cabin for Crusoe, 1943; Waggon for Five, 1944; Hermit in the Hills, 1945; Forest Holiday, 1946; Ponies and Poachers, 1947; Dream Gold, 1948; The Cruise of the Maiden Castle, 1948; Treasure for Three, 1949; My Foreign Correspondent through Africa, 1950; Crazy Castle, 1951; Burglars and Bandicoots, 1952; Drumbeats!, 1953; The Future Took Us, 1958; The Green-eyed Gryphon, 1958; Foxy-boy, 1959; Three at the Sea, 1959; Clouds over the Alberhorn, 1963; Jeff Dickson, Cowhand, 1963; The Girl in the Grove, 1974; The Wishing Bone, 1977. *Recreations:* travel, gardening. *Address:* Garden Flat, 31 Belsize Park, NW3 4DX. *Club:* PEN.

UNWIN, Eric Geoffrey; Chairman: Halma plc, since 2003 (Deputy Chairman, 2002–03); Liberata, since 2003; Omnibus Systems Ltd, since 2005; *b* 9 Aug. 1942; *s* of Maurice Doughty Unwin and Olive Milburn (*née* Watson); *m* 1967, Margaret Bronia Element; one *s* one *d*. *Educ:* Heaton Grammar School, Newcastle upon Tyne; King's College, Durham Univ. (BSc Hons Chemistry). Cadbury Bros, 1963–68; joined John Hoskyns & Co., 1968; Managing Dir, Hoskyns Systems Development, 1978; Dir, 1982, Man. Dir, 1984, Exec. Chm., 1988–93, Hoskyns Group; Chief Operating Officer, 1993–2000, and Vice Chm., Exec. Bd, 1996–2000, Cap Gemini Sogeti, then Cap Gemini; CEO, Cap Gemini, then Cap Gemini Ernst and Young, 2000–01. Chairman: Cap Programmator AB, 1993–2000; United Business Media, 2002–07; Cloud Networks Ltd, 2005–06; non-executive Director: Volmac Software Groep NV, 1992–; Gemini Consulting Hldg SA, 1994–2000; United News & Media plc, 1995–2002; Mem. Bd, Cap Gemini SA, 2000–; Taptu Ltd, 2006–. Pres., Computing Services Assoc., 1987–88. Mem., ITAB, 1988–91. CCMI (CBIM 1984; Mem., Bd., 1990–94). Freeman, City of London, 1987; Founder Mem., and Liveryman, Co. of Information Technologists, 1987. *Recreations:* golf, riding, ski-ing. *Address:* 17 Park Village West, NW1 4AE. *Clubs:* Royal Automobile; Hendon Golf, Hunstanton Golf, Royal West Norfolk Golf, Morfontaine Golf (France).

UNWIN, Sir (James) Brian, KCB 1990 (CB 1986); President, European Investment Bank, 1993–99, now Hon. President; Director, Dexia SA, since 2000; President, European Centre for Nature Conservation, since 2001; Chairman, Asset Trust Housing Ltd, since 2003; *b* 21 Sept. 1935; *s* of Reginald Unwin and Winifred Annie Walthall; *m* 1964, Diana Susan, *d* of Sir D. A. Scott, *qv;* three *s*. *Educ:* Chesterfield School; New College, Oxford (MA; Hon. Fellow, 1997); Yale University (MA). Asst Principal, CRO, 1960; Private Sec. to British High Commissioner, Salisbury, 1961–64; 1st Secretary, British High Commission, Accra, 1964–65; FCO, 1965–68; transferred to HM Treasury, 1968; Private Sec. to Chief Secretary to Treasury, 1970–72; Asst Secretary, 1972; Under Sec., 1976; seconded to Cabinet Office, 1981–83; Dep. Sec., HM Treasury, 1983–85; Dir, Eur. Investment Bank, 1983–85; Dep. Sec., Cabinet Office, 1985–87; Chm., Bd of HM Customs and Excise, 1987–93. Chm., Supervisory Bd, European Investment Fund, 1994–99; Gov., EBRD, 1993–99; Chm., European Task Force on Banking and Biodiversity, 2002–. Pres., Customs Co-operation Council, 1991–92. Chm., Civil Service Sports Council, 1989–93. Member: IMPACT Adv. Bd, 1990–93; Bd of Dirs, ENO, 1993–94, 2000–; (Sec., 1987–93); Bd, Centre d'Etudes Prospectives, 1996–2000; Bd, Foundation Pierre Werner, 1998–2000. Mem. Council, Federal Trust for Educn and Res., 2003–. Pres., New Coll. Soc., 2003–08. Hon. Pres., Euronem, Athens, 2000–. Gold Medal, Fondation du Mérite Européen, 1995. Comdr, Order of Ouissam Aloui (Morocco), 1998; Grand Officier, Ordre de la Couronne (Belgium), 2001; Grand Croix, Ordre Grand-Ducal de la Couronne de Chêne (Luxembourg), 2002. *Recreations:* opera, bird watching, Wellingtoniana, cricket. *Club:* Reform.

UNWIN, Julia, CBE 2006 (OBE 2000); Director, Joseph Rowntree Foundation, since 2007; *b* 6 July 1956; *d* of Peter William Unwin, *qv;* partner, Patrick Kelly; two *d*. *Educ:* Univ. of Liverpool (BA 1978); London Sch. of Econs (MSc 1991). Dir, Homeless Network, 1986–92; consultant, 1992–2006. Member: Bd, Housing Corporation, 1992–2001; Charity Commn, 1998–2003; Dep. Chm., Food Standards Agency, 2003–06. Chairman, Committee of Reference: ISIS Asset Mgt, 2004–06; Friends Provident, 2004–06. FRSA. *Publications:* The Grant Making Tango, 2004; Fruitful Funding, 2005; (jtly) The Voluntary Sector Delivering Public Services: transfer or transformation, 2005. *Address:* c/o Joseph Rowntree Foundation, The Homestead, 40 Water End, York YO30 6WP. *T:* (01904) 629241, *Fax:* (01904) 620072; *e-mail:* julia.unwin@jrf.org.uk. *Clubs:* Royal Commonwealth Society, Reform.

UNWIN, Ven. Kenneth; Archdeacon of Pontefract, 1981–92, now Emeritus; *b* 16 Sept. 1926; *s* of Percy and Elsie Unwin; *m* 1958, Beryl Riley; one *s* four *d*. *Educ:* Chesterfield Grammar School; St Edmund Hall, Oxford (MA Hons); Ely Theological Coll. Assistant Curate: All Saints, Leeds, 1951–55; St Margaret, Durham City (in charge, St John's, Neville's Cross), 1955–59; Vicar: St John Baptist, Dodworth, Barnsley, 1959–69; St John Baptist, Royston, Barnsley, 1969–73; St John's, Wakefield, 1973–82. Hon. Canon, Wakefield Cathedral, 1980–92. RD of Wakefield, 1980–81. Proctor in Convocation, 1972–82. *Address:* 2 Rockwood Close, Skipton, Yorks BD23 1UG. *T:* (01756) 791323. *See also Sir J. D. Acland, Bt.*

UNWIN, Peter Francis; Director General, Natural Environment Group, Department for Environment, Food and Rural Affairs, since 2007; *b* 8 June 1954; *s* of Francis Charles Unwin, MBE and Margaret (Marjorie) Unwin (*née* Caskey); *m* 1978, Margaret Elizabeth Wiseman; two *s* one *d*. *Educ:* George Watson's Coll., Edinburgh; Pembroke Coll., Cambridge (BA Hons Maths 1975; Dip. Mathematical Stats 1976). Asst Statistician, Capital and Co. Taxation, Inland Revenue, 1976–79; Private Sec. to Hd, Govt Statistical Service, 1979–81; Principal, Gen. Finance Div., MoD, 1981–84; Statistician, Local Authy Statistics Div., 1984–87; Principal, Local Authy Capital Finance Div., 1987–90; Hd, Inner Cities Policy Unit, 1990–93, Internat. Envmt Div., 1993–97, DoE; Hd, Global Atmosphere Div., DoE, then DETR, 1997–98; Principal Private Secretary: to Dep. Prime Minister, 1998–2001; to Sec. of State for Local Govt, Transport and the Regions, 2001; Director: Central Policy Gp, Cabinet Office, 2001–02; Corporate Strategy and Resources,

ODPM, 2002–04; Dir Gen., Corporate Strategy and Resources Gp, ODPM, 2004–06; Corporate Delivery Gp, DCLG, 2006–07. *Recreations:* golf, ski-ing, travel, hill walking, wine. *Address:* Department for Environment, Food and Rural Affairs, Nobel House, 17 Smith Square, SW1P 3JR. *Club:* Chislehurst Golf.

UNWIN, Dr (Peter) Nigel (Tripp), FRS 1983; Scientist, Medical Research Council Laboratory of Molecular Biology, Cambridge, 1968–80 and since 1987; Senior Research Fellow, Trinity College, Cambridge, since 1988; *b* 1 Nov. 1942; *s* of Peter Unwin and Cara Unwin (*née* Pinckney); *m* 1968, Janet Patricia Ladd; one *s* one *d*. *Educ:* Univ. of Otago, NZ (BE); Univ. of Cambridge (PhD 1968). Prof. of Structural Biol., then Cell Biol., Stanford Univ. Sch. of Medicine, Calif, 1980–87. Founder FMedSci 1998. Hon. FRMS 1989. Ernst Ruska Award, Ernst Ruska Foundn, 1980; Rosenstiel Award, Brandeis Univ., Mass, 1991; Louis Jeantet Prize for Medicine, Jeantet Foundn, Geneva, 1996; Gregori Aminoff Prize, Royal Swedish Acad. of Scis, 1999. *Recreation:* mountaineering. *Address:* 19/20 Portugal Place, Cambridge CB5 8AF.

UNWIN, Prof. (Peter) Timothy (Holt), PhD; Professor of Geography, since 1999, and UNESCO Chair in Information and Communication Technologies for Development, since 2007, Royal Holloway and Bedford New College, University of London; *b* 11 July 1955; *s* of Thomas Peter Farrer Unwin and Rhoda Patricia Unwin (*née* Vare); *m* 1981, Pamela Julie Cottam; one *s* two *d*. *Educ:* St John's Coll., Cambridge (BA 1976, MA 1980); Univ. of Durham (PhD 1980). Bedford College, subseq. Royal Holloway and Bedford New College, University of London: Lectr, 1981–92; Sen. Lectr, 1992–93; Reader in Geog., 1993–99; Hd, Dept of Geog., 1999–2001; on secondment as Leader, Imfundo: Partnership for Inf. Technol. in Educn, DFID, 2001–04. Commonwealth Scholarship Comr, 2004–. Prog. Dir, 2007, Sen. Advr, 2008, Partnerships for Educn, World Economic Forum. Hon. Sec., RGS (with IBG), 1995–97. Academic Advr and Ext. Examiner, Inst. of Masters of Wine, 2004–. Hon. Mem., Estonian Geographical Soc., 2002. Cuthbert Peek Award, RGS, 1992. *Publications:* Wine and the Vine: an historical geography of viticulture and the wine trade, 1991 (trans. Italian, Greek and Spanish); The Place of Geography, 1992 (trans. Spanish); (ed) Atlas of World Development, 1996; (ed jtly) Environmental Management, 1997; (ed) A European Geography, 1998; (ed jtly) European Landscapes, 2003. *Recreations:* wine, European cultural landscapes, my family. *Address:* Department of Geography, Royal Holloway, University of London, Egham, TW20 0EX. *Clubs:* Athenæum, Geographical.

UNWIN, Peter William, CMG 1981; HM Diplomatic Service, retired; writer; Chairman, David Davies Memorial Institute of International Studies, 2001–07 (Director, 1995–2001); *b* 20 May 1932; *s* of Arnold and Norah Unwin; *m* 1955, Monica Steven; two *s* two *d*. *Educ:* Ampleforth; Christ Church, Oxford (history scholar). Army, 1954–56; FO, 1956–58; British Legation, Budapest, 1958–61; British Embassy, Tokyo, 1961–63; FCO, 1963–67; British Information Services, NY, 1967–70; FCO, 1970–72; Bank of England, 1973; British Embassy, Bonn, 1973–76; Head of Personnel Policy Dept, FCO, 1976–79; Fellow, Center for Internat. Affairs, Harvard, 1979–80; Minister (Economic), Bonn, 1980–83; Ambassador to: Hungary, 1983–86; Denmark, 1986–88; a Dep. Sec. Gen. of the Commonwealth, 1989–93. Chairman: British-Hungarian Soc., 1993–2000 (Pres., 2000–04); Abbeyfield Internat., 1996–2002; Vice Chm., UK Cttee, UNICEF, 1996–2000. Order of Merit (Hungary), 1996. *Publications:* Voice in the Wilderness: Imre Nagy and the Hungarian Revolution, 1991; Baltic Approaches, 1996; Hearts, Minds & Interests: Britain's place in the world, 1998; Where East Met West: a Central European journey, 2000; The Narrow Sea: the history of the English Channel, 2003; 1956: power defied, 2006; contrib. The European, Evening Standard, Guardian, Independent, Independent on Sunday, International Affairs, International Relations, The Observer, The Times and The Tablet. *Address:* 30 Kew Green, Richmond, Surrey TW9 3BH. *T:* (020) 8940 8037. *Club:* Oxford and Cambridge.

See also J. Unwin.

UNWIN, Timothy; *see* Unwin, P. T. H.

UPDIKE, John Hoyer; freelance writer; *b* 18 March 1932; *s* of late Wesley R. and Linda G. Updike; *m* 1st, 1953, Mary E. Pennington (marr. diss.); two *s* two *d*; 2nd, 1977, Martha Bernhard. *Educ:* Harvard Coll. Worked as journalist for The New Yorker magazine, 1955–57. *Publications: poems:* Hoping for a Hoopoe (in America, The Carpentered Hen), 1958; Telephone Poles, 1968; Midpoint and other poems, 1969; Tossing and Turning, 1977; Facing Nature, 1985; Collected Poems, 1993; Americana and other poems, 2001; *novels:* The Poorhouse Fair, 1959; Rabbit, Run, 1960; The Centaur, 1963; Of the Farm, 1966; Couples, 1968; Rabbit Redux, 1972; A Month of Sundays, 1975; Marry Me, 1976; The Coup, 1979; Rabbit Is Rich (Pulitzer Prize), 1982; The Witches of Eastwick, 1984 (filmed 1987); Roger's Version, 1986; S., 1988; Rabbit at Rest, 1990 (Pulitzer Prize 1991); Memories of the Ford Administration, 1993; Brazil, 1994; Rabbit Angstrom: a tetralogy, 1995; In the Beauty of the Lilies, 1996; Toward the End of Time, 1998; Gertrude and Claudius, 2000; Seek My Face, 2003; Villages, 2004; Terrorist, 2006; *short stories:* The Same Door, 1959; Pigeon Feathers, 1962; The Music School, 1966; Bech: A Book, 1970; Museums and Women, 1973; Problems, 1980; Bech Is Back, 1982; (ed) The Year's Best American Short Stories, 1985; Trust Me, 1987; The Afterlife and other stories, 1995; Bech at Bay: a quasi-novel, 1998; Licks of Love, 2001; The Early Stories: 1953–1975, 2004; *miscellanies:* Assorted Prose, 1965; Picked-Up Pieces, 1976; Hugging the Shore, 1983; Just Looking: essays on art, 1989; Odd Jobs: essays and criticism, 1991; Golf Dreams, 1997; More Matter, 1999; Still Looking: essays on American art, 2006; Due Considerations: essays and criticism, 2007; *autobiography:* Self-Consciousness: Memoirs, 1989; *play:* Buchanan Dying, 1974. *Address:* Beverly Farms, MA 01915, USA.

UPRICHARD, Dame Mary (Elizabeth), DBE 1998 (OBE 1983); President, UK Central Council for Nursing, Midwifery and Health Visiting, 1993–98 (Member of Council, 1980–93); *b* 23 March 1938; *d* of late Norman Uprichard and Rebecca Uprichard (*née* Gracey). *Educ:* Grosvenor Grammar Sch., Belfast. RSCN, RGN, RM, MTD. Sch. of Midwifery, Belfast, 1974–83; Dir of Midwifery Educn, NI Coll. of Midwifery, 1983–97. Chairman: Nat. Bd for Nursing, Midwifery and Health Visiting, 1988–93 (Mem. Bd, 1980–93); Nurses Welfare Service, 1999–; Member: EC Adv. Cttee on Training of Midwives, 1984–98; Council for Professions Supplementary to Medicine, 1997–; Council on Social Responsibility, Methodist Church in Ireland, 1994–. *Address:* 29 Glenview Avenue, Belfast BT5 7LZ. *T:* (028) 9079 1466.

UPSHAW, Dawn; American soprano; *b* 17 July 1960; *m* Michael Nott; two *c*. *Educ:* Illinois Wesleyan Univ. (BA Music 1982); Manhattan Sch. of Music (MA 1984). Joined NY Metropolitan Opera, 1984; début, Rigoletto, 1984; other productions include: Magic Flute, Wolf Trap Fest., 1985, Aix-en-Provence Fest., 1988; Death in the Family, Opera Co. of St Louis, 1986; Béatrice et Bénédict, 1993, Theodora, 1996, Glyndebourne Fest.; The Rake's Progress, Stravinsky Fest., Paris, 1996; El Niño, Châtelet, Paris, 2000; Cunning Little Vixen, Royal Opera House, Covent Garden, 2003; numerous recitals and concerts with major orchestras and chamber gps. Numerous recordings (Grammy Awards). (Jtly) Winner, Naumburg Competition, 1985. *Address:* c/o IMG Artists, The Light Box, 111 Power Road, Chiswick, W4 5PY.

UPTON, Prof. Graham, PhD; Vice-Chancellor, Oxford Brookes University, 1997–2007; *b* 30 April 1944; *m* 1st, 1966, Jennifer Ann Clark (marr. diss. 1984); one *s* one *d*; 2nd, 1986, Bebe Speed; one *s* one *d*. *Educ:* Univ. of Sydney (BA, Dip Educn 1966; MA 1969); Univ. of New South Wales (MEd 1973); UC Cardiff, Univ. of Wales (PhD 1978). CPsychol 1988; FBPsS 1996. Teacher, New South Wales, 1966–70; Lectr in Educn, Sydney Teachers' Coll., 1970–71; Lectr in Special Educn, Leeds Poly., 1972–74; University College, Cardiff, 1974–88: Lectr; Sen. Lectr; Reader; Hd of Dept of Educn; Dean, Collegiate Faculty of Educn; Dean, Faculty of Educn and Prof. Studies; University of Birmingham: Prof. of Educnl Psychology and Special Educn and Hd, Sch. of Educn, 1988–93; Pro-Vice-Chancellor, 1993–97. Mem., 2001–, Chm., 2004–, Bd, Oxford Playhouse. Non-exec. Dir, Oxford Expression Technology. Mem. Adv. Council, Oxford Trust, 2001–07. Chm., Oxford Community Partnership, 2002–07. Governor, Headington Sch., 1999–2007. AcSS 2000. FRSA 1999. Hon. Fellow, Birmingham Coll. of Food, Tourism and Leisure Studies, 1997. *Publications:* Physical and Creative Activities for the Mentally Handicapped, 1979; Behaviour Problems in the Comprehensive School, 1980; Educating Children with Behaviour Problems, 1983; Staff Training and Special Educational Needs, 1991; Special Educational Needs, 1992; Special Education in Britain After Warnock, 1993; Emotional and Behavioural Difficulties in Schools, 1994; The Voice of the Child, 1996; Pupils with Severe Learning Difficulties who Present Challenging Behaviour, 1996; Stresses in Special Educational Needs Teachers, 1996; Sound Practice, 1997; Effective Schooling for Pupils with Emotional and Behavioural Difficulties, 1998. *Recreations:* good food, DIY, cycling.

UPTON, Robert Ian William; Secretary-General, Royal Town Planning Institute, since 1996; *b* 20 Aug. 1951; *s* of late Ronald Alfred Upton and of Iris Eveline Upton; *m* 1987, Mary Faith Higgins; two *d*. *Educ:* Dulwich Coll.; Magdalene Coll., Cambridge (MA); Harvard Business Sch. Hong Kong Government, 1972–91: Clerk of Councils, 1982–84; Sec., Educn Commn, 1985–86; Dep. Sec. for Security, 1986–89; Dir of Planning, 1989–91. Chief Exec., Rushmoor BC, 1992–96. *Recreations:* reading, walking, book-hunting. *Address:* Royal Town Planning Institute, 41 Botolph Lane, EC3R 8DL. *T:* (020) 7929 9494.

UPTON, Rt Hon. Simon (David); PC 1999; FRSNZ 1999; Chairman, OECD Round Table on Sustainable Development, 1998–2007 and since 2008; *b* 7 Feb. 1958; *s* of Thomas Wilson Upton and Dorothy Vernon Upton (*née* Hosking); *m* 1984, Bhaady Jane Miller; one *s* one *d*. *Educ:* Southwell Prep. Sch., Hamilton, NZ; St Paul's Collegiate Sch.; Auckland Univ. (BA, LLB Hons); Wolfson Coll., Oxford (Rhodes Schol.; MLitt). MHR (Nat.): Waikato, then Raglan, 1981–96; party list, 1996–99; Minister: for the Envmt, 1990–91 and 1993–99; of Res., Sci. and Technol., 1990–96; of Health, 1990–93; for Crown Res. Insts, 1991–99; of Biosecurity, 1996–97; of State Services, 1998–99; of Cultural Affairs, 1998; Associate Minister of Foreign Affairs, 1996–99; Dir, Global Subsidies Initiative, Internat. Inst. for Sustainable Develt, 2007–08. Dir, Holcim (NZ) Ltd, 2007–. Advr on climate change to PriceWaterhouseCoopers (NZ). Chm., 7th Session of UN Commn on Sustainable Develt, 1999. *Publication:* The Withering of the State, 1986. *Recreations:* gardening and landscaping, NZ geology and botany, music, ski-ing, running, roller-blading. *Address:* OECD Round Table on Sustainable Development, OECD, 2 rue André-Pascal, Paris 75775 Cedex 16, France. *Club:* Wellington (Wellington, NZ).

UPWARD, Mrs Janet; Member, then Chair, Birmingham and Solihull Mental Health Patients' Forum, 2004–08. *Educ:* Newnham College, Cambridge (BA (Geog. Hons) 1961; MA 1966); Univ. of Birmingham (MSocSci 1993). Sec., Nat. Fedn of Consumer Gps, 1972–82; Mem., 1978–84, Dep. Chm., 1978–83, Domestic Coal Consumers' Council; Chm., Nat. Consumer Congress, 1981–83; Chief Officer, S Birmingham CHC, 1983–90; Project Manager, Birmingham FHSA, 1991–96.

URBAN, Mark Lee; Diplomatic and Defence Editor, BBC Newsnight, since 1999; *b* London, 26 Jan. 1961; *s* of Harry and Josephine Urban; *m* 1993, Hilary Jane Rosen; one *s* two *d*. *Educ:* King's College Sch., Wimbledon; London Sch. of Economics (BSc (Econ) Internat. Relns). Asst producer, BBC TV, 1983–86; Defence Corresp., Independent, 1986–90; BBC Television: reporter, Newsnight, 1990–93; Middle East Corresp., 1993–94; Diplomatic Corresp., Newsnight, 1995–98. *Publications:* Soviet Land Power, 1983; War in Afghanistan, 1987; Big Boys' Rules: the secret struggle against the IRA, 1992; UK Eyes Alpha: the inside story of British Intelligence, 1996; The Illegal, 1996; The Linguist, 1998; The Man Who Broke Napoleon's Codes, 2001; Rifles: six years with Wellington's legendary sharpshooters, 2003; Generals: ten British commanders who shaped the world, 2005; Fusiliers: eight years with the Redcoats in America, 2007. *Recreations:* good food, reading, trying to keep fit. *Address:* c/o Newsnight, BBC TV Centre, Wood Lane, W12 7RJ.

URE, James Mathie, OBE 1969; British Council Representative, India, and Minister (Education), British High Commission, New Delhi, 1980–84; *b* 5 May 1925; *s* of late William Alexander Ure, and Helen Jones; *m* 1950, Martha Walker Paterson; one *s* one *d*. *Educ:* Shawlands Acad., Glasgow; Glasgow Univ. (MA); Trinity Coll., Oxford (BLitt). Army Service, 1944–47. Lectr, Edinburgh Univ., 1953–59; British Council: Istanbul, 1956–57; India, 1959–68; Dep. Controller, Arts Div., 1968–71; Rep., Indonesia, 1971–75; Controller, Home Div., 1975–80. *Publications:* Old English Benedictine Office, 1952; (with L. A. Hill) English Sounds and Spellings, 1962; (with L. A. Hill) English Sounds and Spellings—Tests, 1963; (with J. S. Bhandari and C. S. Bhandari) Read and Act, 1965; (with C. S. Bhandari) Short Stories, 1966.

URE, Sir John (Burns), KCMG 1987 (CMG 1980); LVO 1968; HM Diplomatic Service, retired; author; *b* 5 July 1931; *s* of late Tam Ure; *m* 1972, Caroline, *d* of late Charles Allan, Roxburghshire; one *s* one *d*. *Educ:* Uppingham Sch.; Magdalene Coll., Cambridge (MA); Harvard Business Sch. (AMP). Active Service as 2nd Lieut with Cameronians (Scottish Rifles), Malaya, 1950–51; Lieut, London Scottish (Gordon Highlanders) TA, 1952–55. Book publishing with Ernest Benn Ltd, 1951–53; joined Foreign (subseq. Diplomatic) Service, 1956; 3rd Sec. and Private Sec. to Ambassador, Moscow, 1957–59; Resident Clerk, FO, 1960–61; 2nd Sec., Leopoldville, 1962–63; FO, 1964–66; 1st Sec. (Commercial), Santiago, 1967–70; FCO, 1971–72; Counsellor, and intermittently Chargé d'Affaires, Lisbon, 1972–77; Head of South America Dept, FCO, 1977–79; Ambassador to Cuba, 1979–81; Asst Under-Sec. of State, FCO, 1981–84; Ambassador to Brazil, 1984–87, to Sweden, 1987–91. UK Comr Gen., Expo 92, 1990–92. Director: Thomas Cook Group, 1991–99; Sotheby's Scandinavia AB, 1991–99; CSE Aviation, 1992–94; Consultant: Robert Fleming & Co. (merchant bankers), 1995–98; Ecosse Films, 1997–99; European Risk Mgt Consultants, 1997–2000; Sotheby's Scandinavia, 1999–. Chairman: panel of judges, Thomas Cook Travel Book of the Year Award, 1991–2000; Anglo-Swedish Soc., 1992–96; Anglo-Brazilian Chamber of Commerce, 1994–96. Pres., Weald of Kent Protection Soc., 2005–. Trustee, Leeds Castle Foundn, 1995–2006. Life Fellow and Mem. Council, RGS, 1982–84. Regular guest lectr on foreign tours. Comdr, Mil. Order of Christ, Portugal, 1973. *Publications:* Cucumber Sandwiches in the Andes, 1973 (Travel Book Club Choice); Prince Henry the Navigator, 1977 (History Guild Choice); The Trail of Tamerlane, 1980 (Ancient History Club Choice); The Quest for Captain

Morgan, 1983; Trespassers on the Amazon, 1986; Central and South America sections, in RGS History of World Exploration, 1990; A Bird on the Wing: Bonnie Prince Charlie's flight from Culloden retraced, 1992; Diplomatic Bag, 1994; The Cossacks, 1999; In Search of Nomads, 2003; Pilgrimage: the great adventure of the Middle Ages, 2006; (contrib.) The Seventy Great Journeys in History, 2006; travel articles in Daily and Sunday Telegraph; book reviews in TLS and Country Life; biographies for Oxford DNB. *Recreation:* travelling uncomfortably in remote places and writing about it comfortably afterwards. *Address:* Netters Hall, Hawkhurst, Kent TN18 5AS. *T:* (01580) 752191. *Clubs:* Beefsteak, Pilgrims.

URMSON, James Opie, MC 1943; Emeritus Professor of Philosophy, Stanford University; Emeritus Fellow of Corpus Christi College, Oxford; *b* 4 March 1915; *s* of Rev. J. O. Urmson; *m* 1940, Marion Joyce Drage; one *d*. *Educ:* Kingswood School, Bath; Corpus Christi College, Oxford. Senior Demy, Magdalen College, 1938; Fellow by examination, Magdalen College, 1939–45. Served Army (Duke of Wellington's Regt), 1939–45. Lecturer of Christ Church, 1945–46; Student of Christ Church, 1946–55; Professor of Philosophy, Queen's College, Dundee, University of St Andrews, 1955–59; Fellow and Tutor in Philosophy, CCC, Oxford, 1959–78. Visiting Associate Prof., Princeton Univ., 1950–51. Visiting Lectr, Univ. of Michigan, 1961–62, 1965–66, and 1969; Stuart Prof. of Philosophy, Stanford, 1975–80. *Publications:* Philosophical Analysis, 1956; The Emotive Theory of Ethics, 1968; Berkeley, 1982; Aristotle's Ethics, 1988; The Greek Philosophical Vocabulary, 1990; edited: Encyclopedia of Western Philosophy, 1960; J. L. Austin: How to Do Things with Words, 1962; (with G. J. Warnock) J. L. Austin: Philosophical Papers, 2nd edn, 1970; translations from ancient Greek; articles in philosophical jls. *Recreations:* gardening, music.

URQUHART, Sir Brian (Edward), KCMG 1986; MBE 1945; Scholar-in-Residence, Ford Foundation, 1986–96; an Under-Secretary-General, United Nations, 1974–86; *b* 28 Feb. 1919; *s* of Murray and Bertha Urquhart; *m* 1st, 1944, Alfreda Huntington (marr. diss. 1963); two *s* one *d*; 2nd, 1963, Sidney Damrosch Howard; one *s* one *d*. *Educ:* Westminster; Christ Church, Oxford (Hon. Student, 1985). British Army: Dorset Regt and Airborne Forces, N Africa, Sicily and Europe, 1939–45; Personal Asst to Gladwyn Jebb, Exec. Sec. of Preparatory Commn of UN, London, 1945–46; Personal Asst to Trygve Lie, 1st Sec.-Gen. of UN, 1946–49; Sec., Collective Measures Cttee, 1951–53; Mem., Office of Under-Sec.-Gen. for Special Political Affairs, 1954–71; Asst Sec.-Gen., UN, 1972–74; Exec. Sec., 1st and 2nd UN Conf. on Peaceful Uses of Atomic Energy, 1955 and 1958; active in organization and direction of UN Emergency Force in Middle East, 1956; Dep. Exec. Sec., Preparatory Commn of Internat. Atomic Energy Agency, 1957; Asst to Sec.-Gen.'s Special Rep. in Congo, July–Oct. 1960; UN Rep. in Katanga, Congo, 1961–62; responsible for organization and direction of UN peace-keeping ops and special political assignments. Hon. LLD: Yale, 1981; Tufts, 1985; Grinnell, 1986; State Univ. NY, 1986; Warwick, 1989; DUniv: Essex, 1981; City Univ. NY, 1986; Hon. DCL Oxford, 1986; Hon. DHL Colorado, 1987; Hon. DLitt: Keele, 1987; Cambridge, 2005. *Publications:* Hammarskjold, 1972; A Life in Peace and War (autobiog.), 1987; Decolonization and World Peace, 1989; (with Erskine Childers) A World in Need of Leadership: tomorrow's United Nations, 1990; Ralph Bunche: an American life, 1993; (with Erskine Childers) Renewing the United Nations System, 1994; A World in Need of Leadership: tomorrow's United Nations, a fresh appraisal, 1996; various articles and reviews on internat. affairs. *Address:* 50 West 29th Street, Apt 11E, New York, NY 10001, USA; Howard Farm, Tyringham, MA 01264, USA. *T:* (212) 6796358. *Club:* Century (New York).

URQUHART, Rt Rev. David Andrew; *see* Birmingham, Bishop of.

URQUHART, James Graham, CVO 1983; FCILT, FIMH; Chairman, Fiox Ltd, 1990–92 (Director, 1988–90); *b* 23 April 1925; *s* of James Graham Urquhart and Mary Clark; *m* 1949, Margaret Hutchinson; two *d*. *Educ:* Berwickshire High Sch. Served War, RAF, 1941–44. Management Trainee, Eastern Region, BR, 1949–52; Chief Controller, Fenchurch Street, 1956–59; Dist Traffic Supt, Perth, 1960–62; Divl Operating Supt, Glasgow, 1962–64; Divl Manager, Glasgow and SW Scotland, 1964–67; Asst Gen. Man., Eastern Reg., 1967–69; BR Bd HQ: Chief Ops Man., 1969–72; Exec. Dir, Personnel, 1972–75; Gen. Manager, London Midland Reg., BR, 1975–76; BR Bd: Exec. Mem., Operations and Productivity, 1977–83; Mem., Exports, 1983–85; Chairman: British Transport Police, 1977–86; BRE-Metro, 1978–86; BR Engrg Ltd, 1979–85; Freightliners, 1983–85; Transmark, 1983–86. Director: Waterslides PLC, 1987–89; Park Air Electronics Ltd, 1987–91; Systems Connection Group PLC, 1988–92; CVC Ltd, 1988–91; Sonic Tape PLC, 1988–90. Mem., Industrial Tribunal, 1987–90. MIPM, MCIM, CCMI. *Recreations:* golf, travel, gardening. *Address:* 12 Durlston Point, 78 Park Road, Swanage, Dorset BH19 2AE. *T:* (01929) 421574.

URQUHART, Lawrence McAllister, CA; Chairman, BAA plc, 1998–2002 (Director, 1993–2002); *b* 24 Sept. 1935; *s* of Robert and Josephine Urquhart; *m* 1961, Elizabeth Catherine Burns; three *s* one *d*. *Educ:* Strathallan; King's Coll., London (LLB). Price Waterhouse & Co., 1957–62; Shell International Petroleum, 1962–64; P. A. Management Consultants, 1964–68; Charterhouse Gp, 1968–74; TKM Gp, 1974–77; Burmah Oil, subseq. Burmah Castrol, 1977–99: Gp Man. Dir, 1985–88; Chief Exec., 1988–93; Chm., 1990–98; non-exec. Dir, 1998–99. Chairman: English China Clays, 1995–99 (Dir, 1991–99); Scottish Widows plc (formerly Scottish Widows' Fund and Life Assurance Soc.), 1995–2001 (non-exec. Dir, 1992–2001); non-executive Director: Imerys SA, 1999–2002; Lloyds TSB Bank plc, 2000–02; Lloyds TSB Group plc, 2000–02. *Recreations:* golf, music. *Clubs:* Frilford Heath Golf, Royal Mid-Surrey Golf.

URQUHART, His Honour Peter William Gordon; a Circuit Judge, 1992–2001; *b* 18 March 1934; *s* of Gordon Eldridge Urquhart and Constance Margaret (*née* Taylor); *m* 1965, Carolyn Hemingway Hines; one *s* one *d*. *Educ:* Liverpool Coll.; Peterhouse, Cambridge (MA, LLB). Admitted solicitor, 1960. Member: Lord Chancellor's Legal Aid Adv. Cttee, 1974–80; Equal Opportunities Commn, 1977–82. *Recreations:* book collecting, reading, gardening, early music, jazz. *Address:* Braehead, 19 Poplar Road, Prenton, Merseyside CH43 5TB. *T:* (0151) 652 4043. *Club:* Athenæum (Liverpool).

URSELL, Prof. Fritz Joseph, FRS 1972; Emeritus Professor of Applied Mathematics, Manchester University, since 1990 (Beyer Professor of Applied Mathematics, 1961–90); *b* Düsseldorf, 28 April 1923; *m* 1959, Katharina Renate (*née* Zander); two *d*. *Educ:* Clifton; Marlborough; Trinity College, Cambridge (BA 1943; MA 1947; ScD 1958); MSc Manchester, 1965. Admiralty Service, 1943–47; ICI Fellow in Applied Mathematics, Manchester Univ., 1947–50. Fellow (Title A), Trinity Coll., Cambridge, 1947–51; Univ. Lecturer in Mathematics, Cambridge, 1950–61; Stringer Fellow in Natural Sciences, King's Coll., Cambridge, 1954–60. Georg Weinblum Lectr in Ship Hydrodynamics, Hamburg and Washington, 1986; Stewartson Lectr in Fluid Mechanics, 1991. FIMA 1964 (Gold Medal, 1994). *Publication:* Collected Papers 1946–1992, 1994. *Address:* 28 Old Broadway, Manchester M20 3DF. *T:* (0161) 445 5791; *e-mail:* fritz@maths.man.ac.uk.

URSELL, Rev. Canon Philip Elliott; Warden, Society of The Most Holy Trinity, Ascot Priory, since 1985; *b* 3 Dec. 1942; *o* *s* of late Clifford Edwin Ursell and Hilda Jane Ursell

(*née* Tucker). *Educ:* Cathays High Sch.; University Coll. Cardiff (Craddock Wells Exhibnr; BA); St Stephen's House, Oxford. MA Oxon. DD Nashotah House, Wisconsin, 2008. Curate of Newton Nottage, Porthcawl, 1968–71; Asst Chaplain of University Coll. Cardiff, 1971–77; Chaplain of Polytechnic of Wales, 1974–77; Chaplain, Fellow and Dir of Studies in Music, Emmanuel Coll., Cambridge, 1977–82; Principal, Pusey House, Oxford, 1982–2002 (Gov., 2006–). Bishop's Commissary for Province of Canterbury, and Canon of Rio Grande, 2005–. Select Preacher, Harvard Univ., 1982, 1983, 1996, 1997; Univ. Preacher, Harvard Summer Sch., 1985. Examining Chaplain to the Bishop of London, 1987–. Chairman: Number One Trust Fund, 1991–; Soc. for Maintenance of the Faith, 1995–; Anglo-Catholic Ordination Candidates Fund, 2003–. Gov., Heathfield St Mary Sch., 2008–. Mem. Governing Body, Church in Wales, 1971–77. *Recreations:* fine wines, opera, championing lost causes. *Address:* Ascot Priory, Berks SL5 8RT. *T:* (01344) 885157.

URWICK, Sir Alan (Bedford), KCVO 1984; CMG 1978; Serjeant at Arms, House of Commons, 1989–95; *b* 2 May 1930; *s* of late Col Lyndall Fownes Urwick, OBE, MC and Joan Wilhelmina Saunders (*née* Bedford); *m* 1960, Marta, *o* *d* of Adhemar Montagne; three *s*. *Educ:* Dragon Sch.; Rugby (Schol.); New Coll., Oxford (Exhibr). 1st cl. hons Mod. History 1952. Joined HM Foreign (subseq. Diplomatic) Service, 1952; served in: Brussels, 1954–56; Moscow, 1958–59; Baghdad, 1960–61; Amman, 1965–67; Washington, 1967–70; Cairo, 1971–73; seconded to Cabinet Office as Asst Sec., Central Policy Review Staff, 1973–75; Head of Near East and N Africa Dept, FCO, 1975–76; Minister, Madrid, 1977–79; Ambassador to Jordan, 1979–84; Ambassador to Egypt, 1985–87; High Comr to Canada, 1987–89. Chm., Anglo-Jordanian Soc., 1997–2001. KStJ 1982. Grand Cordon, first class, Order of Independence (Jordan), 1984. *Address:* The Moat House, Slaugham Place, near Haywards Heath, Sussex RH17 6AL. *Club:* Garrick.

URWIN, Rt Rev. Lindsay Goodall, OGS; Area Bishop of Horsham, 1993–2009; Priest Administrator, Shrine of Our Lady of Walsingham, Norfolk, from Feb. 2009 (Guardian, since 2006); *b* 13 March 1956. *Educ:* Camberwell GS, Australia; Ripon Coll., Cuddesdon; Heythrop Coll., Univ. of London (MA 2003). Ordained deacon, 1980, priest, 1981; Curate, St Peter, Walworth, 1980–83; Vicar, St Faith, N Dulwich, 1983–88; Diocesan Missioner, Chichester, 1988–93. Nat. Chm., Church Union, 1995–98. Member: OGS, 1991– (UK Provincial, 1996–2005); Coll. of Evangelists, 1999–. Provost, Southern Area, Woodard Corp. of Schs, 2006–; Pres., Sch. Chaplains' Conf., 2007–. *Publication:* (ed jtly) Youthful Spirit, 1999. *Address:* (until Feb. 2009) Bishop's House, 21 Guildford Road, Horsham RH12 1LU. *T:* (01403) 211139, *Fax:* (01403) 217349; *e-mail:* bishhorsham@diochi.co.uk; (from Feb. 2009) The Shrine of Our Lady of Walsingham, Walsingham, Norfolk NR22 6EE. *T:* (01328) 820255, *Fax:* (01328) 824206.

URWIN, Roger John, CBE 2007; PhD; FREng, FIET; Chairman, Alfred McAlpine plc, since 2007 (non-executive Director, since 2006); *b* 8 Feb. 1946. *Educ:* Watford Grammar Sch.; Weston-super-Mare Grammar Sch.; Southampton Univ. (BSc 1964; PhD 1971). CEng; FIET (FIEE 1990). Various appts with CEGB, 1971–85; Dir of Engrg, Midlands Electricity Bd, 1985–90; Man. Dir, subseq. Chief Exec., London Electricity, 1990–95; Dir, 1995–2001, Chief Exec., 2001–02, Nat. Grid Gp; Chief Exec., Nat. Grid Transco plc, 2002–06. Non-executive Director: Special Utilities Investment Trust plc, 1993–2003; TotalFinaElf Exploration UK plc, 1996–2003; Utilico, 2003–. FREng (FEng 1998).

URWIN, (Terence) Peter; public sector consultant, since 2001; Director of Administration and County Solicitor, Northumberland County Council, 1990–2000; *b* 28 Oct. 1948; *s* of John Robson Urwin; *m* 1971, Mary Theresa Smith; one *d*. *Educ:* Durham Johnston Sch.; Liverpool Univ. (LLB Hons). Solicitor. Durham County Council: Asst Solicitor, 1973–74; Asst Clerk of the Council, 1974–86; Dep. County Solicitor, 1986–90. Clerk to the Lieutenancy, Northumberland, 1990–2000. Secretary, Northumberland Advisory Committee: Justices of the Peace, 1990–2000; Gen. Comrs of Income Tax, 1990–2000. Mem. Council, Law Soc., 1997–2001. *Recreations:* Rugby, walking, crosswords. *Address:* Buckburns, Brancepeth Village, Durham City DH7 8DT. *T:* (0191) 378 3086.

USBORNE, Peter; *see* Usborne, T. P.

USBORNE, (Thomas) Peter; Founder and Managing Director, Usborne Publishing Ltd, since 1973; *b* 18 Aug. 1937; *s* of Thomas George Usborne and Gerda (*née* Just); *m* 1964, Cornelie Tücking; one *s* one *d*. *Educ:* Summer Fields Sch., Oxford; Eton Coll.; Balliol Coll., Oxford (BA); INSEAD, Fontainebleau, France (MBA 1966). Co Founder and Man. Dir, Private Eye mag., 1962–65; Sen. Scientist, Metra Sigma Martech, 1967–68; Asst to Chm., BPC Publishing Ltd, 1969–70; Publishing Dir, Macdonald Educnl, 1970–73. *Recreations:* flying, gardening, France. *Clubs:* Garrick, Groucho.

USHER, Sir Andrew (John), 8th Bt *cr* 1899, of Norton, Ratho, Midlothian and of Wells, Hobkirk, Roxburghshire; interior decorator and builder; *b* 8 Feb. 1963; *er* *s* of Sir John Usher, 7th Bt and of Rosemary Margaret, *d* of Col Sir Reginald Houldsworth, 4th Bt, OBE, TD; *S* father, 1998; *m* 1987, Charlotte Louise Alexandra, *o* *d* of R. B. Eldridge; two *s*. *Educ:* Hilton Coll., S Africa. *Recreations:* golf, fishing. *Heir:* *s* Rory James Andrew Usher, *b* 11 June 1991.

USSHER, Kitty; MP (Lab) Burnley, since 2005; Parliamentary Under-Secretary of State, Department for Work and Pensions, since 2008; *b* 18 March 1971; *d* of Patrick Ussher and Susan (*née* Bottomley, now Whitfield); *m* 1999, Peter Colley; one *s* one *d*. *Educ:* Balliol Coll., Oxford (PPE 1993); Birkbeck Coll., London (MSc Econs 1998). Researcher, Labour Party, 1994–97; Economist: EIU, 1997–98; Centre for European Reform, 1998–2000; Chief Economist, Britain in Europe Campaign, 1999–2001; Special Advr to Rt Hon. Patricia Hewitt, MP, at DTI, 2001–04. Economic Sec., HM Treasury, 2007–08. Mem., LBC of Lambeth, 1998–2002. *Publication:* The Spectre of Tax Harmonisation, 2000. *Recreations:* hill walking, supporting Burnley Football Club. *Address:* House of Commons, SW1A 0AA; *e-mail:* ussherk@parliament.uk; (office) 2 Victoria Street, Burnley BB11 1DD. *T:* (office) (01282) 450840, *Fax:* (office) (01282) 839623.

UTEEM, Cassam; President, Republic of Mauritius, 1992–2002; *b* 22 March 1941; *s* of Omar and Aisha Uteem; *m* 1967, Zohra Uteem; one *s* one *d* (and one *s* decd). *Educ:* Univ. of Mauritius (Dip. Soc. Work); Univ. of Paris VII (LèsL, MPsychol). Mem., Municipal Council, Port Louis, 1969, 1977–79, 1986–88 (Lord Mayor, 1986); MLA Port Louis East/Maritime, 1982–92; Minister of Employment, Social Security and National Solidarity, 1982–83; Opposition Whip, 1983–87; Chm., Public Accounts Cttee, 1988–90; Dep. Prime Minister and Minister of Industry and Industrial Technol., 1990–92. Mem. Bd, Internat. Inst. for Democracy and Electoral Assistance. Hon. DCL Mauritius, 1994; Dr *hc* Aix Marseilles III, 1994. Grand Commander, Order of Star and Key of the Indian Ocean (Republic of Mauritius), 1993. *Recreations:* reading, walking. *Address:* c/o State House, Le Reduit, Mauritius. *T:* 4543021.

UTLEY, (Clifton) Garrick; President, Levin Graduate Institute, State University of New York, since 2003; *b* 19 Nov. 1939; *s* of late Clifton Maxwell Utley and Frayn Garrick

Utley; *m* 1973, Gertje Rommeswinkel. *Educ:* Carleton Coll., Northfield, Minn, USA (BA 1961); Free Univ., Berlin. Correspondent, NBC News: Saigon, Vietnam, 1964–65; Berlin, Germany, 1966–68; Paris, France, 1969–71; NY, 1971–72; London (Senior European Correspondent), 1973–79; New York (Chief Foreign Correspondent), 1980–93; Chief Foreign Correspondent, ABC News, London, 1993–96; contributor, CNN, NY, 1996–2003. Numerous documentary films on foreign affairs. Hon. LLD: Carleton Coll., 1979; Pomona Coll., 2001. *Recreations:* music, conversation, languages. *Address:* 19 East 88th Street, New York, NY 10128, USA. *Club:* Century (New York).

UTLEY, Prof. James Henry Paul; Professor of Organic Chemistry, Queen Mary and Westfield College (formerly at Queen Mary College), University of London, 1983–2001, now Emeritus; *b* 11 Sept. 1936; *s* of Victor Eric Utley and Lena Beatrice Utley; *m* 1959, Hazel Wendler (*née* Brown); two *s* two *d. Educ:* E. P. Collier Sch., Reading; Univ. of Hull (BSc, PhD); Technische Hogeschool, Delft; University College London; DSc London. CChem, FRSC. NATO Research Fellowships, 1961–62; Queen Mary, later Queen Mary and Westfield College, London: Lectr, 1963–76; Reader in Organic Chemistry, 1976–83; Head of Chemistry, 1987–91, 1997–99; Dean, Faculty of Natural Scis, 1991–94; Mem. Council, 1991–94. Guest Professor: Univ. of Aarhus, 1973; Univ. of Münster, 1985; Ecole Normale Supérieure, Paris, 1994; Univ. of Texas at Austin, 1995. M. M. Baizer Award, Electrochem. Soc., USA, 2000. *Publications:* research and review articles in internat. learned jls. *Recreations:* walking, bowls, jazz. *Address:* School of Biological and Chemical Sciences, Queen Mary, University of London, Mile End Road, E1 4NS. *Club:* Heathfield (Wandsworth Common).

UTSUMI, Yoshio; Secretary-General, International Telecommunication Union, United Nations, 1999–2006; *b* 14 Aug. 1942; *m* 1970, Masako Okubo; one *s* one *d. Educ:* Univ. of Tokyo (BA Law); Univ. of Chicago (MA Pol Sci.). Joined Min. of Posts and Telecommunications (MPT), Japan, 1966; Prof. of Public Admin, MPT Postal Coll., 1972–73; First Sec., i/c ITU Affairs, Perm. Mission of Japan, Geneva, 1978–81; Dir, Computer Communication Div. and of Policy Div., Communications Policy Bureau, 1982–86; Dir, Fund Mgt Div., Postal Life Insurance Bureau, 1986–88; Dir, Gen. Affairs Div., Broadcasting Bureau, 1988–89; Asst Vice-Minister, 1990–91; Dep. Dir-Gen., Communications Policy Bureau, 1991–93; Dir-Gen., Internat. Affairs Dept, 1993–95; Dep. Minister for Internat. Affairs, 1995–96; Dir-Gen. of Posts, 1996–97; Dep. Minister, 1997–99. Chm., ITU Plenipotentiary Conf., 1994.

UTTING, Sir William (Benjamin), Kt 1991; CB 1985; President, Mental Health Foundation, since 1999 (Trustee, 1988–97; Vice-President, 1997–99); *b* 13 May 1931; *s* of John William Utting and Florence Ada Utting; *m* 1954, Mildred Jackson; two *s* one *d. Educ:* Great Yarmouth Grammar Sch.; New Coll., Oxford (Exhibnr; MA; Hon. Fellow, 1996); Barnett House, Oxford. Probation Officer: Co. Durham, 1956–58; Norfolk, 1958–61; Sen. Probation Officer, Co. Durham, 1961–64; Principal Probation Officer, Newcastle upon Tyne, 1964–68; Lectr in Social Studies, Univ. of Newcastle upon Tyne, 1968–70; Dir of Social Services, Kensington and Chelsea, 1970–76; Chief Social Work Officer, DHSS, 1976–85; Chief Inspector, Social Services Inspectorate, DHSS, subseq. DoH, 1985–91. Member: Chief Scientist's Res. Cttee, DHSS, 1973–76; SSRC, 1979–83; ESRC, 1984; Cttee on Standards in Public Life, 1994–2001. Chm., 1991–97, Pres., 1997–2002, NISW. Chairman: Mary Ward House Trust, 1997–2006; Forum on Children and Violence, 1997–2000; Vice-President: Nat. Family Mediation, 1997–; Nat. Children's Bureau, 2002–07; Member of Council: Caldecott Foundn, 1998–2002; Goldsmiths Coll., London Univ., 1993–2006 (Chair, 2000–06, Hon. Fellow, 2007); Trustee: Joseph Rowntree Foundn, 1991–2006 (Dep. Chm., 2001–05; Chm., 2005–06); CSV, 1991–97; Family Fund Trust, 1996–2000. Pres., New Coll. Soc., 2002–03. Fellow, Centre for Social Policy, Dartington, 2001. Hon. DLitt: UEA, 1992; East London, 1998; Hon. DCL Northumbria, 1997; Hon. DSc Kingston, 2000. *Publications:* Children in the Public Care, 1991; People Like Us, 1997; contribs to professional jls. *Recreations:* literature, music, art. *Address:* 76 Great Brownings, SE21 7HR. *T:* (020) 8670 1201.

UXBRIDGE, Earl of; Charles Alexander Vaughan Paget; *b* 13 Nov. 1950; *s* and *heir* of 7th Marquess of Anglesey, *qv*; *m* 1986, Georganne Elizabeth Elliott, *d* of Col John Alfred Downes, MBE, MC; one *s* one *d. Educ:* Dragon School, Oxford; Eton; Exeter Coll., Oxford; Sussex Univ. (MA, DPhil). *Heir:* *s* Lord Paget de Beaudesert, *qv. Address:* Plâs-Newydd, Llanfairpwll, Gwynedd LL61 6DZ.

V

VADERA, Baroness *cr* 2007 (Life Peer), of Holland Park in the Royal Borough of Kensington and Chelsea; **Shriti Vadera;** Parliamentary Under-Secretary of State, Department for Business, Enterprise and Regulatory Reform, and a Parliamentary Secretary, Cabinet Office, since 2008; *b* Uganda. *Educ:* Somerville Coll., Oxford. With S. G. Warburg, later UBS, 1984–99; Advr to Chancellor of Exchequer and Mem. Council of Econ. Advrs, HM Treasury, 1999–2007; Parly Under-Sec. of State, DFID, 2007–08. Trustee, Oxfam, 2000–05. *Address:* Department for Business, Enterprise and Regulatory Reform, 1 Victoria Street, SW1H 0ET.

VADGAMA, Prof. Pankaj Maganlal, PhD; FRCPath; FRCS; FInstP; FIMMM; Professor of Clinical Biochemistry, and Director, Interdisciplinary Research Centre in Biomedical Materials, Queen Mary, University of London, since 2000; *b* 16 Feb. 1948; *s* of Maganlal Vadgama and Champaben Vadgama (*née* Gajjar); *m* 1977, Dixa Bakrania; one *s* two *d. Educ:* Orange Hill Co. Grammar Sch.; Univ. of Newcastle upon Tyne (MB BS, BSc 1st cl. Hons; PhD 1984). FRCPath 1989; FRSC 1996; FInstP 2000; FIMMM 2001. MRC Trng Fellow, Newcastle Univ., 1978–81; Sen. Registrar in Clin. Biochem., Newcastle Gen. Hosp., 1981–83; Dir, Biosensor Gp, Newcastle Univ., 1983–88; Manchester University: Prof. of Clin. Biochem., 1988–2000; Prof. of Biomed. Materials, 1999–2000. Hon. Consultant Chemical Pathologist: Royal Victoria Infirmary, Newcastle, 1983–88; Hope Hosp., Salford, 1988–2000; Barts and the London NHS Trust, 2000–. *Publications:* (ed) Surfaces and Interfaces for Biomaterials, 2005; contribs on biosensors, *in vivo* monitoring, biomaterials, biocompatibility and membrane technol. *Recreations:* reading, walking. *Address:* 16 Wellfields, Loughton, Essex IG10 1NX. *T:* (office) (020) 7882 5189, *Fax:* (020) 8983 1007. *Club:* Athenæum.

VAEA, Baron of Houma; Chairman: National Reserve Bank Board, since 1989; Shipping Corporation of Polynesia; *b* 15 May 1921; *s* of Viliami Vilai Tupou and Tupou Seini Vaea; *m* 1952, Tuputupu Ma'afu; three *s* three *d. Educ:* Wesley College, Auckland, NZ. RNZAF, 1942–45; Tonga Civil Service, 1945–53; ADC to HM Queen Salote, 1954–59; Governor of Ha'apai, 1959–68; Commissioner and Consul in UK, 1969; High Comr in UK, 1970–72; Minister for Labour, Commerce and Industries, 1973–91; Actg Dep. Prime Minister, 1986; Prime Minister of Tonga, 1991–2000; Minister of Agric. and Forestry, for Marine and Ports, responsible for Telecommunications, 1991–2000. Chairman: Tonga Telecommunications Commn, 1991–2000; Tonga Broadcasting Commn, 1991–2000; Chm., Tonga Investment Ltd, 1991–. Given the title Baron Vaea of Houma by HM The King of Tonga, 1970. *Recreations:* fishing, tennis. *Heir: e s* Albert Tu'ivanuavou Vaea, *b* 19 Sept. 1957. *Address:* PO Box 262, Nuku'alofa, Tonga.

VAILE, Hon. Mark Anthony James; MP (National) for Lyne, NSW, since 1993; Deputy Prime Minister of Australia, 2005–07; Leader, National Party, 2005–07; *b* 18 April 1956; *s* of George and Sue Vaile; *m* 1976, Wendy Duff; three *d. Educ:* Taree High Sch., NSW. Jackaroo, 1973–75; farm machinery retailer, 1975–78; stock, station and real estate agent and auctioneer, 1978–92. Greater Taree City Council: Alderman, 1985–93; Dep. Mayor, 1986–87, 1991–92, 1992–93. Mem., National Party, 1978– (Chm., Wingham Br., 1982–86); Sec., Lyne Electorate Council, 1984–90. Minister: for Transport and Regl Develt, 1997–98; for Agric., Fisheries and Forestry, 1998–99; for Trade, 1999–2006; for Transport and Regl Services, 2006–07. Asst Nat. Party Whip, 1994–96; Nat. Party Whip, 1996–97; Dep. Leader, Fed. Parly Nat. Party, Australia, 1999–2005. *Address:* Parliament House, Canberra, ACT 2600, Australia. *T:* (2) 65525222, *Fax:* (2) 65525835; *e-mail:* mark.vaile.mp@aph.gov.au.

VAISEY, David George, CBE 1996; FSA; FRHistS; Bodley's Librarian, Oxford, 1986–96, now Emeritus; Keeper of the Archives, Oxford University, 1995–2000; Professorial Fellow then Fellow by Special Election, Exeter College, Oxford, 1975–2000, now Emeritus; *b* 15 March 1935; *s* of William Thomas Vaisey and Minnie Vaisey (*née* Payne); *m* 1965, Maureen Anne (*née* Mansell); two *d. Educ:* Rendcomb Coll., Glos (schol.); Exeter Coll., Oxford (Exhibnr; BA Mod. Hist., MA). 2nd Lieut, Glos Regt and KAR, 1955–56. Archivist, Staffordshire CC, 1960–63; Asst then Sen. Asst Librarian, Bodleian Liby, 1963–75; Dep. Keeper, Oxford Univ. Archives, 1966–75; Keeper of Western Manuscripts, Bodleian Liby, 1975–86. Vis. Prof., Liby Studies, UCLA, 1985. Hon. Res. Fellow, Dept of Library, Archive and Information Studies, UCL, 1987–. Member: Royal Commn on Historical Manuscripts, 1986–98; Adv. Council on Public Records, 1989–94; Expert Panel on Museums, Libraries and Archives, Heritage Lottery Fund, 1999–2005; Archive, Libraries and Information Adv. Cttee, English Heritage, 1999–2002; Chm., Nat. Council on Archives, 1988–91. Vice-Pres., British Records Assoc., 1998–2006; Pres., Soc. of Archivists, 1999–2002. FRHistS 1973; FSA 1974. Hon. Fellow, Kellogg Coll., Oxford, 1996. Encomienda, Order of Isabel the Catholic (Spain), 1989. *Publications:* Staffordshire and The Great Rebellion (jtly), 1964; Probate Inventories of Lichfield and District 1568–1680, 1969; (jtly) Victorian and Edwardian Oxford from old photographs, 1971; (jtly) Oxford Shops and Shopping, 1972; (jtly) Art for Commerce, 1973; Oxfordshire: a handbook for students of local history, 1973, 2nd edn 1974; The Diary of Thomas Turner 1754–65, 1984; articles in learned jls and collections. *Address:* 5 Restwood Place, Faringdon Road, Southmoor, Oxon OX13 5BW.

VAIZEY, Lady; Marina Vaizey; writer, lecturer and art critic; Editor, National Art Collections Fund Publications, 1991–94 (Editorial Consultant, 1994–98); *b* 16 Jan. 1938; *o d* of late Lyman and Ruth Stansky; *m* 1961, Lord Vaizey (*d* 1984); two *s* one *d. Educ:* Brearley Sch., New York; Putney Sch., Putney, Vermont; Radcliffe Coll., Harvard Univ. (BA Medieval History and Lit.); Girton Coll., Cambridge (BA, MA). Art Critic: Financial Times, 1970–74; Sunday Times, 1974–92; Dance Critic, Now!, 1979–81. Member: Arts Council, 1976–79 (Mem. Art Panel, 1973–79, Dep. Chm., 1976–79); Advisory Cttee, DoE, 1975–81; Paintings for Hospitals, 1974–90; Cttee, Contemporary Art Soc., 1975–79, 1980–94 (Hon. Sec., 1988–94); Hist. of Art and Complementary Studies Bd, CNAA, 1978–82; Photography Bd, CNAA, 1979–81; Fine Art Bd, CNAA, 1980–83; Passenger Services Sub-Cttee, Heathrow Airport, 1979–83; Visual Arts Adv. Cttee, British Council, 1987–2004; Crafts Council, 1988–94; Art Wkg Gp, National Curriculum, DES, 1990–91; Cttee, 20th Century Soc., 1995–98; Gov., South Bank Bd, 1993–2003; Trustee: Nat. Mus and Galls on Merseyside, 1986–2001; Geffrye Mus., London, 1990–; Imperial War Mus., 1991–2003 (Mem. Council, Friends of Imperial War Mus., 2003–); London Open House, 1996–2008; Internat. Rescue Cttee UK, 1997–2007; Assoc. for Cultural Exchange, 1998–; Mem. Council, Friends of the V&A, 2001– (Chm., 2008–); Gov., Nat. Army Mus., 2001– (Mem. Council, Friends of Nat. Army Mus., 2003–06); Exec. Dir, Mitchell Prize for the Hist. of Art, 1976–87. Governor: Camberwell Coll. of Arts and Crafts, 1971–82; Bath Acad. of Art, Corsham, 1978–81. Curated: Critic's Choice, Tooth's, 1974; Painter as Photographer, touring exhibn, UK, 1982–85; Shining Through, Crafts Council, 1995. Turner Prize Judge, 1997. *Publications:* 100 Masterpieces of Art, 1979; Andrew Wyeth, 1980; The Artist as Photographer, 1982; Peter Blake, 1985; Christiane Kubrick, 1990; Christo, 1990; Sorensen, 1994; Picasso's Ladies, 1998; Sutton Taylor, 1999; Felim Egan, 1999; (with Charlotte Gere) Great Women Collectors, 1999; (ed) Art, the Critics' Choice, 1999; Magdalene Odundo, 2001; The British Museum Smile, 2002; Colin Rose, 2003; Wendy Ramshaw, 2004. *Address:* 24 Heathfield Terrace, Chiswick, W4 4JE. *T:* (020) 8994 7994; *e-mail:* marina@vaizey.demon.co.uk.

See also Hon. E. H. B. Vaizey.

VAIZEY, Hon. Edward Henry Butler, (Ed); MP (C) Wantage, since 2005; *b* 5 June 1968; *s* of Baron Vaizey and of Lady Vaizey, *qv*; *m* 2005, Alexandra Mary Jane Holland; one *s* one *d. Educ:* St Paul's Sch., London; Merton Coll., Oxford (BA 1989, MA 2004); City Univ. (Dip. Law 1992). Desk Officer, Conservative Res. Dept, 1989–91; called to the Bar, Middle Temple, 1993, practised as barrister, 1993–96; Director: Public Policy Unit, 1996–97; Politics Internat., 1997–98; Consolidated Communications, 1998–2003; Chief Speech Writer to Leader of the Opposition, 2004; Opposition frontbench spokesman on the arts, 2006–. Contested (C) Bristol East, 1997. *Publications:* (ed with M. Gove and N. Boles) A Blue Tomorrow, 2001; (ed with M. McManus) The Blue Book on Transport, 2002; (ed) The Blue Book on Health, 2002. *Address:* House of Commons, SW1A 0AA. *T:* (020) 7219 3000; *e-mail:* vaizeye@parliament.uk. *Clubs:* Soho House; Didcot Conservative.

VAJDA, Christopher Stephen; QC 1997; a Recorder, since 2002; *b* 6 July 1955; *s* of late Stephen Vajda and of Heidi Vajda (*née* Schmalhorst). *Educ:* Winchester Coll.; Corpus Christi Coll., Cambridge (MA); Inst d'Etudes Européennes, Brussels (Licence speciale en droit européen). Called to the Bar, Gray's Inn, 1979 (Bencher 2004), NI, 1996. Mem., Supplementary Panel, Treasury Counsel, 1993–97. *Publication:* (contrib.) Bellamy & Child, Common Market Law of Competition, 3rd edn 1987 to 6th edn 2008. *Recreations:* architecture, opera, theatre, tennis. *Address:* Monckton Chambers, 1 Raymond Buildings, Gray's Inn, WC1R 5NR. *T:* (020) 7405 7211. *Club:* Royal Automobile.

VAJPAYEE, Atal Bihari; Member, Lok Sabha, 1957–62, 1967–84 and since 1991; Prime Minister of India, May 1996 and 1998–2004; Leader, Bharatiya Janata Party Parliamentary Party, 1980–84, 1986–91 and 1993–2004; *b* Gwalior, Madhya Pradesh, 25 Dec. 1926; *s* of Shri Krishna Bihari; unmarried. *Educ:* Victoria Coll., Gwalior; D.A.V. Coll., Kanpur (MA). Journalist and social worker. Arrested in freedom movement, 1942; Founder Mem., Jana Sangh, 1951–77; Leader, Jana Sangh Parly Party, 1957–77; Pres., Bharatiya Jana Sangh, 1968–73; detained 26 June 1975, during Emergency; Founder Member: Janata Party, 1977–80; Bharatiya Janata Party, 1980– (Pres., 1980–86). Mem., Rajya Sabha, 1962–67 and 1986–91; Minister of External Affairs, 1977–79; Leader of the Opposition, Lok Sabha, 1993–98; Chairman: Cttee on Govt Assurances, 1966–67; Public Accounts Cttee, 1969–70, 1991–92; Cttee on Petitions, 1990–91. Member: Parly Goodwill Mission to E Africa, 1965; Parly Delegns to Australia, 1967, Eur. Parlt, 1983; Member: Indian Delegation: to CPA meetings in Canada, 1966, Zambia, 1980, IOM, 1984; to IPU Confs in Japan, 1974, Sri Lanka, 1975, Switzerland, 1984; to UN Gen. Assembly, 1988, 1989, 1990, 1991. Mem., Nat. Integration Council, 1958–62, 1967–73, 1986, 1991–. President: All India Station Masters and Asst Station Masters Assoc., 1965–70; Pandit Deen Dayal Upadhyay Smarak Samiti, 1968–84; Pandit Deen Dayal Upadhyaya Janma Bhumi Smarak Samiti, 1979–. Formerly Editor: Rashtra-dharma; Panchajanya; Veer Arjun. *Publications:* Lok Sabha Mein Atalji (collection of speeches); Qaidi Kavirai ki Kundaliyan; New Dimensions of India's Foreign Policy; Sansad Mein Teen Dashak (collection of speeches). *Address:* Shinde ki Chhawni, Gwalior, MP, India; 7 Race Course Road, New Delhi 110001, India. *T:* (11) 3018939.

VALE, Brian, CBE 1994 (OBE 1977); Regional Director for Middle East and North Africa, British Council, 1995; retired; *b* 26 May 1938; *s* of Leslie Vale and May (*née* Knowles); *m* 1966, Margaret Mary Cookson; two *s. Educ:* Sir Joseph Williamson's Mathematical Sch., Rochester; Keele Univ. (BA, DipEd); King's Coll., London (MPhil). HMOCS, N Rhodesia, 1960–63; Assistant to Comr for N Rhodesia, London, 1963–64; Educn Attaché, Zambia High Commn, London, 1964–65; British Council: Rio de Janeiro, 1965–68; Appts Div., 1968–72; Educn and Sci. Div., 1972–75; Rep., Saudi Arabia, 1975–78; Dep. Controller, Educn and Sci. Div., 1978–80; Dir Gen., Tech. Educn and Trng Orgn for Overseas Countries, 1980–81; Controller, Sci., Technol. and Educn Div., 1981–83; Rep. in Egypt, and Cultural Counsellor, British Embassy, Cairo, 1983–87; Asst Dir Gen., 1987–90; Dir, Spain, and Cultural Attaché, British Embassy, Madrid, 1991–95. Chm., Internat. Family Health, 1998–2005; Mem. Council, Navy Records Soc., 2005–. Chm., St Alfege Develt Cttee, Greenwich, 2004–. Medalha Merito Tamandaré (Brazil), 1997. *Publications:* Independence or Death: British sailors and Brazilian independence, 1996; A War Betwixt Englishmen: Argentina versus Brazil in the River Plate 1825–30, 1999; A Frigate of King George: life and duty on HMS Doris

1807–1829, 2001; The Audacious Admiral Cochrane, 2004; Cochrane in the Pacific: fortune and freedom in Spanish America, 2007; contribs to specialist jls on naval hist. *Recreations:* reading, talking, naval history. *Address:* 40 Gloucester Circus, SE10 8RY. *T:* (020) 8858 6233.

VALENTIA, 16th Viscount *cr* 1622 (Ire.); **Francis William Dighton Annesley;** Bt 1620; Baron Mountnorris 1628; *b* 29 Dec. 1959; *s* of 15th Viscount Valentia and of Anita Phyllis Annesley (*née* Joy); *S* father, 2005; *m* 1982, Shaneen Therese Hobbs; two *d. Educ:* Falcon Coll., Bulawayo (DipAg; BCom (Mkting)). *Recreations:* golf, scuba diving. *Heir: b* Hon. Peter John Annesley [*b* 18 Dec. 1967; *m* 1997, Deborah Ann Coelen; three *s*]. *Address:* 3 Ruby Close, Wokingham, Berks RG41 3TX. *T:* (0118) 989 0258; *e-mail:* annesley@onetel.net.

VALENTINE, Baroness *cr* 2005 (Life Peer), of Putney in the London Borough of Wandsworth; **Josephine Clare Valentine;** Chief Executive, London First, since 2003; *b* 8 Dec. 1958; *d* of Michael and Shirley Valentine; *m* 1990, Simon Acland; two *d. Educ:* St Hugh's Coll., Oxford Univ. (BA Hons Maths and Philosophy). Manager, Corporate Finance, Barings, 1981–88; Chief Exec., Blackburn Partnership, 1988–90; Sen. Manager, Planning and Corporate Finance, BOC Gp, 1990–95; Chief Exec., Central London Partnership, 1995–97; London First, 1997–. Bd Mem., New West End Co., 2001–. Comr, Nat. Lottery, 2001–05. Trustee, Teach First, 2005–. *Recreations:* piano, bridge, travel. *T:* (020) 7665 1521, *Fax:* (020) 7665 1537.

VALENTINE, Rt Rev. Barry, MA, BD, LTh, DD; Rector, Parish of Salt Spring Island, British Columbia, 1989–95; *b* 26 Sept. 1927; *s* of Harry John Valentine and Ethel Margaret Purkiss; *m* 1st, 1952, Mary Currell Hayes; three *s* one *d*; 2nd, 1984, Shirley Carolyn Shean Evans. *Educ:* Brentwood Sch.; St John's Coll., Cambridge; McGill Univ., Montreal. Curate, Christ Church Cath., Montreal, 1952; Incumbent, Chateauguay-Beauharnois, 1954; Dir, Religious Educn, Dio. Montreal, 1957; Rector of St Lambert, PQ, 1961; Exec. Officer, Dio. Montreal, 1965; Dean of Montreal, 1968; Bishop Coadjutor of Rupert's Land, 1969; Bishop of Rupert's Land, 1970–82; Chaplain, Univ. of British Columbia, 1984–85; Asst Bishop of Maryland, 1986–89. Interim Rector, St Paul's Parish, Washington, 1997. Chancellor, 1970, Res. Fellow, 1983, St John's Coll., Winnipeg. Hon. DD: St John's Coll., Winnipeg, 1969; Montreal Dio. Theol Coll., 1970. *Publication:* The Gift that is in you, 1984. *Recreations:* music, theatre, walking, reading. *Address:* 111 Carlin Avenue, Salt Spring Island, BC V8K 2J5, Canada.

VALENTINE, Caroline, (Mrs Malcolm Valentine); *see* Charles, Caroline.

VALIANT, Prof. Leslie Gabriel, FRS 1991; T. Jefferson Coolidge Professor of Computer Science and Applied Mathematics, Harvard University, since 2001; *b* 28 March 1949; *s* of Leslie Valiant and Eva Julia (*née* Ujlaki); *m* 1977, Gayle Lynne Dyckoff; two *s. Educ:* Tynemouth High Sch.; Latymer Upper Sch.; King's Coll., Cambridge (MA); Imperial Coll., London (DIC); Warwick Univ. (PhD). Vis. Asst Prof., Carnegie Mellon Univ., Pittsburgh, 1973–74; Lecturer: Leeds Univ., 1974–76; Edinburgh Univ., 1977–81, Reader 1981–82; Gordon McKay Prof. of Computer Sci. and Applied Maths, Harvard Univ., 1982–2001. Vis. Prof., Harvard Univ., 1982; Vis. Fellow, Oxford Univ. Computing Lab. and Merton Coll., Oxford, 1987–88; Guggenheim Fellow, 1985–86. Fellow, Amer. Assoc. for Artificial Intelligence, 1992; Mem., US NAS, 2001. Nevanlinna Prize, IMU, 1986; Knuth Prize, ACM/IEEE, 1997; EATCS Award, 2008. *Publications:* Circuits of the Mind, 1994; research papers in scientific jls. *Address:* School of Engineering and Applied Sciences, Harvard University, 33 Oxford Street, Cambridge, MA 02138, USA. *T:* (617) 4955817.

VALIN, Reginald Pierre; business consultant; *b* 8 March 1938; *s* of Pierre Louis Valin and Molly Doreen Valin; *m* 1960, Brigitte Karin Leister; one *d. Educ:* Emanuel School. Bank of America, 1959–60; Charles Barker & Sons Ltd, later Charles Barker City, 1960–79: Dir, 1971–73; Man. Dir, 1973–76; Chief Exec., 1976–79; Founder Dir, Valin Pollen, subseq. The VPI Gp: Chm. and Chief Exec., 1979–89, Dep. Chm., 1989–90. *Address:* 38 Monckton Court, Melbury Road, W14 8NF. *T:* (020) 7371 1872.

VALIOS, Nicholas Paul; QC 1991; a Recorder of the Crown Court, since 1986; *b* 5 May 1943; *s* of Nicholas William and Elizabeth Joan Valios; *m* 1967, Cynthia Valerie Horton; one *s* one *d. Educ:* Stonyhurst Coll., Lancs. Called to the Bar, Inner Temple, 1964; Mem., SE Circuit. *Recreations:* windsurfing, golf, reading, computers, scuba diving. *Address:* 4 Breams Building, EC4A 1HP. *T:* (020) 7092 1900.

VALLANCE, family name of **Baron Vallance of Tummel**.

VALLANCE OF TUMMEL, Baron *cr* 2004 (Life Peer), of Tummel in Perth and Kinross; **Iain David Thomas Vallance,** Kt 1994; Chairman, Royal Scottish Academy of Music and Drama, since 2006; *b* 20 May 1943; *s* of late Edmund Thomas Vallance and Janet Wright Bell Ross Davidson; *m* 1967, Elizabeth Mary McGonnigill (*see* E. M. Vallance); one *s* one *d. Educ:* Edinburgh Acad.; Dulwich Coll.; Glasgow Acad.; Brasenose Coll., Oxford (Hon. Fellow, 1997); London Grad. Sch. of Business Studies (MSc). FCIBS 2002. Joined Post Office, 1966; Director: Central Finance, 1976–78; Telecommunications Finance, 1978–79; Materials Dept, 1979–81; British Telecommunications: a Corp. Dir, 1981–2001; Board Mem. for Orgn and Business Systems, 1981–83; Man. Dir, Local Communications Services Div., 1983–85; Chief of Operations, 1985–86; Chief Exec., 1986–95; Chm., 1987–2001 (part-time 1998–2001); Pres. Emeritus, 2001–02. Dir, 1993–2005, Vice-Chm., 1994–2005, Royal Bank of Scotland; Dir, Mobil Corp., 1996–99. Chairman: Nations Healthcare Ltd, 2005–07; Amsphere Ltd, 2006–. Pres., CBI, 2000–02 (Mem., Pres.'s Cttee, 1988–); Member, President's Committee: (also Adv. Council), BITC, 1988–2002; Eur. Foundn for Quality Management, 1988–96. Chairman: Eur. Adv. Cttee, New York Stock Exchange, 2000–02 (Mem., 1995–); European Services Forum, 2003–07; Dep. Chm., Financial Reporting Council, 2001–02. Member: Internat. Adv. Bd, British-American Chamber of Commerce, 1991–2002; Bd, Scottish Enterprise, 1998–2001; Internat. Adv. Bd, AllianzSE, 1998–; Supervisory Bd, Siemens AG, 2003–; European Adv. Council, Rothschild Gp, 2003–. Chm., H of L Econ. Affairs Cttee, 2008– (Mem., 2005–07). Vice Pres., Princess Royal Trust for Carers, 1999– (Chm., 1991–98); Trustee, Monteverdi Trust, 1993–2001; Patron, Loughborough Univ., 1996–. Freeman, City of London, 1985; Liveryman, Wheelwrights' Co., 1986–. Hon. Gov., Glasgow Acad., 1993–. Fellow, London Business School, 1989. Hon. DSc: Ulster, 1992; Napier, 1994; City, 1996; Hon. DTech: Loughborough, 1992; Robert Gordon, 1994; Hon. DBA Kingston, 1993; Hon. DEng Heriot-Watt, 1995. *Recreations:* hill walking, music. *Address:* House of Lords, SW1A 0PW.

VALLANCE OF TUMMEL, Lady; *see* Vallance, E. M.

VALLANCE, Air Vice-Marshal Andrew George Buchanan, CB 2003; OBE 1987; FRAeS; Secretary, Defence Press and Broadcasting Advisory Committee, since 2004; *b* 7 April 1948; *s* of George Charles Buchanan Vallance and Dorothy Mabel Vallance (*née* Wooton); *m* 1972, Katharine Ray Fox; one *s* one *d. Educ:* RAF Coll., Cranwell; RAF Staff Coll. (psa 1980); Queens' Coll., Cambridge (MPhil Internat. Relns 1988). Commnd RAF, 1969; sqdn pilot with Nos 9, 617 and 27 Sqdns; Flight Comdr, No 50 Sqdn, 1977–79; Personal SO to Air Mem. for Personnel, 1981; OC No 55 Sqdn, 1982–84; Personal SO to CAS, 1984–87; Dir of Defence Studies, 1988–90; Chief of Mil. Co-op., SHAPE, 1991–93; OC RAF Wyton, 1993–95; Dep. Dir, Nuclear Policy, MoD, 1995; Chief, Special Weapons Br., SHAPE, 1996–98; COS, Reaction Forces Air Staff, NATO, 1998–2000; COS and Dep. C-in-C, RAF Personnel Trng Comd, 2000; Exec. Asst to COS, Comd Gp, SHAPE, 2000–04. FRAeS 1999. Member: RUSI, 1988–; IISS, 1988–. *Publications:* Air Power, 1989; RAF Air Power Doctrine, 1990; The Air Weapon, 1995; contrib. numerous articles to various defence jls. *Recreations:* military history, classical music, structural gardening, strategic studies. *Address:* Ministry of Defence, Main Building, Whitehall, SW1A 2HB. *Club:* Royal Air Force.

VALLANCE, Dr Elizabeth Mary, (Lady Vallance of Tummel); JP; Founder and Chairman, me too, since 1999; Chairman, I CAN, since 2007; *b* 8 April 1945; *e d* of William Henderson McGonnigill and Hon. Jean, *d* of 1st Baron Kirkwood; *m* 1967, Iain David Thomas Vallance (*see* Baron Vallance of Tummel); one *s* one *d. Educ:* Univ. of St Andrews (MA); LSE (MSc); Univ. of London (PhD); London Business Sch. (Sloan Fellow). Queen Mary College, later Queen Mary and Westfield College, University of London: Asst Lectr, Lectr, Sen. Lectr, Reader in Govt and Politics, 1968–85; Head, Dept of Politics, 1985–88; Vis. Prof., 1990–96; Hon. Fellow, 1997. Chm., St George's Healthcare NHS Trust, 1993–99; Director: HMV Group, 1990–97; Norwich Union plc, 1995–2000; Charter European Trust (formerly Charter Pan-European Trust) plc, 1998– (Sen. Ind. Dir, 2006–March 2009); Health Foundn (formerly PPP Healthcare Medical Trust), 1999– (Vice-Chm., 2003–); Aviva plc (formerly CGNU) plc, 2000–05; Medical Protection Soc., 2005–. Chm., NHS Adv. Cttee on Distinction, then Clin. Excellence, Awards, 2000–05; Mem., Cttee on Standards in Public Life, 2004–. Chm. of Govs, James Allen's Girls' Sch., 1991–94; Chm. Council, Inst. of Educn, Univ. of London, 2000–; Gov., Sutton Valence Sch., 2006–. Member: Adv. Council, Citizenship Foundn, 1988–; Council, Dulwich Picture Gallery Trust, 1995–2000; Council, RSA, 1997–2002; Adv. Council, NCVO, 1998–. Trustee: Royal Anniversary Trust, 1994–2004; St George's Hosp. Special Trustees, 1999–2001; Playing Alive Foundn, 2004–; Autism Speaks, 2006–. Patron: Donaldson Coll., Edinburgh, 1998; Marlow Theatre Develt Trust, 2007; Sheriffs' and Recorders' Fund, 2008. FRSA 1991; FCGI 2004. JP Inner London, 1993; High Sheriff, Greater London, 2008–March 2009. *Publications:* (ed) The State, Society and Self-destruction, 1975; Women in the House, 1979; (with Davies) Women of Europe, 1982; (with Radice and Willis) MP: the job of a backbencher, 1988; (with Mahoney) Business Ethics in a New Europe, 1992; Business Ethics at Work, 1995; contribs to other books, academic articles, journalism. *Recreations:* writing, reading novels, ski-ing, opera. *Address:* Institute of Education, 20 Bedford Way, WC1H 0AL. *T:* (020) 7612 6004.

VALLANCE, Michael Wilson; Headmaster of Bloxham School 1982–91; *b* 9 Sept. 1933; *er s* of late Vivian Victor Wilson Vallance and Kate Vallance, Wandsworth and Helston; *m* 1970, Mary Winifred Ann, *d* of John Steele Garnett; one *s* two *d. Educ:* Brighton Coll.; St John's Coll., Cambridge (MA). On staff of United Steel Companies Ltd, 1952–53; awarded United Steel Companies Scholarship (held at Cambridge), 1953; Asst Master, Abingdon School, 1957–61; Asst Master, Harrow School, 1961–72; Headmaster, Durham Sch., 1972–82. Chairman: Cttee of Northern ISIS, 1976–77; NE Div., HMC, 1981–82. World Challenge Expeditions Ltd: Consultant, 1991–; Dir, 1992–96; Chm. Bd, 1995–96. Chm., Council for the Registration of Schools Teaching Dyslexic Pupils, (formerly Nat. Registration Council), 1992–96 (Chm., Trustees, 1996–98). Trustee, Bloxham Project, 1987–91. Oblate of Belmont Abbey (Benedictine), 1999–. FRSA 1997. *Recreations:* reading, cricket, gardens (sitting in), the sea. *Address:* 4 Chalmore Gardens, Wallingford, Oxon OX10 9EP. *T:* (01491) 837321. *Clubs:* MCC, Jesters.

VALLANCE, Prof. Patrick John Thompson, MD; FRCP; FMedSci; Senior Vice-President and Head of Drug Discovery, GlaxoSmithKline, since 2006; *b* 17 March 1960; *s* of Peter John Vallance and Barbara Bickford Vallance (*née* Thompson); *m* 1986, Sophia Ann Dexter; two *s* one *d. Educ:* Truro Sch.; St George's Hosp. Med. Sch., Univ. of London (BSc 1981; MB BS with Dist. 1984; MD 1990). MRCP 1987, FRCP 1995. Lectr, 1986–90, Sen. Lectr and Consultant Physician, 1990–95, St George's Hosp. Med. Sch.; Prof. of Clin. Pharmacol. and Consultant Physician, 1995–2002, Prof. of Medicine and Hd, Div. of Medicine, 2002–06, UCL. Goulstonian Lectr, RCP, 1996. Chm., Wellcome Trust Pharmacol. and Physiology Panel, 2002–05. FMedSci 1999 (Registrar, 2003–06). Hon. Fellow: Faculty of Medicine, Imperial Coll. London, 2006; UCL, 2007. Hon. DSc London, 2007. Graham Bull Prize, RCP, 2002. *Publications:* (ed jtly) Endothelial Function in Hypertension, 1987; (ed jtly) Endothelium in Human Physiology and Pathophysiology, 1989; contribs to learned jls on pharmacol., vascular biol., and exptl and clin. medicine. *Recreations:* mushrooming, cooking, gardening, playing tennis badly. *Address:* GlaxoSmithKline R&D Ltd, Greenford Road, Greenford, Middx UB6 0HE.

VALLANCE, Philip Ian Fergus; QC 1989; in-house counsel, Berrymans Lace Mawer, since 2002; *b* 20 Dec. 1943; *o s* of Aylmer Vallance and Helen Gosse; *m* 1973, Wendy, *d* of J. D. Alston; one *s* one *d. Educ:* Bryanston; New Coll., Oxford (BA Mod. Hist). Called to the Bar, Inner Temple, 1968. *Recreations:* cooking, drystone walling. *Address:* Berrymans Lace Mawer, Salisbury House, London Wall, EC2M 5QN. *Club:* Travellers (Chm., 2006–).

VALLANCE-OWEN, Prof. John, MA, MD, FRCP, FRCPI, FRCPath; Visiting Professor, Imperial College of Science, Technology and Medicine, at Hammersmith Hospital, since 1988; *b* 31 Oct. 1920; *s* of late Prof. E. A. Owen; *m* 1950, Renee Thornton; two *s* two *d. Educ:* Friar's Sch., Bangor; Epsom Coll.; St John's Coll., Cambridge (de Havilland Schol. from Epsom); London Hosp. (Schol.). BA 1943; MA, MB, BChir Cantab, 1946; MD Cantab 1951; FRCP 1962; FRCPath 1971; FRCPI 1973. Various appts incl. Pathology Asst and Med. 1st Asst to Sir Horace Evans, London Hosp., 1946–51; Med. Tutor, Royal Postgrad. Med. Sch., Hammersmith Hosp., 1952–55 and 1956–58; Rockefeller Trav. Fellowship, at George S. Cox Med. Research Inst., Univ. of Pennsylvania, 1955–56; Cons. Phys. and Lectr in Medicine, Univ. of Durham, 1958–64; Cons. Phys., Royal Victoria Infirmary and Reader in Medicine, Univ. of Newcastle upon Tyne, 1964–66; Prof. of Medicine, QUB, 1966–82; Consultant Physician: Royal Victoria Hosp., Belfast, 1966–82 (Chm., Med. Div., 1979–81); Belfast City Hosp., 1966–82; Forster Green Hosp., Belfast, 1975–82 (Chm., Med. Staff Cttee, 1979–82); Dir of Med. Services, Maltese Is, 1981–82; Chinese University of Hong Kong: Foundation Prof. and Chm., Dept of Medicine, 1983–88, now Emeritus Professor of Medicine; Associate Dean, Faculty of Medicine, 1984–88; Hon. Consultant in Medicine: to Hong Kong Govt, 1984–88; to British Army in Hong Kong, 1985–88; Consultant Physician: London Ind. Hosp., 1988–99; Wellington Hosp., London, 1999–2002. Med. Advr on Clinical Complaints, NE Thames RHA, 1989–96, S Thames RHA, 1995–96. Member: Standing Med. Adv. Cttee, Min. of Health and Social Services, NI, 1970–73; Specialist Adv. Cttee (General Internal Medicine) to the Govt; Northern Health and Social Services Bd, Dept of Health and Soc. Services, NI; Mem., Exec. Cttee, Assoc. of Physicians of GB and Ireland, 1976–79; Regional Adviser for N Ire, to RCP, 1970–75 and Councillor, RCP, 1976–79 (Oliver-Sharpey Prize, RCP, 1976); Councillor, RCPI, 1978–82; Mem.

Research Cttee, Brit. Diabetic Assoc.; Brit. Council Lectr, Dept Medicine, Zürich Univ., 1963; 1st Helen Martin Lectr, Diabetic Assoc. of S Calif, Wm H. Mulberg Lectr, Cincinnati Diabetes Assoc., and Lectr, Brookhaven Nat. Labs, NY, 1965; Brit. Council Lectr, Haile Selassie Univ., Makerere UC and S African Univs, 1966; Guest Lecturer: Japan Endocrinological Soc., 1968; Madrid Univ., 1969; Endocrine Soc. of Australia, 1970; Bologna Univ., 1976. Hon. FRCPI 1970; Hon. FHKCP 1996. *Publications:* Essentials of Cardiology, 1961 (2nd edn 1968); Diabetes: its physiological and biochemical basis, 1976; papers in biochem., med., and scientific jls on carbohydrate and fat metabolism and aetiology of diabetes mellitus and related conditions, with special reference to insulin antagonism. *Recreations:* tennis, golf, music. *Address:* 10 Spinney Drive, Great Shelford, Cambridge CB2 5LY. *T:* (01223) 842767; 17 St Matthews Lodge, Oakley Square, NW1 1NB. *T:* (020) 7388 3644; Cuildochart, Killin, Perthshire FK2 8SS. *T:* (01567) 820337. *Clubs:* East India, Royal Society of Medicine (Life Mem.); United Services Recreation (Hong Kong).

VALLANCE WHITE, James Ashton, CB 1997; Fourth Clerk at the Table and Clerk of the Judicial Office, House of Lords, 1983–2002; Clerk to Committee for Privileges (Peerage Claims) 1983–2002; Registrar of Lords' Interests, 1996–2002; *b* 25 Feb. 1938; *s* of Frank Ashton White and Dieudonnée Vallance; *m* 1987, Anne O'Donnell. *Educ:* Allhallows School; Albert Schweitzer College, Switzerland; St Peter's College, Oxford (MA). Clerk, House of Lords, 1961; Clerk of Committees, 1971–78; Chief Clerk, Public Bill Office, 1978–83. *Address:* 14 Gerald Road, SW1W 9EQ. *T:* (020) 7730 7658; Biniparrell, San Luis, Menorca. *T:* (971) 151476. *Clubs:* Brooks's, Beefsteak.

VALLELY, Paul, CMG 2006; writer and broadcaster; Associate Editor, The Independent, since 2000; *b* 8 Nov. 1951; *s* of late Victor Terence Vallely and Mary Frances Mannion; *m* 1st, 1972, Heather Cecilia Neil (marr. diss.); one *d*; 2nd, 2000, Christine Lesley Morgan, *qv*; one *s*. *Educ:* St Mary's Coll. Grammar Sch., Middlesbrough; Univ. of Leeds (BA Philosophy and English). Reporter, Feature Writer, Theatre Critic, Yorkshire Post, 1974–80; Asst Features Editor, Sunday Telegraph Magazine, 1980–82; Radio Critic, The Listener, 1980–82; Feature Writer, Mail on Sunday, 1982–84; Home News Reporter and Corresp. in Africa, Belfast and NY, The Times, 1984–89; Sen. Foreign Writer, Religious Affairs Editor, News Editor and Asst Editor, Sunday Correspondent, 1989–90; Land Reform Study, Philippines, Brazil, Eritrea, Christian Aid, 1990; Editor of Irish edn, Sunday Times, 1991–92; Oped Feature Writer, Daily Telegraph, 1992–94; Dep. Editor, The European, 1994; Editor, News Review, Sunday Times, 1994–95; Feature Writer, Leader Writer and Columnist, The Independent, 1995–; Exec. Editor, Independent on Sunday, 1999–2000; seconded to PM's Commn for Africa, 2004–05 (co-author report, Our Common Interest, 2005). Columnist: The Tablet, 1996–99 (Dir, 2006–); Third Way, 1995–; Church Times, 2002–. Editl Advr, Catholic Bishops' Conf. of England and Wales, 2004. Lectures: La Casas, Blackfriars, Oxford, 2000; Gilpin, Durham, 2004; Newman, London, 2008; Anthony Storey Meml, 2008. Chair, Catholic Inst. for Internat. Relations, 1995–2001 (Trustee, 1993–2001). Media Adviser: Christian Aid, 1990–92; CAFOD, 1993–2001; Trustee, Traidcraft, 1992–95; Chair, Traidcraft Exchange, 1995–99. Gov., St Joseph's RC Primary Sch., Sale, 2006– (Chair, 2007–). *Publications:* (with David Blundy) With Geldof in Africa, 1985; (with Bob Geldof) Is That It?, 1986; Bad Samaritans: First World ethics and Third World debt, 1990; Promised Lands: stories of power and poverty in the Third World, 1992; (for children) Daniel and the Mischief Boy, 1993; (ed) The New Politics: Catholic social teaching for the 21st century, 1999; The Church and the New Age, 2000; (ed) A Place of Redemption: a Christian approach to punishment and prison, 2004; The Fifth Crusade: George Bush and the Christianisation of the war in Iraq, 2004; (with Bob Geldof) Geldof in Africa, 2005; Hello World: the official Live8 book, 2005; New Labour and the New World Order in Remoralising Britain, 2008. *Recreation:* Thomas. *Address:* The Independent, PO Box 165, Sale, Cheshire M33 2YA. *T:* (0161) 973 3456; *e-mail:* p.vallely@independent.co.uk. *Club:* Royal Commonwealth Society.

VAN ALLAN, Richard, CBE 2002; principal bass; Director, National Opera Studio, 1986–2001; *b* 28 May 1935; *s* of Joseph Arthur and Irene Hannah Van Allan; *m* 1976, Elisabeth Rosemary (marr. diss. 1986); one *s* one *d* (and one *s* decd). *Educ:* Worcester College of Education (DipEd Science); Birmingham School of Music. Glyndebourne, 1964; Welsh National Opera, 1968; English National Opera, 1969 (Mem. Bd of Dirs, 1995–98); Royal Opera House, Covent Garden, 1971; performances also: l'Opéra de Paris, Bordeaux, Nice, Toulouse, Rome, Brussels; USA: Boston, San Diego, Phoenix, Houston, Austin, San Antonio, New Orleans, NY; Argentina: Buenos Aires; Spain: Madrid and Barcelona; Hong Kong; Victoria State Opera, Melbourne. Recordings incl. Don Giovanni, Cosi fan tutte (Grammy Award), Luisa Miller, L'Oracolo, Britten's Gloriana. Hon. RAM 1987; Hon. FBC (FBSM 1991). Sir Charles Santley Memorial Award, Musicians' Co., 1996. *Recreation:* shooting.

van ANDEL, Dr Katharine Bridget, (Mrs T. H. van Andel); *see* Pretty, Dr K. B.

VAN CAENEGEM, Baron Raoul Charles Joseph; Ordinary Professor of Medieval History and of Legal History, University of Ghent, Belgium, 1964–92, now Emeritus; *b* 14 July 1927; *s* of Joseph Van Caenegem and Irma Barbaix; created Baron, 1994; *m* 1954, Patricia Mary Carson; two *s* one *d*. *Educ:* Univ. of Ghent (LLD 1951; PhD 1953); Univ. of Paris; London Univ. Ghent University: Assistant to Prof. of Medieval Hist., 1954; Lectr, 1960. Vis. Fellow, UC, Cambridge, 1968; Arthur L. Goodhart Prof. in Legal Science, and Vis. Fellow of Peterhouse, Cambridge Univ., 1984–85; Erasmus Lectr on the History and Civilization of the Netherlands, Harvard Univ., 1991. Corresp. Fellow, Medieval Acad. of Amer., 1971; Corresp. FBA 1982; Sir Henry Savile Fellow, Merton Coll., Oxford, 1989. Mem. Acad. of Scis, Brussels, 1974; For. Mem., Acad. of Scis, Amsterdam, 1977. Hon. Dr: Tübingen, 1977; Catholic Univ., Louvain, 1984; Paris, 1988. Francqui Prize, Brussels, 1974; Solvay Prize, Brussels, 1990. *Publications:* Royal Writs in England from the Conquest to Glanvill: studies in the early history of the common law, 1959; The Birth of the English Common Law, 1973, 2nd edn 1988; Geschiedenis van Engeland (History of England), 1982, 2nd edn 1997; Judges, Legislators and Professors: chapters in European legal history, 1987; An Historical Introduction to Private Law, 1992; An Historical Introduction to Western Constitutional Law, 1995; Introduction aux sources de l'histoire médiévale, 1997; European Law in the Past and Future: unity and diversity over two millennia, 2002; Historical Considerations on Judicial Review and Federalism in the United States of America, 2003; Engeland Wonderland, 2005; (contrib.) International Encyclopaedia of Comparative Law, 1973. *Recreations:* wine (Bordeaux, Alsace), swimming, classical music, bridge. *Address:* Veurestraat 47, 9051 Afsnee, Belgium. *T:* (9) 2226211. *Club:* Universitaire Stichting (Brussels).

VANCE, Charles Ivan; actor, director and theatrical producer; Chairman, Charles Vance Productions Ltd, since 1962; *b* 6 Dec. 1929; *s* of Eric Goldblatt and Sarah (*née* Freeman); *m* 1959, Hon. Imogen Moynihan; one *d*. *Educ:* Royal Sch., Dungannon; Queen's Univ., Belfast. FInstD 1972; FRSA 1975. Early career as broadcaster; acting debut with Anew MacMaster Co., Gaiety, Dublin, 1949; dir, first prodn, The Glass Menagerie, Arts, Cambridge, 1960; founded Civic Theatre, Chelmsford, 1962; i/c rep. cos, Tunbridge Wells, Torquay, Whitby and Hastings, 1962; as Dir of Charles Vance Prodns, created Eastbourne Theatre Co., 1969; dir. own adaptation of Wuthering Heights, 1972; wrote and staged four pantomimes, 1972–75; devised and dir. The Jolson Revue, 1974 (staged revival, Australia, 1978; world tour, 1981); played Sir Thomas More in A Man for All Seasons, and dir, Oh! What a Lovely War, Greenwood, 1975; purchased Leas Pavilion Theatre, Folkestone, 1976 (HQ of own theatre organisation until 1985); prod and dir. world tour of Paddington Bear, 1978; *produced:* Cinderella, Stafford, 1981 (also dir.); Aladdin, Bognor, 1981; (London and national tours): Stop the World—I Want to Get Off (revival), 1976; Salad Days (revival), 1977; (also dir.) In Praise of Love, 1977; Witness for the Prosecution, (revival), 1979, 1992; Hallo Paris, 1980; This Happy Breed (revival), 1980; Starlite Spectacular, 1981; The Kingfisher (revival), 1981; The Hollow (revival), 1982 (also dir.); The Little Hut, Australia (also dir.), 1982; Cinderella, 1982, 1983, 1984, 1992 (also dir.); Aladdin, 1982 (also wrote); Lady Chatterley's Lover, 1983; The Mating Game, 1983; The Sleeping Beauty, The Gingerbread Man, The Wizard of Oz, 1983; Dick Whittington, Jack and the Beanstalk, Pinocchio, Jesus Christ Superstar (revival), 1984; Mr Cinders (revival), 1985; Policy for Murder, 1984 (also dir.); Jane Eyre, 1985 (also wrote and dir.), (revival) 1996; Oh Calcutta! (revival), 1985–86; Wuthering Heights (own adaptation), 1987; The Creeper (revival tour), 1994; (also adapted) A Christmas Carol, Gala Th., Durham, 2002; Who Killed Agatha Christie? (tour), 2002; Whisky Galore (tour), 2003; *directed:* Verdict (revival), 1984; Alice in Wonderland, 1985 (also wrote); Dick Whittington, Aladdin, Jack and the Beanstalk, Cinderella, 1986–87 (also wrote); Dénouement (also prod), 1988; Spiders Web (Agatha Christie Centenary Prodn) (also prod), 1990; The Mousetrap, USA (also prod), 1990; Daisy Pulls it Off (also prod), 1991; Gaslight (also prod), 1991; Time and Time Again (also prod), 1991; My Cousin Rachel (also prod), 1992; Godspell (also prod), 1993–94; Peter Pan, 1993; Dick Whittington, 1994, 1998, 2001; Brideshead Revisited (also prod), 1995; Cinderella, 1995, 1996, 1997, 2001, 2006; Jack and the Beanstalk, 1995, 1998, 2000; Eye Witness (prod), 1996; Babes in the Wood, 1996; Aladdin, 1996, 1997, 1999, 2000; Lettice and Lovage (prod.), 1977; Huckleberry Finn, 1997–98 (tour); Snow White, 1997, 1998, 1999; The Thirty-Nine Steps, 1998, 2000; The Ladykillers, What the Butler Saw, 1999 (tour); Passport to Pimlico, 2000 (tour); The Lady Vanishes, 2001; Oh What a Lovely War, 2001; Me and My Girl (revival), 2001; Bedside Manners, 2001; The Lavender Hill Mob (also prod), 2002 (tour); The Edge of Darkness, 2003 (tour); Goldilocks and the Three Bears, 2003; The Musical Celebration of Yorkshire TV's Heartbeat, 2004; Peter Pan, 2004; Aladdin, 2005; Worms Eye View (revival; tour), 2005; The Titfield Thunderbolt, Queens Th., Hornchurch and Th. Royal, Windsor, 2005; Kind Hearts and Coronets (revival; also prod; Pitlochry Fest. Th. and tour), 2005; Washington Square (adaptation), 2006; Whisky Galore (tour), 2007; celebration of Tennessee Williams' earlier short plays (tour), 2007. Controlled: Floral Hall Th., Scarborough, 1984–86; Beck Th., Hillingdon, 1986–90; Grand Opera House York, 1988–89; controls Summer Th., Manor Pavilion, Sidmouth, 1987–; rep. seasons: Harlow Playhouse, 1993–94; Grand Th., Wolverhampton, 1994–; Wyvern, Swindon, 1996–97, 2003–; Lyceum, Crewe, 1996–; Palace, Westcliff, 1997; Alhambra, Bradford, 1997; Middlesbrough Th., 2001–; Alexandra Th., Birmingham, 2003–; Brewhouse, Taunton, 2005–; Grand Opera House, Belfast, 2006–; launched first UK Dinner Theatre, Imperial Hotel, Torquay, 1990. Theatrical Management Association: Mem. Council, 1969; Pres., 1971–73 and 1973–76; Exec. Vice-Pres., 1976– (also of Council of Reg. Theatre). Advisor to Govt of Ghana on bldg Nat. Theatre, 1969. Director: Theatres Investment Fund, 1975–83; Entertainment Investments Ltd, 1980–82; International Holiday Investments, 1980–87; Southern Counties Television, 1980–87; Channel Radio, 1981–86; Gateway Broadcasting Ltd, 1982; Prestige Plays Ltd, 1987–; Operations Dir, Contemporary Theatre Ltd, 1992–94; Trustee Dir, Folkestone Theatre Co., 1979–85. Chairman: Provincial Theatre Council, 1971–87; Standing Adv. Cttee on Local Authority and the Theatre, 1977–90 (Vice-Chm., 1975–77); Gala and Fund-raising Cttee, British Theatre Assoc., 1986–89; Standing Adv. Cttee on Local Authority and the Performing Arts, 1990–93. Vice-Chairman: Theatres Adv. Council, resp. for theatres threatened by develt, 1974–; (also dir.) Festival of Brit. Theatre, 1975–; Irving Soc., 1972–. Member: Theatres Nat. Cttee, 1971–; Drama Adv. Panel, SE Arts Assoc., 1974–85; Prince of Wales' Jubilee Entertainments Cttee, 1977; Entertainment Exec. Cttee, Artists' Benev. Fund, 1980–; Court, Guild of Thespians, 1998; Adv. Bd, Manor Pavilion Th., Sidmouth, 2006–. Chm. of Trustees (formerly Govs), Acad. of Live and Recorded Arts, 2000–. Mem., Variety Club of GB, 1984–; Life Mem., Equity, 1995; Patron, Voluntary Arts Network, 1992–; Vice-Pres., E Sussex Br., RSPCA, 1975–; Member: Rotary Internat., 1971–; Rotary Club of London, 1986–; Life Pres., Green Room Club. Founded Vance Offord (Publications) Ltd, publishers of British Theatre Directory, British Theatre Review, and Municipal Entertainment, 1971; Chm., Platform Publications Ltd, 1987–; Editor in Chief, Team Publishing, 1986–87; Editor, Amateur Stage, and Preview, 1987–. Chambellan, Ordre des Coteaux de Champagne, 1993. *Publications:* British Theatre Directory, 1972, 1973, 1974, 1975; (ed) Amateur Theatre Yearbook, 1989, 1991, 1993, 1995, 1997, 2000; Agatha Christie, The Theatrical Celebration, 1990; Community Arts Directory, 2003; *plays:* Wuthering Heights, 1992; Jane Eyre, 1996. *Recreations:* sailing (crossed Atlantic single-handed, 1956), cooking (Cordon Bleu, 1957), travelling, animals. *Address:* Hampden House, 2 Weymouth Street, W1W 5BT. *Clubs:* Hurlingham, Royal Automobile, Royal Over-Seas League, Directors', Kennel (Mem. Cttee, 1989–), Groucho, Home House, Lord's Taverners.

VAN CULIN, Rev. Canon Samuel; Secretary General, Anglican Consultative Council, 1983–94; *b* 20 Sept. 1930; *s* of Samuel Van Culin and Susie (*née* Mossman). *Educ:* High School, Honolulu; Princeton University (AB); Virginia Theological Seminary (BD). Ordained 1955; Curate, St Andrew's Cathedral, Honolulu, 1955–56; Canon Precentor and Rector, Hawaiian Congregation, 1956–58; Asst Rector, St John, Washington DC, 1958–60; Gen. Sec., Laymen International, Washington, 1960–61; Asst Sec., Overseas Dept, Episcopal Church, USA, 1962–68; Sec. for Africa and Middle East, Episcopal Church, USA, 1968–76; Executive, World Mission, 1976–83. Hon. Canon: Canterbury Cathedral, 1983; Ibadan, Nigeria, 1983; Jerusalem, 1984; Southern Africa, 1989; Honolulu, 1991. Hon. DD: Virginia Seminary, 1977; Gen. Theol Seminary, 1983. *Recreations:* music, swimming. *Address:* 3900 Watson Place, NW, #5D–B, Washington, DC 20016, USA. *Clubs:* Athenæum, Huguenot Society; Princeton (New York).

van CUTSEM, Hugh Bernard Edward; self-employed; farmer; bloodstock breeder; *b* 21 July 1941; *s* of Bernard van Cutsem and Mary van Cutsem (*née* Compton); *m* 1971, Emilie Elise Christine Quarles van Ufford; four *s*. *Educ:* Sunningdale Sch.; Ampleforth Coll. Lieut Life Guards. Chm., Ecospray Ltd. Member, Council: NT, 1998– (Mem., Exec. Cttee); English Nature, 2002–06; a Vice Pres., Game Conservancy Trust, 1998–. Chm., Norfolk CLA, 2003–. Pres., SW Norfolk Cons. Assoc., 2004–. Knight of Honour and Devotion, SMO Malta (Sec. Gen., British Assoc.). *Address:* Hilborough House, Thetford, Norfolk IP26 5BQ. *T:* (01760) 756586, *Fax:* (01760) 756587; *e-mail:* vancutsem@hilborough.com. *Clubs:* White's, Pratt's, Jockey.

VandeLINDE, Prof. (Vernon) David, PhD; Vice-Chancellor, University of Warwick, 2001–06; *b* Charleston, W Virginia, 9 Aug. 1942; *s* of Vernon Geno VandeLinde and Ava Mae (*née* Scott); *m* 1964, Marjorie Ann Park; two *s*. *Educ:* Carnegie-Mellon Univ. (BS 1964; MS 1965; PhD 1968). Johns Hopkins University: Asst Prof., Elec. Engrg, 1967–74;

Associate Prof., 1974–77; Prof., 1977–92; Dean, Sch. of Engrg, 1978–92; Vice-Chancellor, Univ. of Bath, 1992–2001. Chairman: Overseas Res. Students Awards Scheme Cttee, UUK (formerly CVCP), 1993–2005; Better Regulation Review Gp, DfES, 2003–04; Mem., Council for Science and Technology, 2000–03. Non-exec. Dir, W Midlands S Strategic HA, 2003–06. Hon. LLD Bath, 2001; Hon. DEd West of England, 2001. *Address:* Claremont House, 29 The Rank, North Bradley, Bath BA14 9RP.

VANDEN-BEMPDE-JOHNSTONE; *see* Johnstone.

van den BERGH, Maarten Albert; Chairman, Supervisory Board, Akzo Nobel nv, since 2006 (Deputy Chairman, 2005–06); Deputy Chairman, BT Group plc, since 2006 (non-executive Director, since 2001); *b* 19 April 1942; *s* of Sidney James van den Bergh and Maria van den Bergh (*née* Mijers); *m* 1965, Marjan Désirée Kramer; two *d. Educ:* Univ. of Groningen (Drs Econs). Joined Shell Gp, 1968; East and Australasia Area Co-ordinator, 1981–84; Dep. Gp Treas., Shell Internat., 1984–86; Chm., Shell cos in Thailand, 1987–89; Regl Co-ordinator, Western Hemisphere and Africa, Shell Internat., 1989–92; Royal Dutch/Shell Group plc: Gp Man. Dir, 1992–2000; Dir of Finance, 1994–98; Vice-Chm., Cttee of Man. Dirs, and Pres., Royal Dutch Petroleum Co., 1998–2000; non-exec. Dir, 2000–. Dep. Chm., 2000–01, Chm., 2001–06, Lloyds TSB Gp plc; non-executive Director: British Telecommunications plc, 2000–01; British Airways Plc, 2002–. Advr to Chief Exec., HKSAR, 1998–2002. Member: Internat. Bd of Advisers to Pres. of Philippines, 2001–05; Adv. Council, Amsterdam Inst. of Finance, 2001–05. Mem., Steering Bd, and Dutch Co-Chm., Apeldoorn Conf., 2003–. Advr, Rembrandt Soc., 2001–05. Fellow and Vice-Pres., Inst. of Financial Services, 2001–06; Mem., Guild of Internat. Bankers, 2001–06. *Recreation:* European history. *Address:* c/o BT Group plc, BT Centre, 81 Newgate Street, EC1A 7AJ. *Club:* Soc. De Witte (The Hague).

van den BERGH, Prof. Sidney, OC 1994; FRS 1988; astronomer, Dominion Astrophysical Observatory, Victoria, British Columbia, since 1977; *b* 20 May 1929; *s* of S. J. van den Bergh and S. M. van den Berg; *m* 1st, 1957, Roswitha Koropp (marr. diss.); one *s* two *d*; 2nd, 1978, Gretchen Krause (*d* 1987); 3rd, 1990, Paulette Brown. *Educ:* Princeton Univ. (AB); Ohio State Univ. (MSc); Göttingen Univ. (Dr rer. nat.). Asst Prof., Ohio State Univ., 1956–58; progressively, Asst Prof., Associate Prof., Prof., Univ. of Toronto, 1958–77; Dir, Dominion Astrophys. Observatory, 1977–86. Res. Associate, Mt Wilson and Palomar Observatories, 1967–68. ARAS 1984. Hon. DSc: St Mary's Univ., 1995; Univ. of Victoria, 2001. NRCC President's Research Medal, 1988; Killam Laureate, Killam Trust, 1990; Henry Norris Russel Prize Lecture, Amer. Astron. Soc., 1990; Carlyle S Beals Award, 1998, R. M. Petrie Prize, 1999, Can. Astron. Soc.; Catherine Wolfe Bruce Gold Medal, Astron. Soc. Pacific, 2008. *Publications:* approx. 645 articles in various scholarly jls. *Recreations:* photography, archaeology. *Address:* Dominion Astrophysical Observatory, 5071 West Saanich Road, Victoria, BC V9E 2E7, Canada.

van den BROEK, Hans, Grand Cross Order of Oranje Nassau; Hon. GCMG; President, Netherlands Institute for International Relations, 2000–07; Honorary Minister, since 2005; *b* 11 Dec. 1936; *m* 1965, Josephine van Schendel; two *d. Educ:* Univ. of Utrecht (Law degree). Lawyer, Rotterdam, 1965–68; Enka Bv., Arnhem: Sec., Man. Bd, 1969–73; Commercial Manager, 1973–76. Member: Lower House of Parliament, Netherlands, 1976–78; Exec., Catholic People's Party, 1978–81; State Sec. for Foreign Affairs, 1981–82; Minister for Foreign Affairs, 1982–93. Mem., CEC, later EC, 1993–99. Chm., Radio Netherlands Internat., 2000–; Member: Supervisory Bd, Schiphol Gp, 2000–; Supervisory Council, Utrecht Univ., 2000–07. Pres., Carnegie Foundn, 2000–07; Founding Mem., Global Leadership Foundn, 2000–. Grand Cross: Order of Merit (Italy); Order of Isabel la Católica (Spain); Nat. Order of Merit (France); Order of Merit (Germany); Order of the Rising Sun (Japan). *Address:* Zwiepseweg 158, 7241 PV Lochem, The Netherlands.

VAN DEN HOVEN, Helmert Frans; *see* Hoven.

VAN der BIJL, Nigel Charles; His Honour Judge Van der Bijl; a Circuit Judge, since 2001; *b* 28 April 1948; *s* of late Nicholas Alexander Christian Van der Bijl and of Mollie Van der Bijl; *m* 1974, Loba Nassiri; one *s* one *d. Educ:* Trinity Coll., Dublin (MA Classics, LLB). Called to the Bar, Inner Temple, 1973; Co. Sec., Internat. Div., Beecham Pharmaceutical, 1973–74; Legal Manager, Shahpur Chemical Co. Ltd and Nat. Iranian Oil Co., Tehran, 1974–77; in private practice as barrister, specialising in crime and in European and human rights law, 1977–2001; a Recorder, 1996–2001. Recorder of the City of Canterbury, 2004–. Friend, British Sch. of Athens, 1996–. *Recreation:* cycling. *Address:* c/o The Law Courts, Chaucer Road, Canterbury, Kent CT1 1ZA.

VANDERMARK, Simone; *see* Hochgreb, S.

VANDERMEER, (Arnold) Roy; QC 1978; a Recorder of the Crown Court, 1972–97; a Deputy High Court Judge, 1989–99; *b* London, 26 June 1931; *o s* of late William Arnold Vandermeer and Katherine Nora Vandermeer; *m* 1964, Caroline Veronica (*née* Christopher); one *s* two *d. Educ:* Dame Alice Owen's Sch., Islington; King's Coll., London (LLB). Called to Bar, Gray's Inn, 1955, Bencher, 1988. Flt-Lt, RAF, 1955–58. Chairman: Greater Manchester Structure Plan Examination in Public, 1978; County of Avon Structure Plan Examination in Public, 1983. Inspector, Heathrow Terminal 5 and associated enquiries, 1995–2000. *Recreations:* reading, watching cricket, golf. *Address:* The Dower House, Cheverells Green, Markyate, Herts AL3 8BH. *T:* (01582) 849458. *Club:* MCC.

van der MEER, Dr Simon; Ridder Nederlandse Leeuw, 1985; Senior Engineer, CERN, Geneva (European Organisation for Nuclear Research), 1956–90; *b* 24 Nov. 1925; *s* of Pieter van der Meer and Jetske Groeneveld; *m* 1966, Catharina M. Koopman; one *s* one *d. Educ:* Technical University, Delft, Netherlands; physical engineer. Philips Research Laboratories, Eindhoven, 1952–56. Hon. degrees: Univ. of Geneva, 1983; Amsterdam, 1984; Genoa, 1985. Nobel Prize for Physics (jtly), 1984. *Recreation:* literature. *Address:* 4 chemin des Corbillettes, 1218 Grand-Saconnex, Switzerland. *T:* (22) 7984305.

VANDERMERWE, Prof. Sandra, DBA; Visiting Professor, since 2005 (Professor, 1996–2005) of International Marketing and Services, Tanaka Business School (formerly Management School), Imperial College of Science, Technology and Medicine, University of London; Chairman, Great Minds Consulting Ltd, since 1995; *b* 8 Aug. 1946; *d* of late David Fortes and of Myra Fortes; two *d. Educ:* Univ. of Cape Town (BA 1966); Grad. Sch. of Business, Univ. of Cape Town (MBA 1972); Grad. Sch. of Business, Univ. of Stellenbosch (DBA 1974). Senior Lecturer: Dept of Business Sci., Univ. of Cape Town, 1973–76; Grad. Sch. of Business, Univ. of Stellenbosch, 1976–79; Prof., and Head of Mktg Dept, Univ. of Witwatersrand, 1979–82; Vis. Prof. of Mktg, Internat. Mgt Inst., Geneva, 1983–85; Prof. of Internat. Mktg and Services, IMD-Internat. Inst. for Mgt Develt, Lausanne, 1985–96 (also Dir, several exec. progs). Mem. Bd, Internat. Health Insurance, 2000–05. Consultant on implementing customer-focused growth and transformation, major internat. cos; speaker on Executive progs for business schs incl. INSEAD, Eur. Sch. of Mgt and Technol., Germany, London Business Sch., and Templeton Coll., Oxford. Mem., editl bds, and reviewer for internat. academic and mgt jls. FRSA 1996. Several awards. *Publications:* From Tin Soldiers to Russian Dolls: creating added value through services, 1993; (jtly) Cases in European Marketing Management, 1994; (jtly) Competing Through Services, 1994; The 11th Commandment: transforming to 'own' customers, 1995; Customer Capitalism: getting increasing returns in new market spaces, 1999; Breaking Through: implementing customer focus in enterprises, 2004; numerous articles in prof. jls. *Recreations:* jogging, animals, arts. *Address:* 201 Victoria Court, Long Street, Cape Town 8001, South Africa.

VANDERSTEEN, Martin Hugh; Chairman, Bart's and The London NHS Trust, 2001–03; *b* 9 Aug. 1935; *s* of William Martin Vandersteen and Dorothy Margaret Vandersteen (*née* Leith); *m* 1967, Catherine Susan Mary Webb; two *s. Educ:* Harrow Co. Grammar Sch. for Boys; Open Univ. (BSc 2004). Chartered Accountant, 1957; Allen, Attfield & Co. Chartered Accountants, 1951–57; Andersen Consulting, 1957–97: Partner, 1968; Man. Partner UK, 1973–86; Man. Partner Regl, 1989–94; Man. Partner Resources and Quality, 1994–97. Non-exec. Dir, 1999–, Chm., 2000, Kingston Hosp. NHS Trust. *Recreations:* sailing, fishing, golf, swimming, science. *Address:* 2 Bristol Gardens, Putney Heath, SW15 3TG. *T:* (020) 8788 9026, *Fax:* (020) 8788 9121; *e-mail:* mvanderstn@aol.com. *Clubs:* Arts, Royal Ocean Racing; Royal Southern Yacht; Royal Wimbledon Golf; Otter Swimming.

van der VEEN, Air Vice-Marshal Marten; Senior Bursar, 2000–05 (Bursar, 1998–2000) and Fellow, 1999–2005, Balliol College, Oxford; *b* 22 Jan. 1946; *s* of late Lourens Jan van der Veen and Esmé Lily van der Veen (*née* Edwards); *m* 1968, Susan Mary Wallers; two *s. Educ:* King's Coll. Sch., Wimbledon; Magdalen Coll., Oxford (MA Engrg Sci. and Econs); RAF Coll., Cranwell (Aerosystems course). Exchange Officer with French Air Force, Paris, 1978–79; RAF Staff Coll., 1980; Dir of Defence Studies, RAF, 1985–88; Station Comdr, RAF Cosford, 1989–90; Dir, Support Policy, RAF, 1991–93; Station Comdr, RAF St Athan and Air Officer, Wales, 1994–95; last Commandant, RAF Staff Coll., Bracknell, 1996; DG Support Mgt, RAF, 1997. Gov., Stowe Sch., 2002– (Vice-Chm., 2007–). *Recreations:* travel, classical music, opera, social tennis, inevitable DIY. *Clubs:* Royal Air Force; Phyllis Court (Henley).

VAN der VEER, Jeroen; President, Royal Dutch Petroleum NV, since 2000; a Group Managing Director, since 1997, Chairman, Committee of Managing Directors, since 2004, and Chief Executive, since 2004, Royal Dutch/Shell Group (Vice-Chairman, 2000–04); *b* 1947; *m*; three *d. Educ:* Delft Univ. (MMechE 1976); Rotterdam Univ. (MEcons 1976). Joined Shell Internat. BV, 1971; Refining, Curaçao, 1978; Marketing, UK, 1981; Corporate Planning, UK, 1984; Area Officer, 1990; Pres. and CEO, Shell Chemicals Co., Houston, 1995–97; Gp Res. Advr, 1997. *Recreations:* golf, sailing, ski-ing, visiting museums. *Address:* Royal Dutch Shell plc, PO Box 162, 2501 AN The Hague, The Netherlands. *T:* (70) 3772715, *Fax:* (70) 3772780.

van der WATEREN, Jan Floris, FCLIP; Keeper and Chief Librarian, National Art Library, 1988–2000; *b* 14 May 1940; *s* of late Jacob van der Wateren and Wilhelmina (*née* Labuschagne). *Educ:* Potchefstroom Univ., S Africa (MA); University Coll. London (Postgrad. Dip. Librarianship). ALA 1971, FCLIP (FLA 1995). Lectr in Philosophy, Potchefstroom Univ., 1962–64; Asst Librarian, Univ. of London Inst. of Educn, 1967–71; Dep. Librarian, Sir Banister Fletcher Liby, RIBA, 1971–78; British Architectural Library: Managing Librarian, 1978–83; Dir and Sir Banister Fletcher Librarian, 1983–88. Sec., British Architectural Liby Trust, 1983–88. Hon. FRIBA 1995. FRSA 1994. *Publications:* articles, reviews for librarianship jls. *Address:* 52 Blenheim Crescent, W11 1NY. *T:* (020) 7221 6221.

van der WERFF, His Honour Jonathan Ervine; a Circuit Judge, 1986–2007; Resident Judge, Inner London Crown Court, 1993–2007; *b* 23 June 1935; *s* of H. H. J. van der Werff; *m* 1968, Katharine Bridget, *d* of Major J. B. Colvin, Withypool, Som; two *d. Educ:* St Piran's Sch., Maidenhead; Harrow; RMA, Sandhurst. Commnd in Coldstream Guards, 1955; Adjt 1st Bn, 1962–63; Major 1967, retired 1968. Called to Bar, Inner Temple, 1969; a Recorder, 1986; Resident Judge, Croydon Law Courts, 1989–93; Sen. Circuit Judge, 1993. *Clubs:* Boodle's, Pratt's, Something; Bembridge Sailing.

VANDER ZALM, Hon. William N.; Premier of the Province of British Columbia, 1986–91; MLA (Social Credit Party) for Richmond, British Columbia; *b* Noordwykerhout, Holland, 29 May 1934; *s* of Wilhelmus Nicholaas van der Zalm and Agatha C. Warmerdam; *m* 1956, Lillian Mihalic; two *s* two *d. Educ:* Phillip Sheffield Sen. Secondary Sch., Abbotsford, BC. Purchased Art Knapp Nurseries Ltd, and became Co. Pres., 1956. Alderman 1965, Mayor 1969, Surrey Municipal Council. Minister of Human Resources, BC, 1975; Minister of Municipal Affairs and Minister responsible for Urban Transit Authority, 1978; Minister of Educn and Minister responsible for BC Transit, 1982; Leader, BC Social Credit Party, 1986–. Established Fantasy Garden World, major tourist attraction in Richmond, BC, 1983–. Hon. Dr Law Univ. of the North, Prince George, BC, 2004. *Publication:* The Northwest Gardener's Almanac, 1982. *Recreations:* gardening, fishing, soccer. *Address:* Normandy Manor, 3553 Arthur Drive, Ladner, BC V4K 3N2, Canada. *Clubs:* Union (Victoria, BC); Hon. Member: Victoria Golf, Royal Vancouver Yacht, Royal Victoria Yacht.

VANDEVELDE, Luc Emile; Founder and Managing Director, Change Capital Partners, since 2002; *b* Belgium, 26 Feb. 1951; *s* of Emile Vandevelde and Sylvie Vandevelde (*née* Jacobs); *m* Monique Sapin; one *s*. Administrator, Kraft NV SA, Brussels, 1971–80; Finance Dir, Kraft Leonesas SA, Madrid, 1980–83; Vice-Pres. of Develt and Planning, Kraft Europe, Lausanne, 1983–86; Dir of Finance and Admin, Kraft GmbH, Germany, 1986–88; Vice-Pres. of Finance and Admin, Kraft Internat., USA, 1988–90; Vice-Pres. of Admin and Develt, Kraft General Foods Internat., NY, 1989–90; CEO, France, 1989–93, Italy, 1994–95, Kraft Jacobs Suchard; Pres. and Chief Operating Officer, 1995–99, Chm., 1999–2000, Promodès; Chief Exec., 2000–02, Chm., 2000–04, Marks and Spencer plc; Dir, 2004–07, Chm., 2005–07, Carrefour. Non-exec. Dir, Vodafone, 2003–. *Address:* Change Capital Partners, 2nd Floor, College House, 272 Kings Road, SW3 5AW.

VAN de WALLE, Leslie; Chief Executive, Rexam PLC, since 2007; *b* 27 March 1956; *s* of Philippe Van de Walle and Luce Van de Walle; *m* 1982, Domitille Noel; two *d. Educ:* Hautes Etudes Commerciales, Paris. Managing Director: Schweppes Benelux, 1990–92; Schweppes France and Benelux, 1992–93; Schweppes Spain and Portugal, 1993–94; Snacks Div., Continental Europe UB, 1994–95; Chief Executive Officer: UB Continental Europe, 1996–97; McVities Gp, 1998; Chief Exec., United Biscuits Gp, 1999–2000; CEO, Shell South America and Africa, 2001; Pres., Shell Europe Oil Products; Exec. Vice-Pres., Global Retail, Royal Dutch Shell, 2004–06. Non-exec. Dir, Aegis Gp plc, 2003–. *Recreations:* golf (handicap 6), travel. *Address:* 6 Rose Square, SW3 6RS. *Club:* Lambourne Golf.

VANDYKE PRICE, Pamela Joan; freelance writer and lecturer on wine, since 1956; *b* 21 March 1923; *o c* of Harry Norman Walford, MBE, and Florence Amélie Halliday; *m*

1950, Alan Vandyke Price, MB BS, MRCP (*d* 1955). *Educ:* privately; Somerville Coll., Oxford (MA Hons); Central Sch. of Speech and Drama. Various odd jobs, 1943–53; occasional adult educn lects, S Wales, 1951–52; Household Ed., House & Garden, 1953–55; Ed., Wine & Food, 1967–69; formerly: consumer contributor to Spectator; wine correspondent: The Times; Sunday Times; Observer; contribs to The Guardian, provincial newspapers and trade jls. Has made frequent radio broadcasts. Circle of Wine Writers: Mem.; formerly Cttee Mem., Programme Sec., Chm., and Pres.; Hon. Trustee in Perpetuity; Hon. Mem., Internat. Food & Wine Soc. Glenfiddich Gold Medal and Trophy, 1971, Silver Medal, 1973. Chevalier du Mérite Agricole (France), 1981. *Publications:* Cooking with Wine, Spirits, Beer and Cider, 1959; France: a food and wine guide, 1960; Casserole Cooking, 1961; The Art of the Table, 1962; Cooking with Spices, 1964; Century Companion to the Wines of Bordeaux, 1971, rev. edn 1982 (trans. French, German and Dutch); Eating and Drinking in France Today, 1972; Wine Lovers' Handbook, 1972; Wines and Spirits, 1972; A Dictionary of Wines and Spirits, 1974; The Taste of Wine, 1975 (trans. French, German, Dutch and Japanese); Entertaining with Wine, 1976; Century Companion to the Wines of Champagne, 1979 (trans. French, German and Dutch); The Penguin Book of Spirits and Liqueurs, 1979; Dictionary of Wines and Spirits, 1980, rev. edn 1987; Understanding Wines and Spirits, 1981; Enjoying Wine: a taster's companion, 1982; The Penguin Wine Book, 1984; (with C. Fielden) Alsace Wines and Spirits, 1984; Wine: lore, legends and traditions, 1985 (Book of Year: Wine Mag., 1986; Wine Guild, 1986); Wine's Company, 1986; French Vintage, 1986; France for the Gourmet Traveller, 1988; Wines of the Graves, 1988; (ed) Christie's Wine Companion, 1989; Woman of Taste (autobiog.), 1990; Curiosities of Wine, 2002. *Recreation:* making wine vinegar. *Address:* 8 Queen's Gate, SW7 5EL.

VANE; *see* Fletcher-Vane, family name of Baron Inglewood.

VANE, family name of **Baron Barnard**.

VANE, Amber; *see* Feldman, S. J.

VANE-TEMPEST-STEWART, family name of **Marquess of Londonderry**.

VANE-WRIGHT, Richard Irwin; Keeper of Entomology, 1998–2004, Scientific Associate, since 2004, Natural History Museum; *b* 26 July 1942; *s* of late Gerald, (James), Vane Wright, and Jessie Margaret (*née* Baldwin); *m* 1987, Hazel June Whitehead; two *d*. *Educ:* University Coll. London (BSc 1st Cl. Hons Zool. 1967). British Museum (Natural History), subseq. Natural History Museum: Asst (Scientific), 1961–63; SO, Dept Entomology, 1967–84; Dep. Keeper of Entomology, 1984–90; Individual Merit Researcher (Band 2), 1990–98. Fellow: Wissenschaftskolleg, Berlin, 1993–94; NESTA, 2005–08. Hon. Prof. of Taxonomy, Univ. of Kent, Canterbury, 2006–. Hon. Fellow, Royal Entomol Soc. of London, 2004. Hon. DSc Copenhagen, 2003. Karl Jordan Medal, Lepidopterists' Soc., USA, 1989; Jacob Hübner Award, Assoc. for Tropical Lepidoptera, 2005. *Publications:* (with P. R. Ackery) The Biology of Butterflies, 1984, 2nd edn 1989; (with P. R. Ackery) Milkweed Butterflies, 1984; (jtly) Carcasson's African Butterflies, 1995; Butterflies, 2003; (with Harold Hughes) The Seymer Legacy: Henry Seymer and Henry Seymer Jnr of Dorset, and their entomological paintings, 2005; The Tasks of Taxonomy, 2009; numerous contribs to books and science jls. *Recreations:* jazz, walking, woodwork, books, clocks, craneflies, butterflies, conservation. *Address:* Department of Entomology, Natural History Museum, Cromwell Road, SW7 5BD. *Club:* Tetrapods.

VANEZIS, Prof. Peter Savvas, OBE 2001; MD, PhD; FRCPath, FRCPGlas, FFFLM; Director, Cameron Centre for Forensic Medical Sciences, Queen Mary's School of Medicine and Dentistry, London University, since 2006; *b* 11 Dec. 1947; *s* of Savvas Vanezis and Efrosini Vanezis; *m* 1981, Maria Galatariotis; one *s* one *d*. *Educ:* Wanstead High Sch.; Bristol Univ. (MB ChB, MD); PhD London; DMJ Path; MRCPGlas. FFFLM 2006. Jun. appt, St Olave's Hosp. (Guy's), 1973–74; Jun. Lectr, Lectr and Sen. Lectr in Forensic Medicine, London Hosp. Med. Coll., 1974–90; Reader and Head of Dept of Forensic Medicine and Toxicology, Charing Cross and Westminster Med. Sch. and Hon. Consultant, Riverside AHA, 1990–93; Regius Prof. of Forensic Medicine and Sci., 1993–2003, and Dir, Human Identification Centre, 1994–2003, Univ. of Glasgow; Dir Gen., Centre for Internat. Forensic Assistance, 2001–03; Chief Forensic Med. Officer, Forensic Sci. Service, 2003–06. External Examiner in Forensic Pathology: Postgrad. Med. Inst., Sri Lanka, 1995–; Coll. of Pathologists, Hong Kong, 1999–; Ext. Examiner in Forensic Medicine, Univ. of Malaysia, 2001–. Visiting Professor: Inst. of Forensic Medicine, Singapore, 2000–; London South Bank (formerly S Bank) Univ., 2001–; Univ. of Glasgow, 2003–; Hon. Prof., Dept of Pathology, Univ. of HK, 2003–. Hon. Consultant: Tower Hamlets AHA, 1982–90; the Armed Forces, 1992–; Gtr Glasgow Health Bd, 1993–; Medico-legal Inst., Santiago, 1994–; Govt of Republic of Cyprus, 1984–. Advr in Forensic Medicine to ICRC, 2006–. President: British Acad. of Forensic Scis, 1996–97; British Assoc. in Human Identification, 2001–03; mem., numerous forensic science socs, UK and USA. Mem., Editl Bds (Path), Science and Justice, Jl of Clinical Path, Amer. Jl Forensic Medicine & Path. *Publications:* Pathology of Neck Injury, 1989; Suspicious Death-Scene Investigation, 1996; articles on forensic medicine and science in learned jls. *Recreations:* painting, golf. *Address:* Cameron Centre for Forensic Medical Sciences, Clinical Pharmacology, Barts and the London, Charterhouse Square, EC1M 6BQ.

VAN GELDER, Prof. Gerard Jan Henk, PhD; FBA 2005; Laudian Professor of Arabic, University of Oxford, since 1998; Fellow, St John's College, Oxford, since 1998; *b* 10 June 1947; *s* of Gerard Jan Van Gelder and Hendrika Venmans; *m* 1973, Sheila Maureen Ottway; two *d*. *Educ:* Univ. of Amsterdam (doctoral); Univ. of Leiden (PhD 1982). Librarian, Inst. for Modern Near East, Univ. of Amsterdam, 1973–75; Lectr in Arabic, Univ. of Groningen, 1975–98. Mem., Royal Netherlands Acad. of Arts and Scis, 1997. *Publications:* Beyond the Line: classical Arabic literary critics on the coherence and unity of the poem, 1982; Two Arabic Treatises on Stylistics, 1987; The Bad and the Ugly: attitudes towards invective poetry (Hijā') in classical Arabic literature, 1989; Of Dishes and Discourse, 2000; Close Relationships: incest and inbreeding in classical Arabic literature, 2005; books in Dutch; contrib. articles in learned jls and encyclopaedias. *Recreation:* music and musicology, especially early music. *Address:* The Oriental Institute, Pusey Lane, Oxford OX1 2LE. *T:* (01865) 278200; 48 Merrivale Square, Oxford OX2 6QX.

van GRIETHUYSEN, Dr (Willem) John, CEng, FREng; FRINA; RCNC; Chief Naval Architect, Ministry of Defence, and Director Sea Systems (formerly Sea Technology, then Sea Systems Group Leader), Defence Equipment and Support, Ministry of Defence (formerly Defence Procurement Agency), since 2003; *b* 14 May 1953; *s* of Jean-Pierre van Griethuysen and Margaret Emily (*née* Williams); *m* 1983, Zaida Katharine Gibbs; three *d*. *Educ:* Haberdashers' Aske's Boys' Sch., Elstree; UCL (BSc (Mech. Engrg) 1975; MSc (Nav. Arch.) 1976; PhD 1989). Mem., Type 23 Design Team, 1981–83; Lectr in Naval Architecture, UCL, 1983–86; In-Service Submarine Project, 1986–91; Project Manager, Minehunters, 1991–93; Ship Design Manager, Horizon Jt Project Office, 1993–96; Hd, Business Improvement, DG Surface Ships, 1996–98; Prof. of Naval Architecture, UCL, 1998–2003. Technical Advr to Judge in re-opened formal investigation into loss of MV Derbyshire, 2000. Member: Council, RINA, 1998–2002; Court, Imperial Coll., London, 2001–07. Dep. Hd, RCNC, 2003–. FREng 2003. *Publications:* papers on naval engrg and design. *Address:* Defence Equipment and Support, Ministry of Defence, # 3311, Abbey Wood, Bristol BS34 8JH; *e-mail:* dessesea-d@mod.uk.

VANHANEN, Matti; MP (Centre Party) Uusimaa, since 1991; Prime Minister of Finland, since 2003; *b* Jyväskylä, Finland, 4 Nov. 1955; *s* of Tatu and Anni Vanhanen; *m* (marr. diss.); one *s* one *d*. *Educ:* Helsinki Univ. (Master Soc. Scis). Journalist, 1985–88, Ed.-in-Chief, 1988–91, Kehäsanomat (local newspaper). Vice Chairman: Parly Envmt Cttee, 1991–95; Parly Gp, Centre Party, 1994–2001; Chm., Parly Grand Cttee, 2000–01; Rep. of Parlt, European Convention on Future of EU, 2002–03; Minister of Defence, 2003. Centre Party: Mem. or Dep. Mem., Party Delegn, 1976–2000; Chm., Youth League, 1980–83; Bd Mem., 1980–83; Vice Chm., 2000–03; Chm., 2003–. Espoo City Council, 1981–84; Nurmijärvi Municipal Council, 1989–; Board Member: Helsinki Met. Area Council YTV, 1983–84; Uusimaa Regl Council, 1997–2000. Member Supervisory Board: Neste/Fortum, 1991–2003; Helsingin Osuuskauppa (Cooperative), 2002–03. Chairman: State Youth Council, 1987–90; Housing Foundn for the Young, 1998–2003 (Vice Chm., 1981–97); Union for Rural Educn, 1998–2003; Vice Chairman: Housing Council, 1991–2003; Pro Medi-Heli Assoc., 1995–2003. *Address:* Office of the Prime Minister, Snellmaninkatu 1A, PO Box 23, 00023 Helsinki, Finland.

van HASSELT, Marc; Headmaster, Cranleigh School, 1970–84; *b* 24 April 1924; *s* of Marc and Helen van Hasselt; *m* 1st, 1949, Geraldine Frances Sinclair (marr. diss. 1976); three *s* one *d*; 2nd, 1989, Tessa Carolyn, *d* of Mrs B. Gofton-Salmond. *Educ:* Sherborne; Selwyn Coll., Cambridge (MA); Corpus Christi Coll., Oxford (DipEd). Served War of 1939–45 (despatches): commissioned in Essex Yeomanry, RHA, 1944; served North-West Europe (D-day). Lecturer in Commonwealth Studies, RMA, Sandhurst, 1950–58; Asst Master, Oundle School, 1959–70 (Housemaster, Sanderson House, 1963–70). Member: Admiralty Interview Bd, 1972–86; Army Scholarship Bd, 1972–86. Chairman: Castle Court Sch., 1988–95; Walhampton Sch., 1990–97; Gov., Canford Sch., 1985–95. *Publications:* occasional articles and reviews. *Recreations:* cruising under sail, governing schools. *Address:* Carrick Corner, New Road, Keyhaven, Lymington, Hants SO41 0TN. *T:* (01590) 644690; rue Lyvet, 22690 Vicomte-sur-Rance, France. *Clubs:* Royal Cruising; Royal Lymington Yacht.

van HEYNINGEN, Joanna; Joint Principal, van Heyningen and Haward Architects, since 1982; *b* 22 July 1945; *d* of William Edward Kits van Heyningen and Ruth Eleanor van Heyningen (*née* Treverton); *m* 1977, Birkin Anthony Christopher Haward, *qv*; one *s* one *d*. *Educ:* Oxford High Sch. for Girls; St Anne's Coll., Oxford (BA (French and Russian) 1967); New Hall, Cambridge (BA (Architecture) 1971); Darwin Coll., Cambridge (Dip Arch 1973). RIBA 1981. Estab. private practice, 1977; formed van Heyningen and Haward Architects, 1982. RIBA: Member: Awards Gp, 2000–04; Jt Validation Panel, 2000–; LSC Client Forum, 2003–. Mem., Design Rev. Panel, CABE, 2004–. Governor, Building Centre Trust, 1998–. Award winning buildings include: Haward House, London, 1976; Newnham Coll. Rare Books Liby, Cambridge, 1981; 2nd Haward House, London, 1986; Clovelly Visitor Centre, 1989; Wilson Court, Cambridge, 1994; Jacqueline du Pré Music Building, Oxford, 1995; King Alfred's Sch., London, 1997; Gateway to the White Cliffs (NT), Dover, 1999; West Ham Station, Jubilee Line Extension, 1999; Nat. Centre for Early Music, York, 2000; Polhill Information Centre, Bedford, 2000; Khoan & Michael Sullivan Chinese Painting Gall., Ashmolean Mus., Oxford, 2001; Sutton Hoo Visitor Centre (NT), 2002; RSPB Envmt and Educn Centre, Rainham, 2006; Lewisham Children and Young People's Centre, 2006; Centre for Classical and Byzantine Studies, Oxford Univ., 2006; Trinity Events Centre, Suffolk Showground, 2006; Ysol Ifor Bach, Caerphilly, 2007. Exhibitions: Kent Design, Maidstone, 2000; University Challenge: buildings for higher educn, Building Centre, 2001; New Connections, Municipal Arts Soc. of NY, NY, 2001; Winning Designs, Bristol Arch. Centre, RIBA, and Cube Gall., Manchester, 2002; Diverse City, RIBA, 2003; Celebration of Architectural Competitions, Cube Gall., Manchester, 2003, RIAS, Edinburgh, 2004; Women in Architecture, Paris, 2004. *Recreations:* pottering and seeing friends. *Address:* van Heyningen and Haward Architects, Burghley Yard, 106 Burghley Road, NW5 1AL. *T:* (020) 7482 4454, *Fax:* (020) 7284 0632; *e-mail:* jo@vhh.co.uk.

van HEYNINGEN, Prof. Veronica, DPhil; FMedSci; FRS 2007; FRSE; research scientist in human genetics; Group Leader and Section Head, MRC Human Genetics Unit, Edinburgh, since 1992; *b* 12 Nov. 1946; *d* of Laszlo and Anna Daniel; *m* 1968, Simon van Heyningen; one *s* one *d*. *Educ:* Girton Coll., Cambridge (BA 1968, MA 1971); Northwestern Univ. (MS 1970); DPhil Oxon 1973. Beit Meml Fellow, Oxford and Edinburgh Univs, 1973–76; MRC Human Genetics Unit: postdoctoral scientist, 1977–81; Scientist with tenure, 1981–86; Sen. Scientist, 1986–91; Special Appt grade, 1991. Mem., Human Genetics Commn, 2000–06. Trustee, Nat. Museums of Scotland, 1994–2000. FRSE 1997; FMedSci 1999. *Publications:* contribs to scientific jls. *Recreations:* museums, theatre, feeding people, travelling, novels. *Address:* MRC Human Genetics Unit, Western General Hospital, Edinburgh EH4 2XU; *e-mail:* v.vanheyningen@hgu.mrc.ac.uk.

VAN KLAVEREN, Adrian; Controller, BBC Radio 5 Live and 5 Live Sports Extra, since 2008; *b* 31 Dec. 1961; *s* of late Arthur Van Klaveren and Thelma Van Klaveren; *m* 1990, Julie Stringer; two *s*. *Educ:* Bristol Grammar Sch.; St John's Coll., Oxford (BA Modern Hist.). Joined BBC, 1983; news trainee, 1983–85; producer, TV News, 1985–90; Sen. Producer, Panorama, 1990–91; Deputy Editor: Nine O'Clock News, 1992–94; Newsnight, 1994; Hd, Local Progs, BBC W Midlands, 1995–96; News Ed., 1996–2000, Hd, 2000–05, Newsgathering, Dep. Dir and Controller of Prodn, 2005–08, BBC News. *Recreations:* football (especially Spurs), cricket, political biography. *Address:* BBC Television Centre, Wood Lane, W12 7RJ. *T:* (020) 8624 8938.

van KUFFELER, John Philip de B.; *see* de Blocq van Kuffeler.

van LEUVEN, (John) Nikolas; QC (Guernsey) 2002; HM Procureur (Attorney General) and HM Receiver General, Guernsey, since 2002; *b* 17 July 1947; *s* of John van Leuven and Catherine van Leuven (*née* Horton); *m* 1990, Wendy Sheppard; two *s* one *d*. *Educ:* Elizabeth Coll., Guernsey; Trinity Hall, Cambridge (MA); Caen Univ. (Cert. d'Etudes Juridiques Françaises et Normandes). Called to the Bar, Inner Temple, 1970; called to the Guernsey Bar, 1971; Batonnier, Guernsey Bar, 1994–96; in private practice, Guernsey, 1971–2002; Sen. Partner, Ozannes, 1983–2002. Mem., Chief Pleas of Sark, 1997–2002. FCIArb 1999. Chm., Council of St John, Bailiwick of Guernsey, 2001–08. OStJ 2000. *Recreations:* boating, book collecting. *Address:* Les Truchots, St Andrews, Guernsey GY6 8UD. *T:* (01481) 255146. *Clubs:* Royal Automobile; Sark Yacht.

van LINT, Prof. Theo Maarten, PhD; Calouste Gulbenkian Professor of Armenian Studies, University of Oxford, and Fellow, Pembroke College, Oxford, since 2002; *b* 15 June 1957; *s* of Henk and Coby van Lint. *Educ:* Leiden Univ. (MA Slavic Langs and Lits, 1988; MA Indo-European Comparative Linguistics 1988; PhD Armenian Studies 1996).

Researcher: Netherlands Orgn for Scientific Res., 1996–99; Deutsche Forschungs Gemeinschaft, Westfälische Wilhelms-Universität, Münster, 1999–2001. Mem., Assoc. Internat. des Études Arméniennes, 1986–. *Publications:* articles in Revue des Études Arméniennes. *Recreations:* volleyball, literature. *Address:* The Oriental Institute, University of Oxford, Pusey Lane, Oxford OX1 2LE.

van MAURIK, Ernest Henry, OBE 1944; HM Diplomatic Service, retired; *b* 24 Aug. 1916; *s* of late Justus van Maurik and Sybil van Maurik (*née* Ebert), BEM; *m* 1945, Winifred Emery Ritchie Hay (*d* 1984); one *s* one *d*. *Educ:* Lancing Coll.; Ecole Sup. de Commerce, Neuchatel, Switzerland. Worked in Tea Export, Mincing Lane, 1936–39. Commnd as 2nd Lt, in Wiltshire Regt, 1939; seconded to Special Ops Exec., 1941–46; demob. with hon. rank of Lt-Col (subst. Major), 1946. Joined Foreign Office, 1946; Moscow, 1948–50; West Germany and West Berlin, 1952–56; Buenos Aires, 1958–62; Copenhagen, 1965–67; Rio de Janeiro, 1968–71; FCO, 1971–75. Commemorative Medal (Czech Republic), 2005; Anniversary Medal (Slovak Republic), 2005. Officier de la Couronne (Belgium), 1944; Chevalier, Légion d'Honneur (France), 2002. *Recreations:* gardening, languages. *Address:* Little Cotchford, Cotchford Lane, Upper Hartfield, E Sussex TN7 4DN. *Clubs:* Special Forces, Civil Service.

VAN MIERT, Karel; President, Nyenrode University, Netherlands Business School, 2000–03; *b* 17 Jan. 1942; *m* 1971, Annegret Sinner; one *s*. *Educ:* Univ. of Ghent; European Univ. Centre, Nancy. With Sicco Mansholt, 1968–70; Asst in Internat. Law, New Univ. of Brussels, 1971–73; Office of Vice-Pres. of EC, 1973–75; Head of Private Office of Minister of Economic Affairs, Belgium, 1977; part-time Lectr on European Instns, Free Univ. of Brussels, 1978; Mem., European Parlt, 1979–85; Mem., Belgian Chamber of Reps, 1985–88; Mem., CEC, then EC, responsible for tranport, 1989–92, for competition, 1993–99; Chm., EU high-level gp on transeuropean networks, 2003. Vice-Chm., Socialist Internat., 1986–89. *Publications:* papers on European integration. *Address:* Puttestraat 10, 1650 Beersel, Belgium.

VANN, Ven. Cherry Elizabeth; Archdeacon of Rochdale, since 2008; *b* Whetstone, Leicester, 29 Oct. 1958; *d* of Maurice and Jean Vann. *Educ:* Lutterworth Upper Sch.; Royal Coll. of Music (ARCM 1978; GRSM 1980); Westcott House. Ordained deacon, 1989, priest, 1994; Parish Deacon, St Michael, Flixton, 1989–92; Parish Deacon, 1992–94, Asst Curate, 1994–98, Bolton-le-Moors; Team Vicar, 1998–2004, Incumbent, 2004–08, E Farnworth and Kearsley; Area Dean, Farnworth, 2005–08. Chaplain: Colleges of Higher Educn and Further Educn, Bolton, 1992–98; Deaf Community, 1998–2004. Hon. Canon, Manchester Cathedral, 2007–. *Recreations:* music, gardening, hill-walking. *Address:* 57 Melling Road, Oldham OL4 1PN. *T:* (0161) 678 1454; *e-mail:* parochdale@yahoo.co.uk.

VANN, (William) Stanley, DMus; *b* 15 Feb. 1910; *s* of Frederick and Bertha Vann; *m* 1934, Frances Wilson; one *s* one *d*. *Educ:* Alderman Newton's Grammar Sch. BMus London; FRCO; ARCM. Asst Organist, Leicester Cath., 1931–33; Chorus Master, Leicester Phil. Soc., 1931–36; Organist and Choirmaster, Gainsborough Parish Ch., Dir of Music, Queen Elizabeth Grammar Sch. and High Sch., Gainsborough, Conductor, Gainsborough Mus. and Orch. Socs, also Breckin Choir, Doncaster, 1933–39; Organist and Choirmaster, Holy Trinity PC, Leamington Spa, Founder-Conductor, Leamington Bach Choir and Warwicks Symph. Orch., and Dir of Music, Emscote Lawn Sch., Warwick, 1939–49. Served War of 1939–45, RA, final rank Captain. Master of Music, Chelmsford Cath., Conductor, Chelmsford Singers, Founder Conductor, Essex Symph. Orch., Prof., Trinity Coll. of Music, London, 1949–53; Master of Music, Peterborough Cath., Conductor, Peterborough Phil. Choir and Orch., 1953–77, retired. Conductor, St Mary's Singers, 1984–2002. Examiner, TCL, 1953–77; Mem. Council and Examr RCO, 1972–98; Mem., ISM; Adjudicator, Brit. Fed. of Festivals, Canadian Fed. Fest. and Hong Kong Fest., 1950–84; Chairman: Peterborough Music Fest., 1953–2002; Eastern Area Council, British Fedn of Music Festivals, 1982–90; President: Essex Symph. Orch., 1990–; Peterborough Children's Choir, 1994–2002; Gildenburgh Choir, 1997–. Patron, Precincts Soc., 1985–. DMus Lambeth 1971 (for eminent services to church music); Hon. FTCL 1953. *Publications:* twelve settings of Missa Brevis and Missa Sancti Pauli; Billingshurst Mass; three settings of Rite A Communion Service; two settings of Rite B Communion Service; Evening Services in E minor and C major and for Rochester, Gloucester, Hereford, Lincoln, Lichfield, Peterborough, Chester, Salisbury, York, Chichester, Ripon and Worcester Cathedrals; over 100 anthems, motets, carols, organ works and choral arrangements of folk-songs and of Handel; five sets of Preces and Responses and a Collection of Anglican Chants. *Recreations:* railway modelling, painting.

VANNECK, family name of **Baron Huntingfield**.

VANNET, Alfred Douglas; Sheriff of South Strathclyde, Dumfries and Galloway at Airdrie, since 2003; *b* 31 July 1949; *s* of William Peters Vannet and Jean Farquhar Low or Vannet; *m* 1979, Pauline Margaret Renfrew; one *s* one *d*. *Educ:* High Sch. of Dundee; Univ. of Dundee (LLB 1973). Solicitor in private practice, Oban, 1973–76; Procurator Fiscal Depute, Dundee, 1976–77; Procurator Fiscal Depute, then Sen. Procurator Fiscal Depute, Glasgow, 1977–84; Crown Office, Edinburgh: Head of Appeals Section, 1984–87; Asst Solicitor, Law Officers' Secretariat, 1987–88; Dep. Crown Agent, 1990–94; Solicitor to Public Inquiry into Piper Alpha Disaster, 1988–90; Regional Procurator Fiscal: Grampian Highland and Islands, 1994–97; Glasgow and Strathkelvin, 1997–2000; floating Sheriff, all Scotland, 2000–01; Sheriff at Airdrie and Lanark, 2001–03. Mem., Criminal Courts Rules Council, 1997–2000. Member: Forensic Sci. Soc., 1985–2000; Internat. Assoc. of Prosecutors, 1997–2000; Council, Scottish Medico-Legal Soc., 1997–2000. Hon. Mem., Royal Faculty of Procurators in Glasgow, 1997. FRSA 1995. *Recreations:* music, dog walking, curling. *Address:* Sheriff Court House, Graham Street, Airdrie ML6 6EE. *T:* (01236) 751121; *e-mail:* sheriff.advannet@scotcourts.gov.uk.

VANNI d'ARCHIRAFI, Raniero; Italian Ambassador to Spain, 1983–87 and 1995–98; *b* 7 June 1931; *m*; two *s*. *Educ:* Univ. of Rome (Degree in Law). Joined Italian Diplomatic Service; served on Permanent Representation of Italy to EC, Brussels, 1961–66; Counsellor, Directorate General for Econ. Affairs, 1969–73; 1st Counsellor, Madrid, 1973; Minister Plenipotentiary, EC Summit, Feb. 1980; Head, Cabinet of Minister of Foreign Affairs, 1980–83; Ambassador to FRG, 1987–89; Director General for: Econ. Affairs, 1989–91; Political Affairs, 1991–93; Mem., CEC, later EC, 1993–95. Pres., RCS Ibérica (Rizzoli-Corriere della Sera Gp), 2002–; Mem. Bd, Endesa Italia, 2001. Gran Cruz, Isabela la Católica (Spain), 1986; Cavaliere di Gran Croce della Rep. Italiana, 1990. *Address:* Calle Lagasca 107, 28006 Madrid, Spain.

VAN ORDEN, Brig. Geoffrey Charles, MBE 1973; Member (C) Eastern Region, England, European Parliament, since 1999; *b* 10 April 1945; *s* of Thomas and Mary Van Orden; *m* 1974, Frances Elizabeth Weir; three *d*. *Educ:* Sandown Sch.; Mons OCS; Univ. of Sussex (BA Hons Pol Sci.); Indian Defence Services Staff Coll. (psc). Commnd Intelligence Corps, 1964; operational service in Borneo, NI and BAOR; Directing Staff, Führungs Akademie der Bundeswehr, 1985–88; COS and ACOS, G2 Berlin (British Sector), 1988–90; Assessment Staff, Cabinet Office, 1990; Res. Associate, IISS and Service Fellow, Dept of War Studies, KCL, 1990–91; Head, Internat. Mil. Staff Secretariat, NATO HQ, 1991–94; retd and trans. to Regular Reserve, 1994; Sen. Official, EC (Directorate-Gen. Ext. Relations), 1995–99. European Parliament: Cons. Defence Spokesman, 1999–; Vice-Chm., Foreign Affairs Cttee, 2002–06. Mem., IISS, 1991–. Founder Mem., Anglo-German Officers' Assoc., 1991. Member: Friends of the Union, 1997–; Countryside Alliance, 1999–; Bow Gp, 1999–; Founder Mem., Friends of India, 2003–. Freeman, City of London, 1991; Freeman, Co. of Painter-Stainers, 1991. *Publications:* various articles on foreign and security policy issues. *Address:* 88 Rectory Lane, Chelmsford, Essex CM1 1RF. *T:* (01245) 345188; European Parliament, Rue Wiertz, 1047 Brussels, Belgium. *T:* (2) 2845332. *Club:* Army and Navy.

VAN REENEN, Prof. John Michael, PhD; Director, Centre for Economic Performance, since 2003; Professor, Department of Economics, London School of Economics and Political Science, since 2003; *b* 26 Dec. 1965; *s* of Lionel and Ann Van Reenen; *m* 2001, Sarah Chambers. *Educ:* Queens' Coll., Cambridge (BA 1988; Joshua King Prize, 1988); LSE (MSc 1989; Automation Prize, 1989); University Coll. London (PhD 1992). Res. Fellow, Inst. for Fiscal Studies, 1993–95; Prof., Dept of Econs, UCL, 1995–2003. Vis. Prof., Univ. of Calif, Berkeley, 1999–2000. Sen. Policy Advr to Sec. of State, DoH, 2000–01. *Publications:* over 100 articles in American Econ. Rev., Qly Jl of Econs, Rev. of Econ. Studies and many others. *Recreations:* music, cooking, film, reading, arguing, politics. *Address:* 161 Fentiman Road, SW8 1JZ. *T:* (020) 7955 6976; *e-mail:* j.vanreenen@lse.ac.uk. *Clubs:* Black's, Tuesday.

van RIEMSDIJK, John Theodore; Keeper of Mechanical and Civil Engineering, Science Museum, 1976–84; author and broadcaster; *b* 13 Nov. 1924; *s* of late Adrianus Kors van Riemsdijk and Nora Phyllis van Riemsdijk (*née* James); *m* 1957, Jocelyn Kilma Arfon-Price. *Educ:* University College Sch.; Birkbeck Coll. (BA). Served SOE, 1943–46. Manufacturer of gearing, 1946–54; Science Museum: Asst, 1954; Lectr, 1961; Educn Officer, 1969. Curator i/c setting up Nat. Railway Mus., York, 1973–75. *Publications:* Pregrouping Railways, 1972; Pictorial History of Steam Power, 1980; Compound Locomotives, 1982, 2nd edn 1994; John van Riemsdijk's Contribution (selected articles for GIMRA journal), 2005; Science Museum Books; contribs to: BBC Publications; Newcomen Soc. Trans, Procs of IMechE. *Recreations:* oil painting, making models. *Address:* Le Moulin du Gavot, St Maximin, 30700 Uzès, Gard, France. *T:* 466227378.

van ROIJEN, Jan Herman Robert Dudley; Knight, Order of the Netherlands Lion; Officer, Order of Orange Nassau; Netherlands Ambassador to the Court of St James's, and concurrently to Iceland, 1995–99; *b* 17 Dec. 1936; *s* of late Dr Jan Herman van Roijen and Anne (*née* Jonkvrouw Snouck Hurgronje); *m* 1963, Jonkvrouw Caroline H. W. Reuchlin; one *s* two *d*. *Educ:* Groton Sch., Mass, USA; Univ. of Utrecht (LLM 1961). Mil. service, Platoon Comdr in New Guinea, 1962. Joined Foreign Service, 1963: served Jakarta, Paris (NATO), Brussels (NATO), Saigon (chargé d'Affaires); Counsellor and Dep. Chief of Mission: Athens, 1975; Ottawa, 1978; Minister and Dep. Chief of Mission, Jakarta, 1981; Dep. Dir-Gen., Internat. Co-operation, Min. of Foreign Affairs, 1983; Ambassador, Tel Aviv, 1986; Principal Dir of Personnel, Diplomatic Budget and Buildings, Min. of Foreign Affairs, 1990; Ambassador, Jakarta, 1992. Chm., Netherlands Helsinki Cttee, 1999. *Recreations:* tennis, ski-ing. *Address:* Jagerslaan 9 Zuid, 2243 EH Wassenaar, Netherlands. *T:* (70) 5144470. *Clubs:* Brooks's; The Haagsche (The Hague).

van SCHOONHETEN, Baron Willem Oswald B.; *see* Bentinck van Schoonheten.

VÄNSKÄ, Osmo; Music Director, Minnesota Symphony Orchestra, since 2003; *b* Finland, 1953. *Educ:* trained as clarinettist; Sibelius Acad., Helsinki (conducting, under Jorma Panula). Formerly clarinettist, Helsinki Philharmonic Orch.; Music Dir, 1988–2008, Conductor Laureate, 2008–, Lahti SO; Artistic Dir, Icelandic SO, 1993–96; Chief Conductor, BBC Scottish SO, 1996–2002; Guest Conductor of orchestras in Europe, USA, Australia and Japan. First Prize, Internat. Young Conductors' Competition, Besançon, 1982. *Address:* c/o HarrisonParrott Ltd, 12 Penzance Place, W11 4PA.

van WACHEM, Lodewijk Christiaan; Knight, Order of the Netherlands Lion, 1981; Commander, Order of Orange-Nassau, 1990; Hon. KBE 1988 (Hon. CBE 1977). Chairman: Supervisory Board, Global Crossing Ltd, since 2004; Board of Directors, Maersk (formerly Nedlloyd) Holding BV, since 2005; *b* Pangkalan Brandan, Indonesia, 31 July 1931; *m* 1958, Elisabeth G. Cristofoli; two *s* one *d*. *Educ:* Univ. of Technol., Delft (mech. engr). Joined Royal Dutch/Shell Gp, 1953; worked in Latin America, Africa, FE and Europe; Royal Dutch Petroleum Co.: Man. Dir, 1976–82; Pres., 1982–92; Chm., Supervisory Bd, 1992–2002. Member, Supervisory Board: Akzo Nobel NV, 1992–2002; BMW AG, 1994–2002; Bayer AG, 1997–2002; Member, Board of Directors: IBM Corp., 1992–2002; Philips Electronics NV, 1993–2005 (Chm., 1999–2005); Atco Ltd, 1993–; Zurich Financial Services, 1993–2005 (Vice-Chm., 2001–02; Chm., 2002–05). Hon. Citizen, Singapore, 2004. *Address:* Maersk Holding BV, PO Box 487, 3000 AL Rotterdam, Netherlands.

van ZWANENBERG, Zoë; Chief Executive, Scottish Leadership Foundation, since 2001; *b* Ipswich, 20 Dec. 1952; *d* of David Francis and Aldyth Vincent van Zwanenberg; *m* 1986, Stephen Thompson (marr. diss. 1995); two step *d*. *Educ:* Univ. of Birmingham (BA Eng. Lang. and Lit.); Univ. of Sussex (MA Hist. of Art). MCIPD; MIHM. Gen. mgt, NHS, 1979–86; Force Personnel Officer, Suffolk Constabulary, 1987–90; Dir, Personnel and Trng, Life Span Healthcare, 1990–92; Mgt and Employee Develt Advr, InterCity, 1992–93; Dir, HR, Anglia Railways, 1993–96; Orgn Develt Advr, EA, 1996–99; Hd, Strategic Change Unit, NHS in Scotland, 1999–2001. Chairman: Scottish Youth Dance, 2000–06; Scottish Ballet, 2004–; Dir, Scottish Sculpture Trust. Hon. Professor: Queen Margaret Univ., 2007; De Montfort Univ., 2007. *Recreations:* arts and culture, European travel, ballet, opera, reading, gardens. *Address:* 10 Bielside Gardens, West Barns, Dunbar, Scotland EH42 1WA; *e-mail:* zoe-van-zwanenberg@hotmail.com. *Club:* Art (Glasgow).

VARA, Shailesh Lakhman; MP (C) Cambridgeshire North West, since 2005; *b* 4 Sept. 1960; *s* of Lakhman Arjan Vara and Savita Vara (*née* Gadher); *m* 2002, Beverley Deanne Fear; one *s*. *Educ:* Aylesbury Grammar Sch.; Brunel Univ. (LLB). Admitted Solicitor, 1990; articled, Richards Butler, 1988–90 (in Hong Kong, 1989–90); Crossman Block, 1991–92; Payne Hicks Beach, 1992–93; CMS Cameron McKenna, 1994–2001. Shadow Dep. Leader of the H of C, 2006–. Member: Select Cttee on Envmt, Food and Rural Affairs, 2005–06; Standing Cttee on Company Law Reform Bill, 2006; Treas., BBC All Party Gp, 2005–; Jt Vice Chm., All Party Parly Gp on Trafficking of Women and Children, 2006–; Jt Sec., Cons. Backbench Gp on Foreign Affairs, 2006–. A Vice-Chm., Cons. Party, 2001–05. Contested (C): Birmingham Ladywood, 1997; Northampton S, 2001. Vice Pres., Small Business Bureau, 1998–. Vice Chm., Exec. Cttee, Soc. of Cons. Lawyers, 2006– (Mem., Exec. Cttee, 1990–93, 1994–97, 1998–2001; Treas., 2001–04). Audit Gov., Westminster Kingsway Coll., 2002–05 (Mem., 2002–05, Vice Chm., 2005, Audit Cttee). *Recreations:* travel, cricket, tae kwon do. *Address:* House of Commons, SW1A 0AA. *T:* (020) 7219 3000; *e-mail:* varas@parliament.uk.

VARADHAN, Prof. Srinivasa, PhD; FRS 1998; Professor of Mathematics, Courant Institute of Mathematical Sciences (formerly Courant Institute), New York University, since 1972; *b* 2 Jan. 1940; *s* of S. V. Rangaiyengar and S. R. Janaki; *m* 1964, Vasundara Narayanan; two *s*. *Educ:* Madras Univ. (BSc Hons, MA); Indian Statistical Inst. (PhD 1963). Courant Institute, New York University: Vis. Member, 1963–66; Asst Prof., 1966–68; Associate Prof., 1968–72; Dir, 1980–84 and 1992–94. Fellow, Amer. Acad. Arts and Sci., 1988; Associate Fellow, Third World Acad. Scis, 1988; Mem., NAS, 1995. *Publications:* Multi-dimensional Diffusion Processes, 1979; On Diffusion Problems and Partial Differential Equations, 1980; Large Deviations and Applications, 1984; Probability Theory, 2001; Stochastic Processes, 2007. *Recreations:* travel, tennis, squash, bridge. *Address:* Courant Institute of Mathematical Sciences, New York University, 251 Mercer Street, New York, NY 10012, USA. *T:* (212) 9983334.

VARCOE, (Christopher) Stephen; baritone; *b* 19 May 1949; *s* of Philip William and Mary Northwood Varcoe; *m* 1972, Melinda Davies; two *s* two *d* (and one *s* decd). *Educ:* King's School, Canterbury; King's College, Cambridge (MA). Freelance concert and opera singer, 1970–; on teaching staff, Royal Coll. of Music, 2003–. Calouste Gulbenkian Foundation Fellowship, 1977. *Publications:* Sing English Song: a practical guide to the language and repertoire, 2000; (contrib.) Cambridge Companion to Singing, 2000. *Recreations:* painting, gardening, building. *Address:* c/o Caroline Phillips, 11 Pound Pill, Corsham, Wilts SN13 9HZ.

VARCOE, Jeremy Richard Lovering Grosvenor, CMG 1989; HM Diplomatic Service, retired; part-time Immigration Judge (formerly Adjudicator), 1995–2007; *b* 20 Sept. 1937; *s* of late Ronald A. G. Varcoe and Zoe E. Varcoe (*née* Lovering); *m* 1st, 1961, Wendy Anne Moss (*d* 1991); two *d*; 2nd, 1995, Ruth Murdoch (*née* Wallis). *Educ:* Charterhouse; Lincoln Coll., Oxford (MA). National Service, Royal Tank Regt, 2nd Lieut, 1956–58. HMOCS: District Officer, Swaziland, 1962–65. Called to the Bar, Gray's Inn, 1966; Lectr in Law, Univ. of Birmingham, 1967–70; joined HM Diplomatic Service, 1970; FCO, 1970–72; Dep. Secretary General, Pearce Commn on Rhodesian Opinion, 1972; First Sec., Ankara, 1972–74, Lusaka, 1974–78; FCO, 1978–79; Counsellor, Kuala Lumpur, 1979–82; Head of Southern African Dept, FCO, 1982–84; Counsellor, Ankara, 1984–85; on special leave with Standard Chartered Bank, Istanbul, 1985–87; Ambassador to Somalia, 1987–89; Minister/Dep. High Comr, Lagos, 1989–90; Asst Under-Sec. of State, FCO, 1990–92. Co-ordinator, London Economic Summit, 1991. Dir Gen., United World Colls, 1992–94; Dep. Dir, Develt Office, Oxford Univ., 1995–96. *Publication:* Legal Aid in Criminal Proceedings—a Regional Survey, 1970. *Recreations:* sailing, golf. *Address:* Lemail Quinnies, Egloshayle, Wadebridge, Cornwall PL27 6JQ. *Club:* St Enodoc Golf.

VARCOE, Stephen; *see* Varcoe, C. S.

VARDY, Prof. Alan Edward, PhD, DEng, DSc; FREng, FICE; FRSE; Research Professor of Civil Engineering (part-time), University of Dundee, since 1995 (Professor of Civil Engineering, 1979–95); Engineering Consultant, Dundee Tunnel Research, since 1995; *b* Sheffield, 6 Nov. 1945; *s* of John Moreton Vardy and Margaret Vardy (*née* Thompson); *m* 1991, Susan Janet Upstone; two *s* one *d*. *Educ:* Univ. of Leeds (BSc 1st Cl. Hons Civil Engrg 1967; PhD Civil Engrg 1971; DEng Tunnel Safety 1997); Univ. of Dundee (DSc Transient 1-D Flows 2007). MICE 1975, FICE 1989; Eur Ing 1989; FRSE 2002; FREng 2007. Res. Officer, 1971–72, Lectr in Civil Engrg, 1972–75, Univ. of Leeds; Royal Soc. Warren Res. Fellow, Univ. of Cambridge, 1975–79; University of Dundee: Hd, Dept of Civil Engrg, 1979–85; Dir, Wolfson Bridge Res. Unit, 1980–90; Dep. Principal, 1985–88; Dep. Principal and Vice Principal, 1988–89; Royal Soc./SERC Industrial Fellow, 1990–94; Dir, Lightweight Structures Unit, 1998–2004. FASCE 1995 (MASCE 1980). FRSA 1980; FHEA 2007. *Publications:* Fluid Principles, 1990; 150 papers in jls and confs. *Recreations:* wine, wife, walking.

VARDY, Sir Peter, Kt 2001; DL; Chairman, Vardy Group of Companies, since 2006; *b* 4 March 1947; *s* of late Reginald Vardy and of Sarah Vardy; *m* 1971, Margaret; two *s* one *d* (and one *s* decd.). *Educ:* Chorister Sch.; Durham Sch. Began work in family business, Reg Vardy Ltd (motor dealership), at age of 16; built co. to become one of largest UK motor retail gps; CEO, 1982–2006; floated on Stock Exchange, 1989; sold to Pendragon Plc, 2006. Sponsor and Chairman: Emmanuel Coll., Gateshead (City Tech. Coll.), 1990–; Kings Acad. (City Acad.), Middlesbrough, 2003; Trinity Acad. (City Acad.), Doncaster, 2005; Bede Acad., Blyth, 2009. DL Tyne and Wear, 2002. Hon. DBA Sunderland, 1995. *Address:* (office) Venture House, Aykley Heads, Durham DH1 5TS.

VARDY, Peter, PhD; Vice-Principal, Heythrop College, London, since 1999; *b* 29 July 1945; *s* of Mark and Christa Vardy; *m* 1974, Anne Moore (marr. diss. 2004); two *s* four *d*. *Educ:* Charterhouse; Univ. of Southampton (BA 1979); W Sussex Inst. of Higher Educn (PGCE 1980); KCL (MTh 1982; PhD 1985). FCA 1967. Chm., H. Young Holdings plc, 1979–83. Chm., Bd of Theology, Univ. of London, 1990–93. Pres., London Soc. for the Study of Religion, 1996–98. Ed., Dialogue Australasia, 1997–2008. *Publications:* The Puzzle of God, 1989, 4th edn 1999; (jtly) The Puzzle of Ethics, 1990, 4th edn 1999; The Puzzle of Evil, 1991, 2nd edn 1997; The Puzzle of Sex, 1993, new edn 2009; (jtly) The Puzzle of the Gospels, 1994; (ed) Great Christian Thinkers, 1995; What is Truth, 1999, 2nd edn 2003; (with Julie Arliss) The Thinker's Guide to Evil, 2003; (with Julie Arliss) The Thinker's Guide to God, 2003; Being Human, 2003; Kierkegaard, 2008. *Recreations:* forestry, reading, stillness, anticipating death. *T:* (020) 7795 4212; *e-mail:* petervardy@heythrop.ac.uk.

VARFIS, Grigoris; Member (Socialist), European Parliament, 1984–89; *b* 1927. *Educ:* Univ. of Athens; Univ. of Paris. Journalist, Paris, 1953–58; OECD, 1958–62; Econ. Adviser to perm. Greek delegn to EEC, 1963–74; Dir-Gen., Econ. Min. of Co-ordination, 1974–77; Man. Dir in chemical industry, 1977–81; Vice-Minister of Foreign Affairs, 1981–84; Greek Comr to EC, 1985–88 (responsible for structural funds and consumer protection, 1986–88). *Address:* Kypseli, Aegina 18010, Greece.

VARGAS LLOSA, Mario; writer; *b* Arequipa, Peru, 28 March 1936; *m* 1st, 1955, Julia Urquidi (marr. diss. 1964); 2nd, 1965, Patricia Llosa Urquidi; two *s* one *d*. *Educ:* Univ. Nacional Mayor de San Marcos, Lima (BA); Univ. of Madrid (PhD 1971). Journalist and broadcaster, Lima and Paris; Lectr, QMC, 1967; Writer in Residence, Wilson Center, Smithsonian Instn, 1980; Vis. Fellow, Wissenschaftskolleg, Berlin, 1991–92; Dist. Writer-in-Residence, Georgetown Univ., Washington DC, 2003; Visiting Professor: Washington State Univ., 1968; KCL, 1969; Univ. de Puerto Rico, 1969; Columbia Univ., 1975; Cambridge Univ., 1977; Syracuse Univ., 1988; Florida Internat. Univ., 1991; Harvard Univ., 1992–93; Princeton Univ., 1993; Georgetown Univ., 1994, 1999; Oxford Univ., 2000. Founder of political party, Movimiento Libertad, 1988; Presidential candidate, Peru, 1990. Pres., PEN Club Internat., 1976–79. Member: Acad. Peruana de la Lengua, 1975; Royal Spanish Acad., 1994. Biblioteca Breve prize (Spain), 1963; Rómulo Gallegos Internat. Literature prize (Venezuela), 1967; Ritz Paris Hemingway prize (France), 1985; Asturias prize (Spain), 1986; Planeta prize (Spain), 1993; Cervantes prize (Spain), 1994; Jerusalem prize (Israel), 1995. Congressional Medal of Honour (Peru), 1981; Gran Cruz, Orden El Sol (Peru), 2001; Légion d'honneur (France), 1985; Chevalier, Ordre des Arts et des Lettres (France), 1993. *Publications:* Los jefes (short stories), 1959; *novels:* La ciudad y los perros, 1963; La casa verde, 1966; Los cachorros, 1967; Conversación en la Catedral, 1969; Historia secreta de una novela, 1971; Pantaleón y las visitadoras, 1973; La tía Julia y el escribidor, 1977 (filmed as Tune in Tomorrow, 1990); La guerra del fin del mundo, 1981; La historia de Mayta, 1984; ¿Quién mató a Palomino Molero?, 1986; El hablador, 1987; Elogio de la madrastra, 1988; Lituma en los Andes, 1993; Los cuadernos de Don Rigoberto, 1997; La fiesta del Chivo, 2000 (filmed as The Feast of the Goat, 2006); El paraíso en la otra esquina, 2003; Travesuras de la niña mala, 2006; *plays:* La señorita de Tacna, 1981; Kathie y el hipopótamo, 1983; La Chunga, 1986; El loco de los balcones, 1993; *non-fiction:* Contra viento y marea (essays), vols I and II, 1986, vol. III, 1990; El pez en el agua (autobiog.), 1993; Desafíos a la libertad (essays), 1994; Making Waves (essays), 1996; Touchstones: essays on literature, art and politics, 2007. *Address:* Las Magnolias 295–6° Piso, Barranco, Lima 04, Peru. *Fax:* (1) 4773518; c/o Faber & Faber Ltd, 3 Queen Square, WC1N 3AU. *Fax:* (020) 7465 0034.

VARLEY, Dame Joan (Fleetwood), DBE 1985 (CBE 1974); Director, Local Government Organisation, Conservative Central Office, 1976–84; *b* 22 Feb. 1920; *d* of late F. Ireton and Elizabeth Varley. *Educ:* Cheltenham Ladies' College; London School of Economics (BSc Econ). Section Officer, WAAF, 1944–46. Conservative Agent, Shrewsbury, 1952–56; Dep. Central Office Agent, NW Area, 1957–65; Dep. Dir Orgn, 1966–74, Dir, Central Admin, 1975–76, Cons. Central Office. Chm., Friends of St James Norlands Assoc., 1986–95; Pro Chancellor, Univ. of Greenwich Court of Governors, 1992–94 (Vice-Chm., 1986–91, Chm., 1991–92, Thames Polytechnic Court of Governors); pt-time Mem., Panel of VAT Tribunals, 1986–94. DUniv Greenwich, 1995. *Recreations:* gardening, walking. *Address:* 21 Chartwell House, 12 Ladbroke Terrace, W11 3PG. *T:* (020) 7727 7300.

VARLEY, John Silvester; Group Chief Executive, Barclays Bank plc, since 2004; *b* 1 April 1956; *m* 1981, Carolyn Thorn Pease; one *s* one *d*. *Educ:* Downside Sch.; Oriel Coll., Oxford (MA 1st cl. Hons History). Admitted Solicitor, 1979; Commercial Law Dept, Frere Cholmeley, Solicitors, 1979–82; Asst Dir, Corporate Finance Dept, Barclays Merchant Bank, 1982–86; Barclays de Zoete Wedd: Corporate Finance Div., 1986–89; Man. Dir, BZW Asia, 1989–91; Dep. Chief Exec., Global Equities Div., 1991–94; Dir, Odey Asset Management, 1994–95; Chairman: BZW Asset Management, 1995–96; BZW Property Investment Management, 1995–96; Dir, Barclays Global Investors, 1995–96; Chm., Barclays Asset Management Gp, 1996–98; Barclays Bank plc: Dir, 1998–; Chief Exec., Retail Finance Services, Barclays Bank plc, 1998–2000; Gp Finance Dir, 2000–03. *Address:* c/o Barclays Bank plc, One Churchill Place, E14 5HP. *T:* (020) 7116 3336; *e-mail:* john.varley@barclays.com. *Clubs:* Brooks's, Army and Navy.

VARLEY, Rosemary Margaret, (Rosie), OBE 2007; Chairman: General Optical Council, since 1999; Public Guardian Board, since 2007; *b* 22 Dec. 1951; *d* of late Ratcliffe Bowen Wright, MD, FRCOG and of Dr Margaret Bowen Wright (*née* Williams); *m* 1976, Andrew Iain Varley (*d* 2005); one *s* one *d*. *Educ:* New Hall, Chelmsford; Durham Univ. (BA Hons); Manchester Univ. (MA Econ). Various acad. posts, Manchester Univ., 1978–83; Mem., W Suffolk HA, 1984–92; Chairman: Mid Anglia Community NHS Trust, 1992–97; Anglia and Oxford, then Eastern, Reg., NHS Exec., DoH, 1997–2001; NHS Appointments Comr, Eastern Reg., 2001–06. Ind. Mem., E of England Regl Assembly, 1999–2001. Member: Mental Health Rev. Tribunal, 1995–; Disability Appeal Tribunal, 1992–. Mem., Council for Healthcare Regulatory Excellence (formerly Council for the Regulation of Healthcare Professionals), 2002– (Actg Chm., 2007). FRSocMed 1999. Freeman, City of London, 2005; Liveryman, Co. of Spectacle Makers, 2006–. *Publications:* contrib. various articles in health jls and mgt textbooks. *Recreations:* walking, travel, sailing, extended family. *Address:* 72 Southgate Street, Bury St Edmunds, Suffolk IP33 2BJ. *T:* (01284) 753135; *e-mail:* rosievarley@btinternet.com.

VARMUS, Prof. Harold Eliot, MD; President and Chief Executive Officer, Memorial Sloan-Kettering Cancer Center, New York City; *b* 18 Dec. 1939; *s* of Frank Varmus and Beatrice Barasch Varmus; *m* 1969, Constance Louise Casey; two *s*. *Educ:* Freeport High Sch., NY; Amherst Coll., Mass (BA 1961); Harvard Univ. (MA 1962); Columbia Univ., NY (MD 1966). Surgeon, US Public Health Service, 1968–70; Dept of Microbiology, Univ. of California Medical Center, San Francisco: Lectr, 1970–72; Asst Prof., 1972–74; Associate Prof., 1974–79; Prof. of Microbiology and Immunology, 1979–93 (Dept of Biochem. and Biophys, 1982–93); Amer. Cancer Soc. Prof. of Molecular Virology, 1984–93; Dir, NIH, Bethesda, Md, 1993–99. Scientific Consultant, Chiron Corp., 1982–87; Member, Scientific Adv. Bd: Merck Corp., 1985–88; Gilead Corp., 1988–. Associate Editor: Cell, 1974–78, 1979–; Virology, 1974–84; Genes and Develt, 1986–; Editor, Molecular and Cellular Biol., 1984–88; Mem., Editl Bd, Trends in Genetics, 1989–. Member: Special Grants Cttee, Calif. Div., Amer. Cancer Soc., 1973–76; Breast Cancer Virus Wkg Gp, Virus Cancer Program, 1973–74. Bd of Scientific Counselors, Div. of Cancer Biol. and Diagnosis, 1983–87, Nat. Cancer Inst.; Virology Study Section, NIH, 1976–80. Member: AAAS; Amer. Soc. Microbiology; Amer. Soc. Biochem. and Molecular Biol; Amer. Soc. Virology; Nat. Acad. Scis, 1984; Amer. Acad. Arts and Scis, 1988. Foreign Mem., Royal Soc., 2005. Hon. DSc: Amherst Coll., 1984; Columbia Univ., 1990. Numerous awards and prizes incl. (jtly) Nobel Prize for Physiology or Medicine, 1989. *Address:* Memorial Sloan-Kettering Cancer Center, 1275 York Avenue, New York, NY 10065, USA.

VARNEY, Sir David (Robert), Kt 2006; Chairman, HM Revenue and Customs, 2004–06; *b* 11 May 1946; *s* of Robert Kitchener Frederick Varney and Winifred Gwendoline Williams; *m* 1971, Patricia Ann Billingham; one *s* one *d*. *Educ:* Brockley County Grammar Sch.; Surrey Univ. (BSc); Manchester Univ. (MBA; Alumnus of the Year, 2005). Joined Shell Refining Co., 1968; various appts in UK, Australia, Holland and Sweden, 1968–90; Head of Mkting, Branding and Product Develt, SIPCO, 1990–91; Man. Dir, Downstream Oil, Shell UK, 1991–95; Dir (responsible for Shell's oil products business in Europe), Shell Internat. Petroleum Co., 1996; Chief Exec., BG Group plc, 1997–2000; Chm., BT Wireless, subseq. mmO_2, 2001–04. Non-executive Director: Cable and Wireless, 1999–2000; HM Treasury, 2004–07; Civil Service Steering Bd, 2007–. Member: Bd, Oil, Gas and Petrochemicals Supplies Office, 1997–99; Public Service Productivity Panel, 2000–01; Policy Commn on Future of Farming and Food, 2001–02. Chm., BITC, 2002–04. President: Inst. of Employment Studies, 2003–07; Chartered Mgt Inst., 2005–06. Vice-Chm., Council, Univ. of Surrey, 2001–02 (Mem., 1994–2002). Hon. DTech London Metropolitan, 2005; Hon. LLD Bath, 2006; DUniv Surrey, 2007. *Recreations:* opera, Formula 1 motor racing, Rugby. *Address:* River Thatch, The Abbotsbrook, Bourne End, Bucks SL8 5QU. *Club:* Royal Society of Medicine (Mem. Council, 2003–05).

VARNISH, Peter, OBE 1982; FREng, FIET; Chairman: Definition International Ltd, since 2002; Wrightson Group, since 2002; *b* 30 May 1947; *s* of John Varnish and Ilma Varnish (*née* Godfrey); *m* 1968, Shirley-Anne Bendelow; two *s*. *Educ:* Warwick Sch.; UCNW, Bangor (BSc Hons 1968). CEng 1987; FIET (FIEE 1989); FREng (FEng 1995).

Res., Services Electronics Res. Lab., Baldock, 1968–75; Scientific Advr to MoD, British Embassy, Washington, 1975–79; Res. Area Co-ordinator for Electrical Warfare in UK, ASWE Portsdown, 1979–81; Officer i/c, ASWE Funtington, 1981–84; Head: Radar Div., ASWE Portsdown, 1984–86; Signature Control, ARE Funtington, 1986–88; Electronic Warfare and Weapons Dept, ARE Portsdown, 1988–90; Dir, Above Water Weapons, DRA, 1990–92; RCDS 1992; Dir, SDI Participation Office, 1993; Dir of Sci. for Ballistic Missile Defence, MoD, 1993–95; Defence Evaluation and Research Agency: Dir, Internat. Business Develt, 1995–98; Dir, Business Develt, 1998–2000; Dir of Technology (Partnership), 2000–01; Chief Exec., S3T Ltd, 2001–05. Director: CMB Ltd, 2001–04; Sparks Technology Ltd, 2001–06; Internat. Geopolitical Solutions Ltd, 2001–; Charteris, Mackie, Baillie, 2001–05; Closed Solutions Ltd, 2002–; CMBIE Ltd, 2003–04; ITAG Ltd, 2003–06; Evesham Ltd, 2004–06; Table 27 Ltd, 2004–07; Ipsotek Ltd, 2005; QTEL Europe Plc, 2005–06; Consols Ltd, 2006–08; WPM Ltd, 2008–; 1SH Division, 2003–. Mem., Defence Scientific Adv. Council, 1991–99; Adviser: Home Office, 2003–; MoD Faraday Initiative, 2004–. Chairman: Common Defence Forum, 1988–2004; Military Microwaves, 1990; Stealth Conf., 1990, 2003, 2004; Milcon, Abu Dhabi, biennially, 1995–; Singapore Internat. Defence Conf., 1997, 1999, 2005; Air Missile Conf., 2001, 2002, 2003, 2004, 2005; Global Security Conf., 2002; Interoperability Conf., 2002, 2003, 2004, 2005; Air Launched Weapons Conf., 2002, 2003, 2004, 2005; Military Aviation Repair and Maintenance, 2004, 2005; Asymmetric Warfare, 2004, 2005, 2006; Homeland Defence Conf., Dubai, 2005, 2006; ISNR, London, 2007; EW-AOC, Interlaken, 2007; Networked Public Safety, London, 2008; Vice-Chm., Global Security, Asia Conf., Singapore, 2005, 2007. TV appearances, Horizon and Discovery. Liveryman, Coachmakers' and Coach Harness Makers' Co. SMIEE; MInstD 1995. FRSA 1996. Several patents on stealth technology, electronic devices, radar. *Publications:* numerous papers on electron bombarded semiconductor devices, radar, electronic warfare, Stealth, SDI, ballistic missile defence and res. policy, defence globalisation, technol. of modern warfare, homeland defence, novel threats. *Recreations:* Rugby football, classical music, photography, furtherance of science in UK, travelling, being a grandparent. *Address:* 1 Greatfield Way, Rowlands Castle, Hants PO9 6AG. *T:* (023) 9241 2440; *e-mail:* peter.varnish@btinternet.com. *Clubs:* Army and Navy, Brooks's, Savage.

VASARY, Tamàs; pianist and conductor; Principal Conductor, Budapest Symphony Orchestra, since 1993; Principal Conductor, Bournemouth Sinfonietta, 1989–97, Conductor Laureate, 1997–98; *b* 11 Aug. 1933; *s* of Jozsef Vàsàry and Elizabeth (*née* Baltazàr); *m* 1967, Ildiko (*née* Kovàcs). *Educ:* Franz Liszt Music Academy Budapest. First concert at age of 8 in Debrecen, Hungary; First Prize, Franz Liszt Competition, Budapest, 1947; prizes at internat. competitions in Warsaw, Paris, Brussels, Rio de Janeiro; Bach and Paderewski medals, London, 1961; début in London, 1961, in Carnegie Hall, NY, 1961; plays with major orchestras and at festivals in Europe, USA, Australasia and Far East; 3 world tours. Conducting debut, 1970; Musical Dir, Northern Sinfonia Orch., 1979–82; conducts worldwide. Records Chopin, Debussy, Liszt, Rachmaninov (in Germany), Brahms, Mozart, Honegger, Respighi, Martinu, Beethoven. *Recreations:* yoga, writing, sports. *Address:* c/o Magyar Rádió Zenekari Iroda, Bródy Sándor u. 5–7, 1800 Budapest, Hungary.

VASELLA, Dr Daniel L.; Chairman and Chief Executive Officer, Novartis AG, since 1999 (President and Head of Executive Committee, 1996–99); *b* 15 Aug. 1953; *m*; two *s* one *d*. *Educ:* Univ. of Berne (MD 1979). Former resident physician: Waid Hosp., Zurich; Univ. Hosp., Berne; Inst. of Pathology, Univ. of Berne; attendant physician, C. L. Lory Haus, Univ. Hosp., Berne, 1984–88; Sandoz Group: consecutively, mkt res. and sales, Product Manager for Sandostatin, then Dir of special project mkting, Sandoz Pharmaceuticals Corp., USA, 1988–92; Asst Vice-Pres., 1992; Head of Corp. Mkting, 1993; Sandoz Pharma Ltd: Sen. Vice-Pres. and Hd of Worldwide Develt, 1994; Chief Operating Officer, 1994; CEO, 1995–96. *Address:* Novartis AG, 4002 Basle, Switzerland.

VASEY, Terence, CMG 2004; Chief Executive, British Leprosy Relief Association, since 1991; *b* 5 Sept. 1944; *s* of Thomas William Vasey and Hannah Mary Vasey (*née* Wilkinson); *m* 1976, Margarita Pradera de Mendivil. *Educ:* Heythrop Coll., London (BA (Philos. and Theol.) 1968); Southampton Univ. (Dip. Social Work). CQSW 1976. Principal Social Worker, Emergency Services, London Borough of Hackney, 1969–82; Hd of Therapy and Social Work Co-ordinator, Dartmouth House Centre, London, 1982–85; Country Co-ordinator, Bolivia and Brazil, UNA Internat. Service, 1985–90. KLJ 2005 (CLJ 1998). *Recreation:* diving. *Address:* Wig Cottage, Wig Lane, Boxted, Essex CO4 5QX. *T:* (01206) 272241, *Fax:* (01206) 216700; *e-mail:* terry_vasey@lepra.org.uk. *Club:* New Cavendish.

VASQUEZ, Hon. Sir Alfred (Joseph), Kt 1988; CBE 1974; QC (Gibraltar) 1986; *b* 2 March 1923; *s* of Alfred Joseph Vasquez and Maria Josefa (*née* Rugeroni); *m* 1950, Carmen, *o d* of Lt-Col Robert Sheppard-Capurro, OBE, JP; three *s* one *d*. *Educ:* Mount St Mary's Sch., Millfield; Fitzwilliam Coll., Cambridge (MA). Gibraltar Defence Force, 1943–45; The Gibraltar Regt, 1957–64, Captain. Called to the Bar, Inner Temple, 1950; called to Gibraltar Bar, 1950; Sen. Partner, Vasquez Benady & Co., 1950–91; Consultant, Triay & Triay, barristers and solicitors, 1995–. Speaker, Gibraltar Hse of Assembly, 1970–89; Mayor of Gibraltar, 1970–76. Vice-Chm., Gibraltar Bar Council, 1996–98. Pres., Gibraltar Oxford & Cambridge Soc. Hon. Fellow, World Innovation Foundn, 2000. KHS 1989. *Recreations:* golf, shooting, gardening, bridge. *Address:* St Vincent House, 4a Rosia Parade, Gibraltar. *T:* 73710. *Clubs:* Royal Gibraltar Yacht; Sotogrande Golf (Spain).

VASSAR-SMITH, Sir John (Rathborne), 4th Bt *cr* 1917, of Charlton Park, Charlton Kings, Co. Gloucester; Headmaster, St Ronan's Preparatory School, 1972–97; *b* 23 July 1936; *o s* of Major Sir Richard Rathborne Vassar-Smith, 3rd Bt and Mary Dawn, *d* of Sir Raymond Woods, CBE; *S* father, 1995; *m* 1971, Roberta Elaine, *y d* of Wing Comdr N. Williamson; two *s*. *Educ:* Eton. *Heir: s* Richard Rathborne Vassar-Smith, *b* 29 Dec. 1975. *Address:* 24 Haywards Close, Wantage, Oxon OX12 7AT.

VASSILIOU, Dr George Vassos; Leader, United Democrats (formerly Free Democrats Movement), Cyprus, since 1993; President of Cyprus, 1988–93; *b* 20 May 1931; *s* of Vassos Vassiliou and Fofo Vassiliou; *m* Androulla Georgiades; one *s* two *d*. *Educ:* Univs of Geneva, Vienna and Budapest (DEcon). Market researcher, Reed Paper Group, UK; Founder: Middle East Marketing Research Bureau, 1962 (Chm., 1993–); Middle East Centres for Management and Computing Studies, 1984; Cyprus Branch, Inst. of Directors (Hon. Sec.). Vis. Prof., Cranfield School of Management, 1985–. MP (United Democrats), Cyprus, 1993. Head, Cyprus negotiating team for accession to EU, 1998–2003. Member: Bd and Exec. Cttee, Bank of Cyprus, 1981–88; Econ. Adv. Council, Church of Cyprus, 1982–88; Educn Adv. Council, 1983–88; Inter Action Council, 1994–; Trilateral Commn, 2000–. Chm. Bd, World Inst. for Develt Econ. Res. of UN Univ., Helsinki, 1999–2000 (Mem., 1995–). Mem., Bd of Govs, Shimon Peres Inst. for Peace, 1997–. Dr *hc:* Univ. of Athens; Univ. of Econs, Budapest. Grand Cross of Order of Merit (Cyprus), 2002. Grand Cross: Legion of Honour (France); Order of the Saviour (Greece); Order of Republic of Italy; Standard (Flag) Order (Hungarian People's Republic); Grand Collar, Order of Austria. *Publications:* Marketing in the Middle East, 1976; The Middle East Markets up to 1980, 1977; Towards the Solution of the Cyprus Problem, 1992; Modernisation of the Civil Service, 1992; (with Klaus Schwab) Overcoming Indifference, 1994; numerous articles and contribs in internat. pubns. *Address:* 21 Academia Avenue, Aglandjia, PO Box 22098, Nicosia 1583, Cyprus.

VASSYLENKO, Volodymyr; Adviser, Minister of Foreign Affairs, Ukraine, since 2005; *b* Kyiv, Ukraine, 16 Jan. 1937; *m*; one *s* one *d*. *Educ:* Kyiv State Univ. (PhD 1964; LLD 1977). Teaching Public Internat. Law, Human Rights Law, Internat. Humanitarian Law and Law of Internat. Orgn, Ukrainian Inst. Internat. Relns, Kyiv State Univ., 1964–93 (Prof. 1978); Legal Advr to Min. of Foreign Affairs, Ukraine, 1972–93; Sen. Legal Advr to Parliament of Ukraine and Mem., Constitutional Commn, 1991–93; Ambassador to Belgium, The Netherlands and Luxembourg, and Rep. to EU and N Atlantic Co-operation Council, 1993–95; Ambassador-at-Large, Min. of Foreign Affairs, 1995–98; Ambassador to UK and (non-resident) to Ireland, 1998–2002; Permanent Rep. to IMO, 1999–2002; Judge *ad litem*, Internat. Criminal Tribunal for Former Yugoslavia, 2002–05. Rep. of Ukraine to internat. confs; Rep. to UN Commn on Human Rights, 1989–91, 1996–98, 2005; Rep. to UN Council on Human Rights, 2006–07; Mem., Ukrainian Delegn to CIS summits, 1991, 1992. Member: Consultative Council to Min. of Justice, Ukraine; Supervisory Bd, Ukrainian Legal Foundn. Sec., Adv. and Governing Councils, 1972–78, Mem., 1978–92, Inst. Internat. Relns, Kyiv State Univ. Mem., Grand Council, Popular Democratic People's Movement of Ukraine, 1969–91. Vice-Pres., Ukrainian Assoc. for UN, 1989–98. *Publications:* International Law, 1971; *monographs:* State Responsibility for International Offences, 1976; Sanctions in International Law, 1982; Legal Aspects of Participation of the Ukrainian SSR in International Relations, 1985; Protection Mechanisms for International Law and Order, 1986; Fundamentals of International Law, 1988; contrib. numerous articles in public internat. law and constitutional protection of human rights. *Address:* 4/6 Antonovych St, Apt 23, 01004 Kiev, Ukraine. *T:* (44) 2381518, 2344766.

VAUGHAN, family name of **Earl of Lisburne**.

VAUGHAN, Viscount; David John Francis Malet Vaughan; artist; *b* 15 June 1945; *e s* of 8th Earl of Lisburne, *qv*; *m* 1973, Jennifer Jane Sheila Fraser Campbell, artist, *d* of James and Dorothy Campbell, Invergarry; one *s* one *d*. *Educ:* Ampleforth Coll.

VAUGHAN, David Arthur John, CBE 2002; QC 1981; QC (NI) 1981; a Deputy High Court Judge, since 1997; a Judge of the Courts of Appeal of Jersey and Guernsey, since 2000; *b* 24 Aug. 1938; *s* of late Captain F. H. M. Vaughan, OBE, RN and J. M. Vaughan; *m* 1st, 1967, (marr. diss.); 2nd, 1985, Leslie Anne Fenwick Irwin; one *s* one *d*. *Educ:* Eton Coll.; Trinity Coll., Cambridge (MA). 2nd Lieut, 14th/20th King's Hussars, 1958–59. Called to the Bar, Inner Temple, 1962, Bencher, 1988; a Recorder, 1994–2001. Vis. Prof., 1989–2000, Hon. Vis. Prof., 2000–, European Law, Durham Univ. Leader, European Circuit, Bar of England and Wales, 2001–03. Member: Bar Council, 1968–72, 1984–86; Bar Cttee, 1987–88; International Relations Committee of Bar Council, 1968–86 (Chm., 1984–86); Bar/Law Soc. Working Party on EEC Competition Law, 1977– (Chm., 1978–88); UK Delegation to Consultative Committee of the Bars and Law Societies of the European Communities, 1978–81 (Chm., Special Cttee on EEC Competition Law, 1978–88); Law Adv. Cttee, British Council, 1982–85; Bar European Gp, 1978– (Founder and Chm., 1978–80, Hon. Vice-Pres., 1990–); EEC Section, Union Internationale des Avocats, 1987–91 (Chm., 1987–91); Adv. Bd, Centre for Europ. Legal Studies, Cambridge Univ., 1991–; Council of Management, British Inst. of Internat. and Comparative Law, 1992–2004; Chm., Mgt Cttee, Lord Slynn of Hadley Eur. Law Foundn, 1999– (Man. Trustee, 2004–). Trustee, Wye Foundn, 1997–2000 (Chm., Steering Gp, Wye Habitat Improvement Project, 1999–2000). Chm. Editl Bd, European Law Reports, 1997–; Member, Editorial Board: Eur. Business Law Review, 1998–; Cambridge Yearbook of European Legal Studies, 1999–; Welsh Law Jl, 2001–05; Consulting editor for numerous pubns on EC Law. FRSA 1997. Bronze Medal, Bar of Bordeaux, 1985. *Publications:* co-ordinating editor, vols on European Community Law, Halsbury's Laws of England, 1986; (ed) Vaughan on Law of the European Communities, 2 vols, 1986, 2nd edn 1993–98; Vaughan and Robertson's Law of the European Union, 2003–. *Recreation:* fishing. *Address:* 50 Oxford Gardens, W10 5UN. *T:* (020) 8960 5865, (020) 8969 0707; Brick Court Chambers, 7–8 Essex Street, WC2R 3LD. *T:* (020) 7379 3550; avenue d'Auderghem 36, 1040 Brussels, Belgium. *T:* (2) 2303161. *Clubs:* Brooks's, Pratt's.

VAUGHAN, Elizabeth, (Mrs Ray Brown), FRAM, FRWCMD; international operatic mezzo-soprano (formerly soprano); *b* Llanfyllin, Montgomeryshire; *m* 1968, Ray Brown (former Gen. Manager, D'Oyly Carte Opera); one *s* one *d*. *Educ:* Llanfyllin Grammar Sch.; RAM (ARAM, LRAM); Kathleen Ferrier Prize. Joined Royal Opera House; rôles in: Benvenuto Cellini; La Bohème; Midsummer Night's Dream; Madama Butterfly; Rigoletto; Simon Boccanegra; La Traviata; Il Trovatore; Turandot; Don Giovanni; Un Ballo in Maschera; Ernani; Nabucco; Aida; Cassandra; La Forza del Destino; Tosca; Idomeneo; Macbeth; Gloriana; Salome; Katya Kabanova; Hansel and Gretel; The Carmelites; Suor Angelica. Frequent appearances with: ENO; WNO; Opera North; Scottish Opera; Vienna State Opera; Deutsche Oper, Berlin; Hamburg State Opera; Metropolitan Opera, NY; Paris Opera. Professor of Singing: Guildhall School of Music, 1989–; RNCM, 1994–96. Has toured in: Europe; USA; Australia; Canada; Japan; S America. Hon. DMus Wales, 1989. *Recreations:* tapestry, antiques, cookery. *Address:* c/o IMG, The Light Box, 111 Power Road, W4 5PY.

VAUGHAN, Prof. John Patrick, CBE 1998; MD; FRCPE, FFPH; Professor of Epidemiology and Public Health (formerly Health Care Epidemiology), London School of Hygiene and Tropical Medicine, University of London, 1987–2000, now Emeritus; consultant in international health; *b* 27 Dec. 1937; *s* of Thomas Frances Gerald Vaughan and Ellalline (*neé* Norwood); *m* 1st, 1960, Patricia Elspeth Pooley; two *s*; 2nd, 1975, Pauline Winifred Macaulay; two step *s* one step *d*. *Educ:* Bishop Wordsworth GS, Salisbury (Holgate and Folliott Prizes); Guy's Hosp. Med. Sch. (MB BS 1961; MD 1978). FRCPE 1982; FFPH (FFPHM 1988). Specialist physician, Papua New Guinea, 1966–68; Head, Dept of Epidemiology and Biostats, Univ. of Dar es Salaam, 1969–73; Sen. Lectr in Epidem. and Public Health, Med. Sch., Nottingham, 1973–75; London School of Hygiene and Tropical Medicine: Sen. Lectr, 1975–83; Director: Trop. Epidem. Unit, 1975–79; Evaluation and Planning Centre, 1980–89; Reader, 1983–87; Head of Dept of Public Health and Policy, 1989–93; on secondment as Dir, Public Health Scis Div., Internat. Centre for Diarrhoeal Disease Res., Dhaka, 1995–98. Visiting Professor: Pelotas Fed. Univ., Brazil, 1986–90; Andalucian Sch. of Public Health, Spain, 1994. Specialist Advr in Public Health to World Bank, 1989; hon. consultancies include: NHS, 1975–; MRC; WHO, in foreign countries; Sen. Health and Population Advr, DFID, 1998–99; Adviser in Public Health: Perf. and Innovation Unit, Cabinet Office, 2000–01; WHO Geneva staff, 2001–02. Member: Amnesty Internat.; WWF; Dorset Trust for Nature Conservation; Trustee: Malaria Consortium (UK), 2002–07; BBC World Service Trust (UK), 2003–; BRAC UK, 2006–. Founder and Editor, Health Policy and Planning Jl,

1985–93. Okeke and William Simpson Prizes for best student, LSHTM, 1969. *Publications:* (jtly) Community Health, 1981; (ed jtly and contrib.) Refugee Community Health Care, 1983; (jtly) Community Health Workers: the Tanzanian experience, 1987; (jtly) In the Shadow of the City: community health and the urban poor, 1988; (with R. Morrow) Manual of Epidemiology for District Health Management, 1989 (trans. French, Portuguese, Spanish, Turkish); (jtly) Health System Decentralization: concepts, issues and country experience, 1990 (trans. French, Spanish, Indonesian); (ed with C. Normand) Europe without Frontiers: the implications for health, 1993; (contrib.) Disease Control Priorities in Developing Countries, 1993; monographs on health and medicine; over 120 contribs to learned jls on internat. health and epidemiology. *Recreations:* travel, yachting, reading, art history, wild life, natural history. *Address:* Department of Public Health and Policy, London School of Hygiene and Tropical Medicine, Keppel Street, WC1E 7HT. *T:* (020) 7636 8636; *e-mail:* patrick.vaughan@lshtm.ac.uk.

VAUGHAN, Prof. Leslie Clifford, FRCVS; Professor of Veterinary Surgery, 1974–91, now Emeritus, and Vice-Principal, 1982–91, Royal Veterinary College; *b* 9 Jan. 1927; *s* of Edwin Clifford and Elizabeth Louise Vaughan; *m* 1951, Margaret Joyce Lawson; one *s* one *d. Educ:* Bishop Gore Grammar School, Swansea; Royal Veterinary College, Univ. of London (DVR 1967; DSc 1970; FRVC 1995). FRCVS 1957. Lectr in Veterinary Surgery, RVC, 1951; Reader, London Univ., 1968; Prof. of Vet. Orthopaedics, 1972. Junior Vice-Pres., 1986, Pres., 1987–88, Senior Vice-Pres., 1988–89, 1989–90, RCVS. Vice-Chm., Dogs Home Battersea, 2002–04. Francis Hogg Prize for contribs to small animal medicine and surgery, RCVS, 1962; Simon Award for small animal surgery, 1966, Bourgelat Prize, 1975, British Small Animal Vet. Assoc.; Victory Medal, Central Vet. Soc., 1982; Dalrymple-Champneys Cup and Medal, BVA, 1995. *Publications:* papers in sci jls. *Recreations:* gardening, watching rugby football. *Address:* 26 Burywick, Harpenden, Herts AL5 2AH.

VAUGHAN, Prof. Megan Anne, PhD; FBA 2002; Smuts Professor of Commonwealth History, University of Cambridge, since 2003; Fellow of King's College, Cambridge, since 2003; *b* 1 May 1954; *d* of late Albert Edward Vaughan and of Winifred Margaret Vaughan (*née* Breaman); one *d. Educ:* United World College of the Atlantic; Univ. of Kent (BA Hons); PhD London 1981. Lectr, Univ. of Malawi, 1978–83; Smuts Res. Fellow, Univ. of Cambridge, 1984–86; Rhodes Lectr in Commonwealth Studies, 1986–96, Prof. of Commonwealth Studies, 1996–2003, Univ. of Oxford; Fellow, Nuffield Coll., Oxford, 1986–2003. *Publications:* The Story of an African Famine, 1987; Cutting Down Trees: gender, nutrition and agricultural change in northern Zambia, 1994 (Herskovits Award, 1995); Curing Their Ills: colonial power and African illness, 1991; Creating the Creole Island: slavery in eighteenth century Mauritius, 2005; articles in learned jls. *Recreations:* cooking, dancing, running, writing. *Address:* History Faculty, West Road, Cambridge CB3 9EF.

VAUGHAN, Michael Paul, OBE 2006; cricketer; *b* 29 Oct. 1974; *s* of Graham Vaughan and Deirdre Vaughan (*née* Greenhaugh); *m* 2003, Nichola Shannon; one *s* one *d. Educ:* Silverdale Comprehensive Sch., Sheffield. Cricketer (right-handed batsman): Yorks CCC, 1993–; England: début, 1999; apptd Captain, One Day Internat. and Test teams, 2003, World Cup team, 2007; won Test series: *v* Bangladesh, 2003, 2005; *v* W Indies (home and away), 2004; *v* NZ, 2004; *v* S Africa, 2004–05; *v* Australia, 2005; resigned as Test Captain, 2008. Ranked world number one batsman, 2003. *Publications:* A Year in the Sun, 2003; Calling the Shots: the Captain's story, 2005. *Address:* Yorkshire County Cricket Club, Headingley Cricket Ground, Leeds LS6 7QE; c/o International Sports Management Ltd, Cherry Tree Farm, Cherry Tree Lane, Rostherne, Cheshire WA14 3RZ.

VAUGHAN, Prof. Peter Rolfe, FREng; FICE; Professor of Ground Engineering, Imperial College, London, 1987–94, now Emeritus; *b* 10 March 1935; *s* of Ernest Alfred Vaughan and Clarrice Marjorie Vaughan. *Educ:* Luton Grammar Sch.; Imperial Coll., London (BSc Eng, PhD, DSc). FREng (FEng 1991). Industry; postgraduate studies; work on Kainji Dam, Nigeria, 1964–67; academic staff, Imperial Coll., 1969–. Dir, 1982–99, Sen. Consultant, 1999–, Geotechnical Consulting Group. *Publications:* numerous technical papers. *Recreation:* growing old. *Address:* 101 Angel Street, Hadleigh, Ipswich, Suffolk IP7 5DE.

VAUGHAN, Rt Rev. Peter St George; Area Bishop of Ramsbury, 1989–98; Hon. Assistant Bishop, dioceses of Gloucester and Bristol, since 2002; *b* 27 Nov. 1930; *s* of late Dr Victor St George Vaughan and Dorothy Marguerite Vaughan; *m* 1961, Elisabeth Fielding Parker; one *s* two *d. Educ:* Charterhouse; Selwyn Coll., Cambridge (MA Theology 1959); Ridley Hall, Cambridge; MA Oxon (by incorporation) 1963. Nat. Service, 1949–51, Lt RAPC. Ordained deacon 1957, priest 1958; Asst Curate, Birmingham Parish Church, 1957–62; Chaplain to Oxford Pastorate, 1963–67; Asst Chaplain, Brasenose Coll., Oxford, 1963–67; Vicar of Christ Church, Galle Face, Colombo, 1967–72; Precentor of Holy Trinity Cathedral, Auckland, NZ, 1972–75; Principal of Crowther Hall, CMS Training Coll., Selly Oak Colleges, Birmingham, 1975–83; Archdeacon of Westmorland and Furness, 1983–89. Hon. Asst Bishop, dio. of Bradford, 1998–2001; Hon. Canon: Carlisle Cathedral, 1983–89; Salisbury Cathedral, 1989–98, now Emeritus; Bradford Cathedral, 1998–2001. Commissary for Bishop of Colombo, 1984–. *Recreations:* gardening, reading, people. *Address:* Willowbrook, Downington, Lechlade-on-Thames, Glos GL7 3DL. *T:* (01367) 252216; *e-mail:* P_St-G_VAUGHAN@lineone.net.

VAUGHAN, Prof. Robert Charles, FRS 1990; Professor of Mathematics, Pennsylvania State University, since 1999; *b* 1945. Imperial College, London, 1972–97: Prof. of Pure Maths, 1980–97; EPSRC (formerly SERC) Senior Fellow, 1992–96; Vis. Prof. of Maths, Univ. of Michigan, Ann Arbor, 1997–98. *Publication:* The Hardy-Littlewood Method, 1981, 2nd edn 1997; (with H. L. Montgomery) Multiplicative Number Theory I: classical theory, 2006. *Address:* Department of Mathematics, McAllister Building, Pennsylvania State University, University Park, PA 16802–6401, USA.

VAUGHAN, Roger, PhD; FREng; FRINA; Chairman, Safinah Ltd, since 1999; *b* 14 June 1944; *s* of late Benjamin Frederick Vaughan and Marjorie (*née* Wallace); *m* 1st, 1968 (marr. diss.); three *s* two *d*; 2nd, 1987, Valerie (*née* Truelove); one step *s* (and one step *s* decd). *Educ:* Newcastle Univ. (BSc Hons Naval Architecture and Shipbuilding 1966, PhD 1971). FREng (FEng 1990). Student apprentice, Vickers Gp, 1962; Shipbuilding Develt Engr, Swan Hunter Shipbuilders Ltd, 1970–71; Dir, 1971–81, Man. Dir, 1978–81, A&P Appledore Ltd; Dir, Performance Improvement and Productivity, British Shipbuilders, 1981–86; took part in privatisation of Swan Hunter, 1986; Joint Chief Exec., Swan Hunter, 1988–93; Chief Exec., Sch. of Mgt, Newcastle Univ., 1995–99. Non-exec. Dir, Newcastle City Health NHS Trust, 1996–2001; Dir, Northern Sinfonia Concert Soc. Ltd, 1996–2002. Vis. Prof., 2000–01, 2005–, Res. Fellow, 2001–05, Business Sch. (formerly Sch. of Mgt), Univ. of Newcastle. Member: Nat. Curriculum Council, 1992–94; Council, Newcastle Univ., 1992–95 (Chm., Engrg Design Centre, 1990–94). Pres., Shipbuilders and Shiprepairers Assoc., 1991–93. FRSA 1993. Shipbuilding Gold Medal, NECInst, 1969. *Recreations:* music, theatre, ballet, opera, sailing, walking, reading. *Address:* Correslaw, Netherwitton, Morpeth, Northumberland NE61 4NW.

VAUGHAN, Roger Davison, OBE 1986; FREng; General Manager, Fast Reactor Projects, National Nuclear Corporation Ltd, 1977–88, retired; Director, Fast Reactor Technology Ltd, 1984–88; *b* 2 Oct. 1923; *s* of late David William and Olive Marion Vaughan; *m* 1951, Doreen Stewart; four *s. Educ:* University High Sch., Melbourne; Univ. of Melbourne, Aust. (BMechE). Engineer Officer, RAAF, 1945–46. Chemical Engr, Commonwealth Serum Laboratories, 1946–47; Works apprenticeship, C. A. Parsons & Co., 1948–49; Chief Engr, C. A. Parsons Calcutta, 1950–53; AERE, Harwell, 1954; Chief Engineer: Nuclear Power Plant Co., 1955–59 (Director, 1958); The Nuclear Power Group, 1960–75 (Dir, 1960–75); Manager, Technology Div., Nuclear Power Co., 1976–77. Chairman: Gas-cooled Breeder Reactor Assoc., Brussels, 1970–78; Forum on Cabinet Office Energy Review, 2002; Member: Bd, BSI, 1989–92 (Chm., BSI Engineering Council, 1983–88); BSI Standards Bd, 1992–96. FIMechE (Mem. Council, 1977–81, 1985–89; Chairman: Power Industries Div., 1985–89; Energy Jt Venture Study Gp, Engrg Council, 1996–98); FREng (FEng 1981). *Publications:* papers in jls of IMechE, Brit. Nuc. Energy Soc., World Energy Conf. *Recreations:* ski-ing, mountain walking; questionable performer on piano and clarinet. *Address:* Otterburn House, Manor Park South, Knutsford, Cheshire WA16 8AG. *T:* (01565) 632514. *Club:* Himalayan (Bombay).

VAUGHAN, Tom; *see* Phillips, T. R. V.

VAUGHAN JONES, Sarah Jane, (Mrs Julian O'Halloran); QC 2008; a Recorder, since 2004; *b* London, 20 July 1961; *d* of Dr Ronald Vaughan Jones and Pamela Vaughan Jones; *m* 1986, Julian O'Halloran; three *d. Educ:* Trinity Hall, Cambridge (BA Law 1982). Called to the Bar, Middle Temple, 1983; in practice as barrister specialising in clinical negligence and medical law. *Recreation:* walking the Cornish cliffs. *Address:* 2 Temple Gardens, EC4Y 9AY. *T:* (020) 7822 1200; *e-mail:* svj@2tg.co.uk.

VAUX OF HARROWDEN, 11th Baron *cr* 1523; **Anthony William Gilbey;** *b* 25 May 1940; *e s* of 10th Baron Vaux of Harrowden and Maureen, *d* of Hugh Gilbey; *S* father, 2002; *m* 1964, Beverley Anne, *o d* of Charles Alexander Walton; two *s* two *d. Educ:* Ampleforth. FCA. *Heir: s* Hon. Richard Hubert Gordon Gilbey [*b* 16 March 1965; *m* 1996, Elizabeth Worsley; one *s*].

VAUX, John Esmond George; Speaker's Counsel, House of Commons, 2000–08; *b* 3 Sept. 1948; *s* of Arthur Ernest Vaux and Marjory May Vaux; *m* 1980 Jenny Lennox; one *s* one *d. Educ:* Gosport Co. Grammar Sch.; Selwyn Coll., Cambridge (MA). Legal Dept, MAFF, 1979–90 (on secondment to EC, 1983–85); Cabinet Office Legal Advr, and Hd, European Div., Treasury Solicitor's Dept, 1990–97; Speaker's Counsel (European Legislation), H of C, 1997–2000.

VAUX, Maj.-Gen. Nicholas Francis, CB 1989; DSO 1982; DL; Major General Royal Marines Commando Forces, 1987–90, retired; *b* 15 April 1936; *s* of late Harry and Penelope Vaux; *m* 1966, Zoya Hellings; one *s* two *d. Educ:* Stonyhurst College. Commissioned RM, 1954; served Suez, 1956; Far East, 1958–61; West Indies Frigate, 1962–64; Staff Coll., Camberley, 1969; MoD (Army), 1975–77; Special Advisor, USMC, 1979–81; CO 42 Commando RM, 1981–83; Falklands, 1982; RCDS, 1985. Consultant and Man. Dir, UK-Russia Security Gp, subseq. Internat. Security Co., 1993. DL Devon, 2003. *Publication:* March to the South Atlantic, 1986. *Recreations:* field sports. *Address:* National Westminster Bank, Old Town Street, Plymouth PL1 1DG. *Club:* Farmers'.

VAVALIDIS, Barbara Joan; *see* Donoghue, B. J.

VAVASOUR, Sir Eric (Michel Joseph Marmaduke), 6th Bt *cr* 1828, of Haslewood, Yorkshire; Chief Engineer (formerly Senior Engineer), since 1997, and Director, since 2001, BAL Broadcast Ltd; Director, Faraday Technology Holdings Ltd, since 2001; *b* 3 Jan. 1953; *s* of Hugh Bernard Moore Vavasour (*d* 1989) and Monique Pauline Marie Madeleine (*née* Beck) (*d* 1982); *S* kinsman, 1997; *m* 1976, Isabelle Baudouin Françoise Alain Cécile Cornelie Ghislaine (*née* van Hille); two *s* one *d. Educ:* St Joseph's Coll., Stoke-on-Trent; Manchester Univ. (BSc). MIET. BCRA, 1977; Matthey Printed Products Ltd, 1979; BAL (UK) Ltd, 1985. *Heir: s* Joseph Ian Hugh André Vavasour, *b* 22 Jan. 1978. *Address:* 15 Mill Lane, Earl Shilton, Leicester LE9 7AW.

VAVER, Prof. David, JD; Reuters Professor of Intellectual Property and Information Technology Law, University of Oxford, since 1998; Fellow, St Peter's College, Oxford, and Director, Oxford Intellectual Property Research Centre at St Peter's College, since 1998; *b* 28 March 1946; *s* of Ladislav and Pola Vaver; *m* 1978, Judith Maxine McClenaghan; one *s* one *d. Educ:* Auckland Grammar Sch.; Univ. of Auckland (BA French 1969; LLB Hons 1970); Univ. of Chicago (JD 1971); MA Oxon 1998. Called to the Bar, NZ, 1970; Asst Prof. of Law, Univ. of BC, 1971; Lectr, 1972–74, Sen. Lectr in Law, 1974–78, Univ. of Auckland; Res. Dir, later Dir, Legal Res. Foundn, Auckland, 1972–78; Associate Prof. of Law, Univ. of BC, 1978–85; Prof. of Law, Osgoode Hall Law Sch., York Univ., Toronto, 1985–98. NZ Law Foundn Dist. Vis. Fellow, 2000. Editor-in-Chief, Intellectual Property Jl, 1984–98. Consultant on copyright law reform to Dept of Canadian Heritage, 1989–98; Mem., Intellectual Property Adv. Cttee to Minister of Trade and Industry, 2001–. *Publications:* Intellectual Property Law: copyright, patents, trade-marks, 1997; Copyright Law, 2000; numerous contribs to edited books and legal jls on intellectual property and contract law. *Recreations:* music, art, wine. *Address:* St Peter's College, Oxford OX1 2DL. *T:* (01865) 278900.

VAZ, Rt Hon. (Nigel) Keith (Anthony Standish); PC 2006; MP (Lab) Leicester East, since 1987; *b* Aden, 26 Nov. 1956; *m* 1993, Maria Fernandes; one *s* one *d. Educ:* St Joseph's Convent, Aden; Latymer Upper Sch., Hammersmith; Gonville and Caius Coll., Cambridge (BA 1979); Coll. of Law, Lancaster Gate. Solicitor, Richmond-upon-Thames BC, 1982; Senior Solicitor, Islington BC, 1982–85; Solicitor, Highfields and Belgrave Law Centre, Leicester, 1985–87. Contested (Lab): Richmond and Barnes (gen. election), 1983; Surrey W (European Parlt election), 1984. Opposition front bench spokesman on inner cities and urban areas, 1992–97; PPS to Attorney Gen. and Solicitor Gen., 1997–99; Parly Sec., Lord Chancellor's Dept, 1999; Minister of State (Minister for Europe), FCO, 1999–2001. Member: Home Affairs Select Cttee, 1987–92 (Chm., 2007–); Select Cttee, LCD, 2002–; Constitutional Affairs Select Cttee, 2002–07 (Chm., Sub-Cttee on Courts and Judiciary, 2007–). Chairman: Unison Gp of MPs, 1996–99; Indo-British Parly Gp, 1997–99; Yemen Parly Gp, 1997–99, 2001–; Vice Chairman: PLP Internat. Develt Gp, 1997–99; All Party Parly Gp to Holy See, 2006; Treas., All Party Parly Race and Community Gp, 2006; Chm., Ethnic Minority Taskforce, Labour Party, 2006–. Mem., NEC, Labour Party, 2007–. Pres., India Develt Gp (UK) Ltd, 1992–. Chm., City 2020, Urban Policy Commn, 1993–99; Mem., Nat. Adv. Cttee, Crime Concern, 1989–93; Vice Chm., British Council, 1998–99. Mem., Clothing and Footwear Inst., 1988–94. Vice Pres., Assoc. of Dist Councils, 1993–97. Patron, Gingerbread, 1990–; Founder Patron: Naz Project London, 1999–; Silver Star Appeal, 2006. Jt Patron, UN Year of Tolerance, 1995; EU Ambassador, Year of Intercultural Dialogue, 2008. Pres., Leicester and S Leics RSPCA, 1988–99. Former Columnist: Tribune; Catholic Herald; New Life (Gujarat Samachar). *Address:* 144 Uppingham Road, Leicester LE5 0QF. *T:* (0116) 212 2028. *Clubs:* Safari (Leicester); Scraptoft Valley Working Men's.

VEAL, Group Captain John Bartholomew, CBE 1956; AFC 1940; Civil Aviation Safety Adviser, Department of Trade and Industry, 1972–74, retired; *b* 28 Sept. 1909; *er s* of John Henry and Sarah Grace Veal; *m* 1933, Enid Marjorie Hill (*d* 1987); two *s*. *Educ:* Christ's Hosp. Special trainee, Metropolitan-Vickers, 1926–27; commissioned in RAF as pilot officer, 1927; served in Nos 4 and 501 Squadrons and as flying Instructor at Central Flying School, transferring to RAFO, 1932; Flying-Instructor, Chief Flying Instructor, and Test Pilot, Air Service Training Ltd, 1932–39; recalled to regular RAF service, 1939; commanded navigation and flying training schools, 1939–43; Air Staff No. 46 Transport Group, 1944 and Transport Command, 1945–46 (despatches); released from RAF, 1946, to become Deputy Director of Training, Ministry of Civil Aviation; Director of Air Safety and Training, 1947; Director of Operations, Safety and Licensing, 1952; Deputy Director-General of Navigational Services, Ministry of Transport and Civil Aviation, 1958; Director-General of Navigational Services, Ministry of Aviation, 1959–62; Chief Inspector of Accidents, Civil Aviation Department, Board of Trade (formerly Min. of Aviation), 1963–68; Dir Gen. of Safety and Operations, DTI (formerly BOT), 1968–72. FRAeS 1967 (AFRAeS 1958). *Address:* Woodacre, Horsham Road, Cranleigh, Surrey GU6 8DZ. *T:* (01483) 274490. *Club:* Royal Air Force.

VEAL, Kevin Anthony; Sheriff of Tayside Central and Fife, since 1993; *b* 16 Sept. 1946; *s* of George Algernon Veal and Pauline Grace Short; *m* 1969, Monica Flynn; two *s* two *d*. *Educ:* St Joseph's Primary Sch., Dundee; Lawside Acad., Dundee; Univ. of St Andrews (LLB 1966). Partner, Burns Veal & Gillan, Dundee, 1971–93; Temp. Sheriff, 1984–93. Dean, Faculty of Procurators and Solicitors in Dundee, 1991–93; part-time Tutor, Dept of Law, Univ. of Dundee, 1978–85. Mem., Court, Abertay Dundee Univ., 1998–. Musical Dir, Cecilian Choir, Dundee, 1975–; Hon. Pres., Dundee Operatic Soc., 2003. KCHS with star 2007 (KCHS 1998; KHS 1989); KSG 1993. *Recreations:* choral music, organ playing, classical music, hill-walking. *Address:* Sheriff Court House, Market Street, Forfar, Angus DD8 3LA. *T:* (01307) 462186.

VEASEY, Josephine, CBE 1970; opera singer (mezzo soprano), retired; teaching privately, since 1982; vocal consultant to English National Opera, 1985–94; *b* London, 10 July 1930; *m* (marr. diss.); one *s* one *d*. Joined chorus of Royal Opera House, Covent Garden, 1948; a Principal, on tour, in opera, for Arts Council; a Principal, Royal Opera House, Covent Garden, 1955–. Teacher of voice production, RAM, 1983–84. Has sung at Royal Opera House, Glyndebourne, Metropolitan (NY), La Scala, and in France, Germany, Spain, Switzerland, South America; operatic Roles include: Octavian in Der Rosenkavalier; Cherubino in Figaro; name role in Iphigenie; Dorabella in Cosi fan Tutte; Amneris in Aida, Fricka in Die Walküre; Fricka in Das Rheingold; name role in Carmen; Dido and Cassandra in the Trojans; Marguerite in The Damnation of Faust; Charlotte in The Sorrows of Werther; Eboli, Don Carlos; name role, Orfeo; Adalgesa in Norma; Rosina in The Barber of Seville; Kundry in Parsifal; Gertrude in Hamlet, 1980. Concerts, 1960–70 (Conductors included Giulini, Bernstein, Solti, Mehta, Sargent). Verdi's Requiem; Monteverdi's Combattimento di Tancredi e Clorinda, Aix Festival, 1967; various works of Mahler; two tours of Israel (Solti); subseq. sang in Los Angeles (Mehta); then Berlioz: Death of Cleopatra, Royal Festival Hall, and L'enfance du Christ, London and Paris; Rossini's Petite Messe Solennelle, London and Huddersfield (with late Sir Malcolm Sargent); Handel's Messiah, England, Munich, Oporto, Lisbon; Berlioz' Romeo and Juliette, London, and Bergen Festival; Rossini's Stabat Mater, Festival d'Angers and London, 1971; Berlioz' Beatrice and Benedict, NY, and London; Emperor in 1st perf. Henze's We Come to the River, Covent Garden, 1976. Has sung Elgar's Dream of Gerontius all over England. Hon. RAM, 1972. *Recreations:* grandchildren, gardening. *Address:* 5 Meadow View, Whitchurch, Hants RG28 7BL.

VEDI, Anu Kiran, CBE 2005; Group Chief Executive, Genesis Housing Group, since 1999; *b* 10 Feb. 1955; *s* of late Jagjeet Singh Vedi and Bimla Vedi; *m* 1980, Shobhana Chadha; two *s*. *Educ:* Duke of Gloucester Sch., Nairobi; Cranford Sch., Middlesex. Chartered Accountant, 1980; Director of Finance: Ealing Family Housing Assoc., 1982–86; Sanctuary Housing Assoc., 1986–88; Paddington Churches Housing Assoc., 1988–99. Member: Bd, Dolphin Square Foundn; Adv. Bd, Relationships Foundn. *Recreations:* sports, reading, family. *Address:* 105 The Grove, Isleworth, Middlesex TW7 4JE; Genesis Housing Group, Capital House, 25 Chapel Street, NW1 5DT. *T:* (020) 8150 4111, *Fax:* (020) 8150 4197; *e-mail:* anu.vedi@ghg.org.uk.

VEDRINE, Hubert Yves Pierre; Managing Partner, Hubert Vedrine Conseil, since 2003; *b* 31 July 1947; *s* of Jean and Suzanne Vedrine; *m* 1974, Michèle Froment; two *s*. *Educ:* Lycée Albert-Camus; Univ. of Nanterre; Institute d'Etudes Politiques; Ecole Nationale d'Administration. Chargé de mission, Min. of Culture, 1974–78; Head, Dept of Architecture, Min. of the Envmt, 1978–79; Co-ordinator, Cultural Relations, Near and Middle East, Min. of Foreign Affairs, 1979–81; Head, Dept for Technical Co-operation on Health, Housing, Public Admin and Human Science, 1979–81; Technical Advr, External Affairs, Office of Sec.-Gen. of the Pres., 1981–86; Maître des requêtes, Conseil d'Etat, 1986; Advr and Spokesman, 1988–91, Sec.-Gen., 1991–95, Office of the Pres.; Partner, Jeantet & Associés, barristers, 1996–97; Minister of Foreign Affairs, 1997–2002. *Publications:* Mieux aménager sa ville, 1979; Les Mondes de François Mitterand, 1996; (with D. Moïsi) Les Cartes de la France à l'Heure de la Mondialisation, 2000; Face à l'hyperpuissance, 2003; François Mitterand: un dessein, un destin, 2005; Continuer l'Histoire, 2007; articles in jls. *Address:* 6 rue de Luynes, 75007 Paris, France.

VEEDER, Van Vechten; QC 1986; *b* 14 Dec. 1948; *s* of John Van Vechten Veeder and Helen Letham Townley; *m* 1st, 1970; one *s* one *d*; 2nd, 1991, Marie Lombardi; one *d*. *Educ:* Ecole Rue de la Ferme, Neuilly, Paris; Clifton College, Bristol; Jesus College, Cambridge. Called to the Bar, Inner Temple, 1971, Bencher, 2000; a Recorder, 2000–06. *Recreations:* sailing, travelling, reading. *Address:* Essex Court Chambers, 24 Lincoln's Inn Fields, WC2A 3EG. *T:* (020) 7813 8000, *Fax:* (020) 7813 8080. *Club:* Garrick.

VEIL, Simone Annie, Hon. DBE 1998; Chevalier de l'Ordre national du Mérite; Member, Constitutional Council, 1998–2007; Magistrate; *b* Nice, 13 July 1927; *d* of André Jacob and Yvonne (*née* Steinmetz); *m* 1946, Antoine Veil, Inspecteur des Finances, President, A. V. Consultants; three *s*. *Educ:* Lycée de Nice; Lic. en droit, dipl. de l'Institut d'Etudes Politiques, Paris; qualified as Magistrate, 1956. Deported to Auschwitz and Bergen-Belsen, March 1944–May 1945. Ministry of Justice, 1957–69; Technical Advr to Office of Minister of Justice, 1969; Gen.-Sec., Conseil Supérieur de la magistrature, 1970–74. Minister of Health, France, 1974–76; Minister of Health and Social Security, 1976–79; Minister of Social Affairs, Health and Urban Develt, 1993–95. European Parliament: Member, 1979–93; Pres., 1979–82; Chm., Liberal and Democratic Reformist Gp, 1984–89. Pres., Haut Conseil à l'Intégration, 1997–99. Monismanie Prize, 1978; Onassis Foundn Prize, Athens, 1980; Charlemagne Prize, Prix Louise Weiss, 1981; Louise Michel Prize, 1983; Jabotinsky Prize, 1983; Prize for Everyday Courage, 1984; Special Freedom Prize, Eleanor and Franklin Roosevelt Foundn, 1984; Fiera di Messina Prize, 1984; Living Legacy Award, San Diego, Univ. d'Acadie, 1987; Johanna Lowenherz Prize, Neuwied, 1987; Thomas Dehler Prize, Munich, 1988. Dr *hc*: Princeton, 1975; Institut Weizmann, 1976; Yale, Cambridge, Edinburgh, Jerusalem, 1980; Georgetown, Urbino, 1981; Yeschiva, Sussex, 1982; Free Univ., Brussels, 1984; Brandeis, 1989; Glasgow, 1995; Pennsylvania, 1997. *Publications:* (with Prof. Launay and Dr Soulé) Les Données psycho-sociologiques de l'Adoption, 1969; Les hommes aussi s'en souviennent, 2004; Une Vie (memoir), 2007. *Address: e-mail:* dorothee.guerrin@orange.fr.

VELTMAN, Prof. Dr Martinus Justinus Godefridus; McArthur Professor of Physics, University of Michigan, 1981–97, Emeritus Professor, since 1997; *b* Netherlands, 27 June 1931; *s* of Gerard P. H. Veltman and Goverdina Veltman; *m* 1960, Anna M. M.; two *s* one *d*. *Educ:* Univ. of Utrecht (PhD 1963). Fellow and Staff Mem., CERN, Geneva, 1961–66; Prof. of Theoretical Physics, Univ. of Utrecht, 1966–81. High Energy Physics Prize, Eur. Physics Soc., 1993; Nobel Prize for Physics, 1999. Comdr, Order of Dutch Lion (Netherlands), 1999; Officier, Légion d'Honneur (France), 2000. *Publications:* Diagrammatica, 1994; Facts and Mysteries in Particle Physics, 2002. *Recreation:* billiards. *Address:* Nikhef, PO Box 41882, 1009 DB Amsterdam, Netherlands. *Club:* Probus '83 (Bilthoven, Netherlands).

VENABLES, Prof. Anthony James, DPhil; FBA 2005; BP Professor of Economics and Director, Oxford Centre for the Analysis of Resource Rich Economies, University of Oxford, since 2007; Fellow of New College, Oxford, since 2007; *b* 25 April 1953; *s* of John Stuart Venables and Phyllis (*née* Cox); *m* 1983, Patricia Rice; one *s* one *d*. *Educ:* Clare Coll., Cambridge (MA); St Antony's Coll., Oxford (BPhil); Worcester Coll., Oxford (DPhil 1984). Lecturer in Economics: Univ. of Essex, 1978–79; Univ. of Sussex, 1979–88; Eric Roll Prof. of Econ. Policy, Univ. of Southampton, 1988–92; Prof. of Internat. Econs and Dir, Globalization Prog., Centre for Econ. Perf., LSE, 1992–2007. Ed., Eur. Econ. Rev., 1991–95. Res. Manager, Trade Gp, World Bank, Washington, 1998–99; Chief Economist, DFID, 2005–08. Res. Fellow, 1984–, Co-Dir, Internat. Trade Prog., 1994–2003, Centre for Econ. Policy Res., London. Specialist Advr, H of L Select Cttee on Econ. Affairs, 2001–02; Advr, HM Treasury, 2001–02. Mem., Econs Res. Adv. Bd, GLA, 2003–. Fellow, Econometric Soc., 2003. *Publications:* (jtly) The Spatial Economy: cities, regions and international trade, 1999; (jtly) Multinational Firms in the World Economy, 2004; contrib. acad. jls in internat. econs, econ. geog. and develt econs. *Address:* Department of Economics, Manor Road, Oxford OX1 3UQ.

VENABLES, David; *see* Venables, H. D. S.

VENABLES, Most Rev. Gregory James; *see* Argentina, Bishop of.

VENABLES, (Harold) David (Spenser), CB 1993; Official Solicitor to the Supreme Court, 1980–93; *b* 14 Oct. 1932; *s* of late Cedric Venables and Gladys Venables (*née* Hall); *m* 1964, Teresa Grace, *d* of late J. C. Watts; one *d* one *s*. *Educ:* Denstone College. Admitted Solicitor, 1956. Pilot Officer, Royal Air Force, 1957–58. Legal Assistant, Official Solicitor's Office, 1960; Secretary, Lord Chancellor's Cttee on the Age of Majority, 1965–67; Asst Official Solicitor, 1977–80. *Publications:* A Guide to the Law Affecting Mental Patients, 1975; The Racing Fifteen-Hundreds: a history of voiturette racing 1931–40, 1984; Napier: the first to wear the Green, 1998; First Among Champions: the Alfa Romeo Grand Prix cars, 2000; Bugatti: a racing history, 2002; Brooklands: the official centenary history, 2007; British Racing Green, 2008; contributor, Halsbury's Laws of England, 4th edn. *Recreations:* vintage cars, motoring and military history. *Address:* 11 Onslow Road, Hove, Sussex BN3 6TA. *T:* (01273) 502374.

VENABLES, Jean, OBE 2004 (MBE 1997); CEng, FREng; FICE; Chairman, Crane Environmental, since 1994; Chief Executive, Association of Drainage Authorities, since 2003; President, Institution of Civil Engineers, since 2008 (Vice President, 2007–08); *b* 11 June 1948; *d* of Denis and Zena Edwards; *m* 1970, Roger Kendrick Venables; two *s*. *Educ:* Imperial College, London (BSc(Eng); MSc). CEng 1974, FREng 2006; MCIWEM 1995; FICE 1998; CEnv 2004. Sen. Lectr in Civil Engrg, Kingston Poly., 1975–94; Chm., Venables Consultancy Services Ltd, 1988–. Visiting Lecturer: Southampton Univ., 2006–; Imperial Coll., London, 2007–. Chairman: Thames Regl Flood Defence Cttee, 1994–2003; Thames Estuary Partnership, 2003–. MCIArb 1998; FCGI 2002. Liveryman, Co. of Engrs, 2006–. Hon. DSc Nottingham, 2005; Hon. DEng Kingston, 2006. *Publication:* Preparing for the Professional Reviews of the ICE, 1995. *Recreations:* walking, gardening, seeing friends and family. *Address:* c/o Institution of Civil Engineers, 1 Great George Street, SW1P 3AA.

VENABLES, Robert; QC 1990; *b* 1 Oct. 1947; *s* of Walter Edwin Venables, MM, and Mildred Daisy Robson Venables. *Educ:* Merton Coll., Oxford (MA); London School of Economics (LLM). FTII. Called to Bar, Middle Temple, 1973, Bencher, 1999; private practice as barrister, 1976–. Lecturer: Merton Coll., Oxford, 1972–75; UCL, 1973–75; Official Fellow and Tutor in Jurisprudence, St Edmund Hall, Oxford, and CUF Lectr, Oxford Univ., 1975–80; Fellow, St Edmund Hall, Oxford, 1992–. Chartered Institute of Taxation: Council Mem., 1999–; Chartered Tax Adviser, 1999. Chm., Revenue Bar Assoc., 2001–05. Pres., Key Haven Pubns plc, 1990–. Treasurer, CRUSAID, 1991–96 (Pres. Council, 1996–); Director: Yves Guihannec Foundn, 1992–; Temple Music Foundn, 2004–; Trustee, Morris Venables Charitable Foundn, 2004–. Consulting Editor: Personal Tax Planning Review; Corporate Tax Review; Offshore and Internat. Taxation Review; EC Tax Jl; Taxation Ed., Charities Law and Practice Review. *Publications:* Inheritance Tax Planning, 1986, 4th edn 2000; Preserving the Family Farm, 1987, 2nd edn 1989; Non-Resident Trusts, 1988, 8th edn 2000; Tax Planning and Fundraising for Charities, 1989, 3rd edn 2000; Hold-Over Relief, 1990; The Company Car, 1990; Tax Planning Through Trusts—Inheritance Tax, 1990; National Insurance Contributions Planning, 1990; Capital Gains Tax Planning for Non-UK Residents, 1991, 3rd edn 1999; The Family Home, 2002. *Recreation:* music making. *Address:* 15 Old Square, Lincoln's Inn, WC2A 3UE. *T:* (020) 7242 2744, *Fax:* (020) 7831 8095; *e-mail:* taxchambers@15oldsquare.co.uk. *Clubs:* Athenæum, Travellers.

VENABLES, Robert Michael Cochrane; Consultant, Bircham Dyson Bell (formerly Bircham & Co.), Solicitors, since 1997; *b* 8 Feb. 1939; *s* of late Cdre Gilbert Henry Venables, DSO, OBE, RN and Muriel Joan Haes; *m* 1972, Hazel Lesley Gowing, BSc; two *s* two *d*. *Educ:* Portsmouth Grammar Sch. Admitted solicitor, 1962; in private practice, London, Petersfield and Portsmouth, 1962–70; Treasury Solicitor's Department: Legal Asst, 1970; Sen. Legal Asst, 1973; Asst Treasury Solicitor, 1980; Charity Comr, 1989–97. Adminr, Cobbe Collection Trust, 1997–99. Mem. Council, Law Soc., 1993–2001; Pres., City of Westminster Law Soc., 1997–98. Trustee: Incorp. Council of Law Reporting for Eng. and Wales, 1999–; LawCare (formerly SolCare), 1997– (Chm., 1998–2003, 2005–); Old Portmuthian Charity, 1999–. Mem., FDA, 1974–97 (Chm., Legal Sect., 1981–83; Mem., Exec. Cttee, 1981–83, 1987–92). Ind. Co-opted Mem., Standards Cttee, E Hants DC, 2002–. Vis. Prof. of Charity Law, London S Bank Univ., 2005–. FRSA 1995. *Recreations:* opera, theatre, collecting domestic anachronisms. *Address:* c/o Bircham Dyson Bell, 50 Broadway, SW1H 0BL. *T:* (020) 7227 7000, *Fax:* (020) 7222 3480.

VENABLES, Terence Frederick; Assistant Coach, England football team, 2006–07; *b* 6 Jan. 1943; *m* Yvette; two *d*. *Educ:* Dagenham. Played at football clubs: Chelsea, 1958–66 (Captain, 1962); Tottenham Hotspur, 1966–68 (winners FA Cup 1967); Queen's Park

Rangers, 1968–73; represented England at all levels; Club Manager: Crystal Palace, 1976–80 (took club from 3rd Div. to top of 1st Div.); QPR, 1980–84 (won 2nd Div. title, 1980); Barcelona, 1984–87 (won Spanish championship, 1984); Tottenham Hotspur, 1987–93 (won FA Cup, 1991; Chief Exec., 1991–93); Coach: England football team, 1994–96; Australian football team, 1996–98; Chm., Portsmouth FC, 1996–98; Head Coach, Crystal Palace FC, 1998–99; Coach, Middlesbrough FC, 2000–01; Manager, Leeds Utd FC, 2002–03. *Publications:* They Used to Play on Grass, 1971; (with Gordon Williams) TV detective series Hazell: Hazell plays Solomon, 1974; Hazell and the Three Card Trick, 1975; Hazell and the Menacing Jester, 1976; (with Neil Hanson) Terry Venables: the Autobiography, 1994; (with Jane Nottage) Venables' England, 1996; The Best Game in the World, 1996.

VENABLES-LLEWELYN, Sir John (Michael) Dillwyn-, 4th Bt *cr* 1890; farmer, since 1975; *b* 12 Aug. 1938; *s* of Sir Charles Michael Dillwyn-Venables-Llewelyn, 3rd Bt, MVO, and Lady Delia Mary Dillwyn-Venables-Llewelyn, *g d* of 1st Earl St Aldwyn; *S* father, 1976; *m* 1st, 1963, Nina (marr. diss. 1972), *d* of late Lt J. S. Hallam; two *d*; 2nd, 1975, Nina Gay Richardson Oliver (*d* 1995); one *d* decd; 3rd, 2005, Carolyn I'Anson. *Recreation:* racing vintage cars. *Address:* Llysdinam, Newbridge-on-Wye, Llandrindod Wells, Powys LD1 6NB.

VENDLER, Helen Hennessy, PhD; author and poetry critic; Porter University Professor, Harvard University, since 1990; *b* Boston, Mass, 30 April 1933; *d* of George and Helen Hennessy (*née* Conway); one *s*. *Educ:* Emmanuel Coll., Boston, Mass (AB 1954); Harvard Univ. (PhD 1960). Instructor, Cornell Univ., 1960–63; Lectr, Swarthmore Coll. and Haverford Coll., Pa, 1963–64; Asst Prof., Smith Coll., Northampton, Mass, 1964–66; Associate Prof., 1966–68, Prof., 1968–85, Boston Univ.; Harvard University: Kenan Prof., 1985–90; Associate Acad. Dean, 1987–92; Sen. Fellow, Harvard Soc. Fellows, 1981–93. Fulbright Lectr, Univ. of Bordeaux, 1968–69; Vis. Prof., Harvard Univ., 1981–85. Poetry Critic, New Yorker, 1978–95. Member: Educnl Adv. Bd, Guggenheim Foundn, 1991–2001; Pulitzer Prize Bd, 1991–2000. Jefferson Lectr, NEH, 2004. Overseas Fellow, Churchill Coll., Cambridge, 1980; Stewart Parnell Fellow, Magdalene Coll., Cambridge, 1996, Hon. Fellow, 1996. Holds numerous hon. degrees, including: DLitt: Columbia, 1987; Washington, 1991; DHL: Toronto, 1992; TCD, 1993; Cambridge, 1997; NUI, 1998. Awards include: Nat. Book Critics Award, 1980; Keats-Shelley Assoc. Award, 1994; Truman Capote Award, 1996; Jefferson Medal, APS, 2000. *Publications:* Yeats's Vision and the Later Plays, 1963; On Extended Wings: Wallace Stevens' longer poems, 1969; The Poetry of George Herbert, 1975; Part of Nature, Part of Us, 1980; The Odes of John Keats, 1983; Wallace Stevens: words chosen out of desire, 1984; (ed) Harvard Book of Contemporary American Poetry, 1985; Voices and Visions: the poet in America, 1987; The Music of What Happens, 1988; Soul Says, 1995; The Given and the Made, 1995; The Breaking of Style, 1995; Poems, Poets, Poetry, 1995; The Art of Shakespeare's Sonnets, 1997; Seamus Heaney, 1998; Coming of Age as a Poet, 2003; Poets Thinking, 2004; Invisible Listeners, 2005; Our Secret Discipline, 2007. *Address:* Department of English, Harvard University, Barker Center, Cambridge, MA 02138–3929, USA.

VENESS, Sir David (Christopher), Kt 2005; CBE 2000; QPM 1994; Under-Secretary-General for Safety and Security, United Nations, since 2005; *b* 20 Sept. 1947; *m*; three *c*. *Educ:* Raynes Park Co. Grammar Sch.; Trinity Coll., Cambridge (BA 1975; LLB 1976). Joined Metropolitan Police, 1966; CID officer, 1969; detective in N, E and Central London; Detective Chief Supt in Fraud Squad and Crime Ops Gp; Comdr, 1987, served with Royal and Diplomatic protection, until 1990; rcds, 1990; Comdr, Public Order, Territorial Security and Operational Support; a Dep. Asst Comr, 1991–94; an Asst Comr, 1994–2005. *Address:* United Nations, United Nations Plaza, New York, NY 10017, USA.

VENGEROV, Maxim; violinist, violist and conductor; *b* 20 Aug. 1974; *s* of Alexander Vengerov, oboist, and Larissa Vengerov; studied with Galina Turtschaninova, then Zakhar Bron. Has performed in recitals worldwide; has appeared with major orchestras throughout the world, including: NY Philharmonic, 1991; Berlin Philharmonic; LSO; Chicago SO; LA Philharmonic; Vienna Philharmonic; San Francisco SO; Concertgebouw. Ambassador for UNICEF, 1997–. Numerous recordings. First Prize: Jun. Wieniawski Competition, Lublin, 1985; Carl Flesch Internat. Violin Competition, London, 1990; Grammy Award, best instrumental soloist, 2004.

VENKATARAMAN, Ramaswamy; President of India, 1987–92 (Vice-President, 1984–87); *b* 4 Dec. 1910; *s* of Ramaswami Iyer; *m* 1938, Janaki; three *d*. *Educ:* Madras Univ. (MA, LLB). Formerly in practice as a lawyer, Madras High Court and Supreme Court; prominent trade union leader, also political and social worker. Mem., Provisional Parlt, 1950; Mem., Lok Sabha, 1952–57 and (for Madras S), 1977–84; Leader of the House, Madras Legislative Council, and Minister of Industries, 1957–67; Mem., Planning Commn, Madras, 1967–71. Minister of: Finance and Industry, 1980–82; Defence, 1982–84. Sec., Madras Provincial Bar Fedn, 1947–50. Chm., Nat. Research and Develt Corp. Leader, Indian delegation to ILO, 1958, and delegate, UN Gen. Assembly, 1953–61. Chm., Kalakshetra Foundn; Mem. Internat. Jury, Gandhi Peace Prize Award; Trustee: Jawaharlal Nehru Meml Fund; Indira Gandhi Nat. Centre for the Arts. *Address:* 5 Safdarjang Road, New Delhi 110011, India. *T:* (11) 3794366, *Fax:* (11) 3014925.

VENKITARAMAN, Prof. Ashok Ramakrishnan, PhD; Ursula Zoellner Professor of Cancer Research, University of Cambridge, since 1998; Fellow, Pembroke College, Cambridge, since 2007; Director, Medical Research Council Cancer Cell Unit, Cambridge, since 2006 (Deputy Director, 2001–06); *s* of Prof. Avittathur R. Venkitaraman and Vasanti Venkitaraman; *m* 1984, Dr Rajini Ramana; one *s* one *d*. *Educ:* Christian Med. Coll., Vellore, India (MB BS 1984); University Coll. London (PhD 1988); MA Cantab 1993. House Physician, Christian Med. Coll. Hosp., Vellore, India, 1983–84; Fellow, Lady Tata Meml Trust, UCL and Charing Cross and Westminster Med. Sch., 1985–88; MRC Laboratory of Molecular Biology, Cambridge: Fellow, Beit Meml Trust, 1988–91; Mem., Scientific Staff, 1991–98; Fellow, New Hall, Cambridge, 1991–2007, now Emeritus. Mem., EMBO European Acad., 2004–. FMedSci 2001. *Publications:* numerous contribs to scientific and med. jls. *Address:* University of Cambridge, Hutchison/MRC Research Centre, Hills Road, Cambridge CB2 0XZ. *T:* (01223) 336901.

VENNE, Roger André; Queen's Coroner and Attorney, Master of the Crown Office, Registrar of Criminal Appeals, Registrar of the Courts-Martial Appeal Court and a Master of the Queen's Bench Division, since 2003; *b* 11 June 1946; *s* of Georges and Rose Ellen Venne; *m* 1970, Katherine Winter; one *s* one *d* (and one *d* decd). *Educ:* St Mary's Coll., Southampton; Inns of Court Sch. of Law. Called to the Bar, Gray's Inn, 1972, Bencher, 2000; Legal Asst, Criminal Appeal Office, 1973–78; Sen. Legal Asst and Legal Sec. to Lord Chief Justice, 1978–80; Crown Office, 1980; Asst Registrar, Criminal Appeal Office, 1981–87; Hd, Crown Office, 1987–89; Sen. Lawyer, Civil Appeals Office, and Legal Sec. to Master of the Rolls, 1989; Lord Chancellor's Department: Head: Law Reform and Adv. Div., 1990–93; Judicial Appts Div. 2, 1993–96; Dep. Sec. of Commns, 1996–99; Hd, Civil Appeals Office, and Master, 1999–2003. Mem., Criminal Cttee, Judicial Studies Bd, 2003–. Dep. Ed.-in-Chief, Administrative Court Digest (formerly Crown Office Digest), 1988–; an Ed., Civil Procedure (formerly Supreme Court Practice), 1989–. *Publications:* (jtly) Alderney Annals, 1992; contribs to legal jls. *Recreations:* sailing, book-collecting. *Address:* Criminal Appeal Office, Royal Courts of Justice, Strand, WC2A 2LL. *Clubs:* Bar Yacht; Alderney Sailing.

VENNER, Rt Rev. Stephen Squires; *see* Dover, Bishop Suffragan of.

VENNING, Philip Duncombe Riley, OBE 2003; FSA; Secretary, Society for the Protection of Ancient Buildings, since 1984; *b* 24 March 1947; *s* of late Roger Venning and of Rosemary (*née* Mann); *m* 1987, Elizabeth Frances Ann, *d* of M. A. R. Powers; two *d*. *Educ:* Sherborne Sch.; Trinity Hall, Cambridge (MA). Times Educational Supplement, 1970–81 (Asst Editor, 1978–81); freelance journalist and writer, 1981–84. Mem., Westminster Abbey Fabric Commn, 1998–. Member: Council, Nat. Trust, 1992–2001; Expert Panel, Heritage Lottery Fund, 2005–. Vice-Pres., Nat. Churches Trust (formerly Historic Churches Preservation Trust), 2005–; Founder Trustee, Heritage Link, 2002–03. FSA 1989; FRSA 1990. *Publications:* contribs to books and other pubns on educn and on historic buildings. *Recreations:* exploring Britain, book collecting. *Address:* 17 Highgate High Street, N6 5JT.

VENNING, Robert William Dawe; Principal Establishment and Finance Officer, Cabinet Office, 1993–96; *b* 25 July 1946; *s* of Tom William Dawe and Elsie Lillian Venning; *m* 1969, Jennifer Mei-Ling Jackson; one *s* one *d*. *Educ:* Midhurst Sch.; Univ. of Birmingham (BA Special Hons Philosophy 1968). Tutor in Philosophy, Univ. of Birmingham, 1968; Lectr in Logic and Scientific Method, Lanchester Polytechnic, 1969; Department of Health and Social Security: Admin. Trainee, 1971; Private Sec. to Minister for Disabled, 1974; Principal, 1975; Private Sec. to Minister for Health, 1981; Asst Sec., 1983; Under Sec., HA Personnel Div., DoH, 1990–93. Non-Exec. Dir, Compel plc, 1990–93. *Recreations:* playing classical and flamenco guitar; electronics and computing. *Address:* 49 Coogee Avenue, The Entrance North, NSW 2261, Australia.

VENTER, J. Craig, PhD; Founder, Chairman and President, J. Craig Venter Institute, since 2006; Founder, Chairman and Chief Executive, Synthetic Genomics, since 2005; *b* 14 Oct. 1946; *m* Claire Fraser. *Educ:* UCSD (BS; PhD 1975). Served US Navy, Vietnam, 1967. Asst Prof., subseq. Prof., of Pharmacol. and Therapeutics, SUNY, 1976–84; Section and Lab. Chief, NIH, 1984–92; Founder, Chm. and Chief Scientist, Inst. for Genomic Res., 1992–2006; President and Chairman: Inst. for Biol Energy Alternatives, 2002–06; Center for the Advancement of Genomics, 2002–06; J. Craig Venter Sci. Foundn, 2002–06; Founder, 1998, Pres. and CSO, 1998–2002, Chm., Scientific Adv. Bd, 2002, Celera Genomics Corp. *Publications:* A Life Decoded (autobiog.), 2007; articles in learned jls. *Address:* J. Craig Venter Institute, 9712 Medical Center Drive, Rockville, MD 20850–3343, USA.

VENTERS, June Marion, (Mrs R. P. Brown); QC 2006; Managing Partner, Venters Solicitors, since 1991; a Recorder, since 1999; *b* 25 March 1957; *o d* of Douglas William Walter Venters and Lily Lydia Venters (*née* Grimwood); *m* 1994, Robin Perry Brown; one *d*. *Educ:* Honor Oak Grammar Sch.; College of Law. Admitted solicitor, 1984. Family and Civil Mediator, 2007. *Publications:* Standard Letters and Forms, 1995; (contrib.) Child Care Management. *Recreation:* my family. *Address:* Venters Solicitors, 1–6 Camberwell Green, SE5 7AD. *T:* (020) 7277 0110, *Fax:* (020) 7277 2288; *e-mail:* j.ventersqc@venters.co.uk; Priory House, High Street, Reigate, Surrey RH2 9AE.

VENTRY, 8th Baron *cr* 1800 (Ire.); **Andrew Wesley Daubeny de Moleyns;** Bt 1797; Director, Burgie Lodge Farms Ltd, since 1970; Marketing Manager, Unico (UK) Ltd, since 1994; *b* 28 May 1943; *s* of Hon. Francis Alexander Innys Eveleigh Ross de Moleyns (*d* 1964) (2nd *s* of 6th Baron) and Joan (later Joan Springett), *e d* of Harold Wesley; assumed by deed poll, 1966, surname of Daubeny de Moleyns; *S* uncle, 1987; *m* 1st, 1963, Nelly Renée (marr. diss. 1979), *d* of Abel Chaumillon; one *s* two *d*; 2nd, 1983, Jill Rosemary, *d* of C. W. Oramon; one *d*. *Educ:* Edge Grove; Aldenham. Farmer, 1961–; in electronics, 1986–. *Recreations:* shooting, stalking, photography, sailing, ski-ing. *Heir:* *s* Hon. Francis Wesley Daubeny de Moleyns, *b* 1 May 1965.

VENTURI, Robert; architect; Principal, Venturi, Scott Brown and Associates, Inc., since 1989 (Venturi, Rauch and Scott Brown, 1980–89); *b* 25 June 1925; *s* of Robert Charles Venturi and Vanna Venturi (*née* Lanzetta); *m* 1967, Denise Scott Brown; one *s*. *Educ:* Princeton Univ. (AB 1947, MFA 1950). Designer, Oskar Stonorov, 1950, Eero Saarinen & Assoc., 1950–53; Rome Prize Fellow, Amer. Acad. in Rome, 1954–56; designer, Louis I Kahn, 1957; Principal: Venturi, Cope and Lippincott, 1958–61; Venturi and Short, 1961–64; Venturi and Rauch, 1964–80. Associate Prof., Univ. of Pennsylvania, 1957–65; Charlotte Shepherd Davenport Prof. of Architecture, Yale, 1966–70. Works include: Vanna Venturi House, 1961, Guild House, 1961, Franklin Court, 1972, Inst. for Sci. Inf. Corp. HQ, 1978 (all Philadelphia); Allen Meml Art Museum Addition (Oberlin, Ohio), 1973; Gordon Wu Hall (Princeton), 1980; Seattle Art Mus., 1984; Sainsbury Wing, Nat. Gall., London, 1986; Fisher and Bendheim Halls, 1986, Princeton Campus Center, 1996, Princeton Univ.; Gordon and Virginia MacDonald Med. Res. Labs (with Payette Associates), 1986, Gonda (Goldschmied) Neuroscience and Genetics Res. Center (with Lee, Burkhart, Liu Inc.), 1993, UCLA; Charles P. Stevenson Jr Library, Bard Coll., 1989; Roy and Diana Vagelos Labs (with Payette Associates), Univ. of Penn, 1990; Regl Govt Bldg, Toulouse, France, 1992; Kirifuri resort facilities, Nikko, Japan, 1992; Perelman Quadrangle, Univ. of Pennsylvania, 1995; Frist Campus Center, Princeton Univ., 1996; Baker/Berry Liby, Dartmouth Coll., 1996; Master Plan and buildings for Univ. of Michigan, 1997–; Congress Ave Bldg, Yale Univ. Sch. of Medicine (with Payette Associates), 1998; Woodmere Art Mus., Philadelphia, 2000; Biomed. Res. Bldg, Univ. of Kentucky, 2000; Dumbarton Oaks Liby Expansion, Washington, 2001; Stuart Country Day Sch. Theater, Auditorium and Sanctuary, Princeton, 2001; Lehigh Valley Hosp., Muhlenberg, Allentown, Pennsylvania, 2002. Fellow: Amer. Inst. of Architects; Amer. Acad. in Rome; Accad. Nazionale di San Luca; Amer. Acad. of Arts and Letters; Amer. Acad. of Arts and Scis; Hon. FFRIAS; Hon. RIBA. Hon. DFA: Oberlin Coll., 1977; Yale, 1979; Univ. of Pennsylvania, 1980; Princeton Univ., 1983; Philadelphia Coll. of Art, 1985; Hon. LHD NJ Inst. of Technology, 1984. James Madison Medal, Princeton Univ., 1985; Thomas Jefferson Meml Foundn Medal, Univ. of Virginia, 1983; Pritzker Architecture Prize, Hyatt Foundn, 1991; US Nat. Medal of Arts, 1992; Benjamin Franklin Medal, RSA, 1993. Comdr, Order of Arts and Letters (France), 2000. *Publications:* A View from the Campidoglio: selected essays, 1953–84 (with Denise Scott Brown), 1984; Complexity and Contradiction in Architecture, 1966, 2nd edn 1977 (Classic Book Award, AIA, 1996); Learning from Las Vegas (with Denise Scott Brown and Steven Izenour), 1972, 2nd edn 1977; Iconography and Electronics upon a Generic Architecture, 1996; (with D. Scott Brown) Architecture as Signs and Systems for a Mannerist Time, 2004; articles in periodicals. *Recreation:* travel. *Address:* Venturi, Scott Brown and Associates, Inc., 4236 Main Street, Philadelphia, PA 19127, USA. *T:* (215) 4870400.

VENUGOPAL, Dr Sriramashetty, OBE 1992; FRCGP; Principal in General Practice, Aston, Birmingham, 1967–99; *b* 14 May 1933; *s* of Satyanarayan and Manikyamma

Sriramashetty; *m* 1960, Subhadra Venugopal; one *s* one *d*. *Educ:* Osmania Univ., Hyderabad, India (BSc, MB BS); Madras Univ. (DMRD). MRCGP 1990, FRCGP 1997; MFPHM 1998. Medical posts, Osmania Hosp., State Med. Services, Hyderabad, Singareni Collieries, 1959–65; Registrar, Radiology, Selly Oak Hosp., Birmingham, 1965–66; Registrar, Chest Medicine, Springfield Hosp., Grimsby, 1966–67; Hosp. Practitioner, Psychiatry, All Saints Hosp., Birmingham, 1972–94. Member: Working Group, DHSS, 1984–94; Local Med. Cttee, 1975–99; Dist. Med. Cttee, 1978–88; GMC, 1984–99; West Birmingham HA, 1982–87 (Chm., sub-cttee on needs of ethnic minorities, 1982–85); Birmingham FPC, 1984–88; Birmingham Community Liaison Adv. Cttee, 1985–87. Vice-Chm., Birmingham Div., BMA, 1986–87 (Chm., 1985–86). Mem., Local Review Cttee for Winson Green Prison, 1981–83. Founder Mem., Overseas Doctors' Assoc., 1975–81 (Dep. Treasurer, 1975–81; Nat. Vice-Chm., 1981–87; Inf. and Adv. Service, 1981–99; Nat. Chm., 1987–93; Pres., 1993–99); Founder Mem. and Chm., Link House Council, 1975–89. Founder Mem., Osmania Grad. Med. Assoc. in UK, 1984–99. Vice-Chm., Hyderabad Charitable Trust, 1985–99. FRSocMed 1986; FRIPH (FRIPHH 1988); FRSH 1997. *Publications:* contribs to learned jls on medico-political topics. *Recreations:* medical politics, music, gardening. *Address:* 24 Melville Road, Edgbaston, Birmingham B16 9JT. *T:* (0121) 454 1725. *Club:* Aston Rotary (Pres., 1984–85).

VERANNEMAN de WATERVLIET, Jean-Michel; Ambassador of Belgium to the Court of St James's, since 2006; *b* Bruges, 11 July 1947; *s* of Raymond Veranneman de Watervliet and Manuela van den Bogaerde de Terbrugge; *m* 1981, Maria do Carmo; three *s*. *Educ:* Paris Inst d'Etudes Politiques; Army Reserve Officers course; Univ. Libre de Bruxelles (Soc. Scis degree); Vrije Univ. Brussel (Press and Communication Scis degree). Intern, EC, Brussels, 1976; joined Diplomatic Service, 1976; trng, Foreign Min., Brussels, 1976–77 and 1977–78; Third Sec., Bonn, 1977; Dep. Hd of Mission, Brasilia, 1978–80 and 1980–81; Chargé d'Affaires, La Paz, 1980; Dep. Hd, Pol Mil. Desk, 1981–83; Ambassador, Mozambique and Swaziland, 1983–86; First Secretary: UN, NY, 1986–89; EC, Brussels, 1989–91; Consul Gen., São Paulo, 1991–94; Minister Plenipotentiary and Dep. Hd of Mission, London, 1994–97; Africa Dir, 1997–2000; Ambassador: Brasilia, 2000–03; Tel Aviv, 2003–06. Commandeur: Ordre de Léopold; Ordre de la Couronne; Médaille civique de Première Classe; Grand Cross, Order of Southern Cross (Brazil). *Publications:* Is the Sovereign Nation State Obsolete?, 1997; History of Africa, 2003. *Recreations:* reading history books, archery, ship models. *Address:* Belgian Embassy, 17 Grosvenor Crescent, SW1X 7EE. *T:* (020) 7470 3700; *e-mail:* london@diplobel.be. *Clubs:* Royal Anglo Belgian, Travellers, Royal Automobile, Caledonian; Prince Albert (Brussels).

VERCOE, Miranda Lucy Mary; *see* Carruthers-Watt, M. L. M.

VERDAN, (Hilaire) Alexander; QC 2006; a Recorder, since 2004; *b* 24 May 1963; *s* of Jean Pierre Verdan and late Sonya de Vries (*née* Beasley); *m* 1987, Alexandra Mutch; three *s*. *Educ:* W London Inst. of Higher Educn (BA Hons); Poly. of Central London (Dip. Law). In practice as a barrister, 1987–, specialising in family law (children). *Recreations:* cycling, ski-ing, reading, theatre, cinema, eating and drinking. *Address:* 4 Paper Buildings, Temple, EC4Y 7EX.

VERDI, Prof. Richard Frank, OBE 2007; PhD; Professor of Fine Art, since 1989, and Director, Barber Institute of Fine Arts, since 1990, University of Birmingham; *b* 7 Nov. 1941; *s* of Frank and Anne Verdi. *Educ:* Univ. of Michigan (BA 1963); Univ. of Chicago (MA 1966); Courtauld Inst. of Art, Univ. of London (PhD 1976). Lectr in Hist. of Art, Univ. of Manchester, 1969–71; Lectr, 1971–81, Sen. Lectr, 1981–89, in Hist. of Art, Univ. of York. FRSA 1999. *Publications:* Klee and Nature, 1984; Cézanne and Poussin: the classical vision of landscape, 1990; Cézanne, 1992; Nicolas Poussin 1594–1665, 1995. *Recreations:* music, literature, natural history. *Address:* Barber Institute of Fine Arts, University of Birmingham, Edgbaston, Birmingham B15 2TS. *T:* (0121) 414 3485.

VERE OF HANWORTH, Lord; James Malcolm Aubrey Edward de Vere Beauclerk; *b* 2 Aug. 1995; *s* and *heir* of Earl of Burford, *qv*.

VERE-HODGE, Michael John Davy; QC 1993; a Recorder, since 1989; *b* 2 July 1946; *s* of late Nicholas and Anne Vere-Hodge; *m* 1st; one *s* one *d*; 2nd, 2004, Nicola Anne Heron. *Educ:* Winchester Coll.; Grenoble Univ. Called to the Bar, Gray's Inn, 1970, Bencher, 2005. Head of Chambers, 2001–05. *Recreations:* shooting (GB Helice Shooting team, 2006), fishing. *Address:* 3 Paper Buildings, Temple, EC4Y 7EU.

VEREKER, family name of **Viscount Gort**.

VEREKER, Sir John (Michael Medlicott), KCB 1999 (CB 1992); Governor and Commander-in-Chief of Bermuda, 2002–07; *b* 9 Aug. 1944; *s* of late Comdr C. W. M. Vereker and M. H. Vereker (*née* Whatley); *m* 1971, Judith Diane, *d* of Hobart and Alice Rowen, Washington; one *s* one *d*. *Educ:* Marlborough Coll.; Keele Univ. (BA Hons 1967). Asst Principal, ODM, 1967–69; World Bank, Washington, 1970–72; Principal, ODM, 1972; Private Sec. to successive Ministers of Overseas Develt, 1977–78; Asst Sec., 1978; Prime Minister's Office, 1980–83; Under Sec., 1983–88, and Principal Finance Officer, 1986–88, ODA, FCO; Dep. Sec., DES, then DFE, 1988–93; Perm.-Sec., ODA, subseq. DFID, 1994–2002. Chm., Students Loans Co. Ltd, 1989–91. Non-exec. Dir, XL Capital Ltd, 2007–. Mem. Council, Inst. of Manpower Studies, 1989–92; Member Board: British Council, 1994–2002; IDS, 1994–2001; VSO, 1994–2002; Mem. Adv. Council, British Consultants and Construction Bureau, 2000–05. Gov., Ditchley Foundn for Internat. Relations, 2007–. Hon. Vice-Pres., Raleigh Internat., 2002–. Trustee, Internat. Assoc. for Digital Pubns, 2004–. CCMI (CIMgt 1995). FRSA 1999. KStJ 2002. Hon. DLitt Keele, 1997. *Publications:* Blazing the Trail, 2002; tech. papers for Commonwealth Secretariat and World Bank. *Address:* 23 Richmond Road, SW20 0PG.

VEREY, David John, CBE 2004; Chairman, Blackstone Group UK, 2004–08; *b* 8 Dec. 1950; *s* of late Michael John Verey, TD and Sylvia Mary Verey; *m* 1st, 1974, Luise Jaschke (marr. diss. 1990); two *s* one *d*; 2nd, 1990, Emma Katharine Broadhead (*née* Laidlaw). *Educ:* Eton College; Trinity College, Cambridge (MA). Lazard Brothers: joined 1972; Dir, 1983–2001; Dep. Chief Exec., 1985–90; Chief Exec., 1990–2001; Chm., 1992–2001; Dep. Chm., Cazenove Gp Plc, 2001–02. Director: Pearson plc, 1996–2000; Daily Mail and Gen. Trust plc, 2004–; Sofina S.A., 2004–; Mem., Supervisory Bd, Bank Gutmann AG, 2002–. Mem., Financial Services Practitioner Panel, 2002–05. Special Advr, Fresh Minds Ltd, 2004–. Trustee, Tate Gall., 1992–2004 (Chm., Bd of Trustees, 1998–2004); Chm., The Art Fund, 2004–. Fellow, Eton Coll., 1997–. *Recreations:* stalking, bridge, gardening, travel.

VERHAGEN, Maxime Jacques Marcel; Minister of Foreign Affairs, the Netherlands, since 2007; *b* Maastricht, 14 Sept. 1956; *m* Annemieke Beijlevelt; three *c*. *Educ:* Univ. of Leiden (degree in History 1986). Christian Democratic Alliance: Asst to an MP, 1984–87; joined party staff with responsibility for Eur. affairs, develt cooperation and trade policy. Mem. (CDA) Oegstgeest Municipal Council, until 1989 (Leader, CDA Gp, 1986). Mem., European Parlt, 1989–94. Mem., House of Representatives, Netherlands (Leader, CDA Parly Party, 2002–07). Vice Chairman: ACP-EU Jt Assembly; Perm. Parly Cttee on Foreign Affairs. Member Board: Eduardo Frei Foundn; Netherlands Atlantic Assoc.; European Movement; Parly Hist. Foundn, Nijmegen Univ.; Mem. Supervisory Bd, Free Voice. Grand Officer, Order of the Legion of Merit of O'Higgins (Chile); Grand Cross: Order of Merit (Germany), 2007; Order of the Southern Cross (Brazil), 2008. *Address:* c/o Ministry of Foreign Affairs, PO Box 20061, 2500 EB The Hague, Netherlands.

VERHEUGEN, Günter, Hon. GCVO 1998; Member, European Commission, since 1999; *b* Bad Kreuznach, 28 April 1944; *s* of Leo Verheugen and Leni (*née* Holzhäuser); *m* 1st, Helga (*d* 1983); 2nd, 1987, Gabriele (*née* Reimann). *Educ:* studied history, sociol. and politics in Cologne and Bonn. Trainee, Neue Rhein-Neue Ruhr Zeitung, 1963–65; Head: Public Relns Div., Min. of Interior, W Germany, 1969–74; Analysis and Inf. task force, Foreign Office, 1974–76; Federal Party Manager, 1977–78, Gen. Sec., 1978–82, FDP. Mem. (SPD) Bundestag, 1983–99 (Mem., Foreign Affairs Cttee, 1983–99; Chm., EU special cttee, 1992). Chm., Socialist Internat. Peace, Security and Disarmament Council, 1997–99. Chm., Radio Broadcasting Council, Deutsche Welle, 1990–99. Joined SPD, 1982: spokesman of Nat. Exec., 1986–87; Editor-in-Chief, Vorwärts (SPD newspaper), 1987–88; Dep. foreign policy spokesman and Chm., UN wkg gp of parly gp, 1991–93; Chm., Bavarian SPD gp in Bundestag, 1993–95; Sec., parly gp, 1993; Fed. Party Manager, 1993–95; Dep. Chm., parly gp for foreign, security and develt policy, 1994–97; Chm., Kulmbach-Lichtenfels dist, 1996–99; Mem., Upper Franconia regl exec., 1996–99; Co-ordinator for internat. relns of SPD and SPD parly gp, 1997–99; Mem., Nat. Exec., 1997–. Mem., Cttee for Envmt and Develt, Protestant Ch, Germany, 1998–. Officer's Cross, Order of Merit (Germany), 1994; Order of Merit (Bavaria), 1997; Kt Comdr's Cross, Order of Merit (Italy), 1982. *Publications:* Der Ausverkauf: Macht und Verfall der FDP, 1984; (jtly) Halbzeit in Bonn: die BRD zwei Jahre nach der Wende, 1985; Apartheid, Südafrika und die deutschen interessen am Kap, 1986; and numerous others. *Address:* European Commission, Rue de la Loi 200, 1049 Brussels, Belgium. *T:* (2) 2991111.

VERHOFSTADT, Guy; Prime Minister of Belgium, 1999–2008; *b* 11 April 1953; *s* of Marcel Verhofstadt and Gaby (*née* Stockmans); *m* 1981, Dominique Verkinderen; one *s* one *d*. *Educ:* Koninklijk Atheneum, Ghent; Univ. of Ghent (LLM 1975). Attorney, Ghent Bar, 1975–94. Pol Sec. to Nat. Pres., Party for Freedom and Progress, 1977–81; Mem. (Party for Freedom and Progress) Ghent-Eekklo, House of Reps, Belgium, 1978–84, 1985–95; Dep. Prime Minister and Minister for the Budget, Scientific Res. and the Plan, 1985–88; Pres., shadow cabinet, 1988–91; Minister of State, 1995–2008; Senator (Flemish Liberals and Democrats), and Vice Pres., Senate, 1995–99. Mem., City of Ghent Council, 1976–82, 2007–. Nat. Pres., Party for Freedom and Progress, 1982–85, 1989–92; Nat. Pres., Flemish Liberals and Democrats, 1992–95, 1997–99. Vice-Pres. and Rapporteur, Rwanda Investigation Commn, Senate, 1996–97. *Publications:* Angst, afgunst en het algemeen belang, 1994; De Belgische ziekte, 1997; De Vierde Golf, 2002; De Verenigde Staten van Europa, 2005; Het Vierde Burgermanifest, 2006; pamphlets, articles, contribs to books.

VERITY, Anthony Courtenay Froude, MA; Master, Dulwich College, 1986–95; *b* 25 Feb. 1939; *s* of Arthur and Alice Kathleen Verity; *m* 1962, Patricia Ann Siddall; one *s* one *d*. *Educ:* Queen Elizabeth's Hosp., Bristol; Pembroke Coll., Cambridge (MA). Assistant Master: Dulwich Coll., 1962–65; Manchester Grammar Sch., 1965–69; Head of Classics, Bristol Grammar Sch., 1969–76; Headmaster, Leeds Grammar Sch., 1976–86. Educnl Advr to Emir of Qatar, 1996. Chm., Schools' Arabic Project, 1988–96. Trustee, Dulwich Picture Gallery, 1994–96. Gov., Stonyhurst Coll., 2004–. Editor, Greece and Rome, 1971–76. *Publications:* Latin as Literature, 1971; (trans.) The Idylls of Theocritus, 2002; (trans.) The Odes of Pindar, 2007; contribs to Jl of Arabic Lit. *Recreations:* music, fell-walking. *Address:* The Reddings, Cliburn, Penrith, Cumbria CA10 3AL. *Club:* Athenæum.

VERMA, Baroness *cr* 2006 (Life Peer), of Leicester in the County of Leicestershire; **Sandip Verma;** Senior Partner, Domiciliary Care Services, since 2000; *b* 30 June 1959; *d* of S. S. and R. Rana; *m* 1977, Ashok Kumar Verma; one *s* one *d*. *Educ:* locally. Contested (C): Hull E, 2001; Wolverhampton SW, 2005. Opposition spokesperson on health, educn and skills, H of L, 2006–. Advr, Bright Distributors Ltd, 2006–. Exec. Mem., Ethnic Diversity Council, 2005–. Dep. Chm. (Political), Leics South Cons Assoc., 2006–. Champion, Roko Breast Cancer, 2006–; Patron: Tory Reform Group, 2006–; Cons. British Asian Link, 2006–; Pakistan-India Friendship Soc., 2006–; Bucks Punjabi Internat. Soc., 2006–. *Recreations:* socialising, reading, walking, going to different parts of the world, arranging events, watching cricket. *Address:* House of Lords, SW1A 0PW. *T:* (office) (020) 7219 5216, (home) (0116) 270 1686, *Fax:* (0116) 270 1603; *e-mail:* Vermas@parliament.uk.

VERMES, Prof. Geza, FBA 1985; Professor of Jewish Studies, 1989–91, now Professor Emeritus, and Fellow of Wolfson College, 1965–91, now Fellow Emeritus, Oxford University; Director, Oxford Forum for Qumran Research, Oxford Centre for Hebrew and Jewish Studies (formerly for Postgraduate Hebrew Studies), since 1991; *b* 22 June 1924; *s* of late Ernö Vermes and Terézia Riesz; *m* 1st, 1958, Pamela Hobson (*d* 1993); 2nd, 1996, Margaret Unarska. *Educ:* Univ. of Budapest; Coll. St Albert de Louvain, Louvain Univ. Licencié en Histoire et Philologie Orientales (avec la plus grande distinction), 1952; DTheol 1953; MA Oxon 1965, DLitt 1988. Asst Editor, Cahiers Sioniens, Paris, 1953–55; research worker, CNRS, Paris, 1955–57; Lectr, later Sen. Lectr in Divinity, Newcastle Univ., 1957–65; Reader in Jewish Studies, Oxford Univ., 1965–89; Chm. of Curators of Oriental Inst., Oxford, 1971–74; Chm. Bd of Faculty of Oriental Studies, Oxford, 1978–80; Emeritus Governor, Oxford Centre for Postgrad. Hebrew Studies (Governor, 1972–92). Vis. Prof. in Religious Studies, Brown Univ., 1971; Rosenstiel Res. Fellow, Univ. of Notre Dame, 1972; Dist. Vis. Prof. in Judeo-Christian Studies, Tulane Univ., 1982; Vis. Prof. of History, Univ. of Calif, San Diego, 1995; Vis. Prof. in Hebrew Studies, Peter Pázmány Univ., Budapest, 1996. Lectures: Margaret Harris in Religion, Dundee Univ., 1977; Riddell Meml, Newcastle Univ., 1981; Igor Kaplan Visiting, Toronto Sch. of Theology, 1985, 1987; Inaugural, Geza Vermes Lectures in Hist. of Religions, Univ. of Leicester, 1997; Gunning, Univ. of Edinburgh, 1998. Pres., British Assoc. for Jewish Studies, 1975, 1988; Pres., European Assoc. for Jewish Studies, 1981–84. Editor, Jl of Jewish Studies, 1971–. Fellow, Eur. Acad. of Arts, Scis and Humanities, 2001. Hon. DD: Edinburgh, 1989; Durham, 1990; Hon. DLitt Sheffield, 1994. W. Bacher Medallist, Hungarian Acad. of Scis, 1996; Meml Medallist, City of Mako, Hungary. *Publications:* Les manuscrits du désert de Juda, 1953; Discovery in the Judean Desert, 1956; Scripture and Tradition in Judaism, 1961; The Dead Sea Scrolls in English, 1962, 4th edn 1995 (trans. Portuguese); Jesus the Jew, 1973 (trans. Spanish, French, Japanese, Italian, Portuguese, German, Hungarian, Polish); Post-Biblical Jewish Studies, 1975; (with Pamela Vermes) The Dead Sea Scrolls: Qumran in perspective, 1977 (trans. Spanish), 3rd edn 1994; The Gospel of Jesus the Jew, 1981; (ed jtly) Essays in Honour of Y. Yadin, 1982; Jesus and the World of Judaism, 1983 (trans. Portuguese, Hungarian); (ed and rev., with F. G. B. Millar and M. D. Goodman) E. Schürer, The History of the Jewish People in the Age of Jesus Christ I–III, 1973–87 (trans. Spanish, Italian); (with M. D. Goodman) The Essenes according to the Classical Sources, 1989; The Religion of Jesus the Jew, 1993 (trans. Spanish, Portuguese, Italian); (ed) Pamela Vermes, The Riddle of the Sparks, 1993; The

Complete Dead Sea Scrolls in English, 1997, rev. edn 2004 (trans. Turkish); Providential Accidents (autobiog.), 1998 (trans. Hungarian); (ed with P. S. Alexander) Discoveries in the Judaean Desert, vol. 26, 1998; An Introduction to the Complete Dead Sea Scrolls, 1999; The Dead Sea Scrolls, 2000; The Changing Faces of Jesus, 2000 (trans. Italian, Hungarian, Dutch, French); Jesus in his Jewish Context, 2003; The Authentic Gospel of Jesus, 2003 (trans. Hungarian); The Passion, 2005 (trans. French, Hungarian, German, Portuguese); Who's Who in the Age of Jesus, 2005; The Nativity: history and legend, 2006; The Resurrection, 2008. *Recreations:* watching wild life, correcting proofs. *Address:* Oriental Institute, Pusey Lane, Oxford OX1 2LE; West Wood Cottage, Foxcombe Lane, Boars Hill, Oxford OX1 5DH. *T:* (01865) 735384, *Fax:* (01865) 735034; *e-mail:* geza.vermes@orinst.ox.ac.uk.

VERNEY, family name of **Baron Willoughby de Broke**.

VERNEY, Sir Edmund Ralph, 6th Bt *cr* 1818, of Claydon House, Buckinghamshire; *b* 28 June 1950; *o s* of Sir Ralph Bruce Verney, 5th Bt, KBE and of Mary (*née* Vestey); *S* father, 2001; *m* 1982, Daphne Fausset-Farquhar; one *s* one *d*. *Educ:* Harrow; York Univ. FRICS. Mem., Nat. Council, CLA, 1990–2001 (Chm., Bucks Br., 1996–99). Prime Warden, Dyers' Co., 2001–02. High Sheriff, Bucks, 1998–99. *Heir: s* Andrew Nicholas Verney, *b* 9 July 1983. *Address:* Claydon House, Middle Claydon, Bucks MK18 2EX.

VERNEY, (Sir) (John) Sebastian, (3rd Bt *cr* 1946, of Eaton Square, City of Westminster; *S* father, 1993, but does not use the title and his name does not appear on the Official Roll of the Baronetage). *Heir: cousin* Christopher Ralph Evelyn Verney [*b* 4 Oct. 1948; *m* 1976, Madeliene Lindberg].

VERNEY, His Honour Sir Lawrence (John), Kt 1993; TD 1955; DL; Recorder of London, 1990–98; *b* 19 July 1924; *y s* of Sir Harry Verney, 4th Bt, DSO; *m* 1972, Zoë Auriel, *d* of Lt-Col P. G. Goodeve-Docker. *Educ:* Harrow; Oriel Coll., Oxford. Called to Bar, Inner Temple, 1952, Bencher, 1990. Dep. Chm., Bucks QS, 1962–71; Dep. Chm., Middlesex Sessions, then a Circuit Judge, 1971–90. Governor, Harrow Sch., 1972–87. Master, Co. of Pattenmakers, 1988. Hon. Col 1 (RBY) Signal Sqdn, 1997–99. DL Bucks 1967. Jun. Grand Warden, United Grand Lodge of England, 2001. Hon. LLD London Guildhall, 1998; DUniv Bucks Chilterns UC, 2003. OStJ 1992. *Address:* Windmill House, Church Lane, Oving, Aylesbury, Bucks HP22 4HL.

See also Rt Rev. S. E. Verney.

VERNEY, Sebastian; *see* Verney, (Sir) J. S.

VERNEY, Rt Rev. Stephen Edmund, MBE 1945; Assistant Bishop, diocese of Oxford, since 1991; *b* 17 April 1919; 2nd *s* of late Sir Harry Verney, 4th Bt, DSO and Lady Rachel Verney (*née* Bruce); *m* 1st, 1947, Priscilla Avice Sophie Schwerdt (*d* 1974); one *s* three *d*; 2nd, 1981, Sandra Ann Bailey; (one *s* decd). *Educ:* Harrow School; Balliol College, Oxford (MA). Curate of Gedling, Nottingham, 1950; Priest-in-charge and then first Vicar, St Francis, Clifton, Nottingham, 1952; Vicar of Leamington Hastings and Diocesan Missioner, Dio. Coventry, 1958; Canon Residentiary, Coventry Cathedral, 1964; Canon of Windsor, 1970; Bishop Suffragan of Repton, 1977–85. *Publications:* Fire in Coventry, 1964; People and Cities, 1969; Into the New Age, 1976; Water into Wine, 1985; The Dance of Love, 1989. *Recreations:* conversation and aloneness; music, gardening, travel. *Address:* Cherry Patch, Church Road, Blewbury, Oxon OX11 9PY. *Club:* English-Speaking Union.

See also Sir L. J. Verney.

VERNON, family name of **Baron Lyveden**.

VERNON, 11th Baron *cr* 1762; **Anthony William Vernon-Harcourt;** founder and Chairman, Monks Partnership Ltd, 1980–2002; *b* 29 Oct. 1939; *s* of William Ronald Denis Vernon-Harcourt, OBE and Nancy Everil (*née* Leatham); *S* kinsman, 2000; *m* 1966, Cherry Stanhope, *er d* of T. J. Corbin; three *s* one *d*. *Educ:* Eton; Magdalene Coll., Cambridge. *Publication:* Archibald Sturrock: pioneer locomotive engineer, 2007. *Recreations:* Church of England, railway history, motorcycling, countryside issues. *Heir: s* Hon. Simon Anthony Vernon-Harcourt [*b* 24 Aug. 1969; *m* 1999, Jessica Jane, *e d* of William Eric Faber; one *d*]. *Address:* Monks Farm, Debden Green, Saffron Walden, Essex CB11 3LX.

VERNON, Annette, CBE 2004; Chief Information Officer, Home Office, since 2008; *b* 4 May 1963; *d* of David Richard Willacy and Edith Willacy; partner, Peter Francis Sharkey. *Educ:* Preston Poly. (HND Business Studies (Dist.)). Joined DHSS, 1984; various information technol. and business change roles until 1999 (incl. secondment to Australian DSS, 1992–93); Lord Chancellor's Department, subseq. Department for Constitutional Affairs: IT Dir, Court Service, 1999–2002; Chief Inf. Officer, 2002–06; Interim Dir, Criminal Justice IT, 2003–04; Chief Inf. Officer, Identity and Passport Service, Home Office, 2006–08. *Recreations:* making stained-glass windows, golf, mosaic. *Address:* Home Office, Room 5.2.39 Second Floor, Seacole Building, 2 Marsham Street, SW1A 4DF; *e-mail:* annette.vernon6@homeoffice.gsi.gov.uk. *Club:* Inskip Golf.

VERNON, David Bowater; Under Secretary, Inland Revenue, 1975–84; *b* 14 Nov. 1926; *s* of Lt-Col Herbert Bowater Vernon, MC, and Ivy Margaret Vernon; *m* 1954, Anne de Montmorency Fleming, *d* of late John and Margaret Fleming; three *s* three *d*. *Educ:* Marlborough Coll.; Oriel Coll., Oxford (MA). RA, 1945–48 (Lieut). Inland Revenue, 1951–84. *Recreation:* gardening. *Address:* 6 Hurstwood Park, Tunbridge Wells, Kent TN4 8YE.

VERNON, Diana Charlotte; Headmistress, City of London School for Girls, since 2007; *b* 30 April 1961; *d* of Roderick W. P. Vernon and Jennifer F. F. Vernon (*née* Tyrrell). *Educ:* St Michael's, Burton Park; Durham Univ.; King's Coll., London (PGCE). Editl Asst, John Wiley & Sons Ltd, 1982–84; Account Executive: Business Image PR, 1984–85; Grayling, 1985–87; Corporate Communications Executive: Thorn EMI, 1987–89; London Internat. Gp, 1989–93; Housemistress and Dir of PR, Downe House, Newbury, 1994–2000; Headmistress, Woldingham Sch., 2000–07. Governor: Lilian Baylis, London, 1985–2002; Flexlands Sch., Chobham, 1994–2003; St Christopher's, Hampstead, 2003–; Conifers, Sussex, 2003–06; Notting Hill Prep Sch., 2007–. *Recreations:* theatre, cookery, travel, swimming. *Address:* City of London School for Girls, St Giles' Terrace, Barbican, EC2Y 8BB. *T:* (020) 7847 5500.

VERNON, Sir James (William), 5th Bt *cr* 1914, of Shotwick Park, Chester; business consultant; *b* 2 April 1949; *s* of Sir Nigel Vernon, 4th Bt and Margaret Ellen Vernon (*née* Dobell); S father, 2007; *m* 1981, Davinia Elizabeth Howard; two *s* one *d*. *Educ:* Shrewsbury. FCA. *Recreations:* shooting, fishing, vintage cars, gardening. *Heir: s* George William Howard Vernon, *b* 25 July 1987. *Address:* The Hall, Lygan-y-Wern, Pentre Halkyn, Holywell, Flintshire CH8 8BD. *Clubs:* Army and Navy, Honourable Artillery Company; Liverpool Artists; Chester City; Bentley Drivers, Vintage Sports Car.

VERNON, Kenneth Robert, CBE 1978; Deputy Chairman and Chief Executive, North of Scotland Hydro-Electric Board, 1973–88; *b* 15 March 1923; *s* of late Cecil W. Vernon and Jessie McGaw, Dumfries; *m* 1946, Pamela Hands, Harrow; one *s* three *d* (and one *d* decd). *Educ:* Dumfries Academy; Glasgow University. BSc, FREng, FIET, FIMechE. BTH Co., Edinburgh Corp., British Electricity Authority, 1948–55; South of Scotland Electricity Bd, 1955–56; North of Scotland Hydro-Electric Bd, 1956: Chief Electrical and Mech. Engr, 1964; Gen. Man., 1966; Bd Mem., 1970. Dir, British Electricity International Ltd, 1976–88; Mem. Bd, Northern Ireland Electricity Service, 1979–85. *Publications:* various papers to technical instns. *Recreations:* fishing, gardening. *Address:* 10 Keith Crescent, Edinburgh EH4 3NH. *T:* (0131) 332 4610.

VERNON, Sir (William) Michael, Kt 1995; Chairman, Royal National Lifeboat Institution, 1989–96 (Deputy Chairman, 1980–89; Vice-President, 1975–2001, now Chairman Emeritus); *b* 17 April 1926; *o* surv. *s* of late Sir Wilfred Vernon and Nancy Elizabeth Vernon (*née* Jackson); *m* 1st, 1952, Rosheen O'Meara; one *s*; 2nd, 1977, Mrs Jane Colston (*née* Kilham-Roberts) (*d* 1998); 3rd, 2001, Mrs Penelope Cuddeford (*née* Skelton). *Educ:* Marlborough Coll.; Trinity Coll., Cambridge. MA 1948. Lieut, Royal Marines, 1944–46. Joined Spillers Ltd, 1948: Dir, 1960; Jt Man. Dir, 1962; Chm. and Chief Exec., 1968–80; Chm., Granville Meat Co. Ltd, 1981–94. Director: EMI Ltd, 1973–80; Strong & Fisher (Hldgs) plc, 1980–90; Chm., Famous Names Ltd, 1981–85. Pres., Nat. Assoc. of British and Irish Millers, 1965; Vice-Chm., Millers' Mutual Assoc., 1968–80; Pres., British Food Export Council, 1977–80. CCMI. Bronze Medal, RHS, 1956. *Recreation:* shooting. *Address:* Fyfield Manor, Andover, Hants SP11 8EL. *Clubs:* Royal Ocean Racing (Cdre 1964–68); Royal Yacht Squadron.

VERNON-HARCOURT, family name of **Baron Vernon**.

VERPLAETSE, Viscount Alfons Remi Emiel; Governor, National Bank of Belgium, 1989–99, now Hon. Governor; *b* Zulte, Belgium, 19 Feb. 1930; created Viscount, 1999; *s* of Leon Verplaetse and Alida Baert; *m* 1954, Odette Vanhee; three *s* two *d*. *Educ:* Catholic Univ. of Louvain (Licentiate of Commercial and Consular Scis). Joined National Bank of Belgium, 1953: Attaché, 1960–62; Asst Advr, 1962–66; Advr, 1966–74; Inspector Gen., 1974–80; Sen. Economist, 1980–82; on secondment to Social and Econ. Cabinet of Prime Minister as Dep. Chief of Cabinet, 1982–83, Chief of Cabinet, 1983–88; Dir, 1985–88; Vice-Governor, 1988–89. Gov., IMF, 1989–99; Deputy Governor: IBRD, 1989–99; IFC, 1989–99; IDA, 1989–. Dir, European Fund for Monetary Co-operation, 1989–; Mem. Council, European Monetary Inst., 1994–. Grand Officier, Ordre de la Couronne (Belgium), 1991; Grande Ufficiale, Ordine al Merito (Italy), 1986; Officier de la Légion d'Honneur (France), 1994. *Address:* National Bank of Belgium, Boulevard de Berlaimont 14, 1000 Bruxelles, Belgium. *T:* (2) 2214777.

VERSACE, Donatella; Vice-President and Creative Director, Gianni Versace Group, since 1997; *b* 2 May 1955; *d* of Antonio Versace and Francesca Versace; *m* Paul Beck (marr. diss.); one *s* one *d*. *Educ:* Univ. of Florence. Joined Versace, 1978; designer: Versace Young, 1993; Versus; Isante; launched fragrance, Versace Woman, 2001. *Address:* Gianni Versace SpA, Via Manzoni 38, 20121 Milan, Italy.

VERTOVEC, Prof. Steven Allen, DPhil; Director, Max Planck Institute for the Study of Religious and Ethnic Diversity, Göttingen, since 2007; Hon. Joint Professor of Sociology and Ethnology, University of Göttingen, since 2007; *b* 2 July 1957; *s* of Frank J. Vertovec and Dorothea M. Vertovec; *m* 1994, Astrid Gräfe; one *s* one *d*. *Educ:* Immaculate Conception High Sch., Elmhurst, Ill; Univ. of Colorado, Boulder (BA); Univ. of Calif, Santa Barbara (MA); Nuffield Coll., Oxford (DPhil 1988). Res. Fellow, Sch. of Geography, Oxford Univ., 1991–93; Principal Res. Fellow, Centre for Res. in Ethnic Relns, Univ. of Warwick, 1994–97; Dir, ESRC Transnat. Communities Res. Prog., 1997–2003; University of Oxford: Res. Reader in Anthropology, 1997–2002; Prof. of Transnational Anthropology, 2002–07; Dir, Centre on Migration, Policy and Society, 2003–07; Jt Dir, Internat. Migration Inst., 2006–07; Sen. Res. Fellow, Linacre Coll., Oxford, 1997–2007. Regents' Fellow, Univ. of Calif, 1980–82; Overseas Res. Student Award, CVCP, 1983–86; Res. Fellow, Alexander von Humboldt-Stiftung, 1993–94; Vis. Fellow, Inst. Ethnology, Free Univ., Berlin, and Inst. Eur. Ethnology, Humboldt Univ., Berlin, 1993–94. *Publications:* (jtly) South Asians Overseas: migration and ethnicity, 1990; Aspects of the South Asian Diaspora, 1991; Hindu Trinidad: religion, ethnicity and socio-economic change, 1992; (with A. Rogers) The Urban Context: ethnicity, social networks and situational analysis, 1995; (with C. Peach) Islam in Europe: the politics of religion and community, 1997; (with A. Rogers) Muslim European Youth: reproducing religion, ethnicity and culture, 1998; Migration and Social Cohesion, 1999; (with R. Cohen) Migration, Diasporas and Transnationalism, 1999; The Hindu Diaspora: comparative patterns, 2000; (with R. Cohen) Conceiving Cosmopolitanism, 2002; (with B. Parekh) Culture and Economy in the Indian Diaspora, 2003; (with D. Posey) Globalization, Globalism, Environments and Environmentalism, 2004; (with W. Schiffauer) Civil Enculturation, 2004; (jtly) Citizenship in European Cities, 2004; Transnationalism, 2008; contrib. articles to Religion, Ethnic and Racial Studies, Social and Economic, Ethnology, New Community, Etnolog, Contribs to Indian Sociology, Social Compass, Internat. Social Sci. Jl; Jl of Ethnic and Migration Studies; Internat. Migration Review. *Address:* Max Planck Institut zur Erforschung multireligiöser und multiethnischer Gesellschaften, Hermann Foge Weg 11, 37073 Göttingen, Germany.

VERULAM, 7th Earl of, *cr* 1815; **John Duncan Grimston;** Bt 1629; Baron Forrester (Scot.), 1633; Baron Dunboyne and Viscount Grimston (Ire.), 1719; Baron Verulam (Gt. Brit.), 1790; Viscount Grimston (UK), 1815; Vice-Chairman, Kleinwort Benson Private Bank, since 2001; *b* 21 April 1951; *s* of 6th Earl of Verulam and Marjorie Ray (*d* 1994), *d* of late Walter Atholl Duncan; *S* father, 1973; *m* 1976, Dione Angela (*see* Countess of Verulam), *e d* of Jeremy Fox Eric Smith, *qv*; three *s* one *d*. *Educ:* Eton; Christ Church, Oxford (MA 1976). Dir, Baring Brothers Ltd, 1987–96; Man. Dir, ABN-AMRO Bank NV, 1996–2000. Chm., Grimston Trust Ltd, 1982–. *Heir: s* Viscount Grimston, *qv*. *Address:* Gorhambury, St Albans, Herts AL3 6AH. *T:* (01727) 855000. *Clubs:* White's, Beefsteak.

VERULAM, Countess of; Dione Angela Grimston; Lord Lieutenant of Hertfordshire, since 2007; artist; *b* 19 July 1954; *d* of Jeremy Fox Eric Smith, *qv*; *m* 1976, Earl of Verulam, *qv*; three *s* one *d*. *Educ:* Benenden Sch.; Exeter Univ. (BA Hons Hist. and Archaeol.). Stencilling commns, 1981–2001; exhibns in gp shows, 1994–2005; solo exhibn, Fleming Collection, 2007. Mem., Panel of Acceptance in Lieu, DCMS, 2001–06. Mem., Regl Cttee, NT, 1991–98. Liveryman, Goldsmiths' Co., 2005–. High Sheriff, Herts, 2002–07. Trustee, St Albans Cathedral Fabric Trust, 1995–2004; President: Herts Garden Trust, 1997–; Gade Valley NADFAS, 2004–. *Publications:* (ed) Memories of Strathvaich, 1992; Gorhambury Gardens Guide, 1993. *Recreations:* ski-ing, riding, golf, theatre, opera, reading, sewing, painting, Gorhambury. *Clubs:* Boodle's Ladies' Side; Northern Meeting (Inverness).

VESEY, family name of **Viscount de Vesci**.

VESSEY, Prof. Martin Paterson, CBE 1994; FRS 1991; Professor of Public Health (formerly Social and Community Medicine), University of Oxford, 1974–2000, now Emeritus; Fellow of St Cross College, Oxford, since 1973; *b* 22 July 1936; *s* of Sidney J. Vessey and Catherine P. Vessey (*née* Thomson); *m* 1959, Anne Platt; two *s* one *d. Educ:* University College Sch., Hampstead; University Coll. London (Fellow, 1992); University Coll. Hosp. Med. Sch., London. MB, BS London 1959; MD London 1971; FFCM RCP 1972; MA Oxon 1974; MRCPE 1978; FRCPE 1979; FRCGP 1983; FRCP 1987; FRCOG 1989; FFSRH (FFFP 1995). Scientific Officer, Dept of Statistics, Rothamsted Exper. Stn, 1960–65; House Surg. and House Phys., Barnet Gen. Hosp., 1965–66; Mem. Sci. Staff, MRC Statistical Research Unit, 1966–69; Lectr in Epidemiology, Univ. of Oxford, 1969–74. Chairman: Adv. Cttee on Breast Cancer Screening, DHSS, subseq. DoH, 1987–99; Adv. Cttee on Cervical Cancer Screening, DoH, 1996–2006; Member: Cttee on Safety of Medicines, 1980–92, 1996–98; Royal Commn on Environmental Pollution, 1984–89. Founder FMedSci 1998. *Publications:* many sci. articles in learned jls, notably on med. aspects of fertility control, safety of drugs, and epidemiology of cancer. *Recreations:* fine arts, conservation, model engineering. *Address:* Clifden Cottage, Burford Road, Fulbrook, Burford OX18 4BL.

VEST, Prof. Charles Marstiller, PhD; President, Massachusetts Institute of Technology, 1990–2004, now President Emeritus; *b* 9 Sept. 1941; *m* 1963, Rebecca McCue; one *s* one *d. Educ:* West Virginia Univ.; Univ. of Michigan (MSc 1964; PhD 1967). Asst Prof., then Associate Prof., 1968–77, Prof. of Mechl Engrg, 1977–90, Univ. of Michigan. *Publications:* Holographic Interferometry, 1979; Pursuing the Endless Frontier: essays on MIT and the role of research universities, 2004; The American Research University from World War II to World Wide Web: governments, the private sector, and the emerging meta-university, 2007. *Address:* Massachusetts Institute of Technology, Cambridge, MA 02139–4307, USA.

VESTEY, family name of **Baron Vestey.**

VESTEY, 3rd Baron *cr* 1922, of Kingswood; **Samuel George Armstrong Vestey;** DL; Bt 1913; Master of the Horse, since 1999; *b* 19 March 1941; *s* of late Captain the Hon. William Howarth Vestey (killed in action in Italy, 1944; *o s* of 2nd Baron Vestey and Frances Sarah Howarth) and of Pamela Helen Fullerton, *d* of George Nesbitt Armstrong, *S* grandfather, 1954; *m* 1st, 1970, Kathryn Mary (marr. diss. 1981), *er d* of John Eccles, Moor Park, Herts; two *d*; 2nd, 1981, Celia Elizabeth, *d* of late Major Guy Knight, MC, Lockinge Manor, Wantage, Oxon; two *s* one *d. Educ:* Eton. Lieut, Scots Guards. Chairman: Steeplechase Co. (Cheltenham), 1990–; Vestey Group Ltd, 1995–. Chm., Meat Training Council, 1991–95. President: London Meat Trade and Drovers Benevolent Assoc., 1973; Inst. of Meat, 1978–83; Three Counties Agricl Soc., 1978; Royal Bath and W of England Soc., 1994; BHS, 1994–97; Glos Assoc. of Boys' Clubs, 1979–; Chm., Royal Agricl Soc. of the Commonwealth, 1998–. Patron, Glos CCC, 1997–. Liveryman, Butchers' Co. DL Glos, 1982. GCStJ 1987 (Chancellor of the Order, 1988–91, Lord Prior, 1991–2002). *Recreations:* racing, shooting, cricket. Heir: *s* Hon. William Guy Vestey [*b* 27 Aug. 1983. Page of Honour to the Queen, 1995–97]. *Address:* Stowell Park, Northleach, Glos GL54 3LE. *Clubs:* White's, Turf; Jockey (Newmarket); I Zingari; Melbourne (Melbourne); South Cerney Golf.

VESTEY, Sir Paul (Edmund), 3rd Bt *cr* 1921, of Shirley; *b* 15 Feb. 1944; *s* of Sir (John) Derek Vestey, 2nd Bt and Phyllis Irene Vestey (*née* Brewer); *S* father, 2005; *m* 1971, Victoria Anne Scudamore, *d* of John Salter; three *d. Educ:* Radley. Heir: *cousin:* James Patrick Vestey [*b* 13 April 1954; *m* 1981, Nicola Jane Knight]. *Address:* Manor House Farm, Bishops Sutton, Alresford, Hants SO24 0BA.

VETTRIANO, Jack, OBE 2003; artist, since 1988; *b* Fife, 17 Nov. 1951; *s* of William and Catherine Hoggan; *né* Jack Hoggan. Mining engr, 1966–70; variety of middle mgt posts, 1970–88. Self-taught artist; solo exhibitions: Edinburgh, London, Hong Kong, Johannesburg; Portland Gall., London, 2004, 2006. Hon. DLitt St Andrews, 2003; DUniv Open, 2004. *Publications:* (with W. Gordon Smith) Fallen Angels, 1996; (with Anthony Quinn): Lovers and Other Strangers, 2000; Jack Vettriano: a life, 2004. *Recreations:* antiques, art, classic cars. *Address:* c/o Portland Gallery, 8 Bennet Street, SW1A 1RP.

VIALA, Prof. Alain Bernard Jean; Professor of French Literature and Fellow of Lady Margaret Hall, University of Oxford, since 2002; Professor of French Literature, University of Paris III, Sorbonne Nouvelle, since 1985; *b* 20 Nov. 1947; *s* of Ernest and Marie Viala. *Educ:* Ecole Normale Supérieure, Cachan; (Agregé des lettres; DèsL). Lecturer: Ecole Nationale de Chimie, 1972–78; Ecole d'Artillerie, 1973–74; Asst Prof., Univ. Sorbonne Nouvelle, 1978–84; Prof. of French Studies and Fellow, Wadham Coll., Univ. of Oxford, 1997–2002. Guest Professor: Univ. of Liège, 1988; Univ. of Tel Aviv, 1996. Pres., Commn des Programmes de Lettres, Min. of Educn, France, 1993–. Mem., Lit. Cttee, Presses Universitaires de France, 2007–. Chevalier des Palmes Académiques (France), 1988; Chevalier, Ordre National du Mérite (France), 2006. *Publications:* Savoir-lire, 1982; Naissance de l'écrivain, 1985; Racine: la stratégie du caméléon, 1990; Approches de la réception, 1993; Le théâtre en France, 1996, new edn 2008; Le Dictionnaire du Littéraire, 2002; Le Tragique, 2002; De la Publication, 2002; Lettre à Rousseau sur l'intérêt littéraire, 2005; Histoire du théâtre, 2006; La France galante, 2008. *Address:* Lady Margaret Hall, Oxford OX2 6QA.

VICARY-SMITH, Peter David; Chief Executive, Which?, since 2004; *b* 31 May 1962; *s* of James David Smith and Valerie Ann Smith; changed name by deed poll to Vicary-Smith on marriage, 1991; *m* 1991, Susan Joy Vicary; two *d. Educ:* Dulwich Coll.; Queen's Coll., Oxford (BA PPE 1984). Various mktg appts, Procter and Gamble, Mars Confectionery and Kenner Parker, 1984–88; McKinsey & Co., 1988–91; Hd of Appeals, Oxfam, 1991–96; Dir of Fundraising and Communications, ICRF, 1996–2002; Commercial Dir, CRUK, 2002–04. Non-exec. Dir, Oxfordshire Learning Disabilities NHS Trust, 1994–96. Member: Fundraising Standards Bd, 2006–08; Commercial Panel, Nat. Trust Enterprises, 2007–. Trustee, Methodist Homes for the Aged, 2003–06. *Recreations:* gardening, golf. *Address:* Which?, 2 Marylebone Road, NW1 4DF. *T:* (020) 7770 7000. *Club:* Lansdowne.

VICK, His Honour Arnold Oughtred Russell; QC 1980; a Circuit Judge, 1982–2001; a Designated Family Judge, 1991–2001; *b* 14 Sept. 1933; *yr s* of late His Honour Judge Sir Godfrey Russell Vick, QC and late Lady Russell Vick, JP, *d* of J. A. Compston, KC; *m* 1959, Zinnia Mary, *e d* of Thomas Brown Yates, Godalming; two *s* one *d. Educ:* The Leys Sch., Cambridge; Jesus Coll., Cambridge (MA). Pilot, RAF, 1952–54. Called to Bar, Inner Temple, 1958; Mem. Gen. Council of the Bar, 1964–68; Prosecuting Counsel to the Post Office, 1964–69; Dep. Recorder, Rochester City QS, 1971; a Recorder of the Crown Court, 1972–82; Principal Judge for Civil Matters in Kent, 1990–98. Mem., Lord Chancellor's County Court Rules Cttee, 1972–80; Recorder, SE Circuit Bar Mess, 1978–80. Gov., New Beacon Sch., Sevenoaks, 1982–2000. Master, Curriers' Co., 1976–77. *Publication:* A Hundred Years of Golf at Wildernesse, 1990. *Recreations:* golf, cricket, bridge, flying. *Address:* Little Hermitage, Wildernesse Avenue, Seal, Sevenoaks,

Kent TN15 0ED. *T:* (01732) 761686. *Clubs:* MCC; Hawks (Cambridge); Wildernesse (Captain 1978) (Sevenoaks); Senior Golfers.

VICK, Graham; Founder and Artistic Director, Birmingham Opera Company (formerly City of Birmingham Touring Opera); *b* 30 Dec. 1953. Trained as a singer and conductor. Associate Dir, English Music Theatre; Director of Productions: Scottish Opera, 1984–87; Glyndebourne Fest. Opera, 1994–2000. Hambro Vis. Prof. of Opera Studies, Oxford Univ., 2002–03; Hon. Prof. of Music, Univ. of Birmingham. *Productions* include: Scottish Opera: La vie parisienne, 1985; Hedda Gabler, 1985; Carmen, 1986; Don Giovanni, Billy Budd, 1987; Opera Theatre of St Louis: Die Entführung aus dem Serail, 1986; Vanessa, 1988; City of Birmingham Touring Opera: Falstaff, 1987; The Magic Flute, 1988; Ghanashyam (Ravi Shankar), 1989; The Ring, 1990; Les Boréades, 1992; Silas Marner, 1994; The Adventures of Vixen Sharp-Ears, 1998; The Two Widows, 1999; Birmingham Opera Company: Wozzeck, 2001; Fidelio, 2002; Candide, 2003; Il Ritorno d'Ulisse, 2005; He Had It Coming, 2006; La Traviata, 2007; King Idomeneo, 2008; Royal Opera House, Covent Garden: Un rè in ascolto, 1989; Mitridate, 1991; Die Meistersinger, 1993; King Arthur, 1995; The Midsummer Marriage, 1995; The Merry Widow, 1997; Falstaff, 1999, 2003; English National Opera: Ariadne auf Naxos, 1983; The Rape of Lucretia, Madam Butterfly, 1986; Eugene Onegin, 1989; Timon of Athens, 1991; Figaro's Wedding, 1991; Fidelio, 1996; Tales of Hoffmann, 1998; Musica nel Chiostro, Batignano, Italy: Tolomeo; Zaïde, 1981; King Priam, 1990; Candide, 1993; Glyndebourne Festival Opera: Queen of Spades, 1992; Eugene Onegin, 1994; Ermione, 1995; Lulu, 1996; Manon Lescaut, 1997; Così fan tutte, 1998; Pelléas et Mélisande, 1999; Le Nozze di Figaro, Don Giovanni, 2000; Opera North: Così fan tutte; Katya Kabanova; West Side Story; The Magic Flute; Opéra Bastille, Paris: Un rè in ascolto, 1991; Mahagonny; Peter Grimes, 2001; Parsifal; Don Carlo; Netherlands Opera: Ariadne; Mefistofele; New Israeli Opera: Don Giovanni, 1994; Metropolitan Opera, NY: Lady Macbeth of Mtsensk; Moses und Aron, 1999; War and Peace, Kirov Theatre, Leningrad; Vienna State Opera: Ernani; Florence Maggio Musicale: Mahagonny; Lucia di Lammermoor; Tamerlano; Les Troyens; La Scala, Milan: Outis (Berio), 1996; Macbeth, 1997; Otello, 2001; Eugene Onegin, 2006; Das Rheingold, Teatro Nacional de Sao Carlos, Lisbon, 2006. *Address:* Birmingham Opera Company, 205 The Argent Centre, Frederick Street, Birmingham B1 3HS; c/o Ingpen & Williams, 7 St George's Court, 131 Putney Bridge Road, SW15 2PA.

VICKERMAN, Prof. Keith, FRS 1984; FRSE 1971; Regius Professor of Zoology, University of Glasgow, 1984–98; *b* 21 March 1933; *s* of Jack Vickerman and Mabel Vickerman (*née* Dyson); *m* 1961, Moira Dutton, LLB; one *d. Educ:* King James' Grammar School, Almondbury; University College London (BSc 1955; PhD 1960; DSc 1970; Fellow, 1985). Wellcome Trust Lectr, Zoology Dept, UCL, 1958–63; Royal Soc. Tropical Res. Fellow, UCL, 1963–68; Glasgow University: Reader in Zoology, 1968–74; Prof., 1974–98; Head of Dept of Zoology, 1979–85. Leeuwenhoek Lectr, Royal Soc., 1994. Mem., WHO Panel of Consultant Experts on Parasitic Diseases, 1973–98. Mem. Council, Royal Soc., 1996–97. Founder FMedSci 1998. Gold Medal for Zoology, Linnean Soc., 1996. *Publications:* The Protozoa (with F. E. G. Cox), 1967; numerous papers on protozoa (esp. trypanosomes) in scientific and med. jls. *Recreations:* sketching, gardening. *Address:* Division of Environmental and Evolutionary Biology, Graham Kerr Building, University of Glasgow, Glasgow G12 8QQ. *T:* (0141) 330 4433; *e-mail:* k.vickerman@bio.gla.ac.uk; 16 Mirrlees Drive, Glasgow G12 0SH. *T:* (0141) 586 7794.

VICKERS, Andrew Julian; Assistant Attending Research Methodologist, Memorial Sloan-Kettering Cancer Center, New York, since 1999; *b* 11 Feb. 1967; *s* of Jeffrey Vickers and Angela Vickers; *m* 1996, Caroline Batzdorf; one *s* one *d. Educ:* Girton Coll., Cambridge; Green Coll., Oxford. Joined Res. Council for Complementary Medicine, 1993; Dir of Res., 1997–99; estabd registry of randomised trials in complementary medicine for Cochrane Collaboration, 1995. Ed., Complementary Therapies in Medicine, 1996–99. Principal investigator, NHS funded trial of acupuncture for headache, 1998–. Mem., R&D Cttee, Prince of Wales initiative for Integrated Medicine, 1996–98. *Publications:* Complementary Medicine and Disability, 1993; Health Options: complementary therapies for cerebral palsy and related conditions, 1994; Massage and Aromatherapy: a guide for health professionals, 1996; (ed) Examining Complementary Medicine: the sceptical holist, 1998; (jtly) ABC of Complementary Medicine, 2000; contrib. numerous papers to peer-reviewed health-related jls. *Recreations:* cooking, Ultimate Frisbee, running, guitar. *Address: e-mail:* andrewline@earthlink.net.

VICKERS, Andrew Robert; a District Judge (Magistrates' Courts), since 2004; *b* 18 Jan. 1951; *s* of late Francis Albert Vickers and Barbara Winifred Vickers (*née* Tappenden); *m* 1973, Alison Ayres; one *s* two *d. Educ:* Windsor Grammar Sch.; Univ. of London (ext. BA 1976). Called to the Bar, Gray's Inn, 1987. Assistant: Chamberlain's Dept, City of London Corp., 1977–78; Mansion House and Guildhall Justice Rooms, 1978–83; PSDs, Slough and Windsor, 1983–86; Principal Court Clerk, Hounslow PSA, 1986–89; Dep. Justices' Clerk, Enfield PSA, 1989–92; Clerk to the Justices, Kingston upon Thames PSA, 1992–2004; Justices' Chief Exec., Kingston upon Thames MCC, 1995–2001; Regl Justices' Clerk for Hounslow, Ealing, Richmond, Wimbledon, W London and S Western PSAs, 2003–04. *Recreations:* avid supporter Brentford FC, reading, music. *Address:* High Wycombe Magistrates' Court, Easton Street, High Wycombe, Bucks HP11 1LR. *T:* (01494) 651035.

VICKERS, Sir Brian (William), Kt 2008; PhD; LittD; FBA 1998; Professor of English Literature, and Director, Centre for Renaissance Studies, ETH Zürich, 1975–2003, now Emeritus Professor; *b* 13 Dec. 1937; *s* of William Morgan Davies and Josephine Davies (*née* Grant); *m* 1st, 1962, Ilse-Renate Freiling (marr. diss. 1989); two *d*; 2nd, 1989, Sabine Köllmann; one *s* one *d. Educ:* St Marylebone Grammar Sch.; Trinity Coll., Cambridge (BA 1st Cl. Hons English 1962; Charles Oldham Shakespeare Schol., 1961; Sen. Schol., 1962); PhD 1967, LittD 1996 Cantab. Cambridge University: Res. Fellow, Churchill Coll., 1964–65; Asst Lectr in English, 1964–68; Fellow and Dir of Studies in English, Downing Coll., 1966–71; Univ. Lectr in English, 1968–72; Prof. of English Lit., Univ. of Zürich, 1972–75. Vis. Fellow, All Souls Coll., Oxford, 1980–81; Fellow, Wissenschaftskolleg zu Berlin, 1986–87. Lectures: Shakespeare, British Acad., 1992; John Coffin, London Univ., 2001. Pres., Internat. Soc. for History of Rhetoric, 1977–79; Chm., Soc. for Renaissance Studies, 2004–. Dist. Sen. Fellow, Sch. of Advanced Study, Univ. of London, 2003–; Sen. Res. Fellow, Inst. of English Studies, 2004–. Hon. Fellow, Downing Coll., Cambridge, 2008. Hon. Foreign Mem., Amer. Acad. of Arts and Scis, 2007. Member of Editorial Board: Renaissance Studies, 1994–98; Annals of Science, 1995–; Isis, 1999–2002; Gen. Ed., The Complete Works of John Ford, 2005–. Dr *hc* Fribourg, 2003. *Publications:* (ed) Henry Mackenzie, The Man of Feeling, 1967, 2nd edn 2001; Francis Bacon and Renaissance Prose, 1968; The Artistry of Shakespeare's Prose, 1968, rev. edn 1979; (ed) Essential Articles for the Study of Francis Bacon, 1968; (ed) The World of Jonathan Swift, 1968; (ed) Seventeenth Century Prose, 1969; Classical Rhetoric in English Poetry, 1970, rev. edn 1989 (trans. German 2008); Towards Greek Tragedy, 1973; (ed) Shakespeare: the critical heritage, 6 vols, 1623–1692, 1974, 1693–1733, 1974, 1733–1752, 1975, 1753–1765, 1976, 1765–1774, 1979, 1774–1801, 1981; (ed jtly) Hooker: the laws of ecclesiastical polity, 1976; Shakespeare's Coriolanus, 1976; (ed)

Rhetoric Revalued, 1982; (ed) Occult and Scientific Mentalities in the Renaissance, 1984 (trans. Spanish 1980); (ed) Arbeit, Musse, Meditation: Betrachtungen zur Vita activa und Vita contemplativa, 1985, rev. edn 1991; (ed) Public and Private Life in the Seventeenth Century: the Mackenzie-Evelyn debate, 1986; (ed) English Science: Bacon to Newton, 1987; In Defence of Rhetoric, 1988 (trans. Italian 1994), rev. edn 1997; Returning to Shakespeare, 1989; Appropriating Shakespeare: contemporary critical quarrels, 1993; (ed) Francis Bacon: the major works, 1996, 2nd edn 2002; (ed) Francis Bacon: history of the reign of King Henry VII, 1998; (ed) Francis Bacon: the essays and counsels, civil and moral, 1999; (ed) English Renaissance Literary Criticism, 1999; Counterfeiting Shakespeare: evidence, authorship and John Ford's Funerall Elegye, 2002; Shakespeare, Co-Author: a historical study of five collaborative plays, 2002; (Gen. Ed.) series, Shakespeare: the critical tradition: King John, 1996; Richard II, 1998; A Midsummer Night's Dream, 1999; Measure for Measure, 2001; Coriolanus, 2004; The Merchant of Venice, 2005; articles and reviews in learned jls. *Recreations:* music, sport, film. *Address:* 7 Abbot's Place, NW6 4NP. *T:* (020) 7372 7210.

VICKERS, Eric, CB 1979; Director of Defence Services, Department of the Environment, 1972–81; *b* 25 April 1921; *s* of late Charles Vickers and late Ida Vickers; *m* 1945, Barbara Mary Jones; one *s* one *d. Educ:* King's School, Grantham. Joined India Office, 1938; RAF (Fl/Lt Coastal Command), 1941–46; Ministry of Works, 1948; Principal, 1950; Assistant Secretary, 1962; Imperial Defence College, 1969; Dir of Home Estate Management, DoE, 1970–72. *Recreation:* photography, music, wine appreciation. *Address:* 46 Stamford Road, Oakham, Rutland LE15 6JA. *T:* (01572) 724166.

VICKERS, Hugo Ralph; author, lecturer and broadcaster; Chairman, Jubilee Walkway Trust, since 2002; *b* 12 Nov. 1951; *s* of late Ralph Cecil Vickers, MC, and Dulcie (*née* Metcalf); *m* 1995, Elizabeth Anne Blyth Vickers, *y d* of late (Dennis) Michael Vickers, Montaillac, France; two *s* one *d. Educ:* Eton; Strasbourg Univ. Lay Steward, 1970–, Dep. Vice-Capt., 1996–, St George's Chapel, Windsor Castle (Mem., Adv. Council, later Mgt Cttee, Friends of St George's, 2001–04, 2005–). Worked with London Celebrations Cttee, Queen's Silver Jubilee, 1977; Administrator, Great Children's Party, Hyde Park, 1979. Member: Prince of Wales' Royal Parks Tree Appeal, 1987–2003; Council of Mgt, Windsor Fest., 1999–. Broadcaster including: studio guest, weddings of Prince of Wales and Duke of York, funeral of Diana, Princess of Wales; asstd with commentaries: wedding of Earl of Wessex, Queen Mother's 100th birthday and funeral. Producer and writer, one-man play, The Immortal Dropout, Jermyn St Th., 2008. Golo Mann Dist. Lectr, Claremont McKenna Coll., 2007. Liveryman, Co. of Musicians, 1978. *Publications:* We Want the Queen, 1977; Gladys, Duchess of Marlborough, 1979; Debrett's Book of the Royal Wedding, 1981; (ed) Cocktails and Laughter, 1983; Cecil Beaton, 1985; Vivien Leigh, 1988; Royal Orders, 1994; Loving Garbo, 1994; The Private World of the Duke and Duchess of Windsor, 1995; The Kiss (Stern Silver Pen for non-fiction), 1996; Alice, Princess Andrew of Greece, 2000; (ed) The Unexpurgated Beaton, 2002; (ed) Beaton in the Sixties, 2003; (ed) Alexis: the memoirs of the Baron de Redé, 2005; Elizabeth, The Queen Mother, 2005; (ed) The Rich Spoils of Time, 2006; (ed) Horses and Husbands, 2007; St George's Chapel, Windsor Castle, 2008. *Recreations:* reading, travel, photography. *Address:* Wyeford, Ramsdell, Hampshire RG26 5QL. *T:* (01256) 850044; 62 Lexham Gardens, W8 5JA; *e-mail:* hugovickers@wyeford.co.uk; *web:* www.hugovickers.co.uk.

VICKERS, Sir John (Stuart), Kt 2005; DPhil; FBA 1998; Warden, All Souls College, Oxford, since 2008 (Fellow, 1991–2008); *b* 7 July 1958; *s* of Aubrey and Kay Vickers; *m* 1991, Maureen Freed; one *s* two *d. Educ:* Eastbourne Grammar Sch.; Oriel Coll., Oxford (BA PPE 1979; Hon. Fellow 2005); MPhil Econs Oxon 1983; DPhil Econs Oxon 1985. Financial Analyst, Shell UK, 1979–81; Fellow, All Souls Coll., Oxford, 1979–84; Roy Harrod Fellow in Economics of Business and Public Policy, Nuffield Coll., Oxford, 1984–90; Drummond Prof. of Political Economy, Univ. of Oxford, 1991–2008 (on leave, 1998–2005); Exec. Dir, Chief Economist, and Mem. Monetary Policy Cttee, Bank of England, 1998–2000; Dir Gen., 2000–03, Chm., 2003–05, OFT. Vis. Fellow, Princeton, 1988; Vis. Lectr, Harvard, 1989, 1990; Vis. Prof., London Business Sch., 1996. President: Inst. for Fiscal Studies, 2003–07; REconS, 2007–. Rhodes Trustee, 2006–. Fellow, Econometric Soc., 1998. Hon. DLitt UEA, 2001. *Publications:* (jtly) Privatization: an economic analysis, 1988; (jtly) Regulatory Reform, 1994; articles in econ. jls on industrial organisation, regulation, competition, monetary policy. *Address:* All Souls College, Oxford OX1 4AL. *T:* (01865) 279379.

VICKERS, Jon, CC (Canada) 1969; dramatic tenor; *b* Prince Albert, Saskatchewan, 29 Oct. 1926; *m* 1953, Henrietta Outerbridge; three *s* two *d.* Studied under George Lambert, Royal Conservatory of Music, Toronto. Made debut with Toronto Opera Company, 1952; Stratford (Ontario) Festival, 1956. Joined Royal Opera House, Covent Garden, 1957. First sang at: Bayreuth Festival, 1958; Vienna State Opera, San Francisco Opera, and Chicago Lyric, 1959; Metropolitan, New York, and La Scala, Milan, 1960; Buenos Aires, 1962; Salzburg Festival, 1966; appeared in other opera houses of Argentina, Austria, Brazil, France, Germany, Greece, Mexico and USA. *Films:* Carmen; Pagliacci; Otello; Norma; Peter Grimes; Fidelio; Samson et Delilah. Has made many recordings. Presbyterian. Hon. Dr: University of Saskatchewan, 1963; Bishop's Univ., 1965; Univ. West Ontario, 1970; Brandon Univ., 1976; Laval Univ., 1977; Univ. of Guelph, 1978; Illinois, 1983; Queens, Canada, 1984; Toronto, 1987. RAM 1977. Canada Centennial Medal, 1967; 'Critics' Award, London, 1978; Grammy Award, 1979.

VICKERS, Rt Rev. Michael Edwin; Area Bishop of Colchester, 1988–94; Assistant Bishop, Diocese of Blackburn, since 1994; *b* 13 Jan. 1929; *s* of William Edwin and Florence Alice Vickers; *m* 1960, Janet Cynthia Croasdale; three *d. Educ:* St Lawrence Coll. Ramsgate; Worcester Coll., Oxford (BA Mod. History 1952; MA 1956); Cranmer Hall, Durham (DipTheol with distinction, 1959). Company Secretary, Hoares (Ceylon) Ltd, 1952–56; Refugee Administrator for British Council for Aid to Refugees, 1956–57; Lay Worker, Diocese of Oklahoma, 1959; Curate of Christ Church, Bexleyheath, 1959–62; Sen. Chaplain, Lee Abbey Community, 1962–67; Vicar of St John's, Newland, Hull, 1967–81; Area Dean, Central and North Hull, 1972–81; Archdeacon of E Riding, 1981–88. Chm., York Diocesan House of Clergy, 1975–85; Canon and Prebendary of York, 1981–88. Mem., Gen. Synod, 1975–88 (Proctor in Convocation, 1975–85). *Recreations:* gardening, fell-walking, travel, drama. *Address:* 2 Collingham Park, Lancaster LA1 4PD. *T:* (01524) 848492.

VICKERS, Prof. Michael John, DLitt; FSA 1978; Professor of Archaeology, University of Oxford, since 2002 (Reader in Archaeology, 1996–2002); Senior Research Fellow in Classical Studies, since 1996, and Dean of Degrees, since 2002, Jesus College, Oxford (Garden Master, 2002–08); Senior Assistant Keeper, Department of Antiquities, Ashmolean Museum, since 1988 (Assistant Keeper, 1971–88); *b* 17 Feb. 1943; *s* of late John Fletcher and Agnes Mary Vickers; *m* 1st, 1966, Marie Moley (marr. diss. 1982); one *s* one *d;* 2nd, 1982, Susan Brandes (*d* 1998); two *s;* 3rd, 2001, Manana Odisheli. *Educ:* St Bede's Coll., Manchester (jun. high jump champion, Lancs, 1960); UCNW Bangor (BA (Classics) 1964); Corpus Christi Coll., Cambridge (Dip. Classical Archaeol. 1965); Univ. of Wales (DLitt 1999). Asst Lectr in Ancient Hist. and Classical Archaeol., University

Coll., Dublin, 1966–69; Lectr in Archaeol., Univ. of Libya, Benghazi, 1969–70. Vis. Mem., University Coll., Cambridge, 1970–71; Mem., Inst. for Advanced Study, Princeton, 1976; Vis. Lectr, Univ. of Texas, 1979–80; George Tait Meml Lectr, Eton Coll., 1987; Vis. Scholar, Inst. for Advanced Studies, Hebrew Univ., Jerusalem, 1993; Visiting Professor: Univ. of Catania, 2002; Univ. of Colorado at Boulder, 2003; Kress Lectr, Archaeol Inst. of America, 2002–03. Co-Dir, excavations at Pichvnari, Georgia, 1998–. Chm., Friends of Academic Res. in Georgia, 2005. Corresp. Mem., German Archaeol Inst., 1978; Hon. Mem., Vani Expdn, Centre for Archaeol Studies, Georgian Acad. of Scis, 1995. *Publications:* The Roman World, 1977, 2nd edn as Ancient Rome, 1989; Greek Vases, 1978, 3rd edn 1989; Greek Symposia, 1978; Scythian Treasures in Oxford, 1979; (with K. Branigan) Hellas, 1980; (jtly) From Silver to Ceramic: the potter's debt to metalwork in the Greco-Roman, Chinese and Islamic worlds, 1986; (ed) Pots and Pans, 1986; The Ancient Romans, 1992; (ed with M. Henig) Cameos in Context: the Benjamin Zucker lectures 1990, 1993; (with D. W. J. Gill) Artful Crafts: Ancient Greek silverware and pottery, 1994, 2nd edn 1996; Pericles on Stage: political comedy in Aristophanes' early plays, 1997; Ancient Greek Pottery, 1998; Images on Textiles: the weave of fifth-century Athenian art and society, 1999; Skeuomorphismus, oder die Kunst aus wenig viel zu machen, 1999; Scythian and Thracian Antiquities in Oxford, 2002; (with A. Kakhidze) Pichvnari I, Pichvnari 1998–2002: Greeks and Colchians on the East Coast of the Black Sea, 2004; Oedipus and Alcibiades in Sophocles, 2005; The Arundel and Pomfret Marbles in Oxford, 2006; Sophocles and Alcibiades: Athenian politics in Ancient Greek literature, 2008; articles in jls. *Recreation:* classical philology. *Address:* 87 Lonsdale Road, Oxford OX2 7ET; *e-mail:* michael.vickers@jesus.ox.ac.uk.

VICKERS, Lt-Gen. Sir Richard (Maurice Hilton), KCB 1983; CVO 1998 (LVO 1959); OBE 1970 (MBE 1964); an Extra Gentleman Usher to the Queen, since 1998 (a Gentleman Usher, 1986–98); *b* 21 Aug. 1928; *s* of Lt-Gen. W. G. H. Vickers, CB, OBE; *m* 1957, Gaie, *d* of Maj.-Gen. G. P. B. Roberts, CB, DSO, MC; three *d. Educ:* Haileybury and Imperial Service Coll.; RMA. Commissioned Royal Tank Regt, 1948; 1st RTR, BAOR, Korea, Middle East, 1948–54; Equerry to HM The Queen, 1956–59; Brigade Major, 7 Armd Bde, 1962–64; 4th RTR, Borneo and Malaysia, 1964–66; CO The Royal Dragoons, 1967–68, The Blues and Royals, 1968–69; Comdr, 11th Armd Brigade, 1972–74; Dep. Dir of Army Training, 1975–77; GOC 4th Armoured Div., 1977–79; Comdt, RMA, 1979–82; Dir-Gen. of Army Training, 1982–83. Dir Gen., Winston Churchill Meml Trust, 1983–93. *Recreation:* flyfishing.

VICKERS, Roger Henry, FRCS; Orthopaedic Surgeon, since 1992, and Serjeant Surgeon, since 2007, to the Queen; Consultant Orthopaedic Surgeon: St George's Hospital, 1980–2008; King Edward VII's Hospital Sister Agnes (formerly King Edward VII Hospital for Officers), since 1992; Civilian Consultant Orthopaedic Surgeon to the Army, since 1992; *b* 26 July 1945; *s* of late Dr H. Renwick Vickers, FRCP and of Penelope Evelyn (*née* Peck); *m* 1972, Joanna, *d* of late John Francis Mordaunt; two *s* two *d. Educ:* Winchester Coll.; Magdalen Coll., Oxford (MA); St Thomas's Hosp. (BM, BCh 1970). FRCS 1975. Sen. Orthopaedic Registrar, Charing Cross, St Mary's and Royal Nat. Orthopaedic Hosps, 1977–80; Consultant Orthopaedic Surgeon, St James' Hosp., London, 1980–88. Mem. Council, Med. Defence Union, 1983–; Mem., Adv. Bd, Med. Sickness Soc., 1998–. *Recreations:* sailing, Real tennis. *Address:* 46 Novello Street, SW6 4JB; 5 Devonshire Place, W1G 6HL. *Clubs:* Garrick, Hurlingham; Royal Yacht Squadron.

VICKERS, Dr Tony; Project Manager, UK Human Genome Mapping Project, 1990–92; *b* 6 July 1932; *s* of Harry and Frances Vickers; *m* 1964, Anne Dorothy Wallis (marr. diss. 1986); two *d. Educ:* Manchester Grammar Sch.; Sidney Sussex Coll., Cambridge (MA, PhD). University of Cambridge: Demonstrator, 1956; Lectr in Physiology, 1961–72; Fellow, Sidney Sussex Coll., 1956–70; Headquarters Office, MRC, 1972–84 (Head of Medical Div., 1980–84); UK Administrator, Ludwig Inst. for Cancer Res., 1985–89. Member of Council: BAAS, 1969–72, 1982–85 (Pres., Biomed. Scis Sect., 1977); Cancer Res. Campaign, 1980–85 (Mem., Scientific Cttee, 1979–85); Paterson Labs, Manchester, 1984–85. Chm., Tenovus Sci. Adv. Cttee, 1987–91; Mem. Res. Cttee, Clatterbridge Centre for Oncology and Cancer Res. Trust, 1994–99. Governor, Beatson Inst., Glasgow, 1983–85. *Address:* 42 Bengeo Street, Hertford, Herts SG14 3ET.

VICKERY, Prof. Brian Campbell, FCLIP; Professor of Library Studies and Director, School of Library Archive and Information Studies, University College London, 1973–83, now Professor Emeritus; *b* 11 Sept. 1918; *s* of Adam Cairns McCay and Violet Mary Watson; *m* 1st, 1945, Manuletta McMenamin; one *s* one *d;* 2nd, 1970, Alina Gralewska. *Educ:* King's Sch., Canterbury; Brasenose Coll., Oxford. MA. Chemist, Royal Ordnance Factory, Somerset, 1941–45; Librarian, ICI Ltd, Welwyn, 1946–60; Principal Scientific Officer, Nat. Lending Library for Sci. and Technology, 1960–64; Librarian, UMIST, 1964–66; Head of R&D, Aslib, 1966–73. *Publications:* Classification and Indexing in Science, 1958, 3rd edn 1975; On Retrieval System Theory, 1961, 2nd edn 1965; Techniques of Information Retrieval, 1970; Information Systems, 1973; Information Science, 1987, 3rd edn 2004; Online Search Interface Design, 1993; (ed) Fifty Years of Information Progress, 1994; Scientific Communication in History, 2000; A Long Search for Information, 2004; articles in professional jls. *Recreations:* reading history, poetry, philosophy; music and theatre; personal computing. *Address:* 9 Clover Close, Cumnor Hill, Oxford OX2 9JH. *T:* (01865) 863306.

VICTOR, Ed; Chairman, Ed Victor Ltd, since 1977; *b* 9 Sept. 1939; *s* of Jack Victor and late Lydia Victor; *m* 1st, 1963, Michelene Dinah Samuels (marr. diss.); two *s;* 2nd, 1980, Carol Lois Ryan; one *s. Educ:* Dartmouth Coll. USA (BA *summa cum laude* 1961); Pembroke Coll., Cambridge (MLitt 1963). Began as art books editor, later editorial Dir, Weidenfeld & Nicolson, 1964–67; editorial Dir, Jonathan Cape Ltd, 1967–71; Senior Editor, Alfred A. Knopf Inc., NY, 1972–73; literary agent and Dir, John Farquharson Ltd (lit. agents), 1974–76; founded Ed Victor Ltd (lit. agency), 1977. Council Mem., Aids Crisis Trust, 1986–98. Vice-Chm., Almeida Theatre, 1994–2002 (Dir, 1993–). Trustee: The Arts Foundn, 1991–2004; Hay Literary Fest., 2002–. *Publication:* The Obvious Diet, 2001. *Recreations:* golf, tennis, travel, opera. *Address:* 10 Cambridge Gate, Regent's Park, NW1 4JX. *T:* (020) 7224 3030. *Clubs:* Garrick, Beefsteak.

VICTORY, Louis Eamonn Julian; artist photographer; public services consultant; Chairman, Avon Ambulance NHS Trust, 2005–06; *b* 14 Feb. 1948; *s* of Gerald Louis Victory and Doris Mabel Victory; *m* 1st, 1969, Sian Anne Bees Davies (marr. diss. 1996; she *d* 2002); three *d;* 2nd, 2004, Mary Reville. *Educ:* Cambridge Grammar Sch.; Christ's Coll., Cambridge (MA). DipArch; RIBA 1974. Architect in public and private practice, Birmingham, Oxon and Dyfed, 1972–90; Nottinghamshire County Council: Dep. Co. Architect, 1990; Dep. Dir, 1991, Dir, 1992–95, Construction and Design; Dir, Envmt, 1995–2000; Chief Exec., Cumbria CC, 2000–04. *Recreations:* travelling, observing, recording (and sometimes making) townscape and landscape.

VICUÑA, Francisco O.; see Orrego-Vicuña.

VIDAL, Gore; author; *b* 3 Oct. 1925; *s* of Eugene and Nina Gore Vidal. *Educ:* Phillips Exeter Academy, New Hampshire, USA (grad. 1943). Army of the US, 1943–46: Private to Warrant Officer (jg) and First Mate, Army FS-35, Pacific Theatre Ops. Democratic-Liberal candidate for US Congress, 1960; candidate for Democratic nomination for election to US Senate from California, 1982. Apptd to President Kennedy's Adv. Council of the Arts, 1961–63. Hon. DLitt Brown Univ., 1988, etc. Chevalier de l'Ordre des Arts et des Lettres (France), 1995. *Publications: novels:* Williwaw, 1946; In a Yellow Wood, 1947; The City and the Pillar, 1948; The Season of Comfort, 1949; A Search for the King, 1950; Dark Green, Bright Red, 1950; The Judgment of Paris, 1952; Messiah, 1954; Julian, 1964; Washington, DC, 1967; Myra Breckinridge, 1968 (filmed 1969); Two Sisters, 1970; Burr, 1973; Myron, 1975; 1876, 1976; Kalki, 1978; Creation, 1981; Duluth, 1983; Lincoln, 1984; Empire, 1987; Hollywood, 1989; Live from Golgotha, 1992; The Smithsonian Institution, 1998; The Golden Age, 2000; *essays:* Rocking the Boat, 1962; Reflections upon a Sinking Ship, 1969; Homage to Daniel Shays (collected essays 1952–72), 1972; Matters of Fact and of Fiction, 1977; The Second American Revolution (UK title, Pink Triangle and Yellow Star and other essays (1976–1982)), 1982; Armageddon?, 1987; At Home, 1988; A View from the Diner's Club, 1991; Screening History, 1992; United States: essays 1952–1992, 1993 (Nat. Book Award, 1994); Virgin Islands: essays 1992–1997, 1997; The Last Empire: essays 1992–2000, 2001; Imperial America, 2005; Selected Essays, 2007; *short stories:* A Thirsty Evil, 1956; Clouds and Eclipses, 2006; *travel:* Vidal in Venice, 1987; *memoirs:* Palimpsest, 1995; Point to Point Navigation, 2006; *biography:* Inventing a Nation: Washington, Adams, Jefferson, 2003; *plays:* Visit to a Small Planet (NY prod.), 1957; The Best Man (NY prod.), 1960, 2000; Romulus (adapted from F. Dürrenmatt) (NY prod.), 1962; Weekend (NY prod.), 1968; On the March to the Sea (German prod.), 1962; An Evening with Richard Nixon (NY prod.), 1972; *screenplays:* from 1955: Wedding Breakfast, 1957; Suddenly Last Summer, 1958; The Best Man (Critic's Prize, Cannes), 1964, etc; *television plays:* 1954–56: The Death of Billy the Kid (translated to screen as The Lefthanded Gun, 1959, and as Gore Vidal's Billy the Kid, 1989), etc; *literary and political criticism for:* NY Review of Books, New Yorker, Nation, TLS, etc. *Recreations:* as noted above. *Club:* Athenæum.

VIGARS, Della, (Mrs Paul Vigars); *see* Jones, D.

VIGARS, Robert Lewis; *b* 26 May 1923; *s* of late Francis Henry Vigars and Susan Laurina May Vigars (*née* Lewis); *m* 1962, Margaret Ann Christine, *y d* of late Sir John Walton, KCIE, CB, MC, and Lady Walton; two *d. Educ:* Truro Cathedral Sch.; London Univ. (LLB (Hons)). Served War of 1939–45: RA and Royal Corps of Signals, 1942–47; attached Indian Army (Captain), 1944–47; Captain, Princess Louise's Kensington Regt, TA, 1951–54. Qualified as solicitor (Hons), 1948. Partner, Simmons & Simmons, London, EC2, 1951–75. Member: Kensington Borough Council, 1953–59; London and Home Counties Traffic Adv. Cttee, 1956–58; London Roads (Nugent) Cttee, 1958–59; LCC and GLC Kensington (formerly South Kensington), 1955–86; Environmental Planning Cttee, GLC, 1967–71 (Chm.); Strategic Planning Cttee, GLC, 1971–73 (Chm.); Leader of Opposition, ILEA, 1974–79; Chm. of the GLC, 1979–80; Mem., Standing Conf. on London and SE Regional Planning and SE Economic Planning Council, 1968–75. Gen. Comr of Income Tax (Highbury), 1988–98; Mem., Central London Valuation Tribunal, 1989–95. Dir, Heritage of London Trust, 1985–; Mem., Historic Buildings and Monuments Commn for England, 1986–88 (Mem., London Adv. Cttee, 1986–92 (Chm. 1986–88)); Trustee, Historic Chapels Trust, 1993–2008. Mem. Court, London Univ., 1977–82. Chm., Kensington Soc., 1994–99. *Recreation:* dreaming of past mountain walking. *Club:* Hurlingham.

VIGGERS, Lt-Gen. Sir Frederick (Richard), KCB 2007; CMG 2004; MBE 1988; DL; Adjutant General, 2005–08; *b* 29 June 1951; *m* Jane; one *s* one *d.* Commnd RA, 1972; served in Germany and UK; psc 1983; Comdr, Gun Battery, 3rd Regt, RHA, 1984–85; COS, 1st Infantry Bde, UK Mobile Force, 1986; Staff Coll. Directing Staff, Camberley, 1988; Comdr, 3 RHA, Germany, 1989; 19 Infantry Bde, Colchester, 1990; Central Staff Directorate of Defence Policy, MoD, 1991–93; Defence Costs Study Secretariat, MoD, 1993; Comdr Artillery, 3rd UK Div., 1994; hcsc; Dir of Manning (Army), 1997; Comdr, Multi-Nat. Div. (SW), Stabilisation Force, Bosnia Herzegovina, 1999–2000; COS, HQ Land Comd, 2000–03; Dep. Comdg Gen., Combined Jt Task Force 7, and Sen. British Mil. Rep., Iraq, 2003; Mil. Sec. and Chief Exec., Army Personnel Centre, 2003–05. DL Hants, 2008. *Address:* HQ AG Command, Trenchard Lines, Upavon, Pewsey, Wilts SN9 6BE.

VIGGERS, Sir Peter (John), Kt 2008; MP (C) Gosport, since Feb. 1974; *b* 13 March 1938; *s* of late J. S. Viggers and E. F. Viggers (later Mrs V. E. J. Neal), Gosport; *m* 1968, Jennifer Mary McMillan, MB, BS, LRCP, MRCS, DA, *d* of late Dr R. B. McMillan, MD, FRCP, Guildford, and late Mrs J. T. C. McMillan, MA, MIB; two *s* one *d. Educ:* Portsmouth Grammar Sch.; Trinity Hall, Cambridge (MA 1961). Chm., Cambridge Univ. Cons. Assoc., 1960. Solicitor 1967. Royal Canadian Air Force (pilot), 1956–58; commnd 457 (Wessex) Regt, RA (TA), 1963. PPS to Solicitor-General, 1979–83, to Chief Sec. of HM Treasury, 1983–85; Parly Under-Sec. of State (Industry Minister), NI Office, 1986–89. Chm., Select Cttee on Armed Forces Bill, 1986, 1996; Member: Select Cttee on Members' Interests, 1991–93; Select Cttee on Defence, 1992–97, 2000–01, 2003–05 (Vice-Chm., 2000–01, 2003–05); Exec., British-American Parly Gp, 2000– (Jt Treas., 2003–); Vice-Chm., British-Japanese Parly Gp, 1999– (Chm., 1992–99); UK Delegate: Jt IPU and UN Conf. on Conventional Disarmament, Mexico City, 1985; N Atlantic Assembly, 1981–86, 1992– (Vice-Chm., Political Cttee, 1995–97; Chm., 2000–04). Chm. and dir of public and private cos, 1972–. Underwriting Member of Lloyd's (Council Mem., 1992–96); Chm. Trustees, Lloyd's Pension Fund, 1996–. Mem., Management Cttee, RNLI, 1979–89, Vice-Pres., 1989–. Dir and Trustee, HMS Warrior 1860, 1995–2004. *Recreations:* opera, travel, trees. *Address:* House of Commons, SW1A 0AA. *Clubs:* Boodle's, House of Commons Yacht (Cdre, 1984–85; Adm., 1997–); Gosport Conservative (Pres.).

VIGNOLES, Roger Hutton, ARCM; pianoforte accompanist; *b* 12 July 1945; *s* of late Keith Hutton Vignoles and of Phyllis Mary (*née* Pearson); *m* 1st, 1972, Teresa Ann Elizabeth Henderson (marr. diss. 1982); 2nd, 1982, Jessica Virginia, *d* of late Prof. Boris Ford; one *s* one *d. Educ:* Canterbury Cathedral Choir Sch.; Sedbergh Sch.; Magdalene Coll., Cambridge (BA, BMus); Royal College of Music, London (ARCM). Accompanist of internat. reputation, regularly appearing with the most distinguished internat. singers and instrumentalists (Sir Thomas Allen, Dame Kiri te Kanawa, Dame Felicity Lott, Sarah Walker, etc.), both in London and provinces and at major music festivals (*eg* Aldeburgh, Cheltenham, Edinburgh, Brighton, Bath, Salzburg, Prague, etc.) and broadcasting for BBC Radio 3 and television. International tours incl. USA, Canada, Australia-New Zealand, Hong Kong, Scandinavia, and recitals at Opera Houses of Cologne, Brussels, Frankfurt, Lincoln Center, NY, San Francisco, Tokyo, Carnegie Hall, NY, Venice, Paris, Munich, Berlin, etc. Repetiteur: Royal Opera House, Covent Garden, 1969–71; English Opera Group, 1968–74; Australian Opera Company, 1976. Professor of Accompaniment, 1974–81, Prince Consort Prof. of Piano Accompaniment, 1996–, RCM; Consultant Prof. of Accompaniment, RAM, 1989–. Masterclasses for singers and pianists in Aarhus, Amsterdam, Barcelona, Copenhagen, Stockholm, Vienna, Toronto, Montreal, Ravinia Fest., Santa Fe Opera, Britten-Pears Sch., Snape. Extensive discography of vocal and chamber music. Hon. RAM 1984; Hon. FRCM 1997. *Recreations:* drawing, painting, looking at pictures, swimming, sailing. *Address:* 130 Mercers Road, N19 4PU. *T:* (020) 7272 5325, *Fax:* (020) 7281 1840.

VILAR, Alberto; Founder and President, Amerindo Investment Advisors, 1980–2005; *b* New Jersey, USA, 4 Oct. 1940; *m* 1st (marr. diss.); 2nd, 2002, Karen Painter. *Educ:* schs in Cuba and Puerto Rico; Washington and Jefferson Coll., Penn. Internat. credit officer, Citibank; portfolio manager and analyst, Burnham & Co., 1967. Founder, Amerindo Technology, 1996. Philanthropist; has made donations to opera houses worldwide and funded educnl projects in music and the arts.

VILE, Prof. Maurice John Crawley; Professor Emeritus of Political Science, University of Kent at Canterbury; *b* 23 July 1927; *s* of Edward M. and Elsie M. Vile; two *s. Educ:* London Sch. of Economics (BSc (Econ) 1951); PhD London, 1954; MA Oxford, 1962. FRHistS 1989. Lectr in Politics, Univ. of Exeter, 1954–62; Fellow of Nuffield Coll., Oxford, 1962–65; Lectr in Politics, Magdalen Coll., Oxford, 1963–64; University of Kent: Reader in Politics and Govt, 1965–68; Prof. of Political Sci., 1968–84; Dir of Internat. Progs, 1984–87; Dean of Faculty of Social Scis, 1969–75; Pro-Vice-Chancellor, 1975–81; Dep. Vice-Chancellor, 1981–84; Dir of British Progs, Boston Univ., 1989–94; Dir of Res., Canterbury Christ Church Coll., 1994–99. Visiting Professor: Univ. of Massachusetts, 1960; Smith College, Mass., 1961. Royer Lectr, Univ. of Calif., Berkeley, 1974. Hon. Fellow, Canterbury Christ Church UC, 2003. Hon. DCL Kent, 1993. *Publications:* The Structure of American Federalism, 1961; Constitutionalism and the Separation of Powers, 1967, 2nd edn 1998; Politics in the USA, 1970, 6th edn 2007; Federalism in the United States, Canada and Australia (Res. Paper No 2, Commn on the Constitution), 1973; The Presidency (Amer. Hist. Documents Vol. IV), 1974.

VILIKOVSKÝ, Ján, PhD; Head: Slovak Centre for Literary Translation, 1997–2002; Centre for Information on Literature, 2001–02; Dean, Philological Faculty, Matej Bel University, Banská Bystrica, 2001–04; *b* 13 July 1937; *s* of late Prof. Ján Vilikovský and Dr Júlia Vilikovská (*née* Bárdošová); *m* 1st, 1962, Božica Štúrová (*d* 1985); two *d*; 2nd, 1992, Mária Horváthová. *Educ:* Comenius Univ., Bratislava (BA 1959; MA 1975; PhD 1982). Editor, Slovak Writers' Publishing House, 1959–70; Asst Prof., Inst. of Translators, 1970–74; Asst Prof., Dept of English and American Studies, Comenius Univ., 1974–90; Sec.-Gen., Slovak Translators' Assoc., 1986–90; Dir, Tatran Publishers, 1990–92; Ministry of Foreign Affairs, 1992–96; Ambassador of Czechoslovakia, 1992; Ambassador of Slovak Republic to UK, 1993–96. Asst Gen. Sec., RECIT (European Network of International Centres of Literary Translators), 2000–04. Hon. Dr Constantine the Philosopher Univ., Nitra, 2007. Ján Hollý Prize for Translation, 1969, 1980, 2003. *Publications:* Slovak-English Dictionary, 1959, 5th edn 1992; Preklad ako tvorba (Translation as a creative process), 1984; contribs to learned jls; translations from English and American literature. *Recreations:* classical music, reading, talking. *Address:* Záložická 7, 821 01 Bratislava, Slovakia.

VILJOEN, His Honour (Theo) Leon; a Circuit Judge, 1992–2007; *b* 25 Aug. 1937; *s* of Robert Bartlett Viljoen and Cecilia Jacoba Viljoen (*née* van der Walt); *m* 1967, Dorothy Nina Raybould, *d* of late Prof. S. G. Raybould; two *d. Educ:* Afrikaanse Hoër Seunskool; Univ. of Pretoria. Called to the Bar, Middle Temple, 1972; a Recorder, 1991–92. Legal Assessor, UKCC, 1987–92. Mem., 1997–2003, 2005–, Appraiser, 2004–, Parole Bd. Mem., Mediterranean Garden Soc. *Recreations:* walking, gardening, wine. *Address:* c/o 2 Harcourt Buildings, Temple, EC4Y 9DB. *T:* (020) 7583 9020.

VILLAGE, Peter Malcolm; QC 2002; *b* 3 Feb. 1961; *s* of late Malcolm Rowland Village and of Margaret Village (now Millar); *m* 1992, Alison Helen Wallis; one *s* two *d. Educ:* Repton Sch.; Univ. of Leeds (LLB Hons). Called to the Bar, Inner Temple, 1983, NI, 1997; barrister specialising in planning, compulsory purchase and judicial review, 1985–. Gov., Repton Sch., 1998–. *Recreations:* salmon fishing, shooting, ski-ing, walking the dog. *Address:* 4–5 Gray's Inn Square, Gray's Inn, WC1R 5AH. *T:* (020) 7404 5252, *Fax:* (020) 7242 7803; *e-mail:* pvillage@4-5.co.uk. *Club:* Brooks's.

VILLIERS; *see* Child Villiers, family name of Earl of Jersey.

VILLIERS; *see* de Villiers.

VILLIERS, family name of **Earl of Clarendon.**

VILLIERS, Charles Nigel, FCA; Deputy Chairman, Abbey National plc, 1999–2001; *b* 25 Jan. 1941; *s* of Robert Alexander and Elizabeth Mary Villiers; *m* 1970, Sally Priscilla Magnay; one *s* one *d. Educ:* Winchester Coll.; New Coll., Oxford (MA German and Russian). Arthur Andersen & Co., 1963–67; ICFC, 1967–72; County Bank Ltd, 1972–86; Dir, 1974; Dep. Chief Exec., 1977; Chm. and Chief Exec., 1984–85; Exec. Chm., 1985–86; Exec. Dir, National Westminster Bank, 1985–88; Chief Exec., NatWest Investment Bank Ltd (estab. June 1986 incorporating the business of County Bank Ltd), 1986–88; Chm., County NatWest Ltd, 1986–88; Man. Dir of Corporate Develt, then Abbey Nat. Building Soc.), Abbey National plc, 1988–99. Non-exec. Dir, DTZ Hldgs, 1997–2004. Treas., E Thames Housing Gp, 2001–08. *Recreations:* opera, ski-ing, European history, tennis. *Club:* Reform.

VILLIERS, Theresa Anne; MP (C) Chipping Barnet, since 2005; *b* 5 March 1968; *d* of George and Virginia Villiers; *m* 1999, Sean Wilken. *Educ:* Univ. of Bristol (LLB Hons 1990); Jesus Coll., Oxford (BCL Hons 1991). Called to the Bar, Inner Temple, 1992; Barrister specialising in chancery, insolvency and entertainment law, 1994–95; Lectr in Law, King's Coll., London, 1995–99. MEP (C) London Region, 1999–2005. Treas. and economic spokesman, 1999–2004, Dep. Leader, 2001–02, Cons. delegn to EP; EP Rapporteur for Investment Services Directive, 2002–05. Shadow Chief Sec. to HM Treasury, 2005–07; Shadow Sec. of State for Transport, 2007–. *Publications:* (with Sean Wilken) Waiver, Variation and Estoppel, 1998; Tax Harmonisation: the impending threat, 2001; various articles in legal jls, incl. Lloyd's Maritime and Commercial Law Qly. *Address:* House of Commons, SW1A 0AA. *Club:* Middlesex CC.

VINCENT, family name of **Baron Vincent of Coleshill.**

VINCENT OF COLESHILL, Baron *cr* 1996 (Life Peer), of Shrivenham, in the County of Oxfordshire; **Field Marshal Richard Frederick Vincent,** GBE 1990; KCB 1984; DSO 1972; FIMechE; FRAeS; *b* 23 Aug. 1931; *s* of late Frederick Vincent and Frances Elizabeth (*née* Coleshill); *m* 1955, Jean Paterson, *d* of Kenneth Stewart and Jane (*née* Banks); one *s* one *d* (and one *s* decd). *Educ:* Aldenham Sch.; RMCS. Commnd RA, National Service, 1951; Germany, 1951–55; Gunnery Staff, 1959; Radar Res. Estabt, Malvern, 1960–61; BAOR, 1962; Technical Staff Training, 1963–64; Staff Coll., 1965; Commonwealth Bde, Malaysia, 1966–68; MoD, 1968–70; Comd 12th Light Air Def. Regt, Germany, UK and NI, 1970–72; Instr, Staff Coll., 1972–73; Greenlands Staff Coll., Henley, 1974; Mil. Dir of Studies, RMCS, 1974–75; Comd 19 Airportable Bde, 1975–77; RCDS, 1978; Dep. Mil. Sec., 1979–80; Comdt, Royal Military College of Science, 1980–83; Master-Gen. of the Ordnance, MoD, 1983–87; VCDS, 1987–91; CDS,

1991–92; Chm. of Mil. Cttee, NATO, 1993–96. Master Gunner, St James's Park, 1996–2000. Dir, 1996–2001, Chm., 1998–2001, Hunting Engrg Ltd; Chairman: Hunting Defence Ltd, 1996–2003; Hunting Brae, 1997–2003; non-executive Director: Vickers Defence Systems Ltd, 1997–2002; INSYS Ltd, 2001–05. Mem., Commn on Britain and Europe, RIIA, 1996. Col Commandant: REME, 1981–87; RA, 1983–2000; Hon. Colonel: 100 (Yeomanry) Field Regt RA, TA, 1982–91; 12th Air Defence Regt, 1987–91. Vice Pres., Forces' (formerly Officers') Pension Soc., 1997–2005. President: Combined Services Winter Sports Assoc., 1983–90; Army Ski-ing Assoc., 1983–87. Patron, Nat. Service Veterans Assoc., 2007–. Kermit Roosevelt Lectr, 1988; Vis. Fellow, Australian Coll. of Defence and Strategic Studies, 1995–99. Vice-Pres., 1996–2000, Pres., 2000–05, Defence Manufacturers Assoc. Chancellor, Cranfield Univ., 1998–; Member: Court, Cranfield Inst. of Technol., 1981–83; Court, Greenwich Univ., 1997–2001; Adv. Council, RMCS, 1983–91; Governor: Aldenham Sch., 1987–; Imperial Coll., London (formerly ICSTM), 1995–2004 (Chm., 1996–2004; Fellow, 1996). Freeman: City of London, 1992; Wheelwrights' Co., 1997; Mem., Guild of Freemen, 1992. FRAeS 1990; FIMechE 1990. Hon. DSc Cranfield, 1985. Order of Merit (1st cl.) (Jordan), 1991; Commander, Legion of Merit (USA), 1993. *Publications:* contrib. mil. jls and pubns. *Recreation:* seven grandchildren. *Address:* c/o House of Lords, SW1A 0PW.

VINCENT, Anthony Lionel; Legal Adviser, Department of Foreign Affairs and Trade, Canberra, 1993–97; *b* 18 Oct. 1933; *s* of Harold Francis Vincent and Lesley Allison Vincent; *m* 1958, Helen Frances Beasley; one *s* one *d. Educ:* Univ. of Western Australia, Perth (LLB); Univ. of Oxford (BCL). Joined Dept of Foreign Affairs, Aust., 1958; served: Karachi, 1959–61; Hong Kong, 1963–66; Singapore, 1966–69; Belgrade, 1972–74; Paris, 1977–80; Australian Ambassador to: Iraq, 1981–83; GDR, 1984; Dep. High Comr in London, 1984–87; Asst Sec., Treaties and Sea Law Br., 1987–89, Intelligence and Defence Br., 1989–90, Dept of Foreign Affairs and Trade, Canberra; Ambassador to Czech and Slovak Federal Republic, subseq. to Czech and Slovak Republics, 1990–93. *Recreations:* drawing, painting, reading. *Address:* 56 Blackwall Reach Parade, Bicton, WA 6157, Australia.

VINCENT, Catherine Beatrice Margaret, (Katie); *see* Derham, C. B. M.

VINCENT, Prof. Colin Angus, OBE 2003; Professor of Electrochemistry, 1989–2003, Master of the United College, 1996–2003 and Deputy Principal, 2001–03, University of St Andrews; *b* 4 March 1938; *s* of Harold Frederick Vincent and Helen McEachern Vincent; *m* 1964, Doris Susan Cole; one *s* one *d. Educ:* Oban High Sch.; Univ. of Glasgow (BSc; PhD; DSc). MIEE; CChem, FRSC 1976; FRSE 1992. Assistant, Univ. of Glasgow, 1963–65; Lectr, Univ. of Illinois, 1965–67; University of St Andrews: Lectr, 1967–76; Sen. Lectr; 1976–84; Reader, 1984–89; Head, School of Chemistry, 1990–97; Vice-Principal, 1996–2001; Vice-Chancellor and Acting Principal, 2000. Hon. LLD St Andrews, 2003. Galvani Medal, Italian Chem. Soc., 1998. *Publications:* (jtly) Alkali Metal, Alkaline Earth Metal and Ammonium Halides in Amide Solvents, 1980; Modern Batteries, 1984, 2nd edn 1997; Polymer Electrolyte Reviews, vol. 1, 1987, vol. 2, 1989; more than 120 papers in learned jls. *Recreations:* squash, hill walking, opera. *Address:* 1 Station Brae, Newport-on-Tay, Fife DD6 8DQ. *T:* (01382) 543156.

VINCENT, Prof. Ewart Albert; Professor of Geology, and Fellow of University College, Oxford, 1967–86, now Emeritus; *b* 23 Aug. 1919; *o s* of Albert and Winifred Vincent, Aylesbury; *m* 1944, Myrtle Ablett (*d* 2004); two *d. Educ:* Reading Sch.; Univ. of Reading. BSc (Reading) 1940; PhD 1951; MA (Oxon) 1952; MSc (Manch.) 1966. FGS. Chemist, Min. of Supply, 1940–45; Geologist, Anglo-Iranian Oil Co., 1945–46; Lectr in Mineralogy and Crystallography, Univ. of Durham, 1946–51; Lectr in Geology, Oxford Univ., 1951–56; Reader in Mineralogy, Oxford Univ., 1956–62; Prof. of Geology, Manchester Univ., 1962–66. Visiting Professor: Univ. of Kuwait, 1970; Washington and Lee Univ., Va, 1980. Mem. NERC, 1975–78. Vice-Pres., Internat. Assoc. of Volcanology, 1968–71; Pres., Mineralogical Soc. of GB, 1974–76; Mem. Council, Geol Soc., 1973–76. Fellow, Mineralogical Soc. of Amer. Hon. Corresp. Mem., Soc. Géol. de Belgique. Awarded Wollaston Fund, Geol Soc. London, 1961. *Publications:* scientific papers in learned jls. *Recreations:* music, photography. *Address:* 2 Linch Farm, Wytham, Oxford OX2 8QP. *T:* (01865) 723170; Department of Earth Sciences, Parks Road, Oxford OX1 3PR. *T:* (01865) 272000.

VINCENT, Rev. Irvin James; Supernumerary Minister, Taunton Methodist Church, since 1999; *b* 22 July 1932; *s* of Amy Mary Catharine Vincent (*née* Nye) and Vince Thomas Vincent; *m* 1959, Stella Margaret (*née* Chaplin); one *s* two *d. Educ:* Mitcham Grammar School; Didsbury College (Methodist), Bristol. BA Open Univ. Accountancy, 1948; National Service, RAF, 1950–52; Local Govt, 1952–55; theological training, 1955–59; Methodist Circuit, Stonehouse and Dursley, 1959–61; entered RN as Chaplain, 1961; Malta, 1968–72; exchange with USN, 1976–78; Principal Chaplain, Church of Scotland and Free Churches (Navy), 1984–86; QHC, 1984–86; Minister, Temple Methodist Church, Taunton, 1986–97; Hon. Associate Minister, Westminster Central Hall, 1997–99. *Recreations:* all sport, reading, family. *Address:* 60 Queen's Drive, Sherford Brook, Taunton, Som TA1 4XD.

VINCENT, Rev. Dr John James; writer and lecturer; Methodist Minister, Sheffield Inner City Ecumenical Mission (Superintendent, 1970–97); Director, Urban Theology Unit, 1969–97, Director Emeritus, since 1997; President of the Methodist Conference, 1989–90; *b* 29 Dec. 1929; *s* of late David Vincent and Ethel Beatrice Vincent (*née* Gadd); *m* 1958, Grace Johnston, *d* of late Rev. Wilfred Stafford, Bangor, Co. Down; two *s* one *d. Educ:* Manchester Grammar Sch.; Richmond Coll.; London Univ. (BD 1954); Drew Univ., USA (STM 1955); Basel Univ., Switzerland (DTheol 1960). Sgt, RAMC, 1948–49. Minister, Manchester and Salford Mission, 1956–62; Supt, Rochdale Mission, 1962–69; Founder and Leader, The Ashram Community, 1967–. Visiting Professor of Theology: Boston Univ., and New York Theol Seminary, 1969–70; Drew Univ., 1977; Adjunct Prof. of Theol., New York Theol Seminary, 1979–88. Hon. Lectr in Biblical Studies, 1990–; supervisor, doctoral prog. in Contextual, Urban and Liberation Theologies, 1993–, Sheffield Univ.; Hon. Lectr in Theol. and doctoral supervisor, Birmingham Univ., 2003–. Chairman: NW Campaign for Nuclear Disarmament, 1957–63; Alliance of Radical Methodists, 1970–76; Urban Mission Trng Assoc., 1982–90; Trustee Savings Bank Depositors Assoc. (also litigant in High Court and H of L, TSB *v* Vincent), 1986; Jt Co-ordinator, British Liberation Theol. Inst., 1990–; Co-Chair, Urban Theologians Internat., 1993–; Member: Studiorum Novi Testamenti Societas, 1961–; Council, Christian Orgns for Social, Political and Econ. Change, 1981–91; Exec., Assoc. of Centres of Adult Theol. Educn, 1984–90. Fellow, St Deiniol's Library, Hawarden, 2003. Jt Ed., British Liberation Theology series, 1995, 1997, 1999, 2001. Centenary Achievement Award, Sheffield Univ., 2005. *Publications:* Christ in a Nuclear World, 1962; Christian Nuclear Perspective, 1964; Christ and Methodism, 1965; Here I Stand, 1967; Secular Christ, 1968; The Race Race, 1970; The Jesus Thing, 1973; Stirrings: essays Christian and Radical, 1975; Alternative Church, 1976; Disciple and Lord: discipleship in the Synoptic Gospels, 1976; Starting All Over Again, 1981; Into the City, 1982; OK, Let's Be Methodists, 1984; Radical Jesus, 1986, 2nd edn 2004; Mark at Work, 1986; Britain in the Nineties, 1989; Discipleship in the Nineties, 1991; A Petition of Distress from the Cities (to the Queen and Govt), 1993; (ed jtly) The Cities: Methodist report, 1997; Hope from the City, 2000; (ed jtly) Bible and Practice, 2001; (ed jtly) Methodist and Radical, 2003; (ed) Faithfulness in the City, 2003; (ed) Mark: gospel of action, 2006; (ed) Primitive Christianity, 2007; *relevant publication:* Urban Christ: responses to John Vincent, ed I. K. Duffield, 1997. *Recreations:* jogging, writing. *Address:* 178 Abbeyfield Road, Sheffield S4 7AY. *T:* (0114) 243 6688, *T:* and *Fax:* (Urban Theology Unit) (0114) 243 5342; *e-mail:* john@utu.sheffield.fsnet.co.uk.

VINCENT, Prof. John Russell; Professor of History, University of Bristol, 1984–2002, now Emeritus Professor; *b* 20 Dec. 1937; *s* of late Prof. J. J. Vincent and M. Monica Vincent, MSc, PhD (*née* Watson); *m* 1972, Nicolette Elizabeth Kenworthy; one *s* (and one *s* decd). *Educ:* Bedales Sch.; Christ's Coll., Cambridge. Fellow, Peterhouse, Cambridge, 1962–70; Lectr in Modern British History, Cambridge Univ., 1967–70; Prof. of Modern History, Univ. of Bristol, 1970–84. Vis. Prof., UEA, 2003–. Chm., Bristol Br., NCCL, 1972–74. *Publications:* The Formation of the Liberal Party, 1966 (2nd edn as The Formation of the British Liberal Party 1857–68, 1980); Poll Books: How Victorians voted, 1967; (ed with A. B. Cooke) Lord Carlingford's Journal, 1971; (ed with M. Stenton) McCalmont's Parliamentary Poll Book 1832–1918, 1971; (with A. B. Cooke) The Governing Passion: Cabinet Government and party politics in Britain 1885–86, 1974; (ed) Disraeli, Derby and the Conservative Party: the political journals of Lord Stanley 1849–69, 1978; Gladstone and Ireland (Raleigh Lecture), 1979; (ed) The Crawford Papers: the journals of David Lindsay, Twenty-Seventh Earl of Crawford and Tenth Earl of Balcarres during the years 1892 to 1940, 1984; Disraeli, 1990; (ed) The Derby Diaries 1869–1878, 1995; (contrib.) Twentieth-Century Britain: an encyclopaedia, 1995; An Intelligent Person's Guide to History, 1995; (contrib.) Why Tory Governments Fall, 1996; (ed) The Derby Diaries 1878–1893, 2003. *Recreation:* journalism. *Address:* University of Bristol, Senate House, Bristol BS8 1TH.

VINCENT, Matthew Philip Jude; Editor, Personal Finance, Financial Times, since 2007; *b* 28 Oct. 1966; *s* of Dudley Joseph and Claire Vincent. *Educ:* Salvatorian Coll., Harrow Weald; Univ. of Manchester (BA Hons English Lang. and Lit.). Prodn asst, BBC TV, 1988–89; staff writer: Stately Homes and Gardens mag., 1989–90; Money mag., 1990; Moneywise magazine: staff writer, 1990–92; Chief Sub-ed./Associate Ed., 1992–95; Ed., 1995–2000; Hd of Content, Investors Chronicle Online and FT Business, 2000–02; Editor: Investors Chronicle, 2002–07; FT Business, 2002. BBC TV: reporter, Short Change, 1994; presenter, Pound For Pound, 1998. *Publications:* contrib. articles to various financial jls. *Recreations:* poetry, cricket, sherry. *Address:* 96 Speed House, Barbican, EC2Y 8AU. *Club:* Blackheath Cricket.

VINCENT, Prof. Nigel Bruce, FBA 2006; Mont Follick Professor of Comparative Philology, University of Manchester, since 1987; *b* 24 Sept. 1947; *s* of Denis George Vincent and Peggy Eliza Vincent; *m* 1st, 1971, Janet Elizabeth Hutchinson (marr. diss. 1999); two *d*; 2nd, 1999, Merethe Damsgård Sørensen; one *d. Educ:* Sexey's Sch., Bruton; Trinity Hall, Cambridge (BA 1st cl. hons Mod. and Medieval Langs 1970); Darwin Coll., Cambridge (Dip. Linguistics 1971). Lecturer: Birkbeck Coll., London, 1973–74; Univ. of Lancaster, 1974–76; Univ. of Hull, 1976–81; Univ. of Cambridge, 1981–87 (Fellow, Trinity Hall, 1983–87); University of Manchester: Res. and Graduate Dean of Arts, 1992–96; Associate Dean, Postgrad. Res. in Humanities, 2004–06; Associate Vice-Pres., Graduate Educn, 2006–. British Acad. Res. Reader, 1996–98. Visiting Professor: Univ. of Pavia, 1983; Univ. of Rome, 1986; Ecole Pratique des Hautes Etudes, Paris, 1993; Australian Linguistic Inst., La Trobe Univ., 1994; Univ. of Copenhagen, 1997; Melbourne Univ., 2000; Erskine Fellow, Univ. of Canterbury, NZ, 2000. Member: Res. Grants Bd, ESRC, 1988–91; Council, Philological Soc., 1982–86, 1989–94, 1995–99 (Pres., 2000–03); Res. Gp Leader, EUROTYP Project, ESF, 1990–94; Humanities Res. Bd, 1994–96; Chm., Res. Assessment Panels, HEFCE, 1992, 1996, 2005–. Vice Pres., Società di Linguistica Italiana, 1990–92; Pres., Internat. Soc. of Historical Linguistics, 1993–95. Mem. Bd, British Inst. in Paris, 1999–2002. Editor, Jl of Linguistics, 1984–93. *Publications:* (jtly) Studies in the Romance Verb, 1982; (jtly) The Romance Languages, 1988; (jtly) Parameters of Morphosyntactic Change, 1997; articles in jls. *Recreations:* wine, all things Italian. *Address:* School of Languages, Linguistics and Cultures, University of Manchester, Manchester M13 9PL. *T:* (0161) 275 3194; 48–50 Lower Lane, Chinley, High Peak SK23 6BD. *T:* (01663) 750943; *e-mail:* nigel.vincent@manchester.ac.uk.

VINCENT, Robert Warden; Chief Executive, Kirklees Metropolitan Council, since 2004; *b* 27 Sept. 1951; *s* of Stanley and Joan Vincent; *m* 1974, Heather Hitchen; two *s* two *d. Educ:* King's Coll., Wimbledon; Univ. of Liverpool (BEng 1973; MCD 1975). MRTPI 1977. Town planning and policy posts, Dorset CC, 1973–78 and Tameside MBC, 1978–87; Kirklees Metropolitan Council: Asst Dir of Educn, 1987–90; Hd of Resources, 1990–94; Chief Educn Officer, 1994–98; Exec. Dir and Dep. Chief Exec., 1998–2004. Non-exec. Dir, DCLG. *Recreation:* looking at buildings. *Address:* Kirklees Metropolitan Council, Civic Centre, Huddersfield HD1 1WG. *T:* (01484) 226600; *e-mail:* Rob.Vincent@kirklees.gov.uk.

VINCENT, Robin Anthony, CMG 2006; CBE 2001; senior consultant, international criminal and transitional justice issues, since 2005; Assistant Secretary General, United Nations (Registrar of Special Court for Sierra Leone), 2002–05; *b* 27 Feb. 1944; *s* of late John Kenneth Vincent and of Ivy Elizabeth Ann Vincent (*née* Grayer); *m* 1971, Hazel Ruth Perkins; two *s. Educ:* King's Sch., Worcester. Clerk, Worcs QS, 1962–70; Sen. Asst and Dep. Clerk, Worcs County Justices, 1970–72; Higher Executive Officer: Worcester Crown Court, 1972–76; Worcs County Court, 1976–77; Court Business Officer, 1977–79; Sen. Exec. Officer (Personnel), Circuit Administrator's Office, Birmingham, 1979–80; Chief Clerk, Worcester Crown Court, 1980–82; Principal Chief Clerk, Manchester Crown Court, 1982–86; Head of Division, Lord Chancellor's Department: Court Service Devlt, London, 1986–91; Personnel Mgt, 1991–93; Judicial Appts, 1993; Circuit Administrator, Northern Circuit, LCD, then Court Service Agency, 1993–2001; Internat. Court Mgt Consultant, UN and British Council, 2001–02. *Recreations:* cricket (playing), music, drinking red wine with Steve Baines. *Address:* The Moorings, 33 Grange Road, Bramhall, Stockport, Cheshire SK7 3BD. *T:* (0161) 440 9526. *Clubs:* Old Vigornians (Worcester); Eggington Cricket (Leighton Buzzard); Stockport Georgians (Stockport).

VINCENT, Sir William (Percy Maxwell), 3rd Bt *cr* 1936; Managing Director, Cambridge Associates Ltd, since 1995; *b* 1 Feb. 1945; *o s* of Sir Lacey Vincent, 2nd Bt, and Helen Millicent, *d* of Field Marshal Sir William Robert Robertson, 1st Bt, GCB, GCMG, GCVO, DSO; *S* father, 1963; *m* 1976, Christine Margaret, *d* of Rev. E. G. Walton; three *s. Educ:* Eton College. 2nd Lieutenant, Irish Guards, 1964–67. Director: Save and Prosper Investment Mgt, 1980–85; Touche Remnant & Co., 1985–92; M & G (N America) Ltd, 1992–95. *Recreations:* water ski-ing, sailing. *Heir: s* Edward Mark William Vincent, *b* 6 March 1978. *Address:* Thieves Lane Barn, Thieves Lane, near Clanfield, Hants PO8 0PY.

VINE, David Martin; broadcaster and promotions consultant, since 1960; Presenter, ESPN, since 2006; *b* 3 Jan. 1935; *s* of Dorothy and Harold Vine; *m* Mandy; two *s* two *d.*

Educ: Barnstaple Grammar Sch. Journalist: North Devon Journal-Herald, 1953; Western Morning News, 1956; Westward Television, 1960; presenter, 1965–2001, consultant, 2001–06, BBC TV; programmes include: The Superstars, Question of Sport, Wimbledon, Horse of Year Show, World Snooker Championships, 1976–2000, Ski Sunday, 1977–97, fourteen Summer and Winter Olympic Games, Miss World, Eurovision Song Contest, Jeux Sans Frontières. *Publication:* The Superstars, 1984. *Recreation:* relaxing.

VINE, Prof. Frederick John, FRS 1974; Emeritus Professor, School of Environmental Sciences, University of East Anglia, since 2004 (Professor, 1974–98; Professorial Fellow, 1998–2004); *b* 17 June 1939; *s* of Frederick Royston Vine and Ivy Grace Vine (*née* Bryant); *m* 1964, Susan Alice McCall; one *s* one *d*. *Educ:* Latymer Upper Sch., Hammersmith; St John's Coll., Cambridge (BA, PhD). Instructor, 1965–67, and Asst Professor, 1967–70, Dept of Geological and Geophysical Sciences, Princeton Univ., NJ, USA; Reader, 1970–74, Dean, 1977–80 and 1993–98, School of Environmental Sciences, UEA. *Publications:* (jtly) Global Tectonics, 1990, 3rd edn 2008; articles in Nature, Science, Phil. Trans Roy. Soc. London, etc. *Recreations:* walking, travel.

VINE, Jeremy; Presenter: Jeremy Vine Show, BBC Radio Two, since 2003; Panorama, BBC1, since 2007; *b* 17 May 1965; *s* of Dr Guy and Diana Vine; *m* 2002, Rachel Schofield; one *d*. *Educ:* Epsom Coll.; Durham Univ. (BA Hons English Lit. 1986). Coventry Evening Telegraph, 1986–87; joined BBC, 1987: News Trainee, 1987–89; Programme Reporter, Today, 1989–93; Political Corresp., 1993–97; Africa Corresp., 1997–99; Presenter: Newsnight, 1996–2002, full-time, 1999–2002; Politics Show, BBC TV, 2003–05. *Address:* c/o BBC Radio 2, Western House, W1A 1AA. *T:* (020) 7765 2129. *Clubs:* Reform, Soho House; Chelsea Football.

VINE, Roy; Vice-Chairman, Barclays Bank UK Ltd, 1982–84; *b* 1923; *m* 1945, Dorothy A. Yates; one *s* one *d*. *Educ:* Taunton's Sch., Southampton. Served RAF (Flt Lieut), 1942–46 and 1951–53. Dir, Barclays Bank plc, 1979–84 (Gen. Man., 1972; Senior Gen. Man., 1979–81). Director: First Nat. Finance Corp. plc, 1984–93; First Nat. Bank Plc (formerly First Nat. Securities Ltd), 1985–90; First Nat. Commercial Bank Ltd, 1990–93. FCIB 1951. *Recreations:* golf, football, music. *Address:* Summerfold, Itchen Abbas, Winchester SO21 1AX.

VINEALL, Sir Anthony (John Patrick), Kt 2002; Chairman, School Teachers' Review Body, 1996–2002; *b* 17 March 1932; *s* of George John Charles Vineall and Helen Fairley Vineall (*née* Bradshaw); *m* 1962, Dorothy Earnshaw; two *s*. *Educ:* Leeds Grammar Sch.; New Coll., Oxford (MA PPE). FCIPD (FIPD 1982). Nat. Service, commnd RA, 1951. Unilever: personnel posts in Animal Foods, Frozen Food, and in Ghana, 1955–67; Co. Personnel Manager, Walls Meat, 1967–70; Personnel Dir, SSC&B Lintas, 1970–75; Dir, Unilever UK Hldgs and Nat. Personnel Manager, 1975–81; Head of Corporate Mgt Develt, 1981–92. Chm., Tavistock and Portman NHS Trust, 1993–99. Member: Council, Foundn for Mgt Educn, 1976–92; Doctors' and Dentists' Pay Review Body, 1990–93; Review of Armed Forces Career and Rank Structure, 1994–95; Chairman: Exec. Cttee, Industrial Soc., 1982–85; Careers Res. Adv. Centre, 1991–96 (Mem. Council, 1981–); Vice Pres., Centre for Internat. Briefing, Farnham Castle, 1996– (Chm. Govs, 1987–96). Vice Chm. of Govs, Guildford Royal Grammar Sch., 2004–08 (Gov., 1994–). *Recreations:* gardening, travel, bridge. *Address:* Ways End, 34 Abbotswood, Guildford GU1 1UZ.
See also N. E. J. Vineall.

VINEALL, Nicholas Edward John; QC 2006; *b* 1 May 1963; *s* of Sir Anthony John Patrick Vineall, *qv*; *m* 1992, Kate Jenkins; two *s* one *d*. *Educ:* Royal Grammar Sch., Guildford; Christ's Coll., Cambridge (BA Natural Sci. 1985); Univ. of Pittsburgh (MA Hist. and Philosophy of Sci.); City Univ. (Dip. Law). Harkness Fellow, Univ. of Pittsburgh, 1985–86. Called to the Bar, Middle Temple, 1988; in practice as barrister specialising in commercial and construction law. Mem., Council of Legal Educn, 1990–96. Member: Bar Council, 1990–96 (Chm., Young Bar, 1994); Exec. Cttee, Soc. of Cons. Lawyers, 1999–2007 (Chm., Res., 2003–05). Mem. (C) Southwark LBC, 2006– (Chm., Dulwich Community Council, 2006–). Chm., Dulwich and W Norwood Cons. Assoc., 2000. Contested (C) Dulwich and W Norwood, 2001, Morley and Rothwell, 2005. Gov., Waverley Sch. and Harris Girls' Acad., E Dulwich, 1998–2008. Chm., Free Representation Unit, 1988. *Recreations:* music, microscopy, tennis, bridge. *Address:* 4 Pump Court, Temple, EC4Y 7EL. *T:* (020) 7842 5555.

VINEN, William Frank, (Joe), FRS 1973; Professor of Physics, 1962–74, Poynting Professor of Physics, 1974–97, University of Birmingham, now Emeritus Professor of Physics; *b* 15 Feb. 1930; *o s* of Gilbert Vinen and Olive Maud Vinen (*née* Roach); *m* 1960, Susan-Mary Audrey Master; one *s* one *d*. *Educ:* Watford Grammar Sch.; Clare College, Cambridge. Research Fellow, Clare College, 1955–58. Royal Air Force, 1948–49. Demonstrator in Physics, Univ. of Cambridge and Fellow of Pembroke Coll., 1958–62. Hon. Life Fellow, Coventry Univ. (formerly Poly.), 1989. Hon. FInstP, 2002. Simon Meml Prize, Inst. of Physics, 1963; Holweck Medal and Prize, Inst. of Physics and French Physical Soc., 1978; Rumford Medal, Royal Soc., 1980; Guthrie Medal and Prize, Inst. of Physics, 2005. *Recreation:* good food. *Address:* 52 Middle Park Road, Birmingham B29 4BJ. *T:* (0121) 475 1328.

VINES, Prof. David Anthony, PhD; Professor of Economics, University of Oxford, since 2000; Fellow and Tutor in Economics, Balliol College, Oxford, since 1992; Adjunct Professor of Economics, Research School of Pacific and Asian Studies, Australian National University, since 1991; *b* 8 May 1949; *s* of Robert Godfrey and Vera Frances Vines; *m* 1st, 1979, Susannah Lucy Robinson (marr. diss. 1992); three *s*; 2nd, 1995, Jane Elizabeth Bingham; two step *s*. *Educ:* Scotch Coll., Melbourne; Melbourne Univ. (BA 1971); Cambridge Univ. (BA 1974; MA 1977; PhD 1984). Cambridge University: Fellow, Pembroke Coll., 1976–85; Res. Officer and Sen. Res. Officer, Dept of Applied Econs, 1979–85; Adam Smith Prof. of Political Economy, Univ. of Glasgow, 1985–92; Reader in Econs, Oxford Univ., 1997–2000; Res. Fellow, Centre for Econ. Policy Res., London, 1985–. Board Member: Channel 4 Television, 1987–92; Glasgow Develt Agency, 1990–92. Economic Consultant to Sec. of State for Scotland, 1987–92; Consultant, IMF, 1988, 1989. Economic and Social Research Council: Member: Econ. Affairs Cttee, 1985–87; Res. Progs Bd, 1992–93; Dir, Res. Prog. on Global Econ. Instns, 1994–2000. Mem. Academic Panel, HM Treasury, 1986–95. Mem. Council, Royal Economic Soc., 1988–92. Bd Mem., Analysys, 1989–2002. Comr, BFI Enquiry into the Future of the BBC, 1992. Bd Mem., Scottish Early Music Consort, 1990–. *Publications:* (with J. E. Meade and J. M. Maciejowski) Stagflation, Vol. II: Demand Management, 1983; (with D. A. Currie) Macroeconomic Interactions Between North and South, 1988; (jtly) Macroeconomic Policy: inflation, wealth and the exchange rate, 1989; (with G. Hughes) Deregulation and the Future of Commercial Television, 1989; (with A. Stevenson) Information, Strategy, and Public Policy, 1991; (with D. A. Currie) North South Interactions and International Macroeconomic Policy, 1995; (with Peter Drysdale) Europe, East Asia and APEC, 1998; (ed with Alan Montefiore) Integrity in the public and private domains, 1998; (jtly) The Asian Financial Crises, 1999; (with Chris Gilbert) The World Bank: structure and policies, 2000; (with Chris Gilbert) The IMF and its Critics: reform of global financial architecture, 2004; papers on international macroeconomics, macro-economic policy, in professional jls. *Recreations:* hillwalking, music. *Address:* Balliol College, Oxford OX1 3BJ. *T:* (01865) 271067, *Fax:* (01865) 271094; *e-mail:* david.vines@economics.ox.ac.uk.

VINES, Sir William (Joshua), AC 1987; Kt 1977; CMG 1969; FASA, ACIS; psc; Chairman, ANZ Banking Group, 1982–89 (Director, since 1976); Director, Dalgety Australia Ltd, 1980–91 (Chairman, 1970–80); grazier at Tara, Queensland, 1965–82 and Cliffdale, Currabubula, NSW, 1982–97; *b* 27 May 1916; *s* of P. V. Vines, Canterbury, Victoria, Australia; *m* 1st, 1939, Thelma J. (*d* 1988), *d* of late F. J. Ogden; one *s* two *d*; 2nd, 1990, Judith Anne Ploeg, *d* of late T. E. Raynsford. *Educ:* Haileybury College, Brighton Beach, Victoria. Served War of 1939–45 (despatches, C-in-C's commendation for gallantry, El Alamein), 2nd AIF, 2/23 Aust. Inf. Bn, Middle East, New Guinea and Borneo, Major. Managing Director: Internat. Wool Secretariat, 1961–69 (Board Mem., 1969–79); Berger, Jenson & Nicholson Ltd, 1960 (Dir, 1961–69); Dalgety Australia Ltd, 1971–76 (Chm., 1970–80); Group Managing Director, Lewis Berger & Sons Ltd, 1955–61; Director: Lewis Berger & Sons (Aust.) Pty Ltd & Sherwin Williams Co. (Aust.) Pty Ltd, 1952–55; Goodlass Wall & Co. Pty Ltd, 1947–49; Dalgety Ltd; Dalgety New Zealand Ltd, 1969–80; Port Phillip Mills Pty Ltd, 1969–88; Wiggins Teape Ltd (UK), 1970–79; Tubemakers of Australia Ltd, 1970–86 (Dep. Chm., 1973–86); Associated Pulp & Paper Mills Ltd, 1971–83 (Dep. Chm. 1977, Chm. 1979–83); Conzinc Rio Tinto of Australia, 1977–84; Grindlays Hldgs, subseq. ANZ UK Hldgs, 1985–89; Grindlays Bank, 1987–89; Chm., Thorn Holdings Pty Ltd, 1969–74. Vice-President Melbourne Legacy, 1949–51; Pres. Building Industry Congress, Vic., 1954–55. Chm., Aust. Wool Commn, 1970–72; Mem. Exec., CSIRO, 1973–78; Chm. Council, Hawkesbury Agric. Coll., 1975–85. Mem., Australia New Zealand Foundn, 1979–84. Chm., The Sir Robert Menzies Meml Trust, 1978–92. Hon. DSc Econ Sydney, 1993. *Address:* 1/10 West Street, Balgowlah, NSW 2093, Australia. *T:* (2) 99481147. *Clubs:* Union (Sydney); Royal Automobile of Victoria (Melbourne).

VINET, Dr Luc; Rector, University of Montreal, since 2005; *b* 16 April 1953; *m* Letitia Muresan; three *s* one *d*. *Educ:* Univ. of Montreal (BSc Hons Physics 1970; MSc Theoretical Physics 1974; PhD Theoretical Physics 1980); Dr in Theoretical Physics, Univ. Pierre & Marie Curie, 1979. Res. Associate, Center for Theoretical Physics, MIT, 1980–82; Department of Physics, University of Montreal: NSERC Res. Fellow, 1982–87; Asst Prof., 1987–88; Associate Prof., 1987–88; Prof., 1992–99; Dir, 1993–99, Associate Mem., 1999–2002, Centre de recherches mathématiques; Pres., Network for Computing and Mathematical Modelling (rcm2), 1996–99; Chief Exec., Bell Energis Univ. Lab., 1998; McGill University: Prof., Dept of Maths and Stats and Dept of Physics, 1999–2005; Vice-Principal (Acad.), 1999–2005; Provost, 2001–05. Chair: Panel of Experts, Canadian Foundn for Innovation; Conf. des Recteurs et des Principaux des Univs du Québec; Member: Groupe de travail sur les affaires médicales; Gen. Physics Steering Cttee; Inst. de finance mathématique de Montréal; Bd, Canadian Inst. for Telecommunications Res.; Comité Ministériel sur la pondération des activités; Bd, Maths of Information Technol. and Complex Systems; Bd, Ouranos; Bd, Industries de la science de la vie et biotechnologies. Member: Soc. for Industrial and Applied Maths; Canadian Assoc. Physicists; Canadian Mathematical Soc. Hon. Mem., Golden Key Nat. Honor Soc., 2000. *Address:* Office of the Rector, University of Montreal, PO Box 6128, Station Centre-Ville, Montreal, QC H3C 3J7, Canada. *T:* (514) 3436991, *Fax:* (514) 3432354; *e-mail:* luc.vinet@umontreal.ca.

VINEY, Anne Dorothy; Chief Executive, Cruse Bereavement Care, 2002–08; *b* 29 March 1948; *d* of Edward Walter Totman and Margaret Totman (*née* Fulljames); *m* 1970, Stephen John Viney. *Educ:* Bristol Univ. (BA Hons (French) 1969); King's Coll. London (PGCE 1970); Goldsmiths Coll., London (CQSW 1986); Open Univ. (MBA 2000). Teacher: London Borough of Sutton, 1970–71; Essex CC, 1971–75; London Borough of Barnet, 1975–76; Sec., NABC, 1976; Age Concern, Westminster: Sec., 1977; Welfare Worker, 1977–79; Dep. Organising Sec., 1979–85; Social Worker, Camden Social Services, at Gt Ormond St Hosp., 1986–87; Asst Dir, 1987–99, Hd of R&D, 1999–2001, Victim Support. *Recreations:* music, films, theatre. *Address:* *e-mail:* anne.viney@runbox.com. *Clubs:* Royal Commonwealth Society, Royal Society of Medicine.

VINGT-TROIS, His Eminence Cardinal André Armand; *see* Paris, Archbishop of, (RC).

VINING, Rowena Adelaide, OBE 1979 (MBE 1964); HM Diplomatic Service, retired; *b* 25 Sept. 1921; *er d* of late Col Percival Llewellyn Vining and Phyllis Servante Vining. *Educ:* privately, and at Chiddingstone Castle, Edenbridge, Kent. Foreign Office, 1941–52 (war service in Italy, Indonesia, 1943–45). Commonwealth Relations Office, 1952–55; Second Secretary: Karachi, 1955–58; Sydney, 1958–62; First Sec.: CRO, 1962–65; Canberra, 1965–67; Commonwealth Office (later Foreign and Commonwealth Office), 1967–71; Vienna, 1972–74; Consul, Florence and Consul-General, San Marino, 1974–78; Dep. UK Permanent Rep. to the Council of Europe, 1978–81; Consul-General, Strasbourg, 1979–80. Staff Assessor, FCO, 1983–86. *Recreations:* gardening, music. *Address:* Dorchester Cottage, Greywell, Hook, Hants RG29 1BT.

VINSON, family name of **Baron Vinson.**

VINSON, Baron *cr* 1985 (Life Peer), of Roddam Dene in the County of Northumberland; **Nigel Vinson,** LVO 1979; DL; entrepreneur; Founder, 1952, Chairman, 1952–72, Plastic Coatings Ltd; Founder Director, Centre for Policy Studies, 1974–80; Life Vice-President, Institute of Economic Affairs, 2004; *b* Nettlestead Place, Kent, 27 Jan. 1931; *s* of late Ronald Vinson and Bettina Vinson (*née* Southwell-Sander); *m* 1972, Yvonne Ann Collin; three *d*. *Educ:* Pangbourne Naval Coll. Lieut, Queen's Royal Regt, 1949–51. Plastic Coatings Ltd: started in a Nissen hut, 1952, flotation, 1969; Queen's Award to Industry, 1971. Director: Fleming High Income Growth Trust (formerly Fleming Tech. Trust), 1972–2001; BAA, 1973–80; Electra Investment Trust, 1975–98 (Dep. Chm., 1990–98); Barclays Bank UK, 1982–88. Mem., H of L Select Cttee on Econ. Affairs, 2001–03. Member: Crafts Adv. Cttee, 1971–77; Design Council, 1973–80; Dep. Chm., CBI Smaller Firms Council, 1979–84; Chairman: CoSIRA, 1980–82; Rural Develt Commn, 1980–90 (Mem., 1978–90); Industry Year Steering Cttee, RSA, 1985–87; Pres., Industrial Participation Assoc., 1979–89 (Chm., 1971–78). Institute of Economic Affairs: Trustee, 1972–2004; Chm. of Trustees, 1989–95; Vice-Pres., 1998–2004. Trustee, Civitas, 2005–. Hon. Dir, Queen's Silver Jubilee Appeal, 1976–78; Member: Northumbrian Nat. Parks Countryside Cttee, 1977–89; Regional Cttee, Nat. Trust, 1977–84. Chm., NE Region, PYBT, 1995–98; Pres., NE Civic Trust, 1999–2001. Council Mem., St George's House, Windsor Castle, 1990–96. Foundn Donor, Martinmere Wildfowl Reserve, 1972; gifted a village green to Holburn, Northumberland, 2006. FRSA. DL Northumberland, 1990. *Publications:* Personal and Portable Pensions for All, 1984; Owners All, 1985; Take upon Retiring, 1998. *Recreations:* fine art and craftsmanship, horses, farming. *Address:* 34 Kynance Mews, SW7 4QR. *T:* (01668) 217230. *Clubs:* Boodle's, Pratt's.

VINTON, Alfred Merton; Chairman, Electra Partners Ltd (formerly Electra Kingsway Managers, then Electra Fleming Ltd), since 1995; *b* 11 May 1938; *s* of Alfred Merton Vinton and Jean Rosalie Vinton (*née* Guiterman); *m* 1st, 1963, Mary Bedell Weber; two *s* one *d*; 2nd, 1983, Anna-Maria Hawser (*née* Dugan-Chapman); one *s* one *d*. *Educ:* Harvard College (AB Econs 1960). US Navy Lieut (JG), 1960–62. J. P. Morgan, 1962–88; Chief Operating Officer, N. M. Rothschild & Sons, 1988–92; Chief Exec. Officer, Entreprises Quilmes SA, 1992–94; Director: Sand Aire Investments plc, 1995–; Sagitta Investment Advrs Ltd, 1996–2001; Unipart Ltd, 1998–; Amerindo Internet Fund plc, 2000–06; Lambert Howarth Gp plc, 2000–07; GP Investments Ltd, 2006–. *Recreations:* golf, tennis, riding, music. *Address:* Stoke Albany House, Market Harborough, Leics LE16 8PT. *T:* (01858) 535227. *Clubs:* White's; Sunningdale Golf; Harvard (NY).

VIOT, Jacques Edmond; Commandeur de la Légion d'Honneur; Commandeur de l'Ordre National du Mérite; President: France-Great Britain Association, 1987–2000; French section, Franco-British Council, since 1992; Alliance Française de Paris, 1994–2004; *b* 25 Aug. 1921; *m* 1950, Jeanne de Martimprey de Romécourt. *Educ:* Bordeaux and Paris Lycées; Ecole Normale Supérieure; Ecole Nationale d'Administration. Foreign Office (European Dept), 1951–53; Second Sec., London, 1953–57; First Sec., Rabat, 1957–61; Tech. Advisor to Foreign Minister, 1961–62; Head of Technical Co-operation, FO, 1962–68; Dir for Personnel and Gen. Admin, 1968–72; Ambassador to Canada, 1972–77; Gen. Inspector for Foreign Affairs, 1977–78; Directeur de Cabinet to Foreign Minister, 1978–81; Gen. Inspector for Foreign Affairs, 1981–84; Ambassador to the Court of St James's, 1984–86; Ambassadeur de France, 1986; Chm., Review Cttee on Foreign Affairs, Paris, 1986–87. Chm. Entrance Examination Bd, Ecole Nat. d'Admin, 1987. Fellow, St Antony's College, Oxford. *Address:* 19 rue de Civry, 75016 Paris, France.

VIRANI, Nazmudin Gulamhusein; Chairman and Chief Executive, Control Securities PLC, property and leisure company, 1985–92; *b* 2 March 1948; *s* of Gulamhusein Virani and Fatma Virani; *m* 1970, Yasmin Abdul Rasul Ismail; two *s* one *d*. *Educ:* Aga Khan Sch., Kampala, Uganda. Left Uganda for UK, 1972; founded Virani gp of companies, 1972 (Chm. and Chief Exec.); Chm. and Chief Exec., Belhaven PLC, 1983–86. *Recreations:* cricket, travel, philanthropy.

VIRLEY, Simon James; Head of Renewable Energy and Innovation Unit, Department of Energy and Climate Change (formerly Department for Business, Enterprise and Regulatory Reform), since 2008; *b* 7 June 1969; *s* of Brian Michael Virley and Jean Barbara (*née* Lofts); *m* 2005, Kate Jaggar; one *s*. *Educ:* Jesus Coll., Oxford (BA Hons PPE 1990, MA 1994); London Sch. of Econs (MSc Econs 1995). Econs tutor, Green Coll., Oxford, 1990–91; Economist, Dept of Transport, 1991–93; Policy Advr, 1993–99, Team Leader, 1999–2000, HM Treasury; Private Sec. (Econ. Affairs) to Prime Minister, 2000–03; Dir, Better Regulation Exec., Cabinet Office, 2003–05; Dir, Corporate Finance, KPMG (on secondment from Cabinet Office), 2005–07. Mem., ICA. *Publications:* contrib. to jls incl. Econ. Briefing, Treasury Occasional Papers, Transport Policy. *Recreations:* cricket, football, ski-ing, golf. *Address:* Department of Energy and Climate Change, 1 Victoria Street, SW1H 0ET.

VIS, Dr Rudolf Jan; MP (Lab) Finchley and Golders Green, since 1997; *b* 4 April 1941; *s* of late Laurens and Helena Vis; *m* 1st, 1968, Dr Joan Hanin (marr. diss. 1984); one *s*; 2nd, 2001, Jacqueline Suffling; twin *s*. *Educ:* Univ. of Maryland (BSc Econ 1970); LSE (MSc Econ 1972); Brunel Univ. (PhD Econ 1976). Dutch military service, 1960–64; USAF Base, Spain, 1964–65; Hotel Fleissig, Amsterdam, 1966; Fox Language Inst., USA, 1967; Lectr in Econs, Poly. of East London, later Univ. of East London, 1971–97. Mem., Council of Europe and WEU, 1997–. *Recreations:* walking through London, bridge. *Address:* House of Commons, SW1A 0AA. *T:* (020) 7219 4562.

VISCHER, Vivienne; *see* Cox, V.

VISHNEVSKAYA, Galina; soprano; Founder, Galina Vishnevskaya Opera Centre, Moscow, 2002; *b* 25 Oct. 1926; *m* 1955, Mstislav Rostropovich, Hon. KBE, 'cellist (*d* 2007); two *d*. *Educ:* studied with Vera Garina. Toured with Leningrad Light Opera Co., 1944–48, with Leningrad Philharmonic Soc., 1948–52; joined Bolshoi Theatre, 1952. Concert appearances in Europe and USA, 1950–; first appeared at Metropolitan Opera, NY, 1961. Rôles include: Leonora in Fidelio, Tatiana in Eugene Onegin, Iolanta, Butterfly in Madame Butterfly, Aida, Liza in Queen of Spades, Natasha Rostova in War and Peace, Marguerite in Faust, Violetta in La Traviata, Liù in Turandot, Katerina Izmailova, Tosca, Marfa in The Tsar's Bride, etc. Has sung in Britain at Festival Hall, Aldeburgh Festival, Edinburgh Festival, Covent Garden, Rostropovich Festival, Snape; Dir, Iolanta, Aldeburgh Fest., 1988. Made concert tours with her husband. Has made many recordings. Awarded numerous prestigious internat. awards. *Publication:* Galina (autobiog.), 1984. *Address:* Galina Vishnevskaya Opera Centre, Ostozhenka str., 25 build. 1, Moscow 119034, Russia.

VISSER, John Bancroft; Governor: Powell's School, Cirencester, since 1992 (Chairman, 1999–2005); Cirencester Deer Park School, since 1998; Trustee, Powell's Educational Foundation, since 1991; *b* 29 Jan. 1928; *o s* of late Gilbert and Ethel Visser; *m* 1955, Astrid Margareta Olson; two *s* one *d*. *Educ:* Mill Hill Sch.; New Coll., Oxford (Exhibnr). Entered Civil Service, Asst Principal, Min. of Supply, 1951; Principal, 1956; Min. of Aviation, 1959; Admin. Staff Coll., 1965; Asst Sec., 1965; Min. of Technology, 1967; Royal Coll. of Defence Studies, 1970; Civil Service Dept, 1971; Procurement Exec., MoD, 1971; Under-Sec., 1974; Sec. of Nat. Defence Industries Council, 1971–74; Dir of Admin, SRC, then SERC, 1974–88. *Recreations:* sport, music, gardening, art and antiques. *Address:* 79 Corinium Gate, Cirencester, Glos GL7 2PX. *T:* (01285) 652626. *Club:* Old Millhillians.

VITMAYER, Janet; Chief Executive, Horniman Museum and Gardens, since 1998; *b* 2 Sept. 1952; *d* of Arnost Vitmayer and Maria (*née* Pichler); one *s* one *d*. *Educ:* Univ. of Keele (BA Hons Hist. and American Studies 1976); City Univ. (MA Mus. and Gall. Mgt 1990). Imperial War Mus., 1976–83; Dir, Livesey Mus., 1983–93; Hd, Public Services, Horniman Mus. and Gardens, 1993–98. Visitor, Pitt Rivers Mus., Univ. of Oxford, 2000–. Mem., Expert Panel, Heritage Lottery Fund, 2005–. *Recreations:* family pursuits, travel. *Address:* Horniman Museum, 100 London Road, Forest Hill, SE23 3PQ. *T:* (020) 8699 1872. *Club:* Royal Commonwealth Society.

VITORIA, Dr Mary Christine; QC 1997; *m* Prof. Clive Ashwin. *Educ:* Bedford Coll., London (BSc, PhD Chemistry); LLB (ext.) London Univ. Called to the Bar, Lincoln's Inn, 1975, Bencher, 2004; Lectr in Law, QMC, 1977; in practice at the Bar, 1978–. Editor: Reports of Patent Cases, 1995–; Fleet Street Reports, 1995–. *Publications:* (jtly) Modern Law of Copyright and Designs, 1980, 3rd edn 2000; (contrib.) Halsbury's Laws of England, 4th edn. *Recreations:* opera, bird watching. *Address:* 8 New Square, Lincoln's Inn, WC2A 3QP. *T:* (020) 7405 4321.

VITORINO, António; Member, European Commission, 1999–2004; *b* 12 Jan. 1957; *m*; two *c*. *Educ:* Lisbon Law Sch. (law degree 1981; Master in Law and Pol Sci. 1986). Lawyer, 1982; Asst Prof., Lisbon Law Sch., 1982; Prof., Lisbon Autonomous Univ., 1986; Judge, Constitutional Court of Portugal, 1989–94; Vice-Pres., Portugal Telecom Internacional, 1998–99; Prof., Internat. Univ., 1998–99. Deputy (Socialist Party) Portuguese Parlt, 1980–83, 1985–89; Sec. of State for Parly Affairs, 1984–85, for Admin and Justice, Macao govt, 1986–87; Dep. Prime Minister and Minister of Defence, 1995–97; Mem., European Parlt, 1994–96. Member: Jt EP and Portuguese Parlt Cttee on European Integration, 1980–84; Sino-Portuguese Jt Liaison Gp on Macao, 1987–89. *Publications:* books on European affairs, constitutional law and pol sci.

VIVIAN, family name of **Barons Swansea** and **Vivian**.

VIVIAN, 7th Baron *cr* 1841; **Charles Crespigny Hussey Vivian;** Bt 1828; *b* 20 Dec. 1966; *s* of 6th Baron Vivian and his 1st wife, Catherine Joyce (*née* Hope) (now Countess of Mexborough); *S* father, 2004. Dir, Pelham Public Relations. *Heir: uncle* Hon. Victor Anthony Ralph Brabazon Vivian [*b* 26 March 1940; *m* 1966, Inger Johanne Gulliksen; one *s* one *d*]. *Address:* 28 Walpole Street, SW3 4QS. *Club:* White's.

VIVIAN, James Antony, FRCO; Organist, since 2004, and Director of Music, since 2006, Temple Church; *b* Worcester, 19 June 1974; *s* of Roy John Vivian and Pamela Ann Vivian (*née* Bromley); *m* 2004, Ann Elise Smoot. *Educ:* Malvern Coll. (Music Scholar); King's Coll., Cambridge (BA 1996). FRCO 1994. Actg Asst Organist, Lincoln Cath., 1992–93; A. H. Mann Organ Scholar, King's Coll., Cambridge, 1993–97; Suborganist, Temple Ch, 1997–2004. *Recreations:* American history, cooking, baseball. *Address:* c/o The Master's House, Temple, EC4Y 7BB. *T:* (020) 7353 8559.

VLESSING, Suzanna; *see* Taverne, S.

VOAKE, Charlotte Elizabeth Mary; freelance author and illustrator; *b* 9 Jan. 1957; *d* of Colin and Margaret Voake; *m* 1983, Robert Atkins; one *s* one *d*. *Educ:* Birkenhead High Sch. GPDST; University Coll. London (BA Hons Hist. of Art). *Publications include:* illustrator: The Best of Aesop's Fables by Margaret Clark, 1990; Elsie Piddock Skips in Her Sleep by Eleanor Farjeon, 2000; A Child's Guide to Wild Flowers by Kate Petty, 2004; Collected Poems by Allan Ahlberg, 2008; author and illustrator: Ginger, 1997 (Smarties Award, 1997); Pizza Kittens, 2002 (Smarties Award, 2002); Ginger Finds a Home, 2003; Hello Twins, 2006 (Best Illustrated Children's Bks Award, NY Times, 2006); Tweedle Dee Dee, 2008. *Recreations:* gardening, piano, violin.

VOBE, Helen Mary; *see* Jones, H. M.

VOCKLER, Most Rev. John Charles, (Most Rev. Brother John-Charles); Founder, and Superior, Franciscan Order of the Divine Compassion, since 1990; Archbishop and Metropolitan of the Anglican Catholic Church, 2001–05; Bishop of the Missionary Diocese of Australia, 2004–05, Vicar-General, until 2008; *b* 22 July 1924; *e s* of John Thomas Vockler and Mary Catherine Vockler (*née* Widerberg), Sydney, New South Wales. *Educ:* Sydney Boys' High Sch.; after studying accountancy, matriculated by private study and correspondence (Metropolitan Business Coll. and Internat. Correspondence Schs, Sydney) to the Univ. of Sydney; Moore Theol Coll.; St John's Theol College, Morpeth, NSW; Australian Coll. of Theology (LTh 1948; Hey Sharp Prize for NT Greek); Univ. of Queensland (BA (1st cl. Hons History) 1953; Univ. Gold Medal for outstanding achievement, 1953; Walter and Eliza Hall Foundn Travelling Scholarship, 1953); Fulbright Schol., 1953; BA Univ. of Adelaide, *aegr.*, 1961; Gen. Theol Seminary, NY (MDiv 1954; STM 1956). Junior Clerk, W. R. Carpenter & Co. Ltd, Sydney, NSW, 1939–43. Deacon, 1948; priest, 1948; Asst Deacon, Christ Church Cathedral, Newcastle, 1948; Asst Priest, 1948–50; Vice-Warden of St John's Coll., Univ. of Queensland, 1950–53; Acting Chaplain, C of E Grammar Sch. for Boys, Brisbane, 1953; Acting Vice-Warden, St John's Coll., Morpeth and Lectr in Old Testament, 1953; Asst Priest, Cathedral of S John the Divine, NY and Chaplain, St Luke's Home for Aged Women and the Home for Old Men and Aged Couples, 1953–54; Australian Delegate to Anglican Congress, 1954; Fellow and Tutor, GTS, 1954–56; Asst Priest, St Stephen's Church, West 69th Street, NY, 1955; Priest-in-charge, St Stephen's, New York, 1956; Asst Priest, parish of Singleton, NSW, 1956–59; Lecturer in Theology, St John's Theol Coll., Morpeth, NSW, 1956–59; Secretary, Newcastle Diocesan Board of Education, 1958–59; Titular Bishop of Mount Gambier and Assistant Bishop of Adelaide (Coadjutor, 1959; title changed to Assistant, 1961), until 1962; also Archdeacon of Eyre Peninsula, 1959–62; Vicar-General, Examining Chaplain to Bishop of Adelaide, 1960–62; Bishop of Polynesia, 1962–68. Society of St Francis: entered Soc., 1969; professed, 1972; Chaplain, Third Order, European Province, 1972–74; made life profession, 1975; Guardian, Friary of St Francis, Brisbane, 1975–77, Islington, NSW, 1978–79; Minister Provincial, Pacific Province, 1976–81; Archivist, Amer. Province, 1985–89; left SSF, 1990; Vicar, Trinity Church, Monmouth, Ill, 1990–93; Adjunct Prof. of Ascetical Theology, Nashotah House Seminary, 1991–93; received into Anglican Catholic Church, USA, 1994: Commissary in USA for Bishop of Australia, 1994–98; Hon. Asst Bishop, dio. of Australia, 1994; Asst Bp to the Metropolitan, 1995–97; Chm., Dept of Ministry, 1996, Dept of Evangelism, 1997; VG, dio. of Australia, 1998; Dean, Holyrood Seminary, Liberty, NY, 1995–97 (Sub-Dean for Acad. Affairs, 1994–95); Prof. of Ascetical and Pastoral Theol., 1997; Bishop of New Orleans, 1999–2002, Archbishop, 2001. Warden: Community of St Clare, Newcastle, NSW, 1975–80; Soc. of Sacred Advent, Qld, 1976–80 (Priest Associate, 1975–); Poor Clares of Reparation, Mt Sinai, NY, 1982–83 (Bishop Protector, 1987–93); Spiritual Dir, Community of the Holy Spirit, NY, 1988–89; Bishop Visitor, Order of the Incarnation, NY, 1990–93 (Spiritual Advr, 1988–89); Spiritual Dir to Bishops and Priests of the Catholic and Apostolic Church of N America, 1988–97; Confessor Extraordinary, Soc. of St John the Evangelist, Cambridge, Mass, 1987–89; Chaplain to Monmouth Community Hosp., 1990–93. Collegial Mem., House of Bishops, Episcopal Church, USA, 1983–93; Member: House of Bishops' Cttee on Religious Life, 1986–89; Episcopal Synod of America, 1989–93. President, Harry Charman's All Races Sports and Social Club, Suva, Fiji, 1962–68, Hon. Life Vice-Pres., 1968; Chairman: S Pacific Anglican Council, 1963–68; Council of Pacific Theol Coll., 1963–68; President: Fiji Council of Social Services, 1964–68; Fiji Branch, Royal Commonwealth Soc., 1966–68. Writing Grant, Literature Bd of Australia Council, 1979, 1981. Member: Soc. of Authors; Australian Soc. of Authors; PEN (International), Sydney Br. and New York Br.; Guild of Writers Inc., NY; Christian Writers' Fellowship (USA); Aust. Professional Writers' Services; Penman Club (UK); National Writers' Club (USA); Federated Clerks Union of Aust., 1978–81; Internat. Center for Integrative Studies, NY 1983–93; Internat. Ecumenical Fellowship; Guild of All Souls; Confraternity of the Blessed Sacrament; Soc. of Mary; Catholic and Evangelical Mission; Anglican Pacifist Fellowship; Fellowship of Reconciliation (England & Australia); Fellowship of S Alban and S Sergius; Anglican Fellowship of Prayer, USA; Fellowship of Three Kings, Haddington, Scotland; Amnesty Internat., USA (Mem., Urgent Action Gp); Soc. of the Holy Cross, 1992–94; The Living Rosary of Our Lady and St Dominic, 1992–. Priest Associate, Shrine of Our Lady, Walsingham and Priory of Our Lady of Pew, Westminster Abbey, 1978–96; Associate, Guild of St Vincent, 1985–93; Priest Mem., OGS, 1952–75. Sec., Adv. Council for Religious Communities in Aust. and Pacific, 1976–80. Permission to officiate in various dioceses, UK, NZ, USA, Australia, 1969–93. Vice-Pres. and Mem. Council, USPG, 1973–74; Vice-Pres., Missions to

Seamen, 1963–69; Hon. Asst Bp of Worcester, 1972–73; Assistant Bishop: Chelmsford, 1973–74; Southwark, 1974–75; Assisting Bishop, dio. of Quincy, USA, 1990–93; Hon. Canon of Southwark, 1975, Canon Emeritus 1975; Hon. Mission Chaplain, dio. Brisbane, 1975–79. Examnr for Aust. Coll. of Theology, 1975–76 and 1979. Patron: Monarchist League, 1993–; King Kigali V's Fund for Rwandan Children, 1993–; Mem., Australian Monarchist League, 1998–. ThD (jure dig.) ACT, 1961; STD (hc) Gen. Theological Seminary, NY, 1961; BD (ad eund.) Melbourne College of Divinity, 1960. Bronze Medal, Royal Aust. Life Saving Soc., 1939; Bishop's Cross, dio. of Long Is, 1989; La Croce d'Oro di S Ambrogio, 2003. Publications: Can Anglicans Believe Anything—The Nature and Spirit of Anglicanism, 1961 (NSW); Forward Day by Day, 1962; (ed) Believing in God (by M. L. Yates), 1962 (Australian edn), revd edn 1983 (US); One Man's Journey, 1972; St Francis: Franciscanism and the Society of St Francis, 1980; A School of Prayer, 1998; Seven Deadly Sins, Seven Grace-full Virtues, and Seven Mystical or Spiritual Gifts, 1999; Two Paths to Holiness, 2002; An Introduction to Some Spiritual Classics, 2004; contributions to: Preparatory Volume for Anglican Congress, Toronto, 1963; Anglican Mosaic, 1963; Mutual Responsibility: Questions and Answers, 1964; All One Body (ed T. Wilson), 1968; Australian Dictionary of Biography (4 articles); St Mark's Review, Australian Church Quarterly, The Anglican, The Young Anglican, Pacific Journal of Theology, New Zealand Theological Review, weekly feature, Newcastle Morning Herald, NSW; book reviews in Amer. theol jls; Aust. corresp. to New Fire, 1980–81; book review Editor, New York Episcopalians, 1986–91; Contributing Ed., The Trinitarian, 1995–. Recreations: classical music, detective stories, theatre, films, prints and engravings. Address: Room 767, Benhome, 30 Regent Street, Maitland, NSW 2320, Australia. T: (2) 49320105; e-mail: vockler@networksmm.com.au. Clubs: Tonga (Nukualofa); St John's Coll. (Brisbane) (Hon Mem., 1976–); Returned Services League (Toronto, NSW); Gallipoli Legion (Newcastle, NSW); Royal Commonwealth Society (NSW).

VOELCKER, Christopher David, TD 1967; a District Judge (Magistrates' Courts) (formerly Metropolitan Stipendiary Magistrate), 1982–2001; b 10 May 1933; s of Eric Voelcker and Carmen Muriel Lyon Voelcker (née Henstock); m 1st, 1964, Sybil Russell Stoneham (marr. diss. 1985); two d; 2nd, 1991, Petrina Alexandra Keany (née Holdsworth). Educ: Wellington Coll., Berks. Called to Bar, Middle Temple, 1955. National Service, 8th King's Royal Irish Hussars, 1952–53. 3/4 County of London Yeomanry (Sharpshooters) TA, 1953–60; Kent and County of London Yeomanry (Sharpshooters) TA, 1960–67. An Asst Recorder, 1985–89; a Recorder, 1989–94. Member: Inner London Probation Cttee, 1986–92; Recruitment and Trng Cttee, Central Council of Probation for England and Wales, 1988–91. Recreations: military history, gardening, preserved railways. Address: 6 Pump Court, Temple, EC4Y 7AR. T: (020) 7353 7242. Club: Cavalry and Guards.

VOGEL, Dr Dieter H.; Chairman: Supervisory Board, Bertelsmann AG, 2003–07; Board of Trustees, Bertelsmann Foundation, since 2007; b 14 Nov. 1941; m 1970, Ursula Gross; two c. Educ: primary sch., Berchtesgaden; secondary sch., Frankfurt; Tech. Univ. of Darmstadt (Dip. Mech. Engrg); Tech. Univ. of Munich (Dr.Ing). Asst Prof., Thermic Turbo Engines, Tech. Univ. of Munich, 1967–69; Vice-Pres., Printing Div., Bertelsmann AG, 1970–74; Pegulan Ag, 1975–85 (Chm., 1978); Vice-Chm., Mgt Bd, Batig (BAT Industries), 1978–85; Thyssen Group, 1986–98: Chm., Thyssen Handelsunion AG, 1986–96; Mem., Exec. Bd, 1986–91, Dep. Chm., 1991–96, Chm., 1996–98, Thyssen AG; Chm., Deutsche Bahn AG, 1998–2001. Recreation: ski-ing. Address: Koenigsallee 60A, 40212 Düsseldorf, Germany.

VOGEL, Hans-Jochen, Hon. CBE; Dr jur; Chairman: Social Democratic Party (SPD), Federal Republic of Germany, 1987–91; Gegen Vergessen-Für Demokratie eV; b 3 Feb. 1926; s of Dr Hermann Vogel and Caroline (née Brinz); m 1st, 1950, Ilse Leisnering (marr. diss. 1972); one s two d; 2nd, 1972, Liselotte Sonnenholzer. Educ: Göttingen and Giessen; Univs of Marburg and Munich (Dr jur 1950). Army service, 1943–45 (PoW). Admitted Bavarian Bar, 1951; Legal Asst, Bavarian Min. of Justice, 1952–54; District Court Counsel, Traunstein, 1954–55; staff of Bavarian State Chancellery, 1955–58; Munich City Council, 1958–60; Oberbürgermeister (Chief Executive), Munich, 1960–72 (re-elected, 1966); Vice-Pres., Org. Cttee, Olympic Games, 1972. Mayor of West Berlin, Jan.–June 1981, leader of opposition, 1981–83. Chm., Bavarian SPD, 1972–77; Mem. (SPD) Bundestag, 1972–81, 1983–94; Minister of regional planning, housing and urban develt, 1972–74; Minister of Justice, 1974–81; Leader of the Opposition, 1983–91. Bundesverdienstkreuz; Bavarian Verdienstorden. Publications: Städte im Wandel, 1971; Die Amtskette: Meine 12 Münchner Jahre, 1972; Reale Reformen, 1973; Nachsichten, 1996; Demokratie lebt auch vom Widerspruch, 2001; Politik und Anstand, 2005; Deutschland aus der Vogel Perspektive, 2007. Recreations: mountaineering, swimming, reading history. Address: Gegen Vergessen-Für Demokratie eV, Stauffenbergstrasse 13–14, 10785 Berlin, Germany.

VOGEL, Johannes Christian, PhD; Keeper of Botany, Natural History Museum, since 2004; b 15 May 1963; s of late Erich Vogel and Edith Vogel (née Froböse); m 2003, Sarah Catherine Darwin; two s. Educ: Ratsgymnasium, Bielefeld; Bielefeld Univ. (Vordiplom Biol. 1986); Peterhouse, Cambridge (PhD 1996). Served Armed Forces, FRG, 1982–84. Researcher, Alpeninstitut, Munich, 1989–90; Natural History Museum: Researcher, Dept of Botany, 1995–2004; Hd, UK Biodiversity Prog., 1999–2004. Member: UK Biodiversity Gp, 1999–2001; Biodiversity Res. Adv. Gp, 2001–; DCMS Sustainable Develt Forum, 2001–; Darwin Initiative Adv. Cttee, 2005–. Member Board: Naturwissenschaftlicher Verein für Bielefeld und Umgegend e.V., 1985–90; Dachverband Naturwissenschaftlicher Vereine Deutschlands, 1995–; Council Mem., Systematics Assoc., 1995–98. Trustee: Radio Bielefeld, 1988–2004; Nat. Biodiversity Network, 1999–. Expert Rev. Panel, Deutsche Forschungsgemeinschaft, 2000–. FLS 1994. Strasburger Preis, Deutsche Botanische Gesellschaft, 1996. Publications: scientific papers on fern evolution, genetics, biogeography, systematics and biodiversity conservation in range of learned scientific jls. Recreations: natural history, walking, photography, music. Address: Department of Botany, Natural History Museum, Cromwell Road, SW7 5BD. T: (020) 7942 5093, Fax: (020) 7942 5501; e-mail: J.Vogel@nhm.ac.uk.

VOGENAUER, Prof. Stefan; Professor of Comparative Law, since 2003, and Director, Institute of European and Comparative Law, since 2004, University of Oxford; Fellow, Brasenose College, Oxford, since 2003; b 4 Aug. 1968; s of Gottfried Dieter Vogenauer and Brigitte Maria (née Franz); m 1997, Jutta Greive; two s one d. Educ: Johann-Heinrich-Voß-Gymnasium, Eutin; Kiel Univ. (First State Exam. in Law 1994); Trinity Coll., Oxford (MJur 1995; Clifford Chance Prize; HLA Hart Prize); Regensburg Appeal Court (Second State Exam. in Law 2000). Res. Asst and Lectr (pt-time), Univ. of Regensburg, 1997–2002; Res. Fellow, Max-Planck-Inst. for Foreign Private Law and Private Internat. Law, Hamburg, 2002–03. Lectr (pt-time), Bucerius Law Sch., Hamburg, 2002–04. Publications: Die Auslegung von Gesetzen in England und auf dem Kontinent, 2001 (Max Weber Prize, Bavarian Acad. of Scis and Humanities, 2002; Otto Hahn Medal, Max Planck Soc., 2002); articles on comparative law, European legal hist., German, English and European private law and legal method. Address: Institute of European and Comparative

Law, St Cross Building, St Cross Road, Oxford OX1 3UL. T: (01865) 281615, Fax: (01865) 281611; e-mail: stefan.vogenauer@iecl.ox.ac.uk.

VOLCKER, Paul A.; Frederick H. Schultz Professor of International Economic Policy, Princeton University, 1988–96, now Emeritus; Chairman, James D. Wolfensohn Incorporated, 1988–96; b Cape May, New Jersey, 5 Sept. 1927; s of Paul A. Volcker and Alma Louise Klippel; m 1954, Barbara Marie Bahnson (d 1998); one s one d. Educ: Princeton Univ. (AB summa cum laude); Harvard Univ. (MA); LSE. Special Asst, Securities Dept, Fed. Reserve Bank, NY, 1953–57; Financial Economist, Chase Manhattan Bank, NYC, 1957–62; Vice-Pres. and Dir of Forward Planning, 1965–69; Dir, Office of Financial Analysis, US Treasury Dept, 1962–63; Dep. Under-Sec. for Monetary Affairs, 1963–65; Under-Sec. for Monetary Affairs, 1969–74; Senior Fellow, Woodrow Wilson Sch. of Public and Internat. Affairs, Princeton Univ., 1974–75; Pres. NY Federal Reserve Bank, 1975–79; Chairman: American Federal Reserve Board, 1979–87; J. Rothschild, Wolfensohn & Co., 1992–95. Chairman: Group of Thirty, 1989–2000; Trilateral Commn, 1992–2001; Internat. Accounting Standards Cttee, IASC Foundn, 2001–06; Independent Inquiry Cttee into UN Oil for Food Prog., 2004–06. Address: 151 E 79th Street, New York, NY 10021, USA; (office) 610 Fifth Avenue, Suite 420, New York, NY 10020, USA. T: (212) 2187878.

VOLGER, Dr Hendrik Cornelis; Manager, Sittingbourne Research Centre, and Director, Shell Research Ltd, 1989–93; b 6 March 1932; s of Ferdinand Pieter and Marijtje Spaans Volger; m 1959, Aaltje Roorda; two d. Educ: Univ. of Groningen (PhD). Lieut, Special Branch, Royal Dutch Air Force, 1958–59; Ramsay Fellow, UCL, 1959–60; Shell Research BV, Amsterdam, 1960 and 1969–75; Shell Development Co., USA, 1968–69; Director: Shell Milstead Lab., 1975–77; Shell Biotech. Res., 1977–83; Product Res. Lab., Amsterdam, 1983–89. Mem., Royal Dutch Akademie of Science, 1987. AKZO Prize, 1972. Publications: Organic Chemistry, 1956; Organometal Complexes, 1961; Homogenous Catalysis, 1965. Recreations: tennis, gardening.

VOLHARD, Christiane N.; see Nüsslein-Volhard.

VOLLRATH, Prof. Lutz Ernst Wolf; Professor of Histology and Embryology, University of Mainz, Germany, 1974–2004, now Emeritus; b 2 Sept. 1936; s of Pastor Richard Hermann Vollrath and Rita (née Brügmann); m 1963, Gisela (née Dialer); three d. Educ: Ulrich von Hutten-Schule, Berlin; Univs of Berlin, Kiel (Dr med 1961), and Tübingen. Wissenschaftlicher Assistent, Dept of Anatomy, Würzburg, Germany, 1963; Res. Fellow, Dept of Anatomy, Birmingham, 1964; Wissenschaftlicher Assistent, Dept of Anatomy, Würzburg, 1965–71 (Privatdozent, 1968; Oberassistent, 1969; Universitätsdozent, 1970); King's College London: Reader in Anatomy, 1971; Prof. of Anatomy, 1973–74. Hon. Mem., Romanian Soc. of Anatomists, 1996; Corresp. Mem., Saxonian Acad. of Scis in Leipzig, 1998; Hon. Mem., Anatomy Assoc., Costa Rica, 1999. Editor: Cell & Tissue Research, 1978–96; Annals of Anatomy, 1992–. Publications: (co-editor) Neurosecretion: the final neuroendocrine pathway, 1974; The Pineal Organ, 1981; (ed) Handbook of Microscopic Anatomy (formerly Handbuch der mikr. Anat. des Menschen) (series), 1978–; research publications on histochemistry and ultrastructure of organogenesis and various aspects of neuroendocrinology, in Annals of Anatomy, Z Zellforsch., Histochemie, Phil. Trans Royal Society B, Erg. Anat. Entw.gesch. Recreation: gardening. Address: c/o Anatomisches Institut, 55099 Mainz, Saarstr. 19/21, Germany.

von BERTELE, Maj. Gen. Michael James, OBE 1994; QHS 2008; Commander, Joint Medical Command, since 2008; b 23 Aug. 1956; s of Otto Bertele von Grenadenberg and Monica von Bertele (née Barrett); m 1985, Frances Mary Buist Loudon; one s two d. Educ: St Mary's, Darlington; Welsh Nat. Sch. of Medicine, Cardiff (MB BCh 1979); London Sch. of Hygiene and Tropical Medicine (DAvMed 1986; DIH 1989). MFOM 1991. Peripatetic drayman, Schwechat Brewery, Vienna, 1974–76; commnd RAMC, 1976; MO, Parachute Field Ambulance, 1980–83; Specialist in Aviation Medicine, 1983–91; Commanding Officer: 5 Armd Field Ambulance, 1992–94; British Med. Bn, UN Protection Force, 1993; Comdr, Med. 3 (UK) Div., 1996–98; rcds 2000; Col, Employment Policy (Army), 2001–03; Dir, Med. Operational Capability, MoD, 2004–06; Chief Exec., Defence Medical Educn and Trng Agency, 2006–08. Chairman: NATO Gen. Med. Wkg Gp, 2004–06; NATO Chem., Biol, Radiol and Nuclear Wkg Gp, 2004–06. Chm., Army Lawn Tennis Assoc., 2002–. Recreations: cooking, working with wood, mountains and beaches. Address: Mackenzie Building, Fort Blockhouse, Gosport, Hants PO12 2AB; e-mail: michaelvonbertele@hotmail.com.

von DOHNÁNYI, Christoph; Principal Conductor, Philharmonia Orchestra, London, 1997–2008; Chief Conductor, NDR Symphony Orchestra, Hamburg, since 2004; b 8 Sept. 1929; m 1st, 1957, Renate Zillessen (marr. diss.); one s one d; 2nd, 1979, Anja Silja, qv; one s two d. Educ: 2 years' law study; Musikhochschule, Munich; Florida State Univ.; with grandfather Ernst von Dohnányi in USA. Coach and asst conductor, Frankfurt Opera, 1953; Gen. Music Dir, Lübeck and Kassel, 1957–68; Chief Conductor, Radiosymphonie Orch., Cologne, 1964–70; London début with LPO, 1965; Gen. Music Dir, Frankfurt Opera, 1968–77; Dir, Städtische Bühnen, Frankfurt, 1972–77; Intendant and Chief Conductor, Hamburg Opera, 1977; Music Dir, Cleveland Orch., 1984–2002, Music Dir Laureate, 2002–. Guest Conductor of major orchestras and opera houses in Europe, Israel and USA; Artistic Advr, l'Orchestre de Paris, 1998–2000. Numerous recordings; honours, music prizes and hon. doctorates. Address: c/o HarrisonParrott, 12 Penzance Place, W11 4PA.

von ETZDORF, Georgina Louise, RDI 1997; Artistic Director, Georgina von Etzdorf, since 1981; b 1 Jan. 1955; d of late Roderick Rudiger von Etzdorf and of Audrey von Etzdorf (née Catterns). Educ: Downe House; St Martin's Sch. of Art; Camberwell Sch. of Art (BA Hons 1977). Freelance textile designer, 1978–79; freelance designer, developing designs from paper work and silk screens on to fabric, 1979–80; Founder, Georgina von Etzdorf Partnership, 1981; artistic dir of team producing biannual collections of clothing and accessories, 1992–. Lectures and teaching posts: Cooper Hewitt Mus., NYC; Nova Scotia Sch. of Art and Design; Glasgow Coll. of Art; St Martin's Sch. of Art; Royal Coll. of Art; Crafts Council. Exhibitions: Smithsonian Instn's Nat. Mus. of Design, Washington; Cooper Hewitt Mus., NY; V&A; Manchester City Art Gall. (25 yr retrospective), 2006. Gov., Univ. of the Arts, 2005. Hon. Fellow, London Inst., 2003. Hon. DDes Winchester Sch. of Art, Univ. of Southampton, 1996. Enterprise Award for Small Businesses, Radio 4, 1984; British Apparel Export Award, 1986; Manchester Prize for Art and Industry, British Gas Award, 1988. Recreations: singing, dancing, playing the ukelele. Club: Chelsea Arts.

von HASE, Karl-Günther, Hon. GCVO 1972; Hon. KCMG 1965; Hon. President, Deutsch-Englische Gesellschaft, Düsseldorf, since 1993 (Chairman, 1982–93); b 15 Dec. 1917; m 1945, Renate Stumpff; five d. Educ: German schools. Professional Soldier, 1936–45; War Academy, 1943–44; Training College for Diplomats, 1950–51; Georgetown Univ., Washington DC, 1952. German Foreign Service: German Embassy, Ottawa, 1953–56; Spokesman, Foreign Office Bonn, 1958–61; Head, West European Dept, 1961–62; Spokesman of German Federal Government, 1962–67; State Secretary,

Min. of Defence, German Federal Govt, 1968–69; German Ambassador to the Court of St James's, 1970–77; Dir-Gen., Zweites Deutsches Fernsehen, 1977–82. Hon. LLD Manchester, 1987. Holds German and other foreign decorations. *Recreations:* shooting, music. *Address:* Am Stadtwald 60, 53177 Bonn, Germany.

von KLITZING, Prof. Klaus, PhD; Director, Max-Planck-Institut für Festkörperforschung, Stuttgart, since 1985; *b* 28 June 1943; *s* of Bogislav and Anny von Klitzing; *m* 1971, Renate Falkenberg; two *s* one *d*. *Educ:* Technische Univ., Braunschweig (Dipl Phys); Univ. of Würzburg (PhD; Habilitation (univ. teaching qual.). Prof., Technische Univ., München, 1980–84; Hon. Prof., Univ. of Stuttgart, 1985. Foreign Mem., Royal Soc., 2003. Hon. FInstP 2002. Nobel Prize for Physics, 1985. *Address:* Max-Planck-Institut für Festkörperforschung, Heisenbergstrasse 1, 70569 Stuttgart, Federal Republic of Germany. *T:* (711) 6891570.

von KUENHEIM, Eberhard; Chairman of the Board, Eberhard von Kuenheim Stiftung, since 2000; Chairman: Executive Board, 1970–93, Supervisory Board, 1993–2000, BMW AG, Munich; *b* 2 Oct. 1928, E Prussia. *Educ:* Stuttgart Technical Univ. (Diplom-Ingenieur; MSc). Technical Dir, Machine tool factory, Hanover, 1954–65; joined QUANDT Gp, 1965; Dep. Chm., Exec. Bd., Industriewerke Karlsruhe Augsburg AG, 1968–70. Hon. Senator, Munich Technical Univ. Hon. doctorates: Clausthal-Zellerfeld Technical Univ.; Munich Technical Univ. *Address:* Eberhard von Kuenheim Stiftung, Amiraplatz 3, Luitpoldblock, 80333 Munich, Germany.

von MALLINCKRODT, George Wilhelm, Hon. KBE 1997; President, Schroders plc, since 1995 (Chairman, 1984–95; Director, since 1977); Chairman, Schroders Incorporated, New York, since 1985; Chairman, J. Henry Schroder Bank AG, Zurich, 1984–2003; *b* 19 Aug. 1930; *s* of Arnold Wilhelm von Mallinckrodt and Valentine von Mallinckrodt (*née* von Joest); *m* 1958, Charmaine Schroder; two *s* two *d*. *Educ:* Salem, West Germany. Agfa AG Munich, 1948–51; Münchmeyer & Co., Hamburg, 1951–53; Kleinwort Sons & Co., London, 1953–54; J. Henry Schroder Banking Corp., New York, 1954–55; Union Bank of Switzerland, Geneva 1956–57; J. Henry Schroder Banking Corp., NY, 1957–60; J. Henry Schroder & Co., subseq. J. Henry Schroder Wagg & Co., London, 1960–85, Director, 1967–; Schroders Incorp., NY, 1977–; Chm. and Chief Exec. Officer, J. Henry Schroder Bank & Trust Co., NY, 1984–86. Director: Schroder Asseily & Co., 1981–2000; Schroders Australia Hldgs Ltd, Sydney, 1984–2001; NM UK, 1986–90; Schroder Internat. Merchant Bankers, 1988–2000; Director: Allianz of America Inc. (NY), 1978–84; Banque Privée de Gestion Financière (Paris), 1980–83; Siemens plc, 1989–2000; Euris SA, Paris, 1989–98; Foreign & Colonial German Investment Trust PLC, 1992–98. Vice-Pres., German-British Chamber of Industry and Commerce in UK, 1996– (Dir, 1971–91, Pres., 1992–95); Chm. of Council, World Economic Forum, 1995–97; Mem., Europ. Adv. Cttee, McGraw Hill Inc., USA, 1986–89; Advr, Bain & Co., 1997–2005; Dir, Europ. Arts Foundn, 1987–2002. Member: British N American Cttee, 1988–; City Adv. Gp, CBI, 1990–. Pres., German YMCA, London, 1961–; Member: Ct of Benefactors, Oxford Univ., 1990–; Nat. Art Collection Develt Fund, 1995–2005; BM Develt Trust, 1995–; INSEAD Circle of Patrons, 1995–; Council, John F. Kennedy Sch. of Govt, Harvard Univ., 2005–; Adv. Cttee on Finance, St George's Coll., Windsor; Trustee: Prague Heritage Fund, 1992–2004; Christian Responsibility in Public Affairs; Patron, Three Faiths Forum. Freeman, City of London, 2004. FRSA 1986; CCMI (CBIM 1986). Hon. DCL Bishop's Univ., Canada, 1994. Verdienstkreuz am Bande, 1986, Verdienstkreuz 1 Klasse, 1990, Grosse Verdienstkreuz, 2001, des Verdienstordens (Germany). Awarded Annual Sternberg Interfaith Award, 2005. *Recreations:* music, gardening, shooting, ski-ing. *Address:* Schroders plc, 31 Gresham Street, EC2V 7QA. *T:* (020) 7658 6000.

von MOLTKE, Gebhardt; Chairman, Deutsch-Britische Gesellschaft, since 2003; *b* 28 June 1938; *s* of late Hans-Adolf von Moltke and Davida, Gräfin Yorck von Wartenburg; *m* 1965, Dorothea Bräuer; one *s* one *d*. *Educ:* Univs of Grenoble, Berlin, Freiburg (Law); qualified as lawyer, 1967. German Trade Unions, 1967–68; Fed. Republic of Germany Diplomatic Service, 1968–2003: served Liverpool, Cabinet of Foreign Minister, Moscow, Jaoundé/Cameroon, and Foreign Office Personnel Dept; Washington Embassy, 1982–86; Head, US Desk, Foreign Office, 1986–91; Asst Sec.-Gen. for Political Affairs, NATO HQ, Brussels, 1991–97; Ambassador to UK, 1997–99; Perm. Rep. to NATO, 1999–2003. *Recreations:* music, art (Italian drawings), reading, tennis. *Address:* Deutsch-Britische Ges., Albrechtstrasse 22, 10117 Berlin, Germany.

von OTTER, Anne Sofie; singer (mezzo-soprano); *b* Stockholm, 9 May 1955. *Educ:* Stockholm Acad. of Music; GSMD; vocal studies with Vera Rozsa, 1981–. With Basle Opera, 1983–85; freelance, 1985–; appearances at most major opera houses incl. Royal Opera, Covent Garden, 1985–; Metropolitan Opera, 1985–; La Scala, Milan, 1987–; Glyndebourne, Geneva, Aix-en-Provence, Paris, Vienna, Chicago, Berlin and Munich; has also given recitals worldwide. Rôles include: Mozart: Cherubino, Sextus, Idamante, Dorabella, Ramiro; Strauss: Octavian, Clairon, Componist; Bellini: Romeo; Rossini: Tancredi, Cenerentola; Bizet: Carmen; Gluck: Orfeo; Monteverdi: Nerone; Handel: Ariodante, Xerxes. Major recordings include: Così fan tutte; Orfeo ed Euridice; Hansel and Gretel; Der Rosenkavalier; Le Nozze di Figaro; Idomeneo; Ariodante; Werther; Les Contes d'Hoffmann; La Damnation de Faust; Nuits d'Eté, Mahler cycles, and lieder by Mahler, Brahms, Grieg, Wolf, etc. Hon. RAM 2002. *Address:* c/o IMG, The Light Box, 111 Power Road, W4 5PY. *T:* (020) 7957 5800.

von PLOETZ, Dr Hans-Friedrich; Chairman, Foundation on German-Russian Youth Exchange, since 2006; *b* 12 July 1940; *m* 1971, Päivi Leinonen; two *s*. Diplomatic posts in: Morocco, 1967–68; Helsinki, 1968–73; Min. for Foreign Affairs, 1973–78; Washington, 1978–80; Min. for Foreign Affairs, 1980–88; Dep. Perm. Rep. of Germany, 1988–89, Ambassador and Perm. Rep. of Germany, 1989–93, on NATO Council; Dir-Gen. for Eur. Integration, Bonn, 1993–94; State Sec., Min. for Foreign Affairs, Bonn, 1994–99; Ambassador to UK, 1999–2002; Ambassador in the Russian Federation, 2002–05. *Recreations:* music, golf, gardening. *Address:* Schloßstrasse 5, 14059 Berlin, Germany.

von REITZENSTEIN, Hans-Joachim Freiherr; *see* Leech, John.

von RICHTHOFEN, Baron Hermann, Hon. GCVO 1992; Permanent Representative of the Federal Republic of Germany to NATO, 1993–98; *b* 20 Nov. 1933; *s* of Baron Herbert von Richthofen and Baroness Gisela von Richthofen (*née* Schoeller); *m* 1966, Christa, Countess von Schwerin; one *s* two *d*. *Educ:* Univs of Heidelberg, Munich and Bonn; Dr in law Cologne Univ. 1963. Joined Diplomatic Service of FRG, 1963; served Boston, Mass, 1963–64; FO, 1964–66; Saigon, 1966–68; Jakarta, 1968–70; FO, 1970–74; Dep. Hd, Sect. for Internat. Law, FO, 1974; Hd, Sect. for For. Policy, Perm. Mission to GDR, 1975–78; Hd of Dept for German and Berlin Affairs, FO, 1978–80; seconded to Fed. Chancellery as Hd of Intra-German Policy Unit, 1980–86; Dir Gen. of Legal Div., 1986, of Political Div., and Political Dir, 1986–88, FO; Ambassador to UK, 1988–93. Chm., British-German Assoc., Berlin, 1998–2003 (Hon. Mem.). Gov., Ditchley Foundn, 1988–93, 1996–. Trustee, 21st Century Trust, 1998–. Hon. Prof., Central Connecticut State Univ., 2001. Hon. LLD Birmingham, 2000. ER 1961, RR 1985, Johanniter Orden; Officer's Cross, Order of the Knights of Malta, 1967; Commander's Cross: Order of Merit (Italy), 1979; Legion of Honour (France), 1987; Grand Officer's Cross, Order of Infante D. Henrique (Portugal), 1988; Knight Commander's Cross, 2nd class (Austria), 1989; Grand Cross, Order of Merit (FRG), 1999; Grand Cross, Order of Merit (Luxembourg), 2000; Commander's Cross, Order of Merit (Poland), 2003; Order of Merit of Land Brandenburg (Germany), 2000. *Recreations:* reading history, arts. *Address:* Beckerstrasse 6a, 12157 Berlin, Germany.

von SCHRAMEK, Sir Eric (Emil), Kt 1982; architect; Chairman, von Schramek and Dawes Pty Ltd, 1963–91; Consultant to Hames Sharley International, Architects and Planners, 1989–97; *b* 4 April 1921; *s* of Emil and Annie von Schramek; *m* Edith, *d* of Dipl. Ing. W. Popper; one *s* two *d*. *Educ:* Stefans Gymnasium, Prague; Technical Univ., Prague. DiplIngArch; Life Fellow: RAIA; Inst. of Arbitrators and Mediators of Aust. Town Planner, Bavaria, 1946–48; Sen. Supervising Architect, Dept of Works and Housing, Darwin, NT, 1948–51; Evans, Bruer & Partners (later von Schramek and Dawes), 1951–91: work includes multi-storey office buildings in Adelaide (Nat. Mutual Centre; State Govt Insce Bldg; Wales House; Qantas Bldg, etc); Wesley House, Melbourne; Westpac House, Hobart; AMP Bldg and Qantas Bldg, Darwin; numerous churches throughout Australia and New Guinea. National Pres., Building Science Forum of Aust., 1970–72; President: RAIA (SA Chapter), 1974–76; Inst. of Arbitrators, Aust. (SA Chapter), 1977–80. Vis. Lectr, Univ. of Adelaide; former Vis. Lectr, S Australian Inst. of Technol. Past National Dep. Chm., Austcare; past Councillor, Council of Professions; past Chm., Commn on Worship and other Depts, Lutheran Church of Australia. Hon. Associate (Arch.), SA Inst. of Technology, 1989. KCSJ 2001 (KSJ 1995). *Publications:* Remembrances: Eric von Schramek and his churches, 2007; contribs and articles in architectural pubns. *Recreations:* music, reading, golf. *Address:* 48 Coopers Avenue, Leabrook, SA 5068, Australia. *T:* (8) 84315263.

von WEIZSÄCKER, Richard, Dr jur; President of the Federal Republic of Germany, 1984–94; *b* 15 April 1920; *s* of late Ernst von Weizsäcker; *m* 1953, Marianne von Kretschmann; three *s* one *d*. *Educ:* Berlin and Bern; Univs of Oxford, Grenoble and Göttingen (Dr jur). Army service, 1938–45 (Captain, wounded). Formerly with: Mannesmann; Waldthausen & Co., Essen/Düsseldorf; Boehringer, Ingelheim. Pres., German Protestant Convention, 1964–70, 1979–81; Mem., Synod and Council, German Evangelical Church, 1967–84. Joined Christian Democratic Union, 1954: Mem., Fed. Board; Chm., Gen. Policy Commn, 1971–74; Chm., Basic Prog. Commn, 1974–77; Dep. Chm., CDU/CSU Parlt Gp, 1972–79; Presidential candidate, 1974; First Chm., Berlin CDU, 1981–83. Mem., Bundestag, 1969–81, Vice-Pres., 1979–81; Governing Mayor of West Berlin, 1981–84. Royal Victorian Chain, 1992. *Address:* (office) Am Kupfergraben 7, 10117 Berlin, Germany.

von WINTERFELDT, (Hans) Dominik; Partner, Boyden World Corporation, New York, since 1996; *b* 3 July 1937; *s* of late Curt von Winterfeldt and Anna Franziska Margaretha Luise (*née* Petersen); *m* 1966, Cornelia Waldthausen; one *s* one *d*. *Educ:* German schools; Stanford-INSEAD, Fontainebleau (Industriekaufmann). DipICC. Joined Hoechst AG, Frankfurt/Main, 1957; Asst Manager, Hoechst Colombiana Ltda, 1960; Commercial Manager, Pharmaceuticals, Hoechst Peruana SA, 1963; General Manager, Hoechst Dyechemie W. L. L., Iraq, 1965; Man. Dir, Hoechst Pakistan Ltd and Hoechst Pharmaceuticals Ltd, 1967; Hoechst UK Ltd: Dep. Man. Dir, 1972; Man. Dir and Chief Exec., 1975; Exec. Chm., 1984; Dir (Corporate PR and Communications), 1987–94; Dir, Cassella AG, 1994–95. Mem., British Assoc. for Shooting and Conservation, 1979–. Mem., Rotary Club, Frankfurt, 1990–. KStJ 2008. *Recreations:* music, deer stalking, golf. *Address:* Boyden International GmbH, Ferdinandstrasse 6, 61348 Bad Homburg, Germany. *T:* (6172) 180200.

VORDERMAN, Carol Jean, MBE 2000; broadcaster and author; *b* 24 Dec. 1960; *d* of Anton Joseph Maria Vorderman and Edwina Jean Vorderman; *m* 1st, 1985 (marr. diss. 1987); 2nd, 1990 (marr. diss. 2002); one *s* one *d*. *Educ:* Blessed Edward Jones High Sch., Rhyl; Sidney Sussex Coll., Cambridge (MA). Member: Action into Engrg Task Force, DTI, 1995; Home Office Internet Task Force, 2001–02. Founder Mem. and Trustee, NESTA, 1998–2001. Television programmes include: Countdown, 1982–2008; World Chess Championship (Kasparov *v* Short), 1993; Tomorrow's World, 1994–95; Computers Don't Bite, 1997; Mysteries with Carol Vorderman, 1997–98; Carol Vorderman's Better Homes, 1999–2003; Find a Fortune, 1999–2001; Star Lives (formerly Stars and Their Lives), 1999–2002; Tested to Destruction, 1999; Pride of Britain Awards, 2000–; Britain's Brainiest Kids, 2001–02; Vorderman's Sudoku Live, 2005; Golden Lot, 2005. Columnist: Daily Telegraph, 1996–98; Mirror, 1998–2004. FRSA 1997. Hon. Fellow, Univ. of Wales, Bangor, 1999. Hon. MA Bath, 2000. *Publications:* Dirty, Loud and Brilliant, 1988; Dirty, Loud and Brilliant Too, 1989; How Mathematics Works, 1996; (with R. Young) Carol Vorderman's Guide to the Internet, 1998, 2nd edn 2001; Maths Made Easy, 1999; Science Made Easy, 2000; English Made Easy, 2000; Educating and Entertaining Your Children Online with Carol Vorderman, 2001; (with Ko Chohan) Detox for Life, 2001; Carol Vorderman's Summer Detox, 2003; Carol Vorderman's Detox Recipes, 2003; Carol Vorderman's 30 Day Cellulite Plan, 2004; Carol Vorderman's How to do Sudoku, 2005; Super Brain, 2007. *Address:* c/o John Miles Organisation, Cadbury Camp Lane, Clapton-in-Gordano, Bristol BS20 7SB. *T:* (01275) 854675.

VORHAUS, Jennifer; *see* Dixon, J.

VOS, Geoffrey Charles; QC 1993; Judge of the Courts of Appeal of Jersey and Guernsey, since 2005; Chairman, Bar Council of England and Wales, 2007; *b* 22 April 1955; *s* of Bernard Vos and Pamela Celeste Rose (*née* Heilbuth); *m* 1984, Vivien Mary Fieldhouse (*née* Dowdeswell); one *d* and one step *s* two step *d*. *Educ:* University College Sch., London; Gonville and Caius Coll., Cambridge (BA, MA). Called to the Bar, Inner Temple, 1977; Bencher, Lincoln's Inn, 2000. Chm., Chancery Bar Assoc., 1999–2001 (Hon. Sec., 1994–97; Vice-Chm., 1997–99). Bar Council: Chm., Fees Collection Cttee, 1995–2004; Vice Chm., 2001–03, Chm., 2004–05, Professional Standards Cttee; Mem., Gen. Mgt Cttee, 2004–07; Vice Chm., 2006. Trustee, Social Mobility Foundn, 2007– (Chm., 2008–). *Recreations:* farming, wine, photography. *Address:* 3 Stone Buildings, Lincoln's Inn, WC2A 3XL. *Clubs:* Oxford and Cambridge; Worcestershire Golf.

VOS, His Honour Geoffrey Michael; a Circuit Judge, 1978–94; *b* 18 Feb. 1927; *s* of Louis and Rachel Eva Vos; *m* 1955, Marcia Joan Goldstone (marr. diss. 1977); two *s* two *d*; *m* 1981, Mrs Anne Wilson. *Educ:* St Joseph's College, Blackpool; Gonville and Caius College, Cambridge (MA, LLB). Called to the Bar, Gray's Inn, 1950. A Recorder of the Crown Court, 1976–78. *Recreations:* swimming, walking. *Address:* c/o The Crown Court, The Law Courts, Quayside, Newcastle upon Tyne NE1 3LA. *T:* (0191) 201 2000.

VOSPER, Christopher John; QC 2000; **His Honour Judge Vosper;** a Circuit Judge, since 2006; *b* 4 Oct. 1952; *s* of John Darvel Vosper and Hettie Vosper; *m* 1982, Ann Prosser Bowen; one *s* one *d*. *Educ:* Cowbridge Grammar Sch.; Pembroke Coll., Oxford (MA). Called to the Bar, Middle Temple, 1977; in practice as barrister, 1977–2006; a

Recorder, 1998–2006. *Address:* Swansea Civil Justice Centre, Caravella House, Quay West, Quay Parade, Swansea SA1 1SP.

VOUSDEN, Prof. Karen Heather, (Mrs R. Ludwig), PhD; FRS 2003; FMedSci; Director, Beatson Institute for Cancer Research, and Professor, University of Glasgow, since 2002; *b* 19 July 1957; *d* of William and Erna Vousden; *m* 1986, Robert Ludwig; one *d. Educ:* Queen Mary Coll., Univ. of London (BSc 1978; PhD 1982). Post-Doctoral Fellow, Inst. of Cancer Res., London, 1981–85; Nat. Cancer Inst., USA, 1985–87; Hd, Human Papillomavirus Gp, Ludwig Inst. for Cancer Res., 1987–95; Dir, Molecular Virology and Carcinogenesis Lab., Advanced Biosci. Lab. Basic Res. Prog., USA, 1995–99; Chief, Regulation of Cell Growth Lab., Nat. Cancer Inst., USA, 1999–2002. FMedSci 2006. *Publications:* contrib. numerous articles to learned jls. *Recreation:* hill-walking. *Address:* Beatson Institute for Cancer Research, Garscube Estate, Switchback Road, Bearsden, Glasgow G61 1BD. *T:* (0141) 330 2424, *Fax:* (0141) 943 0372; *e-mail:* k.vousden@beatson.gla.ac.uk.

VOWLES, Paul Foster; Academic Registrar, University of London, 1973–82; *b* 12 June 1919; *s* of late E. F. Vowles and G. M. Vowles, Bristol; *m* 1948, Valerie Eleanor Hickman; one *s* two *d. Educ:* Bristol Grammar Sch.; Corpus Christi Coll., Oxford (schol.; MA). Served Gloucestershire Regt and King's African Rifles, 1939–46 (despatches, Major). Asst Secretary: Appts Bd, Univ. of Birmingham, 1947–48; Inter-University Council for Higher Educn Overseas, 1948–51; Registrar, Makerere University Coll., E Africa, 1951–63; Sen. Asst to Principal, Univ. of London, 1964–68; Warden, Lillian Penson Hall, 1965–69; External Registrar, 1968–73. Mem., 1983–89, Vice-Chm., 1986–89, Westfield Coll. Council. Hon. Fellow, QMW (Fellow, 1991). *Address:* 13 Dale Close, Oxford OX1 1TU. *T:* (01865) 244042.

VRAALSEN, Tom; Commander, Royal Order of Saint Olav 1987; Ambassador and Special Advisor to Norwegian Ministry of Foreign Affairs, since 2004; *b* 26 Jan. 1936; *m* 1977, Viebecke Strøm; two *d. Educ:* Arhus Sch. of Econs and Business Admin, Denmark (MEcon). Entered Norwegian Foreign Service, 1960; served Peking, Cairo, Manila, 1960–71; Head of Div., Min. of Foreign Affairs, 1971–75; Minister-Counsellor, Perm. Mission of Norway to UN, NY, 1975–81; Dir-Gen., Min. of Foreign Affairs, 1981–82; Ambassador, Perm. Mission of Norway to UN, NY, 1982–89; Minister of Develt Assistance, 1989–90; Dir of Information, Saga Petroleum, 1991–92; Asst Sec. Gen., Min. of Foreign Affairs, 1992–94; Ambassador to: UK, 1994–96; USA, 1996–2001; to Finland, 2001–03. Special Envoy of UN Sec.-Gen. for humanitarian affairs, Sudan, 1998–2004. Chm., Assessment and Evaluation Commn, Khartoum, 2005–08. *Address:* Ministry of Foreign Affairs, 7 Juni plassen 1, 0032 Oslo, Norway.

VREDELING, Hendrikus, (Henk); Member, and Vice-President (responsible for Employment and Social Affairs), Commission of European Communities, 1977–80; *b* 20 Nov. 1924. *Educ:* Agricultural Univ., Wageningen. Member: Second Chamber of States-General, Netherlands, 1956–73; European Parliament, 1958–73; Socio-Economic Adviser to Agricultural Workers' Union, Netherlands, 1950–73; Minister of Defence, Netherlands, 1973–76. Member: Dutch Emancipation Council, 1981–85; Dutch Council on Peace and Security, 1987–94. *Address:* Rembrandtlaan 13A, 3712 AJ Huis ter Heide, Netherlands.

VULLIAMY, Edward Sebastian; Senior Correspondent and writer, The Guardian and The Observer, since 1986; *b* 1 Aug. 1954; *s* of late John Sebastian Papendiek Vulliamy and of Shirley Hughes, *qv*; separated; two *d. Educ:* University Coll. Sch., London; Univ. di Firenze (Dip. Italian and Renaissance Studies 1973); Hertford Coll., Oxford (MA PPE 1976). Researcher, World in Action, Granada TV, 1979–85; The Guardian: gen. reporter, 1986–89; corresp. in Italy and Balkans, 1990–96; US corresp., Guardian and Observer, 1994–95 and 1997–2003. RTS Award, 1985; Internat. Reporter of Year, British Press Awards, 1992, 1997; Foreign Corresp. of Year, Granada/What the Papers Say Awards, 1992; Amnesty Internat. Award, 1992; James Cameron Meml Award, 1994. *Publications:* Seasons in Hell: understanding Bosnia's war, 1994; (with David Leigh) Sleaze: the corruption of Parliament, 1996; contrib. chapters in books, incl. Crimes of War, ed Gutman and Reiff; contribs to jls incl. Internat. Affairs, Colombian Journalism Rev., Nat. Geographic. *Recreations:* opera, classical music, rock blues, jazz, history of painting, especially Italian Renaissance, Italy, football, politics, current affairs. *Address:* c/o The Guardian, Kings Place, 90 York Way, N1 9AG; *e-mail:* ed.vulliamy@guardian.co.uk. *Club:* Frontline.

VULLIAMY, Shirley, (Mrs J. S. P. Vulliamy); *see* Hughes, S.

VUONG THUA PHONG; Ambassador of Vietnam to the Czech Republic; *b* 25 Oct. 1956; *m* Ngo Thi Phi Nga; two *s. Educ:* Soviet Union. Dep. Dir, Policy Planning Dept, Min. of Foreign Affairs, Vietnam; Private Sec. to Foreign Minister, 1994–98; Ambassador to the UK, 1998–2003. Member: RIIA; London Diplomatic Assoc. *Recreation:* golf. *Address:* Embassy of Vietnam, Plzeñská 214/2578, Prague 5, Czech Republic. *Club:* London Golf.

VYVYAN, Maj.-Gen. Charles Gerard Courtenay, CB 1998; CBE 1990 (MBE 1974); Gentleman Usher of the Scarlet Rod, Order of the Bath, since 2006; Defence Attaché and Head, British Defence Staff, Washington, 1997–2000; *b* 29 Sept. 1944; *er s* of John Michal Kenneth Vyvyan and Elizabeth Mary Lowder Vyvyan; *m* 1989, Elizabeth Frances (LVO 1998), 3rd *d* of Sir John Paget, 3rd Bt, Haygrass, Taunton. *Educ:* Winchester Coll.; Balliol Coll., Oxford (BA Mod. Hist. 1966; MA 1991). Nat. Defence Coll., Pakistan (MSc, Defence and Strategic Studies). Commnd, Royal Green Jackets (Rifle Bde), 1967; Sultan of Oman's Armed Forces, 1975–76; Staff Coll., 1978; CO 1st Bn RGJ, 1984–86; Col GS Mil. Ops, 1986–87; Comdr 3 Inf. Bde, 1988–90; student, Nat. Defence Coll., Pakistan, 1990–91; DCS, HQ UKLF, 1991–94; COS, HQ UKLF, later Land Command, 1994–97. Col Comdt, 1 RGJ, 1994–2000. Vis. Fellow, Eisenhower Inst., Washington, 2002–06. Gov., Cranleigh Sch., 2000–. *Recreations:* mountains, gardens, travel, fishing, Alexander the Great. *Clubs:* Boodle's, Beefsteak.

VYVYAN, Sir (Ralph) Ferrers (Alexander), 13th Bt *cr* 1645, of Trelowarren, Cornwall; *b* 21 Aug. 1960; *s* of Sir John Stanley Vyvyan, 12th Bt and of his 3rd wife, Jonet Noël, *e d* of Lt-Col Alexander Hubert Barclay, DSO, MC; *S* father, 1995, but his name does not appear on the Official Roll of the Baronetage; *m* 1986, Victoria Arabella, *y d* of M. B. Ogle; five *s. Educ:* Charterhouse; Sandhurst; Architectural Assoc. High Sheriff, Cornwall, 2008. *Heir: s* Joshua Drummond Vyvyan, *b* 10 Oct. 1986. *Address:* Trelowarren, Mawgan, Helston, Cornwall TR12 6AF.

W

WADDELL, Bruce; Editor, Daily Record, since 2003; *b* 18 March 1959; *s* of Ken and Christina Ann Waddell; *m* 1994, Cathy Cullis; one *s*. Johnston Newspapers, 1977–87; Sub Ed., then Chief Sub Ed., Scottish Sun, 1987–90; Dep. Ed., Sunday Scot, 1990–91; Mktg and Sales Exec., Murray Internat., 1991–93; Dep. Ed., 1993–98, Ed., 1998–2003, Scottish Sun. *Recreations:* football, classic cars, cinema, golf. *Address:* Daily Record, One Central Quay, Glasgow G3 8DA. *T:* (0141) 309 3000, *Fax:* (0141) 309 3340.

WADDELL, Gordon Herbert; Chairman, Shanks Group plc (formerly Shanks & McEwan), 1992–2002; *b* Glasgow, 12 April 1937; *s* of late Herbert Waddell; *m* 1st, 1965, Mary (marr. diss. 1971), *d* of Harry Frederick Oppenheimer; 2nd, 1973, Kathy May, *d* of W. S. Gallagher. *Educ:* St Mary's Sch., Melrose; Fettes Coll., Edinburgh; Cambridge Univ. (BA); Stanford Univ. (MBA). Rugby Blue, Cambridge Univ., 1958, 1959, 1961; Member, British Isles Rugby Touring Team: to Australia and NZ, 1959; to South Africa, 1962; eighteen rugby caps for Scotland. MP (Progressive Party) for Johannesburg North, April 1974–Nov. 1977. Dir, E. Oppenheimer & Son Ltd, 1965–87; Exec. Dir, Anglo American Corp. of South Africa Ltd, 1971–87; Chairman: Johannesburg Consolidated Investment Co. Ltd, 1981–87; Rustenburg Platinum Mines Ltd, 1981–87; South African Breweries Ltd, 1984–87; Fairway Group plc (formerly Fairway (London)), 1989–98; Ryan Gp (formerly Digger), 1991–95; Gartmore Scotland Investment Trust, 1991–2001; Tor Investment Trust, 1992–96; Mersey Docks and Harbour Co., 1992–2006; Director: Cadbury Schweppes, 1988–97; Scottish Nat. Trust, 1988–96; London and Strathclyde Trust, 1989–96. *Recreation:* golf. *Address:* 1 Alexander Place, SW7 2SG. *Clubs:* Hawks (Cambridge); Honourable Company of Edinburgh Golfers; Royal and Ancient (St Andrews).

WADDELL, Rear-Adm. William Angus, CB 1981; OBE 1966; *b* 5 Nov. 1924; *s* of late James Whitefield Waddell and Christina Waddell (*née* Maclean); *m* 1950, Thelma Evelyn Tomlins (*d* 2007); one *s* one *d. Educ:* Glasgow Univ. (BSc (Hons) Maths and Nat. Phil.; Cleland Gold Medal). CEng; FIET. Midshipman, Sub Lieut RNVR (Special Branch), HMS Ranee, HMS Collingwood, 1945–47; Instr Lieut, HMS Collingwood, HMS Glasgow, HMS Siskin, HMS Gambia, 1947–59 (RMCS 1956–57); Instr Comdr, HMS Albion, 1959–61; Staff of Dir, Naval Educn Service, 1961–63; Sen. British Naval Officer, Dam Neck, Virginia, 1963–66; Officer i/c RN Polaris Sch., 1966–68; Instr Captain, Staff of SACLANT (Dir, Inf. Systems Gp), 1969–72; Dean, RN Coll., Greenwich, 1973–75; Dir Naval Officer Appointments (Instr), 1975–78; Rear-Adm. 1979; Chief Naval Instructor Officer, 1978–81 and Flag Officer, Admiralty Interview Bd, 1979–81. ADC to HM the Queen, 1976–79. Assoc. Teacher, City Univ., 1973–75; Sec. and Chief Exec., RIPH&H, 1982–90. Hon. FRIPH (Hon. FRIPHH 1990). *Publication:* An Introduction to Servomechanisms (with F. L. Westwater), 1961, repr. 1968. *Address:* c/o National Westminster Bank, 80 Lewisham High Street, SE13 5JJ.

WADDINGTON, family name of **Baron Waddington**.

WADDINGTON, Baron *cr* 1990 (Life Peer), of Read in the County of Lancashire; **David Charles Waddington,** GCVO 1994; PC 1987; DL; QC 1971; Governor and Commander-in-Chief of Bermuda, 1992–97; a Recorder of the Crown Court, 1972–99; *b* 2 Aug. 1929; *o s* of late Charles Waddington and of Mrs Minnie Hughan Waddington; *m* 1958, Gillian Rosemary, *d* of late Alan Green, CBE; three *s* two *d. Educ:* Sedbergh; Hertford Coll., Oxford (Hon. Fellow, 1998). President, Oxford Univ. Conservative Assoc., 1950. 2nd Lieut, XII Royal Lancers, 1951–53. Called to Bar, Gray's Inn, 1951, Bencher, 1985. Contested (C): Farnworth Div., 1955; Nelson and Colne Div., 1964; Heywood and Royton Div., 1966; MP (C): Nelson and Colne, 1968–Sept. 1974; Clitheroe, March 1979–1983; Ribble Valley, 1983–90; a Lord Comr, HM Treasury, 1979–81; Parly Under-Sec. of State, Dept of Employment, 1981–83; Minister of State, Home Office, 1983–87; Parly Sec., HM Treasury and Govt Chief Whip, 1987–89; Sec. of State, Home Office, 1989–90; Lord Privy Seal and Leader of H of L, 1990–92. DL Lancs 1991. *Address:* Old Bailiffs, South Cheriton, Templecombe, Somerset BA8 0BH.

WADDINGTON, Prof. David James; Professor of Chemical Education, University of York, 1978–2000, now Emeritus; *b* 27 May 1932; *s* of late Eric James and Marjorie Edith Waddington; *m* 1957, Isobel Hesketh; two *s* one *d. Educ:* Marlborough College; Imperial College, Univ. of London (BSc, ARCS, DIC, PhD). Head of Chemistry Dept, 1959, Head of Science Dept, 1961, Wellington College; York University: Sen. Lectr, 1965; Head Chemistry Dept, 1983–92; Pro-Vice-Chancellor, 1985–91. Hon. Prof., Mendeleev Univ. of Chem. Technol., Moscow, 1998–; Vis. Prof., Inst. für die Pädagogik der Naturwissenschaften, Univ. Kiel, 2000–. President, Educn Div., Royal Soc. of Chem., 1981–83; Inst. of Sci. Technol., 1995–2000; Sec., 1977, Chm., 1981–86, Cttee on Teaching of Chemistry, IUPAC; Sec., 1986–89, Chm., 1990–94, Cttee on Teaching of Science, ICSU. Liveryman, Salters' Co., 2001–; Freedom, City of London, 2001. Nyholm Medal, RSC, 1985; Brasted Award, ACS, 1988. Nat. Order of Scientific Merit (Brazil), 1997. *Publications:* Organic Chemistry, 1962; (with H. S. Finlay) Organic Chemistry Through Experiment, 1965; (with R. O. C. Norman) Modern Organic Chemistry, 1972; (with A. Kornhauser and C. N. R. Rao) Chemical Education in the 70s, 1980; (ed) Teaching School Chemistry, 1985; (ed) Education, Industry and Technology, 1987; (jtly) Introducing Chemistry: the Salters' approach, 1989; Chemistry: the Salters' approach, 1990; (jtly) Salters' Advanced Chemistry, 1994; (ed) Science for Understanding Tomorrow's World: global change, 1994, 2nd edn 2000; Global Environmental Change Science: education and training, 1995; (with J. N. Lazonby) Partners in Chemical Education, 1996; (jtly) Salters' Higher Chemistry, 1999; (jtly) The Essential Chemical Industry, 1999; Evaluation as a Tool for improving Science Education, 2005; Context Based Learning of Science, 2005; Standards in Science Education, 2007. *Recreation:* gardening. *Address:* Department of Chemistry, University of York, York YO10 5DD.

WADDINGTON, Leslie; Chairman, Waddington Galleries, since 1966; *b* Dublin, 9 Feb. 1934; *s* of late Victor and Zelda Waddington; *m* 1st, 1967, Ferriel Lyle (marr. diss. 1983); two *d*; 2nd, 1985, Clodagh Frances Fanshawe. *Educ:* Portora Royal School; Sorbonne; Ecole du Louvre (Diplômé). Formed Waddington Galleries with father, 1957. Chm., Modern Painting Sect., 1994–2004, Pictura Sect., 1996–2000, Maastricht Art Fair. Sen. Fellow, RCA, 1993. *Recreations:* backgammon, reading. *Address:* 11 Cork Street, W1S 3LT. *T:* (020) 7851 2200.

WADDINGTON, Susan Andrée; European Development Officer, National Institute of Adult Continuing Education, since 2000; *b* 23 Aug. 1944; *m* 1966, Ivan Waddington; one *s* one *d. Educ:* Blyth GS, Norwich; Leicester Univ. (BA; MEd). Assistant Director of Education: Derbys CC, 1988–90; Birmingham CC, 1990–94. Mem. (Lab) Leics CC, 1973–91, 2003–. MEP (Lab) Leicester, 1994–99. Contested (Lab): Leics NW, 1987; E Midlands Reg., EP, 1999. *Address:* 5 Roundhill Road, Leicester LE5 5RJ; *e-mail:* susan.waddington@ntlworld.com.

WADDS, Mrs Jean Casselman, OC 1982; Member, Royal Commission on Economic Union and Development Prospects for Canada, 1983–85; *b* 16 Sept. 1920; *d* of Hon. Earl Rowe and Treva Lennox Rowe; *m* 1st, 1946, Clair Casselman; one *s* one *d*; 2nd, 1964, Robert Wadds (marr. diss. 1977). *Educ:* Univ. of Toronto (BA); Weller Business Coll. First elected to Canadian House of Commons (Riding Grenville-Dundas), 1958; re-elected: 1962, 1963, 1965; defeated (Riding Grenville-Carlton), 1968. Member, Canada's Delegn to United Nations, 1961; Parliamentary Sec. to Minister of Health and Welfare, 1962. National Sec., Progressive Conservative Party, 1971–75; Member, Ontario Municipal Bd, 1975–79. Canadian High Comr to UK, 1980–83. Former Director: Bell Canada; Royal Trustco Ltd; Air Canada; Celanese Canada Inc.; Canadian Pacific Ltd. Adv. Bd, Norman Paterson Sch. of Internat. Affairs, Carleton Univ., Ont. Freeman, City of London, 1981. Hon. DCL Acadia Univ., NS, 1981; Hon. LLD St Thomas Univ., NB, 1983; hon. degrees: Univ. of Toronto, 1985; Dalhousie Univ., NS, 1985. Hon. Fellowship Award, Bretton Hall Coll., W Yorks, 1982; Hon. Patron, Grenville Christian Coll., Brockville, 1981. *Recreations:* walking, swimming. *Address:* PO Box 579, Prescott, ON K0E 1T0, Canada.

WADDY, Rev. Lawrence Heber; retired; Lecturer in Classics, University of California, San Diego, 1969–80; *b* 5 Oct. 1914; *s* of late Archdeacon Stacy Waddy, Secretary of SPG, and Etheldred (*née* Spittal). *Educ:* Marlborough Coll.; Balliol Coll., Oxford (Domus Exhibitioner in Classics, Balliol, 1933; 1st Class Hon. Mods., Oxford, 1935; de Paravicini Scholar, 1935; Craven Scholar, 1935; 2nd Class Lit. Hum., 1937; BA 1937; MA 1945). Deacon, 1940; Priest, 1941; Chaplain, RNVR, 1942–46; Assistant Master: Marlborough Coll., 1937–38; Winchester Coll., 1938–42 and 1946–49 (Chaplain, 1946); Headmaster, Tonbridge Sch., 1949–62; Education Officer, School Broadcasting Council, 1962–63; Chaplain to The Bishop's School, La Jolla, California, 1963–67; Headmaster, Santa Maria Internat. Acad., Chula Vista, Calif, 1967–69; Vicar, Church of the Good Samaritan, University City, 1970–74; Hon. Asst, St James', La Jolla, 1974–94. Examining Chaplain to the Bishop of Rochester, 1959–63; Hon. Canon of Rochester, 1961–63; Hon. Canon of San Diego, 1997. Select Preacher: Cambridge Univ., 1951; Oxford Univ., 1954–56. *Publications:* Pax Romana and World Peace, 1950; The Prodigal Son (musical play), 1963; The Bible as Drama, 1974; Faith of Our Fathers, 1975; Symphony, 1977; Drama in Worship, 1978; Mayor's Race, 1980; A Parish by the Sea, 1988; First Bible Stories, 1994; Shakespeare Remembers, 1994; Florence Nightingale, 1995; Jonah, 1995; Bible Drama, 2005. *Address:* 5910 Camino de la Costa, La Jolla, CA 92037, USA; *e-mail:* lawrencewaddy@yahoo.com.

WADE, family name of **Baron Wade of Chorlton**.

WADE OF CHORLTON, Baron *cr* 1990 (Life Peer), of Chester in the County of Cheshire; **(William) Oulton Wade,** Kt 1982; JP; farmer and cheese master; company director; consultant; Deputy Chairman, Midas Capital plc; Chairman: NIMTECH; RockTron Ltd; RisingStars Growth Fund; *b* 24 Dec. 1932; *s* of Samuel Norman Wade and Joan Ferris Wade (*née* Wild); *m* 1959 Gillian Margaret Leete, Buxton, Derbys; one *s* one *d. Educ:* Birkenhead Sch.; Queen's Univ., Belfast. Jt Treas., Cons. Party, 1982–90; Member: Refreshment Cttee, 2003–; Sci. and Technol. Cttee, 2003–06; European Cttee G, 2007–, H of L. Chm., Internat. Open View. Chairman: Children's Safety Educn Foundn; Cheshire Churches Preservation Trust. Hon. DLaws Liverpool, 2006; Hon. DLit Chester, 2007. JP Cheshire 1967. Freeman, City of London, 1980; Liveryman, Farmers' Co., 1980–. *Publications:* contribs to Dairy Industries Internat., Jl of Soc. of Dairy Technol. *Recreations:* politics, reading, shooting, food, travel. *Address:* House of Lords, Westminster, SW1A 0PW. *Clubs:* Chester City (Chester); St James's (Manchester); Portico Library (Manchester).

WADE, Charles; see Wade, R. C. B.

WADE, Kathryn Jean, (Mrs H. P. Williams); Principal, Outreach Programme, Royal Ballet School, since 2005; *b* 27 Dec. 1945; *d* of George Wade Brown and Sheila (*née* Gilbourne-Stenson); adopted surname Wade, 1965; *m* 1981, Hugh Patrick Williams, FRCS. *Educ:* Royal Ballet Sch., Jun. and Sen. With Royal Ballet Co., 1965–70; Sen. Soloist, London Fest. Ballet, 1970–72; Soloist, Royal Ballet Co., 1970–75; teacher, Royal Ballet Sen. Sch., 1975–88; Ballet Administrator, Jun. and Sen. Royal Ballet Schs, 1988–92; Dir, English Nat. Ballet Sch., 1992–2004. Internat. teacher and adjudicator at internat. ballet and dance comps. Mem., Exec. Cttee, Royal Acad. of Dance (formerly of Dancing), 1990–2005; Exec. Dir, Ashton Trust, 2006–. Trustee: Dance Teachers' Benevolent Fund, 1996– (Chm., 2004–); Voices of British Ballet, 2002–. Adeline Genée Gold Medal, Royal Acad. of Dancing, 1965. *Publications:* (contrib.) The Ballet Goers' Guide, 1981; (tech.

advr) My Ballet Book, 1988; contrib. to Dancing Times, Dance Now. *Recreations:* all performing arts, travelling, fly fishing. *Address:* Royal Ballet School, 46 Floral Street, Covent Garden, WC2E 9DA. *T:* (020) 7845 7061, *Fax:* (020) 7845 7066; *e-mail:* kathrynw@royalballetschool.co.uk.

WADE, Prof. Kenneth, FRS 1989; CChem, FRSC; Professor of Chemistry, Durham University, 1983–98, now Emeritus; *b* Sleaford, Lincs, 13 Oct. 1932; 2nd *s* of Harry Kennington Wade and Anna Elizabeth (*née* Cartwright); *m* 1962, Gertrud Rosmarie Hetzel; one *s* two *d. Educ:* Carre's Grammar Sch., Sleaford; Nottingham Univ. (BSc, PhD; DSc 1970). Postdoctoral research assistant: Cambridge Univ., 1957–59; Cornell Univ. 1959–60; Lectr in Inorganic Chemistry, Derby Coll. of Technology, 1960–61; Durham University: Lectr 1961–71, Sen. Lectr 1971–77, Reader 1977–83, in Chemistry; Chm., Dept of Chemistry, 1986–89. Vis. Res. Fellow, Loker Hydrocarbon Res. Inst., USC, LA, 1979–. Visiting Professor: Technical Univ., Warsaw, 1974; Free Univ., Amsterdam, 1977–78; Univ. of S California, 1979 and 1984–85; Notre Dame Univ., 1983; McMaster Univ., 1984; Western Ontario Univ., 1991. Tilden Lectr, 1987–88, Mond Lectr, 1998–99, RSC; Emanuel Merck Lectr, Darmstadt, 1994. Pres., Dalton Div., RSC, 1995–97. Main Gp Element Award, RSC, 1982. *Publications:* (jtly) Organometallic Compounds: the main group elements, 1967; (jtly) Principles of Organometallic Chemistry, 1968; Electron Deficient Compounds, 1971; (jtly) The Chemistry of Aluminium, Gallium, Indium and Thallium, 1973; (jtly) Organometallic Chemistry, 1976; Hypercarbon Chemistry, 1987; Electron Deficient Boron and Carbon Clusters, 1990; Contemporary Boron Chemistry, 2000; many papers (res. and rev. articles) in learned jls. *Recreations:* (a) musing, (b) musing, (c) walking. *Address:* Chemistry Department, Durham University Science Laboratories, South Road, Durham DH1 3LE. *T:* (0191) 334 2122.

WADE, Martyn John; National Librarian and Chief Executive, National Library of Scotland, since 2002; *b* 24 March 1955; *s* of Albert R. Wade and Nancy Joan Wade; *m* 1978, Anne Patterson. *Educ:* Newcastle Poly. (BA); Univ. of Wales, Aberystwyth (MLib). MCLIP (ALA 1978). Trainee librarian, Northumberland CC, 1976–78; br. librarian, Sunderland MBC, 1978–81; br. librarian and librarian i/c, Sutton LBC, 1981–87; librarian, Northumberland CC, 1987–91; Area Librarian, Leics CC, 1991–93; Area Library Officer, Cambridgeshire CC, 1994–99; Hd, Libraries, Inf. and Learning, Glasgow CC, 1999–2002. Vice Chm., Edinburgh UNESCO City of Literature, 2008. MCMI (MIMgt 1996); FRSA 2006. *Recreations:* motorcycling, reading, the arts, cooking. *Address:* National Library of Scotland, George IV Bridge, Edinburgh EH1 1EW. *T:* (0131) 623 3730, *Fax:* (0131) 623 3702; *e-mail:* m.wade@nls.uk. *Club:* Scottish Motorcycle.

WADE, Prof. Owen Lyndon, CBE 1983; MD; FRCP; FRCPI; FFPM; Professor of Therapeutics and Clinical Pharmacology, 1971–86, now Emeritus, and Pro-Vice-Chancellor and Vice-Principal, 1985–86, University of Birmingham; *b* 17 May 1921; *s* of J. O. D. Wade, MS, FRCS, and Kate Wade, Cardiff; *m* 1948, Margaret Burton, LDS; three *d. Educ:* Repton; Emmanuel Coll., Cambridge (Sen. Scholar, 1941); University College Hospital, London (Achison and Atkinson Morley Schol., 1945). Resident Medical Officer, UCH, 1946; Clinical Assistant, Pneumoconiosis Research Unit of the Medical Research Council, 1948–51; Lecturer and Sen. Lecturer in Medicine, Dept of Medicine, University of Birmingham, 1951–57; Whitla Prof. of Therapeutics and Pharmacology, Queen's Univ., Belfast, 1957–71; Dean, Faculty of Medicine and Dentistry, Univ. of Birmingham, 1978–84. Research Fellow, Columbia Univ. at Department of Medicine, Presbyterian Hospital, New York, 1953–54; Rockefeller Travelling Fellowship in Medicine, 1954–55; Consultant, WHO. Chm., Cttee on the Review of Medicines, 1978–84; Chm., Jt Formulary Cttee for British Nat. Formulary, 1978–86. Mem. GMC, 1981–84. Hon. MD QUB, 1989. *Publications:* (with J. M. Bishop) The Cardiac Output and Regional Blood Flow, 1962; Adverse Reactions to Drugs, 1970, 2nd edn with L. Beeley, 1976; The Romance of Remedies, 1996; When I Dropped the Knife, 1996. *Recreations:* books, travel and sailing. *Address:* 26 West Street, Stratford upon Avon, Warwicks CV37 6DN. *Club:* Athenæum.

WADE, Rebekah; Editor, The Sun, since 2003; *b* 27 May 1968; *d* of late Robert Wade and of Deborah Wade; *m* 2002, Ross Kemp. *Educ:* Appleton Hall, Cheshire; Sorbonne, Paris. Features Editor, then Associate Editor, subseq. Dep. Editor, News of the World, 1989–98; Dep. Ed., The Sun, 1998–2000; Editor, News of the World, 2000–03. Founder Mem. and Pres., Women in Journalism. *Address:* The Sun, 1 Virginia Street, E98 1SN. *T:* (020) 7782 4001.

WADE, (Richard) Charles (Bathurst); His Honour Judge Wade; a Circuit Judge, since 2000; a Designated Family Judge, Swindon, since 2006; *b* 16 Dec. 1946; *s* of David Ison Wade and Margaret Elizabeth Lucy Wade (*née* Wainwright); *m* 1972, Juliet Ann Jehring; one *s* three *d. Educ:* Malvern Coll. Admitted Solicitor, 1972; in private practice, 1972–89; County Court Registrar, 1989–91; Dist Judge, 1991–2000. Trustee: Gloucester Acad. of Music and Performing Arts, 1992–99; Harnhill Centre of Christian Healing, 2001–05. Mem. Council, Cheltenham and Gloucester Coll. of Higher Educn, 1999–2000. Pres., Foundn Fellows, Univ. of Gloucestershire, 2002–08, Hon. Vice-Pres., 2008–. *Recreations:* gardening, music, walking.

WADE, Richard Lawrence; writer, photographer, and campaigner for the modernisation of English orthography; *b* 5 July 1938; *s* of Wilfred George Wade and Frances Mary (*née* Smith); *m* 1st, 1962, Angela Lee Mikhelson (marr. diss. 1995); two *d*; 2nd, 1996, Angela Claire Mills (*née* Thomson). *Educ:* Bedford Sch.; New Coll., Oxford (MA Oriental Studies; Pres., OU Gymnastics Club (Half Blue)). Management Trainee, Unilever Ltd, 1961–63; BBC TV, 1963–75: dir and producer, 1963–70; Editor, Tomorrow's World 1970–75; Chief Asst, Radio 4 and Hd of Radio 4, 1975–83; Chief Asst to Man. Dir, BBC Radio, 1983–86; Marketing Dir, BITC, 1986–88; Man. Dir, Business in the Cities, 1988–89; Dir Gen., Advertising Assoc., 1990–93; Fellow and Dir of Develt, St Edmund Hall, Oxford, 1993–96. Founder, Freespeling.com, 2001. Chm., Direct Marketing Assoc. (UK) Ltd, 1991–92. Mem., Calderdale Partnership, Halifax, 1987–89. Mem., BAFTA, 1968–. Freeman, City of London, 1988. *Recreations:* ski-ing, conversation, photography. *Address:* 49 Park Town, Oxford OX2 6SL. *T:* (01865) 511984. *Club:* Oxford and Cambridge.

WADE, R(obert) Hunter; New Zealand diplomat, retired; *b* 14 June 1916; *s* of R. H. Wade, Balclutha, NZ; *m* 1941, Avelda Grace Petersen (*d* 1990); one *s* two *d* (and one *s* decd). *Educ:* Waitaki; Otago Univ. NZ Treasury and Marketing Depts, 1939; NZ Govt diplomatic appts, Delhi, Simla, Sydney, Canberra, 1941–49; Head of Eastern Political Div., Dept of External Affairs, Wellington, NZ, 1949; NZ Embassy, Washington, 1951; NZ High Commn, Ottawa, 1956; Director of Colombo Plan Bureau, Colombo, 1957; Dir, External Aid, Wellington, 1959; Comr for NZ in Singapore and British Borneo, 1962; High Comr in Malaya/Malaysia, 1963–67; Dep. High Comr in London, 1967–69; NZ Ambassador to Japan and Korea, 1969–71; Dep. Sec.-Gen. of the Commonwealth, 1972–75; NZ Ambassador to Federal Republic of Germany and to Switzerland, 1975–78. Represented New Zealand at Independence of: Uganda, 1962; Botswana, 1966; Lesotho, 1966. Pres., Asiatic Soc. of Japan, 1971. *Address:* 12 Pleasant Place, Howick, Auckland, New Zealand. *Club:* Northern (Auckland).

WADE, (Sarah) Virginia, OBE 1986 (MBE 1969); tennis player; commentator, BBC Television, since 1980; *b* 10 July 1945; *d* of late Eustace Holland Wade and of Joan Barbara Wade. *Educ:* Sussex Univ. (BSc). Won tennis championships: US Open, 1968; Italian, 1971; Australian, 1972; Wimbledon, 1977; played for GB in Wightman Cup and Federation Cup 20 times (record); Captain, GB team. Mem. Cttee, All England Lawn Tennis Club, 1983–91. Hon. LLD Sussex, 1985. Elected into Internat. Tennis Hall of Fame, 1989. *Publications:* Courting Triumph, 1978; Ladies of the Court, 1984. *Address:* c/o IMG, McCormack House, Hogarth Business Park, W4 2TH. *T:* (020) 8233 5000.

WADE-GERY, Sir Robert (Lucian), KCMG 1983 (CMG 1979); KCVO 1983; Fellow, All Souls College, Oxford, since 1997; *b* 22 April 1929; *o s* of late Prof. H. T. Wade-Gery; *m* 1962, Sarah, *er d* of A. D. Marris, CMG; one *s* one *d. Educ:* Winchester; New Coll., Oxford (1st cl. Hon. Mods 1949 and Lit. Hum. 1951; Hon. Fellow, 1985). Fellow, All Souls Coll., Oxford, 1951–73, 1987–89. Joined HM Foreign (now Diplomatic) Service, 1951; FO (Economic Relations Dept), 1951–54; Bonn, 1954–57; FO (Private Sec. to Perm. Under-Sec., later Southern Dept), 1957–60; Tel Aviv, 1961–64; FO (Planning Staff), 1964–67; Saigon, 1967–68; Cabinet Office (Sec. to Duncan Cttee), 1968–69; Counsellor 1969; on loan to Bank of England, 1969; Head of Financial Policy and Aid Dept, FCO, 1969–70; Under-Sec., Central Policy Review Staff, Cabinet Office, 1971–73; Minister, Madrid, 1973–77; Minister, Moscow, 1977–79; Dep. Sec. of the Cabinet, 1979–82; High Comr to India, 1982–87. Dir, Barclays Capital (formerly BZW), 1987–99 (Vice-Chm., 1994–99). Hon. Treas., IISS, 1991–2005. Chm., Anglo-Spanish Soc., 1995–98. Chm. of Govs, SOAS, 1990–99. *Recreations:* walking, sailing, travel, history. *Address:* The Old Vicarage, Cold Aston, Cheltenham GL54 3BW. *T:* (01451) 821115, *Fax:* (01451) 822496; 14 Hill View, 2 Primrose Hill Road, NW3 3AX. *T:* (020) 7722 4754, *Fax:* (020) 7586 5966. *Clubs:* Boodle's, Beefsteak.

WADHAM, John; Group Director, Legal, Equality and Human Rights Commission, since 2007; *b* 24 Jan. 1952; *s* of late Ernest George Wadham and Unity Winifred Wadham (*née* Errington); *m* 2004, Alison Macnair. *Educ:* London School of Economics (BSc 1974); Surrey Univ. (CQSW 1978; MSc 1979). Legal Advr, Wandsworth Law Centres, 1978–86; articled clerk, Birnberg & Co., Solicitors, 1987–90; admitted Solicitor, 1989; Legal Officer, 1990–92, Dir of Law, 1992–95, Dir, 1995–2003, NCCL, later Liberty; Dep. Chm., Indep. Police Complaints Commn, 2003–07. Mem., Human Rights Act Task Force, 1999–2001; Chairman: Forum for Preventing Deaths in Custody; UK Human Rights Coalition, 2001–03; Internat. Network for Indep. Oversight of Policing, 2006–07. Hon. Lectr in Law, Univ. of Leicester; Hon. Fellow of Law, Univ. of Kent at Canterbury. Series Editor, Blackstone's Human Rights Act series, 2000–04. Hon. Fellow of Law, Univ. of Kent at Canterbury, 1992. *Publications:* (contrib.) The Penguin Guide to the Law, 3rd edn, 1992, 4th edn, 2001; (ed) Your Rights: the Liberty guide, 5th edn 1994 to 7th edn 2000; Blackstone's Guide to the Human Rights Act 1998, 1999, 4th edn 2007; Blackstone's Guide to the Freedom of Information Act 2000, 2001, 3rd edn 2007; Blackstone's Guide to the Identity Cards Act 2006, 2006. *Recreation:* flying (private pilot). *Address:* Equality and Human Rights Commission, 3 More London, Tooley Street, SE1 2RG.

WADHAMS, Prof. Peter, ScD; FRGS; Professor of Ocean Physics, Department of Applied Mathematics and Theoretical Physics, Cambridge University, since 2003 (Scott Polar Research Institute, 2001–02); Fellow, Scottish Association of Marine Science, since 2003; *b* 14 May 1948; *s* of late Frank Cecil Wadhams and Winifred Grace Wadhams (*née* Smith); *m* 1980, Maria Pia Casarini. *Educ:* Palmer's Sch., Grays, Essex; Churchill Coll., Cambridge (BA Phys. 1969; MA 1972; ScD 1994); graduate res., Scott Polar Res. Inst. (PhD 1974). Res. Scientist, Bedford Inst. of Oceanography, Dartmouth, Canada, 1969–70 (asst to Sen. Scientist on Hudson '70 expedn, first circumnavigation of Americas); Fellow, NRC Canada, 1974–75 (Inst. Ocean Scis, Victoria, BC); Cambridge University: Scott Polar Research Institute, 1976–2002: leader, Sea Ice Gp, 1976; Asst Dir of Res., 1981; Dep. Dir, 1983–87; Dir, 1987–92; Sen. Res. Fellow, Churchill Coll., 1983–93; Reader in Polar Studies, 1992–2001. Leader, 32 field ops in Arctic, 5 in Antarctic; UK Deleg., Arctic Ocean Scis Bd, 1984–; Member: IAPSO Commn on Sea Ice, 1987– (Pres., 1999–); SCAR Gp of specialists in Antarctic Sea Ice, 1989–; IASC Wkg Gp on Global Change, 1992–; Co-ordinator, Internat. Prog. for Antarctic Buoys, World Climate Res. Prog., 1999–. Vis. Prof., Naval Postgrad. Sch., Monterey, 1980–81; Green Schol Scripps Instn, 1987–88; Walker-Ames Vis. Prof., Univ. of Washington, WA, 1988; Vis. Prof., Nat. Inst. of Polar Res., Tokyo, 1995, 1996–97. W. S. Bruce Prize, RSE 1977; Polar Medal, 1987; Italgas Prize for Envmtl Scis, 1990. *Publications:* (contrib.) The Nordic Seas, 1986; (contrib.) The Geophysics of Sea Ice, 1986; (ed) Ice Technology for Polar Operations, 1990; (contrib.) Microwave Remote Sensing of Sea Ice, 1992; (ed) Advances in Ice Technology, 1992; Marine, Offshore and Ice Technology, 1994; (ed) The Arctic and Environmental Change, 1996; Ice in the Ocean, 2000; numerous sci. papers on glaciology and polar oceanography. *Recreations:* painting, music, sailing. *Address:* Dunstaffnage Marine Laboratory, Oban, Argyll PA37 1QA.

WADHWANI, Sushil Baldev, CBE 2002; PhD; Chief Executive Officer, Wadhwani Asset Management LLP, since 2002; *b* 7 Dec. 1959; *s* of Baldev and Meena Wadhwani; *m* 1st, 1991, Anjali Mirgh (marr. diss. 1994); 2nd, 1996, Renu Sakhrani; one *s* one *d. Educ:* London Sch. of Economics (BSc Econs; MSc Econs 1982; PhD 1986). Lectr, 1984–91, Reader, 1991–92, in Economics, London Sch. of Economics; Dir of Equity Strategy, Goldman Sachs Internat. Ltd, 1991–95; Dir of Res. and Partner, Tudor Gp, 1995–99; Mem., Monetary Policy Cttee, Bank of England, 1999–2002. Visiting Professor: Sir John Cass Business Sch., City of London (formerly City Univ. Business Sch.), 2000–; LSE, 2000–. Mem. Council, NIESR, 2000–. Asst Ed., Economic Policy, 1987–89; Mem. Editl Bd, New Economy, 1996–. *Publications:* articles in academic jls. *Address:* (office) Warwick Court, 5 Paternoster Square, EC4M 7DX. *T:* (020) 7663 3400.

WADIA, Jim, FCA; Chief Operating Officer, Linklaters, 2001–04; *b* 12 April 1948; *m* 1972, Joelle Garnier; one *s* one *d. Educ:* Le Rosey, Rolle, Switzerland; Inns of Court Sch. of Law. Called to the Bar, Inner Temple, 1969. Arthur Andersen: Partner, 1982–2000; Hd, London Tax, 1989–93; Man. Partner, UK, 1993–97; Worldwide Man. Partner, 1997–2000. FRSA 1993. *Recreations:* tennis, theatre. *Address:* 28 Eldon Road, W8 5PT. *T:* (020) 7937 7045.

WADKINS, Lanny; golfer; *b* 5 Dec. 1949; *s* of Jerry Lanston Wadkins and Frances Ann Wadkins (*née* Burnett); *m* 1971, Rachel Irene Strong; one *d. Educ:* Wake Forest Univ., USA. US Amateur Champion, 1970; tournament wins include: US World Series and US PGA, 1977; Tournament Players' Champion, 1979, 1982, 1983; Hawaiian Open, 1988, 1991; mem., US Ryder Cup Team, 1977, Captain, 1995. *Address:* c/o Professional Golfers' Association Tour, 112 PGA Tour Boulevard, Ponte Vedra Beach, FL 32082, USA.

WADLEY, Veronica Judith Colleton; Editor, Evening Standard, since 2002; *b* 28 Feb. 1952; *d* of Neville John Wadley and Anne Colleton Wadley (*née* Bowring); *m* 1985, Thomas Michael Bower, *qv*; one *s* one *d. Educ:* Francis Holland Sch., London; Benenden Sch., Kent. Condé Nast Pubns, 1971–74; Telegraph Mag., 1978–81; Mail on Sunday,

1982–86; Daily Telegraph: Features Ed., 1986–89; Asst Ed., 1989–94; Dep. Ed., 1994–95; Daily Mail: Associate Ed., 1995–98; Dep. Ed., 1998–2002. *Recreations:* tennis, ski-ing, riding, cooking, opera, reading newspapers. *Address:* Evening Standard, Northcliffe House, 2 Derry Street, W8 5EE.

WADSWORTH, Brian; transport and public affairs consultant, since 2008; *b* 18 Jan. 1952; *s* of George David Brian Wadsworth and Betty (*née* Metcalfe); *m* 1987, Anne Jacqueline Beuselinck. *Educ:* Univ. of British Columbia (BA Hons Eng. Lit. 1973). FILog 1998. Entered Department of Transport, 1974; Sec., Review of Main Line Rly Electrification, 1978–79; Sec. to Chief Exec., LB of Hounslow, 1981; Principal: Transport Policy Rev. Unit, 1981–83; London Transport Finance, 1984; Pvte Sec. to Minister of State, 1985; Finance Transport Industries (BA, BAA, NBC privatisations), 1986–89; Sec. to BA plc, 1989–91; Asst Sec., Rlys Policy (BR privatisation), 1991–95; Sec. to British Oxygen plc, 1995; Under Sec., Dir of Finance, 1995–97; Dir, Freight Distbn and Logistics, DETR, 1997–99; Dir, Logistics and Maritime Transport, DETR, subseq. DTLR, then DfT, 1999–2007; Dir, Strategic Roads, Planning and Nat. Networks, DfT, 2007–08. Chm. Admin Bd, European Maritime Safety Agency, 2003–. Freeman, City of London, 1997; Liveryman: Co. of Carmen, 1997– (Mem., Ct of Assistants, 2000–; Jun. Warden, 2007–08); Co. of Shipwrights, 2005–. *Publication:* Best Methods of Railway Restructuring and Privatisation, 1995. *Recreations:* travel, sailing, music.

WADSWORTH, David Grant; Chief Executive, Service Children's Education, Ministry of Defence, since 1997; *b* 30 Dec. 1944; *s* of Fred Wadsworth and Lona Wadsworth (*née* Booth); *m* Marcia Armour (*née* Lyles); one step *s* one step *d. Educ:* Hipperholme Grammar Sch., Yorks; Oriel Coll., Oxford (MA 1970); Univ. of Newcastle upon Tyne (MPhil 1992). Teacher, 1966–73; Educn Admin, Leeds CC, 1973–85; Dep. Dir of Educn, Northumberland CC, 1985–89; Chief Educn Officer, Bedfordshire CC, 1989–96. Hon. DEd De Montfort, 1996. Chevalier, l'Ordre des Palmes Académiques (France), 1992; Cavaliere della Ordine al Merito (Italy), 1994. *Recreations:* Rugby and cricket (passively), travel, music, European food and wine. *Address:* HQ SCE, BFPO 40. *T:* (Germany) (2161) 9082372. *Club:* Oxford and Cambridge.

WADSWORTH, James Patrick; QC 1981; **His Honour Judge Wadsworth;** a Circuit Judge, since 2000; *b* 7 Sept. 1940; *s* of Francis Thomas Bernard Wadsworth, Newcastle, and Geraldine Rosa (*née* Brannan); *m* 1963, Judith Stuart Morrison, *e d* of Morrison Scott, Newport-on-Tay; one *s* one *d. Educ:* Stonyhurst; University Coll., Oxford (MA). Called to the Bar, Inner Temple, 1963, Bencher, 1988; a Recorder, 1980–2000. Member: Bar Council, 1992–95; Bar Professional Standards Cttee, 1993–95. *Address:* Southwark Crown Court, 1 English Grounds, Southwark, SE1 2HU.

WADSWORTH, Prof. Michael Edwin John, PhD; FFPH; Director, Medical Research Council National Survey of Health and Development, 1985–2006, and Professor of Social and Health Life Course Research, Department of Epidemiology and Public Health Medicine, 2003–06, now Emeritus, Royal Free and University College Medical School, University College London (formerly University College London Medical School); *b* 20 Jan. 1942; *s* of Cecil and Amelia Wadsworth; *m* 1st, 1966, Jane Arnott (marr. diss. 1991); one *s* one *d;* 2nd, 2001, Kit Leighton-Kelly; one *d. Educ:* Leeds Univ. (BA, MPhil); London Sch. of Econs (PhD 1976). FFPH 2006 (Hon. MFPHM 1993). Research Asst, Dept of Medicine, Guy's Hosp. Med. Sch., 1963–65; Res. Fellow, Dept of Gen. Practice, Univ. of Edinburgh Med. Sch., 1965–68; Res. Scientist, MRC Nat. Survey Health and Develt, 1968–2007. Vis. Prof., Royal Free and UC Med. Sch., UCL, 1992–2003. *Publications:* (jtly) Health and Sickness, 1971; Roots of Delinquency, 1976; (ed with D. Robinson) Studies in Everyday Medical Life, 1976; (ed with U. Gerhardt) Stress and Stigma, 1985; The Imprint of Time, 1991; (ed with M. G. Marmot) Fetal and Early Childhood Development, 1997; (ed jtly) Changing Britain, Changing Lives, 2003; (ed jtly) Epidemiological Methods in Life Course Research, 2007; numerous articles in learned jls in medicine and social scis. *Recreations:* music, living. *Address:* 12C Kingsdown Parade, Bristol BS6 5UD. *T:* (0117) 924 4906.

WAENA, Sir (Rahumaea) Nathaniel, GCMG 2005; CSI 2003; Governor General, Solomon Islands, since 2004; *b* 1 Nov. 1945; *s* of Joseph Talo and Matilda Tahalata; *m* 1972, Alice Ole; three *s* three *d. Educ:* Alangaula, Pawa and Lae Tech. Trng Inst. Provincial Sec., 1978–82; Chief Admin. Officer, 1982–84; Perm. Sec., 1984–87. MP Solomon Is, 1987–2004; Minister: Provincial Govt and Rural Develt, 1989–90, 2000–01; Health and Medical Services, 1993–94; Nat. Unity, Reconciliation and Peace, 2001–04. Vice-Pres., Honiara Town Council, 1984–86. KStJ 2005. *Recreations:* gardening, reading, watching sports competitions. *Address:* Government House, Honiara, Solomon Islands. *T:* 21777, *Fax:* 22533; c/o National Parliament Office, Honiara, Solomon Islands.

WAGERMAN, Josephine Miriam, OBE 1992; President, Board of Deputies of British Jews, 2000–03 (Senior Vice-President, 1997–2000); *b* 17 Sept. 1933; *d* of Emanuel and Jane Barbanel; *m* 1956, Peter Henry Wagerman; one *s* one *d. Educ:* John Howard Sch., London; Birkbeck Coll., London Univ. (BA Hons 1955); Inst. of Educn, London Univ. (PGCE 1956; Acad. Dipl. 1959; MA (Ed) 1970). Teacher, Battersea, Highgate, Hackney and Singapore, 1956–73; Jews' Free School: Head of Lower Sch., 1973–76; Dep. Head, 1976–85; Headteacher, 1985–93; Chief Exec., Lennox Lewis Coll., 1994–96. Indep. Assessor, NHS non-exec. Appts, 1996–. Former Pres., London Br., AMMA; former Member: Teachers' Pay and Conditions of Service Adv. Cttee, ILEA; London Standing Cttee Adv. Cttee on Religious Educn, ILEA; Council, Selly Oak Coll. Centre for Jewish-Christian Relns; Member: Acad. Panel, Stuart Young Awards, 1991–; Inner Cities Religious Council, DoE, 1994–2006; Bd of Dirs, and Partnership 2000 Policy Cttee, United Jewish Israel Appeal, 1995–. Pres., European Jewish Congress, 2000–02. Trustee and Gov., Central Foundn Schs, London, 1995–2002. *Recreations:* gardening, cooking, entertaining friends, travel, Art Nouveau silver, Victorian painting. *Address:* 38 Crespigny Road, NW4 3DX.

WAGGOTT, Shuna Taylor; *see* Lindsay, S. T.

WAGNER, Erica Augusta; writer; Literary Editor, The Times, since 1996; *b* NYC, 24 Sept. 1967; *d* of Arthur Malcolm Wagner and Ellen Franklin Wagner; *m* 1993, Francis Jonathan Gilbert; one *s. Educ:* Brearley Sch., NYC; St Paul's Girls' Sch., London; Corpus Christi Coll., Cambridge (BA Hons 1989); UEA (MA Creative Writing 1991). Freelance editor/researcher/journalist, 1992–95; The Times: Asst to Literary Editor, 1995; Dep. Literary Editor, 1996. *Publications:* Gravity: stories, 1997; Ariel's Gift: Ted Hughes, Sylvia Plath and the story of Birthday Letters, 2000; Seizure, 2006. *Recreations:* bridges, cooking, fencing. *Address:* c/o Antony Harwood Ltd, 103 Walton Street, Oxford OX2 6EB. *T:* (01865) 559615.

WAGNER, Gerrit Abram, KBE (Hon.) 1977 (CBE (Hon.) 1964); Kt, Order of Netherlands Lion, 1969; Grand Officer, Order of Oranje Nassau, 1983 (Commander 1977); Chairman, Supervisory Board, Royal Dutch Petroleum Co., 1977–87 (President, 1971–77); *b* 21 Oct. 1916; *m* 1946, M. van der Heul; one *s* three *d. Educ:* Leyden Univ. LLM 1939. After a period in a bank in Rotterdam and in Civil Service in Rotterdam and

The Hague, joined Royal Dutch Shell Group, 1946; assignments in The Hague, Curaçao, Venezuela, London and Indonesia; apptd Man. Dir, Royal Dutch Petroleum Co. and Shell Petroleum Co. Ltd; Mem. Presidium of Bd of Directors of Shell Petroleum NV, 1964; Dir, Shell Canada Ltd, 1971–77; Chm., Cttee of Man. Dirs, Royal Dutch/Shell Group, 1972–77; Chm., Shell Oil USA, 1972–77. Former Chairman, Supervisory Board: De Nederlandsche Bank NV; Gist-Brocades NV; KLM; Smit Internat.; Vice-Chm., Supervisory Bd, Hoogovens Gp BV, Beverwijk; Member, International Advisory Committee: Chase Manhattan Bank, NY; Robert Bosch, Stuttgart. Hon. Dr Eindhoven, 1986; Hon. LLD Rochester, USA, 1987. Order of Francisco de Miranda, Grand Officer (Venezuela), 1965; Officier Légion d'Honneur (France), 1974. *Address:* 13 Teylingerhorstlaan 13, 2244 EJ Wassenaar, The Netherlands.

WAGNER, Dame Gillian (Mary Millicent), (Lady Wagner), DBE 1994 (OBE 1977); Chairman, Carnegie UK Trust, 1995–2000 (Trustee, 1980–2002); *b* 25 Oct. 1927; *e d* of late Major Henry Archibald Roger Graham, and of Hon. Margaret Beatrix, *d* of 1st Baron Roborough; *m* 1953, Sir Anthony Wagner, KCB, KCVO; two *s* one *d. Educ:* Cheltenham Ladies' Coll.; Geneva Univ. (Licence ès Sciences Morales); London Sch. of Economics (Dip. Social Admin). PhD London 1977. Mem. Council, Barnardo's, 1969–97 (Chm., Exec./Finance Cttee, 1973–78; Chm. Council, 1978–84); Chairman: Nat. Centre for Volunteering (formerly Volunteer Centre), 1984–89 (Pres., 1990–2002); Review of Residential Care, 1986–88; Ct of Govs, Thomas Coram Foundn for Children, 1990–95; The Leche Trust, 1992–97; Chair, Community Care Inquiry for people with learning difficulties, Mental Health Foundn, 1995–96; President: Skill: Nat. Bureau for Students with Disabilities, 1978–91; IAPS, 1985–90; Abbeyfield, 1995–2002; Abbeyfield UK, 2003–; Trustee, Princess Royal Trust for Carers, 1992–2002. Mem. Exec. Cttee, Georgian Gp, 1970–78. Chm. of Governors, Felixstowe Coll., 1980–87; Gov., Nat. Inst. for Social Work, 1988–96. Governor, LSE, 1991–96. FRSA 1995. Hon. DSc Bristol, 1989; Hon. LLD Liverpool, 1990. *Publications:* Barnardo, 1979; Children of the Empire, 1982; The Chocolate Conscience, 1987; Thomas Coram, 2004; various articles on residential care. *Recreations:* gardening, travelling. *Address:* Flat 31, 55 Ebury Street, SW3W 0PA. *T:* (020) 7730 0040; 46 Lee Road, Aldeburgh, Suffolk IP15 5HG. *T:* (01728) 454550; *e-mail:* wagner934@aol.com. *Club:* Athenæum.

WAGNER, Prof. Leslie, CBE 2000; MA(Econ); Vice-Chancellor (formerly Principal and Chief Executive), and Professor, Leeds Metropolitan University, 1994–2003; *b* 21 Feb. 1943; *s* of Herman and Toby Wagner; *m* 1967, Jennifer Jean Fineberg; one *s* one *d. Educ:* Salford Grammar Sch.; Manchester Univ. (MA Econ). Economic Asst and Economic Advr, DEA, 1966–69; Economic Advr, Min. of Technology, 1969–70; Lectr in Econs, Open Univ., 1970–76; Hd of Social Sciences, 1976–82, Prof., 1980, Polytechnic of Central London; Asst Sec. (Academic), Nat. Adv. Body for Local Authy Higher Educn, 1982–85; Dep. Sec., Nat. Adv. Body for Public Sector Higher Educn, 1985–87; Dir, Poly. of N London, 1987–92, then Vice-Chancellor and Chief Exec., Univ. of N London, 1992–93. Member: Bd, Open Learning Foundn, 1990–96 (Chm., 1990–93); Bd, HEQC, 1992–97; Council for Industry and Higher Educn, 1992–2003; Leeds TEC, 1997–2001; DFEE Skills Task Gp, 1998–2000. Chairman: SRHE, 1994–96; Higher Educn for Capability, 1994–98; Yorks and Humberside Univs Assoc., 1996–99; UUK Wider Participation and Lifelong Learning Gp, 1998–2003; Leeds Common Purpose Adv. Gp, 2000–03; Univ. Vocational Awards Council, 2001–03; Higher Educn Acad., 2003–07; Foundn Degree Task Force, 2003–04; Educn Leeds, 2004–07. Councillor (Lab) London Bor. of Harrow, 1971–78, Chm., Educn Cttee, 1972–74. Contested (Lab) Harrow W, Feb. 1974. Dir, Leeds Business Services Ltd, 2001–03; Mem., Leeds Cares Leadership Gp, 2000–01. Vice-Pres., Utd Synagogue, 1992–93; Chmairman: Jewish Community Allocations Bd, 1994–96; Commn on the Future of Jewish Schs, 2007–08; Mem. Bd, Jewish Chronicle Trust, 1999–2008. Trustee, Chief Rabbinate Trust, 2003–. Chancellor, Univ. of Derby, 2003–08; Mem. Council, Open Univ., 2005–. Hon. Dr of Univ. Middlesex, 2003; DUniv: Leeds Metropolitan, 2003; Open, 2006; Hon. DCL Huddersfield, 2003. *Publications:* (ed) Readings in Applied Microeconomics, 1973, 2nd edn 1981; (ed) Agenda for Institutional Change in Higher Education, 1982; The Economics of Educational Media, 1982; (jtly) Choosing to Learn: a study of mature students, 1987. *Address:* 3 Lakeland Drive, Leeds LS17 7PJ. *T:* (0113) 268 7355.

WAGONER, G. Richard; Chief Executive Officer, since 2000, and Chairman, since 2003, General Motors Corporation; *b* Wilmington, Delaware, 9 Feb. 1953. *Educ:* Duke Univ. (BS 1975); Harvard Univ. (MBA 1977). General Motors Corporation: analyst in treasurer's office, Manager, Latin American financing, Dir, Canadian and overseas borrowing, then Dir, capital analysis and investment, NY, 1977–81; Treas., 1981–84, Exec. Dir of Finance, 1984–87, São Paulo, Brazil; Vice-Pres. and Financial Manager, 1987–88, Gp Dir of strategic business planning, 1988–89, Canada; Vice-Pres. of Finance, Zurich, 1989–91; Pres. and Man. Dir, Brazil, 1991–93; Chief Financial Officer, 1992–94, and Head of Worldwide Purchasing Gp, 1993–94; Exec. Vice-Pres. and Pres. of N American ops, 1994–98; Chief Operating Officer, 1998–2000; Pres., 1998–2003; Mem., Bd of Dirs, 1998–. *Address:* General Motors Corporation, 300 Renaissance Center, Detroit, MI 48265–0001, USA.

WAGSTAFF, Ven. Christopher John Harold; Archdeacon of Gloucester, 1982–2000, now Emeritus; *b* 25 June 1936; *s* of Harold Maurice Wagstaff and Kathleen Mary Wagstaff (*née* Bean); *m* 1964, Margaret Louise (*née* Macdonald); two *s* one *d. Educ:* Bishop's Stortford College, Herts; Essex Inst. of Agriculture, Chelmsford (Dipl. in Horticulture 1959); St David's Coll., Lampeter (BA 1962, Dipl. in Theol. 1963). Deacon 1963, priest 1964; Curate, All Saints, Queensbury, 1963–68; Vicar, St Michael's, Tokyngton, Wembley, 1968–73; Vicar of Coleford with Staunton, 1973–83; RD, South Forest, 1975–82. Diocese of Gloucester: Chairman: House of Clergy, 1983–95; Bd of Social Responsibility, 1983–96; Diocesan Trust, 1983–2000; Diocesan Assoc. for the Deaf, 1989–94; DAC, 1988–2000; Adv. Council for Ministry, 1996–2000. Mem., General Synod, 1988–98. Hon. Canon, St Andrew's Cathedral, Njombe, Tanzania, 1993–. Freeman, City of London; Liveryman, Co. of Armourers and Brasiers (Master, 2000–01). *Recreations:* gardening, entertaining, travel. *Address:* Karibuni, 1 Collafield, Littledean, Glos GL14 3LG. *T:* (01594) 825282.

WAGSTAFF, David St John Rivers; a Recorder of the Crown Court, 1974–94; barrister, retired; *b* 22 June 1930; *s* of late Prof. John Edward Pretty Wagstaff and Dorothy Margaret (*née* McRobie); *m* 1970, Dorothy Elizabeth Starkie; two *d. Educ:* Winchester Coll. (Schol.); Trinity Coll., Cambridge (Schol., MA, LLB). Called to Bar, Lincoln's Inn, 1954. *Publication:* Man's Relationship with God, or Spiritual Adventure, 1996. *Recreations:* mountaineering, fencing. *Address:* 8 Breary Lane East, Bramhope, Leeds LS16 9BJ. *Clubs:* Alpine; Fell and Rock Climbing (Lake District).

WAGSTAFF, (Edward) Malise (Wynter); HM Diplomatic Service, retired; psychotherapist; *b* 27 June 1930; *s* of late Col Henry Wynter Wagstaff, CSI, MC, and Jean Mathieson, MB, BS; *m* 1st, 1957, Eva Margot (marr. diss. 1995), *d* of Erik Hedelius; one *s* two *d;* 2nd, 1995, Vivien Rosemary Manton, *d* of Winston and Marjorie Farrar. *Educ:* Wellington Coll.; RMA Sandhurst; Pembroke Coll., Cambridge (MA; Mech Scis Tripos);

Staff Coll., Camberley; psc. Commissioned RE, 1949; served in UK, Germany and Gibraltar, 1950–62; seconded to Federal Regular Army, Fedn of S Arabia, 1963–65; Asst Mil. Attaché, Amman, 1967–69 (Major, 1962; GSM; South Arabia Radfan bar). Joined FCO, 1969; served Saigon, 1973, FCO, 1975, Oslo, 1976, Copenhagen, 1978, FCO, 1981; Counsellor, FCO, 1982–92; Advr, later Consultant FCO, 1992–95. Qualified as Psychosynthesis psychotherapist, 1993. Kt, First Degree, Order of Dannebrog, 1979. *Recreations:* God, concern for the bewildered, plumbing. *Address:* La Palmera, Calle Alta 7, 29788 Frigiliana, Málaga, Spain.

WAGSTAFF, Sheena Vanessa; Chief Curator, Tate Modern, since 2001; *b* 30 Aug. 1956; *d* of Walton Wynter Wagstaff and Patricia (*née* Hugonin); *m* 1983, Mark Michael Peregrine Francis; one *s* one *d*. *Educ:* Univ. of East Anglia (BA Hons Hist. of Art and Arch. 1980). Postgraduate Fellow, Whitney Mus. of American Art, NY, 1982–83. Asst to Dir, MOMA, Oxford, 1976–77; Asst to Dir, Whitechapel Art Gall., 1980–82; Gall. Manager, Lisson Gall., 1983–84; freelance curator, 1984–93; curated exhibitions for: Whitney Mus. of American Art, NY; Kettle's Yard Gall., Cambridge; ICA; Centre Culturel de Courbevoie, Paris; Mattress Factory, Pittsburgh; Dir of Collection, Exhibns and Educn, Frick Art Mus., Pittsburgh, 1993–98; Hd of Exhibns and Displays, Tate Britain, 1998–2001. Curated, Tate Modern: Edward Hopper, 2004; Jeff Wall Photographs 1978–2004, 2005; Juan Muñoz: a retrospective, 2008. Member: Prog. Adv. Bd, Mattress Factory, Pittsburgh, 1998–; Bd, Internat. Cttee of ICOM for Museums and Collections of Modern and Contemporary Art, 2001–; Internat. Adv. Cttee, Istanbul Modern, 2005–; Adv. Bd, Delfina Foundn, 2007–; Adv. Panel, St Paul's Cathedral, 2007–. *Publications:* numerous exhibition catalogues. *Recreations:* historic and contemporary art, architecture, music, dance, literature, walking, gardening. *Address:* Tate Modern, Bankside, SE1 9TG. *T:* (020) 7401 5196.

WAIARU, Rt Rev. Amos Stanley, OBE 2001; Archbishop of Melanesia, and Bishop of Central Melanesia, 1988–93; *b* 19 April 1944; *s* of late Stanley Qagora and Emma Kaifo; *m* 1976, Mary Marjorie Waiaru (*née* Mwele); one *s* three *d*. *Educ:* Bishop Patteson Theol Coll., Kohimarama, Solomon Is; Pacific Theol Coll., Suva, Fiji Is (DipTh). Tutor, Torgil Training Centre, Vanuatu, 1976; Chaplain, Vureas High School, Vanuatu, 1977–78, Head Master 1979–80; Bishop of Temotu, Solomon Is, 1981–87. Chm., S Pacific Anglican Council, 1991–93. *Recreations:* gardening, fishing. *Address:* Ngafinuatoga Village, Santa Anna, Makira-Ulawa Province, Solomon Islands.

WAIGEL, Dr Theodor; Member for Neu Ulm, Bundestag, 1972–2002; Chairman, CSU, 1988–99; *b* 22 April 1939; *s* of August Waigel and Genoveva Konrad; *m* 1st, 1966, Karin Hönig; one *s* one *d*; 2nd, 1994, Dr Irene Epple; one *s*. *Educ:* Univ. of Munich; Univ. of Würzburg (Dr jur. 1967). Lawyer, 1967–69. Junge Union: Dist Chm., Krumbach, 1961–70; Regl Chm., Schwaben, 1967–71; Chm., Bavaria, 1971–75; Chairman: CSU Basic Commn, 1973–88; Economy wkg gp, CDU/CSU parly gp, 1980–82; Bavaria gp, CSU, 1982–89; First Dep. Chm., CDU/CSU parly gp, 1982–89. Posts in Min. of Finance, and Min. of Economy and Transport, Bavaria, 1969–72; Minister of Finance, Germany, 1989–98. Governor: German Helsinki Human Rights Cttee; German Soc. of For. Policy.

WAIKATO, Bishop of, since 1993; **Most Rev. David John Moxon;** Archbishop and Co-Primate, Anglican Church in Aotearoa, New Zealand and Polynesia, since 2006; *b* 6 Sept. 1951; *s* of John Rosher Moxon and Joan Moxon; *m*; two *s* two *d*. *Educ:* Freyberg High Sch., Palmerston North; Massey Univ. (MA Hons); Oxford Univ. (MA); Univ. of Waikato (Dip. Maori Studies 1991). Volunteer service abroad (school leaver scheme), 1970; Univ. Tutor, Educn Dept, Massey Univ., 1974–75; Curate, St Luke's, Havelock North, 1978–81; Vicar, St George's, Gate Pa, Tauranga, 1981–87; Dir, Theol Educn by Extension Unit, Anglican Church of Aotearoa, NZ and Polynesia, 1987–93. Hon. LTh Aotearoa. Gold Duke of Edinburgh Award, 1969. *Recreations:* playing flute, reading, tramping, swimming. *Address:* Bishop's House, 3 Lake Domain Drive, Hamilton, New Zealand. *T:* (7) 8395308; (office) Anglican Church House, 100 Morrinsville Road, Hamilton, New Zealand. *T:* (7) 8570020.

WAIN, Peter; a District Judge (Magistrates' Courts), since 2004; *b* 3 Sept. 1947; *s* of late Frank and Margaret Wain; *m* 1972, Mary Carolyn Hilditch; two *s* one *d*. *Educ:* Bemrose Sch., Derby; Stamford Sch., Lincs; Univ. of Leeds (LLB Hons 1969). Called to the Bar, Gray's Inn, 1972; Clerk to the Felixstowe, Ipswich and Woodbridge Justices, 1978–87; practising barrister, 1987–2004. Pt-time Legal Mem., Mental Health Review Tribunal, 1995–2005. *Recreations:* bird watching, gardening, sculling on the River Deben. *Address:* Camberwell Green Magistrates' Court, D'Eynsford Road, Camberwell Green, SE5 7UP. *T:* (020) 7805 9802. *Clubs:* Bawdsey Bird; Felixstowe Ferry Sailing.

WAINE, Dr Colin, OBE 1990; FRCGP, FRCPath; Director of Health Programmes and Primary Care Development, Sunderland Health Authority, 1996–2002; Chairman, Council, Royal College of General Practitioners, 1990–93; *b* 12 March 1936; *m* 1959, Gwendoline Jameson; two *d*. *Educ:* King James I Grammar Sch., Bishop Auckland; Medical Sch., King's Coll., Univ. of Durham (MB BS Hons). MRCGP (dist.) 1975, FRCGP 1976, FRCPath 1993. Principal in general practice, Bishop Auckland, 1962–93; Hosp. Practitioner in Paediatrics, Bishop Auckland General Hosp., 1963–88; Gen. Manager, SW Durham HA, 1985–92; Dir of Primary Care, Sunderland Health Commn, 1993–96. Vis. Prof., Primary and Community Care, Univ. of Sunderland, 2002–. Chm., Nat. Obesity Forum, 2005–. Course Organiser (Continuing Educn), Regional Post Grad. Inst., Newcastle upon Tyne, 1978–86. Consultant and UK Delegate, European Health Cttee, Primary Care and Prevention Gp, Council of Europe, Strasbourg, 1983–85. *Publications:* (contrib.) Handbook of Preventative Care for Pre-School Children, 1984; Organisation of Prevention in Primary Care, 1986; Why not care for your diabetic patients?, 1986; (contrib.) Chronic Disease in Medical Audit in General Practice, 1990; Obesity and Weight Management in Primary Care, 2002; contrib. to reports of working parties and papers and articles on diabetes, health care for children, asthma, etc in BMJ, The Practitioner, Cardiology in Practice, Members Reference Books, RCGP. *Recreations:* reading, gardening, music, cricket. *Address:* 42 Etherley Lane, Bishop Auckland, Co. Durham DL14 7QZ. *T:* (01388) 604429.

WAINE, Rt Rev. John, KCVO 1996; Bishop of Chelmsford, 1986–96; Clerk of the Closet to the Queen, 1989–96; *b* June 1930; *s* of late William and Ellen Waine; *m* 1957, Patricia Zena Haikney; three *s*. *Educ:* Prescot Grammar Sch.; Manchester Univ. (BA); Ridley Hall, Cambridge. Deacon 1955, Priest 1956; Curate of St Mary, West Derby, 1955–58; Curate in Charge of All Saints, Sutton, 1958–60; Vicar of Ditton, 1960–64; Vicar of Holy Trinity, Southport, 1964–69; Rector of Kirkby, 1969–75; Bishop Suffragan of Stafford, 1975–78; Bishop of St Edmundsbury and Ipswich, 1978–86. Chm., Churches Main Cttee, 1991–96. Mem., Press Complaints Commn, 1997–. Chairman: Council, Univ. of Essex, 1995–2001; Foundn, Univ. of Essex, 2001–07. Master, Glass Sellers' Co., 1999–2000. Entered H of L, 1985. DUniv Essex, 2002. ChStJ 1983 (Prelate, 1999–2007). *Recreations:* music, gardening. *Address:* Broadmere, Ipswich Road, Grundisburgh, Woodbridge, Suffolk IP13 6TJ. *T:* (01473) 738296. *Club:* Royal Air Force.

WAINE, Stephen Phillip; His Honour Judge Waine; a Circuit Judge, since 2001; Designated Family Judge, Northampton, since 2006; *b* 9 June 1947; *s* of late Dr T. E. Waine and M. F. Waine; *m* 1st, 1976 (marr. diss.); 2nd, 1981, Clare (*née* Pryor); one *s* one *d*. *Educ:* Rugby Sch.; Southampton Univ. (LLB). Called to the Bar, Lincoln's Inn, 1969; a Recorder, Midland and Oxford Circuit, 1992–2001. Chm., Mental Health Tribunals, 2002–. FCIArb 1999. *Recreations:* ski-ing, golf, gardening, watching sports, reading. *Address:* Northampton Combined Court Centre, 85–87 Lady's Lane, Northampton NN1 3HQ. *Club:* MCC.

WAINWRIGHT, Elizabeth-Anne; *see* Gumbel, E.-A.

WAINWRIGHT, (Elizabeth) Jane, MA; Headteacher, Wycombe High School, since 2002; *b* 27 Sept. 1950; *d* of Eric Foster Wainwright and Marie Wainwright. *Educ:* St Hugh's Coll., Oxford (MA; PGCE); Sch. of Oriental and African Studies, Univ. of London (MA). Geography teacher: Sandford Sch., Addis Ababa, 1975–77; Peers Sch., Oxford, 1977–82; Hd of Geog., Plymouth High Sch., 1982–88; Dep. Hd, Lancaster Girls' GS, 1988–92; Headteacher, Aylesbury High Sch., 1992–2002. *Recreations:* travel, friends, photography, feminism, keeping up with information technology. *Address:* Wycombe High School, Marlow Hill, High Wycombe HP11 1TB; *e-mail:* jane_wainwright@btinternet.com.

WAINWRIGHT, Geoffrey John, MBE 1991; PhD; FSA; Founder, Bluestone Partnership, 1999; *b* 19 Sept. 1937; *s* of Frederick and Dorothy Wainwright; *m* 1977, Judith; one *s* two *d*. *Educ:* Pembroke Docks Sch.; Univ. of Wales (BA); Univ. of London (PhD). FSA 1967; MIFA 1984, Hon. MIFA 1999. Prof. of Archaeology, Univ. of Baroda, India, 1961–63; Inspectorate of Ancient Monuments, English Heritage (formerly part of DoE), 1963–99; Principal Inspector, 1963–90; Chief Archaeologist, 1989–99. Chm., Wessex Archaeology, 2004–. Mem., Royal Commn on Ancient and Historical Monuments in Wales, 1987–2000, Vice Chm., 2000–02; President: Cornwall Archaeological Soc., 1980–84; Prehistoric Soc., 1982–86; Cambrian Archaeol Assoc., 2002–03; Vice Pres., 1997–2001, Treasurer, 2001–07, Pres., 2007–, Soc. of Antiquaries (Dir, 1984–90). Visiting Professor: Univ. of Southampton, 1991–; UCL, 1995–. Fellow, University Coll., Cardiff, 1985. FRSA 1991. Hon. Fellow, Univ. of Wales, Lampeter, 1996. Hon. Mem., Europae Archaeologiae Consilium, 1999. Grahame Clark Medal, British Acad., 2006. *Publications:* Stone Age in North India, 1964; Coygan Camp, Carms, 1967; Durrington Walls, Wilts, 1971; Mount Pleasant, Dorset, 1979; Gussage All Saints, Dorset, 1979; The Henge Monuments, 1990; numerous articles in learned jls. *Recreations:* Rugby football, walking, food and drink. *Address:* March Pres, Pontfaen, Pembs SA65 9TT.

WAINWRIGHT, Jane; *see* Wainwright, E. J.

WAINWRIGHT, Prof. Mark Sebastian, AM 2004; PhD, DSc; FIChemE, FIEAust; Professor of Chemical Engineering, 1989–2006, now Emeritus, and Vice-Chancellor and President, 2004–06, University of New South Wales; *b* 20 Oct. 1943; *s* of William Edward and Marjorie Wanda Wainwright; *m* Irene Eve Ruffio; two *d*. *Educ:* S Australia Inst. of Technol. (BAppSc Hons); Univ. of Adelaide (MAppSc); McMaster Univ. (PhD Chem. Engrg); Univ. of S Australia (DSc). University of New South Wales: School of Chemical Technology: Lectr in Industrial Chem., 1974–77; Sen. Lectr, 1978–80; School of Chemical Engineering and Industrial Chemistry: Associate Prof., and Hd, Dept of Industrial Chem., 1981–88; Hd, Dept of Chem. Engrg, 1989–91; Dean, Faculty of Engrg, 1991–2000; Actg Pro-Vice-Chancellor (Inf. Services), 1994; Pro-Vice-Chancellor (Res.), 1998–2000; Dep. Vice-Chancellor (Res. and Internat.), 2001–04. *Publications:* contrib. numerous papers; patents published. *Recreation:* golf. *Club:* Coast Golf.

WAINWRIGHT, Richard Barry; European Law consultant, FIPRA International; Principal Legal Adviser, European Commission, 1992–2005; *b* 10 June 1940; *s* of Denys and Shelagh Wainwright; *m* 1966, Linda Sully; three *s* one *d*. *Educ:* Trinity Coll., Oxford (BA Hons); Inns of Court Sch. of Law. In practice as barrister, 1966–68; Solicitor's Office, Inland Revenue, 1968–69; Legal Advr, British Petroleum Co., 1969–73; with Legal Service, EC, 1973–2005. *Publications:* contribs to Common Market Law Rev., European Law Rev., Oxford Yearbook of European Law, Revue du Marché Commun. *Recreations:* music, reading, sailing, ski-ing, tennis, golf, walking. *Address:* 101 Swains Lane, N6 6PJ. *T:* (020) 8340 2131. *Club:* Château Ste Anne (Brussels).

WAINWRIGHT, Sam, CBE 1982; Member: Monopolies and Mergers Commission, 1985–91; Post Office Audit Committee, 1989–92; Director, BICC, 1985–90; *b* 2 Oct. 1924; *m* Ruth Strom; three *s* one *d*. *Educ:* Regent Street Polytechnic; LSE (MSc Econ). Financial journalist, Glasgow Herald, 1950; Deputy City Editor, 1952–55; Director: Rea Brothers Ltd (Merchant Bankers), 1960–77 (Managing Dir, 1965–77); Furness Withy & Co. Ltd, 1971–77; Stothert & Pitt Ltd, 1970–77 (Chm., 1975–77); Aeronautical & General Instruments Ltd, 1968–77; Lancashire & London Investment Trust Ltd, 1963–77; Scottish Cities Investment Trust Ltd, 1961–77; Scottish & Mercantile Investment Co. Ltd, 1964–77; AMDAHL (UK), 1987–93; Post Office Corporation: Mem. Bd, 1977–85; Dep. Chm., 1981–85; Man. Dir, Nat. Girobank, 1977–85; Dir Postel Investment Ltd, 1982–85; Dir, 1972–87, Dep. Chm., 1985–86, Chm., 1986–87, Manders (Hldgs). Mem. Council, Soc. of Investment Analysts, 1961–75, Fellow, 1980. Chm., Jigsaw Day Nurseries, 1991–95. Hon. Editor, The Investment Analyst, 1961–74. *Publications:* articles in various Bank Reviews. *Recreations:* reading, bridge, walking. *Address:* Flat 5, 29 Warrington Crescent, W9 1EJ. *T:* (020) 7286 8050. *Club:* Reform.

WAIT, John James; His Honour Judge Wait; a Circuit Judge, since 1997; Resident Judge, Derby Combined Court, since 2000; *b* 19 Sept. 1949; *s* of Eric James Wait and Rachel Wait; *m* 1986, Patricia, (Tricia), Ann Hitchcock; two *s*. *Educ:* Queen Mary's Grammar Sch., Walsall; Nottingham Univ. (LLB 1971). Called to the Bar, Inner Temple, 1972; Lectr in Law, UCW, Aberystwyth, 1972–74; in practice at the Bar, 1974–97; Asst Recorder, 1989–93; a Recorder, 1993–97; Midland and Oxford Circuit. *Recreations:* golf, tennis. *Address:* Derby Combined Court, Morledge, Derby DE1 2XE. *Clubs:* Moor Hall Golf (Sutton Coldfield), St Enodoc Golf (N Cornwall).

WAITE, Rt Hon. Sir John (Douglas), Kt 1982; PC 1993; a Lord Justice of Appeal, 1993–97; *b* 3 July 1932; *s* of late Archibald Waite and Betty, *d* of late Ernest Bates; *m* 1966, Julia Mary, *er d* of late Joseph Tangye; three *s* two step *s*. *Educ:* Sherborne Sch.; Corpus Christi Coll., Cambridge (MA). President of Cambridge Union, 1955. Nat. Service, 2nd Lieut, RA, 1951–52. Called to Bar, Gray's Inn, 1956, Bencher, 1981; QC 1975; a Judge of the High Court of Justice, Family Div., 1982–93; Presiding Judge, North Eastern Circuit, 1990–93; Judge, Gibraltar Court of Appeal, 1997–2000. Pres., Employment Appeal Tribunal, 1983–85. Co-Chm., Indep. Asylum Commn, 2006–08. Chairman: UNICEF (UK), 1997–2004; Special Trustees, Middx and UC Hosps, 1997–2004; UCL Hosps Charitable Foundn, 1999–2004. *Recreations:* reading (haphazardly), sailing (uncertainly), gardening (optimistically). *Address:* 33 Cleaver Square, SE11 4EA; 54 Church Street, Orford, Woodbridge, Suffolk IP12 2NT.

WAITE, Jonathan Gilbert Stokes; QC 2002; *b* 15 Feb. 1956; *s* of late Capt. David Waite, RN, and of Joan Waite (*née* Paull). *Educ:* Sherborne Sch.; Trinity Coll., Cambridge (MA). Called to the Bar, Inner Temple, 1978; in practice, specialising in personal injury, industrial diseases and pharmaceutical product liability law, 1979–. *Recreations:* golf, ski-ing, bridge, wines of Bordeaux. *Address:* 76 Forthbridge Road, Battersea, SW11 5NY; Crown Office Chambers, 2 Crown Office Row, Temple, EC4Y 7HJ. *T:* (020) 7228 4488, *Fax:* (020) 7797 8100; *e-mail:* waite@crownofficechambers.com. *Clubs:* Woking Golf, Aldeburgh Golf, Rye Golf, Royal St George's Golf.

WAITE, Judith Mary; *see* Rowe, J. M.

WAITE, Terence Hardy, CBE 1992 (MBE 1982); writer and lecturer; Adviser to Archbishop of Canterbury on Anglican Communion Affairs, 1980–92 (taken captive and held hostage in Lebanon, Jan. 1987–19 Nov. 1991); Fellow Commoner, Trinity Hall, Cambridge, 1992–93, now Emeritus; *b* 31 May 1939; *s* of Thomas William Waite and Lena (*née* Hardy); *m* 1964, Helen Frances Watters; one *s* three *d*. *Educ:* Wilmslow and Stockton Heath, Cheshire; Church Army Coll., London. Lay training adviser to Bishop and Diocese of Bristol, 1964–68; Adviser to Archbishop of Uganda, Rwanda and Burundi, 1968–71; Internat. Consultant working with Roman Catholic Church, 1972–79. Member, National Assembly, Church of England, 1966–68 (resigned on moving to Africa); Co-ordinator, Southern Sudan Relief Project, 1969–71. Vis. Fellow, Magdalen Coll., Oxford, 2006. Founder-Chairman: Y Care International, 1985–2000 (Pres., 2000–); Hostage UK, 2005–; Pres., Emmaus UK, 1998–. Chm., Prison Video Trust, 1998–. Pres., Internat. Eisteddfod of Wales, 2006–; Vice President: Suffolk Assoc. of Local Councils, 1999–; E Cheshire Hospice, Macclesfield, 2001–. Trustee: Butler Trust, 1986–; Freeplay Foundn. Patron: One World Broadcasting Trust, 1987–; Strode Park Foundn for the Disabled, Herne, Kent, 1988–; Bishop Simon Nkoane Trust, 1993–; Bury St Edmunds Volunteer Centre, 1994–; Uganda Soc. for Disabled Children, 1995–; Warrington Male Voice Choir, 1996–; Lewisham Envmt Trust, 1996–; Romany Soc., 1997–; Suffolk Far East Prisoners of War (Pres.); Save our Parsonages, 1999–; Bridge Project, Sudbury, 1999–; Children (and Families) of Far Eastern Prisoners of War, 1999–; Kingswood Foundn, Bristol; Canterbury Oast Trust; Coventry Cathedral Internat. Centre for Reconciliation, 2000–; Friends of the Samaritans, Bury St Edmunds; One to One Children's Fund, 2001–; Under-Privileged Children's Charity, Bristol, 2003–; British Friends of Neve Shalom/Wahat al-Salam, 2003–; Habit for Humanity, 2004–. Ambassador for WWF, 2000–. Hon. DCL: Kent at Canterbury, 1986; City, 1992; Hon. LLD: Liverpool, 1992; Durham, 1992; Sussex, 1992; Yale, 1992; Robert Gordon, 2007; Hon. DHL Virginia Commonwealth Univ., 1996; Hon. LHD Wittenberg, 1992; Hon. DHumLit Southern Florida, 1992; Hon. DPhil Anglia Polytech. Univ., 2001; Hon. DLitt: Nottingham Trent, 2001; De Montfort, 2005. Templeton UK Award, 1985; Franklin D. Roosevelt Four Freedom Award, 1992. *Publications:* Taken on Trust, 1993; Footfalls in Memory, 1995; Travels with a Primate, 2000. *Recreations:* music, travel (esp. in remote parts of the world), Jungian studies, international affairs. *Address:* Trinity Hall, Cambridge CB2 1TJ. *Clubs:* Travellers; Empire (Toronto).

WAJDA, Andrzej; Polish film and theatre director; Senator, Polish People's Republic, 1989–91 (one term); President, Andrzej Wajda Master School of Film Directing; *b* 6 March 1926; *s* of Jakub Wajda and Aniela Wajda; *m* 1st, 1967, Beata Tyszkiewicz (marr. diss.); one *d*; 2nd, 1975, Krystyna Zachwatowicz. *Educ:* Acad. Fine Arts, Cracow; Film Acad., Łódź. Asst Stage Manager, 1953; film dir, 1954–; Stage Manager, Teatr Stary, Cracow, 1973; Man. Dir, Teatr Powszechny, Warsaw, 1989–90. Pres., Polish Film Assoc., 1978–83. Hon. Mem., Union of Polish Artists and Designers, 1977. Dr *hc* American, Washington, 1981; Bologna, 1988; Jagiellonian, Cracow, 1989. British Acad. Award for Services to Film, 1982; BAFTA Fellowship, 1982; Hon. Academy Award for lifetime achievement, 2000. Order of Banner of Labour, 1975; Officer's Cross of Polonia Restituta; Officier, Légion d'Honneur (France), 1982; Order of Kirill and Methodius (Bulgaria). *Films:* Generation, 1954; I'm Going to the Sun, 1955; Kanal, 1956 (Silver Palm, Cannes, 1957); Ashes and Diamonds, 1957; Lotna, 1959; Innocent Sorcerers, 1959; Samson, 1960; Serbian Lady Macbeth, 1961; Love at Twenty, 1961; Ashes, 1965; Gates of Paradise, 1967; Everything For Sale, 1968; Jigsaw Puzzle (for TV), 1969; Hunting Flies, 1969; Macbeth (TV), 1969; Landscape After Battle, 1970; The Birch Wood, 1970; Pilatus (TV), 1971; Master and Margaret (TV), 1972; The Wedding, 1972 (Silver Prize, San Sebastian, 1973); The Promised Land, 1974 (Grand Prix, Moscow Film Festival, 1975); The Shadow Line, 1976; A Dead Class (TV), 1976; Man of Marble, 1977; Rough Treatment, 1978; The Orchestral Conductor, 1979; The Maids of Wilko, 1979 (Oscar nomination, 1980); Man of Iron, 1981 (Palme D'Or, Cannes, 1981); Danton, 1982; Love in Germany, 1985; Chronicle of Love Affairs, 1986; The Possessed, 1987; Korczak, 1990; The Ring with the Crowned Eagle, 1992; Nastasya, 1994; The Great Week, 1995; Miss Nobody, 1996; Pan Tacleusz, 2000; *plays:* Hatful of Rain, 1959; Hamlet, 1960, 1980, 1989; Two on the Seesaw, 1960, 1990; The Wedding, 1962; The Possessed, 1963, 1971, 1975; Play Strindberg, 1969; Idiot, 1971, 1975; Sticks and Bones, Moscow, 1972; Der Mittmacher, 1973; November Night, 1974; The Danton Case, 1975, 1978; When Reason is Asleep, 1976; Emigrés, 1976; Nastasia Philipovna (improvisation based on Dostoyevsky's The Idiot), 1977; Conversation with the Executioner, 1977; Gone with the Years, Gone with the Days …, 1978; Antygone, 1984; Crime and Punishment, 1984, 1986, 1987; Miss Julia, 1988; Dybuk, 1988; Lesson of Polish Language, 1988; Nastasya (adapted from The Idiot), 1989, Osaka, 1993; Hamlet IV, 1989; Romeo and Juliet, 1990; The Wedding, 1991; Sonate of Spectres, 1994; Mishima, 1994; Wrocław's Improvisation, 1996. *Publication:* My Life in Film (autobiog.), 1989. *Address:* Film Polski, ul. Mazowiecka 6/8, Warsaw, Poland.

WAKE, Sir Hereward, 14th Bt *cr* 1621; MC 1942; Vice Lord-Lieutenant of Northamptonshire, 1984–91; Major (retired) King's Royal Rifle Corps; *b* 7 Oct. 1916; *e s* of Maj. Gen. Sir Hereward Wake, 13th Bt, CB, CMG, DSO, and Margaret W. (*d* 1976), *er d* of R. H. Benson; *S* father, 1963; *m* 1952, Julia Rosemary, JP, DL, *yr d* of late Capt. G. W. M. Lees, Falcutt House, near Brackley, Northants; one *s* three *d*. *Educ:* Eton; RMC, Sandhurst. Served War of 1939–45 (wounded, MC). Retired from 60th Rifles, 1947, and studied Estate Management and Agriculture. Fellow, University of Northampton (formerly Nene Coll., later UC, Northampton), 1997–. High Sheriff, 1955, DL 1969, Northants. *Heir: s* Hereward Charles Wake [*b* 22 Nov. 1952; *m* 1st, 1977, Lady Doune Ogilvy (marr. diss. 1995), *e d* of Earl of Airlie, *qv*; two *s* one *d* (and one *s* decd); 2nd, 1998, Mrs Joan Barrow]. *Address:* Old School House, Courteenhall, Northampton NN7 2QD. *Club:* Brooks's.

WAKEFIELD, Bishop of, since 2003; **Rt Rev. Stephen George Platten;** *b* 17 May 1947; *s* of George Henry and Marjory Platten; *m* 1972, Rosslie Thompson; two *s*. *Educ:* Stationers' Company's Sch.; Univ. of London (BEd Hons 1972); Trinity Coll., Oxford (Dip. Theol. 1974; BD 2003); Cuddesdon Theol Coll. Deacon 1975, Priest 1976; Asst Curate, St Andrew, Headington, Oxford, 1975–78; Chaplain and Tutor, Lincoln Theol Coll., 1978–82; Diocesan Dir of Ordinands and Canon Residentiary, Portsmouth Cathedral, 1983–89; Dir, post-ordination trng and continuing ministeriel educn, Dio. Portsmouth, 1984–89; Archbishop of Canterbury's Sec. for Ecumenical Affairs, 1990–95; Dean of Norwich, 1995–2003. Hon. Canon of Canterbury Cathedral, 1990–95. Anglican Sec., ARCIC (II), 1990–95; Chm., Liturgical Commn, 2005–. Chairman: Soc. for Study of Christian Ethics, 1983–88; Govs, Anglican Centre in Rome, 2001–. Minister Provincial, European Province, Third Order, SSF, 1991–96. Dir, SCM Press, 1990– (Chm., 2001–); Mem. Council, Hymns Ancient and Modern, 1997–. Guestmaster, Nikaean Club, 1990–95. Liveryman, Stationers' Co., 2004. Hon. DLitt East Anglia, 2003. *Publications:* (contrib.) Deacons in the Ministry of the Church, 1987; (series editor) Ethics and Our Choices, 1990–; (contrib.) Spirituality and Psychology, 1990; (contrib.) Say One for Me, 1991; (jtly) Spirit and Tradition: an essay on Change, 1996; Pilgrims, 1996; (ed jtly) New Soundings, 1997; Augustine's Legacy: authority and leadership in the Anglican Communion, 1997; (ed jtly) Flagships of the Spirit: cathedrals in society, 1998; (ed and contrib.) Seeing Ourselves: who are the interpreters of contemporary society?, 1998; Pilgrim Guide to Norwich, 1998; Cathedrals and Abbeys of England, 1999; (ed and contrib.) The Retreat of the State, 1999; Ink and Spirit, 2000; (ed and contrib.) Open Government, 2002; (ed and contrib.) Runcie: on reflection, 2002; (ed and contrib.) Anglicanism and the Western Tradition, 2003; (ed jtly and contrib) Dreaming Spires: cathedrals in a new age, 2006; Rebuilding Jerusalem: the Church's hold on hearts and minds, 2007; Vocation: singing the Lord's song, 2007; contribs to theol and educnl jls. *Recreations:* walking, music, literature, Land Rovers, Northumberland. *Address:* Bishop's Lodge, Woodthorpe Lane, Wakefield WF2 6JL. *T:* (01924) 255349, *Fax:* (01924) 250202; *e-mail:* bishop@bishopofwakefield.org.uk. *Club:* Athenæum.

WAKEFIELD, Dean of; *see* Greener, Very Rev. J. D. F.

WAKEFIELD, Her Honour Anne Prudence; a Circuit Judge, 1999–2005; *b* 25 May 1943; *d* of John Arkell Wakefield and Stella Adelaide Wakefield; *m* 1974, James Robert Reid, *qv* (marr. diss. 2002); two *s* one *d*. *Educ:* London Sch. of Economics and Political Science (LLB); Newnham Coll., Cambridge (LLM 1969). Called to the Bar, Gray's Inn, 1968; in practice, 1970–75 and 1987–99; Asst Recorder, 1991–95; a Recorder, 1995–99. Lecturer in Law: LSE, 1969–70; pt-time, QMC, 1983–87. Pt-time Chm., Industrial Tribunals, 1992–99; a Judge of the Employment Appeal Tribunal, 2000–05. Associate, Newnham Coll., Cambridge, 2002–05.

WAKEFIELD, Derek John, CB 1982; Under Secretary, Government Communications Headquarters, 1978–82; *b* 21 Jan. 1922; *s* of Archibald John Thomas and Evelyn Bessie Wakefield; *m* 1951, Audrey Ellen Smith (*d* 2001); one *d*. *Educ:* The Commonweal School. Air Ministry, 1939–42 and 1947–52. Served War, Lieut, Royal Pioneer Corps, 1942–47. Government Communications Headquarters, 1952–82. Mem., Airship Assoc. Governor, Barnwood House Trust, Gloucester, 1973–90. *Recreation:* airships. *Club:* Naval and Military.

WAKEFIELD, Sir (Edward) Humphry (Tyrrell), 2nd Bt *cr* 1962; *b* 11 July 1936; *s* of Sir Edward Birkbeck Wakefield, 1st Bt, CIE, and Constance Lalage, *e d* of Sir John Perronet Thompson, KCSI, KCIE, and *nephew* of 1st Baron Wakefield of Kendal; *S* father, 1969; *m* 1st, 1960, Priscilla (marr. diss. 1964), *e d* of O. R. Bagot; 2nd, 1966, Hon. Elizabeth Sophia (from whom he obt. a divorce, 1971), *e d* of 1st Viscount De L'Isle, VC, KG, PC, GCMG, GCVO, and former wife of G. S. O. A. Colthurst; one *s*; 3rd, 1974, Hon. Katharine Mary Alice Baring, *d* of 1st Baron Howick of Glendale, KG, GCMG, KCVO, and of Lady Mary Howick; one *s* one *d* (and one *s* decd). *Educ:* Gordonstoun; Trinity Coll., Cambridge (MA Hons). Formerly Captain, 10th Royal Hussars. Exec. Vice-Pres., Mallett, America Ltd, 1970–75; Chm., Tyrrell & Moore Ltd, 1978–92; Director: Mallett & Son (Antiques) Ltd, 1971–78; Tree of Life Foundn 1976–. Dir, Spoleto Fest. of Two Worlds, USA and Italy, 1973–80. Chm., Wilderness Trust, 1999–; President: Northumberland Nat. Park Search and Rescue Team; Avison Trust; Tibetan Spaniel Assoc.; Patron: Action North East; Medicine and Chernobyl; Centre for Search Res. UK; Shadow Dance UK; formerly Appeals Consultant, London Br., British Red Cross Soc. Mem., Standing Council of Baronetage. Mem., Soc. of Dilettante. Fellow, Pierpont Morgan Library. Joined NZ Everest Team, 1990, and also in their first ascent of Mount Wakefield; Mem., Norman Vaughan Antarctic Expedn, 1993. Life Mem., Scott-Polar Inst. FRGS. *Recreations:* riding, writing, music, shooting. *Heir: s* Capt. Maximilian Edward Vereker Wakefield [*b* 22 Feb. 1967; *m* 1994, Lucinda Katharine Elizabeth, *d* of Lt-Col and Mrs David Pipe; two *s*. *Educ:* Milton Abbey; RMA Sandhurst]. *Address:* Chillingham Castle, Chillingham, Northumberland NE66 5NJ. *Clubs:* Beefsteak, Cavalry and Guards, Turf; Harlequins Rugby Football (Twickenham) (Hon. Life Mem.).

See also G. H. C. Wakefield.

WAKEFIELD, Gerald Hugo Cropper, (Hady); Chairman, J & H Marsh & McLennan (Holdings) Ltd (formerly Bowring Group), 1996–99; *b* 15 Sept. 1938; *s* of Sir Edward Wakefield, 1st Bt, CIE, and (Constance) Lalage, *e d* of Sir John Perronet Thompson, KCSI, KCIE; *m* 1971, Victoria Rose Feilden; one *s*. *Educ:* Eton; Trinity Coll., Cambridge (MA). Started at Lloyd's, 1961; joined C. T. Bowring & Co., 1968, Dir 1983; Guy Carpenter & Co., NY: Dep. Chm., 1990; Pres., 1993; Chm., 1996. *Recreations:* fishing, shooting, ski-ing, opera. *Address:* Bramdean House, Alresford, Hants SO24 0JU. *T:* (01962) 771214. *Clubs:* White's, Cavalry and Guards, Beefsteak; The Brook (NY).

WAKEFIELD, Hady; *see* Wakefield, G. H. C.

WAKEFIELD, Sir Humphry; *see* Wakefield, Sir E. H. T.

WAKEFIELD, Sir Norman (Edward), Kt 1988; Chairman, Y. J. Lovell (Holdings) plc, 1987–90; *b* 30 Dec. 1929; *s* of Edward and Muriel Wakefield; *m* 1953, Denise Mary Bayliss (*d* 1998); two *s* four *d*. *Educ:* Wallington County Sch.; Croydon and Brixton Technical Colls. Articled student, Wates Ltd, 1947; Man. Dir, Wates Construction Ltd, 1967; Pres., jt venture co., USA, between Wates and Rouse Co., 1970–73; Man. Dir, Holland, Hannen & Cubitts, 1973; Chief Exec., 1977–83, Chm. and Chief Exec., 1983–87, Y. J. Lovell (Holdings). Dep. Chm., Housing Corp., 1990–94. Director: Lloyds Abbey Life, 1986–93; English Estates, 1990–94. Pres., CIOB, 1985–86. Chm., 1995–2003, Dep. Chm., 2003–, Nelson House Recovery Trust. *Recreations:* opera, walking, gardening. *Address:* 12 Rosemary Gate, Esher Park Avenue, Esher, Surrey KT10 9NZ. *Club:* Arts.

WAKEFIELD, Sir Peter (George Arthur), KBE 1977; CMG 1973; HM Diplomatic Service, retired; art management consultant; Life President, Asia House, London, since 2006 (Chairman of Trustees, 1993–2003; Trustee, since 2003); *b* 13 May 1922; *s* of John Bunting Wakefield and Dorothy Ina Stace; *m* 1951, Felicity Maurice-Jones; four *s* one *d*. *Educ:* Cranleigh Sch.; Corpus Christi Coll., Oxford. Army Service, 1942–47; Military Govt, Eritrea, 1946–47; Hulton Press, 1947–49; entered Diplomatic Service, 1949; Middle East Centre for Arab Studies, 1950; 2nd Sec., Amman, 1950–52; Foreign Office, 1953–55; 1st Sec., British Middle East Office, Nicosia, 1955–56; 1st Sec. (Commercial), Cairo, 1956; Administrative Staff Coll., Henley, 1957; 1st Sec. (Commercial), Vienna, 1957–60; 1st Sec. (Commercial), Tokyo, 1960–63; SE Asia Dept, FO, 1964–66; Consul-General and Counsellor, Benghazi, 1966–69; Econ. and Commercial Counsellor, Tokyo, 1970–72; Econ. and Commercial Minister, Tokyo, 1973; seconded as Special Adviser on the Japanese Market, BOTB, 1973–75; Ambassador to the Lebanon, 1975–78, to

Belgium, 1979–82. Director: NACF, 1982–92; UK, Trust for Mus. Exhibns, 1992–99. Chairman: Richmond Theatre Trust, 1989–2001; Heritage Co-ordination Gp, 1992–98. *Recreations:* looking at paintings, collecting pots, restoring ruins. *Address:* Lincoln House, 28 Montpelier Row, Twickenham, Middx TW1 2NQ. *T:* (020) 8892 6390; Cortijo Rosa, Periana 29710, Provincia de Malaga, Spain. *T:* (951) 230229. *Club:* Travellers.

WAKEFIELD, Robert; His Honour Judge Wakefield; a Circuit Judge, since 1996; *b* 14 Feb. 1946; *s* of Dudley James Wakefield and Violet Harriette Hart; *m* 1977, Anne Jennifer Gregory. *Educ:* Birmingham Univ. (LLB); Brasenose Coll., Oxford (BCL). Called to the Bar, Middle Temple, 1969; Recorder, 1993–96. *Address:* Inner London Crown Court, Sessions House, Newington Causeway, SE1 6AZ. *T:* (020) 7234 3100.

WAKEFIELD, William Barry, CB 1990; Deputy Director (Research), National Commission on Education, 1991–95; *b* 6 June 1930; *s* of Stanley Arthur and Evelyn Grace Wakefield; *m* 1953, Elizabeth Violet (*née* Alexander); three *s* one *d*. *Educ:* Harrow County Grammar Sch.; University Coll., London. BSc; FSS. Statistician, NCB, 1953–62; DES, 1962–67; Chief Statistician, MoD, 1967–72, CSO, 1972–75; Asst Dir, CSO, Cabinet Office, 1975–79; Dir of Statistics, DES, 1979–90. Member, United Reformed Church. *Recreations:* horse racing, gardening, family history. *Address:* Egg Hall Cottage, 14 Birch Street, Nayland, Colchester CO6 4JA.

WAKEFORD, David Ewing, MBE 1992; International Trade Director, Commonwealth Business Council, since 2006; Managing Director, Global Trade Knowledge, 1999–2000 and since 2006; *b* 30 Oct. 1944; *s* of Arthur Ewing Wakeford and late Gertrude Ada Wakeford (*née* Hall); *m* 1st, 1968 (marr. diss. 2006); three *s*; 2nd, 2007, SallyAnn Jackson. *Educ:* Hadham Hall Sch.; St Mary's Sch., Welwyn; Univ. of Manchester (MSc Polymer and Fibre Sci.). ICI, 1963–99: Res. Chemist, Plastics Div., 1963–78; Purchasing Manager, Petrochemicals and Plastics, 1978–85; Internat. Trade Manager, Head Office, 1985–99; Chief Exec., Simpler Trade Procedures Board, then SITPRO Ltd, 2000–05. *Recreations:* sailing, bird-watching, country pursuits. *Address:* 18 Pall Mall, SW1Y 5LU. *T:* (020) 7024 8201.

WAKEFORD, Sir (Geoffrey) Michael (Montgomery), Kt 2004; OBE 1995; Clerk to the Worshipful Company of Mercers, 1974–98; Barrister-at-Law; *b* 10 Dec. 1937; *o s* of late Geoffrey and Helen Wakeford; *m* 1966, Diana Margaret Loy Cooper, *y d* of late Comdr W. G. L. Cooper and of Patricia Cooper (*née* Fforde), Aislaby, N Yorks; two *s* two *d*. *Educ:* Downside; Clare Coll., Cambridge (MA, LLB). Called to Bar, Gray's Inn and South Eastern Circuit, 1961; practised at Common Law Bar until 1971. Apptd Dep. Clerk to the Mercers Co., 1971. Director: Portman Settled Estates Ltd, 1998–2007; Alto Film Prodn LLP, 2004–. Governor: London Internat. Film Sch., 1981–85, 1990– (Vice Chm, 1997–); Molecule Theatre, 1986–; Unicorn Children's Theatre, 2005–; Thomas Telford Sch., 1990–2001 (Chm., 1997–2001); Abingdon Sch., 2000–07; Guardian Angels RC Primary Sch., 2000– (Chm., 2000–07); Walsall Acad., 2001– (Chm., 2001–). *Address:* 15 Compton Terrace, N1 2UN. *Club:* Travellers.

WAKEFORD, Richard George; Director-General Environment, Scottish Government (formerly Head, Scottish Executive Environment and Rural Affairs Department), since 2005; *b* 6 Oct. 1953; *s* of (Henry) Eric Wakeford and Mary Elisabeth Wakeford (*née* Parsons); *m* 1976, Susan Mary Beacham; three *s*. *Educ:* Chichester High Sch. for Boys; King's Coll., London (BSc Maths and Physics). Exec. Officer, 1975–80, Asst Private Sec. to Minister of State, 1979–80, DoE; HEO posts, DoE and Dept of Transport, 1980–83; Department of the Environment: Private Sec. to Permt Sec., 1983–85; Planning Inspectorate, 1985; Develt Control, 1985–87; Bill Manager, Water Privatisation, 1988–89; Principal, Envmt White Paper Team, 1990; (last) Chief Exec., Crown Suppliers, 1991; Head of Develt Plans and Policies, 1991–94; Asst Sec., Economic and Domestic Secretariat, Cabinet Office, 1994–96; Chief Executive: Countryside Commn, 1996–99; Countryside Agency, 1999–2004. UK Sustainable Develt Comr, 2000–04. Non-exec. Bd Mem., DEFRA, 2001–04. Mid Career Fellow, Princeton Univ., 1987–88. Hon. MR.TPI. Hon. Dr Glos. *Publications:* Speeding Planning Appeals, 1986; American Development Control: parallels and paradoxes from a British perspective, 1990. *Recreations:* gardening, photography, built and natural landscape. *Address:* Charingworth Court, Broadway Road, Winchcombe, Glos GL54 5JN. *T:* (01242) 603033.

WAKEHAM, family name of **Baron Wakeham.**

WAKEHAM, Baron *cr* 1992 (Life Peer), of Maldon in the County of Essex; **John Wakeham;** PC 1983; JP; DL; FCA; Chairman, Press Complaints Commission, 1995–2002; *b* 22 June 1932; *s* of late Major W. J. Wakeham and Mrs E. R. Wakeham; *m* 1st, 1965, Anne Roberta Bailey (*d* 1984); two *s*; 2nd, 1985, Alison Bridget Ward, MBE, *d* of late Ven. E. J. G. Ward, LVO; one *s*. *Educ:* Charterhouse. Chartered Accountant. MP (C) Maldon, Feb. 1974–1983, Colchester South and Maldon, 1983–92; Asst Govt Whip, 1979–81; a Lord Comr of HM Treasury (Govt Whip), 1981; Parly Under-Sec. of State, DoI, 1981–82; Minister of State, HM Treasury, 1982–83; Parly Sec. to HM Treasury and Govt Chief Whip, 1983–87; Lord Privy Seal, 1987–88; Leader of the H of C, 1987–89; Lord Pres. of the Council, 1988–89; Sec. of State for Energy, 1989–92; Minister responsible for co-ordinating develt of presentation of govt policies, 1990–92; Lord Privy Seal and Leader of the H of L, 1992–94. Chm., Royal Commn on Reform of H of L, 1999. Chm., British Horseracing Bd, 1996–98 (Mem., 1995–98). Chancellor, Brunel Univ., 1998–. Mem., Cttee of Mgt, RNLI, 1995–2005. JP Inner London, 1972; DL Hants, 1997. Hon. PhD Anglia Poly. Univ., 1992; DUniv Brunel, 1998. *Recreations:* sailing, racing, reading. *Address:* House of Lords, SW1A 0PW. *Clubs:* Carlton (Chm. 1992–98), St Stephen's, Buck's, Garrick; Royal Yacht Squadron.

WAKEHAM, Prof. William Arnot, FREng; Vice-Chancellor, University of Southampton, since 2001; *b* 25 Sept. 1944; *s* of Stanley William Wakeham; *m* 1st, 1969, Christina Marjorie Stone (marr. diss. 1974); one *s*; 2nd, 1978, Sylvia Frances Tolley; two *s*. *Educ:* Univ. of Exeter (BSc 1966; PhD 1969; DSc 1985). FREng (FEng 1997). Research Associate, Brown Univ., USA, 1969–71; Imperial College, London University: Lectr in Transport Processes, Dept of Chem. Engrg, 1971–78; Reader in Chemical Physics, 1978–85; Prof. in Chemical Physics, 1985–2001; Hd of Dept of Chem. Engrg and Chem. Technology, 1988–96; Pro Rector (Research), 1996–2001; Dep. Rector, 1997–2001. Chm., Commn of IUPAC, 1993–98. Mem., EPSRC, 2005–. FIC 2003. *Publications:* Intermolecular Forces: their origin and determination, 1981; Forces between Molecules, 1988; The Transport Properties of Fluids, 1987; International Thermodynamic Tables, vol. XI, 1989; Experimental Thermodynamics, vol. III, 1992; numerous articles in learned jls. *Recreations:* water ski-ing, cycling. *Address:* Beacon Down, Rewe, Exeter, Devon EX5 4DX; (office) University of Southampton, Highfield, Southampton SO17 1BJ. *T:* (023) 8059 2801.

WAKEHURST, 3rd Baron *cr* 1934, of Ardingly; **(John) Christopher Loder;** Chairman; Anglo & Overseas Trust PLC (formerly Anglo-American Securities Corporation), 1980–96 (Director, 1968–96); The Overseas Investment Trust PLC (formerly North Atlantic Securities Corporation), 1980–95; Morgan Grenfell Equity Income Trust PLC,

1991–95; *b* 23 Sept. 1925; *s* of 2nd Baron Wakehurst, KG, KCMG, and Dowager Lady Wakehurst, (Dame Margaret Wakehurst), DBE (*d* 1994); *S father*, 1970; *m* 1956, Ingeborg Krumbholz-Hess (*d* 1977); one *s* one *d*; *m* 1983, Brigid, *yr d* of William Noble, Cirencester. *Educ:* Eton; King's School, nr Sydney, NSW; Trinity College, Cambridge (BA 1948, LLB 1949, MA 1953). Served War as Sub Lieut RANVR and RNVR; South West Pacific, 1943–45. Barrister, Inner Temple, 1950. Chm., Morgan Grenfell Trust Managers Ltd, 1991–94; Director: Mayfair & City Properties plc, 1984–87; The Nineteen Twenty-Eight Investment Trust plc, 1984–86; Morgan Grenfell Latin American Cos Trust, 1994–96; Chm. and Dir, Hampton Gold Mining Areas, 1981–86; Chairman: Continental Illinois Ltd, 1973–84; Philadelphia National Ltd, 1985–90; Dep. Chm., London and Manchester Gp, 1981–95 (Dir, 1966–95). Trustee: The Photographers' Gallery Ltd, 1979–90; Photographers' Trust Fund, 1986–91. *Heir: s* Hon. Timothy Walter Loder, *b* 28 March 1958. *Address:* Trillinghurst Oast, Ranters Lane, Goudhurst, Kent TN17 1HL. *Club:* Chelsea Arts.

WAKELAM, Prof. Michael John Owen, PhD; Director, BBSRC Babraham Institute, since 2007; Fellow, Downing College, Cambridge, since 2007; *b* 15 July 1955; *s* of John Wakelam and Sheila Wakelam; *m* 1980, Jane Catherine Fensome; two *s*. *Educ:* Univ. of Birmingham (BSc Med. Biochem. 1977; PhD Biochem. 1980). Res. Fellow, Univ. of Konstanz, 1981–83; Beit Meml Res. Fellow, Imperial Coll., London, 1983–85; Lectr, 1985–90, Sen. Lectr, 1991–92, Reader, 1992–93, in Biochemistry, Univ. of Glasgow; Prof. of Molecular Pharmacology, Univ. of Birmingham, 1993–2006. Mem., MRC, 2004–08 (Chm., Molecular and Cellular Medicine Bd 2004–08). *Publications:* contrib. to learned jls on cell signalling processes. *Recreations:* reading, music. *Address:* Babraham Institute, Babraham Research Campus, Cambridge CB22 4AT.

WAKELEY, Amanda Jane; fashion designer; Creative Director, Amanda Wakeley, since 1990; *b* 15 Sept. 1962; *d* of Sir John Cecil Nicholson Wakeley, 2nd Bt, *qv*. *Educ:* Cheltenham Ladies' Coll. Worked in fashion industry, NY, 1983–85, for private commns, 1987–90; Founder, Amanda Wakeley label, 1990; fashion and jewellery collections sold globally through over 100 outlets and online. Co-Chm., Fashion Targets Breast Cancer Appeal Cttee, 1996– (raised over £10 million). British Fashion Award for Glamour, 1992, 1993 and 1996. *Recreations:* theatre, music, sports, travel, photography. *Address:* 6 Old Park Lane, W1K 1QR.

WAKELEY, Sir John (Cecil Nicholson), 2nd Bt *cr* 1952; FRCS; Consultant Surgeon, West Cheshire Group of Hospitals, 1961–88, retired; *b* 27 Aug. 1926; *s* of Sir Cecil Pembrey Grey Wakeley, 1st Bt, KBE, CB, MCh, FRCS, and Elizabeth Muriel (*d* 1985), *d* of James Nicholson-Smith; *S father*, 1979; *m* 1954, June Leney; two *s* one *d*. *Educ:* Canford Sch.; MB, BS London 1950. LRCP 1950, FRCS 1955 (MRCS 1950); FACS 1973. Lectr in Anatomy, Univ. of London, 1951–52. Sqdn Ldr, RAF, 1953–54. Councillor, RCS, 1971–83; Member: Mersey Regional Health Authority, 1974–78; Editorial Bd, Health Trends, DHSS, 1968–71. Examiner for Gen. Nursing Council for England and Wales, 1954–59; Consultant Adviser in Surgery to RAF, 1981–89, Hon. Consultant Advr, 1990–. Freeman of City of London; Liveryman: Worshipful Soc. of Apothecaries; Worshipful Co. of Barbers. CStJ 1959. *Publications:* papers on leading med. jls, incl. British Empire Cancer Campaign Scientific Report, Vol. II: Zinc 65 and the prostate, 1958; report on distribution and radiation dosimetry of Zinc 65 in the rat, 1959. *Recreations:* music, photography, bird-watching. *Heir: s* Nicholas Jeremy Wakeley [*b* 17 Oct. 1957; *m* 1991, Sarah Ann, *d* of Air Vice-Marshal B. L. Robinson, *qv*]. *Address:* Croxton Green Cottage, Croxton Green, Cholmondley, Malpas, Cheshire SY14 8HG. *T:* (01829) 720530. *Club:* Council Club of Royal College of Surgeons.
See also A. J. Wakeley.

WAKELIN, Michael Paul; Head of Religion and Ethics, BBC, since 2006; *b* 21 April 1961; *s* of Paul Oasland Wakelin and Rosemary Wakelin (*née* Sorrel); *m* 1997, Jacqueline Clare Jouannet; one *s* one *d*. *Educ:* Little Plumstead Primary Sch., Priors Court; Kingswood Sch., Bath; Birmingham Univ. (BA Hons Theol.). English teacher, Mokwon Univ., Taejon, S Korea, 1983–85; BBC Radio: researcher, 1986; producer, 1987; Exec. Producer, 1988–99; Series Producer, BBC TV, 1999–2006. *Publication:* J. Arthur Rank: the man behind the gong, 1996. *Recreations:* playing bass guitar and squash badly, walking, preaching. *Address:* c/o BBC, New Broadcasting House, Oxford Road, Manchester M60 1SJ. *T:* (0161) 200 2020.

WAKELING, Richard Keith Arthur; Chairman, Polar Capital (formerly Henderson) Technology Trust PLC, since 1996; *b* 19 Nov. 1946; *s* of late Eric George Wakeling and Dorothy Ethel Wakeling; *m* 1971, Carmen; three *s*. *Educ:* Churchill Coll., Cambridge (MA). Called to the Bar, Inner Temple, 1971. Group Treasurer, BOC Group, 1973–83; Finance Dir, John Brown, 1983–86; Finance Dir, 1986–88, Acting Chief Exec., 1988–89, Charter Consolidated; Dep. Chief Exec., 1990, Chief Exec., 1991–94, Johnson Matthey. Dep. Chm., Celtic Group Holdings Ltd, 1994–97; Director: Costain, 1992–96; Laura Ashley Holdings, 1994–95; Logica, 1995–2002; Staveley Industries, 1995–99; Henderson Geared Income & Growth Trust (formerly HTR Income and Growth Split Trust), 1995–2003; Oxford Instruments plc, 1995–2001; MG plc, 1999–2000; Brunner Investment Trust plc, 2000–. *Recreations:* mediaeval history and architecture, golf, music, gardening. *Address:* 46 The Bourne, Southgate, N14 6QS.

WAKEMAN, Sir Edward Offley Bertram, 6th Bt *cr* 1828, of Perdiswell Hall, Worcestershire; *b* 31 July 1934; *s* of Captain Sir Offley Wakeman, 4th Bt, CBE and his 2nd wife, Josceline Ethelreda (*d* 1996), *e d* of Maj.-Gen. Bertram Revely Mitford, CB, CMG, DSO; *S half-brother*, 1991, but his name does not appear on the Official Roll of the Baronetage. *Heir:* none.

WAKSMAN, David Michael; QC 2002; **His Honour Judge Waksman;** a Circuit Judge, since 2007; *b* 28 Aug. 1957; *Educ:* Royal Grammar Sch., Newcastle Upon Tyne; Manchester Univ. (LLB Hons); St Catherine's Coll., Oxford (BCL). Called to the Bar, Middle Temple, 1982. Recorder of the Crown and County Courts, 2001–07.

WALBANK, Frank William, CBE 1993; FBA 1953; MA; Rathbone Professor of Ancient History and Classical Archæology in the University of Liverpool, 1951–77, now Professor Emeritus; Dean, Faculty of Arts, 1974–77; *b* 10 Dec. 1909; *s* of A. J. D. and C. Walbank, Bingley, Yorks; *m* 1935, Mary Woodward (*d* 1987), *e d* of O. C. A. and D. Fox, Shipley, Yorks; one *s* two *d*. *Educ:* Bradford Grammar School; Peterhouse, Cambridge (Hon. Fellow, 1984). Scholar of Peterhouse, 1928–31; First Class, Parts I and II Classical Tripos, 1930–31; Hugo de Balsham Research Student, Peterhouse, 1931–32; Senior Classics Master at North Manchester High School, 1932–33; Thirlwall Prize, 1933; Asst Lecturer, 1934–36, Lecturer, 1936–46, in Latin, Professor of Latin, 1946–51, University of Liverpool; Public Orator, 1956–60; Hare Prize, 1939. J. H. Gray Lectr, Univ. of Cambridge, 1957; Andrew Mellon Vis. Prof., Univ. Pittsburgh, 1964; Myres Memorial Lectr, Univ. of Oxford, 1964–65; Sather Prof., Univ. of Calif (Berkeley), 1971. Pres., Cambridge Phil. Soc., 1982–84; Member Council: Classical Assoc., 1944–48, 1958–61 (Pres. 1969–70); Roman Soc., 1948–51 (Vice-Pres., 1953–; Pres., 1961–64); Hellenic Soc., 1951–54, 1955–56; Classical Journals Bd, 1948–66; British Acad., 1960–63; British

Sch. at Rome, 1979–87. Mem., Inst. for Advanced Study, Princeton, 1970–71; Foreign Mem., Royal Netherlands Acad. of Arts and Sciences, 1981–; Corresp. Mem., German Archaeol Inst., 1987–. Hon. Mem., Israel Soc. for Promotion of Classical Studies, 1992–; Foreign Hon. Mem., Amer. Acad. of Arts and Scis, 2002. Hon. DLitt Exeter, 1988; Hon. DHL Louisville, 1996. Kenyon Medal, British Acad., 1989; Steven Runciman Prize, Anglo-Hellenic Soc., 1989. Kentucky Col, 1995. *Publications:* Aratos of Sicyon, 1933; Philip V of Macedon, 1940; Latin Prose Versions contributed to Key to Bradley's Arnold, Latin Prose Composition, ed J. F. Mountford, 1940; The Decline of the Roman Empire in the West, 1946; A Historical Commentary on Polybius, Vol. i, 1957, Vol. ii, 1967, Vol. iii, 1979; The Awful Revolution, 1969; Polybius, 1972; The Hellenistic World, 1981; Selected Papers: Studies in Greek and Roman history and historiography, 1985; (with N. G. L. Hammond) A History of Macedonia, Vol. III: 336–167 BC, 1988; Polybius, Rome and the Hellenistic World, 2002; chapters in: The Cambridge Economic History of Europe, Vol. II, 1952, 2nd edn 1987; A Scientific Survey of Merseyside, 1953; (ed jtly and contrib.) Cambridge Ancient History, Vol. VII pt 1, 1984, pt 2, 1989, Vol VIII 1989; contribs to: the Oxford Classical Dictionary, 1949; Chambers' Encyclopædia, 1950; Encyclopædia Britannica, 1960 and 1974; English and foreign classical books and periodicals. *Address:* 64 Grantchester Meadows, Cambridge CB3 9JL. *T:* (01223) 364350.

See also D. J. Thompson.

WALBY, Christine Mary, OBE 2005; Independent Chair, Local Safeguarding Children Board, Rhondda Cynon Taff, 2006–08; independent consultant in social services and children's services matters, since 1996; *b* 9 Feb. 1940; *d* of late Kathleen Walby (*née* Bradburn) and James Walby. *Educ:* University College of Wales, Aberystwyth (BA, DipEd); Manchester Univ. (Dip. Social Admin and Social Work); University College Cardiff (MSc Econ). Youth Leader Trainer, 1961–64; Social Worker, Children's Dept, Cheshire, 1964–70; Training Officer, Salford; Tutor, Manchester Univ.; Area Officer, Salford Social Services, 1970–74; Principal Officer, S Glam Social Services, 1974–81; Divl Dir, Berks Social Services, 1981–87; Dir, Social Services, Solihull MDC, 1987–91; Dir of Social Services, Staffs CC, 1991–96. Sen. Vis. Res. Fellow, Keele Univ., 1994–; Hon. Res. Fellow, Univ. of Wales Swansea, 1998–. Mem., Human Fertilization and Embryology Authy, 1991–93. Chm., Early Childhood Unit Adv. Gp, Nat. Children's Bureau, 1995–99; Trustee: Office for Children's Rights Comr, 1992–97; Children in Wales, 1998–2007 (Chm., 2002–); Bryn Melyn Gp Foundn, 2001–03; Triangle Trust 1949 Fund, 2004–06; Mem., Nat. Commn of Inquiry into Prevention of Child Abuse, 1994–96; Advr to Chair, Safeguarding Vulnerable Children Review, Welsh Assembly Govt, 2004–06; Chm., Bd of Dirs, Tros Gynnal, 2002–. Mem. (Lab) Monmouthshire CC, 2008–. Hon. Life Mem. Council, NSPCC, 1993–. Chm., Homestart (Wales), 1999–2004. *Publications:* Who Am I?: identity, adoption and human fertilization (with Barbara Symons), 1990; contrib. professional jls. *Recreations:* mountain walking, bird watching, theatre, music.

WALCOTT, Derek Alton; poet and playwright; *b* Castries, St Lucia, 23 Jan. 1930; twin *s* of late Warwick and Alix Walcott; *m* 1954, Fay Moston (marr. diss. 1959); one *s*; *m* 1962, Margaret Ruth Maillard (marr. diss.); two *d*; *m* Norline Metivier (marr. diss.). *Educ:* St Mary's Coll., St Lucia; Univ. of WI (BA 1953). Formerly teacher at schs in St Lucia and Grenada, and at Kingston Coll., Jamaica. Founded Trinidad Theatre Workshop, 1958. Lecturer: Rutgers Univ.; Yale Univ. Visiting Professor: Columbia Univ., 1981; Harvard Univ., 1982; Boston Univ., 1985–. Hon. DLitt Univ. of WI, 1972. Heinemann Award, RSL, 1966, 1983; Cholmodeley Award, 1969; Queen's Gold Medal for Poetry, 1989; Nobel Prize for Literature, 1992. Order of the Hummingbird (Trinidad and Tobago), 1969. *Publications include:* In a Green Night, 1962; Selected Poems, 1964; Castaway, 1965; Gulf and other poems, 1969; Another Life, 1973; Sea Grapes, 1976; Joker of Seville, 1979; Remembrance, and Pantomime, 1980; The Star-Apple Kingdom, 1980; The Fortunate Traveller, 1982; Midsummer, 1984; Collected Poems 1948–84, 1986; The Arkansas Testament, 1988; Three Plays: The Last Carnival, Beef No Chicken, A Branch of the Blue Nile, 1988; Collected Poems, 1990; Poems 1965–80, 1992; Omeros, 1990 (W. H. Smith Literary Award, 1991); Selected Poetry, 1993; Odyssey, 1993; The Bounty, 1997; (jtly) Homage to Robert Frost, 1998; What the Twilight Says (essays), 1998; Tiepolo's Hound, 2000; The Prodigal, 2005. *Address:* c/o Faber & Faber, 3 Queen Square, WC1N 3AU; PO Box GM926, Castries, St Lucia, West Indies.

WALCOTT, Prof. Richard Irving, PhD; FRS 1991; FRSNZ; Professor of Geology, Victoria University, Wellington, New Zealand, 1985–99, now Emeritus; *b* 14 May 1933; *s* of James Farrar Walcott and Lilian Stewart (*née* Irving); *m* 1960, Genevieve Rae Lovatt; one *s* two *d*. *Educ:* Victoria Univ., Wellington (BSc Hons 1962; PhD 1965; DSc 1980). Meteorological Asst, Falkland Is Dependencies Survey, 1955–58; Post-doctoral Fellow, Geophysics Dept, Univ. of BC, 1966–67; Research Scientist: Earth Physics Br., Dept of Energy, Mines and Resources, Ottawa, 1967–74; Geophysics Div., Dept Sci. and Industrial Res., Wellington, NZ, 1975–84. FRSNZ 1982; Fellow, American Geophysical Union, 1993. Hector Medal, Royal Soc. NZ, 1994; Charles Whitten Medal, Amer. Geophysical Union, 1999. *Recreations:* tramping, gardening. *Address:* 24 Mahoe Street, Eastbourne, Wellington, New Zealand. *T:* (4) 5628040.

WALD, Sir Nicholas John, Kt 2008; DSc; FRCP, FFPH, FRCOG, FMedSci; FRS 2004; CBiol, FIBiol; Professor, since 1983, and Director, since 2003, Centre for Environmental and Preventive Medicine, and Chairman, Wolfson Institute of Preventive Medicine, 1991–95 and since 1997, Bart's and The London School of Medicine and Dentistry, Queen Mary (formerly St Bartholomew's Hospital Medical College, then St Bartholomew's and The Royal London School of Medicine and Dentistry, Queen Mary and Westfield College), University of London; Hon. Consultant, St Bartholomew's Hospital, since 1983; *b* 31 May 1944; *s* of Adolf Max Wald and Frieda (*née* Shatsow); *m* 1966, Nancy Evelyn Miller; three *s* one *d*. *Educ:* Owen's Sch., EC1; University Coll. London; University Coll. Hosp. Med. Sch. (MB BS); DSc (Med) London 1987. FRCP 1986 (MRCP 1971); FFPH (FFCM 1982; MFCM 1980); FRCOG 1992; CBiol, FIBiol 2000. VSO, India, 1966. Ho. appts, UCH and Barnet Gen. Hosp., 1968–69; Med. Registrar, UCH, 1970; Member: MRC Sci. Staff, MRC Epidemiology and Med. Care Unit, 1971; Sci. Staff, ICRF (formerly DHSS) Cancer Epidem. and Clin. Trials Unit, 1972–82, Dep. Dir, 1982–83. Wellcome Vis. Prof. in Basic Med. Scis, at Foundn for Blood Res., USA, 1980, then Hon. Sen. Res. Scientist. Hon. Dir, Cancer Screening Gp, CRC, 1989–2000. Chairman: MRC Smoking Res. Rev. Cttee, 1986–89; MRC Study Monitoring Cttee of Randomised Trial of Colo-rectal Cancer Screening, 1986–; MRC Volatile Substance Abuse Wkg Party, 1985–87; NE Thames Reg. Breast Cancer Res. Cttee, 1988–96; Nat. Inst. of Child Health and Human Develt Wkg Gp on Quality Control of Alpha-fetoprotein Measurement, 1978; Steering Cttee for MRC Multicentre Aneurysm Screening Study, 1997–; Member: MRC Neurosciences Bd, 1962–86; MRC Steering Cttee of Randomised Trial of Multivitamins and Neural Tube Defects, 1983–92; DHSS Cttee on Med. Aspects of Contamination of Air, Soil and Water, 1985–89; DHSS Cttee on Carcinogenicity of Chemicals in Food, Consumer Products and the Environment, 1984–89; DHSS Indep. Sci. Cttee on Smoking and Health, 1983–91; DoH (formerly DHSS) Adv. Cttee on Breast Cancer Screening, 1986–99; Central R&D Cttee, 1991–95; CMO's Health of the Nation Wkg Gp, 1991–97; DoH Population Screening Panel, 1992–98; CMO's Scientific Cttee on Tobacco and Health, 1993–2002; Folic Acid Sub-gp, DoH Cttee on Med. Aspects of Food and Nutrition Policy, 1996–2000; Antenatal Sub-gp, DoH Nat. Screening Cttee, 1997–2005; Nat. Screening Cttee, HPV/LBC Pilots Steering Gp, 2000–03; Adv. Gp for Evaluation of UK Colorectal Cancer Screening Pilot, 2000–03; ACOST Med. Res. and Health Cttee, 1991–92; RCP Cttee on Ethical Issues in Medicine, 1988–; RCP Computer Cttee, 1988–92, and special Adv. Gp to the RCP Med. IT Cttee, 1992–; Physiol. and Pharmacol. Panel, Wellcome Trust, 1995–2000; MRC Scientific Adv. Cttee on Gulf War Syndrome, 1996–97; Adv. Gp on Nuclear Test Veterans, 2000–; Council of Trustees, Foundn for Study of Infant Deaths, 2000–04; Cttee on Environmental Tobacco Smoke, Nat. Acad. of Sci., USA, 1985–86. 140th Cutter Lectr on Preventive Medicine, Harvard Sch. of Public Health, 2004. Inaugural Ed., Jl of Medical Screening, 1994–. Pres., Med. Screening Soc., 2002–. William Julius Mickle Fellow, Univ. of London, 1990. Founder FMedSci 1998; Mem., Assoc. of Physicians of GB and Ire. Joseph P. Kennedy Jr Foundn Award for Scientific Res., 2000. *Publications:* (ed) Antenatal and Neonatal Screening, 1984; (ed with Sir Richard Doll) Interpretation of Negative Epidemiological Evidence for Carcinogenicity, 1985, 2nd edn (ed with Ian Leck) 2000; Epidemiological Approach: an approach to epidemiology in medicine, 1985, 4th edn 2004; (ed jtly) UK Smoking Statistics, 1988; (ed with Sir Peter Froggatt) Nicotine, Smoking and the Low Tar Programme, 1989; (ed with J. Baron) Smoking and Hormone Related Disorders, 1990; (jtly) International Smoking Statistics, 1993, 2nd edn (ed jtly) 2000; articles in sci. jls on screening for neural tube defects, Down's Syndrome and other disorders, on health effects of tobacco, on the aetiology and prevention of cancer, cardiovascular disease and congenital malformations. *Recreations:* family, discussion, boating, economics. *Address:* Centre for Environmental and Preventive Medicine, Wolfson Institute of Preventive Medicine, Bart's and The London School of Medicine and Dentistry, Charterhouse Square, EC1M 6BQ. *T:* (020) 7882 6269; 9 Park Crescent Mews East, W1W 5AF. *T:* (020) 7636 2721. *Club:* Athenæum.

WALDECK, Pieter Willem, Grand Cross of Honour, Order of House of Orange (Netherlands), 2006; Ambassador of the Netherlands to the Court of St James's, since 2007; *b* 6 Nov. 1947; *s* of late Dr Karel Waldeck and of Elisabeth Waldeck (*née* Koster); *m* 1976, Jonkvrouw Cordula Catharina Agatha Quarles van Ufford; one *s* two *d*. *Educ:* Vrijzinnig Christelijk Lyceum, The Hague; Univ. of Leiden (Master of Law). Mem. Bd (Sales and Publicity), NBBS Student Travel, 1970–71; 2nd Lieutenant RNR, Naval Intelligence Service, 1973–75; entered Netherlands Foreign Service, 1975; Third Sec. (Political), Moscow, 1976–78; Second Sec., Develt Co-operation, ESCAP, Bangkok, 1978–81; First Sec., Hd of Econ. Section, Cairo, 1981–84; Private Sec. to HM Queen and HRH Prince Claus of Netherlands, 1984–88; Hd of Section, Dept of Eur. Integration, Min. of Foreign Affairs, 1988–92; Counsellor, Perm. Repn to EU, Brussels, 1992–97; Hd, Dept of Information, and Chief Spokesman, Min. of Foreign Affairs, 1997–2000; Principal Sec. to HM Queen of Netherlands, 2000–02; Grand Master of the House of HM Queen of Netherlands, 2002–06. Grand Officer: Order of Isabella la Católica (Spain), 2001; Order of Three Stars (Latvia), 2006; Grand Cross: Order of Southern Cross (Brazil), 2003; Order of Merit (Chile), 2003; Order of White Elephant (Thailand), 2004; Order of Independence (Jordan), 2006; Order of the Crown (Belgium), 2006; Civil and Mil. Order of Merit, Adolf of Nassau (Luxembourg), 2006. *Publications:* articles in Nederlands Juristenblad, Mars Et Historia, Tijdschrift voor Zeegeschiedenis, Jaarboek Die Haghe. *Recreations:* drawing, bird watching, (naval) history, golf, sailing. *Address:* Royal Netherlands Embassy, 38 Hyde Park Gate, SW7 5DP. *T:* (020) 7590 3299; *e-mail:* lon-cdp@minbuza.nl. *Clubs:* Haagsche (Plaats Royaal), Nieuwe Litteraire Sociëteit de Witte (The Hague); Broekpolder Golf.

WALDEGRAVE, family name of **Earl Waldegrave** and **Baron Waldegrave of North Hill.**

WALDEGRAVE, 13th Earl, *cr* 1729; **James Sherbrooke Waldegrave;** Bt 1643; Baron Waldegrave 1685; Viscount Chewton 1729; *b* 8 Dec. 1940; *e s* of 12th Earl Waldegrave, KG, GCVO and Mary Hermione (*d* 1995), *d* of Lt-Col A. M. Grenfell, DSO; *S* father, 1995; *m* 1986, Mary Alison Anthea (marr. diss. 1996), *d* of late Sir Robert Furness, KBE, CMG, and Lady Furness; two *s*. *Educ:* Eton Coll.; Trinity Coll., Cambridge. *Heir: s* Viscount Chewton, *qv*. *Address:* Chewton House, Chewton Mendip, Radstock BA3 4LL. *Clubs:* Beefsteak, Garrick; Leander.

WALDEGRAVE OF NORTH HILL, Baron *cr* 1999 (Life Peer), of Chewton Mendip in the county of Somerset; **William Arthur Waldegrave;** PC 1990; Provost of Eton College, from Feb. 2009 (Fellow, since 2007); *b* 15 Aug. 1946; *yr s* of 12th Earl Waldegrave, KG, GCVO and Mary Hermione (*née* Grenfell); *m* 1977, Caroline Burrows (*see* Caroline Waldegrave); one *s* three *d*. *Educ:* Eton Coll.; Corpus Christi Coll., Oxford (Hon. Fellow, 1991); Harvard Univ. (Kennedy Fellow). Fellow, All Souls Coll., Oxford, 1971–86 and 1999–. Central Policy Review Staff, Cabinet Office, 1971–73; Political Staff, 10 Downing Street, 1973–74; Head of Leader of Opposition's Office, 1974–75; GEC Ltd, 1975–81; a Man. Dir, Dresdner Kleinwort Wasserstein, 1998–2003; a Vice-Chm. and Man. Dir, UBS, 2003–08. MP (C) Bristol West, 1979–97; contested (C) same seat, 1997. Parly Under-Sec. of State, DES, 1981–83, DoE, 1983–85. Minister of State for the Environment and Countryside, 1985–87, for Planning, 1986–88, and for Housing, 1987–88, DoE; Minister of State, FCO, 1988–90; Sec. of State for Health, 1990–92; Chancellor of the Duchy of Lancaster, 1992–94; Minister of Agric., Fisheries and Food, 1994–95; Chief Sec. to HM Treasury, 1995–97. Director: Waldegrave Farms Ltd, 1975–; Bristol and West plc (formerly Bristol and West Bldg Soc.), 1997–2006; Bank of Ireland Financial Services (UK) plc, 2002–06; Henry Sotheran Ltd, 1998–; Biotech. Growth Trust plc (formerly Finsbury Life Scis Investment Trust), 1998–. Member: IBA Adv. Council, 1980–81; Internat. Adv. Bd, Teijin Ltd, 2006–08; Remuneration and Nomination Cttee, Bergesen Worldwide Gas ASA, 2006–08. Chm., Nat. Mus. of Sci. and Industry, 2002–. Trustee: Rhodes Trust, 1992–2002 (Chm., 2002–); Beit Meml Fellowships for Medical Res., 1998–2006; Mandela Rhodes Foundn, 2003–; Dyson Sch. of Design Innovation, 2007–08; Strawberry Hill Trust, 2008–. Founder Trustee and Chm., Bristol Cathedral Trust, 1989–2002. Pres., Royal Bath and West Soc., 2006. JP Inner London Juvenile Court, 1975–79. *Publication:* The Binding of Leviathan, 1977. *Address:* 66 Palace Gardens Terrace, W8 4RR; (from Feb. 2009) Provost's Lodge, Eton College, Windsor, Berks SL4 6DH. *Clubs:* White's, Beefsteak, Pratt's.

WALDEGRAVE, Caroline Linda Margaret, (Lady Waldegrave of North Hill), OBE 2000; Founding Principal, since 1975, and Director, since 1977, Leith's School of Food and Wine Ltd; *b* 14 Aug. 1952; *y d* of Major Philip Richard Miles Burrows and late Molly Burrows (*née* Hollins); *m* 1977, Hon. William Waldegrave (*see* Baron Waldegrave of North Hill); one *s* three *d*. *Educ:* Convent of the Sacred Heart, Woldingham, Surrey. Mem., HEA, 1985–88. Chm., Guild of Food Writers, 1991–93; Pres., Hosp. Caterers Assoc., 2006–08. Trustee, Nat. Life Story Collection, BL, 2005–. Pres., Portobello Trust, 1987–2000. *Publications:* The Healthy Gourmet, 1986; Low Fat Gourmet, 1987; *jointly:* Leith's Cookery Course, 1980; Leith's Cookery School, 1985; Leith's Cookery Bible, 1991, 2nd edn 1996; Leith's Complete Christmas, 1992; Children's Cookery, 1993; Leith's Fish Bible, 1995; Leith's Easy Dinner Parties, 1995; Leith's Healthy Eating, 1996;

Children's Fun to Cook Book, 1996; Sainsbury Book of Children's Cookery, 1997. *Recreations:* bridge, tennis. *Address:* c/o Leith's School of Food and Wine Ltd, 21 St Albans Grove, W8 5BP. *T:* (020) 7229 0177.

WALDEN, (Alastair) Brian; television and radio presenter and journalist; Chairman: Paragon, since 1996; Ten Alps, since 2001; Capital Fund, since 2006; *b* 8 July 1932; *s* of W. F. Walden; *m* Hazel Downes, *d* of William A. Downes; one *s* (and three *s* of former marriages). *Educ:* West Bromwich Grammar School; Queen's College and Nuffield College, Oxford; Pres., Oxford Union, 1957. University Lecturer. MP (Lab): Birmingham, All Saints, 1964–74; Birmingham, Ladywood, 1974–77. Mem., W Midland Bd, Central TV, 1981–84. Pres., Birmingham and Midland Inst., 2006. Columnist: London Standard, 1983–86; Thomson Regional Newspapers, 1983–86; Sunday Times, 1986–90. Presenter: Weekend World, LWT, 1977–86; The Walden Interview, ITV, 1988 and 1989; Walden, LWT, 1990–94; Walden on Labour Leaders, BBC, 1997; Walden on Heroes, BBC, 1998; Walden on Villains, BBC, 1999; A Point of View, BBC Radio 4, 2005–. Shell International Award, 1982; BAFTA Richard Dimbleby Award, 1985; Aims of Industry Special Free Enterprise Award, 1990; TV Times Favourite TV Current Affairs Personality, 1990; Television and Radio Industries Club ITV Personality of the Year, 1991. *Publication:* The Walden Interviews, 1990. *Recreations:* chess, reading. *Address:* Landfall, Fort Road, St Peter Port, Guernsey GY1 1ZU.

WALDEN, David Peter; Director of Strategy, Commission for Social Care Inspection, since 2004; *b* 23 Sept. 1954; *s* of Gerald Walden and Shirley Walden (*née* Rothfield); *m* 1981, Janet Day; one *s* one *d*. *Educ:* Newcastle upon Tyne Royal Grammar Sch.; St John's Coll., Oxford (BA Modern Hist. 1977). DHSS, subseq. DoH, 1977–2004: Principal, 1982; Management Side Secretary: Nurses' and Midwives' Whitley Council, 1982–85; NHS Consultants' Negotiating Body, 1985–86; Private Sec. to Dep. Chm., NHS Mgt Bd, 1986–87; Asst Sec., Doctors' Pay and Conditions, 1989–90; on secondment as Personnel Dir, Poole Hosp. NHS Trust, 1991–93; Head: Community Care Br., 1993–96; Health Promotion Div., 1996–99; Social Care Policy, 1999–2001; Dir, Health Services Devolt, Anchor Trust, 2001–03 (on secondment); Dir, Office of Ind. Regulator for NHS Foundn Trusts, 2003–04. *Address:* Commission for Social Care Inspection, 33 Greycoat Street, SW1P 2QF. *T:* (020) 7979 2050.

WALDEN, George Gordon Harvey, CMG 1981; writer; *b* 15 Sept. 1939; *s* of G. G. Walden; *m* 1970, Sarah Nicolette Hunt; two *s* one *d*. *Educ:* Latymer Upper Sch.; Jesus Coll., Cambridge; Moscow Univ. (post-graduate). Research Dept, Foreign Office, 1962–65; Chinese Language Student, Hong Kong Univ., 1965–67; Second Secretary, Office of HM Chargé d'Affaires, Peking, 1967–70; First Sec., FCO (Soviet Desk), 1970–73; Ecole Nationale d'Administration, Paris, 1973–74; First Sec., HM Embassy, Paris, 1974–78; Principal Private Sec. to Foreign and Commonwealth Sec., 1978–81; sabbatical year, Harvard, 1981; Head of Planning Staff, FCO, 1982–83; retired from HM Diplomatic Service, 1983. MP (C) Buckingham, 1983–97. PPS to Sec. of State for Educn and Science, 1984–85; Parly Under-Sec. of State, DES, 1985–87. Chm. of Judges, Booker Prize, 1995. Columnist, Evening Standard, 1991–2002. *Publications:* Ethics and Foreign Policy, 1990; We Should Know Better: solving the education crisis, 1996; Lucky George (memoir), 1999; The New Elites: making a career in the masses, 2000; Who is a Dandy?, 2002; God won't save America, 2006; Time to Emigrate?, 2006; China: a wolf in the world?, 2008. *Address:* 43 Edwardes Square, W8 6HH.

WALDEN, Rt Rev. Graham Howard; Bishop of The Murray, 1989–2001; *b* 19 March 1931; *s* of Leonard Howard Walden and Mary Ellen Walden (*née* Cahalane); *m* 1964, Margaret Ann (*née* Brett); two *s* one *d*. *Educ:* Univ. of Queensland (BA 1952; MA 1954); Australian Coll. of Theol. (ThL 1954); Christ Church, Oxford (BLitt 1960; MLitt 1980). Ordained deacon 1954, priest 1955; Assistant Curate: West Hackney, 1954–56; St Saviour's, Poplar, 1957–58; permission to officiate, dio. of Oxford, 1955–59; Mem., Bush Brotherhood of the Good Shepherd, NSW, 1959–63; Vice Principal, Torres Strait Mission Theol Coll., 1963–65; Rector of Mudgee, NSW, 1965–70; Archdeacon of Barker, 1968–70; Archdeacon and Vicar-Gen. of Ballarat, 1970–89; Asst Bishop of Ballarat, 1981–89; Rector of Hamilton and Bishop in Hamilton, 1981–84. Nat. Chm., Anglican Men's Soc., 1983–93 (Vice-Pres., 1993–); Anglican Chm., Jt Anglican RC Diocesan Commn, 1977–89; Vice-Chm., Internat. Bishops' Conf., 1992–95; Member: Gen. Bd of Religious Educn, 1970–81; Anglican Lutheran Conversations constituted by Gen. Synod of Anglican Church of Australia, 1989–2001 (Co-Chm., 1993–2001); Gen. Synod Commn on Doctrine, 1989–98 (Chm., 1992–98); Council, Brotherhood of the Good Shepherd, 2003– (Episcopal Visitor to Company of the Good Shepherd, 2003–05). *Publications:* contrib. to jls and church papers. *Address:* 13 O'Connor Place, Dubbo, NSW 2830, Australia.

WALDEN, Ian Mennie, MBE 1972; independent consultant to the voluntary sector; Founder, Mosaic Consultancy Services, since 2004; *b* 23 Oct. 1940; *s* of Col Frank Walden, MBE, DL, and Mollie Walden (*née* Mennie); *m* 1st, 1965, Anne Frances Lacey (marr. diss.); three *s*; 2nd, 1995, Christine Anne Osbourn; one *d*, and two step *d*. *Educ:* Haileybury. Served Royal Marines, 1958–89, including: active service in ME, FE and NI; Temp. Equerry to Duke of Edinburgh, 1976; briefer to CDS, during Falklands War, 1980–82; CO, Commando Logistic Regt, 1983–85; Dep. COS, Trng and Reserve Forces, 1985–87; Dir, Jt Ops Centre, MoD, 1987–89. Campaign Manager, St John Ambulance, 1992–93; Dir, Internat. Spinal Res. Trust, 1993–97; Chief Executive: Br. Lung Foundn, 1997–2001; BLISS, the Premature Baby Charity, 2001–03; Watford & District Mencap, 2003–04. Ind. Mem., Herts Police Authy, 2007–. Chm., St Albans Dist CAB, 2008–. Trustee, Herts and Beds Pastoral Foundn, 2005–. Trustee, Over the Wall Gang Camp, 2000– (Chm., 2000–07; Vice Chm., 2007–). Mem., Lions Clubs Internat., 2000–. *Recreations:* woodwork, ski-ing, badminton, family life. *Address:* 50 Lyndhurst Drive, Harpenden, Herts AL5 5RJ. *T:* (01582) 462067.

WALDER, Edwin James, CMG 1971; NSW Civil Service, retired; *b* 5 Aug. 1921; *s* of Edwin James Walder and Dulcie Muriel Walder (*née* Griffiths); *m* 1944, Norma Cheslin; two *d*. *Educ:* North Newtown High Sch.; Univ. of Sydney (BEc). FRAIPA 1983. Apptd NSW Civil Service, 1938; NSW State Treasury: 1945; Asst Under-Sec. (Finance), 1959–61; Dep. Under-Sec., 1961–63; Under-Sec. and Comptroller of Accounts, 1963–65; Pres., Metrop. Water, Sewerage and Drainage Bd, Sydney, 1965–81. Member: State Pollution Control Commn, 1971–81; Metropolitan Waste Disposal Authority (Sydney), 1971–81; management consultant and co. dir, 1981–92. *Recreations:* genealogy, internet browsing. *Address:* 13 Willowin Close, Green Point, NSW 2251, Australia. *Clubs:* Central Coast League's (Gosford); Avoca Beach Bowling; Probus (Avoca Beach, and Broadwater, Central Coast).

WALDMANN, Prof. Herman, FRS 1990; Professor and Head of Department of Pathology, Oxford University, since 1994; Fellow of Lincoln College, Oxford, since 1994; *b* 27 Feb. 1945; *s* of Leon and Rene Ryfka Waldmann; *m* 1971, Judith Ruth Young. *Educ:* Sir George Monoux Grammar Sch., Walthamstow; Sidney Sussex Coll., Cambridge (BA; Hon. Fellow, 2008); London Hosp. Med Coll. (MB BChir); PhD Cantab. MRCPath, MRCP. Cambridge University: Dept of Pathology, 1971–94; Fellow, King's Coll., 1985–94; Kay Kendall Prof. of Therapeutic Immunology, 1989–93. Founder FMedSci 1998. Hon. Fellow, QMW, 1996. Graham Bull Prize for Clinical Res., RCP, 1991; José Carreras Award, European Hematology Assoc., 2005; JDRF Excellence in Clinical Res. Award, 2005. *Publications:* Limiting Dilution Analysis (with Dr I. Lefkovits), 1977, 2nd edn 1998; The Immune System (with Dr I. McConnell and A. Munro), 1981; (ed) Monoclonal Antibodies, 1988; many scientific papers. *Recreations:* family, (less) food, friends, travel, music. *Address:* Sir William Dunn School of Pathology, South Parks Road, Oxford OX1 3RE; *e-mail:* herman.waldmann@path.ox.ac.uk.

WALDNER, Benita Maria F.; *see* Ferrero-Waldner.

WALDRON, William Francis; QC 2006; a Recorder, since 2000; *b* 27 Oct. 1957; *s* of William Henry Waldron, QC and Rosemary Waldron; *m* 2007, Julie Case; one *s*. *Educ:* St Edward's Coll., Liverpool; University Coll. of Wales, Cardiff (LLB 1979). Disc jockey, 1980–83, Prog. Controller, 1983–85, CBC Commercial Radio Station, Cardiff. Called to the Bar, Gray's Inn, 1986; in practice specialising in catastrophic injury law and crime. *Recreations:* Everton FC (lifelong, fanatical and ever-hopeful fan; ambition to live long enough to see Everton win another trophy!), acoustic guitar, flying (private pilot's licence/IMC). *Address:* Exchange Chambers, Derby Square, Liverpool L2 9XX. *T:* (0151) 236 7747; *e-mail:* waldronqc@exchangechambers.co.uk.

WALDRON-RAMSEY, Waldo Emerson; Barrister and Attorney-at-Law; international consultant; *b* 1 Jan. 1930; *s* of Wyatt and Delcina Waldron-Ramsey; *m* 1954, Shiela Pamella Beresford, Georgetown, Guyana; one *s* two *d*. *Educ:* Barbados; Hague Academy; London Sch. of Economics; Yugoslavia. LLB Hons; BSc (Econ) Hons; PhD. Called to Bar, Middle Temple; practised London Bar and SW Circuit, 1957–60; Marketing Economist, Shell International, 1960–61; Tanzanian Foreign Service, 1961–70; High Comr for Barbados in UK, and Ambassador to France, Netherlands and Germany, 1970–71; Ambassador and Perm. Rep. for Barbados to UN, 1971–76. UN Legal Expert: in field of human rights, 1967–71; on Israel, 1968–71. Chairman: Sunny Investment & Finance Gp of Cos, 1994–; Edutech (Pty) Ltd, Windhoek, Cape Town, and Gaborone, 1994–. Senator, Parlt of Barbados, 1983–85. Member: Amer. Acad. of Political and Social Sciences; Amer. Soc. of Internat. Law; Amer. Inst. of Petroleum (Marketing Div.). Hon. Fellow, Hebrew Univ. of Jerusalem, 1972. DSc (Pol. Econ.) Univ. of Phnom-Penh, 1973; Hon. LLD Chung-Ang Univ., Republic of Korea, 1975. Grand Officer (1st Class), Nat. Order of Honneur et Mérite, Republic of Haiti, 1968; Grand Officier, Ordre Nat. de l'Amitié et Mérite, Khymèr, 1973; Order of Distinguished Diplomatic Service Merit, Gwanghwa (1st Class), Republic of Korea, 1974. *Recreations:* cricket, tennis, bridge, travel. *Address:* (chambers) 50 Swan Street, Bridgetown, Barbados. *T:* 4278280, 4242021; (chambers) 26 Court Street, Brooklyn, New York 11225, USA; The Monticello, 30 Park Avenue, Mount Vernon, New York 10550, USA. *T:* (London) (020) 7229 4870, *T:* (N Carolina) (336) 7650080. *Clubs:* Royal Automobile; Lincoln Lodge (Connecticut).

WALE, Kevin Ernest; President and Managing Director, General Motors China Group, since 2005; *b* 30 Oct. 1954; *m* 1976, Marilyn Joy Baensch; two *s*. *Educ:* Melbourne Univ. (BCom Hons); General Motors Inst., USA. General Motors: joined Finance Dept, Holden, Australia, 1975; Corp. Finance Dept, NY, 1983–85; various posts, Finance Div., subseq. Dir of Finance and Strategic Planning, Holden, Australia, 1985–93; Dir of Sales, Marketing and Aftersales, Holden, Australia, 1993–98; Exec. in Charge, General Motors Asia Pacific (Pte) Ltd, Singapore, 1998–2001; Chm. and Man. Dir, Vauxhall Motors Ltd, and Vice-Pres., General Motors Europe, 2001–05; Mem., European Strategy Bd, 2001–. *Recreations:* golf, cricket, motor sports. *Address:* General Motors China Group, 10th Floor, Jinmao Tower, 88 Century Avenue, Pudong, Shanghai 200121, China.

WALES, Archbishop of, since 2003; **Most Rev. Barry Cennydd Morgan,** PhD; Bishop of Llandaff, since 1999; *b* 31 Jan. 1947; *s* of Rees Haydn Morgan and Mary Gwyneth Morgan; *m* 1969, Hilary Patricia Lewis; one *s* one *d*. *Educ:* Ystalyfera Grammar Sch.; University Coll. London (BA Hons History 1969); Selwyn Coll., Cambridge (BA Hons Theol. 1971); Westcott House, Cambridge. MA Cantab 1974; PhD Wales 1986. Priest, Llandaff, 1973; Curate, St Andrew's Major, Dinas Powis, 1972–75; Chaplain, Bryn-y-Don Community Sch., 1972–75; Chaplain and Lectr, St Michael's Coll., Llandaff, 1975–77; Lectr, University Coll., Cardiff, 1975–77; Warden of Church Hostel, Bangor, Anglican Chap., UCNW and Lectr in Theology, UCNW, 1977–84; Rector of Wrexham, 1984–86; Archdeacon of Merioneth and Rector of Criccieth, 1986–92; Bishop of Bangor, 1993–99. Editor, Welsh Churchman, 1975–82. Exam. Chaplain to Abp of Wales, 1978–82, to Bp of Bangor, 1983; Diocese of Bangor: In-Service Trng Officer, 1979–84; Warden of Ordinands, 1982–84; Canon of Bangor Cathedral, 1983–84. Mem., Archbishop's Doctrinal Commn, 1982–93 (Chm. 1989–93); Chm., Div. of Stewardship, Provincial Bd of Mission, 1988–95. Pres., Welsh Centre for Internat. Affairs, 2004. Vice-Chairman: Nat. Soc., 1999; Bible Soc., 1999. Fellow, Woodard Corp., 2001–. Pro-Chancellor, Univ. of Wales, 2006–. Hon. Fellow: Bangor Univ., 1994; UWIC, 2003; Lampeter Univ., 2004; Cardiff Univ., 2004. *Publications:* O Ddydd i Ddydd, Pwyllgor Darlleniadau Beiblaidd Cyngor Eglwysi Cymru, 1980; History of the Church Hostel and Anglican Chaplaincy at University College of North Wales, Bangor, 1986; Concepts of Mission and Ministry in Anglican University Chaplaincy Work, 1988; Strangely Orthodox: R. S. Thomas and his poetry of faith, 2006. *Recreation:* golf. *Address:* Llys Esgob, The Cathedral Green, Llandaff, Cardiff CF5 2YE.

WALES, Daphne Beatrice; Chairman, Board for Mission and Unity, General Synod of the Church of England, 1983–88; *b* 6 Dec. 1917; *d* of Frederick James Wales and Lilian Frederica (*née* Whitnall). Dep. Principal, Bank of England, retd. Mem., General Synod, 1975–90 (Mem., Panel of Chairmen, 1983); Chm., St Albans Diocese House of Laity, 1979–85. Chm., Highway Trust, 1992–99 (Vice-Chm., 1983–92); Gov., Partnership for World Mission, 1978–90; Trustee, S American Missionary Soc., 1983–97 (Vice-Chm., 1989–97). Mem. Council, Oak Hill Theol Coll., 1981–91. *Address:* 3 Wildwood Court, Cedars Village, Dog Kennel Lane, Chorleywood, Herts WD3 5GG. *T:* (01923) 352072.

WALES, Jimmy; Founder, Wikipedia.org, 2001; Co-Founder and President, Wikia Inc., since 2004; *b* Huntsville, Ala, 7 Aug. 1966; *s* of Jimmy and Doris Wales; one *d*. *Educ:* Auburn Univ. (BA Finance); Univ. of Alabama (MA Finance). Res. Dir, Chicago Options Assoc., 1994–2000; Founder, Nupedia, 2000. Founder and Chm. Emeritus, Wikimedia Foundn, 2003. Board Member: iCommons, 2005; Creative Commons, 2006–. Co-Chm., World Econ. Forum on Middle E, 2008–. Fellow, Berkman Center for Internet and Soc., Harvard Law Sch., 2005. Hon. LLD Knox Coll., Ill, 2006. Young Global Leader, World Econ. Forum, 2007. *Publication:* (contrib.) Advances in Futures and Options Research, 1994. *Recreations:* international travel, free speech supporter, free culture advocate, contributor and active editor on Wikipedia, commerce and technology. *Address:* Wikimedia Foundation, PO Box 78350, San Francisco, CA 94107, USA. *Fax:* (415) 8820495; *e-mail:* jwales@wikia.com.

WALES, Prof. Kathleen Margaret; Special Professor in English, University of Nottingham, since 2008; *b* 8 Feb. 1946; *d* of Richard Derwent and Yvonne Derwent (*née* Atkins); *m* 1st, 1971, Brian Wales (marr. diss. 1988); one *s*; 2nd, 1993, David Bovey. *Educ:*

Darlington High Sch. for Girls; Royal Holloway Coll., Univ. of London (BA 1st Cl. Hons English). Royal Holloway College, later Royal Holloway and Bedford New College, University of London: Lectr in English Lang., 1968–88; Sen. Lectr, 1988–94; Reader, 1994–95; Prof., 1995–96; Hd, English Dept, 1995–96; University of Leeds: Prof. of Modern English Lang., 1996–2005; Dean of Learning and Teaching, Faculty of Arts, 2000–03; Dir, Centre for Medieval Studies, 2002–03; Res. Prof. in English, Univ. of Sheffield, 2005–08. Sen. Res. Fellow, British Acad./Leverhulme Trust, 1992–93; Visiting Research Fellow: Lucy Cavendish Coll., Univ. of Cambridge, 1999–2000, 2004; Centre for Res. in Arts, Social Scis and Humanities, Univ. of Cambridge, 2004–05; Leverhulme Emeritus Res. Fellow, Inst. of English Studies, Univ. of London, 2005–06. Member: Exec. Cttee, Council for Coll. and Univ. English, 1998–2002; Adv. Bd, Inst. of English Studies, Univ. of London, 2000–05; Cttee of Mgt, British Inst. in Paris, 2002–04; Peer Review Coll., AHRC, 2005– (Mem., PG Panel 5, 2007–); Leverhulme Trust Adv. Panel, 2006–. Gov., Trinity and All Saints Coll., Leeds, 2001–04. FRSA 1996; FEA 2001. Ed., Jl Lang. and Lit., 1996–2005. *Publications:* Dictionary of Stylistics, 1989, 2nd rev. edn 2001; The Language of James Joyce, 1992; (ed) Feminist Linguistics in Literary Criticism, 1994; Personal Pronouns in Present-Day English, 1996; (ed jtly) Shakespeare's Dramatic Language: a reader's guide, 2000; Northern English: a cultural and social history, 2006; numerous book chapters; contrib. articles to learned jls and children's joke books. *Recreations:* buying and selling at antique fairs and flea markets, keeping fit, collecting elephants, Fairport Convention. *Address:* 2 The Orchards, Great Shelford, Cambs CB22 5AB. *T:* (01223) 840506.

WALES, Sir Robert Andrew, (Sir Robin), Kt 2000; first elected Mayor of Newham, since 2002; two *c. Educ:* Glasgow Univ. (BSc). With BT, responsible for developing credit and fraud mgt systems (on leave of absence, 2002–). Newham Borough Council: Mem. (Lab), 1982–86 and 1992–; Leader of Council, 1995–2002. Chm., Assoc. of London Govt, 2000–06. *Address:* c/o Newham Town Hall, Barking Road, East Ham, E6 2RP.

WAŁĘSA, Lech, Hon. GCB 1991; Founder and Head of Lech Wałęsa Institute Foundation, since 1995; President of Poland, 1990–95; *b* Popowo, 29 Sept. 1943; *s* of late Bolesław Wałęsa and Feliksa Wałęsa; *m* 1969, Danuta; four *s* four *d. Educ:* Lipno primary and tech. schools; trained as electrician. Lenin Shipyard, Gdańsk, 1966–76, 1980–90 (Chm., Strike Cttees, 1970, 1980); founder Chm., Nat. Co-ordinating Commn of Indep. Autonomous Trade Union Solidarity (NSZZ Solidarność), 1981–82; in custody, 1981–82; returned to Gdańsk Shipyard, 1983; Leader, (outlawed) Solidarity, 1983–88, (re-instated) Solidarity, 1988–90. Founder and Pres., Christian Democratic Party of Third Republic, Poland, 1997–2001. Dr *hc*, including: Alliance Coll., Cambridge, Mass, 1981; Harvard, 1983; Gdańsk, 1990; Connecticut State, 1996. Nobel Peace Prize, 1983. Presidential Medal of Freedom (USA); Grand Cross, Legion of Honour (France); Order of Merit (Italian Republic); Order of Pius, 1st Cl. (Holy See); Grand Ribbon, Order of Leopold (Belgium). *Publication:* A Path of Hope: An Autobiography, 1987. *Address:* Lech Wałęsa Institute Foundation, Al. Jerozdimskie 11/19, 00508 Warsaw, Poland.

WALEY, Daniel Philip, PhD; FBA 1991; Keeper of Manuscripts, British Library, 1973–86 (Keeper of Manuscripts, British Museum, 1972–73); *b* 20 March 1921; *er s* of late Hubert David Waley and Margaret Hendelah Waley; *m* 1945, Pamela Joan Griffiths; one *s* one *d* (and one *d* decd). *Educ:* Dauntsey's Sch.; King's Coll., Cambridge (MA, PhD). Historical Tripos, Cambridge, 1939–40 and 1945–46 (cl. 1). Served War, 1940–45. Fellow of King's Coll., Cambridge, 1950–54. Asst Lectr in Medieval History, London School of Economics and Political Science, Univ. of London, 1949–51, Lectr, 1951–61, Reader in History, 1961–70, Prof. of History, 1970–72. Hon. Res. Fellow, Westfield Coll., London, 1986; Emer. Fellow, Leverhulme Trust, 1986–87. Lectures: British Acad. Italian, 1975; Emil Godfrey Meml, Lewes Priory Trust, 2002. Corresp. Fellow, Deputazione di Storia Patria per l'Umbria, 1991. Prince Consort Award, Cambridge Univ., 1950; Serena Medal, British Acad., 1990. *Publications:* Mediaeval Orvieto, 1952; The Papal State in the 13th Century, 1961; Later Medieval Europe, 1964, 3rd edn (with P. Denley) 2001; The Italian City Republics, 1969, 3rd edn 1988; British Public Opinion and the Abyssinian War, 1935–36, 1975; (ed) George Eliot's Blotter: A Commonplace-Book, 1980; (contrib.) Storia d'Italia, ed by G. Galasso, vol. 7, 1987; Siena and the Sienese in the Thirteenth Century, 1991; (ed) J. K. Hyde, Literacy and Its Uses: studies on late medieval Italy, 1993; (contrib.) Il Libro Bianco di San Gimignano, vol. 1, 1996; A Liberal Life: Sydney, Earl Buxton, 1853–1934, 1999; (introd.) N. Rubinstein, Studies in Italian History in the Middle Ages and the Renaissance, vol. 1, 2004; contributor to: Oxford DNB, Dizionario Biografico degli Italiani, English Hist. Review, Trans Royal Hist. Soc., Papers of British Sch. at Rome, Jl of Ecclesiastical Hist., Jl of the History of Ideas, Rivista Storica Italiana, Rivista di Storia della Chiesa in Italia, Procs Brit. Acad., British Library Jl, Bull. of John Rylands Liby, Sussex Archaeol Collections, etc. *Recreation:* walking. *Address:* 33 Greyfriars Court, Court Road, Lewes, E Sussex BN7 2RF.

WALEY-COHEN, Hon. Joyce Constance Ina; (Joyce, Hon. Lady Waley-Cohen), MA; President, Independent Schools Information Service Council, 1981–85 (Member, 1972–80); *b* 20 Jan. 1920; *o d* of 1st Baron Nathan, PC, TD, and Eleanor Joan Clara, *d* of C. Stettauer; *m* 1943, Sir Bernard Nathaniel Waley-Cohen, 1st Bt, (*d* 1991); two *s* two *d. Educ:* St Felix Sch., Southwold; Girton Coll., Cambridge (MA). Member: Governing Body, St Felix Sch., 1945–83 (Chm., 1970–83); Westminster Hosp. Bd of Governors, 1952–68; Chairman: Westminster Children's Hosp., 1952–68; Gordon Hosp., 1961–68; Governing Bodies of Girls' Schools' Assoc., 1974–79 (Mem., 1963); Ind. Schs Jt Council, 1977–80. Governor: Taunton Sch., 1978–90; Wellington Coll., 1979–90. JP Middx 1949–59, Somerset 1959–86. *Recreations:* hunting, spinning, family life. *Address:* Honeymead, Simonsbath, Minehead, Somerset TA24 7JX. *T:* (01643) 831242.

WALEY-COHEN, Sir Stephen (Harry), 2nd Bt *cr* 1961, of Honeymead, Co. Somerset; Managing Director: Victoria Palace Theatre, since 1989; Mousetrap Productions, since 1994; Ambassador Theatre, since 2007; *b* 22 June 1946; *s* of Sir Bernard Nathaniel Waley-Cohen, 1st Bt and Hon. Joyce Constance Ina Waley-Cohen, *qv*; *S* father, 1991; *m* 1st, 1972, Pamela Elizabeth (marr. diss.), *yr d* of J. E. Doniger; two *s* one *d*; 2nd, 1986, Josephine Burnett, *yr d* of late Duncan M. Spencer; two *d. Educ:* Wellesley House Sch.; Eton (Oppidan Scholar); Magdalene Coll., Cambridge (MA Hons). Financial journalist, Daily Mail, 1968–73; Publisher, Euromoney, 1969–83; Chief Exec., Maybox Theatres, 1984–89; Chairman: Thorndike Holdings, management training, 1989–98; Bridge Underwriting Agents (formerly Willis Faber & Dumas (Agencies)), 1992–99 (Dir, 1988–99); Policy Portfolio, 1993–97; Portsmouth & Sunderland Newspapers, 1998–99 (Dir, 1994–99); First Call Gp, 1996–98; Director: Badgworthy Land Co., 1982–; St Martin's Theatre, 1989–; Theatresoft, 1992–97; Theatre Investment Fund, 1992–; Exeter Selective Assets (formerly Preferred Capital) Investment Trust, 1992–2003; Managing Director: Vaudeville Th., 1996–2001; Savoy Th. Mgt, 1997–2005. Chm., Mousetrap Foundn for the Arts, 1996–; Mem., SOLT (formerly SWET), 1984– (Mem., Finance Cttee, 1989–; Chm., 1996–2002; Pres., 2002–05); Chm., Olivier Awards Cttee, 1995–2002. Pres. Council, JCA Charitable Foundn (formerly Jewish Colonisation Assoc.), 1995– (Mem. Council, 1985–); Chairman: Exec. Cttee, British American Project for Successor Generation, 1986–92; Mowbray Trust for Reproductive Immunology, 1996–. Trustee, Theatres Trust, 1998–2004. Member: Public Affairs Cttee, British Field Sports Soc., 1972–92; Cttee, Devon & Somerset Staghounds, 1974–. Member: UCL Finance Cttee, 1984–89; Council, RADA, 2003– (Chm., 2007–). Governor, Wellesley House Sch., 1974–97. Contested (C) Manchester, Gorton, Feb. and Oct. 1974. *Recreations:* family, theatre, hunting. *Heir: s* Lionel Robert Waley-Cohen [*b* 7 Aug. 1974; *m* 2007, Octavia Green; one *d*]. *Address:* 1 Wallingford Avenue, W10 6QA. *T:* (020) 8968 6268; Honeymead, Simonsbath, Somerset TA24 7JX. *T:* (01643) 831584. *Club:* Garrick.

WALFORD, Sir Christopher (Rupert), Kt 1995; TEM 1972; Lord Mayor of London, 1994–95; *b* 15 Oct. 1935; *s* of John Rupert Charles Walford, MBE and Gladys Irene Walford (*née* Sperrin); *m* 1967, Anne Elizabeth Viggars (*d* 2004); two *s* (and one *s* decd). *Educ:* Charterhouse; Oriel College, Oxford (MA; Hon. Fellow, 1995). Solicitor (Hons). National Service, commissioned RA, 1954–56; HAC 1957–72 (to Warrant Officer). Allen & Overy, 1959–96 (Partner, 1970–96). Councillor, Kensington, 1962–65, Kensington & Chelsea, 1964–82, Dep. Mayor, 1974–75, Mayor, 1979–80; Alderman, Ward of Farringdon Within, 1982–2002; Sheriff, City of London, 1990–91. Member: Council, CGLI, 1984–98; Council, and Policy and Exec. Cttees, Inst. of Directors, 1986–94; Court of Assistants and Finance Cttee, Corp. of Sons of the Clergy, 1989–98; Trustee: St Paul's Cathedral Choir Sch. Foundn, 1985–97; Guildhall Sch., Music and Drama Foundn, 1989–97; Morden Coll., 1991–. Vice-Pres., Bridewell Royal Hosp., 1996–2002 (Gov., 1984–2002). Governor, Hon. Irish Soc., 1997–2000; Mem. Bd of Govs, London Guildhall Univ., 1997–2002. Freeman, City of London, 1964; Liveryman: Makers of Playing Cards Co., 1978 (Master, 1987; Hon. Liveryman, 2002); City of London Solicitors Co., 1983 (Master, 1993). FRSA. Hon. DCL City, 1994; Hon. LLD Ulster, 2000. *Recreations:* listening to music, watching Rugby football and cricket, horse racing. *Clubs:* Athenæum, East India, MCC.

WALFORD, Dr Diana Marion, CBE 2002; Principal, Mansfield College, Oxford, since 2002; *b* 26 Feb. 1944; *d* of late Lt-Col Joseph Norton, LLM, and of Thelma Norton (*née* Nurick); *m* 1970, Arthur David Walford, LLB; one *s* one *d. Educ:* Calder High Sch. for Girls, Liverpool; Liverpool Univ. (George Holt Medal, Physiol.; J. H. Abram Prize, Pharmacol.; BSc (1st C1. Hons Physiol.) 1965; MB ChB 1968; MD 1976); London Univ. (MSc (Epidemiology) 1987); MA Oxon 2003. FRCP 1990 (MRCP 1972); FRCPath 1986 (MRCPath 1974); MFPHM 1989, FFPH (FFPHM 1994). Ho. Officer posts, Liverpool Royal Inf., 1968–69; Sen. Ho. Officer posts and Sen. Registrar, St Mary's Hosp., Paddington, and Northwick Park Hosp., Harrow, 1969–75; MRC Research (Training) Fellow, Clin. Res. Centre, 1975–76; Sen. MO 1976–79, PMO 1979–83, SPMO (Under Sec.), 1983–89, Dep. CMO, 1989–92, DHSS, subseq. Dept of Health; Dir, PHLS, 1993–2002. Hon. Consultant Haematologist, Central Middlesex Hosp., 1977–87. Non-exec. Dir, NHS Blood and Transplant Authy, 2005–. Founder Mem., British Blood Transfusion Soc., 1983–95; Hon. Life Mem., British Assoc. of Med. Managers. Gov., Ditchley Foundn, 2000–. FRSocMed; FRSA. *Publications:* chapters on haematological side effects of drugs in: Meyler's Side Effects of Drugs, 9th edn 1980; Side Effects of Drugs Annual, 1980; Drug-Induced Emergencies, 1980; articles on alpha-thalassaemia. *Recreations:* theatre, painting, travel. *Address:* Mansfield College, Mansfield Road, Oxford OX1 3TF.

WALFORD, Prof. Geoffrey, PhD; Professor of Education Policy, University of Oxford, since 2000; Fellow, Green Templeton College (formerly Green College), Oxford, since 1995; *b* 30 April 1949. *Educ:* Univ. of Kent (BSc Physics 1971; PhD 1975); Open Univ. (BA Sociol. and Educn 1975; MSc 1985; MBA 1996); St John's Coll., Oxford (MPhil Sociol. 1978; MA 1995); Inst. of Educn, Univ. of London (MA Educnl Admin 1986). Aston University: Lectr in Sociol. of Educn, Dept of Educnl Enquiry, 1979–83; Lectr in Educn Policy and Mgt, 1983–90, Sen. Lectr in Sociol. and Educn Policy, 1990–94, Aston Business Sch.; University of Oxford: Lectr in Educnl Studies (Sociol.), 1995–97; Reader in Educn Policy, 1997–2000; Univ. Jun. Proctor, 2001–02. Jt Ed., Brit. Jl Educnl Studies, 1998–2002; Ed., Oxford Review of Educn, 2003–. *Publications:* books include: Life in Public Schools, 1986; Restructuring Universities: politics and power in the management of change, 1987; Privatization and Privilege in Education, 1990; (with H. Miller) City Technology College, 1991; (ed) Doing Educational Research, 1991; Choice and Equity in Education, 1994; (ed) Researching the Powerful in Education, 1994; Educational Politics: pressure groups and faith-based schools, 1995; (ed with R. Pring) Affirming the Comprehensive Ideal, 1997; (ed) Doing Research about Education, 1998; (ed) Studies in Educational Ethnography, annually, 1998–; Policy, Politics and Education: sponsored grant-maintained schools and religious diversity, 2000; Doing Qualitative Educational Research, 2001; Private Education: tradition and diversity, 2005; Markets and Equity in Education, 2006. *Recreations:* travel, walking. *Address:* Department of Education, University of Oxford, 15 Norham Gardens, Oxford OX2 6PY. *T:* (01865) 274141.

WALFORD, John de Guise; His Honour Judge Walford; a Circuit Judge, since 1993; *b* 23 Feb. 1948; *s* of late Edward Wynn Walford and of Dorothy Ann Walford; *m* 1977, Pamela Elizabeth Russell; one *s* one *d. Educ:* Sedbergh Sch.; Queens' Coll., Cambridge (MA). Called to the Bar, Middle Temple, 1971; practice on NE Circuit, 1974; Asst Recorder, 1985–89; Recorder, 1989–93. Standing Counsel (Criminal) to DHSS, NE Circuit, 1991–93. Chancellor, dio. of Bradford, 1999–. *Recreations:* cricket, tennis, opera, watching Middlesbrough FC. *Address:* Law Courts, Russell Street, Middlesbrough TS1 2AE. *Clubs:* Hawks (Cambridge); Free Foresters.

WALFORD, John Thomas, OBE 1985; a Vice President, Multiple Sclerosis Society of Great Britain and Northern Ireland, since 1995 (Deputy General Secretary, 1965–77; General Secretary, 1977–95); *b* 6 Feb. 1933; *s* of Frederick Thomas Walford and Rose Elizabeth Walford; *m* 1st, 1955, June Muriel Harding (marr. diss. 1970); two *s* one *d*; 2nd, 1996, Nansi Yvonne Long. *Educ:* Richmond and East Sheen County Grammar Sch. Served RAF, 1951–53. C. C. Wakefield & Co. Ltd, 1949–51 and 1953–55; Stanley Eades & Co., 1955–60; Moo Cow Milk Bars Ltd, 1960–64. DL Greater London, 1988–95. Editor, MS News (qly jl of Multiple Sclerosis Soc.), 1977–95. *Recreation:* collecting Victorian fairings. *Address:* Rhoslyn, Talley, Llandeilo, Carmarthenshire SA19 7AX. *T:* (01558) 685744. *Club:* Royal Society of Medicine.

WALFORD, Lionel Kingsley, PhD; FInstP; Assessor for Civil Service Fast Stream, since 1999; *b* 19 May 1939; *s* of late Edward Walford and Muriel (*née* Davies); *m* 1963, Linda Jones; one *d* (and one *d* decd). *Educ:* Whitchurch Grammar Sch., Cardiff; Univ. of Wales (BSc 1st Cl. Hons Physics, 1960); St Catharine's Coll., Cambridge (PhD 1963). FInstP 1972. Southern Illinois University, USA: Asst Prof., 1963–67; Associate Prof., 1967–72; Prof. of Physics, 1972–78; Research Consultant, McDonnell Douglas Corp., 1964–72; joined Welsh Office, 1978: Principal, 1978–84; Sen. Principal seconded to WDA, 1984–85; Dir, Manpower Services in Wales, 1985–88; Asst Sec., 1988–94, Under Sec. (Hd, then Dir), 1994–99, Welsh Office Agriculture Dept. *Publications:* numerous articles in jls on applied physics; one US patent. *Address:* *e-mail:* lionel.walford@btinternet.com.

WALKER, family name of **Barons Walker of Aldringham, Walker of Gestingthorpe** and **Walker of Worcester**.

WALKER OF ALDRINGHAM, Baron *cr* 2006 (Life Peer), of Aldringham in the County of Suffolk; **Gen. Michael John Dawson Walker,** GCB 2000 (KCB 1995); CMG 1997; CBE 1990 (OBE 1982); DL; Governor, Royal Hospital Chelsea, since 2006; *b* 7 July 1944; *s* of William Hampden Dawson Walker and Dorothy Helena Walker (*née* Shiach); *m* 1973, Victoria Margaret Holme; two *s* one *d*. *Educ:* Milton Sch., Bulawayo; Woodhouse Grove Sch., Yorks; RMA Sandhurst. Commissioned Royal Anglian Regt, 1966; Regtl and Staff duties, 1966–82; Staff Coll., 1976–77; MA to CGS, 1982–85; CO 1 Royal Anglian Regt, 1985–87; Comdr, 20th Armoured Brigade, 1987–89; COS, 1 (Br) Corps, 1989–91; GOC NE District and Comdr, 2nd Inf. Div., 1991–92; GOC Eastern District, 1992; ACGS, MoD, 1992–94; Comdr, ACE Rapid Reaction Corps, 1994–97; Comdr, Land Component Peace Implementation Force, Bosnia, 1995–96; C-in-C, Land Comd, 1997–2000; CGS, 2000–03. Colonel Commandant: Queen's Div., 1991–2000; AAC, 1994–2004; Col, Royal Anglian Regt, 1997–2002 (Dep. Col, 1991–97); CDS, MoD, 2003–06; ADC Gen. to the Queen, 1997–2006. DL Gtr London, 2007. Hon. LLD UEA, 2002; Hon. DSc Cranfield, 2003. *Recreations:* ski-ing, sailing, shooting, golf, family. *Address:* Royal Hospital, Chelsea, SW3 4SR.

WALKER OF GESTINGTHORPE, Baron *cr* 2002 (Life Peer), of Gestingthorpe in the County of Essex; **Robert Walker,** Kt 1994; PC 1997; a Lord of Appeal in Ordinary, since 2002; *b* 17 March 1938; *s* of late Ronald Robert Antony Walker and Mary Helen Walker (*née* Welsh); *m* 1962, Suzanne Diana Leggi; one *s* three *d*. *Educ:* Downside Sch.; Trinity Coll., Cambridge (BA; Hon. Fellow, 2006). Called to Bar, Lincoln's Inn, 1960, Bencher 1990; QC 1982; in practice at Chancery Bar, 1961–94; a Judge of the High Court of Justice, Chancery Div., 1994–97; a Lord Justice of Appeal, 1997–2002. *Address:* House of Lords, SW1A 0PW.

WALKER OF WORCESTER, Baron *cr* 1992 (Life Peer), of Abbots Morton in the County of Hereford and Worcester; **Peter Edward Walker;** PC 1970; MBE 1960; *b* 25 March 1932; *s* of Sydney and Rose Walker; *m* 1969, Tessa, *d* of G. I. Pout; three *s* two *d*. *Educ:* Latymer Upper Sch. Member, National Executive of Conservative Party, 1956–70; Nat. Chairman, Young Conservatives, 1958–60; contested (C) Dartford, 1955 and 1959. MP (C) Worcester, March 1961–1992. PPS to Leader of House of Commons, 1963–64; Opposition Front Bench Spokesman: on Finance and Economics, 1964–66; on Transport, 1966–68; on Local Government, Housing, and Land, 1968–70; Minister of Housing and Local Govt, June–Oct. 1970; Secretary of State for: the Environment, 1970–72; Trade and Industry, 1972–74; Opposition Spokesman on Trade, Industry and Consumer Affairs, Feb.–June 1974, on Defence, June 1974–Feb. 1975; Minister of Agric., Fisheries and Food, 1979–83; Sec. of State for Energy, 1983–87, for Wales, 1987–90. Chairman: Thornton & Co., 1991–97; Allianz Cornhill Insurance plc (formerly Cornhill Insurance), 1992–2006; English Partnerships, 1992–98; Kleinwort Benson, 1997–99; Vice Chm., Dresdner Kleinwort (formerly Dresdner Kleinwort Benson, later Dresdner Kleinwort Wasserstein), 1999–; non-executive Director: British Gas, 1990–96; Dalgety, 1990–96; Tate & Lyle, 1990–2001; LIFFE, 1995–; ITM Power plc, 2004–. Pres., British German Chamber of Commerce, 1999–2002 (Vice-Pres., 2002–). *Publications:* The Ascent of Britain, 1977; Trust The People, 1987; Staying Power (autobiog.), 1991. *Address:* Abbots Morton Manor, Gooms Hill, Abbots Morton, Worcester WR7 4LT. *Clubs:* Carlton (Chm., 1998–2004); Worcestershire County Cricket; Worcester Rugby Football.

WALKER, Prof. Alan Cyril, PhD; FRS 1999; Evan Pugh Professor of Anthropology and Biology, Pennsylvania State University, since 2002 (Professor of Anthropology and Biology, 1995–96; Distinguished Professor of Anthropology and Biology, 1996–2002); *b* 23 Aug. 1938; *s* of Cyril Walker and Edith (*née* Tidd); *m* 1st, 1963, Patricia Dale Larwood (marr. diss.); one *s*; 2nd, 1976, Patty Lee Shipman. *Educ:* St John's Coll., Cambridge (BA 1962); Royal Free Hosp., London (PhD 1967). BM Scientific Associate, 1963–64; Asst Lectr in Anatomy, Royal Free Hosp. Sch. of Medicine, 1965; Lectr in Anatomy, Makerere UC, Kampala, 1965–69; Hon. Keeper of Paleontology, Uganda Mus., 1967–69; Sen. Lectr in Anatomy, Univ. of Nairobi, 1969–73; Harvard University: Vis. Lectr, Dept of Anatomy, 1973–74, Associate Prof. of Anatomy, 1974–78, Med. Sch.; Associate Prof. of Anthropol., 1974–78; Res. Associate, Peabody Mus., 1974–78; Mem., Cttee of Profs in Evolutionary and Organismic Biol., 1974–78; Prof. of Cell Biol. and Anatomy, Johns Hopkins Univ. Sch. of Medicine, 1978–95 (part-time, 1995–97). Associate Editor: Amer. Jl Physical Anthropol., 1974–79; Jl Human Evolution, 1994–98. John Simon Guggenheim Meml Foundn Fellow, 1986; John D. and Catherine T. MacArthur Foundn Fellow, 1988–93; Phi Beta Kappa Schol., 1995. Mem., American Acad. of Arts and Scis, 1996; Foreign Assoc., NAS, USA, 2003. Hon. DSc Chicago, 2000. Internat. Fondation Fyssen Prize, 1998; Faculty Scholar's Medal, Pennsylvania State Univ., 1999. *Publications:* (ed jtly) Prosimian Biology, 1974; (jtly) Structure and Function of the Human Skeleton, 1985; (ed with R. Leakey) The Nariokotome Homo Erectus Skeleton, 1993; (with P. Shipman) The Wisdom of the Bones, 1996 (Rhône-Poulenc Prize, 1997); (with P. Shipman) The Ape in the Tree, 2005; contrib. numerous papers to jls and edited books. *Address:* Department of Anthropology, 409 Carpenter Building, Pennsylvania State University, University Park, PA 16802–3404, USA. *T:* (814) 8653122.

WALKER, Alexandra Margaret Jane; psychoanalytic psychotherapist; Director, Human Resources, Inland Revenue, 2000–03; *b* 31 Oct. 1945; *d* of late Frederic Douglas Walker and Hertha Julie (*née* Freiin Gemmingen von Massenbach); one *d*. *Educ:* Nikolaus Cusanus Gymnasium, Bonn; Lady Margaret Hall, Oxford (Schol.; BA Lit. Hum.). Joined MoD as admin. trainee, 1973; Principal, 1976; on secondment to: Plessey Co., 1979–81; LSE as Nancy Seear Fellow in Industrial Relns, 1981–82; Asst Sec. and Hd of Civilian Mgt (Industrial Relns), 1983–86; rcds 1987; Counsellor, British Embassy, Bonn, 1988–92; Asst Under-Sec. of State (Service Personnel), 1993–97; Dir Gen. Future Hd Office, 1997–2000. *Recreations:* walking the coastline, geology, amateur cello playing.

WALKER, Andrew Douglas; Senior Partner, Lovells, 2000–04; *b* 6 May 1945; *s* of Malcolm Douglas Walker and Jean Catherine Walker (*née* Ross-Scott); *m* 1973, Hilary Georgina Smith. *Educ:* Giggleswick Sch.; Exeter Coll., Oxford (MA 1966). Admitted Solicitor, England and Wales, 1970, Hong Kong, 1982; articled, 1968–70, Solicitor, 1970–71, Wilkinson Kimbers & Staddon; Lovell, White & King: Solicitor, 1971–75; Partner, 1975; Hong Kong office, 1982–87; Managing Partner, 1987–88; Lovell White Durrant (formed from merger with Durrant Piesse): Managing Partner, 1988–93; Sen. Partner, 1996–2000; Lovells formed 2000, from merger with Boesebeck Droste. *Recreations:* opera, classical music, ornithology. *Address:* 85 Apsley House, 23–29 Finchley Road, NW8 0NZ. *T:* (020) 7586 9697. *Club:* Hong Kong.

WALKER, Andrew John; Chairman, Bioganix plc, since 2004; *b* 27 Sept. 1951; *s* of John Kenneth Walker, MD and Mary Magdaline (*née* Browne); *m* 1981, Pippa Robinson; two *s* one *d*. *Educ:* Ampleforth; Gonville and Caius Coll., Cambridge (MA). FIMechE 2003. Chief Executive: SWALEC, 1993–96; McKechnie plc, 1997–2001; Director: Ultra Electronics Hldgs plc, 1996–; API Gp plc, 2003–; Manganese Bronze Hldgs plc, 2003–; Delta plc, 2005–; Porvair plc, 2005–; Fountains plc, 2005–; Brintons Ltd, 2006–; Plastics Capital plc, 2007–. Liveryman, Engineers' Co. *Address:* Bioganix plc, Wharton Court, Leominster, Herefordshire HR6 0NX. *Club:* Farmers.

WALKER, Andrew John; Director General of Resources, House of Commons, since 2008; *b* 4 Jan. 1955; *s* of Edward Geoffrey Walker and Raymonde Dorothy Walker; *m* 1987, Alison Aitkenhead; two *s* one *d*. *Educ:* Newcastle-under-Lyme High Sch.; Univ. of Birmingham (BA Ancient Near Eastern Studies). Inland Revenue, 1976–89; Principal, Fiscal Policy Gp, HM Treasury, 1989–91; Asst Dir, Human Resources Strategy and Planning, Inland Revenue, 1992–96; Dir of Finance and Admin, H of C, 1997–2007. *Address:* Department of Resources, House of Commons, SW1A 0AA. *T:* (020) 7219 5460.

WALKER, Angus Henry; Senior Consultant, Europe Economics, since 2006; *b* 30 Aug. 1935; *s* of late Frederick William Walker and of Esther Victoria (*née* Wrangle); *m* 1st, 1968, Beverly Phillpotts (*see* B. J. Anderson) (marr. diss. 1976); 2nd, 1979, Ann (*née* Griffiths), *widow* of Richard Snow; two *d* and two step *d*. *Educ:* Erith Grammar Sch., Kent; Balliol Coll., Oxford (Domus Scholar; 1st Cl. Hons BA Mod. Hist. 1959; Stanhope Prize, 1958; MA 1968). Nat. Service, 1954–56 (commnd RA). Senior Scholar, St Antony's Coll., Oxford, 1959–63; HM Diplomatic Service, 1963–68: FO, 1963–65; First Sec., Washington, 1965–68. Lectr, SSEES, London Univ., 1968–70; Univ. Lectr in Russian Social and Political Thought, Oxford, and Lectr, Balliol Coll., 1971–76; Fellow, Wolfson Coll., Oxford, 1971–76; Dir, SSEES, London Univ., 1976–79; British Petroleum Co. Plc, 1979–84; Dir, Corporate Strategy, British Telecom PLC, 1985–88; Managing Director: Strategic Planning Associates, 1988–91; A. T. Kearney, 1991–94; Partner, Mitchell Madison Gp, 1996–98. Co-opted Mem., Arts Sub-Cttee, UGC, for enquiry into Russian in British Univs, 1978–79; Governor, Centre for Economic Policy Res., 1986–89. Chairman: HemiHelp, 2004–; Hampstead Garden Suburb Trust, 2007–. FIET (FIEE 2002; CompIEE 1988). *Publications:* trans. from Polish: Political Economy, by Oskar Lange, vol. 1, 1963; Marx: His Theory in its Context, 1978, 2nd edn 1989. *Address:* Barclays Bank plc, 126 Station Road, Edgware, HA8 7RY. *Club:* Reform.

WALKER, Hon. Anna Elizabeth Blackstock, (Hon. Mrs Walker), CB 2003; Chief Executive, Healthcare Commission, since 2004; *b* 5 May 1951; *d* of Baron Butterworth, CBE; *m* 1983, Timothy Edward Hanson Walker, *qv*; three *d*. *Educ:* Benenden Sch., Kent; Bryn Mawr Coll., USA; Lady Margaret Hall, Oxford (MA History). British Council, 1972–73; CBI, 1973–74; joined Department of Trade, 1975: Commercial Relations and Exports Div. (ME), 1975; Post and Telecommunications Div., 1976; Private Sec. to Sec. of State for Industry, 1977–78; Shipping Policy Div. (Grade 7), 1979–82; Finance Div., 1983–84; Interdeptl Rev. of Budgetary Controls, 1985; Cabinet Office (on secondment), 1986; Personnel Div. (Grade 6), 1987–88; Competition Policy Div. (Grade 5), 1988–91; Dir, Competition, 1991–94, Dep. Dir Gen., 1994–98, Oftel; Dep. Dir Gen., 1998, Dir Gen., 1998–2001, Energy, DTI; Dir Gen., Land Use and Rural Affairs, DEFRA, 2001–03. Mem. Council, NCC, 2008–. *Recreations:* family, travel, theatre, cycling. *Address:* c/o Healthcare Commission, Finsbury Tower, 103–105 Bunhill Row, EC1Y 8TG. *T:* (020) 7448 9246; *e-mail:* anna.walker@healthcarecommission.org.uk.

WALKER, Annabel; *see* Carr, E. A.

WALKER, Gen. Sir Antony (Kenneth Frederick), KCB 1987; Director-General, British Institute of Facilities Management, 1998; *b* 16 May 1934; *o s* of late Kenneth Walker and Iris Walker; *m* 1961, Diana Merran Steward (marr. diss. 1983); one *s* one *d*; *m* 1991, Sqn Ldr Hannah Watts, WRAF. *Educ:* Merchant Taylors' School; RMA Sandhurst. Commissioned into Royal Tank Regt, 1954; served BAOR, Libya, Ghana, Northern Ireland, Hong Kong, Cyprus; Instructor, Staff Coll., 1971–73; CO 1st Royal Tank Regt, 1974–76 (despatches); Col GS HQ UK Land Forces, 1976–78; Comdr Task Force Golf (11 Armd Bde), 1978–80; Dep. Mil. Sec. (A), 1980–82; Comdr, 3rd Armoured Div., 1982–84; Chief of Staff, HQ UKLF, 1985–87; Dep. CDS (Commitments), MoD, 1987–89; Comdt, RCDS, 1990–92. Sec.-Gen., Opsis (Nat. Assoc. for Educn, Trng and Support of Blind and Partially Sighted People), 1992–96. Mil. Advr, Porton Internat. plc, 1992–94; Sen. Mil. Advr, Electronic Data Systems Ltd, 1994; Business Develt Dir, John Mowlem. Col Comdt, Royal Tank Regt, 1983–94 (Rep., 1985–91). Mem. Council, RUSI, 1982–85 and 1990–94. Governor, Centre for Internat. Briefing, Farnham Castle, 1987–91. Chairman: Army Bobsleigh Assoc., 1983–92; British Bobsleigh Assoc., 1992–98 (Mem. Council, 1989–); President: Services' Dry Fly Fishing Assoc., 1988–92; Combined Services' Winter Sports Assoc., 1990–92. Mem., Council of Management, Salisbury Festival, 1988–96 (Vice-Chm., 1990–93; Chm., 1994–96). Trustee, Tank Mus., 1994–. *Recreations:* bird watching, fly-fishing, music, practical study of wine. *Address:* c/o National Westminster Bank plc, PO Box 237, 72–74 High Street, Watford, Herts WD1 2BQ. *Club:* Royal Air Force (Associate).

WALKER, Bill; *see* Walker, W. C.

WALKER, (Brian) Stuart, RDI 1989; freelance film production designer, since 1990; *b* 5 March 1932; *s* of William and Annie Walker; *m* 1st, 1961, Adrienne Elizabeth Atkinson (marr. diss. 1997); two *d*; 2nd, 2000, Francesca Boyd; one *s*. *Educ:* Blackpool Sch. of Art (Intermediate Exam. in Arts and Crafts; Nat. Diploma in Painting (1st cl. Hons)); RA Schs (RA Dip.). BBC Television, 1958–90: Design Assistant, 1958; Designer, 1961; Sen. Designer, 1970. BAFTA Award for TV Design, 1983, 1990; RTS Award for Production Design, 1988. *Address:* c/o Casarotto Marsh Ltd, Waverley House, 7–12 Noel Street, W1F 8GQ. *T:* (020) 7287 4450.

WALKER, Brian Wilson; consultant in ecology and development, since 1996; Executive Director, Earthwatch Europe, 1989–95; *b* 31 Oct. 1930; *s* of Arthur Walker and Eleanor (*née* Wilson); *m* 1954, Nancy Margaret Gawith; one *s* five *d*. *Educ:* Heversham Sch., Westmorland; Leicester Coll. of Technology; Faculty Technology, Manchester Univ. Management Trainee, Sommerville Bros, Kendal, 1952–55; Personnel Manager, Pye Radio, Larne, 1956–61; Bridgeport Brass Ltd, Lisburn: Personnel Manager, 1961–66; Gen. Manager (Develt), 1966–69; Gen. Manager (Manufrg), 1969–74; Dir Gen., Oxfam, 1974–83; Dir, Independent Commn on Internat. Humanitarian Issues, 1983–85; Pres., Internat. Inst. for Envmt and Develt, 1985–89. Chairman: Band Aid—Live Aid Projects Cttee, 1985–90; SOS Sahel, 1988–95. Founder Chm., New Ulster Movt, 1969–74; Founder Pres., New Ulster Movt Ltd, 1974. Member: Standing Adv. Commn on Human Rights for NI, 1975–77; World Commn on Food and Peace, 1989–95; Preparing for Peace, Westmorland Quakers, 2000–07. Mem., Editl Cttee, World Resources Report, 1985–95. Trustee: Cambodia Trust, 1989–95; Internat. Inst. for Environment and Develt, 1989–95; Artizan Trust, 1992–99; Nginn Karet Foundn, 1996–2002; Chm., Arnside Parish Plan Trust, 2003–07. Chm., Kent Estuary Labour Party, 2005–08. Chm. Govs, Dallam Sch., Cumbria, 1996–2003; Chm., Dallam Trust, 2003–. Eponymous annual lecture inaugurated Oxford Univ., 1996. Hon. MA Oxon, 1983. Kt, Sov. Order of St Thomas of Acre; Kentucky Colonel, 1966. *Publications:* Authentic Development—Africa, 1986; various political/religious papers on Northern Ireland problem and Third World subjects. *Recreations:* gardening, Irish politics, classical music, active Quaker. *Club:* Athenæum.

WALKER, Carl, GC 1972; Police Inspector, 1976–82; *b* 31 March 1934; English; *m* 1955, Kathleen Barker; one *s*. *Educ:* Kendal Grammar Sch., Westmorland. RAF Police, 1952–54 (Corporal). Lancashire Police, Oct. 1954–March 1956, resigned; Blackpool Police,

1959–82 (amalgamated with Lancashire Constabulary, April 1968); Sergeant, 1971. Retired 1982, as a result of the injuries sustained from gunshot wounds on 23 Aug. 1971 during an armed raid by thieves on a jeweller's shop in Blackpool (GC). *Recreations:* Cumberland and Westmorland wrestling, photography, walking. *Address:* 9 Lawnswood Avenue, Poulton-le-Fylde, Blackpool FY6 7ED.

WALKER, Catherine Marguerite Marie-Therese; French couturier; Founder: The Chelsea Design Company Ltd, 1977; Catherine Walker Ltd, 2003; *b* Pas de Calais; *d* of Remy Baheux and Agnes (*née* Lefèbvre); *m* John Walker (decd); two *d.* *Educ:* Univ. of Lille; Univ. of Aix-en-Provence. Dir, Film Dept, French Inst., London, 1970; Lecture Dept, French Embassy, London, 1971. Hon. Bd Mem., 1999–, and Donor Patron, Gilda's Club; Founder Sponsor, Haven Trust, Catherine Walker Tree of Life (fund-raising mural/sculpture). FRSA 2000. Designer of the Year Award: for British Couture, 1990–91; for Glamour, 1991–92. *Publications:* Catherine Walker, An Autobiography by the Private Couturier to Diana, Princess of Wales, 1998; Catherine Walker, 25 Years 1977–2002, British Couture, 2002. *Address:* Catherine Walker Ltd, 65 Sydney Street, Chelsea, SW3 6PX. *T:* (020) 7352 4626; *e-mail:* catwalk@catherinewalker.com.

WALKER, Charles Ashley Rupert; MP (C) Broxbourne, since 2005; *b* 11 Sept. 1967; *s* of late Timothy Walker and of Carola Walker (*née* Ashton) (she *m* 1976, Rt Hon. Sir Christopher John Chataway, *qv*); *m* 1995, Fiona Jane Newman; two *s* one *d.* *Educ:* American Sch. of London; Univ. of Oregon (BSc Pol Sci. 1990). Communications Dir, CSG plc, 1997–2001; Director: Blue Arrow Ltd, 1999–2001; LSM Processing Ltd, 2002–04. Mem., Wandsworth LBC, 2002–. Contested (C) Ealing North, 2001. *Recreations:* fishing, cricket. *Address:* House of Commons, SW1A 0AA. *T:* (020) 7219 3000; *e-mail:* walkerca@parliament.uk. *Clubs:* Waltham Cross Conservative; Hoddesdon Conservative.

WALKER, Charls E., PhD; Consultant, Washington, DC, since 1973; *b* Graham, Texas, 24 Dec. 1923; *s* of Pinkney Clay and Sammye McCombs Walker; *m* 1949, Harmolyn Hart, Laurens, S Carolina; one *s* one *d.* *Educ:* Univ. of Texas (MBA); Wharton Sch. of Finance, Univ. of Pennsylvania (PhD). Instructor in Finance, 1947–48, and later Asst and Associate Prof., 1950–54, at Univ. of Texas, in the interim teaching at Wharton Sch. of Finance, Univ. of Pennsylvania; Associate Economist, Fed. Reserve Bank: of Philadelphia, 1953, of Dallas, 1954 (Vice-Pres. and Economic Advr, 1958–61); Economist and Special Asst to Pres. of Republic Nat. Bank of Dallas, 1955–56 (took leave to serve as Asst to Treasury Sec., Robert B. Anderson, April 1959–Jan. 1961); Exec. Vice-Pres., Amer. Bankers Assoc., 1961–69. Under-Sec. of the Treasury, 1969–72, Dep. Sec., 1972–73. Chm., American Council for Capital Formation; Co-founder, Cttee on the Present Danger; Mem. Council on Foreign Relations; Founder Chm., Bretton Woods Cttee. Adjunct Prof. of Finance and Public Affairs, Univ. of Texas at Austin, 1985–; Dist. Vis. Prof., Emory Univ., 2000–. Dist. Alumnus, Univ. of Texas, 1994. Hon. LLD Ashland Coll., 1970. Alexander Hamilton Award, US Treasury, 1973; Award for Outstanding Contribs to Minority Enterprise and Educn, Urban League, 1973; Baker Award, Nat. Council on Econ. Educn, 1991. Co-editor, The Banker's Handbook, 1988–. *Publications:* (ed) New Directions in Federal Tax Policy, 1983; (ed) The Consumption Tax, 1987; (ed) The US Savings Challenge, 1990; contribs to learned jls, periodicals. *Address:* 9426 Thrush Lane, Potomac, MD 20854, USA. *T:* (301) 2995414. *Clubs:* Congressional Country, Burning Tree Golf (Bethesda, Md).

WALKER, Christopher Charles, FRCS; Consultant Plastic and Reconstructive Surgeon, 1983–2008; Medical Director, Mid Essex Hospitals NHS Trust, 2001–07; President, British Association of Plastic, Reconstructive and Aesthetic Surgeons, 2007; *b* 26 April 1945; *s* of Cyril and Evelyn Vera Walker; *m* 1981, Marlene Dawn Menner; one *d.* *Educ:* Univ. of Newcastle upon Tyne (MB BS 1968). FRCS 1974. SHO, Surgery Rotating, United Norwich Hosp., 1971–74; Registrar, Gen. Surgery, Leicester Royal Infirmary, 1974–75; MRC Res. Registrar, Burns Project, Mt Vernon Hosp., 1975–76; Registrar in Plastic Surgery, Mt Vernon Hosp. and UCH, 1976–80; Sen. Registrar in Plastic Surgery, Manchester Hosps, 1980–83; Consultant Plastic Surgeon: St Andrews Centre, Billericay, 1983–2008 (transf. to Broomfield Hosp., Chelmsford, 1998); Queen Elizabeth Children's Hosp. and Royal London Hosp., 1983–2001; Whipps Cross Hosp., 1983–2008. Founder and Chm., Broomfield Hosp. Arts Prog. 1997–. *Recreations:* jazz and classical music, wine and food, travel.

WALKER, Sir Christopher (Robert Baldwin), 5th Bt *cr* 1856, of Oakley House, Suffolk; *b* 25 Oct. 1969; *s* of Sir (Baldwin) Patrick Walker, 4th Bt and of Rosemary Ann Walker (*née* Hollingdrake); *S* father, 2005. *Educ:* Diocesan Coll., Cape Town. Leading Seaman, South African Marine Corps, 1994–96; Sales Manager, 1996–2006; Dir, 2007–08. *Heir: kinsman:* David Christopher Wake-Walker [*b* 11 March 1947; *m* 1979, Jenni Rosemary Vaulkhard; two *s*]. *Address:* 8 Waltham Way, Meadowridge, Cape Town 7806, South Africa; *e-mail:* chris@unilynx.co.za.

WALKER, (Christopher) Roy, CB 1992; Chief Officer, Joint Nature Conservation Committee, 1993–96; *b* 5 Dec. 1934; *s* of late Christopher Harry Walker and Dorothy Jessica Walker; *m* 1961, Hilary Mary Biddiscombe; two *s.* *Educ:* Sir George Monoux Grammar Sch., E17; Sidney Sussex Coll., Cambridge (BA); Université Libre de Bruxelles. National Service, Essex Regt, 1952–54. BoT, 1958; CSD, 1968; Private Sec. to Lord Privy Seal, 1968–71; Treasury, 1973; DTI, 1973; Dept of Energy, 1974; Cabinet Office, 1974; Dept of Energy, 1975; Under Secretary: DES, 1977; Dept. of Employment, 1986; seconded as Dir, Business in the Cities, 1989; Dep. Head of Sci. and Technol. Secretariat, Cabinet Office, 1989–92. Chm., Rockdale Housing Assoc., Sevenoaks, 2003–07. *Recreations:* hill walking, sailing. *Clubs:* Cruising Association; Chipstead Sailing (Sevenoaks); Medway Yacht.

WALKER, Prof. David Alan, PhD, DSc; FRS 1979; Professor of Photosynthesis, University of Sheffield, 1988–93, now Emeritus; *b* 18 Aug. 1928; *s* of Cyril Walker and Dorothy Walker (*née* Dobson); *m* 1956, Shirley Wynne Walker (*née* Mason); one *s* one *d.* *Educ:* King's Coll., Univ. of Durham (BSc, PhD, DSc). Royal Naval Air Service, 1946–48. Lecturer, 1958–63, Reader, 1963–65, Queen Mary Coll., Univ. of London; Reader, Imperial Coll., Univ. of London, 1965–70; University of Sheffield: Prof. of Biology, 1970–84; Prof. and Dir, Res. Inst. for Photosynthesis, 1984–88. Leverhulme Emeritus Fellow, 1991–93. Corresp. Mem., Amer. Soc. Plant Physiol., 1979; MAE 1994. Hon. LittD Sheffield, 2006. Alexander von Humboldt Prize, Alexander von Humboldt Foundn, Bonn, 1991. *Publications:* Energy Plants and Man, 1979, 2nd edn 1992; (with G. E. Edwards) C3, C4—Mechanisms, Cellular and Environmental Regulation of Photosynthesis, 1983; The Use of the Oxygen Electrode and Fluorescence Probes in Simple Measurements of Photosynthesis, 1987, 2nd edn 1990; A Leaf in Time, 1999; Like Clockwork, 2006; A New Leaf in Time, 2007; papers, mostly in field of photosynthesis. *Recreations:* changing the Biddlestone landscape, singing the Sheffield Carols, philosophising in The Cross Keys. *Address:* 6 Biddlestone Village, Morpeth, Northumberland NE65 7DT. *T:* (01669) 630235; *e-mail:* d.a.walker@sheffield.ac.uk.

WALKER, Sir David (Alan), Kt 1991; Executive Chairman, 2004–05, and Senior Adviser, 2001–04 and since 2006, Morgan Stanley International plc (formerly Ltd); *b* 31 Dec. 1939; *m* 1963, Isobel Cooper; one *s* two *d.* *Educ:* Chesterfield Sch.; Queens' Coll., Cambridge (MA; Hon. Fellow, 1989). Joined HM Treasury, 1961; Private Sec. to Joint Permanent Secretary, 1964–66; seconded to Staff of International Monetary Fund, Washington, 1970–73; Asst Secretary, HM Treasury, 1973–77; joined Bank of England as Chief Adviser, then Chief of Economic Intelligence Dept, 1977; a Dir, 1981–93 (non-exec., 1988–93); Chairman: Johnson Matthey Bankers, later Minories Finance, 1985–88; SIB, 1988–92; Agricl Mortgage Corp., 1993–94; Dep. Chm., Lloyds Bank plc, 1992–94; Dir, Morgan Stanley Inc., 1994–97; Exec. Chm., Morgan Stanley Gp (Europe) plc, subseq. Morgan Stanley Dean Witter (Europe) Ltd, 1994–2000; Chm., Morgan Stanley Internat. Inc., 1995–2000; Mem., Mgt Bd, Morgan Stanley Dean Witter, 1997–2000. Chairman: Steering Gp, Financial Markets Gp, LSE, 1986–93; Review of Disclosure and Transparency in Private Equity, 2007–. Bd Mem., CEGB, 1987–89; Chm., RVC Greenhouse Fund, 1999–; non-executive Director: National Power, 1990, 1993–94; British Invisibles, 1993–97; Reuters Holdings, 1994–2000; Legal & General Assce Co., 2002– (Vice-Chm., 2004–). Mem., 1993–, Treas., 1998–, and Trustee, 2007–, The Group of Thirty. Chairman: London Investment Bankers' Assoc., 2002–04; Moroccan British Business Council, 2000–07. Nominated Mem., Council of Lloyd's, 1988–92 (Chm., Inquiry into LMX Spiral, 1992). UK Co. Chm., Univ. of Cambridge 800th Anniversary Campaign, 2005–. Governor, Henley Management Coll., 1993–99. Chm., Community Links, East End charity. FRSA 1987; CCMI (CBIM 1986). Hon. LLD Exeter, 2002. *Recreations:* music, long-distance walking. *Address:* Morgan Stanley International plc, 25 Cabot Square, Canary Wharf, E14 4QA. *Clubs:* Reform, Garrick.

WALKER, Air Vice-Marshal David Allan, OBE 1995; MVO 1992; Master of HM Household, since 2005; an Extra Equerry to the Queen, since 2005; *b* 14 July 1956; *s* of late Allan Walker and of Audrey Walker (*née* Brothwell); *m* 1983, Jane Alison Fraser Calder. *Educ:* City of London Sch.; Univ. of Bradford (BSc). RAF univ. cadet, 1974; RAF Coll., 1977–78; Equerry to the Queen, 1989–92; Loan Service, S Africa, 1994; Comd, RAF Halton, 1997–98; Director: Corporate Communication (RAF), 1998–2002; Personnel and Trng Policy (RAF), 2002–03; AOC RAF Trng Gp and Chief Exec., Trng Gp Defence Agency, 2003–04. Vice-Pres., Royal Internat. Air Tattoo, 2005–. Liveryman, Co. of Bakers, 1991–. *Recreations:* walking dogs, keeping fit(ish), old cars, shooting. *Address:* Buckingham Palace, SW1A 1AA. *T:* (020) 7024 5832. *Clubs:* Royal Over-Seas League, Royal Air Force.

WALKER, David Bruce; Member (part-time), British Coal Corporation, 1988–95; *b* 30 Aug. 1934; *s* of Noel B. Walker and June R. Walker (*née* Sutherland); *m* 1961, Leonora C. Freeman; two *s.* *Educ:* Knox Grammar Sch., Wahroonga, NSW; Univ. of Sydney (BSc (Hons), MSc, Geology). Demonstrator in Geology: Univ. of Sydney, 1956–58; Bristol Univ., 1958–59; British Petroleum Co., 1959–85: worked as geologist in UK, Gambia, Algeria, Libya, Colombia, Kuwait, Iran and US; Vice-Pres., Production Planning, USA, 1974–77; Regional Coordinator, Western Hemisphere, 1977–79; Controller, BP Exploration, 1979–80; Chief Executive, BP Petroleum Development (UK), 1980–82; Dir, Resources Development, BP Australia, 1982–85; Chief Exec., Britoil plc, 1985–88. Chairman: Sun Internat. Exploration and Production Co., 1988–91; Sun Oil Britain, 1988–91. Distinguished Lectr, Soc. of Petroleum Engineers, 1976. President, UK Offshore Operators Assoc., 1982. *Recreations:* music, gardening. *Address:* Spring Cottage, Chetnole, Sherborne, Dorset DT9 6PF. *T:* (01935) 872604.

WALKER, David Critchlow, CMG 1993; CVO 1988 (MVO 1976); HM Diplomatic Service, retired; Chairman, Impact UK, since 2003; *b* 9 Jan. 1940; *s* of John Walker and Mary Walker (*née* Cross); *m* 1965, Tineke van der Leek; three *s.* *Educ:* Manchester Grammar Sch.; St Catharine's Coll., Cambridge (BA, MA, DipEd). Assistant Lecturer, Dept of Geography, Manchester Univ., 1962; Commonwealth Relations Office, 1963; Third Secretary, British Embassy, Mexico City, 1965; Second Secretary, Brussels, 1968; First Secretary: FCO, 1970; Washington, 1973; First Sec., later Counsellor, FCO, 1978–83; Consul General, São Paulo, 1983–86; Minister, Madrid, 1986–89; Counsellor, FCO, 1989–92; High Comr, Ghana, and non-resident Ambassador, Togo, 1992–96; High Comr, Bangladesh, 1996–99. *Address:* 7 The Crescent, Thirsk YO7 1DE.

WALKER, Prof. David Maxwell, CBE 1986; QC (Scot.) 1958; FBA 1976; FRSE 1980; Regius Professor of Law, Glasgow University, 1958–90, now Professor Emeritus and Senior Research Fellow; Dean of the Faculty of Law, 1956–59; Senate Assessor on University Court, 1962–66; *b* 9 April 1920; *o s* of James Mitchell Walker, Branch Manager, Union Bank of Scotland, and Mary Paton Colquhoun Irvine; *m* 1954, Margaret Knox, OBE, MA, *yr d* of Robert Knox, yarn merchant, Brookfield, Renfrewshire. *Educ:* High School of Glasgow (Mackindlay Prizeman in Classics); Glasgow, Edinburgh and London Universities. MA (Glasgow) 1946; LLB (Distinction), Robertson Schol., 1948; Faulds Fellow in Law, 1949–52; PhD (Edinburgh), 1952; Blackwell Prize, Aberdeen Univ., 1955; LLB (London), 1957; LLD (Edinburgh), 1960; LLD (London), 1968; LLD (Glasgow), 1985. Served War of 1939–45, NCO Cameronians; commissioned HLI, 1940; seconded to RIASC, 1941; served with Indian Forces in India, 1942, Middle East, 1942–43, and Italy, 1943–46, in MT companies and as Brigade Supply and Transport Officer (Captain). HQ 21 Ind. Inf. Bde, 8 Ind. Div. Advocate of Scottish Bar, 1948; Barrister, Middle Temple, 1957; QC (Scotland) 1958; practised at Scottish Bar, 1948–53; studied at Inst. of Advanced Legal Studies, Univ. of London, 1953–54; Prof. of Jurisprudence, Glasgow Univ., 1954–58. Dir, Scottish Univs' Law Inst., 1974–80. Trustee, Hamlyn Trust, 1954–93. Vice-Pres., RSE, 1985–88. Governor: Scottish College of Commerce, 1957–64; High School of Glasgow (and Chm., Educational Trust), 1974–2001. Hon. Sheriff of Lanarkshire at Glasgow, 1966–82. FSAScot 1966; FRSA 1991. Hon. LLD Edinburgh, 1974. *Publications:* (ed) Faculty Digest of Decisions, 1940–50, Supplements, 1951 and 1952; Law of Damages in Scotland, 1955; The Scottish Legal System, 1959, 8th edn 2001; Law of Delict in Scotland, 1966, 2nd edn 1981; Scottish Courts and Tribunals, 1969, 5th edn 1985; Principles of Scottish Private Law (2 vols), 1970, 4th edn (4 vols), 1988–89; Law of Prescription and Limitation in Scotland, 1973, 6th edn 2002; Law of Civil Remedies in Scotland, 1974; Law of Contracts in Scotland, 1979, 3rd edn 1995; Oxford Companion to Law, 1980; (ed) Stair's Institutions (6th edn), 1981; (ed) Stair Tercentenary Studies, 1981; The Scottish Jurists, 1985; Legal History of Scotland, 7 vols, 1988–2004; Scottish Part of Topham and Ivamy's Company Law, 12th edn 1955, to 16th edn 1978; contribs to collaborative works; articles in legal periodicals; *festschrift:* Obligations in Context, ed A. J. Gamble, 1990. *Recreations:* motoring, book collecting, Scottish history. *Address:* 1 Beaumont Gate, Glasgow G12 9EE. *T:* (0141) 339 2802.

WALKER, David Ralph, FFPH; Regional Director of Public Health, East Midlands, since 2006; *b* 28 Oct. 1962; *s* of David and Ada Walker; *m* 1995, Elisabeth Ann Martin; two *d.* *Educ:* Nottingham High Sch.; Univ. of Newcastle upon Tyne Med. Sch. (BMedSci 1986; MB BS 1987; MSc 1994). MRCP 1991; MFPHM 1995, FFPH 2006. Trng posts in medicine and public health, Newcastle upon Tyne, 1987–94; Vis. Scientist, Centers for Disease Control, Atlanta, Ga, 1994–95; Consultant in Communicable Disease Control and Dep. Dir of Public Health, Co. Durham and Darlington HA, 1996–2001; Actg Dir of Public Health, Newcastle and N Tyneside HA, 2001–02; Dir of Public Health and Med. Dir, Co. Durham and Tees Valley Strategic HA, 2002–06; Actg Regl Dir of Public Health for NE of England, 2005–06. *Publications:* articles in med. jls. *Recreations:* ski-ing, boogie-woogie piano playing. *Address:* Government Office for the East Midlands, Belgrave Centre, Stanley Place, Nottingham NG1 5GG. *T:* (0115) 971 4750; *e-mail:* David.walker@dh.gsi.gov.uk.

WALKER, Rt Rev. David Stuart; *see* Dudley, Suffragan Bishop of.

WALKER, Maj.-Gen. Derek William Rothwell; Manager, CBI Overseas Scholarships, 1980–89, retired; *b* 12 Dec. 1924; *s* of Frederick and Eileen Walker; *m* 1950, Florence Margaret Panting; two *s* (and one *s* decd). *Educ:* Mitcham County Grammar Sch.; Battersea Polytechnic. FIMechE 1970–89; FIEE 1971–89. Commissioned REME, 1946; served: Middle East, 1947–50 (despatches 1949); BAOR, 1951–53; Far East, 1954–56 (despatches 1957); Near East, 1960–62; Far East, 1964–67; psc 1957. Lt-Col 1964, Col 1970, Brig. 1973. Appts include: Comdr, REME Support Group, 1976–77; Dir, Equipment Engineering, 1977–79. Mem. Council, IEE, 1975–79; Pres., SEE, 1979–81. *Recreations:* fishing, sailing, wine-making. *Address:* 20 Moor Lane, Strensall, York YO32 5UQ.

WALKER, Desmond; *see* Le Cheminant, Air Chief Marshal Sir P. de L.

WALKER, Rt Rev. Dominic Edward William Murray; *see* Monmouth, Bishop of.

WALKER, Prof. Donald, FRS 1985; Professor of Biogeography, Institute of Advanced Studies, Australian National University, Canberra, 1969–88; *b* 14 May 1928; *s* of Arthur Walker and Eva (*née* Risdon); *m* 1959, Patricia Mary Smith; two *d.* *Educ:* Morecambe Grammar School; Sheffield Univ. (BSc); MA, PhD Cantab. Commission, RAF (Nat. Service), 1953–55. Research Scholar and Asst in Res., later Sen. Asst, Sub-Dept of Quaternary Res., Cambridge Univ., 1949–60; Fellow of Clare College, 1952–60 (Asst Tutor, 1955–60); Reader in Biogeography, ANU, 1960–68; Head of Dept of Biogeography and Geomorphology, ANU, 1969–88. Hon. Prof., Chinese Acad. of Science, 1986–. *Publications:* articles on plant ecology, palaeoecology and related topics in sci. jls. *Recreations:* pottery, architecture, prehistory. *Address:* 8 Galali Place, Aranda, ACT 2614, Australia. *T:* (2) 62513136.

WALKER, Edward William F.; *see* Faure Walker.

WALKER, Prof. Frederick, MD, PhD; FRCPath; Regius Professor of Pathology, University of Aberdeen, 1984–2000, now Emeritus; Consultant Pathologist, Grampian Health Board, 1984–2000; *b* 21 Dec. 1934; *s* of Frederick James Walker and Helen Stitt Halliday; *m* 1st, 1963, Cathleen Anne Gordon, BSc (marr. diss.); two *d*; 2nd, 1998, Jean Winifred Keeling, FRCPath, FRCPE, FRCPCH. *Educ:* Kirkcudbright Academy; Univ. of Glasgow. MB ChB 1958; PhD 1964; MD (Hons and Bellahouston Medal) 1971. MRCPath 1966, FRCPath 1978. Lectr in Pathology, Univ. of Glasgow, 1962–67; Vis. Asst Prof., Univ. of Minnesota, 1964–65; Sen. Lectr in Pathology, Univ. of Aberdeen, 1968–73; Foundation Prof. of Pathology, Univ. of Leicester, 1973–84. Chm., Nat. Quality Assurance Adv. Panel (Histopathology and Cytology), 1991–96; Mem. Council, RCPath, 1990–93; Chm. and Gen. Sec., Pathol Soc. of GB and Ireland, 1992–2000 (Mem. Cttee, 1990–92). Editor, Jl of Pathology, 1983–93. *Publications:* papers in scientific and med. jls. *Recreations:* writing, walking. *Address:* 9 Forres Street, Edinburgh EH3 6BJ. *T:* (0131) 225 9673.

WALKER, George Alfred; Chief Executive: Walkers International, 1992; Premier Telesports Plc, since 1994; *b* 14 April 1929; *s* of William James Walker and Ellen (*née* Page); *m* 1957, Jean Maureen Walker (*née* Hatton); one *s* two *d.* *Educ:* Jubilee Sch., Bedford, Essex. Formerly boxer and boxing manager; Amateur Boxing Champion, GB, 1951. *Recreations:* ski-ing, ocean racing, climbing.

WALKER, George Robert, OBE 1992; Director-General, International Baccalaureate Organisation, 1999–2006; *b* 25 Jan. 1942; *s* of William Walker and Celia Walker (*née* Dean); *m* 1968, Jennifer Anne Hill; one *s* one *d.* *Educ:* Watford Boys' Grammar Sch.; Exeter Coll., Oxford (MA, MSc); Univ. of Cape Town (LRSM). Science teacher, Watford Grammar Sch., 1966–68; Salters' Inst. Schol., 1968–69; Lectr in Educn, Univ. of York, 1969–73; Dep. Headmaster, Carisbrooke High Sch., 1973–76; Headmaster: Heathcote Sch., Stevenage, 1977–81; Cavendish Sch., Hemel Hempstead, 1981–91; Dir-Gen., Internat. Sch. of Geneva, 1991–99. Chm., Centre for Study of Comprehensive Schs, 1980–85. Member: HMC, 1982–99; Nat. Curriculum Sci. Working Gp, 1987–88. Educn Advr to ICI plc, 1990–91. Hon. Sen. Vis. Fellow, Univ. of York, 1988–91; Vis. Prof., Univ. of Bath, 1997–. Mem. Council, Univ. of York, 2002–05. Hon. DEd Bath, 2003. *Publications:* (jtly) Modern Physical Chemistry, 1981, 3rd edn 1986; Comprehensive Themes, 1983; (ed jtly) International Education in Practice, 2002; To Educate the Nations, 2002; To Educate the Nations 2, 2004; International Education and the International Baccalaureate, 2004; Educating the Global Citizen, 2006; An A to Z of School Leadership, 2007. *Recreation:* piano-playing. *Address:* Tyebank, Peacocks Close, Cavendish, Suffolk CO10 8DA.

WALKER, Gordon; *see* Walker, T. G.

WALKER, Sir Harold (Berners), KCMG 1991 (CMG 1979); HM Diplomatic Service, retired; President, British Society for Middle Eastern Studies, since 2006; *b* 19 Oct. 1932; *s* of late Admiral Sir Harold Walker, KCB, RN, and Lady Walker (*née* Berners); *m* 1st, 1960, Jane Bittleston (marr. diss.); one *s* two *d*; 2nd, 2004, Anne Savage (*née* Gourlay). *Educ:* Winchester; Worcester Coll., Oxford. BA 1955. 2nd Lieut RE, 1951–52. Foreign Office, 1955; MECAS, 1957; Asst Political Agent, Dubai, 1958; Foreign Office, 1960; Principal Instructor, MECAS, 1963; First Sec., Cairo, 1964; Head of Chancery and Consul, Damascus, 1966; Foreign Office (later FCO), 1967; First Sec. (Commercial), Washington, 1970; Counsellor, Jedda, 1973; Dep. Head, Personnel Operations Dept, FCO, 1975–76, Head of Dept, 1976–78; Corpus Christi Coll., Cambridge, 1978; Ambassador to Bahrein, 1979–81, to United Arab Emirates, 1981–86, to Ethiopia, 1986–90, to Iraq, 1990–91; retd 1992. Member: Commonwealth War Graves Commn, 1992–97; Bd, CARE International UK, 1992–2001 (Chm., 1994–97); Pres., CARE Internat., 1997–2001; Chm., RSAA, 2001–08. Pres., Friends of Imperial War Mus., 1992–97. Chm., Bahrain Soc., 1993–99. Mem. of Corp., Woking Sixth Form Coll., 1996–99. Associate Fellow, RUSI, 1992–97. *Address:* 39 Charlwood Street, SW1V 2DU. *Club:* Oxford and Cambridge.

WALKER, His Honour Judge Harry; *see* Walker, P. H. C.

WALKER, Rev. Dr James Bernard; Chaplain, since 1993, and Associate Director, Student Support Services, since 2005 (Assistant Director, 1998–2005), St Andrews University; *s* of Rev. Dr Robert B. W. Walker and Grace B. Walker; *m* 1972, Sheila Mary; three *s.* *Educ:* Hamilton Academy, Lanarkshire; Edinburgh Univ. (MA 1st cl. Hons Mental Philosophy 1968; BD 1st cl. Hons Systematic Theol. 1971); Merton Coll., Oxford (DPhil 1981). Church of Scotland minister, ordained 1975, Dundee; Associate Minister, Mid Craigie Parish Church linked with Wallacetown Parish Church, Dundee, 1975–78; Minister, Old and St Paul's Parish Church, Galashiels, 1978–87; Principal, Queen's Coll., Birmingham, 1987–93. *Publications:* Israel—Covenant and Land, 1986; (contrib.) Politique et Théologie chez Athanase d'Alexandrie (ed C. Kannengiesser), 1974; (contrib.) God, Family and Sexuality (ed D. W. Torrance), 1997. *Recreations:* golf, tennis, swimming, hill walking. *Address:* The Chaplaincy Centre, University of St Andrews, 3a St Mary's Place, St Andrews, Fife KY16 9UY. *T:* (01334) 462865.

WALKER, Prof. James Johnston, MD; FRCPSGlas, FRCPE, FRCOG; Professor of Obstetrics and Gynaecology, University of Leeds, since 1994; *b* 17 March 1952; *s* of James and Catherine Walker; *m* 1976, Ann Mary Young; two *d.* *Educ:* High Sch. of Dundee; Univ. of Glasgow (MB ChB 1976; MD 1992). MRCOG 1981, FRCOG 1994; MRCP 1981; FRCPSGlas 1991; FRCPE 1994. Jun. doctor, Obstetrics and Gynaecol., Glasgow, 1976–83; University of Glasgow: Res. Fellow in Obstetrics and Gynaecol., 1983–84; Lectr in Obstetrics and Gynaecol., 1984–87; Sen. Lectr, 1987–93; Reader, 1993. Clin. Advr (Obstetrics) to Nat. Patient Agency, 2003–. *Publications:* (with N. F. Gant) Hypertension in Pregnancy, 1997; (jtly) Problem-based Obstetrics and Gynaecology, 2003; (jtly) Pre-eclampsia, 2003; peer-reviewed articles in Obstetrics and Gynaecol. *Recreations:* travelling, cooking, swimming. *Address:* 12 Shire Oak Road, Headingley, Leeds LS6 2DE. *T:* (0113) 278 9599, *Fax:* (0113) 234 3450; *e-mail:* j.j.walker@leeds.ac.uk. *Club:* Royal Society of Medicine.

WALKER, Jane Helen; *see* Darbyshire, J. H.

WALKER, Janet Sheila; Commercial and Finance Director, Ascot Racecourse, since 2003; *b* Felton, 21 April 1953; *d* of David Walker and Sheila Walker (*née* Rapps); partner, Peter Corbett. *Educ:* Somerville Coll., Oxford (BA 1st Cl. PPE 1975); Institut des Hautes Études Internationales, Nice (Dip.). ACA 1979. Price Waterhouse, 1976–79; Financial Controller for Regl Broadcasting, BBC, 1994–96; Financial Dir, Granada Media Gp, 1996–98; Dir, Finance and Business Affairs, Channel 4 Television, 1998–2003. Non-executive Director: Pizza Express plc, 1999–2003; Henderson High Income Trust plc, 2007–. Mem., Design Council, 2006–. Mem. Bd, Young Vic Th., 1997–2005. *Recreations:* walking, gardening, modern fiction. *Address:* Ascot Racecourse, Ascot, Berks SL5 7JX. *T:* (01344) 878522; *e-mail:* janet.walker@ascot.co.uk.

WALKER, Janey Patricia Winifred, (Mrs Hamish Mykura); Managing Editor Commissioning, since 1999, and Head of Education, since 2006, Channel 4 Television; *b* 10 April 1958; *d* of Brig. Harry Walker and Patricia Walker; *m* 1997, Hamish Mykura; twin *d.* *Educ:* Brechin High Sch.; Benenden Sch.; York Univ. (BA Hist./Politics); Univ. of Chicago (Benton Fellow). BBC News and Current Affairs, 1983–89; The Late Show, BBC, 1990–94; Editor, Edge prog., WNET, and dir, BBC NY, 1994–95; Wall to Wall TV, London, 1995–96; Commng Ed. Arts, Channel 4, 1996–99. *Recreations:* walking, art. *Address:* c/o Channel 4 Television, 124 Horseferry Road, SW1P 2TX. *T:* (020) 7396 4444.

WALKER, Jeremy Colin Maclaren; Chairman, Yorkshire Regional Flood Defence Committee, since 2005; *b* 12 July 1949; *m* 1968, Patricia June Lockhart; two *s* one *d.* *Educ:* Brentwood Sch., Essex; Univ. of Birmingham (BA 1971). Dept of Employment, 1971–73; Pvte Sec. to Chm., MSC, 1974–75; HSE, 1975–76; Econ. Secretariat, Cabinet Office, 1976–78; MSC, 1978–82; Exchange Officer, Australian Dept of Employment and Industrial Relations, 1982–84; Manpower Services Commission: Regl Employment Manager, 1984–86; Hd, Community Prog. and New Job Trng Scheme, 1986–88; Regl Dir, Yorks and Humberside, Trng Agency and Dept of Employment, 1988–94; Regl Dir, Govt Office for Yorks and the Humber, 1994–99; Chief Exec., N Yorks CC, 1999–2005. Chm., Adv. Cttee for Yorks and the Humber, Forestry Commn, 2007–. Member: Bd, Yorks and Humberside Arts, 1994–99; N Yorks TEC, 1999–2001; Court, Univ. of York, 2001–; Court, Univ. of Leeds, 2002– (Mem. Council, 1992–2000); Nat. Employment Panel, 2002–05. Trustee: W Yorks Police Community Trust, 1996–99; York and N Yorks Community Trust, 2000–04. *Recreations:* walking, family, gardening.

WALKER, John; *see* Walker, N. J.

WALKER, John; Under Secretary, Scottish Development Department, 1985, retired; *b* 16 Dec. 1929; *s* of John Walker and Elizabeth White Fish; *m* 1952, Rena Robertson McEwan; two *d.* *Educ:* Falkirk High School. Entered Civil Service, Min. of Labour, as clerical officer, 1946. National Service, RAF, 1948–50. Asst Principal, Dept of Health for Scotland, 1958; Scottish Home and Health Dept: Principal, 1960; Secretary, Cttee on General Medical Services in the Highlands and Islands, 1964–67; Asst Sec., 1969; Scottish Development Dept, 1975–78; Under Sec., Scottish Home and Health Dept, 1978–85. Asst Comr, Scottish Local Govt Boundary Commn, 1987–94. *Recreations:* grandparenthood, being cared for and blethering to Rena. *Address:* 8/1 Back Dean, Ravelston Terrace, Edinburgh EH4 3UA. *T:* (0131) 343 3811.

WALKER, His Honour John David; DL; a Circuit Judge, 1972–89; *b* 13 March 1924; *y s* of late L. C. Walker, MA, MB (Cantab), BCh, and late Mrs J. Walker, Malton; *m* 1953, Elizabeth Mary Emma (*née* Owbridge); one *s* two *d.* *Educ:* Oundle (1937–42); Christ's Coll., Cambridge (1947–50); BA 1950, MA 1953. War of 1939–45: commissioned Frontier Force Rifles, Indian Army, 1943; demob., Captain, 1947. Called to the Bar, Middle Temple, 1951; a Recorder, 1972. A Pres., Mental Health Review Tribunals, 1986–96. Mem., Parole Bd, 1992–95. Chm., Standards Cttee, ER of Yorks CC, 1999–. DL Humberside, subseq. ER of Yorks, 1985. *Recreations:* shooting, fishing. *Address:* 7 Waltham Lane, North Bar Within, Beverley, E Yorks HU17 8HB. *Club:* Lansdowne.

WALKER, John Eric Austin; *see* Austin, J. E.

WALKER, Sir John (Ernest), Kt 1999; DPhil; FRS 1995; Director, MRC Dunn Human Nutrition Unit, Cambridge, since 1998; Fellow, Sidney Sussex College, since 1997, and Professor of Molecular Bioenergetics, since 2002, University of Cambridge; *b* Halifax, Yorks, 7 Jan. 1941; *s* of late Thomas Ernest Walker and Elsie (*née* Lawton); *m* 1963, Christina Jane Westcott; two *d.* *Educ:* Rastrick Grammar Sch., W Yorks; St Catherine's Coll., Oxford (BA; DPhil 1969; Hon. Fellow, 1998). Vis. Research Fellow, Univ. of Wisconsin, 1969–71; NATO Res. Fellow, CNRS, Gif-sur-Yvette, France, 1971–72; EMBO Res. Fellow, Pasteur Inst., Paris, 1972–74; Staff Scientist, MRC Lab. of Molecular Biol., Cambridge, 1974–98. Mem., EMBO, 1983. Hon. Prof., Peking Union Med. Coll., Beijing, 2001–. Hon. Member: Biochem. Soc., 1998; British Biophysical Soc., 2000. For. Mem., l'Accademia Nazionale dei Lincei, Rome, 2003–; For. Associate, NAS, 2004–. Founder FMedSci 1998; Millennium Fellow, RSC 2000. Hon. FIBiol 2002. MAE 1998. Hon. DSc: Bradford, 1998; Buenos Aires, 1998; Huddersfield, 1998; UMIST, 1999; Oxon, 1999; Groningen, 1999; Leeds, 1999; London, 2002; Sussex, 2003; Liverpool, 2004; UEA, 2006; Moscow State, 2007; Toyo, Japan, 2007; Dr *hc* Paul Sabatier, France, 2007. Johnson Foundn Prize, Univ. of Pennsylvania, 1994; Ciba Medal and Prize,

Biochem. Soc., 1995; Peter Mitchell Medal, European Bioenergetics Conf., 1996; Nobel Prize for Chemistry, 1997; Messel Medal, SCI, 2000; RSC Award for Biomembrane Chemistry, 2003. *Publications:* research papers and reviews in scientific jls. *Recreations:* cricket, opera music, walking. *Address:* MRC Dunn Human Nutrition Unit, Wellcome Trust/MRC Building, Hills Road, Cambridge CB2 0XY. *T:* (01223) 252701, *Fax:* (01223) 252705.

WALKER, Air Marshal Sir John (Robert), KCB 1992; CBE 1978; AFC; Ministry of Defence, 1989–95; *b* 26 May 1936. rcds; psc. SASO, Strike Comd, 1985–87; Dep. CoS (Ops), HQ AAFCE, 1987–89. Wing Comdr 1970; Gp Capt. 1975; Air Cdre 1980; Air Vice-Marshal 1986; Air Marshal 1991.

WALKER, Julian Fortay, CMG 1981; MBE 1960; HM Diplomatic Service, retired; Director, British Development Group, Iraqi Kurdistan and the Gulf, since 2005; *b* 7 May 1929; *s* of Kenneth Macfarlane Walker, FRCS, and Eileen Marjorie Walker (*née* Wilson); *m* 1983, Virginia Anne Austin (*née* Stevens) (marr. diss. 1995); three step *d. Educ:* Harvey Sch., Hawthorne, New York; Stowe; Bryanston; Cambridge Univ. (MA). National Service, RN, 1947–49; Cambridge, 1949–52; London Univ. Sch. of African and Oriental Studies, 1952. Foreign Service: MECAS, 1953; Asst Political Agent, Trucial States, 1953–55; 3rd and 2nd Sec., Bahrain Residency, 1955–57; FCO and Frontier Settlement, Oman, 1957–60; 2nd and 1st Sec., Oslo, 1960–63; FCO News Dept Spokesman, 1963–67; 1st Sec., Baghdad, 1967; 1st Sec., Morocco (Rabat), 1967–69; FCO, 1969–71; Political Agent, Dubai, Trucial States, 1971, Consul-Gen. and Counsellor, British Embassy, Dubai, United Arab Emirates, 1971–72; Cambridge Univ. on sabbatical leave, 1972–73; Political Advr and Head of Chancery, British Mil. Govt, Berlin, 1973–76; NI Office, Stormont Castle, 1976–77; Dir, MECAS, 1977–78; Ambassador to Yemen Arab Republic and Republic of Jibuti, 1979–84; Ambassador to Qatar, 1984–87. Special Advr on Syria, 1987–93, and on Iraq, 1990–93, Res. and Analysis Dept, FCO. Manager, Kurdish Cultural Centre, 2001–05. *Publications:* (ed) The UAE Internal Boundaries and Boundaries with Oman, 8 vols, 1994; Tyro on the Trucial Coast, 1999. *Recreations:* ski-ing, sailing, tennis, music, cooking.

WALKER, Julian Guy Hudsmith, CB 1991; independent engineering consultant, since 1994; Director General, Policy and Special Projects, Ministry of Defence, 1992–94, retired; *b* 2 Oct. 1936; *s* of Nathaniel and Frieda Walker; *m* 1960, Margaret Burns (*née* Jamieson). *Educ:* Winchester College; Southampton Univ. (BSc Mech Eng). CEng, FIMechE. Hawker Aircraft Co., 1958–61; Logistic Vehicles, FVRDE, WO, subseq. MoD, 1961–69; Ministry of Defence: Special Projects, MVEE, 1970–80; Head, Vehicle Engrg Dept, 1980–84; Scientific Adviser (Land), 1984–87; Dir, Estabts and Research (B), 1987–89; Head, RARDE, Chertsey, 1989–92. *Recreations:* vintage cars, photography, wood-turning, Wombling, solving practical problems.

WALKER, Kathrine S.; *see* Sorley Walker.

WALKER, Linda, (Mrs P. B. Walker); *see* Sutcliffe, L.

WALKER, Lorna Margaret S.; *see* Secker-Walker.

WALKER, Lorna Stuart, CChem, FCIWEM; Director, Lorna Walker Consulting Ltd, since 2004; *b* 2 Jan. 1952; *d* of Eric and Anne Walker; *m* 1992, Gareth James Young. *Educ:* Univ. of Cape Town (BSc Chem. and Maths; MSc Civil Engrg). MRSC; FCIWEM 1978; MCIWM 1993; Specialist in Land Condition. Dir, Ove Arup & Partners Ltd, 1977–2004. Vis. Prof. of Engrg Design for Sustainable Develt, Univ. of Sheffield, 2003–. Mem., CABE, 2006–. Mem., UK Urban Taskforce, 1997–. Hon. DEng Sheffield, 2007. *Publications:* (contrib.) London's Environment: prospects for a sustainable world city, 2001; (contrib.) Manufactured Sites, 2005. *Recreations:* gardening, reading, travelling. *Address:* Lorna Walker Consulting Ltd, 5 Heathfield Road, SW18 3HX. *T:* (020) 8874 3516; *e-mail:* lwalker@lornawalker.co.uk. *Club:* Reform.

WALKER, Malcolm Conrad, CBE 1995; Chief Executive, Iceland Foods Ltd, since 2005; *b* 11 Feb. 1946; *s* of Willie Walker and Ethel Mary Walker; *m* 1969, Nest Rhianydd; one *s* two *d. Educ:* Mirfield Grammar Sch. Trainee Manager, F. W. Woolworth & Co., 1964–71; Jt Founder, Iceland Frozen Foods, 1970; Chief Exec., 1973–2000, Chm., 1973–2001, Iceland Frozen Foods plc, subseq. Iceland Gp plc; Founder and CEO, Cooltrader Ltd, 2001–06. Non-exec. Dir, DFS Furniture Co. plc, 1993–2004. Trustee, Imagine appeal, Alder Hey Children's Hosp., 2006–. *Recreations:* ski-ing, sailing, shooting, stalking, business, home and family.

WALKER, Martin John; a District Judge (Magistrates' Courts), since 2002; *b* 18 Sept. 1952; *s* of Eric and Olive Walker; *m* 1997, Rosalind Ann Jones; one *d*; one *s* one *d* from former marriage. *Educ:* Sheffield Univ. (LLB). Admitted solicitor, 1977; County Prosecutor; in practice as solicitor, Bakewell, 1981–2001. *Recreations:* boating, herbs. *Address:* Magistrates' Court, Teesside Law Courts, Victoria Square, Middlesbrough TS1 2AS. *T:* (01642) 240301.

WALKER, His Honour Michael; a Circuit Judge, 1978–2001; *b* 13 April 1931; *m* 1959, Elizabeth Mary Currie; two *s. Educ:* Chadderton Grammar Sch.; Sheffield Univ. (LLM). Called to the Bar, Gray's Inn, 1956; joined North Eastern Circuit, 1958; a Recorder of the Crown Court, 1972–78; Hon. Recorder of Sheffield, 1996–2001; authorised to sit in Ct of Appeal (Criminal Div.), 1997.

WALKER, Dr Michael John; Headmaster, Felsted School, since 2008; *b* 24 Nov. 1955; *s* of Stephen Thomas Walker and Sheila Walker (*née* Ereaut); *m* 1977, Rita Bridget Carpenter (marr. diss.); one *s* two *d*; *m* 2007, Corinne Anne Francis. *Educ:* Corpus Christi Coll., Cambridge (BA Hons Hist. 1977; CertEd 1979; MA 1980; PhD 1985). Asst Prof. of History, Birmingham-Southern Coll., Birmingham, Alabama, 1977–78; Asst Master, Dulwich Coll., 1982–86; Hd of History, Gresham's Sch., Norfolk, 1986–89; King Edward VI Grammar School, Chelmsford: Sen. Teacher, 1989–90; Dep. Head (Middle Sch.), 1990–92; Dep. Head (Sixth Form), 1992–99; Headmaster, 1999–2008. Member: Leading Edge Prog. Nat. Steering Gp, 2003–05; Forum for Learning and Res. Enquiry in Essex, 2003–05; Evaluation and Knowledge Transfer Wkg Gps, 2003–04; working with DfES Innovations Unit: leading Nat. Heads' Gp, 2004–07; leading Next Practice project on Higher Order Teaching Skills, 2005–06; Mem., Steering Gp, ARIA Project (UK-wide Assessment Reform Gp on evaluation of assessment develt projects), 2006–08. Mem., HMC, 2008. Vice-Pres., Helen Rollason Cancer Care Trust. FRSA 2006. *Recreations:* painting, drawing, tennis, squash, horse-riding, walking, travel. *Address:* Felsted School, Felsted, Essex CM6 3LL. *T:* (01371) 822600, *Fax:* (01371) 822607.

WALKER, Michael John, CBE 2007; District Judge, Wandsworth County Court, since 1994, seconded to Royal Courts of Justice, since 2007; *b* 8 July 1951; *s* of late Albert George Walker and of Joan Walker; *m* 1st, 1974, Jill Sandham (marr. diss. 1980); one *s*; 2nd, 1982, Elaine G. Robinson; two *d. Educ:* Sir John Deane's Grammar Sch., Northwich, Cheshire; Univ. of Kent (BA Hons Law 1972); Law Soc. Finals Hons 1973. Articled clerk, 1973–75, Solicitor, 1975–78, Norton Rose; Solicitor, then Partner, Carpenter & Co., (Solicitors), Wallington, 1979–94. Member: Judges' Council, 2002–; Bd, HM Courts Service, 2008–. Hon. Sec., Assoc. of HM District Judges (formerly Assoc. of Dist Judges), 2000–. Gov., Wallington High Sch. for Girls, 1988–2007. *Publications:* (contrib.) Jordan's Civil Court Service, 3rd edn 2000 to 21st edn 2008; (contrib.) Blackstone's Civil Practice, 5th edn 2004 to 7th edn 2006. *Recreations:* sitting on committees, pottering around in the garden, listening to classical music and, in between times, enjoying food and wine and dreaming of Italy. *Address:* c/o Wandsworth County Court, 76–78 Upper Richmond Road, Putney, SW15 2SU. *T:* (020) 8333 4351.

WALKER, Sir Michael Leolin F.; *see* Forestier-Walker.

WALKER, Hon. Sir Miles Rawstron, Kt 1997; CBE 1991; Chief Minister, Isle of Man, 1986–96; *b* 13 Nov. 1940; *s* of George Denis Walker and Alice (*née* Whittaker); *m* 1966, Mary Lilian Cowell; one *s* one *d. Educ:* Arbory Primary Sch.; Castle Rushen High Sch.; Shropshire Coll. of Agric. Company Dir, farming and retail dairy trade, 1960–. Mem. and Chm., Arbory Parish Comrs, 1970–76; Mem., House of Keys for Rushen, 1976–2001. Hon. LLD Liverpool, 1994. *Address:* Magher Feailley, Main Road, Colby, Isle of Man IM9 4AD. *T:* (01624) 833728.

WALKER, Prof. Neil Craig, PhD; Regius Professor of Public Law and the Law of Nature and Nations, University of Edinburgh, since 2008; *b* 5 July 1960; *s* of William Walker and Catherine Walker; *m* 1993, Gillian Couse; one *s* one *d*, and one *s* from former marriage. *Educ:* Univ. of Strathclyde (LLB 1st cl. 1981; PhD 1991). Lectr in Constitnl Law, 1986–92, Sen. Lectr, 1992–95, Univ. of Edinburgh; Prof. of Legal and Constitnl Theory, Univ. of Aberdeen, 1996–2000; Prof. of Eur. Law, European University Inst., Florence, 2000–08. *Publications:* Managing the Police: law, organisation and democracy, 1986; The Scottish Community Charge, 1989; Policing the European Union, 1996; Policing in a Changing Constitutional Order, 2000; Civilizing Security, 2007; articles and collections on questions of constitnl law and theory. *Recreations:* literature, sport, anything convivial. *Address:* School of Law, University of Edinburgh, Old College, South Bridge, Edinburgh EH8 9YL.

WALKER, Prof. Nigel David, CBE 1979; MA Oxon, PhD Edinburgh, DLitt Oxon; Wolfson Professor of Criminology and Fellow of King's College, Cambridge, 1973–84 (Director, Institute of Criminology, 1973–81); *b* 6 Aug. 1917; *s* of David B. Walker and Violet Walker (*née* Johnson); *m* 1939, Sheila Margaret Johnston; one *d. Educ:* Tientsin Grammar Sch.; Edinburgh Academy; Christ Church, Oxford (Hon. Scholar). Served War, Infantry officer (Camerons and Lovat Scouts), 1940–46. Scottish Office, 1946–61; Gwilym Gibbon Fellow, Nuffield Coll., 1958–59; University Reader in Criminology and Fellow of Nuffield Coll., Oxford, 1961–73. Visiting Professor: Berkeley, 1965; Yale, 1973; Stockholm, 1978; Cape Town, 1984. Chairman: Home Secretary's Adv. Council on Probation and After-care, 1972–76; Study Gp on Legal Training of Social Workers, 1972–73; President: Nat. Assoc. of Probation Officers, 1980–84; British Soc. of Criminology, 1984–87; Member: Home Sec.'s TV Research Cttee, 1963–69; Adv. Council on Penal System, 1969–73; Cttee on Mentally Abnormal Offenders, 1972–75; Working Party on Judicial Training and Information, 1975–78; Floud Cttee on Dangerous Offenders; Hodgson Cttee on Profits of Crime; Parole Bd, 1986–89. Hon. LLD: Leicester, 1976, Edinburgh 1985. Hon. FRCPsych 1987. *Publications:* Delphi, 1936 (Chancellor's Prize Latin Poem); A Short History of Psychotherapy, 1957 (various trans); Morale in the Civil Service, 1961; Crime and Punishment in Britain, 1965; Crime and Insanity in England, 2 vols, 1968 and (jtly) 1972; Sentencing in a Rational Society, 1969 (various trans.); Crimes, Courts and Figures, 1971; Explaining Misbehaviour (inaug. lecture), 1974; Treatment and Justice (Sandoz lecture), 1976; Behaviour and Misbehaviour, 1977; Punishment, Danger and Stigma, 1980; Sentencing Theory Law and Practice, 1985, 2nd edn (jtly) 1997; Crime and Criminology, 1987; (jtly) Public Attitudes to Sentencing, 1988; Why Punish?, 1991; (jtly) Dangerous People, 1996; Aggravation, Mitigation and Mercy, 1999; A Man Without Loyalties, 2003; reports, articles, etc. *Recreation:* chess. *Address:* Flat 32, 5 Oswald Road, Edinburgh EH9 2HE. *T:* (0131) 602 1450. *Club:* Royal Over-Seas League (Edinburgh).

WALKER, (Noel) John; strategic development consultant; Managing Director, John Walker Consultants Ltd, since 1999; *b* 18 Dec. 1948; *s* of Robert and Nora Walker; *m* 1979, Pamela Gordon; two *s. Educ:* Liverpool Univ. (BSc 1970); Trent Polytechnic (DipTP 1972). Planning Officer, Hartlepool BC, 1972–74; Sen. Planner, Cleveland CC, 1974; travelled abroad, 1974–75; Milton Keynes Development Corporation: Employment Planner, 1975–76; Head of Policy Evaluation, 1976–78; Dep. Planning Manager, 1978–79; Planning Manager, 1979–80; Dir of Planning, 1980–87; Dep. Gen. Manager, 1987–92; Chief Exec., Commn for the New Towns, 1992–99; Dir, Competition for future use of Millennium Dome, 1999–2000; Chief Exec., BURA, 2000–02. Chairman: Bucks Manpower Cttee, 1982–83; Milton Keynes IT Exchange, 1983–86; Central Milton Keynes Project Bd, 2003–07; Milton Keynes and S Midlands Funding Gp, 2004–; Eco Towns Challenge Gp, 2008. Founder Mem., Nat. Energy Foundn, 1988– (Trustee, 1999–2005). Dep. Chm., Milton Keynes Housing Assoc., 1986–89; Board Member: Milton Keynes Marketing, 1992–93; Telford Develt Agency, 1992; Peterborough Develt Agency, 1992–94. Trustee: Bletchley Park Trust, 2000–04; Milton Keynes Parks Trust, 2000–; Milton Keynes Theatre and Gallery Co., 2002–. Advr, ODPM, 2002–06; Develt Advr, TCPA, 2003–. FRSA 1997. Hon. DArts De Montfort, 1998. *Recreations:* squash, gardening, travelling. *Address:* Fullers Barn, The Green, Loughton, Milton Keynes MK5 8AW.

WALKER, Sir Patrick (Jeremy), KCB 1990; *b* 25 Feb. 1932; *s* of late Reginald Plumer Walker, sometime Chief Accountant, East African Railways, and Gladys Walker; *m* 1955, Susan Mary Hastings; two *s* one *d. Educ:* King's Sch., Canterbury; Trinity Coll., Oxford (MA). Uganda Admin, 1956–62; Security Service, 1963–92, Dir Gen., 1988–92. Chm., Bd, N Northants Together, 2005–06; Dep. Chm., Bd, N Northants Develt Co., 2007– (Co-Chm., 2006–07). Mem., Iraq Commn, Foreign Policy Centre, 2007. Trustee: Leonard Cheshire Foundn, 1994–2003 (Internat. Chm., 1995–2000; Vice Pres., 2003–); Northants Victoria County Records Trust, 2000–05. Gov., UC Northampton (formerly Nene Coll. of Higher Educn), 1997–2005 (Chm. Govs, 2000–05). Hon. Fellow, Univ. of Northampton, 2006. *Recreations:* music, African history, art. *Clubs:* Oxford and Cambridge, MCC.

WALKER, Paul Ashton; Chief Executive: Sage Group plc, since 1984; Sage Software Ltd; *b* 17 May 1957. *Educ:* Univ. of York (BA). ACA. With Arthur Youngs, 1979–84. Non-exec. Dir, Diageo plc, 2002–. *Address:* Sage Group plc, North Park, Newcastle upon Tyne NE13 9AA.

WALKER, Dr Paul Crawford; Regional Medical Officer, North East Thames Regional Health Authority, 1977–85; Chairman, Transform Drug Policy Foundation, since 2008; *b* 9 Dec. 1940; *s* of Joseph Viccars Walker, KHS, and Mary Tilley (*née* Crawford); *m* 1963, Barbara Georgina Bliss; three *d. Educ:* Queen Elizabeth Grammar Sch., Darlington; Downing Coll., Cambridge (MA); University College Hospital Med. Sch. (MB, BChir); Edinburgh Univ. (DipSocMed); Harvard Bus. Sch. (Program for Health Systems

Management, 1980). FFPH (FFCM 1980). Dep. Medical Officer of Health and Dep. Principal Sch. MO, Wolverhampton County Borough Council, 1972–74; District Community Physician, Staffordshire AHA, 1974–76; Area MO, Wakefield AHA, 1976–77; Dist Gen. Manager, Frenchay HA, 1985–88; Hon. Consultant in Community Medicine, Bristol and Weston HA, 1988–89; Dir of Public Health, Norwich HA, 1989–93; Sen. Lectr in Applied Epidemiology, Univ. of Wales Coll. of Medicine, 1993–94; Dir of Public Health, Powys and Ceredigion Health Bds, 2003–05. Hon. Sen. Lectr, Dept of Community Medicine, LSHTM, 1983–85; Co-Dir, Centre for Health Policy Res., UEA, 1990–93; Vis. Prof., QMC, London Univ., 1985; Visiting Fellow: UWE, 1999–; Univ. of Glamorgan, 2004–. Governor, Moorfields Eye Hosp., 1981–82; Vice-Chm., Professional Adv. Gp, NHS Trng Authy, 1986–88; Member: Bd of Management, LSHTM, 1983–85; Adv. Council on Drug Misuse, 1983–87; Exec. Cttee, Greater London Alcohol Adv. Service, 1978–85; NHS Computer Policy Cttee, 1984–85; Editl Bd, Jl of Management in Medicine, 1985–; Norwich HA, 1989–93; Frenchay Mental Handicap Trust, 1986–88; Frenchay Mental Health Trust, 1986–88; Norwich and Norfolk Care Trust, 1991–; Frenchay Community Care Trust, 1994–97; Peckham Pioneer Health Centre Ltd, 1994–96; Powys Local Health Alliance, 1999–2002; Ceredigion Local Health Gp, 2001–03. Chm., Welsh Food Alliance, 1998–; Director: S Bristol Advice Services, 1998–2000; Bristol Health Co-op., 1999–2000. Pres., Socialist Health Assoc., 2003–; Sec., Public Health Assoc. Cymru, 1998–2004 (Chm., 2004–). Trustee, UK Public Health Assoc., 2006–. Mem. (Lab), Bristol CC, 1995–99; Member: Avon and Som Police Authy, 1998–99; Avon Probation Cttee, 1997–99. JP Epping and Ongar, 1980–85. Captain, RAMC (V). *Publications:* Healthy Norfolk People, 1990; (ed) Helping People with Disabilities in East Anglia, 1991; contribs to medical and health service jls. *Recreations:* music, natural history, railway history. *Address:* Chagford, 8 Church Avenue, Sneyd Park, Bristol BS9 1LD; *e-mail:* paulcrawfordwalker@googlemail.com.

WALKER, Hon. Sir Paul (James), Kt 2004; **Hon. Mr Justice Walker;** a Judge of the High Court of Justice, Queen's Bench Division, since 2004; *b* Wellington, NZ, 1954; *s* of James Edgar Walker and Dawne Walker (*née* McGowan); *m* 1988, Josephine Andrews; one *d*. *Educ:* St Peter's Coll., Adelaide; Magdalen Coll., Oxford (BA Law, BCL). Called to the Bar, Gray's Inn, 1979, Bencher, 2005; barrister in private practice, 1980–2004; QC 1999. Sen. Lectr in Law, Victoria Univ. of Wellington, 1994–96; Dir, NZ Inst. Public Law, 1996. Counsel to BSE Inquiry, 1998–2000. Mem. Adv. Bd, British Inst. of Internat. and Comparative Law, 2001–. Fellow: Arbitrators and Mediators Inst., NZ, 1994; Soc. for Advanced Legal Studies, 1998. *Publications:* (ed with S. Rogers) Studies in Insurance Law, 1996; (ed jtly) Commercial Regulation and Judicial Review, 1998; (ed jtly) Judicial Review, 3rd edn 2005. *Address:* Royal Courts of Justice, Strand, WC2A 2LL.

WALKER, Pauline Ann, (Mrs D. D. Walker); *see* Oliver, P. A.

WALKER, Rt Rev. Peter Knight, MA, DD; Bishop of Ely, 1977–89; an Hon. Assistant Bishop, diocese of Oxford, 1989–95; *b* 6 Dec. 1919; *s* of late George Walker and Eva Muriel (*née* Knight); *m* 1973, Mary Jean, JP 1976, *yr d* of late Lt-Col J. A. Ferguson, OBE. *Educ:* Leeds Grammar Sch. (Schol.); The Queen's Coll., Oxford (Hastings schol.; Cl. 2 Classical Hon. Mods. 1940, Cl. 1 Lit. Hum. 1947; MA Oxon 1947; Hon. Fellow, 1981); Westcott House, Cambridge; MA Cantab by incorporation, 1958. Served in RN (Lieut, RNVR, Atlantic, Indian Ocean, Mediterranean), 1940–45. Asst Master: King's Sch., Peterborough, 1947–50; Merchant Taylors' Sch., 1950–56. Ordained, 1954; Curate of Hemel Hempstead, 1956–58; Fellow, Dean of Chapel and Lectr in Theology, Corpus Christi Coll., Cambridge, 1958–62 (Asst Tutor, 1959–62), Hon. Fellow, 1978; Principal of Westcott House, Cambridge, 1962–72; Commissary to Bishop of Delhi, 1962–66; Hon. Canon of Ely Cathedral, 1966–72; Bishop Suffragan of Dorchester, and Canon of Christ Church, Oxford, 1972–77. Entered H of L, 1984. Select Preacher: Univ. of Cambridge, 1962, 1967 (Hulsean), 1986; Univ. of Oxford, 1975, 1980, 1990, 1996; Examining Chaplain to Bishop of Portsmouth, 1962–72. Chm., Hosp. Chaplaincies Council, 1982–86. Pres., British Sect., Internat. Bonhoeffer Soc., 1987–96. A Governor, St Edward's Sch., Oxford, 1975–96. Hon. Fellow: St John's Coll., Cambridge, 1989; St Edmund's Coll., Cambridge, 1989. Hon. DD Cantab, 1978. *Publications:* The Anglican Church Today: rediscovering the middle way, 1988; contrib. to: Classical Quarterly; Theology, etc. *Address:* 19 St Mark's Court, Barton Road, Cambridge CB3 9LE. *T:* (01223) 363041. *Club:* Cambridge County.

WALKER, Philip Andrew Geoffrey; Editor, Daily Star, 1994–98; *b* 28 July 1944; *m* 1st, 1965, Stella Kaspar; one *s* three *d*; 2nd, 1987, Sharon Ring. *Educ:* Howardian High Sch., Cardiff. South Wales Echo, 1962–64; Daily Sketch, 1964–65; Evening Post, Reading, 1966–68; Daily Mail, 1968–69; Asst Editor, Daily Mirror, 1969–80; Associate Editor, Daily Express, 1980–83; Dep. Editor, Daily Mirror, 1983–88; freelance journalist, 1988–90; Dep. Editor, Daily Star, 1990–94. *Recreation:* natural history.

WALKER, His Honour Philip Henry Conyers, (Harry); a Circuit Judge, 1979–99; *b* 22 Dec. 1926; *o c* of Philip Howard and Kathleen Walker; *m* 1953, Mary Elizabeth Ross; two *s* two *d*. *Educ:* Marlborough; Oriel Coll., Oxford. MA, BCL (Oxon); DipTh (London). Army (6 AB Sigs), 1944–48 (despatches, 1948). Solicitor in private practice, 1954–79; Dep. Coroner for Craven, 1965–74; a Recorder of the Crown Court, 1972–79. Mem., Church Assembly, Nat. Synod of C of E, 1960–80; Reader, C of E, 1965–. Chm., Agricultural Land Tribunal (Yorks & Lancs), 1977–79; Dep. Chm., Agricultural Land Tribunal (Western), 1989–99; Mem., Criminal Law Revision Cttee, 1981–. *Recreations:* fishing, shooting, sailing, walking. *Address:* Pond House, Askwith, Otley, West Yorks LS21 2JN. *T:* (01943) 463196.

WALKER, Dr Ranginui Joseph Isaac, DCNZM 2001; PhD; Professor of Maori Studies and Head of Department, Auckland University, 1993–97, now Professor Emeritus; Amorangi (Executive), Manukau Institute of Technology, 2000–03; *b* 1 March 1932; *s* of Isaac Walker and Wairata Walker; *m* 1953, Deirdre Patricia Dodson; two *s* one *d*. *Educ:* Univ. of Auckland (PhD Anthropol. 1970). Asst teacher (primary), 1953–62; Lectr, Auckland Teachers' Coll., 1962–66; Auckland University: Asst Lectr, 1967–69; Lectr (Contg Educn), 1970–85; Associate Prof., 1986–93; Pro Vice-Chancellor (Maori), 1996–97. Mem., Treaty of Waitangi Tribunal, 2004–. Elsdon Best Meml Medal, Jl of Polynesian Soc., 1997. *Publications:* Years of Anger, 1987; Struggle Without End, 1990, rev. edn 2004; The Walker Papers, 1996; He Tipua: a biography of Sir Apirana Ngata, 2001; Opotiki-Mai Tawhiti, Capital of Whakatohea, 2007; Tohunga Whakairo: a biography of Pakaariki Harrison, 2008. *Recreations:* reading, boating, fishing, diving, skiing.

WALKER, Raymond Augustus; QC 1988; a Recorder, since 1993; *b* 26 Aug. 1943; *s* of Air Chief Marshal Sir Augustus Walker, GCB, CBE, DSO, DFC, AFC and Lady Walker; *m* 1976, June Rose Tunesi; one *s*. *Educ:* Radley; Trinity Hall, Cambridge (MA). Called to the Bar, Middle Temple, 1966. *Recreations:* golf, tennis, ski-ing, sailing, opera. *Address:* Lombard Chambers, 1 Sekforde Street, Clerkenwell, EC1R 0BE. *T:* (020) 7107 2100. *Clubs:* Garrick; Royal West Norfolk Golf, Sunningdale Golf.

WALKER, Raymond James, OBE 1991; Special Adviser on International Electronic Data Interchange to Department of Trade and Industry, 1996; *b* 13 April 1943; *s* of Cyril James Walker and Louie Walker; *m* 1969, Mary Eastwood Whittaker (marr. diss. 1995); one *d*; *m* 1996, Anne Troye. *Educ:* St Audreys', Hatfield; University of Lancaster. BA (Hons). Personnel Director, Saracen Ltd, 1971–73; Jt Man. Dir, Carrington Viyella Exports Ltd, 1973–78; Export Dir, Carrington Viyella Home Furnishings (DORMA), 1978–83; Chief Exec., SITPRO, 1983–96. Co-Chm., Jt Electronic Data Interchange Cttee, UN Econ. Commn for Europe, 1985–87; Rapporteur for Western Europe, UN-Electronic Data Interchange for Admin, Commerce and Transport, 1987–. Amer. Nat. Standards Inst. Award, 1986; Electronic Data Interchange Award, Internat. Data Exchange Assoc., 1988. *Recreations:* collecting wine labels, a fascination for maps, growing clematis. *T:* (office) (020) 8318 7616. *Clubs:* Royal Automobile; Belle Toute (Lancaster).

WALKER, His Honour Richard; a Circuit Judge, 1989–2006; *b* 9 March 1942; *s* of Edwin Roland Walker and Barbara Joan (*née* Swann); *m* 1969, Angela Joan Hodgkinson; two *d*. *Educ:* Epsom Coll.; Worcester Coll., Oxford (MA). Called to the Bar, Inner Temple, 1966; in practise at the Bar, 1966–89; Asst Boundary Comr, 1979–88; a Recorder, 1989. Judicial Mem., Mental Health Review Tribunal, 1991–2005. Commissary Gen., City and Dio. of Canterbury, 1995–. *Publication:* (ed jtly) Carter-Ruck on Libel and Slander, 3rd edn 1985, 4th edn 1992. *Address:* c/o Brick Court, Temple, EC4Y 9BY. *T:* (020) 7353 8845.

WALKER, Richard Alwyne F.; *see* Fyjis-Walker.

WALKER, Richard John Boileau, CVO 2000; MA; FSA; picture cataloguer; *b* 4 June 1916; *s* of Comdr Kenneth Walker and Caroline Livingstone-Learmonth; *m* 1946, Margaret, *d* of Brig. Roy Firebrace, CBE; one *s* two *d*. *Educ:* Harrow; Magdalene Coll., Cambridge (MA); Courtauld Institute of Art. Active service, RNVR, 1939–45. British Council, 1946; Tate Gallery, 1947–48; Min. of Works Picture Adviser, 1949–76; Curator of the Palace of Westminster, 1950–76; Nat. Portrait Gallery Cataloguer, 1976–85; Royal Collection Cataloguer, 1985–91; Nat. Trust Cataloguer, 1990–2001. Trustee: Nat. Maritime Museum, 1977–84; Army Museums Ogilby Trust, 1979–90. *Publications:* Catalogue of Pictures at Audley End, 1950 and 1973; Old Westminster Bridge, 1979; Regency Portraits, 1985; Palace of Westminster: a catalogue, 4 vols, 1988; Royal Collection: the 18th century miniatures, 1992; Miniatures in the Ashmolean Museum, 1997; The Nelson Portraits, 1998 (Anderson Prize, Soc. for Nautical Res.); (with Hugh Tait) The Athenæum Collection, 2000; (with Alastair Laing) Miniatures in National Trust Houses, vol. 1, 2003, vol. 2, 2005. *Recreation:* looking at pictures. *Address:* Green Ash, Chagford, Newton Abbot, Devon TQ13 8EJ. *Clubs:* Athenæum, Oxford and Cambridge.

WALKER, Robert M.; Chairman: WH Smith plc, since 2005; BCA Europe Ltd, since 2007; *b* 3 Feb. 1945; *s* of Arthur Norman Walker and Nancy (*née* Waugh); *m* 1970, Patricia Douglass; one *s* one *d*. *Educ:* Hampton Sch.; Magdalen Coll., Oxford (BA Hons Modern History 1966). Brand Manager, Procter & Gamble Ltd, 1966–70; Engagement Manager, McKinsey & Co. Inc., 1970–76; Div. Pres., PepsiCo Inc., 1976–99; Gp Chief Exec., Severn Trent plc, 2000–05 (non-exec. Dir, 1996–99). Chm., Williams Lea Group Ltd, 2005–06. Non-executive Director: Thomson Travel Gp plc, 1998–2000; Wolseley plc, 1999–2007; Signet Gp plc, 2004–; BAA plc, 2004–05; Tate & Lyle plc, 2006–; Williams Lea Hldgs Plc, 2006–. Advr, Cinven, 2005–07. Gov., Hampton Sch., 2007–. *Club:* Oxford and Cambridge.

WALKER, Sir Rodney (Myerscough), Kt 1996; Chairman: SMC Gp plc, since 2004; Goals Soccer Centres, since 2002; Spice Holdings plc, since 2002; World Snooker Ltd, since 2003; *b* 10 April 1943; *s* of Norman and Lucy Walker; *m* 1974, Anne Margaret Aspinall; two *s*. *Educ:* Thornes House Grammar Sch. CEng. Founder Chm., Myerscough Holdings, 1976; activities incl. civil engrg, motor retail, and develt. Chairman: W Yorks Broadcasting, 1986–2002; Brands Hatch Leisure plc, 1996–99; Leicester City plc, 1997–2002 (now Hon. Life Pres.). Chairman: Rugby Football League, 1993–2002; Sports Council of GB, 1994–96; English Sports Council, 1996–98; UK Sports Council, 1998–2003. Mem., Wakefield HA, 1982–90; Chairman: Bradford Hosps NHS Trust, 1990–96; NHS Trust Fedn, 1993–95 (Pres., 1995–97). Chm., Wakefield Theatre Trust, 1981–99, now Hon. Life Pres.; Vice Chm., Yorks Sculpture Park, 1984–. Trustee: Nat. Mining Mus. for England, 1993–; English Nat. Stadium Trust, 1998–; Chm., Wembley Nat. Stadium Ltd, 2000–02. FInstD; FRSA. KLJ 1997. *Recreations:* golf, theatre, travel. *Address:* Tower House, Bond Street, Wakefield WF1 2QP. *T:* (01924) 374349; Pine Lodge, Home Farm, Woolley, Wakefield WF4 2JS. *T:* (01226) 384089.

WALKER, Comdr Roger Antony Martineau-, LVO 1994; RN; Clerk to Trustees, and Chief Executive, United Westminster Almshouses Foundation, 1997–2007; *b* 15 Oct. 1940; *s* of Antony Philip Martineau-Walker and Sheila Hazeal Mayoh Wilson; *m* Inger Lene Brag-Nielsen; two *s*. *Educ:* Haileybury and Imperial Service College, Hertford; BRNC Dartmouth. Commissioned RN, 1962; served Malta, Singapore and Sarawak, 1962–65; Torpedo and Antisubmarine Course, HMS Vernon, 1968; HMS Galatea, 1973–76; NDC Latimer, 1977–78; Naval and Defence Staff, MoD, 1978–83; Naval Manpower Planning, with special responsibility for introd. of longer career for ratings (2nd Open Engagement), 1983–85; operational staff (UK commitments), 1985–87; Head, Naval Sec's Policy Staff, 1987–90; Pvte Sec. to Duke and Duchess of Kent, 1990–93. Trustee, St Giles in-the-Fields United Charity, 2008–. Bursar, Royal Sch. for Daughters of the Army, 1995–96. Foundn Gov., Burdett Coutts and Townshend C of E Primary Sch., 1998–2002 (Trustee, 2004–). *Recreations:* fishing, photography, music. *Address:* 13 The Peak, Rowlands Castle, Hants PO9 6AH. *Club:* Army and Navy.

WALKER, Ronald Jack; QC 1983; a Recorder, since 1986; *b* 24 June 1940; *s* of Jack Harris Walker and Ann Frances Walker; *m* 1st, 1964, Caroline Fox (marr. diss. 1997); two *s*; 2nd, 1999, Clare Oonagh Jane Devitt; one *s* one *d*. *Educ:* Owen's School, London; University College London. LLB (Hons). Called to the Bar, Gray's Inn, 1962, Bencher, 1993. Mem. Gen. Council of the Bar, 1993–96 (Chm. Professional Conduct Cttee, 1993–94). Mem., Mental Health Review Tribunal, 2000–. *Publications:* English Legal System (with M. G. Walker), 1967, 7th edn 1994; contributing ed., Bullen & Leake & Jacob's Precedents of Pleadings, 13th edn 1990; (ed) Butterworths Professional Negligence Service, 1999. *Address:* 12 King's Bench Walk, Temple, EC4Y 7EL. *T:* (020) 7583 0811.

WALKER, Roy; *see* Walker, C. R.

WALKER, Sir Roy Edward, 6th Bt *cr* 1906, of Pembroke House, City of Dublin; *b* 10 Aug. 1977; *yr s* of Major Sir Hugh Ronald Walker, 4th Bt and of Norma Walker (*née* Baird); *S* brother, 2006, but his name does not appear on the Official Roll of the Baronetage.

WALKER, Sarah Elizabeth Royle, (Mrs R. G. Allum), CBE 1991; mezzo-soprano; *d* of Elizabeth Brownrigg and Alan Royle Walker; *m* 1972, Graham Allum. *Educ:* Pate's Grammar School for Girls, Cheltenham; Royal College of Music. FRCM 1987; LRAM. Prince Consort Prof. of Singing, RCM, 1993–; vocal performance consultant, GSMD,

1999–. Pres., Cheltenham Bach Choir, 1986–. Major appearances at concerts and in recital in Britain, America, Australia, New Zealand, Europe; operatic débuts include: Coronation of Poppea, Kent Opera, 1969, San Francisco Opera, 1981; La Calisto, Glyndebourne, 1970; Les Troyens, Scottish Opera, 1972, Wien Staatsoper, 1980; Principal Mezzo Soprano, ENO, 1972–77; Die Meistersinger, Chicago Lyric Opera, 1977; Werther, Covent Garden, 1979; Giulio Cesare, Le Grand Théâtre, Genève, 1983; Capriccio, Brussels, 1983; Teseo, Sienna, 1985; Samson, NY Metropolitan Opera, 1986; numerous recordings and video recordings, incl. title rôle in Britten's Gloriana. FGSM 2000. *Recreations:* interior design, encouraging her husband with the gardening. *Address:* Cheffings, Witheridge, Devon EX16 8QD. *T:* (01884) 860132; *e-mail:* megamezzo@sarahwalker.com. *Club:* University Women's.

WALKER, Simon Edward John; Chief Executive, British Private Equity and Venture Capital Association, since 2007; *b* 28 May 1953; *s* of Louis Charles Vivian Walker and Joan Wallace Walker (*née* Keith); *m* 1980, Mary Virginia Strang; one *s* one *d*. *Educ:* South African Coll. Sch.; Balliol Coll., Oxford (BA PPE; Pres., Oxford Union, 1974; MA 1978). Personal Asst to Lord Sainsbury, 1974–75; reporter, TV NZ, Wellington, 1975–79; Knight Journalism Fellow, Stanford Univ., 1979–80; Communications Dir, NZ Labour Party, 1980–84; Director: Communicor Govt and PR, 1984–87; NZ Centre for Independent Studies, Auckland, 1987–89; Eur. Public Affairs, Hill & Knowlton PR, London, 1989–90; Man. Dir, Hill & Knowlton, Belgium, 1990–94; Partner, Brunswick PR, 1994–98 (on secondment to Policy Unit, 10 Downing St, 1996–97); Dir of Communications, British Airways, 1998–2000; Communications Sec. to the Queen, 2000–02; Dir of Corporate Mktg and Communications, Reuters, 2003–07. Non-exec. Dir, Comair Ltd (SA), 2000–01. Mem., Better Regulation Commn, 2006–08. Trustee, NZ-UK Link Foundn, 2003–. *Publication:* Rogernomics: reshaping New Zealand's economy, 1989. *Recreations:* family, reading, music, travel. *Address:* 86 Brook Green, W6 7BD. *T:* (020) 7602 3883; *e-mail:* swalker@bvca.co.uk. *Club:* Athenæum.

WALKER, Stuart; *see* Walker, B. S.

WALKER, Susannah Mary; a District Judge, Principal Registry, Family Division, since 2006; *b* 6 Aug. 1948; *d* of Ronald Jack Marsh and Mary Marsh; *m* 1973, Robert Adrian Walker; one *s* one *d*. *Educ:* Univ. of Birmingham (BSocSc 1969; DipSW 1971); City Univ., London (Dip Law 1984). Social worker, 1971–80; called to the Bar, Inner Temple, 1985; an Immigration Judge, 2003–06. Mem., Mental Health Rev. Tribunal, 1996–. *Address:* Principal Registry, Family Division, First Avenue House, 42–49 High Holborn, WC1V 6NP.

WALKER, Terence William, (Terry Walker); *b* 26 Oct. 1935; *s* of William Edwin and Lilian Grace Walker; *m* 1959, Priscilla Dart (marr. diss. 1983); two *s* one *d*; *m* 1983, Rosalie Fripp. *Educ:* Grammar Sch. and Coll. of Further Educn, Bristol. Employed by Courage (Western) Ltd at Bristol for 23 yrs, Mem. Chief Accountant's Dept. MP (Lab) Kingswood, Feb. 1974–1979; Second Church Estates Comr, 1974–79. Contested (Lab): Kingswood, 1983; Bristol NW, 1987. Member: Avon CC, 1981–96 (Vice-Chm., 1992–93; Chm., 1993–94), S Glos Unitary Council, 1996– (Dep. Leader Labour Gp); Chm., Avon Combined Fire Authy, 1996–. *Recreations:* cricket, football. *Address:* 43 The Furlong, Bristol BS6 7TF. *T:* (01454) 864058.

WALKER, Dr (Thomas) Gordon, OBE 2000; FInstP; Chief Executive, Council for the Central Laboratory of Research Councils, 2000–01; retired; *b* 4 Nov. 1936; *s* of James Smart Walker and Mary Margaret McIntosh Walker; *m* 1960, Una May Graham Stevenson; one *s* one *d*. *Educ:* Uddingston Grammar Sch.; Univ. of Glasgow (BSc, PhD). Rutherford High Energy Laboratory, National Institute for Research in Nuclear Science, later Rutherford Appleton Laboratory, Science and Engineering Research Council: Res. Physicist, 1960–71; Gp Leader, 1971–80; Head: Instrumentation Div., 1980–83; Technology Div., 1983–87; Dep. Dir, 1987–94; Head, 1994–96; Dir, R&D, CCLRC, 1996–2000. Mem., Renewable Energy Adv. Cttee, DTI, 1980–2000. Chief Sci. Advr (Civil Defence), Oxfordshire CC, 1983–93. Chm., Mgt Cttee, Didcot CAB, 1991–97; Pres., Didcot Rotary Club, 1977–78. Chm., Harwell Parish Council, 1988–91. *Publications:* papers in sci. jls on experimental particle physics. *Recreations:* golf, gardening. *Address:* 6 Brookside, Harwell, Didcot OX11 0HG. *T:* (01235) 835418. *Club:* Frilford Heath Golf.

WALKER, Ven. Thomas Overington; Archdeacon of Nottingham, 1991–96, now Emeritus; *b* 7 Dec. 1933; *m* 1957, Molly Anne Gilmour; one *s* two *d*. *Educ:* Keble Coll., Oxford (BA 1958; MA 1961); Oak Hill Theol Coll. Ordained 1960. Curate: St Paul, Woking, dio. of Guildford, 1960–62; St Leon, St Leonards, dio. of Chichester, 1962–64; Travelling Sec., Inter-Varsity Fellowship, 1964–67; Succentor, Birmingham Cathedral, 1967–70; Vicar, Harborne Heath, 1970–91; Priest-in-charge, St Germain, Edgbaston, 1983–91; Rural Dean, Edgbaston, 1989–91; Hon. Canon, Birmingham Cathedral, 1980–91. Proctor in Convocation, 1985–92. *Publications:* Renew Us By Your Spirit, 1982; The Occult Web, 1987, 3rd edn 1989; From Here to Heaven, 1987; Small Streams Big Rivers, 1991. *Recreations:* sport, music, reading, dry stone walling. *Address:* 6 Cornbrook, Clee Hill, Ludlow, Shropshire SY8 3QQ. *T:* (01584) 890176.

WALKER, Prof. Thomas William, ONZM 2000; ARCS; DSc; DIC; Professor of Soil Science, Lincoln College, New Zealand, 1961–79, now Emeritus; *b* 22 July 1916; *m* 1940, Edith Edna Bott; four *d*. *Educ:* Loughborough Grammar School; Royal College of Science. Royal Scholar and Kitchener Scholar, 1935–39; Salter's Fellow, 1939–41; Lecturer and Adviser in Agricultural Chemistry, Univ. of Manchester, 1941–46. Provincial Advisory Soil Chemist, NAAS, 1946–51; Prof. of Soil Science, Canterbury Agric. Coll., New Zealand, 1952–58; Prof. of Agric., King's Coll., Newcastle upon Tyne, 1958–61. Bledisloe Medal, Lincoln Univ., 1997; Gold (now Rutherford) Medal, Royal Soc. of NZ, 1998; Inaugural Jubilee Medal, NZ Inst. Agricl Sci., 2003. *Publications:* Vegetable Growers Handbook for New Zealanders, 1992; numerous research. *Recreations:* fishing, gardening. *Address:* 843 Cashmere Road, Christchurch 3, New Zealand.

WALKER, Hon. Sir Timothy (Edward), Kt 1996; a Judge of the High Court of Justice, Queen's Bench Division, and a Judge of the Commercial Court, 1996–2002; *b* 13 May 1946; *s* of George Edward Walker, solicitor, and Muriel Edith Walker; *m* 1968, Mary (*née* Tyndall); two *d*. *Educ:* Harrow Sch. (Totland Entrance Schol.; Clayton Leaving Schol.); University Coll., Oxford (Plumptre Schol., 1965; 1st Cl. Hons Jurisprudence, 1967; MA). Asst Lectr in Law, King's Coll., London, 1967–68; Profumo Schol., Inner Temple, 1968; Eldon Law schol., 1969; called to the Bar, Inner Temple, 1968, Bencher, 1996; QC 1985; a Recorder of the Crown Court, 1986–96. *Address:* c/o Royal Courts of Justice, Strand, WC2A 2LL.

WALKER, Timothy Edward Hanson, CB 1998; Third Church Estates Commissioner, since 2006; *b* 27 July 1945; *s* of late Harris and Elizabeth Walker; *m* 1st, 1969, Judith Mann (*d* 1976); one *d*; 2nd, 1983, Hon. Anna Butterworth (*see* Hon. A. E. B. Walker); two *d*. *Educ:* Tonbridge Sch.; Brasenose Coll., Oxford (BA Chemistry, 1967; MA, DPhil 1969). Weir Jun. Res. Fellow, University Coll., Oxford, and Exhibnr of Royal Commn of 1851, Oxford and Paris, 1969; Harkness Fellow, Commonwealth Fund of New York, 1971, Univ. of Virginia, 1971 and Northwestern Univ., 1972; Strategic Planner, GLC, 1974; Principal, Dept of Trade, 1977; Sloan Fellow, London Business Sch., 1983; Department of Trade and Industry: Asst Sec., 1983; Dir (Admin), Alvey Programme, 1983; Head, Policy Planning Unit, 1985; Principal Private Sec. to successive Secs of State for Trade and Industry, 1986; Under Sec., 1987; Dir, Inf. Engrg Directorate, 1987; Head, Atomic Energy Div., Dept of Energy, then DTI, 1989–95; Dep. Sec., 1995, and Dir Gen., Immigration and Nationality Directorate, 1995–98, Home Office; Comr and Dep. Chm., HM Customs and Excise, 1998–2000; Dir-Gen., HSE, 2000–05. Non-exec. Dir, London Strategic Health Authy, 2006–. UK Gov., IAEA, 1989–94; non-exec. Dir, Govt Div., UKAEA, 1994–95. Chm., Assembly of Donors, Nuclear Safety Account, EBRD, 1993–95. Chm., Accountancy and Actuarial Discipline Bd, 2008–; Exec. Dir, Financial Reporting Council, 2008–. Non-exec. Dir, ICI Chemicals and Polymers Ltd, 1988–89. Governor, St Anne's Sch., Wandsworth, 1977–82; Council Member: Warwick Univ., 2000–06; Inst. of Employment Studies, 2001–05. Trustee: Prostate Cancer Charity, 2006–; Lambeth Palace Library, 2007–; De Morgan Foundation, 2007–; Chm., Arts and Crafts Museum, 2008–. CEng, FIET, FInstP 2003. FRSA 2000; CCMI 2002. Hon. Fellow, Warwick Manufacturing Gp, 2006–. Hon. DSc Cranfield, 2003. *Publications:* contribs to scientific jls. *Recreations:* cookery, travel, African tribal art. *Address:* Church Commissioners for England, Church House, Great Smith Street, SW1P 3AZ.

WALKER, Sir Victor (Stewart Heron), 6th Bt *cr* 1868, of Sand Hutton, York and Beachampton, Bucks; *b* 8 Oct. 1942; *s* of Sir James Heron Walker, 5th Bt and Angela Margaret (*née* Beaufort); *S* father, 2003; *m* 1st, 1969, Caroline Louisa (marr. diss. 1982), *d* of Lt-Col F. E. B. Wignall; two *s* one *d*; 2nd, 1982, Svea, *o d* of Captain Ernst Hugo Gothard Knutson Borg. *Educ:* Eton. 2nd Lt Grenadier Guards, 1962–65; Lt Royal Wilts Yeo., 1965–73. Mem., RYS. *Heir: s* James Frederick Heron Walker, *b* 14 Feb. 1970.

WALKER, Victoria Patricia Ann, (Mrs F. A. Woods Walker); *see* Woods, V. P. A.

WALKER, William Connoll, (Bill), OBE 1998; FIPM; Chairman, Walker Associates, since 1975; *b* 20 Feb. 1929; *s* of Charles and Williamina Walker; *m* 1956, Mavis Evelyn Lambert; three *d*. *Educ:* Logie Sch., Dundee; Trades Coll., Dundee; College for Distributive Trades. FIPM 1968. Message boy, 1943–44; office boy, 1944–46; commissioned RAF, 1946–49; Sqdn Leader, RAFVR, 1949–; salesman, public service vehicle driver, general manager, 1949–59; RAF, 1959–65; training and education officer, furnishing industry, 1965–67; company director, 1967–79; pt-time presenter, TV progs, 1969–75. MP (C) Perth and E Perthshire, 1979–83, Tayside N, 1983–97; contested (C) Tayside N, 1997. Director: Stagecoach Malaŵi, 1989–94; Stagecoach Internat. Services, 1989–94; Chm., Aerotech Marketing, 1995–2002. Dep. Chm., and Mem., UK Party Bd, Scottish Cons. Party, 2000–02. Chm., Scotland and NI Air Cadet Council, 1997–; Vice Pres., British Gliding Assoc., 1992–; Hon. Pres., Air Cadet Gliding, 1994–. FRSA 1970; FCMI. *Recreations:* RAFVR, gliding, caravanning, walking, youth work. *Address:* Longacres, Burrelton, Perthshire PH13 9NY. *T:* (01828) 670407. *Club:* Royal Air Force.

WALKER, William MacLelland; QC (Scot.) 1971; Social Security Commissioner, 1988–2003; a Child Support Commissioner, 1993–2003; *b* 19 May 1933; *s* of late Hon. Lord Walker; *m* 1957, Joan Margaret (*d* 2006), *d* of late Charles Hutchison Wood, headmaster, Dundee; one *d*. *Educ:* Edinburgh Academy; Edinburgh Univ. (MA, LLB). Advocate, 1957; Flying Officer, RAF, 1957–59; Standing Junior Counsel: Min. of Aviation, 1963–68; BoT (Aviation), 1968–71; Min. of Technology, 1968–70; Dept of Trade and Industry (Power), 1971; Min. of Aviation Supply, 1971. Hon. Sheriff, various Sheriffdoms, 1963–71. Chairman: Industrial Tribunals in Scotland, 1972–88; VAT Tribunals, 1985–88. *Recreations:* shooting, travel, photography. *Clubs:* Royal Air Force; New (Edinburgh).

WALKER-ARNOTT, Edward Ian; Consultant, Herbert Smith, since 2000 (Senior Partner, 1992–2000); *b* 18 Sept. 1939; *s* of late Charles Douglas Walker-Arnott and Kathleen Margaret (*née* Brittain); *m* 1971, (Phyllis) Jane Ricketts; one *s* two *d*. *Educ:* Haileybury Coll.; London Univ. (LLB ext.); University Coll. London (LLM; Fellow, 1999; Vis. Prof., 2000–). Admitted solicitor, 1963; Partner, Herbert Smith, 1968–2000. Dir, Sturge Hldgs, 1989–95. Member: Cork Cttee on Review of Insolvency Law, 1977–82; Insolvency Practitioners Tribunal, 1987–. Mem. Council of Lloyds, 1983–88. Mem., Regulation of Investigatory Powers, Guernsey Tribunal, 2006–. Mem. Bd, RNT, 2000–08. Governor: S Bank Bd, 1999–; The Wellcome Trust, 2000–. Member, Governing Body: Haileybury Coll., 1969–98; Benenden Sch., 1987–93. Author, report for Arts Council of England on relationship with Royal Opera House, Covent Garden (Walker-Arnott Report), 1997. *Recreations:* reading, gardening, watching sport. *Address:* Manuden Hall, Manuden, near Bishop's Stortford, Herts CM23 1DY. *Club:* City of London.

WALKER-HAWORTH, John Leigh; Chairman, GB Group plc, since 2002; *b* 25 Oct. 1944; *s* of William and Julia Walker-Haworth; *m* 1976, Caroline Mary Blair Purves; two *s*. *Educ:* Charterhouse; Pembroke College, Oxford. Called to the Bar, Inner Temple, 1967. Dir, 1981–93, Vice Chm., 1993–95, S. G. Warburg & Co.; Man. Dir, 1995–97, Advr, 1997–2000, UBS Warburg; Man. Dir, Integrated Finance Ltd, 2005–07. Chm., Merrill Lynch Greater Europe Investment Trust plc, 2004– (non-exec. Dir, Merrill Lynch European Investment Trust plc, 2000–04). Dep. Chm., Takeover Panel, 1997–2006 (Dir-Gen., City Panel on Takeovers and Mergers, 1985–87). Gov., Sutton's Hosp., Charterhouse, 1997–2003; Mem., Governing Body, Charterhouse, 2000– (Chm., 2004–). *Address:* 7 Chancellor House, Hyde Park Gate, SW7 5DQ.

WALKER-OKEOVER, Sir Andrew Peter Monro, 5th Bt *cr* 1886, of Gateacre Grange, co. Lancaster and Osmaston Manor, co. Derby; *b* 22 May 1978; *s* of Sir Peter Ralph Leopold Walker-Okeover, 4th Bt and of Catherine Mary Maule (*née* Ramsay); *S* father, 2003. *Heir: b* Patrick Ralph Walker-Okeover, *b* 6 May 1982. *Address:* Okeover Hall, Ashbourne, Derbyshire DE6 2DE.

WALKER-SMITH, Sir (John) Jonah, 2nd Bt *cr* 1960, of Broxbourne, Co. Herts; a Recorder of the Crown Court, 1980–2005; *b* 6 Sept. 1939; *s* of Baron Broxbourne (Life Peer), QC, TD and Dorothy (*d* 1999), *d* of late L. J. W. Etherton; *S* to baronetcy of father, 1992; *m* 1974, Aileen Marie Smith; one *s* one *d*. *Educ:* Westminster School; Christ Church, Oxford. Called to Bar, Middle Temple, 1963. Mem., Westminster CC, 1968–86 (Chm. of Social Services, Housing and Finance Cttees). *Heir: s* Daniel Derek Walker-Smith, *b* 26 March 1980. *Club:* Garrick.

WALKINE, Herbert Cleveland, CMG 1990; CVO 1994; OBE 1985; Secretary to the Cabinet, Bahamas, 1987–94; *b* 28 Nov. 1929; *s* of late Herbert Granville Walkine and Rebecca Walkine; *m* 1966, Julliette Pam Maria Sherman; three *d*. *Educ:* Government High Sch., Nassau; Bahamas Teachers' Coll.; Univ. of Manchester. Started career as teacher; served as District Commissioner, 1958–68; Asst Sec., 1968, First Asst Sec., 1969, Dep. Perm. Sec., 1970, Under Sec., 1972, Perm. Sec., 1974–87, Bahamas. *Recreations:* fishing, reading, watching boxing matches. *Address:* PO Box CB 13333, Nassau, Bahamas. *T:* 3255979.

WALL OF NEW BARNET, Baroness *cr* 2004 (Life Peer), of New Barnet in the London Borough of Barnet; **Margaret Mary Wall;** consultant, Department for Education and Skills, since 2004; *b* 14 Nov. 1941; *d* of Thomas and Dorothy Mylott; *m* 1st, 1962, Peter Wall (marr. diss. 1990); one *s*; 2nd, 1992, Edwin Holdsworth. *Educ:* Notre Dame High Sch., Liverpool; Liverpool John Moores Univ. (Dip. Social Studies/Econs/Politics). Amicus (formerly MSF): Nat. Sec., 1995–98; Dir of Political Policy, 1999–2003. Fair Pay Champion, 1995–2003. Chair, Barnet and Chase Farm Hosps NHS Trust, 2005–. Wainwright Trust Equalities Award, 2000. *Recreations:* walking, grandchildren, reading. *Address:* 1 Willow Lodge, Lyonsdown Road, New Barnet EN5 1JJ. *T:* (020) 8275 0828, *Fax:* (020) 8275 0148; *e-mail:* margaret.wall@btconnect.com.

WALL, Alfreda, (Mrs D. R. Wall); *see* Thorogood, A.

WALL, (Alice) Anne, (Mrs Michael Wall), DCVO 1982 (CVO 1972; MVO 1964); Extra Lady in Waiting to HM the Queen (formerly Extra Woman of the Bedchamber), since 1981; *b* 1928; *d* of late Admiral Sir Geoffrey Hawkins, KBE, CB, MVO, DSC and late Lady Margaret Montagu-Douglas-Scott, *d* of 7th Duke of Buccleuch; *m* 1975, Commander Michael E. St Q. Wall, Royal Navy. *Educ:* Miss Faunce's PNEU School. Asst Press Sec. to the Queen, 1958–81. *Address:* Ivy House, Lambourn, Hungerford, Berks RG17 8PB. *T:* (01488) 72348.

WALL, Brian Owen, CEng, FRINA; RCNC; Chief Naval Architect, Ministry of Defence, 1985–90; *b* 17 June 1933; *s* of Maurice Stanley Wall and Ruby Wall; *m* 1960, Patricia Thora Hughes; one *s*. *Educ:* Newport High School, Mon; Imperial Coll. of Science and Technology; RN Coll., Greenwich. BSc Eng. ACGI. MoD Bath: Ship Vulnerability, 1958–61; Submarine Design, 1961–66; Head of Propeller Design, Admiralty Experiment Works, Haslar, 1966–71; Staff of C-in-C Fleet, Portsmouth, 1971–73; Submarine Support and Modernisation Group, MoD Bath, 1973–77; RCDS 1977; MoD Bath: Ship Production Div., 1978–79; Project Director, Vanguard Class, 1979–84; Dir, Cost Estimating and Analysis, 1985. Gov., Imperial Coll., London, 1991–99. *Recreations:* photography, chess, music, walking. *Address:* Wychwood, 39 High Bannerdown, Batheaston, Bath BA1 7JZ.

WALL, Prof. Charles Terence Clegg, FRS 1969; Professor of Pure Mathematics, 1965–99, and Senior Fellow, 1999–2002, Liverpool University; *b* 14 Dec. 1936; *s* of late Charles Wall, schoolteacher; *m* 1959, Alexandra Joy, *d* of late Prof. Leslie Spencer Hearnshaw; two *s* two *d*. *Educ:* Marlborough Coll.; Trinity Coll., Cambridge. PhD Cantab 1960. Fellow, Trinity Coll., 1959–64; Harkness Fellow, Princeton, 1960–61; Univ. Lectr, Cambridge, 1961–64; Reader in Mathematics, and Fellow of St Catherine's Coll., Oxford, 1964–65. SERC Sen. Fellowship, 1983–88. Royal Soc. Leverhulme Vis. Prof., CIEA, Mexico, 1967. Pres., London Mathematical Soc., 1978–80 (Mem. Council, 1973–80 and 1992–96); Hon. Mem., Irish Math. Soc., 2001. Fellow, Royal Danish Academy, 1990. Sylvester Medal, Royal Soc., 1988. *Publications:* Surgery on Compact Manifolds, 1970; A Geometric Introduction to Topology, 1972; (with A. A. du Plessis) The Geometry of Topological Stability, 1995; Singular Points of Plane Curves, 2004; papers on various problems in geometric topology, singularity theory, and related algebra. *Recreations:* reading, walking, gardening. *Address:* 5 Kirby Park, West Kirby, Wirral, Merseyside CH48 2HA. *T:* (0151) 625 5063.

WALL, David (Richard), CBE 1985; Ballet Master, English National Ballet Co., 1994–2007; *b* 15 March 1946; *s* of Charles and Dorothy Wall; *m* 1967, Alfreda Thorogood, *qv*; one *s* one *d*. *Educ:* Royal Ballet Sch. Joined Royal Ballet Co., Aug. 1964. Promotion to: Soloist, Aug. 1966; Junior Principal Dancer, Aug. 1967; Senior Principal Dancer, Aug. 1968; during period of employment danced all major roles and had many ballets created for him; retired from dancing, 1984. Assoc. Dir, 1984–87, Dir, 1987–91, Royal Acad. of Dancing. Guest repetiteur, London City Ballet, 1992–94. Evening Standard Award for Ballet, 1977. *Recreations:* music, theatre. *Address:* 34 Croham Manor Road, South Croydon, Surrey CR2 7BE.

WALL, Rt Rev. Eric St Quintin; Hon. Assistant Bishop, Diocese of Gloucester, since 2002; *b* 19 April 1915; *s* of Rev. Sydney Herbert Wall, MA, and Ethel Marion Wall (*née* Wilkins); *m* 1942, Doreen Clare (*née* Loveley); one *s* one *d*. *Educ:* Clifton; Brasenose Coll., Oxford (MA); Wells Theol. College. Deacon, 1938; priest, 1939; Curate of Boston, 1938–41; Chaplain, RAFVR, 1941–45; Vicar of Sherston Magna, 1944–53; Rural Dean of Malmesbury, 1951–53; Vicar of Cricklade with Latton, 1953–60; Hon. Chaplain to Bp of Bristol, 1960–66; Hon. Canon, Bristol, 1960–72; Diocesan Adviser on Christian Stewardship, Dio. Bristol, 1960–66; Proc. Conv., 1964–69; Vicar, St Alban's, Westbury Park, Bristol, 1966–72; Rural Dean of Clifton, 1967–72; Bp Suffragan of Huntingdon, and Canon Residentiary of Ely, 1972–80. *Recreation:* golf. *Address:* Forest House, Cinder Hill, Coleford, Glos GL16 8HQ. *T:* (01594) 832424.

WALL, James Francis, (Frank), CMG 1999; formerly Head of Shipping Policy 2 Division, Department for Transport; *b* 6 Jan. 1944; *s* of late James Wall, MA and Elizabeth Wall (*née* O'Sullivan); *m* 1970, Eileen Forrester McKerracher; two *d*. *Educ:* Belvedere Coll., SJ; University Coll., Dublin (BA 1966); Univ. of Liverpool (MCD 1968). MRTPI 1970. Asst to Prof. H. Myles Wright, Dublin Regl Planning Consultant, 1965–66; Planner then Sen. Planner, Antrim and Ballymena Develt Commn, 1968–71; Planning Officer, NI Min. of Develt, 1971–72; Asst, S Hants Plan Technical Unit, 1972–74; Sen. Planning Officer, Hants CC, 1974; Planning Officer, then Principal Planning Officer, DoE, 1974–82; Principal, 1982, Asst Sec., 1993, Dept of Transport; Hd of Shipping Policy 3, later 2, Div., Dept of Transport, then DETR, subseq. DTLR, later DfT, 1993–2004. Chairman: UK Search and Rescue Strategy Cttee, 2000; Shipping Task Force, 2001. Internat. Maritime Prize, IMO, 2002; Dist. Public Service Award, US Coast Guard, 2002. *Publications:* contrib. conf. proc. and articles in maritime law jls. *Recreations:* Flower Class Corvettes, the Boeing 707–348C. *Address:* Collingwood, Elvetham Road, Fleet, Hants GU51 4HH.

WALL, Jasper V., PhD; Adjunct Professor, Department of Physics and Astronomy, University of British Columbia, since 2003; *b* 15 Jan. 1942; *s* of late Philip Errington Wall and Lilian Margaret (*née* Blackburn); *m* 1969, Jennifer Anne Lash; one *s* one *d*. *Educ:* Vankleek Hill Collegiate Inst.; Queen's Univ., Kingston (BSc 1963); Univ. of Toronto (MASc 1966); Australian Nat. Univ. (PhD 1970). Res. Scientist, Australian Nat. Radio Astronomy Observatory, Parkes, NSW, 1970–74; Leverhulme Fellow, RAS, 1974–75, Jaffé Donation Fellow, Royal Soc., 1975–79, Cavendish Lab.; Hd, Astrophysics and Astrometry Div., Royal Greenwich Observatory, 1979–87; Officer-in-Charge, Isaac Newton Gp of Telescopes, La Palma, Canary Is, 1987–90; Royal Greenwich Observatory: Hd, Technol. Div., 1990–91; Hd, Astronomy Div., 1991–95; Dep. Dir, 1991–93; Head, 1993–95; Dir, 1995–98. Vis. Reader, Univ. of Sussex, 1980–90; Vis. Prof., Univ. of Oxford, 1998–. FRAS 1975 (Mem. Council, 1992–96; Vice-Pres., 1996); FRSA 1998. Chm., Editl Bd, Astronomy & Geophysics, 1999–2002. *Publications:* (ed jtly) Modern Technology and its Influence on Astronomy, 1986; (ed jtly) Optics in Astronomy, 1993; (ed jtly) The Universe at High Redshifts, 1997; (with C. R. Jenkins) Practical Statistics for Astronomers, 2003, 2nd edn 2009; 150 papers in professional jls on observational cosmology and statistics for astronomers. *Recreations:* hiking, ski-ing, music. *Address:* Department of Physics and Astronomy, University of British Columbia, Vancouver, BC V6T 1Z1, Canada.

WALL, Sir John (Anthony), Kt 2000; CBE 1994; Chairman, Royal National Institute for the Blind, 1990–2000; Partner, Lawrence Graham, solicitors, 1977–93 (Consultant, 1993–95); *b* 4 June 1930; *s* of George and Edith Wall; *m* 1st, 1956, Joan Reeve (*d* 1991); four *s*; 2nd, 1996, Friedel Lawrence (*d* 1999). *Educ:* Worcester Coll. for the Blind; Balliol Coll., Oxford (MA). Legal Officer, NALGO, 1956–74; Partner, Middleton Lewis, 1974–77; Dep. Master of High Court, Chancery Div., 1990–2002. Mem., Supreme Ct Rule Cttee, 1993–99. Pres., European Blind Union, 1996–2003 (Mem. Bd, 1990–2003; Sec.-Gen., 1992–96); Hon. Sec., Soc. of Visually Impaired Lawyers (formerly Blind Lawyers), 1993–. Vice-Pres., British Chess Fedn, 1991–. Hon. DBA Kingston, 2001; DUniv Open, 2003. Gold Medal, IBCA Correspondence Chess Olympiad, 1987. *Publications:* articles in learned periodicals. *Recreation:* chess (Oxford *v* Cambridge 1949 and 1951). *Address:* 36 Broadmead Avenue, Worcester Park, Surrey KT4 7SW. *T:* (020) 8330 2309. *Club:* Reform.

WALL, Sir (John) Stephen, GCMG 2004 (KCMG 1996; CMG 1990); LVO 1983; HM Diplomatic Service, retired; Vice-Chair, Business for New Europe, since 2005; *b* 10 Jan. 1947; *s* of John Derwent Wall and Maria Laetitia Wall (*née* Whitmarsh); *m* 1975, Catharine Jane Reddaway, *d* of late G. F. N. Reddaway, CBE and of Jean Reddaway, OBE; one *s*. *Educ:* Douai Sch.; Selwyn Coll., Cambridge (BA; Hon. Fellow, 2000). FCO 1968; Addis Ababa, 1969–72; Private Sec. to HM Ambassador, Paris, 1972–74; First Sec., FCO, 1974–76; Press Officer, No 10 Downing Street, 1976–77; Asst Private Sec. to Sec. of State for Foreign and Commonwealth Affairs, 1977–79; First Sec., Washington, 1979–83; Asst Head, later Head, European Community Dept, FCO, 1983–88; Private Secretary: to Foreign and Commonwealth Sec., 1988–90; to the Prime Minister, 1991–93; Ambassador to Portugal, 1993–95; Ambassador and UK Perm. Rep. to EU, Brussels, 1995–2000; Head of European Secretariat, Cabinet Office, 2000–04; Principal Advr to Cardinal Archbp of Westminster, 2004–05. Official Govt historian, 2007–. Member: Council, UCL, 2005– (Chm., 2008–); Academic Council, Wilton Park, 2005–. Trustee, Thomson Foundn, 2006–. *Publication:* A Stranger in Europe: Britain and the European Union from Thatcher to Blair, 2008. *Recreations:* walking, photography, reading.

WALL, Malcolm Robert; Chief Executive Officer, Content, Virgin Media, since 2006; *b* 24 July 1956; *s* of Maj. Gen. Robert Percival Walter Wall, CB, and of Patricia Kathleen Wall; *m* 1985, Elizabeth Craxford; three *d*. *Educ:* Allhallows Sch., Lyme Regis; Univ. of Kent (BA Hons). Sales Dir, Anglia TV, 1987; Sales and Mktg Dir, Granada TV, 1988–92; Dep. CEO, Meridian Broadcasting, 1992–94; Man. Dir, Anglia TV, 1994–96; Dep. CEO, 1996–99, CEO, 1999–2000, United Broadcasting and Entertainment; Chief Operating Officer, United Business Media plc, 2000–05; CEO, ntl: Telewest, 2006. Chm., Harlequin FC, 1997–2000. Non-executive Director: Five, 2000–05; ITE plc, 2006–; Creston plc, 2007–. *Recreations:* sport, reading, television. *Address:* The Close, 2 Longfield Drive, SW14 7AU. *Clubs:* Royal Automobile, MCC.

WALL, Mark Arthur; QC 2006; a Recorder, since 2002; *b* 4 March 1963; *s* of Arthur and Phyllis Wall; *m* 1987, Carmel Miriam (*née* Adler); one *s* one *d*. *Educ:* King Charles I Sch., Kidderminster; St John's Coll., Cambridge (BA 1984). Called to the Bar, Lincoln's Inn, 1985; in practice, specialising in criminal law. *Recreations:* driving children around, occasionally escaping to the racecourse or holidaying abroad. *Address:* Citadel Chambers, 190 Corporation Street, Birmingham B4 6QD. *T:* (0121) 233 8500, *Fax:* (0121) 233 8501; *e-mail:* markandcarmel@wall132.fsnet.co.uk.

WALL, Mrs Michael; *see* Wall, A. A.

WALL, Rt Hon. Sir Nicholas (Peter Rathbone), Kt 1993; PC 2004; **Rt Hon. Lord Justice Wall;** a Lord Justice of Appeal, since 2004; *b* 14 March 1945; *s* of late Frederick Stanley Wall and of Margaret Helen Wall; *m* 1973, Margaret Sydee, JP, MSc; four *c*. *Educ:* Dulwich College; Trinity Coll., Cambridge (Scholar; MA). Pres., Cambridge Union Soc., 1967; Mem., combined univs debating tour, USA, 1968. Called to the Bar, Gray's Inn, 1969, Bencher, 1993; QC 1988; Asst Recorder, 1988–90; a Recorder, 1990–93; a Judge of the High Ct of Justice, Family Div., 1993–2004; Family Div. Liaison Judge, Northern Circuit, 1996–2001 (Hon. Mem., Northern Circuit, 2001); a Judge of the Employment Appeal Tribunal, 2001–03; a Judge of the Administrative Ct, 2003–04. Mem., Lord Chancellor's Adv. Bd on Family Law, 1997–2001 (Chm., Children Act Sub-Cttee, 1998–2001). Hershman/Levy Meml Lectr, Assoc. of Lawyers for Children, 2006. *Publications:* (ed jtly) Supplements to Rayden and Jackson on Divorce, 15th edn, 1988–91; (ed jtly) Rayden and Jackson on Divorce, 16th edn, 1991–97, 17th edn 1997; (ed and contrib.) Rooted Sorrows: psychoanalytic contributions to assessments and decisions in the family justice system, 1996; (contrib.) Divided Duties: care planning within the family justice system, 1998; A Handbook for Expert Witnesses in Children Act Cases, 2000, 2nd edn 2007; (contrib.) Delight and Dole: the Children Act ten years on, 2002; (contrib.) Durable Solutions: the collected papers of the 2005 Dartington Hall Conference, 2006; papers in med. and legal jls. *Recreations:* collecting, binding and restoring books, theatre, opera, walking, composing clerihews. *Address:* Royal Courts of Justice, Strand, WC2A 2LL.

WALL, Lt Gen. Peter Anthony, CBE 2002 (OBE 1994); Deputy Chief of Defence Staff (Commitments), Ministry of Defence, since 2007; *b* 10 July 1955; *s* of late John Ramsay Wall and of Dorothy Margaret (*née* Waltho); *m* 1980, Fiona Anne Simpson; two *s*. *Educ:* Whitgift Sch.; Selwyn Coll., Cambridge (BA 1978; MA 1980); psc; hcsc. Commnd RE, 1974; sc 1987; COS 5 AB Bde, 1988–89; OC 9 Para Sqn, RE, 1990–92; CO 32 Engr Regt, 1994–96; Commander: 24 Airmob Bde, 1999; 16 Air Assault Bde, 1999–2001; Chief of Jt Force Ops, 2001–03; GOC 1st (UK) Armoured Div., 2003–05; Dep. Chief of Jt Ops (Ops), MoD, 2005–07. Colonel Commandant: REME, 2002–; RE, 2003–. *Recreation:* sport. *Address:* c/o Ministry of Defence, Main Building, Whitehall, SW1A 2HB.

WALL, Sir Robert (William), Kt 1987; OBE 1980; DL; Pro-Chancellor, University of Bristol, 1990–98; *b* 27 Sept. 1929; *s* of William George and Gladys Perina Wall; *m* 1968, Jean Ashworth; one *d* (and one *s* decd). *Educ:* Monmouth School; Bristol Coll. of Technology. HND MechEng; AMRAeS, TechEng. Student apprentice, Bristol Aeroplane Co., 1947–52; commissioned RAF Eng. Branch, and Mountain Rescue Service, 1955–57; management posts with British Aircraft Corp., 1957–67, Chief Ratefixer, 1969–75, Manager, Cost Control, 1975–88. Bristol City Council: Councillor 1959; Alderman 1971; re-elected Councillor 1974; Leader, Cons. Gp, 1974–97; Chm., Public Works Cttee, 1968–72; Dep. Leader, 1971–72, Council Leader, 1983–84. Mem., Bristol Develt Corp., 1993–96. Chairman: Bristol Cons. Assoc., 1979–88; Western Area Provincial Council, Nat. Union of Cons. and Unionist Assocs, 1988–91. Mem. Council,

Univ. of Bristol, 1974–98 (Chairman: GP Cttee, 1979–87; Buildings Cttee, 1987–91; Audit Cttee, 1991–98); Governor, Bristol Old Vic Theatre Trust, 1974–87, and 1988–93; Mem. Council, SS Great Britain Project, 1975–; Chm., Rail Users' Cons. Cttee for W England, 1982–98. Mem., Audit Commn, 1986–94. Pres., Bristol Soc. of Model and Experimental Engrs, 1972–2000. FCILT (FCIT 1990). DL Bristol, 2002. Freeman, Co. of Watermen and Lightermen. Hon. MA Bristol, 1982; Hon. DEng Bristol, 1999. *Publications:* Bristol Channel Pleasure Steamers, 1973; Ocean Liners, 1978 (trans. German, French, Dutch), 2nd edn 1984; Air Liners, 1980; Bristol: maritime city, 1981; The Story of HMS Bristol, 1986; Quayside Bristol, 1992; Ocean Liner Postcards, 1998; Brabazon, 1999; Bristol Aircraft, 2000; Shipsides Bristol, 2001; Shipsides Slow Boat to Bristol, 2003. *Recreations:* writing maritime history, collecting postcards, hill walking. *Address:* The Glebe, Winsford, Somerset TA24 7JF. *Clubs:* Bristol Savages, Clifton (Bristol).

WALL, Sir Stephen; *see* Wall, Sir J. S.

WALLACE, family name of **Barons Dudley**, **Wallace of Saltaire** and **Wallace of Tankerness**.

WALLACE OF SALTAIRE, Baron *cr* 1995 (Life Peer), of Shipley in the County of West Yorkshire; **William John Lawrence Wallace;** Professor of International Relations, London School of Economics, 1999–2005, now Emeritus; *b* 12 March 1941; *s* of William E. Wallace and Mary A. Tricks; *m* 1968, Helen Sarah Rushworth (*see* H. S. Wallace); one *s* one *d. Educ:* Westminster Abbey Choir School (Sen. Chorister, 1954); St Edward's Sch., Oxford; King's Coll., Cambridge (Exhibnr, 1959; BA Hist 1962); Nuffield Coll., Oxford; Cornell Univ. (PhD Govt 1968). Lectr in Govt, Univ. of Manchester, 1967–77; Dep. Dir, RIIA, 1978–90; Sen. Res. Fellow in European Studies, St Antony's Coll., Oxford, 1990–95; Prof. of Internat. Studies, Central European Univ., Budapest, 1994–97; Reader in Internat. Relns, LSE, 1995–99. House of Lords: Mem., Select Cttee on EU, 1997–2001 (Chair, Sub-Cttee on justice and home affairs, 1997–2000); Lib Dem spokesman: on defence, 1998–2001; on foreign affairs, 2001–; Dep. Leader, Lib Dem Gp, 2004–. Contested (L): Huddersfield West, 1970; Manchester Moss Side, Feb. and Oct. 1974; Shipley, 1983 and 1987. Vice-Chm., Liberal Party Policy Cttee, 1977–87. Editor, Jl of Common Market Studies, 1974–78. Hon. Dr, Free Univ. of Brussels, 1992. Ordre pour la Mérite (France), 1995; Chevalier, Légion d'Honneur (France), 2005. *Publications:* Foreign Policy and the Political Process, 1972; The Foreign Policy Process in Britain, 1977; (ed with Helen Wallace, and contrib.) Policy-making in the European Union, 1977, 5th edn 2005; (with Christopher Tugendhat) Options for British Foreign Policy in the 1990s, 1988; The Transformation of Western Europe, 1990; Regional Integration: the West European experience, 1994; Why vote Liberal Democrat?, 1997. *Address:* House of Lords, SW1A 0PW.

WALLACE OF SALTAIRE, Lady; *see* Wallace, H. S.

WALLACE OF TANKERNESS, Baron *cr* 2007 (Life Peer), of Tankerness in Orkney; **James Robert Wallace;** PC 2000; QC (Scot.) 1997; Member (Lib Dem) Orkney, Scottish Parliament, 1999–2007; *b* 25 Aug. 1954; *s* of John F. T. Wallace and Grace Hannah Wallace (*née* Maxwell); *m* 1983, Rosemary Janet Fraser; two *d. Educ:* Annan Academy; Downing College, Cambridge (BA 1975, MA 1979); Edinburgh University (LLB 1977). Called to the Scots Bar, 1979; practised as Advocate, 1979–83. Contested Dumfriesshire (L), 1979; contested South of Scotland (L), European Parlt election, 1979. Vice-Chm. (Policy), Scottish Liberal Party, 1982–85; Leader, Scottish Liberal Democrats, 1992–2005. MP Orkney and Shetland, 1983–2001 (L 1983–88, Lib Dem 1988–2001). Liberal spokesman on defence, 1985–87; Deputy Whip, 1985–87, Chief Whip, 1987–88; first Lib Dem Chief Whip, 1988–92; Alliance spokesman on Transport, 1987; Lib Dem spokesman on employment and training, 1988–92, on fisheries, 1988–97, on Scottish affairs, 1992–99, on maritime affairs, 1994–97. Scottish Executive: Dep. First Minister, 1999–2005; Minister of Justice, 1999–2003; Minister for Enterprise and Lifelong Learning, 2003–05. Director: Northwind Associates Ltd, 2007–; Jim Wallace Consultancy Ltd, 2007–. Mem. Bd, St Magnus Festival Ltd, 2007–. Hon. Prof., Inst. of Petroleum Engrg, Heriot-Watt Univ., 2007. Hon. DLitt Heriot-Watt, 2007. *Recreations:* golf, music, travel. *Address:* Northwood House, Tankerness, Orkney KW17 2QS. *T:* (01856) 861383; *e-mail:* jr.wallace@virgin.net; House of Lords, SW1A 0PW; *e-mail:* wallacej@parliament.uk. *Clubs:* Caledonian; Scottish Liberal (Edinburgh).

WALLACE, Albert Frederick, CBE 1963 (OBE 1955); DFC 1943; Controller of Manpower, Greater London Council, 1978–82; *b* 22 Aug. 1921; *s* of Major Frederick Wallace and Ada Wallace; *m* 1940, Evelyn M. White (*d* 2005); one *s* one *d. Educ:* Roan School, Blackheath, SE3. MIPM, MCMI, MILGA. Regular Officer, Royal Air Force, 1939–69: served war of 1939–45, with 40 Sqn, 93 Sqn, 214 Sqn, 620 Sqn; overseas service in Egypt (Canal Zone), S Rhodesia, India, Cyprus; sc 1944–45; NDC 1959–60; sowc 1963; retired in rank of Group Captain. Regional Advisory Officer, Local Authorities Management Services and Computer Cttee, 1969–71; Asst Clerk of the Council, Warwickshire CC, 1971–73; County Personnel Officer, W Midlands CC, and Dir, W Midlands PTA, 1973–78. *Recreations:* golf, bridge. *Address:* Flat 14, Kepplestone, Staveley Road, Eastbourne BN20 7JY. *T:* (01323) 730668. *Club:* Royal Air Force.

WALLACE, Angus; *see* Wallace, W. A.

WALLACE, Ben; *see* Wallace, R. B. L.

WALLACE, Charles William, CMG 1983; CVO 1975; HM Diplomatic Service, retired; *b* 19 Jan. 1926; *s* of Percival Francis and Julia Wallace; *m* 1957, Gloria Regina de Ros Ribas (*née* Sanz-Agero). *Educ:* privately and abroad. HM Foreign (later Diplomatic) Service, 1949; served: Asuncion; Barcelona; Bari; Bahrain; Tegucigalpa; Guatemala; Panama; Foreign Office; Baghdad; Buenos Aires; Montevideo; FO, later FCO, Asst Head of American Dept; Counsellor 1969; Rome and Milan; Mexico City; Ambassador: Paraguay, 1976–79; Peru, 1979–83; Uruguay, 1983–86. Freeman, City of London, 1981. *Publication:* The Valedictory, 1992. *Recreations:* sailing, fishing. *Address:* c/o Lloyds Private Banking, 50 Grosvenor Street, W1X 9FH.

WALLACE, Lt-Gen. Sir Christopher (Brooke Quentin), KBE 1997 (OBE 1983; MBE 1978); DL; Commandant, Royal College of Defence Studies, 2001–04; *b* 3 Jan. 1943; *s* of Major Robert Quentin Wallace, RA and Diana Pamela Wallace (*née* Galtrey); *m* 1969, Delicia Margaret Agnes Curtis; one *s* one *d. Educ:* Shrewsbury Sch.; RMA Sandhurst. Commissioned 1962; CO 3rd Bn Royal Green Jackets, 1983–85; Comdr, 7th Armd Brigade, 1986–88; Dir, Public Relations (Army), 1989–90; Comdr, 3rd Armd Div., 1990–93; Comdt, Staff Coll., Camberley, 1993–94; Perm. Jt HQ Implementation Team Leader, 1994–96; Chief of Jt Ops, Perm. Jt HQ (UK), Northwood, 1996–99. Rep. Col Comdt, Royal Green Jackets, 1995–98; Col Comdt, Light Div., 1998–99; Dep. Col Comdt, AGC, 1992–99. Pres., Army Golf Assoc., 1995–2000; Mem., RUSI Council, 1996–2000. Chm. Trustees, RGJ Mus., 1999–; Trustee, Imperial War Mus., 1999–2008 (Dep. Chm., 2006–08). DL Hants, 2004. *Publications:* A Brief History of The King's Royal Rifle Corps 1755–1965, 2005; Focus on Courage: the 59 Victoria Crosses of the Royal Green Jackets, 2006; Rifles and Kukris: Delhi, 1857, 2007. *Recreations:* golf, bird-watching, military history. *Address:* c/o RHQ The Rifles, Peninsula Barracks, Winchester, Hants SO23 8TS. *Clubs:* Army and Navy; Sunningdale Golf.

WALLACE, Sir David (James), Kt 2004; CBE 1996; PhD; FRS 1986; CEng, FREng, FInstP; FRSE; N. M. Rothschild & Sons Professor of Mathematical Sciences and Director, Isaac Newton Institute for Mathematical Sciences, University of Cambridge, since 2006; Master, Churchill College, Cambridge, since 2006; *b* 7 Oct. 1945; *s* of Robert Elder Wallace and Jane McConnell Wallace (*née* Elliot); *m* 1970, Elizabeth Anne Yeats; one *d. Educ:* Hawick High Sch.; Univ. of Edinburgh (BSc, PhD). FRSE 1982; FInstP 1991; FREng (FEng 1998). Harkness Fellow, Princeton Univ., 1970–72; Lecturer in Physics, 1972–78, Reader in Physics, 1978–79, Southampton Univ.; Tait Prof. of Mathematical Physics, 1979–93, Hd of Physics, 1984–87, Edinburgh Univ.; Vice-Chancellor, Loughborough Univ., 1994–2005. Director: Edinburgh Concurrent Supercomputer, 1987–89; Edinburgh Parallel Computing Centre, 1990–93. Science and Engineering Research Council, subseq. Engineering and Physical Sciences Research Council: Chm., Physics Cttee, 1987–90; Chm., Science Bd, 1990–94; Mem. Council, 1990–98; Chm., Technical Opportunities Panel, 1994–98. European Commission: Physics Panel, Human Capital and Mobility Prog., 1991–94; Large Scale Facilities Evaluation Panel, 1995–97; European Sci. and Technol. Assembly, 1997–98. Mem., Royal Commn for Exhibn of 1851, 2001–. Chairman: CVCP/SCOP Task Force on sport in higher educn, 1995–97; Value for Money Steering Gp, HEFCE, 1997–2003; Member: Royal Soc. sci. and industl award Cttees, 1990–95; SHEFC, 1993–97; LINK Bd, OST, 1995–98; LINK/Teaching Co. Scheme Bd, 1999–2001; Chairman: e-Science Steering Cttee, OST, 2001–06; Teaching Co. Scheme Quinquennial Rev., 2001. Non-executive Director: Scottish Life Insurance Co., 1999–2001; Taylor & Francis Gp plc, 2000–04; UK e-Univs Worldwide Ltd, 2001–04. Chm., Council for Mathematical Scis, 2006–. President: Physics Sect., BAAS, 1994; Inst. of Physics, 2002–04. Royal Society: Mem. Council, 2001–07; Treas. and Vice-Pres., 2002–07. Gov., Harrow Sch., 2007–. CCMI (CIMgt 2001). DL Leics, 2001–06. Maxwell Medal of Inst. of Physics, 1980. *Publications:* in research and review jls, in a number of areas of theoretical physics and computing. *Recreations:* exercise, eating well, mycophagy. *Address:* Churchill College, Cambridge CB3 0DS. *T:* (01223) 336142, *Fax:* (01223) 336177; *e-mail:* david.wallace@chu.cam.ac.uk.

WALLACE, (Dorothy) Jacqueline H.; *see* Hope-Wallace.

WALLACE, Fleming; *see* Wallace, J. F.

WALLACE, Graham Martyn, FCMA; Chief Executive, Merryck & Co, since 2006; *b* 26 May 1948; *s* of Ronald and May Wallace; *m* 1974, Denise Margaret Wallace (*née* Dyer); one *s* one *d. Educ:* Imperial College, London (BSc Eng; ACGI); Birkbeck Coll., London (MA London Studies 2005). Graduate trainee, Turner & Newall, 1969–72; Co. Accountant, Brandhurst Co. Ltd, 1972–74; various finance and mgt posts, Rank Xerox, 1974–83; Planning Manager, Imperial Gp, 1983–85; Finance Dir, Imperial Leisure and Retailing, 1985–86; Head of Finance and Planning, 1986–89, Finance Dir, 1989–92, Granada Gp plc; Chief Executive: Granada UK Rental, 1992–95; Granada Restaurants and Services, 1995–97; Cable & Wireless Communications plc, 1997–99; Cable and Wireless plc, 1999–2003. Non-executive Director: Barclays PLC, 2001–03; Barclays Bank PLC, 2001–03.

WALLACE, Helen Richenda, (Mrs D. Papp); Consultant Editor, BBC Music Magazine (Editor, 1999–2004); *b* 19 Nov. 1966; *d* of Dr Ian Wallace and Richenda Ponsonby; *m* 2000, David Papp. *Educ:* St Peter's Coll., Oxford (MA English); Guildhall Sch. of Music and Drama (LGSM); London Coll. of Printing (Dip. Periodical Journalism). Features Ed., The Music Mag., 1991–92; Ed., The Strad, 1992–94; Dep. Ed., BBC Music Mag., 1994–99; Editor-in-Chief, South Bank mag., 2000–. *Publications:* Spirit of the Orchestra, 2006; Boosey & Hawkes: the publishing story, 2007. *Address:* c/o BBC Music Magazine, Origin Publishing Ltd, 14th Floor, Tower House, Fairfax Street, Bristol BS1 3BN.

WALLACE, Prof. Helen Sarah, (Lady Wallace of Saltaire), CMG 2000; PhD; FBA 2000; Centennial Professor, European Institute, London School of Economics and Political Science, since 2007; *b* 25 June 1946; *d* of Edward Rushworth and Joyce Rushworth; *m* 1968, William John Lawrence Wallace (*see* Baron Wallace of Saltaire); one *s* one *d. Educ:* St Anne's Coll., Oxford (MA Classics); Coll. of Europe, Bruges (Dip. Eur. Studies 1968); Univ. of Manchester (PhD 1975). Lectr, UMIST, 1974–78; Lectr, then Sen. Lectr, CS Coll., 1978–85 (on secondment to FCO, 1979–80); Dir, Eur. Programme, RIIA, 1985–92; Dir, 1992–98, Co-Dir, 1998–2001, Sussex European Inst.; Dir, Robert Schuman Centre, European University Inst., 2001–06. Dir, One Europe or Several? Programme, ESRC, 1998–2001. Mem., Better Regulation Commn, 2006–08. Serves on various editl and adv. bds. Chevalier, Ordre Nationale du Mérite (France), 1996. *Publications:* (ed jtly) Policy Making in the European Union, 1977, 5th edn 2005; (jtly) The Council of Ministers of the European Union, 1997, 2nd edn 2006; (ed) Interlocking Dimensions of European Integration, 2001; contrib. numerous articles on European integration. *Recreations:* gardening, travelling.

WALLACE, Ian Bryce, OBE 1983; Hon. RAM; Hon. RCM; singer, actor and broadcaster; *b* London, 10 July 1919; *o s* of late Sir John Wallace, Kirkcaldy, Fife (one-time MP for Dunfermline), and Mary Bryce Wallace (*née* Temple), Glasgow; *m* 1948, Patricia Gordon Black, Edenwood, Cupar, Fife; one *s* one *d. Educ:* Charterhouse; Trinity Hall, Cambridge (MA). Served War of 1939–45, (invalided from) RA, 1944. London stage debut in The Forrigan Reel, Sadler's Wells, 1945. Opera debut, as Schaunard, in La Bohème, with New London Opera Co., Cambridge Theatre, London, 1946. Sang principal roles for NLOC, 1946–49, incl. Dr Bartolo in Il Barbiere di Siviglia. Glyndebourne debut, Masetto, Don Giovanni, Edin. Fest., 1948. Regular appearances as principal *buffo* for Glyndebourne, both in Sussex and at Edin. Fest., 1948–61, incl. perfs as Don Magnifico in La Cenerentola, at Berlin Festwoche, 1954. Italian debut: Masetto, Don Giovanni, at Parma, 1950; also Don Magnifico, La Cenerentola, Rome, 1955, Dr Bartolo, Il Barbiere di Siviglia, Venice, 1956, and Bregenz Fest., 1964–65. Regular appearances for Scottish Opera, 1965–, incl. Leporello in Don Giovanni, Pistola in Falstaff, Duke of Plaza Toro in The Gondoliers. Don Pasquale, Welsh Nat. Opera, 1967, Dr Dulcamara, L'Elisir d'Amore, Glyndebourne Touring Opera, 1968. Devised, wrote and presented three series of adult education programmes on opera, entitled Singing For Your Supper, for Scottish Television (ITV), 1967–70. Recordings include: Gilbert and Sullivan Operas with Sir Malcolm Sargent, and humorous songs by Flanders and Swann. Theatrical career includes: a Royal Command Variety Perf., London Palladium, 1952; Cesar in Fanny, Theatre Royal, Drury Lane, 1956; 4 to the Bar, Criterion, 1960; Toad in Toad of Toad Hall, Queen's, 1964. Regular broadcaster, 1944–: radio and TV, as singer, actor and compere; a regular panellist on radio musical quiz game, My Music; acted in series, Porterhouse Blue, Channel 4 TV, 1987. President: ISM, 1979–80; Council for Music in Hosps, 1987–99. Hon. DMus St Andrews, 1991. Sir Charles Santley Meml Award, Musicians' Co., 1984. *Publications:* Promise Me You'll Sing Mud (autobiog.), 1975; Nothing Quite Like It (autobiog.), 1982; Reflections on Scotland, 1988. *Recreations:* reading, sport watching, going to the theatre, singing a song about a hippopotamus to children of all ages. *Address:* c/o Peters, Fraser & Dunlop, Drury House, 34–43 Russell Street, WC2B 5HA. *T:* (020) 7344 1010. *Clubs:* Garrick, MCC; Stage Golfing Society.

WALLACE, Sir Ian (James), Kt 1982; CBE 1971 (OBE (mil.) 1942); Director, Coventry Motor and Sundries Co. Ltd, 1986–92; Chairman, SNR Bearings (UK) Ltd, 1975–85; *b* 25 Feb. 1916; *s* of John Madder Wallace, CBE; *m* 1942, Catherine Frost Mitchell, *e d* of Cleveland S. Mitchell; one *s* (one *d* decd). *Educ:* Uppingham Sch.; Jesus Coll., Cambridge (BA). Underwriting at Lloyd's, 1935–39. War Service, Fleet Air Arm: Cmdr (A) RNVR, 1939–46. Harry Ferguson Ltd from 1947: Dir 1950; later Massey Ferguson Ltd, Dir Holdings Board until 1970. Coventry Conservative Association: Treas., 1956–68; Chm., 1968–88; Pres., 1988–92; Pres., S Worcs Cons. Assoc., 1992–96; Life Pres., Mid Worcs Cons. Assoc., 1996–; Chm., W Midlands Cons. Council, 1967–70 (Treas., 1962–67); Pres., W Midlands Area Cons. Council. Member: Severn-Trent Water Authority, 1974–82; W Midlands Econ. Planning Council, 1965–75; Vice-Chm., Midland Regional Council, CBI, 1964, Chm., 1967–69; President: Coventry Chamber of Commerce, 1972–74; Birmingham and Midland Inst., 1992–93. Pres., Hereford and Worcester (formerly Worcs County) Rifle Assoc., 1983–2004. *Recreations:* rifle shooting, horology. *Address:* Little House, 156 High Street, Broadway, Worcs WR12 7AJ. *T:* (01386) 852414. *Club:* North London Rifle.

WALLACE, Ivan Harold Nutt, CB 1991; Senior Chief Inspector, Department of Education, Northern Ireland, 1979–95; *b* 20 Feb. 1935; *s* of late Harold Wallace and Annie McClure Wallace; *m* 1962, Winifred Ervine Armstrong; two *d. Educ:* Grosvenor High Sch., Belfast; QUB (BSc 1957). MRSC 1963. School Teacher: Leeds Central High Sch., 1957–60; Foyle Coll., Londonderry, 1960–69; Inspector of Schools, NI, 1969–75; Sen. Inspector, 1975–77; Staff Inspector, 1977–78; Chief Inspector, 1978–79. Hon. Prof., Sch. of Educn, QUB, 1996–2001. *Recreations:* music, walking, bell-ringing.

WALLACE, (James) Fleming; QC (Scot) 1985; Counsel to Scottish Law Commission, 1979–93; *b* 19 March 1931; *s* of James F. B. Wallace, SSC and Margaret B. Gray, MA; *m* 1st, 1964, Valerie Mary (*d* 1986), *d* of Leslie Lawrence, solicitor, and Madge Lawrence, Ramsbury, Wilts; two *d*; 2nd, 1990, Linda Ann, solicitor, *d* of Robert Grant, civil engineer, and Alice Grant. *Educ:* Edinburgh Academy; Edinburgh University (MA 1951; LLB 1954). Served RA, 1954–56 (2nd Lieut); TA 1956–60. Admitted Faculty of Advocates, 1957; practised at Scottish Bar until 1960; Parly Draftsman and Legal Secretary, Lord Advocate's Dept, London, 1960–79. Part-time Chm., Industrial Tribunals, Scotland, 1993–2001. Volunteer, CAB, 2001–. *Publication:* The Businessman's Lawyer (Scottish Section), 1965, 2nd edn 1973. *Recreations:* hill walking, choral singing, golf. *Address:* 24 Corrennie Gardens, Edinburgh EH10 6DB.

WALLACE, Prof. James Stuart, PhD; Team Leader, Floodplain Hydrology Group, Land and Water Division, Commonwealth Scientific and Industrial Research Organisation, since 2004; *b* 20 June 1952; *s* of Joseph Wallace and Anne Wallace (*née* Keenan); *m* 1974, Josephine Marie Richardson; one *s* three *d. Educ:* Lisburn Tech. Coll.; Queen's Univ., Belfast (BSc 1973); Univ. of Nottingham (PhD 1978). NERC Institute of Hydrology: Envmtl Physicist, 1978–2004; Head: Vegetation Water Use Section, 1989–93; Hydrological Processes Div., 1993–96; Dir, 1996–2000; Dep. Dir, and Dir of Hydrology, NERC Centre for Ecol. & Hydrol., 2000–04. Vis. Prof. in Hydrology, Univ. of Reading, 1997–2005. Consultant to UNDP Global Envmt Facility, 1995; Hydrological Advr to UK Perm. Rep. to WMO, 1999–2003. Chairman: Jt UNESCO/WMO Task Force for Hydrology for Envmt, Life and Policy initiative, 1999–2005; UK Inter-Deptl Cttee on Hydrology, 2000–03; Member: Dirs Mgt Bd, EurAqua, 2001–03; Steering Cttee, NERC Centres for Atmospheric Sci., 2002–03; Bd, British Oxygen Co. Foundn, 2003–07. Vice-Pres., Internat. Cttee on Atmosphere-Soil-Vegetation Relns, 1996. FRMetS 2003. *Publications:* (ed jtly) Soil Water Balance in the Sudano-Sahelian Zone, 1991; papers on hydrological processes in Qly Jl RMetS, Proc. Royal Soc., Agric. and Forest Meteorology, etc. *Recreations:* gardening, golf, motorcycling with Gromit. *Address:* CSIRO Land and Water, Davies Laboratory, Private Mail Bag, PO Aitkenvale, Townsville, Qld 4814, Australia; *e-mail:* jim.wallace@csiro.au.

WALLACE, Hon. Sir John (Hamilton), KNZM 1997; Judge of the High Court of New Zealand, 1982–96; *b* 9 Sept. 1934; *s* of G. H. and C. I. Wallace; *m* 1961, Elizabeth Ann Goodwin; one *s* one *d. Educ:* King's Coll., Auckland; Auckland Univ.; Merton Coll., Oxford (MA 1958; Hon. Fellow 2006). Called to the Bar, Gray's Inn, 1958; admitted as Barrister and Solicitor, NZ, 1959; QC 1974. Chairman: Equal Opportunities Tribunal, 1978–82; Human Rights Commn, 1984–89; Royal Commn on the Electoral System, 1985–86; Pres., Electoral Commn, 1994–96; Dep. Pres., Law Commn, 1991–96; Member: Contracts and Commercial Law Reform Cttee, 1974–85; Royal Commn on the Courts, 1976–78. Pres., Auckland Law Soc., 1980–81; Vice Pres., NZ Law Soc., 1981–82. Fellow, Internat. Acad. of Trial Lawyers, 1981. *Recreation:* reading.

WALLACE, John Malcolm Agnew; JP; Vice Lord-Lieutenant, Dumfries and Galloway (District of Wigtown), 1990–2003; *b* 30 Jan. 1928; *s* of John Alexander Agnew Wallace and Marjory Murray Wallace; *m* 1955, Louise Haworth-Booth; one *s* two *d. Educ:* Brooks Sch., USA; Harrow; West of Scotland Agricultural College. Farmer. JP Stranraer, 1970; DL Dumfries and Galloway, 1971. *Address:* Lochryan, Stranraer DG9 8QY. *T:* (01581) 200284.

WALLACE, John Williamson, OBE 1995; Principal, Royal Scottish Academy of Music and Drama, since 2002; freelance soloist, composer, conductor; *b* 14 April 1949; *s* of Christopher Kidd Wallace and Ann Drummond Allan; *m* 1971, Elizabeth Jane Hartwell; one *s* one *d. Educ:* Buckhaven High Sch.; King's Coll., Cambridge (MA); York Univ.; Royal Acad. of Music (ARAM 1983; FRAM 1990). ARCM 1968; FRSAMD 1993; Hon. RCM 1985. Asst Principal Trumpet, LSO, 1974–76; Prin. Trumpet, Philharmonia Orch., 1976–94; founded The Wallace Collection (brass-interest music gp), 1986; Principal Trumpet, London Sinfonietta, 1987–2001; Artistic Dir of Brass, RAM, 1993–2001. Trumpet solo recordings. Mercedes-Benz Prize, 1991. *Publications:* Five Easy Pieces, 1984; First Book of Trumpet Solos, 1985; Second Book of Trumpet Solos, 1985, 2nd edn 1987; Grieg's Seven Lyric Pieces, 1985; Kornukopia, 1986; Prime Number, 1990; Odd Number and Even Number, 1991; (jtly) Music Through Time, 1995; (ed jtly) Cambridge Companion to Brass Instruments, 1997. *Address:* Royal Scottish Academy of Music and Drama, 100 Renfrew Street, Glasgow G2 3DB.

WALLACE, Major Malcolm Charles Robarts; Director of Regulation, British Horseracing Authority (formerly Jockey Club, then Horseracing Regulatory Authority), 1994–2007; Chairman, HPower Group, since 2007; *b* 12 June 1947; *s* of Lionel John Wallace, MBE, TD and Maureen Winefride (*née* Robarts); *m* 1st, 1974, Caroline Anne Doyne-Ditmas (marr. diss. 1990); one *s* one *d*; 2nd, 1991, Mrs Jane Thelwall; two *s. Educ:* Blackrock College, Co. Dublin. Student pupil with Lt-Col J. Hume-Dudgeon at Burton Hall, Co. Dublin, 1965–67; Mons Officer Cadet Sch.; commissioned RA, 1967; gun line officer, 18 Light Regt, Hong Kong; 3rd Regt RHA, 1969; King's Troop RHA, 1970 (long equitation course, RAVC Melton Mowbray); Troop Comdr, 19 Field Regt, 1974; Adjutant 101 Northumbrian Field Artillery, 1976; Staff Officer, HQ UKLF, 1978–82; Comd King's Troop RHA, 1982–85, retired. Dir Gen., BEF, 1985–94. Chef d'Equipe to British Internat. and Olympic Three Day Event Teams, 1979–84; Chef de Mission, Equestrian Team, Olympic Games, Seoul, 1988 and Barcelona, 1992. Chm., Burghley Horse Trials, 2002–. Freeman, Saddlers' Co., 1985. *Publication:* The King's Troop Royal Horse Artillery, 1984. *Recreations:* field and equestrian sports, golf, gardening. *Address:* Fishponds Farm, Stoke Albany, Market Harborough LE16 8PZ. *T:* (01858) 535250, *Fax:* (01858) 535499; *e-mail:* malcolmw@hpower.co.uk. *Club:* Cavalry and Guards.

WALLACE, Margaret; Member (Lab) Kilmarnock and Loudoun, Scottish Parliament, 1999–2007; *b* 6 April 1953; *d* of late George and Margaret Wallace; *m* 1974, Russell Jamieson (marr. diss. 2002); one *d. Educ:* Grange Acad.; Ayr Coll. Official for UNISON (formerly NUPE), 1979–99. Mem. Bd, E Ayrshire Employment Initiative, 1998–. Scottish Parliament: Member: Audit Cttee, 1999–2007; Health and Community Care Cttees, 1999–2003. Convener, Scottish Commn for Public Audit, 2001–07.

WALLACE, Marjorie Shiona, CBE 2008 (MBE 1994); Founder, and Chief Executive, SANE, mental health charity, since 1989; broadcaster, author, journalist; *d* of William Wallace and Doris Tulloch; *m* Count Andrzej Skarbek; three *s* one *d. Educ:* Rodeane; Johannesburg; Parsons' Mead, Ashtead; University College London (BA Hons Psych and Phil; Fellow, 2004). Television: The Frost Programme, 1966–68; ITV religious programmes, 1966–68; LWT current affairs, 1968–69; Dir/reporter, current affairs, BBC TV, 1969–72; Insight team (thalidomide campaign), feature writer, Sunday Times, 1972–89, incl. Forgotten Illness, mental illness campaign, The Times, 1985–89; Guardian Res. Fellow, Nuffield Coll., Oxford, 1989–91. Founded SANE, and Prince of Wales Internat. Centre for SANE Res., Oxford (opened 2003). Institute of Psychiatry: Member: Cttee of Management, 1989–2002; Ethics Cttee (Res.), 1991–2002; Schiz. Adv. Panel, 1991–; Adv. Cttee, 2003–. Chm., Friends of Open Air Theatre, 1991–. Patron, Hay Literary Festival, 2001–. Numerous internat. presentations and speeches, also broadcasts on TV and radio; TV documentaries: Whose Mind Is It?, 1988; Circles of Madness, 1994. Hon. FRCPsych 1997. Hon. DSc City, 2001. Campaigning Journalist of the Year, British Press Awards, 1982, 1986; John Pringle Meml Award, 1986; Book Trust Prize, 1987; Snowdon Special Award, 1988; Medical Journalist of the Year, 1988; Evian Health Award, 1991, and Best Use of Media award, 1995; Public Service award, British Neurosci. Assoc., 2002; Internat. Pioneer and Diversity Award, Muslim community, 2005. *Publications:* (jtly) On Giant's Shoulders, 1976 (also original TV screenplay (Internat. Emmy award), 1979); (jtly) Suffer the Children: the story of Thalidomide, 1978; (jtly) The Superpoison, The Dioxin Disaster, 1980; The Silent Twins, 1986 (also TV screenplay); Campaign and Be Damned, 1991. *Recreations:* poetry, piano, Victorian ballads, opera, musicals, dining out. *Address:* SANE, Cityside House, 40 Adler Street, E1 1EE. *T:* (020) 7422 5554. *Clubs:* Athenæum, Groucho.

WALLACE, Rt Rev. Martin William; *see* Selby, Bishop Suffragan of.

WALLACE, Moira Paul, OBE 1997; Director General, Crime Reduction and Community Safety Group (formerly Crime, Policing and Counter Terrorism), Home Office, since 2005; *b* 15 Aug. 1961; *d* of Prof. and Mrs W. V. Wallace. *Educ:* Coleraine High Sch.; Emmanuel Coll., Cambridge (MA Mod. Langs 1983); Harvard Univ. (Kennedy Schol.; AM Comparative Lit. 1985). Joined HM Treasury, 1985; Private Sec. to Chancellor of Exchequer, 1987–90; Econ. Affairs Private Sec. to Prime Minister, 1995–97; Dir, Social Exclusion Unit, Cabinet Office, 1997–2002; Dir Gen., Criminal Justice Gp, Home Office, 2002–04; Chief Exec., Office for Criminal Justice Reform, 2004–05. Vis. Fellow, Nuffield Coll., Oxford, 1999–. *Address:* Home Office, 2 Marsham Street, SW1P 4DF; *e-mail:* moira.wallace@homeoffice.gsi.gov.uk.

WALLACE, Reginald James, CMG 1979; OBE 1961; Chairman, Abbey National Gibraltar Ltd, 1987–2000; *b* 16 Aug. 1919; *s* of James Wallace and Doris (*née* Welch); *m* 1st, 1943, Doris Barbara Brown, MD, FRCS, MRCOG (decd); one *d*; 2nd, 1973, Maureen Coady (*d* 1983); 3rd, 1983, Marilyn Ryan (*née* Gareze); one *d. Educ:* John Gulson Sch., Coventry; Tatterford Sch., Norfolk; Leeds Univ. (BA); Queen's Coll., Oxford. Served War, 1939–46, 7th Rajput Regt, Indian Army (Major). Gold Coast/Ghana Admin. Service, 1947–58; Sen. District Comr, 1955; Asst Chief Regional Officer, Northern Region, 1957; Regional Sec., 1958; Financial Sec., British Somaliland, 1958–60; War Office, 1961–66; HM Treasury, 1966–78; seconded to Solomon Is, as Financial Sec. (later Financial Adviser), 1973–76; seconded, as British Mem., Anglo/French Mission on Admin. Reform in the Condominium of the New Hebrides, 1977; Governor of Gilbert Is, 1978 to Independence, July 1979; Financial and Develt Sec., Gibraltar, 1979–83. Chm., Norwich Union Fire Insurance Soc. (Gibraltar) Ltd, 1984–99. *Recreations:* walking, music. *Club:* Royal Commonwealth Society.

WALLACE, Richard Alexander; Principal Finance Officer, Welsh Office, 1990–97; *b* 24 Nov. 1946; *s* of Lawrence Mervyn and late Norah Wallace; *m* 1970, Teresa Caroline Harington Smith (*d* 2006); three *c* (and one *c* decd). *Educ:* Bembridge and Sandown C of E Primary Schools; Clifton Coll. Prep. Sch.; Clifton Coll.; King's Coll., Cambridge (MA). Asst Master, Woking County GS for Boys, 1967; Min. of Social Security, 1968; Principal, DHSS, 1972, Asst Sec., 1981; transf. to Welsh Office, 1986; Under Sec., 1988.

WALLACE, Richard David; Editor, Daily Mirror, since 2004; *b* 11 June 1961; *s* of Bill and Maureen Wallace. *Educ:* Ratcliffe Coll., Leics. Leicester Mercury, 1979–83; EMI Records, 1983–84; Oxon Bucks News Agency, 1984–86; Daily Mail, 1986–88; The Sun, 1988–90; Daily Mirror: show business reporter, then show business ed., 1999–2000; Hd of News, 2000–02; US Ed., 2002–03; Dep. Ed., Sunday Mirror, 2003–04. *Recreations:* travel, contemporary American literature. *Address:* c/o Daily Mirror, 1 Canada Square, E14 5AP. *T:* (020) 7293 3000.

WALLACE, (Robert) Ben (Lobban); MP (C) Lancaster and Wyre, since 2005; *b* 15 May 1970; *m* 2001, Liza Cooke; one *s* one *d. Educ:* Millfield Sch., Somerset; RMA Sandhurst. Ski Instructor, Austrian Nat. Ski Sch., 1987–89; advertising, RGSH Boston, USA; commissioned, Scots Guards, 1991; Platoon Comdr, 1991–93 (despatches, 1992); Ops Officer, 1993, Intelligence, 1994–97; Co. Comdr, 1997; served Windsor, London, N Ireland, Central America, BAOR, Egypt, Cyprus; retired 1998. EU Dir, Qinetiq, 2003–05. MSP (C) NE Scotland, 1999–2003; Mem., EU Cttee, health spokesman, Scottish Parlt. Shadow Minister of State for Scotland; Mem., Scottish Select Cttee, 2005–, NI Grand Cttee, H of C. Mem., Queen's Body Guard for Scotland (Royal Co. of Archers), 2006–. *Recreations:* ski-ing, sailing, Rugby, horse racing. *Address:* House of Commons, SW1A 0AA; c/o Lancaster and Wyre Conservative Association, Great Eccleston Village Centre, 59 High Street, Great Eccleston PR3 0YB. *Clubs:* Carlton, Beefsteak.

WALLACE, Sharmila; *see* Nebhrajani, S.

WALLACE, Stephanie Vera; *see* Hilborne, S. V.

WALLACE, Theodore; *see* Wallace, W. T. O.

WALLACE, (Wellesley) Theodore (Octavius); Chairman, VAT and Duties (formerly VAT) Tribunal, since 1989 (part-time, 1989–92); Special Commissioner of Income Tax, since 1992; *b* 10 April 1938; *s* of late Dr Caleb Paul Wallace and Dr Lucy Elizabeth Rainsford (*née* Pigott); *m* 1988, Maria Amelia Abercromby, *d* of Sir Ian Abercromby, 10th Bt; one *s* one *d*. *Educ:* Charterhouse; Christ Church, Oxford. 2nd Lt, RA, 1958; Lt, Surrey Yeomanry, TA, 1959–62. Called to the Bar, Inner Temple, 1963. Mem., Lincoln's Inn (*ad eundem*), 1973. Hon. Sec., Taxation of Sub-cttee, Soc. of Cons. Lawyers, 1974–92. Trustee, Trinity Fields Trust, Wandsworth. Contested (C): Pontypool, Feb. 1974; S Battersea, Oct. 1974, 1979. *Publication:* (jtly with John Wakeham) The Case Against Wealth Tax, 1968. *Recreations:* lawn tennis, ski-ing, golf. *Address:* 46 Belleville Road, SW11 6QT. *T:* (020) 7228 7740; Whitecroft, W Clandon, Surrey GU4 7TD. *T:* (01483) 222574.

WALLACE, Prof. (William) Angus, FRCS, FRCSE; Professor of Orthopaedic and Accident Surgery, School of Medical and Surgical Sciences, University of Nottingham, since 1985; *b* 31 Oct. 1948; *s* of late Dr William Bethune Wallace and Dr Frances Barret Wallace (*née* Early), Dundee; *m* 1971, Jacqueline Vera Studley; two *s* one *d*. *Educ:* Dundee High Sch.; Univ. of St Andrews (MB ChB 1972); FRCSE 1977; Cert. of Orthopaedic Higher Specialist Trng 1984; FRCSE (Orth) 1985; FRCS 1997. Jun. House Officer, Dundee Royal Infirmary and Maryfield Hosp., 1972–73; Sen. House Officer, Derby, 1974–75; Registrar (Basic Surg. Trng), Newcastle and Gateshead Hosps, 1975–77; Orthopaedic Registrar, Nottingham Hosps, 1978–81; MRC Res. Fellow, 1979; Lectr (Hon. Sen. Registrar) in Orthopaedic Surgery, Univ. of Nottingham, 1981–84; Vis. Res. Fellow, Toronto Western Hosp., Canada, 1983; Med. Dir, North Western Orthotic Unit, and Med. Advr, Dept of Orthopaedic Mechanics, Univ. of Salford, 1984–85. Advr, Rail Accident Investigation Bd, 2007. Mem., ABC Club, 1988–. Member: RSocMed 1988; Council, RCSE, 1990–2000, 2004–07 (Vice-Pres., 1997–2000); Council, Faculty of Sport and Exercise Medicine, 2005–; Dean, Faculty of Medical Informatics, RSCE, 2000–05. Chairman: Nat. Sports Medicine Inst. of UK, 1999–2003; Inter-Collegiate Bd in Trauma and Orthopaedic Surgery, 2002–05; Specialist Adv. Cttee for Trauma and Orthopaedic Surgery, 2008–. Pres., British Elbow and Shoulder Soc., 2001–03. Foundn Fellow, Faculty of Sports and Exercise Medicine (UK), 2006. Sir Walter Mercer Gold Medal, RCSE, 1985; Weigelt-Wallace Award for exceptional med. care, Univ. of Texas, 1995; Great Scot Sci. and Medicine Award, Sunday Mail, Scotland, 1995; People of the Year Award, RADAR, 1995. *Publications:* Shoulder Arthroscopy, 1992; Management of Disasters and their Aftermath, 1994; Joint Replacement of the Shoulder and Elbow, 1998; A Handbook of Sports Medicine, 1999; numerous articles in learned jls on osteoporosis, shoulder surgery and sports medicine. *Recreations:* narrow boating, information technology, DIY. *Address:* High Trees, Foxwood Lane, Woodborough, Nottingham NG14 6ED. *T:* (0115) 965 2372, *Fax:* (0115) 965 4638; *e-mail:* Angus.Wallace@rcsed.ac.uk.

WALLACE-HADRILL, Prof. Andrew Frederic, OBE 2004; DPhil; Director: British School at Rome, since 1995; Herculaneum Conservation Project, since 2001; Professor of Classics, University of Reading, since 1987 (on leave of absence); *b* 29 July 1951; *s* of John Michael Wallace-Hadrill and Anne (*née* Wakefield); *m* 1976, Josephine Claire Braddock; one *s* one *d*. *Educ:* Rugby Sch.; Corpus Christi Coll., Oxford (MA); St John's Coll., Oxford (DPhil). Fellow and Dir of Studies in Classics, Magdalene Coll., Cambridge, 1976–83; Lectr in Ancient History, Univ. of Leicester, 1983–87; Head, Dept of Classics, Reading Univ., 1988–94. Editor, Jl of Roman Studies, 1991–95. *Publications:* Suetonius: the scholar and his Caesars, 1983, 2nd edn 1995; (ed) Patronage in Ancient Society, 1989; (ed with J. W. Rich) City and Country in the Ancient World, 1991; Augustan Rome, 1993; Houses and Society in Pompeii and Herculaneum, 1994; (ed with R. Laurence) Domestic Space in the Roman World: Pompeii and beyond, 1997; The British School at Rome: one hundred years, 2001; Rome's Cultural Revolution, 2008. *Address:* The British School at Rome, via Gramsci 61, 00197 Rome, Italy.

WALLARD, Prof. Andrew John, PhD; Director, International Bureau of Weights and Measures, since 2004 (Director Designate, 2002–03); *b* 11 Oct. 1945; *s* of late William John Wallard and of Marjorie Meredith Wallard (*née* Briggs); *m* 1969, Barbara Jean Pritchard; two *s*. *Educ:* Liverpool Inst. High Sch. for Boys; Univ. of St Andrews (BSc Hons 1968; PhD 1971). CPhys 1990; CEng 2000; FInstP 2000. Laser physicist, NPL, 1968–78; Chief Scientist's Unit, DTI, 1978–80; Mktg Unit, NPL, 1980–81; Department of Trade and Industry, 1981–90: Res. and Technol. Policy Div.; Sec. of State's Policy Unit; Electronics Applications Div.; Alvey/Information Engrg Directorate; ESPRIT prog.; Dep. Dir and Chief Metrologist, NPL, 1990–2002. Member: Central Policy Review Staff, 1980–82; Panel, CSSB, 1985–95; Steering Cttee, Ilkley R&D Conf., 1988–2002; Internat. Cttee for Weights and Measures, 1995– (President Consultative Committee: for Photometry and Radiometry, 1995–2002; for Acoustics, Ultrasound and Vibration, 1999–2003); Bd Mem., Nat. Conf. of Standards Labs Internat., 2002–. Council Mem., 1998–2001, Chm., 2001–03, Res. and Develt Soc.; Vice Pres., Inst. of Physics, 2001– (Council Mem., 1996–2001); Member, Science Council: Istituto di Metrologia "Gustavo Colonnetti", 2002–; Istituto Elettrotecnico "Galileo Ferraris", 2002–. Mem., Ext. Panel, Physics Dept, Univ. of Wales, Aberystwyth, 1997– (Hon. Vis. Prof., 2001–). Chm., Alice Ruston Housing Assoc., 1986–95; Mem., Send PCC, 1988–95; Gov., Send First Sch., 1995–99. FRSA. Fellow: Acad. of Scis of Turin, 2003; Russian Acad. of Metrology. Hon. DSc Huddersfield, 1999. Lifetime Achievement Award, Co. of Scientific Instrument Makers, 2000; Gold Medal, NPL, 2002. *Publications:* contribs to various books and over 40 contribs to learned jls. *Recreations:* reading the newspapers, the garden, choosing wines, choral evensong. *Address:* Bureau International des Poids et Mesures, Pavillon de Breteuil, 92312, Sèvres Cedex, France. *T:* (1) 4507 7070, *Fax:* (1) 4534 8670; *e-mail:* awallard@bipm.org. *Club:* Athenæum.

WALLENBERG, Jacob; Chairman of the Board, Investor AB, since 2005; *b* 13 Jan. 1956; *s* of Peter Wallenberg, *qv* and Suzanne Fleming; *m* Marie Wehtje; one *s* two *d*. *Educ:* Wharton Sch., Univ. of Pennsylvania (BSc Econ 1980; MBA 1981). Officer, Swedish Naval Reserve. Joined J. P. Morgan, NY, 1981; Hambros Bank, London, 1983; Enskilda Securities, London, 1984, then with Skandinaviska Enskilda Banken, Sweden, 1985; Exec. Vice Pres., Investor AB, 1990–92; rejoined Skandinaviska Enskilda Bank Gp, 1993: Dep. Chief Operating Officer, 1994, Chief Operating Officer, 1995–97, Enskilda Div.; Pres. and CEO, 1997–98; Chm. of Bd, 1998–2005; Vice-Chm. 2005–. Vice Chairman: SAS; Scandinavian Airlines; Atlas Copco; Board Member: ABB Ltd; Coca-Cola Co. Member: Bd, Knut and Alice Wallenberg Foundn; Bd, Nobel Foundn. *Recreations:* golf, sailing, ski-ing. *Address:* Investor AB, 10332 Stockholm, Sweden. *T:* (8) 6142000.

WALLENBERG, Marcus; Chairman, Skandinaviska Enskilda Banken, since 2005 (a Deputy Chairman, 2002–05); *b* 2 Sept. 1956; *s* of Marc and Olga Wallenberg; *m* Fanny Sachs; four *c*. *Educ:* Georgetown Univ., Washington (BSc Foreign Service). Lieut, Royal Swedish Naval Acad., 1977. Citibank NA, New York, 1980–82; Deutsche Bank AG, Frankfurt and Hamburg, 1983; S. G. Warburg Co. Ltd, London, 1983; Citicorp, Hong Kong, 1984; Skandinaviska Enskilda Banken, Stockholm and London, 1985–90; Dir, Stora Feldmuhle AG, Dusseldorf, 1990–93; Investor AB: Exec. Vice Pres., 1993–99; Pres. and Chief Exec., 1999–2005. Vice Chairman: L. M. Ericsson; Saab AB. Holds numerous directorships. *Recreations:* sports, tennis, sailing, ski-ing, hunting. *Address:* Skandinaviska Enskilda Banken, Kungsträdgårdsgatan 8, 10640 Stockholm, Sweden.

WALLENBERG, Peter, Order of Wasa, 1974; King's Medal 12th Class, 1983; Hon. KBE 1989; First Vice Chairman, Skandinaviska Enskilda Banken, 1984–96 (Vice Chairman, 1980–84); Chairman: Investor AB, 1982–97; Wallenberg Foundation, since 1982; *b* Stockholm, 26 May 1926; *s* of Marcus Wallenberg and Dorothy (*née* Mackay); *m* (marr. diss.); two *s* one *d*. *Educ:* Stockholm Univ. (LLB 1953). Various positions within Atlas Copco Gp, 1953–68; Man. Dir, Atlas Copco MCT AB, 1968–70; Dep. Man. Dir, Atlas Copco AB, 1970–74; Industrial Advr to Skandinaviska Enskilda Banken, 1974–80. Mem. Bd, Stockholm Sch. of Econs, 1976–. Pres., ICC, 1989–90. Hon. Dr: Stockholm Sch. of Econ., 1984; Augustana Coll., Ill, 1985; Upsala Coll., NJ, 1989; Georgetown, Wash, 1990. Seraphime Medal, 2000. Orden de Isabel la Católica (Spain), 1979; Comdr, Légion d'Honneur (France), 1987; Comdr 1st Cl. Order of Lion of Finland, 1988; Comdr l'Ordre de Léopold (Belgium), 1989; Grand Cross, Ordem do Merito e Industrial (Portugal), 1990; Grand Cross, Order of Gregorius the Great (Vatican), 1991; Comdr 1st Cl., Royal Norwegian Order of Merit, 1992. *Recreations:* hunting, sailing, tennis. *Address:* Investor AB, 103 32 Stockholm, Sweden.

See also J. Wallenberg.

WALLER, Gary Peter Anthony; business analyst; *b* 24 June 1945; *s* of late John Waller and Elizabeth Waller. *Educ:* Rugby Sch.; Lancaster Univ. (BA Hons 1967); Open Univ. Business Sch. (MBA 2001). Chairman: Lancaster Univ. Conservative Assoc., 1965; Spen Valley Civic Soc., 1978–80; Vice-Chm., Nat. Assoc. of Cons. Graduates, 1970–73 and 1976–77. Exec. Sec., Wider Share Ownership Council, 1973–76. Contested (C): Kensington, Bor. Council elecns, 1971, 1974; Leyton, GLC elecn, 1973; Rother Valley, parly elecn, Feb. and Oct. 1974. MP (C) Brighouse and Spenborough, 1979–83, Keighley, 1983–97; contested (C) Keighley, 1997. PPS to Sec. of State for Transport, 1982–83. Chm., Select Cttee on Information, 1992–97 (Mem., 1991–97); Member: H of C Select Cttee on Transport, 1979–82; Jt Cttee on Consolidation Bills, 1982–92; Select Cttee on Finance and Services, 1992–97; Chm., All Party Wool Textile Gp, 1984–89 (Sec., 1979–83); Vice-Chairman: Parly Food and Health Forum, 1985–97; Parly IT Cttee, 1987–97 (Treas., 1981–87); Cons. Parly Transport Cttee, 1992–94, 1996–97 (Sec., 1985–87, 1988–92); Secretary: Cons. Parly Sport and Recreation Cttee, 1979–81; Yorkshire Cons. Members, 1979–83; All-Party Rugby League Gp, 1989–97; Chm., Cons. Technology Forum, 2000–04; Hon. Secretary: Parly and Scientific Cttee, 1988–91; Parly Univs Gp, 1995–97. Lay Mem., Dental Complaints Service Adv. Bd, GDC, 2006–. President: Brighouse Citizens Advice Bureau, 1979–83; Harlow Cons. Assoc., 2008–; Vice-President: Newham S Cons. Assoc., 1979–95 (Chm., 1971–74); Keighley Cons. Assoc., 1998–. Vice-President: Trading Standards Inst. (formerly Inst. of Trading Standards Admin), 1988–; Keighley Sea Cadets, 1984–97; Friends of the Settle-Carlisle Railway, 1987–; AMA, 1992–97. Council Mem., Consumers' Assoc., 1995–; Dir, Which? Ltd, 2002–04, 2006–. Mem., Hatfield Heath Parish Council, 2008–. Chm., Southern Gp, Yorks CCC, 2004–06. FRSA 2005. *Recreations:* music, photography, sport, classic cars, 19th and 20th century decorative arts. *Address:* Monksfield, Sawbridgeworth Road, Hatfield Heath, Bishop's Stortford, Herts CM22 7DR. *T:* (01279) 739435; *e-mail:* gary.waller@which.net. *Club:* Carlton.

WALLER, Rt Hon. Sir (George) Mark, Kt 1989; PC 1996; **Rt Hon. Lord Justice Waller;** Lord Justice of Appeal, since 1996; Vice-President, Court of Appeal (Civil Division), since 2006; *b* 13 Oct. 1940; *s* of Rt Hon. Sir George Waller, OBE; *m* 1967, Rachel Elizabeth, *d* of His Honour Christopher Beaumont, MBE; two *s* (and one *s* decd). *Educ:* Oundle Sch.; Durham Univ. (LLB). Called to the Bar, Gray's Inn, 1964, Bencher, 1988 (Vice-Treas., 2008); QC 1979; a Recorder, 1986–89; a Judge of the High Court of Justice, QBD, 1989–96; Presiding Judge, NE Circuit, 1992–95; Judge i/c Commercial List, 1995–96. Chm., Judicial Studies Bd, 1999–2003. Pres., Council of Inns of Court, 2003–06. *Recreations:* tennis, golf. *Address:* Royal Courts of Justice, Strand, WC2A 2LL. *Clubs:* Garrick, MCC; Huntercombe Golf.

WALLER, Guy de Warrenne, MA, MSc; Headmaster, Cranleigh School, since 1997; *b* 10 Feb. 1950; *s* of late Col Desmond de Warrenne Waller and of Angela Mary Waller (*née* Wright); *m* 1980, Hilary Ann Farmbrough; four *d*. *Educ:* Hurstpierpoint Coll.; Worcester Coll., Oxford (MA; Hon. Sec., OUCC; cricket blue, 1974; hockey blue, 1974, 1979); Wolfson Coll., Oxford (MSc). Head of Chemistry and Housemaster, Radley Coll., 1974–93; Headmaster, Lord Wandsworth Coll., 1993–97. *Publications:* Thinking Chemistry, 1980; Advancing Chemistry, 1982; Condensed Chemistry, 1985. *Recreations:* sports, keeping up with family and friends, chess, music. *Address:* Crane House, Cranleigh School, Cranleigh, Surrey GU6 8QQ. *T:* (01483) 542001. *Clubs:* MCC; Vincent's (Oxford); Ladykillers Hockey.

WALLER, Sir (John) Michael, 10th Bt *cr* 1780, of Newport, Co. Tipperary; PhD; Professor of International Communication, Institute of World Politics, Washington, DC, since 2001; *b* 14 May 1962; *s* of Sir Robert William Waller, 9th Bt and Carol Anne Waller (*née* Hines); *S* father, 2000; *m* 1986, Maria Renee Gonzalez; four *s* three *d*. *Educ:* George Washington Univ. (BA 1985); Boston Univ. (MA 1989; PhD 1993). Vice Pres., Center for Security Policy, Washington, DC, 2000–. *Publications:* The Third Current of Revolution, 1991; Secret Empire: the KGB in Russia today, 1994; The Public Diplomacy Reader, 2007; Strategic Influence, 2007. *Heir:* *s* John Michael Waller, *b* 18 Feb. 1990. *Address:* Institute of World Politics, 1521 16th Street NW, Washington, DC 20036, USA.

WALLER, Rt Rev. John Stevens; Bishop Suffragan of Stafford, 1979–87; Assistant Bishop, diocese of Bath and Wells, 1987–2003; *b* 18 April 1924; *m* 1951, Pamela Peregrine; two *s* three *d*. *Educ:* St Edward's School, Oxford; Peterhouse, Cambridge (MA); Wells Theol Coll. War service with RNVR, 1942–46. Deacon 1950, priest 1951, London; Leader, Strood Gp of Parishes, 1967–72, Team Rector of Strood 1972–73; Rector of St Nicholas, Harpenden, Herts, 1973–79; Team Vicar, Long Sutton and Long Load, Som, 1987–89. *Address:* 102 Harnham Road, Salisbury, Wilts SP2 8JW. *T:* (01722) 329739.

WALLER, Rt Hon. Sir Mark; *see* Waller, Rt Hon. Sir G. M.

WALLER, Sir Michael; *see* Waller, Sir J. M.

WALLER, Peter Graham; Director, Energy Group, Department for Business, Enterprise and Regulatory Reform (formerly Department of Trade and Industry), 2004–08; *b* 3 Jan. 1954; *s* of Raymond and Phyllis Waller; *m* 1991, Erica Zimmer. *Educ:* King's Sch., Macclesfield; Mansfield Coll., Oxford (BA Jurisp. 1976). Dept of Prices and Consumer Protection, subseq. Departments of Industry and of Trade, then Department of Trade and Industry, 1976–2001: various posts incl. Private Sec. to Minister of Consumer Affairs, 1981–83; privatisation of Rolls Royce, British Steel and water industry, 1987–91; Dir, Mkt Intelligence Unit, 1990–91; policy on future of PO, 1991–95; Dir, Business Links Services, 1995–97, Business Links, 1997–99; Dep. Chief Exec., Small Business Service, 2000–01; Dep. Dir Gen., Oftel, 2002–03. *Recreations:* watching lower league football, gardening, Shakespeare, walking in London. *Address:* 22 Grove Park, Wanstead E11 2DL; *e-mail:* peteranderica@aol.com.

WALLER, Philip Anthony; Senior District Judge, Principal Registry of the Family Division, since 2004 (District Judge, 1994–2004); *b* 12 Oct. 1952; *s* of late Robert Waller and of Olive (*née* Deakin); *m* 1978, Linda Andrews; two *d*. *Educ:* Whitgift Sch.; Univ. of Exeter (LLB Hons 1974); Inns of Court Sch. of Law. Called to the Bar, Inner Temple, 1975; with Reed, Smith, Shaw & McClay, Attorneys, Pittsburgh, USA, 1976; practised London, 1977–93. *Publication:* (co-ed) Rayden and Jackson's Law and Practice in Divorce and Family Matters, 17th edn 1997, 18th edn 2005. *Recreations:* choral singing, early music, historic houses and gardens, wine, France. *Address:* Principal Registry, Family Division, First Avenue House, 42–49 High Holborn, WC1V 6NP.

WALLER, Rev. Dr Ralph; Principal, and Tutor in Theology, Harris Manchester (formerly Manchester) College, University of Oxford, since 1988; Director, Farmington Institute for Christian Studies, since 2001; *b* 11 Dec. 1945; *s* of Christopher Waller and Ivy (*née* Miller); *m* 1968, Carol Roberts; one *d*. *Educ:* John Leggott Grammar Sch., Scunthorpe; Richmond Coll. Divinity Sch., Univ. of London (BD); Univ. of Nottingham (MTh); King's Coll. London (PhD 1986); MA Oxon. VSO in India, teaching maths and PE, and House Master, Shri Shivajh Mil. Sch., Poona, 1967–68; Maths Master, Riddings Comprehensive Sch., Scunthorpe, 1968–69; Methodist Minister, Melton Mowbray, 1972–75; ordained, 1975; Minister, Elvet Methodist Ch, Durham City, and Methodist Chaplain, Univ. of Durham, 1975–81; Chaplain, St Mary's Coll. and St Aidan's Coll., Univ. of Durham, 1979–81; Chaplain, Tutor in Theol. and Resident Tutor, Westminster Coll., Oxford, 1981–88; University of Oxford: Chm., Faculty of Theol., 1995–97; Chm., Envmtl Cttee, 1997–2000; Mem., Hebdomadal Council, 1997–2000. Hon. DLitt Menlo Coll., Calif, 1994; Hon. DHum: Ball State Univ., Indiana, 1998; St Olaf, 2001; Indianapolis, 2006; Hon. DTheol Uppsala, 1999; Hon. DHL Christopher Newport, 2005; Hon. DD Hartwick, 2003. UK Templeton Prize, 1993. *Publications:* (contrib.) Truth, Liberty and Religion, 1986; (ed with Benedicta Ward) Christian Spirituality, 1999; John Wesley: a personal portrait, 2003; (ed with Benedicta Ward) Joy of Heaven, 2003. *Recreations:* swimming, walking, browsing round second-hand bookshops. *Address:* Harris Manchester College, Mansfield Road, Oxford OX1 3TD. *T:* (01865) 271006. *Club:* Oxford and Cambridge.

WALLER, Stephen Philip; His Honour Judge Stephen Waller; a Circuit Judge, since 1996; *b* 2 Jan. 1950; *s* of Ronald Waller and Susannah Waller; *m* 1st, 1974, Anne Brooksbank (marr. diss.); one *s* one *d*; 2nd, 1986, Jennifer Welch; one *d*. *Educ:* Mill Hill Sch.; University College London (LLB Hons). Called to the Bar, Inner Temple, 1972.

WALLERSTEINER, Dr Anthony Kurt; Headmaster, Stowe School, since 2003; *b* 7 Aug. 1963; *m* 1994, Valerie Anne Macdougall-Jones; one *s* two *d*. *Educ:* King's Sch., Canterbury (Sen. Schol.); Trinity Coll., Cambridge (Open Schol.; BA Hist. Tripos 1985; MA 1993); Univ. of Kent at Canterbury (PhD Hist. and Theory of Art 2001). Crawford Travelling Schol., 1984; Assistant Master: Bancroft's Sch., Woodford Green, 1986; Sherborne, 1986–89; St Paul's Sch., 1989–92; Hd of Hist., 1993–2000, Housemaster, 1999–2003, Tonbridge Sch. Council Mem., Tate St Ives, 2006–. Governor: Ashfold Prep. Sch., 2004–; Winchester House Prep. Sch., 2004–; Summer Fields Prep. Sch., 2006–. *Publications:* contrib. reviews to Burlington Mag. *Recreations:* galleries, music, travel, family and friends. *Address:* Kinloss, Stowe, Buckingham MK18 5EH.

WALLEY, Dr Francis, CB 1978; FREng; consulting engineer; Consultant to the Arup Group (formerly Ove Arup Partnership); *b* 30 Dec. 1918; *s* of late Reginald M. Walley and Maria M. Walley; *m* 1946, Margaret, *yr d* of late Rev. Thomas and Margaret J. Probert; two *d*. *Educ:* Cheltenham Grammar Sch.; Bristol Univ. MSc, PhD; FICE (Mem. Council, 1978–81); FIStructE (Vice-Pres., 1982–83; Hon. Treasurer, 1981; Hon. Sec., 1979–81); FREng (FEng 1985); Lewis Kent Award, IStructE, 1985. Entered Min. of Home Security as Engr, 1941: reported to CIGS on allied bombing of Pantelleria, 1943; Member: British Bombing Survey Unit, France, 1944–45; Jt UK/USA Survey Unit of Nagasaki and Hiroshima, 1945. Min. of Works, 1945; Suptg Civil Engr, 1963; Dep. Dir of Building Devel t, 1965; Dir of Estate Management Overseas, 1969; Dir of Post Office Services, 1971; Under-Sec., Dir of Civil Engineering Services, DoE, 1973–78. I/c of Civil Defence Structures, British Atomic Trials, Aust., 1954; Mem., British Govt team looking at building construction in USSR, 1966. Mem., Standing Cttee on Structural Safety, 1977–88; Chairman: BSI Code Cttee for Structural Use of Concrete, 1987–2002; ISO Cttee of Design of Concrete Structures, 1989–2002. Diamond Jubilee Lecture, British Cement Assoc., 1995; James Sutherland Lecture, IStructE, 2000. *Publications:* Prestressed Concrete Design and Construction, 1954; (with Dr S. C. C. Bate) A Guide to the Code of Practice CP 115, 1960; (contrib.) Historic Concrete, 2000; several papers to ICE and techn. jls. *Recreations:* gardening, furniture-making. *Address:* 13 Julien Road, Coulsdon, Surrey CR5 2DN. *T:* (020) 8660 3290.

WALLEY, Joan Lorraine; MP (Lab) Stoke-on-Trent North, since 1987; *b* 23 Jan. 1949; *d* of late Arthur Walley and Mary Walley; *m* 1980, Jan Ostrowski; two *s*. *Educ:* Biddulph Grammar School; Hull Univ. (BA); University Coll. Swansea (Dip. Community Work). Alcoholics Recovery Project, 1970–73; Swansea City Council, 1974–78; Wandsworth Borough Council, 1978–79; NACRO, 1979–82. Mem., Lambeth Borough Council, 1982–86 (Chair: Health and Consumer Services Cttee, 1982–86; Assoc. of London Authorities Public Protection Cttee, 1982–86). Opposition front-bench spokesman on envmtl protection, 1988–90, on transport, 1990–95; Mem., Envmtl Audit Select Cttee, 1997–; Vice-Chairman: All Party Football Gp, 1997–2000 and 2005–; All Party Eur. Gp, 2001–; Chairman: All Party Lighting Gp, 2000–; All Party Regeneration Gp, 2000–; Associate Envmt Gp, 2002–05; Mem., Speaker's Panel, 2008–. Vice-President: Inst. of Environmental Health Officers, 1987–; Socialist Envmt and Resources Assoc. Member: UNISON; Globe Internat. Hon. Pres., 235 (1st Stoke-on-Trent) Sqn, ATC. *Address:* House of Commons, SW1A 0AA. *Club:* Fegg Hayes Sports and Social.

WALLFISCH, Raphael; 'cellist; *b* 15 June 1953; *s* of Peter Wallfisch, pianist; *m* Elizabeth; two *s* one *d*. *Educ:* Univ. of Southern California; studies with Amaryllis Fleming, Amadeo Baldovino, Derek Simpson and Gregor Piatigorsky. London début, QEH, 1974. 1st recordings of compositions by Bax, Strauss and others; numerous other recordings. Won Gaspar Cassadó Internat. Cello competition, 1977. *Address:* c/o Ikon Arts Management, Suite 111, Office E, Business Design Centre, 52 Upper Street, N1 0QH.

WALLINGER, Mark; artist; *b* Chigwell, 1959. *Educ:* Loughton Coll.; Chelsea Sch. of Art; Goldsmiths' Coll., London (MA 1985). Contemporary artist; work includes painting, sculpture, photography, video and installations. Henry Moore Fellow, British Sch. at Rome, 1998; Artist-in-residence for Year of the Artist, Oxford Univ., 2000–01; represented GB at Venice Biennale, 2001; Artist-in-residence, Edinburgh Coll. of Art, 2008. Work in *group exhibitions* includes: Manchester City Art Galls, 1996; ICA, 1996; Royal Acad., 1997; *solo exhibitions* include: Serpentine Gall., London, Ikon Gall., Birmingham, 1995; Anthony Reynolds Gall., London, 1997, 2003, 2004; Canary Wharf Window Gall., 1997; Palais des Beaux Arts, Brussels, Portikus, Frankfurt, 1999; Ecce Homo, The Fourth Plinth, Trafalgar Sq., 1999; British Sch. at Rome, Tate Liverpool, 2000; Milton Keynes Gall., Southampton City Art Gall., Univ. Mus. of Natural Hist., Oxford, Whitechapel Art Gall., 2001; Christmas Tree, Tate Britain, 2003; Laing Gall., Newcastle, Neue Nat. Gall., Berlin, 2004. *Film:* The Lark Ascending, 2004. Hon. Fellow, London Inst., 2002. Hon. Dr UCE, 2003. Turner Prize, 2007. *Publications:* (with M. Warnock) Art for All?: their policies and our culture; (ed jtly) On the Border: contemporary artists in Essex and Suffolk. *Address:* c/o Anthony Reynolds Gallery, 60 Great Marlborough Street, W1F 7BG.

WALLINGTON, Peter Thomas; QC 2008; barrister; *b* Maidstone, Kent, 25 March 1947; *s* of Thomas Edwin and Doris Evelyn Wallington; *m* 1972, Barbara Alice Rowland. *Educ:* Hemel Hempstead Grammar Sch.; Trinity Hall, Cambridge (BA 1968; LLM 1969); Inns of Court Sch. of Law (Cert. of Hon. and CLE Scholar 1987). Lecturer in Law: Univ. of Edinburgh, 1969–72; Univ. of Liverpool, 1972–73; Asst Lectr, then Lectr in Law, Univ. of Cambridge, and Fellow, Trinity Hall, Cambridge, 1973–79; Prof. of Law, 1979–88, Hd, Dept of Law, 1979–86, Univ. of Lancaster; Prof. of Law and Hd, Dept of Law, Brunel Univ., 1988–91. Called to the Bar, Gray's Inn, 1987; in practice as barrister specialising in employment law. Mem. editl team, Harvey on Industrial Relations and Employment Law, 2000–. *Publications:* Civil Liberties and a Bill of Rights (with Jeremy McBride), 1976; (ed) Butterworths Employment Law Handbook, 1979, 16th edn 2008; (jtly) Labour Law Cases and Materials, 1980; (ed and contrib.) Civil Liberties 1984, 1984; (jtly) The Police, Public Order and Civil Liberties: legacies of the miners strike, 1988; (with R. G. Lee) Blackstone's Public Law Statutes, 1988, 18th edn 2008; (contrib.) Supperstone and Goudie on Judicial Review, 1992, 3rd edn 2005; (contrib.) Tolley's Employment Law Handbook, 9th edn 1995 to 22nd edn 2008. *Recreations:* music, walking, reading. *Address:* 11 KBW Chambers, 11 King's Bench Walk, Temple, EC4Y 7EQ. *T:* (020) 7632 8500, *Fax:* (020) 7583 9123; *e-mail:* wallington@11kbw.com.

WALLINGTON, Susan Margaret; *see* Bullock, S. M.

WALLIS, (Diana) Lynn; Artistic Director, Royal Academy of Dance (formerly of Dancing), since 1994; *b* 11 Dec. 1946; *d* of Dennis Blackwell Wallis and Joan Wallis. *Educ:* Tonbridge Grammar Sch. for Girls; Royal Ballet Upper Sch. FISTD. Royal Ballet Touring Co., 1965–68; Royal Ballet School: Ballet Mistress, 1969–81; Dep. Principal, 1981–84; National Ballet of Canada: Artistic Co-ordinator, 1984–86; Associate Artistic Dir, 1986–87; Co-Artistic Dir, 1987–89; Dep. Artistic Dir, English National Ballet, 1990–94. *Recreations:* music, theatre, cinema.

WALLIS, Diana Paulette; Member (Lib Dem) Yorkshire and the Humber, since 1999, and Vice President, since 2007, European Parliament; *b* 28 June 1954; *d* of John Frederick Wallis and Jean Elizabeth Wallis (*née* Jones); *m* 1989, Stewart David Arnold. *Educ:* N London Poly. (BA Hist.); Univ. of Kent at Canterbury (MA Local Govt); Coll. of Law, Chester. Admitted Solicitor, 1983. Mem. (Lib Dem) Humberside CC, subseq. E Riding of Yorks UA, 1994–99 (Dep. Leader, 1995–99). European Parliament: Mem., Legal Affairs Cttee, 1999–; Vice-Pres., delegn to Switzerland, Iceland and Norway, 1999–2004; Pres., delegn to Switzerland, Iceland, Norway and Eur. Econ. Area, 2004–; Leader: Lib Dems, 2002–04; Lib Dem European Parly Party, 2002–04, 2006–. Pres., Inst. of Translation and Interpreting, 2002–. *Address:* (constituency office) PO Box 176, Brough, E Yorks HU15 1UX. *T:* (01482) 666898. *Club:* National Liberal.

WALLIS, Edmund Arthur, FREng; Chairman, WS Atkins, since 2005 (Director, since 2004); Chairman, Natural Environment Research Council, since 2007; *b* 3 July 1939; *s* of late Reuben Wallis and of Iris Mary Cliff; *m* 1964, Gillian Joan Mitchell; two *s*. CEng 1978; MIET (MIEE 1971); MIMechE 1972; FREng (FEng 1995). Central Electricity Generating Board: Stn Manager, Oldbury Nuclear Power Stn, 1977–79; Dir of System Op., 1981–86; Divl Dir of Ops, 1986–88; PowerGen, subseq. Powergen: Chief Exec., 1988–2001 and 2002–03; Chm., 1996–2002; Dep. Chm., 2002–03. Non-executive Director: BSI, 1992–97; LucasVarity plc, 1995–99 (Chm., 1998–99); London Transport, 1999–2003 (Chm., 2001–03); Ind. non-exec. Dir, Mercury European Privatisation Trust plc, 1994–2004; Mem. Adv. Bd, RWE, Germany, 1994–98. Lay Mem. Council, Aston Univ., 1992–98. Chm., Birmingham Royal Ballet Trust, 1996–2004; Mem. Bd, Birmingham Royal Ballet, 2005–; Gov., Royal Ballet Sch., 2006–. CCMI (CBIM 1991; AMBIM 1973). *Address:* WS Atkins, Euston Tower, 286 Euston Road, NW1 3AT.

WALLIS, Eithne Victoria, CB 2004; Managing Director, Government Business (formerly Central Government Business Unit), Fujitsu Services UK, since 2005; *b* 14 Dec. 1952; *d* of Ewing Walsh and late Marion Walsh; *m* 1st, 1977, Phillip Wallis (marr. diss. 2001); one *s* two *d*; 2nd, 2006, Baron Birt, *qv*. *Educ:* High Sch. for Girls, Dungannon, NI; Manchester Univ. (BA Econ 1973; MA Social Studies 1979). Probation Officer, 1979–87, mgt, 1987–94, Manchester; Asst Chief Probation Officer, Cambs, 1991–94; Dep. Chief Probation Officer, Inner London, 1994–97; Chief Probation Officer, Oxon and Bucks, 1997–2000; on secondment to Home Office, 2000; led team which created Nat. Probation Service for England and Wales, Dir Gen., 2001–04; Sen. Partner, Fujitsu Services UK, 2005. *Recreations:* reading, walking, gardening. *Address:* Grange House, Fotheringhay, Northants PE8 5HZ.

WALLIS, Frederick Alfred John E.; *see* Emery-Wallis.

WALLIS, Jane; *see* Packer, J.

WALLIS, Jeffrey Joseph; retail consultant; *b* 25 Nov. 1923; *s* of Nathaniel and Rebecca Wallis; *m* 1948, Barbara Brickman; one *s* one *d*. *Educ:* Owen's; Coll. Aeronautical Engrg. Man. Dir, Wallis Fashion Group, 1948–80. Mem., Monopolies and Mergers Commn, 1981–85. Formerly Member: CNAA; Clothing Export Council; NEDC (Textiles). Involved in art educn throughout career; various governorships. *Recreations:* motor racing, motor boating, industrial design. *Address:* 37 Avenue Close, NW8 6DA. *T:* (020) 7722 8665.

WALLIS, Prof. Kenneth Frank, FBA 1994; Professor of Econometrics, University of Warwick, 1977–2001, now Emeritus; *b* 26 March 1938; *s* of late Leslie Wallis and Vera Daisy Wallis (*née* Stone); *m* 1963, Margaret Sheila Campbell. *Educ:* Wath-on-Dearne GS; Manchester Univ. (BSc, MScTech); Stanford Univ. (PhD). Mem. Exec., NUS, 1961–63. Lectr, then Reader, in Stats, LSE, 1966–77; Dir, ESRC Macroeconomic Modelling Bureau, 1983–99. Member: HM Treasury Academic Panel, 1980–2001 (Chm., 1987–91); Nat. Statistics Methodology Adv. Cttee, 2001–. Member Council: Royal Stat. Soc., 1972–76; Royal Econ. Soc., 1989–94; Econometric Soc., 1995–97 (Fellow, 1975); British Acad., 2002–05. Fellow, Internat. Inst. of Forecasters, 2003. Hon. Dr Groningen, 1999. *Publications:* Introductory Econometrics, 1972; Topics in Applied Econometrics, 1973; (ed with D. F. Hendry) Econometrics and Quantitative Economics, 1984; Models of the UK Economy 1–4, 1984–87; (ed) Macroeconometric Modelling, 1994; Time Series Analysis and Macroeconometric Modelling, 1995; (ed with D. M. Kreps) Advances in Economics and Econometrics: theory and applications, 1997; articles in learned jls. *Recreations:* travel, music, gardening, swimming. *Address:* Department of Economics, University of Warwick,

Coventry CV4 7AL. *T:* (024) 7652 3055; 4 Walkers Orchard, Stoneleigh, Warwicks CV8 3JG. *T:* (024) 7641 4271.

WALLIS, Lynn; *see* Wallis, D. L.

WALLIS, Maria Assumpta, QPM 2002; Chief Constable, Devon and Cornwall Constabulary, 2002–06; *b* 13 Aug. 1955; *d* of Philip and late Margaret O'Donnell; *m* 1983, Michael Wallis. *Educ:* Bristol Univ. (BSc Jt Hons Sociol. and Social Admin). Metropolitan Police, 1976–94; Asst, then Dep. Chief Constable, Sussex Police, 1994–2002. *Recreations:* gardening, walking, reading. *Address:* c/o Devon and Cornwall Constabulary, Police HQ, Middlemoor, Exeter EX2 7HQ.

WALLIS, Sir Peter (Gordon), KCVO 1992; CMG 1990; HM Diplomatic Service, retired; High Commissioner to Malta, 1991–94; *b* 2 Aug. 1935; *s* of late Arthur Gordon Wallis, DFC, BScEcon, and Winifred Florence Maud Wallis; *m* 1965, Delysia Elizabeth (*née* Leonard); three *s* one *d. Educ:* Taunton and Whitgift Schools; Pembroke Coll., Oxford (MA). Ministry of Labour and National Service, 1958; HM Customs and Excise, 1959 (Private Sec., 1961–64); HM Diplomatic Service, 1968; Tel Aviv, 1970; Nairobi, 1974; Counsellor (Econ. and Comm.), Ankara, 1977; RCDS, 1981; Cabinet Office, 1982; Hd, Perm. Under-Sec.'s Dept, FCO, 1983; Minister, Pretoria, 1987; Minister, British Liaison Office, 1989, and subseq. Acting High Comr, 1990, Windhoek, Namibia; Political Advr to Jt Comdr, British Forces in the Gulf, Jan.–April 1991, to Comdr, British Forces, SE Turkey and N Iraq, May–July 1991. Advr to Learmont Enquiry into Prison Security, 1995. Head, UK delegn to EC monitor mission, Balkans, 1996, 1997, 1998, 1999. Mem., Regl Adv. Council, subseq. Regl Audience Council, BBC West, 2005–. Chm., Taunton and Dist Br., ESU, 2004–07. Vice-Chm., Taunton Area Cttee, Somerset CCC, 2006–. Trustee, Friends of Somerset Churches, 2007–. *Recreations:* reading, music, walking. *Address:* Parsonage Farm, Curry Rivel, Somerset TA10 0HG.

WALLIS, Peter Ralph; Deputy Controller, Aircraft Weapons and Electronics, Ministry of Defence, 1980–84; *b* 17 Aug. 1924; *s* of Leonard Francis Wallis and Molly McCulloch Wallis (*née* Jones); *m* 1949, Frances Jean Patricia Cowie; three *s* one *d. Educ:* University College Sch., Hampstead; Imperial Coll. of Science and Technology, London (BSc(Eng)). CEng 1967; FIET (FIEE 1967); FIMA 1968. Henrici and Siemens Medals of the College, 1944. Joined Royal Naval Scientific Service 1944; work at Admty Signal and Radar Estab. till 1959, Admty Underwater Weapons Estab. till 1968; Asst Chief Scientific Advr (Research), MoD, 1968–71, Dir Gen. Research Weapons, 1971–75, Dir Gen. Guided Weapons and Electronics, 1975–78, Dir Gen. Research A (Electronics) and Dep. Chief Scientist (Navy), 1978–80. Vice Pres., 1992–, Hon. Treas., 1988–, Hampstead Scientific Soc. (Hon. Sec., 1974–90). FCGI. Marconi Award, IERE, 1964. *Publications:* articles in Jl of IEE, IERE and Op. Res. Quarterly. *Recreations:* ski-ing, mountain walking, archæology, sailing, egyptology, geology, travel. *Address:* 22 Flask Walk, Hampstead, NW3 1HE. *Clubs:* Alpine Ski, Eagle Ski.

WALLIS, Peter Spencer; a District Judge (Magistrates' Courts) (formerly Metropolitan Stipendiary Magistrate), since 1993; a Recorder, since 2000; *b* 31 March 1945; *s* of Philip Wallis and Winifred Wallis; *m* 1970, Ann Margaret Bentham; one *s* one *d. Educ:* Maidstone Grammar Sch.; Lincoln Coll., Oxford (MA). Pilot, RAF, 1967–72. Admitted solicitor, 1976. Clerk to: Tonbridge and Malling Justices, 1977–88; Dover and Ashford Justices, 1988–93; Folkestone and Hythe Justices, 1990–93. An Asst Recorder, 1997–2000. Mem. Council, Justices' Clerks' Soc., 1983–93 (Pres., 1993). *Publications:* The Transport Acts 1981 and 1982, 1982, 2nd edn 1985; Road Traffic: guide to Part I of the 1991 Act, 1991; General Editor, Wilkinson's Road Traffic Offences, 13th edn 1987 to 23rd edn 2007. *Recreations:* flying, watching cricket, choral singing. *Address:* c/o Greenwich Magistrates' Court, 9 Blackheath Road, SE10 8PG. *T:* (020) 8694 0033. *Club:* Royal Air Force.

WALLIS, Dame Sheila (Ann), DBE 2002; Director and Education Consultant, Wallis Partnership Ltd, since 2002; *b* 13 Feb. 1942; *d* of John and Lilian Pearson; *m* 1964, Brian Wallis; two *s. Educ:* Chelsea Sch. of Human Movt; Univ. of London (BEd); Univ. of Brighton (MEd). Davison High School for Girls: Teacher, 1962–64, Head, 1964–82, of Physical Educn; Dep. Headteacher, 1982–88; Headteacher, 1988–2002. Comr, NCC Commn into Public Services, 2003–. FRSA 1998. *Publications:* contribs to educn jls and govt papers. *Recreations:* jogging, swimming, travelling, cooking. *Address:* Drake House, River Road, Arundel, W Sussex BN18 9EY. *T:* and *Fax:* (01903) 882171; *e-mail:* innovation@wallispartnership.co.uk.

WALLIS, Stuart Michael; Chairman, Protherics plc, since 1999; *b* 8 Oct. 1945; *s* of Stanley Oswald Wallis and Margaret Ethel Wallis; *m* 1971, Eileen; one *s. Educ:* Hawesdown Sch., West Wickham, Kent. FCA, CTA. Roland Goodman & Co., 1962–68; Chrysler, 1968–71; Shipton Automation, 1971–73; Star Computer Services, 1973–74; Hestair Gp, 1974–85 (Main Board, 1977); Exec. Dir, Octopus, 1985–87; Main Board Dir, Bowater plc, 1988–94; Chief Exec., Fisons plc, 1994–95; Chairman: Sheffield Forgemasters Ltd, 1996–98; LLP Gp, 1996–98; Yorkshire Gp, 1996–2000; SSL Internat., 1996–2001; John Mansfield Gp, then Communisis plc, 1997–2003; Euramax Internat., 1997–2005; Hay Hall Gp Ltd, 1997–2004; Trident Components Gp, 1999–2005; Tetley Group Ltd, 1999–2000; Eleksen Ltd (formerly ElektroTextiles), 2000–03; Worldmark Internat., 2000–02; Simply Smart Gp Ltd, 2004–08; Plethora Solutions Hldgs plc, 2005–; BCS Global Networks Ltd, 2005–; TSL Education Ltd, 2005–07; LGC Hldgs Ltd, 2007–. *Recreations:* golf, swimming, ski-ing. *Address:* Protherics plc, 3rd Floor, 3 Creed Court, 5 Ludgate Hill, EC4M 7AA. *Club:* Ashridge Golf.

WALLIS, Sir Timothy (William), Kt 1994; Managing Director, Alpine Deer Group; *b* 9 Sept. 1938; *s* of Arthur Wallis and Janice Blunden; *m* 1974, Prudence Ann Hazledine; four *s. Educ:* Christ's Coll., Christchurch. Founding Dir, Tourism Holdings Ltd. Mem. Council, NZ Deer Farmers' Assoc., 1977–84 (Hon. Life Mem.); founding Chm. and Hon. Life Mem., NZ Wapiti Soc. DCom (*hc*) Lincoln Univ., 2000. E. A. Gibson Award, 1980, for contribs to NZ aviation; Sir Arthur Ward Award, 1985, for contribs to agric.; Commem. Medal for services to deer industry, 1990; Sir Jack Newman Award, 1999, for outstanding contrib. to NZ tourism industry; Speights Southern Man Award, 2001; Laureate, NZ Business Hall of Fame, 2002; World Wide Gold Medal, RAeS, 2005. *Relevant publications:* Hurricane Tim: the story of Sir Tim Wallis, by Neville Peat, 2005; (for children) Winging It: the adventures of Tim Wallis, by Neville Peat, 2006. *Recreations:* scuba diving, hunting, fly fishing; represented West Coast-Buller 1958, S Canterbury 1959, at Rugby. *Address:* Benfiddich, Mount Barker, Wanaka 9192, New Zealand.

WALLIS-KING, Maj.-Gen. Colin Sainthill, CBE 1975 (OBE 1971); retired; *b* 13 Sept. 1926; *s* of late Lt-Col Frank King, DSO, OBE, 4th Hussars, and Colline Ammabel, *d* of late Lt-Col C. G. H. St Hill; *m* 1962, Lisabeth, *d* of late Swan Swanstrøm, Oslo, Norway; two *d. Educ:* Stowe. Commissioned Coldstream Guards, 1945; Liaison Officer with Fleet Air Arm, 1954; Staff Coll., 1960; Regtl Adjutant, Coldstream Guards, 1961; seconded to Para. Regt, 1963; ACOS HQ Land Norway, 1965; Comdr 2nd Bn Coldstream Guards, 1969; Dep. Comdr 8 Inf. Brigade, 1972; Comdr 3 Inf. Brigade, 1973; BGS Intell., MoD, 1975; Dir of Service Intelligence, 1977–80. Dir, Kongsberg Ltd, 1982–87; UK Agent for Norsk Forsvarsteknologi A/S, 1987–93. *Recreations:* equitation, sailing, music, cross-country ski-ing, fishing. *Address:* c/o Royal Bank of Scotland, Lawrie House, Victoria Road, Farnborough, Hants GU14 7NR. *Club:* Cavalry and Guards.

WALLOP, family name of **Earl of Portsmouth**.

WALLS, Geoffrey Nowell; Executive Director, Pearls of the Orient (International) Ltd, since 2006; *b* 17 Feb. 1945; *s* of Andrew Nowell Walls and Hilda Margaret Thompson; *m* 1975, Vanessa Bodger; one *s* three *d. Educ:* Trinity Grammar Sch., Melbourne; Univ. of Melbourne (BComm 1965). Australian Regular Army, 2nd Lieut RAAOC, 1966–69; Australian Trade Comr Service, 1970–79; served Jakarta, Singapore, Cairo, Beirut, Bahrain, Manila, Baghdad; Regional Dir, Adelaide, Commonwealth Dept of Trade, 1980–83; Gen. Manager, ATCO Industries (Aust) Pty Ltd, 1983–86; Agent Gen. for S Australia in London, 1986–98. CIH Ltd (formerly Clipsal Industries (Holdings) Ltd): Regl Manager, Sharjah, 1998–2000; Regl Dir, 2000–02; Exec. Dir, 2002–05; non-exec. Dir, 2005–07. Mem., S Australian Cricket Assoc. *Recreations:* golf, tennis, gardening. *Address:* Bollards, Ropes Lane, Fernhurst, Surrey GU27 3JD.

WALLS, Rev. Brother Roland Charles; Member, Community of the Transfiguration, since 1965; *b* 7 June 1917; *s* of late Roland William Walls and late Tina Josephine Hayward. *Educ:* Sandown Grammar Sch.; Corpus Christi Coll., Cambridge; Kelham Theological Coll. Curate of St James', Crossgates, Leeds, 1940–42; Curate of St Cecilia's, Parson Cross, Sheffield, 1942–45; Licensed preacher, Diocese of Ely, 1945–48; Fellow of Corpus Christi Coll., Cambridge, 1948–62; Lecturer in Theology, Kelham Theological Coll., 1948–51; Chaplain and Dean of Chapel, Corpus Christi Coll., Cambridge, 1952–58; Canon Residentiary, Sheffield Cathedral, 1958–62; Chaplain of Rosslyn Chapel, Midlothian, 1962–68. Examining Chaplain to Bishop of Edinburgh. Lecturer at Coates Hall Theological Coll.; Lecturer in Dogmatics Dept, New Coll., Edinburgh, 1963–74. Received into RC Church, ordained priest, 1983. *Publications:* (contrib.) Theological Word Book (ed A. Richardson), 1950; Law and Gospel, 1980; (contrib.) Dictionary of Christian Spirituality, 1983; (contrib.) Dictionary of Pastoral Counsel, 1984; The Royal Mysteries, 1990. *Recreations:* botany, music, etc. *Address:* The Hermitage, 23 Manse Road, Roslin, Midlothian EH25 9LF.

WALLS, Stephen Roderick; Partner, Next Wave Partners LLP, since 2007; *b* 8 Aug. 1947; *s* of late R. W. Walls and of D. M. Walls; *m*; two *s.* Accountant. Senior Auditor, Deloitte & Co., 1969; Group Chief Accountant, Lindustries, 1971; Financial Planning Exec., Vernons, 1974; Chesebrough Ponds: Finance Dir, UK and Geneva, 1975; Internat. Finance Dir, Geneva, 1981; Vice-Pres., Finance, 1981–87; Dir of Finance, 1987, Man. Dir, 1988–89, Plessey Co.; Chm., 1990–91, Chief Exec., 1990–92, Wiggins Teape Appleton, later Arjo Wiggins Appleton; Chm., The Albert Fisher Gp, 1992–97; Partner: Compass Partners Internat., 1998–2001; Bridley Capital Partners Ltd, 2001–05. Chairman: VPS Hldgs Ltd, 2003–; Pourshins plc, 2004–07; ITI Energy Ltd, 2006–. Chm., CHASE Children's Hospice, 2004–. Mem., Financial Reporting Council, 1990–95. *Recreations:* running, flying, music, theatre. *Address:* c/o Next Wave Partners LLP, 71 Wimpole Street, W1G 8AY. *Club:* Royal Automobile.

WALLSTRÖM, Margot; Member, since 1999, Vice-President, since 2004, European Commission; *b* 28 Sept. 1954; *m* 1984, Håkan Wallström; two *s.* Adminr, Swedish Social Democratic Youth League, 1974–77; Accountant, 1977–79, Sen. Accountant, 1986–87, Alfa Savings Bank, Karlstad; MP (SDP), Sweden, 1979–85; Minister for: Civil Affairs, 1988–91; Culture, 1994–96; Health and Social Affairs, 1996–98; CEO, TV Värmland, 1993–94; Exec. Vice-Pres., Worldview Global Media, Sri Lanka, 1998–99. Mem. Exec. Cttee, Swedish SDP, 1993–99. Hon. Dr: Chalmers Univ., Sweden, 2001; Mälardalen Univ., Sweden, 2004. *Publication:* (jtly) The People's Europe, or Why is it so Hard to Love the EU?, 2004. *Address:* European Commission, 1049 Brussels, Belgium.

WALLWORK, John, FRCSE; DL; Consultant Cardiothoracic Surgeon, Papworth Hospital, since 1981 (Director of Transplantation, 1989–2006; Medical Director, 1997–2002); *b* 8 July 1946; *s* of Thomas and Vera Wallwork; *m* 1973, Elizabeth Ann Medley; one *s* two *d. Educ:* Accrington Grammar Sch.; Edinburgh Univ. (BSc Hons Pharm. 1966; MB ChB 1970); MA Cantab 1986. FRCSE 1974; FRCS 1992 *ad eundem*, FRCPE 1999, FRCP 2001. Surgical Registrar, Royal Infirmary, Edinburgh, 1975–76; Senior Registrar: Adelaide Hosp., SA, 1977–78; Royal Infirmary, Glasgow, 1978–79; St Bartholomew's Hosp., 1979–81; Chief Resident in Cardiovascular and Cardiac Transplant Surgery, Stanford Univ. Med. Sch., 1980–81. Hon. Prof. of Cardiothoracic Surgery, Cambridge Univ., 2002–. Lister Prof., RCSE, 1985–86. FMedSci 2002. DL Cambs, 2007. *Publications:* (with R. Stepney) Heart Disease: what it is and how it is treated, 1987; (ed) Heart and Heart-Lung Transplantation, 1989; numerous papers on cardiothoracic and cardiopulmonary topics. *Recreations:* tennis, conversation, making phone calls from the bath. *Address:* 3 Latham Road, Cambridge CB2 2EG. *T:* (01223) 352827. *Club:* Sloane.

WALLWORK, John Sackfield, CBE 1982; Director, Daily Mail and General Trust PLC, 1982–91; Managing Director, Northcliffe Newspapers Group Ltd, 1972–82 (General Manager, 1967–71); *b* 2 Nov. 1918; *s* of Peter Wallwork and Clara Cawthorne Wallwork; *m* 1945, Bessie Bray; one *s* one *d. Educ:* Leigh Grammar Sch., Leigh, Lancs. FCIS. General Manager, Scottish Daily Mail, Edinburgh, 1959–62; Asst Gen. Man., Associated Newspapers Gp Ltd, London, 1962–66, Dir, 1973–82. Chm., Press Association Ltd, 1973–74 (Dir, 1969–76); Director: Reuters Ltd, 1973–76; Reuters Founders Share Co. Ltd, 1984–87; Reuters Trustee, 1978–84; Member Press Council, 1974–75; Newspaper Society: Mem. Council, 1967–85; Jun. Vice-Pres. 1975; Sen. Vice-Pres., 1976, Pres., 1977–78. Commander, Order of Merit, Republic of Italy, 1973. *Recreations:* reading, music. *Address:* 14 Bowling Green Court, 2 Brook Street, Chester, CH1 3DP. *T:* (01244) 350299.

WALMSLEY, Baroness *cr* 2000 (Life Peer), of West Derby in the co. of Merseyside; **Joan Margaret Walmsley;** Director, Walmsley Jones Communications, 1999–2003; *b* 12 April 1943; *d* of Leo Watson and Monica Watson (*née* Nolan); *m* 1st, 1966, John Newan Caro Richardson (marr. diss. 1979); one *s* one *d*; 2nd, 1986, Christopher Roberts Walmsley (*d* 1995); one step *s* two step *d*; 3rd, 2005, Baron Thomas of Gresford, *qv*. *Educ:* Notre Dame High Sch., Liverpool; Univ. of Liverpool (BSc Hons Biology); Manchester Poly. (PGCE). Cytologist, Christie Hosp., Manchester, 1966–67; teacher, Buxton Coll., 1979–87; Mkting Officer, Ocean Youth Club, 1987–88; PR Consultant: Intercommunication, Manchester, 1988–89; Hill & Knowlton UK Ltd, 1989–97; Joan Walmsley Public Relations, 1997–99. Lib Dem spokesman on educn and children, H of L, 2004–. *Recreations:* music, theatre, keeping fit, good company. *Address:* House of Lords, SW1A 0PW. *T:* (020) 7219 6047.

WALMSLEY, Brian; Under Secretary, Social Security Policy Group, Department of Social Security, 1990–94; *b* 22 April 1936; *s* of late Albert Edward Walmsley and Ivy Doreen Walmsley (*née* Black); *m* 1st, 1956, Sheila Maybury (marr. diss. 1993); two *d*; 2nd, 1994, Margaret Wilson. *Educ:* Prescot Grammar School. National Service, RAF, 1955–57.

Joined Min. of Pensions and Nat. Insurance, 1957, later Min. of Social Security and DHSS; Sec. to Industrial Injuries Adv. Council, 1978–79; Asst Sec., 1979; Under Sec., 1985; Civil Service Comr, OMCS, Cabinet Office (on secondment), 1988–90. *Recreations:* following cricket, playing golf, reading, gardening. *Clubs:* MCC; Chester Golf.

WALMSLEY, Rt Rev. Francis Joseph, CBE 1979; Roman Catholic Bishop of the Forces, 1979–2002, now Bishop Emeritus; *b* 9 Nov. 1926; *s* of Edwin Walmsley and Mary Walmsley (*née* Hall). *Educ:* St Joseph's Coll., Mark Cross, Tunbridge Wells; St John's Seminary, Wonersh, Guildford. Ordained, 1953; Asst Priest, Woolwich, 1953; Shoreham-by-Sea, Sussex, 1958; Chaplain, Royal Navy, 1960; Principal RC Chaplain, RN, 1975; retired from RN, 1979. Prelate of Honour to HH Pope Paul VI, 1975; ordained Bishop, 1979. *Recreations:* photography, gardening. *Address:* St John's Convent, Kiln Green, Reading, Berks RG10 9XP.

WALMSLEY, Prof. Ian Alexander, PhD; Hooke Professor of Physics, University of Oxford, since 2005; Fellow of St Hugh's College, Oxford, since 2001; *b* 13 Jan. 1960; *s* of Richard M. and Hazel F. Walmsley; *m* 1986, Katherine Frances Pardee; two *s* one *d*. *Educ:* Imperial Coll., Univ. of London (BSc 1980); Univ. of Rochester, NY (PhD 1986). Res. Associate, Cornell Univ., NY, 1986–88; Institute of Optics, University of Rochester, New York: Asst Prof., 1988–94, Associate Prof., 1994–98, Prof., 1998–2000, of Optics; Dir, 2000; Oxford University: Prof. of Exptl Physics, 2001–05; Head, Subdept of Atomic and Laser Physics, 2002–07. Vis. Prof. of Physics, Ulm Univ., 1995; Sen. Vis. Fellow, Princeton Univ., 2002–05. FInstP 2004; Fellow: Optical Soc. of America, 1997; APS, 2000. Dr *hc* Libre de Bruxelles, 2008. Leibinger Innovationspreis, Berthold Leibinger Stiftung, 2006; Wolfson Res. Merit Award, Royal Soc., 2007. *Publications:* contrib. to books and professional jls. *Recreation:* Tae Kwon Do (4th dan, World Assoc.). *Address:* Department of Physics, University of Oxford, Clarendon Laboratory, Parks Road, Oxford OX1 3PU. *T:* (01865) 272205.

WALMSLEY, Nigel Norman; Chairman: Broadcasters' Audience Research Board Ltd, since 2002; Tourism South East, since 2003; *b* 26 Jan. 1942; *s* of late Norman and Ida Walmsley; *m* 1969, Jane Walmsley, broadcaster, author and producer; one *d*. *Educ:* William Hulme's Sch.; Brasenose Coll., Oxford (BA English). Joined the Post Office, 1964; Asst Private Secretary to Postmaster General, 1967; Asst Director of Marketing, Post Office, 1973–75; Asst Sec., Industrial Planning Division of Dept of Industry, 1975–76; Director of Marketing, Post Office, 1977–81, Board Mem. for Marketing 1981–82; Man. Dir, Capital Radio, 1982–91; Chief Exec., 1991–94, Chm., 1994–2001, Carlton TV; Exec. Dir, 1992–2001, Dep. Chief Exec., 2000–01, Carlton Communications plc; Chm., GMTV, 1994–96, 2000–01. Board Member: Ind. Radio News, 1983–91; South Bank Centre, 1985–92 and 1997–2002; Director: The Builder Gp, 1986–92; General Cable plc, 1994–97; non-exec. Chm., Central Television, 1996–2001; non-executive Director: Energis plc, 1997–2002; ONdigital, subseq. ITV Digital, plc, 1997–2001; ITN, 2000–01; Ambassador Theatre Gp, 2001–04; de Vere plc, 2001–06; Eagle Rock, 2007– (Chm., 2002–07). Member Council: ASA, 2004–; Postwatch, 2006–; Mem., Rail Passengers' Council, 2005–. Chm., GLAA, 1985–86; Vice Chm., Advertising Assoc., 1992–2003. *Recreation:* intensive inactivity. *Address:* Broadcasters' Audience Research Board Ltd, 18 Dering Street, W1S 1AQ.

WALMSLEY, Peter James, MBE 1975; Director-General (formerly Director) of Petroleum Engineering Division, Department of Energy, 1981–89; *b* 29 April 1929; *s* of George Stanley and Elizabeth Martin Walmsley; *m* 1970, Edna Fisher; three *s* one *d*. *Educ:* Caterham Sch., Surrey; Imperial Coll., London (BSc; ARSM). Geologist: Iraq Petroleum Co., 1951–59; BP Trinidad, 1959–65; BP London, 1965–72; Exploration Manager, BP Aberdeen, 1972–78; Dep. Chief Geologist, BP London, 1978–79; Regional Exploration Manager, BP London, 1979–81. Chairman, Petroleum Exploration Soc. of Gt Britain, 1971–72; Pres., RSM Assoc., 1995–96. *Publications:* contribs to various learned jls on North Sea geology. *Recreations:* home and garden. *Address:* Elm Tree Cottage, 10 Great Austins, Farnham, Surrey GU9 8JG.

WALMSLEY, Sir Robert, KCB 1995; FREng, FIET; Chief of Defence Procurement, Ministry of Defence, 1996–2003; Chief Executive, Defence Procurement Agency, 1999–2003; *b* Aberdeen, 1 Feb. 1941; *s* of late Prof. Robert Walmsley, TD, FRCPE, FRCSE and Dr Isabel Mary Walmsley; *m* 1967; one *s* two *d*. *Educ:* Fettes Coll.; RN Coll., Dartmouth; Queens' Coll., Cambridge (MA MechScis); RN Coll., Greenwich (MSc Nuclear Sci.). FIET (FIEE 1994); FREng (FEng 1998). HMS Ark Royal, 1962–63; HMS Otus, 1964–66; HMS Churchill, 1968–72; Ship Dept, MoD, 1973–74; HM Dockyard, Chatham, 1975–78; MoD, PE, 1979–80; Chm., Naval Nuclear Technical Safety Panel, 1981–83; Naval Staff, 1984; MoD, PE, 1985–86; Dir Operational Requirements (Sea), 1987–89; ACDS (Communications, Command, Control and Information Systems), 1990–93; Dir Gen. Submarines, Chief Naval Engr Officer and Sen. Naval Rep. in Bath, 1993–94; Controller of the Navy, in rank of Vice-Adm., 1994–96. Non-executive Director: British Energy, 2003–; Cohort plc, 2006–; Independent Director: Gen. Dynamics, USA, 2004–; EDO Corp., USA, 2004–08; Stratos Global, Canada, 2006–08; Chm., Major Projects Assoc., 2004–; Sen. Advr, Morgan Stanley, 2004–. Hon. Col, 71st (Yeomanry) Signal Regt, 2001–07. Freeman, City of London, 1996; Liveryman, Co. of Engrs, 1999; Hon. Freeman, Co. of Shipwrights, 2001. FRSA 1997. Hon. FCIPS 2002. Hon. DSc Cranfield, 2002. *Recreations:* fly fishing, West Ham United FC, Scotland. *Address:* c/o Lloyds TSB, 7 Pall Mall, SW1Y 5NA. *Clubs:* Reform, Army and Navy; Hawks; North Hants Golf.

WALPOLE, family name of **Baron Walpole**.

WALPOLE, 10th Baron *cr* 1723, of Walpole; **Robert Horatio Walpole;** Baron Walpole of Wolterton, 1756; *b* 8 Dec. 1938; *s* of 9th Baron Walpole, TD and Nancy Louisa, OBE, *y d* of late Frank Harding Jones; *S* father, 1989; *m* 1st, 1962, S. Judith Schofield (later S. J. Chaplin, OBE, MP; marr. diss. 1979; she *d* 1993); two *s* two *d*; 2nd, 1980, Laurel Celia, *o d* of S. T. Ball; two *s* one *d*. *Educ:* Eton; King's College, Cambridge (MA, Dip Agric). Member, Norfolk CC, 1970–81 (Chm. of various cttees). Elected Mem., H of L, 1999. Chairman: Area Museums Service for South East England, 1976–79; Norwich School of Art, 1977–87; Textile Conservation Centre, 1981–88 (Pres. 1988); East Anglian Tourist Board, 1982–88. Hon. Fellow, St Mary's UC, Strawberry Hill, 1997. JP Norfolk, 1972. *Heir: s* Hon. Jonathan Robert Hugh Walpole [*b* 16 Nov. 1967; *m* 2006, Eileen Margaret Sean, *d* of Edward James Quinn]. *Address:* Mannington Hall, Norwich NR11 7BB. *T:* (01263) 587763.

WALPORT, Mark Jeremy, PhD; FRCP, FRCPath, FMedSci; Director, Wellcome Trust, since 2003; *b* 25 Jan. 1953; *s* of Samuel Walport and Doreen Walport (*née* Music); *m* 1986, Julia Elizabeth Neild; one *s* three *d*. *Educ:* St Paul's Sch., London; Clare Coll., Cambridge; Middlesex Hosp. Med. Sch., London (MA, MB BChir; PhD 1986). FRCP 1990; FRCPath 1997. House Officer, Middlesex Hosp. and Queen Elizabeth II Hosp., Welwyn, 1977–78; SHO, 1978–80; Hon. Registrar, Brompton Hosp., 1980; Registrar, Hammersmith Hosp., 1980–82; MRC Trng Fellow, MRC Mechanisms in Tumour Immunity Unit, Cambridge, 1982–85; Harrison-Watson Student, Clare Coll., Cambridge, 1982–85; Royal Postgraduate Medical School, subseq. Imperial College Faculty of Medicine: Sen. Lectr in Rheumatology, 1985–90; Reader in Rheumatological Medicine, 1990–91; Prof. of Medicine, 1991–2003; Vice Dean for Res., 1994–97; Hd, Div. of Medicine, 1997–2003; Hon. Cons. Physician, Hammersmith Hosp., 1985–2003; Dir, R&D, Hammersmith Hosps Trust, 1994–98. Member: Scientific Adv. Bd, Cantab Pharmaceuticals, Cambridge, 1989–; R&D Adv. Bd, SmithKline Beecham, 1998–. Member: Council, British Soc. for Rheumatology, 1989–95 (Chm., Heberden Cttee, 1993–95); Wkg Cttee on Ethics of Xenotransplantation, Nuffield Bioethics Council, 1995–96; Council, British Soc. for Immunology, 1998–2000; Council for Sci. and Technol., 2004–; Chairman: Ethics Cttee, Hammersmith and Queen Charlotte's SHA, 1990–94; Molecular and Cell Panel, Wellcome Trust, 1998–2000. Philip Ellman Lecture, RCP, 1995 (Graham Bull Prize in Clin. Sci., 1996). Founder FMedSci 1998 (Registrar, 1998–2003). Gov., Wellcome Trust, 2000–03. Fellow, ICSTM, 2006. Asst Ed., British Jl of Rheumatology, 1990–97; Series Ed., 1998–2001, Chm., Editl Bd, 2001–03, British Med. Bulletin; Ed., Clin. and Exptl Immunology, 1998–2000. Hon. DSc: Sheffield; KCL. Roche Prize for Rheumatology, 1991. *Publications:* (jtly) Immunobiology, 3rd edn 1997, 6th edn 2004; (ed jtly) Clinical Aspects of Immunology, 6th edn 2005; papers in sci. jls on immunology and genetics of rheumatic diseases. *Recreations:* natural history, food. *Address:* Wellcome Trust, 215 Euston Road, NW1 2BE.

WALSALL, Archdeacon of; *see* Jackson, Ven. R. W.

WALSBY, Prof. Anthony Edward, PhD; FRS 1993; Melville Wills Professor of Botany, 1980–2006, now Professor Emeritus, and Senior Research Fellow, since 2006, University of Bristol. *Educ:* Birmingham Univ. (BSc); PhD London. Asst Lectr, then Lectr in Botany, Westfield Coll., London Univ., 1965–71; Miller Fellow, Univ. of Calif at Berkeley, 1971–73; Lectr, then Reader, Department of Marine Science-Marine Biology, UCNW, Bangor, 1973–80. *Address:* School of Biological Sciences, University of Bristol, Woodland Road, Bristol BS8 1UG. *T:* (0117) 928 7490; *e-mail:* a.e.walsby@bristol.ac.uk.

WALSH, Arthur Stephen, CBE 1979; FREng, FIET; Chairman, Simoco International Ltd, 1997–2000; *b* 16 Aug. 1926; *s* of Wilfred and Doris Walsh; *m* 2nd, 1985, Judith Martha Westenborg. *Educ:* Selwyn Coll., Cambridge (MA). FIET (FIEE 1974); FREng (FEng 1980). GEC Group, 1952–79: various sen. appts within the Group; Managing Director: Marconi Space and Defence Systems, 1969–86; Marconi Co., 1982–85; Dir, GEC, 1983; Chief Exec., 1985–91, Chm., 1989–91, STC. Chairman: Telemetrix plc, 1991–97; Nat. Transcommunications Ltd, 1991–96; Dir, FKI plc, 1991–99. Hon. DSc: Ulster, 1988; Southampton, 1993. *Recreations:* ski-ing, golf. *Address:* Aiglemont, Trout Rise, Loudwater, Rickmansworth, Herts WD3 4JS. *T:* (01923) 770883.

WALSH, Colin Stephen, FRCO; Organist Laureate, Lincoln Cathedral, since 2002 (Organist and Master of the Choristers, 1988–2002); *b* 26 Jan. 1955. *Educ:* Portsmouth Grammar Sch.; St George's Chapel, Windsor Castle (Organ Scholar); Christ Church, Oxford (Organ Scholar; MA 1980). DipEd 1978. ARCM 1973; FRCO 1976. Asst Organist, Salisbury Cathedral, 1978–85; Master of the Music, St Alban's Cathedral, 1985–88. Recitals in UK (incl. Royal Festival Hall) and many other countries. Recordings incl. French organ music, esp. by Vierne. *Recreations:* walking, dining out, theatre, travel. *Address:* 12 Minster Yard, Lincoln LN2 1PJ. *T:* (01522) 561646.

WALSH, Rt Rev. (Geoffrey David) Jeremy; Bishop Suffragan of Tewkesbury, 1986–95; *b* 7 Dec. 1929; *s* of late Howard Wilton Walsh, OBE and Helen Maud Walsh (*née* Lovell); *m* 1961, Cynthia Helen, *d* of late F. P. Knight, FLS, VMH, and H. I. C. Knight, BEM; two *s* one *d*. *Educ:* Felsted Sch., Essex; Pembroke Coll., Cambridge (MA Econ.); Lincoln Theological Coll. Curate, Christ Church, Southgate, London, 1955–58; Staff Sec., SCM, and Curate, St Mary the Great, Cambridge, 1958–61; Vicar, St Matthew, Moorfields, Bristol, 1961–66; Rector of Marlborough, Wilts, 1966–76; Rector of Elmsett with Aldham, 1976–80; Archdeacon of Ipswich, 1976–86. Hon. Canon, Salisbury Cathedral, 1973–76. *Recreations:* gardening, golf, bird-watching. *Address:* 6 Warren Lane, Martlesham Heath, Ipswich IP5 3SH. *T:* (01473) 620797.

WALSH, Graham Robert, FCA; Deputy Chairman, Moss Bros Group plc, 1999–2001 (Director, 1988–2001); *b* 30 July 1939; *s* of Robert Arthur Walsh and Ella Marian (*née* Jacks); *m* 1967, Margaret Ann Alexander; one *s* one *d*. *Educ:* Hurstpierpoint Coll., Sussex. Qualified as chartered accountant, 1962; joined Philip Hill Higginson Erlangers (now Hill Samuel & Co. Ltd), 1964; Director, Hill Samuel, 1970, resigned 1973; Dir, 1973–87, Head of Corporate Finance Div., and Mem. Management Cttee, 1981–87, Morgan Grenfell & Co. Ltd; Man. Dir, Bankers Trust Co., 1988–91; Director: Morgan Grenfell Group plc (formerly Morgan Grenfell Holdings), 1985–87; Armitage Shanks Group Ltd, 1973–80; Phoenix Opera Ltd, 1970–87; Ward White Group plc, 1981–89; Rush & Tompkins Gp plc, 1988–90; Haslemere Estates, 1989–92; Rodamco UK BV, 1992–98. Dir Gen., Panel on Takeovers and Mergers, 1979–81; Chm., Issuing Houses Assoc., 1985–87 (Dep. Chm., 1979 and 1983–85). Gov., Dulwich Coll. Prep. Sch., 1995–97. *Recreations:* opera, theatre, music, gardening.

WALSH, Henry George; Deputy Chairman, Building Societies Commission, 1991–95; *b* 28 Sept. 1939; *s* of James Isidore Walsh and Sybil Bertha Bazeley; *m* 1999, Elizabeth Long; one *d*; two *d* by previous *m*. *Educ:* West Hill High Sch., Montreal; McGill Univ.; Churchill Coll., Cambridge. HM Treasury, 1966–74; Private Secretary to Chancellor of the Duchy of Lancaster, 1974–76; HM Treasury, 1976–78; Cabinet Office Secretariat, 1978–80; Counsellor (Economic), Washington, 1980–85; HM Treasury: Hd of Monetary Policy Div., 1985–86; Hd of IMF and Debt Div., 1986–89; Hd of Financial Instns and Markets Gp, 1989–91. *Recreations:* golf, model railways, being taken for walks by Labrador retrievers. *Address:* 60 Roxburgh Road, SE27 0LD. *Clubs:* Model Railway; Dulwich and Sydenham Hill Golf.

WALSH, Rt Rev. Jeremy; *see* Walsh, Rt Rev. G. D. J.

WALSH, Jill P.; *see* Paton Walsh.

WALSH, John; Director, J. Paul Getty Museum, 1983–2000, now Director Emeritus; Vice-President, J. Paul Getty Trust, 1998–2000; *b* 9 Dec. 1937; *s* of John J. Walsh and Eleanor Walsh (*née* Wilson); *m* 1961, Virginia Alys Galston; two *s* one *d*. *Educ:* Yale Univ. (BA 1961); Univ. of Leyden, Netherlands; Columbia Univ. (MA 1965; PhD 1971). Lectr, Research Asst, Frick Collection, NY, 1966–68; Metropolitan Museum of Art, NY: Associate for Higher Educn, 1968–71; Associate Curator and Curator, 1970–75, Vice-Chm., 1974–75, Dept of European Paintings; Columbia University: Adjunct Associate Prof., 1972–75; Prof. of Art History, Barnard Coll., 1975–77; Mrs Russell W. Baker Curator of Paintings, Museum of Fine Arts, Boston, 1977–83. Vis. Prof. of Fine Arts, Harvard, 1979; Mem., Inst. for Advanced Study, Princeton Univ., 2001–02; Adjunct Prof. of History of Art, Yale Univ., 2003. Member: Governing Bd, Yale Univ. Art Gallery, 1975–; Bd of Fellows, Claremont Grad. Sch. and Univ. Center, 1988–2000; Assoc. of Art Museum Dirs, 1983–2001 (Trustee, 1986–90; Pres., 1989); Amer. Antiquarian Soc., 1984–. Mem., Amer. Acad. of Arts and Scis, 1997. Hon. LHD Wheaton Coll., 2000.

Publications: Things in Place: landscapes and still lifes by Sheridan Lord, 1995; Jan Steen, The Drawing Lesson, 1996; (with D. Gribbon) The J. Paul Getty Museum and its Collections: a museum for the new century, 1997; numerous contribs to learned jls. *Address:* c/o J. Paul Getty Museum, 1200 Getty Center Drive, Ste 1000, Los Angeles, CA 90049–1679, USA. *Club:* Century Association (NY).

WALSH, John Henry Martin; Assistant Editor, Independent, since 1998; *b* 24 Oct. 1953; *s* of Martin Walsh and Anne Walsh (*née* Durkin); partner, Carolyn Clare Hart; one *s* two *d. Educ:* Wimbledon Coll.; Exeter Coll., Oxford (BA Hons); University Coll., Dublin (MA). Advertisement Dept, Tablet Magazine, 1977; Publicity Dept, Victor Gollancz, 1978–79; Associate Editor, The Director, 1979–83; freelance writer, 1983–87; Literary Editor, 1987, Features and Literary Editor, 1988, Evening Standard; Literary Editor, Sunday Times, 1988–92; Editor, Independent Magazine, 1993–95; Literary Editor, Independent, 1995–96. Presenter, Books and Company, BBC Radio 4, 1995–97. Artistic Dir, Cheltenham Festival of Literature, 1997–98. Chm. Judges, Forward Poetry Prize, 2000. *Publications:* Growing Up Catholic, 1989; The Falling Angels, 1999; Are You Talking to Me?, 2003; Sunday at the Cross Bones, 2007. *Recreations:* drinking, talking, music. *Address:* 88 Croxted Road, Dulwich, SE21 8NP. *T:* (020) 8670 5859. *Club:* Groucho.

WALSH, Rev. Mgr John Michael; Principal Roman Catholic Chaplain to the Royal Air Force, since 2007; *b* London, 22 June 1959; *s* of Vincent John and Elizabeth Philomena Walsh. *Educ:* St Raphael's RC Prim. Sch., Manchester; St George's RC Sec. Mod. Sch., Manchester; St Joseph's Coll., Upholland; St Cuthbert's Coll., Ushaw, Durham (CTh 1982). Ordained priest, 1983; Assistant Priest: Metropolitan Cath. of Christ the King, 1983–89; St Mary's, Blackbrook, 1989–91; St Joseph's Penketh, 1991–92; Parish Priest, St Elizabeth's, Litherland, 1992–95; Community of St Laurence, Ampleforth, 1995–98; Parish Priest, St Michael's, Ditton, 1999–2003; Commnd as Chaplain, RAF, 2003; RAF Coll. Cranwell, 2003; RAF Brize Norton, 2003–04; RAF Halton, 2004–05; RAF Marham, 2005–07; RAF Coll. Cranwell, 2007; Vicar General, 2007. Prelate of Honour, 2007. *Recreations:* travel, watching movies, Italian food, gadgets. *Address:* Chaplaincy Centre, RAF Halton, Aylesbury, Bucks HP22 5PG. *T:* (01296) 656910. *Club:* Royal Air Force.

WALSH, John P.; *see* Pakenham-Walsh.

WALSH, Dr Julia M.; Chairman: CardioTech International Ltd, since 2000; AVL Holdings, since 1997. Chief Exec., ADAS, 1991–95. Non-executive Director: British Energy, 1996–2002; Southalls Hygiene Services, 1996; David A. Hall Ltd, 1996. Mem., Ct of Regents, RCSE, 2002.

WALSH, (Mary) Noëlle; Editor, The Good Deal Directory, since 1992; Director, The Value for Money Company Ltd, since 1992; *b* 26 Dec. 1954; *d* of late Thomas Walsh and of Mary Kate Ferguson; *m* 1988, David Heslam; one *s* one *d. Educ:* Univ. of East Anglia (BA Hons European Studies (History and German)). Editorial Asst, PR Dept, St Dunstan's Orgn for the War-Blinded, 1977–79; News Editor, Cosmopolitan, 1979–85; Editor, London Week newspaper, 1985–86; freelance writer, 1986; Dep. Editor, 1986–87, Editor, 1987–91, Good Housekeeping; Dep. Editor, You and Your Family, Daily Telegraph, 1992; Editor, The Good Deal Directory monthly newsletter, 1992–97; Founder: gooddealdirectory website, 2000; gooddealhouse website, 2004. Member: Network; 300 Group; Forum UK. FRSA. *Publications:* Hot Lips, the Ultimate Kiss and Tell Guide, 1985; (co-ed) Ragtime to Wartime: the best of Good Housekeeping 1922–39, 1986; (co-ed) The Home Front: the best of Good Housekeeping 1939–1945, 1987; (co-ed) The Christmas Book: the best of Good Housekeeping at Christmas 1922–1962, 1988; (ed jtly) Food Glorious Food: eating and drinking with Good Housekeeping 1922–1942, 1990; Things my Mother Should Have Told Me, 1991; Childhood Memories, 1991; (ed) The Good Deal Directory, annually, 1994–; (ed) The Good Deal Directory Food Guide, 1993; (ed) The Home Shopping Handbook, 1994; Baby on a Budget, 1995; Wonderful Weddings that won't cost a fortune, 1995; The Factory Shopping and Sightseeing Guide to the UK, 1996; The Good Mail Order Guide, 1996; contrib. to Sunday Times annual Good Deal Guide. *Recreation:* medieval Irish history. *Address:* Cottage by the Church, Filkins, Lechlade, Glos GL7 3JG.

WALSH, Michael Jeffrey; Chairman, UK Group, 1990–99 and 2002–05, and Chief Executive Officer, Europe, Africa and Middle East, 1994–2005, Ogilvy & Mather; *b* 1 Oct. 1949; *s* of Kenneth Francis Walsh and Edith Walsh; *m* 1983, Sally Elizabeth Hudson; one *s* one *d. Educ:* Hulme Grammar Sch., Oldham; Durham Univ. (BA Hons Geog.). Joined Young and Rubicam as grad. trainee, 1972; Dir, 1980–83; New Business Dir, 1981–83; Mem., Exec. Cttee, 1982–83; Ogilvy & Mather, 1983–2005: Man. Dir, 1986–89, Chm., 1989–90, UK. Chm., UK Disasters Emergency Cttee, 2005–. Bd Mem., MLA, 2006–. Hon. Vice-Chm. and Trustee, BRCS, 1994–2004; Worldwide Trustee, WWF, 1996–99. *Recreations:* collecting children's books, antiques, golf, tennis, sailing. *Address:* Disasters Emergency Committee, 43 Charlton Street, NW1 1DU. *Clubs:* Royal Automobile, Mark's, Annabel's; Highgate Golf, Royal West Norfolk Golf, Hunstanton Golf.

WALSH, Maj.-Gen. Michael John Hatley; CB 1980; CBE 1996; DSO 1968; Director of Overseas Relations, St John's Ambulance, 1989–95; *b* 10 June 1927; *s* of Captain Victor Michael Walsh, late Royal Sussex, and Audrey Walsh; *m* 1952, Angela, *d* of Col Leonard Beswick; two *d. Educ:* Sedbergh Sch. Commnd, KRRC, 1946; served in Italy, Malaya, Germany, Cyprus, Suez, Aden, Australia and Singapore; Bde Maj. 44 Parachute Bde, 1960–61; GSO1 Defence Planning Staff, 1966; CO 1 Para Bn, 1967–69; Col AQ 1 Div., 1969–71; Comdr, 28 Commonwealth Bde, 1971–73; BGS HQ BAOR, 1973–76; GOC 3rd Armoured Div., 1976–79; Dir of Army Training, MoD, 1979–81. Hon. Col, 1st Bn Wessex Regt, TA, 1981–89. Chief Scout of the UK and Dependent Territories, 1982–88; Vice Pres., Scout Assoc., 1988–. Council Mem., Operation Raleigh, 1984; Royal National Life-boat Institution: Member: Cttee of Management, 1988–2003; Search and Rescue Sub-cttee, 1989–99; Fund Raising Sub-cttee, 1991–2001; Vice Pres., 1998–. Kt Pres., Hon. Soc. of Knights of the Round Table, 1988–95 (Kt 1986–); Mem., St John Council, Wilts, 1989–99, London, 1995–2000. Pres., 1525 Soc., 2004–; Vice Pres., Old Sedberghian Club, 2005–. DL Greater London, 1986–99. Freeman, City of London, 1987. KStJ 1993 (Mem., Chapter Gen., 1989–99). *Publication:* One Man in his Time, 2007. *Recreations:* athletics, boxing (Life Pres., Army Boxing Assoc., 1986), parachuting (Pres., Army Parachute Assoc., 1979–81), sailing, Australian Rules football, photography (LRPS). *Address:* c/o Barclays Bank, James Street, Harrogate.

WALSH, Michael Thomas; Head of Research, Community (formerly Iron and Steel Trades Confederation), since 1999; *b* 22 Oct. 1943; *s* of late Michael Walsh and Bridget (*née* O'Sullivan); *m* 1972, Margaret Patricia Blaxhall; two *s* two *d. Educ:* Gunnersbury Grammar Sch.; Exeter Coll., Oxford (Hons degree PPE). Internat. Dept, TUC, 1966; Deputy Overseas Labour Adviser, FCO, 1977–79; Head, Internat. Dept, TUC, 1980–99. Economic and Social Committee of the European Community: Mem., 1976–77 and 1979–80; Alternate Mem., Consultative Commn on Industrial Change, 2003–; Mem.,

World of Work Cttee, Catholic Bishops' Conf. of England and Wales, 1992–2001; Dep. Mem., Exec. Cttee, Eur. Metalworkers' Fedn, 2003–. Member: Wilton Park Academic Council, 1994–2003; Governing Body, Plater Coll., Oxford, 1995–2001. *Publications:* (ed) Report of International Confederation of Free Trade Unions, 1994–99; (ed) ISTC reports; contrib. professional jls. *Recreations:* cricket, moral philosophy, historical research, music. *Address:* (office) Swinton House, 324 Gray's Inn Road, WC1X 8DD. *T:* (020) 7239 1200; 77 Uvedale Road, Enfield EN2 6HD.

WALSH, Most Rev. Patrick Joseph; *see* Down and Connor, Bishop of.

WALSH, Paul S.; Chief Executive Officer, Diageo plc, since 2000; *b* Manchester, 1 May 1955; *s* of Arthur and Anne Walsh; *m* (marr. diss.); one *s. Educ:* Manchester Poly. (accounting qualifications). GrandMet, subseq. Diageo plc: joined Brewing Div., 1982; Finance Dir, Intercontinental Hotels, 1986–90; Div. Chief Exec., Pillsbury, 1990–92; CEO, Pillsbury Co., 1992–2000; Mem. Bd, 1995–; Chief Operating Officer, 2000. Non-executive Director: Fedex Corp.; Centrica plc. Chm., Scotch Whisky Assoc. Mem. Bd of Trustees, Prince of Wales' Internat. Business Leaders Forum. Gov., Henley Mgt Coll., 2003 (Chm., Court of Govs). *Recreations:* outdoor activities, fishing, riding. *Address:* Diageo plc, 8 Henrietta Place, W1G 0NB.

WALSH, Robin; Controller, BBC Northern Ireland, 1991–94; *b* 6 Feb. 1940; *s* of Charles and Ellen Walsh; *m* 1964, Dorothy Beattie; two *d. Educ:* Foyle College, Londonderry; Royal Belfast Academical Inst. Reporter, Belfast Telegraph, 1958–65; Reporter/News Editor, Ulster TV, 1965–74; BBC: News Editor, NI, 1974–81; Dep. Editor, TV News, 1982–85; Managing Editor, News and Current Affairs—TV, 1985–88; Asst Controller, News and Current Affairs, Regions, 1988–90. *Recreations:* cricket, walking. *Address:* Holly Lodge, 3A Ballymullan Road, Crawfordsburn, Co. Down NI BT19 1JG. *T:* (028) 9185 2709.

WALSH, Simon; JP; barrister in private practice, since 1988; *b* 7 Jan. 1962; *s* of Thomas Walsh and Jean Walsh (*née* Morris). *Educ:* Manchester Grammar Sch.; Balliol Coll., Oxford (BA 1984, MA 1987); City Univ., London (Dip. Law 1986). MCIArb 1999. Called to the Bar, Middle Temple, 1987, Inner Temple, Lincoln's Inn, ad eundem. Chm., Central London Valuation Tribunal, 1998–. City of London: Common Councilman, 1989–2000; Alderman, Ward of Farringdon Without, 2000–; Chairman: Housing Cttee, 1995–98; Police Authy, 2002–05; Licensing Authy, 2007–. Mem., London Fire and Emergency Planning Authy, 2008–. Freeman, City of London, 1987–; Liveryman: Glovers' Co., 1989–; Fletchers' Co., 2001–; Court Assistant: Parish Clerks' Co., 2004– (Under Warden, 2008–09); Guild of Freemen, 2004–06. Parish Clerk, St Augustine Old Change, 1993–; Churchwarden, St Dunstan-in-the-West, 2002–. Chm., City Br., Royal Soc. of St George, 2004–05. Governor: City of London Sch., 1992–2000, City of London Sch. for Girls, 2005–; St Bride Foundn Inst., 1996–; (ex officio): Christ's Hosp., 2000–; Bridewell Royal Hosp., 2000–. Pres., Alumni Assoc., City Univ., 2001–05. JP City of London, 2000. CLJ 1999. *Recreations:* the Commonwealth, civic responsibility, 19th century French novels, municipal tramways, promoting the survival of real ale. *Address:* 5 Essex Court, Temple, EC4Y 9AH. *Clubs:* East India, City Livery, Farringdon Ward; Athenæum (Liverpool).

WALSH, Terence Michael; His Honour Judge Walsh; a Circuit Judge, North East Circuit, since 2001; *b* 10 March 1945; *s* of late Gerrard Walsh and of Freda Alice Walsh (now Kay); *m* 1969, Pauline Totham; two *s* one *d. Educ:* Belle View Boys' Grammar Sch., Bradford. Admitted as solicitor, 1974; Sen. Partner, Chivers Walsh Smith, Solicitors, Bradford, 1991–2001. Dep. Registrar, later Dep. Dist Judge, 1984–94; Asst Recorder, 1989–94; Recorder, 1994–2001. Pres., Bradford Law Soc., 1990–91; Mem., Children's Panel, Law Soc., 1994–2001. Consulting Ed., Practitioner's Guides, 1991–. *Publications:* Child Care and the Courts, 1988; Child Protection Handbook, 1995. *Recreations:* history, cricket, music, walking. *Address:* Leeds Combined Court Centre, Oxford Row, Leeds LS1 3BG. *T:* (0113) 283 0040. *Club:* Bradford.

WALSH, Most Rev. William; *see* Killaloe, Bishop of, (RC).

WALSHAM, Prof. Geoffrey; Professor of Management Studies, University of Cambridge, since 2001; *b* 10 June 1946; *s* of Harry Walsham and Charlotte Gladys Walsham; *m* 1970, Alison Jane Evans; three *s* one *d. Educ:* St Catherine's Coll., Oxford (BA Maths 1966; MA 1971); Warwick Univ. (MSc Maths 1968). Lectr in Maths, Mindanao State Univ., Philippines, 1966–67; OR Analyst, BP Chemicals, 1968–72; Lectr in OR, Univ. of Nairobi, Kenya, 1972–75; Cambridge University: Lectr in Mgt Studies, 1975–94; Fellow, Fitzwilliam Coll., 1979–94; Prof. of Information Mgt, Lancaster Univ., 1994–96; University of Cambridge: Dir, MBA course, 1997–98; Res. Prof. of Mgt Studies, 1998–2001. *Publications:* Interpreting Information Systems in Organizations, 1993; Making a World of Difference: information technology in a global context, 2001; jl articles in information systems, organisational studies, operational res. *Recreations:* mountain walking, travel. *Address:* Judge Business School, University of Cambridge, Cambridge CB2 1AG. *T:* (01223) 339606; *Fax:* (01223) 339701; *e-mail:* g.walsham@jbs.cam.ac.uk.

WALSHAM, Sir Timothy (John), 5th Bt *cr* 1831, of Knill Court, Herefordshire; horticulturalist; *b* 26 April 1939; *o s* of Rear Adm. Sir John Walsham, 4th Bt, CB, OBE and Sheila Christina, *o d* of Comdr B. Bannerman, DSO; *S* father, 1992. *Educ:* Sherborne. Peninsular & Oriental Shipping Company, 1960–67; Royal Fleet Auxiliary Service, 1968–72. *Recreation:* horticulture. *Heir: cousin* Gerald Percy Robert Walsham [*b* 1939; *m* 1984, Evelyn Niebes]. *Address:* c/o Trefelix, Trebetherick, Wadebridge, Cornwall TL27 6SA.

WALSINGHAM, 9th Baron *cr* 1780; **John de Grey,** MC 1952; Lieut-Colonel, Royal Artillery, retired, 1968; *b* 21 Feb. 1925; *s* of 8th Baron Walsingham, DSO, OBE, and Hyacinth (*d* 1968), *o d* of late Lt-Col Lambart Henry Bouwens, RHA; *S* father, 1965; *m* 1963, Wendy, *er d* of E. Hoare, Southwick, Sussex; one *s* two *d. Educ:* Wellington Coll.; Aberdeen Univ.; Magdalen Coll., Oxford; RMCS. BA Oxon, 1950; MA 1959. Army in India, 1945–47; Palestine, 1947; Oxford Univ., 1947–50; Foreign Office, 1950; Army in Korea, 1951–52; Hong Kong, 1952–54; Malaya, 1954–56; Cyprus, Suez, 1956; Aden, 1957–58; Royal Military Coll. of Science, 1958–60; Aden, 1961–63; Malaysia, 1963–65. Co. Dir, 1968–96. FInstD 1978. *Publications:* On the Origins of Speaking, 2006; Lithic Language, 2008. *Heir: s* Hon. Robert de Grey [*b* 21 June 1969; *m* 1995, Josephine Elizabeth, *d* of Richard Haryott; one *s* two *d*]. *Address:* The Hassocks, Merton, Thetford, Norfolk IP25 6QP. *T:* (01953) 885385, *Fax:* (01953) 881431; 19B Calle Palmera, PO Box 202, Los Gigantes, Santiago Del Teide 38683, Tenerife, Canary Islands, Spain. *T:* and *Fax:* 922862486; *e-mail:* hassocks@lineone.net.

WALTER, Harriet Mary, CBE 2000; actress; *b* 24 Sept. 1950; *d* of late Roderick Walter and Xandra Carandini (*née* Lee). *Educ:* Cranborne Chase Sch.; LAMDA. Associate Artist, RSC, 1987–. Hon. DLitt Birmingham, 2001. Pragnell Shakespeare Award, 2007. *Theatre:* Ragged Trousered Philanthropists, Joint Stock Co., 1978; Hamlet, Cloud Nine, Royal

Court, 1980; Nicholas Nickleby, RSC, 1980; Seagull, Royal Court, 1981; RSC seasons, 1981–83: Midsummer Night's Dream; All's Well That Ends Well (also on Broadway, 1983); The Castle, RSC, 1985; Merchant of Venice, Royal Exchange, Manchester, 1987; RSC seasons, 1987–89: Cymbeline; Twelfth Night; Three Sisters; Question of Geography (Best Actress, Olivier Awards, 1988); Duchess of Malfi, RSC, 1989–90; Three Birds Alighting on a Field, Royal Court, 1991–92, NY, 1994; Arcadia, 1993, The Children's Hour, 1994, National; Old Times, Wyndham's, 1995; Hedda Gabler, Chichester, 1996; Ivanov, Almeida, 1997; The Late Middle Classes, Watford and UK tour, 1999; Macbeth, RSC, 1999; Life x 3, RNT, 2000, transf. Old Vic, 2001; The Royal Family, Th. Royal, Haymarket, 2001; Much Ado About Nothing, RSC, 2002; Dinner, RNT, 2002, transf. Wyndham's, 2003; Us & Them, Hampstead, 2003; The Deep Blue Sea, Th. Royal, Bath and UK tour, 2003; Mary Stuart, Donmar Warehouse, 2005 (Best Actress, Evening Standard Th. Awards, 2005); Antony and Cleopatra, RSC, 2006; Fallujah, Old Truman Brewery, London, 2007; *television:* The Imitation Game, 1980; Cherry Orchard, 1981; The Price, 1985; Lord Peter Wimsey, 1987; Benefactors, 1989; The Men's Room, 1991; Ashenden, 1991; Inspector Morse, 1992; A Dance to the Music of Time, 1997; Unfinished Business, 1998; Macbeth, 1999; George Eliot, 2002; Midsomer Murders, 2004; Ballet Shoes, 2007; many radio performances (Sony Award, Best Actress, 1988 and 1992); *films:* Reflections, 1983; Turtle Diary, 1985; The Good Father, 1986; Milou en Mai, 1990; Sense and Sensibility, 1996; The Governess, 1998; Bedrooms and Hallways, 1998; Onegin, 1999; Villa des Roses, 2002; Bright Young Things, 2003; Chromophobia, 2004; Babel, 2005; Atonement, 2007. *Publications:* Other People's Shoes, 1999; contribs to: Clamorous Voices, 1988; Players of Shakespeare, Vol. III, 1993; Mothers by Daughters, 1995; Renaissance Drama in Action, 1999; Actors on Shakespeare: Macbeth, 2002. *Address:* c/o Conway van Gelder Grant Ltd, 18–21 Jermyn Street, SW1Y 6HP. *T:* (020) 7287 0077.

WALTER, Neil Douglas, CNZM 2002; Chair, Environmental Risk Management Authority of New Zealand, 2003–08; *b* 11 Dec. 1942; *s* of Ernest Edward Walter and Anita Walter (*née* Frethey); *m* 1966, Berys Anne (*née* Robertson); one *s* two *d*. *Educ:* New Plymouth Boys' High School; Auckland University (MA). Second Sec., Bangkok, 1966–70; First Sec., NZ Mission to UN, NY, 1972–76; Official Sec., Tokelau Public Service, Apia, 1976–78; Minister, Paris and NZ Permt Deleg. to Unesco, 1981–85; Dep. High Comr for NZ in London, 1985–87; Asst Sec., Ministry of External Relations, NZ, 1987–90; NZ Ambassador to Indonesia, 1990–94; Dep. Sec., Ministry of Foreign Affairs and Trade, NZ, 1994–98; NZ Ambassador to Japan, 1998–99; NZ Sec. of Foreign Affairs and Trade, 1999–2002. *Recreations:* sport, reading. *Address:* c/o ERMA NZ, PO Box 131, Wellington, New Zealand.

WALTER, Robert John; MP (C) Dorset North, since 1997; *b* 30 May 1948; *s* of late Richard and of Irene Walter; *m* 1970, Sally Middleton (*d* 1995); two *s* one *d*. *Educ:* Lord Weymouth Sch., Warminster; Aston Univ. (BSc 1971). Formerly farmer, S Devon; Mem., Stock Exchange, 1983–; internat. banker. Dir and Vice Pres., Aubrey G. Lanston & Co., Inc., 1986–97. Vice Pres., Cons. Gp for Europe, 1995–97 (Vice Chm., 1984–86; Dep. Chm., 1989–92; Chm., 1992–95). Contested (C) Bedwellty, 1979. Opposition spokesman on constitutional affairs and Wales, 1999–2001. Member: Health Select Cttee, 1997–99; Eur. Scrutiny Select Cttee, 1998–99; Internat. Develt Select Cttee, 2001–03; Treasury Select Cttee, 2003–05; Vice-Chm., Cons. Agric. Cttee, 1997–99; Sec., Cons. Eur. Affairs Cttee, 1997–99; Treasurer: All Party British-Japanese Parly Gp, 1997–; All Party Gp on Charities and Vol. Sector, 1997–; British-Caribbean Parly Gp, 1997–; Vice Chairman: All Party Gp on Lupus, 2000–; All Party Human Rights Gp; Mem., British-Irish Parly Body, 1997–; Member: Parly Assembly of Council of Europe, 2001– (Chm., Media Sub-cttee); Assembly of WEU, 2001– (Chm., Defence Cttee, 2006–; Leader, Federated Gp of Christian Democrats and European Democrats, 2006–). Hon. Sec., 1999–, Rear Cdre, 2001–, H of C Yacht Club. Chm. Bd of Governors, Tachbrook Sch., 1980–2000. Freeman, City of London, 1983; Liveryman, Needlemakers' Co., 1983. *Address:* House of Commons, SW1A 0AA. *Clubs:* Constitutional (Blandford); Conservative (Wimborne).

WALTERS, Sir Alan (Arthur), Kt 1983; Professor of Economics, Johns Hopkins University, Maryland, 1976–91; *b* 17 June 1926; *s* of James Arthur Walters and Claribel Walters (*née* Heywood); *m* 1975, Margaret Patricia (Paddie) Wilson; one *d* of former marr. *Educ:* Alderman Newton's Sch., Leicester; University Coll., Leicester (BSc (Econ) London); Nuffield Coll., Oxford (MA). Lectr in Econometrics, Univ. of Birmingham, 1951; Visiting Prof. of Economics, Northwestern Univ., Evanston, Ill, USA, 1958–59; Prof. of Econometrics and Social Statistics, Univ. of Birmingham, 1961; Cassel Prof. of Economics, LSE, 1968–76. Vis. Prof. of Econs, MIT, 1966–67; Vis. Fellow, Nuffield Coll., Oxford, 1982–84; Sen. Fellow, Amer. Enterprise Inst., 1983– (Boyer Lectr, 1983). Vice-Chm. and Dir, AIG Trading Gp Inc., 1991–2003. Economic Adviser to World Bank, 1976–80, 1984–88; Chief Econ. Advr to the Prime Minister (on secondment), 1981–84, 1989. Mem. Commission on Third London Airport (the Roskill Commission), 1968–70. Contested (Referendum) Cities of London and Westminster, 1997. Fellow, Econometric Soc., 1971. Hon. Fellow, Cardiff Univ., 2001. Hon. DLitt Leicester, 1981; Hon. DSocSc: Birmingham, 1984; Francisco Marroquin Univ., Guatemala, 1994. *Publications:* Growth Without Development (with R. Clower and G. Dalton), 1966 (USA); Economics of Road User Charges, 1968; An Introduction to Econometrics, 1969 (2nd edn 1971); Economics of Ocean Freight Rates (with E. Bennathan), 1969 (USA); Money in Boom and Slump, 1970 (3rd edn 1971); Noise and Prices, 1974; (with R. G. Layard) Microeconomic Theory, 1977; (with Esra Bennathan) Port Pricing and Investment Policy for Developing Countries, 1979; Britain's Economic Renaissance, 1986; Sterling in Danger, 1990; The Economics and Politics of Money, 1998. *Recreations:* music, Thai porcelain. *Address:* 3 Chesterfield Hill, W1J 5BJ. *Club:* Political Economy.

WALTERS, Sir Dennis, Kt 1988; MBE 1960; *b* 28 Nov. 1928; *s* of late Douglas L. Walters and Clara Walters (*née* Pomello); *m* 1st, 1955, Vanora McIndoe (marr. diss. 1969); one *s* one *d*; 2nd, 1970, Hon. Celia (*née* Sandys) (marr. diss. 1979); one *s*; 3rd, 1981, Bridgett (marr. diss. 2004), *d* of late J. Francis Shearer; one *s* one *d*. *Educ:* Downside; St Catharine's College (Exhibitioner), Cambridge (MA). War of 1939–45: interned in Italy; served with Italian Resistance Movement behind German lines after Armistice, 1943–44; repatriated and continued normal educn, 1944. Chm., Fedn of Univ. Conservative and Unionist Assocs, 1950; Personal Asst to Lord Hailsham throughout his Chairmanship of Conservative Party, 1957–59; Chm., Coningsby Club, 1959. Contested (C) Blyth, 1959 and Nov. 1960; MP (C) Westbury Div. of Wilts, 1964–92. Jt Hon. Sec., Conservative Parly Foreign Affairs Cttee, 1965–71, Jt Vice-Chm., 1974–78; Jt Chm., Euro-Arab Parly Assoc., 1978–81; Mem., UK Parly Delegn to UN, 1966; UK Deleg. to Council of Europe and Assembly of WEU, 1970–73. Introduced Children and Young Persons (Amendment) Bill, 1985 (Royal Assent, 1986). Pres., Cons. ME Council, 1992– (Chm., 1980–92). Director: The Spectator, 1983–84; Middle East Internat., 1971–90 (Chm., 1990–2006). Chm., Asthma Research Council, 1968–88; Vice Pres., Nat. Asthma Campaign, 1989–2001. Joint Chairman: Council for Advancement of Arab British Understanding, 1970–82 (Jt Vice-Chm., 1967–70); UK/Saudi Cultural Cttee, 1988–2007; Kuwait British Friendship Soc., 1996–2007 (Hon. Pres., 2007–); Mem., Kuwait Investment Adv. Cttee, 1969–. Governor, British Inst. of Florence, 1965–95. Comdr, Order of Cedar of Lebanon, 1969. *Publication:* Not Always with the Pack (autobiographical memoirs), 1989 (trans. Italian, rev. edn, as Benedetti Inglesi Benedetti Italiani, 1991). *Address:* Flat 43, 5 Sloane Court East, SW3 4TQ. *Clubs:* Boodle's, Hurlingham, Queen's.

WALTERS, Sir Donald, Kt 1983; Chairman, Llandough Hospital NHS Trust, 1992–98; *b* 5 Oct. 1925; *s* of Percival Donald and Irene Walters; *m* 1950, Adelaide Jean McQuistin; one *s*. *Educ:* Howardian High Sch., Cardiff; London School of Economics and Political Science (LLB). Called to Bar, Inner Temple, 1946; practised at Bar, Wales and Chester circuit, 1948–59. Dir, 1959–85, Dep. Man. Dir, 1975–85, Chartered Trust plc. Member: Welsh Develt Agency, 1980–93 (Dep. Chm., 1984–92); Develt Bd for Rural Wales, 1984–99; Dir, WNO, 1985–2000 (Vice-Chm., 1990); Chm., Wales Council for Voluntary Action, 1987–93; Mem. Council, Cardiff Univ. (formerly UWCC), 1988– (Chm., 1988–98). High Sheriff, S Glamorgan, 1987–88. Treas., Friends of Llandaff Cathedral, 1998–; Clerk to Dean and Chapter, Llandaff Cathedral, 2001–. Hon. LLD Wales, 1990; Hon. Dr Glamorgan, 1997. *Recreations:* gardening, walking. *Address:* 120 Cyncoed Road, Cardiff CF23 6BL. *T:* (029) 2075 3166.

WALTERS, Ian, FIMechE; Chief Executive, Action Mental Health, since 2002; *b* 20 March 1943; *s* of John and Olive Walters; *m* 1968, Carol Ann Flanders; two *s* one *d*. *Educ:* Moseley Hall Grammar Sch., Cheadle; Univ. of Manchester (BSc; DipTechSc 1966). MIET (MIEE 1970); MIGEM (MIGasE 1972); FIMechE 1997. With Parkinson Cowan Measurement, rising to Factory Manager, Manchester, then Belfast, 1966–72; Dep. Principal, then Principal, Dept of Commerce, NI, 1972–80; Industrial Development Board for Northern Ireland: Dir, then Sen. Dir, IDB N America, NY, 1980–84; Executive Director: Food Div., 1985–89; Internat. Mktg Div., 1989–91; Internat. Repn Div., 1991–92; Corporate Services Group: Actg Dep. Chief Exec., 1992–93; Sen. Exec. Dir, Jan.–Oct. 1993; Dir, Business Support Div., 1993–95, Chief Exec., 1995–2001, Trng and Employment Agency, NI. FCMI (MCMI; MBIM 1980); FRSA 2000. Mem., Governing Body, Belfast Metropolitan Coll., 2007–. Hon. Dr Rocky Mountain Coll., Montana, 1999. *Recreations:* photography, swimming, gardening. *Address:* Action Mental Health, Mourne House, Knockbracken Healthcare Park, Saintfield Road, Belfast BT8 8BH.

WALTERS, John Latimer; QC 1997; *b* 15 Sept. 1948; *o s* of late John Paton Walters and Charlotte Alison Walters (*née* Cunningham); *m* 1st, 1970, Victoria Anne Chambers (marr. diss. 1987; she *d* 1996); 2nd, 1990, Caroline Elizabeth, *d* of late John Vipond Byles and of Doreen Violet Byles, Norwich; two *d*, and one step *s*. *Educ:* Rugby Sch.; Balliol Coll., Oxford (MA; Wylie Prize, 1970). FCA. Called to the Bar, Middle Temple, 1977 (Astbury Scholar); practice at Revenue Bar, 1978–. Special Comr and Chm. (part-time), VAT and Duties Tribunals, 2002–. Local Preacher in the Methodist Church (Diss Circuit). *Recreations:* gardening, painting, design and work embroidery, genealogy, singing, esp. hymns, formerly Lieder. *Address:* Gray's Inn Tax Chambers, Gray's Inn, WC1R 5JA. *T:* (020) 7242 2642.

WALTERS, Joyce Dora; Headmistress, Clifton High School, Bristol, 1985–95; *m* 1st, 1979, Lt-Col Howard C. Walters (*d* 1983); one *s*; 2nd, 2004, Prof. Richard Lynn, *qv*. *Educ:* St Anne's College, Oxford. Headmistress, St Mary's, Calne, 1972–85. *Recreations:* travelling, reading, cooking. *Address:* 4 Longwood House, Failand, Bristol BS8 3TL. *T:* (01275) 392092.

WALTERS, Julie, CBE 2008 (OBE 1999); actress; *b* 22 Feb. 1950; *d* of late Thomas and Mary Walters; *m* 1997, Grant Roffey; one *d*. *Educ:* Holly Lodge Grammar Sch., Smethwick; Manchester Polytechnic (Teaching Certificate). *Theatre:* Educating Rita, 1980 (Drama Critics' Most Promising Newcomer Award; Variety Club Best Newcomer); Having a Ball, Lyric, Hammersmith, 1981; Fool for Love, NT, 1984; Macbeth, Leicester Haymarket, 1985; When I was a Girl I used to Scream and Shout, Whitehall, 1986; Frankie and Johnny in the Clair de Lune, Comedy, 1989; The Rose Tattoo, Playhouse, 1991; All My Sons, RNT, 2000 (Best Actress, Laurence Olivier Awards, 2001); Acorn Antiques the Musical, Th. Royal, Haymarket, 2005. *Films:* Educating Rita, 1983 (Variety Club of GB's Award for best film actress; BAFTA Award for best actress; Hollywood Golden Globe Award); She'll be Wearing Pink Pyjamas, 1985; Car Trouble, 1986; Personal Services, 1987 (British Video Award, Best Actress); Prick Up Your Ears, 1987; Buster, 1988; Killing Dad, 1989; Stepping Out (Variety Club Best Film Actress), 1991; Just Like a Woman, 1992; Clothes in the Wardrobe, 1992; Wide Eyed and Legless, 1993; Bambino Mio, 1994; Pat and Margaret, 1994; Sister My Sister, 1995; Intimate Relations, 1996; Girls' Night, 1998; Titanic Town, 1999; Billy Elliot (Evening Standard Award, Best Actress; BAFTA Award, Best Supporting Actress), 2000; Harry Potter and the Philosopher's Stone, 2001; Before You Go, 2002; Harry Potter and the Chamber of Secrets, 2002; Calendar Girls, 2003; Harry Potter and the Prisoner of Azkaban, 2004; Wah-Wah, 2006; Driving Lessons, 2006; Becoming Jane, 2007; Harry Potter and the Order of the Phoenix, 2007; Mamma Mia!, 2008; *television:* Ahead of the Class, 2005; Ruby in the Smoke, 2006; series include: Wood and Walters, 1981–82; Victoria Wood as Seen on TV, 1984, 2nd series, 1986; The Secret Diary of Adrian Mole, 1985; Victoria Wood Series, 1989; GBH, 1991; Jake's Progress, 1995; Melissa, 1997; dinnerladies, 1998–99; film: Little Red Riding Hood, 1995; serials: Oliver Twist, 1999; Murder, 2002 (BAFTA Award, Best Actress, 2003); Filth: The Mary Whitehouse Story, 2008; also television plays, incl. monologues in series, Talking Heads, 1988, 1998. Show Business Personality of the Year, Variety Club of GB, 2001. *Publications:* Baby Talk, 1990; Maggie's Tree (novel), 2006. *Recreations:* reading, television, travel. *Address:* c/o 41 Warbeck Road, W12 8NS.

WALTERS, Prof. Kenneth, PhD, DSc; FRS 1991; Professor of Applied Mathematics, Aberystwyth University (formerly University of Wales, Aberystwyth), since 1973; *b* 14 Sept. 1934; *s* of late Trevor Walters and Lilian (*née* Price); *m* 1963, Mary Ross Eccles; two *s* one *d*. *Educ:* University Coll. of Swansea (BSc 1956; MSc 1957; PhD 1959; DSc 1984; Hon. Fellow, 1992). Dept of Mathematics, University Coll. of Wales, Aberystwyth: Lectr, 1960–65; Sen. Lectr, 1965–70; Reader, 1970–73. Vis. Fellow, Peterhouse, Cambridge, 1996. Pres., European Soc. of Rheology, 1996–2000; Chm., Internat. Cttee on Rheology, 2000–04. Church Warden, St Michael's, Aberystwyth, 1993–99, 2001–07. For. Associate, NAE, USA, 1995. Dr *hc* Joseph Fourier, Grenoble, 1998. Gold Medal, British Soc. of Rheology, 1984; Weissenberg Award, European Soc. of Rheology, 2002. *Publications:* Rheometry, 1975; (ed) Rheometry: industrial applications, 1980; (with M. J. Crochet and A. R. Davies) Numerical Simulation of non-Newtonian Flow, 1984; (with H. A. Barnes and J. F. Hutton) An Introduction to Rheology, 1989; (with D. V. Boger) Rheological Phenomena in Focus, 1993; (with R. I. Tanner) Rheology: an historical perspective, 1998; The Way it Was, 2003. *Address:* Institute of Mathematical and Physical Sciences, Aberystwyth University, Penglais, Aberystwyth, Ceredigion SY23 3BZ. *T:* (01970) 622750; 8 Pen y Graig, Aberystwyth, Ceredigion SY23 2JA. *T:* (01970) 615276.

WALTERS, Michael Quentin; Senior Partner, Theodore Goddard, Solicitors, 1983–89; *b* 14 Oct. 1927; *s* of late Leslie Walters and Helen Marie Walters; *m* 1st, 1954, Lysbeth Ann Falconer (*d* 1999); 2nd, 2005, Jennifer Anne Burden. *Educ:* Merchant Taylors' School; Worcester College, Oxford (MA). Served Army, 1946–48, 2nd Lieut. Joined

Theodore Goddard, 1951; admitted Solicitor, 1954. Chm., EIS Group plc, 1977–94; Deputy Chairman: Martonair International plc, 1980–86; Tilbury Douglas plc, 1991–96; Dir, Delta plc, 1980–95. Mem., Management Cttee, Inst. of Neurology, 1986–91. *Recreations:* fishing, gardening, reading. *Address:* Woodlarks, Rhinefield Road, Brockenhurst, Hants SO42 7SQ. *T:* (01590) 622340.

WALTERS, Minette Caroline Mary; crime writer, since 1992; *b* 26 Sept. 1949; *d* of Capt. Samuel Henry Desmond Jebb and Minette Colleen Helen Jebb (*née* Paul); *m* 1978, Alex Hamilton Walters; two *s. Educ:* Godolphin Sch.; Durham Univ. (BA). Magazine journalist, 1972–77; freelance journalist and writer, 1977–82. Hon. DLitt: Bournemouth, 2005; Southampton Solent, 2006. John Creasey Award, 1992, Gold Dagger Award, 1994, 2007, CWA; Edgar Allen Poe Award, 1994; Pelle Rosencrantz Prize, 2000; Quick Reads Award, 2006. *Publications:* The Ice House, 1992; The Sculptress, 1993; The Scold's Bridle, 1994; The Dark Room, 1995; The Echo, 1997; The Breaker, 1998; The Shape of Snakes, 2000; Acid Row, 2001; Fox Evil, 2002; Disordered Minds, 2003; The Tinder Box, 2004; The Devil's Feather, 2005; Chickenfeed, 2006; The Chameleon's Shadow, 2007. *Recreations:* crosswords, jigsaw puzzles, DIY, cinema, TV, Radio 4, sailing, reading, wine. *Address:* c/o Gregory & Co., Authors' Agents, 3 Barb Mews, W6 7PA. *T:* (020) 7610 4676.

WALTERS, Sir Peter (Ingram), Kt 1984; non-executive Director, Nomura International plc, since 2004 (Senior Adviser, 2002–04); *b* 11 March 1931; *s* of late Stephen Walters and of Edna Walters (*née* Redgate); *m* 1st, 1960, Patricia Anne (*née* Tulloch) (marr. diss. 1991); two *s* one *d*; 2nd, 1992, Meryl Marshall. *Educ:* King Edward's Sch., Birmingham; Birmingham Univ. (BCom). NS Commn; RASC, 1952–54; British Petroleum Co., 1954–90: Man. Dir, 1973–90; Chm., 1981–90; Vice-Pres., BP North America, 1965–67; Chairman: BP Chemicals, 1976–81; BP Chemicals Internat., 1981; Blue Circle Industries PLC, 1990–96; SmithKline Beecham, subseq. Glaxo SmithKline: Dir, 1989–2000; Chm., 1994–2000; Jt Dep. Chm., 2000–02; Dep. Chm., Thorn EMI, later EMI, 1990–99 (Dir, 1989–99). Dir, 1981–89, Dep. Chm., 1988–89, Nat. Westminster Bank; Chm., Midland Bank, 1991–94; Dep. Chm., HSBC Hldgs, 1992–2001. Member: Indust. Soc. Council, 1975–90; Post Office Bd, 1978–79; Coal Industry Adv. Bd, 1981–85; Inst. of Manpower Studies, 1986–88 (Vice-Pres., 1977–80; Pres., 1980–86); Gen. Cttee, Lloyds Register of Shipping, 1976–90; President's Cttee, CBI, 1982–90; President: Soc. of Chem. Industry, 1978–80; Gen. Council of British Shipping, 1977–78; Inst. of Directors, 1986–92; Inst. Business Ethics, 2001–. Chm. Governors, London Business Sch., 1987–91 (Governor, 1981–91); Governor Nat. Inst. of Economic and Social Affairs, 1981–90; Mem. Foundn Bd, 1982–83, Chm., 1984–86, Internat. Management Inst.; Trustee: Nat. Maritime Museum, 1983–90; E Malling Res. Station, 1983–; Inst. of Economic Affairs, 1986–2007. Pres., Police Foundn, 2001– (Chm., Trustees, 1985–2001). Hon. DSocSc Birmingham, 1986; DUniv Stirling, 1987. Comdr, Order of Leopold (Belgium), 1984. *Recreations:* golf, gardening, sailing. *Address:* 53 Davies Street, W1K 5JH. *Clubs:* Athenæum; West Sussex Golf.

WALTERS, Rhodri Havard, DPhil; Reading Clerk, House of Lords, since 2007; *b* Merthyr Tydfil, 28 Feb. 1950; *s* of late Havard Walters and of Veigan Walters (*née* Hughes). *Educ:* Cyfarthfa Castle Grammar Sch., Merthyr Tydfil; Jesus Coll., Oxford (Meyricke Exhibnr; BA 1971; DPhil 1975). Clerk, Parliament Office, House of Lords, 1975–: on secondment to Cabinet Office as Private Sec. to Leader of the House and Govt Chief Whip, 1986–89; Civil Service Nuffield and Leverhulme Travelling Fellow, attached to US Congress, 1989–90; Clerk to Select Cttee on Sci. and Technol., H of L, 1990–93; Establishment Officer, 1993–2000; Clerk of Public Bills, 2000–02; Sec. to Ecclesiastical Cttee, 2000–03; Clerk: of Cttees, 2002–07; of the Overseas Office, 2002–. *Publications:* How Parliament Works (with Robert Rogers), 1987, 6th edn 2006; (contrib.) The British Constitution in the Twentieth Century, 2003; articles in Econ. Hist. Rev., Welsh Hist. Rev., Govt and Opposition. *Recreations:* rowing, gardening, ski-ing, church music. *Address:* House of Lords, SW1A 0PW. *T:* (020) 7219 3187; *e-mail:* waltersrh@ parliament.uk.

WALTERS, Sir Roger (Talbot), KBE 1971 (CBE 1965); RIBA, FIStructE; architect in private practice, 1979–87; *b* 31 March 1917; 3rd *s* of Alfred Bernard Walters, Sudbury, Suffolk; *m* 1st, 1946, Gladys Evans (marr. diss.); 2nd, 1976, Claire Myfanwy Chappell. *Educ:* Oundle; Architectural Association School of Architecture; Liverpool University; Birkbeck Coll., London Univ. (BA 1980, BSc 2000). Diploma in Architecture, 1939. Served in Royal Engineers, 1943–46. Office of Sir E. Owen Williams, KBE, 1936; Directorate of Constructional Design, Min. of Works, 1941–43; Architect to Timber Development Assoc., 1946–49; Principal Asst Architect, Eastern Region, British Railways, 1949–59; Chief Architect (Development), Directorate of Works, War Office, 1959–62; Dep. Dir-Gen., R&D, MPBW, 1962–67; Dir-Gen., Production, 1967–69; Controller General, 1969–71; Architect and Controller of Construction Services, GLC, 1971–78. Hon. FAIA. *Address:* 46 Princess Road, NW1 8JL. *T:* (020) 7722 3740. *Club:* Reform.

WALTERS, Sam Robert, MBE 1999; Artistic Director, Orange Tree Theatre, since 1971 (Founder, 1971); *b* 11 Oct. 1939; *s* of Denbigh Robert Walters and Elizabeth Walters (*née* Curry); *m* 1964, Auriol Smith; two *d. Educ:* Felsted Sch., Essex; Merton Coll., Oxford (MA PPE); LAMDA. Actor, 1963–67; Resident Dir, Worcester Repertory Co., Swan Theatre, 1967–69; Dir, Jamaica Theatre Co. and Jamaica Theatre Sch., 1970–71; freelance dir, West End, regl theatres, and in Israel and Holland, 1970–; at Orange Tree Theatre has dir. premières of plays by Alan Ayckbourn, Rodney Ackland, Harley Granville Barker, Vaclav Havel and James Saunders, amongst many others. *Recreations:* no time, alas! *Address:* Orange Tree Theatre, 1 Clarence Street, Richmond TW9 2SA. *T:* (020) 8940 0141.

WALTHER, Robert Philippe, FIA; Chairman, Fidelity European Values, since 1999 (Director, since 1993); *b* 31 July 1943; *s* of Prof. D. P. Walther and Barbara (*née* Brook); *m* 1969, Anne Wigglesworth. *Educ:* Charterhouse; Christ Church, Oxford (MA). FIA 1970. Clerical Medical Investment Group: Investment Manager, 1974–85; Investment Dir, 1985–94; Dep. Man. Dir, 1994–95; Gp Chief Exec., 1995–2001; Chm., JP Morgan Fleming (formerly Fleming Claverhouse Investment Trust), 1999–2005 (Dir, 1993–99). Director: Nationwide Bldg Soc., 2002– (Dep. Chm., 2006–); BUPA, 2004–. *Recreations:* hockey, golf, sailing, bridge. *Address:* Ashwells Barn, Chesham Lane, Chalfont St Giles, Bucks HP8 4AS. *T:* (01494) 875575. *Club:* Oxford and Cambridge.

WALTHO, Lynda Ellen; MP (Lab) Stourbridge, since 2005; *b* 22 May 1960; *d* of Charles and Eunice Abbott; *m* Stephen J. Waltho; two *s. Educ:* Keele Univ.; Univ. of Central England (PGCE). School teacher, Birmingham, Sandwell and Dudley LEAs, 1981–94; Assistant to: Simon Murphy, MEP, 1995–97; Sylvia Heal, MP, 1997–2001; Agent, W Midlands Regional Labour Party, 2001–04; Principal Advr to Neena Gill, MEP, 2004–05. PPS to Minister of State, NI Office, 2005–07, Min. of Justice, 2007–. *Address:* (office) The Lawns, Hagley Road, Stourbridge DY8 1QR; House of Commons, SW1A 0AA.

WALTON, family name of **Baron Walton of Detchant.**

WALTON OF DETCHANT, Baron *cr* 1989 (Life Peer), of Detchant in the County of Northumberland; **John Nicholas Walton,** Kt 1979; TD 1962; FRCP; Warden, Green College, University of Oxford, 1983–89; *b* 16 Sept. 1922; *s* of Herbert Walton and Eleanor Watson Walton; *m* 1946, Mary Elizabeth Harrison (*d* 2003); one *s* two *d. Educ:* Alderman Wraith Grammar Sch., Spennymoor, Co. Durham; Med. Sch., King's Coll., Univ. of Durham. MB, BS (1st Cl. Hons) 1945; MD (Durham) 1952; DSc (Newcastle) 1972; MA(Oxon) 1983; FRCP 1963 (MRCP 1950). Ho. Phys., Royal Victoria Inf., Newcastle, 1946–47; service in RAMC, 1947–49; Med. Registrar, Royal Vic. Inf., 1949–51; Research Asst, Univ. of Durham, 1951–56; Nuffield Foundn Fellow, Mass. Gen. Hosp. and Harvard Univ., 1953–54; King's Coll. Fellow, Neurological Res. Unit, Nat. Hosp., Queen Square, 1954–55; First Asst in Neurology, Newcastle upon Tyne, 1956–58; Cons. Neurologist, Newcastle Univ. Hosps, 1958–83; Prof. of Neurology, 1968–83, and Dean of Medicine, 1971–81, Univ. of Newcastle upon Tyne. Numerous named lectureships and overseas visiting professorships. Member: MRC, 1974–78; GMC, 1971–89 (Chm. Educn Cttee, 1975–82; Pres., 1982–89); President: BMA, 1980–82; Royal Soc. of Medicine, 1984–86 (Hon. Fellow, 1988); ASME 1982–94; Assoc. of British Neurologists, 1987–88; World Fedn Neurol., 1989–97 (First Vice-Pres., 1981–89; Chm., Res. Cttee); Chm., Hamlyn Nat. Commn on Educn, 1991–95; UK Rep., EEC Adv. Cttee, Med. Educn, 1975–83; Editor-in-Chief, Jl of Neurological Sciences, 1966–77; Chm., Muscular Dystrophy Gp of GB, 1970–95, etc. Chm., H of L Select Cttee on Med. Ethics, 1993–94; Mem., H of L Select Cttee on Sci. and Technol., 1992–97, 1999–2001 (Chm., Sub-Cttee 1, 1994–96 and 1999–2001). Col (late RAMC) and OC 1 (N) Gen. Hosp. (TA), 1963–66; Hon. Col 201(N) Gen. Hosp. (T&AVR), 1971–77. Freeman, City of London, 1978. Founder FMedSci 1998. Foreign Member: Norwegian Acad. of Sci. and Letters, 1987; Venezuelan Acad. of Medicine, 1992; Russian Acad. of Med. Scis, 1993; Hon. Mem., Osler Club of London; Hon. Foreign Member: Amer. Neurological Assoc., Amer. Acad. of Neurology, Assoc. Amer. Phys., Amer. Osler Soc., Japan Osler Soc., and of Canadian, French, German, Australian, Austrian, Belgian, Spanish, Polish, Venezuelan, Thai, Japanese, Russian and Brazilian Neurological Assocs. Hon. FACP 1980; Hon. FRCPE 1981; Hon. FRCP (Can) 1984; Hon. FRCPath 1993; Hon. FRCPsych 1993; Hon. FRCPCH 1996; Hon. Fellow, Inst. of Educn, Univ. of London, 1994. Dr de l'Univ. (Hon.) Aix-Marseille, 1975; Hon. DSc: Leeds, 1979; Leicester, 1980; Hull, 1988; Oxford Brookes, 1994; Durham, 2002; Hon. MD: Sheffield, 1987; Mahidol, Thailand, 1998; Hon. DCL Newcastle, 1988; Laurea *hc* Genoa, 1992. Hon. Freeman, Newcastle upon Tyne, 1980. Hewitt Award, RSM Foundn Inc., 2006. *Publications:* Subarachnoid Haemorrhage, 1956; (with R. D. Adams) Polymyositis, 1958; Essentials of Neurology, 1961, 6th edn 1989; Disorders of Voluntary Muscle, 1964, 6th edn (ed jtly) 1994; Brain's Diseases of the Nervous System, 7th edn 1969, 10th edn 1993; (with F. L. Mastaglia) Skeletal Muscle Pathology, 1982, 2nd edn 1991, etc; (ed jtly) The Oxford Companion to Medicine, 1986; The Spice of Life (autobiog.), 1993; (ed jtly) The Oxford Medical Companion, 1994; numerous chapters in books and papers in sci. jls. *Recreations:* cricket, golf and other sports, reading, music. *Address:* 15 Croft Way, Belford, Northumberland NE70 7ET. *T:* (01668) 219009. *Clubs:* Athenæum, Oxford and Cambridge, MCC; Bamburgh Castle Golf (Pres., 1998–).

WALTON, Arthur Halsall, FCA; Partner in Lysons, Haworth & Sankey, 1949–85; *b* 13 July 1916; *s* of Arthur Walton and Elizabeth Leeming (*née* Halsall); *m* 1958, Kathleen Elsie Abram; three *s. Educ:* The Leys School. Articled in Lysons & Talbot, 1934; ACA 1940. Military Service, 1939–48: commnd Lancs Fusiliers, 1940. Institute of Chartered Accountants: Mem. Council, 1959; Vice-Pres., 1969; Dep. Pres., 1970; Pres., 1971. *Recreation:* reading. *Address:* 17 Langdale Avenue, Formby, Liverpool L37 2LB.

WALTON, Christopher Thomas; His Honour Judge Walton; a Circuit Judge, since 1997; *b* 20 March 1949; *s* of George Edward Taylor Walton and Margaret Walton; *m* 1992, Brenda Margaret Laws. *Educ:* St Cuthbert's GS, Newcastle upon Tyne; Downing Coll., Cambridge (MA). Called to the Bar, Middle Temple, 1973; a Recorder, 1992–97; North Eastern Circuit. *Publication:* (gen. ed.) Charlesworth & Percy on Negligence, 9th edn 1996, 11th edn 2006. *Recreations:* tennis, golf, suffering with Newcastle United FC, history, music, Scottish art. *Address:* Newcastle Group Manager's Office, North Eastern Circuit, 3rd Floor, Merchant House, 30 The Cloth Market, Newcastle upon Tyne NE1 1EE.

WALTON, Ven. Geoffrey Elmer; Archdeacon of Dorset, 1982–2000, now Archdeacon Emeritus; *b* 19 Feb. 1934; *s* of Harold and Edith Margaret Walton; *m* 1961, Edith Mollie O'Connor; one *s. Educ:* St John's Coll., Univ. of Durham (BA); Queen's Coll., Birmingham (DipTh). Asst Curate, Warsop with Sookholme, 1961–65; Vicar of Norwell, Notts, 1965–69; Recruitment and Selection Sec., ACCM, 1969–75; Vicar of Holy Trinity, Weymouth, 1975–82; RD of Weymouth, 1980–82; Non-Residentiary Canon of Salisbury, 1981–2000. Chairman: E Dorset Housing Assoc., 1991–2003; Dorset County Scout Council, 1995–; Synergy Housing Gp, 2003–05. *Recreations:* conjuring, religious drama. *Address:* Priory Cottage, 6 Hibberds Field, Cranborne, Dorset BH21 5QL. *T:* (01725) 517167.

WALTON, John William Scott; Director of Statistics, Board of Inland Revenue, 1977–85; *b* 25 Sept. 1925; *s* of late Sir John Charles Walton, KCIE, CB, MC, and late Nelly Margaret, Lady Walton, *d* of late Prof. W. R. Scott. *Educ:* Marlborough; Brasenose Coll., Oxford. Army (RA), 1943–47. Mutual Security Agency, Paris, 1952; Inland Revenue, 1954; Central Statistical Office, 1958, Chief Statistician, 1967, Asst Dir, 1972. *Publications:* (contrib. jtly) M. Perlman, The Organization and Retrieval of Economic Knowledge, 1977; articles in The Review of Income and Wealth, Economic Trends, Business Economist, Statistical News. *Club:* Oxford and Cambridge.

WALTON, Peter David; Director, Human Resources and Workplace Services, Department for Communities and Local Government (formerly Office of the Deputy Prime Minister), 2005–06; *b* 24 Feb. 1954; *s* of Kenneth Walton and Sheila Walton; *m* 1997, Margaret Clark. *Educ:* Robert Gordon's Coll., Aberdeen; Univ. of Durham (BA Hons (Geog.) 1975). Joined DoE, administrative trainee, 1975; various policy posts; Grade 7, 1980; various policy and finance posts, incl. secondment to RDA; sen. Civil Service posts in housing, finance, central policy planning and agency sponsorship, 1991–2001; Exec. Dir, Change Mgt, then Human Resources and Business Change, subseq. Orgnl Develt and Resources, ONS, 2001–05. *Recreations:* watching sport, music and opera, DIY, walking, seeing friends.

WALTON, Richard Arthur, CB 2003; PhD; information assurance consultant; *b* 22 Sept. 1947; *s* of Lt Col Gordon Walton and Audrey Mary Walton (*née* Varah); *m* 1st, 1968, Jacqueline Elisabeth Roberts (*d* 1990); one *d*; 2nd, 1992, Mary Elizabeth Mackenzie. *Educ:* Univ. of Nottingham (BSc Hons Maths 1968; PhD 1971); Open Univ. (BA Hons 1987). FIMA 1999; CMath 1999; MBCS 2004; FIET 2005; CEng 2005; CSc 2005. Lectr in Maths, N Staffordshire Poly., 1971–73; GCHQ: various posts, 1973–98; Dir, CESG (Nat. Technical Authy for Inf. Assurance), 1999–2002; Office of the e-Envoy, Cabinet Office, 2002–03. Vis. Prof., Royal Holloway, Univ. of London, 2002–. Mem., Elmley Castle Parish Council, 2004–. Honorary Treasurer: Elmley Castle Cricket Club, 1984–2004;

Elmley Castle PCC, 2001–. *Recreations:* supporting cricket and Rugby, concerts, theatre. *Address: e-mail:* richard@walton-mackenzie.com. *Clubs:* Civil Service; New (Cheltenham).

WALTON, Sarah Louise; *see* Rowland-Jones, S. L.

WALTON, William Stephen; Chief Education Officer, Sheffield, 1985–90; *b* 28 March 1933; *s* of Thomas Leslie Walton and Ena Walton (*née* Naylor); *m* 1964, Lois Elicia Petts; three *d* (incl. twins). *Educ:* King's School, Pontefract; Univ. of Birmingham (BA). RAF, gen. duties (flying), 1951–55. Production Management, Dunlop Rubber Co., 1958–61; Derbyshire Local Educn Authy School Teacher, 1961–67; Educational Administration: Hull, 1967–70; Newcastle upon Tyne, 1970–79; Sheffield 1979–90. Visiting Professor: Univ. of Simon Fraser, BC, 1990–91; Univ. of Portland, Oregon, 1990–91. Pres., Soc. of Educn Officers, 1989–90; Chm., Sch. Curriculum Industry Partnership/Mini Enterprise Schs Project, 1990–95. Dir, Outward Bound, 1989–95. Registered Inspector of Schools, 1993–2003. Hon. Fellow, Sheffield City Polytechnic, 1990. *Recreation:* travel. *Club:* Royal Air Force.

WALWYN, Peter Tyndall; racehorse trainer, 1960–99; *b* 1 July 1933; *s* of late Lt-Col Charles Lawrence Tyndall Walwyn, DSO, OBE, MC, Moreton in Marsh, Glos; *m* 1960, Virginia Gaselee, *d* of A. S. Gaselee, MFH; one *s* one *d*. *Educ:* Amesbury Sch., Hindhead, Surrey; Charterhouse. Leading trainer on the flat, 1974, 1975; leading trainer, Ireland, 1974, 1975; a new record in earnings (£373,563), 1975. Major races won include: One Thousand Guineas, 1970, Humble Duty; Oaks Stakes, 1974, Polygamy; Irish Derby, 1974, English Prince, and 1975, Grundy; King George VI and Queen Elizabeth Stakes, Ascot, 1975, Grundy; Epsom Derby, 1975, Grundy. Chm., Lambourn Trainers' Assoc., 1989–; Member: Jockey Club, 1999–; Council of Mgt, Animal Health Trust, 1998–. Trustee: Lambourn Valley Housing Trust, 1996–; Nat. Horseracing Mus., Newmarket, 2004–. President: Vine and Craven Foxhounds, 1975–; British Racing Sch., Newmarket, 2006–. Freeman, City of London, 2005; Yeoman, Saddlers' Co., 2005. *Publication:* Handy All the Way: a trainer's life, 2000. *Recreations:* foxhunting, shooting, watercolours. *Address:* Windsor House, Lambourn, Berks RG17 8NR. *T:* (01488) 71347. *Club:* Turf.

WAMIRI, Sir Akapite, KBE 1999; *b* 1938; *s* of Wamiri and Okero Simelupo; *m* 1963, Aime Robuna; two *s* three *d* (and one *d* decd). *Educ:* primary sch.; Teaching Cert. Primary sch. teacher, SDA Church, 1962–70; carpenter, 1970–72; public motor vehicle operator, 1972–75; Man. Dir and Proprietor, 1975–2000. PNG Businessman of the Year, 1993. *Recreation:* watching Rugby League games. *Address:* PO Box 477, Goroka, Papua New Guinea. *T:* 7321818, 7321652.

WANAMAKER, Zoë, CBE 2001; actor; *b* 13 May; *d* of late Sam Wanamaker, Hon. CBE, and Charlotte (*née* Holland); acquired British passport, 2001; *m* 1994, Gawn Grainger. *Stage includes:* A Midsummer Night's Dream, 69 Theatre Co., 1970; repertory at Royal Lyceum, 1971–72, Oxford Playhouse, 1974–75 and Nottingham, 1975–76; Royal Shakespeare Company: The Devil's Disciple, Ivanov, Wild Oats, 1976; Captain Swing, The Taming of the Shrew, Piaf, 1978 (NY, 1980); Once in a Lifetime, 1979 (Olivier Award/SWET Award); Comedy of Errors, Twelfth Night, The Time of your Life, 1983; Mother Courage (Drama magazine award), 1984; Othello, 1989; National Theatre: The Importance of Being Earnest, 1982; The Bay at Nice, Wrecked Eggs, 1986; Mrs Klein, 1988, transf. Apollo, 1989; The Crucible, 1990; Battle Royal, 1999; His Girl Friday, 2003; The Rose Tattoo, Much Ado About Nothing, 2007; West End: The Last Yankee, Young Vic, 1993; Dead Funny, Hampstead, transf. Vaudeville, 1994; The Glass Menagerie, Donmar, transf. Comedy, 1995; Sylvia, Apollo, 1996; The Old Neighbourhood, Duke of York's, 1998; Boston Marriage, Donmar, transf. New Ambassadors, 2001; Chichester: Electra, 1997 (Olivier Award, Variety Club Award, and Callaway Award, US Equity, 1998), transf. Princeton and NY, 1998–99; Loot, NY, 1986; Awake and Sing!, NY, 2006; *films include:* Inside the Third Reich, The Hunger, 1982; The Raggedy Rawney, 1987; Amy Foster, 1996; Wilde, 1996; Harry Potter and the Philosopher's Stone, 2001; Five Children and It, 2004; *television includes:* Strike, 1981; Richard III, 1982; Enemies of the State, 1982; The Edge of Darkness, 1984; Paradise Postponed, 1985; Once in a Lifetime, 1987; The Dog it was that Died, 1988; Prime Suspect, 1990; Love Hurts, 1991, 1992, 1993; The Blackheath Poisonings, 1991; Momento Mori, 1991; The Countess Alice, 1991; The Widowing of Mrs Holroyd, 1995; A Dance to the Music of Time, 1997; Leprechauns, 1999; David Copperfield, 1999; Gormenghast, 1999; My Family, 2000–08 (Best Sitcom Actress Rose d'Or, 2005); Adrian Mole: the Cappuccino Years, 2000; Miss Marple: A Murder is Announced, 2004; A Waste of Shame, 2005; Dr Who, 2005, 2006; Poirot: Cards on the Table, 2006; Johnny and the Bomb, 2006; The Old Curiosity Shop, 2007; Poirot: Mrs McGinty's Dead, 2008; Poirot: the Third Girl, 2008; has also appeared in radio plays. Patron, Prisoners of Conscience, 2003–; Vice Patron, The Actors' Centre, 2005–; Hon. Pres., Shakespeare's Globe, 2005–; Hon. Vice-Pres., Dignity in Dying (formerly Voluntary Euthanasia Soc.), 1994. Hon. DLitt: S Bank, 1993; Amer. Internat. Univ., London, 1999. BPG TV Award for Best Actress, 1992; Theatre Sch., DePaul Univ., Chicago, Award for Excellence in the Arts. 2004. *Address:* c/o Peggy Thompson, 1st & 2nd Floor Offices, 296 Sandycombe Road, Kew, Richmond, Surrey TW9 3NG.

WANDSWORTH, Archdeacon of; *see* Roberts, Ven. S. J.

WANG Gungwu, Prof., CBE 1991; FAHA; Chairman, East Asian Institute, Singapore, since 2007 (Director, 1997–2007); University Professor, National University of Singapore, since 2007; Vice-Chancellor, University of Hong Kong, 1986–95; *b* 9 Oct. 1930; *s* of Wang Fo Wen and Ting Yien; *m* 1955, Margaret Lim Ping-Ting; one *s* two *d*. *Educ:* Anderson Sch., Ipoh, Malaya; Nat. Central Univ., Nanking, China; Univ. of Malaya, Singapore (BA Hons, MA); Univ. of London (PhD 1957). University of Malaya, Singapore: Asst Lectr, 1957–59; Lectr, 1959; University of Malaya, Kuala Lumpur: Lectr, 1959–61; Sen. Lectr, 1961–63; Dean of Arts, 1962–63; Prof. of History, 1963–68; Australian National University: Prof. of Far Eastern History, 1968–86, Emeritus Prof., 1988; Dir, Res. Sch. of Pacific Studies, 1975–80; Univ. Fellow, 1996–97. Rockefeller Fellow, 1961–62, Sen. Vis. Fellow, 1972, Univ. of London; Vis. Fellow, All Souls Coll., Oxford, 1974–75; John A. Burns Distinguished Vis. Prof. of History, Univ. of Hawaii, 1979; Rose Morgan Vis. Prof. of History, Univ. of Kansas, 1983; Dist. Professorial Fellow, Inst. of SE Asian Studies, 1999–2007. Dir, East Asian History of Science Foundation Ltd, 1987–95. MEC, Hong Kong, 1990–92. Co-Patron, Asia-Link, Melbourne, 1994–. Chairman: Australia-China Council, 1984–86; Envmt Pollution Cttee, HK, 1988–93; Adv. Council on the Envmt, 1993–95; Council for the Performing Arts, HK, 1989–94; Asia-Pacific Council, Griffith Univ., 1997–2001; Asia Scholarship Foundn, 2002–; Internat. Adv. Council, Universiti Tunku Abdul Rahman, Malaysia, 2002–; Bd of Trustees, Inst. SE Asian Studies, 2002–; Singapore Higher Educn Accreditation Council, 2004–06; Bd, Lee Kuan Yew Sch. for Public Policy, 2005–. Member: Commn of Inquiry on Singapore Riots, 1964–65; Internat. Adv. Panel, E-W Center, Honolulu, 1979–91; Cttee on Aust.-Japan Relations, 1980–81; Regional Council, Inst. of SE Asian Studies, Singapore, 1982–2002; Admin. Bd, Assoc. of SE Asian Instns of Higher Learning, 1986–92; Council, Chinese Univ. of Hong Kong, 1986–95; Exec. Council, WWF, HK, 1987–95; Council, Asia-Aust. Inst., Sydney, 1991–95, 1999–; Council, Asia Soc., HK, 1991–95; Council, IISS, 1992–2001; Nat. Arts Council, Singapore, 1996–2000; Nat. Heritage Bd, Singapore, 1997–2002; Nat. Library Bd, 1997–2003; Bd, Social Sci. Council, NY, 2000–; Council, Nat. Univ. of Singapore, 2000–04; Bd, Inst. of Policy Studies, 2002–; Vice-Chm., Chinese Heritage Centre, Singapore, 2000–. President: Internat. Assoc. of Historians of Asia, 1964–68, 1988–91; Asian Studies Assoc. of Aust., 1979–80; Australian Acad. of the Humanities, 1980–83 (Fellow 1970); Hon. Corresp. Mem. for Hong Kong, RSA, 1987 (Fellow 1987; Chm., Hong Kong Chapter, 1992–95). Mem., Academia Sinica, 1992. For. Hon. Mem., Amer. Acad. of Arts and Scis., 1995; Hon. Mem., Chinese Acad. of Social Scis, 1996. Editor: (also Councillor), Jl of Nanyang Hsueh-hui, Singapore, 1958–68; (also Vice-Pres.), Jl of RAS, Malaysian Br., 1962–68; China, an internat. jl, 2002–; Gen. Editor, East Asian Historical Monographs series for OUP, 1968–95. Hon. Fellow, SOAS, London Univ., 1996. Hon. DLitt: Sydney, 1992; Hull, 1998; Hong Kong, 2002; Hon. LLD: Monash, 1992; ANU, 1996; Melbourne, 1997; DUniv: Soka, 1993; Griffith, 1995. *Publications:* The Nanhai Trade: a study of the early history of Chinese trade in the South China Sea, 1958, 2nd edn 1998; A Short History of the Nanyang Chinese, 1959; Latar Belakang Kebudayaan Pendudok di-Tanah Melayu: Bahagian Kebudayaan China (The Cultural Background of the Peoples of Malaysia: Chinese culture), 1962; The Structure of Power in North China during the Five Dynasties, 1963; (ed) Malaysia: a survey, 1964; (ed jtly) Essays on the Sources for Chinese History, 1974; (ed) Self and Biography: essays on the individual and society in Asia, 1975; China and the World since 1949: the impact of independence, modernity and revolution, 1977; (ed jtly) Hong Kong: dilemmas of growth, 1980; Community and Nation: essays on Southeast Asia and the Chinese, 1981; (ed jtly) Society and the Writer: essays on literature in modern Asia, 1981; Dongnanya yu Huaren (Southeast Asia and the Chinese), 1987; Nanhai Maoyi yu Nanyang Huaren (Chinese Trade and Southeast Asia), 1988; (ed with J. Cushman) Changing Identities of Southeast Asian Chinese since World War II, 1988; Lishi di Gongneng (The Functions of History), 1990; China and the Chinese Overseas, 1991 (Zhongguo yu Haiwai Huaren, 1994); The Chineseness of China: selected essays, 1991; Community and Nation: China, Australia and Southeast Asia, 1992; The Chinese Way: China's position in international relations, 1995; (ed with S. L. Wong) Hong Kong's Transition, 1995; (ed) Global History and Migrations, 1997; (ed) Xianggang shi Xinbian (Hong Kong History: new perspectives), 2 vols, 1997; (ed with S. L. Wong) Hong Kong in the Asia-Pacific Region, 1997; (ed with S. L. Wong) Dynamic Hong Kong: business and culture, 1997; (ed with L. C. Wang) The Chinese Diaspora, 2 vols, 1998; China and Southeast Asia, 1999; (ed with J. Wong) Hong Kong in China, 1999; (ed with J. Wong) China: two decades of reform and change, 1999; The Chinese Overseas: from earthbound China to the quest for autonomy, 2000; Joining the Modern World: inside and outside China, 2000; (ed with Y. Zheng) Reform, Legitimacy and Dilemmas: China's politics and society, 2000; Don't Leave Home: migration and the Chinese, 2001; Sino-Malay Encounters, 2001; (ed) Wang Fo-wen Jinianji (Wang Fo-wen, 1903–1972: a memorial collection of poems, essays and calligraphy), 2002; To Act Is To Know: Chinese dilemmas, 2002; Wang Gengwu zixuanji: selected works, 2002; Bind Us In Time: nation and civilisation in Asia, 2002; Haiwai Huaren Yanjiu di Dashiye yu Xinfangxiang (Overseas Chinese Research: new directions), 2002; (ed with Y. Zheng) Damage Control: the Chinese Communist Party and the era of Jiang Zemin, 2003; (ed with I. Abrahms) The Iraq War and its Consequences, 2003; (ed jtly) Sino-Asiatica, 2003; Anglo-Chinese Encounters since 1800: war, trade, science and governance, 2003; Ideas Won't Keep: the struggle for China's future, 2003; Diasporic Chinese Ventures, 2004; (ed with C. K. Ng) Maritime China in Transition, 2004; (ed) Nation-building: five Southeast Asian histories, 2005; Yimin yu xingqi de Zhongguo, 2005; Divided China: preparing for reunification, 883–947, 2006; Lixiang bietu: jingwai kanzhonghua (China and its Cultures: from the periphery), 2007; Chuka Bunmei to Chugoku no yukue (Chinese Civilization and China's Position), 2007; (ed with Y. Zheng) China and the New International Order, 2008; contribs to collected vols on Asian history; articles on Chinese and Southeast Asian history in internat. jls. *Recreations:* music, reading, walking. *Address:* East Asian Institute, Arts Link, National University of Singapore, Singapore 117571. *T:* 67752033, *Fax:* 67756607; *e-mail:* eaiwgw@nus.edu.sg.

WANLESS, Sir Derek, Kt 2005; FCIB; Chairman, Northumbrian Water Group plc, since 2006 (Director, since 2003); *b* 29 Sept. 1947; *s* of Norman Wanless and Edna (*née* Charlton); *m* 1971, Vera West; one *s* four *d*. *Educ:* Royal Grammar Sch., Newcastle upon Tyne; King's Coll., Cambridge (BA 1st cl. Hons Maths, MA). MIS 1973; ACIB 1978. Joined National Westminster Bank, 1970; appts include: Dir of Personal Banking, 1986–88; Gen. Manager, UK Branch Business, 1989–90; Chief Exec., UK Financial Services, 1990–92; Dir, 1991–99; Dep. Gp Chief Exec., Feb.–March 1992; Gp Chief Exec., 1992–99. Dir, Mastercard Internat., 1989–90; Vice-Chm., Eurocard Internat., 1989–90. Dir, Northern Rock plc, 2000–07. Chairman: Adv. Cttee on Business and Envmt set up by Secs of State for Envmt and Trade and Ind., 1993–95 (Mem., 1991–93); NACETT, 1997–2000; Financial Services NTO, 2000–03; Member: EC Consultative Forum, on the Envmt, 1994–96; World Business Council for Sustainable Develt (formerly World Industry Council for the Envmt), 1993–96; Statistics Commn, 2000–08 (Vice Chm., 2004–08); Bd for Actuarial Standards, Financial Reporting Council, 2006–. President: CIB, 1999–2000; Inst Internat. d'Etudes Bancaires, 1999. Dir, BITC, 1995–2004; Trustee, NESTA, 2000–06. Report on funding health service, Securing our Future Health: taking a long-term view, 2002; report on public health, Securing Good Health for the Whole Population, 2004; report on social care, Securing Good Care for Older People, 2006. FRSA 1991; CCMI (CBIM 1992). Freeman, City of London, 1992. Hon. DSc City, 1995; Hon. DCL Durham, 2005; Hon. DBA: Coventry, 2007; Sunderland, 2007. *Recreations:* all sports, chess, music, walking, gardening. *Club:* Reform.

WANLESS, Peter Thomas, CB 2007; Chief Executive, Big Lottery Fund, since 2008; *b* 25 Sept. 1964; *s* of Thomas and Pam Wanless; *m* 1999, Beccy King; one *s*. *Educ:* Sheldon Sch., Chippenham; Univ. of Leeds (BA Hons Internat. History and Politics). HM Treasury, 1986–94; Private Sec. to Treasury Chief Sec., 1992–94; Head of Information, Dept of Employment, 1994–95; Head of Private Finance Policy, HM Treasury, 1996–98; Dir of Strategy and Communications, DfEE, subseq. DfES, 1998–2003; Dir of Secondary Educn, DfES, 2003–06; Dir of School Perf. and Reform, Sch. Standards Gp, DfES, subseq. DCSF, 2006–07; Dir, Families Gp, DCSF, 2007–08. *Recreations:* cricket, football, good food. *Address:* Big Lottery Fund, 1 Plough Place, EC4A 1DE.

WANSBROUGH, Rev. Dom (Joseph) Henry, OSB; Master, St Benet's Hall, Oxford, 1990–2004; *b* 9 Oct. 1934; *s* of George Wansbrough and Elizabeth Wansbrough (*née* Lewis). *Educ:* Ampleforth Coll.; St Benet's Hall, Oxford (MA 1963); Univ. of Fribourg (STL 1964); Ecole Biblique Française, Jerusalem; Pontifical Biblical Commn, Rome (LSS 1965). Asst Master, 1965–90, Housemaster, 1969–90, Ampleforth Coll.; Chm., Oxford Fac. of Theology, 2001–03; Magister Scholarum of English Benedictines, 2002–. Chairman: Catholic Biblical Assoc. of GB, 1985–91; Mgt Bd, Keston Inst., 1993–2001; Mem., Pontifical Biblical Commn, 1996–2007. Exec. Sec., Internat. Commn for Preparing an English Language Lectionary, 2006–. Cathedral Prior of Norwich, 2004–. *Publications:* The Sunday Word, 1979; New Jerusalem Bible, 1985; The Lion and the Bull, 1996; The Passion and Death of Jesus, 2003; The Story of the Bible, 2006; numerous articles and reviews in The Tablet, Priests & People and TLS. *Recreations:* music, running. *Address:* Ampleforth Abbey, YO62 4EN.

WAPSHOTT, Nicholas Henry; author and journalist; Senior Editor, The Daily Beast; Contributing Editor and columnist, New York Sun; *b* 13 Jan. 1952; *s* of Raymond Gibson Wapshott and Olivia Beryl Darch; *m* 1980, Louise Nicholson; two *s*. *Educ:* Dursley County Primary Sch.; Rendcomb Coll., Cirencester; Univ. of York (BA Hons). The Scotsman, 1973–76; The Times, 1976–84; The Observer, 1984–92, Political Editor, 1988–92; Editor: The Times Magazine, 1992–97; The Saturday Times, 1997–2001; North America Correspondent, The Times, 2001–04. *Publications:* Peter O'Toole, 1982; (with George Brock) Thatcher, 1983; The Man Between: a biography of Carol Reed, 1990; Rex Harrison, 1991; (with Tim Wapshott) Older: a biography of George Michael, 1998; Ronald Reagan and Margaret Thatcher: a political marriage, 2007. *Recreations:* cinema, music, elephants. *Address:* c/o Kathy Robbins, The Robbins Office Inc., 405 Park Avenue, 9th Floor, New York, NY 10022, USA. *Club:* Garrick.

WARBECK, Stephen; freelance film and theatre composer, since 1977; Associate Artist, Royal Shakespeare Co., since 1999; *b* 21 Oct. 1953; *s* of Harold Robert Wood and Olive Patricia Wood; name changed to Warbeck, 1977. *Educ:* Lewes Priory Sch.; Bristol Univ. (BA Hons). Scores composed include: *theatre:* An Inspector Calls, NT, 1992; RSC prodns incl. Alice in Wonderland; Pericles, Globe, 2005; *films:* Mrs Brown, 1997; Shakespeare in Love, 1999 (Oscar for Best Soundtrack); Billy Elliott, Quills, 2000; Captain Corelli's Mandolin, Charlotte Gray, 2001; Deséo, 2002; Blackball, Love's Brother, 2003; Two Brothers, Proof, Mickybo and Me, Oyster Farmer, 2004; On a Clear Day, 2005. *Recreation:* the hKippers (*sic*). *Address:* c/o Linda Mamy, United Agents, 12–26 Lexington Street, W1F 0LE.

WARBOYS, Prof. Brian Charles, CEng, FBCS, CITP; Professor of Software Engineering, University of Manchester, 1985–2007, now Emeritus; *b* 30 April 1942; *s* of Charles Bernard and Vera Beatrice Warboys; *m* 1965, Gillian Whitaker; one *s* one *d*. *Educ:* Univ. of Southampton (BSc Maths). CEng 1990; FBCS 1996; CITP 1998. English Electric, subseq. ICL: Software Engr, 1963–71; Chief Designer, ICL mainframe computer VME operating system, 1971–79; Manager, Systems Strategy, Mainframes Div., 1979–85; first ICL Fellow, 1984–89; Sen. ICL Fellow (pt-time), 1989–96. *Publication:* Business Information Systems: a process approach, 1999. *Recreations:* playing golf badly, supporting Millwall Football Club, reading, spending time with my family. *Address:* School of Computer Science, University of Manchester, Manchester M13 9PL. *T:* (0161) 275 6182, *Fax:* (0161) 275 6204; *e-mail:* brian@cs.man.ac.uk.

WARBRICK, Prof. Colin John; Professor of Law, 2006–08, Barber Professor of Jurisprudence, 2007–08, University of Birmingham; *b* 7 Aug. 1943; *s* of George and Nancy Warbrick; *m* 1974, Rosemary Goodwin; one *s* one *d*. *Educ:* Barrow-in-Furness Grammar Sch.; Corpus Christi Coll., Cambridge (LLB 1966; MA 1969); Michigan (LLM 1969; Fulbright Schol. and Ford Foundn Fellow). Law Department, University of Durham: Lectr, then Sen. Lectr, 1970–96; Prof. of Law, 1996–2006 ; Chm., 1998–2001. Vis. Prof., Coll. of Law, Univ. of Iowa, 1981–82, 1985; Sen. Associate, St Antony's Coll., Oxford, 2001. Consultant on Human Rights, Council of Europe, 1991–; Specialist Advr, Constitution Cttee, H of L, 2005–06. *Publications:* (ed with Vaughan Lowe) The United Nations and the Principles of International Law, 1993; (with David Harris and Michael O'Boyle) Law of the European Convention on Human Rights, 1995; articles on internat. law and human rights. *Recreations:* Rugby, allotment. *Address:* Birmingham Law School, University of Birmingham, Birmingham B15 2TT. *T:* (0121) 414 3637; *e-mail:* c.warbrick@bham.ac.uk.

WARBURTON, Dame Anne (Marion), DCVO 1979 (CVO 1965); CMG 1977; HM Diplomatic Service, 1957–85; President, Lucy Cavendish College, Cambridge, 1985–94; *b* 8 June 1927; *d* of Captain Eliot Warburton, MC and Mary Louise (*née* Thompson), US. *Educ:* Barnard Coll., Columbia Univ. (BA); Somerville Coll., Oxford (BA, MA; Hon. Fellow, 1977); MA Cantab 1985. Economic Cooperation Administration, London, 1949–52; NATO Secretariat, Paris, 1952–54; Lazard Bros, London, 1955–57; entered Diplomatic Service, Nov. 1957; 2nd Sec., FO, 1957–59; 2nd, then 1st Sec., UK Mission to UN, NY, 1959–62; 1st Sec., Bonn, 1962–65; 1st Sec., DSAO, London, 1965–67; 1st Sec., FO, then FCO, 1967–70; Counsellor, UK Mission to UN, Geneva, 1970–75; Head of Guidance and Information Policy Dept, FCO, 1975–76; Ambassador to Denmark, 1976–83; Ambassador and UK Permanent Rep. to UN and other internat. organisations, Geneva, 1983–85. Dep. Leader, UK Delegn to UN Women's Conf., Nairobi, 1985; Leader, EC Investigative Mission: Abuse of Bosnian Muslim Women, 1992–93; Mem., Cttee on Standards in Public Life, 1994–97. Member: Equal Opportunities Commn, 1986–88; British Library Bd, 1989–95; Council, UEA, 1991–97. Governor, ESU, 1992–96. Hon. LLD Arkansas, 1994. Verdienstkreuz, 1st Class (West Germany), 1965; Grand Cross, Order of Dannebrog, 1979; Lazo de Dama, Order of Isabel la Católica (Spain), 1988. *Recreations:* travel, enjoying the arts. *Address:* Ansted, Thornham Magna, Eye, Suffolk IP23 8HB. *Club:* English-Speaking Union.

WARBURTON, David; Senior National Officer: GMB (formerly General, Municipal, Boilermakers and Allied Trades Union), 1973–95; APEX (white collar section of GMB), since 1990; *b* 10 Jan. 1942; *s* of Harold and Ada Warburton; *m* 1966, Carole Anne Susan Tomney; two *d*. *Educ:* Cottingley Manor Sch., Bingley, Yorks; Coleg Harlech, Merioneth, N Wales. Campaign Officer, Labour Party, 1964; Educn Officer, G&MWU, 1965–66, Reg. Officer, 1966–73. Co-Chm., Crazy Horse Investment Trust, 2001–. Secretary: Chemical Unions Council; Rubber Industry Jt Unions, 1980–86; Chm., Paper and Packaging Industry Unions, 1988–92. Mem., Europ. Co-ord. Cttee, Chem., Rubber and Glass Unions, 1975–81. Chm., Chem. and Allied Industries Jt Indust. Council, 1973–86; Mem., Govt Industrial Workers Jt Consultative Cttee, 1988–92; Sec., Home Office Jt Indust. Council, 1989–; Treas., Electricity Supply Nat. Jt Council, 1990–; Member: Industrial Tribunal, 1995–99; Employment Tribunal, 1999–. Vice-Pres., Internat. Fedn of Chemical, Energy and Gen. Workers, 1986–94. Member: NEDC, 1973–86; Commonwealth Develt Corp., 1979–87; TUC Energy Cttee, 1978–92; Nat. Jt Council for Civil Air Transport, 1992–95; Chm., TUC Gen. Purposes Cttee, 1984–95; Dir, Union Liaison Services, 1995–. Nat. Sec., UK Friends of Palestine, 1983–. Campaign Dir, Friends of The Speaker, 1996–2000. *Publications:* Pharmaceuticals for the People, 1973; Drug Industry: which way to control, 1975; UK Chemicals: The Way Forward, 1977; Economic Detente, 1980; The Case for Voters Tax Credits, 1983; Forward Labour, 1985; Facts, Figures and Damned Statistics, 1987. *Recreations:* music, American politics, flicking through reference books, films of the thirties and forties. *Address:* 47 Hill Rise, Chorleywood, Rickmansworth, Herts WD3 7NY. *T:* (01923) 778726.

WARBURTON, Prof. Geoffrey Barratt, FREng; Hives Professor of Mechanical Engineering, University of Nottingham, 1982–89; *b* 9 June 1924; *s* of Ernest McPherson and Beatrice Warburton; *m* 1952, Margaret Coan; three *d*. *Educ:* William Hulme's Grammar School, Manchester; Peterhouse, Cambridge (Open Exhibition in Mathematics, 1942; 1st cl. Hons in Mechanical Sciences Tripos, 1944; BA 1945; MA 1949); PhD Edinburgh, 1949. FREng (FEng 1985). Junior Demonstrator, Cambridge Univ., 1944–46; Asst Lecturer in Engineering, Univ. Coll. of Swansea, 1946–47; Dept of Engineering, Univ. of Edinburgh: Assistant, 1947–48, Lecturer, 1948–50 and 1953–56; ICI Research Fellow, 1950–53; Head of Post-graduate School of Applied Dynamics, 1956–61; Nottingham University: Prof. of Applied Mechanics, 1961–82; a Pro-Vice-Chancellor, 1984–88. Vis. Prof., Dept of Civil Engrg, Imperial Coll., 1990–97. FRSE 1960; FIMechE 1968. Rayleigh Medal, Inst. of Acoustics, 1982. Editor, Earthquake Engineering and Structural Dynamics, 1988–96 (Associate Editor, 1972–88); Member, Editorial Boards: Internat. Jl of Mechanical Sciences, 1967–92; Internat. Jl for Numerical Methods in Engineering, 1969–96; Jl of Sound and Vibration, 1971–96. *Publications:* The Dynamical Behaviour of Structures, 1964, 2nd edn 1976; research on mechanical vibrations, in several scientific journals. *Address:* 18 Grangewood Road, Wollaton, Nottingham NG8 2SH.

WARBURTON, Ivor William; Vice President and General Manager Operations, Tangula Railtours, Shanghai, 2006–09; *b* 13 Aug. 1946; *s* of late Dennis and of Edna Margaret Warburton; *m* 1969, Carole-Ann Ashton (marr. diss. 1982); three *d*. *Educ:* Dulwich Coll.; Queens' Coll., Cambridge (MA); Univ. of Warwick (MSc). FCILT (FCIT 1989); FCIM 1994. British Railways, 1968–97: graduate trainee, 1968–70; local ops posts, London Midland Region, 1970–73; Divl Passenger Manager, Bristol, 1974–78; Overseas Tourist Manager, 1978–82; Regional Passenger Manager, York, 1982–83; Dir, Passenger Marketing Services, 1984–85; Asst Gen. Manager, London Midland Region, 1985–87; Employee Relations Manager, 1987–88; Dir of Operations, 1988–90; Gen. Manager, London Midland Region, 1990–92; Dir, 1992–95, Man. Dir, 1995–97, InterCity West Coast; Dir, Business Develt and Industry Affairs, Virgin Rail Gp, 1997–99. Chm., Assoc. of Train Operating Cos, 1997–99. President: Railway Study Assoc., 1993–94; Retired Railway Officers' Soc., 2003–04. *Recreations:* Chinese language and culture, music, opera, handicapped scouting, Marketors' Livery Company. *Address:* 34 St Clair's Road, Croydon CR0 5NE. *T:* (020) 8681 6421.

WARBURTON, John Kenneth, CBE 1983; Director General, Birmingham Chamber of Commerce and Industry, 1994 (Chief Executive, 1978–94); *b* 7 May 1932; *s* of Frederick and Eva Warburton; *m* 1960, Patricia Gordon; one *d*. *Educ:* Newcastle-under-Lyme High Sch.; Keble Coll., Oxford (MA Jurisprudence). Called to Bar, Gray's Inn, 1977. London Chamber of Commerce, 1956–59; Birmingham Chamber of Commerce and Industry, 1959–94. President, British Chambers of Commerce Executives, 1979–81; Member: Steering Cttee, Internat. Bureau of Chambers of Commerce, 1976–94; Nat. Council, Assoc. of British Chambers of Commerce, 1978–94; European Trade Cttee and Business Link Gp, BOTB, 1979–87; E European Trade Council, BOTB, 1984–93; Review Body on Doctors' and Dentists' Remuneration, 1982–92; MSC Task Gp on Employment Trng, 1987; Lord Chancellor's Birmingham Adv. Cttee, 1993–99; Ind. Remuneration Panel, Birmingham CC, 2001–07; Chm., Adv. Council, W Midlands Industrial Develt Assoc., 1983–86. Mediator, Centre for Dispute Resolution, 1994–. Director: National Garden Festival 1986 Ltd, 1983–87; National Exhibition Centre Ltd, 1989–95. Chm., Birmingham Macmillan Nurses Appeal, 1994–97; Dep. Chm., Birmingham Children's Hosp. Appeal, 1996–98. Vol. advr, BESO, Slovakia, 1994, and Mongolia, 1995. Companion, BITC, 1992–. Trustee, Holy Child Sch., Edgbaston, 1992–96; Gov., Newman Coll., 1993–2002 (Exec. Chm., 1999–2002; Hon. Life Fellow, 2003); Life Mem., Court, Birmingham Univ., 1981 (Gov., 1982–99). Hon. DUniv UCE, 1999. *Address:* 35 Hampshire Drive, Edgbaston, Birmingham B15 3NY. *T:* (0121) 454 6764.

WARBURTON, Richard Maurice, OBE 1987; Director General, Royal Society for the Prevention of Accidents, 1979–90; *b* 14 June 1928; *s* of Richard and Phylis Agnes Warburton; *m* 1952, Lois May Green; two *s*. *Educ:* Wigan Grammar Sch.; Birmingham Univ. (BA 1st Cl. Hons). Flying Officer, RAF, 1950–52. HM Inspector of Factories, 1952–79; Head of Accident Prevention Advisory Unit, Health and Safety Executive, 1972–79. *Recreations:* golf, gardening, fell walking. *Address:* Cornaa, Wyfordby Avenue, Blackburn, Lancs BB2 7AR. *T:* (01254) 56824.

WARBY, Mark David John; QC 2002; *b* 10 Oct. 1958; *s* of David James Warby, FIMechE, and Clare Warby; *m* 1985, Ann Kenrick; one *s* two *d*. *Educ:* Bristol Grammar Sch.; St John's Coll., Oxford (Schol.; MA Jurisprudence). Called to the Bar, Gray's Inn, 1981, Bencher, 2007. *Publication:* (jtly) The Law of Privacy and the Media, 2002. *Recreations:* surfing, guitar, tennis. *Address:* 5 Raymond Buildings, Gray's Inn, WC1R 5BP. *T:* (020) 7242 2902, *Fax:* (020) 7831 2686; *e-mail:* clerks@5rb.co.uk. *Clubs:* Union, Butterfly Tennis; Crackington Haven Tennis; Crackington Haven Surf.

WARCHUS, Matthew; freelance theatre director; *b* 24 Oct. 1966; *s* of Michael Warchus and Rosemary Warchus. *Educ:* Bristol Univ. (BA 1st Cl. Hons Music and Drama). Associate Dir, W Yorkshire Playhouse, 1992–94. Plays directed include: Sejanus: his fall, Edinburgh, 1988; The Suicide, 1989, Coriolanus, 1990–91, NYT; Master Harold and the Boys, Bristol Old Vic, 1990; West Yorkshire Playhouse, 1992–94: Life is a Dream, 1992; Who's Afraid of Virginia Woolf, 1992; Fiddler on the Roof, 1992; The Plough and the Stars, 1993; Death of a Salesman, 1994; Betrayal, 1994; True West, 1994; Much Ado About Nothing, Queen's, 1993; The Life of Stuff, Donmar Warehouse, 1993; Henry V, 1994, The Devil is an Ass, 1995, RSC; Troilus and Cressida, Opera North, 1995; Volpone, RNT, 1995; Peter Pan, W Yorks Playhouse, 1995; The Rake's Progress, WNO, 1996; Art, Wyndham's, 1996, NY, 1998; Falstaff, Opera North and ENO, 1997; Hamlet, 1997, The Unexpected Man, Duchess, 1998, NY 2000, RSC; Life x 3, RNT, transf. Old Vic, 2000, NY, 2003; The Winter's Tale, RSC, 2002; Così fan tutte, ENO, 2002; Our House (musical), Cambridge, 2002; Tell me on a Sunday, Gielgud, 2003; Buried Child, NT, 2004; The Lord of the Rings, Th. Royal, 2007; Boeing Boeing, Comedy, 2007; Speed-the-Plow, Old Vic, 2008; God of Carnage, Gielgud, 2008. Film: Simpatico (also screenplay), 1999. *Address:* c/o Royal Shakespeare Company, Royal Shakespeare Theatre, Stratford-upon-Avon CV37 6BB.

WARD, family name of **Earl of Dudley** and of **Viscount Bangor**.

WARD, Rt Hon. Sir Alan Hylton, Kt 1988; PC 1995; **Rt Hon. Lord Justice Ward;** a Lord Justice of Appeal, since 1995; *b* 15 Feb. 1938; *s* of late Stanley Victor Ward and of Mary Ward; *m* 1st, 1963 (marr. diss. 1982); one *s* two *d*; 2nd, 1983, Helen (*née* Gilbert); one *d* (and one twin *d* decd). *Educ:* Christian Brothers Coll., Pretoria; Univ. of Pretoria (BA, LLB); Pembroke Coll., Cambridge (MA, LLB; Hon. Fellow, 1998). Called to the Bar, Gray's Inn, 1964, Bencher, 1988, Treas., 2006 (Vice-Treas., 2005); QC 1984; a Recorder, 1985–88; a Judge of the High Court, Family Div., 1988–95; Family Div. Liaison Judge, Midland and Oxford Circuit, 1990–95. Formerly an Attorney of Supreme Court of South Africa. Mem., Matrimonial Causes Procedure Cttee, 1982–85. Consulting Editor, Children Law and Practice, 1991–. Hon. LLD East Anglia, 2001. *Recreation:* when not reading and writing boring judgments, trying to remember what recreation is. *Address:* Royal Courts of Justice, Strand, WC2A 2LL. *Clubs:* Garrick, MCC.

WARD, (Albert Joseph) Reginald; Chief Executive, Reg Ward Associates, since 1993; *b* 5 Oct. 1927; *s* of Albert E. and Gwendolene M. E. Ward, Lydbook, Glos; *m* 1954, Betty Anne Tooze; one *s* one *d*. *Educ:* East Dean Grammar Sch., Cinderford, Glos; Univ. of

Manchester (BA Hons History). HM Inspector of Taxes, 1952–65; Chief Administrator, County Architects Dept, Lancashire CC, 1965–68; Business Manager, Shankland Cox & Associates, 1968–69; Corporation Secretary, Irvine New Town Development Corporation, 1969–72; Chief Executive: Coatbridge Borough Council, 1972–74; London Borough of Hammersmith, 1974–76; Hereford and Worcester CC, 1976–80; LDDC, 1981–88; Kent European Enterprise, 1988–89; ISLEF, Danish develt co., 1989–92; Whitegate Develt Corp., St Kitts, 1999–2002. Mem., Duke of Edinburgh's Commn into Housing, 1986–87. Hon. Fellow, QMC, 1987; Fellow, Univ. of London. FRSA. *Recreations:* walking, tennis, music, architecture and urban design. *Address:* Abbot's Court, Deerhurst, Gloucester GL19 4BX. *T:* (01684) 274881.

WARD, Mrs Ann Sarita; non-executive Director, Lambeth, Southwark, Lewisham Family Health Services Authority, 1991–96; *b* 4 Aug. 1923; *d* of Denis Godfrey and Marion Phyllis Godfrey; *m* Frank Ward (*d* 1991); two *s*. *Educ:* St Paul's Girls' Sch., Hammersmith. Professional photographer; photo journalist, Daily Mail, 1962–67, Daily Mirror, 1967–70; award winner, British Press Photographs of Year, 1967. Councillor, London Bor. of Southwark, 1971–86 (Dep. Leader, 1978–83); Chm., ILEA, 1981–82. Pol Advr to Barbara Follett, MP, 1996–2001. Contested (Lab) Streatham, 1970. Associate Mem., Camberwell HA, 1990–93 (Mem., 1982–90). Special Trustee, KCH, 1983–88. Mem., Exec. Cttee, Stevenage, Abbeyfield Soc., 2002–. Bd Mem., Internat. Shakespeare Globe Centre, 1988–92; Hon. Vice Pres., Friends of Shakespeare's Globe, 1992– (Chm., 1987–92). Co-ordinator, Emily's List UK, 1992–96. *Recreations:* theatre, gardening. *Address:* Tadworth Grove Residential and Nursing Home, The Avenue, Tadworth, near Epsom, Surrey KT20 5AT.

WARD, Hon. Sir Austin; *see* Ward, Hon. Sir L. A.

WARD, Caroline Jane; *see* Drummond, C. J.

WARD, Cecil, CBE 1989; JP; Town Clerk, Belfast City Council, 1979–89; *b* 26 Oct. 1929; *s* of William and Mary Caroline Ward. *Educ:* Technical High Sch., Belfast; College of Technology, Belfast. Employed by Belfast City Council (formerly Belfast County Borough Council), 1947–89; Asst Town Clerk (Administration), 1977–79. Mem., Local Govt Staff Commn, 1983–89. Member: Arts Council NI, 1980–85, 1987–89; Bd, Ulster Mus., 1989–95; Dir, Ulster Orchestra Soc., 1980–94 (Chm., 1990–94). Mem., Senate, QUB, 1990–2001. Mem., Bd, Mater Hosp., 1994–2002. JP Belfast, 1988. Hon. MA QUB, 1988. *Recreations:* music, reading, hill walking. *Address:* 24 Thornhill, Malone, Belfast, Northern Ireland BT9 6SS. *T:* (028) 9066 8950; Hatter's Field, Drumawier, Greencastle, Co. Donegal, Ireland.

WARD, (Charles John) Nicholas, FCA; Chairman, Interactive Prospect Targeting Holdings plc, since 2008; *b* 1 Aug. 1941; *s* of late John Newman Ward and Vivienne Grainger Ward; *m* 1967, Deirdre Veronica Shaw; two *d*. *Educ:* Charterhouse; INSEAD (MBA 1968). FCA 1964. Early career spanned several cos engaged in textiles, venture capital, overseas trading, retailing, distribution, healthcare, leisure and property, subseq. Chairman or non-exec. dir of numerous cos in retail, textiles, healthcare, transport, stockbroking and fund mgt, coal mining, student accommodation, and agriculture and envmt sectors. Chairman: NHS Supplies Authy, 1995–98; Ryan Group Ltd, 1995–2004; ADAS Hldgs, 1998–; UPP Projects Ltd, 2006–07; Dep. Chm., Albert E. Sharp Hldgs, 1996–98; non-exec. Dir, Anglia and Oxford RHA, 1990–96. Consultant to: Deutsche Bank, 1995–; 3i, 1998–2007; Swiss Re, 2008–. Ind. Mem., Steering Bd, Insolvency Service, DTI, 2004–06. Chairman: Make a Difference Team, 1994–96; The Volunteering Partnership, 1995–96; British Liver Trust, 1999–2004; CORGI Trust, 2005; Co-Chm., The Volunteering Partnership Forum for England, 1996–97; Pres., Ind. Custody Visiting Assoc. (formerly Nat. Assoc. for Lay Visiting), 1996–2006 (Chm., 1992–96); Chm., Lay Visiting Charitable Trust, 1995–. Fellow, Inst. for Turnaround (formerly Soc. of Turnaround Professionals), 2001. Liveryman, Tylers' and Bricklayers' Co., 1963– (Master, 1991–92). *Address:* Bacon House, Greatworth, Banbury, Oxon OX17 2DX. *T:* (01295) 712732; *e-mail:* nicholasward@variouscompanies.com. Flat 12, 77 Warwick Square, SW1V 2AR. *T:* (020) 7834 9175. *Club:* Royal Society of Medicine.

WARD, Christopher John; Joint Founder, 1983, and Chairman, since 2006, Redwood Publishing (Editorial Director, 1983–2002; Vice-Chairman, 2002–06); *b* 25 Aug. 1942; *s* of John Stanley Ward and Jacqueline Law-Hume Costin; *m* 1st, 1971 (marr. diss.); one *s* two *d*; 2nd, 1990, Nonie Niesewand (*née* Fogarty). *Educ:* King's Coll. Sch., Wimbledon. Successively on staff of Driffield Times, 1959, and Newcastle Evening Chronicle, 1960–63; reporter, sub-editor, then feature writer and columnist, 1963–76, Daily Mirror; Assistant Editor: Sunday Mirror, 1976–79; Daily Mirror, 1979–81; Editor, Daily Express, 1981–83. Dir, Acorn Computer plc, 1983–99. Chm., Redwood Custom Communications, 2007–. WWF: Trustee, 1994–2000; Chm., UK, 2002–08. Mark Boxer award, British Soc. of Magazine Eds, 1995. *Publications:* How to Complain, 1974; Our Cheque is in the Post, 1980. *Recreations:* walking in the Scottish Borders, shooting. *Address:* Glenburn Hall, Jedburgh TD8 6QB. *T:* (01835) 865801; *e-mail:* cj.ward@btinternet.com. *Clubs:* Garrick, Savile.

WARD, Christopher John Ferguson; solicitor; *b* 26 Dec. 1942; *m* Janet Ward, JP, LLB; one *s* one *d* and two *s* one *d* by former marr. *Educ:* Magdalen College Sch.; Law Society Sch. of Law. MP (C) Swindon, Oct. 1969–June 1970; contested (C) Eton and Slough, 1979. Mem., Berks CC, 1965–81 (Leader of the Council and Chm., Policy Cttee, 1979–81). Gov., Chiltern Nursery Trng Coll., 1975–97 (Chm., 1988–91). Treas., United & Cecil Club, 1993 (Hon. Sec., 1982–87). *Address:* Ramblings, Maidenhead Thicket, Berks SL6 3QE. *T:* (office) (01635) 517111.

WARD, (Christopher) John (William); Development Advisor, Welsh National Opera, since 2003; *b* 21 June 1942; *s* of late Thomas Maxfield and Peggy Ward; *m* 1970, Diane Lelliott (marr. diss. 1988); partner, 1982, Susan Corby. *Educ:* Oundle Sch.; Corpus Christi Coll., Oxford (BA LitHum); Univ. of East Anglia (Graduate DipEcon). Overseas and Economic Intelligence Depts, Bank of England, 1965; General Secretary, Bank of England Staff Organisation, 1973; Gen. Sec., Assoc. of First Div. Civil Servants, 1980; Head of Development, Opera North, 1988–94; Dir of Corporate Affairs, W Yorks Playhouse, 1994–97; Develt Dir, ENO, 1997–2002; Dir of Fundraising, Crafts Council, 2003–04. *Recreations:* opera, theatre, football. *Address:* c/o Welsh National Opera, Wales Millennium Centre, Bute Place, Cardiff CF10 5AL. *Club:* Swindon Town Supporters.

WARD, Claire Margaret; MP (Lab) Watford, since 1997; Vice-Chamberlain of HM Household, since 2008; *b* 9 May 1972; *d* of Frank and Catherine Ward; *m* 2003, John Simpson; one *s* one *d*. *Educ:* Loreto Coll., St Albans; Univ. of Hertfordshire (LLB Hons); Brunel Univ. (MA). Trainee Solicitor, Pattinson & Brewer, 1995–97; qualif. Solicitor, 1998–. Mem. (Lab) Elstree and Borehamwood Town Council, 1994–98 (Mayor, 1996–97). PPS to Minister of State for Health, 2001–05; an Asst Govt Whip, 2005–06; a Lord Comr of HM Treasury (Govt Whip), 2006–08. Mem., NEC, Lab. Party, 1991–95. Mem., Select Cttee on Culture, Media and Sports, 1997–2001. Jt Sec., All Party Film Industry Gp, 1997–. Patron, Young European Movement, 1999. *Recreations:* films, Association Football (Watford FC season ticket holder), eating out. *Address:* House of Commons, SW1A 0AA. *Club:* Reform.

WARD, Colin; Associate, Capgemini, since 2003; *b* 23 June 1947; *s* of Simon Myles Ward and Ella May McConnell; *m* 1969, Marjory Hall Milne. *Educ:* Daniel Stewart's Coll., Edinburgh; Heriot-Watt Univ. (BA 1970). CA 1974. Ernst & Young, Edinburgh, 1970–74; Price Waterhouse, Glasgow, 1974–75; BSC, 1975–77; SDA, latterly Chief Accountant, 1977–90; Student Loans Co., 1990–2003: Loans Dir, 1990–92; Asst Man. Dir, 1992–96; Main Board, 1994–2003; Chief Exec., 1996–2003. Loans Scheme consultant to Hungarian Govt, 1999–2000. CCMI 2003. *Recreations:* sailing, gardening, classical music. *Address:* 108 Sinclair Street, Helensburgh, Argyll G84 9QE. *T:* (01436) 676048.

WARD, David; Consultant, Atkinson Ritson (formerly Atkinson & North), Solicitors, Carlisle, since 1998 (Partner, 1964–98); President, The Law Society, 1989–90; *b* 23 Feb. 1937; *s* of Rev. Frank Ward, Darfield, Yorks, and Elizabeth Ward (*née* Pattinson), Appleby, Westmorland; *m* 1978, Antoinette, *d* of Maj.-Gen. D. A. B. Clarke, CB, CBE; two *s* one *d*. *Educ:* Dame Allan's Sch., Newcastle upon Tyne; Queen Elizabeth Grammar Sch., Penrith; St Edmund Hall, Oxford (BA). Admitted solicitor, 1962. Articled Clerk, 1959, Assistant, 1962, Atkinson & North. Mem., Lord Chancellor's Adv. Cttee on Legal Educn and Conduct, 1991–97. Mem. Council, 1972–91, Vice-Pres., 1988–89, Law Soc.; Pres., Carlisle and District Law Soc., 1985–86. Pres., Carlisle Mountaineering Club, 1985–88. Methodist local preacher, 1955–. *Recreations:* mountaineering, choral and church music. *Address:* The Green, Caldbeck, Wigton, Cumbria CA7 8ER. *T:* (01697) 478220.

WARD, Rev. David Conisbee; Non-Stipendiary Minister, St George's, Tolworth, 1995–2006; *b* 7 Jan. 1933; *s* of late Sydney L. Ward and Ivy A. Ward; *m* 1958, Patricia Jeanette (*née* Nobes); one *s* one *d*. *Educ:* Kingston Grammar Sch.; St John's Coll., Cambridge (Scholar, MA). Asst Principal, Nat. Assistance Bd, 1956, Principal, 1961; Asst Sec., DHSS, 1970, Under Sec., 1976–83. Southwark Ordination Course, 1977–80; Deacon, 1980; Priest, 1981; Non-Stipendiary Curate, St Matthew, Surbiton, 1980–83; Curate, Immanuel Church, Streatham Common, 1983–84, parish priest, 1984–87; Vicar, St Paul's, Hook, Surrey, 1987–93; NSM, All Saints, Kingston, 1993–95. Councillor (Lib Dem) Kingston-upon-Thames, 1994–98 (Dep. Mayor, 1996–97). Governor, Kingston GS, 1988–2003. FRSA 2000. *Publication:* (with G. W. Evans) Chantry Chapel to Royal Grammar School: the history of Kingston Grammar School 1299–1999, 2000. *Recreations:* member Kingstonian FC; Pitcairn Islands Study Group (philately). *Address:* 50 Elgar Avenue, Tolworth, Surbiton, Surrey KT5 9JN. *T:* (020) 8399 9679. *Clubs:* Civil Service; Rotary (Kingston upon Thames).

WARD, David Gordon; HM Diplomatic Service, retired; British Consul, Tenerife, 2002–07; *b* 25 July 1942; *s* of late Major Gordon Alec Ward, MBE and Irene Ward; *m* 1st, 1966, Rosemary Anne Silvester (marr. diss. 1979); two *s* one *d*; 2nd, 1980, Margaret (*née* Martin); one *s* one *d*, and one step *s*. *Educ:* Rutlish Sch., Merton. With CRO, 1961–65; entered FCO, 1965; Montevideo, 1967–70; Dakar (also accredited to Nouakchott, Bamako and Conakry), 1970–74; FCO, 1974–76; Victoria, 1977–80; Libreville, 1980; Luxembourg, 1981–83; Consul, Oporto, 1983–87; FCO, 1988–90; Harare, 1990–95; FCO, 1995–98; Ambassador to Dominican Rep., 1998–2002 and (non-resident) to Haiti, 1999–2002. Hon. Cavaleiro da Confrariá do Vinho do Porto, 1986. Grand Silver Cross, Order of Merit of Duarte Sanchez and Mella (Dominican Republic), 2002. *Recreations:* theatre, visual arts, tennis. *Address:* *e-mail:* david_warduk@yahoo.co.uk.

WARD, Graham Norman Charles, CBE 2004; FCA; FEI; Senior Partner, World Energy and Utilities Group, PricewaterhouseCoopers, since 2000; President, International Federation of Accountants, 2004–06; *b* 9 May 1952; *s* of late Ronald Charles Edward Ward and Hazel Winifred Ward (*née* Elis); *m* 1975, Ingrid Imogen Sylvia Baden-Powell (marr. diss. 1981); two *s*; *m* 1993, Ann Mistri; one *s*. *Educ:* Jesus Coll., Oxford (Boxing Blue; MA). ACA 1977, FCA 1983; CIGEM (CIGasE 1997); FEI (FInstE 1999). Price Waterhouse, subseq. PricewaterhouseCoopers: articled clerk, 1974–77; Personal Technical Asst to Chm., Accounting Standards Cttee, 1978–79; on secondment to HM Treasury, 1985; Partner, 1986; Dir, Electricity Services Europe, 1990–94; Direct Business Develt, 1993–94; Chm., World Utilities Gp, 1994–96; Dep. Chm., World Energy Gp, 1996–98; World Utilities Leader, 1998–2000. Member: Panel on Takeovers and Mergers, 2000–01; Financial Reporting Council, 2001–07 (Dep. Chm., 2000–01); Bd, UK India Business Council (formerly Indo British Partnership Network), 2005– (Vice-Chm., 2008–); Financial Services Sector Adv. Bd, UK Trade & Investment, 2006–. Chairman: Consultative Cttee of Accountancy Bodies, 2000–01; Power Sector Adv. Gp, UK Trade & Investment (formerly Trade Partners UK), 2001–04; Mem. Council, Soc. of Pension Consultants, 1988–90; Mem., Auditing Practices Bd, 2001–04 (Vice-Chm., 2003–04); Member: Cttee, British Energy Assoc., 1997–2004 (Vice-Chm., 1998–2001; Chm., 2001–04); Exec. Council, Parly Gp for Energy Studies, 1998–. Chairman: Young Chartered Accountants' Gp, 1980–81; London Soc. of Chartered Accountants, 1989–90 (Mem. Cttee, 1983–91); Chartered Accountants in the Community, 1996–2002; Member: Council, ICAEW, 1991–2003 (Vice-Pres., 1998–99; Dep. Pres., 1999–2000; Pres., 2000–01); Bd, Internat. Fedn of Accountants, 2000–06. Vice-Chm., World Energy Council, 2008–. Vice Pres., Epilepsy Res. UK (formerly Epilepsy Res. Foundn), 1997–. Vice President: Univ. of Oxford Amateur Boxing Club, 1990–; Soc. of Conservative Accountants, 1992–; President: Jesus Coll. Assoc., 1990–91; Chartered Accountant Students' Soc. of London, 1992–96 (Vice-Pres., 1987–92). Governor: Goodenough Coll., 2004–; Dulwich Coll., 2008–. Hon. Financial Advr, St Paul's Cathedral, 2008–. FRSA 1996. Freeman: City of London, 1994; Co. of Chartered Accountants in England and Wales, 1994 (Mem., Ct of Assts, 1997–; Sen. Warden, 2008–Oct. 2009). *Publications:* The Work of a Pension Scheme Actuary, 1987; Pensions: your way through the maze, 1988; (consultant ed) A Practitioner's Guide to Audit Regulation in the UK, 2004. *Recreations:* boxing, Rugby, opera, ballet. *Address:* PricewaterhouseCoopers LLP, 1 Embankment Place, WC2N 6RH. *T:* (020) 7804 3101. *Clubs:* Carlton; Vincent's (Oxford).

WARD, Hubert, OBE 1996; MA; Headmaster (formerly Principal), English College, Prague, 1992–96; *b* 26 Sept. 1931; *s* of Allan Miles Ward and Joan Mary Ward; *m* 1st, 1958, Elizabeth Cynthia Fearn Bechervaise (*d* 2005); one *s* two *d*; 2nd, 2007, Judith Marion Hart (*née* Gay). *Educ:* Westminster Sch.; Trinity Coll., Cambridge. Asst Master (Maths), Geelong C of E Grammar Sch., Victoria, 1955–66; Asst Master (Maths), Westminster Sch., London, 1966–69; Headmaster, King's Sch., Ely, 1970–92. Mem. (L) Cambs CC, 1985–89. JP Cambs, 1976–92. *Publication:* (with K. Lewis) Starting Statistics, 1969. *Recreations:* rowing, sailing, bird-watching. *Address:* 1 The Green, Mistley, Manningtree, Essex CO11 1EU.

WARD, Prof. Ian Macmillan, FRS 1983; FInstP, FIMMM; Research Professor, University of Leeds, since 1994 (Professor of Physics, 1970–94, and Cavendish Professor, 1987–94); *b* 9 April 1928; *s* of Harry Ward and Joan Ward; *m* 1960, Margaret (*née* Linley); two *s* one *d*. *Educ:* Royal Grammar Sch., Newcastle upon Tyne; Magdalen Coll., Oxford (MA, DPhil). FInstP 1965; FIMMM (FPRI 1974). Technical Officer, ICI Fibres, 1954–61; seconded to Division of Applied Mathematics, Brown Univ., USA, 1961–62;

Head of Basic Physics Section, ICI Fibres, 1962–65, ICI Research Associate, 1964; Sen. Lectr in Physics of Materials, Univ. of Bristol, 1965–69; Chm., Dept of Physics, Univ. of Leeds, 1975–78, 1987–89; Dir, Interdisciplinary Res. Centre in Polymer Sci. and Technol., Univs of Leeds, Bradford and Durham, 1989–94. Secretary, Polymer Physics Gp, Inst. of Physics, 1964–71, Chm. 1971–75; Chairman, Macromolecular Physics Gp, European Physical Soc., 1976–81; Pres., British Soc. of Rheology, 1984–86. Hon. DSc Bradford, 1993. A. A. Griffith Medal, Plastics and Rubber Inst., 1982; S. G. Smith Meml Medal, Textile Inst., 1984; Swinburne Medal, Plastics and Rubber Inst., 1988; Charles Vernon Boys Medal, 1993, Glazebrook Medal, 2004, Inst. of Physics; Netlon Medal, IOM^3, 2004. Ed., Polymer, 1974–2002. *Publications:* Mechanical Properties of Solid Polymers, 1971, 2nd edn 1983; (ed) Structure and Properties of Oriented Polymers, 1975, 2nd edn 1997; (ed jtly) Ultra High Modulus Polymers, 1979; (with D. Hadley) An Introduction to the Mechanical Properties of Solid Polymers, 1993, 2nd edn (with J. Sweeney) 2004; (ed jtly) Solid Phase Processing of Polymers, 2000; contribs to Polymer, Jl of Polymer Science, Jl of Materials Science, Proc. Royal Soc., etc. *Recreations:* music, walking. *Address:* Kirskill, 2 Creskeld Drive, Bramhope, Leeds LS16 9EL. *T:* (0113) 267 3637.

WARD, John; *see* Ward, C. J. W.

WARD, Sir John (Devereux), Kt 1997; CBE 1973; BSc; CEng, FICE, FIStructE; *b* 8 March 1925; *s* of late Thomas Edward and Evelyn Victoria Ward; *m* 1955, Jean Miller Aitken; one *s* one *d. Educ:* Romford County Technical Sch.; Univ. of St Andrews (BSc). Navigator, RAF, 1943–47; student, 1949–53. Employed, Consulting Engineers, 1953–58, Taylor Woodrow Ltd, 1958–79; Man. Dir, Taylor Woodrow Arcon, Arcon Building Exports, 1976–78. MP (C) Poole, 1979–97. PPS to: Financial Sec. to Treasury, 1984–86; Sec. of State for Social Security, 1987–89; Prime Minister, 1994–97. UK Rep. to Council of Europe and WEU, 1983–87, 1989–94. Chm., British Gp, IPU, 1993–94 (Mem., Exec. Cttee, 1982–94). Chm., Wessex Area Conservatives, 1966–69; Conservative Party: Mem., Nat. Union Exec., 1965–78 (Mem., Gen. Purposes Cttee, 1966–72, 1975–78); Mem., Central Bd of Finance, 1969–78; Vice-Chm., Cons. Trade and Industry Cttee, 1983–84.

WARD, Sir John (MacQueen), Kt 2003; CBE 1995; FRSE; Chairman, Scottish Enterprise, 2004–Feb. 2009; *b* 1 Aug. 1940; *m* Barbara MacIntosh; one *s* three *d. Educ:* Edinburgh Acad.; Fettes Coll. CA. FRSE 2005. IBM UK Ltd: Plant Controller, 1966–75; Dir, Inf. Systems for Europe, 1975–79; Manufacturing Controller, 1979–81; Dir, Havant Plant, 1982–90 (numerous quality awards); Dir, UK Public Service Business, 1991–95; Res. Dir, Scotland and N England, 1991–96; Chairman: Scottish Homes, 1996–2002; Scottish Post Office Bd, 1997–2001; Macfarlane Gp (Clansman), subseq. Macfarlane Gp plc, 1998–2003. Chm., European Assets Trust, 1995–; non-exec. Chm., Dunfermline Building Soc., 1995–2007. Chairman: Scottish CBI, 1993–95; Scottish Qualifications Authy, 2000–04. Chm. or former Chm., advisory bodies and councils in Scotland. Trustee, Nat. Mus Scotland (formerly Nat. Mus of Scotland), 2005–. *Recreations:* walking, DIY, reading. *Address:* c/o Scottish Enterprise, 150 Broomielaw, 5 Atlantic Quay, Glasgow G2 8LU. *Club:* New (Edinburgh).

WARD, Rev. Prof. (John Stephen) Keith, FBA 2001; Regius Professor of Divinity, University of Oxford, 1991–2003; Canon of Christ Church, Oxford, 1991–2003; *b* 22 Aug. 1938; *s* of John George Ward and Evelyn (*née* Simpson); *m* 1963, Marian Trotman; one *s* one *d. Educ:* UCW, Cardiff (BA 1962); Linacre Coll., Oxford (BLitt 1968); Trinity Hall, Cambridge (MA 1972); Westcott House, Cambridge. DD Oxon, 1998; DD Cantab, 1999. Ordained priest of Church of England, 1972. Lecturer in Logic, Univ. of Glasgow, 1964–69; Lectr in Philosophy, Univ. of St Andrews, 1969–71; Lectr in Philosophy of Religion, Univ. of London, 1971–75; Dean of Trinity Hall, Cambridge, 1975–82; F. D. Maurice Prof. of Moral and Social Theology, Univ. of London, 1982–85; Prof. of History and Phil. of Religion, King's Coll. London, 1985–91. Gresham Prof. of Divinity, 2004–. Jt Editor, Religious Studies, 1990–98. Jt Pres., World Congress of Faiths, 1992–2001. *Publications:* Ethics and Christianity, 1970; Kant's View of Ethics, 1972; The Divine Image, 1976; The Concept of God, 1977; The Promise, 1981; Rational Theology and the Creativity of God, 1982; Holding Fast to God, 1982; The Living God, 1984; Battle for the Soul, 1985; Images of Eternity, 1987; The Rule of Love, 1989; Divine Action, 1990; A Vision to Pursue, 1991; Religion and Revelation, 1994; Religion and Creation, 1996; God, Chance and Necessity, 1996; God, Faith and the New Millennium, 1998; Religion and Human Nature, 1998; Religion and Community, 2000; God: a guide for the perplexed, 2002; The Case for Religion, 2004; What the Bible Really Teaches, 2004; Pascal's Fire, 2006; Is Religion Dangerous?, 2006; Christianity: a guide for the perplexed, 2007; Re-thinking Christianity, 2007; The Big Questions in Science and Religion, 2008; Religion and Human Fulfilment, 2008. *Recreations:* music, walking. *Address:* Church View, Abingdon Road, Cumnor, Oxford OX2 9QN. *T:* (01865) 865513.

WARD, Joseph Haggitt; *b* 7 July 1926; *s* of Joseph G. and Gladys Ward; *m* 1961, Anthea Clemo; one *s* one *d. Educ:* St Olave's Grammar School; Sidney Sussex College, Cambridge. Asst Principal, Min. of National Insurance, 1951; Private Sec. to Minister of Social Security, 1966–68; Asst Sec., 1968; Min. of Housing, later DoE, 1969–72; DHSS, 1972; Under-Sec. (pensions and nat. insce contributions), DHSS, 1976–86. *Recreations:* music, history of music. *Address:* 34 Uffington Road, SE27 0ND. *T:* (020) 8670 1732.

WARD, Sir Joseph James Laffey, 4th Bt *cr* 1911; *b* 11 Nov. 1946; *s* of Sir Joseph George Davidson Ward, 3rd Bt, and Joan Mary Haden (*d* 1993), *d* of Major Thomas J. Laffey, NZSC; *S* father, 1970; *m* 1968, Robyn Allison, *d* of William Maitland Martin, Rotorua, NZ; one *s* one *d. Heir: s* Joseph James Martin Ward, *b* 20 Feb. 1971.

WARD, Keith; *see* Ward, J. S. K.

WARD, Hon. Sir (Lisle) Austin, Kt 2006; Justice of Appeal, Bermuda, since 2004; *b* 14 Nov. 1935; *s* of Sir Erskine Rueul La Tourette Ward, KA; *m* 1961, Francisca Sorhaindo; two *d. Educ:* Harrison Coll., Barbados. Called to the Bar, Middle Temple, 1962; Solicitor Gen., Bermuda, 1981–85; QC Bermuda 1983; Puisne Judge, Bermuda, 1985–93; Chief Justice, 1993–2004. *Publication:* Digest of Judgements of the Court of Appeal, 1985. *Address:* PO Box WK1, Warwick WKBX, Bermuda; c/o Court of Appeal, 21 Parliament Street, Hamilton HM12, Bermuda.

WARD, His Honour Malcolm Beverley; a Circuit Judge, Midland and Oxford Circuit, 1979–97; *b* 3 May 1931; *s* of Edgar and Dora Mary Ward; *m* 1958, Muriel Winifred, *d* of Dr E. D. M. Wallace, Perth; two *s* two *d. Educ:* Wolverhampton Grammar Sch.; St John's Coll., Cambridge (Open Mathematical Schol.; MA, LLM). Called to the Bar, Inner Temple, 1956; practised Oxford (later Midland and Oxford) Circuit; a Recorder of the Crown Court, 1974–79. Governor, Wolverhampton Grammar Sch., 1972– (Chm., 1981–2001). *Recreations:* golf, music, (in theory) horticulture.

WARD, Malcolm Stanley; Group Account Director, JiWin, Dubai, since 2006; *b* 24 Sept. 1951; *s* of Hugh Ward and Rebecca Ward (*née* Rogerson). *Educ:* Gilberd School, Colchester. Dep. Editor, Gulf News, Dubai, 1978–79; Editor, Woodham and Wickford Chronicle, Essex, 1979–81; Dep. Editor, Gulf Times, Qatar, 1981–84; Dep. Editor, 1984–86, Dir and Editor, 1986–91, Daily News, Birmingham; Editor, Metro News, Birmingham, 1991–92; Ed., Evening News, Worcester, 1992–95; Man. Ed., The Peninsula, Qatar, 1995–98; News Ed., Gulf News, Dubai, 1998–2001; Account Dir, MCS Action, Dubai, 2001–06. *Recreations:* writing, travel, soccer, driving, tennis. *Address:* JiWin, PO Box 39333, Dubai Media City, Al Thuraya Tower, Dubai, UAE.

WARD, Mary Angela, MBE 1996; Co-Founder, and Artistic Director, since 1974, Chickenshed (formerly Chicken Shed Theatre Co.); *b* 2 Dec. 1944; *d* of Patrick O'Dwyer and Dot O'Dwyer (*née* Johnson); *m* 1971, Manus Ward; two *s. Educ:* Ilford Ursuline High Sch.; Digby Stuart Coll. Teacher, 1966–85; with Jo Collins, MBE, founded Chicken Shed Th. Co., 1974, with aim of producing pieces of theatrical and musical excellence to open the performing arts to all, incl. those denied access elsewhere. DUniv Middx, 1998. *Recreation:* Chickenshed!! *Address:* Chickenshed, 290 Chase Side, Southgate, N14 4PE. *T:* (020) 8351 6161, ext. 204.

WARD, Michael; Chief Executive, British Urban Regeneration Association, since 2008; *b* 15 Oct. 1949; *s* of late Donald Albert Ward; partner, Hilary Knight; one *s* one *d. Educ:* Wimbledon Coll., London; University Coll., Oxford (BA PPE 1972); Birkbeck Coll., London (MA Social and Econ. Hist. 1980). Mem. (Lab), GLC, 1981–86 (Chm., Industry and Employment Cttee, 1981–86; Dep. Leader, 1985–86). Dir, Centre for Local Econ. Strategies, Manchester, 1987–2000. Chm., Manchester City Labour Party, 1995–2000; Chief Executive: London Develt Agency, 2000–04; QMW Public Policy Seminars, Univ. of London, 2004–05; Kent Thameside Delivery Bd, 2005–08. Member: Poverty and Disadvantage Cttee, Joseph Rowntree Foundn, 2002–06; Bd, London Pensions Fund Authy, 2004– (Dep. Chm., 2005–). *Address:* 30 Clairview Road, SW16 6TX; British Urban Regeneration Association, 63–66 Hatton Garden, EC1N 8LE.

WARD, Michael Jackson, CBE 1980; British Council Director, Germany, 1990–91, retired; *b* 16 Sept. 1931; *s* of late Harry Ward, CBE, and Dorothy Julia Ward (*née* Clutterbuck); *m* 1955, Eileen Patricia Foster; one *s* one *d. Educ:* Drayton Manor Grammar Sch.; University Coll. London (BA); Univ. of Freiburg; Corpus Christi Coll., Oxford. HM Forces, 1953–55; 2nd Lieut Royal Signals. Admin. Officer, HMOCS, serving as Dist Comr and Asst Sec. to Govt, Gilbert and Ellice Is; British Council, 1961–91: Schs Recruitment Dept, 1961–64; Regional Rep., Sarawak, 1964–68; Dep. Rep., Pakistan, 1968–70; Dir, Appointments Services Dept, 1970–72; Dir, Personnel Dept, 1972–75; Controller, Personnel and Appts Div., 1975–77; Representative, Italy, 1977–81; Controller, Home Div., 1981–85; Asst Dir-Gen., 1985–90. Hon. Mem., British Council, 1991. *Recreations:* music, golf. *Address:* 1 Knapp Rise, Haslingfield, Cambridge CB23 1LQ; *e-mail:* mjward@spanner.org. *Club:* Gog Magog Golf.

WARD, Michael John; Chairman, Charlton Triangle Homes Ltd, 1999–2004 (Director, 1999–2006); *b* 7 April 1931; *s* of late Stanley and Margaret Ward; *m* 1953, Lilian Lomas; two *d. Educ:* Mawney Road Jun. Mixed Sch., Romford; Royal Liberty Sch., Romford; Bungay Grammar Sch.; Univ. of Manchester (BA (Admin)). FCIPR. Education Officer, RAF, 1953–57; Registrar, Chartered Inst. of Secretaries, 1958–60; S. J. Noel-Brown & Co. Ltd: O&M consultant to local authorities, 1960–61; Local Govt Officer to Labour Party, 1961–65; Public Relns consultant to local authorities, 1965–70; Press Officer, ILEA, 1970–74 and 1979–80; Public Relns Officer, London Borough of Lewisham, 1980–84; Dir of Information, ILEA, 1984–86; Public Affairs Officer, Gas Consumers Council, 1986–88; Exec. Officer to Rt Hon. Paddy Ashdown, MP, 1988–89; Asst Gen. Sec., Public Relations, Assoc. of Chief Officers of Probation, 1989–95. Administrator, Blackheath Cator Estate Residents Ltd, 1995–2001. Contested: (Lab) Peterborough, 1966, 1970, Feb. 1974; (SDP/Alliance) Tonbridge and Malling, 1987. MP (Lab) Peterborough, Oct. 1974–1979; PPS to Sec. of State for Educn and Science, 1975–76, to Minister for Overseas Develt, 1976, to Minister of State, FCO, 1976–79. Sponsored Unfair Contract Terms Act, 1977. Councillor, Borough of Romford, 1958–65; London Borough of Havering: Councillor, 1964–78; Alderman, 1971–78; Leader of Council, 1971–74. Labour Chief Whip, London Boroughs Assoc., 1968–71; Member: Essex River Authority, 1964–71; Greenwich DHA, 1982–85; Greenwich and Bexley FPC, 1982–85; SE London Valuation Tribunal, 1997–2003; Gov., Medway NHS Foundn Trust, 2007–08. FRSA 1992. *Recreations:* gardens, music, aviation history. *Address:* 55 Bridge House, Valetta Way, Rochester, Kent ME1 1LQ.

See also A. J. Seabeck.

WARD, Neil David; Interim Chief Executive, HM Courts Service, Ministry of Justice, 2007–08; *b* 14 March 1953; *s* of Tom Ward and Vera Ward (*née* Dowd); *m* 1979, Jane Gray; one *s* one *d. Educ:* St Francis Xavier's Coll., Liverpool; Wallasey Grammar Sch. HM Treasury, 1972–73; NI Office, 1973–87; DoH, 1987–89; Sen. Civil Service, 1989–91, 1994–; DSS, 1989–90; Chief Exec., Pegasus Retirement Homes (SE) Ltd, 1991–93; DWP (formerly DSS), 1994–99; Chief Exec., Appeals Service, 1999–2003; Department for Constitutional Affairs, subseq. Ministry of Justice: Dir, Judicial Appts, 2003–04; Dir, Criminal Justice, 2004–05; Dir, Crime, HM Courts Service, 2005–06; Chief Operating Officer, HM Courts Service, 2006–07. *Recreation:* sport (golf, ski-ing and as a spectator of all sports). *Address:* HM Courts Service, Selborne House, 54–60 Victoria Street, SW1E 6QW.

WARD, Nicholas; *see* Ward, C. J. N.

WARD, Peter Simms; a District Judge (Magistrates' Courts), Lancashire, since 2006; *b* 20 June 1943; *s* of Norman and Marie Ward; *m* 1974, Monica Stalker; three *s. Educ:* Bolton Sch.; Bristol Univ. (LLB). Articled to J. J. Rothwell, Solicitor, Salford; admitted Solicitor, 1969; Partner, Rothwell & Evans, Solicitors, Salford, Gtr Manchester, 1969–94; Provincial Stipendiary Magistrate, subseq. Dist Judge (Magistrates' Courts), Merseyside, 1994–2001; Dist Judge (Magistrates' Courts), Manchester, 2001–06. *Recreations:* reading, walking, swimming. *Address:* Preston Magistrates' Court, PO Box 52, Lawson Street, Preston PR1 2RD. *T:* (01772) 208021.

WARD, Phillip David; Director, Waste and Resources Action Programme Ltd, since 2004; *b* 1 Sept. 1950; *s* of Frederick William Ward and Phyllis Mavis Ward; *m* 1974, Barbara Patricia, (Pip), Taylor; two *d. Educ:* Sir John Talbot's GS, Whitchurch; Sheffield Univ. (BJur 1973). Department of the Environment, later Department of the Environment, Transport and the Regions: Admin Trainee, 1973–78; Hackney/Islington Inner City Partnership, 1978–80; Principal, Local Govt Finance Directorate, 1980–85; Asst Sec., Local Govt Finance Review, 1985–90; Principal Private Sec. to Sec. of State for the Envmt, 1990–92; Dir (Under Sec.), Construction Sponsorship, 1992–97; Dir, Energy, Envmt and Waste, 1997–2001; Dir of Finance, then Prin. Finance Officer, DETR, subseq. DTLR, then ODPM, 2001–02; Dir, Local Govt Performance Unit, ODPM, 2002–04. *Recreations:* sailing, Rugby, cinema. *Address:* WRAP, The Old Academy, 21 Horse Fair, Banbury, Oxon OX16 0AH.

WARD, Rear-Adm. Rees Graham John, CB 2002; FIET; Director General, Defence Manufacturers Association, since 2007; *b* 1 Oct. 1949; *s* of John Walter Ward and Helen Burt Ward (*née* Foggo); *m* 1st, 1973, Christina Glen Robertson (marr. diss.); two *s*; 2nd, 1980, Phyllis Gentry Pennington; two *d. Educ:* Queens' Coll., Cambridge (MA); Cranfield Univ. (MSc 1981; MSc (Corp. Mgt) 2001). FIET (FIEE 1998). Joined RN, 1967; served: HMS Russel, 1972–73; HMS Brighton, 1977–79; MoD PE, 1981–83; jsdc 1984; HMS Ark Royal, 1984–87; Naval Asst to Controller of Navy, 1988–89; Asst DOR (Sea), 1990–92; NA to Chief of Defence Procurement, 1992–94; DOR (Sea), 1995–97; rcds 1998; hcsc 1999; ACDS, Operational Requirements (Sea Systems), 1999; Capability Manager (Strategic Deployment), MoD, 1999–2002; Chief Exec., Defence Communications Services Agency, 2002–07; Dir Gen. Inf. Systems and Services, Defence Equipment and Support, 2007. Rep. GB and Scotland at athletics cross country running, 1972–77. CRAeS 2008. *Recreations:* reading, running marathons. *Clubs:* Army and Navy; Hawks (Cambridge).

WARD, Reginald; *see* Ward, A. J. R.

WARD, Reginald George; Director, Analysis and Research (formerly Statistics and Economic Office), Inland Revenue, 1994–2001; *b* 6 July 1942; *s* of Thomas George and Ada May Ward; *m* 1964, Chandan Mistry; two *s* one *d. Educ:* Leicester, Aberdeen and Oxford Universities; London Business Sch. Lectr in Economics, St Andrews Univ., 1965; Analyst, National Cash Register, 1969; Economist, ICL, 1970; DTI, 1971; Chief Statistician: HM Treasury, 1978; Cabinet Office, 1982; Dir, Business Statistics Office, DTI, 1986; Asst Dir, CSO, 1989–94. *Recreation:* sailing.

WARD, Richard Churchill, PhD; Chief Executive, Lloyd's of London, since 2006; *b* 6 March 1957; *s* of Alan and Margaret Ward; *m* 1990, Carol Cole; two *s. Educ:* Wellington Coll.; Univ. of Exeter (BSc 1979; PhD 1982). Scientist, SERC, 1982–88; Sen. Manager, BP Research, 1988–91; Hd of Business Develt, BP Oil Trading Internat., 1991–94; Hd of Mktg, Tradition Financial Services, 1994–95; International Petroleum Exchange, subseq. ICE Futures: Dir, Product Develt and Res., 1995–96; Exec. Vice Pres., 1996–99; Chief Exec., 1999–2005; Vice Chm., 2005–06. *Publications:* scientific res. papers in Chem. Soc. Rev., Jl of Applied Crystallography, Europhysics Letters, Molecular Physics, Nature, etc. *Recreations:* capsizing small dinghies, hockey, ski-ing, tennis. *Address:* Lloyd's of London, One Lime Street, EC3M 7HA. *T:* (020) 7327 6930, *Fax:* (020) 7327 6512; *e-mail:* richard.ward@lloyds.com.

WARD, Prof. Richard Samuel, DPhil; FRS 2005; Professor of Mathematics, since 1991, Head, Department of Mathematical Sciences, 2004–07, University of Durham; *b* 6 Sept. 1951; *s* of late Walter Ward and Eileen Ward (*née* Phillips); *m* 1991, Rebecca Nora, *d* of Horace Basil Barlow, *qv*; one *s* one *d. Educ:* Rhodes Univ. (BSc Hons 1973, MSc 1974); St John's Coll., Oxford (DPhil 1977). Jun. Res. Fellow, Merton Coll., Oxford, 1977–79; Lectr and Fellow, TCD, 1979–82; Mem., Inst. for Theoretical Physics, Stony Brook, NY, 1982; Lectr, Sen. Lectr, then Reader, Univ. of Durham, 1983–91. Life Mem., Clare Hall, Cambridge. Jun. Whitehead Prize, LMS, 1989. *Publications:* (with R. O. Wells, Jr) Twistor Geometry and Field Theory, 1990; articles on mathematical physics in learned jls. *Recreations:* family, music, reading. *Address:* Department of Mathematical Sciences, University of Durham, Durham DH1 3LE. *T:* (0191) 334 3118; *e-mail:* richard.ward@durham.ac.uk.

WARD, Maj.-Gen. Robert William, CB 1989; MBE 1972; DL; plantsman, landscape and garden design consultant, since 1992; *b* 17 Oct. 1935; *s* of late Lt-Col William Denby Ward and Monica Thérèse Ward (*née* Collett-White); *m* 1966, Lavinia Dorothy Cramsie; two *s* one *d. Educ:* Rugby School; RMA Sandhurst. Commissioned Queen's Bays (later 1st Queen's Dragoon Guards), 1955; served Jordan, Libya, BAOR, Borneo, NI, and Persian Gulf; MA to C-in-C BAOR, 1973–75; CO 1st Queen's Dragoon Guards, 1975–77; Col GS Staff Coll., 1977–79; Comdr 22 Armd Brigade, 1979–82; RCDS Canada, 1982–83; Asst Chief of Staff, Northern Army Group, 1983–86; GOC Western Dist, 1986–89, retd. Col, 1st Queen's Dragoon Guards, 1991–97; Hon. Col, Royal Mercian and Lancastrian Yeomanry, 1995–2001. Sec., Game Conservancy, Shropshire, 1993–2000; Chairman: Nat. Meml Arboretum, 1996–98; Shropshire Parks and Gardens Trust, 1996–2002. Pres., SSAFA, Shropshire, 1994–. DL Shropshire, 2000. *Recreations:* gardening, outdoor sports, country pursuits, travel, food, wine. *Clubs:* Army and Navy, MCC, I Zingari.

WARD, Rev. Robin, PhD; Principal, St Stephen's House, Oxford, since 2006; *b* 24 Jan. 1966; *s* of late Peter Herbert Ward and of Maureen Ann Ward; *m* 1997, Ruth Suzanne (*née* Sheard); two *s. Educ:* Hassenbrook Sch.; City of London Sch.; Magdalen Coll., Oxford (BA 1987, MA 1991); St Stephen's House, Oxford; King's Coll. London (PhD 2003). Ordained deacon, 1991, priest, 1992; Assistant Curate: St Andrew Romford, 1991–94; St Andrew and St Francis, Willesden Green, 1994–96; Vicar, St John the Baptist, Sevenoaks, 1996–2006. Hon. Canon, and Hon. Canon Theologian, Rochester Cathedral, 2004–06, Canon Emeritus, 2006–. Proctor in Convocation, 2000–05. *Publications:* reviews in Jl of Theol Studies and Jl of Ecclesiastical Hist. *Recreation:* cultivation of rhododendrons. *Address:* St Stephen's House, 16 Marston Street, Oxford OX4 1JX. *T:* (01865) 247874. *Club:* Travellers.

WARD, Robin William; Director-General, West Yorkshire Passenger Transport Executive, 1976–82; *b* 14 Jan. 1931; *s* of William Frederick and Elsie Gertrude Ward; *m* 1974, Jean Catherine Laird; three *s. Educ:* Colston's Sch., Bristol; University Coll. London. BScEcon, 1st Cl. Hons. Pilot Officer/Flying Officer, RAF Educn Br., 1954–55. Various posts, London Transport Exec., 1955–67; seconded to Brit. Transport Staff Coll. as mem. staff and latterly Asst Principal (incl. course at Harvard Business Sch.), 1967–70; Industrial Relations Officer, London Transport Exec., 1970–74; Dir of Personnel, W Yorks Passenger Transport Exec., 1974–76. *Recreations:* Scottish country dancing; trying to learn the piano. *Address:* 13 Turnbury Street, Little Mountain, Qld 4551, Australia.

WARD, Rt Rev. Simon B.; *see* Barrington-Ward.

WARD, Tony, OBE 1998; Group Services Director, BAA plc, 1999–2007 (Group Human Resources Director, 1997–99); non-executive Director, SThree, since 2006; *b* 20 Feb. 1950; *s* of Kenneth H. Ward and Elsie M. Ward; *m* 1972, Margaret Harrison; one *d. Educ:* Univ. of Leeds (BSc 1st Class Hons 1972). Personnel Manager, Stone Platt Industries, 1972–81; Personnel Director (Divisional), GrandMet, 1981–91; Dir of Human Resources, Kingfisher plc, 1992–97. Mem., 1990–95, Dep. Chm., 1993–95, CRE. Chm., Equal Opportunities Panel, CBI. FCIPD 1991; FRSA 2000. *Recreations:* golf, yoga, art. *Club:* Lambourne.

WARD, William Alan H.; *see* Heaton-Ward.

WARD, William Alec; HM Diplomatic Service, retired; *b* 27 Nov. 1928; *s* of William Leslie Ward and Gladys Ward; *m* 1955, Sheila Joan Hawking; two *s* two *d. Educ:* King's Coll. Sch., Wimbledon; Christ Church, Oxford. HM Forces, 1947–49. Colonial Office, 1952; Private Sec. to Permanent Under-Sec., 1955–57; Singapore, 1960–64; seconded to CRO, 1963; Karachi, 1964–66; Islamabad, 1966–68; joined HM Diplomatic Service, 1968; FCO, 1968–71; Salisbury, 1971–72; Dep. High Comr, Colombo, 1973–76; High Comr, Mauritius, 1977–81. *Recreations:* music, walking. *Address:* Suilven, Frome Vauchurch, Dorchester DT2 0DY.

WARD-JONES, Norman Arthur, CBE 1990; VRD 1959; Chairman, Gaming Board for Great Britain, 1986–92 (Member, 1984–92); *b* 19 Sept. 1922; *s* of Alfred Thomas Ward-Jones and Claire Mayall Lees; *m* 1962, Pamela Catherine Ainslie (*née* Glessing). *Educ:* Oundle Sch.; Brasenose Coll., Oxford. Solicitor 1950. War service, Royal Marines (Captain), 1941–46; RM Reserve, 1948–64, Lt-Col and CO RMR (City of London), 1961–64; Hon. Col 1968–74. Solicitor, Lawrance Messer & Co., Sen. Partner, 1981–85, retired 1989. Hon. Solicitor, Magistrates' Assoc., 1960–85. Chm., East Anglian Real Property Co. Ltd, 1970–80, non-exec. Dir, 1980–89. Pres., Brasenose Soc., 1991–92. JP N Westminster PSD, 1966–92. *Recreation:* wine drinking. *Address:* The Cottage, Barnhorn Manor, 75 Barnhorn Road, Little Common, Bexhill-on-Sea, East Sussex TN39 4QU. *Club:* East India.

WARD-THOMAS, Evelyn, (Mrs Michael Ward-Thomas); *see* Anthony, Evelyn.

WARD THOMAS, Gwyn Edward; *see* Thomas.

WARDALE, Sir Geoffrey (Charles), KCB 1979 (CB 1974); Second Permanent Secretary, Department of the Environment, 1978–80; *b* 29 Nov. 1919; *m* 1944, Rosemary Octavia Dyer; one *s* one *d. Educ:* Altrincham Grammar Sch.; Queens' Coll., Cambridge (Schol.). Army Service, 1940–41. Joined Ministry of War Transport as Temp. Asst Princ., 1942; Private Sec. to Perm. Sec., 1946; Princ., 1948; Asst Sec., 1957; Under-Sec., Min. of Transport, later DoE, 1966; Dep. Sec., 1972. Led inquiry: into the Open Structure in the Civil Service (The Wardale Report), 1981; into cases of fraud and corruption in PSA, 1982–83. Mem. Council, Univ. of Sussex, 1986–92; Chm., Brighton Coll. Council, 1985–90. President: Friends of Lewes Soc., 1992–97; Lewes Area CABx, 1989–99. *Recreations:* transport history, painting, listening to music. *Address:* 89 Paddock Lane, Lewes, East Sussex BN7 1TW. *T:* (01273) 473468.

WARDELL, Gareth Lodwig; environmental and planning consent consultant, since 2007; *b* 29 Nov. 1944; *s* of John Thomas Wardell and Jenny Ceridwen Wardell; *m* 1967, Jennifer Dawn Evans; one *s. Educ:* London Sch. of Econs and Pol. Science (BScEcon, MSc). Geography Master, Chislehurst and Sidcup Technical High Sch., 1967–68; Head of Econs Dept, St Clement Danes Grammar Sch., 1968–70; Sixth Form Econs Master, Haberdashers' Aske's Sch., Elstree, 1970–72; Educn Lectr, Bedford Coll. of Physical Educn, 1972–73; Sen. Lectr in Geography, Trinity Coll., Carmarthen, 1973–82. MP (Lab) Gower, Sept. 1982–1997. A Forestry Comr, 1999–2007. Mem. Bd, Envmt Agency, 1997–2004. Lay Mem., GMC, 1995–2008. *Publications:* articles on regional issues in British Econ. Survey. *Recreations:* cycling, cross-country running.

WARDINGTON, 3rd Baron *cr* 1936, of Alnmouth in the county of Northumberland; **William Simon Pease;** *b* 15 Oct. 1925; *s* of 1st Baron Wardington and Hon. Dorothy Charlotte, *er d* of 1st Baron Forster and *widow* of Hon. Harold Lubbock; *S* brother, 2005; *m* 1962, Hon. Elizabeth Jane Ormsby-Gore (*d* 2004), *d* of 4th Baron Harlech, KG, GCMG, PC. *Educ:* Eton; New Coll., Oxford (MA 1956); St Thomas's Hosp. Med. Sch. (MB BS Lond. 1956). FRCS 1961. Captain, Grenadier Guards, 1947. Consultant ENT Surgeon, Central Middlesex and Northwick Park Hosps., 1967–85. *Recreations:* golf, sailing, gardening. *Heir:* none. *Address:* Lepe House, Exbury, Southampton SO45 1AD. *T:* (023) 8089 3724; Flat 45, Elizabeth Court, 47 Milmans Street, SW10 0DA. *T:* (020) 7351 0954. *Clubs:* Royal Yacht Squadron, Island Sailing (Cowes).

WARDLAW, Sir (Henry) Justin, 22nd Bt *cr* 1631, of Pitreavie; *b* 10 Aug. 1963; *s* of Sir Henry John Wardlaw, 21st Bt, and of Julie-Ann, *d* of late Edward Patrick Kirwan; *S* father, 2005; *m* 1988, Rachel Jane, *y d* of James Kennedy Pitney; two *s* one *d. Heir: s* Henry James Wardlaw, *b* 8 Dec. 1999.

WARDLE, Charles Frederick; immigration policy adviser and international consultant; *b* 23 Aug. 1939; *s* of late Frederick Maclean Wardle and Constance Wardle (*née* Roach); *m* 1964, Lesley Ann, *d* of Sidney Wells; one *d. Educ:* Tonbridge Sch.; Lincoln Coll., Oxford; Harvard Business Sch. MA Oxon 1968; MBA Harvard. Asst to Pres., American Express Co., NY, 1966–69; Merchant Banking, London, 1969–72; Chairman: Benjamin Priest Gp plc, 1977–84 (Dir, 1972–74, Man. Dir, 1974–77); Warne, Wright and Rowland, 1978–84. Mem. Council, CBI, 1980–84. MP (C) Bexhill and Battle, 1983–2001. PPS: to Sec. of State for Social Services, 1984–87; to Sec. of State for Scotland, 1990–92; Parly Under-Sec. of State, and Immigration Minister, Home Office, 1992–94, DTI, 1994–95. Member Select Committee: on Trade and Industry, 1983–84; on Treasury and Civil Service, 1990; on Public Accounts, 1995–2000. Public Affairs Dir, Harrods Ltd, 2000–02; claims settlement for Equitas Ltd with Libya, Iraq and UN Compensation Commn, 2003–06. Chm., Cons. One Nation Forum, 1989–90. Member: Commercial and Econ. Cttee, EEF, 1981–83; Midlands Cttee, InstD, 1981–83. FRGS 1977. *Recreations:* books, sport, travel. *Address:* Shepherds, Cranbrook, Kent TN17 3EN. *Clubs:* Farmers, Travellers.

WARDLE, (John) Irving; Drama Critic, The Independent on Sunday, 1990–95; *b* 20 July 1929; *s* of John Wardle and Nellie Partington; *m* 1958, Joan Notkin (marr. diss.); *m* 1963, Fay Crowder (marr. diss.); two *s; m* 1975, Elizabeth Grist; one *s* one *d. Educ:* Bolton Sch.; Wadham Coll., Oxford (BA); Royal Coll. of Music (ARCM). Joined Times Educational Supplement as sub-editor, 1956; Dep. Theatre Critic, The Observer, 1960; Drama Critic, The Times, 1963–89. Editor, Gambit, 1973–75. Play: The Houseboy, prod Open Space Theatre, 1974, ITV, 1982. *Publications:* The Theatres of George Devine (biog.), 1978; Theatre Criticism, 1992. *Recreation:* piano playing. *Address:* 51 Richmond Road, New Barnet, Herts EN5 1SF. *T:* (020) 8440 3671.

WARDLE, Peter; Chief Executive, Electoral Commission, since 2004; *b* 3 July 1962; *s* of late Alec Peter Wardle and of Rev. Patricia Wardle (*née* Haker); *m* 2005, Jo Gray. *Educ:* Emanuel Sch.; Merton Coll., Oxford (BA Hons 1985). Inland Revenue, 1985–87; Private Sec. to Minister for Higher Educn and Sci., 1987–89; Inland Revenue: Principal, 1989–94; Asst Dir, 1994–98; Dir, Strategy and Planning, 1998–2000; Dir, Corporate Services, Cabinet Office, 2000–04. Non-exec. Dir, Basildon and Thurrock Univ. Hosp. NHS Foundn Trust (formerly Basildon and Thurrock Univ. Hosp.), 2004– (Vice Chm., 2007–). *Recreations:* walking, political biographies, music. *Address:* Electoral Commission, Trevelyan House, Great Peter Street, SW1P 2HW. *T:* (020) 7271 0605; *e-mail:* pwardle@electoralcommission.org.uk.

WARDLE, Robert James; Director, Serious Fraud Office, 2003–08; *b* 23 Dec. 1951; *s* of William James Wardle and late Peggy Mary Wardle. *Educ:* Stamford Sch.; Univ. of Hull (LLB Hons). Admitted solicitor, 1976; articled clerk, 1974–76, asst solicitor, 1976–78, Greenwoods; Prosecuting Solicitor, Essex CC, 1978–80; Cambridgeshire County Council: Prosecuting Solicitor, 1980–86; Sen. Crown Prosecutor, 1986–88; Serious Fraud

Office: Case Controller, 1988–92; Asst Dir, 1992–2003. *Recreations:* walking, shooting. *T:* (01733) 554929; *e-mail:* wardle522@btinternet.com.

WARE, Anna, (Mrs T. D. O. Ware); *see* Pavord, A.

WARE, Cyril George, CB 1981; Under-Secretary, Inland Revenue, 1974–82; *b* 25 May 1922; *s* of Frederick George Ware and Elizabeth Mary Ware; *m* 1946, Gwennie (*née* Wooding); two *s* one *d. Educ:* Leyton County High Sch. Entered Inland Revenue as Tax Officer, 1939; Inspector of Taxes, 1949; Sen. Principal Inspector, 1969. *Recreations:* music, woodwork, gardening, swimming. *Address:* 86 Tycehurst Hill, Loughton, Essex IG10 1DA. *T:* (020) 8508 3588.

WARE, Howard Elliott, FRCS; Consultant Orthopaedic Surgeon, Wellington Knee Surgery Unit, Wellington Hospital, and Chase Farm Hospital, Enfield, since 1994; *b* 2 Nov. 1955; *s* of David Frederick Ware and Ann Julia Ware; *m* 1979, Carol Frances Davis; one *s* two *d. Educ:* Lady Owen's Sch.; St Bartholomew's Med. Sch. (MB BS 1980). FRCS 1985; FRCS(Orth) 1992. Consultant Orthopaedic Surgeon, St Bartholomew's Hosp., 1992–94. Hon. Sen. Lectr, Univ. of Dundee, 2001–. *Publications:* contribs to BMJ, Jl Bone and Joint Surgery. *Recreations:* travel, films, reading, gardening. *Address:* Wellington Knee Surgery Unit, Wellington Hospital South, Wellington Place, NW8 9LE. *T:* (020) 7586 5959.

WARE, Joni; *see* Lovenduski, J.

WARE, Michael John, CB 1985; QC 1988; barrister-at-law; Solicitor and Legal Adviser, Department of the Environment, 1982–92; *b* 7 May 1932; *s* of Kenneth George Ware and Phyllis Matilda (*née* Joynes); *m* 1966, Susan Ann Maitland; three *d. Educ:* Cheltenham Grammar Sch.; Trinity Hall, Cambridge (BA(Law), LLB). Called to Bar, Middle Temple. Nat. Service, 2/Lieut RASC, 1954–56. Board of Trade (later Dept of Trade and Industry): Legal Asst, 1957–64; Sen. Legal Asst, 1964–72; Asst Solicitor, 1972–73; Dir, Legal Dept, Office of Fair Trading, 1973–77; Under Secretary: Dept of Trade, 1977–81; DoE, 1982. Chm., Meat Hygiene Appeals Tribunals for England and Wales, 1993–2002.

WAREING, Robert Nelson; MP (Lab) Liverpool, West Derby, since 1983; *b* 20 Aug. 1930; *s* of late Robert Wareing and late Florence Wareing (*née* Mallon); *m* 1962, Betty Coward (*d* 1989). *Educ:* Ranworth Square Sch., Liverpool; Alsop High Sch., Liverpool; Bolton Coll. of Educn; BSc (Econ) London Univ., 1956. RAF, 1948–50. Administrative Asst, Liverpool City Bldg Surveyor's Dept, 1946–56; Lecturer: Brooklyn Technical Coll., Birmingham, 1957–59; Wigan and Dist Mining and Technical Coll., 1959–63; Liverpool Coll. of Commerce, 1963–64; Liverpool City Inst. of Further Educn, 1964–72; Central Liverpool Coll. of Further Educn, 1972–83. Merseyside County Council: Mem., 1981–86; Chief Whip, Labour Gp, 1981–83; Chm., Economic Develt Cttee, 1981–83; Chm., Merseyside Economic Develt Co. Ltd, 1981–86. A Vice-Pres., AMA, 1984–97. Joined Labour Party, 1947: Pres., Liverpool Dist Labour Party, 1974–81; Mem., MSF. Introduced Chronically Sick and Disabled Persons Bill, 1983; Asst Labour Whip, 1987–92, with responsibility for health and social security, employment, sport, environment and foreign affairs. Mem., Select Cttee on Foreign Affairs, 1992–97. Vice-Chairman: British-Yugoslav Parly Gp, 1985–94, 2001–02 (Chm., 1994–97); Serbia-Montenegro Parly Gp, 2003–; Armenia Parly Gp, 2004–; Sec., British-Russian Parly Gp, 1997– (Vice Pres., 1992–97); Treasurer: British-Azerbaijan Parly Gp, 1997–; British-Ukranian Parly Gp, 1999–; British-German Parly Gp, 2005–. *Recreations:* watching soccer (especially Everton FC), concert-going and ballet, motoring and travel. *Address:* House of Commons, SW1A 0AA.

WARHAM, Mark Francis; Managing Director, since 2000, Chairman, UK Investment Banking, since 2007, and Vice Chairman, since 2008, Morgan Stanley; *b* 2 Jan. 1962; *s* of Joseph Warham and Eileen Warham (*née* Northover); *m* 2000, Olivia Dagtoglou; three *d. Educ:* St Thomas Aquinas Grammar Sch., Leeds; St Catherine's Coll., Oxford (BA PPE 1982). 3i plc, 1982–86; J. Henry Schroder Wagg & Co. Ltd, 1986–2000, Dir, 1995–2000; Dir Gen., The Takeover Panel, 2005–07 (on secondment). *Recreations:* mountaineering, photography, ornithology. *Address:* Morgan Stanley, 20 Bank Street, E14 4AD. *Club:* Alpine.

WARHURST, Alan, CBE 1990; Director, Manchester Museum, 1977–93; *b* 6 Feb. 1927; *s* of W. Warhurst; *m* 1953, Sheila Lilian Bradbury; one *s* two *d. Educ:* Canon Slade Sch., Bolton; Manchester Univ. (BA Hons History 1950). FSA 1958; FMA 1958. Commnd Lancashire Fusiliers, 1947. Asst, Grosvenor Museum, Chester, 1950–51; Asst Curator, Maidstone Museum and Art Gallery, 1951–55; Curator, Northampton Museum and Art Gallery, 1955–60; Director: City Museum, Bristol, 1960–70; Ulster Museum, 1970–77. Vice-Pres., NW Museum and Art Gallery Service, subseq. NW Museums Service, 1997–2002 (Dep. Chm., 1987–92; Chm., 1992–97). Mem., Museums and Galls Commn, 1994–99. Chm., Irish Nat. Cttee, ICOM, 1973–75; President: S Western Fedn Museums and Galls, 1966–68; Museums Assoc., 1975–76; N Western Fedn of Museums and Art Galls, 1979–80; Hon. Sec., Univ. Museums Gp, 1987–93. Trustee, Boat Mus., Ellesmere Port, 1990–92. Chm., Hulme Hall Cttee, Univ. of Manchester, 1986–93; Gov., Hulme Hall Trust Foundn, 1994–2000. Hon. MA Belfast, 1982. *Publications:* various archaeological and museum contribs to learned jls. *Address:* Calabar Cottage, Woodville Road, Altrincham, Cheshire WA14 2AL.

WARHURST, Pamela Janice, CBE 2005; Board Member, Natural England, since 2006; Chair, Pennine Prospects Rural Regeneration Co., since 2006; *b* 12 Sept. 1950; *d* of Fred and Kathleen Short; marr. diss.; one *d. Educ:* Manchester Univ. (BA Hons Econ; MA Econs). Chm., Bear Healthfood Co-operative, 1985–. Mem. (Lab), Calderdale MBC, 1991–99 (Council Leader, 1995–99); Dep. Chair, Regl Assembly for Yorks and Humber, 1997–99; Yorks Rep., Cttee of the Regions in Europe, 1997–99; Dep. Chair, Countryside Agency, 1999–2006. Mem. Bd, Yorks Forward RDA, 1996–99. Chair, Calderdale NHS Trust, 1998–2000. *Recreations:* cooking, travelling, dog walking. *Address:* 21 Mons Road, Todmorden, Lancs OL14 8EF. *T:* (01706) 819803; *e-mail:* pam.warhurst@naturalengland.org.uk, pam@bearco-op.com.

WARING, Sir (Alfred) Holburt, 3rd Bt *cr* 1935; *b* 2 Aug. 1933; *s* of Sir Alfred Harold Waring, 2nd Bt, and Winifred (*d* 1992), *d* of late Albert Boston, Stockton-on-Tees; *S* father, 1981; *m* 1958, Anita, *d* of late Valentin Medinilla, Madrid; one *s* two *d. Educ:* Rossall School; Leeds College of Commerce. Director: SRM Plastics Ltd; Waring Investments Ltd; Property Realisation Co. Ltd. *Recreations:* golf, squash, swimming. *Heir: s* Michael Holburt Waring, *b* 3 Jan. 1964. *Club:* Moor Park Golf (Rickmansworth).

WARK, Prof. David Lee, PhD; FRS 2007; FInstP; Professor of Physics, Imperial College London and Rutherford Appleton Laboratory, since 2004; *b* 8 June 1958; *s* of William L. Wark and Maxine V. Wark; *m* 1988, Sally Annette Martinez; one *s* one *d. Educ:* Indiana Univ. (BSc Physics 1980); California Inst. of Technol. (MS Physics 1982; PhD 1987). FInstP 2003. Postdoctoral Fellow, Los Alamos Nat. Lab., 1987–89; Res. Officer, 1990–92, Lectr in Phys, 1992–99, Oxford Univ.; Fellow, Balliol Coll., Oxford, 1992–99; Prof. of Phys, Univ. of Sussex and Rutherford Appleton Lab., 1999–2003. PPARC Lectr-Fellow, 1996–99. Chm., High Energy and Particle Phys Div., Eur. Phys. Soc., 2005–07. Rutherford Prize, Inst. of Phys, 2003. *Publications:* over 100 articles in learned jls. *Recreations:* reading, cooking, juggling, ski-ing, playing guitar (badly) and blues harp (worse). *Address:* High Energy Physics, Imperial College London, Blackett Laboratory, Prince Consort Road, SW7 2BW. *T:* (020) 7594 7804, *Fax:* (020) 7823 8830; *e-mail:* d.wark@imperial.ac.uk.

WARK, Kirsty Anne; journalist and television presenter, since 1976; *b* 3 Feb. 1955; *d* of James Allan Wark and Roberta Eason Forrest; *m* 1990, Alan Clements; one *s* one *d. Educ:* Wellington Sch., Ayr; Edinburgh Univ. (BA 1976). Joined BBC, 1976: radio then TV producer, politics and current affairs progs, 1977–90; formed independent prodn co., Wark Clements & Co. Ltd, with husband, 1990; Presenter: The Late Show, and Edinburgh Nights, 1990–93; Newsnight, Newsnight Rev. and Newsnight Specials, 1993–; One Foot In The Past, 1993–2000; Words With Wark, 1995–99; Building a Nation, 1998; Gen. Elections, Scottish Gen. Elections and Referendum, and Rough Justice, 1998–; The Kirsty Wark Show, 1999–2001; Tales from Europe, 2004; Tales from Spain, 2005; series of interviews for BBC2 and BBC4, 2002–. Patron: Scottish Blind Golf Soc., 2000–; Maggies Centre, 2001–; Cambodia Trust, 2001–; Crichton Foundn, 2001–; RIAS, 2001–; Ambassador: Nat. AIDS Trust, 2000–; The Prince's Trust, 2004– (Mem. Council, 2000–04). Hon. FRIAS 2000; Hon. FRIBA 2001. Hon. DLitt Abertay, 1995; Dr *hc* Edinburgh, 2000; Hon. LLD Aberdeen, 2001. Scotland Journalist of Year, 1993, Scotland Presenter of Year, 1997, BAFTA; Scot of the Year, Scotland on Sunday, 1998. *Publication:* Restless Nation, 1997. *Recreations:* reading, tennis, beachcombing, architecture, cooking, film, music. *Address:* c/o Black Pepper Media Ltd, PO Box 26323, Ayr KA7 9AY. *T:* (0141) 404 6355; *e-mail:* info@blackpeppermedia.com.

WARKE, Rt Rev. Robert Alexander; Bishop of Cork, Cloyne and Ross, 1988–98; *b* 10 July 1930; *s* of Alexander and Annie Warke; *m* 1964, Eileen Charlotte Janet Minna Skillen; two *d. Educ:* Mountmellick National School; The King's Hospital; Trinity Coll., Dublin (BA 1952, BD 1960); Union Theol Seminary, New York (Dip. in Ecumenical Studies). Ordained, 1953; Curate: St Mark's, Newtownards, 1953–55; St Catherine's, Dublin, 1956–59; Rathfarnham, Dublin, 1959–64; Rector: Dunlavin, Hollywood and Ballymore-Eustace, 1964–67; Drumcondra, North Strand and St Barnabas, 1967–71; Zion, Dublin, 1971–88; Archdeacon of Dublin, 1980–88. *Publications:* St Nicholas Church and Parish, 1967; Light at Evening Time, 1986; The Passion according to St Matthew, 1990; Ripples in the Pool, 1993; In Search of the Living God, 2000; On Being a Bishop, 2004. *Recreations:* following sport, theatre, reading. *Address:* 6 Kerdiff Park, Naas, Co. Kildare, Ireland.

WARKENTIN, Juliet; Content Director, WGSN, since 2007; *b* 10 May 1961; *d* of John and Germaine Warkentin; *m* 1991, Andrew Lamb. *Educ:* Univ. of Toronto (BA History). Editor: Toronto Life Fashion Magazine, 1989–91; Drapers Record Magazine, 1993–96; Marie Claire, 1996–98; Man. Dir, Mktg and Internet Develt, Arcadia Gp plc, 1998–2000; Partner, The Fourth Room, 2000–02; Editl Dir, Redwood, 2002–07. FRSA 2004. National Magazine Award, Canada, 1990; PPA Business Editor of the Year, 1995. *Address:* WGSN, Greater London House, Hampstead Road, NW1 7EJ. *T:* (020) 7874 0200.

WARLOW, Prof. Charles Picton, MD; FRCP, FRCPE, FRCPGlas, FMedSci; FRSE; Professor of Medical Neurology, 1987–2008, now Emeritus, and Hon. Consultant Neurologist, University of Edinburgh, since 1987; *b* 29 Sept. 1943; *s* of Charles Edward Picton Warlow and Nancy Mary McLennan (*née* Hine); *m* (marr. diss.); two *s* one *d*; partner, Cathie Sudlow; one *s* one *d. Educ:* Haileybury and Imperial Service Coll.; Sidney Sussex Coll., Cambridge (BA 1st Cl. Hons 1965; MB BChir with Dist. in Medicine 1968; MD 1975); St George's Hosp. Med. Sch. FRCP 1983; FRCPE 1987; FRCPGlas 1993; FRSE 2006. Clinical Reader in Neurology and Hon. Consultant Neurologist, Univ. of Oxford, 1977–86; Fellow, Green Coll., Oxford, 1979–86; Head, Dept of Clinical Neuroscis, Univ. of Edinburgh, 1990–93 and 1995–98. Pres., Assoc. of British Neurologists, 2001–03. Ed., Practical Neurology, 2001–. Founder FMedSci 1998. *Publications:* Handbook of Clinical Neurology, 1991; (with G. J. Hankey) Transient Ischaemic Attacks of the Brain and Eye, 1994; (jtly) Stroke: a practical guide to management, 1996, 3rd edn 2008; (ed) Lancet Handbook of Treatment in Neurology, 2006. *Recreations:* sailing, photography, mountains, theatre. *Address:* Department of Clinical Neurosciences, Western General Hospital, Crewe Road, Edinburgh EH4 2XU. *T:* (0131) 537 2081.

WARMAN, Oliver Byrne, RBA 1984; ROI 1989; Chief Executive, Federation of British Artists, 1984–96; *b* 10 June 1932. *Educ:* Stowe; Exeter Univ.; Balliol Coll., Oxford. Commissioned Welsh Guards, 1952; GSO3 Cabinet Office; Instructor, Intelligence Centre; Staff College; RMCS; retired 1979. Dir, Exports and Public Relations, 1977–80, Dir, Public Relations, 1980–84, Ship and Boat Builders Fedn. First exhibited RA, 1980; exhib. at RBA, RWA, NEAC, RSMA, ROI; work in public collections, incl. US Embassy, Sultanate of Oman and Crown Commn. Officer, ROI, 1998–. Gold Medal, 1997, Gourlay Prize, 1998, ROI. *Publications:* Arnhem 1944, 1970; Omaha Beach 1944, 2002; articles on wine and military history, 1968–. *Recreations:* France, food, wine, sailing, painting, mongrel dogs. *Address: e-mail:* objwarman@aol.com. *Clubs:* Cavalry and Guards, Chelsea Arts, Special Forces; Royal Cornwall Yacht.

WARMINGTON, Sir Rupert (Marshall), 6th Bt *cr* 1908, of Pembridge Square, Royal Borough of Kensington; Director, Thomson Tradeweb, since 2004; *b* 17 June 1969; *s* of Sir David Marshall Warmington, 5th Bt and Susan Mary Warmington; *S* father, 2005; *m* 2002, Joanne Emma Mewse; two *s. Educ:* Charterhouse; Exeter Univ. (BA Hons). Dir, Fixed Income Dept, ABN AMRO, 1999–2004. *Recreations:* golf, tennis, riding. *Heir: s* Oliver Charles Warmington, *b* 23 Oct. 2004.

WARNE, (Ernest) John (David), CB 1982; Secretary, Institute of Chartered Accountants in England and Wales, 1982–90; *b* 4 Dec. 1926; *m* 1st, 1953, Rena Wolfe (*d* 1995); three *s*; 2nd, 1997, Irene Zajac. *Educ:* Univ. of London (BA(Hons)). Civil Service Commission, 1953; Asst Comr and Principal, Civil Service Commn, 1958; BoT, later DTI and Dept of Industry: Principal, 1962; Asst Sec., 1967; Under-Sec., 1972; Dir for Scotland, 1972–75; Under-Secretary: Personnel Div., 1975–77; Industrial and Commercial Policy Div., 1977–79; Dep. Sec., Dep. Dir-Gen., OFT, 1979–82. *Recreations:* reading, collecting prints, languages. *Address:* 2 Bishops Mill, West Street, Wells, Som BA5 2HH. *T:* (01749) 674271.

WARNE, (Frederick) John (Alford), CB 2000; Staff Counsellor, Security and Intelligence Agencies, since 2004; *b* 7 March 1944; *m* 1st, 1967 (marr. diss. 1979); two *s*; 2nd, 2002, Elaine Carol Smith. *Educ:* Liskeard Grammar Sch., Cornwall. Home Office: Pvte Sec. to Minister of State, 1966–69; Principal, 1974–83; Asst Sec., 1984–93; Under-Sec., Police Dept, 1993–95; Dir, Organised Crime, 1996–98; Dir Gen., Organised Crime, Drugs and Internat. Gp, 1998–2002; Actg Perm. Sec., 2001–02, retd. *Recreations:* Chelsea FC, Surrey Cricket Club, exploring Cornwall. *Address:* c/o Cabinet Office, 70 Whitehall, SW1A 2AS.

WARNER, family name of **Baron Warner**.

WARNER, Baron *cr* 1998 (Life Peer), of Brockley in the London Borough of Lewisham; **Norman Reginald Warner;** PC 2006; Chairman, Provider Development Agency, NHS London, since 2007; *b* 8 Sept. 1940; *s* of Albert Henry Edwin Warner and Laura Warner; *m* 1961, Anne Lesley Lawrence (marr. diss. 1981); one *s* one *d*; *m* 1990, Suzanne Elizabeth Reeve (*see* S. E. Warner); one *s*. *Educ:* Dulwich College; University of California, Berkeley (MPH). Min. of Health, 1959; Asst Private Sec. to Minister of Health, 1967–68, to Sec. of State for Social Services, 1968–69; Executive Councils Div., DHSS, 1969–71; Harkness Fellowship, USA, 1971–73; NHS Reorganisation, DHSS, 1973–74; Principal Private Sec. to Sec. of State for Social Services, 1974–76; Supplementary Benefits Div., 1976–78; Management Services, DHSS, 1979–81; Regional Controller, Wales and S Western Region, DHSS, 1981–83; Gwilym Gibbon Fellow, Nuffield Coll., Oxford, 1983–84; Under Sec., Supplementary Benefits Div., DHSS, 1984–85; Dir of Social Services, Kent CC, 1985–91; Man. Dir, Warner Consultancy and Trng Services Ltd, 1991–97. Advr to Govt on family policy and related matters, 1998–2001. Parly Under-Sec. of State, 2003–05, Minister of State, 2005–06, DoH. Sen. Fellow in European Social Welfare and Chm., European Inst. of Social Services, Univ. of Kent, 1991–97. Chairman: City and E London FHSA, 1991–94; London Sports Bd, Sport England, 2003. Mem., Local Govt Commn, 1995–96. Chm., Expert Panel for UK Harkness Fellowships, 1994–97. Chairman: Nat. Inquiry into Selection, Develt and Management of Staff in Children's Homes, 1991–92 (report, Choosing with Care, 1992); Govt Task Force on Youth Justice, 1997–98; Youth Justice Bd for Eng. and Wales, 1998–2003. Mem. Nat. Mgt Cttee, Carers Nat. Assoc., 1991–94. Trustee: Leonard Cheshire Foundn, 1994–96; MacIntyre Care, 1994–97; Royal Philanthropic Soc., 1992–99 (Chm., 1993–98); Chairman: Residential Forum, 1994–97; Include, 2000–01; NCVO, 2001–03. *Publications:* (ed) Commissioning Community Alternatives in European Social and Health Care, 1993; articles in Jl of Public Admin., Community Care, The Guardian, Local Govt Chronicle, etc. *Recreations:* reading, cinema, theatre, exercise, travel. *Address:* House of Lords, SW1A 0PW.

WARNER, Lady; *see* Warner, S. E.

WARNER, Prof. Anne Elizabeth, FRS 1985; Professor of Developmental Biology, since 1986, and Research Strategy Director, since 2005, Centre for Mathematics and Physics in the Life Sciences and Experimental Biology, University College London (Director, 1999–2005); *b* 25 Aug. 1940; *d* of late James Frederick Crompton Brooks and of Elizabeth Marshall; *m* 1963, Michael Henry Warner. *Educ:* Pate's Grammar School for Girls, Cheltenham; University College London (BSc); Nat. Inst. for Med. Res. (PhD). Res. Associate, Middlesex Hosp. Med. Sch., 1968–71; Lectr in Physiology 1971–75, Sen. Lectr 1975–76, Royal Free Hosp. Sch. of Medicine; Sen. Lectr in Anatomy, 1976–80, Reader in Anatomy, 1980–86, Fellow, 1993, UCL; Royal Soc. Foulerton Res. Prof., 1986–2001. *Publications:* papers in scientific jls. *Address:* University College London, Gower Street, WC1E 6BT.

WARNER, Deborah, CBE 2006; free-lance theatre and opera director, since 1980; *b* 12 May 1959; *d* of Ruth and Roger Warner. *Educ:* Sidcot Sch., Avon; St Clare's Coll., Oxford; Central Sch. of Speech and Drama. Founder, 1980, and Artistic Dir, 1980–86, Kick Theatre Co.; Resident Dir, RSC, 1987–89; Associate Dir, Royal Nat. Theatre, 1989–98. *Productions:* Kick Theatre Co.: The Good Person of Szechwan, 1980; Woyzeck, 1981, 1982; The Tempest, 1983; Measure for Measure, 1984; King Lear, 1985; Coriolanus, 1986; Royal Shakespeare Co.: Titus Andronicus 1987 (Laurence Olivier and Evening Standard Awards for Best Dir); King John, Electra, 1988; Electra (also in Paris), 1991; Royal National Theatre: The Good Person of Sichuan, 1989; King Lear, 1990; Richard II, 1995 (filmed, 1997); The Diary of One Who Vanished (also ENO), 1999; The PowerBook, 2002–03; Happy Days, European and USA tour, 2007–08; other productions: Wozzeck, Opera North, 1993 and 1996; Coriolan, Salzburg Fest., 1993 and 1994; Hedda Gabler, Abbey Theatre, Dublin, and Playhouse, 1991 (Laurence Olivier Award for Best Dir and Best Prodn); Don Giovanni, Glyndebourne Festival Opera, 1994 and 1995 (also Channel 4); Footfalls, Garrick, 1994; The Waste Land, Brussels, Dublin, Paris, Toronto, Montreal, NY, Cork, London, Adelaide, Brighton, Bergen, Perth, 1995–99 (televised, 1995); Une Maison de Poupée, Paris, 1996; The Turn of the Screw, Royal Opera, 1997; Bobigny (S Bank Arts Award; Evening Standard Award), 1998; Tower Project (London Internat. Fest. of Theatre), 1999; St John Passion, ENO, 2000; Medea, Abbey Th., Dublin, 2000, Queen's, 2001, USA tour and NY, 2002–03; The Angel Project, Perth Internat. Arts Festival, 2000 and NY, 2003; Fidelio, Glyndebourne, 2001, Châtelet, Paris, 2002, revived Glyndebourne, 2006; The Rape of Lucrece, Munich, 2004; Julius Caesar, Barbican, 2005; Dido and Aeneas, Vienna, 2006; La Voix Humaine, Opera North, 2006; Death in Venice, ENO, 2007. *Film:* The Last September, 2000. Officier de l'Ordre des Arts et des Lettres (France), 2000 (Chevalier, 1992). *Recreation:* travelling. *Address:* c/o Askonas Holt, Lincoln House, 300 High Holborn, WC1V 7JH. *T:* (020) 7400 1700; c/o The Agency, 24 Pottery Lane, Holland Park, W11 4LZ. *T:* (020) 7727 1346.

WARNER, Edmond William; Chairman, UK Athletics, since 2007; *b* Farnborough, Kent, 17 Aug. 1963; *s* of William John Warner and Kathleen Elizabeth Warner (*née* Rooke-Matthews); *m* 1988, Katharine Louise Wright; two *d*. *Educ:* St Olave's Grammar Sch., Orpington; Worcester Coll., Oxford (BA Hons PPE). Fund Manager, GT Management, 1985–87; Strategy Unit, UBS Phillips & Drew, 1987–89; Sen. Investment Dir, Thornton Management, 1989–91; Hd, Pan European Res., Baring Securities, 1991–93; Hd, Strategy and Econs, and Hd, Global Res., Dresdner Kleinwort Benson, 1993–97; Man. Dir, Natwest Markets, then BT Alex.Brown, 1997–99; Chief Executive: Old Mutual Securities, 1999–2001; Old Mutual Financial Services, 2001–03; IFX Gp, 2003–06; Chm., Cantos Communications, 2007–. Non-exec. Dir, Clarkson plc, 2008–. *Recreation:* running with the Fittleworth Flyers. *Address:* c/o UK Athletics, Athletics House, Central Boulevard, Blythe Valley Park, Solihull, West Midlands B90 8AJ.

WARNER, Sir (Edward Courtenay) Henry, 3rd Bt, *cr* 1910; *m*; three *s*. *Heir:* *s* Philip Courtenay Thomas Warner, *b* 3 April 1951.

WARNER, Francis (Robert Le Plastrier), DLitt; poet and dramatist; Emeritus Fellow, St Peter's College, Oxford, since 1999; Hon. Fellow, St Catharine's College, Cambridge, since 1999; *b* Bishopthorpe, Yorks, 21 Oct. 1937; *s* of Rev. Hugh Compton Warner and Nancy Le Plastrier (*née* Owen); *m* 1st, 1958, Mary Hall (marr. diss. 1972); two *d*; 2nd, 1983, Penelope Anne Davis; one *s* one *d*. *Educ:* Christ's Hosp.; London Coll. of Music; St Catharine's Coll., Cambridge (Choral Exhibitioner; BA, MA); DLitt Oxon 2002. Supervisor in English, St Catharine's Coll., Cambridge, 1959–65; Staff Tutor in English, Cambridge Univ. Bd of Extra-Mural Studies, 1963–65; Oxford University: Fellow and Tutor, 1965–99, Fellow Librarian, 1966–76, Dean of Degrees, 1984–2006, and Vice-Master, 1987–89, St Peter's Coll.; University Lectr (CUF), 1966–99; Pro-Proctor, 1989–90, 1996–97, 1999–2000; Chm., Examiners, English Hon. Mods, 1993. Founder, Elgar Centenary Choir and Orch., 1957; cond. Honegger's King David, King's Coll. Chapel, 1958. Foreign Academician, Acad. de Letras e Artes, Portugal, 1993. Messing Internat. Award for distinguished contribs to Literature, 1972. Benemerenti Silver Medal, Kts of St George, Constantinian Order (Italy), 1990. *Publications: poetry:* Perennia, 1962; Early Poems, 1964; Experimental Sonnets, 1965; Madrigals, 1967; The Poetry of Francis Warner, USA 1970; Lucca Quartet, 1975; Morning Vespers, 1980; Spring Harvest, 1981; Epithalamium, 1983; Collected Poems 1960–84, 1985; Nightingales: poems 1985–96, 1997; Cambridge: a poem, 2001; Oxford: a poem, 2002; By the Cam and the Isis, 2005; *plays:* Maquettes, a trilogy of one-act plays, 1972; Requiem: Pt 1, Lying Figures, 1972, Pt 2, Killing Time, 1976, Pt 3, Meeting Ends, 1974; A Conception of Love, 1978; Light Shadows, 1980; Moving Reflections, 1983; Living Creation, 1985; Healing Nature: the Athens of Pericles, 1988; Byzantium, 1990; Virgil and Caesar, 1993; Agora: an epic, 1994; King Francis 1st, 1995; Goethe's Weimar, 1997; Rembrandt's Mirror, 2000; *edited:* Eleven Poems by Edmund Blunden, 1965; Garland, 1968; Studies in the Arts, 1968; *relevant publications:* by G. Pursglove: Francis Warner and Tradition, 1981; Francis Warner's Poetry: a critical assessment, 1988. *Recreations:* grandchildren, cathedral music, travel. *Address:* St Peter's College, Oxford OX1 2DL. *T:* (01865) 278900; St Catharine's College, Cambridge CB2 1RL. *T:* (01223) 338300. *Club:* Athenæum.

WARNER, Prof. Sir Frederick (Edward), Kt 1968; FRS 1976; FREng; Visiting Professor, Essex University, since 1983; *b* 31 March 1910; *s* of Frederick Warner; *m* 1st, Margaret Anderson McCrea; two *s* two *d*; 2nd, Barbara Ivy Reynolds. *Educ:* Bancrofts Sch.; University Coll., London. Pres., Univ. of London Union, 1933. Chemical Engr with various cos, 1934–56; self-employed, 1956–. Joined Cremer and Warner, 1956, Senior Partner 1963–80. Inst. of Chemical Engrs: Hon. Sec., 1953; Pres., 1966; Mem. Council, Engrg Instns, 1962; President: Fedn Européenne d'Assocs nationales d'Ingénieurs, 1968–71 (European Engr, 1987); Brit. Assoc. for Commercial and Industrial Educn, 1977–89; Inst. of Quality Assurance, 1987–90; Vice-Pres., BSI, 1976–80 and 1983–89 (Chm., Exec. Bd, 1973–76; Pres., 1980–83). Missions and Consultations in India, Russia, Iran, Egypt, Greece, France. Assessor, Windscale Inquiry, 1977. Chairman: Cttee on Detergents, 1970–74; Process Plant Working Party, 1971–77; Sch. of Pharmacy, Univ. of London, 1971–79; CSTI, 1987–90; Member: Royal Commn on Environmental Pollution, 1973–76; Adv. Council for Energy Conservation, 1974–79; Treasurer, SCOPE (Scientific Cttee on Problems of Environment), 1982–88 (Chm., Environmental Consequences of Nuclear Warfare, 1983–88). Visiting Professor: Imperial Coll., 1970–78 and 1993–2001; UCL, 1970–86; Pro-Chancellor, Open Univ., 1974–79; Member Court: Cranfield Inst. of Technology; Essex Univ.; Fellow UCL, 1967. FREng (FEng 1976). Hon. FRSC 1991; Hon. FICE 1998; Hon. Fellow: UMIST, 1986; Sch. of Pharmacy, 1979. Ordinario, Accademia Tiberina, 1969. Hon. DTech, Bradford, 1969; Hon. DSc: Aston, 1970; Cranfield, 1978; Heriot-Watt, 1978; Newcastle, 1979; DUniv: Open, 1980; Essex, 1992. Gold Medal, Czecho-Slovak Soc. for Internat. Relations, 1969; Medal, Insinöö-riliitto, Finland, 1969; Leverhulme Medal, Royal Soc., 1978; Buchanan Medal, 1982; Environment Medal, Technical Inspectorate of the Rheinland, 1984; Gerard Piel Award, 1991; World Fedn of Engrg Organs Medal for World Engrg Excellence, 1993. Hon. Mem., Koninklijk Instituut van Ingenieurs, 1972; Academico Correspondiente, AI Mexico, 1972. *Publications:* Problem in Chemical Engineering Design (with J. M. Coulson), 1949; Technology Today (ed de Bono), 1971; Standards in the Engineering Industries, NEDO, 1977; Risk Assessment, Royal Soc., 1982; (ed jtly) Treatment and Handling of Wastes, 1992; (ed jtly) Radioecology since Chernobyl, 1992; (ed) Risk Analysis, Perception and Assessment, 1992; (ed) Quality 2000, 1992; (ed jtly) Nuclear Test Explosions, 1998; papers on Kuwait oil fires, nuclear winter, underground gasification of coal, air and water pollution, contracts, planning, safety, professional and continuous education. *Recreations:* monumental brasses, ceramics, gardens. *Address:* Essex University, Colchester CO4 3SQ. *T:* (01206) 873370. *Club:* Athenæum.

WARNER, Sir Gerald (Chierici), KCMG 1995 (CMG 1984); HM Diplomatic Service, retired; Intelligence Co-ordinator, Cabinet Office, 1991–96; *b* 27 Sept. 1931; *s* of Howard Warner and Elizabeth (*née* Chierici); *m* 1st, 1956, Mary Wynne Davies (*d* 1998), DMath, Prof., City Univ.; one *s* two *d*; 2nd, 2000, Catherine Mary Humphrey. *Educ:* Univ. of Oxford (BA). 2 Lieut, Green Howards, 1949–50; Flight Lt, RAFVR, 1950–56. Joined HM Diplomatic Service, 1954; 3rd Sec., Peking, 1956–58; 2nd Sec., Rangoon, 1960–61; 1st Sec., Warsaw, 1964–66, Geneva, 1966–68; Counsellor, Kuala Lumpur, 1974–76; FCO, 1976–90, retd. Mem., Police Complaints Authy, 1990–91. Mem., Adv. Bd, Tavistock Inst., 1998–; Chm., Glos Council for Drugs and Alcohol, 1997–. *Address:* c/o Coutts & Co., 440 Strand, WC2R 0QS.

WARNER, Graeme Christopher; Sheriff of Grampian, Highland and Islands, 1992–98; Part-time Sheriff, since 2001 (Temporary Sheriff, 1985–91); *b* 20 Oct. 1948; *s* of Richard James Lewis Warner and Jean McDonald McIntyre or Warner; *m* 1st, 1976, Rachel Kidd Gear (marr. diss. 1994); one *s* one *d*; 2nd, 1996, Jean Raeburn. *Educ:* Belmont House, Glasgow; Strathallan, by Perth; Edinburgh Univ. (LLB). NP, WS. Law Apprentice, 1969–71; Law Assistant, 1971–72; Partner: Boyd, Janson & Young, WS, Leith, 1972–76; Ross Harper & Murphy, WS, Edinburgh, 1976–88; Macbeth, Currie & Co., WS, Edinburgh, 1989–91, Consultant, 1999–2000. Mem., Parole Bd for Scotland, 2003–04. *Recreation:* staying alive! *Address:* 6 Mortonhall Road, Edinburgh EH9 2HW. *T:* (0131) 668 2437.

WARNER, Sir Henry; *see* Warner, Sir E. C. H.

WARNER, Jeremy; Business and City Editor, The Independent, since 1994; *b* 23 Sept. 1955; *s* of Jonathan and Marigold Warner; *m* 1988, Henrietta Jane Franklin; one *s* two *d*. *Educ:* Magdalen Coll. Sch., Oxford; University Coll. London (BA 1st cl. Hons Hist. 1977). Reporter, The Scotsman, 1979–83; Business Correspondent: The Times, 1983–86; The Independent, 1986–91; City Editor, The Independent on Sunday, 1991–94. Specialist Writer of the Year, British Press Awards, 1990; Financial Journalist of the Year, Wincott Foundn, 1992; Special Award for outstanding contribn in defence of freedom of the press, Assoc. of British Editors, 1997. *Address:* The Independent, 191 Marsh Wall, E14 9RS. *T:* (020) 7005 2696, *Fax:* (020) 7005 2098.

WARNER, Jocelyn; textile designer, since 1986; *b* 16 April 1963; *d* of Brian and Jackie Warner; *m* 1993, Simon Bore; one *s*. *Educ:* Lewes Priory Sch.; Brighton Poly. (Foundn in Art); Camberwell Sch. of Arts and Crafts (BA Hons Textile Design); Central St Martin's Sch. of Art (MA Textile Design). Established: Jocelyn Warner Studio for printed textile design, 1986; Jocelyn Warner Ltd (contemporary wallpaper products and consultancy in surface design), 1999. Elle Decoration Award for Best in Wall Coverings, 2003. *Recreations:* looking at things, collecting bits and pieces from nature, taking photographs and scanning plants, walking, being with friends and family. *Address:* Jocelyn Warner Ltd, 3–4 Links Yard, Spelman Street, E1 5LX; *web:* www.jocelynwarner.com.

WARNER, John Charles; His Honour Judge Warner; a Circuit Judge, since 1996; *b* 30 Aug. 1945; *s* of late Frank Charles Warner and Kathleen Moyra Warner; *m* 1975, Kathleen Marion Robinson; one *s* one *d*. *Educ:* King Edward's Sch., Birmingham. Solicitor, 1969; Partner, Adie Evans & Warner, 1971–96; Asst Recorder, 1988–92; Recorder, 1992–96. *Address:* c/o Midlands Regional Office, HMCS, 6th Floor, Temple Court, Bull Street, Birmingham B4 6WF. *T:* (0121) 681 3449.

WARNER, Prof. John Oliver, MD; FRCPCH; Professor of Paediatrics, Imperial College London, since 2006; *b* 19 July 1945; *s* of Henry Paul Warner and Ursula Mina Warner; *m* 1st, 1968, Wendy Margaret Cole (marr. diss. 1989); one *s* two *d*; 2nd, 1990, Jill Amanda Price; two *d*. *Educ*: Sheffield Univ. Med. Sch. (MB ChB 1968; DCH 1970; MD 1979). FRCP 1986 (MRCP 1972); FRCPCH 1997. Gen. prof. trng, Children's Hosp. and Royal Hosp., Sheffield, 1968–72; Great Ormond Street Children's Hospital: Registrar, 1972–74; research, 1974–77; Sen. Registrar, 1977–79; Consultant, 1979–90, Sen. Lectr, 1979–88, Reader, 1988–90, London Cardiothoracic Inst., Brompton Hosp.; Prof. of Child Health, Univ. of Southampton, 1990–2006. FRSocMed; FMedSci 1999. *Publications*: A Colour Atlas of Paediatric Allergy, 1994; The Bronchoscope - Flexible and Rigid - in Children, 1995; (ed jtly) Textbook of Pediatric Asthma: an international perspective, 2001; over 300 papers in med jls. *Recreations*: cricket, horse riding. *Address*: Navaho, Hurdle Way, Compton Down, Winchester SO21 2AN. *Club*: MCC.

WARNER, Keith Reginald; freelance opera and theatre director, since 1989; *b* 6 Dec. 1956; *s* of Gordon Lawrence Warner and Sheila Mary Ann (*née* Collinson); *m* 1984, Emma Belinda Judith Besly. *Educ*: Bristol Univ. (BA Jt Hons English and Drama). Asst Dir, ENO, 1981–84; Associate Director: Scottish Opera, 1984–85; ENO, 1985–89; Associate Artistic Director, Opera Omaha, USA, 1991–94. *Recreations*: movie-going, reading, modern/contemporary art. *Address*: e-mail: KeithRWarner@aol.com.

WARNER, Marina Sarah, CBE 2008; FBA 2005; FRSL; writer and critic; Professor, Department of Literature, Film and Theatre (formerly Literature, Drama and Visual) Studies, University of Essex, since 2004; *b* 9 Nov. 1946; *d* of Esmond Pelham Warner and Emilia (*née* Terzulli); *m* 1st, 1971, Hon. William Shawcross, *qv*; one *s*; 2nd, 1981, John Dewe Mathews (marr. diss. 1999); partner, Graeme Segal, *qv*. *Educ*: Lady Margaret Hall, Oxford (MA Mod. Langs, French and Italian; Hon. Fellow, 2000). FRSL 1985. Getty Schol., Getty Centre for Hist. of Art and Humanities, Calif, 1987–88; Vis. Fellow, BFI, 1992; Whitney J. Oakes Fellow, Princeton Univ., 1996; Tinbergen Prof., Erasmus Univ., Rotterdam, 1991; Mellon Prof., Univ. of Pittsburgh, 1997; Visiting Professor: Univ. of Ulster, 1995; QMW, 1995–; Paris XIII, 2003; Dist. Vis. Prof., Stanford Univ., 2000; Visiting Fellow: Trinity Coll., Cambridge, 1998; Humanities Res. Centre, Warwick Univ., 1999; All Souls Coll., Oxford, 2001; Hon. Res. Fellow, Birkbeck Coll., Univ. of London, 1999–2005; Sen. Fellow, Erich Remarque Inst., NY Univ., 2006. Lectures: Reith, 1994; Tanner, Yale Univ., 1999; Clarendon, Oxford Univ., 2001; Robb, Auckland Univ., 2004; Presidential, Stanford Univ., 2008; Jane Harrison, Cambridge Univ., 2008; Hussey, Oxford Univ., 2008. Mem. Adv. Bd, Royal Mint, 1986–93. Member: Council, Charter 88, 1990–98; Cttee of Management, NCOPF, 1990–99 (Vice-Pres., 2000–); Adv. Council, British Liby, 1992–98; Cttee, London Liby, 1997–2000; Literature Panel, Arts Council, 1992–98; Council, Inst. of Historical Res., Univ. of London, 1999–2000; Cttee, PEN, 2001–04. Jt Curator, Metamorphing, Wellcome Trust exhibn at Sci. Mus., 2002–03; Curator, Only Make Believe: Ways of Playing, Compton Verney, 2004; Adv. Curator, Eyes, Lies and Illusions, Haywood Gall., 2006. Trustee: Artangel, 1997–2004; Orwell Foundn, 2004–. Pres., Virgil Soc., 2004–05. Patron: Med. Foundn for Victims of Torture, 2000–; Soc. for Story-telling, 2003–; Hosking Houses Trust, 2006–. Hon. DLitt: Exeter, 1995; York, 1997; St Andrews, 1998; Kent, 2005; Oxford, 2006; Leicester, 2006; Hon. Dr: Sheffield Hallam, 1995; North London, 1997; East London, 1999; RCA, 2004; Kent, 2005. Chevalier de l'Ordre des Arts et des Lettres (France), 2000; Stella dell'Ordine della Solidarietà (Italy), 2005. Libretti: The Legs of the Queen of Sheba, 1991; In the House of Crossed Desires, 1996. *Publications*: The Dragon Empress, 1972; Alone of All Her Sex: the myth and the cult of the Virgin Mary, 1976; Queen Victoria's Sketchbook, 1980; Joan of Arc: the image of female heroism, 1981; Monuments and Maidens: the allegory of the female form, 1985; L'Atalante, 1993; Managing Monsters: six myths of our time (Reith Lectures), 1994; From the Beast to the Blonde: on fairy tales and their tellers, 1994; The Inner Eye: art beyond the visible, 1996 (touring exhibn catalogue); No Go the Bogeyman: scaring, lulling and making mock, 1998; Fantastic Metamorphoses, Other Worlds (Clarendon Lectures), 2002; Signs and Wonders: essays on literature and culture, 2003; Phantasmagoria: spirit visions, metaphors, and media into the twenty-first century, 2006; *fiction*: In a Dark Wood, 1977; The Skating Party, 1983; The Lost Father, 1988; Indigo, 1992; The Mermaids in the Basement, 1993; (ed) Wonder Tales, 1994; The Leto Bundle, 2001; Murderers I Have Known (short stories), 2002; *children's books*: The Impossible Day, 1981; The Impossible Night, 1981; The Impossible Bath, 1982; The Impossible Rocket, 1982; The Wobbly Tooth, 1984; *juvenile*: The Crack in the Teacup, 1979; pamphlet in Counterblasts series; short stories, arts criticism, radio and television broadcasting. *Recreations*: friends, travels, reading. *Address*: c/o Rogers, Coleridge & White, 20 Powis Mews, W11 1NJ.

WARNER, Rev. Canon Martin Clive, PhD; Canon Residentiary, St Paul's Cathedral, since 2003; *b* 24 Dec. 1958; *s* of John Warner and Anona Warner (now McGeorge). *Educ*: King's Sch., Rochester; Maidstone Grammar Sch.; Durham Univ. (BA 1980, MA 1985; PhD 2003); St Stephen's House, Oxford. Ordained deacon, 1984, priest, 1985; Asst Curate, St Peter, Plymouth, 1984–88; Team Vicar, Parish of the Resurrection, Leicester, 1988–93; Priest Administrator, Shrine of Our Lady of Walsingham, 1993–2002; Associate Vicar, St Andrew, Holborn, 2002–03. *Publications*: Walsingham: an ever-circling year, 1996; Say Yes to God, 1999; (ed) The Habit of Holiness, 2004; Known to the Senses, 2005. *Recreations*: medieval and Renaissance art, contemporary architecture, cinema, modern fiction, travel. *Address*: 3 Amen Court, EC4M 7BU. *T*: (020) 7248 2559; *e-mail*: treasurer@stpaulscathedral.org.uk.

WARNER, Stephen Clifford; His Honour Judge Stephen Warner; a Circuit Judge, since 2006; *b* 5 Aug. 1954; *s* of Jack and Marion; *m* 1979, Dr Amanda Craig; two *s*. *Educ*: Carmel Coll., Wallingford; St Catherine's Coll., Oxford (MA Hons Juris.). Called to the Bar, Lincoln's Inn, 1976; in practice as barrister, 1976–2006; Asst Recorder, 1999–2000; Recorder, 2000–06. Trustee, Finchley Youth Music Centre. *Recreations*: cricket, music, walking, foreign travel. *Address*: c/o St Albans Crown Court, Bricket Road, St Albans, Herts AL1 3JW.

WARNER, Suzanne Elizabeth, (Lady Warner), OBE 2006; Chairman, Botanic Gardens Conservation International, 1999–2005; *b* 12 Aug. 1942; *d* of Charles Clifford Reeder and Elizabeth Joan Armstrong Reeder; *m* 1st, 1967, Jonathan Reeve (marr. diss. 1980); one *s*; 2nd, 1990, Norman Reginald Warner (*see* Baron Warner); one *s*. *Educ*: Badminton Sch., Bristol; Univ. of Sussex (BA Hons History); Univ. of Cambridge (Dip. Criminology). Home Office Res. Unit, 1966–67; Personal Assistant to Sec. of State for Social Services, DHSS, 1968–70; Principal, DHSS, 1970–73; Central Policy Review Staff, 1973–74; Asst Sec., DHSS, 1979–85; Sec., 1985–88, Actg Chm., 1987–88, ESRC; Exec. Dir, Food from Britain, 1988–90; Chief Exec., Foundn for Educn Business Partnerships, 1990–91; Personal Advr to Dep. Chm., BT plc, 1991–93; Hd of Gp Govt Relations, 1993–96, Gp Dir of Govt Relations, 1996–97, Cable and Wireless plc; Dep. Chm., Broadcasting Standards Commn, 1998–2003. Member: Management Bd, Sci. Policy Support Unit, Royal Soc., 1991–93; Technology Foresight Steering Gp, OST, 1994–97; Council, Industry and Parlt Trust, 1994–97; Acad. Council, Wilton Park, 1995–2004 (Chm., 1999–2004); Bd, Envmt Agency, 2006–. University of Sussex: Mem. Adv. Bd,

Sci. Policy Res. Unit, 1998–2007; Mem., Court, 2000–07; Vice-Chm. of Council, 2001–07. Non-executive Director: SE Thames RHA, 1993–94; S Thames RHA, 1994–96; Broadmoor Hosp. Authy, 1996–98. *Recreations*: family life, cooking, gardening, reading, films.

WARNOCK, family name of **Baroness Warnock**.

WARNOCK, Baroness *cr* 1985 (Life Peer), of Weeke in the City of Winchester; **(Helen) Mary Warnock,** DBE 1984; Mistress of Girton College, Cambridge, 1985–91; *b* 14 April 1924; *d* of late Archibald Edward Wilson, Winchester; *m* 1949, Sir Geoffrey Warnock (*d* 1995); two *s* three *d*. *Educ*: St Swithun's, Winchester; Lady Margaret Hall, Oxford (Hon. Fellow 1984). Fellow and Tutor in Philosophy, St Hugh's Coll., Oxford, 1949–66; Headmistress, Oxford High Sch., GPDST, 1966–72; Talbot Res. Fellow, Lady Margaret Hall, Oxford, 1972–76; Sen. Res. Fellow, St Hugh's Coll., Oxford, 1976–84 (Hon. Fellow, 1985). Member: IBA, 1973–81; Cttee of Inquiry into Special Educn, 1974–78 (Chm.); Royal Commn on Environmental Pollution, 1979–84; Adv. Cttee on Animal Experiments, 1979–85 (Chm.); SSRC, 1981–85; UK Nat. Commn for Unesco, 1981–84; Cttee of Inquiry into Human Fertilization, 1982–84 (Chm.); Cttee of Inquiry into Validation of Public Sector Higher Educn, 1984; Cttee on Teaching Quality, PCFC, 1990 (Chm.); European Adv. Gp on Bioethics, 1992–94; Archbishop of Canterbury's Adv. Gp on Medical Ethics, 1992–; Chm., Educn Cttee, GDST (formerly GPDST), 1994–2001. Visitor, RHBNC, 1997–2001. Gifford Lectr, Univ. of Glasgow, 1991–92; Reed Tuckwell Lectr, Univ. of Bristol, 1992. Leverhulme Emeritus Fellow, 1992–94. FRCP 1979; FRSocMed 1989; Hon. FIC 1986; Hon. FBA 2000. Hon. Fellow, Hertford Coll., Oxford, 1997. Hon. degrees: Open, Essex, Melbourne, Manchester, Bath, Exeter, Glasgow, York, Nottingham, Warwick, Liverpool, London, St Andrews and Ulster Univs; Leeds Poly.; Leicester Poly.; King Alfred's Coll., Winchester; Brighton. Albert Medal, RSA, 1999. *Publications*: Ethics since 1900, 1960, 3rd edn 1978; J.-P. Sartre, 1963; Existentialist Ethics, 1966; Existentialism, 1970; Imagination, 1976; Schools of Thought, 1977; (with T. Devlin) What Must We Teach?, 1977; Education: a way forward, 1979; A Question of Life, 1985; Teacher Teach Thyself (Dimbleby Lect.), 1985; Memory, 1987; A Common Policy for Education, 1988; Universities: knowing our minds, 1989; The Uses of Philosophy, 1992; Imagination and Time, 1994; (ed) Women Philosophers, 1996; An Intelligent Person's Guide to Ethics, 1998; A Memoir, 2000; Making Babies, 2002; Nature and Morality: recollections of a philosopher in public life, 2003; (with E. Macdonald) Easeful Death: is there a case for assisted suicide?, 2008. *Recreations*: music, gardening. *Address*: 60 Church Street, Great Bedwyn, Wilts SN8 3PF. *T*: (01672) 870214.

WARNOCK, (Alastair) Robert (Lyon); His Honour Judge Warnock; a Circuit Judge, since 2003; *b* 23 July 1953; *s* of Alexander Nelson Lyon Warnock and Annabel Forest Lyon Warnock; *m* 1993, Sally Mary Tomkinson. *Educ*: Sedbergh Sch.; Univ. of East Anglia (BA History); Coll. of Law. Called to the Bar, Lincoln's Inn, 1977; Jun., Northern Circuit, 1980–81; Asst Recorder, 1996–2000, Recorder, 2000–03. Pres., SW Lancs Magistrates' Assoc., 2006–. Pres., Royal Liverpool Village Play, 2000–; Vice-Pres., Artisan Golfers' Assoc., 2002–. *Recreations*: golf, travel, food and wine, cricket. *Address*: c/o Bolton Combined Court Centre, Blackhorse Street, Bolton BL1 1SU. *T*: (court) (01204) 392881, *Fax*: (home) (0151) 651 2242; *e-mail*: HHJudge.Warnock@judiciary.gsi.gov.uk. *Clubs*: Artists' (Liverpool); Royal Liverpool Golf.

WARNOCK-SMITH, Shân; QC 2002; *b* 13 Sept. 1948; *d* of Thomas John Davies and Denise Dorothy Davies; *m* 1970, Anthony Warnock-Smith (marr. diss. 1993); one *s* one *d*; partner, Andrew de la Rosa. *Educ*: King's Coll., London (LLB Hons 1970, LLM 1972). Called to the Bar, Gray's Inn, 1971; Lectr, Inns of Court Sch. of Law, 1970–72; Sen. Lectr, City of London Poly., 1972–80; in practice as barrister, specialising in trusts, estates and charities, 1979–. *Publications*: (ed) Heywood and Massey Court of Protection Practice, 2002; contrib. articles to private client jls. *Recreations*: interior design, travel. *Address*: 5 Stone Buildings, Lincoln's Inn, WC2A 3XT. *T*: (020) 7242 6201, *Fax*: (020) 7831 8102; *e-mail*: swarnocksmith@5sblaw.com.

WARR, John James; Deputy Chairman, Clive Discount Co. Ltd, 1973–87, retired; President of the MCC, 1987–88; *b* 16 July 1927; *s* of late George and Florence May Warr; *m* 1957, Valerie Powell (*née* Peter) (*d* 2000); two *d*. *Educ*: Ealing County Grammar Sch.; Emmanuel Coll., Cambridge (BA Hons 1952). Served RN, 1945–48. Man. Dir, Union Discount Co., 1952–73. Chm., Racecourse Assoc., 1989–93. Mem., Jockey Club, 1977–. Pres., Berks CCC, 1990–. *Recreations*: racing, cricket, golf, good music. *Address*: Orchard Farm, Touchen End, Maidenhead, Berks SL6 3TA. *T*: (01628) 622994. *Clubs*: Saints and Sinners (Chm., 1991–92), MCC, XL, I Zingari; Temple Golf, Berkshire Golf.

WARRELL, Prof. David Alan, DM, DSc; FRCP, FRCPE, FMedSci; Professor of Tropical Medicine and Infectious Diseases, 1987–2006, now Emeritus, and Head, Nuffield Department of Clinical Medicine, 2002–04 (Deputy Head, 2004–06), University of Oxford; Fellow, St Cross College, Oxford, 1977–2006, Hon. Fellow, since 2007; *b* 6 Oct. 1939; *s* of Alan and late Mildred Warrell; *m* 1975, Dr Mary Jean Prentice; two *d*. *Educ*: Portsmouth Grammar Sch.; Christ Church, Oxford (MA, BCh 1964; DM 1970; DSc 1990). MRCS 1965; FRCP 1977; FRCPE 1999. Oxford Univ. Radcliffe Travelling Fellow, Univ. of Calif at San Diego, 1969–70; Sen. Lectr, Ahmadu Bello Univ., Zaria, Nigeria, 1970–74; Lectr, RPMS, London, 1974–75; Consultant Physician, Radcliffe Infirmary, Oxford, 1975–79; Founding Dir, Wellcome-Mahidol Univ. Oxford Tropical Medicine Research Programme in Bangkok, 1979–86; Founding Dir, Centre for Tropical Medicine, Univ. of Oxford, 1991–2001, now Emeritus. Hon. Clin. Dir, Alistair Reid Venom Res. Unit, Liverpool Sch. of Tropical Med., 1983–; Vis. Prof., Mahidol Univ., 1997–; Hon. Prof., Univ. Nacional Mayor de San Marcos, Lima, 2005–; Principal Fellow, Dept of Pharmacol., Univ. of Melbourne, 1997–. WHO Consultant on malaria, rabies and snake bite, 1979–. Chm., MRC's AIDS Therapeutic Trials Cttee, 1987–93; MRC's China-UK Res. Ethics Cttee, 2007–; Mem., MRC's Tropical Medicine Res. Bd, 1986–89; Advr to MRC on tropical medicine, 2001–; Mem., FCO Pro Bono Medical Panel, 2002–. Hon. Consultant Malariologist to the Army, 1989–; Hon. Med. Advr, RGS, 1993–. Pres., Internat. Fedn of Tropical Medicine, 1996–2000; Pres., RSTM&H, 1997–99. Delegate, OUP, 1999–2006. RCP Lectures: Marc Daniels, 1977; Bradshaw, 1989; Croonian, 1996; College, 1999; Harveian Oration, 2001; Lloyd-Roberts Lectr, RSocMed, 2004. Scientific FZS 1976; FRGS 1989. Founder FMedSci 1998. Hon. Member: Assoc. Physicians of GB & Ireland, 2003; Amer. Soc. of Tropical Medicine and Hygiene, 2003. Hon. Fellow, Ceylon Coll. of Physicians, 1985. Chalmers Medal, RSTM&H, 1981; Ambuj Nath Bose Prize, RCP, 1994; Busk Medal, RGS, 2003; Guthrie Medal, RAMC, 2004; Mary Kingsley Centenary Medal, Liverpool Sch. of Tropical Medicine, 2005. Kt Comdr, Order of White Elephant (Thailand), 2004. *Publications*: Rabies—the Facts, 1977, 2nd edn 1986; (ed) Oxford Textbook of Medicine, 1983, 4th edn 2003; (ed) Essential Malariology, 3rd edn 1993, 4th edn 2002; Expedition Medicine, 1998, 2nd edn 2002; Oxford Handbook of Expedition and Wilderness Medicine, 2008; chapters in textbooks of medicine and herpetology; papers in learned jls (Lancet, New England Jl of Medicine, etc) on respiratory physiology, malaria, rabies, infectious diseases and snake bite. *Recreations*: book collecting, music, bird watching, hill walking. *Address*:

University of Oxford, Nuffield Department of Clinical Medicine, John Radcliffe Hospital, Headington, Oxford OX3 9DU. *T:* (01865) 234664, *Fax:* (01865) 760683.

WARRELL, David Watson, MD; FRCOG; urological gynaecologist, 1969–94; Chairman, Mid-Cheshire Hospitals NHS Trust, 1994–97; *b* 20 June 1929; *s* of late Charles Warrell and Sarah (*née* Gill); *m* 1955, Valerie Jean Fairclough; one *s* one *d. Educ:* Sheffield Univ. MB ChB 1953; MD 1964; FRCOG 1970. Sen. Lectr and Hon. Consultant Obstetrician and Gynaecologist, Jessop Hosp. for Women, 1965–69; St Mary's Hosp., Manchester, 1969–94: established Dept of Urological Gynaecology; Med. Dir, 1991–92, Chief Exec., 1992–94, Central Manchester Health Care Trust. Blair Bell Travelling Fellowship, 1967. *Publications:* chapters and papers on urinary control in women. *Address:* Beudy y Chain, Llanfaglan, Caernarfon, Gwynedd LL54 5RA.

WARRELL, Ernest Herbert, MBE 1991; Organist: King's College, London, 1980–91; Harrow and Wembley Liberal and Progressive Synagogue, since 1992; St Paul's, Deptford, since 2000; *b* 23 June 1915; *er s* of Herbert Henry Warrell and Edith Peacock; *m* 1952, Jean Denton Denton; two *s* one *d. Educ:* Loughborough School. Articled pupil (Dr E. T. Cook), Southwark Cath., 1938; Asst Organist, Southwark Cath., 1946–54; Lectr in Music, KCL, 1953–80; Organist, St Mary's, Primrose Hill, 1954–57; Lectr in Plainsong, RSCM, 1954–59; Organist, St John the Divine, Kennington, SW9, 1961–68; Organist and Dir of Music, Southwark Cathedral, 1968–76; Musical Dir, Gregorian Assoc., 1969–82; Conductor, Lynne Singers, St Paul's, Covent Gdn, 1989–2006. Chief Examiner in Music, Internat. Baccalaureate, 1984–89; Examinations Sec., Guild of Church Musicians, 1991–97. Hon. FTCL 1977; FKC 1979; Hon. FGCM 1988. MA Lambeth, 2006. *Publications:* Accompaniments to the Psalm Tones, 1942; Plainsong and the Anglican Organist, 1943; (ed jtly) An English Kyriale, 1988; (ed jtly) Seriously Silly Hymns, 1999. *Recreation:* sailing. *Address:* 41 Beechhill Road, Eltham, SE9 1HJ. *T:* (020) 8850 7800. *Clubs:* Special Forces, Little Ship; Royal Scots (Edinburgh).

WARREN, Very Rev. Alan Christopher; Provost of Leicester, 1978–92, now Provost Emeritus; *b* 27 June 1932; *s* of Arthur Henry and Gwendoline Catherine Warren; *m* 1957, Sylvia Mary (*née* Matthews); three *d. Educ:* Dulwich College; Corpus Christi Coll., Cambridge (Exhibnr, MA); Ridley Hall, Cambridge. Curate, St Paul's, Margate, 1957–59; Curate, St Andrew, Plymouth, 1959–62; Chaplain of Kelly College, Tavistock, 1962–64; Vicar of Holy Apostles, Leicester, 1964–72; Coventry Diocesan Missioner, 1972–78; Hon. Canon, Coventry Cathedral, 1972–78; Proctor in Convocation, 1977–78, 1980–85. Mem., Cathedral Statutes Commn, 1981–85. Trustee, St Martin's, Birmingham, 1979–. Chm., Leicester Council of Christians and Jews, 1985–92; President: Leicester Council of Churches, 1985–92; Leicester Civic Soc., 1983–92. Tutor, Adult Educn, Norfolk, 1993–99; Dir of Music, W Norfolk Choral Soc., 1993–2000. Chm., Hunstanton Arts Fest. Cttee, 1994–99; Mem., Brancaster Fest. Cttee, 2001–. Mem., MCC, 1960–76. Pres., Alleyn Club, 1991–92 (Vice-Pres., 1990–91). *Publications:* Putting it Across, 1975; The Miserable Warren, 1991; articles on church music, evangelism and sport in Church Times and other journals; *compositions:* Incarnatus for Organ, 1960; Piano Sonata, 1996. *Recreations:* music, golf, steam trains. *Address:* 9 Queens Drive, Hunstanton, Norfolk PE36 6EY. *T:* (01485) 534533. *Clubs:* Free Foresters; Hunstanton Golf.

See also Ven. N. L. Warren, R. H. C. Warren.

WARREN, Prof. Alan John, PhD; FRCP, FRCPath; FMedSci; Professor of Haematology, University of Cambridge, since 2003; Honorary Consultant Haematologist, Cambridge University Hospitals NHS Foundation Trust (formerly Addenbrooke's NHS Trust), since 1997; *b* 22 Nov. 1961; *s* of John Rundle Warren and Marion Wallace Warren; *m* 1989, Nina Louise Johnman; one *s* one *d. Educ:* Univ. of Glasgow (BSc Hons (Biochem.) 1983; MB ChB 1986); Gonville and Caius Coll., Cambridge (PhD (Molecular Biol.) 1995). MRCP 1989, FRCP 2002; MRCPath (Haematol.) 1997, FRCPath (Haematol.) 2005. House officer posts, medicine and surgery, Royal Infirmary, Glasgow, 1986–87; Sen. House Officer, Western Infirmary Med. Rotation, Glasgow, 1987–89; Registrar in Haematol., Hammersmith and Ealing Hosps, London, 1989–91; MRC Laboratory of Molecular Biology, Cambridge: MRC Trng Fellow, 1991–94; MRC Clinician Scientist and Hon. Sen. Registrar, 1994–95; MRC Clinician Scientist, 1997–2000, and Hon. Consultant Haematologist, 1997–2003; MRC Sen. Clinical Fellow, 2000–03; Sen. Registrar in Haematol., Addenbrooke's Hosp., Cambridge, 1995–97. FMedSci 2005. *Publications:* articles of research in peer-reviewed primary scientific jls. *Recreations:* avid camellia collector, golf. *Address:* MRC Laboratory of Molecular Biology, Hills Road, Cambridge CB2 0QH. *T:* (01223) 402245, *Fax:* (01223) 412178; *e-mail:* ajw@mrc-lmb.cam.ac.uk.

WARREN, Rt Rev. Cecil Allan; Rector, Old Brampton and Loundsley Green, 1983–88; Assistant Bishop, Diocese of Derby, 1983–88; *b* 25 Feb. 1924; *s* of Charles Henry and Eliza Warren; *m* 1947, Doreen Muriel Burrows. *Educ:* Sydney Univ. (BA 1950); Queen's Coll., Oxford (MA 1959). Deacon 1950, priest 1951, Dio. of Canberra and Goulburn; appointments in Diocese of Oxford, 1953–57; Canberra, 1957–63; Organising Sec. Church Society, and Director of Forward in Faith Movement, Dio. of Canberra and Goulburn, 1963–65; Asst Bishop of Canberra and Goulburn, 1965–72; Bishop of Canberra and Goulburn, 1972–83. *Publication:* A Little Foolishness: an autobiographical history, 1993. *Address:* 2/19 Sidney Street, Toowoomba, Qld 4350, Australia.

WARREN, David Alexander, CMG 2007; HM Diplomatic Service; Ambassador to Japan, since 2008; *b* 11 Aug. 1952; *s* of late Alister Charles Warren and Celia Warren (*née* Golding); *m* 1992, Pamela, *d* of late Benjamin Ivan Pritchard and of Violet Pritchard (*née* Sherman). *Educ:* Epsom Coll.; Exeter Coll., Oxford (MA English; Pres., Oxford Union Soc., 1973). Entered HM Diplomatic Service, 1975; FCO, 1975–77; Third, later Second, then First Sec., Tokyo, 1977–81; FCO, 1981–87; First Sec. and Hd of Chancery, Nairobi, 1987–90; FCO, 1990–91; on secondment as Hd, Internat. Div., Sci. and Technol. Secretariat, later OST, then OPSS, Cabinet Office, 1991–93; Counsellor (Commercial), Tokyo, 1993–98; Hd, Hong Kong Dept, later China Hong Kong Dept, FCO, 1998–2000; Dir, Business Gp, 2000–02, Internat. Gp, subseq. Internat. Trade Develt Gp, 2002–04, Trade Partners UK, British Trade Internat., subseq. UK Trade and Investment; Dir, HR, FCO, 2004–07. *Recreations:* books, history of theatre and music hall. *Address:* c/o Foreign and Commonwealth Office, King Charles Street, SW1A 2AH. *Club:* Oxford and Cambridge.

WARREN, Frank John; Chief Executive Officer, Sports Network, since 1996; *b* London, 28 Feb. 1952; *s* of Frank and Iris Warren; *m* 1983, Susan Margaret Cox; four *s* two *d. Educ:* Highbury Co. Grammar Sch. Sport and boxing promoter and manager, 1978–; clients have included Nigel Benn, Frank Bruno, Chris Eubank, Mike Tyson, Ricky Hatton, Naseem Hamed, Joe Calzaghe and Amir Khan. *Recreations:* music, reading, art, sport. *Address:* Sports Network, Centurion House, Bircherley Green, Hertford, Herts SG14 1AP. *T:* (01992) 505550, *Fax:* (01992) 505552; *e-mail:* emmahedley@frankwarren.tv. *Club:* Royal Automobile.

WARREN, Sir (Frederick) Miles, ONZ 1995; KBE 1985 (CBE 1974); FNZIA; ARIBA; Senior Partner, Warren & Mahoney, Architects Ltd, 1958–94; *b* Christchurch, 10 May 1929. *Educ:* Christ's Coll., Christchurch; Auckland Univ. DipArch; ARIBA 1952; FNZIA 1965. Founded Warren & Mahoney, 1958. Award-winning designs include: Christchurch Town Hall and Civic Centre; NZ Chancery, Washington; Canterbury Public Library; Michael Fowler Centre, Wellington; St Patrick's Church, Napier; Ohinetahi, Governors Bay; Rotorua Dist Council Civic Offices; Mulholland Hse, Wanganui; Parkroyal Hotel, Christchurch. Pres., Canterbury Soc. of Arts, 1972–76. Gold Medal, NZIA, 1960, 1964, 1969, 1973; Nat. Awards, NZIA, 1980, 1981, 1983–86, 1988, 1989, 1990, 1991. *Publication:* Warren & Mahoney Architects, 1990. *Recreation:* making a garden.

WARREN, Prof. Graham Barry, PhD; FRS 1999; Scientific Director, Max F. Perutz Laboratories, Vienna, since 2007; *b* 25 Feb. 1948; *s* of Joyce Thelma and Charles Graham Thomas Warren; *m* 1966, Philippa Mary Adeline (*née* Temple-Cole); four *d. Educ:* Willesden County Grammar Sch.; Pembroke Coll., Cambridge (MA, PhD). MRC Fellow, Nat. Inst. for Med. Research, 1972–75; Royal Soc. Stothert Research Fellow, Dept of Biochemistry, Cambridge, 1975–77; Research Fellow, Gonville & Caius Coll., Cambridge, 1975–77; Group Leader then Senior Scientist, European Molecular Biology Lab., Heidelberg, 1977–85; Prof. and Hd of Dept of Biochemistry, Dundee Univ., 1985–88; Prin. Scientist, ICRF, 1989–99; Prof. of Cell Biology, Yale Univ. Med. Sch., 1999–2007. Mem., EMBO, 1986. *Publications:* papers in learned jls on cell biology. *Recreation:* woodworking. *Address:* Max. F. Perutz Laboratories, Dr Bohr-Gasse 9, 1030 Vienna, Austria. *T:* (1) 4277 24011, *Fax:* (1) 4277 9240; *e-mail:* graham.warren@mfpl.ac.at.

WARREN, Ian Scott; Senior Master of the Supreme Court (Queen's Bench Division) and Queen's Remembrancer, 1988–90 (Master, 1970–90); *b* 30 March 1917; *er s* of Arthur Owen Warren and Margaret Cromarty Warren (*née* Macnaughton); *m* 1st, 1943, Barbara (marr. diss.), *er d* of Walter Myrick, Tillsonburg, Ont.; four *s* one *d*; 2nd, Jeanne Hicklin (marr. diss.), *d* of late Frederick and Lydia Shaw, Crosland Moor; 3rd, 1987, Olive Sybil, *d* of late James Charles Montgomerie Wilson. *Educ:* Charterhouse (Exhbnr); Magdalene Coll., Cambridge (Exhbnr); BA 1938, MA 1950. Colonial Administrative Service, 1938–41, serving Gold Coast (Asst DC, 1940); RAF, 1942–46; Flying Badge and commissioned, 1943; Flt Lieut, 1944. Called to Bar, Lincoln's Inn, 1947, Bencher 1967; practised at Common Law Bar, London, 1947–70. *Publications:* Verses from Lincoln's Inn (jtly), 1975; Aesop's Fables: a selection, 1982. *Recreations:* ski-ing, walking, poetry. *Clubs:* Garrick, MCC.

WARREN, John; QC 1994; a Recorder, Midland and Oxford Circuit, 1993–2004; *b* 25 Aug. 1945; *s* of Frank Warren and Dora Warren (*née* Thomas); *m* 1968, Anne Marlor; one *s* one *d* (twins). *Educ:* Chadderton Grammar Sch., near Oldham; Univ. of Nottingham (LLB). Called to the Bar, Gray's Inn, 1968. *Recreations:* opera and classical music, supporting Nottingham Forest FC, doing The Times crossword in bed with my wife. *Address:* 11 Parc yr Eglwys, Dinas Cross, Newport, Pembrokeshire SA42 0SH. *T:* (01348) 811214. *Club:* Newport Boat.

WARREN, John; Regional Employment Judge (formerly Regional Chairman, Employment Tribunals), London South, 2003–08; *b* 26 Sept. 1943; *s* of William John Warren and Phyllis Eliza Warren; one *s* one *d.* Solicitor. *Recreations:* walking, photography, gardening.

WARREN, (John) Robin, AC 2007; MD; FAA; FRCPA; Pathologist, Royal Perth Hospital, 1968–99, now Emeritus Consultant Pathologist; Emeritus Professor, University of Western Australia, since 2005; *b* Adelaide, 11 June 1937; *s* of John Roger Hogarth Warren and Helen Josephine Warren (*née* Verco); *m* 1962, Winifred Teresa Williams (*d* 1998); four *s* two *d. Educ:* St Peter's Coll.; Univ. of Adelaide Sch. of Medicine (MB BS 1961; MD 2000). FRCPA 1967; FAA 2006. Jun. RMO, Queen Elizabeth Hosp., Woodville, 1961; Registrar in Haematology and Clinical Pathology, Inst. of Med. and Vet. Sci., Adelaide, 1962; Temp. Lectr in Pathology, Univ. of Adelaide, and Hon. Clinical Asst in Pathology, Royal Adelaide Hosp., 1963; Registrar in Clinical Pathology, 1964–66, in Pathology, 1966–68, Royal Melbourne Hosp. Member: AMA 1960; BMA 1960; Australian Soc. of Cytology, 1975; Internat. Acad. of Pathology, 1975. Honorary Member: Polish Soc. of Gastroenterology, 2006; German Soc. of Pathology, 2007. Hon. FRACP 2006. Hon. MD Western Aust., 1997; DUniv Adelaide, 2006; Dr *hc* Toyama, 2007; Otto-von-Guericke Universität, 2007. (Jtly) Warren Alpert Foundn Prize, Harvard Med. Sch., 1994; Western Aust. Br. Award, AMA, 1995; Dist. Fellows Award, RCPA, 1995; Medal, Univ. of Hiroshima, 1996; Paul Ehrlich and Ludwig Darmstaedter Award, Paul Ehrlich Foundn, 1997; Faulding Florey Medal, 1998; (jtly) Nobel Prize in Physiology or Medicine, 2005; Gold Medal, AMA, 2006; Western Australian of the Year, 2007; Medal of Hirosaki Univ. Sch. of Med., 2007. *Publications:* contrib. numerous letters and articles in learned jls. *Recreations:* photography, philately, computer processing, music, sports (not active at present), rifle shooting and cycling. *Address:* 178 Lake Street, Perth, WA 6000, Australia. *T:* (8) 93289248, *Fax:* (8) 93289248; *e-mail:* jrwarren@aapt.net.au.

WARREN, Sir Kenneth (Robin), Kt 1994; Eur Ing, CEng, FRAeS; FCILT; consultant in engineering; director of a number of companies; *b* 15 Aug. 1926; *s* of Edward Charles Warren and Ella Mary Warren (*née* Adams); *m* 1962, Elizabeth Anne Chamberlain, MA Cantab and MA Lond; one *s* two *d. Educ:* Midsomer Norton; Aldenham; London Univ.; De Havilland Aeronautical Technical Sch. Fulbright Scholar, USA, 1949; Research Engineer, BOAC, 1951–57; Personal Asst to Gen. Manager, Smiths Aircraft Instruments Ltd, 1957–60; Elliott Automation Ltd, 1960–69; Military Flight Systems: Manager, 1960–63; Divisional Manager, 1963–66; Marketing Manager, 1966–69. MP (C) Hastings, 1970–83, Hastings and Rye, 1983–92. Mem., Select Cttee on Science and Technology, 1970–79 (Chm., Offshore Engrg Sub-Cttee, 1975–76); Mem., Council of Europe, 1973–81; Chm., WEU, Science, Technology and Aerospace Cttee, 1976–79; Chm., Cons. Parly Aviation Cttee, 1975–77; PPS to Sec. of State for Industry, 1979–81, to Sec. of State for Educn and Sci., 1981–83; Chairman: Select Cttee on Trade and Industry, 1983–92; British Soviet Parly Gp, 1986–92. Former branch officer, G&MWU. Chairman: Computer Security Adv. Bd, LSE, 1991–2001; Anglo-Japanese Adv. Bd on Financial Regulation, 1999–. President: British Resorts Assoc., 1987–92; Inst. of Travel Mgt, 1999–2002. Liveryman, GAPAN; Freeman, City of London. Hon. Fellow, Exeter Univ., 1994. *Publications:* various papers on aeronautical engineering and management, in USA, UK, Hungary, Netherlands and Japan. *Recreations:* mountaineering, flying, gardening. *Address:* The Garden House, High Street, Cranbrook, Kent TN17 3EN. *T:* (01580) 714464, *Fax:* (01580) 714360. *Clubs:* Athenæum, Garrick, Special Forces.

WARREN, Prof. Lynda May, PhD; FIBiol; Professor of Environmental Law, Aberystwyth University (formerly University of Wales, Aberystwyth), 1996–2003, now Emeritus; Member, Royal Commission on Environmental Pollution, since 2005; *b* Croydon, 26 April 1950; *d* of Leonard Warren and Peggy Warren (*née* Tatnell); *m* 1986, Barry Archie Thomas; one *s. Educ:* Bedford Coll., Univ. of London (BSc 1971; PhD 1973); Univ. of London (LLB 1986 ext.); Univ. of Wales, Cardiff (MSc). FIBiol 1991.

Senior Lecturer: in Marine Biol., Poly. of Central London, 1981–84; in Zool., Goldsmiths' Coll., London, 1984–89; Lectr, then Sen. Lectr in Law, Cardiff Law Sch., Univ. of Wales, Cardiff, 1989–95. Chm., Salmon and Freshwater Fisheries Rev., 1998–2000; Dep. Chm., JNCC, 2008–; Member: Countryside Council for Wales, 1993–2003; Bd, EA, 2000–06; Cttee on Radioactive Waste Mgt, 2003–. Founding Editor: Law, Science and Policy (formerly Internat. Jl of Bioscience and the Law), 1996–; Envmtl Law Rev., 1999–. *Publications:* over 100 articles on law and science. *Recreations:* travel, reading, cinema, fashion. *Address:* Ynys Einion, Eglwys Fach, Machynlleth SY20 8SX. *T:* (01654) 781344, 07764 848230; *e-mail:* lm.warren@btopenworld.com.

WARREN, Maurice Eric; Chairman, Aggregate Industries plc, 1997–2000; *b* 21 June 1933; *s* of Frederick Leonard Warren and Winifred (*née* Gale); *m* 1954, Molly Slater; one *s* one *d*. *Educ:* St Brendan's Coll., Bristol. Certified Accountant, FCCA. Crosfield & Calthrop, 1958–74 (Dir, 1970–74); Managing Director: Dalgety Crosfields, 1974–76; Dalgety Agriculture Ltd, 1976–81; Dalgety UK Ltd, 1981–87; Dalgety PLC: Dir, 1982; Chief Exec., 1989–93; Chm., 1993–96. Chairman: S Western Electricity, 1993–95; CAMAS, 1994–97; Great Western Holdings, 1996–98. *Recreation:* golf.

WARREN, Prof. Michael Donald, MD, FRCP, FFPH; Emeritus Professor of Social Medicine, University of Kent, since 1983; *b* 19 Dec. 1923; *s* of late Charles Warren and Dorothy Gladys Thornton Reeks; *m* 1946, Joan Lavina Peacock; one *s* two *d*. *Educ:* Bedford Sch.; Guy's Hosp.; London Sch. of Hygiene and Tropical Medicine. MB 1946, MD 1952; DPH 1952, DIH 1952. MRCP 1969, FRCP 1975; FFCM 1972; Hon. FFPH (Hon. FFPHM 1991). Sqdn Ldr RAF, Med. Branch, 1947–51; Dep. MOH, Metropolitan Borough of Hampstead, 1952–54; Asst Principal MO, LCC, 1954–58; Sen. Lectr and Hon. Consultant in Social Medicine, Royal Free Hosp. Sch., Royal Free Hosp. and London Sch. of Hygiene and Tropical Medicine, 1958–64; Sen. Lectr in Social Medicine, LSHTM, 1964–67; Reader in Public Health, Univ. of London, 1967–71; Prof. of Community Health, Univ. of London, 1978–80; Dir, Health Services Res. Unit, and Prof. of Social Medicine, Univ. of Kent, 1971–83, jtly with Specialist in Community Medicine (Epidemiology and Health Services Res.), SE Thames RHA, 1980–83. Chm., Soc. of Social Medicine, 1982–83. Academic Registrar, Faculty of Community Medicine, Royal Colls of Physicians, 1972–77. Jt Editor, British Jl of Preventive and Social Medicine, 1969–72. *Publications:* (jtly) Public Health and Social Services, 4th edn 1957, 6th edn 1965; (ed jtly) Management and the Health Services, 1971; (jtly) Physiotherapy in the Community, 1977; (jtly) Physically Disabled People Living at Home, 1978; (ed jtly) Recalling the Medical Officer of Health, 1987; (jtly) Health Services for Adults with Physical Disabilities, 1990; The Genesis of the Faculty of Community Medicine, 1997; A Chronology of State Medicine, Public Health, Welfare and Related Services in Britain 1066–1999, 2000; contribs to BMJ, Lancet, Internat. Jl of Epidemiology. *Recreations:* enjoying gardens, genealogy, reading, listening to music. *Address:* 2 Bridge Down, Bridge, Canterbury, Kent CT4 5AZ. *T:* (01227) 830233. *Club:* Royal Society of Medicine.

WARREN, Sir Miles; *see* Warren, Sir F. M.

WARREN, Nicholas John; a Recorder, since 1992; President, Gambling Appeals Tribunal, since 2007; *b* 24 June 1951; *s* of Stanley and Barbara Warren; *m* 1976, Catherine Mackie; two *s* three *d*. *Educ:* Blessed John Rigby Grammar Sch., Wigan; St Catherine's Coll., Oxford (MA Juris.). Admitted solicitor, 1975; Solicitor: Arthur Smiths, Wigan, 1973–77; Child Poverty Action Gp, 1977–80; Family Rights Gp, 1980–81; Birkenhead Resource Unit, 1981–92; full-time Chm., Social Security Tribunals, 1992–98, Regl Chm., 1998–. Mem., Lord Chancellor's Adv. Cttee on Legal Aid, 1992–95. Trustee, Cafod, 2000–. *Publications:* articles on social security and family law. *Recreations:* watching National Hunt racing and Tranmere Rovers FC. *Address:* Tribunals Service, 36 Dale Street, Liverpool L2 5UZ. *T:* (0151) 243 1415.

WARREN, Hon. Sir Nicholas Roger, Kt 2005; **Hon. Mr Justice Warren;** a Judge of the High Court of Justice, Chancery Division, since 2005; *b* 20 May 1949; *s* of Roger Warren and Muriel (*née* Reeves); *m* 1st, 1978 (marr. diss. 1989); two *s* one *d*; 2nd, 1994, Catherine Graham-Harrison. *Educ:* Bryanston Sch.; University Coll., Oxford. Called to the Bar, Middle Temple, 1972, Bencher, 2001; QC 1993; a Recorder, 1999–2005. *Recreations:* music, sailing. *Address:* c/o Royal Courts of Justice, Strand, WC2A 2LL.

WARREN, Ven. Norman Leonard; Archdeacon of Rochester, 1989–2000; *b* 19 July 1934; *s* of Arthur Henry Warren and Gwendoline Catharine Warren; *m* 1961, Yvonne Sheather; three *s* two *d*. *Educ:* Dulwich College; Corpus Christi Coll., Cambridge (MA). Asst Curate, Bedworth, 1960–63; Vicar, St Paul's, Leamington Priors, 1963–77; Rector of Morden, 1977–89; RD of Merton, 1984–88. Musical Editor: Hymns for Today's Church, 1982; Jesus Praise, 1982; Sing Glory, 1999. *Publications:* Journey into Life, 1964; The Way Ahead, 1965; Directions, 1969; What's the Point?, 1986; The Path of Peace, 1988; A Certain Faith, 1988; Is God there?, 1990; Why Believe?, 1993; (ed) Responsorial Psalms of the Alternative Services Book, 1994; Psalms for the People, 2001. *Recreations:* cricket, soccer and Rugby, walking, music. *Address:* 6 Hillview, Stratford-upon-Avon CV37 9AY. *T:* (01789) 414255.

See also Very Rev. A. C. Warren, R. H. C. Warren.

WARREN, Peter Francis; Chairman, Hammond Communications, 1994; non-executive Chairman, Radio Advertising Bureau, 1995–2001; *b* 2 Dec. 1940; *s* of Francis Joseph Warren and Freda Ruth Hunter; *m* 1962, Susan Poole; two *s* one *d*. *Educ:* Finchley Grammar School. Deputy Managing Dir, Ogilvy Benson & Mather Ltd, 1977; Dir, Ogilvy & Mather International Inc., 1978; Managing Dir, Ogilvy Benson & Mather Ltd, 1978; Chairman: Ogilvy & Mather (Hldgs), subseq. The Ogilvy Gp (Hldgs) Ltd, 1981–90; Ogilvy & Mather Europe, 1988–90; Consultant, Ogilvy & Mather Worldwide, 1991 (Dir, 1985–90). Dir, Abbott Mead Vickers, 1992–99.

WARREN, Prof. Peter Michael, PhD; FSA; FBA 1997; Professor of Ancient History and Classical Archaeology, 1977–2001, now Emeritus, and Senior Research Fellow, since 2001, University of Bristol; *b* 23 June 1938; *s* of Arthur George Warren and Alison Joan Warren (*née* White); *m* 1966, Elizabeth Margaret Halliday; one *s* one *d*. *Educ:* Sandbach Sch.; Llandovery Coll.; University College of N Wales, Bangor (Ellen Thomas Stanford Schol.; BA 1st Cl. Hons Greek and Latin); Corpus Christi Coll., Cambridge (Exhibnr; BA Classical Tripos Pt II 1962; MA 1966; PhD 1966; Fellow, 1965–68); student, British Sch. at Athens, 1963–65. FSA 1973. Research Fellow in Arts, Univ. of Durham, 1968–70; Asst Director, British Sch. at Athens, 1970–72; University of Birmingham: Lectr in Aegean Archaeol., 1972–74; Sen. Lectr, 1974–76; Reader, 1976; Bristol University: Dean, Faculty of Arts, 1988–90; Pro-Vice-Chancellor, 1991–95; Fellow, 1995–96. Vis. Prof., Univ. of Minnesota, 1981; Geddes-Harrower Prof. of Greek Art and Archaeol., Univ. of Aberdeen, 1986–87; Neuberg Lectr, Univ. of Göteborg, 1986. Dir of excavations, Myrtos, Crete, 1967–68; Debla, Crete, 1971; Knossos, 1971–73, 1978–82, 1997. Member: Managing Cttee, British Sch. at Athens, 1973–77, 1978–79, 1986–90, 1994–98, 1999–2004, 2006– (Chm., 1979–83, 2003–04; Vice-Pres., 2005–); Council, Soc. for Promotion of Hellenic Studies, 1978–81; President: Bristol Anglo-Hellenic Cultural Soc., 1987–97; Birmingham and Midlands Br., Classical Assoc., 1996–97. Bristol and Gloucestershire Archaeological Society: Vice-Chm. Council, 1980–81; Chm., 1981–84; Vice-Pres., 1989–93; Pres., 2000–01. Hon. Fellow, Archaeol Soc. of Athens, 1987; Corresp. Fellow, Soc. for Cretan Historical Studies, 1992; Corresp. Mem., Österreichische Akad. der Wissenschaften, 1997; For. Fellow, Onassis Public Benefit Foundn, 2007. Hon. Dr Univ. of Athens, 2000. *Publications:* Minoan Stone Vases, 1969; Myrtos, an Early Bronze Age Settlement in Crete, 1972; The Aegean Civilizations, 1975, 2nd edn 1989; Minoan Religion as Ritual Action, 1988; (with V. Hankey) Aegean Bronze Age Chronology, 1989; (with S. Alexiou) The Early Minoan Tombs of Lebena, Southern Crete, 2004; articles on Aegean Bronze Age, particularly Minoan archaeology, in archaeol, science and classical jls. *Recreations:* growing *Cistaceae* (Nat. Collection), Manchester United, history of Greek botany. *Address:* Claremont House, 5 Merlin Haven, Wotton-under-Edge, Glos GL12 7BA. *T:* (01453) 842290.

WARREN, Peter Tolman, CBE 1998; PhD; Administrator, Livery Schools Link, 2004–06; *b* 20 Dec. 1937; *s* of late Hugh Alan Warren and Florence Christine Warren (*née* Tolman); *m* 1961, Angela Mary (*née* Curtis); two *s* one *d*. *Educ:* Whitgift Sch., Croydon; Queens' Coll., Cambridge (MA, PhD); CGeol. Geological Survey of GB, 1962; Chief Scientific Adviser's Staff, Cabinet Office, 1972; Private Sec. to Lord Zuckerman, 1973–76; Science and Technology Secretariat, Cabinet Office, 1974–76; Safety Adviser, NERC, 1976–77; Dep. Exec. Sec., 1977–85, Exec. Sec., 1985–97, Royal Soc.; Dir, World Humanity Action Trust, 1997–99, then Consultant, 1999–2001, Trustee, 2001–03 and Mem., Exec. Cttee, 2001–05, Stakeholder Forum for our Common Future. Mem. Council, Parly and Scientific Cttee, 1992– (Vice-Pres., 1995–97, 2001–04). Member: Council, GDST (formerly GPDST), 1989–2004; Ct of Governors and Council, Amgueddfa Cymru, Nat. Mus. of Wales (formerly Nat. Mus and Galls of Wales), 2000–06. Vice-President: Geol Soc., 1992–96; BAAS, 1997–2002; Chm., 2000–05, Vice-Pres., 2005–, Cambridge Soc. (Surrey Br.). Pres., Old Whitgiftian Assoc., 2008–Aug. 2009. Mem. Ct, Guild of Educators, 2002– (Middle Warden, 2005–06; Upper Warden, 2006–07; Master, 2007–08). Editor, Monographs of Palaeontographical Soc., 1968–77. *Publications:* (ed) Geological Aspects of Development and Planning in Northern England, 1970; (co-author) Geology of the Country around Rhyl and Denbigh, 1984; papers on geology in learned jls. *Recreations:* geology, gardening. *Address:* 34 Plough Lane, Purley, Surrey CR8 3QA. *T:* (020) 8660 4087. *Club:* Athenæum.

WARREN, Prof. Raymond Henry Charles, MusD; Stanley Hugh Badock Professor of Music, University of Bristol, 1972–94; *b* 7 Nov. 1928; *s* of Arthur Henry Warren and Gwendoline Catherine Warren; *m* 1953, Roberta Lydia Alice Smith; three *s* one *d*. *Educ:* Bancroft's Sch.; Corpus Christi Coll., Cambridge (MA, MusD). Music Master, Woolverstone Hall Sch., 1952–55; Queen's University Belfast: Lectr in Music, 1955–66; Prof. of Composition, 1966–72; Resident Composer, Ulster Orchestra, 1967–72. Compositions incl. 3 symphonies, 3 string quartets and 6 operas. *Publications: compositions:* The Passion, 1963; String Quartet No 1, 1967; Violin Concerto, 1967; Songs of Old Age, 1971; Continuing Cities (oratorio), 1989; Opera Workshop, 1995. *Recreation:* walking. *Address:* 4 Contemporis, Merchants Road, Bristol BS8 4HB. *T:* (0117) 923 7687.

See also Very Rev. A. C. Warren, Ven. N. L. Warren.

WARREN, Robin; *see* Warren, J. R.

WARREN EVANS, (John) Roger; consultant and lecturer, since 1995; *b* 11 Dec. 1935; *s* of Thomas and Mary Warren Evans; *m* 1966, Elizabeth M. James; one *s* one *d*. *Educ:* Leighton Park Sch., Reading; Trinity Coll., Cambridge (BA History, 1st Cl.); London Sch. of Economics. Called to Bar, Gray's Inn, 1962. Television Interviewer, Anglia Television, 1960–61; Research Officer, Centre for Urban Studies, London, 1961; practice at Bar, 1962–69; Legal Correspondent, New Society, 1964–68; general management functions with Bovis Gp, in construction and develt, 1969–74, incl. Man. Dir, Bovis Homes Southern Ltd, 1971–74; Under-Secretary, DoE, 1975; Industrial Advr on Construction, DoE, 1975–76; Man. Dir, Barratt Develts (London), Ltd, 1977–79; Dir, Swansea Centre for Trade and Industry, 1979–85; Man. Dir, Demos Ltd, 1985–87; SavaCentre Property Develt Manager, 1987–88; Regl Property Dir, J. Sainsbury plc, 1988–94. Dir, Estates & Agency Hldgs plc, 1995–2004. Member: Welsh Consumer Council, 1992–95; Cttee, Community Selfbuild Agency, 1995–99. Mem. Bd, Assoc. of Self Employed, 1995–96. Gov., Gillespie Primary Sch., Islington, 1993–96. Trustee: Inst. of Community Studies, 1975–2001; Mutual Aid Centre, 1975–2005 (Chm., 2003–05); Aquaterra Leisure, 1999–2005; Hygeia Trust, 1999–2005; Croeso Trust, 2000–05; Libri Trust, 2000–04; Mumbles Community Leisure Trust, 2003–05; Asylum Justice Trust, 2005–. Sec., Coll. of Questors, 2003–. Member: Hackney BC, 1971–73; Mumbles Community Council, Swansea, 1999–2004. Sec., RBL, Mumbles, 2004–06. Convenor, Fabian Soc., Wales, 1999–2004. FCIOB 1976. Hon. Fellow, Coll. of Estate Mgt, 1982. *Recreations:* walking, talking. *Address:* 23 St Peter's Road, Newton, Swansea SA3 4SB. *T:* (01792) 360673; *e-mail:* roger@warrenevans.net.

WARREN-GASH, Haydon Boyd; HM Diplomatic Service; Ambassador to Colombia, 2005–08; *b* 8 Aug. 1949; *s* of Alexis Patrick and Cynthia Warren-Gash; *m* 1973, Caroline Emma Bowring Leather; one *s* one *d*. *Educ:* Sidney Sussex Coll., Cambridge (MA Econs). Joined Foreign and Commonwealth Office, 1971; language training, SOAS, London Univ., 1972 (on secondment); Third Sec., Ankara, 1973–76; Second, subseq. First, Sec., Madrid, 1977–80; First Sec., FCO, 1980–82; Private Sec. to Minister of State, 1982–85; First Sec. (Commercial), Paris, 1985–89; Asst Head, Southern European Dept, FCO, 1989–91; Dep. High Comr, Nairobi, 1991–94; Hd, Southern European Dept, FCO, 1994–97; Ambassador to Côte d'Ivoire, to Niger, Burkino Faso and Liberia, 1997–2001; FCO, 2001–02; Ambassador to Morocco and Mauritania, 2002–05. *Recreations:* entomology, music, walking, swimming. *Address:* c/o Foreign and Commonwealth Office, King Charles Street, SW1A 2AH. *Club:* Muthaiga (Nairobi).

WARRENDER, family name of **Baron Bruntisfield**.

WARRINGTON, Bishop Suffragan of, since 2000; **Rt Rev. David Willfred Michael Jennings;** *b* 13 July 1944; *s* of late Rev. Willfred Jennings and Nona Jennings (*née* de Winton); *m* 1969, Sarah Catherine Fynn, *d* of late Dr Robert Fynn of Harare, Zimbabwe; three *s*. *Educ:* Radley Coll.; King's Coll., London (AKC 1966). Ordained deacon, 1967, priest, 1968; Assistant Curate: St Mary, Walton on the Hill, Liverpool, 1967–69; Christchurch Priory, Christchurch, Hants, 1969–73; Vicar: Hythe, Southampton, 1973–80; St Edward, Romford, 1980–92; Rural Dean of Havering, 1985–92; Archdeacon of Southend, 1992–2000. Non-residentiary Canon, Chelmsford Cathedral, 1987–92. *Recreation:* exploring the buildings of the British Isles. *Address:* 34 Central Avenue, Eccleston Park, Prescot, Merseyside L34 2QP. *T:* (0151) 426 1897.

WARRINGTON, Archdeacon of; *see* Bradley, Ven. P. D. D.

WARRINGTON, Prof. Elizabeth Kerr, FRS 1986; Professor of Clinical Neuropsychology, 1982–96, now Emeritus, and Hon. Consultant, since 1996, National Hospital for Neurology and Neurosurgery; *d* of late Prof. John Alfred Valentine Butler, FRS and Margaret Lois Butler; one *d*. *Educ:* University College London (BSc 1954; PhD

1960; DSc 1975; Fellow 1994). Research Fellow, Inst. of Neurology, 1956; National Hospital: Senior Clinical Psychologist, 1960; Principal Psychologist, 1962; Top Grade Clinical Psychologist, 1972–82. Dr *hc*: Psicologia, Bologna, 1998; Univ. Louis Pasteur, Strasbourg, 2006; DUniv York, 1999. *Publications:* (with R. A. McCarthy) Cognitive Neuropsychology, 1990; numerous papers in neurological and psychological jls. *Recreations:* gardening, entertaining granddaughters. *Address:* Dementia Research Centre, Institute of Neurology, Queen Square, WC1N 3BG. *T:* 0845 155 5000.

WARRY, Peter Thomas, PhD; CEng, FREng, FIET, FIMechE; FCMA; Chairman: Victrex plc, since 1999; BSS Group plc, since 2004 (non-executive Director, 1999–2003); Chairman, Science and Technology Facilities Council, since 2007; *b* 31 Aug. 1949; *s* of William Vivian Warry and late Pamela Warry; *m* 1981, Rosemary Furbank; one *d*. *Educ:* Clifton Coll., Bristol; Merton Coll., Oxford (MA; Hon. Fellow, 2007); LLB London Univ.; Reading Univ. (PhD 2005). CEng 1979; FIET (FIEE 1995); FIMechE 1995; FCMA 1983; FREng 2006. Man. Dir, Self-Changing Gears Ltd, 1979–82; Gp Man. Dir, Aerospace Engineering plc, 1982–84; Director: Plessey Telecoms, 1986–87; Norcros plc, 1988–94; Nuclear Electric plc, 1995–96; British Energy plc, 1996–98; Chief Exec., Nuclear Electric Ltd, 1996–98. Non-executive Director: Heatherwood & Wexham Park Hosps NHS Trust, 1992–95; PTS Gp plc, 1995–98; Kier Gp plc, 1998–2004 (Chm., 2004–07); Office of the Rail Regulator, 1999–2004; Thames Water Utilities, 2001–05. Chm., PPARC, 2001–07. Special Advr, Prime Minister's Policy Unit, 1984–86; Mem., Deregulation Task Force, DTI, 1993–94; Chm., Econ. Impact Gp (Warry Report), Office of Sci. and Innovation, 2006. Indust. Prof., Warwick Univ., 1993–. Member Council: Reading Univ., 2006–; Royal Acad. of Engrg, 2007–. *Publications:* A New Direction for the Post Office, 1991; Tegulae: manufacture, typology and use in Roman Britain, 2006; contribs to Archaeology, Economics and Engineering Jl and Utilities Jl. *Recreations:* squash, tennis, walking, archeology, history. *Address:* Coxhorne, London Road, Cheltenham GL52 6UY. *T:* (01242) 518552.

WARSI, Baroness *cr* 2007 (Life Peer), of Dewsbury in the County of West Yorkshire; **Sayeeda Hussain Warsi;** Shadow Minister for Community Cohesion and Social Action, since 2007; Shadow Minister for Sheffield; *b* 1971; *m* (marr. diss.); one *d*. *Educ:* Birkdale High Sch.; Dewsbury Coll.; Leeds Univ. (LLB). Admitted Solicitor, 1996. Chm., Savayra Foundn UK, 2002–. Comr, Joseph Rowntree Charitable Trust Destitution Inquiry, 2007. Vice Chm., Cons. Party, 2005–07. Contested (C) Dewsbury, 2005. *Address:* House of Lords, SW1A 0PW; *e-mail:* Sayeeda.Warsi@Conservatives.com.

WARSI, Perween, CBE 2002 (MBE 1997); Managing Director, S&A Foods Ltd, since 1987; *b* 10 Aug. 1956; *m* 1972, Dr Talib Warsi; two *s*. Started S&A Foods from own kitchen, 1986; founded business, 1987; entered partnership with Hughes Foods Gp, 1988; with husband, completed mgt buy-out, 1991; S&A Foods began exporting, 1995; company created 1300 jobs in inner-city Derby, achieved annual growth rate of 40–50%, and has recd 28 awards, 1995–. Member: Govt Adv. Cttee on Competitiveness, 1997–; Nat. Cttee, CBI, 2004–. Hon. MBA Derby, 1997; Hon. DBA: Internat. Mgt Centres, 1999; Coventry, 2005; Hon. LLD Nottingham, 2006. Midlands Business Woman of Year Award, 1994; RADAR People of Year Award, 1995; Woman Entrepreneur of World Award, 1996; First Woman Lifetime Achievement Award, 2005. *Address:* S&A Foods Ltd, Sir Francis Ley Industrial Park, 37 Shaftesbury Street South, Derby DE23 8YH. *T:* (01332) 270670, *Fax:* (01332) 270523.

WARTNABY, Dr John; Keeper, Department of Earth and Space Sciences, Science Museum, South Kensington, 1969–82; *b* 6 Jan. 1926; *o s* of Ernest John and Beatrice Hilda Wartnaby; *m* 1962, Kathleen Mary Barber, MD, MRCP, DPM; one *s* one *d*. *Educ:* Chiswick Grammar Sch.; Chelsea Coll. (BSc 1946); Imperial Coll. of Science and Technology (DIC 1950); University Coll., London (MSc 1967; PhD 1972). FInstP 1971; FRAS 2004. Asst Keeper, Dept of Astronomy and Geophysics, Science Museum, 1951; Deputy Keeper, 1960. *Publications:* Seismology, 1957; The International Geophysical Year, 1957; Surveying, 1968; papers in learned jls. *Recreations:* country walking, Zen. *Address:* 19 Grange Close, Edenbridge, Kent TN8 5LT.

WARWICK; *see* Turner-Warwick.

WARWICK, 9th Earl of, *cr* 1759; **Guy David Greville;** Baron Brooke 1621; Earl Brooke 1746; *b* 30 Jan. 1957; *s* of 8th Earl of Warwick and of Sarah Anne Chester Greville (*née* Beatty; now Mrs Harry Thomson Jones); *S* father, 1996; *m* 1st, 1981, Susan McKinlay Cobbold (marr. diss. 1992); one *s*; 2nd, 1996, Louisa Heenan. *Educ:* Summerfields; Eton; Ecole des Roches. *Recreation:* golf. *Heir:* *s* Lord Brooke, *qv*. *Address:* 4 Walter Street, Claremont, WA 6010, Australia. *Club:* White's.

WARWICK OF UNDERCLIFFE, Baroness *cr* 1999 (Life Peer), of Undercliffe in the county of West Yorkshire; **Diana Warwick;** Chief Executive, Universities UK (formerly Committee of Vice Chancellors and Principals), since 1995; *b* 16 July 1945; *d* of Jack and Olive Warwick; *m* 1969. *Educ:* St Joseph's Coll., Bradford; Bedford Coll., Univ. of London (BA Hons). Technical Asst to the Gen. Sec., NUT, 1969–72; Asst Sec., CPSA, 1972–83; Gen. Sec., AUT, 1983–92; Chief Exec., Westminster Foundn for Democracy, 1992–95. Member: Bd, Lattice plc, 2000–02; Mgt Bd, USS, 2001–. Mem., Cttee on Standards in Public Life, 1994–2000. Member: Bd, British Council, 1985–95; Employment Appeal Tribunal, 1987–99; Exec. and Council, Industrial Soc., 1987–2001; TUC Gen. Council, 1989–92; Council, Duke of Edinburgh's Seventh Commonwealth Study Conf., 1991; Chm., VSO, 1994–2003. Gov., Commonwealth Inst., 1988–95. Trustee: Royal Anniversary Trust, 1991–93; St Catharine Foundn, Windsor, 1996–. FRSA 1984. Hon. DLitt Bradford, 1993; DUniv Open, 1998; Hon. DSSc Royal Holloway, London, 2006. *Recreations:* theatre, looking at pictures. *Address:* Universities UK, Woburn House, 20 Tavistock Square, WC1H 9HQ. *T:* (020) 7419 4111.

WARWICK, Bishop Suffragan of, since 2005; **Rt Rev. John Ronald Angus Stroyan;** *b* 5 May 1955; *s* of His Honour Ronald Angus Ropner Stroyan, *qv*; *m* 1990, Mary (*née* Ferguson); two *d*. *Educ:* St Andrews Univ. (MTh 1976); Queen's Coll., Birmingham; Ecumenical Inst., Geneva; MA (Dist.) Univ. of Wales, 2007. Ordained deacon, 1983, priest, 1984; Curate, Coventry E Team, St Peter's, Hillfields, 1983–87; Vicar: St Matthew with St Chad, Smethwick, 1987–94; Bloxham with Milcombe and S Newington, 1994–2005; Area Dean, Deddington, 2002–05. Chm., Coventry Council of Churches, 1986–87. Pres., Community of Cross of Nails (UK), 2007–. *Publication:* Shakespeare Sermon, 1996. *Recreations:* theatre, cinema, travel, walking. *Address:* Warwick House, 139 Kenilworth Road, Coventry CV4 7AP. *T:* (024) 7641 2627, *Fax:* (024) 7641 5254; *e-mail:* Bishop.Warwick@CovCofE.org.

WARWICK, Archdeacon of; *see* Paget-Wilkes, Ven. M. J. J.

WARWICK, Hannah Cambell Grant; *see* Gordon, H. C. G.

WARWICK, Kenneth Scott; Deputy Chief Economic Adviser and Director of Economics, Department for Business, Enterprise and Regulatory Reform (formerly Department of Trade and Industry), since 2003; *b* 23 April 1955; *s* of John Warwick and Mary Orr Warwick (*née* Osborne); *m* 1978, Susan Eileen Finch; one *s* one *d*. *Educ:* Christ's Coll., Cambridge (BA Hons 1976); Yale Univ. (MPhil 1982). Economist, MAFF, 1976–84; Econ. Advr, FCO, 1984–89; Economist, IMF, 1989–92; Senior Economic Adviser: FCO, 1992–96; DTI, 1996–2003. *Recreations:* golf, music, family past and present. *T:* (office) (020) 7215 6042, *Fax:* (office) (020) 7215 6691; *e-mail:* ken.warwick@btinternet.com. *Club:* West Byfleet Golf.

WARWICK, Prof. Kevin, PhD; FIET; Professor of Cybernetics, University of Reading, since 1988; *b* 9 Feb. 1954; *s* of Stanley and Jessie Allcock; *née* Kevin Warwick Allcock; adopted Warwick as surname by Deed Poll, 1974; *m* 1st, 1974, Sylvia Margaret Walsh (marr. diss. 1991); one *s* one *d*; 2nd, 1991, Irena Vorackova. *Educ:* Lawrence Sheriff Sch., Rugby; Aston Univ. (BSc); Imperial Coll., London (PhD 1982; DIC 1982); DSc (Eng) London 1993. FIET (FIEE 1987). British Telecom Apprentice, 1970–76; Res. Asst, Imperial Coll., London, 1982; Lectr, Newcastle upon Tyne Univ., 1982–85; Res. Lectr, Oxford Univ., 1985–87; Sen Lectr, Warwick Univ., 1987–88. FCGI 1992. Mem., Aventis Books Cttee, Royal Soc., 2000–01. Presenter, Royal Instn Christmas Lectures, 2000. Hon. Mem., Acad. of Scis, St Petersburg, 1999. DrSc Czech Acad. of Scis, 1994; Hon. DSc Aston, 2008. Future of Health Technol. Award, MIT, 2000; Achievement Award, IEE, 2004. *Publications:* (ed jtly) Neural Nets for Control and Systems, 1992; March of the Machines, 1997; In the Mind of the Machine, 1998; QI: The Quest for Intelligence, 2000; I, Cyborg, 2002; contribs to books and jls on control, robotics, machine intelligence and cyborgs. *Recreations:* soccer (Viktoria Zizkov FC supporter), travel, theatre. *Address:* School of Systems Engineering, University of Reading, Whiteknights, Reading RG6 6AY. *T:* (0118) 931 8210, *Fax:* (0118) 931 8220.

WARWICK THOMPSON, Paul; Director, Smithsonian Cooper-Hewitt National Design Museum, New York, since 2001; *b* 9 Aug. 1959; *s* of Sir Michael Thompson, *qv*; *m* 1984, Adline Finlay; one *s* one *d*. *Educ:* Bryanston Sch.; Univ. of Bristol (BA Jt Hons); Univ. of East Anglia (MA, PhD). Design Council, 1987–88; Design Museum, 1988–2001, Dir, 1992–2001. *Recreations:* theatre, cinema, gardening. *Address:* Cooper-Hewitt National Design Museum, Smithsonian Institution, 2 East 91st Street, New York, NY 10128, USA.

WASHINGTON, Denzel; actor; *b* Mt Vernon, NY, 28 Dec. 1954; *s* of late Denzel Washington and of Lennis Washington; *m* 1983, Pauletta Pearson; two *s* two *d* (incl. twin *s* and *d*). *Educ:* Oakland Acad., New Windsor, NY; Fordham Univ. (BA 1977). American Conservatory Theater, San Francisco. *Theatre includes:* Coriolanus, 1979; Spell No 7; The Mighty Gents; One Tiger to a Hill; Ceremonies in Dark Old Men; When the Chickens Come Home to Roost, 1981; A Soldier's Play, 1981; Checkmates, 1988; Split Second; Richard III, 1990; *films include:* Carbon Copy, 1981; A Soldier's Story, 1984; Power, 1986; Cry Freedom, 1987; For Queen and Country, The Mighty Quinn, Glory (Best Supporting Actor, Acad. Awards, 1990), 1989; Heart Condition, Love Supreme, Mo' Better Blues, 1990; Ricochet, 1991; Mississippi Masala, Malcolm X, 1992; Much Ado About Nothing, 1993; The Pelican Brief, Philadelphia, 1994; Crimson Tide, Virtuosity, Devil in a Blue Dress, 1995; Courage Under Fire, 1996; The Preacher's Wife, 1997; Fallen, He Got Game, 1998; The Siege, 1999; The Bone Collector, The Hurricane (Best Actor, Golden Globe Awards), 2000; Remember the Titans, 2001; Training Day (Best Actor, Acad. Awards), 2002; The Manchurian Candidate, Man on Fire, 2004; Inside Man, Déjà Vu, 2006; American Gangster, 2007; *director:* Antwone Fisher, 2002; *television includes:* Wilma, 1977; Flesh and Blood, 1979; St Elsewhere (series), 1982–88; License to Kill, 1984; The George McKenna Story, 1986.

WASHINGTON, Neville James Cameron, OBE 1992; Chief Executive, Coal Authority, 1994–97; *b* 8 May 1948; *s* of Peter Washington and Sybil Joan Washington (*née* Cameron); *m* 1980, Jennifer Anne Frideswide Kekewich; two *s* one *d*. *Educ:* Marlborough Coll.; Trinity Hall, Cambridge (MA). Research on chimpanzee behaviour, Gombe, Tanzania, 1969–70. Joined Queen's Own Highlanders (Seaforth & Camerons), 1971; Army Staff Coll., Camberley, 1982; jsdc 1987; comd 3rd Bn, UDR, 1987–89 (despatches); left Army in rank of Lieut-Col, 1992. Dir of Human Resources, Victoria Infirmary, Glasgow, 1992–94. *Recreations:* sheep, hunting. *Address:* Rottenrow, Crosshands, by Mauchline, Ayrshire KA5 5TN.

WASINONDH, Kitti; Ambassador of Thailand to the Court of St James's, since 2007; *b* 23 Nov. 1951; *m* Nutchanart; one *d*. *Educ:* Chulalongkorn Univ., Bangkok (Bachelor Pol Sci. 1974); Nat. Inst. Develt Admin, Bangkok (Master Develt Admin 1976). Consul-Gen. of Thailand in Sydney, 2000–02; Director-General: Dept of ASEAN Affairs, 2003–06; Dept of Information, and Spokesman of Min. of Foreign Affairs, 2006–07. *Recreation:* golf. *Address:* Royal Thai Embassy, 29 Queen's Gate, SW7 5JB. *T:* (020) 7225 5509, *Fax:* (020) 7823 9695; *e-mail:* kittiw@mfa.go.th.

WASS, Sir Douglas (William Gretton), GCB 1980 (KCB 1975; CB 1971); Senior Adviser, Nomura International plc, 1998–2002 (Chairman, 1986–98); Permanent Secretary to HM Treasury, 1974–83, and Joint Head of the Home Civil Service, 1981–83; *b* 15 April 1923; *s* of late Arthur W. and late Elsie W. Wass; *m* 1954, Dr Milica Pavičić; one *s* one *d*. *Educ:* Nottingham High Sch.; St John's Coll., Cambridge (MA; Hon. Fellow, 1982). Served War, 1943–46: Scientific Research with Admiralty, at home and in Far East. Entered HM Treasury as Asst Principal, 1946; Principal, 1951; Commonwealth Fund Fellow in USA, 1958–59; Vis. Fellow, Brookings Instn, Washington, DC, 1959; Private Sec.: to Chancellor of the Exchequer, 1959–61; to Chief Sec. to Treasury, 1961–62; Asst Sec., 1962; Alternate Exec. Dir, Internat. Monetary Fund, and Financial Counsellor, British Embassy, Washington, DC, 1965–67; HM Treasury: Under-Sec., 1968; Dep. Sec., 1970–73; Second Permanent Sec., 1973–74. Chairman: Equity & Law, subseq. Axa Equity & Law, Life Assurance Soc., 1986–95 (Dir, 1984–95); NCM (Credit Insce), 1991–95; Director: Barclays Bank, 1984–87; De La Rue Company plc, 1984–93; Equitable Cos Inc., 1992–95; Equitable Life Assurance Soc., USA, 1992–93; NCM (NV), Amsterdam, 1992–95; Soho Theatre Co., 1996–2000. Administrateur, Axa SA (formerly Cie du Midi), 1987–95; Consultant to Coopers & Lybrand, 1984–86. Chairman: British Selection Cttee of Harkness Fellowships, 1981–84; UN Adv. Gp on Financial Flows for Africa, 1987–88; SIB Adv. Cttee on Pension Transfers, 1993–94; Syndicate on the Government of Univ. of Cambridge, 1988–89. Pres., Market Res. Soc., 1987–91. Dep. Chm., Council of Policy Studies Inst., 1981–85; Vice-Pres., 1984–91, and Mem. Adv. Bd, Constitutional Reform Centre; Vice Chm., Africa Capacity Building Foundn, 1991–98; Governor, Ditchley Foundn, 1981–2000; Member, Council: Centre for Econ. Policy Res., 1983–90; Employment Inst., 1985–92; Univ. of Bath, 1985–91; British Heart Foundn, 1990–96; ODI, 1991–98. Lectures: Reith, BBC, 1983; Shell, St Andrews Univ., 1985; Harry Street Meml, Univ. of Manchester, 1987. Hon. DLitt Bath, 1985. *Publications:* Government and the Governed, 1984; Decline to Fall, 2008; articles in newspapers and jls. *Address:* 6 Dora Road, SW19 7HH. *T:* (020) 8946 5556. *Club:* Reform.
See also S. Wass.

WASS, Prof. John Andrew Hall, MD; FRCP; Professor of Endocrinology, University of Oxford, since 1998; Fellow of Green Templeton College (formerly Green College), Oxford, since 1995; Consultant Physician, and Head, Department of Endocrinology, Churchill Hospital, Oxford, since 1995; *b* 14 Aug. 1947; *s* of Samuel Hall Wass and June

Mary Vaudine Wass (*née* Blaikie); *m* 1st, 1970, Valerie Vincent (marr. diss. 1997); one *s* one *d*; 2nd, 1998, Sally Smith. *Educ:* Rugby; Guy's Hosp. Med. Sch., Univ. of London (MB BS 1971; MD 1980). FRCP 1986. Sub-Dean, Med. Coll. and Prof. of Clin. Endocrinol., St Bartholomew's Hosp., London, 1989–95. Admissions Tutor, Green Coll., Oxford, 2001–03. Advr, Cancer Bacup, 1985–. Ed., Clin. Endocrinol. Jl, 1991–94. Linacre Fellow, RCP, 1994–98. Chm., Soc. for Endocrinol., 2005–; President: Eur. Fedn of Endocrine Socs, 2001–03; Pituitary Soc. (NY), 2006–07. Co-founder, Pituitary Foundn, 1994. Gov., Purcell Sch., 2000–. Chm., Bart's Choral Soc., 1992–95. *Publications:* (jtly) Clinical Endocrine Oncology, 1997, 2nd edn 2008; Oxford Textbook of Endocrinology, 2002; Oxford Handbook of Endocrinology, 2002; articles and chapters on acromegaly, pituitary tumours and osteoporosis. *Recreations:* music, theatre, wine, Scotland. *Address:* Department of Endocrinology, Churchill Hospital, Oxford OX3 7LJ. *T:* (01865) 227621; *e-mail:* john.wass@noc.anglox.nhs.uk. *Club:* Garrick.

WASS, Sasha, (Mrs N. R. A. Hall); QC 2000; a Recorder, since 2000; *b* 19 Feb. 1958; *d* of Sir Douglas William Gretton Wass, *qv*; *m* 1986, Nigel R. A. Hall; one *s* one *d*. *Educ:* Wimbledon High Sch.; Liverpool Univ. (LLB Hons). Called to the Bar: Gray's Inn, 1981, Bencher, 2003; Gibraltar, 2008; Asst Recorder, 1997–2000. Criminal Bar Association: Mem. Cttee, 1992–; Treas., 1997–99; Dir of Educn, 2002. *Address:* 6 King's Bench Walk, Temple, EC4Y 7DR. *T:* (020) 7583 0410.

WASSALL, Philip Hugh; His Honour Judge Wassall; a Circuit Judge, since 2004; *b* 11 March 1950; *s* of late Derek William Wassall and Avril Mary Holden Wassall; *m* 1991, Julia Lesley; two *d*. *Educ:* Aldridge Grammar Sch.; Chelmsford Coll. (LLB Hons ext. London). Criminal Law Clerk, 1969–75; Articled Clerk, 1976–78; Solicitor, 1979–94; a District Judge (Magistrates' Courts) (formerly Provincial Stipendiary Magistrate, Devonshire), 1994–2004; a Recorder, 2000–04. *Recreations:* golf, cooking, walking, music, fishing. *Address:* Truro Crown Court, 2 Edmund Street, Truro TR1 2PB. *T:* (01752) 206200.

WASSERMAN, Gordon Joshua; Chairman and Chief Executive Officer, Gordon Wasserman Group LLC, since 2003; *b* Montreal, 26 July 1938; *s* of late John J. Wasserman, QC, and Prof. Rachel Chait Wasserman, Montreal; *m* 1964, Cressida Frances, *yr d* of late Rt Hon. Hugh Gaitskell, PC, CBE, MP, and Baroness Gaitskell; two *d*. *Educ:* Westmount High Sch., Montreal; McGill Univ. (BA); New Coll., Oxford (MA). Rhodes Scholar (Quebec and New Coll.), 1959; Sen. Research Scholar, St Antony's Coll., Oxford, 1961–64; Lectr in Economics, Merton Coll., Oxford, 1963–64; Research Fellow, New Coll., Oxford, 1964–67; joined Home Office as Economic Adviser, 1967, Sen. Econ. Adviser, 1972, Asst Sec., 1977–81; Head, Urban Deprivation Unit, 1973–77; Civil Service Travelling Fellowship in USA, 1977–78; Under Sec., Central Policy Review Staff, Cabinet Office, 1981–83; Asst Under Sec. of State, Home Office (Head, Police Science and Technology Gp), 1983–95; Special Advr (Sci. and Technol.) to Police Comr, NYC, 1996–98; COS, 1998–2002, Special Advr to Police Comr, 1998–2003, City of Philadelphia. Chm., Ion Track Inc., 2000–02. Member: Exec., ELITE Gp, 1993–96; Bd, SEARCH Gp Inc., USA, 1994–2000; US Justice Dept Adv. Panel on Sci. and Technol., 1996–2003. Trustee, McGill Univ. (Canada) Trust, 1995–96. Fellow, Koret Inst., USA, 1996–98. Vice-Pres., English Basket Ball Assoc., 1983–86. *Recreations:* walking, opera, music, gardening. *Address:* 201 South 18th Street, Suite 621, Philadelphia, PA 19103–5906, USA. *Clubs:* Reform, Beefsteak.

WASSERSTEIN, Bruce; Chief Executive, since 2001, and Chairman, since 2005, Lazards; *b* 25 Dec. 1947; *s* of Morris and Lola Wasserstein; *m* 1996, Claude Elizabeth Becker; two *s*, and two *s* one *d* from former marriage. *Educ:* Univ. of Michigan (BA Hons 1967); Harvard Univ. (MBA with high distinction 1971; JD cl 1971); Darwin Coll., Cambridge (Dip. Law 1972). Associate, Cravath, Swaine and Moore, 1972–77; Man. Dir, First Boston Corp., 1977–88; Chm. and CEO, Wasserstein Perella & Co., 1988–2000; Exec. Chm., Dresdner Kleinwort Wasserstein, 2000–01. *Publications:* Corporate Finance Law: a guide for the executive, 1978; Big Deal: 2000 and beyond, 2000. *Address:* Lazards, 30 Rockefeller Plaza, New York, NY 10020, USA. *T:* (212) 6326000.

WASTELL, Cyril Gordon, CBE 1975; Secretary General of Lloyd's, 1967–76, retired; *b* 10 Jan. 1916; *s* of Arthur Edward Wastell and Lilian Wastell; *m* 1947, Margaret Lilian (*née* Moore); one *d*. *Educ:* Brentwood Sch., Essex. Joined Staff of Corporation of Lloyd's, 1932; apart from war service (Lieut Royal Corps of Signals), 1939–46, progressed through various depts and positions at Lloyd's, until retirement. *Recreations:* reading, gardening under duress, walking, crosswords, various trivial pursuits.

WATERFALL, Simon, RDI 2008; Creative Director, Poke, London, since 2001; *b* Portsmouth, 1971; *s* of John and Jenny Waterfall. *Educ:* Brunel Univ. (BSc Hons); Royal Coll. of Art (MA). Co-Founder, Deepend Design, 1995–2001. Pres., D&AD, 2007–08. Award for Interactive Design, BAFTA, 2006. *Address:* Poke, Biscuit Building, 10 Redchurch Street, E2 7DD; *e-mail:* simon@pokelondon.com. *Club:* Shoreditch House.

WATERFIELD, Giles Adrian, FSA; writer and curator; *b* 24 July 1949; *s* of late Anthony and Honor Waterfield. *Educ:* Eton College; Magdalen College, Oxford (BA); Courtauld Institute (MA). FSA 1991. Education Officer, Royal Pavilion, Art Gallery and Museums, Brighton, 1976–79; Dir, Dulwich Picture Gall., 1979–96; Jt Dir, Attingham Summer Sch., 1995–2003; Dir, Royal Collection Studies, 1995–. Consultant Curator, Compton Verney, 1996–98. Heritage Advr, Esmée Fairbairn Foundn, 2002–; Associate Lectr, Courtauld Inst. of Art, 2002–. Mem., Museums Expert Panel, 1996–2000, Trustee, 2000–06, Heritage Lottery Fund. Mem. Exec. Cttee, London Library, 1997–2001; Mem. Adv. Cttee, Paul Mellon Centre for British Art. Vice-Pres., NADFAS, 1998–2006. Judge, Mus. of the Year Awards, Nat. Heritage, 1999–2003. Trustee: Holburne Mus., Bath, 1999–2003; Edward James Foundn, 1999–2003; Charleston Trust, 2005– (Chm., 2006–). Paul Mellon Lectr, London and Yale, 2007. *Publications:* Faces, 1983; (ed) Collection for a King (catalogue), 1985; Soane and After, 1987; Rich Summer of Art, 1988; (ed) Palaces of Art, 1991; (ed) Art for the People, 1994; (ed) Soane and Death, 1996; (contrib.) Art Treasures of England (catalogue), 1998; (contrib.) In Celebration: the art of the country house (catalogue), 1998; (ed jtly) Below Stairs (catalogue), 2003; (ed) Opening Doors: learning and the historic environment, 2004; *novels:* The Long Afternoon, 2000; Hound in the Left Hand Corner, 2002; Markham Thorpe, 2006; articles in Apollo, Art Newspaper, Burlington Magazine, Connoisseur, Country Life, London Review, TLS. *Recreations:* historic buildings, theatre. *Address:* 48 Claylands Road, SW8 1NZ.

WATERFIELD, Prof. Michael Derek, PhD; FRCPath, FMedSci; FRS 1991; Courtauld Professor of Biochemistry, 1991–2006, now Emeritus, and Director of Proteomics Unit, Ludwig Institute for Cancer Research, 2004–07, University College London; *b* 14 May 1941; *s* of Leslie N. Waterfield and Kathleen A. (*née* Marshall); *m* 1982, Sally E. James, MB BS, PhD; two *d*. *Educ:* Brunel Univ. (BSc 1963); Univ. of London (PhD 1967). FRCPath 1994. Res. Fellow, Harvard Univ. Med. Sch., 1967–70; Sen. Res. Fellow, CIT, 1970–72; Hd, Protein Chem. Lab., ICRF Labs, 1972–86; Dir of Research, Ludwig Inst. for Cancer Res., UCL, 1986–2004; Head, Dept of Biochem. and Molecular Biology, UCL, 1991–2001. Mem. Scientific Adv. Bd, Baxter Healthcare (US), 1987–2007; Founder and Dir, Piramed, 2003–08. Trustee, Inst. for Cancer Res., 2000–07. Founder FMedSci 1998. Hon. MD Ferrara, Italy, 1991. *Publications:* numerous articles in scientific jls on biochem. and molecular biol. as applied to cancer research. *Recreation:* pottering about the garden and kitchen. *Address:* Chantemerle, Speen Lane, Newbury, Berks RG13 1RN.

WATERFORD, 8th Marquess of, *cr* 1789; **John Hubert de la Poer Beresford;** Baron Le Poer, 1375; Baronet, 1668; Viscount Tyrone, Baron Beresford, 1720; Earl of Tyrone, 1746; Baron Tyrone (Great Britain), 1786; *b* 14 July 1933; *er s* of 7th Marquess and Juliet Mary (who *m* 2nd, 1946, Lieut-Colonel John Silcock), 2nd *d* of late David Lindsay; *S* father, 1934; *m* 1957, Lady Caroline Wyndham-Quin, *yr d* of 6th Earl of Dunraven and Mount-Earl, CB, CBE, MC; three *s* one *d*. *Educ:* Eton. Lieut, RHG Reserve. *Heir: s* Earl of Tyrone, *qv*. *Address:* Curraghmore, Portlaw, Co. Waterford, Ireland. *T:* (51) 387102, *Fax:* (51) 387481. *Club:* White's.

WATERFORD AND LISMORE, Bishop of, (RC), since 1993; **Most Rev. William Lee,** DCL; *b* 2 Dec. 1941; *s* of John Lee and Bridget Ryan. *Educ:* Newport Boys' Nat. Sch.; Rockwell Coll.; Maynooth Coll. (BA, BD, LPh, DCL); Gregorian Univ., Rome. Ordained priest, 1966; Catholic Curate, Finglas, West Dublin, 1969–71; Bursar, 1971–87, President, 1987–93, St Patrick's Coll., Thurles. Sec., Irish Episcopal Conf., 1998–. *Recreations:* reading, walking, golf. *Address:* Bishop's House, John's Hill, Waterford, Ireland. *T:* (51) 874463, *Fax:* (51) 852703.

WATERHOUSE, David Martin; Regional Director for South Asia and Pacific, British Council, 1994–97; *b* 23 July 1937; *s* of Rev. John W. Waterhouse and Dr Esther Waterhouse; *m* 1966, Verena Johnson; one *s* two *d*. *Educ:* Kingswood Sch., Bath; Merton Coll., Oxford (MA). Joined British Council, 1961; Enugu, Nigeria, 1962–65; Glasgow, 1965–68; Ndola, Zambia, 1968–71; Inst. of Educn, London Univ., 1971–72; Representative: Nepal, 1972–77; Thailand, 1977–80; Dir, Personnel Management Dept, 1980–85; Rep., Nigeria, 1985–89; Controller, Home Div., subseq. Dir, Exchanges and Training Div., British Council, 1989–91; Dir, Germany, 1991–93. Chm., Hoffman de Visme Foundn, 1998–2002; Vice-Pres., Royal Asiatic Soc., 2003–06. *Publication:* The Origins of Himalayan Studies: Brian Houghton Hodgson in Kathmandu and Darjeeling 1820–1858, 2004. *Recreations:* walking, music. *Address:* Courtyard Cottage, Council House Court, Shrewsbury SY1 2AU.

WATERHOUSE, Frederick Harry; systems consultant and advisor, since 1995; *b* 3 June 1932; *m* 1954, Olive Carter; two *d*. *Educ:* King Edward's, Aston, Birmingham; London Univ. (BScEcon). Associate Mem., CIMA. Chief Accountant, Copper Div., Imperial Metal Industries, 1967–70; Asst Chief Accountant, Agricl Div., ICI, 1970–72; Chief Accountant, Plant Protection Div., ICI, 1972–78; Dir, Société pour la Protection d'Agriculture (SOPRA), France, 1976–78; Dir, Solplant SA, Italy, 1976–78; Bd Member, Finance and Corporate Planning, The Post Office, 1978–79; Treasurer's Dept, ICI Ltd, Millbank, 1980–82. Partner, Bognor Antiques, 1984–87; Chief Accountant, Jelkeep Ltd, Deerhyde Ltd and Thawscroft Ltd, Selsey, 1988–94. *Recreations:* reading, gardening. *Address:* Pendennis, Fishers, St Lawrence, Ventnor, Isle of Wight PO38 1UU.

WATERHOUSE, Keith Spencer, CBE 1991; FRSL; writer; *b* 6 Feb. 1929; 4th *s* of Ernest and Elsie Edith Waterhouse; *m* 1984, Stella Bingham (marr. diss. 1989); one *s* one *d* (and one *d* decd) from previous marriage. *Educ:* Leeds. Journalist in Leeds and London, 1950–; Columnist with: Daily Mirror, 1970–86; Daily Mail, 1986–; Contributor to various periodicals; Mem. Punch Table, 1979. Mem., Kingman Cttee on Teaching of English Language, 1987–88. Hon. Fellow, Leeds Metropolitan Univ. (formerly Poly.), 1991. Granada Columnist of the Year Award, 1970; IPC Descriptive Writer of the Year Award, 1970; IPC Columnist of the Year Award, 1973; British Press Awards Columnist of the Year, 1978, 1991; Granada Special Quarter Century Award, 1982; Edgar Wallace Trophy, London Press Club, 1996; Gerald Barry Lifetime Achievement Award, What the Papers Say awards, 2000. *Films* (with Willis Hall) include: Billy Liar; Whistle Down the Wind; A Kind of Loving; Lock Up Your Daughters. Plays: Mr and Mrs Nobody, 1986; Jeffrey Bernard is Unwell, 1989 (Evening Standard Best Comedy Award, 1990), revived 1999; Bookends, 1990; Our Song, 1992; Good Grief, 1998; Bing-Bong!, 1999; The Last Page, 2007; *plays* with Willis Hall include: Billy Liar, 1960 (from which musical Billy was adapted, 1974); Celebration, 1961; All Things Bright and Beautiful, 1963; Say Who You Are, 1965; Whoops-a-Daisy, 1968; Children's Day, 1969; Who's Who, 1972; The Card (musical), 1973; Saturday, Sunday, Monday (adaptation from de Filippo), 1973; Filumena (adaptation from de Filippo), 1977; Worzel Gummidge, 1981; Budgie (musical), 1988. *TV series:* Budgie, Queenie's Castle, The Upper Crusts, Billy Liar, The Upchat Line, The Upchat Connection, Worzel Gummidge, West End Tales, The Happy Apple, Charters and Caldicott, Andy Capp; *TV films:* Charlie Muffin, 1983; This Office Life, 1985; The Great Paper Chase, 1988. *Publications: novels:* There is a Happy Land, 1957; Billy Liar, 1959; Jubb, 1963; The Bucket Shop, 1968; Billy Liar on the Moon, 1975; Office Life, 1978; Maggie Muggins, 1981; In the Mood, 1983; Thinks, 1984; Our Song, 1988; Bimbo, 1990; Unsweet Charity, 1992; Good Grief, 1997; Soho, 2001; Palace Pier, 2003; *plays:* Jeffrey Bernard Is Unwell and other plays, 1991; (with Willis Hall) include: Billy Liar, 1960; Celebration, 1961; All Things Bright and Beautiful, 1963; Say Who You Are, 1965; Who's Who, 1974; Saturday, Sunday, Monday (adaptation from de Filippo), 1974; Filumena (adaptation from de Filippo), 1977; *general:* (with Guy Deghy) Café Royal, 1956; (ed) Writers' Theatre, 1967; The Passing of The Third-floor Buck, 1974; Mondays, Thursdays, 1976; Rhubarb, Rhubarb, 1979; Daily Mirror Style, 1980, rev. and expanded edn, Newspaper Style, 1989; Fanny Peculiar, 1983; Mrs Pooter's Diary, 1983; Waterhouse At Large, 1985; Collected Letters of a Nobody, 1986; The Theory and Practice of Lunch, 1986; The Theory and Practice of Travel, 1989; English Our English, 1991; Sharon & Tracy & The Rest, 1992; City Lights, 1994; Streets Ahead, 1995. *Recreation:* lunch. *Address:* 84 Coleherne Court, Old Brompton Road, SW5 0EE. *Club:* Garrick.

WATERHOUSE, Dame Rachel (Elizabeth), DBE 1990 (CBE 1980); PhD; Chairman, Consumers' Association, 1982–90 (Member Council, 1966–96, Deputy Chairman, 1979–82); *b* 2 Jan. 1923; *d* of Percival John Franklin and Ruby Susanna Franklin; *m* 1947, John A. H. Waterhouse; two *s* two *d*. *Educ:* King Edward's High Sch., Birmingham; St Hugh's Coll., Oxford (BA 1944, MA 1948); Univ. of Birmingham (PhD 1950). WEA and Extra-mural tutor, 1944–47. Birmingham Consumer Group: Sec., 1964–65, Chm. 1966–68, Mem. Cttee, 1968–2005; Member: Nat. Consumer Council, 1975–86; Consumers' Consultative Cttee of EEC Commn, 1977–84; Price Commn, 1977–79; Council, Advertising Standards Authority, 1980–85; NEDC, 1981–91; BBC Consultative Gp on Industrial and Business Affairs, 1984–89; Richmond Cttee on Microbiol Safety of Food, 1989–90; HSC, 1990–95; Adv. Cttee on Microbiological Safety of Food, 1991–95. Ministerial nominee to Potato Marketing Bd, 1969–81; Chm., Council for Licensed Conveyancers, 1986–89; Member: Home Office Working Party on Internal Shop Security, 1971–73; Adv. Cttee on Asbestos, 1976–79; Council for the Securities Industry, 1983–85; Securities and Investments Board, 1985–92; Organising Cttee, Marketing of Investments Bd, 1985–86; Council, Office of the Banking Ombudsman, 1985–95; Duke of Edinburgh's Inquiry into British Housing, 1984–85; Adv. Bd, Inst. of Food Res.,

1988–93. Pres., Inst. of Consumer Ergonomics, Univ. of Loughborough, 1980–90 (Chm., 1970–80); Vice-President: Nat. Fedn of Consumer Gps, 1980–96; Birmingham Centre for Business Ethics, 1999–2005; Member: Council, Birmingham and Midland Inst., 1993 (Pres., 1992); Court of Govs, Univ. of Birmingham, 1992–; Provost, Selly Oak Colls, 1997–2000. Chm., Birmingham Gp, Victorian Soc., 1966–67, 1972–74; Vice-Chm., Lunar Soc., 1996–98 (Chm., 1990–96). Trustee: Joseph Rowntree Foundn, 1990–98; Affirming Catholicism, 1991–2001; Gov., Foundn of Lady Katherine Leveson, 2001–04. Hon. FGIA (Hon. CGIA 1988). Hon. DLitt Univ. of Technology, Loughborough, 1978; Hon. DSocSc Birmingham, 1990; Hon. DSc Aston, 1998. *Publications:* The Birmingham and Midland Institute 1854–1954, 1954; A Hundred Years of Engineering Craftsmanship, 1957; Children in Hospital: a hundred years of child care in Birmingham, 1962; (with John Whybrow) How Birmingham became a Great City, 1976; King Edward VI High School for Girls 1883–1983, 1983.

WATERHOUSE, Roger William; Vice-Chancellor, University of Derby, 1992–2004; *b* 29 April 1940; *s* of Ronald Waterhouse and Dorthy May Waterhouse (*née* Holmes); *m* 1st, 1962, Mania Jevinsky (marr. diss.); one *s* two *d*; 2nd, 1979, Jacqueline Mary Dymond; one *s* one *d*. *Educ:* Corpus Christi Coll., Oxford (BA, MA Phil. & Psychol.). Lectr, Shoreditch Coll., 1961–62; Teacher, Kibbutz Ma'abarot, Israel, 1962–64; Hd of Econs, Myers Grove Comprehensive Sch., Sheffield, 1966–68; Asst Lectr, Lectr, Sen. Lectr and Principal Lectr, Hendon Coll. of Technol., 1968–73; Hd, Dept of Humanities and Dean of Humanities, Middx Poly., 1973–86; Dep. Dir (Acad. Planning), Wolverhampton Poly., 1986–89; Dir, Derbys Coll. of Higher Educn, 1989–92. Chairman: Derbyshire Careers Service Ltd, 1995–2001; High Peak Rural Action Zone, 2003–05. FRSA 1993. DUniv Middlesex; Derby 2006. Name inscribed in Keren Hakayemet (Jewish Nat. Fund) Golden Book, 2004. *Publications:* A Heidegger Critique, 1981; jl articles on modern European philosophy, higher educn, credit accumulation and transfer. *Recreation:* wood-turning.

WATERHOUSE, Sir Ronald (Gough), GBE 2002; Kt 1978; Judge of the High Court of Justice, Family Division, 1978–88, Queen's Bench Division, 1988–96; *b* Holywell, Flintshire, 8 May 1926; *s* of late Thomas Waterhouse, CBE, and Doris Helena Waterhouse (*née* Gough); *m* 1960, Sarah Selina, *d* of late Captain E. A. Ingram and Diana Mary Ingram (*née* Leigh-Bennett); one *s* two *d*. *Educ:* Holywell Grammar Sch.; St John's Coll., Cambridge. RAFVR, 1944–48. McMahon Schol., St John's Coll., 1949; Pres., Cambridge Union Soc., 1950; MA, LLM; called to Bar, Middle Temple, 1952 (Harmsworth Schol.), Bencher, 1977, Treas., 1995; Wales and Chester Circuit, Leader, 1978; QC 1969; a Recorder of the Crown Court, 1972–77; Presiding Judge, Wales and Chester Circuit, 1980–84; a Judge, Employment Appeal Tribunal, 1979–87. Mem. Bar Council, 1961–65. Deputy Chairman: Cheshire QS, 1964–71; Flintshire QS, 1966–71. Contested (Lab) West Flintshire, 1959. Chairman: Inter-departmental Cttee of Inquiry on Rabies, 1970; Cttees of Investigation for GB and England and Wales, under Agricultural Mkting Act, 1971–78; Local Govt Boundary Commn for Wales, 1974–78; Tribunal of Inquiry into Child Abuse in N Wales Children's Homes, 1996–2000. Ind. Supervisory Authy for Hunting, 2000–05. Pres., CAB, Royal Courts of Justice, 1992–98 (Chm., 1981–92). A Vice-Pres., Zoological Soc. of London, 1981–84 and 1992–93 (Mem. Council, 1972–89, 1991–93). President: Llangollen Internat. Musical Eisteddfod, 1994–97; St John's Wood Soc., 1994–96. Hon. LLD Wales, 1986. *Recreations:* music, reading. *Address:* Greystone House, Walford, Ross-on-Wye, Herefordshire HR9 5RJ. *Clubs:* Garrick, Pilgrims, MCC; Cardiff and County (Cardiff).

See also J. B. Thompson.

WATERLOW, Anthony John; Chairman and Managing Director, Kodak, 1992–97; *b* 14 July 1938; *s* of George Joseph Waterlow and Sylvia Netta Waterlow; *m* 1st, 1962, Sheila; three *s*; 2nd, 1992, Ann. *Educ:* Harrow County Grammar Sch.; Ealing College; Chartered Inst. of Management Accountants. Joined Kodak as accountant trainee, 1954. *Recreation:* bridge. *Address:* c/o Kodak Ltd, Kodak House, Hemel Hempstead, Herts HP1 1JU.

WATERLOW, Sir Christopher Rupert, 5th Bt *cr* 1873; Lighting Cameraman, QVC, The Shopping Channel; *b* 12 Aug. 1959; *s* of (Peter) Rupert Waterlow (*d* 1969) and Jill Elizabeth (*d* 1961), *e d* of E. T. Gourlay; *S* grandfather, 1973; *m* 2003, Nicola Louise, *yr d* of Robert McDonald, Petts Wood, Kent. *Educ:* Stonyhurst Coll., Lancs; Ravensbourne Coll. (HND Professional Broadcasting Technical Ops, 1999). Fellow and Assessment Officer, Inst. of Videography; Mem., Guild of Television Cameramen. *Recreations:* playing and listening to music, supporting Wasps RFC. *Heir: cousin* Nicholas Anthony Waterlow [*b* 30 Aug. 1941; *m* 1965, Rosemary (*d* 1998), *o d* of W. J. O'Brien; two *s* one *d*]. *Address:* 78 Portland Road, Bromley, Kent BR1 5AZ. *Club:* Stonyhurst Association.

WATERLOW, Sir (James) Gerard, 4th Bt *cr* 1930; former management consultant; *b* 3 Sept. 1939; *s* of Sir Thomas Gordon Waterlow, 3rd Bt, CBE and Helen Elizabeth (*d* 1970), *yr d* of Gerard A. H. Robinson; *S* father, 1982; *m* 1965, Diana Suzanne, *yr d* of Sir Thomas Skyrme, KCVO, CB, CBE, TD and Hon. (Barbara) Suzanne Lyle, *yr d* of 1st Baron Lyle of Westbourne; one *s* one *d*. *Educ:* Marlborough; Trinity College, Cambridge. *Recreations:* tennis, bridge. *Heir: s* (Thomas) James Waterlow [*b* 20 March 1970; *m* 1999, Theresa, *y d* of Captain Francis Walsh; two *d*]. *Address:* Rushall Lodge, Pewsey, Wilts SN9 6EN. *Club:* Lansdowne.

WATERLOW, Prof. John Conrad, CMG 1970; MD, ScD; FRCP; FRS 1982; FRGS; Professor of Human Nutrition, London School of Hygiene and Tropical Medicine, 1970–82, now Emeritus; *b* 13 June 1916; *o s* of Sir Sydney Waterlow, KCMG, CBE, HM Diplomatic Service; *m* 1939, Angela Pauline Cecil Gray; two *s* one *d*. *Educ:* Eton Coll.; Trinity Coll., Cambridge (MD, ScD); London Hosp. Med. College. Mem., Scientific Staff, MRC, 1942; Dir, MRC Tropical Metabolism Research Unit, Univ. of the West Indies, 1954–70. For. Associate Mem., Nat. Acad. of Scis, USA, 1992. *Publications:* numerous papers on protein malnutrition and protein metabolism. *Recreation:* mountain walking. *Address:* 15 Hillgate Street, W8 7SP. *Club:* Savile.

See also S. J. Broadie.

WATERMAN, Adrian Mark; QC 2006; a Recorder, since 2003; *b* 24 March 1964; *s* of Brian and Pamela Waterman; *m* 1992, Dr Amanda Jones; one *s* one *d*. *Educ:* King Edward VI Sch., Stourbridge; QMC, Univ. of London (LLB Hons). Called to the Bar, Inner Temple, 1988. *Recreations:* music, movies, reading, cycling. *Address:* c/o KBW Chambers, 3 Park Court, Leeds LS1 2QH.

WATERMAN, Dame Fanny, DBE 2005 (CBE 2000; OBE 1971); FRCM; Chairman, Leeds International Pianoforte Competition, since 1963, also Chairman of Jury, since 1981; *b* 22 March 1920; *d* of Myer Waterman and Mary Waterman (*née* Behrmann); *m* 1944, Dr Geoffrey Michael de Keyser (*d* 2001); two *s*. *Educ:* Allerton High Sch., Leeds; Tobias Matthay, Cyril Smith, Royal College of Music, London (FRCM 1972). Concert pianist, teacher of international reputation. Vice-President: European Piano-Teachers Assoc., 1975–; World Fedn of Internat. Music Competitions, 1992–2000; Trustee, Edward Boyle Meml Trust, 1981–96. Governor, Harrogate Fest., 1983–99; Vice-Pres., Harrogate Internat. Fest., 1999–. Founded (with Marion Harewood) Leeds International

Pianoforte Competition, 1961. Member of International Juries: Beethoven, Vienna, 1977, 1993; Casagrande, Terni, 1978, 1994; Munich, 1979, 1986; Bach, Leipzig, 1980, 1984, 1988; Calgary, 1982; Gina Bachauer, Salt Lake City, 1982, 1984; Viña del Mar (Chm.), 1982, 1987, 1992; Maryland, 1983; Cologne, 1983, 1986, 1989, 1996; Pretoria, 1984, 1992; Santander, 1984; Rubinstein, Israel (Vice-Pres.), 1986, 1989; Tchaikowsky, Moscow, 1986; Vladigerov, Bulgaria, 1986; Lisbon, 1987, 1991; Canadian Broadcasting Corp., Toronto, 1989; first Internat. Pianoforte Competitions, China, 1994, and Korea, 1995; Casagrande, Italy, 2002; Hong Kong (Asia) Piano Open Comp., 2005 (Chm.); Clara Haskil Comp., 2005; International Piano Competitions: Horowitz, 2005; Chopin, 2005; Dublin, 2006; Hamamatsu, 2006. Piano Progress series on ITV Channel 4. Hon. MA 1966, Hon. DMus 1992, Leeds; DUniv York, 1995. Hon. Freeman, City of Leeds, 2004. Dist. Musician Award, ISM, 2000; World Fedn of Internat. Comps Lifetime Achievement Award, 2002; Yorks Soc. Lifetime Achievement Award, 2003. *Publications:* (with Marion Harewood): series of Piano Tutors, 1967–: 1st Year Piano lessons: 1st Year Repertoire; 2nd Year Piano lessons: 2nd Year Repertoire; 3rd Year Piano lessons: 3rd Year Repertoire; Duets and Piano Playtime, 1978; Recital Book for pianists, Book 1, 1981; Sonatina and Sonata Book, 1982; Four Study Books for Piano (Playtime Studies and Progress Studies), 1986; (with Paul de Keyser) Young Violinists Repertoire books, 1–4; Fanny Waterman on Piano Playing and Performing, 1983; Music Lovers Diary, 1984–86; Merry Christmas Carols, 1986; Christmas Carol Time, 1986; Nursery Rhyme Time, 1987; Piano for Pleasure, Bks 1 and 2, 1988; Me and my Piano series, Book 1, 1988, Book 2, 1989, repertoire and duets, Books 1 and 2, 1992, superscales for the young pianist, 1995; Animal Magic, 1989; Monkey Puzzles, Books 1 and 2, 1990; (with Wendy Thompson) Piano Competition: the story of the Leeds, 1990; Young Pianist's Dictionary, 1992. *Recreations:* travel, reading, voluntary work, cooking. *Address:* Woodgarth, Oakwood Grove, Leeds LS8 2PA. *T:* (0113) 265 5771.

WATERMAN, Peter Alan, OBE 2005; record producer; Chairman, PWL Empire, since 1983; *b* 15 Jan. 1947; *s* of John Waterman and Stella Waterman; *m* 1st, 1970, Elizabeth Reynolds (marr. diss. 1974); (one *s* decd); 2nd, 1980, Julie Reeves (marr. diss. 1984); one *s*; 3rd, 1991, Denise Gyngell (marr. diss. 2000); two *d*. *Educ:* Frederick Bird Secondary Sch. Disc jockey at local pubs and Mecca dance hall, 1961–83; arts and repertoire man for various record cos, 1973–; formed Loose Ends Prodns with Peter Collins, 1977–83; Founder Partner with M. Stock and M. Aitken, Stock Aitken Waterman, 1984–93. Judge, TV series, Pop Idol, 2000, 2003. Has produced numerous charity records. Waterman Railway Trust formed 1994. Hon. DBA Coventry, 2001; Hon. DMus Liverpool, 2004. Awards for songwriting and for records produced include: BPI Best British Producer Award, 1988; Music Week Top Producers Award, 1987, 1988 and 1989; Ivor Novello Award, 1987, 1988 and 1989. *Publication:* I Wish I Was Me: Pete Waterman (autobiog.), 2000. *Recreation:* railways: models and the real thing. *Address:* (office) Open Studios, County Hall, Belvedere Road, SE1 7PB.

WATERPARK, 7th Baron *cr* 1792; **Frederick Caryll Philip Cavendish**; Bt 1755; Director, D. T. Dobie (East Africa) Ltd, 1995–2000; *b* 6 Oct. 1926; *s* of Brig.-General Frederick William Laurence Sheppard Hart Cavendish, CMG, DSO (*d* 1931) and Enid, Countess of Kenmare (she *m* 3rd, 1933, as his 3rd wife, 1st Viscount Furness, who *d* 1940; 4th, as his 2nd wife, 6th Earl of Kenmare), *d* of Charles Lindeman, Sydney, New South Wales, and *widow* of Roderick Cameron, New York; *S* uncle, 1948; *m* 1951, Daniele, *e d* of Roger Guirche, Paris; one *s* two *d*. *Educ:* Eton. Lieut, 4th and 1st Bn Grenadier Guards, 1944–46. Served as Assistant District Commandant Kenya Police Reserve, 1952–55, during Mau Mau Rebellion. Man. Dir, Spartan Air Services, 1955–60; Dep. Chm. and Man. Dir, CSE International Ltd, 1984–90; Dep. Chm., 1984–90, Chief Exec., 1990, CSE Aviation Ltd; Director: Handley Page Ltd, 1968–70; Airborn Group plc, 1990–93. Trustee, RAF Mus., 1994–2000. Founder Mem., Air Sqdn. *Heir: s* Hon. Roderick Alexander Cavendish [*b* 10 Oct. 1959; *m* 1989, Anne, *d* of Hon. Luke Asquith; two *s*]. *Club:* Cavalry and Guards.

WATERS, Alan Victor; HM Diplomatic Service, retired; High Commissioner, Solomon Islands, 1998–2001; *b* 10 April 1942; *s* of late George and Ruth Waters; *m* 1977, Elizabeth Ann Newman; one *s* one *d*. *Educ:* Judd Sch., Tonbridge. Joined CO, 1958, CRO, 1961; Freetown, 1963–66; UKDEL to ECSC, Luxembourg, 1967–68; Prague, 1968–70; Anguilla, 1970–71; Peking, 1971–73; FCO, 1973–76; Second Secretary: Kinshasa, 1976–80; Bombay, 1980–83; FCO, 1984–86; First Secretary: FCO, 1986–87; Copenhagen, 1987–91; FCO, 1991–95; acting Adminr, Tristan da Cunha, 1995–96; First Sec., Islamabad, 1996–98. *Recreations:* walking, cricket, golf, philately.

WATERS, Gen. Sir (Charles) John, GCB 1995 (KCB 1988); CBE 1981 (OBE 1977); DL; Deputy Supreme Allied Commander, Europe, 1993–94; Aide-de-Camp General to The Queen, 1992–95; *b* 2 Sept. 1935; *s* of Patrick George Waters and Margaret Ronaldson Waters (*née* Clark); *m* 1962, Hilary Doyle Nettleton; three *s*. *Educ:* Oundle; Royal Military Academy, Sandhurst. Commissioned, The Gloucestershire Regt, 1955; GSO2, MO1 (MoD), 1970–72; Instructor, GSO1 (DS), Staff Coll., Camberley, 1973–74; Commanding Officer, 1st Bn, Gloucestershire Regt, 1975–77; Colonel General Staff, 1st Armoured Div., 1977–79; Comdr 3 Infantry Bde, 1979–81; RCDS 1982; Dep. Comdr, Land Forces, Falkland Islands, May–July 1982; Comdr 4th Armoured Div., 1983–85; Comdt, Staff Coll., Camberley, 1986–88; GOC and Dir of Ops, NI, 1988–90; C-in-C, UKLF, 1990–93. Col, The Gloucestershire Regt, 1985–91; Col Comdt, POW Div., 1988–91; Hon. Colonel: Royal Wessex Yeomanry, 1991–97; Royal Devonshire Yeomanry, 1991–97. President: (Army) Officers' Assoc., 1997–2006; Devon RBL, 1998–2002. Mem. Adv. Council, Victory Meml Mus., Arlon, Belgium 1989–97; Mem. Council, Cheltenham Coll., 1991–2002; Chm. Council, Nat. Army Mus., 1997–2005; Gov., Colyton Primary Sch., 1997–2003. Pres., Honiton and Dist Agricl Assoc., 2004–05; Patron, Royal Albert Meml Mus., Exeter, 2006–. Admiral: Army Sailing Assoc., 1990–93; Infantry Sailing Assoc., 1990–93. Kermit Roosevelt Lectr, USA, 1992. FRSA 1993. JP: Axminster and Honiton, 1998; Central Devon, 1998–2006; DL Devon, 2001. *Recreations:* sailing, ski-ing, painting, gardening. *Address:* c/o Lloyds TSB, Colyton, Devon EX13 6JS. *Clubs:* Army and Navy; British Keil Yacht.

WATERS, David Ebsworth Benjamin; QC 1999; a Recorder, since 1990; *b* 24 April 1945; *s* of William Thomas Ebsworth Waters and Esther Jane Waters; *m* 1996, Sonia Jayne Bound. *Educ:* Greenhill Grammar Sch., Tenby. Admitted Solicitor, 1969; called to the Bar, Middle Temple, 1973; Junior Treasury Counsel, 1989–94, Sen. Treasury Counsel, 1994–99, CCC. *Recreations:* golf, fishing. *Address:* 2 Hare Court, Temple, EC4Y 7BH. *T:* (020) 7353 3982. *Clubs:* MCC; Royal Wimbledon Golf, Woking Golf.

WATERS, David Watkin; Lt-Comdr RN; *b* 2 Aug. 1911; *s* of Eng. Lt William Waters, RN, and Jessie Rhena (*née* Whitemore); *m* 1946, Hope Waters (*née* Pritchard); one step *s* one step *d*. *Educ:* RN Coll., Dartmouth. Joined RN, 1925; Cadet and Midshipman, HMS Barham, 1929; specialised in Aviation (Pilot), 1935. Served War of 1939–45: Fleet Air Arm, Malta (PoW, Italy, Germany, 1940–45). Admlty, 1946–50; retd, 1950. Admlty Historian (Defence of Shipping), 1946–60; Head of Dept of Navigation and Astronomy, Nat. Maritime Museum, 1960–76, and Sec. of Museum, 1968–71; Dep. Dir, 1971–78.

Pres., British Soc. for Hist. of Sci., 1976–78 (Vice-Pres., 1972–74, 1978–81). Vis. Prof. of History, Simon Fraser Univ., Burnaby, BC, 1978; Regents' Prof., UCLA, 1979; Caird Res. Fellow, Nat. Maritime Museum, 1979–83; Alexander O. Victor Res. Fellow, John Carter Brown Library, Brown Univ., Providence, RI, 1990. Chm., Japan Animal Welfare Soc., 1972–80. Gold Medal, Admiralty Naval History, 1936, and Special Award, 1946; FRHistS 1951; Fellow, Inst. Internacional da Cultura Portuguesa, 1966; FSA 1970. Hon. Fellow, Royal Inst. of Navigation, 1989 (Fellow 1959); Hon. Member: Scientific Instrument Soc., 1989; Acad. de Marinha Portuguesa, 1989; Soc. for Nautical Res., 1996. *Publications:* The True and Perfect Newes of Syr Francis Drake, 1955; (with F. Barley) Naval Staff History, Second World War, Defeat of the Enemy Attack on Shipping, 1939–1945, 1957, 2nd edn 1997; The Art of Navigation in England in Elizabethan and Early Stuart Times, 1958, 2nd edn 1978; The Sea—or Mariner's Astrolabe, 1966; The Rutter of the Sea, 1967; (with Hope Waters) The Saluki in History, Art, and Sport, 1969, 2nd edn 1984; (with G. P. B. Naish) The Elizabethan Navy and the Armada of Spain, 1975; Science and the Techniques of Navigation in the Renaissance, 1976; (with Thomas R. Adams) English Maritime Books relating to ships and their construction and operation at sea printed before 1801, 1995; contrib.: Jl RIN; RUSI; Mariners' Mirror; American Neptune; Jl RN Scientific Service; Jl British Soc. of History of Science; Navy International; Revista da Universidade de Coímbra. *Recreations:* maritime history, history of technology (medieval, Renaissance and Scientific Revolution, and Chinese sailing craft). *Address:* Gatekeeper's Lodge, Rhodes Road, Otahuna Valley, RD2 Christchurch, New Zealand. *Club:* English-Speaking Union.

WATERS, Donald Henry, OBE 1994; CA; Chief Executive, 1987–97, and Deputy Chairman, 1993–97, Grampian Television PLC; *b* 17 Dec. 1937; *s* of late Henry Lethbridge Waters, WS, and Jean Manson Baxter; *m* 1962, June Leslie, *d* of late Andrew Hutchison; one *s* two *d*. *Educ:* George Watson's, Edinburgh; Inverness Royal Acad. Mem. ICA(Scot.) 1961; CA 1961. Dir, John M. Henderson and Co. Ltd, 1972–75; Grampian Television: Company Sec., 1975; Dir of Finance, 1979. Chairman: Glenburnie Properties, 1993–97 (Dir, 1976–93); Central Scotland Radio Ltd, 1994–96; Director: Scottish TV and Grampian Sales Ltd, 1980–98; Blenheim Travel, 1981–91; Moray Firth Radio, 1982–97; Independent Television Publications Ltd, 1987–90; Cablevision (Scotland) PLC, 1987–91; GRT Bus Group, 1994–96; British Linen Bank, 1995–99; British Linen Bank Gp, 1995–99; Aberdeen Royal Hosp. NHS Trust, 1996–99; Scottish Post Office Bd, 1996–2003; Digital 3 and 4 Ltd, 1997–98; Scottish Media Group plc, 1997–2005; James Johnston of Elgin Ltd, 1999–; North Bd, Bank of Scotland, 1999–2001; Aberdeen Asset Mgt plc, 2000–. Vis. Prof. of Film and Media Studies, Stirling Univ., 1991–. Mem., BAFTA, 1980– (Scottish Vice Chm., 1992–); Chm., Celtic Film and Television Assoc., 1994–96 (Trustee for Scotland, 1990–96); Dir, ITVA, 1994–97. Mem. Council, CBI Scotland, 1994–2001. Chairman: Police Dependent Trust, Aberdeen, 1991–96; Project Steering Gp, New Royal Aberdeen Children's Hosp., 1999–2002; Jt Chm., Grampian Cancer MacMillan Appeal, 1999–2003; Member: Council, Cinema and Television Benevolent Fund, 1986–99; Grampian & Islands Family Trust, 1986–2005. Gov., Univ. of Aberdeen, 1998–99. Burgess of Guild, Aberdeen, 1979– (Assessor, 1998–2001). FRTS 1998 (Mem., 1988); FRSA 1990. *Recreations:* gardening, travel, hill-walking. *Address:* Balquhidder, Milltimber, Aberdeen AB13 0JS. *T:* (01224) 867131; *e-mail:* donaldwaters@btinternet.com. *Club:* Royal Northern and University (Aberdeen) (Chm., 1987–88).

WATERS, Emily; *see* Watson, E.

WATERS, Gen. Sir John; *see* Waters, Gen. Sir C. J.

WATERS, Keith Stuart, FCA; Clerk, Fishmongers' Company, since 1994 (Assistant Clerk, 1987–93); *b* 18 March 1951; *s* of late Thomas Charles Waters and of Elsie Lillian (*née* Addison); *m* 1976, Elizabeth Jane Weeks; one *s* two *d*. *Educ:* Leigh GS; Wigan Tech. Coll.; Univ. of Newcastle upon Tyne (BA 1973). FCA 1976. Deloitte Haskins & Sells, Manchester, 1973–77; audit senior, Peat Marwick Mitchell, Kingston, Jamaica, 1978; with Price Waterhouse: audit senior, Miami, Fla, 1979–80; Manager, Melbourne, Aust., 1980–82; Sen. Manager, London, 1982–85; Gp Financial Accountant, Guinness plc, 1985–87. Chm., Livery Cos Mutual Ltd, 1999–. Clerk to Govs, Gresham's Sch., Holt, 1993–; Sec., Bd of Trustees, City and Guilds of London Art Sch., 1993–. *Recreations:* theatre, concerts, ballet, tennis, watersports, running, food and wine. *Address:* The Cow Shed, Bard Hill, Salthouse, Norfolk NR25 7XB. *T:* (01263) 740227.

WATERS, Malcolm Ian; QC 1997; *b* 11 Oct. 1953; *s* of late Ian Power Waters and Yvonne Waters (*née* Mosley); *m* 2002, Setsuko Sato. *Educ:* Whitgift Sch.; St Catherine's Coll., Oxford (MA, BCL). Called to the Bar, Lincoln's Inn, 1977; in practice, 1978–. *Publications:* (jtly) The Building Societies Act 1986, 1987; (ed jtly) Wurtzburg & Mills, Building Society Law, 15th edn, 1989 (with annual updates); (ed jtly) The Law of Investor Protection, 2nd edn, 2003; (Cons. Ed.) Friendly Societies, 2007, Mutual Societies, 2008, Halsbury's Laws of England. *Recreations:* music, opera. *Address:* Radcliffe Chambers, 11 New Square, Lincoln's Inn, WC2A 3QB. *T:* (020) 7831 0081.

WATERS, Sarah, PhD; author, since 1995; *b* 21 July 1966; *d* of Ron and Mary Waters. *Educ:* Univ. of Kent (BA Hons English and American Lit. 1987); Univ. of Lancaster (MA Contemp. Literary Studies 1988); Queen Mary and Westfield Coll., London (PhD 1995). Tutor, Open Univ., 1996–2000. *Publications:* Tipping the Velvet, 1998 (televised 2002); Affinity, 1999; Fingersmith, 2002 (televised 2005); The Night Watch, 2006. *Recreations:* cinema, theatre. *Address:* c/o Greene & Heaton (Authors' Agents) Ltd, 37 Goldhawk Road, W12 8QQ. *T:* (020) 8749 0315.

WATERS, Sir (Thomas) Neil (Morris), Kt 1995; PhD; DSc; FRSNZ; Vice-Chancellor, Massey University, 1983–95, now Emeritus Professor; *b* New Plymouth, 10 April 1931; *s* of Edwin Benjamin Waters and Kathleen Emily (*née* Morris); *m* 1959, Joyce Mary (ONZM 2006), *d* of Ven. T. H. C. Partridge. *Educ:* Auckland Univ. (BSc 1953; MSc 1954; PhD 1958; DSc 1969); FNZIC 1977; FRSNZ 1982. Sen. Res. Fellow, UKAEA, 1958–60; Auckland University: Lectr in Chemistry, 1961–62; Sen. Lectr, 1963–65; Associate Prof., 1966–69; Prof., 1970–83, Emeritus Prof., 1984–; Asst Vice-Chancellor, 1979–81; Acting Vice-Chancellor, 1980. Visiting Scientist: Univ. of Oxford, 1964, 1971; Northwestern Univ., Illinois, 1976. Chm., NZ Vice-Chancellors' Cttee, 1985–86, 1994 (Mem., 1983–95). Hon. DSc East Asia, Macao, 1988; Hon. DLitt Massey, 1995. *Address:* Box 25–463, St Heliers, Auckland 1740, New Zealand.

WATERSON, Prof. Michael John, PhD; Professor of Economics, University of Warwick, since 1991; *b* 29 July 1950; *s* of Geoffrey and Christine Mary Waterson; *m* 1972, Sally Ann Davis; one *s* one *d*. *Educ:* Univ. of Warwick (BA 1971; PhD 1977); London Sch. of Econs (MSc Econ 1972). Lectr in Econs, 1974–86, Reader in Econs, 1986–88, Univ. of Newcastle upon Tyne; Prof. of Econs, Univ. of Reading, 1988–91. Gen. Ed., Jl Industrial Econs, 1994–99. Mem., UK Competition Commn, 2005–. Specialist Advr, H of L Subcttee B, 2005, 2006. Chm., Utilities Appeals Panel, States of Guernsey, 2002–07. Pres., Eur. Assoc. for Res. in Industrial Econs, 1999–2001. FRSA 1989. *Publications:* Economic Theory of the Industry, 1984; Regulation of the Firm and Natural Monopoly, 1988; (jtly) Buyer Power and Competition in European Food Retailing, 2002; contrib. jls incl. Amer. Econ. Rev., Qly Jl Econs, Econ. Jl, Eur. Econ. Rev. *Recreations:* walking, playing musical instruments, travel. *Address:* Department of Economics, University of Warwick, Coventry CV4 7AL. *T:* (024) 7652 3427, *Fax:* (024) 7652 3032; *e-mail:* michael.waterson@warwick.ac.uk.

WATERSON, Nigel Christopher; MP (C) Eastbourne, since 1992; *b* 12 Oct. 1950; *s* of James Waterson and Katherine (*née* Mahon); *m* 1999, Dr Barbara Judge. *Educ:* Leeds Grammar Sch.; Queen's Coll., Oxford (MA Jurisprudence); College of Law. Called to the Bar, Gray's Inn, 1973; admitted solicitor, 1979. Pres., Oxford Univ. Cons. Assoc., 1970. Res. Asst to Sally Oppenheim, MP, 1972–73. Cllr, London Borough of Hammersmith, 1974–78. Chairman: Bow Gp, 1986–87 (Hon. Patron, 1993–95); Hammersmith Cons. Assoc., 1987–90; Hammersmith and Fulham Jt Management Cttee, 1988–90; Member: Cons. Gtr London Area Exec. Cttee, 1990–91; Soc. of Cons. Lawyers Exec. Cttee, 1993–97; Conservative Political Centre: Mem., Adv. Cttee, 1986–90; Mem., Gtr London Gen. Purposes Cttee, 1990–91. PPS to Minister of State, DoH, 1995, to Dep. Prime Minister, 1996–97; an Opposition Whip, 1997–99; Opposition spokesman on local govt and housing, 1999–2001, on trade and industry, 2001–02, on pensions, 2003–. Mem., Select Cttee on Nat. Heritage, 1995–96; Vice Chairman: Cons. Backbench Tourism Cttee, 1992–97; Cons. Backbench Transport Cttee, 1992–97; Sec., Cons. Backbench Shipping and Shipbuilding Cttee, 1992–97; Vice Chairman: All-Party Daylight Extra Gp, 1993–97; All-Party British Greek Gp, 1993–; Sec., British Cyprus Gp, CPA, 1992–. Member: London West European Constituency Council, 1987–91; Management Cttee, Stonham Housing Assoc. Hostel for Ex-Offenders, 1988–90. *Publications:* papers on an Alternative Manifesto, 1973, the future of Hong Kong, and on shipping. *Recreations:* walking on Downs, reading, music. *Address:* House of Commons, SW1A 0AA. *Clubs:* Coningsby; Eastbourne Constitutional.

WATERSTON, Dr Charles Dewar, FRSE; formerly Keeper of Geology, Royal Scottish Museum; *b* 15 Feb. 1925; *s* of Allan Waterston and Martha Dewar (*née* Robertson); *m* 1965, Marjory Home Douglas. *Educ:* Highgate Sch., London; Univ. of Edinburgh (BSc 1st Cl. Hons 1947; Vans Dunlop Scholar, PhD 1949; DSc 1980). FRSE 1958. Asst Keeper, Royal Scottish Museum, 1950–63, Keeper, 1963–85. Member: Scottish Cttee, Nature Conservancy, 1969–73; Adv. Cttee for Scotland, Nature Conservancy Council, 1974–82; Chairman's Cttee, 1978–80, Exec. Cttee, 1980–82, Council for Museums and Galleries in Scotland; Adv. Cttee on Sites of Special Scientific Interest, 1992–95; Gen. Sec., RSE, 1986–91 (Mem. Council, 1967–70; Vice-Pres., 1980–83; Sec., 1985–86); Hon. Sec., Edinburgh Geol Soc., 1953–58 (Pres., 1969–71). Chm., Judges Panel, Scottish Mus. of Year Award, 1999–2000. Keith Prize, 1969–71, Bicentenary Medal, 1992, RSE; Clough Medal, Edinburgh Geol Soc., 1984–85; (first) A. G. Brighton Medal, Geol Curators' Gp, 1992. *Publications:* (with G. Y. Craig and D. B. McIntyre) James Hutton's Theory of the Earth: the lost drawings, 1978; (with H. E. Stace and C. W. A. Pettitt) Natural Science Collections in Scotland, 1987; Collections in Context, 1997; (with D. Guthrie) The Royal Society Club of Edinburgh 1820–2000, 1999; (with A. Macmillan Shearer) Biographical Index of Former Fellows of the Royal Society of Edinburgh 1783–2002, 2 vols, 2006; Perth Entrepreneurs: the Sandemans of Springland, 2008; technical papers in scientific jls, chiefly relating to extinct arthropods and the history of geology. *Address:* 9/7 Trinity Way, East Trinity Road, Edinburgh EH5 3PY.

WATERSTONE, David George Stuart, CBE 1991; UK Chairman, Ansaldo Ltd, 1995–98; Chairman, ADAS Holdings Ltd, 1997–98; *b* 9 Aug. 1935; *s* of Malcolm Waterstone and Sylvia Sawday; *m* 1st, 1960, Dominique Viriot (marr. diss.); one *s* two *d*; 2nd, 1988, Sandra Packer (*née* Willey). *Educ:* Tonbridge; St Catharine's Coll., Cambridge (MA). HM Diplomatic Service, 1959–70; Sen. Exec., IRC, 1970–71; BSC, 1971–81: Board Mem., 1976–81; Man. Dir, Commercial, 1972–77; subseq. Executive Chairman, BSC Chemicals, 1977–81, and Redpath Dorman Long, 1977–81; Chief Exec., Welsh Develt Agency, 1983–90; Chief Exec., Energy and Technical Services Gp plc, 1990–95. Director: Portsmouth and Sunderland Newspapers, 1983–99; Hunting, 1995–2000; Precoat Internat., 1995–2003. Chm., Combined Heat and Power Assoc., 1993–95. *Publications:* (ed) Waste in Wales: a national resource, 2000; (ed) World Best Practice in Economic Development, 2002. *Recreations:* sailing, walking, painting, furniture making. *Address:* 1 Prior Park Buildings, Prior Park Road, Bath BA2 4NP. *T:* (01225) 427346. *Club:* Reform.

See also T. J. S. Waterstone.

WATERSTONE, Timothy John Stuart; Founder, Waterstone's Booksellers, 1982; *b* 30 May 1939; *s* of Malcolm Waterstone and Sylvia Sawday; *m* 1st, Patricia Harcourt-Poole (marr. diss.); two *s* one *d*; 2nd, Clare Perkins (marr. diss.); one *s* two *d*; 3rd, Mary Rose, (Rosie), *d* of Rt Hon. Michael Alison, PC and of Sylvia (*née* Haigh); two *d*. *Educ:* Tonbridge; St Catharine's College, Cambridge (MA). Carritt Moran, Calcutta, 1962–64; Allied Breweries, 1964–73; W. H. Smith, 1973–81; Founder, Chm. and Chief Exec., Waterstone's Booksellers Ltd, 1982–93; Dep. Chm., Sinclair-Stevenson Ltd, 1989–92; Chairman: Priory Investments Ltd, 1990–95; Golden Rose Radio (London Jazz FM), 1992–93; Founder and Exec. Chm., Chelsea Stores Ltd (Daisy & Tom), 1996–2007 (acquired Early Learning Centre Hldgs, 2004); Founder Chm., HMV Media Gp plc (merged businesses of Waterstone's and HMV), 1998–2001; Member of Board: Yale Univ. Press, 1992–; Future Start, 1992–; Virago Press., 1995–96; Hill Samuel UK Emerging Cos Investment Trust PLC, 1996–2000; National Gallery Co. Ltd, 1996–2003; Downing Classic VCT, 1998–2003. Chm., DTI Working Gp on Smaller Quoted Cos and Private Investors, 1999. Chm., Shelter 25th Anniversary Appeal Cttee, 1991–92. Member: Bd of Trustees, English International (Internat. House), 1987–92; Bd, London Philharmonic Orch., 1990–97 (Trustee, 1995–98); Portman House Trust, 1994–96; Chairman: Acad. of Ancient Music, 1990–95; London Internat. Festival of Theatre, 1991–92; Elgar Foundn, 1992–98; Library Bd, KCL, 2000–02; Vis. Cttee, Cambridge Univ. Library, 2007–. Co-Founder BOOKAID, 1992–93. Adv. Mem., Booker Prize Management Cttee, 1986–93; Chm. of Judges, Prince's Youth Business Trust Awards, 1990. Chancellor, Napier Univ., 2007–. *Publications: novels:* Lilley & Chase, 1994; An Imperfect Marriage, 1995; A Passage of Lives, 1996; *non-fiction:* Swimming Against the Stream, 2006. *Recreation:* talking with Rosie Alison. *Address:* 64 Portland Road, W11 4LQ. *Club:* Garrick.

See also D. G. S. Waterstone.

WATERWORTH, Sir Alan (William), KCVO 2007; JP; Lord-Lieutenant of Merseyside, 1993–2006 (Vice Lord-Lieutenant, 1989–93); *b* 22 Sept. 1931; *s* of late James and Alice Waterworth, Liverpool; *m* 1955, Myriam, *d* of late Edouard Baete and Magdelaine Baete, formerly of Brussels; three *s* one *d*. *Educ:* Uppingham Sch.; Trinity Coll., Cambridge (MA). National Service, commnd King's Regt, 1950. Waterworth Bros Ltd: progressively, Dir, Man. Dir, Chm., 1954–69. Gen. Comr, Inland Revenue, 1965–72. Dir, NHS Hosp. Trust, Liverpool, 1992–93. Member: Skelmersdale Develt Corp., 1971–85 (Dep. Chm., 1979–85); Merseyside Police Authority, 1984–92; Cttee, Merseyside Br., Inst. of Dirs, 1965–77 (Chm., 1974–77). Chm., IBA Adv. Cttee for Radio on Merseyside, 1975–78. Chairman: Liverpool Boys' Assoc., 1967–75; Merseyside Youth Assoc., 1971–75; Everton FC, 1973–76 (Dir, 1970–93). Mem. Council, Liverpool Univ.,

1993–2004. Trustee, Nat. Museums and Galls on Merseyside, 1994–2004. Mem. Council, Liverpool Cathedral, 2004–. JP Liverpool 1961 (Chm., Juvenile Panel, 1974–83; Chm. of Bench, 1985–89); DL Co. Merseyside 1986, High Sheriff, Co. Merseyside, 1992. Hon. Col, Merseyside Cadet Force, 1994–2007; Pres., RFCA, NW England and I of M, 2004–07. Hon. Fellow, Liverpool John Moores, 1995. Hon. LLD Liverpool, 2001. KStJ 1994. *Recreations:* local history, bibliomania. *Address:* Crewood Hall, Kingsley, Cheshire WA6 8HR. *T:* (01928) 788316. *Clubs:* Army and Navy; Athenæum, Artists' (Liverpool).

WATERWORTH, Peter Andrew; HM Diplomatic Service; Governor of Montserrat, since 2007; *b* 15 April 1957; *s* of Bobby and Betty Waterworth; *m* 1994, Catherine Margaret. *Educ:* Univ. of Durham (BA Hons); Downing Coll., Cambridge (LLB Hons 1982); Inns of Court Sch. of Law. Standing Adv. Commn on Human Rights, NI, 1979–81; called to the Bar; barrister, 1983–87; joined FCO, 1987; Asst Legal Advr, FCO, 1987–90; Legal Advr, Bonn, 1990–94; Middle Eastern Dept, FCO, 1994–96; First Sec., Rome, 1996–2000; NI Office, 2000–03; Pol Counsellor, Islamabad, 2003–05, Iraq, 2005; Dep. High Comr and Consul-Gen., Lagos, 2005–07. *Recreations:* ski-ing, football, cooking, golf, reading. *Address:* Government House, Montserrat, West Indies. *T:* 4912688, 4912689, *Fax:* 4918867; *e-mail:* Peter.Waterworth@fco.gov.uk.

WATES, Andrew Trace Allan; DL; Chairman: Wates Group (formerly Wates Ltd), 2000–06; Wates Family Holdings, since 2000; *b* 16 Nov. 1940; 4th *s* of Sir Ronald Wallace Wates and Phyllis Mary Wates (*née* Trace); *m* 1965, Sarah Mary de Burgh Macartney; four *s* (and one *s* decd). *Educ:* Oundle Sch.; Emmanuel Coll., Cambridge (BA Estate Mgt 1960). Joined Wates, 1964; Dir, Wates Construction, 1972–2000; Chairman: Wates Leisure Gp, later Pinnacle Leisure Gp, 1972–99; Wates Estate Agency Services, 1976–2000; Director: Wates Ltd, 1973–2000; Wates Hldgs, 1973–. Chairman: United Racecourses Ltd, 1996–; Leisure and Media plc, 2001–; Director: Racecourse Hldgs Trust, 1996; Fontwell Park plc, 1991–2001. Chm., Inst. for Family Business, 2007–. Vice-Chm., Bd of Mgt, Royal Albert and Alexandra Sch., 2000–. Mem., Jockey Club, 1977–. High Sheriff, Surrey, 2003–04; DL Surrey, 2006. *Recreations:* horse-racing, shooting, fishing, golf. *Address:* Henfold House, Beare Green, Dorking, Surrey RH5 4RW. *T:* (01306) 631324. *Clubs:* White's, Turf.

See also M. E. Wates, P. C. R. Wates.

WATES, Sir Christopher (Stephen), Kt 1989; BA; FCA; Chairman, Wates Holdings, 2000–05; Chief Executive, Wates Group (formerly Wates Building Group), 1984–2000; *b* 25 Dec. 1939; *s* of Norman Edward Wates and Margot Irene Sidwell; *m* 1965, Sandra Mouroutsos (marr. diss. 1975); three *d*; *m* 1992, Georgina Ferris McCallum. *Educ:* Stowe School; Brasenose College, Oxford (BA 1962; Rugby blue, 1961; Hon. Fellow, 1993). FCA 1975 (ACA 1965). Financial Director, Wates Ltd, 1970–76. Chm., Criterion Hldgs, 1981–96. Director: Electra Investment Trust, 1980–93; Equitable Life Assurance Society, 1983–94; Scottish Ontario Investment Co. Ltd, 1978–83; 3i Smaller Quoted Cos Trust (formerly North British Canadian Investment Co., then NB Smaller Cos Trust), 1983–98 (Chm., 1996–98); Wates City of London Properties plc, 1984–2000; Mem., 1980–89, Chm., 1983–89, English Industrial Estates Corp.; Chm., Keymer Brick & Tile Co. Ltd, 1985–89. A Church Comr, 1992–96. Gov. of Council, 1984–2006, Chm., 1997–, Goodenough Coll. (formerly London House for Overseas Graduates, then London Goodenough Trust) (Dep. Chm., 1989–96); Gov., Frewen Coll., 2004–06. Trustee: Chatham Historic Dockyard Trust, 1984–87; Science Museum, 1987–2002; Lambeth Palace Library, 1990–2005. Chm., Industrial Soc., 1998. FRSA 1988. Hon. Mem., RICS, 1990. *Address:* Tufton Place, Northiam, Rye, East Sussex TN31 6HL. *T:* (01797) 252125.

WATES, Michael Edward, CBE 1998; Chairman, Wates Group (formerly Wates Ltd), 1974–2000; *b* 19 June 1935; 2nd *s* of Sir Ronald Wallace Wates and Phyllis Mary Wates (*née* Trace); *m* 1959, Caroline Josephine Connolly; four *s* one *d*. *Educ:* Oundle School; Emmanuel College, Cambridge (MA); Harvard Business Sch. (PMD 1963). Served RM, 1953–55. Joined Wates 1959; Director: Wates Construction, 1963; Wates Built Homes, 1966. Mem., Nat. Housebuilding Council, 1974–80. Chm., British Bloodstock Agency plc, 1986–92; Member: Council, Thoroughbred Breeders Assoc., 1978–82 (Chm., 1980–82); Horserace Betting Levy Bd, 1987–90. King's College Hospital: Deleg., Sch. of Medicine and Dentistry, 1983–2004; Chm., Equipment Cttee, 1983–91; Special Trustee, 1985 (Chm., Trustees, 1985). Hon. FRIBA. *Address:* Manor House, Langton Long, Blandford Forum, Dorset DT11 9HS. *T:* (01258) 455241.

See also A. T. A. Wates, P. C. R. Wates.

WATES, Paul Christopher Ronald, FRICS; Managing Director, 1984–94, Chairman, 1994–2001, Wates City of London Properties plc; *b* 6 March 1938; 3rd *s* of Sir Ronald Wallace Wates and Phyllis Mary Wates (*née* Trace); *m* 1965, Annette Beatrice Therese Randag; three *s* three *d*. Chesterton & Sons, 1958–59; Nat. Service, 14th/20th King's Hussars, 1959–61; joined Wates Ltd, 1962; Director: Wates Gp, 1969–2006; Wates Holdings (formerly Wates Family Holdings), 1973–. Chm., C&G, 1991–99 (Vice Pres., 2006–; Hon. FCGI). Mem. Court, Clothworkers' Co. (Master, 2003). *Address:* Bellasis House, Mickleham, Dorking, Surrey RH5 6DH. *Clubs:* White's, Turf, Cavalry & Guards, MCC.

See also A. T. A. Wates, M. E. Wates.

WATHEN, Julian Philip Gerard; Chairman: Hall School Charitable Trust, 1972–97; City of London Endowment Trust for St Paul's Cathedral, 1983–2002; *b* 21 May 1923; *s* of late Gerard Anstruther Wathen, CIE, and Melicent Louis (*née* Buxton); *m* 1948 Priscilla Florence Wilson; one *s* two *d*. *Educ:* Harrow. Served War, 60th Rifles, 1942–46. Third Secretary, HBM Embassy, Athens, 1946–47. Barclays Bank DCO, 1948; Ghana Director, 1961–65; General Manager, 1966; Sen. Gen. Manager, Barclays Bank International, 1974; Vice Chm., 1976; Vice Chairman: Barclays Bank, 1979–84; Banque du Caire, Barclays International, 1976–83; Dep. Chm., Allied Arab Bank, 1977–84; Director: Barclays Australia International, 1973–84; Barclays Bank of Kenya, 1975–84; Mercantile & General Reinsurance Co., 1977–91. Pres., Royal African Soc., 1984–89 (Chm., 1978–84). Member Council: Goodenough Coll. (formerly London House for Overseas Graduates, then London Goodenough Trust), 1971–2001 (Vice-Chm., 1984–89); Book Aid Internat., 1988–; Governor: St Paul's Sch., 1981–99 (Chm., 1995–99); St Paul's Girls' Sch., 1981–2003; SOAS, 1983–92; Overseas Develt Inst., 1984–96; Dauntsey's Sch., 1985–2005; Abingdon Sch., 1985–95; Dep. Chm., Thomas Telford Sch., 1990–97. Mem. Cttee, GBA, 1986–94. Master, Mercers' Co., 1984–85. *Address:* Woodcock House, Owlpen, Dursley, Glos GL11 5BY. *T:* (01453) 860214. *Club:* Travellers.

WATHERSTON, John Anthony Charles, CBE 2005; Registrar of the Privy Council, 1998–2005; *b* 29 April 1944; *yr s* of Sir David Watherston, KBE, CMG and Lady Watherston; *m* 1976, Jane (*née* Chaytor), *widow* of John Atkinson; one *s*, and one step *s* one step *d*. *Educ:* Winchester Coll.; Christ Church, Oxford (BA Jurisp. 1966; MA 1970). Called to the Bar, Inner Temple, 1967; Lord Chancellor's Department: Legal Asst, 1970–74; Sec., Phillimore Cttee on Law of Contempt of Court, 1971–74; Sen. Legal Asst, 1974–80; Private Sec. to Lord Chancellor, 1975–77; Asst Solicitor (Grade 5), 1980–85, 1988–98; Sen. Crown Counsel, Attorney Gen.'s Chambers, Hong Kong, 1985–88. Consultant Registrar, Dubai Internat. Financial Centre Courts, 2005–06. Lay Reader, Chelsea Old Church, Dio. of London, 1995–; Mem., London Diocesan Synod, 2000–. *Publication:* (contrib.) Halsbury's Laws of England, vol. 10, 4th edn, 2002. *Club:* Reform.

See also Baron Freyberg.

WATKIN, Prof. David John, LittD; FSA; Fellow of Peterhouse, Cambridge, 1970–2008; Professor of History of Architecture, 2001–08, now Emeritus, University of Cambridge; *b* 7 April 1941; *o s* of late Thomas Charles and Vera Mary Watkin. *Educ:* Farnham Grammar Sch.; Trinity Hall, Cambridge (Exhibnr; BA (1st Cl. Hons Fine Arts Tripos); PhD; LittD 1994). University of Cambridge: Librarian, Fine Arts Faculty, 1967–72; University Lectr in History of Art, 1972–93; Head, Dept of History of Art, 1989–92; Reader in Hist. of Architecture, 1993–2001. Mem., Historic Bldgs Council for England, then Historic Bldgs Adv. Cttee, Historic Bldgs and Monuments Commn for England, 1980–95. Hon. FRIBA 2001. Hon. DArts De Montfort Univ., 1996. *Publications:* Thomas Hope (1769–1831) and the Neo-Classical Idea, 1968; (ed) Sale Catalogues of Libraries of Eminent Persons, vol. 4, Architects, 1970; The Life and Work of C. R. Cockerell, RA, 1974 (Alice Davis Hitchcock medallion, 1975); The Triumph of the Classical, Cambridge Architecture 1804–34, 1977; Morality and Architecture, 1977 (trans. French, Italian, Japanese and Spanish); English Architecture, a Concise History, 1979, 2nd edn 2001; The Rise of Architectural History, 1980; (with Hugh Montgomery-Massingberd) The London Ritz, a Social and Architectural History, 1980; (with Robin Middleton) Neo-Classical and Nineteenth-century Architecture, 1980 (trans. French, German and Italian); (jtly) Burke's and Savills Guide to Country Houses, vol. 3, East Anglia, 1981; The Buildings of Britain, Regency: a Guide and Gazetteer, 1982; Athenian Stuart, Pioneer of the Greek Revival, 1982; The English Vision: The Picturesque in Architecture, Landscape and Garden Design, 1982; (contrib.) John Soane, 1983; The Royal Interiors of Regency England, 1984; Peterhouse: an architectural record 1284–1984, 1984; A History of Western Architecture, 1986 (trans. German, Italian, Dutch, Greek and Polish), 4th edn 2005; (with Tilman Mellinghoff) German Architecture and the Classical Ideal: 1740–1840, 1987 (trans. Italian); (contrib.) The Legacy of Rome: a new appraisal, 1992; (contrib.) Public and Private Doctrine: essays in English history presented to Maurice Cowling, 1993; (contrib.) The Golden City: essays on the architecture and imagination of Beresford Pite, 1993; Creations and Recreations: Alec Cobbe, thirty years of design and painting, 1996; Sir John Soane: enlightenment thought and the Royal Academy lectures, 1996 (Sir Banister Fletcher Award, 1997); Sir John Soane: the Royal Academy lectures, 2000; The Age of Wilkins: the architecture of improvement, 2000; Morality and Architecture Revisited, 2001; (ed) Alfred Gilbey: a memoir by some friends, 2001; (contrib.) New Offerings, Ancient Treasures: studies in medieval art for George Henderson, 2001; (contrib.) William Beckford, 1760–1844: an eye for the magnificent, 2001; (with Richard John) John Simpson: The Queen's Gallery, Buckingham Palace, and other works, 2002; (contrib.) Royal Treasures: a golden jubilee celebration, 2002; The Architect King: George III and the culture of the enlightenment, 2004; Radical Classicism: the architecture of Quinlan Terry, 2006; (contrib.) James "Athenian" Stuart: the rediscovery of antiquity, 2007; (contrib.) A History of St Mary le Bow, 2007; (contrib.) Carl Laubin: paintings, 2007; (ed and contrib.) Thomas Hope: Regency designer, 2008; The Roman Forum, 2009. *Address:* Peterhouse, Cambridge CB2 1RD; Albany, Piccadilly, W1J 0AU; St Margaret's Place, King's Lynn, Norfolk PE30 5DL. *Clubs:* Beefsteak, Brooks's; University Pitt (Cambridge).

WATKINS, Dr Alan Keith; Chairman, Senior plc (formerly Senior Engineering Group), 1996–2001 (Director, 1994–2001; Deputy Chairman, 1995–96); *b* 9 Oct. 1938; *s* of late Wilfred Victor Watkins and Dorothy Hilda Watkins; *m* 1963, Diana Edith Wynne (*née* Hughes); two *s*. *Educ:* Moseley Grammar School, Birmingham; Univ. of Birmingham (BSc Hons, PhD). FIMMM (Mem. Council, 1990–95); CEng; FIMfgE (Vice-Pres., 1991). Lucas Research Centre, 1962; Lucas Batteries, 1969, subseq. Manufacturing Dir; Lucas Aerospace, 1975; Man. Dir, Aerospace Lucas Industries, 1987–89; Man. Dir and Chief Exec., Hawker Siddeley Gp, 1989–91; London Transport: Chief Exec., 1992–94; Vice-Chm., 1992–93; Dep. Chm., 1993–94. Director: Dobson Park Industries plc, 1992–95; Hepworth plc, 1995–98; Chm., High Duty Alloys Ltd, 1997–2000. Member: DTI Aviation Cttee, 1985–89; Review Bd for Govt Contracts, 1993–2002. Member Council: SBAC, 1982–89 (Vice-Pres., 1988–89); CBI, 1992–94. Vice-Pres., EEF, 1989–91, 1997–2001. *Recreations:* tennis, veteran and vintage cars, hot-air ballooning, photography.

WATKINS, Alan (Rhun); journalist; Political Columnist, Independent on Sunday, since 1993; *b* 3 April 1933; *o c* of late D. J. Watkins, teacher, Tycroes, Carmarthenshire, and Violet Harris, teacher; *m* 1955, Ruth Howard (*d* 1982); one *s* one *d* (and one *d* decd). *Educ:* Amman Valley Grammar Sch., Ammanford; Queens' Coll., Cambridge (MA, LLM). Chm., Cambridge Univ. Labour Club, 1954. National Service, FO, Educn Br., RAF, 1955–57. Called to Bar, Lincoln's Inn, 1957. Research Asst to W. A. Robson, LSE, 1958–59; Editorial Staff, Sunday Express, 1959–64 (New York Corresp., 1961; Actg Political Corresp., 1963; Crossbencher Columnist, 1963–64); Political Columnist: Spectator, 1964–67; New Statesman, 1967–76; Sunday Mirror, 1968–69; Observer, 1976–93; Columnist, Evening Standard, 1974–75; Rugby Columnist: Field, 1984–86; Independent, 1986–2006; Drink Columnist, Observer Magazine, 1992–93. Scriptwriter, BBC 3 and The Late Show, 1966–67. Mem. (Lab) Fulham Bor. Council, 1959–62. Dir, The Statesman and Nation Publishing Co. Ltd, 1973–76. Chm., Political Adv. Gp, British Youth Council, 1978–81. Hon. Fellow, Univ. of Wales, Lampeter, 1999. Awards: Political Columnist, 1973, Gerald Barry, 2007, What the Papers Say; British Press, Columnist, 1982, commended 1984; Edgar Wallace, London Press Club, 2005. *Publications:* The Liberal Dilemma, 1966; (contrib.) The Left, 1966; (with A. Alexander) The Making of the Prime Minister 1970, 1970; Brief Lives, 1982, reissued 2004; (contrib.) The Queen Observed, 1986; Sportswriter's Eye, 1989; A Slight Case of Libel, 1990; A Conservative Coup, 1991, 2nd edn 1992; (contrib.) The State of the Nation, 1997; The Road to Number 10, 1998; (contrib.) Secrets of the Press, 1999; A Short Walk Down Fleet Street, 2000; (contrib.) Roy Jenkins, 2004; contrib. Oxford DNB. *Recreation:* watching cricket. *Address:* 54 Barnsbury Street, N1 1ER. *T:* (020) 7607 0812. *Clubs:* Beefsteak, Garrick.

WATKINS, Barbara Janet; *see* Fontaine, B. J.

WATKINS, Brian, CMG 1993; HM Diplomatic Service, retired; Immigration Judge, 1993–2007; *b* 26 July 1933; *s* of late James Edward Watkins and late Gladys Anne Watkins (*née* Fletcher); *m* 1st, 1957 (marr. diss. 1978); one *s*; 2nd, 1982, Elisabeth Arfon-Jones, *qv*; one *d*. *Educ:* London School of Economics (BSc Econ); Worcester College, Oxford. Solicitor. Flying Officer, RAF, 1955–58. HMOCS, Sierra Leone, 1959–63; Local Govt, 1963–66; Administrator, Tristan da Cunha, 1966–69; Lectr, Univ. of Manchester, 1969–71; HM Diplomatic Service, 1971; FCO, 1971–73; New York, 1973–75; seconded to N Ireland Office, 1976–78; FCO, 1978–81; Counsellor, 1981; Dep. Governor, Bermuda, 1981–83; Consul General and Counsellor (Economic, Commercial, Aid), Islamabad, 1983–86; Consul Gen., Vancouver, 1986–90; High Comr to Swaziland, 1990–93. First Pres., Council of Immigration Judges, 1997–2000, now Emeritus. Swazi Rep., 1993–2002, Royal Canadian Legion, Rep., 2002–, on Council, Royal

Commonwealth Ex-Services League (Mem. Exec. Cttee, 1996–; Hon. Legal Advr, 2001–); Patron, Friends of Swaziland Hospice (UK), 1997–; Chm., Swaziland Soc., 1998–2002; Trustee, S Asian Assoc. for Regl Co-operation Foundn (UK), 2001–07. Patron, Vancouver Welshmen's Choir, 1987–92; Pres., Chepstow Rifle Club, 2006–. High Sheriff Gwent, 2004–05. OStJ 1994 (Chm., Monmouthshire Council, 1996–2002; Mem., Welsh Chapter, 1996–2002). *Recreations:* reading history and spy stories, watching theatre, dancing. *Address:* c/o Royal Bank of Scotland, Drummonds Branch, Charing Cross, SW1A 2DX. *Clubs:* Athenæum, Royal Over-Seas League.

WATKINS, David James; CB 2002; Director, DJW Consulting (Northern Ireland) Ltd, since 2004; *b* 3 Aug. 1948; *s* of John Walter Watkins and Elizabeth Watkins (*née* Buckley); *m* 1974, Valerie Elizabeth Graham; one *s* one *d. Educ:* Royal Belfast Academical Instn; Trinity Coll., Dublin (BA Hons Modern Langs). Public Expenditure Control Div., NI Dept of Finance and Personnel, 1972–77; State Aids Directorate, DGIV, Eur. Commn, 1978–79; NI Dept of Econ. Develt, 1979–86; Private Sec. to Sec. of State for NI, 1986–88; Dep. Chief Exec., IDB, 1989–92; Dir, Central Secretariat, 1992–98; Sen. Dir, and Dir of Policing and Security, NI Office, 1998–2004. *Recreations:* reading, gardening, holidays in France.

WATKINS, David John; Director, Council for the Advancement of Arab-British Understanding, 1983–90 (Joint Chairman, 1979–83; Hon. Treasurer, 1983–2004); *b* 27 Aug. 1925; *s* of Thomas George Watkins and Alice Elizabeth (*née* Allen); unmarried. *Educ:* S Bristol Central and Merrywood Grammar Sch., Bristol. National Service, RAF, 1945–48. Member: Bristol City Council, 1954–57; Bristol Educn Cttee, 1958–66; Labour Party, 1950–; UNITE (formerly Amalgamated Engineering Union, later AEEU, then AMICUS), 1942–; Sec., AEU Gp of MPs, 1968–77. Contested Bristol NW, 1964. MP (Lab) Consett, 1966–83; Mem., House of Commons Chairmen's Panel, 1978–83. Sponsored Employers Liability (Compulsory Insurance) Act, 1969, and Industrial Common Ownership Act, 1976 as Private Member's Bills; introd Drained Weight Bill, 1973, and Consett Steel Works Common Ownership Bill, 1980. Chm., Labour Middle East Council, 1974–83; Treas., Internat. Co-ord Cttee, UN Meeting of Non-Governmental Organisations on Question of Palestine, 1985–90. Dir, 1987–2004, Chm., 1990–2004, Courtlands Estate (Richmond) Ltd (Vice Chm., 1988–90). Hon. Treas., Med. Aid for Palestinians, 1995–2004 (Trustee, 1984–2004). *Publications:* Labour and Palestine, 1975; Industrial Common Ownership, 1978; The World and Palestine, 1980; The Exceptional Conflict, 1984; Palestine: an inescapable duty, 1992; Seventeen Years in Obscurity, 1996; Class and Consequence, 2007. *Recreations:* reading, listening to music. *Address:* 1 Carisbrooke House, Courtlands, Sheen Road, Richmond, Surrey TW10 5AZ. *Club:* Royal Commonwealth Society.

WATKINS, Prof. David John; Professor and Head, Department of Goldsmithing, Silversmithing, Metalwork and Jewellery, Royal College of Art, since 1984; sculptor and jewellery designer; *b* 14 Nov. 1940; *s* of Jack Watkins and Dorothy May Watkins (*née* Burgwin); *m* 1962, Wendy Anne Jopling Ramshaw, *qv*; one *s* one *d. Educ:* Wolverhampton Grammar Sch.; Reading Univ. (BA Fine Art 1963). Sculptor, musician, special effects model maker (incl. 2001: A Space Odyssey) and jewellery designer, 1963–71; own studios for jewellery and sculpture, 1971–. Artist in Residence, Western Australian Inst. for Technol., 1978. Vis. Lectr, Berks Coll. of Art and Guildford Sch. of Art, 1964–66; Vis. Prof., Bezalel Acad., Jerusalem, 1984. *Solo exhibitions* include: American Inst. of Architects, Philadelphia, 1973; Goldsmiths' Hall, Electrum Gall., London, 1973; Arnolfini Gall., Bristol, 1977; Nat. Gall. of Victoria, Melbourne, 1978; Gall. Am Graben, Vienna, 1980; City Art Gall., Leeds, 1985; Stedelijk Mus., Amsterdam, 1986; Contemporary Applied Art, London, 1989; City Art Gall., Birmingham, 1990; Mikimoto Hall, Tokyo, 1993; Handwerkmesse, Munich, 1999; Galerie Louise Smit, Amsterdam, 2000; *group exhibitions* include: V&A Mus., 1976; Kunstlerhaus, Vienna, 1980; Crafts Council, London, 1982 and 1996; NMOMA, Tokyo, 1983; Barcelona, 1987; Nat. Mus of Scotland, 1998; American Crafts Mus., NY, 2001; *work in major collections* including: American Craft Mus.; Australian Nat. Gall.; Birmingham City Mus. and Art Gall.; Crafts Council, London; Kunstgewerbe Mus., Berlin; Musee des Arts Decoratifs, Paris; Nat. Gall. of Victoria; Nat. Mus. of Modern Art, Tokyo; Nat. Mus of Scotland; Science Mus., London; V&A Mus. Crafts Council: Member: Membership Cttee, 1976–78; Collection Cttee, 1983–84. Mem., Bd of Trustees, Haystack Mt Sch. of Crafts, Maine, 1999–. FCSD 1984; FRSA 1991. Freeman, 1988, Liveryman, 1989, Co. of Goldsmiths. Diamonds Today Award, De Beers, 1974; Art for Architecture Award, RSA, 1995. *Publications:* The Best in Contemporary Jewellery, 1994; A Design Sourcebook: Jewellery, 1999; The Paper Jewelry Collection, 2000. *Recreations:* being in my studio, listening to jazz and classical music. *Address:* Royal College of Art, Kensington Gore, SW7 2EU. *T:* (020) 7590 4261; *e-mail:* david.watkins@rca.ac.uk.

WATKINS, Elisabeth; *see* Arfon-Jones, E.

WATKINS, Prof. (Eric) Sidney, OBE 2002; MD; FRCSE; President, FIA Institute for Motor Sport Safety, since 2004; Consultant Neurosurgeon, Princess Grace Hospital, since 1999; Professor of Neurosurgery, University of London, 1972–93, now Emeritus; *b* 6 Sept. 1928; *s* of Wallace and Jessica Watkins; four *s* two *d. Educ:* Prescot Grammar Sch.; Univ. of Liverpool Med. Sch. (BSc Hons Neurophysiol. 1949; MB ChB 1952; MD 1956); MD New York 1962. FRCSE 1969. House physician and house surgeon, Walton and Stanley Hosps, Liverpool, 1952–53; Capt., RAMC, 1953–56; Specialist in Physiol., W African Council for Med. Res., Lagos, 1954–56; Registrar in Gen. Surgery and Orthopaedic Surgery, Weston-super-Mare Gen. Hosp. and Winford Orthopaedic Hosp., Bristol, 1956–58; Registrar in Neurosurgery, Radcliffe Infirmary, Oxford, 1958–61; MRC Res. Fellow, Middx and Maida Vale Hosp., 1961–62; Prof. of Neurosurgery, SUNY, Upstate Med. Center, 1962–70; Consultant Neurosurgeon, London Hosp., 1970–93. Consultant Surgeon, Formula One Constructors' Assoc., 1978–2004. Pres., Med., Safety and Res. Commns, Fedn Internat. de l'Automobile (World Governing Body of Motor Sport), 1981–2004. Hon. DSc Liverpool, 2004. Prince Michael of Kent RAC Centennial Award for Contributions to Motor Sport, 1998. *Publications:* Stereotaxic Anatomy of Thalmus and Basal Ganglia, 1969; Stereotaxic Anatomy of Cerebellum and Brain Stem, 1976; Life at the Limit: triumph and tragedy in Formula One, 1996; Beyond the Limit, 2001. *Recreation:* fly fishing. *Address:* FIA Institute for Motor Sport Safety, 8 Place de la Concorde, 75008 Paris, France. *Clubs:* Athenæum, Royal Automobile.

WATKINS, Dr George Edward, CBE 2000; Chairman and Managing Director, Conoco (UK) Ltd, 1993–2002; *b* 19 Aug. 1943; *s* of George Robert Leonard Watkins and Laura Watkins; *m* 1966, Elizabeth Mary Bestwick; two *s. Educ:* Leeds Univ. (BSc Mining, MSc Geophysics, PhD Geophysics 1968); Stanford Univ., Calif (MS Mgt 1985). Geophysicist, Shell Internat. Petroleum Co., 1968–73; Conoco (UK) Ltd: Geophysicist, 1973–80; Dir, Exploration, 1980–84; Dir, Prodn, 1985–90; Vice Pres., Exploration Prodn, Conoco Inc., Houston, 1990–93. Non-executive Director: Abbot Gp plc, 2002–08; ITI Scotland Ltd, 2003–; Petroleum Services Network Ltd, 2006–; Bridge Resources Corp., 2006–. Sloan Fellow, Stanford Univ., 1984–85. Chm., Scottish Enterprise Grampian, 2002–04. Chm., UK Oil & Gas Industry Safety Leadership Forum,

1997–2000. Pres., UKOOA, 1996. Gov., Robert Gordon Univ., Aberdeen, 2005–. Hon. DEng Heriot-Watt, 2001. Van Weelden Award, Eur. Assoc. Exploration Geophysicists, 1967. *Recreations:* cinema, gardening, walking, fishing. *Address:* 12 Rubislaw Den South, Aberdeen AB15 4BB. *T:* (01224) 208706.

WATKINS, Gerwyn Rhidian; a District Judge (Magistrates' Courts) (formerly Stipendiary Magistrate), South Glamorgan, since 1993; *b* 22 Jan. 1943; *s* of late William Watkins and Margaret Watkins (*née* Evans); *m* 1966, Eleanor Margaret Hemingway; two *s. Educ:* Ardwyn Grammar Sch., Aberystwyth; University Coll. of Wales, Aberystwyth (LLB). Articled to Thomas Andrews, Bracknell, 1966–68; Court Clerk, Cardiff Magistrates' Court, 1968–71; Justices' Clerk: Bromsgrove and Redditch, 1971–74; Vale of Glamorgan, 1974–93. Pres., Barry Rotary Club, 1990–91. *Address:* Magistrates' Court, Fitzalan Place, Cardiff CF24 0RZ. *T:* (029) 2046 3040.

WATKINS, Rev. Gordon Derek; Secretary, London Diocesan Advisory Committee, 1984–94; *b* 16 July 1929; *s* of Clifford and Margaret Watkins; *m* 1957, Beryl Evelyn Whitaker. *Educ:* St Brendan's College, Clifton. Nat. Service, RAOC, 1947–49. Staff of W. D. & H. O. Wills, 1944–51; deacon 1953, priest 1954; Curate, Grafton Cathedral, NSW, 1953–56; Vicar of Texas, Qld, 1957–61; Curate, St Wilfrid's, Harrogate, 1961–63; Vicar of Upton Park, 1963–67; Rector: Great and Little Bentley, 1967–73; Great Canfield, 1973–78; Pastoral Sec., Dio. London, 1978–84; Vicar, St Martin-within-Ludgate, City and Dio. of London, 1984–89; Priest Vicar, Westminster Abbey, 1984–90; Priest in Ordinary to the Queen, 1984–96. Freeman, City of London, 1984. *Recreations:* reading, music, country life.

WATKINS, Maj.-Gen. Guy Hansard, CB 1986; OBE 1974; Chief Executive, Royal Hong Kong Jockey Club, 1986–96; *b* 30 Nov. 1933; *s* of Col A. N. M. Watkins and Mrs S. C. Watkins; *m* 1958, Sylvia Margaret Grant; two *s* two *d. Educ:* The King's Sch., Canterbury; Royal Military Academy, Sandhurst. Commissioned into Royal Artillery, 1953; CO 39 Medium Regt RA, 1973; Comd Task Force 'B'/Dep. Comd 1 Armd Div., 1977; Director, Public Relations (Army), 1980; Maj. Gen. RA and GOC Artillery Div., 1982; Dir Gen., Army Manning and Recruiting, 1985; retd 1986. Hon. Col, The Royal Hong Kong Regt (The Volunteers), 1993–95. Director: British Bloodstock Agency, 1996–2001; Racecourse Holdings Trust, 1996–2003. *Recreations:* racing, golf, fishing, ski-ing. *Address:* The Mill House, Fittleworth, near Pulborough, West Sussex RH20 1EP. *T:* (01798) 865717, *Fax:* (01798) 865684. *Clubs:* Hong Kong Jockey, Shek O (Hong Kong); W Sussex Golf.

WATKINS, Prof. Hugh Christian, MD, PhD; FRCP, FMedSci; Field Marshal Alexander Professor of Cardiovascular Medicine, University of Oxford, since 1996; Fellow, Exeter College, Oxford, since 1996; *b* 7 June 1959; *s* of David Watkins, MB, BCh, and late Gillian Mary Watkins; *m* 1987, Elizabeth Bridget Hewett; one *s* one *d. Educ:* Gresham's Sch., Norfolk; St Bartholomew's Hosp. Med. Sch., London (BSc 1st Cl. Hons; MB, BS; Brackenbury & Bourne Prize in Gen. Medicine, 1984); PhD 1995, MD 1995, London. MRCP 1987, FRCP 1997. House Physician, Professorial Med. Unit, St Bartholomew's Hosp., 1984–85; Senior House Officer: in Medicine, John Radcliffe Hosp., Oxford, 1985–87; in Neurology, St Bartholomew's, 1987; Registrar, Medicine and Cardiology, St Thomas' Hosp., London, 1987–89; Lectr in Cardiological Scis, St George's, London, 1990–94; Hon. Sen. Lectr, 1995; Res. Fellow in Medicine, Harvard Med. Sch. and Brigham & Women's Hosp., Boston, 1990–94; Asst Prof. of Medicine, Harvard Med. Sch. and Associate Physician, Brigham & Women's Hosp., 1995. BHF Clinical Scientist Fellow, 1990. Goulstonian Lectr, RCP, 1998; Thomas Lewis Lectr, British Cardiac Soc., 2004. FMedSci 1999. Young Res. Worker Prize, British Cardiac Soc., 1992; Graham Bull Prize, RCP, 2003. *Publications:* papers in scientific jls incl. New England Jl Medicine, Jl Clinical Investigation, Cell, Nature Genetics. *Recreations:* photography, Oriental porcelain. *Address:* Department of Cardiovascular Medicine, John Radcliffe Hospital, Oxford OX3 9DU. *T:* (01865) 220257, *Fax:* (01865) 768844.

WATKINS, Prof. Jeffrey Clifton, PhD; FMedSci; FRS 1988; FIBiol; Hon. Professor of Pharmacology, 1989–99, and Leader of Excitatory Amino Acid Group, Department of Pharmacology, 1973–99, School of Medical Sciences (formerly The Medical School), Bristol (Hon. Senior Research Fellow, 1983–89), now Professor Emeritus; *b* 20 Dec. 1929; *s* of Colin Hereward and Amelia Miriam Watkins; *m* 1973, Beatrice Joan Thacher; one *s* one *d. Educ:* Univ. of Western Australia (MSc 1954); Univ. of Cambridge (PhD 1954). Research Fellow, Chemistry Department: Univ. of Cambridge, 1954–55; Univ. of Yale, 1955–57; Res. Fellow, 1958–61, Fellow, 1961–65, Physiology Dept, ANU; Scientific Officer, ARC Inst. of Animal Physiology, Babraham, Cambridge, 1965–67; Res. Scientist, MRC Neuropsychiatry Unit, Carshalton, Surrey, 1967–73; Senior Research Fellow, Depts of Pharmacology and Physiology, The Med. Sch., Bristol, 1973–83. MAE 1989; FIBiol 1998; FMedSci 1999. *Publications:* The NMDA Receptor, 1989, 2nd edn 1994; approx. 250 pubns in learned jls, eg Jl of Physiol., Brit. Jl of Pharmacol., Nature, Brain Res., Exptl Brain Res., Eur. Jl of Pharmacol., Neuroscience, Neuroscience Letters, Jl of Neuroscience. *Address:* 8 Lower Court Road, Lower Almondsbury, Bristol BS32 4DX. *T:* (01454) 613829.

WATKINS, Paul Rhys; 'cellist and conductor; Member ('cellist), Nash Ensemble, since 1998; Associate Conductor, English Chamber Orchestra, since 2007; *b* 4 Jan. 1970; *s* of John Watkins and Esther Elizabeth Picton Watkins; *m* 1993, Jennifer Laredo; two *d. Educ:* Yehudi Menuhin Sch.; St Catharine's Coll., Cambridge. Finalist, BBC Young Musician of Year, 1988; Principal 'Cellist, BBC SO, 1990–98. Prof., RAM, 1996–2002. Featured soloist, Masterworks, BBC TV, 1999. Solo and conducting appearances with LSO, LPO, Philharmonia and English Chamber Orch., 2005–06; soloist, First Night of the Proms, 2007. Recordings: two solo recordings, 2001; début recording as conductor, BBC SO, 2004. Winner, Leeds Conducting Competition, 2002. *Recreations:* procrastination, tax avoidance. *Address:* c/o Sulivan Sweetland, 1 Hillgate Place, SW12 9ER. *T:* (020) 8772 3470, *Fax:* (020) 8673 8959; *e-mail:* es@sulivansweetland.co.uk.

WATKINS, Penelope Jill, (Mrs M. J. Bowman); a District Judge (Magistrates' Courts) (formerly Stipendiary Magistrate), Mid-Glamorgan, since 1995, and South Wales, since 1996; a Recorder, since 2000; *b* 19 April 1953; *d* of Laurence Gordon Watkins and Dorothy Ernestine Watkins; *m* 1977, Michael James Bowman. *Educ:* Howell's Sch., Llandaff; Henbury Sch., Bristol; Somerville Coll., Oxford (BA Jurisp. 1974; MA). Called to the Bar, Lincoln's Inn, 1975; Inner London Magistrates' Courts Service: Dep. Chief Clerk, serving at London Courts, 1976–90; Dep. Training Officer, 1983–86; Justices' Clerk: Wells Street, 1990–91; Camberwell Green, 1991–95. An Asst Recorder, 1998–2000. *Recreations:* reading, music, travel. *Address:* Pontypridd Magistrates' Court, Union Street, Pontypridd CF37 1SD. *T:* (01443) 480750.

WATKINS, Peter Derek, CBE 2004; Director General Typhoon, Ministry of Defence, since 2007; *b* 8 Feb. 1959; *s* of Vivian Derek Watkins and Eunice Mary Watkins (*née* Wilkinson). *Educ:* Strode's Sch., Egham; Peterhouse, Cambridge (BA Hist. 1980). Joined MoD, 1980; various posts, 1980–90; Private Sec. to Minister for Defence Procurement, 1990–93; Dir (Finance and Secretariat) Air, 1994–96; Counsellor (Defence Supply and

Aerospace), Bonn/Berlin, 1996–2000; Team Leader, Smart Acquisition, 2000–01; Private Sec. to Defence Sec., 2001–03; Comd Sec., RAF Strike Comd, 2004–06; Fellow, Weatherhead Center for Internat. Affairs, Harvard Univ., 2006–07. *Recreations:* overseas travel, historic buildings. *Address:* Level 2, Zone E, Ministry of Defence, Main Building, Whitehall, SW1A 2HB; *e-mail:* peter.watkins262@mod.uk.

WATKINS, Peter Rodney; Office for Standards in Education Inspector, 1993–98; *b* 8 Oct. 1931; *s* of late Frank Arthur Watkins and Mary Gwyneth Watkins (*née* Price); *m* 1971, Jillian Ann Burge (marr. diss. 1998); two *d. Educ:* Solihull Sch.; Emmanuel Coll., Cambridge (Exhibnr; Hist. Tripos Pts I and II 1952, 1953; Cert. in Educn 1954; MA 1957). Flying Officer, RAF, 1954–56; History Master, East Ham Grammar Sch., 1956–59; Sixth Form Hist. Master, Brentwood Sch., 1959–64; Sen. Hist. Master, Bristol Grammar Sch., 1964–69; Headmaster, King Edward's Five Ways Sch., Birmingham, 1969–74; Headmaster, Chichester High Sch. for Boys, 1974–79; Principal, Price's Sixth Form Coll., Fareham, 1980–84; Dep. Chief Exec., Sch. Curriculum Develt Cttee, 1984–88, Nat. Curriculum Council, 1988–91. Exec., SHA, 1980–84. Chm., Christian Educn Movement, 1980–87. Reader, St Peter's, Bishop's Waltham, dio. of Portsmouth, 1989–. Gov., St Luke's C of E Aided Sch., Portsmouth, 1992–2003 (Chm., 1998–2003). *Publications:* The Sixth Form College in Practice, 1982; Modular Approaches to the Secondary Curriculum, 1986; St Barnabas' Church, Swanmore 1845–1995, 1995; Swanmore since 1840, 2001; Jerusalem or Athens?, 2005; Not Like Uncle Tom: an autobiography, 2006; Bishop's Waltham: parish, town and church, 2007. *Recreations:* travel, walking, writing, local history, theology, cooking. *Address:* 7 Crofton Way, Swanmore, Southampton SO32 2RF. *T:* (01489) 894789.

WATKINS, Wendy Anne Jopling; *see* Ramshaw, W. A. J.

WATKINSON, Angela Eileen; MP (C) Upminster, since 2001; *b* 18 Nov. 1941; *m* 1961, Roy Michael Watkinson (marr. diss.); one *s* two *d. Educ:* Wanstead County High Sch.; Anglia Poly. (HNC 1989). Bank of NSW, 1958–64; Special Sch. Sec., Essex CC, 1976–88; Cttee Clerk, Barking and Dagenham BC, 1988–89; Cttee Manager, Basildon DC, 1989–94. Member (C): Havering BC, 1994–98; Essex CC, 1997–2001. An Opposition Whip, 2002–04 and 2006–; Shadow Minister: for Health and Educn in London, 2004–05; for Local Govt and Communities, 2005. *Address:* (office) 23 Butts Green Road, Hornchurch, Essex RM11 2JS; c/o House of Commons, SW1A 0AA.

WATLING, His Honour Rev. (David) Brian; QC 1979; a Circuit Judge, 1981–2001; Resident Judge, Chelmsford Crown Court, 1997–2001; *b* 18 June 1935; *o s* of late Russell and Stella Watling; *m* 1964, Noelle Louise Bugden. *Educ:* Charterhouse; King's Coll., London (LLB). Sub-Lieut RNR. Called to Bar, Middle Temple, 1957, Lincoln's Inn, 1998; Advocate, Gibraltar, 1980. Various Crown appts, 1969–72; Treasury Counsel, Central Criminal Court, 1972–79; a Recorder of the Crown Court, 1979–81. Vis. Lectr, 1978–80, Vis. Prof. in Criminal Law, 1980–84, University Coll. at Buckingham (now Univ. of Buckingham). Judicial Mem., Parole Bd, 2002–07; Legal Assessor, GMC, 2002–07. Reader, dio. of St Edmundsbury and Ipswich, 1985; ordained deacon 1987, priest 1988; Hon. Curate: Lavenham, 1987–90; Nayland with Wissington, 1990–2002; Boxford with Groton etc., 2002–03 (retd); permission to officiate, 2003–. Pres., Dedham Vale Soc., 1994–2002. *Publication:* (contrib.) Serving Two Masters, 1988. *Recreations:* sailing, theatre and ballet, fireside reading, the company of old friends. *Address:* Howe's House, 5 High Street, Nayland, Suffolk CO6 4JE. *Clubs:* Sloane; Aldeburgh Yacht.

WATMORE, Ian Charles; Permanent Secretary, Department for Innovation, Universities and Skills, since 2007; *b* 5 July 1958; *s* of late Dr Kenneth Watmore and of Kathleen Watmore; *m* 1987, Georgina; four *s. Educ:* Trinity Sch. of John Whitgift, Croydon; Trinity Coll., Cambridge (BA 1980). UK Man. Dir, Accenture, 2000–04; Govt CIO and Hd, e-Govt Unit, Cabinet Office, 2004–05; Chief Advr to Prime Minister on Delivery and Hd, Prime Minister's Delivery Unit, 2005–07. Board Member: e-skills uk, 2000–06; English Inst. for Sport, 2002–. Pres., Mgt Consultants Assoc., 2003–04. *Recreations:* away scheme season ticket holder for Arsenal FC, golf, new technology, rock music. *Address:* Department for Innovation, Universities and Skills, Kingsgate House, 66–74 Victoria Street, SW1E 6SW.

WATSON, family name of **Barons Manton** and **Watson of Richmond**.

WATSON OF INVERGOWRIE, Baron *cr* 1997 (Life Peer), of Invergowrie in Perth and Kinross; **Michael Goodall Watson;** *b* 1 May 1949; *s* of late Clarke Watson and Senga (*née* Goodall); *m* 2004, Clare Thomas. *Educ:* Invergowrie Primary Sch., Dundee; Dundee High Sch.; Heriot-Watt Univ., Edinburgh (BA 2nd Cl. Hons Econs and Industrial Relns). Development Officer, WEA, E Midlands Dist, 1974–77; full-time official, ASTMS, then MSF, 1977–89. Director: PS Communications Consultants Ltd, Edinburgh, 1997–99; Dundee United FC, 2003–05. MP (Lab) Glasgow Central, 1989–97. Mem., Public Accounts Cttee, 1995–97. Mem., Scottish Exec. Cttee, Labour Party, 1987–90; Chm., PLP Overseas Develt Aid Cttee, 1991–97. Mem. (Lab) Glasgow Cathcart, Scottish Parlt, 1999–2005; Minister for Tourism, Culture and Sport, 2001–03. *Publications:* Rags to Riches: the official history of Dundee United Football Club, 1985; Year Zero: an inside view of the Scottish Parliament, 2001. *Recreations:* Dundee United FC, reading, especially political biographies, running. *Address:* House of Lords, SW1A 0PW.

WATSON OF RICHMOND, Baron *cr* 1999 (Life Peer), of Richmond in the London Borough of Richmond-upon-Thames; **Alan John Watson,** CBE 1985; Chairman: Corporate Television Networks (CTN), since 1992; Burson-Marsteller UK, 1994–2004; Burson-Marsteller Europe, 1996–2007; Raisin Social, since 2005; Director, Burson-Marsteller Worldwide, 1992–2004; *b* 3 Feb. 1941; *s* of Rev. John William Watson and Edna Mary (*née* Peters); *m* 1965, Karen Lederer; two *s. Educ:* Diocesan Coll., Cape Town, SA; Kingswood Sch., Bath, Somerset; Jesus Coll., Cambridge (Open Schol. in History 1959, State Schol. 1959; MA Hons; Hon. Fellow 2004). Vice-Pres., Cambridge Union; Pres., Cambridge Univ. Liberal Club. Research Asst to Cambridge Prof. of Modern History on post-war history of Unilever, 1962–64. General trainee, BBC, 1965–66; Reporter, BBC TV, The Money Programme, 1966–68; Chief Public Affairs Commentator, London Weekend Television, 1969–70; Reporter, Panorama, BBC TV, 1971–74; Presenter, The Money Programme, 1974–75; Head of TV, Radio, Audio-Visual Div., EEC, 1975–79; Dir, Charles Barker City Ltd, 1980–85 (Chief Exec., 1980–83); Dep. Chm., Sterling PR, 1985–86; Chairman: City and Corporate Counsel Ltd, 1987–94; Threadneedle Publishing Gp, 1987–94; Corporate Vision Ltd, 1989–98. Mem. Bd, Y & R Partnership, 1999–2002; Chm., Coca-Cola European Adv. Bd, 2003–06; Mem., Havas Media Adv. Bd. Mem., Exec. Bd, Unicef, 1985–92; Mem. Bd, POW Business Leaders Forum, 1996–; non-exec. Dir, Community and Charities Cttee, BT Bd, 1996–2004. Pres., Liberal Party, 1984–85. Vice Chm., European Movt, 1995–2001. Chm., Jt Commonwealth Socs Council, 2003–. Chairman: UK Koenigswinter Steering Cttee, 2003–; British Accreditation Council, 2007–. Presenter: You and 1992, BBC 1 series, 1990; The Germans, Channel 4, 1992; Key Witness, Radio 4, 1996. Vis. Prof. in English Culture and European Studies, Louvain Univ., 1990–; Vis. Fellow, Oriel Coll., Oxford, 2003–; Hon. Professor: German Studies, Birmingham Univ., 1997–; Political Studies, St Petersburg State Univ., 2003–; Business Studies, Korea Univ., 2004–. Chairman: RTS, 1992–94 (Mem. Council, 1989–95; FRTS 1992); CBI Media Industries Gp, 1995–98. Pres., British-German Assoc., 2000– (Chm., 1992–2000). Pres., Heathrow Assoc. for Control of Aircraft Noise, 1992–95. Co-Chair, British Jamestown Cttee, 2006–08. Chairman: Chemistry Adv. Bd, Cambridge Univ., 1999–; Cambridge Foundn, 2005–; Mem. Adv. Council, John Smith Meml Trust, 1998–2002. Chm. of Govs, Westminster Coll., Oxford, 1988–94; Governor: Kingswood Sch., 1984–90; ESU, 1993– (Internat. Dep. Chm., 1995–99; Chm., 2000–05, now Emeritus; Churchill Medal, 2005); Trustee, British Studies Centre, Humboldt Univ., Berlin, 1998–; Patron: Richmond Soc., 2001–; Mus. of Richmond, 2002–. Fellow, Internat. Visual Communications Assoc., 1997. Hon. FCIPR (Hon. FIPR 1998). Hon. DHL: St Lawrence Univ., 1992; Richmond American Internat. Univ., 2007; Hon Dr: Moldova Univ., 2007; Richmond American Internat. Univ., 2008. Grand Prix Eurodiaporama of EC for European TV Coverage, 1974. Order of Merit (Germany), 1995, Grand Cross, 2001, Knight's Grand Cross, 2007; Order of Merit, Grand Cross (Romania), 2004; Commonwealth of Virgina Cert. of Public Recognition, 2007. *Publications:* Europe at Risk, 1972; The Germans: who are they now?, 1992 (German, US, Japanese, Polish and Chinese edns); Thatcher and Kohl: old rivalries renewed, 1996; Jamestown: the voyage of English, 2007. *Recreations:* historical biography, wine, the Thames. *Address:* Cholmondeley House, 3 Cholmondeley Walk, Richmond upon Thames, Surrey TW9 1NS; Somerset Lodge, Nunney, Somerset BA11 4NP. *Clubs:* Brooks's, Royal Automobile, Kennel.

WATSON, Alan; *see* Watson, W. A. J.

WATSON, Alan, CBE 2001; Deputy Parliamentary Commissioner for Administration, 2000–03; Deputy Scottish Parliamentary Commissioner for Administration, 2000–02; Deputy Welsh Administration Ombudsman, 2000–03; *b* 23 Nov. 1942; *s* of late Dennis Watson and of Dorothy Watson; *m* 1st, 1966, Marjorie Eleanor Main (marr. diss.); one *s* one *d*; 2nd, 1991, Susan Elizabeth Beare (*née* Dwyer); one step *s. Educ:* King Edward VI Grammar Sch., Morpeth. Min. of Pensions and Nat. Insce, later Min. of Social Security, then DHSS, 1962–76; Staff Inspection, CSD, 1976–80; Mgt Trng, DSS, 1980–84; Investigations Manager with Parly Comr for Admin, 1984–89; Personnel, DSS, 1989–92; Dir, Field Ops, with Contributions Agency, 1992–94; Dir of Investigations, with Parly Comr for Admin, 1994–2000. Dep. Ind. Football Ombudsman, 2008– (Dir, 2002–08, Dep. Chm., 2004–08, Ind. Football Commn). *Recreations:* cricket, football, football referee, walking, books.

WATSON, Prof. Alan Andrew, FRS 2000; FRAS, FInstP; Professor of Physics, 1984–2003, now Emeritus, and Research Professor, since 2003, University of Leeds; *b* 26 Sept. 1938; *s* of William John Watson and Elsie Robinson; *m* 1973, Susan Lorraine Cartman; one *s* one *d. Educ:* Daniel Stewart's College, Edinburgh; Edinburgh Univ. (BSc 1st cl. hons Physics 1960; PhD 1964). FInstP 1998. Asst Lectr, Univ. of Edinburgh, 1962–64; University of Leeds: Lectr, 1964–76; Reader in Particle Cosmic Physics, 1976–84; Chm., Physics Dept, 1989–93; Pro Vice-Chancellor, 1994–97; Hd, Dept of Physics and Astronomy, 1997–2000. Science and Engineering Research Council: Member: Astronomy and Planetary Science Bd, 1986–90; Nuclear Physics Bd, 1987–90; Chm., Ground Based Facilities Cttee, PPARC, 1996–99. Mem., Cosmic Ray Commn, IUPAP, 1991–95. Spokesman, Pierre Auger Observatory, Argentina, 2001–07, now Emeritus. Member, Editorial Board: Astroparticle Physics, 1992–2005; Nuclear Instruments and Methods, 1993–. *Publications:* contribs to Physical Review Letters, Astrophysical Jl, Jl of Physics, Nuclear Instruments and Methods, Astroparticle Physics, Nature. *Recreations:* malt whisky tasting, golf, watching Scotland win Calcutta Cup games, theatre. *Address:* School of Physics and Astronomy, University of Leeds, Leeds LS2 9JT. *T:* (0113) 343 3888; *e-mail:* a.a.watson@leeds.ac.uk. *Club:* Crail Golfing Society.

WATSON, Alistair Gordon; Sheriff of North Strathclyde at Kilmarnock, since 2005; *b* Dundee, 1 July 1959; *s* of Robert and Isobel Watson; *m* 1985, Susan Gibson; one *s* two *d. Educ:* High Sch. of Dundee; Univ. of Dundee (LLB 1980; DipLP 1981). NP 1982. Solicitor, 1981–2005; Dir, Public Defence Solicitors' Office, 1998–2005. *Recreations:* family, photography, walking, gardening. *Address:* Kilmanock Sheriff Court, St Marnock Street, Kilmarnock, Ayrshire KA1 1ED.

WATSON, Sir Andrew; *see* Watson, Sir J. A.

WATSON, Prof. Andrew James, PhD; FRS 2003; Professor of Environmental Science, School of Environmental Science, University of East Anglia, since 1996; *b* 30 Nov. 1952; *s* of Leslie John Watson and Ena Florence Watson (*née* Bence); *m* 1978, Jacqueline Elizabeth Pughe; two *s. Educ:* Steyning Grammar Sch.; Imperial Coll., London (BSc Physics 1975); Univ. of Reading (PhD 1978). Research Scientist: Dept of Atmospheric and Oceanic Sci., Univ. of Michigan, Ann Arbor, 1978–81; Marine Biological Assoc., Plymouth, 1981–88; Res. Scientist and Project Leader, Plymouth Marine Lab., 1988–95. Visiting Scientist: Lamont-Doherty Geol Observatory, Columbia Univ., 1985, 1987; Woods Hole Oceanographic Inst., 2000. *Publications:* numerous articles and papers in scientific jls. *Recreations:* acoustic and electric guitar, cycling, gardening. *Address:* School of Environmental Science, University of East Anglia, Norwich NR4 7TJ. *T:* (01603) 456161, *Fax:* (01603) 507714.

WATSON, Maj.-Gen. Andrew Linton, CB 1981; Lieutenant Governor and Secretary, Royal Hospital, Chelsea, 1984–92; *b* 9 April 1927; *s* of Col W. L. Watson, OBE, and Mrs D. E. Watson (*née* Lea); *m* 1952, Mary Elizabeth, *d* of Mr and Mrs A. S. Rigby, Warrenpoint, Co. Down; two *s* one *d. Educ:* Wellington Coll., Berks. psc, jssc, rcds. Commnd The Black Watch, 1946; served, 1946–66: with 1st and 2nd Bns, Black Watch, in UK, Germany, Cyprus and British Guiana; with UN Force, Cyprus; as GSO 2 and 3 on Staff, UK and Germany; GSO 1 HQ 17 Div./Malaya Dist, 1966–68; CO 1st Bn The Black Watch, UK, Gibraltar and NI, 1969–71; Comdr 19 Airportable Bde, Colchester, 1972–73; RCDS, 1974; Comdr British Army Staff, and Military Attaché, Washington, DC, 1975–77; GOC Eastern District, 1977–80; COS, Allied Forces, Northern Europe, 1980–82. Col, The Black Watch, 1981–92. Chm., Inner London Br., Army Benevolent Fund, 1983–2000; Trustee, Royal Cambridge Home for Soldiers' Widows, 1992–2001. *Recreations:* golf, walking, classical music. *Address:* c/o Royal Bank of Scotland, 12 Dunkeld Road, Perth PH1 5RB. *T:* (01738) 21777. *Club:* Pitt.

See also T. D. H. Davies.

WATSON, Sir Andrew Michael M.; *see* Milne-Watson.

WATSON, (Angus) Gavin; Secretary, Buildings Books Trust, since 2002; *b* 14 April 1944; *s* of late H. E. and M. Watson; *m* 1967, Susan Naomi Beal (marr. diss. 1991); two *s* (and one *d* decd). *Educ:* Carlisle Grammar School; Merton College, Oxford; Peterhouse, Cambridge. Joined Dept of the Environment, 1971; Private Office, Secretary of State, 1975–77; Asst Sec., 1980–86; Under Secretary, 1986–97; Head: Directorate of Public Housing Mgt and Resources, 1986–91; Water Directorate, June–July 1991; Directorate of Envmtl Policy and Analysis, 1991–94; Cities, Countryside and Private Finance Directorate, 1994–95; Govt Offices Central Unit, 1995–97; Chm., Fortunegate

Community Housing, 1998–2004. Hon. Ed., Llanfair Railway Jl, 1998–2006. *Publication:* contribs to Pevsner Architectural Guides. *Recreations:* looking at buildings, industrial archaeology, fell walking. *Address:* 19 Castle Street, Bishop's Castle, Shropshire SY9 5BU. *T:* (01588) 630444.

WATSON, Anthony; Chairman, Marks & Spencer Pension Trust Ltd, since 2006; *b* 2 April 1945; *s* of Lt Comdr Andrew Patrick Watson and Harriet Watson; *m* 1972, Heather Jane Dye; two *s* one *d*. *Educ:* Campbell Coll., Belfast; Queen's Univ., Belfast (BSc Hons Econ). AIIMR 1972. Called to the Bar, Lincoln's Inn, 1976, Bencher, 2002. Dir, Touche, Remnant & Co., 1980–85; Chief Investment Officer, Citibank NA, 1985–91; Dir Internat. Investments, 1991–95, Man. Dir, 1995–98, AMP Asset Management plc; Chief Investment Officer, 1998–2001, Chief Exec., 2002–06, Hermes Pensions Mgt Ltd. Chm., Asian Infrastructure Fund Ltd, 1998–; Director: Virgin Direct Ltd, 1995–98; Innisfree plc, 1996–98; MEPC, 2000–06 (Chm., 2003–06); Securities Inst., 2000–06; Edinburgh Fund Managers plc, 2001–02; Investment Mgt Assoc. Ltd, 2002–05; Vodafone Gp PLC, 2006–; Hammerson Gp PLC, 2006–; Witan Investment Trust PLC, 2006–; Mem. Adv. Bd, Norges Bank Investment Mgt, 2006–; Mem. Adv. Gp, Shareholder Exec., BERR, 2008–. Chm., Strategic Investment Bd (NI), 2002–. Mem., Financial Reporting Council, 2004–07. Dir, Queen's Univ. Foundn Bd, 2003–. Trustee: Women Caring Trust, 1996–; Lincoln's Inn Pension Fund, 2002–; Investment Property Educnl Trust, 2004–06. Hon. FSI 2006. Freeman, City of London, 2008; Liveryman, Leathersellers' Co., 2008. *Recreations:* golf, ski-ing, history, tennis, Rugby. *Address: e-mail:* tonywatson11@btinternet.com. *Clubs:* Royal Automobile; Royal St Davids Golf (Harlech).

WATSON, Anthony David F.; *see* Forbes Watson.

WATSON, Anthony Gerard; Editor in Chief, Press Association, since 2007; *b* 28 May 1955; *s* of George Maurice Watson and Ann (*née* McDonnell); *m* 1st, 1982, Susan Ann Gutteridge (marr. diss. 1994); two *s* one *d*; 2nd, 1994, Sylvie Helen Pask; one *s* one *d*. *Educ:* St John Fisher Sch., Peterborough; N Staffs Polytechnic (BA Pol. and Internat. Relns). Journalist with E Midlands Allied Press, Peterborough, 1977–79; joined Westminster Press—Evening Despatch, Darlington, 1979, News Editor, 1983–84; Yorkshire Post, 1984–86; Researcher, World in Action, Granada TV, 1986–88; Dep. Editor, 1988–89, Editor, 1989–2002, Yorkshire Post; Head of Business Develt, 2003–04, Editl Dir, 2004–06, Press Assoc. Provincial Journalist of the Year, British Press Awards, 1987. *Address:* The Press Association, 292 Vauxhall Bridge Road, SW1V 1AE.

WATSON, Antony Edward Douglas; QC 1986; *b* 6 March 1945; *s* of William Edward Watson and Margaret Watson (*née* Douglas); *m* 1972, Gillian Mary Bevan-Arthur; two *d*. *Educ:* Sedbergh School; Sidney Sussex College, Cambridge (MA). Called to the Bar, Inner Temple, 1968. Dep. Chm., Copyright Tribunal, 1994–97. *Publication:* (jtly) Terrell on Patents (1884), 13th edn 1982, 14th edn 1994. *Recreations:* wine, opera, country pursuits. *Address:* The Old Rectory, Milden, Suffolk IP7 7AF. *T:* (01449) 740227. *Club:* Boodle's.

WATSON, Barbara Joan; Her Honour Judge Watson; a Circuit Judge, since 2000; *b* 13 Oct. 1950; *d* of Gordon Smith Watson and Joan Watson; *m* 1975, James David Heyworth (marr. diss. 1982); one *s*. *Educ:* Nelson Grammar Sch., Lancs; Southampton Univ. (LLB Hons 1972). Called to the Bar, Gray's Inn, 1973; in practice as barrister, Northern Circuit, 1973–75 and 1981–2000; Lectr in Law, Manchester Poly., 1973–80; Asst Recorder, 1992–97; Recorder, 1997–2000; Hon. Recorder, Bor. of Burnley, 2004–; Designated Family Judge for Lancs, 2007–. *Recreations:* opera, travel, watching Rugby Union. *Address:* Blackburn County Court, 64 Victoria Street, Blackburn BB1 6DT. *T:* (01254) 299840.

WATSON, Sir Bruce (Dunstan), AC 2004; Kt 1985; Chairman, M.I.M. Holdings Limited, 1983–91 (Chief Executive Officer, 1981–90); *b* 1 Aug. 1928; *s* of James Harvey and Edith Mary (Crawford); *m* 1952, June Kilgour; one *s* two *d*. *Educ:* University of Queensland (BE (Elec) 1949, BCom 1957). Engineer, Tasmanian Hydro Electricity Commn, 1950–54, Townsville Regional Electricity Board, 1954–56; MIM Group of Companies: Engineer, Copper Refineries Pty Ltd, Townsville, 1956–69; Mount Isa Mines Ltd, 1970–73; Group Industrial Relations Manager, MIM Group, Brisbane, 1973–75; First Gen. Manager, Agnew Mining Co., WA, 1975–77; M.I.M. Holdings Ltd, Brisbane: Director, 1977; Man. Dir. 1980; Man. Dir and Chief Exec. Officer, 1981. Director: Asarco Inc., 1985–90; National Australia Bank, 1984–91, 1992–98; Boral, 1990–99; Mem., Supervisory Bd, Metallgesellschaft AG, 1988–93. Member: Business Council of Australia, 1983–90; Exec. Cttee, Australian Mining Industry Council, 1980–90 (Pres., 1985–87); President: Australian Inst. of Mining and Metallurgy, 1992; Australian Inst. of Co. Dirs, 1992–95. Mem., Qld Corrective Services Commn, 1997–99 (Chm., 1998–99); Chm. Council, Qld Inst. of Med. Res., 1998–. Bd Mem., Australian Management Coll., Mt Eliza, 1980–91. Pres., Qld Art Gall. Foundn, 1985–2008. Hon. DEng Queensland, 1989; DUniv Griffith 1992. *Recreation:* golf. *Address:* 272 Jesmond Road, Fig Tree Pocket, Brisbane, Qld 4069, Australia. *T:* (7) 33781536.

WATSON, (Daniel) Stewart, CB 1967; OBE 1958; *b* 30 Dec. 1911; *s* of Reverend Dr William Watson, DD, DLitt, and Mary Mackintosh Watson; *m* 1939, Isabel (*née* Gibson) (*d* 1991); one *s*. *Educ:* Robert Gordon's Coll.; Aberdeen University. Student Apprentice, British Thomson Houston, Rugby, 1933, Research Engr, 1936. Scientific Officer, Admiralty, 1938–; Dir, Admiralty Surface Weapons Establishment, 1961–68; Dep. Chief Scientist (Naval), MoD, 1968–72; Dir Gen. Establishments, Resources Programme A, MoD, 1972–73. *Publications:* contribs to IEEJ. *Recreations:* thoroughbred cars, caravanning. *Address:* 28 Longhope Drive, Wrecclesham, Farnham, Surrey GU10 4SN. *T:* (01252) 733126.

WATSON, Sir David (John), Kt 1998; Professor of Higher Education Management, Institute of Education, University of London, since 2005; *b* 22 March 1949; *s* of late Lewis James Watson and Berenice Nichols; *m* 1975, Betty Pinto Skolnick; one *d* one *s*. *Educ:* Cheshunt Grammar School; Eton College; Clare College, Cambridge (MA); Univ. of Pennsylvania (PhD). ITLM 1999; CCMI 2001; FHEA 2007. Sen. Lectr, Principal Lectr in Humanities, Crewe and Alsager Coll. of Higher Educn, 1975–81; Dean, Modular Course, Asst Dir, Dep. Dir, Oxford Polytechnic, 1981–90; Dir, then Vice-Chancellor, and Prof. of Hist. of Ideas, Brighton Poly., later Univ. of Brighton, 1990–2005. Member: Council, CNAA, 1989–93 (Mem., 1977–93); PCFC, 1988–93; HEFCE, 1992–96; Paul Hamlyn Foundn Nat. Commn on Educn, 1991–93; Open Univ. Validation Bd, 1992–2001; Nat. Cttee of Inquiry into Higher Educn (Dearing Cttee), 1996–97; Council, ILT, 2000–02; Bd, QCA, 2003–07; Chairman: Univs Assoc. for Contg Educn, 1994–98; Steering Cttee for ESRC Teaching and Learning Prog., 1998–2003; SE England Cultural Consortium, 1999–2002; UUK Longer Term Strategy Gp, 1999–2005; Nat. Inquiry into Future of Lifelong Learning, 2007–Sept. 2009. Pres., SRHE, 2005–. Trustee, Nuffield Foundn, 2005–. Chm., Brighton Fest. Soc., 2002–05. Hon. RCM 2007. DUniv: Open, 2002; Oxford Brookes, 2003; Hon. DSocSc Southampton, 2004; Hon. LLD Sussex, 2005; Hon. DEd Bath, 2005; Hon. DLitt: Manchester Metropolitan, 2006; Brighton, 2006. *Publications:* Margaret Fuller, 1988; Managing the Modular Course, 1989; (jtly) Developing Professional Education, 1992; Arendt, 1992; (jtly) Managing the University Curriculum, 1994; (jtly) Continuing Education in the Mainstream, 1996; (jtly) Lifelong Learning and the University, 1998; Managing Strategy, 2000; (jtly) New Directions in Professional Higher Education, 2000; (jtly) Higher Education and the Lifecourse, 2003; (jtly) Managing Institutional Self-study, 2005; Managing Civic and Community Engagement, 2007; (jtly) The Dearing Report: ten years on, 2007; Morale, 2009; papers on history of American and British ideas, higher education policy. *Recreations:* cricket, tennis, music (piano). *Address:* Institute of Education, University of London, 20 Bedford Way, WC1H 0AL. *T:* (020) 7612 6363.

WATSON, Very Rev. Derek Richard; Dean of Salisbury, 1996–2002; *b* 18 Feb. 1938; *s* of Richard Goodman and Honor Joan Watson; *m* 1985, Sheila Anne Atkinson (*see* Ven. S. A. Watson). *Educ:* Uppingham Sch.; Selwyn Coll., Cambridge (MA 1965); Cuddesdon Coll., Oxford. Ordained deacon, 1964, priest, 1965; Asst Curate, All Saints, New Eltham, 1964–66; Chaplain, Christ's Coll., Cambridge, 1966–70; Domestic Chaplain to Bishop of Southwark, 1970–73; Vicar, St Andrews and St Mark's, Surbiton, 1973–78; Canon Treasurer, Southwark Cathedral and Diocesan Dir of Ordinands and Post Ordination Training, 1978–82; Rector, St Luke and Christchurch, Chelsea, 1982–96. Preacher of Lincoln's Inn, 2007–. Chm., Chelsea Festival, 1993–96. *Recreations:* cycling, croquet. *Address:* 29 The Precincts, Canterbury, Kent CT1 2EP. *Club:* Hurlingham.

WATSON, Sir Duncan (Amos), Kt 1993; CBE 1986; Principal Assistant Treasury Solicitor, Common Law, 1978–86; Chairman, Executive Council, Royal National Institute for the Blind, 1975–90; *b* 10 May 1926; *m* 1954, Mercia Casey (*d* 2002), Auckland, NZ; *m* 2007, Anthea Nicholson-Cole. *Educ:* Worcester College for the Blind; St Edmund Hall, Oxford (BA). Solicitor. Chm., Access Cttee for England, 1989–93; Pres., World Blind Union, 1988–92.

WATSON, Prof. Elaine Denise, PhD, DSc; FRCVS; Professor of Veterinary Reproduction, since 1999, and Dean, Royal (Dick) School of Veterinary Studies, since 2003, University of Edinburgh; *b* Ayrshire, 8 Sept. 1955; *d* of Alexander and Isabel Watson; *m* 1989, Dr Christopher Clarke; one *s*. *Educ:* Univ. of Glasgow (BVMS 1978; MVM 1979); Univ. of Bristol (PhD 1987); Univ. of Edinburgh (DSc 2002). FRCVS 1990. Res. Officer, MAFF Cattle Breeding Centre, Shinfield, 1979–82; Veterinary Res. Officer, AFRC Inst. for Res. on Animal Diseases, Compton, 1982–84; Res. Asst, Univ. of Bristol Sch. of Veterinary Sci., 1984–87; Asst Prof. of Equine Reproduction, Univ. of Pennsylvania, 1987–91; Royal (Dick) School of Veterinary Studies: Sen. Lectr and Hd of Reproduction, 1991–95; Reader, 1995–99. *Publications:* (ed jtly) Equine Medicine, Surgery and Reproduction, 1997; contrib. scientific papers and abstracts. *Recreations:* cycling, walking, travel, cinema, books, good food and wine. *Address:* Royal (Dick) School of Veterinary Studies, University of Edinburgh, Easter Bush, Roslin, Midlothian EH25 9RG. *T:* (0131) 650 6235, *Fax:* (0131) 650 8838; *e-mail:* elaine.watson@ed.ac.uk.

WATSON, (Elizabeth) Joyce; Member (Lab) Wales Mid and West, National Assembly for Wales, since 2007; *b* 2 May 1955; *d* of late William Roberts and Jean Roberts (*née* Rennie); *m* 1986, Colin Watson; one *s* two *d*. *Educ:* Manorbier Sch.; Cosheston Sch.; Cardigan Comprehensive Sch.; Pembroke Coll.; Univ. of Wales, Swansea (BScEcon Politics). Self-employed, retail and hospitality trade, 1980–2002; Manager, Women's Voice, 2002–07. *Publications:* Not Bad for a Woman, 2002; From Governess to Government, 2007. *Recreations:* coastal path walking with dog, reading, bird watching, family meals. *Address:* National Assembly for Wales, Cardiff CF99 0NA. *T:* (029) 2089 8972, *Fax:* (029) 2089 8419. *Club:* Soroptimist.

WATSON, Emily, (Mrs J. Waters); actress; *b* 14 Jan. 1967; *m* 1995, Jack Waters; one *d*. *Educ:* Bristol Univ. (BA Hons English). *Films:* Breaking the Waves, 1997 (Best Actress, Variety Club); Metroland, 1998; The Boxer, 1998; Hilary and Jackie, 1998 (Best Actress, British Ind. Film Awards); Cradle Will Rock, 1999; Angela's Ashes, 2000; The Luzhin Defense, 2000; Trixie, 2000; Equilibrium, 2001; Punch-Drunk Love, 2002; Gosford Park, 2002; Red Dragon, 2002; The Life and Death of Peter Sellers, 2004; Separate Lies, 2005; Wah Wah, 2006; The Proposition, 2006; Corpse Bride, 2006; Miss Potter, 2006; The Water Horse: Legend of the Deep, 2007; Fireflies in the Garden, 2008; Synecdoche, New York, 2008; *television:* Mill on the Floss, 1997; The Memory Keeper's Daughter, 2008; *theatre:* Uncle Vanya, Twelfth Night, Donmar Warehouse, 2002. *Address:* c/o Independent Talent Group Ltd, Oxford House, 76 Oxford Street, W1D 1BS.

WATSON, (Francis) Paul; QC 2002; a Recorder, since 1998; *b* 10 Sept. 1953; *s* of Ray and Hilda Watson; *m* 1980, Sally; one *s*. *Educ:* Churcher's Coll., Petersfield; Leeds Poly. (BA Hons). Called to the Bar, Gray's Inn, 1978; Magistrate's Clerk, 1978–80; Army Officer, Army Legal Corps, 1980–85, retd in rank of Major; in practice as barrister, 1986–. *Recreations:* sailing, avid supporter of Middlesbrough FC. *Address:* Paradise Chambers, Sheffield S1 2DE.

WATSON, Gavin; *see* Watson, A. G.

WATSON, George William P.; *see* Pascoe-Watson.

WATSON, Gerald Walter; Chairman, Centaur Trust, since 1999; *b* 13 Dec. 1934; *s* of Reginald Harold Watson and Gertrude Hilda Watson (*née* Ruffell); *m* 1961, Janet Rosemary (*née* Hovey); one *s* two *d*. *Educ:* King Edward VI, Norwich School; Corpus Christi Coll., Cambridge (MA). National Service, RAF Regt, 1953–55. War Office, 1958–64; MoD, 1964–69; Civil Service Dept, 1969–73; Northern Ireland Office, 1973–75; CSD, 1975–81; HM Treasury, 1981–86; Dir, Central Computer and Telecommunications Agency, 1978–82; Dep. Chm., Building Socs Commn, 1986–88; Partner, Banking Gp, Ernst & Young (formerly Arthur Young), 1989–98. *Recreations:* opera and theatre going, equestrian sports. *Address:* Topcroft Lodge, Bungay, Suffolk NR35 2BB.

WATSON, Graham Robert; Member (Lib Dem) South West Region, England, since 1999, also Gibraltar, since 2004, European Parliament (Somerset and North Devon, 1994–99); Leader, Alliance of Liberals and Democrats for Europe (formerly European Liberal Democrat and Reform Group), since 2002; *b* 23 March 1956; *s* of late Gordon Graham Watson and of Stephanie Revill-Johnson; *m* 1987, Rita Giannini; one *s* one *d*. *Educ:* City of Bath Boys' Sch.; Heriot-Watt Univ. (BA Hons Mod. Langs). Freelance interpreter and translator, 1979–80; Administrator, Paisley Coll. of Tech., 1980–83; Head, Private Office of Rt Hon. David Steel, MP, 1983–87; Sen. Press Officer, TSB Group, 1987–88; HSBC Holdings: Public Affairs Manager, 1988–91; Govt Affairs Manager, 1992–94. Chm., Justice and Home Affairs Cttee, EP, 1999–2002. *Publications:* (ed) The Liberals in the North-South Dialogue, 1980; (ed) To the Power of Ten, 2000; (ed) Liberalism and Globalisation, 2001; Liberal Language, 2003; EU've Got Mail, 2004; Liberal Democracy and Globalisation, 2006; The Power of Speech, 2006; articles on politics in magazines and nat. newspapers. *Recreations:* sailing, walking. *Address:* European Parliament, 1040 Brussels, Belgium. *T:* (2) 2845626; Liberal Democrat Office, Bagehot's Foundry, Beard's Yard, Langport, Som TA10 9PS. *T:* (01458) 252265. *Club:* Royal Commonwealth Society.

WATSON, Maj.-Gen. (Henry) Stuart (Ramsay), CBE 1973 (MBE 1954); *b* 9 July 1922; *yr s* of Major H. A. Watson, CBE, MVO and Mrs Dorothy Bannerman Watson, OBE; *m* 1965, Susan, *o d* of Col W. H. Jackson, CBE, DL; two *s* one *d*. *Educ:* Winchester College. Commnd 2nd Lieut 13th/18th Royal Hussars, 1942; Lieut 1943; Captain 1945; Adjt 13/18 H, 1945–46 and 1948–50; psc 1951; GSO2, HQ 1st Corps, 1952–53; Instr RMA Sandhurst, 1955–57; Instr Staff Coll. Camberley, 1960–62; CO 13/18 H, 1962–64; GSO1, MoD, 1964–65; Col GS, SHAPE, 1965–68; Col, Defence Policy Staff, MoD, 1968; idc 1969; BGS HQ BAOR, 1970–73; Dir Defence Policy, MoD, 1973–74; Sen. Army Directing Staff, RCDS, 1974–76. Col, 13th/18th Royal Hussars, 1979–90. Exec. Dir, 1977–85, Dep. Dir Gen., 1985–88, Inst. of Dirs; Dir, Treasurers' Dept, Cons. Central Office, 1992–94. *Recreations:* golf, gardening. *Address:* The White Cross, Askett, Princes Risborough, Bucks HP27 9LR. *T:* and *Fax:* (01844) 347601. *Clubs:* Cavalry and Guards; Huntercombe Golf; St Enodoc Golf.

WATSON, Dr Iain Arthur; Director, Information Superiority, Defence Procurement Agency, 2004–07; *b* 21 Nov. 1947; *s* of Alastair Cameron Watson and Lilian Ellen Watson (*née* Smith); *m* 1st, 1968, Janet Marshall (marr. diss. 1995); one *s* one *d*; 2nd, 1998, Pamela Chambers (*née* Low). *Educ:* Stratford Grammar Sch.; Dundee Univ. (BSc Pure Maths 1970; MSc Maths 1972; PhD 1976). Ministry of Defence: Underwater Research, Portland, 1974–89; Director: IT Systems, 1989–91; IT Strategy, 1991–92; Fleet Support (Communications and Inf. Systems), 1992–97; Dir Gen., Command Inf. Systems, 1997–99; Integrated Project Team Leader, BOWMAN and Land Digitization, 1999–2002; Dep. Tech. Dir, Thales Underwater Systems, 2002–03; Exec. Dir, Defence Procurement Agency, 2003–04. *Recreations:* dinghy sailing, basketball, car restoration, skiing, history.

WATSON, Ven. Ian Leslie Stewart; Archdeacon of Coventry, since 2007; *b* Carlton, Nottingham, 17 Sept. 1950; *s* of Leslie Arthur Watson and Joan Harrison Watson (*née* Bramley); *m* 1972, Denise Macpherson; one *s* one *d*. *Educ:* Nottingham High Sch.; Britannia Royal Naval Coll. (French Interpreter); Army Staff Coll.; Wycliffe Hall, Oxford. Officer, RM, 1969–79; ordained deacon, 1981, priest, 1982; Curate, St Andrew's, Plymouth, with St Paul's, Stonehouse, 1981–85; Vicar (and Methodist Minister), Matchborough, 1985–89; Vicar, 1989–92, Team Rector, 1992–95, Woodley; Anglican Chaplain, Amsterdam and Noord Holland, 1995–2001; Chief Exec., Intercontinental Church Soc., 2001–07. Canon, Gibraltar Cathedral, 2002–. Dir of Ordinands, Benelux, 1998–2001; Mem., Archbishop's Bd of Mission and Partnership in World Mission, 2001–07. Officiating Chaplain, RN, 1981–85; Chaplain, City of Coventry Freeman's Guild, 2008–. Asst Mechanic, RNLI Plymouth Lifeboat, 1983–85; Retained Firefighter, Royal Berks Fire and Rescue Service, 1991–93. Bishop Kirkby's Meml Lect., Australia, 2003. GSM (NI) 1973; Silver Jubilee Medal, 1977; Vellum Service Cert., RNLI, 1985. *Recreations:* sport (Rugby, cricket, golf, rock climbing and potholing, now sedentary due to disability), music (singing, cellist), fishing. *Address:* 9 Armorial Road, Coventry CV3 6GH. *T:* (024) 7641 7750; *e-mail:* i.watson440@btinternet.com.

WATSON, Sir (James) Andrew, 5th Bt *cr* 1866; *b* 30 Dec. 1937; *s* of Sir Thomas Aubrey Watson, 4th Bt and Ella Marguerite, *y d* of late Sir George Farrar, 1st Bt, DSO; *S* father, 1941; *m* 1965, Christabel Mary, *e d* of K. R. M. Carlisle and Hon. Mrs Carlisle; two *s* one *d*. *Educ:* Eton. Called to the Bar, Inner Temple, 1966; a Recorder, 1985–2003. Gov., RSC, 1990–2003. *Heir: s* Roland Victor Watson, *b* 4 March 1966. *Address:* Talton House, Newbold-on-Stour, Stratford-upon-Avon, Warwickshire CV37 8UB.

WATSON, Prof. James Dewey, Hon. KBE 2002; Chancellor, Cold Spring Harbor Laboratory, 2003–07 (Director, 1968–94; President, 1994–2003); *b* 6 April 1928; *s* of James D. and Jean Mitchell Watson; *m* 1968, Elizabeth Lewis; two *s*. *Educ:* Univ. of Chicago (BS); Indiana Univ. (PhD); Clare Coll., Cambridge (Hon. Fellow, 1967). Senior Res. Fellow in Biology, California Inst. of Technology, 1953–55; Harvard University: Asst Prof. of Biology, 1956–58; Associate Prof., 1958–61; Prof. of Molecular Biology, 1961–76. Dir, Nat. Center for Human Genome Res., NIH, 1989–92. Newton-Abraham Vis. Prof., Oxford, 1994. Member: US National Acad. Sciences, 1962–; Amer Acad. of Arts and Sciences, 1958; Royal Danish Acad. 1962; Amer. Philosophical Soc., 1977; Foreign Member: Royal Soc., 1981; Acad. of Scis, Russia (formerly USSR), 1989; NAS, Ukraine, 1995; Hon. Member: Nat. Acad. of Scis, India, 2001; Internat. Acad. of Humanism, 2004 (Humanist Laureate 2005); RIA, 2005. Hon. FIBiol 1995; Hon. Fellow, Tata Inst. of Fundamental Res., Bombay, 1996. Hon. degrees include: Hon. DSc: Chicago, 1961; Indiana, 1963; Long Island, 1970; Adelphi, 1972; Brandeis, 1973; Albert Einstein Coll. of Medicine, 1974; Hofstra, 1976; Harvard, 1978; Rockefeller, 1980; Clarkson Coll., 1981; SUNY, 1983; Rutgers, 1988; Bard Coll., 1991; Univ. of Stellenbosch, S Africa, 1993; Fairfield Univ., Conn, 1993; Cambridge, 1993; Oxford, 1995; Melbourne, 1996; Univ. of Judaism, LA, 1999; London, Illinois Wesleyan, 2000; Widener, Dartmouth, TCD, 2001; Barcelona, 2005; Hon. MD: Buenos Aires, 1986; Charles Univ., Prague, 1998; Hon. LLD Notre Dame, 1965; Dhc Barcelona, 2005. Awards include: Nobel Prize for Physiology or Medicine (jointly), 1962; Carty Medal, US NAS, 1971; Kaul Foundn Award for Excellence, 1992; Copley Medal, Royal Soc., 1993; Mendel Nat. Biotechnol. Venture Award, 1993; Nat. Medal of Science, USA, 1997; Mendel Medal, Czechoslovakia, 1998; Univ. of Chicago Medal, 1998; Heald Award, Illinois Inst. of Technol., 1999; NY Acad. of Medicine Award, 1999; Univ. Medal, SUNY, 2000; UCL Prize, 2000; (jtly) Benjamin Franklin Medal, APS, 2001; Gairdner Award, 2002; Lotos Club Medal of Merit, 2004; Othmer Medal, Chemical Heritage Foundn, 2005. US Presidential Medal of Freedom, 1977. Liberty Medal, City of Philadelphia, 2000. US Presidential Medal of Freedom, 1977. *Publications:* (jtly) Molecular Biology of the Gene, 1965, 4th edn 1986; The Double Helix, 1968; (with John Tooze) The DNA Story, 1981; (with others) The Molecular Biology of the Cell, 1983, 3rd edn 1994; (with John Tooze and David T. Kurtz) Recombinant DNA: a short course, 1984, 2nd edn (with others) 1992; A Passion for DNA, 2000; Genes, Girls and Gamow (autobiog.), 2001; DNA: the secret of life, 2003; (ed and commentary) Darwin: the indelible stamp, 2005; Avoid Boring People: and other lessons from a life in science (autobiog.), 2007; scientific papers on the mechanism of heredity. *Recreation:* tennis. *Clubs:* Century, Piping Rock, Lotos, River (New York).

WATSON, James Kay Graham, PhD; FRS 1987; FRSC 1990; Principal Research Officer, National Research Council of Canada, 1987–2007, now Researcher Emeritus (Senior Research Officer, 1982–87); *b* Denny, Stirlingshire, 20 April 1936; *s* of Thomas Watson and Mary Catherine (*née* Miller); *m* 1981, Carolyn Margaret Landon Kerr, *e d* of late Robert Reid Kerr. *Educ:* Denny High Sch.; High School of Stirling; Univ. of Glasgow (BScChem, PhD). Postdoctoral Fellow: UCL, 1961–63; Nat. Res. Council, Ottawa, 1963–65; Univ. of Reading, 1965–66; Lectr in Chem. Physics, Univ. of Reading, 1966–71; Vis. Associate Prof. of Physics, Ohio State Univ., Columbus, 1971–75; SRC Sen. Res. Fellow in Chemistry, Univ. of Southampton, 1975–82. Fellow, American Physical Soc., 1990. Award for Theoretical Chemistry and Spectroscopy, Chemical Soc., 1974; Plyler Prize, Amer. Phys. Soc., 1986; Joannes Marcus Marci Medal, Czech and Slovak Spectroscopic Soc., 1996; H. M. Tory Medal, Royal Soc. of Can., 1999; E. Bright Wilson Award in Spectroscopy, Amer. Chem. Soc., 2004. *Publications:* 163 articles on molecular physics and spectroscopy in learned jls. *Recreations:* music, golf, tree-watching. *Address:* 183 Stanley Avenue, Ottawa, ON K1M 1P2, Canada. *T:* (613) 7457928; (business) Steacie Institute for Molecular Sciences, National Research Council of Canada, Ottawa, ON K1A OR6, Canada. *T:* (613) 9900739; *e-mail:* james.watson@nrc-cnrc.gc.ca.

WATSON, James Kenneth, FCA; Chairman: Alldays (formerly Watson & Philip) plc, 1994–99; NFC plc (formerly National Freight Consortium), 1991–94 (Finance Director, 1982–84; Deputy Chairman, 1985–90); *b* 16 Jan. 1935; *s* of James and Helen Watson; *m* 1st, 1959, Eileen Fay Waller (marr. diss. 1998); two *s* one *d*; 2nd, 2001, Sylvia Grace Bailey. *Educ:* Watford Grammar Sch.; Stanford Univ., California, USA. Baker Sutton & Co., Chartered Accountants, 1964; Financial Controller, Times Group, 1968; Finance Director: British Road Services Ltd, 1970–76; Nat. Freight Corp., later Nat. Freight Co., 1977–82. Non-executive Director: Gartmore, 1993–96; Henlys Group, 1994–2000; National Express, 1994–2001. Chm., Chairmen's Forum Ltd, 2001–. Chm., Inst. of Management, 1993–96. *Publications:* contribs to transport, management and financial press. *Recreations:* cricket, theatre, history. *Address:* Benton Potts, Hawridge Common, near Chesham, Bucks HP5 2UH. *Clubs:* Royal Automobile, MCC.

WATSON, Prof. James Patrick; Professor of Psychiatry, Guy's, King's and St Thomas' School of Medicine of King's College London (formerly UMDS), 1974–2000, now Emeritus; *b* 14 May 1936; *e s* of Hubert Timothy Watson and Grace Emily (*née* Mizen); *m* 1962, Dr Christine Mary Colley; four *s*. *Educ:* Roan Sch. for Boys, Greenwich; Trinity Coll., Cambridge; King's Coll. Hosp. Med. Sch., London. MA, MD; FRCP, FRCPsych, DPM, DCH. Qualified, 1960. Hosp. appts in Medicine, Paediatrics, Pathology, Neurosurgery, at King's Coll. Hosp. and elsewhere, 1960–64; Registrar and Sen. Registrar, Bethlem Royal and Maudsley Hosps, 1964–71; Sen. Lectr in Psychiatry, St George's Hosp. Med. Sch., and Hon. Consultant Psychiatrist, St George's Hosp., 1971–74. *Publications:* (ed jtly) Personal Meanings, 1982; papers on gp, family, marital and behavioural psychotherapy, treatment of phobias, hospital ward environmental effects on patients, postnatal depression, community psychiatry, in BMJ, Lancet, British Jl of Psychiatry, British Jl of Med. Psychology, British Jl of Clin. Psychology, Behaviour Research and Therapy. *Recreations:* mountains; music, especially opera, especially Mozart.

WATSON, Ven. Jeffrey John Seagrief; Archdeacon of Ely, 1993–2004, now Archdeacon Emeritus; *b* 29 April 1939; *s* of late John Cole Watson and Marguerite Freda Rose Watson; *m* 1969, Rosemary Grace Lea; one *s* one *d*. *Educ:* University College Sch., Hampstead; Emmanuel Coll., Cambridge (MA Hons Classics); Clifton Theol Coll., Bristol. Curate: Christ Church, Beckenham, 1965–69; St Jude, Southsea, 1969–71; Vicar: Christ Church, Winchester, 1971–81; Holy Saviour, Bitterne, 1981–93; Examining Chaplain to Bishop of Winchester, 1976–93; RD of Southampton, 1983–93; Hon. Canon: Winchester Cathedral, 1991–93; Ely Cathedral, 1993–2004. Mem., Gen. Synod, 1985–95; Chm., C of E Vocations Adv. Sub-Cttee, 1991–99; Chm., Ministry Div. Candidates' Panel, 1999–. *Recreations:* photography, barbershop singing, walking, travel. *Address:* 7 Ferry Road, Hythe, Southampton SO45 5GB. *T:* (023) 8084 1189.

WATSON, Jennifer, (Jenny); Chairman, Electoral Commission, since 2009; *b* 25 Jan. 1964; *d* of Ronald Watson and Phyllis Watson (*née* Avery). *Educ:* Coopers' Co. and Coborn Sch., Upminster; Sheffield Hallam Univ. (BA Communications Studies); Univ. of Westminster (MA 20th Century British Hist.). Promotions Manager, Liberty (NCCL), 1993–95; Campaign and Communications Manager, Charter 88, 1996–98; Media and PR Manager, Victim Support, 1999; Develt Dir, Human Rights Act Res. Unit, KCL, 2000–01; Dir and Co-Founder, 2004–05, Associate, 2007–08, Global Partners and Associates. Equal Opportunities Commission: Comr, 1999–2000; Dep. Chair, 2000–05; Chair, 2005–07. Member: Banking Code Standards Bd, 2001–06 (Dep. Chair, 2005–06); Cttee on Radioactive Waste Mgt, 2003–06; Audit Commn, 2007–; Chair, Indep. Transparency Rev. Panel, Nirex UK, 2001–03. Dir, WRAP, 2007–. Chm., Fawcett Soc., 1997–2001. Mem., Mgt Cttee, Liby of Women, London Guildhall Univ., 2001–. *Publication:* (jtly) Human Rights Act Toolkit, 2003. *Recreations:* gardening, singing (Mem., London Philharmonic Choir), reading, walking. *Address:* Electoral Commission, Trevelyan House, Great Peter Street, SW1P 2HW.

WATSON, John, FRCS, FRCSE; Consultant Plastic Surgeon to: Queen Victoria Hospital, East Grinstead, 1950–77, now Hon. Consultant; King Edward VII Hospital for Officers, 1963–87; London Hospital, 1963–82; *b* 10 Sept. 1914; *s* of late John Watson; *m* 1941, June Christine Stiles; one *s* three *d*. *Educ:* Leighton Park, Reading; Jesus Coll., Cambridge; Guy's Hospital. MRCS, LRCP 1938; MA, MB, BChir (Cantab) 1939; FRCS(Ed.) 1946; FRCS 1963. Served as Sqdn Ldr (temp.) RAF, 1940–46 (despatches twice). Marks Fellow in Plastic Surgery, Queen Victoria Hosp., E Grinstead, 1947–50; Consultant Plastic Surgeon, Queen Victoria Hospital, East Grinstead, and Tunbridge Wells Gp of Hospitals, 1950–77. Gen. Sec., Internat. Confedn for Plastic and Reconstructive Surgery, 1971–75; Hon. Mem. Brit. Assoc. of Plastic Surgeons, 1979– (Hon. Sec., 1960–62, Pres., 1969); Hon. MRSocMed. *Publications:* numerous articles on plastic surgery in techn. jls and scientific periodicals. Chapters in: Textbook of Surgery, Plastic Surgery for Nurses, Modern Trends in Plastic Surgery, Clinical Surgery. *Recreations:* fishing, astronomy. *Address:* Iddons, Henley's Down, Catsfield, Battle, East Sussex TN33 9BN. *T:* (01424) 830226.

WATSON, John Grenville Bernard, OBE 1998; Member (C), North Yorkshire County Council, since 2005 (Executive Member for Schools, since 2005); *b* 21 Feb. 1943; *s* of Norman V. Watson and Ruby E. Watson; *m* 1965, Deanna Wood; one *s* two *d*. *Educ:* Moorlands Sch., Leeds; Bootham Sch., York; College of Law, Guildford. Articled, 1962, qualified as solicitor, 1967; joined John Waddington Ltd as managerial trainee, 1968; Export Director, Plastona John Waddington Ltd, 1972; Marketing Dir, 1975, Man. Dir, 1977, Waddington Games Ltd, responsible for Security Printing Div., 1984–89, for Johnsen & Jorgensen, 1988–89; Director: John Waddington PLC, 1979–89; Goddard Kay Rogers (Northern) Ltd, 1989–92; Yorkshire Bldg Soc., 1995–2004; Chief Exec., Bradford City Challenge Ltd, 1992–97. Chm., Bradford Community NHS Trust, 1996–2002. Mem., Leeds Develt Corp., 1988–92; Chm., Heritage Lottery Fund, Yorks and Humber, 2005–. Joined Young Conservatives, 1965; Chairman, Yorkshire YC, 1969; Personal Asst to Rt Hon. Edward Heath, 1970; Chm., Nat. YC, 1971; contested (C) York, general elections, Feb. and Oct. 1974. MP (C): Skipton, 1979–83; Skipton and Ripon, 1983–87. Chm., Conservative Candidates Assoc., 1975–79. Mem., Parly Select Cttee on Energy, 1980–82; PPS, NI Office, 1982–83; PPS, Dept of Energy, 1983–85. Chm., British Atlantic Gp of Young Political Leaders, 1982–84; Nat. Vice Pres., Young Conservative Orgn, 1984–86. Pres., British Youth Council, 1980–83. *Recreations:* travel, property renovation. *Address:* Evergreen Cottage, Main Street, Kirk Deighton, Leeds LS22 4DZ. *T:* (01937) 588273.

See also V. H. Watson.

WATSON, Joyce; *see* Watson, E. J.

WATSON, Julian Howard R.; *see* Richmond-Watson.

WATSON, (Leslie) Michael (Macdonald) S.; *see* Saunders Watson.

WATSON, Lynn Deborah; *see* Roberts, L. D.

WATSON, Paul; *see* Watson, F. P.

WATSON, Dr Peter, OBE 1988; FREng; Executive Chairman, AEA Technology, 2002–05 (Chief Executive, 1994–2001); *b* 9 Jan. 1944; *m* 1966, Elizabeth Buttery; two *s*. *Educ:* Univ. of Leeds (BSc 1966); Univ. of Waterloo, Canada (MSc 1968; PhD 1971). FIMechE; FREng (FEng 1998); FCIPS. PSO, British Railways Res., 1971–76; GKN Technology Ltd, 1976–89 (Chm., 1982–89); Chm., GKN Axles Ltd, 1986–91; Technical Dir, British Railways, 1991–94. Chm., Lontra Ltd, 2006–; non-executive Director: Spectris (formerly Fairey) Plc, 1997–2003; Martin Currie Enhanced Income Trust, 2000–; HSL Ltd, 2006–; SVL Ltd, 2007–. Vis. Prof., Imperial Coll., London, 2005–. Pres., Engrg Integrity Soc., 1988–. Mem. Bd, Univ. of Wolverhampton, 1993–2004. Hon. FAPM. FRSA 1988. *Publications:* numerous articles on metal fatigue and management. *Address:* 49 Suckling Green Lane, Codsall, Wolverhampton, W Midlands WV8 2BT. *T:* (01902) 845252.

WATSON, Rt Rev. Peter Robert; Archbishop of Melbourne and Metropolitan of the Province of Victoria, 2000–05; *b* 1 Jan. 1936; *s* of Noel Frederick and Helen Elizabeth Watson; *m* 1962, Margo Eleanor Deans; three *d*. *Educ:* Canterbury Boys' High Sch., Sydney; Sydney Univ. (BEc); Moore Theological Coll., Sydney (ThL). Asst Priest, St Paul's, Chatswood, 1961–63; Curate-in-Charge, Lalor Park and Seven Hills, 1963–73; Rector, Lalor Park and Seven Hills, 1973–74; RD of Prospect, 1968–74; Canon, Prov. Cathedral of St John, Parramatta, 1969–74; Rector: St Luke's, Miranda, 1974–84; St Thomas, North Sydney, 1984–89; Area Dean, North Sydney, 1986–89; Bishop of Parramatta, 1989–93, of South Sydney, 1993–2000; an Asst Bp of Sydney, 1989–2000. *Recreations:* caravanning, walking, travel, swimming. *Address:* c/o The Anglican Centre, 209 Flinders Lane, Melbourne, Vic 3000, Australia.

WATSON, Vice-Adm. Sir Philip (Alexander), KBE 1976; LVO 1960; *b* 7 Oct. 1919; *yr s* of A. H. St C. Watson; *m* 1948, Jennifer Beatrice Tanner; one *s* two *d*. *Educ:* St Albans School. FIET (FIEE 1963). Sub-Lt RNVR, 1940; qual. Torpedo Specialist, 1943; transf. to RN, 1946; Comdr 1955; HM Yacht Britannia, 1957–59; Captain 1963; MoD (Ship Dept), 1963; Senior Officers' War Course, 1966; comd HMS Collingwood, 1967; Dep. Dir of Engrg (Ship Dept), MoD, 1969; Dir Gen. Weapons (Naval), MoD, 1970–77; Chief Naval Engineer Officer, 1974–77. Rear-Adm. 1970; Vice-Adm. 1974. Director: Marconi International Marine Co. Ltd, 1977–86; Marconi Radar Systems Ltd, 1981–86 (Chm., 1981–85); Consultant, GEC-Marconi Ltd, 1986–87. Mem. Council, IEE, 1975–78, 1982–91, Chm. South East Centre, 1982–83. Adm. Pres., Midland Naval Officers Assoc., 1979–85, Vice Pres., 1985–. CCMI (CBIM 1973). *Address:* The Hermitage, Bodicote, Banbury, Oxon OX15 4BZ. *T:* (01295) 263300.

WATSON, Philip Stuart, CBE 2006; RIBA; FCIH; public sector consultant; Chief Executive, Blackburn with Darwen Unitary Authority, 1996–2006; *b* Blackburn, 22 Feb. 1946; *s* of late Herbert and Aimée Watson; *m* 1973, Shirley Clark; one *s* two *d*. *Educ:* Wensley Fold Primary Sch., Blackburn; Queen Elizabeth's Grammar Sch., Blackburn; Sheffield Univ. (BArch Hons 1968). Chartered Architect 1970; RIBA 1970; FCIH 1976. Blackburn Borough Council: various posts from architect to Dep. Borough Architect, 1968–85; Asst Chief Exec., 1985–96; Dep. Chief Exec., 1994–96. Gov., Blackburn Coll., 2005–. *Recreations:* Blackburn Rovers, running, crown green bowling, golf. *Address:* Westleigh, Lawley Road, Blackburn BB2 6SG. *Clubs:* Blackburn Golf; Alexandra Bowling.

WATSON, Richard (Eagleson Gordon) Burges, CMG 1985; HM Diplomatic Service, retired; Ambassador to Nepal, 1987–90; *b* 23 Sept. 1930; *er s* of late Harold Burges Watson and Marjorie Eleanor (*née* Gordon); *m* 1966, Ann Rosamund Clarke; two *s* three *d*. *Educ:* King Edward VI Sch., Bury St Edmunds; St John's Coll., Cambridge. RA, 1948–50. Joined HM Foreign (subseq. Diplomatic) Service, 1954; Tokyo, 1954–60; FO, 1960–63; Bamako (Mali), 1963–66; British Delegn to OECD, 1966–69; FCO, 1969–71; Vis. Student, Woodrow Wilson Sch., Princeton, 1971–72; Tokyo, 1972–76; Brussels, 1976–78; FCO, 1978–81; Foundn for Internat. Research and Studies, Florence, 1981–82; FCO, 1982–83; Minister (Commercial) and Consul-Gen., Milan, 1983–86. *Recreations:* travel, bridge. *Address:* Highfield House, Gloucester Road, Painswick GL6 6QN. *T:* (01452) 814763. *Club:* Hurlingham.

WATSON, Sir Ronald (Mathew), Kt 1997; CBE 1989; Member (C), Sefton Metropolitan Borough Council, 1974–91 and since 1992; *b* 24 May 1945; *s* of Ralph and Rheta Mary Watson; *m* 1966, Lesley Ann McLean; one *s* one *d*. *Educ:* South Shields GS; Waterloo GS. General Manager: Laycock Travel Services, 1972–79; Morrisons Travel Agents, 1979–92. Mem. (C), Southport CBC, 1969–74; Leader, Sefton MBC, 1983–87. Leader, Cons. Gp, AMA, 1992–97. Director: Southport Mktg and Enterprise Bureau, 1983–97; Liverpool Airport plc, 1993–97; non-exec. Dir, Southport & Formby, subseq. Sefton, HA, 1991–2001; Dep. Chairman: Cheshire and Merseyside Strategic HA, 2002–06; Cheshire W PCT, 2006–; Southport and Ormskirk Hosp. NHS Trust, 2006–. Mem. Bd, Merseyside Develt Corp., 1993–97; Consultant, NW Trng Council, 1996–. Local Government Association: Dep. Leader, Cons. Gp, 1996–2000; Vice-Chm., 1997–2000; Chm., Tourism Exec., 1998–2003; Chm., Envmt and Regeneration Exec., 2003–04; Dep. Chm., Regeneration Bd, 2005–; Vice Chm., Urban Commn, 2006–. Mem., EU Cttee of the Regions, 1998–. Consultant, Eur. Advice Unit, Barnetts, Solicitors, Southport, 1994–2007. Member: Audit Commn, 1995–2001; Mental Health Tribunal, 2002–; Standards Bd for England, 2006–. Vice-Pres., British Resorts Assoc., 1998–. Founder Mem. and Fellow, Tourism Soc., 1978; Fellow, Inst. of Travel and Tourism, 1989. *Recreation:* writer on jazz and blues. *Address:* 7 Carnoustie Close, Oxford Road, Birkdale, Southport PR8 2FB.

WATSON, Ven. Sheila Anne; Archdeacon of Canterbury, since 2007; *b* 20 May 1953; *d* of William Calderhead Atkinson and Margaret Atkinson (*née* Gray); *m* 1985, Derek Richard Watson, *qv*. *Educ:* Ayr Acad.; St Andrews Univ. (MA 1975, MPhil 1980); Corpus Christi Coll., Oxford; Edinburgh Theol Coll. Ordained deaconess, 1979, deacon, 1987, priest, 1994; Deaconess: St Saviour, Bridge of Allan and St John's, Alloa, 1979–80; St Mary, Monkseaton, 1980–84; Adult Educn Officer, Kensington Episcopal Area, 1984–87; Hon. Curate, St Luke and Christchurch, Chelsea, 1987–96; Selection Sec., 1992–93, Sen. Selection Sec., 1993–96, ABM; Advr, CME, 1997–2002, Dir of Ministry, 1998–2002, dio. Salisbury; Hon. Canon, Salisbury Cathedral, 2000–02; Archdeacon of Buckingham, 2002–07. *Recreations:* theatre, cycling. *Address:* 29 The Precincts, Canterbury, Kent CT1 2EP. *T:* (01227) 865238, *Fax:* (01227) 785209; *e-mail:* archdeacon@canterbury-cathedral.org.

WATSON, Sir Simon (Conran Hamilton), 6th Bt *cr* 1895, of Earnock, co. Lanarks; *b* 11 Aug. 1939; *s* of Leslie Dundas Watson, *g s* of 1st Bt, and Enid Margaret Watson (*née* Conran); *S* cousin, Lt-Col Sir John Inglefield-Watson, 5th Bt, 2007; *m* 1971, Madeleine Stiles Dickerson (*d* 1998); *m* 2007, Patricia Wheatley Burt, *d* of Anthony Wheatley. *Educ:* Harrow Sch. Balfour Williamson Co. Ltd, 1958–62; Bank of London & S America and Lloyds Bank International, 1962–83; Managing Director: Gulf Trust & Credit Ltd, 1984; Yelverton Investments plc, 1984–88; Chairman: Southend Stadium plc, 1985–87; QuillWills plc, 1991–92; Director: Steaua Romana plc, 1985–88; Clabir Internat. Corp., 1985–87; Imperial Waterproofing Systems Ltd, 1995–97; Bloxham Gp Ltd, 1996–2002; Internet Research Co. Ltd, 1997–2002; Netpoll Ltd, 1997–02; Imperial Roofing Systems Ltd, 1996–; Independent Telecommunications Mgt Co., 1997–. *Recreations:* travel, theatre, opera, cooking, eating. *Heir: cousin* Julian Frank Somerled Watson, *b* 12 Nov. 1931. *Address:* 2 Old Brompton Road, SW7 3DQ. *T:* 07966 167115; *e-mail:* simonwatsonbt@aol.com.

WATSON, Prof. Stephen Roger; Principal, Henley Management College, 2001–05; Fellow of Emmanuel College, Cambridge, since 1968; *b* 29 Aug. 1943; *s* of John C. Watson and Marguerite F. R. Watson; *m* 1969, Rosemary Victoria Tucker; one *s* one *d*. *Educ:* University College Sch., Hampstead; Emmanuel Coll., Cambridge (BA 1964, MA 1968, PhD 1969). Research Fellow, Emmanuel Coll., Cambridge, 1968–70; Shell International, 1970–71; Cambridge University: Univ. Lectr in Operational Research, Engineering Dept, 1971–86; Tutor, Emmanuel Coll., 1973–85; Peat, Marwick Prof. of Management Studies, 1986–94; Dir, Judge Inst. of Management Studies, 1990–94; Dean, Lancaster Univ. Mgt Sch., 1994–2001. Director: Cambridge Decision Analysts Ltd, 1984–95; Environmental Resources Management, 1989–95. Assoc. Dean, Reims Mgt Sch., Reims, 2005–. Special Advr to Pres., Assoc. to Advance Collegiate Schs of Business, Tampa, Florida, 2005–. Chm., Practical Action, 2006–. *Publications:* Decision Synthesis (with D. M. Buede), 1987; papers in learned jls. *Recreations:* singing, development issues. *Address:* 33 De Freville Avenue, Cambridge CB4 1HW.

WATSON, Stewart; *see* Watson, D. S.

WATSON, Maj.-Gen. Stuart; *see* Watson, Maj.-Gen. H. S. R.

WATSON, Thomas; MP (Lab) West Bromwich East, since 2001; a Parliamentary Secretary, Cabinet Office, since 2008; *b* 8 Jan. 1967; *s* of Tony and Linda Watson; *m* 2000, Siobhan Corby. *Educ:* Hull Univ. Fundraiser, Save the Children, 1988–89; Chair, Nat. Orgn of Labour Students, 1992–93; Dep. Gen. Election Co-ordinator, Labour Party, 1993–97; Nat. Political Organiser, AEEU, 1997–2001. An Asst Govt Whip, 2004–05 and 2007–08; a Lord Comr of HM Treasury (Govt Whip), 2005–06; Parly Under-Sec. of State, MoD, 2006. *Recreation:* gardening. *Address:* House of Commons, SW1A 0AA. *Club:* Friar Park and West Bromwich Labour.

WATSON, Thomas Sturges; professional golfer, since 1971; *b* 4 Sept. 1949; *s* of Raymond Etheridge Watson and Sarah Elizabeth Watson (*née* Ridge); *m* 1973, Linda Tova Rubin (marr. diss. 1998); one *s* one *d*. *Educ:* Stanford Univ. (BS 1971). Championships include: Open, 1975, 1977, 1980, 1982, 1983; US Open, 1982; Masters, 1977, 1981; Mem., Ryder Cup team, 1977, 1981, 1983, 1989, Captain, 1993. *Address:* 1901 W 47th Place, Suite 200, Shawnee Mission, KS 66205, USA.

WATSON, Victor Hugo, CBE 1987; DL; *b* 26 Sept. 1928; *s* of Norman Victor and Ruby Ernestine Watson; *m* 1952, Sheila May Bryan; two *d*. *Educ:* Clare Coll., Cambridge (MA). Served Royal Engineers (2nd Lieut), 1946–48. Joined John Waddington Ltd, 1951; Chm., 1977–93, retired. Director: Leeds & Holbeck Building Soc., 1985–99 (Pres., 1989–91); Stylo PLC, 1993–99; Topps Tiles PLC, 1997–; Black i Ltd, 1998–2003; Swivel Technologies, 2001–04. Pres., Inst. of Packaging, 1984–2004. DL West Yorks, 1991. Hon. LLD Leeds, 1994; DUniv Leeds Metropolitan, 2001. *Recreations:* music, golf, sailing. *Address:* Moat Field, Moor Lane, East Keswick, Leeds LS17 9ET.

WATSON, William Albert, CB 1989; PhD; FRCVS; international veterinary consultant, 1990–2003; *b* 8 March 1930; *s* of Henry Watson and Mary Emily Watson; *m* 1956, Wilma, *d* of Rev. Theodorus Johannas Henricus Steenbeck; one *s* one *d*. *Educ:* Preston Grammar School; University of Bristol (PhD, BVSc). Private practice, Garstang, Lancs, 1954–55; Asst Vet. Investigation Officer, Weybridge, 1954–56, Leeds, 1956–66; Animal Health Expert, FAO, Turkey, 1966–67; Vet. Investigation Officer, Penrith, 1967–71; Dep. Regional Vet. Officer, Nottingham, 1971–75; Regional Vet. Officer, Edinburgh, 1975–77; Asst Chief Vet. Officer, Tolworth, 1977–84; Dep. Dir, 1984–86, Dir, 1986–90, Vet. Labs, MAFF, Weybridge. External Examr, London, Liverpool, Dublin and Edinburgh Univs. *Publications:* contribs to vet. jls and textbooks. *Recreations:* fishing, gardening, restoration of listed property, farming.

WATSON, Prof. William Alexander Jardine, (Alan); Ernest P. Rogers Professor of Law, University of Georgia, since 1989; *b* 27 Oct. 1933; *s* of James W. and Janet J. Watson; *m* 1st, 1958, Cynthia Betty Balls, MA, MLitt (marr. diss.); one *s* one *d*; 2nd, 1986, Harriett Camilla Emanuel, BA, MS, JD, LLM; one *d*. *Educ:* Univ. of Glasgow (MA 1954, LLB 1957); Univ. of Oxford (BA (by decree) 1957, MA 1958, DPhil 1960, DCL 1973). Lectr, Wadham Coll., Oxford, 1957–59; Lectr, 1959–60, Fellow, 1960–65, Oriel Coll., Oxford; Pro-Proctor, Oxford Univ., 1962–63; Douglas Prof. of Civil Law, Univ. of Glasgow, 1965–68; Prof. of Civil Law, Univ. of Edinburgh, 1968–79; University of Pennsylvania: Prof. of Law and Classical Studies, 1979–84; Dir, Center for Advanced Studies in Legal Hist., 1980–89; Nicholas F. Gallichio Prof. of Law, 1984–86; Univ. Prof. of Law, 1986–89. Visiting Professor of Law: Tulane Univ., 1967; Univ. of Virginia, 1970 and 1974; Univ. of Cape Town, 1974 and 1975; Univ. of Michigan, 1977. Mem. Council, Stair Soc., 1970–; Hon. Mem., Speculative Soc., 1975. Corresp. FRSE 2004. Hon. LLD: Glasgow, 1993; Pretoria, 2002; Edinburgh, 2002; Palermo, 2003; Belgrade, 2004; Stockholm, 2005. *Publications:* (as Alan Watson): Contract of Mandate in Roman Law, 1961; Law of Obligations in Later Roman Republic, 1965; Law of Persons in Later Roman Republic, 1967; Law of Property in Later Roman Republic, 1968; Law of the Ancient Romans, 1970; Roman Private Law Around 200 BC, 1971; Law of Succession in Later Roman Republic, 1971; Law Making in Later Roman Republic, 1974; Legal Transplants, An Approach to Comparative Law, 1974, 2nd edn 1993; (ed) Daube Noster, 1974; Rome of the Twelve Tables, 1975; Society and Legal Change, 1977; The Nature of Law, 1977; The Making of the Civil Law, 1981; Sources of Law, Legal Change, and Ambiguity, 1984; The Evolution of Law, 1985, enlarged edn as The Evolution of Western Private Law, 2000; (ed) The Digest of Justinian (4 vols), 1986; Failures of the Legal Imagination, 1988; Slave Law of the Americas, 1989; Roman Law and Comparative Law, 1991; The State, Law and Religion: pagan Rome, 1991; Studies in Roman Private Law, 1991; Legal Origins and Legal Change, 1991; The State, Law and Religion: archaic Rome, 1992; Joseph Story and the Comity of Errors, 1993; International Law in Archaic Rome, 1993; The Spirit of Roman Law, 1995; Jesus and the Jews, 1995; The Trial of Jesus, 1995; Jesus and the Law, 1996; The Trial of Stephen, 1996; Jesus: a profile, 1998; Ancient Law and Modern Understanding, 1989; Law Out of Context, 2000; Legal History and a Common Law for Europe, 2002; Authority of Law and Law, 2003; Shame of American Legal Education, 2005; Comparative Law: law, reality and society, 2007; various articles. *Recreations:* Roman numismatics, shooting. *Address:* School of Law, University of Georgia, Herty Drive, Athens, GA 30602–6012, USA.

WATT, Very Rev. Alfred Ian; Dean of the United Diocese of St Andrews, Dunkeld and Dunblane, 1989–98; *b* 1934. *Educ:* Edinburgh Theol Coll. Deacon, 1960, priest 1961, Diocese of Brechin; Curate, St Paul's Cathedral, Dundee, 1960–63; Precentor, 1963–66; Rector of Arbroath, 1966–69; Provost of St Ninian's Cathedral, Perth, 1969–82; Canon, 1982–89; Rector, St Paul's, Kinross, 1982–95. Convenor, Mission Bd of General Synod, 1982–87. *Address:* 33 Stirling Road, Milnathort, Kinross KY13 9XS.

WATT, Alison Jane, OBE 2008; artist; *b* 11 Dec. 1966; *d* of James Watt and Annie Watt (*née* Sinclair); *m* 2000, Ruaridh Nicoll. *Educ:* Glasgow Sch. of Art (BA Fine Art 1987, MA Fine Art 1989). Associate Artist, Nat. Gall., 2006–08. *Solo exhibitions:* Contemporary Art Season, Glasgow Art Gall. and Mus., 1990; New Paintings, 1993, Paintings, 1995, Monotypes, 1997, Flowers East, London; New Paintings, Charles Belloc Lowndes, Chicago, 1996; Fold, Fruitmarket Gall., Edinburgh, 1997, Aberdeen Art Gall. and Mus. and Leeds Metropolitan Gall., 1998; Shift, Scottish Nat. Gall. of Modern Art, 2000; New Paintings, Dulwich Picture Gall., 2002; Still (installation), Old St Paul's Ch, Edinburgh, 2004. First Prize for Painting, RA, 1986; BP Portrait Award, 1987; City of Glasgow Lord Provost Prize, 1993; Scottish Arts Council Award, 1996; Creative Scotland Award, 2004. *Publications:* catalogues for exhibitions and monographs. *Recreations:* visiting the Highlands, eating in great restaurants, cooking, walking. *Address:* c/o Ingleby Gallery, 6 Carlton Terrace, Edinburgh EH7 5DD. *T:* (0131) 556 4441, *Fax:* (0131) 556 4454; *e-mail:* mail@inglebygallery.com.

WATT, Prof. David Anthony, PhD; Professor of Computing Science, University of Glasgow, since 1995; *b* 5 Nov. 1946; *s* of Francis Watt and Mary Watt (*née* Stuart); *m* 1974, Helen Dorothy Day; one *s* one *d*; *m* 2000, Carol Ann Laing. *Educ:* Univ. of Glasgow (BSc (Eng) 1st Cl. Hons; Dip. Comp. Sci. (Dist.); PhD 1974). University of Glasgow: programmer, Computing Service, 1969–72 and 1974; Department of Computing Science: Lectr, 1974–85; Sen. Lectr, 1985–90; Reader, 1990–95; Head of Dept, 1993–96; Vice-Dean, Faculty of Sci., 1996–. Vis. Associate Prof., Univ. of Calif, Santa Cruz, 1981–82; Vis. Res. Associate, Univ. of Calif, Berkeley, 1985. *Publications:* (with W. Findlay) Pascal: an introduction to methodical programming, 1978, 3rd edn 1985; (jtly) Ada: language and methodology, 1987; Programming Language Concepts and Paradigms, 1990; Programming Language Syntax and Semantics, 1991; Programming Language Processors: compilers and interpreters, 1993; (with D. Brown) Programming Language Processors in Java, 2000; (with D. Brown) Java Collections, 2001. *Recreations:* chess, running, science, history, politics. *Address:* Department of Computing Science, University of Glasgow, Glasgow G12 8QQ. *T:* (0141) 330 4470.

WATT, Prof. Donald C.; *see* Cameron Watt.

WATT, Prof. Fiona Mary, FRS 2003; Herchel Smith Professor of Molecular Genetics, since 2006, and Deputy Director, Wellcome Trust Centre for Stem Cell Research, University of Cambridge; Deputy Director, Cancer Research UK Cambridge Research Institute, since 2005; *b* 28 March 1956; *d* of David Mackie Watt and Janet Elizabeth Watt (*née* MacDougall); *m* 1979, James Cuthbert Smith, *qv*; two *s* one *d*. *Educ:* New Hall, Cambridge (BA Hons); Univ. of Oxford (DPhil 1979). Postdoctoral Associate, MIT, 1979–81; Head: Molecular Cell Biol. Lab., Kennedy Inst. of Rheumatology, 1981–86; Keratinocyte Lab., ICRF, then CRUK, London Res. Inst. 1987–2006. *Publications:* numerous contribs to learned jls. *Recreations:* fishing, reading novels, playing flute, modern art. *Address:* CR-UK Cambridge Research Institute, Li Ka Shing Centre, Robinson Way, Cambridge CB2 0RE; *e-mail:* fiona.watt@cancer.org.uk.

WATT, Hamish; writer, politician, retired farmer; Rector of Aberdeen University, 1985–88; *b* 27 Dec. 1925; *s* of Wm Watt and Caroline C. Allan; *m* 1948, Mary Helen Grant (marr. diss. 1989; she *d* 2007); one *s* two *d*. *Educ:* Keith Grammar Sch.; St Andrews Univ. Engaged in farming (dairy and sheep), until 2007; sometime company director, quarries. Contested (C), Caithness, 1966; contested (SNP): Banff, 1970; Moray, 1983. MP (SNP) Banff, Feb. 1974–1979. Regional and Dist Councillor (SNP), Moray, 1985–90 (Chm., Educn Cttee, 1986–90). Columnist, after-dinner speaker, story writer. JP Moray, 1984. Hon. LLD Aberdeen, 1988. *Address:* Jorglyn, Richmond Place, Portgordon, Buckie, Banffshire AB56 5QX. *T:* (01542) 832591. *Clubs:* Farmers', Whitehall Court.
See also M. Watt.

WATT, Surgeon Vice-Adm. Sir James, KBE 1975; MS, FRCS; Medical Director-General (Navy), 1972–77; *b* 19 Aug. 1914; *s* of Thomas Watt and Sarah Alice Clarkson. *Educ:* King Edward VI Sch., Morpeth; Univ. of Durham. MB, BS 1938; MS 1949; FRCS 1955; MD 1972; FRCP 1975. Served War, RN, FE and N Atlantic, 1941–46 (despatches, 1945). Surgical Registrar, Royal Vic. Infirm., Newcastle upon Tyne, 1947; Surgical Specialist: N Ire., 1949; RN Hosp., Hong Kong, 1954; Consultant in Surgery, RN Hospitals: Plymouth, 1956; Haslar, 1959; Malta, 1961; Haslar, 1963; Jt Prof. of Naval Surgery, RCS and RN Hosp., Haslar, 1965–69; Dean of Naval Medicine and MO i/c, Inst. of Naval Medicine, 1969–72. Chm. Bd of Trustees, Naval Christian Fellowship, 1968–75; President: Royal Naval Lay Readers Soc., 1973–83; Inst. of Religion and Medicine, 1989–91. QHS 1969–77. Surg. Comdr 1956; Surg. Captain 1965; Surg. Rear-Adm. 1969; Surg. Vice-Adm. 1972. Thomas Vicary Lectr, RCS, 1974; Vis. Prof. in Naval History, Univ. of Calgary, 1980; University House Vis. Fellow, ANU, 1986. FICS 1964; Fellow: Assoc. of Surgeons of GB and Ire.; Med. Soc. of London (Mem. Council, 1976; Lettsomian Lectr, 1979; Pres., 1980–81; Vice-Pres., 1981–83); RSocMed (Pres., 1982–84; Hon. FRSocMed 1998); FSA 1991; Hon. FRCSE; Hon. Fellow, Royal Acad. of Medicine in Ireland, 1983; Member: Brit. Soc. for Surgery of the Hand; Internat. Soc. for Burns Injuries; Corr. Mem., Surgical Research Soc., 1966–77. FRGS 1982; Mem. Council, RGS, 1985–88. Pres., ECHO, 1989–2003; Vice-Pres., Churches' Council for Health and Healing, 1987–99. Trustee: Marylebone Centre Trust, 1989–93; Medical Soc. of London, 1986–. Gov., Epsom Coll., 1990–2001 (Vice Pres., 2001–). Pres., Smeatonian Soc. of Civil Engineers, 1996 (Hon. Mem., 1978–). Hon. Freeman, Co. of Barbers, 1978. Hon. DCh Newcastle, 1978. Errol-Eldridge Prize, 1968; Gilbert Blane Medal, 1971. CStJ 1972. *Publications:* edited: Starving Sailors, 1981; Talking Health, 1988; What is Wrong with Christian Healing?, 1993; The Church, Medicine and the New Age, 1995; papers on: burns, cancer chemotherapy, peptic ulceration, hyberbaric oxygen therapy, naval medical history, contemporary Christianity. *Recreations:* mountain walking, music. *Address:* 10 The Firs, Stockbridge Road, Winchester, Hants SO22 6BD. *Clubs:* Royal Over-Seas League, Naval and Military.

WATT, Sir James H.; *see* Harvie-Watt.

WATT, James Wilfrid, CVO 1997; HM Diplomatic Service; Ambassador to Jordan, since 2006; *b* 5 Nov. 1951; *s* of late Anthony James MacDonald Watt and Sona Elvey (*née* White); *m* 1st, 1980, Elizabeth Ghislaine Villeneuve (*d* 1998), *d* of Marcel Villeneuve and Lorna Oliver Tudsbery; one *s* one *d*; 2nd, 2004, Amal Saad, *d* of Ibrahim and Alice Saad. *Educ:* Ampleforth Coll., York; Queen's Coll., Oxford (MA Mod. Langs 1974). Kleinwort Benson, 1974–75; freelance broadcaster and interpreter, Madrid, 1975–77; entered HM Diplomatic Service, 1977; MECAS, 1978; FCO, 1979–80; Abu Dhabi, 1980–83; FCO, 1983–85; UK Permanent Mission to UN, NY, 1985–89; Dep. Hd, UN Dept and Hd, Human Rights Unit, FCO, 1989–92; Dep. Hd of Mission and Consul Gen., Amman, 1992–96; Dep. High Comr, Islamabad, 1996–98; Res. Studentship, SOAS, 1999–2000; Head, Consular Div., then Dir for Consular Services, FCO, 2000–03; Ambassador to Lebanon, 2003–06. *Address:* c/o Foreign and Commonwealth Office, King Charles Street, SW1A 2AH. *Club:* Athenæum.

WATT, John Gillies McArthur; QC (Scot.) 1992; *b* 14 Oct. 1949; *s* of Peter Julius Watt and Nancy (*née* McArthur); *m* 1st, 1972, Catherine (marr. diss. 1988), *d* of Robert Russell, Toronto, Canada; two *d*; 2nd, 1988, Susan, *d* of Dr Tom C. Sparks, Ardmore, Oklahoma, and Breckenridge, Colorado, USA. *Educ:* Clydebank High Sch.; Glasgow Univ.; Edinburgh Univ. (LLB 1971). Solicitor, 1974–78; Advocate at Scottish Bar, 1979; Advocate Depute *ad hoc*, 1990; Temporary Sheriff, 1991; called to the Bar, Middle Temple, 1992. *Recreations:* shooting, ski-ing, sailing, opera. *Address:* 25 Eagle Ranch Road, PO Box 3188, Eagle, CO 81631, USA. *T:* (970) 3902791, *Fax:* (970) 3280130; *e-mail:* jgmwatt1@eagleranch.com. *Clubs:* Lansdowne; Royal Western Yacht (Glasgow).

WATT, Maureen, (Mrs Bruce Donaldson); Member (SNP) North-East Scotland, Scottish Parliament, since April 2006; Minister for Schools and Skills, since 2007; *b* 23 June 1951; *d* of Hamish Watt, *qv*; *m* 1987, Bruce Donaldson; one *s* one *d*. *Educ:* Univ. of Strathclyde (BA Hons Politics 1972); Univ. of Birmingham (PGCE 1973). Teacher, Bulmershe Sch., Woodley, Reading, 1974–76; Personnel Asst, then Personnel Mgr, Deutag Drilling, Aberdeen, 1977–91; Assessor for Office of Comr for Public Appts in Scotland, 1999–2006. *Recreations:* gardening, yoga, swimming. *Address:* SNP Parliamentary Office, 825–827 Great Northern Road, Aberdeen AB24 2BR. *T:* (Scottish Parliament) (0131) 348 6675, *Fax:* (0131) 348 5563; *e-mail:* Maureen.watt.msp@scottish.parliament.uk. *T:* (constituency office) (01224) 697182, *Fax:* (01224) 695397.

WATT, Miranda Lucy Mary C.; *see* Carruthers-Watt.

WATT, Peter Martin; General Secretary, Labour Party, 2006–07; *b* 20 July 1969; *s* of David Watt and Sandra Watt; *m* 2003, Vilma Bermudez; one *s* one *d*, and one step *d*. *Educ:* Inst. of Health, Bournemouth Univ. (RGN 1992); Open Univ. Business Sch. (Professional Cert. in Mgt 2004). Student nurse, Inst. of Health, Bournemouth Univ., 1989–92; Staff Nurse, then Sen. Staff Nurse, Poole Hosp. NHS Trust, 1992–96; Labour Party: Local Organiser, Battersea/Wandsworth, 1996–98; Nat. Elections Delivery and Local Recruitment Officer, 1998–2001; Membership Taskforce Leader, 2000–01; Regl Dir, Labour East, 2001–02; Taskforce Leader, Financial and Legal Compliance, 2003–05; Dir of Finance and Compliance, 2005. Foster carer (with wife), Kingston-upon-Thames BC. *Recreations:* watching sport (cricket and Liverpool Football Club in particular), reading crime novels.

WATT, His Honour Robert; QC (NI) 1964; County Court Judge, 1971–89; *b* 10 March 1923; *s* of John Watt, schoolmaster, Ballymena, Co. Antrim; *m* 1951, Edna Rea; one *d*. *Educ:* Ballymena Academy; Queen's Univ., Belfast (LLB). Called to Bar, Gray's Inn, 1946; called to Bar of Northern Ireland, 1946; Sen. Crown Prosecutor Counties Fermanagh and Tyrone. *Recreation:* sailing. *Address:* 12 Deramore Drive, Belfast BT9 5JQ. *Club:* Royal North of Ireland Yacht.

WATT, Thorhilda Mary Vivia A.; *see* Abbott-Watt.

WATT-PRINGLE, Jonathan Helier; QC 2008; barrister; *b* 8 June 1958; *s* of Louis Roy Watt-Pringle and Molly Alleyne Watt-Pringle (*née* Payn). *Educ:* Queen's Coll., Queenstown; Univ. of Stellenbosch (BA 1978; LLB 1980); Keble Coll., Oxford (Rhodes Scholar; BA 1983; BCL 1984). Advocate, Supreme Court of South Africa, 1984–86; called to the Bar, Middle Temple, 1987; in practice at London Bar, 1988–. *Recreations:* bridge, tennis, theatre, travel. *Address:* Farrar's Building, Temple, EC4Y 7BD. *T:* (020) 7583 9241; *e-mail:* jwpringle@farrarsbuilding.co.uk. *Club:* Reform.

WATTERS, David George; Executive Director, International Patient Organisation for Primary Immunodeficiencies, since 2005; *b* 14 Jan. 1945. *Educ:* Stromness Acad., Orkney Is. Church of Scotland lay worker, 1964–68; Social Worker, St Martin-in-the-Fields, 1968–73; Director: Threshold Centre, 1973–78; Alone In London Service, 1978–81; Primary Gen. Sec., Haemophilia Soc., 1981–93; Gen. Sec., subseq. Chief Exec., Primary Immunodeficiency Assoc., 1994–2005. Churchwarden, All Saints, Tooting, 1978–84 and 1994–98. JP Inner London, 1980–2000. *Recreations:* music, photography, birdwatching, travel, Cornwall, Orkney, theology, reading, cooking, wine. *Address:* Firside, Main Road, Downderry, Cornwall PL11 3LE. *Club:* Rotary (Torpoint Eddystone).

WATTLEY, Graham Richard; Director, Driver and Vehicle Licensing Directorate, Department of Transport, 1985–90, retired; *b* 12 March 1930; *s* of R. C. H. Wattley and Sylvia Joyce Wattley (*née* Orman); *m* 1st, 1953, Yvonne Heale (*d* 1990); one *s* two *d*; 2nd, 1997, M. Rose Daniel (*née* Dawson). *Educ:* Devonport High School. Pilot Officer, RAF, 1949–50. Min. of Works, 1950–71; Dept of the Environment, 1971–73; Department of Transport, 1973–90: Asst Sec., DVLC Computer Div., 1978–85; Dir, DVLC, 1985; Under Sec., 1986. Treas., Dewi Sant Housing Assoc., 1991–95. Mem., Governing Body, Church in Wales, 1992–94. Warden, St Paul's Church, Sketty, 1991–96. Walk Leader, HF Holidays, 1994–2004. *Recreations:* walking, cooking, bird-watching. *Address:* 36 The Ridge, Derwen Fawr, Swansea SA2 8AG. *T:* (01792) 290408. *Club:* Civil Service.

WATTS, Prof. Anthony, PhD; DSc; Professor of Biochemistry, University of Oxford, since 1996; C. W. Maplethorpe Fellow in Biological Sciences, St Hugh's College, Oxford, since 1983; *b* 7 Jan. 1950; *s* of late Wilfred Thomas Watts and of Ingrid Hiltraud Watts; *m* 1972, Valerie Maud Lewis; one *s* two *d*. *Educ:* Ludlow Grammar Sch.; Leeds Univ. (BSc; PhD 1976); St Hugh's Coll., Oxford (MA; DSc 1995). Max Planck Res. Fellow, Göttingen, 1976–80; University of Oxford: Deptl Demonstrator, 1980–83; New Blood Lectr, 1983–88; BBSRC Sen. Res. Fellow, 1997–2002; Rutherford Appleton Laboratory, Didcot: Sen. Scientist, ISCis (formerly ISIS) Facility, 1996–; Dir, Nat. Biol Solid State NMR Facility, 1997–. Fulbright Fellow and Vis. Prof., Harvard Univ., 1987; Fellow, IACR, 1998; Willsmore Fellow, Melbourne Univ., 2000. Lectr, Aust. and NZ Magnetic Resonance Soc., 1998. Moses Gomberg Lectr, Univ. Michigan, 2001. Chm., ESF Network on Molecular Dynamics of Biomembranes, 1990–92; UK rep., Membrane Commn, IUPAB, 1994–; Mem. Cttee, then Chm., BBSRC Biol Neutron Adv. Panel and Mem., ISIS Scheduling Panels, 1995–99. Member: Cttee, Biochem. Soc. of GB, 1989–98; Cttee, Biophysical Soc., 1998– (Chm., 2002–). Principal Ed., Biophysical Chem., 1994–; Managing Ed., European Biophysics Jl, 1997–. 350th Commemorative Medal, Helsinki Univ., 1990; SERC-CNRS Maxime Hanss Prize for Biophysics, 1992; Morton Medal, British Biochem. Soc., 1999; Award for Biomembrane Chem., Royal Soc. Chem., 2001. *Publications:* (with J. J. H. H. M. de Pont) Progress in Protein-Lipid Interactions, Vol. 1 1985, Vol. 2 1986; Protein-Lipid Interactions, 1993; numerous contribs to learned jls. *Address:* Biomembrane Structure Unit, Department of Biochemistry, South Parks Road, Oxford OX1 3QU. *T:* (01865) 275268; *e-mail:* anthony.watts@bioch.ox.ac.uk.

WATTS, Prof. Anthony Brian, PhD, DSc; Professor of Marine Geology and Geophysics, University of Oxford, since 1990; *b* 23 July 1945; *s* of Dennis Granville Watts and of late Vera (née Fisher); *m* 1970, Mary Tarbit; two *d. Educ:* University Coll. London (BSc); Univ. of Durham (PhD); DSc Oxon 2003. Post-Doctoral Fellow, Nat. Res. Council of Canada, 1970–71; Res. Scientist, Lamont-Doherty Geol Observatory, Palisades, NY, 1971–81; Arthur D. Storke Meml Prof. of Geol Scis, Columbia Univ., NY, 1981–90. Fellow: Amer. Geophysical Union, 1986; Geol Soc. of Amer., 2006; Eur. Geoscis Union, 2008 (Arthur Holmes Medal, 2008); MAE 1999. A. I. Levorsen Meml Award, Amer. Assoc. Petroleum Geologists, 1981; Rosenstiel Award, Univ. of Miami, 1982; Murchison Medal, Geol Soc., 1993; George P. Woollard Award, Geol Soc. of America, 2005. *Publications:* Isostasy and flexure of the lithosphere, 2001; numerous articles in scientific jls. *Recreations:* cricket, carpentry. *Address:* Department of Earth Sciences, University of Oxford, Parks Road, Oxford OX1 3PR. *T:* (01865) 272032. *Club:* Geological Society.

WATTS, Prof. Colin, DPhil; FRS 2005; FRSE; Professor of Immunobiology, University of Dundee, since 1998; *b* 28 April 1953; *s* of George Watts and Kathleen Mary Watts (née Downing); *m* 1979, Susan Mary Light; one *s* two *d. Educ:* The Friends Sch., Saffron Walden; Univ. of Bristol (BSc Hons 1975); Univ. of Sussex (DPhil 1980). EMBO Fellow, UCLA, 1980–82; Beit Meml Fellow, MRC Lab. of Molecular Biol., Cambridge, 1982–85; Lectr, 1986–92, Reader, 1992–98, Univ. of Dundee. Mem., Basel Inst. for Immunology, 1991; E. de Rothschild & Y. Mayent Fellow, Institut Curie, 1999. Mem., EMBO, 1996. FRSE 1999. Margaret Maclellan Prize, Tenovus Scotland, 2000; (jtly) Descartes Prize, EU, 2002. *Publications:* res. papers, reviews and commentaries in scientific jls. *Recreations:* music, cities, armchair sport. *Address:* Wellcome Trust Biocentre, School of Life Sciences, University of Dundee, Dundee DD1 5EH. *T:* (01382) 344233, *Fax:* (01382) 345783; *e-mail:* c.watts@dundee.ac.uk.

WATTS, David Leonard; MP (Lab) St Helens North, since 1997; a Lord Commissioner of HM Treasury (Government Whip), since 2005; *b* 26 Aug. 1951; *s* of Leonard and Sarah Watts; *m* 1972, Avril Davies; two *s. Educ:* Huyton Hey Secondary Sch. Labour Party Orgnr, until 1992; Researcher for John Evans, MP, 1992–97. PPS to Minister of State, MoD, 2000–01, to Minister of State (Minister of Transport), DfT (formerly DTLR), 2001–03, to Dep. Prime Minister, 2003–05. *Recreations:* reading, football, travel. *Address:* 1st Floor, Century House, Hardshaw Street, St Helens, Merseyside WA10 1QU.

WATTS, Diana; *see* Ellis, D.

WATTS, Donald Walter, AM 1998; PhD; FTSE; FRACI; FACE; FAIM; Senior Policy Adviser to the Vice Chancellor, University of Notre Dame Australia, since 2004; *b* 1 April 1934; *s* of late Horace Frederick Watts and Esme Anne Watts; *m* 1960, Michelle Rose Yeomans; two *s. Educ:* Hale Sch., Perth; University of Western Australia (BSc Hons, PhD); University College London. FRACI 1967. Post-Doctoral Fellow, UCL, 1959–61; University of Western Australia: Sen. Lectr, 1962; Reader, 1969; Associate Prof., 1971; Personal Chair in Physical and Inorganic Chemistry, 1977–79; Dir, W Australian Inst. of Tech., 1980–86, renamed Vice-Chancellor, Curtin Univ. of Tech., Jan.–June 1987; Pres. and Vice-Chancellor, Bond Univ., Australia, 1987–90, now Emeritus; Dean, Res. and Postgraduate Studies, Univ. of Notre Dame Australia, 1995–2003. Vis. Scientist, Univ. of S California, 1967; Visiting Professor: Australian National Univ., 1973; Univ. of Toronto, 1974; Japan Foundn Vis. Fellow, 1984. Chairman: Aust. Cttee of Dirs and Principals in Advanced Education Ltd, 1986–87; NT Employment and Trng Authy, 1991–93; NT Trade Develt Zone Authy, 1993–95. Member: Aust. Science and Technol. Council, 1984–90; Technology Develt Authority of WA, 1984–87; Chm., Australian Space Council, Canberra, 1993–95. Chairman: Advanced Energy Systems Ltd, 1997–2003 (Dir, 1995–2003); Technical Trng Inst. Pty Ltd, 2001–03; Woodside Valley Foundn, 2003–. Hon. Fellow, Marketing Inst. of Singapore, 1987. Hon. DTech Curtin, 1987; Hon. DEd WA, 2001. *Publications:* Chemical Properties and Reactions (jtly) (Univ. of W Aust.), 1978 (trans. Japanese, 1987); (jtly) Chemistry for Australian Secondary School Students (Aust. Acad. of Sci.), 1979; (jtly) The School Chemistry Project—a secondary school chemistry syllabus for comment, 1984; Earth, Air, Fire and Water, and associated manuals (Aust. Acad. of Sci. Sch. Chem. Project), 1984; numerous papers on phys. and inorganic chemistry in internat. jls; several papers presented at nat. and internat. confs. *Recreations:* tennis (Mem. Interstate Tennis Team, 1952–53), squash (Mem. Interstate Squash Team, 1957–66), golf. *Address:* University of Notre Dame Australia, 19 Mouat Street, Fremantle, WA 6160, Australia. *Clubs:* Royal Kings Park Tennis (Perth); Nedlands Tennis (Nedlands); Lake Karrinyup Golf (Karrinyup); Vines Resort (Swan Valley).

WATTS, Edward, (Ted), FRICS; property advisor; Chairman, Blackheath Preservation Trust Ltd, since 2001; Director: Avilla Developments Ltd, since 1999; Cedar Rydal Ltd, since 2006; *b* 19 March 1940; *s* of Edward Samuel Window Watts and Louise Coffey; *m* 1960, Iris Josephine Frost; two *s* (one *d* decd). *Educ:* SW Essex Technical Coll. FRICS 1971 (ARICS 1962). Established own practice, Watts & Partners, 1967 (surveyors, architects and engineers), Chm., 1967–99. Founder Chm., Hyde Housing Assoc., 1967–70 (Mem., 1967–85; Hon. Life Pres., 2007). Director: Surveyors Hldgs, 1983–88; People Need Homes, 1991–97; WASP, 1994–98; Buildingcare, 1994–97; non-executive Director: WSP Gp, 1993–2002; Thamesmead Town, 1994–2000; Mem. Adv. Bd, Property Hldgs, 1992–96. Chairman: Technical Cttee, Bldg Conservation Trust, 1984–86; Empty Homes Agency, 1997–2002; Tilfen Ltd, 1999–2001. Member: ARCUK, 1991–97; Urban Villages Gp, 1992–96; Bd, Coll. of Estate Management, 1994–96; Ministerial Adv. Bd, Property Advrs to the Civil Estate. Royal Institution of Chartered Surveyors: Pres., 1991–92; Mem., Gen. Council, 1982–95; Dir, RICS Journals Ltd, 1982–88 (Chm., 1986–88). FCMI (FBIM 1982). Freeman, City of London, 1985; Liveryman, Chartered Surveyors' Co., 1985–2002. Hon. DSc South Bank, 1992. *Recreations:* sailing, cruising, local races. *Address:* Flexford Farm, South Sway Lane, Sway, Lymington, Hants SO41 6DP. *T:* (01590) 681053, *Fax:* (01590) 681170; *e-mail:* ted.watts@flexfordfarm.co.uk. *Clubs:* Royal Cruising; Royal Lymington Yacht (Hants).

WATTS, Graham Clive, OBE 2008; Chief Executive, Construction Industry Council, since 1991 (Director, since 1989); Performance Director, British Fencing, since 2000; dance writer; *b* 5 Aug. 1956; *s* of Clifford Bertie Watts and Monica Kathleen Watts; *m* 1981, Tamara Jemima Ingrid Esposito; two *d. Educ:* Bedford Modern Sch.; Westfield Coll., London (BA Hons Hist. 1979); University Coll., Chichester (MA module, dance writing and criticism, 2005). Society of Architectural and Associated Technicians: Sec. for Educn and Membership, 1979–82; Chief Exec., 1983–86; Chief Exec., British Inst. of Architectural Technicians, 1986–91. Director: Nat. Centre for Construction, 1996–; Considerate Constructors Scheme, 2001–; Construction Umbrella Body (Hldgs) Ltd, 2003–. Chm., Construction Skills Standards and Qualifications Strategic Cttee, 2007–; Sec., Strategic Forum for Construction, 2002–; Mem. Council and Strategic Partnership Panel, Sector Skills Council for Construction, 2006–; Trustee: Interbuild Fund, 1997–2003; Sir Ian Dixon Meml Trust, 2001–; Happold Trust, 2002–. Vis. Prof., Univ. of Northumbria, 2000–. Manager, British Fencing Team, 1995–; Olympic Team Manager for Fencing, 2001–; Team Manager, 2004 and 2008 Olympic Games; Commonwealth Bronze Medal, 1990; British Sabre Capt., 1992 Olympic Games and 7 World Championships; Chm., Sabre Club, 1988–2008; Internat. Fencing Referee, 1991–.

Consultant Editor, PSA and Local Government Rev., 1993; columnist: Atrium, 1987–90; New Civil Engineer, 1996–99; dance writer and critic for Dance Europe, Ballet Co. mag., Londondance, Sky Arts and Soc. of Dance Research. Mem., Chichester Gp of Dance Writers, 2005–. MCMI 1983; FRSA 1983. Hon. Member: Chartered Inst. of Architectural Technologists, 1991; RICS, 2001; Hon. Fellow: RIBA, 2000; Assoc. of Building Engrs, 2000; Inst. of Building Control, 2000–01; Faculty of Building, 2003; CIBSE, 2006. Peter Stone Award, Assoc. of Building Engrs, 1996; President's Medal, Chartered Inst. of Building, 2000; Silver Medal, British Fencing Assoc., 2005. *Publications:* (jtly) Architectural Technology: the constructive link, 1984; contrib. articles in Building and many other jls and mags associated with built envmt. *Recreations:* ballet and all forms of contemporary dance, dance writing, fencing, modern history and politics, reading (especially modern literature and biographies), a cocker spaniel called Romeo Blue, being in N Norfolk or the Lake District, voice and life of Maria Callas. *Address:* c/o Construction Industry Council, The Building Centre, 26 Store Street, WC1E 7BT. *T:* (020) 7399 7402, *Fax:* (020) 7399 7425; *e-mail:* gwatts@cic.org.uk.

WATTS, Helen Josephine, (Mrs Michael Mitchell), CBE 1978; concert, lieder and opera singer (contralto), retired 1985; *b* 7 Dec. 1927; *d* of Thomas Watts and Winifred (née Morgan); *m* 1980, Michael Mitchell. *Educ:* Sch. of St Mary and St Anne, Abbots Bromley; Royal Academy of Music (LRAM). Began career with Glyndebourne Fest. Chorus and BBC Chorus; Proms début, 1958; with Royal Opera, Covent Gdn, 1965–71; with WNO, 1969–83; worked with world's leading conductors, notably Solti, Giulini, Haitink and von Karajan; has sung in all major cities in Europe and USA; toured Australia, 1967, NZ, 1972; many recordings of oratorio, opera and songs (Grand Prix du Disque, 1959). Hon. FRAM 1961. Mem., Musicians' Co., 1978. *Recreations:* gardening, reading.

WATTS, Jane Angharad, (Mrs C. D. G. Ross), FRCO; concert organist, since 1980; *b* 7 Oct. 1959; *d* of J. Maldwyn Watts and J. Leonora Watts; *m* 1985, Callum David George Ross; one *s. Educ:* Royal Coll. of Music (ARCM 1978, LRAM 1979); postgrad. studies with Mme Marie-Claire Alain, Paris. FRCO 1980; GRSM 1981. Mem. Council, RCO, 1994–. Débuts: BBC Radio, 1980; BBC TV, 1981; RFH, with LPO, 1983; recital, 1986; BBC Prom. Concerts, 1988; Organist and accompanist, Bach Choir, 1991–. Numerous engagements throughout UK, 1980–, with orchestras incl. BBC Nat. Orch. of Wales, LPO, Ulster Orch., London Mozart Players, etc; recital series incl. complete cycle of Widor Organ Symphonies, Brangwyn Hall, Swansea, 1999 and 2000 and St John's Smith Square, 2001; Duruflé series, Brangwyn Hall, 2002; has performed in USA, Europe, Hong Kong, Barbados, Australia and NZ, 1991–. Jury Mem., St Albans Internat. Organ Festival, 2005. Numerous recordings incl. recitals in Westminster Abbey, Salisbury Cathedral, Chartres Cathedral, Orleans Cathedral, Belfast, Glasgow, Sydney, Brisbane and Wellington; Handel organ concertos. Performer of Year, RCO, 1986. *Recreations:* cookery, maintaining links with Wales and Welsh-speaking community. *Address:* c/o Callum Ross, Yr Ysgubor, 10 Bury Farm Close, Horton Road, Slapton, Bucks LU7 9DS. *T:* (01525) 222729; c/o Phillip Truckenbrod Concert Artists, PO Box 331060, West Hartford, CT 06133–1060, USA. *T:* (860) 5607800. *Club:* London Welsh.

WATTS, John Arthur, FCA; *b* 19 April 1947; *s* of late Arthur and Ivy Watts; *m* 1974, Susan Jennifer Swan; one *s* three *d. Educ:* Bishopshalt Grammar Sch., Hillingdon; Gonville and Caius Coll., Cambridge (MA). Qual. as chartered accountant, 1972; FCA 1979. Chairman: Cambridge Univ. Cons. Assoc., 1968; Uxbridge Cons. Assoc., 1973–76; Mem., Hillingdon Bor. Council, 1973–86 (Leader, 1978–84). MP (C) Slough, 1983–97; contested (C) Reading E, 1997. PPS to Minister for Housing and Construction, 1984–85; to Minister of State, Treasury, 1985; Minister of State, Dept of Transport, 1994–97. Chm., Treasury and CS Select Cttee, 1992–94 (Mem., 1986–94). *Recreation:* reading. *Address:* The Hustings, 34 West Lane Close, Keeston, Haverfordwest, Pembs SA62 6EW.

WATTS, Sir John (Augustus Fitzroy), KCMG 2000; CBE 1988; President of the Senate, Grenada, 1967, 1985–90 and since 1995; *b* 31 May 1923; *s* of Cecil and Pearl Watts; *m* 1963, Dorothy Paterson. *Educ:* Michigan State Univ. (BSc); New York Univ. (DDS 1952). Founder and Leader, Grenada Nat. Party, 1955; Mem. and Dep. Speaker, Grenada Legislative Council, 1962–67; Leader of Opposition, Senate, 1968–72. Director: Caribbean Hotel Assoc., 1965–67; Grenada Airports Authy, 1985–90; Chairman: Grenada Tourist Bd, 1959–67, 1980–90; Carnival Develt Cttee, 1960–65; Pres., Caribbean Tourist Assoc., 1965–67. Pres., Granada Dental Assoc., 1998–2000. Charter Pres., Rotary Club of Grenada, 1968–69; Gov., Dist 404, Rotary Internat., 1974–79. *Recreations:* music, golf, politics. *Address:* Church Street, St George's, Grenada, West Indies. *T:* 4402606. *Clubs:* Rotary of Grenada, Grenada Golf and Country (St George's) (Pres., 1966).

WATTS, Col John Cadman, OBE 1959; MC 1946; FRCS 1949; first Professor of Military Surgery, Royal College of Surgeons, 1960–64; *b* 13 April 1913; *s* of John Nixon Watts, solicitor, and Amy Bettina (née Cadman); *m* 1938, Joan Lilian (née Inwood); three *s* one *d. Educ:* Merchant Taylors' Sch.; St Thomas's Hospital. MRCS, LRCP, 1936; MB, BS, 1938. Casualty Officer, Resident Anæsthetist, House Surgeon, St Thomas's Hospital, 1937; Surgical Specialist, RAMC, 1938–60, serving in Palestine, Egypt, Libya, Syria, Tunisia, Italy, France, Holland, Germany, Malaya, Java, Japan, and Cyprus. Hunterian Professor, RCS, 1960; Conslt Surgeon, Bedford Gen. Hosp., 1966–76. Co. Comr, St John Ambulance Brigade, 1970. British Medical Association: Chm., N Beds Div., 1971; Mem. Council, 1972–74; Chm., Armed Forces Cttee, 1978–82; Pres., Ipswich Div., 1982–83. OStJ 1970. *Publications:* Surgeon at War, 1955; Clinical Surgery, 1964; Exploration Medicine, 1964. *Recreations:* sailing, gardening. *Address:* Grove Court, 17 Beech Way, Woodbridge, Suffolk IP12 4BW. *T:* (01394) 382618. *Clubs:* Deben Yacht (Woodbridge); United Hospitals Sailing (Burnham-on-Crouch).

WATTS, Mark Francis; Associate Director, The Waterfront Partnership, since 2004; *b* 11 June 1964; *s* of Albert Charles Watts and Carole Emmah Watts (née Fleischman); *m* 1st, 1988, Kim McEachan (marr. diss. 2003); two *s*; 2nd, 2003, Jessica D'Souza. *Educ:* Maidstone Grammar Sch.; LSE (BSc Econ; MSc Econ). Planning Officer, Royal Borough of Kingston-upon-Thames, 1988–94. MEP (Lab) Kent E, 1994–99, SE Region, 1999–2004; Spokesman on transport, EP, 1995–2004. Co-Chm., Eur. Transport Safety Council, 1996–2004. Maidstone Borough Council: Councillor, 1986–96; Leader, Lab. Gp, 1990–94. Pres., E Kent Eur. Movt, 1999–. Mem. Council, Univ. of Kent at Canterbury, 2006–. Pres., Old Maidstonians Soc., 1996–97. *Recreations:* walking, enjoying the countryside, spending time with my family, cycling. *Address:* The Waterfront Partnership, 130–132 Tooley Street, SE1 2TU. *T:* (020) 7787 1200; 39 Imperial Way, Ashford, Kent TN23 5HA. *T:* and *Fax:* (01233) 665933; *e-mail:* markwatts@thewaterfront.co.uk. *Club:* Whitstable Labour.

WATTS, Sir Philip (Beverley), KCMG 2003; FInstP, FRGS, FGS; Group Managing Director, 1997–2004, and Chairman, Committee of Managing Directors, 2001–04, Royal Dutch/Shell Group; Managing Director, 1997–2004, and Chairman, 2001–04, Shell Transport and Trading plc; *b* 25 June 1945; *s* of Samuel Watts and Phillippa (née Wale); *m* 1966, Janet Lockwood; one *s* one *d. Educ:* Wyggeston Grammar Sch., Leicester; Univ. of Leeds (BSc Hons Physics, MSc Geophysics). FInstP 1980; FInstPet 1990; FRGS 1998; FGS 1998. Sci. teacher, Methodist Boys High Sch., Freetown, Sierra Leone, 1966–68;

joined Shell International, 1969: seismologist, Indonesia, 1970–74; geophysicist, UK/Europe, 1974–77; Exploration Manager, Norway, 1978–81; Div. Head, Malaysia, Brunei, Singapore, London, 1981–83; Exploration Dir, UK, 1983–85; Head, Exploration & Production Liaison—Europe, The Hague, 1986–88; Head, Exploration & Production Econs and Planning, The Hague, 1989–91; Man. Dir, Nigeria, 1991–94; Regl Co-ordinator—Europe, The Hague, 1994–95; Dir, Planning, Envmt and Ext. Affairs, London, 1996–97. Member: Exec. Cttee, World Business Council for Sustainable Develt, 1998–2003 (Chm., 2002–03); Governing Body, ICC UK, 1997–2004 (Chm., 1998–2004); ICC Exec. Bd (Worldwide), 1997–2000. *Recreations:* travel, gardening, reading. *Club:* Travellers.

WATTS, Rolande Jane Rita; *see* Anderson, R. J. R.

WATTS, Vincent Challacombe, OBE 1998; Founding Chairman, East of England Development Agency, 1998–2003; Vice-Chancellor, University of East Anglia, 1997–2002; *b* 11 Aug. 1940; *s* of Geoffrey Watts and Lilian Watts (*née* Pye); *m* 1967, Rachel Rosser (*d* 1998), Prof. of Psychiatry, UCL Med. Sch.; one *s* one *d*; partner, Hilary Coutts. *Educ:* Sidcot Sch.; Peterhouse, Cambridge (MA 1966); Birmingham Univ. (MSc 1967). FCA 1976. Joined Andersen Consulting, 1963, Partner, 1976–97; seconded to: Dept of Health as Founder Mem., Operational Res. Unit, 1970–71; HM Treasury, 1974; Financial Management Unit, Cabinet Office/HM Treasury, 1982–85. Mem. Council, John Innes Centre, 1997–; Mem. Council and Chair, Audit Cttee, LSC, 2002–03. FIMC 1986; CCMI 2001. Hon. LittD East Anglia, 2002. *Publications:* papers on performance evaluation in health services. *Recreations:* sailing, gardening, exploring. *Clubs:* Oxford and Cambridge; Jesters.

WATTS, William Arthur, ScD; MRIA; Provost, Trinity College, Dublin, 1981–91; *b* 26 May 1930; *s* of William Low Watts and Bessie (*née* Dickinson); *m* 1954, Geraldine Mary Magrath; two *s* one *d*. *Educ:* Trinity Coll., Dublin (MA, ScD). Lecturer in Botany, Univ. of Hull, 1953–55; Trinity College, Dublin: Lectr in Botany, 1955–65; Fellow, 1970; Professor of Botany, 1965–80; Prof. of Quaternary Ecology, 1980–81. Adjunct Prof. of Geology, Univ. of Minnesota, 1975–. Pres., RIA, 1982–85; Governor: National Gallery of Ireland, 1982–85; Marsh's Library, 1981–91; Member: Dublin Inst. for Advanced Studies, 1981–91; Scholarship Exchange Bd, Ireland, 1982–. Chairman: Federated Dublin Voluntary Hosps, 1983–89; Mercer's Hosp., 1975–83; Mercer's Hosp. Foundn, 1983–; Health Res. Bd, Ireland, 1987–89; Fota Trust, Co. Cork, 1992–; Dublin Dental Hosp., 1999–2007. Hon. LLD QUB, 1990; Hon. DSc NUI, 1991. *Publications:* numerous articles on aspects of quaternary ecology. *Recreations:* walking, conservation studies, music. *Address:* Room 24.02, Trinity College, Dublin 2, Ireland. *T:* (home) (1) 2887130.

WAUCHOPE, Sir Roger Hamilton D.; *see* Don-Wauchope.

WAUGH, Andrew Peter; QC 1998; *b* 6 Nov. 1959; *m* 1980, Catrin Prys Davies; four *s*. *Educ:* City Univ. (BSc 1st Cl. Hons 1980; DipLaw 1981). Called to the Bar, Gray's Inn, 1982; in practice as barrister, 1982–; specialist in Intellectual Property Law. *Address:* 3 New Square, Lincoln's Inn, WC2A 3RS. *T:* (020) 7405 1111.

WAUGH, Rev. Eric Alexander; Consultant on Christian Education and Theology, Every Nation Leadership (formerly His People Christian Education) Institute, Cape Town, South Africa, 2003–06 (Dean, 1996–98, Vice-Chancellor, 1998–2003, His People Institute); *b* 9 May 1933; *s* of Hugh Waugh and Marion Waugh (*née* McLay); *m* 1955, Agnes-Jean (Sheena) Saunders; two *s*. *Educ:* Glasgow Univ.; Edinburgh Univ. (LTh). Local government officer, 1948–64. Assistant Minister, High Church, Bathgate, 1969–70; Missionary, Kenya Highlands, 1970–73; Minister, Mowbray Presbyterian Church, Cape Town, 1973–78; Missioner, Presbyterian Church of Southern Africa, 1978–85; Minister, City Temple, URC, 1986–91; Missioner, Kingdom Communications Trust, S Africa, 1992–95. *Recreations:* hill walking, gardening. *Address:* Rose Cottage, 1 Eildonbank, Eildon, Melrose TD6 9HH. *T:* (01835) 824165; Every Nation Leadership Institute, PO Box 75, Century City 7441, Cape Town, South Africa; *e-mail:* eric.eawaugh@btinternet.com.

WAUGH, Stephen Rodger, AO 2003; cricketer; Captain, Australian Test Cricket Team, 1999–2004; *b* Sydney, NSW, 2 June 1965; *s* of Rodger and Beverley Waugh; *m* Lynette; one *s* two *d*. *Educ:* East Hills High Sch. Cricketer: with NSW, 1984–2004; with Somerset CCC, 1987–88; Mem., Australian Cricket Team, 1985–2004; Captain, One Day Internats team, 1997–2002; Mem. of winning team, World Cup, 1987; Captain of winning team, World Cup, 1999. Passed 10,000 Test runs, 2003. Life Member: BCCI, India; Bankstown Canterbury CC, NSW; Hon. Member: SCG; MCG. Allan Border Medal, 2001; Steve Waugh Medal, 2003. *Publications:* South African Tour Diary, 1995; Steve Waugh's West Indies Tour Diary, 1996; Steve Waugh's World Cup Diary, 1997; Steve Waugh's 1997 Ashes Diary, 1997; (with Nasser Hussain) Ashes Summer, 1997; Images of Waugh, 1998; Steve Waugh: no regrets—a captain's diary, 2000; Never Satisfied, 2000; Ashes Diary, 2001; Steve Waugh—Captain's Diary, 2002. *Address:* c/o TEAM-Duet, 3 Winnie Street, Cremorne, NSW 2090, Australia; *e-mail:* robert@duetgroup.com; *web:* www.stevewaughfoundation.com.au.

WAUMSLEY, Lance Vincent; a Senior Immigration Judge, Asylum and Immigration Tribunal (formerly a Vice President, Immigration Appeal Tribunal), since 2003; *b* 30 July 1947; *s* of Leslie Vincent Waumsley and Cecilia Daisy Waumsley (*née* Burden); *m* 2006, Sherrie Lee (*née* McCargar); two step *s* one step *d*. *Educ:* Wycliffe Coll., Glos; Selwyn Coll., Cambridge (MA, LLM). Admitted solicitor, 1972; with Collyer-Bristow and Co., 1970–76; Partner: Halsey Lightly and Hemsley, 1976–84; Macdonald Stacey, subseq. incorporated in Kidd Rapinet, 1984–97; Adjudicator of Immigration Appeals, 1997–2003. Mem., Special Immigration Appeals Commn, 2005–. Hon. Treas., Council of Immigration Judges, 2001–03. Sec., Yapp Welfare Trust and Yapp Educn and Res. Trust, 1987–97; Trustee and Founder Mem., Arts and Entertainment (formerly Comic Heritage) Charitable Trust, 1993–2001. *Recreations:* genealogy, music, reading, crosswords. *Address:* Asylum and Immigration Tribunal, Field House, 15 Bream's Buildings, EC4A 1DZ.

WAVERLEY, 3rd Viscount *cr* 1952, of Westdean; **John Desmond Forbes Anderson;** *b* 31 Oct. 1949; *s* of 2nd Viscount Waverley and of Myrtle Ledgerwood; *S* father, 1990; *m* 1994; one *s*. *Educ:* Malvern. Elected Mem., H of L, 1999. Jubilee Medal, Kazakhstan, 2002. Grand Cross, Order of San Carlos (Colombia), 1998. *Recreations:* golf, walking. *Heir:* *s* Hon. Forbes Alastair Rupert Anderson, *b* 15 Feb. 1996. *Address:* c/o House of Lords, SW1A 0PW.

WAVERLEY, Viscountess; *see* Barrow, U. H.

WAWRZYNSKI, Dana R.; *see* Ross-Wawrzynski.

WAX, Ruby; actor and comedian; *b* 19 April 1953; *d* of Edward Wax and Berta Wax (*née* Goldmann); *m* 1988, Edward Richard Morison Bye; one *s* two *d*. *Educ:* Evanston High Sch.; Berkeley Univ.; RSAMD. *Theatre:* Crucible, 1976; Royal Shakespeare Co., 1978–82; Stressed (one-woman show), UK, Australia and NZ tour, 2000; The Witches, Wyndhams Th., 2005; *television:* Not the Nine O'Clock News, 1982–83; Girls on Top, 1983–85; Don't Miss Wax, 1985–87; Hit and Run, 1988; Full Wax, 1987–92; Ruby Wax Meets…, 1996, 1997, 1998; Ruby, 1997, 1998, 1999, 2000; Ruby's American Pie, 1999, 2000; Hot Wax, 2001; The Waiting Game (quiz show), 2001, 2002; Life with Ruby (chat show), 2002; Commercial Breakdown, 2002; Ruby Wax With…, 2003; Ruby Does the Business, 2004; *films:* Miami Memoirs, 1987; East Meets Wax, 1988; Class of '69; Ruby Takes a Trip, 1992. *Publication:* How Do You Want Me?, 2002. *Address:* c/o United Agents, 12–26 Lexington Street, W1F 0LE.

WAXMAN, Prof. Jonathan Hugh, MD; FRCP; Professor of Oncology, Imperial College, University of London, since 1999; *b* 31 Oct. 1951; *s* of David Waxman and Shirley Waxman (*née* Friedman); *m*; one *s* one *d*. *Educ:* Haberdashers' Aske's Sch., Elstree; University Coll. London (BSc); University Coll. Hosp. (MB BS 1975; MD 1986). MRCP 1978, FRCP 1988. House Officer, UCH and Addenbrooke's Hosp., Cambridge, 1975–76; SHO, UCH, London Chest Hosp. and St Mary's Hosp., London, 1976–78; Registrar, St Mary's Hosp., 1979–81; ICRF Res. Fellow, St Bartholomew's Hosp., 1981–86; Consultant Physician, Hammersmith Hosp., 1986–99. Founder Mem., All Party Gp on Cancer, 1998–. Founder Chm., Prostate Cancer Charity, 1996–. *Publications:* The New Endocrinology of Cancer, 1987; The Molecular Biology of Cancer, 1989; Urological Oncology, 1992; Interleukin 2, 1992; Molecular Endocrinology of Cancer, 1996; The Fifth Gospel, 1997; Cancer Chemotherapy Treatment Protocols, 1998; Cancer and the Law, 1999; Treatment Options in Urological Oncology, 2002; The Prostate Cancer Book, 2002; Lecture Notes in Oncology, 2006; contrib. various scientific papers on cancer res. *Recreations:* family and friends. *Address:* Department of Oncology, Hammersmith Hospital, Du Cane Road, W12 0NN. *T:* (020) 8383 4651.

WAY, Andrew Mark; Chief Executive, Royal Free Hampstead NHS Trust, since 2005; *b* 27 Feb. 1959; *s* of Maxwell Andrew Way and Jane Kathleen Way (*née* Palliser). *Educ:* Bournemouth Sch.; Bristol Sch. of Nursing (RN); City Univ. (BSc Hons 1990); Keele Univ. (MBA 1994). Gen. Manager, St George's Hosp., London, 1993–95; Gen. Manager, 1995–2000, Chief Operating Officer, 2000–02, Hammersmith Hosps NHS Trust; Chief Exec., Heatherwood & Wexham Park Hosps NHS Trust, 2002–05. *Recreations:* swimming, ski-ing, bridge. *Address:* Royal Free Hospital, Pond Street, NW3 2QG. *T:* (020) 7830 2176, *Fax:* (020) 7830 2961; *e-mail:* andrew.way@royalfree.nhs.uk.

WAY, Col Anthony Gerald, MC 1944; Member, HM Body Guard of the Honourable Corps of Gentlemen at Arms, 1972–90 (Standard Bearer, 1988–90); *b* 5 Nov. 1920; *s* of Roger Hill Way and Brenda Lathbury; *m* 1st, 1946, Elizabeth Leslie Richmond (*d* 1986); one *s* one *d*; 2nd, 1989, Mrs Anthea Methven, St Martin's Abbey, by Perth. *Educ:* Stowe Sch.; RMC Sandhurst. Joined Grenadier Guards, 1939, 2nd Lieut; served in N Africa and Italy; CO, 3rd Bn, 1960–61; Lt-Col comdg Grenadier Guards, 1961–64. *Recreations:* shooting, gardening. *Address:* Kincairney, Dunkeld, Perthshire PH8 0RE. *T:* (01738) 710304.

WAY, Nicholas John; Director General, Historic Houses Association, since 2005; *b* 28 Aug. 1955; *s* of John Francis Way and Margaret (*née* Ewins); *m* 1987, Susan Clark; two *s* one *d*. *Educ:* Clare Coll., Cambridge (BA Econs 1978). MAFF, 1978–89; CLA, 1989–2005, Dir of Policy, 2001–05. Board Member: English Rural Housing Assoc., 1999–2005; Heritage Link, 2005–; Attingham Trust, 2005–; Sec., Heritage Conservation Trust, 2005–. Member: Adv. Council, Sch. of Rural Economy and Land Mgt, RAC, 2002–05; Charlbury Sch. Assoc., 2004–06. *Recreations:* family, countryside, history, football (watching). *Address:* Historic Houses Association, 2 Chester Street, SW1X 7BB. *T:* (020) 7259 5688, *Fax:* (020) 7259 5590; *e-mail:* nick.way@hha.org.uk.

WAYWELL, Prof. Geoffrey Bryan, FSA 1979; Professor of Classical Archaeology, King's College, University of London, 1987–2004; Director, Institute of Classical Studies, University of London, 1996–2004; *b* 16 Jan. 1944; *s* of Francis Marsh Waywell and Jenny Waywell; *m* 1970, Elisabeth Ramsden; two *s*. *Educ:* Eltham Coll.; St John's Coll., Cambridge (BA, MA, PhD). Walston Student, Cambridge Univ., 1965–67; School Student, British Sch. at Athens, 1966–67; King's College, London: Asst Lectr in Classics, 1968; Lectr in Classics, 1970; Reader in Classical Archaeology, 1982; Hon. Curator, Ashmole Archive, 1985; FKC 2004. Dir of excavations at ancient Sparta, 1989–98. *Publications:* The Free-Standing Sculptures of the Mausoleum at Halicarnassus in the British Museum, 1978; The Lever and Hope Sculptures, 1986; Sculptors and Sculpture of Caria and the Dodecanese, 1997; numerous articles and reviews in archaeol and classical jls. *Recreations:* music, excavating. *Address:* 47 Bird-in-Hand Lane, Bickley, Bromley, Kent BR1 2NA.

WEAIRE, Prof. Denis Lawrence, PhD; FRS 1999; Erasmus Smith's Professor of Natural and Experimental Philosophy, 1984–2007, Fellow, since 1987, Trinity College, Dublin; *b* 17 Oct. 1942; *s* of Allen Maunder Weaire and Janet Eileen (*née* Rea); *m* 1969, Colette Rosa O'Regan; one *s*. *Educ:* Belfast Royal Acad.; Clare Coll., Cambridge (MA Maths; PhD 1968). Harkness Fellow, Calif and Chicago, 1964–66; researcher, Cavendish Lab., Univ. of Cambridge, 1966–69; Fellow, Clare Coll., Cambridge, 1967–69; Res. Fellow, Harvard Univ., 1969–70; Yale University: Instructor, 1970–72; Asst Prof., 1972–73; Heriot-Watt University: Associate Prof., 1973–74; Sen. Lectr, 1974–77; Reader, 1977–79; Prof. of Exptl Physics, UC Dublin, 1980–84 (Hd of Dept, 1983–84); Trinity College, Dublin: Hd of Dept, 1984–89, 2003–05; Dean of Science, 1989–92. Ed., Jl Physics: Condensed Matter, 1994–97. Pres., Eur. Physical Soc., 1997–99 (Vice Pres., 1996–97 and 1999–2000). MRIA 1987; MAE 1998 (Vice Pres., 2005–). Dr *hc* Tech. Univ., Lisbon, 2001. *Publications:* (ed jtly) Tetrahedrally Bonded Amorphous Semiconductors, 1974; (ed with D. Pettifor) The Recursion Method, 1985; (with P. G. Harper) Introduction to Physical Mathematics, 1985; (ed with C. Windsor) Solid State Science, 1987; (ed jtly) Tradition and Reform, 1988; (ed jtly) Epioptics, 1995; (ed) The Kelvin Problem, 1997; (ed with J. Banhart) Foams and Films, 1999; (ed jtly) Richard Helsham's Course of Lectures on Natural Philosophy, 1999; (with S. Hutzler) The Physics of Foams, 1999; (with T. Aste) The Pursuit of Perfect Packing, 2000; contrib. numerous scientific papers. *Recreations:* theatre, humorous writing. *Address:* 26 Greenmount Road, Terenure, Dublin, Republic of Ireland. *T:* (1) 4902063.

WEALE, Prof. Albert Peter, PhD; FBA 1998; Professor of Government, University of Essex, since 1992; *b* 30 May 1950; *s* of Albert Cecil and Margaret Elizabeth Weale; *m* 1st, 1976, Jane Leresche (marr. diss. 1987); 2nd, 1994, Janet Felicity Harris. *Educ:* St Luke's Primary Sch., Brighton; Varndean Grammar Sch., Brighton; Clare Coll., Cambridge (BA Theol.; PhD Social and Political Scis 1977). Sir James Knott Fellow, Dept of Politics, Univ. of Newcastle upon Tyne, 1974–76; University of York: Lectr, Dept of Politics, 1976–85; Asst Dir, Inst. for Res. in Social Scis, 1982–85; Prof. of Politics, UEA, 1985–92. Mem., Nuffield Council on Bioethics, 1998–2004. Chm., King's Fund, 2008– (Chm. Grants Cttee, 1997–2001; Mem. Mgt Cttee, 1997–2001). FRSA 1993. *Publications:* Equality and Social Policy, 1978; Political Theory and Social Policy, 1983; The New Politics of Pollution, 1992; Democracy, 1999, 2nd edn 2007; Democratic Citizenship and the European Union, 2005; *jointly:* Lone Mothers, Paid Work and Social Security, 1984; Controlling Pollution in the Round, 1991; The Theory of Choice, 1992; Environmental

Governance in Europe, 2000; *edited:* Cost and Choice in Health Care, 1988; (with L. Roberts) Innovation and Environmental Risk, 1991; (jtly) Environmental Standards in the European Community in an Interdisciplinary Framework, 1994; (with P. Lehning) Citizenship, Democracy and Justice in the New Europe, 1997; (with Michael Nentwich) Political Theory and the European Union, 1998; Risk, Democratic Citizenship and Public Policy, 2002; articles in learned jls. *Recreations:* walking, music, the company of friends. *Address:* Department of Government, University of Essex, Wivenhoe Park, Colchester, Essex CO4 3SQ. *T:* (01206) 872127.

WEALE, Anthony Philip; Secretary of Faculties, 1984–2005 and Academic Registrar, 1999–2005, University of Oxford; Fellow of Worcester College, Oxford, 1982–2005, now Emeritus; *b* 4 Dec. 1945; *s* of Geoffrey Arthur Weale and Jocelyn Mary Weale (*née* Weeks); *m* 1975, Katharine O'Connell; two *d. Educ:* Kimbolton Sch.; University Coll., Oxford (Scholar; MA 1st Cl., Honour Sch. of Jurisprudence; Martin Wronker Prize for Law, 1967). GKN Ltd, 1967–71; Admin. Service, Oxford Univ., 1971–2005; Sec., Medical Sch., 1977–84. Treas., Historic Towns Trust, 1975–. Governor: Pusey House, Oxford, 1977–85; Kimbolton Sch., 2001–; Bishop Wordsworth's Sch., 2008–. Trustee, St Bartholomew's Sch. Foundn, Newbury, 2006–. *Recreations:* family, dabbling in military and political history. *Address:* 40 Harnwood Road, Salisbury, Wilts SP2 8DB.

WEALE, Martin Robert, CBE 1999; Director, National Institute of Economic and Social Research, since 1995; *b* 4 Dec. 1955; *s* of Prof. R. A. Weale and M. E. Weale. *Educ:* Clare Coll., Cambridge (BA 1977; ScD 2006). ODI Fellow, Nat. Statistical Office, Malawi, 1977–79; University of Cambridge: Research Officer, Dept of Applied Econs, 1979–87; Lectr, Faculty of Econs and Politics, 1987–95; Fellow, Clare Coll., 1981–95. Houblon-Norman Fellow, Bank of England, 1986–87. Member: Stats Commn, 2000–08; Bd of Actuarial Standards, 2006–. Hon. Treasurer, Alzheimer's Trust, 1992–2008. Hon. FIA 2001. Hon. DSc City, 2007. *Publications:* (with J. Grady) British Banking, 1986; (jtly) Macroeconomic Policy: inflation, wealth and the exchange rate, 1989; (with J. Sefton) Reconciliation of National Income and Expenditure, 1995; articles in learned jls. *Recreations:* bridge, music, travel. *Address:* 63 Noel Road, N1 8HE. *T:* (020) 7359 8210. *Club:* Athenæum.

WEARE, Trevor John, OBE 1990; PhD; Chairman, 1999–2007, Member of Board, since 2007, HR Wallingford Group, Ltd; *b* 31 Dec. 1943; *s* of Trevor Leslie Weare and Edna Margaret (*née* Roberts); *m* 1964, Margaret Ann Wright; two *s. Educ:* Aston Technical Coll.; Imperial College of Science and Technology (BSc Physics, PhD). Post-doctoral Research Fellow: Dept of Mathematical Physics, McGill Univ., Montreal, 1968–70; Dept of Theoretical Physics, Univ. of Oxford, 1970–72; Sen. Scientific Officer, Hydraulics Res. Station, 1972; Principal Scientific Officer, 1975; Sen. Principal Scientific Officer, Head of Estuaries Div., 1978; Chief Scientific Officer, DoE, 1981; Chief Exec., Hydraulics Res. Ltd, then HR Wallingford Gp Ltd, 1984–99. *Publications:* numerous contribs to scientific jls on theoretical High Energy Nuclear Physics, and on computational modelling in Civil Engineering Hydraulics; archaeological paper in Oxoniensia. *Recreations:* music, walking, archaeology, golf, sailing. *Address:* 14 Trenithick Meadow, Mount Hawke, Truro, Cornwall TR4 8GN. *T:* (01209) 890082.

WEARING, Gillian; artist; *b* 1963; Goldsmiths' Coll., Univ. of London (BA Hons Fine Art 1990). *Solo exhibitions:* Maureen Paley/Interim Art, London, 1994, 1996–97, 1999; Hayward Gall., 1995; Le Consortium, Dijon, 1996; Jay Gorney Modern Art, NY, Chisenhale Gall., London, Kunsthaus Zürich, 1997; Centre d'Art Contemporain, Geneva, 1998; De Vleeshal, Middleburg, The Netherlands, 1999; Serpentine Gall., Regen Projects, LA, Contemp. Art Center, Cincinnati, 2000; Bluecoat Gall., Liverpool, la Caixa, Madrid, Musée d'Art Moderne, Paris, Museo do Chiado, Lisbon, Kunstverein München, Angel Row Gall., Nottingham, 2001; Trilogy, Vancouver, 2002; Mass Observation, MCA Chicago, Kunsthaus Glarus, and tour, 2002; Regen Projects, LA, 2004; Snapshot, Bloomberg Space, London, 2005; Aust. Center for Contemp. Art, 2006; Family History, Ikon, Birmingham, 2006; Family Monument, Galleria Civica di Arte Contemporanea, Trento, 2007; *group exhibitions* include: BT Young Contemporaries, UK tour, 1993; Brilliant! New Art from London, Walker Art Center, Minneapolis, 1995; Life/Live, Musée d'Art Moderne, Paris, 1996; Pandaemonium, London Fest. of Moving Images, ICA, 1996; Sensation, RA, and Mus. für Gegenwart, Berlin, 1998; Real/Life: new British art, Japanese Mus. tour, 1998; Let's Entertain, Walker Art Centre, Minneapolis, 2000; New British Art, Tate Britain, London, 2000; Century City, Tate Modern, London, 2001; ABBILD recent portraiture and depiction, Graz, Birmingham, 2001; I Promise it's Political, Cologne, 2002; Remix: Contemporary Art and Pop, Tate Liverpool, São Paulo, 2002; Of Mice and Men, Berlin Biennial for Contemp. Art, A Short History of Performance Part IV, Whitechapel Art Gall., 2006; Local Stories, Modern Art Oxford, 2006; Aftershock, Contemporary British Art 1990–2006, Guangdong Mus. of Art, Guangzhou, Capital Mus., Beijing, 2006; Global Feminisms, Brooklyn Mus., NY, 2007; The Turner Prize: a retrospective, Tate Britain, 2007; exhibns in Europe. Trustee, Tate Gall., 1999–. Turner Prize, 1997. *Address:* c/o Maureen Paley, 21 Herald Street, E2 6JT. *T:* (020) 7729 4112.

WEATHERALL, Sir David (John), Kt 1987; DL; MD, FRCP; FRCPE 1983; FRS 1977; Chancellor, University of Keele, since 2002; Regius Professor of Medicine, University of Oxford, 1992–2000; Student of Christ Church, Oxford, 1992–2000; Hon. Director: Molecular Haematology Unit, Medical Research Council, 1980–2000; Institute for Molecular Medicine, University of Oxford, 1988–2000 (renamed Weatherall Institute of Molecular Medicine, 2000); *b* 9 March 1933; *s* of late Harry and Gwendoline Weatherall; *m* 1962, Stella Mayorga Nestler; one *s. Educ:* Calday Grange Grammar Sch.; Univ. of Liverpool (MB, ChB 1956; MD 1962); MA Oxon 1974. FRCP 1967; FRCPath 1969. Ho. Officer in Med. and Surg., United Liverpool Hosps, 1956–58; Captain, RAMC, Jun. Med. Specialist, BMH, Singapore, and BMH, Kamunting, Malaya, 1958–60; Research Fellow in Genetics, Johns Hopkins Hosp., Baltimore, USA, 1960–62; Sen. Med. Registrar, Liverpool Royal Infirmary, 1962–63; Research Fellow in Haematology, Johns Hopkins Hosp., 1963–65; Consultant, WHO, 1966–70; Univ. of Liverpool: Lectr in Med., 1965–66; Sen. Lectr in Med., 1966–69; Reader in Med., 1969–71; Prof. of Haematology, 1971–74; Consultant Physician, United Liverpool Hosps, 1966–74; Nuffield Prof. of Clinical Medicine, Univ. of Oxford, 1974–92; Fellow, Magdalen Coll., Oxford, 1974–92, Emeritus 1992–. Mem. Soc. of Scholars, and Centennial Schol., Johns Hopkins Univ., 1976; Physician-in-Chief *pro tem.*, Peter Bent Brigham Hosp., Harvard Med. Sch., 1980. RSocMed Foundn Vis. Prof., 1981; Sims Commonwealth Vis. Prof., 1982; Phillip K. Bondy Prof., Yale, 1982. K. Diamond Prof., Univ. of Calif in San Francisco, 1986; HM Queen Elizabeth the Queen Mother Fellow, Nuffield Prov. Hosps Trust, 1982; Fogarty Scholar, NIH, USA, 2003. Lectures: Watson Smith, RCP, 1974; Foundn, RCPath, 1979; Darwin, Eugenics Soc., 1979; Croonian, RCP, 1984; Fink Meml, Yale, 1984; Sir Francis Frazer, Univ. of London, 1985; Roy Cameron, RCPath, 1986; Hamm Meml, Amer. Soc. of Haematology, 1986; Still Meml, BPA, 1987; Harveian, RCP, 1992. President: British Soc. for Haematology, 1980; Internat. Soc. of Haematology, 1992; BAAS, 1992–93; Chm., Med. and Scientific Adv. Panel, Leukaemia Res. Fund, 1985–89; Mem. Council, Royal Soc., 1989– (Vice Pres., 1990–91); Mem., MRC, 1994–96; Trustee: Wellcome Trust, 1990–2000; Wolfson Foundn, 2001–. Founder FMedSci 1998. DL Oxfordshire, 2000. Foreign Member: Nat. Acad. of Scis, USA, 1990; Inst. of Medicine, Nat. Acad. of Scis, USA, 1991; Amer. Philosophical Soc., 2005; Hon. Member: Assoc. of Physicians of GB and Ireland, 1968 (Pres., 1989); Assoc. of Amer. Physicians, 1976; Amer. Soc. of Haematology, 1982; Eur. Molecular Biology Orgn, 1983; Amer. Acad. of Arts and Scis, 1988; Alpha Omega Alpha Honor Med. Soc., USA, 1988; Hon. Fellow, Royal Coll. Physicians, Thailand, 1988; Hon. FRACP 1986; Hon. FRCOG 1988; Hon. FIC 1989; Hon. FACP 1991; Hon. FRSocMed 1998. Hon. Fellow, Green Coll., Oxford, 1993. Hon. DSc: Manchester, 1988; Edinburgh, 1989; Leicester, 1991; Aberdeen, 1991; London, 1993; Keele, 1993; Oxford Brookes, 1995; South Bank, 1995; Exeter, 1998; Cambridge, 2004; Hon. MD: Leeds, 1988; Sheffield, 1989; Nottingham, 1993; Hon. DHL Johns Hopkins, 1990; Hon. LLD: Liverpool, 1992; Bristol, 1994. Ambuj Nath Bose Prize, RCP, 1980; Ballantyne Prize, RCPE, 1982; Stratton Prize, Internat. Soc. Haematology, 1982; Feldberg Prize, 1984; Royal Medal, Royal Soc., 1989; Gold Medal, RSM, 1992; Conway Evans Prize, RCP and Royal Soc., 1992; Buchanan Medal, Royal Soc., 1994; (jtly) Helmut Horten Res. Award, 1995; Manson Medal, 1998; Prince Mahidol Award, Thailand, 2002; Gold Medal, BMA, 2002; Allen Award, Amer. Soc. of Human Genetics, 2003; Mendel Medal, Genetics Soc., 2006. Commandeur de l'Ordre de la Couronne (Belgium), 1994. *Publications:* (with J. B. Clegg) The Thalassaemia Syndromes, 1965, 4th edn 2001; (with R. M. Hardisty) Blood and its Disorders, 1973, 2nd edn 1981; The New Genetics and Clinical Practice, 1982, 3rd edn 1991; (ed, with J. G. G. Ledingham and D. A. Warrell) Oxford Textbook of Medicine, 1983, 3rd edn 1995; Science and the Quiet Art, 1995; many papers on Abnormal Haemoglobin Synthesis and related disorders. *Recreations:* music, oriental food. *Address:* 8 Cumnor Rise Road, Cumnor Hill, Oxford OX2 9HD. *T:* (01865) 222360.

WEATHERALL, Vice-Adm. Sir James (Lamb), KCVO 2001; KBE 1989; DL; an Extra Equerry to the Queen, since 2001; HM Marshal of the Diplomatic Corps, 1992–2001; *b* 28 Feb. 1936; *s* of Alwyn Thomas Hirst Weatherall and Olive Catherine Joan Weatherall (*née* Cuthbert); *m* 1962, Hon. Jean Stewart Macpherson, *d* of 1st Baron Drumalbyn, KBE, PC; two *s* three *d. Educ:* Glasgow Academy; Gordonstoun School. Joined RN 1954; commanded HM Ships: Soberton, 1966–67; Ulster, 1970–72; Tartar, 1975–76; Andromeda, 1982–84 (incl. Falklands conflict); Ark Royal, 1985–87; with SACEUR, 1987–89; Dep. Supreme Allied Comdr Atlantic, 1989–91. Chairman: Sea Cadet Council, 1992–98; Sea Cadet Assoc., 1992–98 (Sea Cadet Medal, 1998). Pres., Internat. Social Service (UK), 1996–2001 (Vice Pres., 2001–). Patron, Marwell Preservation Trust, 2007– (Trustee, 1992–2007; Chm., 1999–2007). Chm., Lord Mayor of London's Appeal, 1997–98. Chairman, Board of Governors: Box Hill Sch., 1993–2003 (Trustee, 1992–; Warden, 2003–); Gordonstoun Schs, 1996–2003 (Gov., 1994–; Warden, 2004–). Member: Ct of Assts, Shipwrights' Co., 1989– (Prime Warden, 2001–02); Incorp. of Hammermen of Glasgow, 1998–; HM Lieut, City of London, 2001–. Younger Brother, Corp. of Trinity House, 1986–. Fellow, WWF (UK), 2008– (Trustee, 2001–07). DL Hampshire, 2004. *Recreations:* stamp collecting, fishing. *Address:* Craig House, Street End, Bishop's Waltham, Hampshire SO32 1FS. *Clubs:* Royal Over-Seas League, Royal Navy of 1765 and 1785.

WEATHERBY, Jonathan Roger; Chairman, Weatherbys Group Ltd, since 1993; *b* 30 Nov. 1959; *s* of late Christopher Nicholas Weatherby and of Alison Beatrix (*née* Pease); *m* 1993, Sophie Frances Cliffe-Jones; two *s* two *d. Educ:* Eton Coll. Joined Weatherbys, 1979; Dir, 1988–. Chairman: Gazelle Investments Ltd, 1992–; Weatherbys Bank Ltd, 1993–; Wild Boar Inns Ltd, 1994–2001. Mem., Jockey Club, 1997–. Trustee, Ascot Authority, 1998–. *Recreations:* horse-racing, soccer, hunting. *Address:* Weatherbys, Sanders Road, Wellingborough, Northants NN8 4BX. *T:* (01933) 440077. *Clubs:* White's, Turf.

WEATHERHEAD, Alexander Stewart, (Sandy), OBE 1985; TD 1964 (clasp 1973); Partner, 1960–97 and Senior Partner, 1992–97, Tindal Oatts & Rodger, then Tindal Oatts Buchanan and McIlwraith, subsequently Tindal Oatts, and Brechin Tindal Oatts, Solicitors, Glasgow (Consultant, 1997–98); *b* Edinburgh, 3 Aug. 1931; *er s* of Kenneth Kilpatrick Weatherhead and Katharine Weatherhead (*née* Stewart); *m* 1972, Harriett Foye, *d* of Rev. Dr Arthur Organ, Toronto, Canada; two *d. Educ:* Glasgow Acad.; Glasgow Univ. MA 1955, LLB 1958. Served in RA, 1950–52, 2nd Lieut, 1950. Solicitor, 1958; Temp. Sheriff, 1985–92. Hon. Vice-Pres., Law Society of Scotland, 1983–84 (Mem. Council, 1971–84); Member: Royal Faculty of Procurators in Glasgow, 1960– (Mem. Council, 1992–2001; Dean, 1992–95; Hon. Mem., 1997); Council, Soc. for Computers and Law, 1973–86 (Vice-Chm., 1973–82; Chm., 1982–84; Hon. Mem., 1986); Mem., Royal Commn on Legal Services in Scotland, 1976–80. Trustee, Nat. Technol. and Law Trust (formerly Nat. Law Library Trust), 1979–86; Examr in Conveyancing, Univ. of Aberdeen, 1984–86. Dir, Glasgow Chamber of Commerce, 1992–95. Member: Local Res. Ethics Cttee, Royal Infirmary, Glasgow, 1999–06; Multi Centre Res. Ethics Cttee for Scotland (B), 2005–06. Mem. Business Cttee, Gen. Council, Univ. of Glasgow, 2001–05 and 2007–. Joined TA, 1952; Lt-Col Comdg 277 (A&SH) Field Regt, RA (TA), 1965–67; The Lowland Regt (RA(T)), 1967 and Glasgow & Strathclyde Univs OTC, 1971–73; Col 1974; TAVR Col Lowlands (West), 1974–76; ADC (TAVR) to the Queen, 1977–81; Member: TAVR Assoc. Lowlands, 1967–2000 (Vice-Chm., 1987–90; Chm., 1990–93); RFCA Lowlands, 2000–; RA Council for Scotland, 1972– (Vice Chm., 1997–2001; Patron, 2001–). Hon. Col, Glasgow and Strathclyde Univs OTC, 1982–98. Commodore, Royal Western Yacht Club, 1995–98 (Vice Cdre, 1991–95; Hon. Sec., 1981–84). *Recreations:* sailing, reading, music, tennis. *Address:* 52 Partickhill Road, Glasgow G11 5AB. *T:* (0141) 334 6277. *Clubs:* New (Edinburgh); Royal Highland Yacht (Oban); Royal Western Yacht, Clyde Cruising (Glasgow).

WEATHERHEAD, Very Rev. James Leslie, CBE 1997; Principal Clerk of the General Assembly of the Church of Scotland, 1985–93 and 1994–96 (Moderator, 1993–94); Chaplain to the Queen in Scotland, 1991–2001, Extra Chaplain, since 2001; *b* 29 March 1931; *s* of Leslie Binnie Weatherhead, MBE, MM and Janet Hood Arnot Smith or Weatherhead; *m* 1962, Dr Anne Elizabeth Shepherd; two *s. Educ:* High Sch., Dundee; Univ. of Edinburgh (MA, LLB; Senior Pres., Students' Repr. Council, 1953–54); New Coll., Univ. of Edinburgh (Pres., Univ. Union, 1959–60). Temp. Acting Sub-Lieut RNVR (Nat. Service), 1955–56. Licensed by Presb. of Dundee, 1960; ordained by Presb. of Ayr, 1960; Asst Minister, Auld Kirk of Ayr, 1960–62; Minister, Trinity Church, Rothesay, 1962–69; Minister, Old Church, Montrose, 1969–85. Convener, Business Cttee of Gen. Assembly, 1981–84. Mem., Broadcasting Council for Scotland, BBC, 1978–82. Gov., Fettes Coll., Edinburgh, 1994–99. Hon. DD Edinburgh, 1993. *Publication:* (ed) The Constitution and Laws of the Church of Scotland, 1997. *Recreations:* sailing, music. *Address:* Newton Park, 59 Brechin Road, Kirriemuir DD8 4DE. *Clubs:* Victory Services; RNVR Yacht.

WEATHERHEAD, Sandy; *see* Weatherhead, A. S.

WEATHERILL, Barry Nicholas Aubrey, CBE 2005; Consultant, Wedlake Bell, solicitors, since 2003; Chairman, Guide Dogs for the Blind Association, 2000–07 (Trustee, since 1975); *b* 17 July 1938; *s* of Percival Aubrey and Flora Evelyn Weatherill; *m* 1965, Wouterina Johanna Cornelia van den Bovenkamp; one *s* two *d*. *Educ:* Caldicott Sch.; Felsted Sch.; Clare Coll., Cambridge (BA 1962). Admitted solicitor, 1966; Wedlake Bell: Partner, 1966–2003; Finance Partner, 1975–81; Sen. Partner, 1984–94. All England Lawn Tennis Club: Mem., Cttee of Mgt, 1981–2002; Vice Pres., 2002–; Trustee, 2003–; Pres., Council of Internat. Lawn Tennis Clubs, 2008– (Chm., 1991–2008). *Recreations:* tennis, golf, gardening, music, investment. *Clubs:* Travellers; Jesters; Hawks (Cambridge); All England Lawn Tennis and Croquet; International Lawn Tennis Clubs of GB, France, USA and the Netherlands; Berkshire Golf.

WEATHERILL, Hon. Bernard Richard; QC 1996; a Recorder, since 2000; *b* 20 May 1951; *er s* of Baron Weatherill, PC and of Lyn Weatherill; *m* 1977, Sally Maxwell Fisher (marr. diss. 2001); one *s* one *d*; *m* 2005, Diana Clare Forsyth. *Educ:* Malvern Coll.; Principia Coll., Illinois, USA; Kent Univ. (BA Hons). Called to the Bar, Middle Temple, 1974, Bencher, 2002; an Asst Recorder, 1998–2000. Non-exec. Dir, A. Cohen & Co. plc, 1989–2000. Mem., General Council of the Bar, 1990–95 (Mem., Professional Conduct Cttee, 1998–99); Chm., Bar Services Co. Ltd, 2000–08. FCIArb 1999. *Recreations:* lawn tennis, Real tennis, golf, wine, avoiding gardening. *Address:* Enterprise Chambers, 9 Old Square, Lincoln's Inn, WC2A 3SR. *Clubs:* Hurlingham; All England Lawn Tennis, Royal Tennis Court, Bar Lawn Tennis Society, Jesters; Royal Wimbledon Golf, Lucifer Golfing Society.

WEATHERILL, Rt Rev. Garry John; *see* Willochra, Bishop of.

WEATHERILL, Prof. Nigel Peter, PhD, DSc; CEng, FREng; FRAeS; FIMA; CSci; CMath; Head, College of Engineering and Physical Sciences, University of Birmingham, since 2008; *b* 1 Nov. 1954; *s* of Ernest and Barbara Weatherill; *m* 1976, Dr Barbara Ann Hopkins; one *s* one *d*. *Educ:* Whitcliffe Mount Grammar Sch., Cleckheaton, Yorks; Southampton Univ. (BSc 1st Cl. Hons Maths; PhD Maths 1979; DSc 1994). CEng 1996, FREng 2003; FIMA 1987; CMath 1991; FRAeS 1996; CSci 2005. Asst Team Leader, Regl Res. Team, Anglian Water Authy, Cambridge, 1979–81; Sen. Project Supervisor, Aircraft Res. Assoc., Bedford, 1981–87; Swansea University (formerly University of Wales, Swansea): Department of Civil Engineering: Lectr, 1987–90; Sen. Lectr, 1990–92; Reader, 1992–95; Prof. of Civil Engineering, 1995–2008; Hd of Dept, 1996–2001; Dir, Centre of Excellence in Computation and Simulation, 2000–08; Hd, Sch. of Engineering, 2001–07; Pro-Vice-Chancellor (Research), 2002–08. Vis. Res. Fellow, Dept of Mechanical and Aerospace Engrg, Princeton Univ., 1985; Res. Consultant, Nat. Grid Generation Project, USA, NSF Engrg Res. Center, Mississippi State Univ., 1991–92, Adjunct Prof., 1992–98; Vis. Scientist-in-Residence, Inst. of High Performance Computing, A*Singapore, 2006–. Ed., Internat. Jl Numerical Methods in Fluids, 1999–. *Publications:* (jtly) Multiblock Grid Generation, 1993; (jtly) Handbook of Grid Generation, 1999; (jtly) Probabilistic Methods in Fluids, 2003. *Recreations:* fly fishing, gardening, travelling. *Address:* College of Engineering and Physical Sciences, University of Birmingham, Edgbaston, Birmingham B15 2TT. *T:* (0121) 414 9029; *e-mail:* n.p.weatherill@bham.ac.uk.

WEATHERILL, Prof. Stephen Robson; Jacques Delors Professor of European Community Law, University of Oxford, since 1998; Fellow, Somerville College, Oxford, since 1998; *b* 21 March 1961. *Educ:* Queens' Coll., Cambridge (MA); Univ. of Edinburgh (MSc). Brunel Univ., 1985; Reading Univ., 1986–87; Manchester Univ., 1987–90; Nottingham Univ., 1990–97, Jean Monnet Prof. of European Law, 1995–97. *Publications:* Cases and Materials on EC Law, 1992, 8th edn as Cases and Materials on EU Law, 2007; (with P. Beaumont) EC Law, 1993, 3rd edn 1999; Law and Integration in the European Union, 1995; (with G. Howells) Consumer Protection Law, 1995, 2nd edn 2004; EC Consumer Law and Policy, 1997, 2nd edn 2005; (with H. Micklitz) European Economic Law, 1997. *Address:* Somerville College, Oxford OX2 6HD. *T:* (01865) 270600.

WEATHERLEY, Christopher Roy, MD; FRCS, FRCSE, FRCSE (Orth); Consultant Spinal Surgeon, Royal Devon & Exeter Hospital, since 1987; *b* 26 Sept. 1943; *s* of Dudley Graham Weatherley and Hilda Ada Weatherley (*née* Wilson). *Educ:* Queen Elizabeth's Sch., Crediton; Liverpool Univ. Med. Sch. (MB ChB; MD 1968). FRCSE 1973; FRCS 1974; FRCSE (Orth) 1984. Sen. Res. Associate, MRC Decompression Sickness Unit, Newcastle upon Tyne, 1973–76; Sen. Registrar in Orthopaedics, Robert Jones and Agnes Hunt Orthopaedic Hosp., 1979–87. Eur. Res. Fellow, Inst. Calôt, Berck-Plage, France, 1981–82; Consultant Spinal Surgeon, St Vincent's Hosp., Melbourne, 1985–86. Hon. Civilian Consultant, RN, 1991. Fellow, Brit. Orthopaedic Assoc., 1983; FRSocMed 1991. Member: Exec. Cttee, Brit. Scoliosis Soc., 1993– (Sec. and Treas., 1996–99; Pres., 2006–07); Council, Brit. Scoliosis Res. Foundn, 1998–; Eur. Cervical Spine Soc., 1984. Gold Medal Lectr, Old Oswestrians Annual Meeting, 2000. *Publications:* contrib. chapters in books, editorials and papers on: decompression sickness and dysbaric osteonecrosis; spinal tumours; scoliosis; back pain; surgical approaches to the spine; spinal fusion; ankylosing spondylitis; stress fractures in fast bowlers. *Recreations:* the fine line, the creation of myths. *Address:* 1 The Quadrant, Wonford Road, Exeter, Devon EX2 4LE. *T:* (01392) 272951. *Club:* Royal Society of Medicine.

WEATHERSTON, (William) Alastair (Paterson), CB 1993; Under Secretary, Scottish Office Education Department, 1989–95; *b* 20 Nov. 1935; *s* of William Robert Weatherston and Isabella (*née* Paterson); *m* 1961, Margaret Jardine (*d* 2004); two *s* one *d*. *Educ:* Peebles High Sch.; Edinburgh Univ. (MA Hons History). Asst Principal, Dept of Health for Scotland and Scottish Educn Dept, 1959–63; Private Sec. to Permanent Under Sec. of State, Scottish Office, 1963–64; Principal, Scottish Educn Dept, 1964–72, Cabinet Office, 1972–74; Assistant Secretary: SHHD, 1974–77; Scottish Educn Dept, 1977–79; Central Services, Scottish Office, 1979–82; Dir, Scottish Courts Admin, 1982–86; Fisheries Sec., Dept of Agric. and Fisheries for Scotland, 1986–89. Sec., Gen. Council, Univ. of Edinburgh, 1997–2001. Mem., Murrayfield Community Council, 2005–. *Recreations:* reading, music. *Address:* 1 Coltbridge Terrace, Edinburgh EH12 6AB. *T:* (0131) 337 3339.

WEATHERSTONE, Robert Bruce, TD 1962; CA; Chairman, Lothian Health Board, 1986–90; *b* 14 May 1926; *s* of Sir Duncan Mackay Weatherstone, MC, TD, and late Janet Pringle; *m* 1954, Agnes Elaine Jean Fisher; one *s* one *d*. *Educ:* Edinburgh and Dollar Academies. CA 1951. Served Royal Marines, 44 Commando, 1944–47. Dir/Sec., J. T. Salvesen Ltd, 1954–62; Dir and Mem., Management Cttee, Christian Salvesen Ltd, 1962–83; Dir, Lothian Region Transport plc, 1986–92. Chm., Leith Enterprise Trust, 1983–88; Vice-Pres., Leonard Cheshire Foundn, 1996– (Trustee, 1973–96). *Recreations:* hill-walking, ornithology. *Address:* Strachan House, 93 Craigcrook Road, Edinburgh EH4 3PE. *Club:* New (Edinburgh).

WEATHERUP, Hon. Sir Ronald Eccles, Kt 2001; **Hon. Mr Justice Weatherup;** a Judge of the High Court of Justice, Northern Ireland, since 2001. *Educ:* Methodist Coll.; Queen's Univ., Belfast. Called to the Bar, NI, 1971; QC (NI) 1993. Jun. Crown Counsel, 1989–93, Sen. Crown Counsel, 1997–2001, for NI. Mem., NI Judicial Appts Commn, 2005–. *Address:* Royal Courts of Justice, Chichester Street, Belfast BT1 3JF.

WEAVER, (Christopher) Giles (Herron), FCA; Chairman: Charter Pan European Trust, since 2003; Helical Bar plc, since 2005 (non-executive Director, since 1993); Kenmore European Property Fund, since 2006; *b* 4 April 1946; *s* of Lt Col John Weaver and Ursula (*née* Horlick); *m* 1975, Rosamund Betty Mayhew; two *s* two *d*. *Educ:* Eton Coll.; London Business Sch. (MSc 1973). FCA 1978. Dir, UK and Pensions Investment, Ivory & Sime, 1976–86; Man. Dir, Pension Mgt, Prudential Corp., 1986–90; Murray Johnstone Ltd, 1990: Chief Investment Officer, 1990–93; Man. Dir, 1993–99; Chm., 1999–2000. Chm., Murray Emerging Growth & Income Trust plc, 2001–05; non-executive Director: James Finlay, 1996–; Aberdeen Asset Management plc, 2000–; Investec High Income Trust plc, 2004–; Anglo & Overseas Trust plc, 2004–; ISIS Property Trust II Ltd, 2004–. Trustee and Dep. Chm., Nat. Galls of Scotland, 1998–2005; Chm., HHA in Scotland, 1999–2004. *Recreations:* ski-ing, golf, tennis, bridge. *Address:* Greywalls, Gullane, E Lothian EH31 2EG. *T:* (01620) 842144. *Clubs:* Boodle's, Hurlingham, Queen's; New (Edinburgh); Hon. Company of Edinburgh Golfers (Muirfield).

WEAVER, Susan Alexandra, (Sigourney); actress; *b* New York, 8 Oct. 1949; *d* of late Sylvester Laflin, (Pat), Weaver and Elizabeth Weaver (*née* Inglis); *m* 1984, James Simpson; one *d*. *Educ:* Stanford Univ. (BA); Sch. of Drama, Yale Univ. (MFA). Founder, Goat Cay Productions. *Theatre includes:* Gemini, 1976, Crazy Mary, 2007, Playwrights Horizons, NY; Beyond Therapy, Marymount Manhattan Th., NY, 1981; Hurlyburly, Ethel Barrymore Th., NY, 1984; The Merchant of Venice, Classic Stage Co., NY, 1986; The Guys, 2002, Mrs Farnsworth, 2004, Flea Th., NY; The Mercy Seat, Acorn Th., NY, 2002. *Films include:* Annie Hall, 1977; Madman, 1978; Alien, 1979; Eyewitness, 1981; The Year of Living Dangerously, 1982; Deal of the Century, 1983; Ghostbusters, 1984; Walls of Glass, Une Femme ou Deux, 1985; Half Moon Street, Aliens, 1986; Gorillas in the Mist (Best Actress, Golden Globe Awards, 1989), Working Girl (Best Supporting Actress, Golden Globe Awards, 1989), 1988; Ghostbusters II, 1989; Alien^3 (also co-prod.), 1492: Conquest of Paradise, 1992; Dave, 1993; Death and the Maiden, 1995; Jeffrey, Copycat, 1996; Snow White: a Tale of Terror, Alien: Resurrection (also co-prod.), 1997; Ice Storm, 1998; A Map of the World, Galaxy Quest, 1999; Company Man, 2000; Heartbreakers, 2001; The Guys, 2002; Tadpole, Holes, 2003; The Village, 2004; Imaginary Heroes, 2005; Snow Cake, The TV Set, Infamous, 2006; Vantage Point, 2008. *Address:* c/o William Morris Agency, 1 William Morris Place, Beverly Hills, CA 90212, USA; Goat Cay Productions, PO Box 38, New York, NY 10150, USA.

WEBB, Sir Adrian (Leonard), Kt 2000; DLitt; Chairman, Pontypridd & Rhondda NHS Trust, 2005–08; Vice-Chancellor, University of Glamorgan, 1993–2004; *b* 19 July 1943; *s* of Leonard and Rosina Webb; *m* 1st, 1966, Caroline Williams (marr. diss. 1995); two *s*; 2nd, 1996, Monjulee Dass. *Educ:* Birmingham Univ. (1st cl. Hons BSocSci 1965); LSE (MSc (Econ) 1966); DLitt Loughborough 1993. Lectr, LSE, 1966–74; Res. Dir, Personal Social Services Council, 1974–76; Loughborough University: Prof. of Social Policy, 1976–93; Dir, Centre for Res. in Social Policy, 1983–90; Dean, then Pro Vice-Chancellor, subseq. Sen. Pro Vice-Chancellor, 1986–93. Member: Nat. Cttee of Inquiry into Higher Educn (Dearing Cttee), 1996–97; BBC Broadcasting Council for Wales, 1998–2001; HM Treasury Public Sector Productivity Panel, 2000–06; Nat. Council, Educn and Learning in Wales, 2001–06; Beecham Review of Public Services in Wales, 2005–06; Administrative Justice and Tribunals Council, 2008– (Chair, Wales Cttee); Wales Comr, UK Commn for Employment and Skills, 2008– (Chair, Welsh Employment and Skills Bd); Chairman: Welsh Review Group (Nursing, Midwifery and Health Workers), 1999–2002; Higher Educn Wales, 2000–02; Rev. of Further and Post-14 Educn in Wales, 2006–07; Webb Rev. of Further Educn, 2007. Non-executive Director: E Glamorgan NHS Trust, 1997–99; Exec. Bd, Nat. Assembly for Wales, 2003–. Founder Mem., Bevan Foundn, 2002–. Gov., Thames Valley Univ., 2006–. FRSA. *Publications:* Change, Choice and Conflict in Social Policy, 1975; Planning Need and Scarcity: essays on the personal social services, 1986; The Economic Approach to Social Policy, 1986; Social Work, Social Care and Social Planning, 1987; Joint Approaches to Social Policy: rationality and practice, 1988; contribs on social policy to scholarly and professional periodicals. *Recreations:* walking, painting (water colour), ornithology.

WEBB, Rear-Adm. Arthur Brooke, CB 1975; retired; *b* 13 June 1918; *m* 1949, Rachel Marian Gerrish; three *d*. Joined Royal Navy, 1936; Comdr 1954, Captain 1963, Rear-Adm. 1973. *Recreations:* gardening, walking, survival.

WEBB, Prof. Colin Edward, MBE 2000; DPhil; FRS 1991; FInstP; Professor, Department of Physics, University of Oxford, 1992–2002, now Emeritus; Senior Research Fellow, Jesus College, Oxford, 1988–2005, now Emeritus; Founder and Chairman, Oxford Lasers Ltd, since 1977; *b* 9 Dec. 1937; *s* of Alfred Edward Webb and Doris (*née* Collins); *m* 1st, 1964, Pamela Mabel Cooper White (*d* 1992); two *d*; 2nd, 1995, Margaret Helen (*née* Dewar); two step *d*. *Educ:* Univ. of Nottingham (BSc 1960); Oriel Coll., Oxford (DPhil 1964). FInstP 1985. Mem., Technical Staff, Bell Labs, Murray Hill, NJ, 1964–68; University of Oxford: AEI Res. Fellow in Physics, Clarendon Lab., 1968–71; Univ. Lectr, 1971–90; Tutorial Fellow, Jesus Coll., 1973–88; Reader, 1990–92, Prof., 1992, Dept of Physics; Hd of Atomic and Laser Physics, 1995–99. Visiting Professor: Dept of Pure and Applied Physics, Univ. of Salford, 1987–2002; Dept of Mechanical Engrg, Cranfield Univ., 1999–. Fellow, Optical Soc. of America, 1988. Hon. DSc Salford, 1996. Duddell Medal and Prize, 1985, Glazebrook Medal and Prize, 2001, Inst. of Physics; Clifford Paterson Lect. and Medal, Royal Soc., 1999. *Publications:* (Ed-in-Chief) Handbook of Laser Technology and Applications, 2003; contribs on lasers, laser mechanisms and applications to learned jls. *Recreations:* travel, photography, music, reading. *Address:* Clarendon Laboratory, Parks Road, Oxford OX1 3PU. *T:* (01865) 272254.

WEBB, Colin Thomas; Editor-in-Chief, Press Association, 1986–94 (Director, 1989–96; General Manager, 1994–96); *b* 26 March 1939; *e s* of late William Thomas and Ada Alexandra Webb; *m* 1970, Margaret Frances, *y d* of late Maurice George and Joan Rowden Cheshire; two *s* one *d*. *Educ:* Portsmouth Grammar School. Reporter, Portsmouth Evening News, Surrey Mirror, Press Assoc., Daily Telegraph, The Times; Royal Army Pay Corps Short Service Commission (to Captain), 1960–64; Home News Editor, The Times, 1969–74; Editor, Cambridge Evening News, 1974–82; Dep. Editor, The Times, 1982–86; Journalist Dir, Times Newspaper Holdings, 1983–86. Member: Core Cttee, British Executive Internat. Press Inst., 1984–96; Council, Commonwealth Press Union, 1985–96; Lord Chancellor's Adv. Bd on Family Law, 1997–2001; Consultative Council, BBFC, 2000–08. Chair, UK Coll. of Family Mediators, 2003–06. Nat. Trustee, Lloyds TSB Foundn for England and Wales, 2000–05. Gov., Univ. of Portsmouth, 2001–08 (Hon. Fellow, 1991). Lay Reader, Dio. Chichester, 2005–. *Publication:* (co-author with The Times News Team) Black Man in Search of Power, 1968. *Recreations:* family, walking, history books. *Address:* Fairfield House, Pine Grove, West Broyle, Chichester, West Sussex PO19 3PN. *T:* (01243) 771870. *Club:* Garrick.

WEBB, Prof. David Charles, PhD; Professor of Finance, and Director, Financial Markets Group Research Centre, since 1991, and Director, UBS Pensions Research Programme, since 2001, London School of Economics; *b* 13 July 1953; *s* of Charles Ronald Webb and Margaret Jane Webb (*née* Oldham). *Educ:* Hurworth Secondary Sch., Darlington; Grangefield Grammar Sch., Stockton upon Tees; Univ. of Manchester (BA Econs 1974; MA Econs 1975); London School of Economics (PhD 1979). Lectr, Univ. of Bristol, 1978–84; Lectr, 1984–90, Reader in Economics, 1991, LSE. Vis. Associate Prof., Queen's Univ., Canada, 1982–84; Vis. Prof. of Economics, Univ. of Iowa, 1991. Consultant, Asian Develt Bank, 1998–; Mem., Adv. Bd, Centro de Estudios Monetarios y Financieros, Madrid, 1998–. Mem. Council, Royal Economic Soc., 2008–. Editor, Economica, 1989–97. *Publications:* articles in Econs and Finance, Qly Jl of Econs, Rand Jl of Econs, Internat. Econ. Review, Econ. Jl and Jl of Public Econs. *Recreation:* ski-ing. *Address:* Financial Markets Group, London School of Economics, Houghton Street, WC2A 2AE. *T:* (020) 7955 6301.

WEBB, Prof. David John, MD, DSc; FRCPE, FRCP, FFPM, FMedSci; FRSE; Christison Professor of Therapeutics and Clinical Pharmacology, since 1995, Director, Education Programme, Wellcome Trust Clinical Research Facility, since 1998, University of Edinburgh; Consultant Physician, Lothian University Hospitals NHS Trust, since 1990; *b* 1 Sept. 1953; *s* of Alfred William Owen Webb and Edna May Webb (*née* Parish); *m* 1984, Margaret Jane Cullen; three *s*. *Educ:* Dulwich Coll. (Kent Schol.); Royal London Hosp.; MB BS 1977, MD 1990, London; DSc Edinburgh 2000. MRCP 1980, FRCP 1994; FRCPE 1992; FFPM (FFPHM 1993); FBPharmacolS 2004. House Officer posts, Royal London Hosp. scheme, 1977–78; Senior House Officer: Chelmsford Hosps, 1978–79; Stoke Mandeville Hosp., 1979–80; Registrar: Royal London Hosp., 1980–82; in Medicine, and MRC Clin. Scientist, MRC BP Unit, Western Infirmary, Glasgow, 1982–85; Lectr in Clin. Pharmacol., St George's Med. Sch., London, 1985–89; Sen. Registrar in Medicine, St George's Hosp., London, 1985–89; University of Edinburgh: Sen. Lectr in Medicine, 1990–95; Dir, Clin. Res. Centre, 1990–96; Head: Dept of Medicine, 1997–98; Dept of Med. Scis, 1998–2001; Wellcome Trust Res. Leave Fellow, and Leader, Wellcome Trust Cardiovascular Res. Initiative, 1998–2001; Convenor, Cardiovascular Interdisciplinary Gp, 1999–2000; Hd, Centre for Cardiovascular Sci., 2000–04. Chm., Scottish Medicines Consortium, 2005–08 (Chm., New Drugs Cttee, 2001–05); Dir, Wellcome Trust Scottish Translational Medicine and Therapeutics Initiative, 2008. Councillor, Clin. Div., Internat. Union for Pharmacol., 2004–. Res. Dir, High Blood Pressure Foundn, 1993– (Trustee, 1991–). Pres., Eur. Assoc. for Clin. Pharmacol. and Therapeutics, July 2009–; Vice-Pres., RCPE, 2006–; Mem., Exec. Cttee, British Hypertension Soc., 1991–94; British Pharmacological Society: Mem., Exec. Cttee, 1994–98; Clin. Vice-Pres., 1995–98; Dir and Trustee, 1996–99 and 2004–; Chm., Cttee of Profs and Hds of Clin. Pharmacol. & Therapeutics, 2004–; Mem., Sectional Cttee 1, Acad. Med. Scis, 2000–02. Internat. Fellow, Amer. Heart Assoc., 1998; FMedSci 1999; FESC 2001; FRSE 2004. *Publications:* (with G. A. Gray) The Molecular Biology and Pharmacology of the Endothelins, 1995; (ed with P. J. T. Vallance) The Endothelium in Hypertension, 1996; (ed with P. J. T. Vallance) Vascular Endothelium in Human Physiology and Pathophysiology, 1999; (jtly) The Year in Therapeutics, Vol. 1, 2005. *Recreations:* summer and winter mountaineering, scuba diving, reading late at night. *Address:* Queen's Medical Research Institute, Centre for Cardiovascular Science, University of Edinburgh, E3.22, 47 Little France Crescent, Edinburgh EH16 4TJ. *T:* (0131) 242 9215, *Fax:* 0870 134 0897; *e-mail:* d.j.webb@ed.ac.uk; 75 Great King Street, Edinburgh EH3 6RN. *T:* (0131) 556 7145, 07770 966786. *Club:* Scottish Mountaineering.

WEBB, Prof. Joseph Ernest, PhD (London) 1944, DSc (London) 1949; CBiol, FIBiol; FLS; FZS; Professor of Zoology, 1960–80, and Vice-Principal, 1976–80, Westfield College, University of London, now Emeritus Professor; *b* 22 March 1915; *s* of Joseph Webb and Constance Inman Webb (*née* Hickox); *m* 1940, Gwenllian Clara Coldwell (*d* 1994); three *s*. *Educ:* Rutlish School; Birkbeck College, London (BSc 1940). FZS 1943; CBiol, FIBiol 1963; FLS 1972. Research Entomologist and Parasitologist at The Cooper Technical Bureau, Berkhamsted, Herts, 1940–46; Lecturer, Univ. of Aberdeen, 1946–48; Senior Lecturer, 1948–50, Professor of Zoology, 1950–60, University Coll., Ibadan, Nigeria. Hon. Fellow, QMW (formerly Westfield Coll.), 1986. *Publications:* (jointly): Guide to Invertebrate Animals, 1975, 2nd edn 1978; Guide to Living Mammals, 1977, 2nd edn 1979; Guide to Living Reptiles, 1978; Guide to Living Birds, 1979; Guide to Living Fishes, 1981; Guide to Living Amphibians, 1981; various on insect physiology, insecticides, systematics, populations, tropical ecology, marine biology and sedimentology. *Recreations:* art, music, photography, gardening. *Address:* 43 Hill Top, NW11 6EA. *T:* (020) 8458 2571. *Club:* Athenæum.

WEBB, Justin Oliver; North America Editor, BBC, since 2007; *b* 3 Jan. 1961; *s* of Charles Webb and late Gloria (*née* Crocombe); *m* 1996, Sarah Gordon; one *s* two *d*. *Educ:* London Sch. of Econs (BSc Econ 1983). BBC: Reporter: Radio Ulster, 1985–87; Today Prog., 1987–89; Foreign Affairs Corresp., TV News, 1989–94; Presenter: Breakfast TV News, 1994–98; One O'Clock TV News, 1998–99; Chief Europe Corresp., 1999–2002; Chief Washington Corresp., 2002–07. Part-time Presenter, BBC Radio: Today Prog.; World This Weekend. *Publication:* Have a Nice Day, 2008. *Recreation:* falling in love with America and preparing to write a book about it. *Address:* BBC News, Television Centre, Wood Lane, W12 7RJ; *e-mail:* justin.webb@bbc.co.uk.

WEBB, Prof. (Leslie) Roy, AO 2003; Vice-Chancellor, Griffith University, 1985–2001, Emeritus Professor, 2002; *b* 18 July 1935; *s* of Leslie Hugh Charles Webb and Alice Myra Webb; *m* 1966, Heather, *d* of late H. Brown; one *s* one *d*. *Educ:* Wesley College, Univ. of Melbourne (BCom 1957); Univ. of London (PhD 1962). FASSA 1986; FAIM 1989; FACE 1997. Sen. Lectr in Economics, Univ. of Melbourne, 1964–68; Reader in Economics, La Trobe Univ., 1968–72; University of Melbourne: Truby Williams Prof. of Economics, 1973–84, Prof. Emeritus, 1984; Pro-Vice-Chancellor, 1982–84; Chm., Academic Bd, 1983–84. Vis. Prof., Cornell, 1967–68. Chairman: Bd, Qld Tertiary Admissions Centre, 1986, 1991, 1992 (Mem., 1985–2001); Australian-Amer. Educnl Foundn (Fulbright Program), 1986–90 (Mem., 1985–89); Qld Non-State Schs Accreditation Bd, 2001–; Library Bd of Qld, 2002–08; Member: Bd of Dirs, Australian Vice-Chancellors' Cttee, 1991–94; Cttee, Sir Robert Menzies Australian Studies Centre, Univ. of London, 1990–92; Bd of Govs, Foundn for Develt Co-operation, 1990–2007. Consultant, UN Conf. on Trade and Develt, 1974–75; Chm., Cttee of Inquiry into S Australian Dairy Industry, 1977; Mem., Council of Advice, Bureau of Industry Economics, 1982–84; Pres., Victoria Branch, Econ. Soc. of Aust. and NZ, 1976. DUniv: Qld Univ. of Technol., 2002; Griffith, 2002; Hon. DLitt Southern Qld, 2002. Award for outstanding achievement, US Inf. Agency, 1987. Joint Editor, The Economic Record, 1973–77. Cavaliere dell'Ordine al Merito (Italy), 1995. *Publication:* (ed jtly) Industrial Economics: Australian studies, 1982. *Recreations:* music, art. *Address:* 3 Davrod Street, Robertson, Qld 4109, Australia.

WEBB, Lynn Margaret; *see* Tayton, L. M.

WEBB, Margaret Elizabeth Barbieri; *see* Barbieri, M. E.

WEBB, Michael Alfred Healey, OBE 2002; Consultant in Occupational Medicine; Deputy Chief Commander, St John Ambulance, 1999–2002; *b* 10 Oct. 1934; *s* of Alfred Webb and Lily Margaret Webb (*née* Beeson); *m* 1962, Shirley Ann Parsons; one *s* one *d*. *Educ:* Sir Walter St John's Grammar Sch.; King's Coll., London; King's Coll. Hosp. Med. Sch. MRCS, LRCP 1961; DIH 1978; FFOM 1996. Various posts as occupational health physician to: EMAS, 1973–78; Commonwealth Smelting Ltd, 1978–81; Post Office, 1981–94. Med. Dir, St John Ambulance Assoc., 1991–96; Dir-Gen., St John Ambulance, 1996–99. KStJ 1996. *Publication:* (jtly) First Aid Manual, 7th edn 1997. *Recreations:* gardening, home maintenance. *Address:* 48 Offington Avenue, Worthing, W Sussex BN14 9PJ.

WEBB, Nicholas John David; His Honour Judge Webb; a Circuit Judge, since 2003; *b* 13 Oct. 1949; *s* of late David Frederick and of Joyce Mary Webb; *m* 1973, Jane Elizabeth; two *s*. *Educ:* Nottingham High Sch.; Downing Coll., Cambridge (BA 1971). Called to the Bar, Middle Temple, 1972; barrister, Midland and Oxford, later Midland Circuit, 1972–2003, specialising in crime and personal injury; Asst Recorder, 1996–2001, Recorder, 2001–03. Chairman: Cambridge Univ. Conservative Assoc., 1971; Edgbaston Constituency Conservative Assoc., 1989–93; Dep. Chm., West Midlands Area Conservative Assoc., 1992–94. Contested (C) Birmingham Sparkbrook, 1979. *Recreations:* jazz (New Orleans to be-bop), cricket, medieval and modern history. *Address:* Wolverhampton Crown Court Centre, Pipers Row, Wolverhampton WV1 3LQ.

WEBB, Dame Patricia M.; *see* Morgan-Webb.

WEBB, Pauline Mary, FKC; retired; author and broadcaster; *b* 28 June 1927; *d* of Rev. Leonard F. Webb. *Educ:* King's Coll., London Univ. (BA English Hons 1948; AKC, FKC 1985); Teacher's Diploma, London Inst. of Educn, 1949; Union Theological Seminary, New York (STM). Asst Mistress, Thames Valley Grammar Sch., 1949–52; Editor, Methodist Missionary Soc., 1955–66; Vice-Pres., Methodist Conf., 1965–66; Dir, Lay Training, Methodist Church, 1967–73; Area Sec., Methodist Missionary Soc., 1973–79; Chm., Community and Race Relns Unit, BCC, 1976–79; Organiser, Religious Broadcasting, BBC World Service, 1979–87. Vice-Chm., Central Cttee, WCC, 1968–75; Jt Chm., World Conf. on Religion and Peace, 1989–93. Pres., Feed the Minds, 1998–2003. Hon. Life Mem., World Assoc. of Christian Communication, 1998. Hon. Dr in Protestant Theology, Univ. of Brussels, 1984; Hon. DSL Victoria Univ., Toronto, 1985; Hon. DHL Mt St Vincent Univ., Nova Scotia, 1987; Hon. DD Birmingham, 1997. *Publications:* Women of Our Company, 1958; Women of Our Time, 1960; Operation-Healing, 1964; All God's Children, 1964; Are We Yet Alive?, 1966; Agenda for the Churches, 1968; Salvation Today, 1974; Eventful Worship, 1975; Where are the Women?, 1979; Faith and Faithfulness, 1985; Celebrating Friendship, 1986; Evidence for the Power of Prayer, 1987; Candles for Advent, 1989; (ed jtly) Dictionary of the Ecumenical Movement, 1991; She Flies Beyond, 1993; (ed) The Long Struggle: the World Council of Churches' involvement with South Africa, 1994; (ed) All Loves Excelling, 1997; Worship in Every Event, 1998; (compiler) Living by Grace (anthol.), 2001; World-Wide Webb, 2006. *Address:* 14 Paddocks Green, Salmon Street, NW9 8NH. *Club:* BBC.

WEBB, Richard Murton Lumley; Chairman, Morgan Grenfell & Co. Ltd, 1989–96; *b* 7 March 1939; *s* of Richard Henry Lumley Webb and Elizabeth Martin (*née* Munro Kerr); *m* 1966, Juliet Wendy English Devenish; one *s* one *d*. *Educ:* Winchester Coll.; New Coll., Oxford (BA Modern Hist.). Mem., Inst. Chartered Accountants of Scotland, 1965. Brown Fleming & Murray, 1961–68; Director: Morgan Grenfell & Co. Ltd, 1973–96; Morgan Grenfell Gp PLC, 1988–96. Chairman: Medway Housing Society Ltd, 1996–2004; Wax Lyrical Ltd, 1997–99; Dir, Scottish Provident Instn, 1997–2001. *Address:* 12 Gwendolen Avenue, Putney, SW15 6EH. *Club:* Hurlingham.

WEBB, Robert Stopford; QC 1988; General Counsel, British Airways, since 1998; *b* 4 Oct. 1948; *s* of late Robert Victor Bertram Webb, MC and Isabella Raine Webb (*née* Hinks); *m* 1975, Angela Mary Freshwater; two *s*. *Educ:* Wycliffe Coll.; Exeter Univ. (LLB 1970). Called to the Bar, Inner Temple, 1971 (Bencher, 1997), and Lincoln's Inn, 1996; a Recorder, 1993–98; Western Circuit. Director: Air Mauritius, 1998–2005; London Stock Exchange, 2001–; London First, 2002–; Hakluyt and Co. Ltd, 2005–; Emerging Health Threats Forum CIC (formerly Forum for Global Health Protection), 2006–. Non-exec. Dir, BBC, 2007–. Chm., Air Law Gp, RAeS, 1988–93 (FRAeS 1992); English Bar Rep., Internat. Bar Assoc., 1994–99; Chm., Internat. Relations Cttee, Bar Council, 1997–98. Trustee, Migratory Salmon Fund, 1997–. Fellow, Internat. Acad. of Trial Lawyers, 1990 (Mem. Bd, 1994–2008). Hon. Fellow, UNICEF, 2006. *Recreations:* golf, conservation. *Address:* British Airways PLC, Waterside (HBB3), PO Box 365, Harmondsworth UB7 0GB. *T:* (020) 8738 6870, *Fax:* (020) 8738 9647. *Clubs:* Royal Automobile, Reform; Royal Wimbledon Golf, Royal Lytham St Anne's Golf, Prestbury Golf.

WEBB, Roy; *see* Webb, L. R.

WEBB, Simon, CBE 1991; Director General, International Networks and Environment, Department for Transport, since 2007; *b* 21 Oct. 1951; *s* of Rev. Canon Bertie Webb and Jane Webb (*née* Braley); *m* 1975, Alexandra Jane Culme-Seymour; one *s* one *d*. *Educ:* King's Sch., Worcester (Schol.); Hertford Coll., Oxford (Meeke Schol.; MA). Entered MoD, 1972: Asst Private Sec. to Minister of State, 1975; Principal, 1977; Public Enterprises, HM Treasury, 1982–85; Dir of Resources and Progs (Warships), MoD, 1985–88; Rand Corp., Santa Monica, Calif, 1988–89; Head, Agency Team, MoD, 1989; Private Sec. to Sec. of State for Defence, 1989–92; Minister (Defence Materiel), Washington, 1992–96; Dir Gen. Resources, PE, MoD, 1996–98; Team Leader, Smart Procurement, 1998–99; Asst Under Sec. of State (Home & Overseas), subseq. Dir Gen., Operational Policy, MoD, 1999–2001; Policy Dir, MoD, 2001–04; Dir Gen., Delivery and Security, DfT, 2004–07. Edgell Sheppee Prize for Engrg and Econs. *Publication:* Defense Acquisition and Free Markets, 1990. *Recreations:* cycling, gardens, golf. *Address:* Department for Transport, Great Minster House, 76 Marsham Street, SW1P 4DR. *Club:* Reform.

WEBB, Steven John; MP (Lib Dem) Northavon, since 1997; *b* 18 July 1965; *s* of Brian and Patricia Webb; *m* 1993, Rev. Helen Edwards; one *s* one *d*. *Educ:* Hertford Coll., Oxford (1st Cl. BA Hons PPE). Economist, Inst. for Fiscal Studies, 1986–95; Prof. of Social Policy, Bath Univ., 1995–97. Lib Dem spokesman on health, 2005–07, on envmt, energy, food and rural affairs, 2008–; Lib Dem Manifesto Chair, 2007. *Publication:* (with Alissa Goodman and Paul Johnson) Inequality in the UK, 1997. *Recreations:* internet issues, church organ, oboe. *Address:* (constituency office) Poole Court, Poole Court Drive, Yate BS37 5PP.

WEBB-CARTER, Maj. Gen. Sir Evelyn (John), KCVO 2000; OBE 1989; Controller, Army Benevolent Fund, since 2003; *b* 30 Jan. 1946; *s* of Brig. Brian Webb-Carter, DSO, OBE and Rosemary Webb-Carter (*née* Hood); *m* 1973, Hon. Anne Celia Wigram, *yr d* of Baron Wigram, *qv*; one *s* two *d*. *Educ:* Wellington Coll.; RMA Sandhurst. Commissioned

Grenadier Guards, 1966; Commanded: 1st Bn Grenadier Guards, 1985–88; 19 Mechanised Bde, 1991–93; Multi National Div. (SW) in Bosnia, 1996–97; GOC London Dist and Maj. Gen. Comdg Household Div., 1997–2000. Special Advr to CRE, 2001–03. Regtl Lt-Col, Grenadier Guards, 1995–2000; Col, Duke of Wellington's Regt, 1999–2006; Hon. Regtl Col, King's Troop, RHA, 2001–. Chairman: Mounted Infantry Club, 1993–; Assoc. of Friends of Waterloo Cttee, 2002–; Commemoration Cttee, 200th Anniversary of Battle of Waterloo; Adv. Council, First Aid Nursing Yeomanry, 2003–. Patron, Burnaby Blue Foundn, 2001–. Mem. Ct of Assts, Farriers' Co., 2004– (Liveryman, 2003–). *Recreations:* hunting, military history, riding in foreign parts. *Address:* Army Benevolent Fund, Mountbarrow House, 6–20 Elizabeth Street, SW1W 9RB. *Clubs:* Boodle's; Banja Luka Hunt (Bosnia).

WEBBER; *see* Lloyd Webber.

WEBBER, Prof. Bryan Ronald, PhD; FRS 2001; CPhys, FInstP; Professor of Theoretical Physics, University of Cambridge, since 1999; Fellow, Emmanuel College, Cambridge, since 1973; *b* 25 July 1943; *s* of Frederick Ronald Webber and Iris Evelyn Webber (*née* Hutchings); *m* 1968, Akemi Horie. *Educ:* Colston's Sch., Bristol; Queen's Coll., Oxford (MA); Univ. of Calif, Berkeley (PhD 1969). CPhys, FInstP 1987. Physicist, Lawrence Berkeley Nat. Lab., Calif, 1969–71; Department of Physics, University of Cambridge: Res. Asst, 1971–73; Demonstrator, 1973–78; Lectr, 1978–94; Reader, 1994–99. *Publications:* (jtly) QCD and Collider Physics, 1996; contrib. articles on high energy physics. *Address:* Cavendish Laboratory, J. J. Thomson Avenue, Cambridge CB3 0HE. *T:* (01223) 337200.

WEBBER, Howard Simon; Chief Executive, Postwatch, 2006–08; *b* 25 Jan. 1955; *s* of Manny and Josie Webber; *m* 1978, Sandra Wagman; one *s*. *Educ:* Univ. of Birmingham (LLB 1976); Harvard Univ. (MPA 1987). Joined Home Office, 1976; seconded to Royal Commn on Criminal Procedure, 1979–80 and Cabinet Office, 1986; Harkness Fellow, USA, 1986–87; Prison Bldg Budget Manager, Home Office, 1987–88; Dir, Incentive Funding, 1988–91, Hd, Policy and Planning, 1991–94, Arts Council; Manager, Public Sector MBA, Cabinet Office, 1994; Hd, Voluntary Services Unit/Active Community Unit, Home Office, 1995–99; Chief Exec., Criminal Injuries Compensation Authy, 1999–2006. *Publication:* (jtly) A Creative Future: a national strategy for the arts and media, 1993. *Recreations:* travel, the arts. *Address: e-mail:* howardwebber@gmail.com.

WEBBER, Rev. Lionel Frank; Chaplain to the Queen, 1994–2001; Hon. Curate, St Mary, Burnham-on-Crouch, since 2005; *b* 12 July 1935; *s* of Nellie and Sydney Webber; *m* 1961, Jean Thomas; one *d*. *Educ:* Danetree Road Co. Secondary Sch., Ewell; Kelham Theol Coll.; St Michael's Theol Coll., Llandaff. Ordained deacon, 1960, priest, 1961; Curate: The Saviour, Bolton, 1960–63; Holy Trinity, Aberavon, 1963–65; Rector, Stowell Meml Parish Ch, Salford, 1965–69; Vicar, Holy Trinity, Aberavon, 1969–74; Team Vicar, Stantonbury, Milton Keynes, 1974–76; Rector of Basildon, 1976–2001. Hon. Canon, Chelmsford Cathedral, 1984–2001. Chaplain: Vintage Sports Car Club; RNSA. *Recreations:* motor racing, sailing.

WEBBER, Roy Seymour, FCCA; Town Clerk and Chief Executive, Royal Borough of Kensington and Chelsea, 1979–90; *b* 8 April 1933; *s* of A. E. and A. M. Webber; *m* 1960, Barbara Ann (*née* Harries); one *s* three *d*. *Educ:* Ipswich School. Ipswich CBC, 1949–55; Coventry CBC, 1955–58; St Pancras BC, 1958–61; IBM (UK) Ltd, 1961–62; Woolwich BC, 1962–65; Greenwich LBC, 1965–68; Royal Borough of Kensington and Chelsea: Dep. Borough Treasurer, 1968–73; Director of Finance, 1973–79. *Recreation:* walking. *Address:* 11 River Park, Marlborough, Wilts SN8 1NH. *T:* (01672) 511426.

WEBBON, Peter Michael, PhD; Chief Executive, Animal Health Trust, since 2007; *b* Leicester, 9 Jan. 1948; *s* of late Robert Ernest Webbon and Grace Webbon (*née* Salt); *m* 1970, Phyllis Mary Christine (marr. diss. 2008), *d* of late Major John Frederick Langdon, MC; one *s* three *d*. *Educ:* Wyggeston Boys' Grammar Sch.; Royal Veterinary Coll., London (BVetMed Hons 1971; DVR 1975; PhD 1989). MRCVS. Res. Trng Scholar, Horserace Betting Levy Bd, 1971–74; Lectr, 1974–83, Sen. Lectr, 1983–96, RVC, London; Chief Vet. Advr, 1996–2001, Vet. Dir, 2002–06, Jockey Club; Chief Exec., HRA, 2006. Hon. Prof., RVC, 2007. Official veterinarian, FEI. *Publications:* (ed and contrib.) A Guide to Diagnostic Radiography in Small Animal Practice, 1981; chapters in books on diagnostic imaging and equine medicine; articles in scientific and gen. jls; contrib. professional and lay societies. *Recreations:* keeping Ryeland sheep, gardening, skiing, golf. *Address:* Animal Health Trust, Lanwades Park, Kentford, Newmarket, Suffolk CB8 7UU. *T:* (01638) 555656; *e-mail:* peter.webbon@aht.org.uk.

WEBER, Prof. Axel Alfred; President, Deutsche Bundesbank, and Member, Governing Council, European Central Bank, since 2004; *b* Kusel, 8 March 1957; *m*; two *c*. *Educ:* Univ. of Constance (degree Econs and Mgt 1982); Univ. of Siegen (Doctorate 1987; Habilitation Econs 1994). Prof. of Econ. Theory, Rheinische Friedrich Wilhelms Univ., Bonn, 1994–98; Prof. of Applied Monetary Econs, Johann Wolfgang Goethe Univ., Frankfurt am Main, 1998–2001; Dir, Center for Financial Studies, Frankfurt am Main, 1998–2002; Prof. of Internat. Econs, Univ. of Cologne, 2001–04. Mem., German Council of Economic Experts, 2002–04. *Address:* Deutsche Bundesbank, Wilhelm-Epstein-Strasse 14, 60431 Frankfurt am Main, Germany. *T:* (69) 95661, *Fax:* (69) 5601071; *e-mail:* presse-information@bundesbank.de.

WEBER, Catherine Elisabeth Dorcas; *see* Bell, C. E. D.

WEBER, Prof. Jonathan Norden, PhD; FRCP, FRCPath, FMedSci; Jefferiss Professor of Genito-Urinary Medicine and Communicable Diseases, Imperial College and St Mary's Hospital, since 1991; Head, Division of Medicine, Imperial College London, since 2004; Director of Research, Imperial College Healthcare NHS Trust, since 2007; *b* 29 Dec. 1954; *s* of Dr Geoffrey Norden Weber and Rosalie Weber; *m* 1996, Dr Sophie Elisabeth Day; three *s*. *Educ:* Gonville and Caius Coll., Cambridge (BA 1976; PhD 2003); St Bartholomew's Med. Sch. (MB BChir 1979). FRCP 1993; FRCPath 1997. Wellcome Trust Res. Fellow, St Mary's Hosp. Med. Sch., 1982–85; Wellcome Trust Lectr in Cell and Molecular Biol., Inst. Cancer Res., 1985–88; Sen. Lectr, Dept of Medicine, RPMS, 1988–91; Chm., Wright-Fleming Inst., 2000–04, Dean, St Mary's Campus, 2001–04, Imperial Coll. London. FMedSci 2000. *Publications:* The Management of AIDS Patients, 1986; contribs to The Lancet, etc. *Recreations:* motor-bikes, boats. *Address:* 50 St Paul's Road, Islington, N1 2QW. *T:* (020) 7226 4579; *e-mail:* j.weber@imperial.ac.uk.

WEBER, Jürgen; Chairman, Supervisory Board, Lufthansa German Airlines, since 2003; *b* 17 Oct. 1941; *m* 1965, Sabine Rossberg; one *s* one *d*. *Educ:* Stuttgart Tech. Univ. (Dipl. Ing. Aeronautical Engrg 1965); MIT (Sen. Mgt Trng 1980). Joined Lufthansa, 1967: Engrg Div., 1967–74; Director: Line Maintenance Dept, 1974–78; Aircraft Engrg Sub-div., 1978–87; Chief Operating Officer (Tech.), 1987–89; Dep. Mem., Exec. Bd, 1989–90; Chief Exec., Tech., 1990–91; Chm., Exec. Bd, 1991–2003. *Recreations:* jogging, ski-ing. *Address:* c/o Deutsche Lufthansa AG, Flughafen-Bereich West, 60546 Frankfurt/Main, Germany. *T:* (69) 6962200.

WEBER, Prof. Richard Robert, Jr, PhD; Churchill Professor of Mathematics for Operational Research, since 1994, and Director, Statistical Laboratory, since 2001, Cambridge University; Fellow, Queens' College, Cambridge, since 1978; *b* 25 Feb. 1953; *s* of Richard Robert Weber and Elizabeth Bray. *Educ:* Walnut Hills High Sch., USA; Solihull Sch.; Downing Coll., Cambridge (BA 1974; MA 1978; PhD 1980). Cambridge University: Asst Lectr and Lectr in Engrg, 1978–92; Reader in Management Sci., Engrg, 1992–94; Queens' College: Res. Fellow, 1977–78; Tutor, 1979–92; Dir of Studies (Maths), 1985–94; Vice Pres., 1996–2007. *Publications:* (with C. Courcoubetis) Pricing Communication Networks, 2003; numerous articles on stochastic systems, scheduling and queueing theory. *Recreations:* hiking, travel. *Address:* Queens' College, Cambridge CB3 9ET; Statistical Laboratory, Centre for Mathematical Sciences, Wilberforce Road, Cambridge CB3 0WB. *T:* (01223) 335570, 337944.

WEBLEY, Prof. Paul, PhD; Director and Principal, School of African and Oriental Studies, University of London, since 2006; *b* Hayes, Middx, 19 Nov. 1953; *s* of Reginald Sidney Webley and Sylvia Mary Webley; *m* 1976, Julie Dawick; two *s* one *d*. *Educ:* London Sch. of Econs (BSc Soc. Psychol. 1976; PhD 1981). Lectr in Soc. Psychol., Univ. of Southampton, 1979–80; University of Exeter: Lectr, 1980–91, Sen. Lectr, 1991–95, in Psychol.; Reader in Econ. Psychol., 1995–98; Prof. of Econ. Psychol., 1998–2006; Hd, Sch. of Psychol., 1998–2003; Dep. Vice-Chancellor, 2003–06. Visiting Professor: of Sociol. of Law, Erasmus Univ., Rotterdam, 1988; Agder University Coll., Kristiansand, 2002–06; Visiting Research Fellow: Univ. of Tilburg, 1994, 1998; Internat. Centre for Econ. Res., Turin, 1999. *Publications:* (jtly) The Individual in the Economy, 1987; (jtly) Tax Evasion: an experimental approach, 1991; (ed jtly) New Directions in Economic Psychology: theory, experiment and application, 1992; (with Edmund Sonuga-Barke) Children's Saving, 1993; (jtly) The New Economic Mind, 1995; (ed with Catherine Walker) Handbook for the Teaching of Economic and Consumer Psychology, 1999; (jtly) The Economic Psychology of Everyday Life, 2001; (jtly) Psicologia economica della vita quotidiana, 2004. *Recreations:* fell-walking, eating, conversation. *Address:* School of Oriental and African Studies, Thornhaugh Street, WC1H 0XG. *T:* (020) 7898 4014; *e-mail:* pw2@soas.ac.uk.

WEBLIN, Harold; Chairman, Liberty's, 1984–95 (Chief Executive, 1984–93); *b* 10 April 1930; *s* of E. W. Weblin and B. Weblin; *m* 1954, June Weblin (decd); two *s*. *Educ:* Walpole Grammar School, London. General Manager, Way-In, Harrods, 1948–71; General Manager, Liberty's, 1971–84. *Recreation:* gardening. *Address:* Weston Hill House, Weston Road, Helmdon, Northants NN13 5QB.

WEBSTER, Alec, FCCA; CIGEM; Regional Chairman, British Gas Wales, 1989–92; *b* 22 March 1934; *s* of Clifford Webster and Rose Webster (*née* Proctor); *m* 1958, Jean Thompson; one *s* two *d*. *Educ:* Hull Univ. (BScEcon Hons). Chief Accountant, British Gas Southern, 1974; Controller of Audit and Investigations, British Gas, 1979; Treas., British Gas, 1981; Reg. Dep. Chm., British Gas Southern, 1984. Pres., Chartered Assoc. of Certified Accountants, 1989–90. Chairman: Hendref Building Preservation Trust, 1992–2000; Darwin Centre for Biology and Medicine, 1993–2000. FRSA 1990. *Recreations:* sailing, mountaineering, wood carving. *Address:* Tŷ Carreg, 2 Maillards Haven, Penarth, S Glam CF64 5RF.

WEBSTER, Alistair Stevenson; QC 1995; a Recorder, since 1996 (an Assistant Recorder, 1992–96); *b* 28 April 1953; *s* of His Honour Ian Stevenson Webster; *m* 1977, Barbara Anne Longbottom; two *d*. *Educ:* Hulme Grammar Sch., Oldham; Brasenose Coll., Oxford (BA Hons Jurisp.). Called to the Bar, Middle Temple, 1976; practice on Northern Circuit, 1976–. Hon. Sec., Northern Circuit, 1988–93; Mem., Bar Council, 1995–96. *Recreations:* cricket, tennis, ski-ing, football. *Address:* Lincoln House Chambers, 1 Brazennose Street, Manchester M2 5EL. *T:* (0161) 832 5701. *Clubs:* Manchester Racquets; Rochdale Racquets; I Volenti CC.

WEBSTER, Maj.-Gen. Bryan Courtney, CB 1986; CBE 1981; Director of Army Quartering, 1982–86; *b* 2 Feb. 1931; *s* of Captain H. J. Webster, Royal Fusiliers (killed in action, 1940) and late M. J. Webster; *m* 1957, Elizabeth Rowland Waldron Smithers, *d* of Prof. Sir David Smithers; two *s* one *d*. *Educ:* Haileybury College; RMA Sandhurst. Commissioned Royal Fusiliers, 1951; ADC to GOC, 16 Airborne Div., 1953–55; served BAOR, Korea, Egypt, Malta, Gibraltar, Hong Kong; Directing Staff, Staff Coll., 1969–70; Comd 1st Bn Royal Regt of Fusiliers, 1971–73; Comd 8th Inf. Brigade, 1975–77 (despatches); Dep. Col, Royal Regt of Fusiliers (City of London), 1976–89; Nat. Defence Coll., India, 1979; Staff appts, Far East, MoD, incl. Dir of Admin Planning (Army), 1980–82. Chm., Army Benevolent Fund, Surrey, 1986–2000. Mem. Council, Wine Guild of UK, 1995–2001. Pres., CPRE Hants, 2001–08. FCMI. Freeman, City of London, 1984. *Recreations:* ornithology, shooting, wine. *Address:* c/o HSBC, 69 High Street, Sevenoaks, Kent TN13 1LB.

WEBSTER, Charles, DSc; Senior Research Fellow, All Souls College, Oxford, 1988–2004, now Emeritus Fellow. Reader in the History of Medicine, University of Oxford, 1972–88; Director, Wellcome Unit for the History of Medicine, 1972–88; Fellow of Corpus Christi College, Oxford, 1972–88. FBA 1982–99. *Publications:* (ed) Samuel Hartlib and the Advancement of Learning, 1970; The Great Instauration, 1975; From Paracelsus to Newton, 1982; Problems of Health Care: the National Health Service before 1957, 1988; (ed) Aneurin Bevan on the National Health Service, 1991; (ed) Caring for Health, History and Diversity, 1993; Government and Health Care: the British National Health Service 1958–1979, 1996; The National Health Service: a political history, 1998. *Address:* All Souls College, Oxford OX1 4AL. *T:* (01865) 279379.

WEBSTER, David Gordon Comyn; Chairman: InterContinental Hotels Group, since 2004 (Director, since 2003); Makinson Cowell, since 2004; *b* 11 Feb. 1945; *s* of Alfred Edward Comyn Webster and Meryl Mary Clutterbuck; *m* 1972, Pamela Gail Runnicles; three *s*. *Educ:* Glasgow Acad.; Glasgow Univ. (LLB). Lieut, RNR, retd 1970. Admitted Solicitor, 1968; Corporate Finance Manager, Samuel Montagu & Co., 1969–72; Finance Dir, Oriel Foods Ltd, 1973–76; Co-Founder and Finance Dir, 1977–89, Dep. Chm., 1989–97, Chm., 1997–2004, Argyll Gp, subseq. Safeway plc. Non-executive Director: Reed International plc, 1992–2002; Reed Elsevier, 1993–2002; Elsevier NV, 1999–2002. Mem., Nat. Employers Liaison Cttee, 1992–2002. Pres., Inst. of Grocery Distribn, 2001–02. Dir, Nat. Life Story Collection, 2005–. KStJ 2004. *Recreations:* military history, ski-ing, sailing, gardening, walking. *Address:* InterContinental Hotels Group, 67 Alma Road, Windsor, Berks SL4 3HD.

WEBSTER, His Honour David MacLaren; QC 1980; a Circuit Judge, 1987–2003 (Resident Judge, Salisbury); Hon. Recorder of Salisbury, since 2002; *b* 21 Dec. 1937; *s* of late John MacLaren Webster and Winning McGregor Webster (*née* Rough); *m* 1964, Frances Sally McLaren, RE, *o d* of late Lt-Col J. A. McLaren and of Mrs H. S. Scammell; three *s*. *Educ:* Hutchesons', Glasgow; Christ Church, Oxford (MA (Eng. Lang. and Lit.)); Conservatoire d'Art Dramatique and Sorbonne (French Govt Schol. 1960–61). Radio and television work in drama and current affairs, Scotland, incl. Dixon of Dock Green, A Nest of Singing Birds, and Muir of Huntershill, 1949–64; called to the Bar, Gray's Inn, 1964;

Western Circuit; a Dep. Circuit Judge, 1976–79; a Recorder, 1979–87. Chairman: Salisbury & Dist Family Mediation Service, 1987–2001; Area Criminal Justice Liaison Cttee for Hants, Dorset and IoW, 1994–99; Area Criminal Justice Strategy Cttee, Hants and IoW, 2000–01. Member: Bar Council, 1972–74; Senate of Inns of Court and Bar, 1974–79, 1982–85 (Senate Representative, Commonwealth Law Conf., Edinburgh, 1977). Chm., Salisbury Safety Partnership, 1998–2004. Gold Medal, LAMDA, 1954; LRAM 1955. President, Oxford Univ. Experimental Theatre Club, 1958–59; Secretary, Mermaid's, 1958; Chm., Bar Theatrical Soc., 1976–86. Governor, Port Regis Sch., 1983–94. *Recreations:* theatre, sailing, cricket, reading, still training Jupiter and Juno. *Clubs:* Garrick, MCC; Bar Yacht.

WEBSTER, Derek Adrian, CBE 1979; Chairman and Editorial Director, Scottish Daily Record and Sunday Mail Ltd, 1974–86; *b* 24 March 1927; *s* of James Tulloch Webster and Isobel Webster; *m* 1966, Dorothy Frances Johnson; two *s* one *d*. *Educ:* St Peter's, Bournemouth. Served RN, 1944–48. Reporter, Western Morning News, 1943; Staff Journalist, Daily Mail, 1949–51; joined Mirror Group, 1952; Northern Editor, Daily Mirror, 1964–67; Editor, Daily Record, 1967–72; Director: Mirror Gp Newspapers, 1974–86; Clyde Cable Vision, 1983–87. Mem., Press Council, 1981–84 (Jt Vice-Chm., 1982–83). Vice-Chm., Age Concern (Scotland), 1977–83; Hon. Vice-Pres., Newspaper Press Fund, 1983–; Mem. Council, CPU, 1984–86. *Recreations:* travel, photography. *Address:* 6 Park Circus Place, Glasgow G3 6AN. *T:* (0141) 353 6330.

WEBSTER, Janice Helen, WS; Secretary, Scottish Law Agents Society, 1998–2004; part-time Chairman, Appeals Service, since 1996; legal expert to Council of Europe, 1993–97; *b* 2 April 1944; *d* of James Bell Reid and Janet (*née* Johnston); *m* 1968, R. M. Webster; two *d*. *Educ:* Edinburgh Univ. (LLB 1964). Solicitor and Notary Public. Legal Asst, then Sen. Solicitor, Falkirk Town Council, 1967–71; in private practice, Alston Nairn & Hogg, Edinburgh, 1971–74; Dep. Sec., Law Soc. of Scotland, 1974–80; Crown Counsel, then Magistrate, Govt of Seychelles, 1980–82; Law Society of Scotland, 1982–90 (Dep. Sec., Dir, European Affairs and Sec., Scottish Lawyers' European Gp); Dir Gen., CCBE, 1991–93; Consultant, Bell & Scott, WS, Edinburgh, 1994–96. Mem., Scottish Records Adv. Council, 1995–2000. Director: Scottish Archive Network, 1998–2002; Franco-British Lawyers' Soc. Ltd, 1998–2000; Chm., Scottish Soc. for Computers and Law, 2001–04. Member: Council, WS Soc., 1998–2000; Governing Council, Erskine Stewart's Melville, 1998–2002. Ed., Human Rights and UK Practice, 1999–. *Publication:* (with R. M. Webster) Professional Ethics and Practice for Scottish Solicitors, 3rd edn 1996, 4th edn 2004. *Recreations:* singing, walking, gardening. *Club:* New (Edinburgh).

WEBSTER, Rev. Prof. John Bainbridge, PhD; Professor of Systematic Theology, University of Aberdeen, since 2003; *b* 20 June 1955; *s* of Gordon and Ruth Webster; *m* 1978, Jane Goodden; two *s*. *Educ:* Clare Coll., Cambridge (MA, PhD 1982). Stephenson Fellow, Dept of Biblical Studies, Univ. of Sheffield, 1981–82; ordained deacon, 1983, priest, 1984; Dep. Sen. Tutor, Tutor in Systematic Theology, and Chaplain, St John's Coll., Univ. of Durham, 1982–86; Wycliffe College, University of Toronto: Associate Prof. of Systematic Theology, 1986–93; Professor, 1993–95; Ramsay Armitage Prof., 1995–96; Lady Margaret Prof. of Divinity, Univ. of Oxford, and Canon of Christ Church, Oxford, 1996–2003. FRSE 2005. Hon. DD Aberdeen, 2003. *Publications:* Eberhard Jüngel: an introduction to his theology, 1986; (ed) The Possibilities of Theology, 1994; Barth's Ethics of Reconciliation, 1995; Barth's Moral Theology, 1998; (ed) Theology after Liberalism, 2000; (ed) The Cambridge Companion to Karl Barth, 2000; Karl Barth, 2000; Word and Church, 2001; Holiness, 2002; Holy Scripture, 2003; Confessing God, 2005; Barth's Earlier Theology, 2005; (ed) Oxford Handbook of Systematic Theology, 2007. *Address:* King's College, University of Aberdeen, Aberdeen AB24 3FX.

WEBSTER, John Lawrence Harvey, CMG 1963; *b* 10 March 1913; *s* of late Sydney Webster, Hindhead, and Elsie Gwendoline Webster (*née* Harvey); *m* 1st, 1940, Elizabeth Marshall Gilbertson (marr. diss. 1959); two *d*; 2nd, 1960, Jessie Lillian Royston-Smith. *Educ:* Rugby Sch.; Balliol College, Oxford (MA). District Officer, Colonial Administrative Service, Kenya, 1935–49; Secretary for Development, 1949–54; Administrative Sec., 1954–56; Sec. to Cabinet, 1956–58; Permanent Sec., Kenya, 1958–63; on retirement from HMOCS, with the British Council, 1964–80, in Thailand, Sri Lanka, Hong Kong, Istanbul and London. *Recreations:* travel, reading, swimming. *Clubs:* Royal Commonwealth Society; Leander; Nairobi (Kenya).

WEBSTER, Vice-Adm. Sir John (Morrison), KCB 1986; RSMA; painter; President, Royal Naval Benevolent Trust, 1991–98; *b* 3 Nov. 1932; *s* of late Frank Martin Webster and Kathleen Mary (*née* Morrison); *m* 1962, Valerie Anne Villiers (*d* 2005); two *d* (one *s* decd). *Educ:* Pangbourne College. Joined RN, 1951; specialised navigation, 1959; RAN, 1959–61; HMS Lowestoft, 1961–63; BRNC Dartmouth, 1963–65; HMS Dido, 1965–67; RN Tactical Sch., 1967–69; in command HMS Argonaut, 1969–71; MoD Navy, 1971–73; RNLO Ottawa, 1974–76; in command HMS Cleopatra and 4th Frigate Sqdn, 1976–78; MoD, Director Naval Warfare, 1980–82; Flag Officer Sea Trng, 1982–84; C of S to C-in-C Fleet, 1984–86; Flag Officer Plymouth, Naval Base Comdr Devonport, Comdr Central Sub Area Eastern Atlantic and Comdr Plymouth Sub Area Channel, 1987–90; retired. Lt-Comdr 1963, Comdr 1967, Captain 1973, Rear-Adm. 1982, Vice-Adm. 1985. Younger Brother of Trinity House, 1970–. Life Mem., Armed Forces Art Soc., 2008 (Mem., 1967–2008; Chm., 1990–96). One-man exhibitions of paintings: Canada, 1976; Winchester, 1980; London, 1982, 1984, 1986, 1988, 1991, 1993, 1996, 1999, 2002, 2004, 2007; Jersey, 2006. Governor: Canford Sch., 1984–2003; Pangbourne College, 1990–2000 (Chm., 1992–2000); FBA, 2002–08. Associate, RSMA, 1998, RSMA 2001. *Recreations:* painting, travel. *Address:* Old School House, Soberton, Hants SO32 3PF. *Clubs:* Royal Cruising, Royal Naval Sailing Association.

WEBSTER, Prof. (John) Paul (Garrett), PhD; Emeritus Professor of Agricultural Business Management, Imperial College London, since 2005; *b* 16 July 1942; *s* of Leonard Garrett Webster and Dorothy Agnes Webster (*née* White); *m* 1972, Dr Amanda Jane Hetigin; one *s* one *d*. *Educ:* Reading Univ. (BSc); Wye Coll., London Univ. (PhD). FIAgrM 1995; FRAgS 2003. Wye College (merged with Imperial College of Science, Technology and Medicine, 2000): Department of Agricultural Economy, 1965–2005: Asst Lectr, 1965–67; Lectr in Agricl Econs, 1967–76; Sen. Lectr, 1976–81; Reader, 1981–91; Prof. of Agricl Business Mgt, 1991–2005. Visiting appointments: Makerere Univ., Uganda, 1970–71; Drapers Lectr, Univ. of New England, Australia, 1974–75; Economist, Internat. Rice Res. Inst., Philippines, 1980–81; Prof., Lincoln Univ., NZ, 1999–2000. Indep. Mem., Adv. Cttee on Pesticides, MAFF, 1992–99. Pres., Agricl Econs Soc., 1999–2000. President: City of Canterbury Swimming Club, 2004–06; E Invicta Amateur Swimming Assoc., 2007–08. FCMI (FBIM 1985); FRSA 1987. Hon. Freeman, Farmers' Co., 2000. *Publications:* articles in Jl Agricl Econs, Amer. Jl Agricl Econs, Farm Mgt, etc. *Recreation:* masters swimming (UK rankings). *Address:* Imperial College London, Wye Campus, Ashford, Kent TN25 5AH. *T:* (020) 7594 2857. *Club:* Farmers'.

WEBSTER, Prof. Keith Edward, PhD; Professor of Anatomy and Human Biology (formerly Professor of Anatomy), King's College, University of London, 1975–2000; *b* 18 June 1935; *e s* of Thomas Brotherwick Webster and Edna Pyzer; 1st marr. diss. 1983; two *s*; 2nd marr. diss. 1990. *Educ:* UCL (BSc 1957, PhD 1960); UCH Med. Sch. (MB, BS 1962). University Coll. London: Lectr in Anatomy, 1962–66; Sen. Lectr in Anat., 1966–74; Reader in Anat., 1974–75. Symington Prize, British Anatomical Soc., 1966. *Publications:* A Manual of Human Anatomy, Vol. 5: The Central Nervous System (with J. T. Aitken and J. Z. Young), 1967; papers on the nervous system in Brain Res., Jl of Comp. Neurol., Neuroscience and Neurocytology. *Recreation:* Mozart, Wagner and language: the deification of the unspeakable.

WEBSTER, Leslie Elizabeth, FSA; Keeper, Department of Prehistory and Europe, British Museum, 2003–07; *b* 8 Nov. 1943; *d* of James Lancelot Dobson and Elizabeth Marjorie Dobson (*née* Dickenson); *m* 1966, William Ian Webster; one *s* two *d*. *Educ:* Central Newcastle High Sch.; Westfield Coll., Univ. of London (Open Exhibnr; BA 1st Cl. Hons 1964). British Museum: Asst Keeper, Dept of British and Medieval Antiquities, 1964–69; Asst Keeper, 1969–85, Dep. Keeper, 1985–2002, Dept of Medieval and Later Antiquities, subseq. Dept of Medieval and Modern Europe; Actg Keeper, Dept of Medieval and Modern Europe, 2002–03. Vis. Prof., Inst. of Archaeol., UCL, 2002–. Pres., Soc. for Medieval Archaeol., 2007–; Vice-Pres., Royal Archaeol Inst., 2007–. UK rep., Koordinierend Ausschuss der Internationalen Arbeitsgemeinschaft für Sachsenforschung, 1986–99. FSA 1973. *Publications:* (ed) Aspects of Production and Style in Dark Age Metalwork, 1982; (jtly) The Golden Age of Anglo-Saxon Art 966–1066, 1984; (with J. Backhouse) The Making of England: Anglo-Saxon art and culture AD 700–900, 1991; (ed with M. Brown) The Transformation of the Roman World, 1997; contrib. numerous articles to learned jls and chapters in monographs, on Anglo-Saxon material culture. *Recreations:* books, music, walking, cooking, France. *Address:* c/o Department of Prehistory and Europe, British Museum, Great Russell Street, WC1B 3DG.

WEBSTER, Maj. Michael; *see* Webster, R. M. O.

WEBSTER, Michael George Thomas; Chairman, DRG plc (formerly Dickinson Robinson Group), 1985–87 (Director, 1976–87; Deputy Chairman, 1983–85); *b* 27 May 1920; *s* of late J. A. Webster, CB, DSO, and late Constance A. Webster, 2nd *d* of late Richard and Lady Constance Combe; *m* 1947, Mrs Isabel Margaret Bucknill, *d* of late Major J. L. Dent, DSO, MC; three *d*. *Educ:* Stowe; Magdalen Coll., Oxford (MA). Commnd Grenadier Guards, 1940–46: NW Europe Campaign, 1944–45 (despatches). Joined Watney Combe Reid & Co. Ltd, 1946; Chm., Watney Combe Reid, 1963–68; Watney Mann Ltd: Vice-Chm., 1965–70; Chm., 1970–72; Chm., Watney Mann & Truman Holdings, 1974; Director: Grand Metropolitan Ltd, 1972–74; National Provident Instn, 1973–85; Chm., Fitch Lovell PLC, 1977–83. Master of Brewers' Co., 1964–65; a Vice-Pres., The Brewers' Soc., 1975–. Gov., Gabbitas Truman & Thring, 1986–90 (Chm., Truman and Knightley Educnl Trust, 1985–87). Chm., Aldenham Sch. Governing Body, 1977–84. High Sheriff, Berks, 1971; DL Berks, 1975–90. *Recreations:* fishing, golf. *Address:* Little Manor Farm, Dummer, Basingstoke, Hants RG25 2AD. *Clubs:* Cavalry and Guards, MCC.

See also Viscount Torrington.

WEBSTER, Patrick; a Chairman, Industrial, then Employment, Tribunals, Cardiff Region, 1965–2000 (full-time Chairman, 1976–93); a Recorder, 1972–93; *b* 6 Jan. 1928; *s* of late Francis Glyn Webster and Ann Webster; *m* 1955, Elizabeth Knight; two *s* four *d*. *Educ:* Swansea Grammar Sch.; Rockwell Coll., Eire; St Edmund's Coll., Ware; Downing Coll., Cambridge (BA). Called to Bar, Gray's Inn, 1950. Practised at Bar, in Swansea, 1950–75; Chm., Medical Appeals Tribunal (part-time), 1971–75. *Recreations:* listening to music, watching rowing and sailing. *Address:* Langland, 24 Maillard's Haven, Penarth, South Glam CF64 5RF. *T:* (029) 2070 4758. *Clubs:* Penarth Yacht; Beechwood (Swansea).

WEBSTER, Paul; Film Producer, Kudos Pictures, since 2004; *b* 19 Sept. 1952. Co-Dir, Osiris Film, London, 1979–81; Founder, Palace Pictures, 1982–88; launched Working Title Films, LA, 1990–92; Head of Prodn, Miramax Films, 1995–97 (films incl. The English Patient, Welcome to Sarajevo, Wings of the Dove); Head of Film Div., Channel 4, subseq. Chief Exec., FilmFour Ltd, 1998–2002. Producer: The Tall Guy, 1988; Drop Dead Fred, 1990; Bob Roberts, 1992; Romeo is Bleeding, 1993; Little Odessa, 1994; The Pallbearer, 1995; Gridlock'd, 1996; The Yards, 1998; Pride and Prejudice, 2005; Atonement, 2007; Eastern Promises, 2007; Executive Producer: The Motorcycle Diaries, 2004; Crimson Wing, 2007; Miss Pettigrew Lives for a Day, 2008. Member: UK Film Council, 2000–03; Council and Film Council, BAFTA. *Address:* Kudos Pictures, 12–14 Amwell Street, EC1R 1UQ. *T:* (020) 7812 3270.

WEBSTER, Paul; *see* Webster, J. P. G.

WEBSTER, Sir Peter (Edlin), Kt 1980; a Judge of the High Court of Justice, Queen's Bench Division, 1980–92; *b* 16 Feb. 1924; *s* of Herbert Edlin Webster and Florence Helen Webster; *m* 1955, Susan Elizabeth Richards (marr. diss.); one *s* two *d*; *m* 1968, Avril Carolyn Simpson, *d* of Dr John Ernest McCrae Harrisson. *Educ:* Haileybury; Merton Coll., Oxford (MA). RNVR, 1943–46 and 1950, Lieut (A). Imperial Tobacco Co., 1949; Lectr in Law, Lincoln Coll., Oxford, 1950–52; called to Bar, Middle Temple, 1952; Bencher, 1972; Standing Jun. Counsel to Min. of Labour, 1964–67; QC 1967; a Recorder of the Crown Court, 1972–80. Mem., Council of Justice, 1955–60, 1965–70; Mem., General Council of the Bar, 1967–74, and of Senate of the Inns of Court and the Bar, 1974–81 (Vice-Chm. 1975–76; Chm., 1976–77); Chairman: London Common Law Bar Assoc., 1975–79; Judicial Studies Bd, 1980–83 (Mem., 1979–83); Review Bd for Govt Contracts, 1993–; Mem., City Disputes Panel, 1994–. Dir, Booker McConnell, 1978–79. FCIArb 1993. *Address:* West Stowell Place, Oare, Marlborough SN8 4JU.

WEBSTER, Philip George; Political Editor, The Times, since 1993; *b* 2 June 1949; *s* of Bertie and Eva Webster; *m* 1974, Gill Bloomfield. *Educ:* Rockland St Mary Primary Sch.; County GS; Wymondham Coll.; Harlow Coll. (NCTJ Cert.). Eastern Counties Newspapers, 1967–73; The Times: Parly Reporter, 1973–81; Pol Reporter, 1981–86; Chief Pol Correspondent, 1986–93. *Recreations:* golf, ski-ing, cricket, squash, football. *Address:* 3 Wyke Close, Syon Lane, Osterley TW7 5PE. *T:* (020) 8847 1210. *Clubs:* Richmond Golf, Rookery Park Golf.

WEBSTER, Maj. (Richard) Michael (Otley); Secretary, The Royal Hampshire Regiment Trust, 2004–06; one of HM Body Guard, Honourable Corps of Gentlemen-at-Arms, since 1993; *b* 11 Aug. 1942; *s* of Brig. Frederick Richard Webster and Beryl Helena Sellars (*née* Otley); *m* 1971, Joanna Gay Enid Simpson, *d* of Lt-Col R. H. O. Simpson, DSO; two *s*. *Educ:* Charterhouse; RMA, Sandhurst. Commnd RA, 1962; Army Staff Coll., 1975; CO, King's Troop, RHA, 1976–78. United Racecourses, 1979–96; Clerk of the Course: Kempton Park, 1980–96; Lingfield Park, 1986–87; Epsom, 1988–95; Chester, 2001–03; Clerk of the Course and Manager, Bangor-on-Dee, 1996–2003. Member: Horseracing Adv. Council, 1987–90; Nat. Jt Pitch Council, 2000–03. *Recreations:* cricket, racing, shooting, Soay sheep. *Address:* Coopers Farm, Hartley Wespall, Hook, Hants RG27 0BQ. *Club:* Army and Navy.

WEBSTER, Prof. Robert Gordon, FRS 1989; Professor of Virology and Molecular Biology, St Jude Children's Research Hospital, Memphis, USA; *b* 5 July 1932; *s* of Robert Duncan Webster and Mollie Sherriffs; *m* 1957, Marjorie Freegard; two *s* one *d*. *Educ:* Otago Univ., NZ (BSc, MSc); Australian Nat. Univ., Canberra (PhD). Virologist, NZ Dept of Agric., 1958–59; Postdoctoral Fellow, Sch. of Public Health, Univ. of Michigan, Ann Arbor (Fulbright Schol.), 1962–63; Res. Fellow, then Fellow, Dept of Microbiology, John Curtin Med. Sch., ANU, 1964–67; Associate Mem., then Mem., Dept of Virology and Molecular Biol., 1968–88, apptd Head of Dept and Rose Marie Thomas Prof., 1988, St Jude Children's Res. Hosp. Fogarty Internat. Sen. Fellow, Nat. Inst. for Med. Res., MRC, London, 1978–79. Mem., Nat. Acad. of Sci., USA, 1998. *Publications:* contribs on influenza viruses etc to learned jls, incl. Virology, Nature, and Cell. *Recreations:* gardening, sea-fishing, walking. *Address:* Department of Infectious Diseases, St Jude Children's Research Hospital, 332 N Lauderdale Street, Memphis, TN 38105, USA. *T:* (901) 5220403. *Club:* Royal Society of Medicine.

WEBSTER, Prof. Robin Gordon MacLennan, OBE 1999; RSA (ARSA 1995); RIBA; FRIAS; Partner, cameronwebster architects, since 2005; Professor of Architecture, Scott Sutherland School of Architecture, Robert Gordon University, Aberdeen, 1984–2004; *b* 24 Dec. 1939; *s* of Gordon Webster and Sheila Webster; *m* 1967, Katherine Crichton (*d* 2003); one *s* two *d*. *Educ:* Glasgow Acad.; Rugby Sch.; St John's Coll., Cambridge (MA); University Coll., London (MA Arch). ARIBA 1967; FRIAS 1996. Partner, Spence & Webster, 1972–84; Principal, Robin Webster Associates, 1984–2004. Comr, Royal Fine Art Commn for Scotland, 1990–98. Winner, internat. competition for new Parly bldg at Westminster, 1972; Joint Winner: internat. competition for Manhattan West Side, NY, 1991; Sci. and Engrg Liby and Inf. Centre, Univ. of Edinburgh, 1997. *Publication:* Stonecleaning, and the nature, soiling and decay mechanisms of stone, 1992. *Recreations:* looking at buildings, drawing. *Address:* 7 Walmer Crescent, Glasgow G51 1AT. *T:* and *Fax:* (0141) 427 4494; *e-mail:* robin.webster@mac.com.

WEBSTER, Toby Crawford Gordon; Founding Director, The Modern Institute, since 1998; *b* Glasgow, 4 Dec. 1968; *s* of Martyn and Shery Webster; *m* 2007, April; one *s* two *d*. *Educ:* Glasgow Sch. of Art (BA 1st Cl. Hons 1993). Mem. Cttee, Transmission Gall., 1995–97; Gall. Manager and Curator, Centre for Contemporary Arts, Glasgow, 1996–98. Board Member: Grizdale Arts, 2004–08; Common Guild, 2006–08. *Publications:* My Head is on Fire but My Heart is Full of Love, 2002; Strange I've Seen that Face Before, 2006. *Recreations:* walking, sailing, ski-ing, reading, raising children, talking to varied people, collecting art and looking at it. *Address:* The Modern Institute, 73 Robertson Street, Glasgow G2 8QD. *T:* (0141) 248 3711, *Fax:* (0141) 248 3280; *e-mail:* mail@themoderninstitute.com.

WECHSLER, David Keith; Chief Executive, London Borough of Croydon, 1993–2007; *b* 17 June 1946; *s* of Bernard James Victor Wechsler and late Kathleen Nora Wechsler (*née* Ramm); *m* 1968, Muriel-Anne (Polly) Stuart; one *s* one *d*. *Educ:* Sloane Sch., Chelsea; Leicester Univ. (BA Social Sci.). London Borough of Croydon: grad. trainee, 1970–72; Corporate Planner, 1972–79; Hd, Exec. Office, 1979–87; Dep. Chief Exec., 1987–91; Dir, Econ. and Strategic Develt, 1991–93. Director: S London TEC, 1993–99; Croydon Business Venture, 1993–2007. Chm., Emergency Planning Sub-cttee, London Local Authorities, 2002–07. Dep. Regl Returning Officer, EP elections, 2004. Dir, London Mozart Players, 2007–. *Publications:* articles on corporate planning and local govt mgt in specialist jls. *Recreations:* sailing, music, swimming, making ice cream.

WEDD, George Morton, CB 1989; South-West Regional Director, Departments of the Environment and Transport, Bristol, 1983–90; *b* 30 March 1930; *s* of Albert Wedd and Dora Wedd; *m* 1953, Kate Pullin; two *s* one *d*. *Educ:* various schs in Derbyshire; St John's Coll., Cambridge (BA 1951). Joined Min. of Housing and Local Govt, later DoE, 1951; Principal, 1957; Asst Sec., 1966; Under Sec., 1976. *Address:* The Lodge, Church Hill, High Littleton, Somerset BS39 6HG.

WEDDERBURN, family name of **Baron Wedderburn of Charlton.**

WEDDERBURN OF CHARLTON, Baron *cr* 1977 (Life Peer), of Highgate; **(Kenneth) William Wedderburn;** QC 1990; FBA 1981; Cassel Professor of Commercial Law, London School of Economics, University of London, 1964–92, now Professor Emeritus and Hon. Fellow; *b* 13 April 1927; *o s* of Herbert J. and Mabel Wedderburn, Deptford; *m* 1st, 1951, Nina Salaman; one *s* two *d*; 2nd 1962, Dorothy E. Cole; 3rd, 1969, Frances Ann Knight; one *s*. *Educ:* Aske's Hatcham School; Whitgift School; Queens' College, Cambridge (MA 1951; LLB 1949; George Long Prize for Jurisprudence; Chancellor's Medal for English Law). Royal Air Force, 1949–51. Called to the Bar, Middle Temple, 1953, Bencher, 2008. Fellow, 1952–64, Tutor, 1957–60, Hon. Fellow, 1997, Clare College, Cambridge; Asst Lectr, 1953–55, Lectr 1955–64, Faculty of Law, Cambridge University. Visiting Professor: UCLA Law Sch., 1967; Harvard Law Sch., 1969–70. Staff Panel Mem., Civil Service Arbitration Tribunal; Chm., Independent Review Cttee, 1976–; Mem., Cttee on Industrial Democracy, 1976–77. Independent Chm., London and Provincial Theatre Councils, 1973–93. Hon. Pres., Industrial Law Soc., 1997–. Gen. Editor, Modern Law Review, 1971–88; Mem. Editl Bd, Internat. Labour Law Reports, 1975–. Hon. Doctor of Jurisprudence, Pavia, 1987; Hon. Doctor of Econs, Siena, 1991; Hon. LLD Stockholm, 1995. *Publications:* The Worker and the Law, 1965, 3rd edn 1986; Cases and Materials on Labour Law, 1967; (with P. Davies) Employment Grievances and Disputes Procedures in Britain, 1969; (ed) Contracts, Sutton and Shannon, 1956, 2nd edn 1963; (Asst Editor) Torts, Clerk and Lindsell, 1969, 1975, 1982, 1989, 1995, 2000; (ed with B. Aaron) Industrial Conflict, 1972; (with S. Sciarra *et al*) Democrazia Politica e Democrazia Industriale, 1978; (ed with Folke Schmidt) Discrimination in Employment, 1978; (with R. Lewis and J. Clark) Labour Law and Industrial Relations, 1983; (ed with W. T. Murphy) Labour, Law and the Community, 1983; (with S. Ghimpu and B. Veneziani) Diritto del Lavoro in Europa, 1987; Social Charter, European Company and Employment Rights, 1990; Employment Rights in Britain and Europe, 1991; (with M. Rood *et al*) Labour Law in the post-Industrial Era, 1994; Labour Law and Freedom, 1995; I Diritti del Lavoro, 1998; articles in legal and other jls. *Recreation:* Charlton Athletic Football Club. *Address:* 29 Woodside Avenue, N6 4SP. *T:* (020) 8444 8472.

WEDDERBURN, Sir Andrew John Alexander O.; *see* Ogilvy-Wedderburn.

WEDDERBURN, Prof. Dorothy Enid Cole; Senior Research Fellow, Imperial College, London, 1981–2003; Principal, Royal Holloway and Bedford New College, 1985–90, and a Pro-Vice-Chancellor, 1986–88, University of London; *b* 18 Sept. 1925; *d* of Frederick C. Barnard and Ethel C. Barnard. *Educ:* Walthamstow High Sch. for Girls; Girton Coll., Cambridge (MA). Research Officer, subseq. Sen. Res. Officer, Dept of Applied Economics, Cambridge, 1950–65; Imperial College of Science and Technology: Lectr in Industrial Sociology, 1965–70, Reader, 1970–77, Prof., 1977–81; Dir, Industrial Sociol. Unit, 1973–81; Head, Dept of Social and Economic Studies, 1978–81; Principal, Bedford Coll., 1981–85. Mem. Court, Univ. of London, 1981–90. Vis. Prof., Sloan Sch. of Management, MIT, 1969–70. Mem. SSRC, 1976–82; Chm., SERC/SSRC Jt Cttee, 1980–82. Chm., Cttee of Inquiry into Women Imprisonment, Prison Reform Trust, 1998–2000. Member: Govt Cttee on the Pay and Condition of Nurses, 1974–75; (part-time), Royal Commn on the Distribution of Income and Wealth, 1974–78; Council, Advisory Conciliation and Arbitration Service, 1976–82; Cttee of Vice-Chancellors and Principals, 1988–90; Bd, Anglo-German Foundn, 1987–2004; Bd of Governors, London Guildhall Univ. (formerly City of London Polytechnic), 1989–99; Council, Loughborough Univ., 1990–93; Court, City Univ., 1992–; Council, Goldsmiths Coll., London Univ., 1993–2000. Mem., Kensington, Chelsea and Westminster DHA, 1993–2002. Hon. Pres., Fawcett Soc., 1986–2002. Hon. Fellow: Ealing Coll. of Higher Educn, 1985; RHBNC, 1991; Goldsmiths Coll., London Univ., 2001; Hon. FIC 1986. Hon. DLitt: Warwick, 1984; Loughborough, 1989; DUniv Brunel, 1990; Hon. LLD Cambridge, 1991; Hon. DSc City, 1991; Hon. DSocSc Southampton, 1999; Hon. PhD London Guildhall, 2000. *Publications:* White Collar Redundancy, 1964; Redundancy and the Railwayman, 1964; Enterprise Planning for Change, 1968; (with J. E. G. Utting) The Economic Circumstances of Old People, 1962; (with Peter Townsend) The Aged in the Welfare State, 1965; (jtly) Old Age in Three Industrial Societies, 1968; (with Rosemary Crompton) Workers' Attitudes and Technology, 1972; (ed) Poverty, Inequality and Class Structure, 1974; Justice for Women: the case for reform, 2000; contrib. Jl of Royal Statistical Soc.; Sociological Review; New Society, etc. *Recreations:* politics, cooking. *Address:* Flat 5, 65 Ladbroke Grove, W11 2PD.

WEDDERSPOON, Very Rev. Alexander Gillan; Dean of Guildford, 1987–2001, now Emeritus; *b* 3 April 1931; *s* of Rev. Robert John Wedderspoon and Amy Beatrice Woolley; *m* 1968, Judith Joyce Wynne Plumptre; one *s* one *d*. *Educ:* Westminster School; Jesus Coll., Oxford (MA, BD); Cuddesdon Theological Coll. Nat. Service, 1949–51; commnd, RA. Ordained deacon 1961, priest 1962; Curate, Kingston Parish Church, 1961–63; Lectr in Religious Education, Univ. of London, 1963–66; Education Adviser, C of E Schools Council, 1966–69; Sec. of Commn on Religious Education, 1966–69; Priest in charge, St Margaret's, Westminster, 1969–70; Canon Residentiary, Winchester Cathedral, 1970–87. *Publication:* A City Set on a Hill: a selection of sermons, 2001. *Recreations:* walking, travel. *Address:* 1 Ellery Close, Cranleigh GU6 8DF.

WEDELL, Prof. (Eberhard Arthur Otto) George; Professor of Communications Policy, University of Manchester, 1983–92, Professor Emeritus since 1992; Vice President, European Institute for the Media, 1993–97 (Director, 1983–90; Director-General, 1991–93); *b* 4 April 1927; *er s* of late Rev. Dr H. Wedell and Gertrude (*née* Bonhoeffer); *m* 1948, Rosemarie (*née* Winckler); three *s* one *d*. *Educ:* Cranbrook; London School of Economics (BSc Econ., 1947). Ministry of Education, 1950–58; Sec., Bd for Social Responsibility, Nat. Assembly of Church of England, 1958–60; Dep. Sec., ITA, 1960–61, Secretary, 1961–64; Prof. of Adult Educn and Dir of Extra-Mural Studies, Manchester Univ., 1964–75; Vis. Prof. of Employment Policy, Manchester Business Sch., 1975–83; Head, Employment Policy Div., European Commn, 1973–82. Emeritus Fellow, Leverhulme Trust, 1994–96. Contested (L) Greater Manchester West, 1979, (L-SDP Alliance) Greater Manchester Central, 1984, European Parly elections; Chm., British Liberals in EEC, 1980–82; Vice-President: Greater Manchester Liberal Party, 1984–88; EC-ACP Cultural Foundn, 1992–94. Chairman: Wyndham Place Trust, 1983–2001; Beatrice Hankey Foundn, 1984–2001; Christians and the Future of Europe, 1997–99. Director, Royal Exchange Theatre Company, 1968–89, Hon. Mem., 1989. Patron, Mosscare Housing Assoc., 1998–. FRSA; FRTS. Hon. MEd Manchester, 1968; Dr *hc* Internat. Journalistics Inst., Kazakstan, 1994. Lord of the Manor of Clotton Hoofield in the County Palatine of Chester. Letters Patent of Armorial Ensigns, 1997. Chevalier de l'Ordre des Arts et des Lettres (France), 1989; Verdienstkreuz (1 Klasse) des Verdienstordens (Germany), 1991; Comdr, Order of Merit (Portugal), 1993. *Publications:* The Use of Television in Education, 1963; Broadcasting and Public Policy, 1968; (with H. D. Perraton) Teaching at a Distance, 1968; (ed) Structures of Broadcasting, 1970; (with R. Glatter) Study by Correspondence, 1971; Correspondence Education in Europe, 1971; Teachers and Educational Development in Cyprus, 1971; (ed) Education and the Development of Malawi, 1973; (with E. Katz) Broadcasting in the Third World, 1977 (Nat. Assoc. of Educational Broadcasters of USA Book of the Year Award, 1978); (with G. M. Luyken and R. Leonard) Mass Communications in Western Europe, 1985; (ed) Making Broadcasting Useful, 1986; (with G. M. Luyken) Media in Competition, 1986; (ed and contrib.) Europe 2000: what kind of television?, 1988; (with P. Crookes) Radio 2000, 1991; (with R. Rocholl) Vom Segen des Glaubens, 1995 (trans. as A Memoir of Troubled Times, 2008); (ed and contrib.) No Discouragement, 1997; (with A. J. Tudesq) Television and Democracy in Africa, 1998; (with B. Luckham) Television at the Crossroads, 2001; contrib. Oxford DNB; general editor, Media Monographs, 1985–93. *Recreations:* gardening, theatre, reading. *Address:* 18 Cranmer Road, Manchester M20 6AW. *T:* (0161) 445 5106; Vigneau, Lachapelle, 47350 Seyches, France. *T:* (5) 53838871. *Club:* Athenæum.

WEDGWOOD, family name of **Baron Wedgwood.**

WEDGWOOD, 4th Baron *cr* 1942, of Barlaston; **Piers Anthony Weymouth Wedgwood;** Director, Waterford Wedgwood, since 2000; *b* 20 Sept. 1954; *s* of 3rd Baron Wedgwood and of Lady Wedgwood (Jane Weymouth, *d* of W. J. Poulton, Kenjockety, Molo, Kenya); *S* father, 1970; *m* 1985, Mary Regina Margaret Kavanagh Quinn, *d* of late Judge Edward Thomas Quinn and of Helen Marie Buchanan Quinn of Philadelphia; one *d*. *Educ:* Marlborough College; RMA Sandhurst. Royal Scots, 1973–80. GSM for N Ireland, 1976. Freeman, City of London, 2006. Hon. DLitt Chicago, 2000. *Heir: cousin* Antony John Wedgwood [*b* 31 Jan. 1944; *m* 1970, Angela Margaret Mary Page; one *s* two *d*]. *Address:* Waterford Wedgwood plc, Barlaston, Stoke-on-Trent, Staffordshire ST12 9ES.

WEDGWOOD, Sir (Hugo) Martin, 3rd Bt *cr* 1942, of Etruria, Co. Stafford; *b* 27 Dec. 1933; *s* of Sir John Hamilton Wedgwood, 2nd Bt, TD and Diana Mildred (*d* 1976), *d* of late Col Oliver Hawkshaw, TD; *S* father, 1989; *m* 1963, Alexandra Mary Gordon Clark, *er d* of late Judge Alfred Gordon Clark; one *s* two *d*. *Educ:* Eton; Trinity Coll., Oxford. Mem., Stock Exchange, 1973–91; Partner, Laurence, Prust and Co., 1973–84; Dir, Smith New Court Far East Ltd, 1986–91. *Recreation:* ceramics. *Heir: s* Ralph Nicholas Wedgwood, *b* 10 Dec. 1964. *Club:* Oriental.

WEDGWOOD, Sir Martin; *see* Wedgwood, Sir H. M.

WEDGWOOD, Pamela, Lady, (Pamela Tudor-Craig), PhD; FSA; Medieval art historian; *b* 26 June 1928; *d* of Herbert Wynn Reeves and Madeline Marion Wynn Reeves (*née* Brows); *m* 1st, 1956, Algernon James Riccarton Tudor-Craig (*d* 1969); one *d*; 2nd, 1982, Sir John Hamilton Wedgwood, 2nd Bt (*d* 1989). *Educ:* Courtauld Inst. Fine Art (BA 1st Cl. Hons Hist. of Art London 1949; PhD 1952). FSA 1958. Lectr at American Colls in UK, 1969–96. Mem., Cathedrals Adv. Commn, 1973–88; Chm., Wall Paintings Cttee, and Vice-Chm., Panel Paintings Cttee, 1975–92, Vice Chm., Paintings Cttee, 1992–96, Council for Care of Churches; Mem., Wells Cathedral West Front Cttee, 1973–86; Member, Architectural Advisory Panel: Westminster Abbey, 1979–98; Exeter Cathedral, 1985–90; Member, Fabric Committee: Lincoln Cathedral, 1986–92; Peterborough Cathedral, 1987–96; Southwell Minster, 1984–2001. Founder, Cambs Historic Churches

Trust, 1982; Chm. Friends, Sussex Historic Churches Trust, 2002–. Founder, Annual Harlaxton Symposium of English Medieval Studies, 1984. Hon. Member: SPAB; Richard III Soc. TV broadcasts, incl. series, The Secret Life of Paintings, 1986–87; contribs to numerous radio programmes. Hon. DHum William Jewell Coll., USA, 1983. *Publications:* Richard III (exhibn catalogue), 1973; (with R. Foster) The Secret Life of Paintings, 1986; 'Old St Paul's': the Society of Antiquaries' Diptych, 1616, 2004; contrib. numerous chapters and articles in books and exhibn catalogues; contrib. to History Today, Church Times and other scholarly jls. *Recreations:* walking dogs on Downs, swimming. *Address:* 9 St Anne's Crescent, Lewes, E Sussex BN7 1SB. *T:* (01273) 479564.

WEDZICHA, Prof. Jadwiga Anna, (Wisia), MD; FRCP; Professor of Respiratory Medicine, University College London, since 2005; *b* 17 Sept. 1953; *d* of Karol and Irena Wedzicha. *Educ:* Somerville Coll., Oxford (BA 1975); St Bartholomew's Hosp. Med. Coll., London Univ. (MB BS 1978; MD 1985). FRCP 1994. Consultant Physician, London Chest Hosp., 1988–96; Reader in Respiratory Medicine, 1996–2000, Prof. of Respiratory Medicine, 2000–05, Bart's and The London, Queen Mary's Sch. of Medicine and Dentistry. Editor in Chief, Thorax, 2002–. *Publications:* (ed with M. Pearson) Chronic Obstructive Pulmonary Disease: critical debates, 2003; papers in BMJ, American Jl of Respiratory and Critical Care Medicine, Thorax. *Recreations:* gardening, tennis, music. *Address:* Academic Unit of Respiratory Medicine, Royal Free and University College Medical School, Rowland Hill Street, Hampstead, NW3 2PF. *T:* (020) 7317 7510, *Fax:* (020) 7472 6141; *e-mail:* j.a.wedzicha@medsch.ucl.ac.uk.

WEEDEN, John, CB 2003; Member, Criminal Cases Review Commission, since 2002; *b* 21 June 1949; *s* of Denis Claude Weeden and Winifred Marion Weeden; *m* 1971, Marjanne Dita De Boer; three *s* two *d*. *Educ:* Brighton Coll.; Univ. of Bristol (LLB Hons). SSC 1973. Articled to Griffith Smith, Brighton, 1971–73, Asst Solicitor, 1973–74; joined RAF Legal Br. as Flight Lieut, 1974; worked in UK and Europe, undertaking court martial prosecutions and gen. legal work involving administrative, internat. and operational law; Deputy Director: Cyprus, 1984–87; Germany, 1991–92; Legal Services (RAF), MoD, 1992–97; Dir of Legal Services (RAF) and RAF Prosecuting Authy, MoD, 1997–2002; retd in rank of Air Vice Marshal. Trustee, RAF Benevolent Fund, 2004–. *Recreations:* golf, photography, cars. *Address:* Criminal Cases Review Commission, Alpha Tower, Suffolk Street, Queensway, Birmingham B1 1TT. *T:* (0121) 633 1800.

WEEDY, Maj.-Gen. Michael Anthony C.; *see* Charlton-Weedy.

WEEKES, Rt Rev. Ambrose Walter Marcus, CB 1970; FKC; Assistant Bishop, Diocese in Europe, since 1988; *b* 25 April 1919; *s* of Lt-Comdr William Charles Tinnoth Weekes, DSO, RNVR, and Ethel Sarah Weekes, JP. *Educ:* Cathedral Choir Sch., Rochester; Sir Joseph Williamson's Sch., Rochester; King's Coll., London (Plumptre prize, Barry prize; AKC 1941, FKC 1972); Scholae Cancellarii, Lincoln. Asst Curate, St Luke's, Gillingham, Kent, 1942–44; Chaplain, RNVR, 1944–46, RN 1946–72; HMS: Ganges, 1946–48; Ulster, 1948–49; Triumph, 1949–51; Royal Marines, Deal, 1951–53; 45 Commando, RM, 1953–55; HMS: Ganges, 1955–56; St Vincent, 1956–58; Tyne, 1958–60; Ganges, 1960–62; 40 Commando, RM, 1962–63; MoD, 1963–65; HMS: Eagle, 1965–66; Vernon, 1966–67; Terror, and Staff of Comdr Far East Fleet, 1967–68; HMS Mercury, 1968–69; Chaplain of the Fleet and Archdeacon for the Royal Navy, 1969–72; QHC, 1969–72; Chaplain of St Andrew, Tangier, 1972–73; Dean of Gibraltar, 1973–77; Assistant Bishop, Diocese of Gibraltar, 1977, until creation of new diocese, 1980; Suffragan Bishop of Gibraltar in Europe, 1980–86; Dean, Pro-Cathedral of the Holy Trinity, Brussels, 1980–86; Hon. Asst Bishop of Rochester, 1986–88; Hon. Canon of Rochester Cathedral, 1986–88; Chaplain at Montreux, Switzerland, 1988–92. Freeman, City of London, 2000. *Recreations:* yachting, music. *Address:* Charterhouse, Charterhouse Square, EC1M 6AN. *Club:* MCC.

WEEKES, Anesta Glendora; QC 1999; a Recorder, since 2000; *b* 10 June 1955; *d* of late Joseph Weekes and of Sarah Weekes. *Educ:* Keele Univ. (BA Hons). Called to the Bar, Gray's Inn, 1981, Bencher, 2003; in practice at the Bar, specialising in criminal law and public inquiries; Counsel to Stephen Lawrence Inquiry, 1999; Asst Recorder, 1999–2000. Arbitrator (part-time), Commonwealth Secretariat Arbitral Tribunal, 2000–. Dir, ENO, 2000–. *Recreations:* music, opera, dance, travel books. *Address:* 23 Essex Street, WC2R 3AA. *T:* (020) 7413 0353. *Club:* Royal Commonwealth Society.

WEEKES, Sir Everton (de Courcy), KCMG 1995; GCM; OBE; international bridge player; former international cricketer; *b* Bridgetown, Barbados, 26 Feb. 1925. *Educ:* St Leonard's Sch., Bridgetown. First class début, 1944, for Barbados; played for Barbados, 1944–64 (Captain), for West Indies, 1947–58 (48 Test matches; 15 centuries, incl. 5 double centuries in England, 1950); on retirement from Test cricket, held world record for five consecutive centuries (*v* England and India), 1948–49, and for seven consecutive half-centuries. *Address:* c/o West Indies Cricket Board of Control, Letchworth Complex, The Garrison, St Michael, Barbados, West Indies.

WEEKES, Mark K.; *see* Kinkead-Weekes.

WEEKS, His Honour John Henry; QC 1983; a Circuit Judge, 1991–2006; *b* 11 May 1938; *s* of Henry James and Ada Weeks; *m* 1970, Caroline Mary, *d* of Lt Col J. F. Ross; one *s* two *d*. *Educ:* Cheltenham Coll.; Worcester Coll., Oxford (MA). Called to Bar, Inner Temple, 1963, Bencher, 1996; in practice in Chancery, 1963–91. *Publication:* Limitation of Actions, 1989. *Recreation:* walking the dog. *Address:* 18 Centrepoint House, 15A St Giles High Street, WC2H 8LW. *T:* (020) 7497 9560.

WEEKS, Wilfred John Thomas, OBE 2006; Chairman, European Public Affairs, Weber Shandwick, since 2002; *b* 8 Feb. 1948; *s* of late William Weeks and Kathleen Weeks (*née* Penhale); *m* 1981, Anne Veronica Harrison; three *s*. *Educ:* Shebbear Coll.; KCL (BD Hons). Private Sec. to Rt Hon. Edward Heath, 1976–80; Jt Founder, GJW Govt Relns, 1980–2000; Chm., BSMG UK, 2000–02. Non-exec. Dir, Helical Bar, 2005–. Chm., Friends of the Tate, 1990–99, Mem. Council, Tate Britain, 2000–03; Chairman: Dulwich Picture Gall., 2000–06 (Trustee, 1994–2006); Spitalfields Fest., 2006–; Heritage Educn Trust, 2002–08; Trustee: LAMDA, 2000– (Chm. Develt Bd, 2002–06); City Parochial Foundn and Trust for London, 2007–. Hon. Treas., Hansard Soc., 1996–2007. Goodman Award, Arts and Business, 2004. *Recreations:* gardening, collecting. *Address:* 25 Gauden Road, SW4 6LR. *T:* (020) 7622 0532. *Club:* Garrick.

WEEPLE, Edward John, CB 2004; Head of Lifelong Learning Group, Scottish Executive Enterprise, Transport and Lifelong Learning (formerly Enterprise and Lifelong Learning) Department, 1999–2003; *b* 15 May 1945; *s* of Edward Weeple and Mary Catherine (*née* McGrath); *m* 1970, Joan (*née* Shaw); three *s* one *d*. *Educ:* St Aloysius' Coll., Glasgow; Glasgow Univ. (MA). Asst Principal, Min. of Health, 1968–71; Private Sec. to Minister of Health, 1971–73; Principal: DHSS, 1973–78; Scottish Econ. Planning Dept, 1978–80; Assistant Secretary: SHHD, 1980–85; Dept of Agriculture and Fisheries for Scotland, 1985–90; Under Sec., Scottish Office Industry Dept, 1990–95; Hd of Further and Higher Educn, Trng and Sci., then Lifelong Learning, Gp, Scottish Office Educn and Industry Dept, 1995–99. First Minister's Assessor, Carnegie Trust for Univs of Scotland, 2005–; non-exec. Dir, Interactive Univ., 2005–07. Member: Bd of Mgt, Edinburgh's Telford Coll., 2003–07 (Chm., 2007–); Court, Heriot-Watt Univ., 2005–; Special Advr, Paisley Univ., 2005–07. Sec., Goodison Gp in Scotland, 2003–05. *Address:* 19 Lauder Road, Edinburgh EH9 2JG. *T:* (0131) 668 1150.

WEETCH, Kenneth Thomas; *b* 17 Sept. 1933; *s* of Kenneth George and Charlotte Irene Weetch; *m* 1961, Audrey Wilson; two *d*. *Educ:* Newbridge Grammar Sch., Mon; London School of Economics (MSc(Econ)), London Inst. of Educn (DipEd). National Service: Sgt, RAEC, Hong Kong, 1955–57; Walthamstow and Ilford Educn Authorities and Research at LSE, 1957–64; Head of History Dept, Hockerill Coll. of Educn, Bishop's Stortford, 1964–74. Contested (Lab): Saffron Walden, 1970; Ipswich, 1987. MP (Lab) Ipswich, Oct. 1974–1987. PPS to Sec. of State for Transport, 1976–79. Member: Lab Select Cttee on Home Affairs, 1981–83; Select Cttee on Parly Comr for Administration, 1983–87. *Recreations:* walking, reading, watching Association football, playing the piano in pubs, eating junk food. *Club:* Silent Street Labour (Ipswich).

WEETMAN, Prof. Anthony Peter, MD, DSc; FRCP, FRCPE; FMedSci; Sir Arthur Hall Professor of Medicine, since 1991, and Pro-Vice-Chancellor for Medicine, since 2008, University of Sheffield; *b* 29 April 1953; *s* of Kenneth Weetman and Evelyn Weetman (*née* Healer); *m* 1982, Sheila Thompson; one *s* one *d*. *Educ:* Univ. of Newcastle upon Tyne (BMedSci 1974; MB BS 1977; MD 1983; DSc 1991). FRCP 1990; FRCPE 2004. MRC Trng Fellow, Welsh Nat. Sch. of Medicine, 1980–84; MRC Travelling Fellow, NIH, Bethesda, USA, 1984–85; Wellcome Trust Sen. Res. Fellow in Clin. Sci., RPMS and Univ. of Cambridge, 1985–89; Lectr in Medicine, Univ. of Cambridge, 1989–91; Dean, Medical Sch., Univ. of Sheffield, 1999–2008. Hon. Consultant Physician: Hammersmith Hosp., 1986–87; Addenbrooke's Hosp., 1987–91; Northern Gen. Hosp., Sheffield, 1991–2001; Sheffield Teaching Hosps NHS Trust, 2001–. Pres., British Thyroid Assoc., 2005–08. FMedSci 1998. *Publications:* Autoimmune Endocrine Disease, 1991; papers on endocrine autoimmunity and disease, esp. concerning the thyroid. *Recreations:* fell walking (Munroist number 2342), squash, ski-ing. *Address:* School of Medicine and Biomedical Sciences, University of Sheffield, Beech Hill Road, Sheffield S10 2RX. *T:* (0114) 271 2570, *Fax:* (0114) 271 3960; *e-mail:* a.p.weetman@sheffield.ac.uk.

WEIDENBAUM, Murray Lew, PhD; Hon. Chairman, Weidenbaum Center on the Economy, Government and Public Policy, since 2001; Mallinckrodt Distinguished University Professor, Washington University, since 1971; *b* 10 Feb. 1927; *m* 1954, Phyllis Green; one *s* two *d*. *Educ:* City Coll., NY; Columbia Univ. (MA); Princeton Univ. (PhD 1958). Fiscal Economist, Budget Bureau, Washington, 1949–57; Corp. Economist, Boeing Co., Seattle, 1958–63; Sen. Economist, Stanford Res. Inst., 1963–64; Washington University, St Louis, 1964–81, 1982–: Prof. and Chm. of Dept of Econs, 1966–69; Dir, 1975–81 and 1983–95, and Chm., 1995–2000, Center for the Study of Amer. Business (renamed Weidenbaum Center on the Economy, Govt and Public Policy, 2001). Asst Sec., Treasury Dept, Washington, 1969–71 (on secondment). Chairman: Council of Economic Advisers, USA, 1981–82; Congressional Commn on Trade Deficit, 1999–2000. Hon. LLD: Baruch Coll., 1981; Evansville, 1983. Mem., Free Market Hall of Fame, 1983. Nat. Order of Merit, Republic of France, 1985. *Publications:* Federal Budgeting, 1964; Economic Impact of the Vietnam War, 1967; Modern Public Sector, 1969; Economics of Peacetime Defense, 1974; Government-Mandated Price Increases, 1975; Business, Government, and the Public, 1977, 7th edn (as Business and Government in the Global Marketplace), 2004; The Future of Business Regulation, 1980; Rendezvous with Reality: the American economy after Reagan, 1988; Small Wars, Big Defense, 1992; The Bamboo Network, 1996; One-armed Economist, 2004; Advising Reagan: making economic policy 1981–82, 2005; The Competition of Ideas, 2008. *Address:* Weidenbaum Center, Washington University, Campus Box 1027, St Louis, MO 63130–4899, USA.

WEIDENFELD, family name of **Baron Weidenfeld.**

WEIDENFELD, Baron *cr* 1976 (Life Peer), of Chelsea; **Arthur George Weidenfeld,** Kt 1969; Chairman, Weidenfeld & Nicolson Ltd, since 1948; *b* 13 Sept. 1919; *o s* of late Max and Rosa Weidenfeld; *m* 1st, 1952, Jane Sieff; one *d*; 2nd, 1956, Barbara Connolly (*née* Skelton) (marr. diss. 1961; she *d* 1996); 3rd, 1966, Sandra Payson Meyer (marr. diss. 1976); 4th, 1992, Annabelle Whitestone. *Educ:* Piaristen Gymnasium, Vienna; University of Vienna (Law); Konsular Akademie (Diplomatic College). BBC Monitoring Service, 1939–42; BBC News Commentator on European Affairs on BBC Empire & North American service, 1942–46. Wrote weekly foreign affairs column, News Chronicle, 1943–44; Founder: Contact Magazine and Books, 1945; Weidenfeld & Nicolson Ltd, 1948. One year's leave as Political Adviser and Chief of Cabinet of President Weizmann of Israel. Consultant, Bertelsmann Foundn, 1992–; Mem. Bd, Herbert-Quandt-Foundn, Bad Homburg, 1999–; Dir, Cheyne Capital, 2000–; Trustee, Alfred Herrhausen Ges. (Deutsche Bank), 2004–. Consultant, Burda Medien, 1983–. Columnist, Die Welt and Die Welt am Sonntag, 1999–. Vice Chm., EU-Israel Forum, 2002–08. Jt Vice-Pres., Campaign for Oxford, 1992–95; Vice-Chm., Oxford Develt Prog., 1995–. Chm., Trialogue Educnl Trust, 1999–. Chm., Bd of Governors, Ben Gurion Univ. of the Negev, Beer-Sheva, 1996–2004 (Vice-Chm., 1976–96; Hon. Chm., 2004–); Governor: Weizmann Inst. of Science, 1964–; Univ. of Tel Aviv, 1980–; Hon. Senator, Univ. of Bonn, 1997; Hon. Gov., Diplomatic Acad., Vienna, 1998. Member: South Bank Bd, 1986–99; ENO Bd, 1988–98; Trustee, Nat. Portrait Gall., 1988–95. Founder and Pres., Weidenfeld Inst. for Strategic Dialogue, 2006–. FKC 2005. Hon. Fellow: St Peter's Coll., Oxford, 1992; St Anne's Coll., Oxford, 1994. Hon. PhD Ben Gurion Univ. of the Negev, 1984; Hon. MA Oxon, 1992; Hon. DLitt Exeter, 2001. Charlemagne Medal for European Media, Aachen, Germany, 2000; Lifetime Achievement Award, London Book Fair/ Trilogy, 2007. Golden Kt's Cross with Star, Order of Merit (Austria), 1989; Chevalier, Légion d'Honneur (France), 1990; Kt Comdr, Cross, Badge and Star, Order of Merit (Germany), 1991; Cross of Merit for Arts and Science (Austria), 2002; Grande Ufficiale, Ordine del Merito (Italy), 2005. *Publications:* The Goebbels Experiment, 1943 (also publ. USA); Remembering My Good Friends (autobiog.), 1994. *Recreations:* travel, opera. *Address:* 9 Chelsea Embankment, SW3 4LE. *Club:* Garrick.
See also C. A. Barnett.

WEIGHTMAN, Michael William, DPhil; HM Chief Inspector of Nuclear Installations, and Director, Health and Safety Executive, since 2005; *b* 6 Feb. 1949; *s* of William Henry Weightman and Hilda Weightman; *m* 1974, Elizabeth Anne; two *s*. *Educ:* Lutterworth Grammar Sch.; Univ. of Sussex; Univ. of Bristol. BSc, MSc; DPhil. CEng; MInstP. HM Principal Inspector of Nuclear Installations, 1988; Hd, Nuclear Policy, HSE, 1995; HM Dep. Chief Inspector of Nuclear Installations, 2000–05. Chm., Potters Bar Rail Crash Investigation Bd, 2002. MIOM. *Recreations:* family, Rugby Union, village community, arts. *Address:* HM Nuclear Installations Inspectorate, 4N.1 Redgrave Court, Merton Road, Bootle, Merseyside L20 7HS. *T:* (0151) 951 4168, *Fax:* (0151) 951 4821; *e-mail:* mike.weightman@hse.gsi.gov.uk. *Club:* Chester Rugby Union Football.

WEIGHTMAN, Prof. Peter, PhD; Professor of Physics, University of Liverpool, since 1989; *b* Alfreton, Derbys, 21 Oct. 1944; *s* of Arthur and Gertrude Edith Weightman; *m*

1st, 1974, Anne Susan Kirby (marr. diss. 1993); two *s*; 2nd, 2001, Susan Clare Nobay. *Educ:* Univ. of Keele (BA 1st Cl. Hons Phys and Maths 1967; PhD 1970). Res. Fellow, Phys Dept, Univ. of Essex, 1970–71; University of Liverpool: Lectr, 1971–81, Sen. Lectr, 1981–85, Reader, 1985–89, Dept of Phys; Dep. Dir, 1988–98, Dir, 1998–2001, Interdisciplinary Res. Centre in Surface Sci.; Dir, Grad. Sch. in Engrg and Physical Sci., 1994–98. Fulbright Sen. Res. Scholar, Chem. Dept, Oregon State Univ., 1980–81. Mem. of numerous cttees of UK res. councils, SERC, EPSRC, CCLRC, STFC and MRC; UK Mem., High Technol. Panel, 1993–98, Physical and Engrg Sci. and Technol. Panel, 1999–2000, NATO; European Synchrotron Radiation Facility: Mem., Sci. Adv. Cttee, 1995–97, 1997–99; Mem. Council, 2000–03; Chm., Scientific Steering Cttee, UK Fourth Generation Light Source, 2000–08. Chm., Condensed Matter Physics Div., Inst. of Physics, 2008–. Council, European Physical Soc., 2007–. Mott Medal and Prize, Inst. of Physics, 2006. *Publications:* 240 res. papers in learned jls. *Recreations:* reading history books, listening to music. *Address:* Physics Department, University of Liverpool, Oxford Street, Liverpool L69 3BX. *T:* (0151) 794 3871, *Fax:* (0151) 794 3441; *e-mail:* peterw@liverpool.ac.uk.

WEILER, Terence Gerard, OBE 1993; *b* 12 Oct. 1919; *s* of Charles and Clare Weiler; *m* 1952, Truda, *d* of Wilfrid and Mary Woollen; two *s* two *d*. *Educ:* Wimbledon College; University College, London. Army (RA and Queen's Royal Regiment, Chindit), 1940–45; UCL, 1937–39 and 1945–47; Home Office: Asst Principal, 1947; Principal, 1948; Asst Sec., 1958; Asst Under-Sec. of State, 1967–80; Mem., Prisons Board, 1962–66, 1971–80; Chm., Working Party: on Habitual Drunken Offenders, 1967–70; on Adjudication Procedures in Prisons, 1975. *Recreations:* cinema, crime fiction. *Address:* 4 Vincent Road, Isleworth, Middx TW7 4LT. *T:* (020) 8560 7822.

WEILL, Michel Alexandre D.; *see* David-Weill.

WEINBERG, Prof. Anton; solo clarinettist; teacher of music; woodwind consultant; *b* 25 Nov. 1944; *s* of Louis and Gladys Weinberg; *m* 1987, Brenda Teresa Douglas; three *s* one *d*. *Educ:* Royal Acad. of Music (Associated Bd, Royal Schs of Music Schol.; 1st clarinettist to hold both Hawkes and Solomon prizes; LRAM). ARCM; ARAM 1987. Prof., GSMD, 1979–86, Prof. of Performance and Communication Skills course, 1983–85; Prof. of Music, Indiana Univ., 1984–90. Artistic Dir, Capitol Prodns Ltd, 1984–87; Music Dir, New Music Prodns, 1984–87; Founding Prof., Nat. Youth Orch. of Spain, 1984–86; Consultant: Jumping Sideways Ltd, 2002–; in woodwind and mouthpiece design, Dawkes Music Ltd, 2002–. Visiting Professor: Nat. Centre of Orchestral Studies, NY; Dartington Internat. Summer Sch. Various lecture progs, BBC Radio 3, 1970–84, incl. writer/presenter, Contrasting Styles of Playing, 1974; writer/presenter, The Keller Instinct (TV prog.). Solo clarinettist, Wallfisch/Weinberg Trio, 1974–86. Distinguished Teacher, White House Commn on Presidential Scholars, USA, 1989. *Publications:* Unfinished Sentences, 1987; Mouthpieces: what you need to know, 2008; numerous articles in the Listener, Classical Music Mag. and Musical Times, 1970–84. *Recreation:* supporting my wife who is Founder and Chair of United Families and Friends Campaign (Deaths in Custody). *Address:* 78 Smallwood Road, SW17 0TW. *T:* (020) 8672 5903; *e-mail:* anton@antonweinberg.com.

WEINBERG, Prof. Felix Jiri, FRS 1983; CPhys, FInstP; Emeritus Professor of Combustion Physics, University of London, since 1993; Senior Research Fellow, Imperial College London, since 1993 (Professor of Combustion Physics, 1967–93); consultant to numerous industrial and government research organisations in UK and USA; *b* 2 April 1928; *s* of Victor Weinberg and Nelly Marie (*née* Altschul); *m* 1954, Jill Nesta (*née* Piggott) (*d* 2006); three *s*. *Educ:* Univ. of London (BSc ext.); Imperial Coll., London (PhD, DIC, DSc). Lecturer 1956–60, Sen. Lectr 1960–64, Reader in Combustion, 1964–67, Dept of Chemical Engrg and Chem. Technology, Imperial Coll. Director, Combustion Inst., 1978–88 (Chm. British Sect., 1975–80); Founder and first Chm., Combustion Physics Gp, Inst. of Physics, 1974–77, and Rep. on Watt Cttee on Energy, 1979–85; Mem. Council, Inst. of Energy, 1976–79; Mem., Royal Institution. Leverhulme Emeritus Fellow, 1994. FCGI 1998. Foreign Associate, Amer. NAE, 2001. DSc *hc* Israel Inst. of Technol., Haifa, 1990. Combustion Inst. Silver Combustion Medal 1972, Bernard Lewis Gold Medal 1980; Rumford Medal, Royal Soc., 1988; ItalGas Prize for Res. and Innovation in Energy Scis, Turin Acad., 1991; Lifetime Achievement Award, Inst. of Physics, 2005. *Publications:* Optics of Flames, 1963; Electrical Aspects of Combustion, 1969; (ed) Combustion Institute European Symposium, 1973; Advanced Combustion Methods, 1986; over 200 papers in Proc., jls and symposia of learned socs. *Recreations:* Eastern philosophies, travel, archery. *Address:* Department of Chemical Engineering, Imperial College London, SW7 2AZ. *T:* (020) 7594 5580; 59 Vicarage Road, SW14 8RY. *T:* (020) 8876 1540.

WEINBERG, Prof. Julius Rolf, DM; FRCP, FFPH; Deputy Vice Chancellor, City University, since 2006; *b* 27 Dec. 1954; *s* of Willy Wolfgang Weinberg and Jose Letitia Weinberg; two *s* one *d*. *Educ:* Queen's Coll., Oxford (BM BCh; MA; DM 1990); Radcliffe Infirmary; MSc London. FRCP 2001; FFPH (FFPHM 2002). Lectr and Sen. Registrar, Charing Cross Hosp. Sch. of Medicine, 1984–89; Lectr and Hon. Consultant, Univ. of Zimbabwe Sch. of Medicine, 1989–93; Consultant, WHO Mission to Bosnia, 1993–94; Consultant Epidemiologist, PHLS, 1994–99; Pro Vice-Chancellor (Res.), 1999–2006, Dir, Inst. of Health Scis, 2002–06, City Univ. Vis. Prof., of Health Policy, City Univ., 1996–99. *Publications:* (jtly) Communicable Disease Control Handbook, 2001, 2nd edn 2005; contrib. peer-reviewed jls on physiol. of shock, internat. outbreak control, modelling hosp. services and health informatics. *Recreations:* pottery, cycling, ski-ing. *Address:* City University, Northampton Square, EC1V 0HB. *T:* (020) 7040 5060, *Fax:* (020) 7040 8890; *e-mail:* j.r.weinberg@city.ac.uk.

WEINBERG, Sir Mark (Aubrey), Kt 1987; Chairman: St James's Place Group (formerly J Rothschild Assurance), 1991–2004 (President, since 2004); Synergy Insurance Holdings, since 2005; Pension Insurance Corporation Holdings, since 2006; *b* 9 Aug. 1931; *s* of Philip and Eva Weinberg; *m* 1st, 1961, Sandra Le Roith (*d* 1978); three *d*; 2nd, 1980, Anouska Hempel; one *s*. *Educ:* King Edward VII Sch., Johannesburg; Univ. of the Witwatersrand (BCom, LLB); London Sch. of Econs (LLM). Called to the Bar, South Africa, 1955. Barrister, S Africa, 1955–61; Man. Dir, Abbey Life Assurance Co., 1961–70; Hambro Life Assurance, subseq. Allied Dunbar Assurance: Man. Dir, 1971–83; Chm., 1984–90; Chm., Life Assce Hldg Corp., 1994–2003. Chm., Organizing Cttee, Marketing of Investments Bd, 1985–86; Dep. Chm., Securities and Investment Bd, 1986–90 (Mem., 1985–90); Trustee, Tate Gall., 1985–92. Hon. Treas., NSPCC, 1983–91. *Publication:* Take-overs and Mergers, 1962, 5th edn 1989. *Recreations:* bridge, ski-ing. *Address:* Spencer House, 27 St James's Place, SW1A 1NR. *T:* (020) 7514 1909. *Club:* Portland.

WEINBERG, Prof. Steven, PhD; Josey Regental Professor of Science, University of Texas, since 1982; *b* 3 May 1933; *s* of Fred and Eva Weinberg; *m* 1954, Louise Goldwasser; one *d*. *Educ:* Cornell Univ. (AB); Copenhagen Institute for Theoretical Physics; Princeton Univ. (PhD). Instructor, Columbia Univ., 1957–59; Research Associate, Lawrence Berkeley Laboratory, 1959–60; Faculty, Univ. of California at Berkeley, 1960–69; full prof., 1964; on leave: Imperial Coll., London, 1961–62; Loeb Lectr, Harvard, 1966–67; Vis. Prof., MIT, 1967–69; Prof., MIT, 1969–73; Higgins Prof. of Physics, Harvard Univ., and concurrently Senior Scientist, Smithsonian Astrophysical Observatory, 1973–83 (Sen. Consultant, 1983–). Morris Loeb Vis. Prof., Harvard Univ., 1983–; Dir, Jerusalem Winter Sch. of Theoretical Physics, 1983–94. Lectures: Richtmeyer, Amer. Assoc. of Physics Teachers, 1974; Scott, Cavendish Lab., 1975; Silliman, Yale Univ., 1977; Lauritsen, Calif Inst. of Technol., 1979; Bethe, Cornell, 1979; Schild, Texas, 1979; de Shalit, Weizmann Inst., 1979; Henry, Princeton, 1981; Harris, Northwestern, 1981; Cherwell-Simon, Oxford, 1983; Bampton, Columbia, 1983; Einstein, Israel Acad. of Arts and Sciences, 1984; Hilldale, Wisconsin, 1985; Dirac, Cambridge, 1986; Klein, Stockholm, 1989; Brittin, Colorado, 1992; Gibbs, Amer. Math. Soc., 1996; Bochner, Rice, 1997; Witherspoon, Washington, 2001; Messenger, Cornell, 2007; Phi Beta Kappa Oration, Harvard, 2008. Mem., Science Policy Cttee, Superconducting Supercollider Lab., 1989–93. Mem., Bd of Dirs, Daedalus, 1990–. Fellow, Amer. Acad. of Arts and Scis; Member: US Nat. Acad. of Scis; Amer. Philosophical Soc.; Phil Soc. of Texas (Pres., 1994); IAU; Texas Inst. of Letters; For. Mem., Royal Soc.; Hon. MRIA. Hon. ScD: Knox Coll. 1978; Chicago, 1978; Rochester, 1979; Yale, 1979; City Univ. of New York, 1980; Clark, 1982; Dartmouth Coll., 1984; Columbia, 1990; Salamanca, 1992; Padua, 1992; Barcelona, 1996; Bates Coll., 2002; McGill, 2003; Hon. PhD Weizmann Inst., 1985; Hon. DLitt, Washington Coll., 1985. J. R. Oppenheimer Prize, 1973; Heinemann Prize in Mathematical Physics, 1977; Amer. Inst. of Physics—US Steel Foundn Science Writing Award, 1977; Elliott Cresson Medal of Franklin Inst., 1979; (jtly) Nobel Prize in Physics, 1979; Madison Medal, Princeton, 1991; US Nat. Medal of Sci., 1991; Gemant Prize, Amer. Inst. of Physics, 1997; Piazz Prize, govts of Sicily and Palermo, 1998; Lewis Thomas Prize, Rockefeller Univ., 1999; Humanist of the Year Award, Amer. Humanist Assoc., 2002; Benjamin Franklin Medal, Amer. Philosophical Soc., 2004; Trotter Prize, Texas A & M Univ., 2008. Hon. Citizen, Padua, 2007. *Publications:* Gravitation and Cosmology: principles and applications of the general theory of relativity, 1972; The First Three Minutes: a modern view of the origin of the universe, 1977; The Discovery of the Subatomic Particles, 1982; (jtly) Elementary Particles and the Laws of Physics, 1988; Dreams of a Final Theory, 1993; The Quantum Theory of Fields, vol. I, 1995, vol. II, 1996, vol. III, 2000; Facing Up, 2001; Glory & Terror, 2004; Cosmology, 2008; numerous articles in learned jls. *Recreation:* reading history. *Address:* Physics Department, University of Texas, Austin, TX 78712, USA. *T:* (512) 4714394. *Clubs:* Saturday (Boston, Mass); Cambridge Scientific (Cambridge, Mass); Headliners, Tuesday (Austin, Texas).

WEINER, Edmund Simon Christopher; Deputy Chief Editor, Oxford English Dictionary, 1993–98 and since 2001 (Co-Editor, 1984–93; Principal Philologist, 1998–2001); Supernumerary Fellow, Kellogg College (formerly Rewley House), Oxford, since 1991; *b* 27 Aug. 1950; *s* of late Prof. Joseph Sidney Weiner and Marjorie Winifred (*née* Daw); *m* 1973, Christine Mary, (Clare), Wheeler; two *s* one *d*. *Educ:* Westminster; Christ Church, Oxford (BA Eng. Lang. and Lit.; MA). Lectr, Christ Church, Oxford, 1974–77; Mem. Staff, A Supplement to The Oxford English Dictionary, 1977–84. *Publications:* Oxford Guide to English Usage, 1983, 2nd edn (with A. Delahunty) 1993; (ed with John Simpson) The Oxford English Dictionary, 2nd edn, 1989; (with Sylvia Chalker) The Oxford Dictionary of English Grammar, 1994; (with Sidney Greenbaum) The Oxford Reference Grammar, 2000; (with Peter Gilliver and Jeremy Marshall) The Ring of Words: J. R. R. Tolkien and the Oxford English Dictionary, 2006. *Recreations:* language, music, family life, the Church, history. *Address:* Oxford University Press, Great Clarendon Street, Oxford OX2 6DP. *T:* (01865) 556767.

WEINSTEIN, Harvey, Hon. CBE 2004; film producer; Co-Chairman, The Weinstein Company, since 2005; *b* 19 March 1952; *s* of late Max Weinstein and of Miriam Weinstein; *m* 1986, Eve (marr. diss. 2004); two *d*; *m* 2007, Georgina Chapman. Co-Chm., Miramax Films Corp., 1979–2005. Films produced include: Playing for Keeps, 1986; Scandal, 1989; Strike it Rich, Hardware, 1990; A Rage in Harlem, 1991; The Crying Game, 1992; The Night We Never Met, Benefit of the Doubt, True Romance, 1993; Mother's Boys, Like Water for Chocolate, Pulp Fiction, Pret-a-Porter, 1994; Smoke, A Month by the Lake, The Crossing Guard, The Journey of August King, Things To Do In Denver When You're Dead, The Englishman Who Went Up A Hill But Came Down A Mountain, Blue in the Face, Restoration, 1995; Scream, The Pallbearer, The Last of the High Kings, Jane Eyre, Flirting with Disaster, The English Patient, Emma, The Crow: City of Angels, Beautiful Girls, 1996; Addicted to Love, Air Bud, Cop Land, Good Will Hunting, Scream 2, Jackie Brown, 1997; Velvet Goldmine, Shakespeare in Love, Rounders, The Prophecy II, A Price Above Rubies, Playing by Heart, The Mighty, Little Voice, Heaven, Halloween H20: Twenty Years Later, The Faculty, B. Monkey, Phantoms, Senseless, Ride, Wide Awake, Night Watch, 54, Talk of Angels, 1998; Guinevere, Allied Forces, Wasteland, She's All That, My Life So Far, The Yards, 1999; Scary Movie, Boys and Girls, The Crow: Salvation, Reindeer Games, Love's Labour's Lost, Scream 3, About Adam, Highlander: Endgame, Chocolat, Dracula, 2000; Bounce, Spy Kids, Texas, Scary Movie 2, The Others, The Fellowship of the Ring, 2001; Iris, Shipping News, Spy Kids 2, Equilibrium, Waking up in Reno, The Two Towers, Gangs of New York, Chicago, 2002; Human Stain, Kill Bill: Vol. 1, Confessions of a Dangerous Mind, Spy Kids 3-D, Scary Movie 3, The Return of the King, Cold Mountain, 2003; Kill Bill: Vol. 2, Fahrenheit 9/11, Shall We Dance, 2004; The Aviator, The Brothers Grimm, 2005; An Unfinished Life, Proof, Derailed, Scary Movie 4, 2006; Miss Potter, 2007; The No 1 Ladies' Detective Agency (TV), Crossing Over, 2008. *Publication:* (with Robert Weinstein) The Art of Miramax: the inside story. *Address:* The Weinstein Company, 345 Hudson Street, 13th Floor, New York, NY 10014, USA.

WEINSTOCK, Anne Josephine, CBE 1993; Head, Youth Task Force, Department for Children, Schools and Families, since 2008; *b* 28 Dec. 1950; *d* of late Dr Kevin Maher and Brenda Maher; *m* 1976, Dr Harold Weinstock; one *s* two *d*. *Educ:* Manchester Victoria Univ. (BA Hons Econs). Manager: Stopover hostel for homeless girls, 1972–73; Lance Project for Single Homeless, 1973–75; Regl Manager, then Principal Organiser, NACRO, 1975–79; Mem., Home Office Parole Bd, 1979–84; Chief Exec., Rathbone Soc., later Community Industry, then Rathbone CI, 1985–99; Dir, Millennium Volunteers, 1999–2000 (on secondment); Chief Exec., Connexions Service, DfES, 2000–03; Dir, Supporting Children and Young People Gp, DfES, subseq. DCSF, 2003–08. Director: Manchester TEC, 1989–98; Manchester Careers Partnership, 1995–98; Member: NW FEFC, 1995–98; Govt Skills Task Force, 1998–2000. Fellow, Univ. of Central Lancs, 2001. *Publications:* contrib. articles on raising standards in educn and trng, impact of league tables, alternative educn for disaffected youth, and encouraging young people to become volunteers. *Recreations:* running, walking, swimming, friends and family, reading. *Address:* 12 Warwick Drive, Hale, Cheshire WA15 9DY. *T:* (0161) 980 5070.

WEIR, family name of **Baron Inverforth** and **Viscount Weir**.

WEIR, 3rd Viscount *cr* 1938; **William Kenneth James Weir;** Chairman: The Weir Group PLC, 1983–99; Balfour Beatty (formerly BICC) plc, 1996–2003; CP Ships Ltd, 2001–03; Director: St James's Place Capital (formerly J. Rothschild Holdings) plc, 1985–2004 (Vice-Chairman, 1985–95); Canadian Pacific Railway Co., 1989–2004; *b* 9 Nov. 1933; *e s* of 2nd Viscount Weir, CBE, and Lucy (*d* 1972), *d* of late James F. Crowdy,

MVO; *S* father, 1975; *m* 1st, 1964, Diana (marr. diss.), *o d* of Peter L. MacDougall; one *s* one *d*; 2nd, 1976, Mrs Jacqueline Mary Marr (marr. diss.), *er d* of late Baron Louis de Chollet; 3rd, 1989, Marina, *d* of late Marc Sevastopoulo; one *s*. *Educ:* Eton; Trinity Coll., Cambridge (BA). Dir, BSC, 1972–76; Dir, 1977–91, Dep. Chm., 1991–96, BICC Ltd. Dir, 1970, Chm., 1975–82, Great Northern Investment Trust Ltd; Co-Chm., RIT and Northern plc, 1982–83; Chairman: Major British Exporters, 1992–2003; British Water, 1998–2000. Member: London Adv. Cttee, Hongkong & Shanghai Banking Corp., 1980–92; Court, Bank of England, 1972–84; Export Guarantees Adv. Council, 1992–98. Chm., Engrg Design Res. Centre, 1989–91; Pres., BEAMA, 1988–89, 1994–95; Vice Pres., China-Britain Business Council, 1994–2003. Chm., Patrons of Nat. Galls of Scotland, 1985–95. Mem., Queen's Body Guard for Scotland (Royal Co. of Archers). FRSA. Hon. FREng (Hon. FEng 1993). Hon. DEng Glasgow, 1993. *Recreations:* shooting, golf, fishing. *Heir: s* Hon. James William Hartland Weir [*b* 6 June 1965; *m* 2001, Benedicte Marie Françoise, *d* of Louis Virard]. *Address:* Rodinghead, Mauchline, Ayrshire KA5 5TR. *T:* (01563) 884233. *Club:* White's.

WEIR, Hon. Lord; David Bruce Weir; a Senator of the College of Justice in Scotland, 1985–97; *b* 19 Dec. 1931; *yr s* of late James Douglas Weir and Kathleen Maxwell Weir (*née* Auld); *m* 1964, Katharine Lindsay, *yr d* of Hon. Lord Cameron, KT, DSC; three *s*. *Educ:* Kelvinside Academy; Glasgow Academy; The Leys Sch., Cambridge; Glasgow Univ. (MA, LLB). Royal Naval Reserve, 1955–64, Lieut RNR. Admitted to Faculty of Advocates, 1959; Advocate Depute for Sheriff Court, 1964; Standing Junior Counsel: to MPBW, 1969; to DoE, 1970; QC (Scot.) 1971; Advocate Depute, 1979–82; Justice of Ct of Appeal, Botswana, 1999–2002; Hon. Sheriff, N Strathclyde at Campbeltown, 2004–. Chairman: Medical Appeal Tribunal, 1972–77; Pensions Appeal Tribunal for Scotland, 1978–84 (Pres., 1984–85); NHS Tribunal, Scotland, 1983–85; Member: Criminal Injuries Compensation Bd, 1974–79 and 1984–85; Transport Tribunal, 1979–85; Parole Bd, Scotland, 1989–92. Mem., Law Adv. Cttee, 1988–95, Chm., Scottish Law Cttee, 1994–95, British Council. Governor, Fettes Coll., 1986–95 (Chm., 1989–95). Mem. Bd, Scottish Internat. Piano Competition, 1997–2007. Vice-Chm., S Knapdale Community Council, 1998–2004. Mem. Council, RYA, 2005–. *Publication:* (contrib.) The Laws of Scotland: Stair Memorial Encyclopaedia, 1990. *Recreations:* sailing, music. *Clubs:* New (Edinburgh); Royal Cruising; Royal Highland Yacht.

WEIR, Rear-Adm. Alexander Fortune Rose, CB 1981; DL; Consultant, McMullen Associates (formerly Captain Colin McMullen and Associates), Marine Consultants, since 2006 (Senior Associate, 1982–2006); *b* 17 June 1928; *s* of late Comdr Patrick Wylie Rose Weir and Minna Ranken Forrester Weir (*née* Fortune); *m* 1953, Ann Ross Hamilton Crawford, Ardmore, Co. Londonderry; four *d*. *Educ:* Royal Naval Coll., Dartmouth. Cadet, 1945–46; Midshipman, 1946–47; Actg Sub-Lieut under trng, HMS Zephyr, Portland, 1947; Sub-Lieut professional courses, 1947–48; Sub-Lieut and Lieut, HMS Loch Arkaig, Londonderry Sqdn, 1949–51; ADC to Governor of Victoria, Aust., 1951–53; HMS Mariner, Fishery Protection Sqdn, Home waters and Arctic, 1953–54; qual. as Navigating Officer, 1954; HMS St Austell Bay, WI, Navigating Officer, 1955–56; HMS Wave, Fishery Protection Sqdn, Home, Arctic and Iceland, 1956–58; Lt-Comdr, advanced navigation course, 1958; Staff ND Officer, Flag Officer Sea Trng at Portland, Dorset, 1958–61; HMS Plymouth, Staff Officer Ops, 4th Frigate Sqdn, Far East Station, 1961–62; Comdr 1962; Trng Comdr, BRNC Dartmouth, 1962–64; Comd, HMS Rothesay, WI Station, 1965–66; Staff of C-in-C Portsmouth, Staff Officer Ops, 1966–68; 2nd in Comd and Exec. Officer, HMS Eagle, 1968–69; Captain 1969; jssc 1969–70; Pres., Far East Comd Midshipman's Bd, 1970; Asst Dir Naval Operational Requirements, MoD(N), 1970–72; Captain (F) 6th Frigate Sqdn (8 ships) and HMS Andromeda, 1972–74; NATO Def. Coll., Rome, 1974–75; ACOS Strategic Policy Requirements and Long Range Objectives, SACLANT, 1975–77; Captain HMS Bristol, 1977–78; Rear-Adm. 1978; Dep. Asst Chief of Staff (Ops) to SACEUR, 1978–81. FCMI (FBIM 1979); AVCM 1982. Member: Nautical Inst.; Royal Inst. of Navigation. Licensed Royal Naval Lay Reader, 1981; Licensed Lay Reader: Westbourne Parish, dio. Chichester, 1982; St Kew Parish, dio. Truro, 1984–; Warden of Readers, dio. Truro, 1995–2000; Lay Canon, Truro Cathedral, 1996–2001, now Emeritus. JP: Chichester, 1982–84; Bodmin, 1985–97; DL Cornwall, 1993. *Recreations:* sailing, shooting, golf. *Address:* Tipton, St Kew, Bodmin, Cornwall PL30 3ET. *T:* (01208) 841289; *e-mail:* weiralec@madasafish.com. *Clubs:* Naval, Institute of Directors; Royal Yachting Association, Royal Naval Sailing Association.

WEIR, Alison; historian and novelist; *d* of Ronald James Matthews and Doreen Ethel (*née* Marston, now Cullen); *m* 1972, Rankin Alexander Lorimer Weir; one *s* one *d*. *Educ:* City of London Sch. for Girls; N Western Poly., London. Civil Service, 1974–83; Principal and Proprietor, Henry Tudor Sch. for Children with Special Needs, 1991–97. FRSA 2003. *Publications:* Britain's Royal Families, 1989; The Six Wives of Henry VIII, 1991; The Princes in the Tower, 1992; Lancaster and York, 1995; Children of England: the heirs of Henry VIII, 1996; Elizabeth the Queen, 1998; Eleanor of Aquitaine, 1999; Henry VIII: King and Court, 2001; Mary, Queen of Scots and Murder of Lord Darnley, 2003; Isabella, She Wolf of France, Queen of England, 2005; Innocent Traitor, 2006; Katherine Swynford: the story of John of Gaunt and his scandalous Duchess, 2007; The Lady Elizabeth, 2008; The Lady in the Tower, 2009. *Recreations:* royal and aristocratic genealogy, reading, music, foreign travel, art, poetry.

WEIR, David Bruce; *see* Weir, Hon. Lord.

WEIR, Prof. David Thomas Henderson; Professor of Intercultural Management, Liverpool Hope University, since 2007; Affiliate Professor of Management, Ecole Supérieure de Commerce, Rennes, since 2007; *b* 10 April 1939; *s* of late Johnstone Mather Weir and Irene Florence Brooks; *m* 1st, 1959, Janeen Elizabeth Whitson Fletcher; one *s* one *d*; 2nd, 1967, Mary Willows; one *s*. *Educ:* Ilkley Grammar Sch.; Bradford Grammar Sch.; Queen's Coll., Oxford (Hastings Scholar, Sir William Akroyd's Scholar, MA, Dip PSA). Research and lecturing, Univs of Aberdeen, Leeds, Hull, Manchester, 1961–72; Sen. Lectr, Manchester Business Sch., 1972–74; University of Glasgow: Prof. of Organizational Behaviour, 1974–89; Head, Dept of Management Studies, 1981–89; Dean, Scottish Business Sch., 1977–79; Chm., Glasgow Business Sch., 1985–89; Dir and Prof. of Mgt, Univ. of Bradford Sch. of Mgt, 1989–97; Dean and Dir, Newcastle Business Sch., and Prof. of Mgt, Univ. of Northumbria at Newcastle, 1998–2000, now Prof. Emeritus; Prof. of Mgt, Centre for Educn and Res. Applied to Mgt, France, 2001–07. Visiting Professor: Bolton Inst., 1993; Southampton Inst., 1994; (in Mgt Develt) Lancaster Sch. of Mgt, 2000–; Bristol Business Sch., 2002; Dist. Vis. Prof., eTQM Coll., Dubai, 2007; Sen. Enterprise Fellow, Essex Univ., 2005–; Barrie Turner Meml Lectr, Middlesex Univ., 1998. Keynote address, Gulf Economic Summit, 2002. Dir, Gulliver Foods, 1980–81; Arbitrator, Dairy Industry, Scotland, 1985–89; Chm., Forever Broadcasting, Yorks, 2000–01. Consultant, World Bank, Unesco, SDA, Arthur Andersen and many companies; Strategic Advr, Emerald Gp, 2000–. Member: Sociology and Social Admin Cttee, SSRC, 1976–78; Cttee of Inquiry, Engrg Profession (Finniston Cttee), 1977–79; Teaching Co. Cttee, SERC, 1983–87 (Chm., 1986–87); CNAA, 1986–89; Incorp. of Gardeners of Glasgow, 1985; Conseil Scient. de l'Univ. des eaux de vie, Segonzac, 1989; Strategic Audit Panel for Review of Dutch Business Educn, Eur. Foundn for Mgt Educn, 1994–95. Chm., Assoc. of Business Schs, 1994–96; Mem. Council, Nat. Forum for Management Educn and Develt, 1994–96. Member Council: Prague Internat. Business Sch., 1992–99; Cyprus Internat. Business Sch., 1990–99. Pres., Emerald Acad. for Online Action and Learning, 2006–. CCMI (FBIM 1984); FRSA. Burgess, City of Glasgow, 1985; Ambassador for Bradford, 1996–. *Publications:* with Eric Butterworth: Sociology of Modern Britain, 1970, 3rd edn 1980; Social Problems of Modern Britain, 1972; New Sociology of Modern Britain, 1984; Men and Work in Modern Britain, 1973; (with Camilla Lambert) Cities in Modern Britain, 1974; (jtly) Computer Programs for Social Scientists, 1972; (with Gerald Mars) Risk Management: theories and models, 2000; (with Gerald Mars) Risk Management: practice and prevention, 2000; (jtly) Critical Management into Critical Practice, 2009; Management in the Arab World, 2009. *Recreations:* playing cricket, supporting Leeds United FC, listening to music, fell walking, wine appreciation. *Address:* Deanery of Business, Liverpool Hope University, Liverpool L16 9JD; *e-mail:* dweir@runbox.com. *Clubs:* Athenæum, Groucho, Ebury Court; Cabris Cricket.

WEIR, Fiona; Chief Executive, One Parent Families | Gingerbread, since 2008; *b* Bellshill, N Lanarks, 20 Oct. 1959; *d* of John Morrison Weir and Wendy Elisabeth Christine Weir; partner, 1986, Toby Peter Shelley; two *s*. *Educ:* Lady Margaret Hall, Oxford (BA Hons PPE). Nat. organiser, Eur. Nuclear Disarmament, 1984–87; Sen. Climate Change and Air Pollution Campaigner, Friends of the Earth, 1988–95; Dir of Campaigns, Amnesty Internat. UK, 1995–2000; Hd, Public Affairs, Consumers' Assoc., 2000–02; Dir, Policy and Communications, Save the Children, 2002–07; freelance consultant to charities on strategy, communications and campaigning, 2007. Mem., BBC Appeals Adv. Cttee, 2007–. Mem. RSA. *Recreations:* family, food, films, travel, football (Arsenal). *Address:* One Parent Families | Gingerbread, 255 Kentish Town Road, NW5 2LX. *T:* (020) 7428 5400.

WEIR, Dame Gillian (Constance), DBE 1996 (CBE 1989); concert organist; Prince Consort Professor, Royal College of Music, since 1999; *b* 17 Jan. 1941; *d* of Cecil Alexander Weir and Clarice M. Foy Weir; *m* 1st, 1967, Clive Rowland Webster (marr. diss. 1971); 2nd, 1972, Lawrence Irving Phelps (*d* 1999). *Educ:* Royal College of Music, London. LRSM, LRAM, LTCL; Hon. FRCO. Winner of St Albans Internat. Organ Competition, 1964; Début, 1965: Royal Festival Hall, solo recital; Royal Albert Hall, concerto soloist, opening night of Promenade Concerts; since then, worldwide career solely as touring concert organist; concerto appearances with all major British orchestras, also with Boston Symphony, Seattle Symphony, Württemberg Chamber Orch., and others; solo appearances at leading internat. Festivals, incl. Bath, Aldeburgh, Edinburgh, English Bach, Europalia, Europe and USA (AGO Nat. Conventions, RCCO Diamond Jubilee Nat. Convention, etc). Frequent radio and television appearances: BBC Third Prog., USA, Australasia, Europe, Far East; TV film, Toccata: two weeks in the life of Gillian Weir, 1981 (shown NZ TV 1982); presenter and performer, The King of Instruments, TV series BBC2 and Europe, Australia etc, 1989; many first performances, incl. major works by Fricker, Connolly, Camilleri, Messiaen. Dist. Vis. Artist, Peabody Conservatory of Music, Baltimore, 2004–; master-classes, adjudicator internat. competitions, UK, Europe, N America, Japan; exponent of and authority on Messiaen. President: Incorp. Assoc. of Organists, 1981–83; ISM, 1992–93; RCO, 1994–96 (Hon. Fellow and Mem. Council, 1977–); Hon. RAM, 1989; Hon. FRCM 2000. Hon. Fellow, Royal Canadian Coll. of Organists, 1983. Hon. DMus: Victoria Univ. of Wellington, NZ, 1983; Hull, 1999; Exeter, 2001; Leicester, 2003; Aberdeen, 2004; Hon. DLitt Huddersfield, 1997; DUniv UCE, 2001. Internat. Performer of the Year Award, NY Amer. Guild of Organists, 1981; Internat. Music Guide's Musician of the Year Award, 1982; Turnovsky Prize for outstanding achievement in the arts, Turnovsky Foundn for the Arts, NZ, 1985; Silver Medal, Albert Schweitzer Assoc., Sweden, 1998; Evening Standard Award for outstanding performance, 1999; award-winning recordings include complete organ works of Messiaen, 1994, and of Franck, 1997. *Publications:* contributor to: Grove's Internat. Dictionary of Music and Musicians, 1980; The Messiaen Companion; musical jls and periodicals. *Recreation:* theatre. *Address:* c/o Rayfield Artists, Southbank House, Black Prince Road, SE1 7ST.

See also Sir R. B. Weir.

WEIR, Col James Mathieson Knight, OBE (mil.) 1988; TD 1971 (clasp 1977); FRICS; Vice Lord-Lieutenant of Rutland, 1997–2006; Chairman, Rutland County Council, 1997–99; *b* 3 March 1931; *s* of James Weir and Elspet Mathieson Weir (*née* Knight); *m* 1961, Mary, *d* of Thomas Maden; two *s*. *Educ:* George Heriot's Sch., Edinburgh; Heriot-Watt Coll. FRICS 1954. Nat. Service, 1954–57; RSME; commnd RE; served UK, Germany, Belgium and Holland. Territorial Army: RE in Scotland, 1958–74; attached 4 Armd Div., 1974–81; Territorial, Auxiliary & Volunteer Reserve Association: Mem., Council, 1996–2000; Mem. for E Midlands, 1983–2000; Chm., Leics and Rutland Cttee, 1996–2000; Chm., ACF Cttee, E Midlands, 1998–2000; Co. Comdt, Leics and Northants ACF, 1982–92 (Hon. Col, Leics, Northants and Rutland ACF, 1995–2002); Mem., ACFA Council, 1998–2002. Director: Mitchell Construction Kinnear Moodie Gp, 1966–73; Jeakins Weir Ltd, 1973–. Mem. Bd, Anglian Water Authy, 1981–87. Mem. (C), Leics CC, 1981–93 (Chm., Public Protection Cttee, 1989–93); Mem., Leics Police Authy, 1986–93; Chm., Rutland & Melton Police/Community Consultative Cttee, 1990–93; Mem. (C), Rutland DC, 1991–97 (Vice Chm., 1996–97). DL: Leics, 1984–97; Rutland, 1997. Chm., Leics and Rutland Campaign Army Benevolent Fund, 1989–99. Constituency Conservative Association: Chm., Rutland & Stamford, 1982–83; Rutland & Melton, 1983–85 and 1991–94. Trustee: Peterborough Cathedral Preservation Trust, 1988–; Oakham Sch., 1989–; Governor: C of E Co. Primary Sch., Oakham, 1984–92; Rutland Sixth Form Coll., 1985–93; Vale of Catmose Coll., 1986–95. *Recreations:* golf, visual arts, Rugby Union. *Address:* Swooning House, Oakham, Rutland LE15 6JD. *T:* (01572) 724273. *Club:* Army and Navy.

WEIR, Judith, CBE 1995; composer; *b* 11 May 1954; *d* of Jack and Ishbel Weir. *Educ:* King's Coll., Cambridge (MA). Cramb Fellow, Glasgow Univ., 1979–82; Fellow-Commoner, Trinity Coll., Cambridge, 1983–85; Composer-in-Residence, RSAMD, Glasgow, 1988–91; Fairbairn Composer in assoc. with CBSO, 1995–98; Artistic Dir, Spitalfields Fest., 1998–2000 (Jt Artistic Dir, 1994–97). Hambro Vis. Prof. of Opera Studies, Oxford Univ., 1999; Vis. Prof. of Composition, Princeton Univ., 2001; Fromm Foundn Vis. Prof., Harvard Univ., 2004; Vis. Res. Prof., Cardiff Univ., 2006–. Critics' Circle Award, 1994; Lincoln Center Stoeger Award, 1996; South Bank Show Award, 2000; Queen's Medal for Music, 2007. *Publications include: compositions:* King Harald's Saga, 1979; The Consolations of Scholarship, 1985; Missa Del Cid, 1988; Heaven Ablaze In His Breast, 1989; Music Untangled, 1991–92; Heroic Strokes of the Bow, 1992; Moon and Star, 1995; Forest, 1995; Piano Concerto, 1997; Storm, 1997; We are Shadows, 2000; The Welcome Arrival of Rain, 2002; Tiger under the Table, 2003; Piano Trio Two, 2004; Vertue, 2005; *operas:* A Night at the Chinese Opera, 1987; The Vanishing Bridegroom, 1990; Blond Eckbert, 1994; Armida, 2005. *Address:* c/o Chester Music, 14–15 Berners Street, W1T 3LJ. *T:* (020) 7612 7400.

WEIR, Michael; MP (SNP) Angus, since 2001; *b* 24 March 1957; *s* of James and Elizabeth Weir; *m* 1985, Anne Jack; two *d*. *Educ:* Arbroath High Sch.; Aberdeen Univ. (LLB).

Solicitor: Charles Wood and Son, Kirkcaldy, 1981–83; Myers and Wills, Montrose, 1983–84; J. & D. G. Shiell, Brechin, 1984–2001. Dean, Faculty of Procurators and Solicitors in Angus, 2001. Mem. (SNP), Angus DC, 1984–88. Contested (SNP) Aberdeen S, 1987. Pres., Aberdeen Univ. Student Nationalist Assoc., 1979; Mem., Nat. Exec., Young Scottish Nationalists, 1982. *Address:* House of Commons, SW1A 0AA; (office) 16 Brothock Bridge, Arbroath, Angus DD11 1NG. *T:* (01241) 874522.

WEIR, Peter James; barrister; Member, North Down, Northern Ireland Assembly, since 1998 (UU, 1998–2001, DemU, since 2002); *b* 21 Nov. 1968; *s* of James Weir and Margaret Lovell Weir. *Educ:* Ballyholme Primary Sch.; Bangor Grammar Sch.; Queen's Univ., Belfast (LLB Law and Accountancy; MSSc; Cert. Professional Legal Studies). Called to the Bar, NI, 1992; Lectr in Constitutional and Admin. Law, Univ. of Ulster, 1993. Mem., NI Forum, 1996–98. Mem., Finance Cttee, 2007–, and Envmt Cttee, 2007–, NI Assembly. Chm., Ulster Young Unionist Council, 1993–95. Mem., North Down BC, 2005–. Pres., NI LGA, 2005–06; Member: S Eastern Educn and Liby Bd, 2005–; NI Police Bd, 2006–. Mem., Senate, QUB, 1997–2005. *Publications:* (jtly) The Anglo-Irish Agreement: three years after, 1988; (jtly) Unionism, National Parties and Ulster, 1991. *Recreations:* sport, history, reading. *Address:* 6 Vernon Park, Bangor, Co. Down BT20 4PH; (office) 94 Abbey Street, Bangor, Co. Down BT20 4JB. *T:* and *Fax:* (028) 9145 4500.

WEIR, Peter Lindsay, AM 1982; film director, since 1969; *b* 21 Aug. 1944; *s* of Lindsay Weir and Peggy Barnsley Weir; *m* 1966, Wendy Stites; one *s* one *d*. *Educ:* Scots Coll., Sydney; Vaucluse High Sch.; Sydney Univ. Short Film: Homesdale, 1971; Feature Films: The Cars That Ate Paris, 1973; Picnic at Hanging Rock, 1975; Last Wave, 1977; The Plumber (for TV), 1979; Gallipoli, 1980; The Year of Living Dangerously, 1982; Witness, 1985; The Mosquito Coast, 1986; Dead Poets Society, 1989; Green Card, 1991; Fearless, 1994; The Truman Show, 1998; Master and Commander, 2003.

WEIR, Sir Roderick (Bignell), Kt 1984; JP; Chairman, Rod Weir Co. Ltd; Director, New Zealand Enterprise Trust; *b* 14 July 1927; *s* of Cecil Alexander Weir and Clarice Mildred Foy; *m* 1952, Loys Agnes Wilson (*d* 1984); one *d*; *m* 1986, Anna Jane Mcfarlane. *Educ:* Wanganui Boys' Coll., NZ. Various positions to regional manager, Dalgety NZ Ltd, Wanganui, 1943–63; formed stock and station co., Rod Weir & Co. Ltd, 1963; formed Crown Consolidated Ltd, 1976; Dir, 1980–98, Chm., 1988–98, McKechnie Pacific Ltd; Chm., Danaflex Packaging Corp. Ltd, 1990–98; former Chm., Rangatira Ltd; former Dir, NZ SO. Patron, Massey Coll. Business & Property Trust. Past President: NZ Stock and Station Agents' Assoc.; ASEAN Business Council. Mem., NZ Inst. of Econ. Res. Inc.; Board Member and Patron: Massey Univ. Foundn; Medic Alert; Wellington Sch. of Medicine; Wellington Med. Res. Foundn. Trustee: Link Foundn; Wanganui Old Boys' Assoc. Almoner, Wellington Cathedral of St Paul, 2000–. Hon. Consul-Gen., Austria, 1982–87. Dist. Fellow, Inst. of Dirs in NZ, 2002; FNZIM 1982. JP NZ 1972. Hon. DSc Massey, 1993. *Recreations:* fishing, shooting, boxing. *Address:* The Grove, 189 Main Road, Waikanae, New Zealand. *T:* and *Fax:* (4) 2936373. *Clubs:* Wellington (Wellington); Levin (Levin).

See also Dame Gillian Weir.

WEIR, Stuart Peter; Director, Democratic Audit, and Senior Research Fellow, Human Rights Centre, Essex University, since 1991; Visiting Professor, Essex University, since 1999; *b* 13 Oct. 1938; *e s* of Robert Hendry Weir, CB and Edna Frances (*née* Lewis); *m* 1st, 1963, Doffy Burnham; two *s*; 2nd, 1987, Elizabeth Ellen Bisset; one *s* two *d*. *Educ:* Peter Symonds Sch., Winchester; Brasenose Coll., Oxford (BA Hons Modern History). Feature writer, Oxford Mail, 1964–67; diarist, The Times, 1967–71; Dir, Citizens Rights Office, CPAG, 1971–75; Founding Editor, Roof magazine, 1975–77; Dep. Editor, New Society, 1977–84; Editor: New Socialist, 1984–87; New Statesman, 1987–88, New Statesman and Society, 1988–90. WEA and Adult Educn lectr, 1969–73. Founder Chair, Family Rights Gp, 1975; Founder, Charter 88, 1988, Exec. Mem., 1988–95 and 1997–; Chm., Charter 88 Trust, 1991–92. Associate Consultant, British Council, 1997–2001; Consultant, State of Democracy Project, Inst. for Democracy and Electoral Assistance, Stockholm, 1998–2002. Member: Exec., CPAG and Finer Jt Action Cttee, 1970–84; (Founding), Labour Co-ordinating Cttee, 1979. Active in anti-racist and community groups, Oxford and Hackney, 1964–72; Mem. (Lab), London Bor. of Hackney Council, 1972–76. Mem., Human Rights Commn, Helsinki Citizens Assembly, 1990–92; Sen. Internat. Facilitator, EU Democracy and Governance Project, Namibia, 1994–95; Facilitator, Parly Reform Project, Zimbabwe, 1996–98; Head, UNDP Parly Assessment, Zimbabwe, 2002–03; consultant on Parly reform, Malawi, 2004–06. Special Advr, Public Admin Select Cttee, H of C, 2000–01, 2002–03. Trustee: Civil Liberties Trust, 1990–97; The Scarman Trust, 1997–99. Columnist: Community Care, 1973–75; London Daily News, 1987; script consultant: Spongers, BBC TV, 1977; United Kingdom, BBC TV, 1980–81; editorial consultant: The People's Parliament, 1994–96; C4 Dispatches, Behind Closed Doors, 1995. *Publications:* (contrib.) Towards Better Social Services, 1973; Social Insecurity, 1974; Supplementary Benefits: a social worker's guide, 1975; (ed and contrib.) Manifesto, 1981; (contrib.) The Other Britain, 1982; (contrib.) Consuming Secrets, 1982; (with W. Hall) EGO-TRIP, 1994; (with W. Hall) Behind Closed Doors, 1995; Consolidating Parliamentary Democracy in Namibia, 1995; (with F. Klug and K. Starmer) The Three Pillars of Liberty: political rights and freedoms in the UK, 1996; (jtly) Making Votes Count, 1997; (with D. Beetham) Political Power and Democratic Control in Britain, 1998; (jtly) Voices of the People, 2001, 2nd edn 2005; (jtly) The IDEA Handbook on Democracy Assessment, 2001; (jtly) The State of Democracy, 2002; (jtly) Democracy Under Blair, 2003; (jtly) Not in Our Name, 2005; Unequal Britain: the human rights route to social justice, 2006; (jtly) Power and Participation in Modern Britain, 2008. *Recreations:* cooking, football, being with my family.

WEISKRANTZ, Lawrence, FRS 1980; Professor of Psychology, Oxford University, 1967–93, now Emeritus; Fellow, Magdalen College, Oxford, 1967–93, now Emeritus; *b* 28 March 1926; *s* of Dr Benjamin Weiskrantz and Rose (*née* Rifkin); *m* 1954, Barbara Collins; one *s* one *d*. *Educ:* Girard College; Swarthmore; Univs of Oxford and Harvard. Part-time Lectr, Tufts University, 1952; Research Assoc., Inst. of Living, 1952–55; Sen. Postdoctoral Fellow, US Nat. Res. Council, 1955–56; Research Assoc., Cambridge Univ., 1956–61; Asst Dir of Research, Cambridge Univ., 1961–66; Reader in Physiological Psychology, Cambridge Univ., 1966–67. Dep. Editor, Brain, 1981–; Co-Editor, Oxford Psychology Series, 1979–. Member: US Nat. Acad. of Scis, 1987; Council, Royal Soc., 1988–89. Ferrier Lectr, Royal Soc., 1989; Hughlings Jackson Lectr/Medallist, RSM, 1990; Camp Lectr, Stanford Univ., 1997; Heisenberg Lectr, Bavarian Acad. of Sci., 1998. Kenneth Craik Research Award, St John's Coll., Cambridge, 1975–76; Williams James Award, Amer. Psychol Soc., 1992; McGovern Prize Lecture, AAAS, 2002. *Publications:* (jtly) Analysis of Behavioural Change, 1967; The Neuropsychology of Cognitive Function, 1982; Animal Intelligence, 1985; Blindsight, 1986; Thought Without Language, 1988; Consciousness Lost and Found, 1997; articles in Science, Nature, Quarterly Jl of Experimental Psychology, Jl of Comparative and Physiological Psychology, Animal Behaviour, Brain. *Recreations:* music, walking. *Address:* Department of Experimental Psychology, South Parks Road, Oxford OX1 3UD.

WEISMAN, Malcolm, OBE 1997; Barrister-at-law; a Recorder of the Crown Court, since 1980; *s* of David and Jeanie Pearl Weisman; *m* 1958, Rosalie, *d* of Dr and Mrs A. Spiro; two *s*. *Educ:* Harrogate Grammar Sch.; Parmiter's Sch.; London School of Economics; St Catherine's Coll., Oxford (MA). Blackstone Pupillage Prize. Chaplain (Sqdn Ldr), Royal Air Force, 1956; called to Bar, Middle Temple, 1961; Head of Chambers, 1982–90. Asst Comr of Parly Boundaries, 1976–85; Special Adjudicator, Immigration Appeals, 1998–. Mem., Bar Disciplinary Cttee, Inner Temple, 1990–. Senior Jewish Chaplain, HM Forces, 1972; Religious advisor to small congregations, and Hon. Chaplain, Oxford, Cambridge and new universities, 1963–; Chm. and Sec.-Gen., 1981–92, Pres., 1993–, Allied Air Forces in Europe Chief of Chaplains Cttee; Sec., Former Chiefs of Chaplains Assoc., 1994; Mem. Exec., USA Jewish Chaplains Assoc., 1992–; Member: MoD Adv. Cttee on Chaplaincy, 1972–; Exec. Council, CCJ, 1998–; Exec. Council, Three Faiths Forum, 1998–. Mem., Cabinet of the Chief Rabbi, 1967–; Hon. Chaplain to: Lord Mayor of Westminster, 1992–93; Mayor of Barnet, 1994–95; Assoc. of Jewish Ex-Servicemen and Women, 1999–; Chaplain to Mayor of Montgomery, 2006–07. Hon. Vice-Pres., Monash Br., RBL, 1992–. Mem., Senior Common Room, Essex, Kent and Lancaster Univs, 1964–; Fellow, Centre for Theol. and Soc. (formerly Inst. of Theology), Univ. of Essex, 1992– (Mem. Council, 2000–). Member of Court: Univ. of Lancaster, 1970–; Univ. of Kent, 1970–; Warwick Univ., 1983–; Univ. of East Anglia, 1985–; Essex Univ., 1990–; Sussex Univ., 1992–; Mem. Council, Selly Oak Coll., Birmingham, 1992–; Gov., 1980–, Trustee, 1994–, Parmiter's Sch.; Gov., Carmel Coll., 1995–98. Trustee: B'nai B'rith Music Fest., 1995–; Internat. Multi-faith Chaplaincy, Univ. of Derby, 2000. Patron, Jewish Nat. Fund (formerly Holy Land Trust), 1993–. Hon. Fellow, Univ. of Lancaster, 2006. B'nai B'rith Award for Outstanding Communal Service, 1980; Chief Rabbi's Award for Excellence, 1993; US Jewish Military Special Chaplains' Chaplain Award, 1998; Inter-faith Gold Medallion, Internat. CCJ, 2001; Outstanding Leadership Award, United Synagogue Rabbinic Conf., 2005. Editor, Menorah Jl, 1972–. *Recreations:* travelling, reading, doing nothing. *Address:* 1 Gray's Inn Square, WC1R 5AA. *T:* (020) 7405 8946, *Fax:* (020) 7405 1617.

WEISS, Althea McNish; *see* McNish, A. M.

WEISS, John Roger, CB 2004; Deputy Chief Executive and Member of Management Board, Export Credits Guarantee Department, 2004–05; *b* 27 Dec. 1944; *s* of Ernst Weiss, Basel, and Betsy Weiss (*née* Hallam); *m* 1967, Hazel Kay Lang. *Educ:* St Helen's Coll., Thames Ditton. Tax Officer, Inland Revenue, 1961–64; ECGD, 1964–2005: Dir, Asset Management Gp, 1990–95; Gp Dir, Underwriting, 1995–2001; Dir, Business Gp, 2001–04. Adminr, Dorking Chamber Orch., 2006–. *Recreations:* music, walking. *Address:* 17 Portland Square, E1W 2QR.

WEISS, Prof. Nigel Oscar, FRS 1992; Professor of Mathematical Astrophysics, Cambridge University, 1987–2004, now Emeritus; Fellow of Clare College, Cambridge, since 1965; *b* 16 Dec. 1936; *s* of Oscar and Molly Weiss; *m* 1968, Judith Elizabeth Martin; one *s* two *d*. *Educ:* Hilton College, Natal; Rugby School; Clare College, Cambridge (BA 1957; PhD 1962; ScD 1993). Research Associate, UKAEA Culham Lab., 1962–65; Cambridge University: Lectr, Dept of Applied Maths and Theoretical Physics, 1965–79; Reader in Astrophysics, 1979–87; Sen. Fellow, SERC, 1987–92; Chm., Sch. of Physical Scis, 1993–98. Visiting Professor: Sch. of Math. Scis, QMC, then QMW, London, 1986–96; Dept of Applied Maths, Univ. of Leeds, 2001–07; temporary appointments: MIT; Max Planck Inst. für Astrophysik, Munich; Nat. Solar Observatory, New Mexico; Harvard-Smithsonian Center for Astrophysics; Sci. Univ. of Tokyo. Pres., Royal Astronomical Soc., 2000–02. Gold Medal, RAS, 2007. *Publications:* Sunspots and Starspots, 2008; papers on solar and stellar magnetic fields, astrophysical and geophysical fluid dynamics and nonlinear systems. *Recreation:* travel. *Address:* Department of Applied Mathematics and Theoretical Physics, Centre for Mathematical Sciences, Wilberforce Road, Cambridge CB3 0WA. *T:* (01223) 337910; 10 Lansdowne Road, Cambridge CB3 0EU. *T:* (01223) 355032.

WEISS, Prof. Robert Anthony, (Robin), PhD; FRCPath; FRS 1997; Professor of Viral Oncology, University College London, since 1999; *b* 20 Feb. 1940; *s* of Hans Weiss and Stefanie Löwinsohn; *m* 1964, Margaret Rose D'Costa; two *d*. *Educ:* University College London (BSc, PhD; Fellow, 2006). Lecturer in Embryology, University Coll. London, 1963–70; Eleanor Roosevelt Internat. Cancer Research Fellow, Univ. of Washington, Seattle, 1970–71; Visiting Associate Prof., Microbiology, Univ. of Southern California, 1971–72; Staff Scientist, Imperial Cancer Research Fund Laboratories, 1972–80, Gustav Stern Award in Virology, 1973; Institute of Cancer Research: Dir, 1980–89; Prof. of Viral Oncology, 1984–98; Dir of Res., 1990–96; Hon. Fellow, 1999. Researching into viruses causing cancer and AIDS. Chm., Governing Body, Inst. of Animal Health, 2003–06. Pres., Soc. of Gen. Microbiol., 2006. Founder FMedSci 1998. Hon. Fellow, LSHTM, 2003. Hon. FRCP 1998. Hon. MD Uppsala, 2003. *Publications:* RNA Tumour Viruses, 1982, 2nd edn (2 vols) 1985; various articles on cell biology, virology and genetics. *Recreations:* music, natural history. *Address:* Division of Infection and Immunity, University College London, 46 Cleveland Street, W1T 4JF. *T:* (020) 7679 9554, *Fax:* (020) 7679 9555; *e-mail:* r.weiss@ucl.ac.uk.

WEISSBERG, Prof. Peter Leslie, MD; FRCP, FMedSci; Medical Director, British Heart Foundation, since 2004; Fellow of Wolfson College, Cambridge University, since 1993; *b* 4 Oct. 1951; *s* of Edmund and Dorcas Alfreda Weissberg; *m* 1976, Alison (*née* Prowse), MB ChB; two *s*. *Educ:* Warwick Sch.; Univ. of Birmingham (MB ChB Hons 1976; MD 1985). MRCP 1978, FRCP 1992; FRCPE 1996. Lectr in Cardiovascular Medicine, Univ. of Birmingham, 1983–88; MRC Res. Fellow, Baker Inst., Melbourne, Australia, 1985–87; University of Cambridge: BHF Sen. Res. Fellow, 1988–92; Lectr in Medicine, 1993–94; BHF Prof. of Cardiovascular Medicine, 1994–2004. FESC 1994; FMedSci 1999. *Publications:* numerous contribs to sci. jls. *Address:* British Heart Foundation, 14 Fitzhardinge Street, W1H 6DH. *T:* (020) 7487 7105, *Fax:* (020) 7486 1273.

WEITZ, Dr Bernard George Felix, OBE 1965; DSc; MRCVS; FIBiol; Chief Scientist, Ministry of Agriculture, Fisheries and Food, 1977–81; *b* London, 14 Aug. 1919; *m* 1945, Elizabeth Shine; one *s* one *d*. *Educ:* St Andrew, Bruges, Belgium; Royal Veterinary College, London. MRCVS 1942; DSc London, 1961. Temp. Research Worker, ARC Field Station, Compton, Berks, 1942; Research Officer, Veterinary Laboratory, Min. of Agric. and Fisheries, 1942–47; Asst Bacteriologist, Lister Inst. of Preventive Medicine, Elstree, Herts, 1947; Head of Serum Dept, 1952; Dir, Nat. Inst. for Res. in Dairying, Univ. of Reading, Shinfield, Berks, 1967–77. Vis. Prof., Dept of Agriculture and Horticulture, Univ. of Reading, 1980–88. Member: ARC, 1978–81; NERC, 1978–81. Hon. FRASE 1977. *Publications:* many contribs to scientific journals on immunology and tropical medicine. *Recreations:* music, croquet. *Address:* 21 Hartley Close, Charlton Kings, Cheltenham, Glos GL53 9DN.

WEITZENHOFFER, (Aaron) Max; producer; President: Weitzenhoffer Productions, New York and London, since 1965; Weitzenhoffer Theatres Ltd, since 2001; Chairman, Nimax Theatres Ltd, since 2005; *b* 30 Oct. 1939; *s* of Aaron and Clara Weitzenhoffer; *m*

1st, Frances (*d* 1991); 2nd, 2000, Ayako Takanashi; one *s* one *d*. *Educ:* Univ. of Oklahoma (BFA Drama 1962). Productions include: Dracula, NY (Tony Award), 1978; Song and Dance, NY, 1985; The Will Rogers Follies (Tony Award), NY, 1991; Defending the Caveman, Apollo (Olivier Award), 2000; Feel Good, Garrick, 2001; One Flew over the Cuckoo's Nest, Gielgud, 2004; Who's Afraid of Virginia Woolf, Apollo, 2006; A Moon for the Misbegotten, NY, 2007. Member: Amer. League of Theatres and Producers, 1977–; SOLT, 2001–. Regent, Univ. of Oklahoma, 2003–. Hon. DHL Oklahoma, 2000. *Recreation:* trying to keep up with my children. *Address:* Nimax Theatres Ltd, 1 Lumley Court, off 402 Strand, WC2R 0NB. *T:* 0845 434 9290, *Fax:* (020) 7240 4540; *e-mail:* mweitzenhoffer@cox.net. *Clubs:* Friars, Century Association, Players (New York).

WEITZMAN, Peter; QC 1973; a Recorder of the Crown Court, 1974–98; *b* 20 June 1926; *s* of late David Weitzman, QC, and Fanny Weitzman (*née* Galinski); *m* 1954, Anne Mary Larkam; two *s* two *d*. *Educ:* Cheltenham Coll.; Christ Church, Oxford (Gibbs Schol. in Mod. Hist., Newdigate Prize, 1949; BA 1950). Lt RA, 1945–48. Called to Bar, Gray's Inn, 1952; Bencher, 1981; Leader, Midland and Oxford Circuit, 1988–92 (Dep. Leader, 1985–88). Mem., Senate of Inns of Court, 1980–81, 1984–92. Member: Mental Health Review Tribunal, 1986–98; Criminal Injuries Compensation Bd, 1986–2000; Criminal Injuries Compensation Appeals Panel, 2000–02. *Recreations:* hedging and ditching. *Address:* 21 St James's Gardens, W11 4RE; Little Leigh, Kingsbridge, Devon TQ7 4AG.

WEITZMAN, Thomas Edward Benjamin; QC 2003; *b* 11 Sept. 1959; *s* of Peter Weitzman, *qv*; *m* 1995, Maria Villegas; one *s* one *d*. *Educ:* St Paul's Sch.; New Coll., Oxford (BA Hons). Called to the Bar, Gray's Inn, 1984; in practice, specialising in commercial, insurance and reinsurance and professional negligence law. *Recreations:* looking, reading, walking. *Address:* 3 Verulam Buildings, Gray's Inn, WC1R 5NT. *T:* (020) 7831 8441.

WELANDER, Rev. Canon David Charles St Vincent; Canon Residentiary and Librarian, Gloucester Cathedral, 1975–91, now Emeritus; *b* 22 Jan. 1925; *s* of late Ernest Sven Alexis Welander, Orebro and Uppsala, Sweden, and Louisa Georgina Downes Welander (*née* Panter); *m* 1952, Nancy O'Rorke Stanley; two *s* three *d*. *Educ:* Unthank Coll., Norwich: London Univ. (BD 1947, Rubie Hebrew Prize 1947); ALCD (1st Cl.) 1947; Toronto Univ., 1947–48 (Hon. Mem. Alumni, Wycliffe Coll., 1948). FSA 1981. Deacon 1948, Priest 1949; Asst Curate, Holy Trinity, Norwich, 1948–51; Chaplain and Tutor, London Coll. of Divinity, 1952–56; Vicar: of Iver, Bucks, 1956–62; of Christ Church, Cheltenham, 1963–75; Rural Dean of Cheltenham, 1973–75. Member: Council, St Paul's and St Mary's Colls of Educn, Cheltenham, 1963–78; Council, Malvern Girls' Coll., 1982–91; Bishops' Cttee on Inspections of Theol Colls, 1967–81; Sen. Inspector of Theol Colls, 1970–84; Mem., Gen. Synod of C of E, 1970–85. Mem., Cathedrals Cttee, English Heritage, 1990–94. Trustee: Church Patronage Trust, 1969–78; Stained Glass Mus., 1986–95. *Publications:* History of Iver, 1954; Gloucester Cathedral, 1979; The Stained Glass of Gloucester Cathedral, 1984; Gloucester Cathedral: its history, art and architecture, 1990; Gloucester Cathedral, A Visitor's Handbook, 2001; contrib. Expository Times, etc. *Recreations:* walking, church architecture, music. *Address:* 1 Sandpits Lane, Sherston Magna, near Malmesbury, Wilts SN16 0NN. *T:* (01666) 840180.

WELBY, Very Rev. Justin Portal; Dean of Liverpool, since 2007; *b* 6 Jan. 1956; *s* of late Gavin Welby and of Jane Gillian Welby (*née* Portal, now Lady Williams of Elvel); *m* 1979, Caroline Eaton; two *s* three *d* (and one *d* decd). *Educ:* Eton Coll.; Trinity Coll., Cambridge (BA 1978); St John's Coll., Durham (BA 1991). Manager, Project Finance, Société Nationale Elf Aquitaine, Paris, 1978–83; Treas., Elf UK, 1983–84; Gp Treas., Enterprise Oil plc, 1984–89; ordained deacon, 1992, priest, 1993; Curate, All Saints, Chilvers Coton, Nuneaton, with St Mary the Virgin, Astley, 1992–95; Rector: St James, Southam, 1995–2002; St Michael and All Angels, Ufton, 1996–2002; Coventry Cathedral: Co-Dir of Internat. Ministry and Canon Residentiary, 2002–05; Sub-Dean and Canon for Reconciliation Ministry, 2005–07. Non-exec. Dir, S Warwicks Gen. Hosps NHS Trust, 1998–2000 (Chm., 2000–02). Mem., Cttee of Reference, F&C Stewardship Funds, 2006–. Mem., ACT, 1983. *Publications:* numerous articles on treasury mgt, finance and ethics, and reconciliation. *Recreations:* anything French, sailing. *Address:* 1 Cathedral Close, Liverpool L7 1BR. *T:* (0151) 702 7202; *e-mail:* dean@liverpoolcathedral.org.uk.

WELBY, Sir (Richard) Bruno (Gregory), 7th Bt *cr* 1801; *b* 11 March 1928; *s* of Sir Oliver Charles Earle Welby, 6th Bt, TD, and Barbara Angela Mary Lind (*d* 1983), *d* of late John Duncan Gregory, CB, CMG; *S* father, 1977; *m* 1952, Jane Biddulph, *y d* of late Ralph Wilfred Hodder-Williams, MC; three *s* one *d*. *Educ:* Eton; Christ Church, Oxford (BA 1950). *Heir: s* Charles William Hodder Welby [*b* 6 May 1953; *m* 1978, Suzanna, *o d* of Major Ian Stuart-Routledge, Harston Hall, Grantham; three *d*]. *Address:* Denton Manor, Grantham, Lincs NG32 1JX.

WELCH, Andrew Richard; theatre producer; Managing Director, Andrew Welch Ltd, since 2005; *b* 5 Feb. 1949; *s* of Richard Joseph Welch and Ruth Jordan Welch; *m* 1980, Louisa Mary Emerson; two *s*. *Educ:* Bedford Sch., Bedford; UC of Swansea, Univ. of Wales (BA). Dir, Arts Centre, Univ. of Warwick, 1977–81; General Manager: Hong Kong Arts Centre, 1981–84; Theatre Royal, Plymouth, 1984–90; Producer, Carnival Films and Theatre Ltd, 1990–95; Chief Exec., Theatre of Comedy Ltd, 1996–98; Fest., subseq. Theatre, Dir, Chichester Fest. Th., 1998–2002; Gen. Dir, Dance Umbrella, 2002–04 (Mem. Bd, 1985–88). Man. Dir, Armada Prodns, 1987–; Chairman: Paines Plough Th. Co., 1979–81; Michael Clark Dance Co., 2003–; Bd, Wimbledon Th. Prodns Ltd, 2004–; Bd, Milton Keynes Th. Prodns Ltd, 2004–; Member: Watermill Th. Ltd, 1984–96; Arts Council Touring Bd, 1984–91; Bd, Goodnights Entertainment Ltd, 2005–; Bd, Richmond Th. Prodns Ltd, 2006–. Mem., Bd of Govs, GSMD, 2001–08. FRSA 2004. Hon. MA UC Chichester, 2002. *Recreations:* music, walking. *Address:* 12 Westwood Road, SW13 0LA. *T:* (020) 8876 9292. *Club:* Garrick.

WELCH, Rear Adm. John Edwin Nugent, CB 1996; Chief of Naval Staff, New Zealand, 1994–97; *b* 14 Jan. 1941; *s* of Robert Nugent Welch and Mary Helen Anne Welch; *m* 1966, Adrienne Sandford Cox; three *s*. *Educ:* King's High Sch., Dunedin, NZ; Britannia Royal Naval Coll., Dartmouth. Service at sea, Pacific and Far East, 1961–66; Long Gunnery Course, HMS Excellent, 1967–68; i/c HMNZS Mako, 1968–69; service at sea, Far East, 1969–70; ashore, 1971–72; service at sea, 1972–75; i/c HMNZS Inverell, 1976–77; jssc, Australia, 1978; i/c HMNZS Otago, Far East and USA, 1978–80; staff appts, 1981–82; i/c HMNZS Canterbury, 1983–84; Capt. 1985; staff appts, Wellington, 1985–87; NZ Defence Advr, Ottawa, 1988–90; staff appts, 1991–97; Cdre 1992; Rear Adm. 1994. Naval Gen. Service Medal, 1964; NZ Armed Forces Award, 1985. Silver Jubilee Medal, 1977. *Recreations:* trout fishing, golf, reading, sailing. *Address:* 9 Rangitira Avenue, Takapuna, Auckland, New Zealand. *T:* (9) 4891237; *e-mail:* welchfam@clear.net.nz. *Clubs:* Auckland Central Rotary; Waitemata Golf.

WELCH, Sir John K.; *see* Kemp-Welch.

WELCH, Sir John (Reader), 2nd Bt *cr* 1957; Partner, Wedlake Bell, 1972–96; Chairman, John Fairfax (UK) Ltd, 1977–90; *b* 26 July 1933; *s* of Sir (George James) Cullum Welch, 1st Bt, OBE, MC, and Gertrude Evelyn Sladin Welch (*d* 1966); *S* father, 1980; *m* 1962, Margaret Kerry, *o d* of late K. Douglass, Killara, NSW; one *s* twin *d*. *Educ:* Marlborough College; Hertford Coll., Oxford (MA). National service in Royal Signals, 1952–54 (2nd Lt); TA, 1954–62 (Capt., Middlesex Yeomanry). Admitted a solicitor, 1960. Partner, Bell Brodrick & Gray, 1961–71. Ward Clerk of Walbrook Ward, City of London, 1961–74, Common Councilman, 1975–86 (Chm., Planning and Communications Cttee, 1981, 1982); Chm., Walbrook Ward Club, 1978–79; Registrar of Archdeaconry of London, 1964–99. Governor: City of London Sch. for Girls, 1977–82; Haberdashers' Aske's Schs, Elstree, 1981–85 and 1990–91. FRSA. Liveryman, Haberdashers' Co., 1955 (Court of Assistants, 1973; Master, 1990–91); Freeman, Parish Clerks' Co. (Master, 1967, now Past Master Emeritus). Chm., Cttee of Management, London Homes for the Elderly, 1980–90; Pres., Freemasons' Grand Charity, 1985–95; Sen. Grand Warden, United Grand Lodge of England, 1998–2000. CStJ 1981. *Recreations:* piano, walking. *Heir: s* James Douglass Cullum Welch, *b* 10 Nov. 1973. *Address:* 28 Rivermead Court, Ranelagh Gardens, SW6 3RU. *Clubs:* City Livery (Hon. Solicitor, 1983–90, Pres., 1986–87), Hurlingham.

WELCH, Prof. Robert Anthony, PhD; MRIA, FEA; Professor of English, since 1984 and Dean, Faculty of Arts, since 2000, University of Ulster; *b* 25 Nov. 1947; *s* of Patrick Welch and Kathleen Kearney; *m* 1970, Angela O'Riordan; three *s* one *d*. *Educ:* University Coll., Cork (BA Hons 1968; MA 1971); Univ. of Leeds (PhD 1974). Lecturer: Sch. of English, Univ. of Leeds, 1971–73; in English, Univ. of Ife, Nigeria, 1973–74; Sch. of English, Univ. of Leeds, 1974–84; Head of Dept of English, 1984–94, Dir, Centre for Irish Lit. and Bibliography, 1994–2000, Univ. of Ulster. Mem. 1990–96, Vice Chm. 1992–93, Arts Council of NI. Chm., Internat. Assoc. for Study of Ireland's Literatures, 1988–91. Founding FEA, 2000. *Publications:* Irish Poetry from Moore to Yeats, 1980; A History of Verse Translation from the Irish, 1988; Changing States: transformations in modern Irish literature, 1993; Muskerry (poems), 1993; The Kilcolman Notebook (novel), 1994; (ed) Oxford Companion to Irish Literature, 1996; Secret Societies (poems), 1997; Groundwork (novel), 1997; The Blue Formica Table (poems), 1998; The Abbey Theatre: 1899–1999, 1999; (ed) The Concise Oxford Companion to Irish Literature, 2000; (trans.) Forty Four: Dana Podracka - poems from the Slovak, 2005; The Evergreen Road (poems), 2006; Protestants (play), 2006; (gen. ed.) Oxford History of the Irish Book, vol. III, 2006. *Recreations:* gardening, fishing. *Address:* Faculty of Arts, University of Ulster, Coleraine, Northern Ireland BT52 1SA. *Club:* Kildare Street and University (Dublin).

WELCH, Ven. Stephan John; Archdeacon of Middlesex, since 2006; *b* 16 Oct. 1950; *s* of Ernest Ian Welch and Regina Welch; *m* 1990, Jennifer Clare (*née* Gallop); three *s*. *Educ:* Hull Univ. (BA French Lang. and Lit. 1974); Birmingham Univ. (Postgrad. Dip. in Theol. 1976); London Univ. (MTh 1998). Ordained deacon, 1977, priest, 1978; Curate, Christ Church, Waltham Cross, 1977–80; Priest-in-charge: Reculver, 1980–86; St Bartholomew, Herne Bay, 1982–86; Vicar: Reculver and St Bartholomew, Herne Bay, 1986–92; Hurley and Stubbings, 1992–2000; Priest-in-charge, St Peter, Hammersmith, 2000–06. Area Dean, Hammersmith and Fulham, 2001–06. *Recreations:* French language and literature, French wine, sailing, patristic theology. *Address:* 98 Dukes Avenue, W4 2AF. *T:* (020) 8742 8308; *e-mail:* archdeacon.middlesex@london.anglican.org.

WELCHMAN, Charles Stuart; His Honour Judge Welchman; a Circuit Judge, since 1998; *b* 7 April 1943; *s* of late Edward James Welchman and Marjorie (*née* Williams, later Parsons); *m* 1972, Rosemary Ann Fison, *d* of late Dr Thomas Notley Fison and of Nancy Jean Laird Fison; one *s* one *d*. *Educ:* W Buckland Sch.; Exeter Tech. Coll.; University Coll. London (LLB Hons 1965). Called to the Bar, Gray's Inn, 1966 (Mould Scholar 1966); an Asst Recorder, 1990–94; a Recorder, 1994–98. Mem., Restricted Patients Panel, Mental Health Review Tribunal, 2002–. Mem., Exec. Cttee, Professional Negligence Bar Assoc., 1996–98. Contested (L): Esher, Oct. 1974, 1979; Putney, 1982. Best Individual Speaker, Observer Mace Nat. Debating Competition, 1965. *Recreations:* inland waterways, theatre, jazz. *Address:* Kingston Crown Court, 6–8 Penrhyn Road, Kingston-upon-Thames, Surrey KT1 2BB. *Club:* Surrey County Cricket.

WELD FORESTER, family name of **Baron Forester.**

WELDON, Sir Anthony (William), 9th Bt *cr* 1723; *b* 11 May 1947; *s* of Sir Thomas Brian Weldon, 8th Bt, and of Marie Isobel (who *m* 1984, 6th Earl Cathcart, CB, DSO, MC), *d* of Hon. William Joseph French; *S* father, 1979; *m* 1980, Mrs Amanda Wigan (marr. diss. 2006), *d* of Major Geoffrey and Hon. Mrs North; two *d*. *Educ:* Sherborne. Formerly Lieutenant, Irish Guards. Dir, Bene Factum Publishing Ltd, 1983–; Asst Dir and Gen. Manager, ViRSA Educnl Trust, 2003–05. *Publications:* (ed) Breakthrough: handling career opportunities and changes, 1994; (jtly) Numeroids: any number of things you didn't know, 2008. *Recreations:* stalking, fishing, antiquarian books, champagne. *Heir: cousin* Kevin Nicholas Weldon [*b* 19 April 1951; *m* 1973, Catherine Main; one *s*]. *Clubs:* White's, Pratt's, Stranded Whales.

WELDON, Duncan Clark; theatrical producer; Chairman and Managing Director, Duncan C. Weldon Productions Ltd, since 1964; *b* 19 March 1941; *s* of Clarence Weldon and Margaret Mary Andrew; *m* 1967, Helen Shapiro; *m* 1974, Janet Mahoney; one *d*; *m* 2005, Ann Sidney. *Educ:* King George V School, Southport. Formerly a photographer; first stage production, A Funny Kind of Evening, with David Kossoff, Theatre Royal, Bath, 1965; co-founder, Triumph Entertainment Ltd, 2000; Director: Triumph Proscenium Productions Ltd, 1994–; Malvern Festival Theatre Trust Ltd, 1997–; Artistic Dir, Chichester Festival Theatre, 1995–97. First London production, Tons of Money, Mayfair Theatre, 1968; productions in the West End include: When We are Married, 1970 (also 1996); The Chalk Garden, Big Bad Mouse, The Wizard of Oz, 1971; Lord Arthur Savile's Crime, Bunny, The Wizard of Oz, 1972; Mother Adam, Grease, The King and I, 1973; Dead Easy, 1974; The Case in Question, Hedda Gabler (RSC), Dad's Army, Betzi, On Approval, 1975; 13 Rue de l'Amour, A Bedful of Foreigners, Three Sisters, The Seagull, Fringe Benefits, The Circle, 1976; Separate Tables, Stevie, Hedda Gabler, On Approval, The Good Woman of Setzuan, Rosmersholm, Laburnum Grove, The Apple Cart, 1977; Waters of the Moon, Kings and Clowns, The Travelling Music Show, A Family, Look After Lulu, The Millionairess, 1978; The Crucifer of Blood, 1979; Reflections, Rattle of a Simple Man, The Last of Mrs Cheyney, Early Days, 1980; Virginia, Overheard, Dave Allen, Worzel Gummidge, 1981; Murder In Mind, Hobson's Choice (also 1995), A Coat of Varnish, Captain Brassbound's Conversion, Design for Living, Uncle Vanya (also 1996), Key for Two, The Rules of the Game, Man and Superman, 1982; The School for Scandal, DASH, Heartbreak House (also 1992), Call Me Madam, Romantic Comedy, Liza Minnelli, Beethoven's Tenth, Edmund Kean, Fiddler on the Roof, A Patriot for Me, Cowardice, Great and Small, The Cherry Orchard, Dial 'M' for Murder, Dear Anyone, The Sleeping Prince, Hi-De-Hi!, 1983; Hello, Dolly!, The Aspern Papers, Strange Interlude, Serjeant Musgrave's Dance, Aren't We All?, American Buffalo, The Way of the World, Extremities, 1984; The Wind in the Willows, The Lonely Road, The Caine Mutiny Court-Martial, Other Places, Old Times (also 1995), The Corn is Green, Waste, Strippers, Guys and Dolls, Sweet Bird of Youth, Interpreters, Fatal Attraction, The Scarlet Pimpernel, 1985; The Apple Cart, Across From the Garden of Allah, Antony and Cleopatra, The Taming of the Shrew, Circe & Bravo, Annie Get

Your Gun, Long Day's Journey Into Night, Rookery Nook, Breaking the Code, Mr and Mrs Nobody, 1986; A Piece of My Mind, Court in the Act!, Canaries Sometimes Sing, Kiss Me Kate (RSC), Melon, Portraits, Groucho: a Life In Review, A Man for All Seasons, You Never Can Tell, Babes in the Wood, 1987; A Touch of the Poet, The Deep Blue Sea, The Admirable Crichton, The Secret of Sherlock Holmes, A Walk in the Woods, Richard II, Orpheus Descending, 1988; Richard III (also RSC, 1999), The Royal Baccarat Scandal, Ivanov, Much Ado About Nothing, The Merchant of Venice, Frankie & Johnny, Veterans Day, Another Time, The Baker's Wife, London Assurance, 1989; Salome (RNT), Bent (RNT), An Evening with Peter Ustinov (also 1994), The Wild Duck, Henry IV, Kean, Love Letters (also 1999), Time and the Conways, 1990; The Homecoming, The Philanthropist, The Caretaker, Becket, Tovarich, The Cabinet Minister, 1991; Talking Heads (also 1996), A Woman of No Importance (RSC), Lost in Yonkers, Trelawny of the "Wells", Cyrano de Bergerac, 1992; Relative Values, Two Gentlemen of Verona, Macbeth, 1993; Travesties (RSC), A Month in the Country, Rope, Arcadia (RNT), Home, Saint Joan, Lady Windermere's Fan, The Rivals, 1994; Dangerous Corner, Cell Mates, The Duchess of Malfi, Taking Sides, Communicating Doors, The Hothouse, 1995; The Cherry Orchard (RSC), 1996; Live and Kidding, The Herbal Bed (RSC), Life Support, A Letter of Resignation, The Magistrate, Electra, 1997; New Edna—The Spectacle, Rent, 1998; The Prisoner of Second Avenue, Hay Fever, The Importance of Being Earnest (also 2001), Collected Stories, 1999; Enigmatic Variations, Napoleon, God Only Knows, 2000; Peggy Sue Got Married, Private Lives, My One and Only, 2002; The Tempest, Coriolanus (RSC), The Merry Wives of Windsor (RSC), The Master Builder, Thoroughly Modern Millie, 2003; Rattle of a Simple Man, Suddenly Last Summer, 2004; The Birthday Party, The Philadelphia Story, As You Desire Me, 2005; Stones in his Pockets, 2006; The Last Confession, Macbeth, Nicholas Nickleby, 2007; presented on Broadway: Brief Lives, 1974; Edmund Kean, Heartbreak House, 1983; Beethoven's Tenth, 1984; Strange Interlude, Aren't We All?, 1985; Wild Honey, 1986; Blithe Spirit, Pygmalion, Breaking the Code, 1987; Orpheus Descending, The Merchant of Venice, 1989; Taking Sides, 1996; Electra, 1999; Stones in his Pockets, 2001; Private Lives, 2002; Macbeth, 2008; has also presented in Europe, Australia, Canada and Hong Kong. *Television:* Co-producer, Into the Blue, 1997. *Address:* 1 Lumley Court, Strand, WC2R 0NB. *T:* (020) 7836 0186.

WELDON, Fay, CBE 2001; writer; *b* 22 Sept. 1931; *d* of Frank Birkinshaw and Margaret Jepson; *m* 1962, Ron Weldon (*d* 1994); four *s*; *m* 1994, Nicolas Fox. *Educ:* Hampstead Girls' High Sch.; St Andrews Univ. (MA 1952). Has written or adapted numerous television and radio plays, dramatizations, and series, and ten stage plays. Chm. of Judges, Booker McConnell Prize, 1983. Hon. DLitt St Andrews, 1990. *Libretto:* A Small Green Space, 1989. *Publications:* The Fat Woman's Joke, 1967; Down Among the Women, 1972; Female Friends, 1975; Remember Me, 1976; Little Sisters, 1977 (as Words of Advice, NY, 1977); Praxis, 1978 (Booker Prize Nomination); Puffball, 1980; Watching Me, Watching You (short stories), 1981; The President's Child, 1982; The Life and Loves of a She-Devil, 1984 (televised, 1986; filmed as She-Devil, 1990); Letters to Alice—on First Reading Jane Austen, 1984; Polaris and other Stories, 1985; Rebecca West, 1985; The Shrapnel Academy, 1986; Heart of the Country, 1987 (televised, 1987); The Hearts and Lives of Men, 1987; The Rules of Life, 1987; Leader of the Band, 1988; (for children) Wolf the Mechanical Dog, 1989; The Cloning of Joanna May, 1989 (televised, 1992); (for children) Party Puddle, 1989; Darcy's Utopia, 1990; (contrib.) Storia 4: Green, 1990; Moon over Minneapolis or Why She Couldn't Stay (short stories), 1991; Life Force, 1992; Growing Rich, 1992; Affliction, 1994; Splitting, 1995; (with David Bailey) The Lady is a Tramp: portraits of Catherine Bailey, 1995; Wicked Women (short stories), 1995; Worst Fears, 1996; (for children) Nobody Likes Me!, 1997; Big Women, 1998 (televised, 1998); A Hard Time to Be a Father (short stories), 1998; Godless in Eden: a book of essays, 1999; Rhode Island Blues, 2000; The Bulgari Connection, 2001; Auto Da Fay (autobiog.), 2002; Nothing to Wear & Nowhere to Hide (short stories), 2003; Mantrapped, 2004; She May Not Leave, 2005; What Makes Women Happy, 2006; The Spa Decameron, 2007; The Stepmother's Diary, 2008. *Address:* c/o Capel & Land Ltd, 29 Wardour Street, W1D 6PS.

WELEMINSKY, Judith Ruth; Chief Executive, Mental Health Providers Forum, since 2005; *b* 25 Oct. 1950; *d* of Dr Anton Weleminsky and Gerda Weleminsky (*née* Loewenstamm); *m* 2003, Robert James Armstrong Smith; two *d*. *Educ:* Birmingham Univ. (BSc Hons Psych); Lancaster Univ. (MA Organisational Psych). Personnel and Training Officer, Lowfield (Storage and Distbn), 1973–75; Community Relations Officer, Lambeth, 1975–78; Equal Opportunities Officer, Wandsworth, 1978–80; Employment Development Officer, NACRO, 1980–82; Dir, Nat. Fedn of Community Orgns, 1982–85; Dir, Nat. Schizophrenia Fellowship, 1985–90; Dir, NCVO, 1991–94; Associate, Centre for Voluntary Sector and Not for Profit Mgt, City Univ. Bus. Sch., 1994–97; Sen. Consultant, Compass Partnership, 1994–2005. Partner, Mentoring Dirs, 1995–97. Member: Bd, Children and Family Court Adv. Support Service, 2001–04; Gen. Social Care Council, 2001–04. Trustee, Makaton Vocabulary Develt Project, 1998–. Council Mem., Wimbledon and Dist Synagogue, 2005–06. FRSA. *Recreations:* family, friends, food. *Address:* *e-mail:* judywele@aol.com.

WELFARE, Jonathan William; Chief Executive, Elizabeth Finn Care (formerly Distressed Gentlefolk's Aid Association, then Elizabeth Finn Trust), since 1998; *b* 21 Oct. 1944; *s* of late Kenneth William Welfare and of Dorothy Patience Athol Welfare (*née* Ross); *m* 1969, Deborah Louise Nesbitt; one *s* three *d*. *Educ:* Bradfield Coll., Berks; Emmanuel Coll., Cambridge (MA Econs and Land Economy 1969; boxing blue). Economist, Drivers Jonas & Co., 1966–68; Consultant, Sir Colin Buchanan and Partners, 1968–70; Economist and Corporate Planning Manager, Milton Keynes Develt Corp., 1970–74; Economist, then Dep. Chief Exec., S Yorks CC, 1974–84; Director: Landmark Trust, 1984–86; Oxford Ventures Gp, 1986–90; Man. Dir, Venture Link Investors, 1990–95; Chief Exec., Bristol 2000, 1995–96; mgt consultant, 1995–98. Director: Oxford Innovation, 1987–96; Granite TV, 1988–2003; Interconnect Ltd, 1990–94; Calidair Ltd, 1990–95; Meridian Software, 1990–95; English Community Care Assoc., 1999–; Elizabeth Finn Homes Ltd, 2005–. Trustee: Oxford Trust, 1985– (Chm., 1985–95); Northmoor Trust, 1986–99 (Chm., 1986–95); Turn2Us, 2007–. FRSA 1992. Freeman: City of London, 1991; Co. of Information Technologists, 1991. *Recreations:* family, cricket, fishing, gardening. *Address:* Wilton House, High Street, Hungerford, Berks RG17 0NF. *T:* (01488) 684228; (office) 1 Derry Street, W8 5HY. *T:* (020) 7396 6700. *Club:* Hawks (Cambridge).

WELLAND, Colin, (Colin Williams); actor, playwright; *b* 4 July 1934; *s* of John Arthur Williams and Norah Williams; *m* 1962, Patricia Sweeney; one *s* three *d*. *Educ:* Newton-le-Willows Grammar Sch.; Bretton Hall Coll.; Goldsmiths' Coll., London (Teacher's Dip. in Art and Drama; Hon. Fellow, 2000). Art teacher, 1958–62; entered theatre, 1962; Library Theatre, Manchester, 1962–64; television, films, theatre, 1962–. Freelance sports writer: The Observer; The Independent. Films (actor): Kes; Villain; Straw Dogs; Sweeney; Dancing through the Dark; (original screenplay): Yanks, 1978; Chariots of Fire, 1980 (won Oscar, Evening Standard and Broadcasting Press Guild Awards, 1982); Twice in a Lifetime, 1986; A Dry White Season, 1989; War of the Buttons, 1994; television (actor): Blue Remembered Hills; The Fix; Bramwell, 1998. Plays (author): Say Goodnight to Grandma, St Martin's, 1973; Roll on Four O'clock, Palace, 1981. Award winning TV plays include: Roll on Four O'clock, Kisses at 50, Leeds United, Jack Point, Your Man from Six Counties, Bambino Mio. Best TV Playwright, Writers Guild, 1970, 1973 and 1974; Best TV Writer, and Best Supporting Film Actor, BAFTA Awards, 1970; Broadcasting Press Guild Award (for writing), 1973. *Publications:* Northern Humour, 1982; plays: Roomful of Holes, 1972; Say Goodnight to Grandma, 1973. *Recreations:* sport, theatre, cinema, politics, dining out. *Address:* c/o United Agents, 12–26 Lexington Street, W1F 0LE.

WELLAND, Prof. Mark Edward, PhD; FRS 2002; FREng, FIET, FInstP; Professor of Nanotechnology, University of Cambridge, since 1999; Fellow, St John's College, Cambridge, since 1986; Chief Scientific Adviser, Ministry of Defence, since 2008; *b* 18 Oct. 1955; *s* of John Michael Welland and Pamela June Welland (*née* Davey); *m* 1981, Dr Esme Lynora Otun; two *s* two *d*. *Educ:* Univ. of Leeds (BSc Physics 1979); Univ. of Bristol (PhD Physics 1984); MA Cambridge 1988. FInstP 2001; FREng 2002; FIET (FIEE 2002). Lectr in Electrical Engrg, 1986–95, Reader in Nanoscale Sci., 1995–99, Univ. of Cambridge. World Trade Vis. Scientist, IBM Res. Div., Yorktown Heights, USA, 1985–86. *Publications:* numerous contribs to learned jls, Trans Royal Soc. and NATO pubns; 5 patents. *Recreations:* squash, running, rowing, ski-ing. *Address:* 32 Wingate Way, Trumpington, Cambridge CB2 2HD. *T:* (01223) 760305, *Fax:* (01223) 760306; *e-mail:* mew10@cam.ac.uk.

WELLBELOVED, James; commercial consultant; Director General, National Kidney Research Fund, 1984–93; *b* 29 July 1926; *s* of Wilfred Henry Wellbeloved, Sydenham and Brockley (London), and Paddock Wood, Kent; *m* 1948, Mavis Beryl Ratcliff; two *s* one *d*. *Educ:* South East London Technical College. Boy seaman, 1942–46; building maintenance operative, 1946–50; marketing electrical appliances, 1950–56; marketing, sales and merchandising, 1956–65. TU Branch Officer, activist in CLP and Mem. Jt Mgt Cttee, LCC, 1946–50; Mem., Erith BC, 1950–56 (Chm., Estabt Cttee); first Leader, Bexley LBC, 1965–66. MP (Lab 1965–81, SDP 1981–83) Erith and Crayford, Nov. 1965–1983; Parly Private Secretary: Minister of Defence (Admin), 1967–69; Sec. of State for Foreign and Commonwealth Affairs, 1969–70; an Opposition Whip, 1972–74; Parly Under-Sec. of State for Defence (RAF), MoD, 1976–79. UK Rep., North Atlantic Assembly, 1972–76, 1979–82. Dep. Chm., London MPs Parly Gp, 1970–81; Chairman: River Thames Gp; All Party Parly Camping and Caravanning Gp, 1967–74; Nat. Whitley Council, MoD, 1976–79; Member: Ecclesiastical Cttee, 1971–76; RACS Political Purposes Cttee, 1973–83; PLP Liaison Cttee, 1974–78; Defence Council, 1976–79; Unrelated Live Transplant Regulatory Authority, 1990–97; Vice Chm., Labour Party Defence Gp, 1970–81. Contested (SDP) 1983, (SDP/Alliance) 1987, Erith and Crayford. Dir, Greenwich and Bexley Cottage Hospice, 1998–2006. Pres., British Transplant Organ Donor Soc., 1992–97. Nat. Vice-Pres., Camping and Caravanning Club, 1974–. Former Governor, Greenwich Hosp. Sch. *Publication:* Local Government, 1971. *Recreations:* camping, travel. *Address:* 9 Woodstock Close, Bexley, Kent DA5 3JT.

WELLER, Sir Arthur (Burton), Kt 1997; CBE 1988; Chairman, Citadel Reinsurance Company Ltd, since 1984; *b* 9 Nov. 1929; *s* of Thomas Burton Weller and Mary Johnston Weller (*née* Norman); *m* 1962, Margaret Marea Piper (*née* Callinan); one *s* one *d*. *Educ:* Trinity Acad., Edinburgh. Master Mariner, 1957. Chm., Sirius Insurance Co., 1969–91. Chairman: Britain-Australia Bicentennial Schooner Trust, 1986–2003; Maritime Trust, 1989–96 (Mem. Council, 1977; Hon. Warden, 1996–); HM Bark Endeavour Foundn, 1991–2000; Trustee, 1990–97, Hon. Cdre, 2006, Nat. Maritime Mus. *Recreations:* reading, breeding Angus cattle. *Address:* 1503 Quay Grand, 61–69 Macquarie Street, Sydney, NSW 2000, Australia; *e-mail:* sirarthurweller@acenet.com.au. *Clubs:* Hong Kong Yacht (Hong Kong); Royal Sydney Yacht Squadron (Sydney).

WELLER, Prof. Ian Vincent Derrick, MD; FRCP; Professor, Centre for Sexual Health and HIV Research, University College London, since 1991 (formerly at University College London Medical School, then Royal Free and University College Medical School of University College London); *b* 27 March 1950; *s* of Derrick Charles William Weller and Eileen Weller; *m* 1972, Darryl McKenna; two *d*. *Educ:* Westlain Grammar Sch., Brighton; St Bartholomew's Hosp. Med. Sch. (BSc 1st Cl. Hons 1971; MB BS 1974; MD 1983). MRCP 1977, FRCP 1990. House physician, Med. Unit, St Bartholomew's Hosp. and house surgeon, Hackney Hosp., 1975; SHO rotation, Northwick Park Hosp., 1976–77; Med. Registrar rotation, St Mary's Hosp., London, 1977–79; Ingram Res. Fellow, then Hon. Lectr and MRC Trng Fellow, Acad. Dept of Medicine, Royal Free Hosp., 1979–82; Lectr and Hon. Sen. Registrar, Acad. Dept of Genito-Urinary Medicine, 1982–84, Wellcome Trust Sen. Lectr in Infectious Diseases, 1984–88, Middx Hosp. Med. Sch.; Reader in Genito-Urinary Medicine, UCL Med. Sch., 1988–91; Hd, Dept of Sexually Transmitted Diseases, UCL Med. Sch., subseq. Royal Free and University Coll. Med. Sch. of UCL, 1994–2003. Dir, Camden PCT, 2002–. Member: UK Adv. Panel for Health Care Workers Infected with Blood Borne Viruses, DoH, 1993–2005; Genito-Urinary Specialist Cttee, RCP, 1994–2005; Adv. Gp to HEA, 1994–97; Jt Med. Adv. Cttee to HEFC, 2000–06; MRC Committees: AIDS Res. Co-ordinating Cttee, 1994–; AIDS Therapeutics Cttee, 1987–2000 (Dep. Chm.; Chm., Anti-viral Sub-gp); Vice Co-Chair, Commn on Human Medicines (formerly Cttee on Safety of Medicines), 1999–; Chairman: Steering Gp, N Thames Regl AIDS/HIV Educn Prog., 1994–2001; HIV/Viral Diseases Scientific Adv. Gp, Cttee for Human Medicinal Products, EMEA, 2005–; Collaboration of Observational HIV Epidemiology Res. Europe, 2005–; Chm. of Scientific Cttee and organiser, Internat. Congress on Drug Therapy in HIV Infection, 1992–2008. Member: Eur./Australian Internat. Co-ordinating Cttee for trials in HIV infection and AIDS, 1989–2000; Internat. Sci. Adv. Gp, Agence Nationale de Recherches sur le SIDA, 2000–; Bd, Internat. AIDS Soc., 2001–08 (Treas.); Indep. Expert Mem., Strategic Working Gp, Div. of AIDS, NIH, 2007–. Mem. and Chm. of Bd, Terrence Higgins Trust, 1998–2001. *Publications:* contrib. chapters in proc. and books; numerous papers in peer reviewed jls and articles. *Recreations:* golf, walking, farming. *Address:* Centre for Sexual Health and HIV Research, University College London, Mortimer Market Centre, Mortimer Market, off Capper Street, WC1E 6AU.

WELLER, Walter; Music Director, National Orchestra of Belgium, 2007–08; Principal Guest Conductor, National Orchestra of Spain, 1987–2004; *b* 30 Nov. 1939; *s* of Walter and Anna Weller; *m* 1966, Elisabeth Samohyl; one *s*. *Educ:* Realgymnasium, Vienna; Akademie für Musik, Vienna (degree for violin and piano). Founder of Weller Quartet, 1958–69; Member, Vienna Philharmonic, 1958–69. First Leader, 1960–69; Conductor, Vienna State Opera, 1969–75; Guest Conductor with all main European and American Orchestras, also in Japan and Israel, 1973–; Principal Conductor and Artistic Adviser, Royal Liverpool Philharmonic Orch., 1977–80; Principal Conductor, RPO, 1980–85; Principal Conductor and Music Dir, Royal Scottish Nat. Orch., 1992–97, now Conductor Emeritus; Artistic Dir, Allgemeine Musikges. Basel, 1994–95; Associate Dir, Orch. of Valencia; Conductor Laureate, Stuttgart Philharmonic Orch., 2004–. Many recordings (Grand Prix du disque Charles Cros). Medal of Arts and Sciences, Austria, 1968; Great Silver Cross of Honour, Austria, 1998. *Recreations:* magic, model railway, sailing, swimming, stamp-collecting, ski-ing. *Address:* c/o HarrisonParrott Ltd, 12 Penzance Place, W11 4PA.

WELLESLEY, family name of **Earl Cowley** and of **Duke of Wellington.**

WELLINGS, Sir Jack (Alfred), Kt 1975; CBE 1970; Chairman, 1968–87, Managing Director, 1963–84, The 600 Group Ltd; *b* 16 Aug. 1917; *s* of Edward Josiah and Selina Wellings; *m* 1946, Greta (*d* 2005), *d* of late George Tidey; one *s* two *d*. *Educ:* Selhurst Grammar Sch.; London Polytechnic. Vice-Pres., Hawker Siddeley (Canada) Ltd, 1954–62; Dep. Man. Dir, 600 Group Ltd, 1962. Member: NCB, 1971–77; NEB, 1977–79; part-time Mem., British Aerospace, 1980–87; non-exec. Dir, Clausing Corp., USA, 1982–84. *Address:* F115, Sunrise of Chorleywood, High View, Chorleywood, Rickmansworth, Herts WD3 5TQ.

WELLINGS, Prof. Paul William, PhD; Vice Chancellor and Professor of Population Ecology, Lancaster University, since 2002; *b* 1 Nov. 1953; s of late William and Beryl Wellings; *m* 1990, Annette Frances Schmidt. *Educ:* Royal Grammar Sch., Lancaster; King's Coll. London (BSc Hons); Durham Univ. (MSc); Univ. of E Anglia (PhD 1980). NERC Res. Fellow, 1980–81; Res. Scientist, 1981–95, Chief of Div. of Entomol., 1995–97, CSIRO; First Asst Sec., Dept of Industry, Sci. and Resources, Australia, 1997–99; Dep. Chief Exec., CSIRO, Australia, 1999–2002. Board Member: Australian Nuclear Sci. and Technol. Orgn, 1996–99; Australian Centre for Internat. Agricl Res., 2000–02; HEFCE, 2006–; UUK, 2006–. Mem. Bd, Cumbria Rural Regeneration Co., 2003–06. FAICD 2001; CCMI 2005; FRSA 2005. *Publications:* numerous contribs in fields of insect ecology and pest mgt. *Recreations:* cricket, fell-walking, visual arts. *Address:* University House, Lancaster University, Lancaster LA1 4YW. *T:* (01524) 592025, *Fax:* (01524) 36841; *e-mail:* p.wellings@lancaster.ac.uk.

WELLINGTON, 8th Duke of, *cr* 1814; **Arthur Valerian Wellesley,** KG 1990; LVO 1952; OBE 1957; MC 1941; DL; Baron Mornington, 1746; Earl of Mornington, Viscount Wellesley, 1760; Viscount Wellington of Talavera and Wellington, Somersetshire, Baron Douro, 1809; Earl of Wellington, Feb. 1812; Marquess of Wellington, Oct. 1812; Marquess Douro, 1814; Prince of Waterloo, 1815, Netherlands; Count of Vimeiro, Marquess of Torres Vedras and Duke of Victoria in Portugal; Duke of Ciudad Rodrigo and a Grandee of Spain, 1st class; *b* 2 July 1915; *s* of 7th Duke of Wellington, KG, and Dorothy Violet (*d* 1956), *d* of Robert Ashton, Croughton, Cheshire; *S* father, 1972; *m* 1944, Diana Ruth (MBE 2007), *o d* of Maj.-Gen. D. F. McConnel; four *s* one *d*. *Educ:* Eton; New Coll., Oxford. Served War of 1939–45 in Middle East (MC), CMF and BLA. Lt-Col Comdg Royal Horse Guards, 1954–58; Silver Stick-in-Waiting and Lt-Col Comdg the Household Cavalry, 1959–60; Comdr 22nd Armoured Bde, 1960–61; Comdr RAC 1st (Br.) Corps, 1962–64; Defence Attaché, Madrid, 1964–67, retired; Col-in-Chief, The Duke of Wellington's Regt, 1974–; Hon. Col 2nd Bn, The Wessex Regt, 1974–80; Dep. Col, The Blues and Royals, 1998–2002. Director: Massey Ferguson Holdings Ltd, 1967–89; Massey Ferguson Ltd, 1973–84. President: Game Conservancy, 1976–81 (Dep. Pres., 1981–87); SE Branch, Royal British Legion, 1978; BSJA, 1980–82; Rare Breeds Survival Trust, 1984–87; Council for Environmental Conservation, 1983–87; Atlantic Salmon Trust, 1983–; Thames Salmon Trust, 1986–2002; Labrador Retriever Club, 1997–; Nat. Canine Defence League, 1999–; Vice-President: Zool Soc. of London, 1983–89; Kennel Club, 1985–; Mem. Council, RASE, 1976– (Dep. Pres., 1993). HM's Rep. Trustee, Bd of Royal Armouries, 1983–95; Trustee, WWF (UK), 1985–90. Hampshire CC 1967–74; DL Hants, 1975. Pres., Hampshire Assoc. of Parish and Town Councils, 1994–99. Governor of Wellington Coll., 1964–. Pres., Pitt Club. OStJ. Officier, Légion d'Honneur (France); Kt Grand Cross: Order of St Michael of the Wing (Portugal), 1984; Order of Isabel the Catholic (Spain), 1986. *Heir:* *s* Marquess of Douro, *qv*. *Address:* Park Corner House, Heckfield, Hook, Hants RG27 0LJ; Apsley House, 149 Piccadilly, W1J 7NT. *Club:* Cavalry and Guards.

WELLINGTON (NZ), Archbishop of, (RC), since 2005; **Most Rev. John Atcherley Dew;** Metropolitan, and Military Ordinary, for New Zealand, since 2005; *b* 5 May 1948; *s* of Alfred George Dew and Joan Theresa Dew (*née* McCarthy). *Educ:* St Joseph's Coll., Masterton; Holy Name Seminary, Christchurch; Holy Cross Coll., Mosgiel (BTh 1975). Ordained deacon, 1975, priest, 1976; Asst Priest, St Joseph's Parish, Upper Hutt, 1976–79; Parish Priest, St Joseph's Cathedral Parish, Dio. Rarotonga, Cook Is, 1980–82; Leader, Archdiocesan Youth Ministry Team and Chaplain to Cook Is Maori Community, 1983–87; Dir, First Year Formation, Holy Cross Coll., Mosgiel, 1988–91; study leave, St Anselm, Kent, England, 1991–92; Parish Priest, St Anne's, Newtown, 1993–95; Auxiliary Bishop, Archdio. Wellington, 1995–2005. *Address:* Archdiocese of Wellington, PO Box 1937, Wellington 6140, New Zealand. *T:* (4) 4961766, *Fax:* (4) 4961330; *e-mail:* j.dew@wn.catholic.org.nz.

WELLINGTON (NZ), Bishop of, since 1998; **Rt Rev. Dr Thomas John Brown;** *b* 16 Aug. 1943; *s* of Ernest Robert Brown and Abby Brown; *m* 1965, Dwyllis Lyon; one *s* two *d*. *Educ:* Otago Univ.; St John's Theol Coll., Auckland (LTh, STh); Graduate Theol Union, Berkeley, Univ. of California (DMin). Curate: St Matthew, Christchurch, NZ, 1972–74; St James the Greater, Leicester, UK, 1974–76; Vicar: Upper Clutha, 1976–79, St John, Roslyn, 1979–85, Dio. Dunedin, NZ; St James, Lower Hutt, Dio. Wellington, 1985–91; Archdeacon of Belmont, 1987–91; Asst Bishop and Vicar General, Diocese of Wellington, 1991–98. *Publications:* Ministry At The Door, 1981; Learning From Liturgy, 1984; (contrib.) Growing in Newness of Life, 1993; (contrib.) Designer Genes, 2000; (contrib.) Gene Technology in New Zealand: scientific issues and implications, 2000. *Recreations:* golf, fly-fishing, reading, swimming. *Address:* Bishopscourt, 20 Eccleston Hill, Thorndon, Wellington, New Zealand.

WELLINK, Arnout Henricus Elisabeth Maria; Executive Director, since 1982, President, since 1997, De Nederlandsche Bank; *b* 27 Aug. 1943; *m* 1989, Monica Victoria Volmer; three *s* two *d*. *Educ:* Gymnasium B; Leyden Univ. (law degree 1968); Univ. of Rotterdam (PhD Econs 1975). Teaching asst in econs, and staff mem., Leyden Univ., 1965–70; Ministry of Finance: staff mem., 1970–75; Hd, Directorate Gen. for Financial and Econ. Policy, 1975–77; Treas. Gen., 1977–81. Mem. Bd of Dirs, 1997–, Pres., 2002–04, BIS, Basle; Member: Council, Eur. Monetary Inst., 1997–98; Governing Council, European Central Bank, 1998–. Chm., Bd of Trustees, Nederlands Openlucht Mus., 2003–; Bd of Trustees, Mus. of Mauritius. Chm., King William I Foundn, 1997–; Member: Bd, Foundn for Orthopaedic Patients' Interests, 1995–; Foundn for Postgrad. Med. Trng in Indonesia, 1997–; N. G. Pierson Fund Foundn, 1997–. Kt, Order of Lion (Netherlands), 1981. *Address:* De Nederlandsche Bank NV, PO Box 98, 1000 AB Amsterdam, The Netherlands. *T:* (20) 5242150, *Fax:* (20) 5242525.

WELLINS, Robert Coull; freelance improvising saxophonist and composer; *b* 24 Jan. 1936; *s* of Maximillian and Catherine Wellins; *m* 1966, Isabella Brotherston Teer; two *d*. *Educ:* Carnwadric Primary Sch., Glasgow; Shawlands Acad.; RAF Sch. of Music, Uxbridge. Teacher, Chichester Coll. of Further Educn. Big bands, 1950s; joined, 1960s: Buddy Featherstonhaugh's Quintet; Tony Crombie Jazz Inc.; Stan Tracey Quartet; toured with Charlie Watts Orch., E Coast USA, 1986, W Coast USA, 1987. Best tenor sax, British Jazz Awards, 1994, 1998, 2000. *Recreation:* walking. *Address:* 30 Frith Road, Bognor Regis, W Sussex PO21 5LL. *T:* (01243) 863882; *web:* www.bobbywellins.co.uk.

WELLS, Dean of; *see* Clarke, Very Rev. J. M.

WELLS, Archdeacon of; *see* Sullivan, Ven. N. A.

WELLS, Andrew Mark; Director, New Homes and Sustainable Communities (formerly New Housing and Communities, then New Homes and Sustainable Development), Department for Communities and Local Government (formerly Director, Sustainable Communities, Office of the Deputy Prime Minister), since 2003; *b* 22 Feb. 1955; *s* of Richard Frederick Wells and Eunice Mary Wells (*née* Williams); partner, Pam Temple; one *d*. *Educ:* Bristol Grammar Sch.; St John's Coll., Cambridge (MA Maths 1976). Grad. trainee, 1976–83, Principal, Local Govt Finance, 1983–87, DoE; on loan as Principal, Econ. Secretariat, Cabinet Office, 1987–90; Department of the Environment: Divl Manager, Local Govt Rev. Team, 1990–92; Hd, London Policy Unit, 1992–93; Divisional Manager: Local Authy Housing, 1993–96; Water Supply and Regulation, 1996–99; on loan as Dir, Modernising Govt, Cabinet Office, 1999–2000; Dir, Regl Co-ordination Unit, Cabinet Office, then ODPM, 2000–03. *Recreations:* walking, squash. *Address:* Department for Communities and Local Government, Eland House, Bressenden Place, SW1E 5DU. *T:* (020) 7944 3025.

WELLS, Bowen; international development specialist, since 2001; *b* 4 Aug. 1935; *s* of late Reginald Laird Wells and of Agnes Mary Wells (*née* Hunter); *m* 1975, Rennie Heyde; two *s*. *Educ:* St Paul's School; Univ. of Exeter (BA Hons); Regent St Polytechnic School of Management (Dip. Business Management). National Service, RN (promoted to Sub Lt), 1954–56. Schoolmaster, Colet Court, 1956–57; sales trainee, British Aluminium, 1957–58; Univ. of Exeter, 1958–61; Commonwealth Development Corporation, 1961–73; Owner Manager, Substation Group Services Ltd, 1973–79. Board Member: CARE UK, 2001–07; AMREF UK, 2001–07. MP (C) Hertford and Stevenage, 1979–83, Hertford and Stortford, 1983–2001. Parliamentary Private Secretary: to Minister of State for Employment, 1982–83; to Minister of State at Dept of Transport, 1992–94; an Asst Govt Whip, 1994–95; a Lord Comr of HM Treasury (Govt Whip), 1994–97. Member: For. Affairs Select Cttee, 1981–92; European Legislation Select Cttee, 1983–92; Chairman: Select Cttee on Internat. Develt, 1997–2001; UN Parly Gp, 1983–92; British-Caribbean Gp, 1983–95; Jt Hon. Sec., Parly Cons. Trade and Industry Gp, 1984–91 (Vice-Chm., 1983–84); Sec., All Party Overseas Develt Gp., 1984–94; Sec., Cons. Envmt Cttee, 1991–92; Mem., 1922 Exec.; Mem., British-American Gp, 1985. Mem., Assoc. of Former MPs, 2004–. Member: UK Br. Exec., CPA, 1984–2001 (Treas., 1997–2001); Exec. Cttee, Internat. CPA, 1994–98 (Treas., 1998–2001). Trustee, Industry and Parlt Trust, 1985–2001. Gov., Inst. of Development Studies, 1980–94; Mem. Bd, ODI, 1997–2008. Rep. of BVI, 2002–03. *Recreations:* music, walking, gardening, cooking, sailing. *Address:* Saltings, Harbour Road, Bosham, Chichester, W Sussex PO18 8JE. *Clubs:* Naval; Bosham Sailing.

WELLS, Brigid; *see* Wells, J. B. E.

WELLS, Christopher; *see* Wells, J. C. D.

WELLS, Sir Christopher (Charles), 3rd Bt *cr* 1944, of Felmersham, co. Bedford; *b* 12 Aug. 1936; *s* of Sir Charles Maltby Wells, 2nd Bt and of Katharine Boulton Wells; *S* father, 1996; *m* 1st, 1960, Elizabeth Florence Vaughan (marr. diss. 1983), *d* of I. F. Griffiths; two *s* two *d*; 2nd, 1985, Lynda Ann Cormack; one *s*. *Educ:* McGill Univ., Montreal (BSc); Univ. of Toronto (MD). MD in family practice, retired 1995. Assoc. Prof., Faculty of Medicine, Univ. of Toronto, 1975–95. *Heir:* *s* Michael Christopher Gruffydd Wells, *b* 24 Oct. 1966. *Address:* 1268 Seaforth Crescent, RR#3, Lakefield, ON K0L 2H0, Canada.

WELLS, Hon. Clyde (Kirby); Chief Justice of Newfoundland, since 1999; *b* 9 Nov. 1937; *s* of Ralph Pennell Wells and Maude Wells (*née* Kirby); *m* 1962, Eleanor, *d* of Arthur and Daisy Bishop; two *s* one *d*. *Educ:* All Saints Sch., Stephenville Crossing; Memorial Univ., Newfoundland (BA 1959); Dalhousie Univ. Law Sch. (LLB 1962). Served with Canadian Army, JAG's Office, 1962–64; called to the Bar, Nova Scotia, 1963, Newfoundland, 1964; Partner, Barry and Wells, and successor law firms, 1964–81; Senior Partner, Wells & Co., 1981–87; QC (Can.) 1977; Counsel, O'Reilly, Noseworthy, 1996–98; Justice, Court of Appeal, Newfoundland, 1998–99. Dir, 1978–87, and Chm., 1985–87, Newfoundland Light & Power Co. Ltd. MHA (L): Humber East, 1966–71; Windsor-Buchans, Dec. 1987–1989; Bay of Islands, 1989–96; Minister of Labour, 1966–68; Leader of Liberal Party, 1987; Premier of Newfoundland and Labrador, 1989–96. Hon. LLD Memorial, Newfoundland, 1996. *Address:* Court of Appeal, 287 Duckworth Street, PO Box 937, St John's, NL A1C 5M3, Canada; 305–25 Bonaventure Avenue, St John's, NL A1C 1T4, Canada; *e-mail:* cwells@judicom.gc.ca.

WELLS, Prof. David Arthur; Professor of German, Birkbeck College, University of London, 1987–2006, now Emeritus; *b* 26 April 1941; *s* of Arthur William Wells and Rosina Elizabeth (*née* Jones). *Educ:* Christ's Hosp., Horsham; Gonville and Caius Coll., Cambridge; Univs of Strasbourg, Vienna and Münster. Mod. and Med. Langs Tripos, BA 1963, Tiarks Studentship 1963–64, MA, PhD Cantab 1967. Asst Lectr 1966–67, Lectr 1967–69, in German, Univ. of Southampton; Lectr in German, Bedford Coll., Univ. of London, 1969–74; Sec., London Univ. Bd of Staff Examiners in German, 1973–74; Tutor, Nat. Extension Coll., Cambridge, 1966–74; Prof. of German, QUB, 1974–87. Lecture tour of NZ univs, 1975. Mem., Managing Body, Oakington Manor Jun. Mixed and Infant Sch., London Bor. of Brent, 1972–74. Hon. Treasurer: Assoc. for Literary and Linguistic Computing, 1973–78; MHRA, 2001–09 (Hon. Sec., 1969–2001); Pres., Internat. Fedn for Modern Langs and Lits, 2005–08 (Sec.-Gen., 1981–2005). Jt Editor, The Year's Work in Modern Language Studies, 1976–2004 (Editor, 1982). FRSA 1983. *Publications:* The Vorau Moses and Balaam: a study of their relationship to exegetical tradition, 1970; The Wild Man from the Epic of Gilgamesh to Hartmann von Aue's Iwein, 1975; A Complete Concordance to the Vorauer Bücher Moses (Concordances to the Early Middle High German Biblical Epic), 1976; (contrib.) MHRA Style Guide: a handbook for authors, 2002; The Central Franconian Rhyming Bible, 2004; articles, monographs and reviews in learned jls. *Recreations:* travel, theatre, music. *Address:* School of Languages, Linguistics and Culture, Birkbeck College, 43 Gordon Square, WC1H 0PD. *T:* (020) 7631 6103.

WELLS, David George; Managing Director, Service, British Gas plc, 1993–96; *b* 6 Aug. 1941; *s* of George Henry Wells and Marian (*née* Trolley); *m* 1967, Patricia Ann Fenwick; two *s*. *Educ:* Market Harborough Grammar Sch.; Reading Univ. (BA). FCA 1966. Hancock, Gilbert & Morris, 1962–67; Esso Chemical Ltd, 1967–69; joined Gas Council, 1969; Investment Accountant (Investment Appraisal), 1970–73; British Gas Corporation: Chief Accountant, Admin, 1973–76; Chief Investment Accountant, 1976; Dir of Finance, SE Reg., 1976–83; Dep. Chm., W Midlands Reg., 1983–88; Regl Chm., S Eastern, 1988–93; Man. Dir, Regl Services, 1993. Director: Metrogas Bldg Soc., 1978–86 (Dep. Chm., 1979–83); Port Greenwich Ltd, 1989–. Chm., S London Trng and Enterprise Council, 1989–93. CIGEM (CIGasE 1988); CCMI (CBIM 1990); FRSA 1991.

Recreations: world travel, walking, reading, photography, bridge, U3A activities, gardening. *Address:* 11 Parklands, Ice House Wood, Oxted, Surrey RH8 9DP.

WELLS, Dominic Richard Alexander; Editor, Saturday Times, The Knowledge (formerly The Eye) magazine, 2003–07; *b* 7 March 1963; *s* of Prof. Colin M. Wells and Catherine Wells; partner, Liz Hitchcock; two *s*. *Educ:* Winchester Coll.; New Coll., Oxford (BA Hons Modern History). Gofer, Muller, Blond & White Publishing Ltd, 1985–86; Sub-Editor, London's Alternative Magazine, 1986–87; Time Out magazine: Sub-Editor, then Chief Sub-Editor, subseq. Dep. Editor, 1987–92; Editor, 1992–98; Editorial Dir, AOL Bertelsmann Online, 1999–2001; Editor in Chief, AOL UK, 2001–02; Ed., Saturday Times Play mag., 2002–03. Editor of the Year, BSME, 1992, 1994, 1995, 1998. *Recreation:* anything with my family. *Address:* 52 Drewstead Road, SW16 1AG. *T:* (020) 3133 2060; *e-mail:* DominicRAWells@aol.com.

WELLS, Doreen Patricia, (Doreen, Marchioness of Londonderry); dancer and actress; Ballerina of the Royal Ballet, 1955–74; *m* 9th Marquess of Londonderry, *qv* (marr. diss. 1989); two *s*. *Educ:* Walthamstow; Bush Davies School; Royal Ballet School. Engaged in Pantomime, 1952 and 1953. Joined Royal Ballet, 1955; became Principal Dancer, 1960; has danced leading roles in Noctambules, Harlequin in April, Dance Concertante, Sleeping Beauty, Coppelia, Swan Lake, Sylvia, La Fille mal Gardée, Two Pigeons, Giselle, Invitation, Rendezvous, Blood Wedding, Raymonda, Concerto, Nutcracker, Romeo and Juliet, Concerto No 2 (Ballet Imperial); has created leading roles in Toccata, La Création du Monde, Sinfonietta, Prometheus, Grand Tour; also starred in musical shows. Choreographer and Co-Dir, Canterbury Pilgrims for the Canterbury Fest., 2000; Reader, 600th anniv. of Geoffrey Chaucer, Southwark Cathedral and Westminster Abbey, 2000; Consultant, Images of Dance performing gp, London Studio Centre, 2005–. Founder Mem., Foundn of Purcell Sch., 2004–. Patron: British Ballet Orgn; ISTD Ballet; Chelmsford Ballet Co.; Liverpool Proscenium Youth Ballet Co.; Liverpool Th. Sch. and Coll. Ltd; Tiffany Sch. of Dancing; Hon. Chm., London Children's Ballet, 2003–04; Hon. Patron, London ArtFest. Pres., Radionic Assoc., 2004–; Reiki Master, 1997. Adeline Genée Gold Medal, 1954. *Recreations:* music, theatre-going, charity fundraising.

WELLS, Prof. George Albert, MA, BSc, PhD; Professor of German, Birkbeck College, University of London, 1968–88, now Emeritus; *b* 22 May 1926; *s* of George John and Lilian Maud Wells; *m* 1969, Elisabeth Delhey. *Educ:* University College London (BA, MA German; PhD Philosophy; BSc Geology). Lecturer in German, 1949–64, Reader in German, 1964–68, University Coll. London. Hon. Associate, Rationalist Press Assoc., 1989–2002 (Dir, 1974–89). Mem., Acad. of Humanism, 1983– (Humanist Laureate, 1983). *Publications:* Herder and After, 1959; The Plays of Grillparzer, 1969; The Jesus of the Early Christians, 1971; Did Jesus Exist?, 1975, 2nd edn 1986; Goethe and the Development of Science 1750–1900, 1978; The Historical Evidence for Jesus, 1982; The Origin of Language: aspects of the discussion from Condillac to Wundt, 1987; (ed and contrib.) J. M. Robertson (1856–1933), Liberal, Rationalist and Scholar, 1987; Religious Postures, 1988; Who Was Jesus? a critique of the New Testament record, 1989; Belief and Make Believe: critical reflections on the sources of credulity, 1991; What's in a Name?: reflections on language, magic and religion, 1993; The Jesus Legend, 1996; The Jesus Myth, 1998; The Origin of Language, 1999; Can We Trust the New Testament?: reflections on the reliability of Early Christian Testimony, 2004; Cutting Jesus Down to Size: what higher criticism has achieved and where it leaves Christianity, 2009; articles in Jl of History of Ideas, Jl of English and Germanic Philology, German Life and Letters, Question, Trivium, Wirkendes Wort. *Recreation:* walking. *Address:* 35 St Stephen's Avenue, St Albans, Herts AL3 4AA. *T:* (01727) 851347.

WELLS, Howard James Cowen; Chief Executive Officer, Irish Football Association, since 2005; *b* 9 Jan. 1947; *s* of late Harold Arthur James Wells and Joan Wells (*née* Cowen, later Moore); *m* 1971, Linda Baines; one *s* one *d*. *Educ:* Leeds Univ. (BEd, Cert Ed); Carnegie Coll. (Dip. in Phys. Educn). Head of Boys' Phys. Educn, Brooklands Sch., Leighton Buzzard, 1970–72; Lectr-in-Charge of Phys. Recreation, Hitchin Coll., 1972–74; Dep. Dir, Bisham Abbey Nat. Sports Centre, 1975–81; Operations Manager, 1981–84, Chief Exec., 1984–89, Jubilee Sports Centre, Hong Kong; Chief Executive: Hong Kong Sports Develt Bd, 1989–96; UK Sports Council, 1996–98; Watford Assoc. FC, 1998–99; Ipswich Town FC, 1999–2000; Chm., CCPR, 2001–05. Director: Premier Sport & Media Ltd, 2000–05; Sportsgate Ltd, 2002–05; Chm., Rebben Ltd, 2007–. Mem., Saudi Arabian-UK Memorandum of Understanding Gp in Sport, 1996–. Governor, Ashlyns Sch., Berkhamsted, 1996–2003. *Publication:* Start Living Now, 1979. *Recreations:* Football Association (full qualifying coaching licence, 1973), theatre, travel. *Address:* Irish Football Association, 20 Windsor Avenue, Belfast BT9 6EG. *Clubs:* Oriental, Scribes.

WELLS, Jack Dennis; Executive Director, Aircraft Owners and Pilots Association, since 1991 (Vice-Chairman, 1996–98); Assistant Director, Central Statistical Office, 1979–88; *b* 8 April 1928; *s* of late C. W. Wells and H. M. Wells (*née* Clark); *m* 1st, 1953, Jean Allison; one *s* one *d*; 2nd, 1987, Cynthia Palmer. *Educ:* Hampton Grammar Sch.; Polytechnic of Central London. AIS 1955. Ministry of Fuel and Power, 1947; Royal Air Force, 1947–49; Min. of (Fuel and) Power, 1949–69; Private Secretary to Paymaster General, 1957–59; Chief Statistician, Dept of Economic Affairs, 1969; Min. of Technology, 1969; HM Treasury, 1970; Dept of (Trade and) Industry, 1971–79. Pres., CS Aviation Assoc., 1988–2008. Sec. and Dir, 1997–2002, Vice Pres., 2003–, Gen. Aviation Awareness Council. Past Chairman, Old Hamptonians Assoc. *Publications:* contribs to Long Range Planning, Economic Trends, Statistical News, Review of Income and Wealth, Jl of Banking and Finance, BIEC Yearbook. *Recreations:* cricket, jazz, travel. *Clubs:* Civil Service, United Services, MCC.

WELLS, James Henry; Member (DemU) South Down, Northern Ireland Assembly, since 1998; *b* 27 April 1957; *s* of Samuel Henry Wells and Doreen Wells; *m* 1983, Violet Grace Wallace; one *s* two *d*. *Educ:* Lurgan Coll.; Queen's Univ., Belfast (BA Hons Geog. 1979; DipTP 1981). Mem. (DemU) South Down, NI Assembly, 1982–86; research asst, RSPB, 1987–88; Asst Regl Public Affairs Manager, NI Reg., NT, 1989–98. *Recreations:* birdwatching, hill-walking. *Address:* 12 Bridge Street, Kilkeel, Newry BT34 4AD.

WELLS, (Jennifer) Brigid (Ellen), (Mrs Ian Wells); Chairman Assessor, Civil Service Selection Board, 1989–95; *b* 18 Feb. 1928; *d* of Dr Leonard John Haydon, TD, MA Cantab, MB BCh and Susan Eleanor Haydon (*née* Richmond), actress; *m* 1962, Ian Vane Wells; three *d*. *Educ:* schools in UK, USA, Canada; Edinburgh Univ.; Lady Margaret Hall, Oxford (scholar; BA Mod. Hist.; MA); PG Dip. Couns., Univ. of Brighton, 1995. Commonwealth Relations Office, 1949; UK High Commn, NZ, 1952–54; Private Sec. to Parly Under-Sec. of State, CRO, 1954–56; MAFF, 1956–62; teaching: LCC, 1962–63; Haringey, 1967; Camden Sch. for Girls, 1969–75 (to Head of Dept); Head of Dept, St David's and St Katharine's, Hornsey, 1975–77; Headmistress, Brighton and Hove High Sch., GPDST, 1978–88. Qualified team inspector: OFSTED, 1994; ISI (formerly ARCS), 1995–2003. Chm. designate, W Sussex Ambulance NHS Trust, 1992–93. Member: Local Radio Council, 1980–82; Broadcasting Complaints Commn, 1986–93 (Chm., Jan.–June 1992); Chairman: Educn Cttee, GSA, 1987–88; SE Region, GSA, 1984–86. Project Manager (USA), GAP, 1989–91; Mem., British Atlantic Council, 1988–93; Governor, Woldingham Sch., 1989–97; Comr, Duke of York's Royal Mil. Sch., Dover, 1993–2004. Chm., Friends of GPDST (now GDST), 1991–2003. JP Inner London, 1972–77, Brighton and Hove, 1980–98. *Publications:* (ed jtly) The First Crossing, 2007; articles in learned jls. *Recreations:* gardening, travel. *Address:* Cherry Trees, Bradford Road, Lewes, E Sussex BN7 1RD. *T:* (01273) 477491.

WELLS, Prof. John Christopher, PhD; FBA 1996; FCIL; Professor of Phonetics, University College London, 1988–2006, now Emeritus; *b* 11 March 1939; *s* of Rev. Philip Cuthbert Wells and Winifred May (*née* Peaker); civil partnership 2006, Gabriel Parsons. *Educ:* St John's Sch., Leatherhead; Trinity Coll., Cambridge (BA 1960; MA 1964); University Coll., London (MA 1962; PhD 1971). FCIL (FIL 1982). University College London: Asst Lectr in Phonetics, 1962–65; Lectr, 1965–82; Reader, 1982–88; Head, Dept of Phonetics and Linguistics, 1990–2000. Sec., Internat. Phonetic Assoc., 1973–86 (Pres., 2003–); President: World Esperanto Assoc., 1989–95; Simplified Spelling Soc., 2003–. Mem., Esperanto Acad., 1971–. Editor, Jl Internat. Phonetic Assoc., 1971–87. Contribs to radio and TV programmes. *Publications:* Concise Esperanto and English Dictionary, 1969; (with G. Colson) Practical Phonetics, 1971; Jamaican Pronunciation in London, 1973; (jtly) Jen Nia Mondo 1, 1974 (trans. Italian, Icelandic, Swedish, Finnish); (jtly) Jen Nia Mondo 2, 1977; Lingvistikaj aspektoj de Esperanto, 1978, 2nd edn 1989 (trans. Danish, Korean, German); Accents of English (three vols and cassette), 1982; Geiriadur Esperanto/Kimra vortaro, 1985; (pronunciation editor) Universal Dictionary, 1987; (pronunciation editor) Hutchinson Encyclopedia, 8th edn 1988, and subsequent editions; Longman Pronunciation Dictionary, 1990, 3rd edn 2008; English Intonation: an introduction, 2006; articles in learned jls and collective works. *Recreations:* reading, walking, running. *Address:* 5 Poplar Road, SW19 3JR. *T:* (020) 8542 0302; *e-mail:* j.wells@ucl.ac.uk.

WELLS, (John) Christopher (Durant), FRCA; Consultant in Pain Relief, since 1982; *b* 5 Oct. 1947; *s* of late Colin Durant Wells and of Barbara Gwynneth Wells; *m* 1st, 1971, Sheila Frances Murphy (marr. diss. 2000); two *d*; 2nd, 2004, Susan Lynn Corness. *Educ:* Manchester Grammar Sch.; Liverpool Univ. (MB ChB 1970). LRCP 1970; MRCS 1970; LMCC 1974; FRCA (FFARCS 1978). Consultant in Pain Relief: Guy Pilkington Meml Hosp., St Helens, 1996–; Spire (formerly BUPA N) Cheshire Hosp., Stretton, 2000–. Hon. Consultant: Clatterbridge Hosp., Wirral, 1994–; Pain Res. Inst., Liverpool, 1995–. Dir, Pain Relief Res. Foundn, 1984–95. Director: Pain Matters Ltd, 2000–; Pain Management Co., 2006–. Hon. Mem., British Pharmacological Soc., 2008–. Hon. Fellow of Interventional Pain Practice, 2001. *Publications:* (with C. Woolf) Pain Mechanisms and Management, 1991; (with G. Nown) In Pain?, 1993, 2nd edn as The Pain Relief Handbook, 1996; (with D. Jankowicz) Regional Blockade, 2001; contrib. to British Med. Bull. *Recreations:* curling (for Wales), ski-ing, boating. *Address:* (office) 25 Rodney Street, Liverpool L1 9EH. *T:* (0151) 708 9344, *Fax:* (0151) 707 0609; *e-mail:* cxwells@aol.com.

WELLS, Sir John (Julius), Kt 1984; DL; *b* 30 March 1925; *s* of A. Reginald K. Wells, Marlands, Sampford Arundel, Som; *m* 1948, Lucinda Meath-Baker; two *s* two *d*. *Educ:* Eton; Corpus Christi College, Oxford (MA). War of 1939–45: joined RN as ordinary seaman, 1942; commissioned, 1943, served in submarines until 1946. Contested (C) Smethwick Division, General Election, 1955. MP (C) Maidstone, 1959–87. Chairman: Cons. Party Horticulture Cttee, 1965–71, 1973–87; Horticultural sub-Cttee, Select Cttee on Agriculture, 1968; Parly Waterways Group, 1974–80; Vice-Chm., Cons. Party Agriculture Cttee, 1970; Mem., Mr Speaker's Panel of Chairmen, 1974. Hon. Freeman, Borough of Maidstone, 1979. DL Kent, 1992. Kt Comdr, Order of Civil Merit (Spain), 1972; Comdr, Order of Lion of Finland, 1984. *Recreations:* country pursuits. *Address:* Mere House Barn, Mereworth, Kent ME18 5NB.

WELLS, Malcolm Henry Weston, FCA; Director, Carclo Engineering Group PLC, 1982–97 (Deputy Chairman, 1987–93); *b* 26 July 1927; *s* of late Lt-Comdr Geoffrey Weston Wells; *m* 1952, Elizabeth A. Harland, *d* of late Rt Rev. M. H. Harland, DD; one *s* one *d*. *Educ:* Eton Coll. ACA 1951, FCA 1961. Served RNVR, 1945–48. Peat, Marwick Mitchell, 1948–58; Siebe Gorman and Co. Ltd, 1958–63; Charterhouse Japhet, 1963–80 (Chm., 1973–80); Dir, Charterhouse Gp, 1971–80; Chairman: Charterhouse Petroleum PLC, 1977–82; Granville Business Expansion Funds, 1983–93; BWD Securities, 1987–95; London rep., Bank in Liechtenstein, 1981–85; Director: Bank in Liechtenstein (UK) Ltd, 1985–90; Nat. Home Loans Corp., 1989–93. Mem., CAA, 1974–77. Mem. Solicitors' Disciplinary Tribunal, 1975–81. *Recreation:* sailing. *Address:* Willow Cottage, The Wad, West Wittering, Chichester PO20 8AH.

WELLS, Prof. Peter Neil Temple, PhD, DSc; FMedSci; FRS 2003; FREng; Distinguished Research Professor, Cardiff University, since 2004; Professor of Physics and Engineering in Medicine, Bristol University, 2000–01, now Emeritus; *b* 19 May 1936; *s* of Sydney Parker Temple Wells and Elizabeth Beryl Wells; *m* 1960, Valerie Elizabeth Johnson; three *s* one *d*. *Educ:* Clifton Coll., Bristol; Aston Univ., Birmingham (BSc 1958); Bristol Univ. (MSc 1963; PhD 1966; DSc 1978). FInstP 1970; FIET (FIEE 1978); FREng (FEng 1983). Res. Asst, United Bristol Hosps, 1960–71; Prof. of Medical Physics, Welsh Nat. Sch. of Medicine, 1972–74; Area Physicist, Avon AHA, 1975–82; Chief Physicist, Bristol and Weston HA, subseq. United Bristol Healthcare NHS Trust, 1982–2000. Hon. Prof. in Clinical Radiology, Bristol Univ., 1986–2000. FMedSci 2005. Editor-in-Chief, Ultrasound in Medicine and Biology, 1992–2006. *Publications:* Physical Principles of Ultrasonic Diagnosis, 1969; Biomedical Ultrasonics, 1977. *Recreation:* cooking. *Address:* The Old Meeting House, Silver Street, Weston in Gordano, N Somerset BS20 8QA. *T:* (01275) 848348; *e-mail:* WellsPNT@aol.com.

WELLS, Petrie Bowen; *see* Wells, B.

WELLS, Richard Burton, QPM 1987; Chief Constable of South Yorkshire, 1990–98; Director, E-Quality Leadership, 1998–2007; *b* 10 Aug. 1940; *s* of Walter Percival Wells and Daphne Joan Wells (*née* Harris); *m* 1970, Patricia Ann Smith; one *s* one *d*. *Educ:* Sir Roger Manwood's Grammar Sch., Sandwich; Priory Sch. for Boys, Shrewsbury; St Peter's Coll., Oxford (Open Exhibnr 1959; BA 1962; MA 1965); principal educn, 36 yrs with the police service. Constable, Bow Street, 1962–66; Sergeant, Notting Hill, 1966–68; Special Course, Police Staff Coll., 1966–67; Inspector, Leman St, and Hendon Police Trng Sch., 1968–73; Chief Inspector, Notting Hill, 1973–76; Supt, Hampstead, 1976–79; Chief Supt, Hammersmith and New Scotland Yard, 1979–82; Sen. Command Course, Police Staff Coll., 1981; Comdt, Hendon Training Sch., 1982–83; Dep. Asst Comr, Dir of Public Affairs, New Scotland Yard, 1983–86; Dep. Asst Commissioner, OC NW London, 1986–90. Chairman: Media Adv. Gp, ACPO, 1992–98; Nat. Conf. of Police Press and PROs, 1994–98; Personnel and Trng Cttee, ACPO, 1996–98 (Sec., 1993–96). Sec., Provincial Police Award Selection Cttee, 1990–98. Member: Rathbone Corporate Partnership Gp, 1993–98; Selection Cttee, Fulbright Fellowship in Police Studies, 1991–98; Forensic Psychotherapy Course Adv. Gp, 1990–98; Barnsley City Challenge Bd, 1992–98; Sheffield Common Purpose Adv. Gp and Council, 1993–98. President: Young Enterprise Bd for S Yorks and S Humberside, 1993–98; Deepcar Brass Band, 1992–98; Patron: S Yorks Br., RLSS, 1990–98; Weston Park Hosp. Cancer Care Appeal, 1993–98. President: St Peter's Soc., Oxford Univ., 1989–96; Police Athletics Assoc. Men's Hockey, 1996–98 (Vice Pres., 1989–96). Mem., St John Council for S and W

Yorks, 1990–98. Freeman, City of London, 1992. CCMI (CBIM 1991; Pres., Exeter & Torbay Br., 2004). Chm. Editl Bd, Policing Today, 1994–98. *Publications:* (contrib.) Leaders on Leadership, 1996; (contrib.) Learning Organisations in the Public Sector, 1997; (contrib.) On Work and Leadership, 1999. *Recreations:* walking, painting (watercolour, gloss and emulsion), T'ai Chi, genealogy, local history. *Address:* Bidwell Farm, Upottery, Devon EX14 9PP. *T:* (01404) 861122.

WELLS, Ven. Roderick John; Archdeacon of Stow, 1989–2001, and of Lindsey, 1994–2001, now Archdeacon Emeritus; *b* 17 Nov. 1936; *s* of Leonard Arthur and Dorothy Alice Wells; *m* 1969, Alice Louise Scholl; one *s* two *d*. *Educ:* Durham Univ. (BA Hons Theol.); Hull Univ. (MA). Insurance clerk, 1953–55 and 1957–58. RAF, 1955–57 (Radar Mechanic). Asst Master, Chester Choir School, 1958–59; Asst Curate, St Mary at Lambeth, 1965–68, Priest-in-Charge 1968–71; Rector of Skegness, 1971–78; Team Rector, West Grimsby Team Ministry (Parish of Great and Little Coates with Bradley), 1978–89; Area Dean of Grimsby and Cleethorpes, 1983–89. *Recreations:* music (pianist and organist), walking, geology, golf. *Address:* 9 Hardwick Close, Oakham, Rutland LE15 6FF.

WELLS, Rosemary; writer and illustrator of children's books, since 1968; *b* 29 Jan. 1943; *m* Thomas M. Wells; two *d*. Mem., Soc. of Illustrators, NY. Best Illustrated Book of the Year, New York Times (twice); Horn Best Book of the Year; Notable Book, American Library Assoc. (40 times); numerous other awards. *Publications* include: Noisy Nora, 1973; Benjamin and Tulip, 1973; Timothy Goes to School, 1981; Voyage to the Bunny Planet, 1992; Edward Unready for School, 1995; My Very First Mother Goose, 1996; Bunny Cakes, 1997; Bunny Money, 1997; The Bear Went Over the Mountain, 1998; The Itsy-Bitsy Spider, 1998; Max's Toys, 1998; Max's Bath, 1998; Yoko, 1998; Morris's Disappearing Bag, 1999; Max Cleans Up, 2000; Emily's First 100 Days of School, 2000; Timothy Goes to School, 2000; Mama, Don't Go!, 2001; The School Play, 2001; The Halloween Parade, 2001; Bunny Party, 2001; Ruby's Beauty Shop, 2003; Max Drives Away, 2003; Ruby's Tea for Two, 2003; My Kindergarten, 2004; Bunny Mail, 2004; The Gulps 2007.

WELLS, Prof. Stanley William, CBE 2007; Professor of Shakespeare Studies, and Director of the Shakespeare Institute, University of Birmingham, 1988–97, now Emeritus Professor and Hon. Fellow; General Editor of the Oxford Shakespeare since 1978; *b* 21 May 1930; *s* of Stanley Cecil Wells and Doris Wells; *m* 1975, Susan Elizabeth Hill, *qv*; two *d* (and one *d* decd). *Educ:* Kingston High Sch., Hull; University Coll., London (BA; Fellow, 1995); Shakespeare Inst., Univ. of Birmingham (PhD). Fellow, Shakespeare Inst., 1962–77: Lectr, 1962; Sen. Lectr, 1971; Reader, 1973–77; Hon. Fellow, 1979–88; Head of Shakespeare Dept, OUP, 1978–88. Sen. Res. Fellow, Balliol Coll., Oxford, 1980–88; Vis. Fellow, UCL, 2006–07. Consultant in English, Wroxton Coll., 1964–80. Chm., Membership Cttee, 1991–99, Collections Cttee, 1992–99, RSC; Mem., Exec. Council, 1976–, Exec. (formerly F and GP) Cttee, 1991–, Educn Cttee, Royal Shakespeare Theatre (Gov., 1974–, Vice Chm. of Govs, 1991–2003, Hon. Gov. Emeritus, 2004–); Dir, Royal Shakespeare Theatre Summer Sch., 1971–98. Pres., Shakespeare Club of Stratford-upon-Avon, 1972–73; Chm., Internat. Shakespeare Assoc., 1996–2001, Mem. Exec., 2001– (Vice-Chm., 1991–96); Member: Council, Malone Soc., 1967–90; Exec. Cttee, Shakespeare Birthplace Trust, 1976–78, 1988– (Trustee, 1975–81, 1984–2004; Chm. Trustees, 1991–, Life Trustee, 2003–); Trustee, Rose Theatre, 1991–; Dir, Globe Theatre, 1992– (Trustee, 1998–2004); President: Wolverhampton Shakespeare Soc., 1992–93; Birmingham and Midland Inst. Governor, King Edward VI Grammar Sch. for Boys, Stratford-upon-Avon, 1973–77. Guest lectr, British and overseas univs; Lectures: British Acad. Annual Shakespeare, 1987; Hilda Hulme Meml, 1987; first annual Globe, 1990; Melchiori, Rome, 1991; Walter Clyde Curry Annual Shakespeare, Vanderbilt Univ., 1998. Hon. DLitt: Furman Univ., SC, 1978; Hull, 2005; Durham, 2005; Craiova, 2008; Warwick, 2008; Hon. DPhil Munich, 1999. Walcott Award, LA, 1995. Associate Editor: New Penguin Shakespeare, 1967–; Oxford DNB, 1998–; Editor, Shakespeare Survey, 1980–99; Gen. Editor, Penguin Shakespeare, 2005–. *Publications:* (ed) Thomas Nashe, Selected Writings, 1964; (ed, New Penguin Shakespeare): A Midsummer Night's Dream, 1967, Richard II, 1969, The Comedy of Errors, 1972; Shakespeare, A Reading Guide, 1969 (2nd edn 1970); Literature and Drama, 1970; (ed, Select Bibliographical Guides): Shakespeare, 1973 (new edn 1990), English Drama excluding Shakespeare, 1975; Royal Shakespeare, 1977, 2nd edn 1978; (compiled) Nineteenth-Century Shakespeare Burlesques (5 vols), 1977; Shakespeare: an illustrated dictionary, 1978, 2nd edn 1985, revised as Oxford Dictionary of Shakespeare, 1998; Shakespeare: the writer and his work, 1978; (ed with R. L. Smallwood) Thomas Dekker, The Shoemaker's Holiday, 1979; (with Gary Taylor) Modernizing Shakespeare's Spelling, with three studies in the text of Henry V, 1979; Re-Editing Shakespeare for the Modern Reader, 1984; (ed) Shakespeare's Sonnets, 1985; (ed with Gary Taylor *et al*) The Complete Oxford Shakespeare, 1986; (ed) The Cambridge Companion to Shakespeare Studies, 1986; (with Gary Taylor *et al*) William Shakespeare: a textual companion, 1987; An Oxford Anthology of Shakespeare, 1987; Shakespeare: a dramatic life, 1994, rev. edn as Shakespeare: the poet and his plays, 1997; (ed with E. A. Davies) Shakespeare and the Moving Image, 1994; (ed with R. Warren) Twelfth Night, 1994; (ed) Shakespeare in the Theatre: an anthology of criticism, 1997; (ed) Summerfolk, 1997; William Shakespeare: the quiz book, 1998; (ed) King Lear, 2000; (ed with C. M. S. Alexander) Shakespeare and Race, 2001; (ed with M. de Grazia) The Cambridge Companion to Shakespeare, 2001; (ed with Michael Dobson) The Oxford Companion to Shakespeare, 2001; (ed with C. M. S. Alexander) Shakespeare and Sexuality, 2001; Shakespeare For All Time, 2002; (ed with Lena Orlin) A Shakespeare Study Guide, 2002; Looking for Sex in Shakespeare, 2004; (with Paul Edmondson) Shakespeare's Sonnets, 2004; Shakespeare and Co., 2006; Is It True What They Say About Shakespeare?, 2007; (ed with Alec Cobbe) Shakespeare's 'Lovely Boy': the poet and his patron, 2008; (with P. Edmondson) Coffee with Shakespeare, 2008; contrib. Shak. Survey, Shak. Qly, Shak. Jahrbuch, Theatre Notebook, Stratford-upon-Avon Studies, TLS, etc. *Recreations:* music, theatre, the countryside. *Address:* Longmoor Farmhouse, Ebrington, Glos GL55 6NW. *T:* (01386) 593352; *e-mail:* Stanley.Wells@shakespeare.org.uk.

WELLS, Susan Elizabeth, (Mrs Stanley Wells); *see* Hill, S. E.

WELLS, Sir William (Henry Weston), Kt 1997; FRICS; Chairman: Covenant Healthcare, since 2005; Pure Sports Medicine plc, since 2007; *b* 3 May 1940; *s* of Sir Henry Wells, CBE, and Lady Wells; *m* 1966, Penelope Jean Broadbent; two *s* (and one *s* decd). *Educ:* Radley Coll.; Magdalene Coll., Cambridge (BA). Joined Chesterton, 1959, Partner, 1965–92; Chairman: Land and House Property Gp, 1977 (Dir, 1972–76); Frincon Holdings Ltd, 1977–87; Chesterton plc, 1992–97; Pres., Chesterton Internat. plc, London, 1998–2004. Chairman: ADL plc, 2006–; CMG plc, 2007–; Ashley House plc, 2007–; Director: London Life Assoc., 1984–89; AMP (UK) plc, 1994–2002; Pearl Gp Ltd (formerly Pearl Assurance), 1994–2005; Norwich and Peterborough Bldg Soc., 1994–2003; NFC plc, 1996–2000; AMP (UK) Holdings, 1997–2005; NPI Ltd, 1999–2005; Nat. Provident Life Ltd, 1999–2005; Exel plc, 2000–05; Hillgate (220) Ltd, 2002–; HHG plc, 2003–05; ARC Fund Mgt, 2006–. Mem. Council, NHS Trust Fedn, 1991–93 (Vice Chm., 1992–93). Chairman: Hampstead HA, 1982–90; Royal Free Hampstead NHS Trust, 1990–94; S Thames RHA, 1994–96; S Thames Region, NHS Exec., DoH, 1996–99; NHS Appointments Commn, 2001–07; Commercial Adv. Bd, DoH, 2003–07; Regl Chm., SE, NHS Exec., 1999–2001. Member: Board of Governors, Royal Free Hosp., 1968–74; Camden and Islington AHA, 1974–82; Chm., Special Trustees of Royal Free Hosp., 1979–2001; Member, Council: Royal Free Hosp. Sch. of Medicine, 1977–91; UMDS, Guy's and St Thomas' Hosps, 1994–98; St George's Hosp. Med. Sch., 1994–98; Univ. of Surrey, 1998– (Vice Chm., 1999–2000, Chm., 2001–06); KCL, 1998–2001; City Univ., 1999–2001; Member: Delegacy, King's Coll. Sch. of Medicine and Dentistry, 1994–98; Council and Mgt Cttee, King's Fund, 1995–. Pro-Chancellor, Univ. of Surrey, 2007–. Trustee: Nat. Mus. of Science and Industry, 2003–; Action Med. Res., 2005–. Pres., Royal Free Hosp. Retirement Fellowship, 1994–; Vice President: RCN, 2006– (Hon. Treas., 1988–2005); Attend (formerly Nat. Assoc. of Leagues of Hosp. Friends), 2004– (Hon. Treas., 1992–2004). Mem. Council, Priory of England and the Is, 2000–02. Hon. FRCP 2002. *Recreations:* family, philately, gardening. *Club:* Boodle's.

WELSBY, John Kay, CBE 1990; President, Institute of Logistics and Transport, 1999–2002; *b* 26 May 1938; *s* of late Samuel and Sarah Ellen Welsby; *m* 1964, Jill Carole Richards; one *s* one *d*. *Educ:* Heywood Grammar Sch.; Univ. of Exeter (BA); Univ. of London (MSc). FCILT (FCIT 1990). Govt Economic Service, 1966–81; British Railways Board: Dir, Provincial Services, 1982–84; Managing Dir, Procurement, 1985–87; Mem. Bd, 1987–99; Chief Exec., 1990–98; Chm., 1995–99; Director: London & Continental Rlys Ltd, 1999–2007; LCR Finance plc, 1999–2007. Chm., CIT, 1998–99. Member: Business Adv. Council, Northwestern Univ., Evanston, Ill., 1995–2000. CCMI (CIMgt 1991). Freeman, City of London, 1992; Liveryman, Carmen's Co., 1992. *Publications:* articles on economic and transport matters. *Recreations:* walking, music, swimming. *Address:* Higher Burston Farm, Bow, Crediton, Devon EX17 6LB.

WELSER-MÖST, Franz; Music Director, Cleveland Orchestra, since 2002; General Music Director designate, Vienna State Opera, since 2007; *b* 16 Aug. 1960. Music Dir, LPO, 1990–96; Chief Conductor, 1995–2002, Principal Conductor, 2002–05, Gen. Music Dir, 2005–08, Zürich Opera; conducts Bayerischer Rundfunk, Vienna Philharmonic, Salzburg Fest., Berlin Philharmonic and all major US orchestras; numerous recordings. Awards from USA and UK. *Address:* c/o IMG Artists, The Light Box, 111 Power Road, W4 5PY.

WELSH, Andrew Paton; Member (SNP) Angus, Scottish Parliament, since 1999; *b* 19 April 1944; *s* of William and Agnes Welsh; *m* 1971, Sheena Margaret Cannon; one *d*. *Educ:* Univ. of Glasgow (MA (Hons) History and Politics; DipEd, 1980); Open Univ. (Dip. French 2005). Teacher of History, 1972–74; Lectr in Public Admin and Economics, Dundee Coll. of Commerce, 1979–83; Sen. Lectr in Business and Admin. Studies, Angus Technical Coll., 1983–87. MP (SNP) South Angus, Oct. 1974–1979; contested (SNP) Angus E, 1983; MP (SNP) Angus E, 1987–97, Angus, 1997–2001. SNP Parly Chief Whip, 1978–79, 1987–97; SNP spokesman on: housing, 1974–78; self employed affairs and small businesses, 1975–79, 1987–2001; agriculture, 1976–79, 1987–2001; local govt, 1987–97; local govt, housing and educn, 1997–2001. Member: Scottish Affairs Select Cttee, 1992–2001; Speaker's Panel of Chairmen, 1997–2001. Scottish Parliament: Member: Corporate Body, 1999–2006; Commn of Accounts, 2000–07; Audit Cttee, 2007– (Convener, 1999–2003; Dep. Convener, 2004–07); Dep. Convener, Local Govt and Transport Cttee, 2003–04; Convener, Finance Cttee, 2007–. SNP Exec. Vice Chm. for Admin, 1979–87; SNP Vice-Pres., 1987–2004. Mem., Angus District Council, 1984–87; Provost of Angus, 1984–87. *Recreations:* music, horse riding, languages. *Address:* 31 Market Place, Arbroath, Angus DD11 1HR. *T:* (01241) 439369, *Fax:* (01241) 871561. *Club:* Glasgow University Union.

WELSH, Prof. Dominic; *see* Welsh, J. A. D.

WELSH, Frank Reeson, FRHistS; writer; Director, Grindlays Bank, 1971–85; *b* 16 Aug. 1931; *s* of F. C. Welsh and D. M. Welsh; *m* 1954, Agnes Cowley; two *s* two *d*. *Educ:* Gateshead and Blaydon Grammar Schools; Magdalene Coll., Cambridge (schol.; MA). With John Lewis Partnership, 1954–58; CAS Group, 1958–64; Man. Dir, William Brandt's Sons & Co. Ltd, 1965–72; Chairman: Hadfields Ltd, 1967–79; Jensen Motors Ltd, 1968–72; Cox & Kings, 1972–76; Dir, Henry Ansbacher & Co., 1976–82. Member: British Waterways Board, 1975–81; Gen. Adv. Council, IBA, 1976–80; Royal Commn on Nat. Health Service, 1976–79; Health Educn Council, 1978–80. Dir, Trireme Trust, 1983–. Vis. Lectr and Alcoa Schol., Graduate Sch. of Business Studies, Univ. of Tennessee, Knoxville, 1979–85. CCMI. *Publications:* The Profit of the State, 1982; (contrib.) Judging People, 1982; The Afflicted State, 1983; First Blood, 1985; (with George Ridley) Bend'Or, Duke of Westminster, 1985; Uneasy City, 1986; Building the Trireme, 1988; Companion Guide to the Lake District, 1989, 2nd edn 1997; Hong Kong: a history (US edn as A Borrowed Place), 1993, 2nd edn 1997; A History of South Africa, 1998; Dangerous Deceits, 1999; The Four Nations, 2002; Great Southern Land: a new history of Australia, 2004; (jtly) Victoria's Empire, 2007; The Battle for Christendom, 2008. *Recreation:* sailing. *Address:* 33 rue St Bartélémy, 16500 Confolens, France. *Club:* Oxford and Cambridge.

WELSH, Ian; Director, UK Services Rehab Group, since 2007; *b* 23 Nov. 1953; *m* 1977, Elizabeth McAndrew; two *s*. *Educ:* Prestwick Acad.; Ayr Acad.; Glasgow Univ. (MA Hons Eng. Lit. and Hist.); Jordanhill Coll. (Dip. in Educnl Mgt); Open Univ. (MA). Former professional football player, Kilmarnock FC; English teacher: James Hamilton Acad., Kilmarnock, 1977–80; Auchinleck Acad., 1980–97 (Dep. Head Teacher, 1992–97); Dir of Human Resources and Public Affairs, Prestwick Internat. Airport, 1997; Chief Executive: Kilmarnock FC, 1997–99 and 2000–01; Momentum Scotland, 2001–07. Member (Lab): Kyle and Carrick Council, 1984–95 (Leader, 1990–92); S Ayrshire Council, 1995–99 (Leader); MSP (Lab) Ayr, 1999. Chairman: Scottish Adv. Cttee to Voluntary Sector NTO, 2002–05; Ayrshire Business in the Community, 2007–; Ayr United Football Acad., 2007–; Member of Board: Scottish Enterprise, Ayrshire, 2002–07; Irvine Bay Regeneration Co., 2007–. Director: Borderline Theatre Co., 1990– (Chm., 2002–07); Prestwick Internat. Airport, 1992–97. Mem. Ct, Univ. of W Scotland, 2007–. FRSA. *Address:* 35 Ayr Road, Prestwick, Ayrshire KA9 1SY.

WELSH, Prof. (James Anthony) Dominic, DPhil; Professor of Mathematics, 1992–2005, and Chairman of Mathematics, 1996–2001, Oxford University; Fellow of Merton College, Oxford, 1966–2005, now Emeritus; *b* 29 Aug. 1938; *s* of late James Welsh and Teresa Welsh (*née* O'Callaghan); *m* 1966, Bridget Elizabeth Pratt; two *s* (and one *s* decd). *Educ:* Bishop Gore Grammar Sch., Swansea; Merton Coll., Oxford (MA DPhil); Carnegie Mellon Univ. (Fulbright Scholar). Bell Telephone Labs, Murray Hill, 1961; Oxford University: Jun. Lectr, Mathematical Inst., 1963–66; Tutor in Maths, Merton Coll., 1966–90; Reader in Maths, 1990–92. Vis. appts, Univs of Michigan, Waterloo, Calgary, Stockholm, North Carolina; John von Neumann Prof., Univ. of Bonn, 1990–91; Vis. Oxford Fellow, Univ. of Canterbury, NZ, 2005; Res. Visitor, Centre de Recerca Matemàtica, Barcelona, 2006–07. Chm., British Combinatorial Cttee,

1983–87. Hon. Dr Math. Waterloo, 2006. *Publications:* (ed) Combinatorial Mathematics and its Applications, 1971; (ed jtly) Combinatorics, 1973; Matroid Theory, 1976; (with G. R. Grimmett) Probability: an introduction, 1986; Codes and Cryptography, 1988, German edn 1991, Japanese edn 2004; (ed jtly) Disorder in Physical Systems, 1990; Complexity: knots, colourings and counting, 1993; (with J. Talbot) Complexity and Cryptography: an introduction, 2006; articles in math. jls. *Recreations:* most sports, walking. *Address:* Merton College, Oxford OX1 4JD. *T:* (01865) 276310.

WELSH, Michael Collins; *b* 23 Nov. 1926; *s* of Danny and Winnie Welsh; *m* 1950, Brenda Nicholson; two *s*. *Educ:* Sheffield Univ. (Dept of Extramural Studies, Day Release Course, three years); Ruskin Coll., Oxford. Miner from age of 14 years. Member, Doncaster Local Authority, 1962–69. MP (Lab) Don Valley, 1979–83, Doncaster North, 1983–92. *Club:* Carcroft Village Workingmen's (Carcroft, near Doncaster).

WELSH, Michael John; Member (C) Lancashire County Council, since 1997 (Leader, Conservative Group, 2003–08); *b* 22 May 1942; *s* of Comdr David Welsh, RN, and Una Mary (*née* Willmore); *m* 1963, Jennifer Caroline Pollitt; one *s* one *d*. *Educ:* Dover Coll.; Lincoln Coll., Oxford (BA (Hons) Jurisprudence). Proprietors of Hays Wharf Ltd, 1963–69; Levi Strauss & Co. Europe Ltd, 1969–79 (Dir of Market Development, 1976). Chm., Chorley and S Ribble NHS Trust, 1994–98. MEP (C) Lancashire Central, 1979–94; contested (C) Lancashire Central, Eur. Parly elecns, 1994; Chm., Cttee for Social Affairs and Employment, Eur. Parlt, 1984–87. Chm., Positive Europe Gp, 1988–94; Chief Exec., Action Centre for Europe Ltd, 1995–2004. *Recreations:* sailing, rough walking. *Address:* Watercrook, 181 Town Lane, Whittle le Woods, Chorley, Lancs PR6 8AG. *T:* (01257) 276992. *Club:* Carlton.

WELSH, Peter, OBE 2001; CEng, FIET; Executive Director, United Kingdom Atomic Energy Authority (Dounreay Division), 1998–2003; *b* 25 March 1941; *s* of late Robert Welsh and Florence Welsh (*née* Gollege; later Armory); *m* 1964, Margaret Philips; two *s*. *Educ:* Sunderland Poly. (BSc 1st Cl. Hons Electrical Engrg 1966). CEng 1966; FIET (FIEE 2000). Manager: Dungeness A Power Station, CEGB, 1987–91; Hinkley Point A and B Power Station, Nuclear Electric Plc, 1991–95; Dir, Business Improvement, Magnox Electric Plc, 1995–98. Chm., Somerset TEC, 1994–96; Dir, Somerset Careers Bd, 1994–96; non-exec. Director: Trng Standards Council, 1998–2001; Sector Skills Develt Agency, 2002–06. Mem. Council, SW Reg., CBI, 1998–2001. Gov., Somerset Coll. of Art and Technol., 1995–98. *Recreations:* walking, ski-ing, golf, travel.

WELSH, Maj.-Gen. Peter Miles, OBE 1983; MC 1967; President, Regular Commissions Board, 1983–85; *b* 23 Dec. 1930; *s* of William Miles Moss O'Donnel Welsh and Mary Edith Margaret Gertrude Louise Welsh (*née* Hearn); *m* 1974, June Patricia McCausland (*née* Macadam); two step *s* one step *d*. *Educ:* Winchester College; RMA Sandhurst. Commissioned, KRRC, 1951; Kenya Regt, 1958–60; student, Staff Coll., 1961; Malaya and Borneo, 1965–66; Royal Green Jackets, 1966; JSSC, 1967; Instructor, Staff Coll., 1968–71; CO 2 RGJ, 1971–73; Comd 5 Inf. Bde, 1974–76; RCDS, 1977; HQ BAOR, 1978–80; Brig., Light Div., 1980–83. *Recreations:* shooting, fishing, vegetable gardening, cooking, golf. *Clubs:* MCC, Free Foresters, I Zingari, Jesters; Berks Golf.

WELTEKE, Ernst; President, Deutsche Bundesbank, 1999–2004; *b* Korbach, 21 Aug. 1942. *Educ:* Univ. of Marburg; Univ. of Frankfurt am Main (grad. in econs). Apprentice agricl machine mechanic, 1959–62; Office of Prime Minister of Hesse, 1972–74; MP (SDP) Hesse, 1974–95; Minister of Econs, Transport and Technol., 1991–94; Minister of Finance, 1994–95; Pres., Land Central Bank, Hesse, and Mem., Central Bank Council, Deutsche Bundesbank, 1995–99. Chm., Parly Gp, SDP, 1984–Apr. 1987 and Feb. 1988–1991. Mem. Governing Council, European Central Bank, 1999–2004.

WEMYSS, 12th Earl of *cr* 1633, **AND MARCH,** 8th Earl of *cr* 1697; **Francis David Charteris,** KT 1966; Lord Wemyss of Elcho, 1628; Lord Elcho and Methil, 1633; Viscount Peebles, Baron Douglas of Neidpath, Lyne and Munard, 1697; Baron Wemyss of Wemyss (UK), 1821; President, The National Trust for Scotland, 1967–91, now President Emeritus (Chairman of Council, 1946–69); Lord Clerk Register of Scotland and Keeper of the Signet, 1974–2007; *b* 19 Jan. 1912; *s* of late Lord Elcho (killed in action, 1916) and Lady Violet Manners (she *m* 2nd, 1921, Guy Holford Benson (decd), and *d* 1971), 2nd *d* of 8th Duke of Rutland; *S* grandfather, 1937; *m* 1st, 1940, Mavis Lynette Gordon, BA (*d* 1988), *er d* of late E. E. Murray, Hermanus, Cape Province; one *s* one *d* (and one *s* and one *d* decd); 2nd, 1995, Shelagh Kathleen Kennedy, *d* of George Ernest Thrift, Vancouver. *Educ:* Eton; Balliol College, Oxford. Assistant District Commissioner, Basutoland, 1937–44. Served with Basuto Troops in Middle East, 1941–44. Lieut, Queen's Body Guard for Scotland, Royal Company of Archers; Lord High Comr to Gen. Assembly of Church of Scotland, 1959, 1960, 1977; Chairman: Scottish Cttee, Marie Curie Meml Foundn, 1952–86; Royal Commn on Ancient and Historical Monuments, Scotland, 1949–84; Scottish Churches Council, 1964–71; Hon. Pres., The Thistle Foundn; Mem., Central Cttee, WCC, 1961–75; Mem., Royal Commn on Historical Manuscripts, 1975–85. Consultant, Wemyss and March Estates Management Co. Ltd; formerly Director: Standard Life Assurance Co. Ltd; Scottish Television Ltd. Lord-Lieut, E Lothian, 1967–87. Hon. LLD St Andrews, 1953; DUniv Edinburgh, 1983. *Heir: s* Lord Neidpath, *qv*. *Address:* Gosford House, Longniddry, East Lothian EH32 0PX. *Club:* New (Edinburgh).

See also D. H. Benson.

WEMYSS, Rear-Adm. Martin La Touche, CB 1981; *b* 5 Dec. 1927; *s* of late Comdr David Edward Gillespie Wemyss, DSO, DSC, RN, and Edith Mary Digges La Touche; *m* 1st, 1951, Ann Hall (marr. diss. 1973); one *s* one *d*; 2nd, 1973, Elizabeth Loveday Alexander; one *s* one *d*. *Educ:* Shrewsbury School. CO HMS Sentinel, 1956–57; Naval Intell. Div., 1957–59; CO HMS Alliance, 1959–60; CO Commanding Officers' Qualifying Course, 1961–63; Naval Staff, 1963–65; CO HMS Cleopatra, 1965–67; Naval Asst to First Sea Lord, 1967–70; CO 3rd Submarine Sqdn, 1970–73; CO HMS Norfolk, 1973–74; Dir of Naval Warfare, 1974–76; Rear-Adm., 1977; Flag Officer, Second Flotilla, 1977–78; Asst Chief of Naval Staff (Ops), 1979–81. Clerk to Brewers' Co., 1981–91. *Recreation:* gardening. *Address:* The Old Post House, Emberton, near Olney, Bucks MK46 5BX. *T:* (01234) 713838. *Clubs:* White's, Army and Navy.

WEN, Eric Lewis; lecturer, freelance writer and music producer; Chairman of Musical Studies, Curtis Institute of Music, Philadelphia, since 2002; *b* 18 May 1953; *s* of Adam and Mimi Wen; *m* 1999, Rachel Stadlen; one *s*, and two *d* from former marr. *Educ:* Columbia Univ. (BA); Yale Univ. (MPhil); Cambridge Univ. Lecturer: Guildhall Sch. of Music, 1978–84; Goldsmiths' Coll., Univ. of London, 1980–84; Mannes Coll. of Music, NY, 1984–86; Editor: The Strad, 1986–89; The Musical Times, 1988–90; Man. Dir, Biddulph Recordings, 1990–99; Lectr, Curtis Inst. of Music, 1999–2002. *Publications:* (contrib.) Schenker Studies, 1989; (contrib.) Trends in Schenkerian Research, 1990; (ed) The Fritz Kreisler Collection, 1990; (contrib.) Cambridge Companion to the Violin, 1992; (ed) The Heifetz Collection, 1995; (contrib.) Schenker Studies 2, 1999; (ed) The Joseph Szigeti Collection, 2000; (ed) Hebrew Melodies, 2001; (ed) Masterpieces for Violin, 2005; (contrib.) Structure and Meaning in Tonal Music, 2006; (contrib.) Essays from the Third Schenker Symposium, 2006; (ed) Masterworks for Violin, 2006; contrib. various music jls. *Recreations:* music, chess, cooking.

WENBAN, Sarah Ann; *see* Thane, S. A.

WENBAN-SMITH, (William) Nigel, CMG 1991; HM Diplomatic Service, retired; Secretary General, Commonwealth Magistrates' and Judges' Association, 1993–94; *b* 1 Sept. 1936; *s* of William Wenban-Smith, CMG, CBE; *m* 1st, 1961, Charlotte Chapman-Andrews (marr. diss 1975; she *m* 2nd, Sir Peter Evelyn Leslie); two *s* two *d*; 2nd, 1976, Charlotte Susanna Rycroft (*d* 1990); two *s*; 3rd, 1993, Frances Catharine Barlow; two step *d*. *Educ:* King's Sch., Canterbury; King's Coll., Cambridge (BA); MA Buckingham 2000. National Service, RN. Plebiscite Supervisory Officer, Southern Cameroons, 1960–61; Asst Principal, CRO, 1961–65 (Private Sec. to Parly Under Sec., 1963–64); Second Sec., Leopoldville, 1965–67; First Sec. and (1968) Head of Chancery, Kampala, 1967–70; FCO, 1970–74; Dublin, 1975; Commercial Sec., 1976–78, Commercial Counsellor, 1978–80, Brussels; on loan to Cabinet Office, 1980–82; Hd of E Africa Dept and Comr, British Indian Ocean Territory, FCO, 1982–85; National Defence Coll. of Canada, 1985–86; Deputy High Comr, Ottawa, 1986–89; High Comr, Malaŵi, 1990–93. Chm., Friends of the Chagos Assoc., 1996–2002. *Recreations:* walking, gardening. *Address:* Highbank, The Quarry, Brockhampton, Cheltenham GL54 5XL.

WENDT, Henry, Hon. CBE 1995; Chairman: SmithKline Beecham, 1989–94; Global Health Care Partners, DLJ Merchant Banking, 1997–2002; Arrail Dental (China) Ltd, since 1999; *b* 19 July 1933; *s* of Henry Wendt and Rachel L. (*née* Wood); *m* 1956, Holly Peterson; one *s* one *d*. *Educ:* Princeton Univ. (AB 1955). Joined SmithKline & French Labs, 1955: various positions in Internat. Div.; Pres., 1976–82; Chief Exec. Officer, 1982–87; Chm., 1987–89 (merger of SmithKline Beckman and Beecham, 1989). Director: Arjo Wiggins Appleton plc, 1990–92; Cambridge Labs plc, 1996–; West Marine Inc., 1997–2001; Wilson Greatbatch Ltd, 1997–2003; Computerised Med. Systems, 1997–; Charles River Labs, 2000–01; Prometheus Labs, 2000–03; Focus Technologies Inc., 2000–03. Chairman: Healdsburg Performing Arts Theatre, 2000–03; Sonoma County Community Foundn, 2001–04. Trustee: Philadelphia Museum of Art, 1979–94; Amer. Enterprises Inst., 1987–96. Order of the Rising Sun with Gold and Silver Star (Japan), 1994. *Publication:* Global Embrace, 1993. *Recreations:* sailing, flyfishing, tennis, viticulture. *Address:* 560 Warbass Way, Friday Harbor, WA 98250, USA. *Clubs:* Flyfishers'; New York Yacht (NYC).

WENDT, Robin Glover, CBE 1996; DL; Vice-Chairman, Action for Children (formerly NCH), since 2000; *b* 7 Jan. 1941; *er s* of late William Romilly Wendt and Doris May (*née* Glover), Preston, Lancs; *m* 1965, Prudence Ann Dalby; two *d*. *Educ:* Hutton GS, Preston; Wadham Coll., Oxford Univ. (BA 1962; MA 1992). Asst Principal 1962, Principal 1966, Min. of Pensions and Nat. Insurance; Principal Private Sec. to Sec. of State for Social Services, 1970; Asst Sec., DHSS, 1972; Dep. Sec., 1975, Chief Exec., 1979–89, Cheshire CC; Clerk of Cheshire Lieutenancy, 1979–90; Sec., ACC, 1989–97; Chief Exec., Nat. Assoc. of Local Councils, 1997–99. Member: Social Security Adv. Cttee, 1982–2002; PCFC, 1989–93; Council, RIPA, 1989–92; Council for Charitable Support, 1991–97; DoH Wider Health Working Gp, 1991–97; Adv. Bd, Fire Service Coll., 1992–96; Citizenship Foundn Adv. Council, 1993–97; Joseph Rowntree Foundn Income and Wealth Inquiry, 1993–95; Royal Commn on Long-Term Care of the Elderly, 1997–99; Bd, FAS, 1997–99; Council, Action for Children (formerly NCH Action for Children, then NCH), 1997–; Bd, YMCA Chester, 1997–; Benefits Agency Standards Cttee, 1999–2002; Joseph Rowntree Foundn Adv. Gp on Long-Term Care of the Elderly, 2003–06; NCH/Nat. Family and Parenting Inst./Joseph Rowntree Foundn Family Commn, 2005–06. Non-exec. Dir, NIMTECH, 2000–. Mem., S Cheshire HA, 2001–02; Vice-Chm., Cheshire and Merseyside Strategic HA, 2002–04. Chairman: Cheshire Rural Forum, 2000–04; Chester in Partnership, 2001–06. Mem. Exec., Chester Music Soc., 1999–; Chairman: Chester Summer Music Fest., 2001–08; Chester Fests, 2003–06; Dir, Chester Performing Arts Centre Ltd, 2006–. Pres., Cheshire Assoc. of Town and Parish Councils, 1997–2004. Sec., NW Says No Campaign, 2003–04. Trustee, Indep. Living Funds, 1993–2000. DL Cheshire, 1990. Contributor (as Ted Browning), Tribune, 1999–2004. *Publications:* various articles and reviews on public service issues; occasional music reviews. *Recreations:* music, swimming, following sport, travel. *Address:* 28 Church Lane, Upton, Chester CH2 1DJ. *T:* (01244) 382786; *e-mail:* robin.wendt@tstnet.co.uk.

WENGER, Arsène, Hon. OBE 2003; Chevalier, Légion d'Honneur, 2002; Manager, Arsenal Football Club, since 1996; *b* 22 Oct. 1949. *Educ:* Strasbourg Univ. (BEc 1974). Amateur football player, Mutzig, then Mulhouse, 1969–78; professional football player, Strasbourg, 1978–83 (Coach, Youth team, 1981–83); Player/Coach, Cannes, 1983; Manager: AS Nancy, 1984–87; AS Monaco, 1987–94; Nagoya Grampus Eight, Japan, 1995–96. Arsenal won Premier League and FA Cup, 1998, 2002, FA Cup, 2003, 2005, Premier League, 2004; Champions League finalists, 2006. *Address:* Arsenal Football Club, Highbury House, 75 Drayton Park, N5 1BU.

WENGER, (John) Patrick; Chairman, Stoke Further Education College; *b* 23 Nov. 1943; *s* of Richard John Wenger and Hilda Wenger (*née* Hardy); *m* 1969, Sheila Ann Baddeley; one *s* one *d*. *Educ:* Repton; N Staffs Tech. Coll. (Pottery Managers Dip.; Ceramic Technicians Dip.); Harvard (AMP). Allied English Potteries: Mgt trainee, 1960–65; works manager, 1966; PA to Man. Dir, 1967–68; Gen. Works Manager, 1969–70; Asst Chief Exec., Paragon Div., 1971; Exec. i/c Paragon, following merger with Royal Doulton, 1972–84; Chief Executive: Hotel and Airlines Div., 1985–86; Ext. Sales Div., 1986–89; Internat. Sales Dir, 1989–93; Chief Operating Officer (following demerger from Pearson PLC), 1993–97; Chief Exec., Royal Doulton plc, 1997–99. Retired due to serious car accident whilst in Australia in business. Dir, North Staffs Risk Capital Fund plc. Chm., Newcastle Sch. *Recreations:* sailing, golf, tennis, hockey, cricket, travel. *Address:* Foxley, Mill Lane, Standon, near Eccleshall, Staffs ST21 6RP. *Club:* British Pottery Manufacturers (Stoke-on-Trent).

WENNER, Michael Alfred; HM Diplomatic Service, retired; President, Wenner Communications Co. (formerly Wenner Trading Co.), 1982–2002; *b* 17 March 1921; *s* of Alfred E. Wenner and of Simone Roussel; *m* 1st, 1950, Gunilla Cecilia Ståhle (*d* 1986), *d* of Envoyé Nils K. Ståhle, CBE, and Birgit Olsson; four *s*; 2nd, 1990, Holly (Raven) Adrianne Johnson, *d* of Adrian W. Johnson and Ophelia A. Matley. *Educ:* Stonyhurst; Oriel College, Oxford (Scholar). Served E Yorks Regt, 1940; Lancs Fusiliers and 151 Parachute Bn, India, 1941–42; 156 Bn, N Africa, 1943; No 9 Commando, Italy and Greece, 1944–45. Entered HM Foreign Service, 1947; 3rd Sec., Stockholm, 1948–51; 2nd Sec., Washington, 1951–53; Foreign Office, 1953–55; 1st Sec., Tel Aviv, 1956–59; Head of Chancery, La Paz, 1959–61, and at Vienna, 1961–63; Inspector of Diplomatic Establishments, 1964–67; Ambassador to El Salvador, 1967–70. Commercial Advr, Consulate-Gen. of Switzerland in Houston, 1974–91. Hon. Mem., Consular Corps of Houston, 1992–. *Publications:* Advances in Controlled Droplet Application, Agrichemical Age, 1979; So It Was (memoirs), 1993; Telephone Tales, 1996. *Recreations:* fly-fishing, old maps, choral singing, elocution. *Address:* The Old Coach House, 32 Bostock Road,

Broadbottom, Hyde, Cheshire SK14 6AH; Laythams Farm, Slaidburn, Clitheroe, Lancs BB7 3AJ. *T:* (01200) 446677.

WENSLEY, Prof. (John) Robin (Clifton), PhD; Director, Advanced Institute of Management Research, since 2004; Professor of Policy and Marketing, University of Warwick, since 1986; *b* 26 Oct. 1944; *s* of George Leonard Wensley and Jeannette Marion Wensley; *m* 1970, Susan Patricia Horner; one *s* two *d. Educ:* Perse Sch., Cambridge; Queens' Coll., Cambridge (BA 1966); London Business Sch. (MSc; PhD). Lectr, then Sen. Lectr, London Business Sch., 1974–85; University of Warwick: Chm., Warwick Business Sch., 1989–94; Chair, Faculty of Soc. Studies, 1993–99; Dep. Dean, Warwick Business Sch., 2001–04. Chm. Council, Tavistock Inst. of Human Relns, 1998–2003; Council Mem., ESRC, 2001–04. Member: Warwickshire Wildlife Trust, 1997–; Sustrans, 1997–. *Publications:* Strategic Marketing: planning, implementation and control, 1983; Interface of Marketing and Strategy, 1990; Rethinking Marketing, 1994; Handbook of Marketing, 2002. *Recreations:* walking, DIY, reading, cycling. *Address:* 147 Leam Terrace, Leamington Spa, CV31 1DF. *T:* (01926) 425022, *Fax:* 0870 734 3001; *e-mail:* robin.wensley@warwick.ac.uk.

WENT, David; Chairman, Irish Times Ltd, since 2007; *b* 25 March 1947; *s* of Arthur Edward James Went and Phyllis (*née* Howell); *m* 1972, Mary Christine Milligan; one *s* one *d. Educ:* High Sch., Dublin; Trinity Coll., Dublin (BA Mod; LLB). Called to the Bar, King's Inns, Dublin, 1970. Graduate Trainee, Citibank, Dublin, 1970; Gen. Manager, Citibank, Jeddah, 1975–76; Dir 1976, Chief Exec. 1982, Ulster Investment Bank; Ulster Bank: Dep. Chief Exec., 1987; Chief Exec., 1988–94; Chief Exec., Coutts Gp, 1994–97; Man. Dir, Irish Life, 1998, Gp Chief Exec., 1999–2007, Irish Life & Permanent PLC. Non-exec. Dir, Vhi Healthcare, 2007–; Goldman Sachs Bank (Europe) Ltd, 2007–. Chm., NI Bankers' Assoc., 1988–89; President: Irish Bankers' Fedn, 1991–92; Inst. of Bankers in Ireland, 1993–94. Chm., Trinity Foundn, 2002–. *Recreations:* tennis, reading. *Address:* Irish Times Building, PO Box 74, 24–28 Tara Street, Dublin 2, Ireland. *Clubs:* Kildare Street and University (Dublin); Fitzwilliam Lawn Tennis; Killiney Golf; Royal North of Ireland Yacht.

WENT, Rt Rev. John Stewart; *see* Tewkesbury, Bishop Suffragan of.

WENTWORTH, Stephen, CB 2003; Fisheries Director, Department for Environment, Food and Rural Affairs (formerly Fisheries Secretary, Ministry of Agriculture, Fisheries and Food), 1993–2003; *b* 23 Aug. 1943; *s* of Ronald Wentworth, OBE and Elizabeth Mary Wentworth (*née* Collins); *m* 1970, Katharine Laura Hopkinson; three *d. Educ:* King's College Sch., Wimbledon; Merton Coll., Oxford (MA, MSc). Joined Ministry of Agriculture, Fisheries and Food, 1967; seconded to CSSB, 1974, and to FCO, as First Sec., UK Perm. Repn to EEC, Brussels, 1976; Head of Beef Div., 1978; seconded to Cabinet Office, 1980; Head of: Milk Div., 1982; European Communities Div., 1985; Under-Sec. and Head of Meat Gp, 1986; Head of Livestock Products Gp, 1989; Head of EC and External Trade Policy Gp, 1991. *Recreations:* Yorkshire dales, William Shakespeare, Japan.

WERNER, Ronald Louis, AM 1980; MSc, PhD; President, New South Wales Institute of Technology, 1974–86; Emeritus Professor, University of Technology Sydney, since 1988; *b* 12 Sept. 1924; *s* of Frank Werner and Olive Maude Werner; *m* 1948, Valerie Irene (*née* Bean) (*d* 2002); two *s* one *d. Educ:* Univ. of New South Wales (BSc (1st Cl. Hons; Univ. Medal); MSc; PhD). FRACI. Sen. Lectr, 1954–60, Associate Prof., 1961–67, Head of Dept of Phys. Chemistry, 1964–67, Univ. of New South Wales; Dep. Dir, 1967–68, Director, 1968–73, NSW Inst. of Technology. Chm., NSW Advanced Educn Bd, 1969–71; Trustee, Mus. of Applied Arts and Scis, 1973–86 (Pres., Bd of Trustees, 1976–84); Chairman: Conf. of Dirs of Central Insts of Technology, 1975; ACDP, 1982–83; Member: Science and Industry Forum, Aust. Acad. of Science, 1971–76; Council for Tech. and Further Educn, 1970–85; Hong Kong UPGC, 1972–90; NSW Bicentennial Exhibition Cttee, 1985–88; Adv. Council, Univ. of Western Sydney, 1986–88; Governor, College of Law, 1972–76. Director: NRMA Ltd, 1977–95; NRMA Life Ltd, 1985–95; NRMA Travel Ltd, 1986–95; Open Road Publishing Co., 1986–95; NRMA Sales & Service, 1986–95; NRMA Finance Ltd, 1992–95. Councillor, Nat. Roads and Motorists Assoc., 1977–95. DUniv Univ. of Tech. Sydney, 1988. *Publications:* numerous papers in scientific jls. *Recreations:* yachting, golf. *Address:* 13 Capri Close, Clareville, NSW 2107, Australia.

WERNICK, Jane Melville, CEng, FIStructE; Director, Jane Wernick Associates Ltd, since 1998; *b* 21 April 1954; *d* of Doreen and Irving Wernick. *Educ:* Christchurch Primary Sch., Hampstead; Haberdashers' Aske's Sch., Acton; Southampton Univ. (BSc Civil Engrg). CEng 1985; MICE 1989; FIStructE 1993. Grad. engr, Ove Arup & Partners, 1976–80; project engr, Birdair Structures Inc., 1980–81; Ove Arup & Partners, 1981–98: Associate, 1984; Principal i/c LA Office, 1986–89; Associate Dir, London Office, 1989–98. Visiting Professor: Harvard Univ. Grad. Sch. of Design, 1995; Architecture Dept, Oxford Brookes Univ., 1999–; Bedford Vis. Prof., Rensselaer Poly. Inst., 1998; RAEng Vis. Prof. of Design, Civil Engrg Dept, Univ. of Southampton, 2001–. Diploma Unit Master, AA, 1998–2003. Mem., Design Rev. Panel, CABE, 2001–06. Liveryman, Co. of Engrs, 2000–. F.R.S.A. Hon. FRIBA 2006. *Publications:* (contrib.) Lunar Bases and Space Activities of the 21st Century, Vol. 2, 1988; (contrib.) Arups on Engineering, 1996; contribs to Structural Engr, Architectural Research Qly. *Recreations:* making music, making art, making things, gardening, reading, socializing, travelling, snorkelling. *Address:* c/o Jane Wernick Associates Ltd, Unit 10D, Printing House Yard, Hackney Road, E2 7PR. *T:* (020) 7749 1066.

WERRETT, Dr David John; Chief Executive, Forensic Science Service, since 2001; *b* 24 Oct. 1949; *s* of Kenneth John Werrett and Heather Victoria Werrett; *m* 2004, Rebecca Lesley; one *s* one *d*, and one step *s* one step *d. Educ:* Univ. of Birmingham (BSc; PhD 1974). With Forensic Sci. Service, 1974– (Mem. Bd, 1986–). MInstD 2002. *Publications:* contrib. numerous scientific papers to jls, incl. Nature. *Recreations:* good food, good wine, good company, preferably on a sail boat. *Address:* Forensic Science Service, Trident Court, 2920 Solihull Parkway, Birmingham Business Park, Solihull B37 7YN. *T:* (0121) 329 8594, *Fax:* (0121) 329 8405; *e-mail:* Dave.Werrett@fss.pnn.police.uk. *Club:* Lyme Regis Yacht.

WESKER, Sir Arnold, Kt 2006; FRSL 1985; playwright; director; Founder Director of Centre Fortytwo, 1961 (dissolved 1970); Chairman, British Centre of International Theatre Institute, 1978–82; President, International Playwrights' Committee, 1979–83; *b* 24 May 1932; *s* of Joseph Wesker and Leah Perlmutter; *m* 1958, Dusty Bicker; two *s* two *d. Educ:* Upton House School, Hackney. Furniture Maker's Apprentice, Carpenter's Mate, 1948; Bookseller's Asst, 1949 and 1952; Royal Air Force, 1950–52; Plumber's Mate, 1952; Farm Labourer, Seed Sorter, 1953; Kitchen Porter, 1953–54; Pastry Cook, 1954–58. Former Mem., Youth Service Council. Hon. Fellow, QMW, 1995. Hon. LittD UEA, 1989; Hon. DHL Denison, Ohio, 1997. Author of plays: The Kitchen, produced at Royal Court Theatre, 1959, 1961, 1994 (filmed, 1961; adapted for film, 2005); Trilogy of plays (Chicken Soup with Barley, Roots, I'm Talking about Jerusalem) produced Belgrade Theatre (Coventry), 1958–60, Royal Court Theatre, 1960; Chips with Everything, Royal

Court, 1962, Vaudeville, 1962 and Plymouth Theatre, Broadway, 1963; The Four Seasons, Belgrade Theatre (Coventry) and Saville, 1965; Their Very Own and Golden City, Brussels and Royal Court, 1966 (Marzotto Drama Prize, 1964); The Friends, Stockholm and London, 1970 (also dir); The Old Ones, Royal Court, 1972; The Wedding Feast, Stockholm, 1974, Leeds 1977; The Journalists, Coventry (amateur), 1977, Yugoslav TV, 1978, Germany, 1981; The Merchant, subseq. entitled Shylock, Stockholm and Aarhus, 1976, Broadway, 1977, Birmingham, 1978 (adapted for radio, 2005); Love Letters on Blue Paper, Nat. Theatre, 1978 (also dir); Fatlips (for young people), 1978; Caritas (Scandinavian Project commission), 1980, Nat. Theatre, 1981, adapted as opera libretto (music by Robert Saxton), 1991; Sullied Hand, 1981, Edinburgh Festival and Finnish TV, 1984; Four Portraits (Japanese commn), Tokyo, 1982, Edinburgh Festival, 1984; Annie Wobbler, Suddeutscher Rundfunk, Germany, Birmingham and New End Theatre, 1983; Fortune Theatre, 1984, New York, 1986; One More Ride on the Merry-Go-Round, Leicester, 1985; Yardsale, Edinburgh Fest. and Stratford-on-Avon (RSC Actors' Fest.), 1985 (also dir); When God Wanted A Son, 1986; Whatever Happened to Betty Lemon (double-bill with Yardsale), Lyric Studio, 1987 (also dir); Little Old Lady (for young people), Sigtuna, Sweden, 1988; The Mistress, 1988, Rome (also dir); Beorhtel's Hill, Towngate, Basildon, 1989; Three Women Talking, 1990, Chicago, 1992; Letter to a Daughter, 1990; Blood Libel, 1991; Wild Spring, 1992, Tokyo, 1994; Denial, Bristol Old Vic, 2000; Groupie, Fest. di Todi, Italy, 2001; Longitude, 2002, Greenwich Th., 2005; Letter To Myself, Studio Th., Univ. of Aberystwyth, 2004; GRIEF (libretto for one-woman opera), 2004; abridged version of Much Ado About Nothing and Henry V, NYT, Hackney Empire, 2005. *Film scripts:* Lady Othello, 1980; Homage to Catalonia, 1990; Maudie, 1995 (adapted from Diary of Jane Somers, by Doris Lessing). *Television:* (first play) Menace, 1963; Breakfast, 1981; (adapted) Thieves in the Night, by A. Koestler, 1984; (adapted) Diary of Jane Somers, by Doris Lessing, 1989; Barabbas, 2000. *Radio:* Yardsale, 1984; Bluey (Eur. Radio Commn), Cologne Radio 1984, BBC Radio 3, 1985 (adapted as stage play, 1993); Groupie, 2001; Amazed and Surprised, BBC Radio 3, 2006; The Rocking Horse, 2007 (commnd for 75th Anniv. of BBC World Service). *Publications:* Chicken Soup with Barley, 1959; Roots, 1959; I'm Talking about Jerusalem, 1960; The Wesker Trilogy, 1960; The Kitchen, 1961; Chips with Everything, 1962; The Four Seasons, 1966; Their Very Own and Golden City, 1966; The Friends, 1970; Fears of Fragmentation (essays), 1971; Six Sundays in January, 1971; The Old Ones, 1972; The Journalists, 1974 (in Dialog; repr. 1975); Love Letters on Blue Paper (stories), 1974, 2nd edn 1990; (with John Allin) Say Goodbye! You May Never See Them Again, 1974; Words—as definitions of experience, 1976; The Wedding Feast, 1977; Journey Into Journalism, 1977; Said the Old Man to the Young Man (stories), 1978; The Merchant, 1978; Fatlips (for young people), 1978; The Journalists, a triptych (with Journey into Journalism and A Diary of the Writing of The Journalists), 1979; Caritas, 1981; The Merchant, 1983; Distinctions, 1985; Yardsale, 1987; Whatever Happened to Betty Lemon, 1987; Little Old Lady, 1988; Shoeshine, 1989; Collected Plays: vols 1 and 5, 1989, vols 2, 3, 4 and 6, 1990, vol. 7, 1994; As Much As I Dare (autobiog.), 1994; Circles of Perception, 1996; Break, My Heart, 1997; Denial, 1997; The Birth of Shylock and the Death of Zero Mostel (journals), 1997; The King's Daughters (stories), 1998; Honey (novel), 2005; Longitude, 2006; All Things Tire of Themselves (poetry), 2008; Wesker's Love Plays, 2008; Wesker's Monologues, 2008. *Address:* Hay-on-Wye, Hereford HR3 5RJ.

WESSELY, Prof. Simon Charles, MD; FRCP, FRCPsych, FMedSci; Professor of Epidemiological and Liaison Psychiatry, since 1996, and Head, Department of Psychological Medicine, since 2005, Institute of Psychiatry, King's College London; *b* 23 Dec. 1956; *s* of Rudi and Wendy Wessely; *m* 1989, Dr Clare Gerada; two *s. Educ:* King Edward VII Sch., Sheffield; Trinity Hall, Cambridge (BA 1978); University Coll., Oxford (BM BCh 1981); London Sch. of Hygiene and Tropical Medicine (MSc 1989); MD London 1993. MRCP 1984, FRCP 1997; MRCPsych 1986, FRCPsych 2000. SHO in Gen. Medicine, Freeman Hosp., Newcastle upon Tyne, 1982–84; SHO, then Registrar, Maudsley Hosp., 1984–87; Sen. Registrar, Nat. Hosp. for Neurol., 1987–88; Wellcome Res. Trng Fellow in Epidemiol., 1988–91; Sen. Lectr, Dept of Psychol Medicine, GKT, 1991–96; Director: Chronic Fatigue Syndrome Res. Unit, KCL, 1994–; Gulf War Illness Res. Unit, later King's Centre for Mil. Health Res., KCL, 1996–. Civilian Consultant Advr in Psychiatry, British Army, 2001–; Sen. Investigator, NIHR, 2008–. FMedSci 1999. *Publications:* (jtly) Psychosis in the Inner City, 1998; Chronic Fatigue and its Syndromes, 1998; Clinical Trials in Psychiatry, 2003; From Shellshock to PTSD: a history of military psychiatry, 2005; Psychological Reactions to the New Terrorism: a NATO Russia dialogue, 2005; numerous contribs to learned jls on epidemiol., schizophrenia, chronic fatigue syndrome, unexplained symptoms and syndromes, somatisation, deliberate self-harm, Gulf War illness, military health, psychol aspects of terrorism, risk communication and med. history. *Recreations:* modern history, ski-ing, wasting time in Viennese cafes. *Address:* Department of Psychological Medicine, Weston Education Centre, Cutcombe Road, Camberwell, SE5 9RJ. *T:* (020) 7848 5411, *Fax:* (020) 7848 5408; *e-mail:* s.wessely@iop.kcl.ac.uk.

WESSON, Jane Louise; Independent Public Appointments Assessor, since 2001; Chairman, Council for Healthcare Regulatory Excellence (formerly Council for the Regulation of Healthcare Professionals), 2003–07; *b* 26 Feb. 1953. *Educ:* Univ. of Kent (BA Hons Law). Solicitor of the Supreme Court; Solicitor, Hepworth & Chadwick, 1978–89; Consultant, Ashworth Tetlow & Co., 1995–2005. Chairman: Ind. Tribunal Service, 1992–99; Nat. Clinical Assessment Authy, 2000–02. Chm., Harrogate Healthcare NHS Trust, 1993–2000; Board Member: Northern Counties Housing Assoc., 1993–96; Anchor Housing, 2003–; Nuffield Hosps, 2005–. FRSA. *Club:* Royal Automobile.

WEST; *see* Sackville-West, family name of Baron Sackville.

WEST, family name of **Baron West of Spithead.**

WEST OF SPITHEAD, Baron *cr* 2007 (Life Peer), of Seaview in the County of Isle of Wight; **Adm. Alan William John West,** GCB 2004 (KCB 2000); DSC 1982; Parliamentary Under-Secretary of State for Security and Counter Terrorism, Home Office, since 2007; *b* 21 April 1948; *m* 1973, Rosemary Anne Linington Childs; two *s* one *d. Educ:* Windsor Grammar Sch.; Clydebank High Sch. Joined RN 1965; seagoing appts, 1966–73; CO HMS Yarnton, 1973; qualified Principal Warfare Officer, 1975; HMS Juno, 1976; HMS Ambuscade, 1977; RN Staff Course, 1978; qualified Advanced Warfare Officer, 1978; HMS Norfolk, 1979; CO HMS Ardent, 1980; Naval Staff, 1982; CO HMS Bristol, 1987; Defence Intell. Staff, 1989; RCDS 1992; Higher Comd and Staff Course, Camberley, 1993; Dir, Naval Staff Duties, 1993; Naval Sec., 1994–96; Comdr UK Task Gp, and Comdr Anti Submarine Warfare Striking Force, 1996–97; Chief of Defence Intelligence, 1997–2001; C-in-C Fleet, C-in-C E Atlantic and Comdr Allied Naval Forces N, 2001–02; Chief of Naval Staff and First Sea Lord, 2002–06; First and Principal Naval ADC to the Queen, 2002–06. Chm., Defence Adv. Bd, QinetiQ, 2006–07. Trustee, Imperial War Mus., 2006–. Chm., Cadet Vocational Qualification Orgn, 2006–. Chancellor, Southampton Solent Univ., 2006–. Yr Brother, Trinity House. President: Bollington Sea Cadet Corps; Ardent Assoc.; Ship Recognition Corps. President:

Destroyer Club; Merchant Navy Medal Fund. Mem., Master Mariners' Co.; Hon. Mem., Soc. of Merchants Trading to the Continent; Hon. Freeman, Watermen and Lightermen's Co., 2005. *Recreations:* sailing, military and local history. *Address:* Home Office, 2 Marsham Street, SW1P 4DF. *Clubs:* Army and Navy, Royal Navy of 1765 and 1785, Anchorites; Royal Yacht Squadron.

WEST, Brian John; media consultant; Director and Chief Executive, Association of Independent Radio Companies, 1983–95; *b* 4 Aug. 1935; *s* of Herbert Frank West and Nellie (*née* Painter); *m* 1st, 1960, Patricia Ivy White (marr. diss. 1986); 2nd, 1987, Gillian Bond. *Educ:* Tiffin Sch., Kingston upon Thames. Sub-Lt (O), Fleet Air Arm, RN, 1956–58. Journalist, Richmond Herald, Surrey Comet and Western Morning News, 1952–60; Surrey Comet: Asst Editor, 1960–64; Editor, 1964–70; Editor, Leicester Mercury, 1970–74; Head of Advertising and PR, Littlewoods Orgn Plc, 1974–83. Founder Pres., Assoc. of European Radios, 1992–93; Council Mem., Advertising Assoc., 1987–95; Dir, Radio Jt Audience Res. Ltd, 1992–94. Churchill Fellow, 1995; Beaverbrook Foundn Fellow, 1995; Fellow, Radio Acad., 1995. *Publication:* Radio Training in the United States, 1996. *Recreations:* voluntary work for the blind and partially-sighted in N Wales, computers, music, horses and dogs, walking, gardening, photography, cherishing my wife. *Address:* Melrose, 33 Cwm Road, Dyserth, Denbighshire LL18 6BA. *T:* and *Fax:* (01745) 570568; *e-mail:* brigil9@tiscali.co.uk.

WEST, Prof. Christopher David; Chief Executive Officer, Royal Zoological Society of South Australia, since 2006; Professor of Zoology, University of Adelaide, since 2006; *b* 16 Aug. 1959; *s* of Donald Frank Hartley West and Delia Handford West; *m* 1993, Diane Linda Keetch; two *s* three *d*. *Educ:* Poole Grammar Sch.; Purbeck Sch.; Royal Veterinary Coll., London (BVetMed 1983; Cert. Lab. Animal Sci. 1986). CBiol, MIBiol 1985. Houseman, 1983, Registrar, 1985, Surgery Dept, RVC; Vet. Surgeon and Res. Scientist, Clinical Res. Centre, MRC, 1985–87; Gp Manager, ICI Pharmaceuticals, 1987–91; Named Vet. Surgeon, Zeneca-CTL, 1991–97; Chief Curator, Chester Zoo, 1997–2001; Zool Dir, Zool Soc. of London, 2001–05. Vis. Prof. in Conservation Medicine, Vet. Faculty, Univ. of Liverpool, 2001; Vis. Lectr, Univ. of Gothenburg, 2002. Chm. Trustees, Wildlife Vets Internat., 2005–. *Publications:* papers in Animal Behaviour, Animal Welfare, etc. *Recreations:* organic gardening, visiting deserts, tree planting (to offset international travel), cooking curries, worrying about climate change. *Address:* Royal Zoological Society of South Australia, Adelaide Zoo, Frome Road, Adelaide, SA 5000, Australia.

WEST, Christopher John, CBE 2002; Solicitor to HM Land Registry, 1991–2006; *b* 4 May 1941; *s* of late George William West and of Kathleen Mary West; *m* 1978, Susan Elizabeth Kirkby; one *d*. *Educ:* Raynes Park County Grammar Sch.; Inns of Court Sch. of Law. Called to the Bar, Lincoln's Inn, 1966. Exec. Officer, Charity Commn, 1961; HM Land Registry, 1969–2006: Sen. Land Registrar, 1983; Dist Land Registrar, Tunbridge Wells Dist Land Registry, 1987. *Publications:* (contrib.) Land Registration (jtly) and Land Charges, to Halsbury's Laws of England, 4th edn, 1977; (contrib.) Atkin's Court Forms, 1978, 1987; (with T. B. F. Ruoff) Concise Land Registration Practice and Land Registration Forms, 1982; (ed jtly) Ruoff and Roper's Registered Conveyancing, 5th edn 1986, looseleaf edn updated bi-annually 1991–2003, 2nd looseleaf edn, 2003. *Recreations:* theatre, jazz, watching cricket. *Address:* 1 Brooklands Park, Blackheath, SE3 9BN. *T:* (020) 8852 0667.

WEST, David Arthur James; Assistant Under Secretary of State (Naval Personnel), Ministry of Defence, 1981–84, retired; *b* 10 Dec. 1927; *s* of Wilfred West and Edith West (*née* Jones). *Educ:* Cotham Grammar Sch., Bristol. Executive Officer, Air Ministry, 1946; Higher Executive Officer, 1955; Principal, 1961; Assistant Secretary, 1972; Asst Under Sec. of State, 1979. *Address:* 66 Denton Road, East Twickenham TW1 2HQ. *T:* (020) 8892 6890.

WEST, David Thomson, CBE 1982; *b* 10 March 1923; *m* 1958, Marie Sellar; one *s* one *d*. *Educ:* Malvern Coll.; St John's Coll., Oxford. Served in RNVR, 1942–45; HM Diplomatic Service, 1946–76; served in Foreign Office, Office of Comr General for UK in SE Asia, HM Embassies, Paris, Lima, and Tunis; Counsellor, 1964; Commercial Inspector, 1965–68; Counsellor (Commercial) Berne, 1968–71; Head of Export Promotion Dept, FCO, 1971–72; seconded to Civil Service Dept as Head of Manpower Div., 1972–76; transf. to Home Civil Service, 1976, retired 1983. *Publication:* Admiral Edward Russell and the Rise of British Naval Supremacy, 2005. *Address:* 14 Newbiggen Street, Thaxted CM6 2QR. *T:* (01371) 830228.

WEST, Prof. Donald James; Professor of Clinical Criminology 1979–84, now Emeritus, and Director 1981–84, University of Cambridge Institute of Criminology; Fellow of Darwin College, Cambridge, 1967–91, now Emeritus; Hon. Consultant Psychiatrist, National Health Service, 1961–86, retired; *b* 9 June 1924; *s* of John Charles and Jessie Mercedes West. *Educ:* Merchant Taylors' Sch., Crosby; Liverpool Univ. (MD). LittD Cambridge. FRCPsych. Research Officer, Soc. for Psychical Research, London, and pt-time graduate student in psychiatry, 1947–50; in hospital practice in psychiatry, 1951–59; Sen. Registrar, Forensic Psychiatry Unit, Maudsley Hosp., 1957–59; Inst. of Criminology, Cambridge, 1960–. Leverhulme Emeritus Fellow, 1988–89. Mental Health Act Comr, 1989–97. Vice Pres., 1981–, and former Pres., British Soc. of Criminology; Pres., Soc. for Psychical Research, 1963–65, 1984–87, 1998–; Chm., Forensic Section, World Psychiatric Assoc., 1983–89; Chm., Streetwise Youth, 1986–92. *Publications:* Psychical Research Today, 1954 (revd edn 1962); Eleven Lourdes Miracles (med. inquiry under Parapsych. Foundn Grant), 1957; The Habitual Prisoner (for Inst. of Criminology), 1963; Murder followed by Suicide (for Inst. of Criminology), 1965; The Young Offender, 1967; Homosexuality, 1968; Present Conduct and Future Delinquency, 1969; (ed) The Future of Parole, 1972; (jtly) Who Becomes Delinquent?, 1973; (jtly) The Delinquent Way of Life, 1977; Homosexuality Re-examined, 1977; (ed, jtly) Daniel McNaughton: his trial and the aftermath, 1977; (jtly) Understanding Sexual Attacks, 1978; Delinquency: its roots, careers and prospects, 1982; Sexual Victimisation, 1985; Sexual Crimes and Confrontations, 1987; (jtly) Children's Sexual Encounters with Adults, 1990; Male Prostitution, 1992; (ed) Sex Crimes, 1994; (ed with R. Green) Sociolegal Controls on Homosexuality: a multi-nation comparison, 1997; various contribs to British Jl of Criminology, Criminal Behaviour and Mental Health and Jl Soc. for Psychical Res. *Recreations:* travel, parapsychology. *Address:* Flat 1, 11 Queen's Gate Gardens, SW7 5LY. *T:* (020) 2581 2875; *e-mail:* donjwest@dsl.pipex.com.

WEST, Edward Mark, CMG 1987; Deputy Director-General, Food and Agriculture Organization of the United Nations, 1982–86; *b* 11 March 1923; *m* 1948, Lydia Hollander; three *s*. *Educ:* Hendon County Sch.; University Coll., Oxford (MA). Served RA (W/Lieut), 1943; ICU BAOR (A/Captain), 1945. Asst Principal, Colonial Office, 1947; Private Sec., PUS, Colonial Office, 1950–51, Principal, 1951–58; Head of Chancery, UK Commn, Singapore, 1958–61; Private Secretary to Secretary of State, Colonial Affairs, 1961–62; Private Secretary to Secretary of State for Commonwealth and Colonial Affairs, 1963; Asst Sec., ODM, 1964–70; Food and Agriculture Organization: Director, Programme and Budget Formulation, 1970; Asst Dir-Gen., Administration and Finance Dept, 1974; Asst Dir-Gen., Programme and Budget Formulation, 1976; Special Rep., Internat. Conf. on Nutrition, 1992. *Address:* 10 Warwick Mansions, Cromwell Crescent, SW5 9QR.

WEST, Emma Louise; *see* Johnson, E. L.

WEST, Lt-Col George Arthur Alston-Roberts-, CVO 1988; DL; Comptroller, Lord Chamberlain's Office, 1987–90 (Assistant Comptroller, 1981–87); an Extra Equerry to the Queen, since 1982; *b* 1937; *s* of Major W. R. J. Alston-Roberts-West, Grenadier Guards (killed in action 1940) and late Mrs W. R. J. Alston-Roberts-West; *m* 1970, Hazel, *d* of late Sir Thomas and Lady Cook. *Educ:* Eton Coll.; RMA, Sandhurst. Commissioned into Grenadier Guards, Dec. 1957; served in England, Northern Ireland, Germany and Cyprus; retired, 1980. Dir, Care Ltd, 1991–95. DL Warwicks, 1988. *Address:* Atherstone Hill Farm, Stratford-on-Avon, Warwicks CV37 8NF. *Club:* Boodle's.

WEST, Rev. Jeffrey James, OBE 2006; Curate, St Mary's, Banbury, since 2007; *b* 15 Oct. 1950; *s* of Walter Edward West and (Frances) Margaret West (*née* Tatam); *m* 1987, Juliet Elizabeth Allan. *Educ:* Bedford Modern Sch.; Worcester Coll., Oxford (BA PPE 1972; BPhil Politics 1974; MA 1976); Ripon Coll., Cuddesdon (Postgrad. DipTh 2006, DipMin 2007). Joined Ancient Monuments Inspectorate, Department of Environment, 1974: Asst Inspector, 1974–79; Inspector, 1979–81; seconded as Principal, Local Govt Finance, DoE, 1981–83; Principal Inspector of Historic Buildings, DoE, later English Heritage, 1983–86; English Heritage: Regl Dir of Historic Properties (Midlands and E Anglia), 1986–97; Actg Dir of Historic Properties, 1997–98; Dep. Dir of Conservation, and Dir, Conservation Mgt, 1998–2002; Policy Dir, 2002–05. Ordained deacon, 2007, priest, 2008. Member: Council, Royal Archaeol Inst., 1980–83; Exec. Cttee, ICOMOS (UK), 2006– (Mem., Res. and Recording Cttee, 1997–2004). Dir, BURA, 2004–07; Vice-Chm., Cotswolds Area of Outstanding Natural Beauty Conservation Bd, 2005–. FRSA 2001. *Publications:* contrib. articles, notes and reviews on individual historic bldgs and theory and practice of conservation in learned jls. *Recreation:* architectural and landscape history. *Address:* c/o St Mary's Centre, Horsefair, Banbury, Oxon OX16 0AA.

WEST, Prof. John Clifford, CBE 1977; PhD, DSc; FREng; Vice-Chancellor and Principal, University of Bradford, 1979–89; *b* 4 June 1922; *s* of J. H. West and Mrs West (*née* Ascroft); *m* 1946, Winefride Mary Turner; three *d*. *Educ:* Hindley and Abram Grammar School; Victoria Univ., Manchester (PhD 1953; DSc 1957). Matthew Kirtley Entrance Schol., Manchester Univ., 1940. Electrical Lieutenant, RNVR, 1943–46. Lecturer, University of Manchester, 1946–57; Professor of Electrical Engineering, The Queen's University of Belfast, 1958–65; University of Sussex: Prof. of Electrical and Control Engineering, 1965–78; Founder Dean, Sch. of Applied Scis, 1965–73, Pro-Vice-Chancellor, 1967–71; Dir, Phillips' Philatelic Unit, 1970–78. Director, A. C. E. Machinery Ltd, 1966–79. Member: UGC, 1973–78 (Chm., Technology Sub-Cttee, 1973–78); Science Res. Council Cttee on Systems and Electrical Engineering, 1963–67; Science Res. Council Engrg Bd, 1976–79; Vis. Cttee, Dept of Educn and Science, Cranfield; Civil Service Commn Special Merit Promotions Panel, 1966–72; Naval Educn Adv. Cttee, 1965–72; Crawford Cttee on Broadcasting Coverage, 1973–74; Inter-Univ. Inst. of Engrg Control, 1967–83 (Dir, 1967–70); Chairman: Council for Educnl Technology, 1980–85; Educn Task Gp, IStructE, 1988–89. Pres., IEE, 1984–85 (Dep. Pres. 1982–84); Chm., Automation and Control Div., IEE, 1970–71. Vice-Chm., Yorkshire Cancer Res. Campaign, 1989– (Treas., 1989–97). Chm., Internat. Commn on Higher Educn, Botswana, 1990; UK deleg., Conf. on Higher Educn, Madagascar, 1992. Member: Royal Philatelic Soc., 1960–; Sociedad Filatélica de Chile, 1970–2001; Chm., British Philatelic Council, 1980–81; Trustee, Nat. Philatelic Trust, 1989–2002; Keeper of the Roll of Distinguished Philatelists, 1992–2004, Signatory, 2000. FRPSL 1970; Fellow, Inst. of Paper Conservation, 1980; FREng (FEng 1983). Hon. FInstMC 1984; Hon. FIET (Hon. FIEE 1992). Hon. DSc Sussex, 1988; DUniv Bradford, 1990. Hartley Medal, Inst. Measurement and Control, 1979; International Philatelic Gold Medal: Seoul, 1994; Seville, 1996. *Publications:* Textbook of Servomechanisms, 1953; Analytical Techniques for Non-Linear Control Systems, 1960; The Postmarks of Valparaiso, 1997; The Postal History of Chile, 2002; Tierra del Fuego, 2004; papers in Proc. IEE, Trans Amer. IEE, Brit. Jl of Applied Physics, Jl of Scientific Instruments, Proc. Inst. Measurement and Control. *Recreations:* philately, postal history. *Address:* North End House, 19 The Street, Stedham, West Sussex GU29 0NQ. *T:* (01730) 810833, *Fax:* (01730) 810834; *e-mail:* johncwest@btinternet.com. *Club:* Athenæum.

WEST, John James; Member (Lab), 1981–2001, Leader, 1997–2001, Lancashire County Council (Deputy Leader, 1989–97); *b* 19 April 1939; *s* of John West and Teresa West (*née* Campbell); two *s*. *Educ:* St Mary's RC Sch., Dublin; Dublin Univ. (BA Econs and Hist. 1961); Harris Coll., Preston and Poole Tech. Coll. (Dip. Business Studies 1974); Open Univ. MInstTA 1976; MCIT 1978. Dep. Manager/Dep. Chm. of Bd, Preston Borough Transport Ltd, 1961–92. Freelance pt-time Lectr in Econs and History. Lancashire County Council: Chair: Superannuation Panel, 1984–2001; Finance Cttee, 1985–2001; Hon. Alderman, 2001. Exec. Mem., LGA, 1994–2001. Chairman: Lancashire Waste Services Ltd, 1991–2001; Lancashire Co-op Devlt Agency, 1991–2001; non-executive Director: Preston and S Ribble Devlt Agency, 1997–2001; Preston Acute Hosp. NHS Trust, 1997–2001; Lancashire Teaching Hosps NHS Trust, 2002–. *Recreations:* reading (especially ancient history), watching most sports. *Address:* 17 Carlton Drive, Frenchwood, Preston PR1 4PP.

WEST, Kenneth, CChem, FRSC; Deputy Chairman, ICI Fibres Division, 1980–84 (Technical Director, 1977–80); *b* 1 Sept. 1930; *s* of Albert West and Ethel Kirby (*née* Kendall); *m* 1980, Elizabeth Ann Borland (*née* Campbell); one step *s*, and three *d* by a previous marriage. *Educ:* Archbishop Holgate's Grammar Sch., York; University Coll., Oxford (BA). Customer Service Manager, ICI Fibres, 1960; Res. and Engrg Manager, FII, 1967; Director: South African Nylon Spinners, Cape Town, 1970; Fibre Industries Inc., N Carolina, 1974; Man. Dir, TWA, 1984–85; Dir, Water Res. Council, 1984–85. Dir, Seahorse Internat. Ltd, 1987–89. Mem., British Assoc. of the Var, 2000–. FRSA. *Recreations:* sailing, flying, music, wine, amateur dramatics. *Address:* La Salamandre, Route de Repenti, 83340 Le Luc, France. *Clubs:* Don Mills Variety; Oxford and Cambridge (Var Br.); Yacht International (Bormes les Mimosas).

WEST, Lawrence Joseph; QC 2003; a Recorder, since 2000; *b* 6 July 1946; *s* of Lionel Chaffey West and Catherine Agnes (*née* Daly); *m* 1972, Cathryn Hudson; two *s*. *Educ:* De La Salle Oaklands Sch., Toronto; Univ. of Toronto (BA 1967; LLB 1970); London Sch. of Econs (LLM 1971). MCIArb. Called: to Law Soc. of Upper Canada, 1973; to the Bar, Gray's Inn, 1979. *Recreations:* golf, music, travel, religion. *Address:* Henderson Chambers, 2 Harcourt Buildings, Temple, EC4Y 9DB. *T:* (020) 7583 9020, *Fax:* (020) 7583 2686; *e-mail:* lwest@hendersonchambers.co.uk.

WEST, Martin Litchfield, DPhil, DLitt; FBA 1973; Senior Research Fellow, All Souls College, University of Oxford, 1991–2004, now Emeritus Fellow; *b* 23 Sept. 1937; *s* of Maurice Charles West and Catherine Baker West (*née* Stainthorpe); *m* 1960, Stephanie Roberta Pickard (*see* S. R. West); one *s* one *d*. *Educ:* St Paul's Sch.; Balliol Coll., Oxford (MA 1962; DPhil 1963; DLitt 1994; Hon. Fellow, 2004). Chancellor's Prizes for Latin

Prose and Verse, 1957; Hertford and de Paravicini Schols, 1957; Ireland Schol., 1957; Conington Prize, 1965. Woodhouse Jun. Research Fellow, St John's Coll., Oxford, 1960–63 (Hon. Fellow 2007); Fellow and Praelector in Classics, University Coll., Oxford, 1963–74 (Hon. Fellow 2001); Prof. of Greek, Bedford Coll., then at RHBNC, London Univ., 1974–91. Corresp. Mem., Akademie der Wissenschaften zu Göttingen, 1991; MAE 1998; Foreign Mem., Accademia Nazionale dei Lincei, 2007. Editor of Liddell and Scott's Greek-English Lexicon, 1965–81. Hon. DLitt Cyprus, 2008. Internat. Balzan Prize for Classical Antiquity, 2000; Kenyon Medal for Classical Studies, British Acad., 2002. *Publications:* (ed) Hesiod, Theogony, 1966; (ed with R. Merkelbach) Fragmenta Hesiodea, 1967; Early Greek Philosophy and the Orient, 1971; Sing Me, Goddess, 1971; (ed) Iambi et Elegi Graeci, 1971–72; Textual Criticism and Editorial Technique, 1973; Studies in Greek Elegy and Iambus, 1974; (ed) Hesiod, Works and Days, 1978; (ed) Theognidis et Phocylidis fragmenta, 1978; (ed) Delectus ex Iambis et Elegis Graecis, 1980; Greek Metre, 1982; The Orphic Poems, 1983; (ed) Carmina Anacreontea, 1984; The Hesiodic Catalogue of Women, 1985; (ed) Euripides, Orestes, 1987; Introduction to Greek Metre, 1987; Hesiod (trans.), 1988; (ed) Aeschyli Tragoediae, 1990; Studies in Aeschylus, 1990; Ancient Greek Music, 1992; Greek Lyric Poetry (trans.), 1993; The East Face of Helicon, 1997; (ed) Homeri Ilias, 2 vols, 1998 and 2000; Studies in the Text and Transmission of the Iliad, 2001; (with E. Pöhlmann) Documents of Ancient Greek Music, 2001; (ed and trans.) Homeric Hymns, Homeric Apocrypha, Lives of Homer, 2003; (ed and trans.) Greek Epic Fragments, 2003; Indo-European Poetry and Myth, 2007; articles in classical periodicals. *Recreation:* strong music. *Address:* All Souls College, Oxford OX1 4AL.

WEST, Mary Cecilia; *see* Kenny, M. C.

WEST, Prof. Michael, PhD; Professor of Organisational Psychology, since 2001, and Executive Dean, since 2007, Aston Business School, Aston University; *b* Loughborough, 6 March 1951; *m* 2006, Gillian Hardy; one *s* two *d*; one *s* from previous marriage. *Educ:* Univ. of Wales Inst. of Sci. and Technol. (BSc Econ Hons 1973; PhD 1977). Res. Dir, Aston Business Sch., Aston Univ., 2001–06. Dir, Aston Organisational Development Ltd, 2004–. FRSA. *Publications:* (jtly) The Transition from School to Work, 1983; (ed) The Psychology of Meditation, 1987; (jtly) Managerial Job Change: men and women in transition, 1988; (ed jtly) Innovation and Creativity at Work, 1990; (ed jtly) Women at Work: psychological and organizational perspectives, 1990; Effective Teamwork: practical lessons from organisational research, 1994, 2nd edn 2004; (ed) Handbook of Work Group Psychology, 1996; Developing Creativity in Organizations, 1997; (jtly) Effective Top Management Teams, 2001; (ed jtly) International Handbook of Organizational Teamwork and Cooperative Working, 2003; (with L. Markiewicz) Building Team-based Working: a practical guide to organizational transformation, 2004; The Secrets of Successful Team Management, 2004; (ed jtly) The Essentials of Teamworking: international perspectives, 2005; (jtly) Teamwork, teamdiagnose, teamentwicklung, 2005; (jtly) Aston Team Performance Inventory: management set, 2006. *Address:* Executive Dean's Office, Aston Business School, Aston University, Birmingham B4 7ET. *T:* (0121) 204 3234; *e-mail:* m.a.west@aston.ac.uk.

WEST, Nigel; *see* Allason, R. W. S.

WEST, Norman; Member (Lab) Yorkshire South, European Parliament, 1984–98; *b* 26 Nov. 1935; *m*; two *s*. *Educ:* Barnsley; Sheffield Univ. Miner. Mem., South Yorks CC (Chm., Highways Cttee; Mem., anti-nuclear working party). Member: NUM; CND. Mem., Energy, Research and Technology Cttee, European Parlt, 1984–98. *Address:* 43 Coronation Drive, Birdwell, Barnsley, South Yorks S70 5RJ.

WEST, Paul, QPM 2004; Chief Constable, West Mercia Constabulary, since 2003; *b* 29 March 1958; *s* of Derrick and Constance West; *m* 1993, Rosemary Helen Goundry; three *s* three *d*. *Educ:* Durham Johnston Sch.; Pembroke Coll., Oxford (BA (Physics) 1979, MA 1983); Michigan State Univ. (MSc (Criminal Justice) 1987); Durham Univ. (MA (Human Resource Mgt and Develt) 1998). Joined Durham Constabulary, 1979: Constable, 1979–83; Sergeant, 1983–85; Insp., 1985–90; Harkness Fellow, 1986; Chief Insp., 1990–92; Supt, 1992–98; Thames Valley Police: Asst Chief Constable, 1998–2000; Dep. Chief Constable, 2000–03. *Recreations:* classical music, sports (partic. football), gardening, poultry and small animal rearing, family. *Address:* West Mercia Constabulary, Hindlip Hall, PO Box 55, Hindlip, Worcs WR3 8SP. *T:* 08457 444888, *Fax:* (01905) 331806; *e-mail:* chief@westmercia.pnn.police.uk.

WEST, Peter Bernard; HM Diplomatic Service; Consul-General, Melbourne, since 2004; *b* 29 June 1958; *s* of late Bernard West and Alice West (*née* Bowen); *m* 1980, Julia Anne Chandler; two *s* (twins) one *d*. Joined FCO, 1977; Third Secretary: Buenos Aires, 1980–83; Auckland, 1984–85; Second, then First, Sec., FCO, 1986–91; First Sec. (Political/EU), Copenhagen, 1992–97; Dep. Hd, S Asian Dept, FCO, 1997–99; Counsellor and Dep. Hd of Mission, Bangkok, 2000–04. *Recreations:* family, sport, travel. *Address:* c/o Foreign and Commonwealth Office, King Charles Street, SW1A 2AH. *Club:* Melbourne Football (Melbourne).

WEST, Prof. Peter Christopher, PhD; FRS 2006; Professor, Department of Mathematics, King's College, London, since 1986; *b* 4 Dec. 1951; *s* of Ronald West and Martha West (now Williams); *m* 1980, Susan Amanda Back; one *s* one *d*. *Educ:* Imperial Coll., London (BSc 1973; PhD 1976). Postdoctoral Fellow: Ecole Normale Superieure, Paris, 1976–77; Imperial Coll., London, 1977–78; Lectr, 1978–85, Reader, 1985–86, KCL. Visiting appointments: CIT, 1984; CERN, 1986–89, 2000; Chalmers 150th Anniv. Prof., Sweden, 1992. FKC 2007. *Publications:* Introduction to Supersymmetry and Supergravity, 1983, 2nd edn 1990; more than 190 scientific papers. *Recreations:* classical music, cycling, travelling in remote regions, gardening. *Address:* Department of Mathematics, King's College London, Strand, WC2R 2LS. *T:* (020) 7848 2224, *Fax:* (020) 7848 2017; *e-mail:* peter.west@kcl.ac.uk.

WEST, Prunella Margaret Rumney, (Mrs T. L. West); *see* Scales, Prunella.

WEST, Prof. Richard Gilbert, FRS 1968; FSA; FGS; Fellow of Clare College, Cambridge, since 1954; Professor of Botany, University of Cambridge, 1977–91; *b* 31 May 1926; *m* 1st, 1958; one *s*; 2nd, 1973, Hazel Gristwood (*d* 1997); two *d*. *Educ:* King's School, Canterbury; Univ. of Cambridge. Cambridge University: Demonstrator in Botany, 1957–60; Lecturer in Botany, 1960–67; Dir, Subdept of Quaternary Research, 1966–87; Reader in Quaternary Research, 1967–75; Prof. of Palaeoecology, 1975–77. Member: Council for Scientific Policy, 1971–73; NERC, 1973–76; Ancient Monuments Bd for England, 1980–84. Darwin Lecturer to the British Association, 1959; Lyell Fund, 1961, Bigsby Medal, 1969, Lyell Medal, 1988, Geological Society of London. Hon. MRIA. *Publications:* Pleistocene Geology and Biology, 1968, 2nd edn 1977; (jtly) The Ice Age in Britain, 1972, 2nd edn 1981; The Pre-glacial Pleistocene of the Norfolk and Suffolk coasts, 1980; Pleistocene Palaeoecology of Central Norfolk, 1991; Plant Life in the Quaternary Cold Stages, 2000. *Address:* 3A Woollards Lane, Great Shelford, Cambs CB2 5LZ. *T:* (01223) 842578; Clare College, Cambridge CB2 1TL.

WEST, Prof. Richard John, FRCP, FRCPCH; Medical Postgraduate Dean to South West Region, Hon. Professor of Postgraduate Medical Education, University of Bristol, and Hon. Consultant Paediatrician, Royal Hosp. for Sick Children, Bristol, 1991–99, retired; *b* 8 May 1939; *s* of late Cecil J. West and of Alice B. West (*née* Court); *m* 1962, Jenny Winn Hawkins; one *s* two *d*. *Educ:* Tiffin Boys' Sch.; Middlesex Hospital Medical School (MB, BS; MD 1975). MRCP 1967, FRCP 1979; FRCPCH 1997. Research Fellow, Inst. of Child Health, London, 1971–73; Sen. Registrar, Hosp. for Sick Children, London, 1973–74; Lectr, Inst. of Child Health, 1974–75; Sen. Lectr, 1975–91, Dean, 1982–87, St George's Hosp. Med. Sch.; Consultant Paediatrician, St George's Hosp., 1975–91. Member: Wandsworth HA, 1981–82, 1989–90; SW Thames RHA, 1982–88. Member: DoH Clinical Outcomes Gp, 1991–96; Steering Gp on Undergraduate Med. and Dental Educn and Res., 1992–97. Mem. Governing Body, Inst. of Med. Ethics, 1985–96 (Gen. Sec., 1989–96); Governor: Tiffin Boys' Sch., 1983–86; Wimbledon High Sch., 1988–91. *Publications:* Family Guide to Children's Ailments, 1983; Royal Society of Medicine Child Health Guide, 1992; research papers on metabolic diseases, incl. lipid disorders. *Recreations:* windmills, medical history, travel, archaeology.

WEST, Samuel Alexander Joseph; actor and director; Artistic Director, Sheffield Theatres, 2005–07; *b* 19 June 1966; *s* of Timothy Lancaster West, *qv* and Prunella Margaret Rumney West (*see* Prunella Scales). *Educ:* Alleyn's Sch., Dulwich; Lady Margaret Hall, Oxford (BA Hons Eng. Lit.). First professional stage appearance, The Browning Version, Birmingham Rep., 1985; London début, Les Parents Terribles, Orange Tree, Richmond, 1988; West End début, A Life in the Theatre, Haymarket, 1989; *theatre* includes: Hidden Laughter, Vaudeville, 1990; Royal National Theatre: The Sea, 1991; Arcadia, 1993; Antony and Cleopatra, 1998; Cain (Byron), Chichester, 1992; The Importance of Being Earnest, Manchester, 1993; Henry IV parts I & II, English Touring Th., 1996; Richard II, 2000, Hamlet, 2001, RSC; Dr Faustus, The Master and Margarita, Chichester, 2004; Much Ado About Nothing, Crucible Th., Sheffield, 2005; Betrayal, Donmar Warehouse, 2007; Drunk Enough To Say I Love You?, NY, 2008; director: The Lady's Not For Burning, Chichester, 2002; Les Liaisons Dangereuses, Bristol Old Vic, 2003; Cosi fan tutte, ENO, 2003; Three Women and a Piano Tuner, Chichester, 2004, Hampstead, 2005; Insignificance, Lyceum, Sheffield, 2005; The Romans in Britain, The Clean House, 2006, As You Like It, 2007, Crucible Th., Sheffield; Dealer's Choice, Menier, 2007; Waste, Almeida, 2008; *television* includes: serials: Stanley and the Women, 1990; Over Here, 1995; Out of the Past, 1998; Hornblower, 1998; Waking the Dead, 2002; Cambridge Spies, 2003; Foyle's War, 2004; E=mc^2, 2005; The Inspector Lynley Mysteries, 2006; The Long Walk to Finchley, 2008; films: Frankie and Johnny, 1985; Voices in the Garden, 1991; A Breed of Heroes, 1995; Persuasion, 1995; Longitude, 2000; Random Quest, 2006; *films* include: Reunion, 1989; Howards End, 1991; Archipel (in French), 1992; Carrington, 1994; A Feast at Midnight, 1995; Jane Eyre, 1995; Stiff Upper Lips, 1996; The Ripper, 1997; Rupert's Land, 1997; Notting Hill, 1998; Pandæmonium, 1999; Iris, 2001; Van Helsing, 2003; *radio* includes: more than thirty plays; regular reader for Poetry Please. Reciter and reader for concerts with orchs incl. LSO, BBC SO and CBSO. Member: Council, Equity, 1996–2000; Bd, Nat. Campaign for the Arts, 2006–. *Recreations:* birding, travelling, poker, supporting AFC Wimbledon. *Address:* c/o United Agents, 12–26 Lexington Street, W1F 0LE. *T:* (020) 3214 0800. *Clubs:* Century, Groucho.

WEST, Shani; *see* Rhys-James, S.

WEST, Dr Stephanie Roberta, FBA 1990; Senior Research Fellow in Classics and Fellow Librarian, Hertford College, Oxford, 1990–2005, now Emeritus Fellow; *b* 1 Dec. 1937; *d* of Robert Enoch Pickard and Ruth (*née* Batters); *m* 1960, Martin Litchfield West, *qv*; one *s* one *d*. *Educ:* Nottingham High Sch. for Girls; Somerville Coll., Oxford (1st cl. Classics Mods 1958, 1st cl. Lit. Hum. 1960; Gaisford Prize for Greek Verse Composition 1959; Ireland Scholar 1959, Derby Scholar 1960); MA 1963, DPhil 1964, Oxon. Oxford University: Mary Ewart Res. Fellow, Somerville Coll., 1965–67; Lecturer: in Classics, Hertford Coll., 1966–90; in Greek, Keble Coll., 1981–2005. Mem. Council, GPDST, 1974–87. *Publications:* The Ptolemaic Papyri of Homer, 1967; Omero, Odissea 1 (libri I–IV), 1981; (with A. Heubeck and J. B. Hainsworth) A commentary on Homer's Odyssey 1, 1988; Demythologisation in Herodotus, 2002; articles and reviews in learned jls. *Recreations:* opera, curious information. *Address:* 42 Portland Road, Oxford OX2 7EY. *T:* (01865) 556060.

WEST, Dr Stephen Craig, FMedSci; FRS 1995; Principal Scientist, Cancer Research UK (formerly Imperial Cancer Research Fund), since 1989; *b* 11 April 1952; *s* of Joseph and Louise West; *m* 1985, Phyllis Fraenza. *Educ:* Univ. of Newcastle upon Tyne (BSc 1974; PhD 1977). Post-doctoral Research Associate: Univ. of Newcastle upon Tyne, 1977–78; Dept of Molecular Biophysics and Biochemistry, and Therapeutic Radiology, Yale Univ., 1978–83 (Res. Scientist, Dept of Therapeutic Radiology, 1983–85); Sen. Scientist, ICRF, 1985–89. Mem., EMBO, 1994; FMedSci 2000. Hon. Prof., UCL, 1997–. Louis-Jeantet Prize for Medicine, 2007; Novartis Lect. and Prize, Biochem. Soc., 2008. *Publications:* numerous res. papers in biochem. and molecular biol. *Recreations:* squash, ski-ing, music. *Address:* Cancer Research UK, Clare Hall Laboratories, South Mimms, Potters Bar, Herts EN6 3LD.

WEST, Prof. Thomas Summers, CBE 1988; FRS 1989; FRSE, FRSC; Director, Macaulay Institute for Soil Research, Aberdeen, 1975–87; Honorary Research Professor, University of Aberdeen, 1983–87, now Emeritus; *b* 18 Nov. 1927; *s* of late Thomas West and Mary Ann Summers; *m* 1952, Margaret Officer Lawson, MA; one *s* two *d*. *Educ:* Tarbat Old Public Sch., Portmahomack; Royal Acad., Tain; Aberdeen Univ. (BSc 1st Cl. Hons Chemistry, 1949); Univ. of Birmingham (PhD 1952, DSc 1962). FRSC (FRIC 1962); FRSE 1979. Univ. of Birmingham: Sen. DSIR Fellow, 1952–55; Lectr in Chem., 1955–63; Imperial Coll., London: Reader in Analytical Chem., 1963–65; Prof. of Analytical Chem., 1965–75. Royal Society: Mem., British National Cttee for Chem., and Chm., Analytical Sub-cttee, 1965–82; Mem., Internat. Cttee, 1990–92; Mem., Internat. Exchanges Cttee, 1992– (Chm. Panel III). Sec. Gen., IUPAC, 1983–91 (Pres., Analytical Div., 1977–79); Pres., Soc. for Analytical Chem., 1969–71; Chm., Finance Cttee, ICSU, 1990–92; Mem., British Nat. Cttee for IUPAC, RSC, 1990–98; Hon. Sec., Chemical Soc., 1972–75 (Redwood Lectr, 1974); Hon. Member: Bunseki Kagakukai (Japan), 1981; Fondation de la Maison de la Chimie (Paris), 1985. Meldola Medal, RIC, 1956; Instrumentation Medal, 1976, and Gold Medal, 1977, Chemical Soc.; Johannes Marcus Medal for Spectroscopy, Spectroscopic Soc. of Bohemia, 1977. *Publications:* Analytical Applications of Diamino ethane tetra acetic acid, 1958, 2nd edn 1961; New Methods of Analytical Chemistry, 1964; Complexometry with EDTA and Related Reagents, 1969. *Recreations:* gardening, motoring, reading, music, family history research. *Address:* 31 Baillieswells Drive, Bieldside, Aberdeen AB15 9AT. *T:* (01224) 868294.

WEST, Timothy Lancaster, CBE 1984; actor and director; *b* 20 Oct. 1934; *s* of late Harry Lockwood West and Olive Carleton-Crowe; *m* 1st, 1956, Jacqueline Boyer (marr. diss.); one *d*; 2nd, 1963, Prunella Scales, *qv*; two *s*. *Educ:* John Lyon Sch., Harrow; Regent Street Polytechnic. Entered profession as asst stage manager, Wimbledon, 1956; first

London appearance, Caught Napping, Piccadilly, 1959; Mem., RSC, 1964–66; Prospect Theatre Co., 1966–72: Dr Samuel Johnson, Prospero, Bolingbroke, young Mortimer in Edward II, King Lear, Emerson in A Room with a View, Alderman Smuggler in The Constant Couple, and Holofernes in Love's Labour's Lost; Otto in The Italian Girl, 1968; Gilles in Abelard and Heloise, 1970; Robert Hand in Exiles, 1970; Gilbert in The Critic as Artist, 1971; Sir William Gower in Trelawny (musical), Bristol, 1972; Falstaff in Henry IV Pts I and II, Bristol, 1973; Shpigelsky in A Month in the Country, Chichester, 1974 (London, 1975); Brack in Hedda Gabler, RSC, 1975; Iago in Othello, Nottingham, 1976; with Prospect Co.: Harry in Staircase, 1976, Claudius in Hamlet, storyteller in War Music, and Enobarbus in Antony and Cleopatra, 1977; Ivan and Gottlieb in Laughter, and Max in The Homecoming, 1978; with Old Vic Co.: Narrator in Lancelot and Guinevere, Shylock in The Merchant of Venice, 1980; Beecham, Apollo, 1980, NZ, 1983, Dublin, 1986; Uncle Vanya, Australia, 1982; Stalin in Master Class, Leicester, 1983, Old Vic, 1984; Charlie Mucklebrass in Big in Brazil, 1984; The War at Home, Hampstead, 1984; When We Are Married, Whitehall, 1986; The Sneeze, Aldwych, 1988; Bristol Old Vic: The Master Builder, 1989; The Clandestine Marriage, Uncle Vanya, 1990; James Tyrone, in Long Day's Journey into Night, 1991, also at NT; Andrew in It's Ralph, Comedy, 1991; King Lear, Dublin, 1992; Willie Loman in Death of a Salesman, Theatr Clwyd, 1993; Christopher Cameron in Himself, Southampton, 1993; Sir Anthony Absolute in The Rivals, Chichester, 1994; Macbeth, Theatr Clwyd, 1994; Mail Order Bride, 1994, Getting On, 1995, W Yorks Playhouse; Twelve Angry Men, Comedy, 1996; Falstaff, in Henry IV Pts 1 and 2, Old Vic, 1997; Gloucester, in King Lear, RNT, 1997; The Birthday Party, Piccadilly, 1999; The Master Builder, tour, 1999; The External, tour, 2001; Luther, RNT, 2001; Lear in King Lear, tour, 2002, Old Vic, 2003; National Hero, Edinburgh and tour, 2005; The Old Country, Trafalgar Studio, 2006; Menenius in Coriolanus, RSC, 2007; The Collection, Comedy, 2008. *Directed*: plays for Prospect Co., Open Space, Gardner Centre, Brighton, and rep. at Salisbury, Bristol, Northampton and Cheltenham; HMS Pinafore, Carl Rosa Co., 2003; own season, The Forum, Billingham, 1973; Artistic Dir, Old Vic Co., 1980–81. *Television includes*: Edward VII, 1973; Hard Times, 1977; Crime and Punishment, 1979; Brass, 1982–84, 1990; The Last Bastion, 1984; The Nightingale Saga, Tender is the Night, 1985; The Monocled Mutineer, 1986; The Train, 1987; A Shadow on the Sun, 1988; The Gospels, Framed, 1992; Bramwell, 1998; Midsomer Murders, 1999; Murder in Mind, 2000; Bedtime, 2001, 2002, 2003; *plays*: Richard II, 1969; Edward II, The Boswell and Johnson Show, 1970; Horatio Bottomley, 1972; Churchill and the Generals, 1979 (RTS Award); The Good Doctor Bodkin Adams, 1986; What the Butler Saw, Harry's Kingdom, When We are Married, Breakthrough at Reykjavik, 1987; Strife, The Contractor, 1988; Blore, MP, Beecham, 1989; Survival of the Fittest, 1990; Bye Bye Columbus, 1991; Reith to the Nation, Smokescreen, 1993; Hiroshima, Eleven Men Against Eleven, Cuts, 1995; The Place of the Dead, 1996; King Lear, 1997; Bleak House, 2005; A Room with a View, 2007. *Films*: The Looking-Glass War, 1968; Nicholas and Alexandra, 1970; The Day of the Jackal, 1972; Hedda, 1975; Joseph Andrews, and The Devil's Advocate, 1976; William Morris, 1977; Agatha, and The 39 Steps, 1978; The Antagonists, 1980; Murder is Easy, and Oliver Twist, 1981; Cry Freedom, 1986; Consuming Passions, 1987; Ever After, 1997; Joan of Arc, 1998; Iris, 2001; Beyond Borders, 2002; Villa des Roses, 2002; The Endgame, 2008. Compiles and dir. recital progs; sound broadcaster. Dir, All Change Arts Ltd, 1986–2006; Dir and Trustee, Nat. Student Drama Fest., 1990–; Pres., LAMDA, 2003– (Gov., 1992–). Pres., Soc. for Theatre Res., 1999–. FRSA 1992. DUniv Bradford, 1993; Hon. DLitt: West of England, 1994; East Anglia, 1996; Westminster, 1999; London, 2004; Hull, 2004. Hon. Dr Drama, RSAMD, 2004. *Publications*: I'm Here, I Think, Where are You? (collected letters), 1994; A Moment Towards the End of the Play, 2001; (with Prunella Scales) So You Want to be an Actor?, 2005. *Recreations*: theatre history, travel, music, old railways. *Address*: c/o Gavin Barker Associates Ltd, 2D Wimpole Street, W1G 0EB. *Clubs*: Garrick, Groucho.

See also S. A. J. West.

WEST CUMBERLAND, Archdeacon of; *see* Hill, Ven. C.

WEST HAM, Archdeacon of; *see* Cockett, Ven. E. W.

WEST INDIES, Archbishop of, since 1998; **Most Rev. Drexel Wellington Gomez**, CMG 1994; Bishop of the Bahamas and the Turks and Caicos Islands (formerly Nassau and the Bahamas), since 1995; *b* Jan. 1937; *s* of late Rueben and Wealthy Gomez; *m* Carrol Gomez; four *c. Educ*: Codrington Coll., Barbados (DipTh 1957); Durham Univ. (BA 1959). Ordained 1959; parochial work, Bahamas, 1962–64; Tutor, Codrington Coll., 1964–68; Sec. and Treas., dio. of Bahamas, 1970–72; Bishop of Barbados, 1972–93; Asst Bishop, dio. of Bahamas, 1993–95. *Address*: PO Box N–7107, Nassau, Bahamas; *e-mail*: primate@batelnet.bs.

WEST-KNIGHTS, Laurence James; QC 2000; a Recorder, since 1999; *b* 30 July 1954; *o s* of late Major Jan James West-Knights and Amy Winifred West-Knights (*née* Gott); *m* 1st, 1979 (marr. diss. 1983); 2nd, 1992, Joanne Anita Florence Ecob; one *s* two *d. Educ*: Perse Sch., Cambridge; Hampton Sch.; Emmanuel Coll., Cambridge (MA 1976). FCIArb 1993. RNR, 1979–94 (Lt Comdr 1993, retd). Called to the Bar, Gray's Inn, 1977, Bencher, 2004; W Circuit; in practice at the Bar, 1977–; Asst Recorder, 1994–99. Chm., Steering Cttee, IT Industry Enquiry into Govt IT Contracts, 2000; Member: IT Cttees, Bar Council, 1996–2001; Incorporated Council of Law Reporting, 1997–2005; IT and the Courts, 1998– (Mem., Civil Litigation Wkg Party, 1997–2005); Founding Trustee and Exec. Dir, British and Irish Legal Information Inst. Jt Chm., Soc. for Computers and Law, 2001–02 (Mem. Council, 1995–2001; Vice-Chm., 1996–2001). Lay Chm., PCC, Christ Church, Turnham Green, 1998–2001. Mem. Editl Bd, Jl of Judicial Studies Bd, 1997–2003. Writer, LawOnLine.cc legal web site, 1997–. Winner, Kennett Shoot Trophy, 2003. *Publications*: (contrib.) Researching the Legal Web, 1997; (contrib.) Jordan's Civil Court Service, 1999–; numerous papers and articles on free access to the law via the Internet. *Recreations*: motorcycling, sailing, scuba diving, ski-ing, cricket, shooting, family. *Address*: Hailsham Chambers, 4 Paper Buildings, Temple, EC4Y 7EX. *T*: (020) 7643 5000, *Fax*: (020) 7353 5778; *e-mail*: laurie.west-knightsqc@hailshamchambers.com. *Clubs*: Whitefriars, MCC; Royal Naval Volunteer Reserve Yacht; Bar Yacht.

WESTABY, Prof. Stephen, FRCS; Senior Cardiac Surgeon, John Radcliffe Hospital, since 1986; Professor of Biomedical Sciences, University of Wales, since 2006; *b* 27 July 1948; *s* of Kenneth and Doreen Westaby; *m*; one *s* one *d. Educ*: Charing Cross Hosp. Med. Sch., Univ. of London (BSc Biochemistry 1969; MB BS 1972; MS 1986); PhD (Bioeng). FRCS 1986; FESC, FETCS, FICA. Surgical training: Addenbrooke's Hosp., Hammersmith Hosp., RPMS, Hosp. for Sick Children, Great Ormond Street, Harefield Hosp., Middlesex Hosp., Univ. of Alabama. Dist. Ralph Cicerone Prof., Univ. of California, 2006; adult and paediatric surgeon; specialist surgeon in congenital heart disease, thoracic aortic surgery, valvular and coronary heart disease; designated a pioneer in artificial heart technology by Jl of Amer. Heart Assoc.; developed first artificial heart res. prog., UK; established Oxford Heart Centre, John Radcliffe Hosp., internat. teaching centre for valve and aortic surgery; has performed over 10,000 open heart ops on adults and children. Member: Soc. for Thoracic Surgery, USA, 1995; Amer. Assoc. for Thoracic Surgery, 1998; European Assoc. for Cardiothoracic Surgery, 1998. Editor, Jl of Heart Failure Clinics of N Amer., surgical edn. *Publications*: editor/joint author: Wound Care, 1985; Stentless Bioprosthesis, 1995, 2nd edn 1999; Landmarks in Cardiac Surgery, 1997; Surgery of Acquired Aortic Valve Disease, 1997; Principles and Practice of Critical Care, 1997; Trauma Pathogenesis and Treatment, 1998; Ischemic Heart Disease: surgical management, 1998; Cardiothoracic Trauma, 1999; more than 50 chapters in books, and over 260 scientific papers. *Recreations*: writing, shooting. *Address*: Oxford Heart Centre, John Radcliffe Hospital, Headley Way, Headington, Oxford OX3 9DU. *T*: (01865) 220269; *e-mail*: swestaby@ahf.org.uk.

WESTBROOK, Michael John David, OBE 1988; composer, pianist and band-leader; *b* 21 March 1936; *s* of Philip Beckford Westbrook and Vera Agnes (*née* Butler); *m* 1976, Katherine Jane (*née* Duckham), singer, songwriter and painter; one *s* one *d* of previous marriage. *Educ*: Kelly Coll., Tavistock; Plymouth Coll. of Art (NDD); Hornsey Coll. of Art (ATD). Formed first band at Plymouth Art Sch., 1958; moved to London, 1962, and has since led a succession of groups incl. The Mike Westbrook Brass Band, formed with Phil Minton in 1973, The Mike Westbrook Orch., 1974–, Westbrook Trio (with Kate Westbrook and Chris Biscoe), formed in 1982, Kate Westbrook Mike Westbrook Duo, 1995–, Westbrook & Company, 1998–, The New Westbrook Orchestra, 2001–, and The Village Band, 2004–. Has toured extensively in Britain and Europe, and performed in Australia, Canada, NY, Singapore and Hong Kong. Has written commissioned works for fests in Britain, France and other European countries, composed music for theatre, radio, TV and films, and made numerous LPs. Principal compositions/recordings include: Marching Song, 1967; Metropolis, 1969; Tyger: a celebration of William Blake (with Adrian Mitchell), 1971, also The Westbrook Blake, 1980 and Glad Day, 1999; Citadel/Room 315, 1974; On Duke's Birthday (dedicated to the memory of Duke Ellington), 1984; Off Abbey Road, 1988; Bean Rows and Blues Shots (saxophone concerto), 1991; Coming Through Slaughter (opera), 1994; Bar Utopia (lyrics by Helen Simpson), 1995; Blues for Terenzi, 1995; Cable Street Blues, 1997; The Orchestra of Smith's Academy, 1998; Classical Blues, 2001; TV scores incl. Caught on a Train, 1983; film scores: Moulin Rouge, 1990; Camera Makes Whoopee, 1996; with Kate Westbrook: concert works incorporating European poetry and folk song, notably The Cortège, for voices and jazz orch., 1979, London Bridge is Broken Down, for voice, jazz orch. and chamber orch., 1987, and Chanson Irresponsable, 2001; Turner in Uri, 2003; also a succession of music-theatre pieces, including: Mama Chicago, 1978; Westbrook-Rossini, 1984; The Ass (based on poem by D. H. Lawrence), 1985; Pier Rides, 1986; Quichotte (opera), 1989; Goodbye Peter Lorre, 1991; Measure for Measure, 1992; Good Friday 1663 (TV opera), 1994; Stage Set, 1996; Love Or Infatuation, 1997; Platterback, 1998; Jago (opera), 2000; L'Ascenseur/The Lift, 2002; Art Wolf, 2003; The Nijinska Chamber, 2005; Waxeywork Show, 2006; Cape Gloss (opera), 2007; English Soup or the Battle of the Classic Trifle, 2008. Hon. DMus Plymouth, 2004. *Recreation*: walking by the sea. *Address*: Flat 17, Tamar House, 12 Tavistock Place, WC1H 9RD; *e-mail*: admin@westbrookjazz.co.uk.

WESTBROOK, Sir Neil (Gowanloch), Kt 1988; CBE 1981; Chairman and Managing Director: Central Manchester Holdings Ltd, 1960–2005; Trafford Park Estates PLC, 1963–98; *b* 21 Jan. 1917; *s* of Frank and Dorothy Westbrook; *m* 1945, Hon. Mary Joan Fraser (*d* 2004), *o d* of 1st Baron Strathalmond, CBE; one *s* one *d. Educ*: Oundle Sch.; Clare Coll., Cambridge (MA). FRICS. Served War of 1939–45: Sapper, 1939; Actg Lt-Col 1945 (despatches). Chm., NW Industrial Council, 1982–87; Member: Council, CBI North West Region, 1982–88 (Chairman: NW Inner Cities Studies Gp, 1985; NW Working Party on Derelict Land Clearance, 1986); Inst. of Directors Greater Manchester Branch Cttee, 1972–86. Treas., Manchester Conservative Assoc., 1964–73, Dep. Chm., 1973–74, Chm., 1974–83; Chairman: Greater Manchester Co-ordinating Cttee, NW Area Cons. Assoc., 1977–86; Exchange Div. Cons. Assoc., 1973; Manchester Euro South Cons. Assoc., 1978–84; Member: NW Area F and GP Cttee, Cons. Party, 1974–87; Nat. Union Exec. Cttee, 1975–81; Cons. Bd of Finance, 1984–87. Mem., Manchester City Council, 1949–71; Dep. Leader 1967–69; Lord Mayor 1969–70. Chm., North Western Art Galleries and Museums Service, 1965–68; Mem., Exec. Cttee, Museums Assoc., 1965–69. Pres., Central Manchester Br., Arthritis and Rheumatism Council, 1970. Member: Duke of Edinburgh's Award Scheme Cttee, Manchester Area, 1972–75; Bd, Manchester YMCA, 1960–73. Mem., Chartered Auctioneers & Estate Agents Agricl Cttee, 1949–70; Mem., ABCC Rating Cttee, 1971–74. Hon. Mem., Magdalene Coll., Cambridge. *Recreations*: football, fishing, horse racing. *Address*: 1E Middlemede, Wigan Lane, Ballasalla, Isle of Man IM9 3EP. *Club*: Carlton.

WESTBROOK, Roger, CMG 1990; HM Diplomatic Service, retired; Chief Hon. Steward, Westminster Abbey, since 2006; *b* 26 May 1941; *e s* of Edward George Westbrook and Beatrice Minnie Westbrook (*née* Marshall). *Educ*: Dulwich Coll.; Hertford Coll., Oxford (MA Modern History). Foreign Office, 1964; Asst Private Sec. to Chancellor of Duchy of Lancaster and Minister of State, FO, 1965; Yaoundé, 1967; Rio de Janeiro, 1971; Brasilia, 1972; Private Sec. to Minister of State, FCO, 1975; Head of Chancery, Lisbon, 1977; Dep. Head, News Dept, FCO, 1980; Dep. Head, Falkland Is Dept, FCO, 1982; Overseas Inspectorate, FCO, 1984; High Comr, Negara Brunei Darussalam, 1986–91; Ambassador to Zaire, 1991–92; High Comr, Tanzania, 1992–95; Ambassador to Portugal, 1995–99. UK Comr, EXPO 98, Lisbon. Chm., Spencer House, 2000–06. Chairman: Anglo-Portuguese Soc., 2000–04; FCO Assoc., 2003–. Mem. Council, Book Aid Internat., 2002–. *Recreations*: doodling, sightseeing, theatre, reading, dining. *Address*: 33 Marsham Court, Marsham Street, SW1P 4JY.

WESTBURY, 6th Baron *cr* 1861, of Westbury, co. Wilts; **Richard Nicholas Bethell**, MBE 1979; *b* 29 May 1950; *e s* of 5th Baron Westbury, CBE, MC and Ursula Mary Rose (*née* James); *S* father, 2001; *m* 1st, 1975, Caroline Mary Palmer (marr. diss. 1991); one *s* two *d*; 2nd, 1993, Charlotte Sara Jane, *d* of John Temple Gore. *Educ*: Harrow; RMA Sandhurst. Major, Scots Guards, retd. *Heir*: *s* Hon. Alexander Bethell, *b* 21 Dec. 1986.

WESTBURY, Prof. Gerald, OBE 1990; FRCP, FRCS; Professor of Surgery, 1982–89, now Professor Emeritus, and Dean, 1986–92, Institute of Cancer Research; Hon. Consultant Surgeon, Royal Marsden Hospital, 1982–89; *b* 29 July 1927; *s* of Lew and Celia Westbury; *m* 1965, Hazel Frame; three *d. Educ*: St Marylebone Grammar Sch.; Westminster Med. Sch., Univ. of London (MB, BS (Hons) 1949). FRCS 1952; FRCP 1976. House Surg., Westminster and Royal Northern Hosps, 1949–50; RAF Med. Service, 1950–52; RSO, Brompton Hosp., 1952–53; Registrar and Sen. Registrar, Westminster Hosp., 1953–60; Fellow in Surgery, Harvard Med. Sch., 1957; Cons. Surg., Westminster Hosp., 1960–82 (Hon. Cons. Surgeon, 1982–89); Hon. Cons. in Surgery to the Army, 1980–89. Pres., British Assoc. of Surgical Oncology, 1989–92. Examiner, Univs of London, Edinburgh, Cambridge, Hong Kong; Hunterian Prof., RCS, 1963; Honyman Gillespie Lectr, Univ. of Edinburgh, 1965; Semon Lectr and Haddow Lectr, RSM, 1982; Gordon-Taylor Lectr, RCS, 1989. Fellow, Inst. of Cancer Res., 2000; Hon. FRCSE, 1993. Walker Prize, RCS, 1990. *Publications*: medical articles and contribs to text books. *Recreations*: music, bird watching. *Club*: Athenæum.

WESTCOTT, David Guy; QC 2003; *b* 14 May 1957; *s* of Walter Dennis Wetscott and Eileen Patricia Westcott; *m* Sara Paterson-Brown; one *s* one *d*. *Educ:* Cranleigh Sch.; Brasenose Coll., Oxford (BA Juris; BCL). Called to the Bar, Middle Temple, 1982. Captain, GB Men's Hockey team (winners of Bronze Medal), LA Olympics, 1984. Vice-Chm., Governing Body, Cranleigh Sch., 2006–. *Recreations:* outdoor sports, theatre.

WESTCOTT, Prof. John Hugh, DSc(Eng), PhD, DIC; FRS 1983; FREng; FCGI, FInstD; Professor of Control Systems, Imperial College of Science and Technology, 1961–84, now Emeritus; Chairman, Feedback plc, 1958–99; *b* 3 Nov. 1920; *s* of John Stanley Westcott and Margaret Elisabeth Westcott (*née* Bass); *m* 1950, Helen Fay Morgan; two *s* one *d*. *Educ:* Wandsworth Sch.; City and Guilds Coll., London; Massachusetts Inst. of Technology. Royal Commission for the Exhibition of 1851 Senior Studentship; Apprenticeship BTH Co., Rugby. Radar Research and Develt Estabt, 1941–45; Imperial College, London: Lectr, 1950; Reader, 1956; Head of Computing and Control Dept, 1970–79; Sen. Res. Fellow, 1984–94. Control Commn for Germany, 1945–46. Consultant to: Bataafsche Petroleum Maatschappij (Shell), The Hague, Holland, 1953–58; AEI, 1955–69; ICI, 1965–69; George Wimpey & Son, 1975–80; Westland plc, 1983–85. Chm., Control and Automation Div., Instn of Electrical Engrs, 1968–69. Mem., Exec. Council of Internat. Fedn of Automatic Control, 1969–75; Chm., United Kingdom Automation Council, 1973–79; Pres., Inst. of Measurement and Control, 1979–80. Mem., Adv. Council, RMCS, 1986–2001; Governor, Kingston Polytechnic, 1974–80. FREng (FEng 1980). Hon. FIET; Hon. FInstMC. *Publications:* An Exposition of Adaptive Control, 1962; monographs and papers, mainly on Control Systems and related topics. *Recreations:* gardening, reading. *Address:* (home) 8 Fernhill, Oxshott, Surrey KT22 0JH; Department of Electrical Engineering, Imperial College, SW7 2BT. *T:* (020) 7594 6240.
See also N. J. Westcott.

WESTCOTT, Dr Nicholas James, CMG 1999; HM Diplomatic Service; High Commissioner to Côte d'Ivoire, Ghana, and (non-resident) Ambassador to Togo, Niger and Burkina Faso, since 2007; *b* 20 July 1956; *s* of Prof. John Hugh Westcott, *qv* and Helen Fay Westcott (*née* Morgan); *m* 1989, Miriam Pearson; one *s* one *d*. *Educ:* Epsom Coll.; Sidney Sussex Coll., Cambridge (MA; PhD History 1982). Entered Foreign and Commonwealth Office, 1982; on secondment to EC, 1984–85; UK Perm. Rep. to EC, Brussels, 1985–89; FCO, 1989–93; Head of Common Foreign and Security Policy Unit, 1992–93; Dep. High Comr, Dar es Salaam, 1993–96; Head of Economic Relations Dept, FCO, 1996–98; Minister-Counsellor (Trade and Transport), Washington, 1999–2002; Head of IT Strategy, subseq. Chief Information Officer, FCO, 2002–07. *Publications:* (contrib.) Africa and the Second World War, 1986; (with P. Kingston and R. G. Tiedemann) Managed Economies in World War II, 1991; articles in jls. *Recreations:* cycling, reading, world music, story-telling. *Address:* c/o Foreign and Commonwealth Office, King Charles Street, SW1A 2AH.

WESTENRA, family name of **Baron Rossmore**.

WESTERN AUSTRALIA, Metropolitan of; *see* Perth, Archbishop of.

WESTGARTH, Peter Allen; Chief Executive, Duke of Edinburgh's Award, since 2005; *b* 17 May 1953; *s* of Allen and Elizabeth Westgarth; *m* 2007, Rachael Molsom; three *d* from previous marriage. *Educ:* City of Birmingham Sch. of Educn (Cert Ed). Secondary sch. teacher, Walbottle High Sch., 1974–75; advertising sales exec., Newcastle Chronicle, 1976; Exec. Manager, Help the Aged, 1976–80; Fundraising Manager, MIND, 1980–83; PR Officer, NE Co-op., 1983–86; UK Dir, Livewire, 1986–90; Chief Exec., Young Enterprise UK, 1990–2005. Hon. Pres., Young Enterprise Europe, 1991–98. Bata Lifetime Achievement Award for Young Enterprise Achievement, 2004; Queen's Award for Enterprise Promotion, 2006. *Recreations:* playing guitar, hill-walking, travel, BBQ, red wine, reading, and work. *Address:* Duke of Edinburgh's Award, Gulliver House, Madeira Walk, Windsor SL4 1EU. *T:* (01753) 727400; *e-mail:* peter.westgarth@theaward.org.

WESTHEIMER, Prof. Gerald, FRS 1985; Professor of Neurobiology, University of California, Berkeley, since 1989 (Professor of Physiology, 1967–89; Head of Division of Neurobiology, 1989–92); *b* Berlin, 13 May 1924; *s* of late Isaac Westheimer and Ilse Westheimer (*née* Cohn); Australian citizen, 1945. *Educ:* Sydney Tech. Coll. (Optometry dip. 1943, Fellowship dip. 1949); Univ. of Sydney (BSc 1947); Ohio State Univ. (PhD 1953); postdoctoral training at Marine Biol. Lab., Woods Hole, 1957 and at Physiolog. Lab., Cambridge, 1958–59. Practising optometrist, Sydney, 1945–51; faculties of Optometry Schools: Univ. of Houston, 1953–54; Ohio State Univ., 1954–60; Univ. of California, Berkeley, 1960–67. Associate: Bosch Vision Res. Center, Salk Inst., 1984–92; Neurosciences Res. Program, NY, 1985–95; Chairman: Visual Scis Study Sect., NIH, 1977–79; Bd of Scientific Counsellors, Nat. Eye Inst., 1981–83; Bd of Editors, Vision Research, 1986–91; service on numerous professional cttees. Adjunct Prof., Rockefeller Univ., NY, 1992–. Fellow or Member, scientific socs, UK and overseas; Fellow, Amer. Acad. of Arts and Scis. Lectures: Sackler, in Med. Sci., Tel Aviv Univ., 1989; Perception, Eur. Conf. on Visual Perception, 1989; D. O. Hebb, McGill Univ., Canada, 1991; Ferrier, Royal Soc., 1992; Wertheimer, Frankfurt Univ., 1998. Hon. DSc: New South Wales, 1988; SUNY, 1990; Hon. MD Tübingen, 2005. Tillyer Medal, Optical Soc. of America, 1978; Proctor Medal, Assoc. for Res. in Vision and Ophthalmology, 1979; von Sallmann Prize, Coll. of Physicians and Surgeons, Columbia Univ., 1986; Prentice Medal, Amer. Acad. of Optometry, 1986; Bicentennial Medal, Aust. Optometric Assoc., 1988. *Publications:* research articles in sci. and professional optometric and ophth. jls; edtl work for sci. jls. *Recreations:* chamber music (violin), foundation and history of sensory physiology. *Address:* 582 Santa Barbara Road, Berkeley, CA 94707, USA; *e-mail:* gwestheimer@berkeley. edu. *Club:* Cosmos (Washington).

WESTLEY, Stuart Alker, MA; Master of Haileybury, 1996–Aug. 2009; *b* 21 March 1947; *s* of Arthur Bancroft Westley and Gladys Westley; *m* 1979, Mary Louise Weston; one *d*. *Educ:* Lancaster Royal GS; Corpus Christi Coll., Oxford (BA 1969; MA 1972). Professional cricketer, 1969–71; Mathematics Teacher, King Edward VII Sch., Lytham, 1969–72; Housemaster and Dir of Studies, Framlingham Coll., 1973–84; Dep. Headmaster, Bristol Cathedral Sch., 1984–89; Principal, King William's Coll., IOM, 1989–96. *Recreations:* golf, fly fishing, gardening, architecture, choral and classical music, computers. *Address:* (until Aug. 2009) The Master's Lodge, Haileybury, Hertford SG13 7NU. *T:* (01992) 706222. *Club:* East India, Devonshire, Sports and Public Schools.

WESTMACOTT, Sir Peter John, KCMG 2003 (CMG 2000); LVO 1993; HM Diplomatic Service; Ambassador to France, since 2007; *b* 23 Dec. 1950; *s* of late Rev. Prebendary Ian Field Westmacott and of Rosemary Patricia Spencer Westmacott; *m* 1st, 1972, Angela Margaret Lugg (marr. diss. 1999); two *s* one *d*; 2nd, 2001, Susan Nemazee. *Educ:* Taunton Sch.; New Coll., Oxford (MA). Entered FCO 1972; served Tehran 1974, Brussels, 1978; First Sec., Paris, 1980; Private Sec. to Minister of State, FCO, 1984; Head of Chancery, Ankara, 1987; Dep. Private Sec. to Prince of Wales, 1990; Counsellor, Washington, 1993; Dir, Americas, FCO, 1997; Dep. Under-Sec. of State, FCO, 2000–01; Ambassador to Turkey, 2002–06. *Recreations:* tennis, ski-ing. *Address:* c/o Foreign and Commonwealth Office, SW1A 2AH.

WESTMACOTT, Richard Kelso; Chairman, Hoare Govett Ltd, 1975–90; *b* 20 Feb. 1934; *s* of Comdr John Rowe Westmacott, RN and Ruth Pharazyn; *m* 1965, Karen Husbands; one *s* one *d*. *Educ:* Eton College. Royal Navy, 1952–54. Hoare & Co., 1955; Mem., Stock Exchange, 1960; Chm., Security Pacific Hoare Govett (Holdings) Ltd, 1985–90; Dep. Chm., Maritime Trust, 1992–99. Dir, Prudential-Bache Internat. Bank Ltd, 1996–2002; Chm., Country Gardens plc, 1998–2001. Master, Mercers' Co., 1998–99; Younger Brother, Trinity House, 2000–. *Recreations:* sailing, shooting. *Address:* 9 Alexander Square, SW3 2AY. *Clubs:* White's; Royal Yacht Squadron.

WESTMEATH, 13th Earl of, *cr* 1621; **William Anthony Nugent;** Baron Delvin, by tenure temp. Henry II; by summons, 1486; Senior Master, St Andrew's School, Pangbourne, 1980–88; *b* 21 Nov. 1928; *s* of 12th Earl of Westmeath and Doris (*d* 1968), 2nd *d* of C. Imlach, Liverpool; *S* father, 1971; *m* 1963, Susanna Margaret, *o d* of His Honour James Leonard; two *s*. *Educ:* Marlborough Coll. Captain, RA, retired. Staff of St Andrew's Sch., Pangbourne, 1961–88. *Heir: s* Hon. Sean Charles Weston Nugent, *b* 16 Feb. 1965. *Address:* Farthings, Rotten Row Hill, Bradfield, Berks RG7 6LL. *T:* (0118) 974 4426.

WESTMINSTER, 6th Duke of, *cr* 1874; **Gerald Cavendish Grosvenor,** KG 2003; CB 2008; OBE 1995; TD 1994; DL; Bt 1622; Baron Grosvenor, 1761; Earl Grosvenor and Viscount Belgrave, 1784; Marquess of Westminster, 1831; *b* 22 Dec. 1951; *s* of 5th Duke of Westminster, TD, and Viola Maud (*d* 1987), *d* of 9th Viscount Cobham, KCB, TD; *S* father, 1979; *m* 1978, Natalia, *d* of Lt-Col H. P. J. Phillips; one *s* three *d*. *Educ:* Harrow. Commnd Queen's Own Yeomanry, RAC, TA, 1973; Captain, 1979; Major, 1985; Lt-Col, 1992; Comd, 1993–95; Col, 1995–97; Dep. Comdr, 143 W Midlands Bde, 1997–99; Brig., TA HQ Adjt Gen., 2000–02; Dir, Reserve Forces and Cadets, 2002–04; Maj. Gen., ACDS (Reserves and Cadets), 2004–07 (on unposted list 2007–). Chairman: Grosvenor, 1979–2007; Grosvenor Gp (formerly Grosvenor Gp Hldgs) Ltd, 1999–2007; Chm. of Trustees, Grosvenor Estate, 1974–; Director: Internat. Students Trust, 1976–93; Suttonridge Pty (Aust.), 1979–2000; Claridges Hotel Ltd, 1981–93; Marcher Sound Ltd, 1982–97; Westminster Christmas Appeal Trust Ltd, 1989–94; NW Business Leadership Team Ltd, 1990–97; BITC, 1991–95; Manchester Olympic Games Co-ordinating Cttee Ltd, 1991–94. Life Gov., RASE; Pro-Chancellor, Univ. of Keele, 1986–93; Chancellor, Manchester Metropolitan Univ., 1992–2002; first Chancellor, Univ. of Chester, 2005–. President: NW Industrialists' Council, 1979–93; London Fedn of Boys' Clubs, later of Clubs for Young People, 1979–2000; SCOPE (formerly Spastics Soc.), 1982–2005; Nat. Kidney Res. Fund, 1985–97; RNIB, 1986–; N of England Zool Soc., 1987–; Drug and Alcohol Foundn, 1987–97; Holstein UK & Ireland (formerly British Holstein Soc.,), 1988–; Country Trust, 1989–; Abbeyfield Soc., 1989–95; Inst. of Envmtl Scis, 1989–; BLESMA, 1992–; British Assoc. for Shooting and Conservation, 1992–2000; Youth Sports Trust, 1996–2004; Manchester Commonwealth Games, 1998–2002; Life Educn Centres (Drug Prevention), 2000–; Tank Mus., 2002–; Atlantic Salmon Trust, 2004–; Yeomanry Benevolent Fund, 2005–; Vice-President: Fountain Soc., 1985–; Freshwater Biol Assoc., 1985–; Royal Soc. of St George, 1987–; Royal Engrs Mus. Foundn, 1990–; RUSI, 1993–; RBL, 1993–; Royal Assoc. of British Dairy Farmers, 1995–; Reserve Forces, Ulysses Trust, 1995–; CLA, 1999–; Game and Wildlife Conservation Trust (formerly Game Conservancy Trust), 2000– (Pres., 1987–2000); Youth Fedn, 2000–; Royal Soc. of Friends of St George's and Descendants of the Knights of the Garter, 2003–; Not Forgotten Soc., 2004–; Royal Smithfield Club, 2004–; Community Network Foundn UK, 2005–; Life Vice-Pres., NSPCC, 1988–. Member, Committee: Nat. Army Mus., 1988–97; PYBT, 1989–; Rural Target Team, 1992; N Amer. Adv. Gp, BOTB, 1994; Nuffield Hosps, 1995–; Supporters of Nuclear Energy, 1998–; Special Appeal, St George's House, Windsor Castle, 2000–; Mem., Prince's Council, Duchy of Cornwall, 2001–; Chm., RICS Foundn, 2000–02. Patron: Worcs CCC (Pres., 1984–86); British Kidney Patients Assoc., 1979–84 (Mem. Council, 1984–2007); MIND, 1984–; Royal Fine Art Commn, 1988–; Dyslexia Inst., 1989–98; Inst. for Rural Health, 1989–; Rural Stress Inf. Network, 1996–; Royal Ulster Agricl Soc., 1997–2003; The Prince's Trust in the NW, 2001–; Emeka Anyaoku Chair in Commonwealth Studies, 2001–; Changing Faces, 2001–; Blue Cross Animal Hosp., 2001–; Barrowmore, 2002–; Arthritis Care, 2003– (Pres., 1987–2003); Emmaus, 2003–; Soil Assoc., 2004–; Vice-Patron, Animals in War Meml Fund, 2002–. Chm. Trustees, Nuffield Trust for Forces of the Crown, 1992–; Trustee: TSB Foundn for England and Wales, 1986–97; Westminster Abbey Trust; Westminster Foundn; Westminster Housing Trust; Falcon Trust; Habitat Res. Trust. Freeman: Chester, 1973; England, 1979; City of London, 1980. Liveryman: GAPAN; Gunmakers' Co.; Weavers' Co.; Armourers' and Braziers' Co.; Marketors' Co.; Goldsmiths' Co.; Fishmongers' Co. DL Cheshire, 1982. FIStructE 1997; FRSA; FRAS; FCIM; FCIOB; Fellow, Liverpool John Moores Univ., 1990. Hon. MRICS; Hon. Fellow: Liverpool Poly., 1990; Univ. of Central Lancs, 2001. Hon. LLD: Keele, 1990; Liverpool, 2000; Hon. DLitt: Manchester Metropolitan, 1993; Salford, 2000. Hon. Colonel: 7 Regt AAC, 1993–; Northumbrian Univs OTC, 1995–2003; Northumberland OTC; Royal Mercian and Lancastrian Yeomanry, 2001–08; Col in Chief, Royal Westminster Regt, 1991; Col Comdt, Yeomanry Assoc., 2005–. KStJ 1991. Knight Grand Cross, Royal Order of Francis I, 2005. *Recreations:* shooting, fishing, scuba diving. *Heir: s* Earl Grosvenor, *qv*. *Address:* Eaton Hall, Chester, Cheshire CH4 9EJ. *Clubs:* Brooks's, Cavalry, MCC; Royal Yacht Squadron.
See also Lady J. M. Dawnay.

WESTMINSTER, Archbishop of, (RC), since 2000; **His Eminence Cardinal Cormac Murphy-O'Connor;** *b* 24 Aug. 1932; *s* of late Dr P. G. Murphy-O'Connor and Ellen (*née* Cuddigan). *Educ:* Prior Park Coll., Bath; English Coll., Rome; Gregorian Univ. PhL, STL. Ordained Priest, 1956. Asst Priest, Portsmouth and Fareham, 1956–66; Sec. to Bp of Portsmouth, 1966–70; Parish Priest, Parish of the Immaculate Conception, Southampton, 1970–71; Rector, English College, Rome, 1971–77; Bishop of Arundel and Brighton, 1977–2000. Cardinal, 2001. Chairman: Bishops' Cttee for Europe, 1978–83; Cttee for Christian Unity, 1983–2000; Dept for Mission and Unity, Bishops' Conf. of England and Wales, 1993–2001; Jt Chm., ARCIC-II, 1983–2000; Pres., Catholic Bps' Conf. of England and Wales, 2000–. Member: Congregation for the Sacraments and Divine Worship, 2001–; Admin of Patrimony of Holy See, 2001–; Council for Study of Orgnl and Econ. Problems of the Holy See, 2001–; Presidential Cttee, Pontifical Council for the Family, 2002–; Pontifical Council for Culture, 2002–. DD Lambeth, 1999. *Publications:* At the Heart of the World, 2004; The Human Face of God, 2004. *Recreations:* music, sport. *Address:* Archbishop's House, Westminster, SW1P 1QJ.

WESTMINSTER, Auxiliary Bishops of, (RC); *see* Arnold, Rt Rev. J. S. K.; Hopes, Rt Rev. A. S.; Longley, Rt Rev. B.; Stack, Rt Rev. G.

WESTMINSTER, Dean of; *see* Hall, Very Rev. J. R.

WESTMORLAND, 16th Earl of, *cr* 1624; **Anthony David Francis Henry Fane;** Baron Burghersh, 1624; independent art adviser; Director: Phillips Auctioneers, 1994–2001; Bonhams Auctioneers, 2001–04; *b* 1 Aug. 1951; *s* of 15th Earl of Westmorland, GCVO and of Jane, *d* of Lt-Col Sir Roland Lewis Findlay, 3rd Bt; *S* father, 1993; *m* 1985, Caroline Eldred, *d* of Keon Hughes; one *d*. *Educ:* Eton. Mem., Orbitex North Pole Expedn, 1990. *Heir: b* Hon. Harry St Clair Fane [*b* 19 March 1953; *m* 1984, Tessa, *d* of Captain Michael Philip Forsyth-Forrest; one *s* one *d*]. *Address:* London SW7. *Club:* Turf.

WESTMORLAND AND FURNESS, Archdeacon of; *see* Howe, Ven. G. A.

WESTON, Prof. Arthur Henry, PhD, DSc; FMedSci, FBPharmacolS; Leech Professor of Pharmacology, University of Manchester, since 1990; *b* 31 May 1944; *s* of Arthur Edward Weston and Betty Nutt Weston (*née* Wetherell); *m* 1967, Kathleen Margaret Goodison; one *s* one *d*. *Educ:* Hymers Coll., Hull; Univ. of Manchester (BSc 1st Cl. Hons 1966, MSc 1968; PhD 1970; DSc 1994). Lectr in Pharmacol., 1970–75, Sen. Lectr, 1975–88, Reader, 1988–90, Univ. of Manchester. Alexander von Humboldt Fellow, Univ. of Marburg, 1974, Univ. of Heidelberg, 1985; Vis. Prof., Univ. of Kyushu, 1987. Trustee and Hon. Treas., British Pharmacol Soc., 2000–07; Pres., Fedn of Eur. Pharmacol Socs, 2006–08; Hon. Mem., Finnish Pharmacol Soc., 2008. FMedSci 2001; FBPharmacolS 2004. Gaddum Memorial Award, British Pharmacol Soc., 2008. *Publications:* (jtly) Pharmacology of the Hypothalamus, 1978; (with T. C. Hamilton) Potassium Channel Modulators, 1992; contrib. original papers to British Jl Pharmacol., Jl Pharmacol. and Exptl Therapeutics, Nature, Naunyn Schmiedeberg's Archives of Pharmacol. *Recreations:* gardening, mechanical watches, visiting Germany; early British postage stamps. *Address:* Faculty of Life Sciences, University of Manchester, 2nd Floor, CTF Building, 46 Grafton Street, Manchester M13 9NT. *T:* (0161) 275 5490, *Fax:* (0161) 275 5600; *e-mail:* arthur.weston@manchester.ac.uk.

WESTON, Christopher John; Life President, Phillips Son & Neale (Chairman and Chief Executive, 1972–98); Chairman and Chief Executive Officer, Plaxbury Group, since 1998; *b* 3 March 1937; *s* of Eric Tudor Weston and Evelyn Nellie Weston; *m* 1969, Josephine Annabel Moir; one *d*. *Educ:* Lancing Coll. FIA (Scot.). Director: Phillips, 1964–98; Foreign and Colonial Pacific Investment Trust, 1984–99; Hodder Headline Plc (formerly Headline Book Publishing PLC), 1986–99 (Chm., 1997–99); Foreign & Colonial Enterprise Trust plc, 1987–99. Vice-Pres., Quit - Soc. of Non Smokers, 1993–. Freeman, Painters-Stainers' Co. FRSA (Mem. Council, 1985). *Recreations:* theatre, music. *Address:* 5 Hillside Close, Carlton Hill, NW8 0EF. *T:* (020) 7372 5042. *Club:* Oriental.

WESTON, Rev. Canon David Wilfrid Valentine, PhD; Residentiary Canon of Carlisle Cathedral, 1994–2006; Canon Librarian, 1995–2006; *b* 8 Dec. 1937; *s* of Rev. William Valentine Weston and Mrs Gertrude Hamilton Weston; *m* 1984, Helen Strachan Macdonald, *d* of James and Barbara Macdonald; two *s*. *Educ:* St Edmund's Sch., Canterbury; Lancaster Univ. (PhD 1993). Entered Nashdom Abbey, 1960; deacon, 1967, priest, 1968; Novice Master, 1969–74; Prior, 1971–74; Abbot, 1974–84; Curate, St Peter's, Chorley, 1984–85; Vicar, St John the Baptist, Pilling, 1985–89; Domestic Chaplain to Bishop of Carlisle, 1989–94; Actg Dean, Carlisle, 2003–04. Chm., Carlisle Tourism Forum, 1996–98. Freeman, City of London; Liveryman of Salters' Co. *Publications:* Carlisle Cathedral History, 2000; (ed jtly) Carlisle and Cumbria, 2004. *Address:* 40 St James' Road, Carlisle, Cumbria CA2 5PD.

WESTON, Galen; *see* Weston, W. G.

WESTON, George Garfield; Chief Executive, Associated British Foods plc, since 2005; *b* 4 March 1964; *s* of late Garfield Howard Weston and Mary Ruth Weston (*née* Kippenberger); *m* 1996, Katharine Mary Acland; three *s* one *d*. *Educ:* Westminster Sch.; New Coll., Oxford (MA PPE); Harvard Business Sch. (MBA). N. B. Love Mills, 1988–92; Managing Director: Westmill Foods, 1992–98; Allied Bakeries, 1999–2003; Chief Exec., George Weston Foods Ltd (Australia), 2003–05. *Recreations:* tennis, gardening. *Address:* Associated British Foods plc, 10 Grosvenor Street, W1K 4QY. *T:* (020) 7399 6500.

WESTON, Hon. Hilary Mary, CM 2003; OOnt 2001; Lieutenant Governor of Ontario, 1997–2002; *b* 12 Jan. 1942; *d* of Michael Frayne and Noel Elizabeth Guerrini; *m* 1966, Willard Galen Weston, *qv*; one *s* one *d*. *Educ:* Loretto Abbey, Dalkey. Dep. Chm., Holt, Renfrew & Co., 1986–96; Design Dir, Windsor, Florida, 1988–96. Founder, Ireland Fund of Canada, 1979. Hon. Col, 437 Transport Sqdn, CFB Trenton & The Princess of Wales' Own Regt, Kingston, 1998–2002. Hon. DLitts Univ. of St Michael's Coll., Toronto, 1997; Hon. LLD: Western Ontario, 1997; UC of Cape Breton, 1999; Toronto, 2000; Niagara, York, 2002; Dublin, 2004. DStJ 1997. *Publications:* (jtly) In a Canadian Garden, 1989; (jtly) At Home in Canada, 1995. *Recreations:* tennis, riding. *Address:* 22 St Clair Avenue East, Toronto, ON M4T 2S3, Canada. *T:* (416) 9354050; Fort Belvedere, Ascot, Berks SL5 7SD. *Club:* National (Toronto).

WESTON, Sir John; *see* Weston, Sir P. J.

WESTON, John Pix, BSc(Eng), BSc(Econ); CEng, FIET; investment consultant, since 1984; *b* 3 Jan. 1920; *s* of John Pix Weston and Margaret Elizabeth (*née* Cox); *m* 1948, Ivy (*née* Glover); three *s*. *Educ:* King Edward's Sch., Birmingham, 1931–36; Univ. of Aston, 1946–50 (BSc(Eng), Hons); Univ. of London (LSE), 1954–57 (BSc(Econ), Hons). CEng 1953, FIET (FIEE 1966); FSS 1958; FREconS 1958. Mil. Service, 1939–46, S Africa and Albania. City of Birmingham: Police Dept, 1936–39; Electricity Supply Dept, 1939–48; Midlands Electricity Bd, 1948–50; English Electricity Co., 1950–51; NW Elec. Bd, 1951–58; Eastern Elec. Bd, 1958–60; Dep. Operating Manager, Jamaica Public Services Co., 1960–61; Principal Asst Engr, Midlands Elec. Bd, 1961–64; Asst Ch. Commercial Officer, S of Scotland Elec. Bd, 1964–66; Sen. Econ. Adviser to Mrs Barbara Castle, MoT, 1966–69; Sen. Econ. and Chartered Engr, IBRD, 1968–70; Michelin Tyre Co., France, 1970–72; Dir of Post Experience Courses, Open Univ., 1972–75; Dir Gen., RoSPA, 1975–77; Gen. Sec., Birmingham Anglers' Assoc., 1977; Industrial Develt Officer, Argyll and Bute, 1977–79; Health, Safety and Welfare Officer, Newcastle Polytechnic, and Central Safety Advr, Northants CC, 1979; Chief Admin. Officer and Clerk to Governors, W Bromwich Coll. of Comm. and Tech., 1979–85. Hon. Sec. and Treasurer, Assoc. of Coll. Registrars and Administrators (W Midlands), 1982–85. Council Mem., Midlands Counties Photographic Fedn, 1984–86; Hon. Prog., Competition and Outings Sec. and Council Mem., Birmingham Photographic Soc., 1981–86; MIES 1963; Mem., Assoc. of Public Lighting Engrs, 1962. FCMI (FBIM 1977). Chm., Upper Marlbrook Residents' Assoc., 1982–87; Treasurer, Laugharne Cons. Assoc., 1991–94 (Asst Treasurer, 1990–91). Member: Narbeth and Dist Probus Club, 1988–96; St Clears Probus Club, 1989–96 (Pres., 1990–91); Tenby Probus Club, 1990–96. Page Prize, IEE, 1950; Rosebery Prize, Univ. of London, 1957. SBStJ 1962. *Publications:* papers, reports and other contribs on electricity, highways, educn (espec. function and progress of the Open University), safety, etc, to public bodies, congresses and conferences, UK and abroad. *Recreations:* cine photography, gardening, swimming, fell walking. *Address:* Brook Mill & Woodside, Brook, Pendine, Carmarthenshire SA33 4NX. *T:* (01994) 427477. *Clubs:* Farmers', St John House; Birmingham Press.

See also J. P. Weston.

WESTON, John Pix, CBE 1994; FRAeS; FREng; Chairman: Acra Controls, since 2003; Ufi, since 2004; iSoft plc, since 2005; Insensys Ltd, since 2007; MB Aerospace, since 2007; *b* 16 Aug. 1951; *s* of John Pix Weston, *qv* and Ivy (*née* Glover); *m* 1974, Susan West; one *s* one *d*. *Educ:* King's Sch., Worcester; Trinity Hall., Cambridge (MA Eng.). CEng 1992, FRAeS 1992. British Aerospace, subseq. BAE SYSTEMS: undergrad. apprenticeship, 1970–74; sales appts on Jaguar and Tornado projects, 1974–82; on secondment to MoD Sales Orgn, 1982–85; Military Aircraft Division, Warton: ME Sales Manager, Project Manager, Al Yamamah Project and Exec. Dir, Saudi Ops, 1985–89; Dir, 1989–92; Man. Dir, 1990–92; Chm. and Man. Dir, British Aerospace Defence Ltd, 1992–96; Dir, 1994–2002; Gp Man. Dir, 1996–98; Chief Exec., 1998–2002. Chairman: Spirent plc, 2002–06; INBIS plc, 2004–05. Mem., President's Cttee, 2000–, Chm., Europe Cttee, 2001–, CBI; Vice-Pres., RUSI, 2000–. FREng 2000; FRSA. *Recreations:* ski-ing, photography, hill-walking. *Address: e-mail:* johnpweston@btinternet.com.

WESTON, Dame Margaret (Kate), DBE 1979; BScEng (London); CEng, FIET, FINucE; FMA; Director of the Science Museum, 1973–86; *b* 7 March 1926; *o c* of late Charles Edward and Margaret Weston. *Educ:* Stroud High School; College of Technology, Birmingham (now Univ. of Aston). Engineering apprenticeship with General Electric Co. Ltd, followed in 1949 by development work, very largely on high voltage insulation problems. Joined Science Museum as an Assistant Keeper, Dept of Electrical Engineering and Communications, 1955; Deputy Keeper, 1962; Keeper, Dept of Museum Services, 1967–72. Member: Ancient Monuments Bd for England, 1977–84; 1851 Commission, 1987–96; Museums and Galleries Commission, 1988–96; Steering Gp, Museum in Docklands, 1986–90. Member: SE Elec. Bd, 1981–90; BBC Sci. Consultative Gp, 1986–89. Chairman: Brunel Goods Shed Cttee, Stroud, 2004–07; Heritage Network (formerly Heritage Forum), Stroud, 2005–; Trustee: Hunterian Mus., RCS, 1981–; Brooklands, 1987–2002; Fleet Air Arm Mus., 1992–2000; British Empire and Commonwealth Mus., Bristol, 1999–2002 (Chm., 1999–2002); Museum in the Park, Stroud, 2004– (Chm. Trustees, 2004–05). Horniman Public Museum and Public Park: Chm. Trust, 1990–96; Mem. Develt Cttee, 1996–2002; Pres., Friends, 1996–2003; Chm. Trustees, Horniman Mus., Trust, 1997–2002. Patron, Stroudwater Textile Trust, 2002–. Governor: Imperial Coll., 1974–90 (FIC 1975); Ditchley Foundn, 1984– (Mem., Mgt Council, 1984–2003). Pres., Heritage Railways Assoc. (formerly Assoc. of Railway Preservation Socs, then Assoc. of Independent Railways and Preservation Socs), 1985–. FMA 1976; Sen. Fellow, RCA, 1986; FRSA (Mem. Council, 1985–90); CCMI. Hon. Fellow, Newnham Coll., Cambridge, 1986. Hon. DEng Bradford, 1984; Hon. DSc: Aston, 1974; Salford, 1984; Leeds, 1987; Loughborough, 1988; DUniv Open, 1987. *Address:* 7 Shawley Way, Epsom, Surrey KT18 5NZ. *T:* (01737) 355885.

WESTON, Sir Michael (Charles Swift), KCMG 1991; CVO 1979; JP; HM Diplomatic Service, retired; UK Permanent Representative to Conference on Disarmament, Geneva (with personal rank of Ambassador), 1992–97; *b* 4 Aug. 1937; *s* of late Edward Charles Swift Weston and Kathleen Mary Weston (*née* Mockett); *m* 1st, 1959, Veronica Anne Tickner (marr. diss. 1990); two *s* one *d*; 2nd, 1990, Christine Julia Ferguson; one *s* one *d*. *Educ:* Dover Coll.; St Catharine's Coll., Cambridge (Exhibitioner; BA, MA). Joined HM Diplomatic Service, 1961; 3rd Sec., Kuwait, 1962; 2nd Sec., FCO, 1965; 1st Secretary: Tehran, 1968; UK Mission, New York, 1970; FCO, 1974; Counsellor, Jedda, 1977; RCDS, 1980; Counsellor (Information), Paris, 1981; Counsellor, Cairo, 1984; Head of Southern European Dept, FCO, 1987; Ambassador to Kuwait, 1990–92. Member: UN Sec.-Gen.'s Gp of Experts on Small Arms, 1998–99; Special Immigration Appeals Commn, 1999–. JP West Kent, 2002. *Recreations:* tennis, squash, walking. *Address:* Beech Farm House, Beech Lane, Matfield, Kent TN12 7HG. *T:* and *Fax:* (01892) 824921. *Club:* Oxford and Cambridge.

WESTON, Sir (Philip) John, KCMG 1992 (CMG 1985); HM Diplomatic Service, retired; British Permanent Representative to the United Nations, 1995–98; *b* 13 April 1938; *s* of late Philip George Weston and Edith Alice Bray (*née* Ansell); *m* 1967, Margaret Sally Ehlers; two *s* one *d*. *Educ:* Sherborne; Worcester Coll., Oxford (1st Cl. Hons Honour Mods Classics and Lit. Hum.; Hon. Fellow, 2003). Served with Royal Marines, 1956–58. Entered Diplomatic Service, 1962; FO, 1962–63; Treasury Centre for Admin. Studies, 1964; Chinese Language student, Hong Kong, 1964–66; Peking, 1967–68; FO, 1969–71; Office of UK Permanent Representative to EEC, 1972–74; Asst Private Sec. to Sec. of State for Foreign and Commonwealth Affairs (Rt Hon. James Callaghan, Rt Hon. Anthony Crosland), 1974–76; Counsellor, Head of EEC Presidency Secretariat, FCO, 1976–77; Vis. Fellow, All Souls Coll., Oxford, 1977–78; Counsellor, Washington, 1978–81; Hd Defence Dept, FCO, 1981–84; Asst Under-Sec. of State, FCO, 1984–85; Minister, Paris, 1985–88; Dep. Sec. to Cabinet, Cabinet Office, 1988–89 (on secondment); Dep. Under-Sec. of State (Defence), FCO, 1989–90; Political Dir, FCO, 1990–91; Ambassador and UK Perm. Rep. to N Atlantic Council (NATO), 1992–95, to Perm. Council of WEU, 1992–95. Non-executive Director: BT Gp, 1998–2002; Rolls Royce, 1998–2004; Hakluyt and Co. Ltd, 2001–07. Trustee: NPG, 1999–2008; Poetry Soc., 2005–08; Chm. Trustees, The Poetry Sch., 2005–08. Council Mem., IISS, 2001–05. Governor: Sherborne Sch., 1995–2007 (Chm., 2002–07); Ditchley Foundn, 1999–. Trustee, Amer. Associates of the Royal Acad. Trust, 1998–2004. Pres., Worcester Coll. Soc., 2003–. Hon. Pres., Community Foundn Network, 1999–2008. *Publications:* (contrib.) Take Five 04 (anthol.), 2004; Chasing The Hoopoe (poems), 2005; poems in many magazines (various prizes). *Recreations:* poetry, fly-fishing, birds, running. *Address:* 13 Denbigh Gardens, Richmond, Surrey TW10 6EN. *Club:* Garrick.

WESTON, Simon, OBE 1992; writer and performer, since 1985; *b* 8 Aug. 1961; *s* of Harold Hatfield and Pauline Hatfield; *m* 1990, Lucy Veronica (*née* Titherington); two *s* one *d*. *Educ:* Lewis Boys' Sch., Pengam, Mid Glam. Joined Welsh Guards, 1978; served Berlin, NI, Kenya and Falklands; Co-Founder and Vice Pres., Weston Spirit, 1988–. Vice Pres. and advocate, Royal Star and Garter Home, 1991. Pres., Fleming Fulton Special Needs Sch. Poultry Club, 1990. A Freemason. Freedom, City of Liverpool, 2002. Hon. Fellow: John Moore's Univ., Liverpool, 2003; Open Univ., 2003; Cardiff Univ., 2005. Hon. degree in humanities, 1994, Hon. DHum, 2002, Glamorgan. *Publications: autobiography:* Walking Tall, 1989; Going Back, 1992; Moving On, 2003; *novels:* Cause of Death, 1995; Phoenix, 1996. *Recreations:* reading, keeping fit, music, watching sport, jogging. *Address:* Abingdon Management Company, Rosedale House, Rosedale Road, Richmond, Surrey TW9 2SZ. *T:* (020) 8939 9019, *Fax:* (020) 8939 9080.

WESTON, Susan Elizabeth; *see* Murray, S. E.

WESTON, W(illard) Galen, OC 1990; Chairman, since 1978, and President, George Weston Ltd, Toronto; former Executive Chairman, Loblaw Companies Ltd; *b* England, 29 Oct. 1940; *s* of W. Garfield Weston and Reta Lila (*née* Howard); *m* 1966, Hon. Hilary Mary Frayne (*see* Hon. H. M. Weston); one *s* one *d*. Chairman: Selfridges & Co.; Holt Renfrew & Co. Ltd; Brown Thomas; Wittington Investments Ltd; Vice-Chm., Fortnum & Mason plc (UK); Director: Associated British Foods plc (UK); Brown Thomas Group Ltd (Eire). Pres. and Trustee, W. Garfield Weston Foundation, Canada. Hon. LLD Univ. of Western Ont. *Recreations:* outdoor sports, contemporary arts. *Address:* Suite 2001,

George Weston Ltd, 22 St Clair Avenue East, Toronto, ON M4T 2S7, Canada. *T:* (416) 9222500, *Fax:* (416) 9224394. *Clubs:* Guards' Polo; Toronto, York (Toronto); Windsor (Florida); Deep Dale (NY).

WESTON, William John, MVO 2002; independent management consultant to cultural, heritage and leisure sectors; *b* 4 July 1949; *s* of Eric Gordon and Pauline Violet Weston; *m* 1978, Patricia April (decd); two *d*; *m* 1995, Jane Henriques; one step *s* one step *d*. *Educ:* Wymondham Coll., Norfolk; Royal Manchester Coll. of Music; Poly. of Central London. Concerts Manager, Bournemouth SO, 1971–73; City Arts Administrator, Southampton CC, 1973–77; Administrator, Irish Th. Co., Dublin, 1977–80; Exec. Dir and Creator, W Yorks Playhouse, Leeds, 1980–93; freelance TV producer, 1993–95; Gen. Manager, RSC, 1995–2000; Chief Exec., Royal Parks Agency, 2000–05. Non-exec. Dir, England Nat. Cttee, Forestry Commn. Member: Yorks Regl Arts Council, 2005–; Yorks Dales Nat. Park Authy, 2006–. *Recreations:* the arts, walking, gardening, open spaces, jazz, sailing. *Address:* Brignall Mill, Brignall, Barnard Castle, County Durham DL12 9SQ.

WESTWELL, Alan Reynolds, OBE 1996; PhD, MSc; CEng, MIMechE, MIET; FCILT; Managing Director and Chief Executive, Dublin Buses Ltd, 1997–2005; *b* 11 April 1940; *s* of Stanley Westwell and Margaret (*née* Reynolds); *m* 1967, Elizabeth Aileen Birrell; two *s* one *d*. *Educ:* Old Swan Coll.; Liverpool Polytechnic (ACT Hons); Salford Univ. (MSc 1983); Keele Univ. (PhD 1991). Liverpool City Transport Dept: progressively, student apprentice, Technical Asst, Asst Works Manager, 1956–67; Chief Engineer: Southport Corporation Transport Dept, 1967–69; Coventry Corp. Transport Dept, 1969–72; Glasgow Corp. Transport Dept, 1972–74; Director of Public Transport (responsible for bus/rail, airport, harbours), Tayside Regional Council, 1974–79; Dir Gen., Strathclyde PTE, 1979–86; Chm., Man. Dir and Chief Exec., Strathclyde Buses Ltd, 1987–90; Man. Dir and Chief Exec., Greater Manchester Buses Ltd, 1990–93, Greater Manchester Buses North Ltd, 1993–97. Professional Advr, COSLA, 1976–86. President: Scottish Council of Confedn of British Road Passenger Transport, 1982–83 (Vice-Pres., 1981–82); Bus and Coach Council, UK, 1989–90 (Vice Pres., 1985–88; Sen. Vice-Pres., 1988–89). Mem., Parly Road Transport Cttee, 1986–97. Chm., IMechE, Automobile Div., Scottish Centre, 1982–84; Mem. Council, CIT, UK, 1986–89 (Chm. Scottish Centre, 1983–84). International Union of Public Transport: Vice Pres., 1997; Member: Management Cttee, 1991–; Internat. Metropolitan Railway Cttee, 1979–86; Internat. Gen. Commn on Transport and Urban Life (formerly Internat. Commn, Traffic and Urban Planning), 1986–; UITP-EU (formerly European Action) Cttee, 1988–; Chm., UK Members, 1993–97. Hon. Vice Pres., UITP, 2003. *Publications:* various papers. *Recreations:* swimming, music, reading. *Address:* 6 Amberley Drive, Hale Barns, Altrincham, Cheshire WA15 0DT. *T:* (0161) 980 3551.

WESTWOOD, family name of **Baron Westwood**.

WESTWOOD, 3rd Baron *cr* 1944, of Gosforth; **William Gavin Westwood;** *b* 30 Jan. 1944; *s* of 2nd Baron Westwood and of Marjorie, *o c* of Arthur Bonwick; *S* father, 1991; *m* 1969, Penelope, *e d* of Dr C. E. Shafto; two *s*. *Educ:* Fettes. *Recreations:* music, reading. *Heir:* *s* Hon. (William) Fergus Westwood, *b* 24 Nov. 1972. *Address:* 9 Princes Close, Brunton Park, Newcastle upon Tyne NE3 5AS; *e-mail:* lordwestwood@hotmail.com.

WESTWOOD, Dr Albert Ronald Clifton, FREng; consultant in research and technology management, since 2000; Vice President, Research and Exploratory Technology, Sandia National Laboratories, 1993–96, now Emeritus; *b* 9 June 1932; *s* of Albert Sydney Westwood and Ena Emily (*née* Clifton); *m* 1956, Jean Mavis Bullock; two *d*. *Educ:* Univ. of Birmingham (BSc Hons 1953; PhD 1956; DSc 1968). FInstP 1967; FIMMM (FIM 1998). Joined Research Institute for Advanced Studies, subseq. Martin Marietta Labs, Baltimore, 1958, Dir, 1974–84; Martin Marietta Corporation: Corporate Dir, R&D, 1984–87; Vice Pres., R&D, 1987–90; Corporate Vice Pres., Res. and Technol., 1990–93. Chm. and Chief Exec., CCLRC, UK, 1998–2000. Chairman: Commn on Engrg and Technical Systems, Nat. Res. Council, 1992–97; Cttee on Global Aspects of Intellectual Properties Rights in Sci. and Technol., Nat. Res. Council, 1992–93; and numerous govt, academic, civic, music and humanities councils and adv. bds. Mem. Bd, US Civilian R&D Foundn, 1995–. President: Industrial Res. Inst., US, 1989–90; Minerals, Metals and Materials Soc., 1990 (Fellow, 1990). Fellow, Amer. Soc. for Materials Internat., 1974; FAAAS 1986; FREng (FEng 1996). Member: US NAE, 1980; Royal Swedish Acad. Engrg Scis, 1989; Russian Acad. Engrg, 1995; Georgia Acad. of Engrg. Pianist and arranger accompanying wife in concerts and recitals in US and around world. Has received numerous awards, prizes and lectureships in recognition of scientific and managerial contribs. *Publications:* (ed) Environment Sensitive Mechanical Behavior, 1966; (ed) Mechanisms of Environment Sensitive Cracking of Materials, 1977; about 125 scientific papers. *Recreations:* music, theatre, arts, travel. *Address:* 13539 Canada Del Oso, High Desert, Albuquerque, NM 87111, USA; *e-mail:* arwestwood@aol.com.

WESTWOOD, Dr David, QPM 2001; Chief Constable, Humberside Police, 1999–2005; *b* 1 April 1948; *s* of late Sqdn Ldr William Westwood and Judith Westwood (*née* Green); *m* 1969, Wendy Stevenson; three *s* one *d*. *Educ:* Collyers Sch., Horsham; Lady Margaret Hall, Oxford (MA Juris.); Bristol Poly. (PhD 1991). Constable, Sussex Police, 1963–73; Constable to Supt, Avon and Somerset Police, 1973–92; Chief Supt, Humberside Police, 1992–95; Asst Chief Constable, Merseyside Police, 1995–97; Dep. Chief Constable, Humberside Police, 1997–99. Hd, Business Area for Race and Community Relns, ACPO, 2000–03. *Recreations:* theatre, organic gardening. *Address:* c/o Humberside Police Headquarters, Priory Road, Kingston upon Hull HU5 5SF. *T:* (01482) 578204.

WESTWOOD, Dame Vivienne (Isabel), DBE 2006 (OBE 1992); RDI 2001; fashion designer; *b* 8 April 1941; *née* Vivienne Isabel Swire; two *s*. In partnership with Malcolm McLaren, designed a series of influential avant-garde collections showcased at World's End (formerly named Let It Rock, Too Fast to Live Too Young to Die, Sex, Seditionaries), 430 King's Rd, Chelsea, 1971–82; opened Vivienne Westwood shop, 6 Davies St, W1, 1990, flagship shop, 44 Conduit St, W1, 1992, head office Milan, 1998, and stores worldwide; collections include: Anglomania, 1993–; Vivienne Westwood Man (Milan), 1996–; Red Label, London, 1997–, Paris, 1998–, New York, 2000–; Gold Label, 1999–. Launched fragrances: Boudoir, 1998; Libertine, 2000; Boudoir Sin City, 2007; Let It Rock, 2007. Exhibitions at V & A Museum: (contrib.) Radical Fashion, 2001; (contrib.) Men in Skirts, 2002; (contrib.) Tiaras, 2002; Vivienne Westwood 36 Years in Fashion, 2004 and subseq. world tour; launched manifesto at Wallace Collection, 2007. Professor of Fashion: Acad. of Applied Arts, Vienna, 1989–91; Hochschule der Künste, Berlin, 1993–. Trustee, Civil Liberties Trust, 2007–. Hon. Sen. FRCA 1992; Hon. FKC 2008; Dr *hc* Heriot Watt, 2008; RCA, 2008. British Designer of the Year, 1990, 1991, Outstanding Achievement in Fashion, 2007, British Fashion Council; Queen's Award for Export, 1998; Moët & Chandon Red Carpet Dresser, 2006. *Address:* Vivienne Westwood Ltd, Westwood Studios, 9–15 Elcho Street, Battersea, SW11 4AU. *T:* (020) 7924 4747.

WETHERED, Julian Frank Baldwin; Director, International Division, United States Banknote Corporation, 1992–94; *b* 9 Nov. 1929; *s* of late Comdr Owen Francis McTier Wethered, RN retd and Betty (*née* Baldwin); *m* 1st, 1952, Britt Eva Hindmarsh (marr. diss. 1971); one *s* one *d*; 2nd, 1973, Antonia Mary Ettrick Roberts; two *s*. *Educ:* Eton Coll.; Jesus Coll., Cambridge (BA Hons Hist. 1952; MA); BA Hons Open Univ. 2002. National Service, RM, HMS Diadem, 1948–49. Trainee, Expandite Ltd, 1952–54; Sales Rep., Remington Rand, 1955–56; Thomas De La Rue and Co.: trainee, 1956; Mem., PA Study Team, 1957; Printing Preliminaries Manager, Currency Div., 1958–62; Special Rep., Africa, 1963–67; Manager, Banknote Printing Co., 1968–69; Regl Manager, FE, 1970–75; Associate Dir of Sales, Africa and FE, 1976–83; Regl Dir, FE, De La Rue Co. plc, 1984–88; Associate Dir of Sales, Thomas De La Rue & Co., 1989. Dir Gen., RoSPA, 1990–91. Chm., Riding for the Disabled Assoc. of Singapore, 1987–88. Pres., British Business Assoc. of Singapore, 1988. FInstD; FRSA. *Recreations:* sailing, riding, the arts. *Address:* Brunton Barn, Collingbourne Kingston, Marlborough, Wilts SN8 3SE. *Club:* Travellers.

WETHERELL, Gordon Geoffrey; HM Diplomatic Service; Governor, Turks and Caicos Islands, since 2008; *b* 11 Nov. 1948; *s* of Geoffrey and late Georgette Maria Wetherell; *m* 1981, Rosemary Anne Myles; four *d*. *Educ:* Bradfield Coll., Berks; New Coll., Oxford (BA 1969; MA 1975); Univ. of Chicago (MA 1971). Joined HM Diplomatic Service, 1973; FCO (concurrently British Embassy, Chad), 1973–74; E Berlin, 1974–77; First Sec., FCO, 1977; UK Delegn to Comprehensive Test Ban Negotiations, Geneva, 1977–80; New Delhi, 1980–83; FCO, 1983–85; on secondment to HM Treasury, 1986–87; Asst Head, European Communities Dept (External), FCO, 1987–88; Counsellor and Dep. Head of Mission, Warsaw, 1988–92; Counsellor (Politico-Military), Bonn, 1992–94; Hd, Personnel Services Dept, FCO, 1994–97; Ambassador: to Ethiopia and (non-resident) to Eritrea and Djibouti, 1997–2000; to Luxembourg, 2000–04; High Comr to Ghana, and (non-resident) Ambassador to Togo, Niger, Burkina Faso and Côte d'Ivoire, 2004–07. *Recreations:* tennis, reading, travel, Manchester United Football Club. *Address:* c/o Foreign and Commonwealth Office, King Charles Street, SW1A 2AH. *Club:* Oxford and Cambridge.

WETTON, Hilary John D.; *see* Davan Wetton.

WETTON, Philip Henry Davan, CMG 1993; HM Diplomatic Service, retired; Consul-General, Milan, 1990–96; *b* 21 Sept. 1937; *s* of late Eric Davan Wetton, CBE and Kathleen Valerie Davan Wetton; *m* 1983, Roswitha Kortner. *Educ:* Westminster; Christ Church, Oxford (MA). Unilever Ltd, 1958–65; FCO, 1965–68; served Tokyo, Osaka and FCO, 1968–73; Head of Division, later Director, Secretariat of Council of Ministers of European Communities, 1973–83; Counsellor, Seoul, 1983–87; FCO, 1987–90. Founded Philip Wetton Chair of Astrophysics, Oxford Univ., 2000; endowed Grad. Scholarship in Astrophysics, Christ Church, Oxford, 2005. *Recreations:* rowing, music, astronomy. *Address:* Aller's End, East Kennett, Marlborough, Wilts SN8 4EY.
See also H. J. Davan Wetton.

WETZEL, Dave; Managing Director, Transforming Communities Consultancy, since 2008; *b* 9 Oct. 1942; *s* of Fred Wetzel and Ivy Donaldson; *m* 1973, Heather Allman; two *d*. *Educ:* Spring Grove Grammar Sch.; Southall Technical Coll., Ealing Coll., and the Henry George Sch. of Social Sciences (part-time courses). Student apprentice, Wilkinson Sword/Graviner, 1959–62; Bus Conductor/Driver, 1962–65, Bus Official, 1965–69, London Transport; Br. Manager, Initial Services, 1969–70; Pilot Roster Officer, British Airways, 1970–74 (ASTMS Shop Steward); Political Organiser, London Co-op., 1974–81; Proprietor, Granny's Attic Antique Shop, Mevagissey, 1994–99; Partner, family restaurant, 1997–2008. Member (Lab): for Hammersmith N, GLC, 1981–86 (Transport Cttee Chair, 1981–86); Hounslow Borough Council, 1964–68, 1986–94 (Dep. Leader and Chair, Environmental Planning, 1986–87; Leader, 1987–91). Vice-Chair, Transport for London, 2000–08 (Chair, Safety, Health and Envmt Cttee, 2004–08); Chair: London Buses, 2000–01; Transport Trading Ltd, 2000–01. Contested (Lab): Richmond upon Thames, Twickenham, 1979; Mevagissey, Restormel DC, 1995; St Austell West, Cornwall CC, 1997. Vice-Chm., Public Transport Cttee, AMA, 1993–94; Mem. Management Cttee, Hounslow Community Transport and Central London Dial-a-Ride, 1991–94. Dir, DaRT (Dial-a-Ride and Taxicard Users), 1989–94. Pres., W London Peace Council, 1982–94; Pres., Labour Land Campaign, 1982–; Chair, Professional Land Reform Gp, 2004–. Mem. Bd, Riverside Studios, Hammersmith, 1983–86. Founder and co-ordinator, Trade Union and Co-op Esperanto Gp, 1976–80. Pres., Thames Valley Esperanto Soc., 1982–94; Vice-Pres., Transport Studies Soc., London Univ., 1992–99 (Pres., 1991–92). Vice Chm., Mevagissey Chamber of Commerce, 1996–98. Member: Cttee, Mevagissey Folk Mus., 1995–99; Bd, London Transport Mus., 2007–. Mem. Editl Bd, Voice of the Unions, 1975–79; Editor, Civil Aviation News, 1978–81. FRSA 2001; FCILT (FCIT 2002; FILT 2002). *Recreations:* politics, Esperanto, land campaigning. *Address:* 40 Adelaide Terrace, Great West Road, Brentford, Middlesex TW8 9PQ. *T:* (020) 8568 9004, 07715 322926.

WEYLAND, Joseph; Ambassador of Luxembourg to United States of America, since 2005; *b* 24 April 1943; *s* of Adolphe Weyland and Marie Kox; *m* 1st, 1969, France Munhowen; two *s*; 2nd, 1993, Bénédicte Boucqueau. *Educ:* LLD, and Dip. of Inst. d'Etudes Politiques, Univ. of Paris. Foreign Ministry, Luxembourg, 1968; served Bonn and EEC, Brussels; Ambassador to UN, NY, 1982; Perm. Rep. to EEC, Brussels, 1985 (Mem., Intergovt. Conf. leading to Single European Act, 1985, later Chm., Intergovt Conf. on Political Union leading to Treaty of Maastricht, 1991; Sec.-Gen., Foreign Ministry, Luxembourg, 1992; Ambassador to UK, 1993–2002; Ambassador to NATO and to Belgium, 2003–05. Mem., Reflection Gp, IGC, 1995. *Publication:* (jtly) Le Traité de Maastricht, 1993. *Recreations:* art, sports, music. *Address:* Luxembourg Embassy, 2200 Massachusetts Avenue NW, Washington, DC 20008, USA. *Club:* Rotary.

WEYMAN, Anne Judith, OBE 2000; FCA; Chief Executive, fpa (Family Planning Association), 1996–2008; *b* 1 Feb. 1943; *d* of Stanley Weyman and Rose Weyman; *m* 1977, Christopher Leonard Bulford; one *d*. *Educ:* Tollington GS; Bristol Univ. (BSc Physics); London Sch. of Econs (BScSoc). FCA 1973. Articled Clerk and Audit Manager, Finnie, Ross, Welch & Co., Chartered Accts, 1964–68; Audit Manager, Foster Weyman & Co., Chartered Accts, 1968–69; Research Officer: LSE, 1972–74; Queen Mary's Hosp., Roehampton, 1974–77; Hd of Finance and Admin, Internat. Secretariat, Amnesty Internat., 1977–86; Dir of Inf. and Public Affairs and Co. Sec., Nat. Children's Bureau, 1986–96. Chm., Pinter Publishers Ltd, 1989–95. Mem. (Lab), Westminster CC, 1978–82. Mem., NW Thames RHA, 1978–80; non-exec. Dir, Islington PCT, 2002–. Vice-Chair: Sexual Health Strategy Reference Gp, 1999–2000; Ind. Adv. Gp on Sexual Health and HIV, 2003–; Member: Ind. Adv. Gp on Teenage Pregnancy, 2000–07; Women's Nat. Commn, 1999–2003; Chm., Programme Develt Gp in Personal Social and Health Educn, NICE, 2007–. Trustee, Family & Parenting Inst., 2006–. Hon. Pres., Sex Educn Forum (Founder, 1987). Hon. LLD Bristol, 2005. *Publications:* (with J. Westergaard and P. Wiles) Modern British Society: a bibliography, 1977; (with J. Unell) Finding and Running Premises, 1985; (with S. Capper and J. Unell) Starting and Running a Voluntary Group, 1989; (jtly) RCGP Handbook of Sexual Health in Primary Care, 1998, 2nd edn 2006; (with M. Duggan) Individual Choices, Collective Responsibility: sexual health, a public health issue, 1999; (jtly) Sexual and Reproductive Health and Rights in the UK: 5 years on from Cairo, 1999; articles on health, mental health and sex educn. *Recreations:* reading, gardening.

WEYMES, John Barnard, OBE 1975; HM Diplomatic Service, retired; Managing Director, Cayman Islands News Bureau, Grand Cayman, 1981–83; *b* 18 Oct. 1927; *s* of William Stanley Weymes and Irene Innes Weymes; *m* 1978, Beverley Pauline Gliddon; three *c* by a previous marr. *Educ:* Dame Allan's Sch., Newcastle upon Tyne; King's Coll., Durham Univ., Newcastle upon Tyne. Served HM Forces, 1945–48. Foreign Office, 1949–52; 3rd Sec., Panama City, 1952–56; 2nd Sec., Bogotá, 1957–60; Vice-Consul, Berlin, 1960–63; Dep-Consul, Tamsui, Taiwan, 1963–65; 1st Sec., FCO, 1965–68; Prime Minister's Office, 1968–70; Consul, Guatemala City, 1970–74; 1st Sec., FCO, 1974–77; Consul-Gen., Vancouver, 1977–78; Ambassador to Honduras, 1978–81. *Recreations:* outdoor sport, partic. cricket; chess, reading. *Address:* Holmesdale, Lower Lane, Dalwood, Axminster, Devon EX13 7EG. *T:* (01404) 881114. *Clubs:* MCC; Sedlescombe Cricket.

WEYMOUTH, Viscount; Ceawlin Henry Laszlo Thynn; *b* 6 June 1974; *s* and *heir* of Marquess of Bath, *qv.*

WHALEN, Sir Geoffrey (Henry), Kt 1995; CBE 1989; FIMI, FIPD; Chairman, Camden Ventures (formerly Camden Motors) Ltd, since 1996; *b* 8 Jan. 1936; *s* of Henry and Mabel Whalen; *m* 1961, Elizabeth Charlotte; two *s* three *d. Educ:* Magdalen College, Oxford (MA Hons Modern History). National Coal Board, Scotland (industrial relations), 1959–66; Divl Personnel Manager, A. C. Delco Div., General Motors, Dunstable, 1966–70; British Leyland, 1970–78; Personnel Dir, Leyland Cars, 1975–78; Personnel Dir, Rank Hovis McDougall Bakeries Div., 1978–80; Personnel and Indust. Rel. Dir, 1980–81, Asst Man. Dir, 1981–84, Talbot Motor Co.; Man. Dir, 1984–95, Dep. Chm., 1990–2003, Peugeot Motor Co. plc. Director: Coventry Bldg Soc., 1992–2006 (Chm., 1999–2005); Novar (formerly Caradon) plc, 1996–2005; Chm., Hills Precision Components Ltd, 1990–2001. Pres., SMMT, 1988–90 and 1993; Vice Pres., Inst. of Motor Industry, 1986–; Chm., Coventry and Warwicks TEC, 1990–94. FIMI 1986; FCGI 1989; CCMI (CBIM 1987). Hon. DBA Coventry Univ., 1995. Midlander of the Year Award, Bass Mitchells & Butlers Ltd, 1988; Midlands Businessman of the Year, 1992. Chevalier de la Légion d'Honneur (France), 1990. *Address:* Victoria Lodge, 8 Park Crescent, Abingdon, Oxon OX14 1DF. *Club:* Oxford and Cambridge.

WHALLEY, Jeffrey; Chairman and Chief Executive, Gartland Whalley & Barker plc, since 2005 (Director, since 1995); *b* 20 Nov. 1942; *s* of William Henry and Elsie Whalley; *m* 1st, 1965; three *s*; 2nd, 1996, Karn Jane Jamieson. *Educ:* Grammar School and Polytechnic. Managing Director: Dynamo Electrical Services, 1970–75; Whipp & Bourne Switchgear, 1975–80; FKI Electricals, 1980–87; Man. Dir and Dep. Chm., FKI Babcock, 1987–89; Jt Dep. Chm., Babcock International, 1989–95; Man. Dir, Gartland & Whalley Securities, later Gartland Whalley & Barker Ltd, 1989–95; Chairman: FKI, 1991–99; British Aluminium plc, 1996–2006. Non-exec. Dir, Towcester Racecourse Ltd, 1998–2006. FRSA; FInstD. *Recreations:* tennis, fishing, football.

WHALLEY, John Mayson, FRTPI; FRIBA; PPLI; Principal, JMW International, since 1994; *b* 14 Sept. 1932; *s* of George Mayson Whalley and Ada Florence Cairns; *m* 1966, Elizabeth Gillian Hide; one *s* two *d. Educ:* Grammar Sch., Preston; Univ. of Liverpool (BArch, 1st Cl. Hons; Sir Charles Reilly Medal and Prize for thesis design, 1956; MCivic Des.); Univ. of Pennsylvania (MLandscape Arch). Leverhulme and Italian Govt Fellowships for study in Scandinavia and Univ. of Rome, 1957; Fulbright Schol., 1958; Manchester Soc. of Architects Winstanley Fellowship, 1965. Asst architect to Sir Frederick Gibberd, Harlow, 1956; architect/landscape architect: Oskar Stonorov, Philadelphia, 1958–60; Grenfell Baines and Hargreaves Building Design Partnership, Preston, 1960–62; Associate, 1963–68, Sen. Partner, 1968–93, Derek Lovejoy & Partners. Design Co-ordinator, Kishiwada Port Develt Corp., Osaka, Japan, 1997–2001. Chm., NW Region, RIBA, 1984–85; President: Manchester Soc. of Architects, 1980–81; Landscape Inst., 1985–87; Mem. Council, National Trust, 1989–94; Trustee and Dir, Rural Heritage (formerly Rural Bldgs Preservation) Trust, 1996–2002; Chm., Rivington Heritage Trust, 1997–2004. Civic Trust awards: W Burton Power Stn, 1968; Cheshire Constabulary HQ, 1969; Rochdale Canal, 1973; Royal Life Offices, Peterborough, 1992; design competitions 1st prizes: Cergy-Pontoise Urban Park, 1970; La Courneuve Regional Park, Paris, 1972; Liverpool Anglican Cathedral precinct, 1982; Urban Park, Vitoria-Gasteiz, 1991; Regional Park, Mito City, Japan, 1992; Garden Festivals: Liverpool, 1982; Stoke-on-Trent, 1983; Glasgow, 1985. Civic Trust awards assessor, 1970–94; UN Tech. Expert, Riyadh, 1975. Mem., Ordre des Architectes de France; FRSA. Contribs to radio and TV. *Publications:* Selected Architects Details, 1958; articles in professional jls. *Recreation:* using imagination - to play jazz piano, opening for Lancashire and England, playing twenty pounds salmon and owning French vineyard! *Address:* Dilworth House, Longridge, Preston, Lancs PR3 3ST. *T:* and *Fax:* (01772) 783262; *e-mail:* johnmwhalley@aol.com. *Clubs:* Ronnie Scott's; St James's (Manchester).

WHALLEY, Robert Michael, CB 2005; Independent Reviewer, Justice and Security (Northern Ireland) Act 2007, since 2008; *b* 17 Feb. 1947; *s* of William Lambert Whalley and Edith Mary Whalley; *m* 1981, Teresa Jane, *yr d* of Dr D. W. Hall; three *d. Educ:* King Edward's Sch., Birmingham; Pembroke Coll., Cambridge (MA). Home Office, 1970–72; Private Sec. to Sec. of State for NI, 1972–73; Principal, 1975, Private Sec. to Perm. Sec., 1978–80, Home Office; Cabinet Office, 1980–82; Private Sec. to Lord President of the Council, 1983; Home Office: Asst Sec., Prison Dept, 1984–87; Emergency Planning Div., 1987–89; Sec., Hillsborough Stadium Disaster Inquiry, 1989–90; Personnel Dept, 1990–93; Dir, Immigration and Nationality Policy, 1993–2000; Hd of Unit, Organised and Internat. Crime Directorate, 2000–03; Dir, Crime Reduction and Community Safety Gp, 2003–05. Consulting Sen. Fellow, IISS, 2006–. *Recreations:* gardens, music. *Address:* c/o Home Office, 2 Marsham Street, SW1P 4DF.

WHALLEY, Maj.-Gen. William Leonard, CB 1985; *b* 19 March 1930; *m* 1955, Honor Mary (*née* Golden); one *d. Educ:* Sir William Turner's Sch., Coatham. Joined Army (Nat. Service), 1948; sc 1962; Commander, RAOC, 1st Div., 1968–71; Dir of Ordnance Services, BAOR, 1980–83; Dir Gen. of Ordnance Services, MoD, 1983–85. Colonel Commandant: RAOC, 1986–93; RLC, 1993. Life Vice-Pres., Army Boxing Assoc. (Chm., 1983–85). Pres., Little Aston Br., Conservative Assoc., 1996– (Chm., 1987–96, 1998–2005). Chm. of Govs, Brooke Weston (formerly Corby) City Technol. Coll., 1991–96 (Project Dir, 1989–91). Pres., RAOC Charitable Trust, 1996–2000. *Recreations:* bridge, computers, cabinet making. *Address:* HSBC, 67 The Parade, Sutton Coldfield, West Midlands B72 1PU.

WHARMBY, Debbie; *see* Wiseman, D.

WHARNCLIFFE, 5th Earl of, *cr* 1876; **Richard Alan Montagu Stuart Wortley;** Baron Wharncliffe 1826; Viscount Carlton 1876; *b* 26 May 1953; *s* of Alan Ralph Montagu-Stuart-Wortley (*d* 1986) and Virginia Anne (*d* 1993), *d* of W. Martin Claybaugh; *S* cousin, 1987; *m* 1979, Mary Elizabeth Reed; three *s. Heir: s* Viscount Carlton, *qv. Address:* 310 Main Street, Cumberland, ME 04021–3903, USA.

WHARTON, 12th Baron *cr* 1544–45; **Myles Christopher David Robertson;** *b* 1 Oct. 1964; *e s* of Baroness Wharton (11th in line) and Henry McLeod Robertson; *S* mother, 2000; *m* 2003, Barbara Kay, *d* of Colin Paul Marshall; one *d. Educ:* King's Coll., Wimbledon. *Heir: d* Hon. Meghan Ziki Mary Robertson, *b* 8 March 2006.

WHARTON, Rt Rev. John Martin; *see* Newcastle, Bishop of.

WHATELY, Kevin; actor; *b* 6 Feb. 1951; *s* of late Richard Whately and of Mary Whateley (*née* Pickering); *m* 1984, Madelaine Newton; one *s* one *d. Educ:* Barnard Castle Sch.; Central Sch. of Speech and Drama. Rep. theatre, incl. Old Vic Co., 1975–82; *television:* rôles include: Neville in Auf Wiedersehen Pet, 1992–2002; Sgt Lewis in Inspector Morse, 1986–2001; Jack Kerruish in Peak Practice, 1992–95; Inspector Lewis in Lewis, 2005–; *films:* rôles include: Hardy in The English Patient, 1996. Ambassador for: Prince's Trust, 1992–; Alzheimer's Soc., 2007–; Vice-Pres., NCH, 2003–; Patron, Sparks, 1993–. Ambassador for: Newcastle and Gateshead, 2002–; City of Sunderland, 2005–. Hon. DCL Northumbria, 2000. *Recreation:* charity golf. *Address:* c/o Caroline Dawson Associates, 125 Gloucester Road, SW7 4TE. *T:* (020) 7373 3323, *Fax:* (020) 7373 1110. *Club:* Bamburgh Castle Golf.

WHATLEY, Prof. Frederick Robert, FRS 1975; Sherardian Professor of Botany, Oxford University, 1971–91; Fellow of Magdalen College, Oxford, since 1971; *b* 26 Jan. 1924; *s* of Frederick Norman Whatley and Maud Louise (*née* Hare); *m* 1951, Jean Margaret Smith Bowie; two *d. Educ:* Bishop Wordsworth's Sch., Salisbury; (Scholar) Selwyn Coll., Cambridge University (BA, PhD). Benn W. Levy Student, Cambridge, 1947. Sen. Lectr in Biochemistry, Univ. of Sydney, 1950–53; Asst Biochemist, Univ. of California at Berkeley, 1954–58; Associate Biochemist, 1959–64; Guggenheim Fellowship (Oxford and Stockholm), 1960; Prof. of Botany, King's Coll., London, 1964–71. Vis. Fellow, ANU, 1979. *Publications:* articles and reviews in scientific jls. *Address:* 50 Church Road, Sandford-on-Thames, Oxford OX4 4XZ.

WHATMORE, Prof. Sarah Jane, PhD, DSc; Professor of Environment and Public Policy, University of Oxford, since 2004; *b* 25 Sept. 1959; *d* of late Col Denys Edwin Whatmore and of (Freda) Pauline Whatmore. *Educ:* University Coll. London (BA Hons 1st cl. (Geog.) 1981; PhD (Geog.) 1988); Bartlett Sch., UCL (MPhil Town Planning 1983); Univ. of Bristol (DSc 2000). Policy Res. Officer, GLC, 1983–84; Res. Associate, Dept of Geog., UCL, 1984–87; University of Leeds: Res. Fellow, Sch. of Econ. Studies, 1988; Lectr, Dept of Geog., 1988–89; University of Bristol: Lectr, 1989–93, Reader, 1993–99, in Human Geog.; Prof. of Human Geog., 1999–2001; Prof. of Envmtl Geog., OU, 2001–04. Visiting Scholar: Univs of Calif, Santa Cruz, Wisconsin, Madison and Monash, 1993; Univ. of Newcastle, 1997; Vis. Res. Prof., Univ. of Trondheim, 1994–97. FRGS 1994 (Mem. Council, 2004–07); AcSS 2002; FRSA 2003. Cuthbert Peek Award, RGS, 2003. *Publications:* Farming Women: gender, work and family enterprise, 1991; Hybrid Geographies: natures, cultures, spaces, 2002; (ed jtly) Using Social Theory: thinking through research, 2003; (with Thrift) Cultural Geography: critical concepts, 2004; numerous other ed vols, book chapters, papers in learned jls and policy reports. *Recreations:* gardening, antiquarian books, reading, modern art and architecture. *Address:* Oxford University Centre for the Environment, Dyson Perrins Building, South Parks Road, Oxford OX1 3QY.

WHATMOUGH, Rev. Michael Anthony, (Tony); Teacher of Religious Education, Fair Oaks Business and Enterprise College, Rugeley, since 2005; *b* 14 Oct. 1950; *s* of Derrick and Molly Whatmough; *m* 1st, 1975, Jean Macdonald Watt (marr. diss. 2004); two *s* two *d*; 2nd, 2006, Catherine, *d* of Richard and Margaret Ainley. *Educ:* Exeter Univ. (BA 1972); Edinburgh Univ. (BD 1981). ARCO 1972. Teacher of music, Forrester High Sch., Edinburgh, 1973–74; Sub-Organist, Old St Paul's Church, Edinburgh, 1973–78; Music Master, George Watson's Coll., Edinburgh, 1974–78; ordained deacon, 1981, priest, 1982; Curate, St Hilda and St Fillan, Edinburgh, 1981–84; Vis. Lectr in Music, Faculty of Divinity, Edinburgh Univ., 1981–84; Curate and Rector, Salisbury St Thomas, 1984–93; Rural Dean, Salisbury, 1990–93; Vicar, St Mary Redcliffe, Bristol, 1993–2005. *Recreations:* playing clavichord and organ, cooking, hill walking, singing. *Address:* 30 Gaia Lane, Lichfield, Staffs WS13 7LW. *T:* (01543) 257019; *e-mail:* tony@whatmough.org.uk.

WHEADON, Richard Anthony; Principal, Elizabeth College, Guernsey, 1972–88, retired; *b* 31 Aug. 1933; *s* of Ivor Cecil Newman Wheadon and Margarita Augusta (*née* Cash); *m* 1961, Ann Mary (*née* Richardson); three *s. Educ:* Cranleigh Sch. Balliol Coll., Oxford (MA (Physics)). Commissioned RAF, 1955 (Sword of Honour); Air Radar Officer, 1955–57; Asst Master, Eton Coll., 1957–66; Dep. Head Master and Head of Science Dept, Dauntsey's Sch., 1966–71. Mem., Wilts Educn Cttee's Science Adv. Panel, 1967–71. Rowed bow for Oxford, 1954, for GB in European Championships and Olympic Games, 1956; Captain RAF VIII, 1956 and 1957; Olympic Selector and Nat. Coach, 1964–66. Contingent Comdr, Dauntsey's Sch. CCF, 1969–70; Sqdn Leader, RAFRO, 1970–. Reader, C of E, dio. of Winchester, 1995–; Member: Guernsey Standing Adv. Council for Religious Educn, 1997–2003; Diocesan Readers' Selection Bd, 1998–; Admin Sec., 2001–03, Hon. Sec., 2003–05, Guernsey Readers' Centre. *Publication:* The Principles of Light and Optics, 1968. *Recreations:* French horn, photography, electronics, singing, sailing, words. *Address:* L'Enclos Gallienne, Rue du Court Laurent, Torteval, Guernsey, Channel Islands GY8 0LH. *T:* (01481) 264988.

WHEARE, Thomas David, MA; Headmaster of Bryanston School, 1983–2005; *b* 11 Oct. 1944; *s* of late Sir Kenneth Wheare, CMG, FBA, and of Lady (Joan) Wheare; *m* 1977, Rosalind Clare Spice; two *d. Educ:* Dragon Sch.; Magdalen College Sch., Oxford; King's Coll., Cambridge (BA, MA); Christ Church, Oxford (DipEd). Assistant Master, Eton College, 1967–76; Housemaster of School House, Shrewsbury School, 1976–83. Chm., HMC, 2000 (Hon. Treas., 1993–98). Ed., Conference & Common Room, 2005–. FRSA 1989. *Recreations:* music, supporting Arsenal FC. *Address:* 63 Chapel Lane, Zeals, Warminster, Wilts BA12 6NP.

WHEAT, Rev. Fr (Charles Donald) Edmund, SSM; Assistant Curate (Non-Stipendiary Minister), St John, South Bank, diocese of York, 2003–07; *b* 17 May 1937; *s* of Charles and Alice Wheat. *Educ:* Kelham Theol Coll.; Nottingham Univ. (BA); Sheffield Univ. (MA). Curate, St Paul's, Arbourthorne, Sheffield, 1962–67; licensed, Dio. Southwell, 1967–70; Mem., SSM, 1969–; Chaplain, St Martin's Coll., Lancaster, 1970–73; Prior, SSM Priory, Sheffield, 1973–75; Curate, St John, Ranmoor and Asst Chaplain, Sheffield Univ., 1975–77, Chaplain 1977–80; Provincial, English Province, 1981–91, Dir, 1982–89, Provincial Bursar, 1992–98, Provincial of European Province, 1999–2001, SSM; Vicar, All Saints', Middlesbrough, 1988–95; Prior, St Antony's Priory, Durham, 1998–2001; Vicar, St Thomas', Middlesbrough, 2001–03. Chaplain: Whitelands Coll., 1996–97; Order of the Holy Paraclete, Whitby, 1997–98. Mem., Gen. Synod, 1975–80. *Recreations:* reading, watching soap operas. *Address:* St Clare, Sneaton Castle, Whitby YO21 3QN.

WHEATCROFT, Geoffrey Albert; author; freelance journalist, since 1997; *b* 23 Dec. 1945; *s* of Stephen Frederick Wheatcroft, *qv* and late Joy Wheatcroft (*née* Reed); *m* 1990, Sally, *d* of late Frank Muir, CBE and Polly Muir; one *s* one *d*. *Educ:* University Coll. Sch.; New Coll., Oxford (Schol.; MA Modern Hist.); London Coll. of Printing. In publishing, 1968–75: prodn asst, then publicity manager, Hamish Hamilton, 1968–70; editor: Michael Joseph, 1971–73; Cassell & Co., 1974–75; asst ed., 1975–77, Literary Ed., 1977–81, Spectator; reporting and researching in S Africa, 1981–84; Ed., Londoner's Diary, Evening Standard, 1985–86; columnist, Sunday Telegraph, 1987–91; feature writer, Daily Express, 1996–97. *Publications:* The Randlords, 1985; Absent Friends, 1989; The Controversy of Zion, 1996 (Amer. Nat. Jewish Book Award); Le Tour: a history of the Tour de France, 2003, 2nd edn 2007; The Strange Death of Tory England, 2005; Yo, Blair!, 2007. *Recreations:* bibliophily and hypochondria. *Address:* 11 Southstoke Road, Combe Down, Bath BA2 5SJ. *T:* (01225) 835540; *e-mail:* wheaty@compuserve.com. *Clubs:* Garrick, Beefsteak, Colony Room, MCC.

WHEATCROFT, Patience Jane, (Mrs A. Salter); Editor, The Sunday Telegraph, 2006–07; *b* 28 Sept. 1951; *d* of Anthony Wheatcroft and Ruth Wheatcroft (*née* Frith); *m* 1976, Anthony Salter; two *s* one *d*. *Educ:* Univ. of Birmingham (LLB). Dep. City Ed., The Times, 1984–86; Asst City Ed., Daily Mail, 1986–88; Ed., Retail Week, 1988–93; Dep. City Ed., Mail on Sunday, 1994–97; Business and City Ed., The Times, 1997–2006. Non-executive Director: Barclays plc, 2008–; Shaftesbury plc, 2008–. *Recreations:* ski-ing, opera, talking.

WHEATCROFT, Stephen Frederick, OBE 1974; Director, Aviation and Tourism International Ltd, since 1983; *b* 11 Sept. 1921; *s* of late Percy and Fanny Wheatcroft; *m* 1st, 1943, Joy (*d* 1974), *d* of late Cecil Reed; two *s* one *d*; 2nd, 1974, Alison, *d* of late Arnold Dessau; two *s*. *Educ:* Latymer Sch., N9; London Sch. of Economics (BSc(Econ) 1942; Hon. Fellow, 1998). Served War, Pilot in Fleet Air Arm, 1942–45. Commercial Planning Manager, BEA, 1946–53; Simon Research Fellow, Manchester Univ., 1953–55; private practice as Aviation Consultant, 1956–72; retained as Economic Adviser to BEA. Commns for Govts of: Canada, India, W Indies, E African Community, Afghanistan; Consultant to World Bank; Assessor to Edwards Cttee on British Air Transport in the Seventies; Mem. Bd, British Airways (Dir of Economic Develt), 1972–82. Governor, London Sch. of Economics, 1970–2003, (first) Emeritus Governor, 2003. FRAeS, FCILT (Pres., CIT, 1978–79); FAIAA. *Publications:* Economics of European Air Transport, 1956; Airline Competition in Canada, 1958; Air Transport Policy, 1966; Air Transport in a Competitive European Market, 1986; European Liberalisation and World Air Transport, 1990; Europe's Senior Travel Market, 1993; Aviation and Tourism Policies, 1994; Europe's Youth Travel Market, 1995; articles in professional jls. *Recreation:* travel. *Address:* 49 Dovehouse Street, SW3 6JY. *T:* (020) 7351 1511. *Club:* Reform.
See also G. A. Wheatcroft.

WHEATER, Prof. Howard Simon, PhD; FREng; FICE; CEng; Professor of Hydrology, Department of Civil and Environmental Engineering, Imperial College London, since 1993; *b* 24 June 1949; *s* of late Claude and Marjorie Wheater; *m* 1970 (marr. diss. 2004); two *s*; *m* 2007, Prof. Valerie Susan Isham. *Educ:* Nottingham High Sch.; Queens' Coll., Cambridge (BA 1971, MA Engrg Scis); Univ. of Bristol (PhD 1977). CEng 1978; FICE 1999. Grad. apprentice, Aero Engine Div., Rolls-Royce Ltd, 1967–72; Res. Asst, Dept of Civil Engrg, Univ. of Bristol, 1972–78; Department of Civil and Environmental Engineering, Imperial College London: Lectr, 1978–87; Sen. Lectr, 1987–90; Reader, 1990–93; Hd, Envmtl and Water Resource Engrg, 1995–; Chm., Centre for Envmtl Control and Waste Mgt, 1995–. Mem. and Chair, nat. and internat. adv. panels and cttees, incl. MAFF, DEFRA, Envmt Agency, NERC, UNESCO. Consultant: Northern Oman Flood Study, 1981; to State of Nevada concerning proposed Yucca Mt nuclear waste repository, 2003–; Counsel and Advocate for Republic of Hungary at Internat. Court of Justice concerning GNBS Danube barrage system, 1993–97. Pres., British Hydrological Soc., 1999–2001. Life Mem., Internat. Water Acad., Oslo. FREng 2003. Prince Sultan bin Abdulaziz Internat. Water Prize, 2006. *Publications:* (ed jtly) Hydrology in a Changing Environment, 3 vols, 1998; (jtly) Rainfall-Runoff Modelling in Gauged and Ungauged Catchments, 2004; (jtly) Biosphere Implications of Deep Disposal of Nuclear Waste: the upwards migration of radionuclides in vegetated soils, 2007; (jtly) Hydrological Modelling in Arid and Semi-Arid Areas, 2008; 200 refereed papers. *Recreations:* sailing (dinghy racing and yacht cruising), music (orchestral trumpet player). *Address:* Department of Civil and Environmental Engineering, Imperial College London, SW7 2AZ. *T:* (020) 7594 6066, *Fax:* (020) 7594 1511; *e-mail:* h.wheater@imperial.ac.uk.

WHEATER, Roger John, OBE 1991; CBiol, FIBiol; FRSE; Chairman, National Trust for Scotland, 2000–05; *b* 24 Nov. 1933; *m* 1963, Jean Ord Troup; one *s* one *d*. *Educ:* Brighton, Hove and Sussex Grammar Sch.; Brighton Tech. Coll. FRSE 1985; FIBiol 1987. Commnd Royal Sussex Regt, 1953; served Gold Coast Regt, 1953–54; 4/5th Bn, Royal Sussex Regt (TA), 1954–56. Served Colonial Police, Uganda, 1956–61; Chief Warden, Murchison Falls Nat. Park, 1961–70; Director: Uganda Nat. Parks, 1970–72; RZSScot, 1972–98. Hon. Prof., Univ. of Edinburgh, 1993–. Mem. Editl Bd, Internat. Zoo Year Book, 1987–99. Consultant, World Tourist Orgn, UN, 1980–. Mem., Sec. of State for Scotland's Wkg Gp on Envmtl Educn, 1990–94. Mem., Co-ordinating Cttee, Nuffield Unit of Tropical Animal Ecol. Member: Council, NT for Scotland, 1973–78 and 2000– (Mem., Exec. Cttee, 1982–87); Bd, Scottish Natural Heritage, 1995–99 (Dep. Chm., 1997–99); Assessor, Council, Scottish Wildlife Trust, 1973–92 (Pres., 2007–). Chm., Wkg Party on Zoo Licensing Act, 1981–84. Pres., Assoc. of British Wild Animal Keepers, 1984–99 (Chm., Membership and Licensing Cttee, 1984–91); Chairman, Advisory Committee: Whipsnade Wild Animal Park, 1999–2002; London Zoo, 2002–03. Chm., Fedn of Zool Gardens of GB and Ireland, 1993–96. Dep. Chm., Zoo Forum, 1999–2002; Chairman: Access Forum, 1996–2000; Tourism and Envmt Forum, 1999–2003. Chm., Eur. Assoc. of Zoos and Aquaria, 1994–97; Mem. Council, 1980, Pres., 1988–91, Internat. Union of Dirs of Zool Gdns. Vice-President: Eur. Network of Nat. Heritage Orgns, 2000–05; Scottish Heritage USA, 2001–05. Chm., Cammo Estate Adv. Cttee, 1980–95; Dir, Nat. Park Lodges Ltd; Mem., Uganda Nat. Res. Council; Vice-Chm., Uganda Tourist Assoc. Chm., Anthropoid Ape Adv. Panel, 1977–91. Mem. Council, 1991–92, 1995–99, 2000–03, Vice Pres., 1999, Zool Soc. of London. Vice-Pres., World Pheasant Assoc., 1994–. Vice Chm., Edinburgh Br., ESU, 1977–81. Trustee: The Gorilla Orgn (formerly Dian Fossey Gorilla Fund), 1995–; Thyne Scholarship, 1997– (ESU William Thyne Schol., 1975); and Founder Patron, Dynamic Earth, 1999–; Tweed Foundn, 2007–; Chm., Heather Trust, 1999–2002. Pres., Tweedale Soc., 2007–. Gov., Mweka Coll. of Wildlife Mgt, Tanzania, 1970–72. FRSA 1995. Hon. FRSGS 1995; Hon. FRZSScot 1999. DUniv Open, 2004. *Publications:* numerous papers on wildlife mgt and conservation to professional jls. *Recreations:* country pursuits, painting, gardening. *Address:* 17 Kirklands, Innerleithen, Peeblesshire EH44 6NA. *T:* (01896) 830403; *e-mail:* roger.wheater@btinternet.com. *Clubs:* Edinburgh Special Mobile Angling (Pres., 1982–86), Cockburn Trout Angling (Pres., 1997–).

WHEATLEY, Rt Hon. Lord; Rt Hon. John Francis Wheatley; PC 2007; a Senator of the College of Justice in Scotland, since 2000; *b* 9 May 1941; *s* of John Thomas Wheatley (Baron Wheatley, PC) and late Agnes Nichol; *m* 1970, Bronwen Catherine Fraser; two *s*. *Educ:* Mount St Mary's Coll., Derbyshire; Edinburgh Univ. (BL). Called to the Scottish Bar, 1966; Standing Counsel to Scottish Develt Dept, 1971; Advocate Depute, 1975; Sheriff of Tayside Central and Fife, at Dunfermline, 1979–80, at Perth, 1980–2000; Temp. High Ct Judge, 1992; QC (Scot.) 1993. Chm., Judicial Studies Cttee, 2002–06. *Recreations:* gardening, music. *Address:* Braefoot Farmhouse, Crook of Devon, Fossoway, Kinross-shire KY13 7UL. *T:* (01577) 840212.

WHEATLEY, Alan Edward, FCA; Chairman, Emigré Consulting Ltd, since 2006; Vice-Chairman, Carlton Financial Group Ltd, since 2005; *b* 23 May 1938; *s* of late Edward and of Margaret Wheatley (*née* Turner); *m* 1962, Marion Frances (*née* Wilson); two *s* one *d*. *Educ:* Ilford Grammar School. Chartered Accountant. Norton Slade, 1954–60, qualified 1960; joined Price Waterhouse, 1960; admitted to partnership, 1970; Mem., Policy Cttee, 1981–92; Sen. Partner (London Office), 1985–92; Chm., 3i Gp, 1992–93; Dep. Chm., Ashtead Gp, 1994–2003; Chm., Foreign and Colonial Special Utilities, subseq. Special Utilities, Investment Trust plc, 1993–2003. Non-executive Director: EBS Investments (Bank of England sub.), 1977–90; British Steel plc (formerly BSC), 1984–94; Babcock International Gp, 1993–2002; Legal & General Gp, 1993–2002; Forte, 1993–96; N M Rothschild & Sons, 1993–99; Chairman: New Court Financial Services Ltd, 1996–99; Utilico Investment Trust plc, 2003–07; Govt Dir, Cable & Wireless, 1981–84, non-exec. Dep. Chm., 1984–85. Mem., Ind. Develt Adv. Bd, 1985–92. Trustee, V&A Mus., 1996–99. Governor, Solefield School, 1985–95. *Recreations:* golf, bridge. *Club:* Wildernesse (Seal, Kent).

WHEATLEY, Rear-Adm. Anthony, CB 1988; General Manager, National Hospital for Neurology and Neurosurgery, Queen Square, 1988–96; *b* 3 Oct. 1933; *yr s* of late Edgar C. Wheatley and Audrey G. Barton Hall; *m* 1962, Iona Sheila Haig; one *d*. *Educ:* Berkhamsted School. Entered RN Coll., Dartmouth, 1950; RNEC, Manadon, 1953–57; HMS Ceylon, 1958–60; HMS Ganges, 1960–61; HMS Cambrian, 1962–64; Staff of RNEC, Manadon, 1964–67; Staff of Comdr British Navy Staff, Washington, 1967–69; HMS Diomede, 1970–72; Staff of C-in-C Fleet, 1972–74; Exec. Officer, RNEC Manadon, 1975–76; MoD Procurement Exec., 1977–79; British Naval Attaché, Brasilia, 1979–81; RCDS course 1982; HMS Collingwood (in Command), 1982–85; Flag Officer, Portsmouth, Naval Base Comdr and Head of Establishment of Fleet Maintenance and Repair Orgn, Portsmouth, 1985–87. Dir, Queen Square Enterprises, 1988–. Trustee, Friends of the Elderly, 1997–2008; Vice-Pres., Nat. Soc. for Epilepsy, 2004– (Trustee, 1996–2003, Chm., 1998–2003). *Recreations:* cricket, golf, music. *Address:* 7 The Hollies, New Barn, Kent DA3 7HU. *Clubs:* Army and Navy (Chm., 2006–); Free Foresters, Incogniti, Royal Navy Cricket (Vice-Pres.).

WHEATLEY, Prof. David John, MD; British Heart Foundation Professor of Cardiac Surgery, University of Glasgow, 1979–2006; Hon. Consultant Cardiac Surgeon, Glasgow Royal Infirmary, 1979–2006; *b* 2 Aug. 1941; *s* of John Henry Wheatley and Dorothy Wheatley (*née* Price); *m* 1964, Ann Marie Lamberth; two *d*. *Educ:* South African Coll., Cape Town; Univ. of Cape Town Med. Sch. (MB ChB 1964; ChM 1976; MD 1979). FRCSE 1969; FRCSGlas 1979; FRCPE 1997; FRCS 1998. Senior Registrar: Nat. Heart Hosp., London, 1972–73; Mearnskirk Hosp., Glasgow, 1974–76; Sen. Lectr, Royal Infirmary, Edinburgh, 1976–79. Mem. Council, RCSE, 1986–90, 1992–97, 1997–2002; President: Soc. of Cardiothoracic Surgeons of GB and Ireland, 1996–98; European Assoc. for Cardiothoracic Surgery, 1998–99. Founder FMedSci 1998; FECTS 2002. *Publications:* Surgery of Coronary Artery Disease, 1986, 2nd edn 2003; author or jt author of 175 articles on cardiac surgery. *Recreations:* piano, classical music, opera. *Address:* 13 Lochend Drive, Bearsden, Glasgow G61 1ED. *T:* (0141) 942 1381.

WHEATLEY, Derek Peter Francis; QC 1981; Barrister-at-Law; Member, Joint Law Society/Bar Council Working Party on Banking Law, 1976–94; 3rd *s* of late Edward Pearse Wheatley, company director, and Gladys Wheatley; *m* 1955, Elizabeth Pamela, *d* of John and Gertrude Reynolds; two *s* one *d*. *Educ:* The Leys Sch., Cambridge; University Coll., Oxford (MA). Served War of 1939–45, Army, 1944–47: (short univ. course, Oxford, 1944); commissioned into 8th King's Royal Irish Hussars, 1945, Lieut. University Coll., Oxford, 1947–49; called to the Bar, Middle Temple, 1951; Deputy Coroner: to the Royal Household, 1959–64; for London, 1959–64; Recorder of the Crown Court, 1972–74. Chief Legal Advr to Lloyds Bank, 1976–89. Member: Commercial Court Cttee, 1976–90; Senate of Inns of Court and the Bar, 1975–78, 1982–85; Exec. Cttee, Bar Council, 1982–85; Bar Council, 1986–90, 1995–96, 1999–2000 (Member: Professional Standards Cttee, 1986–88; F and GP Cttee, 1988–); Chm., Bar Assoc. for Commerce, Finance and Industry, 1982–83 and 1999–2000 (Vice-Pres., 1986–). Chm., Legal Cttee, Cttee of London and Scottish Bankers, 1985–87. FRSA 1994. *Publications:* The Silent Lady (novel), 2008; articles in legal jls and The Times, etc. *Recreation:* sailing. *Address:* Three The Wardrobe, Old Palace Yard, Richmond, Surrey TW9 1PA. *T:* (020) 8940 6242, *Fax:* (020) 8332 0948; *e-mail:* derek.wheatley@virgin.net. *Clubs:* Roehampton, Sloane; Bar Yacht.

WHEATLEY, John Derek, CBE 1993; Member, National Rivers Authority, 1989–96 (Chief Executive, 1991–92); *b* 24 July 1927; *s* of Leslie Sydney and Lydia Florence Wheatley; *m* 1956, Marie Gowers; one *s* one *d*. *Educ:* Sir Thomas Rich's Sch., Gloucester; Loughborough Coll., 1944–46 (Teacher's Cert.); Carnegie College of Physical Educn, 1952–53 (DipPE). Served RAF, 1946–52; Surrey Education Authority, 1953–54; Central Council of Physical Recreation: London and SE, 1954–58; Secretary, Northern Ireland, 1959–69; Principal Regional Officer, SW, 1970–72; Sports Council: Regional Director, SW, 1972–80; Director of Administrative Services, Headquarters, 1980–83; Dir Gen., 1983–88. Chm., Nat. Small-Bore Rifle Assoc., 1989–95. *Recreations:* gardening, music.

WHEATLEY, Rt Hon. John Francis; *see* Wheatley, Rt Hon. Lord.

WHEATLEY, Oswald Stephen, (Ossie), CBE 1997; Chairman, Sports Council for Wales, 1990–99; company director; *b* 28 May 1935; *s* of late Harold Wheatley and Laura Wheatley (*née* Owens); *m* 1964, Christine Mary Godwin (*d* 2000); one *s* (two *d* decd). *Educ:* King Edward's Sch., Birmingham; Caius Coll., Cambridge (MA Econs and Law). 2nd Lieut, RA, 1954. Cambridge Cricket Blue, 1957–58; played for Warwicks CCC, 1957–60; Glamorgan CCC, 1961–69 (Captain, 1961–66); Chm., Glamorgan CCC, 1977–84. Test and County Cricket Board: Test Selector, 1972–74; Chairman: Discipline Cttee, 1978–83; Cricket Cttee, 1987–95; Mem., England Cttee, 1989–93; Chm., Cricket Foundn, 1996–2008. Member: Sports Council of GB, 1984–88 and 1990–96; UK Sports Council, 1997–99; Broadcasting Council for Wales, 1990–95; Sch. Exam and Assessment Council, 1992–93. Chm., Nat. Sports Medicine Inst., St Bartholomew's Hosp., 1991–96. Hon. Fellow, Univ. of Wales Inst., 1995. Freeman, City of Newcastle-upon-Tyne, 1976. *Recreations:* sport, art. *Address:* 3 Heritage Coast House, Main Road, Ogmore-by-Sea, Vale of Glamorgan CF32 0PR. *Clubs:* MCC, Free Foresters; Cardiff and County; Glamorgan CC.

WHEATLEY, Ven. Paul Charles; Archdeacon of Sherborne and Priest in Charge of West Stafford with Frome Billet, 1991–2003, now Archdeacon Emeritus; *b* 27 May 1938; *s* of Charles Lewis and Doris Amy Wheatley; *m* 1963, Iris Mary Lacey; two *s* one *d*. *Educ:* Wycliffe Coll.; St John's Coll., Durham (BA 1961); Lincoln Theol Coll. Ordained deacon 1963, priest 1964; Curate, Bishopston, Bristol, 1963–68; Youth Chaplain, dio. of Bristol, 1968–73; Team Rector, Dorcan, Swindon, 1973–79; Rector, Ross, Hereford, 1979–81; Team Rector, Ross with Brampton Abbots, Bridstow, Peterstow, 1979–91; Prebendary, Hereford Cathedral, 1987–91; Ecumenical Officer, Hereford, 1987–91; Hon. Canon, Salisbury Cathedral, 1991–2003, now Hon. Canon Emeritus. *Recreations:* travel, gardening, opera, model railways. *Address:* The Farthings, Bridstow, Herefordshire HR9 6QF.

WHEATLEY, Rt Rev. Peter William; *see* Edmonton, Area Bishop of.

WHEATLEY, Philip Martin, CB 2004; Chief Executive, National Offender Management Service, Ministry of Justice, since 2008; *b* 4 July 1948; *s* of Alan Osborne Wheatley and Ida Mary Wheatley; *m* 1st, 1969, Merryll Angela Francis (marr. diss. 1989); one *s* one *d*; 2nd, 1990, Anne Eleanor Roy. *Educ:* Leeds Grammar Sch.; Sheffield Univ. (LLB Hons). HM Prison Service: Prison Officer, 1969–70; Asst Gov., 1970; Hull Prison, 1971–74; Prison Service Coll., 1974–78; Leeds Prison, 1978–82; Dep. Gov., Gartree Prison, 1982–86; Governor, Hull Prison, 1986–90; Prison Service Area Manager for E Midlands, 1990–92; Asst Dir, Custody Gp, Prison Service HQ, 1992–95; Dir of Dispersals, i/c 6 highest security prisons, 1995–99; Dep. Dir Gen., 1999–2003; Dir Gen., 2003–08. Mem., Nat. Offender Mgt (formerly Prisons) Bd, 1995–. *Recreations:* good wine, good food and holidays to enjoy them. *Address:* National Offender Management Service, Cleland House, Page Street, SW1P 4LN.

WHEATON, Rev. Canon David Harry; Vicar of Christ Church, Ware, 1986–96; Chaplain to The Queen, 1990–2000; *b* 2 June 1930; *s* of Harry Wheaton, MBE, and Kathleen Mary (*née* Frost); *m* 1956, Helen Joy Forrer; one *s* two *d*. *Educ:* Abingdon Sch.; St John's Coll., Oxford (Exhibnr; MA); London Univ. (BD (London Bible Coll.)); Oak Hill Theol Coll. NCO, Wiltshire Regt, 1948–49. Deacon, 1959; priest, 1960; Tutor, Oak Hill Coll., 1954–62; Rector of Ludgershall, Bucks, 1962–66; Vicar of St Paul, Onslow Square, S Kensington, 1966–71; Chaplain, Brompton Chest Hosp., 1969–71; Principal Oak Hill Theol Coll., 1971–86; RD of Hertford, 1988–91. Hon. Canon, Cathedral and Abbey Church of St Alban, 1976–96, now Canon Emeritus. *Publications:* (jtly) Witness to the Word, 2002; *contributed to:* Baker's Dictionary of Theology, 1960; New Bible Dictionary, 1962; New Bible Commentary (rev.), 1970, 21st century edn 1994; Lion Handbook to the Bible, 1973, 3rd edn 1999; Evangelical Dictionary of Theology, 1984; Here We Stand, 1986; Restoring the Vision, 1990. *Recreations:* walking, carpentry and do-it-yourself. *Address:* 43 Rose Drive, Chesham, Bucks HP5 1RR. *T:* (01494) 783862.

WHEELER, Rev. Andrew Charles; Mission Pastor and Director of Mission Education, St Saviour's Church, Guildford, since 2002; World Mission Advisor, Guildford Diocese, since 2006; *b* 14 April 1948; *s* of Charles Hildred Wheeler and Ruth Goss Wheeler (*née* Rhymes); *m* 1979, Susan Jane Snook; one *s* one *d*. *Educ:* Corpus Christi Coll., Cambridge (MA); Makerere Univ., Kampala (MA); Leeds Univ. (PGCE); Trinity Coll., Bristol (BA Theol.). Asst Master in Hist., Harrogate Granby High Sch., 1972–75; theol teacher, for CMS, Bishop Gwynne Coll., Mundri, Sudan, 1977–86; ordained deacon, 1988, priest, 1988; Asst Curate, Aldbourne, Salisbury dio., 1988–89; Hon. Curate, with resp. for care of Sudanese refugees, 1989–92, Hon. Canon, 2005, All Saints Cathedral, Cairo; Theol Trng Co-ordinator, New Sudan Council of Churches, 1992–96; Sudan Church Res. Project Dir, 1996–2000; Archbishop's Sec. for the Anglican Communion, 2000–01. *Publications:* (Gen. Ed.) Faith in Sudan series, 13 vols, 1997–2000 (ed and contrib. to vols 1, 5 and 6); (jtly) Day of Devastation, Day of Contentment: the history of the Sudanese Church across 2000 years, 2000; (ed) Voices from Africa, 2002; Bombs, Ruins and Honey: journeys of the spirit with Sudanese Christians, 2006. *Recreations:* music, walking, squash.

WHEELER, Sir Anthony; *see* Wheeler, Sir H. A.

WHEELER, Anthony Ian; Co-founder and Joint Director, Lonely Planet Publications, since 1973; *b* 20 Dec. 1946; *s* of late Ian James Wheeler and of Hilary Audrey Wheeler; *m* 1971, Maureen Dixon; one *s* one *d*. *Educ:* Warwick Univ. (BSc); London Business Sch. (MSc). *Publications:* Across Asia on the Cheap, 1973; South-East Asia on a Shoestring, 1975; Australia, 1977; New Zealand, 1977; West Asia on a Shoestring, 1978; Papua New Guinea, 1978; Burma, 1979; Sri Lanka, 1979; India, 1981; Malaysia, Singapore and Brunei, 1981; Bali and Lombok, 1984; Rarotonga and the Cook Islands, 1986; Islands of Australia's Great Barrier Reef, 1990; Nepal, 1990; Japan, 1991; Dublin, 1993; Britain, 1995; San Francisco, 1996; Tahiti and French Polynesia, 1996; Chasing Rickshaws, 1998; Tahiti and French Polynesia: diving and snorkeling, 2001; Time and Tide: the Islands of Tuvalu, 2001; Rice Trails, 2004. *Recreations:* walking, trekking, scuba diving, running, travel (as much as possible). *Address:* Lonely Planet Publications, 90 Maribyrnong Street, Footscray, Vic 3011, Australia; *e-mail:* tony.wheeler@lonelyplanet.com.au.

WHEELER, Captain Arthur Walter; RN retd; CEng; Keeper, HMS Belfast, 1983–88; *b* 18 Oct. 1927; *s* of Walter Sidney Wheeler and Annie Ethel Marsh; *m* 1st, 1957, Elizabeth Jane Glendinning Bowman (marr. diss. 1968); two *s*; 2nd, 1968, Mary Elvis Findon; one *s*. *Educ:* Woodhouse Sch., Finchley; HMS Fisgard, Torpoint; RN Engineering Coll., Manadon. FIMechE, MIMarEST. Joined Royal Navy as artificer apprentice, 1943; served in cruiser Birmingham, 1947–50. Progressively, Sub Lieut 1950 to Captain 1974. Served in frigate Palliser and aircraft carriers Bulwark, Hermes and Ark Royal 1954–74; Sea Trng Staff at Portland, 1961–63; MoD, Ship Dept, 1966–70 and 1975–78; CSO(Engrg) to Flag Officer Third Flotilla, 1979–80; HMS Daedalus in comd, 1980–82, retired. Received into RC Church, 1987; returned to C of E, 2008. *Recreations:* music, reading, painting and trying to remember.

WHEELER, Arthur William Edge, CBE 1979 (OBE 1967); Chairman, Foreign Compensation Commission, 1983–2001; a Social Security Commissioner, 1992–98; a Child Support Commissioner, 1993–98; *b* 1 Aug. 1930; *e s* of Arthur William Wheeler and Rowena (*née* Edge); *m* 1956, Gay; two *s* one *d*. *Educ:* Mountjoy Sch.; Trinity Coll., Dublin (Reid Prof.'s Prize, MA, LLB). Called to the Irish Bar, King's Inns, 1953; called to the Bar, Gray's Inn, 1960; practised at Irish Bar, 1953–55; Crown Counsel, Nigeria, 1955; Legal Sec. (Actg), Southern Cameroons, and Mem. Exec. Council and House of Assembly, 1958; Principal Crown Counsel, Fedn of Nigeria, 1961; Northern Nigeria: Dep. Solicitor Gen., 1964; Dir of Public Prosecutions, 1966; High Court Judge, 1967; Chief Judge (formerly Chief Justice), Kaduna State of Nigeria, 1975; Comr for Law Revision, northern states of Nigeria, 1980. Mem., Body of Benchers, Nigeria, 1975; Associate Mem., Commonwealth Parly Assoc. *Recreations:* sport (university colours for hockey and assoc. football; Nigerian hockey internat.), music. *Clubs:* Royal Commonwealth Society, MCC.

WHEELER, (Belinda) Christian; *see* Rucker, B. C.

WHEELER, Frank Basil, CMG 1990; HM Diplomatic Service, retired; *b* 24 April 1937; *s* of late Harold Gifford Wheeler and Winifred Lucy Wheeler (*née* Childs); *m* 1st, 1959, Catherine Saunders Campbell (*d* 1979); one *s*; 2nd, 1984, Alyson Ruth Lund (*née* Powell) (marr. diss. 1989); 3rd, 1991, Susana Plaza Larrea. *Educ:* Mill Hill Sch. HM Forces, 1956–58. HM Foreign Service, 1958–: Foreign Office, 1958–61; Third Sec., Moscow, 1961–63; Asst Private Sec. to Minister of State, FO, 1963–65; Second Sec., Berne, 1965–67; First Sec., FO (later FCO), 1967–72; Wellington, 1972–75; FCO, 1975–77; Counsellor and Head of Chancery, Prague, 1977–79; Inspector, 1979–82; Head of Personnel Policy Dept, FCO, 1982–84; Counsellor and Head of Chancery, UK Delegn to NATO, Brussels, 1984–86; Counsellor, on loan to DTI, 1986–89; Ambassador: to Ecuador, 1989–93; to Chile, 1993–97; Chm., British-Chilean Chamber of Commerce, 1997–2003. Internat. Advr, FA, 1997–2000. Grand Cross, Order of Merit (Chile), 1998. *Recreations:* music, tennis. *Address:* 53 Shelton Street, WC2H 9JU.

WHEELER, Fraser William; HM Diplomatic Service; High Commissioner to Guyana, and concurrently Ambassador to Suriname and the Caribbean Community, since 2006; *b* 23 March 1957; *s* of Albert, (Bill), and Janet Wheeler; *m* 1988, Sarah Humphreys; one *s* one *d*. *Educ:* Univ. of Warwick (BA Hons Politics). Trainee accountant, Deloitte Touche, 1979–80; entered FCO, 1980; Finance Dept, FCO, 1980–82; Third Secretary: Accra, 1982–85; UK Mission to UN, Geneva, 1986–89; Desk Officer, Soviet Dept, 1990–91; Dep. Hd, Trade Section, Moscow, 1991–94; Dep. Consul Gen., Vancouver, 1995–2000; PR Consultant, Vancouver, 2000–01 (on special leave); Policy Planning Staff, 2001–03, Hd, Partnerships and Networks Gp, 2003–05, FCO; Hd, British Embassy Office, Basra, Iraq, 2005–06. *Recreations:* the fruitless pursuit of the life of old Reilly, travel with a point to it, playing with a Harley Davidson, country walking in bad weather, smokey and cramped jazz bars, sport for fun, banter with the best of them over fine wine or good coffee. *Address:* c/o Foreign and Commonwealth Office, King Charles Street, SW1A 2AH; *e-mail:* fraser.wheeler@fco.gov.uk. *Club:* Royal Commonwealth Society.

WHEELER, Sir (Harry) Anthony, Kt 1988; OBE 1973; RSA, FRIBA, FRIAS; President, Royal Scottish Academy, 1983–90; Senior Partner, 1954–86, Consultant, 1986–89, Wheeler & Sproson, Architects and Planning Consultants, Edinburgh and Kirkcaldy; *b* 7 Nov. 1919; *s* of Herbert George Wheeler and Laura Emma Groom; *m* 1944, Dorothy Jean Campbell; one *d*. *Educ:* Stranraer High Sch.; Royal Technical Coll., Glasgow; Glasgow School of Art; Univ. of Strathclyde (BArch). DipTP. Glasgow Sch. of Architecture, 1937–48 (war service, Royal Artillery, 1939–46); John Keppie Scholar and Sir Rowand Anderson Studentship, 1948; RIBA Grissell Gold Medallist, 1948, and Neale Bursar, 1949. Assistant: to City Architect, Oxford, 1948; to Sir Herbert Baker & Scott, London, 1949; Sen. Architect, Glenrothes New Town, 1949–51; Sen. Lectr, Dundee Sch. of Arch., 1952–58; commenced private practice in Fife, 1952. Principal works include: Woodside Shopping Centre and St Columba's Parish Church, Glenrothes; Reconstruction of Giles Pittenweem; Redevelopment of Dysart and of Old Buckhaven; Town Centre Renewal, Grangemouth; Students' Union, Univ. of St Andrews; Hunter Building, Edinburgh Coll. of Art; St Peter's Episcopal Ch, Kirkcaldy; Leonard Horner Hall, and Students' Union, Heriot-Watt Univ.; Bank of Scotland, and Royal Bank of Scotland, Dunfermline; Community and Outdoor Centre, Linlithgow. Member: Royal Fine Art Commn for Scotland, 1967–86; Scottish Housing Adv. Cttee, 1971–75; Trustee, Scottish Civic Trust, 1970–83; Pres., Royal Incorpn of Architects in Scotland, 1973–75; Vice-Pres., RIBA, 1973–75. FRSA; RSA 1975 (ARSA 1963; Treasurer, 1978–80; Sec., 1980–83); Hon. RA 1983; Hon. RHA 1983; Hon. RGI 1987. Hon. DDes Robert Gordon's Inst. of Technology, 1991. Hon. Pres., Saltire Soc., 1995. 22 Saltire Awards and Commendations for Housing and Reconstruction; 12 Civic Trust Awards and Commendations. *Publications:* articles on civic design and housing in technical jls. *Recreations:* making gardens, sketching and water colours, fishing, music and drama. *Address:* South Inverleith Manor, 31/6 Kinnear Road, Edinburgh EH3 5PG. *T:* (0131) 552 3854. *Clubs:* New, Scottish Arts (Edinburgh).

WHEELER, Air Chief Marshal Sir (Henry) Neil (George), GCB 1975 (KCB 1969; CB 1967); CBE 1957 (OBE 1949); DSO 1943; DFC 1941 (Bar 1943); AFC 1954; *b* 8 July 1917; *s* of late T. H. Wheeler, South African Police; *m* 1942, Elizabeth, *d* of late W. H. Weightman, CMG; two *s* one *d*. *Educ:* St Helen's College, Southsea, Hants. Entered Royal Air Force College, Cranwell, 1935; Bomber Comd, 1937–40; Fighter and Coastal Comds, 1940–45; RAF and US Army Staff Colls, 1943–44; Cabinet Office, 1944–45; Directing Staff, RAF Staff Coll., 1945–46; FEAF, 1947–49; Directing Staff, JSSC, 1949–51; Bomber Comd, 1951–53; Air Min., 1953–57. Asst Comdt, RAF Coll., 1957–59; OC, RAF Laarbruch, 1959–60; IDC, 1961; Min. of Defence, 1961–63; Senior Air Staff Officer, HQ, RAF Germany (2nd TAF), Sept. 1963–66; Asst Chief of Defence Staff (Operational Requirements), MoD, 1966–67, Deputy Chief of Defence Staff, 1967–68; Commander, FEAF, 1969–70; Air Mem. for Supply and Organisation, MoD, 1970–73; Controller, Aircraft, MoD Procurement Exec., 1973–75. ADC to the Queen, 1957–61. Director: Rolls-Royce Ltd, 1977–82; Flight Refuelling (Holdings) Ltd, 1977–85. Chm., Anglo-Ecuadorian Soc., 1986–88. Vice-Pres., Air League; Liveryman, GAPAN, 1980, Master, 1986–87. FRAeS; CCMI. *Address:* Boundary Hall, Cooksbridge, Lewes, East Sussex BN8 4PT. *Clubs:* Royal Air Force, Flyfishers'.

WHEELER, Rt Hon. Sir John (Daniel), Kt 1990; PC 1993; JP; DL; Chairman, Service Authorities for National Criminal Intelligence Service and National Crime Squad, 1997–2002; *b* 1 May 1940; *s* of late Frederick Harry Wheeler and of Constance Elsie (*née* Foreman); *m* 1967, Laura Margaret Langley; one *s* one *d*. *Educ:* county sch., Suffolk; Staff Coll., Wakefield. Home Office: Asst Prison Governor, 1967–74; Res. Officer (looking into causes of crime and delinquency and treatment of offenders), 1974–76; Dir-Gen., BSIA, 1976–88 (Hon. Mem., 1990). Dir, National Supervisory Council for Intruder Alarms, 1977–88. Chairman: Nat. Inspectorate of Security Guard Patrol and Transport Services, 1982–92; Security Systems Inspectorate, 1987–90; Inspectorate of the Security Industry, 1992–93; govt review of airport security, 2002; Airport Security and Policing Review, Fed. Govt of Aust., 2005; Dep. Chm., UK Border Security Adv. Cttee, 2007–08. Chm. and non-exec. dir, various cos, 1976–93, 1997–. Chm., Capital Link, 1997–2002. MP (C) City of Westminster, Paddington Div., 1979–83, Westminster N, 1983–97. Minister of State, NI Office, 1993–97. Member: Home Office Crime Prevention Cttee, 1976–92; Cons. Party National Adv. CPC Cttee, 1978–80; Home Affairs Select Cttee, 1979–92 (Chm., 1987–92); Chairman: Home Affairs Sub-Cttee, Race Relations and Immigration, 1980–87; All Party Penal Affairs Gp, 1986–93 (Vice-Chm., 1979–86); Vice-Chairman: Cons. Home Affairs Cttee, 1987–92 (Jt Sec., 1980–87); British Pakistan Parly Gp, 1987–93; Chm., Cons. Greater London Area Members' Cttee, 1983–90 (Jt Sec., 1980–83). Mem., Lloyd's, 1986–97. Pres., Paddington Div., St John Ambulance, 1998–99 (Vice Pres., 1990–98). Trustee, Police Foundn, 2004–. Freeman, City of London, 1987. JP Inner London, 1978; DL Greater London, 1989; Rep. DL, LB of Merton, 1997. James Smart Lecture, SHHD, 1991 (Silver Medal). KStJ 1997 (Mem. Council, Order of St John for London, 1990–; Mem., Chapter Gen., 1993–99; Registrar, 1997–99, Sub-Chancellor, 1999–2002, Order of St John; Trustee and Mem., 1999–2008, Chancellor, 2002–08, Priory Chapter of England and the Islands). Hilal-i-Quaid-i-Azam (Pakistan), 1991. *Publications:* Who Prevents Crime?, 1980; (jtly) The Standard Catalogue of the Coins of the British Commonwealth, 1642 to present day, 1986. *Recreation:* enjoying life. *Address:* PO Box 890, SW1P 1XW.

WHEELER, Sir John (Frederick), (Jim), 4th Bt *cr* 1920, of Woodhouse Eaves, co. Leicester; *b* 3 May 1933; *s* of Sir John Hieron Wheeler, 3rd Bt and Gwendolen Alice Wheeler (*née* Oram); *S* father, 2005; *m* 1963, Barbara Mary, *d* of Raymond Flint; two *s* one *d. Educ:* Bedales; London Sch. of Printing. *Heir: s* Lt-Col John Radford Wheeler [*b* 27 Dec. 1965; *m* 1991, Sarah, *d* of Comdr Tim Howard-Jones; two *s* two *d*]. *Address:* Round Hill, Aldeburgh, Suffolk IP15 5PG.

WHEELER, (John) Stuart; Founder, IG Group (formerly IG Index), 1985 (Chief Executive, 1974–2002; Chairman, 1985–2003); *b* 30 Jan. 1935; adopted by late Capt. Alexander Hamilton Wheeler and Betty Lydia Wheeler; *m* 1979, Teresa Anne Codrington; three *d. Educ:* Eton Coll.; Christ Church, Oxford (LLB Hons). Nat Service, 2nd Lieut, Welsh Guards, 1953–55. Called to the Bar, Inner Temple, 1959, in practice as barrister, 1959–62; Asst Manager, Investment Dept, Hill Samuel, 1962–68; Manager, Investment Dept, J. H. Vavasseur, 1968–73; First Nat. Finance Corp., 1973. Coronation Medal, 1953. *Recreations:* tennis, bridge, poker. *Address:* Penthouse A, 21 Davies Street, W1K 3DE. *T:* (020) 7499 1630; Chilham Castle, Canterbury, Kent CT4 8DB. *T:* (01227) 733100. *Clubs:* White's, Portland.

WHEELER, Air Vice-Marshal Leslie William Frederick; Independent Inspector for Public Inquiries and Chairman of Appointments Boards for Civil Service Commissioners and Ministry of Defence, 1984–94; *b* 4 July 1930; *s* of late George Douglas and Susan Wheeler; *m* 1961, Joan, *d* of late Harry and Evelyn Carpenter; two *d. Educ:* Creighton School, Carlisle. Commnd, 1952; Egypt and Cyprus, 1954–56; Specialist in Signals, 1958; Aden, 1958–60; V-force (Valiants), 1961–65; India (Staff Coll.), 1965–66; Headquarters Signals Command, 1966–69; OC 360 Sqdn, 1970–72; Dir, RAF Staff Coll., 1972–74; Electronic Warfare and Recce Operations, MoD, 1975–77; Stn Comdr, RAF Finningley, 1977–79; Air Cdre Policy & Plans, Headquarters RAF Support Comd, 1979–83; Dir-Gen., Personal Services (RAF), MoD, 1983–84, retired. *Recreations:* walking, golf, philately. *Address:* c/o HSBC, Brampton, Cumbria CA8 1NQ. *Club:* Royal Air Force.

WHEELER, Dame Margaret Anne; *see* Brain, Dame M. A.

WHEELER, Sir Neil; *see* Wheeler, Sir H. N. G.

WHEELER, Nicholas Charles Tyrwhitt; Chairman, Charles Tyrwhitt, since 1986; *b* 20 Jan. 1965; *s* of John Vashon Tyrwhitt Wheeler and Geraldine Noel Wheeler; *m* 1995, (Belinda) Christian Rucker, *qv*; one *s* three *d. Educ:* Eton Coll.; Univ. of Bristol (BSc 1987). Charles Tyrwhitt, 1986–; Bain & Co., 1987–89. *Recreations:* tennis, ski-ing, photography. *Address: e-mail:* nickw@ctshirts.co.uk. *Club:* Hurlingham.

WHEELER, Prof. Quentin D., PhD; Vice President and Dean, College of Liberal Arts and Sciences, and Professor of Natural History and the Environment, School of Life Sciences, Arizona State University, since 2006; *b* 31 Jan. 1954; *s* of Quentin Wheeler and Hattie (*née* Philips); *m* 2004, Darlene Marie Platt; one *s* four *d. Educ:* Ohio State Univ., Columbus (BS 1976, MS 1977; PhD 1980). Cornell University: Prof., 1980–2004; Chm., Entomology, 1989–93; Dir, L. H. Bailey Hortorium, 1988–89. US National Science Foundation: Prog. Officer, 2001; Dir, Div. of Envmtl Biology, 2001–04; Keeper and Hd of Entomol., Natural History Mus., 2004–06; Dir, Internat. Inst. for Species Exploration, Arizona State Univ., 2007–. Mem., Willi Hennig Soc. FAAAS 2003; FLS 2003; FRES 2004. *Publications:* Fungus/Insect Relationships: perspectives in ecology and evolution, 1984; Extinction and Phylogeny, 1992; Species Concepts and Phylogenetic Theory: a debate, 2000; more than 100 articles in scientific jls. *Recreations:* furniture making, insect collecting, hiking, photography, wines and coffees. *Address:* College of Liberal Arts and Sciences, Arizona State University, PO Box 87 6505, Tempe, AZ 85287–6505, USA.

WHEELER, Raymond Leslie, RDI 1995; FRAeS; FRINA; *b* 25 Oct. 1927; *s* of Edmund Francis Wheeler and Ivy Geraldine Wheeler; *m* 1950, Jean McInnes; one *s* two *d. Educ:* Southampton Univ. (BSc (Eng) 1949); Imperial Coll., London (MSc (Eng) 1953; DIC). FRAeS 1974; FRINA 1975. Apprentice, 1945–48, Aircraft stressman, 1953–62, Chief Stressman, 1962–65, Saunders Roe Ltd, then Saunders Roe Div. of Westland Aircraft Ltd; Chief Structural Designer and Project Engr, SRN4 (world's largest hovercraft), 1965; British Hovercraft Corp. Ltd, subseq. Westland Aerospace Ltd: Chief Designer, 1966–85; Technical Dir, 1972–85; Dir, 1985–91. *Publications:* (with A. E. Tagg) From Sea to Air: the heritage of Sam Saunders, 1989; From River to Sea: the marine heritage of Sam Saunders, 1993; Saunders Roe, 1998; (with J. B. Chaplin) In the Beginning: the SRNI hovercraft, 2007. *Recreations:* gardening, photography, pottery, painting, archaeology, sport. *Address:* Brovacum, 106 Old Road, East Cowes, Isle of Wight PO32 6AX.

WHEELER, Gen. Sir Roger (Neil), GCB 1997 (KCB 1993); CBE 1983; Constable, HM Tower of London, since 2001; Chief of the General Staff, 1997–2000; Aide-de-camp General to the Queen, 1996–2000; *b* 16 Dec. 1941; *s* of Maj.-Gen. T. N. S. Wheeler, CB, CBE; *m* 1980, Felicity Hares; three *s* one *d* by former marriage. *Educ:* All Hallows Sch., Devon. Early Army service in Borneo and ME, 1964–70; Bde Major, Cyprus Emergency, 1974; Mem., Lord Carver's Staff, Rhodesia talks, 1977; Bn Comd, Belize, Gibraltar, Berlin and Canada, 1979–82; COS, Falkland Is, June–Dec. 1982; Bde Comd, BAOR, 1985–86; Dir, Army Plans, 1987–89; Comdr, 1st Armoured Div., BAOR, 1989–90; ACGS, MoD, 1990–92; GOC and Dir of Military Ops, NI, 1993–96; C-in-C, Land Comd, 1996–97. Col, Royal Irish Regt, 1996–2001; Col Comdt, Intell. Corps, 1996–2000. Hon. Colonel: QUB OTC, 2000–; Oxford Univ. OTC, 2000–06. President: Army RFU, 1995–99; Army Rifle Assoc., 1995–2000; Mem. Council, NRA, 2000–02. Non-executive Director: Thales plc, 2001–; Aegis Defence, 2003–; Serious Organised Crime Agency, 2005–. President: Ex Services Mental Welfare Soc., Combat Stress, 2001–; Forces Pension Soc., 2006–. Patron, Police Foundn, 2001–. Pres. and Patron, Lady Grover's Fund, 2003–. Chm. Trustees, Tank Mus., Bovington, 2002–. FRGS 2000. Liveryman, Painter-Stainers' Co. Hon. Fellow, Hertford Coll., Oxford. *Recreations:* fly-fishing, cricket, shooting, ornithology. *Clubs:* Army and Navy, Beefsteak; Stragglers of Asia CC.

WHEELER, Sara Diane, FRSL; writer; *b* 20 March 1961; *d* of John Wilfred Wheeler and Diane Pauline Wheeler (*née* Vernon, now Price); partner, Peter Graham; two *s. Educ:* Redland High Sch., Bristol; Brasenose Coll., Oxford (BA Hons). FRSL 1999 (Mem. Council, 2000–05). Trustee, London Liby, 2006–. *Publications:* An Island Apart: travels in Evia, 1992; Travels in a Thin Country: a journey through Chile, 1994; Terra Incognita: travels in Antarctica, 1996; (ed jtly) Amazonian: the Penguin Book of women's new travel writing, 1998; Cherry: a biography of Apsley Cherry-Garrard, 2001; Too Close to the Sun: a biography of Denys Finch Hatton, 2006. *Address:* c/o Aitken Alexander Associates, 18–21 Cavaye Place, SW10 9PT; *e-mail:* reception@aitkenalexander.co.uk. *Club:* Academy.

WHEELER, Stuart; *see* Wheeler, J. S.

WHEELER, Prof. Timothy Jerome, PhD; CPsychol; DL; Vice-Chancellor, University of Chester, since 2005; *b* 22 Oct. 1950; *s* of George Edward Wheeler and Mary Wheeler (*née* Carter); *m* 1975, Marilyn Sutton Jones; three *d. Educ:* Colwyn Bay Grammar Sch.; University Coll. of N Wales, Bangor (BA; PhD 1977); Llandrillo Coll. (FE Teacher's Cert.). CPsychol 1988. Lectr, then Sen. Lectr, Sheffield Poly., 1974–80; Hd of Sch. and Dean of Faculty, Dublin City Univ., 1980–85; Hd, Sch. of Social Scis, Robert Gordon's Inst. of Technol., Aberdeen, 1985; Hd, Communication and Media, Dorset Inst., subseq. Bournemouth Poly., 1986–91; Southampton Institute: Dir, Envmt Sch., 1991–96; Dep. Dir, 1996–97; Dir, 1997–98; Principal, Chester Coll., subseq. UC Chester, 1998–2005. Vis. Prof., Communication Studies, Calif State Univ., Sacramento, 1982; Sen. Schol., St John's Coll., Oxford, 1988. Dep. Chm., UCAS, 1999–2005. Member: LLSC Cheshire and Warrington, 2001–; Cheshire & Warrington Econ. Alliance, 2001–. Lay Canon, 2003–, Mem. Chapter, 2004–, Chester Cathedral. DL Cheshire, 2003. Member Editorial Boards: Dyslexia: an Internat. Jl of Res. and Practice; Internat. Jl of Corporate Communications. *Publications:* Handbook of Safety Management, 1989; contribs to scientific jls, chapters in books, reviews. *Recreations:* collector of antique oriental ceramics, keen interest in contemporary film, catholic tastes in music, active in a number of charities. *Address:* Old College, University of Chester, Parkgate Road, Chester, Cheshire CH1 4BJ. *T:* (01244) 511000, *Fax:* (01244) 392808; *e-mail:* t.wheeler@chester.ac.uk.

WHEELER-BENNETT, Richard Clement; Chairman of the Council, Marie Curie Cancer Care (formerly Marie Curie Memorial Foundation), 1990–2000; *b* 14 June 1927; *s* of Dr Clement Wheeler-Bennett and Enid Lucy (*née* Boosey); *m* 1st, 1954, Joan Ellen Havelock (marr. diss. 2000); two *d* (one *s* decd); 2nd, 2001, Hon. Lady Smith-Ryland. *Educ:* Radley; Christ Church, Oxford (MA); Harvard Business Sch. Served Royal Marines, 1944–48. First Nat. City Bank of NY, 1951–66, Manager 1960–66; Australia and New Zealand Banking Group, 1966–80; Exec. Dir, 1967–78; Gen. Manager Europe, 1978–80; Chm., Thomas Borthwick & Sons Ltd, 1980–85; Director: Fleming Technology Trust, 1983–90; Fleming Internat. High Income Investment Trust, 1990–92; ANZ Grindlays Bank, 1993–96. Pres. Dir Gen., Boucheries Bernard SA, Paris, 1980–85. Chm., British Overseas and Commonwealth Banks Assoc., 1980. Founder Chm., Prospect Housing Assoc., 1965–77. Chm. of Govs, Springfields Sch., Calne, 1991–2007. Chm., Roehampton Club Ltd, 1988–92. Freeman, City of London; Liveryman, Butchers' Co. *Recreations:* flyfishing, golf, shooting, viticulture. *Address:* The Old Hall, Medbourne, Market Harborough, Leics LE16 8DZ. *T:* (01858) 565543. *Clubs:* Brooks's, Pratt's, MCC.

WHEELER-BOOTH, Sir Michael (Addison John), KCB 1994; Special Lecturer in Politics, Magdalen College, Oxford, 1998–June 2009; Clerk of the Parliaments, 1991–97; *b* 25 Feb. 1934; *s* of Addison James Wheeler and Mary Angela Wheeler-Booth (*née* Blakeney-Booth); *m* 1982, Emily Frances Smith; one *s* two *d. Educ:* Leighton Park Sch.; Magdalen Coll., Oxford (Exhibnr; MA; Hon. Fellow, 2003). Nat. Service, Midshipman (Sp.) RNVR, 1952–54. A Clerk, House of Lords, 1960–97; seconded to HM Treasury as Private Secretary to Leader of House and Government Chief Whip, 1965; seconded as Jt Sec., Inter-Party Conference on House of Lords Reform, 1967–69; Clerk of the Journals, 1970–74, 1983–90; Chief Clerk, Overseas and European Office, 1972, Principal Clerk, 1978; Reading Clerk, 1983; Clerk Asst, 1988. Treas. and Co-Ed. Jl, Soc. of Clerks at the Table in Commonwealth Parlts, 1962–65. Comr, Welsh Nat. Assembly Standing Orders, 1998–99. Chm., 1984–87, Pres., 2004–, Study of Parliament Gp; Member: Royal Commn on H of L reform, 1999–2000; Fabian Commn on the Monarchy, 2002–03; Commn on Powers and Electoral Arrangements of Nat. Assembly for Wales, (Richard Commn), 2002–04; Chm., Ind. Review Panel on Salaries, Pensions and Allowances for Welsh Assembly Mems, 2007–08. Waynflete Lectr, 1998, Vis. Fellow, 1997–98, Magdalen Coll., Oxford. Trustee: History of Parliament Trust, 1991–97; Industry and Parliament Trust, 1994–97. Gov., Magdalen Coll. Sch., 2001– (Chm., F and GP Cttee, 2004–). *Publications:* (contrib.) Griffith and Ryle, Parliament, 1989, 2nd edn 2003; (ed jtly) Halsbury's Laws of England on Parliament, 4th edn 1997; contribs to parly jls. *Recreations:* reading, ruins, pictures, swimming, opera, the countryside. *Address:* Magdalen College, Oxford OX1 4AU. *T:* (01865) 276108; Northfields, Sandford St Martin, Chipping Norton, Oxon OX7 7AG. *T:* (01608) 68632; 4 Polstead Road, Oxford OX2 6TN. *T:* (01865) 514040, *Fax:* (01865) 516048. *Clubs:* Brooks's, Garrick.

WHEELHOUSE, Keith Oliver B.; *see* Butler-Wheelhouse.

WHEEN, Francis James Baird; author and journalist; *b* 22 Jan. 1957; *s* of James Francis Thorneycroft Wheen and Patricia Winifred Wheen (*née* Ward); *m* 1985, Joan Smith (marr. diss. 1993); partner, Julia Jones; two *s. Educ:* Copthorne Sch.; Harrow; Royal Holloway Coll., London (BA 1978; Hon. Fellow, 2008). Office boy, The Guardian, 1974–75; reporter: New Statesman, 1978–84; Private Eye, 1987–; columnist: Independent, 1986–87; Independent on Sunday, 1990–91; Observer, 1993–95; Esquire, 1993–98; Guardian, 1994–2001; Evening Standard, 2006–07. Panellist, News Quiz, BBC Radio, 1989–. Columnist of Year, Granada/What the Papers Say awards, 1997. *Publications:* The Sixties, 1982; World View, 1982; The Battle for London, 1985; Television: a history, 1985; Tom Driberg: his life and indiscretions, 1990; (ed) The Chatto Book of Cats, 1993; (ed) Lord Gnome's Literary Companion, 1994; Karl Marx, 1999 (Isaac Deutscher Prize); Hoo-Hahs and Passing Frenzies, 2002 (George Orwell Prize); Who Was Dr Charlotte Bach?, 2002; How Mumbo-Jumbo Conquered the World, 2004; Marx's Das Kapital: a biography, 2006. *Recreation:* cricket. *Address:* Sokens, Green Street, Pleshey, Chelmsford, Essex CM3 1HT. *T:* (01245) 231566, *Fax:* (01245) 231857; *e-mail:* fwheen@netcomuk.co.uk. *Clubs:* Academy, MCC; Essex CC.

WHEEN, Natalie Kathleen; broadcaster and writer; *b* Shanghai, China, 29 July 1947; *d* of late Edward Leslie Lee Wheen and Galina (*née* Yourieff). *Educ:* Downe House, Newbury; London Univ. (BMus 1967); Royal Coll. of Music (ARCM). BBC, 1968–80: radio studio manager; attachments as Asst Producer, BBC TV Music and Arts, 1970; Radio 3 Music Producer, Manchester and London, 1971–72; Asst Producer, Music Now, Radio 3, 1972–73; Producer, Music Now, Talking About Music and various documentaries, 1973–80 (Best Music Documentary, Imperial Tobacco Soc. Authors Awards for Radio, 1978); London Arts Corresp., Canadian Broadcasting; freelance broadcaster, 1980–; Presenter: Kaleidoscope, Radio 4, 1980–95; Mainly for Pleasure, subseq. In Tune, Radio 3, 1980–97; Music Review, World Service; Cardiff Singer of the World, BBC2, 1993, 1995 and 1997; presenter, Classic FM: Week-end Afternoons, 1999–2008; Access All Areas, 2000–01; Tonight at 11, 2001–03; The Full Works, week-ends, 2008–; contributor: The Food Programme, R4; The Influence of Effluent, R4, 1998; Compère, Gramophone Awards, 1995 and 1996; interviews, Third Ear, etc; interviewer and co-producer: Tippett's Time, C4, 1995; Visions of Paradise Intervals, R3, 1995; documentaries on arts subjects. Partner, Worsley Wheen prodns, 1983–88; indep. media prodn with Natalie Wheen & Associates. Contributing Editor, 3 mag., 1983–86. Jury Member: Sony Awards for Radio, 1994, 2003; Prudential Awards for the Arts, 1996; Masterprize, 2003; Kathleen Ferrier Scholarship, 2003; David Parkhouse Award, 2005. Director/Trustee: Hackney Music Develt Trust, 1995–2002; Creative Dance Artists Trust, 1995–96; Matthew Hawkins and the Fresh Dances Gp, 1995–97. Lectr and Workshop Leader in presentation and communication skills; Consultant, GSMD,

1991–92; Presenter, British Airways In-flight Light Classics Channel, 1991–95. Mem. Council, ENO Works, 1996–98. Governor, Downe House Sch., 1986–98. *Publications:* (jtly) A Life on the Fiddle: Max Jaffa's Autobiography, 1991; publications on trng and employment for Careers and Occupational Information Centre, and Dept of Employment; contribs to Spectator, Independent (Travel), Classic FM mag., Opera Now. *Recreations:* olives, fishing, laughter, anarchy. *Address:* c/o Arlington Enterprises Ltd, 1–3 Charlotte Street, W1T 1RD.

WHELAN, Michael George; Director, Whelan Associates Ltd, since 2006; Chief Executive, Institute of Optometry, since 2007; *b* 13 Oct. 1947; *s* of George Henry Whelan and Vera Frances Whelan (*née* Davies); *m* 1st, 1968, Veronica Gemma Merron (marr. diss. 1986); one *s* one *d*; 2nd, 1987, Anne Vivien Williams, JP; one *s*. *Educ:* Univ. of London (BSc(Econ) Hons, MSc(Econ)). Operational Manager, Walton Hosp., Liverpool, then Good Hope Hosp., Sutton Coldfield, and Hope Hosp., Salford, 1964–72; Tutor in Management, and Principal Trng Officer, N Western RHA, 1972–74; Deputy Chief Officer: Tameside and Glossop HA, 1974–78; Surrey AHA, 1978–80; Chief Officer, SW Surrey HA, 1980–85; Gp Manager, Healthcare, KPMG Management Consultants, 1985–90; Partner, Pannell Kerr Forster, 1990–92; Chief Exec., Parkinson's Disease Soc., 1992–94; healthcare business consultant, 1994–97; Principal, Watson Wyatt Actuaries and Consultants, 1997–98; Chief Exec., Thomson, Snell & Passmore, Solicitors, 1998–2000; Practice Dir, T. V. Edwards (Solicitors), 2000–02; healthcare mgt consultant, 2002–03; Project Dir, Surrey and Sussex SHA, 2003–05; Registrar, Faculty of Dental Surgery, RCS, 2005. AIPM 1975; FHSM 1980. *Recreations:* music, entertaining, family, gardening, literature. *Address:* Chambord, 46 Pewley Way, Guildford, Surrey GU1 3QA.

WHELAN, Prof. Michael John, MA, PhD, DPhil; FRS 1976; FInstP; Professor of Microscopy of Materials, Department of Materials, University of Oxford, 1992–97, now Emeritus Professor; Fellow of Linacre College, Oxford, since 1967; *b* 2 Nov. 1931; *s* of William Whelan and Ellen Pound. *Educ:* Farnborough Grammar Sch.; Gonville and Caius Coll., Cambridge. FInstP 1976. Fellow of Gonville and Caius Coll., 1958–66; Demonstrator in Physics, Univ. of Cambridge, 1961–65; Asst Dir of Research in Physics, Univ. of Cambridge, 1965–66; Reader, Dept of Materials, Univ. of Oxford, 1966–92. Hon. Prof., Univ. of Sci. and Technol. Beijing, China, 1995. Hon. FRMS 2001; Hon. Fellow, Japanese Soc. of Microscopy, 2003. C. V. Boys Prize, Inst. of Physics, 1965; Hughes Medal, Royal Soc., 1988; Distinguished Scientist Award, Microscopy Soc. of Amer., 1998. *Publications:* (jtly) Electron Microscopy of Thin Crystals, 1965; Worked Examples in Dislocations, 1990; (jtly) High-Energy Electron Diffraction and Microscopy, 2004; numerous papers in learned jls. *Recreation:* gardening. *Address:* 18 Salford Road, Old Marston, Oxford OX3 0RX. *T:* (01865) 244556.

WHELAN, Prof. William Joseph, PhD, DSc; FRS 1992; Professor of Biochemistry and Molecular Biology, University of Miami Miller School of Medicine (formerly University of Miami School of Medicine), since 1967 (Chairman of Department, 1967–91); *b* 14 Nov. 1924; *s* of William Joseph Whelan and Jane Antoinette Whelan (*née* Bertram); *m* 1951, Margaret Miller Birnie (*d* 1993). *Educ:* Univ. of Birmingham, England (BSc Hons 1944; PhD 1948; DSc 1955). Asst Lectr, Univ. of Birmingham, 1947–48; Asst Lectr, Lectr and Sen. Lectr, UCNW, Bangor, 1948–55; Sen. Mem., Lister Inst. of Preventive Medicine, Univ. of London, 1956–64; Prof. and Head, Dept of Biochemistry, Royal Free Hosp. Sch. of Medicine, Univ. of London, 1964–67. Co-Dir, Miami Winter Symposia, 1968–. Dir, Enterprise Florida Technol. Develt Bd (formerly Enterprise Florida Innovation Partnership), 1993–98. President: Portland Press Inc., 1994–98; Frontiers of Knowledge Inc., 1999–2003. Pres., Internat. Union of Biochemistry and Molecular Biol., 1997–2000. FAAAS 1989. Hon. MRCP 1985; Hon. Mem., Biochemical Soc., 1993. Hon. DSc La Trobe, 1997. Alsberg Medal, 1967; Ciba Medal, 1968; Saare Medal, 1979; FEBS Millennium Medal, 2000. Editor-in-Chief: Trends in Biochemical Sciences, 1975–78; BioEssays, 1984–89; Fedn Procs, 1986–87; FASEB Jl, 1987–96; IUBMB Life, 2000–. *Recreations:* publishing, travel. *Address:* Department of Biochemistry and Molecular Biology, University of Miami Miller School of Medicine (M823), PO Box 016129, Miami, FL 33101–6129, USA. *T:* (305) 2436267, *Fax:* (305) 3245665; *e-mail:* wwhelan@miami.edu. *Club:* Athenæum.

WHELDON, Dame Juliet (Louise), DCB 2004 (CB 1994); Chief Legal Adviser and Adviser to the Governor of the Bank of England, since 2006; *b* 26 March 1950; *d* of late John Wheldon and of Ursula Mabel Caillard. *Educ:* Sherborne School for Girls; Lady Margaret Hall, Oxford (1st Cl. Hons Mod. Hist.). Called to the Bar, Gray's Inn, 1975, Bencher 1999. Treasury Solicitor's Dept, 1976–83; Law Officers Dept, 1983–84; Treasury Solicitor's Dept, 1984–86; Asst Legal Sec. to the Law Officers, 1986–87; Legal Advr to HM Treasury, Treasury Solicitor's Dept, 1987–89; Legal Sec. to the Law Officers, 1989–97; Legal Advr to Home Office, 1997–2000; HM Procurator Gen., Treasury Solicitor and Hd of Govt Legal Service, 2000–06. Hon. QC 1997. *Address:* Bank of England, Threadneedle Street, EC2R 8AH; *e-mail:* juliet.wheldon@bankofengland.co.uk.

WHELER, Sir Trevor (Woodford), 15th Bt *cr* 1660, of City of Westminster; *b* 11 April 1946; *s* of Sir Edward Woodford Wheler, 14th Bt, and Molly Ashworth, *e d* of Thomas Lever, Devon; *S* father, 2008; *m* 1974, Rosalie Margaret, *d* of late Ronald Thomas Stunt; two *s*. *Educ:* St Edmund's Sch., Canterbury; St Mary's Sch., Nairobi. Air Traffic Control, RAF, 1966–71, CAA, 1971–2006. *Heir: s* Edward William Wheler [*b* 14 June 1976; *m* 2004, Monika Polešáková; one *s*]. *Address:* 83 Middle Park, Inverurie, Aberdeenshire AB51 4QW. *T:* (01467) 622642; *e-mail:* trevor.wheler@sky.com.

WHELON, (Charles) Patrick (Clavell); a Recorder of the Crown Court, 1978–97; *b* 18 Jan. 1930; *s* of Charles Eric Whelon and Margaret Whelon; *m* 1968, Prudence Mary (*née* Potter); one *s* one *d*. *Educ:* Wellington Coll.; Pembroke Coll., Cambridge (MA Hons). Called to Bar, Middle Temple, 1954. Liveryman of Vintners' Co., 1952–. *Recreations:* gardening, cartooning. *Address:* Russets, Pyott's Hill, Old Basing, Hants RG24 8AP. *T:* (01256) 469964.

WHELTON, David William; pianist, organist, music administrator; Managing Director, Philharmonia Orchestra, since 1988; *b* 16 June 1954; *s* of William and Nora Whelton; *m* 1977, Caroline Rachel Gardner; one s. Mem. of Staff, GSMD, 1978–83; Dir of Music, Royal GS, Guildford, 1979–83; Music Officer, Yorks Arts Assoc., 1983–85; Principal Arts Officer, Leeds CC, 1985–86; Music Officer, Arts Council of GB, 1986–88. Director: Assoc. of British Orchestras, 1997–; Internat. Musicians Seminar, Prussia Cove, 1998–. Chm., Leeds Internat. Conductors' Comp., 2005, 2009. Trustee: Mayfield Valley Arts Trust, 1986–; Philharmonia Trust, 1988–. Hon. Vice Pres., Ernst Bloch Soc. FRSA. Freeman, City of London, 2005; Mem., Musicians' Co. *Recreations:* gardening, architecture, history. *Address:* Philharmonia Orchestra, 6th Floor, The Tower Building, 11 York Road, SE1 7NX. *T:* (020) 7921 3901.

WHETNALL, Andrew Donard, CB 1996; Director for Local Government, Office of the Deputy Prime Minister (formerly Department of the Environment, Transport and the Regions, then Department for Transport, Local Government and the Regions), 1996–2003; *b* 18 May 1948; *s* of late Donard and of Joan Whetnall (*née* Mummery); *m* 1972, Jane Lepel Glass; two *s* two *d*. *Educ:* King's Norton Grammar Sch.; Univ. of Sussex (MA). Joined DoE, 1975; Principal, Dept of Transport, 1980–83; Department of the Environment: Principal, 1983–87, Asst Sec., 1987–88, Inner Cities; Water Legislation, 1988–89; Head, Machinery of Govt Div., Cabinet Office, 1989–96 (Under Sec., 1993). *Recreations:* reading, music. *Address:* *e-mail:* andrew.whetnall@tiscali.co.uk.

WHETSTONE, Rear-Adm. Anthony John, CB 1982; Chairman, Bridgeworks Trust, 1999–2004; *b* 12 June 1927; *s* of Albert and Anne Whetstone; *m* 1951, Elizabeth Stewart Georgeson; one *s* two *d*. *Educ:* King Henry VIII School, Coventry. Joined RN, 1945; specialised in submarines, 1949; Commanded: HMS Sea Scout, 1956–57; HMS Artful, 1959–61; HMS Repulse, 1968–70; HMS Juno, 1972–73; HMS Norfolk, 1977–78; Flag Officer Sea Training, 1978–80; Asst Chief of Naval Staff (Operations), 1981–83. Director-General: Cable TV Assoc., 1983–86; Nat. Television Rental Assoc., 1983–87. Dep. Sec., Defence Press and Broadcasting Cttee, 1987–92. Dir, DESC Ltd, 1991–96. Mem., Adv. Cttee on Historic Wreck Sites, 1996–2002. Nat. Pres., Submariners Assoc., 1988–2002. Chm. Trustees, Royal Navy Submarine Mus., 1990–98. FCMI (FBIM 1979). *Recreations:* fishing, gardening, theatre (Chm., Civil Service Drama Fedn, 1985–92). *Address:* 17 Anglesey Road, Alverstoke, Hants PO12 2EG. *Club:* Army and Navy.

WHICHER, Peter George, CEng; FRAeS; MIET; Principal, INECO, since 1994; *b* 10 March 1929; *o s* of late Reginald George Whicher and Suzanne (*née* Dexter); *m* 1st, 1962, Susan Rosemary Strong (*d* 1989); one *s* one *d*; 2nd, 1992, Margaret Rosemary (*née* Rickman). *Educ:* Chichester High Sch.; BSc(Eng) London 1948. CEng, MIET (MIEE 1957). STC, 1948–51; Flying Officer, RAF, 1951–53; Min. of Aviation, 1953; Principal Expert in Telecommunications, Eurocontrol Agency, Paris, 1962–64; Cabinet Office, 1964–66; Asst Dir, Telecommunications R & D, and Manager, Skynet Satellite Communications Project, Min. of Technology, 1967–71; Superintendent, Communications Div., RAE, 1971–73; Dir, Air Radio, MoD(PE), 1973–76; RCDS, 1977; Dir, Defence Sci. (Electronics), MoD, 1978–81; Dep. Dir, RAE, 1981–84. Consultant, Logica, 1985–94. FRAeS 1985. *Publications:* reports and papers for professional instns. *Recreations:* sailing, innovation, arts. *Address:* Widgers Wood, Sheets Health, Brookwood, Woking, Surrey GU24 0EJ. *Club:* Offshore Cruising.

WHICKER, Alan Donald, CBE 2005; television broadcaster (Whicker's World); writer; *b* 2 Aug. 1925; *o s* of late Charles Henry Whicker and late Anne Jane Cross. *Educ:* Haberdashers' Aske's Sch. Capt., Devonshire Regt; Dir, Army Film and Photo Unit, with 8th Army and US 5th Army. War Corresp. in Korea, Foreign Corresp., novelist, writer, television and radio broadcaster. Joined BBC TV, 1957: Tonight programme (appeared nightly in filmed reports from around the world, studio interviews, outside broadcasts, Eurovision, and Telstar, incl. first Telstar two-way transmission at opening of UN Assembly, NY, 1962); TV Series: Whicker's World, 1959–60; Whicker Down Under, 1961; Whicker on Top of the World!, 1962; Whicker in Sweden, Whicker in the Heart of Texas, Whicker Down Mexico Way, 1963; Alan Whicker Report series: The Solitary Billionaire (J. Paul Getty), etc; wrote and appeared in own series of monthly documentaries on BBC 2, subseq. repeated on BBC 1, under series title, Whicker's World, 1965–67 (31 programmes later shown around the world); BBC radio programmes and articles for The Listener, etc; left BBC, 1968. Various cinema films, incl. The Angry Silence. Mem., successful consortium for Yorkshire Television, 1967. Completed 16 Documentaries for Yorkshire TV during its first year of operation, incl. Whicker's New World series, and Specials on Gen. Stroessner of Paraguay, Count von Rosen, and Pres. Duvalier of Haiti; Whicker in Europe; Whicker's Walkabout; Broken Hill—Walled City; Gairy's Grenada; documentary series, World of Whicker; Whicker's Orient; Whicker within a Woman's World, 1972; Whicker's South Seas, Whicker way out West, 1973; Whicker's World, series on cities, 1974–77; Whicker's World—Down Under, 1976; Whicker's World: US, 1977 (4 progs); India, 1978 (7 progs); Indonesia, 1979; California, 1980 (6 progs); Peter Sellers Meml programme, 1980; Whicker's World Aboard the Orient Express, 1982; Around Whicker's World in 25 Years (3 YTV retrospect. progs), 1982; BBC TV, 1982–92; Whicker's World—the First Million Miles (6 retrospect. progs), 1982; Whicker's World—a Fast Boat to China (4 QE2 progs), 1984; Whicker! (10 talk shows), 1984; Whicker's World—Living with Uncle Sam (10 progs), 1985; Whicker's World—Living with Waltzing Matilda (10 progs), 1987–88; Whicker's World—Hong Kong (8 progs), 1990; Whicker's World—a Taste of Spain (8 progs), 1992; returned to ITV for: Around Whicker's World—the Ultimate Package! (4 progs), 1992; Whicker's World—The Absolute Monarch (the Sultan of Brunei), 1992; South Africa: Whicker's Miss World, and Whicker's World—The Sun King, 1993; South-East Asia: Whicker's World Aboard the real Orient Express; Whicker—the Mahathir Interview (Dr Mahathir Mohammed, PM of Malaysia); Pavarotti in Paradise, 1994; updated 27 progs for Travel Channel, 1996 and 4 for Yorkshire-Tyne Tees, 1997; Auntie's Greatest Hits, 1998, One-On-One, 2002, BBC TV; Whicker's War (2 progs), Channel 4, 2004; Comedy Map of Britain (12 progs), 2007, (6 progs), 2008, BBC TV; Whicker's World—The Journey of a Lifetime (4 progs), BBC TV, 2008. BBC Radio: Chm., Start the Week; Whicker's Wireless World (3 series), 1983; Around Whicker's World (6 progs), 1998; Whicker's Week, 1999; Whicker's New World (7 progs), 1999; Whicker's World Down Under (6 progs), 2000; The Fabulous Fifties (4 progs), 2000; The History of Television—It'll Never Last! (6 progs), 2001; Fifty Royal Years (6 progs), Around Whicker's World, 3 essays, 2002; Archive Hour, 2005. FRSA 1970. Various awards, 1963–, incl. Screenwriters' Guild, best Documentary Script, 1963; Guild of Television Producers and Directors Personality of the Year, 1964; Silver Medal, Royal Television Soc., 1968; Dumont Award, Univ. of California, 1970; Best Interview Prog. Award, Hollywood Festival of TV, 1973; Dimbleby Award, BAFTA, 1978; TV Times Special Award, 1978; first to be named in RTS Hall of Fame for outstanding creative contribution to British TV, 1993; Travelex travel writers' Special Award for outstanding achievement in travel journalism, 1998; Grierson Documentary Award, BAFTA Tribute, 2001; NFT Tribute, 6 TV Fest., 2002; War Reporter of the Year and Lifetime Achievement Award, Official Airline Guide, 2006. *Publications:* Some Rise by Sin, 1949; Away—with Alan Whicker, 1963; Best of Everything, 1980; Within Whicker's World: an autobiography, 1982; Whicker's Business Traveller's Guide (with BAA), 1983; Whicker's New World, 1985; Whicker's World Down Under, 1988; Whicker's World—Take 2, 2000; Whicker's War, 2005; Sunday newspaper columns; contrib. various internat. pubns. *Recreations:* people, photography, writing, travel, and reading (usually airline timetables). *Address:* Trinity, Jersey.

WHINERAY, Sir Wilson (James), KNZM 1998; OBE 1961; Chairman, National Bank of New Zealand Ltd, 1998–2004 (Director, 1993–2004); *b* 10 July 1935; *s* of Bruce Ludlow Whineray and Ida Cecilia Whineray (*née* Billany); *m* 1959, Elisabeth Eve Seymour; one *s* two *d*. *Educ:* Auckland GS; Auckland Univ. (BCom 1964); Grad. Sch. of Business Admin, Harvard Univ. (MBA 1969). Played Rugby for All Blacks, 1957–65, Capt., 1958–65; 32 Tests, 30 as Captain. State Advances Corp. of NZ, 1958–64; Dominion Breweries Ltd, 1964–67; joined Alex Harvey Industries Ltd, 1969; became Carter Holt Harvey Ltd, 1985: Dir, 1987–2003; Dep. Man. Dir, 1987–93; Chm., 1993–2003. Chm., Hillary Commn, 1993–98. Gov., NZ Sports Fedn, 1981–95. Col

Comdt, NZ SAS, 1997–2001. NZ Sportsman of the Year, 1965. *Address:* 2/422 Remuera Road, Remuera, Auckland, New Zealand.

WHINNEY, Rt Rev. Michael Humphrey Dickens; Hon. Assistant Bishop, Diocese of Birmingham, since 1996 (Assistant Bishop, 1988–95); Canon Residentiary, Birmingham Cathedral, 1992–95; *b* 8 July 1930; *s* of late Humphrey Charles Dickens Whinney and Evelyn Lawrence Revell Whinney (*née* Low); great-great-grandson of Charles Dickens; *m* 1958, Veronica (*née* Webster); two *s* one *d*. *Educ:* Charterhouse; Pembroke Coll., Cambridge (BA 1955, MA 1958); Ridley Hall, Cambridge; General Theological Seminary, NY (STM 1990). National Service commission, RA, 1949 (served in 5th Regt, RHA and Surrey Yeo. Queen Mary's Regt). Articled clerk to Chartered Accountants, Whinney Smith & Whinney (now Ernst Young), 1950–52. Curate, Rainham Parish Church, Essex, 1957–60; Head, Cambridge University Mission Settlement, Bermondsey, 1960–67, Chaplain, 1967–72; Vicar, St James' with Christ Church, Bermondsey, 1967–73; Archdeacon and Borough Dean of Southwark, 1973–82; Bishop Suffragan of Aston, 1982–85; Bishop of Southwell, 1985–88. *Address:* Moorcroft, 3 Moor Green Lane, Moseley, Birmingham B13 8NE.

WHISH, Prof. Richard Peter; Professor of Law, King's College London, since 1991; *b* 23 March 1953; *s* of Thomas Stanton Whish and Avis Mary Whish (*née* Sullivan). *Educ:* Clifton Coll., Bristol; Worcester Coll., Oxford (BA 1st Cl. Hons 1974; BCL 1st Cl. Hons 1978). Qualified as solicitor, 1977; University of Bristol: Lectr in Law, 1978–88; Reader in Commercial Law, 1988–90; Partner, Watson, Farley and Williams (Solicitors), London, 1989–98. Mem., Exec. Council, Centre for European Law, KCL, 1991–. Chm., Adv. Body to Dir Gen. of Gas and Electricity Mgt, 2000–01. Member: Adv. Cttee, Centre for Study of Regulated Industries, 1991–; Adv. Panel, Dir Gen. of Fair Trading, 2001–03; non-executive Director: OFT, 2003–; Energy Mkts Authy of Singapore, 2005–. Member: Editl Bd, European Business Law Review, 1994–; Adv. Bd, Competition Law Jl, 2002–. FRSA 1995. *Publications:* (jtly) Conveyancing Solutions, 1987; (Gen. Ed.) Butterworth's Competition Law, 1991; Competition Law, 3rd edn 1993, to 5th edn 2003; (jtly) Merger Cases in the Real World: a study of merger control procedures, 1994; (ed) Halsbury's Laws of England, Vol. 47, 4th edn 1994; The Competition Act, 1998; numerous articles, case-notes and book reviews in legal periodicals and books. *Recreations:* opera and music, travelling (in particular in the sub-continent), gardening, conservation, Bristol Rovers FC. *Address:* 14 Glebe House, 15 Fitzroy Mews, W1T 6DP; *e-mail:* richard.whish@kcl.ac.uk.

WHISHAW, Anthony Popham Law, RA 1989 (ARA 1980); RWA 1992; *b* 22 May 1930; *s* of Robert Whishaw and Joyce (*née* Wheeler); *m* 1957, Jean Gibson; two *d*. *Educ:* Tonbridge Sch. (Higher Cert.); Chelsea Sch. of Art; Royal College of Art (ARCA 1955). Travelling Schol., RCA; Abbey Minor Schol.; Spanish Govt Schol.; Abbey Premier Schol., 1982; Lorne Schol., 1982–83. John Moores Minor Painting Prize, 1982; (jtly) 1st Prize, Hunting Group Art Awards, 1986. *One-man exhibitions:* Libreria Abril, Madrid, 1957; Rowland Browse and Delbranco, London, 1960, 1961, 1963, 1965, 1968; ICA, 1971; New Art Centre, 1972; Folkestone Arts Centre, 1973; Hoya Gall., London, 1974; Oxford Gall., Oxford, 1974; ACME, London, 1978; Newcastle upon Tyne Polytech. Gall., 1979; (with Martin Froy) New Ashgate Gall., Farnham, 1979; Nicola Jacobs Gall., London 1981; From Landscape, Kettle's Yard, Cambridge, Ferens Gall., Hull, Bede Gall., Jarrow, 1982–84; Works on Paper, Nicola Jacobs Gall., 1983; Paintings, Nicola Jacobs Gall., 1984; Mappin Art Gall., Sheffield, 1985; Large Paintings, RA 1986; Reflections after Las Meninas (touring): Royal Acad., and Hatton Gall., Newcastle upon Tyne, 1987; Mead Gall., Warwick Univ., John Hansard Gall., Southampton Univ., and Spacex Gall., Exeter, 1988; Infaust Gall., Shanghai and Hamburg, 1989; Blason Gall., London, 1991; artspace, London, 1992, 1994 and 1995; RWA Bristol, 1993; Barbican, 1994 and tour, Mappin Gall., Sheffield, Royal Albert Meml Mus., Exeter, 1994, Newport Mus. and Art Gall., Bolton Metropolitan Mus. and Art Gall., 1995; Maclaurin Gall., Ayr, Huddersfield Gall., Royal Hibernian Acad. of Arts, Gallagher Gall., Dublin, Hatton Gall., Newcastle, 1994; Art First, London, 1997; Friends' Room, Royal Acad., 2000; Stephen Lacey Gall., London, 2000; Osborne Samuel Gall., London, 2007. *Group exhibitions:* Gimpel Fils, AIA Gall., Café Royal Centen., Towards Art (RCA), Camden Arts Centre, London, Ashmoleum Mus., Oxford, 1957–72; Brit. Drawing Biennale, Teesside, 1973; British Landscape, Graves Art Gall., Sheffield, Chichester Nat. Art, 1975; Summer Exhibn, RA, 1974–81; British Painting, 1952–77, RA, 1977; London Group, Whitechapel Open, 1978, A Free Hand, Arts Council (touring show), 1978; The British Art Show, Arts Council (touring), Recent Arts Council Purchases and Awards, Serpentine Gall., First Exhibition, Nicola Jacobs Gall., Tolly Cobbold (touring), 55 Wapping Artists, London, 1979; Four Artists, Nicola Jacobs Gall., Sculpture and Works on Paper, Nicola Jacobs, Wapping Open Studios, Hayward Annual, Hayward Gall., Whitechapel Open, Whitechapel Gall., John Moore's Liverpool Exhibn 12, 1980, Exhibn 13, 1982, Walker Art Gall., Liverpool; London Gp, S London Art Gall., Wapping Artists, 1981; Images for Today, Graves Art Gall., Sheffield, 1982; Nine Artists (touring), Helsinki, 1983; Tolly Cobbold/Eastern Arts Fourth (touring), 1983; Three Decades 1953–83, RA, 1983; Romantic Tradition in Contemporary British Painting (touring), Murcia and Madrid, Spain, and Ikon Gall., Birmingham, 1988. *Works in collections:* Arts Council of GB, Tate Gall., Coventry Art Gall., Leicester Art Gall., Nat. Gall. of Wales, Sheffield City Art Galls, Financial Times, Shell-BP, Museo de Bahia, Brazil, Nat. Gall. of Victoria, Melb., Seattle Mus. of Art, Bank of Boston, Chantrey Bequest, W Australia Art Gall., Bayer Pharmaceuticals, DoE, Nat. Westminster Bank, Power Art Gall., Aust. European Parlt, Ferens Art Gall., Museum, Murcia, Spain, Alliance & Leicester, Rosehaven PLC, Royal Academy, Linklater and Paines, Mus. of Contemp. Art, Helsinki, Christchurch, Kensington, Long Term Credit Bank of Japan, Andersen Consulting, Ashikaga Bank of Tokyo, Tetrapak, Zeneca, RWA, Deutsche Morgan-Grenfell, Mercury Asset Mgt, Ladbrokes, Crown Commodities, Stanhope, Baring Asset Mgt, St Anne's Coll., Oxford. Hon. RWA 2003. *Recreations:* chess, badminton. *Address:* 7a Albert Place, Victoria Road, W8 5PD. *T:* (020) 7937 5197; *web:* www.anthonywhishaw.com.

WHISTON, John Joseph; Director of ITV Productions, since 2006; *b* 10 Oct. 1958; *s* of Peter Rice Whiston and Kathleen Whiston (*née* Parker); partner, Kate Symington; one *s* two *d*. *Educ:* Edinburgh Acad.; Balliol Coll., Oxford (BA Eng.). Follow spot operator, for Rowan Atkinson, 1982; joined BBC, 1982: gen. trainee, 1983–85; Producer, Music and Arts, 1985–94; Head: Youth and Entertainment Features, 1994–96; Entertainment and Features, 1996–98; Director of Programmes: Yorkshire Tyne Tees Prodns, 1998–2001; Granada Content (North), 2001–02; Dir, Drama, Children's, Arts and Features, Granada Content, subseq. Drama, Kids and Arts, Granada, 2002–05. Motoring corresp., Vogue, 1991–93. *Recreations:* collecting power tools, watching bad television. *Address:* 68 Stamford Road, Bowdon, Cheshire WA14 2JF. *T:* (0161) 928 6979.

WHITAKER, family name of **Baroness Whitaker**.

WHITAKER, Baroness *cr* 1999 (Life Peer), of Beeston in the county of Nottinghamshire; **Janet Alison Whitaker;** Deputy Chair, Independent Television Commission, 2001–03; *b* 20 Feb. 1936; *d* of late Alan Harrison Stewart and Ella Stewart (*née* Saunders); *m* 1964, Benjamin Charles George Whitaker, *qv*; two *s* one *d*. *Educ:* Nottingham High Sch. for Girls; Girton Coll., Cambridge (Major Scholar); Bryn Mawr Coll., USA (Farley Graduate Fellow); Harvard Univ. (Radcliffe Fellow). Teacher, Lycée Français de Londres, 1958–59; Editor, André Deutsch Ltd, 1961–66; Health and Safety Executive, 1974–88: Hd of Gas Safety, 1983–86; Hd of Nuclear Safety Admin, 1986–88; Department of Employment: Hd of Health and Safety Br., 1988–92; Hd of Sex Equality Div., 1992–96; Leader, UK delegn to Fourth UN Conf. on Women, 1995. Chair, Working Men's Coll. for Men and Women Corp., 1998–2001. Member: Sub Cttee on Social Affairs, Educn and Home Affairs, EU Select Cttee, H of L, 1999–2002; Jt Parly Cttee on Human Rights, 2000–03; Jt Parly Cttee on Corruption Bill; Vice-Chair, All-Party Groups: on Ethiopia, 2003–; on Overseas Develt, 2005–; on Landmine Eradication, 2005–07; on Gypsy and Traveller Law Reform, 2006–; Vice-Chair: PLP Civil Rights Cttee, 2002–05; PLP Internat. Develt Cttee, 2003–; Member: OECD Wkg Pty on Rôle of Women in the Economy, 1992–96; Employment Tribunals, 1996–2000; ACORD Gender Cttee, 1996–2002; SOS Sahel Mgt Cttee, 1997–2004 (Council, 2004–); Immigration Audit Complaints Cttee, 1998–99; Opportunity Internat., 2001–; Council, Overseas Develt Inst., 2003–. Chair, Camden Racial Equality Council, 1999. Assessor, Citizen's Charter Chartermark Unit, 1996. Dir, Tavistock & Portman NHS Trust, 1997–2001. Member: Friends Provident Cttee of Reference, 2000–08; Adv. Council, Transparency Internat. (UK), 2001–; Adv. Council, British Inst. of Human Rights, 2005–; Council, African and W Eur. Parly Assoc., 2005–08; UNA-UK Adv. Panel, 2006–. Patron: Runnymede Trust, 1997–; British Stammering Assoc., 2003–; Student Partnerships Worldwide, 2005–. Trustee: One World Trust, 2000–04 (Vice-Pres., 2004–); UNICEF UK, 2003–. Member: Fabian Soc., 1970; British Humanist Assoc., 1970 (Vice-Pres., 2004–). FRSA 1993. *Recreation:* travelling hopefully. *Address:* House of Lords, SW1A 0PW. *Club:* Reform.

WHITAKER, Benjamin Charles George, CBE 2000; author; *b* 15 Sept. 1934; 3rd *s* of late Maj.-Gen. Sir John Whitaker, 2nd Bt, CB, CBE, and late Lady Whitaker (*née* Snowden), Babworth, Retford, Notts; *m* 1964, Janet Alison Stewart (*see* Baroness Whitaker); two *s* one *d*. *Educ:* Eton; New Coll., Oxford (BA Modern History). Nat. Service, Coldstream Guards, 1952–54 (2nd Lt, 1953–54, Lt, 1954). Called to Bar, Inner Temple, 1959 (Yarborough-Anderson Scholar). Practised as Barrister, 1959–67. Extra-mural Lectr in Law, London Univ., 1963–64. Executive Director: Minority Rights Group, 1971–88; Gulbenkian Foundn (UK), 1988–99. MP (Lab) Hampstead, 1966–70; PPS to Minister of: Overseas Development, 1966; Housing and Local Govt, 1966–67; Parly Sec., ODM, 1969–70. Member: UN Human Rights Sub-Commn, 1975–88 (Vice-Chm., 1979); Goodman Cttee on Charity Law Reform, 1974–76; UK Nat. Commn for UNESCO, 1978–85; Speaker's Commn on Citizenship, 1989–90; Nat. Lottery Charities Bd, subseq. Community Fund, 2000–04; Chm., SE Reg., Big Lottery (formerly Community) Fund, 2003–06; Chairman: UN Working Gp on Slavery, 1976–78; Defence of Literature and Arts Soc., 1976–82; City Poverty Cttee, 1971–83; Friends of Regent's Park, 1991–93; Foundns Forum, 1996–98. Judge: NCR Book Award, 1990; RIBA Architecture Awards, 1992. Gen. Service Medal (Canal Zone), 2004. Lieut, Order of Merit (Portugal), 1993. *Publications:* The Police, 1964; (ed) A Radical Future, 1967; Crime and Society, 1967; Participation and Poverty, 1968; Parks for People, 1971; (ed) The Fourth World, 1972; The Foundations, 1974; The Police in Society, 1979; (contrib.) Human Rights and American Foreign Policy, 1979; UN Report on Slavery, 1982; (ed) Teaching about Prejudice, 1983; A Bridge of People, 1983; (ed) Minorities: a question of human rights?, 1984; UN Report on Genocide, 1985; The Global Connection, 1987; (contrib.) The United Kingdom—The United Nations, 1990; Gen. Editor, Sources for Contemporary Issues series (7 vols), 1973–75. *Address:* 16 Adamson Road, NW3 3HR.

WHITAKER, David Haddon, OBE 1991; Chairman, J. Whitaker & Sons, Ltd, 1982–97 (Director, 1966–97; Editorial Director, 1980–91); *b* 6 March 1931; *s* of late Edgar Haddon Whitaker, OBE and of Mollie Marian, *y d* of George and Louisa Seely; *m* 1st, 1959, Veronica Wallace (decd); two *s* two *d*; 2nd, 1976, Audrey Miller (marr. diss. 1979); 3rd, 1994, Marguerite van Reenen. *Educ:* Boscastle Infants' Sch.; Marlborough Coll.; St John's Coll., Cambridge. Joined family firm of publishers, J. Whitaker & Sons, Ltd, 1955; Dir, 1966; Editor, The Bookseller, 1977–79. Member: Adv. Panel, Internat. Standard Book Numbering Agency (Berlin), 1979–97 (Chm., 1990–97); Adv. Panel, Registrar for Public Lending Right, 1983–93 (Chm., 1989–93); Standing Cttee on Technology, Booksellers' Assoc., 1984–89; Library and Information Services Council, 1985–89; Chairman: Information and Library Services Lead Body for Nat. Vocational Qualifications, 1992–95; British Nat. Bibliography Res. Fund, 1992–2001. Chairman: Soc. of Bookmen, 1984–86; Book Trade Electronic Data Interchange Standards Cttee, 1987–90. Trustee, 2002–07, Chm., 2005–07, Laser Foundn. Hon. Vice-Pres., LA, 1990. Hon. Fellow, Amer. Nat. Inst. of Standards Orgns, 1997. *Recreations:* reading, walking. *Address:* 4 Ufton Grove, N1 4HG. *T:* (020) 7241 3501, *Fax:* (020) 7241 5177. *Clubs:* Beefsteak, Garrick, Thames Rowing; Leander (Henley-on-Thames); Boscastle and Crackington Haven Gig.

WHITAKER, (Edwin) John, MBE 1991; show-jumper; *b* 5 Aug. 1955; *er s* of Donald Whitaker and Enid (*née* Lockwood); *m* 1979, Claire Barr; one *s* two *d*. British champion, 1992, 1993; other European championship wins: team and individual silver medals, 1983 (Ryan's Son); team gold and individual bronze, 1985 (Hopscotch); team gold and individual silver, 1987 (Milton); individual and team gold, 1989 (Milton); team bronze, 2007 (Peppermill). World Cup gold medals, 1990, 1991 (Milton); Olympic individual and team silver medals, 1980, and team silver medal, 1984 (Ryan's Son); jumping Derby, 1983 (Ryan's Son), 1998 (Gammon), 2000 (Virtual Village Welham); King George V Gold Cup, 1986 (Ryan's Son), 1990 (Milton), 1997 (Virtual Village Welham); Aachen Grand Prix, 1997 (Virtual Village Welham); Rome Grand Prix, 2007 (Peppermill). Leading Jumper of the Year, Horse of the Year Show, 1993, 1998; numerous other wins and awards. *Address:* c/o British Show Jumping Association, Stoneleigh, Warwicks CV8 2LR.

See also M. Whitaker.

WHITAKER, John; *see* Whitaker, E. J.

WHITAKER, Sir John James Ingham, (Sir Jack), 4th Bt *cr* 1936, of Babworth, Nottinghamshire; farmer; *b* 23 Oct. 1952; *o s* of Sir James Herbert Ingham Whitaker, 3rd Bt, OBE and Mary Elisabeth Lander Whitaker (*née* Johnston); *S* father, 1999; *m* 1981, Elizabeth Jane Ravenscroft Starke; one *s* three *d*. *Educ:* Eton; Bristol Univ. (BSc). FCA; MIET. Treas., Royal Forestry Soc., 1993–2008. High Sheriff, Notts, 2001. *Heir: s* Harry James Ingham Whitaker, *b* 16 March 1984. *Address:* Babworth Hall, Retford, Notts DN22 8EP. *T:* (01777) 860964.

WHITAKER, Michael; show-jumper; *b* 17 March 1960; *yr s* of Donald Whitaker and Enid (*née* Lockwood); *m* 1980, Veronique Dalems, *d* of Dino Vastapane. British champion, 1984, 1989; other European championship wins: Junior, 1978; team gold medal, 1985 (Warren Point); team gold, 1987 (Amanda); team gold and individual silver, 1989 (Monsanta); team silver and individual silver, 1995; team bronze, 1997; Olympic silver medal, 1984 (Amanda); Jumping Derby: 1980 (Owen Gregory); 1991 and 1992 (Monsanta); 1993 (My Messieur); King George V Gold Cup: 1982 (Disney Way); 1989 (Didi); 1992, 1994 (Midnight Madness); bareback high jump record, Dublin, 1980.

Address: c/o British Show Jumping Association, Stoneleigh, Warwicks CV8 2LR.
See also E. J. Whitaker.

WHITAKER, Sheila; Director, London Film Festival, 1987–96; *b* 1 April 1936; *d* of Hilda and Charles Whitaker. *Educ:* Cathays High Sch. for Girls, Cardiff; Kings Norton Grammar Sch. for Girls, Birmingham; Univ. of Warwick (BA Hons). Secretarial and admin. posts in commerce and industry, 1956–68; Chief Stills Officer, National Film Archive, 1968–74; Univ. of Warwick, 1975–78; Dir, Tyneside Cinema, Tyneside Film Festival, Newcastle upon Tyne, 1979–84; Head, Programming: NFT, 1984–90; Article 27, 2000. Director: Film London Ltd, 1997–2001; Metropolis Films Ltd, 2002–03. Adv. Ed., I. B. Tauris Contemp. Cinema pubns, 2001–. Mem., Programming Commn, Locarno Internat. Film Fest., 2002–05; consultant/programming adviser, 2004–, Dir of Internat. Programming, 2008–, Dubai Internat. Film Fest.; Mem., Bd of Dirs, Engaged Events (Palestine Fest. of Literature), 2007–. Dir, Free Form Arts Trust, 2000–. Mem. Jury, Venice Internat. Film Festival, 1992. Co-Editor, Framework Jl, 1976–78; Founder and Co-Editor, Writing Women, 1981–84; Gen. Editor, Tyneside Publications, 1984; Dir, Vertigo Mag., 2007–. Hon. DLitt Newcastle, 1997; Hon. LLD Warwick, 2005. Chevalier des Arts et des Lettres (France), 1996. *Publications:* (ed jtly) Life and Art: the new Iranian cinema, 1999; An Argentine Passion: Maria Luisa Bemberg and her films, 2000; contribs to Framework, Screen, Sight and Sound, Guardian, Observer, New Statesman, TES. *Recreation:* reading. *Address:* 3.7 The Ziggurat Building, 60–66 Saffron Hill, EC1N 8QX.

WHITAKER, Steven Dixon; Senior Master of the Supreme Court, Queen's Bench Division, and Queen's Remembrancer, since 2007; *b* 28 Jan. 1950; *s* of George and Elsie Whitaker; partner, Tereska Anita Christiana Stawarz; one *s* one *d*. *Educ:* Burnley Grammar Sch.; Churchill Coll., Cambridge (MA). Called to the Bar, Middle Temple, 1973; in practice as a barrister, specialising in property and professional negligence law, 1973–2002; Dep. Dist Judge, 1998–2002; Master of Supreme Court, QBD, 2002–07. Mem., Civil Procedure Rules Cttee, 2002–08. *Recreations:* horses, music, poetry. *Address:* Royal Courts of Justice, Strand, WC2A 2LL; *e-mail:* seniormaster@hmcourts-service.gsi.gov.uk.

WHITAKER, Thomas Kenneth; Chancellor, National University of Ireland, 1976–96; Member, Council of State, Ireland, 1991–97; Chairman, Constitution Review Group, 1995–96; President, Royal Irish Academy, 1985–87; *b* 8 Dec. 1916; *s* of Edward Whitaker and Jane O'Connor; *m* 1st, 1941, Nora Fogarty (*d* 1994); five *s* one *d*; 2nd, 2005, Mary Moore. *Educ:* Christian Brothers' Sch., Drogheda; London Univ. (External Student; BScEcon, MScEcon). Irish CS, 1934–69 (Sec., Dept of Finance, 1956–69); Governor, Central Bank of Ireland, 1969–76; Dir, Bank of Ireland, 1976–85. Dir, Arthur Guinness Son & Co. Ltd, 1976–84. Chairman: Bord na Gaeilge, 1975–78; Agency for Personal Service Overseas, 1973–78; Mem., Seanad Éireann, 1977–82. Jt Chm., Anglo-Irish Encounter, 1983–89. Former Pres., Econ. and Social Res. Inst.; Chm. Council, Dublin Inst. for Advanced Studies. Freeman of Drogheda, 1999. Hon. DEconSc National Univ. of Ireland, 1962; Hon. LLD: Univ. of Dublin, 1976; Queen's Univ. of Belfast, 1980; Hon. DSc NUU, 1984; Hon. PhD Dublin City Univ., 1995. Commandeur de la Légion d'Honneur, France, 1976. *Publications:* Financing by Credit Creation, 1947; Economic Development, 1958; Interests, 1983. *Recreations:* fishing, golf, music. *Address:* 148 Stillorgan Road, Donnybrook, Dublin 4, Ireland. *T:* (1) 2693474.

WHITBREAD, Jasmine; Chief Executive, Save the Children UK, since 2005; *b* 1 Sept. 1963; *d* of Gerald and Ursula Whitbread; *m* 1994, Howard Exton-Smith; one *s* one *d*. *Educ:* Bristol Univ. (BA Hons English); Stanford Univ. (Exec. Prog.). Dir, Global Mktg, Cortex Corp., 1986–90; Mgt Trainer, Nat. Union of Disabled Persons of Uganda/VSO, 1990–92; Man. Dir, Thomson Financial, 1994–99; Regl Dir, W Africa, 1999–2002, Internat. Dir, 2002–05, Oxfam GB. *Recreations:* spending time with family and friends, W African music, learning to ride. *Address:* Save the Children UK, 1 St John's Lane, EC1M 4AR. *T:* (020) 7012 6400; *e-mail:* chiefexecutive@savethechildren.org.uk.

WHITBREAD, Samuel Charles; JP; Director: Whitbread plc, 1972–2001 (Chairman, 1984–92); Whitbread Farms Ltd (formerly S. C. Whitbread Farms), since 1985; Lord-Lieutenant of Bedfordshire, since 1991; *b* 22 Feb. 1937; *s* of late Major Simon Whitbread and Helen Beatrice Margaret (*née* Trefusis); *m* 1961, Jane Mary Hayter; three *s* one *d*. *Educ:* Eton College. Beds and Herts Regt, 1955–57. Joined Board, Whitbread & Co., 1972, Dep. Chm., Jan. 1984. Director: Whitbread Investment Co., 1977–93; Sun Alliance Gp, 1989–92; Chm., Hertfordshire Timber Supplies, 2000–. Chm., Mid-Beds Conservative Assoc., 1969–72 (Pres., 1986–91). President: Shire Horse Soc., 1990–92; E of England Agricl Soc., 1991–92; St John Council for Beds, 1991–; Beds RFCA (formerly Beds TA&VRA), 1991–; Vice-Pres., E Anglia RFCA (formerly E Anglia TA&VRA), 1991–2000, 2005– (Pres., 2000–05). Bedfordshire: JP, 1969–83, 1991; High Sheriff, 1973–74; DL, 1974; County Councillor, 1974–82. FRSA 1986; FLS 1994; FSA 2007. Hon. LLD: De Montfort, 2002; Bedfordshire, 2007. Bledisloe Gold Medal, RASE, 1989. KStJ 1992. *Publications:* Straws in the Wind, 1997; Plain Mr Whitbread: seven centuries of a Bedfordshire family, 2007. *Recreations:* shooting, painting, music. *Address:* Glebe House, Southill, Biggleswade, Beds SG18 9LL. *T:* (01462) 813272. *Club:* Brooks's.

WHITBURN, Vanessa Victoria; Editor, The Archers, BBC Radio, since 1991; additional responsibility for Radio Drama in the Midlands, BBC, since 1995, and for Silver Street, since 2004; *b* 12 Dec. 1951; *d* of Victor D. Whitburn and Eileen Whitburn. *Educ:* Mount St Mary's Convent, Exeter; Univ. of Hull (BA Hons). Studio Manager, BBC, 1974–76; Asst Floor Manager, BBC TV, 1976–77; Producer and Sen. Producer, Radio Drama, Pebble Mill, 1977–88; Producer, Brookside, Channel 4, 1988–90; Producer and Director, BBC TV, Pebble Mill, 1990–91. *Publication:* The Archers: the official inside story, 1996. *Recreations:* opera, theatre, spending time with friends, travel. *Address:* Radio Drama Department, BBC Birmingham, The Mailbox, Birmingham B1 1RF.

WHITBY, Bishop Suffragan of, since 1999; **Rt Rev. Robert Sidney Ladds,** SSC; *b* 15 Nov. 1941; *s* of late Sidney Ladds and of Joan Dorothy Ladds (*née* Cant); *m* 1964, Roberta Harriet Sparkes; three *s*. *Educ:* Christ Church Coll., Canterbury (CertEd 1970, BEd Hons 1971, London Univ.); Canterbury Sch. of Ministry. LRSC 1972; FRSC (FCS 1972). Industrial res. chemist, 1959–68; schoolmaster, 1971–80; ordained deacon, 1980, priest, 1981; Asst Curate, St Leonard, Hythe, 1980–83; Rector of Bretherton, 1983–91; Chaplain, Bishop Rawstorne Sch., 1983–86; Bishop of Blackburn's Chaplain for Ministry, 1986–90; Bishop's Audit Officer, 1990–91; Rector of Preston, 1991–97; Hon. Canon, Blackburn, 1993–97; Archdeacon of Lancaster, 1997–99. Commissary for Northern Province to Bp of Taejon, S Korea, 1997–99; Vice-Pres., Korea Mission Partnership, 1999–. Superior-Gen., Soc. of Mary, 2000–. *Recreations:* gardening, fell-walking, bonsai, church architecture. *Address:* 60 West Green, Stokesley, Middlesbrough TS9 5BD.

WHITBY, Mrs Joy; Director, Grasshopper Productions Ltd; *b* 27 July 1930; *d* of James and Esther Field; *m* 1954, Anthony Charles Whitby (*d* 1975); three *s*. *Educ:* St Anne's Coll., Oxford. Schools Producer, BBC Radio, 1956–62; Children's Producer, BBC Television, 1962–67; Executive Producer, Children's Programmes, London Weekend Television, 1967–70; freelance producer and writer, 1970–76; Head of Children's Programmes, Yorkshire TV, 1976–85. Dir, Bd of Channel 4, 1980–84; Member: Adv. Panel for Youth, Nat. Trust, 1985–89; Bd, Unicorn Theatre, 1987–92. Trustee, Internat. Childcare Trust, 1995–97. Devised for television: Play School, 1964; Jackanory, 1965; The Book Tower, 1979; Under the Same Sky (EBU Drama Exchange), 1984. Independent film productions: Grasshopper Island, 1971; A Pattern of Roses, 1983; Emma and Grandpa, 1984; East of the Moon, 1988; The Angel and the Soldier Boy, 1989 (ACE Award, 1991); On Christmas Eve, 1992; The Mousehole Cat, 1993; The Story of Arion and the Dolphin, 1996; Mouse and Mole (series), 1997–; A Small Miracle, 2002; (stage prodn) Grasshopper Rhymes from Other Times, 2004. BAFTA Award and Prix Jeunesse: for Play School, 1965; for The Book Tower, 1980 (also BAFTA Award, 1983); Eleanor Farjeon Award for Services to Children's Books, 1979. *Publications:* Grasshopper Island, 1971; Emma and Grandpa (4 vols), 1984. *Address:* *e-mail:* whitby165@btinternet.com.

WHITBY, Mark, FICE, FREng; Director, whitbybird Engineers (formerly Whitby Bird & Partners), since 1984; *b* 29 Jan. 1950; *s* of George Whitby, MBE, FRIBA and Rhona Carmian Whitby (*née* Butler); one *s* by Alison Scott; *m* 1991, Janet Taylor; two *s* two *d*. *Educ:* Ealing Grammar Sch. for Boys; King's Coll., London (BSc). FICE 1992; FREng 1996. Major projects include: York and Lancaster Millennium Bridges, 2000; British Embassies in Dublin, 1995, Berlin, 2000, and Sana, 2006. Chairman: Urban Design Alliance, 2001–02; Sustainability and Urban Renaissance Sector Gp, SEEDA, 2002–. Pres., ICE, 2001–02. Gov., Building Centre Trust, 1997–. Hon. FRIBA 1999. *Recreations:* canoeing (Mem., Olympic Team, 1968), running (London Marathon 2001), 20th Century engineering history, the children. *Address:* whitbybird, 60 Newman Street, W1T 3DA. *T:* (020) 7631 5291, *Fax:* (020) 7323 4645; *e-mail:* mark.whitby@whitbybird.com.

WHITCHURCH, Sir Graeme (Ian), Kt 2006; OBE 1984; Senior Advisor, Leaders Benefits, National Parliament of Papua New Guinea, since 1970; Officer of the Parliamentary Service, Papua New Guinea, since 1970; *b* 8 Dec. 1945; *s* of late Roy Frederick Whitchurch and Alpha Aimee Whitchurch; *m* 1967, Kaia Edith Heni; three *s* three *d*. *Educ:* Punchbowl State Sch., Launceston, Tasmania; Launceston State High Sch. Civil Servant: PMG's Dept, Australia, 1961–64; Public Service of PNG, 1964–70. Mem., Rotary Club of Boroko, PNG, 1990–2007 (Pres., 1995–96). *Recreation:* Australian Rules Football (Life Mem., Koboni FC, Port Moresby). *Address:* PO Box 413, Konedobu, Papua New Guinea. *T:* (home) 6753211255, (office) 6753277789, *Fax:* 6753254346; *e-mail:* gwhit@daltron.com.pg. *Clubs:* Papua (1912) (Mem. Cttee, 2002–07), Aviat Social and Sporting (Life Mem., 1994, Pres., 1984–98), Royal Papua Yacht (Port Moresby).

WHITE, family name of **Baron Annaly** and **Baroness James of Holland Park**.

WHITE, Adrian Edwin, CBE 1993; CSci; DL; Founder Chairman, Biwater plc, since 1968; Governor of the BBC, 1995–2000; *b* 25 July 1942; *s* of Raymond Gerard White and Lucy Mildred White (*née* Best); *m* 1971, Gillian Denise Evans; four *s* one *d*. *Educ:* Cray Valley Technical High; City of London Coll. Chartered Water Engineer; FCIWEM; CSci 2005. Biwater plc (holding co. for Cascal NV, Biwater International and other cos), 1968–. Gp Chm., British Water Industries Gp, 1992–93; Founder Chm., British Water, 1993–98. Vice-Pres., Small Business Bureau, 1980–90; Governor, Engineering, World Economic Forum, 1989–2006; Mem., Overseas Projects Bd, DTI, 1993–95. Chm., Epsom Healthcare NHS Trust, 1990–94, 1997–99. Pres., Epsom Medical Equipment Fund, 1999–. Founder, Denbies and St Kilda Charitable Trusts; Chm., The Children's Trust, Tadworth, 2008–. Founder and owner, Denbies Wine Estate, 1985–. Governor: Stanway Sch., 1984–94; Queen Elizabeth's Foundn (formerly Queen Elizabeth's Foundn for Disabled People), 1989–; Parkside Sch., 1994–96; Chm. Bd of Governors, Millfield Schs, 1997–2009. Hon. Fellow, Regent's Park Coll., Oxford, 2005. DL, 2002, High Sheriff, 2006–07, Surrey. Winner, Free Enterprise Award, 1985. *Recreations:* family, golf, theatre. *Address:* Biwater plc, Biwater House, Station Approach, Dorking, Surrey RH4 1TZ. *T:* (01306) 740740; Denbies, Ranmore Common, Dorking, Surrey RH5 6SP. *T:* (01306) 886640. *Club:* Wisley Golf.
See also Rev. B. R. White.

WHITE, Aidan Patrick; General Secretary, International Federation of Journalists, since 1987; *b* 2 March 1951; *s* of Thomas White and Kathleen Ann McLaughlin. *Educ:* King's Sch., Peterborough. Dep. Gp Editor, Stratford Express, 1977–79; journalist, The Guardian, 1980–87. Mem., Press Council, 1978–80. National Union of Journalists: Mem. Exec. Council, 1974, 1976, 1977; Treasurer, 1984–86; Chm., National Newspapers Council, 1981. Chm., EC Inf. Soc. Forum Wkg Gp, 1996–98. Member: Exec. Council, Global Union Council (formerly ICFTU), 1989–; Steering Cttee, ETUC, 1997–. *Publications:* Making a World of Difference, 2006; Journalism, Civil Liberties and the War on Terror, 2006; contribs on ethics of journalism for UNESCO, UNICEF and Council of Europe. *Address:* Avenue de Montalembert 23, 1330 Rixensart, Belgium. *T:* (2) 6541016; *e-mail:* aidan.white@ifj.org.

WHITE, Alan, CMG 1985; OBE 1973; HM Diplomatic Service, retired; Ambassador to Chile, 1987–90; *b* 13 Aug. 1930; *s* of William White and Ida (*née* Hall); *m* 1st, 1954, Cynthia Maidwell (*d* 2004); two *s* one *d*; 2nd, 1980, Clare Corley Smith. SSC Army 1954 (Capt.); Hong Kong, 1959–63; MoD (Central), 1965; First Sec., FO (later FCO), 1966; Mexico City, 1969; First Sec., UK Disarmament Delegn, Geneva, 1974; Counsellor (Commercial), Madrid, 1976; Counsellor and Head of Chancery, Kuala Lumpur, 1980–83; Hd, Trade Relns and Exports Dept, FCO, 1983–85; Ambassador to Bolivia, 1985–87. *Recreations:* reading, travel. *Address:* c/o Foreign and Commonwealth Office, SW1A 2AH.

WHITE, Alan, FCA; Chief Executive, N Brown Group plc, since 2002; *b* 15 April 1955; *s* of Ronald and Margaret White; *m* 1979, Helen Caygill (marr. diss.); one *s* one *d*. *Educ:* Warwick Univ. (LLB). FCA 1979. Audit Senior, Arthur Andersen, 1976–79; Gen. Manager, Finance, Sharp Electronics, 1979–85; Finance Dir, N Brown Gp, 1985–99; Gp Finance Dir, Littlewoods plc, 1999–2002. *Recreations:* tennis, squash, ski-ing, waterski-ing, Manchester United. *Address:* N Brown Group plc, 40 Lever Street, Manchester M60 6ES.

WHITE, Andrew; QC 1997; *b* 25 Jan. 1958; *s* of Peter White and late Sandra Jeanette White (*née* Lovelace); *m* 1987, Elizabeth Denise Rooney; two *s*. *Educ:* University Coll. Cardiff (LLB Hons). Called to the Bar, Lincoln's Inn (Hardwick Schol., Megarry Schol.), 1980, Bencher, 2003; in practice at the Bar, 1981–. *Publication:* (contrib.) Encyclopaedia of Forms and Precedents, vol. 5: Building and Engineering Contracts, 5th edn (1986). *Recreations:* farming, sailing, music. *Address:* 1 Atkin Building, Gray's Inn, WC1R 5AT. *T:* (020) 7404 0102.

WHITE, Air Vice-Marshal Andrew David, CB 2003; Chief Executive, National Security Inspectorate, since 2006; *b* 2 Jan. 1952; *s* of Edward and Margaret White; *m* 1975, Christine Ann Spratt; two *s*. *Educ:* Loughborough Univ. (BTech Hons Aeronautical Engrg); RAF Cranwell. Joined RAF, 1970; served Nos 17, 151, 20 Sqdns, 1977–84; Flt Comdr, No 14 Sqdn, 1984–85; NATO staff, 1985–88; jsdc 1988; MoD staff, 1988–91; Sqdn Comdr, Nos 15 and 9 Sqdns, 1991–94; PSO to CAS, 1994–96; Station Comdr, RAF Cottesmore, 1996–99; Staff Officer, HQ Strike Comd, 1999–2003; AOC No 3 Gp, 2003–06. Non-exec. Dir, NATS, 2006–. Chm. Govs, Cottesmore Co. Primary Sch.,

1996–99. *Recreations:* golf, private aviation, ski-ing, walking. *Address:* National Security Inspectorate, Sentinel House, 5 Reform Road, Maidenhead, Berks SL6 8BY. *Clubs:* Royal Air Force, Commonwealth.

WHITE, Rev. Canon Andrew Paul Bartholomew; President and Chief Executive Officer, Foundation for Reconciliation in the Middle East, and Anglican Chaplain to Iraq, since 2005; Vicar of St George's, Baghdad, since 2007; Director, US Department of Defense and Iraqi Government Religious Sectarianism Programme, since 2007; *b* 29 June 1964; *s* of Maurice and Pauline White; *m* 1991, Caroline Spreckley; two *s*. *Educ:* Picardy Sch.; St Thomas' Hosp., London; Ridley Hall, Cambridge; Hebrew Univ., Jerusalem. Student Operating Dept Practitioner, St Thomas' Hosp., London, 1981–84; Operating Department Practitioner: Obstetrics, Derby City Hosp., 1984; St Thomas' Hosp., 1985–86 (Hon. Operating Dept Practitioner, 1990–97); ordained deacon, 1990, priest, 1991; Asst Curate, St Mark's Ch, Battersea Rise, London, 1990–93; Vicar, Ch of the Ascension, Balham Hill, London, 1993–98; Canon, Coventry Cathedral, and Dir, Internat. Centre for Reconciliation, 1998–2005. Archbishop of Canterbury's Special Representative: to Middle East, 2002–04; to Alexandria Process, 2004–; Internat. Dir, Iraqi Inst. of Peace, 2003–. Sen. Inter-religious Advr to Iraqi Prime Minister, 2006, to Iraqi Presidency, 2006–. Vis. Lectr, Wheaton Coll., Illinois, 1999–; Vis. Fellow, Harvard Univ., 2008. Chm., Young Leadership Section, Internat. CCJ, 1990–95 (Prize for Intellectual Contribn to Jewish Christian Relns, 1993). Mem. for Balham, Wandsworth BC, 1998 (Dep. Chm., Social Services, 1998). Eric Lane Fellow, Clare Coll., Cambridge, 2003. Anglo Israel Assoc. Prize, 1998; Sternberg Inter Faith Prize, Three Faith Forum, 2003; Tannenbaum Peace Prize, 2005; Cambridge Centre for Jewish Christian Relations Peacemaker Award, 2007; Prize for Peace, Woolf Inst., Cambridge, 2007. Grand Comdr and Companion of Honour, OSMTH, 2003; Cross of Valour, American OSMTH, 2005. *Publications:* Iraq: people of hope, land of despair, 2003; Iraq: searching for hope, 2005 (Christian Book Award, 2006), rev. edn 2007; Fighting for Peace in the Middle East, 2009; various newspaper articles and chapters in books on conflict resolution, Jewish Christian relns, interfaith issues, Israel/Palestine and the Middle East. *Recreations:* angora goats, cleaning, cooking, collecting crosses from around the world. *Address:* The Croft, Shepherds Way, Liphook, Hants GU30 7HH. *T:* (01428) 723939; *e-mail:* apbw2@cam.ac.uk. *Clubs:* Royal Over-Seas League; Alwyah (Baghdad).

WHITE, Antony Dennis Lowndes; QC 2001; *b* 22 Jan. 1959; *s* of Albert Dennis White and Marion Seymour White; partner, Kate Ursula Macfarlane; one *s* two *d*. *Educ:* Huish's Grammar Sch., Taunton; Clare Coll., Cambridge (MA). Called to the Bar, Middle Temple, 1983; called to the Gibraltar Bar, 1998. *Publications:* (with S. Greer) Abolishing the Diplock Courts, 1986; *contributed to:* Justice Under Fire, 1988; The Jury Under Attack, 1988; Bullen & Leake & Jacob's Precedents of Pleadings, 14th edn, 2001 to 16th edn, 2007; Privacy and the Media: the developing law, 2002; Civil Appeals, 2002; Enforcing Contracts in Transition Economies, 2005; Freedom of Information Handbook, 2006, 2nd edn 2008. *Recreations:* classic cars and motorcycles, walking, swimming, cooking, wine, modern literature, contemporary art. *Address:* Matrix Chambers, Griffin Building, Gray's Inn, WC1R 5LN. *T:* (020) 7404 3447.

WHITE, Rev. Barrington Raymond; Principal, Regent's Park College, Oxford, 1972–89, now Principal Emeritus (Senior Research Fellow and Tutor in Ecclesiastical History, 1989–99); *b* 28 Jan. 1934; *s* of Raymond Gerard and Lucy Mildred White; *m* 1957, Margaret Muriel Hooper; two *d*. *Educ:* Chislehurst and Sidcup Grammar Sch.; Queens' Coll., Cambridge (BA Theol, MA); Regent's Park Coll., Oxford (DPhil). Ordained, 1959; Minister, Andover Baptist Church, 1959–63; Tutor in Ecclesiastical History, Regent's Park Coll., Oxford, 1963–72. First Breman Prof. of Social Relations, Univ. of N Carolina at Asheville, 1976. FRHistS 1973. *Publications:* The English Separatist Tradition, 1971; Association Records of the Particular Baptists to 1660, Part I, 1971, Part II, 1973, Part III, 1974; Authority: a Baptist view, 1976; Hanserd Knollys and Radical Dissent, 1977; contrib. Reformation, Conformity and Dissent, ed R. Buick Knox, 1977; The English Puritan Tradition, 1980; contrib. Biographical Dictionary of British Radicals in the Seventeenth Century, ed Greaves and Zaller, 1982–84; The English Baptists of the Seventeenth Century, 1983; (contrib.) A Transcription of the Glasshouse Yard Church Book 1832 to 1857, 2000; contribs to Baptist Qly, Jl of Theological Studies, Jl of Ecclesiastical History, Welsh Baptist Studies. *Recreation:* recorded music. *Address:* Regent's Park College, Oxford OX1 2LB.

See also A. E. White.

WHITE, Brian Arthur Robert; consultant on technology, energy and regulatory issues; Chairman of Trustees, National Energy Foundation, since 2007; *b* 5 May 1957; *s* of Edward and Jean White; *m* 1984, Leena Lindholm; two step *s*. *Educ:* Methodist Coll., Belfast. Systems analyst: HM Customs, 1977–83 (consultant, 1983–84); Canada Life Assurance, 1984–86; Abbey National, 1986–97. MP (Lab) Milton Keynes NE, 1997–2005. Contested (Lab) Milton Keynes NE, 2005. *Address: e-mail:* brian@brianwhite.org.uk.

WHITE, Bryan Oliver; HM Diplomatic Service, retired; *b* 3 Oct. 1929; *s* of Thomas Frederick White and Olive May Turvey; *m* 1958, Helen McLeod Jenkins; one *s* two *d*. *Educ:* The Perse Sch.; Wadham Coll., Oxford (Lit.Hum.). HM Forces, 1948–49; FO, 1953; Kabul, Vienna, Conakry, Rio de Janeiro, the Cabinet Office, and Havana, 1953–79; Counsellor, Paris, 1980–82; Head of Mexico and Central America Dept, FCO, 1982–84; Ambassador to Honduras and (non-resident) to El Salvador, 1984–87; Consul-Gen., Lyon, 1987–89. *Recreation:* the Romance languages. *Address:* 14 Stonebridge Lane, Fulbourn, Cambridge CB21 5BW.

WHITE, (Charles) John (Branford); HM Diplomatic Service, retired; Director for Development, Marine Stewardship Council, since 2006; *b* 24 Sept. 1946; *s* of Frederick Bernard White and Violet Phyllis White (*née* Palmer); *m* 1975, Judith Margaret Lewis. *Educ:* Taunton Sch.; Brentwood Sch.; Pembroke Coll., Cambridge (Trevelyan Schol., MA); University Coll. London (MSc 1983). ODI Fellow, Govt of Botswana, 1968–71; ODA, 1971–77; Economic Advr, E Africa Develt Div., ODM, 1977–82; ODA, 1983–86; Asst Head, Economic Relations Dept, FCO, 1986–90; First Sec., Lagos, 1990–93; Dep. Hd of Mission, Consul Gen. and Counsellor, Tel Aviv, 1993–97; Hd, S Atlantic and Antarctic, subseq. UK Overseas Territories, Dept, FCO, and Comr (non-resident), British Antarctic Territory and British Indian Ocean Territory, 1997–2001; High Comr, Barbados and the Eastern Caribbean States, 2001–05. *Recreations:* golf, ski-ing. *Address:* 26 Turner House, Clevedon Road, Twickenham, Middx TW1 2TE. *Clubs:* Ski Club of Great Britain; Royal Mid-Surrey Golf.

WHITE, Prof. Sir Christopher (John), Kt 2001; CVO 1995; PhD; FBA 1989; Director, Ashmolean Museum, Oxford, 1985–97; Fellow of Worcester College, 1985–97, and Professor of the Art of the Netherlands, 1992–97, now Professor Emeritus, Oxford University; *b* 19 Sept. 1930; *s* of late Gabriel Ernest Edward Francis White, CBE and Elizabeth Grace Ardizzone; *m* 1957, Rosemary Katharine Desages; one *s* two *d*. *Educ:* Downside Sch.; Courtauld Institute of Art, London Univ. BA (Hons) 1954, PhD 1970. Served Army, 1949–50; commnd, RA, 1949. Asst Keeper, Dept of Prints and Drawings, British Museum, 1954–65; Director, P. and D. Colnaghi, 1965–71; Curator of Graphic Arts, Nat. Gall. of Art, Washington, 1971–73; Dir of Studies, Paul Mellon Centre for Studies in British Art, 1973–85; Adjunct Prof. of History of Art, Yale Univ., 1976–85; Associate Dir, Yale Center for British Art, 1976–85. Dutch Govt Schol., 1956; Hermione Lectr, Alexandra Coll., Dublin, 1959; Adjunct Prof., Inst. of Fine Arts, New York Univ., 1973 and 1976; Conference Dir, European-Amer. Assembly on Art Museums, Ditchley Park, 1975; Visiting Prof., Dept of History of Art, Yale Univ., 1976. Trustee: V & A Mus., 1997–2004; NACF, 1998–2005; Mauritshuis, The Hague, 1999–2007. Gov., British Inst. of Florence, 1994–2002. Dir, Burlington Magazine, 1981– (Chm., 1996–2002). Reviews Editor, Master Drawings, 1967–80. *Publications:* Rembrandt and his World, 1964; The Flower Drawings of Jan van Huysum, 1965; Rubens and his World, 1968; Rembrandt as an Etcher, 1969, 2nd edn 1999; (jtly) Rembrandt's Etchings: a catalogue raisonné, 1970; Dürer: the artist and his drawings, 1972; English Landscape 1630–1850, 1977; The Dutch Paintings in the Collection of HM The Queen, 1982; (ed) Rembrandt in Eighteenth Century England, 1983; Rembrandt, 1984; Peter Paul Rubens: man and artist, 1987 (Eugène Baie Prize, 1983–87); (jtly) Drawing in England from Hilliard to Hogarth, 1987; (jtly) Rubens in Oxford, 1988; (jtly) One Hundred Old Master Drawings from the Ashmolean Museum, 1991; (jtly) The Dutch and Flemish Drawings at Windsor Castle, 1994; Anthony van Dyck: Thomas Howard, the Earl of Arundel, 1995; Dutch, Flemish and German Paintings in the Ashmolean Museum, 1999; (ed jtly) Rembrandt by Himself, 1999; The Later Flemish Pictures in the Collection of HM The Queen, 2007; film (script and commentary), Rembrandt's Three Crosses, 1969; various exhibn catalogues; contribs to Burlington Mag., Master Drawings, etc. *Recreation:* husbandry. *Address:* 34 Kelly Street, NW1 8PH. *T:* (020) 7485 9148; Shingle House, St Cross, Harleston, Norfolk IP20 0NT. *T:* (01986) 782264.

WHITE, Sir Christopher (Robert Meadows), 3rd Bt *cr* 1937, of Boulge Hall, Suffolk; *b* 26 Aug. 1940; *s* of Sir (Eric) Richard Meadows White, 2nd Bt, and Lady Elizabeth Mary Gladys (*d* 1950), *o d* of 6th Marquess Townshend; *S* father, 1972, but his name does not appear on the Official Roll of the Baronetage; *m* 1st, 1962, Anne Marie Ghislaine (marr. diss. 1968), *yr d* of Major Tom Brown, OBE; 2nd, 1968, Dinah Mary Sutton (marr. diss. 1972), Orange House, Heacham, Norfolk; 3rd, 1976, Ingrid Carolyn Jowett, *e d* of Eric Jowett, Great Baddow; two step *s*. *Educ:* Bradfield Coll., Berks. Imperial Russian Ballet School, Cannes, France, 1961; schoolmaster, 1961–72; Professore, Istituto Shenker, Rome, and Scuola Specialisti Aeronauta, Macerata, 1962–63; Housemaster, St Michael's Sch., Ingoldisthorpe, Norfolk, 1963–69. Hon. Pres., Warnborough House, Oxford, 1973–. Lieutenant, TA, Norfolk, 1969. *Recreations:* dogs, vintage cars, antiques. *Address:* c/o Mrs Edwin Steinschaden-Silver, Pinkney Court, Malmesbury, Wilts SN16 0PD.

WHITE, Dr Colin Saunders, FSA, FRHistS; Director, Royal Naval Museum, Portsmouth, since 2006; *b* 28 Aug. 1951; *s* of Philip Saunders White and Margaret Joyce White (*née* Gummer). *Educ:* Culford Sch., Bury St Edmunds; Southampton Univ. (BA Hons); King's Coll., London (MA). FRHistS 2005. Royal Naval Museum, Portsmouth: Asst Curator, 1975–82; Chief Curator, 1982–96; Dep. Dir and Hd, Mus. Services, 1996–2001; Dir, Trafalgar 200, Nat. Maritime Mus., 2001–06. Chm., Official Nelson Commemorations Cttee, 2001–06. FSA 2003. Hon. DLitt Portsmouth, 2004; Hon. MA Chichester, 2005. *Publications:* The End of the Sailing Navy 1815–1870, 1981; The Heyday of Steam 1870–1910, 1983; The Nelson Companion, 1995, 2nd edn 2005; 1797: Nelson's Year of Destiny, 1998; The Nelson Encyclopaedia, 2002, 2nd edn 2005; Nelson: the new letters, 2005, 2nd edn 2006 (Dist. Book Award, Soc. for Mil. Hist. 2006); The Trafalgar Captains: their lives and memorials, 2005; Nelson the Admiral, 2005; articles in Mariners' Mirror, Jl Maritime Res., History Today, BBC History, Trafalgar Chronicle, Nelson Dispatch. *Recreations:* Church of England (passionate liberal catholic), amateur drama (mem., Southsea Shakespeare Actors), historical novels, the Mediterranean, messing about in boats. *Address:* Royal Naval Museum, HM Naval Base, Portsmouth PO1 3NH. *T:* (023) 9272 7574; *e-mail:* colin.white@royalnavalmuseum.org. *Clubs:* Army and Navy, Naval.

WHITE, Prof. David Clifford Stephen, DPhil; Director, Institute of Food Research, since 2004; *b* 8 March 1941; *s* of late Clifford George White and of Joyce Beatrice White (*née* Lawley); *m* 1st, 1965, Ailsa Pippin (marr. diss.); one *s* one *d*; one *s*; 2nd, 1987, Patricia Spallone. *Educ:* Berkhamsted Sch.; New Coll., Oxford (BA 1962; MA 1967; DPhil 1967). Deptl Demonstrator, Dept of Zool., Univ. of Oxford, 1967–71; Department of Biology, University of York: Lectr, 1971–86; Sen. Lectr, 1986–90; Reader, 1990–95; Prof., 1995–97; Head of Dept, 1990–97; Dir of Sci. and Technol., BBSRC, 1997–2004. *Publications:* Biological Physics, 1973; The Kinetics of Muscle Contraction, 1973. *Recreations:* walking, photography. *Address:* Institute of Food Research, Norwich Research Park, Colney, Norwich NR4 7UA. *T:* (01603) 255119.

See also A. F. Moore-Gwyn.

WHITE, Sir David Harry, Kt 1992; DL; Chairman, Mansfield Brewing, 1993–2000; Director, 1970–88, a Deputy Chairman, 1988–90, Chairman of Trustees, 1986–2000, National Freight Consortium; *b* 12 Oct. 1929; *s* of late Harry White, OBE, FCA, and Kathleen White; *m* 1971, Valerie Jeanne White; one *s* four *d*. *Educ:* Nottingham High Sch.; HMS Conway. Master Mariner's F. G. Certificate. Sea career, apprentice to Master Mariner, 1944–56; Terminal Manager, Texaco (UK) Ltd, 1956–64; Operations Manager, Gulf Oil (GB) Ltd, 1964–68; Asst Man. Dir, Samuel Williams Dagenham, 1968–70; Trainee to Gp Managing Director, British Road Services Ltd, 1970–76; Group Managing Director: British Road Services, 1976–82; Pickfords, 1982–84; NFC Property Gp, 1984–87; Chm., Nottingham HA, 1986–98; Director (non-executive): BR Property Bd, 1985–87; Y. J. Lovell Ltd, 1987–94; Hilda Hanson Ltd, 1996–; James Bell (Nottingham) Ltd, 1997–; Nottingham Forest FC, 1999–2004; Alkane Energy plc, 2000–04; non-exec. Chm., EPS Ltd, 1997–2000. Mem., British Coal Corp., 1993–94; Chm., Coal Authy, 1994–99. Mem. Editorial Bd, Nottingham Evening Post, 2003–. Chairman: Nottingham Develt Enterprise, 1987–93; Bd of Governors, Nottingham Trent Univ. (formerly Nottingham Poly.), 1989–99. Trustee, Djanogly City Technology Coll., 1989–99. Hon. Pres., Notts County Branch, RSPCA, 1987–. Governor, Nottingham High Sch., 1987–99. DL Notts, 1989. Hon. DBA Nottingham Trent, 1999. *Recreations:* football supporter (Nottingham Forest), walking. *Address:* Whitehaven, 6 Croft Road, Edwalton, Nottingham NG12 4BW.

WHITE, David Thomas, (Tom), CBE 1990; Principal and Chief Executive, NCH Action for Children (formerly National Children's Home), 1990–96; *b* 10 Oct. 1931; *s* of Walter Henry White and Annie White; *m* 1956, Eileen May Moore; two *d* (and one *s* decd). *Educ:* Council Primary and Maesydderwen Grammar Sch., Ystradgynlais, Swansea Valley; University Coll., Swansea (Social Sci.); London School of Economics (Social Work). Clerical Officer, CS, 1947–54; National Service, RAF, 1951–53. Social work and management posts, Devon CC, 1957–61; Dep. Children's Officer, Monmouthshire, 1961–65; Dep. County Children's Officer, Lancs, 1965–70; Dir of Social Services, Coventry, 1970–85; Dir of Social Work, Nat. Children's Home, 1985–90. Past President: Assoc. of Child Care Officers; Assoc. of Directors of Social Services; Gov., Nat. Inst. of Social Work, 1973–96 (Hon. Fellow, 1996); Chm., Nat. Foster Care Assoc., 1996–99.

Mem. (Lab), Coventry CC, 1996–2004. Hon. DBA Coventry, 1998. Coventry Award of Merit, Coventry CC, 2002. *Publication:* (contrib.) Social Work, the Media and Public Relations, 1991. *Recreations:* gardening, golf, walking. *Address:* Heathcote House, Little Tew, Chipping Norton, Oxon OX7 4JE. *T:* (01608) 683873. *Club:* Coventry Golf (Finham, Coventry).

WHITE, David Vines; Somerset Herald of Arms, since 2004; *b* 27 Oct. 1961; *s* of late Peter Vines White and of Sheila White (*née* Chatterton, *widow* of Lt Comdr (E.) John William Windley Baker, RN). *Educ:* Kelvinside Acad.; Marlborough Coll.; Pembroke Coll., Cambridge (MA); Courtauld Inst. (MA). Res. Asst, College of Arms, 1988–95; Rouge Croix Pursuivant, 1995–2004. Member, Council: British Record Soc., 1998–; Heraldry Soc., 2000– (Chm., 2006–08). Hon. Vice Pres., Cambridge Univ. Heraldic and Genealogical Soc., 2002–. *Address:* College of Arms, Queen Victoria Street, EC4V 4BT. *T:* and *Fax:* (020) 7248 1766; *e-mail:* somerset@college-of-arms.gov.uk. *Club:* Travellers.

WHITE, Derek Leslie; HM Diplomatic Service, retired; *b* 18 April 1933; *s* of John William and Hilda White; *m* 1989, Elisabeth Denise Marcelle Lemoine; one *d* from previous marr. *Educ:* Catshill Secondary Sch., Bromsgrove; RAF Apprentice Sch. Served RAF, 1950–63. For. Office (later HM Diplomatic Service), 1963; served Helsinki, Sofia, Algiers; Vice Consul, Tripoli, 1970; FCO, 1972; Commercial Officer, Baghdad, 1975, Second Sec., 1977; Port Louis, 1979; Antananarivo, 1983; FCO, 1984, First Sec., 1985; Consul, Marseilles and Principality of Monaco, 1986; FCO, 1989; High Comr to Kiribati, 1990–93, and concurrently Ambassador to Federated States of Micronesia and to Marshall Is, 1992–93. *Recreations:* sailing, cooking, music. *Address:* Cansargue, 83470 Pourcieux, France. *T:* 494597879.

WHITE, Edward George, OBE 1976; HM Diplomatic Service, retired; *b* 30 June 1923; *s* of late George Johnson White, OBE, ISO, and Edith (*née* Birch); *m* 1st, 1945, Sylvia Shears; two *d*; 2nd, 1966, Veronica Pauline Crosling. *Educ:* Bec Secondary Sch., London SW. Served RAF, 1941–47. Various consular and diplomatic appts in Guatemala, USA, Madagascar, Burma, Thailand and India; Dep. Head of Finance Dept, FCO, 1976–78; Counsellor (Admin), Bonn, 1978–79. Specialist Adviser, Foreign Affairs Cttee, H of C, 1980–87. *Publication:* Nightfighter Navigator, 1994. *Address:* 13 Elvestone, Fore Street Hill, Budleigh Salterton, Devon EX9 6HD. *T:* (01395) 443008.

WHITE, Rt Rev. Francis; *see* Brixworth, Bishop Suffragan of.

WHITE, His Honour Sir Frank (John), Kt 1997; a Senior Circuit Judge, 1994–97 (a Circuit Judge, 1974–94); *b* 12 March 1927; *s* of late Frank Byron White and Marie-Thérèse Renée White (*née* Cachou); *m* 1953, Anne Rowlandson, MBE, *d* of late Sir Harold Gibson Howitt, GBE, DSO, MC and Dorothy Howitt (*née* Radford); two *s* two *d*. *Educ:* Reading Sch.; King's Coll., London (LLB, LLM; FKC 1999). Sub-Lt, RNVR, 1945–47; called to the Bar, Gray's Inn, 1951, Bencher, 1997; Dep. Chm., Berkshire QS, 1970–72; a Recorder of the Crown Court, 1972–74. Pres., Council of HM Circuit Judges, 1990–91. Member: Lord Chancellor's Adv. Cttee on Legal Aid, 1977–83; Judicial Studies Bd, 1985–89; County Court Rule Cttee, 1991–97 (Chm., 1993–97). Mem., General Council of the Bar, 1969–73. Pres., KCL Assoc., 2000–02. Pres., Le Demi-Siècle de Londres, 1997–2002. *Publication:* Bench Notes and Exercises for Assistant Recorders, 1988. *Recreations:* walking, photography. *Address:* 8 Queen's Ride, SW13 0JB. *T:* (020) 8788 8903. *Clubs:* Athenæum, Roehampton.

WHITE, Frank Richard; JP; former executive director and industrial relations adviser; Director, National Training College, GMB (formerly General, Municipal, Boilermakers and Allied Trades Union), 1988–2000; *b* Nov. 1939; *m*; three *c*. *Educ:* Bolton Tech. Coll. Member: Bolton CC, 1963–74; Greater Manchester CC, 1973–75; Bolton MBC (formerly DC), 1986– (Cabinet Mem. for HR, Perf. Mgt and Community Cohesion, 2001–; Mayor, 2005–06). Member: GMB; IPM; Inst. of Management Services. Contested (Lab): Bury and Radcliffe, Feb. 1974; Bury North, 1983; Bolton NE, 1987. MP (Lab) Bury and Radcliffe, Oct. 1974–1983; PPS to Minister of State, Dept of Industry, 1975–76; Asst Govt Whip, 1976–78; Opposition Whip, 1980–82; opposition spokesman on church affairs, 1980–83. Chairman: All Party Paper Industry Gp, 1979–83; NW Lab Gp, 1979–83; Mem., NW Regional Exec., Labour Party, 1986–88. Director: Lancs Co-op. Develt Agency, 1984–; Bolton/Bury TEC, 1995–2004; Mem., Greater Manchester Police Authy, 1997–2004; Mem. Area Bd, United Norwest Co-op., 1994–2004. Chairman: Bolton FM Community Radio, 2005–; Age Concern, Bolton, 2008–. President: Bolton United Services Veterans' Assoc., 1988–; Bolton Male Voice Choir, 1992–2004; Vice-Pres., E Lancs Railway Preservation Soc., 1983–2005. JP Bolton, 1968 (Chm. Bench, 1993–95). Hon. Fellow, Bolton Inst., 1993. *Address:* 23 Dovedale Road, Bolton, Lancs BL2 5HT.

WHITE, Air Vice-Marshal George Alan, CB 1984; AFC 1973; FRAeS; Commandant, Royal Air Force Staff College, 1984–87; *b* 11 March 1932; *s* of James Magee White and Evangeline (*née* Henderson); *m* 1955, Mary Esmé (*née* Magowan); two *d*. *Educ:* Wallace High Sch., Lisburn, NI; Queen's Univ., Belfast; University of London (LLB). Pilot, 1956; served in RAF Squadrons and OCUs, 1956–64; RAF Staff College, 1964; HQ Middle East Command, 1966–67; 11 Sqn, 1968–70; 5 Sqn, 1970–72; Nat. Defence Coll., 1972–73; in command, RAF Leuchars, 1973–75; Royal Coll. of Defence Studies, 1976; Dir of Ops (Air Defence and Overseas), 1977–78; SASO No 11 Group, 1979–80; Air Cdre Plans, HQ Strike Comd, 1981–82; Dep. Comdr, RAF Germany, 1982–84. FRAeS 1985. *Recreations:* sailing, hill walking, bridge. *Address:* The Grange, Pulham St Mary, Diss, Norfolk IP21 4QZ. *Club:* Royal Air Force.

WHITE, Sir George (Stanley James), 4th Bt *cr* 1904, of Cotham House, Bristol; FSA; clockmaker and horological consultant; Keeper of the Collection of the Worshipful Company of Clockmakers, since 1988; *b* 4 Nov. 1948; *s* of Sir George Stanley Midelton White, 3rd Bt, and Diane Eleanor, *d* of late Bernard Abdy Collins, CIE; *S* father, 1983; *m* 1st, 1974; one *d*; 2nd, 1979; one *s* one *d*; 3rd, 2006, Joanna, *d* of Kazimierz Migdal. *Educ:* Harrow School. Pres., Gloucestershire Soc., 1993; Chm., Adv. Gp on Bldg Conservation, Bristol Univ., 1996–; Member: Gloucester DAC for Care of Churches, 1985– (Clocks Advr, 1986–); Council, Bristol and Glos Archaeological Soc., 1987–2000 (Chm., 1992–95); Council, Nat. Trust, 1998. Pres., British Horological Inst., 2001 (Pres., Bristol Br., 1993–). Liveryman, Co. of Clockmakers, 1986– (Asst, 1994–; Master, 2001). High Sheriff, Avon, 1989; JP Bristol, 1991–95. FSA 1988. *Publications:* English Lantern Clocks, 1989; Tramlines to the Stars, 1995; The Clockmakers of London, 1998; contrib. Antiquaries' Jl, Antiquarian Horology, etc. *Heir:* *s* George Philip James White, *b* 19 Dec. 1987.

WHITE, Graham Brian Newton; His Honour Judge Graham White; a Circuit Judge, since 2007; *b* London, 6 Dec. 1942; *s* of Pat and Molly White; *m* 1971, Lesley Williams; five *s* two *d*. *Educ:* Uxendon Manor Co. Prim. Sch., Wembley; Haberdashers' Aske's Hampstead Sch.; College of Law; Univ. of London (LLB by private study 1966). Admitted solicitor, 1965; Dep. District Judge, 1979–2007; Asst Recorder, 1992–96; Recorder, 1996–2007. Mem. Council, Law Soc., 1989–2007; Pres., Herts Law Soc., 1995. *Recreation:* rock 'n' roll drummer. *Address:* c/o Portsmouth Combined Court, Courts of Justice, Winston Churchill Avenue, Portsmouth PO1 2EB. *T:* (023) 9289 3000, *Fax:* (023) 9285 6212; *e-mail:* gwhitesol@btinternet.com.

WHITE, Graham John; Deputy Chairman, Lloyd's of London, since 2007; Managing Director, Argenta Private Capital Ltd, since 2008 (Director, since 2006); *b* 4 June 1946; *s* of William Kenneth White and Evelyn White (*née* Marshall); *m* 1989, Rosemary Maude Hadow; four *d* (and one *d* decd). *Educ:* University Coll. Sch., Hampstead; Gonville and Caius Coll., Cambridge (BA 1968); Cranfield Sch. of Mgt (MBA). Willis Faber Gp, 1968–83 (Gp Co. Sec., 1980); Man. Dir, Richard Beckett Underwriting Agencies Ltd, 1983–86; NY Rep., Merrett Syndicates Ltd, 1987–88; Dir, Jardine Thompson Graham Ltd, 1989–96; Chairman: Bankside Members' Agency Ltd, 1996–97; Murray Lawrence Members' Agency, 1997–98; Chief Exec., Amlin Pvte Capital Ltd, 1998–2000; Chm., CBS Pvte Capital Ltd, 2000–06; Dir, CBS Insce Hldgs Ltd, 2000–07. Director: English Pocket Opera Ltd, 2002–; Children's Music Workshop Ltd, 2006–. *Recreations:* ski-ing, golf, tennis, theatre, opera, watching Tottenham Hotspur. *Address:* Argenta Private Capital Ltd, 130 Fenchurch Street, EC3M 5DJ. *T:* (020) 7825 7200, *Fax:* (020) 7825 7299; *e-mail:* graham.white@argentaplc.com. *Clubs:* Travellers, City of London; Kandahar Ski (Mürren).

WHITE, Harvey, DM; FRCS; Consulting Surgeon: Royal Marsden Hospital, since 1976; King Edward VII Hospital for Officers, since 1983; *b* 10 March 1936; *s* of Arthur White and Doris (*née* Dunstan); *m* 1965, Diana Mary Bannister; one *s* one *d*. *Educ:* Winchester Coll.; Magdalen Coll., Oxford (DM, MCh); St Bartholomew's Hosp. FRCS 1970. St Bartholomew's Hospital: Lectr in Physiol., 1966–71; Sen. Surgical Registrar, 1971–76; Chm., Div. of Surgery, Royal Marsden Hosp., 1987–89. Editor: Oxford Med. Gazette, 1956–57; St Bartholomew's Hosp. Jl, 1960–61; Clinical Oncology, 1983–84; European Jl of Surgical Oncology, 1985–87; Chm., Royal Society of Medicine Press Ltd, 1997–. Hunterian Prof., RCS, 1988; Hunterian Oration, 1993. Vice-President: Brit. Assoc. of Surgical Oncology, 1984; RSocMed, 2008; President: Med. Soc. of London, 1995–96; Hunterian Soc., 2004–05. Mem. Council, Cancer Relief Macmillan Fund, 1991–95. Chm., Brendoncare Foundn of Elderly, 1986–2003; Trustee, Duchess of Somerset's Almshouses, 1992–. Ernest Miles Medal, Brit. Assoc. of Surgical Oncology, 1989. *Publications:* (jtly) The Greater Omentum, 1983, Russian edn 1989; (jtly) The Omentum and Malignant Diseases, 1984; An Atlas of Omental Transposition, 1987; contrib. to: History of Surgery, 1974; Royal Hospital St Bartholomew, 1974; Surgical Oncology for Nurses, 1978; The Laser in General Surgery, 1979; Oxford Companion to Medicine, 1986; European Handbook of Oncology, 1989; Aird's Companion to Surgery, 1992; contrib. various learned surgical and cancer jls. *Recreations:* dog-walking, rackets and Real tennis, sailing, fishing. *Address:* (office) 67 Harley Street, W1G 8QZ. *T:* (020) 7935 2021; 7 Arlington Square, N1 7DS. *T:* (020) 7226 4628; Carley Cottage, Bapton, Wylye, Wilts BA12 0SD. *T:* (01985) 850759. *Clubs:* Garrick, Royal Society of Medicine, Flyfishers'.

WHITE, Adm. Sir Hugo (Moresby), GCB 1995 (KCB 1991); CBE 1985; DL; Governor and Commander-in-Chief, Gibraltar, 1995–97; *b* 22 Oct. 1939; *s* of late Hugh Fortescue Moresby White, CMG and Betty Sophia Pennington White; *m* 1966, Josephine Mary Lorimer Pedler; two *s*. *Educ:* Dragon School; Nautical Coll., Pangbourne; Britannia RN Coll., Dartmouth. HMS Blackpool, 1960; submarine training, 1961; HM Submarines Tabard, Tiptoe, Odin, 1961–65; Long Navigation Course, HMS Dryad, 1966; Navigator, HMS Warspite, 1967; First Lieut, HMS Osiris, 1968–69; in Comd, HMS Oracle, 1969–70; Staff, BRNC Dartmouth, 1971–72; Submarine Sea Training, 1973–74; in Comd, HMS Salisbury (cod war), 1975–76; Naval Sec.'s Dept, 1976–78; Naval Plans, 1978–80; in Comd, HMS Avenger (Falklands) and 4th Frigate Sqn, 1980–82; Principal Staff Officer to Chief of Defence Staff, 1982–85; in Comd, HMS Bristol and Flag Captain, 1985–87; Flag Officer Third Flotilla, and Comdr Anti-Submarine Warfare Striking Force, 1987–88; ACNS, 1988–91; Flag Officer Scotland and NI, 1991–92; C-in-C Fleet, Allied C-in-C, Eastern Atlantic, 1992–95, also Allied C-in-C, Channel, 1991–94; Naval Comdr, NW Comd, 1994–95. DL Devon, 1999. *Recreations:* sailing, travelling, gardening, reading. *Address:* c/o Naval Secretary, Fleet Headquarters, Whale Island, Portsmouth PO2 8BY. *Club:* Army and Navy.

WHITE, Ian; Member (Lab) Bristol, European Parliament, 1989–99; former Partner, McCarthy and White, solicitors. Contested (Lab) SW Reg., EP elecn, 1999.

WHITE, Prof. Ian Hugh, PhD; CEng, FREng, FIET; Van Eck Professor of Engineering, and Fellow, Jesus College, University of Cambridge, since 2001; *b* 6 Oct. 1959; *s* of Oliver Morrow White and Emily Greenaway White; *m* 1983, Margaret Rosemary Hunt; one *s* one *d*. *Educ:* Belfast Royal Acad.; Jesus Coll., Cambridge (BA 1980, MA 1984; PhD 1984). FREng 2006. Res. Fellow, 1983–84, Asst Lectr, 1984–90, Univ. of Cambridge; Prof. of Physics, Univ. of Bath, 1990–96; University of Bristol: Prof. of Optical Communication Systems, 1996–2001; Hd, Dept of Electrical and Electronic Engrg, 1998–2001. Royal Soc. Leverhulme Res. Fellow, Univ. of Bath, then Bristol, 1995–96. *Publications:* numerous contribs on semiconductor optoelectronic components, optical communications and sensors to learned jls. *Recreations:* church, music. *Address:* Electrical Engineering Division, Department of Engineering, Cambridge University, 9 J. J. Thomson Avenue, Cambridge CB3 0FA. *T:* (01223) 748340, *Fax:* (01223) 748342; *e-mail:* ihw3@cam.ac.uk.

WHITE, Rev. Ian Thomas; President of the Methodist Conference, 2002–03; *b* 6 July 1939; *s* of Sydney White and Annie (*née* Heathcote); *m* 1967, Diana (*née* Casson); two *d*. *Educ:* Manchester Coll. of Sci. and Technol.; Hartley Victoria Theol Coll., Manchester. Methodist Minister: Hull Trinity Circuit, 1965–69; Retford Circuit, 1969–72; Bristol South Circuit, 1972–78; Bristol Kingswood Circuit, 1978–87 (Supt Minister, 1981–87); Sec., Bristol Dist Synod, 1978–87; Chairman: Bristol Dist, 1987–98; Channel Is Dist, 1998–2004; Supt Minister, Jersey Circuit, 1998–2004. Moderator, Bristol Free Ch Council, 1989–93. *Recreations:* reading, jigsaws, current affairs, theatre, walking, music. *Address:* 26 Aln Crescent, Newcastle upon Tyne NE3 2LU. *T:* (0191) 285 5975.

WHITE, James; Managing Director, Glasgow Car Collection Ltd, 1959–87; *m*; one *s* two *d*. *Educ:* Knightswood Secondary School. Served Eighth Army, War of 1939–45 (African and Italian Stars; Defence Medal). MP (Lab) Glasgow (Pollok), 1970–87. Mem. Commonwealth Parly Assoc. Delegns, Bangladesh, 1973, Nepal, 1981. *Address:* 23 Alder Road, Glasgow G43 2UU.

WHITE, James Ashton V.; *see* Vallance White.

WHITE, Sir Jan Hew D.; *see* Dalrymple-White.

WHITE, Jeremy Nigel; Chairman, Newfound International Resorts NV, since 2006; President, White Foundation, since 2001; *b* 20 Jan. 1955; *s* of Colin Lawrence White and Drusilla Marie Goodman; *m* 1989, Kim-Marie Klinger; one *s* three *d*. *Educ:* Leeds Grammar Sch.; Leeds Polytechnic (Dip. Management, Accounting and Finance, Marketing); City Univ. (MBA); Pepperdine Univ. (MA Educn and Psychology; Dist Alumni 1995). Man. Dir, RSS Gp, 1975–79; Chm., White Gp Electronics, 1979–85

Britannia Group: Jt Man. Dir, 1985–86; Pres., 1986–88; Chm., Data Safe Inc., 1988–94; Chief Exec. and Dep. Chm., Prince's Youth Business Trust, 1994–95; Dep. Chm., Youthnet UK, 1995–2000; Chm., Nettec plc, 1995–2001, 2003–06; Dir, Vizual Business Tools Ltd, subseq. OneclickHR plc, 1997–2003. Mem., Bd, British-Amer. Chamber of Commerce, S Calif, 1993–94, and other LA orgns, 1992–94. Member: Council, Industry and Parlt Trust, 1984–88 and 1995–2000; Young Enterprise Nat. Council, 1986–98; Adv. Council Educn and Trng, Inst. of Econ. Affairs, 1996–2000; DoI Business Links Accreditation Adv. Bd, 1996–98; Small and Medium Size Enterprises Task Gp and Basic Skills Gp, Univ. for Industry, 1999–2000. Trustee: Prince of Wales Award for Innovation, 1995–; Technology Coll. Trust, 1998–2000. Gov., Pepperdine Univ., 1993–; Mem. Council, City Univ. Business Sch., 1995–99; Mem. Ct Govs, Univ. of Westminster, 1999–2002. Founder and Judge, World Sax Competition, Montreux, 2002–. Produced film, Virtuosic Saxophones, 2002. Mem., BSES exp. to W Himalayas, 1989; flying records: Lisbon to LA, 1990; LA to Albuquerque, 1990; Buenos Aires to LA, 1991; La Paz to LA, 1991. FRGS. *Publications:* The Retail Financial Services Sector, 1985; 21st Century Schools—Educating for the Information Age, 1997. *Recreations:* private flying, collecting, jazz music. *Address: e-mail:* info@whitefoundation.com. *Clubs:* Brooks's, Pilgrims', Royal Geographical.

WHITE, Jeremy Richard, (Jerry); Commissioner for Local Administration in England (Local Government Ombudsman), since 1995; *b* 23 March 1949; *s* of John Robert White and Molly Loiseau; *m* 1st, 1981, Sandra Margaret Smith (marr. diss. 1995); two *s* one *d*; 2nd, 1995, Rosie Cooper; one *d*. *Educ:* Swanage Grammar Sch.; Cosham and Hackney Technical Colls. Sen. Public Health Inspector, Islington, 1970–81; Asst Borough Housing Officer, Haringey, 1981–84; London Borough of Hackney: Head, Environmental Health, 1984–87; Dir, Environmental Health and Consumer Protection, 1987–89; Chief Exec. and Town Clerk, 1989–95. Vis. Prof., Sch. of Arts, Middlesex Univ., 1996–; Vis. Prof. in London History, Birkbeck Coll., London, 2004–. Associate Fellow, Centre for Social History, Univ. of Warwick, 1997–. Hon. DLitt London, 2005. *Publications:* Rothschild Buildings: life in an East End tenement block 1887–1920, 1980; The Worst Street in North London: Campbell Road, Islington, between the wars, 1986; Fear of Voting: local democracy and its enemies 1894–1994, 1994; (with Michael Young) Governing London, 1996; London in the Twentieth Century: a city and its people (Wolfson History Prize), 2001; London in the Nineteenth Century: a human awful wonder of God, 2007. *Recreations:* reading, music, London. *Address:* Commission for Local Administration, 2 The Oaks, Westwood Way, Coventry CV4 8JB. *T:* (024) 7669 5999. *Club:* Reform.

WHITE, John; *see* White, C. J. B.

WHITE, Rev. Canon John Austin, LVO 2004; Canon, since 1982, and Vice-Dean, since 2004, Windsor; *b* 27 June 1942; *s* of Charles White and Alice Emily (*née* Precious). *Educ:* The Grammar Sch., Batley, W Yorkshire; Univ. of Hull (BA Hons); College of the Resurrection, Mirfield. Assistant Curate, St Aidan's Church, Leeds, 1966–69; Asst Chaplain, Univ. of Leeds, 1969–73; Asst Dir, post ordination training, Dio. of Ripon, 1970–73; Chaplain, Northern Ordination Course, 1973–82. Dir of Clergy Courses, 1998–, Warden, 2000–03, St George's House, Windsor Castle; European Dep. for Dio. Mexico, Anglican Ch of Mexico, 2003–. *Publications:* (with Julia Neuberger) A Necessary End: attitudes to death, 1991; (with L. R. Muir) Nicholas Ferrar: materials for a life, 1997; Phoenix in Flight, 1999; (with Mark Stenning) Spoken Light, 2007; various articles. *Recreations:* medieval iconography, drama, Italy, cooking, poetry. *Address:* 4 The Cloisters, Windsor Castle SL4 1NJ.

WHITE, Hon. Sir John (Charles), Kt 1982; MBE (mil.) 1942; Judge of High Court of New Zealand, retired 1981, sat as retired Judge, 1982–84; *b* 1 Nov. 1911; *s* of Charles Gilbert White and Nora Addison Scott White; *m* 1st, 1943, Dora Eyre Wild (*d* 1982); one *s* three *d*; 2nd, 1987, Margaret Elspeth Maxwell Fletcher. *Educ:* Wellesley Coll., Wellington; John McGlashan Coll., Dunedin; Victoria University Coll., Wellington; Univ. of New Zealand (LLM Hons). Barrister and Solicitor of Supreme Court of New Zealand. Judge's Associate, 1937–38; served War, Middle East, Greece, Crete, N Africa, Italy, 1940–45, ADC to Gen. Freyberg, 2nd NZEF, ME, 1940–45 (final rank Major); formerly Dominion Vice-Pres., New Zealand Returned Services Assoc.; Private practice as barrister and solicitor, Wellington, 1945–66; Pres., Wellington Law Soc., Vice-Pres., NZ Law Soc., 1966; QC and Solicitor General of New Zealand, 1966; Judge of the Supreme Court (now High Court), 1970, retd 1981; Judge Advocate General of Defence Forces, 1966–87. Actg Chief Justice, Solomon Islands, 1984. Pres., Solomon Is Court of Appeal, 1985–87. Royal Comr, Inquiry into 1982 Fiji Gen. Election, 1983. Asst Editor, Sim's Practice & Procedure, 9th edn, 1955, and 10th edn 1966. *Publications:* letters and commentaries in mil. pubns and the press on hist. of NZ Forces in ME during World War II, and world peace through rule of law. *Recreations:* formerly Rugby, cricket, tennis, golf, bowls. *Address:* 23 Selwyn Terrace, Wellington 6001, New Zealand. *T:* (4) 4725502. *Clubs:* Wellington; Dunedin; Melbourne.

WHITE, Prof. John Edward Clement Twarowski, CBE 1983; FSA; Durning-Lawrence Professor of the History of Art, University College London, 1971–90 (Vice-Provost, 1984–88; Pro Provost, 1990–95); *b* 4 Oct. 1924; *s* of Brigadier A. E. White and Suzanne Twarowska; *m* 1950, Xenia Joannides (*d* 1991). *Educ:* Ampleforth College; Trinity College, Oxford; Courtauld Institute of Art, University of London. Served in RAF, 1943–47. BA London 1950; Junior Research Fellow, Warburg Inst., 1950–52; PhD Lond. 1952; MA Manchester 1963. Lectr in History of Art, Courtauld Inst., 1952–58; Alexander White Vis. Prof., Univ. of Chicago, 1958; Reader in History of Art, Courtauld Inst., 1958–59; Pilkington Prof. of the History of Art and Dir of The Whitworth Art Gallery, Univ. of Manchester, 1959–66; Vis. Ferens Prof. of Fine Art, Univ. of Hull, 1961–62; Prof. of the History of Art and Chm., Dept of History of Art, Johns Hopkins Univ., USA, 1966–71. Member: Adv. Council of V&A, 1973–76; Exec. Cttee, Assoc. of Art Historians, 1974–81 (Chm., 1976–80); Art Panel, Arts Council, 1974–78; Vis. Cttee of RCA, 1977–86; Armed Forces Pay Review Body, 1986–92; Chm., Reviewing Cttee on Export of Works of Art, 1976–82 (Mem., 1975–82). Trustee: Whitechapel Art Gall., 1976–93 (Vice-Chm., 1985–93); Japan Arena, 2003–. Mem., Cttee, Burma Campaign Soc., 2003–. Membre Titulaire, 1983–95, Membre du Bureau, 1986–92, Comité International d'Histoire de l'Art. *Publications:* Perspective in Ancient Drawing and Painting, 1956; The Birth and Rebirth of Pictorial Space, 1957, 3rd edn 1987 (Italian trans. 1971; French trans. 1992; Spanish trans. 1994); Art and Architecture in Italy, 1250–1400, 1966, 3rd edn 1993 (Spanish trans. 1989); Duccio: Tuscan Art and the Medieval Workshop, 1979; Studies in Renaissance Art, 1983; Studies in Late Medieval Italian Art, 1984; Poems Poèmes Poesie, 1992; Quartet Quartett Quartetto Quatuor, 1993; Trinity Trinita Trinité, 1994; You that I love, 1998; The Breath in the Flute, 2001 (English/Japanese bilingual text); On the Razor's Edge, 2004; New Moon, Old Moon, 2006; articles in Art History, Art Bulletin, Burlington Magazine, Jl of Warburg and Courtauld Institutes. *Address:* 25 Cadogan Place, SW1X 9SA. *Club:* Athenæum.

WHITE, John William, CMG 1981; DPhil; FRS 1993; FRSC; FAA; Professor of Physical and Theoretical Chemistry, Australian National University, Canberra, since 1985 (Pro Vice-Chancellor and Chairman, Board of Institute of Advanced Studies, 1992–94; Dean, Research School of Chemistry, 1995–98); *b* Newcastle, Australia, 25 April 1937; *s* of late George John White and of Jean Florence White; *m* 1966, Ailsa Barbara, *d* of A. A. and S. Vise, Southport, Qld; one *s* three *d*. *Educ:* Newcastle High Sch.; Sydney Univ. (MSc); Lincoln Coll., Oxford (1851 Schol., 1959; MA, DPhil). ICI Fellow, Oxford Univ.; Research Fellow, Lincoln Coll., 1962; University Lectr, Oxford, 1963–85, Assessor, 1981–82; Fellow, St John's Coll., Oxford, 1963–85 (Vice-Pres. 1973; Hon. Fellow, 1995). Neutron Beam Coordinator, AERE, Harwell, 1974; Asst Director, 1975, Director 1977–80, Institut Laue-Langevin, Grenoble. Argonne Fellow, Argonne Nat. Lab. and Univ. of Chicago, 1985; Christensen Fellow, St Catherine's Coll., Oxford, 1991. President: Soc. of Crystallographers, Aust., 1989–92; Aust. Inst. of Nuclear Sci. and Engrg, 2004– (Vice Pres., 2002–04); Chairman: Nat. Cttee for Crystallography, Aust., 1992–2001; Neutron Scattering Commn, Internat. Union of Crystallography, 1994–; Internat. Adv. Cttee, J-PARC project, Japan, 2001–; Mem., Internat. Adv. Cttee, Central Lab. of the Res. Councils, 2002–. Sec. for Sci. Policy, and Mem. Council, Aust. Acad. of Sci., 1997–2001. Chm., Dirs' Adv. Council, Intense Pulsed Neutron Source, Argonne Nat. Lab., and Univ of Chicago, 1989–92. Pres., ISCAST Australia, 1991–. Chm., James Fairfax-Oxford Australia Scholarship Cttee, 1997–. Lectures: Tilden, Chemical Soc., 1975; Liversidge, Sydney Univ., 1985; Hinshelwood, Oxford Univ., 1991; Foundn, Assoc. of Asian Chemical Socs, 1991; H. G. Smith, RACI, 1997–98; T. G. H. Jones Meml, Univ. of Qld, 1998; Hudnall-Cars Distinguished, Univ. of Chicago, 1998; 50th Anniversary, Internat. Union of Crystallography, 1998. Member of Council: Epsom Coll., 1981–85; Wycliffe Hall, Oxford, 1983–85; St Mark's Nat. Theol Centre, Canberra, 1997–. FRSC 1982; FRACI 1985; FAIP 1986; FAA 1991. Marlow Medal, Faraday Soc., 1969; H. G. Smith Medal and Prize, 1997, Leighton Medal, 2005, RACI; Craig Medal, Aust. Acad. of Sci., 2005. *Publications:* various contribs to scientific jls. *Recreations:* family, squash, ski-ing. *Address:* 2 Spencer Street, Turner, ACT 2612, Australia. *T:* (2) 62486836.

WHITE, Sir John (Woolmer), 4th Bt *cr* 1922; *b* 4 Feb. 1947; *s* of Sir Headley Dymoke White, 3rd Bt and Elizabeth Victoria Mary (*d* 1996), *er d* of late Wilfrid Ingram Wrightson; *S* father, 1971; *m* 1987, Joan Borland; one *s*. *Educ:* Hurst Court, Hastings; Cheltenham College; RAC, Cirencester. *Heir:* *s* Kyle Dymoke Wilfrid White, *b* 16 March 1988. *Address:* Salle Park, Norwich, Norfolk NR10 4SG. *Clubs:* Athenæum, MCC.

WHITE, Keith George, FCILT; Chief Executive, Crown Agents for Overseas Governments and Administrations Ltd, since 2005; *b* 12 Oct. 1948; *s* of Arthur and Rose White; *m* 1971, Philomena Smith; one *s* one *d*. *Educ:* Bec Sch.; Kingston Poly. (BA London); City of London Poly. (MA Business Law). Crown Agents: Corporate Sec., 1980–98; Dir, 1997–; Chief Operating Officer, 1997–2005. Pres., HF Holidays Ltd, 1987–; Chm., St Helena Line Ltd, 1992–2005; Dir, SITPRO Ltd, 2000–05. FCILT 2005; MInstRE 2007. FRSA. *Recreations:* family, walking, browsing in walking kit shops, playing guitar. *Address:* Crown Agents, St Nicholas House, Sutton, Surrey SM1 1EL. *T:* (020) 8643 3311, *Fax:* (020) 8643 6518. *Club:* Royal Over-Seas League.

WHITE, Kenneth James; District Judge, Principal Registry of Family Division, since 1991; *b* 24 March 1948; *s* of Kenneth William John White and Pamela Blanche Emily White (*née* Seth); *m* 1971, Anne Christine Butcher; one *s* one *d*. *Educ:* Gosport County Grammar Sch., Hants; QMC, Univ. of London (LLB Hons 1969). Qualified as Solicitor, 1972; Partner, R. V. Stokes & Co., Solicitors, Portsmouth, 1974, Sen. Partner, 1991. Mem., Family Cttee, Judicial Studies Bd, 1999–2004. Mem., Portsmouth & Southsea Voluntary Lifeguards, 1968– (Pres. 1985–); Royal Life Saving Society UK: Vice-Pres., 1994–98; Pres., 1998–2004; Chm., Nat. Lifeguard Cttee, 1992–98; Mem., Commonwealth Council, 1998–2004; Pres., Wessex Br., 1981; Dir, Internat. Life Saving Fedn, 2000–. *Publications:* (consulting editor) Family Court Reporter, 1992; (contrib.) Atkin's Court Forms, 1994–. *Recreations:* swimming, reading, travel, lifesaving. *Address:* First Avenue House, High Holborn, WC1V 6HA. *T:* (020) 7936 6000.

WHITE, Kevin Charles Gordon, CB 2003; *b* 20 July 1950; *s* of John Gordon White and Dorothy Marion White; *m* 1977, Louise Sarah Watt; three *s*. *Educ:* Haberdashers' Aske's, Elstree; Univ. of E Anglia (BA Hons); Univ. of Warwick (MA). Senior CS posts in Dept for Employment, 1977–95; Human Resources Dir, Employment Service, 1995–2001; Gp Dir of Human Resources, DWP, 2001–07. Associate MCIPD 1996. FRSA 2002. *Recreations:* family, music, cooking. *Club:* Druidston (Broadhaven, Pembrokeshire).

WHITE, Malcolm D.; *see* Davis-White.

WHITE, Marco Pierre; chef and restaurateur; *b* 11 Dec. 1961; *s* of late Frank and Maria Rosa White; *m* 1st, 1988, Alexandra McCarthy (marr. diss.); one *d*; 2nd, 1992, Lisa Butcher (marr. diss.); 3rd, 2000, Matilda Conejero-Caldera; two *s* one *d*. *Educ:* Firtree Primary Sch.; Allarton High Sch., Leeds. Commis: Hotel St George, Harrogate, 1978; Box Tree, Ilkley, 1979; Chef de Partie: Le Gavroche, 1981; Tante Claire, 1983; Sous Chef, Manoir aux Quat' Saisons, 1984–85; Proprietor and Chef: Harveys, 1986–93; The Canteen Restaurant, Chelsea Harbour, 1992–96; Restaurant Marco Pierre White, 1993–; Marco Pierre White's Criterion, 1995–; Quo Vadis, 1996–; Oak Room, Le Meridien, 1997–99; MPW Canary Wharf, 1997–; Café Royal Grill Room, 1997–; Mirabelle Restaurant, Curzon St, 1998–; Belvedere, 1999–; Wheelers of St James, 2002; Luciano, 2005–; Jt Proprietor, Frankie's, 2004–. Michelin Stars 1988, 1990, 1995 (youngest and first GB winner of 3 Michelin stars). Television series: Hell's Kitchen, 2007; Marco's Great British Feast, 2008. *Publications:* White Heat, 1990; Wild Food from Land and Sea, 1994; Canteen Cuisine, 1995; Glorious Puddings, 1998; The Mirabelle Cookbook, 1999; White Slave: the autobiography, 2006; Marco Pierre White's Great British Feast, 2008. *Recreations:* shooting, fishing, bird watching. *Address:* Mirabelle Restaurant, 56 Curzon Street, W1Y 7PF.

WHITE, Martin Andrew C.; *see* Campbell-White.

WHITE, Maj.-Gen. Martin Spencer, CB 1998; CBE 1991; Lord-Lieutenant of the Isle of Wight, since 2006 (Vice Lord-Lieutenant, 1999–2006); *b* 25 March 1944; *s* of Harold Spencer White and Mary Elizabeth White; *m* 1966, Fiona Margaret MacFarlane; three *s* one *d*. *Educ:* Sandown GS, IoW; Welbeck Coll.; RMA Sandhurst. FCIT 1992; FILog 1993. Commnd, RASC/RCT, 1966; Staff Coll., Camberley, 1977–78; Comd 4 Div., Transport Regt, 1983–85; Directing Staff, Army Staff Coll., 1985–87; Command: Logistic Support Gp, 1987–89; Force Maintenance Area (Gulf), 1990–91; Transport 1(BR) Corps, 1991–92; RCDS, 1993; Dir of Support, HQ Allied Land Forces Central Europe, 1993–95; Dir-Gen., Logistic Support (Army), 1995–98. Senior Military Adviser: Ernst & Young, subseq. Cap Gemini Ernst & Young, 1999–2003; Deloittes, 2003–08. Col Comdt, RLC, 1998–2009. Hon. Colonel: Southampton Univ. OTC, 1999–2004; 165 Regt RLC, 2001–09. Governor, Ryde Sch., 1997–2006. Liveryman, Co. of Carmen, 1996–2007. DL Isle of Wight, 1998. *Publication:* Gulf Logistics: Black Adder's war, 1995. *Recreations:* cricket, sailing. *Address:* Grove House, Old Seaview Lane, Seaview, Isle of Wight PO34 5BJ. *Clubs:* Army and Navy; Royal Yacht Squadron; Sea View Yacht.

WHITE, Michael Charles; Associate Editor, since 1989, and Assistant Editor (Politics), since 2006, The Guardian; *b* 21 Oct. 1945; *y s* of Henry Wallis White, master mariner of St Just in Penwith, Cornwall and of Kay (*née* Wood); *m* 1973, Patricia Vivienne Gaudin; three *s*. *Educ:* Bodmin Grammar Sch.; University Coll. London (BA Hist. 1966; Fellow, 2002). Reporter: Reading Evening Post, 1966–70; London Evening Standard, 1970–71; The Guardian, 1971–: Parly Sketchwriter, 1977–84; Washington Corresp., 1984–88; Political Ed., 1990–2006. Columnist, Health Service Jl, 1977–84, 1992–. Chm., Parly Press Gall., 1994, and Lobby, 1997. Vis. Fellow, Woodrow Wilson Foundn, Princeton, NJ, 1990–. Hon. Fellow, UC Falmouth, 2006. What the Papers Say Sketchwriter of the Year Award, 1982; Political Writer Award, House Magazine, 2003. *Recreation:* dashing about. *Address:* Press Gallery, House of Commons, SW1A 0AA. *T:* (020) 7219 4700; 7 The Avenue, Chiswick, W4 1HA. *T:* (020) 8995 5055. *Club:* Garrick.

WHITE, Michael John; broadcaster and author; *b* 4 April 1955; *s* of Albert E. White and Doris M. White (*née* Harvey). *Educ:* Langdon Sch., London; Mansfield Coll., Oxford (MA Jurisp.). Called to the Bar, Middle Temple, 1978 (non-practising) (Harmsworth Scholar and Middle Temple Advocacy Prize). Contribs to Observer and Guardian; joined Independent, 1986; Music Critic, The Independent on Sunday, 1990–2000. Broadcasts for BBC Radio and TV, Channel 4, Classic FM (voted Britain's least boring music critic); presenter: Best of 3, R3, 1998–2000; Opera in Action, R3; Sound Barrier series, R4, 1999; opera libretti writer; awards judge. Member, Board of Directors: Spitalfields Fest., 1992–2000; London Internat. Piano Comp., 2002–. *Publications:* Wagner for Beginners, 1995; Opera and Operetta, 1997. *Recreations:* travel, Church of England (occasionally). *Address:* c/o BBC Radio 3, Broadcasting House, W1A 1AA.

WHITE, Michael Simon; theatre and film producer; *b* 16 Jan. 1936; *s* of Victor R. and Doris G. White; *m* 1965, Sarah Hillsdon (marr. diss. 1973); two *s* one *d*; 2nd, 1985, Louise M. Moores, *d* of late Nigel Moores; one *s*. *Educ:* Lyceum Alpinum, Zuoz, Switzerland; Pisa University; Sorbonne, Paris. Asst to Sir Peter Daubeny, 1956–61; *stage:* London productions include: The Connection, 1961; Blood Knot, 1966; American Hurrah, 1967; Oh, Calcutta!, 1970; Joseph and the Technicolor Dreamcoat, 1972; Rocky Horror Show, 1973; Loot, 1975; A Chorus Line, 1976; Sleuth, 1978; Deathtrap, 1978; Annie, 1978; Pirates of Penzance, 1982; On Your Toes, 1984; Metropolis, 1989; Bus Stop, 1990; Crazy for You, 1993; Me and Mamie O'Rourke, 1994; She Loves Me, 1994; Fame, 1995; Voyeurz, 1996; Boys in the Band, 1997; Disney's Beauty and the Beast, 1997; Black Goes with Everything, 2000; Notre-Dame de Paris, 2000; Contact, 2002; The Harder They Come, 2008; *films:* include: Monty Python and the Holy Grail, 1974; Rocky Horror Picture Show, 1975; The Comic Strip Presents…, 1983; My Dinner with André, 1984; Ploughman's Lunch, 1984; Moonlighting, 1984; Stranger's Kiss, 1985; The Supergrass, 1985; High Season, 1986; Eat the Rich, 1987; White Mischief, 1987; The Deceivers, 1988; Nuns on the Run, 1989; The Pope Must Die, 1991; Robert's Movie, 1993; Widow's Peak, 1994; Enigma, 2000. *Publication:* Empty Seats, 1984. *Recreations:* art, skiing, racing. *Address:* 13 Duke Street, St James's, SW1Y 6DB.

WHITE, Neville Helme; Stipendiary Magistrate for Humberside, 1985–99; *b* 12 April 1931; *s* of Noel Walter White and Irene Helme White; *m* 1958, Margaret Jennifer Catlin; two *s* one *d*. *Educ:* Newcastle-under-Lyme High School. RAF, 1949–51. Partner, Grindey & Co., Solicitors, Stoke-on-Trent, 1960–85. Pres., N Staffs Law Soc., 1980–81. Pres., Hull Boys' Club, 1985–99. *Recreations:* music, walking, gardening, reading, all sports, paintings. *Address:* Chestnut Cottage, Tunwells Lane, Great Shelford, Cambridge CB22 5LJ.

WHITE, Prof. Nicholas John, OBE 1999; MD, DSc; FRCP, FMedSci; FRS 2006; Chairman, Wellcome Trust Southeast Asian Tropical Medicine Research Programmes, since 2001; Professor of Tropical Medicine, Mahidol University, Bangkok, since 1995, and University of Oxford, since 1996; *b* 13 March 1951; *s* of John Carlisle White and Eileen Margaret White (*née* Millard); *m* 1997, Jitda; three *d*. *Educ:* Guy's Hosp. Med. Sch., London (BSc Pharmacol. 1971; MB BS 1st Cl. Hons 1974); MD 1984, DSc 1995, London Univ. Dir, Wellcome Trust Mahidol Univ.-Oxford Tropical Medicine Res. Prog., 1986–2001. Hon. Consultant Physician, John Radcliffe Hosp., Oxford, 1986–. Chm., WHO Antimalarial Treatment Guidelines Cttee, 2004. FMedSci 2001. *Publications:* over 700 scientific articles in jls. *Recreations:* cricket, squash, guitar, gardening. *Address:* Faculty of Tropical Medicine, Mahidol University, 420/6 Rajvithi Road, Bangkok 10400, Thailand. *T:* (2) 3549171, *Fax:* (2) 3549169; *e-mail:* nickw@tropmedres.ac. *Clubs:* British (Bangkok); Royal Bangkok Sports.

WHITE, Sir Nicholas (Peter Archibald), 6th Bt *cr* 1802, of Wallingwells, Nottinghamshire; *b* 2 March 1939; *s* of Captain Richard Taylor White, DSO (2 bars), RN (*d* 1995) and Gabrielle Ursula White (*née* Style) (*d* 1996); *S* uncle, 1996; *m* 1st, 1970, Susan (*d* 1995); two *s* one *d*; 2nd, 2007, Elaine Jeanne Hume, *d* of Irene (*d* 2002), *d* of G. W. B. Pollock; two *s* one *d*; 2nd, 2007, Elaine Jeanne Hume, *d* of R. J. Dickson. *Educ:* Eton. Nat. Service, 2nd Lt 2/10th PMO Gurkha Rifles, 1957–59. Courage Ltd, 1959–84; wine trade, 1984–94; Gulf Eternit Industries, Dubai, UAE, 1994–2000; Future Pipe Industries Gp, 2001–06. *Recreations:* tennis, travelling, music. *Heir:* *s* Christopher David Nicholas White, *b* 20 July 1972. *Address:* Wateringbury Place Stables, Canon Lane, Wateringbury, Kent ME18 5PQ.

WHITE, Norman Arthur, PhD; CEng, FIMechE; Eur Ing; corporate executive, international consultant and management academic; *b* Hetton-le-Hole, Durham, 11 April 1922; *s* of late Charles Brewster White and Lillian Sarah (*née* Finch); *m* 1st 1944, Joyce Marjorie Rogers (*d* 1982); one *s* one *d*; 2nd, 1983, Marjorie Iris Rushton. *Educ:* Luton Tech. Coll. (HNC); Manchester Inst. of Sci. and Technol. (AMCT Hons); London Univ. (BSc Eng (Hons)); Univ. of Philippines (MSc); London Polytechnic (DMS); Harvard Business Sch. (grad. AMP 1968); LSE (PhD 1973). CEng; MRAeS; FEI; FIMechE; FIMMM. Industrial apprentice, George Kent, and D. Napier & Son, 1936–43; Flight Test Engr, Mil. Aircraft develt, 1943–45. Royal Dutch/Shell Gp, 1945–72: Petroleum Res. Engr, Thornton Res. Centre, 1945–51; Tech. Manager, Shell Co. of Philippines, 1951–55; Shell International Petroleum: Div. Hd, later Dep. Manager, Product Develt Dept, 1955–61; special assignments in various countries, 1961–63; Gen. Manager, Lubricants, Bitumen and LPG Divs, 1963–66; Dir of Marketing Develt, 1966–68; Chief Exec., New Enterprises Div., London and The Hague, 1968–72; Chm. and Dir, Shell oil and mining cos, UK and overseas, 1963–72. Established Norman White Associates (specialists in technology based enterprises and international resources), 1972, Director and Principal Executive, 1972–94; Energy Adviser: Hambros Bank, 1972–76; Tanks Consolidated Investments, Nassau, 1974–85; Chm./Dir, various petroleum exploration and prodn cos in UK, Netherlands, Canada and USA, 1974–92; Chairman: KBC Advanced Technologies, 1979–90; Tesel plc, 1983–85 (Dir, 1980–85); Ocean Thermal Energy Conversion Systems, 1982–; Process Automation and Computer Systems, 1985–94; Andaman Resources plc, 1986–90; Technology Transfer Centre Surrey Ltd, 1990–97; SpaceLink Learning Foundn (formerly Millennium Satellite Centre Ltd), 1995–; Director: Environmental Resources, 1973–87; Henley Centre for Forecasting, 1974–92 (Dep. Chm., 1974–87); Proscyon Partners, 1992–2000 (Chm., 2000–04); Corporate Adviser: Placer Dome, Vancouver, 1973–78; Kennedy & Donkin Gp, 1986–94; Alcatel-Alsthom, Paris, 1993–96. Mem., Parly and Scientific Cttee, House of Commons, 1977–83, 1987–92. World Energy Council, Member: British Nat. Cttee, 1977–88; Conservation Commn, 1979–87; Internat. Exec. Assembly, 1987–94; World Petroleum Congress: Chm., British Nat. Cttee, 1987–94 (Dep. Chm., 1977–87); Permanent Council, 1979–97; Treasurer, 1983–91, 1994–97; Chm., Develt Cttee, 1989–97; Vice-Pres., 1991–94; Presidential Award, 1997; Member: Bd and World Council, Internat. Road Fedn, Geneva and Washington, 1964–72; UK CAA Cttee of Enquiry on Flight Time Limitations (Bader Cttee), 1972–73; Internat. Energy/Petroleum Delegn to Russia, Rumania, E Germany, Hungary, Venezuela, Japan, Korea, People's Republic of China, Indonesia, India, Mexico, Argentina, Brazil, Iran and Southern Africa, 1979–97; Royal Soc./Inst. of Petroleum Delegn to People's Republic of China, 1985; Chm., China Technical Exchange Cttee, 1985–89. Visiting Professor: Arthur D. Little Management Educn Inst., Boston, USA, 1977–79; Henley Management Coll., 1979–89 (Vis. Fellow 1976–79); Manchester Business Sch., 1981–90 (Vis. Industrial Dir 1971–81); City Univ., 1990–96 (ext. examnr, 1983–89); Vis. Lectr, RCDS, 1981–85. London University: Member: Senate, 1974–87; External Council, 1974–84; Governing Bd, Commerce Degree Bureau, 1975–84; Academic Adv. Bd in Engrg, 1976–85; Collegiate Council, 1984–87; Cttee of Mgt, Inst. of US Studies, 1984–92; Mem., Council of Mining and Metallurgical Instns, 1981–87; Member Council: Inst. of Petroleum, 1975–81 (Vice-Pres., 1978–81; Council Award for Meritorious Service, 1996); IMechE, 1980–85, 1987–91 (Chm., Engrg Management Div., 1980–85, Southern Br., 1987–89; Presidential Award for Meritorious Service, 1994); Founder Chm., Jt Bd for Engrg Management, 1990–93 (Chm. Academic Bd, 1994–97; Hon. DipEM 1997). FRSA 1944; FCMI; MRI; Mem., RIIA; Founder Mem., British Inst. of Energy Econs. Associate, St George's House, Windsor Castle, 1972. Governor: King Edward VI Royal Grammar Sch., Guildford, 1976–2002; Reigate Grammar Sch., 1976–93. Freeman, City of London, 1983; Liveryman: Worshipful Co. of Engineers, 1984; Co. of Spectacle Makers, 1986; Member: Guild of Freemen, 1986; Co. of World Traders, 1989. *Publications:* Financing the International Petroleum Industry, 1978; The International Outlook for Oil Substitution to 2020, 1983; (contrib.) Handbook of Engineering Management, 1988; Space-based Learning Service for Schools Worldwide, 2002; contribs to professional jls in UK, Philippines and Canada, on fluid mechanics, petroleum utilization, energy resources, R&D management, project financing and engrg management. *Recreations:* family and various others in moderation, country and coastal walking, wild life, browsing, international affairs, comparative religions, domestic odd-jobbing. *Address:* 9 Park House, 123–125 Harley Street, W1G 6AY. *T:* (020) 7935 7387; Green Ridges, 6 Downside Road, Guildford, Surrey GU4 8PH. *T:* (01483) 567523, *Fax:* (01483) 504314. *Clubs:* Athenæum, City Livery, Inst. of Directors; Harvard Business (USA).

WHITE, Rt Rev. Paul Raymond; an Assistant Bishop, Diocese of Melbourne (Bishop of the Southern Region), since 2007 (Bishop of the Western Region, 2002–07); *b* Sydney, 31 March 1949; *s* of Ronald and Betty White; *m* 1970, Robyn Jamieson, *d* of Robert Jamieson and Maxine Jamieson (*née* Lang); one *s* one *d*. *Educ:* Cronulla High Sch.; Bathurst Teachers' Coll.; St Mark's Coll., Canberra (BTh 1985, Dip. Min., 1986, ACT); Heythrop Coll., Univ. of London (MTh 1989). Teacher, NSW Dept of Educn, 1968–71; voluntary work in community-based progs made poss. by periods of paid work in business, industry and educn, 1971–82. Ordained deacon, 1985, priest, 1986; Asst Curate, N Goulburn, NSW, 1985–87; Lucas-Tooth Schol. and Acting Priest i/c, Reigate, UK, 1987–89; Rector, Queanbeyan, NSW, 1989–92; Vicar: Redhill, UK, 1992–96; E Ivanhoe, Vic, 1996–2000. Dir, Theol Educn, dio. Melbourne, 2000–07. *Address:* The Anglican Centre, 209 Flinders Lane, Melbourne, Vic 3000, Australia.

WHITE, Adm. Sir Peter, GBE 1977 (KBE 1976; CBE 1960; M BE 1944); *b* 25 Jan. 1919;
s of William White, Amersham, Bucks; *m* 1947, Audrey Eil en (*d* 1991), *d* of Ernest
Wallin, Northampton; two *s*. *Educ:* Dover College. Secretary to Chief of Staff, Home
Fleet, 1942–43; to Flag Officer Comdg 4th Cruiser Sqdn, 1944- 45; to Asst Chief of Naval
Personnel, 1946–47; to Flag Officer, Destroyers, Mediterranea , 1948–49; to Controller
of the Navy, 1949–53; to C-in-C Home Fleet and C-in-C I astern Atlantic, 1954–55;
Naval Asst to Chm. BJSM, Washington, and UK Rep. of tanding Group, NATO,
1956–59; Supply Officer, HMS Adamant, 1960–61; Dep. Dir f Service Conditions and
Fleet Supply Duties, Admty, 1961–63; idc 1964; CO HMS R leigh, 1965–66; Principal
Staff Officer to Chief of Defence Staff, 1967–69; Dir-Gen. Fle : Services, 1969–71; Port
Admiral, Rosyth, 1972–74; Chief of Fleet Support, 1974–7 . Consultant, Wilkinson
Match Ltd, 1978–79; Associate Director: The Industrial Soc., 980–88; BITC, 1988–96.
Underwriting Member of Lloyd's, 1979–97. Chm., Officers ension Society, 1982–90.
Mem. Foundn Cttee, Gordon Boys' Sch., 1979–89.

WHITE, Peter Richard; non-executive Director, Reckitt Ber kiser (formerly Reckitt &
Colman), 1997–2008 (Chairman, Audit Committee, 19 3–2006, and Member,
Nomination Committee, 1999–2008); *b* 11 Feb. 1942; *m* 1968, lary Angela Bowyer; one
s one *d*. *Educ:* St Paul's School. FCA; FCIB, FCT. Pri Waterhouse, 1965–69;
Management Accountant, Chief Internal Auditor, Financial C troller, Treasurer, Abbey
National Building Soc., 1970–82; Gen. Manager (Finance a Management Services),
Alliance Building Soc., 1982–85; Alliance & Leicester Build Society: Gen. Manager
(Admin. and Treasury), 1985–87; Dir and Gen. Manager (Dev and Treasury), 1987–89;
Dep. Group Chief Exec. and Man. Dir, 1989–91; Gp Chief c., Alliance & Leicester
Bldg Soc., subseq. Alliance & Leicester plc, 1991–99. Dir, 0–99, Chm., 1996–99,
Girobank plc; Dir, Alliance & Leicester Pensions Investmen d, 1989–99. Chairman:
Metropolitan Assoc. of Buildings Socs, 1994–95; Council of gage Lenders, 1995–98;
Dep. Chm., BSA, 1995–96; Mem. Council, BBA, 1996- rustee: Crimestoppers
Trust, 1997–98; Develt Trust (for the Mentally Handicapp 97–99. Freeman, City
of London, 1996. MInstD; CCMI. *Recreations:* golf, oper *Address:* 21 Clareville
Grove, South Kensington, SW7 5AU.

WHITE, Peter Robert, OBE 2006; FSA; Secretary, Roy sion on the Ancient
and Historical Monuments of Wales, 1991–2005; *b* 28 No of late John Edward
White and Lily Agnes Lois White (*née* Powell); *m* 19 ine Margaret Joyce
Robertson; two *d*. *Educ:* Eastbourne Grammar Sch.; Univ (BA History); Univ.
of Southampton. FSA 1988; IHBC 1998. Asst Insp. of A Monuments, MPBW,
1966–71; Insp., 1971–82, Prin. Insp., 1982–89, DoE; Hea oric Buildings Listing,
English Heritage, 1989–91. Member: Res. Cttee on Indu Archaeol., Council of
British Archaeol., 1969–91; Wkg Party on Industrial Archa ol., Council of Europe,
1984–89; Industrial Archaeol. Panel, English Heritage, 1991–; Exec. Cttee, Soc. of Antiquaries of London, 1994–2002 (Mem. Council, 1992–94); Editl Bd, Cardiganshire County History, 1997–2005; Nat. Adv. Panel, Eur. Assoc. of Archaeologists, 1998–99. Hon. Res. Fellow, Univ. of Wales Lampeter, 2007–. Vice-Pres., Royal Archaeol Inst., 1994–99 (Mem. Council, 1975–78, 1991–94). Chairman: Hafod Adv. Panel, Forestry Commn Wales, 2006–; Wales Cttee, Assoc. of Preservation Trusts, 2007–; Vice-Chm., Ethical Standards Cttee, Dyfed-Powys Police Authy, 2007–. Trustee/Dir, Ironbridge Heritage Foundn Ltd, 2005–. FRSA 1999. Hon. Fellow, UC, Northampton, 1999. *Publications:* contribs to learned jls, particularly on industrial archaeol. *Recreations:* walking, orchestral music. *Address:* *e-mail:* peterrw@lineone.net.

WHITE, Richard Michael, MBE 1983; HM Diplomatic Service, retired; Head, Foreign and Commonwealth Outplacement Service, since 2007; b 12 July 1950; s of late Geoffrey Richard White and Frances Kathleen (née Kendrick); m 1979, Deborah Anne Lewis; one s one d. Educ: King's Sch., Pontefract; Richmond Sch., Yorkshire. VSO, Senegal, 1968–69; entered HM Diplomatic Service, 1969: Attaché, UK Delegn to EEC, Brussels, 1971–74; Persian lang. studies, SOAS, and Yazd, Iran, 1974–75; Third Sec. (Commercial), Tehran, 1975–77; Second Sec. and Asst Private Sec. to Minister of State, Lord Privy Seal, FCO, 1978–79; FCO, 1979–80; Second Sec. (Commercial/Admin) and Consul, Dakar, 1980–84; First Secretary: (Technol.), Paris, 1984–88; FCO, 1988–92; Dep. High Comr, Valletta, 1992–95; FCO, 1996–2002, Hd, Migration and Visa Div., 1997–2000, Asst Dir, Personnel Services, 2000–02; Counsellor (Mgt), Paris, 2003–07. Recreations: family history, French cuisine, walking. Address: c/o Foreign and Commonwealth Office, King Charles Street, SW1A 2AH; e-mail: richard.white@fco.gov.uk.

WHITE, Prof. Robert George, PhD, DSc; FREng; Professor of Vibration Studies, University of Southampton, 1983–98, now Emeritus; b 11 Dec. 1939; s of N. A. J. White and G. M. White; m 1988, Patricia Margaret (née Sidley); one step s one step d. Educ: Farnborough Coll. of Technology; Southampton Univ. (PhD 1970; DSc 1992). FInstP 1981; FIOA 1985; FRAeS 1986; FREng (FEng 1995). RAE, Farnborough, 1957–67; Dir, Inst. of Sound and Vibration Res., 1982–89, Inst. of Transducer Technol., 1989–93, Hd of Dept of Aeronautics and Astronautics, 1995–98, Southampton Univ. Hon. FIOA 2003. (Jtly) Simms Prize, RAeS, 1982; Tyndall Medal, Inst. of Acoustics, 1984. Publications: (ed jtly) Noise and Vibration, 1982; 210 conf. papers and contribs to jls. Recreations: flying, walking. Address: 41 Lower Bere Wood, Waterlooville, Hants P07 7NQ.

WHITE, Prof. Robert Stephen, FRS 1994; FGS; Professor of Geophysics, Cambridge University, since 1989; Fellow of St Edmund's College, Cambridge, since 1988; b 12 Dec. 1952; 2nd s of James Henry White and Ethel Gladys (née Cornick); m 1976, Helen Elizabeth (née Pearce); one s one d. Educ: Market Harborough and West Bridgford Comprehensive Schs; Emmanuel Coll., Cambridge (Sen. Schol., 1972–74; Bachelor Schol., 1974–77; BA, MA, PhD). FRAS 1979; FGS 1989. Research Assistant: Berkeley Nuclear Labs, CEGB, 1970–71; Dept of Geodesy and Geophysics, Cambridge, 1978; postdoctoral schol., Woods Hole Oceanographic Instn, USA, 1978–79; Res. Fellow, Emmanuel Coll., Cambridge, 1979–82; Sen. Asst in Res., 1981–85, Asst Dir of Res., 1985–89, Dept of Earth Scis, Cambridge Univ. Cecil and Ida H. Green Schol., Scripps Instn of Oceanography, UCSD, USA, 1987; Guest Investigator, Woods Hole Oceanographic Instn, 1988. Bigsby Medal, Geol Soc., 1991; George P. Woollard Award, Geol. Soc. Amer., 1997. Publications: (with D. Alexander) Beyond Belief: science, faith and ethical challenges, 2004; (with N. Spencer) Christianity, Climate Change and Sustainable Living, 2007; papers in many internat. jls. Recreations: building radio-controlled models, walking. Address: Bullard Laboratories, Madingley Road, Cambridge CB3 0EZ. T: (01223) 337187, Fax: (01223) 360779.

WHITE, Robin Bernard G.; see Grove-White.

WHITE, Roger, FSA 1986; Executive Secretary, Garden History Society, 1992–96; b 1 Sept. 1950; s of Geoffrey and Zoë White. Educ: Ifield Grammar School; Christ's College, Cambridge (1st class Hons, Hist. of Art Tripos); Wadham College, Oxford. GLC Historic Buildings Div., 1979–83; Sec., Georgian Gp, 1984–91; Mem., Chiswick House Adv. Panel, 1991–. Trustee, Pell Wall Preservation Trust, 1994–98. Curator: John Piper: Georgian Arcadia, Marlborough Fine Art, 1987; Nicholas Hawksmoor and the Replanning of Oxford, RIBA, 1997, Ashmolean Mus., 1998. Chichele Lectr, All Souls Coll., Oxford, 1999. Contributing Ed., House and Garden, 1994–. Publications: John Vardy, 1985; Georgian Arcadia: architecture for the park and garden, 1987; The Architectural Evolution of Magdalen College, Oxford, 1993; Chiswick House and Gardens, 2001; The Architectural Drawings of Magdalen College, Oxford, 2001; Witley Court and Gardens, 2003, rev. edn 2008; Belsay Hall, Castle and Gardens, 2005; (with Graham Byfield) Oxford Sketchbook, 2005; (ed) A Life of Frederick, Prince of Wales 1707–1751, 2007; contribs to Architectural Hist., Jl of Garden Hist., Country Life, World of Interiors. Recreation: visiting and writing about historic buildings. Address: 142 Weir Road, SW12 0ND.

WHITE, Sandra; Member (SNP) Glasgow, Scottish Parliament, since 1999; b 17 Aug. 1951; d of Henry Harley and Elizabeth Rodgers; m 1971, David White; two s one d. Educ: Garthamlock Sen. Sec. Sch.; Cardonald Coll. of Further Educn; Glasgow Coll. (Social Science degree). Clerkess, Gray Dunn, 1966–68; Timothy Whites, then Boots Chemist, 1968–73; Littlewoods Pools, 1973–88. Member (SNP): Renfrew DC, 1989; Renfrewshire CC, 1995–99. Recreations: walking, reading, gardening. Address: Scottish Parliament, Edinburgh EH99 1SP. T: (0131) 348 5000.

WHITE, Sharon Michele, (Mrs R. W. Chote); Director of Welfare to Work, Department for Work and Pensions, since 2006; b 21 April 1967; d of Curtis Gustavus White and Bernice White; m 1997, Robert William Chote, qv; one s. Educ: Fitzwilliam Coll., Cambridge (BA Hons Econs 1988); University Coll. London (MSc Econs 1993). HM Treasury, 1990–95; First Sec., Econ., Washington, 1995–97; Advr on Welfare Reform to the Prime Minister, 1997–99; Sen. Economist, World Bank, 1999–2002; Dir of Policy, DFID, 2003–06. Recreations: running, art. Address: Department for Work and Pensions, The Adelphi, 1–11 John Adam Street, WC2N 6HT.

WHITE, Prof. Simon David Manton, PhD; FRS 1997; Director, Max Planck Institute for Astrophysics, since 1994; b 30 Sept. 1951; s of David and Gwynneth White; m 1st, 1984, Judith Dianne Jennings (marr. diss. 1990); 2nd, 1994, Guinevere Alice Mei-Ing Kauffmann; one s. Educ: Christ's Hosp.; Jesus Coll., Cambridge (BA 1973; MA 1976; PhD 1977); Univ. of Toronto (MSc 1974). Lindemann Fellow, 1977–78, Sen. Res. Fellow, 1980–83, Univ. of Calif at Berkeley; Res. Fellow, Churchill Coll., Cambridge, 1978–80; Associate Prof., 1983–87, Prof., 1987–90, Univ. of Arizona; Sheepshanks Reader, Univ. of Cambridge, 1990–94. Scientific Mem., Max Planck Soc., 1994–. Publication: Morphology and Dynamics of Galaxies, 1983. Recreations: ski-ing, singing, violin, Morris Dancing. Address: Max Planck Institut für Astrophysik, Karl Schwarzschild Strasse 1, 85740 Garching bei München, Germany. T: (89) 300002211.

WHITE, Stephen Fraser; consulting engineer; b 13 May 1922; s of Robert and Iola White; m 1953, Judith Hamilton Cox; two s one d. Educ: Friars, Bangor; Nottingham Univ. BSc; FICE, MIWEM. War Service in Indian Electrical and Mechanical Engineers, discharged 1947. G. H. Hill and Sons, Consulting Civil Engineers, 1947–59; Cardiff Corporation, 1959–62; Engineering Inspector, Min. of Housing and Local Govt, 1962–70; Dir of Water Engineering, Dept of the Environment, 1970–77; Sen. Technical Advr to Nat. Water Council, 1977–83. Recreations: golf, bridge. Address: Rosehill, 4 Goodens Lane, Great Doddington, Northants NN29 7TY.

WHITE, Air Vice-Marshal Terence Philip, CB 1987; DL; CEng, FIET; at leisure; b 1 May 1932; s of Horace Arthur White and Evelyn Annie White (née Simpson); m 1956, Sheila Mary (née Taylor); three d. Educ: Wellingborough Technical Inst.; Rugby Coll. of Technology and Arts; RAF Engineering College. Electrical engineering apprentice, BTH Co., 1948–53; Junior Design Engineer, BTH Co., 1953; commissioned RAF Signals Officer, 1954–56; RAF Permt commn, Elect. Engr, 1957; attached RAAF, 1958–60; RAF weapons, communications and radar appts, 1963–67; OC Wing, RAF, Fylingdales, 1967–70; RAF Staff Coll., 1971; commanded RAF N Luffenham, 1972–74; Mem., RCDS, 1975; Senior Elect. Engr, HQ RAF Strike Command, 1976–77; Dir, Engineering Policy MoD (Air), 1978–80; Air Officer, Engrg and Supply, HQ RAF Germany, 1981–82; AOC Maintenance Units and AO Maintenance, RAF Support Comd, 1983–87. Vice Chm. (Air), E Midlands TAVRA, 1988–98. Hon. Air Cdre, County of Lincoln RAuxAF Sqn, 1992–2005; Hon. County Rep., Lincs, RAF Benevolent Fund, 1995–2003. DL Lincoln, 1994. Publications: contribs to RAF and professional jls. Recreations: rough shooting, antiques, travel. Address: c/o HSBC, Grantham, Lincs NG31 6LF. Club: Royal Air Force.

WHITE, Tom; see White, D. T.

WHITE, Sir Willard Wentworth, Kt 2004; CBE 1995; singer, actor; b 10 Oct. 1946; s of Egbert and Gertrude White; m 1972, Gillian Jackson; three s one d. Educ: Excelsior High Sch., Kingston, Jamaica; Juilliard Sch. of Music. BM. Guest singer, recitalist and recording artist, UK and overseas; singing rôles include Sarastro, Osmin, Sprecher, Leporello, Banquo, King Philip, Grand Inquisitor, Ferrando, Wotan, Klingsor, Hunding, Fafner, King Henry, Orestes, Porgy, Golaud, Pizarro, Prince Khovansky, Mephistopheles (Gounod's Faust and Berlioz's Damnation of Faust); Nekrotzar, Moses, four villains in Tales of Hoffman, Wanderer; stage: title rôle, Othello, RSC, 1989. Prime Minister of Jamaica's Medal of Appreciation, 1987; OM (Jamaica). Address: c/o IMG Artists Europe, The Light Box, 111 Power Road, Chiswick, W4 5PY.

WHITE, William Kelvin Kennedy, CMG 1983; HM Diplomatic Service, retired; b 10 July 1930; y s of late Kennedy White, JP, Caldy, Cheshire, and Violet White; m 1957, Susan Margaret, y d of late R. T. Colthurst, JP, Malvern, Worcs; three s. Educ: Birkenhead Sch.; Merton Coll., Oxford. 2nd Lieut Manchester Regt, 1949–50; Lieut 13th (Lancs) Bn, Parachute Regt, TA, 1950–54. Entered HM Foreign (later Diplomatic) Service, 1954; Foreign Office, 1954–56, attending UN Gen. Assemblies, 1954 and 1955; 3rd Sec., Helsinki, 1956–57; 2nd Sec., Commissioner-General's Office, Singapore, 1957–61; 2nd Sec., then 1st Sec., FO, 1961–66; 1st Sec. (Commercial), Stockholm, 1966–69; 1st Sec., then Counsellor and Head of Republic of Ireland Dept, FCO, 1969–74; Counsellor, New Delhi, 1974–77; Head of South Asian Dept, FCO, 1978–80; Minister, Canberra, 1980–81; Dep. Chief Clerk and Chief Inspector, FCO, 1982–84; High Comr to Zambia, 1984–87; Ambassador to Indonesia, 1988–90. Mem. Council, Univ. of Surrey, 1991–97. Address: Church Farm House, North Moreton, near Didcot, Oxon OX11 9BA. Club: Moreton CC.

WHITE-COOPER, (William) Robert (Patrick), FCII; Director, Marsh & McLennan Companies, 1998–2000; b 17 March 1943; s of William Ronald White-Cooper and Alison Mary White-Cooper; m 1965, Jennifer Margaret Hayward; one s three d. Educ: Diocesan Coll., Cape Town. FCII 1970. Various exec. posts, Price Forbes Gp, S Africa, 1962–83; Chairman: Sedgwick UK Ltd, 1986–89; Sedgwick Europe Ltd, 1989–93; Sedgwick Noble Lowndes Gp, 1993–96; Chief Exec., Sedgwick Gp plc, 1997–98. Chm., Adv. Bd, Sapiens, 2004–07. Past President: Insce Inst. of London; Insce Inst. of Cape of Good Hope. Dep. Chm., Addaction, 2001–. Recreations: tennis, golf, spectating cricket and Rugby, biographies, antiques. Clubs: MCC; Wentworth; Kelvin Grove, Steenberg Golf, Western Province Cricket (Cape Town).

WHITE-SPUNNER, Maj. Gen. Barney William Benjamin, CBE 2002; General Officer Commanding 3rd (UK) Division, 2007–Aug. 2009; b 31 Jan. 1957; s of Benjamin Nicholson, (Tommy), White-Spunner and Elizabeth, (Biddy), White-Spunner; m 1989, Amanda Faulkner; one s two d. Educ: Eton; Univ. of St Andrews (MA 1978). Commnd Blues and Royals, 1979; Dep. Leader, British-Chinese Taklamakan Expedn, 1993; MA to CDS, 1994–96; CO Household Cavalry Regt, 1996–98; Dep. Dir Defence Policy, 1998–2000; Commander: 16 Air Assault Bde, 2000–02; NATO Op. Harvest Macedonia, 2001; Kabul Multi-Nat. Bde, 2002; Chief of Jt Force Ops UK, 2003–05; COS HQ Land Comd, 2005–07. Corresp., The Field, 1992–; Ed., Baily's Hunting Directory, 1996–. Hon. Legionnaire 1st Cl., French Foreign Legion. Publications: Baily's Hunting Companion, 1994; Our Countryside, 1996; Great Days, 1997; Horse Guards, 2006. Recreations: Central Asia, hunting, fishing. Address: Headquarters 3rd (UK) Division, Bulford, Salisbury, Wilts SP4 9NY. Club: Turf.

WHITEFIELD, Gavin; Chief Executive, North Lanarkshire Council, since 2000; b 7 Feb. 1956; s of late Gavin Whitefield and of Annie Whitefield; m 1981, Grace Tait; two d. Educ: DPA 1990; CPFA 1996. Audit Asst, Exchequer and Audit Dept, 1974–76; Clydesdale District Council: Asst Auditor, 1976–84; Computer Develt Officer, 1984–86; Principal Housing Officer (Finance and Admin), 1986–89; Asst Dir of Housing (Finance and Admin), Motherwell DC, 1989–95; Dir, Housing and Property Services, N Lanarks Council, 1995–2000. Chm., Solace Scotland, 2007–. Recreations: hill walking, football. Address: North Lanarkshire Council, PO Box 14, Civic Centre, Motherwell ML1 1TW. T: (01698) 302252, Fax: (01698) 230265; e-mail: chief.executive@northlan.gov.uk.

WHITEFIELD, Karen; Member (Lab) Airdrie and Shotts, Scottish Parliament, since 1999; b 8 Jan. 1970; d of William and Helen Whitefield. Educ: Calderhead High Sch.; Glasgow Poly. (BA Hons Public Admin and Mgt). Civil Servant, Benefits Agency, 1992; Personal Asst to Rachel Squire, MP, 1992–99. Mem., Girls' Bde, Scotland. Recreations: reading, travel, swimming. Address: (office) 3 Sandvale Place, Shotts, N Lanarks ML7 5EF. T: (01501) 822200, Fax: (01501) 823650; e-mail: Karen.Whitefield.msp@scottish.parliament.uk.

WHITEHEAD, Dr Alan Patrick Vincent; MP (Lab) Southampton Test, since 1997; b 15 Sept. 1950; m; one s one d. Educ: Southampton Univ. (BA 1973, PhD 1976). Dep. Dir, 1976–79, Dir, 1979–83, Outset; Dir, British Inst. of Industrial Therapy, 1983–92; Prof. of Public Policy, Southampton Inst., 1992–97. Mem. (Lab), Southampton CC, 1980–92 (Leader, 1984–92). Parly Under-Sec. of State, DTLR, 2001–02. Mem., Select Cttee on Envmt, Transport and Regions, 1997–99, on constitutional affairs, 2003–; Chairman: All Party Ports Gp, 1998–2001; Parly Renewable and Sustainable Energy Gp, 2003–; Parly Sustainable Waste Gp, 2003–. Address: House of Commons, SW1A 0AA. T: (020) 7219 3000.

WHITEHEAD, Edward Anthony, (Ted); playwright; b 3 April 1933; s of Edward Whitehead and Catherine Curran; m 1st, 1958, Kathleen Horton (marr. diss. 1976); two d; 2nd, 1976, Gwenda Bagshaw. Educ: Christ's Coll., Cambridge (MA). Military Service, King's Regt (Infantry), 1955–57. TV plays: Under the Age; The Peddler; The Proofing Session; The Blonde Bombshell; TV adaptations: The Detective; Jumping the Queue; The Life and Loves of a She-Devil; Firstborn; The Free Frenchman; The Cloning of Joanna May; A Question of Guilt; Tess of the D'Urbervilles; The Mayor of Casterbridge; stage adaptation: The Dance of Death; radio play: Features Like Mine, 2005. Evening Standard

Award, and George Devine Award, 1971; BAFTA Award, 1986. *Publications:* The Foursome, 1972; Alpha Beta, 1972; The Sea Anchor, 1975; Old Flames, 1976; The Punishment, 1976; Mecca, 1977; World's End, 1981; The Man Who Fell in Love with his Wife, 1984; Collected Plays, 2005. *Recreations:* soccer, pubs, cats. *Address:* c/o Jenne Casarotto, Waverley House, 7–12 Noel Street, W1F 8GQ. *T:* (020) 7287 4450.

WHITEHEAD, Frank Ernest; Deputy Director (Statistics), Office of Population Censuses and Surveys, 1987–89; *b* 21 Jan. 1930; *s* of Ernest Edward Whitehead and Isabel Leslie; *m* 1961, Anne Gillian Marston; three *s*. *Educ:* Leyton County High School; London School of Economics. BSc (Econ). National Service, RAF, 1948–49. Rio Tinto Co. Ltd, 1952–54; Professional Officer, Central Statistical Office, Fedn of Rhodesia and Nyasaland, 1955–64; Statistician, General Register Office, 1964–68; Chief Statistician, Min. of Social Security, later DHSS, 1968–77; Head of Social Survey Div., Office of Population Censuses and Surveys, 1977–82; Under Secretary, 1982; Dep. Dir, OPCS, 1982–87. Vice-Pres., Royal Statistical Soc., 1988–89 (Council, 1987–92). *Publications:* Social Security Statistics: reviews of United Kingdom statistical sources, vol. II (ed W. F. Maunder), 1974; contribs to Statistical News, Population Trends. *Recreations:* family history, gardening.

WHITEHEAD, Godfrey Oliver, CBE 1987; FICE; Chairman: Minerva plc, since 2007; Norland Managed Services Ltd, since 2008; *b* 9 Aug. 1941; *s* of late Clarence Whitehead and Mary Whitehead (*née* Gartside); *m* 1965, Stephanie McAllister; three *s* one *d*. *Educ:* Hulme Grammar Sch., Oldham; Univ. of Bradford (BSc Civil Engrg). FICE 1992. John Laing Plc, 1963–86: Man. Dir, John Laing Construction Ltd, 1982–86; Exec. Dir, John Laing Plc 1983–86; Chm., Jt Venture (Laing-Mowlem-ARC) which built Mt Pleasant Airport, Falkland Is, 1983–86; Chm., John Laing Internat., 1986; Exec. Dir, AMEC Plc, 1986–89; Gp Chief Exec., Babcock Internat. Gp PLC, 1989–93; Chief Exec., 1993–2003, Chm., 2002–07 (non-exec. Chm., 2003–07), Alfred McAlpine plc. Non-exec. Dir, PSA, 1989–91. Manchester Ringway Developments PLC: Chm., 1987–89; Pres., 1989–2002. Col, 1996, CO, 2001, Engr and Logistics Staff Corps, TA (Major, 1984; Chm., Liaison Cttee, 1991–2000). Liveryman, Paviors' Co., 1986–. *Recreations:* gardening, shooting, opera. *Address:* Minerva plc, 42 Wigmore Street, W1U 2RY.

WHITEHEAD, Graham Wright, CBE 1977; President, Jaguar Cars Inc., 1983–90; Chairman, Jaguar Canada Inc., Ontario, 1983–90; Director: Jaguar Cars Ltd, 1982–90; Jaguar plc, 1984–90; *m* Gabrielle Whitehead, OBE; one *s* one *d*. Joined Wolseley Motors, 1945; moved to US, 1959; Pres., BL Motors Inc., later Jaguar Rover Triumph Inc., NJ, 1968–83; Chm., Jaguar Rover Triumph Canada Inc., Ont, 1977–83. President: British-American Chamber of Commerce, NY, 1976–78; British Automobile Manufacturers Assoc., NY; St George's Soc. of NY; Governor, Nat. Assoc. of Securities Dealers, 1987–90. *Address:* 20 Meadow Place, Old Greenwich, CT 06870, USA. *Club:* Riverside Yacht (Conn).

WHITEHEAD, Ian Richard; HM Diplomatic Service, retired; Counsellor (Management), Paris, 1999–2003; *b* 21 July 1943; *s* of Alexander Guthrie Whitehead and Mary Helen (*née* Crosby-Milligan); *m* 2nd, 1996, Pamela Denise Mitchison; one *d*, and one *d* from previous marriage. *Educ:* Parmiter's Grammar Sch., London. Entered Foreign Office, 1960: 3rd Secretary: Addis Ababa, 1965–69; UK Delegn, NATO, Brussels, 1969–71; Consular Officer, Dubai, 1971–72; Vice Consul, Casablanca, 1972–75; FCO, 1975–78; 2nd Sec., Bridgetown, 1978–83; First Secretary: Paris, 1983–88; FCO, 1988–91; Dep. High Comr, Dar-es-Salaam, 1991–93; Head of Mission, Skopje, 1993–94; Counsellor, FCO, 1994–98; High Comr to Guyana and Ambassador to Suriname, 1998. *Recreations:* football, tennis, reading. *Address:* Ashview, 5 Lawrence's Lane, Cold Ash, Berks RG18 3LF.

WHITEHEAD, Sir John (Stainton), GCMG 1992 (KCMG 1986; CMG 1976); CVO 1978; HM Diplomatic Service, retired; Chairman, Japaninvest, since 2004; *b* 20 Sept. 1932; *s* of late John William and Kathleen Whitehead; *m* 1964, Carolyn (*née* Hilton); two *s* two *d*. *Educ:* Christ's Hospital (Almoner, 2005–); Hertford Coll., Oxford (MA; Hon. Fellow 1991); Open Univ. (BA Hons 2004). HM Forces, 1950–52; Oxford, 1952–55; FO, 1955–56; Tokyo, 1956–61; FO, 1961–64; 1st Sec., Washington, 1964–67; 1st Sec. (Economic), Tokyo, 1968–71; FCO, 1971–76, Head of Personnel Services Dept, 1973–76; Counsellor, Bonn, 1976–80; Minister, Tokyo, 1980–84; Dep. Under-Sec. of State (Chief Clerk), FCO, 1984–86; Ambassador to Japan, 1986–92. Chm., Deutsche Morgan Grenfell Trust Bank Ltd (Japan), 1996–99; non-executive Director: Cadbury Schweppes, 1993–2001; Serco Group, 1994–96; BPB, 1995–2002; Senior Adviser: Morgan Grenfell, later Deutsche Morgan Grenfell, Gp, 1992–99; Deutsche Asset Mgt Gp Ltd, 1996–2000; Adviser: Cable and Wireless plc, 1992–2002; Sanwa Bank Ltd, 1993–2000; Tokyo Electric Power Co. Inc., 1993–2002; Adviser to Board: Inchcape plc, 1992–96; Guinness plc, 1992–97; Mem. Adv. Bd, PowerGen International, 1996–2001. Exec. Consultant, WDA, 1992–94; Advr to Pres. of BoT, 1992–95; Mem. Adv. Panel, All Nippon Airways Co. Ltd, 2000–03. Member: UK-Japan 2000 Gp, 1992–2000, UK Japan 21st Century Gp, 2001– (Dir, 1995–2006); Council, Japan Soc., 1992–2006 (Mem. Exec. Cttee, 1996–2000, Jt Chm., 2000–04, Chm., 2004–06); Management Council, GB Sasakawa Foundn, 1993–96. Trustee: Monteverdi Choir and Orchestra, 1991–2000; Daiwa Anglo-Japanese Foundn, 2004– (Chm., 2008–); Member: Royal Opera House Trust, 1992–93; Council, Buckingham Univ., 1992–95. Pres., Hertford Soc., 1991–97. Bundes Verdienst Kreuz (FRG), 1978; Grand Cordon, Order of Rising Sun (Japan), 2006. *Recreations:* new challenges, music, travel, golf, woodland management. *Address:* Bracken Edge, High Pitfold, Hindhead, Surrey GU26 6BN. *Clubs:* Oxford and Cambridge, London Capital, MCC; Liphook Golf (Hants).

WHITEHEAD, Sir Philip Henry Rathbone, 6th Bt *cr* 1889, of Highfield House, Catford Bridge, Kent; *b* 13 Oct. 1957; *s* of Sir Rowland John Rathbone Whitehead, 5th Bt and of Marie-Louise (*née* Gausel); *S* father, 2007; *m* 1987, Emma Charlotte Milne Home (marr. diss. 2002); two *s*. *Educ:* Eton; Bristol Univ. *Heir:* *s* Orlando James Rathbone Whitehead, *b* 8 Oct. 1994.

WHITEHEAD, Dr Roger George, CBE 1992; nutrition consultant; Director, Dunn Nutrition Centre, Medical Research Council, Cambridge and Keneba, The Gambia, 1973–98; Fellow of Darwin College, Cambridge, 1973–2001, now Emeritus Fellow; *b* 7 Oct. 1933; *s* of late Arthur Charles Sanders Whitehead and Eleanor Jane Whitehead (*née* Farrer); *m* 1958, Jennifer Mary Lees; two *s* one *d*. *Educ:* Ulverston Grammar Sch.; Univ. of Leeds (BSc 1956; PhD 1959); MA Cantab 1973. FIBiol 1973; Hon. MRCP 1986, Hon. FRCP 1993; Hon. FRCPCH 1997. Scientific Staff, MRC, 1959–98; Dir, Child Nutrition Unit, Kampala, 1968–73; Vice Master, Darwin Coll., Cambridge, 1989–97. Visiting Professor: KCL, 1992–; Oxford Brookes Univ., 2002–; Hon. Professor: Shenyang Univ., China, 1995–; Chinese Acad. of Preventive Medicine, 1995–; Fellow, Internat. Union of Nutritional Scis, 1997; Mem. Internat. Staff, Makerere Univ., Uganda, 2003–. Committee on Medical Aspects of Food Policy: Mem., 1975–91; Chm., Dietary Reference Panel, 1987–91; Mem., MAFF Food Adv. Cttee, 1988–95. Hon. Sen. Scientist, Human Nutrition Res., MRC, Cambridge, 1999–. FAO consultant, 2004–06. Pres., Nutrition Soc., 1989–92 (Hon. Mem., 2000); Chm., British Nutrition Foundn, 1994–96 (Vice-Chm., 1993–94). Hon. DSc Ulster, 2000. Drummond Prize, Nutrition Soc., 1968; Unesco Science Prize, 1983; British Nutrition Foundn Prize, 1990; Nutricia Internat. Award for Nutritional Sci., 1994. *Publications:* (jtly) Protein-Energy Malnutrition, 1977; (ed) Maternal Nutrition during Pregnancy and Lactation, 1980; (ed) New Techniques in Nutritional Research, 1991; contribs to learned jls. *Recreations:* photography, licensed amateur radio operator, G3ZUK, 5X5NA, C53U. *Address:* Church End, Weston Colville, Cambridge CB1 5PE. *T:* (01223) 290524; *e-mail:* rogergwhitehead@aol.com.

WHITEHEAD, Simon Christopher, PhD; Partner and Co-Head of Trial (Europe), Dorsey & Whitney LLP, since 2003; *b* Castle Donnington, 31 Jan. 1963; *s* of John Whitehead and late Patricia Helena Whitehead; *m* 1991, Frances Mary Somers; two *d*. *Educ:* Cranbrook Sch.; Univ. of Sydney (BA 1st cl. Hons 1985; LLB 1987; PhD 1993). St Paul's Coll. Council Scholar, 1985; Australian and Commonwealth Postgrad. Res. Award, 1987–91. Admitted solicitor, England and Wales, 1991, NSW, 1987, High Court of Australia, 1998; Partner and Hd of Civil Litigation, Saunders & Co., 1994–98; solicitor, NSW, 1998–2000; returned to practice in England, 2000; Partner and Hd of Litigation, PricewaterhouseCoopers Legal, 2002–03. *Publications:* (contrib.) Roman Crossings: theory and practice in the Roman Republic, 2005; articles in EC Tax Rev., Tax Jl, Solicitors' Jl, Taxation, Internat. Tax Rev., Tax Notes Internat., New Law Jl. *Recreations:* reading Latin poetry and prose, watching Australia win at cricket and Rugby. *Address:* Dorsey & Whitney LLP, 21 Wilson Street, EC2M 2TD. *T:* (020) 7826 4581, *Fax:* (020) 7588 0555; *e-mail:* whitehead.simon@dorsey.com.

WHITEHEAD, Ted; *see* Whitehead, E. A.

WHITEHORN, Katharine Elizabeth, (Mrs Gavin Lyall); Columnist, The Observer, 1960–96 (Associate Editor, 1980–88); Agony Aunt, Saga Magazine, since 1997; *b* London; *d* of late A. D. and E. M. Whitehorn; *m* 1958, Gavin Tudor Lyall (*d* 2003); two *s*. *Educ:* Blunt House; Roedean; Glasgow High School for Girls, and others; Newnham Coll., Cambridge. Publisher's Reader, 1950–53; Teacher-Secretary in Finland, 1953–54; Grad. Asst, Cornell Univ., USA, 1954–55; Picture Post, 1956–57; Woman's Own, 1958; Spectator, 1959–61. Member: Latey Cttee on Age of Majority, 1965–67; BBC Adv. Gp on Social Effects of Television, 1971–72; Board, British Airports Authority, 1972–77; Council, RSocMed, 1982–85. Director: Nationwide Building Soc., 1983–91; Nationwide Anglia Estate Agents, 1987–90. Vice-Pres., Patients Assoc., 1983–96. Rector, St Andrews Univ., 1982–85. Advr, Inst. for Global Ethics, 1993–. Mem., ESU. Hon. LLD St Andrews, 1985; Hon. DLitt London Guildhall, 2000. Woman That Makes A Difference Award, Internat. Women's Forum, 1992. *Publications:* Cooking in a Bedsitter, 1960; Roundabout, 1961; Only on Sundays, 1966; Whitehorn's Social Survival, 1968; Observations, 1970; How to Survive in Hospital, 1972; How to Survive Children, 1975; Sunday Best, 1976; How to Survive in the Kitchen, 1979; View from a Column, 1981; How to Survive your Money Problems, 1983; Selective Memory (autobiog.), 2007. *Address:* 14 Provost Road, NW3 4ST. *Clubs:* University Women's (Hon. Mem.), Royal Society of Medicine, Royal Commonwealth Society; Forum UK.

WHITEHOUSE, Prof. Colin Ralph, PhD; CPhys, FInstP; FIMMM; FREng; Deputy Chief Executive and Member, since 2007, Head of Daresbury Laboratory, since 2007, and Director of Campus Strategy, since 2008, Science and Technology Facilities Council; *b* 21 Aug. 1949; *s* of Clifford William Whitehouse and Edith Elizabeth Whitehouse (*née* Pearson); *m* 1973, Mary Elizabeth Wilks; two *d*. *Educ:* Queen Elizabeth Coll., London (BSc Physics 1970); Univ. of Birmingham (MSc Physics 1971); Univ. of Brighton/GEC Hirst Res. Centre (PhD Semiconductor Growth 1978). CPhys 1994; FInstP 1994; FREng 2002; FIMMM 2002. Res. Scientist, GEC Hirst Res. Centre, Wembley, 1974–77; Sen. Res. Associate, Univ. of Newcastle upon Tyne, 1977–80; Higher SO, 1980–83, SSO, 1983–87, PSO, 1987–93, RSRE Malvern; University of Sheffield: Prof. of Electronic Materials, 1993–2003; Dir, EPSRC Nat. Facility for III–V Semiconductors, 1993–2003; Hd, Electronic and Electrical Engrg Dept, 1994–2000; Dir of Res., Engrg and Physical Scis Res. Div., 1996–99; Pro-Vice-Chancellor: for Res. and Internat. Affairs, 1999–2001 for Res. and Res. Exploitation, 2001–03; Council for the Central Laboratory of the Research Councils: Dir of Engrg, 2003–04; Dir, Daresbury Lab., 2004–06; Chief Technologist, 2005–06; Dep. Chief Exec., 2006–07. Dep. Dir, UK IRC for Semiconductor Materials, 1993–98. Visiting Professor: in Materials Sci., Univ. of Oxford, 2003–; Sch. of Engrg, Univ. of Birmingham, 2005–. Member: MoD/DTI Nat. Adv. Cttee for Electronic Materials and Devices, 2000–; IET (formerly IEE) Internat. Technical Adv. Panel on Electronic Material and Devices, 2002–; UK North West Sci. Council, 2004–; UK Yorks and Humber Sci. and Innovation Council, 2005–; Knowledge Transfer and Economic Impact Gp, Res. Councils UK, 2006–08; Technology Strategy Bd, Res. Council UK Strategy Gp, 2007–; Northern Way Innovation Strategy Gp, 2008–. Member Board: Sheffield Univ. Enterprises Ltd, 1999–2003; White Rose Univs Res. Ltd, 1999–2003; Malvern Girls' Coll., 2000–06; CLIK, 2004–; Microvisk, 2004–06; Halton Borough Chamber of Commerce and Enterprise, 2005–07; Didcot First, 2007–; Quadrant, 2007–; Oxford Economic Partnership, 2007–; STEMNET, 2008–; Res. and Develt Soc., 2008. *Publications:* numerous contribs to learned jl and prestigious conf. papers, relating to semiconductor materials, semiconductor processing, nanotechnology and nanoscience, next-generation devices and sensors, and innovation. *Recreations:* classical music, theatre, sports, walking, cycling. *Address:* STFC Daresbury Laboratory, Daresbury, Cheshire WA14 4AD. *T:* (01925) 603119, *Fax:* (01925) 603601; *e-mail:* c.r.whitehouse@stfc.ac.uk.

WHITEHOUSE, Dr David Bryn; Executive Director and Trustee, The Corning Museum of Glass, Corning, USA, since 1992 (Chief Curator, 1984–88; Deputy Director, 1988–92); Trustee, The Rockwell Museum, since 1992; *b* 15 Oct. 1941; *s* of Brindley Charles Whitehouse and Alice Margaret Whitehouse; *m* 1st, 1963, Ruth Delamain Ainger; one *s* two *d*; 2nd, 1975, Elizabeth-Anne Ollemans; one *s* two *d*. *Educ:* King Edward's Sch., Birmingham; St John's Coll., Cambridge. MA, PhD; FSA; FRGS. Scholar, British Sch. at Rome, 1963–65; Wainwright Fellow in Near Eastern Archaeology, Univ. of Oxford, 1966–73; Dir, Sīrāf Expedn, 1966–73; Dir, British Inst. of Afghan Studies, 1973–74; Dir, British Sch. at Rome, 1974–84. President: Internat. Union of Institutes, 1980–81; Internat. Assoc. for Hist. of Glass, 1991–95 (Mem. Management Cttee, 1988–95 and 1998–); Mem. Council, Internat. Assoc. for Classical Archaeology, 1974–84. Mem., Steering Cttee, Dublin Blaschka Congress, 2006. Trustee, Amer. Friends of Chartres Cathedral, 2005–. Corresp. Mem., German Archaeological Inst.; Academician, Accademia Fiorentina dell'Arte del Disegno; Fellow: Pontificia Accademia Romana di Archeologia; Accademia di Archeologia, Lettere e Belle Arti, Naples. Ed., Jl of Glass Studies, 1988–. *Publications:* (jtly) Background to Archaeology, 1973; (jtly) The Origins of Europe, 1974; (with Ruth Whitehouse) Archaeological Atlas of the World, 1975; (ed jtly) Papers in Italian Archaeology I, 1978; Siraf III: The Congregational Mosque, 1980; (with David Andrews and John Osborne) Papers in Italian Archaeology III, 1981; (with Richard Hodges) Mohammed, Charlemagne and the Origins of Europe, 1983; (jtly) Glass of the Caesars, 1987; Glass of the Roman Empire, 1988; (jtly) Treasures from The Corning Museum of Glass, 1992; Glass: a pocket dictionary, 1993, rev. edn 2006; English Cameo Glass, 1994; Roman Glass in The Corning Museum of Glass, Vol. I, 1997, Vol. II, 2001,

Vol. III, 2003; Ancient Glass from Ed-Dur, 1998; The Corning Museum of Glass: a decade of glass collecting 1990–1999, 2000; (with Stefano Carboni) Glass of the Sultans, 2001; Sasanian and Post-Sasanian Glass in The Corning Museum of Glass, 2005; (jtly) Drawing upon Nature: studies for the Blaschkas' glass models, 2007; Reflecting Antiquity, 2007; many papers in Iran, Antiquity, Med. Archaeol., Papers of Brit. Sch. at Rome, Jl of Glass Studies, etc. *Address:* The Corning Museum of Glass, One Museum Way, Corning, NY 14830–2253, USA. *T:* (607) 9748424; *e-mail:* whitehoudb@cmog.org. *Club:* Athenæum.

WHITEHOUSE, David Rae Beckwith, QC 1990; a Recorder, since 1987; *b* 5 Sept. 1945; *s* of late (David) Barry Beckwith Whitehouse, MA, MD, FRCS, FRCOG and Mary Beckwith Whitehouse, JP; *m* 1971, Linda Jane, *d* of Eric Vickers, CB and Barbara Mary Vickers; one *s*. *Educ:* Ellesmere College; Choate Sch., Wallingford, Conn., USA; Trinity College, Cambridge (MA). English-Speaking Union Scholarship, 1964. Called to the Bar, Gray's Inn, 1969; in practice on SE Circuit, specialising in criminal law, licensing and tribunals. Criminal cases include: Last Tango in Paris (obscene pubns); George Davis (five robbery trials and two appeals); Handless Corpse Murder; Cyprus Spy trial; murder trial of Lennie The Guv'nor McLean; Colombian Cartel and Mafia drug trials; Thomas Ap Rhys Pryce murder trial; Christopher Langham case; defence of Adams, Arif, McAvoy, Richardson, Tibbs and Tobin families. Fraud cases include: Barlow Clowes (investment and co. takeover fraud); Norton plc (rights issue fraud); Abbey National plc (corruption); local authy frauds involving W Wilts and Brent Councils; John (Goldfinger) Palmer (timeshare fraud); read The Sun for defamation and contempt, 1969–76. Member: Criminal Bar Assoc., 1969–; Central Criminal Court Bar Mess, 1970. *Recreations:* the arts, esp. architecture, music and cinema; walking, wild gardening. *Address:* 3 Raymond Buildings, Gray's Inn, WC1R 5BH. *T:* (020) 7400 6400, *Fax:* (020) 7400 6464. *Club:* Reform.

WHITEHOUSE, Elly; *see* Jansen, E.

WHITEHOUSE, Prof. (Julian) Michael (Arthur), MD; FRCP, FRCR, FRCPEd, FMedSci; Professor Emeritus, Imperial College School of Medicine, London, 2000; Vice Principal for Undergraduate Medicine, Imperial College School of Medicine and Professor of Medical Oncology, University of London, 1997–2000; *b* 2 June 1940; *s* of Arthur Arnold Keer Whitehouse and Kathleen Ida Elizabeth (*née* Elliston); *m* 1965, Diane France de Saussure; one *s* two *d. Educ:* Queens' Coll., Cambridge (BA 1963; MB, BChir 1966; MA 1967; MD 1975); St Bartholomew's Hosp. Med. Coll., London. FRCP 1979; FRCR 1992; FRCPEd 1994. Sen. Lectr and Actg Dir, ICRF Dept of Med. Oncology, and Hon. Consultant Physician, St Bartholomew's Hosp., London, 1975–76; Prof. of Med. Oncology and Dir, CRC Wessex Regl Med. Oncology Unit, Univ. of Southampton, and Hon. Consultant Physician, Southampton Gen. Hosp., 1976–97; Dean, Charing Cross and Westminster Med. Sch., 1997. Chm., Educn Trng Bd, Eur. Orgn for Res. and Treatment of Cancer, 1997–2001. Chm. Council, Paterson Inst., Christie Hosp., Manchester, 1997–2002; Member: Council, CRC, 1997–2002; GMC Fitness to Practise panel, 2000–. Governor: Canford Sch., Dorset, 1998–; (and Mem. Council) St Swithun's Sch., Winchester, 1996–; City of London Sch., 2000–. FMedSci 2000. *Publications:* CNS Complications of Malignant Disease, 1979; Recent Advances in Clinical Oncology, 1982, 2nd edn 1986; A Pocket Consultant in Clinical Oncology, 1983; Cancer Investigation and Management, 1984; Cancer: the facts, 1996; contrib. numerous papers in various jls on res. and treatment of cancer. *Recreations:* devising projects, ski-ing, sailing, travelling. *Address: e-mail:* m.whitehouse@imperial.ac.uk. *Club:* Athenæum.

WHITEHOUSE, Michael, *see* Whitehouse, J. M. A.

WHITEHOUSE, Michael; Assistant Auditor General, National Audit Office, since 2002; *b* 14 Nov. 1957; *s* of Bernard Joseph Whitehouse and late Margaret Whitehouse (*née* Hutchings). *Educ:* King Edward VI Grammar Sch., Birmingham; Univ. of Exeter (BA Hons). Joined Exchequer and Audit Dept, 1979; Dir, 1990–92; Min. of Finance, Zambia, 1992–94; Office of Auditor Gen., NZ, 1994–95; Dir, Value for Money Develt and Modernising Govt, 1996–2002. *Recreations:* sport, travel, reading, theatre, history. *Address:* National Audit Office, 157–197 Buckingham Palace Road, SW1W 9SP. *T:* (020) 7798 7078; *e-mail:* michael.whitehouse@nao.gsi.gov.uk.

WHITEHOUSE, Paul; writer, actor and producer; *m* Fiona (separated); two *d. Educ:* Univ. of E Anglia. Formerly plasterer. Dir, Tomboy Films Ltd. *Television includes:* writer (with Charlie Higson) and actor: Harry Enfield's Television Programme, 1990, 1992; Harry Enfield and Chums, 1994, 1997; The Fast Show, 1994–97 (also co-producer; Best Light Entertainment Perf., BAFTA Awards, 1998); Randall and Hopkirk, 1999; Happiness (also co-producer), 2001, 2003; writer (with Chris Langham) and actor, Help, 2005; writer and actor, Ruddy Hell! It's Harry and Paul, 2007; Harry and Paul, 2008; actor, David Copperfield, 1999. *Films include:* Love's Labour's Lost, 2000; Kevin and Perry Go Large, 2000. *Theatre:* The Fast Show Live, Apollo, Hammersmith, 2002; The Fast Show Live: shamelessly plugging the DVD, Dominion, 2007. *Address:* c/o Curtis Brown Group Ltd, Haymarket House, 28–29 Haymarket, SW1Y 4SP.

WHITEHOUSE, Paul Chapple, QPM 1993; Chairman, Gangmasters Licensing Authority, since 2005; Chief Constable, Sussex Police, 1993–2001; *b* 26 Sept. 1944; *s* of Beatrice and Jack Whitehouse, Cambs; *m* 1970, Elizabeth Dinsmore; one *s* one *d. Educ:* Ipswich Sch.; Emmanuel Coll., Cambridge (BA 1967; MA 1969). VSO, Starehe Boys' Centre, Nairobi, 1963–64; Durham Constabulary, 1967–74; Northumbria Police, 1974–83; Asst Chief Constable, Greater Manchester Police, 1983–87; Dep. Chief Constable, W Yorkshire Police, 1987–93. Association of Chief Police Officers: Chairman: Communications Gp, 1995–2001; Personnel Mgt (formerly Personnel and Trng) Cttee, 1998–2001; Vice Chm., Media Adv. Group, 1994–2001; Member: Finance and Resources Cttee, 1994–2001; Inf. Mgt Cttee, 1995–2001. Chm., Brighton and Hove Common Purpose Adv. Gp, 1994–2001; Member Council: IAM, 1993–2002; NACRO, 1994– (Vice-Chm., 2003–); Centre for Crime and Justice Studies, 1997–2002. Chm., Starehe Endowment Fund (UK), 1994–. Treasurer: Ludlow Assembly Rooms, 2002–07; Dutch Barge Assoc., 2002–. *Recreations:* collecting people, IT, steam, disputation, keeping the peace. *Address:* 1 Slate Cottages, Abbots Leigh, Bristol BS8 3RX. *T:* 07813 802783, *Fax:* 0870 796 4033; *e-mail:* paul@dunstanburgh.net. *Club:* Oxford and Cambridge.

WHITEHOUSE-JANSEN, Elly; *see* Jansen, E.

WHITELAW, Billie, CBE 1991; actress; *b* 6 June 1932; *d* of Perceval and Frances Whitelaw; *m* Robert Muller (*d* 1998), writer; one *s. Educ:* Thornton Grammar Sch., Bradford. Appeared in: *plays:* Hotel Paradiso, Winter Garden, 1954 and Oxford Playhouse, 1956; Progress to the Park, Theatre Workshop and Saville, 1961; England our England, Prince's, 1962; Touch of the Poet, Venice and Dublin, 1962; National Theatre, 1963–65: Othello, London and Moscow; Hobson's Choice; Beckett's Play; Trelawny of the Wells; The Dutch Courtesan; After Haggerty, Criterion, 1971; Not I, Royal Court, 1973 and 1975; Alphabetical Order, Mayfair, 1975; Footfalls, Royal Court, 1976; Molly,

Comedy, 1978; Happy Days, Royal Court, 1979; The Greeks, Aldwych, 1980; Passion Play, Aldwych, 1981; Rockaby and Enough, NY, 1981, with Footfalls, 1984, NT 1982, Riverside, 1986, Adelaide Fest., 1986, Purchase Fest., NY, 1986; Tales from Hollywood, NT, 1983; Who's Afraid of Virginia Woolf?, Young Vic, 1987; *films:* No Love for Johnny; Charlie Bubbles; Twisted Nerve; The Adding Machine; Start the Revolution Without Me; Leo the Last; Eagle in a Cage; Gumshoe; Frenzy; Night Watch; The Omen; Leopard in the Snow; The Water Babies; An Unsuitable Job for a Woman; Slayground; Shadey; The Chain; The Dressmaker; Maurice; Joyriders; The Krays; Deadly Advice; Jane Eyre; Canterbury Tales (animated film); Quills; Hot Fuzz; *television:* No Trams to Lime Street; Lena Oh My Lena; Resurrection; The Skin Game; Beyond the Horizon; Anna Christie; Lady of the Camellias; The Pity of it all; Love on the Dole; A World of Time; You and Me; Poet Game; Sextet (8 plays); Napoleon and Love (9 plays: Josephine); The Fifty Pound Note (Ten from the Twenties); The Withered Arm (Wessex Tales); The Werewolf Reunion (2 plays); Ghost Trio, and But the Clouds, by Samuel Beckett; Not I; Eustace and Hilda (2 plays); The Serpent Son; Happy Days (dir. by Beckett); Private Schulz; Last Summer's Child; A Tale of Two Cities; Jamaica Inn; Camille; Old Girlfriends; The Secret Garden; Imaginary Friends (mini-series); The Picnic; Three Beckett plays; The 15 Streets; Lorna Doone; The Entertainer; A Murder of Quality; The Cloning of Joanna May; Firm Friends I and II (mini-series); Born to Run; Shooting the Past; A Dinner of Herbs; *radio plays:* The Master Builder; Hindle Wakes; Jane Eyre; The Female Messiah; Alpha Beta; The Cherry Orchard; Vassa Zheleznova; Filumena; The Wireless Lady. Lecturer on Beckett: in USA at univs of Santa Barbara, Stanford and Denver, 1985, Smith and Dartmouth Colls, 1992, Franklyn and Marshall Colls, 1993, Albany Univ., NY, 1997; at Balliol Coll., Oxford, 1986; An Informal Evening with Samuel Beckett and lecture tours, USA, 1992–95 and 1996; one-woman Beckett Evening, NY, 1997 and QEH, 1999. Annenberg/Beckett Fellow, Reading Univ., 1993. Silver Heart Variety Club Award, 1961; TV Actress of Year, 1961, 1972; British Academy Award, 1968; US Film Critics Award, 1968; Variety Club of GB Best Film Actress Award, 1977; Evening News Film Award as Best Actress, 1977; Sony Best Radio Actress Award, 1987; Evening Standard Film Award for Best Actress, 1988. Hon. DLitt: Bradford, 1981; St Andrews, 1997; Birmingham, 1997. *Publication:* Billie Whitelaw: who he? (autobiog.), 1995, USA 1996. *Recreation:* pottering about the house. *Address:* c/o Michael Foster, Independent Talent Group Ltd, Oxford House, 76 Oxford Street, W1D 1BS.

WHITELEY, family name of **Baron Marchamley.**

WHITELEY, Sir Hugo Baldwin H.; *see* Huntington-Whiteley.

WHITELEY, Dame Jane (Elizabeth), DBE 1990; *b* 14 July 1944; *d* of Major Charles Packe (killed in action, July 1944) and Hon. Margaret (*née* Lane Fox); *m* 1st, 1966, Ian Gow, TD, MP (*d* 1990); two *s*; 2nd, 1994, Lt-Col Michael Whiteley. *Educ:* St Mary's School, Wantage. Governor: three special schs in S London, 1968–72; Hankham CP Sch., 1976–85; St Bede's Sch., Eastbourne, 1980–87; Park Coll., Eastbourne, 1985–88; Grenville Coll., Bideford, 1997–2005; Mem. Council, Cheltenham Coll., 1996–98. Trustee: Ian Gow Meml Fund, 1990–2003; Exeter Cathedral Music Foundn Trust, 2005–; Visitor: Henry Smith Charity, 2001–07; Trusthouse Charitable Foundn, 2005–07. Freeman, Bor. of Eastbourne, 1992. *Recreations:* playing organ and piano, reading. *Address:* Lower Lewer, Hatherleigh, Okehampton, Devon EX20 3LF.

WHITELEY, Gen. Sir Peter (John Frederick), GCB 1979 (KCB 1976); OBE 1960; DL; Lieutenant-Governor and Commander-in-Chief, Jersey, 1979–84; *b* 13 Dec. 1920; *s* of late John George Whiteley; *m* 1948, Nancy Vivian, *d* of late W. Carter Clayden; two *s* two *d. Educ:* Bishop's Stortford Coll.; Bembridge Sch.; Ecole des Roches. Joined Royal Marines, 1940; 101 Bde, 1941; HMS: Resolution, 1941; Renown, 1942; HMNZS Gambia, 1942; seconded to Fleet Air Arm, 1946–50; Adjt 40 Commando, 1951; Staff Coll., Camberley, 1954; Bde Major 3rd Commando Bde, 1957; Instructor, Staff Coll., Camberley, 1960–63; CO 42 Commando, 1965–66 (despatches, Malaysia, 1966); Col GS Dept of CGRM, 1966–68; Nato Defence Coll., 1968; Comdr 3rd Commando Bde, 1968–70; Maj.-Gen. Commando Forces, 1970–72; C of S, HQ Allied Forces Northern Europe, 1972–75; Commandant General, Royal Marines, 1975–77; C-in-C Allied Forces Northern Europe, 1977–79. Col Comdt, RM, 1985–87; Hon. Col, 211 (Wessex) Field Hosp. RAMC (Volunteers), TA, 1985–90. Mem., Council, Union Jack Club, 1985–91; Vice Chm., Theatre Royal, Plymouth, 1991–97; Pres., W Devon Area, 1985–87, Pres., Devon, 1987–96, St John's Ambulance Bde; Vice-Pres., Devon Care Trust, 1995–2003. Life Trustee, Durrell Wildlife Conservation Trust. Governor: Bembridge Sch., 1981–95; Kelly Coll., 1985–94; St Michael's Sch., Tavistock, 1985–89. Member: Royal Commonwealth Soc., 1981–; Anglo Norse Soc., 1980–; Anglo Danish Soc., 1980–; Jersey Soc. in London, 1984–. Liveryman, Fletchers' Co., 1982 (Hon. Life Liveryman, 1999); Guild of Freemen of City of London: Mem. Ct of Assistants, 1980–; Master, 1987–88. DL Devon, 1987. CCMI. KStJ 1980; Chevalier, Ordre de la Pléaiade, Assoc. of French Speaking Parliaments, 1984. *Publications:* contribs to Jane's Annual, NATO's Fifteen Nations, RUSI Jl, Nauticus. *Recreations:* music, painting, wood carving, sailing, dogs. *Clubs:* Royal Commonwealth Society; Royal Naval Sailing Assoc.

WHITEMAN, Hon. Burchell Anthony, OJ 2006; High Commissioner of Jamaica in the United Kingdom, since 2007; *b* May Pen, Jamaica, 21 Feb. 1938; *s* of Edgar James Whiteman and Merab Wilhelmina Whiteman (*née* Morgan); *m* 1970, Joline Ann Davis; two *d. Educ:* Munro Coll., Jamaica; University Coll. of the West Indies (BA Hons); Univ. of London; Univ. of Birmingham (MEd 1965; Dip. Educnl Admin 1974). Principal, York Castle High Sch., Jamaica, 1959–75; Principal, Brown's Town Community Coll., Jamaica, 1975–89; Minister of State, Jamaican Govt, 1989–91; Minister of Educn, 1992–2002; Minister of Information, 2002–06; Sen. Advr to the Gov. Gen. of Jamaica, 2006. Mem., Electoral Adv. Cttee, Jamaica, 2002–06. Mem. Bd of Govs, Commonwealth of Learning, Vancouver, 2001–08 (Actg Chm., 2007–08). Hon. Mem., Order of the Southern Cross (Brazil), 1998. *Recreation:* occasional writing. *Address:* Jamaican High Commission, 1–2 Prince Consort Road, SW7 2BZ. *T:* (020) 7808 8001; *e-mail:* whitemanb@jhcuk.com, burchell.whiteman@gmail.com.

WHITEMAN, Prof. John Robert, PhD; CMath, FIMA; Distinguished Professor of Numerical Analysis, since 2004 (Professor, since 1981), and Public Orator, since 1999, Brunel University; Director, Brunel Institute of Computational Mathematics, since 1976; *b* 7 Dec. 1938; *s* of Robert Whiteman and Rita (*née* Neale); *m* 1964, Caroline Mary Leigh; two *s* (one *d* decd). *Educ:* Bromsgrove Sch.; Univ. of St Andrews (BSc); Worcester Coll., Oxford (DipEd); Univ. of London (PhD). FIMA 1970. Sen. Lectr, RMCS, Shrivenham, 1963–67; Assistant Professor: Univ. of Wisconsin, 1967–68; Univ. of Texas, Austin, 1968–70; Reader in Numerical Analysis, Brunel Univ., 1970–76; Richard Merton Gästprofessor, Univ. of Münster, 1975–76; Brunel University: Hd of Dept of Maths and Statistics, 1982–90; Vice Principal, 1991–96. Visiting Professor: Univ. of Pisa, 1975; Univ. of Kuwait, 1986; Texas A & M Univ., 1986, 1988, 1989, 1990, 1992; Univ. of Stuttgart, 1989, 1992; Vis. Prof., 1996, Dist. Res. Fellow, 1997–2007, Univ. of Texas at Austin. Lectures: Geary, City Univ., 1986; Robert Todd Gregory, Univ. of Texas, Austin, 1990; Collatz Gedenkkolloquium, Hamburg Univ., 1991; Univ. of Stuttgart, 1995; Brunel,

Brunel Univ., 2004; Ravenscroft, Co. of Glass Sellers, 2004. Vice Pres., UK Inst. of Maths and Its Applications, 2004–05. Member: SERC Maths Cttee, 1981–86 and Science Bd, 1989–91; Bd of Dirs, Eur. Scientific Assoc. for Forming Processes, 1997–. Renter Ward, 2002, Prime Warden, 2003, Master, 2004, Co. of Glass Sellers. FRSA. Hon. DSc West Bohemia Univ., 1995. Editor, Numerical Methods for Partial Differential Equations, 1985–; Member, Editorial Board: Computer Methods in Applied Mechanics and Engrg; Communications in Applied Numerical Methods; Internat. Jl for Numerical Methods in Fluids; Jl of Mathematical Engrg in Industry; Jl of Engrg Analysis; Computational Mechanics Advances. *Publications:* (ed) The Mathematics of Finite Elements and Applications, vols 1–10, 1973, 1976, 1979, 1982, 1985, 1988, 1991, 1994, 1997, 2000, 2003; numerous works on numerical solution of partial differential equations, particularly finite element methods for singularities in elliptic problems and for problems of linear and non linear solid mechanics, incl. viscoelasticity and applications to problems of thermoforming. *Recreations:* walking, swimming, golf, orchestral and choral music. *Address:* Brunel Institute of Computational Mathematics, Brunel University, Uxbridge, Middx UB8 3PH. *T:* (01895) 203270; *e-mail:* john.whiteman@brunel.ac.uk.

WHITEMAN, Joslyn Raphael; Ambassador for Grenada to the People's Republic of China, since 2005; *b* 19 Oct. 1939; *s* of Francis Ignatius and Veronica Whiteman; *m* 1964, Lydia Theodora Purcell; three *s* two *d. Educ:* Presentation Brothers Coll., Grenada. General Post Office, 1968–74; gen. insce consultant, 1974–77; Br. Manager, Amer. Life Insce Co., 1977–2000. Government of Grenada, 1995–2003: Minister: of Agriculture, 1995–96; of Tourism, 1996–2000; of Information, 2000–01; of Implementation, 2001–03. High Comr for Grenada in UK, 2004–05. *Recreations:* golf, table tennis, snooker. *Address:* Embassy of Grenada, T3–2–52, Ta Yuan Diplomatic Office Building, Beijing, China.

WHITEMAN, Peter George; QC 1977; barrister-at-law; a Recorder, since 1989; a Deputy High Court Judge, since 1994; Attorney and Counselor at Law, State of New York; *b* 8 Aug. 1942; *s* of David Whiteman and Betsy Bessie Coster; *m* 1971, Katherine Ruth (*née* Ellenbogen); two *d. Educ:* Warwick Secondary Modern Sch.; Leyton County High Sch.; LSE (LLB, LLM with Distinction). Called to the Bar, Lincoln's Inn, 1967, Bencher, 1985; *ad eundem* Middle Temple, 1977. Lectr, London Univ., 1966–70; Prof. of Law, Univ. of Virginia, 1980. Mem., Faculty of Laws, Florida Univ., 1977; Visiting Professor: Virginia Univ., 1978; Univ. of California at Berkeley, 1980. Mem. Cttee, Unitary Tax Campaign (UK), 1982–. Pres., Dulwich Village Preservation Soc., 1987–97; Chairman: Dulwich against the Rail Link, 1988–97; Dulwich Jt Residents' Cttee, 1991–97. Member: Cttee, Dulwich Picture Gall., 1989–97; Adv. Cttee, Dulwich Estate Govs' Scheme of Management, 1988–97. FRSA. Mem. Bd, Univ. of Virginia Jl of Internat. Law, 1981–. *Publications:* Whiteman on Capital Gains Tax, 1967, 4th edn 1988; Whiteman on Income Tax, 1971, 3rd edn 1988; contrib. British Tax Encyc. *Recreations:* tennis, squash, mountain-walking, jogging, croquet. *Address:* Hollis Whiteman Chambers, Queen Elizabeth Building, Temple, EC4Y 9BS. *T:* (020) 7936 3131.

WHITEMAN, Robert Arthur; Chief Executive, London Borough of Barking and Dagenham, since 2005; *b* 4 Dec. 1961; *s* of late William Whiteman and of Joan Whiteman (*née* Elliott); *m* 1988, Hilary Barbara Cannon; two *s* one *d. Educ:* Univ. of Essex (BA Hons). IRRV 1988; CPFA 1995. W. H. Smith plc, 1983–86; London Borough of Newham, 1986–88; Corp. of London, 1988; Head of Revenues, London Borough of Camden, 1988–96; London Borough of Lewisham: Asst Dir of Finance, 1996–99; Exec. Dir for Resources, 1999–2005; Dep. Chief Exec., 2001–05. Mem. Council, CIPFA, 2004–06. JP Newham, 1996–2005. *Publications:* regular contribs to local authy jls. *Recreations:* DIY, music, gardening. *Address:* (office) Civic Centre, Dagenham, Essex RM10 7BN; *e-mail:* Rob.whiteman@lbbd.gov.uk.

WHITEMAN, Ven. Rodney David Carter; Archdeacon of Cornwall, 2000–05, now Archdeacon Emeritus; *b* Par, Cornwall, 6 Oct. 1940; *s* of Leonard Archibald Whiteman and Sybil Mary (*née* Morshead); *m* 1969, Christine Anne Chelton; one *s* one *d. Educ:* St Austell Grammar School; Pershore Coll. of Horticulture; Ely Theological Coll. Deacon 1964, priest 1965; Curate of Kings Heath, Birmingham, 1964–70; Vicar: St Stephen, Rednal, Birmingham, 1970–79; St Barnabas, Erdington, 1979–89; RD of Aston, 1981–89; Hon. Canon of Birmingham Cathedral, 1985–89; Priest-in-charge of Cardinham with Helland, 1989–94; Hon. Canon of Truro Cathedral, 1989–2005, now Canon Emeritus; Archdeacon of Bodmin, 1989–99. *Recreations:* gardening, music, historic buildings and monuments, walking. *Address:* 22 Treverbyn Gardens, Sandy Hill, St Austell, Cornwall PL25 3AW.

WHITEMORE, Hugh John; dramatist; *b* 16 June 1936; *s* of late Samuel George Whitemore and Kathleen Alma Whitemore (*née* Fletcher); *m* 1st, Jill Brooke (marr. diss.); 2nd, 1976, Sheila Lemon (marr. diss.); one *s*; 3rd, 1998, Rohan McCullough. *Educ:* King Edward VI School, Southampton; RADA. FRSL 1999. Vis. Prof. in Broadcasting Media, Oxford Univ., 2003–04. Hon. Fellow, KCL, 2006. *Stage:* Stevie, Vaudeville, 1977; Pack of Lies, Lyric, 1983; Breaking the Code, Haymarket, 1986, transf. Comedy, 1987 (Amer. Math. Soc. Communications Award, 1990); The Best of Friends, Apollo, 1988, Hampstead, 2006; It's Ralph, Comedy, 1991; A Letter of Resignation, Comedy, 1997, transf. Savoy, 1998; Disposing of the Body, Hampstead, 1999; God Only Knows, Vaudeville, 2000; (adaptation) As You Desire Me, Playhouse, 2005; *television:* plays and dramatisations include: Elizabeth R (Emmy award, 1970); Cider with Rosie (Writer's Guild award, 1971); Country Matters (Writer's Guild award, 1972); Dummy (RAI Prize, Prix Italia, 1979); Concealed Enemies (Emmy award, Neil Simon Jury award, 1984); The Final Days, 1989; A Dance to the Music of Time, 1997 (Script Prize, Monte Carlo Fest., 1998); The Gathering Storm, 2002 (Emmy award, Golden Globe, Writers' Guild of America Award, Peabody Award, 2002); *films:* Stevie, 1980; The Return of the Soldier, 1982; 84 Charing Cross Road, 1986 (Scriptor Award, Los Angeles, 1988); Utz, 1992; Jane Eyre, 1996. *Publications:* (contrib.) Elizabeth R, 1972; Stevie, 1977, new edn 1984; (contrib.) My Drama School, 1978; (contrib.) Ah, Mischief!, 1982; Pack of Lies, 1983; Breaking the Code, 1986; The Best of Friends, 1988; It's Ralph, 1991; A Letter of Resignation, 1997; Disposing of the Body, 1999; God Only Knows, 2001; As You Desire Me (from Pirandello), 2005. *Recreations:* music, movies, reading. *Address:* 67 Peel Street, W8 7PB.

WHITEN, Prof. (David) Andrew, PhD; FBA 2000; AcSS; FRSE; FBPsS; Professor of Evolutionary and Developmental Psychology, since 1997, and Wardlaw Professor, since 2000, University of St Andrews; *b* 20 April 1948; *s* of Bernard Wray Whiten and Maisie (*née* Gathercole); *m* 1973, Dr Susie Challoner; two *d. Educ:* Sheffield Univ. (BSc 1st Cl. Hons Zool. 1969); Bristol Univ. (PhD 1973). FBPsS 1991. SSRC Conversion Fellow, Queen's Coll., Oxford, 1972–75; St Andrew's University: Lectr in Psychol., 1975–90; Reader, 1991–97; Leverhulme Res. Fellow, 1997, 2003–06; Royal Soc. Leverhulme Trust Sen. Res. Fellow, 2006–07. Vis. Prof., Zurich Univ., 1992; F. M. Bird Prof., Emory Univ., 1995–96; British Acad. Res. Reader, 1999–2001. FRSE 2001; AcSS 2003. Jean-Marie Delwart Internat. Scientific Prize, Acad. Royale des Scis de Belgique, 2001; Rivers Meml Medal, RAI, 2007. *Publications:* (ed) Natural Theories of Mind: evolution, development and simulation of everyday mindreading, 1991; (ed with E. Widdowson) Natural Diet and Foraging Strategy of Monkeys, Apes and Humans, 1992; (ed with R. Byrne) Machiavellian Intelligence: social expertise and the evolution of intellect, 1988; Machiavellian Intelligence II: extensions and evaluations, 1997 (trans. Japanese 2000); contrib. many articles on evolution and develt of social intelligence and cultural transmission to learned jls. *Recreations:* friends, family, art, painting, film, music, garden. *Address:* School of Psychology, University of St Andrews, St Andrews, Fife KY16 9JP.

WHITEOAK, John Edward Harrison, MA, CPFA; Managing Director (formerly Managing Partner), WA (formerly Whiteoak) Associates Ltd (Public Sector Consultancy), since 1998; *b* 5 July 1947; *s* of Frank Whiteoak, farmer, and Marion Whiteoak; *m* 1st, 1969, Margaret Elizabeth Blakey (decd); one *s* two *d*; 2nd, 1983, Karen Lynne Wallace Stevenson, MB ChB, BSc (marr. diss. 2004); two *d. Educ:* Sheffield Univ. (MA). CIPFA 1971. Cheshire County Council: Dep. County Treas., 1979–81; County Treas., 1981–94; Gp Dir, Resources, 1994–98; Treas., Cheshire Police Authy, 1995–98. Non-exec. Director: VALPAK Ltd, 1998–2004; Industrial Properties Ltd, 1997–. Financial Advr, ACC, 1984–97. Lead negotiator on local govt finance for local authorities in England, 1994–97; lead finance advr to English County Councils, 1994–98. Member: Soc. of County Treasurers, 1981–98 (Pres., 1997–98); Accounting Standards Cttee, 1984–87. Chartered Institute of Public Finance and Accountancy: Mem., Technical Cttee, 1986–87 and 1991–; Mem., Accounting Panel, 1984–87 (Chm., 1987); Chm., Financial Reporting Panel, 1991–94; Chm., Corporate Governance Panel, 1994–; Pres., NW Region, 1994–95. *Publications:* (jtly) Public Sector Accounting and Financial Control, 1992; contrib. various professional and management journals. *Recreations:* social golf, tennis. *Address:* West Mount, Chester CH3 5UD. *Clubs:* Royal Automobile; City (Chester); Eaton Golf.

WHITEREAD, Rachel, CBE 2006; artist, sculptor; *b* 20 April 1963. *Educ:* Brighton Poly. (BA 1st Cl. Hons); Slade Sch. of Art (DipHE). *Solo exhibitions* include: Ghost, Chisenhale Gall., London, 1990; Stedelijk Van-Abbemuseum, Eindhoven, 1992; Mus. of Contemporary Art, Chicago, 1993; Kunsthalle, Basel, ICA, Philadelphia, ICA, Boston, 1994–95; retrospective, Tate Gall., Liverpool, 1996–97; Reina Sofia, Madrid, 1997; Venice Biennale (Award for Best Young Artist), 1997; Anthony d'Offay Gall., 1998; Serpentine Gall. and Scottish Nat. Gall. of Modern Art, 2001; Deutsche Guggenheim, Berlin, and Solomon Guggenheim Mus., NY, 2001–02; Room 101, V&A Mus., 2003–04; Mus. de Arte Moderna, Rio de Janeiro and São Paulo, 2004; Kunsthaus Bregenz, Austria, Gagosian Gall., London, Embankment for Turbine Hall, Tate Modern, 2005; Luhring Augustine Gall., NY, 2006; Donnaregina Mus. of Contemp. Art, Naples, 2007; Galleria Lorcan O'Neill, Rome, 2007; Centro Arte Contemporaneo, Málaga, 2007. *Public sculptures:* Water Tower Project, NY, 1998; Holocaust Meml, Judenplatz, Vienna, 2000; Monument, Fourth Plinth, Trafalgar Sq., 2001. Deutscher Akademischer Austauschdienst, Berlin, 1992; Turner Prize, 1993; Herbert von Karajan Prize, Salzburg, 1996; Nord LB Art Prize, 2004. *Address:* c/o Lawrence Luhring, Luhring Augustine Gallery, 531 West 24th Street, New York, NY 10011, USA. *T:* (212) 206 9100, *Fax:* (212) 206 9055; c/o Gagosian Gallery, 6–24 Britannia Street, WC1X 9JD. *T:* (020) 7841 9960, *Fax:* (020) 7841 9961.

WHITESIDE, Bernard Gerrard, MBE 1994; HM Diplomatic Service, retired; Ambassador to Ecuador, 2007–08; *b* 3 Oct. 1954; *s* of late Joseph Whiteside and Phoebe Anna (*née* Cummings). *Educ:* St Michael's Coll., Kirkby Lonsdale; Westfield Coll., Univ. of London (BA Hons French and Latin 1977). Entered HM Diplomatic Service, 1979; Moscow, 1983–86; UK Disarmament Delegn, Geneva, 1986–89; FCO, 1989–91; Bogotá, 1991–95; FCO, 1995–99; DFID, 1999–2001; Ambassador to Moldova, 2002–06. *Recreations:* reading, music, travel. *Address: e-mail:* bernardwhiteside@hotmail.com.

WHITEWAY, Paul Robin; HM Diplomatic Service, retired; independent consultant; *b* 1 Dec. 1954; *s* of Frank Whiteway and Patricia (*née* Callaway); *m* 1st, 1980, Melanie Jane Blew (marr. diss.); one *d*; 2nd, 1996, Maha Georges Yannieh; one *s. Educ:* Henley Grammar Sch.; Merton Coll., Oxford (BA Hons Mod. History; MA). Joined FCO, 1977; Far Eastern Dept, 1977–79; Third, later Second Sec., Dublin, 1980–83; First Secretary: Nuclear Energy Dept, 1984–86; Port Stanley, 1986–87; Mexico and Central America Dept, 1987–88; seconded to MoD (Navy), 1988–90; Dep. High Comr, Uganda, 1990–93; Asst Head, Southern Africa Dept, 1993–96; Counsellor and Deputy Head of Mission: Syria, 1996–99; Chile, 2000–03; Dir Internat., Inward Investment Gp, 2003–06, Dir Internat. Sales, Business Gp, 2006–08, UK Trade and Investment. *Recreations:* riding, tennis, history, travel. *Address:* c/o GDP Global Development, St James House, 13 Kensington Square, W8 5HD.

WHITFIELD, family name of **Baron Kenswood**.

WHITFIELD, Adrian; QC 1983; a Recorder of the Crown Court, 1981–2000; *b* 10 July 1937; *s* of Peter Henry Whitfield and Margaret Mary Burns; *m* 1st, 1962, Lucy Caroline Beckett (marr. diss.); two *d*; 2nd, 1971, Niamh O'Kelly; one *s* one *d. Educ:* Ampleforth Coll.; Magdalen Coll., Oxford (Demy; MA). 2nd Lieut, KOYLI (Nat. Service), 1956–58. Called to the Bar, Middle Temple, 1964, Bencher 1990, Treasurer 2005; Member of Western Circuit. *Publications:* contribs on legal matters in legal and medical pubns. *Recreations:* reading, visual arts, travel. *Address:* 47 Faroe Road, W14 0EL. *T:* (020) 7603 8982; 3 Serjeants' Inn, EC4Y 1BQ. *T:* (020) 7427 5000.

WHITFIELD, Alan; transport consultant, 1998–2007; *b* 19 April 1939; *s* of John J. Whitfield and Annie Fothergill-Rawe; *m* 1964, Sheila Carr; two *s. Educ:* Consett Grammar Sch., Durham; Sunderland and Newcastle Colls of Advanced Technology. MICE 1968; MIMunE 1969; FIHT 1984. Surveyor/Engr, NCB, 1956–62; Engrg Asst, Northumberland CC, 1962–70; Department of Transport: Main Grade Engr, 1970–73; Prin. Professional, 1973–76; Suptg Engr, 1976–80; Dep. Dir, Midlands Road Construction Unit, 1980–83; Dir (Transport), W Midlands Reg. Office, 1983–89; Regl Dir, Eastern Region, DoE and Dept of Transport, 1989; Road Prog. Dir, Dept of Transport, 1989–94, Highways Agency, 1994–95. Director: Ove Arup & Partners, 1995–98; Ove Arup & Partners Internat., 1995–98. Associate Consultant, Waterfront Partnership, 1998–2002. *Publications:* papers on cost benefit analysis, centrifugal testing soils, road design and construction, etc. to IHT, ICE, Inst. Geo. Sci., etc. *Recreations:* restoration of old property, golf, music, travel.

WHITFIELD, Prof. Charles Richard, MD; FRCOG; FRCPGlas; Regius Professor of Midwifery in the University of Glasgow, 1976–92, now Emeritus; *b* 21 Oct. 1927; *s* of Charles Alexander and Aileen Muriel Whitfield; *m* 1953, Marion Douglas McKinney; one *s* two *d. Educ:* Campbell Coll., Belfast; Queen's Univ., Belfast (MD). House Surg. and Ho. Phys. appts in Belfast teaching hospitals, 1951–53; Specialist in Obstetrics and Gynaecology, RAMC (Lt-Col retd), 1953–64; Sen. Lectr/Hon. Reader in Dept of Midwifery and Gynaecology, Queen's Univ., Belfast, 1964–74; Consultant to Belfast teaching hosps, 1964–74; Prof. of Obstetrics and Gynaecology, Univ. of Manchester, 1974–76. Mem. Council, RCOG, 1985–91 (Chairman: Subspecialty Bd, 1984–89; Scottish Exec. Cttee, 1985–91; Higher Trng Cttee, 1989–92). *Publications:* (ed)

Dewhurst's Obstetrics and Gynaecology for Postgraduates, 4th edn 1985, 5th edn 1995; papers on perinatal medicine, pregnancy anaemia and other obstetric and gynaec. topics in med. and scientific jls. *Recreations:* food, travel, sun-worship. *Address:* 7 Grange Road, Bearsden, Glasgow G61 3PL.

WHITFIELD, Clovis; Director, Whitfield Fine Art Ltd, since 1979; *b* 21 Oct. 1940; *s* of late Prof. John Humphreys Whitfield; *m* 1st, 1964, Sarah Oppenheim (marr. diss. 1986); two *d*; 2nd, 1986, Dr Irene Cioffi; one *s* one *d*. *Educ:* Corpus Christi Coll., Cambridge (MA 1962); Courtauld Inst. of Art, London. Vis. Prof., Indiana Univ., 1967–68; Associate Dir, Thomas Agnew & Sons Ltd, London, 1970–77; Director: Colnaghi, London, 1978–81, NY, 1983–84; Walpole Gall., London, 1987–91. Cavaliere al Merito (Italy), 1978. Exhibitions: (co-ordinator and joint editor): Painting in Naples: Caravaggio to Giordano, RA and Nat. Gall., Washington, 1982; Classicismo e Natura: la lezione di Domenichino, Capitoline Gall., (joint editor) Rome, 1996. *Publications:* contrib. Burlington mag. *Recreation:* bee-keeping. *Address:* Whitfield Fine Art Ltd, 211 Piccadilly, W1J 9HF. *T:* (020) 7917 1890; *e-mail:* fineart@whitfieldfineart.com. *Club:* Brooks's.

WHITFIELD, Hugh Newbold, FRCS; Consultant Urological Surgeon: London Clinic, since 1979; King Edward VII Hospital, since 1988; *b* 15 June 1944; *s* of George Joshua Newbold Whitfield and Audrey Priscilla Whitfield; *m* 1969, Penelope Joy Craig; two *s*. *Educ:* Gonville and Caius Coll., Cambridge (BA 1965, MA 1969; MB BChir 1968); St Bartholomew's Med. Coll., London (MA 1969, MChir 1978). FRCS 1972. Short service commn, RAMC, 1969–74; Res. Registrar, Inst. of Urology, London, 1974–76; Sen. Registrar, St Bartholomew's Hosp., 1976–79; Consultant Urological Surgeon: St Bartholomew's Hosp., 1979–93; Central Middlesex Hosp., 1993–2000; Reader in Urol., Inst. of Urol. and Nephrol., UCL, 1993–2001; Consultant Urol Surgeon, Royal Berks Hosp., 2001–06. Hon. Consultant: in Urol. to the Army, 1997–; in Paediatric Urol., Hosp. for Sick Children, Gt Ormond St, 1999–2006. Ed., British Jl Urol. Internat., 1994–2002. *Publications:* Urology Pocket Consultant, 1985; Textbook of Genito-Urinary Surgery, 1985, 2nd edn 1998; Rob & Smith's Operative Surgery: Genito-Urinary Surgery, 1992; ABC in Urology, 1996, 2nd edn 2006; articles in urological jls. *Recreations:* music, golf, country pursuits, veteran rowing. *Address:* King Edward VII Consulting Rooms, Emmanuel Kaye House, 37a Devonshire Street, W1G 6QA. *T:* (020) 7935 3095, *Fax:* (020) 7935 3147; *e-mail:* urology@whitfield.uk.net. *Clubs:* Garrick; Leander (Henley).

WHITFIELD, John; solicitor; Senior Partner, Whitfield Hallam Goodall, of Batley, Dewsbury and Mirfield, since 1997; *b* 31 Oct. 1941; *s* of Sydney Richard Whitfield and Mary Rishworth Whitfield; *m*; three *s*; *m* 1999, Janet Gissing (*née* Oldroyd). *Educ:* Sedbergh Sch.; Leeds Univ. (LLB). Solicitor: Bird & Bird, 1966–67; Whitfield Son and Hallam, then Whitfield Hallam Goodall, 1967–. MP (C) Dewsbury, 1983–87. Contested (C): Hemsworth, 1979; Dewsbury, 1987 and 1992. Dir, Leeds Rugby Union Football Club Ltd, 1998–2007. *Recreations:* fishing, shooting, walking with dogs, supporting Leeds Carnegie (Rugby Union). *Address:* Haugh Top Farm, Krumlin, Barkisland, Halifax HX4 0EL. *T:* (01422) 822994. *Clubs:* Mirfield Constitutional; Tanfield Angling (Hon. Sec.); West Park Leeds Rugby Union Football; Octave (Elland).

WHITFIELD, John Flett; JP; DL; Chairman, Surrey Police Authority, 1985–89; Chairman of Police Committee, Association of County Councils, 1985–88; *b* 1 June 1922; *s* of John and Bertha Whitfield; *m* 1946, Rosemary Elisabeth Joan Hartman; two *d*. *Educ:* Epsom Coll., Surrey. Served War, King's Royal Rifle Corps, 1939–46. HM Foreign Service, 1946–57; Director, Materials Handling Equipment (GB) Ltd, 1957–61; London Director, Hunslet Holdings Ltd, 1961–64. Director, Sunningdale Golf Club, 1973–77. Councillor: Berkshire CC, 1961–70; Surrey CC, 1970–89 (Chm., 1981–84). Contested (C) Pontefract, General Election, 1964. JP Berkshire 1971–, Chm. Windsor County Bench, 1978–80; DL Surrey 1982, High Sheriff, 1985–86. Chm., Surrey Univ. Council, 1986–88 (Vice-Chm., 1983–86). *Recreations:* golf, foreign languages, bookbinding. *Address:* Moor Cottage, Chobham Road, Sunningdale, Berks SL5 0HU. *T:* (01344) 620997. *Clubs:* Royal and Ancient Golf of St Andrews; Royal Cinque Ports Golf; Sunningdale Golf; Rye Golf; Woking Golf.

WHITFIELD, June Rosemary, (Mrs T. J. Aitchison), CBE 1998 (OBE 1985); actress; *b* 11 Nov. 1925; *d* of John Herbert Whitfield and Bertha Georgina Whitfield; *m* 1955, Timothy John Aitchison (*d* 2001); one *d*. *Educ:* Streatham Hill High School; RADA (Diploma 1944). Revue, musicals, pantomime, TV and radio; worked with Arthur Askey, Benny Hill, Frankie Howerd, Dick Emery, Bob Monkhouse, Leslie Crowther, Ronnie Barker; first worked with Terry Scott in 1969; *radio:* JW at the BBC, 1997; June Whitfield at the Beeb, 1999; series include: Take It From Here (with Dick Bentley and Jimmy Edwards, 1953–60; The News Huddlines (with Roy Hudd and Chris Emmett), 1984–2000; JW Radio Special, 1992; Like They've Never Been Gone (with Roy Hudd), 1998–; Not Talking, 2007; serials (as Miss Marple): Murder at the Vicarage, 1993; A Pocketful of Rye, 1994; At Bertram's Hotel, 1995; The 4.50 from Paddington, 1996; The Caribbean Mystery, 1997; Nemesis, The Mirror Cracked, 1998; The Body in the Library, 1999; A Murder is Announced, 1999; The Moving Finger, 2001; They Do It With Mirrors, 2001; musical, Gigi, 1997; *films:* Carry on Nurse, 1959; Carry on Abroad, 1972; Bless This House, 1972; Carry on Girls, 1973; Carry On Columbus, 1992; Jude the Obscure, 1996; The Last of the Blonde Bombshells, 2000; *television:* This Is Your Life, 1976 and 1995; South Bank Show, 2007; guest appearance, Amer. TV series, Friends, 1998; series include: Fast and Loose (with Bob Monkhouse), 1954; Faces of Jim (with Jimmy Edwards), 1962, 1963; Beggar My Neighbour, 1966, 1967; Scott On… (with Terry Scott), 1969–73; Happy Ever After, 1974–78; Terry and June, 1979–87; Cluedo, 1990; Absolutely Fabulous, 1993–96, 2001, 2003; What's My Line?, 1994, 1995; Common As Muck, 1996; Family Money, 1997; The Secret, 2000; Last of the Summer Wine, 2005, 2006, 2007, 2008; Green Green Grass, 2007, 2008; Kingdom, Harley Street, 2008; *stage:* An Ideal Husband, Chichester, 1987; Ring Round the Moon, Chichester, 1988; Over My Dead Body, Savoy, 1989; Babes in the Wood, Croydon, 1990, Plymouth, 1991, Cardiff, 1992; Cinderella, Wimbledon, 1994; Bedroom Farce, Aldwych, 2002; On the Town, ENO, 2007. Freeman, City of London, 1982. Lifetime Achievement Award, British Comedy Awards, 1994; RTS Hall of Fame, 1999. *Publication:* And June Whitfield (autobiog.), 2000. *Address:* c/o Maureen Vincent, United Agents, 12–26 Lexington Street, W1F 0LE.

WHITFIELD, Dr Michael, CChem, FRSC; CBiol, FIBiol; FGS; Vice President, Marine Biological Association, since 2000 (Director and Secretary, 1987–99); Director, Plymouth Marine Laboratory, 1994–96 (Deputy Director, 1988–94); *b* 15 June 1940; *s* of Arthur and Ethel Whitfield; *m* 1961, Jean Ann Rowe (*d* 1984); one *s* three *d*. *Educ:* Univ. of Leeds (BSc 1st cl. Hons Chem.; PhD Chem.). FRSC 1980; FIBiol 1994; FGS 2001. Research Scientist, CSIRO Div. of Fisheries and Oceanography, Cronulla, NSW, 1964–69; Vis. Res. Fellow, KTH Stockholm, 1969, Univ. of Liverpool, 1970; Res. Scientist, Marine Biolog. Assoc., 1970–87. Vice Pres., Sir Alister Hardy Foundn for Ocean Science, 1991–99; Pres., Challenger Soc. for Marine Science, 1996–98. FRSA 1992. Dr (*hc*): Göteborg, 1991; Plymouth, 2000. *Publications:* Ion-selective electrodes for the analysis of natural waters, 1970; Marine Electrochemistry, 1981; Tracers in the Ocean, 1988; Light and Life in the Sea, 1990; Aquatic Life Cycle Strategies, 1999; numerous papers in professional jls. *Recreations:* hill walking, bird watching, photography. *Address:* The Laboratory, Citadel Hill, Plymouth PL1 2PB. *T:* (01752) 633331.

WHITFIELD, Prof. Roderick; Percival David Professor of Chinese and East Asian Art, University of London, 1993–2002, now Professor Emeritus (Professor of Chinese and East Asian Art, and Head of Percival David Foundation of Chinese Art, 1984–93); *b* 20 July 1937; *s* of late Prof. John Humphreys Whitfield and Joan Herrin, ARCA; *m* 1st, 1963, Frances Elizabeth Oldfield, PhD (marr. diss 1983), *e d* of late Prof. R. C. Oldfield and Lady Kathleen Oldfield; one *s* two *d*; 2nd, 1983, Youngsook Pak, PhD, art historian, *e d* of late Pak Sang-Jon, Seoul. *Educ:* Woodbourne Acad.; King Edward's Sch., Birmingham; Sch. of Oriental and African Studies (Civil Service Interpreter, 2nd cl.); St John's Coll., Cambridge (BA Hons 1960, Oriental Studies Tripos; MA 1966); Princeton Univ. (MFA 1963, PhD 1965). Research Associate and Lectr, Princeton, 1965–66; Research Fellow, St John's Coll., Cambridge, 1966–68; Asst Keeper I, Dept of Oriental Antiquities, British Museum, 1968–84. Visiting Professor: Univ. of Heidelberg, 1996; Univ. of Helsinki, 1997; Univ. of Barcelona, 1998; Univ. of Oslo, 2002; City Univ. of Hong Kong, 2003; Univ. of Hong Kong, 2004; Yale Univ., 2007. Teetzel Lectr, Univ. of Toronto, 1995. Pres., Circle of Inner Asian Art, 1996–. Trustee, Inst. of Buddhist Studies, 1987–. Corresp. Fellow, Dunhuang Res. Acad., 1999–; Fellow, Palace Mus., Beijing, 2003–. Mem. Editl Bd, Artibus Asiae, 1992–. *Publications:* In Pursuit of Antiquity: Chinese paintings of Ming and Ch'ing dynasties in collection of Mr and Mrs Earl Morse, 1969; The Art of Central Asia: the Stein collection at the British Museum, 3 vols, 1983–85; (ed) Treasures from Korea, 1984; (ed) Korean Art Treasures, 1986; (ed) Early Chinese Glass, 1988; Caves of the Thousand Buddhas, 1990; (ed) Problems in Meaning in Early Chinese Ritual Bronzes, 1993; Fascination of Nature: plants and insects in Chinese paintings and ceramics of the Yuan dynasty, 1993; Dunhuang, Caves of the Singing Sands: Buddhist Art from the Silk Road, 2 vols, 1995; (trans. jtly) The Arts of Central Asia: the Pelliot Collection in the Musée Guimet, 1996; (ed jtly) Exploring China's Past: new researches and discoveries in Chinese archaeology, 2000; (jtly) The Mogao Caves, 2000; (jtly) Handbooks of Korean Art: pottery and celadon, 2002; (jtly) Buddhist Sculpture, 2002; (ed) Folk Painting, 2002; (contrib.) New Perspectives on China's Past: Chinese archaeology in the twentieth century, 2004; (trans. and ed jtly) Korean True-View Landscape: paintings by Chŏng Sŏn (1676–1759), 2005; articles in Asiatische Studien, Artibus Asiae, Buddhica Britannica, Orientations, Burlington Magazine, British Liby Jl, Bukkyo Geijutsu (Ars Buddhica), Zijincheng and other jls. *Address:* 7 St Paul's Crescent, NW1 9XN. *T:* (020) 7267 2888.

WHITFIELD, Sir William, Kt 1993; CBE 1976; RIBA; Senior Partner, Whitfield Partners, architects. DipArch; DipTP. Prof. of Architecture, Victoria Univ. of Manchester, 1981. Surveyor to the Fabric, St Paul's Cathedral, 1985–90. Formerly: Mem., Royal Fine Art Commn; Trustee, British Museum.

WHITFIELD LEWIS, Herbert John; *see* Lewis.

WHITHAM, Prof. Gerald Beresford, FRS 1965; Charles Lee Powell Professor of Applied Mathematics, at the California Institute of Technology, Pasadena, Calif, 1983–98, now Emeritus Professor of Applied Mathematics; *b* 13 Dec. 1927; *s* of Harry and Elizabeth Ellen Whitham; *m* 1951, Nancy (*née* Lord); one *s* two *d*. *Educ:* Elland Gram. Sch., Elland, Yorks; Manchester University (PhD Maths 1953). Lectr in Applied Mathematics, Manchester Univ., 1953–56; Assoc. Prof., Applied Mathematics, New York Univ., 1956–59; Prof., Mathematics, MIT, 1959–62; Prof. of Aeronautics and Maths, 1962–67, Prof. of Applied Maths, 1967–83, CIT. FAAAS 1959. Wiener Prize in Applied Mathematics, 1980. *Publications:* Linear and Nonlinear Waves, 1974; Lectures on Wave Propagation, 1979; research papers in Proc. Roy. Soc., Jl Fluid Mechanics, Communications on Pure and Applied Maths.

WHITING, Alan; Managing Director, Merlan Financial, since 2004; *b* 14 Jan. 1946; *s* of Albert Edward and Marjorie Irene Whiting; *m* 1968, Annette Frances Pocknee; two *s* two *d*. *Educ:* Acklam Hall Grammar Sch., Middlesbrough; Univ. of East Anglia (BA Hons); University College London (MSc Econ). Research Associate and Asst Lectr, Univ. of East Anglia, 1967; Cadet Economist, HM Treasury, 1968; Economic Asst, DEA, and Min. of Technology, 1969; Economist, EFTA, Geneva, 1970; Economist, CBI, 1972; Economic Adviser, DTI, 1974; Sen. Econ. Adviser, 1979; Industrial Policy Div., Dept of Industry, 1983–85; Under Sec., Economics Div., DTI, 1985; Finance and Resource Management Div., DTI, 1989–92; Under Sec., Securities and Investment Services, later Financial Regulation, HM Treasury, 1992–97; Exec. Dir, Regulation and Compliance, London Metal Exchange, 1997–2004. Director: Nymex Europe Ltd, 2005–07; NYSE/Euronext/LIFFE, 2006–. Dep. Chm., Mortgage Code Compliance Bd (formerly Council of Mortgage Code Register Intermediaries), 1999–2005; Mem., Gibraltar Financial Services Commn, 2005–; Dir, Banking Code Standards Bd, 2005–. *Publications:* (jtly) The Trade Effects of EFTA and the EEC 1959–1967, 1972; (ed) The Economics of Industrial Subsidies, 1975; articles in economic jls. *Recreations:* building, gardening, music, sailing, tennis. *Address:* The Willows, Larges Lane, Bracknell, RG12 9AN. *Clubs:* Bracknell Lawn Tennis; Mill Ride Golf (Ascot).

WHITING, Prof. Brian, MD; FRCPGlas, FRCPE, FMedSci; Professor of Clinical Pharmacology, 1986–2001, Dean, Faculty of Medicine, and Head of Clinical Medicine Planning Unit, 1992–2000, University of Glasgow; *b* 6 Jan. 1939; *s* of late Leslie George Whiting and of Evelyn Irene Edith Whiting (*née* Goss); *m* 1st, 1967, Jennifer Mary Tait (marr. diss. 1983); two *d*; 2nd, 1990, Marlene Shields (*née* Watson); two step *s*. *Educ:* Univ. of Glasgow (MB ChB 1964; MD 1970). FRCPGlas 1979; FRCPE 1996. House Officer, Western Infirmary and Stobhill Gen. Hosp., Glasgow, 1964; University of Glasgow: Department of Materia Medica: Hutchison Res. Schol., 1965; Registrar in Medicine, 1966–68; Lectr and Sen. Registrar in Clinical Pharmacol., 1969–77; Sen. Lectr and Consultant Physician, 1977–82; Reader in Clinical Pharmacol., 1982–86; Hd, Div. of Clinical Pharmacol., Dept of Medicine and Therapeutics, 1989–91. Dir, Clinical Pharmacokinetics Lab., Stobhill Gen. Hosp., Glasgow, 1980–90. Vis. Scientist, Div. of Clinical Pharmacol., Univ. of Calif, San Francisco, 1978–79; Internat. Union of Pharmacol. Vis. Consultant, India and Nepal, 1985; Visiting Professor of Clinical Pharmacology: Univ. of Auckland, 1987; (British Council) Japan, 1988; British Council and Internat. Union of Pharmacol., India and Nepal, 1990. Non-exec. Mem., Gtr Glasgow Health Bd, 1994–2000. Member: Assoc. of Physicians of GB and Ireland, 1985–; GMC, 1991–96. Founder FFPM (by Dist.) 1990; Founder FMedSci 1998. *Publications:* (ed jdy) Lecture Notes on Clinical Pharmacology, 1982, 6th edn 2001; contrib. numerous articles or book chapters, principally in field of clinical pharmacology. *Recreations:* painting, music (listening and composition), mountaineering. *Address:* 2 Milner Road, Glasgow G13 1QL. *T:* (0141) 959 2324.

WHITING, Clifford Hamilton, ONZ 1999; artist; Kaihautu (Leader), Te Papa Tongarewa Museum of New Zealand, 1993–2000; *b* 6 May 1936; *s* of Frank Whiting and Huriana Herewini (Whanau A-Apanui Tribal Gp); *m* 1957, Heather Leckie; three *s*. *Educ:* Wellington Teachers' Coll.; Dunedin Teachers' Coll. (Trained Teachers' Cert.). Art

Advr, Dept of Educn, 1958–71; Lectr in Art, Palmerston North Teachers' Coll., 1972–81; freelance artist, multi media murals, illustrations, photography, print-making, carving, engraving and painting, 1981–. Mem. and Chm., Maori and S Pacific Arts Council and TeWakaToi, 1980–94; Vice-Chm., QEII Arts Council, 1990–93. Hon. DLitt Massey, 1996. *Publication:* Mataora, 1996. *Recreations:* fishing, yachting, diving. *Address:* 24 Gould Street, Russell 0202, Bay of Islands, New Zealand. *T:* (9) 4037726.

WHITING, Maj.-Gen. Graham Gerald M.; *see* Messervy-Whiting.

WHITING, Rev. Peter Graham, CBE 1984; Minister, Beechen Grove Baptist Church, 1985–95; *b* 7 Nov. 1930; *s* of late Rev. Arthur Whiting and Olive Whiting; *m* 1960, Lorena Inns; two *s* three *d. Educ:* Yeovil Grammar Sch.; Irish Baptist Theol Coll., Dublin. Ordained into Baptist Ministry, 1956. Minister, King's Heath, Northampton, 1956–62; commnd RAChD, 1962; Regtl Chaplain, 1962–69 (Chaplain to 1st Bn The Parachute Regt, 1964–66); Sen. Chaplain, 20 Armd Bde and Lippe Garrison, BAOR, 1969–72; Staff Chaplain, HQ BAOR, 1973–74; Sen. Chaplain, 24 Airportable Bde, 1974–75; Dep. Asst Chaplain Gen., W Midland Dist, Shrewsbury, 1975–78 (Sen. Chaplain, Young Entry Units, 1976–78); Asst Chaplain Gen., 1st British Corps, BAOR, 1978–81; Dep. Chaplain Gen. to the Forces (Army), 1981–84. QHC 1981–85. *Address:* 5 Pook Lane, Warblington, Havant, Hants PO9 2TH.

WHITLAM, Hon. (Edward) Gough, AC 1978; QC 1962; Member: Executive Board of Unesco, 1985–89 (Australian Ambassador to Unesco, 1983–86); Constitutional Commission, 1986–88; Prime Minister of Australia, 1972–75; *b* 11 July 1916; *s* of late H. F. E. Whitlam, Australian Crown Solicitor and Aust. rep. on UN Human Rights Commission; *m* 1942, Margaret Elaine, AO, *d* of late Mr Justice Dovey, NSW Supreme Court; three *s* one *d. Educ:* University of Sydney. BA 1938; LLB 1946. RAAF Flight Lieut, 1941–45. Barrister, 1947; MP for Werriwa, NSW, 1952–78; Mem., Jt Parly Cttee on Constitutional Rev., 1956–59; Leader, 1973 and 1975, Dep. Leader, 1977, Constnl Conventions; Deputy Leader, Aust. Labor Party, 1960, Leader, 1967–77; Leader of the Opposition, 1967–72 and 1976–77; Minister for Foreign Affairs, 1972–73. Vis. Fellow, 1978–79, First Nat. Fellow, 1980–81, ANU; Fellow, Univ. of Sydney Senate, 1981–83, 1986–89; Visiting Professor: Harvard Univ., 1979; Univ. of Adelaide, 1983. Chairman: Australia-China Council, 1986–91; Australian Nat. Gall., 1987–90. Pres., Australian Sect., Internat. Commn of Jurists, 1982–83. Founder, Hanoi Architectural Heritage Foundn, 1993. FAHA 1993. Corresp. Mem., Acad. of Athens, 1992. Hon. DLitt: Sydney, 1981; Wollongong, 1989; La Trobe, Wodonga, 1992; Univ. of Technol., Sydney, 1995; Univ. of Western Sydney, 2002; Hon. LLD Philippines, 1974. Silver Plate of Honour, Socialist Internat., 1976; Mem. of Honour, IUCN, 1988; Redmond Barry Award, Australian Library and Info. Assoc., 1994; Dunlop Asia Award, 2001; Friendship Ambassador, China, 2002. Grand Cross of Apostle Andrew, Greek Orthodox Archdio. of Australia, 2002. Grand Cross, Order of Makarios III (Cyprus), 1983; Grand Comdr, Order of Honour (Greece), 1996; Order of the Phoenix (Greece), 1998; Grand Officer, Order of Merit (Italy), 1999 (Comdr, 1997); Grand Comdr, Order of Logohu (PNG), 2005; Grand Cordon, Order of the Rising Sun (Japan), 2006. *Publications:* The Constitution *versus* Labor, 1957; Australian Foreign Policy, 1963; Socialism within the Constitution, 1965; Australia, Base or Bridge?, 1966; Beyond Vietnam: Australia's Regional Responsibility, 1968; An Urban Nation, 1969; A New Federalism, 1971; Urbanised Australia, 1972; Australian Public Administration and the Labor Government, 1973; Australia's Foreign Policy: New Directions, New Definitions, 1973; Road to Reform: Labor in Government, 1975; The New Federalism: Labor's Programs and Policies, 1975; Government of the People, for the People—by the People's House, 1975; On Australia's Constitution, 1977; Reform During Recession, 1978; The Truth of the Matter, 1979, 3rd edn 2005; The Italian Inspiration in English Literature, 1980; A Pacific Community, 1981; The Cost of Federalism, 1983; The Whitlam Government 1972–75, 1985; International Law-Making, 1989; Australia's Administrative Amnesia, 1990; Living with the United States: British Dominions and New Pacific States, 1990; National and International Maturity, 1991; Human Rights in One Nation, 1992; Abiding Interests, 1997; My Italian Notebook, 2002. *Address:* 100 William Street, Sydney, NSW 2011, Australia.

See also N. R. Whitlam.

WHITLAM, Michael Richard, CBE 2000; charity consultant; Director and Owner, Mike Whitlam - Solutions for Charity, consultancy, since 2001; *b* 25 March 1947; *s* of late Richard William Whitlam and Mary Elizabeth Whitlam (*née* Land); *m* 1968, Anne Jane McCurley; two *d. Educ:* Morley Grammar Sch.; Tadcaster Grammar Sch.; Coventry Coll. of Educn, Univ. of Warwick (Cert. of Educn); Home Office Prison Dept Staff Coll. (Qual. Asst Governor Prison Dept); Cranfield Coll. of Technology (MPhil 1988). Biology teacher, Ripon, 1968–69; Asst Governor, HM Borstal, Hollesley Bay and HM Prison, Brixton, 1969–74; Dir, Hammersmith Teenage Project, NACRO, 1974–78; Dep. Dir/Dir, UK ops, Save the Children Fund, 1978–86; Chief Exec., RNID, 1986–90; Dir-Gen., BRCS, 1991–99; Chief Exec., Mentor Foundn (Internat.), 1999–2001; Chief Executive Officer: Internat. Agency for the Prevention of Blindness, 2002–05; Vision 2020 the Right to Sight, 2002–05. Special Charity Advr to Russam GMS, 2005–. Board Member: Britcross Ltd, 1991–99; British Red Cross Events Ltd, 1991–99; British Red Cross Trading, 1991–99; REACH, 1997–; Chm., Sound Advantage plc, 1988–90. Chm., Ofcom Adv. Cttee for Older and Disabled People, 2004–. Non-exec. Dir, Hillingdon PCT, 2004–. Member: Exec. Council, Howard League, 1974–84; Community Alternative Young Offenders Cttee, NACRO, 1979–82; Exec. Council, Nat. Children's Bureau, 1980–86; Bd, City Literary Inst., 1989–90; Bd, Charity Appointments Ltd, 1990–99; Dir, Watford FC Community Educn Trust, 2007–; Chairman: London Intermediate Treatment Assoc., 1980–83; and Founder, ACEVO (formerly ACENVO), 1988– (Mem. Policy and Res. Gp, 1994–99); Prisoners Abroad, 1999–2003; Chalker Foundn for Africa, 2007–. FRSA 1995; CCMI (CIMgt 1997). Mem., St Giles Church, Ickenham. *Publications:* numerous papers on juvenile delinquency and charity management. *Recreations:* painting, walking, family activities, voluntary organisations, politics, visiting France, cooking, motorcaravanning. *Address:* 40 Pepys Close, Ickenham, Middx UB10 8NY. *T:* (01895) 678169; *e-mail:* m.whitlam@btinternet.com. *Club:* New Cavendish.

WHITLAM, Nicholas Richard; banker and company director; Chairman, Whitlam & Co., 1990–2002 and since 2003; proprietor, Mount Kembla Hotel, 2004–07; *b* 6 Dec. 1945; *s* of Hon. (Edward) Gough Whitlam, *qv*; *m* 1973, Sandra Judith Frye; two *s* one *d. Educ:* Sydney High Sch.; Harvard Coll. (AB Hons); London Business Sch. (MBA). Morgan Guaranty Trust Co., 1969–75; American Express Co., 1975–78; Banque Paribas, 1978–80; Comr, Rural Bank of New South Wales, 1980–81, then Man. Dir, State Bank of New South Wales, 1981–87; Man. Dir, Whitlam Turnbull & Co. Ltd, 1987–90; Dep. Chm., Export Finance and Insurance Corp., 1991–94; Advr, Asian Capital Partners, 1993–96. Director: Port Kembla Port Corp., 2004– (Chm., 2005–); WorkCover Insurance Fund Investment Bd, 2005– (Dep. Chm., 2004–). Board Member: Aust. Trade Commn, 1985–91; Integral Energy Aust., 1996–99. Dir, Lifetime Care and Support Authy of NSW, 2006–. Pres., NRMA, 1996–2002 (Dep. Pres., 1995–96); Chm., NRMA Insce Ltd, 1996–2001. Board Member: Aust. Graduate Sch. of Management, 1982–97 (Chm., 1988–97; Chm., Adv. Council, 1997–99; Mem., Adv. Council, 1999–); Aust. Sports Foundn, 1986–95; Chm., Sydney Symphony Orch., 1991–96; Mem. Symphony Council, 1996–2005; Trustee, Sydney Cricket and Sports Ground, 1984–88. DUniv NSW, 1996. *Publications:* (with John Stubbs) Nest of Traitors, 1974; Still Standing, 2004. *Recreations:* swimming, cycling. *Address:* PO Box 72, Austinmer, NSW 2515, Australia. *Fax:* (2) 42682566. *Clubs:* Hong Kong; Tattersall's (Sydney) (Chm., 1993–96).

WHITLEY, Edward Thomas; Chief Executive Officer, International Financial Services, London, 2001–07; *b* 6 May 1954; *s* of John Caswell Whitley and Shirley Frances Whitley (*née* Trollope); *m* 1984, Hon. Tara Olivia Chichester-Clark, *d* of Baron Moyola, PC (NI); one *s. Educ:* Harrow Sch.; Univ. of Bristol (BSc). Chartered accountant; Price Waterhouse, 1976–81; Cazenove & Co., 1981–2001, Partner, 1988–2001. Dir, Henderson Strata Investments plc, 1990–2005. Chm., Financial Services Sector Adv. Gp, 2005–06. Mem., Council of Mgt, Restoration of Appearance and Function Trust, 1999–; Trustee, World Trade Center Disaster Fund, 2001–06. Hon. Pres., S Derry Wildfowl and Game Preservation Soc., 2002–.

WHITLEY, Elizabeth Young, (Mrs H. C. Whitley); social worker and journalist; *b* 28 Dec. 1915; *d* of Robert Thom and Mary Muir Wilson; *m* 1939, Henry Charles Whitley (Very Rev. Dr H. C. Whitley, CVO; *d* 1976); two *s* two *d* (and one *s* decd). *Educ:* Laurelbank School, Glasgow; Glasgow University. MA 1936; courses: in Italian at Perugia Univ., 1935, in Social Science at London School of Economics and Glasgow School of Social Science, 1938–39. Ran Girls' Clubs in Govan and Plantation, Glasgow, and Young Mothers' Clubs in Partick and Port Glasgow; Vice-Chm. Scottish Association of Girls' Clubs and Mixed Clubs, 1957–61, and Chm. of Advisory Cttee, 1958–59. Broadcast regular programme with BBC (Scottish Home Service), 1953. Member: Faversham Committee on AID, 1958–60; Pilkington Committee on Broadcasting, 1960–62. Columnist, Scottish Daily Express. Adopted as Parly candidate for SNP by West Perth and Kinross, 1968. *Publications:* Plain Mr Knox, 1960; The Two Kingdoms: the story of the Scottish covenanters, 1977; descriptive and centenary articles for Scottish papers, particularly Glasgow Herald and Scotland's Magazine. *Recreations:* listening to Radio 4 and Radio Scotland, gardening. *Address:* The Glebe, Southwick, by Dumfries DG2 8AR. *T:* (01387) 780276.

WHITLEY, His Honour John Reginald; a Circuit Judge, 1986–96; Resident Judge, Portsmouth Combined Court Centre, 1988–96; *b* 22 March 1926; *o s* of late Reginald Whitley and of Marjorie Whitley (*née* Orton); *m* 1966, Susan Helen Kennaway; one *d. Educ:* Sherborne Sch.; Corpus Christi Coll., Cambridge. Served War, Army, Egypt, Palestine, 1944–48; commissioned, KRRC, 1945. Called to the Bar, Gray's Inn, 1953; Western Circuit, 1953; a Recorder, 1978–86. *Recreation:* golf. *Address:* Kingsrod, Friday's Hill, Kingsley Green, near Haslemere, Surrey GU27 3LL.

WHITLEY, Susan Alison; *see* Bradbury, S. A.

WHITMORE, Sir Clive (Anthony), GCB 1988 (KCB 1983); CVO 1983; Director, N. M. Rothschild & Sons Ltd, since 1994; *b* 18 Jan. 1935; *s* of Charles Arthur Whitmore and Louisa Lilian Whitmore; *m* 1961, Jennifer Mary Thorpe; one *s* two *d. Educ:* Sutton Grammar Sch., Surrey; Christ's Coll., Cambridge (BA). Asst Principal, WO, 1959; Private Sec. to Permanent Under-Sec. of State, WO, 1961; Asst Private Sec. to Sec. of State for War, 1962; Principal, 1964; Private Sec. to Permanent Under-Sec. of State, MoD, 1969; Asst Sec., 1971; Asst Under-Sec. of State (Defence Staff), MoD, 1975; Under Sec., Cabinet Office, 1977; Principal Private Sec. to the Prime Minister, 1979–82; Dep. Sec., 1981; Permanent Under-Secretary of State: MoD, 1983–88; Home Office, 1988–94. Director: Racal Electronics, 1994–2000; Boots Co., 1994–2001; Morgan Crucible Co. PLC, 1994–2004. Mem., Security Commn, 1998–. Chancellor, De Montfort Univ., 1995–97; Chm. Council, Inst. of Educn, Univ. of London, 1995–2000. *Recreations:* gardening, listening to music. *Address:* c/o N. M. Rothschild & Sons Ltd, New Court, St Swithin's Lane, EC4P 4DU.

WHITMORE, David John Ludlow, FCA; Chief Executive, Compass Management Consulting Group, since 2007; *b* 20 July 1959; *s* of Dr John L. Whitmore and Joan C. Whitmore (*née* Hale); *m* 1984, Monica Mary Boyd; two *s* one *d. Educ:* Carisbrooke High Sch., IoW; Univ. of Warwick (BSc Hons Accounting and Financial Analysis). ACA 1984, FCA 1989; CPA(US) 1988. Joined Arthur Andersen, 1980; worked in: London, 1980–84; LA, 1984–86; World HQ, Chicago, 1986–87; LA, 1987–89; London, 1989–2002; Partner, 1991; Head, Commercial Assurance and Business Adv. Practice, 1995–97; Managing Partner: UK Assurance and Business Adv. Practice, 1997–2001; Global Assurance and Business Adv. Markets, 2001–02; Pres., Europe, Proudfoot Consulting, 2004; Chief Exec., 4 Future Gp, 2005–06. Mem. Adv. Bd, Warwick Business Sch., 2001–. *Recreations:* golf, tennis, reading. *Clubs:* Royal Automobile; Liphook Golf.

WHITMORE, Sir John (Henry Douglas), 2nd Bt *cr* 1954; Senior Partner, Performance Consultants, since 1998; *b* 16 Oct. 1937; *s* of Col Sir Francis Henry Douglas Charlton Whitmore, 1st Bt, KCB, CMG, DSO, TD, and Lady Whitmore (*née* Ellis Johnsen); *S* father, 1961; *m* 1st, 1962, Gunilla (marr. diss. 1969), *e d* of Sven A. Hansson, OV, KLH, Danderyd, and *o d* of Mrs Ella Hansson, Stockholm, Sweden; one *d*; 2nd, 1977, Diana Elaine, *e d* of Fred A. Becchetti, California, USA; one *s. Educ:* Stone House, Kent; Eton; Sandhurst; Cirencester. Active in personal development and social change; retired professional racing driver; business trainer and sports psychologist. *Publications:* The Winning Mind, 1987; Superdriver, 1988; Coaching for Performance, 1992; Need, Greed or Freedom, 1997; Mind Games, 1998. *Recreations:* ski-ing, squash. *Heir: s* Jason Whitmore, *b* 26 Jan. 1983. *Address:* Unit 6, Park Lane, Crowborough, E Sussex TN6 2QN; *e-mail:* Johnwhitmore@performanceconsultants.com. *Club:* British Racing Drivers.

WHITMORE, Mark Graham; Director of Collections, Imperial War Museum, since 2003; *b* 8 July 1952; *s* of Prof. Raymond L. Whitmore, AM and Ruth H. Whitmore; *m* 1975, Laura Diane Vincent; one *s* three *d. Educ:* Univ. of Queensland (BRTP Hons 1975); Univ. of Melbourne (MEnvS 1986). Urban and Envmtl Planner, Gutteridge, Haskins and Davey, 1983–87; Sen. Curator, Hist. of Technol., Qld Mus., 1987–90; Australian War Memorial: Sen. Curator, Military Technol., 1990–95; Asst Dir (Nat. Collection), 1995–2003. Museums Australia: Pres., ACT Br., 2000–03; Mem., Nat. Council, 2000–03. Trustee, Sir Winston Churchill Archive, 2006–. *Publication:* 'Mephisto' A7V Sturmpanzerwagen 506, 1989. *Recreations:* music, photography, art, travel, operating antique steam machinery, restoring classic cars. *Address:* Imperial War Museum, Lambeth Road, SE1 6HZ.

WHITNEY, Prof. David John; Director, Clinical Management Unit, Keele University, since 2001; *b* 1 Sept. 1950; *s* of Leonard and Joyce Susannah Whitney; *m* 1979, Pauline Jane; one *s* two *d. Educ:* Exeter Univ. (BA Hons); London Univ. (MA). Dep. House Governor, Moorfields Eye Hosp., 1982–85; Regl Dir of Planning, Trent RHA, 1985–90; Chief Exec., Central Sheffield Univ. Hosps NHS Trust, 1991–2001. Prof. Associate, Sheffield Centre for Health and Related Res., Univ. of Sheffield, 1995–. FRSA.

Recreations: soccer, tennis, squash, art, music. *Address:* Clinical Management Unit, Darwin Building, Keele University, Keele, Staffs ST5 5SR.

WHITNEY, John Norton Braithwaite, CBE 2008; Chairman: Friends Provident Charitable Foundation, 2002–06; Council, Royal Academy of Dramatic Art, 2003–07; *b* 20 Dec. 1930; *s* of Dr Willis Bevan Whitney and Dorothy Anne Whitney; *m* 1956, Roma Elizabeth Hodgson; one *s* one *d*. *Educ:* Leighton Park Friends' Sch. Radio producer, 1951–64; formed Ross Radio Productions, 1951, and Autocue, 1955; founded Radio Antilles, 1963; Founder Dir, Sagitta Prodns, 1968–82; Man. Dir, Capital Radio, 1973–82; Dir Gen., IBA, 1982–89; Dir, The Really Useful Group Ltd, 1990–97 (Man. Dir, 1989–90; Chm., 1990–95); Chm., Trans World Communications plc, 1992–94. Dir, Duke of York's Theatre, 1979–82. Chm., Friends' Provident Ethical Investment Trust plc, 1992–; Dir, Friends' Provident Life Office, 1982–2002 (Chm., Friends' Provident Stewardship Cttee of Reference, 1985–2000); Chairman: Radio Joint Audience Research Ltd, 1992–2002; Sony Music Pace Partnership (National Bowl), 1992–95; Enterprise Radio Hldgs Ltd, 1994–96; Radio Partnership, 1996–99; Caspian Publishing Ltd, 1996–2002; Director: VCI plc, 1995–98; Galaxy Media Corp. plc, 1997–2000; Far Pavilions Ltd, 1997–; Bird & Co. International, 1999–2001 (Chm.). Chm., Assoc. of Indep. Local Radio Contractors, 1973, 1974, 1975 and 1980. Wrote, edited and devised numerous television series, 1956–82. Chm., Sony Radio Awards Cttee, 1991–97; Vice Pres., Japan Festival 1991, 1991–92 (Chm., Festival Media Cttee, 1991); Trustee, Japan Educn Trust, 1993–; Member: Bd, NT, later RNT, 1982–94 (Trustee, Pension and Life Assce, RNT, 1994–2003); Films, TV and Video Adv. Cttee, British Council, 1983–89; RCM Centenary Develt Fund (formerly Appeals Cttee), 1982– (Chm., Media and Events Cttee, 1982–94); Bd, Open Coll., 1987–89; Council for Charitable Support, 1989–92; Bd, City of London Sinfonia, 1994–2001; Exec. Cttee, Musicians Benevolent Fund, 1995–2001; Council: Royal London Aid Society, 1966–90; TRIC, 1979–89 (Pres., 1985–86; Companion, 1989–); Fairbridge (formerly Drake Fellowship, then Fairbridge Drake Soc.), 1981–96 (Vice Pres., 1996–); RSA, 1994–99; Chm., British Amer. Arts Assoc., 1992–95. Pres., London Marriage Guidance Council, 1983–90; Vice President: Commonwealth Youth Exchange Council, 1982–83; RNID, 1988–; Chm., Trustees, Soundaround (National Sound Magazine for the Blind), 1981–2000 (Life Pres., 2000); Chm., Artsline, 1983–2000 (Life Pres., 2001); Trustee: Venture Trust, 1982–86; Hosp. Broadcasting Assoc. Patron, MusicSpace Trust, 1990–; Governor: English Nat. Ballet (formerly London Festival Ballet), 1989–91; Bd, Performing Arts and Technol. Sch., 1992–2001; Chm., Theatre Investment Fund, 1990–2001. Fellow and Vice Pres., RTS, 1986–89; Fellow, Radio Acad., 1996. FRSA; Hon. RCM. *Recreations:* chess, photography, sculpture. *Address:* 5 Church Close, Todber, Dorset DT10 1JH. *Clubs:* Army and Navy, Garrick, Pilgrims, Whitefriars.

WHITNEY, Sir Raymond (William), Kt 1997; OBE 1968; *b* 28 Nov. 1930; *o s* of late George Whitney, Northampton; *m* 1956, Sheila Margot Beswick Prince; two *s*. *Educ:* Wellingborough Sch.; RMA, Sandhurst; London Univ. (BA (Hons) Oriental Studies). Commnd Northamptonshire Regt, 1951; served in Trieste, Korea, Hong Kong, Germany; seconded to Australian Army HQ, 1960–63; resigned and entered HM Diplomatic Service, 1964; First Sec., Peking, 1966–68; Head of Chancery, Buenos Aires, 1969–72; FCO, 1972–73; Dep. High Comr, Dacca, 1973–76; FCO, 1976–78, Hd of Information Res. Dept and Hd of Overseas Inf. Dept, 1976–78. MP (C) Wycombe, April 1978–2001. PPS to Treasury Ministers, 1979–80; Parly Under-Sec. of State, FCO, 1983–84, DHSS, 1984–86. Vice-Chm., Cons. Employment Cttee, 1980–83; Chm., Cons. For. Affairs Cttee, 1981–83; Mem., Public Accounts Cttee, 1981–83; Vice-Chairman: Parly Latin-America Gp, 1997–2001 (Chm., 1987–97); All-Party China Gp, 1997–2001; All-Party Hospice Gp, 1997–2001; Sec., All-Party Parly Argentine Gp, 1997–2001; Chm., Positive European Gp, 1993–2001. Chm., Mountbatten Community Trust (formerly Mountbatten Training), 1987–. Chm., The Cable Corp., 1989–96. Licensed Lay Minister, Oxford Dio., 1999–. *Publications:* National Health Crisis—a modern solution, 1988; articles on Chinese and Asian affairs in professional jls. *Recreations:* theatricals, golf, bridge, walking. *Address:* The Dial House, Sunninghill, Berks SL5 0AG. *T:* (01344) 623164.

WHITROW, Benjamin John; actor; *b* 17 Feb. 1937; *s* of Philip and Mary Whitrow; *m* 1972, Catherine Cook; one *s* one *d*. *Educ:* RADA (Leverhulme Schol.). *Stage:* Nat. Theatre, 1967–74; West End productions: Otherwise Engaged, Queen's, 1975; Dirty Linen, Arts, 1976; Ten Times Table, Globe, 1978; Passion Play, Aldwych, 1980; Uncle Vanya, Vaudeville, 1986; Noises Off, Savoy, 1983; Man for All Seasons, Savoy, 1987; Falstaff, Merry Wives of Windsor, RSC, 1992; Wild Oats, RNT, 1996; The Invention of Love, RNT, 1998; The Rivals, RSC, 2000; Henry IV Part II, 2001; Tom and Viv, Almeida, 2006; Entertaining Angels, Chichester, 2006; *films:* Quadrophenia, 1979; Clockwise; Personal Services, 1987; Scenes of a Sexual Nature, 2007; Bomber, 2008; *television* includes: Pride and Prejudice, 1995; Tom Jones, 1997; Henry VIII, 2003; Island at War, 2004. *Recreations:* golf, reading, bridge. *Address:* c/o Lou Coulson, 37 Berwick Street, W1F 8RS. *T:* (020) 7734 9633.

WHITSEY, Fred; Gardening Correspondent, Daily Telegraph, 1971–2006; *b* 18 July 1919; *m* 1947, Patricia Searle. *Educ:* outside school hours, and continuously ever since. Assistant Editor, Popular Gardening, 1948–64, Associate Editor, 1964–67, Editor, 1967–82. Gardening correspondent, Sunday Telegraph, 1961–71. Vice-Pres., RHS, 1996–. Gold Veitch Meml Medal, RHS, 1979; VMH 1986; Lifetime Achievement Award, Garden Writers' Guild, 1994. *Publications:* Sunday Telegraph Gardening Book, 1966; Fred Whitsey's Garden Calendar, 1985; Garden for All Seasons, 1986; The Garden at Hidcote, 2007; contribs to Country Life and The Garden. *Recreations:* gardening, music. *Address:* Avens Mead, 20 Oast Road, Oxted, Surrey RH8 9DU.

WHITSON, Sir Keith (Roderick), Kt 2002; Group Chief Executive, HSBC Holdings plc, 1998–2003 (Director, 1994–2003); *b* 25 March 1943; *s* of William Cleghorn Whitson and Ellen (*née* Wade); *m* 1968, Sabine Marita, *d* of Ulrich Wiechert; one *s* two *d*. *Educ:* Alleyn's Sch., Dulwich. FCIB. Joined Hong Kong and Shanghai Banking Corporation Ltd, 1961; Manager, Frankfurt, 1978–80; Manager, Indonesia, 1981–84; Asst Gen. Manager, Finance, Hong Kong, 1985–87; Chief Exec. Officer, UK, 1987, Exec. Dir, Marine Midland Bank, NY, 1990–92; Midland Bank: Dep. Chief Exec., 1992–94; Chief Exec., 1994–98; Dep. Chm., 1998–2003. Chairman: Merrill Lynch HSBC, 2000–02; HSBC Bank AS, 2001–03; Vice-Chm., HSBC Bank North America Inc., 2002–03; Director: HSBC Bank Argentina, 1997–2003; HSBC Bank USA, 1998–2003; HSBC Bank Canada, 1998–2003; Dep. Chm. Supervisory Bd, HSBC Trinkaus und Burkhardt Dusseldorf, 1993–2003. Non-executive Director: FSA, 1998–2003; Tetra Laval, 2005–.

WHITTAKER, Air Vice-Marshal David, CB 1988; MBE 1967; Air Officer Administration and Air Officer Commanding Directly Administered Units, RAF Support Command, 1986–89, retired; *b* 25 June 1933; *s* of Lawson and Irene Whittaker; *m* 1956, Joyce Ann Noble (*d* 2006); two *s*. *Educ:* Hutton Grammar School. Joined RAF, 1951; commissioned 1952; served No 222, No 3, No 26 and No 1 Squadrons, 1953–62; HQ 38 Group, 1962–63; HQ 24 Bde, 1963–65; Comd Metropolitan Comms Sqdn, 1966–68; RAF Staff Coll., 1968; Asst Air Adviser, New Delhi, 1969–70; RAF Leeming, 1971–73; Coll. of Air Warfare, 1973; Directing Staff, RNSC Greenwich, 1973–75; Staff of CDS, 1975–76; DACOS (Ops), AFCENT, 1977–80; RCDS 1980; Defence and Air Adviser, Ottawa, 1983–86. *Recreations:* fishing, gardening, travel. *Address:* Seronera, Copgrove, Harrogate, North Yorks HG3 3SZ. *T:* (01423) 340459. *Club:* Royal Air Force.

WHITTAKER, Geoffrey Owen, OBE 1974 (MBE 1962); Governor of Anguilla, 1987–89; retired 1990; *b* 10 Jan. 1932; *s* of late Alfred James Whittaker and Gertrude (*née* Holvey); *m* 1959, Annette Faith Harris; one *s* one *d*. *Educ:* Nottingham High Sch.; Bristol Univ. (BA). Auditor: Tanganyika, 1956–58; Dominica, 1958–60; Principal Auditor, Windward Is, 1960–64; Dir of Audit, Grenada, 1964–67; Audit Adviser, British Honduras, 1967–69; Colonial Treas., St Helena, 1970–75; Financial Sec. and Actg Governor, Montserrat, 1975–78; Financial Sec., British Virgin Is, 1978–80; Admin Officer, Hong Kong, 1980–87; Finance Br., 1980–83; Principal Asst Sec., Lands and Works Br., 1983–85; Gen. Man., Hong Kong Industrial Estates Corp., 1985–87. *Recreations:* music, Basset hounds, heraldry. *Address:* Ashley, near Market Harborough, Leics.

WHITTAKER, John, PhD; Member (UK Ind) North West Region, European Parliament, since 2004; *b* 7 June 1945; *m*; four *s*. *Educ:* Queen Mary Coll., Univ. of London (BSc Physics 1966); Univ. of Cape Town (PhD Physics 1980; BA Econs 1982). Industrial Engr, Magnesium Elektron Ltd, Manchester, 1966–68; Sales Engr, 1968–72, Manager Controls Div., 1972–75, Bestobell Engrg Ltd, Cape Town; University of Cape Town: Lectr in Physics, 1978–85, in Econs, 1984–90; Associate Prof., Econs, 1990–93; Prin. Lectr, Econs, Staffs Univ., 1994–96; Sen. Lectr, Econs, 1996–2004, Vis. Fellow, 2004–, Univ. of Lancaster. Contested (UK Ind): Littleborough and Saddleworth, July 1995; Lancaster and Wyre, 1997; Wigan, Sept. 1999, 2005; NW Reg., EP, 1999. *Publications:* articles in jls. *Address:* (office) 7 King Street, Lancaster LA1 1JN. *T:* (01524) 387690; *e-mail:* northwest@ukip.org; European Parliament, Rue Wiertz, 1047 Brussels, Belgium.

WHITTAKER, Prof. John Brian, PhD, DSc; FRES; Professor of Ecology, University of Lancaster, 1987–2004, now Emeritus; *b* 26 July 1939; *s* of Roland Whittaker and Freda (*née* Lord); *m* 1st, 1964, Helen May Thorley (*d* 1998); two *s*; 2nd, 2007, Kathleen Wendy Cann. *Educ:* Bacup and Rawtenstall Grammar Sch.; Univ. of Durham (BSc, PhD, DSc). FRES 1979. Res. Officer, Univ. of Oxford, 1963–66; University of Lancaster: Lectr, then Sen. Lectr, 1966–87; Hd, Dept of Biol Scis, 1983–86 and 1991–94. Mem., Adv. Cttee on Sci., NCC, 1978–81; Chm., Terrestrial Life Scis Cttee, NERC, 1991–95. Pres., British Ecol Soc., 2000–01 (Vice-Pres., 1987–89; Mem. Council, 1970–75, 1984–86); Member: Council, Freshwater Biol Assoc., 1988–91; Exec. and Council, UK Bioscis Fedn, 2002–06; Council, Royal Entomol Soc., 2005– (Vice-Pres., 2007–08). Hon. Fellow, Lancaster Univ., 2006. British Ecol Soc. Award, 2004. *Publications:* Practical Demonstration of Ecological Concepts, 1988; (ed jtly) Toward a More Exact Ecology, 1989; (with D. T. Salt) Insects on dock plants, 1998; contribs to books and jls in insect ecology. *Recreations:* 18th century English furniture, fell-walking, family. *Address:* Department of Biological Sciences, Lancaster University, Lancaster LA1 4YQ. *T:* (01524) 65201.

WHITTAKER, Nigel; corporate consultant; Chairman, ReputationInc Ltd, since 2002; *b* 7 Nov. 1948; *s* of late Phillip Whittaker and Joan Whittaker; *m* 1972, Joyce Cadman; three *s*. *Educ:* Caterham Sch.; Clare Coll., Cambridge (MA); Yale Law Sch. (JD). Called to the Bar, Middle Temple, 1974. Roche Products, 1974–77; British Sugar, 1977–82; Woolworth Holdings, subseq. Kingfisher plc, 1982–95 (Exec. Dir, 1983–95). Chairman: Retail Decisions (formerly Card Clear) plc, 1996–2006; Burson-Marsteller UK, 1997–99; MTI Partners Ltd, 1997–2002; Gourmet Hldgs (formerly City Gourmets Hldgs, later Madisons Coffee) plc, 1998–2007; Edelman Public Relations Worldwide, 1999–2002; Eagle Eye Telematics plc, 2000–04; Dir, Wickes plc, 1996–2000. Chm., CBI Distributive Trades Survey, 1986–94; Chm., British Retail Consortium (formerly Retail Consortium), 1995; Mem., UK Ecolabelling Bd (formerly Nat. Adv. Gp on Environmental Labelling), 1993–98. *Recreation:* cricket. *Address:* 176 Bickenhall Mansions, Bickenhall Street, W1U 6BU.

WHITTAKER, Sandra Melanie; *see* Smith, S. M.

WHITTAKER, Stanley Henry, FCA; Director of Finance and Planning, British Railways Board, 1988–91; *b* 14 Sept. 1935; *s* of Frederick Whittaker and Gladys Margaret (*née* Thatcher); *m* 1959, Freda Smith; two *s*. *Educ:* Bec School. ACA 1958, FCA 1969; ACMA 1971. Articled clerk, G. H. Attenborough & Co., Chartered Accountants, 1953–57; Sen. Assistant, Slater, Chapman & Cooke, 1960–62; Partner, Tiplady, Brailsford & Co., 1962–65; Finance Manager, NCB, 1965–68; British Railways: Finance Manager, 1968–74; Corporate Budgets Manager, 1974–78; Sen. Finance Manager, 1978–80; Chief Finance Officer, Western Reg., 1980–82; Director: Budgetary Control, 1982–86; Finance Develt, 1986–87; Group Finance, 1987–88. *Recreations:* flying, ski-ing, industrial archaeology, travel. *Address:* 12 Kennylands Road, Sonning Common, Reading, Berks RG4 9JT. *T:* (0118) 972 2951.

WHITTALL, (Harold) Astley, CBE 1978; CEng; Chairman: B.S.G. International Ltd, 1981–94; Ransomes plc (formerly Ransome, Sims & Jefferies Ltd), 1983–93 (Director 1979–93; Deputy Chairman, 1981–83); *b* 8 Sept. 1925; *s* of Harold and Margaret Whittall; *m* 1952, Diana Margharita Berner. *Educ:* Handsworth Grammar Sch., Birmingham; Handsworth and Birmingham Technical Colls. Gen. Manager, Belliss & Morcom, 1962; Managing Dir, Amalgamated Power Engineering, 1968, Chm., 1977–81; Director: LRC Internat., 1982–85; APV (formerly APV Baker and APV plc), 1982–95; R. Platnauer Ltd, 1984–; Sykes Pickervant, 1987–94; Inchcape Insurance Hldgs, 1988–90; Qualifications for Industry Ltd, 1997–; RTITB Ltd, 1999– (Dep. Chm., 2005–). Pres., Engineering Employers' Fedn, 1976–78; Chairman: Engrg ITB, 1985–91; ETA, 1990–94; British Iron and Steel Consumers Council, 1987–91. Freeman, City of London, 1984. Liveryman, Engineers' Co., 1984–. *Address:* Brook Farmhouse, Whelford, near Fairford, Glos GL7 4DY. *T:* (01285) 712393. *Clubs:* Royal Automobile, St James'.

WHITTALL, Michael Charlton, CMG 1980; OBE 1963; HM Diplomatic Service, retired; First Secretary, then Counsellor, Foreign and Commonwealth Office, 1963–81; *b* 9 Jan. 1926; *s* of Kenneth Edwin Whittall and Edna Ruth (*née* Lawson); *m* 1953, Susan Olivia La Fontaine one *d*. *Educ:* Rottingdean; Rugby; Trinity Hall, Cambridge. Served RAF, 1944–48. Foreign Office, 1949; Salonika, 1949; British Middle East Office, 1952; Vice-Consul, Basra, 1953; FO, 1955; Second Secretary, Beirut, 1956; FO, 1958; First Secretary, Amman, 1959. *Recreations:* railways (GWR), birdwatching, photography.

WHITTAM, Richard; *see* Whittam, W. R. L.

WHITTAM, Prof. Ronald, FRS 1973; Emeritus Professor, Leicester University, since 1983 (Professor of Physiology, 1966–83); *b* 21 March 1925; *e s* of Edward Whittam and May Whittam (*née* Butterworth), Oldham, Lancs; *m* 1957, Christine Patricia Margaret,

2nd *d* of Canon J. W. Lamb; one *s* one *d*. *Educ:* Council and Technical Schools, Oldham; Univs of Manchester and Sheffield and King's College, Cambridge. BSc 1st Class Hons (Manchester); PhD (Sheffield and Cambridge); MA (Oxon). Served RAF, 1943–47. John Stokes Fellow, Dept of Biochem., Univ. of Sheffield, 1953–55; Beit Memorial Fellow, Physiological Lab., Cambridge, 1955–58; Mem. Scientific Staff, MRC Cell Metabolism Research Unit, Oxford, 1958–60; Univ. Lectr in Biochemistry, Oxford, 1960–66; Bruno Mendel Fellow of Royal Society, 1965–66; Dean of Fac. of Science, Leicester Univ., 1979–82. Mem. Editorial Bd of Biochem. Jl, 1963–67; Hon. Sec., 1969–74, Hon. Mem., 1986, Physiological Soc.; Mem. Biological Research Bd of MRC, 1971–74, Co-Chm., 1973–74; Member: Biological Sciences Cttee, UGC, 1974–82; Educn Cttee, Royal Soc., 1979–83; Chm., Biological Educn Cttee, Royal Soc. and Inst. Biol., 1974–77. *Publications:* Transport and Diffusion in Red Blood Cells, 1964; scientific papers dealing with cell membranes. *Recreation:* walking. *Address:* 9 Guilford Road, Leicester LE2 2RD.

WHITTAM, (William) Richard (Lamont); QC 2008; Senior Treasury Counsel, Central Criminal Court, since 2006; *b* 23 Nov. 1959; *s* of late William Wright Whittam and of Elizabeth Mary Whittam (*née* Lamont); *m* 1987, Carol Rosemary van Herwaarden; one *s* one *d*. *Educ:* Marple Hill Sch.; University Coll. London (LLB Hons); Inns of Court Sch. of Law. Called to the Bar, Gray's Inn, 1983; Jun. Treasury Counsel, 1998–2002, First Jun. Treasury Counsel, 2002–06, Central Criminal Court. Member: S Eastern Circuit Cttee, 1991–93; CPS Bar Standards Cttee, 2000–05. Keynote address, 1st Nat. Baby Shaking Conf., Sydney, Australia, 2001. *Recreations:* wakeboarding, pyrotechnics, men's lacrosse, Rugby, golf. *Address:* Furnival Chambers, 32 Furnival Street, EC4A 1JQ. *Club:* Garrick.

WHITTAM SMITH, Andreas, CBE 2003; First Church Estates Commissioner, since 2002; *b* 13 June 1937; *s* of Canon J. E. Smith and Mrs Smith (*née* Barlow); *m* 1964, Valerie Catherine, *d* of late Wing Comdr J. A. Sherry and of Mrs N. W. H. Wyllys; two *s*. *Educ:* Birkenhead Sch., Cheshire; Keble Coll., Oxford (BA) (Hon. Fellow, 1990). With N. M. Rothschild, 1960–62; Stock Exchange Gazette, 1962–63; Financial Times, 1963–64; The Times, 1964–66; Dep. City Editor, Daily Telegraph, 1966–69; City Editor, The Guardian, 1969–70; Editor, Investors Chronicle and Stock Exchange Gazette, and Dir, Throgmorton Publications, 1970–77; City Editor, Daily Telegraph, 1977–85; Editor, The Independent, 1986–94; Editor-in-Chief, Independent on Sunday, 1991–94. Dir, 1986–98, Chief Exec., 1987–93, Chm., 1994–95, Newspaper Publishing plc; Dir, Ind. News & Media (UK), 1998–; Pres., BBFC, 1998–2002; Chairman: Financial Ombudsman Service Ltd, 1999–2003; With Profits Cttee, Prudential Assurance, 2005–; Children's Mutual, 2006–. Vice Pres., Nat. Council for One Parent Families, 1991– (Hon. Treas., 1982–86). Chm., Sir Winston Churchill Archive Trust, 1995–2000. Trustee, Architecture Foundn, 1994–2000. Hon. Fellow: UMIST, 1989; Liverpool John Moores, 2001. Hon. DLitt: St Andrews; Salford; City; Liverpool, 1992; Hon. LLD Bath. Wincott award, 1975; Marketing Man of the Year, Inst. of Marketing, 1987; Journalist of the Year, British Press Awards, 1987; Hemingway Europa Prize, 1988; Editor of the Year, Granada TV What the Papers Say award, 1989. *Recreations:* music, history, walking. *Address:* 154 Campden Hill Road, W8 7AS. *Club:* Garrick.

WHITTELL, James Michael Scott, CMG 1998; OBE 1984; Chief Executive, Interstate Programmes (2000) Ltd, since 2004 (Founder and Chief Executive, Interstate Programmes Ltd, 1999–2004); Founder and Director, The Physics Factory, since 2008; *b* 17 Feb. 1939; *s* of late Edward Arthur Whittell and Helen Elizabeth Whittell (*née* Scott); *m* 1962, Eleanor Jane Carling; three *s*. *Educ:* Gresham's School, Holt; Magdalen College, Oxford (MA, BSc); Manchester Univ. Teaching, Sherborne School, 1962–68, Nairobi School, 1968–72; British Council: Ibadan, Nigeria, 1973–76; Enugu, Nigeria, 1976–78; Director General's Dept, 1978–81; Rep., Algiers, 1981–85; Sec. to the British Council and Head of Dir Gen's Dept, 1985–88; seconded to PM's Efficiency Unit, 1988; Rep., subseq. Dir, Nigeria, 1989–92; Dir, Africa and ME Div., 1992; Regl Dir, EC, later EU, 1993–96; Dir, British Council in Europe, 1996–99. *Recreations:* walking, mountaineering, books, music. *Address:* 15 Stratford Grove, SW15 1NU. *Club:* Alpine.

WHITTEMORE, Prof. Colin Trengove; Professor of Agriculture and Rural Economy, University of Edinburgh, 1990–2007, now Emeritus (Postgraduate Dean, College of Science and Engineering, 2002–07); *b* 16 July 1942; *s* of Hugh Ashcroft Whittemore and Dorothea Whittemore (*née* Nance); *m* 1966, Mary Christine Fenwick; one *s* three *d*. *Educ:* Rydal Sch.; Harper Adams Agricl Coll. (NDA); Univ. of Newcastle upon Tyne (BSc, PhD, DSc). FIBiol 1989; FRSE 1994. Lectr, Univ. of Edinburgh, 1970–79; Head, Animal Production Adv. and Develt, E of Scotland Coll. of Agric., 1979–84; University of Edinburgh: Prof. of Animal Prodn, 1984–90; Head, Dept of Agric., 1989–90; Head, Inst. of Ecology and Resource Mgt, 1990–2000. Pres., British Soc. of Animal Sci., 1998–99. Sir John Hammond Award, British Soc. of Animal Prodn, 1983; Res. Gold Medal, RASE, 1984; Oscar della Suinicoltura, Assoc. Mignini, 1987; David Black Award, Meat and Livestock Commn, 1990. *Publications:* Practical Pig Nutrition (with F. W. H. Elsley), 1976; Lactation, 1980; Pig Production, 1980; Elements of Pig Science, 1987; The Science and Practice of Pig Production, 1993, 3rd edn 2006. *Recreations:* ski-ing, horses. *Address:* Rowancroft, 17 Fergusson View, West Linton, Peeblesshire EH46 7DJ. *Club:* Farmers'.

WHITTING, Ian Robert; HM Diplomatic Service; Ambassador to Iceland, since 2008; *b* 2 April 1953; *s* of Robert Stanley Whitting, ARIBA, and Mary Elizabeth (*née* Tindall); *m* 1986, Tracy Gallagher; two *d*. *Educ:* Chichester High Sch. for Boys. Joined FCO, 1972; Attaché, Moscow, 1975–76; Third Sec., Tunis, 1976–79; Press Attaché, Athens, 1980–83; FCO, 1983–85; Second Sec., Moscow, 1985–88; FCO, 1988–90; First Sec., Dublin, 1990–94; Dep. Hd of Mission, Abidjan, 1994–97; Dep. Hd, Africa Dept (Equatorial), and Sec. of State's Special Rep. for Great Lakes, 1998–2002; Hd, EU Dept (Bilateral), FCO, 2002–03; Dir, EU and Econ. Affairs, Athens, 2003–04; Counsellor, Dep. Hd of Mission and HM Consul-Gen., Athens, 2005–08. *Recreations:* tennis, sailing, hill walking, reading. *Address:* c/o Foreign and Commonwealth Office, King Charles Street, SW1A 2AH.

WHITTINGDALE, John Flasby Lawrance, OBE 1990; MP (C) Maldon and Chelmsford East, since 1997 (Colchester South and Maldon, 1992–97); *b* 16 Oct. 1959; *s* of late John Whittingdale and of Margaret Esmé Scott Napier; *m* 1990, Ancilla Campbell Murfitt (separated 2007); one *s* one *d*. *Educ:* Sandroyd Sch.; Winchester Coll.; University Coll. London (BScEcon). Head of Political Section, Conservative Research Dept, 1982–84; Special Adviser to Sec. of State for Trade and Industry, 1984–87; Manager, N. M. Rothschild & Sons, 1987; Political Sec. to the Prime Minister, 1988–90; Private Sec. to Rt Hon. Margaret Thatcher, 1990–92. PPS to Minister of State for Educn, 1994–95, for Educn and Employment, 1995–96; an Opposition Whip, 1997–98; Opposition Treasury spokesman, 1998–99; PPS to Leader of the Opposition, 1999–2001; Shadow Sec. of State for Trade and Industry, 2001–02, for Culture, Media and Sport, 2002–03 and 2004–05, for Agriculture, Fisheries and Food, 2003–04. Member, Select Committee: on Health, 1993–97; on Trade and Industry, 2001; Chm., Select Cttee on Culture, Media and Sport, 2005–. Sec., Conservative Parly Home Affairs Cttee, 1992–94; Mem. Exec., Cons. 1922 Cttee, 2005– (Vice Chm., 2006–). Parly Mem., Cons. Party Bd, 2006–. *Recreations:* cinema, music. *Address:* c/o House of Commons, SW1A 0AA. *Club:* Essex.

WHITTINGHAM, Charles Percival, BA, PhD Cantab; Head of Department of Botany, Rothamsted Experimental Station, 1971–82; *b* 1922; *m* 1946, Alison Phillips; two *d*. *Educ:* St John's College, Cambridge. Professor of Botany, London University, at Queen Mary College, 1958–64; Head of Dept of Botany, 1967–71, and Prof. of Plant Physiology, 1964–71, Imperial Coll., Univ of London; Dean, Royal Coll. of Science, 1969–71; Hon. Dir, ARC Unit for Plant Physiology, 1964–71. Vis. Prof., Univ. of Nottingham, 1978. *Publications:* Chemistry of Plant Processes, 1964; (with R. Hill) Photosynthesis, 1955; The Mechanism of Photosynthesis, 1974; contrib. to scientific journals. *Recreations:* music, travel. *Address:* Red Cottage, The Green, Brisley, Dereham, Norfolk NR20 5LN.

WHITTINGSTALL, Hugh Christopher Edmund F.; *see* Fearnley-Whittingstall.

WHITTINGTON, Prof. Dorothy Allan, CPsychol; Professor of Health Psychology, University of Ulster, 1999–2003, Professor Emeritus, 2005; *b* 14 Dec. 1941; *d* of Eric George Whittington and Margaret Cowan Whittington (*née* Allan). *Educ:* Hutchesons' Girls' Grammar Sch., Glasgow; Univ. of Glasgow (MA, MEd, Teaching Cert.). AFBPsS 1970; CPsychol 1988. Infant teacher, Glasgow primary schs, 1962–67; Lectr in Psychol., Callendar Park Coll. of Educn, Falkirk, 1967–72; Sen. Lectr in Educn, 1972–73, Principal Lectr in Psychol., 1973–84, Ulster Poly.; University of Ulster: Sen. Lectr in Psychol., 1984–94; Dir, Centre for Health and Social Res., 1990–95; Hd, Sch. of Health Scis, 1994–96; Dir, Health Care Distance Learning, 1997–2003. Mem., Nat. Council, Assoc. for Quality in Health Care, 1989–92; Dir, Trustee and Mem. Academic Council, Higher Educn Acad., 2008–; Partner, Postgrad. Med. Educnl Trng Bd, 2008–. Chairman, Advisory Group: Centre for Health Scis and Practice, Learning and Teaching Support Network, 2002–05; Centre for Medicine, Dentistry, Vet. Medicine and Health Scis, Higher Educn Acad., 2005–. Dir of Educn, R&D, N Bristol NHS Trust, 2003–07; non-exec. Dir, Northern Health and Social Care Trust, NI, 2007–. Co-founder, NI Parents' Advice Centre, 1978. *Publications:* (jtly) Quality Assurance: a workbook for health professionals, 1992 (trans. Italian and Portuguese); with R. Ellis: A Guide to Social Skill Training, 1981; New Directions in Social Skill Training, 1983; Quality Assurance in Health Care, 1993; Quality Assurance in Social Care: an introductory workbook, 1998; contrib. papers and book chapters on social skill, communication in professional contexts, quality and governance in health and social care, needs assessment and prog. evaluation in primary and community care, patient and public involvement in health and social care planning. *Recreations:* sailing, music.

WHITTINGTON, Prof. Geoffrey, CBE 2001; Member, Accounting Standards Board, 1994–2001 and since 2006; Price Waterhouse Professor of Financial Accounting, Cambridge University, 1988–2001, now Emeritus; Fellow of Fitzwilliam College, Cambridge, 1966–72 and 1988–2001, now Life Fellow; *b* 21 Sept. 1938; *s* of late Bruce Whittington and Dorothy Gwendoline Whittington (*née* Gent); *m* 1963, Joyce Enid Smith; two *s*. *Educ:* Dudley Grammar Sch.; LSE (Leverhulme Schol.; BSc Econ); MA, PhD Cantab. FCA. Chartered Accountancy training, 1959–62; research posts, Dept of Applied Econ., Cambridge, 1962–72; Dir of Studies in Econs, Fitzwilliam Coll., Cambridge, 1967–72; Prof. of Accountancy and Finance, Edinburgh Univ., 1972–75; University of Bristol: Prof. of Accounting and Finance, 1975–88; Head of Dept of Econs, 1981–84; Dean, Faculty of Social Scis, 1985–87. Professorial Res. Fellow, Inst. of Chartered Accountants of Scotland, 1996–2001. Part-time Econ. Adviser, OFT, 1977–83; part-time Mem., Monopolies and Mergers Commn, 1987–96; Academic Advr, Accounting Standards Bd, 1990–94; Member: Adv. Body on Fair Trading in Telecommunications, 1997–98; Internat. Accounting Standards Bd, 2001–06. Hon. DSc (SocSci) Edinburgh, 1998. Chartered Accountants Founding Societies Centenary Award, 2003. *Publications:* Growth, Profitability and Valuation (with A. Singh), 1968; The Prediction of Profitability, 1971; Inflation Accounting, 1983; (with D. P. Tweedie) The Debate on Inflation Accounting, 1984; (ed jtly) Readings in the Concept and Measurement of Income, 1986; The Elements of Accounting, 1992; Profitability, Accounting Theory and Methodology, 2007; contribs to jls and books in accounting, economics and finance. *Recreations:* music, walking, usual academic pursuits of reading my own books and laughing at my own jokes. *Address:* Fitzwilliam College, Cambridge CB3 0DG. *Club:* Athenæum.

WHITTINGTON, Prof. Harry Blackmore, FRS 1971; Woodwardian Professor of Geology, Cambridge University, 1966–83; *b* 24 March 1916; *s* of Harry Whittington and Edith M. (*née* Blackmore); *m* 1940, Dorothy E. Arnold; no *c*. *Educ:* Handsworth Gram. Sch.; Birmingham Univ. Commonwealth Fund Fellow, Yale Univ., 1938–40; Lectr in Geology, Judson Coll., Rangoon, 1940–42; Prof. of Geography, Ginling Coll., Chengtu, W China, 1943–45; Lectr in Geology, Birmingham Univ., 1945–49; Harvard Univ.: Vis. Lectr, 1949–50; Assoc. Prof. of Geology, 1950–58; Prof. of Geology, 1958–66. Trustee: British Museum (Nat. History), 1980–89; Uppingham Sch., 1983–91. Hon. Fellow, Geol Soc. of America, 1983. Hon. AM, Harvard Univ., 1950. Medal, Paleontol Soc., USA, 1983; Lyell Medal, 1986, Wollaston Medal, 2001, Geological Soc.; Mary Clark Thompson Medal, US Nat. Acad. of Scis, 1990; Lapworth Medal, Palaeontol Assoc., 2000; Medal, Geol Assoc. of Canada, 2000; Internat. Prize for Biology, Japan, 2001. *Publications:* The Burgess Shale, 1985; Trilobites, 1992; articles in Jl of Paleontology, Bulletin Geol. Soc. of Amer., Quarterly Jl Geol. Soc. London, Phil. Trans. Royal Soc., etc. *Club:* Geological.

WHITTINGTON, Prof. Richard C., PhD; Professor of Strategic Management, University of Oxford, since 2002; Fellow of New College, Oxford, since 1996. *Educ:* Aston Univ. (MBA); Univ. of Manchester (PhD); MA Oxon. Lectr, Sen. Lectr, then Reader in Marketing and Strategic Mgt, Warwick Business Sch., Univ. of Warwick; Lectr in Mgt Studies, Univ. of Oxford, 1996–2002. *Publications:* Corporate Strategies in Recession and Recovery, 1989; (jtly) Rethinking Marketing, 1999; What is Strategy - and Does it Matter?, 2000; (jtly) The European Corporation: strategy, structure, and social science, 2000; (jtly) The Handbook of Strategy and Management, 2001; (jtly) Innovative Forms of Organising, 2003; (jtly) Exploring Corporate Strategy, 7th edn 2004; (jtly) Strategy as Practice: research directions and resources, 2007; articles in learned jls. *Address:* Saïd Business School, University of Oxford, Park End Street, Oxford OX1 1HP.

WHITTINGTON-SMITH, Marianne Christine, (Mrs C. A. Whittington-Smith); *see* Lutz, M. C.

WHITTLE, Prof. Alasdair William Richardson, DPhil; FBA 1998; Professor of Archaeology, School of History and Archaeology, Cardiff University (formerly University of Wales College of Cardiff), since 1997; *b* 7 May 1949; *s* of late Charles and of Grizel Whittle; *m* 1971, Elisabeth Sampson; three *d*. *Educ:* Christ Church, Oxford (MA; DPhil 1976). Lectr, UC Cardiff, then Univ. of Wales Coll. of Cardiff, 1978–97. Jt Ed., Proc. Prehistoric Soc., 1988–94. Leader, Avebury Area Excavation Project, 1987–93. Member: Panel for Archaeol., RAEs, 1996, 2001; Ancient Monuments Adv. Bd for Wales, 2000–. *Publications:* Neolithic Europe, 1985; Scord of Brouster, 1986; Problems in Neolithic Archaeology, 1988; Europe in the Neolithic, 1996; Sacred Mound, Holy Rings, 1997; The Harmony of Symbols, 1999; The Archaeology of People, 2003; Places of Special Virtue, 2004; Histories of the Dead, 2007; Building Memories, 2007; Neolithic on the

Great Hungarian Plain, 2007. *Recreations:* golf, fishing, travel. *Address:* Cardiff School of History and Archaeology, Cardiff University, Humanities Building, Colum Drive, Cardiff CF10 3EU.

WHITTLE, Kenneth Francis, CBE 1987; Chairman, South Western Electricity Board, 1977–87; *b* 28 April 1922; *s* of Thomas Whittle and May Whittle; *m* 1945, Dorothy Inskip; one *s* one *d.* *Educ:* Kingswood Sch., Bath; Faculty of Technol., Manchester Univ. (BScTech). Served War, Electrical Lieut, RNVR, 1943–46. Metropolitan Vickers Elec. Co. Ltd, 1946–48; NW Div., CEGB, 1948–55; North West Electricity Board: various posts, 1955–64; Area Commercial Officer, Blackburn, 1964–69; Manager, Peak Area, 1969–71; Manager, Manchester Area, 1971–74; Chief Commercial Officer, 1974–75; Dep. Chm., Yorks Elec. Bd, 1975–77. Chairman: British Electrotechnical Approvals Bd, 1985–96; British Approvals Bd for Telecommunications, 1985–96. *Recreation:* golf. *Address:* 8 Cambridge Road, Clevedon, N Somerset BS21 7HX. *T:* (01275) 874017.

WHITTLE, Prof. Martin John, MD; FRCPGlas, FRCOG; Professor of Fetal Medicine, 1991–2006, and Associate Dean for Education, 2004–06, University of Birmingham (Head, Division of Reproductive and Child Health, 1998–2003), now Professor Emeritus; Consultant, Birmingham Women's Hospital, 1991–2006; Clinical Co-Director, National Collaborating Centre for Women and Children's Health, National Institute for Health and Clinical Excellence, since 2006; *b* 6 July 1944; *s* of Bruce and Eveline Whittle. *Educ:* William Grimshaw Secondary Modern Sch., London; Univ. of Manchester Med. Sch. (MB ChB 1972; MD 1980). FRCOG 1988; FRCPGlas 1988. House Physician and Surgeon, Manchester Royal Infirmary, 1972–73; Res. Fellow, LAC-USC Med. Center, Los Angeles, 1978–79; Lectr, Queen Mother's Hosp., Glasgow, 1979–82; Consultant Obstetrician and Gynaecologist, Queen Mother's Hosp. and Royal Samaritan Hosp., Glasgow, 1982–91. *Publications:* (with J. M. Connor) Prenatal Diagnosis in Obstetric Practice, 1989, 2nd edn 1995; (with C. H. Rodeck) Fetal Medicine: Basic Science and Clinical Practice, 1999; contrib. articles on fetal medicine and high-risk obstetric practice. *Recreations:* sailing, flying, diving, art. *Address: e-mail:* mwhittle@ncc-wch.org.uk.

WHITTLE, Prof. Peter, FRS 1978; Churchill Professor of Mathematics for Operational Research, University of Cambridge, 1967–94, now Professor Emeritus; Fellow of Churchill College, Cambridge, since 1967; *b* 27 Feb. 1927; *s* of Percy and Elsie Whittle; *m* 1951, Käthe Hildegard Blomquist; three *s* three *d.* *Educ:* Wellington Coll., New Zealand. Docent, Uppsala Univ., 1951–53; employed New Zealand DSIR, 1953–59, rising to Senior Principal Scientific Officer; Lectr, Univ. of Cambridge, 1959–61; Prof. of Mathematical Statistics, Univ. of Manchester, 1961–67. Sen. Fellow, SERC, 1988–91. Mem., Royal Soc. of NZ, 1981–. Hon. DSc Victoria Univ. of Wellington, NZ, 1987. *Publications:* Hypothesis Testing in Time Series Analysis, 1951; Prediction and Regulation, 1963; Probability, 1970; Optimisation under Constraints, 1971; Optimisation over Time, 1982; Systems in Stochastic Equilibrium, 1986; Risk-sensitive Optimal Control, 1990; Probability via Expectation, 1992; Optimal Control: basics and beyond, 1996; Neural Nets and Chaotic Carriers, 1998; Networks: optimisation and evolution, 2007; contribs to Jl Roy. Statistical Soc., Proc. Roy. Soc., Jl Stat. Phys, Systems and Control Letters. *Recreations:* variable. *Address:* 268 Queen Edith's Way, Cambridge CB1 8NL; Statistical Laboratory, University of Cambridge CB3 0WB.

WHITTLE, Stephen Charles, OBE 2006; Chairman, Broadcast Training and Skills Regulator, since 2007; Controller of Editorial Policy, BBC, 2001–05; *b* 26 July 1945; *s* of Charles William Whittle and Vera Lillian Whittle (*née* Moss); *m* 1988, Claire Walmsley (marr. diss. 1999); *m* 2004, Eve Salomon. *Educ:* St Ignatius College, Stamford Hill; University College London (LLB Hons). Asst Editor, New Christian, 1968–70; Communications Officer, World Council of Churches, Geneva, 1970–73; Editor, One World, WCC, 1973–77; Asst Head, Communications Dept, WCC, 1975–77; BBC: Sen. Producer, Religious Programmes, Manchester, 1977–82; Producer, Newsnight, 1982; Editor, Songs of Praise and Worship, 1983–89; Hd of Religious Progs, 1989–93; Chief Advr, Editl Policy, Policy and Planning Directorate, 1993–96; Director: Broadcasting Standards Council, 1996–97; Broadcasting Standards Commn, 1997–2001. Mem., Regulation Bd, Law Soc., subseq. SRA, 2005–. Gov., Eur. Inst. for the Media, 1997–2004. Trustee, Sandford St Martin Trust, 2002–. Vis. Fellow, Reuters Inst. for Study of Journalism, Oxford Univ., 2007–. FRSA. Freeman, City of London, 1990. Sandford St Martin Award for contrib. to religious broadcasting, 1993. *Publications:* Tickling Mrs Smith, 1970; contribs to Media Guardian and The Tablet. *Recreations:* cinema, theatre, music, reading, walking. *Address:* Flat 4, 34A Sydenham Hill, SE26 6LS.

WHITTON, David Forbes; Member (Lab) Strathkelvin and Bearsden, Scottish Parliament, since 2007; *b* 22 April 1952; *s* of David Whitton and May Whitton (*née* Hoy); *m* 1971, Marilyn MacDonald; one *s* one *d.* *Educ:* Morgan Acad., Dundee. Journalist on Scottish weekly and daily and nat. newspapers, 1970–86; various posts at Scottish Television, 1986–96, incl. Hd of Public Affairs, 1994–96; Dir, Media House, PR firm, 1996–98; Special Advr to Scottish Sec. and First Minister of Scotland, 1998–2000; Man. Dir, Whitton pr Ltd, 2000–07. *Recreations:* golf, music (listening and playing my electric drum kit), playing with my grandchildren. *Address:* c/o Scottish Parliament, Edinburgh EH99 1SP. *T:* (0131) 348 6747, *Fax:* (0131) 348 6749; *e-mail:* David.Whitton.msp@scottish.parliament.uk. *Club:* Crail Golfing Society.

WHITTON, Prof. Peter William; Deputy Vice-Chancellor, University of Melbourne, 1979–84, retired; *b* 2 Sept. 1925; *s* of William Whitton and Rosa Bungay; *m* 1950, Mary Katharine White; two *s* three *d.* *Educ:* Latymer Upper Sch., London; Southampton Univ. (BScEng); Imperial College of Science and Technology, London (DIC, PhD); ME Melbourne 1965. Engineering Cadet, English Electric Co., Preston, 1942–46; Wireless Officer, Royal Signals, Catterick and Singapore, 1946–48; Sen. Lectr in Mech. Engrg, Univ. of Melbourne, 1953–56; Head, Engrg Sect., ICI Metals Div. Research Dept, Birmingham, 1956–60; Foundation Prof. and Dean, Faculty of Engrg, Univ. of the West Indies, 1960–64; University of Melbourne: Prof. of Mech. Engrg, 1965–77, Emeritus Prof., 1977–; Dean, Faculty of Engrg, 1966; Principal, Royal Melbourne Inst. of Technology, 1977–78. *Publications:* various papers on metal forming, in Proc. IMechE, London, and Jl of Inst. of Metals, London. *Recreation:* reading. *Address:* 7 Surf Avenue, Beaumaris, Vic 3193, Australia.

WHITTY, family name of **Baron Whitty**.

WHITTY, Baron *cr* 1996 (Life Peer), of Camberwell in the London Borough of Southwark; **John Lawrence Whitty, (Larry);** PC 2005; Chairman, National Consumer Council, since 2006; *b* 15 June 1943; *s* of Frederick James and Kathleen May Whitty; *m* 1969, Tanya Margaret (marr. diss. 1986); two *s*; *m* 1993, Angela Forrester. *Educ:* Latymer Upper School; St John's College, Cambridge (BA Hons Economics). Hawker Siddeley Aviation, 1960–62; Min. of Aviation Technology, 1965–70; Trades Union Congress, 1970–73; General, Municipal, Boilermakers and Allied Trade Union (formerly GMWU), 1973–85; Gen. Sec., 1985–94, European Co-ordinator, 1994–97, Labour Party. A Lord in Waiting (Govt Whip), 1997–98; Parly Under-Sec. of State, DETR, subseq. DEFRA, 1998–2005. Member: Nat. Water Services Regulation Authy, 2006; Bd, Envmt Agency, 2006–. *Recreations:* theatre, cinema, swimming. *Address:* 61 Bimport, Shaftesbury, Dorset SP7 8AZ. *T:* (01747) 854619, (0171) 834 8890.

See also G. J. Whitty.

WHITTY, Prof. Geoffrey James; Director, Institute of Education, University of London, since 2000; *b* 31 Dec. 1946; *s* of Frederick James Whitty and Kathleen May Whitty; *m* 1st, 1969, Gillian Patterson (marr. diss. 1989); one *s* one *d*; 2nd, 1989, Marilyn Toft; one *d.* *Educ:* Latymer Upper Sch.; St John's Coll., Cambridge (BA, MA); Inst. of Educn, London Univ. (PGCE, MA, DLit). Teacher: Lampton Sch., Hounslow, 1969–70; Thomas Bennett Sch., Crawley, 1970–73; Lecturer: Univ. of Bath, 1973–80; KCL, 1981–84; Prof. of Educn, Bristol Poly., 1985–89; Goldsmiths' Prof. of Policy and Mgt, Goldsmiths Coll., Univ. of London, 1990–92; Karl Mannheim Prof. of Sociol. of Educn, Inst. of Educn, 1992–2000. Vis. Prof., Univ. of Wisconsin-Madison, 1979–80. Chairman: Bristol Educn Partnership Bd, 2001–03; Educn Adv. Cttee, British Council, 2002–07. President: Coll. of Teachers, 2005–; British Educnl Res. Assoc., 2005–07. Hon. FCT 2001. Hon. EdD UWE, 2001. *Publications:* (jtly) Society, State and Schooling, 1977; Sociology and School Knowledge, 1985; (jtly) The State and Private Education, 1989; (jtly) Specialisation and Choice in Urban Education, 1993; (jtly) Devolution and Choice in Education, 1998; (jtly) Teacher Education in Transition, 2000; Making Sense of Education Policy, 2002; (jtly) Education and the Middle Class, 2003. *Recreations:* travel, football, reading, politics. *Address:* Institute of Education, 20 Bedford Way, WC1H 0AL. *T:* (020) 7612 6004.

See also Baron Whitty.

WHITTY, Niall Richard, FRSE; Member, Scottish Law Commission, 1995–2000; *b* 28 Oct. 1937; *s* of Richard Hazleton Whitty and Muriel Helen Margaret Scott or Whitty; *m* 1977, Elke Mechthild Maria Gillis; three *s* one *d.* *Educ:* John Watson's Sch., Edinburgh; Morrison's Acad., Crieff; St Andrews Univ. (MA Hons 1960); Edinburgh Univ. (LLB 1963). Admitted solicitor, 1965. Legal Officer, 1967–70, Sen. Legal Officer, 1970–77, Asst Solicitor, 1977–94, Scottish Office; seconded to legal staff, Scottish Law Commn, 1971–94. Vis. Prof., Sch. of Law, Univ. of Edinburgh, 2000–. Gen. Editor, The Laws of Scotland, Stair Memorial Encyclopaedia, 2000–. FRSE 2003. *Publications:* contrib. Stair Memorial Encyclopaedia, and legal jls. *Address:* St Martins, Victoria Road, Haddington, East Lothian EH41 4DJ. *T:* (01620) 822234.

WHITWAM, Derek Firth, CEng, FRINA; RCNC; Director of Quality Assurance, Ministry of Defence, 1985–88; *b* 7 Dec. 1932; *s* of Hilton and Marion Whitwam; *m* 1954, Pamela May (*née* Lander); one *s* one *d.* *Educ:* Royds Hall Sch., Huddersfield; Royal Naval Coll., Dartmouth; Royal Naval Engineering Coll., Manadon; Royal Naval Coll., Greenwich. Work on ship design, MoD (N) Bath, 1957–65; Rosyth Dockyard, 1965–68; Singapore Dockyard, 1968–70; DG Ships Bath, 1970–77; RCDS 1978; Production Manager, Rosyth Dockyard, 1979–80; Gen. Manager, Portsmouth Dockyard, 1981–84; Principal Dir of Planning and Policy, Chief Exec. Royal Dockyards, 1984–85. *Publications:* papers for Trans Royal Inst. of Naval Architects. *Recreations:* golf, music, walking. *Club:* Bath Golf.

WHITWELL, Stephen John, CMG 1969; MC; HM Diplomatic Service, retired; *b* 30 July 1920; *s* of Arthur Percy Whitwell and Marion Whitwell (*née* Greenwood). *Educ:* Stowe; Christ Church, Oxford. Coldstream Guards, 1941–47; joined HM Foreign Service (now Diplomatic Service), 1947; served: Tehran, 1947; FO, 1949; Belgrade, 1952; New Delhi, 1954; FO, 1958; Seoul, 1961. Polit. Adv. to C-in-C Middle East, Aden, 1964; Counsellor, Belgrade, 1965; Ambassador to Somalia, 1968–70; Head of East-West Contacts Dept, FCO, 1970–71. *Recreations:* reading, painting, looking at buildings. *Club:* Travellers.

WHITWORTH, Diana Storey; Consultant, The Young Foundation, since 2008; *b* 5 April 1949; *d* of Barrington Allen Whitworth and Rosemary Whitworth (*née* Braithwaite); one *d* by Anthony Beauchamp; *m* 2008, Guy Dehn. *Educ:* Badminton Sch.; King's High Sch., Warwick; South Bank Poly. (MA Applied Eur. Studies). Consumer Advr, London Borough of Hillingdon, 1973–77; Sen. R&D Officer, NACAB, 1980–88; Sen. Policy and Develt Officer, then Hd, Public Affairs, NCC, 1988–99; Chief Exec., Carers Nat. Assoc., subseq. Carers UK, 1999–2003; Jt Chief Exec., Grandparents plus, 2004–08. Chair, Consumer Congress, 1983–85; Member: Adv. Cttee on Work Life Balance, DFEE, 2000–02; Commng Bd, NHS Service Delivery and Orgn R&D, 2000–; NHS Mental Health Task Force, 2000–02; NHS Older People's Task Force, 2002–03; Appeals Adv. Cttee, BBC, 2002–07; Strategic Res. Bd, ESRC, 2003–06; Council, ASA, 2005–; Chair, External Ref. Gp, Nat. Service Framework for Long term Conditions, 2002–05. Mem., Indep. Complaints Panel, Portman Gp, 1998–2003; Bd Mem., Big Lottery Fund, 2004–. Trustee, Cranstoun Drug Services (formerly Odyssey Trust), 2000–. Gov., Stoke Newington Sch., 1996–2001. *Recreations:* reading, gardening, cycling. *Address: e-mail:* dianawhitworth@aol.com.

WHITWORTH, Francis John, OBE 1994; Member, Economic and Social Committee of the European Communities, 1986–98; *b* 1 May 1925; *s* of late Captain Herbert Francis Whitworth, OBE, RNVR, and Helen Marguerite Whitworth (*née* Tait); *m* 1956, Auriol Myfanwy Medwyn Hughes; one *s* one *d.* *Educ:* Charterhouse (Jun. Schol.); Pembroke Coll., Oxford (Holford Schol.; MA Jurisprudence 1949). Served War, Royal Marines, 1943–46. Called to Bar, Middle Temple, 1950. Joined Cunard Steam-Ship Co., 1950; Personnel Director, 1965, Managing Dir Cunard Line, 1968, Group Admin Dir, 1969; joined British Shipping Fedn as Dir, Industrial Relations, 1972; Dep. Dir-Gen., Gen. Council of British Shipping, 1980–87; Dir, Internat. Shipping Fedn, 1980–88; Mem., Nat. Maritime Bd, 1962–87. Chairman: Internat. Cttee of Passenger Lines, 1968–71; Atlantic Passenger Steamship Conf., 1970–71; Employers' Gp, Jt Maritime Commn of ILO, 1980–88; Employers' Gp, Internat. Maritime (Labour) Conf. of ILO, 1986–87; Social Affairs Cttee, Comité des Assocs d'Armateurs des Communautés Européennes, 1983–88; Nat. Sea Training Schs, 1980–87; Merchant Navy Officers' Pension Fund Trustees, 1987–93; Member: Industrial Tribunals for England and Wales, 1978–94; Council, Mission to Seafarers (formerly Missions to Seamen), 1988–; Vice-Pres., Marine Soc. and Sea Cadets, 2004–. FCMI (FBIM 1980; MBIM 1967). Freeman, City of London, 1999; Liveryman, Shipwrights' Co., 1999–. *Recreations:* racing, opera, music, cricket. *Address:* 5 Beaumond Green, Winchester SO23 8GF. *Club:* Oxford and Cambridge.

WHITWORTH, Prof. Judith Ann, AC 2001; DSc, MD, PhD; FRACP; Director, John Curtin School of Medical Research, Australian National University, 1999; *b* 1 April 1944; *d* of Arthur Howard Whitworth and Margaret Edith Wilson Whitworth (*née* Dobbs); *m* 1981, John Ludbrook (marr. diss. 1992); partner, Colin Nicholson Chesterman. *Educ:* St Michael's C of E Girls' Grammar Sch.; Univ. of Melbourne (BS; MD 1974; PhD 1978; DSc 1992). FRACP 1975. RMO/Registrar, Royal Melbourne Hosp., 1968–71; Sen. Registrar, Queen Elizabeth Hosp., Adelaide, 1972; Winthrop Travelling Fellow, RACP, 1973; Vis. Registrar, Guy's Hosp., London, 1974–75; NHMRC Schol., Howard Florey Inst., 1975–77; Physician, 1978–81; Chm. Bd, Postgrad. Educn, 1983–91, Dep. Dir, Dept of Nephrology, 1990–91, Royal Melbourne Hosp.; Professorial Associate, Univ. of Melbourne, 1987–91; Prof. of Medicine, Univ. of NSW, 1991–99; CMO, Dept of Health and Family Services, 1997–99. Vis. Scientist, MRC Blood Pressure Unit, Glasgow, 1985; Naturalia et Biologia Fellow, Hosp. Tenon, Paris, 1985. Mem., NH&MRC Med. Res. Cttee, 1991–94 (Chm., 1994–97); Pres., High Blood Pressure Res. Council of Australia, 1998–2001. Mem. Council, RACP, 1984–93; Pres., Australian Soc. for Med. Res., 1984. Member: WHO Global Adv. Cttee on Health Res., 2000– (Chm., 2004–07); Nominating Cttee, Internat. Soc. for Nephrology, 1990–93; Councillor, Internat. Soc. of Hypertension, 1992–2000. Member: Council, Charles Darwin Univ., 2003–06; Bd, Menzies Sch. of Health Res., 2004–06; Bd, Menzies Res. Inst., Tasmania, 2005–. MD *hc* Sydney, 2004; NSW, 2005. Smith Kline and French Award, Internat. Soc. for Hypertension, 1984; Howard Florey Inst. Medal, 1990; RACP Medal, 1994; ACT Australian of the Year, 2004. Centenary Medal, Australia, 2003. *Publications:* Dictionary of Medical Eponyms, 1987, 2nd edn 1996; The Kidney, 2nd edn 1987; Textbook of Renal Disease, 1987, 2nd edn 1994; Hypertension Management, 1990; Clinical Nephrology in Medical Practice, 1992; numerous contribs to med. and scientific pubns. *Recreations:* books, cricket, ski-ing, film. *Address:* John Curtin School of Medical Research, Australian National University, GPO Box 334, Canberra, ACT 2601, Australia. *T:* (2) 61252597, *Fax:* (2) 61252337. *Clubs:* Melbourne Cricket, Lord's Taverners.

WHITWORTH-JONES, Anthony; General Director, Garsington Opera, since 2005; *b* 1 Sept. 1945; *s* of Henry Whitworth-Jones and Patience Martin; *m* 1974, Camilla (*née* Barlow); one *d. Educ:* Wellington College. Mem., Inst. of Chartered Accountants of Scotland. Thomson McLintock & Co., 1970–72; Administrative Dir, London Sinfonietta, 1972–81; Administrator, Glyndebourne Touring Opera and Opera Manager, Glyndebourne Fest. Opera, 1981–89; Gen. Adminr, then Gen. Dir, Glyndebourne Fest. Opera, 1989–98; Gen. Dir, The Dallas Opera, 2000–02; Artistic Dir, Casa da Musica, Porto, Portugal, 2004–05. Dir, SE Arts Bd, 1993–96. Chm., Michael Tippett Musical Foundn, 1998–. Member: Adv. Bd, Voices of Change, Dallas, 2001–02; Exec. Bd, Meadows Sch. of the Arts, Southern Methodist Univ., Dallas, 2001–02; Council, Spitalfields Fest., 2003–06 (Hon. Advr, 2006–). Trustee, Young Concert Artists Trust, 2007–. *Recreation:* enjoying the spirit and countryside of Wales and Greece. *Address:* 81 St Augustine's Road, NW1 9RR. *T:* (020) 7284 0908, *Fax:* (020) 7482 7017; *e-mail:* awjones@onetel.com.

WHOMERSLEY, Christopher Adrian; HM Diplomatic Service; Deputy Legal Adviser, Foreign and Commonwealth Office, since 2002; *b* 18 April 1953; *s* of Harry and Doreen Whomersley; *m* 1977, Jeanette Diana Szostak; one *s* two *d. Educ:* London Sch. of Economics (LLB); Christ's Coll., Cambridge (LLM). Called to the Bar, Middle Temple, 1981; Asst Legal Advr, 1977–91, Legal Counsellor, 1991–94, FCO; Legal Secretariat to Law Officers, 1994–97; Legal Counsellor, FCO, 1997–2002. Mem., UK Delegn to Channel Tunnel Intergovtl Commn, 1986–94, 1997–; Legal Advr to UK Delegn to Bermuda II Negotiations, 1991–94, 1997–2004; Govt Agent before the European Court of Human Rights, 2000–04. Mem., Finance Cttee, Internat. Sea-Bed Authy, 2007–. *Recreations:* reading modern literature and history, philately, following Coventry City FC and Warwickshire CCC. *Address:* c/o Foreign and Commonwealth Office, King Charles Street, SW1A 2AH. *Club:* MCC.

WHYBREW, Edward Graham, (Ted), CBE 2002; employment arbitrator, since 2000; Partner, Museum Replicas, 1997–2004; Certification Officer for Trade Unions and Employers' Associations, 1992–2001; *b* 25 Sept. 1938; *s* of Ernest Whybrew and Winifred (*née* Castle); *m* 1967, Julia Helen Baird (OBE 2001); one *s* two *d. Educ:* Hertford Grammar Sch.; Balliol Coll., Oxford (BA 1961); Nuffield Coll., Oxford. Economist: NEDO, 1963; DEA, 1964–69; Dept of Employment, subseq. EDG, 1969–92; Asst Sec., Employment, Trng and Industrial Relations, 1977–85; Under Sec., Industrial Relations Div., 1985–89; Dir, Personnel and Staff Develt, 1989–92. ACAS Arbitrator. Associate Partner, Jamieson Scott (Exec. Search), 1993–98. *Publication:* Overtime Working in Great Britain, 1968. *Recreations:* watching cricket, ceramic restoration, gardening. *Address:* Grangelea, Grange Park, Steeple Aston, Bicester, Oxon OX25 4SR.

WHYBROW, Christopher John; QC 1992; *b* 7 Aug. 1942; *s* of Herbert William Whybrow, OBE and Ruby Kathleen Whybrow (*née* Watson); *m* 1st, 1969, Marion Janet Macaulay (marr. diss. 1976); 2nd, 1979, Susan Younge (marr. diss. 1990). *Educ:* Colchester Royal Grammar Sch.; King's Coll., London (LLB). Called to the Bar, Inner Temple, 1965. A Dep. Social Security Comr, 1996–. *Publications:* (contrib.) Atkins Court Forms; contribs to Jl of Planning and Environment Law. *Recreations:* history, cricket, tennis, gardening, country life. *Address:* Landmark Chambers, 180 Fleet Street, EC4A 2HG. *Clubs:* Lansdowne, MCC; Leavenheath Cricket.

WHYBROW, John William; Chairman, Wolseley PLC, since 2002 (Director, since 1997); *b* 11 March 1947; *s* of Charles Ernest James Whybrow and Doris Beatrice Whybrow (*née* Abbott); *m* 1968, Paula Miriam Hobart; one *s* one *d. Educ:* Hatfield Tech. GS; Imperial Coll., London (BSc Hons Mech. Engrg); Manchester Business Sch. (MBA); ACGI. English Electric, Rugby, 1968–70; Philips Electronics: Northern Operational Res. Gp, 1970–78; Ind. Engrg Head, Mullard Simonstone, 1979–82; Div. Manager, 1982–83, Plant Dir, 1983–87, Mullard Blackburn; Plant Dir, Hazel Grove, 1987–88; Man. Dir, TDS Circuits plc, 1988–90; Tech. Dir, Philips Components, 1990–91; Industrial Dir, 1991–93, Chm. and Man. Dir, 1993–95, Philips Electronics UK; Pres. and CEO, Philips Lighting Holding BV, 1995–2001; Exec. Vice-Pres., Main Bd, Royal Philips Electronics, 1998–2002. Chairman: Lumileds Lighting BV, 1997–2000; CSR plc, 2004–07 (Dir, 2003–07); non-executive Director: Teletext Hldgs, 1993–95; DSG Internat. (formerly Dixons) PLC, 2003–. MInstD 1993. Order of Merit (Poland), 2002. *Recreation:* sailing. *Address:* Wolseley PLC, Parkview 1220, Arlington Business Park, Theale, Reading RG7 4GA. *Club:* East India.

WHYTE, Duncan; consultant; Chairman, Wales and West Utilities Ltd, since 2005; *b* 27 July 1946; *s* of Andrew Montgomery Whyte and Margaret Steedman Whyte; *m* 1971, Marion McDonald McCready; one *s. Educ:* Kilsyth Acad. CA 1968; ATII 1968. Trainee Chartered Accountant, Paterson and Benzies, 1963–69; Arthur Andersen & Co., 1969–83 (Man. Partner, Edinburgh office, 1980–83); Financial Dir, Kwikfit Hldgs plc, 1983–88; Scottish Power: Exec. Dir, 1988–99; Finance Dir, 1988–93; Chief Operating Officer, 1993–95; Exec. Dir, Multi Utility, 1995–99; Chief Exec., Weir Gp plc, 1999–2000. Non-exec. Dir, Motherwell Bridge Hldgs Ltd, 1997–2003. *Recreations:* golf, badminton, reading history.

WHYTE, Prof. Iain Boyd, PhD; FRSE; Professor of Architectural History, University of Edinburgh, since 1996; *b* 6 March 1947; *s* of Thomas Boyd Whyte and Mary Whyte (*née* Macpherson); *m* 1973, Deborah Smart; one *s* one *d. Educ:* Nottingham Univ. (BA 1969; MPhil 1971); Cornell Univ.; Jesus Coll., Cambridge (PhD 1979); Leeds Univ. (MA 1987). FRSE 1998. British Acad./Wolfson Fellow, 1976–77; Alexander von Humboldt-Stiftung Fellow, 1979–82; Leverhulme Trust Res. Fellow, 1985–87; University of Edinburgh: Lectr in Architecl Hist., 1988–93; Reader, 1993–95. Getty Schol., 1989–90; Getty Sen. Schol., 1998–2000; Sen. Prog. Officer, Getty Grant Prog., LA, 2002–04. Trustee, Nat. Galls of Scotland, 1998–2002. Co-Curator, Council of Europe Exhibn, Art and Power - Europe under the Dictators 1930–46, Hayward Gall., London, Centre de Cultura Contemporánea, Barcelona, Deutsches Historisches Mus., Berlin, 1995–96. FRSA. *Publications:* Bruno Taut and the Architecture of Activism, 1982 (German edn, 1981); (ed) The Crystal Chain Letters, 1985 (trans. German, 1986); Emil Hoppe, Marcel Kammerer, Otto Schönthal, 1989; (introd and co-trans.) Hendrik Petrus Berlage on Style 1886–1909, 1996; (jtly) John Fowler, Benjamin Baker: The Forth Bridge, 1997; Modernism and the Spirit of the City, 2003. *Recreations:* violin playing, sculling. *Address:* 44 North Castle Street, Edinburgh EH2 3BN. *T:* (0131) 220 5510. *Clubs:* Leander (Henley-on-Thames); New (Edinburgh); Akademischer Ruderclub zu Berlin (Berlin).

WHYTE, (John) Stuart Scott, CB 1986; Under Secretary, Department of Health and Social Security, 1978–86; *b* 1 April 1926; *er s* of late Thomas and Mysie Scott Whyte, Sandycove, Co. Dublin; *m* 1950, Jocelyn Margaret, *o d* of late George Hawley, CBE, Edinburgh; two *s* one *d. Educ:* St Andrew's Coll., Dublin; Trinity Coll., Univ. of Dublin. BA 1947; LLB 1948. Asst Principal, Dept of Health for Scotland, 1948; Principal, 1955; Principal Private Sec. to Sec. of State for Scotland, 1959; Asst Sec., Scottish Develt Dept, 1962; Asst Sec., Cabinet Office, 1969; Asst Under-Sec. of State, Scottish Office, 1969–74; Under Sec., Cabinet Office, 1974–78. *Address:* La Bâtisse, Bonin, 47120 Duras, France. *T:* 553837031.

WHYTE, Prof. Moira Katherine Brigid, (Mrs D. Crossman), PhD; FRCP, FMedSci; Professor of Respiratory Medicine, since 1996, and Head, Section of Infection, Inflammation and Immunity, since 2006, University of Sheffield; *b* 25 Sept. 1959; *d* of Maurice and Anne Whyte; *m* 1988, David Crossman; two *s. Educ:* Convent of Notre Dame, Plymouth; Plymouth Coll.; St Bartholomew's Hosp. Med. Coll., London (BSc 1st cl. Hons Anatomy 1981; MB BS 1984); Royal Postgraduate Med. Sch., London (PhD 1993). MRCP 1987, FRCP 1997. Jun. med. posts, London, 1984–87; Registrar in Respiratory Medicine, Dept of Medicine, Hammersmith Hosp., 1987–89; MRC Trng Fellow, RPMS, 1989–92; Sen. Registrar in Respiratory Medicine, Hammersmith Hosp., 1992–94; Wellcome Advanced Fellow and Hon. Consultant Physician, Univ. of Nottingham and ICRF, London, 1994–95. Member: Wellcome Trust Clinical Interest Gp, 1997–2002; Wellcome Trust Physiol Scis Panel, 2002–05. Chm., Scientific Cttee, British Lung Foundn, 2003–06. Mem., Dorothy Hodgkin Grants Panel, Royal Soc., 2006–. FMedSci 2005. *Publications:* papers on cell death in inflammation and inflammatory lung disease. *Recreations:* reading, my children's current hobbies. *Address:* Academic Unit of Respiratory Medicine, Section of Infection, Inflammation and Immunity, School of Medicine and Biomedical Sciences, University of Sheffield, Royal Hallamshire Hospital, Sheffield S10 2JF. *T:* (0114) 271 2830, *Fax:* (0114) 226 8898; *e-mail:* m.k.whyte@sheffield.ac.uk.

WHYTE, Stuart Scott; *see* Whyte, J. S. S.

WIBLIN, Derek John, CB 1992; Under Secretary, Principal Establishment and Finance Officer, Crown Prosecution Service, 1988–93; *b* 18 March 1933; *s* of late Cyril G. H. Wiblin and of Winifred F. Wiblin; *m* 1960, Pamela Jeanne Hamshere; one *s* one *d. Educ:* Birmingham University (BSc Hons Chem 1954). RAF, 1954–57. Courtaulds Ltd, 1957–58; joined DSIR Building Research Station, 1958; Civil Service Commission, 1967–71; Asst Sec., Local Govt Div., DoE, 1971–79; Ports Div., Dept of Transport, 1979–81; Estabs Div., DoE, 1981–83; Under Sec., Principal Estabt and Finance Officer, Lord Chancellor's Dept, 1984–88. Chm., First Division Pensioners' Gp, 1993–98. *Recreations:* making violins, collecting books. *Address:* 19 Woodway, Oxhey, Watford, Herts WD19 4NN. *T:* (01923) 228615. *Clubs:* Athenæum, Royal Air Force.

WICKENS, Prof. Alan Herbert, OBE 1980; FREng, FIMechE; Visiting Industrial Professor, Wolfson School of Mechanical and Manufacturing Engineering (formerly Department of Mechanical Engineering), Loughborough University (formerly Loughborough University of Technology), since 1993; *b* 29 March 1929; *s* of late Herbert Leslie Wickens and of Sylvia Wickens; *m* 1st, 1953, Eleanor Joyce Waggott (*d* 1984); one *d*; 2nd, 1987, Patricia Anne McNeil. *Educ:* Ashville Coll., Harrogate; Loughborough Univ. of Technol. (DLC Eng, BScEng London, 1951; DSc Loughborough, 1978). CEng, FIMechE 1971; MRAeS. Res. Engr, Sir W. G. Armstrong Whitworth Aircraft Ltd, Coventry, 1951–55; Gp Leader, Dynamics Analysis, Canadair Ltd, Montreal, 1955–59; Head of Aeroelastics Section, Weapons Res. Div., A. V. Roe & Co., Ltd, Woodford, 1959–62; British Rail: Supt, Res. Dept, 1962–67; Advanced Projs Engr, 1967–68; Dir of Advanced Projs, 1968–71; Dir of Labs, 1971–78; Dir of Research, 1978–84; Dir of Engrg Develt and Research, 1984–89. Loughborough University of Technology: Industrial Prof. of Transport Technol., 1972–76; Prof. of Dynamics, Dept of Mechanical Engrg, 1989–92. Vis. Prof., Dept of Mech. Engrg, Design and Manufacture, Manchester Metropolitan Univ., 1998–2001. Pres., Internat. Assoc. of Vehicle System Dynamics, 1981–86 (Hon. Mem., 2001); Chm., Office of Res. and Experiments, Union Internationale de Chemins de fer, 1988–90. Mem., Amer. Inst. Aeronautics and Astronautics, 1958. FBIS; FRSA. Hon. Fellow, Derbyshire Coll. of Higher Educn, 1984. Hon. DTech: CNAA, 1978; Loughborough, 2006; Hon. Dr Open Univ., 1980. George Stephenson Res. Prize, IMechE, 1966; (jtly) MacRobert Award, 1975. *Publications:* Fundamentals of Rail Vehicle Dynamics, 2003; papers on dynamics of railway vehicles, high speed trains and future railway technology, publ. by IMechE, Amer. Soc. of Mech. Engrs, Internat. Jl of Solids and Structures, and Jl of Vehicle System Dynamics. *Recreations:* gardening, travel, music. *Address:* Ecclesbourne Farmhouse, Ecclesbourne Lane, Idridgehay, Derbys DE56 2SB. *T:* (01773) 550368. *Club:* Royal Air Force.

WICKER-MIURIN, Fields, OBE 2007; Co-Founder and Partner, Leaders' Quest Ltd, since 2002; *b* 30 July 1958; *d* of Warren Jake Wicker and Marie Peachee Wicker; *m* 1994, Dr Paolo Miurin. *Educ:* Univ. of Virginia (BA *cum laude* Foreign Affairs and French); L'Institut d'Etudes Politiques, Paris (Cert. d'Etudes Politiques); Johns Hopkins Sch. of Advanced Internat. Studies (MA Econs and Pol Affairs). Vice Pres., Philadelphia Nat. Bank, 1982–89; Partner and Hd Financial Services Practice, Europe, Strategic Planning Associates, 1989–94; Finance Dir and Dir of Strategy, London Stock Exchange, 1994–97; Partner and Vice Pres., Hd Global Financial Markets, AT Kearney, 1998–2000; Chief Operating Officer and Partner, Vesta Capital Advisors Ltd, 2000–02. Non-exec. Dir, 2002–, Chm. Investment Cttee, 2002–06, BERR (formerly DTI); Member: Technol. Adv. Council, NASDAQ, 2000–; Panel of Experts, Econ. and Monetary Affairs Cttee, EP, 2002–06. Non-executive Director: Utd Business Media plc, 1998–2004; Savills plc, 2002–; Royal London Gp, 2003–06 Carnegie & Co. AB, 2003–07; CDC Gp plc, 2004–. Trustee: London Internat. Fest. of Theatre, 1997–2004; Arts & Business UK, 1998–2001; London Musici, 2000–03; Council, Tate Members, 2000–06; Brogdale Horticultural Trust, 2002–04. Governor, KCL, 2002–. FRSA 1997. Global Leader for Tomorrow, World Econ. Forum, 1997. *Publications:* numerous articles in financial press. *Recreations:* seeing the open countryside, my horse Max, opera, exploring new ideas and ways of seeing the world. *Address:* Leaders' Quest Ltd, 3–5 Richmond Hill, Richmond, Surrey TW10 6RE. *T:* (020) 8948 5202, *Fax:* (020) 8332 6423.

WICKERSON, Sir John (Michael), Kt 1987; Partner, 1962–98, Consultant, since 1998, Ormerods (previously Ormerod, Morris & Dumont, later Ormerod Wilkinson Marshall, then Ormerod Heap & Marshall); President, Law Society, 1986–87; *b* 22 Sept. 1937; *s* of

Walter and Ruth Wicl rson; *m* 1963, Shirley Maud Best; one *s*. *Educ:* Christ's Hospital; London University (Ll). Admitted solicitor, 1960; Mem. Council, Law Society, 1969 (Chm., Contentious B iness Cttee; Vice-Pres., 1985–86). Member: Matrimonial Causes Rules Cttee, 1982–86 Royal Commn on Criminal Justice, 1991–93. Pres., London Criminal Courts Solici rs Assoc., 1980–81. Chairman: Mansell plc (formerly R. Mansell Ltd), 1994–2002; Inve ors' Compensation Scheme Ltd, 1996–2001; United Healthcare (Farnborough Hospita Ltd, 2000–; Hospital Co. (Darenth) Ltd, 2001–; United Healthcare (Farnborou h Hospital) Ltd, 2000–; Hospital Co., (Darenth) Ltd, 2001–; Hospital Co., (Swindo and Marlborough) Ltd, 2002–. Chm., Croydon Community NHS Trust, 1991–98. Hon. Member: Amer. Bar Assoc., 1986; Canadian Bar Assoc., 1986; NZ Law Soc., 987. *Publication:* Motorist and the Law, 1975, 2nd edn 1982. *Recreation:* golf. *Addres* : c/o Ormerods, Green Dragon House, 64–70 High Street, Croydon, Surrey CR0 9XN. *T:* (020) 8686 5000.

WICKES, Charles G.; *see* Goodson-Wickes.

WICKHAM, Prof. Christopher John, DPhil; FBA 1998; Chichele Professor of Medieval History, University of Oxford, since 2005; Fellow of All Souls College, Oxford, since 2005; *b* 18 May 1950; *s* of Cyril George Wickham and Katharine Brenda Warington Wickham (*née* Moss); *m* 1990, Prof. Leslie Brubaker. *Educ:* Millfield Sch.; Keble Coll., Oxford (BA 1971; DPhil 1975). University of Birmingham: Lectr, 1977–87; Sen. Lectr, 1987–89; Reader, 1989–93; Prof. of Early Medieval History, 1993–2005. Jt Ed., Past & Present, 1994–. *Publications:* Early Medieval Italy, 1981; The mountains and the city, 1988; (with J. Fentress) Social memory, 1992; Land and power, 1994; Community and Clientele, 1998 (Italian edn, 1995); Courts and Conflict, 2003 (Italian edn, 2000); Framing the Early Middle Ages, 2005. *Recreations:* politics, travel. *Address:* All Souls College, Oxford OX1 4AL.

WICKHAM, Daphne Elizabeth, (Mrs J. K. A. Alderson); a District Judge (Magistrates' Courts) (formerly Metropolitan Stipendiary Magistrate), since 1989; a Recorder, since 1997; Deputy Chief Magistrate and Deputy Senior District Judge (Magistrates' Courts), since 2003; *b* 31 Aug. 1946; *d* of late Major Harry Temple Wickham and Phyllis Wickham (*née* Roycroft); *m* 1983, John Keith Ameers Alderson. *Educ:* Sydenham High Sch.; Chislehurst and Sidcup Girls' Grammar School. Called to the Bar, Inner Temple, 1967. *Recreation:* laughter. *Address:* City of Westminster Magistrates' Court, 70 Horseferry Road, SW1P 2AX. *T:* (020) 7805 1035. *Club:* Reform.

WICKHAM, David Ian; Chairman: Telecom Direct Ltd, since 2003; Synchronica plc, since 2006; *b* 23 Oct. 1957; *s* of Edwin and Betty Wickham; *m* 1982, Joanne Frances Carter; two *s*. *Educ:* St Olave's Grammar Sch., Orpington; S London Coll. (HND Business Studies). Various devel roles in UK, Europe and S Pacific to 1985; Mktg Dir, C&W Systems Ltd, Hong Kong, 1985–87; Mercury Communications Ltd: Gen. Manager, Residential and Operator Services, 1987–91; Mktg Dir, Business and Consumer Services, 1991–94; Man. Dir, Partner Services, 1994–96; Ops Dir, 1996–97; Man. Dir, Internat. and Partner Services, Cable & Wireless Communications Ltd, 1997–98; Chief Exec., Global Network, Cable and Wireless plc, 1998–99; Energis plc: Chief Operating Officer, 1999–2001; Chief Exec., 2001–02; Dep. Chief Exec., 2002. Chairman: 3c plc, 2004–06; YAC Ltd, 2005–06 (non-exec. Dir, 2003–04, 2006–07). *Recreations:* golf, theatre, family, travel. *Club:* London Golf.

WICKHAM, Janie; *see* Dee, J.

WICKHAM, John Ewart Alfred, FRCS; specialist in minimally invasive surgery and urology; Surgeon and Senior Research Fellow, Guy's Hospital, 1993–98; Director, Academic Unit, Institute of Urology, University of London, 1979–98; Surgeon: St Peter's Hospital, 1967–95; King Edward VII Hospital, 1972–98; Middlesex Hospital, 1973–95; *b* 10 Dec. 1927; *s* of Alfred James Wickham and Hilda May Wickham (*née* Cummins); *m* 1961, (Gwendoline) Ann Loney; three *d*. *Educ:* Chichester Grammar Sch.; London Univ.; St Bartholomew's Hosp. Med. Coll. (BSc Hons 1953; MB BS 1955; MS 1966). FRCS 1959. Nat. Service, RAF, 1947–49. St Bartholomew's Hosp. and RPMS, 1955–66; Sen. Consultant Urological Surgeon, St Bart's, 1966–85; Sen. Lectr, 1967–92, and Sub Dean, 1967–79, Inst. of Urology; Civilian Consultant Urologist, RAF, 1973–98. Director: Lithotripter Units of London Clinic, 1984–98, and of NE Thames Region, 1987–95; Minimally Invasive Therapy, London Clinic, 1989–99. First Pres., Internat. Soc. of Urological Endoscopy, 1982; President: Urological Sect., RSM, 1984–85; Internat. Soc. of Minimally Invasiv herapy, 1989–2000; Founder Mem., Europ. Soc. of Urology, 1969; Member: Inte oc. of Urology, 1970; Italian-Belgian Soc. of Urology, 1980; Irish Soc. of Urolog American Soc. of Urology, 1990; Japanese Soc. of Urology, 1993. Hon. FRCP n. FRCR 1993; Hon. FRSocMed 2008. Freeman, City of London; Liverym r Surgeon's Co., 1971. Hon. MD Gothenburg, 1994. Hunterian Prof. a RCS, 1967; Cutlers Prize and Medal, Assoc. of Surgeons, 1984; James Berry CS, 1985; St Peter's Medal, British Assoc. of Urological Surgeons, 1985; J. er Medal, Amer. Urological Assoc., 1990; Cecil Joll Prize, RCS, 1993; Rovsi , Danish Soc. of Surgery, 1993; Cook Medal, RCR, 1998; Galen Medal, Soc. thecaries, 1998. Editor, Jl of Minimally Invasive Therapy, 1990–2000. *Publicati* rinary Calculus Disease, 1979; Percutaneous Renal Surgery, 1983; Intrarenal Surg 984; Lithotripsy II, 1987; Urinary Stone Metabolic Basis and Clinical Practice, 19 ver 150 papers on urology and minimally invasive surgery. *Recreations:* mechanic gineering, tennis. *Address:* The Cottage, 18 Rose Hill, Dorking, Surrey RH4 2EA. *T:* 306) 882451. *Club:* Athenæum.

WICKHAM, His Hon r William Rayley; a Circuit Judge, 1975–97; Hon. Recorder of Liverpool and Seni Circuit Judge, Liverpool, 1992–97; *b* 22 Sept. 1926; *s* of late Rayley Esmond Wicl and Mary Joyce Wickham; *m* 1957, Elizabeth Mary (*née* Thompson); one *s* tw . *Educ:* Sedbergh Sch.; Brasenose Coll., Oxford (MA, BCL). Served War of 1939–4 Army, 1944–48. Called to Bar, Inner Temple, 1951. Magistrate, Aden, 1953; Chief M strate, Aden, 1958; Crown Counsel, Tanganyika, 1959; Asst to Law Officers, Tangany , 1961–63; practised on Northern Circuit, 1963–75; a Recorder of the Crown Court, 1 2–75. *Recreations:* fell walking, music, amateur dramatics. *Address:* 115 Vyner Road Soutl Prenton CH43 7PP.

WICKRAMASINGHE Prof. (Nalin) Chandra, PhD, ScD; Professor and Director, Cardiff Centre for robiology, since 2000, and Emeritus Professor of Applied Mathematics and Astro omy, since 2006, Cardiff University; *b* 20 Jan. 1939; *s* of Percival Herbert Wickramasing e and Theresa Elizabeth Wickramasinghe; *m* 1966, Nelum Priyadarshini Pereira; e *s* two *d*. *Educ:* Royal Coll., Colombo, Sri Lanka; Univ. of Ceylon (BSc); Univ. o Cambridge (MA, PhD, ScD). Commonwealth Scholar, Trinity Coll., Cambridge, 196 Powell Prize for English Verse, 1961; Jesus College, Cambridge: Research Fellow, 196 –66; Fellow, 1967–73; Tutor, 1970–73; Staff Mem., Inst. of Theoretical Astronomy Univ. of Cambridge, 1968–73; Prof. and Hd of Dept of Applied Maths and Astronomy UC, Cardiff, 1973–88; Prof., Sch. of Maths, UWCC, subseq. Cardiff Univ., 1988–2 00. Visiting Professor: Vidyodaya Univ. of Ceylon, Univ. of Maryland, USA, Univ. of Arizona, USA, Univ. of Kyoto, Japan, 1966–70; Univ. of W Ontario, 1974, 1976; Inst. of Space and Astronautical Studies, Japan, 1993; Univ. of WI, Kingston, Jamaica, 1994; UNDP Cons. and Scientific Advisor to President of Sri Lanka, 1970–81; Dir, Inst. of Fundamental Studies, Sri Lanka, 1982–83 (Vis. Prof., 1997–). Collaborator with Prof. Sir Fred Hoyle, and propounder with Hoyle of the theory of the space origin of life and of microorganisms. Hon. Prof., Glamorgan Univ., 2007. Hon. DSc: Soka Univ., Japan, 1996; Ruhana Univ., Sri Lanka, 2004. Dag Hammarskjöld Gold Medal in science, Académie Diplomatique de la Paix, 1986; Scholarly Achievement Award, Inst. of Oriental Philosophy, Japan, 1989; Internat. Peace and Culture Award, Soka Gakkai, 1993; Sahabdeen Internat. Award for Science, A. M. M. Sahabdeen Trust Foundn, 1996; John Snow Lecture Medal, Assoc. of Anaesthetists of GB and Ire., 2004. Vidya Jyothi (Sri Lanka), 1992. *Publications:* Interstellar Grains, 1967; (with F. D. Kahn and P. G. Mezger) Interstellar Matter, 1972; Light Scattering Functions for Small Particles with Applications in Astronomy, 1973; The Cosmic Laboratory, 1975; (with D. J. Morgan) Solid State Astrophysics, 1976; Fundamental Studies and the Future of Science, 1984; (with F. Hoyle and J. Watkins) Viruses from Space, 1986; (with Daisaku Ikeda) Emergent Perspectives for 2000 AD, 1992; (with D. Ikeda) The Wonders of Life and the Universe, 1993; Glimpses of Life, Time and Space: an anthology of poetry, 1994; Cosmic Dragons: life and death of our planet, 2001; A Journey with Fred Hoyle, 2005; (with F. Hoyle): Lifecloud: the origin of life in the universe, 1978; Diseases From Space, 1979; The Origin of Life, 1980; Evolution From Space, 1981; Space Travellers, the Bringers of Life, 1981; From Grains to Bacteria, 1984; Living Comets, 1985; Archaeopteryx, the Primordial Bird: a case of fossil forgery, 1986; Cosmic Life Force, 1987; Theory of Cosmic Grains, 1991; Our Place in the Cosmos: the unfinished revolution, 1993; Life on Mars?: the case for a cosmic heritage, 1997; (with F. Hoyle) Astronomical Origins of Life: steps towards panspermia, 2000; over 300 articles and papers in astronomical and scientific jls; contributor to anthologies of Commonwealth Poetry, incl. Young Commonwealth Poets '65, ed P. L. Brent, 1965. *Recreations:* photography, poetry—both writing and reading, history and philosophy of science. *Address:* Cardiff Centre for Astrobiology, Cardiff University, 2 North Road, Cardiff CF10 3DY. *T:* (029) 2075 2146, *Fax:* (029) 2075 3173; *e-mail:* wickramasinghe@cardiff.ac.uk; (home) 24 Llwynypia Road, Lisvane, Cardiff CF14 0SY.

See also S. N. Wickramasinghe.

WICKRAMASINGHE, Prof. Sunitha Nimal, PhD, ScD; FRCP, FRCPath; FIBiol; Professor, and Head of Department of Haematology, Imperial College, University of London, 1979–2000, Professor Emeritus, since 2000; *b* 2 July 1941; *s* of Percival Herbert Wickramasinghe and Theresa Elizabeth Wickramasinghe; *m* 1968, Priyanthi Soummia Fernando; one *s* two *d*. *Educ:* Royal Coll., Colombo; Univ. of Ceylon (MB BS); PhD 1968, ScD 1984, Cantab. FRCPath 1986; FRCP 1991; FIBiol 1982. Gulbenkian Res. Student, Churchill Coll., Cambridge, 1966–68; John Lucas Walker Sen. Student, Univ. of Cambridge, 1968; Clin. Res. Fellow, Univ. of Leeds, 1969; Lectr, 1970–73, Sen. Lectr, 1973–78, Reader in Haematol., 1978–79, St Mary's Hosp. Med. Sch., Univ. of London; Dep. Dean, ICSM at St Mary's, 1995–97; Hon. Consultant Haematologist: St Mary's Hosp., London, 1979–; Oxford Radcliffe Hosps, 2000–05. Vis. Prof. in Haematol., Univ. of Oxford, 2000–08. Guest Lectr, Univ. degli Studi di Ferrara, Italy, 1993–97. Hon. Fellow, Sri Lanka Coll. of Haematologists, 1999; E. H. Cooray Meml Orator, Coll. of Pathologists, Sri Lanka, 1995; Sri Lanka Med. Assoc. Orator, 2005. Guest Editor: Megaloblastic Anaemia, 1995; Haematological Aspects of Infection, 2000. *Publications:* Human Bone Marrow, 1975; (ed) Blood and Bone Marrow: systemic pathology, 3rd edn 1986; (with N. C. Hughes-Jones) Lecture Notes on Haematology, 5th edn 1991, 6th edn 1996, (with N. C. Hughes-Jones and C. Hatton) 7th edn 2004, 8th edn 2008; (ed with J. McCullough) Blood and Bone Marrow Pathology, 2003; contrib. papers on abnormal erythropoiesis. *Recreations:* photography, travel, biology. *Address:* 32 Braywick Road, Maidenhead, Berks SL6 1DA. *T:* (01628) 621665.

See also N. C. Wickramasinghe.

WICKREMESINGHE, Sarath Kusum; Chairman, National Development Bank Ltd, Colombo, 1999–2008; *b* 26 Jan. 1928; *m* 1953, Damayantha Hulugalle. *Educ:* St Thomas' Coll., Mt Lavinia; Univ. of Ceylon (BSc Hons Physics). Exec. in ICI (Export) Ltd, Colombo, 1951–66; Chief Exec., 1966–80, Chm., 1966–94, ICI associate co. in Sri Lanka; Chm., subsid. and associate cos, Coates Internat., 1982–84, BAT, 1985–91, and Standard Chartered Bank, 1989–94; High Comr for Sri Lanka in London, 1995–99; Chm., Sri Lanka Airlines Ltd, 1999–2002. *Address:* 8 Claessen Place, Colombo 5, Sri Lanka. *Clubs:* Hill (Sri Lanka); Ceylon Rugby Football.

WICKS, Allan, CBE 1988; Organist, Canterbury Cathedral, 1961–88; *b* 6 June 1923; *s* of late Edward Kemble Wicks, priest, and Nancie (*née* Murgatroyd); *m* 1955, Elizabeth Kay Butcher; two *d*. *Educ:* Leatherhead; Christ Church, Oxford. Sub-organist, York Minster, 1947; Organist, Manchester Cathedral, 1954. MusDoc Lambeth, 1974; Hon. DMus Kent, 1985. *Address:* 27 Chequers Park, Wye, Ashford, Kent TN25 5BB. *T:* (01233) 813920.

WICKS, Geoffrey Leonard; a District Judge (Magistrates' Courts) (formerly Metropolitan Stipendiary Magistrate), 1987–2002; Immigration Adjudicator (part-time), since 1996; *b* 23 July 1934; *s* of late Leonard James Wicks and Winifred Ellen Wicks; *m* 1st, 1959, Catherine Margaret Shanks (marr. diss. 1977); one *s* one *d*; 2nd, 1978, Maureen Evelyn Neville. *Educ:* Tollington Sch., N10; Law Society's Sch. of Law, London. Admitted Solicitor, 1957. National Service, 1957–59. Asst Solicitor, LCC, 1959–60; Asst Solicitor, 1960–61, Partner, 1961–79 (Abu Dhabi office, 1978), Oswald Hickson, Collier & Co., Solicitors, London, Chesham, Amersham, Slough; Principal, Geoffrey Wicks & Co., Solicitors, Chesham, Hemel Hempstead, 1979–82; Partner, Iliffes, Solicitors, London, Chesham, 1982–87. Chairman: Family Courts, 1991–97; Youth Courts, 1991–2002; Mem., Inner London Magistrates' Courts Cttee, 1995–99, 2000–01. Mem., Home Sec.'s Task Force for Youth Justice, 1997–98. Member: Chesham Round Table, 1962–75 (Chm. 1968–69, Area Chm. Area 42, 1972–73); Chesham Rotary Club, 1974–77. *Recreations:* walking, opera, ballet. *Address:* c/o Chief Magistrate's Office, Westminster City Magistrates' Court, 70 Horseferry Road, SW1P 2AX.

WICKS, Rt Hon. Malcolm (Hunt); PC 2008; MP (Lab) Croydon North, since 1997 (Croydon North West, 1992–97); *b* 1 July 1947; *s* of Arthur Wicks and late Daisy (*née* Hunt); *m* 1968, Margaret Baron; one *s* two *d*. *Educ:* Norfolk House; Elizabeth Coll., Guernsey; NW London Poly.; LSE (BSc Hons Sociology). Fellow, Dept of Social Admin, York Univ., 1968–70; res. worker, Centre for Envmtl Studies, 1970–72; Lectr in Social Admin, Dept of Govt Studies, Brunel Univ., 1970–74; Social Policy Analyst, Urban Deprivation Unit, Home Office, 1974–77; Lectr in Social Policy, Civil Service Coll., 1977–78; Res. Dir and Sec., Study Commn on the Family, 1978–83; Dir, Family Policy Studies Centre, 1983–92; Co-Dir, European Family and Social Policy Unit, 1992. Parliamentary Under-Secretary of State: DFEE, 1999–2001; DWP, 2001–03; Minister of State: for Pensions, DWP, 2003–05; for Energy, DTI, 2005–06; for Science and Innovation, DTI, 2006–07; for Energy, BERR, 2007–08; Special Rep. of the Prime Minister on internat. energy issues, 2008–. Sec., PLP Social Security Cttee, 1994–96. Mem., Family Policy Observatory, Eur. Commn, 1987–92. Chm., Winter Action on Cold Homes, 1986–92. Trustee, Nat. Energy Foundn, 1987–. *Publications:* Old and Cold:

hypothermia and social policy, 1978; (jtly) Government and Urban Policy, 1983; A Future for All: do we need a welfare state?, 1987; (jtly) Family Change and Future Policy, 1990; The Active Society: defending welfare, 1994; contribs to books and periodicals. *Recreations:* walking, music, writing. *Address:* House of Commons, SW1A 0AA. *T:* (020) 7219 3000. *Club:* Ruskin House Labour (Croydon).

WICKS, Sir Nigel (Leonard), GCB 1999 (KCB 1992); CVO 1989; CBE 1979; Chairman, Euroclear plc, since 2006 (Deputy Chairman, 2002–06); non-executive Director, Edinburgh Investment Trust plc, since 2005; Commissioner, Jersey Financial Services Commission, since 2007; *b* 16 June 1940; *s* of late Leonard Charles and Beatrice Irene Wicks; *m* 1969, Jennifer Mary (*née* Coveney) three *s*. *Educ:* Beckenham and Penge Grammar Sch.; Portsmouth Coll. of Technology; Univ. of Cambridge (MA); Univ. of London (MA). The British Petroleum Co. Ltd, 1958–68; HM Treasury, 1968–75; Private Sec. to the Prime Minister, 1975–78; HM Treasury, 1978–83; Economic Minister, British Embassy, Washington, and UK Exec. Dir, IMF and IBRD, 1983–85; Principal Private Sec. to the Prime Minister, 1985–88; Second Perm. Sec. (Finance), HM Treasury, 1989–2000. Chm., CRESTCo, 2001–02; Mem. Bd, BNOC, 1980–82; non-exec. Dir, Morgan Stanley Bank Internat. Ltd, 2004–06. Chairman: Cttee on Standards in Public Life, 2001–04; Scrutiny Cttee, Actuarial Profession, 2004–06; Selection Panel for Appts, Judicial Appts Commn, 2005–06. Gov., King's Coll. Sch., Wimbledon, 1993–2005. Hon. LLD: Bath, 1999; Portsmouth, 2002. *Address:* c/o Euroclear SA/NV, 33 Cannon Street, EC4M 5SB.

WICKSTEAD, Cyril; Chairman, Eastern Electricity Board, 1978–82; Member, Electricity Council, 1978–82; *b* 27 Sept. 1922; *s* of John William and Mary Caroline Wickstead; *m* 1948, Freda May Hill; two *s*. *Educ:* Rowley Regis Central Sch.; City of Birmingham Commercial Coll. FCIS. Served War, Royal Navy (Lieut RNVR), 1942–46. Midland Electric Corporation for Power Distribution Ltd: various positions, 1937–42; Asst Sec., 1946–48; Midlands Electricity Board: Sec., S Staffs and N Worcs Sub-Area, 1948–59; Dep. Sec. of Bd, 1959–63; Sec., 1964–72; Dep. Chm., 1972–77. Freeman, City of London, 1979. *Recreations:* music, reading, gardening, sport (spectator, alas).

WICKSTEAD, Myles Antony, CBE 2006; Visiting Professor of International Relations, Open University, since 2005; *b* 7 Feb. 1951; *s* of John Horace Wickstead and Eva Mary Wickstead (*née* Fouracre); *m* 1990, Shelagh Paterson; one *s* one *d*. *Educ:* Blundell's Sch.; St Andrews Univ. (MA 1st Cl. Hons Eng. Lang. and Lit. 1974); New Coll., Oxford (MLitt). Joined ODM, 1976; Asst Private Sec. to Lord Privy Seal, FCO, 1979–80; Asst to UK Exec. Dir, IMF/IBRD, 1980–84; Principal, ODA, 1984–88; Private Sec. to Minister for Overseas Develt, 1988–90; Head: EC and Food Aid Dept, ODA, 1990–93; British Develt Div. in Eastern Africa, 1993–97; UK Alternate Exec. Dir, World Bank, and Counsellor (Develt), Washington, 1997–2000; Ambassador to Ethiopia and (non-res.) to Djibouti, 2000–04; Hd of Secretariat, Commn for Africa, 2004–05. Senior Advisor: Africa Unit, ACU; Business Action for Africa. Chm. Bd, Concern UK; Member: Council, British Inst. in E Africa; Council, Baring Foundn; Council, Crown Agents Foundn; Adv. Council, Wilton Park; Gov., Westminster Foundn for Democracy; Trustee, Tropical Health and Educn Trust. *Address:* The Manor House, Great Street, Norton sub Hamdon, Som TA14 6SJ. *T:* (01935) 881385. *Club:* Muthaiga (Nairobi).

WICKSTEED, Elisabeth Helen; Registry Officer, Institute of Cancer Research, since 2008; *b* 24 June 1964; *d* of Andrew and Monica Hutchinson; *m* 2001, Michael Wicksteed. *Educ:* Univ. of York (BA Hons). Lord Chancellor's Dept, 1987–98; Private Sec. to Lord Chancellor, 1997–98; Dep. Sec., Sierra Leone Arms Investigation, June–July 1998; Econ. and Domestic Secretariat, 1998–2002, Legislative Prog. Manager, 2000–02, Cabinet Office; Home Office: Hd, Crime Reduction Progs and Partnership Unit, subseq. Asst Dir, Crime Reduction Delivery Team, 2002–04; Hd, Violent Crime Unit, 2004–06; Hd, HR Strategy and Policy, 2006–07. *Address:* Institute of Cancer Research, Cotswold Road, Sutton, Surrey SM2 5NG.

WIDDAS, Prof. Wilfred Faraday, MB, BS; BSc; PhD; DSc; Professor of Physiology in the University of London, and Head of the Department of Physiology, Bedford College, 1960–81, now Professor Emeritus; *b* 2 May 1916; *s* of late Percy Widdas, BSc, mining engineer, and Annie Maude (*née* Snowdon); *m* 1940, Gladys Green (*d* 1983); one *s* two *d*. *Educ:* Durham School; University of Durham College of Medicine and Royal Victoria Infirmary, Newcastle upon Tyne. MB, BS 1938; BSc 1947; PhD 1953; DSc 1958. Assistant in General Practice, 1938–39. Served in RAMC, 1939–47; Deputy Assistant Director-General Army Medical Services, War Office (Major), 1942–47. Research Fellow, St Mary's Hospital Medical School, 1947–49; Lecturer and Sen. Lecturer in Physiology, St Mary's Hospital Medical School, 1949–55; Senior Lecturer in Physiology, King's College, 1955–56; University Reader in Physiology at King's College, 1956–60. FRSocMed. Mem., Royal Institution of Gt Britain; Hon. Mem., Physiological Society. *Publications:* papers on membrane transporters for glucose, the red cell anion exchanger and bicarbonate permeability; other research papers. *Address:* Honeysuckle Farm, Jarvis Gate, Sutton St James, Lincs PE12 0EU.

WIDDECOMBE, Rt Hon. Ann (Noreen); PC 1997; MP (C) Maidstone and The Weald, since 1997 (Maidstone, 1987–97); *b* 4 Oct. 1947; *d* of late James Murray Widdecombe, CB, OBE and Rita Noreen (*née* Plummer). *Educ:* La Sainte Union Convent, Bath; Univ. of Birmingham; Lady Margaret Hall, Oxford (BA Hons, MA). Marketing, Unilever, 1973–75; Senior Administrator, Univ. of London, 1975–87. Contested (C): Burnley, 1979; Plymouth, Devonport, 1983. PPS to Tristan Garel-Jones, MP, Nov. 1990; Parly Under-Sec. of State, DSS, 1990–93, Dept of Employment, 1993–94; Minister of State: Dept of Employment, 1994–95; Home Office, 1995–97. *Publications:* Layman's Guide to Defence, 1984; novels: The Clematis Tree, 2000; An Act of Treachery, 2002; Father Figure, 2005; An Act of Peace, 2005. *Recreations:* reading, researching Charles II's escape. *Address:* Widdecombe's Rest, Haytor, Newton Abbot, Devon TQ13 9XT. *T:* (01364) 661154.

WIDDICOMBE, David Graham; QC 1965; a Recorder, 1985–96; a Deputy High Court Judge, 1983–96; *b* 7 Jan. 1924; *s* of Aubrey Guy Widdicombe and Margaret (*née* Puddy); *m* 1961, Anastasia Cecilia (*née* Leech) (marr. diss. 1983); two *s* one *d*. *Educ:* St Albans Sch.; Queens' Coll., Cambridge (BA 1st cl. Hons; LLB 1st cl. Hons; MA). Called to the Bar, Inner Temple, 1950, Bencher, 1973; Attorney at Law, State Bar of California, 1986; retired from legal practice, 2004. Mem., Cttee on Local Govt Rules of Conduct, 1973–74; Chairman: Oxfordshire Structure Plan Examination in Public, 1977; Cttee of Inquiry into Conduct of Local Authority Business, 1985–86. *Publication:* (ed) Ryde on Rating, 1968–83. *Address:* 5 Albert Terrace, NW1 7SU. *T:* (020) 7586 5209. *Club:* Athenæum.

WIDDOWS, Air Commodore (Stanley) Charles, CB 1959; DFC 1941 (despatches); RAF retired; People's Deputy, States of Guernsey, 1973–79; *b* 4 Oct. 1909; *s* of P. L. Widdows, Southend, Bradfield, Berkshire; *m* 1939, Irene Ethel, *d* of S. H. Rawlings, Ugley, Essex; two *s*. *Educ:* St Bartholomew's School, Newbury; No 1 School of Technical Training, RAF, Halton; Royal Air Force College, Cranwell. Commissioned, 1931; Fighting Area, RAF, 1931–32; RAF Middle East, Sudan and Palestine, 1933–37; Aeroplane and Armament Experimental Estab., 1937–40; OC 29 (Fighter) Sqdn, 1940–41; OC RAF West Malling, 1941–42; Gp Capt., Night Ops, HQ 11 and 12 Gp, 1942; SASO, No 85 (Base Defence) Gp, 1943–44, for Operation Overlord; Gp Capt. Organisation, HQ, Allied Expeditionary Air Force, 1944; OC, RAF Wahn, Germany, 1944–46; RAF Directing Staff, Sen. Officers War Course, RNC, Greenwich, 1946–48; Fighter Command, 1948–54: SASO HQ No 12 Gp; Chief Instructor, Air Defence Wing, School of Land/Air Warfare; Sector Commander, Eastern Sector. Imperial Defence College, 1955; Director of Operations (Air Defence), Air Ministry, 1956–58. Bailiwick Rep., RAF Benevolent Fund, 1973–93. Vice-Pres., Guernsey Scout Assoc., 1990– (Chm., 1974–90). *Address:* Les Granges de Beauvoir, Rohais, St Peter Port, Guernsey GY1 1QT. *T:* (01481) 720219.

WIDDOWSON, Prof. Henry George; Professor of English Linguistics, University of Vienna, 1998–2001, now Hon. Professor; *b* 28 May 1935; *s* of George Percival Widdowson and Edna Widdowson; *m* 1st, 1966, Dominique Dixmier (marr. diss.); two *s*; 2nd, 1997, Barbara Seidlhofer. *Educ:* Alderman Newton's Sch., Leicester; King's Coll., Cambridge (MA); Univ. of Edinburgh (PhD). Lectr, Univ. of Indonesia, 1958–61; British Council Educn Officer, Sri Lanka, 1962–63; British Council English Language Officer, Bangladesh, 1963–64, 1965–68; Lectr, Dept of Linguistics, Univ. of Edinburgh, 1968–77; Prof. of Educn, Univ. of London, at Inst. of Educn, 1977–2000, now Prof. Emeritus; Prof. of Applied Linguistics, Univ. of Essex, 1993–98. Chm., English Teaching Adv. Cttee, British Council, 1982–91; Mem., Kingman Cttee of Inquiry into Teaching of English Language, 1986–88. Editor, Jl of Applied Linguistics, 1980–85. Dr *hc* Oulu, 1994. *Publications:* Stylistics and the Teaching of Literature, 1975 (Japanese edn 1989); Teaching Language as Communication, 1978 (French edn 1981, Ital. edn 1982, Japanese edn 1991); Explorations in Applied Linguistics I, 1979; Learning Purpose and Language Use, 1983 (Italian edn 1986); Explorations in Applied Linguistics II, 1984; (with Randolph Quirk) English in the World, 1985; Aspects of Language Teaching, 1990; Practical Stylistics, 1992 (Japanese edn 2004); Linguistics, 1996 (Korean edn 2000); Defining Issues in English Language Teaching, 2003; Text, Context, Pretext, 2004; Discourse Analysis, 2007; editor of series: English in Focus; Communicative Grammar; Language Teaching: a scheme for teacher education; Oxford Introductions to Language Study; papers in various jls. *Recreations:* poetry, bird-watching, walking. *Address:* Institut für Anglistik, Universität Wien, Universitätcampus AAKH/Hof 8, Spitalgasse 2–4, 1090 Vienna, Austria. *T:* (1) 427742441.

WIDE, Charles Thomas; QC 1995; **His Honour Judge Wide;** a Circuit Judge, since 2001; Resident Judge, Northampton, since 2003; *b* 16 April 1951; *s* of late Nicholas Scott Wide, MC, and of Ruth Mildred Norton Wide; *m* 1979, Hon. Ursula Margaret Bridget Buchan, *qv*; one *s* one *d*. *Educ:* The Leys Sch., Cambridge; Exeter Univ. (LLB). Called to the Bar, Inner Temple, 1974; Midland and Oxford Circuit Junior, 1983; Standing Counsel to: HM Customs and Excise (Crime), 1989–95; Inland Revenue (Crime), 1991–95; Asst Recorder, 1991–95; Recorder, 1995–2001. Mem., Criminal Procedure Rule Cttee, 2004–. Reader, Dio. of Peterborough, 2007–. *Recreations:* fell walking, bee keeping. *Address:* Northampton Combined Court Centre, 85/87 Lady's Lane, Northampton NN1 3HQ. *Club:* Travellers.

WIDE, Hon. Ursula Margaret Bridget; *see* Buchan, Hon. U. M. B.

WIEMAN, Prof. Carl Edwin, PhD; Distinguished Professor of Physics, University of Colorado, Boulder, since 1997; Fellow, Joint Institute for Laboratory Astrophysics, Boulder, since 1985 (Chairman, 1993–95); *b* Oregon, 26 March 1951; *s* of N. Orr Wieman and Alison Wieman; *m* 1984, Sarah Gilbert. *Educ:* MIT (BS 1973); Stanford Univ. (PhD 1977). Asst Res. Scientist, Dept of Physics, 1977–79, Asst Prof. of Physics, 1979–84, Univ. of Michigan; Associate Prof., 1984–87, Prof., 1987–, of Physics, Univ. of Colorado, Boulder. (Jtly) Nobel Prize for Physics, 2001. *Address:* Joint Institute for Laboratory Astrophysics, University of Colorado, Campus Box 440, Boulder, CO 80309–0440, USA.

WIENER, Elizabeth Anne, (Libby); Political Correspondent, ITN, since 2003; *b* Stockton-on-Tees, 2 March 1959; *d* of Hans and Irene Wiener; *m* 1995, Dr Bruce Kirkham; one *s* two *d*, and one step *s*. *Educ:* Hendon Sch.; Univ. of Leeds (BA Hons Hist. 1981); Centre for Journalism Studies, Cardiff (Postgrad. Dip. Journalism 1982). Reporter, Southern Evening Echo, Southampton, 1982–85; producer, BBC TV South, 1985–87; ITN: producer, 1987–88; Home Affairs Corresp., 1988–91; Europe Corresp., 1991–94; Australia Corresp., 1995–2000; Royal Corresp., 2000–02. *Recreations:* reading, art, theatre, swimming, ski-ing, travelling to the antipodes. *Address:* ITN, Press Gallery, House of Commons, SW1A 0AA. *T:* (020) 7430 4990; *e-mail:* libby.wiener@itn.co.uk.

WIESCHAUS, Prof. Eric Francis, PhD; Professor of Molecular Biology, since 1987, and Squibb Professor, since 1993, Princeton University; *b* 8 June 1947; *s* of Leroy Wieschaus and Marcella Wieschaus (*née* Carner); *m* 1983, Trudi Schüpbach; three *d*. *Educ:* Univ. of Notre Dame, Indiana (BS 1969); Yale Univ. (PhD 1974); Univ. of Zürich. Postdoctoral Fellow, Zool. Inst., Univ. of Zürich, 1975–78; EMBO Fellowship, France, 1976; Vis. Researcher, Center of Pathology, Univ. of California, Irvine, 1977; Group Leader, EMBL, Heidelberg, 1978–81; Asst Prof., 1981–83, and Associate Prof., 1983–87, Princeton Univ. Fellow, Amer. Acad. of Arts and Scis; Mem., Nat. Acad. of Scis. Awards include: John Spangler Niclaus Prize, Yale, 1974; NIHHD Merit Award, 1989; Nobel Prize in Physiology or Medicine (jtly), 1995. *Publications:* From Molecular Patterns to Morphogenesis: the lessons from Drosophila, in the Nobel Prize 1995 (ed T. Fransmyr), 1996; numerous contribs to Jl of Cell Biology and other sci. jls. *Address:* Department of Molecular Biology, Princeton University, Washington Road, Princeton, NJ 08544, USA.

WIESEL, Prof. Elie, Hon. KBE 2006; Andrew W. Mellon Professor in the Humanities and Professor of Religious Studies, Boston University, since 1976, Professor of Philosophy, since 1988; *b* 30 Sept. 1928; naturalised US citizen, 1963; *m* 1969, Marion Erster; one *s*, one step *d*. *Educ:* The Sorbonne, Univ. of Paris. Distinguished Prof. of Judaic Studies, City Coll., City Univ. of New York, 1972–76; Dist. Vis. Prof. of Literature and Philosophy, Florida Internat. Univ., 1982; Henry Luce Vis. Scholar in the Humanities and Social Thought, Whitney Humanities Center, Yale Univ., 1982–83. Founder and Pres., Elie Wiesel Foundn for Humanity, 1987. Chairman: US Holocaust Meml Council, 1980–86; US President's Commn on the Holocaust, 1979–80; Adv. Bd, World Union of Jewish Students, 1985–; Member, Board of Directors: Nat. Cttee on Amer. Foreign Policy, 1983– (Special Award, 1987); Internat. Rescue Cttee, 1985– (Internat. Vice Pres.); HUMANITAS; Member, Board of Trustees: Yeshiva Univ., 1977–; Elaine Kaufman Cultural Center (formerly Hebrew Arts Sch.), 1980–; Amer. Jewish World Service, 1985–; Member, Board of Governors: Tel-Aviv Univ., 1976–98 (Hon. Mem., 1998); Haifa Univ., 1977–. Fellow: Jewish Acad. of Arts and Sciences; Amer. Acad. of Arts and Sciences, 1986; Member: Amnesty Internat.; Writers Guild of America (East); Authors' Guild; Writers and Artists for Peace in ME; Royal Norwegian Soc. of Sciences and Letters, 1987; Hon. Life Mem., Foreign Press Assoc., 1960. Holds over 100 hon. degrees from univs and colls. Elie Wiesel Chair in Judaic Studies endowed at Connecticut Coll., 1990.

Nobel Peace Prize, 1986; other awards include: Anatoly Shcharansky Humanitarian Award, 1983; US Congressional Gold Medal 1985; US Medal of Liberty Award, 1986; Achievement Award, Israel, 1987. Grand Cross: Légion d'Honneur (France), 2001 (Commandeur, 1984; Grand Officier, 1990); Order of the Southern Cross (Brazil), 1987; Comdr's Cross, Order of Merit (Hungary), 2004; King Hussein Award (Jordan), 2005. *Publications:* Night (memoir), 1960; The Jews of Silence (personal testimony), 1966; Legends of Our Time (essays and stories), 1968; One Generation After (essays and stories), 1970; Souls on Fire: portraits and legends of the Hasidic masters, 1972; Messengers of God: portraits and legends of Biblical heroes, 1976; (with Harry James Cargas) In Conversation with Elie Wiesel, 1976, expanded edn 1992; A Jew Today (essays, stories and dialogues), 1978; Four Hasidic Masters and their Struggle Against Melancholy, 1978; Images from the Bible, 1980; The Testament, 1981 (Prix Livre-Inter, and Bourse Goncourt, France, 1980; Prix des Bibliothèquaires, France, 1981); Five Biblical Portraits, 1981; Paroles d'étranger (essays, stories and dialogues), 1982; Somewhere a Master: further Hasidic portraits and legends, 1982; The Golem, 1983; Signes d'Exode (essays, stories and dialogues), 1985; Against Silence: the voice and vision of Elie Wiesel (collected shorter writings, ed Irving Abrahamson), 3 vols, 1985; Job ou Dieu dans la Tempête (dialogue and commentary with Josy Eisenberg), 1986; The Nobel Address, 1987; (with Albert Friedlander) The Six Days of Destruction, 1988; Silences et Mémoire d'hommes (essays), 1989; From the Kingdom of Memory (reminiscences), 1990; Evil and Exile (dialogues with Philippe-Michaël de Saint-Cheron), 1990; (with John Cardinal O'Connor) A Journey of Faith, 1990; Sages and Dreamers: portraits and legends from the Bible, the Talmud, and the Hasidic tradition, 1991; Célébration talmudique: portraits et légendes, 1991; A Passover Haggadah (commentaries), 1993; (with Shlomo Malka) Monsieur Chouchani: l'énigme d'un maître du XXe siècle, 1994; Tout les Fleuves vont à la Mer (memoirs), vol. I, 1994, English trans., as All Rivers Run to the Sea, 1995; (with Jorge Semprun) Se taire est impossible, 1995; Et la mer n'est pas remplie (memoirs) vol. II, 1996, English trans., as And the Sea is Never Full, 1999; Memoir in Two Voices (with François Mitterrand), 1996; Célébration Prophétique, Portraits et légendes, 1998; King Soloman and His Magic Ring (for children), 1999; Le Mal et L'Exil, Dix ans après (dialogues with Philippe-Michaël de Saint-Cheron), 1999; D'où viens-tu? (essays), 2001; (with Richard Heffner) Conversations with Elie Wiesel, 2001; After the Darkness: reflections on the Holocaust, 2002; (ed Robert Franciosi) Elie Wiesel: conversations, 2002; Wise Men and Their Tales, 2003; Et où vas-tu? (essays), 2004; (with Kofi A. Annan) Confronting Anti-Semitism (essays), 2006; *novels:* Dawn, 1961; The Accident, 1962; The Town beyond the Wall, 1964; The Gates of the Forest, 1966; A Beggar in Jerusalem, 1970; The Oath, 1973; The Fifth Son, 1985 (Grand Prix de la Littérature, Paris); Twilight, 1988; L'Oublié, 1989 (The Forgotten, 1992); The Judges, 2002; Le Temps des Déracinés, 2003 (The Time of the Uprooted, 2005); Un désir fou de danser, 2006; *cantatas:* Ani Maamin, 1973; A Song for Hope, 1987; *plays:* Zalmen, or the Madness of God, 1974; The Trial of God, 1979. *Address:* Boston University, 147 Bay State Road, Boston, MA 02215, USA. *Clubs:* PEN, Lotos.

WIESEL, Prof. Torsten Nils, MD; Secretary-General, Human Frontier Science Program, since 2000; Vincent & Brooke Astor Professor and Head of Laboratory of Neurobiology, 1983–98, and President, 1992–98, now Emeritus, Rockefeller University; *b* 3 June 1924; *s* of Fritz S. Wiesel and Anna-Lisa Wiesel (*née* Bentzer); *m* 1st, 1956, Teeri Stenhammar (marr. diss. 1970); 2nd, 1973, Ann Yee (marr. diss. 1981); one *d*; 3rd, 1995, Jean Stein. *Educ:* Karolinska Inst., Stockholm (MD 1954). Instructor, Dept of Physiol., Karolinska Inst., 1954–55; Asst, Dept of Child Psychiatry, Karolinska Hosp., Stockholm, 1954–55; Fellow in Ophthalmol., 1955–58, Asst Prof. of Ophthalmic Physiol., 1958–59, Johns Hopkins Univ. Med. Sch., Baltimore; Harvard Medical School: Associate in Neurophysiol. and Neuropharmacol., 1959–60; Asst Prof., 1960–67; Prof. of Physiol., 1967–68; Prof. of Neurobiol., 1968–74; Chm., Dept of Neurobiol., 1973–82; Robert Winthrop Prof. of Neurobiol., 1974–83. Dir, Leon Levy and Shelby White Center for Mind, Brain & Behavior, Rockefeller Univ., 1999–. Scientific Advr, Bristol Myers-Squibb Corp. Lectures: Ferrier, Royal Soc., 1972; Grass, Soc. for Neurosci., 1976. Member: Amer. Physiol Soc.; AAAS; Amer. Acad. of Arts and Scis; Amer. Philosophical Soc.; Soc. for Neurosci. (Pres. 1978–79); Nat. Acad. of Scis; Swedish Physiol Soc.; Harvard Bd of Overseers; Foreign Mem., Royal Soc., 1982; Hon. Mem., Physiolog. Soc., 1982. Has received hon. degrees from univs in Sweden, Norway, Italy and USA. Awards and Prizes: Dr Jules C. Stein, Trustees for Research to Prevent Blindness, 1971; Lewis S. Rosenstiel, Brandeis Univ., 1972; Friedenwald, Assoc. for Res. in Vision and Ophthalmology, 1975; Karl Spencer Lashley, Amer. Phil. Soc., 1977; Louisa Gross Horwitz, Columbia Univ., 1978; Dickson, Pittsburgh Univ., 1979; Ledlie, Harvard Univ., 1980; Soc. for Scholars, Johns Hopkins Univ., 1980; Nobel Prize in Physiology or Medicine, 1981. *Publications:* (contrib.) Physiological and Biochemical Aspects of Nervous Integration, 1968; (contrib.) The Organization of the Cerebral Cortex, 1981; (with David Hubel) Brain and Visual Perception: the story of a 25 year collaboration, 2004; contribs to professional jls, symposia and trans of learned socs. *Address:* Rockefeller University, 1230 York Avenue, New York, NY 10021–6399, USA. *T:* (212) 3277093. *Club:* Harvard (Boston).

WIGAN, Sir Michael (Iain), 6th Bt *cr* 1898, of Clare Lawn, Mortlake, Surrey and Purland Chase, Ross, Herefordshire; journalist and author; *b* 3 Oct. 1951; *s* of Sir Alan Lewis Wigan, 5th Bt, and of Robina, 2nd *d* of Sir Iain Colquhoun of Luss, 7th Bt, KT, DSO; *S* father, 1996, but his name does not appear on the Official Roll of the Baronetage; one *s* by Lady Alexandra Hay; *m* 1989, Julia Teresa, *d* of late John de Courcy Ling, CBE; three *s* one *d*. *Educ:* Eton; Exeter Coll., Oxford. *Publications:* The Scottish Highland Estate: preserving an environment, 1991; Stag at Bay, 1993; The Last of the Hunter Gatherers, 1998; Grimersta: the story of a great fishery, 2001. *Recreations:* deer stalking, fishing, literature. *Heir:* *s* Fergus Adam Wigan, *b* 30 April 1990. *Address:* Borrobol, Kinbrace, Sutherland KW11 6UB. *T:* (01431) 831264.

WIGDOR, Lucien Simon, CEng, FRAeS; President, L. S. Wigdor Inc., New Hampshire, 1984; Managing Director, L. S. Wigdor Ltd, 1976; *b* Oct. 1919; *s* of William and Adèle Wigdor; *m* 1951, Marion Louise, *d* of Henry Risner; one *s* one *d*. *Educ:* Highgate Sch.; College of Aeronautical Engineering (Dip. 1939). CEng 1989; FRAeS 2001. Served War, RAF, early helicopter pilot, 1940–46 (Sqn Ldr; FAI Helicopter Aviators Cert. No 10); Operational Research, BEA: Research Engr, 1947–51; Manager, Industrial and Corporate Develt, Boeing Vertol Corp., USA, 1951–55; Managing Dir, Tunnel Refineries Ltd, 1955–69, Vice-Chm., 1969–72; Corporate Consultant, The Boeing Company, 1960–72; Dep. Dir-Gen., CBI, 1972–76; Chief Exec., Leslie & Godwin (Holdings) Ltd, 1977–78, Dir 1977–81; Chm., Weir Pumps Ltd, 1978–81; Director: The Weir Group, 1978–81; Rothschild Investment Trust, 1977–82; Zambian Engineering Services Ltd, 1979–84; Rothschild Internat. Investments SA, 1981–82. Special Adviser on Internat. Affairs, Bayerische Hypotheken-SPTund Wechsel-SPTBank AG, 1981–83; Consultant: Lazard Bros, 1982–84; Manufacturing and Financial Services Industries (L. S. Wigdor Inc.), 1984. *Publications:* papers to Royal Aeronautical Soc., American Helicopter Soc. *Recreations:* ski-ing, experimental engineering. *Address:* Indian Point, Little Sunapee Road, PO Box 1035, New London, NH 03257, USA. *T:* (603) 5264456, *Fax:* (603) 5264963. *Club:* Royal Air Force.

WIGFIELD, Timothy B.; *see* Byram-Wigfield.

WIGGHAM, Hon. (Edward) Barrie, CBE 1991; JP; Hong Kong Commissioner, USA, 1993–97; *b* 1 March 1937; *s* of Edward and Agnes Wiggham; *m* 1961, Mavis Mitson (*d* 2003); two *d* (one *s* decd). *Educ:* Woking Grammar Sch.; Queen's Coll., Oxford (MA Mod. Langs). Hong Kong Government: Admin. Officer, 1961–63; Dist Officer, New Territories, 1963–71; postings in finance, econ., security and information branches, 1971–79; Comr for Recreation and Culture, 1979–83; Regl Sec., 1983–86; seconded to British Embassy, Peking, 1986; Sec., General Duties, 1986–90; Mem. Gov's Exec. Council, 1989–92; Sec. for CS, 1990–93. JP Hong Kong, 1973. *Recreations:* music, people. *Address:* Bauhinia, Litlington, Polegate, E Sussex BN26 5RA. *Clubs:* Royal Commonwealth Society; Hong Kong, Foreign Correspondents, United Services (Hong Kong); George Town, National Press (Washington).

WIGGIN, Sir Alfred William, (Sir Jerry Wiggin), Kt 1993; TD 1970; *b* 24 Feb. 1937; *e s* of late Col Sir William H. Wiggin, KCB, DSO, TD, DL, JP, and late Lady Wiggin, Worcestershire; *m* 1st, 1964, Rosemary Janet (marr. diss. 1982), *d* of David L. D. Orr; two *s* one *d*; 2nd, 1991, Morella Bulmer (*née* Kearton). *Educ:* Eton; Trinity Coll., Cambridge. 2nd Lieut, Queen's Own Warwickshire and Worcestershire Yeomanry (TA), 1959; Major, Royal Yeomanry, 1975–78. Contested (C) Montgomeryshire, 1964 and 1966. MP (C) Weston-super-Mare, 1969–97. PPS to Lord Balniel, at MoD, later FCO, 1970–74, and to Ian Gilmour, MoD, 1971–72; Parly Sec., MAFF, 1979–81; Parly Under-Sec. of State for Armed Forces, MoD, 1981–83. Chm., Select Cttee on Agriculture, 1987–97. Jt Hon. Sec., Conservative Defence Cttee, 1974–75; Vice-Chm., Conservative Agricultural Cttee, 1975–79; Chm., West Country Cons. Gp, 1978–79; Pres., Wells Cons. Assoc., 2000–06. Promoted Hallmarking Act, 1973. Chm., Economic Cttee, North Atlantic Assembly, 1990–94. Hon. Col, Warwickshire and Worcs Yeomanry (A) Sqn, Royal Mercian and Lancastrian Yeomanry, 1992–99. Mem. Ct of Assts, Goldsmiths' Co., 1995– (Prime Warden, 2006–07). *Address:* The Square House, 36 Avenue Road, Malvern, Worcs WR14 3BJ. *T:* (01684) 565232. *Clubs:* Beefsteak, Pratt's; Royal Yacht Squadron.

See also W. D. Wiggin.

WIGGIN, Sir Charles Rupert John, 5th Bt *cr* 1892, of Metchley Grange, Harborne, Staffs; *b* 2 July 1949; *s* of Sir John Wiggin, 4th Bt, MC and his 1st wife, Lady Cecilia Evelyn Anson (*d* 1963), *yr d* of 4th Earl of Lichfield; *S* father, 1992; *m* 1979, Mrs Mary Burnett-Hitchcock; one *s* one *d*. *Educ:* Eton. Civil Service; Major (retd), Grenadier Guards. *Heir:* *s* Richard Edward John Wiggin, *b* 1 July 1980. *Address:* c/o Child & Co., 1 Fleet Street, EC4Y 1BD.

WIGGIN, Sir Jerry; *see* Wiggin, Sir A. W.

WIGGIN, William David; MP (C) Leominster, since 2001; *b* 4 June 1966; *s* of Sir A. W., (Jerry), Wiggin, *qv* and of Rosemary Janet (*née* Orr, now Dale Harris); *m* 1999, Camilla Chilvers; two *s* one *d*. *Educ:* Eton; UCNW, Bangor (BA Hons Pure Econs). Trader: Rayner Coffee Internat., 1988–90; Mitsubishi Corp., 1990–91; Union Bank of Switzerland, 1991–94; Associate Dir, Dresdner Kleinwort Benson, 1994–98; Manager, Commerzbank, 1998–2001. Opposition spokesman on envmt, 2003, on agric. and fisheries, 2005–; Shadow Sec. of State for Wales, 2003–05. *Recreations:* motor bikes, Hereford cattle, poultry. *Address:* House of Commons, SW1A 0AA. *Clubs:* Hurlingham, Annabel's.

WIGGINS, (Anthony) John, CMG 2002; consultant on financial management, control and audit, since 2002; *b* 8 July 1938; *s* of late Rev. Arthur Wiggins and of Mavis Wiggins (*née* Brown); *m* 1962, Jennifer Anne Walkden; one *s* one *d*. *Educ:* Highgate Sch.; The Hotchkiss Sch., Lakeville, Conn, USA; Oriel Coll., Oxford (MA). Assistant Principal, HM Treasury, 1961; Private Sec. to Permanent Under Sec., Dept of Economic Affairs, 1964–66; Principal: Dept of Economic Affairs, 1966–67; HM Treasury, 1967–69; Harkness Fellow, Harvard Univ., 1969–71 (MPA 1970); Asst Sec., HM Treasury 1972–79; Principal Private Sec. to Chancellor of the Exchequer, 1980–81; Under Sec., Dept of Energy, 1981–84 (Mem. of BNOC, 1982–84); Under Sec., Cabinet Office, 1985–87; Under Sec., 1987–88, Dep. Sec., 1988–92, DES, subseq. DFE, on secondment to HM Treasury, 1992; Mem., Ct of Auditors of European Communities, 1993–2001. Sec. to Royal Opera House Develt Bd, 1987–93 (Sec. to cttees, 1982–87). *Recreations:* mountaineering, ski-ing, opera. *Address:* Clayhanger Farm, Wadeford, Chard, Somerset TA20 3BD. *T:* (01460) 61610.

WIGGINS, Bernard; *see* Cornwell, B.

WIGGINS, Prof. David, FBA 1978; Wykeham Professor of Logic, and Fellow of New College, Oxford University, 1994–2000, now Emeritus Fellow; *b* 8 March 1933; *s* of late Norman Wiggins and Diana Wiggins (*née* Priestley); *m* 1979, Jennifer Hornsby. *Educ:* St Paul's Sch.; Brasenose Coll., Oxford. BA 1955; MA 1958. Asst Principal, Colonial Office, London 1957–58. Jane Eliza Procter Vis. Fellow, Princeton Univ., 1958–59; Lectr, 1959, then Fellow and Lecturer, 1960–67, New College, Oxford; Prof. of Philosophy, Bedford Coll., Univ. of London, 1967–80; Fellow and Praelector in Philosophy, University Coll., Oxford, 1981–89; Prof. of Philosophy, Birkbeck Coll., Univ. of London, 1989–94. Visiting appointments: Stanford, 1964 and 1965; Harvard, 1968 and 1972; All Souls College, 1973; Princeton, 1980; New York Univ., 1988; Boston Univ., 2001; Fellow, Center for Advanced Study in the Behavioral Sciences, Stanford, 1985–86. Mem., Indep. Commn on Transport, 1973–74; Chm., Transport Users' Consultative Cttee for the South East, 1977–79. Pres., Aristotelian Soc., 1999–2000. Mem., Institut International de Philosophie. For. Hon. Mem., Amer. Acad. of Arts and Scis, 1992. DUniv York, 2005. *Publications:* Identity and Spatio-Temporal Continuity, 1967; Truth, Invention and the Meaning of Life, 1978; Sameness and Substance, 1980; Needs, Values, Truth, 1987, 3rd edn 1998, rev. 2002; Sameness and Substance Renewed, 2001; Ethics: twelve lectures on the philosophy of morality, 2006; Solidarity and the Root of the Ethical, 2008; philosophical articles in Philosophical Review, Analysis, Philosophy, Synthèse, Phil Qly, Ratio, Proc. Aristotelian Soc., Mind; articles on environmental and transport subjects in Spectator, Times, Tribune, and ed collections.

WIGGINS, John; *see* Wiggins, A. J.

WIGGLESWORTH, Jack; Chairman, London International Financial Futures Exchange, 1995–98; Deputy Chairman, Durlacher Corp. plc, 2002–05; *b* 9 Oct. 1941; *s* of Jack Wigglesworth and Gladys Maud Wigglesworth; *m* 1970, Carlota Josefina Paéz; one *s* one *d*. *Educ:* Jesus Coll., Oxford (MA). Gilt Desk Economist and Bond Salesman, Phillips & Drew, 1963–71; Gilt Desk Bond Salesman, 1971–86, Partner, 1973–86, W. Greenwell & Co.; London International Financial Futures and Options Exchange: Member: Founder Wkg Party, 1980–81; Steering Cttee, 1981–82; Dir, 1982–98; Designed Gilt Contract, 1982; Chm., Membership and Rules Cttee, 1988–92; Dep. Chm., 1992–95. Dir of Marketing, Citifutures Ltd, 1993–97; Chairman: ABN Amro Futures Ltd, 1997–99;

CableNet Internat., 2001–03; LitComp plc, 2002–03; London Asia Capital plc, 2003–. Director: Stace Barr Angerstein plc, 1997–2001; Clivia Ltd, 1998–2002; Capital Value Brokers Ltd, 1998–2005. Mem., London Stock Exchange, 1968–91; Director: Securities Inst., 1992–2003; Futures and Options Assoc., 1995–2000; Financial Services NTO, 2001–04. Mem., Financial Services Adv. Gp, QCA, 1999–2001. Chm., Hackney Educn Action Zone, 1999–2004; Member: Business Sch. Council, London Guildhall Univ., 1998–2002; Council, Gresham Coll., 1999–. Master, World Traders' Co., 2006–07. Hon. DSc City, 1998. *Recreations:* music, films, computers, gardening. *Address:* 3 Deacons Heights, Elstree, Herts WD6 3QY. *T:* (020) 8953 8524. *Clubs:* Athenæum, City of London.

WIGGLESWORTH, Mark Harmon; orchestral conductor; *b* 19 July 1964; *s* of Martin Wigglesworth and Angela (*née* Field). *Educ:* Bryanston Sch.; Manchester Univ. (BMus); Royal Acad. of Music. Winner, Kondrashin Comp., 1989. Founder and Music Dir, Première Ensemble, 1989–; Associate Conductor, BBC SO, 1991–93; Music Director: Opera Factory, 1991–94; BBC Nat. Orch. of Wales, 1996–2000; Prin. Guest Conductor, Swedish Radio SO, 1998–2001. Débuts: Glyndebourne Fest. Opera, 2000; ENO, 2001; Royal Opera House, Covent Gdn, 2002; has conducted many orchestras incl. Berlin Philharmonic, Royal Concertgebouw, NY Philharmonic, Cleveland, Philadelphia, Chicago Symphony, LA Philharmonic, London Philharmonic, London Symphony, Santa Cecilia, Bayerische Staatsoper; also at BBC Proms and Hollywood Bowl. *Address:* c/o Intermusica Artists' Management, 16 Duncan Terrace, N1 8BZ.

WIGGLESWORTH, Raymond; QC 1999; a Recorder, since 1990; *b* 24 Dec. 1947; *s* of Kenneth Holt Wigglesworth and Marguerite (*née* Lonsdale); *m* 1982, Amanda Jane Littler; two *s* one *d*. *Educ:* Manchester Univ. (LLB). Called to the Bar, Gray's Inn, 1974; in practice on Northern Circuit, 1974–; Asst Recorder, 1987–90; Standing Counsel to HM Customs and Excise, 1995–99. *Recreations:* mountaineering, ski-ing, golf, sailing. *Address:* 18 St John Street, Manchester M3 4EA. *T:* (0161) 278 1800. *Club:* Wilmslow Golf.

WIGGLESWORTH, William Robert Brian; Director, Reedheath Ltd, since 1994; Joint Director, International Institute for Regulations in Telecommunications, Westminster University, 1998–2006 (City University, 1994–98); *b* 8 Aug. 1937; *s* of Sir Vincent Wigglesworth, CBE, FRS; *m* 1969, Susan Mary, *d* of late Arthur Baker, JP, Lavenham; one *s* one *d*. *Educ:* Marlborough; Magdalen College, Oxford (BA). Nat. Service, 2nd Lieut, Royal Signals, 1956–58. Ranks, Hovis McDougall Ltd, 1961–70: trainee; Gen. Manager, Mother's Pride Bakery, Cheltenham; PA to Group Chief Exec.; Gen. Manager, Baughans of Colchester; Board of Trade, 1970; Fair Trading Div., Dept of Prices and Consumer Protection, 1975; Posts and Telecommunications Div., 1978, Inf. Tech. Div., 1982, Dept of Industry; Dep. Dir Gen. of Telecommunications, 1984–94, Actg Dir, 1992–93. Prin. Advr, Telecoms Forum, Internat. Inst. of Communications, 1994–97; Mem. Bd, UKERNA, 1994–98. *Recreations:* fishing, gardening, history. *Address:* Millfield House, Heath Road, Polstead, Colchester CO6 5AN. *T:* (01787) 210590, *Fax:* (01787) 210592; *e-mail:* ww@reedheath.keme.co.uk.

WIGGS, (John) Samuel; His Honour Judge Wiggs; a Circuit Judge, Western Circuit, since 1995; Resident Judge, Bournemouth and Dorchester, since 2007 (Bournemouth, 1999–2007); *b* 23 Nov. 1946; *s* of late Kenneth Ingram Wiggs and of Marjorie Ruth Wiggs (*née* Newton); *m* Elizabeth Jones (decd); *m* Kerry Martley; two *d*, and two step *d*. *Educ:* Chigwell Sch.; Southampton Univ. (LLB). Called to the Bar, Middle Temple, 1970; in practice, London, 1971–95; Recorder, 1991. Chancellor, Dio. of Salisbury, 1997–. *Recreations:* playing the bassoon, church choir singing, gardening, hill walking. *Address:* Courts of Justice, Deansleigh Road, Bournemouth, Dorset BH7 7DS. *T:* (01202) 502800, *Fax:* (01202) 502801.

WIGGS, Roger Sydney William Hale; Group Chief Executive, Securicor plc, 1996–2001, non-executive Director, 2001–03; *b* 10 June 1939; *s* of Sydney Thomas Wiggs and Elizabeth Alice Wiggs (*née* Coomber); *m* 1963, Rosalind Anne Francis; four *s*. *Educ:* Tiffin Sch., Kingston upon Thames. Admitted Solicitor, 1962; Partner, Hextall, Erskine & Co., 1963–74; Overseas Dir, Securicor Ltd, 1974–80; Man. Dir, Securicor Internat. Ltd, 1980–89; Dir, 1977, Dep. Gp Chief Exec., 1985–88, Gp Chief Exec., 1988–96, Securicor Gp plc, and Security Services plc. Non-exec. Dir, Crown Agents for Oversea Govts and Admins Ltd, 1997. *Recreations:* sport, particularly soccer, Rugby, motor racing.

WIGGS, Samuel; *see* Wiggs, J. S.

WIGHT, Robin, CVO 2000; Chairman, WCRS, since 1983; Founder and Chairman, The Ideas Foundation, since 2002; *b* 6 July 1944; *s* of late Brig. I. L. Wight and of C. P. Wight; *m* 1st (marr. diss.); two *s* one *d*; 2nd (marr. diss.); one *s* one *d*; 3rd, 2003, Mrs Jane Morgan; two step *c*. *Educ:* Wellington Coll.; St Catharine's Coll., Cambridge. Copywriter: Robert Sharp and Partners, 1966; CDP and Partners, 1967; Creative Director: Richard Cope and Partners, 1968; Euro Advertising, 1968; Creative Partner, Wight, Collins, Rutherford, Scott, 1979. Marketing Adviser to Rt Hon. Peter Walker, 1982–84. Chm., Duke of Edinburgh Award Charter for Business, 1992–2000. Mem. Council, Arts & Business (formerly ABSA), 1994–97 (Chm., 1997–2005). Contested (C) Bishop Auckland, 1987. *Publication:* The Day the Pigs Refused to be Driven to Market, 1972. *Address:* 5 Golden Square, W1F 9BS.

WIGHTMAN, (Andrew Norman) Scott; HM Diplomatic Service; Director, Asia, since 2008; *b* 17 July 1961; *s* of Andrew James Scott Wightman and Joan MacDonald Wightman (*née* Campbell); *m* 1988, Anne Margaret Roberts; two *d*. *Educ:* George Heriot's Sch., Edinburgh; Edinburgh Univ. (MA Hons French and Contemp. European Instns). FCO, 1983; Second Sec., Peking, 1986; Cabinet Office, 1989; FCO, 1991; First Sec., Paris, 1994; Asst Dir, Personnel Policy, FCO, 1998; Minister and Dep. Hd of Mission, Rome, 2002–06; Dir for Global and Econ. Issues, FCO, 2006–08. *Address:* Foreign and Commonwealth Office, King Charles Street, SW1A 2AH.

WIGHTMAN, Very Rev. David; *see* Wightman, Very Rev. W. D.

WIGHTMAN, John Watt, CVO 1998; CBE 1986; RD; WS; Chairman, Craig & Rose plc, 1994–2000; Solicitor to the Queen in Scotland, 1983–99; *b* 20 Nov. 1933; *s* of Robert Johnson Wightman and Edith Wilkinson (*née* Laing); *m* 1962, Isla Fraser MacLeod; one *s* two *d*. *Educ:* Daniel Stewart's Coll.; Univ. of St. Andrews (MA); Univ. of Edinburgh (LLB). Partner, Morton Fraser, WS, 1961–99. Cdre, RNR, 1982–85; Chairman: Lowland TAVRA, 1992–95; Regl Adv. Cttee for S Scotland, Forestry Commn, 1998–2004. Director: Douglas Haig Memorial Homes, 1998–2007; Earl Haig Fund Scotland, 2000–04. *Recreations:* sailing, fishing, ornithology. *Address:* 58 Trinity Road, Edinburgh EH5 3HT. *T:* (0131) 551 6128. *Clubs:* Naval; Royal Scots (Edinburgh).

WIGHTMAN, Scott; *see* Wightman, A. N. S.

WIGHTMAN, Very Rev. (William) David; Provost of St Andrew's Cathedral, Aberdeen, 1991–2002; Priest in charge of St Ninian, Aberdeen, 1991–2002; *b* 29 Jan. 1939; *s* of William Osborne Wightman and Madge Wightman; *m* 1963, Karen Elizabeth Harker; two *s* two *d*. *Educ:* Alderman Newton's GS, Leicester; George Dixon GS, Birmingham; Univ. of Birmingham (BA Hons Theol.); Wells Theol Coll. Ordained deacon, 1963; priest, 1964; Curate: St Mary and All Saints, Rotherham, 1963–67; St Mary, Castlechurch, Stafford, 1967–70; Vicar: St Aidan, Buttershaw, Bradford, 1970–76; St John the Evangelist, Cullingworth, Bradford, 1976–83; Rector: St Peter, Peterhead, 1983–91; St John Longside, St Drostan, Old Deer and All Saints, Strichen, 1990–91; Chaplain, HM Prison, Peterhead, 1989–91; Dir, Training for Ministry, Dio. of Aberdeen and Orkney, 1989–94. Hon. Canon, Christ Church Cathedral, Hartford, Conn, USA, 1991. *Recreations:* fishing, choral music, swimming, gardening. *Address:* 66 Wold Road, Pocklington, E Yorks YO42 2QG. *T:* (01759) 301369.

WIGHTWICK, Charles Christopher Brooke, MA; educational consultant, since 1991; *b* 16 Aug. 1931; *s* of Charles Frederick Wightwick and Marion Frances Wightwick (*née* Smith); *m* 1st, 1955, Pamela Layzell (marr. diss. 1986); one *s* two *d*; 2nd, 1986, Gillian Rosemary Anderson (*née* Dalziel). *Educ:* St Michael's, Otford Court; Lancing Coll.; St Edmund Hall, Oxford. BA 1954, MA 1958. Asst Master, Hurstpierpoint Coll., 1954–59; Head of German, Denstone Coll., 1959–65; Head of Languages, then Director of Studies, Westminster Sch., 1965–75; Head Master, King's College Sch., Wimbledon, 1975–80; HM Inspector of Schs, 1980–91; Staff Inspector for Mod. Langs, 1988–91. Series Editor, Berlitz Language Reference Handbooks, 1992–. *Publications:* (co-author) Longman Audio-Lingual German, 3 vols, 1974–78; Berlitz German Grammar Handbook, 1993. *Recreations:* photography, computer programming, running, judo, language learning, inventing. *Address:* 19 Nottingham Road, SW17 7EA. *T:* and *Fax:* (020) 8767 6161; *e-mail:* ccbwightwick@aol.com.

WIGLEY, Rt Hon. Dafydd; PC 1997; industrial economist; President, National Library of Wales, since 2007; Hon. President, Plaid Cymru, since 2006; *b* 1 April 1943; *s* of late Elfyn Edward Wigley, sometime County Treasurer, Caernarfonshire CC; *m* 1967, Elinor Bennett (*née* Owen), *d* of late Emrys Bennett Owen, Dolgellau; one *s* one *d* (and two *s* decd). *Educ:* Caernarfon Grammar Sch.; Rydal Sch., Colwyn Bay; Manchester Univ. Ford Motor Co., 1964–67; Chief Cost Accountant and Financial Planning Manager, Mars Ltd, 1967–71; Financial Controller, Hoover Ltd, Merthyr Tydfil, 1971–74. Chm., ADC Ltd, 1981–91. Mem., Merthyr Tydfil Borough Council, 1972–74. MP (Plaid Cymru) Caernarfon, Feb. 1974–2001. Mem., Select Cttee on Welsh Affairs, 1983–87. Vice-Chairman: Parly Social Services Gp, 1985–88; All-Party Disablement Gp, 1992–2001; British-Slovene Parly Gp, 1993–2001; Mem., Standing Cttee on Eur. Legislation, 1991–96. Sponsor, Disabled Persons Act, 1981. Pres., Plaid Cymru, 1981–84 and 1991–2000. National Assembly for Wales: Mem. (Plaid Cymru) Caernarfon, 1999–2003; Leader, Plaid Cymru, 1999–2000; Chm., Audit Cttee, 2002–03. Contested (Plaid Cymru), N Wales, Eur. Parly elecns, 1994. Vice-Pres., Nat. Fedn of Industrial Develt Authorities, 1981–2001. Chairman: Ymddiriedolaeth Hybu Gwyddoniaeth Cyf, 2002–06; Una Cyf, 2004–08; non-exec. Dir, Gwernafalau Cyf, 2001–; Member: Adv. Bd for Wales, BT, 2003–07; S4C Authority, 2003–06. Pres., CAB, Gwynedd, 2003–; Chm., N Wales Crimebeat, 2003–. Pro-Chancellor, Univ. of Wales, 2003–06; Chm., Adv. Bd, Sch. of Business (formerly Sch. of Business and Regl Develt), Bangor Univ. (formerly Univ. of Wales, Bangor), 2003–. Pres., Spastic Soc. of Wales, 1985–90; Jt Pres., Mencap Wales, 1997–; Trustee, Hope House, 2003–. Pres. (unpaid), S Caernarfonshire Creamery, 1988–2003. Mem., Writers' Guild, 2000–. Fellow, UCNW, Bangor, 1994. Hon. LLD: Wales, 2002; Glamorgan, 2003. *Publications:* An Economic Plan for Wales, 1970; O Ddifri, 1992; Dal Ati, 1993; A Democratic Wales in a United Europe, 1995; A Real Choice for Wales, 1996; Maen i'r Wal, 2001. *Address:* Hen Efail, Bontnewydd, Caernarfon, Gwynedd LL54 7YH; *e-mail:* dafydd_wigley@hotmail.com.

WIGLEY, Dale Brian, PhD; FRS 2004; Principal Scientist, Cancer Research UK, Clare Hall Laboratories, since 2000; *b* 10 May 1961; *s* of Brian Wigley and Joan Wigley. *Educ:* Univ. of York (BSc Hons (Biochem.) 1985); Univ. of Bristol (PhD (Biochem.) 1988). Post-doctoral Fellow: Univ. of Leicester, 1988–90; Univ. of York, 1990–92; Lectr, 1993–97, Reader, 1997–2000, Univ. of Oxford. Mem., EMBO, 2002. *Recreation:* fly-fishing. *Address:* Cancer Research UK, Clare Hall Laboratories, Blanche Lane, South Mimms, Potters Bar, Herts EN6 3LD. *T:* (020) 7269 3930, *Fax:* (020) 7269 3803; *e-mail:* Dale.Wigley@cancer.org.uk.

WIGLEY, Robert Charles Michael; Chairman, Europe, Middle East and Africa, Merrill Lynch, since 2004; *b* 4 Feb. 1961; *s* of Harold and Elizabeth Margaret Wigley; *m* 1996, Sarah Joan Molony; three *s*. *Educ:* Sch. of Mgt, Univ. of Bath (BSc Business Admin 1983). FCA 1986. Dir, Morgan Grenfell plc, until 1996; Man. Dir, Merrill Lynch Internat., 1996–2004; Chm., Merrill Lynch Internat. Bank Ltd, 2005–. Non-executive Director: Royal Mail Gp plc, 2003–06 (Chm., Audit Cttee, 2003–06); Court, 2006–, Risk Policy Cttee, 2006–, Bank of England; LCH Clearnet Gp Ltd, 2005–; Euroclear plc, 2007–. Dep. Chm., BITC, 2005– (Chm., Educn Leadership Team); Member: Sen. Practitioner Cttee, FSA, 2005–; Panel on Takeovers and Mergers, 2007– (Mem., Remuneration Cttee); Adv. Bd, London Corp., 2005–; Adv. Council, Business for New Europe, 2006–; Chancellor's High Level Gp of Key London Financial Stakeholders, 2006–; Nat. Council for Educnl Excellence, 2007–. Vis. Fellow, Saïd Business Sch., 2008–, Chm., Global Adv. Gp, Centre for Corporate Reputation, 2007–, Univ. of Oxford. Mem. Court, Guild of Internat. Bankers, 2006–. FRSA. Hon. DBA Bath, 2008. *Recreations:* flying light aircraft, vintage cars, entertaining. *Address:* Merrill Lynch, 2 King Edward Street, EC1A 1HQ. *T:* (020) 7628 1000. *Clubs:* Royal Automobile, Queen's, Walbrook; Goodwood Golf; Aston Martin Owners.

WIGRAM, family name of **Baron Wigram**.

WIGRAM, 2nd Baron *cr* 1935, of Clewer; **George Neville Clive Wigram,** MC 1945; JP; DL; *b* 2 Aug. 1915; *s* of Clive, 1st Baron Wigram, PC, GCB, GCVO, CSI, and Nora Mary (*d* 1956), *d* of Sir Neville Chamberlain, KCB, KCVO; *S* father, 1960; *m* 1941, Margaret Helen (*d* 1986), *yr d* of late General Sir Andrew Thorne, KCB, CMG, DSO; one *s* two *d*. *Educ:* Winchester and Magdalen College, Oxford. Page of Honour to HM King George V, 1925–32; served in Grenadier Guards, 1937–57: Military Secretary and Comptroller to Governor-General of New Zealand, 1946–49; commanded 1st Bn Grenadier Guards, 1955–56. Governor of Westminster Hospital, 1967–74. JP Gloucestershire, 1959, DL 1969. *Heir:* *s* Major Hon. Andrew (Francis Clive) Wigram, MVO, late Grenadier Guards [*b* 18 March 1949; *m* 1974, Gabrielle Diana, *y d* of late R. D. Moore; three *s* one *d*]. *Address:* 20 Courtbrook, Fairford, Gloucestershire GL7 4BE. *T:* (01285) 711356, *Fax:* (01285) 711596. *Club:* Cavalry and Guards.

See also Sir E. J. Webb-Carter.

WIGRAM, Sir John (Woolmore), 9th Bt *cr* 1805, of Walthamstow, Essex; Director, Rise Communications, since 2004; *b* 25 May 1957; *s* of late Peter Woolmore Wigram and of Sylvia Mary Wigram; *S* cousin, 2003, but his name does not appear on the Official Roll of the Baronetage; *m* 1996, Sally Jane Winnington; three *s*. *Educ:* Bedford Coll., London

Univ. (BA Hons Hist.); Insead, Fontainebleau (MBA). Davidson Pearce, 1981–84; Leo Burnett, 1984–87; Davis Wilkins, 1987–91; CLK, 1993–96; Doner Cardwell Hawkins, 1996–98; ARC, 1998–2003. *Heir: s* James Woolmore Wigram, *b* 10 Feb. 1997. *Address: e-mail:* johnw@risecommunications.co.uk.

WIIN-NIELSEN, Aksel Christopher, Fil.Dr; Professor, Geophysical Institute, University of Copenhagen, 1988–94, now Emeritus; *b* 17 Dec. 1924; *s of* Aage Nielsen and Marie Petre (*née* Kristoffersen); *m* 1953, Bente Havsteen (*née* Zimsen); three *d. Educ:* Univ. of Copenhagen (MSc 1950); Univ. of Stockholm (Fil.Lic. 1957; Fil.Dr 1960). Danish Meteorol Inst., 1952–55; Staff Member: Internat. Meteorol Inst., Stockholm, 1955–58; Jt Numerical Weather Prediction Unit, Suitland, Md, USA, 1959–61; Asst Dir, Nat. Center for Atmospherical Research, Boulder, Colorado, 1961–63; Prof., Dept of Atmospheric and Oceanic Sci., Univ. of Michigan, 1963–73; Dir, European Centre for Medium-Range Weather Forecasts, Reading, 1974–79; Sec.-Gen., WMO, 1980–83; Dir, Danish Meteorol Office, 1984–87. Pres., European Geophysical Soc., 1988–90; Vice-Pres., Danish Acad. of Technical Scis, 1989–92 (Mem., 1984–); Member: Finnish Acad. of Arts and Scis; Royal Swedish Acad. of Sci.; Danish Royal Soc., 1986–; Hon. Member: RMetS; Amer. Meteorol Soc., 1994; European Geophysical Soc., 1998. Hon. DSc: Reading, 1982; Copenhagen, 1986. Buys Ballot Medal, Royal Netherlands Acad., 1982; Wihuri Internat. Prize, Finland, 1983; Rossby Prize, Sweden, 1987; Friedman Rescue Award, Friedman Foundn, Calif., 1993. *Publications:* Dynamic Meteorology, 1970; Predictability, 1987; Fundamentals of Atmospheric Energetics, 1993; over 100 scientific publications. *Address:* C. F. Richs Vej 101A, 2000 Frederiksberg, Denmark.

WILBRAHAM; *see* Bootle-Wilbraham, family name of Baron Skelmersdale.

WILBRAHAM, Sir Richard B.; *see* Baker Wilbraham.

WILBY, David Christopher; QC 1998; a Recorder, since 2000; a Deputy High Court Judge, since 2008; *b* 14 June 1952; *s* of Alan and June Wilby; *m* 1976, Susan Arding; one *s* three *d. Educ:* Roundhay Sch., Leeds; Downing Coll., Cambridge (MA). Called to the Bar, Inner Temple, 1974, Bencher, 2002; Mem., North Eastern Circuit. Member: Judicial Studies Bd, 2005–; Criminal Injuries Compensation Appeals Panel, 2007–. Member: Exec. Cttee, Professional Negligence Bar Assoc., 1995–; Bar Council, 1996–99; Chm., Bar Conf., 2000. Member: Commonwealth Lawyers Assoc., 1995; Internat. Assoc. of Defense Counsel, 1998; Associate Mem., American Bar Assoc., 1996. Editor: Professional Negligence and Liability Law Reports, 1995–; Professional Negligence Key Cases, 1999–; HSE sect., Atkin's Court Forms, 2002 and 2006. *Publications:* The Law of Damages, 2003, 2008; (contrib.) Munkman, Employers Liability, 14th edn 2006. *Recreations:* being in France, golf, Rugby, Association Football. *Address:* Old Square Chambers, 10–11 Bedford Row, WC1R 4BU. *T:* (020) 7269 0300; Park Lane Plowden Chambers, 19 Westgate, Leeds LS1 2RD. *T:* (0113) 228 5000. *Clubs:* Royal Over-Seas League; Headingley Taverners; Pannal Golf.

WILBY, Peter John; Editor, New Statesman, 1998–2005; *b* 7 Nov. 1944; *s* of Lawrence Edward Wilby and Emily Lavinia Wilby; *m* 1967, Sandra James; two *s. Educ:* Kibworth Beauchamp Grammar Sch., Leics; Univ. of Sussex (BA Hons). Reporter, Observer, 1968–72; Education Correspondent: Observer, 1972–75; New Statesman, 1975–77; Sunday Times, 1977–86; Educn Editor, Independent, 1986–89; Independent on Sunday: Home Editor, 1990–91; Dep. Editor, 1991–95; Editor, 1995–96; Books Editor, New Statesman, 1997–98. Columnist, Guardian and New Statesman, 2005–. *Publications:* Parents' Rights, 1983; Sunday Times Good University Guide, 1984; Sunday Times Good Careers Guide, 1985; (ed with Henry Pluckrose): The Condition of English Schooling, 1981; Education 2000, 1982; Eden, 2006. *Recreations:* reading, cooking, lunching. *Address:* 51 Queens Road, Loughton, Essex IG10 1RR.

WILCOCK, Christopher Camplin, CB 1997; Director, Financial Advisory Services, PricewaterhouseCoopers (formerly Price Waterhouse), 1997–99; *b* 13 Sept. 1939; *s* of late Arthur Camplin Wilcock and Dorothy (*née* Haigh); *m* 1965, Evelyn Clare Gollin; two *d. Educ:* Berkhamsted and Ipswich Schs; Trinity Hall, Cambridge (BA 1st Cl. Hons; MA). FO, 1962–63; MECAS, 1963–64; 3rd Sec., Khartoum, 1964–66; FO, 1966–68; 2nd Sec., UK Delegn to NATO, 1968–70; FO, 1970–72; Hosp. Bldg Div., DHSS, 1972–74; Petroleum Prodn, subseq. Continental Shelf Policy Div., Dept of Energy, 1974–78, Asst Sec. 1976; Electricity Div., 1978–81; on secondment to Shell UK Ltd, 1982–83; Department of Energy, subseq. of Trade and Industry: Hd of Finance Br., 1984–86; Dir of Resource Management (Grade 4), 1986–88; Grade 3, 1988; Hd of Electricity Div. A, 1988–91; Hd of Electricity Div., 1991–94; Hd of Electricity and Nuclear Fuels Div., 1994–95; Hd of Nuclear Power Privatization Team, 1995–96. Order of the Two Niles, Fifth Cl. (Sudan), 1965.

WILCOCK, Prof. Gordon Keith, DM; FRCP; Professor of Clinical Geratology, University of Oxford, since 2006; *b* 5 Sept. 1945; *m* 1969, Louise Molden; three *s* two *d. Educ:* St Catherine's Coll., Oxford; London Hosp. Med. Coll. (BSc 1st cl. Hons. 1967); Oxford Univ. Med. Sch. (BM BCh 1970; DM 1977). FRCP 1984. MRC Clinical Res. Fellow, Dept of Regius Prof. of Medicine, Oxford, 1973–75; Sen. Registrar in Geriatric Medicine, Cambridge, 1976; Consultant Physician to Depts of Geriatric and Gen. Medicine, Oxfordshire HA (Teaching), 1976–84; Clinical Lectr in Geriatric and Gen. Medicine, Univ. of Oxford, 1978–84; Prof. of Care of the Elderly, Univ. of Bristol, and Hon. Consultant Physician, N Bristol NHS Trust, at Frenchay Hosp., 1984–2006. Hon. DSc UWE, 2006. *Publications:* (with J. M. Gray) Our Elders, 1981; (with A. Middleton) Geriatric Medicine, 1980, 2nd edn 1989; (jtly) Geriatric Problems in General Practice, 1982, 2nd edn 1991; Living with Alzheimer's Disease, 1990, 2nd edn 1999 (Italian edn 1992); (ed jtly) Oxford Textbook of Geriatric Medicine, 2000; contrib. numerous articles on Alzheimer's disease and dementia in med. and scientific jls. *Recreations:* ornithology, photography, beekeeping. *Address:* Department of Geratology, Nuffield Department of Medicine, Level 4, John Radcliffe Hospital, Oxford OX3 9DU; *e-mail:* gordon.wilcock@ndm.ox.ac.uk.

WILCOCKS, Rear-Adm. Philip Lawrence, CB 2007; DSC 1991; Chief of Staff (Capability) and Rear Admiral Surface Ships to Commander-in-Chief Fleet, 2007–08; *b* 14 April 1953; *s* of Lt Comdr Arthur Wilcocks, RN and Marjorie Wilcocks; *m* 1976, Kym; two *s. Educ:* Oakham Sch.; Wallington County Grammar Sch.; Univ. of Wales (BSc). Navigation Officer, HMS Torquay, 1977–78; CO, HMS Stubbington, 1978–80; Warfare Officer, HMS Ambuscade (incl. Falklands Campaign), 1980–84; HMS Newcastle/York, 1984–89; CO, HMS Gloucester (incl. Gulf War), 1990–92; MoD, 1992–98; Capt., 3rd Destroyer Sqdn, HMS Liverpool, 1998–99; Dir Naval Ops, MoD, 1999–2001; Cdre, Maritime Warfare Sch., 2001–04; Dep. Chief of Jt Ops (Operational Support), PJHQ, 2004–06; FO Scotland, Northern England and NI, and FO Reserves, 2006. *Recreations:* walking, power boating, cycling. *Clubs:* Royal Navy of 1765 and 1785, Destroyer.

WILCOX, Baroness *cr* 1995 (Life Peer), of Plymouth in the County of Devon; **Judith Ann Wilcox;** Director, Cadbury Schweppes plc, since 1997; *d* of John and Elsie Freeman; *m*

1st, 1961, Keith Davenport; one *s*; 2nd, 1986, Sir Malcolm George Wilcox, CBE (*d* 1986). *Educ:* St Dunstan's Abbey, Devon; St Mary's Convent, Wantage; Plymouth Polytechnic. Management of family business, Devon, 1969–79; Financial Dir, Capstan Foods, Devon, 1979–84; Chm., Channel Foods, Cornwall, 1984–89; Pres. Dir Gen., Pecheries de la Morinie, France, 1989–91; Chm., Morinie et Cie, France, 1991–94. Chm., Nat. Consumer Council, 1990–96; Comr, Local Govt Commn, 1992–95; Mem., Prime Minister's Adv. Panel to Citizen's Charter Unit, 1992–97; Chm., Citizen's Charter Complaints Task Force, 1993–95. Board Member: AA, 1991–; Inland Revenue, 1991–96; PLA, 1993– (Vice-Chm., 2000–); non-executive Director: Carpetright plc, 1997–; Johnson Services PLC, 2004–. Chm., H of L Sci. Select Cttee Enquiry into Aircraft Cabin Envmt, 2000–01; Member: H of L European Select Cttee, Envmt, Public Health and Consumer Affairs, 1996–; Lord Chancellor's Review of Court of Appeal, 1996–; Tax Law Review Cttee. President: NFCG; Inst. of Trading Standards Admin; Mem., Governing Body, Inst. of Food Res. Vice-Pres., Guide Assoc. Gov., Imperial Coll. London, 2006–. FRSA. *Recreations:* sailing, walking, calligraphy. *Address:* House of Lords, SW1A 0PW. *Clubs:* Athenæum; St Mawes Sailing.

WILCOX, Claire, (Mrs J. F. Stair); Acting Head of Contemporary Programmes, Victoria and Albert Museum, 2008–June 2009; *b* London, 7 Oct. 1954; *d* of Sydney William and Margaret Jean Wilcox; *m* 1992, Julian Francis Stair, *qv*; two *d* (one *s* decd). *Educ:* Godolphin and Latymer Sch.; Exeter Univ. (BA Hons English Lit. 1977); Gerrit Rietveld Acad. of Art, Amsterdam; Camberwell Sch. of Art (BA Hons 1987). Curatorial Asst, V&A Mus., 1979–83; Curator, Brixton Artists' Collective, 1987; freelance artist, writer and curator, 1987–99; Curator, 1999–2004, Sen. Curator, Modern Fashion, 2004–08, V&A Mus. Mem. Mgt Council, British Fashion Council, 2006–. *Publications:* (with V. Mendes) Modern Fashion in Detail, 1991, 5th edn 2009; A Century of Style: bags, 1997; Handbags, 1999, 2nd edn 2008; exhibition catalogues. *Recreations:* reading, houses, looking into the past, writing fiction. *Address:* c/o Victoria and Albert Museum, SW7 2RL. *T:* (020) 7942 2000; *e-mail:* c.wilcox@vam.ac.uk.

WILCOX, David John Reed; His Honour Judge David Wilcox; a Judge of the Technology and Construction Court of the High Court, since 1998; *b* 8 March 1939; *s* of Leslie Leonard Kennedy Wilcox and Margaret Ada Reed Wilcox (*née* Rapson); *m* 1st, 1962, Wendy Feay Christine Whiteley (*d* 2003); one *s* one *d*; 2nd, 2005, Roberta Piera Prosio de Pardo. *Educ:* Wednesbury Boys' High Sch.; King's Coll., London (LLB Hons). Called to the Bar, Gray's Inn, 1962. Directorate, Army Legal Services (Captain): Legal Staff, 1962–63; Legal Aid, Far East Land Forces, Singapore, 1963–65. Crown Counsel, Hong Kong, 1965–68; Member, Hong Kong Bar, 1968; in practice, Midland and Midland and Oxford Circuits, 1968–85; a Recorder of the Crown Court, 1979–85; a Circuit Judge, 1985–98; an Official Referee, 1996–98. Resident Judge, Great Grimsby Combined Court Centre, 1989–94; County Court Judge: Lincs and S Humberside, 1989–94; Birmingham, 1994–96; Care Judge, Birmingham, 1994–96. Lord Chancellor's Rep., Humberside Probation Cttee, 1989–94. Chm., Nottingham Friendship Housing Assoc., 1970–75. *Recreations:* pugs, gardening, travel. *Address:* St Dunstan's House, 133–137 Fetter Lane, EC4A 1HD.

WILCOX, Rt Rev. David Peter; Assistant Bishop, diocese of Chichester, since 1995; *b* 29 June 1930; *s* of John Wilcox and Stella Wilcox (*née* Bower); *m* 1956, Pamela Ann Hedges; two *s* two *d. Educ:* Northampton Grammar School; St John's Coll., Oxford (MA); Lincoln Theological Coll. Deacon 1954, priest 1955; Asst Curate, St Peter's, St Helier, Morden, Surrey, 1954–56; Asst Curate, University Church, Oxford and SCM Staff Secretary in Oxford, 1956–59; on staff of Lincoln Theological Coll., 1959–64; USPG Missionary on staff of United Theological Coll., Bangalore, and Presbyter in Church of S India, 1964–70; Vicar of Great Gransden with Little Gransden, dio. Ely, 1970–72; Canon Residentiary, Derby Cathedral and Warden, E Midlands Joint Ordination Training Scheme, 1972–77; Principal of Ripon College, Cuddesdon and Vicar of All Saints', Cuddesdon, 1977–85; Bishop Suffragan of Dorking, dio. Guildford, 1986–95. *Recreations:* walking, music, art, painting. *Address:* 4 The Court, Hoo Gardens, Willingdon, Eastbourne BN20 9AX. *T:* (01323) 506108.

WILCOX, Esther Louise, (Mrs Desmond Wilcox); *see* Rantzen, E. L.

WILCZEK, Prof. Frank Anthony, PhD; Herman Feshbach Professor of Physics, Massachusetts Institute of Technology, since 2000; *b* 15 May 1951; *s* of Frank John Wilczek and Mary Rose Wilczek (*née* Cona); *m* 1973, Elizabeth Jordan Devine; two *d. Educ:* Univ. of Chicago (BS 1970); Princeton Univ. (MA 1972; PhD 1974). Princeton University: Asst Prof., 1974–76; Vis. Fellow, Inst. for Advanced Study, 1976–77; Asst Prof., 1977–78; Associate Prof., 1978–80; Prof., 1980–81, 1989–2000; Prof., Univ. of Calif, Santa Barbara, 1980–88. (Jtly) Nobel Prize in Physics, 2004. *Publications:* articles in learned jls. *Address:* Center for Theoretical Physics, Massachusetts Institute of Technology, 77 Massachusetts Avenue, Cambridge, MA 02139–4307, USA; (home) 4 Wyman Road, Cambridge, MA 02138–2218, USA.

WILD, Dr David; Director of Public Health, South West Thames Regional Health Authority, 1989–90, retired; *b* 27 Jan. 1930; *s* of Frederick and Lena Wild; *m* 1954, Dr Sheila Wightman; one *s* one *d. Educ:* Manchester Grammar Sch.; Univ. of Manchester (MB, ChB); Univ. of Liverpool (DPH; FFCM, DMA). Deputy County Medical Officer, 1962, Area Medical Officer, 1974, West Sussex; Regional MO, 1982–86, Dir of Prof. Services, 1986–89, SW Thames RHA. Non-exec. Dir, Worthing DHA, 1990–95. Dir, Inf. Unit for Conf. of Med. Royal Colls and their Faculties in UK, 1991–93. Editor (with Dr Brian Williams), Community Medicine, 1978–84. *Publications:* contribs Jl Central Council of Health Educn, Medical Officer, Archives of Disease in Childhood. *Recreation:* conversation. *Address:* 16 Brandy Hole Lane, Chichester, Sussex PO19 4RY. *T:* (01243) 527125.

WILD, Dr (John) Paul, AC 1986; CBE 1978; FRS 1970; FAA; FTSE; Chairman and Chief Executive, Commonwealth Scientific and Industrial Research Organization, 1978–85 (Associate Member of Executive, 1977; Chief, Division of Radiophysics, 1971); *b* 17 May 1923; *s* of late Alwyn Howard Wild and late Bessie Delafield (*née* Arnold); *m* 1st, 1948, Elaine Poole Hull (*d* 1991); two *s* one *d*, 2nd, 1991, Margaret Lyndon. *Educ:* Whitgift Sch.; Peterhouse, Cambridge (ScD 1962; Hon. Fellow 1982). FAA 1962; FTSE (FTS 1978). Radar Officer in Royal Navy, 1943–47; joined Research Staff of Div. of Radiophysics, 1947, working on problems in radio astronomy, esp. of the sun, later also radio navigation (Interscan aircraft landing system). Dep. Chm., 1973–75, 1980–82, Chm., 1975–80, Anglo-Australian Telescope Bd; Mem. Bd, Interscan (Australia) Pty Ltd, 1978–84. For. Sec., Australian Acad. of Science, 1973–77. For. Hon. Mem., Amer. Acad. of Arts and Scis, 1961; For. Mem., Amer. Philos. Soc., 1962; Corresp. Mem., Royal Soc. of Scis, Liège, 1969. Hon. FIE(Aust), 1991; Hon. FRSA 1991. Hon. DSc: ANU, 1979; Newcastle (NSW), 1982. Edgeworth David Medal, 1958; Hendryk Arctowski Gold Medal, US Nat. Acad. of Scis, 1969; Balthasar van der Pol Gold Medal, Internat. Union of Radio Science, 1969; 1st Herschel Medal, RAS, 1974; Thomas Ranken Lyle Medal, Aust. Acad. of Science, 1975; Royal Medal, Royal Soc., 1980; Hale Medal, Amer. Astronomical Soc., 1980; ANZAAS Medal, 1984; Hartnett Medal, RSA, 1988; Centenary

Medal, Australia, 2003. *Publications:* numerous research papers and reviews on radio astronomy in scientific jls. *Address:* (Dec.–March) 4/1 Grant Crescent, Griffith, ACT 2603, Australia; (April–Nov.) 800 Avon Road, Ann Arbor, MI 48104, USA.

WILD, (John) Robin; JP; Chief Dental Officer, Department of Health, 1997–2000; Consultant in Dental Public Health, Dumfries and Galloway Health Board, 2005–07; *b* 12 Sept. 1941; *s* of John Edward Brooke Wild and Teresa (*née* Ballance); *m* 1965, Eleanor Daphne Kerr; two *d* (one *s* decd). *Educ:* Sedbergh Sch., Cumbria; Edinburgh Univ. (BDS); Dundee Univ. (DPD). DGDP RCS; FDS RCSE. Dental practice, 1965–71; Dental Officer, E Lothian CC, 1971–74; Chief Admin. Dental Officer, Borders Health Bd, 1974–87; Regl Dental Postgrad. Advr, SE Scotland, 1982–87; Dep. Chief Dental Officer, Scottish Office, 1987–93; Chief Dental Officer and Dir of Dental Services, NHS, Scottish Office, 1993–97. Pres., Council of European Chief Dental Officers, 1999–2000; Vice Pres., Commonwealth Dental Assoc., 1997–2003. JP Scottish Borders, 1982; Chairman: Scottish Borders Justices Cttee, 2000–05; Dist Courts Assoc., 2002–04; Mem., Judicial Council for Scotland, 2007–. Life FRSocMed. *Publications:* contribs to Scottish Office Health Bulletin. *Address:* Braehead House, St Boswells, Roxburghshire TD6 0AZ. *T:* (01835) 823203. *Club:* Royal Society of Medicine.

WILD, John Vernon, CMG 1960; OBE 1955; Colonial Administrative Service, retired; *b* 26 April 1915; *m* 1st, 1942, Margaret Patricia Rendell (*d* 1975); one *d* (one *s* decd); 2nd, 1976, Marjorie Mary Lovatt Robertson. *Educ:* Taunton School; King's College, Cambridge. Senior Optime, Cambridge Univ., 1937; Cricket Blue, 1938. Colonial Administrative Service, Uganda: Assistant District Officer, 1938; Assistant Chief Secretary, 1950; Establishment Secretary, 1951; Administrative Secretary, 1955–60; Chairman, Constitutional Committee, 1959. Teacher and Lectr in Mathematics, 1960–76. *Publications:* The Story of the Uganda Agreement; The Uganda Mutiny; Early Travellers in Acholi; Uganda Long Ago. *Recreation:* gardening. *Club:* Hawks (Cambridge).

WILD, Paul; *see* Wild, J. P.

WILD, Prof. Raymond, DSc, PhD; CEng, FIMechE; Principal, Henley Management College, 1990–2001; *b* 24 Dec. 1940; *s* of Alice Wild and Frank Wild; *m* 1965, Carol Ann Mellor; one *s* one *d*. *Educ:* Stockport College; Bradford University (PhD (Mgt), MSc (Eng), MSc (Mgt)); DSc Brunel, 1988; WhF. Engineering apprentice, Crossley Bros, 1957–62, design engineer, 1962–63, research engineer, 1963–65; postgrad. student, Bradford Univ., 1965–66; production engineer, English Electric, 1966–67; Res. Fellow then Senior Res. Fellow, Bradford Univ., 1967–73; Dir of Grad. Studies, Admin. Staff Coll., Henley, 1973–77, Mem., Senior Staff, Henley Management Coll., 1973–2001; Brunel University: Dir, Special Engineering Programme, 1977–84; Hd, Dept of Engrg and Management Systems, 1977–86; Hd, Dept of Prodn Technology, 1984–86; Hd, Dept of Manufacturing and Engrg Systems, 1986–89; Pro-Vice-Chancellor, 1988–89. CCMI. DUniv Brunel, 2001. Editor-in-Chief, Internat. Jl of Computer Integrated Manufacturing Systems, 1988–91. *Publications:* The Techniques of Production Management, 1971; Management and Production, 1972, trans. Greek 1984; (with A. B. Hill and C. C. Ridgeway) Women in the Factory, 1972; Mass Production Management, 1972; (with B. Lowes) Principles of Modern Management, 1972; Work Organization, 1975; Concepts for Operations Management, 1977; Production and Operations Management, 1979, 5th edn 1994; Operations Management: a policy framework, 1980; Essentials of Production and Operations Management, 1980, 5th edn 2002; (ed) Management and Production Readings, 1981; Read and Explain (4 children's books on technology), 1982 and 1983, trans. French, Swedish, German, Danish; How to Manage, 1983, 2nd edn 1995; (ed) International Handbook of Production and Operations Management, 1989; (ed) Technology and Management, 1990; Operations Management, 2001; Essentials of Operations Management, 2001; papers in learned jls. *Recreations:* writing, restoring houses, travel, painting. *Address:* Broomfield, New Road, Shiplake, Henley on Thames, Oxon RG9 3LA. *T:* (0118) 940 4102.

WILD, Robert; Director, Project Underwriting Group, Export Credits Guarantee Department, 1989–92; *b* 19 April 1932; *s* of Thomas Egan Wild and Janet Wild; *m* 1955, Irene Whitton Martin; two *d*. *Educ:* King Edward VII Sch., Lytham. Board of Trade, 1950; Export Credits Guarantee Dept, 1959. *Recreations:* bird watching, archaeology, reading.

WILD, Robin; *see* Wild, J. R.

WILDASH, Richard James, LVO 1997; HM Diplomatic Service; High Commissioner to Malaŵi, 2006–Feb. 2009; *b* 24 Dec. 1955; *s* of Arthur Ernest Wildash and Sheila Howard Wildash; *m* 1981, Elizabeth Jane Walmsley; two *d*. *Educ:* Corpus Christi Coll., Cambridge (MA). Joined HM Diplomatic Service, 1977; FCO, 1977–79: Third Secretary: E Berlin, 1979–81; Abidjan, 1981–84; Second Sec., FCO, 1984–88; First Secretary: Harare, 1988–92; FCO, 1992–94; New Delhi, 1994–98; Dep. High Comr, Kuala Lumpur, 1998–2002; High Comr, Cameroon and Ambassador (non-res.), Equatorial Guinea, Gabon, Central African Republic and Chad, 2002–06. AIL 1977, MCIL (MIL 1990). FRGS 1991. *Recreations:* the arts, travel. *Address:* c/o Foreign and Commonwealth Office, King Charles Street, SW1A 2AH; *e-mail:* wildash@fish.co.uk.

WILDBLOOD, Stephen Roger; QC 1999; **His Honour Judge Wildblood;** a Circuit Judge, since 2007; *b* 18 Aug. 1958; *s* of F. R. J. Wildblood and late P. A. M. Wildblood; *m*; one *s* one *d*; *m* 2003, Emma Jane Bassett; one *s*. *Educ:* Sheffield Univ. (LLB). Called to the Bar, Inner Temple, 1980; Asst Recorder, 1997–2000; Recorder, 2000–07; Dep. High Court Judge, 2004–07. Legal Mem., Mental Health Review Tribunal, 2003–. *Publication:* (ed jtly) Encyclopedia of Financial Provision in Family Matters, 1998. *Recreations:* sport, reading, languages. *Address:* Exeter Combined Court Centre, Southernhay Gardens, Exeter, Devon EX1 1UH.

WILDE, Imogen; Director, Education Practice, Harvey Nash plc, since 2007; *b* 22 Jan. 1949; *d* of late John William Luxton and of Eva Luxton; *m* 1978, Patrick John Wilde (*d* 1999); two *d*. *Educ:* Colston's Girls' Sch., Bristol; Durham Univ. (BA Hons Hist. 1969). Postgrad. res., Inst. of Historical Research, 1969–71; joined Department of Education and Science, 1971; Sec. to Warnock Cttee on Educn of Children with Special Educnl Needs, 1975–78; Principal Private Sec. to Sec. of State for Educn and Sci., 1982–83; DES, subseq. DFE, 1983–91; Asst Sec., UGC (on secondment), 1986–88; British Petroleum plc (on secondment), 1988–91; various posts DFE, subseq. DfEE, 1991–99, incl. Divl Manager, HE Funding and Orgn, 1997–99; Dir, Curriculum and Communications, subseq. Assessment, Curriculum and e Learning in Schools, DfEE, subseq. DfES, 1999–2002; Dir, Norman Broadbent, 2003. FRSA 2000. *Address:* Harvey Nash plc, 13 Bruton Street, W1J 6QA. *T:* (020) 7333 1503; *e-mail:* imogen.wilde@harveynash.com.

WILDE, John; HM Diplomatic Service, retired; High Commissioner to Botswana, 1998–2001; *b* 6 Oct. 1941; *s* of John William and Clara Wilde; *m* 1965, Jeanette Grace Reed; one *s* one *d*. *Educ:* Malet Lambert Sch., Hull. Foreign Office, 1959; served Conakry, Pretoria, Kuwait, Tripoli, FCO and Zagreb, to 1976; Singapore, 1976–79; FCO, 1979–82; Asst to Dep. Governor, Gibraltar, 1982–85; jsdc, 1985; First Sec., FCO, 1985–87; Dep. High Comr, Lilongwe, 1987–91; FCO, 1991–95 (Mem., EC Monitor to former Yugoslavia, 1991; ECMM Service Medal, 1994); High Comr, The Gambia, 1995–98. *Recreations:* golf, music, reading. *Address:* 115 Main Street, Willerby, E Yorks HU10 6DA.

WILDE, Peter Appleton; HM Diplomatic Service, retired; *b* 5 April 1925; *m* 1950, Frances Elisabeth Candida Bayliss; two *s*. *Educ:* Chesterfield Grammar Sch.; St Edmund Hall, Oxford. Army (National Service), 1943–47; Temp. Asst Lectr, Southampton, 1950; FO, 1950; 3rd Sec., Bangkok, 1951–53; Vice-Consul, Zürich, 1953–54; FO, 1954–57; 2nd Sec., Baghdad, 1957–58; 1st Sec., UK Delegn to OEEC (later OECD), Paris, 1958–61; 1st Sec., Katmandu, 1961–64; FO (later FCO), 1964–69; Consul-Gen., Lourenço Marques, 1969–71; Dep. High Comr, Colombo, 1971–73. Mem., Llanfihangel Rhosycorn Community Council, 1974–83. Member: Management Cttee, Carmarthenshire Pest Control Soc. Ltd, 1974–82; Council, Royal Forestry Soc., 1977–86; Regional Adv. Cttee, Wales Conservancy, Forestry Commn, 1985–87 (Mem., Regional Adv. Cttee, S Wales Conservancy, 1983–85). *Recreation:* forestry. *Address:* Nantyperchyll, Gwernogle, Carmarthen SA32 7RR. *T:* (01267) 223181.

WILDGOOSE, James Richmond, DPhil; Head, Scotland Office, 2005–07; *b* 17 April 1949; *s* of Thomas Wildgoose and Annie Wildgoose; *m* 1982, (Charlotte) Dorothy Campbell; one *s* one *d*. *Educ:* Melville Coll., Edinburgh; Univ. of Edinburgh (BSc 1971); DPhil Oxon 1978. Economist and policy postings, MAFF, 1975–90; Chief Economist, Agric. and Fisheries Dept, Scottish Office, 1990–96, Hd of Profession, 1994–95; Rural Affairs Department, Scottish Office, then Scottish Executive: Hd, Food Safety Animal Health and Welfare Div., 1996–2000; Hd, CAP Mgt Div., 2000–02; Hd, Agricl Policy and Food Div., 2002–05. *Recreations:* bridge, piano, travel, Morningside Baptist Church (Edinburgh).

WILDING, Alison, RA 1999; sculptor; *b* Blackburn, Lancs, 7 July 1948; *m*. *Educ:* Nottingham Coll. of Art; Ravensbourne Coll. of Art and Design, Bromley, Kent; Royal Coll. of Art. Solo exhibitions include: Serpentine Gall., London, 1985; MOMA, NY, 1987; retrospective, Tate Gall., Liverpool, 1991; New Art Centre, Roche Court, Wilts, 1997, 2000; Northern Gall. for Contemp. Art, Sunderland, 1998; Henry Moore Foundn Studio, Dean Clough Galls, Halifax, 2000; group exhibitions in UK, Ireland and Canada. Sculpture in public places incl. Ambit, Sunderland, 1999. *Address:* c/o Karsten Schubert, 5–8 Lower John Street, Golden Square, W1F 9DR.

WILDING, Barbara, CBE 2006; QPM 2000; Chief Constable, South Wales Police Authority, since 2004; *m* Jeff Rees, QPM; two *d*. *Educ:* London Sch. of Econs (Dip. Criminology, 1980). WPC, States of Jersey Police; Detective, Metropolitan Police; Asst Chief Constable, Personnel, 1994–96, Crime, 1996–98, Kent Constabulary; Dep. Asst Comr, Corporate Strategic Resourcing, 1998–2000, Security and Protection Comd, 2000–03, Metropolitan Police. Member: RIIA, 2001–; RCDS, 2003–; Nat. Exec. Inst., FBI, 2005–; Adv. Bd, BITC Wales, 2006–; Council, Prince's Trust Cymru, 2006–; Bd., Big Lottery Cymru, 2006–. Mem., Welsh Livery Guild, 2006. CCMI 2005. FRSA 2006; Hon. Fellow, Cardiff Univ., 2007. Hon. Dr Glamorgan, 2008. *Address:* South Wales Police Authority, Cowbridge Road, Bridgend CF31 3SU.

WILDING, Christine Mary; Director, British Institute of Florence, 1998–2003; *b* 7 Oct. 1941; *d* of Lionel Walter Haines and Marjorie Gibson Haines (*née* Hall); *m* 1964, Malcolm David Wilding (marr. diss. 1999); two *s* one *d*. *Educ:* Univ. of Leeds (BA Italian 1962). Various teaching posts, 1963–78; Res. Asst, Univ. of Aston, 1979–82; Sec., Jt Council of Lang. Assocs, 1982–89; Dir, Assoc. for Lang. Learning, 1989–97. Vis. Lectr, Univs of Warwick and Aston in Birmingham, 1977–79. Co-ordinator, Fest. of Langs and Young Linguists Awards, 1982–92. Chevalier, Ordre des Palmes Académiques (France), 1988. *Publications:* research papers and articles to promote use of foreign langs in business, and to motivate language learning. *Recreations:* cooking, walking, the sea, meeting people. *Address:* Les Cèdres, 1 rue des Tilleuls, 74500 Amphion-les-Bains, Haute Savoie, France. *T:* (04) 50810868.

WILDING, Richard William Longworth, CB 1979; Head of Office of Arts and Libraries, Cabinet Office, 1984–88; *b* 22 April 1929; *er s* of late L. A. Wilding; *m* 1954, Mary Rosamund de Villiers; one *s* two *d*. *Educ:* Dragon Sch., Oxford; Winchester Coll.; New Coll., Oxford (MA). HM Foreign Service, 1953–59; transf. to Home Civil Service, 1959; Principal, HM Treasury, 1959–67; Sec., Fulton Cttee on Civil Service, 1966–68; Asst Sec., Civil Service Dept, 1968–70; Asst Sec., Supplementary Benefits Commn, DHSS, 1970–72; Under-Sec., Management Services, 1972–76, Pay, 1976, CSD; Deputy Secretary: CSD, 1976–81; HM Treasury, 1981–83. Review of Structure of Arts Funding in England, 1989; Review of Redundant Churches Fund, 1990. Trustee, Nat. Museums and Galleries on Merseyside, 1989–97. *Publications:* (with L. A. Wilding) A Classical Anthology, 1954; Key to Latin Course for Schools, 1966; The Care of Redundant Churches, 1990; Civil Servant - a memoir, 2006; articles in Jl Public Administration, Social Work Today, Studies. *Recreations:* music, gardening. *Address:* 19 Stuart Court, Butt Street, Minchinhampton, Glos GL6 9JB. *Club:* Athenæum.

WILDISH, Vice-Adm. Denis Bryan Harvey, CB 1968; *b* 24 Dec. 1914; *s* of late Engr Rear-Adm. Sir Henry William Wildish, KBE, CB; *m* 1941, Leslie Henrietta Jacob; two *d*. *Educ:* RNC Dartmouth; RNEC. Entered Royal Navy, 1932; sea service HM Ships Ramillies, Revenge, Nelson, 1932–39; War service, Atlantic, Mediterranean, FE, HM Ships Prince of Wales, Kedah and Isis (despatches); subseq. various Admiralty appts; HMS Implacable, 1946–48; Planning Staff, Exercise Trident, 1948–49; Asst Naval Attaché, Rome, Berne, 1951–53; HMS Eagle, 1953–56; Asst Dir, then Dir, Fleet Maintenance, 1960–64; Commodore Naval Drafting and i/c HMS Centurion, 1964–66; Adm. Supt, HM Dockyard, Devonport, 1966–70; Dir Gen. of Personal Services and Trng (Navy) and Dep. Second Sea Lord, 1970–72; retired. Rep. RN at cricket, also RN, Combined Services, Devon, and W of England (Divisional Trials), at hockey. *Recreations:* walking, cricket, painting (Mem., Armed Forces Art Soc.). *Address:* 57 The Gatehouse, 354 Seafront, Hayling Island, Hants PO11 0AT. *Clubs:* Army and Navy, MCC; I Zingari, XL, Incogniti, Devon Dumplings, Royal Navy Cricket.

WILDMAN, Maj. Gen. Murray Leslie, CBE 2001; Eur Ing; CEng, FIET; Director, Defence Business Solutions Limited, since 2001; *b* 10 Feb. 1947; *s* of Peter Wildman and late Margery Wildman (*née* Littlechild) and step *s* of Elizabeth Susan Wildman (*née* White); *m* 1974, Lindsay Anne Johnson. *Educ:* Reading Sch.; Royal Military Coll. of Sci. (BSc (Eng) 1969). CEng 1987; Eur Ing 1991; FIET (FIEE 1991). Army service, 1968–2001, mainly in engrg and equipt support field; rcds 1993; Dir, Equipt Support, MoD, 1993–96; Defence Advr, Pretoria, S Africa, 1996–99; Dir Gen., Whole Fleet Mgt, MoD, 1999–2001. Non-exec. Dir, G3 Systems Ltd, 2003–. Chm., CCF Assoc., 2004–. Chm., ABF Fundraising Cttee, Wilts, 2001–. Pres., TA Rifle Assoc., 2006–. FCMI (FIMgt 1989); MInstD 2001. *Recreations:* ski-ing, classic cars. *Club:* Army and Navy.

WILDOR, Sarah; ballet dancer; *b* 1972; *m* Adam Cooper, *qv. Educ:* Royal Ballet Sch. Royal Ballet, 1991–2001: soloist, 1994; Principal, 1999; main rôles include: Juliet, in Romeo and Juliet; Giselle; Ondine; Manon; Anastasia; Cinderella; Titania, in The Dream; Lise, in La Fille Mal Gardée; with Adventures in Motion Pictures, Cinderella, 1998; The Two Pigeons, Scottish Ballet, 2002; (and acted) Contact, Queen's, 2002; On Your Toes, RFH, 2003; Les Liaisons Dangereuses, Japan, then Sadler's Wells, 2005; You Can't Take It With You, Southwark Playhouse, 2007.

WILDS, Ven. Anthony Ronald; Archdeacon of Plymouth, since 2001; *b* 4 Oct. 1943; *s* of Ernest and Eva Wilds; *m* 1967, Elizabeth Mary Prince; three *d. Educ:* Univ. of Durham (BA 1964); Bishops' Coll., Cheshunt. Ordained deacon, 1966, priest, 1967, Asst Curate, Newport Pagnell, 1966–72; Priest in charge, Chipili, Zambia, 1972–75; Vicar: Chandlers Ford, Hants, 1975–85; Andover, Hants, 1985–97; Rector, Solihull, W Midlands, 1997–2001. *Recreations:* theatre, Rugby union, walking, gardening. *Address:* 46a Cambridge Road, Ford, Plymouth PL2 1PU. *T:* (01752) 793397.

WILDSMITH, Brian Lawrence; artist and maker of picture books for young children; *b* 22 Jan. 1930; *s* of Paul Wildsmith and Annie Elizabeth Oxley; *m* 1955, Aurelie Janet Craigie Ithurbide; one *s* three *d. Educ:* de la Salle Coll.; Barnsley Sch. of Art; Slade Sch. of Fine Arts. Art Master, Selhurst Grammar School for Boys, 1954–57; freelance artist, 1975–. Exhibitions include: World of Seven English Picture Book Artists, tour of Japan, 1998–99; one-man shows: Hong Kong, Kobe, Yokohama, Mihara, Imabari, 1992; Nakano, Sumida (both Tokyo), Fukuoka, Sendai, Kuwana, Yamaguchi, 1993; World of Brian Wildsmith, Tokyo and tour of Japan, 1995; New World of Brian Wildsmith, Tokyo and tour of Japan, 1997; World of Nursery Tales, Fukui, 1997; Brian Wildsmith Mus. of Art, Kohoku Tokyu, 1998; Kyoto Mus., 2000; Okazaki Mus. for Children, 2001; Taiwan Mus. of Fine Art and tour of Japan, 2004; retrospective exhibn, Fantasia from a Fairy Land, Tokyo Fuji Art Mus., and tour of Japan, 2003. Production design, illustrations, titles and graphics for first USA-USSR Leningrad film co-production of the Blue Bird, 1974. Brian Wildsmith Museum opened Izukogen, Japan, 1994. Mem. Bd of Visitors, Mazza Galleria, Univ. of Findlay, USA, 1999–. Kate Greenaway Medal, 1962; Soka Gakkai Japan Educn Medal, 1988; USHIO Publication Culture Award, 1991; Gold Medal, Tokyo Fuji Mus., 2003. *Publications:* ABC, 1962; The Lion and the Rat, 1963; The North Wind and the Sun, 1964; Mother Goose, 1964; 1; 2; 3;, 1965; The Rich Man and the Shoemaker, 1965; A Child's Garden of Verses (Lewis Carroll Shelf Award, 1966); The Hare and the Tortoise, 1966; Birds, 1967; Animals, 1967; Fish, 1968; The Miller, the Boy and the Donkey, 1969; The Circus, 1970; Puzzles, 1970; The Owl and the Woodpecker, 1971; The Twelve Days of Christmas, 1972; The Little Wood Duck, 1972; The Lazy Bear, 1973; Squirrels, 1974; Pythons Party, 1974; The Blue Bird, 1976; The True Cross, 1977; What the Moon Saw, 1978; Hunter and his Dog, 1979; Animal Shapes, 1980; Animal Homes, 1980; Animal Games, 1980; Animal Tricks, 1980; The Seasons, 1980; Professor Noah's Spaceship, 1980; Bears Adventure, 1981; The Trunk, 1982; Cat on the Mat, 1982; Pelican, 1982; The Apple Bird, 1983; The Island, 1983; All Fall Down, 1983; The Nest, 1983; Daisy, 1984; Who's Shoes, 1984; Toot Toot, 1984; Give a Dog a Bone, 1985; Goats Trail, 1986; My Dream, 1986; What a Tail, 1986; If I Were You, 1987; Giddy Up…, 1987; Carousel, 1988; The Christmas Story, 1989; The Snow Country Prince, 1990; The Cherry Tree, 1991; The Princess and the Moon, 1991; Over the Deep Blue Sea, 1992; The Easter Story, 1993; Noah's Ark Pop Up, 1994; Saint Francis, 1995; The Creation (pop up), 1995; Brian Wildsmith's Amazing World of Words, 1996; (with HIH Princess Hisako Takamodo) Katie and the Dream Eater, 1996; Joseph, 1997; Exodus, 1998; The Bremen Town Band, 1999; The Seven Ravens, 2000; My Flower, 2000; If Only, 2000; Knock Knock, 2000; Not Here, 2000; Can You Do This?, 2000; How Many, 2000; Jesus, 2000; Mary, 2002; The Road to Bethlehem, 2003; with Rebecca Wildsmith: Wake Up Wake Up, 1993; Whose Hat Was That?, 1993; Look Closer, 1993; What Did I Find?, 1993; Jack and the Meanstalk, 1995; Christmas Crib: a nativity pop up and story, 2003. *Recreations:* squash, tennis, music (piano). *Address:* 11 Castellaras, 06370 Mouans-Sartoux, France. *T:* 493752411. *Club:* Reform.

WILDSMITH, Prof. John Anthony Winston, (Tony), MD; FRCA, FRCPE, FRCSE; Foundation Professor and Head of Department of Anaesthesia, University of Dundee, 1995–2007; Hon. Consultant Anaesthetist, Tayside University (formerly Dundee Teaching) Hospitals NHS Trust, 1995–2007; *b* 22 Feb. 1946; *s* of Winston Wildsmith and Phyllis Wildsmith (*née* Jones); *m* 1969, Angela Fay Smith; three *d. Educ:* King's Sch., Gloucester; Edinburgh Univ. Med. Sch. (MB ChB 1969; MD 1982). FRCA (FFARCS 1973); FRCPE 1996; FRCSE 2005. Grad. Res. Fellow, Dept of Physiology and Anaesthetics, Univ. of Edinburgh, 1971–72; Rotating Registrar in Anaesthesia, Edinburgh Trng Scheme, 1972–75; Lectr in Anaesthesia, 1975–77; Royal Infirmary of Edinburgh: Consultant Anaesthetist, 1977–95; part-time Sen. Lectr, 1977–95; Clin. Dir of Anaesthesia, Theatres and Intensive Care, 1992–95. Vis. Lectr in Anaesthesia, Harvard Med. Sch., 1983–84. Pres., Scottish Soc. of Anaesthetists, 2003–04. Mem. Council, RCAnaes, 1997–2007. *Publications:* edited jointly: Principles and Practice of Regional Anaesthesia, 1987 (trans. German 1991), 3rd edn 2002; Induced Hypotension, 1991; Conduction Blockade for Postoperative Analgesia, 1991; Anaesthesia for Vascular Surgery, 2000; chapters and papers on aspects of regional anaesthesia, acute pain relief, induced hypotension and history of anaesthesia. *Recreations:* golf, travel, wine. *Address:* 6 Castleroy Road, Broughty Ferry, Dundee DD5 2LQ. *T:* (01382) 732451. *Clubs:* Royal Automobile; Royal Burgess Golfing Soc.

WILEMAN, Margaret Annie, MA; Honorary Fellow, Hughes Hall, Cambridge, since 1973 (President (formerly Principal), 1953–73); *b* 19 July 1908; *e d* of Clement Wileman and Alice (*née* Brinson). *Educ:* Lady Margaret Hall, Oxford, and the University of Paris. Scholar of Lady Margaret Hall, Oxford, 1927; First in Hons School of Mod. Langs, 1930; Zaharoff Travelling Scholar, 1931; Assistant, Abbey School, Reading, 1934; Senior Tutor, Queen's College, Harley Street, 1937; Lecturer, St Katherine's Coll., Liverpool, 1940; Resident Tutor, Bedford College, Univ. of London, 1944–53; Univ. Lectr, and Dir of Women Students, Dept of Educn, Cambridge Univ., 1953–73. Officier, Ordre des Palmes Académiques (France), 2000. *Address:* 5 Drosier Road, Cambridge CB1 2EY. *T:* (01223) 351846. *Club:* University Women's.

WILES, Sir Andrew (John), KBE 2000; PhD; FRS 1989; Professor of Mathematics, 1982–88 and since 1990, Eugene Higgins Professor, since 1994, Princeton University; *b* 11 April 1953; *s* of Rev. Prof. Maurice Frank Wiles, FBA; *m*; two *d. Educ:* Merton Coll., Oxford (BA 1974; MA 1988; Hon. Fellow); Clare Coll., Cambridge (MA 1977; PhD 1980). Jun. Res. Fellow, Clare Coll., Cambridge, 1977–80; IAS, Princeton Univ., 1981; Guggenheim Fellow, Paris, 1985–86; Royal Society Res. Prof. in Maths and Professorial Fellow of Merton Coll., Oxford Univ., 1988–90. Solved and proved Fermat's Last Theorem, 1994. For. Mem., US NAS, 1996; Hon. Mem., LMS, 2001. Hon. DSc Oxon, 1999. (Jtly) Jun. Whitehead Prize, LMS, 1988; Royal Medal, Royal Soc., 1996; IMU Silver Plaque, 1998. *Publications:* Modular elliptic curves and Fermat's Last Theorem, in Annals of Mathematics, 1995; contrib. to learned jls. *Address:* Department of Mathematics, Princeton University, Fine Hall, Washington Road, Princeton, NJ 08544, USA.

WILES, Clive Spencer; a District Judge (Magistrates' Courts) (formerly Stipendiary Magistrate), Middlesex, since 1996; *b* 1 Dec. 1942; *s* of late Ernest George Wiles and of Emily Louise Wiles (*née* Cummings); *m* 1966, Marie Susan Glasgow; two *s. Educ:* Leggatts Sch., Watford. Articled clerk to Clerk to Justices, Watford, 1962–67; admitted Solicitor, 1968; Solicitor, subseq. Partner, Ellis Hancock, Watford, later Hancock Quins, 1968–96. *Recreations:* walking, gardening, reading, photography. *Address:* The Court House, The Hyde, Hendon, NW9 7BY. *T:* (020) 8441 9042.

WILES, Harry; HM Diplomatic Service, retired; Ambassador to Nicaragua, 2000–02; *b* 17 June 1944; *s* of John Horace Wiles and Margaret, (Peggy), Wiles; *m* 1966, Margaret Bloom; two *d. Educ:* Hull Grammar Sch. Joined Foreign Office, 1964: Ankara, 1966–68; Paris, 1969–72; Algiers, 1972–75; FCO, 1975–78; Vice Consul, Bilbao, 1978–81; Third Sec. (Admin), Jedda, 1981–83; Second Secretary: (Admin), Riyadh, 1983–84; (Commercial), Abu Dhabi, 1984–88; Second, later First, Sec., on loan to ECGD, 1988–90; Consul (Commercial) and Dep. Consul Gen., Barcelona, 1990–94; First Sec. (Commercial), Buenos Aires, 1994–98; Dep. Hd of Security Comd, FCO, 1998–2000. *Recreations:* golf, Rugby League (spectating), music, reading.

WILES, Air Vice-Marshal Matthew John Gethin, CBE 2008; FCILT; Director General Joint Supply Chain, Defence Equipment and Support, since 2008; Head, RAF Supply Branch, since 2007; *b* 9 Feb. 1961; *s* of Wallace and Elizabeth Anne Wiles; *m* 1989, Rebecca White; one *d. Educ:* Fakenham Grammar Sch.; Open Univ. (MBA 2000). Jun. logistics roles, 1982–90; PSO to DG Support Mgt (RAF), 1990–92; OC Supply and Movts Sqn, RAF Odiham, 1992–94; RAF Advanced Staff Course, 1995; Wing Comdr Resources, HQ Strike Comd, 1995–96; Head of Tri Star/Royal Sqn Support Authy, 1996–98; Prog. Dir, Defence Logistics Orgn, 1998–2001; RCDS, 2002; Asst Dir Internat., MoD (Air Staff), 2002–04; Dir Supply Chain Support, Defence Logistics Orgn, 2004–06; HCSC 2005; ACOS Personnel and Logistics, UK Perm. Jt HQ, 2006–07. FCILT 1998. *Recreations:* collecting (and sampling) fine wine, occasionally playing tennis, travel, keeping up with my family. *Address:* Director General Joint Supply Chain, Defence Equipment and Support, Monxton Road, Andover, Hants SP11 8HT. *T:* (01264) 382999; *e-mail:* matthew.wiles112@mod.uk. *Club:* Royal Air Force (Chm., Bd of Trustees, 2008–).

WILES, Paul Noel Porritt, CB 2005; Chief Scientific Adviser, and Director of Research, Development and Statistics, Home Office, since 2002 (Director of Research, 1999–2002); Government Chief Social Scientist, since 2007; *b* 24 Dec. 1944; *m* 1989, Merlyn Alice Greenhalgh (*née* Morton); one *s* one *d*, and three step *s. Educ:* London Sch. of Economics (BSc Econ. 1967); Trinity Hall, Cambridge (Dip Criminol. 1968). Lectr in Sociology, LSE, 1969–70; Res. Fellow, Inst. of Criminology, Univ. of Cambridge, 1970–72; University of Sheffield: Lectr in Criminology, 1972–76, Sen. Lectr, 1976–88; Dir, Centre for Criminological and Socio-legal Studies, 1985–89; Prof. of Criminology, 1988–99; Dean, Faculty of Law, 1990–96. Mem., Mechanics Inst., Eyam, 1979–. *Publications:* monographs, contribs to books, and papers in learned jls on criminology and socio-legal studies. *Recreation:* fell walking. *Address:* Science and Research Group, Home Office, 2 Marsham Street, SW1P 4DF.

WILFORD, Daisy Georgia; *see* Goodwin, D. G.

WILFORD, Michael James, CBE 2001; RIBA; architect; Senior Partner, Michael Wilford Architects, since 2000; *b* 9 Sept. 1938; *s* of James Wilford and Kathleen Wilford; *m* 1960, Angela Spearman; two *s* three *d. Educ:* Kingston Tech. Sch.; Northern Poly. Sch. of Architecture; Regent St Poly Planning Sch. (Hons DipArch with Dist.). Sen. Asst to James Stirling and James Gowan, 1960–63; Associate Partner, with James Stirling, 1964–71; Partner, James Stirling, Michael Wilford and Associates, 1971–92; Sen. Partner, Michael Wilford and Partners, 1993–2000. Major projects include: Staatsgalerie, Stuttgart, 1983; Clore Gall., Tate Gall., 1986; Tate Gall., Liverpool, 1988; No 1 Poultry, 1996; The Lowry, Salford, 2000; British Embassy, Berlin, 2000; Esplanade, Theatres on the Bay, Singapore, 2001; History Mus., Stuttgart, 2002; Carnegie Liby and Acad., Peace Palace, The Hague, 2007. Hon. DLitt: Sheffield, 1987; Salford, 2002; Hon. DSc Newcastle, Australia, 1993. *Publications:* Recent Work of James Stirling, Michael Wilford and Associates, 1990; James Stirling, Michael Wilford and Associates Design Philosophy and Recent Projects, 1990; The Museums of James Stirling and Michael Wilford, 1990; James Stirling and Michael Wilford Architectural Monograph, 1993; James Stirling, Michael Wilford and Associates Buildings and Projects 1975–1992, 1994; Wilford-Stirling-Wilford, 1996; Michael Wilford and Partners, 1999. *Recreation:* earth moving and landscaping. *Address:* Lone Oak Hall, Chuck Hatch, Hartfield, E Sussex TN7 4EX. *T:* (01892) 770980, *Fax:* (01892) 770040; *e-mail:* michaelwilford@michaelwilford.com.

WILIAM, Eurwyn, PhD; FSA; Director of Collections and Research, and Deputy Director-General, Amgueddfa Cymru – National Museum Wales (formerly National Museums and Galleries of Wales), 1999–March 2009 (Acting Director-General, 2002–03); *b* 26 Feb. 1949; *s* of Griffith Owen Williams and Morfudd (*née* Griffith); surname changed to Wiliam, 1970; *m* 1974, Mary Middleton; one *s* one *d. Educ:* Botwnnog Grammar Sch.; Univ. of Wales Cardiff (BA Hons Archaeol. 1970); Univ. of Manchester (MA 1972; PhD 1980). FSA 1993. Welsh Folk Museum, National Museum of Wales: Asst Keeper, 1971–76, Asst Keeper in charge, 1976–80, Keeper, 1980–84, Dept of Buildings; Keeper, Dept of Buildings and Domestic Life, 1984–91; Curator, 1991–94; National Museum of Wales: Assistant Director: Museums Develt, 1994–96; Collections and Res., 1996–99. Vice-Chm., Royal Commn on Ancient and Historical Monuments in Wales, 2003–06 (Mem., 1993–2006); Mem., Historic Buildings Council for Wales, 1994–2004; non-exec. Dir, Council of Museums in Wales, 2003–04. Pres., Welsh Mills Soc., 1990–; Chm., Ethnology and Folk Life Section, Guild of Grads, Univ. of Wales, 1993–2005 (Pres., 2005–). Hon. Prof., Sch. of Hist. and Archaeol., Univ. of Wales Cardiff, 1993–2005. *Publications:* Traditional Farm Buildings in North-East Wales 1550–1900, 1982; The Historical Farm Buildings of Wales, 1986; Home-made Homes, 1988; Hen Adeiladau Fferm, 1992; Welsh Long-houses, 1992; Welsh Cruck Barns, 1994; numerous articles in learned jls. *Recreations:* books, antiques, art, travel. *Address:* (until March 2009) Amgueddfa Cymru - National Museum Wales, National Museum and Gallery, Cardiff CF10 3NP. *T:* (029) 2057 3334; 42 St Fagans Drive, St Fagans, Cardiff CF5 6EF.

WILK, Christopher David; Keeper, Furniture, Textiles and Fashion Department, Victoria & Albert Museum, since 2001; *b* 28 Dec. 1954; *s* of Maurice Wilk and Norma Wilk (*née* Bloomberg); *m* 1st, 1980, Susan Harris (marr. diss. 1983); 2nd, 1984, Ann Curtis (marr. diss. 1997); two *d*; 3rd, 2002, Carolyn Sargentson; one *s. Educ:* Vassar Coll. (AB 1976); Columbia Univ. (MA 1979). Researcher, 1976–78, Curatorial Asst, 1978–79, NY Mus. of Modern Art; freelance curator and writer, 1979–82; Asst Curator, 1982–87, Associate Curator, 1987–88, Brooklyn Mus.; Victoria and Albert Museum: Asst Keeper, 1988–90; Curator and Head of Dept, 1990–96; Chief Curator, Furniture and Woodwork Dept, and British Galls Project, 1996–2001. Mem., Adv. Council, NACF, 1992–; Member Council: Attingham Trust, 1989–2003; 20th Century Soc., 1990–97; Furniture History Soc., 1992–2002 (Chm., Ingram Fund, 1995–2002, Reviews Ed., 1995–2006);

Trustee, Emery Walker Trust, 2007–. Editl Advr, Studies in the Decorative Arts, 1993–. *Publications:* Thonet: 150 years of furniture, 1980; Marcel Breuer: furniture and interiors, 1981; Frank Lloyd Wright: the Kaufmann Office, 1993; (ed) Western Furniture, 1996; (ed) Creating the British Galleries at the V&A: a study in museology, 2004; (ed) Modernism: designing a new world, 2006; contribs to learned jls. *Recreations:* cycling, soccer, music. *Address:* Furniture, Textiles and Fashion Department, Victoria and Albert Museum, SW7 2RL. *T:* (020) 7942 2286.

WILKES, Rev. David Edward, CB 2008; OBE 1995; Chaplain-General to the Land Forces, 2004–08; *b* 7 June 1947; *s* of Edward and Mary Wilkes; *m* 1967, Dianne Butters; one *s* two *d. Educ:* Sandbach Sch., Cheshire; Hartley Victoria Coll. (Methodist Ch Theol Coll.), Manchester. Ordained Methodist minister, 1976; Worsley, 1973–78, Kettering and Corby, 1978–80, Methodist Circuit; Chaplain, HM Forces, 1980–: Sen. Chaplain, NI, 1993–95; Dep. Chaplain-Gen., 2000–04. Ecumenical Canon, Ripon Cathedral, 2005–08. QHC, 2000–08. *Recreations:* fly-fishing, power walking, reading, travelling, Rugby Union supporter. *Address:* 18 Terrys Mews, Bishopthorpe Road, York YO23 1NA. *T:* (01904) 633811. *Club:* Army and Navy.

WILKES, Prof. Eric, OBE (civil) 1974 (MBE (mil.) 1943); DL; FRCP, FRCGP, FRCPsych; Professor of Community Care and General Practice, Sheffield University, 1973–83, now Emeritus; *b* 12 Jan. 1920; *s* of George and Doris Wilkes; *m* 1953, Jessica Mary Grant; two *s* one *d. Educ:* Royal Grammar Sch., Newcastle upon Tyne; King's Coll., Cambridge (MA); St Thomas' Hosp., SE1 (MB, BChir). Lt-Col, Royal Signals, 1944. General Medical Practitioner, Derbyshire, 1954–73. High Sheriff of S Yorkshire, 1977–78. Med. Director, St Luke's Nursing Home, later St Luke's Hospice, Sheffield, 1971–86; Emeritus Consultant, Centre for Palliative and Continuing Care, Trent RHA, 1993. Chairman: Sheffield and Rotherham Assoc. for the Care and Resettlement of Offenders, 1976–83; Sheffield Council on Alcoholism, 1976–83; Prevention Cttee, Nat. Council on Alcoholism, 1980–83; Trinity Day Care Trust, 1979–83; Sheffield Victim Support Scheme, 1983–84; Mem., Nat. Cancer sub cttee, 1979–88; President: Inst. of Religion and Medicine, 1982–83; Thornhill House, Great Longstone, Derbyshire, 1992–2004; Co-Pres., St Luke's Hospice, Sheffield, 1986–; Hon. Vice-Pres., Nat. Hospice Council, 1992–2007; Trustee, Help the Hospices, 1984–95 (Vice-Chm., 1993–95; Co-Chm., 1984–93). DL Derbys, 1984. Hon. Fellow, Sheffield City Polytechnic, 1985. Hon. MD Sheffield, 1986. *Publications:* The Dying Patient, 1982; Long-Term Prescribing, 1982; various chapters and papers, mainly on chronic and incurable illness. *Recreations:* gardening, walking, natural history. *Address:* Curbar View Farm, Calver, Hope Valley S32 3XR. *T:* (01433) 631291.

WILKES, Prof. John Joseph, FSA; FBA 1986; Yates Professor of Greek and Roman Archaeology, University College London, 1992–2001, Professor Emeritus, since 2001; *b* 12 July 1936; *s* of Arthur Cyril Wilkes and Enid Cecilia Eustance; *m* 1980, Dr Susan Walker; one *s. Educ:* King Henry VIII Grammar Sch., Coventry; Harrow County Grammar Sch.; University Coll. London (BA); Univ. of Durham (St Cuthbert's Society) (PhD). FSA 1969. Research Fellow, Univ. of Birmingham, 1961–63; Asst Lectr in History and Archaeology, Univ. of Manchester, 1963–64; Lectr in Roman History, 1964–71, Sen. Lectr 1971–74, Univ. of Birmingham; Prof. of Archaeology of the Roman Provinces, Univ. of London, 1974–92. Chm., Faculty of Archaeology, Hist. and Letters, British Sch. at Rome, 1979–83. Vis. Fellow, Inst. of Humanistic Studies, Pennsylvania State Univ., 1971. Mem., Ancient Monuments Bd for Scotland, 1981–91. Vice-Pres., Soc. for Promotion of Roman Studies, 1978; Pres., London and Middx Archaeological Soc., 1982–85. Corresp. Mem., German Archaeol Inst., 1976. Governor, Mus. of London, 1981–95. Member: Council, British Sch. at Rome, 1988–96; Man. Cttee, British Sch. at Athens, 1990–97. Editor, Britannia, 1980–84. *Publications:* Dalmatia (Provinces of Roman Empire series), 1969; (jtly) Diocletian's Palace: joint excavations in the southeast quarter, Pt 1, Split, 1972; (ed jtly) Victoria County History of Cambridgeshire, vol. VII, Roman Cambridgeshire, 1978; Rhind Lectures (Edinburgh), 1984; Diocletian's Palace, Split (2nd Ian Saunders Meml Lecture, expanded), 1986; (jtly) Strageath: excavations within the Roman Fort 1973–1986, 1989; The Illyrians, 1992; (jtly) Excavations at Sparta 1988–95, reports 1994–98; papers, excavation reports and reviews in learned jls of Britain, Amer., and Europe. *Recreations:* listening to music, watching Association football.

WILKES, Sir Maurice (Vincent), Kt 2000; PhD; FRS 1956; FREng, FIET, FBCS; Professor of Computer Technology, 1965–80, now Emeritus, and Head of Computer Laboratory, 1970–80, University of Cambridge; Fellow of St John's College, Cambridge, since 1950; *b* 26 June 1913; *s* of late Vincent J. Wilkes, OBE; *m* 1947, Nina Twyman (*d* 2008); one *s* two *d. Educ:* King Edward's School, Stourbridge; St John's College, Cambridge (Mathematical Tripos (Wrangler); MA, PhD 1938). Research in physics at Cavendish Lab.; Univ. Demonstrator, 1937. Served War of 1939–45, Radar and Operational Research. Univ. Lectr and Acting Dir, 1945, Dir, 1946–70, Mathematical Laboratory, Univ. of Cambridge. Computer Engr, Digital Equipment Corp., USA, 1980–86; Mem. for Res. Strategy, Olivetti Res. Bd, 1986–96; Advr on Res. Strategy, Olivetti and Oracle Res. Lab., 1996–99; Staff Consultant, AT&T Laboratories, 1999–2002. Adjunct Prof. of Computer Sci. and Elect. Engrg, MIT, 1981–85. Member: Measurement and Control Section Committee, IEE, 1956–59; Council, IEE, 1973–76; First President British Computer Soc., 1957–60, Distinguished Fellow 1973. Mem. Council, IFIP, 1960–63; Chm. IEE E Anglia Sub-Centre, 1969–70; Turing Lectr Assoc. for Computing Machinery, 1967. Foreign Hon. Mem., Amer. Acad. of Arts and Sciences, 1974; Foreign Corresponding Member: Royal Spanish Acad. of Sciences, 1979; Royal Spanish Acad. of Engrg, 1999; Foreign Associate: US Nat. Acad. of Engrg, 1977; US Nat. Acad. of Scis, 1980. FREng (FEng 1976). Hon. DSc: Newcastle upon Tyne, 1972; Hull, 1974; Kent, 1975; City, 1975; Amsterdam, 1978; Munich, 1978; Bath, 1987; Pennsylvania, 1996; Hon. ScD Cantab, 1993; Hon. DTech Linköping, 1975. Harry Goode Award, Amer. Fedn of Inf. Processing Socs, 1968; Eckert-Mauchly Award, Assoc. for Computing Machinery and IEEE Computer Soc., 1980; McDowell Award, 1981, 60th Anniversary Award, 2007, IEEE Computer Soc.; Faraday Medal, IEE, 1981; Pender Award, Univ. of Pennsylvania, 1982; C & C Prize, Foundn for C & C Promotions, Tokyo, 1988; Italgas Prize for Computer Science, 1991; Kyoto Prize, Inamori Foundn, 1992; John von Neumann Medal, IEEE, 1997; Mountbatten Medal, Nat. Electronics Council, 1997. *Publications:* Oscillations of the Earth's Atmosphere, 1949; (joint) Preparations of Programs for an Electronic Digital Computer, Addison-Wesley (Cambridge, Mass), 1951, 2nd edn 1958; Automatic Digital Computers, 1956; A Short Introduction to Numerical Analysis, 1966; Time-sharing Computer System, 1968, 3rd edn 1975; (jtly) The Cambridge CAP Computer and its Operating System, 1979; Memoirs of a Computer Pioneer, 1985; Computing Perspectives, 1995; papers in scientific jls. *Address:* Computer Laboratory, University of Cambridge, William Gates Building, J. J. Thomson Avenue, Cambridge CB3 0FD. *T:* (01223) 763699. *Club:* Athenæum.

WILKES, Ven. Michael Jocelyn James P.; *see* Paget-Wilkes.

WILKES, Gen. Sir Michael (John), KCB 1991; CBE 1988 (OBE 1980); Lieutenant-Governor and Commander-in-Chief, Jersey, 1995–2000; *b* 11 June 1940; *s* of late Lt-Col Jack Wilkes, OBE, MC and of Phyllis Wilkes; *m* 1966, Anne Jacqueline Huelin; two *s. Educ:* King's Sch., Rochester; RMA Sandhurst. Commnd RA, 1960; joined 7 Para Regt, RHA, 1961; Special Forces, 1964–67, Radfan, S Arabia, Borneo; Staff Coll., 1971–72; Bde Major RA, HQ3 Armd Div., 1973–74; Battery Comdr Chestnut Troop, 1 RHA (BAOR), 1975–76, CO 22 SAS Regt, 1977–79; Mil. Asst to CGS, 1980–81; COS, 3 Armd Div., 1982–83; Comdr, 22 Armd Bde, 1984–85; Arms Dir, Dir Special Forces, MoD, 1986–88; GOC 3 Armd Div., 1988–90; Comdr UK Field Army and Inspector Gen., TA, 1990–93; ME Advr to MoD, 1992–95; Adjutant Gen., 1993–95. Col Comdt and Pres., HAC, 1992–98; Hon. Col, Field Sqn RE (Royal Jersey Militia), 2005–. Pres., ACFA, 1999–2005. Kermit Roosevelt Lectr, 1995. MInstD 2001. Freeman, City of London, 1993. KStJ 1995. Order of Mil. Merit, 1st class (Jordan), 1994. *Recreations:* sailing, ski-ing, military history. *Clubs:* Travellers; Royal Channel Islands Yacht, St Helier Yacht, Royal Artillery Yacht (Adm., 2002–07).

WILKES, Richard Geoffrey, CBE 1990 (OBE (mil.) 1969); TD 1959; DL; FCA; company director; Director, Cassidy, Davis Insurance Group, 1989–99 (Chairman, 1998–99); Partner, Price Waterhouse, Chartered Accountants, 1969–90; *b* 12 June 1928; *s* of Geoffrey W. Wilkes and Kathleen (*née* Quinn); *m* 1953, Wendy Elaine, *d* of Rev. C. Ward; one *s* three *d. Educ:* Repton (Exhibnr). ACA 1952; FCA 1957. Partner, Bolton Bullivant, Chartered Accountants, Leicester, 1953–69. Pres., Leics and Northants Soc. of Chartered Accountants, 1967–68; Mem. Council, Inst. of Chartered Accountants in England and Wales, 1969–90 (Dep. Pres., 1979–80; Pres., 1980–81); Chairman: UK Auditing Practices Cttee, 1976–78; CA Compensation Scheme, 1990–98; International Federation of Accountants: UK Rep; Mem. Council, 1983–87; Dep. Pres., 1985–87; Pres., 1987–90; Mem., Internat. Auditing Practices Cttee, 1978–79; Adviser on self-regulation, Lloyd's of London, 1983–85. Governor, CARE for the Mentally Handicapped, 1972–98 (Chm., 1995–98). Commnd RHA, 1947; served TA, RA and Royal Leics Regt, 1948–69; CO 4/5th Bn Royal Leics Regt (TA), 1966–69; Col TAVR E Midlands Dist, 1969–73; ADC (TAVR) to the Queen, 1972–77. Dep. Hon. Col, Royal Anglian Regt (Leics), 1981–88; Vice Chm., E Midlands TA&VRA, 1980–89 (Chm., Leics Co. Cttee, 1980–89); Chm., E Midlands TAVRA Employers Liaison Cttee, 1990–98. Comdt, Leics Special Constab., 1972–79. Chm., Leics SSAFA, 1991–98 (Treas., 1969–91). Mem., Court, Worshipful Co. of Chartered Accountants in England and Wales, 1977–98 (Master, 1991–92). DL Leics, 1967. Internat. Award, ICA, 1990. *Recreations:* shooting, sailing, gardening. *Club:* Army and Navy.

WILKES, Very Rev. Robert Anthony; Dean of Birmingham, since 2006; *b* 2 Sept. 1948; *s* of Leslie Robert Wilkes and Diana Napier Wilkes; *m* 1974, Sheila Katherine Hare; one *s* three *d. Educ:* Pocklington Sch., York; Trinity Coll., Oxford (MA Lit.Hum.); Wycliffe Hall, Oxford. Ordained deacon, 1974, priest, 1975; Curate, 1974–77, Vicar, 1977–81, St Oswald, Netherton, Bootle; Chaplain and Press Officer to Rt Rev. David Sheppard, Bp of Liverpool, 1981–85; Mission Partner, then Regl Sec., CMS, ME and Pakistan, 1985–98; Priest-in-charge, then Team Rector, Mossley Hill, Liverpool, 1998–2006. Chm., Ch of Pakistan Partners Forum, 1987–97; Focal person, ME Forum, CTBI, 1993–97; Pres., Internat. Assistance Mission, Afghanistan, 1992–97. Chairman: Lifelong Learning, Liverpool Dio., 2000–03; Merseyside Council of Faiths, 2005–06. *Recreations:* singing, fell walking, swimming. *Address:* Birmingham Cathedral, Colmore Row, Birmingham B3 2QB. *T:* (0121) 262 1840; *e-mail:* dean@birminghamcathedral.com.

WILKIE, Hon. Sir Alan (Fraser), Kt 2004; **Hon. Mr Justice Wilkie;** a Judge of the High Court, Queen's Bench Division, since 2004; Presiding Judge North Eastern Circuit, since 2007; *b* 26 Dec. 1947; *s* of James and Helen Wilkie; *m* 1972, Susan Elizabeth Musgrave; one *s* one *d. Educ:* Hutcheson's Grammar Sch., Glasgow; Manchester Grammar Sch.; Balliol Coll., Oxford (BA, BCL). Lecturer in Law: Exeter Coll., Oxford, 1971–72; Southampton Univ., 1972–74; called to the Bar, Inner Temple, 1974, Bencher, 2001; QC 1992; an Asst Recorder, 1992–95; a Recorder, 1995–97; a Circuit Judge, 1997–2004; a Law Comr, 2000–04. *Recreations:* music, films, watching football, playing tennis, cycling. *Address:* Royal Courts of Justice, Strand, WC2A 2LL.

WILKIE, Prof. Alex James, FRS 2001; PhD; Fielden Professor of Pure Mathematics, University of Manchester, since 2007; *b* 1 Aug. 1948; *s* of late Alan George Wilkie and Hilda Grace Wilkie (*née* Mitchell); *m* 1987, Catrin Roberts; one *s* one *d. Educ:* University Coll. London (BSc); Bedford Coll., London (MSc, PhD 1972). Lectr in Maths, Univ. of Leicester, 1972–73; Res. Fellow in Maths, Open Univ., 1973–78; Jun. Lectr in Maths, Oxford Univ., 1978–80 and 1981–82; Res. Fellow in Maths, Univ. Paris VII, 1982–83; SERC Advanced Res. Fellow, 1983–84, Lectr in Maths, 1984–86, Univ. of Manchester; Reader in Math. Logic, 1986–2007, and titular Prof., 1996–2007, Univ. of Oxford; Fellow, Wolfson Coll., Oxford, 1986–2007, now Emeritus. Vis. Asst Prof. in Maths, Yale Univ., 1980–81. Carol Karp Prize, Assoc. for Symbolic Logic, 1993. *Publications:* contrib. numerous papers in maths and mathematical logic jls. *Address:* School of Mathematics, Alan Turing Building, University of Manchester, Manchester M13 9PL. *T:* (0161) 275 5800.

WILKIE, Prof. Andrew Oliver Mungo, FRCP; FMedSci; Nuffield Professor of Pathology, University of Oxford, since 2003; *b* 14 Sept. 1959; *s* of late Douglas Robert Wilkie, FRS and June Rosalind Wilkie (*née* Hill); *m* 1989, Jane Elizabeth Martin; two *s. Educ:* Arnold House Sch.; Westminster Sch.; Trinity Coll., Cambridge (BA 1980, MA 1984); Merton Coll., Oxford (BM BCh 1983; DM 1992). MRCP 1986, FRCP 1998; DCH 1987. MRC Trng Fellow, Univ. of Oxford, 1987–90; Clinical Res. Fellow, Inst. of Child Health, London, 1990–91; Sen. Registrar, Inst. of Medical Genetics, Cardiff, 1992–93; Wellcome Trust Advanced Trng Fellow, 1993–95, then Sen. Res. Fellow in Clinical Sci., 1995–2003, Univ. of Oxford. Hon. Consultant in Clinical Genetics, Oxford Radcliffe Hosps NHS Trust, 1993–. Mem., EMBO, 2006. FMedSci 2002. *Publications:* articles on genetics and mutation (especially on skull and limb malformations) in learned jls, inc. Nature, Cell, Nature Genetics, Science. *Recreations:* ornithology, mountains, wild camping, visual arts, Test Match Special. *Address:* Weatherall Institute of Molecular Medicine, John Radcliffe Hospital, Headington, Oxford OX3 9DS. *T:* (01865) 222619, *Fax:* (01865) 222500; *e-mail:* awilkie@hammer.imm.ox.ac.uk.

WILKIE, Kim Edward Kelvin; Principal, Kim Wilkie Associates, since 1989; *b* 30 Oct. 1955; *s* of Mr and Mrs E. H. Wilkie. *Educ:* Winchester Coll.; New Coll., Oxford (MA); Univ. of California, Berkeley (MLA). MLI (ALI 1987). Marketing Manager, Unilever, 1978–81; Associate, Land Use Consultants, 1984–89. Awards: Amer. Soc. of Landscape Architects, 1984; Francis Tibbalds, RTPI, 1994; Landscape Inst., 1995; RTPI, 1996; Centenary, Country Life, 1997; for Place Design, Envmtl Design Res. Assoc., US, 1999. Hon. FRIBA 2002. *Publications:* Thames Landscape Strategy: Hampton to Kew, 1994; Indignation!, 2000. *Recreations:* earth sculpting, exhausting the dog, bonfires, sea kayaking. *Address:* 34 Friars' Stile Road, Richmond TW10 6NE. *T:* (020) 8332 0304.

WILKIN, Richard Cecil, LVO 1979; MBE (mil.) 1976; Secretary, Estates Business Group, since 2005; *b* 17 Sept. 1944; *s* of late Comdr Henry Egbert Peter Wilkin, RN, and Frances Anne Wilkin (*née* Chichester; she *m* 1984, Vice Adm. Sir (Robert) Alastair Ewing, KBE, CB, DSC); *m* 1st, 1983, Jane Susan Elliott (marr. diss. 1989), *d* of Sir Roger James Elliott, *qv*; 2nd, 2002, Sally Ashley Brown, *d* of Col Ashley Brown, OBE, RM. *Educ*: Eton; RMA Sandhurst. Commnd HM Armed Forces 17th/21st Lancers, 1964; served Rhine Army, Berlin, Libya, British Forces Gulf, Cyprus; Captain 1968; GSOIII HQ NI, 1973 (despatches 1974); retired 1975. Joined HM Diplomatic Service, 1975; UK Delegn to Rhodesia Constitutional Conf., Geneva, 1976; First Sec. (Political and Press), Lusaka, 1978; E Caribbean, 1988; attached MoD, 1990; Counsellor, FCO, 1992; retired 1996. Dir Gen., HHA, 1996–2005. Member: Country Land and Business Assoc. Tax Cttee, 1998–; Council, Attingham Trust, 1999–2005; British Tourism Develt Cttee, 2000–05; Exec. Cttee, Historic Envmt Review, 2001–05; NT Wessex Cttee, 2003– (Chm., 2006–). Trustee: Heritage Link, 2002–05; Nat. Heritage Meml Fund, 2006–. *Recreations*: fishing, painting, fine art and architecture, restoring historic buildings, motor cars. *Address*: c/o Messrs C. Hoare & Co., 37 Fleet Street, EC4P 4DQ. *Clubs*: Farmers'; New (Edinburgh).

WILKIN, Rev. Rose Josephine H.; *see* Hudson-Wilkin.

WILKINS, Baroness *cr* 1999 (Life Peer), of Chesham Bois in the county of Buckinghamshire; **Rosalie Catherine Wilkins**; *b* 6 May 1946; *d* of late Eric Frederick Wilkins and Marjorie Phyllis Elizabeth Wilkins. *Educ*: Univ. of Manchester (BA). PA to Dir, Central Council for the Disabled, 1971–74; Information Officer, MIND (Nat. Assoc. for Mental Health), 1974–78; presenter/researcher, Link magazine programme and documentaries, ATV Network and Central Television, 1975–88; freelance video and documentary producer/presenter on disability issues, 1988–96; Information Officer, Nat. Centre for Independent Living, 1997–99. Vice-Chairman: All Party Parly Gp on Disability, 2004–; All Party Parly Gp on Deafness, 2005–. Snowdon Award (for outstanding work for the benefit of disabled people), Action Research, 1983. *Recreations*: friends, gardening, theatre, cinema. *Address*: 74 Inglethorpe Street, Fulham, SW6 6NX.

WILKINS, John Anthony Francis, MBE 1998; Editor of The Tablet, 1982–2003; *b* 20 Dec. 1936; *s* of Edward Manwaring Wilkins and Ena Gwendolen Francis. *Educ*: Clifton Coll., Bristol (Scholar); Clare Coll., Cambridge (State Scholar, 1954; Major Scholar and Foundn Scholar; Classical Tripos 1959, Theol Tripos 1961; BA 1961; MA 2004). Served 1st Bn Glos Regt, 1955–57 (2nd Lieut). Planning Div., Marine Dept, Head Office of Esso Petroleum, London, 1962–63; Asst Editor: Frontier, 1964–67; The Tablet, 1967–72; features writer, BBC External Services, 1972–81; Producer, Radio 4, 1978. Vis. Fellow, Clare Coll., Cambridge, 1996. MA Lambeth, 2004. Ondas Radio Prize, 1973; John Harriott Meml Prize, ITC, 1996; Christian Culture Gold Medal, Assumption Univ., Windsor, Canada, 2001. *Publications*: (ed) How I Pray, 1993; (ed) Understanding Veritatis Splendor, 1994; (ed jtly) Spiritual Stars of the Millennium, 2001. *Recreation*: ornithology.

WILKINS, Prof. Malcolm Barrett, FRSE 1972; Regius Professor of Botany, University of Glasgow, 1970–2000; *b* 27 Feb. 1933; *s* of Barrett Charles Wilkins and Eleanor Mary Wilkins (*née* Jenkins); *m* 1959, Mary Patricia Maltby; one *s* (one *d* decd). *Educ*: Monkton House Sch., Cardiff; King's Coll., London. BSc 1955; PhD London 1958; AKC 1958; DSc 1972. Lectr in Botany, King's Coll., London, 1958–64; Rockefeller Foundn Fellow, Yale Univ., 1961–62; Research Fellow, Harvard Univ., 1962–63; Lectr in Biology, Univ. of East Anglia, 1964–65; Prof. of Biology, Univ. of East Anglia, 1965–67; Prof. of Plant Physiology, Univ. of Nottingham, 1967–70; Glasgow University: Dean, Faculty of Science, 1984–87; Chm., Sch. of Biol Scis, 1988–92. Darwin Lectr, British Assoc. for Advancement of Science, 1967. Member: Biol. Sci. Cttee of SRC, 1971–74; Governing Body: Hill Farming Res. Orgn, 1971–80; Scottish Crops Research Inst., 1974–89; Glasshouse Crops Res. Inst., 1979–88; W of Scotland Agricl Coll., 1983–92; Exec. Cttee, Scottish Field Studies Assoc.; British Nat. Cttee for Biology, 1977–82; Life Science Working Gp, ESA, 1983–89 (Chm., 1987–89); Microgravity Adv. Cttee, ESA, 1985–89; NASA Lifesat Science Cttee, 1986–91; Court, Glasgow Univ., 1993–97. Vice-Pres., RSE, 1994–97 (Mem. Council, 1989–92). Trustee, Royal Botanic Gdn, Edinburgh, 1990–99 (Chm., 1994–99; Hon. Fellow, 1999); Adv. Council, Scottish Agricl Coll. Corresp. Mem., Amer. Soc. of Plant Physiologists, 1985. Dir, West of Scotland Sch. Co.; Chm., Laurel Bank Sch. Co. Ltd. Cons. Editor in Plant Biology, McGraw-Hill Publishing Co., 1968–80; Managing Editor, Planta, 1977–2001. *Publications*: (ed) The Physiology of Plant Growth and Development, 1969; (ed) Advanced Plant Physiology, 1984; Plantwatching, 1988; papers in Jl of Experimental Botany, Plant Physiology, Planta, Nature, Proc. Royal Soc. *Recreations*: fishing, model engineering. *Address*: 5 Hughenden Drive, Glasgow G12 9XS. *T*: (0141) 334 8079; *e-mail*: Profmwilkins@hotmail.com. *Clubs*: Caledonian; New (Edinburgh).

WILKINS, Nancy; barrister-at-law; *b* 16 June 1932; three *s* one *d*. *Educ*: School of St Helen and St Katharine, Abingdon, Berkshire. Called to the Bar, Gray's Inn, Nov. 1962; in practice, Midland Circuit, 1962–85; Dep. Circuit Judge, 1974–78; a Recorder, 1978–85; practised in solicitors' office, 1986–90; retired. *Publications*: An Outline of the Law of Evidence (with late Prof. Sir Rupert Cross), 1964, 5th edn 1980; Thomas of Moulton, 2002; Ayscoughfee: a great place in Spalding, 2007. *Recreation*: failing to grow old gracefully.

WILKINSON; *see* Browne-Wilkinson.

WILKINSON, Rev. Canon Alan Bassindale, PhD, DD; lecturer and writer; honorary priest, Portsmouth Cathedral, since 1988 (Cathedral Chaplain, 1994–2001; diocesan theologian, 1993–2001); *b* 26 Jan. 1931; *s* of late Rev. J. T. Wilkinson, DD; *m* 1975, Fenella Holland; two *s* one *d* of first marriage. *Educ*: William Hulme's Grammar Sch., Manchester; St Catharine's Coll., Cambridge; College of the Resurrection, Mirfield. MA 1958, PhD 1959, DD 1997 Cambridge. Deacon, 1959; priest, 1960; Asst Curate, St Augustine's, Kilburn, 1959–61; Chaplain, St Catharine's Coll., Cambridge, 1961–67; Vicar of Barrow Gurney and Lecturer in Theology, College of St Matthias, Bristol, 1967–70; Principal, Chichester Theol. Coll., 1970–74; Canon and Prebendary of Thorney, 1970–74, Canon Emeritus, 1975; Warden of Verulam House, Dir of Training for Auxiliary Ministry, dio. of St Albans, 1974–75; Lectr in Theology and Ethics, Crewe and Alsager Coll. of Higher Educn, 1975–78; Dir of Training, Diocese of Ripon, 1978–84; Hon. Canon, Ripon Cathedral, 1984; Priest-in-Charge, Darley with Thruscross and Thornthwaite, 1984–88; Tutor, Open Univ., 1988–96. Vis. Fellow, Chichester Inst. of Higher Educn, 1995–97; Fellow, George Bell Inst., Chichester, 1996–; Vis. Lectr, Portsmouth Univ., 1998–2005. Hulsean Preacher, 1967–68; Select Preacher, Oxford Univ., 1982. Mem., Bd of Educn, Gen. Synod, 1981–85; Vice-Chm., Leeds Marriage and Personal Counselling Service, 1981–83. Governor: SPCK, 1982–91; Coll. of Ripon and York St John, 1985–88. Scott Holland Trustee, 1993–95, 1998– (Scott Holland Lectr, 1998). *Publications*: The Church of England and the First World War, 1978, 2nd edn 1996; Would You Believe It?, 1983; More Ready to Hear, 1983; Christian Choices, 1983; Dissent or Conform?, 1986; The Community of the Resurrection: a centenary history, 1992; (jtly) An Anglican Companion: words from the heart of faith, 1996, 2nd edn 2001; Christian Socialism: Scott Holland to Tony Blair, 1998; contributor to: Cambridge Sermons on Christian Unity, 1966; Catholic Anglicans Today, 1968; A Work Book in Popular Religion, 1986; Chesterton and the Modernist Crisis, 1990; Britain and the Threat to Stability in Europe, 1993; Forever Building, 1995; The Changing Face of Death, 1997; The Impact of New Labour, 1999; Piety and Learning: the Principals of Pusey House 1884–2002, 2002; Walter Frere, 2009; also to: Faith and Unity, Sobornost, Preacher's Quarterly, London Quarterly Holborn Review, Theology, Clergy Review, New Fire, Church Times, Chesterton Review, Internat. Christian Digest, Modern Hist. Rev., Oxford DNB, Expository Times, Humanitas. *Recreations*: gardening, walking, cinema, Victorian architecture. *Address*: 17a High Street, Old Portsmouth PO1 2LP. *T*: (023) 9273 6270.

WILKINSON, Alexander Birrell; QC (Scot.) 1993; Sheriff of Lothian and Borders at Edinburgh, 1996–2001; *b* 2 Feb. 1932; *o s* of late Captain Alexander Wilkinson, MBE, The Black Watch and Isabella Bell Birrell; *m* 1965, Wendy Imogen, *d* of late Ernest Albert Barrett and R. V. H. Barrett; one *s* one *d*. *Educ*: Perth Academy; Univs of St Andrews and Edinburgh. Walker Trust Scholar 1950, Grieve Prizeman in Moral Philosophy 1952, MA(Hons Classics) 1954, Univ. of St Andrews. National Service, RAEC, 1954–56. Balfour Keith Prizeman in Constitutional Law 1957, LLB (with distinction) 1959, Univ. of Edinburgh. Admitted to Faculty of Advocates, 1959; in practice at Scottish bar, 1959–69; Lecturer in Scots Law, Univ. of Edinburgh, 1965–69; Sheriff of Stirling, Dunbarton and Clackmannan at Stirling and Alloa, 1969–72; Prof. of Private Law, 1972–86, and Dean of Faculty of Law, 1974–76 and 1986, Univ. of Dundee; Sheriff of: Tayside, Central and Fife at Falkirk, 1986–91; Glasgow and Strathkelvin, 1991–96; Temp. Judge of Court of Session and High Court of Justiciary, 1993–2003. Chancellor: Dio. of Brechin, 1982–98; Dio. of Argyll and the Isles, 1985–98. Chairman: Central Scotland Marriage Guidance Council, 1970–72; Scottish Marriage Guidance Council, 1974–77; Legal Services Gp, Scottish Assoc. of CAB, 1979–83. Pres., Sheriffs' Assoc., 1997–2000 (Vice-Pres., 1995–97). Trustee, Scottish Episcopal Ch, 2005–. *Publications*: (ed jtly) Gloag and Henderson's Introduction to the Law of Scotland, 8th edn 1980, 9th edn 1987; The Scottish Law of Evidence, 1986; (jtly) The Law of Parent and Child in Scotland, 1993; (contrib.) Macphail's Sheriff Court Practice, 2nd edn 1998; articles in legal periodicals. *Recreations*: collecting books and pictures, reading, travel. *Address*: 1 Weston Gardens, Haddington, East Lothian EH41 3DD. *T*: (01620) 822891. *Club*: New (Edinburgh).

WILKINSON, Prof. Andrew Robert, FRCP, FRCPCH; Professor of Paediatrics, University of Oxford, since 1997; Fellow, All Souls College, Oxford, since 1992; Director of Neonatal Medicine, John Radcliffe Hospital, Oxford, since 1981; *b* 30 Oct. 1943; *s* of late Rev. Thomas Richard Wilkinson and of (Winifred) Frances Wilkinson (*née* Steel). *Educ*: Heath Grammar Sch., Halifax; Univ. of Birmingham Med. Sch. (MB ChB 1968); Univ. of Calif, San Francisco; MA Oxon 1992. FRCP 1986; FRCPCH 1997. House officer: in medicine and surgery, Dudley Rd Hosp., Birmingham, 1968–69; in paediatrics, Warwick Hosp., 1969; Registrar: in medicine, Stratford-on-Avon, 1971–72; in paediatrics, Gt Ormond St Hosp., Oxford and Southampton, 1973–74; Nuffield Med. Res. Fellow, Univ. of Oxford, 1974–75; Fellow, Cardiovascular Res. Inst., Univ. of Calif, San Francisco, 1975–77; Clin. Lectr in Paediatrics, Univ. of Oxford, 1978–81; Consultant Paediatrician, Oxfordshire HA, 1981–92; Clin. Reader in Paediatrics, Univ. of Oxford, 1992–97. President: British Assoc. of Perinatal Medicine, 1999–2002; Neonatal Soc., 2003–06. Chm., Acad. Bd, RCPCH, 1997–98. *Publications*: papers and articles on develts in care of children and specifically neonatal medicine. *Recreations*: sailing, lawn maintenance. *Address*: All Souls College, Oxford OX1 4AL.
    See also C. R. Wilkinson.

WILKINSON, Brian; *see* Wilkinson, W. B.

WILKINSON, Prof. Christopher David Wicks, PhD; FRSE; James Watt Professor of Electrical Engineering, Glasgow University, 1992–2005, now Professor Emeritus; *b* 1 Sept. 1940; *s* of Charles Norman Wilkinson and Doris Margaret (*née* Wicks); *m* 1963, Dr Judith Anne Hughes; one *s* two *d*. *Educ*: Balliol Coll., Oxford (BA Physics; MA); Stanford Univ. (PhD Applied Physics). FRSE 1987. Engr, English Electric Valve Co., Chelmsford, 1968; Department of Electronics and Electrical Engineering, Glasgow University: Lectr, 1969–75; Sen. Lectr, 1975–79; Reader, 1979–82; Titular Prof., 1982–92. Vis. Scientist, IBM Res. Centre, Yorktown Heights, USA, 1975–76; Vis. Prof., NTT Labs, Tokyo, 1982. *Publications*: 220 papers on nanoelectronics, optoelectronics and bioelectronics, in learned jls. *Recreations*: hill walker, allotment holder, cooking, theatre. *Address*: 31 Hyndland Road, Glasgow G12 9UY. *T*: (0141) 357 0204.

WILKINSON, Christopher John, OBE 2000; RA 2006; Chairman, Wilkinson Eyre (formerly Chris Wilkinson) Architects Ltd, since 1989; *b* 1 July 1945; *s* of Edward Anthony Wilkinson and Norma Doreen Wilkinson; *m* 1976, Diana Mary Edmunds; one *s* one *d*. *Educ*: St Albans Sch.; Regent Street Poly. (DipArch). RIBA; FCSD. Architect: Foster Associates, 1973–74; Michael Hopkins Architects, 1975–79; Richard Rogers Partnership, 1979–83; founded Chris Wilkinson Architects, 1983; partnership with James Eyre, 1986–; formed Wilkinson Eyre Architects, 1999. *Projects include*: Stratford Market Depot, 1997 (FT Architecture Award, British Construction Industry Building Award, RIBA Commercial Architecture Award, Structural Steel Design Awards, Industrial Buildings Award, 1997; Civic Trust Design Award, 1998) and Stratford Station, for Jubilee Line Extension, 1998 (RIBA Category Award, 1999; Civic Trust Award, 2000); South Quay Footbridge, 1997 (AIA Excellence in Design Award, 1997; Civic Trust Design Award, 1998); Hulme Arch, 1997; Challenge of Materials Gall., Science Mus., 1997; HQ for Dyson Appliances Ltd, 1999; Explore at Bristol, 2000 (RIBA Award, 2001); Gateshead Millennium Bridge, 2002 (RA/Bovis Grand Award, 1997; RIBA Stirling Prize, 2002); Magna Millennium Project, Rotherham (RIBA Stirling Prize, 2001); Liverpool Arena and Conf. Centre, King's Dock (RIBA Award); Nat. Waterfront Mus., Swansea (RIBA Award); Anglia Poly. Univ. Campus and Business Sch., Chelmsford; City & Islington Coll.; Audi Regl HQ, Hammersmith; Empress State Bldg, Earls Court; John Madejski Acad., Reading, 2007; *current projects*: Guangzhou W Tower, China; Mary Rose Final Voyage Mus., Portsmouth; Earth Scis Faculty, Univ. of Oxford; Humanities Bldg, QMC, Univ. of London; Dyson Sch. of Innovation, Bath; Gardens by the bay, Singapore; Apraksin Dvor redevelt, St Petersburg. Mem. Council, Steel Construction Inst., 1998–2001; Comr, English Heritage, 2007– (Mem. Urban Panel, 2000–); Chm., RA Works Cttee; Founding Cttee, London Festival of Architecture, 2004–. RIBA Lectr, 1996, 2001; Vis. Prof., 1997–98; Mies van der Rohe Lectr, 2003; Illinois Inst. of Technol., Chicago; Vis. Prof., Harvard Grad. Sch. of Design, 2004. Work exhibited: IX Venice Biennale; Royal Acad.; Science Mus.; RIBA; Architecture Foundn; Design Council Millennium Products touring exhibn. Hon FAIA 2007. Hon. DLit Westminster, 2002; Hon Dr Oxford Brookes, 2007. Designer of the Year, CSD, 1996; FX Designer of the Year, 2001; Stirling Prize, 2001, 2002; over 150 design awards. *Publications*: Supersheds, 1991, 2nd edn 1995 (trans. Japanese 1995); (with James Eyre) Bridging Art and Science, 2001; Exploring Boundaries, 2007; contribs World Architecture, Architects Jl. *Recreations*: golf, painting, travel, olive farm in Tuscany. *Address*: 52 Park Hall Road, SE21 8BW. *T*: (020) 8761 7021. *Club*: Dulwich and Sydenham Golf.

WILKINSON, Christopher Richard; Adviser, Internet Governance, Directorate General, Information Society (formerly Telecommunications Information Market and Exploitation of Research) (DG XIII), Commission of the European Communities, 1993–2005, now Hon. Director, European Commission; Head of Secretariat, Governmental Advisory Committee, Internet Corporation for Assigned Names and Numbers, 2002–05 (EU Representative, 1999–2002; Vice-Chairman, 2001–02); *b* 3 July 1941; *s* of late Rev. Thomas Richard Wilkinson and of Winifred Frances Wilkinson (*née* Steel). *Educ:* Hymers Coll., Kingston upon Hull; Heath Grammar Sch., Halifax; Selwyn Coll., Cambridge (MA). Commonwealth Economic Cttee, 1963–65; OECD, Paris and Madrid, 1965–66; World Bank, Washington DC and Lagos, 1966–73; EEC: Head of Division: Directorate Gen. for Regional Policy, 1973–78; Directorate Gen. for Internal Market and Industrial Affairs, 1978–82; Directorate Gen. for Telecommunications, Information Industries and Innovation, 1983–93. Mem., Internet Policy Oversight Cttee, 1997–2000; Chm., Internet Soc. European Co-ordinating Council, 2008–09. Vis. Fellow, Center for Internat. Affairs, Harvard Univ., 1982–83. Vice-Pres., European School Parents Assoc., Brussels, 1974, 1976–77, Alicante, 2005–06; Pres., Interparents, Assoc. of the Parents' Assocs of European Schs, 2008–09. *Recreations:* mountain walking, gardening, cooking.

See also A. R. Wilkinson.

WILKINSON, Clive Victor; Chairman, Heart of England NHS Foundation Trust (formerly Birmingham Heartlands and Solihull NHS Trust), since 2001; *b* 26 May 1938; *s* of Mrs Winifred Jobson; *m* 1961, Elizabeth Ann Pugh; two *d*. *Educ:* Four Dwellings Secondary Sch., Quinton; Birmingham Modern Sch. Birmingham City Council: Member, 1970–84; Leader, 1973–76 and 1980–82; Leader of Opposition, 1976–80, 1982–84. Dir, Nat. Exhibn Centre, 1973–84; Financial and Commercial Dir, Birmingham Rep. Theatre, 1983–87. Chm., CoSIRA, 1977–80; Dep. Chairman: AMA, 1974–76; Redditch Develt Corp., 1977–81. Chairman: Sandwell DHA, 1986–94; Wolverhampton Health Care NHS Trust, 1995–97; W Midlands Region, NHS Exec., DoH, 1997–2001. Member: Develt Commn, 1977–86; Electricity Consumers Council, 1977–80; Audit Commn, 1987–96; Black Country Develt Corp., 1989–92; Local Govt Commn, 1992–95; Midlands Industrial Assoc., 1978– (Chm., 1980–88). Non-exec. Dir, FSA, 2001–. Chairman: Birmingham Civil Housing Assoc., 1979–; Customer Services Cttee, Severn Trent Region, Office of Water Services, 1990–2001. Mem. Council, Univ. of Birmingham, 1974–84. Trustee, Bournville Village Trust, 1982–. Hon. Alderman, City of Birmingham, 1984. *Recreations:* watching Birmingham City Football Club, playing squash. *Address:* 53 Middle Park Road, Birmingham B29 4BH.

WILKINSON, Rev. David Adam, PhD; Principal, St John's College, University of Durham, since 2006; *b* 16 May 1963; *s* of late Adam and Margaret Wilkinson; *m* 1992, Alison Mary Russell; one *s* one *d*. *Educ:* Greencroft Comprehensive Sch., Co. Durham; Univ. of Durham (BSc 1984, PhD 1987 and 2004); Fitzwilliam Coll., Cambridge (MA 1989); Wesley House, Cambridge. FRAS 1989. Methodist Minister, Letchworth, 1990–91; Methodist Minister and Univ. Chaplain, Liverpool, 1991–99; University of Durham: Fellow in Christian Apologetics, St John's Coll., 1999–2004; Wesley Res. Lectr in Theol. and Science, Dept of Theol. and Religion, 2004–06. *Publications:* God, the Big Bang and Stephen Hawking, 1993, 2nd edn 1996; Thinking Clearly About God and Science, 1996, 2nd edn 1997; Alone in the Universe: the X-Files, aliens and God, 1997; A New Start: hopes and dreams for the millennium, 1999; The Power of the Force: the spirituality of the Star Wars films, 2000; Holiness of the Heart, 2000; God, Time and Stephen Hawking, 2001; Creation, 2002; The Case Against Christ, 2006. *Recreations:* Star Wars, the Simpsons, Newcastle United. *Address:* St John's College, 3 South Bailey, Durham DH1 3RJ. *T:* (0191) 334 3500, *Fax:* (0191) 334 3501; *e-mail:* david.wilkinson@durham.ac.uk.

WILKINSON, David Anthony, CB 1994; public administration consultant, since 2004; *b* 27 Nov. 1947; *s* of Ambrose Wilkinson and Doreen (*née* Durden); *m* 1973, Meryl, *d* of Edison and Margaret Pugh; three *d*. *Educ:* Boteler Grammar Sch., Warrington; Wigan and District Mining and Technical Coll.; Bedford Coll., Univ. of London (BA History); London School of Economics; Moscow State Univ. Department of Education and Science, 1974–92: Under Sec., and Hd of Sci. Br., 1989–92; Under Sec., OST, then OPSS, Cabinet Office, 1992–94; RCDS, 1995; Dir, Machinery of Govt and Standards Gp, OPS, 1996–98, Hd of Central Secretariat, 1998–2000, Cabinet Office; Dir of Regl Policy, DETR, 2000–01; Business Co-ordinator, Civil Contingencies Secretariat, Cabinet Office, 2001–02; Sec., Govt Communication Review Gp, Cabinet Office, 2002–03. Lay Mem., Information Tribunal, 2005–. *Address:* 15 Rayleigh Road, Wimbledon, SW19 3RE. *Clubs:* Wimbledon Squash and Badminton, AFC Wimbledon.

WILKINSON, Dr David George; Head, Division of Developmental Neurobiology, and Genetics and Development (formerly Genes and Cellular Controls) Group, National Institute for Medical Research, since 2000; *b* 8 March 1958; *s* of George Arthur Wilkinson and Barbara May Wilkinson (*née* Hayton); *m* 1991, Qiling Xu. *Educ:* Aylesbury Grammar Sch.; Hymers Coll., Hull; Univ. of Leeds (BSc Hons 1979, PhD 1983). Postdoctoral Fellow, Fox Chase Cancer Center, Philadelphia, 1983–86; National Institute for Medical Research: Postdoctoral Fellow, 1986–88; scientific staff, 1988–. Mem., EMBO, 2000. FMedSci 2000. *Publications:* (ed) In Situ Hybridisation, 1992, 2nd edn 1998; (ed jtly) Extracellular Regulators of Differentiation and Development, 1996; contrib. numerous scientific articles to various jls. *Recreations:* natural history, music, poetry. *Address:* Division of Developmental Neurobiology, National Institute for Medical Research, The Ridgeway, Mill Hill, NW7 1AA. *T:* (020) 8959 3666.

WILKINSON, Sir David Graham Brook; *see* Wilkinson, Sir Graham.

WILKINSON, Prof. David Gregor, (Greg), FRCPE; FRCPsych; Professor of Liaison Psychiatry, Liverpool University, 1994–2005; *b* 17 May 1951; *s* of David Pryde Wilkinson and Joan (*née* McCabe); *m* 1984, Christine Mary Lewis; three *s* one *d*. *Educ:* Lawside Acad., Dundee; Edinburgh Univ. (BSc, MB ChB); MPhil London. FRCPE 1989; FRCPsych 1991. House Physician and Surgeon, Royal Infirmary, Edinburgh, 1975–76; Sen. House Physician, Leith Hosp., 1976–78; Registrar, Maudsley Hosp., 1978–81; Sen. Registrar, Maudsley Hosp. and KCH, 1981–83; Res. Worker and Lectr, then Sen. Lectr, Inst. of Psychiatry, Univ. of London, 1983–89; Sen. Lectr and Reader, Academic Sub-dept of Psychol Medicine in N Wales, 1989–91; Prof. of Psychiatry, London Hosp. Med. Coll., London Univ., 1992–94. Editor, Brit. Jl of Psychiatry, 1993–2003. *Publications:* Mental Health Practices in Primary Care Settings, 1985; (jtly) Mental Illness in Primary Care Settings, 1986; (jtly) The Provision of Mental Health Services in Britain, 1986; Coping with Stress, 1987, 2nd edn as Understanding Stress, 1993; Depression, 1989; Recognising and Treating Depression in General Practice, 1989; (jtly) The Scope of Epidemiological Psychiatry, 1989; Recognising and Treating Anxiety in General Practice, 1992; Talking About Psychiatry, 1993; (jtly) Psychiatry and General Practice Today, 1994; (jtly) A Carers Guide to Schizophrenia, 1996, 2nd edn 2000; (ed jtly) Textbook of General Psychiatry, 1998, 2nd edn 2007; (jtly) Critical Reviews in Psychiatry, 1998, 2nd edn 2000; (jtly) Seminars in Psychosexual Disorders, 1998; (jtly) Treating People with Depression, 1999; Treating People with Anxiety and Stress, 1999; articles in general and specialist med. jls. *Recreations:* family, rural pursuits. *Address:* Craig y Castell, Bryniau, Dyserth, Denbighshire LL18 6DE. *T:* (01745) 571858.

WILKINSON, David Lloyd; Chief Executive and General Secretary, Co-operative Union, 1975–99; *b* 28 May 1937; *m* 1960; one *s* one *d*. *Educ:* Royds Hall Grammar Sch. ACIS; CSD. *Address:* 2 Old House, Marsden, Huddersfield HD7 6AS. *T:* (01484) 844580.

WILKINSON, Sir Denys (Haigh), Kt 1974; FRS 1956; Vice-Chancellor, University of Sussex, 1976–87 (Emeritus Professor of Physics, 1987); *b* Leeds, Yorks, 5 Sept. 1922; *o s* of late Charles Wilkinson and Hilda Wilkinson (*née* Haigh); *m* 1st, 1947, Christiane Andrée Clavier (marr. diss. 1967); three *d*; 2nd, 1967, Helen Sellschop; two step *d*. *Educ:* Loughborough Gram. Sch.; Jesus Coll. Cambridge (Fellow, 1944–59, Hon. Fellow 1961). BA 1943, MA, PhD 1947, ScD 1961. British and Canadian Atomic Energy Projects, 1943–46; Univ. Demonstrator, Cambridge, 1947–51; Univ. Lecturer, 1951–56; Reader in Nuclear Physics, Univ. of Cambridge, 1956–57; Professor of Nuclear Physics, Univ. of Oxford, 1957–59; Prof. of Experimental Physics, Univ. of Oxford, 1959–76, Head of Dept of Nuclear Physics, 1962–76; Student, Christ Church, Oxford, 1957–76, Emeritus Student, 1976, Hon. Student, 1979. Dir, Internat. Sch. of Nuclear Physics, Erice, Sicily, 1975–83. Mem. Governing Board of National Institute for Research in Nuclear Science, 1957–63 and 1964–65; Member: SRC, 1967–70; Wilton Park Acad. Council, 1979–83; Council, ACU, 1980–87; Royal Commn for the Exhibn of 1851, 1983–90 (Chm., Science Scholarships Cttee, 1983–90); British Council, 1987– (Chm., Sci. Adv. Panel and Cttee, 1977–86); Chairman: Nuclear Physics Board of SRC, 1968–70; Physics III Cttee, CERN, Geneva, 1971–75; Radioactive Waste Management Adv. Cttee, 1978–83; Pres., Inst. of Physics, 1980–82; Vice-Pres., IUPAP, 1985–93. Lectures: Welch, Houston, 1957; Scott, Cambridge Univ., 1961; Rutherford Meml, Brit. Physical Soc., 1962; Graham Young, Glasgow Univ., 1964; Queen's, Berlin, 1966; Silliman, Yale Univ., 1966; Cherwell-Simon, Oxford Univ., 1970; Distinguished, Utah State Univ., 1971, 1983, 1988; Goodspeed-Richard, Pennsylvania Univ., 1973 and 1986; Welsh, Toronto Univ., 1975; Tizard Meml, Westminster Sch., 1975; Lauritsen Meml, Cal. Tech., 1976; Herbert Spencer, Oxford Univ., 1976; Schiff Meml, Stanford Univ., 1977; Racah Meml, Hebrew Univ. Jerusalem, 1977; Cecil Green, Univ. of BC, 1978; Distinguished, Univ. of Alberta, 1979; Wolfson, Oxford Univ., 1980; Waterloo-Guelph Distinguished, Guelph Univ., 1981; Herzberg, Ottawa, 1984; Solly Cohen Meml, Hebrew Univ., Jerusalem, 1985; Peter Axel Meml, Univ. of Illinois, 1985; Breit Meml, Yale Univ., 1987; Moon, Birmingham Univ., 1987; Rochester, Durham Univ., 1988; Pegram, Brookhaven Nat. Lab., 1989; W. B. Lewis Meml, Chalk River, Ont, 1989; Humphry Davy, Académie des Sciences, Paris, 1990; Rutherford Meml, Royal Soc., 1991; W. V. Houston Meml, Rice Univ., 1994; Hudspeth, Univ. of Texas at Austin, 1994; Anna McPherson, McGill Univ., 1995; Pickavance Meml, Rutherford Lab., 1997; B. W. Sargent, Queen's Univ., Canada, 1998; Director's Distinguished, Livermore Nat. Lab., 1999; Meghnad Saha Meml, Calcutta, 2001; Glenn Knoll, Univ. of Michigan, 2002. Walker Ames Prof., Univ. of Washington, 1968; Battelle Distinguished Prof., Univ. of Washington, 1970–71; Vis. Prof., Tokyo Univ., 1995; Visiting Scientist: Brookhaven Nat. Lab., 1954–80; TRIUMF, Vancouver, 1987–; Los Alamos Nat. Lab., 1990–93. For. Mem., Royal Swedish Acad. of Scis, 1980; Mem. Acad. Europaea, 1990. Holweck Medal, British and French Physical Socs, 1957; Rutherford Prize, British Physical Soc., 1962; Hughes Medal, Royal Society, 1965; Bruce-Preller Prize, RSE, 1969; Bonner Prize, American Physical Soc., 1974; Royal Medal, Royal Soc., 1980; Guthrie Medal and Prize, Inst. of Physics, 1986; Gold Medal, Centro Cultura Scientifica Ettore Majorana, Sicily, 1988. Hon. Mem., Mark Twain Soc., 1978. Hon. DSc: Saskatchewan, 1964; Utah State, 1975; Guelph, 1981; Queen's, Kingston, 1987; William and Mary, Va, 1989; Hon. FilDr Uppsala, 1980; Hon. LLD Sussex, 1987. Comm. Bontemps Médoc et Graves, 1973. *Publications:* Ionization Chambers and Counters, 1951; (ed) Isospin in Nuclear Physics, 1969; (ed) Progress in Particle and Nuclear Physics, 1978–84; (ed jtly) Mesons in Nuclei, 1979; Our Universes, 1991; papers on nuclear physics and bird navigation. *Recreations:* mediæval church architecture and watching birds. *Address:* Gayles Orchard, Friston, Eastbourne, East Sussex BN20 0BA. *T:* (01323) 423333.

WILKINSON, Endymion Porter, PhD; Associate, Fairbank Center for East Asian Research, Harvard University, since 2007 (Senior Fellow, Asia Center, 2001–07); *b* 15 May 1941; *s* of George Curwen Wilkinson and Pamela Algernon Wilkinson (*née* Black). *Educ:* King's Coll., Cambridge (BA 1964; MA 1967); Princeton Univ. (PhD 1970). Teacher, Peking Inst. of Languages, 1964–66; Lectr in History of Far East, SOAS, London Univ., 1970–74; joined European Commn, 1974: Head of Economic and Commercial Section, Tokyo, 1974–79; China Desk, Brussels, 1979–82; Dep. Head, SE Asia Repn, Bangkok, 1982–88; Head, Asia Div., Brussels, 1988–94; Ambassador and Hd of Delegn to China, EC, 1994–2001. *Publications:* The History of Imperial China: a research guide, 1973; Studies in Chinese Price History, 1980; Japan versus Europe: a history of misunderstanding, 1982 (trans. Japanese, Chinese, French, German and Italian); Japan versus the West, 1991; Chinese History: a manual, 1998, 2nd edn 2000; *translations:* The People's Comic Book, 1973; Landlord and Labour in Late Imperial China, by Jing Su and Luo Lun, 1978. *Recreations:* Chinese history, tropical gardening, swimming. *Address:* e-mail: endymion121@yahoo.com.

WILKINSON, Sir Graham, 3rd Bt *cr* 1941; Managing Director, S.E.I.C. Services (UK) Ltd, 1985–89; *b* 18 May 1947; *s* of Sir David Wilkinson, 2nd Bt, DSC, and of Sylvia Anne, *d* of late Professor Bosley Alan Rex Gater; *S* father, 1972; *m* 1977, Sandra Caroline Rossdale (marr. diss. 1996); two *d*; *m* 1998, Hilary Jane Griggs, *d* of late W. H. C. Bailey, CBE. *Educ:* Millfield; Christ Church, Oxford. Orion Royal Bank Ltd, 1971–85 (Dir 1979–85); non-executive Director: Galveston-Houston Co., USA, 1986–89; Sovereign Management Corp., USA, 1987–94; Lamport Gilbert Ltd, 1992–97. Dep. Pres., Surrey County Agricultural Soc., 2004–06; Mem. Council, RASE, 2005. Gov., Queen's Gate Sch. Trust, 1989–2005. Master, Farmers' Co., 2006–07. KStJ 2003 (Council Mem., Order of St John for Surrey). *Clubs:* White's, Royal Ocean Racing; Royal Yacht Squadron.

WILKINSON, Greg; *see* Wilkinson, David Gregor.

WILKINSON, Rev. Guy Alexander; National Inter Faith Relations Adviser, 2004; Archdeacon of Bradford, 1999–2003; *b* 13 Jan. 1948; *m* 1971, Tessa Osbourn; two *s*. *Educ:* Magdalene Coll., Cambridge (BA 1969); Ripon Coll., Cuddesdon. Commn of Eur. Communities, 1973–80; Dir, 1980–85, non-exec. Dir, 1985–87, Express Foods Gp.; ordained deacon 1987, priest 1988; Curate, Caludon, Coventry, 1987–90; Priest i/c, 1990–91, Rector, 1991–94, Ockham with Hatchford; Domestic Chaplain to Bishop of Guildford, 1990–94; Vicar, Small Heath, Birmingham, 1994–99.

WILKINSON, Rt Hon. Dame Heather; *see* Hallett, Rt Hon. Dame H. C.

WILKINSON, James Hugh; freelance journalist and broadcaster; *b* 19 Sept. 1941; *s* of Hugh Davy Wilkinson and Marjorie Wilkinson (*née* Prout); *m* 1978, Rev. Elisabeth Ann Morse; two *s*. *Educ:* Westminster Abbey Choir Sch.; Sutton Grammar Sch.; King's Coll. London (BSc Hons); Churchill Coll., Cambridge (CertEd). Health and Sci. Corresp.

Daily Express, 1964–74; Sci. and Air Corresp., BBC Radio News, 1974–83; Sci. Corresp., BBC News and Current Affairs, 1983–99. Vis. Fellow, Inst. of Food Res., 1992–96. Mem., Educn Cttee, CRC, 1977–82; Mem., Adv. Bd, CIBA Foundn Media Resource Service, 1994–99 (Mem., Steering Cttee, 1985–94). Hon. Steward, Westminster Abbey, 1999– (Sec., Brotherhood of St Edward, 1984–99). Mem., Editl Cttee, Sci. and Public Affairs Jl, 1989–99. Founder Mem., Med. Journalists' Assoc. (Chm., 1972–74). Glaxo Wellcome Sci. Writers' Award, 1996. *Publications:* The Conquest of Cancer, 1973; Tobacco: the truth behind the smokescreen, 1986; Green or Bust, 1990; Westminster Abbey: 1000 years of music and pageant, 2003; booklets about aspects of Westminster Abbey incl. Poet's Corner and the Coronation Chair. *Recreations:* music, singing, bookbinding, editing The Westminster Abbey Chorister. *Club:* Oxford and Cambridge.

WILKINSON, Jeffrey Vernon; management consultant; Consultant, Apax Partners & Co. (formerly Alan Patricof Associates), 2000–07 (Director, 1986–2000; Partner, 1988–2000); Chairman of several private companies, since 1985; *b* 21 Aug. 1930; *s of late* Arthur Wilkinson and Winifred May Allison; *m* 1955, Jean Vera Nurse; two *d. Educ:* Matthew Humberstone Foundation Sch.; King's Coll., Cambridge (BA Hons, MA; Fellow Commoner, 2001–); Sorbonne. FBCS. Joined Joseph Lucas as graduate apprentice, 1954; Director, CAV, 1963; Director and General Manager, Diesel Equipment, CAV, 1967; Director: Simon Engineering, 1968; Joseph Lucas, 1974; Dir and Gen. Manager, Lucas Electrical, 1974; Divisional Man. Dir, Joseph Lucas Ltd, 1978; Jt Gp Man. Dir, Lucas Industries plc, 1979–84; Chm. and CEO, Spear & Jackson plc, 1992–2000. Chairman: Automotive Components Manufacturers, 1979–84; Plastics Processing EDC, 1985–87; Mem. Council and Exec., SMMT, 1979–84. CCMI. Liveryman, Wheelwrights Company, 1971–2006. Mem., 2002–, Chm., 2004–07, Devlt Cttee, King's Coll., Cambridge. *Recreations:* water ski-ing, swimming, tennis, reading, theatre, art. *Address:* Hillcroft, 15 Mearse Lane, Barnt Green, Birmingham B45 8HG. *T:* (0121) 447 7750.

WILKINSON, John Arbuthnot Du Cane; *b* 23 Sept. 1940; 2nd *s* of late Denys Wilkinson and Gillian Wilkinson, Eton College; *m* 1st, 1969 (marr. diss. 1987); one *d*; 2nd, 1987, Cecilia Cienfuegos, *d* of late Raul Cienfuegos Lyon, Santiago, Chile; one *s. Educ:* Eton (King's Scholar); RAF Coll., Cranwell; Churchill Coll., Cambridge (2nd cl. Hons Mod. Hist.; MA). Flight Cadet, RAF Coll., Cranwell, 1959–61 (Philip Sassoon Meml Prize, qualified French Interpreter); commnd 1961; Flying Instructor, No 8 FTS, Swinderby, 1962. Churchill Coll., Cambridge, Oct. 1962–65. Trooper, 21st Special Air Service Regt (Artists'), TA, 1963–65; rejoined RAF 1965; Flying Instructor, RAF Coll., Cranwell, 1966–67; Tutor, Stanford Univ.'s British Campus, 1967; ADC to Comdr 2nd Allied Tactical Air Force, Germany, 1967; resigned RAF, 1967. Head of Universities' Dept, Conservative Central Office, 1967–68; Aviation Specialist, Cons. Research Dept, 1969; Senior Administration Officer (Anglo–French Jaguar Project), Preston Div., British Aircraft Corp., 1969–70; Tutor, Open Univ., 1970–71; Vis. Lectr, OCTU RAF Henlow, 1971–75; Chief Flying Instructor, Skywork Ltd, Stansted, 1974–75; Gen. Manager, General Aviation Div., Brooklands Aviation Ltd, 1975–76; PA to Chm., BAC, 1975–77; Senior Sales Executive, Eagle Aircraft Services Ltd, 1977–78; Sales Manager, Klingair Ltd, 1978–79. MP (C) Bradford W, 1970–Feb. 1974; contested same seat, Feb. and Oct. 1974; MP (C) Ruislip Northwood, 1979–2005. PPS to Minister of State for Industry, 1979–80, to Sec. of State for Defence, 1981–82. Chairman: Cons. Parly Aviation Cttee, 1983–85, and 1992–93 (Jt Sec., 1972–74; Vice-Chm., 1979); Cons. Parly Defence Cttee, 1993–94, 1996–97 (Vice-Chm., 1983–85, 1990–91, 1992–93; Sec., 1972–74 and 1980–81); Special Select Cttee on Armed Forces Bill, 1991; Member Select Committee on: Race Relations and Immigration, 1972–74; Sci. and Technol., 1972–74; Defence, 1987–90. Chairman: Anglo-Asian Cons. Soc., 1979–82; European Freedom Council, 1982–90; Cons. Space Sub Cttee, 1986–90 (Vice-Chm., 1983–85). Chm., Horn of Africa Council, 1984–88. Delegate to Council of Europe (Chm., Space Sub-Cttee, 1984–88, Migration Sub-Cttee, 2001–04; Chm., Cttee on Migration, Refugees and Demography, 2004–05) and WEU (Chm., Cttee on Scientific, Technological and Aerospace Questions, 1986–89), 1979–90, 2000–05; Leader, EDG/EPP Gp, Assembly of WEU, 2000–02; Chief Whip, EDG Gp, Council of Europe, 2001–04; Vice-Chm., British Gp, 2001–04, Vice-Pres., Cttee on Peace and Security, 2004–05, IPU; Chm., Defence Cttee, WEU, 2002–05. Parly Industrial Fellow, GKN plc, 1989–90; Postgrad. Fellow, TI plc, 1993; Parly Armed Forces Scheme attachment, RM, 1993–94; Metropolitan Police attachment, Parly Police Service Scheme, 2002–03. Mem., Commonwealth War Graves Commn, 1997–2003. Pres., London Green Belt Council, 1997–2005. CRAeS 1997. HQA (Pakistan), 1989; Order of Terra Mariana, 3rd cl. (Estonia), 1999; Order of Three Stars (Latvia), 2005; Order of Bernardo O'Higgins (Chile), 2005. *Publications:* (jtly) The Uncertain Ally, 1982; British Defence: a blueprint for reform, 1987; pamphlets and articles on defence and politics. *Recreation:* travel in South America. *Address:* c/o Barclays International Banking, PO Box 9, Barclays House, Douglas, Isle of Man IM99 1AJ. *Club:* Royal Air Force. *See also* R. D. Wilkinson.

WILKINSON, John Francis; Director of Public Affairs, BBC, 1980–85; *b* 2 Oct. 1926; *s* of late Col W. T. Wilkinson, DSO, and Evelyn S. Wilkinson (*née* Ward); *m* 1951, Alison, *d* of late Hugh and Marian Malcolm; two *s* one *d. Educ:* Wellington Coll.; Edinburgh Univ. Naval Short Course, 1944–45; Cambridge and London Univs Colonial Course, 1947–48. Served Royal Navy (Fleet Air Arm trainee pilot, 1945), 1945–47; HM Colonial Service, N Nigeria, 1949; Asst District Officer, Bida, 1949; Asst Sec., Lands and Mines, Kaduna, 1950; Private Sec. to Chief Comr, N Nigeria, 1951; transf. to Nigerian Broadcasting Corp., 1952; Controller: Northern Region, 1952–56; National Programme, Lagos, 1956–58; joined BBC African Service as African Programme Organiser, 1958; East and Central African Programme Organiser, 1961; BBC TV Production Trng Course and attachment to Panorama, 1963; Asst Head, 1964, Head, 1969, BBC African Service; attachment to Horizon, 1972; Head of Production and Planning, BBC World Service, 1976; Secretary of the BBC, 1977–80. Dir, 1986–90, Trustee, 1990–99, The One World Broadcasting Trust. Chm. of Governors, Centre for Internat. Briefing, Farnham Castle, 1977–87, Vice-Pres., 1987–2004. Vice-Pres., Royal African Soc., 1978–82. MUniv Open, 1989. *Publications:* Broadcasting in Africa, in African Affairs (Jl of Royal African Soc.), 1972; (contrib.) Broadcasting in Africa, a continental survey of radio and television, 1974; (contrib.) Was it Only Yesterday, Northern Nigerian Administration Service anthology, 2002. *Address:* Compass Cottage, Box, Minchinhampton, near Stroud, Glos GL6 9HD. *T:* (01453) 833072. *Club:* New Cavendish.

WILKINSON, Jonathan Peter, OBE 2004 (MBE 2003); Rugby Union football player; *b* 25 May 1979; *s* of Philip Wilkinson and Philippa Wilkinson. *Educ:* Lord Wandsworth Coll., Hants. Player (fly half), Newcastle Falcons RFU Club, 1997–; member, England Rugby Team, 1998–; member, winning team: Five Nations Championship, 1999; Six Nations Championship, 2000, 2001, 2003; World Cup, 2003. Member, British Lions tour, Australia, 2001, NZ, 2005. Player of the Year, Internat. Rugby Players Assoc., 2002, 2003; Player of the Year, Internat. Rugby Bd, 2003; BBC Sports Personality of the Year, 2003. *Publications:* Lions and Falcons: my diary of a remarkable year, 2001; My World (autobiog.), 2004; How to Play Rugby My Way, 2005; (with Steve Black) Tackling Life, 2008. *Address:* c/o Wasserman Media Group, 5th Floor, 33 Soho Square, W1D 3QU; c/o

Newcastle Falcons Rugby Club, Kingston Park Stadium, Brunton Road, Newcastle upon Tyne NE13 8AF.

WILKINSON, Rev. Canon Keith Howard; Conduct, Eton College, since 2008; *b* 25 June 1948; *s* of Kenneth John Wilkinson and Grace Winifred (*née* Bowler); *m* 1972, Carolyn Gilbert; two *d. Educ:* Beaumont Leys Sch.; Gateway Sch., Leicester; Univ. of Hull (BA Hons); Emmanuel Coll., Cambridge (Lady Romney Exhibnr, MA status); Westcott House, Cambridge. Hd of Religious Studies, Bricknell High Sch., 1970–72; Hd of Faculty (Humanities), Kelvin Hall Comprehensive Sch., Kingston upon Hull, 1972–74; Deacon 1976; Priest 1977; Asst Priest, St Jude, Westwood, Peterborough, 1977; Asst Master and Chaplain, Eton Coll., Windsor, 1979–84; Sen. Chaplain and Hd of Religious Studies, Malvern Coll., 1984–89; Sen. Tutor, Malvern Coll., 1988–89; Headmaster: Berkhamsted Sch., 1989–96; King's Sch., Canterbury, 1996–2007. Hon. Canon, Canterbury Cathedral, 1996–. *Publications:* various articles and reviews. *Recreations:* films, theatre, music, walking, buildings and building, ecology. *Address:* Eton College, Windsor SL4 6DW. *Clubs:* East India, Lansdowne.

WILKINSON, His Honour Kenneth Henry Pinder; a Circuit Judge, 1996–2005; Designated Family Judge, Merseyside, 2002–05; *b* 5 Aug. 1939; *s* of late Henry Wilkinson and Alice Wilkinson; *m* 1966, Margaret Adams; two *s* one *d. Educ:* Wigan GS; Univ. of Manchester (LLB Hons). Admitted solicitor, 1965; in private practice, 1965–80; Dep. Dist Registrar, 1977–80; Dist Judge, 1980–96; Asst Recorder, 1990–93; Recorder, 1993–96. Chm. (part-time), Industrial Tribunal, 1977–80; Member: Matrimonial Causes Rule Cttee, 1978–80; County Court Rule Cttee, 1988–92. Mem., Family Law Cttee, Law Soc., 1976–80. *Publications:* (jtly) A Better Way Out, 1979; (contrib.) Personal Injury Litigation Service, 1984; (with I. S. Goldrein) Commercial Litigation: pre-emptive remedies, 1987, 3rd edn 1996; (with M. De Haas) Property Distribution on Divorce, 1989; (Consult. Ed.) County Court Litigation, 1993. *Recreations:* gardening, music, walking, watching sport, birdwatching. *Address:* School House, Chorley Road, Bispham, Ormskirk, Lancs L40 3SL.

WILKINSON, Leon Guy, FCIB; a General Commissioner of Income Tax, City of London, 1989–2003; part-time Member, VAT Tribunal, 1989–2004; *b* 6 Nov. 1928; *s* of Thomas Guy and Olive May Wilkinson; *m* 1953, Joan Margaret; one *s* one *d. Educ:* Bude Grammar Sch. CMS Oxon. Lloyds Bank: Regional Gen. Man., N and E Midlands, 1976–79; Asst Gen. Man., 1979–83; Gen. Man. (Finance), 1984–86; Chief Financial Officer, 1986–88. *Recreation:* sports. *Clubs:* MCC, Royal Over-Seas League; Nevill Golf (Tunbridge Wells).

WILKINSON, Rear-Adm. Nicholas John, CB 1994; Press Complaints Commissioner, since 2005; *b* 14 April 1941; *s* of late Lt-Col Michael Douglas Wilkinson, RE and Joan Mary Wilkinson (*née* Cosens); *m* 1st, 1969, Penelope Ann Stephenson (marr. diss. 1996; she *d* 2003); three *s* one *d*; 2nd, 1998, Juliet Rayner (*née* Hockin). *Educ:* English School, Cairo; Cheltenham College; BRNC Dartmouth. Served HM Ships Venus, Vidal and Hermes, 1960–64; RN Air Station, Arbroath, 1964–65; HMS Fife, 1965–67; Asst Sec. to Vice-Chief of Naval Staff, 1968–70; HMS Endurance, 1970–72; Army Staff Course, 1973 (Mitchell Prizewinner); Clyde Submarine Base, 1974–75; Sec. to ACNS (Policy), 1975–77; HMS London, 1977–78; Asst Dir, Naval Officer Appts (SW), 1978–80; Trng Comdr, HMS Pembroke, 1980–82; NATO Defence Coll., Rome, 1982–83; MA to Dir, NATO Internat. Mil. Staff, 1983–85; RCDS, 1986; Dir, Defence Logistics, 1986; Sec. to First Sea Lord, 1989–90; Sen. Mil. Mem., Defence Organisation Study and Project Team, 1991–92; Dir Gen. of Naval Manpower and Trng, 1992–94; Chief Naval Supply and Secretariat Officer, 1993–97; Comdt, JSDC, 1994–97; mgt consultant, 1998–99; Maj.-Gen., RCDS, 1999; Sec., Defence, Press and Broadcasting Adv. Cttee (DA Notice Sec.), 1999–2004. Chm., Assoc. RN Officers, 1998–2004; Member Council: Forces Pension Soc., 1994–2005; Victory Services Assoc., 1998–2008 (Chm., 2001–08). Trustee, Greenwich Foundn, 2003–. Mem., Devlt Council, Trinity Coll. of Music, 2001–; Chm., Adv. Cttee, Maritime Inst., Univ. of Greenwich, 2003–. Gov., Princess Helena Coll., 1994–2004. *Publications:* Secrecy and the Media, 2009; articles in The Naval Review and media publications. *Recreations:* cricket, opera. *Address:* 37 Burns Road, SW11 5GX. *Clubs:* Savile (Chm., 2008–), Victory Services, MCC (Mem., Memship Cttee, 2000–03, 2005–08).

WILKINSON, Nigel Vivian Marshall; QC 1990; a Recorder, since 1992; a Deputy High Court Judge, since 1997; *b* 18 Nov. 1949; *s* of late John Marshall Wilkinson and of Vivien Wilkinson; *m* 1974, Heather Carol Hallett (*see* Rt Hon. Dame Heather Hallett); two *s. Educ:* Charterhouse; Christ Church, Oxford (Holford exhibnr; MA). Called to the Bar, Middle Temple, 1972, Bencher, 1997; Astbury Scholar, 1972; Midland and Oxford Circuit, 1972–; an Asst Recorder, 1988–92. Dep. Chm., Appeals Cttee, Cricket Council, 1991–97. Gov., Brambletye Sch., 1992–98. *Recreations:* cricket, golf, theatre. *Address:* 1 Temple Gardens, Temple, EC4Y 9BB. *T:* (020) 7583 1315. *Clubs:* MCC; Vincent's (Oxford); I Zingari, Butterflies CC, Invalids CC, Armadillos CC, Rye Golf, Royal Wimbledon Golf, Hon. Co. of Edinburgh Golfers.

WILKINSON, Prof. Paul; Professor of International Relations, 1990–2007, Emeritus Professor, 2008, and Chairman (formerly Director), Advisory Board, Centre for the Study of Terrorism and Political Violence, since 1999, University of St Andrews; *b* 9 May 1937; *s* of late Walter Ross Wilkinson and of Joan Rosemary (*née* Paul); *m* 1960, Susan Flook; two *s* one *d. Educ:* Lower School of John Lyon; University Coll., Swansea, Univ. of Wales (BA (jt Hons Mod. Hist. and Politics), MA; Hon. Fellow, 1986). Royal Air Force regular officer, 1959–65. Asst Lecturer in Politics, 1966–68, Lectr in Politics, 1968–75, Sen. Lectr in Politics, 1975–77, University Coll., Cardiff; Reader, Univ. of Wales, 1978–79; Prof., Internat. Relations, 1979–89, Hd, Dept of Politics and Internat. Relations, 1985–89, Univ. of Aberdeen; Dir, Res. Inst. for Study of Conflict and Terrorism, 1989–94; Hd, Sch. of History and Internat. Relations, Univ. of St Andrews, 1994–96. Vis. Fellow, Trinity Hall, Cambridge, 1997–98. Mem., IBA Scottish Adv. Cttee, 1982–85. Special Consultant, CBS Broadcasting Co., USA, 1986–91; Advr, Commonwealth Scholarships Commn, 2002–. FRSA 1995. Joint Editor: Terrorism and Political Violence Jl, 1988–2006; Cass Political Violence series, 1990–; Emeritus Editor, Handbook of Security, 1991–; Co-Chm., Praeger International series, 2004–. *Publications:* Social Movement, 1971; Political Terrorism, 1974; Terrorism versus Liberal Democracy, 1976; Terrorism and the Liberal State, 1977, rev. edn 1986; (jtly) Terrorism: theory and practice, 1978; (ed) British Perspectives on Terrorism, 1981; The New Fascists, 1981, rev. edn 1983; Defence of the West, 1983; (jtly) Contemporary Research on Terrorism, 1987; Lessons of Lockerbie, 1989; Terrorist Targets and Tactics: new risks to world order, 1990; Northern Ireland: reappraising Republican violence, 1991; (ed) Technology and Terrorism, 1993; (ed) Terrorism: British perspectives, 1993; Lloyd Inquiry into Legislation against Terrorism, vol. 2 (research report), 1996; (jtly) Aviation Terrorism and Security, 1998; Terrorism Versus Democracy: the liberal state response, 2000, rev. edn 2006; (jtly) Addressing the New International Terrorism, 2003; (ed) UK Homeland Security, 2007; International Relations - a very short introduction, 2007; contribs to wide range of jls in Britain, USA and Canada. *Recreations:* modern art, poetry, walking. *Address:* Department of International Relations, North Street, St Andrews, Fife KY16 9AL. *T:* (01334) 462936. *Club:* Savile.

WILKINSON, Vice Adm. Peter John, CVO 2007; Deputy Chief of Defence Staff (Personnel), since 2007; *b* 28 May 1956; *s* of Sir Philip (William) Wilkinson; *m* 1981, Tracey Kim Ward; two *d. Educ:* Royal Grammar Sch., High Wycombe; St David's Coll., Lampeter, Univ. of Wales (BA 1978). FCIPD 2003. Joined RN, 1975; trng, 1975–80; qualified submarines, 1980; Torpedo Officer, HMS Onslaught, 1981; Staff, C-in-C Fleet, 1982; trng courses, 1983; Tactics and Sonar Officer, HMS Resolution, 1984–86; Navigating Officer, HMS Churchill, 1986–87; submarine comd course, 1987; CO, HMS Otter, 1988–89; Staff of Captain (SM) Sea Trng, 1989–90; CO, HMS Superb, 1991–92; Comdr (SM), Maritime Tactical Sch., 1992–94; CO, HMS Vanguard, 1994–96; Asst Dir, Nuclear Policy, MOD, 1996–99; Capt., 2nd Submarine Sqn, 1999–2001; Director: RN Service Conditions, 2001–03; RN Life Mgt, 2003–04; Naval Sec., and Dir Gen., Human Resources (Navy), 2004–05; Defence Services Sec., 2005–07. Pres., RN Football Assoc., 2004–; Hon. Vice Pres., FA, 2004–. *Recreations:* genealogy, gardening, watching all sports. *Address:* c/o Naval Secretary, Leach Building, Whale Island, Portsmouth, Hants PO2 8ER. *Club:* Army and Navy.

WILKINSON, Richard Denys, CVO 1992; HM Diplomatic Service, retired; Head of Spanish, Winchester College, since 2007; *b* 11 May 1946; *y s* of late Denys and Gillian Wilkinson; *m* 1982, Maria Angela Morris; two *s* one *d. Educ:* Eton Coll. (King's Schol.); Trinity Coll., Cambridge (MA, MLitt, Wace Medallist); Ecole Nat. des Langues Orientales Vivantes, Univ. de Paris; Ecole des Langues Orientales Anciennes, Inst. Catholique de Paris. Hayter Postdoctoral Fellow in Soviet Studies, SSEES, London, 1971; joined Diplomatic Service, 1972: Madrid, 1973; FCO, 1977; Vis. Prof., Univ. of Michigan, Ann Arbor, 1980; FCO, 1980; Ankara, 1983; Mexico City, 1985; Counsellor (Information), Paris, 1988; Head of Policy Planning Staff, FCO, 1993–94; Head of Eastern Dept, FCO, 1994–96; Ambassador to Venezuela, 1997–2000; Dir, Americas and Overseas Territories, FCO, 2000–03; Ambassador to Chile, 2003–05. *Publications:* articles and reviews in learned jls. *Recreations:* sightseeing, oriental studies. *Address:* 1 Westley Close, Winchester, Hants SO22 5LA. *Club:* Oxford and Cambridge.

See also J. A. D. Wilkinson.

WILKINSON, Dr Robert Edward; Principal, Hills Road Sixth Form College, Cambridge, 2002–08; *b* 23 Jan. 1950; *s* of Sydney Arthur Wilkinson and Winifred Wilkinson (*née* Hawker); *m* 1974, Diana Viader; one *s* two *d. Educ:* Bexley-Erith Tech. High Sch. for Boys, Bexley; University Coll., Swansea (BA; PhD 1982); PGCE Oxford. Teacher of hist., Scarborough Sixth Form Coll., 1975–82; Hd of Hist., John Leggott Coll., Scunthorpe, 1982–89; Vice Principal, Hills Rd Sixth Form Coll., Cambridge, 1989–94; Principal, Wyggeston & Queen Elizabeth I Coll., Leicester, 1994–2002. Registered Inspector, FEFC, 1995–2001; Addnl Inspector, Ofsted, 2001–04. *Recreations:* bird-watching, walking, history, theatre, music.

WILKINSON, Robert Purdy, OBE 1990; *b* 23 Aug. 1933; *s* of Robert Purdy and Lily Ingham Wilkinson; *m* 1957, June (*née* Palmer); two *d. Educ:* Univ. of Durham (BA; DipEd 1957). Kleinwort Sons & Co., 1958–62; Estabrook & Co., 1962–64; Partner, W. I. Carr Sons & Co., 1966–81. Stock Exchange: Mem. Council, 1978–81; Cttee Chm., 1980–81; Stock Exchange Inspector, 1981–84; Dir of Surveillance, Stock Exchange, 1984–90; Dir of Enforcement and Dep. Chief Exec., Securities Assoc., 1987–90. Dir, Tradepoint, 1994–2001; Chm., Bovill Ltd, 2003–05. Consultant: Morgan Grenfell Internat., 1991; S Africa Financial Markets Bd, 1991; Johannesburg Stock Exchange, 1991; DTI Inspector, 1987, 1989, 1991; Invesco Gp, 1997–2003 (Dir, 1994–97). Mem., Financial Services Tribunal, 1991–94; Special Advisor: Assoc. of Swiss Stock Exchanges, 1991; Czech Ministry of Finance, 1995; Bulgarian Ministry of Finance, 1997–99; Romanian Securities Commn, 1997–99; Tallinn Stock Exchange, 1999; Jordan Securities Commn, 1999–2002. Testified US Congress Cttee, 1988. Chm. of Govs, Sevenoaks Sch., 1992–2002; Chm., Sevenoaks Sch. Foundn, 1993–. *Publications:* various articles on securities regulation and insider dealing. *Recreations:* walking, schools' sport.

WILKINSON, Tom, OBE 2005; actor; *b* 5 Feb. 1948; *m* 1998, Diana Hardcastle; two *d. Educ:* Univ. of Kent (BA); Royal Acad. of Dramatic Art. *Theatre includes:* The Cherry Orchard (tour); Peer Gynt; Brand; Three Sisters; Uncle Vanya; Henry IV; Henry V; Julius Caesar; The Merchant of Venice; As You Like It; Hamlet, RSC, 1981; King Lear, Tom and Viv, 1983, My Zinc Bed, 2000, Royal Court; Ghosts, 1986 (Critics' Circle Award, 1986), An Enemy of the People, 1988 (Critics' Circle Award, 1988), Young Vic; The Crucible, White Chameleon, 1991, RNT. *Films include:* Sylvia, Wetherby, 1985; Sharma and Beyond, 1986; Paper Mask, 1990; In the Name of the Father, 1993; Priest, A Business Affair, 1994; Sense and Sensibility, 1995; The Ghost and the Darkness, 1996; Jilting Joe, Oscar and Lucinda, Smilla's Sense of Snow, Wilde, The Full Monty, 1997; The Governess, Shakespeare in Love, Rush Hour, 1998; Molokai: The Story of Father Damien, Ride with the Devil, 1999; The Patriot, Essex Boys, Chain of Fools, 2000; In the Bedroom, Another Life, Black Knight, 2001; The Importance of Being Earnest, Before You Go, 2002; Girl with a Pearl Earring, 2003; If Only, Eternal Sunshine of the Spotless Mind, Stage Beauty, Piccadilly Jim, A Good Woman, 2004; Ripley Under Ground, Batman Begins, The Exorcism of Emily Rose, A Good Woman, Separate Lies, 2005; The Night of the White Pants, The Last Kiss, 2006; Dedication, Michael Clayton, 2007; Cassandra's Dream, RocknRolla, 2008. *Television includes:* Prime Suspect, 1991; All Things Bright and Beautiful, 1994; Martin Chuzzlewit, 1994; The Gathering Storm, 2002. *Address:* c/o Lou Coulson Associates Ltd, 1st Floor, 37 Berwick Street, W1F 8RS.

WILKINSON, Prof. Tony James, FBA 2008; Professor of Archaeology, University of Durham, since 2006; landscape archaeologist; *b* Braintree, Essex, 14 Aug. 1948; *s* of James Wesley Wilkinson and Maggie Wilkinson; *m* 1995, Eleanor Rose Barbanes. *Educ:* Birkbeck Coll., London (BSc Geog.); McMaster Univ. (MSc Geog.). Consultant landscape archaeologist, 1972–89; Asst Dir, British Sch. of Archaeol. in Iraq, 1989–91; Res. Associate (Associate Prof.), Oriental Inst., Univ. of Chicago, 1992–2003; Lectr, 2003–05, Prof. of Near Eastern Archaeol., 2005–06, Univ. of Edinburgh. *Publications:* (with S. Duhon) Excavations at Franchthi Cave, Greece Franchthi Paralia, 1990; Town and Country in SE Anatolia, vol. 1, 1990; (with P. Murphy) The Archaeology of the Essex Coast, vol. 1, 1995; (with D. J. Tucker) Settlement Development in the North Jazira, Iraq, 1995; Archaeological Landscapes of the Near East, 2003 (Book Award, Soc. for Amer. Archaeol., 2004; James R. Wiseman Book Award, Archaeol. Inst. of America, 2005); Settlement and Land Use at Tell Sweyhat, and in the Upper Lake Tabqa, Syria, 2004. *Recreations:* blues: listening and playing (mem., Bamboo Beat Band, Lincoln, 1982–90), walking. *Address:* Department of Archaeology, Durham University, South Road, Durham DH1 3LE.

WILKINSON, Prof. (William) Brian, PhD; FGS; FICE; FCIWEM; Senior Consultant, Solutions to Environmental Problems, since 1999; *b* 20 Jan. 1938; *s* of James Edmund Wilkinson and Gladys (*née* Forster); *m* 1962, Gillian Warren; two *s* one *d. Educ:* Univ. of Durham (BSc Hons Civil Engrg, BSc Hons Geol.); Univ. of Manchester (PhD 1968). FGS 1974; FCIWEM (FIWEM 1984); FICE 1989. Asst engr, Babtie Shaw and Morton, Consulting Engrs, 1961–63; Lectr, Dept of Civil Engrg, Univ. of Manchester, 1963–69; Sen. Engr, Water Resources Bd, 1969–74; Sen. Principal Hydrologist, Severn Trent Water Authy, 1974–75; Hd, Water Resources Div., Water Res. Centre, 1975–83; Prof. of Civil Engrg, RMCS, Cranfield Univ., 1983–88; Dir, Inst. of Hydrology, 1988–94, Dir, Centre for Ecology and Hydrology, 1995–99, NERC. Visiting Professor: in Hydrol., Univ. of Reading, 1989–; in Dept of Civil Engrg, Univ. of Newcastle upon Tyne, 2000–. Dir, Oxford Vacs, 1997–99. Mem. and Project Co-ordinator, Indep. Rev. Gp for Decommissioning Brent N Sea Platforms, 2007–; Advr, Safety Health and Envmt Cttee, Transport for London, 2007–. Fellow, Russian Acad. of Nat. Sci., 1997. *Publications:* (ed) Groundwater Quality, Measurement, Prediction and Protection, 1976; (ed jtly) Applied Groundwater Hydrology, 1991; (ed) Groundwater Problems in Urban Areas, 1994; numerous articles covering geotechnics and envmtl sci. *Recreations:* classical music, French wines, water colour painting, karate. *Address:* Millfield House, High Street, Leintwardine, Craven Arms, Shropshire SY7 0LB. *T:* (01547) 540356; *e-mail:* gb.wilk@dsl.pipex.com. *Club:* Club de la Fondation Universitaire (Brussels).

WILKINSON, Dr William Lionel, CBE 1987; FRS 1990; FREng; a Director, British Nuclear Fuels plc, 1984–94; *b* 16 Feb. 1931; *s* of Lionel and Dorothy Wilkinson; *m* 1955, Josephine Anne Pilgrim; five *s. Educ:* Christ's Coll., Cambridge (MA, PhD, ScD). Salters' Res. Schol., Christ's Coll., Cambridge, 1953–56; Lectr in Chem. Engrg, UC Swansea, 1956–59; UKAEA Production Gp, 1959–67; Prof. of Chem. Engrg, Univ. of Bradford, 1967–79; British Nuclear Fuels Ltd: Dep. Dir, 1982–84; Technical Dir, 1984–86; Dep. Chief Exec., 1986–92; non-exec. Dir, 1992–94; Dep. Chm., Allied Colloids plc, 1992–98. Vis. Prof. of Chemical Engrg, Imperial Coll., London, 1980–2004. Chm., British Nuclear Industry Forum, 1992–97; Pres., Eur. Atomic Forum, 1994–96. Member: SRC, 1981–85; ACOST, 1990–95. FIChemE (Pres., 1980); FREng (FEng 1980). Liveryman, Salters' Co., 1985. Hon. DEng Bradford, 1989. *Publications:* Non-Newtonian Flow, 1960; contribs to sci. and engrg jls on heat transfer, fluid mechanics, polymer processing and process dynamics. *Recreation:* fell-walking. *Address:* Tree Tops, Legh Road, Knutsford, Cheshire WA16 8LP. *T:* (01565) 653344. *Club:* Athenæum.

WILKS, Ann; *see* Wilks, M. A.

WILKS, (David) Michael (Worsley); President, Standing Committee of European Doctors, since 2008; *b* 26 May 1949; *s* of Dennis Worsley Wilks and Bridget Wilks (*née* Chetwynd-Stapylton, later Sewter); *m* 1972, Patricia Hackforth (marr. diss. 1992); one *s* two *d. Educ:* St John's Sch., Leatherhead; St Mary's Hosp. Med. Sch., London (MB BS 1972). DObstRCOG 1975. House officer posts at St Mary's Hosp., Paddington and Wembley Hosp., 1972–74; GP trng, London, 1974; Principal in gen. practice, Kensington and Richmond, 1975–92; Metropolitan Police: Sen. Police Surgeon, 1992–97; Principal Forensic Med. Examr, 1997–. Vis. Lectr, Kingston Univ., 1997–. Asst Med. Advr, Richmond Council Housing Dept, 1991–; Med. Referee and Trustee, Sick Doctors' Trust, 1997–; Chm. of Trustees, Rehabilitation of Addicted Prisoners Trust, 2006–. British Medical Association: Member: Trainees Sub-Cttee, 1974–75; Gen. Med. Services Cttee, 1977–89; New Charter Wkg Gp, 1982; Council, 1997–; Mem., 1979–86, 1995, Chm., 1997–2006, Med. Ethics Cttee; Chm., Representative Body, 2004–07 (Dep. Chm., 2001–04). Observer, Standards Cttee, GMC, 1997–; Mem., Ethics in Medicine Cttee, 1998–, Euthanasia wkg party (jtly with RCGP), 1999–, RCP. *Publications:* contribs to med. jls on ethical issues, addiction medicine, forensic medicine. *Recreations:* photography, theatre, art, literature, cinema, walking, Mozart. *Address:* c/o Standing Committee of European Doctors, Rue Grimard 15, 1040 Brussels, Belgium; *e-mail:* mwilks@bma.org.uk. *Club:* Royal Society of Medicine.

WILKS, Jean Ruth Fraser, CBE 1977; Chairman of Council and Pro-Chancellor, Birmingham University, 1985–89; *b* 14 April 1917; *d* of Mark Wilks. *Educ:* North London Collegiate Sch.; Somerville Coll., Oxford (MA; Hon. Fellow, 1985). Assistant Mistress: Truro High Sch., 1940–43; James Allen's Girls' Sch., Dulwich, 1943–51; Head Mistress, Hertfordshire and Essex High Sch., Bishop's Stortford, Hertfordshire, 1951–64; Head Mistress, King Edward VI High Sch. for Girls, Birmingham, 1965–77. Pres., Assoc. of Head Mistresses, 1972–74; Member: Public Schools Commn, 1968–70; Governing Council of Schools Council, 1972–75; Adv. Council on Supply and Trng of Teachers, 1973–78; Educn Cttee, Royal Coll. of Nursing, 1973–79; University Authorities Panel, 1982–89. University of Birmingham: Mem. Council, 1971–89; Life Mem. Court, 1977; Chm., Academic Staffing Cttee, 1978–85; Dep. Pro-Chancellor, 1979–85. Pres., ASM, Somerville Coll., Oxford, 1982–85. Chm. Governors, Ellerslie, Malvern, 1982–89; Mem. Council, Malvern Coll., 1992–93. FCP 1978. Hon. LLD Birmingham, 1986. *Address:* 4 Hayward Road, Oxford OX2 8LW.

WILKS, (Margaret) Ann, CBE 2004; Secretary, Financial Reporting Council, and Financial Reporting Review Panel, 1998–2004; *b* 11 May 1943; *d* of Herbert Robson and Margaret Robson (*née* Culbert); *m* 1977, Victor Wilks; two *d. Educ:* Putney High Sch., GPDST; Lady Margaret Hall, Oxford (BA Modern Hist., BPhil American Hist.); Univ. of Pennsylvania (Thouron Schol.). Asst Principal, Min. of Power and DTI, 1968–71; Department of Trade and Industry: Private Sec. to Perm. Sec. (Trade) and Parly Sec., 1971–72; Principal, 1972–73; journalist, Economist, 1973–74; Principal: DTI, 1974–76; Cabinet Office, 1976–78; (pt-time) DTI, 1982–84; (pt-time) Asst Sec., DTI, 1984–96 (Hd, Industrial Develt Unit, and Sec., Industrial Develt Adv. Bd, 1991–96); Dir, Metals, Minerals and Shipbuilding, DTI, 1996–98. Mem., Tribunal Panel, Accountancy and Actuarial Discipline Bd (formerly Accountancy Investigation and Discipline Bd), 2004–. Dep. Chm., Hornsey Town Hall Community Partnership Bd and Creative Trust, 2007–. Mem. Cttee, Thouron Scholarship, 1974–80. Trustee, 2002–, and Chm. of Govs, 2004–, Nat. Centre for Young People with Epilepsy, London. *Recreations:* tennis, cookery, theatre, walking, sightseeing. *Address:* 28 Berkeley Road, N8 8RU.

WILKS, Michael; *see* Wilks, D. M. W.

WILKS, Prof. Stephen Robert Mark, PhD; FCA; Professor of Politics, since 1990, and Deputy Vice Chancellor, 1999–2002 and 2004–05, University of Exeter; *b* 2 Jan. 1949; *s* of late Ernest Gordon Fawcett Wilks and of Florence Wilks (*née* Wilson); *m* 1976, Philippa Mary Hughes; three *d. Educ:* Buckhurst Hill Co. High Sch.; City of Westminster Coll.; Univ. of Lancaster (BA); Univ. of Manchester (PhD 1980). FCA 1978. Chartered Accountant, Fryer Whitehill and Co., London, 1968–72; University of Liverpool, Department of Political Theory and Institutions: Lectr, 1978–86; Sen. Lectr, 1986–89; Reader, 1989–90. Vis. Prof., Faculty of Law, Kyoto Univ., 1989. Member: ESRC, 2001–05 (Chm., Res. Priorities Bd, 2001–05); Competition Commn, 2001–. *Publications:* Industrial Crisis (ed with K. Dyson), 1983; Industrial Policy and the Motor Industry, 1984, 2nd edn 1988; (ed with M. Wright) Comparative Government-Industry Relations, 1987; (ed with B. Doern) Comparative Competition Policy, 1996; (ed with B. Doern) Regulatory Institutions in Britain and North America, 1998; In the Public Interest: competition policy and the Monopolies and Mergers Commission, 1999; (ed jtly) Reforming Public and Corporate Governance, 2002. *Recreations:* walking, wine, gardening, tea. *Address:* Department of Politics, University of Exeter, Amory Building, Rennes Drive, Exeter EX4 4RJ. *T:* (01392) 263168; *e-mail:* s.r.m.wilks@exeter.ac.uk.

WILL, Prof. Robert George, CBE 2000; MD; FRCP; Professor of Clinical Neurology, University of Edinburgh, since 1998; Consultant Neurologist, Western General Hospital, Edinburgh, since 1987; Co-ordinator, European Creutzfeldt-Jakob Disease Surveillance, since 2002; *b* 30 July 1950; *s* of George and Margaret Will; *m* 1976, Jayne; one *s* one *d*. *Educ:* Glenalmond Coll.; St John's Coll., Cambridge (MB BChir 1974; MA, MD 1985); London Hosp. Med Coll. FRCP 1994. London Hosp., Nat. Hosp., Queen Sq. and N Middx Hosp., 1974–79; res. at Univ. of Oxford, 1979–82; Registrar, St Thomas' Hosp., 1982–84; Sen. Registrar, Nat. Hosp., Queen Sq. and Guy's Hosp., 1994–97. Dir, Nat. CJD Surveillance Unit, 1990–2002. FMedSci 2001. FRSA 1998. *Publications:* contrib. articles on Creutzfeldt-Jakob Disease. *Address:* 4 St Catherine's Place, Edinburgh EH9 1NU. *T:* (0131) 667 3667.

WILL, Ronald Kerr; Deputy Keeper of Her Majesty's Signet, 1975–83; formerly Senior Partner, Dundas & Wilson, CS, Edinburgh; *b* 22 March 1918; 3rd *s* of late James Alexander Will, WS and late Bessie Kennedy Salmon, Dumfries; *m* 1953, Margaret Joyce, *d* of late D. Alan Stevenson, BSc, FRSE; two *s*. *Educ:* Merchiston Castle Sch.; Edinburgh Univ. Commnd King's Own Scottish Borderers, 1940; served with 1st Bn and in Staff appts (despatches); psc; GSO2. Writer to the Signet, 1950. Director: Scottish Equitable Life Assce Soc., 1965–88 (Chm., 1980–84); Scottish Investment Trust PLC, 1963–88; Standard Property Investment PLC, 1972–87. Mem. Council on Tribunals, 1971–76 and Chm. of Scottish Cttee, 1972–76. Governor, Merchiston Castle Sch., 1953–76. *Recreations:* fishing, gardening. *Address:* 4 Waverley South, East Links Road, Gullane, East Lothian EH31 2AF. *T:* (01620) 845380. *Club:* New (Edinburgh).

WILLACY, Michael James Ormerod, CBE 1989; Managing Director (formerly Managing Partner), Michael Willacy Associates Ltd, since 1990; *b* 7 June 1933; *s* of James and Marjorie Willacy (*née* Sanders); *m* 1st, 1961, Merle Louise de Lange; two *s* one *d*; 2nd, 1985, Victoria Stuart John; three *s* one *d*. *Educ:* Taunton Sch., Somerset. FCIPS. Purchasing Agent, Shell Venezuela, 1964–73; Procurement Advr, Shell Internat., The Hague, 1974–77; Supt., Shell Stanlow, 1978–80; Manager, Shell Wilmslow, 1981–83; Gen. Man., Shell Materials Services, 1983–85; Dir, Central Unit on Purchasing, 1985–90, Procurement Advr, 1991–92, HM Treasury. Chairman: Macclesfield Chamber of Commerce, 1981–83; Macclesfield Business Ventures, 1982–83. Old Tauntonian Association: Gen. Sec., 1978–91; Pres., 1988–89; Vice-Pres., 1990–; Gov., Taunton Sch., 1993–2008; Chm., St Dunstan's Abbey Sch., Plymouth, 1997–2004; Hon. Vice-Pres., Plymouth Coll., 2005–. *Recreations:* golf, travel, gardening. *Address:* Michael Willacy Associates, PO Box 20, Ivybridge PL21 9XS. *Clubs:* Royal Commonwealth Society; Old Tauntonian Association (Taunton); Bigbury Golf (Chm., 2007–).

WILLASEY-WILSEY, Timothy Andrew, CMG 2007; HM Diplomatic Service; Counsellor, Foreign and Commonwealth Office, since 2002; *b* 12 Sept. 1953; *s* of Maj.-Gen. Anthony Patrick Willasey-Wilsey, CB, MBE, MC, and of Dorothy Willasey-Wilsey (*née* Yates); *m* 1983, Alison Middleton Mackie; three *s*. *Educ:* Shrewsbury Sch.; Univ. of St Andrews (MA 1st Cl. Hons Mod. Hist. 1976). Metal Box Ltd, 1976–81: Export Sales Manager, 1977–79; Factory Mgt, 1979–81; joined HM Diplomatic Service, 1981; FCO, 1981–83; First Sec., Luanda, 1983–86; Hd of Chancery, later Dep. Hd of Mission, San Jose, Costa Rica, 1986–89; also Consul, San Jose and Managua, 1986–89; FCO, 1989–93; Counsellor (Political), Islamabad, 1993–96; FCO, 1996–99; Counsellor, UK Mission to UN, Geneva, 1999–2002. *Recreations:* history, travel, reading, cricket. *Address:* c/o Foreign and Commonwealth Office, King Charles Street, SW1A 2AH. *Clubs:* Royal Over-Seas League, MCC.

WILLBY, Christopher Roy, CEng; Director, Hazardous Installations Directorate, Health and Safety Executive, 2003–05; *b* 11 March 1945; *s* of Brian George Willby and Jean Marjorie Willby; *m* 1967, Sheila Burton (marr. diss. 1991); two *d*. *Educ:* Temple Moor Grammar Sch., Leeds; Univ. of Manchester Inst. of Sci. and Technol. (BSc Hons); Leeds Poly. (DMS). CEng, MInstE 1983. Asst Engr, Southern Project Gp, CEGB, 1966–70; Section Hd, UKAEA Risley, later NNC, 1970–78; Engrg Manager for subsid. co., Hickson Gp, 1978–82; Health and Safety Executive: Principal Inspector, 1982–87, Superintendent Inspector, 1987–91, NII; Dep. Chief Inspector, Nuclear and Radioactive Waste Policy, 1991–98; Regl Dir, Yorks and NE, 1998–2002. *Recreations:* gardening, walking, theatre, renovating old motorcycles.

WILLCOCK, His Honour Kenneth Milner; QC 1972; a Circuit Judge, 1972–94. *Educ:* Pembroke Coll., Oxford (BCL 1950; MA 1953). Called to Bar, Inner Temple, 1950. Dep. Chm., Somerset QS, 1969–71; a Recorder of the Crown Court, 1972.

WILLCOCKS, Sir David (Valentine), Kt 1977; CBE 1971; MC 1944; conductor; Musical Director of the Bach Choir, 1960–98, Conductor Laureate, since 1998; General Editor, OUP Church Music, since 1961; *b* 30 Dec. 1919; *s* of late T. H. Willcocks; *m* 1947, Rachel Gordon, *d* of late Rev. A. C. Blyth, Fellow of Selwyn Coll., Cambridge; one *s* two *d* (and one *s* decd). *Educ:* Clifton Coll.; King's Coll., Cambridge (MA; MusB). Chorister, Westminster Abbey, 1929–33; Scholar, Clifton Coll., 1934–38; FRCO, 1938; Scholar at College of St Nicolas (RSCM), 1938–39; Organ Scholar, King's Coll., Cambridge, 1939–40; Open Foundation Scholarship, King's Coll., Cambridge, 1940; Stewart of Rannoch Scholarship, 1940. Served War of 1939–45, 5th Bn DCLI, 1940–45. Organ Scholar, King's Coll., Cambridge, 1945–47; Fellow of King's Coll., Cambridge, 1947–51, Hon. Fellow, 1979–; Organist of Salisbury Cathedral, 1947–50; Master of the Choristers and Organist, Worcester Cathedral, 1950–57; Fellow and Organist, King's Coll., Cambridge, 1957–73; Univ. Lectr in Music, Cambridge Univ., 1957–74; Univ. Organist, Cambridge Univ., 1958–74; Dir, RCM, 1974–84. Conductor: Cambridge Philharmonic Soc., 1947; City of Birmingham Choir, 1950–57; Bradford Festival Choral Soc., 1957–74; Cambridge Univ. Musical Soc., 1958–73. President: RCO, 1966–68; ISM, 1978–79; Old Cliftonian Soc., 1979–81; Nat. Fedn of Music Socs, 1980–89; Assoc. of British Choral Dirs, 1993–. Mem. Council, Winston Churchill Trust, 1980–90. Freeman, City of London, 1981. FRSCM 1965; FRCM 1971; FRNCM 1977; FRSAMD 1982; Hon. RAM 1965; Hon. FTCL 1976; Hon. GSM 1980; Hon. FRCCO 1967. Hon. MA Bradford, 1973; Hon. DMus: Exeter, 1976; Leicester, 1977; Westminster Choir Coll., Princeton, 1980; Bristol, 1981; St Olaf Coll., Minnesota, 1991; RCM, 1998; Victoria, BC, 1999; Rowan, 2007; Hon. DLitt: Sussex, 1982; Newfoundland, 2003; Hon. Dr of Sacred Letters, Trinity Coll., Toronto, 1985; Hon. Dr of Fine Arts, Luther Coll., Iowa, 1998; Hon. LLD Toronto, 2001. *Publications:* miscellaneous choral and instrumental works. *Address:* 13 Grange Road, Cambridge CB3 9AS. *T:* (01223) 359559. *Club:* Athenæum.

WILLCOCKS, Prof. Dianne, CBE 2008; Vice-Chancellor, York St John University (formerly Principal, York St John College, subseq. York St John University College), since 1999; *b* 5 May 1945; *d* of late Jack and Georgina Kitson; *m* 1965, Peter Willcocks (marr. diss. 1984); two *d*. *Educ:* Ealing Coll. of Higher Educn (DipM 1966); Univ. of Surrey (BSc Hons Human Scis 1976). Dir of Res., then Dean, Envmtl and Social Scis, Poly., then Univ., of N London, 1980–93; Prof. of Social Gerontology, Univ. of N London, 1992–93; Asst Principal, Sheffield Hallam Univ., 1993–99. Mem. Bd, HEFCE, 2006–. *Publications:* (jtly) Private Lives in Public Places, 1987; (jtly) Residential Care Revisited, 1997. *Recreations:* family, friends, fitness. *Address:* 61 Rowntree Wharf, York YO1 9XA. *T:* (01904) 670884; *e-mail:* d.willcocks@yorksj.ac.uk.

WILLCOCKS, Lt-Gen. Sir Michael (Alan), KCB 2000 (CB 1997); Gentleman Usher of the Black Rod and Serjeant-at-Arms, House of Lords, and Secretary to the Lord Great Chamberlain, since 2001; *b* 27 July 1944; *s* of late Henry Willcocks and Georgina Willcocks (*née* Lawton); *m* 1966, Jean Paton Weir; one *s* two *d*. *Educ:* St John's Coll.; RMA Sandhurst; London Univ. (BSc Hons). Commnd RA, 1964; served Malaya, Borneo, NI, Germany, 1965–72; Instructor, RMA Sandhurst, 1972–74; MoD, 1977–79; Comd M Battery, RHA, 1979–80; Directing Staff, Staff Coll., 1981–83; CO, 1st Regt, RHA, 1983–85; Dep. ACOS, HQ UKLF, 1985–87; ACOS, Intelligence/Ops, HQ UKLF, 1988; CRA, 4th Armd Div., 1989–90; rcds 1991; ACOS, Land Ops, Joint War HQ, Gulf War, 1991; Dir Army Plans and Programme, 1991–93; Dir Gen. Land Warfare, 1993–94; COS Allied Command Europe Rapid Reaction Corps, 1994–96; COS Land Component Implementation Force, Bosnia-Herzegovina, 1995–96; ACGS, MoD, 1996–99; Dep. Comdr (Ops), Stabilisation Force, Bosnia-Herzegovina, 1999–2000; UK Mil. Rep. to NATO and the EU, 2000–01. Comr, Royal Hosp., Chelsea, 1996–99. Col Comdt, RA, 2000–05; Representative Col Comdt, RA, 2004–05. Hon. Col, 1 RHA, 1999–2006. Mem., European-Atlantic Gp, 1994–. Member: Pilgrims, 2002–; Pitt Club, 2003–; Saints and Sinners, 2007–. Trustee, Freeplay Foundn, 2006–. MSM (USA), 1996, 2000. Hon. DLitt Hull, 2008. Kt Comdr, Sacred Military Order of St George, 2006; PJK 2006. *Publications:* Airmobility and the Armoured Experience, 1989. *Recreations:* books, music, tennis, fishing, sailing, shooting. *Address:* House of Lords, SW1A 0PW. *Clubs:* Beefsteak, Honourable Artillery Company, National Liberal.

WILLCOX, James Henry, CB 1988; Clerk of Public Bills, House of Commons, 1982–88, retired; *b* 31 March 1923; *s* of George Henry and Annie Elizabeth Willcox; *m* 1st, 1950, Winsome Rosemarie Adèle Dallas Ross (*d* 1984); one *s* one *d*; 2nd, 1985, Pamela, *widow* of Col John Lefroy Knyvett. *Educ:* St George's Coll., Weybridge; St John's Coll., Oxford (Schol.; MA). Served RNVR, HMS Laforey, 1942–43 and Offa, 1943–45. Assistant Clerk, House of Commons, 1947; Sen. Clerk, 1951; Clerk of Standing Committees, 1975–76; Clerk of Overseas Office, 1976–77; Clerk of Private Bills, Examiner of Petitions for Private Bills and Taxing Officer, 1977–82. *Recreations:* walking, gardening. *Address:* Ibthorpe Farm House, Hurstbourne Tarrant, Hants SP11 0BN. *T:* and *Fax:* (01264) 736575; *e-mail:* awillcox@toucansurf.com. *Club:* Garrick.

WILLEMS, Lodewijk; Director of External Affairs, Fortis Bank, since 2006; *b* 6 April 1948; *s* of Frans and Leona Willems-Hendrickx; *m* 1976, Lindsay Edwards; three *s* one *d*. *Educ:* Univ. of Brussels (Licentiate Pol. Science and Internat. Relns 1971); Yale Univ. (MA Pol. Science 1975). Entered Belgian Diplomatic Service, 1976; Dep. Perm. Rep., IAEA, Vienna, 1977; Advr to Dep. Prime Minister and Minister for Econ. Affairs, 1977–81; Dep. Sec. Gen., Benelux Econ. Union, 1981–85; Political Counsellor, Kinshasa, 1985–88; Chef de Cabinet to Minister for Econ. Affairs, 1988–91; Dep. Perm. Rep. to EU, 1991–92; Chef de Cabinet to Minister of Foreign Affairs, 1992–94; Perm. Rep. (Ambassador rank), UN, Geneva, 1994–97; Ambassador: to UK, 1997–2002; to Germany, 2002–06. Mem., Anglo-Belgian Soc., 1997–. Commn for Relief of Belgium Fellow, Belgian-American Educnl Foundn, 1973. Grand Officier, Order of Leopold II (Belgium), 2005. *Recreations:* theatre, classical music. *Address:* (office) Rue Royale 20, 1000 Brussels, Belgium.

WILLESDEN, Area Bishop of, since 2001; **Rt Rev. Peter Alan Broadbent;** *b* 31 July 1952; *s* of Philip and Patricia Broadbent; *m* 1974, Sarah Enderby; one *s*. *Educ:* Merchant Taylors' Sch., Northwood, Middx; Jesus Coll., Cambridge (MA 1978); St John's Coll., Nottingham (DipTh 1975). Ordained deacon, 1977, priest 1978; Assistant Curate: St Nicholas, Durham City, 1977–80; Emmanuel, Holloway, 1980–83; Chaplain, Poly. of N London, 1983–89; Vicar, Trinity St Michael, Harrow, 1989–94; Archdeacon of Northolt, 1995–2001. Proctor in Convocation, London, 1985–2001. Member: Archbishops' Council, C of E, 1999–2000; Central Governing Body, City Parochial Foundn, 1999–2003. Chm. Council, St John's Coll., Nottingham, 2002–. Trustee, Church Urban Fund, 2002–. Mem. (Lab) Islington BC, 1982–89. *Publications:* contrib. to theol books and jls. *Recreations:* football, theatre and film, railways. *Address:* 173 Willesden Lane, NW6 7YN. *T:* (020) 8451 0189, *Fax:* (020) 8451 4606; *e-mail:* bishop.willesden@btinternet.com.

WILLETT, Allan Robert, CMG 1997; Lord-Lieutenant of Kent, since 2002; Chairman, Willett International Ltd, 1983–2002 (Chief Executive, 1983–91); *b* 24 Aug. 1936; *s* of Robert Willett and Irene Willett; *m* 1st, 1960, Mary Hillman (marr. diss. 1993); 2nd, 1993, Anne Boardman (*née* Stead). *Educ:* Eastbourne Coll. Commnd Royal E Kent Regt, 1955–57; seconded, KAR, 1955–56. Man. Dir, G. D. Peters Ltd, 1969–71; Chm., Northampton Machinery Co., 1970–74; Dep. Chm., Rowen & Boden, 1973–74; formed Willett Cos, 1974. Chm., SE England Develt Agency, 1998–2002. President: Kent Br., SSAFA, 2002–; County Cttee, Army Benevolent Fund, 2002–; Assoc. of Men of Kent and Kentish Men, 2002–; Patron: Kent Community Foundn, 2002–; Kent Br., RBL, 2002–; Trustee: Rochester Cathedral Trust, 2002–; Canterbury Cathedral Trust Fund, 2002– (Chm., 2006–). Hon. Fellow, Canterbury Christ Church Coll., 2003. Hon. DCL Kent, 2002; Hon. LLB Greenwich, 2003. *Recreations:* military history, golf, walking. *Address:* Cumberland Cottage, Chilham, Kent CT4 8BX. *T:* (01227) 738800, *Fax:* (01227) 738855; *e-mail:* allan@allanwillett.org.

WILLETT, Prof. Keith Malcolm, FRCS; Professor of Orthopaedic Trauma Surgery, University of Oxford, since 2004; Fellow, Wolfson College, Oxford, since 2004; *b* 9 Sept. 1957; *s* of Aubrey and Ruth Willett; *m* 1980, Lesley Kiernan; three *s* two *d*. *Educ:* Charing Cross Hosp. Med. Sch., Univ. of London (MB BS 1981). LRCP, MRCS 1981, FRCS 1985. Fellow in Trauma, Sunnybrook Health Sci. Center, Toronto, 1991–92; Consultant, Nuffield Orthopaedic Centre, Oxford, 1992–95; Consultant Orthopaedic and Trauma Surgeon, John Radcliffe Hospital, 1992–2004, Hon. Consultant, 2004–. *Publications:* research papers on child accident prevention, functional outcomes after injury and surgical trng. *Recreation:* football. *Address:* Kadoorie Centre for Critical Care Research and Education, John Radcliffe Hospital, Oxford OX3 9DU. *T:* (01865) 851021, *Fax:* (01865) 857611.

WILLETT, Michael John, FRAeS; Board Member, Civil Aviation Authority and Group Director, Safety Regulation, 1992–97; *b* 2 Oct. 1944; *s* of Reginald John Willett and Nora Else Willett; *m* 1st, 1967, Gillian Margaret Pope (marr. diss. 1998); two *s* one *d*; 2nd, 1998, Paulene Ann Parkinson. *Educ:* Grammar Sch., Tottenham; Open Univ. (BA Hons); Open Business Sch. (MBA). RAF, 1963–71; Airline Captain, Laker Airways, 1973–82; Flight Ops Inspectorate, CAA, 1982–92. Mem. (C), W Sussex CC, 1999–2001. Liveryman, GAPAN, 1991– (Master, 2003–04). *Recreations:* horse riding, guitar playing. *Club:* Royal Air Force.

WILLETT, Prof. Peter, PhD, DSc; Professor of Information Science, University of Sheffield, since 1991; *b* 20 April 1953; *s* of David and Patricia Willett; *m* 1978, Marie-Therese Gannon; one *d*. *Educ:* Exeter Coll., Oxford (MA); Univ. of Sheffield (MSc 1976;

PhD 1979; DSc 1997). Lectr, 1979–86, Sen. Lectr, 1986–88, Reader, 1988–91, Univ. of Sheffield. Pres., Chemical Structure Assoc., 1998–2002. Chm., Bd of Govs, Cambridge Crystallographic Data Centre, 2001–03. *Publications:* Similarity and Clustering in Chemical Information Systems, 1987; (with J. Ashford) Text Retrieval and Document Databases, 1988; (with E. M. Rasmussen) Parallel Database Processing, 1990; Three-Dimensional Chemical Structure Handling, 1991; (jtly) Readings in Information Retrieval, 1997; (with Y. C. Martin) Designing Bioactive Molecules, 1998; over 460 articles, reports, and book chapters. *Recreations:* classical music, current affairs, military history. *Address:* Department of Information Studies, University of Sheffield, 211 Portobello Street, Sheffield S7 4DP. *T:* (0114) 222 2633, *Fax:* (0114) 278 0300; *e-mail:* p.willett@sheffield.ac.uk.

WILLETTS, David Lindsay; MP (C) Havant, since 1992; *b* 9 March 1956; *s* of John Roland Willetts and Hilary Sheila Willetts; *m* 1986, Hon. Sarah Harriet Ann, *d* of Lord Butterfield; one *s* one *d. Educ:* King Edward's Sch., Birmingham; Christ Church, Oxford (BA 1st cl. Hons PPE). Res. Asst to Nigel Lawson, MP, 1978; HM Treasury, 1978–84: Pvte Sec. to Financial Sec., 1981–82; Principal Monetary Policy Div., 1982–84; Prime Minister's Downing Street Policy Unit, 1984–86; Dir of Studies, Centre for Policy Studies, 1987–92. PPS to Chm. of Cons. Party, 1993–94; an Asst Govt Whip, 1994–95; a Lord Comr of HM Treasury (Govt Whip), 1995; Parly Sec., Office of Public Service, Cabinet Office, 1995–96; HM Paymaster General, 1996; Opposition front bench spokesman on employment, 1997–98, on educn and employment, 1998–99, on social security, 1999–2001, on work and pensions, 2001–05; Shadow Secretary of State: DTI, 2005; for Educn and Skills, 2005–07; for Innovation, Univs and Skills, 2007–. Consultant Dir, 1987–92, Chm., 1997, Cons. Res. Dept; Hd of Policy Co-ordination, Cons. Party, 2003–04. Director: Retirement Security Ltd, 1988–94; Electra Corporate Ventures Ltd, 1988–94; Economic Advr, Dresdner Kleinwort Benson, 1997–2007; Sen. Advr, Punter Southall, 2005–. Mem. Adv. Bd, British Council, 2001–05. Vis. Fellow, Nuffield Coll., Oxford, 1999–2007; Vis. Prof., Pensions Inst., Cass Business Sch., 2005–. Member: Social Security Adv. Cttee, 1989–92; Global Commn on Ageing, 2000–. Member: Parkside HA, 1988–90; Lambeth, Lewisham and Southwark FPC, 1987–90. Mem., Prog. Cttee, 1998–, Gov., 2004–, Ditchley Foundn. Mem. Council, Inst. for Fiscal Studies, 2003–. Mem., Sen. Common Room, Christ Church, Oxford, 2007–. *Publications:* Modern Conservatism, 1992; Civic Conservatism, 1994; Blair's Gurus, 1996; Why Vote Conservative?, 1997; (jtly) Is Conservatism Dead?, 1997; Welfare to Work, 1998; After the Landslide, 1999; Tax Credits: do they add up?, 2002; Old Europe? demographic change and pension reform, 2003; paper, The Role of the Prime Minister's Policy Unit, 1987 (Haldane Medal, RIPA); various pamphlets. *Recreations:* swimming, reading. *Address:* c/o House of Commons, SW1A 0AA. *T:* (020) 7219 4570. *Club:* Hurlingham.

WILLI, Prof. Andreas Jonathan, DPhil; Diebold Professor of Comparative Philology, University of Oxford, since 2005; Fellow of Worcester College, Oxford, since 2005; *b* Altstätten, Switzerland, 17 Dec. 1972; *s* of Thomas Willi and Ina Willi-Plein; *m* 2005, Helen Kaufmann; one *s. Educ:* Primarschule Peters, Basel; Humanistisches Gymnasium, Basel; Universität Basel (lic.phil. Classics, Slavonic Langs/Lits 1997); Université de Lausanne; Univ. of Michigan; Univ. de Fribourg (lic.phil. Comparative Philology 1998); Corpus Christi Coll., Oxford (DPhil Classics 2001). Oberassistent, Classics, 2001–04, Privatdozent für Klassische Philologie, 2007–, Univ. of Basel. *Publications:* (ed) The Language of Greek Comedy, 2002; The Languages of Aristophanes, 2003; Sikelismos: Sprache, Literatur und Gesellschaft im griechischen Sizilien, 2008. *Address:* Worcester College, Oxford OX1 2HB.

WILLIAMS; *see* Rees-Williams.

WILLIAMS; *see* Sims-Williams.

WILLIAMS, family name of **Baron Williams of Elvel** and **Baroness Williams of Crosby**.

WILLIAMS OF CROSBY, Baroness *cr* 1993 (Life Peer), of Stevenage in the County of Hertfordshire; **Shirley Vivian Teresa Brittain Williams;** PC 1974; Co-founder, Social Democratic Party, 1981, President, 1982–88; Leader, Liberal Democrats, House of Lords, 2001–04; Public Service Professor of Elective Politics, John F. Kennedy School of Government, Harvard University, 1988–2000, now Emeritus; *b* 27 July 1930; *d* of late Prof. Sir George Catlin, and late Mrs Catlin, (Vera Brittain); *m* 1st, 1955, Prof. Bernard Arthur Owen Williams, FBA (marr. diss. 1974; he *d* 2003); one *d*; 2nd, 1987, Prof. Richard Elliott Neustadt (*d* 2003). *Educ:* eight schools in UK and USA; Somerville Coll., Oxford (scholar; MA, Hon. Fellow, 1970); Columbia Univ., New York (Smith-Mundt Scholar, 1952). General Secretary, Fabian Soc., 1960–64 (Chm., 1980–81). Contested: (Lab) Harwich, Essex, 1954 and 1955, and Southampton Test, 1959; (SDP) Crosby, 1983; (SDP/Alliance) Cambridge, 1987. MP: (Lab) Hitchin, 1964–74; (Lab) Hertford and Stevenage, 1974–79; (first-elected SDP MP) Crosby, Nov. 1981–1983; PPS, Minister of Health, 1964–66; Parly Sec., Min. of Labour, 1966–67; Minister of State: Education and Science, 1967–69; Home Office, 1969–70; Opposition spokesman on: Social Services, 1970–71, on Home Affairs, 1971–73; Prices and Consumer Protection, 1973–74; Sec. of State for Prices and Consumer Protection, 1974–76; Sec. of State for Educn and Science, 1976–79; Paymaster General, 1976–79. Bd Mem., Rand Corp., Europe, 1993–2001. Chm., OECD study on youth employment, 1979; Member: Council of Advrs to Praesidium, Ukraine, 1991–97; Adv. Council to UN Sec.-Gen. for Fourth World Women's Conf., Beijing, 1995; EC Comité des Sages, 1995–96; Council, Internat. Crisis Gp, 1998–2004; Internat. Adv. Cttee, Council on Foreign Relns, NY. Mem., Labour Party Nat. Exec. Cttee, 1970–81. Dep. Leader, Liberal Democrat Party, H of L, 1999–2001. Visiting Fellow, Nuffield College, Oxford, 1967–75; Res. Fellow, PSI, 1979–85; Visiting Faculty, Internat. Management Inst., Geneva, 1979–88; Fellow, Inst. of Politics, Harvard, 1979–80 (Mem., Sen. Adv. Council, 1986–99; Acting Dir, 1989–90); Director: Turing Inst., Glasgow, 1985–90; Learning by Experience Trust, 1986–94; Educn Develt Centre, Newton, Mass, 1991–98; Internat. Mgt Inst., Kiev, 1990–2000; Project Liberty, 1990–98; Bd Mem., Moscow Sch. of Political Studies, 1993–. Trustee, The Century Foundn (formerly Twentieth Century Fund), NY, 1978–. Lectures: Godkin, Harvard, 1980; Rede, Cambridge, 1980; Janeway, Princeton, 1981; Regents', Univ. of Calif., Berkeley, 1991; Erasmus, Notre Dame, 2001–02. Hon. Fellow, Newnham Coll., Cambridge, 1977. Hon. DEd CNAA, 1969; Hon. Dr Pol. Econ.: Univ. of Leuven, 1976; Radcliffe Coll., Harvard, 1978; Leeds, 1980; Bath, 1980; Hon. LLD: Sheffield, 1980; Southampton, 1981; Hon. DLitt Heriot-Watt, 1980; Hon. DSc: Aston, 1981; Monterey Inst., Calif, 2006. *Publications:* Politics is for People, 1981; Jobs for the 1980s; Youth Without Work, 1981; (jtly) Unemployment and Growth in the Western Economies, 1984; A Job to Live, 1985; Snakes and Ladders: a diary of a political life, 1996; (contrib.) Realizing Human Rights, ed Power and Alison, 2000; (contrib.) Making Globalization Good, 2003; God and Caesar, 2003. *Recreations:* music, poetry, hill walking.

WILLIAMS OF ELVEL, Baron *cr* 1985 (Life Peer), of Llansantffraed in Elvel in the County of Powys; **Charles Cuthbert Powell Williams,** CBE 1980; *b* 9 Feb. 1933; *s* of late Dr Norman Powell Williams, DD, and Mrs Muriel de Lérisson Williams (*née* Cazenove); *m* 1975, Jane Gillian (*née* Portal), DL; one step *s. Educ:* Westminster Sch.; Christ Church, Oxford (MA); LSE. British Petroleum Co. Ltd, 1958–64; Bank of London and Montreal, 1964–66; Eurofinance SA, Paris, 1966–70; Baring Brothers and Co. Ltd, 1970–77 (Man. Dir, 1971–77); Chm., Price Commn, 1977–79; Man. Dir 1980–82, Chm. 1982–85, Henry Ansbacher & Co. Ltd; Chief Exec., Henry Ansbacher Holdings PLC, 1982–85. Parly Candidate (Lab), Colchester, 1964. House of Lords: Dep. Leader of Opposition, 1989–92; Opposition spokesman on trade and industry, 1986–92, on energy, 1988–90, on defence, 1990–97, on the envmt, 1992–97. Founder Mem., Labour Econ. Finance and Taxation Assoc. (Vice-Chm., 1975–77, 1979–83). Director: Pergamon Holdings Ltd, 1985–91; Mirror Group Newspapers Ltd, 1985–91, Mirror Group Newspapers PLC, 1991–92. Pres., Campaign for Protection of Rural Wales, 1989–95 (Vice-Pres., 1995–). *Publications:* The Last Great Frenchman: a life of General de Gaulle, 1993; Bradman: an Australian hero, 1996; Adenauer, the Father of the new Germany, 2000; Pétain, 2005. *Recreations:* cricket (Oxford Univ. CC, 1953–55, Captain 1955; Essex CCC, 1953–59), music. *Address:* 48 Thurloe Square, SW7 2SX. *T:* (020) 7581 1783; Pant-y-Rhiw, Llansantffraed in Elvel, Powys LD1 5RH. *Clubs:* Beefsteak, Reform, MCC.

See also Very Rev. J. P. Welby.

WILLIAMS, Adèle; *see* Williams, J. A.

WILLIAMS, Adrian Spencer Vaughan, CBE 2003; Headteacher, Bury St Edmunds County Upper School, 1985–2005; *b* 23 May 1945; *s* of Bill and Eileen Williams; *m* 1972, Janet Daniels; one *s* two *d. Educ:* Colston's Sch., Bristol; St Catharine's Coll., Cambridge (BA 1967, MA 1971; DipEd). Asst teacher, King's Coll. Sch., Wimbledon, 1968–74; Hd, History Dept, Frome Coll., Som., 1974–79; Dep. Headteacher, Eggbuckland Sch., Plymouth, 1979–84. St Edmundsbury Cathedral: Lay Canon, 2005–; Diocesan Discerner, 2004–. Chairman: Guildhall Feoffment Trust, 2006–, West Suffolk Cruse, 2006–; Chm., Suffolk Educn Business Partnership, 2007–; Trustee: St Nicholas' Hospice, 1998–; Lund Trust, 2005–. *Recreations:* (nearly) all things French, relentless pursuit of the misuse of the apostrophe. *Address:* Gatehouse, 1 Byfield Way, Bury St Edmunds, Suffolk IP33 2SN. *T:* (01284) 763339; *e-mail:* williams@byfieldway.plus.com. *Club:* Bury St Edmunds Rotary.

WILLIAMS, Rt Hon. Alan John; PC 1977; MP (Lab) Swansea West since 1964; *b* 14 Oct. 1930; *m* 1957, Mary Patricia Rees, Blackwood, Mon; two *s* one *d. Educ:* Cardiff High Sch.; Cardiff College of Technology; University College, Oxford. BSc (London); BA (Oxon). Lecturer in economics, Welsh College of Advanced Technology; Free-lance Journalist. Joined Labour Party, 1950. Member: Fabian Society; Co-operative Party; National Union of Students delegation to Russia, 1954. Advr, Assoc. of First Div. Civil Servants, 1982–93. Contested (Lab) Poole, 1959. PPS to Postmaster General, 1966–67; Parly Under-Sec., DEA, 1967–69; Parly Sec., Min. of Technology, 1969–70; Opposition Spokesman on Consumer Protection, Small Businesses, Minerals, 1970–74; Minister of State: Dept of Prices and Consumer Protection, 1974–76; DoI, 1976–79; Opposition spokesman on Wales, 1979–80; Shadow Minister for CS, 1980–83; opposition spokesman on: trade and industry, 1983–87; Wales, 1987–89; Dep. Shadow Leader of the House, 1983–89 and 1988–89; Shadow Sec. of State for Wales, 1987–88. Member: Public Accts Cttee, 1966–67, 1990– (Sen. Mem., 1997–); Standards and Privileges Cttee, 1994–95, 1997–2003; Lord Chancellor's Adv. Council on Public Records, 1995–2001; Jt Cttee on Parly Privilege, 1997–98; Chairman: Public Accounts Commn, 1997–; Liaison Cttee, 2001–; Sec., British Amer. Parly Gp, 2001–; Jt Chm., All-Party Minerals Cttee, 1979–86; Chairman, Welsh PLP, 1966–67; Delegate, Council of Europe and WEU, 1966–67. Sponsored by TSSA (Mem., 1984–95). *Address:* House of Commons, SW1A 0AA. *Club:* Clyne Golf.

WILLIAMS, Alan Lee, OBE 1973; Director, Atlantic Council, 1993–2007 (Director, 1972–74 and 1992–93, Chairman, 1980–83, British Atlantic Committee); *b* 29 Nov. 1930; *m* 1st, 1954, Molly Steer (marr. diss. 1958); 2nd, 1963, Karen Holloway (marr. diss. 1971); two *s*; 3rd, 1974, Jennifer Ford (*née* Bunnett); two step *d. Educ:* Roan Sch., Greenwich; Ruskin Coll., Oxford. National Service, RAF, 1951–53; National Youth Officer, Labour Party, 1956–62. Dir-Gen., E-SU, 1979–86; Warden and Chief Exec., Toynbee Hall, 1987–92. MP (Lab) Hornchurch, 1966–70, Havering, Hornchurch, Feb. 1974–1979; PPS to Sec. of State for Defence, 1969–70, 1976; PPS to Sec. of State for NI, 1976–78; Chm., Parly Lab. Party Defence Cttee, 1976–79. Member: Parly Assembly, Council of Europe and WEU, 1967–70; N Atlantic Parly Assembly, 1974–79; FO Adv. Cttee on Disarmament and Arms Control, 1975–79; Council, RUSI, 1975–78; Adv. Council on Public Records, 1977–84; Chm., Delegn to 4th Cttee of UN, NY, 1969; Chm., Transport on Water Assoc.; Deputy Director, European Movement, 1970–71; Vice Pres., European-Atlantic Gp, 1983–; Pres., Atlantic Treaty Assoc., 2000–; Chm., European Working Gp of Internat. Centre for Strategic and Internat. Studies, Washington, 1987–99 (Mem., 1974–); Member: Council, RUSI, 1968–79; Trilateral Commn, 1976–2002. Chm., Beveridge Foundn, 2006–. Vis. Prof., Queen Mary Univ. of London, 2003–. Chairman: Cedar Centre, Isle of Dogs, 1991–2008; Toynbee Housing Assoc., 1993–99. Chm. of Govs, City Coll., 1990–. Freeman: City of London, 1969; Co. of Watermen and Lightermen, 1952–. Fellow, QMW, 1993. FRSA. DLitt (*hc*) Schiller Internat. Univ., 1987. Golden Laurel Branch (Bulgaria), 2002. *Publications:* Radical Essays, 1966; Europe or the Open Sea?, 1971; Crisis in European Defence, 1973; The European Defence Initiative: Europe's bid for equality, 1985; The Decline of Labour and the Fall of the SDP, 1989; Islamic Resurgence, 1991; Prospects for a Common European Foreign and Security Policy, 1995; NATO's Future in the Balance: time for a rethink, 1995; NATO and European Defence: a new era of partnership, 1997; NATO's Strategy for Securing the Future, 1999. *Recreations:* reading, history, walking. *Address:* 6 North Several, Blackheath, SE3 0QR. *Clubs:* Reform, Pilgrims, Mid-Atlantic (Chm., 2006–).

WILLIAMS, Dr Alan Wynne; freelance solar energy research; *b* 21 Dec. 1945; *s* of late Tom and Mary Hannah Williams; *m* 1973, Marian Williams. *Educ:* Carmarthen Grammar School; Jesus College, Oxford (BA Chem. 1st cl. hons; DPhil). Senior Lecturer in Environmental Science, Trinity College, Carmarthen, 1971–87. MP (Lab) Carmarthen, 1987–97, Carmarthen E and Dinefwr, 1997–2001; contested Carmarthen E and Dinefwr, 2001. *Recreations:* reading, watching sport. *Address:* 79 Parklands Road, Ammanford, Carmarthenshire SA18 3TD.

WILLIAMS, Sir Alastair Edgcumbe James D.; *see* Dudley-Williams.

WILLIAMS, (Albert) Trevor; management scientist; *b* 7 April 1938; *s* of Ben and Minnie Williams; *m* 1st, 1970, Mary Lynn Lyster; three *s*; 2nd, 1978, Deborah Sarah Fraser Duncan (*née* Milne); one *s*, and one step *s* two step *d. Educ:* King George V Sch., Southport; Queens' Coll., Cambridge (Open Exhibr; MA); Univ. of Ghana (Rotary Foundn Fellow); Cranfield Institute of Technology (MSc). Commnd RA, 1957. Director: Business Operations Research Ltd, 1965–68; Novy Eddison and Partners, 1971–74; Dep.-Dir for Futures Research, Univ. of Stellenbosch, 1974–78; Dep. Chief Scientific Officer, Price Commission, 1978–79; Advisor on Technology Projects, Scottish Development Agency, 1979; Dir, Henley Centre for Forecasting, 1980–81. Consultant and Sen. Industrial Advr, Monopolies and Mergers Commn, 1982–90; advr to cos in Europe, S

Africa and USA, 1989–2005. Various academic appointments, 1968–95, incl. visiting and hon. professorships: Graduate Sch. of Business, Cape Town Univ.; Sussex Univ.; INSEAD; Wisconsin Univ.; Hong Kong Univ.; LSE. Mem., Editl Adv. Bd, Futures, 1984–98. FInstD; AMRI. *Publications:* A Guide to Futures Studies, 1976; (contrib.) Futures, 1985–98; (contrib.) Foresight. *Recreation:* reviewing the last fifty years. *Address:* Wyebeere, Ruckhall Common, Hereford HR2 9QU. *T:* (01981) 251439. *Club:* Athenæum.

WILLIAMS, Alexander, CB 1991; FInstP; Government Chemist, 1987–91; *b* 30 March 1931; *s* of Henry and Dorothy Williams; *m* 1957, Beryl Wynne Williams (*née* Williams); one *s*. *Educ:* Grove Park Grammar Sch., Wrexham; University College of North Wales, Bangor (BSc). National Service, REME, 1953–55; Monsanto Chemicals, 1955–56; Southern Instruments, Camberley, 1956–59; National Physical Laboratory: Div. of Radiation Science, 1959–78; Head, Div. of Mechanical and Optical Metrology, 1978–81; Under Sec., Res. and Technology Policy Div., DTI 1981–87. Dir, Assoc. of Official Analytical Chemists, 1989–93. Pres., British Measurement and Testing Assoc., 1995–2001. Freeman, City of London, 1997; Liveryman, Co. of Scientific Instrument Makers, 1997–. *Publications:* (with P. J. Campion and J. E. Burns) A Code of Practice for the Detailed Statement of Accuracy, 1973; (ed with H. Günzler) Handbook of Analytical Techniques, 2001; numerous papers on measurements of radio-activity etc, to Internat. Jl of Applied Radiation and Isotopes, Nucl. Instruments and Methods, etc. *Recreations:* bell-ringing, music, opera, walking.

WILLIAMS, Angela Joy, CMG 2005; Consultant, Music in Me, since 2005; *b* 24 Sept. 1944; *d* of Douglas Granville Needham and Annie Needham (*née* Balshaw); *m* 1984, Edward Hunter Williams; two step *s* one step *d*. *Educ:* Girls' Div., Bolton Sch.; Univ. of Birmingham (BSocSci Hons 1966); American Univ. of Beirut (Middle Eastern studies). VSO, Ghana, 1966–68; Asst Educn Officer, Community Relns Commn, 1969–71; UN Relief and Works Agency for Palestine Refugees in the Near East, 1971–2004: Chief of Secretariat, 1980–83; Chief of External Relns, 1984–85; Dep. Dir of Ops, Gaza, 1985–88; Dir, Relief and Social Services, 1988–98; Dir, UNRWA Affairs, Syrian Arab Rep., 1998–2004. Trustee, Damask Rose Trust, 2008–. *Recreations:* exploring cultural diversity and cross-cultural communication through reading, writing, music, photography and travel. *Address:* Grafenegg 1, Wallhaus Süd-Ost, 3485 Haitzendorf, Austria. *T:* (1) 4782086; 3–111 Echo Drive, Ottawa, ON K1S 5K8, Canada. *T:* (613) 2308610; *e-mail:* ajwilliams_241@hotmail.com.

WILLIAMS, Anna Maureen, (Mrs G. H. G. Williams); *see* Worrall, A. M.

WILLIAMS, Anthony Neville; Managing Partner (formerly Managing Director), Jomati Consultants LLP (formerly Jomati Ltd), since 2002; *b* 8 July 1956; *s* of late David Leslie Williams and Rose Williams (*née* Mingay); *m* 1979, Johannah McDonnell; one *s* one *d*. *Educ:* Southampton Univ. (LLB 1978). Admitted Solicitor, England, 1981, Hong Kong, 1985; Solicitor and Barrister, Victoria, Australia, 1986. Solicitor: Turner Garrett & Co., 1981; Coward Chance, 1981–87, Clifford Chance (following merger), 1987–2000: Hong Kong office, 1984–90; Partner, 1988–2000; Man. Partner, Moscow office, 1995–97; Man. Partner, 1998–2000; Man. Partner Worldwide, Andersen Legal, 2000–02. *Publications:* (jtly) Intellectual Property in the People's Republic of China, 1986; (jtly) The Hong Kong Banking Ordinance, 1987; numerous articles on law firm mgt strategy. *Recreations:* horse racing, cricket, wine. *Address:* Jomati Consultants LLP, 3 Amen Lodge, Warwick Lane, EC4M 7BY; *e-mail:* tony.williams@jomati.com.

WILLIAMS, Dr Anthony Peter; HM Inspector of Constabulary (non-police), 1993–96; *b* 18 June 1936; *s* of late Dr Emlyn Williams, OBE, Principal, Hendon Coll. of Technology, and Gwyneth Mair Williams (*née* Williams); *m* 1964, Vera Georgiadou; one *s* one *d*. *Educ:* St Paul's Sch., London; Keble Coll., Oxford (BA 1961; MA 1965); Birkbeck Coll., London (PhD 1971). Research and teaching, 1961–67; Principal Psychologist, CSSB, 1967–71; Consultant, Hay-MSL Ltd, 1971–76; Head of Personnel, BOC Gases, 1976–78; Consultant and Manager, Hay Associates, NY, 1979–84; Dir of Personnel, World Bank, 1984–88; Worldwide Partner and Dir, Hay Management Consultants, 1989–93. Vis. Sen. Fellow, 1997–2003, Vis. Prof., 2003–, Sir John Cass Business Sch., City of London (formerly City Univ. Business Sch.). Mem., Corporate Governance Wkg Party, Assoc. of Investment Trust Cos, 1999–2000. *Publications:* Just Reward?: the truth about top executive pay, 1994; Who Will Guard the Guardians?: corporate governance in the Millennium, 1999; (with Bill Pitkeathley) Executive Express: a swift and practical route to tomorrow's top jobs, 2006; numerous articles in professional and management jls. *Recreations:* international affairs, use of language, travel, cultural diversity, opera, good food and wine, intelligent conversation, asking difficult questions. *Address:* 49 Talbot Road, W2 5JJ. *Clubs:* Athenæum, Oxford and Cambridge.

WILLIAMS, Sir Arthur (Dennis Pitt), Kt 1991; Chairman, Williams Holdings Ltd, since 1965; *b* 15 Oct. 1928; *s* of Arthur Henry Williams and Dora Ruth Williams; *m* 1st, 1951, Ngaire Garbett; three *s* two *d*; 2nd, 1989, Jeanne Brinkworth; one *s*. *Educ:* Salmerston; Margate College. Served RN, 1944–46. Apprentice carpenter, 1942–44 and 1946–47; carpenter, NZ, 1951–53; builder, 1953–, and property owner. Govt Appointee, Govt Property Services Ltd, 1991. Fellow: NZ Inst. of Builders; Aust. Inst. of Builders; NZ Inst. of Management. NZ Commemorative Medal, 1990. *Recreations:* horse breeding and racing. *Address:* Cranbrook, Cranbrook Grove, Waikanae, New Zealand. *T:* (business) (6) 3647739, *Fax:* (6) 3647605. *Club:* Wellesley (Wellington, NZ).

WILLIAMS, (Arthur) Ronald, OBE 1991; Chief Executive, Publishers Association, 1998–2007; *b* 29 Oct. 1942; *s* of late Alfred Arthur Williams, OBE and Marjory Williams (*née* Heenan); *m* 1st, 1968, Lynne Diana Merrin; two *d*; 2nd, 1993, Antoinette Catherine Naldrett. *Educ:* Rossall Sch., Lancs; Selwyn Coll., Cambridge (MA). HM Diplomatic Service, 1964–79, served Jakarta, Singapore, Budapest and Nairobi (First Sec.); Chief Exec., Timber Growers UK, 1981–87; Exec. Dir, Forestry Industry Council of GB, 1987–97. Mem., Exec. Cttee, Fedn of European Publishers, 1998–2007; Dir, Digital Content Forum (UK), 2003–07. FRSA. *Publications:* Montrose: cavalier in mourning, 1975; The Lords of the Isles, 1985; The Heather and the Gale, 1997; Sons of the Wolf, 1998. *Recreations:* fly-fishing, Real tennis, walking, writing, reading. *Address:* Starlings, Wildhern, Andover, Hants SP11 0JE. *T:* (01264) 735389.

WILLIAMS, Betty; *see* Williams, Elizabeth.

WILLIAMS, Betty Helena; MP (Lab) Conwy, since 1997; *b* 31 July 1944. *Educ:* Ysgol Dyffryn Nantlle; Coleg y Normal, Bangor (BA (Hons) Wales, 1995). Member (Lab): Arfon BC, 1970–91 (Mayor, 1990–91); Gwynedd CC, 1976–93. Contested (Lab) Caernarfon, 1983, Conwy, 1987 and 1992. Mem., Welsh Affairs Select Cttee, 1997–2001. Vice Pres., Univ. of Wales, Bangor, 2001–06 (Hon. Fellow, 2000). *Address:* House of Commons, SW1A 0AA.

WILLIAMS, Brian Owen, MD; FRCP, FRCPE, FRCPGlas; President, Royal College of Physicians and Surgeons of Glasgow, 2006–Nov. 2009; *b* 27 Feb. 1947; *s* of William and Joan Williams; *m* 1970, Martha Carmichael; two *d*. *Educ:* Kings Park Sch., Glasgow; Univ. of Glasgow (MD 1984). FRCPGlas 1983; FRCP 1989; FRCPE 1991; FCPS 1996; FRCSLT 1996; FRCPI 1999; FRACP 2007. Consultant Geriatrician, 1977–; Consultant Geriatrician, Gartnavel Gen. Hosp., Glasgow, 1982–. President: British Geriatric Soc., 1998–2000; EU Geriatric Medicine Soc., 2000–02. Hon. Prof., Univ. of Glasgow, 2007–. Hon. DSc Glasgow Caledonian, 2007. *Recreations:* music, literature, gardening. *Address:* 15 Thorn Drive, High Burnside, Glasgow G73 4RH. *T:* (0141) 634 4480; *e-mail:* b.williams4@btinternet.com. *Club:* Caledonian.

WILLIAMS, Prof. Sir Bruce (Rodda), KBE 1980; Professor of the University of Sydney, since 1967, Fellow of the Senate, 1994–98 and Vice-Chancellor and Principal, 1967–81; *b* 10 Jan. 1919; *s* of late Rev. W. J. Williams and Helen Baud; *m* 1942, Roma Olive Hotten (*d* 1991); five *d*. *Educ:* Wesley College; Queen's College, University of Melbourne (BA 1939). MA Adelaide 1942; MA(Econ) Manchester, 1963. FASSA 1968. Lecturer in Economics, University of Adelaide, 1939–46 and at Queen's University of Belfast, 1946–50; Professor of Economics, University College of North Staffordshire, 1950–59; Robert Otley Prof., 1959–63, and Stanley Jevons Prof., 1963–67, Univ. of Manchester; Dir, Technical Change Centre and Vis. Prof., Imperial Coll., London, 1981–86. Vis. Fellow, ANU, 1987, 1988, 1990, 1992–94. Secretary and Joint Director of Research, Science and Industry Committee, 1952–59. Member, National Board for Prices and Incomes, 1966–67; Econ. Adviser to Minister of Technology, 1966–67; Member: Central Advisory Council on Science and Technology, 1967; Australian Reserve Bank Board, 1969–81; Chairman: NSW State Cancer Council, 1967–81; Australian Vice Chancellors Cttee, 1972–74; Aust. Govt Cttee of Inquiry into Educn and Trng, 1976–79; (Australian) Review of Discipline of Engrg, 1987–88; Dep. Chm., Parramatta Hosps Bd, 1979–81. President: Sydney Conservatorium of Music Foundn, 1994–98; Sydney Spring Fest. of New Music, 1999–2003; Chm., Internat. Piano Comp. of Australia, 1986–2004. Editor, The Sociological Review, 1953–59, and The Manchester Sch., 1959–67. President Economics Section of British Assoc., 1964. Hon. FIEAust 1989; CPEng 1989. Hon. DLitt: Keele, 1973; Sydney, 1982; Hon. DEcon Qld, 1980; Hon. LLD: Melbourne, 1981; Manchester, 1982; Hon. DSc Aston, 1982. Kirby Meml Award, IProdE, 1988. *Publications:* The Socialist Order and Freedom, 1942; (with C. F. Carter): Industry and Technical Progress, 1957, Investment in Innovation, 1958, and Science in Industry, 1959; Investment Behaviour, 1962; Investment Proposals and Decisions, 1965; Investment, Technology and Growth, 1967; (ed) Science and Technology in Economic Growth, 1973; Systems of Higher Education: Australia, 1978; Education, Training and Employment, 1979; Living with Technology, 1982; (ed) Knowns and Unknowns in Technical Change, 1985; Attitudes to New Technologies and Economic Growth, 1986; Review of the Discipline of Engineering, 1988; Academic Status and Leadership, 1990; University Responses to Research Selectivity, 1991; Higher Education and Employment, 1994; Liberal Education and Useful Knowledge, 2002; Making and Breaking Universities, 2005; Fortune's Favours, 2006. *Address:* 24 Mansfield Street, Glebe, NSW 2037, Australia; 31 Queen Anne's Gardens, Ealing, W5 5QD. *Club:* Athenæum.

WILLIAMS, Brynle; Member (C) North Wales, National Assembly for Wales, since 2003; *b* 9 Jan. 1949; *s* of George and Maenwen Williams; *m* 1970, Frances Mary Shawcross; one *s* one *d*. *Educ:* Ysgol Uwchradd Maes Garmon, Mold. Farmer. Chm., 2002–03, Pres., 2003–04, Flintshire County, Farmers Union of Wales; Council Member: Royal Welsh Agricl Soc., 1988–; Welsh Ponies and Cobs Soc., 1997–. *Recreations:* showing and judging cobs and ponies. *Address:* National Assembly for Wales, Cardiff Bay, Cardiff CF99 1ND. *T:* (029) 2089 8755, *Fax:* (029) 2089 8416; *e-mail:* brynle.williams@wales.gov.uk.

WILLIAMS, Rear-Adm. Charles Bernard, CB 1980; OBE 1967; Flag Officer Medway and Port Admiral Chatham, 1978–80, retired; *b* 19 Feb. 1925; *s* of Charles Williams and Elizabeth (*née* Malherbe); *m* 1946, Patricia Mary (*d* 2008), *d* of Henry Brownlow Thorp and Ellen Thorp; one *s* one *d*. *Educ:* Graeme Coll., Grahamstown, SA; Royal Naval Engineering Coll., Plymouth. Served in HM Ships Nigeria, Hornet, Triumph, 1946–53; in charge: Flight deck trials unit, 1953; Naval Wing, Nat. Gas Turbine Estabt, 1956; Sen. Engr, HMS Cumberland, 1958; in charge Admiralty Fuel Experimental Station, 1960; Comdr 1960; Engineer Officer, HMS London, 1962; Staff Engr, Flag Officer ME, 1964; Duty Comdr, Naval Ops MoD (N), 1967; Captain 1969; Dep. Manager, Portsmouth Dockyard, 1969; Supt, Clyde Submarine Base, 1972; Captain, HMS Sultan, 1975; Rear-Adm. 1978. Chairman: RYA Yachting Qualifications Cttee, 1976–86; Whitbread Round the World Race, 1978–90. *Recreations:* sailing, walking, music, bridge. *Address:* Green Shutters, Montserrat Road, Lee-on-Solent PO13 9LT. *T:* (023) 9255 0816. *Clubs:* Royal Yacht Squadron; Royal Ocean Racing; Royal Naval Sailing Association (Life Vice Cdre); Royal London Yacht (Hon. Mem.); Royal Southern Yacht (Hon. Mem.); Hornet Sailing.

WILLIAMS, Sir Charles (Othniel), Kt 2000; Executive Chairman, C. O. Williams Construction and group of companies, since 1969; *b* 24 Nov. 1932; *s* of Elliot Williams and Lillian Williams; *m* 1st, 1956, Diane Walcott (marr. diss. 1999); two *s* one *d*; 2nd, 2000, Mary-Ann Gemmell (*née* Stewart-Richardson). *Educ:* Lodge Secondary Sch., Barbados. Overseer, Brighton Plantation, St George, 1951–54; Under Manager: Hothersall Plantation, St John, 1954–56; Guinea Sugar Factory, St John, 1956; Manager, Foster Hall Plantation, St Joseph, 1956–60; leased Foster Hall, 1960–75; founded: C. O. Williams, 1960; C. O. Williams Construction Co. Ltd, 1969. Master Entrepreneur of the Year, Ernst & Young Awards, 1997. *Recreations:* polo, deep-sea fishing, horse-racing. *Address:* Bromefield Plantation House, St Lucy, Barbados. *Clubs:* Barbados Polo, Barbados Turf, Barbados Yacht, Carlton Cricket, Wanderers Cricket (all Barbados).

WILLIAMS, Chris Morgan; Chief Executive, Buckinghamshire County Council and Clerk to the Lieutenancy, since 2000; *b* 26 Nov. 1948; *s* of Harold and May Williams; two *d*. *Educ:* Lanchester Poly., Coventry (BA Hons); Univ. of Sussex (MA). MRTPI 1976. Co. Planning Officer, E Sussex, 1989–96; Dir, Envmtl Services, Bucks CC, 1996–2000. Vis. Res. Fellow, Univ. of Sussex, 1992–. Pres., Co. Planning Officers' Soc., 1993–94. MCMI. *Recreations:* travel, wine, surfing. *Address:* Buckinghamshire County Council, County Hall, Walton Street, Aylesbury, Bucks HP20 1UA.

WILLIAMS, Rt Rev. Christopher; *see* Williams, Rt Rev. J. C. R.

WILLIAMS, Christopher Beverley, FRCP, FRCS; Consultant Physician in Gastrointestinal Endoscopy: Endoscopy Unit, London Clinic, since 1975; Wolfson Unit for Endoscopy, St Mark's Hospital for Colorectal and Intestinal Disorders, 1975–2003; *b* 8 June 1938; *s* of late Denis John Williams, CBE, MD, FRCP and Dr Joyce Beverley Williams (*née* Jewson); *m* 1970, Christina Janet Seymour, MB, FRCP, *d* of Reginald S. Lawrie, MD, MS, FRCS, FRCP, and Jean E. Lawrie, CBE, MB; one *s* one *d*. *Educ:* Dragon Sch.; Winchester Coll.; Trinity Coll., Oxford (BA Hons Physiol., BM BCh, MA); UCH. MRCS 1965, FRCS 1999; LRCP 1965, MRCP 1968, FRCP 1983. House appointments: UCH, 1965; Whittington and Brompton Hosps, 1966; SHO, Nat. Hosp. for Nervous Diseases, and Hammersmith Hosp., 1966–67; Registrar, UCH, 1968–70; Registrar, 1970–72, Res. Fellow and Hon. Sen. Registrar, 1972–74, St Mark's Hosp.; Consultant Physician, St Bartholomew's Hosp., 1975. Hon. Consultant Physician (Endoscopy): Royal Free Hosp.; Great Ormond Street Hosp. for Sick Children; King

Edward VII Hosp. for Officers; St Luke's Hosp. for the Clergy. Vis. Prof., Sydney Univ., 1973; demonstrations, teaching courses and invited lectures world-wide on colonoscopy and colorectal cancer prevention; Foundn Lectr, British Soc. of Gastroenterology, 1976, 1995 (Vice-Pres., Endoscopy, 1987). Member: Soc. of Apothecaries, 1956–; Medical Soc. of London, 1983–; FRSocMed 1970. Mem., several internat. editl bds. *Publications:* (ed jtly) Colorectal Disease, 1981; (jtly) Practical Gastrointestinal Endoscopy, 1983, 6th edn 2008 (trans. Italian 1980, German 1985, French 1986, Spanish 1992, Portuguese, 1998, Korean, 2003); (jtly) Annual of Gastrointestinal Endoscopy, annually 1988–97; (ed jtly) Colonoscopy: principles and practice, 2003; numerous articles and chapters on colonoscopy, colorectal disease and teaching methodology. *Recreations:* travel, fine wine and food. *Address:* 11 Frognal Way, Hampstead, NW3 6XE. *T:* (020) 7435 4030, *Fax:* (020) 7435 5636; *e-mail:* christopherbwilliams@btinternet.com; London Clinic, 20 Devonshire Place, W1N 2DH. *T:* (020) 8616 7781, *Fax:* (020) 8616 7684.

WILLIAMS, Dr Christopher John Hacon, FRCP; Consultant Medical Oncologist, Bristol Haematology and Oncology Centre, since 2003 (Clinical Director, 2003–07); *b* 3 Aug. 1946; *s* of Owen Henry Williams and Joyce May Hacon Deavin; *m* 1970, Susan Tennant (marr. diss. 1995); two *d. Educ:* Reed's Sch., Surrey; London Univ., St Mary's Hosp. (MBBS); DM Southampton 1980. Jun. posts, London Hosps, 1971–74; Jun. Registrar, Med. Oncology, St Bartholomew's, 1974–75; Postdoctoral Res. Fellow, Stanford Univ., 1975–77; Res. Fellow, 1977–80, Sen. Lectr and Hon. Consultant Physician in Medical Oncology, 1980–96, Southampton Univ.; Dir, Cochrane Cancer Network, Inst. of Health Scis, Oxford, 1996–2003. Chairman: MRC Gynaecol Cancer Working Party, 1989–93; MRC Cancer Therapy Cttee, 1994–97; steering cttees and ind. data monitoring cttees for large-scale trials in breast and ovarian cancer; Member: Protocol Rev. Cttee, EORTC, 1993–2003; Oncology Trials Adv. Cttee, MRC, 1997–2003; Steering Gp, Cochrane Collaboration, 1998–2002; Co-ordinator, ICON trials for ovarian carcinoma, 1991–. Mem., Council, Inst. of Health Scis, Oxford, 1997. Mem. Bd of Editors, Annals of Oncology, 1996; Co-ordinating Ed., Cochrane Gynaecol Cancer Collaborative Rev. Gp, 1997–. *Publications:* Recent Advances in Clinical Oncology, 1982; All About Cancer, 1983; Lung Cancer: the facts, 1984; Cancer Investigations and Management, 1985; Cancer: a guide for patients and family, 1986; (with R. B. Buchanan) Medical Management of Breast Cancer, 1987; Textbook of Uncommon Cancer, 1988; Cancer Biology and Management, 1989; (with J. S. Tobias) Cancer: a colour atlas, 1991; Introducing New Treatments for Cancer, 1992 (Medical Textbook of the Year, 1993); Supportive Care of the Cancer Patient, 1997; (jtly) Cancer: a comprehensive guide, 1998; Evidence-based Oncology, 2003; papers on new therapies for cancer, esp. clinical trials and systematic reviews. *Recreations:* active participation in painting and sculpture, writing, gentle walking, wildlife and landscape photography; passive participation in theatre, music, films, books; gathering art objects. *Address:* Spring Vale, Mill Hill, Brockweir, Chepstow, NP16 7NW. *T:* (01291) 680060; *e-mail:* christopher.williams@ubht.swest.nhs.uk.

WILLIAMS, Colin; *see* Welland, C.

WILLIAMS, Colin Hartley; Partner, Williams & Williams, PR consultants, since 1992; *b* 7 Dec. 1938; *s* of late Gwilym Robert Williams and Margaret (*née* Hartley); *m* 1st, 1964, Carolyn (*née* Bulman) (*d* 1993); one *s* two *d*; 2nd, 1997, Shirley Ann (*née* Lavers). *Educ:* Grangefield Grammar Sch., Stockton-on-Tees; University College of Wales, Aberystwyth (BA). Journalist: Evening Gazette, Middlesbrough, 1960–63; Today Magazine, Odhams Press, 1964; Daily Sketch, 1964–66; Senior Lecturer, International Press Inst., Nairobi, 1967–68; Corporate and Public Relations Executive, 1969–74; Press Officer, Corporation of City of London, 1975–76; Asst Dir, City Communications Centre, 1977, Exec. Dir, 1979–83; Exec. Dir, Cttee on Invisible Exports, 1982–83; Chief Press Relations Manager, 1983–90, Hd of Corporate Communications, 1990–91, Hd of PR Gp, 1991–92, Nat. Westminster Bank. *Recreations:* writing, wine, golf. *Address:* Goodacres House, Goodacres Lane, Lacey Green, Princes Risborough, Bucks HP27 0QD. *T:* (01844) 347271.

WILLIAMS, Ven. Colin Henry; General Secretary, Conference of European Churches, since 2005; Archdeacon of Lancaster, 1999–2005, now Emeritus; *b* 12 Aug. 1952; *s* of William Henry Williams and Blanche Williams. *Educ:* King George V Grammar Sch. for Boys, Southport; Pembroke Coll., Oxford (BA 1973; MA 1977); Coll. of Law, Chester; St Stephen's House, Oxford (BA Oxon 1981). Asst Solicitor, Gibson, Russell & Adler, solicitors, Wigan, 1974–78; ordained deacon 1981, priest 1982; Asst Curate, St Paul Stoneycroft, Liverpool, 1981–84; Team Vicar, St Aidan, Walton, 1984–89; Domestic Chaplain to Bishop of Blackburn, and Chaplain, Whalley Abbey Retreat and Conf. Centre, 1989–94; Vicar, St Chad, Poulton-le-Fylde, 1994–99. Mem., Gen. Synod of C of E, 1995–2005. Mem., Meissen Commn, 1996–2005. Mem., Council for Christian Unity, 2003–05. *Recreations:* walking, singing, developing knowledge of all things German. *Address:* Conference of European Churches, General Secretariat, PO Box 2100, 150 route de Ferney, 1211 Geneva 2, Switzerland. *T:* (22) 7916226, *Fax:* (22) 7916227; *e-mail:* hcw@cec-kek.org.

WILLIAMS, Sir Daniel (Charles), GCMG 1996; QC 1996; Governor-General of Grenada, since 1996; *b* 4 Nov. 1935; *s* of Adolphus D. Williams and Clare Stanislaus; *m* 1960, Cecilia Patricia Gloria Modeste; one *s* three *d. Educ:* Primary and comprehensive schs, Grenada; LLB London Univ.; Council of Legal Educn, London. Called to the Bar, Lincoln's Inn, 1968; Barrister, 1969–70, 1974–84, 1990–96; Magistrate, St Lucia, 1970–74; MP (New Nat. Party) St David's, Grenada, 1984–89; Minister of Health, Housing and Envmt, 1984–89; Minister of Legal Affairs, and Attorney Gen., 1988–89; Acting Prime Minister, July 1988. Sec., Grenada Bar Assoc., 1977–81. Held several lay positions in RC Ch, incl. Chm., Dio. Pastoral Council. Was active Scout, incl. Dist Comr and Dep. Chief Comr; now Chief Scout. Founder and Mem., Grenada Foundn for Needy Students, 1996–. *Publications:* Index of Laws of Grenada 1959–79; (contrib.) Modern Legal Systems Cyclopedia: Central America and the Caribbean, vol. 7, 1985; The Office and Duties of the Governor-General of Grenada, 1998; A Synoptic View of the Public Service of Grenada, 1999; Prescriptions for a Model Grenada, 2000; God Speaks, 2001; The Layman's Lawbook, 2002; The Love of God, 2004; Government of the Global Village. *Recreations:* lawn tennis, gardening. *Address:* Governor-General's Residence, Westerhall, St David's, Grenada. *Clubs:* St George's Lions (Pres.) (St George's); Vieux Fort Lions (Pres.) (St Lucia).

WILLIAMS, Prof. David, FRS 1984; (part-time) Research Professor of Mathematics, Swansea University (formerly University of Wales Swansea), since 1999; Professor of Mathematical Sciences, Bath University, 1992–99, now Emeritus; *b* 9 April 1938; *s* of Gwyn Williams and Margaret Elizabeth Williams; *m* 1966, Sheila Margaret Harrison; two *d. Educ:* Jesus College, Oxford (DPhil); Grey College, Durham. Instructor, Stanford Univ., 1962; Lectr, Durham Univ., 1963; Shell Research Lectr, Statistical Lab., and Res. Fellow, Clare Coll., Cambridge, 1966; Lectr, 1969, Prof. of Maths, 1972, University Coll., Swansea; Prof. of Mathematical Stats and Professorial Fellow, Clare Coll., Cambridge Univ., 1985–92. Vis. Fellow, Bath Univ., 1991–92. Hon. Fellow, UC, Swansea, 1991–. *Publications:* Diffusions, Markov processes, and martingales, vol. 1, Foundations, 1979, 2nd edn (with L. C. G. Rogers) 1994, vol. 2 (with L. C. G. Rogers), Itô calculus, 1987; Probability with martingales, 1991; Weighing the odds, 2001; papers in Séminaire de probabilités and other jls. *Recreations:* music, cycling, walking.

WILLIAMS, Adm. Sir David, GCB 1977 (KCB 1975); DL; Governor and Commander-in-Chief, Gibraltar, 1982–85; a Gentleman Usher to The Queen, 1979–82, an Extra Gentleman Usher, since 1982; *b* 22 Oct. 1921; 3rd *s* of A. E. Williams, Ashford, Kent; *m* 1947, Philippa Beatrice Stevens; two *s. Educ:* Yardley Court Sch., Tonbridge; RN College, Dartmouth. Cadet, Dartmouth, 1935. Graduate, US Naval War Coll., Newport, RI. Served War of 1939–45 at sea in RN. Qual. in Gunnery, 1946; Comdr, 1952; Captain, 1960; Naval Asst to First Sea Lord, 1961–64; HMS Devonshire, 1964–66; Dir of Naval Plans, 1966–68; Captain, BRNC, Dartmouth, 1968–70; Rear-Adm. 1970; Flag Officer, Second in Command Far East Fleet, 1970–72; Vice-Adm. 1973; Dir-Gen. Naval Manpower and Training, 1972–74; Adm. 1974; Chief of Naval Personnel and Second Sea Lord, 1974–77; C-in-C Naval Home Comd, and ADC to the Queen, 1977–79, retired. Pres., Ex Services Mental Welfare Soc., 1979–91; Chm. of Council, Missions to Seamen, 1989–93. Member: Commonwealth War Graves Commn, 1980–89 (Vice Chm., 1985–89); Museums and Galleries Commn, 1987–93. Hon. Liveryman, Fruiterers' Co.; KStJ 1982. DL Devon, 1981. *Recreation:* gardening. *Address:* Barnhill, Stoke Gabriel, Totnes, Devon TQ9 6SJ. *Clubs:* Army and Navy; Royal Dart Yacht; Royal Naval Sailing Association; Royal Yacht Squadron.

WILLIAMS, David; Group Chief Executive, SIG plc, since 2002; *b* 22 Nov. 1950; *s* of Stanley and Ethel Williams; *m* 1972, Joan Elizabeth Martin; three *s. Educ:* Sheffield Coll. of Further Educn (HNC Business Studies 1972). Joined Sheffield Insulations Ltd, 1983, Sales and Mktg Dir, 1988; Dir, Main Bd, 1993, Dep. Chief Exec., 2001, Sheffield Insulations Gp plc, subseq. SIG plc. Mem. Adv. Bd, Sheffield Univ. Business Sch., 2006–. Non-exec. Dir, Sheffield Children's Hosp. Foundn Trust, 2007–. Member: Northern, RSPB; I of M Marshalls Assoc. *Recreations:* motorcycling, bird watching, shooting, walking, travel, gardening, golf, music of Bob Dylan, control of grey squirrels and magpies. *Address:* SIG plc, Signet House, 17 Europa View, Sheffield Business Park, Sheffield S9 1XH. *T:* (0114) 285 6306, *Fax:* (0114) 285 6449. *Club:* Rotherham Golf.

WILLIAMS, Prof. David Arnold, OBE 2000; PhD, DSc; CPhys, FInstP; FRAS; Perren Professor of Astronomy, University College London, 1994–2002; *b* 9 Sept. 1937; *s* of James Arnold Williams and Frances Barbara Williams (*née* Begg); *m* 1964, Doreen Jane Bell; two *s. Educ:* Larne Grammar Sch.; Queen's Univ., Belfast (BSc, PhD); Manchester (DSc). CPhys 1968; FInstP 1994; FRAS 1967. Maths Dept, Manchester Coll. of Sci. and Technol., 1963–65; NASA Goddard Space Flight Centre, Md, USA, 1965–67; Lectr, Sen. Lectr, Reader, Maths Dept, 1967–84, Prof. of Theoretical Astrophysics, 1984–94, UMIST. Pres., RAS, 1998–2000. *Publications:* (with J. E. Dyson) The Physics of the Interstellar Medium, 1980, 2nd edn 1997; (with W. W. Duley) Interstellar Chemistry, 1984; (with T. W. Hartquist) The Chemically Controlled Cosmos, 1995; (with T. W. Hartquist) The Molecular Astrophysics of Stars and Galaxies, 1998; contrib. numerous articles in learned jls. *Recreations:* hill-walking, choral singing, beer and wine. *Address:* Department of Physics and Astronomy, University College London, Gower Street, WC1E 6BT.

WILLIAMS, David Beverley; QC 2003; a Recorder, since 2002; *b* 11 Feb. 1949; *s* of Daniel David Williams and late Gwyneth Williams (*née* Davies); *m* 1995, Christine Seaman; one *s. Educ:* Beaudesert Park; Cheltenham Coll.; Inns of Court Sch. of Law; City Univ. (LLM 1999). Called to the Bar, Middle Temple, 1972; in practice, specialising in criminal law, fraud, and money laundering. *Recreations:* field sports, gardening, theatre. *Address:* 9 Bedford Row, WC1R 4AZ. *T:* (020) 7489 2727. *Club:* National Liberal.

WILLIAMS, David Claverly, CVO 1970; CBE 1977; *b* 31 July 1917; *s* of late Rev. Canon Henry Williams, OBE, and late Ethel Florence Williams; *m* 1944, Elizabeth Anne Fraser; three *d. Educ:* Christ's Coll., Christchurch, NZ; Victoria Univ. of Wellington. Professional Exam. in Public Administration. Inland Revenue Dept, 1936–39. Served War, NZTF, 1939–41, 2NZEF, Pacific and Middle East, 1941–46. NZ Forest Service, 1946–60; Official Sec. to the Governor-General of NZ, 1960–77; Sec./Manager, The Wellington Club (Inc.), 1978–82. *Address:* 20 Bellbird Crescent, Woodlands, Waikanae 5036, New Zealand. *Clubs:* Wellington (Wellington).

WILLIAMS, Prof. David Edward, PhD; FRSC; Professor of Chemistry, University of Auckland, since 2006; *b* 6 Feb. 1949; *s* of William and Gertrude Williams; *m* 1972, Lindsay Mary Sutherland; one *s* one *d. Educ:* Lynfield Coll., Auckland; Univ. of Auckland (BSc, MSc Hons; PhD 1974). CChem 1977, FRSC 1986. Gp Leader, Solid State Chemistry, Harwell Lab., UKAEA, 1980–90; Chief Scientist in Applied Electrochemistry, AEA Technol., 1990–91; University College London: Thomas Graham Prof. of Chemistry, 1991–2002; Hd, Dept of Chemistry, 1999–2002; Vis. Prof. of Chemistry, 2002–; Chief Scientist, Unipath Ltd, 2002–06. Hon. Prof., Royal Instn of GB, 2002–. *Publications:* (ed jtly) Techniques and Mechanisms in Gas Sensing, 1991; approx. 200 papers in jls of chemistry and materials sci. *Recreations:* ski-ing, yachting. *Address:* Department of Chemistry, University of Auckland, Private Bag 92019, Auckland, New Zealand; *e-mail:* david.williams@auckland.ac.nz.

WILLIAMS, Prof. David Franklyn, PhD, DSc; FREng; Professor of Tissue Engineering, since 2001, and Director, UK Centre for Tissue Engineering, since 2004, University of Liverpool; *b* 18 Dec. 1944; *s* of late Henry Sidney and Margaret Williams; *m* 2001, Margaret Mary O'Donnell; three *s. Educ:* Thornbury Grammar Sch.; Univ. of Birmingham (BSc 1965; PhD 1969; DSc 1982). CEng, FIPEM 1982; FIMMM (FIM 1982). University of Liverpool: Department of Clinical Engineering: Lectr, 1968–78; Sen. Lectr, 1978–84; Prof., 1984–; Hd of Clinical Engrg, 1984–; Pro-Vice-Chancellor, 1997–2001. Hon. Consultant Scientist, Royal Liverpool Univ. Hosp., 1990–. Mem., CCLRC, 2001–04. FREng 1999; MAE 1999; Fellow, American Inst. for Med. and Biol Engrg 2000. Ed.-in-Chief, Biomaterials, 1996–. *Publications:* include: Implants in Surgery, 1973; Biocompatibility of Implant Materials, 1976; Materials in Clinical Dentistry, 1979; Biocompatibility, 14 vols, 1981–86; Definitions in Biomaterials, 1987; Concise Encyclopaedia of Medical and Dental Materials, 1990; The Williams Dictionary of Biomaterials, 1999; over 350 papers in learned jls. *Recreations:* painting, photography, travel. *Address:* UK Centre for Tissue Engineering, Department of Clinical Engineering, University of Liverpool, PO Box 147, Liverpool L69 3GA. *T:* (0151) 706 4203, *Fax:* (0151) 706 5920; *e-mail:* dfw@liv.ac.uk. *Club:* Athenæum.

WILLIAMS, David Frederick, PhD; Director General, British National Space Centre, since 2006; *b* 21 Sept. 1951; *s* of Frederick Sefton Williams and Dorothy Williams (*née* Banks); *m* 1985, Jeannie Elizabeth Rickards; one *s* two *d. Educ:* Hutton Grammar Sch., Preston; Univ. of Reading (BSc 1974; PhD 1978). Lectr, Dept of Geography, Reading Univ., 1977–78; Clyde Surveys, 1978–82; NERC, 1982–89; BNSC, DTI, 1989–96; Hd, Strategy and Internat. Relns, Eur. Orgn for the Exploitation of Meteorol Satellites, Darmstadt, 1996–2006. Mem. Steering Cttee, Global Climate Observing System, 2000–. Trustee, Nat. Space Centre, Leicester, 2006–. *Publications:* various articles in jls. *Recreations.*

football, gardening, renovation. *Address:* British National Space Centre, Kingsgate House, 66–74 Victoria Street, SW1E 6SW. *T:* (020) 3300 8778.

WILLIAMS, Sir David (Glyndwr Tudor), Kt 1991; DL; Vice-Chancellor, Cambridge University, 1989–96; Fellow of Emmanuel College, Cambridge, since 1996; Chancellor (formerly President), Swansea University (formerly University of Wales, Swansea), since 2001; *b* 22 Oct. 1930; *s* of late Tudor Williams, OBE (Headmaster of Queen Elizabeth Grammar Sch., Carmarthen, 1929–55), and late Anne Williams; *m* 1959, Sally Gillian Mary Cole; one *s* two *d*. *Educ:* Queen Elizabeth Grammar Sch., Carmarthen; Emmanuel Coll., Cambridge (MA, LLB, Hon. Fellow 1984). LLM Calif. Nat. Service, RAF, 1949–50. Called to the Bar, Lincoln's Inn, 1956, Hon. Bencher, 1985. Commonwealth Fund Fellow of Harkness Foundn, Berkeley and Harvard, 1956–58; Lecturer: Univ. of Nottingham, 1958–63; Univ. of Oxford, 1963–67 (Fellow of Keble Coll.); University of Cambridge: Fellow, 1967–80, Sen. Tutor and Tutor for Admissions, 1970–76, Emmanuel Coll.; Reader in Public Law, 1976–83; Rouse Ball Prof. of English Law, 1983–92; Pres., Wolfson Coll., 1980–92 (Hon. Fellow, 1993); Prof. of Law, 1996–98. Vis. Fellow, 1974, Dist. Anniv. Fellow, 1996, ANU, Canberra; Allen, Allen and Hemsley Vis. Fellow, Law Dept, Univ. of Sydney, 1985; George P. Smith Dist. Visiting Professor: Indiana Univ., 2000; Univ. of Hong Kong, 2007; Hon. Prof., Chinese Univ. of Hong Kong, 2006–. Lectures: Stevens, Cornell, 1984; Martland, Alberta and Calgary, 1988; Read, Dalhousie, 1989; Fuchs, Indiana, 1993; Laskin, Osgoode Hall, 1993; Samuel Gee, RCP, 1993; Morris of Borth-y-Gest, Bangor, 1993; Wynne Baxter Godfree, Sussex, 1994; Spencer Mason, Auckland, 1994; Harry Street, Manchester, 1999; Shann, Hong Kong, 2004; Austen Owen, Richmond, Va, 2006; Jamestown, Gray's Inn, 2006. Pres., Nat. Soc. for Clean Air, 1983–85; Chairman: Animal Procedures Cttee, 1987–90; RAC Adv. Gp on Cars and the Envmt, 1991–92. Member: Clean Air Council, 1971–79; Royal Commn on Environmental Pollution, 1976–83; Commn on Energy and the Environment, 1978–81; Council on Tribunals, 1972–82; Justice/All Souls Cttee on Administrative Law, 1978–88; Berrill Cttee of Investigation, SSRC, 1982–83; Marre Cttee on Future of Legal Profession, 1986–88; Sen. Salaries Review Body, 1998–2004; Univ. Comr, 1988–93. Pres., Cambridge Soc., 1997–2004. Mem., Amer. Law Inst., 1986; For. Hon. Mem., Amer. Acad. of Arts and Scis, 1994. Mem., Internat. Jury, Indira Gandhi Prize, 1992–2002. DL Cambs, 1995. Hon. Fellow: Keble Coll., Oxford, 1992; Pembroke Coll., Cambridge, 1993; Trinity Coll., Carmarthen, 1994; Hon. QC 1994. Hon. DLitt: William Jewell Coll., 1984; Loughborough Univ. of Technology, 1988; Davidson Coll., 1992; Hon. LLD: Hull, 1989; Sydney 1990; Nottingham, 1991; Liverpool, 1994; McGill, De Montfort, 1995; Duke, 1996; Cambridge, 1997; Victoria Univ. of Technol., Melbourne, 2003; Hon. DCL Western Ontario, 2008. *Publications:* Not in the Public Interest, 1965; Keeping the Peace, 1967; articles in legal jls. *Address:* Emmanuel College, Cambridge CB2 3AP. *T:* (01223) 334200.

WILLIAMS, David Huw Anthony; QC 2008; *b* Neath, W Glamorgan, 26 Feb. 1964; *s* of Thomas Brinley Williams and late Mair E. Williams (*née* Anthony); *m* 1994, Denise Dolan; two *s*. *Educ:* Gnoll Prim. Sch., Neath; Cefn Saeson Sch., Neath; Univ. of Wales, Swansea (BSc Hons 1983). Called to the Bar, Inner Temple, 1988; in practice as barrister specialising in crime and fraud. *Publications:* (contrib.) Fraud: law, practice and procedure, 2004; Smith's Law of Theft (with David Ormerod), 9th edn 2007. *Recreations:* tennis, Welsh Rugby, film, reading, theatre (particularly the work of Stephen Sondheim). *Address:* 18 Red Lion Court, EC4A 3EB. *T:* (020) 7520 6000, *Fax:* (020) 7520 6248/9.

WILLIAMS, Sir David Innes, Kt 1985; MD, MChir Cambridge, FRCS; Consulting Urologist: Hospital for Sick Children, Great Ormond Street (Urologist, 1952–78); St Peter's Hospital, London (Surgeon, 1950–78); *b* 12 June 1919; *s* of late Gwynne E. O. Williams, MS, FRCS; *m* 1944, Margaret Eileen Harding; two *s*. *Educ:* Sherborne Sch.; Trinity Hall, Cambridge; Univ. College Hospital (Hon. Fellow, 1986). RAMC, 1945–48 (Major, Surg. Specialist). Urologist, Royal Masonic Hosp., 1963–72; Civilian Consultant Urologist to RN, 1974–84; Dir, BPMF, 1978–86, Pro-Vice-Chancellor, 1985–87, Univ. of London. Mem., 1975–91, Chm., 1982–91, Council, ICRF; Chm., Council for Postgrad. Med. Educn in England and Wales, 1985–88. Mem., Home Sec's Adv. Cttee on Cruelty to Animals, 1975–79. Mem., GMC, 1979–89 (Chm., Overseas Cttee, 1981–88); Vice-Pres., RCS, 1983–85 (Mem. Council, 1974–86; Mem. Jt Consultants Cttee, 1983–85; Hon. Medal, 1987); President: BMA, 1988–89; RSocMed, 1990–92 (Past Pres., Urology Sect.). Pres., Friends of the Wellcome Inst. for History of Medicine, 1998–2003. Hon. Member: British Assoc. Paediatric Surgeons (Denis Browne Medal, 1977); British Assoc. Urological Surgeons (Past Pres.; St Peter's Medal, 1967); Assoc. Française d'Urologie; Amer. Surgical Assoc.; British Paediatric Assoc.; Amer. Acad. Pediatrics (Urology Medal, 1986). Hon. FACS 1983; Hon. FRCSI 1984; Hon. FDSRCS; Hon. FRSocMed 1993; Hon. FRCPCH 1996. *Publications:* Urology of Childhood, 1958; Paediatric Urology, 1968, 2nd edn 1982; Scientific Foundations of Urology, 1976, 2nd edn 1982; The London Lock, 1995; various contributions to medical journals. *Address:* 66 Murray Road, SW19 4PE. *T:* (020) 8879 1042.

WILLIAMS, David John; *b* 10 July 1914; *s* of late James Herbert Williams and late Ethel (*née* Redman); unmarried. *Educ:* Lancing College; Christ Church, Oxford (MA). Called to Bar, Inner Temple, 1939. Postgrad. Dip. in Social Anthropology, LSE, 1965. Served War of 1939–45, Royal Artillery. Practised as Barrister, Norwich, 1946–51; Resident Magistrate, Tanganyika, 1951–56; Senior Resident Magistrate, 1956–60; Judge of High Court of Tanganyika, 1960–62; Lord Chancellor's Office, 1966–79. *Recreations:* the arts and travelling. *Clubs:* Travellers, Hurlingham.

WILLIAMS, David John, QPM 1992; Chief Constable, British Transport Police, 1997–2001; Associate Director, Reliance Security Services Ltd, 2001–02; *b* 7 April 1941; *s* of late John Isaac Williams and Edith (*née* Stoneham); *m* 1962, Johanna Murphy; two *s*. *Educ:* Ystalyfera Grammar Sch.; University Coll. London (LLB Hons). Called to the Bar, Middle Temple, 1977. Metropolitan Police, 1960–84; FBI Nat. Acad., 1982; on secondment to Home Office Inspectorate, 1983; Herts Constabulary, 1984–89; Dep. Chief Constable, 1989–91, Chief Constable, 1991–97, Surrey Police; Nat. Exec. Inst., USA, 1994. Chm., Traffic Cttee, ACPO, 1995–97. Mem. Council, St John Ambulance, Herts, 2004–; Dir and Trustee, Relate, N London, 2004–07; Chm., Child Accident Prevention Trust, 2007–; Gov./Trustee, Corps of Commissionaires Trust, 2008–; Patron, Isabel Hospice, 2006–. OStJ 1995. Queen's Commendation for Bravery, 1976; Police Long Service and Good Conduct Medal, 1982. *Recreations:* music, Rugby football, walking, golf.

WILLIAMS, David John, FRCP, FRCPE, FRCS, FRCSE, FRCA, FCEM; JP; Clinical Director, Accident & Emergency Services, Guy's and St Thomas' Hospitals NHS Trust, 1993–2000; *b* 23 April 1938; *s* of Frank Williams, CBE and Kathleen Williams; *m* 1977, Ann Andrews (*née* Walker-Watson); one *s* one *d*, and one step *s* one step *d*. *Educ:* Highgate Sch.; Hotchkiss Sch., USA; Trinity Coll., Cambridge (MA, MB, BChir); St Thomas' Hosp. Med. Sch. MRCP 1970, FRCP 1982; MRCGP 1972; FCEM (FFAEM 1993); FRCS 1997; FRCPE 1998; FRCSE 1999; FRCA 2000. Jun. med. posts, St Thomas' Hosp., Kingston Hosp., Guy's-Maudsley Neurosurgical Unit, 1964–65; RMO, Nat. Heart Hosp., 1966, Middlesex Hosp., 1967–70; Registrar, Maudsley Hosp., 1970–71; GP, 1971–72; Consultant, Accident and Emergency Medicine: Middlesex Hosp., 1973–84; St Thomas' Hosp., 1984–2000. Clin. Advr, Health Service Comr, 2000–05; Mem., Criminal Injuries Compensation Appeals Panel, 2000–; Medical Mem., Appeals Tribunals, 2006–. Sec., Casualty Surgeons Assoc., 1978–84; President: British Assoc. for A&E Medicine, 1987–90; Intercollegiate Faculty of A&E Medicine, 1993–97; Eur. Soc. for Emergency Medicine, 2004– (Vice-Pres., 2000–04); Invited Member Council: RCP, 1994–2000; RCS, 1994–2000; Royal Coll. of Anaesthetists, 1994–2000. JP Sutton, 2004. Fellow, Internat. Fedn of Emergency Medicine, 2000; Hon. Mem., Amer. Coll. Emergency Physicians, 1990; Hon. Life Mem., British Assoc. for A&E Medicine, 1998; Hon. FRSocMed 2001. *Recreations:* reading, collecting books, theatre, travel. *Address:* 13 Spencer Hill, Wimbledon, SW19 4PA. *T:* (020) 8946 3785.

WILLIAMS, (David John) Delwyn; company director; *b* 1 Nov. 1938; *s* of David Lewis Williams and Irena Violet Gwendoline Williams; *m* 1963, Olive Elizabeth Jerman; one *s* one *d*. *Educ:* Welshpool High School; University College of Wales, Aberystwyth. LLB. Sometime Solicitor and company director. MP (C) Montgomery, 1979–83; former Member: Select Cttee on Wales; Statutory Instruments Cttee; Jt Sec., All-Party Leisure and Recreation Industry Cttee. Contested (C) Montgomery, 1983. Former Mem., British Field Sports Soc. *Recreations:* race horse owner; cricket, golf, small bore shooting.

WILLIAMS, David Lincoln; Chairman and Managing Director, Costa Rica Coffee Co. Ltd, 1988–2002; *b* 10 Feb. 1937; *s* of Lewis Bernard Williams and Eileen Elizabeth Cadogan; *m* 1959, Gillian Elisabeth, *d* of Dr William Phillips; one *s* one *d*. *Educ:* Cheltenham College. Served RA Gibraltar, 1955–57. Chairman: Allied Windows (S Wales) Ltd, 1971–85; Cardiff Broadcasting PLC, 1979–84; Allied Profiles Ltd, 1981–96; Chm. and Man. Dir, John Williams of Cardiff PLC, 1983–88 (Dir, 1968–88). Chm., Cox (Penarth), 1987–94. President, Aluminium Window Assoc., 1971–72. Member: CBI Welsh Council, 1986–89; Welsh Arts Council, 1987–94 (Chm., Music Cttee, 1988–94). Pres., Vale of Glamorgan Festival, 1995– (Chm., 1978–95); Director: Cardiff Bay Opera House Trust, 1994–97; WNO, 1994–2001 (Nat. Chm., 1980–2000, Vice-Pres., 2005–, Friends of WNO). Freeman, City of London, 1986; Liveryman, Founders' Co., 1986. *Recreations:* opera, gardening, fine weather sailing. *Address:* Rose Revived, Llantrithyd, Cowbridge, Vale of Glamorgan CF71 7UB. *T:* (01446) 781357. *Club:* Cardiff and County (Cardiff).

WILLIAMS, Prof. David Michael, PhD; FRCPath, FDSRCS; Professor of Pathology, and Dean, Faculty of Medicine, Health and Life Sciences, University of Southampton, since 2004; Hon. Consultant, since 2004 and non-executive Director, since 2005, Southampton University Hospitals NHS Trust; *b* 4 Nov. 1946; *s* of late Reginald Albert Williams and of Mary Williams (*née* Holland); *m* 1970, Gillian Elizabeth Regester; one *s* one *d*. *Educ:* Plymouth Coll.; London Hosp. Med. Coll., Univ. of London (BDS Hons 1969; MSc 1972; PhD 1976). FRCPath 1991; FDSRCS 1994. London Hospital Medical College: Sen. Lectr in Oral Pathology, 1982–89; Reader in Oral Pathology, 1989–93; Prof. of Oral Pathology, 1994–2004, Dean of Clinical Dentistry, 1994–98, Dep. Warden, 1998–2001, St Bartholomew's and Royal London Sch. of Medicine and Dentistry, QMW, Univ. of London, subseq. Bart's and The London, Queen Mary's Sch. of Medicine and Dentistry; Vice-Principal, Queen Mary, Univ. of London, 2001–04; Hon. Consultant, Bart's and the London NHS Trust (formerly Royal London Hosp., then Royal Hosps NHS Trust), 1982–2004. Chm., Dentistry Sub-panel 2008 RAE. Mem., GDC, 1998–2003 (Chm., Registration Sub-Cttee, 1999–2003). President: British Soc. for Dental Res., 2002–04; Pan-European Fedn, IADR, 2004–05; Vice-Pres., IADR, 2007–. Mem., several edtl bds. *Publications:* (jtly) Pathology of Periodontal Disease, 1992; numerous articles in learned jls. *Recreations:* golf, scuba diving, hill walking, sailing. *Address:* University of Southampton, Biomedical Sciences Building, Bassett Crescent East, Southampton SO16 7PX. *T:* (023) 8059 6702. *Clubs:* Athenæum; Bigbury Golf.

WILLIAMS, David Michael; JP; Clerk to the General Synod, Church of England, since 1999; Head of the Central Secretariat, Archbishops' Council, since 2002 (Director of Central Services, 1999–2002); *b* 6 April 1950; *s* of David Woodget Williams and Edith Olive Williams (*née* Hance); *m* (marr. diss.). *Educ:* Exeter Univ. (BA Hons 1971); UCL (Dip. Liby and Inf. Studies 1974); London Univ. (MA 1977). On staff, Council for the Care of Churches, 1972–73, 1974–87; on staff, 1987–94, Sec., 1994–99, Central Bd of Finance, C of E. FSA 1981; FRSA 1982. JP SE Surrey, 1986. *Publications:* articles in jls on hist. of English parochial libraries. *Recreations:* numismatics, ecclesiology, art and architecture, horticulture, cycling, walking. *Address:* Archbishops' Council, Church House, Great Smith Street, Westminster, SW1P 3AZ. *T:* (020) 7898 1559, *Fax:* (020) 7898 1369; *e-mail:* david.williams@c-of-e.org.uk.

WILLIAMS, David Oliver; General Secretary, Confederation of Health Service Employees, 1983–87; *b* 12 March 1926; *m* 1949, Kathleen Eleanor Jones, Dinorwic; two *s* five *d* (and one *s* decd). *Educ:* Brynrefail Grammar Sch.; North Wales Hospital, Denbigh (RMN 1951). COHSE: full-time officer, Regional Secretary, Yorkshire Region, 1955; National Officer, Head Office, 1962; Sen. National Officer, 1969; Asst General Secretary, 1974. Chairman: Nurses and Midwives Whitley Council Staff Side, 1977–87; General Whitley Council Staff Side, 1974–87. Member: NEC, Labour Party, 1981–83; TUC Gen. Council, 1983–87. Occasional Tech. Advr to WHO. Jubilee Medal, 1977. *Recreations:* walking, birdwatching, swimming, music. *Address:* 1 King's Court, Beddington Gardens, Wallington, Surrey SM6 0HR. *T:* (020) 8647 6412.

WILLIAMS, Air Vice-Marshal David Owen C.; *see* Crwys-Williams.

WILLIAMS, Prof. David Raymond, OBE 1993; Emeritus Professor, Cardiff University; *b* 20 March 1941; *s* of Eric Thomas and Amy Gwendoline Williams; *m* 1964, Gillian Kirkpatrick Murray; two *d*. *Educ:* Grove Park Grammar Sch., Wrexham, Clwyd; Univ. of Wales, Bangor (BSc (1st Cl. Hons Chemistry); PhD); DSc St Andrews. CChem, FRSC, 1976; EurChem 1992. NATO Postdoctoral Fellowship, Univ. of Lund, 1965–66; Lectr in Chemistry, Univ. of St Andrews, 1966–77; Prof. of Applied Chemistry, UWIST, then Speciation and Analytical Chemistry, now Chemistry, UC, Cardiff, later UWCC, now Cardiff Univ., 1977–2006. Chm., Sci. Adv. Cttee, British Council, 1986–94; Member: Radioactive Waste Management Adv. Cttee, DoE, 1980–95; Cttee on Medical Aspects of Radiation in the Environment, DHSS, later Dept of Health, 1985–89; Adv. Cttee on Hazardous Substances, DEFRA (formerly DETR), 2000–05. FRSA 1978. Jeyes Silver Medal, RSC, 1987; Wolfson Foundn Res. Award, 1988. *Publications:* The Metals of Life, 1970; An Introduction to Bioinorganic Chemistry, 1976; The Principles of Bioinorganic Chemistry, 1977; Laboratory Introduction to Bioinorganic Chemistry, 1979; Analysis Using Glass Electrodes, 1984; Trace Metals in Medicine and Chelation Therapy, 1995; What is Safe?: the risks of living in a nuclear age, 1998; 500 res. papers. *Recreations:* cycling, swimming, other outdoor pursuits, public speaking. *Address:* Cerrig Llwydion, St Fagans, Cardiff CF5 6EF. *T:* (029) 2056 8178.

WILLIAMS, Sir David (Reeve), Kt 1999; CBE 1990; Member (Lib Dem), Richmond upon Thames Borough Council, since 1974 (Cabinet Member, 2001–02 and since 2006);

b 8 June 1939; *s* of Edmund George Williams and May Williams (*née* Partridge); *m* 1964, Christine Margaret Rayson. *Educ:* St Cuthbert's Soc.; Univ. of Durham (BA Hons Politics and Econs). Computer systems analyst, 1961–95: IBM UK Ltd, 1961–70; Insurance Systems and Services, 1970–78; David Williams and Associates, 1978–91; Teleglobe Insce Systems Ltd, 1991–95. Leader of Opposition, 1978–83, Leader, 1983–2001, Richmond upon Thames BC. Dep. Chm., and Leader, Lib Dem Gp, LGA, 1996–2001. *Recreations:* collecting books, particularly about Lloyd George, listening to jazz, particularly Charlie Parker. *Address:* 8 Arlington Road, Petersham, Richmond, Surrey TW10 7BY. *T:* (020) 8940 9421.

WILLIAMS, David Wakelin, (Lyn), MSc, PhD; CBiol, FIBiol; retired as Director, Department of Agriculture and Fisheries for Scotland, Agricultural Scientific Services, 1963–73; *b* 2 Oct. 1913; *e s* of John Thomas Williams and Ethel (*née* Lock); *m* 1948, Margaret Mary Wills, BSc (*d* 1993), *d* of late Rev. R. H. Wills; one *s*. *Educ:* Rhondda Grammar School, Porth; University College, Cardiff. Demonstrator, Zoology Dept, Univ. Coll., Cardiff, 1937–38; Lectr in Zoology and Botany, Tech. Coll., Crumlin, Mon., 1938–39; research work on nematode physiology, etc. (MSc, PhD), 1937–41; biochemical work on enzymes (Industrial Estate, Treforest), 1942–43. Food Infestation Control Inspector (Min. of Food), Glasgow; Sen. Inspector, W Scotland, 1945; Scotland and N Ireland, 1946. Prin. Scientific Officer, Dept Agriculture for Scotland, 1948; Sen. Prin. Scientific Officer, 1961; Dep. Chief Scientific Officer (Director), 1963. Chairman, Potato Trials Advisory Cttee, 1963–; FIBiol 1966 (Council Mem. Scottish Br., 1966–69). MBIM, 1970–76. *Publications:* various papers, especially for the intelligent layman, on the environment, and on pest control and its side effects. *Recreations:* writing, music, Hi-Fi, photography, natural history. *Address:* 8 Hillview Road, Edinburgh EH12 8QN. *T:* (0131) 334 1108.

WILLIAMS, David Whittow; Chief Executive, Amari Plastics plc, since 2004; *b* 18 Aug. 1957; *s* of David Whittow Williams and Eileen Williams; *m* 1992, Helle Nordensgaard. *Educ:* Birkenhead Sch.; Mansfield Coll., Oxford (MA). Exec. Vice Pres., Melwire Inc., 1982–86; Mkting Dir, Vickers Healthcare, 1986–88; Eur. Business Develt Manager, Blue Circle Cement, 1988–90; Business Develt Dir, Blue Circle Home Products plc, 1991–94; Man. Dir, Potterton/Myson, 1994–96; Chief Executive: Magnet, 1996–99; Berisford, subseq. Enodis plc, 1999–2001. *Recreations:* Rugby, tennis, cricket.

WILLIAMS, Dr David William; Social Security and Child Support Commissioner, since 1998; Deputy Special Commissioner of Income Tax, and part-time Chairman, VAT and Duties Tribunal, since 2003; *b* 13 Feb. 1946; *s* of J. W. (Bill) Williams, DFC, and Joan Adair (*née* Wallis); *m* 1968, Elisabeth Jones Pierce; three *s*. *Educ:* Queen Elizabeth's Grammar Sch., Faversham; Univ. of Bristol (LLB; LLM; PhD 1979). ATII 1970. Admitted Solicitor, 1970; Lectr, Faculty of Law, Univ. of Bristol, 1969–76; Faculty of Law, University of Manchester: Lectr, then Sen. Lectr, 1976–86; Reader, 1986–87; Dean of Faculty, 1984–86; Queen Mary and Westfield College, University of London: Prof. of Tax Law, 1987–98; Vis. Prof., 1998–; Dean, Faculty of Laws, 1991–93. Vis. Lectr, Univ. of Liverpool, 1978–80; Visiting Professor: Univ. of Buckingham, 1992–93; Univ. of Sydney, 1997; Tech. Univ. of Vienna, 1997–2001; Sorbonne, Paris, 1998–99. Consultant, OECD Fiscal Affairs Dept, 1993–97. Pt-time Chairman: Medical Appeal Tribunals, 1990–98; Social Security Appeal Tribunals, 1984–96; Dep. Social Security Comr, 1996–98. Member: Educn Cttee, Chartered Inst. Taxation, 1988–92; Revenue Law Cttee, Law Soc., 1992–97; Perm. Scientific Cttee, Internat. Fiscal Assoc., 1996–98; Tax Law Rewrite Consultative Cttee, 1997–. Mem. Bd, Centre for Juridico-Economic Investigation, Univ. of Porto, 1997–. *Publications:* Maladministration: remedies for injustice, 1979; (with G. K. Morse) Profit Sharing, 1979; Running Your Own Business, 1979; Tax for the Self-Employed, 1980; Social Security Taxation, 1982; National Insurance Contributions Handbook, 1987; Trends in International Taxation, 1991; Taxation Principles and Practice, 1993; EC Tax Law, 1998; editor: (with G. K. Morse) Introduction to Revenue Law, 1985; Tax on International Transfers of Information, 1991; Principles of Tax Law, 1996, 6th edn 2008; Practical Application of Double Tax Conventions, 1998; (with N. Wikeley) Social Security Legislation: tax credits, 2007; consulting editor: Reader's Digest Guide to the Law, 8th–10th edn, 1986–92; Reader's Digest Know Your Rights, 1997; contrib. articles to legal jls. *Address:* (office) Third Floor, Procession House, 55 Ludgate Hill, EC4M 7JW.

WILLIAMS, Dr (David) Wynford, CB 2007; Chief Executive, United Kingdom Hydrographic Office, and United Kingdom National Hydrographer, 2001–06; *b* 19 July 1946; *s* of late Thomas Elwyn Williams and of Nancy Williams; *m* 1969, Dilys Arthur; one *s* one *d*. *Educ:* Amman Valley Grammar Sch., Ammanford; University Coll., Swansea (BSc 1967, PhD 1971). CPhys 1987, CEng 1987; FInstP 1981; FRAeS 1981; FIMarEST 2006. Scientist: ASWE, MoD, 1971–81; British Naval Staff, Washington, 1981–84; Ministry of Defence: ACOS (Operational Analysis), C-in-C Fleet, 1984–87; Supt, RAE Ranges, 1987–91; Dir, A&AEE Boscombe Down, 1991–95; rcds 1996; Dir, Sea Systems Sector, DERA, 1997–2000. Pres., Inst. of Marine Engrg, Sci. and Technol., 2007–08. *Recreations:* Rugby, golf, music (orchestral and choral). *Address:* Rhos Colwyn, Welsh St Donats, Vale of Glamorgan CF71 7SS. *T:* (01446) 771243; *e-mail:* wyn.dil@talktalk.net.

WILLIAMS, Delwyn; *see* Williams, D. J. D.

WILLIAMS, Sir Denys (Ambrose), KCMG 1993; Kt 1987; Gold Crown of Merit, Barbados, 1981; Chief Justice of Barbados, 1987–2001; *b* 12 Oct. 1929; *s* of George Cuthbert and Violet Irene Williams; *m* 1954, Carmel Mary Coleman; two *s* four *d*. *Educ:* Combermere and Harrison College, Barbados; Worcester College, Oxford (BCL, MA). Called to the Bar, Middle Temple, 1954. Asst Legal Draftsman, Barbados, 1957; Asst to Attorney General, 1959; Asst Legal Draftsman, Fedn of West Indies, 1959; Senior Parly Counsel, Barbados, 1963; Judge of the Supreme Court, 1967. *Recreations:* horse racing, tennis, walking. *Address:* No 9, Garrison, St Michael, Barbados. *T:* 4271164. *Clubs:* Carlton, Barbados Turf (Barbados).

WILLIAMS, Derrick; *see* Williams, R. D.

WILLIAMS, Sir Dillwyn; *see* Williams, Sir E. D.

WILLIAMS, Rev. Doiran George; Non-Stipendiary Minister, Greater Whitbourne, since 1993; *b* 27 June 1926; *s* of Rev. Dr Robert Richard Williams and Dilys Rachel Williams; *m* 1st, 1949, Flora Samitz (decd); one *s* one *d*; 2nd, 1977, Maureen Dorothy Baker; one *d*. *Educ:* Hereford Cathedral Sch.; Colwyn Bay Grammar Sch.; Liverpool Coll.; John F. Hughes Sch., Utica, NY. Served Army (Infantry), 1944–47. Called to the Bar, Gray's Inn, 1952; practised in Liverpool, 1952–58; Dept of Dir of Public Prosecutions, 1959, Asst Dir, 1977–82, Principal Asst Dir of Public Prosecutions, 1982–86; Chm., Med. Appeal Tribunals, 1987–98. Sec., Liverpool Fabian Soc., 1956–58. Reader: Liverpool Dio., 1953–58; London Dio., 1959–63; Southwark Dio., 1963–88; Hereford Dio., 1988–93; Mem., Southwark Readers' Bd, 1977–88. Ordained deacon, 1993, priest, 1994. *Recreations:* arts, mountains, sport, wine. *Address:* Howberry, Whitbourne, Worcester WR6 5RZ.

WILLIAMS, Sir Donald Mark, 10th Bt *cr* 1866; *b* 7 Nov. 1954; *s* of Sir Robert Ernest Williams, 9th Bt, and of Ruth Margaret, *d* of Charles Edwin Butcher, Hudson Bay, Saskatchewan, Canada; *S* father, 1976; *m* 1982, Denise, *o d* of Royston H. Cory; three *d* (one *s* decd). *Educ:* West Buckland School, Devon. *Heir:* *b* Barton Matthew Williams [*b* 21 Nov. 1956; *m* 1st, 1980, Karen Robinson (marr. diss.); one *s* one *d*; 2nd, 1985, Sarah (marr. diss.); one *d*]. *Address:* Upcott House, Barnstaple, N Devon EX31 4DR.

WILLIAMS, Prof. Dudley Howard, PhD, ScD; FRS 1983; Professor of Biological Chemistry, University of Cambridge, 1996–2004, now Professor Emeritus; Fellow of Churchill College, Cambridge, since 1964; *b* 25 May 1937; *s* of Lawrence Williams and Evelyn (*née* Hudson); *m* 1963, Lorna Patricia Phyllis, *d* of Anthony and Lorna Bedford; two *s*. *Educ:* Grammar Sch., Pudsey, Yorks; Univ. of Leeds (state schol.; BSc, PhD); MA, ScD Cantab. Fulbright Schol., Post-doctoral Fellow and Research Associate, Stanford Univ., Calif, 1961–64; University of Cambridge: Sen. Asst in Research, 1964–66; Asst Dir of Research, 1966–74; Reader in Organic Chemistry, 1974–96. Visiting Professor: Univ. of California, Irvine, 1967, 1986, 1989 and 1997; Univ. of Cape Town, 1972; Univ. of Wisconsin, 1975; Univ. of Copenhagen, 1976; ANU, 1980; Lee Kuan Yew Dist. Visitor, Singapore, 2000. Lectures: Nuffield Vis., Sydney Univ., 1973; Arun Guthikonda Meml Award, Columbia Univ., 1985; Dist. Vis., Texas A & M Univ., 1986; Rohrer, Ohio State Univ., 1989; Foundn, Univ. of Auckland, 1991; Pacific Coast, 1991; Steel, Univ. of Queensland, 1994; Marvin Carmack Dist., Indiana Univ., 2001; Paul Ehrlich, France, 2001; James Sprague, Univ. of Wisconsin, 2002; Merck Res., RSC, 2002. Mem. Acad. Europaea. Meldola Medal, RIC, 1966; Corday-Morgan Medal, 1968; Tilden Medal and Lectr, 1983; Structural Chemistry Award, 1984, Bader Award, 1991, RSC; Leo Friend Award, ACS, 1996. *Publications:* Applications of NMR in Organic Chemistry, 1964; Spectroscopic Methods in Organic Chemistry, 1966, 6th edn 2008; Mass Spectrometry of Organic Compounds, 1967; Mass Spectrometry—Principles and Applications, 1981; papers in chemical and biochemical jls, incl. co-discovery of human hormone (1,25-dihydroxyvitamin D) responsible for calcium absorption, and chemistry and action of antibiotics vancomycin and teicoplanin. *Recreations:* music, gardening. *Address:* 7 Balsham Road, Fulbourn, Cambridge CB21 5BZ. *T:* (01223) 740971.

WILLIAMS, Dr Dyfri John Roderick, FSA; Research Keeper, Department of Greek and Roman Antiquities, British Museum, since 2008; *b* 8 Feb. 1952; *s* of Roderick Trevor Williams and Eira Williams (*née* Evans); *m* 1980, Korinna Pilafidis; one *s* one *d*. *Educ:* Repton Sch.; University Coll. London (BA); Lincoln Coll., Oxford (DPhil). FSA 1987. Shuffrey Jun. Res. Fellow, Lincoln Coll., Oxford, 1976–79; Department of Greek and Roman Antiquities, British Museum, 1979–: Res. Asst, 1979–83; Asst Keeper, 1983–93; Keeper, 1993–2008. Corresp. Mem., German Archaeol Inst., 1984. *Publications:* Greek Vases, 1985, rev. and enlarged edn 1999; Corpus Vasorum Antiquorum, BM fasc. 9, 1993; Greek Gold: jewellery of the classical world, 1994; (ed) The Art of the Greek Goldsmith, 1998. *Recreations:* family, reading, music. *Address:* Department of Greek and Roman Antiquities, British Museum, Great Russell Street, WC1B 3DG. *T:* (020) 7323 8411.

WILLIAMS, Prof. Sir (Edward) Dillwyn, Kt 1990; FRCP, FRCPath, FMedSci; Professor of Histopathology, University of Cambridge, 1992–96, now Emeritus; *b* 1 April 1929; *s* of Edward Williams and Ceinwen Williams (*née* James); *m* 1st, 1954, Ruth Hill; one *s* two *d* (and one *s* decd); 2nd, 1976, Olwen Williams; one *s* one *d*. *Educ:* Christ's Coll., Cambridge (MA, MD; Hon. Fellow, 1991); London Hospital Med. Coll. Jun. appts, London Hosp. and RPMS; successively Lectr, Sen. Lectr, Reader, in Morbid Anatomy, RPMS; Prof. of Pathology, 1969–92, Vice-Provost, 1982–84, Univ. of Wales Coll. of Medicine. Consultant Pathologist, Cardiff, 1969–92. Res. Fellowship, Harvard Univ., 1962–63. President: RCPath, 1987–90; BMA, 1998–99; Hd and Prin. Investigator of WHO's Internat. Reference Centre for Endocrine Tumours, 1972–; Chm., Welsh Sci. Adv. Cttee, 1985–92; Mem., GMC, 1987–90. Chm., Scientific Project Panel of Chernobyl Tissue Bank, 1998–2004. Mem., Sci. Scholarships Cttee, Royal Commn for Exhibn of 1851, 2000–. Corresp. Mem., Amer. Thyroid Assoc.; President: Thyroid Club of GB, 1987–90; European Thyroid Assoc., 1993–96. Founder FMedSci 1998. *Publications:* International Histological Classification of Tumours: histological typing of endocrine tumours, 1980; Pathology and Management of Thyroid Disease, 1981; Current Endocrine Concepts, 1982; numerous contribs to learned jls in field of endocrine pathology and carcinogenesis, in particular recently on thyroid carcinoma following Chernobyl nuclear accident. *Recreations:* natural history in general, birdwatching in particular, mountain walking. *Address:* Cow Lane, Fulbourn, Cambs CB21 5HB. *T:* (01223) 880738.

WILLIAMS, Air Cdre Edward Stanley, CBE 1975 (OBE 1968); *b* 27 Sept. 1924; *s* of late William Stanley Williams and Ethel Williams; *m* 1947, Maureen Donovan; two *d*. *Educ:* Wallasey Central Sch.; London Univ. Sch. of Slavonic and E European Studies; St John's Coll., Cambridge (MPhil (Internat. Relations), 1982). Joined RAF, 1942; trained in Canada; service in flying boats, 1944; seconded BOAC, 1944–48; 18 Sqdn, Transport Comd, 1949; Instr, Central Navigation Sch., RAF Shawbury, 1950–52; Russian Language Study, 1952–54; Flying Appts MEAF, A&AEE, 216 Sqdn Transport Comd, 1954–61; OC RAF Element, Army Intell. Centre, 1961–64; Asst Air Attaché, Moscow, 1964–67; first RAF Defence Fellow, UCL, 1967–68; comd Jt Wing, Sch. of Service Intell., 1968–71; Chief, Target Plans, HQ Second ATAF, 1971–73; Chief Intell. Officer, HQ British Forces Near East, 1973–75; comd Jt Air Reconn. Intell. Centre, 1976–77; Defence and Air Attaché, Moscow, 1978–81, retired RAF, 1981. Vice-Chm. (Air), NW Area, TAVRA, 1988–93. *Publications:* The Soviet Military, 1986; Soviet Air Power: prospects for the future, 1990; Cold War, Hot Seat, 2000; various articles in professional jls. *Recreations:* Russian studies, photography. *Address:* c/o HSBC, 2 Liscard Way, Wallasey, Merseyside CH44 5TR. *Club:* Royal Air Force.

WILLIAMS, Elizabeth, (Betty), (Mrs J. T. Perkins); working for peace, since 1976; Founder and President, World Centers of Compassion for Children International, since 1997; *b* 22 May 1943; *m* 1st, 1961, Ralph Williams (marr. diss.); one *s* one *d*; 2nd, 1982, James T. Perkins. *Educ:* St Dominic's Grammar School. Office Receptionist. Co-founder and Leader, NI Peace Movement, 1976–78; Chm., Inst. for Asian Democracy, Washington, DC; Patron, Internat. Peace Foundn, Vienna. Hon. LLD, Yale Univ., 1977; Hon. HLD, Coll. of Sienna Heights, Michigan, 1977. Nobel Peace Prize (jtly), 1976; Carl-von-Ossietzky Medal for Courage, 1976; Eleanor Roosevelt Award; Frank Foundn Child Assistance Internat. Oliver Award; Peace Building Award, Together for Peace Foundn, 1995. Paul Harris Fellow, Rotary Internat., 1995. *Recreation:* gardening.

WILLIAMS, Evelyn Faithfull M.; *see* Monier-Williams.

WILLIAMS, Felicity Ann; General Secretary, Wales Trade Union Congress, 2004–08 (Assistant General Secretary, 2000–04); *b* 29 Oct. 1960; *d* of Ivan and Doris Parker; *m* 1981, David Williams. *Educ:* Univ. of Bristol. FIBMS 1988. Biomed. scientist, then Dep. Hd of Microbiology 1988–97, Welsh Blood Service. *Recreations:* travel, reading, good food and wine, theatre.

WILLIAMS, Francis Julian, CBE 1986; JP; Vice Lord-Lieutenant, Cornwall, 1998–2002; Member of Prince of Wales' Council, Duchy of Cornwall, 1969–85; *b* 16 April 1927; 2nd *s* of late Alfred Martyn Williams, CBE, DSC; *m* Delia Fearne Marshall, *e d* of Captain and Mrs Campbell Marshall, St Mawes; two *s*. *Educ:* Eton; Trinity Coll., Cambridge (BA). RAF, 1945–48. Chm., Cambridge Univ. Conservative Assoc., 1950; Pres., Cambridge Union, 1951. Contested (C) All Saints Div. of Birmingham, 1955. Chm., Royal Instn of Cornwall, 1998–2005. Succeeded to Caerhays, 1955. Pres., Cornwall Cricket Club. Mem., Cornwall CC, 1967–89 (Vice-Chm., 1974; Chm., 1980–89). JP 1970, DL 1977, Cornwall. *Recreation:* gardening. *Address:* Caerhays Castle, Gorran, St Austell, Cornwall PL26 6LY. *T:* (01872) 501250. *Clubs:* Brooks's, White's.

WILLIAMS, Sir Francis Owen Garbett, (Sir Frank), Kt 1999; CBE 1987; Managing Director, Williams Grand Prix Engineering Ltd; *b* 16 April 1942; *s* of Owen Garbett Williams; *m* 1974, Virginia Jane, *d* of Raymond Berry; three *c*. *Educ:* St Joseph's Coll., Dumfries. Racing driver to 1966, competing first in Austin A40; grand prix team management, 1969–; Formula One with Brabham BT 26A; founded Frank Williams Racing Cars, 1975; first Grand Prix race, with FW07, Silverstone, 1979; won Constructors' Cup, 1980, 1981, 1986, 1987, 1992, 1993, 1994, 1996, 1997; introduced active ride system, 1988, semi-automatic 6-speed gear box, 1991. *Address:* Williams Grand Prix Engineering, Grove, Wantage, Oxon OX12 0DQ.

WILLIAMS, Frank John; actor and playwright; *b* 2 July 1931; *s* of William Williams and Alice (*née* Myles). *Educ:* Ardingly Coll.; Hendon County Sch. *Theatre* includes: Stage Manager and actor, Gateway Theatre, London, 1951; *writer:* No Traveller, 1952; The TV Murders, 1960; The Substitute, 1961; Murder by Appointment, 1985; Alibi for Murder, 1989; Murder Weekend, 1993; Mask for Murder, 1993; The Playing Fields, 2003; *actor:* The Cresta Run, Royal Court, 1965; The Waiters, Watford, 1967; Dad's Army, Shaftesbury, and tour, 1975–76; The Editor Regrets, tour, 1978; Stage Struck, 1980, The Winslow Boy, 1982, Vienna; Lloyd George Knew My Father, tour, Middle East and Far East, 1993; A Midsummer Night's Dream, Almeida, and tour, 1996–97; *television* includes: The Call Up, 1952; The Queen came by, 1955; The Army Game, 1958–61; Anna Karenina, 1961; Diary of a Young Man, 1964; After Many a Summer, 1967; Dad's Army, 1969–77; How Many Miles to Babylon, 1981; Grey Granite, 1982; Love's Labour Lost, 1984; You Rang M'Lord, 1989–92; *films* include: Shield of Faith, 1954; The Extra Day, 1955; The Square Peg, 1958; The Bulldog Breed, 1960; Dad's Army, 1970; Jabberwocky, 1976; The Human Factor, 1979. Member: Gen. Synod, 1985–2000; Crown Appts Commn, 1992–97; Trustee, Annunciation Trust, 1995–2006. Mem., Equity Council, 1984–88, 1990–94, 1998–; Dir, Equity Trust Fund, 1992–. *Publication:* Vicar to Dad's Army, 2002. *Recreations:* theatre, cinema, collecting boys' school stories. *Address:* 31 Manor Park Crescent, Edgware, Middx HA8 7NE. *T:* (020) 8952 4871.

WILLIAMS, Prof. Gareth, MD, ScD; FRCP, FRCPE; Professor of Medicine, and Dean, Faculty of Medicine and Dentistry, University of Bristol, since 2003; *b* 17 March 1952; *s* of Sir Alwyn Williams, FRS, and of Joan Williams (*née* Bevan); *m* 1983, Caroline Anne Evans; one *s* one *d*. *Educ:* Royal Belfast Academical Instn (Sir Hans Sloane Medal 1970); Clare Coll., Cambridge (Open and Foundn Scholar); Middlesex Hosp. Med. Sch. (MB BChir Hons Medicine and Pharmacol. 1977); Univ. of Cambridge (MD 1986; ScD 2003). FRCP 1991; FRCPE 1999. Jun. hosp. posts, Middlesex, Hammersmith and Brompton Hosps, London, and Hôpital Cantonal, Geneva, 1977–79; Res. Registrar, Guy's Hosp., London, 1980–83; Med. Registrar, Ealing and Hammersmith Hosps, 1983–85; R. D. Lawrence Res. Fellow, British Diabetic Assoc., 1986–88; University of Liverpool: Sen. Lectr, 1988–92, Reader, 1992, in Medicine; Prof. of Medicine, 1995–2003; Hon. Consultant Physician, Royal Liverpool Univ. Hosp., 1988–92; Foundn Prof. of Medicine and Hon. Consultant Physician, Univ. Hosp. Aintree, Liverpool, 1995–2003. Non-exec. Dir, United Bristol Healthcare Trust, 2005–07. Vis. Prof., Fac. of Medicine, Univ. of Alberta, 1988–89. UK Pres., Anglo-French Med. Soc., 1993–2000; Mem. Council, Europ. Soc. for Clinical Investment, 1996–2000 (Vice-Pres., 2000); Chm., MEDINE (Med. Educn in Europe), 2004–07. Editl Bd, Peptides, 1994–2003. Mem. Cttee, Med. Writers' Gp, Soc. of Authors, 2001– (Chm., 2007). Dr *hc* Angers, 2007. Novartis UK Award for Achievement in Diabetes, 1999. *Publications:* (ed jtly) Textbook of Diabetes, 1990, 2nd edn 1995 (BMA Medicine Book of the Yr; Soc. of Authors prize), 3rd edn 2004; (ed jtly) Handbook of Diabetes, 1992, 3rd edn 2004; (contrib.) Oxford Textbook of Medicine, 4th edn 2004 to 5th edn 2008; (ed jtly) Obesity: science to practice, 2009; papers on diabetes and obesity in sci. and med. jls, and articles of gen. medicine interest. *Recreations:* playing music (reputable and disreputable), exploring Gloucestershire by bike, bird-watching, French, writing fiction and hoping to complete a collection of rejection slips. *Address:* Vellow, Rockhampton, Berkeley, Glos GL13 9DY. *T:* (0117) 331 1690, *Fax:* (0117) 331 1687; *e-mail:* Gareth.Williams@bris.ac.uk. *Clubs:* Bristol Savages; Twenty (Liverpool).

WILLIAMS, Prof. Gareth Howel; Professor of Chemistry, University of London, 1967–84 (Head of Department of Chemistry, Bedford College, 1967–84), now Emeritus Professor; *b* 17 June 1925; *s* of Morgan John and Miriam Williams, Treherbert, Glam; *m* 1955, Marie, BA, *yr d* of William and Jessie Mary Mitchell, Wanlockhead, Dumfriesshire; one *d* (one *s* decd). *Educ:* Pentre Grammar Sch.; University Coll., London. BSc, PhD, DSc London; FRSC 1960. Asst Lectr, then Lectr in Chemistry, King's Coll., Univ of London, 1947–60; Research Fellow, Univ. of Chicago, 1953–54; Reader in Organic Chemistry, Birkbeck Coll., Univ. of London, 1960–67. Vis. Lectr, Univ. of Ife, Nigeria, 1965; Rose Morgan Vis. Prof., Univ. of Kansas, 1969–70; Vis. Prof., Univ. of Auckland, NZ, 1977. External Examr: Univ. of Rhodesia, 1967–70; Univ. of Khartoum, 1967–73, 1976–80; City Univ., 1968–74; Univ. of Surrey, 1974–76; Brunel Univ., 1980–85. Chm., London Welsh Assoc., 1987–90. JP Brent, 1979 (Dep. Chm., 1989–91). *Publications:* Homolytic Aromatic Substitution, 1960; Organic Chemistry: a conceptual approach, 1977; (Editor) Advances in Free-Radical Chemistry, Vol. I, 1965, Vol. II, 1967, Vol. III, 1969, Vol. IV, 1972, Vol. V, 1975, Vol. VI, 1980; numerous papers in Jl Chem. Soc. and other scientific jls. *Recreation:* music. *Address:* 4 Dovey Court, North Common, Bristol BS30 8YX. *T:* (0117) 907 9092. *Club:* Athenæum.

WILLIAMS, Prof. Gareth Lloyd; Professor of Educational Administration, Institute of Education, University of London, 1984–2001, now Emeritus; *b* 19 Oct. 1935; *s* of Lloyd and Katherine Enid Williams; *m* 1960, Elizabeth Ann Peck; two *s* one *d*. *Educ:* Creeting St Mary; Framlingham; Cambridge Univ. (MA). Res. Officer, Agricl Econs Res. Inst., Oxford Univ., 1959–62; Res. Fellow, OECD, Athens, 1962–64; Principal Administrator, OECD, Paris, 1964–68; Associate Dir, Higher Educn Res. Unit, LSE, 1968–73; Prof. of Educnl Planning, Univ. of Lancaster, 1973–84. Visiting Professor: Melbourne Univ., 1981–82; Coll. of Europe, 1994–. Specialist Adviser to Arts and Educn Sub-Cttee to House of Commons Cttee on Expenditure, 1972–76; Consultant to OECD, ILO, UNESCO, and World Bank. Member: Council, Policy Studies Inst., 1979–85; Governing Council for Soc. for Res. into Higher Educn, 1970– (Chm., 1978–80, 1986–88). Mem. Bd, Red Rose Radio PLC, 1981–92. FRSA 1982. *Publications:* (with Greenaway) Patterns of Change in Graduate Employment, 1973; (with Blackstone and Metcalf) The Academic Labour Market in Britain, 1974; Towards Lifelong Learning, 1978; (with Zabalza and Turnbull) The Economics of Teacher Supply, 1979; (with Woodhall) Independent Further Education, 1979; (with Blackstone) Response to Adversity, 1983; Higher Education in Ireland, 1985; (with Woodhall and O'Brien) Overseas Students and their Place of Study, 1986; Changing Patterns of Finance in Higher Education, 1992; The Enterprising University, 2004. *Address:* 11 Thornfield, Ashton Road, Lancaster LA1 5AG. *T:* (01524) 66002.

WILLIAMS, Sir Gareth R.; *see* Rhys Williams, Sir A. G. L. E.

WILLIAMS, Geoffrey; QC 2003; Senior Partner, Geoffrey Williams & Christopher Green, Solicitor Advocates, since 1998; *b* 29 April 1954; *s* of Trevor and Eunice Williams; partner, Kathy Wiley; two *s*. *Educ:* Jones' W Monmouth Grammar Sch., Pontypool; Trent Polytech., Nottingham (BA Hons Law); Coll. of Law, Chester (2nd cl. Hons Solicitors' Finals). Admitted solicitor, 1978; Partner, specialising in regulatory and disciplinary law, solicitors' firm, 1980–98. Higher Rights of Audience (Civil), 1997. *Recreations:* follows cricket, racing, Rugby, motoring, current affairs. *Address:* The Mews, 38 Cathedral Road, Cardiff CF11 9LL. *T:* (office) (029) 2034 3377, *Fax:* (office) (029) 2034 3388; *e-mail:* law@gwcg.globalnet.co.uk. *Clubs:* Royal Automobile; Pontypool Rugby Football; Cheltenham Racecourse, Newbury Racecourse.

WILLIAMS, Geoffrey Guy; Public Works Loan Commissioner, 1990–98; *b* 12 July 1930; *s* of late Captain Guy Williams, OBE, and Mrs Margaret Williams (*née* Thomas). *Educ:* Blundell's Sch.; Christ's Coll., Cambridge (MA, LLM). Slaughter and May, Solicitors, 1952–66, Partner 1961; Dir, J. Henry Schroder Wagg & Co. Ltd, 1966–90, Vice-Chm. 1974, Dep. Chm., 1977–90. Chm., National Film Finance Corp., 1976–85 (Dir, 1970). Director: Bass plc, 1971–91; Schroders plc, 1976–90; John Brown plc, 1977–85; Standard Chartered plc, 1990–94. Chm., Issuing Houses Assoc., 1979–81. *Recreations:* reading, theatre, cinema. *Address:* 18G Eaton Square, SW1W 9DD. *T:* (020) 7235 5212. *Club:* Brooks's.

WILLIAMS, (George Haigh) Graeme; QC 1983; barrister; a Recorder of the Crown Court, 1981–2002; *b* 5 July 1935; *s* of Dr Leslie Graeme Williams, MC, and Joan Haigh Williams (*née* Iago); *m* 1963, Anna Maureen Worrall, *qv*; two *d*. *Educ:* Tonbridge Sch. (Scholar); Brasenose Coll., Oxford (MA). Nat. Service, RA, England and Hong Kong, 1953–55. Called to the Bar, Inner Temple, 1959 (Entrance Scholar; Bencher, 1996). Hd of Chambers, 1988–98. Mem., No 3 Legal Aid Area Cttee, 1980–2000; Legal Pres., Mental Health Review Tribunals (Restricted Cases), 1996–2008. Legal Assessor, GMC and GDC, 1998–2007. *Publication:* Death of a Circuit, 2006. *Address:* 13 King's Bench Walk, Temple, EC4Y 7EN. *T:* (020) 7353 7204; King's Bench Chambers, 32 Beaumont Street, Oxford OX1 2NP. *T:* (01865) 311066. *Club:* Orford Sailing.

WILLIAMS, George Mervyn, CBE 1977; MC 1944; TD; Vice Lord-Lieutenant of Mid Glamorgan, 1986–94; *b* 30 Oct. 1918; *yr s* of late Owain Williams and late Mrs Williams; *m* 1st, 1940, Penelope (marr. diss. 1946), *d* of late Sir Frank Mitchell, KCVO; 2nd, 1950, Grizel Margaretta Cochrane, DStJ, *d* of late Major Walter Stewart, DSO; one *s*. *Educ:* Radley Coll. Served Royal Fusiliers, N Africa and Italy, 1939–46; Major, British Military Mission to Greece, 1945. Great Universal Stores, 1946–49; Christie-Tyler PLC: Sales Dir, 1949; Man. Dir, 1950–80; Chm., 1959–85; Director: Lloyds Bank plc, 1972–77; Lloyds Bank UK Management Ltd, 1975–85; Chm., S Wales Regl Bd, Lloyds Bank, 1977–87. Governor, United World Coll. of Atlantic, 1980–88. JP 1965–70, High Sheriff 1966, DL 1967–86, Glamorgan. CStJ. *Address:* Tretower House, Tretower, near Crickhowell, Powys NP8 1RF. *T:* (01874) 730953; Llanharan House, Llanharan, Mid Glamorgan CF72 9NR. *T:* (01443) 226253. *Clubs:* Brooks's; Cardiff and County (Cardiff).

WILLIAMS, Prof. Geraint Trefor, MD; FRCP, FRCPath, FMedSci; Professor of Pathology, Wales College of Medicine, Cardiff University, since 1991; *b* 10 Sept. 1949; *s* of late Rev. William Trefor Williams and of Eleanor Doris Williams (*née* Evans), Cefngorwydd; *m* 1974, Vivienne Elizabeth Jones; two *d*. *Educ:* Builth Wells Grammar Sch.; Univ. of Wales, Cardiff, and Welsh National Sch. of Medicine (BSc 1st cl. Hons Physiol. 1970; MB BCh Hons 1973; MD 1981). MRCP 1975, FRCP 1991; FRCPath 1991. Jun. med. appts, Univ. Hosp. of Wales, Cardiff, and Hammersmith and Brompton Hosps, London, 1973–76; Lectr in Pathology, St Bartholomew's Hosp. and St Mark's Hosp., London, 1976–79; Sen. Lectr, 1980–88, Reader, 1988–91, Univ. of Wales Coll. of Medicine; Admissions Sub-Dean, Cardiff Univ. Medical Sch., 2004–. Hon. Consultant Histopathologist, Cardiff and Vale NHS Trust, 1980–. Mem., Cttee on Carcinogenicity of Chemicals in Food, Consumer Products and the Envmt, DoH, 1993–2003; Chm., Welsh Scientific Adv. Cttee, Welsh Assembly Govt, 2000–04. Mem. Council, RCPath, 2004–07; Mem. Council, 1985–88, Vice Pres., 1999–2002, Assoc. of Clinical Pathologists; Chm., Pathology Sect., British Soc. of Gastroenterology, 1996–99; Member, Executive Committee: Pathological Soc. of GB and Ire., 1996–99; Europ. Soc. of Pathology, 1991–95; Councillor, 2004–06, Pres. elect, 2006–08, Pres., 2008–, British Div., Internat. Acad. of Pathology. FMedSci 2002. Hon. Mem. RCR, 2003. *Publications:* (jtly) Morson and Dawson's Gastrointestinal Pathology, 3rd edn 1990 to 4th edn 2003; (ed) Current Topics in Pathology: Gastrointestinal Pathology, 1990; (jtly) Tumors of the Intestines, 2003; numerous contribs to learned jls on gut pathology and carcinogenesis. *Recreations:* ornithology, photography, music, cat watching. *Address:* Department of Pathology, Wales College of Medicine, Cardiff University, Heath Park, Cardiff CF14 4XN. *T:* (029) 2074 5316, *Fax:* (029) 2074 2701; *e-mail:* WilliamsGT@cf.ac.uk.

WILLIAMS, Rev. Gethin A.; *see* Abraham-Williams.

WILLIAMS, Prof. Glynn Anthony, FRBS, FRCA; sculptor; Professor of Sculpture, since 1990, and Head, School of Fine Art, since 1995, Royal College of Art; *b* 30 March 1939; *s* of Idris Merion Williams and Muriel Elizabeth Purslow; *m* 1963 (marr. diss. 2001); two *d*. *Educ:* Wolverhampton Grammar Sch.; Wolverhampton Coll. of Art (NDD Sculpture Special Level); British Sch. in Rome (Rome Scholar). Head of Sculpture Departments: Leeds Coll. of Art, later Leeds Polytechnic, 1968–75; Wimbledon Sch. of Art, 1976–90. 24 one-man exhibns incl. retrospective, Margam Park, S Wales, 1992; numerous group exhibns incl. British Sculpture of 20th Century, Whitechapel Gall., 1981; rep. GB, Kotara Takamura Grand Prize Exhibn, Japan, 1984; work in collections: Arts Council of GB; Bottisham Village Coll., Cambridge; Bradford City Art Gall.; British Sch. in Rome; Grisedale Theatre in the Forest, Cumbria; Hakone Open Air Mus., Japan; Hampshire Sculpture Trust; Haroldwood Hosp., Essex; Hemel Hempstead Arts Trust; Henry Moore Centre for Sculpture, Leeds; Hove Mus. and Art Gall.; Hull City Art Gall.; Leeds City Council; Lincoln City Council; London Borough of Hounslow; Middlesbrough Council; Milton Keynes Develt Corp.; Nat. Portrait Gall.; Newport (Gwent) Educn Cttee; Northern Arts Assoc.; Peterborough Develt Corp.; Southern Arts Assoc.; Tate Gall.; V & A; Welsh Arts Council; Welsh Sculpture Trust; Wolverhampton Educn Cttee; Yorkshire Arts Assoc. Commissions: 14′ bronze meml to Henry Purcell, Flowering of the English Baroque, City of Westminster, 1995; Lloyd George Meml, Parliament Sq., 2007. FRCA 1991; FRBS 1992. FRSA 1996. Hon. Fellow, Wolverhampton Polytechnic, 1989. *Publications:* contribs to arts magazines, jls, TLS.

Recreations: cooking, crosswords, music. *Address:* c/o Bernard Jacobson Gallery, 6 Cork Street, W1S 3EE. *Club:* Chelsea Arts.

WILLIAMS, Gordon; *see* Williams, J. G.

WILLIAMS, Prof. Gordon, FRCS; Professor of Surgery, and Dean, St Paul's Millennium Medical School, Addis Ababa, since 2007; *b* 27 June 1945; *s* of Charles and Marjorie Williams; *m* 1st, 1968, Susan Gubbins (marr. diss. 1989); two *d*; 2nd, 1989, Clare Forbes (marr. diss. 2005). *Educ:* Bishop Vesey's Grammar Sch., Sutton Coldfield; University Coll. London (MB BS 1968). FRCS 1973; FRCSE *ad eundem* 2001; FRCSGlas *ad eundem* 2004. Consultant Urologist and the surgery of renal failure, Hammersmith Hosp., 1978–2007. Chairman: Specialist Adv. Cttee Urology, 2000–04; Jt Cttee of Higher Surgical Trng, 2003–07. Mem. numerous editl bds. King James IV Professor of Surgery, RCSE, 2005. Albert Schweitzer Internat. Teaching Award, Internat. Soc. of Urology, 2006; St Peter's Medal, British Assoc. of Urological Surgeons, 2008. *Publications:* Urological Oncology (with J. Waxman), 1991; contrib. 32 chapters in books and over 200 articles. *Recreations:* playing tennis badly, eating Indian food, helping the developing world provide surgical care to rural areas and with such poverty and deprivation trying to understand how there could possibly be a God. *Address:* St Paul's Hospital Medical School, St Paul's Hospital, PO Box 1271, Addis Ababa, Ethiopia.

WILLIAMS, Graeme; *see* Williams, George H. G.

WILLIAMS, Air Vice-Marshal Graham Charles, AFC 1970 and Bar 1975; FRAeS; Director, Lockheed Martin UK (formerly Loral International Inc., then Lockheed Martin International), 1993–2004; Commandant General, RAF Regiment and Director General of Security (RAF), 1990–91; *b* 4 June 1937; *s* of Charles Francis Williams and Molly (*née* Chapman); *m* 1962, Judith Teresa Ann Walker; one *s* one *d*. *Educ:* Marlborough College; RAF College, Cranwell. FRAeS 1984. 54 Sqn, 229 OCU, 8 Sqn, Empire Test Pilots' School, A Sqn, A&AEE, 1958–70; RAF Staff Coll., 1971; OC 3 Sqn, Wildenrath, 1972–74; Junior Directing Staff (Air), RCDS, 1975–77; OC RAF Brüggen, 1978–79; Group Captain Ops, HQ RAF Germany, 1980–82; CO Experimental Flying Dept, RAE, 1983; Comdt, Aeroplane and Armament Exptl Estabt, 1983–85; Dir, Operational Requirements, MoD, 1986; ACDS, Operational Requirements (Air), 1986–89. Harmon Internat. Trophy for Aviators, USA, 1970. *Recreations:* old cars, golf. *Address:* Aldgate House, Aldgate, Ketton, Stamford, Lincs PE9 3TD. *Club:* Royal Air Force.

WILLIAMS, Gwyneth; Director, English Networks and News, BBC World Service, since 2007; Editor, Reith Lectures, since 1999; *b* 14 July 1953; *d* of Prof. Owen Williams and Beryl Williams (*née* Harrett); *m* 1982, David Nissan; one *s* one *d*. *Educ:* St John's High Sch., Pietermaritzburg, Natal; St Hugh's Coll., Oxford (BA Hons PPE 1975; Dip. Soc. Anth. 1976). Current affairs talks writer, BBC Bush House, 1976; Res. Asst, ODI, 1977; BBC: Prod., The World Tonight, 1979; break from formal employment to be with children, 1984–89; Prod. and Ed., various progs on Radio 4 and Radio Five Live, 1989–94; Editor: Foreign Affairs Radio, 1994; Home Current Affairs, Bi-media, 1996; various special series and progs on Radio 4 and World Service; Hd, Radio Current Affairs, BBC News, 2004. Mem. Editl Bd, Political Qly, 1996–2004. *Publications:* Third World Political Organizations, 1981, 2nd edn 1987; (with Brian Hackland) The Contemporary Political Dictionary of Southern Africa, 1988. *Recreations:* reading, music. *Address:* (home) 13 King Henry's Road, NW3 3QP. *T:* (020) 7586 2748; (office) BBC, 320 Centre Block, Bush House, Strand, WC2B 4PH. *T:* (020) 7557 3822, *Fax:* (020) 7240 1104; *e-mail:* gwyneth.williams@bbc.co.uk.

WILLIAMS, Heather Jean; QC 2006; barrister; *b* 1963; *d* of Leonard Archibald Williams and Dorothy Jean Williams; *m* 1997, Trevor William Bragg; one *s* one *d*. *Educ:* King's Coll. London (LLB 1st cl. Hons 1984). Called to the Bar, Gray's Inn, 1985 (Scarman Scholarship 1985); in practice as a barrister, 1987–. Pt-time Judge (formerly Chm.), Employment Tribunals, 2005–. *Publication:* (jtly) Police Misconduct: legal remedies, 4th edn 2005. *Recreations:* supporting Portsmouth FC, playing with my children, reading, yoga, iPod listening. *Address:* Doughty Street Chambers, 10–11 Doughty Street, WC1N 29L. *T:* (020) 7404 1313, *Fax:* (020) 7404 2283/4; *e-mail:* h.williams@doughtystreet.co.uk.

WILLIAMS, Helen Elizabeth Webber, MA; Principal, RNIB New College, Worcester, 1995–2000; *b* 28 April 1938; *o d* of Alwyn and Eleanor Thomas; *m* 1962, Dr Peter Williams (marr. diss. 1974); one *s* one *d*. *Educ:* Redland High Sch., Bristol; Girton Coll., Cambridge (MA; DipEd). Assistant English Mistress: St Paul's Girls' Sch., 1962–63; St George's Sch., Edinburgh, 1963–64; Edinburgh University: Asst Lectr, Dept of English, 1964–67; Lectr in English and Dir of Studies, Faculty of Arts, 1967–78; Headmistress, Blackheath High Sch., 1978–89; High Mistress, St Paul's Girls' Sch., 1989–92; Trevelyan Fellow, Trevelyan Coll., Univ. of Durham, 1993; English teacher, The Brearley Sch., NY, 1993–94. Member: HMC, 1994–2000; Governing Body, SOAS, 1988–96; Council, City Univ., 1990–92; Governing Body, Stowe Sch., 1992–. *Publication:* (ed) T. S. Eliot: The Wasteland, 1968. *Recreations:* music, drama, cookery, gardening. *Address:* 4/2 Advocates Close, The Royal Mile, Edinburgh EH1 1PS.

WILLIAMS, Helen Mary, (Mrs D. M. Forrester), CB 2006; Director, School Curriculum and Pupil Well-Being, Department for Children, Schools and Families (formerly Department for Education and Skills), since 2006; *b* 30 June 1950; *d* of late Graham Myatt and of Mary (*née* Harrison); *m* 1st, 1975, Ian Vaughan Williams (marr. diss. 1982); 2nd, 1993, David Michael Forrester, *qv*; one *s* one *d*. *Educ:* Allerton High Sch., Leeds; St Hilda's Coll., Oxford (BA Hons Mod. Hist.). Joined DES, 1972; Private Sec. to Joan Lester and to Margaret Jackson, 1975–76; Asst Sec., DES, subseq. DFE, 1984–93; Under-Sec., then Dir, OST, Cabinet Office, subseq. DTI, 1993–98; Dir, Sch. Orgn and Funding, DFEE, subseq. DFES, 1999–2002; Department for Education and Skills: Dir, Primary Educn and e Learning, 2002–04; Co-Dir, Sch. Standards, 2004–06. *Recreations:* family life, walking, bell-ringing. *Address:* Department for Children, Schools and Families, Sanctuary Buildings, Great Smith Street, SW1P 3BT.

WILLIAMS, Ven. Henry Leslie; Archdeacon of Chester, 1975–88; *b* 26 Dec. 1919; *m* 1949, Elsie Marie (*d* 2002); one *s*. *Educ:* Bethesda County Sch.; St David's Coll., Lampeter (BA); St Michael's Coll., Llandaff. Deacon 1943, priest 1944, Bangor; Curate of Aberdovey, 1943–45; St Mary's, Bangor, 1945–48; Chaplain, HMS Conway, 1948–49; Curate, St Mary-without-the-Walls, Chester, 1949–53; Vicar of Barnston, Wirral, 1953–84. RD of Wirral North, 1967–75; Hon. Canon of Chester Cathedral, 1972–75. Mem., General Synod, 1978–80, 1985–88. CF (TA), 1953–62. *Recreations:* fly-fishing, grandparenthood. *Address:* 1 Bartholomew Way, Westminster Park, Chester CH4 7RJ. *T:* (01244) 675296.

WILLIAMS, (Henry) Nigel, FRSL; author and broadcaster; *b* 20 Jan. 1948; *s* of late David Ffrancon Williams and of Sylvia Margaret Williams (*née* Hartley); *m* 1973, Suzan Elizabeth Harrison; three *s*. *Educ:* Highgate Sch.; Oriel Coll., Oxford (MA Hist.). BBC: gen. trainee, 1969–73; Producer/Dir, Arts Dept, 1973–85; Editor: Bookmark, 1985–92; Omnibus, 1992–96; writer/presenter, 1997–2000. *Plays:* Class Enemy, Royal Court, 1978 (Most Promising Playwright Award, Plays and Players mag.); Sugar and Spice, Royal Court, 1980; Line 'Em, NT, 1980; Trial Run, Oxford Playhouse, 1980; My Brother's Keeper, Greenwich, 1985; Country Dancing, RSC, 1987; Lord of the Flies (adapted), RSC, 1996; *television plays* include: Charlie, 1980; Breaking Up, 1986; The Last Romantics, 1990; Skallagrig, 1994 (BAFTA Award); Dirty Tricks, 2000 (Internat. Emmy Award); Bertie and Elizabeth, 2002; Uncle Adolf, 2005; Elizabeth I, 2005 (Emmy Award for outstanding mini-series, 2006; Golden Globe Award for best mini-series, 2007); Footprints in the Snow, 2005; HR, 2006. FRSL 1994. *Publications:* (novels): My Life Closed Twice, 1978 (Somerset Maugham Award); Jack Be Nimble, 1980; Star Turn, 1985; Witchcraft, 1987; Black Magic, 1988; The Wimbledon Poisoner, 1990; They Came from SW19, 1992; East of Wimbledon, 1993; 2½ Men in a Boat, 1993; Scenes from a Poisoner's Life, 1994 (televised); From Wimbledon to Waco, 1995; Stalking Fiona, 1997; Fortysomething, 1999 (adapted for television, 2003); Hatchett and Lycett, 2002. *Recreations:* swimming, drinking, walking, talking, family, dogs. *Address:* 18 Holmbush Road, Putney, SW15 3LE.

WILLIAMS, Hilary a'Beckett E.; *see* Eccles-Williams.

WILLIAMS, Hugo Mordaunt; writer; *b* 20 Feb. 1942; *s* of late Hugh Williams, actor and playwright, and Margaret Vyner; *m* 1965, Hermine Demoriane; one *d*. *Educ:* Eton College. Asst Editor, London Magazine, 1961–70; Arts Editor, New Review, 1973–74; television critic, 1983–88, and poetry editor, 1984–93, New Statesman; theatre critic, The Sunday Correspondent, 1989–91; columnist, TLS, 1988–; film critic, Harpers & Queen, 1993–98. Henfield Writer's Fellowship, Univ. of East Anglia, 1981. Awards (for poetry): Eric Gregory, 1965; Cholmondeley, 1970; Geoffrey Faber Memorial Prize, 1979; Queen's Gold Medal for Poetry, 2004. *Publications: poems:* Symptoms of Loss, 1965; Sugar Daddy, 1970; Some Sweet Day, 1975; Love-Life, 1979; Writing Home, 1985; Selected Poems, 1989; Self-Portrait With A Slide, 1990; Dock Leaves, 1994; Billy's Rain (T. S. Eliot Prize), 1999; Collected Poems, 2002; Dear Room, 2006; *travel:* All the Time in the World, 1966; No Particular Place to Go, 1981; *journalism:* Freelancing, 1995; *edited:* Curtain Call, 101 Portraits in Verse, 2001; John Betjeman, Selected Poems, 2006. *Address:* 3 Raleigh Street, N1 8NW. *T:* (020) 7226 1655.

WILLIAMS, Hywel; MP (Plaid Cymru) Caernarfon, since 2001; *b* 14 May 1953; *s* of late Robert Williams and of Jennie Page Williams; *m* 1977, Sian Davies (marr. diss. 1998); three *d*. *Educ:* Ysgol Glan y Mor, Pwllheli, Gwynedd; UC Cardiff (BSc Hons Psychol. 1974); UCNW, Bangor (CQSW 1980). Approved Social Worker (Mental Health), 1984. Social Worker: Child Care and Long Term Team, Social Services Dept, Mid Glam CC, 1974–76; Mental Health Team, Social Services Dept, Gwynedd CC, 1976–78 and 1980–84; Welsh Office funded project worker, 1985–91, Hd of Centre, 1991–93, N and W Wales Practice Centre, UCNW, Bangor; freelance lectr, consultant and author in social work and social policy, 1994–2001. CCETSW Cymru: Mem. Welsh Cttee and Chm., Welsh Lang. Sub-cttee, 1989–92; Mem., Welsh Lang. Pubns Adv. Panel, 1992–93. *Publications:* (contrib.) Social Work in Action in the 1980s, 1985; (compiled and ed) A Social Work Vocabulary, 1988; (gen. ed.) Child Care Terms, 1993; (contrib. and gen ed.) Social Work and the Welsh Language, 1994; (compiled and ed) An Index of Trainers and Training, 1994; (contrib. and ed jtly) Gofal: a training and resource pack for community care in Wales, 1998; Speaking the Invisible, 2002. *Recreations:* walking, cinema, reading. *Address:* House of Commons, SW1A 0AA. *T:* (020) 7219 5021; 8 Stryd Y Castell, Caernarfon, Gwynedd LL15 1SE. *T:* (01286) 672076.

WILLIAMS, Prof. (James) Gordon, FRS 1994; FREng; Professor of Mechanical Engineering, Imperial College, London, 1990–2003, now Emeritus (Head, Department of Mechanical Engineering, 1990–2000); *b* 13 June 1938; *s* of John William and Eira Williams; *m* 1960, Ann Marie Joscelyne; two *s* one *d*. *Educ:* Imperial Coll. (BScEng, PhD, DScEng); FCGI; FREng (FEng 1982). RAE, Farnborough, 1956–61; Imperial College: Asst Lectr, 1962–64; Lectr, 1964–70; Reader, 1970–75; Prof. of Polymer Engrg, 1975–90. *Publications:* Stress Analysis of Polymers, 1973, 2nd edn 1981; Fracture Mechanics of Polymers, 1984. *Recreations:* gardening, mountains (walking and ski-ing), golf. *Address:* Mechanical Engineering Department, Imperial College London, Exhibition Road, South Kensington, SW7 2BX. *T:* (020) 7594 7200.

WILLIAMS, Jane; Executive Director for Further Education, Regeneration and Delivery (formerly Skills and Regeneration), Becta, (British Education Communications Technology Agency), since 2007; *b* 13 April 1953; *d* of John and Gwenllian Williams; *m* 1993, Robert Walker; one *s* one *d*. *Educ:* Univ. of Bristol (BA Hons); Univ. of Birmingham (Cert Ed). Teacher, Swanshurst Sch., 1975–78; Lectr, Bournville Coll., 1979–81; Sen. Lectr, Telford Coll., 1981–84; Principal Lectr, Accredited Training Centre, Telford, 1984–89; Asst Principal, Solihull Coll., 1989–92; Vice Principal, North Warwickshire Coll., Nuneaton, 1992–96; Principal: Wulfrun Coll., Wolverhampton, 1996–99; City of Wolverhampton Coll., 1999–2002; Dir, Teaching and Learning, and Head, Standards Unit, subseq. Dir, Improvement Gp, DFES, 2003–07. Chairman: Focus Housing Assoc., 2000–02; Wolverhampton Strategic Partnership, 2002. Mem. Bd, Ufi Ltd, 2008. FRSA 1999. Hon. DEd Wolverhampton, 2003. *Recreations:* music, travel. *Address:* Becta, Millburn Hill Road, Science Park, Coventry CV4 7JJ. *T:* (024) 7679 7300; *e-mail:* jane.williams@becta.org.uk.

WILLIAMS, (Jean) Adèle, (Mrs A. Patience); Her Honour Judge Williams; a Circuit Judge, since 2000; *b* 28 July 1950; *d* of David James Williams and Dorothy Williams; *m* 1975, Andrew Patience, *qv*; one *s* one *d*. *Educ:* Llanelli Girls' Grammar Sch.; University Coll. London (LLB). Called to the Bar, Gray's Inn, 1972; in practice on S Eastern Circuit, 1972–2000; a Recorder, 1995–2000. Sen., Kent Bar Mess, 1997–2000. *Recreations:* cinema, theatre, holidays, conversation. *Address:* Canterbury Crown Court, Chaucer Road, Canterbury, Kent CT1 1ZA. *T:* (01227) 819200.

WILLIAMS, Jennifer Mary, (Jenny); Commissioner and Chief Executive, Gambling Commission (formerly Gaming Board for Great Britain), since 2004; *b* 26 Sept. 1948; *d* of Baron Donaldson of Lymington, PC, and Dame (Dorothy) Mary Donaldson, GBE; *m* 1970, Michael Lodwig Williams, *qv*; three *s*. *Educ:* New Hall, Cambridge (BA 1970). Joined Home Office, 1973; Dir, PSA Privatisation and Strategy, DoE, 1990–93; Hd, Railways Privatisation and Regulation Directorate, Dept of Transport, 1993–97; Dir, Local Govt Finance Policy, DoE, later DETR, 1997–98; Dir, Company, later Business, Tax Div., Bd of Inland Revenue, 1998–2000; Dir Gen., Judicial Gp, and Sec. of Commns, LCD, 2001–03. Non-exec. Dir, Northumbrian Water Gp PLC, 2004–. Board Member: The Connection at St Martin's, 2004–; Nat. Campaign for the Arts, 2004–07. Non-exec. Dir, Morley Coll., 1993–2000. *Address:* 46 Durand Gardens, SW9 0PP.

WILLIAMS, John, AO 1987; OBE 1980; guitarist; *b* Melbourne, 24 April 1941. Studied with father, Segovia and at the Accademia Musicale Chigiana, Siena and RCM, London; since when has given recitals, concerts, and made TV and radio appearances worldwide. Artistic Dir, South Bank Summer Music, 1984 and 1985; Artistic Dir, Melbourne Arts Fest., 1987. Wide range of recordings with other musicians including Julian Bream, John Dankworth and Cleo Laine, NYJO, Itzhak Perlman, Inti Illimani, etc, and many orchestras. Hon. FRCM; Hon. FRNCM. *Recreations:* people, living, chess, table-tennis, music. *Address:* c/o Askonas Holt Ltd, Lincoln House, 300 High Holborn, WC1V 7JH.

WILLIAMS, John; Director, Communications, Foreign and Commonwealth Office, 2004; *b* 20 Feb. 1954; *s* of Roy and Barbara Williams; *m* 1976, Pamela Blackburn; two *s* one *d*. *Educ:* Sir Roger Manwood's Sch., Sandwich. Reporter: Chatham News, 1973–77; Birmingham Evening Mail, 1977–80; Industrial Corresp., 1980–85, Political Corresp., 1985–93, London Evening Standard; political columnist, Daily Mirror, 1993–98; Dep. Hd, News Dept, FCO, 1998–2000; Press Sec., FCO, 2000–04. *Publication:* Victory, 1997. *Recreations:* gardening, guitar, books, family, walking. *Address:* Cherry Trees, Fore Street, Weston, Hitchin, Herts SG4 7AS. *T:* (01462) 790536.

WILLIAMS, John, FRICS; Director, Aston Rose Chartered Surveyors, since 2000; *b* 18 March 1968; *s* of David and Chantal Williams. *Educ:* Epsom Coll.; Univ. of Reading (BSc Hons Est. Mgt 1990). ARICS 1992, FRICS 1998. Dir, Ernest Owers & Williams, 1986–2000. Royal Institution of Chartered Surveyors: Nat. Jun. Org. Cttee, 1988–2003, Chm., Nat. Jun. Org., 2000–01; Member: Gen. Council, 1999–2001; Internat. Governing Council, 2001–; Sen. Vice Pres., 2004–05. Lionheart: Steward, 1988–2000; Fundraising Cttee, 1989–2001; Trustee, 2000–07. Liveryman, Chartered Surveyors' Co., 2002– (Property, Advertising, Mktg and Design Awards Cttee (PAMADA), 2002–). *Recreations:* ski-ing, reading, film. *Address:* Aston Rose, 35c North Row, W1K 6DH. *T:* (020) 7629 1533, *Fax:* (020) 7409 0876; *e-mail:* johnwilliams@astonrose.co.uk.

WILLIAMS, (John Bucknall) Kingsley; solicitor, retired; *b* 28 July 1927; *s* of Charles Kingsley Williams and Margaret Elizabeth (*née* Bucknall); *m* 1st, 1961, Brenda (*née* Baldwin) (marr. diss. 2001); two *s*; 2nd, 2001, Eleanor Marion Yates. *Educ:* Kingswood Sch., Bath; Trinity Hall, Cambridge (MA, LLB). Partner, Dutton Gregory & Williams, Solicitors, Winchester, 1956–91. Chm., Wessex RHA, 1975–82. Member: Winchester City Council, 1966–73; Hampshire CC, 1973–75; Assoc. of County Councils, 1973–75. Chairman: Exec. Cttee, NHS Supply Council, 1980–82; Adv. Cttee, Wessex Inst. of Public Health Medicine, 1991–96. Chm. Council, Southampton Univ., 1987–98 (Mem., 1977–98); Chm. of Governors, Winchester Sch. of Art, 1986–96. DUniv Southampton, 1999. *Address:* Danesacre, Worthy Road, Winchester, Hants SO23 7AD. *T:* (01962) 852594.

WILLIAMS, John Charles, OBE 1997; PhD; FREng; Secretary and Chief Executive, Institution of Electrical Engineers, 1989–99; *b* 17 July 1938; *s* of Frank and Miriam Williams; *m* 1968, Susan Winifred Ellis; one *s* one *d*. *Educ:* High Wycombe Royal GS; Queen Mary Coll. (BScEng (1st Cl. Hons), 1960; PhD 1964; Fellow, 1995). Philips Research Labs, 1964–78; GEC Marconi Space and Defence Systems, Stanmore, 1978–80; GEC Central Res. Labs, Wembley, 1980–82; GEC Marconi Res. Centre, Gt Baddow, 1982–88. Freeman, City of London, 1996. FREng (FEng 1990). Hon. FIEE 2000. *Recreations:* traditional jazz, contract bridge, walking, tennis, gardening, listening to his family play classical music. *Address:* Beightons, Bassetts Lane, Little Baddow, Chelmsford, Essex CM3 4DA. *T:* (01245) 225092, *Fax:* (01245) 226314; *e-mail:* johnchaswilliams@btinternet.com.

WILLIAMS, Rt Rev. (John) Christopher (Richard); Bishop of The Arctic, 1991–2002; *b* 22 May 1936; *s* of Frank Harold and Ceridwen Roberts Williams; *m* 1964, Rona Macrae (*née* Aitken); one *s* one *d*. *Educ:* Manchester Grammar Sch.; Univ. of Manchester (BA Comm); Univ. of Durham, Cranmer Hall (DipTh). Ordained: deacon, Stretford, England, 1960; priest, Sugluk, PQ, 1962; Missionary, Diocese of The Arctic: Sugluk, PQ, 1961–72; Cape Dorset, NWT, 1972–75; Baker Lake, NWT, 1975–78; Archdeacon of The Keewatin, 1975–87; Rector, Yellowknife, NWT, 1978–87; Bp Suffragan, 1987–90, Coadjutor Bp, 1990, Dio. of The Arctic. Hon. DD: Emmanuel and St Chad Coll., Saskatoon, 1997; Wycliffe Coll., Toronto Univ. *Recreations:* stage and piano. *Address:* 4916–44th Street, Yellowknife, NT X1A 1J8, Canada.

WILLIAMS, John Eirwyn F.; *see* Ffowcs Williams.

WILLIAMS, Hon. Sir John G.; *see* Griffith Williams.

WILLIAMS, John Leighton; QC 1986; a Recorder of the Crown Court, since 1985; a Deputy High Court Judge, since 1995; *b* 15 Aug. 1941; *s* of Reginald John Williams and Beatrice Beynon; *m* 1969, Sally Elizabeth Williams; two *s*. *Educ:* Neath Boys' Grammar School; King's College London (LLB); Trinity Hall, Cambridge (MA). Called to the Bar, Gray's Inn, 1964, Bencher, 1994. Mem., Criminal Injuries Compensation Bd, 1987–2002. Mem. Council, Med. Protection Soc., 1998–2007. *Address:* Farrar's Building, Temple, EC4Y 7BD. *T:* (020) 7583 9241.

WILLIAMS, John Llewellyn, CBE 1999; FRCS, FRCSE, FDSRCS, FDSRCSE, FRCA; Consultant Oral and Maxillofacial Surgeon, St Richard's Hospital, Chichester, Worthing and Southlands Hospitals, Worthing and St Luke's Hospital, Guildford, 1973–2003, now Hon. Consultant Emeritus; Vice-President, Royal College of Surgeons of England, 1997–99; *b* 24 Jan. 1938; *s* of David John Williams and Anne Rosamund Williams (*née* White); *m* 1960, Gillian Joy Morgan; three *d*. *Educ:* Christ's Hosp.; Guy's Hosp. Med. Sch. (MB BS, BDS). FDSRCS 1966; FRCSE 1991; FRCS 1996; FRCA 2000; FDSRCSE *ad hominem* 2000. Registrar in Oral and Maxillofacial Surgery, Plymouth, 1970; Sen. Registrar, Westminster Hosp., UCH and Queen Mary's, Roehampton, 1970–73; Postgrad. Tutor, BMPF, 1973–95; Hon. Consultant: Queen Mary's, Roehampton, 1974–2003; King Edward VII Hosp., Midhurst, 1974–2006; Hon. Clinical Tutor, Guy's and St Thomas', subseq. Guy's, King's and St Thomas' Hosps' Med. and Dental Sch. of KCL, 1976–2003. Hon. Consultant to Army, Cambridge Hosp., 1992–. Chairman: Nat. Cttee of Enquiry into Perio-operative Deaths, 1998–2003; Cttee on Safety of Devices, Med. Devices Agency, DoH, 2001–. Dean, Faculty of Dental Surgery, RCS, 1996–99; Vice Chm., Acad. of Med. Royal Colls, 1998–2000; President: Eur. Assoc. for Cranio-Maxillofacial Surgery, 1998–2000; BAOMS, 2000; Internat. Assoc. of Oral and Maxillofacial Surgeons, 2005–07 (Pres.-elect, 2003–05); Chm., Oral and Maxillofacial Surgery Foundn, 2007–. Mem. Ct of Patrons, RCS, 2004–. Hon. Fellow, Amer. Assoc. Oral and Maxillofacial Surgeons, 1998. Evelyn Sprawson Prize, RCS, 1961; Down Surgical Prize, BAOMS, 1996; John Tomes Medallist, BDA, 1998; Colyer Gold Medallist, RCS, 2000. *Publications:* (with N. L. Rowe) Maxillofacial Injuries, Vols I and II, 1985, 2nd edn 1994; contribs to Brit. Dental Jl, RCS Annals. *Recreations:* gardening (garden open under Nat. Gardens Scheme), sailing (RYA Race Training Instructor). *Address:* Cookscroft, Bookers Lane, Earnley, Chichester, W Sussex PO20 7JG. *T:* (01243) 513671. *Clubs:* Oral Surgery of Great Britain; Hayling Island Sailing.

WILLIAMS, Prof. (John) Mark (Gruffydd), DSc; FBPsS; FBA 2008; Wellcome Principal Research Fellow, since 2003, and Professor of Clinical Psychology, since 2004, Department of Psychiatry, University of Oxford; Fellow of Linacre College, Oxford, since 2004; Director, Oxford Mindfulness Centre, since 2008; *b* 23 July 1952; *s* of John Howard Williams and Anna Barbara Mary Williams (*née* Wright); *m* 1973, Phyllis Patricia Simpson; one *s* two *d*. *Educ:* Stockton-on-Tees Grammar Sch.; St Peter's Coll., Oxford (BA 1973; MSc 1976; MA 1977; DPhil 1979; DSc 1998); E Anglian Ministerial Trng Course. FBPsS 1984. Lecturer in: Psychology, Magdalen Coll., Oxford, 1977–79; Applied Psychology, Univ. of Newcastle upon Tyne, 1979–82; Scientist, then Sen. Scientist, MRC Applied Psychol. Unit, Cambridge, 1983–91; University College of North Wales (Bangor) subseq. University of Wales, Bangor: Prof. of Clinical Psychology, 1991–97; Dir, Centre for Medical and Health Scis, subseq. Inst. for Med. and Social Care Res., 1997–2002; Pro Vice-Chancellor, 1997–2001. Member: Grants Cttee, Neuroscis Bd, MRC, 1992–96; Neuroscis & Mental Health Panel, Wellcome Trust, 1997–2001; Panel Mem. for Psychology, RAE 2001. Ordained deacon, Ely, 1989, priest 1990; Asst Curate (NSM), Girton, 1989–91; permission to officiate, dio. of Bangor, 1991–2003; Asst Curate (NSM), Wheatley, 2003–. Gov., NE Wales Inst. of Higher Educn, 1999–2001. FMedSci 2004. *Publications:* Psychological Treatment of Depression, 1983, 2nd edn 1992; (jtly) Cognitive Psychology and Emotional Disorders, 1988, 2nd edn 1997; (with F. Watts) The Psychology of Religious Knowing, 1988; (jtly) Cognitive Therapy and Clinical Practice, 1989; Cry of Pain: understanding suicide and self-harm, 1997; (with Z. Segal and J. D. Teasdale) Mindfulness-based Cognitive Therapy for Depression: a new approach to preventing relapse, 2002; Suicide and Attempted Suicide, 2002; (jtly) The Mindful Way Through Depression: freeing yourself from chronic unhappiness, 2007; papers in scientific jls on psychological models and treatment of depression and suicidal behaviour. *Recreation:* piano and organ playing. *Address:* Department of Psychiatry, University of Oxford, Warneford Hospital, Oxford OX3 7JX. *T:* (01865) 226445; *e-mail:* mark.williams@psych.ox.ac.uk.

WILLIAMS, John Melville; QC 1977; a Recorder, 1986–94; *b* 20 June 1931; *o s* of late Baron Francis-Williams and late Lady (Jessie Melville) Francis-Williams; *m* 1955, Jean Margaret (*d* 1995), *d* of Harold and Hilda Lucas, Huddersfield; three *s* one *d*. *Educ:* St Christopher Sch., Letchworth; St John's Coll., Cambridge (BA). Called to the Bar, Inner Temple, 1955, Bencher, 1985. A legal assessor to GMC (and formerly to GDC), 1983–2007; first Pres., Assoc. of Personal Injury Lawyers, 1990–94; Co-Chm., Internat. Practice Sect., Assoc. of Trial Lawyers of Amer., 1991–92; Mem., Indep. Review Body Under New Colliery Review Procedure, 1985. Member: Criminal Injuries Compensation Bd, 1998–2000; Criminal Injuries Compensation Appeals Panel, 2000–08. Chm., The ClaimRoom.com Ltd. Chm., Y2K Lawyers' Assoc., 1999. *Recreations:* mountain scrambling and walking, grandchildren and photography. *Address:* 9 Nanhurst Park, Cranleigh, Surrey GU6 8JX. *T:* (01483) 274846; *e-mail:* jmwqc@dial.pipex.com; Cnoclochan, Scourie, by Lairg, Sutherland IV27 4TE;

WILLIAMS, Very Rev. Monsignor John Noctor, CBE 1989; Prelate of Honour, 1985; Parish Priest, Our Lady and St John's, Heswall, 1993–2005; *b* 9 Aug. 1931; *s* of Thomas Williams and Anne Williams (*née* Noctor). *Educ:* St Anselm's Grammar School, Birkenhead; Ushaw College, Durham. Curate: St Laurence's, Birkenhead, 1956; St Joseph's, Sale, 1958; Sacred Heart, Moreton, 1958; Our Lady's, Birkenhead, 1959–66; Army, Chaplains' Dept, 1966–89: 7 Armd Bde, 1966; Singapore, 1969; 6 Armd Bde, 1971; UN, Cyprus, 1972; Senior Chaplain: Hong Kong, 1976; 1 Div., 1978; N Ireland, 1980; HQ BAOR, 1982; SE District, 1984; Prin. RC Chaplain, 1985–89, retd. VG 1986–89. *Recreations:* bridge, golf, motoring. *Club:* Conwy (Caernarvonshire) Golf.

WILLIAMS, John Peter Rhys, MBE 1977; FRCSEd; Consultant in Trauma and Orthopaedic Surgery, Princess of Wales Hospital, Bridgend, 1986–2004; *b* 2 March 1949; *s* of Peter Williams, MB, BCh and Margaret Williams, MB, BCh; *m* 1973, Priscilla Parkin, MB, BS, DObst, RCOG, DA; one *s* three *d*. *Educ:* Bridgend Grammar School; Millfield; St Mary's Hosp. Med. School. MB, BS London 1973; LRCP, MRCS, 1973; Primary FRCS 1976; FRCSEd 1980. University Hosp., Cardiff, Battle Hosp., Reading, St Mary's Hosp., London, 1973–78; Surgical Registrar, 1978–80, Orthopaedic Registrar, 1980–82, Cardiff Gp of Hosps; Sen. Orthopaedic Registrar, St Mary's Hosp., London, 1982–86. Played Rugby for Bridgend, 1967–68, 1976–79 (Captain, 1978–79), 1980–81, for London Welsh, 1968–76; 1st cap for Wales, 1969 (Captain, 1978); British Lions tours, 1971, 1974; a record 55 caps for Wales, to 1981; won Wimbledon Lawn Tennis Junior Championship, 1966. *Publications:* JPR (autobiog.), 1979; JPR: Given the Breaks - My Life in Rugby (autobiog.), 2006. *Recreations:* sport and music. *Address:* Llansannor Lodge, Llansannor, near Cowbridge, South Glamorgan CF71 7RX. *Club:* Lord's Taverners.

WILLIAMS, John Towner; composer of film scores; *b* 8 Feb. 1932. *Educ:* Juilliard Sch., NY. Conductor, Boston Pops Orchestra, 1980–. Hon. DMus: Berklee Coll. of Music, Boston, 1980; St Anselm Coll., Manchester, NH, 1981; Boston Conservatory of Music, 1982; Hon. DHL S Carolina, 1981; Hon. Dr of Fine Arts Northeastern Univ. (Boston), 1981; Hon. DMus: William Woods Coll., USA, 1982; Juilliard Sch., 2004. Awards include Oscars for: Fiddler on the Roof (filmscore arrangement), 1971; Jaws, 1976; Star Wars, 1978; E. T., 1983; Schindler's List, 1994; 14 Grammies, 2 Emmys and many other awards; 42 Academy Award nominations. Kennedy Center Honor, 2004. *Composer of film scores* including: The Secret Ways, 1961; Diamond Head, 1962; None but the Brave, 1965; How to Steal a Million, 1966; Valley of the Dolls, 1967; The Cowboys, 1972; The Poseidon Adventure, 1972; Tom Sawyer, 1973; Earthquake, 1974; The Towering Inferno, 1974; Jaws, 1975; Jaws 2, 1976; The Eiger Sanction, 1975; Family Plot, 1976; Midway, 1976; The Missouri Breaks, 1976; Black Sunday, 1977; Star Wars, 1977; Close Encounters of the 3rd Kind, 1977; The Fury, 1978; Superman, 1978; Dracula, 1979; The Empire Strikes Back, 1980; Raiders of the Lost Ark, 1981; E. T. (The Extra Terrestrial), 1982; Return of the Jedi, 1983; Indiana Jones and the Temple of Doom, 1984; Empire of the Sun, 1988; Indiana Jones and the Last Crusade, Born on the Fourth of July, 1989; Home Alone, 1990; Hook, JFK, 1991; Home Alone 2, Far and Away, 1992; Jurassic Park, 1993; Schindler's List, 1994; The Lost World, Seven Years in Tibet, 1997; Amistad, Saving Private Ryan, 1998; Star Wars, Episode I: The Phantom Menace, Angela's Ashes, 1999; The Patriot, 2000; AI, Harry Potter and the Philosopher's Stone, 2001; Star Wars, Episode II: Attack of the Clones, Minority Report, Harry Potter and the Chamber of Secrets, 2002; Catch Me if You Can, 2003; The Terminal, Harry Potter and the Prisoner of Azkaban, 2004; Star Wars, Episode III: Revenge of the Sith, War of the Worlds, 2005; Memoirs of a Geisha, 2006; many TV films. *Address:* c/o Breslauer and Rutman LLC, Suite 550, 11400 West Olympic Boulevard, Los Angeles, CA 90064–1551, USA.

WILLIAMS, Rev. Prof. John Tudno, PhD; Professor of Biblical Studies, 1973–2003, Principal, 1998–2003, United Theological College, Aberystwyth; Moderator of the General Assembly, Presbyterian Church of Wales, 2006–07 (Moderator of the Association in the South, 2002–03); *b* 31 Dec. 1938; *s* of late Rev. Arthur Tudno Williams and Primrose (*née* Hughes Parry); *m* 1964, Ina Lloyd-Evans; one *s* one *d*. *Educ:* Liverpool Inst. High School; Colfe's GS, Lewisham; Jesus Coll., Oxford (MA); UCW, Aberystwyth (PhD); United Theol Coll., Aberystwyth. Ordained as Welsh Presbyterian Minister, 1963; Minister in Borth, Cards, 1963–73; Part-time Lecturer: United Theol Coll., 1966–73; UCW (Religious Studies), 1976–87; Tutor responsible for Religious Studies, external degree through medium of Welsh, UCW, 1984–2003; Dean, Aberystwyth and Lampeter Sch. of Theology, 1985–87, 1994–97. Vis. Prof., Acadia Divinity Coll., Nova Scotia, 1997. Margaret and Ann Eilian Owen Fellow, Nat. Liby of Wales, 2001–; Hon. Res.

Fellow, Univ. of Wales Lampeter, 2003–. Moderator, Free Church Federal Council, 1990–91. Secretary: Theology Section, Univ. of Wales Guild of Graduates, 1967–2003; Bd of Educn Cttee, Gen. Assembly of Presbyterian Church of Wales, 1979–2000; Bd of Trustees, Davies Lecture, 1983– (Lectr, 1993). External examnr, QUB, Sheffield Univ., Univ. of Glos and Univ. of Wales, Bangor; examiner in religious studies and member of various educn cttees. Mem., Aberystwyth Town Council, 1979–87. Hon. DD Wales, 2006. *Publications:* Cewri'r Ffydd (Heroes of the Faith), 1974, 2nd edn 1979; Problem Dioddefaint a Llyfr Job (The Problem of Suffering and the Book of Job), 1980; Yr Epistol Cyntaf at y Corinthiaid (Commentary on I Corinthians), 1991; Y Llythyrau at y Galatiaid a'r Philipiaid (Commentary on the Letters to the Galatians and to the Philippians), 2001; contrib. to: Studia Biblica, 1978, Vol. ii 1980; C. H. Dodd, The Centenary Lectures, 1985; You Shall Be My Witnesses: festschrift for A. A. Trites, 2003; Protestant Nonconformity in the Twentieth Century, 2003; Ecumenical and Eclectic: festschrift for Alan Sell, 2007; articles in Welsh jls, Expository Times. *Recreations:* music (singing), Welsh language and culture. *Address:* Brynawel, Capel Seion, Aberystwyth SY23 4EF. *T:* (01970) 880489. *Club:* Penn.

WILLIAMS, Dr Jonathan Hugh Creer, FSA, FRHistS; Keeper, Department of Prehistory and Europe, British Museum, since 2007; *b* 19 Aug. 1967; *s* of Hugh and Ann Williams; *m* 2001, Konstanze Scharring; one *d. Educ:* Birkenhead Sch.; University Coll., Oxford (MA Classics); St Hugh's Coll., Oxford (DPhil Ancient Hist. 1994). Lectr in Ancient Hist., St Anne's Coll., Oxford, 1992–93; Curator, Iron Age and Roman Coins, 1993–2005, Internat. Policy Manager, 2006–07, British Mus. Hon. Res. Fellow, Sch. of Hist. and Archaeol., Univ. of Cardiff, 2006–. Mem. Bd, ICOM UK, 2007–. Sec., Royal Numismatic Soc., 2001–05. FRHistS 2005; FSA 2007. *Publications:* (ed jtly) Money, A History, 1997, 2nd edn 2007; (with C. Cheesman) Rebels, Pretenders and Imposters, 2000; Beyond the Rubicon: Gauls and Romans in Republican Italy, 2001; articles on ancient hist. and coins in learned jls. *Address:* Department of Prehistory and Europe, British Museum, Great Russell Street, WC1B 3DG; *e-mail:* jwilliams@thebritishmuseum.ac.uk.

WILLIAMS, Jonathan R.; *see* Rees-Williams.

WILLIAMS, Dame Josephine, DBE 2007 (CBE 2000); Chief Executive, Royal Mencap Society, 2002–08; *b* 8 July 1948; *d* of Frank Heald and Catherine Heald; *m* 1980, Robert Williams; two step *s. Educ:* Univ. of Keele (BA Hons Sociol. and Soc. Studies 1970; Dip. Applied Soc. Work 1971). Social Services in North West, for 20 yrs; Director Social Services: Wigan MBC, 1992–97; Cheshire CC, 1997–2002. Pres., Assoc. of Dirs of Social Services, 1999–2000. *Recreations:* running, tennis, ballet, travel, cooking for family and friends.

WILLIAMS, Dame Judi; *see* Dench, Dame J. O.

WILLIAMS, Juliet Susan Durrant; Chairman, National Forum Regional Studio Partnerships, since 2006; Founder Director, Strategic Management Resources Ltd, since 1991; *b* 17 April 1943; *d* of Robert Noel Williams and Frances Alice Williams (*née* Durrant). *Educ:* Cheltenham Ladies' Coll.; Bedford Coll., Univ. of London (BSc Hons Geog. with Econs); Hughes Hall, Cambridge (PGCE (Dist.)). Commng Ed., Macmillan, 1966–68; Ed., Geographical Mag., 1968–73; Marketing Dir and Gen. Manager, Readers' Union, 1973–78; CEO, Marshall Cavendish Mail Order, 1978–82; Man. Dir, Brann Direct Marketing, 1983–89; CEO, Marketing Communications Div., BIS Gp, 1985–91; Chairman: Alden Gp Ltd, 1993–2007; Waddie & Co., Edinburgh, 1996–99. Chm., SW RDA, 2002–08; Dir, VisitBritain, 2005–. Non-exec. Dir, Oxfam, 1984–90. Mem., Industrial Develt Adv. Bd, DTI, 2003–May 2009. FRGS 1968. DUniv Oxford Brookes, 2005. *Publications:* papers and articles in jls, magazines and newspapers. *Recreations:* writing, sport (esp. sailing, motorsport, Welsh Rugby), the sea, the countryside, walking, gundogs. *Address:* PO Box 54, Newton Abbot, Devon TQ12 5AP. *T:* (01626) 361655, *Fax:* (01626) 361936; *e-mail:* juliet@strategic-management-resources.co.uk.

WILLIAMS, Kathryn Jean; *see* Wade, K. J.

WILLIAMS, Katrina Jane; Director, Food and Farming (formerly Transmissable Spongiform Encephalopathies), Department for Environment, Food and Rural Affairs, since 2006; *b* 30 July 1962; *d* of Ian Clive Williams and June Elizabeth Williams (*née* Dedman); *m* 2005, Paul Allen Green. *Educ:* Cheadle Hulme Sch.; Lady Margaret Hall, Oxford (BA Hons English Lang. and Lit.). MAFF, London, 1983–93; First Sec. (Agriculture), UK Perm. Representation to EU, 1993–96; Hd of Br., EU Div., MAFF, 1996–98; Principal Private Sec. to Minister of Agriculture, Fisheries and Food, 1998–99; Counsellor (Agric., Fisheries and Food), UK Perm. Repn to EU, Brussels, 1999–2003; Dep. Hd, Eur. Secretariat, Cabinet Office, 2003–06. Hon. Nat. Chm., Civil Service Retirement Fellowship, 2004–. *Address:* Department for Environment, Food and Rural Affairs, 1A Page Street, SW1P 4PQ. *T:* (020) 7904 6089.

WILLIAMS, Keith Ronald, RIBA; architect; Design Director and Founder, Keith Williams Architects, since 2001; *b* 21 April 1958; *s* of Ronald Albert Williams and Sheila Lillian Grace Williams (*née* Dobson); *m* 2002, Vanessa Lillian Shrimpton. *Educ:* Kingston Grammar Sch.; Kingston Sch. of Architecture (BA Hons 1979); Greenwich Sch. of Architecture (DipArch Hons 1982). RIBA 1983; MRIAI 2004. Sheppard Robson, 1984–85; Terry Farrell & Partners, 1985–87; Partner, Pawson Williams Architects, 1987–2000. Major works include: Earth Galls Masterplan, Natural Hist. Mus., London, 1995–96; remodelling of Birmingham Repertory Th., 1996–99; Athlone Civic Centre, Co. Westmeath, Ire., 2001–04; Unicorn Th., London, 2001–05; The Long House, St John's Wood, London, 2001–06; Clones Liby and County HQ, Co. Westmeath, 2004–08; new Wexford Opera House, 2005–; new Marlowe Th., Canterbury, 2007–; Chichester District Mus., 2007–. FRSA 2005. Richmond Soc. Award, 2004; RIAI Awards, 2005, 2006, 2007; RIBA Awards, 2005, 2006, 2008; OPUS Arch. and Construction Award, Bank of Ireland, 2005; Irish Concrete Soc. Award, 2005; Public Bldg Architect of the Yr, BD, 2006; AIA Award, 2006; Chicago Athenaeum Prize, 2006; Merit Award, US Inst. for Th. Technol., 2007; Copper in Arch. Award, 2008. *Publications:* numerous internat. and nat. articles, etc. *Recreations:* running, ski-ing, sailing, opera, travel, art, food. *Address:* Keith Williams Architects, 17–21 Emerald Street, WC1N 3QN. *T:* (020) 7841 5810, *Fax:* (020) 7841 5811; *e-mail:* studio@keithwilliamsarchitects.com.

WILLIAMS, Kenneth Robert, CVO 2003; CBE 2002; QPM 1992; HM Inspector of Constabulary, North of England and Northern Ireland, 2002–April 2009; *b* 28 April 1944; *s* of Sydney Williams and Margaret Elizabeth Williams (*née* Howell); *m* 1969, Jean Margaret Ballantyne; two *d. Educ:* Wellacre Sch., Flixton; BA Soc. Scis Open Univ. Greater Manchester Police: Constable, Salford S Div., Salford City Police, 1963–68; Sergeant, N Manchester Div., 1968–72; Patrol Inspector, Salford Div., 1973–74; Inspector, then Chief Inspector, HQ, 1974–76; Sub-Divl Comd, Bolton Div., 1976–78; N Manchester Div., 1978–79; directing staff, Police Staff Coll., Bramshill, 1979–81; Greater Manchester Police: Sub-Divisional Command: Manchester Central Div., 1981; Manchester Internat. Airport, 1981–84; Departmental Command: Computer Project Branch HQ, 1984–85; Ops Support Branch HQ, 1985–86; Divl Comd, N Manchester, 1986–87; Sen. Comd course, Police Staff Coll., Bramshill, 1987; Asst Chief Constable, Greater Manchester Police, 1987–90; Dep. Chief Constable, Durham Constabulary, 1990–93; Chief Constable, Norfolk Constabulary, 1993–2002. *Recreations:* swimming, walking, reading, music. *Address:* (until April 2009) HM Inspectorate of Constabulary, Unit 2, Wakefield Office Village, Fryers Way, Silkwood Park, Wakefield WF5 9TJ. *T:* (01924) 237700, *Fax:* (01924) 237705.

WILLIAMS, Kingsley; *see* Williams, J. B. K.

WILLIAMS, Kirsty; *see* Williams, V. K.

WILLIAMS, Laurence Glynn, CEng, FREng, FIMechE, FINucE; Chief Engineer and Director, Nuclear Safety, Security and Environment (formerly Nuclear Safety and Security), Nuclear Decommissioning Authority, 2005–08; *b* 14 March 1946; *s* of Hugh Williams and Ruby Williams (*née* Lawrence); *m* 1976, Lorna Susan Rance (marr. diss. 1997); one *s* one *d. Educ:* Liverpool Poly. (BSc Hons Mech. Engrg); Univ. of Aston in Birmingham (MSc Nuclear Reactor Technol. 1972). CEng 1976; FIMechE 1991; FINucE 1998; FREng 2004. Design engr, Nuclear Power Gp, 1970–71; nuclear engr, CEGB, 1973–76; Health and Safety Executive: Nuclear Installations Inspectorate: Inspector, 1976–78; Principal Inspector, 1978–86; Superintending Inspector, 1986–91; Dep. Chief Inspector, 1991–96; Div. Head, Safety Policy Directorate, 1996–98; HM Chief Inspector of Nuclear Installations and Dir, Nuclear Safety Directorate, 1998–2005. Member: Defence Nuclear Safety Cttee, 2006–; Civil Nuclear Police Authy, 2007–08. Chm., UN/IAEA Commn on Safety Standards, 2000–05; Pres., UN Jt Convention on Safety of Spent Fuel and Radioactive Waste Mgt, 2003–06; Advr on Nuclear Safety, EBRD, 1996–. Chm., Internat. Nuclear Regulators' Assoc., 1999–2001. *Recreations:* cycling, keeping fit, music, theatre, supporting Liverpool Football Club. *Address: e-mail:* laurence776williams@btinternet.com.

WILLIAMS, Sir Lawrence (Hugh), 9th Bt *cr* 1798, of Bodelwyddan, Flintshire; farmer; *b* 25 Aug. 1929; *s* of Col Lawrence Williams, OBE, DL (*d* 1958) (*gs* of 1st Bt), and his 2nd wife, Elinor Henrietta (*d* 1980), *d* of Sir William Williams, 4th Bt of Bodelwyddan; *S* half-brother, 1995; *m* 1952, Sara Margaret Helen, 3rd *d* of Sir Harry Platt, 1st Bt; two *d. Educ:* Royal Naval Coll., Dartmouth. Commnd Royal Marines, 1947; served Korea 1951, Cyprus 1955, Near East 1956; Captain, 1959, retired 1964. Chm., Parciau Caravans Ltd, 1964–. Underwriting Mem., Lloyds, 1977–96. Lieut Comdr, RNXS, 1965–87. High Sheriff, Anglesey, 1970. *Recreations:* enjoying all aspects of country life, gentle sailing. *Heir:* none. *Address:* Old Parciau, Marianglas, Anglesey LL73 8PH. *Clubs:* Army and Navy; Royal Naval Sailing Association.

See also Baron Suffield.

WILLIAMS, Lyn; *see* Williams, D. W.

WILLIAMS, Marjorie Eileen, CB 2005; Tax Expert, International Monetary Fund, since 2006; *b* 18 Dec. 1946; *d* of Leslie Vernon Cuttle and Mary Fleming Cuttle (*née* Howie); *m* 1970, Graham Terence Williams. *Educ:* Reading Univ. (BSc Hons Geog. with Geol. 1968); Centre for W African Studies, Birmingham Univ. (postgrad. studies). Joined Inland Revenue, 1972; Regl Dir, SW Reg., 1994–96; Dir, Large Business Office, 1996–2000, Capital and Savings Tax Policy, 2000–03; Dir, Local Services, Bd of Inland Revenue, subseq. HM Revenue and Customs, 2003–06. *Publication:* Birdwatching in Lesbos, 1992. *Recreations:* birdwatching, gardening, Romanian needlework. *Address: e-mail:* Marjorie@gandmwilliams.plus.com.

WILLIAMS, Mark; *see* Williams, J. M. G.

WILLIAMS, Mark Fraser; MP (Lib Dem) Ceredigion, since 2005; *b* 24 March 1966; *s* of Ronald and Pauline Williams; *m* 1997, Helen Refna Wyatt; one *s* three *d. Educ:* University Coll. of Wales, Aberystwyth (BSc Econ 1987); Rolle Faculty of Educn, Univ. of Plymouth (PGCE 1993). Res. Asst to Lib, then Lib Dem, Peers and Asst to Geraint Howells, MP, 1987–92; Teacher: Madron Daniel Sch., Penzance, 1993–96; Forches Cross Sch., Barnstaple, 1997–2000; Dep. Hd, Llangors Sch., Brecon, 2000–05. Lib Dem spokesman on schools, 2005–06, on Wales, 2005–. Contested (Lib Dem): Monmouth, 1997; Ceredigion, Feb. 2000, 2001. Pres., Ceredigion Lib Dems, 1999–2000. *Recreations:* gardening, reading, biographies, walking. *Address:* 32 North Parade, Aberystwyth, Ceredigion SY23 2NF. *T:* (01970) 615880; *e-mail:* williamsmf@parliament.uk.

WILLIAMS, Martin John, CVO 1983; OBE 1979; HM Diplomatic Service, retired; High Commissioner, New Zealand, Governor (non-resident) of Pitcairn, Henderson, Ducie and Oeno Islands, and High Commissioner (non-resident), Samoa, 1998–2001; *b* 3 Nov. 1941; *s* of John Henry Stroud Williams and Barbara (*née* Benington); *m* 1964, Susan Dent; two *s. Educ:* Manchester Grammar Sch.; Corpus Christi Coll., Oxford (BA). Joined Commonwealth Relations Office, 1963; Private Sec. to Permanent Under Secretary, 1964; Manila, 1966; Milan, 1970; Civil Service College, 1972; FCO, 1973; Tehran, 1977; FCO, 1980; New Delhi, 1982; Rome, 1986; Hd of S Asian Dept, FCO, 1990; on secondment to NI Office as Asst Under-Sec. of State (Political), Belfast, 1993; High Comr, Zimbabwe, 1995–98. UK Consultant to NZ Antarctic Heritage Trust, 2002–; Chm., NZ-UK Link Foundn, 2004–. *Recreations:* music, gardening. *Address:* Russet House, Lughorse Lane, Yalding, Kent ME18 6EG. *Clubs:* Royal Commonwealth Society, Royal Over-Seas League.

WILLIAMS, Sir Max; *see* Williams, Sir W. M. H.

WILLIAMS, Prof. Michael, FBA 1989; Professor of Geography, 1996–2002, Fellow of Oriel College, 1993–2002 (Vice Provost, 2000–02), now Emeritus and Distinguished Research Associate, and Lecturer, St Anne's College, 1978–2002, University of Oxford; *b* 24 June 1935; *s* of Benjamin Williams and Ethel (*née* Marshell); *m* 1955, Eleanore Lerch; two *d. Educ:* Emmanuel Grammar Sch.; Dynevor Grammar Sch., Swansea; Swansea UC (BA 1956; PhD 1960; DLitt 1991); St Catharine's Coll., Cambridge (DipEd 1960). Deptl Demonstrator in Geography, Swansea, 1957–60; University of Adelaide: Lectr in Geog., 1960–66; Sen. Lectr, 1966–69; Reader, 1970–77; Oxford University: Lectr in Geog., 1978–89; Reader, 1990–96; Dir, MSc course, Envmtl Change Unit, 1994–98; Sir Walter Ralegh Fellow, Oriel Coll., 1993–2002. Visiting Professor: Univ. of Wisconsin-Madison, 1973 and 1994; Univ. of Chicago, 1989; UCLA, 1994; Vis. Lectr, UCL, 1966, 1973. Mem., State Commn on Uniform Regl Boundaries, SA, 1974–75; Chm., Histl Geog. Res. Gp, Inst. of British Geographers, 1983–86; Sec., Inst. of Aust. Geographers, 1969–72; Pres., SA Br., RGS, 1975–76 (Ed. of Procs, 1962–70). Mem. Council, British Acad., 1993–96 (Chm., Sect. N, Geog. and Social Anthropology, 1994–97). Editor: Trans of Inst. of British Geographers, 1983–88; Progress in Human Geography, 1991–2001; Global Environmental Change, 1993–97. John Lewis Gold Medal, RGS, SA, 1979; Lit. Prize, Adelaide Fest. of Arts, 1976; Hidy Award, 1987, Weyerhaeuser Prize, 1990 and 2004, Forest Hist. Soc., Durham, NC (Hon. Fellow, 1990); Meridian Award, Assoc. of American Geog., 2004. *Publications:* South Australia from the Air, 1969; The Draining of the Somerset Levels, 1970; The Making of the South Australian Landscape, 1974; (ed jtly) Australian Space, Australian Time, 1975; The Changing Rural Landscape of South

Australia, 1977, 2nd edn 1992; Americans and their Forests, 1989; (ed) Wetlands: a threatened landscape, 1991; (ed) Planet Management, 1992; (ed jtly) The Relations of History and Geography, 2002; Deforesting the Earth: prehistory to global crisis, 2003, 2nd edn 2006; (ed jtly) A Century of British Geography, 2003; edited vols of essays; contribs to geogl and histl jls. *Recreations:* walking, music. *Address:* Westgates, Vernon Avenue, Harcourt Hill, Oxford OX2 9AU. *T:* (01865) 243725.

WILLIAMS, Dr Michael Charles; United Nations Special Co-ordinator for Lebanon, since 2008; *b* 11 June 1949; *s* of Emlyn Glyndwr Williams and Mildred May Williams (*née* Morgan); *m* 1st, 1974, Margaret Rigby (marr. diss. 1984); one *d*; 2nd, 1992, Isobelle Jaques; one *s*. *Educ:* UCL (BSc (Internat. Relns) 1971); SOAS, London (MSc (Politics) 1973; PhD (Politics) 1984). Researcher, Amnesty Internat., 1977–78; Lectr in Politics, UEA, 1978–80; Hd, Asia Res., Amnesty Internat., 1980–84; Sen. Commentator/Ed., E Asia, BBC World Service, 1984–92; Director: of Human Rights, UN Mission to Cambodia, 1992–93; of Inf., UN Mission to Former Yugoslavia, 1993–95; Sen. Fellow, IISS, 1996–98; Dir, Office for Children and Armed Conflict, UN, NY, 1998–99; Special Advr to Sec. of State for Foreign Affairs, 2000–05; Dir, ME and Asia, 2005–06, and Asst Sec.-Gen. and Special Advr on the Middle East, 2006–07, UN, NY; UK Special Rep. on Middle East and Special Projects, FCO, 2007–08. Consultant, UNHCR, 1998–. Sen. Fellow, 21st Century Trust, 2000–. Member: RIIA, 1978–; IISS, 1990–. Mem., Exec. Cttee and Council, Chatham House, 2000–06. *Publications:* Communism, Religion and Revolt in Banten, West Java, 1990; Vietnam at the Crossroads, 1992; Civil Military Relations and Peacekeeping, 1998. *Recreations:* reading, travel, history and politics of Southeast Asia, military history, food and wine. *Address:* Oakes House, The Crescent, Steyning, W Sussex BN44 3GD; *e-mail:* drmcwilliams@gmail.com.

WILLIAMS, Rev. Canon Michael Joseph; Vicar of Bolton, 1999–2007, and Priest-in-charge, St Philip, Bolton le Moors, 2004–07; *b* 26 Feb. 1942; *s* of James and Edith Williams; *m* 1971, Mary Miranda Bayley; one *s* one *d*. *Educ:* St John's College, Durham (BA in Philosophy 1968). Apprentice Mechanical Engineer, then Engineer, with W & T Avery, Birmingham, 1958–63 (HNC in Mech. Eng 1962). Deacon 1970, priest 1971; Curate, then Team Vicar, St Philemon, Toxteth, 1970–78; Director of Pastoral Studies, St John's Coll., Durham, 1978–88; Principal, Northern Ordination Course, 1989–99; Area Dean, Bolton, 2001–05. Hon. Tutor in Pastoral Theology, Univ. of Manchester, 1990–2000. Hon. Canon: Liverpool Cathedral, 1992–99; Manchester Cathedral, 2000–07, now Canon Emeritus. Part-time Lectr, Liverpool Hope Univ., 2007–. Chaplain, Bolton Normandy Veterans Assoc., 2004–; Hon. Mem., Bolton Royal Artillery Assoc., 2008–. Pres., Northern Fedn for Trng in Ministry, 1991–93. *Publication:* The Power and the Kingdom, 1989. *Address:* 51 Cotswold Drive, Horwich, Bolton BL6 7DE.

WILLIAMS, Michael Lodwig, CB 2003; economics consultant, since 2003; Chief Executive, UK Debt Management Office, 1998–2003; *b* 22 Jan. 1948; *s* of John and Eileen Williams; *m* 1970, Jennifer Mary Donaldson (*see* J. M. Williams); three *s*. *Educ:* Wycliffe Coll., Stonehouse, Glos; Trinity Hall, Cambridge (BA 1969; MA); Nuffield Coll., Oxford. Min. of Finance, Lusaka, Zambia, 1969–71; HM Treasury, 1973–2003: on secondment to Price Waterhouse, 1980–81; Under Sec., then Dep. Dir, Industry, 1992–98. Non-exec. Dir, Euroclear UK and Ireland Ltd (formerly CRESTCo Ltd), 1998–2002, 2004–. *T:* (020) 7735 8694; *e-mail:* mike.williams@mj-w.net.

WILLIAMS, Prof. Michael Maurice Rudolph; consultant engineer; Professor of Nuclear Engineering, University of Michigan, 1987–89; Professor of Nuclear Engineering, 1970–86, now Emeritus, and Head of Department, 1980–86, Queen Mary College, London University; *b* 1 Dec. 1935; *s* of late M. F. Williams, RAFVR and G. M. A. Williams (*née* Redington); *m* 1958, Ann Doreen Betty; one *s* one *d*. *Educ:* Ewell Castle Sch.; Croydon Polytechnic; King's Coll., London; Queen Mary Coll., London. BSc, PhD, DSc; CEng; FINucE (Vice-Pres., 1971–73); CPhys, FInstP. Asst Experimental Officer, AWRE, Fort Halstead, 1954–55; Engr with Central Electricity Generating Board, 1962; Research Associate at Brookhaven Nat. Lab., USA, 1962–63; Lectr, Dept of Physics, Univ. of Birmingham, 1963–65; Reader in Nuclear Engrg, 1965–70, Dir, Nuclear Reactor, 1980–83, QMC, London Univ.; Prin. Scientist, Electrowatt Engrg Services (UK) Ltd, 1989–95. Vis. Prof., Imperial Coll., London, 2002–. Augustin-Frigon Lecture, École Polytechnique de Montréal, 2001. Mem., Adv. Cttee on Safety of Nuclear Installations, 1983–86. UN Advr on Engrg Educn in Argentina, 1979–89. Mem., Electrical Engrg Coll., EPSRC, 1995–97. Chm. of Governors, Ewell Castle Sch., 1976–79; Mem., Academic Bd, RNC, Greenwich, 1975–86. Exec. Editor, Annals of Nuclear Energy. Fellow American Nuclear Soc. (Arthur Holly Compton Award, 1994). Eugene P. Wigner Award, Amer. Nuclear Soc., 2000. *Publications:* The Slowing Down and Thermalization of Neutrons, 1966; Mathematical Methods in Particle Transport Theory, 1971; Random Processes in Nuclear Reactors, 1974; Aerosol Science, 1991; contribs to Proc. Camb. Phil. Soc., Nucl. Science and Engrg, Jl Nuclear Energy, Jl Physics. *Address:* 2A Lytchgate Close, South Croydon, Surrey CR2 0DX.

WILLIAMS, Sir Michael Osmond; *see* Williams, Sir Osmond.

WILLIAMS, Michael Roger; Director, Personal Tax and Welfare Reform, HM Treasury, since 2008; *b* 2 July 1957; *s* of Roger Williams and Margaret Laura Williams (*née* Dawes). *Educ:* Bradford Grammar Sch.; Balliol Coll., Oxford (MA Physics 1978). Entered Inland Revenue, 1978: various tax inspector posts, 1978–93; Principal Inspector, Large Business Office, 1993–97; Asst Dir, Company Tax, then Personal Tax, 1997–99; Hd, Social Security Team, HM Treasury, 1999–2001; Dep. Dir, Internat., IR, 2001–04; Dir, Internat. Tax, HM Treasury, 2004–07. *Recreations:* visiting France, reading, ice skating, going to the gym. *Address:* HM Treasury, 1 Horse Guards Road, SW1A 2HQ. *T:* (020) 7270 5000; *e-mail:* mike.williams@hm-treasury.x.gsi.gov.uk.

WILLIAMS, Nicholas James Donald; *b* 21 Oct. 1925; *s* of late Nicholas Thomas Williams and Daisy Eustace (*née* Hollow); *m* 1st, 1947, Dawn Vyvyan (*née* Hill); one *s* one *d*; 2nd, 1955, Sheila Mary (*née* Dalgety) (decd); two *s* one *d*; 3rd, Betty Edwards (*née* Danby). *Educ:* St Erbyn's Sch., Penzance; Rugby Sch. (Scholar). Admitted Solicitor 1949. Served Royal Marines, 1943–47 (Captain). Partner, Nicholas Williams & Co., Solicitors, London, 1950; Senior Partner, Surridge & Beecheno, Solicitors, Karachi, 1955; Burmah Oil Co. Ltd: Legal Adviser, 1961; Co-ordinator for Eastern ops, 1963; Dir, 1965; Asst Man. Dir, 1967; Man. Dir and Chief Exec., 1969–75; Man. Dir and Chief Exec., Don Engineering, 1977–84. Director: Flarebay Ltd, 1978–85; EBC Gp PLC, 1986–90; Ranvet Ltd, 1986–92. *Recreation:* sailing. *Club:* Royal Ocean Racing.

WILLIAMS, Nicholas Michael Heathcote; QC 2006; a Recorder, since 2000; *b* 5 Nov. 1954; *s* of Sir Edgar Trevor Williams, CB, CBE, DSO, and Gillian Williams (*née* Gambier-Parry); *m* 1987, Corinna Mary Mitchell; two *s* one *d*. *Educ:* St Catharine's Coll., Cambridge (Briggs Scholar; BA 1975); RMA Sandhurst. Commnd and served Royal Green Jackets, 1977–80. Called to the Bar, Inner Temple, 1976; in practice at the Bar, 1980–. *Recreations:* reading, art, film, sport (particularly cricket). *Address:* 12 King's Bench Walk, Temple, EC4Y 7EL. *T:* (020) 7583 0811, *Fax:* (020) 7583 7228; *e-mail:* clerks@12kbw.co.uk. *Clubs:* Royal Green Jackets, MCC.

WILLIAMS, Nigel; *see* Williams, H. N.

WILLIAMS, Nigel Christopher Ransome, CMG 1985; HM Diplomatic Service, retired; UK Permanent Representative to the Office of the United Nations and other international organisations, Geneva, 1993–97; *b* 29 April 1937; *s* of late Cecil Gwynne Ransome Williams and Corinne Belden (*née* Rudd). *Educ:* Merchant Taylors' Sch.; St John's Coll., Oxford. Joined Foreign Service and posted to Tokyo, 1961; FO, 1966; Private Secretary: to Minister of State, 1968; to Chancellor of Duchy of Lancaster, 1969; UK Mission to UN, New York, 1970; FCO, 1973; Counsellor (Economic), Tokyo, 1976; Cabinet Office, 1980; Hd of UN Dept, FCO, 1980–84; Minister, Bonn, 1985–88; Ambassador to Denmark, 1989–93. *Address:* Frederiksberg Allé 45, 1.Th, 1820 Frederiksberg C, Denmark.

WILLIAMS, Norman; *see* Williams, R. N.

WILLIAMS, Prof. Norman Stanley, FRCS, FMedSci; Professor of Surgery and Head, Centre for Academic Surgery, Barts and The London School of Medicine and Dentistry, Queen Mary, University of London (formerly London Hospital Medical College, London University), since 1986; *b* 15 March 1947; *s* of Jules Williams and Mabel Sundle; *m* 1977, Linda Feldman; one *s* one *d*. *Educ:* Roundhay Sch., Leeds; London Hosp. Med. Coll., Univ. of London (MB BS, MS). LRCP, MRCS. House and Registrar appts, London Hosp., 1970–76; Registrar, Bristol Royal Infirmary, 1976–78; Res. Fellow and Lectr, Leeds Gen. Infirmary, 1978–80; Res. Fellow, UCLA, 1980–82; Sen. Lectr, Leeds Gen. Infirmary, 1982–86. Fulbright Scholar, UCLA, 1980; Ethicon Foundn Fellow, RCS, 1980; Moynihan Fellow, Assoc. of Surgeons of GB and Ireland, 1985. President: Ileostomy and Internal Pouch Support Group, 1992–2008; European Digestive Surgery, 1997–98; Chm., UK Co-ordinating Cttee of Cancer Res. Sub-Cttee on Colorectal Cancer, 1996–2001. Mem., Steering Gp, Nat. Cancer Res. Network, 2001–03. Mem. Council, 2005–, Chm., Acad. and Res. Bd, 2006–, RCS. Pres., Soc. of Academic and Res. Surgery, 2009–. Vice-Chm., British Jl of Surgery, 1995–2001. FMedSci 2004. Hon. Fellow, Amer. Surgical Assoc., 2008. Patey Prize, Surgical Res. Soc., 1978; Nessim Habif Prize, Univ. of Geneva, 1995; Galen Medal in Therapeutics, Soc. of Apothecaries, 2002. *Publications:* (jtly) Surgery of the Anus, Rectum and Colon, 1993 (BUPA and Soc. of Authors Med. Writer's Gp Prize), 2nd edn 1999; (ed jtly) Bailey and Love's Short Practice of Surgery, 22nd edn 1995, 25th edn 2008; (ed) Colorectal Cancer, 1996; scientific papers. *Recreations:* long distance swimming, Rugby football, cinema, reading about crime, fact and fiction. *Address:* Centre for Academic Surgery, Royal London Hospital, Whitechapel, E1 1BB. *T:* (020) 7377 7079. *Club:* Royal Society of Medicine.

WILLIAMS, Sir Osmond, 2nd Bt *cr* 1909; MC 1944; JP; *b* 22 April 1914; *s* of late Captain Osmond T. D. Williams, DSO, 2nd *s* of 1st Bt, and Lady Gladys Margaret Finch Hatton, *o d* of 13th Earl of Winchilsea; *S* grandfather, 1927; *m* 1947, Benita Mary (*d* 2003), *yr d* of G. Henry Booker, and Mrs Michael Burn; two *d*. *Educ:* Eton; Freiburg Univ. Royal Scots Greys, 1935–37, and 1939–45; served Palestine, Africa, Italy and NW Europe. Chm., Quarry Tours Ltd (Llechwedd Slate Caverns), 1973–77. Vice-Chm., Amnesty Internat. (British Sect.), 1971–74. Mem., Merioneth Park Planning Cttee, 1971–74. Governor, Rainer Foundn Outdoor Pursuits Centre, 1964–76. MRI 1976. JP 1960 (Chairman of the Bench, Ardudwy-uwch-Artro, Gwynedd, 1974–84). Chevalier, Order of Leopold II with Palm; Croix de Guerre with Palm (Belgium), 1940. *Recreations:* music, travelling. *Heir:* none. *Address:* Borthwen, Penrhyndeudraeth, Gwynedd LL48 6EN. *Club:* Travellers.

WILLIAMS, Paul Maurice, RDI 2005; RIBA; Director, Stanton Williams Architects, since 1985; *b* 8 Oct. 1949; *s* of Maurice Williams and Joan Williams (*née* Neighbour); *m* 1984, Beth Stockley; one *s* one *d*. *Educ:* Birmingham Coll. of Art (BA; HDipAD). RIBA 2002. V&A Museum, 1975–80, Hd of Design, 1978–80: exhibns incl. Fabergé, Biedermeier, Renaissance Jewels and Tudor Miniatures; Design Consultant, Royal Liby, Windsor, 1978–87 (worldwide touring exhibns, Leonardo da Vinci Anatomical and Nature Study Drawings); private practice, 1980–85: exhibns incl. Romanesque, Matisse, Renoir, Hayward Gall.; Japanese Gall., V&A; formed partnership Stanton Williams Architects with Alan Stanton, 1985. *Award-winning projects* include: Design Mus. Galls, London, 1989; Issey Miyake Retail Shops, London, 1990–99; Triforium Mus., Winchester Cath., 1992; Leo Burnett Office Bldg, 60 Sloane Ave, London, 1994; Four Brindley Place, Birmingham, 1999; Wellcome Trust Millennium Seed Bank, Sussex, 2000; Whitby Abbey Visitor Centre, Yorks, 2002; Compton Verney Art Gall., 2004; Tower Hill Environs Scheme, London, 2004; Casa Fontana, Switzerland, 2004; Belgrade Th. Extension, 2008. Exhibitions include: Art of Ancient Mexico, Yves Klein, Jasper Johns, Leonardo da Vinci, Romanesque Art, Hayward Gall.; Gothic Exhibn, RA; Bridget Riley, Tate Britain. Architectural Advr, Heritage Lottery Fund, 1998–2002; Advr/Enabler, CABE, 2002–; Mem., Architectural Adv. Panel, Kensington and Chelsea, 2008–. External Examiner, Schools of Architecture: Westminster Univ., 1993–96; Plymouth Univ., 2000–04; Dundee Univ., 2005–07; lectured and taught in Europe and USA. Trustee, Whitechapel Art Gall., 1994–99. FRSA. *Publications:* work published and exhibited widely in architectural books and jls. *Recreations:* the arts, all sports. *Address:* Stanton Williams, 36 Graham Street, Islington, N1 8GJ. *T:* (020) 7880 6400, *Fax:* (020) 7880 6401; *e-mail:* p.williams@stantonwilliams.com.

WILLIAMS, Dr Paul Randall, CBE 1996; DL; FInstP; Chairman and Chief Executive, Council for Central Laboratory of Research Councils, 1995–98; *b* 21 March 1934; *s* of Fred and Eileen Westbrook Williams; *m* 1957, Marion Frances Lewis; one *s* one *d*. *Educ:* Baines' Grammar School; Loughborough College (BSc London external); Liverpool Univ. (PhD). DLC. ICI Research Fellow, Liverpool Univ., 1957; Research Physicist, British Nat. Bubble Chamber, 1958–62; Rutherford Lab., SRC, 1962–79 (Dep. Div. Head, Laser Div., 1976–79); Science and Engineering Research Council: Head, Astronomy, Space and Radio Div., 1979–81; Head, Engineering Div., 1981–83; Dep. Dir, 1983–87, Dir, 1987–94, Rutherford Appleton Lab.; Dir, Daresbury and Rutherford Appleton Lab., EPSRC, 1994–95. Chm., Abingdon Coll. Corp., 1993–95. Local Preacher, Methodist Church. DL Oxfordshire, 1998. Hon. DSc Keele, 1996. Glazebrook Medal, Inst. of Physics, 1994. *Recreations:* sailing, choral singing, ski-ing. *Address:* 5 Tatham Road, Abingdon, Oxon OX14 1QB. *T:* (01235) 524654.

WILLIAMS, Penry Herbert; Fellow and Tutor in Modern History, New College, Oxford, 1964–92, Hon. Fellow, 1998; *b* 25 Feb. 1925; *s* of late Douglas Williams and Dorothy Williams (*née* Murray); *m* 1952, June Carey Hobson (*d* 1991), *d* of late George and Kathleene Hobson; one *s* one *d*. *Educ:* Marlborough Coll.; New Coll., Oxford, 1947–50; St Antony's Coll., Oxford, 1950–51. MA, DPhil Oxon. Served Royal Artillery, 1943–45, Royal Indian Artillery, 1945–47. Asst Lecturer in History, 1951–54, Lectr, 1954–63, Sen. Lectr, 1963–64, Univ. of Manchester. Sexual Harassment Officer and Dir, Graduate Studies, Faculty of Modern History, Univ. of Oxford, 1989–90. Fellow of Winchester Coll., 1978–93. Chairman: New Coll. Develt Cttee, 1992–97; Thomas Wall Trust, 1995–99. Jt Editor, English Historical Review, 1982–90; Editor, New College Record, 1993–2003. *Publications:* The Council in the Marches of Wales under Elizabeth I, 1958; Life in Tudor England, 1963; The Tudor Regime, 1979; (ed with John Buxton) New College, Oxford 1379–1979, 1979; The Later Tudors: England 1547–1603, 1995;

contribs to learned jls. *Recreations:* travel, theatre. *Address:* Flat 3, Ockham Mews, 24 Bardwell Road, Oxford OX2 6SR. *T:* (01865) 558701.

WILLIAMS, Maj. Gen. Peter Gage, CMG 2005; OBE 1994 (MBE 1984); Head of NATO Military Liaison Mission, Moscow, 2002–05; *b* 25 June 1951; *s* of Col G. T. G. Williams; *m* 1982, Anne Rankine; one *s* two *d. Educ:* Eton; Magdalene Coll., Cambridge (BA 1972). Commnd Coldstream Guards, 1969; Sultan of Oman's Forces, 1976–78; served NI and Berlin; psc; MA to SACEUR, 1990–92; OC 1st Coldstream Guards, 1992–94; served NI (despatches), Bosnia, with MoD Intelligence; ocds (Aust.), 1999; Dep. Mil. Rep., EU Mil. Cttee, 2001–02. Mem., Chartered Inst. of Linguists, 1996 (Associate Mem., 1981). FCMI 2006. Legion of Merit (USA), 2005. *Recreations:* tourism, military history. *Address:* Fradds Meadow, St Tudy, Bodmin, Cornwall PL30 3NA.

WILLIAMS, Peter Keegan, CMG 1992; HM Diplomatic Service, retired; Chairman, Vietnam Enterprise Investments Ltd, since 1997; Director, Prudential Vietnam Ltd, since 1999; Senior Advisor: Prudential Corp. Ltd, since 1997; Tate & Lyle, since 1997; *b* 3 April 1938; *s* of William Edward Williams and Lilian (*née* Spright); *m* 1969, Rosamund Mary de Worms; two *d. Educ:* Calday Grange Grammar Sch.; Collège de Marcq-en-Baroeul (Nord); Univ. de Lille; Pembroke Coll., Oxford (MA). Joined Diplomatic Service, 1962; language student, MECAS, Lebanon, 1962; Second Sec., Beirut, 1963, Jedda, 1964; Commonwealth Office, 1967; First Sec., FCO, 1969; Director, Policy and Reference Div., British Information Services, New York, 1970; First Sec., FCO, 1973; First Sec., Head of Chancery and Consul, Rabat, 1976 (Chargé d'Affaires, 1978 and 1979); Counsellor, GATT, UK Mission, Geneva, 1979–83 (Chm. Panel, USA/Canada, 1980–81; Chm., Cttee on Finance, 1981–83); Ambassador, People's Democratic Republic of Yemen, 1983–85; Hd of UN Dept, FCO, 1986–89; RCDS, 1989; Ambassador to Socialist Republic of Vietnam, 1990–97. Sen. Advr, Scottish Enterprise, 1997–2002. Chm., Internat. Council, Christina Noble Children's Foundn, 1998–99. *Recreations:* wine, walking. *Address:* Lhoob Dhoo, Dalby, Isle of Man IM5 3BS. *Clubs:* Travellers, Oxford and Cambridge.

WILLIAMS, Sir Peter (Michael), Kt 1998; CBE 1992; PhD; FRS 1999; FREng; Chairman, National Physical Laboratory, since 2002; *b* 22 March 1945; *s* of Cyril Lewis and Gladys Williams; *m* 1970, Jennifer Margaret Cox; one *s. Educ:* Hymers College, Hull; Trinity College, Cambridge (MA, PhD). Mullard Research Fellow, Selwyn College, Cambridge, 1969–70; Lectr, Dept of Chemical Engineering and Chemical Technology, Imperial College, 1970–75; VG Instruments Group, 1975–82 (Dep. Man. Dir, 1979–82); Oxford Instruments Group plc, 1982–99: Man. Dir, 1983–85; Chief Exec., 1985–98; Chm., 1991–99; Master, St Catherine's Coll., Oxford, 2000–02. Chm., Isis Innovation Ltd, Oxford Univ., 1997–2001; non-executive Director: GKN plc, 2001–; WS Atkins plc, 2004–. Chairman: PPARC, 1994–99; Trustees, Science Mus., 1996–2002; Engrg and Technol. Bd, 2002–06. Mem., Council for Sci. and Technology, 1993–98; President: Inst. of Physics, 2000–02; BAAS, 2002–03. Supernumerary Fellow, St John's Coll., Oxford, 1988–2000. Chancellor, Univ. of Leicester, 2005–. FREng (FEng 1996). FIC 1997; FCGI 2002. Hon. FIChemE 2003; Hon. FIET (Hon. FIEE 2004); Hon. FCMI 2007. Hon. Fellow: Selwyn Coll., Cambridge, 1997; UCL, 1997; St Catherine's Coll., Oxford, 2002. Hon. DSc: Leicester, 1995; Nottingham Trent, 1995; Loughborough, 1996; Brunel, 1997; Wales, 1999; Sheffield, 1999; Salford, 2003; Staffordshire, 2004; City, 2007. Guardian Young Business Man of the Year, 1986. *Publications:* numerous contribs to jls relating to solid state physics. *Recreations:* ski-ing, walking. *Address:* Kews, Oxford Road, Frilford Heath, Oxon OX13 5NN.

WILLIAMS, Dr Peter Orchard, CBE 1991; FRCP; Director: The Wellcome Trust, 1965–91; Wellcome Institute for the History of Medicine, 1981–83; *b* 23 Sept. 1925; *s* of Robert Orchard Williams, CBE, and Agnes Annie Birkinshaw; *m* 1949, Billie Innes Brown (*d* 2007); two *d. Educ:* Caterham Sch.; Queen's Royal College, Trinidad; St John's Coll., Cambridge (MA); St Mary's Hospital Medical School. MB, BChir 1950; MRCP 1952; FRCP 1970. House Physician, St Mary's Hospital, 1950–51; Registrar, Royal Free Hospital, 1951–52; Medical Specialist, RAMC, BMH Iserlohn, 1954; Medical Officer, Headquarters, MRC, 1955–60; Wellcome Trust: Asst and Dep. Scientific Secretary, 1960–64; Scientific Secretary, 1964–65. Vice-Pres., Royal Soc. of Tropical Med. and Hygiene, 1975–77, Pres., 1991–93; Member: Nat. Council of Soc. Services Cttee of Enquiry into Charity Law and Practice, 1974–76; BBC, IBA Central Appeals Adv. Cttee, 1978–83; DHSS Jt Planning Adv. Cttee, 1986–; Chairman: Foundations Forum, 1977–79; Assoc. of Med. Res. Charities, 1974–76, 1979–83; Hague Club (European Foundns), 1981–83. Hon. Vis. Fellow, Green Coll., Oxford, 1993. Hon. Fellow, LSHTM, 1986. Hon. DSc: Birmingham, 1989; West Indies, 1991; Glasgow, 1992; Hon. DM: Nottingham, 1990; Oxford, 1993. Mary Kingsley Medal for Services to Tropical Medicine, Liverpool Sch. of Trop. Med., 1983. *Publications:* Careers in Medicine, 1952; The Exotic Fruits of My Life (autobiog.), 2003; papers in scientific journals. *Recreations:* garden, history of science. *Address:* Courtyard House, Bletchingdon, Kidlington, Oxon OX5 3DL.

WILLIAMS, Peter Robert; Chief Executive, Quality Assurance Agency for Higher Education, since 2002 (Acting Chief Executive, 2001–02); *b* 20 April 1948; *s* of Gilbert David Williams and Phyllis Williams, Oxford; *m* 1st, 1979, Katherine Pickles (marr. diss.); 2nd, 1987, Fiona Pollock-Gore; two *s. Educ:* City of Oxford High Sch.; Univ. of Exeter (BA Hons English 1969). Mgt trainee, Hazell, Watson and Viney Ltd, 1969–70; Admin. Asst, Univ. of Surrey, 1970–74; University of Leicester: Sen. Admin. Asst, 1974–79; Asst Registrar, 1979–82, Sec., 1982–84, Medical Sch.; Dep. Sec., British Acad., 1984–90; Director: CVCP Academic Audit Unit, 1990–92; of Quality Audit, 1992–94, of Quality Assurance, 1994–97, HEQC; of Institutional Review, QAA, 1997–2001. Mem., Council, 1998–, Exec. Cttee, 2000–, British Accreditation Council for Ind. Further and Higher Educn; European Association (formerly European Network) for Quality Assurance in Higher Education: Mem., Steering Cttee, 2000–04; Mem. Bd, 2004–; Vice-Pres., 2004–05, Pres., 2005–08. Mem. Cttee, 1981–84, Chm., Leicester Gp, 1981–84, Victorian Soc. FRSA 2002. Hon. LLD Higher Educn Trng and Awards Council, Ireland, 2008. Freeman, Guild of Educators, 2002. *Publications:* articles in jls on quality assurance and higher educn. *Recreations:* music, books, pictures, English topography. *Address:* Quality Assurance Agency for Higher Education, Southgate House, Southgate Street, Gloucester GL1 1UB. *T:* (01452) 557000, *Fax:* (01452) 557002; *e-mail:* p.williams@qaa.ac.uk.

WILLIAMS, Peter Wodehouse; Chief Executive, Alpha Group (formerly Alpha Airports), since 2006; *b* 18 Dec. 1953; *s* of John and Claire Williams; *m* 1981, Gwen Knight; two *s. Educ:* Univ. of Bristol (BSc Maths). ACA 1978. Audit Senior, Arthur Andersen, 1975–78; Consultant, Accenture, 1978–82; Financial Controller, Aiwa (UK) Ltd, 1982–84; Finance Dir, Bandive Ltd, 1984–87; Finance Divl Manager, Freemans plc, 1987–91; Finance Dir, 1991–2003, Chief Exec., 2003–04, Selfridges plc. Non-executive Director: Capital Radio plc, 2003–05; GCap Media plc, 2005–; Asos plc, 2006–; Cineworld Gp plc, 2006–. Member: Bd of Mgt, British Retail Consortium, 2003–04; Design Council, 2006–. Member: Business Adv. Bd, Comic Relief, 2002–; Finance Cttee, British Red Cross, 2002–. Trustee: GCap Charities (formerly Capital Charities), 2003–. *Recreations:* film, tennis, ski-ing, Southampton Football Club, shopping. *Address:* 3 Rayners Road, SW15 2AY. *T:* (020) 8788 5346; *e-mail:* Williams5000@hotmail.com. *Clubs:* Home House; Bank of England Sports; Putney Lawn Tennis.

WILLIAMS, Sir Philip; *see* Williams, Sir R. P. N.

WILLIAMS, Raymond Lloyd, CBE 1987; DPhil, DSc; CChem, FRSC; Director, Metropolitan Police Laboratory, 1968–87; Visiting Professor in Chemistry, University of East Anglia, 1968–93; *b* Bournemouth, 27 Feb. 1927; *s* of late Walter Raymond Williams and Vera Mary Williams; *m* 1956, Sylvia Mary Lawson Whitaker; one *s* one *d. Educ:* Bournemouth Sch.; St John's Coll., Oxford (schol.). Gibbs Univ. Schol. 1948, BA 1st Cl. Hons Nat Sci-Chem, MA, DPhil, DSc Oxon. Research Fellow, Pressed Steel Co., 1951–53; Commonwealth Fund Fellow, Univ. of California, Berkeley, 1953–54; progressively, Sen. Res. Fellow, Sen. Scientific Officer, Principal Sci. Officer, Explosives R&D Estab., 1955–60; PSO, Admiralty Materials Lab., 1960–62; Explosives R&D Establishment: SPSO, 1962; Supt, Analytical Services Gp, 1962–65; Supt, Non-metallic Materials Gp, 1965–68. External Examiner: Univ. of Strathclyde, 1983–85; KCL, 1986–88. Vis. Lectr, Univ. of Lausanne, 1989; Lectures: Theophilus Redwood, RSC, 1984; Schools, RSC, 1988; Public, RSC, 1990; Dalton, RSC, 1995. Jt Editor: Forensic Science International, 1978–97; Forensic Science Progress, 1984–92. Pres., Forensic Science Soc., 1983–85; Hon. Mem., Assoc. of Police Surgeons of GB, 1980. Adelaide Medal, Internat. Assoc. of Forensic Scis, 1993. *Publications:* papers in scientific jls on spectroscopy, analytical chemistry, and forensic science. *Recreations:* lawn tennis (played for Civil Service and Oxfordshire: representative colours), carpentry. *Address:* 9 Meon Road, Bournemouth, Dorset BH7 6PN. *T:* (01202) 423446.

WILLIAMS, (Reginald) Norman, CB 1982; Assistant Registrar of Friendly Societies, 1984–93; *b* 23 Oct. 1917; *s* of Reginald Gardnar Williams and Janet Mary Williams; *m* 1956, Hilary Frances West; two *s. Educ:* Neath Grammar Sch.; Swansea Univ. Served War: Captain RA and later Staff Captain HQ 30 Corps, 1940–46. Solicitor in private practice, 1947–48. Dept of Health and Social Security (formerly Min. of Nat. Insurance): Legal Asst, 1948; Sen. Legal Asst, 1959; Asst Solicitor, 1966; Principal Asst Solicitor, 1974; Under Sec., 1977–82. Member of Law Society. *Recreations:* golf, photography, reading. *Address:* Brecon, 23 Castle Hill Avenue, Berkhamsted, Herts HP4 1HJ. *T:* (01442) 865291.

WILLIAMS, Richard Charles John; Founder Director, Williams Murray Hamm Ltd, since 1997; *b* 19 Oct. 1949; *s* of Herbert Charles Lionel Williams and Barbara Dorothy Williams; *m* 1973, Agnieszka Wanda Skrobanska; one *s* one *d. Educ:* Highgate Sch.; London College of Printing (DipAD 1973). Founder Dir, Designbridge, 1986–95. Dir, Design Business Assoc., 1989 and 2005; Mem., Design Council, 2005–. *Publication:* (with Richard Murray and Garrick Hamm) The Little Book of Don'ts in Brand Design, 2002. *Recreations:* motor sport, sailing. *Address:* Williams Murray Hamm Ltd, 10 Dallington Street, EC1V 0DB. *T:* (020) 3217 0000, *Fax:* (020) 3217 0002; *e-mail:* richardw@creatingdifference.com.

WILLIAMS, (Richard) Derrick, MA; Principal, Gloucestershire College of Arts and Technology, 1981–89; *b* 30 March 1926; *s* of Richard Leslie Williams and Lizzie Paddington; *m* 1949, Beryl Newbury Stonebanks; four *s. Educ:* St John's Coll., Cambridge (MA). Asst Master, Lawrence Sheriff Sch., Rugby, 1950–51; Lectr, University Coll., Ibadan, Nigeria, 1951–52; Adult Tutor, Ashby-de-la-Zouch Community Coll., Leicestershire, 1952–54; Further Educn Organising Tutor, Oxfordshire, 1954–60; Asst Educn Officer: West Suffolk, 1960–65; Bristol, 1965–67; Dep. Chief Educn Officer, Bristol, 1967–73; Chief Educn Officer, County of Avon, 1973–76; Dir, Glos Inst. of Higher Educn, 1977–80. *Recreations:* cricket, music. *Address:* Glan y Nant, Bryniau, Brithdir, Dolgellau, Gwynedd LL40 2TY.

WILLIAMS, Richard Evan Huw; a District Judge (Magistrates' Courts), South Wales, since 2004; *b* 17 Feb. 1959; *s* of Evan Howell Williams, FIChemE and Muriel Maynard Williams (*née* Cooke); *m* 1991, Lindsey Ann Duckworth; two *d. Educ:* Ysgol Gyfun Rhydfelen, Pontypridd; Univ. of Bristol (LLB Hons 1991). Metropolitan Police, 1978–88; called to the Bar, Lincoln's Inn, 1992; a barrister, 1992–2004; a Dep. Dist Judge (Magistrates' Courts), 2000–04. *Recreations:* family, music. *Address:* Cardiff Magistrates' Court, Fitzalan Place, Cardiff CF24 0RZ. *T:* (029) 2046 3040, *Fax:* (029) 2046 0264; *e-mail:* districtjudgerichard.williams@judiciary.gsi.gov.uk.

WILLIAMS, Richard Hall; Under Secretary, Agriculture Department, Welsh Office, Cardiff, 1981–86; Deputy Chairman, Local Government Boundary Commission for Wales, 1989–96; *b* 21 Oct. 1926; *s* of late Edward Hall Williams and Kitty Hall Williams; *m* 1949, Nia Wynn (*née* Jones); two *s* two *d. Educ:* Barry Grammar Sch., Glamorgan; University College of Wales, Aberystwyth (BScEcon Hons). Career within Welsh Office included service in Health and Economic Planning Groups before entering Agriculture Dept, 1978. Treasurer, Ministerial Bd, Presbyterian Church of Wales, 1986–95. Vice Chm., Age Concern Wales, 1990–93. Moderator, E Glam Presbytery (Welsh), Presbyterian Ch of Wales, 2000–01. *Recreation:* enjoying all things Welsh. *Address:* Argoed, 17 West Orchard Crescent, Llandaff, Cardiff CF5 1AR. *T:* (029) 2056 2472.

WILLIAMS, Prof. Richard James Willson, TD 1995; FRCPsych, FRCPCH; Professor of Mental Health Strategy, Welsh Institute for Health and Social Care, University of Glamorgan, and Consultant Child and Adolescent Psychiatrist, Gwent Healthcare NHS Trust, since 1998; Professor of Child and Adolescent Mental Health, Lancashire School of Postgraduate Medicine, University of Central Lancashire, since 2006; *b* 5 Feb. 1949; *s* of Ernest James Williams and Eleanor Mary Willson Williams; *m* 1971, Janet May Simons; one *s* two *d. Educ:* Bristol Grammar Sch.; Univ. of Birmingham (MB ChB 1972); DPM 1976. MRCPsych 1976, FRCPsych 1990; MRCPCH 1996, FRCPCH 1997. House Physician, Selly Oak Hosp., Birmingham, 1972–73; House Surgeon, Worcester Royal Infirmary, 1973; Sen. House Officer in Psychiatry, Whitchurch Hospital Mgt Cttee, Cardiff, 1973–74; Registrar in Psychiatry, S Glamorgan AHA (T), 1974–77; Sen. Registrar in Child and Adolescent Psychiatry, S Glamorgan AHA (T) and Welsh Nat. Sch. of Medicine, 1977–80; Consultant Child and Adolescent Psychiatrist, Bristol Royal Hosp. for Sick Children, 1980–98. Director: NHS Health Adv. Service, 1992–96; Drugs Adv. Service, 1992–96; Vice Chm., Mental Health Act Commn, 1997–2001. Special Advr on Child and Adolescent Mental Health to Welsh Assembly Govt, 1999–; Mem., Adv. Bd for Healthcare Standards in Wales, 2004– (Chm., Ethics Cttee, 2005–); Chm., Wales Collaboration in Mental Health, 2003–; Member: Emergency Planning Clinical Leadership Adv. Gp, DoH, 2005–; Cttee on the Ethical Aspects of Pandemic Influenza, UK Govt, 2006–; Exec. Cttee, Fac. of Conflict and Catastrophe Medicine, Soc. of Apothecaries, 2006–; Scientific Adviser on Psychosocial and Mental Healthcare: to Dir of Emergency Preparedness, DoH, 2006–; to Jt Med. Cttee, NATO, 2007–. Chm., Assoc. for Psychiatric Study of Adolescents, 1989–92. Gov. and Mem. Exec. Cttee, Inst. of Child Health, Univ. of Bristol, 1988–94 (Treas., 1989–91); Sen. Fellow, Health Services Mgt Centre, Univ. of Birmingham, 1996–99. Dir of Confs, RCPsych, 2001–07. Chm., Acad. of Med. Royal Colls in Wales, 2004–06; Mem., Acad. of Med. Royal Colls, 2002–08.

MIHM 1994; MInstD 1995. *Publications:* (ed jtly) A Concise Guide to the Children Act 1989, 1992; (ed and contrib.) Comprehensive Mental Health Services, 1994; (ed and contrib.) Clinicians in Management, 1994; (ed jtly) Suicide Prevention, 1994; (ed and contrib.) Comprehensive Health Services for Elderly People, 1994; (ed and contrib.) Drugs and Alcohol, 1994; (ed jtly and contrib.) Together We Stand, 1995; (ed jtly and contrib.) A Place in Mind, 1995; (ed jtly and contrib.) The Substance of Young Needs, 1996; (ed jtly) Safeguards for Young Minds, 1996, 2nd edn 2004; (ed jtly and contrib.) Heading for Better Care, 1996; (ed jtly and contrib.) Addressing the Balance, 1997; (ed jtly) Voices in Partnership, 1997; (ed jtly and contrib.) Forging New Channels, 1998; (jtly) Promoting Mental Health in a Civil Society, 2001; (jtly) Deaths of Detained Patients in England and Wales, 2001; (ed jtly) Child and Adolescent Mental Health Services, 2005; contrib. chapters in books, major reports, and leading articles, editorials and papers in learned jls. *Recreations:* walking on Bodmin Moor, licensed radio amateur, preserved steam railways, military history. *Address:* Welsh Institute for Health and Social Care, University of Glamorgan, Ty Bryn, St Cadoc's Hospital, Lodge Road, Caerleon, Gwent NP18 3XQ. *T:* (01633) 436832, *Fax:* (01633) 436834; *e-mail:* rjwwilli@glam.ac.uk. *Club:* Athenæum.

WILLIAMS, Dr Richard Wynne; Chief Executive Officer, Rathbone, since 2004; *b* 28 March 1954; *m* 1981, Sandra Hauxwell; one *s*. *Educ:* Thames Poly. (BA Hons 1972); Univ. of London (PGCE 1979); DMan Univ. of Herts 2005. Lectr, City & E London Coll., 1979–84; Sen. Lectr, Paddington Coll., 1984–87; Head of Faculty, 1987–91, Dep. Principal, 1987–96, Hendon Coll.; Principal: Kingsway Coll., 1996–2000; Westminster Kingsway Coll., 2000–04. *Publications:* contributor: A Complexity Perspective on Researching Organizations, 2005; Complexity and the Experience of Leading Organisations, 2005; Experiencing Emergence in Organizations, 2005; Complexity and the Experience of Managing in Public Sector Organizations, 2005. *Recreations:* theatre, modern jazz, walking. *Address:* Rathbone, Churchgate House, Manchester M1 6EU. *T:* (0161) 238 6301; *e-mail:* richard.williams@rathboneuk.org.

WILLIAMS, Prof. Robert Hughes, (Robin), CBE 2004; FRS 1990; CPhys, FInstP; Research Professor, School of Engineering, Swansea University (formerly University of Wales, Swansea), 2003, now Emeritus Professor; *b* 22 Dec. 1941; *s* of Emrys and Catherine Williams; *m* 1967, Gillian Mary Harrison; one *s* one *d*. *Educ:* Bala Boys' Grammar Sch.; University College of North Wales, Bangor (BSc, PhD, DSc). Res. Fellow, Univ. of Wales, 1966–68; Lectr, then Reader and Prof., New University of Ulster, 1968–83; Prof. and Hd of Dept of Physics, later Physics and Astronomy, 1984–94, Dep. Principal, 1993–94, Univ. of Wales Coll. of Cardiff; Vice-Chancellor, Univ. of Wales, Swansea, 1994–2003. Visiting Professor: Max Planck Inst., Stuttgart, 1975; Xerox Res. Labs, Palo Alto, USA, 1979; IBM Res. Labs, Yorktown Heights, USA, 1982; Distinguished Res. Fellow, La Trobe Univ., Melbourne, 2003. Mott Lectr, Inst. of Physics, 1992. Hon. DSc Ulster, 2003; Hon. DLaws Wales, 2005. Silver Medal, British Vacuum Council, 1988; Max Born Medal and Prize, German Physics Soc. and Inst. of Physics, 1989. *Publications:* Metal-Semiconductor Contacts (with E. H. Rhoderick), 1988; over 300 pubns in field of solid state physics and semiconductor devices. *Recreations:* walking, fishing, soccer. *Address:* Dolwerdd, Trerhyngyll, Cowbridge, Vale of Glamorgan CF71 7TN. *T:* (01446) 773402.

WILLIAMS, Prof. Robert Joseph Paton, DPhil; FRS 1972; Emeritus Fellow, Wadham College, Oxford, since 1995 (Fellow, 1955–95, Senior Research Fellow, 1991–95); Royal Society Napier Research Professor at Oxford, 1974–91; *b* 25 Feb. 1926; *m* 1952, Jelly Klara (*née* Büchli); two *s*. *Educ:* Wallasey Grammar Sch.; Merton Coll., Oxford (MA, DPhil; Hon. Fellow, 1991). FRSC. Rotary Foundn Fellow, Uppsala, 1950–51; Jun. Res. Fellow, Merton Coll., Oxford, 1951–55; Lectr, 1955–72, Reader in Inorganic Chemistry, 1972–74, Univ. of Oxford. Associate, Peter Bent Brigham Hosp., Boston, USA; Commonwealth Fellow, Mass, 1965–66; Vis. Prof., Royal Free Hosp., London Univ., 1991–. Lectures: Liversidge, Chem. Soc., 1979; Commem., Biochem. Inst., Univ. of Zurich, 1981; Bakerian, 1981, Rutherford, 1996, Royal Soc.; Cohn, Univ. of Philadelphia, 1997; Birchall, Univ. of Keele, 1999; Huxley, Univ. of Birmingham, 2000. President: Chem. Sect., BAAS, 1985–86; Dalton Div., RSC, 1991–93. Foreign Member: Acad. of Science, Portugal, 1981; Royal Soc. of Science, Liège, 1981; Royal Swedish Acad. of Sciences, 1983; Czechoslovak Acad. of Science, 1989. Hon. DSc: Liège, 1980; Leicester, 1985; East Anglia, 1992; Keele, 1993; Instituto Superior Tecnico, Lisbon, 1997. Tilden Medal, Chem. Soc., 1970; Keilin Medal, Biochem. Soc., 1972; Hughes Medal, Royal Soc., 1979; Claire Bruylants Medal, Louvain, 1980; Krebs Medal, Europ. Biochem. Soc., 1985; Linderstrøm-Lang Medal, Carlsberg Foundn, Copenhagen, 1986; Sigillum Magnum (Medal), Univ. of Bologna, 1987; Heyrovsky Medal, Internat. Union of Biochem., 1988; Frederick Gowland Hopkins Medal, Biochem. Soc., 1989; Royal Medal, Royal Soc., 1995; Longstaff Medal, Chem. Soc., 2002; Certificate of Honour, Oxford City, 2003. *Publications:* (with C. S. G. Phillips) Inorganic Chemistry, 1965; (jtly) Nuclear Magnetic Resonance in Biology, 1977; (ed jtly) New Trends in Bio-Inorganic Chemistry, 1978; (with S. Mann and J. Webb) Biomineralization, 1989; with J. J. R. Frausto da Silva: The Biological Chemistry of the Elements, 1991, 2nd edn 2001; The Natural Selection of the Chemical Elements, 1996; Bringing Chemistry to Life, 1999; The Chemistry of Evolution, 2006; papers in Jl Chem. Soc., biochemical jls, etc. *Recreation:* walking in the country. *Address:* Wadham College, Oxford OX1 3QR. *T:* (01865) 242564.

WILLIAMS, Robert Martin, CB 1981; CBE 1973; retired; Chairman, State Services Commission, New Zealand, 1975–81; *b* 30 March 1919; *s* of late Canon Henry Williams; *m* 1944, Mary Constance, *d* of late Rev. Francis H. Thorpe; one *s* two *d*. *Educ:* Christ's Coll., NZ; Canterbury University College, NZ; St John's Coll., Cambridge. MA. 1st Class Hons Mathematics, Univ. Sen. Schol., Shirtcliffe Fellow, NZ, 1940; BA, 1st Class Hons Mathematics Tripos, Cantab, 1947; PhD Math. Statistics, Cantab, 1949. Mathematician at Radar Development Laboratory, DSIR, NZ, 1941–44; Member UK Atomic Group in US, 1944–45; Member, 1949–53, Director, 1953–62, Applied Mathematics Laboratory, DSIR, NZ; Harkness Commonwealth Fellow and Vis. Fellow, at Princeton Univ., 1957–58; State Services Commissioner, NZ Public Service, 1963–67; Vice-Chancellor: Univ. of Otago, Dunedin, 1967–73; ANU, 1973–75. Mem., NZ Metric Adv. Bd, 1969–73. Mem., Internat. Statistical Inst., 1961–97. Chairman: Cttee of Inquiry into Educnl TV, 1970–72; Policy Cttee, Dictionary of NZ Biography, 1983–90. President: NZ Book Council, 1989–92; Nat. Liby Soc., 1992–95. Carnegie Travel Award, 1969. Hon. LLD Otago, 1972. *Publications:* papers mainly on mathematical statistics and related topics. *Address:* 21 Wadestown Road, Wellington, New Zealand. *Club:* Wellington (Wellington, NZ).

WILLIAMS, Sir (Robert) Philip (Nathaniel), 4th Bt *cr* 1915; JP; DL; *b* 3 May 1950; *s* of Sir David Philip Williams, 3rd Bt and of Elizabeth Mary Garneys, *d* of late William Ralph Garneys Bond; *S* father, 1970; *m* 1979, Catherine Margaret Godwin, *d* of Canon Cosmo Pouncey, Tewkesbury; one *s* three *d*. *Educ:* Marlborough; St Andrews Univ. MA Hons. JP W Dorset PSA (formerly Dorchester), 1992; DL Dorset, 1995. *Heir: s* David Robert Mark Williams, *b* 31 Oct. 1980. *Address:* Bridehead, Littlebredy, Dorchester, Dorset DT2 9JA. *T:* (01308) 482232. *Club:* MCC.

WILLIAMS, Robin; *see* Williams, Robert H.

WILLIAMS, Maj.-Gen. Robin Guy, CB 1983; MBE 1969; retired; Chief Executive Officer, Auckland Regional Trust Board, Order of St John, 1993–98; *b* 14 Aug. 1930; *s* of John Upham and Margaret Joan Williams; *m* 1953, Jill Rollo Tyrie; one *s* two *d*. *Educ:* Nelson Coll., New Zealand. psc(UK) 1963, jssc(AS) 1972, rcds(UK) 1976. Commissioned RMC, Duntroon, 1952; 1 Fiji Inf. Regt Malaya, 1953–54; Adjt/Coy Comd 2 NZ Regt Malaya, 1959–61 Chief Instructor Sch. of Inf. (NZ), 1964–65; BM 28 Comwel Inf. Bde, Malaysia, 1965–68; CO 1 Bn Depot (NZ), 1969; CO 1 RNZIR (Singapore), 1969–71; GSO1 Field Force Comd (NZ), 1972–73; CofS Field Force Comd (NZ), 1973–74; Col SD, Army GS, 1974–75; Comd Field Force, 1977–79; ACDS (Ops/Plans), 1979–81; DCGS 1981; CGS, 1981–84. Hon. Col 1 RNZIR, 1986–88; Col, RNZIR, 1988–90. Chm., Bell Helicopter (BH) Pacific, 1988–90. Vice-Chm., 1985–86, Chm., 1986–88, Operation Raleigh, NZ; Chief Executive: Order of St John (NZ), 1986–87; Auckland Div., Cancer Soc. of NZ, 1988–93. *Recreations:* golf, swimming, walking. *Address:* Apt 1A, 463 Remuera Road, Remuera, Auckland 1050, New Zealand. *T:* (9) 5201547. *Clubs:* Northern (Auckland); Auckland Golf (Middlemore, NZ).

WILLIAMS, Sir Robin (Philip), 2nd Bt *cr* 1953; Insurance Broker, 1952–91; Lloyd's Underwriter, 1961–99; 2nd Lieut, retired, RA; *b* 27 May 1928; *s* of Sir Herbert Geraint Williams, 1st Bt, MP, MSc, MEngAssoc, MInstCE; *S* father, 1954; *m* 1955, Wendy Adèle Marguerite, *o d* of late Felix Joseph Alexander, London and Hong Kong; two *s*. *Educ:* Eton Coll.; St John's Coll., Cambridge (MA). 2nd Lieut, Royal Artillery, 1947. Vice-Chairman, Federation of Univ. Conservative and Unionist Assocs, 1951–52; Acting Chairman, 1952; Chairman of Bow Group (Conservative Research Society), 1954. Called to Bar, Middle Temple, 1954; Chm., Anti-Common Market League, 1969–84; Dir, Common Market Safeguards Campaign, 1973–76; Hon. Secretary: Safeguard Britain Campaign, 1976–89; Campaign for an Independent Britain, 1989–2008. Councillor, Haringey, 1968–74. *Publication:* Whose Public Schools?, 1957. *Heir: s* Anthony Geraint Williams [*b* 22 Dec. 1958; *m* 1990, Rachel Jane, *e d* of Norman Jennings; three *s* one *d*]. *Address:* 1 Broadlands Close, Highgate, N6 4AF.

WILLIAMS, Prof. Sir Roger, Kt 2006; Vice-Chancellor of The University of Reading, 1993–2002; Chairman, Higher Education Funding Council for Wales, 2002–08 (Member, 1995–2008; Acting Chairman, 2000–02); *b* 21 March 1942; *s* of late M. O. Williams, MBE and W. Williams; *m* 1967, Rae Kirkbright; two *d*. *Educ:* Tredegar Grammar Sch.; Worcester Coll., Oxford (BA Nat. Scis (Physics), MA; Hon. Fellow, 1999); Univ. of Manchester (MA). Operational Res. Br., Nat. Coal Bd, 1963–64; Department of Government, University of Manchester: Res. Student, 1964–66; Asst Lectr, Lectr, Sen. Lectr, 1966–78; Prof. of Govt and Sci. Policy, 1979–93; Founding Dir, Policy Res. in Engrg, Sci. and Technol., 1979–93; Hd of Dept, 1984–88; Dean of Economic and Social Studies, 1989–92. NATO Envtl Fellowship, 1977–79; Aust. Univs Fellowship, 1984; Vis. Prof., Univ. of Montreal, 1981. Sci. Advr, Sci. Council of Canada (on secondment), 1974–75; Advr, OECD, 1980–81; Specialist Advr, H of L Select Cttees on Sci. and Technology, 1986–92, on European Communities, 1990; Member: Adv. Bd, Sci. Policy Res. Unit, 1987–97; Cabinet Office Wkg Gp on internat. collaboration in sci. and technol., 1989–91. Chm., Jt SERC-ESRC Cttee, 1991–93; Member: ESRC, EPSRC and NERC Cttees; Quality Assurance Agency for Higher Educn, 1997–2002. Mem. Editl Bd, Government and Opposition, 1994–. Associate, Technical Change Centre, 1981–85. British Council Delegn to China, 1985. Hon. Fellow, Cardiff Univ., 2008. Hon. DCL Reading, 2002; Hon. DSc Glamorgan, 2008. *Publications:* Politics and Technology, 1972; European Technology, 1973; The Nuclear Power Decisions, 1980; Public Acceptability of New Technology, 1986; contrib. to approx. 22 books and more than 20 acad. articles. *Club:* Athenæum.

WILLIAMS, Roger Hugh; MP (Lib Dem) Brecon Radnorshire, since 2001; farmer, since 1969; *b* 22 Jan. 1948; *s* of Morgan Glyn Williams and Eirlys Williams; *m* 1973, Penelope James; one *s* one *d*. *Educ:* Llanfilo Co. Primary Sch.; Christ Coll., Brecon; Selwyn Coll., Cambridge (BA). Mem. (Lib Dem) Powys CC, 1981–2001. Dir, Develt Bd for Rural Wales, 1989–97. Chm., Brecon Beacons Nat. Park, 1991–96. *Recreations:* sport, walking. *Address:* House of Commons, SW1A 0AA; Tredomen Court, Llanfilo, Brecon, Powys LD3 0RL.

WILLIAMS, Prof. Roger Stanley, CBE 1993; MD; FRCP, FRCS, FMedSci; Professor of Hepatology, University of London, since 1994; Director, Institute of Hepatology, University College London Medical School, and Hon. Consultant Physician, University College Hospitals NHS Trust, since 1996; *b* 28 Aug. 1931; *s* of Stanley George Williams and Doris Dagmar Clatworthy; *m* 1st, 1954, Lindsay Mary Elliott (marr. diss. 1977); two *s* three *d*; 2nd, 1978, Stephanie Gay de Laszlo; one *s* two *d*. *Educ:* St Mary's Coll., Southampton; London Hosp. Med. Coll., Univ. of London. MB, BS (Hons), MD; LRCP, MRCP, FRCP 1966; MRCS, FRCS 1988; FRCPE 1990; FRACP 1991. House appointments and Pathology Asst, London Hospital, 1953–56; Jun. Med. Specialist, Queen Alexandra Hospital, Millbank, 1956–58; Medical Registrar and Tutor, Royal Postgrad. Med. Sch., 1958–59; Lectr in Medicine, Royal Free Hospital, 1959–65; Consultant Physician, Royal South Hants and Southampton General Hospital, 1965–66; Consultant Physician, KCH, 1966–96; Dir, Liver Res. Unit, then Inst. of Liver Studies, KCH and Med Sch., then King's Coll. Sch. of Medicine and Dentistry, 1966–96. Hon. Consultant: Foundn for Liver Res., 1974–; in medicine to the Army, 1988–. Member: Clinical Standards Adv. Gp, 1994–; Adv. Gp on Hepatitis, DHSS, 1980–; Transplant Adv. Panel, DHSS, 1974–83; WHO Scientific Gp on Viral Hepatitis, Geneva, 1972. Rockefeller Travelling Fellowship in Medicine, 1962; Legg Award, Royal Free Hosp. Med. Sch., 1964; Sir Ernest Finch Vis. Prof., Sheffield, 1974; Hans Sloane Fellow, RCP, 2004–; Lectures: Melrose Meml, Glasgow, 1970; Goulstonian, RCP, 1970; Searle, Amer. Assoc. for the Study of Liver Diseases, 1972; Fleming, Glasgow Coll. of Physicians and Surgeons, 1975; Sir Arthur Hurst Meml, British Soc. of Gastroenterology, 1975; Skinner, Royal Coll. of Radiologists, 1978; Albert M. Snell Meml, Palo Alto Med. Foundn, 1981; Milford Rouse, Baylor Med. Center, Dallas, 1989; Norman Tanner Meml, St George's Hosp., 1992; Searle Special, St Bartholomew's Hosp., 1992; Datta Meml Oration, India, 1984; Quadrennial Review, World Congress of Gastroenterol., Sydney, 1990; Sir Jules Thorn, RCP, 1994. Vice-Pres., RCP, 1991–93; President: Internat. Med. Club, 1989–99; British Liver Trust, 2002–; Member: European Assoc. for the Study of the Liver, 1966– (Cttee Mem., 1966–70; Pres., 1983; Hon. Pres., 2008); Harveian Soc. of London (Sec., Councillor and Vice-Pres., 1963–70, Pres., 1974–75); British Assoc. for Study of Liver (formerly Liver Club) (Sec. and Treasurer, 1968–71; Pres., 1984–86); Royal Soc. of Medicine (Sec. of Section, 1969–71); British Soc. of Gastroenterology (Pres., 1989). FKC 1992; FMedSci 1999. Hon. FACP 1992; Hon. FRCPI 2001. Hon. Fellow, UCL, 2008. Gold Medal, Canadian Liver Foundn, 1992; Lifetime Achievement Award, British Assoc. for the Study of the Liver, 2003; Wyeth Senior Achievement Award for Clinical Transplantation, Amer. Soc. of Transplantation, 2004; Hans Popper Life Achievement Award, Internat. Liver Congress, Hong Kong, 2008. *Publications:* (ed) Fifth Symposium on Advanced Medicine, 1969; (ed) International Developments in Health Care, 1995; edited jointly: Immunology of the Liver, 1971; Artificial Liver Support, 1975; Immune Reactions in Liver Disease, 1978; Drug Reactions and the Liver, 1981; Variceal Bleeding, 1982; Antiviral Agents in Chronic Hepatitis B Virus Infection, 1985; The Practice of Liver

Transplantation, 1995; International Developments in Health Care, 1995; Acute Liver Failure, 1996; Fulminant Hepatic Failure: seminars in liver disease, 2003; author of over 2000 scientific papers, review articles and book chapters. *Recreations:* tennis, sailing, opera. *Address:* Brickworth Park, Whiteparish, Wilts SP5 2QE; 30 Devonshire Close, W1N 1LY; Institute of Hepatology, University College London Medical School, 69–75 Chenies Mews, WC1E 6BT. *Clubs:* Athenæum, Saints and Sinners, Royal Ocean Racing; Royal Yacht Squadron (Cowes).

WILLIAMS, Ronald; *see* Williams, A. R.

WILLIAMS, Rt Rev. Ronald John Chantler; Bishop of the Southern Region, and an Assistant Bishop, Diocese of Brisbane, 1993–2007; *b* 19 July 1938; *s* of Walter Chantler Williams and Constance Bertha Williams (*née* Pool); *m* 1963, Kathryn Rohrsheim; two *s* one *d. Educ:* Prince Alfred Coll., Adelaide; St John's Coll., Morpeth (ThL); St Mark's Coll., Adelaide Univ. (BA); Bristol Univ. (MSc 1974); Australian Management Coll., Mt Eliza (AMP). Ordained deacon, 1963, priest, 1964; Curate, Toorak Gardens, 1963–64; Australian Bd of Missions, Sydney, 1965; Domestic Chaplain, Bishop of Polynesia, 1966–67; Priest, Labasa, Fiji, 1967–71; Hon. Priest, Bedminster, Bristol, 1972–74; Dean of Suva, Fiji, 1974–79; Rector, Campbelltown, Adelaide, 1979–84; Priest to City of Adelaide and founding Dir, St Paul's Centre, 1984–93; Hon. Canon, St Peter's Cathedral, Adelaide, 1986–93. *Recreation:* jazz musician—double bass. *Address:* 42 Princess Street, Bulimba, Qld 4171, Australia. *T:* (7) 33999818; *e-mail:* rkwill@bigpond.net.au.

WILLIAMS, Ronald Millward, CBE 1990; DL; Member, Essex County Council, 1970–93 and 1997–2005 (Chairman, 1983–86); *b* 9 Dec. 1922; *s* of George and Gladys Williams; *m* 1943, Joyce; one *s* two *d. Educ:* Leeds College of Technology. Electrical Engineer, then Industrial Eng Superintendent, Mobil Oil Co. Ltd, 1954–82. Member: Benfleet Urban Dist Council, 1960–74 (Chm. 1963–66, 1972–74); Castle Point Dist Council, 1974–87 (Chm. 1980–81; Leader, 1981–87); Essex County Council: Leader Cons. Gp, 1977–83, 1986–87; Chairman: County Planning Cttee, 1981–83; County Highways Cttee, 1989–93; Envmtl Services Bd, 1998–2000; Exec. Mem., with strategic planning and transportation portfolio, 2000–01; Cabinet Mem., Highways and Transportation, 2001–03; Hon. Alderman, 2005. Chm., Southend Health Authority, 1982–90, Southend Health Care Services, NHS Trust, 1990–96. Chm., SE Essex Abbeyfield Soc., 1983–88. DL Essex, 1983. Hon. Freeman, Borough of Castle Point, 2006. *Recreations:* supporter, football, cricket, bowls, tennis; video filming of countryside.

WILLIAMS, Ronald William; Senior Adviser, PricewaterhouseCoopers (formerly Coopers & Lybrand), 1986–2001; Director, Office of Manpower Economics, 1980–86 (on secondment); *b* 19 Dec. 1926; *yr s* of late Albert Williams and Katherine Teresa Williams (*née* Chilver). *Educ:* City of London Sch.; Downing Coll., Cambridge (MA, LLB). RN, 1945–48. Iraq Petroleum Co. Ltd, 1956–58; Philips Electrical Industries Ltd, 1958–64; Consultant, later Sen. Consultant, PA Management Consultants Ltd, 1964–69; Asst Sec., NBPI, 1969–71; Sen. Consultant, Office of Manpower Economics, 1971–73; Asst Sec., CSD, 1973–80 (UK Govt rep., ILO Tripartite Conf. on Public Servs, 1975); Under Sec. 1980; HM Treasury, 1982; Dept of Employment, 1986. *Recreations:* music, history. *Address:* 10 Pine Park Mansions, 1–3 Wilderton Road, Branksome Park, Poole, Dorset BH13 6EB. *T:* (01202) 769736.

WILLIAMS, Most Rev. and Rt Hon. Rowan Douglas; *see* Canterbury, Archbishop of.

WILLIAMS, Roy, CB 1989; Deputy Secretary, Department of Trade and Industry, 1984–94; *b* 31 Dec. 1934; *s* of Eric Williams and Ellen Williams; *m* 1959, Shirley, *d* of Captain and Mrs O. Warwick; one *s* one *d. Educ:* Liverpool Univ. (1st Cl. BA Econs). Asst Principal, Min. of Power, 1956; Principal, 1961; Harkness Commonwealth Fellow, Univs of Chicago and Berkeley, 1963–64; Principal Private Sec., Minister of Power and subseq. Paymaster Gen., 1969; Asst Sec., DTI, 1971; Principal Private Sec., Sec. of State for Industry, 1974; Under-Sec., DoI, later DTI, 1976–84. Dir, EIB, 1991–94. Chm., EU High Level Gp on Eureka prog., 1995–96; Mem., Design Council, 1995–2001. Chm. Trustees, Nat. Centre for Young People with Epilepsy, St Pier's, Lingfield, 1995–; Trustee, Victorian Soc., 2005–. *Address:* Darl Oast, The Street, Ightham, Sevenoaks, Kent TN15 9HH. *T:* (01732) 883944.

WILLIAMS, Rev. Samuel Lewis; Minister, St Columba's United Reformed Church, Gosport, 1991–96; *b* 8 Jan. 1934; *s* of Thomas John Williams and Miriam Mary Williams (*née* West); *m* 1958, Mary Sansom (*née* Benjamin); one *s* one *d. Educ:* Pagefield College Public Day School, Newport, Gwent; Memorial Coll. (Congregational), Brecon. Local government officer, 1950–52; RAF, 1952–55; theol. training, 1955–58. Ordained Congregational (URC) Minister, 1958; Mill Street Congregational Church, Newport, Gwent, 1958–63; Bettws Congregational Church, 1963–68; Llanvaches Congregational Church, 1966–68; Free Churches Chaplain, St Woolas Hosp., Newport, 1964–68. Entered RN as Chaplain, 1968; served HMS: Seahawk, 1968–69; Hermes, 1969–70; Raleigh, 1970–71; Seahawk, 1971–73; Daedalus, 1973–74; served Malta, 1974–76; C-in-C Naval Home Comd staff, 1977–81; HMS Sultan, 1981–84; Flag Officer Scotland and NI staff, 1984–86; HMS Heron, 1986; Prin. Chaplain (Navy), Ch. of Scotland and Free Churches, 1986–91; RN retired, 1991. QHC, 1986–91. *Recreations:* oil painting, golf, hill walking, music, gardening, Rugby. *Address:* 18 Brodrick Avenue, Gosport, Hants PO12 2EN. *T:* (023) 9258 1114.

WILLIAMS, Sara Ann, (Sally); *see* Muggeridge, S. A.

WILLIAMS, Sarah Rosalind; *see* Palmer, S. R.

WILLIAMS, Sean Mountford Graham; Strategy Advisor, BT Group plc, since 2008; *b* London, 1 June 1963; *s* of Tony Williams and Sheelagh Williams; *m* 1989, Anne-Marie Louise Kauffmann; three *s* one *d. Educ:* Charterhouse; Worcester Coll., Oxford (BA 1986); Kennedy Sch. of Govt, Harvard Univ. (MPA 1990). Man. Dir, Williams Lea & Co., 1990–92; Gp Finance Dir, Williams Lea Gp, 1993–95; Special Advr, Prime Minister's Policy Unit, 1995–97; Partner, LEK Consulting LLP, 1997–2003; Exec. Dir, OFCOM, 2003–07; Exec. Dir, Markets and Projects, OFT, 2007–08. Non-exec. Dir, Williams Lea Hldgs plc, 1995–2008. Chm., Adv. Bd, Transact, 2006–08. *Recreations:* cycling, singing, reading, family. *Address:* 17 Fielding Road, W14 0LL. *T:* (020) 7603 2104; *e-mail:* smgwilliams@btinternet.com.

WILLIAMS, Serena Jameka; tennis player; *b* Mich, USA, 26 Sept. 1981; *d* of Richard and Oracene Williams. *Educ:* Fort Lauderdale Art Inst. (degree in fashion design). Professional tennis player, 1995–: Grand Slam wins: (singles): US Open, 1999, 2002, 2008; French Open, 2002; Wimbledon, 2002, 2003; Australian Open, 2003, 2005; (doubles, with Venus Williams): French Open, 1999; US Open, 1999; Wimbledon, 2000, 2002, 2008; Australian Open, 2001, 2003; (mixed doubles, with Max Mirnyi) Wimbledon, US Open, 1998. Member: US Fedn Cup Team, 1999; US Olympic Team, Sydney, 2000 (Gold Medallist, doubles, with Venus Williams); ranked world No 1, 2002. Founder and designer, fashion label, Aneres, 2004–; launched Serena Williams Collection by Nike, apparel and footwear collection, 2005; numerous appearances as actress on TV progs. *Publication:* (with Venus Williams and Hilary Beard) Venus & Serena – Serving from the Hip: 10 rules for living, loving and winning, 2005. *Address:* c/o William Morris Agency, 1 William Morris Place, Beverly Hills, CA 90212, USA; c/o US Tennis Association, 70 West Red Oak Lane, White Plains, NY 10604, USA.

See also V. E. S. Williams.

WILLIAMS, Sian Mary; Main Presenter, BBC1 Breakfast, since 2001; Presenter, BBC News at Six, since 1999; *b* London, 28 Nov. 1964; *d* of John Price Williams and Katherine Elizabeth Rees; partner, Paul Woolwich; one *s;* two *s* from previous marriage. *Educ:* Oxford Brookes Univ. (BA Hons English and History). BBC Radio trng scheme, 1987–88; reporter, BBC Radio Merseyside, 1988–90; Sen. Producer, BBC Radio 4 World at One/PM, 1990–97; Editor, 1997, Sen. Presenter, 1997–99, BBC News 24; Special Corresp., BBC 6 O'Clock News, 1999–2001; occasional presenter, BBC Radio and BBC1 progs. Pres., Television and Radio Industries Club, 2007–08. Patron: Sparks; Link. *Recreations:* cinema, wine, walking. *Address:* BBC Breakfast, BBC Television Centre, Wood Lane, W12 7RJ. *T:* (020) 8734 8000; *e-mail:* sian.williams@bbc.co.uk.

WILLIAMS, Stephen Michael; HM Diplomatic Service; Ambassador to Bulgaria, since 2007; *b* 20 July 1959; *s* of Very Rev. H. C. N. Williams and of Pamela Williams; *m* 1983, Fiona Michele Hume; one *s* two *d. Educ:* Sidney Sussex Coll., Cambridge (BA 1980, MA). Entered Foreign and Commonwealth Office, 1981; Third, later Second, Sec., Sofia, 1984–87; EU Dept (Ext.), FCO, 1987–90; on secondment to Barclays Bank, 1990–91; Hd, Econ. and Commercial Sect., Oslo, 1991–95; First Sec. (Ext. Relns), UK Perm. Repn to EU, Brussels, 1995–98; Dep. Hd, EU Dept (Int.), FCO, 1998–2000; Minister and Dep. Hd of Mission, Buenos Aires, 2001–03; Hd, Latin America & Caribbean Dept, FCO, 2003–05; Dir, Americas, FCO, 2005–07. *Recreations:* walking, sport, music. *Address:* c/o Foreign and Commonwealth Office, King Charles Street, SW1A 2AH.

WILLIAMS, Stephen Roy; MP (Lib Dem) Bristol West, since 2005; *b* 11 Oct. 1966. *Educ:* Mountain Ash Comprehensive Sch., Glamorgan; Univ. of Bristol (BA 1988). Coopers and Lybrand, Bristol, 1988–95; Tax Manager: Kraft Jacobs Suchard Ltd, 1995; Grant Thornton, Cheltenham, 1996–98, Bristol, 1998–2001; Tax Accountant for Orange plc, Wincanton plc and RAC plc, 2001–05. Member (Lib Dem): Avon CC, 1993–96; Bristol CC, 1995–99. Contested (Lib Dem): Bristol S, 1997; Bristol W, 2001. Shadow Minister: for Public Health, 2005–06; for Further and Higher Education, 2006–07; for Schools, 2007; Shadow Sec. of State for Innovation, Univs and Skills, 2007–. Member: Educn Select Cttee, 2005–07; Public Accounts Cttee, 2005–06; Children, Schs and Families Select Cttee, 2007–08. *Address:* (office) PO Box 2500, Bristol BS6 9AH; House of Commons, SW1A 0AA.

WILLIAMS, Susan Elizabeth, OBE 2000; Director of Nursing, Lanarkshire Primary Care NHS Trust, 2001–03; *b* 30 Oct. 1942; *d* of late Ernest George Fost and of Kathleen Beatrice Maud Fost; *m* 1st, 1964, Dennis Norman Carnevale (decd); one *s* one *d;* 2nd, 1977, Keith Edward Williams (marr. diss. 1996). *Educ:* Grammar School for Girls, Weston-super-Mare; Wolverhampton Polytechnic (Post-grad. DipPsych); Bristol Royal Hosps (RSCN, RGN, RNT); BEd (Hons), DipN London. Ward Sister, Royal Hosp. for Sick Children, Bristol, 1972–76; Nurse Tutor, Salop Area Sch. of Nursing, 1976–80; Sen. Tutor, Dudley AHA, 1980–83; Reg. Nurse (Educn and Res.), W Midlands RHA, 1983–87; Chief Nurse Advr/Dir of Nurse Educn, Bromsgrove and Redditch HA, 1987–88; Regl Dir of Nursing and Quality Assurance, W Midlands RHA, 1988–93; Dep. Dir of Nursing Management Exec., DoH, 1993–94; Dir of Nursing, Greater Glasgow Community and Mental Health NHS Trust, 1994–98; Nurse Advr to Greater Glasgow Health Bd, 1998–2001. Board Member: Erskine Hospital, 2001; Prince and Princess of Wales Hospice, 2003–05. *Recreations:* hill walking, photography, reading, listening to music, foreign travel.

WILLIAMS, Mrs Susan Eva, MBE 1959; Lord-Lieutenant of South Glamorgan, 1985–90; *b* 17 Aug. 1915; *d* of Robert Henry Williams and Dorothy Marie Williams; *m* 1950, Charles Crofts Llewellyn Williams (*d* 1952). *Educ:* St James's, West Malvern. WAAF, 1939–45. JP 1961, High Sheriff 1968, DL 1973, Glamorgan; Lieut, S Glam, 1981–85. DStJ 1990. *Recreation:* National Hunt racing. *Address:* Caercady, Welsh St Donats, Cowbridge, Vale of Glamorgan CF71 7ST. *T:* (01446) 772346.

WILLIAMS, Susan Frances; a District Judge, Magistrates' Courts, West London, since 2002; a Recorder, since 2006; *b* 27 Nov. 1955; *d* of Major John Trelawny Williams and Joyce Williams. *Educ:* Kent Coll.; Bristol Univ. (LLB Hons). Called to the Bar, Middle Temple, 1978; barrister in private practice specialising in criminal law, 1978–2002. Mem., Criminal Bar Assoc., 1987–2002. Member: Hall Cttee, Middle Temple, 1984–94; N London Bar Mess, 1994–2002 (Jun. for Wood Green Crown Court). *Recreations:* gardening (Mem., RHS), malt whisky tasting (Mem., Scotch Malt Whisky Soc.). *Address:* West London Magistrates' Court, 181 Talgarth Road, W6 8DN. *T:* (020) 8700 9303.

WILLIAMS, Rt Rev. Thomas Anthony; Auxiliary Bishop of Liverpool, (RC), Vicar General, and Titular Bishop of Mageo, since 2003; *b* Liverpool, 10 Feb. 1948; *s* of late Richard and Margaret Williams. *Educ:* Christleton Hall, Chester; English Coll., Lisbon; St Joseph's Coll., Upholland. Ordained priest, 1972; Curate: St Francis of Assisi, Garston, 1972–75; Sacred Heart, Liverpool, 1975–83 (Chaplain to Royal Liverpool Hosp.); Our Lady of Walsingham, Netherton, 1983–84; Parish Priest, Liverpool: Our Lady Immaculate, 1984–89 and 1999–2003; St Anthony's, 1989–2003. Mem., Catholic Bishops' Conf. of England and Wales, 2003– (Bishop responsible for Hosp. Chaplaincy, 2003–). Member: Archdiocesan Finance Adv. Cttee, 1977–; George Andrew Fund Cttee, 1994–; Liverpool City Centre Ecumenical Team, 1996–; Trustee: Archdiocese of Liverpool, 2003–; Nugent Care Soc., 2003–. Mem., Archdiocese of Liverpool Chapter of Canons, 2001. *Recreations:* music, golf. *Address:* (office) 14 Hope Place, Liverpool L1 9BG.

WILLIAMS, His Eminence Cardinal Thomas Stafford, ONZ 2000; DD; Archbishop of Wellington, (RC), and Metropolitan of New Zealand, 1979–2005, now Emeritus Archbishop; *b* 20 March 1930; *s* of Thomas Stafford Williams and Lillian Maude Kelly. *Educ:* Holy Cross Primary School, Miramar; SS Peter and Paul Primary School, Lower Hutt; St Patrick's Coll., Wellington; Victoria University Coll., Wellington; St Kevin's Coll., Oamaru; Holy Cross Coll., Mosgiel; Collegio Urbano de Propaganda Fide, Rome (STL); University Coll., Dublin (BSocSc); Hon. DD. Assistant Priest, St Patrick's Parish, Palmerston North, 1963–64; Director of Studies, Catholic Enquiry Centre, Wellington, 1965–70; Parish Priest: St Anne's Parish, Leulumoega, W Samoa, 1971–75; Holy Family Parish, Porirua, NZ, 1976–79. Cardinal, 1983. *Address:* 40 Walton Avenue, Waikanae 6010, New Zealand. *T:* (4) 2934684.

WILLIAMS, Trevor; *see* Williams, A. T.

WILLIAMS, Venetia Mary; racehorse trainer, since 1996; *b* 10 May 1960; *d* of John Williams and Patricia Williams. *Educ:* Downe House Sch., Newbury. Trained winners of: King George VI Gold Cup, Kempton Park; Hennessy Gold Cup, Newbury; Welsh Grand Nat., Chepstow; Scottish Champion Hurdle, Ayr; Grand Annual Chase, Cleeve Hurdle

(3 times), Coral Cup, Racing Post Plate, Cheltenham; Ascot Chase. *Recreations:* ski-ing (snow and water), travel. *Address:* Aramstone, Kings Caple, Hereford HR1 4TU. *T:* (01432) 840646, *Fax:* (01432) 840830.

WILLIAMS, Venus Ebony Starr; tennis player; *b* Calif, USA, 17 June 1980; *d* of Richard and Oracene Williams. Professional tennis player, 1994–: Grand Slam wins: (singles): Wimbledon, 2000, 2001, 2005, 2007, 2008; US Open, 2000, 2001; (doubles, with Serena Williams): French Open, 1999; US Open, 1999; Wimbledon, 2000, 2002, 2008; Australian Open, 2001, 2003; (mixed doubles, with Justin Gimelstob) Australian Open, French Open, 1998. Member: US Fedn Cup Team, 1995, 1999, 2003; US Olympic Team, Sydney, 2000 (Gold Medallist, singles and doubles), Athens, 2004; ranked world No 1, 2002. Pres. and CEO, V Starr Interiors, 2002–. *Publication:* (with Serena Williams and Hilary Beard) Venus & Serena - Serving from the Hip: 10 rules for living, loving and winning, 2005. *Address:* V Starr Interiors, 1102 W Indiantown Road, Suite 11, Jupiter, FL 33458, USA; c/o US Tennis Association, 70 West Red Oak Lane, White Plains, NY 10604, USA.

See also S. J. Williams.

WILLIAMS, Victoria Kirstyn, (Kirsty); Member (Lib Dem) Brecon and Radnorshire, National Assembly for Wales, since 1999; *b* 19 March 1971; *d* of Edward G. Williams and Pamela M. Williams (*née* Hall); *m* 2000, Richard John Rees; three *d. Educ:* St Michael's Sch., Llanelli; Univ. of Manchester (BA Hons Amer. Studies 1993); Univ. of Missouri. Marketing and PR Exec., 1994–97. National Assembly for Wales: Chm., Health and Social Services Cttee, 1999–2003, Standards Cttee, 2003–; Mem., Health and Social Services Cttee, 2003–05, Local Govt and Public Services Cttee, 2003–04; Economic Develt and Transport Cttee, 2005–. Lib Dem Business Manager, 2000–. Dep. Pres., Welsh Liberal Democrats, 1997–99. *Recreations:* horse riding, sport, farming. *Address:* National Assembly for Wales, Crickhowell House, Cardiff CF99 1NA. *T:* (029) 2089 8358.

WILLIAMS, Sir (William) Max (Harries), Kt 1983; solicitor; Senior Partner, Clifford Chance, 1989–91 (Joint Senior Partner, 1987–89); *b* 18 Feb. 1926; *s* of Llwyd and Hilary Williams; *m* 1951, Jenifer (*d* 1999), *d* of late Rt Hon. E. L. Burgin, LLD, and Mrs Burgin, JP; two *d. Educ:* Nautical Coll., Pangbourne. Served 178 Assault Field Regt RA, Far East (Captain), 1943–47. Admitted Solicitor, 1950. Sen. Partner, Clifford Turner, 1984–87. Mem. Council, 1962–85, Pres., 1982–83, Law Society. Mem., Crown Agents for Oversea Govts and Administration, 1982–86; Lay Mem., Stock Exchange Council, 1984–93; Mem., Stock Exchange Appeals Cttee, 1989–2000. Director: Royal Insurance plc, 1985–95 (Dep. Chm., 1992–95); 3i Group plc, 1988–96 (Dep. Chm., 1993–96; Chm. Audit Cttee, 1991–96); Garden Pension Trustees Ltd, 1990–96; Royal Insurance Co. of Canada, 1991–95. Chairman: Review Bd for Govt Contracts, 1986–93; Police Appeals Tribunal, 1993–99. Member: Royal Commission on Legal Services, 1976–79; Cttee of Management of Inst. of Advanced Legal Studies, 1980–86; Council, Wildfowl Trust (Hon. Treasurer, 1974–80). Pres., City of London Law Soc., 1986–87. Mem., Amer. Law Inst., 1985–; Hon. Member: Amer. Bar Assoc.; Canadian Bar Assoc. Master, Solicitors' Co., 1986–87. Hon. LLD Birmingham, 1983. *Recreations:* golf, fishing, ornithology. *Address:* Orinda, Holly Lane, Harpenden, Herts AL5 5DY. *Clubs:* Garrick; Brocket Hall Golf.

WILLIAMS, Hon. Sir Wyn (Lewis), Kt 2007; **Hon. Mr Justice Wyn Williams;** a Judge of the High Court of Justice, Queen's Bench Division, since 2007; *b* 31 March 1951; *s* of Ronald and Nellie Williams; *m* 1973, Carol Ann Bosley; one *s* one *d. Educ:* Rhondda County Grammar Sch.; Corpus Christi Coll., Oxford (MA). Called to the Bar, Inner Temple, 1974; in practice at the Bar, Cardiff, 1974–88, and London, 1998–2004; QC 1992; a Recorder, 1992–2004; a Circuit Judge (specialist Chancery Circuit Judge for Wales and Chester Circuit), 2004–07. Pres., Pendyrus Male Choir, 2008–. *Recreations:* sport, particularly Rugby, music, reading. *Address:* Royal Courts of Justice, Strand, WC2A 2LL. *Clubs:* Cardiff and County; Tylorstown Rugby Football.

WILLIAMS, Wynford; *see* Williams, D. W.

WILLIAMS-BULKELEY, Sir Richard (Thomas), 14th Bt *cr* 1661 of Penrhyn, Caernarvonshire; Vice Lord-Lieutenant of Gwynedd, 2006; *b* 25 May 1939; *s* of Sir Richard Harry David Williams-Bulkeley, 13th Bt, TD and Renée Arundell (*d* 1994), *yr d* of Sir Thomas Neave, 5th Bt; *S* father, 1992; *m* 1964, Sarah Susan, *er d* of Rt Hon. Sir Henry Josceline Phillimore, OBE; twin *s* one *d. Educ:* Eton. FRICS 1989. Captain, Welsh Guards, 1964. High Sheriff, 1993, DL 1998, Gwynedd. *Recreation:* astronomy. *Heir: s* Major Richard Hugh Williams-Bulkeley, Welsh Guards [*b* 8 July 1968; *m* 1995, Jacqueline, *er d* of David Edwards; two *s* one *d*].

WILLIAMS-WYNN, Sir (David) Watkin, 11th Bt *cr* 1688, of Gray's Inn; DL; *b* 18 Feb. 1940; *s* of Sir Owen Watkin Williams-Wynn, 10th Bt, CBE and Margaret Jean (*d* 1961), *d* of late Col William Alleyne Macbean, RA; *S* father, 1988; *m* 1st, 1967, Harriet Veryan Elspeth (marr. diss. 1981), *d* of Gen. Sir Norman Tailyour, KCB, DSO; two *s* twin *d*; 2nd, 1983, Victoria Jane Dillon (marr. diss. 1998), *d* of late Lt-Col Ian Dudley De-Ath, DSO, MBE; twin *s. Educ:* Eton. Lt Royal Dragoons, 1958–63; Major Queen's Own Yeomanry, 1970–77. DL 1970, High Sheriff, 1990, Clwyd. *Recreations:* foxhunting and other field sports. *Heir: s* Charles Edward Watkin Williams-Wynn, *b* 17 Sept. 1970. *Address:* Plas-yn-Cefn, St Asaph, N Wales LL17 0EY. *T:* (01745) 582200. *Clubs:* Pratt's, Cavalry and Guards.

WILLIAMSON, family name of **Barons Forres** and **Williamson of Horton**.

WILLIAMSON OF HORTON, Baron *cr* 1999 (Life Peer), of Horton in the county of Somerset; **David Francis Williamson,** GCMG 1998; CB 1984; PC 2007; Secretary-General, Commission of the European Communities, 1987–97; *b* 8 May 1934; *s* of late Samuel Charles Wathen Williamson and Marie Eileen Williamson (*née* Denney); *m* 1961, Patricia Margaret Smith; two *s. Educ:* Tonbridge Sch.; Exeter Coll., Oxford (MA). Entered Min. of Agriculture, Fisheries and Food, 1958; Private Sec. to Permanent Sec. and to successive Parly Secs, 1960–62; HM Diplomatic Service, as First Sec. (Agric. and Food), Geneva, for Kennedy Round Trade Negotiations, 1965–67; Principal Private Sec. to successive Ministers of Agric., Fisheries and Food, 1967–70; Head of Milk and Milk Products Div., Marketing Policy Div. and Food Policy Div., 1970–74; Under-Sec., Gen. Agricultural Policy Gp, 1974–76, EEC Gp, 1976–77; Dep. Dir Gen., Agriculture, European Commn, 1977–83; Dep. Sec., Cabinet Office, 1983–87. Mem., Select Cttee on EU, H of L, 2001–04. Convenor of crossbench peers, 2004–07. Non-exec. Dir, Whitbread plc, 1998–2005; Chm., Somerset Strategic Partnership, 2001–04. Vis. Prof., Univ. of Bath, 1997–2000. Pres., Univs Assoc. for Contemp. Eur. Studies, 2001–03. Trustee, Thomson Foundn, 2001–06. Hon. DEconSc Limerick, 1996; Hon. DCL Kent, 1998; Hon. Dr of Laws: Robert Gordon, 1999; Bath, 1999. Kt Commander's Cross, Order of Merit (Germany), 1991; Commander Grand Cross, Royal Order of Polar Star (Sweden), 1998; Commandeur, Légion d'Honneur (France), 1999. *Address:* 58 St Joseph's Field, Taunton, Somerset TA1 3TF.

WILLIAMSON, Adrian John Gerard Hughes; QC 2002; a Recorder, since 2004; *b* 25 Nov. 1959; *s* of late Dennis Walter Williamson and of Margaret Teresa Williamson; *m* 1983, Gillian Herrod; two *s* one *d. Educ:* Highgate Sch.; Trinity Hall, Cambridge (BA 1st Cl. Hons Law 1982, MA 1985). Called to the Bar, Middle Temple, 1983; in private practice as barrister, specialising in construction law, 1985–. Pt-time Supervisor in Law, Churchill Coll., Cambridge, 1982–84. Gov., St Thomas More Primary Sch., Saffron Walden, 1996–2003. *Publications:* (contrib.) Keating on Building Contracts, 5th edn 1991 to 8th edn 2005; (ed jtly) Halsbury's Laws of England, vol. 4(3): Building Contracts, Building Societies, 2002; (gen. ed.) Keating on JCT Contracts, 2006. *Recreations:* family, Arsenal FC, squash. *Address:* Keating Chambers, 15 Essex Street, WC2R 3AU. *T:* (020) 7544 2600, *Fax:* (020) 7240 7722; *e-mail:* awilliamson@keatingchambers.com.

WILLIAMSON, Aldon Thompson; Head, Dame Alice Owen's School, 1994–2005; *b* 19 June 1944; *d* of Gordon Anderson Baxter and Margaret Sophia Baxter; *m* 1966, Prof. James Williamson; one *s* one *d. Educ:* Aberdeen Univ. (MA Hons); Inst. of Educn, Univ. of London (PGCE). Maths teacher, S Hampstead High Sch. (GPDST), 1967–69, Head of Maths, 1969–71; Dep. Head, Dame Alice Owen's Sch., 1983–89; Head, Leventhorpe Sch., Herts, 1989–94. FRSA 1997. *Recreations:* opera, art, reading.

WILLIAMSON, Andrew George, CBE 1999; Chairman, Cornwall and Isles of Scilly Primary Care Trust, since 2006; *b* 29 Feb. 1948; *s* of Albert and Jocelyn Williamson; *m* 1972, Mary Eleanor White; one *s* one *d. Educ:* Southern Grammar Sch., Portsmouth; Oxford Poly. (Dip. in Social Work; CQSW); Birmingham Univ. (Advanced Management Develt Prog., 1982). Residential Child Care, Portsmouth, 1967; Child Care Officer, Hants, 1969; social work management positions in Northumberland and Wandsworth; Asst Dir of Social Services, East Sussex, 1983; Dep. Dir, West Sussex, 1986; Dir of Social Services, Devon CC, 1990–99. Chm., N and E Devon HA, 2000–02; non-exec. Dir, SW Peninsular Strategic HA, 2002–06 (Vice-Chm., 2006); Dir, Initiatives in Care, 2000–. Member: Top Mgt Programme, 1992–; Criminal Justice Consultative Council, 1992–95; Sec. of State for the Home Dept's Youth Justice Task Force, 1997–; Co-Chm., MoJ/DCFS Inquiry into use of restraint in secure accommodation, 2008. Chm., Devon and Cornwall Workforce Confedn, 2001–04. Advr, Nat. Authy for Child Protection, Govt of Rumania, 2000–. Hon. Sec., Assoc. of Dirs of Social Services, 1996–99. FRSA 1995. *Recreations:* reading, cricket, music, theatre. *Address:* Randolls, Victoria Road, Topsham, Exeter EX3 0EU. *T:* (01392) 877458.

WILLIAMSON, Sir Brian; *see* Williamson, Sir R. B.

WILLIAMSON, Prof. Edwin Henry, PhD; King Alfonso XIII Professor of Spanish Studies, University of Oxford, since 2003; Fellow, Exeter College, Oxford, since 2003; *b* 2 Oct. 1949; *s* of Henry Alfred Williamson and Renée Williamson (*née* Clarembaux); *m* 1976, Susan Jane Fitchie; two *d. Educ:* Edinburgh Univ. (MA; PhD 1980). Jun. Lectr in Spanish, TCD, 1974–77; Lectr in Spanish, Birkbeck Coll., Univ. of London, 1977–90; Forbes Prof. of Hispanic Studies, Univ. of Edinburgh, 1990–2003. Leverhulme Res. Fellow, 1995–96; Visiting Professor: Univ. of São Paulo, Brazil, 1997; Stanford Univ., Calif, 1999; Brettschneider Vis. Scholar, Cornell Univ., 2006. Comdr, Orden de Isabel la Católica (Spain). *Publications:* The Half-way House of Fiction: Don Quixote and Arthurian romance, 1984, 2nd edn 1986; El Quijote y los libros de caballerías, 1991; The Penguin History of Latin America, 1992, 2nd edn 2003; Cervantes and the Modernists, 1994; Borges: a life, 2004 (trans. Spanish and Dutch, 2006); articles in learned jls. *Recreations:* hill-walking, cinema, theatre, visual arts, exploring cities, going abroad. *Address:* Exeter College, Turl Street, Oxford OX1 3DP. *T:* (01865) 270476, *Fax:* (01865) 270757; *e-mail:* edwin.williamson@exeter.ox.ac.uk.

WILLIAMSON, Elizabeth Ann; Architectural Editor, Victoria History of the Counties of England, since 1997; Reader in Architectural History, University of London; *b* 10 May 1950; *d* of late Walter Felce Williamson and of Elizabeth Joan (*née* Ford); *m* 1995, Malcolm Slade Higgs. *Educ:* High Sch., Stamford; Courtauld Inst. of Art, London (BA Hons (Hist. of European Art) 1973). Asst, then Dep. Ed., Buildings of England, Ireland, Scotland and Wales, Penguin Books, 1976–97. Comr, English Heritage, 2003– (Chm., Historic Parks and Gardens Panel, 2007–). FSA 1998. *Publications:* The Buildings of England: revisions of 5 vols in series, 1978, 1979, 1983, 1984, 1994, London Docklands, 1998; (with Anne Riches and Malcolm Higgs) The Buildings of Scotland: Glasgow, 1990; contribs to vols in Victoria History of the Counties of England, 1998–. *Recreation:* fiction. *Address:* Institute of Historical Research, University of London, Senate House, WC1E 7HU.

WILLIAMSON, Sir (George) Malcolm, Kt 2007; FCIB; Chairman: National Australia Group Europe Ltd, since 2004; Clydesdale Bank plc, since 2004; CDC Group plc, since 2004; *b* 27 Feb. 1939; *s* of George and Margery Williamson; *m* Hang Thi Ngo; one *s* one *d*, and one *s* one *d* by a previous marriage. *Educ:* Bolton School. FIB. Barclays Bank: Local Director, 1980; Asst Gen. Manager, 1981; Regional Gen. Manager, 1983–85; Bd Mem., Post Office, and Man. Dir, Girobank plc, 1985–89; Gp Exec. Dir, Standard Chartered Bank, 1989–91; Gp Man. Dir, 1991–93, Gp Chief Exec., 1993–98, Standard Chartered PLC; Pres. and CEO, Visa Internat., San Francisco, 1998–2004. Chairman: Britannic Gp plc, 2004–05; Signet Gp plc, 2006–; non-executive Director: National Grid Group, 1995–99; British Invisibles, 1996–98; Gp 4 Securicor, subseq. G4S, plc, 2004–08; Nat. Australia Bank, 2004–; JP Morgan Cazenove Hldgs, 2005–; Resolution plc, 2005–08 (Dep. Chm., 2005–08); Internat. Business Leaders Forum, 2006–. UK Chm., British-Thai Business Gp, 1997–; Chm., Youth Business Internat. Adv. Bd, 2005–. Mem. Council, Industrial Soc., 1996–98. Chm., Strategy and Develt Bd, Cass Business Sch., 2008–. *Recreations:* mountaineering, golf, chess. *Address:* National Australia Group Europe Ltd, 3rd Floor, 88 Wood Street, EC2V 7QQ. *Clubs:* Rucksack, Pedestrian (Manchester).

WILLIAMSON, Hazel Eleanor; *see* Marshall, H. E.

WILLIAMSON, Helen Sheppard, (Sarah); *see* Kay, H. S.

WILLIAMSON, Prof. Hugh Godfrey Maturin, FBA 1993; Regius Professor of Hebrew, and Student of Christ Church, Oxford University, since 1992; *b* 15 July 1947; *s* of Thomas Broadwood Williamson and Margaret Frances (*née* Davy); *m* 1971, Julia Eiluned Morris; one *s* two *d. Educ:* Rugby Sch.; Trinity Coll., Cambridge (BA 1st cl. Hons Theol., 1969; MA); St John's Coll., Cambridge; PhD 1975, DD 1986, Cantab. Cambridge University: Asst Lectr in Hebrew and Aramaic, 1975–79; Lectr, 1979–89; Reader, 1989–92; Fellow of Clare Hall, 1985–92. Chm., Anglo-Israel Archaeol Soc., 1990–. Pres., SOTS, 2004. Corresp. Mem., Göttingen Akademie der Wissenschaften, 2008. *Publications:* Israel in the Books of Chronicles, 1977; 1 and 2 Chronicles, 1982; Ezra, Nehemiah, 1985; Ezra and Nehemiah, 1987; Annotated Key to Lambdin's Introduction to Biblical Hebrew, 1987; (ed jtly) The Future of Biblical Studies, 1987; (ed jtly) It is Written: essays in honour of Barnabas Lindars, 1988; Jesus is Lord, 1993; The Book Called Isaiah, 1994; (ed jtly) Wisdom in Ancient Israel: essays in honour of J. A. Emerton, 1995; Variations on a Theme: King, Messiah and Servant in the Book of Isaiah, 1998; (ed jtly) Reading from Right to Left: essays in honour of David J. A. Clines, 2003; (ed jtly) Prophetie in Israel, 2003; Studies in Persian Period History and Historiography, 2004; Confirmation or

Contradiction?: archaeology and Biblical history, 2004; (ed jtly) Dictionary of the Old Testament Historical Books, 2005; Isaiah 1–5: a critical and exegetical commentary, 2006; (ed) Understanding the History of Ancient Israel, 2007; contrib. to learned jls incl. Vetus Testamentum, Jl of Theol Studies, Jl of Biblical Lit., Jl of Semitic Studies, Jl for Study of OT, Palestine Exploration Qly, Zeitschrift für die alttestamentliche Wissenschaft, Oudtestamentische Studiën. *Recreations:* allotment tending, model yacht sailing. *Address:* 7 Chester Road, Southwold, Suffolk IP18 6LN. *T:* (01502) 722319; Christ Church, Oxford OX1 1DP.

WILLIAMSON, Prof. James, CBE 1985; FRCPE; Professor of Geriatric Medicine, University of Edinburgh, 1976–86, now Emeritus; *b* 22 Nov. 1920; *s* of James Mathewson Williamson and Jessie Reid; *m* 1945, Sheila Mary Blair; three *s* two *d*. *Educ:* Wishaw High Sch., Lanarkshire; Univ. of Glasgow (MB ChB 1943); FRCPE 1959 (MRCPE 1949). Training in general medicine, incl. two years in general practice, later specialising in respiratory diseases, then in medicine of old age; Consultant Physician, 1954–73; Prof. of Geriatric Medicine in newly established Chair, Univ. of Liverpool, 1973–76. Pres., British Geriatrics Soc., 1986–88; Chairman: Age Concern Scotland, 1987–90; Chest Heart Stroke Assoc., Scotland, 1993–98. Hon. DSc Rochester, USA, 1989. *Publications:* chapters in various textbooks; numerous articles in gen. med. jls and in jls devoted to subject of old age. *Recreations:* walking, reading. *Address:* 8 Chester Street, Edinburgh EH3 7RA. *T:* (0131) 477 0282.

WILLIAMSON, Marshal of the Royal Air Force Sir Keith (Alec), GCB 1982 (KCB 1979); AFC 1968; Chief of the Air Staff, 1982–85; Air ADC to the Queen, 1982–85; *b* 25 Feb. 1928; *s* of Percy and Gertrude Williamson; *m* 1953, Patricia Anne, *d* of W/Cdr F. M. N. Watts; two *s* twin *d*. *Educ:* Bancroft's Sch., Woodford Green; Market Harborough Grammar Sch.; RAF Coll., Cranwell. Commissioned, 1950; flew with Royal Australian Air Force in Korea, 1953; OC 23 Sqdn, 1966–68; Command, RAF Gütersloh, 1968–70; RCDS 1971; Dir, Air Staff Plans, 1972–75; Comdt, RAF Staff Coll., 1975–77; ACOS (Plans and Policy), SHAPE, 1977–78; AOC-in-C, RAF Support Comd, 1978–80; AOC-in-C, RAF Strike Command and C-in-C, UK Air Forces, 1980–82. *Recreation:* golf.

WILLIAMSON, Sir Malcolm; *see* Williamson, Sir G. M.

WILLIAMSON, Martin Charles; HM Diplomatic Service; Head, Research Analysts, Foreign and Commonwealth Office, since 2007; *b* 28 Jan. 1953; *s* of Charles Frederick Williamson and Marie Williamson; *m* 1978, Elizabeth Michelle Darvill; two *s*. *Educ:* Univ. of Keele (BA Hons 1975); London Sch. of Econs (MSc 1977). Entered FCO, 1977; FCO, 1977–84; Res. Dept, IMF, 1984–87; Econ. Advr, FCO, 1987–89; Cabinet Office, 1989–91; OECD, 1991–94; Foreign and Commonwealth Office: Sen. Econ. Advr, 1994–99; Dep. Hd, Econ. Policy Dept, 1999; Hd, Resource Budgeting Dept, 1999–2003; Prism Team, 2003–04; Dep. High Comr, Wellington, 2004–06. *Publication:* Acquisition of Foreign Assets by Developing Countries, 1986. *Recreations:* walking, gym, reading, music. *Address:* c/o Foreign and Commonwealth Office, King Charles Street, SW1A 2AH; *e-mail:* martinwilliamson@dsl.pipex.com.

WILLIAMSON, Nicol; actor; *b* Hamilton, Scotland, 14 Sept. 1938. Dundee Rep. Theatre, 1960–61; Royal Court: That's Us, Arden of Faversham, 1961; A Midsummer Night's Dream, Twelfth Night, 1962; Royal Shakespeare Company, 1962; Nil Carborundum, The Lower Depths, Women Beware Women; Spring Awakening, Royal Court, 1962; Kelly's Eye, The Ginger Man, Royal Court, 1963; Inadmissible Evidence, 1964, 1978, Royal Court, Wyndham's 1965 (Evening Standard Best Actor Award), NY 1965 (NY Drama Critics Award); A Cuckoo in the Nest, Waiting for Godot, Miniatures, 1964; Sweeney Agonistes, Globe, 1965; Diary of a Madman, Duchess, 1967; Plaza Suite, NY, 1968; Hamlet, Round House, 1969 (Evening Standard Best Actor Award), NY and US tour, 1969; Midwinter Spring, Queen's, 1972; Circle in the Square, Uncle Vanya, NY, 1973; Royal Shakespeare Company, 1973–75: Coriolanus, Midwinter Spring, Aldwych, 1973; Twelfth Night, Macbeth, Stratford 1974, Aldwych 1975; dir and title role, Uncle Vanya, Other Place, Stratford, 1974; Rex, NY, 1975; Inadmissible Evidence, NY, 1981; Macbeth, NY, 1983; The Entertainer, NY, 1983; The Lark, USA, 1983; The Real Thing, NY, 1985; Jack—A Night on the Town with John Barrymore, Criterion, 1994; King Lear, Clwyd Th. Cymru, 2001. *Films:* Inadmissible Evidence, 1967; The Bofors Gun, 1968; Laughter in the Dark, 1968; The Reckoning, 1969; Hamlet, 1970; The Jerusalem File, 1971; The Wilby Conspiracy, 1974; The Seven Per Cent Solution, 1975; The Cheap Detective, The Goodbye Girl, Robin and Marion, 1977; The Human Factor, 1979; Excalibur, Venom, 1980; I'm Dancing as Fast as I Can, 1981; Return to Oz, 1984; Black Widow, 1986; The Hour of the Pig, 1994; The Wind in the Willows, 1996; Spawn, 1997; Return to Oz, 1998. *Television:* The Word, 1977; Macbeth, BBC Shakespeare series, 1982; Christopher Columbus, 1983; Lord Mountbatten—the Last Viceroy, 1985; Passion Flower, 1985. *Publication:* Ming's Kingdom, 1996.

WILLIAMSON, Nigel; writer; *b* 4 July 1954; *s* of Neville Albert and Anne Maureen Williamson; *m* 1976, Magali Patricia Wild; two *s*. *Educ:* Chislehurst and Sidcup Grammar School; University College London. Tribune: Journalist, 1982–84; Literary Editor, 1984; Editor, 1984–87; Editor: Labour Party News, 1987–89; New Socialist, 1987–89; The Times: political reporter, 1989–90; Diary Editor, 1990–92; Home News Editor, 1992–95; Whitehall correspondent, 1995–96; freelance interviewer and music writer, 1996–; contrib. ed., Uncut mag., 1997–; weekly columnist and contrib. ed., Billboard, 1999–; specialist music advr, British Council, 2002–. A Judge, Mercury Music Prize, 1999–2004. *Publications:* The SDP (ed), 1982; The New Right, 1984; (contrib.) The Rough Guide to World Music, 2000; Journey Through the Past: the stories behind the songs of Neil Young, 2002; The Rough Guide to Bob Dylan, 2004; (ed and contrib.) The Rough Guide Book of Playlists, 2005; The Rough Guide to the Blues, 2007; The Rough Guide to Led Zeppelin, 2007. *Recreations:* world music, cricket, gardening. *Address:* Long Tilings, Hever Lane, Hever, Kent TN8 7ET. *T:* (01342) 851472.

WILLIAMSON, Dr Paul, FSA; Keeper of Sculpture, Metalwork, Ceramics and Glass, Victoria and Albert Museum, since 2001; *b* 4 Aug. 1954; *s* of late Peter Williamson and Mary Teresa Williamson (*née* Meagher); *m* 1984, Emmeline Mary Clare Mandley, MBE; one s. *Educ:* Wimbledon Coll.; Univ. of East Anglia (BA Hons; MPhil; LittD). Res., British Sch. at Rome, 1978; Major State Student, DES, 1978–79; Department of Sculpture, Victoria and Albert Museum: Asst Keeper, 1979–89; acting Keeper, 1989; Chief Curator, 1989–2001; Sen. Chief Curator, 1995–98; Dir of Collections, 2004–07. Member: Wells Cathedral West Front Specialist Cttee, 1981–83; Wall Paintings Sub-Cttee, Council for the Care of Churches, 1987–90; Cttee, British Acad. Corpus of Romanesque Sculpture in Britain and Ireland, 1990–97; Lincoln Cathedral Fabric Adv. Council, 1990–2001; Cosmati Pavement Adv. Cttee, Westminster Abbey, 1996–99; Internat. Adv. Bd, Courtauld Inst. of Art (Wall Paintings Conservation), 2005–; Expert Advr on Sculpture, Reviewing Cttee on Export of Works of Art, 1989–. Member, Consultative Committee: Sculpture Jl, 1997–; Burlington Mag., 2003–; Walpole Soc., 2004–. Lansdowne Vis. Prof., Univ. of Victoria, BC, 2001; Diskant Lectr, Philadelphia Mus. of Art, 2001. FSA 1983 (Mem. Council, 1997–2003; Vice-Pres., 1999–2003). Trustee, Stained Glass Mus., Ely, 2005–. *Publications:* An Introduction to Medieval Ivory Carvings, 1982 (trans. German); Catalogue of Romanesque Sculpture in the Victoria and Albert Museum, 1983; (ed) The Medieval Treasury: the art of the Middle Ages in the Victoria and Albert Museum, 1986, 3rd edn 1998; The Thyssen-Bornemisza Collection: medieval sculpture and works of art, 1987; Northern Gothic Sculpture 1200–1450, 1988; (ed jtly) Early Medieval Wall Painting and Painted Sculpture in England, 1990; Gothic Sculpture 1140–1300, 1995 (trans. Spanish, 1997, trans. Portuguese, 1998); (ed) European Sculpture at the Victoria and Albert Museum, 1996; Netherlandish Sculpture 1450–1550, 2002; (ed jtly) Wonder: painted sculpture from medieval England, 2002; Medieval and Renaissance Stained Glass in the Victoria and Albert Museum, 2003; (ed jtly) Gothic: art for England 1400–1547, 2003; Medieval and Later Treasures from a Private Collection, 2005; (ed jtly) Medieval and Renaissance Treasures from the V&A, 2007; contribs to numerous exhibn catalogues; articles and book reviews in learned jls. *Recreation:* travel. *Address:* Victoria and Albert Museum, SW7 2RL. *T:* (020) 7942 2611; *e-mail:* p.williamson@vam.ac.uk.

WILLIAMSON, Peter John; Chairman of the Board, Solicitors Regulation Authority (formerly Regulation Board, Law Society of England and Wales), since 2005 (President, 2003–04); *b* 20 Aug. 1947; *s* of late John Reginald Williamson and Margaret Audrey Williamson (*née* Morrison); *m* 1974, Patricia Anne Mitchell Miller; one *s* one *d*. *Educ:* Berkhamsted Sch. Admitted as Solicitor, 1972; Partner: Kenneth Brown Baker Baker, subseq. Turner Kenneth Brown, 1974–91 (Man. Partner, 1986–90); Dawson & Co., subseq. Dawsons, 1991–98 (Consultant, 1998–2007). Dep. Dist Judge, 1995–2001; Asst Recorder, 1996–2000; Recorder, 2000–08. Law Society: Chm., Associate Mems Gp, 1970; Mem. Council, 1992–2005; Dep. Vice-Pres., 2001–02; Vice-Pres., 2002–03. Dir, Solicitors Indemnity Fund Ltd, 1995–2002 (Chm., 1997–2002). Pres., Holborn Law Soc., 1989–90. Berkhamsted Collegiate School: Pres., Old Berkhamstedians Assoc., 1979–81; Gov., 1991– (Chm. Govs, 1995–); Gov., Coll. of Law, 2002–05. *Recreations:* watching and reading about sport, particularly cricket, listening to classical music, travel. *Address:* Solicitors Regulation Authority, 8 Dormer Place, Leamington Spa CV32 5AE. *T:* (01926) 439748, *Fax:* (01926) 487109; *e-mail:* peter.williamson@sra.org.uk. *Clubs:* Travellers, MCC.

WILLIAMSON, Peter Roger; HM Diplomatic Service, retired; Consultant on Sub-Sahara Africa; *b* 20 April 1942; *s* of Frederick W. and Dulcie R. Williamson; *m* 1977, Greta Helen Clare Richards; one *s* one *d*. *Educ:* Bristol Grammar Sch.; St John's Coll., Oxford (MA). Journalist and teacher, Far East, 1965–66; joined FCO, 1966; Kuala Lumpur, 1970; 1st Sec., FCO, 1973; Hong Kong, 1975; FCO, 1979; Counsellor: Kuala Lumpur, 1985–88; FCO, 1988–92; on loan to Cabinet Office, 1992–94; Counsellor, Nairobi, 1994–97. *Recreations:* tennis, travel, theatre, cinema.

WILLIAMSON, Philip Frederick, CBE 2008; Chief Executive, Nationwide Building Society, 2002–07; Chairman, Investors in People UK, since 2006; *b* 11 Dec. 1947; *s* of late Philip Gordon Williamson and of Elsie May Williamson; *m* 1993, Theresa Taylor; two *d*. *Educ:* Calday Grange Grammar Sch.; Newcastle Univ. (BA Hons Econ); Harvard Business Sch. FCIB 2002. Joined Lloyds Bank as grad. trainee, 1970; Dir, UK Land plc, 1988–91; Nationwide Building Society, 1991–: Divisional Director: Business Planning, 1994–95; Corporate Devlt, 1996; Marketing and Commercial Dir, 1996–99; Retail Ops Dir, 1999–2001; Chm., Nationwide Life, 1999–2001. Non-exec. Dir, Visa Europe, 2006–. Chairman: Council of Mortgage Lenders, 2000–01; Corporate Forum for Internat. Service, 2004–; BSA, 2005–06; Founder Dir, Regulatory and Retail Faculty Bd, Inst. of Financial Services; UK Vice-Pres., Eur. Mortgage Fedn, 2004–. *Recreations:* hockey, proficient golfer (7 handicap), stamp collecting. *Address:* Gable House, Sandridge Lane, Lindfield, Haywards Heath, West Sussex RH16 1XY.

WILLIAMSON, Richard Arthur; Director, Midland Region, Crown Prosecution Service, 1987–89; *b* 9 Jan. 1932; *s* of George Arthur and Winifred Mary Williamson; *m* 1957, Christina Elizabeth, *d* of Harry Godley Saxton, Worksop, Notts, and Helena Saxton; two *s*. *Educ:* King Edward VI Grammar Sch., East Retford; Sheffield Univ. (statutory year). Solicitor, 1956. National Service, RN (Sub-Lieut), 1956–58. Asst Solicitor, Lancs CC, 1958–61; Sen. Asst Solicitor, Lincs (Lindsey) CC, 1961–65; private practice, Partner in Hetts, Solicitors, Scunthorpe, 1965–76; Prin. Prosecuting Solicitor, Greater Manchester, 1976–83; Chief Prosecuting Solicitor, Lincs, 1983–85; Asst Hd of Field Management, Crown Prosecution Service, 1985–87. Prosecuting Solicitors Soc. of England and Wales: Mem. Exec. Council, 1978–85; Treas., 1978–85; Chm., Hds of Office, 1984–85. Mem., York and the Humber War Pensions Cttee, 1997–. *Recreations:* family, theatre, gardening. *Address:* The Lookout, Back Street, Alkborough, near Scunthorpe, North Lincolnshire DN15 9JN. *T:* (01724) 720843.

WILLIAMSON, Prof. Robert, AO 2004; FRCP, FRCPath; FRS 1999; Director, Murdoch Childrens Research Institute (formerly Murdoch Research Institute), Royal Children's Hospital, Melbourne, 1995–2006, now Honorary Senior Research Fellow; Research Professor of Medical Genetics, University of Melbourne School of Medicine, 1995–2005; *b* 14 May 1938; *s* of John and Mae Williamson; *m* 1st, 1962, Patricia Anne Sutherland (marr. diss. 1994); one *s* one *d*; 2nd, 1994, Robyn Elizabeth O'Hehir; one *s* one *d*. *Educ:* Bronx High School of Science, NY; Wandsworth Comprehensive School; University College London (BSc, MSc, PhD). FRCP 1990; FAA 2001. Lectr, Univ. of Glasgow, 1963–67; Sen. Scientist (Molecular Biol.), Beatson Inst. for Cancer Research, Glasgow, 1967–76; Prof. of Biochem., St. Mary's Hosp. Med. Sch., London Univ., 1976–95. Sen. Fellow, Carnegie Instn of Washington, Baltimore, 1972–73. External Examnr, Malaysia, Saudi Arabia. Member: UK Genetic Manipulation Adv. Cttee, 1976–91; Grants Cttees, MRC Cancer Research Campaign, 1976–95, Action Research for Crippled Child, Cystic Fybrosis Research Trust. Francqui Hon. Prof., Belgian Univs, 1995. Hon. MRCP 1986. Hon. MD Turku, 1987. Wellcome Award, Biochem. Soc., 1983; King Faisal Internat. Prize for Medicine, 1994. *Publications:* (ed) Genetic Engineering, vol. 1, 1981, vol. 2, 1982, vol. 3, 1982, vol. 4, 1983; articles in Nature, Cell, Procs of US Nat. Acad. of Scis, Biochemistry, Nucleic Acids Research. *Recreations:* reading, sport. *Address:* The Dean's Ganglion, Faculty of Medicine, University of Melbourne, 4/766 Elizabeth Street, Melbourne, Vic 3010, Australia. *T:* (3) 83444181; *e-mail:* r.williamson@unimelb.edu.au.

WILLIAMSON, Sir (Robert) Brian, Kt 2001; CBE 1989; Chairman: London International Financial Futures and Options Exchange, 1985–88 and 1998–2003 (Director, 1982–89); Electra Private Equity PLC (formerly Electra Investment Trust plc), since 2000 (Director, since 1994); Resolution PLC (formerly Resolution Life Group), 2004–05 (Director, 2004–08); *b* 16 Feb. 1945; *m* 1986, Diane Marie Christine de Jacquier de Rosée. *Educ:* Trinity College, Dublin (MA). Personal Asst to Rt Hon. Maurice Macmillan (later Viscount Macmillan), 1967–71; Editor, International Currency Review, 1971; Man. Dir, Gerrard & National Hldgs, 1978–89; Chairman: GNI Ltd, 1985–89; Gerrard & Nat. Hldgs, later Gerrard Gp PLC, 1989–98; Fleming Worldwide Investment Trust, 1998 (Dep. Chm., 1996–98); MT Fund Management Ltd, 2004–. Director: Fleming Internat. High Income Investment Trust plc, 1990–96; Court, Bank of Ireland, 1990–98; Barlows plc, 1997–98; HSBC Hldgs plc, 2002–; Templeton Emerging Markets

Investment Fund plc, 2002–03; Liv-Ex Ltd, 2005–; Open Europe, 2005–. Member: Bd, Bank of Ireland Britain Hldgs, 1986–90; Council, 1985–88, Council, Eur. Cttee, 1988–90, British Invisible Exports Council; FSA (formerly SIB), 1986–98; Supervisory Bd, NYSE Euronext (formerly Euronext NV), 2002–. Sen. Advr, Fleming Family and Partners, 2003–. Dir, Politeia, 1999–. Chm., Adv. Bd, Armed Forces (formerly Army) Common Investment Fund, 2002–. Gov. at Large, Nat. Assoc. of Securities Dealers, USA, 1995–98; Mem., Internat. Markets Adv. Bd, NASDAQ Stock Market, 1993–98 (Chm., 1996–98). Mem. Governing Council, Centre for Study of Financial Innovation, 2000–. Mem. HAC, commissioned 1975. Dir, Rowing Mus., Henley Foundn, 1992–94. Mem., Royal Opera House Develt Cttee, 2004–; Mem. Council, St George's House, 1996–2002, Dir, St George's House Trust (Windsor Castle), 1998–2002; Trustee, St Paul's Cathedral Foundn, 1999–2005. Freeman, 1994, HM Lieut, 2003, City of London. Contested (C) Sheffield Hillsborough, Feb. and Oct. 1974; prosp. parly cand., Truro, 1976–77. FRSA 1991. Hon. Bencher, Inner Temple, 2006. *Clubs:* Pratt's, White's, Flyfishers'; Kildare and University (Dublin); Brook (New York).

WILLIAMSON, Rt Rev. Robert Kerr, (Roy); Bishop of Southwark, 1991–98; *b* 18 Dec. 1932; *s* of James and Elizabeth Williamson; *m* 1956, Anne Boyd Smith (*d* 2004); three *s* two *d*. *Educ:* Elmgrove School, Belfast; Oak Hill College, London. London City Missionary, 1955–61; Oak Hill Coll., 1961–63; Asst Curate, Crowborough Parish Church, 1963–66; Vicar: St Paul, Hyson Green, Nottingham, 1966–71; St Ann w. Emmanuel, Nottingham, 1971–76; St Michael and All Angels, Bramcote, 1976–79; Archdeacon of Nottingham, 1978–84; Bishop of Bradford, 1984–91. Chm., Central Religious Adv. Cttee to BBC and ITC, 1993–97; Co-Chm., Inter-Faith Network for the UK, 1994–99. *Publications:* Can You Spare a Minute?, 1991; Funny You Should Say That, 1992; For Such a Time as This, 1996; Joyful Uncertainty, 1999; Open Return, 2000; Not Least in the Kingdom, 2001; Wholly Alive, 2002; Loved By Love, 2004. *Recreations:* walking, bird watching, reading, music.

WILLIAMSON, Prof. Robin Charles Noel, FRCS; President, Royal Society of Medicine, since 2008 (Associate Dean, 2001–02; Dean, 2002–06, Emeritus Dean, 2006–08); Consultant Surgeon, Hammersmith Hospital, since 1987; Professor of Surgery, Imperial College School of Medicine (formerly Professor and Head of Department of Surgery, Royal Postgraduate Medical School), University of London, since 1987; *b* 19 Dec. 1942; *s* of James Charles Frederick Lloyd Williamson and Helena Frances Williamson (*née* Madden); *m* 1967, Judith Marjorie (*née* Bull); three *s*. *Educ:* Rugby School; Emmanuel College, Cambridge; St Bartholomew's Hosp. Med. Coll. MA, MD, MChir (Cantab). Surgical Registrar, Reading, 1971–73; Sen. Surgical Registrar, Bristol, 1973–75; Res. Fellow, Harvard, 1975–76; Consultant Sen. Lectr, Bristol, 1977–79; Prof. of Surgery, Univ. of Bristol, 1979–87. Mem., Cell Biology and Disorders Bd, MRC, 1987–91. Fulbright-Hays Sen. Res. Scholar, USA, 1975; Sen. Penman Vis. Fellow, South Africa, 1985; Paul Grange Vis. Fellow, Univ. of Monash, 1986; Hunterian Prof., RCS, 1981–82; Raine Vis. Prof., Univ. of Western Australia, 1983; Richardson Prof., Mass Gen. Hosp., 1985; Visiting Professor: Univ. of Lund, Sweden, 1985; Univ. of Hong Kong, 1987; Univ. of Hamburg, 1999; Johnson and Johnson Vis. Prof., Univ. of Calif, San Francisco, 1989; Edwin Tooth Guest Prof., Royal Brisbane Hosp., Qld, 1989; Totalisator Bd Vis. Prof., Nat. Univ. of Singapore, 1994. Lectures: Arris and Gale, RCS, 1977–78; Finlayson Meml, RCPSG, 1985; Sir Gordon Bell Meml, RACS, NZ, 1988; Stuart, RSocMed and RCSE, 2007; Farndon Meml, Soc. of Acad. and Res. Surgery, 2008. Association of Surgeons of GB and Ireland: Moynihan Fellow, 1979; Mem. Council, 1993–99; Chm., Scientific Cttee, 1995–97; Vice Pres., 1997–98; Pres., 1998–99. President: Pancreatic Soc. of GB and Ireland, 1984–85; Internat. HepatoPancreatoBiliary Assoc., 1996–98 (Sec. Gen., 1994–96); Assoc. of Upper Gastrointestinal Surgeons, 1996–98; European Soc. of Surgery, 1998; James IV Assoc. of Surgeons, 2002–06; Chm., Educn Cttee, British Soc. of Gastroenterology, 1981–87; Member: Med. Adv. Cttee, British Council, 1988–94; Clin. Res and Trng and Career Panel, MRC, 1997–2003; Internat. Adv. Bd, Nat. Univ. of Singapore, 1998–2000; Res. Cttee, Mason Med. Res. Foundn, 1999– (Chm., 2004–); Sec. Gen., World Assoc. of HepatoPancreatoBiliary Surgery, 1990–94 (Treas., 1986–90). Examiner: Primary FRCS, 1981–87; Intercollegiate Bd in General Surgery, 1994– (Mem., Intercollegiate Examng Bd in Gen. Surg., 1998–). FRSocMed 2000. Hon. FRCS Thailand, 1992. Hon. DSc Med. Mahidol Univ., Thailand, 1994. Hallett Prize, RCS, 1970; Research Medal, British Soc. of Gastroenterology, 1982; Bengt Ihre Medal, Swedish Soc. of Gastroenterology, 1998; Gold Medal, IHPBA, 2004. Sen. Ed., British Jl of Surgery, 1991–96 (Co. Sec., 1983–91); Ed., HPB, 1999–2003; Ed.-in-Chief, HPB Surgery, 2006–. *Publications:* edited jointly: Colonic Carcinogenesis, 1982; General Surgical Operations, 2nd edn 1987; Emergency Abdominal Surgery, 1990; Surgical Management, 2nd edn 1991; Clinical Gastroenterology: gastrointestinal emergencies, 1991; Scott, An Aid to Clinical Surgery, 6th edn 1998; Hepatobiliary and Pancreatic Tumours, 1994; Upper Digestive Surgery: oesophagus, stomach and small intestine, 1999; Surgery, 2000; numerous papers in surgical and med. jls. *Recreations:* travel, military uniforms and history. *Address:* The Barn, 88 Lower Road, Gerrards Cross, Bucks SL9 8LB. *T:* (01753) 889816; *e-mail:* r.williamson@imperial.ac.uk. *Club:* Oxford and Cambridge.

WILLIAMSON, Rt Rev. Roy; *see* Williamson, Rt Rev. Robert K.

WILLIAMSON, Prof. Stephen, FREng; Professor of Electrical Engineering, since 2000, and Head, School of Electrical Engineering and Electronics, since 2003, University of Manchester (formerly UMIST); *b* 15 Dec. 1948; *s* of Donald Williamson and Patricia K. M. Williamson (*née* Leyland); *m* 1970, Zita Mellor; one *s* two *d*. *Educ:* Burnage Grammar Sch., Manchester; Imperial Coll. of Science and Technology (scholarship, 1968; Sylvanus P. Thompson Prize, 1969; BScEng, ACGI, PhD, DIC; DScEng 1989). FIEEE 1995; FREng (FEng 1995). Lectr in Engineering, Univ. of Aberdeen, 1973–81; Sen. Lectr, 1981–85, Reader, 1985–89, Dept of Electrical Engineering, Imperial College; Prof. of Engineering, 1989–97, and Fellow, St John's Coll., 1990–97, Cambridge Univ.; Technical Dir, Brook Hansen, later Invensys Brook Crompton, 1997–2000. FCGI 1989. Institution of Electrical Engineers: John Hopkinson Premium, 1981; Crompton Premium, 1987, 1996, 1998; Swan Premium, 1989; Science, Educn and Technol. Div. Premium, 1991; Power Div. Premium, 1995; Achievement Medal, 2000; Nikola Tesla Award, IEEE, 2001. *Publications:* papers relating to induction machines. *Recreations:* reading, walking, gardening. *Address:* School of Electrical and Electronic Engineering, University of Manchester, PO Box 88, Manchester, M60 1QD. *T:* (0161) 200 4683.

WILLIAMSON, Prof. Timothy, FRSE; FBA 1997; Wykeham Professor of Logic, and Fellow of New College, Oxford University, since 2000; *b* 6 Aug. 1955; *er s* of late Colin Fletcher Williamson and of Karina Williamson (*née* Side; she *m* 2nd, Prof. Angus McIntosh, FBA, FRSE); *m* 1st, 1984, Elisabetta Perosino (marr. diss. 2003); one *s* one *d*; 2nd, 2004, Ana Mladenović; one *s*. *Educ:* Henley Grammar Sch.; Balliol Coll., Oxford; Christ Church, Oxford (MA 1981; DPhil 1981); MA *aeg* Dublin 1986. FRSE 1997. Sen. Scholar, Christ Church, Oxford, 1976–80; Lectr in Philosophy, TCD, 1980–88; Fellow and Praelector in Philosophy, University Coll., and CUF Lectr in Philosophy, Univ. of Oxford, 1988–94; Prof. of Logic and Metaphysics, Edinburgh Univ., 1995–2000. Visiting Professor: MIT, 1994; Princeton, 1998–99; Visiting Fellow: ANU, 1990, 1995; Centre for Advanced Study, Oslo, 2004; Vis. Erskine Fellow, Univ. of Canterbury, NZ, 1995; Nelson Dist. Prof., Univ. of Michigan, 2003; Townsend Visitor in Philos., Berkeley, 2006; Tang Chun-I Vis. Prof., Chinese Univ. of Hong Kong, 2007. Lectures: Henriette Herz, British Acad., 1996; Weatherhead, Tulane Univ., 1998; Jacobsen, UCL, 2001; Skolem, Oslo Univ., 2004; Jack Smart, ANU, 2005; Wedberg, Stockholm Univ., 2006; Gaos, Nat. Autonomous Univ. of Mexico, 2006; Hempel, Princeton, 2006; Amherst, Amherst Coll., 2009. President: Aristotelian Soc., 2004–05; Mind Assoc., 2006–07. For. Mem., Norwegian Acad. of Sci. and Letters, 2004; For. Hon. Mem., Amer. Acad. of Arts and Scis, 2007. *Publications:* Identity and Discrimination, 1990; Vagueness, 1994; Knowledge and its Limits, 2000; The Philosophy of Philosophy, 2007; articles in Jl of Phil., Phil Rev., Mind, Jl of Symbolic Logic, etc. *Address:* New College, Oxford OX1 3BN. *T:* (01865) 279555.

WILLING, Maria Paula Figueiroa, (Mrs Victor Willing); *see* Rego, M. P. F.

WILLINK, Sir Charles (William), 2nd Bt *cr* 1957; *b* 10 Sept. 1929; *s* of Rt Hon. Sir Henry Urmston Willink, 1st Bt, MC, QC (*d* 1973), and Cynthia Frances (*d* 1959), *d* of H. Morley Fletcher, MD, FRCP; *S* father, 1973; *m* 1954, Elizabeth, *d* of Humfrey Andrewes, Highgate, London; one *s* one *d*. *Educ:* Eton College (scholar); Trinity College, Cambridge (scholar; MA, PhD). Assistant Master: Marlborough College, 1952–54; Eton College, 1954–85 (Housemaster, 1964–77). *Publications:* (ed) Euripides' Orestes, 1986; articles in Classical Quarterly. *Recreations:* bridge, field botany, music (bassoon). *Heir:* *s* Edward Daniel Willink, *b* 18 Feb. 1957. *Address:* 22 North Grove, Highgate, N6 4SL. *T:* (020) 8340 3996.

WILLIS, (George) Philip; MP (Lib Dem) Harrogate and Knaresborough, since 1997; *b* 30 Nov. 1941; *s* of George Willis and Hannah (*née* Gillespie); *m* 1974, Heather Elizabeth Sellars; one *s* one *d*. *Educ:* City of Leeds and Carnegie Coll.; Univ. of Leeds (Cert Ed 1963); Univ. of Birmingham (BPhil 1978). Asst teacher, Middleton Co. Secondary Boys' Sch., 1963–65; Head of History, Moor Grange Co. Secondary Boys' Sch., 1965–67; Sen. Master, Primrose Hill High Sch., Leeds, 1967–74; Dep. Hd, W Leeds Boys' GS, 1974–78; Head Teacher: Ormsby Sch., Cleveland, 1978–82; John Smeaton Community Sch., 1983–97. Front bench spokesman on further and higher educn, 1997–99, on educn and employment, 1999–2001, on educn and skills, 2001–05. Mem., Educn and Employment Select Cttee, 1999–2001; Chm., Sci. and Technol. Select Cttee, 2005–. Chm., All-Party Gp on mobile telecommunications, 2001–; Treas., All-Party Gp on medical res., 2005–. *Recreations:* Leeds United season ticket holder, dance (ballet), current affairs, fishing. *Address:* House of Commons, SW1A 0AA. *T:* (020) 7219 5709. *Club:* National Liberal.

WILLIS, Air Vice-Marshal Gerald Edward; Director, Projects Defence Estates, 2003–04; *b* 25 Oct. 1949; *s* of John Morris Willis and Dorothy Maud Willis; *m* 1st, 1973, Janet Seaman (marr. diss. 1995); one *s* one *d*; 2nd, 1996, Angela Suter. *Educ:* Cardiff High Sch. for Boys; Univ. of Bristol (BSc Hons 1971). Asst Prodn Manager, GKN, 1971–73; commnd Engr Br., RAF, 1973; Dir, Corporate Develt, RAF Trng Gp Defence Agency, 1999–2000; Asst Comdt, Jt Services Comd and Staff Coll., 2000–01; Dir, Project Alexander Implementation Team, 2001–03. *Recreations:* choral singing, badminton, squash, amateur dramatics. *Address:* The Nook, Fairford, Glos GL7 4HU. *T:* (01285) 712656; *e-mail:* gerrywillis@mail.com.

WILLIS, Jane; Director, Public Service Agreement Delivery, Health and Safety Executive, since 2002; *b* 26 Aug. 1955; *d* of Ernest and Lena England; *m* 1974, Howard Willis; one *s* one *d*. *Educ:* Watford Grammar Sch. for Girls; Open Univ. (BA Hons 1987). Joined Civil Service, 1973; Health and Safety Executive, 1988–: Head: Safety Policy Div., 1998–2002; Planning Efficiency and Finance Div., 2002–03; Strategic Policy, subseq. Strategic Prog., Dir, 2003–. *Recreations:* Girlguiding UK, Bushey Amateur Swimming Club. *Address:* Health and Safety Executive, Rose Court, 2 Southwark Bridge, SE1 9HS. *T:* (020) 7717 6200; *e-mail:* jane.willis@hse.gsi.gov.uk.

WILLIS, Maj.-Gen. John Brooker, CB 1981; *b* 28 July 1926; *s* of late William Noel Willis and of Elaine Willis; *m* 1959, Yda Belinda Jane Firbank; two *s* two *d*. *Educ:* privately, until 1941; Redhill Technical Coll. ptsc, jssc. Enlisted in Royal Navy (Fleet Air Arm) as Trainee Pilot; basic training in USA, 1944; transf. to Indian Army, attended Armoured OTS Ahmed Nagar, 1945; commnd 1947, joined 10th Royal Hussars; attended 13 Technical Staff Course, RMCS, 1958–60; Bt Lt-Col 1965, in comd 10th Hussars Aden and BAOR; GSO1 (Armour) DS RMCS, 1968–69; Col GS MGO Secretariat, MoD, 1969–71; Dep. Comdt, RAC Centre, 1971–74; Sen. Officers' War Course, Greenwich, 1974; Dir, Projects (Fighting Vehicles), 1974–77; Dir Gen., Fighting Vehicles and Engr Equipment, 1977–81, retd. *Recreations:* gardening, aviation.

WILLIS, John Edward; Chief Executive, Mentorn and Creative Director, Tinopolis Group, since 2006 (Director, Tinopolis plc, since 2006); *b* 4 April 1946; *s* of Baron Willis and of Lady (Audrey Mary) Willis (*née* Hale); *m* 1972, Janet Ann Sperrin; one *s* one *d*. *Educ:* Eltham Coll.; Fitzwilliam Coll., Cambridge (MA); Bristol Univ. (PG Cert. in Film and TV). Yorkshire Television: journalist, 1970–75; Documentary Dir, 1975–82; Controller of Documentaries and Current Affairs, 1982–88; Channel Four Television: Controller of Factual Progs, 1988–89; Dep. Dir of Progs, 1990–92; Dir of Progs, 1993–97; Man. Dir, 1997–98, Chief Exec., 1998–2000, United (formerly United Film and Television) Productions; Man. Dir, LWT and United Prodns, 2000–01; Vice-Pres. for Nat. Programming, WGBH, 2002–03; Dir, Factual and Learning, BBC, 2003–06. Member, Board: Channel 5 Broadcasting, 1998–2000; ITN, 1999–2000. Chairman: Broadcasting Support Services, 1997–2002; Edinburgh Internat. Television Fest., 1998–2002; Internat. Television Enterprises Ltd Distributors, 1999–2000; Granada Wild (formerly United Wildlife), 1999–2001; Cosgrove Hall Ltd, 1999–2001; Dir, Sheffield Internat. Documentary Fest., 2007–. Vis. Industrial Prof. in Television, Univ. of Bristol, 1999–2006; Hon. Prof., Univ. of Stirling, 1997–. Ombudsman, 1998–2002, External Ombudsman, 2006–, The Guardian. Mem., Ind. Football Commn, 2002. Advr, Convergence Think Tank, DCMS and BERR, 2007–. Trustee: Future Lab, 2006–; BAFTA, 2007–. FRTS 1993; FRSA 1997. Numerous prizes and awards. *Publications:* Johnny Go Home, 1976; Churchill's Few: the Battle of Britain remembered, 1985. *Recreations:* cycling, soccer, cinema, theatre. *Address:* Mentorn Productions, Elsinore House, 77 Fulham Palace Road, W6 8JA.

WILLIS, Prof. John Raymond, PhD; FRS 1992; FIMA; Professor of Theoretical Solid Mechanics, University of Cambridge, 1994–2000 and 2001–07, now Emeritus; Fellow of Fitzwilliam College, Cambridge, 1966–72, 1994–2000 and 2001–07; *b* 27 March 1940; *s* of John V. G. and L. Gwendoline Willis; *m* 1964, Juliette Louise Ireland; three *d*. *Educ:* Imperial Coll., London (BSc, PhD); MA Cantab 1966. ARCS, DIC; FIMA 1966. Asst Lectr, Imperial Coll., 1962–64; Res. Associate, NY Univ., 1964–65; Cambridge University: Sen. Asst in Research, 1965–67; Asst Dir of Research, 1968–72; Dir of Studies in Maths, Fitzwilliam Coll., 1966–72; Bath University: Prof. of Applied Maths, 1972–94; Prof. of Maths, 2000–01. Editor-in-Chief, 1982–92, Jt Editor, 1992–, Jl Mechanics and Physics of Solids. For. Associate, NAE, 2004. Hon. DSc Bath, 2007. Timoshenko Medal, ASME, 1997; Prager Medal, Soc. of Engrg Sci., 1998. *Publications:* papers on mechanics of solids in learned jls. *Recreations:* swimming, hiking, music. *Address:* Department of Applied Mathematics and Theoretical Physics, Centre for Mathematical Sciences, Wilberforce Road, Cambridge CB3 0WA. *T:* (01223) 339251.

WILLIS, Norman David; General Secretary, Trades Union Congress, 1984–93; *b* 21 Jan. 1933; *s* of Victor J. M. and Kate E. Willis; *m* 1963, Maureen Kenning; one *s* one *d*. *Educ:* Ashford County Grammar Sch.; Ruskin and Oriel Colls, Oxford, 1955–59 (Hon. Fellow, Oriel Coll., 1984). Employed by TGWU, 1949; Nat. Service, 1951–53; PA to Gen. Sec., TGWU, 1959–70; Nat. Sec., Research and Educn, TGWU, 1970–74; TUC: Asst Gen. Sec., 1974–77, Dep. Gen. Sec., 1977–84. Councillor (Lab) Staines UDC, 1971–74. Member: NEDC, 1984–92; Council, ODI, 1985–93; Council, Motability, 1985–93; Employment Appeal Tribunal, 1995–; Chm., Nat. Pensioners' Convention Steering Cttee, 1979–93; Vice-President: IMS, 1985–93; ICFTU, 1984–93; WEA, 1985–93; Trades Union Adv. Cttee to OECD, 1986–93; Pres., ETUC, 1991–93 (Vice-Pres., 1984–91). Member: Exec. Bd, UNICEF, 1986–90; Council for Charitable Support, 1988–93; Trustee: Duke of Edinburgh's Commonwealth Study Conf., 1986–93; Anglo-German Foundn for the Study of Industrial Soc., 1986–95; Council, Prince of Wales Youth Business Trust, 1986–93; Patron, West Indian Welfare (UK) Trust, 1986–93. Member: Norfolk Naturalist Trust; Wildfowl and Wetlands Trust; Nat. Trust; Spelthorne Natural History Soc.; Thames Valley Horticultural Soc.; The Arthur Ransome Soc. (Pres., 2000–); Cley Bird Club; New Chalet Club; Embroiderers' Guild; Cross Stitch Guild; Friends of Royal Sch. of Needlework; Fordbridge Centre, 2002–; Dir and Trustee, Royal Sch. of Needlework, 1999–2007; Trustee and Black Bin Bag Operative (Grade 2), Sunbury-on-Thames Millennium Embroidery Gallery, 2007–. Columnist, CrossStitcher magazine, 1998–. Hon. Member: Writers' Guild of GB; Poetry Soc. (former Vice-Pres.). Fellow, RSPB. Gold Star Award, Ashford (Middx) WI, 2003. *Recreations:* painting, poetry, embroidery, birdwatching, snooker. *Address:* c/o Trades Union Congress, Congress House, Great Russell Street, WC1B 3LS.

WILLIS, Philip; *see* Willis, G. P.

WILLIS, Hon. Ralph; Chairman, C+BUS Industry Superannuation Fund, since 2000; Treasurer of Australia, Dec. 1990 and 1993–96; *b* 14 April 1938; *s* of S. Willis; *m* 1970, Carol Dawson; one *s* two *d*. *Educ:* Footscray Central Sch.; University High Sch.; Melbourne Univ. (BCom). Australian Council of Trade Unions: Research Officer, 1960–70; Industrial Advocate, 1970–72. MP (ALP) Gellibrand, Vic, 1972–98; instrumental in developing econ., finance and ind. relns policies for Opposition, 1976–83; Opposition spokesperson on: Ind. Relns, 1976–77; Econ. Affairs, 1977–83; Econ. Develt, Jan.–March 1983; Minister for Employment and Ind. Relns and Minister Assisting the Prime Minister for Public Service Matters, 1983–88; Minister for Transport and Communications, 1988–90; Minister of Finance, 1990–93. *Recreations:* tennis, reading, football. *Address:* 24a Gellibrand Street, Williamstown, Vic 3016, Australia.

WILLIS, Rebecca; environmental consultant, since 2004; Vice Chairman, Sustainable Development Commission, since 2004; *b* 20 Feb. 1972; *d* of Dave and Jane Willis; *m* 2003, James Wilsdon; two *s*. *Educ:* King's Coll., Cambridge (BA Hons Social and Pol Scis 1994); Univ. of Sussex (MA Envmt, Develt and Policy 1996). Policy Advr, EP, Brussels, 1997–98; Green Alliance: Hd of Policy, 1998–2001; Dir, 2001–04; Associate, 2004–. Freelance writer and policy consultant. Associate, Demos, 2006–. *Publications:* See-through Science: why public engagement needs to move upstream (with James Wilsdon), 2004; Grid 2.0: the next generation, 2006. *Recreations:* fell-walking, riding. *Address:* 5 Bankfield, Kendal, Cumbria LA9 5DR; *web:* www.rebeccawillis.co.uk.

WILLIS, Very Rev. Robert Andrew; Dean of Canterbury, since 2001; *b* 17 May 1947; *s* of Thomas Willis and Vera Rosina Willis (*née* Britton). *Educ:* Kingswood Grammar Sch.; Warwick Univ. (BA); Worcester Coll., Oxford (DipTheol); Cuddesdon Coll., Oxford. Ordained deacon, 1972, priest, 1973; Curate, St Chad's, Shrewsbury, 1972–75; Vicar Choral, Salisbury Cathedral and Chaplain to Cathedral Sch., 1975–78; Team Rector, Tisbury, Wilts, 1978–87; Chaplain, Cranborne Chase Sch. and RAF Chilmark, 1978–87; RD, Chalke, 1982–87; Vicar, Sherborne with Castleton and Lillington, 1987–92; Chaplain, Sherborne Sch. for Girls, 1987–92; RD, Sherborne, 1991–92; Dean of Hereford, 1992–2001; Priest-in-charge, St John the Baptist, Hereford, 1992–2001. Canon and Prebendary of Salisbury Cathedral, 1988–92; Proctor in Convocation, 1985–92, 1994–. Member: Council, Partnership for World Mission, 1990–2002; Cathedrals' Fabric Commn for England, 1994–; C of E Liturgical Commn, 1994–98; Chm., Deans' (formerly Deans' and Provosts') Conf., 1999–. Governor: Cranborne Chase Sch., 1985–87; Sherborne Sch., 1987–92; Chairman of Governors: Hereford Cathedral Sch., 1993–2001; King's Sch., Canterbury, 2001–. Mem. Council, Univ. of Kent, 2003–. FRSA 1993. Hon. Fellow, Canterbury Christ Ch Univ., 2004; Hon. FGCM 2006. CStJ 2001 (Sub ChStJ 1991; Sub Dean, 1999). *Publications:* (contrib.) Hymns Ancient and Modern, New Standard edn, 1983; (jtly) The Chorister's Companion, 1989; (contrib.) Common Praise, 2000; (contrib.) New English Praise, 2006. *Recreations:* music, literature, travel. *Address:* The Deanery, The Precincts, Canterbury, Kent CT1 2EP. *T:* (01227) 762862, *Fax:* (01227) 865222. *Club:* Oxford and Cambridge.

WILLIS, His Honour Stephen Murrell; a Circuit Judge, 1986–95; *b* 21 June 1929; *s* of late John Henry Willis and late Eileen Marian (*née* Heard), Hadleigh, Suffolk; *m* 1st, 1953; one *s* three *d*; 2nd, 1975, Doris Florence Davies (*née* Redding); two step *d*. *Educ:* (chorister) Christ Church Cathedral, Oxford; Bloxham Sch. (scholar). Admitted solicitor, 1955; Partner: Chamberlin Talbot & Bracey, Lowestoft and Beccles, Suffolk, 1955–63; Pearless, de Rougemont & Co., East Grinstead, Sussex, 1964–85; a Recorder, 1980–85. Chm., Lord Chancellor's Adv. Cttee for SE London, 1987–95. Founder Chm., Friends' Hospice, Paphos, Cyprus, 2006–. Founded The Suffolk Singers, 1960; Founder and Director, The Prodigal Singers and Gallery Band, 1964–96; Chm., Renaissance Singers, 1969–95 (Vice-Pres., 1995–). *Compositions:* mediaeval song settings for radio and theatre plays. *Recording:* (with The Prodigal Singers) Christmas Tree Carols. *Recreations:* performing early music, travel, walking. *Address:* Villa Callisto, 49 Melissovounou Avenue, Tala Paphos, 8577, Cyprus.

WILLISON, Lt-Gen. Sir David (John), KCB 1973; OBE 1958; MC 1945; Director General of Intelligence (Deputy Under-Secretary of State), Ministry of Defence, 1975–78; Chief Royal Engineer, 1977–82; *b* 25 Dec. 1919; *s* of Brig. A. C. Willison, DSO, MC; *m* 1st, 1941, Betty Vernon Bates (*d* 1989); one *s* two *d*; 2nd, 1994, Trisha Clitherow. *Educ:* Wellington; RMA Woolwich. 2/Lt RE, 1939; First Instructor, Bailey Bridge SME Ripon, 1942–43; OC 17 and 246 Field Cos, 1944–45; Staff Coll., Camberley 1945; Brigade Major, 1 Indian Inf. Brigade, Java, 1946; Malaya, 1947; WO, 1948–50; OC 16 Field Sqn, Egypt, 1950–52; SO, MGA, 1952–53; GHQ MELF, 1952–53; OC, RE Troops, Berlin, 1953–55; Directing Staff, Staff Coll., Camberley, 1955–58; AQMG (Ops), HQ British Forces Aden, 1958–60; CO, 38 Engr Regt, 1960–63; Col GS MI/DI4, MoD, 1963–66; idc 1966; BGS (Intell.), MoD, 1967–70; BGS (Intell. and Security)/ACOS, G2, HQ NORTHAG, 1970–71; Dir of Service Intelligence, MoD, 1971–72; Dep. Chief Defence Staff (Int.), 1972–75. Col Comdt RE, 1973–82. Chm., RE Widows Soc., 1987–91. Consultant on Internat. Affairs, Nat. Westminster Bank Gp, 1980–84; Consultant: County Natwest Investment Bank, 1985–91; Pareto Partners, 1991–95. Pres., Western Area, Hants, St John's Ambulance, 1987–94; Freeman, City of London, 1981. *Recreations:* sailing, shooting, fishing, gardening. *Clubs:* Naval and Military; Royal Lymington Yacht.

WILLISON, Ian Roy, CBE 2005; Senior Research Fellow, Institute of English Studies, School of Advanced Study, University of London, since 1999; *b* 17 Aug. 1926; *s* of Charles Walter Willison and Daisy Willison (*née* Farmer). *Educ:* Colfe's Grammar Sch.; Peterhouse, Cambridge (BA 1948, MA 1953); Sch. of Librarianship and Archive Admin, UCL (Postgrad. Dip. 1953). Asst Keeper, Dept of Printed Books, BM, 1953–74; Dep. Keeper and Hd, Rare Books Br., then Hd, English Lang. Br., BL, 1974–87. Vis. Prof. of Histl Bibliography, Grad. Liby Sch., Univ. of Chicago, 1959; Kline Vis. Prof., Univ. of Texas at Austin, 1989. Jt Ed., Cambridge History of the Book in Britain, 1999–. Sec., then Chm., Rare and Precious Books and Documents Section, Internat. Fedn of Liby Assocs, 1978–86; Chm., UK Book Trade Hist. Gp, 1985–98; Mem., Colloque d'Histoire Mondiale du Livre et de l'Edition, 2001–. Hon. FCLIP (Hon. FLA 1988). *Publications:* (ed jtly) The New Cambridge Bibliography of English Literature, vol. 4 1900–1950, 1972; (ed jtly) Modernist Writers and the Marketplace, 1996; (ed jtly) Literary Cultures and the Material Book, 2007. *Recreation:* classical music. *Address:* Institute of English Studies, School of Advanced Study, University of London, Senate House, Malet Street, WC1E 7U. *T:* (020) 7862 8675, *Fax:* (020) 7862 8720; *e-mail:* ian.willison@sas.ac.uk.

WILLISON, Prof. Keith Robert, PhD; molecular biologist; *b* 12 Oct. 1953; *s* of Dr Robin Gow Willison and Gillian Margaret Willison (*née* Caven-Irving); *m* 1979, Jennifer Anne Bardsley; two *s*. *Educ:* New College Sch., Oxford; St Edward's Sch., Oxford (Schol.); Univ. of Sussex (BSc Hons 1975); St John's Coll., Cambridge (PhD 1979). MRC Schol., MRC Lab. of Molecular Biol., Cambridge, 1975–78; Postdoctoral Fellow, Cold Spring Harbor Labs, NY, 1979–81; Institute of Cancer Research: Res. Scientist, 1981–; Hd, Chester Beatty Labs, 1996–2005; Hd, Haddow Labs, 2002–05; Personal Chair in Molecular Cell Biol., at BPMF, subseq. Inst. of Cancer Res., Univ. of London, 1995–. Vis. Prof., Osaka Univ., 1990–91. Institute of Cancer Research: Member: Exec. Cttee, 1994–2000; Bd of Mgt, 1997–2000; Corp. Mgt Gp, 2000–05; Mem., Jt Res. Cttee, Royal Marsden NHS, subseq. NHS Foundn, Trust and Inst. Cancer Res., 2000–. Mem. Council, Royal Marsden NHS, subseq. NHS Foundn, Trust, 2003–. Mem., Governing Body, Charterhouse, 2004–. *Publications:* contrib. papers to scientific jls on topics in genetics and protein biochem. *Recreations:* cricket (Mem., Presidents XI CC, Wimbledon, 1983–99), football, Japan. *Address:* Chester Beatty Laboratories, Institute of Cancer Research, 237 Fulham Road, SW3 6JB. *T:* (020) 7878 3855. *Club:* Athenæum.

WILLMAN, John; UK Business Editor, since 2006, and Associate Editor, since 2002, Financial Times; *b* 27 May 1949; *s* of late John Willman and Kate Willman (*née* Thornton); *m* 1978, Margaret Shanahan; one *s* two *d*. *Educ:* Bolton Sch.; Jesus Coll., Cambridge (MA); Westminster Coll., Oxford (CertEd). Teacher, Brentford Sch. for Girls, Brentford, Middx, 1972–76; Financial Researcher, Money Which?, 1976–79; Editor, Taxes and Assessment (Inland Revenue Staff Fedn pubn), 1979–83; Pubns Manager, Peat, Marwick, Mitchell & Co., 1983–85; Gen. Sec., Fabian Soc., 1985–89; Jt Editor, New Socialist, 1989; Editor, Consumer Policy Review, 1990–91; Financial Times: Public Policy Editor, 1991–94; Features Editor, 1994–97; Consumer Industries Editor, 1997–2000; Banking Editor, 2000–01; Chief Leader Writer, 2002–06. Visiting Research Fellow: IPPR, 1990–91; Social Market Foundn, 1997. Journalist of the Year, Financing Healthcare, Norwich Union, 1998; Financial Journalist of the Year, British Press Awards, 2001; Business Journalist of the Year, Best Banking Submission, 2002. *Publications:* Lloyds Bank Tax Guide, annually, 1987–2000; Make Your Will, 1989; Labour's Electoral Challenge, 1989; Sorting Out Someone's Will, 1990; The Which? Guide to Planning and Conservation, 1990; Work for Yourself, 1991; A Better State of Health, 1998. *Address:* (office) 1 Southwark Bridge, SE1 9HL. *T:* (020) 7873 3854.

WILLMAN, Prof. Paul William, DPhil; Professor of Management, London School of Economics, since 2006; *b* 24 Aug. 1953; *s* of late William and Marjorie Willman; *m* 1997, Kathleen Pickett. *Educ:* St Catharine's Coll., Cambridge (BA, MA); Trinity Coll., Oxford (DPhil 1979). Lectr in Industrial Sociol., Imperial Coll., London, 1979–83; Lectr, Sch. of Mgt, Cranfield Inst. of Technol., 1983–84; London Business School: Asst, 1984–88; Associate Prof., 1988–91; Prof. of Organisational Behaviour, 1991–2000; Ernest Butten Prof. of Mgt Studies, Saïd Business Sch., Univ. of Oxford, 2000–06; Fellow, Balliol Coll., Oxford, 2000–06. *Publications:* Fairness, Collective Bargaining and Incomes Policy, 1982; (jtly) Power Efficiency and Institutions, 1983; (ed jtly and contrib.) The Organisational Failures Framework and Industrial Sociology, 1983; (jtly) Innovation and Management Control, 1985; (jtly) The Car Industry: labour relations and industrial adjustment, 1985; Technological Change, Collective Bargaining and Industrial Efficiency, 1986; (jtly) The Limits to Self-Regulation, 1988; Union Business, Trade Union Organisation and Financial Reform in the Thatcher Years, 1993; (jtly) Union Organisation and Activity, 2004; (jtly) Traders: managing risks and decisions in financial markets, 2004; contrib. books and learned jls on industrial relations etc. *Recreations:* opera, parish churches, dogs. *Address:* Department of Management, London School of Economics and Political Science, Houghton Street, WC2A 2AE. *T:* (020) 7955 6739.

WILLMER, John Franklin; QC 1967; Lloyd's Appeal Arbitrator in Salvage Cases, 1991–2000; *b* 30 May 1930; *s* of Rt Hon. Sir (Henry) Gordon Willmer, OBE, TD and Barbara, *d* of Sir Archibald Hurd; *m* 1st, 1958, Nicola Ann Dickinson (marr. diss. 1979); one *s* three *d*; 2nd, 1979, Margaret Lilian, *d* of Chester B. Berryman. *Educ:* Winchester; Corpus Christi Coll., Oxford. National Service, 2nd Lieut, Cheshire Regt, 1949–50; TA Cheshire Regt, 1950–51; Middlesex Regt, 1951–57 (Captain). Called to Bar, Inner Temple, 1955, Bencher, 1975. A Gen. Comr of Income Tax for Inner Temple, 1982–2005. Member: panel of Lloyd's Arbitrators in Salvage Cases, 1967–91; panel from which Wreck Commissioners appointed, 1967–79, reapptd 1987–2000; Admiralty Court Cttee, 1980–95. Leader, Admiralty Bar, 1992–95. Retired from practice at Bar, 1995, from practice as Arbitrator, 2003. Freeman, Arbitrators' Co., 1992. *Recreations:* walking, visiting ancient sites and buildings, amateur dramatics. *Address:* Flat 4, 23 Lymington Road, NW6 1HZ. *T:* (020) 7435 9245. *Club:* Oxford and Cambridge.

WILLMORE, Prof. (Albert) Peter, FRAS; Professor of Space Research, University of Birmingham, 1972–97, now Emeritus; *b* 28 April 1930; *s* of Albert Mervyn Willmore and Kathleen Helen Willmore; *m* 1st, 1963, Geraldine Anne Smith; two *s*; 2nd, 1972, Stephanie Ruth Alden; one *s* one *d*. *Educ:* Holloway Sch.; University Coll. London (BSc, PhD). Research interests: fusion res., AERE, 1954–57; upper atmosphere, using sounding rockets and satellites, esp. Ariel I (launched 1962), UCL, 1957–70; X-ray astronomy, using sounding rockets and satellites, UCL, 1970–72, Univ. of Birmingham, 1972–. Academician, Internat. Acad. of Astronautics, 1996. Tsiolkovsky Medal, USSR, 1987; Vikram Sarabhai Medal, COSPAR, 2004. *Publications:* approx. 150 papers in learned jls, together with many other articles and reviews. *Recreations:* music, playing the violin (though this may not be music), literature, Bronze Age history, travel, sailing. *Address:* 38 Grove Avenue, Moseley, Birmingham B13 9RY. *T:* (0121) 449 2616.

WILLMOTT, Prof. Andrew John, PhD; Director, NERC Proudman Oceanographic Laboratory, since 2005; *b* 1 Aug. 1954; *s* of David Edward Willmott and Margaret Ethel Willmott (*née* Punt); *m* 1979, Sasithorn Aranuvachapun; two *d*. *Educ:* Bristol Univ. (BSc 1st Cl. Hons Maths); Univ. of E Anglia (MSc; PhD Applied Maths 1978). Res. Fellow, Univ. of BC, 1978–81; Asst Prof., Naval Post-grad. Sch., Monterey, 1981–83; Lectr in Applied Maths, 1983–96, Reader in Geophysical Fluid Dynamics, 1991–96, Univ. of Exeter; Prof. of Applied Maths and Hd, Sch. of Computing and Maths, Keele Univ., 1996–2005. Visiting Professor: Dept of Earth and Ocean Scis, Univ. of Liverpool, 2005–; in Applied Maths, Keele Univ., 2005–. *Publications:* numerous contribs to refereed jls, and book chapters, on ocean dynamics and sea ice processes relating to polynya modelling. *Recreations:* racquet sports, hiking, gardening, wine tasting. *Address:* Proudman Oceanographic Laboratory, 6 Brownlow Street, Liverpool L3 5DA. *T:* (0151) 795 4848, *Fax:* (0151) 795 4918; *e-mail:* ajwillmott@pol.ac.uk. *Club:* Oceanography.

WILLMOTT, Dennis James, CBE 1988; QFSM 1981; Group Contingency Manager, 1988–93, and Fire Safety Consultant, 1993–98, Avon Rubber plc; *b* 10 July 1932; *s* of James Arthur Willmott and Esther Winifred Maude Willmott (*née* Styles); *m* 1958, Mary Patricia Currey; three *s*. *Educ:* St Albans County Grammar School. MIFireE. Regular Army Service, East Surrey Regt, 1950–51, Royal Norfolk Regt, 1951–57. London, Bucks, Hants and Isle of Wight Fire Brigades, 1957–74; Dep. Chief Officer, Wilts Fire Brigade, 1974–76; Chief Staff Officer, 1976–81, Dep. Chief Officer, 1981–83, London Fire Brigade; Chief Fire Officer, Merseyside Fire Brigade, 1983–88. Member: Kennet DC, 1991– (Leader, 1999–2003; Chm., 2008–09); (C) Wilts CC, 1993– (Chm., 2003–04). Chairman: Devizes Constituency Cons. Assoc., 1999–2002; Wilts and Swindon Combined Fire Authy, 2000–; SW Regl Mgt Bd, 2004–05; Chm. Bd of Dirs, SW Local Authy Controlled Co., 2007–. *Recreation:* walking. *Address:* 27 Highlands, Potterne, Devizes, Wilts SN10 5NS. *T:* (01380) 730115; *e-mail:* djwillmott@btinternet.com. *Clubs:* Victory Services, Union Jack; Conservative (Devizes); Royal British Legion (Potterne).

WILLMOTT, Maj.-Gen. Edward George, CB 1990; OBE 1979; CEng, FICE; Independent Special Adviser, Healthcare Purchasing Consortium, since 2007; *b* 18 Feb. 1936; *s* of late T. E. Willmott and E. R. Willmott (*née* Murphy); *m* 1960, Sally Penelope (*née* Banyard); two *s* one *d*. *Educ:* Gonville and Caius Coll., Cambridge (MA). FICE 1989; CEng 1990. Commissioned RE 1956; psc 1968; active service, N Borneo 1963, N Ireland 1971, 1972, 1977; comd 8 Field Sqdn, 1971–73; 23 Engr Regt, 1976; 2 Armd Div. Engr Regt, 1977–78; 30 Engr Bde, 1981–82; RCDS 1983; Dep. Comdt RMCS, 1984–85; Vice-Pres. (Army), Ordnance Bd, 1985–86; Pres., Ordnance Bd, 1986–88; Dir Gen., Weapons (Army), 1988–90. Chief Exec., CITB, 1991–98. Col Comdt, RE, 1987–97. Hon. Col 101 (London) Engr Regt (V), 1990–97. Chm., Herefordshire Primary Care Trust, 2000–06; non-exec. Dir, ESG Hereford, 2006–. Pres., Instn of Royal Engrs, 1987–90. Master, Engineers' Co., 2004–05 (Warden, 2001–04). Mem. Council, Roedean Sch., 1994–2004. *Recreations:* gardening, fishing. *Club:* Oriental.

WILLMOTT, Glenis; Member (Lab) East Midlands Region, European Parliament, since 2006; *b* 4 March 1951; *d* of Cyril Montgomery Barden and Lily Barden; *m* 1999, Edward Charles Willmott; one *d*, and one step *s* one step *d*. *Educ:* Trent Poly. (HNC Med. Scis, Clin. Chem.; HNC Med. Scis, Haematol.). Med. scientist, King's Mill and Mansfield Hosps, 1968–87; Parly Asst, 1987–90; Pol Officer, 1990–2006, Organiser, 1992–95, Sen. Organiser, 1995–2006, GMB. Mem. (Lab), Notts CC, 1989–93. Sec., E Midlands Regl Trade Union and Labour Party Orgn, 1990–2006. *Recreations:* reading, pilates, cooking, crosswords and sudoku. *Address:* (office) Harold Wilson House, 23 Barratt Lane, Attenborough, Nottingham NG9 6AD. *T:* (0115) 922 9717, *Fax:* (0115) 922 4439; *e-mail:* office@gleniswillmott.org.uk.

WILLMOTT, Prof. Hugh Christopher, PhD; Research Professor of Organization Studies, Cardiff University, since 2005; *b* 17 Sept. 1950; *s* of David P. T. Willmott and Mary Elizabeth Willmott (*née* Kitchen); *m* 1977, Irena Niezgoda; three *d*. *Educ:* Univ. of Manchester (BSc 1st Cl. 1972; PhD 1977). Univ. of Aston, 1977–85; Prof. of Organizational Analysis, Manchester Sch. of Mgt, UMIST, 1995–2001; Diageo Prof. of Mgt Studies, Judge Inst. of Mgt, Cambridge Univ., 2001–05. Visiting Professor: Copenhagen Business Sch., 1989; Uppsala Business Sch., 1990; Univ. of Lund, Sweden, 1999–2004; Cranfield Univ., 2000–03. *Publications:* (with M. Alvesson) Making Sense of Management, 1996; (with D. Knights) Management Lives, 1999; (ed jtly) Managing Knowledge, 2000; contrib. numerous articles to acad. jls. *Recreations:* cycling, walking, gardening, swimming. *Address:* Cardiff Business School, Cardiff University, Colum Drive, Cardiff CF10 3EU.

WILLMOTT, Prof. John Charles, CBE 1983; PhD; Professor of Physics, University of Manchester, 1964–89 (Director of the Physical Laboratories, 1967–89; a Pro-Vice-Chancellor, 1982–85; Adviser to Vice-Chancellor on Research Exploitation, 1988–93); *b* 1 April 1922; *s* of Arthur George Willmott and Annie Elizabeth Willmott; *m* 1952, Sheila Madeleine Dumbell; two *s* one *d*. *Educ:* Bancroft's Sch., Woodford; Imperial Coll. of Science and Technol. (BSc, PhD). ARCS. Lectr in Physics, Liverpool Univ., 1948–58, Sen. Lectr, 1958–63, Reader, 1963–64. Member: SERC (formerly SRC), 1978–82; Science for Stability Cttee, NATO, 1981–97. *Publications:* Tables of Coefficients for the Analysis of Triple Angular Correlations of Gamma-rays from Aligned Nuclei, 1968; Atomic Physics, 1975; articles on nuclear structure in learned jls. *Address:* 37 Hall Moss Lane, Bramhall, Cheshire SK7 1RB. *T:* (0161) 439 4169.

WILLMOTT, Rt Rev. Trevor; *see* Basingstoke, Bishop Suffragan of.

WILLOCHRA, Bishop of, since 2001; **Rt Rev. Garry John Weatherill;** *b* 3 Oct. 1956; *s* of Trevor Donald and Lorna Beryl Weatherill. *Educ:* Univ. of Adelaide (BA Hons 1978; DipEd 1979); St Barnabas' Theol Coll.; Flinders Univ. of SA (BTh 1991). Asst Master, Pulteney Grammar Sch., Adelaide, 1980–81; ordained deacon 1986, priest 1987; Asst Curate, St Jude's Ch, Brighton, 1986–88; Asst Priest, St Peter's Cathedral, Adelaide, 1988–90; Rector, Semaphore, 1990–97 and Area Dean, Western Suburbs of Adelaide, 1995–97; Ministry Develt Officer, 1997–2000, Archdeacon, 1999–2000, Willochra. Chm., Australia Council of the Mission to Seafarers, 2006–. *Recreations:* contemporary fiction, poetry, drama, garden, godchildren. *Address:* Bishop's House, PO Box 96, Gladstone, SA 5473, Australia. *T:* (8) 86622249, *Fax:* (8) 86622027, *T:* and *Fax:* (home) (8) 86622057; *e-mail:* bishop@diowillochra.org.au.

WILLOTT, Jennifer Nancy; MP (Lib Dem) Cardiff Central, since 2005; *b* 29 May 1974; *d* of (William) Brian Willott, *qv*. *Educ:* Univ. of Durham (BA Hons Classics 1996); London Sch. of Econs (MSc Develt Studies 1997). Consultant, Adithi NGO, Bihar, 1995; Hd of Office, Lembit Öpik, MP, 1997–2000; Researcher, Nat. Assembly for Wales, 2000–01; Project Adminr, Derwen Fostering and Adoption Project, Barnardo's, 2001; Hd of Advocacy, UNICEF UK, 2001–03; Chief Exec., Victim Support S Wales, 2003–05. Mem., Merton BC, 1998–2000. Contested (Lib Dem) Cardiff Central, 2001. Member: Work and Pensions Select Cttee, 2005–; Public Admin Select Cttee, 2005–. *Recreations:* travelling, music, singing, reading. *Address:* House of Commons, SW1A 0AA. *T:* (020) 7219 8418, *Fax:* (020) 7219 0694; *e-mail:* jenny@jennywillott.com. *T:* (029) 2066 8558.

WILLOTT, (William) Brian, CB 1996; PhD; Chair, Gwent Healthcare NHS Trust, since 2003; *b* 14 May 1940; *s* of late Dr William Harford Willott and Dr Beryl P. M. Willott; *m* 1970, Alison Leyland Pyke-Lees; two *s* two *d*. *Educ:* Trinity Coll., Cambridge (MA, PhD). Research Associate, Univ. of Maryland, USA, 1965–67; Asst Principal, Board of Trade, 1967–69; Principal: BoT, 1969–73; HM Treasury, 1973–75; Asst Sec., Dept of Industry, 1975–78; Secretary: Industrial Development Unit, DoI, 1978–80; NEB, 1980–81; Chief Exec., British Technology Gp (NEB and NRDC), 1981–84; Head of IT Div., DTI, 1984–87; Hd of Financial Services Div., DTI, 1987–92; Chief Exec., ECGD, 1992–97; Chief Exec., WDA, 1997–2000. Dir, Dragon Internat. Studios Ltd, 2002–. Dir, Wales Mgt Council, 2000–03. Mem. Council, Nat. Museums and Galls of Wales, subseq. Trustee, Nat. Museum Wales, 2001–. Vis. Prof., Univ. of Glamorgan, 2000–. *Recreations:* music, reading, gardening. *Address:* Coed Cefn, Tregare, Monmouth NP25 4DT.
See also J. N. Willott.

WILLOUGHBY, family name of **Baron Middleton**.

WILLOUGHBY DE BROKE, 21st Baron *cr* 1491; **Leopold David Verney;** DL; *b* 14 Sept. 1938; *s* of 20th Baron Willoughby de Broke, MC, AFC, AE and Rachel (*d* 1991), *d* of Sir Bourchier Wrey, 11th Bt; *S* father, 1986; *m* 1st, 1965, Petra (marr. diss. 1989), 2nd *d* of Sir John Aird, 3rd Bt, MVO, MC; three *s*; 2nd, 2003, Alexandra, Comtesse du Luart. *Educ:* Le Rosey; New College, Oxford. Chairman: S. M. Theatre Co. Ltd, 1992–; Compton Verney Opera and Ballet Project, 1992–2002; St Martins Magazines plc, 1992–2008. President: Heart of England Tourist Bd, 1996–2005; CPRE Warwicks, 2005–; Patron, Warwicks Assoc. of Boys' Clubs, 1991–2004; Chm., Warwicks Hunt Ltd, 2005–. Mem. Council, Anglo-Hong Kong Trust, 1989–2006. Mem., H of L Select Cttee on EC, 1996–2001; elected Mem., H of L, 1999. DL Warwickshire, 1999. *Heir: s* Hon. Rupert Greville Verney, *b* 4 March 1966. *Address:* Ditchford Farm, Moreton-in-Marsh, Glos GL56 9RD.

WILLOUGHBY DE ERESBY, Baroness (27th in line), *cr* 1313 (by some reckonings 28th in line); **Nancy Jane Marie Heathcote-Drummond-Willoughby;** DL; *b* 1 Dec. 1934; *d* of 3rd Earl of Ancaster, KCVO, TD, and Hon. Nancy Phyllis Louise Astor (*d* 1975), *d* of 2nd Viscount Astor; *S* to Barony of father, 1983. Trustee, Nat. Portrait Gall., 1994–2004. Mem. (Ind.), South Kesteven DC, 1969–82. DL Lincs, 1993. DStJ 2000. *Heir: co-heirs:* Carola Eloise Philippi [*b* 26 Oct. 1938; *m* 1st, 1961, George Fillmore Miller III; one *s*; 2nd, 1974, Robert E. J. Philippi; one *s*]; Sir John Aird, Bt, *qv*. *Address:* Grimsthorpe, Bourne, Lincs PE10 0LZ.

WILLS, family name of **Baron Dulverton**.

WILLS, Arthur William, OBE 1990; DMus (Dunelm), FRCO (CHM), ADCM; composer; Organist, Ely Cathedral, 1958–90; *b* 19 Sept. 1926; *s* of Violet Elizabeth and Archibald Wills; *m* 1953, Mary Elizabeth Titterton; one *s* one *d*. *Educ:* St John's Sch., Coventry. Sub. Organist, Ely Cathedral, 1949; Director of Music, King's School, Ely, 1953–64; Prof., Royal Academy of Music, 1964–92. Mem. Council, RCO, 1966–95; Examr to Royal Schs of Music, 1966–2002. Recital tours in Canada, Europe, USA, Australia and New Zealand; recording artist. Hon. RAM, Hon. FLCM, FRSCM. *Publications:* (contrib.) English Church Music, 1978; Organ, 1984, 2nd edn 1993; Full with Wills (memoir), 2006; numerous musical *compositions* include: *organ:* Sonata, Trio Sonata, Christmas Meditations, Prelude and Fugue (Alkmaar), Tongues of Fire, Variations on Amazing Grace, Symphonia Eliensis, Concerto (organ, strings and timpani), The Fenlands (symphonic suite: for brass band and organ; for orchestral brass and organ), Etheldreda Rag (organ or piano); Wondrous Machine! A Young Person's Guide to the Organ; *brass band:* Overture: A Muse of Fire; *guitar:* Sonata, Pavane and Galliard, Hommage à Ravel, Four Elizabethan Love Songs (alto and guitar), Moods and Diversions, The Year of the Tiger, Suite Africana, Concerto Lirico for Guitar Quartet; Concerto for guitar and organ; *chamber:* Sacrae Symphoniae: Veni Creator Spiritus; A Toccata of Galuppi's (counter-tenor and string quartet); *piano:* Sonata; *choral:* Missa Eliensis, The Child for Today (carol sequence), The Light Invisible (double choir, organ and percussion), Missa in Memoriam Benjamin Britten, An English Requiem, Jerusalem Luminosa (choir and organ), Ely (part-song for treble voices), Caedmon: a children's cantata, The Gods of Music (choral concerto), Missa Sancti Stephani; Missa Incarnationis; That Wondrous Birthday: three carols and a coda; Crossing the Bar; Remembrance: the world of light; *vocal:* When the Spirit Comes (four poems of Emily Brontë), The Dark Lady (eight Shakespeare Sonnets); Eternity's Sunrise (three poems of William Blake); *opera:* '1984'; *orchestra:* Symphony No 1 in A minor. *Recreations:* travel, antique collecting, Eastern philosophy. *Address:* Paradise House, 26 New Barns Road, Ely, Cambs CB7 4PN. *T:* (01353) 662084.

WILLS, Brian Alan, PhD; FRPharmS, CChem, FRSC; Chief Pharmacist, Department of Health (formerly of Health and Social Security), 1978–89, retired; *b* 17 Feb. 1927; *s* of late William Wills and Emily (*née* Hibbert); *m* 1955, Barbara Joan Oggelsby; one *d*. *Educ:* Univ. of Nottingham (BPharm); PhD London 1955; MA Leeds 1997. FRPharmS (MPS 1949; FPS 1972); FRSC (ARIC 1957; FRIC 1967); CChem 1975. Lecturer in Pharmaceutics, Sch. of Pharmacy, Univ. of London, 1951–57; Head of Research and Control Dept, Allen & Hanburys (Africa) Ltd, Durban, S Africa, 1957–62; Head of Control Div., Allen & Hanburys Ltd, London, E2, 1962–78. Member: British Pharmacopoeia Commn, 1973–94; UK delegn to European Pharmacopoeia Commn, 1975–94; UK delegn to Council of Europe Public Health Cttee (Partial Agreement) on Pharmaceutical Questions, 1979–89; WHO Expert Adv. Panel on Internat. Pharmacopoeia and Pharmaceutical Preparations, 1979–89. Visiting Professor: Univ. of Bath, 1979–83; Univ. of Bradford, 1984–. Member: Jt Formulary Cttee for British Nat. Formulary, 1979–89; Pharmacy Working Party, Nat. Adv. Body for Local Authy Higher Educn, 1982–89; Bd of Studies in Pharmacy, London Univ., 1979–87; Council, Sch. of Pharmacy, London Univ., 1981–89. Hon. Auditor, RPSGB, 1990–2005. Mem. Ct of Assts, Soc. of Apothecaries of London, 1987–98, Emeritus Asst, 1998–. *Publications:* papers on sterilisation and disinfection and on the preservation, stability and quality control of pharmaceutical preparations. *Address:* 5 Spa Court, Park Street, Ripon, N Yorks HG4 2BX. *T:* (01765) 604469.

WILLS, Sir David James Vernon, 5th Bt *cr* 1923 of Blagdon, co. Somerset; *b* 2 Jan. 1955; *s* of Sir John Vernon Wills, 4th Bt, KCVO, TD and of Diana Veronica Cecil, (Jane), (*née* Baker); *S* father, 1998; *m* 1999, Mrs Paula Burke. *Heir: b* Anthony John Vernon Wills [*b* 10 Dec. 1956; *m* 1983, Katherine Wilks]. *Address:* Langford Court, Langford, Bristol BS40 5DA.

WILLS, Sir (David) Seton, 5th Bt *cr* 1904, of Hazelwood and Clapton-in-Gordano; FRICS; *b* 29 Dec. 1939; *s* of Major George Seton Wills (*d* 1979) (*yr s* of 3rd Bt) and Lilah Mary, *y d* of Captain Percy Richard Hare; *S* uncle, 1983; *m* 1968, Gillian, twin *d* of A. P. Eastoe; one *s* three *d*. *Educ:* Eton. FRICS 1976. *Heir: s* James Seton Wills [*b* 24 Nov. 1970;

m 2003, Katy Gascoigne-Pees]. *Address:* Eastridge House, Ramsbury, Marlborough, Wilts SN8 2HJ.

WILLS, Dean Robert, AO 1994 (AM 1986); Chairman: Transfield Services Ltd, 2001–05; John Fairfax Holdings Ltd, 2002–05 (Director since 1994); *b* 10 July 1933; *s* of Walter William Wills and Violet Wills (*née* Kent); *m* 1955, Margaret Florence Williams, *d* of E. G. Williams; one *s* two *d*. *Educ:* Sacred Heart Coll., S Aust.; SA Inst. of Technology. AASA. Dir, 1974, Man. Dir, 1977–83, Chm., 1983–86, W. D. & H. O. Wills (Australia) Ltd; Amatil Ltd, later Coca-Cola Amatil Ltd: Dir, 1975–99; Dep. Chm., 1983–84; Man. Dir, 1984–94; Chm., 1984–99; Chm., Australian Eagle Insurance Co., 1986–89. Chairman: Nat. Mutual Life Assoc., 1997–2000 (Dir, 1991; Vice Chm., 1992–97); Nat. Mutual Hldgs Ltd, 1997–2000 (Dep. Chm., 1995–97); Coca-Cola Australia Foundn Ltd, 2002–05; Director: Australian Grand Prix Corp., 1994–2002 (Dep. Chm., 1994–2002); Westfield Hldgs/Westfield America Trust, 1994–. Member: Business Council of Aust., 1984–94 (Vice Pres., 1987–88, Pres., 1988–90); Bd of Aust. Graduate Sch. of Management, Univ. of NSW, 1985–. Pres., 1991, Gov., 1992–94, Med. Foundn. Trustee, Mus. of Applied Arts and Sciences (Powerhouse Mus.), NSW, 1986–90. *Recreations:* tennis, performance cars. *Address:* 71 Circular Quay East, Sydney, NSW 2000, Australia.

WILLS, Rt Hon. Michael David; PC 2008; MP (Lab) Swindon North, since 1997; Minister of State, Ministry of Justice, since 2007; *b* 20 May 1952; *s* of Stephen Wills and Elizabeth Wills (*née* McKeowen); *m* 1984, Jill Freeman; three *s* two *d*. *Educ:* Haberdashers' Aske's Sch., Elstree; Clare Coll., Cambridge (BA 1st cl. Hons Hist.). HM Diplomatic Service, 1976–80; Researcher, 1980–82, Producer, 1982–84, LWT; Dir, Juniper Productions, 1985–97. Parliamentary Under-Secretary of State: DTI, 1999; DFEE, 1999–2001; Parly Sec., LCD, 2001–02; Parly Under-Sec. of State, Home Office, 2002–03. *Publications:* as David McKeowen: Grip, 2005; Trapped, 2007. *Address:* House of Commons, SW1A 0AA. *T:* (020) 7219 3000.

WILLS, Nicholas Kenneth Spencer, FCA; international consultant and company director; *b* 18 May 1941; *s* of Sir John Spencer Wills and Elizabeth Drusilla Alice Clare Garcke; *m* 1st, 1973, Hilary Ann Flood (marr. diss. 1983); two *s* two *d*; 2nd, 1985, Philippa Trench Casson, *d* of Rev. Donald and Marion Casson; one *d*. *Educ:* Rugby Sch.; Queens' Coll., Cambridge (MA; Hon. Fellow, 1990). Binder Hamlyn & Co., 1963–67; Morgan Grenfell, 1967–70; BET plc, 1970–92 (Director, 1975–92; Man. Dir, 1982–91; Chief Exec., 1985–91; Chm., 1991–92). Managing Director: Birmingham & Dist Investment Trust, 1970–91; Electrical & Industrial Investment, 1970–91; National Electric Construction, 1971–91; Chairman: Argus Press Hldgs, 1974–83; Electrical Press, 1974–83; Boulton & Paul plc, 1979–84; Initial plc, 1979–87; BET Building Services Ltd, 1984–87; Dep. Chm., Nat. Mutual Home Loans, 1994–96; Director: Bradbury, Agnew & Co. Ltd, 1974–83; National Mutual Life Assce Soc., 1974–85, 1991–2002 (Dep. Chm., 1992–99; Chm., 1999–2002; Chm. Supervisory Bd, 2002–08); St George Assce Co. Ltd, 1974–81; Colonial Securities Trust Co. Ltd, 1976–82; Cable Trust Ltd, 1976–77; Globe Investment Trust plc, 1977–90; Drayton Consolidated, 1982–92; Tribune (formerly Barings Tribune) Investment Trust, 1992–2004; Hitchin Priory Ltd, 1992–2002 (Dep. Chm., 1994–99; Chm., 1999–2002); Onslow Trading and Commercial, 1994–99; Manchester Trading and Commercial, 1995–2000; Toye & Co., 1996–; SMC Gp plc, 1999–; American Chamber of Commerce (UK), 1985–2000 (Vice-Pres., 1988–2000); United World Colls (Internat.) Ltd, 1987–95; IQ-Ludorum plc, 2000–05; Solid Terrain Modeling Inc., 2000–; Member, Advisory Board: City and West End, National Westminster Bank, 1982–91; Charterhouse Buy-Out Funds, 1990–98. Member: Council, CBI, 1987–92 (Member: Overseas Cttee, 1987–90; Public Expenditure Task Force, 1988; Economic Affairs Cttee, 1991–96); Council, Business in the Community, 1987–92; Advisory Board: Fishman-Davidson Center for Study of Service Sector, Wharton Sch., Univ. of Pennsylvania, 1988–92; Centre of Internat. Studies, Cambridge Univ., 1999–2006 (Hon. Fellow, 2000). Mem. Adv. Council, Prince's Youth Business Trust, 1988–2004 (Hon. Treas., 1989–92; Mem., Investment Cttee, 1992–98); Chm., Internat. Trustees, Internat. Fedn of Keystone Youth Orgns, 1990–2002. Chm., Involvement & Participation Assoc., 1991–96. Chm., Mgt Cttee, Cambridge Rev. of Internat. Affairs, 1998–2003. Treasurer and Churchwarden, Church of St Bride, Fleet Street, 1978–2001; Asst, Co. of Haberdashers, 1981– (Master, 1997–98); Gov., Haberdashers' Aske's Schs, Elstree, 1989–98 (Chm., Girls' Sch. Cttee, 1994–97). Hon. Mem., Clan McEwan. CCMI; FCIM; FCT; FRSA. *Recreations:* ski-ing on blue runs, trying to farm in the Highlands. *Address:* The Great House, Great Milton, Oxon OX44 7PD. *Clubs:* White's, Royal Automobile, City Livery; Clyde Cruising; Beaver Creek, Arrowhead Alpine (Colorado, USA).

WILLS, Peter Gordon Bethune, TD 1967; Director: Hambro Clearing Ltd (formerly Sheppards and Chase Options Ltd), 1977–93 (Chairman, 1977–92); BCW Stock Lending Consultants Ltd, 1992–93; *b* 25 Oct. 1931; *s* of P. L. B. Wills and E. W. Wills (*née* Stapledon); *m* 1st, Linda Hutton; two *s* one *d*; 2nd, Gloria Hart; 3rd, Faith Hines. *Educ:* Malvern Coll.; Corpus Christi Coll., Cambridge, 1952–55 (MA). National Service with Royal Inniskilling Fusiliers, N Ireland and Korea, 1950–52; TA, London Irish Rifles, 1952–67. Joined Sheppards & Co. (later Sheppards and Chase), 1955, Partner, 1960–85; Chm., Sheppards Moneybrokers Ltd, 1985–89. Mem., Stock Exchange Council, 1973–87 (Dep. Chm., 1979–82); Chm., Stock Exchange Money Brokers' Cttee, 1985–89. Director: Wills Group plc, 1969–87 (Vice Chm.); LIFFE, 1982; BAII Holding, 1986–89; The Securities Assoc., 1986–89 (Chm., Membership Cttee); London Clear, 1986–89; The Securities Inst., 1992–93 (Chm., Membership Cttee; Fellow, 1993). Specialist Advr to Social Security Cttee, H of C, 1993. *Address:* 5 Old Court, Bull Lane, Long Melford, Sudbury, Suffolk CO10 9HA.

WILLS, Sir Seton; *see* Wills, Sir D. S.

WILLSON, Prof. (Francis Michael) Glenn; Vice-Chancellor, 1978–84, Emeritus Professor, since 1985, Murdoch University, Western Australia; *b* 29 Sept. 1924; *s* of late Christopher Glenn Willson and late Elsie Katrine (*née* Mattick); *m* 1945, Jean (*née* Carlyle); two *d*. *Educ:* Carlisle Grammar Sch.; Manchester Univ. (BA Admin); Balliol and Nuffield Colls, Oxford (DPhil, MA). Merchant Navy, 1941–42; RAF, 1943–46; BOAC 1946–47. Research Officer, Royal Inst. of Public Admin, 1953–60; Res. Fellow, Nuffield Coll., Oxford, 1955–60; Lectr in Politics, St Edmund Hall, Oxford, 1958–60; Prof. of Govt, UC Rhodesia and Nyasaland, 1960–64; Dean, Faculty of Social Studies, UC Rhodesia and Nyasaland, 1962–64; University of California, Santa Cruz: Prof. of Govt/Politics, 1965–74; Provost of Stevenson Coll., 1967–74; Vice-Chancellor, College and Student Affairs, 1973–74; Vis. Prof., 1985–92; Warden, Goldsmiths' Coll., London, 1974–75; Principal of Univ. of London, 1975–78. *Publications:* (with D. N. Chester) The Organization of British Central Government 1914–56, 2nd edn 1914–64, 1968; Administrators in Action, 1961; A Strong Supporting Cast: the Shaw Lefevres 1789–1936, 1993; Our Minerva: the men and politics of the University of London 1836–1858, 1995; In Just Order Move: the progress of the Laban Centre for Movement and Dance, 1997; The University of London 1858–1900: the politics of Senate and Convocation, 2004; contrib. Public Admin, Polit. Studies, Parly Affairs, etc. *Address:* 32 Digby Mansions, Hammersmith Bridge Road, W6 9DF.

WILLSON, John Michael, CMG 1988; HM Diplomatic Service, retired; High Commissioner in Zambia, 1988–90; *b* 15 July 1931; *e s* of late Richard and Kathleen Willson; *m* 1954, Phyllis Marian Dawn, *o c* of late William and Phyllis Holman Richards, OBE; two *s* two *d*. *Educ:* Wimbledon Coll.; University Coll., Oxford (MA); Trinity Hall, Cambridge. National Service, 1949–51. HM Colonial Service, N Rhodesia, 1955–64; Min. of Overseas Development, 1965–70 (seconded to British High Commn, Malta, 1967–70); joined HM Diplomatic Service, 1970; British Consulate-General, Johannesburg, 1972–75; FCO (W Indian and N American Depts), 1975–78; Special Counsellor for African Affairs, 1978; Secretary-General, Rhodesian Independence Conf., 1979; Salisbury (on staff of Governor of Rhodesia), 1979–80; Counsellor, Bucharest, 1980–82; Ambassador to Ivory Coast, Burkina (formerly Upper Volta) and Niger, 1983–87; seconded to RCDS, 1987. *Recreations:* gardening, photography, music. *Address:* 34 The Playing Close, Charlbury, Oxon OX7 3RJ.

WILMERS, Mary-Kay; Editor, London Review of Books, since 1992; *b* 19 July 1938; *d* of Charles Wilmers and Cesia (*née* Eitingon); *m* 1968, Stephen Arthur Frears, *qv* (marr. diss. 1975); two *s*. *Educ:* Athénée Royal d'Uccle, Brussels; Badminton Sch., Bristol; St Hugh's Coll., Oxford (BA; Hon. Fellow 2002). Editor, Faber & Faber, 1961–68; Dep. Ed., The Listener, 1968–73; Fiction Ed., TLS, 1974–79; Dep. Ed., then Co-Ed., London Rev. of Books, 1979–92. *Recreation:* thinking about writing a book. *Address:* c/o London Review of Books, 28 Little Russell Street, WC1A 2HN. *T:* (020) 7209 1101.

WILMOT, Sir David, Kt 2002; QPM 1989; DL; Chief Constable, Greater Manchester Police, 1991–2002; *b* 12 March 1943; *m* Ann Marilyn (*née* Doyle). *Educ:* Southampton Univ. (BSc). Lancashire Constabulary, 1962; Merseyside Police, 1974; W Yorkshire Police, 1983; Deputy Chief Constable, Greater Manchester Police, 1987. Trustee, Broughton House, home for disabled ex-servicemen, 2005–. Pres., Greater Manchester Fedn of Clubs for Young People, 2006–. Hon. RNCM 2001. Greater Manchester: DL 1996; High Sheriff, 2005–06. Hon. DSc Salford, 2000. *Recreations:* wine, travel. *Club:* Army and Navy.

WILMOT, Sir Henry Robert, 9th Bt *cr* 1759; *b* 10 April 1967; *s* of Sir Robert Arthur Wilmot, 8th Bt, and of Juliet Elvira, *e d* of Captain M. N. Tufnell, RN; *S* father, 1974; *m* 1995, Susan Clare, *er d* of John Malvern, *qv*; two *s* one *d* (of whom one *s* one *d* are twins). Mem., TGWU. *Heir:* *s* Oliver Charles Wilmot, *b* 12 July 1999.

WILMOT, Sir Michael John Assheton E.; *see* Eardley-Wilmot.

WILMOT, Robert William, (Robb Wilmot), CBE 1985; Founder and Chairman: Wilmot Consulting Inc., since 1994; WAM Communications Inc., since 1994; Poqet Computer Inc., since 1987; Voicewaves Inc., since 1993; *b* 2 Jan. 1945; *s* of Thomas Arthur William Wilmot and Frances Mary Hull; *m* 1969, Mary Josephine Sharkey; two *s*. *Educ:* Royal Grammar Sch., Worcester; Nottingham Univ. (BSc (1st cl. Hons) Electrical Engrg). Texas Instruments, 1966–81: European Technical Dir, France, 1973–74; Div. Dir USA, 1974–78; Man. Dir, 1978–81; Asst Vice Pres., 1980; International Computers (ICL): Man. Dir, 1981–83; Chief Exec., 1983–84; Chm., 1985. Chairman: Virtual Vineyards Inc., 1995–; Euroventures BV, 1993–; Sonim Technologies, Inc.; Founder Dir, Movid Technology Inc., 1986–; Director: Sequent Inc., 1990–; Com 21 Inc., 1995–; First Virtual Communications, 1998–. Hon. DSc: Nottingham, 1983; City, 1984; Cranfield, 1988. *Recreations:* music, theatre, walking, vintage boats.

WILMOT-SITWELL, Peter Sacheverell; Joint Chairman, 1986–90, Chairman, 1990–94, Consultant, 1995–98, S. G. Warburg (formerly S. G. Warburg, Akroyd, Rowe & Pitman, Mullens) Securities Ltd; *b* 28 March 1935; *s* of late Robert Bradshaw Wilmot-Sitwell and Barbara Elizabeth Fisher; *m* 1960, Clare Veronica Cobbold (LVO 1991); two *s* one *d*. *Educ:* Eton Coll.; Oxford Univ., 1955–58 (BA, MA). Commnd Coldstream Guards, 1953–55. Trainee, Hambros Bank Ltd, 1958–59; Partner 1959–82, Sen. Partner 1982–86, Rowe & Pitman; Vice-Chm., S. G. Warburg Gp, 1987–94. Chm., Merrill Lynch (formerly Mercury) World Mining Trust, 1993–2006; non-executive Director: W. H. Smith Ltd, 1987–96; Stock Exchange Bd, 1991–94; Minorco, 1993–99; Foreign & Colonial Income Growth Investment Trust, 1994–; Close Bros, 1995–2004; Southern Africa Investors, 1996–98; Anglo American plc, 1999–2002. *Recreations:* shooting, golf, tennis. *Address:* Portman House, Dummer, near Basingstoke, Hants RG25 2AD. *Clubs:* White's; Swinley Forest (Ascot).

WILMOT-SMITH, Richard James Crosbie; QC 1994; a Recorder, since 2000; *b* 12 May 1952; *s* of late John Patrick Wilmot-Smith and Rosalys Wilmot-Smith (*née* Massy); *m* 1978, Jenny (marr. diss. 2005), *d* of late R. W. Castle and L. M. Castle; one *s* two *d*. *Educ:* Charterhouse; Univ. of N Carolina (Morehead Schol.; AB 1975). Called to the Bar, Middle Temple, 1978 (Benefactors Law Schol.; Bencher, 2003). Trustee, Free Representation Unit, 1997–2007. *Publications:* Encyclopedia of Forms and Precedents, 5th edn: (contrib. and ed) Vol. 5, Building and Engineering Contracts, 1986; (contrib.) Vol. 12, Contracts for Services, 1994; (ed jtly) Human Rights in the United Kingdom, 1996; Construction Contracts: law and practice, 2006. *Recreations:* music, theatre, cinema, cricket. *Address:* 39 Essex Street, WC2R 3AT. *T:* (020) 7832 1111. *Club:* Kent CC.

WILMOTT, Peter Graham, CMG 1996; consultant on customs, tax and trade matters, since 1996; *b* 6 Jan. 1947; *s* of John Joseph Wilmott and Violet Ena Wilmott; *m* 1969, Jennifer Carolyn Plummer; two *d*. *Educ:* Hove Grammar Sch.; Trinity Coll., Cambridge (MA). Asst Principal, Customs and Excise, 1968; Second Sec., UK Delegn to EEC, Brussels, 1971; Principal, Customs and Excise, 1973; First Sec., UK Perm. Rep.'s Office to EEC, Brussels, 1977; Asst to UK Mem., European Ct of Auditors, Luxembourg, 1980; Asst Sec., Customs and Excise, 1983; a Comr of Customs and Excise, 1988; Dir-Gen. (Customs and Indirect Taxation), Commn of the EC, 1990–96; Partner, Prisma Consulting Gp SA, 1996–2000; First Vice-Prés., Office de Dévelt par l'Automatisation et la Simplification du Commerce Extérieur, Paris, 2004–08 (Prés., 2000–04). Director: Ad Valorem Internat. Ltd, 2000–08; SITPRO Ltd, 2001–07; GlobalLink Border Solutions Ltd, 2006–. Chm., Internat. VAT Assoc., 1998–2000. *Recreations:* travelling, building and mending things. *Address:* 31 Wilbury Avenue, Hove, East Sussex BN3 6HS.

WILMSHURST, Elizabeth Susan, CMG 1999; Associate Fellow, International Law (formerly Head of International Law Programme, then Senior Fellow, International Law), Royal Institute of International Affairs, since 2004; *b* 28 Aug. 1948; *d* of Owen David Wilmshurst and Constance Hope Wilmshurst (*née* Brand). *Educ:* Clarendon Sch., N Wales; King's Coll., London (LLB 1969, AKC 1969). Admitted Solicitor, 1972. Asst Lectr, Bristol Univ., 1973–74; HM Diplomatic Service, 1974–2003: Asst Legal Advr, FCO, 1974–86; Legal Counsellor: Attorney-Gen.'s Chambers, 1986–91; FCO, 1991–94, 1997–99; Legal Advr, UKMIS to UN, NY, 1994–97; Dep. Legal Advr, FCO, 1999–2003.

WILMSHURST, Jon Barry; Under Secretary, Economic and Social Division, and Chief Economist, Overseas Development Administration, 1990–96; *b* 25 Oct. 1936; *s* of Edwin and Sylvia Wilmshurst (*née* Munson); *m* 1960, June Taylor; four *d*. *Educ:* Beckenham and Penge Grammar Sch.; Manchester Univ. (BA Econ.). Statistician, Fedn of Rhodesia and Nyasaland, 1960–63; Inst. of Economic and Social Research, 1964; Statistician and Economic Adviser, ODA, 1964–71; Senior Economic Adviser: ODA, 1971–79; Dept of Transport, 1979–83; Monopolies and Mergers Commn, 1983–85; ODA, 1985–90. *Recreations:* golf, gardening. *Address:* 87 Harvest Bank Road, West Wickham, Kent BR4 9DP. *Club:* Langley Park Golf.

WILMUT, Sir Ian, Kt 2008; OBE 1999; PhD; FRS 2002; Director, Scottish Centre for Regenerative Medicine, University of Edinburgh, since 2006; *b* 7 July 1944; *s* of Leonard (Jack) and Eileen Mary Wilmut; *m* 1967, Vivienne Mary Craven; two *d*, one adopted *s*. *Educ:* Nottingham Univ. (BSc 1967); Darwin Coll., Cambridge (PhD 1971). Post-doctoral Fellow, Unit of Reproductive Physiol. and Biochem., Cambridge, 1971–73; Animal Breeding Research Organisation, ARC, subseq. BBSRC Roslin Institute: res. posts, 1973–81; Principal Investigator, 1981–2000; Hd, Dept of Gene Expression and Develt, 2000–05; Prof. of Reproductive Sci., Univ. of Edinburgh, 2005. Hon. Prof., Edinburgh Univ., 1998. Hon. DSc Nottingham, 1998. FRSE 2000. *Publications:* (jtly) The Second Creation, 2000; (with Roger Highfield) After Dolly: the uses and misuses of human cloning, 2006; contrib. papers to Nature and Science on cloning of Dolly the sheep, first animal produced from an adult cell, using procedure developed at Roslin Inst. and use of this procedure to introduce genetic changes in sheep. *Recreations:* walking in countryside, photography, music, curling, gardening. *Address:* Scottish Centre for Regenerative Medicine, University of Edinburgh, GU.426 Chancellor's Building, 49 Little France Crescent, Edinburgh EH16 4SB. *T:* (0131) 242 6630.

WILSDON, Rebecca; *see* Willis, R.

WILSEY, Gen. Sir John (Finlay Willasey), GCB 1996 (KCB 1991); CBE 1985 (OBE 1982); DL; Chairman, Western Provident Association, since 1996; *b* 18 Feb. 1939; *s* of Maj.-Gen. John Harold Owen Wilsey, CB, CBE, DSO and Beatrice Sarah Finlay Wilsey; *m* 1975, Elizabeth Patricia Nottingham; one *s* one *d*. *Educ:* Sherborne Sch.; RMA Sandhurst. Commissioned, Devonshire and Dorset Regt, 1959; regtl service in Cyprus, Libya, British Guyana, Germany, Malta, UK; Instructor, RMA, 1967–68; Great Abbai (Blue Nile) Expedition, 1968; Staff Coll., 1973, Defence Policy Staff, MoD, 1974–75; Co. Comdr, 1976–77, BAOR and NI (despatches 1976); Directing Staff, Staff Coll., 1978–79; Comd 1st Bn Devonshire and Dorset Regt, 1979–82 (despatches 1981); COS, HQ NI, 1982–84; Comdr 1st Inf. Brigade, 1984–86; RCDS 1987; COS, HQ UKLF, 1988–90; GOC NI, 1990–93; C-in-C, UK Land Forces then Land Comd, 1993–96; Jt Comdr, British Forces in Former Republic of Yugoslavia, 1993–96; ADC Gen. to the Queen, 1994–96. Col, Devonshire and Dorset Regt, 1990–97; Col Comdt, POW Div., 1991–94. Hon. Col, Royal Jersey Militia Sqdn, RE, 1993–2006. Mem., Commonwealth War Graves Commn, 1998–2005 (Vice Chm., 2001–05). President: Army Winter Sports Assoc., 1993–97; Army Catering Corps Assoc., 1996–; Wilts ACF, 2006–. Governor: Sherborne Sch., 1994–2001 (Vice-Chm., 1996–2001); Sherborne Sch. for Girls, 1996–2001; Sutton's Hosp., Charterhouse, 1996–2001; Comr, Royal Hosp. Chelsea, 1996–2002. Chm., Salisbury Cathedral Council, 2001–. Patron, Hope and Home for Children, 1996–2006. Mem., Scientific Exploration Soc. DL Wilts, 1996. *Publications:* Service for the Nation: Seaford papers, 1987; H. Jones, VC, the Life and Death of an Unusual Hero, 2002. *Recreations:* sailing, ski-ing, fishing, breeding alpacas. *Address:* c/o Lloyds TSB, 9 Broad Street, St Helier, Jersey, CI. *Clubs:* Army and Navy; Royal Yacht Squadron, Royal Channel Islands Yacht.

WILSEY, Timothy Andrew W.; *see* Willasey-Wilsey.

WILSHAW, Sir Michael (Norman), Kt 2000; Principal, Mossbourne Community Academy, since 2004; *b* 3 Aug. 1946; *s* of Norman and Verna Wilshaw; *m*; one *s* two *d*. *Educ:* Birkbeck Coll., London Univ. (BA Hons). Teacher, later Head of Department, Inner London comprehensive schools, 1968–81: St Michael's, Bermondsey; Edith Cavell, Hackney; St Thomas the Apostle, Peckham; Dep. Headteacher, Trinity High Sch., Redbridge, 1981–85; Headteacher, St Bonaventure's RC Comp. Sch., 1985–2004. *Recreations:* sport of all kinds, reading, theatre and cinema. *Address:* Mossbourne Community Academy, Downs Park Road, E5 8NP; 3 Brand Street, Greenwich, SE10 8SP. *T:* (020) 8265 1744.

WILSHIRE, David; MP (C) Spelthorne, since 1987; *b* 16 Sept. 1943; *m* 1967, Margaret Weeks (separated 2000); one *s* (one *d* decd). *Educ:* Kingswood School, Bath; Fitzwilliam College, Cambridge. Partner, Western Political Research Services, 1979–2000; Co-Director, Political Management Programme, Brunel Univ., 1986–91; Partner, Moorlands Res. Services, 2000–. Mem., Avon CC, 1977–81; Leader, Wansdyke DC, 1981–87. Parliamentary Private Secretary: to Minister for Defence Procurement, 1991–92; to Minister of State, Home Office, 1992–94; an Opposition Whip, 2001–05. Leader, Cons. Parly Delegn to Parly Assembly of Council of Europe, 2005–. *Recreations:* gardening, cider making. *Address:* 55 Cherry Orchard, Staines, Middx TW18 2DQ. *T:* (01784) 450822.

WILSON; *see* Marslen-Wilson.

WILSON, family name of **Barons Moran, Nunburnholme, Wilson, Wilson of Dinton** and **Wilson of Tillyorn.**

WILSON, 2nd Baron *cr* 1946, of Libya and of Stowlangtoft; **Patrick Maitland Wilson;** *b* 14 Sept. 1915; *s* of Field-Marshal 1st Baron Wilson, GCB, GBE, DSO, and Hester Mary (*d* 1979), *d* of Philip James Digby Wykeham, Tythrop House, Oxon; *S* father, 1964; *m* 1945, Violet Storeen (*d* 1990), *d* of late Major James Hamilton Douglas Campbell, OBE. *Educ:* Eton; King's College, Cambridge. Served War of 1939–45 (despatches). *Heir:* none. *Address:* c/o Barclays Bank, Cambridge CB2 3PZ.

WILSON OF DINTON, Baron *cr* 2002 (Life Peer), of Dinton in the County of Buckinghamshire; **Richard Thomas James Wilson,** GCB 2001 (KCB 1997; CB 1991); Master, Emmanuel College, Cambridge, since 2002; *b* 11 Oct. 1942; *s* of late Richard Ridley Wilson and Frieda Bell Wilson (*née* Finlay); *m* 1972, Caroline Margaret, *y d* of Rt Hon. Sir Frank Lee, GCMG, KCB and Lady Lee; one *s* one *d*. *Educ:* Radley Coll.; Clare Coll., Cambridge (Exhibnr; BA 1964, LLB 1965). Called to the Bar, Middle Temple, 1965. Joined BoT as Asst Principal, 1966; Private Sec. to Minister of State, BoT, 1969–71; Principal: Cabinet Office, 1971–73; Dept of Energy, 1974; Asst Sec., 1977–82; Under Sec., 1982; Prin. Estabt and Finance Officer, Dept of Energy, 1982–86; on loan to Cabinet Office (MPO), 1986–87; Dep. Sec., Cabinet Office, 1987–90; Dep. Sec. (Industry), HM Treasury, 1990–92; Perm. Sec., DoE, 1992–94; Perm. Under-Sec. of State, Home Office, 1994–97; Sec. of the Cabinet and Head, Home Civil Service, 1998–2002. Chm., C. Hoare & Co., Bankers, 2006–. Non-executive Director: BSkyB, 2003–; Xansa plc, 2003–07. Trustee: Ewing Foundn, 1994–; Leeds Castle Foundn, 2002–06; Royal Anniversary Trust, 2003–06; Cicely Saunders Foundn, 2004–. Chm., Prince's Teaching Inst., 2006–. Pres., CIPD, 2004–06. Mem. Council, Radley Coll., 1995– (Chm., 2004–). Hon. Fellow: Univ. of Cardiff, 1999; LSE, 2000; Univ. of Wales Coll., Newport, 2002. Hon. LLD: Birmingham, 2000; City, 2001; Exeter, 2003. *Recreations:* movies, small gardens. *Address:* Master's Lodge, Emmanuel College, Cambridge CB2 3AP. *Clubs:* Athenæum, Brooks's.

WILSON OF TILLYORN, Baron *cr* 1992 (Life Peer), of Finzean in the District of Kincardine and Deeside and of Fanling in Hong Kong; **David Clive Wilson,** KT 2000; GCMG 1991 (KCMG 1987 CMG 1985); PhD; FRSE; Master of Peterhouse, Cambridge, 2002–08; Deputy Vice-Chancellor, University of Cambridge, 2005–08; President, Royal Society of Edinburgh, since 2008; Registrar, Order of Saint Michael and Saint George, since 2001; *b* 14 Feb. 1935; *s* of Rev. William Skinner Wilson and Enid Wilson; *m* 1967, Natasha Helen Mary Alexander; two *s*. *Educ:* Trinity Coll., Glenalmond; Keble Coll., Oxford (schol., MA); PhD London 1973. FRSE 2000. National Service, The Black Watch, 1953–55; entered Foreign Service, 1958; Third Secretary, Vientiane, 1959–60; Language Student, Hong Kong, 1960–62; Second, later First Secretary, Peking, 1963–65; FCO, 1965–68; resigned, 1968; Editor, China Quarterly, 1968–74; Vis. Scholar, Columbia Univ., New York, 1972; rejoined Diplomatic Service, 1974; Cabinet Office, 1974–77; Political Adviser, Hong Kong, 1977–81; Hd, S European Dept, FCO, 1981–84; Asst Under-Sec. of State, FCO, 1984–87; Governor and C-in-C, Hong Kong, 1987–92. Chm., Scottish Hydro-Electric, then Scottish and Southern Energy, 1993–2000; Dir, Martin Currie Pacific Trust plc, 1993–2003. Mem. Board, British Council, 1993–2002 (Chm., Scottish Cttee, 1993–2002). Chm., Scottish Peers Assoc., 2000–02 (Vice Chm., 1998–2000). Chm. Trustees, Nat. Museums of Scotland, 2002–06 (Trustee, 1999–2006); Trustee: Scotland's Churches Scheme, 1999–2002; Carnegie Trust for the Univs of Scotland, 2000–. Member: Council, CBI Scotland, 1993–2000; Adv. Cttee on Business Appts, 2000– (Chm., 2008–). Chancellor's Assessor, Court, Univ. of Aberdeen, 1993–97; Chancellor, Univ. of Aberdeen, 1997–; Member: Governing Body, SOAS, 1992–97; Council, Glenalmond Coll., 1994–2005 (Chm. Council, 2000–05). Oxford Univ. Somaliland Expedn, 1957; British Mt Kongur Expedn (NW China), 1981. President: Bhutan Soc. of UK, 1993–; Hong Kong Assoc., 1994–; Hong Kong Soc., 1994–; Vice Pres., RSGS, 1996–. Burgess, Guild of City of Aberdeen, 2004. Hon. LLD: Aberdeen, 1990; Chinese Univ. of Hong Kong, 1996. Hon. DLitt: Sydney, 1991; Abertay Dundee, 1994; Hong Kong, 2006. KStJ 1987. *Recreations:* hill-walking, theatre, reading. *Address:* c/o House of Lords, SW1A 0PW; The Royal Society of Edinburgh, 22–24 George Street, Edinburgh EH2 2PE. *Clubs:* Alpine; New (Edinburgh); Royal Northern and University (Aberdeen).

WILSON, Sir Alan (Geoffrey), Kt 2001; FRS 2006; FBA 1994; Professor of Urban and Regional Systems, University College London, since 2007; *b* 8 Jan. 1939; *s* of Harry Wilson and Gladys (*née* Naylor); *m* 1987, Sarah Caroline Fildes. *Educ:* Corpus Christi Coll., Cambridge (MA; Hon. Fellow, 2004). Scientific Officer, Rutherford High Energy Lab., 1961–64; Res. Officer, Inst. of Econs and Statistics, Univ. of Oxford, 1964–66; Math. Adviser, MoT, 1966–68; Asst Dir, Centre for Environmental Studies, London, 1968–70; University of Leeds: Prof. of Urban and Regl Geog., 1970–2004; Pro-Vice-Chancellor, 1989–91; Vice-Chancellor, 1991–2004; Dir-Gen., Higher Educn, DfES, 2004–06; Master of Corpus Christi Coll., Cambridge, 2006–07. Hon. Prof., Urban and Regl Geog., Univ. of Cambridge, 2006–07. Mem., Kirklees AHA, 1979–82; Vice-Chm., Dewsbury HA, 1982–85; non-exec. Mem., Northern and Yorks RHA, 1994–96. Chm., AHRC, 2007–; Mem., ESRC, 2000–04 (Vice-Chm. Environment and Planning Cttee, 1986–88). Dir, GMAP Ltd, 1991–2001. MAE 1991; AcSS 2000. FCGI 1997. Honorary Fellow: UCL, 2003; Regional Sci. Assoc. Internat., 2007–. Hon. DSc Pennsylvania State, 2002; DUniv Bradford, 2004; Hon. DEd Leeds Metropolitan, 2004; Hon. LLD: Leeds, 2004; Teesside, 2006. Gill Meml Award, RGS, 1978; Honours Award, Assoc. of Amer. Geographers, 1987; Founder's Medal, RGS, 1992; Lauréat d'Honneur, IGU, 2004; European Prize, Regl Sci. Assoc., 2004. *Publications:* Entropy in Urban and Regional Modelling, 1970; Papers in Urban and Regional Analysis, 1972; Urban and Regional Models in Geography and Planning, 1974; (with M. J. Kirkby) Mathematics for Geographers and Planners, 1975, 2nd edn 1980; (with P. H. Rees) Spatial Population Analysis, 1977; (ed with P. H. Rees and C. M. Leigh) Models of Cities and Regions, 1977; Catastrophe Theory and Bifurcation: applications to urban and regional systems, 1981; (jtly) Optimization in Locational and Transport Analysis, 1981; Geography and the Environment: Systems Analytical Methods, 1981; (with R. J. Bennett) Mathematical Methods in Geography and Planning, 1985; (ed jtly) Urban Systems, 1987; (ed jtly) Urban Dynamics, 1990; (ed jtly) Modelling the City, 1994; (jtly) Intelligent Geographical Information Systems, 1996; Complex Spatial Systems, 2000. *Recreation:* writing. *Address:* Centre for Advanced Spatial Analysis, University College London, 1–19 Torrington Place, WC1E 7HB. *T:* (020) 7679 1914. *Club:* Athenæum.

WILSON, (Alan) Martin; QC 1982; a Recorder of the Crown Court, 1979–2005; *b* 12 Feb. 1940; *s* of late Joseph Norris Wilson and Kate Wilson; *m* 1st, 1966, Pauline Frances Kibart (marr. diss. 1975); two *d*; 2nd, 1976, Julia Mary Carter; one *d*. *Educ:* Kilburn Grammar Sch.; Nottingham Univ. (LLB Hons). Called to the Bar, Gray's Inn, 1963. Occasional Mem., Hong Kong Bar, 1988–; admitted to Malaysian Bar, 1995; Temp. Advocate, IOM Bar, 2004. *Address:* 7 Bedford Row, WC1R 4BU.

WILSON, Rt Rev. Alan Thomas Lawrence; *see* Buckingham, Area Bishop of.

WILSON, Alastair James Drysdale; QC 1987; a Recorder, since 1996; *b* 26 May 1946; *s* of late A. Robin Wilson and of Mary Damaris Wilson; *m* (marr. diss.); one *s* two *d*. *Educ:* Wellington College; Pembroke College, Cambridge. Called to the Bar, Middle Temple, 1968. *Recreations:* gardening, restoring old buildings. *Address:* Hogarth Chambers, 5 New Square, Lincoln's Inn, WC2A 3RJ. *T:* (020) 7404 0404, *Fax:* (020) 7404 0505; *e-mail:* alastairwilson@hogarthchambers.com; Rainthorpe Hall, Tasburgh, Norfolk NR15 1RQ.

WILSON, Allan; Member (Lab) Cunninghame North, Scottish Parliament, 1999–2007; *b* 5 Aug. 1954; *s* of Andrew Wilson and Elizabeth (*née* Lauchlan); *m* 1981, Alison Isabel Melville Liddell; two *s*. *Educ:* Spiers Sch., Beith. Trainee Officer, 1972–75, Area Officer, 1975–93, NUPE; Sen. Regl Officer, UNISON, 1993–94; Head of Higher Educn, UNISON (Scotland), 1994–99. Contested (Lab) Cunninghame N, Scottish Parlt, 2007. Dep. Minister for Sport, the Arts and Culture, 2001, for Envmt and Rural Devel t, 2001–04, for Enterprise and Lifelong Learning, 2004–07, Scottish Exec. *Recreations:* football, reading, golf. *Address:* 44 Stoneyholm Road, Kilbirnie, Ayrshire KA25 7JS. *Clubs:* Garnock Labour, Place Golf (Kilbirnie).

WILSON, Air Chief Marshal Sir Andrew; *see* Wilson, Air Chief Marshal Sir R. A. F.

WILSON, Prof. Andrew Ian, DPhil; Professor of the Archaeology of the Roman Empire, University of Oxford, and Fellow of All Souls College, Oxford, since 2004; *b* 29 Feb. 1968; *s* of Anthony Keith Wilson, *qv*; *m* 1994, Heather Mary Claire Grabbe; two *d*. *Educ:* Corpus Christi Coll., Oxford (BA (Lit.Hum.) 1991; MA 1996); Magdalen Coll., Oxford (DPhil 1998). Fellow by Exam., Magdalen Coll., Oxford, 1996–2000; Univ. Lectr in Roman Archaeol., Univ. of Oxford, and Fellow, Wolfson Coll., Oxford, 2000–04. Hon. Sec., Soc. for Libyan Studies, 2001–; Foreign Corresp. Mem., Soc. Nat. des Antiquaires de France, 2004. Ed., Libyan Studies, 1998–2002. *Publications:* numerous articles in archaeol jls. *Recreation:* moderate hedonism. *Address:* Institute of Archaeology, 36 Beaumont Street, Oxford OX1 2PG.

WILSON, Andrew James; *see* Wilson, Snoo.

WILSON, Andrew John; Head, Group Corporate Affairs, Royal Bank of Scotland Group, since 2008 (Head of Group Media Relations, 2003–05; Deputy Chief Economist, 2005–08); *b* Lanark, 27 Dec. 1970; *s* of Harry Arthur Wilson and Dorothy Wilson (*née* Bunting); *m* 2004, Karen Isabella Doyle; one *s*. *Educ:* Coltness High Sch., Wishaw; Univ. of St Andrews; Univ. of Strathclyde (BA Hons Econs and Politics). Economist, Government Economic Service: Forestry Commn, 1993–95; Scottish Office, 1995–96; Economist: and Sen. Researcher, SNP, 1996–97; Royal Bank of Scotland, 1997–98. MSP (SNP) Central Scotland, 1999–2003; Scottish Parliament: Shadow Minister: Finance, 1999–2001; Economy and Transport, 2001; Economy, Enterprise and Lifelong Learning, 2001–03; contested (SNP) Cumbernauld and Kilsyth, 2003. Columnist: Sunday Mail, 1999–2003; Scots Independent, 2001–03. Mem., Inst. of Fiscal Studies, 2002–. Mem., Develt Bd, Barnardo's (Scotland), 2008–. Trustee and Hon. Treas., John Smith Meml Trust, 2005–. FCIBS 2004. *Publications:* contribs to various jl and conf. papers. *Recreations:* football, golf, swimming, reading, films. *Address:* Royal Bank of Scotland, RBS Gogarburn, Edinburgh EH12 1HQ.

WILSON, Andrew N.; author; *b* 27 Oct. 1950; *s* of late Norman Wilson, Lt-Col RA, potter and industrialist, and Jean Dorothy Wilson (*née* Crowder); *m* Katherine Duncan-Jones, *qv*; two *d*; *m* 1991, Dr Ruth Alexandra Guilding; one *d*. *Educ:* Rugby; New College, Oxford (MA). Chancellor's Essay Prize, 1971, and Ellerton Theological Prize, 1975. Asst Master, Merchant Taylors' Sch., 1975–76; Lectr, St Hugh's Coll. and New Coll., Oxford, 1976–81; Literary Editor: Spectator, 1981–83; Evening Standard, 1990–97. Mem., AAIL, 1988. FRSL 1981. *Publications: novels:* The Sweets of Pimlico, 1977 (John Llewellyn Rhys Memorial Prize, 1978); Unguarded Hours, 1978; Kindly Light, 1979; The Healing Art, 1980 (Somerset Maugham Award, 1981; Arts Council National Book Award, 1981; Southern Arts Prize, 1981); Who was Oswald Fish?, 1981; Wise Virgin, 1982 (W. H. Smith Literary Award, 1983); Scandal, 1983; Gentlemen in England, 1985; Love Unknown, 1986; Stray, 1987; Incline Our Hearts, 1988; A Bottle in the Smoke, 1990; Daughters of Albion, 1991; The Vicar of Sorrows, 1993; Hearing Voices, 1995; A Watch in the Night, 1996; (for children) Hazel the Guinea-pig, 1997; Dream Children, 1998; My Name is Legion, 2004; A Jealous Ghost, 2005; Winnie and Wolf, 2007; *non fiction:* The Laird of Abbotsford, 1980 (John Llewellyn Rhys Memorial Prize, 1981); A Life of John Milton, 1983; Hilaire Belloc, 1984; How Can We Know?, 1985; (jtly) The Church in Crisis, 1986; The Lion and the Honeycomb, 1987; Penfriends from Porlock, 1988; Tolstoy, 1988 (Whitbread Biography Award); Eminent Victorians, 1989; C. S. Lewis, a biography, 1990; Against Religion, 1991; Jesus, 1992; (ed) The Faber Book of Church and Clergy, 1992; The Rise and Fall of the House of Windsor, 1993; (ed) The Faber Book of London, 1993; Paul: the mind of the apostle, 1997; God's Funeral, 1999; The Victorians, 2002; Iris Murdoch as I Knew Her, 2003; London: a short history, 2004; After the Victorians, 2005; Betjeman, 2006; Our Times, 2008. *Address:* 5 Regent's Park Terrace, NW1 7EE. *Clubs:* Travellers, Beefsteak, Chelsea Arts.
See also Viscount Runciman of Doxford.

WILSON, Andrew Thomas, CMG 1982; Consultant, Agricultural Sciences Division, Rockefeller Foundation, 1987–98; Chief Natural Resources Adviser, Overseas Development Administration, 1983–87; *b* 21 June 1926; *s* of John Wilson, farmer, and Gertrude (*née* Lucas); *m* 1954, Hilda Mary (*née* Williams) (*d* 1996); two *d*. *Educ:* Cowley Sch.; Leeds Univ. (BSc); St John's Coll., Cambridge (DipAg); Imperial College of Tropical Agriculture (DTA). Colonial Service/HMOCS, Northern Rhodesia/Zambia, 1949–66: Agricultural Officer, 1949; Chief Agricl Officer, 1959; Chief Agricl Research Officer, 1961; Dep. Director of Agriculture, 1963; ODM/ODA: Agricl Adviser, British Development Div. in the Caribbean, 1967; FCO: Agricl Adviser, Nairobi and Kampala, 1969; ODM/ODA: Agricl Adviser, E Africa Development Div., 1974; Agricl Adviser, Middle East Development Div., 1976; Head of British Develt Div. in S Africa, 1979. *Recreations:* sport, gardening. *Address:* 16 Henley Court, Henley Road, Brighton, East Sussex BN2 5NA. *Clubs:* Farmers'; Nairobi (Kenya).

WILSON, Angela Christine; *see* Smith, A. C.

WILSON, Sir Anthony, Kt 1988; FCA; Head of Government Accountancy Service and Chief Accounting Adviser to HM Treasury, 1984–88; *b* 17 Feb. 1928; *s* of late Charles Ernest Wilson and Martha Clarice Wilson (*née* Mee); *m* 1955, Margaret Josephine Hudson; two *s* one *d*. *Educ:* Giggleswick School. Royal Navy, 1946–49. John Gordon Walton & Co., 1945–46 and 1949–52; Price Waterhouse, 1952, Partner, 1961–84; HM Treasury, 1984–88. Non-exec. Dir, Capita Gp plc, 1989–92. Chm., Jt Disciplinary Scheme of UK Accountancy Profession, 1990–93; Member: UK Govt Production Statistics Adv. Cttee, 1972–84; Accounting Standards Cttee, 1984–88; Auditing Practices Cttee, 1987–88; Rev. Body on Sen. Salaries, 1989–98; Council, Inst. of Chartered Accountants in England and Wales, 1985–88. Mem. Management Cttee, SW Regl Arts Assoc., 1983–91 (Chm., 1988–91); Member: English Ceramic Circle, 1983–; Northern Ceramic Soc., 1976–89. Pres., Chandos Chamber Choir, 1986–88; Chairman: Dorset Opera, 1988–93; Dorset Musical Instruments Trust, 1994–; Vice Chm., Sherborne House Trust, 1995–2000; Dir, Opera-80 Ltd, 1989–91. Liveryman, Chartered Accountants' Co., 1977–2004; Master, Needlemakers' Co., 1999–2000. FRSA 1983. *Recreations:* fishing, gardening, collecting pottery. *Address:* The Barn House, 89 Newland, Sherborne, Dorset DT9 3AG. *T:* (01935) 815674. *Club:* Reform.

WILSON, Anthony Joseph, (Joe); Member (Lab) North Wales, European Parliament, 1989–99; *b* 6 July 1937; *s* of Joseph Samuel Wilson and Eleanor Annie (*née* Jones); *m* 1st, 1959, June Mary Sockett (marr. diss. 1987); one *s* two *d*; 2nd, 1998, Sue Bentley. *Educ:* Birkenhead Sch.; Loughborough Coll. (DLC); Univ. of Wales (BEd Hons). National Service, RAPC, 1955–57. Teacher: Vauvert Sec. Mod. Sch., Guernsey, 1960–64; Les Beaucamps Sec. Mod. Sch., Guernsey, 1964–66; Man., St Mary's Bay Sch. Journey Centre, Kent, 1966–69; Lectr in PE, Wrexham Tech. Coll., subseq. NE Wales Inst. of Higher Educn, 1969–89. Contested (Lab) Wales, EP elecn, 1999. *Recreations:* basketball, camping, boules, tennis. *Address:* 79 Ruabon Road, Wrexham, North Wales LL13 7PU. *T:* (01978) 352808.

WILSON, Anthony Keith; Chief Executive of the Press, University Printer and Secretary, Press Syndicate, Cambridge University Press, 1992–99; Fellow of Wolfson College, Cambridge, 1994–2006, now Emeritus; *b* 28 Sept. 1939; *s* of late Sidney Walter Wilson and Doris Jessie Wilson (*née* Garlick), Streatham; *m* 1963, Christina Helen, *d* of late Ivor Gray Nixon and Margaret Joan Nixon (*née* Smith); two *s* one *d*. *Educ:* Lexden House Sch.; Dulwich Coll.; Corpus Christi Coll., Cambridge (Maj. Scholar; BA Hons Modern and Medieval Langs 1961; MA 1966). Longmans Green & Co. Ltd, 1961–64; Thomas Nelson & Sons Ltd, 1964–68; George Allen & Unwin Ltd, 1968–72; Cambridge University Press, 1972–99: Sen. Editor, R&D, 1972–73; Publishing Ops Dir, 1973–82; Dep. Sec., Press Syndicate, 1979–92; Actg Man. Dir, 1982–83, Man. Dir, 1983–92, Publishing Div.; Dep. Chief Exec., 1991–92. Royal Shakespeare Company: Gov., 1983–; Mem. Council, 1991–2000; Mem., Exec. Cttee, 1991–2000; Mem. Bd, 2001–06; Chm., Budget Cttee, 1991–96; Chm., Budget and Audit Cttee, 1996–2000; Chm., Audit Cttee, 2000–06. Gov., Perse Sch. for Girls, Cambridge, 1979–99 (Chm. Govs, 1988–99); Hon. Treas., Westcott House, Cambridge, 2000–. FInstD 1978 (Life-Mem.). *Recreations:* walking, talking, walking and talking. *Address:* Wolfson College, Cambridge CB3 9BB.
See also A. I. Wilson.

WILSON, Arthur Andrew; Director of Planning and Finance, Bristol South & West Primary Care Trust, 2002–06; *b* 23 July 1946; *s* of Arthur James Wilson and late Hilda Mellor Wilson (*née* Kennedy); *m* 1968, Susan Ann Faulkner; one *s* one *d*. *Educ:* Moulton Sch., Northampton; Bath Spa Univ. (MA 2007). CIPFA; IHSM. W. H. Grigg & Co., 1963; Calne and Chippenham RDC, 1963–66; Berkshire CC, 1966–67; Bath City Council, 1967–73; Chief Accountant, Avon CC, 1973–76; Principal Asst Regl Treasurer, SW RHA, 1976–82; Dist Treasurer, Plymouth HA, 1982–84; South Western RHA: Regl Treasurer, 1984–91; Dep. Regl Gen. Manager, 1991–93; Chief Exec., Plymouth Hosps NHS Trust, 1993–2000; Prog. Dir, Avon, Glos and Wilts HA, 2000–02. Mem. Mgt Council, 1997–2000, Chm. Exec. Cttee, 1998–2000, UC of St Mark and St John, Plymouth. *Recreations:* golf, reading, listening to music, musical theatre, first editions of modern novels. *Address:* 38 Cambridge Road, Clevedon, N Som BS21 7DW. *T:* (01275) 342238.

WILSON, Barbara Ann, OBE 1998; PhD; Senior Scientist and Clinical Psychologist, MRC Cognition and Brain Science Unit, since 1990; *b* 23 Oct. 1941; *d* of William David Forester and Miriam Clara Forester; *m* 1962, Michael John Wilson; one *s* one *d* (and one *d* decd). *Educ:* Univ. of Reading (BA 1st Cl. Hons 1975); MPhil 1977, PhD 1985, London. Sen. Clinical Psychologist, Rivermead Rehab. Centre, Oxford, 1979–85; Principal Clinical Psychologist, Charing Cross Hosp., London, 1985–87; Reader in Rehabilitation Studies, 1987–90, Hon. Prof. of Rehabilitation Studies, 1995–, Univ. of Southampton; Dir of Res., Oliver Zangwill Centre, Princess of Wales Hosp., Ely, 1996–. Hon. ScD UEA, 2005. May Davidson Award for Clin. Psychol., 1984; Dist. Scientist Award, British Psychol Soc., 2000; Professional of the Yr, Encephalitis Soc., 2002; Robert L. Moody Prize for Services to Rehabilitation, Univ. of Texas, 2006. *Publications:* (jtly) Families in Other Places, 1974; Rehabilitation of Memory, 1987; (jtly) Selecting, Administering and Interpreting Cognitive Tests, 1996; (jtly) Coping with Memory Problems, 1997; Case Studies in Neuropsychological Rehabilitation, 1999 (Book of the Yr Award, British Psychol Soc., 2003); (jtly) The Handbook of Memory Disorders, 2002; (ed) Neuropsychological Rehabilitation: theory and practice, 2003; (jtly) Behavioural Approaches in Neuropsychological Rehabilitation, 2003; (jtly) The Essential Handbook of Memory Disorders for Clinicians, 2004; First Year: Worst Year: coping with the unexpected death of our grown up daughter, 2004; *edited jointly:* Clinical Management of Memory Problems, 1984, 2nd edn 1992; Self-Injurious Behaviour, 1985; Everyday Cognition in Adulthood and Late Life, 1989; Developments in the Assessment and Rehabilitation of Brain-damaged Patients, 1993; Handbook of Memory Disorders, 1995; Rehabilitation Studies Handbook, 1997; 8 neuropsychological tests; over 250 book chapters and articles in jls. *Recreation:* travel. *Address:* MRC Cognition and Brain Sciences Unit, Box 58, Addenbrooke's Hospital, Cambridge CB2 2QQ. *T:* (01223) 355294, *Fax:* (01223) 516630; *e-mail:* barbara.wilson@mrc-cbu.cam.ac.uk.

WILSON, Barbara Jolanta Maria, PhD; Director of Organisational Development and Personnel, Catholic Agency for Overseas Development, since 2005; *b* 26 June 1947; *d* of late Edward Szczepanik and Anne Szczepanik (*née* Janikowska); *m* 1971, Peter Brian Wilson (*d* 1996); one *s* one *d*. *Educ:* King George V Sch., Hong Kong; Convent of Sacred Heart, Tunbridge Wells; St Anne's Coll., Oxford (MA Maths); Keele Univ. (PhD 1975). Statistical Res. Unit in Sociol., Keele Univ., 1969–73; Welsh Office, 1974–99: Sen. Asst Statistician, 1974–76; Statistician, 1976–84; Principal, Local Govt Finance, 1984–86; Educn Dept, 1986–89; Head of: Resource and Quality Mgt Div., 1989–92; Community Care Div., 1992–96; Personnel, 1996–99; Principal Estabts Officer, April–Aug. 1999; Dep. Clerk, Nat. Assembly for Wales, 1999–2000; Dir of Res. and Develt, 2000–03, Dir for Public Service Develt, 2003–05, Welsh Assembly Govt. Founder Trustee and Treas., WAY (Widowed and Young) Foundn, 1997–2002. *Recreations:* walking, music, cooking. *Address:* Catholic Agency for Overseas Development, Romero Close, Stockwell Road, SW9 9TY.

WILSON, Vice-Adm. Sir Barry (Nigel), KCB 1990; Deputy Chief of Defence Staff (Programmes and Personnel), 1989–92; *b* 5 June 1936; *s* of Rear-Adm. G. A. M. Wilson, CB, and of Dorothy Wilson; *m* 1961, Elizabeth Ann (*née* Hardy); one *s* one *d*. *Educ:* St Edward's Sch., Oxford; Britannia Royal Naval Coll. Commanded: HMS Mohawk, 1973–74; HMS Cardiff, 1978–80; RCDS 1982; Dir Navy Plans, 1983–85; Flag Officer Sea Training, 1986–87; ACDS (Progs), 1987–89. Chairman: Council, SSAFA Forces Help (formerly SSAFA), 1994–2000; Trustees, Royal Naval Mus., Portsmouth, 1994–2003. Chm. Bd of Visitors, Guys Marsh HMP/YOI, 1997–99; Chm., Friends of Guys Marsh, 2004–08. *Recreations:* campanology, gardening. *Address:* Green Bough, Child Okeford, Blandford Forum, Dorset DT11 8HD.

WILSON, Lt-Col Sir Blair Aubyn S.; *see* Stewart-Wilson.

WILSON, Brian Alfred Samuel; Member (Green) North Down, Northern Ireland Assembly, since 2007; *b* 15 May 1943; *s* of Alfred and Sheila Wilson; *m* 1979, Anne Campbell; three *s* one *d*. *Educ:* Bangor Grammar Sch.; Open Univ. (BA Hons); Univ. of Strathclyde (MSc). Lectr, Belfast Inst. of Further and Higher Educn, 1976–2003. Mem., N Down BC, 1981– (Alliance 1981–96, Ind. 1996–2004, Green 2004–07). *Recreations:* sports, walking. *Address:* 1 Innisfayle Drive, Bangor BT19 1DN. *T:* (028) 9145 5189; *e-mail:* brian.wilson@northdown.gov.uk.

WILSON, Rt Hon. Brian David Henderson; PC 2003; Director, West Highland Publishing Co., 1972–97 and since 2005; Chairman, Airtricity UK, since 2005; *b* 13 Dec. 1948; *s* of late John Forrest Wilson and Marion MacIntyre; *m* 1981, Joni Buchanan; two *s* one *d*. *Educ:* Dunoon Grammar School; Dundee Univ. (MA Hons); University College Cardiff (Dip. Journalism Studies). Publisher and founding editor, West Highland Free Press, 1972–97. MP (Lab) Cunninghame N, 1987–2005. Opposition front bench spokesman on Scottish affairs, 1988–92, on transport, 1992–94 and 1995–96, on trade and industry, 1994–95, on election planning, 1996–97; Minister of State: Scottish Office, 1997–98 and 1999–2001; (Minister for Trade), DTI, 1998–99; FCO, Jan.–June 2001; (Minister for Industry and Energy, then for Energy and Construction), DTI, 2001–03; Prime Minister's Special Rep. on Overseas Trade, 2003–06. Director: Amec Nuclear, 2005–; Celtic plc, 2005–; Scottish Resources Gp, 2005–; Chm., Harris Tweed Hebrides, 2007–. Vis. Prof. in Govt and Media, Glasgow Caledonian Univ., 2007–. Hon. Pres., Industrial Power Assoc., 2005–. Chm., Scottish Venezuelan Soc., 2007–. First winner, Nicholas Tomalin Meml Award, 1975. *Publications:* Celtic: a century with honour, 1988; contribs to various periodicals. *Address:* 219 Queen Victoria Drive, Glasgow G13 1UU; Cnoc nam Bean, Mangersta, Isle of Lewis. *e-mail:* brianwilson@mangersta.net. *Clubs:* Soho House; Stoke Park; Archerfield.

WILSON, Prof. Brian Graham, AO 1995; Vice-Chancellor, University of Queensland, 1979–95; *b* 9 April 1930; *s* of Charles Wesley Wilson and Isobel Christie (*née* Ferguson); *m* 1st, 1959, Barbara Elizabeth Wilkie; two *s* one *d*; 2nd, 1978, Margaret Jeanne Henry; 3rd, 1988, Joan Patricia Opdebeeck; three *s* (incl. twins). *Educ:* Queen's Univ., Belfast (BSc Hons); National Univ. of Ireland (PhD Cosmic Radiation). Post-doctoral Fellow, National Research Council, Canada, 1955–57; Officer in Charge, Sulphur Mt Lab., Banff, 1957–60, Associate Res. Officer, 1959–60; Associate Prof. of Physics, Univ. of Calgary, 1960–65, Prof., 1965–70, Dean of Arts and Science, 1967–70; Prof. of Astronomy and Academic Vice-Pres., Simon Fraser Univ., 1970–78. Pres., Internat. Develt Program of Australian Univs and Colls, 1991–93; Chairman: Australian Vice-Chancellors' Cttee, 1989–90 (Dep. Chm., 1987–88); Quality Assurance in Higher Educn, 1993–95. Member: Council, Northern Territory Univ., 1988–93; Council, Univ. of South Pacific, 1991–95. FTS 1990. Hon. LLD Calgary, 1984; DUniv Queensland Univ. Tech., 1995; Hon. DSc Queensland, 1995. *Publications:* numerous, on astrophysics and on higher educn issues, in learned jls. *Recreations:* golf, swimming. *Address:* Les Tisseyres, Fanjeaux 11270, France.

WILSON, Brian William John Gregg, MA; Deputy Head, St Mary's School, Wantage, 1989–97; *b* 16 June 1937; *s* of late Cecil S. and Margaret D. Wilson; *m* 1969, Sara Remington (*née* Hollins); two *d*. *Educ:* Sedbergh Sch., Yorks; Christ's Coll., Cambridge (MA; Otway Exhibnr and Scholar). NI short service commn, RIrF, 1955–57; Flt Lt, RAFVR (T), 1964–71. Asst Master, Radley Coll., 1960–65; Housemaster, King's Sch., Canterbury, 1965–73; Dir of Studies, Eastbourne Coll., 1973–76; Headmaster, Campbell Coll., Belfast, 1977–87. Project Manager, Navan Fort Initiative Gp, 1987–88. Chief Examiner, Latin A Level, NI Schs Examinations Council, 1987–88. Mem., and Chm. Planning Cttee, Wantage Town Council, 1999–2000. Member: Mgt Cttee, NISTRO, 1980–87; Central Religious Adv. Cttee, BBC/ITV, 1982–86; Researcher and Cttee Mem., Progressive Christianity Network, 2007–08. Hon. Sec., Ancient History Cttee, JACT, 1967–77; Treas., JACT Ancient History Bureau, 1998–2000. Secretary: Wantage PCC, 1999–2000; Cleeve PCC, 2001–04; Mem., Cleeve Parish Council, 2002–03; Chm., N Som Neighbourhood Watch Assoc., 2004–05. *Publications:* (with W. K. Lacey) Res Publica, 1970; (with D. J. Miller) Stories from Herodotus, 1973; (jtly) The Age of Augustus, 2003; A Faith Unfaithful, 2004; Experience is an Arch, 2007. *Recreations:* fives, squash, golf, cricket, hockey, etc; translating, theology, stock market, drama, walking, birds, trees. *Address:* 30 Warner Close, Cleeve, Bristol BS49 4TA.

WILSON, Rt Rev. Bruce Winston; Bishop of Bathurst (NSW), 1989–2000; *b* 23 Aug. 1942; *s* of Alick Bruce Wilson and Maisie Catherine (*née* Pye); *m* 1966, Zandra Robyn Parkes; one *s* one *d*. *Educ:* Canterbury Boys' High School; Univ. of Sydney (MA); London Univ. (BD); Univ. of NSW (BA); Australian Coll. of Theology (ThL). Curacies, Darling Point and Beverly Hills, Sydney, 1966–69; Anglican Chaplain, Univ. of NSW, 1970–75; Rector of St George's, Paddington, Sydney, 1975–83; Director, St Mark's Theol Coll., Canberra, 1984–89; Asst Bishop, Diocese of Canberra and Goulburn, 1984–89. Exec., Nat. Council of Churches in Australia, 1994–97. Co-editor, Market Place, 2005–. *Publications:* The Human Journey: Christianity and Modern Consciousness, 1981; Can God Survive in Australia?, 1983; Reasons of the Heart, 1998. *Recreations:* jogging, motor car restoration, reading, cooking. *Address:* 48 Mount Piddington Road, Mount Victoria, NSW 2786, Australia.

WILSON, Catherine Mary, (Mrs P. J. Wilson), OBE 1996; FMA, FSA; Director, Norfolk Museums Service, 1991–98; *b* 10 April 1945; *d* of Arthur Thomas Bowyer and Kathleen May (*née* Hawes); *m* 1968, Peter John Wilson. *Educ:* Windsor County Grammar Sch. FMA 1984 (AMA 1972); FSA 1990. Museum Asst, Lincoln City Museums, 1964; Curator, Museum of Lincolnshire Life, 1972; Asst Dir (Museums), Lincs CC, 1983. Member: Museums and Galleries Commn, 1996–2000; Railway Heritage Cttee, 2000–; E Midlands Regl Cttee, Heritage Lottery Fund, 2002–08. President: Soc. for Folklife Studies, 2000–02; Soc. for Lincs History and Archaeol., 2005–. FRGS 1998. *Recreations:* industrial archaeology, vernacular architecture, all local history. *Address:* Penates et Lares, 5 Station Road, Reepham, Lincoln LN3 4DN.

WILSON, Cedric Gordon; Member, Strangford, Northern Ireland Assembly, 1998–2003 (UKU 1998–99, NIU 1999–2003); Leader, Northern Ireland Unionist Party, 1999–2003; *b* 6 June 1948; *s* of Samuel Wilson and Elizabeth Wilson; *m* 1975, Eva Kverneland; one *s* two *d*. *Educ:* Hillcrest Prep. Sch.; Belmont Primary Sch.; Orangefield High Sch. Dir, Hollymount Develts Ltd, 1988–. Mem., 1981–89, Dep. Mayor, 1982–83, Mayor, 1983–84, Castlereagh BC. *Recreations:* art, music, photography. *Address:* 12 Sandylands, Ballyhalbert, Newtownards, Co. Down BT22 1BT.

WILSON, Prof. Charles Crichton, (Chick), PhD, DSc; FInstP, FRSC; Regius Professor of Chemistry, University of Glasgow, since 2003; *b* 11 Oct. 1961; *s* of David Cherrie Wilson and Isabella Kennedy Wilson; *m* 2002, Victoria Marie Nield, DPhil. *Educ:* Craigbank Secondary Sch., Glasgow; Univ. of Glasgow (BSc Hons Chem. Physics 1982; DSc Chemistry 2004); PhD Physics Dundee 1985. FInstP 2002; FRSC 2002. Council for the Central Laboratory of the Research Councils: Sen. Scientist and Hd, ISIS Crystallography Gp, 1992–2004; Associate Scientist, 2004–. Vis. Lectr, J. J. Thomson Physical Lab., Univ. of Reading, 1993–96; Vis. Prof. in Chemistry, Univ. of Durham, 2001–06; Adjunct Prof. of Chemistry, Univ. of Tennessee, Knoxville, 2006–. Dep. Dir, WestCHEM, 2006–. Pres., British Crystallographic Assoc., 2003–06. *Publications:* Single Crystal Neutron Diffraction from Molecular Materials, 2000; over 230 articles in learned scientific jls. *Recreations:* walking, running, reading, music (listening, not making), restoring a Victorian walled garden. *Address:* Department of Chemistry, University of Glasgow, Glasgow G12 8QQ. *T:* (0141) 330 8522, *Fax:* (0141) 330 8775; *e-mail:* c.c.wilson@chem.gla.ac.uk.

WILSON, Charles Martin; Managing Director, Mirror Group (formerly Mirror Group Newspapers) plc, 1992–98 (Editorial Director, 1991–92); Managing Director and Editor-in-chief, The Sporting Life, 1990–98; *b* 18 Aug. 1935; *s* of Adam and Ruth Wilson; *m* 1st, 1968, Anne Robinson, *qv* (marr. diss. 1973); one *d*; 2nd, 1980, Sally Angela O'Sullivan, *qv* (marr. diss. 2001); one *s* one *d*; 3rd, 2001, Rachel, *d* of Baroness Pitkeathley, *qv*. *Educ:* Eastbank Academy, Glasgow. News Chronicle, 1959–60; Daily Mail, 1960–71; Dep. Northern Editor, Daily Mail, 1971–74; Asst Editor, London Evening News, 1974–76; Editor, Glasgow Evening Times, Glasgow Herald, Scottish Sunday Standard, 1976–82; The Times: Exec. Editor, 1982; Dep. Editor, 1983; Editor, 1985–90; Internat. Develts Dir, News Internat. plc, 1990. Non-exec. Dir, Chelsea and Westminster NHS Trust, 2000–. Mem., Newspaper Panel, Competition Commn, 1999–2006; Board Member: Youth Justice, 1998–2004; Countryside Alliance, 1998–2005, 2008–. Mem., Jockey Club, 1993–. Trustee: WWF-UK, 1996–2002; Royal Naval Mus., 1999–. *Recreations:* reading, riding, horse racing, countryside. *Address:* 23 Campden Hill Square, W8 7JY. *T:* (020) 7727 3366.

WILSON, Maj. Gen. Christopher Colin, CBE 2004; Capability Manager (Battlespace Manoeuvre) and Master General of the Ordnance, since 2006; *b* 14 Sept. 1953; *s* of Brig. Colin David Hastings Wilson and Eileen Edna Wilson (*née* Fort); *m* 1988, Marguerite Rose Laurraine Stewart; two *d*. *Educ:* Sedbergh Sch.; RMA, Sandhurst. Commnd RA, 1973; Staff Coll., 1986; CO 47 Regt RA, 1993–95; CRA Land and Comdr 1st Artillery Bde, 1998–2000; Dir Capability Integration (Army), 2001–03; Dir RA, 2004; ADC, 2004; Sen. Directing Staff, RCDS, 2005–06; Dep. Comdr, Coalition Forces Comd (Afghanistan), 2006. Col Comdt, RA, 2005–. CGIA Mil. Technol. *Recreations:* sailing, gardening. *Address:* c/o Army and Navy Club, 36–39 Pall Mall, SW1Y 5JN. *Clubs:* Army and Navy; Royal Artillery Yacht (Rear Cdre, 1993–95).

WILSON, (Christopher) David, CBE 1968; MC 1945; Chairman: Southern Television Ltd, 1976–81 (Managing Director, 1959–76); Southstar Television International, 1976–81; Beaumont (UK) Ltd, 1979–81; *b* 17 Dec. 1916; *s* of late James Anthony Wilson, Highclere, Worplesdon, Surrey; *m* 1947, Jean Barbara Morton Smith (*d* 1997); no *c*. *Educ:* St George's Sch., Windsor; Aldenham. Served War of 1939–45: Captain RA, in India, Middle East and Italy. Business Manager, Associated Newspapers Ltd, 1955–57; Dir, Associated Rediffusion Ltd, 1956–57; Gen. Manager, Southern Television Ltd, 1957–59; Chm., ITN Ltd, 1969–71. Mem. Council, Southampton Univ., 1980–89; Trustee, Chichester Festival Theatre Trust Ltd. FCA 1947. *Recreations:* sailing, music. *Address:* 1 Hamble Manor, The Green, Hamble, Southampton SO31 4GB. *T:* (023) 8045 5824. *Clubs:* MCC; Royal Southern Yacht.

WILSON, Christopher G.; *see* Grey-Wilson.

WILSON, Clive Hebden; Independent Complaints Reviewer, Lottery Forum, since 2005; *b* 1 Feb. 1940; *s* of Joseph and Irene Wilson; *m* 1976, Jill Garland Evans; two *d*. *Educ:* Leeds Grammar Sch.; Corpus Christi Coll., Oxford. Joined Civil Service, 1962; Ministry of Health: Asst Principal, 1962–67; Asst Private Sec. to Minister of Health, 1965–66; Principal, 1967–73; Assistant Secretary: DHSS, 1973–77; Cabinet Office, 1977–79; DHSS, 1979–82; Under Sec., DHSS, later DoH, 1982–98: Dir of Estabs (HQ), 1982–84; Child Care Div., 1984–86; Children, Maternity, Prevention Div., 1986–87; Medicines Div., 1987–90; Priority Health Services Div., subseq. Health Care (A) Div., 1990–92; on secondment from Department of Health: Hd of Health and Community Care Gp, NCVO, 1992–95; Dir, Office of Health Service Comr, 1995–96; Dep. Health Service Comr, 1996–98; Clerk Advr, H of C, 1998–2001; Independent Complaints Reviewer: Nat. Lottery Charities Bd, subseq. Community Fund, 1998–2004; New Opportunities Fund, 2000–04; Awards for All Scheme, 2000–05; Arts Council England, 2003–05; Big Lottery Fund, 2004–05. *Recreations:* walking, gardening, tennis.

WILSON, Colin Alexander Megaw; First Scottish Parliamentary Counsel, since 2006; *b* 4 Jan. 1952; *s* of James Thompson Wilson and Sarah Elizabeth Howard Wilson (*née* Megaw); *m* 1987, Mandy Esca Clay; one *s* one *d*. *Educ:* Glasgow High Sch.; Edinburgh Univ. (LLB Hons 1973). Admitted solicitor, Scotland, 1975; Asst Solicitor, then Partner, Archibald Campbell & Harley, WS, Edinburgh, 1975–79; Asst, later Depute, Parly Draftsman for Scotland, 1979–93; Asst Legal Sec. to Lord Advocate, 1979–99; Scottish Parly Counsel, 1993–2006. *Recreations:* choral singing, hill walking, reading. *Address:* Office of the Scottish Parliamentary Counsel, Victoria Quay, Edinburgh EH6 6QQ. *T:* (0131) 244 1670.

WILSON, Colin Henry; author; *b* Leicester, 26 June 1931; *s* of Arthur Wilson and Annetta Jones; *m* Dorothy Betty Troop; one *s*; *m* Joy Stewart; two *s* one *d*. *Educ:* The Gateway Secondary Technical School, Leicester. Left school at 16. Laboratory Asst (Gateway School), 1948–49; Civil Servant (collector of taxes), Leicester and Rugby, 1949–50; national service with RAF, AC2, 1949–50. Various jobs, and a period spent in Paris and Strasbourg, 1950; came to London, 1951; various labouring jobs, long period in plastic factory; returned to Paris, 1953; labouring jobs in London until Dec. 1954, when began writing The Outsider: has since made a living at writing. Visiting Professor: Hollins Coll., Va, 1966–67; Univ. of Washington, Seattle, 1967; Dowling Coll., Majorca, 1969; Rutgers Univ., NJ, 1974. Plays produced: Viennese Interlude; The Metal Flower Blossom; Strindberg. *Publications:* The Outsider, 1956; Religion and the Rebel, 1957; The Age of Defeat, 1959; Ritual in the Dark, 1960; Adrift in Soho, 1961; An Encyclopædia of Murder, 1961; The Strength to Dream, 1962; Origins of the Sexual Impulse, 1963; The Man without a Shadow, 1963; The World of Violence, 1963; Rasputin and the Fall of the Romanovs, 1964; The Brandy of the Damned (musical essays), 1964; Necessary Doubt, 1964; Beyond the Outsider, 1965; Eagle and Earwig, 1965; The Mind Parasites, 1966; Introduction to The New Existentialism, 1966; The Glass Cage, 1966; Sex and the Intelligent Teenager, 1966; The Philosopher's Stone, 1968; Strindberg (play), 1968; Bernard Shaw: A Reassessment, 1969; Voyage to a Beginning, 1969; Poetry and Mysticism, 1970; The Black Room, 1970; A Casebook of Murder, 1970; The God of the Labyrinth, 1970; Lingard, 1970; (jtly) The Strange Genius of David Lindsay, 1970; The Occult, 1971; New Pathways in Psychology, 1972; Order of Assassins, 1971; Tree by Tolkien, 1973; Hermann Hesse, 1973; Strange Powers, 1973; The Schoolgirl Murder Case, 1974; Return of the Lloigor, 1974; A Book of Booze, 1974; The Craft of the Novel, 1975; The Space Vampires, 1976 (filmed as Lifeforce, 1985); Men of Strange Powers, 1976; Enigmas and Mysteries, 1977; The Geller Phenomenon, 1977; Mysteries, 1978; Mysteries (play), 1979; The Quest for Wilhelm Reich, 1979; The War Against Sleep: the philosophy of Gurdjieff, 1980; Starseekers, 1980; Frankenstein's Castle, 1981; (ed with John Grant) The Directory of Possibilities, 1981; Poltergeist!, 1981; Access to Inner Worlds, 1982; The Criminal History of Mankind, 1983; (with Donald Seaman) Encyclopaedia of Modern Murder, 1983; Psychic Detectives, 1983; The Janus Murder Case, 1984; The Essential Colin Wilson, 1984; The Personality Surgeon, 1985; Spider World: the tower, 1987; (with Damon Wilson) Encyclopedia of Unsolved Mysteries, 1987; Spider World: the delta, 1987; (ed with Ronald Duncan) Marx Refuted, 1987; Aleister Crowley: the nature of the beast, 1987; (with Robin Odell) Jack the Ripper: summing up and verdict, 1987; The Magician from Siberia, 1988; The Misfits: a study of sexual outsiders, 1988; Beyond the Occult, 1988; Written in Blood, 1989; (with Donald Seaman) The Serial Killers, 1990; Mozart's Journey to Prague (play), 1991; Spider World: the magician, 1992, new edn 2002; The Strange Life of P. D. Ouspensky, 1993; From Atlantis to the Sphinx, 1996; Atlas of Sacred Sites and Holy Places, 1996; Alien Dawn, 1998; The Devil's Party, 2000; (with Rand Fle'math) Atlantis Blueprint, 2000; Spider World: shadowland, 2003; Dreaming to Some Purpose (autobiog.), 2004; Atlantis and the Neanderthals, 2006; The Angry Years: the rise and fall of the angry young men, 2007; Super Consciousness, 2008; contribs to: The Times, Daily Mail, etc. *Recreations:* collecting gramophone records, mainly opera; mathematics. *Club:* Savage.

WILSON, Maj.-Gen. Dare; *see* Wilson, Maj.-Gen. R. D.

WILSON, David; *see* Wilson, C. D.

WILSON, Sir David, 3rd Bt *cr* 1920; *b* 30 Oct. 1928; *s* of Sir John Mitchell Harvey Wilson, 2nd Bt, KCVO, and Mary Elizabeth (*d* 1979), *d* of late William Richards, CBE; *S* father, 1975; *m* 1955, Eva Margareta, *e d* of Tore Lindell, Malmö, Sweden; two *s* one *d*. *Educ:* Deerfield Acad., Mass., USA; Harrow School; Oriel Coll., Oxford (Brisco Owen Schol.). Barrister, Lincoln's Inn, 1954–61; admitted Solicitor, 1962; Partner, Simmons & Simmons, EC2, 1963–92. *Heir:* *s* Thomas David Wilson [*b* 6 Jan. 1959; *m* 1st, 1984, Valerie Stogdale (marr. diss. 2002); two *s*; 2nd, 2006, Briony Jane Roberts (*née* Clark)].

Address: Tandem House, Queens Drive, Oxshott, Leatherhead, Surrey KT22 0PH. *Club:* Royal Southern Yacht.

WILSON, Prof. David, PhD; Professor of Criminology, Birmingham City University (formerly University of Central England, Birmingham), since 1997; *b* 24 April 1957; *s* of late William and Margaret Wilson; *m* 1990, Anne Maguire; one *s* one *d*. *Educ:* Univ. of Glasgow (MA Hons 1979); Selwyn Coll., Cambridge (PhD 1984). Prison Governor, various prisons incl. HM Prisons Wormwood Scrubs, Grendon and Woodhill, 1983–97. Vice Chm., Howard League for Penal Reform, 2004–. Presenter, BBC Television series: Crime Squad, 1999–2001; Leave No Trace, 2006. Editor, Howard Jl, 1999–. *Publications:* (jtly) The Prison Governor: theory and practice, 1998; The Longest Injustice: the strange story of Alex Alexandrowicz, 1999; Prison(er) Education: stories of change and transformation, 2000; (jtly) What Everyone in Britain Should Know about Crime and Punishment, 2001; (jtly) What Everyone in Britain Should Know about the Police, 2001; (jtly) Innocence Betrayed, 2002; (jtly) Images of Incarceration, 2004; (jtly) Student Handbook of Criminal Justice and Criminology, 2004; Death at the Hands of the State, 2005; Serial Killers: hunting Britons and their victims 1960–2006, 2007; (with P. Harrison) Hunting Evil, 2008. *Recreations:* Rugby, tennis. *Address:* c/o Curtis Brown, 28–29 Haymarket, SW1Y 4SP. *T:* (020) 7393 4460; *e-mail:* profw@globalnet.co.uk.

WILSON, David; Director of Policy and Strategy, Institute of Chartered Secretaries and Administrators, since 2008. *Educ:* Colchester Inst. of Higher Educn; Anglia Ruskin Univ. (BA Hons); Univ. of West of England; London Sch. of Econs and Pol Sci. (LLM). Chartered Sec. 1996; FCIS 1996. Solicitor's clerk and articled clerk, Farrer & Co., 1983–86; admitted solicitor, Supreme Court, 1986; Solicitor: Holman, Fenwick & Willan, 1987–88; Gouldens, 1988–90; BAT Industries plc: Asst Solicitor, 1990–93; Gp Co. Sec., 1993–97; Dir, subsidiary cos; Co. Sec. and Gen. Counsel, Debenhams plc and Dir, Debenhams Retail plc, 1998–99; Co. Sec., PIA and IMRO, 2000–01; Registrar, Stock Exchange Quotations Cttee, 2000–01; self-employed contractor to Cazenove and Co., 2001; Gp Co. Sec. and Legal Dir, Safeway plc, and Dir and Sec., Safeway Stores plc, 2001–04; Robert Woof Dir and Chief Exec., Wordsworth Trust, 2006–08. Antiquarian, art historian and writer. FRSA 1998; FSA 2007. *Publications:* Guide to Best Practice for Annual General Meetings, 1996; articles on legal issues and corporate governance; papers on history and art of 18th and 19th centuries in acad. jls. *Recreations:* music, sport, art, history, literature. *Address:* Institute of Chartered Secretaries and Administrators, 16 Park Crescent, W1B 1AH. *T:* (020) 7580 4741; *e-mail:* dwilson@icsa.co.uk.

WILSON, David Geoffrey, OBE 1986; DL; Chairman, East Manchester Partnership, 1996–2006; Vice Lord-Lieutenant, Greater Manchester, 2003–08; *b* 30 April 1933; *s* of late Cyril Wilson and Winifred Wilson (*née* Sutton); *m* 1980, Dianne Elizabeth Morgan. *Educ:* Leeds Grammar Sch.; Oldham Hulme Grammar Sch. Williams Deacon's Bank, 1953–70 (Co. Sec., 1965–70); Co. Sec., 1970–72, Sen. Manager, 1973–81, Williams & Glyn's Bank; Regl Dir (NW), NEB, 1981–85; Dir of Banking (NW), British Linen Bank, 1986–91. Non-executive Director: Lancastrian Building Soc., 1991–92; Healthsure Gp Ltd, 1998–2003. Chm., Manchester Business Link Ltd, 1993–2000; Dir, 1998–2001, and Chm., 1999–2001, Business Link Network Co. Chairman: N Manchester HA, 1991–93; N Manchester Healthcare NHS Trust, 1993–97; Dir, Manchester Chamber of Commerce and Industry, 1974–2001 (Pres., 1978–80); non-exec. Dir, Manchester TEC, 1998–2001. Non-executive Director: Halle Concerts Soc., 1980–97 (Treas., 1986–92; Dep. Chm., 1992–97); NW Arts Bd, 1991–96. Pres., Manchester Literary and Philosophical Soc., 1981–83. Chairman: Manchester Settlement, 1999–; Manchester Outward Bound Assoc., 2002–; Pres., Gtr Manchester Victim Support and Witness Service, 2001–; Vice-Pres., St Ann's Hospice, 1991– (Sec., 1968–72; Treas., 1975–91). Mem. Court, Manchester Univ., 1980–99; Mem. Council, Salford Univ., 1996–2005; Governor: Salford Coll. of Technol., 1988–96; Manchester Coll. of Arts and Technol., 1999–2008. Hon. Consul for Iceland, 1981–. High Sheriff, 1991–92, DL 1985, Gtr Manchester. Hon. MA: Manchester, 1983; Salford, 1995. *Recreations:* gardening, music. *Address:* 28 Macclesfield Road, Wilmslow, Cheshire SK9 2AF. *T:* (01625) 524133, *Fax:* (01625) 520605; *e-mail:* wilsondg@talk21.com. *Clubs:* Army and Navy; Lancashire County Cricket.

WILSON, Sir David (Mackenzie), Kt 1984; FBA 1981; Director of the British Museum, 1977–92; *b* 30 Oct. 1931; *e s* of Rev. Joseph Wilson; *m* 1955, Eva, *o d* of Dr Gunnar Sjögren, Stockholm; one *s* one *d*. *Educ:* Kingswood Sch.; St John's Coll., Cambridge (LittD; Hon. Fellow, 1985); Lund Univ., Sweden. Research Asst, Cambridge Univ., 1954; Asst Keeper, British Museum, 1954–64; Reader in Archaeology of Anglo-Saxon Period, London Univ., 1964–71; Prof. of Medieval Archaeology, Univ. of London, 1971–76; Jt Head of Dept of Scandinavian Studies, UCL, 1973–76 (Hon. Fellow, 1988). Slade Prof., Cambridge, 1985–86. Member: Ancient Monuments Bd for England, 1976–84; Historic Bldgs and Monuments Commn, 1990–97. Governor, Museum of London, 1976–81; Trustee: Nat. Museums of Scotland, 1985–87; Nat. Museums of Merseyside, 1986–2001. Crabtree Orator 1966. Member: Royal Swedish Acad. of Sci.; Royal Acad. of Letters, History and Antiquities, Sweden; Norwegian Acad. of Science and Letters; German Archaeological Inst.; Royal Gustav Adolf's Acad. of Sweden; Royal Soc. of Letters of Lund; Vetenskapssocieteten, Lund; Royal Soc. of Sci. and Letters, Gothenburg; Royal Soc. of Sci., Uppsala; Royal Norwegian Soc. of Sci. and Letters; FSA; MAE; Hon. MRIA; Hon. Mem., Polish Archaeological and Numismatic Soc.; Hon. FMA. Sec., Soc. for Medieval Archaeology, 1957–77; Pres., Viking Soc., 1968–70; Pres., Brit. Archaeological Assoc., 1962–68. Mem. Council, Nottingham Univ., 1988–94. Foundn Fellow, Birmingham Univ. Hon. Fil.Dr Stockholm; Hon. Dr Phil: Aarhus; Oslo; Hon. DLitt: Liverpool; Birmingham; Nottingham; Leicester; Hon LLD Pennsylvania. Félix Neubergh Prize, Gothenburg Univ., 1978; Gold Medal, Soc. of Antiquaries, 1995. Order of Polar Star, 1st cl. (Sweden), 1977. *Publications:* The Anglo-Saxons, 1960, 3rd edn 1981; Anglo-Saxon Metalwork 700–1100 in British Museum, 1964; (with O. Klindt-Jensen) Viking Art, 1966; (with G. Bersu) Three Viking Graves in the Isle of Man, 1969; The Vikings and their Origins, 1970, 2nd edn 1980; (with P. G. Foote) The Viking Achievement, 1970; (with A. Small and C. Thomas) St Ninian's Isle and its Treasure, 1973; The Viking Age in the Isle of Man, 1974; (ed) Anglo-Saxon Archaeology, 1976; (ed) The Northern World, 1980; The Forgotten Collector, 1984; Anglo-Saxon Art, 1984; The Bayeux Tapestry, 1985, 2nd edn 2004; The British Museum: purpose and politics, 1989; Awful Ends, 1992; Showing the Flag, 1992; Vikingatidens Konst, 1995; Vikings and Gods in European Art, 1997; The British Museum: a history, 2002; (ed jtly) The Hoen Hoard, 2006; The Vikings in the Isle of Man, 208. *Address:* The Lifeboat House, Castletown, Isle of Man IM9 1LD. *T:* (01624) 822800. *Club:* Athenæum.

WILSON, David William; DL; Chairman: Wilson Bowden PLC, 1987–2007; Eastern Range Ltd and subsidiaries, Go Plant Ltd and Davidsons Ltd; *b* 5 Dec. 1941; *s* of Albert Henry Wilson and Kathleen May Wilson; *m* 1st, 1964, Ann Taberner; one *s* one *d*; 2nd, 1985, Laura Isobel Knifton; two *s*. *Educ:* Ashby Boys' Grammar Sch.; Leicester Polytechnic. Created from scratch what is now Wilson Bowden PLC. Pres., Leics CCC. DL Leics, 2008. *Recreation:* farming. *Address:* Lowesby Hall, Lowesby, Leics LE7 9DD. *T:* (0116) 259 5321.

WILSON, Prof. Deirdre Susan Moir, PhD; FBA 1990; Professor of Linguistics, University College London, since 1991; *b* 1941; *m* 1975, Dr Theodore Zeldin, *qv*. *Educ:* Somerville Coll., Oxford (BA 1964); BPhil Oxon 1967; PhD 1973. Lectr in Philosophy, Somerville Coll., Oxford, 1967–68; Harkness Fellow, MIT, 1968–70; University College London: Lectr in Linguistics, 1970–85; Reader, 1985–91; British Acad. Res. Reader, 1988. *Publications:* Presuppositions and Non-truth Conditional Semantics, 1975; (with Neil Smith) Modern Linguistics: the result of Chomsky's Revolution, 1979; (with Dan Sperber) Relevance: communication and cognition, 1995; contrib. to learned jls. *Address:* Department of Phonetics and Linguistics, University College London, Gower Street, WC1E 6BT.

WILSON, Derek Robert; Chief Executive, Slough Estates, 1996–2002; *b* 10 Oct. 1944; *m* 1972, Maureen Thorpe; one *s* one *d*. *Educ:* Bristol Univ. (BA Econs and Accounting). FCA 1970. Deloitte Haskins & Sells, London and Geneva, 1966–72; Cavenham, 1973–78; Wilkinson Match, 1978–83; Dir of Finance, Cadbury Schweppes, 1983–86; Finance Dir, 1986, Group Managing Dir, 1992–96, Slough Estates. Director: Candover Investments, 1994–2005; Westbury, 1996–2005. Gov., Nat. Soc. for Epilepsy, 2003–. Gov., St Mary's Sch., Gerrards Cross, 1996–. *Recreation:* golf.

WILSON, Des; author; public affairs adviser; *b* 5 March 1941; *s* of Albert H. Wilson, Oamaru, New Zealand; *m* 1985, Jane Dunmore; one *s* one *d* by a previous marriage. *Educ:* Waitaki Boys' High Sch., New Zealand. Journalist-Broadcaster, 1957–67; Director, Shelter, Nat. Campaign for the Homeless, 1967–71; Head of Public Affairs, RSC, 1974–76; Editor, Social Work Today, 1976–79; Dep. Editor, Illustrated London News, 1979–81; Chm., 1981–85, Project Advr, 1985–89, CLEAR (Campaign for Lead-Free Air); Dir of Public Affairs, 1993–94, World Wide Vice Chm., Public Affairs, 1994, Burson-Marsteller; Dir of Corporate and Public Affairs, BAA plc, 1994–2000. Non-executive Director: Carphone Warehouse plc, 2000–03; Earls Court and Olympia Holdings, 2001–04. Chairman: Friends of the Earth (UK), 1982–86; Campaign for Freedom of Information, 1984–91; Citizen Action, 1983–91; Parents Against Tobacco, 1990. Member: Nat. Exec., Nat. Council for Civil Liberties, 1971–73; Cttee for City Poverty, 1972–73; Bd, Shelter, 1982–86 (Trustee, 1982–86); Council, Nat. Trust, 2001–02; Trustee, Internat. Year of Shelter for the Homeless (UK), 1985–87. Member: Bd, BTA, 1997–2004; UK Sports Council, 2000–02; Mgt Bd, ECB, 2003–04; Sen. Vice Chm., Sport England, 1999–2002 (Chm., Lottery Panel, 1999–2002). Columnist: The Guardian, 1968–70; The Observer, 1971–75; New Statesman, 1997–; regular contributor, Illustrated London News, 1972–85. Contested (L) Hove, 1973, 1974; Liberal Party: Mem. Council, 1973–74 and 1984–85; Mem., Nat. Exec., 1984–85; Pres., 1986–87; Pres., NLYL, 1984–85; Mem. Federal Exec., SLD, 1988; Gen. Election Campaign Dir, Lib Dems, 1990–92. *Publications:* I Know It Was the Place's Fault, 1970; Des Wilson's Minority Report (a diary of protest), 1973; So you want to be Prime Minister: a personal view of British politics, 1979; The Lead Scandal, 1982; Pressure, the A to Z of Campaigning in Britain, 1984; (ed) The Environmental Crisis, 1984; (ed) The Secrets File, 1984; The Citizen Action Handbook, 1986; Battle for Power - Inside the Alliance General Election Campaign, 1987; Costa Del Sol (novel), 1990; Campaign (novel), 1992; Campaigning, 1993; (with Sir John Egan) Private Business, Public Battleground, 2002; Swimming with the Devilfish: under the surface of professional poker, 2006; Ghosts at the Table: a history of poker, 2007. *Address:* Pryors Cottage, Nancegollan, Helston, Cornwall TR13 0A2.

WILSON, Prof. Edward Osborne, PhD; Pellegrino University Research Professor, 1997–2002, now Emeritus, and Hon. Curator in Entomology, since 1997, Harvard University (Curator in Entomology, 1972–97); *b* 10 June 1929; *s* of Edward O. Wilson, Sen. and Inez Freeman; *m* 1955, Irene Kelley; one *d*. *Educ:* Univ. of Alabama (BS 1949; MS 1950); Harvard Univ. (PhD 1955). Harvard University: Jun. Fellow, Soc. of Fellows, 1953–56; Asst Prof. of Biology, 1956–58; Assoc. Prof. of Zoology, 1958–64; Prof. of Zoology, 1964–76; Baird Prof. of Sci., 1976–94; Mellon Prof. of the Scis, 1990–93; Pellegrino University Prof., 1994–97. Hon. DSc Oxon, 1993; 32 other hon. doctorates. Nat. Medal of Sci., USA, 1978; Tyler Prize for Envmtl Achievement, 1984; Crafoord Prize, Swedish Royal Acad. of Sci., 1990; Internat. Prize for Biol., Japan, 1994; King Faisal Internat. Prize for Sci., 2000; Franklin Medal, Amer. Philosophical Soc., 2000, etc. *Publications:* (with R. H. MacArthur) The Theory of Island Biogeography, 1967; (jtly) A Primer of Population Biology, 1971; The Insect Societies, 1971; Sociobiology: the new synthesis, 1975; On Human Nature, 1978 (Pulitzer Prize, 1979); (jtly) Caste and Ecology in the Social Insects, 1978; (jtly) Genes, Mind and Culture, 1981; (jtly) Promethean Fire, 1983; Biophilia, 1984; (with Bert Hölldobler) The Ants, 1990 (Pulitzer Prize, 1991); Success and Dominance in Ecosystems, 1990; The Diversity of Life, 1992; Naturalist (autobiog.), 1994; (with Bert Hölldobler) Journey to the Ants, 1994; In Search of Nature, 1996; Consilience, 1998; Biological Diversity, 1999; The Future of Life, 2002; Pheidole in the New World: a hyperdiverse ant genus, 2003; Nature Revealed, 2006; The Creation, 2006; contrib. learned jls. *Address:* Museum of Comparative Zoology, Harvard University, 26 Oxford Street, Cambridge, MA 02138–2902, USA. *T:* (617) 4952315.

WILSON, Elizabeth Alice, (Mrs W. I. Wilson), OBE 1995; Chairman, Dumfries and Galloway Community NHS Trust, 1995–97; *b* 26 May 1937; *née* Edwards; *m* 1996, William Iain Wilson, MBE. *Educ:* Coleraine High Sch.; Univ. of Edinburgh (BSc Soc. Sci.); SRN, SCM. Staff Nurse, Midwife, Ward Sister and nurse management posts, 1958–72; Principal Nursing Officer, Edinburgh Northern Hosps Gp, 1972–74; Dist Nursing Officer, N Lothian, Lothian Health Bd, 1974–80; Chief Area Nursing Officer: Dumfries and Galloway Health Bd, 1980–88; Tayside Health Bd, 1988–94. Mem., Nat. Bd for Nursing, Midwifery and Health Visiting, Scotland, 1983–93 (Dep. Chm., 1985–93). Chm., Stranraer Cancer Drop In Centre Assoc., 1998–2008. Hon. Sen. Lectr, Univ. of Dundee, 1988–94. SSStJ 2003. *Publications:* papers on nursing.

WILSON, Lt-Col Eric Charles Twelves, VC 1940; *b* 2 Oct. 1912; *s* of Rev. C. C. C. Wilson; *m* 1943, Ann (from whom he obtained a divorce, 1953), *d* of Major Humphrey Pleydell-Bouverie, MBE; two *s*; *m* 1953, Angela Joy, *d* of Lt-Col J. McK. Gordon, MC; one *s*. *Educ:* Marlborough; RMC, Sandhurst. Commissioned in East Surrey Regt, 1933; seconded to King's African Rifles, 1937; seconded to Somaliland Camel Corps, 1939; Long Range Desert Gp, 1941–42; Burma, 1944; seconded to N Rhodesia Regt, 1946; retd from Regular Army, 1949; Admin Officer, HM Overseas Civil Service, Tanganyika, 1949–61; Dep. Warden, London House, 1962, Warden, 1966–77. Hon. Sec., Anglo-Somali Soc., 1972–77 and 1988–90. *Publication:* Stowell in the Blackmore Vale, 1986. *Recreation:* country life. *T:* (01963) 370264.

WILSON, Fraser Andrew, MBE 1980; HM Diplomatic Service; Ambassador to Albania, since 2006; *b* 6 May 1949; *s* of William McStravick Wilson and Mary McFadyen Wilson (*née* Fraser); *m* 1981, Janet Phillips; two *s*. *Educ:* Bellahouston Acad.; Surrey Univ. (Dip. Russian Studies). Joined Diplomatic Service, 1967; served: FCO, 1967–70; Havana, 1970–71; SE Asia, 1971–73; Seoul, 1973–77; Salisbury, 1977–80; FCO, 1980–84; Moscow, 1984–85; First Sec. (Commercial), Rangoon, 1986–90; FCO, 1990–94; Dep. Consul Gen., São Paulo, 1994–98; Ambassador to Turkmenistan, 1998–2002; High

Comr, Seychelles, 2002–04; Dep. Hd, Overseas Territories, FCO, 2004–06. *Recreations:* travelling, reading. *Address:* c/o Foreign and Commonwealth Office, King Charles Street, SW1A 2AH.

WILSON, Geoffrey; Chairman, Wells, O'Brien & Co., 1972–82; *b* 11 July 1929; *m* 1962, Philomena Mary Kavanagh; one *s* one *d. Educ:* Bolton County Grammar Sch.; Univ. of Birmingham; Linacre Coll., Oxford. PE Consulting Group, 1958–63; British Railways, 1963–71; Mem., BR Bd, 1968–71, Chief Exec. (Railways), 1971. Member: Council, Royal Inst. of Public Admin, 1970–71; Council, Inst. of Transport, 1970–71. *Recreations:* golf, gardening, painting. *Address:* 10 Montpellier Grove, Cheltenham, Glos GL50 2XB.

WILSON, Geoffrey Alan, OBE 2004; Chairman, Equity Land Ltd, since 1994; *b* 19 Feb. 1934; *s* of Lewis Wilson and Doris Wilson (*née* Shrier); *m* 1963, Marilyn Helen Freedman; one *s* two *d. Educ:* Haberdashers' Aske's School; College of Estate Management. FRICS. 2nd Lieut RA, 1955–56. Private practice, 1957–60; Director: Amalgamated Investment & Property Co., 1961–70; Sterling Land Co., 1971–73 (and co-founder); Greycoat, 1976–94 (Chm., 1985–94, and co-founder); Perspectives on Architecture (formerly Perfect Harmony) Ltd, 1993–98. Member: W Metropolitan Conciliation Cttee, Race Relations Bd, 1969–71; Council, Central British Fund for World Jewish Relief, 1993–97. Trustee: ORT Trust, 1980–; Public Art Develt Trust, 1990–95; British Architectural Liby Trust, 1996–2000; AA Foundn, 1998–; Buildings at Risk Trust, 1998–2001. English Heritage: Comr, 1992–98; Chm., London Adv. Cttee, 1995–98; Chm., Urban Panel, 2000–03; Chm., Heritage Protection Review Steering Cttee, DCMS, 2004–08. Mem., Governing Council, UCS, 1991–95. Governor: Peabody Trust, 1998–2004; City Literary Inst., 1998–2002; Mus. of London, 2000–. Hon. FRIBA 1995. *Recreations:* reading, architecture, art. *Address:* (office) 87 Wimpole Street, W1G 9RL. *T:* (020) 7935 8204. *Club:* Reform.

WILSON, Hon. Geoffrey Hazlitt, CVO 1989; FCA, FCMA; Chairman, Southern Electric plc, 1993–96 (Director, 1989–96); *b* 28 Dec. 1929; *yr s* of 1st Baron Moran, MC, MD, FRCP, and Lady Moran, MBE; *m* 1955, Barbara Jane Hebblethwaite; two *s* two *d. Educ:* Eton; King's Coll., Cambridge (BA Hons). JDipMA. Articled to Barton Mayhew (now Ernst & Young), 1952; Chartered Accountant 1955; joined English Electric, 1956; Dep. Comptroller, 1965; Financial Controller (Overseas), GEC, 1968; joined Delta Group as Financial Dir, Cables Div., 1969; elected to Main Board as Gp Financial Dir, 1972; Jt Man. Dir, 1977; Dep. Chief Executive, 1980; Chief Exec., 1981–88; Chm., 1982–94. Director: Blue Circle Industries plc, 1980–97; Drayton English & International Trust, 1978–95; W Midlands and Wales Regl Bd, Nat. Westminster Bank PLC, 1985–92 (Chm., 1990–92); Johnson Matthey plc, 1990–97 (Dep. Chm., 1994–97); UK Adv. Bd, National Westminster Bank, 1990–92. Member: Council, Inst. of Cost and Management Accountants, 1972–78; Accounting Standards Cttee, 1978–79; Financial Reporting Council, 1990–93; London Metal Exchange, 1982–94; Chm., 100 Gp of Chartered Accountants, 1979–80 (Hon. Mem., 1985). Mem. Management Bd, Engineering Employers Fedn, 1979–83 (Vice-Pres., 1983–86 and 1990–94; Dep. Pres., 1986–90); Chm., EEF Cttee on Future of Wage Bargaining, 1980; Dep. Pres., 1986–87, Pres., 1987–88, Counsellor, 1989–94, BEAMA; Member: Administrative Council, Royal Jubilee Trusts, 1979–88, Hon. Treas., 1980–89; Council, Winchester Cathedral Trust, 1985–93; Council, St Mary's Hosp. Med. Sch., 1985–88. Vice-Chm., Campaign Appeal, 1994–97, Fellow Commoner, 1996–, King's Coll., Cambridge. CCMI. Mem. Ct of Assistants, Chartered Accountants' Co., 1982–95 (Master, 1988–89). OStJ 1996. *Recreations:* family, reading, walking, ski-ing, vintage cars. *Club:* Boodle's.

WILSON, Prof. Geoffrey Victor Herbert, AM 1998; PhD; Vice Chancellor and President, Deakin University, 1996–2002; *b* 23 Sept. 1938; *s* of Victor Hawthorne Wilson and Dorothy Eleanor Wilson (*née* Spooner); *m* 1961, Beverley Wigley; two *s* two *d. Educ:* Univ. of Melbourne (BSc 1958; MSc 1960; DSc 1977); PhD Monash Univ. 1964. FAIP, MACE, FTSE, FAIM. Postgrad. Schol., Univ. of Melbourne, 1958–60; Teaching Fellow, Monash Univ., 1960–63; Nuffield Foundn Travelling Fellow, Oxford Univ., 1963–65; Sen. Lectr in Physics, Monash Univ., 1965–71; University of New South Wales: Prof. of Physics, 1971–85, Dean, Faculty of Mil. Studies, 1978–86, Royal Mil. Coll.; Rector of University Coll., Aust. Defence Acad., 1984–91; Vice Chancellor, Central Queensland Univ., 1991–96. Vis. Prof., Free Univ. of Berlin, 1977–78. *Recreations:* gardening, theatre, physical recreation. *Address:* 102/159 Beach Street, Port Melbourne, Vic 3207, Australia.

WILSON, George; *see* Wilson, W. G.

WILSON, Gerald Robertson, CB 1991; FRSE; Chairman, Scottish Biomedical Foundation, 1999–2004; Director (non-executive), ICL (Scotland) Ltd, 2000–02; Special Adviser, Royal Bank of Scotland, since 2000; Adviser, ScottishJobs.com, 2004–05; *b* 7 Sept. 1939; *s* of late Charles Robertson Wilson and Margaret Wilson (*née* Early); *m* 1963, Margaret Anne (*d* 2005), *d* of late John S. and Agnes Wight; one *s* one *d. Educ:* Holy Cross Academy, Edinburgh; University of Edinburgh. (MA). FRSE 1999. Asst Principal, Scottish Home and Health Dept, 1961–65; Private Sec. to Minister of State for Scotland, 1965–66; Principal, Scottish Home and Health Dept, 1966–72; Private Sec. to Lord Privy Seal, 1972–74, to Minister of State, Civil Service Dept, 1974; Asst Sec., Scottish Economic Planning Dept, 1974–77; Counsellor, Office of the UK Perm. Rep. to the European Communities, Brussels, 1977–82; Asst Sec., Scottish Office, 1982–84; Under Sec., Industry Dept for Scotland, 1984–88; Sec., Scottish Office Educn, later Educn and Industry, Dept, 1988–99. Chm., Scottish Biomed. Res. Trust, 1999–2003. Chm., E Scotland, RIPA, 1990–92. Vice Chm., Royal Scottish Nat. Orchestra, 2002–06 (Bd Mem., 1999–2002). Chm., Scottish Eur. Educnl Trust, 2006–. Mem. Ct, Strathclyde Univ., 1999–2008 (Vice Chm., 2008–); Gov., George Watson's Coll., Edinburgh, 2000–. Mem., Bd of Mgt, St Andrew's Children's Soc., 2002–. Mem. Council, Fairbridge in Scotland, 2000–06 (Chm., 2006–). DUniv Stirling, 1999. *Recreation:* music. *Address:* 4 Inverleith Avenue South, Edinburgh EH3 5QA.

WILSON, Gillian Brenda, (Mrs Kenneth Wilson); *see* Babington-Browne, G. B.

WILSON, Gordon; *see* Wilson, Robert G.

WILSON, Guy Murray, MA; FSA; museum and historical consultant; Director, Genesis Trio Ltd, since 2005; *b* 18 Feb. 1950; *s* of late Rowland George Wilson and Mollie (*née* Munson; later Mrs Youngs); *m* 1972, Pamela Ruth McCredie; two *s* two *d. Educ:* New Coll., Oxford (MA); Manchester Univ. (Dip. Art, Gallery and Museum Studies). FSA 1984. Joined Royal Armouries, 1972; Keeper of Edged Weapons, 1978; Dep. Master of the Armouries, 1981–88; Master of the Armouries, 1988–2002. Member: British Commn for Military History, 1978–; Adv. Cttee on History Wreck Sites, 1981–99; Arms and Armour Soc. of GB, 1973– (Vice-Pres., 1995–); Arms and Armour Soc. of Denmark, 1978–; Meyrick Soc., 1980–; Internat. Napoleonic Soc., 2001–; Pres., Internat. Assoc. of Museums of Arms and Military Hist., 2002–03; Chairman: Internat. Cttee of Museums and Collections of Arms and Mil. Hist., 2003–; Battle of Crécy Trust, 2007–. Writer, Arms in Action (TV series), 1998, 2000. FRSA 1992. *Publications:* Treasures of the Tower: Crossbows, 1975; (with A. V. B. Norman) Treasures from the Tower of London, 1982; (with D. Walker) The Royal Armouries in Leeds: the making of a museum, 1996; contribs to museum and exhibn catalogues and to Jl of Arms and Armour Soc., Internat. Jl of Nautical Archaeol., Connoisseur, Burlington, Country Life, Museums Jl, Guns Rev., etc. *Recreations:* theatre, music, reading, walking. *Address:* Yeoman's Course House, Thornton Hill, Easingwold, York YO61 3PY.

WILSON, His Honour Harold, AE 1963; a Circuit Judge, 1981–2000 (Midland and Oxford Circuit); a Deputy Circuit Judge, 2001–03; *b* 19 Sept. 1931; *s* of late Edward Simpson Wilson; *m* 1st, Diana Marion (marr. diss.), *d* of late (Philip) Guy (Dudley) Sixsmith; three *s* one *d*; 2nd, Jill Ginever, *d* of late Charles Edward Walter Barlow; one step *s* one step *d. Educ:* St Albans Sch.; Sidney Sussex Coll., Cambridge (State Scholar; MA). Pilot Officer, RAF, 1950–51; Flying Officer, RAFVR, 1951–54; Flt Lt, RAuxAF, 1954–63. Administrative Trainee, KCH, 1954–56; Schoolmaster, 1957–59. Called to the Bar, Gray's Inn, 1958 (Holker Exhibnr; runner-up, Lee Essay Prize, 1959), Bencher, 1998; Oxford Circuit, 1960–70 (Circuit Junior, 1964–65); Midland and Oxford Circuit, 1971–75; Dep. Chm., Monmouthshire Quarter Sessions, 1969–70; a Recorder, Midland and Oxford Circuit, 1971–75; Chm. of Industrial Tribunals, Birmingham, 1976–81; Resident Judge, Coventry Crown Ct, 1983–92; Liaison Judge, 1986–92; Hon. Recorder of Coventry, 1986–93; designated Care Centre Judge, Coventry, 1991–92, Oxford, 1993–2000; Resident Judge, Oxford Crown Ct, 1993–2000; Liaison Judge to Oxfordshire Magistrates, 1993–96; Hon. Recorder of Oxford, 1999–2001; a Judge of the Employment Appeal Tribunal, 1999–2000; an Additl Judge, Supreme Ct of Gibraltar, 2003. Pres., Transport Tribunal, 1991–96; Chairman: Coventry Reparation Unit Adv. Cttee, 1991–92; Thames Valley Area Criminal Justice Strategy (formerly Liaison) Cttee, 1996–2000. Member: Matrimonial Causes Rules Cttee, 1984–88; W Midlands Probation Cttee, 1985–92. Shrieval Remembrancer, Oxon, 2004–. *Recreations:* watching Rugby football, reading and listening to music. *Address:* 2 Harcourt Buildings, Temple, EC4Y 9DB. *T:* (020) 7353 6961. *Club:* Royal Air Force (Trustee, 2005–).

WILSON, Prof. Henry Wallace, PhD; CPhys, FInstP; FRSE; physicist; Director, Scottish Universities' Research and Reactor Centre, 1962–85; Personal Professor of Physics, Strathclyde University, 1966–85, now Emeritus; *b* 30 Aug. 1923; *s* of Frank Binnington Wilson and Janet (*née* Wilson); *m* 1955, Fiona McPherson Martin, *d* of Alfred Charles Steinmetz Martin and Agnes Mary (*née* McPherson); three *s. Educ:* Allan Glen's Sch., Glasgow; Glasgow Univ. (BSc, PhD Physics). AInstP 1949, FInstP 1962; FRSE 1963. Wartime work as Physicist, Explosives Res. Div., ICI, Ardeer. Asst Lectr, Natural Philosophy Dept, Glasgow Univ., 1947–51; post-doctoral Res. Fellow, Univ. of Calif, Berkeley, 1951–52; Lectr, Nat. Phil. Dept, Glasgow Univ., 1952–55; Leader of Physical Measurements Gp, UKAEA, Aldermaston, 1955–62 (Sen. Principal Scientific Officer, 1958). Hon. Scientific Advr, Nat. Mus. of Antiquities of Scotland, 1969; Scientific Advr, Scottish Office, 1975–93. Mem., Nuclear Safety Cttee, 1964–89, and Consultant, SSEB; Mem., Radioactive Substances Adv. Cttee, 1966–70. Inst. of Physics: Mem. Council, 1970–71; Chm., Scottish Br., 1969–71; mem. several cttees; Royal Soc. of Edinburgh: Mem. Council, 1966–69, 1976–79; Vice Pres., 1979–81. Member: Brit. Nuclear Energy Soc.; British Mass Spectrometry Soc. (Chm., 1977–79). FRSA 1996. *Publications:* contributions to: Alpha, Beta and Gamma-ray Spectroscopy, ed K. Siegbahn, 1965; Activation Analysis, ed Lenihan and Thomson, 1965; Modern Aspects of Mass Spectrometry, ed R. I. Reed, 1968; Encyclopaedic Dictionary of Physics, ed J. Thewlis, 1973; (ed) Nuclear Engineering sect., Chambers' Science and Technology Dictionary, 1988; papers on radioactivity, low energy nuclear physics, meson physics, mass spectrometry, isotope separation, effects of radiation, and reactor physics, in scientific jls. *Recreations:* walking, industrial archaeology, bookbinding, photography. *Address:* Ashgrove, The Crescent, Busby, Glasgow G76 8HT. *T:* (0141) 644 3107.

WILSON, (Iain) Richard, OBE 1994; actor and director; *b* 9 July 1936; *s* of John Boyd Wilson and Euphemia (*née* Colquhoun). *Educ:* Greenock High Sch.; Royal Acad. of Dramatic Art. Associate Director, Royal Court, 2000–07. *Theatre* includes: Normal Service, Hampstead, 1979; Operation Bad Apple, 1982, An Honourable Trade, 1984, May Days, 1990, Royal Court; The Weekend, Strand, 1994; What the Butler Saw, NT, 1995; Waiting for Godot, Manchester Royal Exchange, 1999; The Play What I Wrote, West End, 2001–02; Whipping It Up, Bush Th., 2006, transf. New Ambassadors and tour, 2007; Uncle Vanya, Edinburgh Traverse Th.; *plays directed:* Heaven and Hell, 1981, Other Worlds, 1983, Royal Court; An Inspector Calls, Manchester Royal Exchange, 1986; A Wholly Healthy Glasgow, Manchester Royal Exchange, Royal Court and Edinburgh Fest., 1987, 1988; Prin, Lyric, Hammersmith, 1989; Imagine Drowning, Hampstead, 1991; Women Laughing, Manchester Royal Exchange, transf. Royal Court, 1992; Simply Disconnected, Chichester, 1996; Tom and Clem, Aldwych, 1997; Primo, NT, Hampstead and NY, 2004; East Coast Chicken Supper, Traverse Th., 2005; Astronaut Wives Club, NYT, 2006; Royal Court: Four, 1998; Toast, 1999; Mr Kolpert, I Just Stopped By to See the Man, 2000; Nightingale and Chase, 2001; Where Do We Live, Day in Dull Armour, Graffiti, 2002; Under the Whaleback, Playing the Victim, 2003; The Woman Before, 2005; Rainbow Kiss, 2006; *television series* include: My Good Woman, 1972; Crown Court, 1973–84; A Sharp Intake of Breath, 1979–81; Only When I Laugh, 1979–82; High and Dry, 1987; Tutti Frutti, 1987; One Foot in the Grave, six series, 1989–2000; High Stakes, 2001; Life - As We Know It, 2001; Jeffrey Archer: The Truth, 2002; King of Fridges, 2004; Born and Bred, two series, 2004–05; Doctor Who, 2005; A Harlot's Progress, 2006; The True Voice of Prostitution, 2006; Reichenbach Falls, 2007; Kingdom, two series, 2007–08; The Last Van Helsing; (dir) Primo, 2008; *films* include: A Passage to India, 1984; Whoops Apocalypse, 1986; Prick Up Your Ears, 1987; How to Get Ahead in Advertising, 1989; Fellow Traveller, 1990; Carry on Columbus, 1992; The Man Who Knew Too Little, 1998; Women Talking Dirty, 2001; Love and Other Disasters. Rector, Glasgow Univ., 1996–99. Hon. DLitt Glasgow Caledonian, 1995. Top TV Comedy Actor, British Comedy Awards, 1991; Light Entertainment Award, BAFTA, 1991 and 1993. *Recreations:* squash, collecting work of living Scottish painters. *Address:* c/o Conway van Gelder Grant Ltd, 18–21 Jermyn Street, SW1Y 6HP. *T:* (020) 7287 0077. *Clubs:* Royal Automobile, Groucho.

WILSON, Prof. Ian Andrew, DPhil, DSc; FRS 2000; Professor of Molecular Biology and Skaggs Institute for Chemical Biology, Scripps Research Institute, since 1982; *b* 22 March 1949; *s* of George Alexander Wilson and Margaret Stewart Wilson (*née* McKillop). *Educ:* Perth Acad.; Univ. of Edinburgh (BSc 1st Cl. Hons 1971); Corpus Christi Coll., Oxford (DPhil 1976; DSc 2000). Jun. Res. Fellow, Corpus Christi Coll., Oxford, 1975–77; Res. Fellow in Biochem., 1977–80, Res. Associate, 1980–82, Harvard Univ.; Asst Mem., 1982–84, Associate Mem., 1984–90, Scripps Clinic and Res. Foundn. Adjunct Prof., UCSD, 1998–. *Recreations:* scuba diving, tennis, golf, opera. *Address:* Department of Molecular Biology, BCC206, Scripps Research Institute, 10550 North Torrey Pines Road, La Jolla, CA 92037, USA. *T:* (858) 7849706. *Club:* La Jolla Beach and Tennis.

WILSON, Ian D.; *see* Douglas-Wilson.

WILSON, Ian Matthew, CB 1985; Under Secretary, Scottish Education Department, 1977–86; *b* 12 Dec. 1926; *s* of Matthew Thomson Wilson and Mary Lily Barnett; *m* 1st,

1953, Anne Chalmers (*d* 1991); three *s*; 2nd, 1996, Joyce Town. *Educ:* George Watson's Coll.; Edinburgh Univ. (MA). Asst Principal, Scottish Home Dept, 1950; Private Sec. to Perm. Under-Sec. of State, Scottish Office, 1953–55; Principal, Scottish Home Dept, 1955; Asst Secretary: Scottish Educn Dept, 1963; SHHD, 1971; Asst Under-Sec. of State, Scottish Office, 1974–77. Sec. of Commns for Scotland, 1987–92. Dir, Scottish Internat. Piano Competition, 1997–2004. Mem., Bd of Govs, RSAMD, 1992–2000. Pres., Univ. of Edinburgh Graduates' Assoc., 1995–97. *Address:* 47 Braid Hills Road, Edinburgh EH10 6LD. *T:* (0131) 447 1802. *Club:* New (Edinburgh).

WILSON, Ivan Patrick; Lay Member, Information Tribunal, since 2003; *b* 24 Aug. 1941; *s* of William Wilson and Jessie (*née* Bateson); *m* 1966, Kathleen Mary Price; three *s*. *Educ:* Royal Sch., Dungannon; Academy, Omagh; Queen's Univ., Belfast. HM Treasury, 1965–95; Private Sec. to Perm. Sec., Overseas Finance, 1971–73; Press Office, 1973–76; Defence Policy and Budget Div., 1981–84; RCDS 1985; Information Systems, 1986–89; Under-Sec., Industry and Employment Gp, 1989–90; Dir, Govt Centre for Information Systems, 1990–93; Under Sec., Public Enterprises Gp, HM Treasury, 1993–95; Exec. Advr, ICL Enterprises, 1995–98; Partnership Sec., Freshfields, 1998–99; Interim Chief Exec., NI Policing Bd, 2001–02. *Recreations:* foreign travel, sport, walking. *Address:* 88 Redhill Wood, New Ash Green, Longfield, Kent DA3 8QP. *T:* (01474) 874740.

WILSON, Dame Jacqueline, DBE 2008 (OBE 2002); author; Children's Laureate, 2005–07; *b* 17 Dec. 1945; *d* of late Harry Aitken and of Margaret Aitken (*née* Clibbons); *m* 1965, William Millar Wilson (marr. diss. 2004); one *d*. *Educ:* Coombe Girls' Sch. Journalist, D. C. Thomsons, 1963–65. Ambassador, Reading is Fundamental, UK, 1998–; Cttee Mem., Children's Writers and Illustrators Gp, Soc. of Authors, 1997–; Adv. Mem., Costa (formerly Whitbread) Book Awards Panel, 1997–; Judge: Rhône-Poulenc Prizes for Jun. Sci. Books, 1999; Orange Prize for Fiction, 2006; Prince Maurice Prize, 2006; Patron, Children's Film and TV Foundn, 2000–06; Pres., Book Trade Benevolent Soc., 2007–. FRSL 2006. Hon. DEd: Kingston, 2001; Winchester, 2006; Roehampton, 2007; Hon. DLit Bath, 2006; Hon. DLaws Dundee, 2007. *Publications* include: *fiction:* Hide and Seek, 1972; Truth or Dare, 1973; Snap, 1974; Let's Pretend, 1975; Making Hate, 1977; *for children:* Nobody's Perfect, 1982; Waiting for the Sky to Fall, 1985; Other Side, 1990; Take a Good Look, 1990; The Story of Tracy Beaker, 1991 (adapted for television, 2002); The Suitcase Kid, 1992 (Children's Book of the Year Award, 1993); Video Rose, 1992; Mark The Mum-minder, 1993; The Werepuppy, 1993; The Bed and Breakfast Star, 1994; Mark Spark in the Dark, 1994; Twin Trouble, 1995; Glubbslyme, 1995; Jimmy Jelly, 1995; Dinosaur's Packed Lunch, 1995; Cliffhanger, 1995; Double Act, 1995 (Children's Book of the Year Award; Smarties Prize); My Brother Bernadette, 1995; Werepuppy on Holiday, 1995; Bad Girls, 1996; Mr Cool, 1996; Monster Story-teller, 1997; The Lottie Project, 1997; Girls in Love, 1997; Connie and the Water Babies, 1997; Buried Alive!, 1998; Girls Under Pressure, 1998; The Illustrated Mum (Guardian Children's Book of the Year Award), 1999 (adapted for television, 2003); Girls Out Late, 1999; The Dare Game, 2000; Vicky Angel, 2000; The Cat Mummy, 2001; Sleepovers, 2001; Dustbin Baby, 2001; Girls In Tears, 2002; Secrets, 2002; The Worry Website, 2002; Lola Rose, 2003; Midnight, 2003 (adapted for stage, 2005); The Diamond Girls, 2004; Best Friends, 2004 (adapted for television, 2006); Clean Break, 2005; Love Lessons, 2005; Candyfloss, 2006; Starring Tracy Beaker, 2006; Jacky Daydream (autobiog.), 2007; Kiss, 2007; My Sister Jodie, 2008. *Recreations:* talking to my daughter, reading, swimming, going to art galleries and films. *Address:* c/o David Higham Associates, 5–8 Lower John Street, Golden Square, W1F 9HA. *T:* (020) 7434 5900.

WILSON, James Millar; Member (UU) Antrim South, Northern Ireland Assembly, 1998–2007; *b* 15 Dec. 1941; *s* of James Millar Wilson and Isobel Wilson; *m* 1965, Muriel Smyth; one *s* one *d*. *Educ:* Ballyclare High Sch.; Belfast Coll. of Technol. Engineer: Port Line Ltd, Merchant Navy, 1962–64; British Enkalon Ltd, 1964–73; partner, retail grocery business, 1972–88. Chief Exec., UU Party, 1987–98. Chief UUP Whip, 1998–2002, Dep. Speaker, 2002, NI Assembly. Dir, Bann System Ltd, 2002–. Mem., NI Water Council, 2000–. Dir, Countryside Alliance, NI, 2003–. Mem., UU Council, 1982–87 and 1998– (Mem. Exec. Cttee, 1985–87 and 1998–); Vice Pres., S Antrim UU Assoc., 1996–. *Recreations:* gardening, angling. *Address:* 83 Clare Heights, Ballyclare, Co. Antrim BT39 9SB. *T:* (028) 9332 4477; *e-mail:* jim.wilson83@btopenworld.com.

WILSON, Sir James (William Douglas), 5th Bt *cr* 1906; farmer; *b* 8 Oct. 1960; *s* of Captain Sir Thomas Douglas Wilson, 4th Bt, MC, and of Pamela Aileen, *d* of Sir Edward Hanmer, 7th Bt; *S* father, 1984; *m* 1985, Julia Margaret Louise, fourth *d* of J. C. F. Mutty, Mulberry Hall, Melbourn, Cambs; two *s* two *d*. *Educ:* London Univ. (BA Hons French). *Heir:* *s* Thomas Edward Douglas Wilson, *b* 15 April 1990.

WILSON, Jill Christine; *see* Rubery, J. C.

WILSON, Joe; *see* Wilson, A. J.

WILSON, John; *see* Moran, Baron.

WILSON, John Gordon; Member (SNP) Scotland Central, Scottish Parliament, since 2007; *b* 28 Nov. 1956; *s* of Thomas Wilson and Elizabeth Murray; *m* 1982, Frances M. McGlinchey; one *d*. *Educ:* Univ. of Glasgow (MA Social Scis 1987). Coachbuilder, W. Alexanders Co. Ltd, 1972–82; Project Co-ordinator, Castlemilk Housing Involvement Project, 1987–94; Dir, Glasgow Council of Tenant Assocs, 1994–97; Manager, Glasgow Tenants Resource Centre, 1997–98; Fieldwork Manager, Poverty Alliance, 1998–2001; Dir, Scottish Low Pay Unit, 2001–07. *Address:* Scottish Parliament, Edinburgh EH99 1SP. *T:* (0131) 348 6684, *Fax:* (0131) 348 6686; *e-mail:* john.wilson.msp@scottish.parliament.uk.

WILSON, John Richard; Member, Covent Garden Market Authority, since 2004; *b* 8 March 1946; *s* of Kenneth Charles Wilson and Mary Edith Wilson (*née* Dalladay); *m* 1968, Anne Margaret Saville; two *s*. *Educ:* Lewes Co. Grammar Sch. for Boys. MCIH 2002. Ministry of Defence: Exec. Officer, Navy Dept, 1965–68; Secretariat Divs, 1968–85; Directing Staff, JSDC, 1985–87; Hd, Br. Personnel and Logistics Div., 1987–89; Project Manager, Quality Assce Relocation, 1989–92; Hd, Plans and Budgets, for Dir Gen. Support Systems (RAF), 1992–94; Hd, Plans and Budgets, for AO CIS, HQ RAF Logistics Comd, 1994–95; Dir, Finance and Secretariat, 1995–99, Chief Exec., 1999–2004, Defence Housing Exec. *Recreations:* walking, DIY, classic cars. *Address:* 20 Rowanwood Avenue, Sidcup, Kent DA15 8WN. *T:* (020) 8300 0916.

WILSON, John Veitch D.; *see* Drysdale Wilson.

WILSON, His Honour John Warley; a Circuit Judge, 1982–2001; *b* 13 April 1936; *s* of late John Pearson Wilson and Nancy Wade Wilson (*née* Harston); *m* 1962, Rosalind Mary Pulford. *Educ:* Warwick Sch.; St Catharine's Coll., Cambridge (MA). Served RA, 1954–56. Called to the Bar, Lincoln's Inn, 1960, in practice, 1960–82; a Recorder of the Crown Court, 1979–82. Dep. Chairman, West Midlands Agricultural Land Tribunal, 1978–82. *Recreations:* gardening, National Hunt racing. *Address:* Victoria House, Farm Street, Harbury, Leamington Spa CV33 9LR. *T:* (01926) 612572.

WILSON, Rt Rev. Dr John Warwick; Bishop of the Southern Region (Assistant Bishop, Diocese of Melbourne), 1985–2007; Vicar General, Diocese of Melbourne, 2001–07 (Bishop Administrator, 2006–07); Chairman, Acorn Press Ltd, since 2007; *b* 12 July 1937; *s* of Walter and Norma Wilson; *m* 1963, Jill Brady; two *d*. *Educ:* Bathurst Coll., NSW; Ridley Coll., Parkville, Victoria (ThL, ThSchol); London Univ. (BD (Hons)); Yale Univ. (STM); Duke Univ. (PhD). Educn Officer, Papua New Guinea, 1957–59. Ordained deacon and priest, 1964; Asst, St Cyprian's, Narrabri, 1964–67; Vicar, St Andrew, Tingha, 1967–68; Priest in charge, St John's Henderson, North Carolina, USA, 1969–72; Lectr in OT, Ridley Coll., 1973–85. *Publications:* The Old Testament and Christian Living, 1981, 2nd edn 1985; Ezekiel: God's Communicator, 1990; The Old Testament on the Way to the Cross, 1994. *Recreations:* reading, music, cinema. *Address:* 3 Sunview Place, Berwick, Vic 3806, Australia. *T:* (3) 87869938, *Fax:* (3) 87869940.

WILSON, John Willoughby; QC (NI) 1988; Master, Queen's Bench and Appeals, Supreme Court of Northern Ireland, 1993–2006; Clerk of the Crown for Northern Ireland, 1993–2006; *b* 4 Sept. 1933; *s* of late Willoughby Wilson and Martha (*née* Wood); *m* 1st, 1963, Rosemary Frances Turner (*d* 1999); one *s* two *d*; 2nd, 2006, Irenèe Sarah, *widow* of Gordon Roger Cree; one step *s* one step *d*. *Educ:* Leys Sch.; Magdalene Coll., Cambridge (MA); Queen's Univ., Belfast (LLB). Called to the Bar, NI, 1960; in practice, 1960–66; Private Sec., 1966–79, Legal Sec., 1979–80, to Lord Chief Justice of NI; Asst Dir, NI Court Service, 1980–85; Master, High Court, Supreme Court of NI, 1985–93. Under Treas., Inn of Court of NI, 1997–. Gov., Victoria Coll., Belfast, 1970– (Chm., 1990–95). Chancellor, Dio. Connor, 1982–2007. *Recreations:* music, reading, cycling.

WILSON, Joseph Albert; Secretary to the Cabinet, Sierra Leone Government, 1968–69; Barrister-at-Law; Solicitor of High Court of Sierra Leone; Notary Public; Commissioner for Oaths; *b* 22 Jan. 1922; *e s* of late George Wilson; *m* 1947, Esther Massaquoi; two *s* four *d* (and one *s* decd). *Educ:* St Edward's Secondary Sch., Freetown, Sierra Leone; University of Exeter (DPA); Middle Temple. Graded Clerical Service, Sierra Leone Government, 1941–47; family business, 1948–51; Secretary, Bonthe District Council, 1951–59; Administrative Officer, Sierra Leone Government, rising to rank of Cabinet Secretary, 1959; High Comr from Sierra Leone to UK, 1967–68. Manager (Special Duties), SLST Ltd, 1959. Comdr of the Republic, CR. *Recreations:* tennis, golf.

WILSON, Julian David Bonhôte; freelance journalist and broadcaster; Racing Correspondent, BBC Television, 1966–97; *b* 21 June 1940; *s* of Peter Jardine Bonhôte Wilson, OBE and Helen Angela Josephine Mann; *m* 1st, 1970, Carolyn Anne Michael (marr. diss. 1980); one *s*; 2nd, 1981, Alison Christian Findlay Ramsay. *Educ:* Harrow. Writer and reporter, Mirror Group Newspapers, 1958–64; Editor, Tote Racing Annual, 1965. *Publications:* Lester Piggott: the pictorial biography, 1985; 100 Greatest Racehorses, 1987; The Racing World, 1991; Some You Win (autobiog.), 1998. *Recreation:* cricket. *Address:* Home Farm Cottage, Burrough Green, Newmarket, Suffolk CB8 9LY; 10 Windsor Lane, Tokai 7945, Cape Town, South Africa. *Clubs:* Turf, St Moritz Tobogganing.

WILSON, Mrs (Katherine) Muriel (Irwin), OBE 1985; Chairman and Chief Executive, Equal Opportunities Commission for Northern Ireland, 1981–84; *b* 3 Dec. 1920; *d* of Francis Hosford and Martha Evelyn (*née* Irwin); *m* 1949, William George Wilson; one *s*. *Educ:* Methodist Coll., Belfast; The Queen's University of Belfast (DPA). Northern Ireland Civil Service, 1939–49; N Ireland Health Service, 1949–73: Eastern Special Care Management Cttee (Services for the Mentally Handicapped): Asst Sec., 1963–71; Gp Sec. and Chief Admin. Officer, 1971–73; Asst Chief Admin. Officer (Personnel and Management Services), Northern Health and Social Services Board, 1973–81. Chm. NI Div., 1977–79, National Vice-Pres. 1979–81, United Kingdom Fedn of Business and Professional Women; Member: Bd, Labour Relations Agency (NI), 1976–81; Fair Employment Agency for NI, 1981–84; NI Adv. Cttee, IBA, 1978–83; NI Council, RIPA, 1985–88; Women's Forum, NI, 1990–. Dir, Ulster Telethon Trust, 1989–2000. Chairman, Board of Governors: Glenravel Special Sch., Belfast, 1987–93; Hill Croft Sch., Newtownabbey, 1987–89; Glenveagh Sch., Belfast, 1993–97; Chm., Whiteabbey Hosp. League of Friends, 1989–92. MCMI. *Recreations:* swimming, reading.

WILSON, Rev. Dr Kenneth Brian, OBE 1993; Senior Research Consultant, Research Centre, The Queen's Foundation, Birmingham, 2001–04 (Director of Research, 1996–2001); *b* 10 April 1937; *s* of Norman Harold Wilson and Violet Frances Sarah Wilson; *m* 1962, Jennifer Rosemary Floyd; one *s* two *d*. *Educ:* Kingswood Sch., Bath; Trinity Hall, Cambridge (BA 1961; MA); Univ. of Bristol (MLitt; PhD); MA Oxon. Ordained Minister in Methodist Church; Asst Minister, Hinde Street Methodist Church, London, 1964–66; Asst Chaplain, 1966–69, Chaplain, 1969–73, Kingswood Sch., Bath; Rowbotham Prof. of Philosophy and Ethics, Wesley Coll., Bristol, 1973–80; Principal, Westminster Coll., Oxford, 1981–96. Fernley Hartley Lectr, 1973; Hon. Vis. Fellow, UC Chichester, 2004–; Hon. Res. Fellow, Canterbury Christ Church Univ., 2005–; Fellow, Southlands Coll., Univ. of Roehampton, 2007–. Dir, Methodist Newspaper Co., 1991–2002. Director: Hinksey Network, 1981–; Ammerdown Christian Study Centre, Radstock, 1986–. Chairman: Science and Religion Forum, 1979–81; Nat. Primary Centre, Oxford, 1987–93; Christian Educn Movt, 1995; Member: Council, CNAA, 1982–92; Cttee, Ian Ramsey Centre, Oxford, 1985–99; Council, Inst. of Educn, Univ. of London, 1991–96 (Chm., 1993–95); CATE, 1992–94; Council, Sarum Coll., 2001–07. Trustee, Higher Educn Foundn, 1985–96. Gov., The Leys Sch., Cambridge, 1990–2002. FRSA. Hon. DTh Lycoming, 1994; Hon. DLL High Point Univ., 1995. *Publications:* Making Sense of It, 1973; Living it Out, 1975; (ed) Experience of Ordination, 1979; (with F. Young) Focus on God, 1986; (ed with N. Timms) Governance and Authority in the Roman Catholic Church, 2000; (ed jtly) Readings in Church Authority, 2003; Learning to Hope, 2005; (ed jtly) Christian Community Now, 2008; Dying to Live?, 2008. *Recreations:* books, poetry, art, religion. *Address:* Knapp Cottage, West Bradley, Glastonbury, Som BA6 8LT. *Club:* Oxford and Cambridge.

WILSON, Prof. Kenneth Geddes, PhD; Professor of Physics, Ohio State University, since 1988; *b* 8 June 1936; *s* of Edgar Bright Wilson and Emily Fisher Buckingham; *m* 1982, Alison Brown. *Educ:* Harvard Univ. (AB); Calif Inst. of Technol. (PhD). Cornell University: Asst Prof. of Physics, 1963; Prof. of Physics, 1963–88; Dir, Center for Theory and Simulation in Sci. and Engrg, 1985–88. Co-Prin. Investigator, Nat. Sci. Foundn Statewide Systematic Initiative, Project Discovery, Ohio, to reform sci. and math. educn, 1991–96. Hon. PhD: Harvard, 1981; Chicago, 1976. Nobel Prize for Physics, 1982. *Publications:* (ed jtly) Broken Scale Invariance and the Light Cone, 1971; Quarks and Strings on a Lattice, 1975; (contrib.) New Pathways in High Energy Physics, Vol. II 1976; (contrib.) New Developments in Quantum Field Theory and Statistical Mechanics, 1977; (contrib.) Recent Developments in Gauge Theories, 1980; (with Bennett Daviss) Redesigning Education, 1994; contrib. Jl of Math. Phys, Nuovo Cimento, Acta Phys. Austriaca, Phys Rev., Jl of Chem. Phys, Comm. Math. Phys, Phys Reports, Advances in Maths, Rev. of Mod. Phys, Scientific American; symposia and conf. papers. *Address:* Department of Physics, Ohio State University, 174 West 18th Avenue, Columbus, OH 43210–1106, USA. *T:* (614) 2929396.

WILSON, Prof. Louise, OBE 2008; Director, MA Fashion Course, Central Saint Martins College of Art and Design, since 1992; *b* Cambridge, 23 Feb. 1962; *d* of William Wilson and Pamela Elizabeth, (Tebbs), Wilson; partner, Thomas Kwamina Aggrey; one *s*. *Educ:* Preston Poly. (BA Hons 1st cl. 1984); St Martins School of Art (MA Fashion with Distn 1986). Worked for designers in Italy, France and Los Angeles; Consultant, Krizia, Italy, 1996; Design Dir, Women's Collection and Licensing, Donna Karan International, NY, 1997–2002; Consultant: Ghost, London, 2000; Hugo Boss Womenswear, 2000. Mem., British Fashion Council, 2007. *Recreations:* going out, staying in, eating, sleeping, my profession, voicing one's opinion. *Address:* School of Fashion and Textile Design, Central Saint Martins College of Art and Design, 107–109 Charing Cross Road, WC2H 0DU. *T:* (020) 7514 7154, *Fax:* (020) 7514 7152; *e-mail:* l.wilson@csm.arts.ac.uk.

WILSON, Lynton Ronald, OC 1997; Chairman, CAE Inc., since 1999; Chancellor, McMaster University, since 2007; *b* Port Colborne, Canada, 3 April 1940; *s* of Ronald Alfred and Blanche Evelyn Wilson; *m* 1968, Brenda Jean Black; one *s* two *d*. *Educ:* Port Colborne High Sch.; McMaster Univ. (BA Hons 1962); Cornell Univ. (MA 1967). Dep. Minister, Min. of Industry and Tourism, Govt of Ontario, 1978–81; Pres. and CEO, 1981–88, Chm., 1988–89, Redpath Industries Ltd, Toronto; Man. Dir, North America, Tate & Lyle plc, 1986–89; Vice-Chm., Bank of Nova Scotia, Toronto, 1989–90; BCE Inc.: Chief Operating Officer, 1990–92; Pres., 1990–96; CEO, 1992–98; Chm., 1993–2000; Chm., Nortel Networks Corp., 2001–05 (now Chm. Emeritus). Dir, Supervisory Bd, Daimler AG (formerly DaimlerChrysler AG), 1998–; Chm., Daimler Chrysler Canadian Adv. Council, 2005–. Hon. *Dhc* Montreal, 1995; Hon. LLD: McMaster, 1995; UC of Cape Breton, 1998; Mount Allison, 2000; Brock, 2003; Hon. DCL Bishop's Univ., 1997. *Recreations:* golf, ski-ing. *Address:* BCE Inc., 483 Bay Street, 7th Floor, North Tower, Toronto, ON M5G 2C9, Canada. *Clubs:* York, Toronto (Toronto); Rideau (Ottawa); Toronto Golf, Mount Royal, Mount Bruno Golf.

WILSON, Rev. Canon Mark John Crichton; Priest therapist, Guildford Diocese, since 2005; *b* 14 Jan. 1946; *s* of Rev. William Hubert Wilson and Gladys Margaret Wilson; *m* 1970, Rev. Canon Mavis Kirby Wilson; one *s* three *d*. *Educ:* St Paul's Cathedral Choir Sch.; St John's Sch., Leatherhead; Clare Coll., Cambridge (BA, MA 1970); Ridley Hall, Cambridge; Univ. of E London (Cert. Psychosynthesis Counselling 2003; Postgrad. Dip. Psychosynthesis Psychotherapy 2006). Ordained deacon, 1969, priest, 1970; Assistant Curate: Luton with East Hyde, 1969–72; Ashtead, Surrey, 1972–77; Chaplain, Epsom Coll., 1977–81; Vicar, Christ Church, Epsom Common, 1981–96; Archdeacon of Dorking, 1996–2005. Rural Dean of Epsom, 1987–92. Warden, St Peter's Convent, Woking, 2003–07. *Recreation:* gardening (growing fuchsias). *Address:* The Rectory, 3 Parsonage Way, Frimley, Camberley, Surrey GU16 8HZ. *T:* (01276) 62820.

WILSON, Martin; *see* Wilson, A. M.

WILSON, Martin Joseph, FCA; Deputy Chairman, Ulster Bank, 2004–06 (Group Chief Executive, 1998–2004); *b* 13 March 1950; *s* of Michael and Elizabeth Wilson; *m* Paulette Palmer; one *s* two *d*. *Educ:* Oatlands Coll., Dublin. ACA 1975, FCA 1985; FIBI 1991. Articled Clerk, Fay McMahon & Co., Chartered Accountants, 1969–75; Sen. Audit Manager, KPMG, 1975–78; Chief Accountant, Bell Lines Ltd, 1978–80; Financial Controller, 1980–89, Head of Treasury, 1984–89, Ulster Investment Bank; Ulster Bank: Gp Treas., 1989–95; Dir, 1991–; Dep. Gp Chief Exec., 1997–98; Chief Exec., Ulster Bank Mkts, 1995–97. *Recreations:* golf, reading, music. *Address:* Ulster Bank Ltd, Group Head Office, Donegall Square East, Belfast BT1 5UB. *T:* (028) 9027 6000.

WILSON, Sir Mathew John Anthony, 6th Bt *cr* 1874, of Eshton Hall, Co. York; OBE 1979 (MBE 1971); MC 1972; President, Dolphin Voyaging Inc., since 1995; *b* 2 Oct. 1935; *s* of Anthony Thomas Wilson (*d* 1979; 2nd *s* of Sir Mathew Richard Henry Wilson, 4th Bt) and Margaret (*d* 1980), *d* of late Alfred Holden; *S* uncle, 1991; *m* 1962, Janet Mary, *e d* of late E. W. Mowll, JP; one *s* one *d*. *Educ:* Trinity Coll. Sch., Ontario. Brig. KOYLI, retired 1983. Exec. Dir, Wilderness Foundn (UK), 1983–85. Former Vice-Pres., Internat. Wilderness Leadership Foundn. *Publications:* Taking Terrapin Home: a love affair with a small catamaran, 1994; The Bahamas Cruising Guide with the Turks and Caicos Islands, 1998; The Land of War Elephants: travels beyond the pale—Afghanistan, Pakistan, India, 2003. *Heir: s* Mathew Edward Amcotts Wilson [*b* 13 Oct. 1966; *m* 1995, Imogen Nancy, *yr d* of Richard Thomas Wilson; one *s* one *d*].

WILSON, Michael; *see* Wilson, T. M. A.

WILSON, Michael Anthony, FRCGP; general practitioner; *b* 2 June 1936; *s* of late Charles Kenneth Wilson and Bertha Wilson; *m* 1959, Marlene (*née* Wilson); two *s*. *Educ:* Roundhay Grammar Sch., Leeds; Medical Sch., Univ. of Leeds (MB ChB 1958). DObst RCOG 1961; MRCGP 1965, FRCGP 1980. British Medical Association: Chm., Gen. Med. Services Cttee, 1984–90 (Dep. Chm., 1979–84); Pres., Yorkshire Regional Council, 1975–79; Mem. Council, 1977–90, 1992–2000; Vice-Pres., 2001–; Fellow, 1979. Member: GMC, 1989–2003; Standing Med. Adv. Cttee to DHSS, 1967–69, 1978–90 (Dep. Chm., 1986–90); NHS Clinical Standards Adv. Gp, 1990–93; Code of Practice Authy, Assoc. of British Pharmaceutical Industry, 1990–; Jt Consultants Cttee, 1991–97. Chm., BMA Pension Trustees Ltd, 1994–2000; Dir, Professional Affinity Group Services Ltd, 1987–2000. Sec., Ampleforth Coll. Golf Club. *Recreations:* golf, Rotary. *Address:* Longueville, Mill Hill, Huntington, York YO32 9PY. *T:* (01904) 768861. *Clubs:* East India; York Golf.

WILSON, Michael Anthony; JP; Managing Director, Mike Wilson Associates Ltd, since 2002; Director, JVM Consultants Ltd, since 2007; *b* 19 Feb. 1948; *s* of Alan Wilson and Christina Wilson (*née* McFarlane); *m* 1972, Aileen Athey (marr. diss. 1991); one *s* two *d*. *Educ:* Aston Univ. (BSc Hons Behavioural Sci. 1972); DipTP 1977. MRTPI 1979; AIH 1984. Planning Asst, London Borough of Barnet, 1972–74; Res. and Inf. Officer, Harlow Develt Corp., 1974–80; Housing Manager, City of Glasgow, 1980–84; Dir of Housing and Envmtl Services, London Borough of Brent, 1984–92; Chief Exec., Waltham Forest Housing Action Trust, 1992–2002; Dir of Regeneration, NE London Strategic HA, 2002–06. Chairman: Sports Club Orient, 2003–; Ocean Estate New Deal for Communities, 2004–07; Member Board: Waltham Forest Community-Based Housing Assoc., 2002–; Leyton Orient Community Sports Prog., 2003–07. FRSA. JP Waltham Forest, 1999. *Recreations:* watching football (Spurs), cinema, theatre, good food and wine, the children. *Address:* 4 Dry Dock, Wivenhoe, Colchester CO7 9TE.

WILSON, Michael Gregg, OBE 2008; producer; Chairman, EON Productions, since 1983; *b* NY, 1942; *s* of Lewis Wilson and Dana Broccoli, and step *s* of Albert R., (Cubby), Broccoli; *m* 1965, Coila Jane Wilson; two *s*. *Educ:* Harvey Mudd Coll., Claremont, Calif (BS); Stanford Univ. (DJur). Legal Advr, Dept of Transportation, Washington, 1966–67; Partner, law firm, Surrey and Morse, Washington, 1967–74; joined legal dept, EON Productions, 1974; asst to Cubby Broccoli, The Spy Who Loved Me, 1977; Executive Producer: Moonraker, 1979; (and screenplay) For Your Eyes Only, 1981; (and screenplay) Octopussy, 1983; Producer: (and screenplay) A View to Kill, 1985; (and screenplay) The Living Daylights, 1987; (and writer) Licence to Kill, 1989; GoldenEye, 1995; Tomorrow Never Dies, 1997; The World is Not Enough, 1999; Die Another Day, 2002; Casino Royale, 2006. Trustee, NMSI, 2004–May 2008; Chm. Trustees, Media Mus. (formerly Nat. Mus. of Photography, Film and TV), 2004–. Founder, Wilson Centre for Photography, London, 1998. Trustee, Harvey Mudd Coll., Claremont, CA. *Address:* c/o EON Productions Ltd, 138 Piccadilly, W1J 7NR.

WILSON, Maj.-Gen. Michael Peter Bruce Grant; Chief Executive, Security Industry Authority, since 2007; *b* 19 Aug. 1943; *s* of Ian Henry Wilson and Catherine Collingwood Wilson; *m* 1967, Margaret Ritchie; two *s* one *d*. *Educ:* Duke of York's Sch., Nairobi; Dip. Photogrammetry, UCL. FRICS 1995 (ARICS 1988); FRGS 1990. Commnd RE, 1966; served UK, Kenya, Uganda, Nigeria, BAOR, MoD; UK Exchange Officer, US Defense Mapping Agency, 1978; Sen. Instructor in Air Survey and Cartography, Sch. of Mil. Survey, 1981; Asst Dir, Mil. Survey Systems and Techniques Unit, 1983; CO 512 Special Team RE and Comdr, Geographic Staff, Washington, 1986; Comdr, 42 Survey Engr Gp, 1987; Dir, Geographic Ops, MoD, 1990; Dir-Gen., Mil. Survey and Chief Exec., Mil. Survey Defence Agency, 1993; Dir-Gen. Intelligence and Geographic Resources, MoD, 1995–96; Chief Executive: Defence Vetting Agency, 1996–2004; Gangmasters Licensing Authy, 2005–07. Col Comdt RE, 1997–2002. Mole catcher to the Vicar of Old Malton. FCMI. *Recreations:* mountaineering, rock climbing, shooting, stalking, fishing, golf, cricket. *Clubs:* Geographical; North Wolds Gun.

WILSON, Michael Sumner; Chairman, St James's Place (formerly St James's Place Capital), since 2004 (Director, since 1997; Chief Executive, 1992–2004); *b* 5 Dec. 1943; *s* of late Peter and Margaret Wilson; *m* 1975, Mary Drysdale (marr. diss. 1997); one *d*. *Educ:* St Edward's School, Oxford. Equity & Law, 1963–68; Abbey Life, 1968–71; Allied Dunbar (Hambro Life until 1985, when name was changed), 1971–91: Exec. Dir, 1973; Board Dir, 1976; Dep. Man. Dir, 1982; Man. Dir, 1984; Gp Chief Exec., 1988–91. Director: BAT Industries, 1989–91; Vendôme Luxury Gp, 1993–98. *Recreations:* tennis, racing. *Clubs:* Raffles, Annabel's.

WILSON, Muriel; *see* Wilson, K. M. I.

WILSON, Prof. Nairn Hutchison Fulton, CBE 2004; PhD; FDS; Professor of Restorative Dentistry and Dean and Head of King's College London Dental Institute (formerly Guy's, King's and St Thomas' Dental Institute, King's College London), since 2001; *b* 26 April 1950; *s* of William Fulton Wilson and Anne Hutchison Wilson (*née* Stratton); *m* 1st, 1971, Madeleine Christina Munro (marr. diss. 1981); two *d*; 2nd, 1982, Margaret Alexandra Jones; one *s* one *d*. *Educ:* Strathallan Sch.; Univ. of Edinburgh (BDS 1973); Univ. of Manchester (MSc 1979; PhD 1985); Royal Coll. of Surgeons of Edinburgh (FDS 1977; DRD 1980). FACD 1990; FADM 1991; FDS RCS (*ad eundem*) 1994; FFGDP (UK) (*ad eundem*) 2002. Lectr in Restorative Dentistry (Prosthetics), Univ. of Edinburgh, 1974–75; University of Manchester: Lectr in Conservative Dentistry, 1975–81; Sen. Lectr, 1981–86; Prof. of Restorative Dentistry, 1986–2001; Head, Dept of Conservative Dentistry, 1986–88, Dept of Restorative Dentistry, 1988–92; University Dental Hospital: Head, Unit of Operative Dentistry and Endodontology (formerly of Conservative Dentistry), 1982–2001; Dep. Dean, 1991–92; Dean and Clin. Dir, 1992–95; Pro Vice-Chancellor, Univ. of Manchester, 1997–99. Hon. Vis. Prof. of Restorative Dentistry, Univ. of Manchester, 2001–04. Hon. Consultant in Restorative Dentistry: Central Manchester Healthcare NHS Trust (formerly Central Manchester HA), 1982–2001; King's Coll. Hosp. NHS Trust, 2001–. Non-exec. Dir, N Manchester Healthcare NHS Trust, 1994–97. Chairman: Jt Cttee for Specialist Trng in Dentistry, 1998–99, 2007–; Oral and Dental Res. Trust, 2003–; British Dental Editors Forum, 2004–; Council of Hds and Deans of Dental Schs, 2006–08. Dean, Faculty of Dental Surgery, RCSE, 1995–98. President: British Assoc. of Teachers of Conservative Dentistry, 1992; Sect. of Odontology, Manchester Med. Soc., 1993–94; British Soc. for Restorative Dentistry, 1994–95; Eur. Sect., Acad. of Operative Dentistry, 1998–2000; Educn Res. Gp, IADR, 1998–2000; GDC, 1999–2003; Eur. Fedn of Conservative Dentistry, 2003–05; Sect. of Odontology, Royal Soc. of Med., 2008–Sept. 2009. FKC 2006. Hon. Fellow, Coll. of Dental Surgeons of HK, 1999. Ed., Jl of Dentistry, 1986–2000. Ed. in Chief, Quintessentials in Dental Practice Series (44 vols), 2003–08. *Publications:* (jtly) Advances in Operative Dentistry, vol. 1: contemporary clinical practice, 2001; vol. 2: challenges of the future, 2001; Minimally Invasive Dentistry, 2007; contrib. chaps in contemporary texts and numerous papers in jls. *Recreation:* landscape gardening. *Address:* Central Offices, King's College London Dental Institute, Floor 18, Guy's Tower, Guy's Campus, SE1 9RT. *T:* (020) 7188 1164. *Club:* Athenæum.

WILSON, Rt Hon. Sir Nicholas (Allan Roy), Kt 1993; PC 2005; **Rt Hon. Lord Justice Wilson;** a Lord Justice of Appeal, since 2005; *b* 9 May 1945; *s* of late Roderick Peter Garratt Wilson and of Dorothy Anne Wilson (*née* Chenevix-Trench); *m* 1974, Margaret (*née* Higgins); one *s* one *d*. *Educ:* Bryanston School; Worcester College, Oxford (BA 1st cl. hons Jurisp. 1966). Eldon Scholar, 1967. Called to the Bar, Inner Temple, 1967, Bencher, 1993; QC 1987; a Recorder, 1987–93; a Judge of the High Court, Family Div., 1993–2005. Pres., Family Mediators Assoc., 1998–. Hon. Dr Staffordshire, 2004. Editor-in-Chief, Family Court Practice, 2008–. *Address:* Royal Courts of Justice, Strand, WC2A 2LL.

WILSON, Nigel Guy, FBA 1980; Fellow and Tutor in Classics, Lincoln College, Oxford, 1962–2002; *b* 23 July 1935; *s* of Noel Wilson and Joan Lovibond; *m* 1996, Hanneke Marion Wirtjes. *Educ:* University Coll. Sch.; Corpus Christi Coll., Oxford (1st Cl. Classics (Mods) 1955; 1st Cl. Lit. Hum. 1957; Hertford Scholar 1955; Ireland and Craven Scholar 1955; Derby Scholar 1957). Lectr, Merton Coll., Oxford, 1957–62. Jt Editor, Classical Rev., 1975–87. Ospite Linceo, Scuola normale superiore, Pisa, 1977; Visiting Professor: Univ. of Padua, 1985; Ecole Normale Supérieure, Paris, 1986. James P. R. Lyell Reader in Bibliog., Oxford Univ., 2002–03. Gaisford Lectr, 1983. Hon. DLitt Uppsala, 2001. Gordon Duff Prize, 1968; Premio Anassilao, Reggio Calabria, 1999. *Publications:* (with L. D. Reynolds) Scribes and Scholars, 1968, 3rd edn 1991; An Anthology of Byzantine Prose, 1971; Medieval Greek Bookhands, 1973; St Basil on the Value of Greek Literature, 1975; Scholia in Aristophanis Acharnenses, 1975; (with D. A. Russell) Menander Rhetor, 1981; Scholars of Byzantium, 1983; (with Sir Hugh Lloyd-Jones) Sophoclea, 1990; (ed with Sir Hugh Lloyd-Jones) Sophocles: Fabulae, 1990; From Byzantium to Italy, 1992; Photius: the Bibliotheca, 1994; Aelian: Historical Miscellany, 1997; Pietro Bembo: Oratio pro litteris graecis, 2003; Aristophanes: Comoediae, 2007; Aristophanea, 2007; articles and reviews in various learned jls. *Recreations:* bridge, real tennis. *Address:* Lincoln College, Oxford OX1 3DR. *T:* (01865) 279800, *Fax:* 279802.

WILSON, Sir Patrick Michael Ernest David McN.; *see* McNair-Wilson.

WILSON, Pete; Governor of California, 1991–98; Of Counsel, Bingham McCutcheon, and Principal, Bingham Consulting Group, since 2004; *b* 23 Aug. 1933; *m* Betty Robertson (marr. diss.); *m* 1983, Gayle Edlund. *Educ:* Yale Univ. (BA); Univ. of California at Berkeley (JD). Admitted to California Bar, 1962. Mayor of San Diego, 1971–73; US Senator (Republican) from California, 1983–91. Former Man. Dir, Pacific Capital Gp Inc.

Address: Bingham Consulting Group, 355 South Grand Avenue, Los Angeles, CA 90071–3106, USA.

WILSON, Peter James, OBE 2001; Transformation Project Director, Royal Shakespeare Co., since 2005; *b* 19 Sept. 1947; *s* of James Arthur Wilson and Edith Mary Wilson (*née* Sillick); *m* 1971, Angela Mary Hawkes; one *s* two *d*. *Educ:* Eltham Coll.; Pembroke Coll., Cambridge (BA 1970). Tate Gallery: DES Studentship in Conservation, 1972–76 (Dip. Conservation, 1976); picture restorer, 1976–80; Head: Tech. Services, 1980–88; Gall. Services, 1988–94; Dir, Projects and Estates, 1994–2005. Associate Consultant, Lord Cultural Resources, Toronto, 2006–. Member: CABE Enabling Panel, 2001–04; Steering Cttee, Laban, 2001–04. Chm., Mus. Documentation Assoc., 1988–95. Mem. Bd, Lightbox, Woking, 2001–. FRSA. Hon. FRIBA 2007. *Recreations:* sitting on the juries of architecture competitions, discussing garden history whilst driving on the M40 between London and Stratford-upon-Avon, gardening, drawing, cycling, cooking, theatre-going, visiting museums. *Address:* Royal Shakespeare Co., Courtyard Theatre, Southern Lane, Stratford-upon-Avon, Warwicks CV37 6BH. *T:* (01789) 201760; *e-mail:* peter.wilson@rsc.org.uk.

WILSON, Peter Michael; Chairman, Gallaher Group Plc, 1997–2004 (Chief Executive, 1997–99); Chairman, Gallaher Ltd, 1994–2004 (Deputy Chairman, 1987–94; Chief Executive, 1994–99); *b* 9 June 1941; *s* of late Michael Wilson and Mary Wilson; *m* 1964, Lissa Trab; one *s* one *d*. *Educ:* Downside Sch.; Oriel Coll., Oxford (MA Hons Law). Marketing appts, Reckitt & Colman and Beecham Gp, 1963–69; joined Gallaher Ltd, 1969: Gen. Manager, Cigarette Marketing, 1974–79; Man. Dir, Gallaher (Dublin), 1979–81; Marketing Dir, Gallaher Tobacco Ltd, 1981–84; Jt Man. Dir, 1984–85, Dep. Chm., 1986, Gallaher Tobacco (UK) Ltd. Non-executive Director: Fortune (formerly American) Brands Inc., 1994–; Powergen plc, 2001–03; Somerfield plc, 2002–05; Kesa Electricals plc, 2003–. *Address:* The Stable, Old Odiham Road, Alton, Hants GU34 4BW. *T:* (01420) 543892.

WILSON, Philip; MP (Lab) Sedgefield, since July 2007; *b* 31 May 1959; *s* of Bernard Wilson and Ivy Wilson (*née* Woods); *m* (marr. diss. 1999); two *s*; partner, Margaret Brown. *Educ:* Trimdon Secondary Modern Sch.; Sedgefield Comprehensive Sch. Civil Servant, Dept for Nat. Savings, 1978–87; res. asst to Rt Hon. Tony Blair, MP, 1987–94; Labour Party organiser, 1994–97; Political Asst to Gen. Sec., Labour Party, 1997–99; Consultant, Brunswick Gp, 1999–2002; Dir, Fellows' Associates, 2002–07. *Recreations:* jazz, reading, writing. *Address:* House of Commons, SW1A 0AA. *T:* (020) 7219 3000; *e-mail:* wilsonphil@parliament.uk. *Club:* Trimdon Labour.

WILSON, Philip Alexander P.; *see* Poole-Wilson.

WILSON, Most Rev. Philip Edward; *see* Adelaide, Archbishop of, (RC).

WILSON, Primrose Eileen, CBE 2007 (OBE 1997); engaged in voluntary projects; *b* 21 April 1947; *d* of Anthony and Sheelagh Clarke; *m* 1969, Edward Brice Wilson (CBE 2003); one *s* two *d*. *Educ:* Glengara Park Sch., Dunlaoghaire, Co. Dublin; Royal Victoria Hosp., Belfast (SRN); Open Univ. (BA Hons). SRN, Royal Victoria Hosp., Belfast, 1969–75. Voluntary Co-ordinator, Eur. Heritage Open Days, 1997–2000. Chairman: Ulster Architectural Heritage Soc., 1987–94; Historic Bldgs Council (NI), 1994–2000. Trustee, Nat. Heritage Meml Fund, 2000–06; Chairman: Assoc. Preservation Trusts (NI), 2004–; Follies Trust, 2006–. Hon. Mem., RSUA, 2000. *Publication:* (jtly) The Buildings of Armagh, 1992. *Recreations:* admiring, enjoying, conserving and restoring Ireland's and Britain's built heritage. *Address:* Marlacoo House, Portadown, Co. Armagh. *T:* (028) 3887 1238, *Fax:* (028) 3887 9548.

WILSON, Richard; *see* Wilson, I. R.

WILSON, Richard Henry, RA 2006; sculptor; Visiting Research Professor, University of East London, since 2004; *b* 24 May 1953; *s* of Arthur and Ivy Wilson; partner, Miyako Narita; one *s* one *d* with Silvia Ziranek, writer and performance artist. *Educ:* London Coll. of Printing (Foundn); Hornsey Coll. of Art (DipAD 1st 1974); Univ. of Reading (MFA 1976). Formed Bow Gamelan Ensemble with Anne Bean and Paul Burwell, 1983–91. Mem., Artistic Records Cttee, Imperial War Mus., London, 1999. DAAD Residency, Berlin, 1992; Henry Moore Fellowship in Sculpture, Univ. of East London, 2002–04; Maeda Vis. Artist, AA, London, 2003. *Solo exhibitions and commissions* include: 11 Pieces, 1976, 12 Pieces, 1978, Coracle Press Gall., London; Viaduct, Aspex Gall., Portsmouth, 1983; Sheer Fluke, 1985, 20:50, 1987, She Came in Through the Bathroom Window, 1990, Watertable, 1994, Matt's Gall., London; Hopperhead, Café Gall., London, 1985; Halo, The Aperto, Venice Biennale, 1986; Heatwave, Ikon Gall., Birmingham, 1986; One Piece at a Time, Tyne Bridge, Newcastle upon Tyne, 1987; Up a Blind Alley, Trigon Biennale, Graz, 1987; Leading Lights, Kunsthallen Brandts Klaedefabrik, Odense, 1989; Sea Level, Arnolfini Gall., Bristol, 1990; High-Tec, MOMA, Oxford, 1990; High Rise, São Paulo Biennial, Brazil, Great Britain/USSR, Kiev, Moscow, 1990; All Mod Cons, Edge Biennial, Newcastle, 1990; Take Away, Centre of Contemp. Art, Warsaw, 1990; Lodger, Valeria Belvedere, Milan, 1991; Swift Half and Return to Sender, Gal. de l'Ancienne Poste, Calais, 1992; Installation, Kunsterhaus Bethanien, Berlin, 1993; Deep End, LA/UK, Fest. MOCA, Los Angeles, 1994; Room 6 Channel View Hotel, Towner Art Gall., Eastbourne, 1996; Formative Processes, 1996, Set North for Japan (74° 33' 2"), 2000, Gimpel Fils, London; Jamming Gears, Serpentine Gall., London, 1996; Going In/Off, Château de Sacy, Picardie, 1997; Hung, Drawn and Quartered, Stadtsches Mus., Zwickau, 1997, Ha'Mumche Gall., Tel Aviv, 1999; Irons in the Fire, Globe Gall., South Shields, 1997, UK tour, 2002, Wapping Proj., London, 2003; Tate Christmas Tree, Tate Gall., London, 1997; Pipe Dreams, AA, London, 1999; Turbine Hall Swimming Pool, Clare Coll. Mission Ch, London, 2000; Butterfly, Wapping Proj., London, 2003; Queen & Gantry, Storey Gall., Lancaster, 2005; Curve Gall., London, 2006; 5 Piece Kit, Matthew Bown Gall., London, 2006; RIBA Drawing Show, Liverpool, 2007; Chris Westbrook Gall., London, 2007; Turning the Place Over (lead work for Liverpool, Europ. Capital of Culture 2008), Liverpool, 2007; RA Summer Show, 2007; Objects of Art, Matthew Brown Gall., London, 2007; Galleria Fumagalli, Bergamo, Italy, 2007; Meter's Running, Pula, Croatia, 2007; *group exhibitions* include: Art of Our Time, Saatchi Collection, Royal Scottish Acad., Edinburgh, 1987; Saatchi Collection, London, 1991; Close Encounters of the Art Kind, V&A, 2001; Butterfly, Platform China, Beijing, 2006; Edinburgh Fest., 2008; Folkestone Triennial, 2008; *permanent works:* entrance to Utility Tunnel, Tachikawa Public Art Proj., Tokyo, 1994; Over Easy, The Arc, Stockton, 1999; Slice of Reality, North Meadow Sculpture Proj., Millennium Dome, London, 2000; Set North for Japan (74° 33' 2"), Echigo Tsumari Proj., Japan, 2000; Off Kilter, Millennium Sq., Leeds, 2001; Final Corner, World Cup Proj., Fukuroi City, 2002; Rock n' hole, Lincoln City and Archaeol. Mus., 2005; work in public collections inc. Weltkunst Collection at Irish Mus. of Mod. Art, Boise, BM, Govt Art, Arts Council England, British Council, Ulster Mus., Leeds Mus and Galls, Centre of Contemp. Art, Warsaw and Museet for Samstidskunst, Oslo. Hon. Dr Middx, 2008. *Recreations:* percussion, cinema, world musics, exhibitions. *Address:* 44 Banyard Road, SE16 2YA. *T:* (020) 7231 7312; *e-mail:* richardwilson-sculptor@virgin.net.

WILSON, Robert, OBE 2008; Presenter, ITV football, 1994–2002; *b* 30 Oct. 1941; *s* of William Smith Wilson and Catherine Wingate (*née* Primrose); *m* 1964, Margaret Vera Miles; two *s* (one *d* decd). *Educ:* Tapton House Grammar Sch.; Chesterfield Grammar Sch.; Loughborough Coll. (DipPE). PE teacher, 1963–64; represented England Schoolboys, 1957, Derbyshire Schs, 1957–60, and British Univs, 1960–63, at football; Mem., England Amateur Squad, 1960–63; professional footballer (goalkeeper), Arsenal FC, 1964–74 (winner: Euro Fairs Cup, 1970; League and Cup Double, 1971); internat. appearances for Scotland, 1971–72. BBC presenter, 1974–94. Chm., London Football Coaches Assoc., 1990–2007. Co-founder, Willow Foundn Charity, 1999–. Gov., Univ. of Hertfordshire, 1997–2006. Hon. DLitt Loughborough, 1989; DUniv: Derby, 2001; Middlesex, 2004. *Publications:* Goalkeeping, 1970; The Art of Goalkeeping, 1973; You've Got to be Crazy, 1989; Behind the Network (autobiog.), 2003; Googlies, Nutmegs and Bogies, 2006; Rucks, Pucks and Sliders, 2007; Life in the Beautiful Game, 2008. *Recreations:* reading, golf, boating, theatre.

WILSON, (Robert) Gordon; solicitor in private practice, with Gordon Wilson, 1960–74 and 1987–2005; politician, retired; *b* 16 April 1938; *s* of R. G. Wilson; *m* 1965, Edith M. Hassall; two *d*. *Educ:* Douglas High Sch.; Edinburgh Univ. (BL). Scottish National Party: Nat. Sec., 1963–71; Exec. Vice-Chm., 1972–73; Sen. Vice-Chm., 1973–74; Dep. Leader, 1974–79; Nat. Convener (formerly Chm.), 1979–90; Vice-Pres., 1992–98. Contested (SNP) Dundee E, 1987. MP (SNP) Dundee E, Feb. 1974–1987. Parly Spokesman: on Energy, 1974–79; on Home Affairs, 1975–76; on Devolution (jt responsibility), 1976–79; SNP spokesman: on energy, 1992–93; on Treasury affairs, 1993–94. Rector, Dundee Univ., 1983–86. Chm., Marriage Counselling (Tayside) (formerly Dundee Marriage Guidance Council), 1989–92; temp. Chm., Couple Counselling, Dundee, 2006; Dir, Dundee Age Concern, 2001–05. Mem., Church and Nation Cttee, C of S, 2000–03. Gov., Dundee Inst. of Technology, subseq. Univ. of Abertay, 1991–97. Hon. LLD Dundee, 1986. *Recreations:* reading, writing, photography, sailing. *Address:* 48 Monifieth Road, Broughty Ferry, Dundee DD5 2RX. *T:* (01382) 779009.

WILSON, Prof. (Robert James) Timothy, PhD; Vice-Chancellor and Chief Executive, University of Hertfordshire, since 2003; *b* 2 April 1949; *s* of John and Joan Wilson; *m* 1972, Jackie Hinds; two *d*. *Educ:* Univ. of Reading (BSc Hons); Univ. of Lancaster (MA); Walden Univ., USA (PhD 1997). Lectr, then Sen. Lectr, Operational Res., Leeds Poly., 1974–84; Dir of Studies, Cranfield Inst. of Technol., 1984–87; Asst Dir, Leicester Poly., 1987–91; Hatfield Polytechnic, later University of Hertfordshire, 1991–: formerly: Dep. Dir; Pro Vice Chancellor and Dep. Chief Exec.; Prof., 2002–. Chm., Herts Prosperity Forum, 2002–; Board Member: E of England Develt Agency, 2003–; HEFCE, 2004–. FOR 1986; MInstD 2002; CCMI 2004; FRSA 2008. *Publications:* numerous articles in jls relating to mathematical modelling and higher educn mgt. *Recreations:* Rugby Union, golf, dog-walking. *Address:* University of Hertfordshire, College Lane, Hatfield, Herts AL10 9AB. *T:* (01707) 284030, *Fax:* (01707) 284046; *e-mail:* R.J.T.Wilson@herts.ac.uk.

WILSON, Robert Julian, (Robin), MA; Headmaster, Trinity School of John Whitgift, Croydon, 1972–94; *b* 6 July 1933; *s* of late Prof. Frank Percy Wilson, FBA, and Joanna Wilson (*née* Perry-Keene); *m* 1957, Caroline Anne (*née* Maher); two *d* (and one *s* one *d* decd). *Educ:* St Edward's Sch., Oxford; Trinity Coll., Cambridge (MA). Lektor, Univ. of Münster, Westphalia, 1955–58; Assistant Master: St Peter's, York, 1958–62; Nottingham High Sch. (Hd of English), 1962–72. Mem. Cttee, HMC, 1987–94 (Chm., 1993); Vice-Chm., Academic Policy Cttee, 1990–92; Member: Council, GDST (formerly GPDST), 1994–; Cttee, GBA, 1999–2002. Governor: Brentwood Sch., 1995–; St Peter's Sch., York, 1996–2002. FRSA 1982. *Publications:* (jtly) Bertelsmann Sprachkursus English, 1959; (ed) The Merchant of Venice, 1971; articles on the teaching of English. *Recreations:* drama, travel, golf. *Address:* 22 Beech House Road, Croydon, Surrey CR0 1JP. *T:* (020) 8686 1915. *Clubs:* East India, Devonshire, Sports and Public Schools; Addington Golf.

WILSON, Prof. Robert McLachlan, FBA 1977; Professor of Biblical Criticism, University of St Andrews, 1978–83; *b* 13 Feb. 1916; *er s* of Hugh McL. Wilson and Janet N. (*née* Struthers); *m* 1945, Enid Mary (*d* 2003), *d* of Rev. and Mrs F. J. Bomford, Bournemouth, Hants; two *s*. *Educ:* Greenock Acad.; Royal High Sch., Edinburgh; Univ. of Edinburgh (MA 1939, BD 1942); Univ. of Cambridge (PhD 1945). Minister of Rankin Church, Strathaven, Lanarkshire, 1946–54; Lectr in New Testament Language and Literature, St Mary's Coll., Univ. of St Andrews, 1954, Sen. Lectr, 1964, Prof., 1969–78. Vis. Prof., Vanderbilt Divinity Sch., Nashville, Tenn, 1964–65. Pres., Studiorum Novi Testamenti Societas, 1981–82. Hon. Mem., Soc. of Biblical Literature, 1972–. Associate Editor, New Testament Studies, 1967–77, Editor 1977–83; Mem., Internat. Cttee for publication of Nag Hammadi Codices, and of Editorial Bd of Nag Hammadi Studies monograph series. Hon. DD Aberdeen, 1982. Burkitt Medal for Biblical Studies, British Academy, 1990. *Publications:* The Gnostic Problem, 1958; Studies in the Gospel of Thomas, 1960; The Gospel of Philip, 1962; Gnosis and the New Testament, 1968; (ed) English trans., Hennecke-Schneemelcher, NT Apocrypha: vol. 1, 1963 (3rd edn, completely revised, 1991); vol. 2, 1965 (3rd edn 1993); (ed) English trans., Haenchen, The Acts of the Apostles, 1971; (ed) English trans., Foerster, Gnosis: vol. 1, 1972; vol. 2, 1974; (ed and trans., jtly) Jung Codex treatises: De Resurrectione, 1963, Epistula Jacobi Apocrypha, 1968, Tractatus Tripartitus, pars I, 1973, partes II et III, 1975; (ed) Nag Hammadi and Gnosis, 1978; (ed) The Future of Coptology, 1978; (ed jtly) Text and Interpretation, 1979; (ed) English trans., Rudolph, Gnosis, 1983; Commentary on Hebrews, 1987; Commentary on Colossians and Philemon, 2005; articles in British, Amer. and continental jls. *Recreation:* golf. *Address:* 10 Murrayfield Road, St Andrews, Fife KY16 9NB. *T:* (01334) 474331.

WILSON, Robert Nelson; Chairman, A. Nelson & Co. Ltd, since 2001; *b* 23 July 1962; *s* of Robert Wiseman Wilson and Anne Wilson; *m* 1994, Nicola Jane Petrie; two *s* two *d*. *Educ:* St Columba's Coll., Dublin; Trinity Coll., Dublin (BA Hons Hist., MA); Harvard Business Sch. A. Nelson & Co.: Mktg Dir, 1990–93; Man. Dir, 1993–2001. Dir, Wigmore Pubns, 1991–. Trustee: Scottish Civic Trust, 2002–; Prince's Foundn for Integrated Health, 2005–; Chairman: Prostate Scotland, 2006–; Barcapel Foundn, 2006–; Co-Founder, Jupiter Artland Foundn, 2006–. Gov., Kilgraston Sch., 2005–. *Recreations:* shooting, art, golf, travel. *Address:* A. Nelson & Co., Nelson House, 83 Parkside, Wimbledon SW19 5LP. *T:* (020) 8780 4200, *Fax:* (020) 8789 0141; *e-mail:* RobertWilson@Nelsons.net. *Clubs:* Oriental, Sloane; Kildare Street and University (Dublin).

WILSON, Robert O.; MP (C) Reading East, since 2005; *b* 4 Jan. 1965; *m* Jane; four *c*. *Educ:* Wallingford Sch.; Univ. of Reading. Entrepreneur, health and communications. Mem. (C), Reading BC, 1992–96, 2004–06. Contested (C): Bolton NE, 1997; Carmarthen W and S Pembs, 2001. *Address:* (office) 12a South View Park, Marsack Street, Reading RG4 5AF; House of Commons, SW1A 0AA.

WILSON, Sir Robert (Peter), KCMG 2000; Chairman: BG Group plc, since 2004 (Director, since 2002); The Economist Group (formerly Economist Newspaper Ltd), since 2003 (Director, since 2002); *b* 2 Sept. 1943; *s* of late Alfred Wilson and Dorothy (*née* Mathews); *m* 1975, Shirley Elisabeth Robson; one *s* one *d*. *Educ:* Epsom Coll.; Sussex

Univ. (BA); Harvard Business Sch. (AMP). With Dunlop Ltd, 1966–67; Mobil Oil Co. Ltd, 1967–70; RTZ Corporation plc, later Rio Tinto plc, 1970–2003: Dir, Main Bd, 1987–2003; Dir, Planning and Develt, 1987–89, Mining and Metals, 1989–91; Chief Exec., 1991–97; Chairman: Rio Tinto plc, 1997–2003; Rio Tinto Ltd, 1999–2003. Non-executive Director: The Boots Co. PLC, 1991–98; Diageo plc, 1998–2003; BP plc (formerly British Petroleum, then BP Amoco), 1998–2002; GlaxoSmithKline plc, 2003–. Chm., Internat. Council for Mining & Metals, 2002–03. FEI 2006; CCMI; FRSA. Hon. DSc: Exeter, 1993; Birmingham, 2002; Sussex, 2004; Hon. LLD Dundee, 2001. *Recreations:* theatre, opera, reading, wine. *Address:* BG Group plc, Eagle House, 108–110 Jermyn Street, SW1Y 6RP.

WILSON, Robert William Gordon; Principal Clerk of Select Committees, and Deputy Head, Committee Office, House of Commons, since 2001; *b* 8 July 1946; *s* of late Gordon Chamberlain Wilson, CBE, and Winifred Wilson (*née* Low). *Educ:* Lancing Coll.; Christ Church, Oxford (MA). A Clerk, H of C, 1967–: Clerk: of Europ. Legislation Cttee, 1981–86; of Envmt Cttee, 1986–87; of Foreign Affairs Cttee, 1987–91; Principal Clerk: of Financial Cttees and Treasury and Civil Service Cttee, 1991–92; of Domestic Cttees and Sec., H of C Commn, 1992–95; of Overseas Office, 1995–2001. Jt Sec., Assoc. of Secretaries-General of Parlts, 1977–84. Hon. Steward, Westminster Abbey, 1981–98. Dep. Chm., Decorative Arts Soc., 2004–. Trustee, Erskine May Meml Fund, 2001–. *Publication:* Guide to the Houses of Parliament, edns from 1988 to 2006. *Recreations:* theatre, opera, travel, swimming. *Address:* Committee Office, House of Commons, SW1A 0AA.

WILSON, Dr Robert Woodrow; Senior Scientist, Harvard-Smithsonian Center for Astrophysics, since 1994; *b* 10 Jan. 1936; *s* of Ralph Woodrow Wilson and Fannie May Willis; *m* 1958, Elizabeth Rhoads Sawin; two *s* one *d*. *Educ:* Rice Univ. (BA Physics, 1957); Calif Inst. of Technol. (PhD 1962). Post-doctoral Fellowship, Calif Inst. of Technol., 1962–63; Mem. Technical Staff, Bell Labs, Holmdel, NJ, 1963–76; Head, Radio Physics Res. Dept, Bell Telephone Labs, Inc., later AT&T Bell Labs, 1976–94. Member: Phi Beta Kappa; Amer. Acad. of Arts and Sciences, 1978; US Nat. Acad. of Science, 1979. Hon. degrees: Monmouth Coll., 1979; Jersey City State Coll., 1979; Thiel Coll., 1980. Henry Draper Award, 1977; Herschel Award, RAS, 1977; (jtly) Nobel Prize for Physics, 1978. *Publications:* contrib. to Astrophys. Jl. *Address:* 9 Valley Point Drive, Holmdel, NJ 07733–1320, USA. *T:* (201) 6717807; Harvard-Smithsonian Center for Astrophysics, 60 Garden Street #42, Cambridge, MA 02138–1516, USA.

WILSON, Robin; *see* Wilson, R. J.

WILSON, Robin Lee, CBE 1992; FREng; consulting engineer; *b* 4 March 1933; *s* of late Henry Eric Wilson, OBE and Catherine Margaret Wilson; *m* 1956, Gillian Margaret, *d* of late L. J. N. Kirkby and Margaret Kirkby; one *s* two *d*. *Educ:* Glenalmond College; Univ. of Glasgow (BSc Eng. 1955). FICE 1966; FIHT 1966. Joined R. Travers Morgan & Partners, 1956, Partner, 1966, Sen. Partner, 1985; Dir and Gp Chm., Travers Morgan Ltd, Consulting Engineers, 1988–91; Chairman: New Builder Publications Ltd, 1989–94; Thomas Telford Ltd, publishers, 1990–94. Dir, Mid Kent Hldgs, 1994–97. Member Council: ICE, 1977–80, 1983–86, 1987–93 (Pres., 1991–92); ACE, 1985–88; Construction Industry Council, 1990–97 (Chm., 1994–96); Engrg Council, 1991–99 (Chm., Bd for Engineers' Regulation, 1994–99); Glenalmond Coll., 1985–2001 (Chm. Cttee, 1995–2001). Minister's nominee, SE Council for Sport and Recreation, 1987–90. Chm., Coultershaw Trust, 2002–. Master, Paviors' Co., 2003–04. DSc *hc* City Univ., 1991. Coopers Hill Meml Prize, ICE, 1989; Instn of Highways and Transportation Award, 1990. *Publications:* papers in learned jls on highway engineering and related subjects. *Recreations:* sailing, golf. *Address:* The Grove House, Little Bognor, Pulborough, Sussex RH20 1JT. *T:* (01798) 865569. *Clubs:* Royal Thames Yacht; Itchenor Sailing, West Sussex Golf.

WILSON, Rodney Herbert William; Executive Producer for BBC Classical Music, Television, since 1998; *b* 21 June 1942; *s* of Herbert Herman Wilson and Vera Anne Faulkner. *Educ:* Windsor Grammar Sch. for Boys; Berkshire Coll. of Art (Intermediate Diploma); Camberwell Sch. of Art (NDD); Hornsey Coll. of Art (ATD). Asst Lectr, Loughborough Coll. of Art, 1965–69; Film Officer, 1970, Head of Film Section, 1980, Arts Council of GB; Dir, Dept of Film, Video and Broadcasting, Arts Council of England, 1986–98. Member: Film, Video and Television Adv. Cttee, British Council, 1983–98; Council, Edinburgh Film Festival, 1984–94; Festival Council, Art Film Fest., Slovakia, 1995–; RTS, 1994. Exec. Producer for Arts Council Films, 1970. *Recreations:* walking, doodling, photography. *Address:* Classical Music, Television, BBC Television Centre, Wood Lane, W12 7RJ.

WILSON, Air Chief Marshal Sir (Ronald) Andrew (Fellowes), (Sir Sandy), KCB 1991 (CB 1990); AFC 1978; Air Member for Personnel and Air Officer Commanding-in-Chief Personnel and Training Command, 1993–95; Air Aide-de-Camp to the Queen, 1993–95; *b* 27 Feb. 1941; *s* of late Ronald Denis Wilson and Gladys Vera Groombridge; *m* 1979, Mary Christine Anderson; one *d*, and one step *s* one step *d*. *Educ:* Tonbridge Sch.; RAF Coll., Cranwell. Flying Instr, 1963–65; No 2 Sqn, 1966–68; ADC to C-in-C, RAF Germany, 1967–68; Flt Comdr No 2 Sqn, 1968–72; RAF Staff Coll., 1973; HQ STC, 1974–75; CO No 2 Sqn, 1975–77; Air Plans, MoD, 1977–79; CO RAF Lossiemouth, 1980–82; Air Cdre Falkland Islands, 1982–83; Central Staff, MoD, 1983–85; Dir Ops Strike, MoD, 1985; Dir Air Offensive, MoD, 1986–87; SASO, HQ, RAF Strike Comd, 1987–89; AOC No 1 Group, 1989–91; Comdr, British Forces during Op. Granby, ME, Aug.–Dec. 1990; C-in-C, RAF Germany and Comdr Second ATAF, 1991–93. Pres., Aircrew Assoc., 1997–2003. Vice-Chm., Air League, 1997–2005. Mem. Council, Lord Kitchener Meml Fund, 1998–. Freeman, City of London, 1966; Liveryman, 1970, Mem. Court, 1984–87, 1994–, Master, 1999–2000, Worshipful Co. of Skinners. CCMI (CIMgt 1993); FRAeS 1994. *Recreations:* painting, antique restoration, genealogy, golf. *Club:* Royal Air Force.

WILSON, Maj.-Gen. (Ronald) Dare, CBE 1968 (MBE 1949); MC 1945; MA Cantab; DL; retired; current interests farming, forestry and writing; *b* 3 Aug. 1919; *s* of Sydney E. D. Wilson and Dorothea, *d* of George Burgess; *m* 1973, Sarah, *d* of Sir Peter Stallard, KCMG, CVO, MBE; two *s*. *Educ:* Shrewsbury Sch.; St John's Coll. Cambridge (Part I 1939, BA 1972). Commissioned into Royal Northumberland Fusiliers, 1939; served War, 1939–45: BEF 1940, ME and NW Europe (MC, despatches 1945); 6th Airborne Div., Palestine, 1945–48; 1st Bn Parachute Regt, 1949; MoD, 1950; Royal Northumberland Fusiliers: Korea, 1951; Kenya, 1953; GSO2, Staff Coll., Camberley, 1954–56; Brevet Lt-Col 1958; AA&QMG, 3rd Div., 1958–59; comd 22 Special Air Service Regt, 1960–62; Canadian Nat. Defence Coll., 1962–63; Col GS 1(BR) Corps BAOR, 1963–65; comd 149 Infantry Bde (TA), 1966–67; Brig. 1966; Brig., AQ ME Comd, 1967; Maj.-Gen. 1968; Dir, Land/Air Warfare, MoD, 1968–69; Dir, Army Aviation, MoD, 1970–71. Exmoor Nat. Park Officer, 1974–78. Formerly Consultant to Fedn of Nature and Nat. Parks of Europe. Speaker for E-SU in USA. Church Warden, Church of St George, Morebath, Devon, 1980–93. Helicopter and light aircraft pilot; Mem., Army Cresta Run Team and Army Rifle VIII; captained British Free-Fall Parachute Team, 1962–65; Chm., British Parachute Assoc., 1962–65. Mem. Council, Cambridge Soc., 1989–2002 (Pres., Somerset br.). FRGS. DL Somerset, 1979. Royal Humane Soc. Award, 1953; Royal Aero Club Silver Medal, 1967. *Publications:* Cordon and Search, 1948, reissued USA, 1984, republished as Cordon and Search: with 6th Airborne Division in Palestine, 2008; Tempting the Fates (autobiog.), 2006; contribs to military jls. *Recreations:* country pursuits, music, travelling. *Address:* Combeland, Dulverton, Somerset TA22 9LJ. *Clubs:* Flyfishers'; Hawks (Cambridge); St Moritz Tobogganing.

WILSON, Roy Vernon, CEng, MICE; Director, Eastern Region, Property Services Agency, Department of the Environment, 1980–82; *b* 23 July 1922; *s* of late Alfred Vincent Wilson and Theresa Elsie Wilson; *m* 1951, Elsie Hannah Barrett; three *s*. *Educ:* Cheadle Hulme Sch.; Manchester Univ. (BScTech Hons). Served Royal Engineers, 1942–44. Civil Engineer, local govt, 1945–51; Harlow Develt Corp., 1951–54; Air Ministry Works Directorate: Warrington, 1954–59; Newmarket, 1959–62; Germany, 1962–65; District Works Officer: Wethersfield, 1965–67; Mildenhall, 1967–72; Area Officer, Letchworth (PSA), 1972–76; Regional Director, Cyprus (PSA), 1976–79; Chief Works Officer, Ruislip, 1979. *Recreations:* lacrosse and tennis (earlier years), golf. *Address:* 12 Diomed Drive, Great Barton, Bury St Edmunds, Suffolk IP31 2TD. *Club:* Civil Service.

WILSON, Samuel; MP (DemU) Antrim East, since 2005; Member (DemU) East Antrim, Northern Ireland Assembly, since 2003 (Belfast East, 1998–2003); *b* 4 April 1953; *s* of Alexander and Mary Wilson. *Educ:* Methodist Coll., Belfast; The Queen's Univ., Belfast (BScEcon; PGCE). Teacher of Economics, 1975–83; Researcher in N Ireland Assembly, 1983–86. Councillor, Belfast CC, 1981–; Lord Mayor of Belfast, 1986–87 and 2000–01. Press Officer for Democratic Unionist Party, 1982–96. Contested (DemU) Antrim E, 2001. *Publications:* The Carson Trail, 1982; The Unionist Case—The Forum Report Answered, 1984; Data Response Questions in Economics, 1995. *Recreations:* reading, motor cycling, windsurfing. *Address:* DUP Advice Centre, 116 Main Street, Larne BT40 1RG. *T:* (028) 2826 7722, *Fax:* (028) 28269922; *e-mail:* lewis@parliament.uk.

WILSON, Air Chief Marshal Sir Sandy; *see* Wilson, Air Chief Marshal Sir R. A. F.

WILSON, Sandy; composer, lyric writer, playwright; *b* 19 May 1924; *s* of George Walter Wilson and Caroline Elsie (*née* Humphrey). *Educ:* Elstree Preparatory School; Harrow School; Oriel College, Oxford (BA Eng. Lit.). Contributed material to Oranges and Lemons, Slings and Arrows, 1948; wrote lyrics for touring musical play Caprice, 1950; words and music for two revues at Watergate Theatre, 1951 and 1952; (musical comedy) The Boy Friend for Players' Theatre, 1953, later produced in West End and on Broadway, 1954, revival, Comedy, 1967 (also directed), revival, Old Vic, 1984, 40th anniv. production, Players' Theatre, 1994; (musical play) The Buccaneer, 1955; Valmouth (musical play, based on Firbank's novel), Lyric, Hammersmith and Savile Theatre, 1959, New York, 1960, revival, Chichester, 1982; songs for Call It Love, Wyndham's Theatre, 1960; Divorce Me, Darling! (musical comedy), Players' Theatre, 1964, Globe, 1965, revival, Chichester, 1997; music for TV series, The World of Wooster, 1965–66; music for As Dorothy Parker Once Said, Fortune, 1969; songs for Danny la Rue's Charley's Aunt (TV), 1969; wrote and performed in Sandy Wilson Thanks the Ladies, Hampstead Theatre Club, 1971; His Monkey Wife, Hampstead, 1971; The Clapham Wonder, Canterbury, 1978; Aladdin, Lyric, Hammersmith, 1979. *Publications:* This is Sylvia (with own illustrs), 1954; The Boy Friend (with own illustrs), 1955; Who's Who for Beginners (with photographs by Jon Rose), 1957; Prince What Shall I Do (illustrations, with Rhoda Levine), 1961; The Poodle from Rome, 1962; I Could Be Happy (autobiog.), 1975; Ivor, 1975; Caught in the Act, 1976; The Roaring Twenties, 1977. *Recreations:* cinema, travel, reminiscing. *Address:* 2 Southwell Gardens, SW7 4SB. *T:* (020) 7373 6172.

WILSON, Simon Charles Hartley; HM Diplomatic Service; Deputy High Commissioner to Eastern India, at Kolkata, since 2006; *b* 9 Aug. 1957; *s* of late Charles William Wilson and of Brenda Christine Wilson (*née* Hartley); *m* 1984, Heather Graine Richardson; two *s*. *Educ:* Newborough Sch., Liverpool; Liverpool Coll. Entered FCO, 1975; Attaché: Johannesburg, 1978–81; Helsinki, 1981–83; FCO, 1984–87; Vice Consul: Tehran, 1987; Riyadh, 1987–92; Second Sec. (Political), Lisbon, 1992–96; SE Asia Dept, FCO, 1997–2001; Dep. Hd of Mission, Bahrain, 2001–05. *Recreations:* birding, taxidermy, philately, ambulist, nargileh, Edward VIII memorabilia, tennis, ski-ing. *Address:* c/o Foreign and Commonwealth Office, King Charles Street, SW1A 2AH. *Clubs:* Naval; Tollygunge, Bengal (Calcutta).

WILSON, Snoo; writer, since 1969; *b* 2 Aug. 1948; *s* of late Leslie Wilson and Pamela Mary Wilson; *m* 1976, Ann McFerran; two *s* one *d*. *Educ:* Bradfield Coll.; Univ. of East Anglia (BA English and American Studies). Associate Director, Portable Theatre, 1970–75; Dramaturge, Royal Shakespeare Co., 1975–76; Script Editor, Play for Today, 1976; Associate Prof. of Theatre, Univ. of Calif at San Diego, 1987. Henfield Fellow, Univ. of E Anglia, 1978; US Bicentennial Fellow in Playwriting, 1981–82. Hon. Texan, 1992. *Filmscripts:* Shadey, 1986; The Touch, 1989; Eichmann, 2007; *opera:* (adapted) Gounod's La Colombe, 1983; *radio plays:* Poonsh, 1993; The Good Doctor, 1994; Johnson's Xmas Interlude, 1994; I'll be George, 2001; Hippomania, 2004; Pack Up Your Troubles (musical), 2006. *Publications: plays:* Layby (jtly), 1972; Pignight, 1972; The Pleasure Principle, 1973; Blowjob, 1974; Soul of the White Ant, 1976; England England, 1978; Vampire, 1978; The Glad Hand, 1978; A Greenish Man, 1978; The Number of the Beast, 1982; Flaming Bodies, 1982; Grass Widow, 1983; Loving Reno, 1983; Hamlyn, 1984; More Light, 1987; Lynchville, 1989; Callas, 1990; Erofeyev's Walpurgis Night (adaptation), 1991; HRH, 1994; Darwin's Flood, 1994; Bedbug (adaptation, after Mayakovsky), 1995; Framing Faust (adaptation, after Ernst), 1996; Sabina, 1998; Moonshine, 1999; *novels:* Spaceache, 1984 (adapted for radio, 1990); Inside Babel, 1985; I, Crowley, 1997; The Works of Melmont, 2004; *opera:* Orpheus in the Underworld (new version), 1984; *musical:* 80 Days, 1988. *Recreations:* beekeeping, space travel. *Address:* 41 The Chase, SW4 0NP.

WILSON, Prof. Thomas Michael Aubrey, PhD; CBiol, FIBiol; FIHort; FRSE; Honorary Professor, Warwick-HRI, University of Warwick, since 2007 (Professor of Biological Sciences, 2004–07); *b* 10 Oct. 1951; *s* of Basil Francis Aubrey Wilson and Elisabeth Mathew Wilson (*née* Hogg); *m* 1975, Judith Lindsey Dring; two *s* one *d*. *Educ:* Univ. of Edinburgh (BSc 1st Cl. Hons Biol Scis 1973); St John's Coll., Cambridge (PhD Biochem. 1976). CBiol 1995; FIBiol 1998; FIHort 1999; FRSE 1999. MRC Res. Fellow, Univ. of Nottingham, 1976–78; Lectr in Biochem., Univ. of Liverpool, 1979–83; SSO, 1983–86, PSO, 1986–89, John Innes Inst., Norwich; Prof., Rutgers Univ., NJ, 1989–92; Head of Virology, 1992–95, Dep. Dir, 1995–99, Scottish Crop Res. Inst., Dundee; Sci. Dir, 1999, CEO, 1999–2004, Horticulture Res. Internat. Hon. Lectr, UEA, 1985–92; Hon. Professor: Univ. of Dundee, 1993–99; Zhejiang Acad. Agricl Scis, China, 1993–; Univ. of Birmingham, 1999–2004; Univ. of Warwick, 1999–2004. FRSA 2003. *Publications:* (with J. W. Davies) Genetic Engineering with Plant Viruses, 1992; Engineering Genesis, 1998; contrib. approx. 100 papers in specialist jls; also over 100 abstracts, proceedings and invited seminars. *T:* (024) 7657 5529; *e-mail:* michael.wilson@warwick.ac.uk.

WILSON, Timothy; *see* Wilson, R. J. T.

WILSON, Timothy Hugh, FSA; Keeper of Western Art, Ashmolean Museum, Oxford, since 1990; Professorial Fellow, Balliol College, Oxford, since 1990; *b* 8 April 1950; *s* of late Col Hugh Walker Wilson and Lilian Rosemary (*née* Kirke); *m* 1984, Jane Lott; two *s* one *d*. *Educ:* Winchester Coll.; Mercersburg Acad., USA; Corpus Christi Coll., Oxford (BA 1973; MA); Warburg Inst., London Univ. (MPhil 1976); Dept of Museum Studies, Leicester Univ. FSA 1989. Res. Asst, Dept of Weapons and Antiquities, Nat. Maritime Mus., Greenwich, 1977–79; Asst Keeper (Renaissance collections), Dept of Medieval and Later Antiquities, BM, 1979–90. Trustee: Ruskin Foundn, 1994–2000; Oxford Preservation Trust, 2006–. Fellow: Harvard Univ. Center for Renaissance Studies, Villa I Tatti, Florence, 1984; Accademia Raffaello, Urbino, 2003; Hon. Fellow, Royal Soc. Painter-Printmakers, 1991. *Publications:* (jtly) The Art of the Jeweller, 1984; Flags at Sea, 1986, 2nd edn 1999; Ceramic Art of the Italian Renaissance, 1987; Maiolica, 1989, 2nd edn 2003; (ed) Italian Renaissance Pottery, 1991; (jtly) Systematic Catalogue of the National Gallery of Art: Western Decorative Arts, Part 1, 1993; (ed jtly) C. D. E. Fortnum and the Collecting and Study of Applied Arts and Sculpture in Victorian England, 1999; (jtly) Le maioliche rinascimentali nelle collezioni della Fondazione Cassa di Risparmio di Perugia, 2006–07; articles in Apollo, Burlington Mag., Faenza, Jl Warburg and Courtauld Insts, Jl of Hist. of Collections, Ceramic Review, etc; contribs exhibition and museum catalogues. *Address:* Balliol College, Oxford OX1 3BJ; 6 Longworth Road, Oxford OX2 6RA. *T:* (01865) 511029.

WILSON, William; DL; *b* 28 June 1913; *s* of Charles and Charlotte Wilson; *m* 1939, Bernice Wilson; one *s*. *Educ:* Wheatley St Sch.; Cheylesmore Sch.; Coventry Jun. Technical Sch. Qual. as solicitor, 1939, retired 1999. Entered Army, 1941; served in N Africa, Italy and Greece; demobilised, 1946 (Sergeant). Contested (Lab) Warwick and Leamington, 1951, 1955, March 1957, 1959. MP (Lab) Coventry S, 1964–74, Coventry SE, 1974–83; Mem., Commons Select Cttee on Race Relations and Immigration, 1970–79. Mem., Warwicks CC, 1958–70 (Leader Labour Group), 1972–93. DL County of Warwick, 1967. *Recreations:* gardening, theatre, watching Association football, voluntary work in Warwickshire CC Record Office. *Address:* Avonside House, High Street, Barford, Warwickshire CV35 8BU. *T:* (01926) 624278.

WILSON, William Desmond, OBE 1964 (MBE 1954); MC 1945; DSC (USA) 1945; HM Diplomatic Service, retired; Deputy High Commissioner, Kaduna, Nigeria, 1975–81; *b* 2 Jan. 1922; *s* of late Crozier Irvine Wilson and Mabel Evelyn (*née* Richardson); *m* 1949, Lucy Bride; two *s*. *Educ:* Royal Belfast Acad. Instn; QUB; Trinity Coll., Cambridge. Joined Indian Army, 1941; served with 10 Gurkha Rifles, India and Italy, 1942–46 (Major). Colonial Admin. Service: Northern Nigeria, 1948–63 (MBE for Gallantry, 1954); retd as Permanent Sec.; joined Foreign (subseq. Diplomatic) Service, 1963; First Sec., Ankara, 1963–67; UN (Polit.) Dept, FO, 1967; First Sec. and Head of Chancery, Kathmandu, 1969–74; Counsellor, 1975; Sen. Officers' War Course, RNC Greenwich, 1975. *Recreations:* shooting, riding. *Address:* 19 The Haven, Hythe, Kent CT21 4PJ. *T:* (01303) 260767. *Club:* East India.

WILSON, (William) George, OBE 1960; Associate Director, PA Consulting Group, 1989–92; *b* 19 Feb. 1921; *s* of late William James Wilson and late Susannah Wilson; *m* 1948, Freda Huddleston; three *s*. Min. of Health, 1939. Served War, Army, in India and Ceylon, 1940–46. Min. of Nat. Insurance, 1947; Asst Principal, Colonial Office, 1947; Principal, CO, 1950–57 (Adviser, UK Delegn to UN Gen. Assembly, 1951); Financial Sec., Mauritius, 1957–60; Asst Sec., MoH, 1962; Consultant, Hosp. Design and Construction, Middle East and Africa, 1968–70; Asst Sec., DHSS, 1971; Under-Sec., DHSS, 1972–81. Chm., Paul James & George Wilson Ltd, Health Service Develt Advrs, 1986–89 (Dir, 1983–86). *Recreations:* Border history and genealogy. *Address:* Beck House, Burgh by Sands, Carlisle, Cumbria CA5 6BT. *Club:* Royal Commonwealth Society.

WILSON, Dr William Laurence; Member (SNP) Scotland West, Scottish Parliament, since 2007; *b* 11 Dec. 1963; *s* of Samuel and Mary Wilson; *m* 2002, Julieta A. Pineda. *Educ:* Glasgow Univ. (BSc Hons Zool.; MSc IT); Aberdeen Univ. (MSc Ecol.); Queen's Univ., Belfast (PhD). Biologist: Glasgow Univ., 1987; Berks, Bucks and Oxon Wildlife Trust and Oxford Univ., 1987–89; Res. Asst, QUB, 1989–91; Res. Officer, Ulster Univ., 1993–96; Res. Fellow, 1996–98, Project Manager, 1998–99, Glasgow Univ.; IT Asst, Glasgow Caledonian Univ., 2001; Systems Developer, Prudent/Standard Life, 2001–05; Statistician, Scottish Funding Council, 2005–07. *Publications:* series of training booklets for researchers, 1999; (contrib.) Is There a Scottish Road to Socialism?, 2007; contrib. scientific jls. *Recreations:* reading, hill walking, travel. *Address:* Scottish Parliament, Edinburgh EH99 1SP. *T:* (0131) 348 6805, *Fax:* (0131) 348 6806; *e-mail:* Bill.Wilson.msp@scottish.parliament.uk.

WILSON, William Napier M.; *see* Menzies-Wilson.

WILSON-BARNETT, Dame Jenifer, (Dame Jenifer Trimble), DBE 2003; Professor of Nursing, since 1986, and Head of Florence Nightingale School of Nursing and Midwifery, 1999–2004, King's College, London (Head of Division of Nursing and Midwifery, 1994–99); *b* 10 Aug. 1944; adopted by Edith M. Barnett and Barbara M. Wilson; *m* 1975, Michael Robert Trimble. *Educ:* Chichester High School for Girls; St George's Hosp., London (student nurse), 1963–66; Univ. of Leicester, 1967–70 (BA Politics); Edinburgh Univ., 1970–72 (MSc); Guy's Hosp. Med. Sch., London (PhD 1977). FRCN 1984; FKC 1995. Staff Nurse, 1966, Nursing Sister, 1972–74, St George's Hosp.; Researcher, Guy's Hosp., 1974–77; Chelsea College: Lectr in Nursing, 1977; Sen. Lectr, 1983; Reader and Hd of Dept, 1984. Ed.-in-Chief, Internat. Jl of Nursing Studies, 2000–05. Hon. DSc: Hull, 2004; Kingston, 2006. *Publications:* Stress in Hospital: patients' psychological reactions to illness and health care, 1979; (with Morva Fordham) Recovery from Illness, 1982; Patient Teaching, 1983; Nursing Research: ten studies in patient care, 1983; Nursing Issues and Research in Terminal Care, 1988; Patient Problems: a research base for nursing care, 1988; (with Sarah Robinson) Directions in Nursing Research, 1989; (with Jill Macleod Clark) Health Promotion and Nursing Research, 1993; (with Alison Richardson) Nursing Research in Cancer Care, 1996. *Recreations:* music, writing, 'singing'. *Address:* Florence Nightingale School of Nursing and Midwifery, King's College London, James Clerk Maxwell Building, 57 Waterloo Road, SE1 8WA. *Clubs:* Royal Automobile, Royal College of Nursing, Royal Society of Medicine.

WILSON-JOHNSON, David Robert; baritone; Professor of Singing, Amsterdam Conservatorium, since 2005; Director, Ferrandou Singing School; *b* 16 Nov. 1950; *s* of Sylvia Constance Wilson and Harry Kenneth Johnson. *Educ:* Wellingborough School; British Institute, Florence; St Catharine's College, Cambridge (BA Hons 1973); Royal Acad. of Music. NFMS Award, 1977; Gulbenkian Fellowship, 1978–81. Royal Opera House, Covent Garden: We Come to the River (début), 1976; Billy Budd, 1982; L'Enfant et les Sortilèges, 1983; Le Rossignol, 1983; Les Noces, Boris Godunov, 1984; Die Zauberflöte, 1985; Werther, Turandot, 1987; Madam Butterfly, 1988; title rôle, St François d'Assise (Messiaen), 1988–89; Wigmore Hall recital début, 1977; BBC Proms début, 1981; Paris Opera début (Die Meistersinger), 1989; US début, Cleveland Orch., 1990; appearances at Netherlands Opera, Geneva, Houston, New York, Turin, Salzburg, etc; numerous recordings, including works by Bach, Schönberg and Schubert. FRAM 1988 (ARAM 1982). *Recreations:* swimming, slimming, gardening and growing walnuts at Dordogne house. *Address:* 28 Englefield Road, N1 4ET. *T:* (020) 7254 0941; Prinsengracht 455, 1016 HN Amsterdam, Netherlands.

WILSON JONES, Prof. Edward, FRCP, FRCPath; Professor of Dermatopathology, Institute of Dermatology, University of London, 1974–91, now Emeritus (Dean, 1980–89); *b* 26 July 1926; *s* of Percy George Jones and Margaret Louisa Wilson; *m* 1952, Hilda Mary Rees; one *s* one *d*. *Educ:* Oundle Sch.; Trinity Hall, Cambridge (MB, BChir 1951); St Thomas' Hosp., London. FRCP 1970; FRCPath 1975. National Service, Army, 1953–54. House Surgeon (Ophthalmic), St Thomas' Hosp., 1951; House Physician (Gen. Medicine), St Helier Hosp., Carshalton, 1951–52; House Physician (Neurology and Chest Diseases), St Thomas' Hosp., 1955; Registrar (Gen. Medicine), Watford Peace Meml Hosp., 1955–57; Registrar (Derm.), St Thomas' Hosp., 1957–60; Inst. of Dermatology, St John's Hosp. for Diseases of the Skin: Sen. Registrar (Derm.), 1960–62; Sen. Registrar (Dermatopath.), 1962–63; Sen. Lectr (Dermatopath.), 1963–74; Hon. Consultant, St John's Hosp. for Diseases of Skin, 1974–. Non-exec. Dir, Crockett & Jones Ltd. Founders Award, Amer. Soc. of Dermatopathology; Gray Medal, British Assoc. of Dermatology. *Publications:* (contrib.) Textbook of Dermatology, ed Rook, Wilkinson and Ebling, 3rd edn 1979; articles on dermatopath. subjects in British Jl of Derm., Arch. of Derm., Acta Dermatovenereologica, Dermatologica, Clin. and Exptl Derm., Histopath., and in Human Path. *Recreations:* art history, watercolour painting. *Address:* Featherstone House, 89 Wise Lane, NW7 2RH.

WILTON, 8th Earl of, *cr* 1801; **Francis Egerton Grosvenor;** Viscount Grey de Wilton 1801; Baron Ebury 1857; *b* 8 Feb. 1934; *s* of 5th Baron Ebury, DSO and Ann Acland-Troyte; *S* to Barony of father, 1957; *S* to Earldom of kinsman, 1999; *m* 1st, 1957, Gillian Elfrida (Elfin) (marr. diss. 1962), *d* of Martin Soames, London; one *s*; 2nd, 1963, Kyra (marr. diss. 1973), *d* of late L. L. Aslin; 3rd, 1974, Suzanne Jean, *d* of Graham Suckling, Christchurch, NZ; (one *d* decd). *Educ:* Eton; Univ. of Melbourne (PhD). *Recreation:* ornithology. *Heir:* *s* Viscount Grey de Wilton, *qv*. *Address:* PO Box 466, Mt Macedon, Vic 3441, Australia. *Clubs:* Oriental; Melbourne, Melbourne Savage (Melbourne); Hong Kong.

WILTON, Andrew; *see* Wilton, J. A. R.

WILTON, Sir (Arthur) John, KCMG 1979 (CMG 1967); KCVO 1979; MC 1945; MA; HM Diplomatic Service, retired; *b* 21 Oct. 1921; *s* of Walter Wilton and Annetta Irene Wilton (*née* Perman); *m* 1950, Maureen Elizabeth Alison Meaker; four *s* one *d*. *Educ:* Wanstead High School; Open Schol., St John's Coll., Oxford, 1940. Commissioned, Royal Ulster Rifles, 1942; served with Irish Brigade, N Africa, Italy and Austria, 1943–46 (despatches). Entered HM Diplomatic Service, 1947; served Lebanon, Egypt, Gulf Shaikhdoms, Roumania, and Yugoslavia; Dir, Middle East Centre for Arabic Studies, Shemlan, 1960–65; Dep. High Comr, Aden, 1966–67; Ambassador to Kuwait, 1970–74; Asst Under-Sec. of State, FCO, 1974–76; Ambassador to Saudi Arabia, 1976–79. Dir, London House for Overseas Graduates, 1979–86. Chm., Arab-British Centre, 1981–86; Pres., Plymouth Br., ESU, 1991–2006 (Vice-Pres., 1988–91); Trustee, Arab-British Chamber Charitable Foundn, 1989–. Gov., Hele Sch., Plympton, 1988–92. Churchwarden, St Maurice, Plympton, 1992–2004. Hon. LLD New England Coll., NH, 1986. *Recreations:* reading, gardening. *Address:* 25 Worcester Road, Chichester, W Sussex PO19 5DW.

See also C. E. J. Wilton.

WILTON, Christopher Edward John, CMG 2003; HM Diplomatic Service, retired; Director, DCW Consultants Ltd, since 2007; *b* 16 Dec. 1951; *s* of Sir (Arthur) John Wilton, *qv*; *m* 1975, Dianne Hodgkinson; one *s* one *d*. *Educ:* Tonbridge Sch.; Manchester Univ. (Hons Near Eastern Studies). Production Supervisor, Esso Petroleum, 1975–77; HM Diplomatic Service, 1977–98: FCO, 1977; Bahrain, 1978–81; FCO, 1981–84; Tokyo, 1984–88; on loan to Cabinet Office, 1988–90; Commercial Counsellor, Riyadh, 1990–94; Consul Gen., Dubai, 1994–97; Counsellor, FCO, and Comr (non-resident), British Indian Ocean Territories, 1998; Regl Man. Dir, GEC, later BAE Systems, 1999–2001 (on special leave); Counsellor, FCO, 2001–02; Ambassador to Kuwait, 2002–05. Middle East Advisor: to RBS, 2005–; Selex Sensors and Airborne Systems Ltd, 2005–. Dir, Arab-British Chamber of Commerce, 2005–; Chm. Adv. Council, London Middle East Inst., 2007–. Chm., Raleigh Internat., 2007–. *Recreations:* tennis, golf, piano. *Club:* Athenæum.

WILTON, (James) Andrew (Rutley), FSA; Visiting Research Fellow, Tate Gallery, since 2003 (Keeper and Senior Research Fellow, 1998–2002); *b* 7 Feb. 1942; *s* of Herbert Rutley Wilton and Mary Cecilia Morris (*née* Buckerfield); *m* 1976, Christina Frances Benn (marr. diss.); one *s*. *Educ:* Dulwich Coll.; Trinity Coll., Cambridge (MA). Assistant Keeper: Walker Art Gallery, Liverpool, 1965; Dept of Prints and Drawings, BM, 1967; Curator of Prints and Drawings, Yale Center for British Art, 1976; Asst Keeper, Turner Collection, BM, 1981; Curator, Turner Collection, 1985–89, Keeper of British Art, 1989–98, Tate Gallery. Hon. Curator of Prints and Drawings, Royal Acad., 2003. Hon. Curator and Hon. Liveryman, Painter-Stainers' Co., 2003. FRSA 1973; FSA 2000. Hon. RWS 1985. *Publications:* Turner in Switzerland (with John Russell), 1976; British Watercolours 1750–1850, 1977; The Wood Engravings of William Blake, 1977; The Life and Work of J. M. W. Turner, 1979; The Art of Alexander and John Robert Cozens, 1979; William Pars: journey through the Alps, 1979; Turner and the Sublime, 1980; Turner Abroad, 1982; Turner in his Time, 1987; Painting and Poetry, 1990; The Swagger Portrait, 1992; The Great Age of British Watercolour, 1992; (ed jtly) Grand Tour, 1996; (ed jtly) Pictures in the Garrick Club: a catalogue, 1997; (ed jtly) The Age of Rossetti, Burne-Jones and Watts: symbolism in Britain, 1997; Five Centuries of British Painting, 2001; American Sublime, 2002; Turner as Draughtsman, 2006; contribs to arts magazines. *Recreations:* music, architecture, travel. *Address:* Tate Gallery, SW1P 4RG. *Clubs:* Athenæum, Chelsea Arts.

WILTON, Sir John; *see* Wilton, Sir A. J.

WILTON, Maxwell William M.; *see* Moore-Wilton.

WILTON, Penelope Alice, OBE 2004; actress; *b* 3 June 1946; *m* 1st, Daniel Massey, actor (marr. diss.; he *d* 1998); one *d*; 2nd, 1991, Sir Ian Holm, *qv* (marr. diss. 2002). *Educ:* Drama Centre. *Theatre* includes: National Theatre, later Royal National Theatre: The Philanderer; Betrayal; Much Ado About Nothing; Man and Superman; Major Barbara, 1982; Sisterly Feelings; The Secret Rapture, 1988; Piano, 1990; Landscape, 1994; Sketches, 2002; The House of Bernarda Alba, 2005; Greenwich Theatre: Measure for Measure; All's Well That Ends Well; The Norman Conquests; King Lear, Nottingham Playhouse; The Deep Blue Sea, Almeida, 1992, transf. Apollo, 1993; Vita and Virginia, Chichester, 1992, transf. Ambassadors, 1993; The Cherry Orchard, RSC, 1995; Long Day's Journey into Night, Young Vic, 1996; A Kind of Alaska, Dublin, 1997, Donmar

Warehouse, 1998; The Seagull, RSC, 2000; The Little Foxes, Donmar, 2001; Afterplay, Gielgud, 2002; Women Beware Women, RSC, 2006; Eh Joe, Duke of York's, 2006; John Gabriel Borkman, Donmar, 2007; The Chalk Garden, Donmar, 2008; *television* includes: Othello; King Lear; Country; The Norman Conquests, 1977; The Tale of Beatrix Potter, 1983; Ever Decreasing Circles; Screaming; The Borrowers, 1992; The Deep Blue Sea, 1994; Landscapes, 1995; Talking Heads (Nights in the Gardens of Spain), 1998; Wives and Daughters, 1999; Victoria and Albert, 2001; Bob and Rose, 2001; Lucky Jim, 2003; *radio* includes: Jane and Prudence, 1994; *films* include: The French Lieutenant's Woman, 1981; Clockwise, 1986; Cry Freedom, 1987; The Secret Rapture, 1993; Carrington, 1995; Iris, 2002; Calendar Girls, 2003; Shaun of the Dead, 2003; Pride and Prejudice, 2005; Match Point, 2006; The History Boys, 2006. *Address:* c/o Independent Talent Group Ltd, Oxford House, 76 Oxford Street, W1D 1BS.

WILTS, Archdeacon of; *see* Wraw, Ven. J. M.

WILTSHIRE, Earl of; Christopher John Hilton Paulet; *b* 30 July 1969; *s* and *heir* of Marquess of Winchester, *qv*; *m* 1992, Christine, *d* of Peter Town; one *s* one *d*. *Heir: s* Lord St John, *qv*.

WIMBORNE, 4th Viscount *cr* 1918; **Ivor Mervyn Vigors Guest;** Baron Wimborne 1880; Baron Ashby St Ledgers 1910; Bt 1838; *b* 19 Sept. 1968; *o s* of 3rd Viscount Wimborne and of his 1st wife, Victoria Ann, *o d* of Col Mervyn Vigors, DSO, MC; *S* father, 1993. *Educ:* Eton. *Heir: uncle* Hon. Julian John Guest [*b* 12 Oct. 1945; *m* 1st, 1970, Emma Jane Arlette (marr. diss. 1978), *e d* of Cdre Archibald Gray, RN; 2nd, 1983, Jillian, *d* of late N. S. G. Bannatine]. *Address: e-mail:* pa@wimbornehq.com.

WINCH, Prof. Donald Norman, FBA 1986; FRHistS; Emeritus Research Professor, University of Sussex, since 2000 (Professor of History of Economics, 1969–2000); *b* 15 April 1935; *s* of Sidney and Iris Winch; *m* 1983, Doreen Lidster. *Educ:* Sutton Grammar Sch.; LSE (BSc Econ 1956); Princeton Univ. (PhD 1960). Vis. Lectr, Univ. of California, 1959–60; Lectr in Economics, Univ. of Edinburgh, 1960–63; University of Sussex: Lectr, 1963–66; Reader, 1966–69; Dean, Sch. of Social Scis, 1968–74; Pro-Vice-Chancellor (Arts and Social Studies), 1986–89. Visiting Fellow: Sch. of Social Sci., Inst. for Advanced Study, Princeton, 1974–75; King's Coll., Cambridge, 1983; History of Ideas Unit, ANU, 1983; St Catharine's Coll., Cambridge, 1989; All Souls Coll., Oxford, 1994; British Council Distinguished Vis. Fellow, Kyoto Univ., 1992. Carlyle Lectr, Oxford Univ., 1995. Vice-Pres., British Acad., 1993–94. Publications Sec., Royal Economic Soc., 1971–; Review Editor, Economic Jl, 1976–83. Fellow, Hist. of Econs Soc., 2007. Hon. DLitt Sussex, 2006. *Publications:* Classical Political Economy and Colonies, 1965; James Mill: selected economic writings, 1966; Economics and Policy, 1969; (with S. K. Howson) The Economic Advisory Council 1930–1939, 1976; Adam Smith's Politics, 1978; (with S. Collini and J. W. Burrow) That Noble Science of Politics, 1983; Malthus, 1987; Riches and Poverty, 1996. *Address:* Arts B, University of Sussex, Brighton BN1 9QN. *T:* (01273) 678634.

WINCHESTER, 18th Marquess of, *cr* 1551; **Nigel George Paulet;** Baron St John of Basing, 1539; Earl of Wiltshire, 1550; Premier Marquess of England; *b* 23 Dec. 1941; *s* of George Cecil Paulet (*g g g s* of 13th Marquess) (*d* 1961), and Hazel Margaret (*d* 1976), *o d* of late Major Danvers Wheeler, RA, Salisbury, Rhodesia; *S* kinsman, 1968; *m* 1967, Rosemary Anne, *d* of Major Aubrey John Hilton; two *s* one *d*. *Heir: s* Earl of Wiltshire, *qv*. *Address:* 6A Main Road, Irene, Centurian, 0062 Gauteng, South Africa.

WINCHESTER, Bishop of, since 1995; **Rt Rev. Michael Charles Scott-Joynt;** *b* 1943; *m* 1965, Louise White; two *s* one *d*. *Educ:* King's College, Cambridge (BA 1965, MA 1968); Cuddesdon Theological College. Deacon 1967, priest 1968; Curate, Cuddesdon, 1967–70; Tutor, Cuddesdon Coll., 1967–71, Chaplain 1971–72; Team Vicar, Newbury, 1972–75; Priest-in-charge: Caversfield, 1975–79; Bicester, 1975–79; Bucknell, 1976–79; Rector, Bicester Area Team Ministry, 1979–81; RD of Bicester and Islip, 1976–81; Canon Residentiary of St Albans, 1982–87; Dir of Ordinands and In-Service Training, Diocese of St Albans, 1982–87; Suffragan Bishop of Stafford, 1987–95. *Address:* Wolvesey, Winchester, Hants SO23 9ND. *T:* (01962) 854050.

WINCHESTER, Dean of; *see* Atwell, Very Rev. J. E.

WINCHESTER, Archdeacon of; *no new appointment at time of going to press.*

WINCHESTER, Simon Bernard Adrian, OBE 2006; writer and journalist, since 1967; *b* 28 Sept. 1944; *s* of Bernard Austin William Winchester and Andrée Freda Winchester (*née* de Wael); *m* 1st, 1966, Isobel Judith Brown (marr. diss. 1988); three *s*; 2nd, 1989, Catherine Evans (marr. diss. 1998); 3rd, 2007, Setsuko Sato; also one *d*. *Educ:* Hardye's Sch., Dorchester; St Catherine's Coll., Oxford (BA 1966, MA 1974). Geologist: Falconbridge of Africa Ltd, Kilembe, 1966; Amoco Offshore Exploration, North Sea, 1967; reporter, then Science Corresp., The Journal, Newcastle upon Tyne, 1967–70; correspondent, variously NE England, NI, Washington, New Delhi, The Guardian, 1970–78; America Corresp., Daily Mail, 1978–80; Chief Foreign Feature Writer, then Asia Corresp., Sunday Times, 1980–84; Hong Kong Corresp., The Guardian, 1985–92; freelance journalist and writer, 1992–; Publisher, Art AsiaPacific, 2005–07. FRGS 1984; FGS 2000. *Publications:* In Holy Terror, 1974; American Heartbeat, 1976; Their Noble Lordships, 1981; Stones of Empire (photography), 1983; Prison Diary, Argentina, 1984; Outposts, 1985; Korea, 1988; The Pacific, 1991; Pacific Nightmare, 1992; Hong Kong: here be dragons, 1994; Small World, 1996; The River at the Centre of the World, 1997; The Surgeon of Crowthorne, 1998 (US edn as The Professor and the Madman); The Fracture Zone, 1999; America's Idea of a Good Time, 2001; The Map that Changed the World, 2001; The Meaning of Everything, 2003; Krakatoa, 2003; A Crack in the Edge of the World, 2005; Bomb, Book and Compass, 2008 (US edn as The Man Who Loved China). *Recreations:* bee-keeping, astronomy, stamp collecting, hill-walking, being in Scotland west of the Caledonian Canal, being at sea anywhere. *Address:* c/o William Morris Agency, 1325 Avenue of the Americas, New York, USA. *Clubs:* Century (New York); China (Hong Kong).

WINCHILSEA, 17th Earl of, *cr* 1628, **AND NOTTINGHAM,** 12th Earl of, *cr* 1681; **Daniel James Hatfield Finch Hatton;** Bt 1611; Viscount Maidstone 1623; Bt 1660; Baron Finch, 1674; Custodian of the Royal Manor of Wye; *b* 7 Oct. 1967; *s* of 16th Earl of Winchilsea and 11th Earl of Nottingham, and of Shirley (*née* Hatfield); *S* father, 1999; *m* 1994, Shelley Amanda, *d* of Gordon Gillard; two *s* one *d*. *Educ:* Univ. of the West of England, Bristol. *Recreations:* interior design, motor racing, swimming, cycling. *Heir: s* Viscount Maidstone, *qv*.

WINDEATT, Prof. Barry Alexander Corelli, PhD, LittD; Professor of English, University of Cambridge, since 2001; Fellow of Emmanuel College, Cambridge, since 1978; *b* 5 April 1950; *s* of Edwin Peter Windeatt and Queenie Gladys Windeatt (*née* Rusbridge). *Educ:* Sutton County GS, Surrey; St Catharine's Coll., Cambridge (BA 1971; MA 1975; PhD 1975; LittD 1996). Cambridge University: Res. Fellow, Gonville and Caius Coll., 1974–78; Asst Lectr in English, 1983–87; Lectr in English, 1987–95; Reader in Medieval Lit., 1995–2001; Tutor, 1982–95, Dir of Studies in English, 1979–98, Emmanuel Coll. *Publications:* (ed and trans.) Chaucer's Dream Poetry: sources and analogues, 1982; (ed) Geoffrey Chaucer, Troilus and Criseyde: A New Edition of The Book of Troilus, 1984, 2nd edn 1990; (trans.) The Book of Margery Kempe, 1985, new edn 2000; (ed with Ruth Morse) Chaucer Traditions, 1990; Troilus and Criseyde, 1992, 2nd edn 1995; (ed) English Mystics of the Middle Ages, 1994; articles on medieval English, French and Italian lit. *Recreations:* opera, gardens, visual arts. *Address:* Emmanuel College, Cambridge CB2 3AP. *T:* (01223) 334200.

WINDELER, John Robert; Chairman, Alliance & Leicester plc, 1999–2005; *b* 21 March 1943; *s* of Alfred Stewart Windeler and Ethela Windeler (*née* Boremuth); *m* 1965, Judith Lynn Taylor; two *s*. *Educ:* Ohio State Univ. (BA, MBA). Exec. Vice Pres., Irving Trust Co., 1969–89; Chief Financial Officer, Nat. Australia Bank, 1989–94; Dir, Alliance & Leicester Building Soc., subseq. Alliance & Leicester plc, 1995–2005, Dep. Chm., 1998–99. Chm., Millen Gp, 2006–; Non-executive Director: BMS Associates Ltd, 1995–2005; RM plc, 2002–. Gov., De Montfort Univ., 2005–. *Recreations:* tennis, ski-ing, antiques. *Address:* c/o RM plc, New Mill House, 183 Milton Park, Abingdon, Oxon OX14 0XE. *Club:* Hurlingham.

WINDER, Robert James; writer; Section Editor, Independent on Sunday, 1998–2001; *b* 26 Sept. 1959; *s* of Herbert James Winder and Mary Nina (*née* Dalby); *m* 1989, Hermione Davies; two *s*. *Educ:* Bradfield Coll.; St Catherine's Coll., Oxford (BA English). Euromoney Publications, 1982–86; Dep. Lit. Ed., 1986–89, Lit. Ed., 1989–95, The Independent; Dep. Ed., Granta Publications, 1996–98. *Publications:* No Admission, 1988; The Marriage of Time and Convenience, 1994; Hell for Leather, 1996; Bloody Foreigners, 2004. *Recreations:* reading, writing, walking, talking, etc. *Address:* 125 Elgin Crescent, W11 2JH.

WINDHAM, William Ashe Dymoke; Chairman, Skelmersdale Development Corporation, 1979–85; (Deputy Chairman, 1977); *b* 2 April 1926; *s* of late Lt-Col Henry Steuart Windham and Marjory Russell Dymock; *m* 1956, Alison Audrey, *d* of late Maj. P. P. Curtis, MC and Ellinor Kidston; two *s* one *d*. *Educ:* Bedford; Christ's Coll., Cambridge (schol.; University prize; MA). Gen. Manager, Runcorn Div., Arthur Guinness Son & Co. (GB), 1972–84. Mem., Runcorn Develt Corp., 1975–77. Steward, Henley Royal Regatta, 1953– (Mem. Cttee of Mgt, 1972–94); rowed for: Cambridge, 1947 and 1951; England, Empire Games, 1950; GB, European Championships, 1950 and 1951 (Gold Medal); Olympic Games, 1952. High Sheriff, Powys, 1996. *Recreations:* shooting, fishing. *Clubs:* Hawks (Cambridge); Leander (Henley) (Pres., 1993–98).

WINDLE, Prof. Alan Hardwick, FRS 1997; FIMMM, FInstP; Professor of Materials Science, University of Cambridge, since 1992; Fellow, Trinity College, Cambridge, since 1978; Director, Pfizer Institute for Pharmaceutical Materials Science, since 2005; *b* 20 June 1942; *s* of Stuart George Windle and Myrtle Lillian (*née* Povey); *m* 1968, Janet Susan Carr; one *s* three *d*. *Educ:* Whitgift Sch.; Imperial Coll., London (BSc Eng. 1963; ARSM 1963); Trinity Coll., Cambridge (PhD 1966). FIMMM (FIM 1992); FInstP 1997. Imperial College, University of London: ICI Res. Fellow, 1966–67; Lectr in Metallurgy, 1967–75; Cambridge University: Lectr in Metallurgy and Materials Sci., 1975–92; Hd of Dept of Materials Sci. and Metallurgy, 1996–2001; Trinity College, Cambridge: Lectr and Dir of Studies in Natural Scis, 1978–92; Tutor, 1983–91. Exec. Dir, Cambridge-MIT Inst., 2000–03. Vis. Prof., N Carolina State Univ., 1980. Vice-Pres., Inst. of Materials, 2001–. Comr, Royal Commn for Exhibition of 1851, 2001–. Chm. Trustees, Mission Aviation Fellowship Europe, 2001–03. Gov., Whitgift Foundn, 1997–2001. Fellow, APS, 2001. Foreign Fellow, Nat. Acad. of Scis, India, 2007. Bessemer Medal, Imperial Coll., 1963; Silver Medal, RSA, 1963; Rosenhain Medal and Prize, Inst. Metals, 1987; Swinburne Medal and Prize, PRI, 1992; Founders' Prize, Polymer Physics Gp, Inst. of Physics, RSC and IMMM, 2007; Armourers' and Brasiers' Co. Prize, Royal Soc., 2007. *Publications:* A First Course in Crystallography, 1978; (with A. M. Donald) Liquid Crystalline Polymers, 1992, (with A. M. Donald and S. Hanna) 2nd edn 2006; contribs to learned jls mainly on polymer morphology, polymer glasses, polymer diffusion, liquid crystalline polymers, polymer modelling and the science and technology of carbon nanotubes. *Recreation:* flying light aircraft. *Address:* Department of Materials Science and Metallurgy, Pembroke Street, Cambridge CB2 3QZ. *T:* (01223) 334321.

WINDLE, Terence Leslie William, CBE 1991; Director, Directorate General for Agriculture, European Commission, 1980–91; *b* 15 Jan. 1926; *s* of Joseph William Windle and Dorothy Windle (*née* Haigh); *m* 1957, Joy Winifred Shield; one *s* two *d*. *Educ:* Gonville and Caius College, Cambridge (MA); London University (Colonial Course). Colonial/HMOCS: Nigeria, 1951–59; Zambia, 1959–69 (Under Sec., Min. of Natural Resources and Tourism); Home Civil Service, MAFF, 1969–73; Commn of EC, 1973–91. *Address:* rue du Fond Agny 20, 1380 Lasne, Belgium. *T:* (2) 6334410.

WINDLESHAM, 3rd Baron *cr* 1937; **David James George Hennessy,** CVO 1981; PC 1973; DLitt; Bt 1927; Baron Hennessy (Life Peer), 1999; Principal, Brasenose College, Oxford, 1989–2002, Hon. Fellow 2002; Chairman, Trustees of the British Museum, 1986–96 (Trustee, 1981–96); *b* 28 Jan. 1932; *s* of 2nd Baron Windlesham; *S* father, 1962; *m* 1965, Prudence Glynn (*d* 1986); one *s* one *d*. *Educ:* Ampleforth; Trinity Coll., Oxford (MA; DLitt 1995; Hon. Fellow 1982). Chairman, Bow Group, 1959–60, 1962–63; Member, Westminster City Council, 1958–62. Minister of State, Home Office, 1970–72; Minister of State for Northern Ireland, 1972–73; Lord Privy Seal and Leader of the House of Lords, 1973–74. Mem., Cttee of Privy Counsellors on Ministerial Memoirs, 1975. Man. Dir, Grampian Television, 1967–70; Jt Man. Dir, 1974–75, Man. Dir, 1975–81, Chm., 1981, ATV Network; Director: The Observer, 1981–89; W. H. Smith Gp, plc, 1986–95. Vis. Fellow, All Souls Coll., Oxford, 1986; Weinberg/Goldman Sachs Vis. Prof., 1997, and Vis. Prof., Public and Internat. Affairs, 2002–03, Princeton Univ. Chm., The Parole Bd for England and Wales, 1982–88. Pres., Victim Support, 1992–2001; Vice-Pres., Royal Television Soc., 1977–82; Jt Dep. Chm., Queen's Silver Jubilee Appeal, 1977; Dep. Chm., The Royal Jubilee Trusts, 1977–80; Chairman: Oxford Preservation Trust, 1979–89; Oxford Society, 1985–88; Mem., Museums and Galleries Commn, 1984–86. Ditchley Foundation: Governor and Mem., Council of Management, 1983–; Vice-Chm., 1987–; Trustee: Charities Aid Foundn, 1977–81; Community Service Volunteers, 1981–2000; Royal Collection Trust, 1993–2000; Chm., Butler Trust, 2004–06. Hon. Bencher, Inner Temple, 1999. Hon. FBA 2005. Hon. LLD London, 2002. Commendatore, Order of Merit, (Italian Republic), 2003. *Publications:* Communication and Political Power, 1966; Politics in Practice, 1975; Broadcasting in a Free Society, 1980; Responses to Crime, Vol. 1 1987, Vol. 2 1993, Vol. 3 1996, Vol. 4 2001; (with Richard Rampton) The Windlesham/Rampton Report on Death on the Rock, 1989; Politics, Punishment, and Populism, 1998. *Heir: s* Hon. James Hennessy [*b* 9 Nov. 1968; *m* 2004, Deborah Jane Wallace; one *s*]. *Address:* c/o House of Lords, SW1A 0PW.

WINDSOR, Viscount; Ivor Edward Other Windsor-Clive; *b* 19 Nov. 1951; *s* and *heir* of 3rd Earl of Plymouth, *qv*; *m* 1979, Caroline, *d* of Frederick Nettlefold and late Hon. Mrs Juliana Roberts; three *s* one *d*. *Educ:* Harrow; Royal Agricl Coll., Cirencester. Co-founder, and Dir, Centre for the Study of Modern Art, 1973. Chairman: Earl of Plymouth

Estates Ltd, 1997–; Ludlow Food Centre Ltd, 2006–. Chm., Heart of England Reg., HHA, 1996–2001. FRSA. *Recreation:* cricket. *Heir:* *s* Hon. Robert Other Ivor Windsor-Clive, *b* 25 March 1981. *Address:* Oakly Park, Ludlow, Shropshire SY8 2JW; Flat 3, 6 Oakley Street, SW3 5NN. *Club:* Brooks's.

WINDSOR, Dean of; *see* Conner, Rt Rev. D. J.

WINDSOR, Barbara Anne, MBE 2000; actress; *b* 6 Aug. 1937; *d* of John Deeks and Rose Deeks (*née* Ellis). *Educ:* Our Lady's Convent, London; Aida Foster Stage Sch. *Theatre includes:* Love from Judy, Palace; Fings Ain't Wot They Used T' Be, Garrick, 1959; Oh What a Lovely War, NY; Come Spy with Me, Whitehall; Sing a Rude Song, Garrick; The Threepenny Opera, Prince of Wales, 1972; The Owl and the Pussycat; Carry on London, Victoria Palace; A Merry Whiff of Windsor (one women show, UK and world tour); Twelfth Night, Chichester; Calamity Jane (UK tour); Entertaining Mr Sloane, Lyric, Hammersmith, 1981; The Mating Game; Guys and Dolls (tour). *Television includes:* The Rag Trade, 1961–63; Carry on Laughing, 1975; Worzel Gummidge, 1979; Peggy Mitchell in EastEnders, 1994–2003, 2005–. *Films include:* Lost, 1956; Too Hot to Handle, 1959; Flame in the Street, 1961; On the Fiddle, 1961; Sparrers Can't Sing, 1963; Crooks in Cloisters, 1963; Carry on Spying, 1964; A Study in Terror, 1965; Carry on Doctor, 1968; Carry on Camping, Hair of the Dog, Chitty Chitty Bang Bang, 1969; Carry on Girls, 1971; The Boyfriend, 1971; Carry on Dick, 1974; Comrades, 1987; Double Vision. Numerous albums and radio performances. Variety Club of GB Award, 1998; Best Actress, Manchester Evening News Awards, 1998; Best Actress, Nat. Soap Awards, 1999; RADAR People of the Year Award, 1999; BBC Hall of Fame Award, 2000; Gold Badge of Merit, BASCA, 2000; Outstanding Contrib. to Entertainment Award, Inside Soap, 2001. *Publications:* Laughter and Tears of a Cockney Sparrow; All of Me: my extraordinary life (autobiog.), 2000. *Address:* c/o Burnett Granger Associates Ltd, 3 Clifford Street, W1S 2LF.

WINDSOR, Dr Colin George, FRS 1995; FInstP, FInstNDT; Consultant, United Kingdom Atomic Energy Authority, Fusion, since 1998; *b* 28 June 1938; *s* of late George Thomas Macdonald Windsor and Mabel (*née* Rayment); *m* 1st, 1963, Margaret Lee (marr. diss. 2005); one *s* two *d*; 2nd, 2005, Mo Watkins. *Educ:* Beckenham Grammar Sch.; Magdalen Coll., Oxford (BA 1st Cl. Hons Physics; DPhil 1963). FInstP 1975; FInstNDT 1993. Magnetic resonance research, Clarendon Lab., Oxford, 1963; Res. Fellow, Yale Univ., 1964; Neutron scattering research, Harwell, 1964–96; Sen. Scientist, Nat. Non-Destructive Testing Centre, AEA Technology, 1988–96; Programme Area Manager, UKAEA, Fusion, 1996–98; Sen. Consultant, Penop, 1998–2001. Fellow: Japanese Soc. for Promotion of Sci., 1980; Neural Network Applications, 1987–. Hon. Prof. of Physics, Birmingham Univ., 1990. Mem., Oxford Naturist Soc. *Publications:* Pulsed Neutron Scattering, 1981; Four Computer Models, 1982; (ed jtly) Solid State Science, Past, Present and Predicted, 1987; contrib. to learned jls. *Recreations:* cycling to work, table tennis, sketching, singing, piano, organ, composing. *Address:* D3, Culham Laboratory, Abingdon, Oxon OX14 3DB. *T:* (01235) 466306; *e-mail:* colin.windsor@ukaea.org.uk; *web:* freespace.virgin.net/colin.windsor; (home) 116 New Road, East Hagbourne, Oxon OX11 9LD.

WINDSOR-CLIVE, family name of **Earl of Plymouth**.

WINEGARTEN, Jonathan Isaac; Chief Master of the Supreme Court, Chancery Division, since 1998 (a Master, since 1991); *b* 10 Dec. 1944; *s* of late Moshe Winegarten and Hannah Deborah Winegarten (*née* Cohen). *Educ:* Hasmonean Grammar Sch., Hendon; Gateshead Yeshiva; University Coll. London (LLB Hons 1967); Slabodka Yeshiva, Israel. Chm., Yavneh, 1966. Winston Churchill Award and called to the Bar, Middle Temple, 1969, *ad eundem* Lincoln's Inn, 1972 (Bencher, 1990); in practice, Chancery Bar, 1970–91. Member: Chancery Bar Assoc. Cttee, 1982, 1983; Supreme Court Procedure Cttee, 1992–. Member: Bd of Deputies, 1973–79; Council, Jews' Coll., 1989–2000; Vice Pres., Fedn of Synagogues, 1989–2001. Pres., Shomrei Hadath Synagogue, 1982–2003 (Hon. Life Pres., 2004). Freeman, City of London, 1992. Adv. Editor, Atkin's Court Forms, 1993–; Editor: Tristram and Coote's Probate Practice, 1995–; Civil Procedure (The White Book), 1999–. *Publications:* (ed) Collected works of Rabbi Z. H. Ferber (11 vols), 1983–92. *Recreations:* violin playing, painting, esp. glass painting and etching, music, reading, publishing. *Address:* Thomas More Building, Royal Courts of Justice, Strand, WC2A 2LL.

WINFIELD, Rev. Canon Flora Jane Louise; Secretary for International Affairs, Churches Together in Britain and Ireland, since 2006; Archbishop of Canterbury's Secretary for Anglican Relations, since 2007; Priest-in-charge, St Mary-at-Hill, City of London, since 2008; *m* 1985, Rev. Canon Jonathan Robin Blanning Gough, *qv. Educ:* Portsmouth High Sch. for Girls, GPDST; St David's Univ. Coll., Lampeter (BA Hons 1985); Ripon Coll., Cuddesdon, Oxford (Cert. Theol. 1989); Westminster Coll., Oxford (Dip. Applied Theol. 1996). Lay Worker, Christ Church Abbeydale, Glos, 1986–87; ordained deacon, 1989, priest, 1994; Parish Deacon, Stantonbury and Willen Ecumenical Parish, Milton Keynes, 1989–92; County Ecumenical Officer, Glos, 1992–94; Chaplain and Tutor, Mansfield Coll., Oxford, 1994–97; Sec. for Local Unity, and Advr to House of Bishops, C of E Archbishop's Council, 1997–2002; Canon Residentiary, Winchester Cathedral, 2002–05, now Canon Emerita. Asst Sec. Gen., 2005–06, Special Advr, 2006–, World Conference of Religions for Peace; Special Advr, St Ethelburga's Centre for Reconciliation and Peace, 2005–. Mem., Faith and Order Adv. Gp, C of E, 1991–2005. Chaplain: to HM Forces (V), 1997–; to Farriers' Co., 2004–; to Princess Royal's Volunteer Corps, 2007–; to Playing Card Makers' Co., 2008–. Trustee, St Andrew's Trust, 2003–. Gov., Sch. of St Helen and St Katharine, Abingdon, 1993–. FRSA 1998. Dame, Order of Francis (First Class). *Publications:* (with Elizabeth Welch) Travelling Together: a handbook on local ecumenical partnerships, 1995; Releasing Energy: how Methodists and Anglicans can grow together, 2000; Growing Together: working for unity locally, 2002; Working with Partner Churches in the Diocese: a handbook for new Bishops, 2002; It's the Thought that Counts in Unpacking the Gift: Anglican resources for theological reflection on the gift of authority, 2003; contributed to: European Women's Experience in the Church, 1991; Reconciliation in Religion and Society, 1994; Community, Unity, Communion: essays in honour of Mary Tanner, 1998; The Table of God's Generosity in Voices of this Calling: experiences of the first generation of woman priests, 2002; articles in Midstream, Ecumenical Review. *Recreations:* country pursuits, gardening, food, music. *Address:* Lambeth Palace, SE1 7JU. *T:* (020) 7898 1200. *Club:* Nikæan.

WINFIELD, William Richard, MA; Headmaster, Mill Hill School, 1995–2007; *b* 19 March 1947; *s* of William Arthur and Paula Constance Winfield; *m* 1986, Margaret Ruth Richards; one *s* one *d*. *Educ:* William Ellis Sch.; Royal Acad. of Music (Jun. Exhibnr); Clare Coll., Cambridge (BA Mod. and Med. Langs 1968; PGCE 1970; MA 1972). Lectr, Maison de l'Europe, Bordeaux, 1968–69; Mill Hill School: Asst Master, 1970–75; Head of Modern Langs, 1975–87; Dir of Studies, 1982–92; Dep. Headmaster, 1992–95. Chief Examr, French Studies, JMB, 1980–87. Governor: Keble Sch., 1999–; Berkhamsted Collegiate Sch., 2007–. *Publications:* (jtly) Vocational French, 1985; contribs to jls on Section Bilingue and intensive language teaching. *Recreations:* playing chamber music, hill walking. *Address:* The Old School House, Church Road, Slapton, Leighton Buzzard LU7 9BX.

WING, Prof. John Kenneth, CBE 1990; MD, PhD; DPM; FRCPsych; Director of Research Unit, Royal College of Psychiatrists, 1989–94; Professor of Social Psychiatry, Institute of Psychiatry and London School of Hygiene and Tropical Medicine, 1970–89, now Emeritus Professor, University of London; *b* 22 Oct. 1923; *m* 1950, Lorna Gladys Tolchard (*see* L. G. Wing); one *d*. *Educ:* Strand Sch.; University College London (MB, BS, MD, PhD). Served RNVR, 1942–46, Lieut (A). Dir, MRC Social Psychiatry Unit, 1965–89. Mem., MRC, 1985–89 (Chm., Neurosciences Bd, 1985–87; Chm., Health Services Res. Cttee, 1987–89). Hon. Consultant Psychiatrist, Maudsley and Bethlem Royal Hosp., 1960–89. Advr to H of C Social Services Cttee, 1984–85 and 1990. Founder FMedSci 1998. Hon. MD Heidelberg, 1977. *Publications:* (ed) Early Childhood Autism, 1966, 2nd edn 1975 (trans. Italian 1970, German 1973); (with G. W. Brown) Institutionalism and Schizophrenia, 1970; (with J. E. Cooper and N. Sartorius) Description and Classification of Psychiatric Symptoms, 1974 (trans. German 1978, French 1980, Japanese 1981); Reasoning about Madness, 1978 (trans. Portuguese 1978, German 1982, Italian 1983); ed, Schizophrenia: towards a new synthesis, 1978; ed (with R. Olsen), Community Care for the Mentally Disabled, 1979; (with J. Leach) Helping Destitute Men, 1979; (ed jtly) What is a Case?, 1981; (ed jtly) Handbook of Psychiatric Rehabilitation, 1981; (with L. G. Wing) Psychoses of Uncertain Aetiology, vol. III of Cambridge Handbook of Psychiatry, 1982; (ed) Contributions to Health Services Planning and Research, 1989; (ed) Measurement for Mental Health, 1995; (jtly) Diagnosis and Clinical Measurement in Psychiatry, 1998; (with P. Lelliott) Progress on Health of the Nation Outcome Scales, 2000; Epidemiological Needs Assessment: severe mental illness, 2000.

WING, Dr Lorna Gladys, OBE 1995; FRCPsych; Consultant Psychiatrist to National Autistic Society, since 1990; *b* 7 Oct. 1928; *d* of Bernard Newbury Tolchard and Gladys Ethel Tolchard (*née* Whittell); *m* 1950, John Kenneth Wing, *qv*; one *d*. *Educ:* Chatham Grammar Sch.; University Coll. Hosp. (MD). Scientific Staff, MRC Social Psychiatry Unit, 1964–90; Hon. Consultant Psychiatrist, Maudsley Hosp., 1972–90; Hon. Sen. Lectr, Inst. of Psychiatry, 1974–90. *Publications:* Autistic Children, 1971, 2nd edn 1980; (ed) Early Childhood Autism, 1976; (ed) Aspects of Autism, 1988; Hospital Closure and the Resettlement of Residents, 1989; The Autistic Spectrum, 1996; papers in sci. jls. *Recreations:* reading, gardening, walking. *Address:* Elliot House, 113 Masons Hill, Bromley, Kent BR2 9HT. *T:* (020) 8466 0098.

WINGATE, Rev. Canon Andrew David Carlile, PhD; Director of Inter-Faith Relations (formerly Director of Ministry and Training and Bishop's Inter-Faith Adviser), Diocese of Leicester, since 2000 (Co-ordinator of Lay Training, 2000–04); Director, St Philip's Centre for Study and Engagement in a Multifaith Society, Leicester, since 2004; Canon Theologian of Leicester Cathedral, since 2000; Chaplain to the Queen, since 2007; *b* 2 Aug. 1944; *s* of Rev. Canon David Wingate and late Olga Wingate; *m* 1967, Angela Beever; one *s* two *d*. *Educ:* Worcester Coll., Oxford (BA 1st class, MA, MPhil); Lincoln Theol Coll.; Univ. of Birmingham (PhD 1995). Asst Master, King Edward's Sch., Birmingham, 1968–70; ordained deacon, 1972, priest, 1973; Asst Curate, Halesowen Parish Church, 1972–75; Lectr, Tamil Nadu Theol Seminary, Madurai, S India, 1975–82; Principal: W Midlands Ministerial Training Course, Queen's Coll., Birmingham, 1982–90; United Coll. of the Ascension, Selly Oak, Birmingham, 1990–2000. Hon. Lectr in Theol., Univ. of Birmingham, 1998–. Dr *hc* De Montfort, 2007. *Publications:* Encounter in the Spirit: Muslim Christian dialogue in practice, 1988, 2nd edn 1991; The Church and Conversion, 1997; (ed) Anglicanism: a global communion, 1998; Does Theological Education Make a Difference?, 1999; Free to Be, 2002; Celebrating Difference: staying faithful - how to live in a multifaith world, 2005; articles in theol jls. *Recreations:* tennis, swimming, golf, painting, mountain walking. *Address:* 23 Roundhill Road, Evington, Leicester LE5 5RJ.

WINGATE, Captain Sir Miles (Buckley), KCVO 1982; FNI; Deputy Master and Chairman of the Board of Trinity House, London, 1976–88, retired; *b* 17 May 1923; *s* of Terrence Wingate and Edith Wingate; *m* 1947, Alicia Forbes Philip; three *d*. *Educ:* Taunton Grammar Sch.; Southampton and Prior Park Coll., Somerset. Master Mariner. Apprenticed to Royal Mail Lines Ltd, 1939; first Comd, 1957; elected to Bd of Trinity House, 1968. Commonwealth War Graves Comr, 1986–91. Vice-President: Seamen's Hosp. Soc., 1980–; Royal Alfred Seafarers Soc., 1980–; British Maritime Charitable Foundn, 1983–; Pres., Internat. Assoc. of Lighthouse Authorities, 1985–88 (Vice-Pres., 1980–85); Dep. Chm., Gen. Council, King George's Fund for Sailors, 1983–93; Mem., Cttee of Management, RNLI, 1976–98; Council, Missions to Seamen, 1982–93. Liveryman: Hon. Co. of Master Mariners, 1970–; Shipwrights' Co., 1977–90; Freeman, Watermen and Lightermen's Co., 1984. Governor, Pangbourne Coll., 1982–91. *Recreation:* golf. *Address:* Trinity House, Tower Hill, EC3N 4DH. *T:* (020) 7481 6900.

WINGFIELD, family name of **Viscount Powerscourt**.

WINGHAM, Prof. Duncan John, PhD; Professor and Head, Department of Earth Sciences, University College London, since 2005; Director, NERC Centre for Polar Observation and Modelling, since 2001; *b* 12 Oct. 1957; *s* of Philip and Margaret Wingham; *m* 1987, Ivana Azanjac; one *d*. *Educ:* City of Bath Boys Sch.; Univ. of Leeds (BSc Hons Phys 1979); Univ. of Bath (PhD 1985). Res. Seismologist, Seismograph Service Ltd, Kent, 1979–81; Res. Officer, Dept of Phys, Univ. of Bath, 1981–84; University College London: Res. Associate, Mullard Space Sci. Lab., 1985–86; Lectr, 1986–89, Sen. Lectr, 1989–93, Dept of Electronic and Electrical Engrg; Sen. Lectr, 1993–96, Prof. of Climate Phys, 1996–2005, Dept of Space and Climate Phys. Lead Investigator, CryoSat Mission, ESA, 1999–. *Publications:* articles in Nature, Science, Geophysical Res. Letters, Jl of Geophys Res., Jl of Glaciology, Earth & Planetary Sci. Letters, etc. *Address:* Department of Earth Sciences, University College London, Gower Street, WC1E 6BT.

WINKELMAN, Joseph William, PPRE (RE 1982; ARE 1979); free-lance painter-printmaker, since 1971; President, Royal Society of Painter-Printmakers (formerly Royal Society of Painter-Etchers and Engravers), 1989–95; *b* 20 Sept. 1941; *s* of George William Winkelman and Cleo Lucretia (*née* Harness); *m* 1969, Harriet Lowell Belin; two *d*. *Educ:* Univ. of the South, Sewanee, Tenn (BA English 1964); Wharton School of Finance, Univ. of Pennsylvania; Ruskin Sch. of Drawing; Univ. of Oxford (Cert. of Fine Art 1971). Royal Society of Painter-Etchers and Engravers: Hon. Sec., 1982; Vice-Pres., 1986; Fellow, Printmakers' Council of GB, 1978 (Hon. Fellow, 1988). Former tutor for: Sch. of Architecture, Oxford Polytechnic; Ruskin Sch. of Drawing, Oxford Univ.; Dept for External Studies, Oxford Univ. Artist in Residence, St John's Coll., Oxford, 2004. Mem., Bd of Dirs, Bankside Gall., London, 2002–06. Chm., Oxford Art Soc., 1987–93 (Vice Pres., 1994–). Chm., Nat. Assoc. of Blood Donors, 1994–95. Gov., Windmill First Sch., Headington, Oxford, 1994–98. RWA, 1990–2006 (ARWA 1983). Hon. RWS 1997. *Recreations:* gardening, theatre, hill walking. *Address:* The Hermitage, 69 Old High Street,

Headington, Oxford OX3 9HT. *T:* (01865) 762839; *e-mail:* Winkelman@ukgateway.net; *web:* www.winkelman.co.uk.

WINKETT, Rev. Canon Lucy Clare; Residentiary Canon and Precentor, St Paul's Cathedral, since 2003; *b* 8 Jan. 1968; *d* of Bryan and Cecilia Winkett. *Educ:* Dr Challoner's High Sch.; Selwyn Coll., Cambridge (BA (Hons) Hist. 1990); RCM (ARCM 1992); Queen's Coll., Birmingham (BD 1994). Ordained deacon, 1995, priest, 1996; Asst Curate, St Michael and All Angels, Manor Park, 1995–97; Minor Canon, St Paul's Cathedral, 1997–2003. *Recreations:* reading, singing, cycling. *Address:* Chapter House, St Paul's Churchyard, EC4M 8AD. *T:* (020) 7236 4128; *e-mail:* precentor@stpaulscathedral.org.uk.

WINKLER, Jan; Ambassador of the Czech Republic to the Court of St James's, since 2005; *b* 7 May 1957; *s* of Otto and Helena Winkler; *m* 1979, Jana Zajícová; one *s* two *d*. *Educ:* Charles Univ., Prague (JUD). Company lawyer, 1981–90; Registrar, Charles Univ., Prague, 1990–95; Ministry of Foreign Affairs: Hd, Policy Planning, 1995–97; Vice-Minister, 1997–99; Consultant: for Andersen Consulting, then Accenture, 1999–2002; for PricewaterhouseCoopers, 2002–03; Vice-Minister, Min. of Foreign Affairs, 2003–05. *Publications:* jointly: Obnova ideje university, 1993; Rethinking University, 1994; Uniqueness in Unity, 1995; The Future Development of CEFTA, 1996; The Pilsen Talks, 1997; contrib. many articles to Perspectives, Universidad Futura, Higher Education Mgt, International Politik, Europäische Rundschau, Mezinárodni Vztahy, Aula, etc. *Recreations:* reading, exhibitions, biking, ski-ing, roller blades. *Address:* (office) 26 Kensington Palace Gardens, W8 4QY. *T:* (020) 7243 7902, *Fax:* (020) 7727 9654; *e-mail:* jan_winkler@mzv.cz. *Clubs:* Athenæum, Travellers.

WINKLEY, Sir David (Ross), Kt 1999; DPhil; Founder and President, National Primary Trust, 1986–2006; *b* 30 Nov. 1941; *s* of late Donald Joseph Winkley and Winifred Mary Winkley; *m* 1967, Dr Linda Mary Holland; one *s* one *d*. *Educ:* King Edward's Sch., Birmingham; Selwyn Coll., Cambridge (MA); Wadham Coll., Oxford (DPhil 1975; Hon. Fellow 2006). Mem., Centre for Contemporary Cultural Studies, Univ. of Birmingham, 1965; Dep. Head, Perry Common Sch., 1968–71; Head, Grove Primary Sch., 1974–97. Fellow, Nuffield Coll., Oxford, 1981–82. Vis. Prof., Univ. of Huddersfield, 2003–; Hon. Professor: Univ. of Birmingham, 1999–; Univ. of Warwick, 2004–. Member: CATE, 1985–90; Stevenson Cttee on Information and Communication Technol., 1996. Founder and Chm., Birmingham Children's Community Venture, 1967–; Founder, Children's Univ., 1992. DLitt Birmingham, 1999; DUniv UCE, 2000. *Publications:* Diplomats and Detectives, 1986; Handsworth Revolution, 2002; numerous academic articles on educational and philosophical issues. *Recreations:* reading, music, piano playing, writing fiction.

WINKLEY, Dr Stephen Charles, MA; Headmaster, Rossall School, since 2008; *b* 9 July 1944; *e s* of late George Winkley and Eunice Winkley (*née* Golding); *m* 1st, 1968, Georgina Smart; two *s*; 2nd, 1983, Jennifer Burt; two *d*. *Educ:* St Edward's School, Oxford; Brasenose College, Oxford (MA 1967; DPhil 1973). Asst Master, Cranleigh Sch., 1969–85; Second Master, Winchester College, 1985–91; Headmaster, Uppingham Sch., 1991–2006. *Recreations:* music, water colours. *Address:* Headmaster's House, Rossall School, Fleetwood, Lancs FY7 8JW; Le Peyré, 47170 St Pé St Simon, France.

WINKWORTH-SMITH, (Michael) John; mediator; Regional Managing Partner, Leeds Office, Dibb Lupton Alsop (formerly Dibb Lupton Broomhead), 1995–99; *b* 4 May 1944; *s* of late Frank Winkworth-Smith and of Marjorie Beaumont Winkworth-Smith (*née* Smith); *m* 1974, Sarah Elisabeth Jackson; two *s* (one *d* decd). *Educ:* Ermysted's Grammar Sch., Skipton. Admitted solicitor, 1970; Partner, Broomhead Wightman & Reed, later Dibb Lupton Broomhead, then Dibb Lupton Alsop, 1972–99; Man. Partner, Birmingham Office, 1993–95. Treas., Royal Sheffield Instn for the Blind, 1972–78; Mem., Sheffield CVS, 1978–90; Dir, Broomgrove Trust, 1980–; Chairman: Taptonholme Ltd, 1984–2000; Champion Hse, Derby Diocesan Youth Centre, 1988–93. Director: CEDR, 1991–99; Japan Adv. Services Ltd, 1991–97; Consensus Mediation Ltd, 2004–. Trustee, Sheffield Royal Soc. for the Blind, 2003–. FRSA 1997. *Recreations:* family, farming, shooting. *Address:* Churchdale Farm, Ashford-in-the-Water, Bakewell, Derbys DE45 1NX. *T:* (01629) 640269.

WINN, family name of **Baron St Oswald**.

WINN, Allan Kendal, FRAeS, FCILT; Director, Brooklands Museum, since 2003; *b* 19 March 1950; *s* of Atkinson Winn and Janet Winn; *m* 1994, Jacqueline Christina Worsley; one step *s* one step *d*. *Educ:* Nelson Coll., NZ; Univ. of Canterbury, Christchurch, NZ (BEng, Diploma in Journalism). FCILT (FCIT 1992); FRAeS 1996. Technical Editor, Consulting Engineer, 1975–77; Technical Editor, Editor, Man. Editor, Engineering Today, later New Technology, 1977–85; Editor: Commercial Motor, 1985–88; Flight International, 1989–98; Publisher, Flight International and Airline Business, 1998–2003. Chm., Assoc. of Friends of Brooklands Mus., 1995–2003. Liveryman, GAPAN, 1999–. Sir Peter Masefield Gold Medal, British Assoc. Aviation Consultants, 2006. *Recreation:* vintage motor vehicles. *Address:* Brooklands Museum, Brooklands Road, Weybridge, Surrey KT13 0QN. *T:* (01932) 857381; 39 Heathcote, Tadworth, Surrey KT20 5TH. *T:* (01737) 362760. *Clubs:* Aviation of UK (Chm., 1991–97), Vintage Sports Car, Bentley Drivers'.

WINNER, Michael Robert; Chairman: Scimitar Films Ltd, Michael Winner Ltd, Motion Picture and Theatrical Investments Ltd, since 1957; *b* 30 Oct. 1935; *s* of late George Joseph and Helen Winner. *Educ:* St Christopher Sch., Letchworth; Downing Coll., Cambridge Univ. (MA). Film critic and Fleet Street journalist and contributor to: The Spectator, Daily Express, London Evening Standard, Daily Mail, etc; columnist, Sunday Times. Panellist, Any Questions, BBC radio; presenter, Michael Winner's True Crimes, LWT. Entered Motion Pictures, 1956, as Screen Writer, Asst Director, Editor. Films include: Play It Cool (Dir), 1962; The Cool Mikado (Dir and Writer), 1962; West Eleven (Dir), 1963; The System (Prod. and Dir), 1963; You Must Be Joking (Prod., Dir, Writer), 1965; The Jokers (Prod., Dir, Writer), 1966; I'll Never Forget What's 'isname (Prod. and Dir), 1967; Hannibal Brooks (Prod., Dir, Writer), 1968; The Games (Prod. and Dir), 1969; Lawman (Prod. and Dir), 1970; The Nightcomers (Prod. and Dir), 1971; Chato's Land (Prod. and Dir), 1971; The Mechanic (Dir), 1972; Scorpio (Prod. and Dir), 1972; The Stone Killer (Prod. and Dir), 1973; Death Wish (Prod. and Dir), 1974; Won Ton Ton The Dog That Saved Hollywood (Prod. and Dir), 1975; The Sentinel (Prod., Dir, Writer), 1976; The Big Sleep (Prod., Dir, Writer), 1977; Firepower (Prod., Dir), 1978; Death Wish Two (Prod., Dir, Writer), 1981; The Wicked Lady (Prod., Dir, Writer), 1982; Scream for Help (Prod., Dir), 1984; Death Wish Three (Prod. and Dir), 1985; Appointment with Death (Prod., Dir, Writer), 1988; A Chorus of Disapproval (Prod., Dir, Jt screenplay writer), 1989; Bullseye! (Prod., Dir, jt screenplay writer), 1990; Dirty Weekend (Prod., Dir, jt screenplay writer), 1993; Parting Shots (Prod., Dir, Writer), 1997; actor: For the Greater Good, 1990; Decadence, 1993; radio play: The Flump, 2000; actor/dir, several television commercials. Theatre productions: The Tempest, Wyndhams, 1974; A Day in Hollywood A Night in the Ukraine, 1978. Founder and Chm., Police Meml Trust, 1984–. *Publications:* Winner's Dinners, 1999, rev. edn 2000; Winner Guide, 2002; Winner Takes All (autobiog.), 2004; The Fat Pig Diet, 2007. *Recreations:* walking around art galleries, museums, antique shops, eating, being difficult, making table mats, washing silk shirts, doing Pilates badly. *Address:* 219 Kensington High Street, W8 6BD. *T:* (020) 7734 8385.

WINNICK, David Julian; MP (Lab) Walsall North, since 1979; *b* Brighton, 26 June 1933; *s* of late Eugene and Rose Winnick; one *s*; *m* 1968, Bengi Rona (marr. diss.), *d* of Tarik and Zeynep Rona. *Educ:* secondary school; London Sch. of Economics (Dip. in Social Admin). Army National Service, 1951–53. Branch Secretary, Clerical and Administrative Workers' Union, 1956–62 (later APEX GMB; Mem. Exec. Council, 1978–88, Vice-Pres., 1983–88); Advertisement Manager, Tribune, 1963–66; employed by UKIAS, 1970–79 (Chm., 1984–90). Member: Willesden Borough Council, 1959–64; London Borough of Brent Council, 1964–66 (Chair, Children Cttee, 1965–66). Contested (Lab) Harwich, 1964; MP (Lab) Croydon South, 1966–70; contested (Lab): Croydon Central, Oct. 1974; Walsall N, Nov. 1976. Member: Select Cttee on the Environment, 1979–83; Home Affairs Cttee, 1983–87, 1997–; Select Cttee on Procedure, 1989–97; Co-Chm., British-Irish Inter-Parly Body, 1997–2005 (Vice-Chm., 1993–97). *Recreations:* walking, cinema, theatre, reading. *Address:* House of Commons, SW1A 0AA.

WINNIFRITH, Charles Boniface, CB 1998; Clerk of Committees, House of Commons, 1995–2001; *b* 12 May 1936; *s* of Sir John Winnifrith, KCB and late Lesbia Margaret Winnifrith; *m* 1st, 1962, Josephine Poile, MBE (*d* 1991); one *s* two *d*; 2nd, 1993, Sandra (*née* Stewart). *Educ:* Tonbridge Sch.; Christ Church, Oxford (MA). 2nd Lieut, RAEC, 1958–60. Joined Dept of the Clerk of the House of Commons, 1960; Second Clerk of Select Cttees, 1983; Clerk of Select Cttees, 1987; Principal Clerk of the Table Office, 1989. Mem., General Synod of C of E, 1970–90. Member: Soc. of Clerks-at-the-Table in Commonwealth Parlts, 1989–; Assoc. of Secs Gen. of Parlts, 1996–. Governor, Ashford Sch., Kent, 1973–93. *Recreations:* cricket, American soap opera. *Address:* Gale Lodge Farm, Long Buckby, Northants NN6 7PH. *T:* (01604) 770396. *Club:* MCC.

WINNINGTON, Sir Anthony (Edward), 7th Bt *cr* 1755, of Stanford Court, Worcestershire; *b* 13 May 1948; *s* of Col Thomas Foley Churchill Winnington, MBE and of Lady Betty Marjorie Anson, *d* of 4th Earl of Lichfield; *S* uncle, 2003; *m* 1978, Karyn (marr. diss. 2007), *d* of F. H. Kettles; one *s* two *d*. *Educ:* Eton. FSI. *Heir: s* Edward Alan Winnington, *b* 15 Nov. 1987. *Address:* *e-mail:* winnington@aol.com. *Clubs:* Boodle's, White's, Hurlingham.

WINNINGTON-INGRAM, Edward John; Managing Director, Mail Newspapers Plc (formerly Associated Newspapers Group), 1986–89, retired; *b* 20 April 1926; *s* of Rev. Preb. Edward Francis and Gladys Winnington-Ingram; *m* 1st, 1953, Shirley Lamotte (marr. diss. 1968); two *s*; 2nd, 1973, Elizabeth Linda Few Brown. *Educ:* Shrewsbury; Keble Coll., Oxford (BA). Served RN (Sub-Lieut), 1944–47. Joined Associated Newspapers, 1949; Circulation Manager, Daily Mail, 1960–65; Gen. Manager, Daily Mail Manchester, 1965–70; helped create Northprint Manchester Ltd, a jt printing consortium with Manchester Guardian and Evening News and Associated, 1969; Dir, Associated Newspapers, 1971; Managing Director: Harmsworth Publishing, 1973; Mail on Sunday, 1982; Dir, Associated Newspapers Holdings, 1983; non-executive Director: NAAFI, 1987–93; Burlington Gp, 1988–92. *Recreations:* tennis, shooting, beagling, gardening, music, defending the 1662 Prayer Book. *Address:* Old Manor Farm, Cottisford, Brackley, Northants NN13 5SW. *T:* (01280) 848367. *Clubs:* Buck's, Roehampton.

WINSHIP, Sir Peter (James Joseph), Kt 2004; CBE 1998; QPM 1990; HM Inspector of Constabulary, 1995–2005; *b* 21 July 1943; *s* of late Francis Edward Winship and Iris May (*née* Adams); *m* 1st, 1963, Carol Ann McNaughton; two *s* one *d*; 2nd, 1989, Janet Mary Bird; one *d*. *Educ:* Bicester Grammar Sch.; St John's Coll., Oxford (BA Eng. Lang. and Lit.; MA). Oxfordshire Constabulary, 1962; Sergeant to Supt, Thames Valley Police, 1968–79; Graduate, FBI Acad., 1980; Chief Supt, Metropolitan Police, 1982; Asst Chief Constable, Thames Valley Police, 1984; Metropolitan Police: Dep. Asst Comr, Policy & Planning, 1987, No 1 Area HQ, 1988; Asst Comr, 1989–95; Management Support and Strategy Dept, 1989–91; Inspection and Review Dept, 1992–95. Dir, Police Extended Interviews, 1993–95. Chm., Technical and Res. Cttee, ACPO, 1992–95. Member: Exec. Council, London Fedn of Boys' Clubs, 1988–95; Exec. Cttee, Royal Humane Soc., 1989–95; Governing Bd, Revolving Doors Agency, 1993–95. Trustee, Police Rehabilitation Trust, 2002–. FCMI. *Publications:* articles in police jls and other periodicals on professionally related subjects, travel, and treatment of police in literature; essay on delinquency and social policy (Queen's Police Gold Medal, Essay Competition, 1969). *Recreations:* reading, riding, gardening, music.

WINSKEL, Prof. Glynn, ScD, PhD; Professor of Computer Science, University of Cambridge, since 2000; Fellow, Emmanuel College, Cambridge, since 2000; *b* 23 May 1953; *s* of Thomas Francis Winskel and Helen Juanita Winskel (*née* McCall); *m* 1982, Kirsten Krog Jensen; two *d*. *Educ:* Emmanuel Coll., Cambridge (BA, MA Maths, ScD Computer Sci. 1995); St Catherine's Coll., Oxford (MSc Maths); Univ. of Edinburgh (PhD Computer Sci. 1980). Res. Scientist, Carnegie-Mellon Univ., Pittsburgh, 1982–83; University of Cambridge: Lectr in Computer Sci., 1984–87; Reader, 1987–88; Fellow, King's Coll., 1985–88; Prof. of Computer Sci., 1988–2000, Dir, Basic Res. in Computer Sci., 1994–2000, Aarhus Univ., Denmark. Ed., Jl of Mathematical Structures in Computer Science. *Publications:* Formal Semantics of Programming Languages: an introduction, 1993; (contrib.) Handbook of Logic in Computer Science, 1994. *Recreations:* music, art, running, swimming. *Address:* University of Cambridge, Computer Laboratory, 15 JJ Thomson Avenue, Cambridge CB3 0FD.

WINSLET, Kate Elizabeth; actress; *b* 5 Oct. 1975; *d* of Roger and Sally Winslet; *m* 1st, 1998, Jim Threapleton (marr. diss. 2001); one *d*; 2nd, 2003, Samuel Alexander Mendes, *qv*; one *s*. *Educ:* Theatre Sch., Maidenhead. *Films include:* Heavenly Creatures, 1995; Sense and Sensibility, Jude, 1996; Hamlet, 1997; Titanic, 1998; Hideous Kinky, 1999; Holy Smoke, 2000; Quills, Enigma, 2001; Iris, 2002; The Life of David Gale, 2003; Eternal Sunshine of the Spotless Mind, Finding Neverland, 2004; Romance & Cigarettes, All the King's Men, Little Children, The Holiday, 2006. *Address:* c/o United Agents, 12–26 Lexington Street, W1F 0LE. *T:* (020) 3214 0800, *Fax:* (020) 3214 0801.

WINSOR, Thomas Philip; Partner, White & Case, since 2004; *b* 7 Dec. 1957; twin *s* of late Thomas Valentine Marrs Winsor and Phyllis Margaret Winsor (*née* Bonsor); *m* 1989, Sonya Elizabeth Field; two *d*. *Educ:* Grove Acad., Broughty Ferry; Univ. of Edinburgh (LLB Scots Law 1979); Univ. of Dundee (Postgrad. Dip. Petroleum Law 1983). Admitted solicitor, 1981, NP 1981, WS 1984, Scotland; admitted solicitor, England and Wales, 1991; in general practice, Dundee, 1981–83; Assistant Solicitor: Dundas & Wilson, CS, 1983–84; Norton Rose, 1984–91; Partner, Denton Hall, 1991–99; Chief Legal Advr and Gen. Counsel, Office of Rail Regulator, 1993–95; Rail Regulator and Internat. Rail Regulator, 1999–2004. Hon. Lectr, Centre for Energy, Petroleum and Mineral Law and Policy, Univ. of Dundee, 1993–. Member: Law Soc. of Scotland, 1981–; Internat. Bar Assoc., 1983–; Univ. of Dundee Petroleum and Mineral Law Soc., 1987– (Pres., 1987–89); Soc. of Scottish Lawyers in London, 1987– (Pres., 1987–89); Law Soc. of

England and Wales, 1991–. *Publications:* (with M. P. G. Taylor) Taylor and Winsor on Joint Operating Agreements, 1989; contrib. Legal Lines, articles in Modern Railways mag., 1996–99; contrib. articles in newspapers, books and learned jls on oil and gas, electricity and railways law and regulation. *Recreations:* family, literature, theatre, opera, music, hill-walking, swimming, gardening, chess, cycling, Scottish constitutional history, law. *Address:* White & Case, 5 Old Broad Street, EC2N 1DW. *T:* (020) 7532 1000; *e-mail:* twinsor@whitecase.com.

WINSTANLEY, Rt Rev. Alan Leslie; Vicar of Whittle-le-Woods, and Hon. Assistant Bishop, diocese of Blackburn, since 2003; *b* 7 May 1949; *s* of John Leslie Winstanley and Eva Winstanley; *m* 1972, Vivien Mary Parkinson; one *s* one *d* (one *s* decd). *Educ:* St John's College, Nottingham (BTh, ALCD). Deacon 1972, priest 1973, Blackburn; Curate: St Andrew's, Livesey, Blackburn, 1972–75; St Mary's, Great Sankey, dio. Liverpool, with responsibility for St Paul's, Penketh, 1975–77; Vicar of Penketh, 1978–81; SAMS Missionary in Peru: Lima, 1981–85; Arequipa, 1986–87; Bishop of Peru and Bolivia, 1988–93; Vicar of Eastham, and Hon. Asst Bp, dio. Chester, 1994–2003. *Recreations:* vintage aircraft, caravanning, steam locomotives. *Address:* The Vicarage, Preston Road, Whittle-le-Woods, Chorley, Lancs PR6 7PS.

WINSTANLEY, Charles Jeffery, TD 1990; JP; DL; DBA; Chairman, NHS Lothian, since 2007; *b* London, 6 March 1952; *s* of Jeffery and Elizabeth Winstanley; *m* 1987, Columbine Hobart; one *s* one *d*. *Educ:* Wellington Coll.; RMA Sandhurst; Henley Management Coll. (MBA 1992; DBA 1997). Major, Royal Yeomanry, 1977–92. Chm., Fitness to Practice Panel, GMC, 2000–07; Member: Nat. Consumer Council for Postal Services, 2002–; Asylum and Immigration Tribunal, 2003–. Non-exec. Dir, Norfolk and Norwich Univ. Hosp. NHS Trust, 1999–2006; Chm., Norfolk Probation Bd, 2001–06. JP Thames and Central Norfolk, 1993; DL Gtr London, 1997. *Recreations:* motorcycling, sailing, fly fishing. *Address:* Lothian NHS Board, Deaconess House, 148 Pleasance, Edinburgh EH8 9RS. *T:* (0131) 536 9002, *Fax:* (0131) 536 9011; *e-mail:* cjwinstanley@aol.com.

WINSTANLEY, Robert James; His Honour Judge Winstanley; a Circuit Judge, since 1996; *b* 4 Nov. 1948; *s* of late Morgan James Winstanley and of Joan Martha Winstanley; *m* 1972, Josephine Langhorne; two *s*. *Educ:* St Catharine's Coll., Cambridge (MA 1970). Admitted Solicitor, 1973; Asst Solicitor, Dawson & Co., 1973–75; Partner, Winstanley-Burgess, Solicitors, 1975–96. Mem. Council, Law Soc., 1985–96. *Recreations:* golf, cricket, motorcycling, bridge. *Address:* c/o The Court Service, 2nd Floor, Rose Court, 2 Southwark Bridge, SE1 9HS. *T:* (020) 7921 2109. *Clubs:* MCC; Sudbury Golf.

WINSTON, family name of **Baron Winston**.

WINSTON, Baron *cr* 1995 (Life Peer), of Hammersmith in the London Borough of Hammersmith and Fulham; **Robert Maurice Lipson Winston;** Professor of Science and Society, Imperial College London, since 2008; Professor of Fertility Studies, University of London at Imperial College School of Medicine (formerly at the Institute of Obstetrics and Gynaecology, Royal Postgraduate Medical School), 1987–2005, now Professor Emeritus; formerly Consultant Obstetrician and Gynaecologist, Hammersmith Hospital; Director of NHS Research and Development, Hammersmith Hospitals NHS Trust, 1998–2005; *b* 15 July 1940; *s* of late Laurence Winston and Ruth Winston-Fox, *qv*; *m* 1973, Lira Helen Feigenbaum; two *s* one *d*. *Educ:* St Paul's Sch., London; London Hosp. Med. Coll., London Univ. (MB, BS 1964). MRCS, LRCP 1964; FRCOG 1983 (MRCOG 1971); FRCP 2002. Jun. posts, London Hosp., 1964–66; Registrar and Sen. Registrar, Hammersmith Hosp., 1970–74; Wellcome Res. Sen. Lectr, Inst. of Obs and Gyn., 1974–78; Sen. Lectr, Hammersmith Hosp., 1978–81; Reader in Fertility Studies, RPMS, 1982–86. Vis. Prof., Univ. of Leuven, Belgium, 1976–77; Prof. of Gyn., Univ. of Texas at San Antonio, 1980–81; Clyman Vis. Prof., Mt Sinai Hosp., New York, 1985. Member, Steering Cttee, WHO: on Tubal Occlusion, 1975–77; on Ovum Transport, 1977–78; Mem., EPSRC, 2007– (Chm., Societal Issues Panel, 2007–). Pres., Internat. Fallopius Soc., 1987–88. Mem. Council, Cancer Res. UK (formerly ICRF), 1998–2004. Vice Pres., Progress (all-party parly campaign for res. into human reprodn), 1992 (Chm., 1988–91). Mem. Bd, POST, 1998–; Mem., Select Cttee on Sci. and Technol., H of L, 1997–2001 (Chm., 1998–2001), 2003–. Founder Mem., British Fertility Soc., 1975–; Mem. Bd, Internat. Soc. for Stem Cell Res., 2004–; Pres., BAAS, 2004–05. Dir, Atazoa Ltd, 2004–. Hon. Member: Georgian Obs Soc., 1983–; Pacific Fertility Soc., 1983–; Spanish Fertility Soc., 1985–. Mem. Council, RPMS, 1992–97; Chm. Council, Royal Coll. of Music, 2008–. Chancellor, Sheffield Hallam Univ., 2001–; Mem. Council, Univ. of Surrey, 2008–. Presenter, BBC TV: Your Life in their Hands, 1979–87; The Human Body, 1998; The Secret Life of Twins, 1999; A Child of Our Time, 2000–; Superhuman, 2000; Threads of Life, BBC TV, 2001; Human Instinct, BBC TV, 2002; Walking with Cavemen, 2003; The Human Mind, 2003; Frankenstein: birth of a monster, 2003; The Story of God, 2005; Child Against All Odds, 2006; Super Doctors, 2008; Frontiers of Medicine, 2008. Member, Editorial Board: Internat. Jl of Microsurgery, 1981–; Clinical Reproduction and Fertility, 1985–. Founder FMedSci 1998. Hon. Fellow, QMW, 1996. Hon. FRCSE 2006; Hon. FIBiol 2006; Hon. FRCPSGlas, 2007; Hon. FREng, 2008. Hon. DSc: Cranfield, 2001; UMIST, 2001; Oxford Brookes, 2001; Strathclyde, 2002; St Andrews, 2002; Salford, 2003; Middlesex, 2003; Sunderland, 2003; Exeter, 2004; Southampton Inst., 2004; QUB, 2005; TCD, 2005; East Anglia, 2006; Auckland, 2008; De Montfort, 2008; Aberdeen, 2008. Chief Rabbinate Award for Contribn to Society, 1992–93; Victor Bonney Prize, RCS, 1991–93; Cedric Carter Medal, Clinical Genetics Soc., 1993; Michael Faraday Gold Medal, Royal Soc., 1999; Gold Medal, RSH, 1999; Gold Medal for Medicine in the Media, BMA, 1999; Wellcome Award for Sci. in the Media, 2001; Edwin Stevens Gold Medal, RSocMed, 2003; Viewers' and Listeners' Award for Best Individual Contrib. to Television, 2003; Maitland Medal, Inst. of Engineers, 2004; Gold Medal, N of England Zool Soc., 2004; Al-Hammadi Medal, RCSE, 2007. *Publications:* Reversibility of Sterilization, 1978; (jtly) Tubal Infertility, 1981; Infertility, a Sympathetic Approach, 1987; Getting Pregnant, 1990; The IVF Revolution, 2000; (jtly) Superhuman: the awesome power within, 2000; Human Instinct, 2002; The Human Mind, 2003; What Makes Me Me, 2004 (Aventis Prize, Royal Soc.); The Story of God, 2005; Child Against All Odds, 2006; It's Elementary, 2008; Evolution Revolution from Darwin to DNA, 2009; scientific pubns on human and experimental reproduction. *Recreations:* theatre (directed award-winning Pirandello production, Each in his Own Way, Edinburgh Fest., 1969), festering, music, wine. *Address:* 11 Denman Drive, NW11 6RE. *T:* (020) 8455 7475. *Clubs:* Athenæum, Garrick, MCC.

WINSTON, Prof. Brian Norman, PhD; Lincoln Professor of Communications, University of Lincoln, since 2007 (Dean, Faculty of Media and Humanities, 2002–05; Pro-Vice-Chancellor, 2005–07); *b* 7 Nov. 1941; *s* of Reuben and Anita Winston; *m* 1978, Adèle Paul; one *s* one *d*. *Educ:* Kilburn Grammar Sch.; Merton Coll., Oxford (BA Laws; MA); Univ. of Lincoln (PhD 2007). Researcher, 1963–66, Prod. and Dir, 1963–66, 1969–71, Granada TV; Prod. and Dir, BBC TV, 1966–69; Lectr, Bradford Coll. of Art, 1972–73; Head of Gen. Studies, Nat. Film Sch., 1973–79; Res. Dir, Dept of Sociology, Glasgow Univ., 1974–76; Vis. Prof., 1976–77, Prof., 1979–86, Sch. of the Arts, NY Univ.; writer, WNET-TV, NY, 1984–85; Dean, Coll. of Communications, Pennsylvania State Univ., 1986–92; Dir, Centre for Journalism Studies, UWCC, then Univ. of Wales, Cardiff, 1992–97; Hd, Dept of Communication, Media and Design, then Sch. of Communication and Creative Industries, Westminster Univ., 1997–2002. Gov., BFI, 1995–2001. Emmy Award for documentary script writing, 1985. *Publications:* Dangling Conversations, vol. 1, the image of the media, 1973, vol. 2, hardware/software, 1974; (jtly) Bad News, 1976; (jtly) More Bad News, 1980; Misunderstanding Media, 1986; (jtly) Working with Video, 1986; Claiming the Real, 1995; Technologies of Seeing, 1996; Media, Technology and Society: a history, 1998; Fires Were Started, 1999; Lies, Damn Lies and Documentaries, 2000; Messages, 2005. *Recreations:* cooking, theatre. *Address:* 24a Minster Yard, Lincoln LN2 1PY; University of Lincoln, Brayford Pool, Lincoln LN6 7TS.

WINSTON, Clive Noel; Assistant Director, Federation Against Copyright Theft Ltd, 1985–88; *b* 20 April 1925; *s* of George and Alida Winston; *m* 1952, Beatrice Jeanette; two *d*. *Educ:* Highgate Sch.; Trinity Hall, Cambridge (BA). Admitted solicitor, 1951. Joined Metropolitan Police, 1951; Dep. Solicitor, Metropolitan Police, 1982–85. Chairman, Union of Liberal and Progressive Synagogues, 1981–85 (Vice-Pres., 1985–); Treas., Eur. Bd, World Union of Progressive Judaism, 1990–95. *Recreations:* golf, gardening.

WINSTON-FOX, Mrs Ruth, MBE 1996; JP; Co-Chairman, Women's National Commission, 1979–81 (Member, 1971); *b* 12 Sept. 1912; *d* of Major the Rev. Solomon Lipson, Hon. SCF, and Tilly Lipson (*née* Shandel); *m* 1st, 1938, Laurence Winston (*d* 1949); two *s* one *d*; 2nd, 1960, Goodwin Fox (*d* 1974). *Educ:* St Paul's Girls' Sch.; London Univ. BSc Household and Social Sci.; Home Office Child Care Cert. Mental Hosps Dept and Child Care Dept, LCC, 1936–39; Dep. Centre Organiser, WVS, Southgate, 1941–45; Southgate Borough Council: Member, 1945–65; Alderman, 1955–65; Mayor of Southgate, 1958–59, Dep. Mayor, 1959–61; Sen. Officer, Adoptions Consultant, Social Services Dept, Herts CC, 1949–77. Member: London Rent Assessment Panel and Tribunals, 1975–83; Review Cttee for Secure Accommodation, London Borough of Enfield, 1982; Bd of Deputies of British Jews, 1960– (Chm. Educn Cttee, 1974–80; voluntary nat. organiser, exhibn Jewish Way of Life, 1978, which visited 44 communities in Britain); Vice-Pres., Internat. Council of Jewish Women, 1974–81 (Chairman: Status of Women Cttee, 1966–75; Inter-Affiliate Travel Cttee, 1975–81); Mem. Governing Body, World Jewish Congress, 1981–; Co-Chm., Jewish Community Exhibn Centre, 1984–. Founder, one of first Day Centres for the Elderly in GB, Ruth Winston House, Southgate Old People's Centre, opened by Princess Alexandra, 1961, and again, 1972; Vice-President: Southgate Old People's Welfare Cttee, 1974–; Southgate Horticultural Soc.; President: League of Jewish Women, 1969–72; First Women's Lodge, England, 1972–74; Enfield Relate (formerly Enfield Marriage Guidance Council), 1984–. JP Middx Area GLC, 1954. *Publications:* articles only. *Recreations:* five grandchildren, travel, voluntary service. *Address:* 4 Morton Crescent, Southgate, N14 7AH. *T:* (020) 8886 5056. *Clubs:* University Women's, Bnai Brith.

See also Baron Winston.

WINSTONE, Dame Dorothy (Gertrude), DBE 1990; CMG 1976; *b* 23 Jan. 1919; *d* of Stanley Fowler and Constance May Fowler (*née* Sherwin); *m* 1941, Wilfrid Frank Winstone (*d* 2000); three *s* one *d*. *Educ:* Auckland Girls' Grammar Sch.; Auckland Teachers' Coll.; Auckland University Coll. (BA 1940; DipEd 1943); Univ. of Auckland (BTh 1998). Primary School Teacher, 1938; Asst Mistress, Seddon Memorial Tech. Coll., 1939–45; voluntary community worker, 1945–. Mem., Royal Commn on Contraception, Sterilisation and Abortion, 1975–77. Foundn Mem., NZ Envmtl Council, 1970–81. Dir, Virginia Gildersleeve Fund, Internat. Fedn of Univ. Women, 1993–2002. Member Emerita, NZ Fedn of Univ. Women, 1973; Life Mem., Nat. Council of Women of NZ, 1980. Hon. LLD Univ. of Auckland, 1983. Adelaide Ristori Medal, Centro Culturale Italiano, 1975; New Zealand Suffrage Centennial Medal, 1993. *Publications:* Everyday Words and Phrases, 1975; A Century of Service, 1985; Wesley Methodist Church 1938–1993, 1996. *Recreations:* reading, gardening, 13 grandchildren, 2 great grandsons. *Address:* 2A, 416 Remuera Road, Remuera, Auckland 1050, New Zealand. *T:* (9) 5203407.

WINTER, Rev. Canon David Brian; Team Minister, Hermitage Team Ministry, 1995–2000; Hon. Canon, Christ Church Cathedral, Oxford, 1995–2000, now Canon Emeritus; *b* 19 Nov. 1929; *s* of Walter George Winter and Winifred Ella Winter; *m* 1st, 1961, Christine Ellen Martin (*d* 2001); two *s* one *d*; 2nd, 2004, Rosalind Anne Lee. *Educ:* Machynlleth County Sch.; Trinity County Grammar Sch., Wood Green; King's Coll., Univ. of London (BA, PGCE). Nat. Service, RAF, 1948–50. Teacher: Ware CE Secondary Sch., 1954–58; Tottenham County Grammar Sch., 1958–59; Editor, Crusade, 1959–70; freelance writer and broadcaster, 1970–71; BBC: Producer, Religious Broadcasting, 1971–75, Sen. Producer, 1975–82; Hd of Religious Progs, Radio, and Dep. Hd, Religious Broadcasting, 1982–87; Hd of Religious Broadcasting, 1987–89. Chm., Arts Centre Gp, 1976–82. Oak Hill Ministerial Trng Course, 1985–87. Deacon, 1987, priest, 1988. Hon. Asst Curate, St Paul and St Luke, Finchley, 1987–89; Priest-in-Charge, Ducklington, 1989–95; Bishop's Officer for Evangelism, Dio. of Oxford, 1989–95. Editor, Bible Reading Fellowship, 1997–2001; Consulting Ed., People's Bible Commentary, 1998–2006. *Publications:* Ground of Truth, 1964; New Singer, New Song (biog. of Cliff Richard), 1967; (with S. Linden) Two a Penny, 1968; Closer than a Brother, 1971; Hereafter, 1972; (ed) Matthew Henry's Commentary on the New Testament, 1974; After the Gospels, 1977; But this I can believe, 1980; The Search for the Real Jesus, 1982; Truth in the Son, 1985; Living through Loss, 1985; Walking in the Light (confessions of St Augustine), 1986; Believing the Bible, 1987; Battered Bride, 1988; What happens after Death?, 1992; You Can Pray, 1993; What's in a Word, 1994; Mark for Starters, 1995; Where do we go from here?, 1996; Forty Days with the 'Messiah', 1996; Message for the Millennium, 1998; (ed) The Master Haunter (anthol.), 1998, re-issued as The Poets' Christ, 2000; Winter's Tale (autobiog.), 2001; With Jesus in the Upper Room, 2001; Hope in the Wilderness, 2003; Making Sense of the Bible, 2004; Old Words, New Life, 2005; The Nation's Favourite Prayers (anthol.), 2006; Journey to Jerusalem, 2007; Seasons of the Son, 2008; Pilgrim's Way, 2008. *Recreations:* watching cricket, opera, talking. *Address:* 47A Station Road, Thatcham, Berks RG19 4PU. *T:* 07971 534988.

WINTER, Prof. (David) Michael, OBE 2005; PhD; Professor of Rural Policy and Director, Centre for Rural Policy Research (formerly Centre for Rural Research), University of Exeter, since 2002; *b* 10 Nov. 1955; *s* of David Winter and Nanette Winter (*née* Wellsteed); *m* 1979, Hilary Susan Thomas; one *s* one *d*. *Educ:* Peter Symonds Coll., Winchester; Wye Coll., London (BSc Rural Envmt Studies 1977); Open Univ. (PhD 1986). Res. Asst, Univ. of Exeter, 1980–82; Res. Officer, Univ. of Bath, 1983–87; Dir, Centre for Rural Studies, RAC, Cirencester, 1987–93; Reader, then Prof., Countryside and Community Res. Unit, Cheltenham and Gloucester Coll. of Higher Educn, 1993–2001; Hd, Sch. of Geog., Archaeol. and Earth Resources, Univ. of Exeter, 2003–05. Member Board: Countryside Agency, 2005–06; Commn for Rural Communities, 2006–. Chm., 2001–04, Vice-Chm., 2004–, Hatherleigh Area Proj.; Chm., South West Rural Affairs Forum, 2002–07; Pres., Devon Rural Network, 2006– (Chm., 2002–06); Vice

Pres., Community Council of Devon, 2008–. Res. Associate, Inst. of Grassland and Envmtl Res., 1998– (Mem., Bd of Govs, 2006–08). Lay Canon, Exeter Cathedral, 2008–. *Publications:* (ed jtly) Agriculture: people and policies, 1986; (jtly) Countryside Conflicts, 1986; (ed with M. Bouquet) Who From Their Labours Rest, 1987; (jtly) The Voluntary Principle in Conservation, 1990; (jtly) Church and Religion in Rural England, 1991; Rural Politics, 1996; (with P. Gaskell) The Effects of the 1992 Reform of the Common Agricultural Policy on the Countryside of Great Britain, 1998. *Recreations:* gardening, sheep, hedge-laying, walking, choral singing, music, Church, community, reading, family. *Address:* Centre for Rural Policy Research, University of Exeter, Department of Politics, Amory Building, Rennes Drive, Exeter EX4 4RJ. *T:* (01392) 263837; *e-mail:* d.m.winter@exeter.ac.uk. *Club:* Royal Over-Seas League.

WINTER, Sir Gregory (Paul), Kt 2004; CBE 1997; PhD; FRS 1990; FTSE; Deputy Director: Medical Research Council Laboratory of Molecular Biology, since 2006 (Acting Director, 2007–08); Centre for Protein Engineering, since 1990; Senior Research Fellow, Trinity College, Cambridge, since 1991; *b* 14 April 1951; *m* 1974, Fiona Jane Winter (marr. diss. 2002); one *s* three *d*. *Educ:* Royal Grammar Sch., Newcastle-upon-Tyne; Trinity College, Cambridge (BA Natural Scis 1973; MA; PhD 1976). FTSE 2002. Postgrad. studies in protein chem., Cambridge, 1973–76; Fellow, Trinity College, Cambridge (structure of genes and influenza virus), 1976–80; MRC-LMB (protein and antibody engineering), 1981–, Jt Hd, Div. of Protein and Nucleic Acid Chemistry, 1994–2008. FMedSci 2006. Hon. FRCP 2003. Dr *hc* Nantes, 2001; Hon. Dr rer. nat. ETH Zurich, 2002. Novo Biotechnology Award, Denmark, 1986; Colworth Medal, Biochem. Soc., 1986; Behring Prize, FRG, 1989; Louis Jeantet Foundn Award for Medicine, Switzerland, 1989; Pfizer Award, 1989; Milano Award, Italy, 1990; Scheele Award, Swedish Acad. of Pharmaceutical Scis, 1994; Biochemical Analysis Prize, German Soc. for Clin. Chem., 1995; King Faisal Internat. Prize in Medicine, 1995; William B. Coley Award, Cancer Res. Inst., USA, 1999; Jacob Heskel Gabbay Award in Biotechnol. and Medicine, Brandeis Univ., 2002; Jean-Pierre Lecocq Award, Acad. of Scis, France, 2002; Nat. Biotechnology Ventures Award, USA, 2004; Baly Medal, RCP, 2005; Biochemical Soc. Award, 2006. *Publications:* articles in learned jls on protein and gene structure, enzymes, viral proteins and antibodies. *Address:* Medical Research Council Laboratory of Molecular Biology, Hills Road, Cambridge CB2 0QH.

WINTER, Henry Oliver; Football Correspondent, Daily Telegraph, since 1994; *b* London, 18 Feb. 1963; *s* of John and Valerie Winter; *m* 1992, Catriona Elliott; one *s* one *d*. *Educ:* The Hall, Hampstead; Westminster Sch.; Edinburgh Univ. (MA Hist.); London Coll. of Printing (Cert. Journalism). Sports journalist, The Independent, 1987–94. Columnist, 4-4-2 Mag., 2000–; contrib. Sky Sports, BBC TV and Radio. *Publications:* (with D. Davies) FA Confidential, 2008; ghost writer: Kenny Dalglish: My Autobiography, 1997; John Barnes: The Autobiography, 1999; Steven Gerrard: The Autobiography, 2006. *Recreations:* marathon-running, visiting WW II museums, cycling round Rutland Water, singing out of tune. *Address:* Daily Telegraph, 111 Buckingham Palace Road, SW1W 0DT. *T:* (020) 7931 2600.

WINTER, Michael; *see* Winter, D. M.

WINTER, Peter John, MA; Head, Latymer Upper School, since 2002; *b* 10 July 1950; *s* of Jack Winter and Ursula Winter (*née* Riddington); *m* 1979, Jennifer Adwoa; one *s* one *d*. *Educ:* Trinity Sch., Croydon; Wadham Coll., Oxford (MA French); Univ. of Reading (PGCE). Asst teacher, French and German, Latymer Upper Sch., 1973–79; Head of Modern Langs, Magdalen Coll. Sch., Oxford, 1979–86; Head of Modern Langs, 1986–90, Housemaster, Internat. Centre, 1987–93, Sevenoaks Sch.; Headmaster, King Edward's Sch., Bath, 1993–2002. *Recreations:* Chelsea FC, Test Match cricket, playing golf, France. *Address:* Latymer Upper School, King Street, Hammersmith, W6 9LR.

WINTER, Robert; Lord-Lieutenant and Lord Provost of Glasgow, since 2007; *b* 31 March 1937; *s* of Thomas Rickaby Winter and Dona Smillie McKendrick Winter; *m* 1983, Sheena Morgan Duncan; four *s* one *d*. CSW; DPA. Dir of Social Work, Greenock and Port Glasgow, 1969–75; Dep. Dir of Social Work, 1975–95, Dir of Social Work, 1995–96, Strathclyde Regl Council; Sec., Assoc. of Dirs of Social Work, 1996–99. Mem., GMC, 1996–2005. Mem., Gtr Glasgow Health Bd PCT, 1996–2005 (Chm. Panel, until 2007). Convener, Risk Mgt Authy, 2004–. Mem. (Lab), Glasgow City Council, 1999–2007. *Recreations:* walking, swimming, reading, football spectation. *Address:* Glasgow City Council, City Chambers, George Square, Glasgow G2 1DU. *T:* (0141) 287 4201, *Fax:* (0141) 287 0127; *e-mail:* robert.winter@councillors.glasgow.gov.uk.

WINTER, Dr Robert James David, FRCP; Consultant Respiratory Physician, Addenbrooke's Hospital and Papworth Hospital, Cambridge, since 2000; Medical Director, NHS East of England, since 2008; *b* 11 March 1953; *s* of David Winter and Margery Joan Winter; *m* 1984, Elizabeth Jane Sowton (marr. diss. 2005); two *d*. *Educ:* Clifton Coll., Bristol; Royal Free Hosp. Sch. of Medicine, Univ. of London (BSc 1974; MB BS 1977; MD 1987). MRCP 1979, FRCP 1995. Registrar, UCL, 1981–84; MRC Trng Fellow, 1984–86; Sen. Registrar, Hammersmith Hosp., 1986–91; Consultant Physician, Barnet Hosp., 1991–2000; Med. Dir, Addenbrooke's NHS Trust, subseq. Cambridge Univ. Hosps NHS Foundn Trust, 2002–08. Associate Lectr, Univ. of Cambridge, 2001–. Mem. Exec. Cttee, and Trustee, British Lung Foundn, 1992–2002; Trustee, Fund for Addenbrooke's, 2002–. *Publications:* chapters and articles in med. books and jls on gen. medicine, respiratory medicine and respiratory physiol. *Recreations:* music, walking. *Address:* Box 149, Addenbrooke's Hospital, Hills Road, Cambridge CB2 2QQ. *T:* (01223) 217996, *Fax:* (01223) 216056; *e-mail:* robert.winter@addenbrookes.nhs.uk; 29 High Street, Barrington, Cambridge CB22 7QX.

WINTER, Sophie; *see* Raworth, S.

WINTERBOTTOM, Prof. Michael, MA, DPhil; FBA 1978; Corpus Christi Professor of Latin, University of Oxford, 1993–2001; Fellow, Corpus Christi College, Oxford, 1993–2001, now Emeritus; *b* 22 Sept. 1934; *s* of Allan Winterbottom and Kathleen Mary (*née* Wallis); *m* 1st, 1963, Helen Spencer (marr. diss. 1983); two *s*; 2nd, 1986, Nicolette Janet Streatfeild Bergel. *Educ:* Dulwich Coll.; Pembroke Coll., Oxford. 1st Cl. Hon. Mods and Craven Schol., 1954; 1st Cl. Lit. Hum. and Derby Schol., 1956; Domus Sen. Schol., Merton Coll., 1958–59; MA 1959, DPhil 1964 (Oxon). Research Lectr, Christ Church, 1959–62; Lectr in Latin and Greek, University Coll. London, 1962–67; Fellow and Tutor in Classics, Worcester Coll., Oxford, 1967–92; Reader in Classical Langs, Univ. of Oxford, 1990–92. D*hc* Besançon, 1985. *Publications:* (ed) Quintilian, 1970; (with D. A. Russell) Ancient Literary Criticism, 1972; Three Lives of English Saints, 1972; (ed and trans.) The Elder Seneca, 1974; (ed with R. M. Ogilvie) Tacitus, *Opera Minora*, 1975; (ed and trans.) Gildas, 1978; Roman Declamation, 1980; (ed with commentary) The Minor Declamations ascribed to Quintilian, 1984; (with D. C. Innes) Sopatros the Rhetor, 1988; (with M. Brett and C. N. L. Brooke) rev. edn of Charles Johnson (ed), Hugh the Chanter, 1990; (ed) Cicero, *De Officiis*, 1994; (ed with R. A. B. Mynors and R. M. Thomson) William of Malmesbury, *Gesta Regum Anglorum*, 1998; (ed with R. M. Thomson) William of Malmesbury, Saints' Lives, 2002; (ed with T. Reinhardt) Quintilian Book 2, 2006; (ed) William of Malmesbury, *Gesta Pontificum Anglorum*, vol. 1, 2007; articles and reviews in jls. *Recreations:* hill walking, geology. *Address:* 53 Thorncliffe Road, Oxford OX2 7BA. *T:* (01865) 513066.

WINTERFLOOD, Brian Martin; Founder, 1988, and Chairman, since 2002, Winterflood Securities Ltd (Managing Director, 1988–99; Chief Executive Officer, 1999–2002); Chief Executive Officer, Winterflood Gilts, 1999–2002 (Managing Director, 1994–99); Chairman, Gilts and Securities, since 2001; *b* 31 Jan. 1937; *s* of late Thomas G. Winterflood and of Doris M. Winterflood; *m* 1966, Doreen Stella McCartney; two *s* one *d*. *Educ:* Fray's Coll., Uxbridge. National Service, 1955–57. Greener Dreyfus & Co., 1953–55; Bisgood Bishop & Co. Ltd, 1957–85: Partner, 1967–71; Dir, 1971–81; Man. Dir, 1981–85; Man. Dir, County Bisgood, 1985–86; County NatWest Securities Ltd: Dir, 1986–87; Exec. Dir, 1986–88, resigned, 1988. Director: Union Discount Co. of London, 1991–93; Close Brothers Group, 1993–2002; PROSHARE, 1998–; Monument Securities, 2002–. Jt Chm., Cttee of USM Initiative, Prince's Youth Bus. Trust, 1989–92. Member: City Gp for Smaller Cos, now Quoted Cos Alliance, 1992– (Mem. Exec. Cttee, 1992–96); City Disputes Practitioners Panel, 1994–; AIM Adv. Cttee, 1995–; AIM Appeals Cttee, 1995–98; Non FTSE 100 Wkg Party Cttee, 1996–; Secondary Markets Cttee, 1996–; UK Adv. Bd, EASD, 2000–; Market Adv. Cttee, EASD, 2000–. Mem. Cttee, October Club, 1993–; Trustee, Stock Exchange Benevolent Fund, 1995–; Pres., Securities Industry Mgt Assoc., 2004. Pres., Rehabilitation and Med. Res. Trust, 1998– (Vice Pres., 1989); Vice-Pres., Save the Children, 2004; Vice-Chm., Lord Mayor's Appeal, 2004. Gov., Reeds Sch., 2002– (Pres., Sch. Appeal, 1997–98). Member: Guild of Internat. Bankers, 2002–; Order of St George, 2002–; Heart of the City, 2003–. Freeman, City of London, 2002. FSI 1997. PLC Achievement Award, Price Waterhouse Coopers, 1994. *Recreations:* family, work, travel. *Address:* Winterflood Securities Ltd, The Atrium Building, Cannon Bridge, 25 Dowgate Hill, EC4R 2GA. *T:* (020) 7621 0004. *Club:* City of London.

WINTERSGILL, Dr William, FFPH; Examining Medical Officer (part-time), Department of Health, since 1989; Member, Research and Advisory Committee, Cambridge Applied Nutrition, Toxicology and Biosciences Ltd, since 1984; *b* 20 Dec. 1922; *s* of Fred Wintersgill and May Wintersgill; *m* 1952, Iris May Holland; three *d*. *Educ:* Barnsley Holgate Grammar Sch.; Leeds Medical Sch., Univ. of Leeds (MB, ChB). MRCGP; MFCM, FFCM 1983. House Surgeon, 1948, and Registrar, 1948–49, Pontefract Infirmary; Principal, Gen. Practice, Snaith, Yorks, 1950–66; Dept of Health and Social Security (formerly Min. of Health): Reg. MO, 1967–70; SMO, 1970–72; PMO, 1972–76; SPMO, 1976–83. Specialist in Community Medicine, York HA, 1983–89. Pt-time MO, Cttee on Safety of Medicines, 1987–; Mem., Health Adv. Service Vis. Team, 1987–90; Dist Med. Advr, 1987–88. Chm., British Assoc. of Community Physicians, 1985–89. *Recreations:* gardening, antique collecting, playing the piano, choral singing, painting, old buildings. *Address:* The Latchetts, Eardisland, Leominster HR6 9BE.

WINTERSON, Jeanette, OBE 2006; writer; *b* 27 Aug. 1959. *Educ:* St Catherine's Coll., Oxford (BA Hons English). Internat. Fiction Award, Fest. Letteratura, Italy, 1999. *Publications:* Oranges are not the only fruit, 1985 (Whitbread Prize, 1st Novel; numerous awards for screenplay, televised 1990); The Passion, 1987 (John Llewellyn Rhys Prize); Sexing the Cherry, 1989 (E. M. Forster Award, Amer. Acad. and Inst. of Arts and Letters); Written on the Body, 1992; Art and Lies, 1994; Great Moments in Aviation (screenplay), 1994; Art Objects: essays on ecstasy and effrontery, 1995; Gut Symmetries, 1997; The World and Other Places (short stories), 1998; The Powerbook, 2000 (adapted for stage, 2002); The King of Capri (for children), 2002; Lighthousekeeping, 2004; Weight, 2005; Tanglewreck (for children), 2006; The Stone Gods, 2007; The Lion, the Unicorn, and Me (for children), 2009; (ed) Midsummer Nights: new stories/old dreams (short stories), 2009. *Recreations:* opera, ballet, champagne. *Address:* c/o Great Moments Ltd, 40 Brushfield Street, E1 6AG; *e-mail:* mail@jeanettewinterson.com.

WINTERTON, 8th Earl *cr* 1766 (Ire.); **(Donald) David Turnour;** Baron Winterton 1761 (Ire.); Viscount Turnour 1766 (Ire.); *b* 13 Oct. 1943; *s* of Cecil Noel Turnour, DFM, CD (*d* 1987), *yr b* of 7th Earl Winterton and of Evelyn Isabel, *d* of Dr C. A. Oulton; *S* uncle, 1991; *m* 1st, 1968, Jill Pauline (marr. diss. 1997), *d* of late John Geddes Esplen; two *d*; 2nd, 2004, Vecide Brigitte Aktelligul. *Educ:* Waterloo Lutheran Univ., Ontario (BA). *Heir: b* Robert Charles Turnour [*b* 30 Jan. 1950; *m* 1st, 1974, Sheila (marr. diss. 1976), *d* of G. H. Stocking; 2nd, 1983, Patricia Ann, *d* of William Avery; two *d*].

WINTERTON, (Jane) Ann, (Lady Winterton); MP (C) Congleton, since 1983; *b* 6 March 1941; *d* of late Joseph Robert Hodgson and Ellen Jane Hodgson; *m* 1960, Nicholas Raymond Winterton (*see* Sir N. R. Winterton); two *s* one *d*. *Educ:* Erdington Grammar Sch. for Girls. Opposition spokesman on nat. drug strategy, 1998–2001; Shadow Minister for Agriculture and Fisheries, 2001–02. Mem., Chairmen's Panel, 1992–98, 2005–. Chm., 1992–2002, Vice-Chm., 2002–, All Party Parly Pro-Life Gp. Fellow, Industry and Parlt Trust, 1987–. Pres., Congleton Div., St John Ambulance, 1984–; Vice Pres., Townswomen's Guilds, 1994–2004. *Recreations:* music, theatre, tennis, ski-ing. *Address:* House of Commons, SW1A 0AA.

WINTERTON, Nicholas Hugh, OBE 2003; Executive Director (formerly Administrative Secretary), Medical Research Council, since 1995; *b* 1 May 1947; *s* of Deryck Winterton and Margaret Winterton (*née* Simms). *Educ:* Chislehurst and Sidcup GS for Boys; Sidney Sussex Coll., Cambridge (BA 1968, MA 1971; DipEcon 1969). Medical Research Council: various admin. posts, 1969–81; Head of Personnel, 1981–88; on secondment to Wellcome Foundn, Dartford, 1988–89; Director: Corporate Affairs, 1989–94; Finance, 1994–95. Director: UK Med. Ventures Mgt Ltd, 1998–2006; Hammersmith Imanet (formerly Imaging Research Solutions) Ltd, 2001–; RCUK Shared Services Centre Ltd; Chm. Bd, MRC Technol., 2000–. Non-exec. Dir, Royal Free Hampstead NHS Trust, 1998– (Vice-Chm., 2003–). Chairman, Trustees: Bridge Theatre Trng Co., 1995–2006; Vinjeru (Educn Concern Malawi), 1999–. *Recreations:* gardening, travel, walking, theatre. *Address:* Medical Research Council, 20 Park Crescent, W1B 1AL. *T:* (020) 7637 6016.

WINTERTON, Sir Nicholas (Raymond), Kt 2002; DL; MP (C) Macclesfield, since Sept. 1971; *b* 31 March 1938; *o s* of late N. H. Winterton, Lysways House, Longdon Green, near Rugeley, Staffs; *m* 1960, Jane Ann Hodgson (*see* J. A. Winterton); two *s* one *d*. *Educ:* Bilton Grange Prep. Sch.; Rugby Sch. Commnd 14th/20th King's Hussars, 1957–59. Sales Exec. Trainee, Shell-Mex and BP Ltd, 1959–60; Sales and Gen. Manager, Stevens and Hodgson Ltd, Birmingham (Co. engaged in sale and hire of construction equipment), 1960–71. Chairman: CPC Cttee, Meriden Cons. Assoc., 1966–68; Midland Branch, Contractors Mech. Plant Engrs Assoc., 1968–69. Member: W Midlands Cons. Council, 1966–69, 1971–72; Central Council, Nat. Union of Cons. and Unionist Assocs, 1971–72. Contested (C) Newcastle-under-Lyme, Oct. 1969, 1970. Chairman: Select Cttee on Health, 1991–92; Select Cttee on Procedure, 1997–2005; Member: Social Services Select Cttee, 1980–90; Select Cttee on Modernisation of H of C, 1997–; Liaison Select Cttee, 1997–2005; Chairmen's Panel, 1986–. Additional Dep. Speaker, for sittings in Westminster Hall, 1998–2005. Chairman, All Party Parliamentary: Gp for Cotton and

Allied Textiles, 1979–97; Gp for Media, 1992–2000; British Danish Gp, 1992–; British Falklands Is Gp, 1997–; British Bahamas Gp, 1997–; British Austria Gp, 1999–; Joint Chairman: All Party Parly British Taiwan Gp, 1997–; W Coast Mainline Gp, 2001–; Vice Chairman, All Party Parliamentary: British Swedish Gp, 1992–; British Indonesian Gp, 1992–2000; Anglo S Pacific Gp, 1997–; Road Transport Study Gp, 1997–2001; Clothing and Textiles Gp, 1997–; Manchester 2002 XVII Commonwealth Games Gp, 2000–02. Member Executive: 1922 Cttee, 1997–2001 (Vice-Chm., 2001–05; Treas., 2005–); UK Br., CPA, 1997–; Mem., Exec. Cttee, IPU, 2001– (Treas., 2007–). Member: Exec. Cttee, Anglo-Austrian Soc., 1987–2000 (Chm., 1998–2000); Nat. Adv. Cttee, Duke of Edinburgh Award Scheme, 1973–99; Imperial Soc. of Knights Bachelor, 2002–. County Councillor, Atherstone Div. Warwickshire CC, 1967–72. President: Macclesfield Fermain Club, 1973–; Poynton Youth and Community Centre, 1971–; Upton Priory Youth Club, Macclesfield, 1992–2001; Vice-President: Macclesfield and Congleton District Scout Council; Cheshire Scout Assoc.; E Cheshire Hospice; Nat. Assoc. of Local Councils, 1979–2001; Royal Coll. of Midwives; Nat. Assoc. of Master Bakers, Confectioners and Caterers; N Cheshire Cruising Club. Hon. Mem., Macclesfield Lions Club; Hon. Life Mem., Macclesfield Rugby Union Football Club; Pres., Macclesfield Hockey Club; Patron: Macclesfield and District Sheep Dog Trials Assoc., 1972–; Internat. Centre for Child Care Studies, 1980–94; Civit Hills Open Air Theatre, 1996–2001; Elizabeth Trust, 1983–94; E Cheshire Br., Alzheimer's Soc., 1998–. President, Macclesfield Branch: Riding for the Disabled, 1987–; Multiple Sclerosis Soc., 1987–. Founder Pres., Bollington Light Opera Gp, 1978–. Life Mem., Poynton Gilbert and Sullivan Soc. Liveryman, Past Upper Bailiff and Mem. of Court, Weavers' Co.; Freeman of the City of London. Hon. Freeman, Borough of Macclesfield, 2002. DL Cheshire, 2006. *Recreations:* Rugby football, squash, hockey, tennis, swimming, horse riding, reading, walking. *Address:* House of Commons, SW1A 0AA. *Clubs:* Cavalry and Guards, Lighthouse; Lords and Commons Tennis; Old Boys and Park Green (Macclesfield).

WINTERTON, Rt Hon. Rosalie, (Rt Hon. Rosie); PC 2006; MP (Lab) Doncaster Central, since 1997; Minister of State, Department for Work and Pensions, and Minister for Yorkshire and the Humber, since 2008; *b* 10 Aug. 1958; *d* of Gordon and Valerie Winterton. *Educ:* Doncaster Grammar Sch.; Hull Univ. (BA Hons Hist.). Asst to John Prescott, MP, 1980–86; Parliamentary Officer: London Borough of Southwark, 1986–88; RCN, 1988–90; Man. Dir, Connect Public Affairs, 1990–94; Hd, private office of John Prescott, MP, 1994–97. Parly Sec., LCD, 2001–03; Minister of State: DoH, 2003–07; DfT, 2007–08. *Recreations:* sailing, reading. *Address:* House of Commons, SW1A 0AA.

WINTLE, Rev. Canon Ruth Elizabeth; Hon. Assistant Priest, St John-in-Bedwardine, 1994–2006 (Parish Deacon, 1984–94); Canon Emeritus, Worcester Cathedral, since 1998 (Hon. Canon, 1987–97); *b* 30 Sept. 1931; *d* of John Wintle and Vera (*née* Lane). *Educ:* Clarendon Sch., Malvern, and Abergele, Wales; Westfield Coll., London (BA Hons French 1953); St Hugh's Coll., Oxford (MA Theol. 1972); St Michael's House, Oxford (IDC 1966). Teacher, St Hilda's Sch., Jamaica, 1953–60; Travelling Sec., Inter-Varsity Fellowship and Technical Colls Christian Fellowship, 1960–63; Accredited Lay Worker, St Andrew's Church, N Oxford, 1967–69; Tutor, St John's Coll., Durham, 1969–74; Deaconess (C of E), 1972; Selection Sec., ACCM, 1974–83; Organiser, Internat. Diakonia Conf., Coventry, 1983; Diocesan Dir of Ordinands, Worcester, 1984–92; ordained deacon, 1987, priest 1994; Bishop's Advr on Women's Ministry, Worcester, 1995–97. Mem., Third Order, SSF, 1990–. Mem., Bishop's Staff Meeting, Worcs, 1993–97. Member: Church Army Bd, 1985–2000; Crown Appointments Commn, 1990–95; Gen. Synod of C of E, 1990–95; Council, Retired Clergy Assoc., 1998–2004. Mem. Council, Malvern Coll., 1991–2000. Chm., Li Tim-Oi Foundn, 1993–2006. *Recreations:* reading, driving, ornithology. *Address:* 6 Kenswick Manor, Lower Broadheath, Worcester WR2 6QB. *T:* (01905) 641470.

WINTON, Alexander, CBE 1993; QFSM 1987; HM Chief Inspector of Fire Services for Scotland, 1990–93; *b* 13 July 1932; *s* of Alexander and Jean Winton; *m* 1957, Jean Dowie; two *s*. MIFireE. Fireman, Perth, 1958–64; Station Officer: Perth, 1964–67; Lancashire, 1967–69; Assistant Divisional Officer: E Riding, 1969–72; Angus, 1972–73; Divisional Officer III: Angus, 1973–75; Tayside, 1975–76; Divl Comdr (DOI), Tayside, 1976–80; Temp. Sen. Divl Officer, 1980–81; Dep. Firemaster, 1981–85; Firemaster, Tayside Fire Bde, 1985–89. *Recreations:* golf, curling, reading. *Address:* 5 Ferndale Drive, Broughty Ferry, Dundee DD5 3DB. *T:* (01382) 778156.

WINTON, Sir Nicholas (George), Kt 2003; MBE 1983; *b* 19 May 1909; *s* of Rudolf and Barbara Winton; *m* 1948, Grete Gjelstrup; one *s* one *d* (and one *s* decd). *Educ:* Stowe Sch. (founder mem. 1923). Banking, 1928–31; Mem., Stock Exchange, 1931–39; Internat. Refugee Orgn, 1946–48; International Bank, 1948–49; company director, 1950–68. President: Maidenhead Mencap, 1972–; Abbeyfield Maidenhead, 1986–. Mem., Probus Club. Freedom of Borough, Windsor and Maidenhead, 1999. Order of Tomas Masaryk (Czech Republic), 1998. *Recreations:* gardening, music, tapestry, travelling. *Address:* New Ditton, Pinkneys Green, Maidenhead SL6 6NT. *T:* (01628) 626613. *Club:* Rotary (Maidenhead) (Pres., 1972–73).

WINTOUR, Anna, OBE 2008; Editor, US Vogue, since 1988; *b* 3 Nov. 1949; *d* of late Charles Vere Wintour, CBE; *m* 1984, Dr David Shaffer (marr. diss.); one *s* one *d*. *Educ:* Queen's College Sch., London; North London Collegiate Sch. Dep. Fashion Editor, Harpers and Queen Magazine, 1970–76; Fashion Editor, Harpers Bazaar, NY, 1976–77; Fashion and Beauty Editor, Viva Mag., 1977–78; Contributing Editor for Fashion and Style, Savvy Mag., 1980–81; Sen. Editor, New York Mag., NY, 1981–83; Creative Dir, US Vogue, 1983–86; Editor-in-Chief, Vogue, 1986–87; Editor, House and Garden, New York, 1987–88.

See also P. Wintour.

WINTOUR, Patrick; Political Editor, The Guardian, since 2006; *b* 1 Nov. 1954; *s* of late Charles Vere Wintour, CBE and Eleanor Trego Wintour (*née* Baker); *m* 2002, Rachel Sylvester; two *s*, and one *s* one *d* by a previous marriage. *Educ:* Hall Sch., London; Westminster Sch.; Corpus Christi Coll., Oxford (BA). Journalist, New Statesman, 1976–82; The Guardian: Chief Labour Correspondent, 1983–88; Chief Political Correspondent, 1988–96 and 2000–06; Political Ed., The Observer, 1996–2000. *Publications:* Eddie Shah and the Newspaper Revolution, 1985; Labour Rebuilt, 1990. *Recreations:* piano, gardening. *Address:* The Guardian, Kings Place, 90 York Way, N1 9AG; *e-mail:* Patrick.Wintour@guardian.co.uk. *Club:* Soho House.

See also A. Wintour.

WINYARD, Dr Graham Peter Arthur, CBE 1999; FRCP; FFPH; Consultant Adviser to Defence Medical Services, 2001–07; *b* 19 Jan. 1947; *s* of Lyonel Arthur Winyard and Dorothy Elizabeth Payne; *m* 1st, 1979, Sandra Catherine Bent (*d* 2002); one *s* two *d*; 2nd, 2006, Jill Saltmarsh. *Educ:* Southend High Sch.; Hertford Coll., Oxford (MA); Middlesex Hosp. (BM, BCh). Sen. House Officer, United Oxford Hosps, 1973–75; Registrar in Community Medicine, 1975–77; Provincial Health Officer, Madang, PNG, 1977–79; Sen. Registrar in Community Medicine, Oxford RHA, and Lectr, LSHTM, 1979–82; Dist MO, Lewisham and N Southwark HA, 1982–87; SPMO, DHSS, later Dept of Health, 1987–90; Regl Med. Dir and Dir of Public Health, Wessex RHA, 1990–93; Dep. CMO and Dir Health Services, NHS Exec., DoH, 1993–98; Postgrad. Dean, Wessex Deanery, DoH, 1999–2007. Hon. Prof. of Public Health Mgt, Univ. of Southampton, 1999–2007. Vice-Pres., FPH, 2004–07; Chm., Cttee of Postgrad. Deans UK, 2004–07. *Publications:* various on med. care in med. jls. *Recreations:* meditation, gardening, DIY, music.

WISBECH, Archdeacon of; *see* McCurdy, Ven. H. K.

WISDOM, Sir Norman, Kt 2000; OBE 1995; actor/comedian; *b* 4 Feb. 1915. Has starred regularly on stage and screen, since 1952. First film Trouble in Store, in 1953 (winning an Academy Award) since which has starred in 19 major films in both England and America; two Broadway awards for stage musical, Walking Happy; numerous Royal Performances, both film and stage. Freeman: Tirana, Albania, 1995; City of London, 1995. Lifetime Achievement Award for Comedy, British Comedy Awards, 1991. *Publication:* (with William Hall) Don't Laugh at Me, 1992. *Recreations:* all sports. *Address:* c/o Johnny Mans, Johnny Mans Productions Ltd, PO Box 196, Hoddesdon, Herts EN10 7WG.

WISE, family name of **Baron Wise**.

WISE, 2nd Baron *cr* 1951, of King's Lynn; **John Clayton Wise;** farmer; *b* 11 June 1923; *s* of 1st Baron Wise and Kate Elizabeth (*d* 1987), *e d* of late John Michael Sturgeon; *S* father, 1968; *m* 1st, 1946, Margaret Annie (marr. diss. 1986), *d* of Frederick Victor Snead, Banbury; two *s*; 2nd, 1993, Janice Harman Thompson (marr. diss. 1998). *Heir:* *s* Hon. Christopher John Clayton Wise, PhD, BSc Hons [*b* 19 March 1949. *Educ:* Norwich School; Univ. of Southampton. Plant Scientist].

WISE, Prof. Christopher Mark, RDI 1998; FREng; Co-founder and Director, Expedition Engineering, since 1999; *b* 2 Nov. 1956; *s* of Jeffery and Jean Wise; one *s* by Elspeth Beard; two *s* by Catherine Ramsden. *Educ:* Reigate Grammar Sch.; Univ. of Southampton (BSc Hons 1979). MIStructE 1985; FREng 2003. Joined Ove Arup and Partners, Consulting Engrs, 1979; Dir, Ove Arup Partnership, 1993–99; *projects* include: Torre de Collserola, Barcelona, 1992; Channel 4 HQ, 1995; Commerzbank HQ, Frankfurt, 1996; American Air Mus., Duxford, 1997; Millennium Bridge, London, 2000. Prof. of Civil Engrg Design, ICSTM, 1998–99; Davenport Prof., Sch. of Architecture, Yale Univ., 2006. Mem., Design Council, 2005–. Reconstructions of Roman technology, for Secrets of Lost Empires series, BBC2: Colosseum, 1996; Caesar's Bridge, 1999. Master, Faculty of RDI, 2007–09. FRSA 1995. Guthrie Brown Award, 1993, Oscar Faber Medal, 1996, IStructE; Silver Medal, RAEng, 2007. *Publications:* papers on engrg educn projects in IStructE jl. *Recreations:* abstract painting, guitar, rock and ice climbing, soccer. *Address:* Expedition Engineering, Morley House, 1st Floor, 320 Regent Street, W1B 3BB.

WISE, Prof. Douglass, OBE 1980; FRIBA; Principal, Douglass Wise & Partners, Architects, since 1959; Director, Institute of Advanced Architectural Studies, University of York, 1975–92; *b* 6 Nov. 1927; *s* of Horace Watson Wise and Doris Wise; *m* 1958, Yvonne Jeannine Czeiler (marr. diss. 1985); one *s* one *d*. *Educ:* King's Coll., Newcastle, Durham Univ. (BArch; DipTP). Lecturer in Architecture, 1959–65, Prof. of Architecture, 1965–69, Head of Dept of Architecture, 1969–75, Newcastle Univ. RIBA: Chm., Moderators, 1969–75; Chm., Examinations Cttee, 1969–75; Mem. Council, 1976–79; Chm., Heads of Schools Cttee, 1971–73; Mem. Bd of Management, North Eastern Housing Assoc., 1967–76 (Vice-Chm., 1974–76); Mem. Council, Newcastle Polytechnic, 1974–77; past Mem. Council, Senate and Court, Newcastle Univ.; Governor, Building Centre Trust, London, 1976–92; Chairman: NE Civic Trust, 1993–2002; Northern Regl Centre for the Built Envmt, 1994–98. Hon. LittD Sheffield, 1992. *Publications:* contribs to various technical jls on housing, continuing educn and architectural theory. *Recreations:* painting, natural history. *Address:* Welburn, Kirkwhelpington, Newcastle upon Tyne NE19 2SA. *T:* (01830) 540219.

WISE, Fiona; Chief Executive, North West London Hospitals NHS Trust, 2007; *b* 1 Aug. 1954; *d* of Duncan and Doreen Lamond; *m*; two *s*. *Educ:* Haberdashers' Aske's Girls' Sch., Acton; St Mary's Grammar Sch., Northwood. DipHSM. Dep. Unit Gen. Manager, Royal Free Hosp., 1984–88; Unit Gen. Manager, Enfield Priority and Community Care, 1988–93; Chief Exec., Enfield Community Care NHS Trust, 1993–2001; interim Chief Exec., Stoke Mandeville Hosp. NHS Trust, 2001–03; Actg Dir of Modernisation, Beds and Herts Strategic HA, 2003; Chief Exec., Ealing Hosp. NHS Trust, 2003–07. *Recreations:* family, tennis, cooking. *Address:* North West London Hospitals NHS Trust, Northwick Park Hospital, Watford Road, Harrow, Middx, HA1 3UJ.

WISE, Prof. Michael John, CBE 1979; MC 1945; PhD; FRGS; Emeritus Professor of Geography, University of London; *b* Stafford, 17 Aug. 1918; *s* of Harry Cuthbert and Sarah Evelyn Wise; *m* 1942, Barbara Mary (*d* 2007), *d* of C. L. Hodgetts, Wolverhampton; one *d* one *s*. *Educ:* Saltley Secondary School, Birmingham; University of Birmingham (BA (Hons Geography) and Mercator Prize in Geography, 1939; DipEd 1940; PhD 1951). Served War, Royal Artillery, 80th LAA Regt, 1941–44, 5th Bn The Northamptonshire Regt, 1944–46, in Middle East and Italy; commissioned, 1941, Major, 1944. Assistant Lecturer, Univ. of Birmingham, 1946–48, Lecturer in Geography, 1948–51; London School of Economics: Lecturer in Geography, 1951–54; Sir Ernest Cassel Reader in Economic Geography, 1954–58; Prof. of Geography, 1958–83; Pro-Director, 1983–85; Hon. Fellow, 1988. Chm., Departmental Cttee of Inquiry into Statutory Smallholdings, 1963–67; Mem., Dept of Transport Adv. Cttee on Landscape Treatment of Trunk Roads, 1971–90 (Chm., 1981–90). Mem., UGC for Hong Kong, 1966–73. Recorder, Sect. E, Brit. Assoc. for Advancement of Science, 1955–60 (Pres., 1965); Founder Pres., Transport Studies Soc., 1962; President: Inst. of British Geographers, 1974 (Hon. Mem., 1989); IGU, 1976–80 (Vice-Pres., 1968–76); Geographical Assoc., 1976–77 (Hon. Treasurer, 1967–76, Hon. Mem., 1983); Vice-Pres., Nat. Assoc. for Envmtl Educn, 1977–; Mem., SSRC, 1976–82; Chm., Council for Extra-Mural Studies, Univ. of London, 1976–83; Chm., Exec. Cttee, Assoc. of Agriculture, 1972–83 (Vice-Pres., 1983–93); Mem. Adv. Cttees, UN Univ., 1976–82; Hon. Sec., RGS, 1963–73, Vice-Pres., 1975–78, Hon. Vice-Pres., 1978–80, 1983–, Pres., 1980–82. Chm., Birkbeck Coll., 1983–89 (Governor, 1968–89; Fellow, 1989); Mem. Delegacy, Goldsmiths' Coll., 1984–88. Chm., Dudley Stamp Meml Trust, 1988–2005 (Hon. Sec., 1966–88; Hon. Pres., 2006). Erskine Fellow, Univ. of Canterbury, NZ, 1970. Hon. Life Mem., Univ. of London Union, 1977. Hon. Member: Geog. Soc. of Russia, 1975; Assoc. of Japanese Geographers, 1980; Geog. Soc. of Mexico, 1984; Geog. Soc. of Poland, 1986; Membre d'Honneur, Société de Géographie, 1983. FInstEnvSci 1980; FRSA 1983. Hon. FLI 1991. DUniv Open, 1978; Hon. DSc Birmingham, 1982. Received Gill Memorial award of RGS, 1958; RGS Founder's Medal, 1977; Alexander Körösi Csoma Medal, Hungarian Geographical Soc., 1980; Tokyo Geographical Soc. Medal, 1981; Lauréat d'Honneur, IGU, 1984. *Publications:* Hon. Editor, Birmingham and its Regional Setting, 1951; A Pictorial Geography of the West Midlands, 1958; General Consultant, An Atlas of Earth Resources, 1979; The Great Geographical Atlas, 1982; (consultant and contrib.) The Ordnance Survey Atlas of Great Britain, 1982; numerous articles on economic and urban geography.

Recreations: music, gardening. *Address:* 45 Oakleigh Avenue, N20 9JE. *T:* (020) 8445 6057. *Club:* Athenæum.

WISE, Morag Barbara; QC (Scot.) 2005; *b* 22 Jan. 1963; *d* of Leslie James Wise and Barbara Gillies or Wise; *m* 1994, Alastair John Angus McEwan; one *s* two *d*. *Educ:* Univ. of Aberdeen (LLB 1st Cl. Hons 1985; DipLP 1986); McGill Univ., Montreal (LLM 1995). Solicitor in private practice, 1989–92; admitted Advocate, 1993; Temp. Judge, Ct of Session, 2008. Chair, Advocates Family Law Assoc., 2007–. *Publications:* (ed jtly) Gloag and Henderson, The Law of Scotland, 12th edn 2007; (contrib.) A Practical Guide to Human Rights Law in Scotland, ed Lord Reed, 2001. *Recreations:* singing, ski-ing (badly), socialising. *Address:* Advocates' Library, Parliament House, Edinburgh EH1 1RF. *T:* (0131) 226 5071; *e-mail:* morag.wise@advocates.org.uk.

WISE, Dr Richard, FMedSci; Consultant Medical Microbiologist, City Hospital, Birmingham, 1974–2005; *b* 7 July 1942; s of late James Wise and Joan Wise; *m* 1979, Jane M. Symonds; one *d* (one *s* decd). *Educ:* Univ. of Manchester (MB ChB; MD 1980). Hon. Prof. of Clin. Microbiol., Univ. of Birmingham, 1995–; Civilian Consultant, Army, 1997–. Advr, Sci. and Technol. Cttee, H of L, 1997–99. Chm., Specialist Adv. Cttee on Antimicrobial Resistance, 2001–07; Mem., Nat. Expert Cttee on New and Emerging Diseases, 2003–07. Non-executive Director: Centre for Applied Microbiol Res., Porton Down, 1999–2003; Health Protection Agency, 2003–07. Pres., British Soc. Antimicrobial Chemotherapy, 1997–2000. Advr, European Centre for Disease Control, Stockholm, 2005–. Trustee, Hereford Nature Trust, 2002– (Dep. Chm., 2007–). FMedSci 2003. Hon. FRCP 1997. *Publications:* numerous contribs on antibiotic therapy. *Recreations:* gardening, wine, food, France, walking. *Address:* Springfield House, Breinton, Hereford HR4 7PB. *Club:* East India.

WISE, Thomas Harold; Member (UK Ind) Eastern Region, European Parliament, since 2004; *b* 13 May 1948; *s* of Harold Stanley and Helen Wise; *m* 1974, Janet Featherstone; one *s* one *d*. *Educ:* Bournemouth Grammar Sch.; Bournemouth Coll. Police cadet, 1965, PC, 1967–70, Dorset Police; salesman, 1970–73, Nat. Accounts Exec., 1973–74, Aspro-Nicholas; Regl Manager, Cavenham Confectionery, 1974–78; salesman, 1978–82, Nat. Account Sales Manager, 1982–84, Melitta Benz; National Account Manager: Nestlé, 1984–85; Spillers, 1985–87; Pasta Foods, 1987–89; Sales and Mktg Manager, Chineham Internat., 1989–91; Man. Dir, Ostmann Spices, Brynmawr, 1991–94; Retail Sales Manager, Rio Pacific Foods, Watford, 1994–97; Sales Dir, Brand Mktg Internat., 1997–98; portfolio mgt, 1998–2000; Special Projects Manager, Itswine.com, 2000–01; Office Manager and Regl Organiser, E of England, UKIP, 2001–04. *Recreations:* travel, numismatics, wine appreciation. *Address:* (office) 21A High Street, Leighton Buzzard LU7 1DN. *T:* (01525) 385900, *Fax:* (01525) 376038; *e-mail:* tomw@tomwisemep.co.uk.

WISEMAN, Debbie, MBE 2004; composer and conductor, film and television scores, since 1984; *b* 10 May 1963; *d* of Paul Wiseman and Barbara Wiseman; *m* 1987, Tony Wharmby. *Educ:* Henrietta Barnett Sch.; Trinity Coll. of Music, London (Saturday Exhbnr); Kingsway-Princeton Morley Coll., London; GSMD (GGSM 1984). *Film scores include:* Tom and Viv, 1994; Haunted, 1995; Wilde, 1997; Lighthouse, 1998; Tom's Midnight Garden, 1999; Before You Go, 2002; Freeze Frame, 2004; Arsène Lupin, 2004; The Truth About Love, 2005; Middletown, 2006; Flood, 2007; *television scores include:* The Good Guys, 1992–93; Warriors, 2000; Judge John Deed, 2001–06; My Uncle Silas, 2001; Othello, 2001; He Knew He Was Right, 2004; The Man-eating Leopard of Rudraprayag, 2005; Beaten, 2005; The Inspector Lynley Mysteries, 2005; Johnny and the Bomb, 2006; Jekyll, 2007; The Passion, 2008; *theatre:* Feather Boy: the musical, NT, 2006. Vis. Prof., Composition for Screen course, RCM, 1998–. Hon. FTCL 2006; Hon. FGSM 2007. *Recreations:* swimming, table tennis. *Address:* c/o Music Matters International Ltd, Crest House, 102–104 Church Road, Teddington, Middlesex TW11 8PY. *T:* (020) 8979 4580, *Fax:* (020) 8979 4590; *e-mail:* wisemaninfo@aol.com.

WISEMAN, Prof. Donald John, OBE 1943; DLit; FBA 1966; FSA; Professor of Assyriology in the University of London, 1961–82, Emeritus 1982; *b* 25 Oct. 1918; *s* of Air Cdre Percy John Wiseman, CBE, RAF; *m* 1948, Mary Catherine (*d* 2006), *d* of P. O. Ruoff; three *d*. *Educ:* Dulwich College; King's College, London. BA (London); AKC, McCaul Hebrew Prize, 1939; FKC 1982. Served War of 1939–45, in RAFVR. Ops, 11 Fighter Group, 1939–41; Chief Intelligence Officer, Mediterranean Allied Tactical Air Forces with Rank of Group Capt., 1942–45. Heap Exhibitioner in Oriental Languages, Wadham Coll., Oxford, 1945–47; MA 1949. Asst Keeper, Dept of Egyptian and Assyrian, later Western Asiatic, Antiquities, British Museum, 1948–61. Epigraphist on archæological excavations at Nimrud, Harran, Rimah; Jt Dir of British School of Archæology in Iraq, 1961–65, Chm. 1970–88, Vice-Pres., 1988–93, Pres., 1993–2001. Trustee, British Sch. of Archæology in Jerusalem, 1984–92. Pres., Soc. for Old Testament Studies, 1980; Chm., Tyndale House for Biblical Research, Cambridge, 1957–86. Corresp. Mem., German Archæological Inst., 1961. Editor, Journal IRAQ, 1953–78; Joint Editor, Reallexikon der Assyriologie, 1959–83. Bronze Star (USA), 1944. *Publications:* The Alalakh Tablets, 1953; Chronicles of Chaldaean Kings, 1956; Cuneiform Texts from Cappadocian Tablets in the British Museum, V, 1956; Cylinder-Seals of Western Asia, 1958; Vassal-Treaties of Esarhaddon, 1958; Illustrations from Biblical Archæology, 1958; Catalogue of Western Asiatic Seals in the British Museum, vol. I, 1963; Peoples of Old Testament Times, 1973; Archaeology and the Bible, 1979; Essays on the Patriarchal Narratives, 1980; Nebuchadrezzar and Babylon, 1985; I and II Kings (commentary), 1993; Nimrud Literary Texts, 1996; Memoirs, 2003; contrib. to journals. *Address:* Low Barn, 26 Downs Way, Tadworth, Surrey KT20 5DZ. *T:* (01737) 813536.

WISEMAN, Sir John William, 11th Bt *cr* 1628; *b* 16 March 1957; *o s* of Sir William George Eden Wiseman, 10th Bt, CB, and of Joan Mary, *d* of late Arthur Phelps, Harrow; *S* father, 1962; *m* 1980, Nancy, *d* of Casimer Zyla, New Britain, Conn; two *d*. *Educ:* Millfield Sch.; Univ. of Hartford, Conn, USA. *Heir: kinsman* Thomas Alan Wiseman [*b* 8 July 1921; *m* 1946, Hildemarie Domnik (*d* 1991); (one *s* one *d* decd)].

WISEMAN, Julian Paul Geoffrey, CMG 2000; Director, Penumbra Partners Ltd, since 2002; *b* 3 Oct. 1944; *s* of Norman William Thomas Wiseman and Joan Marion Allen Wiseman; *m* 1973, Diana Christine Spooner; two *d*. *Educ:* Cranleigh Sch.; Australian Nat. Univ. (Dip. in Mod. Langs, 1969). Royal Marines, 1963–75: Troop Comdr, 40 Cdo; ADC to Gov. of Qld, 1967–69; Adjt, 42 Cdo, 1972–74; Bde Signal Officer, 3 Cdo Bde, 1975; HM Diplomatic Service, 1976–99: First Secretary: FCO, 1976–78; UKMIS to UN, Geneva, 1978–82; SOAS, 1982–83; FCO, 1982–84; Dhaka, 1984–87; FCO, 1987–90; Counsellor: Islamabad, 1990–92; FCO, 1992–99. Dir, Retainagroup Ltd, 1999–2002. Mem., Sussex Cttee and London Reg. Adv. Cttee, Duke of Edinburgh's Award, 2000–. Liveryman, Coachmakers' and Coach Harness Makers' Co., 2000. FRGS. *Recreations:* ski-ing, fishing, golf, music, travel. *Address:* Penumbra Partners Ltd, 51 Catherine Place, SW1E 6DY. *Clubs:* Boodle's, Army and Navy; Piscatorial Society; West Sussex Golf.

WISEMAN, Prof. Timothy Peter, DPhil; FSA; FBA 1986; Professor of Classics, University of Exeter, 1977–2001, now Emeritus; *b* 3 Feb. 1940; *s* of Stephen Wiseman and Winifred Agnes Wiseman (*née* Rigby); *m* 1962, Doreen Anne Williams. *Educ:* Manchester Grammar Sch.; Balliol Coll., Oxford (MA 1964; DPhil 1967). FSA 1977. Rome Schol. in Classical Studies, British Sch. at Rome, 1962–63; University of Leicester: Asst Lectr in Classics, 1963–65; Lectr, 1965–73; Reader in Roman History, 1973–76. Vice-Pres., British Acad., 1992–94; President: Roman Soc., 1992–95; Jt Assoc. of Classical Teachers, 1998–99; Classical Assoc., 2000–01. Chm. Council, British Sch. at Rome, 2002–07. Vis. Associate Prof., Univ. of Toronto, 1970–71; Lansdowne Lectr, Univ. of Victoria (BC), 1987; Whitney J. Oates Fellow, Princeton, 1988; Webster Lectr, Stanford, 1993. Hon. DLitt Durham, 1988. *Publications:* Catullan Questions, 1969; New Men in the Roman Senate, 1971; Cinna the Poet, 1974; Clio's Cosmetics, 1979; (with Anne Wiseman) Julius Caesar: The Battle for Gaul, 1980; (ed) Roman Political Life, 1985; Catullus and his World, 1985; Roman Studies Literary and Historical, 1987; trans., Flavius Josephus, Death of an Emperor, 1991; Talking to Virgil, 1992; Historiography and Imagination, 1994; Remus: a Roman myth, 1995; Roman Drama and Roman History, 1998; (ed) Classics in Progress, 2002; The Myths of Rome, 2004; Unwritten Rome, 2008. *Address:* Classics Department, Amory Building, The University, Exeter EX4 4RJ. *T:* (01392) 264202.

WISHART, Maureen; *see* Lehane, M.

WISHART, Peter; MP (SNP) Perth and North Perthshire, since 2005 (North Tayside, 2001–05); *b* 9 March 1962; *s* of Alex and Nan Wishart; *m* 1990, Carrie Lindsay (separated 2003); one *s*. *Educ:* Moray House Coll. of Educn. Community worker, 1984–85; musician with rock band, Runrig, 1985–2001. Chief Whip, SNP Gp, 2001–07. *Recreations:* music, hillwalking. *Address:* (office) 35 Perth Street, Blairgowrie PH10 6DL; (office) 9 York Place, Perth PH2 8EP.

WISTRICH, Enid Barbara, PhD; Visiting Professor, School of Social Sciences (formerly of History and Politics), Middlesex University, since 1997; *b* 4 Sept. 1928; *d* of Zadik Heiber and Bertha Brown; *m* 1950, Ernest Wistrich, *qv*; two *c* (and one *c* decd). *Educ:* Froebel Institute Sch.; Brackley High Sch.; St Paul's Girls' Sch.; London School of Economics (BScEcon, PhD). Research Asst, LSE, 1950–52; Instructor, Mt Holyoke Coll., Mass, USA, 1952–53; Research Officer, Royal Inst. of Public Administration, 1954–56; Sen. Res. Officer, LSE, 1969–72; NEDO, 1977–79; Prin. Lectr, 1979–91, Reader in Politics and Public Admin, 1991–94, Middlesex Poly., subseq. Middlesex Univ. Vis. Lectr, Univ. of Waikato, NZ, 1989. Councillor (Lab): Hampstead Metropolitan Bor. Council, 1962–65; London Bor. of Camden, 1964–68 and 1971–74; GLC, ILEA, 1973–77. Mem., Hampstead Community Health Council, 1984–92 (Chm., 1986–88). Governor: British Film Inst., 1974–81 (also Actg Chm., 1977–78); National Film Sch., 1978–82. Chm. of Governors, Heathlands Sch. for Autistic Children, 1976–86. *Publications:* Local Government Reorganisation: the first years of Camden, 1972; I Don't Mind the Sex, It's the Violence: film censorship explored, 1978; The Politics of Transport, 1983; (jtly) The Migrants' Voice in Europe, 1999; (jtly) Regional Identity and Diversity in Europe, 2007; chapters and articles in various books and jls. *Recreations:* experiencing the arts, admiring nature, fussing round the family. *Address:* 37B Gayton Road, NW3 1UB. *T:* (020) 7419 1742.

WISTRICH, Ernest, CBE 1973; Vice-President, European Movement (British Council), since 2000 (Director, 1969–86); *b* 22 May 1923; *s* of Dr Arthur and Mrs Eva Wistrich; *m* 1950, Enid Barbara (*née* Heiber), *qv*; two *c* (and one *c* decd). *Educ:* Poland; University Tutorial Coll., London. Served in RAF, 1942–46; Timber Merchant, 1946–67; Dir, Britain in Europe, 1967–69; Councillor, Hampstead Borough Council, 1959–65; Camden Borough Council, Alderman 1964–71, Councillor 1971–74; Chm., Camden Cttee for Community Relations, 1964–68; Mem., Skeffington Cttee on Public Participation in Planning, 1968–69. Contested (Lab): Isle of Thanet, 1964; Hendon North, 1966; Cleveland, 1979; contested (SDP) London Central, 1984, European Parly elections. Editor of various jls, incl. The European, 1986–88. *Publications:* After 1992, 1989; The United States of Europe, 1994; contrib. Into Europe, Facts, New Europe and other jls. *Recreations:* music, walking. *Address:* 37B Gayton Road, NW3 1UB. *T:* (020) 7419 1686.

WITCHELL, Nicholas Newton Henshall; Diplomatic Correspondent, since 1995, Royal Correspondent, since 1998, BBC News; *b* 23 Sept. 1953; *s* of William Joseph Henshall Witchell and late Barbara Sybil Mary Witchell (*née* Macdonald); two *d*. *Educ:* Epsom Coll.; Leeds Univ. (LLB). Joined BBC, 1976: grad. news trainee, 1976–78; reporter: TV and radio, NI, 1978–82; TV Network News, 1982–83; Ireland Corresp., 1983–84; Presenter: Six O'Clock News, 1984–89; BBC Breakfast News, 1989–94; Associate Producer: News '39, 1989; News '44, 1994; News '45, 1995; Corresp., Panorama, 1994–95. Gov., Queen Elizabeth's Foundn (formerly Queen Elizabeth's Foundn for Disabled People), 1992–. Hon. Patron, Queen Alexandra Hosp. Home, 2006–. FRGS 1990. Sony Radio Acad. Event Award, 2002. OStJ 1995. *Publication:* The Loch Ness Story, 1974. *Address:* BBC News, BBC TV Centre, W12 7RJ. *T:* (020) 8743 8000. *Club:* Reform.

WITCHER, Sally Anne, OBE 2006; PhD; Deputy Director, Office for Disability Issues, Department for Work and Pensions, since 2006; *b* 11 July 1960; *d* of late Michael James Witcher and of Janet Mary Witcher (*née* Ashford). *Educ:* Slade Sch. of Fine Art (BA Hons); University Coll. London; Edinburgh Univ. (MSc Policy Studies, PhD Social Policy 2006). Teacher, English as a Foreign Language, British Inst., Lisbon, 1984–85; freelance sculptor, 1985–87; Homeless Families Liaison Worker, Earls Court Homelessness Project, 1987–89; Campaign Worker, Disability Alliance, 1989–93; Dir, CPAG, 1993–98; freelance mgt and social policy consultant, 1998–2006. Chair, Disability Employment Adv. Cttee, DWP, 2002–06. *Publications:* (jtly) A Way out of Poverty and Disability, 1991; (jtly) Letters, Lobbies, Legislation: a guide to Parliamentary campaigning in Scotland, 1999; (jtly) Direct Payments: the impact on choice and control for disabled people, 2000; (jtly) Bodies Politic: a guide for voluntary organisations lobbying in Holyrood, Westminster and Brussels, 2002; Reviewing the terms of inclusion: transactional processes, currencies and context, 2003. *Address:* 2 Montague Street, Edinburgh EH8 9QU. *T:* (0131) 662 8855; Department for Work and Pensions, The Adelphi, 1–11 John Adam Street, WC2N 6HT.

WITHALL, Maj.-Gen. William Nigel James, CB 1982; Marketing Director, and Member, Board of Directors, Link-Miles Ltd, 1985–93 (Consultant, 1984); *b* 14 Oct. 1928; *s* of late Bernard Withall and Enid (*née* Hill); *m* 1952, Pamela Hickman; one *s* one *d*. *Educ:* St Benedict's. Army Engr Cadet, 1947–50; Mons OCS, 1950; Commnd RE, 1950; served in Hong Kong, Gulf States, Aden, Germany and India; Staff Coll., 1961; Sqdn Comd, 73 Fd Sqdn, 1964–66; Jt Services Staff Coll., Latimer, 1967; Mil. Asst to MGO, 1968–70; CO 26 Engr Regt, BAOR, 1970–72; Bde Comd, 11 Engr Bde, 1974–76; NDC, India, 1977; No 259 Army Pilots Course, 1978; Dir, Army Air Corps, 1979–83. Col Comdt RE, 1984–97. Chm., Army Football Assoc., 1980–81; Pres., Army Cricket Assoc., 1981–83; Hon. Life Vice Pres., Aircrew Assoc., 1986; Chm., RE Assoc., 1993–97. Chm., Chute Parish Council, 1995–2002. Freeman, City of London, 1981; Liveryman, GAPAN, 1981. *Recreations:* cricket, squash, all games, reading, walking. *Address:* Linden Cottage, Upper Chute, near Andover, Hants SP11 9EL. *Clubs:* MCC, I Zingari, Band of Brothers, Free Foresters, Stragglers of Asia.

WITHERIDGE, Rev. John Stephen, MA; Headmaster of Charterhouse, since 1996; *b* 14 Nov. 1953; *s* of late Francis Edward Witheridge and Joan Elizabeth Witheridge (*née* Exell); *m* 1975, Sarah Caroline, *d* of Rev. Peter Phillips; two *s* two *d*. *Educ:* St Albans Sch.; Univ. of Kent at Canterbury (BA 1st cl. Eng. and Theol.); Christ's Coll., Cambridge (BA 2nd cl. Theol Tripos; MA); Ridley Hall, Cambridge. Ordained deacon, 1979, priest, 1980; Curate, Luton Parish Church, 1979–82; Head of Religious Studies and Asst Chaplain, Marlborough Coll., 1982–84; Chaplain to Archbishop of Canterbury, 1984–87; Conduct (Sen. Chaplain), Eton Coll., 1987–96. Chm., Lomans Trust, 2000–07; Vice-Pres., Eyeless Trust, 2001–07. FRSA 1998. *Publications:* Frank Fletcher: a formidable headmaster, 2005; articles and reviews. *Recreations:* family, history, gardening, Somerset. *Address:* Charterhouse, Godalming, Surrey GU7 2DJ. *T:* (01483) 291600. *Club:* Travellers.

WITHEROW, David Michael Lindley, CBE 2004; Executive Chairman, Radio Authority, 2003 (Member, 1998–2003; Deputy Chair, 2000–03); *b* 19 July 1937; *s* of Dr James Witherow and Greta (*née* Roberts); *m* 1st, 1960, Ragnhild Kadow (marr. diss. 1994); two *d*; 2nd, 1994, Elizabeth Anne Wright. *Educ:* King Edward's Sch., Birmingham (Foundn Schol.); Pembroke Coll., Cambridge (BA Hons 1960). Nat. service, RCS, 1955–57. Press Assoc., 1960–63; BBC, 1963–96: Ext. Services News, 1963–77, Editor, 1973–77; Editor, Weekly Progs, TV News, 1977–79; Chief Assistant, Regions, 1980; Head, then Gen. Manager, Monitoring Service, Caversham, 1980–85; Controller, Resources and Admin, Ext. Services, 1985–89; Dep. Man. Dir, 1989–94, Policy Consultant, 1994–96, World Service; Project Dir, Digital Audio Broadcasting Services, 1994–96. Pres., World (formerly Europ.) DAB Forum, 1995–97. FRSA 1992. *Recreations:* travel, music, crime fiction. *Address:* 6 Northfield Hall, 59 North Road, N6 4BJ.

WITHEROW, John Moore; Editor, The Sunday Times, since 1995; *b* Johannesburg, 20 Jan. 1952; *m* 1985, Sarah Linton; two *s* one *d*. *Educ:* Bedford Sch.; York Univ. (BA Hons Hist.). Reuters trainee, London and Madrid, 1977–80; home and foreign corresp., The Times, 1980–83; Sunday Times: Defence corresp., 1984–85; Diplomatic Corresp., 1985–87; Focus Ed., 1987–89; Foreign Ed., 1989–92; Man. Ed. (News), 1992–94; Actg Ed., 1994. *Publications:* (with Patrick Bishop) The Winter War: the Falklands, 1982; The Gulf War, 1993. *Recreations:* tennis, sailing. *Address:* The Sunday Times, 1 Pennington Street, E98 1ST. *T:* (020) 7782 5640; *e-mail:* john.witherow@sunday-times.co.uk. *Clubs:* Hospital, Hurlingham, Ivy; Campden Hill Tennis.

WITHERS, Prof. Charles William John, PhD; FBA 2006; FRSE, FRGS, FRHistS; Professor of Historical Geography, since 1994, and Head, Institute of Geography, since 2006, University of Edinburgh; *b* 6 Dec. 1954; *s* of John Alastair Withers and Mary Alicia Withers (*née* Green); *m* 1980, Anne Marshall Hamilton; two *s* one *d*. *Educ:* St Andrews Univ. (BSc Hons); Downing Coll., Cambridge (PhD 1982). FRGS 1978; AcSS 2001; FRHistS 2002; CGeog 2003. University of Gloucestershire: Lectr, 1981–84; Principal Lectr, 1984–92; Prof., 1992–94; Hd of Dept, 1991–94; Associate Dean, 1992–94. MAE 2000. FRSE 2006. FRSA 2000. *Publications:* Gaelic in Scotland 1698–1981, 1984; The Highland Communities of Dundee and Perth 1797–1891, 1986; Gaelic Scotland, 1988; Discovering the Cotswolds, 1990; Urban Highlanders, 1998; Geography, Science and National Identity: Scotland since 1520, 2001; Placing the Enlightenment, 2007; joint editor: Urbanising Britain, 1991; Geography and Enlightenment, 1999; Science and Medicine in the Scottish Enlightenment, 2002; Georgian Geographies, 2004; Geography and Revolution, 2005; numerous articles in learned jls. *Recreations:* hill-walking, theatre, reading, food and wine. *Address:* Institute of Geography, University of Edinburgh, Drummond Street, Edinburgh EH8 9XP. *T:* (0131) 650 2559, *Fax:* (0131) 650 2524; *e-mail:* c.w.j.withers@ed.ac.uk.

WITHERS, Googie, (Mrs John McCallum), AO 1980; CBE 2001; actress, since 1932; *b* Karachi, India, 12 March 1917; *d* of late Captain E. C. Withers, CBE, CIE, RIM, and late Lizette Catherine Wilhelmina van Wageningen; *m* 1948, John Neil McCallum, *qv*; one *s* two *d*. *Educ:* Fredville Park, Nonnington, Kent; Convent of the Holy Family, Kensington. Started as dancer in Musical Comedy. First film contract at age of 17; has acted in over 50 pictures, starring in 30. *Films include:* One of our Aircraft is Missing, 1941; The Silver Fleet, 1941; On Approval, 1942; Loves of Joanna Godden, 1946; It Always Rains on Sunday, 1947; White Corridors, 1950; Nickel Queen, 1970; Country Life, 1994; Shine, 1995. *Plays include:* They Came to a City; Private Lives; Winter Journey; The Deep Blue Sea; Waiting for Gillian; Janus; Stratford on Avon Season, 1958: Beatrice in Much Ado About Nothing; Gertrude in Hamlet; The Complaisant Lover, New York, 1962; Exit the King, London, 1963; Getting Married, Strand, 1967; Madame Renevsky in The Cherry Orchard, Mrs Cheveley in An Ideal Husband, 1972; Lady Kitty in The Circle, Chichester Festival Theatre, 1976, Haymarket, 1977 (nominated for SWET best actress award), Toronto, 1978; Lady Bracknell in The Importance of Being Earnest, Chichester, 1979; Time and the Conways, Chichester, 1983; Lady Sneerwell in The School for Scandal, Duke of York's, 1984 (also European tour); The Chalk Garden, Chichester, 1986; Hay Fever, Ring Round the Moon, Chichester, 1988; An Ideal Husband, Old Vic, 1995–96, Australia, 1997–98; Lady Windermere's Fan, Chichester, 1997, Haymarket, 2002. Tours: Roar Like a Dove, The Constant Wife and Woman in a Dressing Gown, Australia and NZ, 1959; excerpts Shakespeare (Kate, Margaret of Anjou, Beatrice, Portia, Rosalind, Cleopatra), 1964; Beekman Place, Australia and NZ, 1965; Relatively Speaking, Australia, 1968; Plaza Suite, Australia and NZ, 1969–70; The Kingfisher, Australia, NZ and Far East, 1978–80, FE, ME and Gulf, 1987; The Cherry Orchard, The Skin Game, Dandy Dick, UK, 1981; Stardust, UK and Australia, 1984–85; The Cocktail Hour, Australia and UK, 1989–90; High Spirits, Australia, 1991, 1993; On Golden Pond, UK, 1992; The Chalk Garden, Australia, 1995; An Ideal Husband, Australia, 1998. *Television* appearances in drama including The Public Prosecutor; Amphitryon 38; The Deep Blue Sea (Best Actress, 1954); Last Year's Confetti, Court Circular, 1971; Knightsbridge, 1972; The Cherry Orchard, 1973; series Within These Walls, 1974–76 (Best Actress of the Year, 1974); Time after Time (TV film), 1985 (Best Actress ACE Award, USA, 1988); Hotel du Lac (TV film), 1985; Northanger Abbey (TV film), 1986; Ending Up, 1989. *Recreations:* music, travel, reading, interior decorating. *Address:* c/o Coutts & Co., 440 Strand, WC2R 0QS.

WITHERS, Rt Hon. Reginald (Greive); PC 1977; Senator (L) for Western Australia, 1966–87; Lord Mayor of Perth, Western Australia, 1991–93; *b* 26 Oct. 1924; *s* of late F. J. Withers and I. L. Greive; *m* 1953, Shirley Lloyd-Jones; two *s* one *d*. *Educ:* Bunbury; Univ. of WA (LLB). Barrister-at-law 1953. Served War, RAN, 1942–46. Councillor, Bunbury Municipal Council, 1954–56; Mem., Bunbury Diocesan Council, 1958–59, Treasurer, 1961–68. State Vice-Pres., Liberal and Country League of WA, 1958–61, State Pres., 1961–65; Mem., Federal Exec. of Liberal Party, 1961–65; Fed. Vice-Pres., Liberal Party, 1962–65. Govt Whip in Senate, 1969–71; Leader of Opposition in Senate, 1972–75; Special Minister of State, Minister for Capital Territory, Minister for Media, and Minister for Tourism and Recreation, Nov.–Dec. 1975; Vice-Pres. of Exec. Council, Leader of Govt in Senate, and Minister for Admin. Services, 1975–78. Sec., SW Law Soc., 1955–68. *Recreations:* swimming, reading, painting. *Address:* 23 Malcolm Street, West Perth, WA 6005, Australia. *T:* (8) 93241322; *e-mail:* reg@withers.pn.

WITHEY, Anthony George Hurst, CBE 1997; FCMA; Chief Executive, Remploy Ltd, 1988–2000; *b* 4 Oct. 1942; *s* of Walter Ronald Withey and Laura Maria Withey (*née* Thomas); *m* 1967, Yvonne Jeanette Price Thomas; one *s* one *d*. *Educ:* Bishop Gore Grammar Sch., Swansea; Wadham Coll., Oxford (BA Hons Modern Hist.). FCMA 1986. Gen. Manager, BXL Plastics Ltd, various divs, and Dir, various subsids, 1976–83; Gp Exec., Tarmac Bldg Products Ltd, 1983–85; Chief Exec., Polymers Div., Evered Holdings PLC, 1985–88. Director: Pan Graphics Industries Ltd, 1991–94; Linx Printing Technologies PLC, 1994–2005; Océ (UK) Ltd, 2000–; Chm., Electron Technologies Ltd, 2003–. Director: Morriston Hosp. NHS Trust, 1997–99; Swansea NHS Trust, 1999–2002. Dir, Internat. Orgn for Provision of Work to Disabled People, 1993–2000. Mem., S Wales Police Selection Panel, 1998–2002. Mem. Council, Industrial Soc., 1989–2000. *Recreations:* squash, gardening, antiques, theatre. *Address:* Westwoods, Caswell Bay, Swansea SA3 3BS. *T:* (01792) 363068. *Club:* Swansea Lawn Tennis and Squash Racquets.

WITNEY, Nicholas Kenneth James; Senior Policy Fellow, European Council on Foreign Relations, since 2008; *b* 14 Dec. 1950; *s* of Kenneth Witney and Joan Witney (*née* Tait); *m* 1977, Ann Margaret Ruskell; one *s* one *d*. *Educ:* Tonbridge Sch.; Corpus Christi Coll., Oxford (MA Lit Hum). Joined Foreign and Commonwealth Office, 1973: E European and Soviet Dept, 1973; Arabic lang. trng, Lebanon and Jordan, 1974–76; Third, later Second, Sec., Baghdad, 1976–78; Second, later First, Sec. and Private Sec. to Ambassador, Washington, 1978–82; EC Dept, FCO, 1982–83; on secondment, later perm. transfer, to MoD, 1983–: Principal: defence policy Africa/Asia, 1983–85; Army budget and plans, 1985–87; Director: (Ops), Saudi Armed Forces Project, 1987–90; Nuclear Policy and Security, 1990–93; sabbatical at Rand Corp., Santa Monica, 1993–94; Hd, Housing Project Team, 1994–96; Dir-Gen., Mgt and Orgn, 1996–98; Asst Under-Sec. of State, Systems, 1998–99; Director-General: Equipment, 1999–2002; Internat. Security Policy, 2002–04; Chief Exec., European Defence Agency, 2004–07. *Publications:* The British Nuclear Deterrent after the Cold War, 1994; (jtly) Western European Nuclear Forces, 1995; Re-energising Europe's Security and Defence Policy, 2008. *Recreations:* Rugby, sailing, modern fiction. *Address:* European Council on Foreign Relations, 71 Boulevard Raspail, 75006 Paris, France.

WITT, Karsten; Joint Founder, and Managing Director, Karsten Witt Musik Management GmbH, since 2004; *b* Hamburg, 5 March 1952; *s* of Reimer Witt and Hilde Witt (*née* Vöge); *m* 1st, 1982, Anna Zeijl; three *s*; 2nd, 1996, Marie-Annick Le Blanc. *Educ:* Univ. of Hamburg (BA Philosophy of Sci.); Univ. of Constance (MA). Founder: Junge Deutsche Philharmonie (Nat. Student Orch.), 1974 (Manager, 1974–87); Deutsche Kammerphilharmonie, 1980 (Manager, 1980–89); Ensemble Modern, 1980 (Manager, 1980–91); Manager, ISCM (German Br.), 1986–90; Gen. Sec., Vienna Konzerthaus, 1991–96; Pres., Deutsche Grammophon, 1996–99; CEO, S Bank Centre, London, 1999–2002; Artistic Advisor: Chamber Orch. of Europe, 2002; Megaron Athens, 2005–08; touring projects with Shaksfin Asia, 2002–04. Governor: Deutsche Ensemble Akad., 1999–; GSMD, 2000–03; Wiener Konzerthausges., 2002–. Curator, Allianz Cultural Foundn, 2001–. Ehrenkreuz für Wissenschaft und Kunst (Austria), 1996; Silbernes Ehrenzeichen für Verdienste um das Land Wien, 1997; Cross of Merit (Hungary), 1999. *Address:* (office) Leuschnerdamm 13, 10999 Berlin, Germany.

WITTEVEEN, Dr (Hendrikus) Johannes, Commander, Order of Netherlands Lion; Commander, Order of Orange Nassau; Chairman, Internationale Nederlanden Group, 1991–93 (Mem. Supervisory Board, 1979–90); Board Member: Royal Dutch Petroleum Co., 1971–73 and 1978–89; Robeco, 1971–73 and 1979–91 (Adviser, 1971–73); *b* Zeist, Netherlands, 12 June 1921; *m* 1949, Liesbeth de Vries Feyens; two *s* one *d*. *Educ:* Univ. Rotterdam (DrEcons). Central Planning Bureau, 1947–48; Prof., Univ. Rotterdam, 1948–63; Mem. Netherlands Parlt, First Chamber, 1959–63 and 1971–73, and Second Chamber, 1965–67; Minister of Finance, Netherlands, 1963–65 and 1967–71; First Deputy Prime Minister, 1967–71; Managing Director, IMF, 1973–78. Chm., Group of Thirty, 1979–85, Hon. Chm., 1985–; Member: Internat. Council, Morgan Guaranty Trust Co. of NY, 1978–85; European Adv. Council, General Motors, 1978–91; Bd Mem., Thyssen-Bornemisza NV, 1978–86; Advr for Internat. Affairs, Amro Bank, Amsterdam, 1979–90. Vice-Pres., Internat. Sufi Movt, 1957–. Grand Cross, Order of Crown (Belgium); Order of Oak Wreath (Luxemburg); Order of Merit (Fed. Republic Germany). *Publications:* Loonshoogte en Werkgelegenheid, 1947; Growth and Business Cycles, 1954; Universal Sufism, 1994; Soefisme en Economie, 2001 (Sufism in Action, 2003); Tot de Ene, 2006; articles in Economische Statistische Berichten, Euromoney. *Recreation:* hiking. *Address:* 2243 HL Wassenaar, Waldeck Pyrmontlaan 15, The Netherlands.

WITTY, (John) David, CBE 1985; Director, Great Portland Estates PLC, 1987–97; *b* 1 Oct. 1924; *s* of late Harold Witty and Olive Witty, Beverley; *m* 1955, Doreen Hanlan (*d* 2007); one *s*. *Educ:* Beverley Grammar Sch.; Balliol Coll., Oxford (MA). Served War, RN, 1943–46. Asst Town Clerk, Beverley, 1951–53; Asst Solicitor: Essex CC, 1953–54; Hornsey, 1954–60; Dep. Town Clerk: Kingston upon Thames, 1960–65; Merton, 1965–67; Asst Chief Exec., Westminster, 1967–77, Chief Exec., 1977–84. Hon. Sec., London Boroughs Assoc., 1978–84. Chm., London Enterprise Property Co., 1984–85. Lawyer Mem., London Rent Assessment Panel, 1984–92. Order of Infante D. Henrique (Portugal), 1978; Order of Right Hand (Nepal), 1980; Order of King Abdul Aziz (Saudi Arabia), 1981; Order of Oman, 1982; Order of Orange-Nassau, 1982. *Recreation:* golf. *Address:* 14 River House, 23–24 The Terrace, Barnes, SW13 0NR.

WITTY, Mark F.; *see* Featherstone-Witty.

WIX, Ethel Rose; Special Commissioner of Income Tax, 1977–86; *b* 1 Nov. 1921; *d* of Michael Wix and Anna Wix (*née* Snyder). *Educ:* Henrietta Barnett Sch.; Cheltenham Ladies' Coll.; University Coll. London (BA Hons 1942); Hull University Coll. (Cert Ed 1943). Special Operations Executive, 1944–45; lived in S Africa, 1948–54; work for S African Inst. of Race Relations, 1950–54; Africa Bureau, London, 1955–56; Solicitor of Supreme Court, 1960; Partner, Herbert Oppenheimer, Nathan & Vandyk, 1960–75; General Commissioner of Income Tax, 1976–78. Mem., Arbitrators Panel, The Securities and Futures Authy Consumer Arbitration Scheme, 1988–94. Member: Exec. Cttee, Jewish Mus., 1987–93 (Hon. Treas., 1987–89); Exec. Cttee, Inst. of Jewish Affairs, 1990–92; Liby Cttee, Oxford Centre for Postgrad. Hebrew Studies, 1990–94. Mem. Council: Richmond Fellowship, 1975–85; Trinity Hospice, Clapham, 1981–90; Cheltenham Ladies' Coll., 1983–93 (Vice-Chm., 1990–92); St Christopher's Hospice, 1985–95; Clifton Coll., 1987–91; Governor, Warwick Schs Foundn, 1988–90, and 1992–96 (Vice-Chm., 1994–96). *Publications:* papers on Cost of Living, 1951, and Industrial Feeding Facilities, 1953, for S African Inst. of Race Relations; summary of Royal Commn Report on E Africa, 1956, for Africa Bureau. *Recreations:* reading, cooking, theatre. *Club:* Special Forces.

WODEHOUSE, family name of **Earl of Kimberley**.

WODEHOUSE, Lord; David Simon John Wodehouse; *b* 10 Oct. 1978; *s* and *heir* of Earl of Kimberley, *qv*.

WOGAN, Sir Michael Terence, (Sir Terry), KBE 2005 (OBE 1997); DL; jobbing broadcaster; *b* 3 Aug. 1938; *s* of late Michael Thomas and Rose Wogan; adopted British citizenship, 2005; *m* 1965, Helen Joyce; two *s* one *d*. *Educ:* Crescent Coll., Limerick, Ireland; Belvedere Coll., Dublin. Joined RTE as Announcer, 1963, Sen. Announcer, 1964–66; various programmes for BBC Radio, 1965–67; Late Night Extra, BBC Radio, 1967–69; The Terry Wogan Show, BBC Radio One, 1969–72, BBC Radio Two, 1972–84 and 1993–; television shows include: Lunchtime with Wogan, ATV, 1972–73; BBC: The Eurovision Song Contest, 1972–2008; Song for Europe; Come Dancing, 1973–79; Blankety-Blank, 1979–83; Children in Need, 1980–; Wogan's Guide to the BBC, 1982–; Wogan; Terry Wogan's Friday Night; Auntie's Bloomers, 1991–; Do the Right Thing, 1994; Auntie's Sporting Bloomers; Wogan's Island, 1994; Points of View, 2000–; The Terry and Gaby Show, 2003; Wogan Now and Then, UKTV, 2006–. Freedom of City of Limerick, 2007. DL Bucks, 2007. Hon. DLitt Limerick, 2004. Awards include: Pye Radio Award, 1980; Radio Industries Award (Radio Personality 3 times; TV Personality, 1982, 1984, 1985, 1987); TV Times TV Personality of the Year (10 times); Daily Express Award (twice); Carl Alan Award (3 times); Variety Club of GB: Special Award, 1982; Showbusiness Personality, 1984; Radio Personality of last 21 yrs, Daily Mail Nat. Radio Awards, 1988; Sony Radio Award, 1993, 1994, 2002, Sony Gold Award, 2006; Radio Prog. of the Year, TRIC Award, 1997. *Publications:* Banjaxed, 1979; The Day Job, 1981; To Horse, To Horse, 1982; Wogan on Wogan, 1987; Wogan's Ireland, 1988; Is it Me? (autobiog.), 2000; Musn't Grumble, 2006; Wogan's Twelve, 2008. *Recreations:* tennis, golf, swimming, reading, writing. *Address:* c/o Jo Gurnett, 12 Newburgh Street, W1F 7RP. *Clubs:* Garrick, Lord's Taverners, Saints and Sinners; London Irish Rugby Football; Lambourn Golf, Doonbeg Golf, Lahinch Golf.

WOGAN, Patrick Francis Michael, CMG 1991; HM Diplomatic Service, retired; Officer of the House of Lords, 1999–2004; *m* 1st, 1960, Rosmarie Diederich (marr. diss. 1988); two *s* one *d*; 2nd, 1988, Afsaneh Khalatbari. Joined FO, subseq. FCO, 1959; Second Sec., Bahrain, 1970; Second, then First, Sec., FCO, 1972; Brussels, 1976; FCO, 1981; Counsellor, FCO, 1983, Tehran, 1984; RCDS, 1987; Consul-Gen. and Dep. High Comr, Karachi, 1988; Ambassador to Iceland, 1991–93; Ambassador and Consul-Gen., Qatar, 1993–97. *Address:* 7 Orchard Rise, Pwllmeyric, Chepstow NP16 6JT.

WOGAN, Sir Terry; *see* Wogan, Sir M. T.

WOJNAROWSKA, Prof. Fenella Theta, DM; FRCP; Professor of Dermatology, University of Oxford, since 1999; Consultant Dermatologist, Oxford Radcliffe NHS Trust, since 1984; *b* Oxford, 23 Oct. 1947; *d* of Kostek Wojnarowski and Muriel Wojnarowska; one *s*; *m* 2008, John Gardiner. *Educ:* Oxford High Sch. for Girls; Tonbridge Girls' Grammar Sch.; Somerville Coll., Univ. of Oxford (BA Animal Physiol.; MSc 1971; DM 1995); St Mary's Hosp. Med. Sch., London (BM BCh 1973). FRCP 1993. Dermatology trng, St John's Hosp. for Diseases of the Skin and St Mary's Hosp., London, 1977–84; Sen. Clin. Lectr, 1992–2002, Reader in Dermatol., 1996–99, Univ. of Oxford; Hon. Sen. Res. Fellow, Somerville Coll., Oxford, 2005–. Founder Mem., British Soc. for the Study of Vulval Disease, 1998– (Chm. and Pres., 2000–); Mem. Bd, Eur. Women's Dermatologic Soc., 1999– (Pres., 2007–). Chm., Tumour Site Specific Cancer Gp for skin, Thames Valley Cancer Gp, 2002–08. European Academy of Dermatology and Venereology: UK Bd Mem., 2004–; Chm., Fostering Dermatology and Venereology Cttee, 2004–; Member: Membership Cttee, 2004–06; CME Cttee; Jt Ed., EADV News, 2004–07; Lead for Skin Diseases in Pregnancy Task Force, 2006–. Mem., Guidelines Cttee, 2005–, Lead on Eur. Guidelines for Safety of Topical Steroids in Pregnancy, 2006–, Eur. Dermatology Forum. Maria M. Duran Lect., Internat. Soc. of Dermatology, 2006. *Publications: contributions to:* Textbook of Dermatology, 3rd edn 1979 to 5th edn 1992; Oxford Textbook of Medicine, 2005; Textbook of Paediatric Dermatology, 2000, 2nd edn 2005; Dermatology, 2 vols, 2003, 2nd edn 2008; Kidney Transplantation, 5th edn 2001, 6th edn 2008; more than 280 articles in med. and scientific jls on autoimmune bullous disease, transplant dermatology and women's health (vulval disease). *Recreations:* gardening, walking, travel. *Address:* Department of Dermatology, Churchill Hospital, Old Road, Headington, Oxford OX3 7LJ. *T:* (01865) 228266, *Fax:* (01865) 228260; *e-mail:* Fenella.Wojnarowska@orh.nhs.uk.

WOLF, Prof. (Charles) Roland, PhD; FMedSci; FRSE; Director, University of Dundee Biomedical Research Centre and Hon. Director, Cancer Research UK (formerly ICRF) Molecular Pharmacology Unit, since 1992; *b* 26 Feb. 1949; *s* of Werner Max Wolf and Elizabeth Wolf; *m* 1975, Helga Loth; one *s* one *d*. *Educ:* Univ. of Surrey (BSc Chem.; PhD Biochem. 1975). Vis. Fellow, Nat. Inst. of Envmtl Health Scis, N Carolina, 1977–80; Vis. Scientist, ICI Central Toxicology Labs, Macclesfield, 1980–81; Hd of Biochemistry, Inst. of Toxicology, Univ. of Mainz, W Germany, 1981–82; Sen. Scientist, ICRF Med. Oncology Unit, Western Gen. Hosp., Edinburgh, 1982–86; Head, ICRF Molecular Pharmacology Gp, Univ. of Edinburgh, 1986–92. FRSE 1995; FRSA 1999; FMedSci 2000. *Publications:* (ed jtly) Molecular Genetics of Drug Resistance, 1997; numerous scientific papers. *Recreations:* weaving, piano playing, gardening, poetry, hiking. *Address:* University of Dundee Biomedical Research Centre, Level 5, Ninewells Hospital and Medical School, Dundee DD1 9SY. *T:* (01382) 632621.

WOLF, Martin Harry, CBE 2000; Associate Editor, since 1990, and Chief Economics Commentator, since 1996, Financial Times; *b* 16 Aug. 1946; *s* of Edmund Wolf and Rebecca Wolf (*née* Wijnschenk); *m* 1970, Alison Margaret Potter; two *s* one *d*. *Educ:* University College Sch.; Corpus Christi Coll., Oxford (MA 1st cl. Hons Mods 1967; 1st cl. Hons PPE 1969); Nuffield Coll., Oxford (MPhil (BPhil Econs 1971)). World Bank: Young Professional, 1971; Sen. Economist, India Div., 1974–77, Internat. Trade Div., 1979–81; Dir of Studies, Trade Policy Res. Centre, 1981–87; Chief Economics Leader Writer, Financial Times, 1987–96. Special Prof., Economics Dept, Univ. of Nottingham, 1993–; Vis. Fellow, Nuffield Coll., Oxford, 1999–2007. Member: NCC, 1987–93; Council, REconS, 1991–96. Advr and Rapporteur, Eminent Persons Gp on World Trade, 1990. Hon. DLitt Nottingham, 2006; Hon. DSc (Econs) LSE, 2006. (Jtly) Sen. Prize, Wincott Foundn, 1989 and 1997; RTZ David Watt Meml Prize, 1994; Decade of Excellence Award, 2003, Commentator of the Year, 2008, Business Journalist of the Year Awards; Newspaper Feature of the Year Award, 2003, AMEC Lifetime Achievement Award, 2007, Workworld Media Awards; Journalism Prize, Fundació Catalunya Oberta, 2006. Commemoration Medal (NZ), 1990. *Publications:* India's Exports, 1982; Why Globalization Works, 2004; Fixing Global Finance, 2008; numerous articles, mainly on internat. econ. policy. *Recreations:* opera, theatre. *Address:* 27 Court Lane, SE21 7DH. *T:* (020) 8299 0199. *Club:* Reform.

WOLF, Roland; *see* Wolf, C. R.

WOLFE, Prof. Charles David Alexander, MD; FRCOG, FFPH; Professor of Public Health Medicine, King's College London School of Medicine (formerly Guy's, King's and St Thomas' School of Medicine at King's College London), since 2002; Head, Division of Health and Social Care, King's College London, since 2004; *b* 30 July 1954; *s* of Kenneth Wolfe and Doreen Hibbert Wolfe (*née* Anderson). *Educ:* Highgate Sch.; Royal Free Hosp. Sch. of Medicine, Univ. of London (MB BS 1978); MD London 1990. MRCOG 1985, FRCOG 1998; MFPHM 1991, FFPH (FFPHM 1996). Regtl MO, RAMC, 1980–85; United Medical and Dental Schools of Guy's and St Thomas' Hospitals: Res. Fellow in Obstetrics, 1985–87; Lectr in Public Health Medicine, 1988–92; Sen. Lectr, 1992–98; Reader, GKT, 1998–2002; Guy's and St Thomas' Hospital: Hon. Consultant in Public Health Medicine, 1992–; Clinical Dir, Women's Health, 1995–2000; Dir, R&D, 2000–. Mem. Bd, Stanley Thomas Johnson Foundn, Switzerland, 2003–. *Publications:* Stroke Service and Research, 1996; Stroke Services: policy and practice across Europe, 2001; articles in med. jls on health service res. in stroke and women's health. *Recreations:* furniture restoration, classical music, opera. *Address:* Holly Lodge, Queen Street, New Buckenham, Norfolk NR16 2AL. *T:* (office) (020) 7848 6608; *e-mail:* charles.wolfe@kcl.ac.uk.

WOLFE, Gillian Anne, CBE 2005 (MBE 1995); Head of Education, Dulwich Picture Gallery, since 1984 (part-time, since 1990); freelance education consultant, since 1990; *b* 25 March 1946; *d* of late Noel Henry Humphrey and Anne (*née* Nicholls); *m* 1974, Dr Kenneth Maurice Wolfe; one *s* one *d*. *Educ:* Sydenham Girls' Sch.; Central Sch. of Art (Pre Diploma 1968); Stockwell Coll. (BEd Hons London 1972). Teacher: Rushey Gn Primary Sch., 1974; Greenwich Pk Secondary Sch., 1974–84. Advisory Teacher: for ILEA, 1984–89; for Southwark, 1989–2008; British Deleg., EC Council of Europe, Saltzburg, 1989; Advr, Kyoto and Tokyo Mus. Educn Project, 1996; Mem., Exec. Cttee, Nat. Heritage, 1997–2000; Judge, Mus. of Year Award, 1997–2000; Project Advr, American Fedn of Arts, 1998; Consultant, Royal Collection, 1999–2000; Specialist Advr, Clore Foundn, 2001–; Comr, CABE, 2000–03, now Emeritus (Trustee, Educn Foundn, 2003–); Mem., Steering Gp, Attingham Trust Survey on Learning in Historic Envmt, 2001–03; Chm., jt DCMS-DfES Adv. Cttee on developing envmt as an educn resource, 2003–04. Trustee: Gilbert Mus., Somerset House, 1998–2001; Historic Royal Palaces, 2002–05. FRSA 2004. Hon. HLD St Norbert Coll., USA, 2006. NACF Award for Educn, 1987; Southwark Achievement Award, 1998. *Publications:* (contrib.) Oxford Children's Encyclopaedia, 7 vols, 1991; Children's Art and Activity Books, 1997 (Gulbenkian Prize); (contrib.) Oxford Children's Pocket Encyclopaedia, 1999; Oxford First Book of Art, 1999 (Parent Choice Silver Hon. Award, USA); Look!: zoom in on art, 2002 (English Assoc. Award for Best Children's non-fiction book); Look!: body language in art, 2004; Look!: seeing the light in art, 2006; Look!: drawing the line in art, 2008. *Recreations:* gardening, classic cars, music. *Address:* Dulwich Picture Gallery, Gallery Road, SE21 7AD; 31 Calton Avenue, SE21 7DE. *T:* (020) 8299 8730; *e-mail:* g.wolfe@dulwichpicturegallery.org.uk.

WOLFE, John Henry Nicholas, FRCS; Consultant Vascular Surgeon, St Mary's Hospital, London, since 1984; Hon. Consultant Vascular Surgeon, Royal Brompton Hospital, Great Ormond Street Hospital for Children and Edward VII Hospital for Officers, London, since 1984; *b* 4 June 1947; *s* of late Herbert Robert Inglewood Wolfe and Lesley Winifred (*née* Fox); *m* 1st, 1973, Jennifer Sutcliffe; three *s* two *d*; 2nd, 1994, Dorothy May Sturgeon. *Educ:* Eastbourne Coll.; St Thomas's Hosp. Med. Sch., London (MB BS 1971); MS 1981. FRCS 1975. Res. Fellow, Harvard Medical Sch., Brigham Hosp., 1981–82; Sen Registrar, St Thomas' Hosp., 1982–84; Consultant Surgeon, RPMS, Hammersmith, 1984. Hunterian Prof., RCS, 1983; Moynihan Fellow, Assoc. of Surgeons, 1985. Member: Speciality Adv. Bd, Assoc. of Surgeons, 1993–96; Specialities Board of Surgery: RCS, 1994–95; RCSE, 1994–96; Chm., Continuing Med. Educn Cttee, Div. Vascular Surgery, 1998–2001, Pres., Bd of Vascular Surgery, 2001–04, European Union of Med. Specialists, Brussels; Council Member: Vascular Soc. of GB and Ire., 1992–96 (Chm., Vascular Adv. Cttee, 1992–96; Pres., 2005–06); Assoc. of Surgeons of GB and Ire., 1998–2002; Pres., European Soc. of Vascular Surgery, 2007–08. Trustee, British Vascular Foundn, 1999–. Honorary Member: Vascular Soc. of India, 2002–; Swiss Vascular Soc., 2004–; Soc. of Vascular Technologists, 2004–; Vascular Soc. of Germany, 2005–; Assoc. of Surgeons of India, 2007–. FRGS 1996. Freedom, City of London, 2007. *Publications:* (associate ed) Rutherfords's Vascular Surgery, 1984; ABC of Vascular Diseases, 1992, Czech edn 1994, Italian edn 1995; articles on arterial, venous and lymphatic disease, and surgical training. *Recreations:* sailing, painting, rudimentary pond management, walking with children. *Address:* Emmanuel Kaye House, 37A Devonshire Street, W1G 6AA. *T:* (020) 7467 4364, *Fax:* (020) 7467 4376; *e-mail:* jwolfe@uk-consultants.co.uk. *Club:* Royal Ocean Racing.

WOLFE, Hon. Lensley Hugh, OJ 1996; Chief Justice of Jamaica, 1996–2007; *b* 19 June 1938; *s* of Ernest Wolfe and Lucille Wolfe (*née* Hewitt); *m* 1965, Audrey Yvonne Pink; three *d*. *Educ:* St Jago High Sch.; Univ. of West Indies (DMS); Council of Legal Educn Law Sch. Called to the Bar, Lincoln's Inn, 1967, Hon. Bencher, 2006. Asst Clerk of Courts, Jamaica, 1958–66; Dep. Clerk of Courts, 1966–67; Clerk of Courts, 1967–70; Crown Counsel, DPP's Office, 1970–71; practised at private Bar, 1971–77; Resident Magistrate, 1977–81; Judge of Supreme Court, 1981–93; Judge of Appeal, 1993–96; Chancellor, Dio. Jamaica, 1996–. Chm., Nat. Task Force on Crime, 1992–93. *Recreations:* walking, music, browsing on the Internet. *Address:* c/o Supreme Court of Jamaica, Public Buildings (East), King Street, Kingston, Jamaica. *T:* 9228300, 9222933.

WOLFE, Thomas Kennerly, Jr; author and journalist; *b* 2 March 1930; *m* Sheila; one *s* one *d*. *Educ:* Washington and Lee Univ.; Yale Univ. (PhD 1957). Reporter, Springfield (Mass) Union, 1956–59; Reporter and Latin America correspondent, Washington Post, 1959–62; Reporter and magazine writer, New York Herald Tribune, 1962–66; magazine writer, New York World Journal Tribune, 1966–67; Contributing Editor: New York, magazine, 1968–76; Esquire, 1977–. Contributing artist, Harper's, 1978–81; one-man exhibns of drawings, Maynard Walker Gall., NY, 1965, Tunnel Gall., NY, 1974, Forbes Gall., NY, 2000. *Publications:* The Kandy-Kolored Tangerine-Flake Streamline Baby, 1965; The Electric Kool-Aid Acid Test, 1968; The Pump House Gang, 1968; Radical Chic and Mau-mauing the Flak Catchers, 1970; The New Journalism, 1973; The Painted Word, 1975; Mauve Gloves and Madmen, Clutter and Vine, 1976; The Right Stuff, 1979; In Our Time, 1980; From Bauhaus to Our House, 1981; Bonfire of the Vanities, 1987; A Man in Full, 1998; Hooking Up (essays), 2000; I am Charlotte Simmons, 2004. *Address:* c/o Janklow & Nesbit Associates, 445 Park Avenue, New York, NY 10022, USA.

WOLFE, William Cuthbertson; Member, National Council, Scottish National Party, since 1991; *b* 22 Feb. 1924; *s* of late Major Tom Wolfe, TD, and Katie Cuthbertson; *m* 1st, 1953, Arna Mary (marr. diss. 1989), *d* of late Dr Melville Dinwiddie, CBE, DSO, MC; two *s* two *d*; 2nd, 1993, Catherine Margaret, *d* of late James Parker, and *widow* of John McAteer. *Educ:* Bathgate Academy; George Watson's Coll., Edinburgh. CA. Army service, 1942–47, NW Europe and Far East; Air OP Pilot. Hon. Publications Treas., Saltire Society, 1953–60; Scout County Comr, West Lothian, 1960–64; Hon. Pres. (Rector), Students' Assoc., Heriot-Watt Univ., 1966–69. Contested (SNP): West Lothian, 1962, 1964, 1966, 1970, Feb. and Oct. 1974, 1979; North Edinburgh, Nov. 1973; Scottish National Party: Chm., 1969–79; Pres., 1980–82; Mem., NEC, 1998–2002. Treas., Scottish CND, 1982–85; Sec., Scottish Poetry Liby, 1985–91. Mem., Forestry

Commn Nat. Cttee for Scotland, 1974–87. *Publication:* Scotland Lives, 1973. *Address:* 17 Limekilnburn Road, Quarter, Hamilton ML3 7XA. *T:* (01698) 281072.

WOLFENDALE, Sir Arnold (Whittaker), Kt 1995; PhD, DSc; FRS 1977; FInstP, FRAS; Professor of Physics, University of Durham, 1965–92, now Emeritus; Astronomer Royal, 1991–95; *b* 25 June 1927; *s* of Arnold Wolfendale and Doris Wolfendale; *m* 1951, Audrey Darby (*d* 2007); twin *s. Educ:* Univ. of Manchester (BSc Physics 1st Cl. Hons 1948, PhD 1953, DSc 1970). FInstP 1958; FRAS 1973. Asst Lectr, Univ. of Manchester, 1951, Lectr, 1954; University of Durham: Lectr, 1956; Sen. Lectr, 1959; Reader in Physics, 1963; Head of Dept, 1973–77, 1980–83, 1986–89. Vis. Lectr, Univ. of Ceylon, 1952; Vis. Prof., Univ. of Hong Kong, 1977–78; Kan Tong Po Vis. Prof. of Physics, City Univ. of Hong Kong, 1995; Prof. of Experimental Physics, Royal Instn of GB, 1996–2002. Lectures: H. C. Bhuyan Meml, Gauhati Univ., 1978 and 1993; B. B. Roy Meml, Calcutta Univ., 1978; Norman Lockyer, Exeter Univ., 1978; E. A. Milne, Oxford Univ., 1982; Rochester, Durham Univ., 1990 and 2006; A. W. Mailvaganam Meml, Colombo Univ., 1990; Perren, QMW, 1991; O'Neill, Glasgow, 1991; Durham Observatory Anniversary, 1992; Cormack, RSE, 1992; Robinson, Armagh, 1992; David Martin, Royal Soc./British Acad., 1992; Preston Guild, Univ. of Central Lancs, 1992; J. H. Holmes Meml, Newcastle Univ., 1993; Irvine Meml, Stirling, 1993; Tompion, Clockmakers' Co., 1993; Courtauld, Manchester Lit. and Phil., 1993; Minerva, Scientific Instrument Makers' Co., 1993; Hess, IUPAP Cosmic Ray Commn, 1993; Poynting, Univ. of Birmingham, 1994; Mme Curie, Inst. of Physics, 1995; Dee, Glasgow Univ., 1995; Harland, Univ. of Exeter, 1996; Temple Chevallier, Univ. of Durham, 1996; Carter Meml, Nat. Observatory of NZ, 1997; Charter, Inst. of Biology, 1997; Manley Meml, Univ. of Durham, 1997; Cockroft & Walton, Inst. of Physics, India, 1998; Wdowczyk Meml, Univ. of Lodz, Poland, 1998; Bakerian, Royal Soc., 2002; Appapillai Meml, Univ. of Peradeniya, 2003; Pniewski, Tech. Univ. of Warsaw, Plock, 2003. Home Office, Civil Defence, later Regl Scientific Advr, 1956–84. Chm., Northern Reg. Action Cttee, Manpower Services Commn's Job Creation Prog., 1975–78; Mem., SERC, 1988–94 (Chm., Astronomy and Planetary Sci. Bd, 1988–93; Chm., Particles, Space and Astronomy Bd, 1993–94). Chm., Cosmic Ray Commn, IUPAP, 1982–84. President: RAS, 1981–83; Antiquarian Horological Soc., 1993–; Inst. of Physics, 1994–96; European Physical Soc., 1999–2001. Pres., Durham Univ. Soc. of Fellows, 1988–94. Freeman: Clockmakers' Co., 1991 (Liveryman, 2006; Harrison Medal, 2006); Sci. Instrument Makers' Co., 1993. MAE 1998. Foreign Fellow: INSA, 1990; Indian Nat. Acad. Scis; For. Associate, RSSAf, 1995; Hon. Fellow, Lancashire Poly., 1991; Hon. Professor: Univ. of Yunnan, China, 1995; Univ. of Sci. and Technology, Hefei, China, 1995; Tata Inst. of Fundamental Res., 1996. Hon. DSc: Univ. of Potchefstroom for Christian Higher Educn, 1989; Lodz, 1989; Teesside, 1993; Newcastle upon Tyne, 1994; Paisley, 1996; Lancaster, 1996; Bucharest, 2000; DUniv: Open, 1995; Durham, 2001; SW Bulgaria, 2001; Dip. *hc* Romanian Acad., 2000. Univ. of Turku Medal, 1987; Armagh Observatory Medal, 1992; Marian Smoluchowski Medal, Polish Phys. Soc., 1993; Powell Meml Medal, EPS, 1996. Silver Jubilee Medal, 1977; Fiorino d'Oro, Comune di Firenze, 2004. *Publications:* Cosmic Rays, 1963; (ed) Cosmic Rays at Ground Level, 1973; (ed) Origin of Cosmic Rays, 1974; (ed jtly and contrib.) Origin of Cosmic Rays, 1981; (ed) Gamma Ray Astronomy, 1981; (ed) Progress in Cosmology, 1982; (with P. V. Ramana Murthy) Gamma Ray Astronomy, 1986, 2nd edn 1993; (with F. R. Stephenson) Secular Solar and Geomagnetic Variations in the last 1,000 years, 1988; (ed jtly) Observational Tests of Cosmological Inflation, 1991; original papers on studies of cosmic radiation and aspects of astrophysics. *Recreations:* walking, gardening, foreign travel. *Address:* Ansford, Potters Bank, Durham DH1 3RR. *T:* (0191) 384 5642.

WOLFENSOHN, James David, Hon. KBE 1995; Chairman and Chief Executive Officer, Wolfensohn & Co. LLC, since 2007; President, International Bank for Reconstruction and Development, 1995–2005; *b* Sydney, 1 Dec. 1933; *s* of Hyman Wolfensohn and Dora Weinbaum; *m* 1961, Elaine Botwinick; one *s* two *d. Educ:* Univ. of Sydney (BA, LLB); Harvard Business Sch. (MBA). Lawyer, Allen Allen & Hemsley; Officer, RAAF; former Exec. Dep. Chm. and Man. Dir, Schroders Ltd, London; former Man. Dir, Darling & Co., Australia; Pres., J. Henry Schroder Banking Corp., 1970–76; Chm., Salomon Brothers Internat., 1977–81; Pres., James D. Wolfensohn Inc., 1981–95. Special Envoy for Gaza Disengagement, 2005–06. Mem. Bd, Carnegie Hall, NY, 1970 (Chm. Bd, 1980–91, now Chm. Emeritus); Chm., Kennedy Center for the Performing Arts, 1990–95, now Chm. Emeritus. Trustee: Inst. for Advanced Study, Princeton Univ., 1979– (Chm., 1986–2007, now Chm. Emeritus); Rockefeller Univ., 1985–94; Fellow: American Acad. of Arts and Scis; American Philosophical Soc. David Rockefeller Prize, Mus. of Modern Art, NY. *Address:* Wolfensohn & Co. LLC, 1350 Avenue of the Americas, 29th Floor, New York, NY 10019, USA.

WOLFF, Prof. Heinz Siegfried, FIBiol; FIET; Director, Brunel Institute for Bioengineering, Brunel University, 1983–95, Emeritus Professor, since 1995; *b* 29 April 1928; *s* of Oswald Wolff and Margot (*née* Saalfeld); *m* 1953, Joan Eleanor Stephenson; two *s. Educ:* City of Oxford Sch.; University Coll. London (BSc (Hons) Physiology; Fellow, 1987). FIET (FIEE 1993); FIPEMB (FBES 1994). National Institute for Medical Research: Div. of Human Physiology, 1954–62; Hd, Div. of Biomedical Engrg, 1962–70; Hd, Bioengrg Div., Clinical Res. Centre of MRC, 1970–83. European Space Agency: Chm., Life Science Working Gp, 1976–82; Mem., Sci. Adv. Cttee, 1978–82; Chm., Microgravity Adv. Cttee, 1982–91. Chm., Microgravity Panel, Brit. Nat. Space Centre, 1986–87. Bd Dir, Edinburgh Internat. Science Fest., 1995–. Vice-President: Coll. of Occupational Therapy, 1990–; Rehabilitation Engrg Movt Adv. Panel, 1995–; Disabled Living Foundn, 1997–. FRSA; Hon. Fellow, Ergonomics Soc., 1991. *Television series:* BBC TV Young Scientist of the Year (contributor), 1968–81; BBC2: Royal Instn Christmas Lectures, 1975; Great Egg Race, 1978–; Great Experiments, 1985–86. Hon. FRCP 1999. DUniv: Open, 1993; De Montfort, 1995; Oxford Brookes, 1999; Hon. Dr Middlesex, 1999; Hon. DSc Brunel, 2003. Harding Award, Action Res. for the Crippled Child/RADAR, 1989; Edinburgh Medal, Edinburgh Internat. Sci. Fest., 1992; Donald Julius Groen Prize, IMechE, 1994; Medal, 1996, Keith Medal for Innovation, 2001, Royal Scottish Soc. of Arts. *Publications:* Biomedical Engineering, 1969 (German, French, Japanese and Spanish trans, 1970–72); about 120 papers in sci. jls and contribs to books. *Recreations:* working, lecturing to children, dignified practical joking. *Address:* Heinz Wolff Building, Brunel University, Uxbridge, Middx UB8 3PH.

WOLFF, Prof. Jonathan; Professor of Philosophy, University College London, since 2000; *b* 25 June 1959; *s* of Herbert Wolff and Doris Wolff (*née* Polakoff); *m* 2004, Elaine Collins; one *s. Educ:* University Coll. London (BA; MPhil). Lectr, 1986–92, Sen. Lectr, 1992–96, Reader, 1996–2000, in Philosophy, UCL; Founding Dir, Philosophy Programme, Sch. of Advanced Study, Univ. of London, 1995–98. Mem., Nuffield Council on Bioethics, 2008–. Mem., Gambling Review Body, 2000–01; Trustee, Gambling Industry Charitable Trust, subseq. Responsibility in Gambling Trust, 2003–. Hon. Sec., Aristotelian Soc., 2001–07; Sec., British Philosophical Assoc., 2004–07. Editor, Procs of Aristotelian Soc., 1994–2000; columnist, Guardian, 2005–. *Publications:* Robert Nozick: property, justice and the minimal state, 1991; An Introduction to Political Philosophy, 1996; Why Read Marx Today?, 2002; (with Avner de-Shalit) Disadvantage, 2007. *Recreations:* reading, music, spectator sport, film, television. *Address:* Department of Philosophy, University College London, Gower Street, WC1E 6BT. *T:* (020) 7679 3067; *e-mail:* j.wolff@ucl.ac.uk.

WOLFF, Michael, PPCSD; President, Michael Wolff and Company (formerly Newhouse Associates), since 1993; Member, Board of Trustees, the Hunger Project, since 1979; *b* 12 Nov. 1933; *s* of Serge Wolff and Mary (*née* Gordon); *m* 1st, 1976, Susan Kent (marr. diss.); one *d*; 2nd, 1989, Martha Newhouse. *Educ:* Gresham's Sch., Holt, Norfolk; Architectural Association Sch. of Architecture. Designer: Sir William Crawford & Partners, 1957–61; BBC Television, 1961–62; Main Wolff & Partners, 1964–65; with Wolff Olins Ltd as a founder and Creative Director, 1965–83; Chm., Addison Design Consultants, 1987–92. Design Consultant to: W. H. Smith Gp, 1990–98; MFI Gp, 2000–; Mothercare, 2000–; Consultant to: Citigroup, 1998–; Insead, 2003–. Non-exec. Dir, Newell & Sorrell, 1995–98. President: D&AD, 1971; SIAD, then CSD, 1985–87. FRSA. *Recreations:* enjoying a family, seeing. *Address:* 9 Cumberland Gardens, WC1X 9AG. *T:* (020) 7833 0007.

WOLFF, Prof. Otto Herbert, CBE 1985; MD, FRCP; Nuffield Professor of Child Health, University of London, 1965–85, now Emeritus Professor; Dean of the Institute of Child Health, 1982–85; *b* 10 Jan. 1920; *s* of Dr H. A. J. Wolff; *m* 1952, Dr Jill Freeborough (*d* 2002); one *s* one *d. Educ:* Peterhouse, Cambridge; University College Hospital, London. Lieut and Capt. RAMC, 1944–47. Resident Medical Officer, Registrar and Sen. Med. Registrar, Birmingham Children's Hospital, 1948–51; Lecturer, Sen. Lectr, Reader, Dept of Pædiatrics and Child Health, Univ. of Birmingham, 1951–64. Senator, London Univ.; Representative of London Univ. on GMC. Past Pres., British Pædiatric Assoc.; Member: Royal Society of Medicine; American Pædiatric Society; New York Academy of Sciences; Amer. Academy of Pediatrics; European Soc. for Paediatric Research; European Soc. for Paediatric Gastroenterology; Deutsche Akad. der Naturforscher Leopoldina. Corresp. Member: Société Française de Pédiatrie; Société Suisse de Pédiatrie; Österreichische Gesellschaft für Kinderheilkunde; Società Italiana di Pediatria; Deutsche Gesellschaft für Kinderheilkunde; Fellow, Indian Acad. of Pediatrics. Chm. of Trustees, Child-to-Child Charity, 1989–93. Hon. FRCPCH 1996. Dawson Williams Meml Prize, BMA, 1984; Medal, Assoc. Française pour le Dépistage et la Prévention des Maladies Métaboliques et des Handicaps de l'Enfant, 1986; Harding Award, Action Res. for Crippled Child, 1987; James Spence Medal, BPA, 1988. *Publications:* chapter on Disturbances of Serum Lipoproteins in Endocrine and Genetic Diseases of Childhood (ed L. I. Gardner); chapter on Obesity in Recent Advances in Paediatrics (ed David Hull); articles in Lancet, British Medical Journal, Archives of Disease in Childhood, Quarterly Jl of Medicine, etc. *Recreation:* music. *Address:* 53 Danbury Street, N1 8LE. *T:* (020) 7226 0748.

WOLFFE, (Walter) James; QC (Scot.) 2007; *b* Dumfries, 20 Dec. 1962; *s* of Antony C. Wolffe and Alexandra L. Wolffe (*née* Graham); *m* 1987, Sarah Poyntell LaBudde; two *s. Educ:* Univ. of Edinburgh (LLB Hons; DipLP); Univ. of Oxford (BCL). Legal Asst to the Lord Pres. of the Court of Session, 1990–91; Advocate, 1992; First Standing Jun. Counsel to the Scottish Ministers, 2002–07; Advocate Depute, 2007–; Sen. Advocate Depute, 2007–. Mem., Scottish Council of Law Reporting, 2008–. Trustee, Nat. Liby of Scotland, 2008–. *Publications: contributions to:* Finnie et al's Edinburgh Essays in Public Law, 1991; Stair Memorial Encyclopaedia of the Laws of Scotland; Gloag and Henderson's The Law of Scotland, 11th edn; Johnston and Zimmermann's Unjustified Enrichment Key Issues in Comparative Perspective, 2002; Macfadyen's Court of Session Practice; articles in Public Law, Scots Law Times and Edinburgh Law Review. *Address:* Advocates Library, Parliament House, Parliament Square, Edinburgh EH11 1RF. *T:* (0131) 226 5071; *e-mail:* james.wolffe@axiomadvocates.com. *Club:* Waverley Tennis.

WOLFSON, family name of **Barons Wolfson** and **Wolfson of Sunningdale**.

WOLFSON, Baron *cr* 1985 (Life Peer), of Marylebone in the City of Westminster; **Leonard Gordon Wolfson,** Kt 1977; Bt 1962; Chairman, since 1972, and Founder Trustee, since 1955, Wolfson Foundation; Chairman: Great Universal Stores, 1981–96 (Managing Director, 1962–81; Director, 1952); Burberrys Ltd, 1978–96; *b* London, 11 Nov. 1927; *s* of Sir Isaac Wolfson, 1st Bt, FRS (*d* 1991) and Lady (Edith) Wolfson (*d* 1981); *m* 1st, 1949 (marr. diss. 1991); four *d*; 2nd, 1991, Estelle (*née* Feldman), *widow* of Michael Jackson, FCA; one step *s* one step *d. Educ:* King's School, Worcester. President: Jewish Welfare Bd, 1972–82; Shaare Zedek UK, 2006–. Hon. Pres., British Technion Soc., 2006. Trustee, Imperial War Mus., 1988–94. Fellow: Royal Albert Hall, 2003; Birkbeck Coll., Univ. of London, 2006. Hon. Fellow: St Catherine's Coll., Oxford; Wolfson Coll., Cambridge; Wolfson Coll., Oxford; Worcester Coll., Oxford; UCL; LSHTM 1985; QMC 1985; Poly. of Central London, 1991; Imperial Coll., 1991; LSE, 1999; Somerville Coll., Oxford, 1999; Inst. of Educn, London Univ., 2001; RAM, 2003; Hon. Mem., Emmanuel Coll., Cambridge, 1996. Hon. Fellow: Israel Mus., 2001; Royal Instn, 2002. Hon. FRCP 1977; Hon. FRCS 1988; Hon. FBA 1986; Hon. FREng (Hon. FEng 1997); Hon. FRS 2005; Hon. MRCSEd 1997, Companion, RCSE, 2006. Hon. DCL Oxon, 1972; Hon. LLD: Strathclyde, 1972; Dundee, 1979; Cantab, 1982; London, 1982; Hon. DSc: Hull, 1977; Wales, 1984; E Anglia, 1986; Sheffield, 2005; Cape Town, 2008; Hon. PhD: Tel Aviv, 1971; Hebrew Univ., 1978; Bar Ilan, 1983; Weizmann Inst., 1988; DUniv: Surrey, 1990; Glasgow, 1997; Hon. MD Birmingham, 1992; Dr *hc:* Technion, 1995; Edinburgh, 1996; Hon. DLitt Loughborough, 2003. Sir Winston Churchill Award, British Technion Soc., 1989; President's Award, Hebrew Univ., 2005. *Address:* 8 Queen Anne Street, W1G 9LD.

See also Hon. J. F. W. de Botton.

WOLFSON OF SUNNINGDALE, Baron *cr* 1991 (Life Peer), of Trevose in the County of Cornwall; **David Wolfson,** Kt 1984; Chairman: Next plc, 1990–98; Great Universal Stores, 1996–2000; *b* 9 Nov. 1935; *s* of Charles Wolfson and Hylda Wolfson; *m* 1st, 1962, Patricia E. Rawlings (*see* Baroness Rawlings) (marr. diss. 1967); 2nd, 1967, Susan E. Davis; two *s* one *d. Educ:* Clifton Coll.; Trinity Coll., Cambridge (MA); Stanford Univ., California (MBA). Great Universal Stores, 1960–78, 1993–2000, Director, 1973–78 and 1993–2000; Secretary to Shadow Cabinet, 1978–79; Chief of Staff, Political Office, 10 Downing Street, 1979–85. Chm., Alexon Group PLC (formerly Steinberg Group PLC), 1982–86; non-executive Director: Stewart Wrightson Holdings PLC, 1985–87; Next, 1989–90; Compco Hldgs plc, 1995–2004; Fibernet Gp plc, 2001–06 (Chm., 2002–). Hon. Fellow, Hughes Hall, Cambridge, 1989. Hon. FRCR 1978; Hon. FRCOG 1989. *Recreations:* golf, bridge. *Clubs:* Portland; Sunningdale; Woburn Golf; Trevose Golf (N Cornwall).

See also S. A. Wolfson.

WOLFSON, (Geoffrey) Mark, OBE 2002; *b* 7 April 1934; *s* of late Captain V. Wolfson, OBE, VRD, RNVR, and Dorothy Mary Wolfson; *m* 1965, Edna Webb (*née* Hardman); two *s. Educ:* Eton Coll.; Pembroke Coll., Cambridge (MA). Served Royal Navy, 1952–54; Cambridge, 1954–57; Teacher in Canada, 1958–59; Warden, Brathay Hall Centre, Westmorland, 1962–66; Head of Youth Services, Industrial Soc., 1966–69; Hd of Personnel, 1970–85, Dir, 1973–88, Hambros Bank. MP (C) Sevenoaks, 1979–97. PPS to

Minister of State for NI, 1983–84, to Minister of State for Defence Procurement, 1984–85, to Minister of State for Armed Forces, 1987–88. Mem., NI Select Cttee, 1994–97. Officer, Cons. Backbench Employment Cttee, 1981–83. Mem., Parly Human Rights Delegns to Nicaragua, 1982, El Salvador and Baltic States, 1990, and St Helena, 1996. Associate Advr, Industrial Soc., 1997–98. Cttee Mem. and Trustee, Brathay Hall Trust, 1968–2002; Dir, McPhail Charitable Settlement, 1996–. *Address:* 6 Fynes Street, Westminster, SW1P 4NH.

WOLFSON, Mark; *see* Wolfson, G. M.

WOLFSON, Hon. Simon Adam; Chief Executive, Next plc, since 2001; *b* 27 Oct. 1967; *e s* of Lord Wolfson of Sunningdale, *qv. Educ:* Radley Coll.; Trinity Coll., Cambridge. Dir, 1997–, Man. Dir, 1999–2001, Next plc. *Address:* Next plc, Desford Road, Enderby, Leicester LE19 4AT. *T:* (0116) 284 2308.

WOLL, Prof. Bencie, PhD; Professor of Sign Language and Deaf Studies, and Director, Deafness, Cognition and Language Research Centre, University College London, since 2005; *b* 22 Feb. 1950; *d* of Lazar Benzion Woll and Fannie Zifkin Woll. *Educ:* Univ. of Pennsylvania (BA 1970); Univ. of Essex (MA 1971); Univ. of Bristol (PhD 1991). Sen. Lectr/Res. Fellow, Univ. of Bristol, 1973–95; Prof. of Sign Language and Deaf Studies, City Univ., London, 1995–2005. Vice Chm., Royal Assoc. for Deaf People, 2002–; Mem., Sign Language Adv. Cttee, Council for Advancement of Communication with Deaf People, 2003–. *Publications:* (with J. Kyle) Sign Language: the study of deaf people and their language, 1985; (with R. Sutton-Spence) The Linguistics of BSL, 1999. *Recreations:* cats, Yiddish language and culture. *Address:* Deafness, Cognition and Language Research Centre, 49 Gordon Square, WC1H 0PD. *T:* (020) 7679 8670, *Fax:* (020) 7679 8691; *e-mail:* b.woll@ucl.ac.uk. *Club:* Penn (New York).

WOLMER, Viscount; William Lewis Palmer; Managing Director, Blackmoor Estate; *b* 1 Sept. 1971; *s* and *heir* of 4th Earl of Selborne, *qv; m* 2001, Victoria Baum; two *s* one *d. Educ:* Eton Coll.; Christ Church, Oxford (BA 1993); Sch. of Oriental and African Studies, London Univ. (MA 1996); Univ. of Sussex (PhD 2001). Res. Officer, then Fellow, Inst. of Develt Studies, Univ. of Sussex, 1997–2007. *Publication:* From Wilderness Vision to Farm Invasions, 2007.

WOLPERT, Prof. Daniel Mark, DPhil; FMedSci; 1875 Professor of Engineering, University of Cambridge, since 2005; Fellow, Trinity College, Cambridge, since 2005; *b* 8 Sept. 1963; *s* of Prof. Lewis Wolpert, *qv* and Elizabeth Wolpert (*née* Brownstein); *m* 1990, Mary Anne Shorrock; two *d. Educ:* Hall Sch.; Westminster Sch.; Trinity Hall, Cambridge (BA Hons Med. Scis 1985); Magdalene Coll., Univ. of Oxford (BM BCh Clinical Medicine 1988); Lincoln Coll., Univ. of Oxford (DPhil Physiol. 1992). Med. House Officer, Oxford, 1988–89; MRC Trng Fellow, Univ. Lab. of Physiol., Univ. of Oxford, 1989–92; Fulbright Scholarship, 1992–95, Postdoctoral Associate, 1992–94, McDonnell-Pew Fellow in Cognitive Neurosci., 1994–95, Dept of Brain and Cognitive Sci., MIT; Institute of Neurology, University College London: Lectr, 1995–99, Reader in Motor Neurosci., 1999–2002; Prof. of Motor Neurosci. and Vice Chm., Sobell Dept of Motor Neurosci., 2002–05; Co-Dir, Inst. of Movt Neurosci., 1999–2005; Hon. Sen. Res. Fellow, UCL, 2005–. Francis Crick Prize Lect., Royal Soc., 2005. FMedSci 2004. *Publications:* articles on neuroscience in learned jls. *Recreations:* gadgets and games. *Address:* Department of Engineering, University of Cambridge, Trumpington Street, Cambridge CB2 1PZ. *T:* (01223) 748530, *Fax:* (01223) 332662; *e-mail:* wolpert@eng.cam.ac.uk; *web:* www.wolpertlab.com.

WOLPERT, Prof. Lewis, CBE 1990; DIC, PhD; FRS 1980; FRSL; Professor of Biology as Applied to Medicine, London University, at University College London Medical School (formerly at Middlesex Hospital Medical School), 1966–2004, now Emeritus; *b* 19 Oct. 1929; *s* of William and Sarah Wolpert; *m* 1961, Elizabeth Brownstein; two *s* two *d. Educ:* King Edward's Sch., Johannesburg; Univ. of Witwatersrand (BScEng); Imperial Coll., London (DIC; FIC 1996); King's Coll., London (PhD; FKC 2001). Personal Asst to Director of Building Research Inst., S African Council for Scientific and Industrial Research, 1951–52; Engineer, Israel Water Planning Dept, 1953–54; King's College, London: Asst Lectr in Zoology, 1958–60; Lectr in Zoology, 1960–64; Reader in Zoology, 1964–66; Hd of Dept of Biology as Applied to Medicine, later Dept of Anatomy and Biology as Applied to Medicine, Middlesex Hosp. Med. Sch., 1966–87. MRC: Mem. Council, 1984–88; Mem., 1982–88, Chm., 1984–88, Cell Bd; Chairman: Scientific Inf. Cttee, Royal Soc., 1983–88; COPUS, 1994–98; Biology Concerted Action Cttee, EEC, 1988–91. President: British Soc. for Cell Biology, 1985–91; Inst. of Information Scientists, 1986–87. Lectures: Steinhaus, Univ. of California at Irvine, 1980; van der Horst, Univ. of Witwatersrand, Johannesburg, 1981; Bidder, Soc. for Experimental Biology, Leicester, 1982; Swirling, Dana-Faber, Boston, 1985; Lloyd-Roberts, RCP, 1986; Royal Instn Christmas Lectures, 1986; R. G. Williams, Univ. of Pennsylvania, 1988; Bernal, Birkbeck Coll., 1989; Radcliffe, Warwick Univ., 1990; Redfearn, Leicester, 1991; Wade, Southampton, 1991; Robb, Univ. of Auckland, 1994; Samuel Gee, RCP, 1995; Hunterian Oration, 1996; Gerald Walters Meml, Bath Univ., 1997; Medawar, 1998, Faraday (also Award), 2000, Royal Soc.; Rose, Marine Biol. Lab., Woods Hole, Mass., 2001. Presenter: Antenna, BBC2, 1987–88; A Living Hell, BBC2, 1999; interviews with scientists, Radio 3, 1981–; radio documentaries: The Dark Lady of DNA, 1989; The Virgin Fathers of the Calculus, 1991. FRSL 1999. Mem., Amer. Philos. Soc., 2002. For. Mem., Polish Acad. of Arts and Scis, 1998. Hon. MRCP, 1986. Hon. Fellow, UCL, 1995. Hon. DSc: CNAA, 1992; Leicester, 1996; Westminster, 1996; Bath, 1997; DUniv Open, 1998. Scientific Medal, Zoological Soc., 1968; Hamburger Award, Amer. Soc. of Develtl Biol., 2003. *Publications:* A Passion for Science (with A. Richards), 1988; Triumph of the Embryo, 1991; The Unnatural Nature of Science, 1992; (with A. Richards) Passionate Minds, 1997; Principles of Development, 1998; Malignant Sadness: the anatomy of depression, 1999; Six Impossible Things Before Breakfast, 2006; articles on cell and developmental biology in scientific jls. *Recreation:* tennis. *Address:* Cell and Developmental Biology, University College London, Gower Street, WC1E 6BT.
See also D. M. Wolpert.

WOLSELEY, Sir Charles Garnet Richard Mark, 11th Bt *cr* 1628; Partner, Smiths Gore, Chartered Surveyors, 1979–87 (Associate Partner, 1974); *b* 16 June 1944; *s* of Capt. Stephen Garnet Hubert Francis Wolseley, Royal Artillery (*d* 1944, of wounds received in action) and Pamela (*d* 2002), *yr d* of late Capt. F. Barry and Mrs Lavinia Power, Wolseley Park, Rugeley, Staffs; *S* grandfather, Sir Edric Charles Joseph Wolseley, 10th Bt, 1954; *m* 1st, 1968, Anita Maria (marr. diss. 1984), *er d* of late H. J. Fried, Epsom, Surrey; one *s* three *d*; 2nd, 1984, Mrs Imogene Brown. *Educ:* St Bede's School, near Stafford; Ampleforth College, York. FRICS. *Recreations:* shooting, fishing, gardening, painting. *Heir: s* Stephen Garnet Hugo Charles Wolseley, *b* 2 May 1980. *Club:* Shikar.

WOLSELEY, Sir James Douglas, 13th Bt *cr* 1745 (Ire.), of Mount Wolseley, Co. Carlow; *b* 17 Sept. 1937; *s* of James Douglas Wolseley (*d* 1960), and Olive, *d* of Carroll Walter Wofford; *S* kinsman, Sir Garnet Wolseley, 12th Bt, 1991, but his name does not appear on the Official Roll of the Baronetage; *m* 1st, 1965, Patricia Lynn (marr. diss. 1971), *d* of William R. Hunter; 2nd, 1984, Mary Anne, *d* of Thomas G. Brown. *Heir: kinsman* John Walter Wolseley [*b* 21 April 1938; *m* 1964, Patricia Ann Newland (marr. diss. 1978); two *s*].

WOLSTENCROFT, Ven. Alan; Archdeacon of Manchester, Canon Residentiary of Manchester Cathedral, and Fellow of the College, 1998–2004, now Archdeacon and Canon Emeritus; *b* 16 July 1937; *s* of John Wolstencroft and Jean (*née* Miller); *m* 1968, Christine Mary Hall; one *s* one *d. Educ:* Wellington Tech. Sch., Altrincham; St John's Coll. of Further Educn, Manchester; Cuddesdon Coll., Oxford. Nat. Service, RAF, Nat. Mountain Rescue Team, 1955–57. Trainee Manager, W. H. Smith & Co., 1957–59; Regl Wine and Spirit Manager, Bass/Charrington Co., 1959–67; ordained deacon, 1969, priest, 1970; Assistant Curate: St Thomas, Halliwell, 1969–71; All Saints, Stand, 1971–73; Vicar, St Martin, Wythenshawe, 1973–80; Asst Chaplain, Wythenshawe Hosp., 1973–91; Rural, then Area, Dean of Withington, 1978–91; Vicar: St John the Divine, Brooklands, 1980–91; St Peter, Bolton, 1991–98. Clerical Sec., York Convocation, 2007–. Theatre Chaplain, Actors' Church Union, 1975–; Religious Advr, Granada TV, 2000–. *Recreations:* squash, watching football, sport, theatre, reading, wines, beers, walking. *Address:* The Bakehouse, 1 Latham Row, Horwich, Bolton, Lancs BL6 6QZ. *T:* and *Fax:* (01204) 469985. *Clubs:* Royal Air Force; Bolton Wanderers FC.

WOLSTENHOLME, (John) Scott; His Honour Judge Wolstenholme; a Circuit Judge, since 1995; *b* 28 Nov. 1947; *s* of Donald Arthur Wolstenholme and Kaye (*née* Humphrys); *m* 1972, Lynne Harrison; three *s* one *d. Educ:* Roundhay Sch., Leeds; University Coll., Oxford (MA). Called to the Bar, Middle Temple, 1971; practised North Eastern Circuit, 1971–92; Chm., Industrial Tribunals, Leeds Region, 1992–95; a Recorder, 1992–95. *Recreations:* playing the drums, walking, golf, photography. *Address:* Leeds Combined Court Centre, Oxford Row, Leeds LS1 3BG.

WOLSTENHOLME, Roy; Investment Consultant, Mercury Asset Management, since 1994; *b* 1 Jan. 1936; *m* 1959, Mary R. Wolstenholme; one *s* two *d. Educ:* Stretford Grammar Sch.; Manchester College of Commerce. Stretford Bor. Council, 1952–61; Worcs CC, 1961–63; Worthing Bor. Council, 1963–65; Glos CC, 1965–68; Holland (Lincs) CC, 1968–74; Lincs CC, 1974–77; County Treasurer: Northumberland CC, 1977–88; Surrey CC, 1988–94. *Recreations:* music, walking, gardening. *Address:* 39 Foxhill Crescent, Camberley, Surrey GU15 1PR. *Club:* Royal Over-Seas League.

WOLSTENHOLME, Scott; *see* Wolstenholme, J. S.

WOLTERS, Gwyneth Eleanor Mary; a Commissioner of Inland Revenue, 1971–78; *b* 21 Nov. 1918; *d* of late Prof. and Mrs A. W. Wolters. *Educ:* Abbey Sch., Reading; Reading Univ.; Newnham Coll., Cambridge (Class. Tripos; Hilda Richardson Prize). Temp. Admin. Asst, Min. of Works, 1941–47; Asst Principal, 1947–49, Principal, 1949–57, Asst Sec., 1957–71, Inland Revenue. *Address:* 45 Albert Road, Caversham, Reading RG4 7AW. *T:* (0118) 947 2605.

WOLTON, Harry; QC 1982; a Recorder, 1985–2003; *b* 1 Jan. 1938; *s* of late Harry William Wolton and Dorothy Beatrice Wolton; *m* 1971, Julie Rosina Josephine Lovell (*née* Mason); three *s. Educ:* King Edward's Sch., Birmingham (Foundn Scholar); Univ. of Birmingham. Called to the Bar, Gray's Inn, 1969; authorised to sit as a Dep. High Court Judge, 1990–2003. Dir, Bar Mutual Insurance Fund, 1997–2004. Hon. Legal Advr, John Groom's Charity, 2004–. *Recreations:* cattle breeding, dendrology. *Address:* The Black Venn, Edwyn Ralph, Bromyard, Herefordshire HR7 4LU. *T:* (01885) 483302. *Club:* Garrick.

WOLTZ, Alan Edward; Chairman, London International Group, 1985–93 (Chief Executive, 1985–91); *b* 29 Feb. 1932; *s* of Robert Woltz and Rose Woltz Katz; *m* 1977, Barbara Howell, writer (*d* 1994); three *s* one *d. Educ:* Dwight Morrow High Sch., Eaglewood, NJ; Wagner Coll., Staten Is, NY. Served US Army, Korea, 1952–54. Schmid Laboratories Inc.: Exec. Vice-Pres., 1971–74; Pres., 1974–78; Pres., LRC N America, 1978–79; Man. Dir and Chief Exec., London Internat. Gp, 1979–85. *Recreations:* golf, swimming. *Club:* Metropolitan (NY).

WOLVERHAMPTON, Bishop Suffragan of, since 2007; **Rt Rev. Clive Malcolm Gregory;** *b* 25 Nov. 1961; *s* of John and Aurea Gregory; *m* 1997, Jenny Hyde; one *s* one *d. Educ:* Lancaster Univ. (BA Hons English 1984); Queens' Coll., Cambridge (BA Theology 1987, MA 1989); Westcott House Theol Coll. Ordained deacon, 1988, priest, 1989; Asst Curate, St John the Baptist, Margate, 1988–92; Sen. Chaplain, Univ. of Warwick, 1992–98; Team Rector, Coventry E, 1998–2007. Hon. MA Warwick, 1999. *Recreations:* walking, playing cricket, contemporary music. *Address:* 61 Richmond Road, Wolverhampton WV3 9JH. *T:* (01902) 824503, *Fax:* (01902) 824504; *e-mail:* bishop.wolverhampton@lichfield.anglican.org.

WOLVERTON, 7th Baron *cr* 1869; **Christopher Richard Glyn,** FRICS; *b* 5 Oct. 1938; *s* of 6th Baron Wolverton, CBE and Audrey Margaret, *d* of late Richard Stubbs; *S* father, 1988; *m* 1st, 1961, Carolyn Jane (marr. diss. 1967), *yr d* of late Antony N. Hunter; two *d*; 2nd, 1975, Mrs Frances S. E. Stuart Black (marr. diss. 1989); 3rd, 1990, Gillian Konig (marr. diss. 1994). *Educ:* Eton. *Heir: nephew* Miles John Glyn, *b* 1966. *Address:* 97 Hurlingham Road, SW6 3NL.

WOLZFELD, Jean-Louis; Ambassador of Luxembourg to Italy, since 2007; *b* 5 July 1951; *s* of late Gustave Wolzfeld and of Marie Thérèse (*née* Normand). *Educ:* Univ. of Paris I (Master Internat. Law). Entered Luxembourg Foreign Service, 1976; Internat. Econ. Relns Dept, Min. of Foreign Affairs, 1977–80; Dep. Perm. Rep., Geneva, 1981–86; Ambassador: Japan, 1986–93; Perm. Rep. to UN, 1993–98; Dir for Pol Affairs, Min. of Foreign Affairs, 1998–2002; Ambassador to the UK and concurrently to Ireland and Iceland, 2002–07. Officer, Ordre du Mérite (Luxembourg), 1995; Comdr, Ordre de la Couronne de Chêne (Luxembourg), 2001. *Recreations:* travel, painting. *Address:* c/o Luxembourg Embassy, 90 Via di Santa Croce in Gerusalemme, Rome 00185, Italy. *Clubs:* Athenæum, Travellers.

WOMACK, Joanna Mary; Fellow, Bursar and Development Director, Clare Hall, Cambridge, since 2003; *b* 12 Sept. 1947; *d* of Laurence Paul Hodges and Mary Elizabeth Hodges (*née* Lyon); *m* 1971, Michael Thomas Womack; three *s. Educ:* James Allen's Girls' Sch., Dulwich; New Hall, Cambridge (MA 1st Cl. Hons Law). Admitted solicitor, 1972; solicitor, Herbert Smith & Co., 1972–75; New Hall, Cambridge: Coll. Lectr in Law, 1975–83; Fellow, 1975–90; Bursar, 1983–90; Emeritus Fellow, 1996; Trinity Hall, Cambridge: Bursar and Steward, 1990–93; Fellow, 1990–2003; Treasurer, Cambridge Univ., 1993–2003. Gen. Comr of Tax, 1987–. Dir, Cambridge Building Soc., 1994–2006. Trustee: Sir Halley Stewart Trust, 2003–; The Varrier-Jones Foundn, 2005–; The Papworth Trust, 2006–. Gov., Long Road VI Form Coll., Cambridge, 1992–2001. *Recreations:* family life, photography, music, hill-walking. *Address:* Clare Hall, Herschel Road, Cambridge CB3 9AL. *T:* (01223) 332362.

WOMBELL, Paul David; Festival Director, Hereford Photography Festival, 2006–07; *b* 8 Oct. 1948; *s* of Clifford and Katherine Wombell; *m* 1995, Tricia Coral Buckley. *Educ:* St Martin's Sch. of Art, London (BA Fine Art). Midland Gp Art Centre, 1983–86; Director: Impressions Gall., York, 1986–94; The Photographers' Gall., London, 1994–2005. Vis. Prof., 2003–07, Res. Prof., 2007–, Univ. of Sunderland. Chm., Citigroup Photography Prize, 2003–05. *Publications:* Battle, Passchendale 1917, 1981; Photovideo: photography in the age of the computer, 1991; Sportscape, the evolution of sport photography, 2000; Blink, 2002; Local: the end of globalisation, 2007. *Recreation:* life. *Address:* 238 Brick Lane, E2 7EB.

WOMBWELL, Sir George (Philip Frederick), 7th Bt *cr* 1778; *b* 21 May 1949; *s* of Sir (Frederick) Philip (Alfred William) Wombwell, 6th Bt, MBE, and late Ida Elizabeth, *er d* of Frederick J. Leitch; *S* father, 1977, but his name does not appear on the Official Roll of the Baronetage; *m* 1974, (Hermione) Jane, *e d* of T. S. Wrightson; one *s* one *d. Educ:* Repton. *Heir: s* Stephen Philip Henry Wombwell, *b* 12 May 1977. *Address:* Newburgh Priory, Coxwold, York YO61 4AS.

WOMERSLEY, Prof. David John, PhD; FRHistS; Thomas Warton Professor of English Literature, University of Oxford, since 2002; Fellow, St Catherine's College, Oxford, since 2002; *b* 29 Jan. 1957; *s* of John Crossley Womersley and late Joyce Womersley; *m* 1982, Carolyn Jane Godlee; one *s* two *d. Educ:* Strodes Sch., Egham; Trinity Coll., Cambridge (BA 1979; PhD 1983). FRHistS 1997; FEA 2003. Drapers' Co. Res. Fellow, Pembroke Coll., Cambridge, 1981–83; Lectr, Sch. of English, Univ. of Leeds, 1983–84; Fellow and Tutor in English Lit., Jesus Coll., Oxford, 1984–2002; Sen. Proctor, Univ. of Oxford, 2001–02. Governor: Dragon Sch., Oxford, 1998–; Harrow Sch., 2001–. *Publications:* The Transformation of the Decline and Fall of the Roman Empire, 1988; Gibbon and the 'Watchmen of the Holy City': the historian and his reputation 1776–1814, 2002; *edited:* Edward Gibbon, The Decline and Fall of the Roman Empire, 3 vols, 1994, 7th edn 2004, facsimile edn, 6 vols, 1997, abridged edn 2000, 10th edn 2004; Edward Gibbon, Reflections on the Fall of Rome, 1995; Religious Scepticism: contemporary responses to Gibbon, 1997; Augustan Critical Writing, 1997; Edmund Burke, Pre-Revolutionary Writings, 1998; Restoration Drama: an anthology, 2000; Samuel Johnson, Selected Essays, 2003; James Boswell, Life of Johnson, 2009; *edited collections of essays:* Gibbon: bicentenary essays, 1997; A Companion to English Literature from Milton to Blake, 2000; Cultures of Whiggism, 2005; Literary Milieux, 2009. *Recreations:* wine, yachting, cooking, dogs. *Address:* St Catherine's College, Manor Road, Oxford OX1 3UJ. *T:* (01865) 271714, *Fax:* (01865) 271768; *e-mail:* david.womersley@ell.ox.ac.uk.

WOMERSLEY, (Denis) Keith, CBE 1974; HM Diplomatic Service, retired; *b* 21 March 1920; *s* of late Alfred Womersley, Bradford, Yorks, and late Agnes (*née* Keighley); *m* 1st, 1955, Eileen Georgina (*d* 1990), *d* of late George and Margaret Howe; 2nd, 1992, Gillian Anne, *widow* of Dr Gerard O'Donnell; three step *s* one step *d. Educ:* Christ's Hospital; Caius Coll., Cambridge (Hons, MA). Served War, HM Forces, 1940–46. Entered Foreign (later Diplomatic) Service, 1946; Foreign Office, 1948, Control Commn Germany, 1952; Vienna, 1955; Hong Kong, 1957, FO, 1960; Baghdad, 1962; FO, 1963; Aden, 1966; Beirut, 1967; FCO, 1969–71; Bonn, 1971–74; Counsellor, FCO, 1974–77. FRSA 1976. Gov., Christ's Hosp., 1991–. *Recreations:* violin-playing, Abbeyfield Soc. work. *Club:* Christ's Hospital (Horsham).

See also J. A. O'Donnell.

WOMERSLEY, Sir Peter (John Walter), 2nd Bt *cr* 1945; JP; human resources consultant; *b* 10 Nov. 1941; *s* of Capt. John Womersley (*o s* of 1st Bt; killed in action in Italy, 1944), and of Betty, *d* of Cyril Williams, Elstead, Surrey; *S* grandfather, 1961; *m* 1968, Janet Margaret Grant; two *s* two *d. Educ:* Aldro; Charterhouse; RMA, Sandhurst. Entered Royal Military Academy (Regular Army), 1960; Lt, King's Own Royal Border Regt, 1964; Captain, 1967; retd 1968; Personnel, then Human Resources, Manager, later Evaluation Project Manager, Human Resources, SmithKline Beecham, 1968–97. JP Steyning, 1991, Worthing and Dist, 1996. *Publication:* (with Neil Grant) Collecting Stamps, 1980. *Heir: s* John Gavin Grant Womersley, *b* 7 Dec. 1971. *Address:* Broomfields, 23 Goring Road, Steyning, W Sussex BN44 3GF.

WONDRAUSCH, Mary, OBE 2000; potter, since 1975; painter; *b* 17 Dec. 1923; *d* of Harold Lambert and Margaret (*née* Montgomery); *m* 1st, 1943, Kenneth Fyfe (marr. annulled); 2nd, 1946, Basil Harthan (marr. diss.); 3rd, 1954, Witold Wondrausch (marr. diss.); one *s* two *d. Educ:* Convent IBVM, St Mary's, Ascot; Convent FCJ, Ware, Herts; Kingston Sch. of Art. WAAF (invalided out), 1943. Flibertygibbet, waitress, cook; professional painter, exhibited, Women's Internat. Art Club, FBA, etc; art teacher, Barrow Hills Sch., 1960–75; set up pottery, Godalming, 1975, later Farncombe, then stables at Brickfields, 1984. Lectures on Continental slipware to BM, Fitzwilliam Mus., Cambridge, and Nat. Ethnographic Mus., Budapest. Pots in private and public collections incl. V&A Mus.; pottery exhibitions: Heidelberg Gall.; Craftsman Potters' Assoc.; British Craft Centre; Farnham Gall.; Amalgam; Univ. of Aberystwyth; Stoke-on-Trent Mus.; BM; Abbots Hall, Kendall; Primavera, Cambridge; Haslemere Mus.; painting exhibitions: Canon Gall., Petworth; Farnham Mus.; Cricket Gall., Chelsea. Hon. Fellow, Craft Potters' Assoc., 2005. *Publications:* Mary Wondrausch on Slipware, 1986, 2nd edn 2001; Brickfields: my life as a potter, painter, gardener, writer and cook, 2004, 2nd edn 2005; contrib. articles on Continental slipware to Ceramic Rev., Antique Collector; contribs on history of food to Oxford Encyclopaedia of Food, Petits Propos Culinaires, Oxford DNB, Oxford Symposium of Food. *Recreations:* reading, eating and drinking good food and wine, making wacky fountains from found materials, wild mushroom gathering. *Address:* The Pottery, Brickfields, Compton, Guildford, Surrey GU3 1HZ. *T:* (01483) 414097.

WONG Kin Chow, Michael, GBS 2001; JP; Chairman, Equal Opportunities Commission of Hong Kong, 2003; a Justice of Appeal of the High Court of Hong Kong, 1999–2001; *b* 16 Aug. 1936; *s* of late Wong Chong and Au Ting; *m* 1963, Mae (*née* Fong); two *s* two *d. Educ:* Univ. of Liverpool (LLB Hons 1961). Called to the Bar, Middle Temple, 1962; private practice, Hong Kong, 1962–65; Hong Kong Government: Crown Counsel, Legal Dept, 1966–69; Senior Crown Counsel, 1969–72; Asst Principal Crown Counsel, 1973; Presiding Officer, Labour Tribunal, 1973–75; Asst Registrar, Supreme Court, 1975–77; District Judge, 1977; a Judge of the High Court, then of the Court of First Instance of the High Court, Hong Kong, 1985–99. Chm., Release Under Supervision Bd, 1988–94. JP Hong Kong, 2002. *Address:* House 12, River North, 4th Street Section P, Fairview Park, Yuen Long, New Territories, Hong Kong. *Clubs:* Chinese, Hong Kong, Hong Kong Jockey, Kowloon Cricket (Hong Kong).

WONNACOTT, John Henry, CBE 2000; artist; *b* 15 April 1946; *s* of John Alfred Wonnacott and Ethel Gwendoline Wonnacott (*née* Copeland); *m* 1974, Anne Rozalia Wesolowska; one *s* two *d. Educ:* Slade Sch. of Fine Art, London. *Solo exhibitions* include: Minories, Colchester, 1977; Rochdale Art Gall. and tour, 1978; Marlborough Fine Art, London, 1980, 1985, 1988; Scottish NPG, Edinburgh, 1986; Agnew's, London, 1992, 1996; Wolsey Art Gall., Christchurch Mansion, Ipswich, 1998; Hirschl & Adler, NY and Agnew's, London, 1999–2000; NPG (Royal Family etc), 2000; *group exhibitions* include: Painting and Perception, MacRoberts Arts Centre Gall., Univ. of Sterling, 1971; British Painting '74, Haywood Gall.; British Painting 1952–77, RA, 1977; Britain Salutes New York, Marlborough Fine Art, 1983; The Hard-Won Image, Tate Gall., 1984; Foundn Veranneman invites Marlborough, Foundn Veranneman, Kruishoutem, 1986–87; Monet to Freud, Sotheby's, London, 1989; Salute to Turner, Agnew's, London, 1989; The Pursuit of the Real, British Figurative Painting from Sickert to Bacon, Manchester City Art Galls, Barbican Art Gall. and Glasgow City Art Gall., 1990; The New Patrons, Twentieth Century Art from Corporate Collections, Christie's, London, 1992; Contemp. Portraits from Suffolk to Essex, Gainsborough's House, Sudbury, 1995; Contemp. British Artists Celebrate One Hundred Years of the Nat. Trust, Christie's, London, 1995; Painting the Century, NPG, 2001; A Sea of Faces, Nat. Maritime Mus., London, 2001; Visions of London, Art Space Gall., 2004; Annual Exhibn, RP (Ondaatje Prize for Portraiture), 2005; work in public collections including: Arts Council, British Council, Imperial War Mus., H of C, NPG, Nat. Maritime Mus., Nat. Trust, Tate Gall., DTI, London; Metropolitan Mus., NY; Christchurch Mus., Ipswich; Scottish NPG; Norwich Castle Mus.; Rochdale Art Gall. Hon. RP 2001. *Address:* 5 Cliff Gardens, Leigh on Sea, Essex SS9 1EY.

WOO, Kwok-Hing, GBS 2002; CBE 1996; **Hon. Mr Justice Woo;** Vice-President, Court of Appeal, Hong Kong, since 2004; *b* 13 Jan. 1946; *s* of late Woo Leung and Leung Yuk-Ling; *m* 1973, Rowena Tang; two *s* two *d. Educ:* Univ. of Birmingham (LLB); University College, London (LLM). Called to the Bar, Gray's Inn, 1969; QC (Hong Kong), 1987; in private practice, Hong Kong, 1970–92; a High Court Judge, then Judge of the Ct of First Instance, High Ct, 1992–2000; a Justice of Appeal, 2000–03. Chairman: Boundary and Election Commn, Hong Kong, 1993–97; Electoral Affairs Commn, 1997–2006; Commn of Inquiry on New Airport, 1998–99; Commissioner: of Inquiry into Garley Bldg Fire, 1997; on Interception of Communications and Surveillance, 2006–. *Address:* High Court, 38 Queensway, Hong Kong. *Clubs:* Hong Kong Jockey, Hong Kong, Hong Kong Country.

WOO, Sir Leo (Joseph), Kt 1993; MBE 1984; Chairman and Chief Executive, Dragon Resources Ltd, since 2006; *b* 17 Oct. 1952; *s* of Gabriel Bernard Woo and Molly Woo; *m* 1973, Emilyn Cha; one *s* two *d. Educ:* De La Salle Oakhill Coll., Sydney. Former Chm. and Chief Exec., Woo Hldgs Gp. *Address:* PO Box R399, Royal Exchange, NSW 1225, Australia.

WOO, Prof. Patricia Mang Ming, CBE 2005; PhD; FRCP, FRCPCH, FMedSci; Professor of Paediatric Rheumatology, University College London, since 1994; Consultant Physician, Great Ormond Street and University College London Hospitals, since 1994; *b* 12 Feb. 1948; *d* of Woo Hing Tak and Woo Lam Chiu Wah. *Educ:* Charing Cross Hosp. Med. Sch., Univ. of London (BSc 1969; MB BS 1972); Darwin Coll., Cambridge (PhD 1979). FRCP 1991; FRCPCH 1997. House physician and house surgeon, Charing Cross Hosp., 1973–74; Senior House Officer: Brompton Hosp., 1974; Northwick Park Hosp., 1974–75; MRC Clin. Trng Fellow and Hon. SHO, Cambridge Univ., 1975–78; Registrar, Northwick Park Hosp., 1979–81; Sen. Registrar, Guy's Hosp., 1981–83; Res. Fellow, Harvard Med. Sch., 1983–85; MRC Clin. Scientist and Consultant Physician, Northwick Park Hosp., 1985–94. FMedSci 2001. *Publications:* Paediatric Rheumatology Update, 1989; Oxford Textbook of Rheumatology, 1993, 3rd edn 2004; numerous original contribs to Jl of Rheumatology and scientific jls. *Recreations:* music, ski-ing, tennis. *Address:* Windeyer Institute of Medical Sciences, University College London, 46 Cleveland Street, W1T 4JF. *T:* (020) 7679 9148, *Fax:* (020) 7679 9255.

WOO, Sir Po-Shing, Kt 1999; FCIArb; Founder, Woo Kwan Lee & Lo, Solicitors & Notaries, Hong Kong, 1973; *b* 19 April 1929; *s* of late Seaward Woo, JP, and of Ng Chiu Man; *m* 1956, Helen Woo Fong Shuet Fun; four *s* one *d. Educ:* La Salle Coll., Hong Kong; King's Coll., London (LLB 1956; FKC 1995). Admitted Solicitor, England and Hong Kong, 1960; NP 1966; admitted as Barrister and Solicitor, Supreme Court of Victoria, Australia, 1983. Hon. Prof., Nankai Univ. of Tianjin, China, 1995. Dir of numerous companies in Hong Kong. Member: Inst. Admin. Mgt, 1975; Inst. Trade Mark Agents, 1978. Founder, Po-Shing Woo Charitable Foundn, 1994. Patron: Woo Po-Shing Gall. of Chinese Bronze, Shanghai Mus., 1996–; Sir Po-Shing Woo Auckland Observatory Bldg, 1998–. Fellow, Hong Kong Mgt Assoc., 2000. FCIArb 1966; FCMI (FIMgt 1975); FInstD 1975; World Fellow, Duke of Edinburgh's Award, 1994. Hon. LLD City Univ. of Hong Kong, 1995. Chevalier, Ordre des Arts et des lettres (France), 2004. *Recreations:* travelling, antiques (incl. Chinese paintings, bronze and ceramic), race-horse owner (incl. Derby winner, Helene Star, 1993). *Clubs:* Royal Automobile; Hong Kong Jockey, Hong Kong (Hong Kong).

WOOD; *see* Muir Wood.

WOOD, family name of **Earl of Halifax.**

WOOD, Adam Kenneth Compton; Director (Africa), Foreign and Commonwealth Office, since 2008; *b* 13 March 1955; *s* of Kenneth Wood and Cynthia Wood; *m* 1993, Katie Richardson; one *d. Educ:* Oriel Coll., Oxford (BA Hons). Kenya Programme Manager, ODA, Nairobi, 1988–93; Advr to Dir Gen., EC, 1993–96; Hd, DFID SE Asia, Bangkok, 1996–2000; Counsellor (Devlt), UKREP, Brussels, 2000–02; High Commissioner: Uganda, 2002–05; Kenya, 2005–08. *Recreations:* birding, golf, tennis. *Address:* c/o Foreign and Commonwealth Office, King Charles Street, SW1A 2AH; *e-mail:* adam.wood@fco.gov.uk.

WOOD, Prof. Adrian John Bickersteth, CBE 2005; Professor of International Development, University of Oxford, since 2005; *b* 25 Jan. 1946; *s* of John Henry Francis Wood and Mary Eva Bickersteth Wood (*née* Ottley, now Brain); *m* 1971, Joyce Miriam Teitz; two *d. Educ:* King's Coll., Cambridge (BA, PhD 1973); Harvard Univ. (MPA). Fellow, King's College, Cambridge, 1969–77; Asst Lectr, then Lectr, Cambridge Univ., 1973–77; Economist, then Sen. Economist, World Bank, 1977–85; Professorial Fellow, Inst. Devélt Studies, Univ. of Sussex, 1985–2000; Chief Economist, DFID, 2000–05. *Publications:* A Theory of Profits, 1975; A Theory of Pay, 1978; (jtly) China: long-term development issues and options, 1985; North-South Trade, Employment and Inequality, 1994; contrib. articles to learned jls. *Recreations:* music, tennis. *Address:* Department of International Development, Queen Elizabeth House, Mansfield Road, Oxford OX1 3TB.

WOOD, Alan John, CBE 1971; Tan Sri (Malaysia) 1972; Chief Executive Officer (formerly Executive Vice President), Malwood Global, Inc., Simpsonville, 1993–2007; *b* 16 Feb. 1925; *s* of late Lt-Col Maurice Taylor Wood, MBE; *m* 1950 (marr. diss.); one *s* one *d*; *m* 1978, Marjorie Anne (*née* Bennett). *Educ:* King Edward VI Royal Grammar Sch., Guildford, Surrey, UK; Indian Mil. Acad., Dehra Dun (grad 1945). Served Army, 1943–47; demobilised rank Captain. Various exec. and managerial positions with Borneo Motors Ltd, Singapore and Malaya, 1947–64 (Dir, 1964); Dir, Inchcape Bhd, 1968–73, Exec. Dep. Chm. 1973–74; Exec. Vice Pres., Sowers, Lewis, Wood Inc., Old Greenwich, Conn, 1975–78; Gen. Man., India, Singer Sewing Machine Co., 1979–82; Asst Dir, Delaware River Port Authority, World Trade Div., then World Trade and Econ. Devélt

Div., 1983–93. Pres., Malaysian Internat. Chamber of Commerce, 1968–72; Chairman: Nat. Chambers of Commerce of Malaysia, 1968 and 1972; Internat. Trade Cttee, Chamber of Commerce of Southern NJ, 1990–93. Mem. Bd, Malaysia-US Business Council, 2003–. Panglima Setia Mahkota (Hon.), 1972. *Recreation:* tennis. *Address:* 205 Lost Tree Lane, Simpsonville, SC 29681, USA. *Clubs:* Lake (Kuala Lumpur); Penang (Penang).

WOOD, Alan John, CBE 2005; FREng; Chairman, Siemens Holdings plc, since 2007; *b* 20 March 1947; *s* of Joseph Wood and Ivy Wood (*née* Larcombe); *m* 1973, Jennifer Margaret Lynn; two *d*. *Educ:* King Edward VII Sch., Sheffield; Manchester Univ. (BSc 1st Cl. Hons 1968; Hon. LLD 2003); Harvard Univ. (MBA 1975). MIMechE 1973, FIMechE 2002. Unilever plc, 1968–73; Head of Production, Crittall Construction, 1975–78; Man. Dir, Small Electric Motors, 1978–81; joined Siemens, 1981: Siemens AG, 1981–82; Production Dir, 1982–84, Man. Dir, 1984–87, Siemens Measurements Ltd; Managing Director: Electronic Components & Telecom Networks, 1987–91; Energy & Industry, 1991–98; Chief Exec., Siemens plc, 1998–2007. Chairman: North West Reg., CBI, 1996–98; Nat. Mfg Council, CBI, 2000–02; German-British Chamber of Industry and Commerce, 2001–; Econ. Policy Cttee, EEF, 2003–05; South East Reg., CBI, 2005–07. Pres., EEF, 2005– (Chm., 2007). FREng 2005. *Recreations:* family, swimming, opera, tennis, gardening. *Address:* Siemens Holdings plc, Sir William Siemens Square, Frimley, Camberley GU16 8QD. *T:* (01276) 696101.

WOOD, Sir Andrew (Marley), GCMG 2000 (KCMG 1995; CMG 1986); HM Diplomatic Service, retired; Senior Adviser: BP, since 2002; ITE, since 2003; *b* 2 Jan. 1940; *s* of Robert George Wood; *m* 1st, 1972, Melanie LeRoy Masset (*d* 1977); one *s*; 2nd, 1978, Stephanie Lee Masset; one *s* one *d*. *Educ:* Ardingly Coll.; King's Coll., Cambridge (MA 1965). Foreign Office, 1961; Moscow, 1964; Washington, 1967; FCO, 1970; seconded to Cabinet Office, 1971; First Sec., FCO, 1973; First Sec. and Hd of Chancery, Belgrade, 1976; Counsellor, 1978; Hd of Chancery, Moscow, 1979; Hd of W European Dept, 1982, Hd of Personnel Operations Dept, 1983, FCO; Ambassador to Yugoslavia, 1985–89; Minister, Washington, 1989–92; Chief Clerk, FCO, 1992–95; Ambassador to Russian Fedn and to Moldova, 1995–2000. Director: The PBN Co., 2002– (Chm., 2007–); Mechel, 2004–06. Director: Foreign and Colonial Trust, 2000–07; Russo-British Chamber of Commerce, 2000–07 (Chm., 2005–06); Member, Advisory Council: British Expertise (formerly British Consultants Bureau), 2000–; Renaissance Capital, 2003–08; European Round Table, 2004–; Toyota Europe, 2007–; Citibank, 2008–.

WOOD, Anne, CBE 2000; Founder, and Creative Director, Ragdoll Ltd, since 1984; *b* 18 Dec. 1937; *d* of Jack Savage and Eleanor Savage (*née* Thomson); *m* 1959, Barrie Wood; one *s* one *d*. *Educ:* Tudhoe Colliery Primary Sch.; Alderman Wraith Grammar Sch.; Bingley Teachers' Trng Coll. Teacher, Spennymoor Secondary Modern Sch., 1959–65; Founder: Books for Your Children mag., 1965, Ed. and publisher, 1965–95; Fedn of Children's Book Gps, 1969; Consultant, Tyne Tees TV, 1977–79; Children's Producer, Yorkshire TV (The Book Tower, Ragdolly Anna), 1979–82; Hd, Children's Progs, TV-am (originator of Rub a dub tub, Roland Rat), 1982–84. FRTS 1998. Eleanor Farjeon Award, 1969; Ronald Politzer Award, 1974; BAFTA Awards, 1979 and 1982, Prix Jeunesse, 1980, for The Book Tower; BAFTA Awards, 1996 and 1997, for Tots TV; Japan Prize, 1997 and BAFTA Award, 1998, for Teletubbies, and 2002 for Teletubbies Everywhere; Veuve Clicquot Business Woman of Year Award, 1998; Olswang Business Award, Women in Film & Television, 2003; Japan Foundn President's Prize, 2004, for Open a Door. *Recreations:* reading, gardening. *Address:* Ragdoll Ltd, Timothy's Bridge Road, Stratford upon Avon, Warwickshire CV37 9NQ. *T:* (01789) 404100.

WOOD, Sir Anthony John P.; *see* Page Wood.

WOOD, Anthony Richard; HM Diplomatic Service, retired; *b* 13 Feb. 1932; *s* of late Rev. T. J. Wood and of Phyllis Margaret (*née* Bold); *m* 1st, 1966, Sarah Drew (marr. diss 1973); one *s* one *d*; 2nd, 2006, Charlotte Olivia Ryder (*née* Strutt). *Educ:* St Edward's Sch.; Worcester Coll., Oxford (BA). HM Forces, 1950–52. British Sch. of Archaeology in Iraq, Nimrud, 1956; joined HM Foreign Service, 1957; served: Beirut, 1957; Bahrain, 1958; Paris, 1959; Benghazi, 1962; Aden, 1963; Basra, 1966; Tehran, 1970; Muscat, 1980; Counsellor, FCO, 1984–87. *Recreations:* walking, singing. *Clubs:* Army and Navy, Rifle Officers'.

WOOD, Prof. Bernard Anthony, PhD, DSc; Director, Center for the Advanced Study of Human Paleobiology, and University Professor of Human Origins, since 2006, and Professor of Human Evolutionary Anatomy, since 1997, George Washington University (Henry R. Luce Professor of Human Origins, 1997–2006); Hon. Senior Scientist, Smithsonian Institution, since 1997; *b* 17 April 1945; *s* of Anthony Wood and Joan Wood (*née* Slocombe); *m* 1st, 1965, Hazel Francis (marr. diss. 1980); one *s* one *d*; 2nd, 1982, Alison Richards (marr. diss. 2003); one *d*. *Educ:* King's Sch., Gloucester; Middlesex Hosp. Med. Sch., Univ. of London (BSc 1966; MB BS 1969; PhD 1975; DSc 1996). Lectr, Charing Cross Hosp. Med. Sch., 1973–74; Middlesex Hospital Medical School: Asst Lectr, 1971–73; Lectr, subseq. Sen. Lectr, 1974–78; Reader in Anatomy, 1978–82; S. A. Courtauld Prof. of Anatomy, 1982–85; Derby Prof. of Anatomy, 1985–97, and Dean, Faculty of Medicine, 1996–97, Univ. of Liverpool. Non-executive Director: Royal Liverpool and Broad Green NHS Trust, 1994–96; Liverpool HA, 1996–97. West Meml Lecture, Univ. of Wales, Cardiff, 1996. Chairman: Science-based Archaeol. Cttee, SERC, 1992–95; Science-based Archaeol. Strategy Gp, NERC, 1995–96; President: Primate Soc., 1986–89; Anatomical Soc. of GB and Ireland, 1996–97; Vice-Pres., Royal Anthropological Inst., 1989–92. *Publications:* (ed) Food Acquisition and Processing in Primates, 1984; (ed) Major Topics in Primate and Human Evolution, 1986; Koobi Fora Research Project: hominid cranial remains, 1991; articles on palaeoanthropology, hominid palaeobiology, and human morphology in scientific jls. *Recreations:* English salt glaze stoneware, Verdi. *Address:* 2110 G Sreet NW, Washington, DC 20052, USA. *T:* (202) 4200042.

WOOD, Prof. Bernard John, PhD; FRS 1998; Research Professor, University of Oxford, since 2007; *b* 10 May 1946; *s* of Sidney James Wood and Marjorie Ethel Wood; *m* 1st, 1968, Susan Brightmore (marr. diss.); two *d*; 2nd, 1982, Kristin Vala Ragnarsdottir (marr. diss.); one *s* one *d*; 3rd, 2004, Susan Prosser. *Educ:* Northern Poly. (BSc London); Univ. of Leeds (MSc); Univ. of Newcastle upon Tyne (PhD 1971). Lectr in Geol., 1973–78, Reader, 1978–79, Univ. of Manchester; Principal Scientist, Rockwell Hanford Ops, Richland, Washington, 1980–81; Prof., Northwestern Univ., 1982–89; Prof. of Earth Sciences, Univ. of Bristol, 1989–2005; Fedn Fellow, Nat. Key Centre for Geochem. Evolution and Metallogeny of Continents, Macquarie Univ., 2005–07. Vis. Prof., Univ. of Chicago, 1979–80. Award, Mineralogical Soc. of America, 1984; Schlumberger Medal, Mineralogical Soc. of GB, 1991; Holmes Medal, Eur. Union of Geoscis, 1997; Murchison Medal, Geol. Soc., 1997; Goldschmidt Medal, Geochem. Soc., 2003. *Publications:* (with D. G. Fraser) Elementary Thermodynamics for Geologists, 1976; (with J. R. Holloway) Simulating the Earth, 1988. *Address:* Department of Earth Sciences, University of Oxford, Parks Road, Oxford OX1 3PR.

WOOD, Charles; Chief Executive, London Borough of Brent, 1986–95; *b* 16 May 1950; *s* of Sir Frank Wood, KBE, CB and Lady (Olive May) Wood (*née* Wilson); *m* Carolyn Hall; three *s* two *d*. *Educ:* King's College London (BSc Hons); Polytechnic of Central London (DipTP). Engineer, GLC, 1971–76; Planner, and Dep. Dir of Housing, London Borough of Hammersmith and Fulham, 1976–82; Dir of Develt, London Borough of Brent, 1982–86. *Recreations:* walking, tennis. *Address:* Aux Deux Soeurs, St Etienne du Grès, France.

See also W. J. Wood.

WOOD, Charles Gerald, FRSL 1984; writer for films, television and the theatre, since 1962; *b* 6 Aug. 1932; *s* of John Edward Wood, actor and Catherine Mae (*née* Harris), actress; *m* 1954, Valerie Elizabeth Newman, actress; one *s* one *d*. *Educ:* King Charles I Sch., Kidderminster; Birmingham Coll. of Art. Corp., 17/21st Lancers, 1950–55; Factory worker, 1955–57; Stage Manager, advertising artist, cartoonist, scenic artist, 1957–59; Bristol Evening Post, 1959–62. Member: Drama Adv. Panel, South Western Arts, 1972–73; Council, BAFTA, 1991–93. Consultant to Nat. Film Develt Fund, 1980–82. *Wrote plays:* Prisoner and Escort, John Thomas, Spare, (Cockade), Arts Theatre, 1963; Meals on Wheels, Royal Court, 1965; Don't Make Me Laugh, Aldwych, 1966; Fill the Stage with Happy Hours, Nottingham Playhouse, Vaudeville Theatre, 1967; Dingo, Bristol Arts Centre, Royal Court, 1967; H, National Theatre, 1969; Welfare, Liverpool Everyman, 1971; Veterans, Lyceum, Edinburgh, Royal Court, 1972; Jingo, RSC, 1975; Has 'Washington' Legs?, Nat. Theatre, 1978; Red Star, RSC, 1984; Across from the Garden of Allah, Comedy, 1986; adapted Pirandello's Man, Beast and Virtue, Nat. Theatre, 1989 and The Mountain Giants, Nat. Theatre, 1993; Dumas's The Tower, Almeida, 1995. *Screenplays include:* The Knack, 1965 (Grand Prix, Cannes; Writers Guild Award for Best Comedy); Help!, 1965; How I Won the War, 1967; The Charge of the Light Brigade, 1968; The Long Day's Dying, 1969; Cuba, 1980; Wagner, 1983; Red Monarch, 1983; Puccini, 1984; Tumbledown, 1988 (Prix Italia, RAI Prize, 1988; BAFTA, Broadcasting Press Guild and RTS awards, 1989); Shooting the Hero, 1991; An Awfully Big Adventure, 1995; (with Richard Eyre) Iris, 2001; (with Richard Eyre) The Other Man, 2008; *adapted:* Bed Sitting Room, 1973. Numerous *television* plays incl. Prisoner and Escort, Drums Along the Avon, Drill Pig, A Bit of a Holiday, A Bit of an Adventure, Do As I Say, Love Lies Bleeding, Dust to Dust; creator of Gordon Maple in series, Don't Forget to Write; Company of Adventurers (series for CBC), 1986; My Family and Other Animals (series for BBC), 1987; The Settling of the Sun, 1987; Sharpe's Company, 1994; A Breed of Heroes, 1994; (with John Osborne) England My England, 1996; Sharpe's Regiment, 1996; Sharpe's Waterloo, 1997; Mute of Malice, 1997; Briefs Trooping Gaily, 1998; Monsignor Renard, 2000. Evening Standard Awards, 1963, 1973. *Publications:* plays: Cockade, 1965; Fill the Stage with Happy Hours, 1967; Dingo, 1967; H, 1970; Veterans, 1972; Has 'Washington' Legs?, 1978; Tumbledown, 1987; Man, Beast and Virtue, 1990; The Mountain Giants, 1993; (trans.) Dumas, The Tower, or Marguerite of Bourgogne, 1995; Plays One, 1997; Plays Two, 1997; Plays Three, 2005. *Recreations:* military and theatrical studies; gardening. *Address:* c/o Sue Rodgers, Independent Talent Group Ltd, Oxford House, 76 Oxford Street, W1D 1BS. *T:* (020) 7636 6565; *e-mail:* charles@wood4760.fsnet.co.uk. *Clubs:* Royal Over-Seas League, British Playwrights' Mafia.

WOOD, Christopher Edward Russell; art historian, dealer and consultant; *b* 31 Oct. 1941; *s* of Russell Wood and Muriel Wood; *m* (marr. diss.); two *s* one *d*. *Educ:* Sedbergh Sch.; St John's Coll., Cambridge (BA 1963). Dir, Christie's, 1969–76; Man. Dir, Christopher Wood Gall., 1977–; Dir, Mallett plc, 1988–95. Prof. of Art Hist., Southampton Inst. Antiques Roadshow, 1999–2004. *Publications:* The Dictionary of Victorian Painters, 2 vols, 1971, 6th edn 1999; Victorian Panorama: paintings of Victorian life, 1976; The Pre-Raphaelites, 1981; Olympian Dreamers, 1983; Tissot, 1986; (with Penelope Hobhouse) Painted Gardens: English watercolours 1850–1914, 1988; Paradise Lost: paintings of English country life and landscape 1850–1914, 1988; Victorian Painting in Oils and Watercolours, 1996; The Great Art Boom 1970–1997, 1997; Burne-Jones, 1998; Victorian Painting, 1999; Fairies in Victorian Art, 2000; William Powell Frith, RA: painter of modern life, 2006. *Recreations:* gardening, music, collecting. *Address:* 10 St James's Place, SW1A 1NP. *T:* (020) 7409 7081; *e-mail:* cwood@christopherwoodgallery.com. *Clubs:* Brooks's, Beefsteak, Chelsea Arts.

See also D. R. Wood.

WOOD, Rear Adm. Christopher Lainson, CB 1991; *b* 9 Feb. 1936; *s* of Gordon and Eileen Wood; *m* 1962, Margot Price; two *s* (one *d* decd). *Educ:* Pangbourne College. Seaman Officer, RN, 1954; joined submarine service, 1958; CO's qualifying course, 1966; in comd, HMS Ambush, 1966–68; JSSC, 1970; nuclear submarine training, 1971; in comd, HMS Warspite, 1971–73; Staff of FO Submarines, 1973–75; Staff of Dir, Naval Op. Requirements, 1975–77; Underwater Weapons Acceptance, 1978–81; Dep. Dir, Naval Op. Requirements, 1981–83; Dir Gen., Underwater Weapons, 1983–85; Dir Gen., Fleet Support, 1986–88; ACDS, Operational Requirements (Sea Systems), 1988–91. Dir, ALVA, 1992–96. *Recreations:* reading, fishing, sporting interests, voluntary service.

WOOD, Christopher Terence; HM Diplomatic Service; Deputy Head of Mission, Beijing, since 2008; *b* Wolverhampton, 19 Jan. 1959; *s* of Terry and Joyce Wood. *Educ:* Cotwall End Prim. Sch., Sedgley; High Arcal Grammar Sch., Sedgley; Fitzwilliam Coll., Cambridge (BA Hons Mod. and Medieval Langs 1981). Desk Officer, W Eur. Dept, FCO, 1981–82; lang. trng, London and Hong Kong, 1982–84; Asst Pol Advr, Hong Kong Govt, 1984–87; Hong Kong Dept, FCO, 1987–89; Security Co-ordination Dept, FCO, 1989–91; DoE, subseq. DETR, 1992–98, Private Sec. to Minister of State, 1995–98; Econ. and Domestic Secretariat, Cabinet Office, 1998–2001; ODPM, 2001–02; Consul-Gen., Guangzhou, 2003–06; Dir, Americas, FCO, 2007–08. *Recreations:* cinema, theatre, swimming. *Address:* c/o Foreign and Commonwealth Office, King Charles Street, SW1A 2AH.

WOOD, Rt Rev. Clyde Maurice, BA, ThL; Bishop of North Queensland, 1996–2002; *b* 7 Jan. 1936; *s* of Maurice O. Wood and Helen M. Wood; *m* 1957, Margaret Joan Burls; two *s* one *d*. *Educ:* Perry Hall, Melbourne (ThL 1964); Monash Univ. (BA 1974). Deacon 1965, priest 1965; Curate: St John's, Bentleigh, 1965–66; St Paul's, Ringwood, 1966–67; in Dept of Evangelism and Extension, 1967–70; Curate-in-Charge: St Philip's, Mount Waverley, 1967–70; Armadale/Hawksburn, 1970–73; Rector and Canon Res., Christ Church Cathedral, Darwin, 1974, Dean 1978–83; on leave, Rector St Timothy's Episcopal Church, Indianapolis, USA, 1981; Bishop of the Northern Territory, 1983–92; Bishop of the Western Region, and Asst Bishop, dio. of Brisbane, 1992–96. OStJ 1980; ChStJ 1985. *Recreations:* golf, sailing. *Address:* PO Box 2394, Humpty Doo, NT 0836, Australia.

WOOD, David, OBE 2004; actor, playwright, writer, composer, theatrical producer and director; *b* 21 Feb. 1944; *s* of Richard Edwin Wood and Audrey Adele Wood (*née* Fincham); *m* 1975, Jacqueline Stanbury; two *d*. *Educ:* Chichester High Sch. for Boys; Worcester Coll., Oxford. BA (Hons). Acted with OUDS and ETC at Oxford; first London appearance in ETC prodn, Hang Down Your Head and Die (also co-writer),

Comedy, 1964; later performances include: A Spring Song, Mermaid, 1964; Dr Faustus (OUDS), 1966; Four Degrees Over, Edinburgh Festival and Fortune, 1966 (also contrib. lyrics and sketches); repertory, 1966–69; RSC's After Haggerty, Aldwych 1970, and Criterion 1971; A Voyage Round My Father, Greenwich, 1970, Toronto, 1972; Me Times Me, tour, 1971; Mrs Warren's Profession, 1972, and revue Just the Ticket, 1973, Thorndike, Leatherhead; The Provok'd Wife, Greenwich, 1973; Jeeves, Her Majesty's, 1975; Terra Nova, Chichester, 1980. *Films include:* If…, 1968; Aces High, 1975; Sweet William, 1978; North Sea Hijack, 1979. *TV plays and series include:* Mad Jack, Fathers and Sons, Cheri, The Vamp, Sporting Scenes, Disraeli, The Avengers, Van der Valk, Danger UXB, Huntingtower, Enemy at the Door, Jackanory, Jim'll Fix It, When the Boat Comes In, The Brack Report, Tricky Business, Watch, Longitude. Wrote various theatre revues in collaboration with John Gould; music and lyrics, The Stiffkey Scandals of 1932, Queen's, 1967 (revived as The Prostitutes' Padre, Norwich Playhouse, 1997); with John Gould formed Whirligig Theatre, touring children's theatre company, 1979; has directed one of own plays on tour and at Sadler's Wells Theatre, annually 1979–, also nat. tours and West End productions for Clarion Productions, including The BFG, 1991–92, 1993–94 and 2001–03, The Witches, 1992–93 and 1996–97, Noddy, 1993–94, and More Adventures of Noddy, 1995–96; has performed David Wood Magic and Music Show in theatres all over UK, incl. Polka Theatre, Arts Theatre and Purcell Room, 1983–; wrote The Queen's Handbag, for children's Party at the Palace for the Queen's 80th birthday, 2006 (also televised). Chm., Action for Children's Arts, 1998–. Formed, jointly: Verronmead Ltd, indep. TV producing co., 1983; Westwood Theatrical Productions Ltd, 1986; W2 Productions Ltd, 1995. *TV series scripts:* Chips' Comic; Chish 'n' Fips; Seeing and Doing; The Gingerbread Man; Watch; *screenplays:* Swallows and Amazons, 1974; Back Home, 1989; Tide Race, 1989; *radio play:* Swallows and Amazons, 1999. Hon. MA Chichester, 2005. *Publications: musical plays for children:* (with Sheila Ruskin) The Owl and the Pussycat went to see…, 1968; (with Sheila Ruskin) Larry the Lamb in Toytown, 1969; The Plotters of Cabbage Patch Corner, 1970; Flibberty and the Penguin, 1971; The Papertown Paperchase, 1972; Hijack over Hygenia, 1973; Old Mother Hubbard, 1975; The Gingerbread Man, 1976; Old Father Time, 1976; (with Tony Hatch and Jackie Trent) Rock Nativity, 1976; Nutcracker Sweet, 1977; Mother Goose's Golden Christmas, 1977; Tickle, 1978; Babes in the Magic Wood, 1978; There Was an Old Woman…, 1979; Cinderella, 1979; Aladdin, 1981; (with Dave and Toni Arthur) Robin Hood, 1981; Dick Whittington and Wondercat, 1981; Meg and Mog Show, 1981; The Ideal Gnome Expedition, 1982; Jack and the Giant, 1982; The Selfish Shellfish, 1983; (with ABBA and Don Black) Abbacadabra, 1984; (with Dave and Toni Arthur) Jack the Lad, 1984; (with Peter Pontzen) Dinosaurs and all that Rubbish, 1985; The Seesaw Tree, 1986; The Old Man of Lochnagar (based on book by HRH the Prince of Wales), 1986; (with Dave and Toni Arthur) The Pied Piper, 1988; Save the Human, 1990; The BFG (based on book by Roald Dahl), 1991; The Witches (based on book by Roald Dahl), 1992; Rupert and the Green Dragon, 1993; Noddy (based on books by Enid Blyton), 1994; More Adventures of Noddy, 1995; Babe, the Sheep-Pig (based on book by Dick King-Smith), 1998; The Forest Child (children's opera based on book by Richard Edwards), 1998; The Twits (based on book by Roald Dahl), 1999; David Wood Plays 1, 1999; David Wood Plays 2, 1999; Spot's Birthday Party (based on books by Eric Hill), 2000; Tom's Midnight Garden (based on book by Philippa Pearce), 2000; Fantastic Mr Fox (based on book by Roald Dahl), 2001; James and the Giant Peach (based on book by Roald Dahl), 2001; Clockwork (opera, based on book by Philip Pullman), 2004; The Lighthouse Keeper's Lunch (based on book by Ronda and David Armitage), 2005; Danny the Champion of the World (based on book by Roald Dahl), 2005; Fimbles Live! (based on TV series), 2006; The Tiger Who Came to Tea (based on book by Judith Kerr), 2008; *books for children:* The Gingerbread Man, 1985; (with Geoffrey Beitz) The Operats of Rodent Garden, 1984; (with Geoffrey Beitz) The Discorats, 1985; Chish 'n' Fips, 1987; Sidney the Monster, 1988; Save the Human, 1991; The BFG: plays for children, 1993; Meg and Mog: plays for children, 1994; The Christmas Story, 1996; (with Peters Day) The Phantom Cat of the Opera, 2000; The Witches: plays for children, 2001; The Twits: plays for children, 2003; (with Dana Kubick) A Present for Father Christmas, 2008; Danny the Champion of the World: plays for children, 2009; with Richard Fowler: Play-Theatres, 1987; Happy Birthday, Mouse, 1991 (USA 1990); Baby Bear's Buggy Ride, 1993; Pop-up Theatre (Cinderella), 1994; Bedtime Story, 1995; The Magic Show, 1995; Mole's Summer Story, 1997; Silly Spider, 1998; Mole's Winter Story, 1998; Funny Bunny, 2000; The Toy Cupboard, 2000; Lady Lollipop: the play (based on book by Dick King-Smith), 2005; Under the Bed, 2006; *book for adults:* (with Janet Grant) Theatre for Children: guide to writing, adapting, directing and acting, 1997; articles in Drama, London Drama, Stage, ArtsBusiness, Encore. *Recreations:* crosswords, conjuring (Mem. of the Inner Magic Circle with Gold Star), collecting old books. *Address:* c/o Casarotto Ramsay Ltd, Waverley House, 7–12 Noel Street, W1F 8GQ. *T:* (020) 7287 4450, *Fax:* (020) 7287 9128.

WOOD, Rear-Adm. David John, CB 1998; CEng, FRAeS; defence aviation consultant; *b* 12 June 1942; *s* of John Herbert Wood and Nesta (*née* Jones); *m* 1966, Hilary Jolly; two *s* one *d*. *Educ:* St Paul's Sch.; BRNC Dartmouth; RNEC Manadon (BScEng 1965). Joined BRNC 1960; service in 892, 846, 707 Sqdns and HMS Ark Royal, 1967–73; Aircraft Dept (Navy), 1973–76; Air Engineer Officer, Lynx IFTU, 1976–77; Army Staff Course, 1978; Helicopter Procurement, MoD (PE), 1979–81; Naval Sec's Dept, MoD, 1981–84; Staff of FONAC, 1984–86; NATO Defence Coll., 1986–87; Asst Dir, EH101, MoD (PE), 1987–89; Dir, Aircraft Support Policy (Navy), 1989–91; Dir, Maritime Projects, MoD (PE), 1991–95; DG Aircraft (Navy), MoD, 1995–98. Mem. Council, RAeS, 1996. *Recreations:* cross-country and long distance running, choral singing. *Club:* Army and Navy.

WOOD, David Russell; His Honour Judge David Wood; a Circuit Judge, since 1995; *b* 13 Dec. 1948; *s* of Christopher Russell Wood and Muriel Wynn Wood (*née* Richardson); *m* 1979, Georgina Susan Buckle; two *s* one *d*. *Educ:* Sedbergh Sch.; Univ. of East Anglia (BA). Called to the Bar, Gray's Inn, 1973; Recorder, 1989–95. Pres., Council of Circuit Judges, 2008–. *Recreations:* country pursuits, tennis, walking, music. *Address:* Newcastle upon Tyne Crown Court, Quayside, Newcastle upon Tyne NE1 3LA. *Club:* Northern Counties (Newcastle upon Tyne).

See also C. E. R. Wood.

WOOD, Maj.-Gen. Denys Broomfield, CB 1978; Independent Inquiry Inspector, 1984–93; General Commissioner for Taxes, 1986–98; *b* 2 Nov. 1923; *s* of late Percy Neville Wood and Meryl Broomfield; *m* 1948, Jennifer Nora Page (*d* 1999), *d* of late Air Cdre William Morton Page, CBE; one *s* two *d*. *Educ:* Radley; Pembroke Coll., Cambridge (MA). CEng, FIMechE. Commissioned into REME, 1944; war service in UK and Far East, 1944–47; Staff Captain, WO, 1948–49; Instructor, RMA, Sandhurst, 1949–52; Staff Coll., 1953; DAA&QMG, 11 Infantry Bde, 1955–57; OC, 10 Infantry Workshop, Malaya, 1958–60; jssc 1960; Directing Staff, Staff Coll., 1961–63; Comdr, REME, 3rd Div., 1963–65; Operational Observer, Viet Nam, 1966–67; Col GS, Staff Coll., 1967–69; idc 1970; Dir, Administrative Planning, 1971–73; Dep. Military Sec. (2), 1973–75; Dir of Army Quartering, 1975–78. Exec. Sec., 1978–82, Sec., 1982–84, CEI. Col Comdt, REME, 1978–84. Lay Mem., Law Soc. Adjudication Cttee, 1986–92. Volunteer Speaker for Nat. Trust, 1999–. FRSA. *Recreations:* walking, gardening, reading. *Address:* 20 Franklin Court, Brook Road, Wormley, Godalming, Surrey GU8 5US. *T:* (01428) 681829.

WOOD, Derek Alexander, CBE 1995; QC 1978; a Recorder, since 1985; Principal, St Hugh's College, Oxford, 1991–2002, now Hon. Fellow; *b* 14 Oct. 1937; *s* of Alexander Cecil Wood and Rosetta (*née* Lelyveld); *m* 1st 1961, Sally Teresa Clarke (marr. diss. 2001); two *d*; 2nd, 2001, Barbara Kaplan (*née* Spector). *Educ:* Tiffin Boys' Sch., Kingston-upon-Thames; University Coll., Oxford (MA, BCL; Hon. Fellow, 2002). Called to the Bar, Middle Temple, 1964 (Bencher, 1986; Treas., 2006). Department of the Environment: Mem., Adv. Gp on Commercial Property Develt, 1975–78; Mem., Property Adv. Gp, 1978–94; Mem., Working Party on New Forms of Social Ownership and Tenure in Housing, 1976; Chairman: Review of Rating of Plant and Machinery, 1991, 1997–98; Property Industry's Working Gp on Code of Practice for Commercial Leases, 1995; Standing Adv. Cttee on Trunk Road Assessment, Dept of Transport, 1987–94. Author of new Code of Statutes, 2002, and Regulations, 2002–04, Univ. of Oxford. Dep. Chm., Soc. of Labour Lawyers, 1978–90. Chm., Chislehurst Constituency Labour Party, 1972–76, 1979–84. Chm., Oxfordshire Community Foundn, 1995–2001; Trustee, Attlee Foundn, 2003– (Chm., 2004–). Mem. Council, London Bor. of Bromley, 1975–78. Gov., Quintin Kynaston Sch., 2003–. Fellow, CAAV, 1988; FCIArb 1993. FRSA 1992. Hon. RICS (Hon. ARICS 1991; Mem., Governing Council, 2003–06). *Publication:* (jtly) Handbook of Arbitration Practice, 2nd edn 1993, 3rd edn 1997; (contrib.) Landlord and Tenant Law: past, present and future, 2006. *Recreation:* music. *Address:* Falcon Chambers, Falcon Court, EC4Y 1AA. *Clubs:* Athenæum, Royal Automobile, Architecture; Kent Valuers' (Hon. Mem.).

WOOD, Donald Edward, CBE 2005; Group Chief Executive (formerly Chief Executive), London & Quadrant Housing Trust, 1987–2008; Chairman, London Housing Foundation, since 2008 (Director, 1999–2008); *b* 10 May 1945; *s* of Thomas Wood and Mary (*née* Burton); *m* 1970, Barbara Schumacher; three *s* three *d*. *Educ:* King's Coll. Sch., Wimbledon; Bristol Univ. (BSc Hons (Civil Engrg) 1966); Manchester Business Sch. (DipBA 1970). W S Atkins & Partners, 1966–69; Rio Tinto Zinc Corp., 1970–73; Circle 33 Housing Trust, 1973–74; GEP Property Management, 1974–76; Dir, New Islington & Hackney Housing Assoc., 1976–87. Mem. Nat. Council, Nat. Housing Fedn, 1985–91; Chm., London Connection, 1991–99; Board Member: Focus Housing Gp, 1995–98; English Churches Housing Gp, 1999–2002. Trustee, Orders of St John Care Trust, 2007–. Member Management Committee: community centre, St Luke's House, 1980–85; Carr-Gomm Soc., 1988–91. Cttee Mem., Catholic Inst. for Internat. Relns, 1976–81. Chm., Barn Educn Assoc., 1977–82; Gov., Queen's Sch., Kew, 1979–83; Mem. Bd of Govs, St Mary's Coll., Twickenham, 2000–03. *Recreations:* music, family. *Address:* 6 The Avenue, Kew Gardens, Richmond, Surrey TW9 2AJ. *T:* (020) 8940 1471; *e-mail:* don.wood@lhf.org.uk.

WOOD, Dudley Ernest, CBE 1995; Secretary, Rugby Football Union, 1986–95; *b* 18 May 1930; *s* of Ernest Edward and Ethel Louise Wood; *m* 1955, Mary Christina Blake; two *s*. *Educ:* Luton Grammar School; St Edmund Hall, Oxford (MA Modern Languages). Sen. Manager, ICI, 1954–86. Rugby Football: Oxford Blue, 1952, 1953; played Rugby for Bedford, Rosslyn Park, Waterloo, and Streatham-Croydon, 1949–65; Pres., Surrey County RFU, 1983–85. Pres., St Edmund Hall Assoc., 1996–99. Pres., Bedfordshire CCC, 1998–2006; Hon. Life Mem., Squash Rackets Assoc., 1984. Hon. DArts De Montfort, 1999. *Recreations:* walking with dogs, watching cricket, attending reunions and socializing. *Address:* Mead Hall, Little Walden, Saffron Walden, Essex CB10 1UX. *Clubs:* East India, Lord's Taverners.

WOOD, Eric; Finance Director (formerly Finance Officer), University of Bristol, 1979–91; *b* 22 Sept. 1931; *s* of late Herbert Francis and Eva Wood; *m* 1955, Erica Twist; three *d*. *Educ:* West Hartlepool Grammar Sch.; Blandford Grammar Sch.; St Peter's Coll., Oxford (MA). CPFA. National Service, Army, 1950–51. Finance Depts, Cheshire, Durham and Notts County Councils, 1954–65; Finance Dept, London Transport, 1965–67; Asst Treasurer, GLC, 1967–73; Dir, CIPFA, 1973–79. *Publications:* articles in prof. accountancy press. *Recreations:* ski-ing, squash, hill-walking, bridge. *Address:* 6 Royal York Mews, Royal York Crescent, Clifton, Bristol BS8 4LF. *T:* (0117) 946 6311.

WOOD, His Honour Frank; Deputy Senior Judge, Sovereign Base Areas of Akrotiri and Dhekelia, 1995–2006 (Resident Judge, 1986–95); *b* 10 June 1929; *s* of late Robert Wood and Marjorie Edith Park Wood (*née* Senior); *m* 1951, Diana Mae Shenton; two *s* one *d*. *Educ:* Berkhamsted; RMA Sandhurst. Called to the Bar, Lincoln's Inn, 1969. Commissioned RASC, 1949–52. Bechuanaland Protectorate Police, 1953–65 (Supt 1965), Acting Dist Comr, 1957–58, 1959–60; Crown Counsel, Bechuanaland, 1965–66, State Counsel, 1966–67; Magistrate, Seychelles, 1970, Sen. Magistrate, 1974; Puisne Judge and Justice of Appeal, Seychelles, 1977–85, Acting Chief Justice, 1982–84; Chief Justice and Justice of Appeal, Solomon Islands, 1985–86; Justice of Appeal, Vanuatu, 1985–87. Chancellor, Dio. of Seychelles, 1973–84. Mem. Council, Commonwealth Magistrates' Assoc., 1973–77. *Publication:* Sovereign Base Areas Law Reports 1960–87, 1988. *Recreations:* reading, philately. *Address:* Pooh Corner, 2 Erimi Gardens, Erimi 4630, Limassol, Cyprus. *Clubs:* Royal Commonwealth Society, Civil Service.

WOOD, Gillian, (Mrs R. Wood); *see* Tishler, G.

WOOD, Prof. Graham Charles, FRS 1997; FREng; Professor of Corrosion Science and Engineering, University of Manchester Institute of Science and Technology, 1972–97, now Emeritus and Visiting Professor, University of Manchester; *b* 6 Feb. 1934; *s* of Cyril Wood and Doris Hilda Wood (*née* Strange); *m* 1959, Freda Nancy Waithman; one *s* one *d*. *Educ:* Bromley Grammar Sch., Kent; Christ's Coll., Cambridge (MA 1960, PhD 1959, ScD 1972). CChem 1969; FRSC 1969; FIMMM (FIM 1969); FICorr (FICorrST 1968); FIMF 1972; FREng (FEng 1990). University of Manchester Institute of Science and Technology: Lectr, 1961, Sen. Lectr, 1966; Reader in Corrosion Sci., 1970–72; Hd, Corrosion and Protection Centre, 1972–82; Vice-Principal for Acad. Develt, 1982–84; Dep. Principal, 1983; Dean, Faculty of Technol., 1987–89; Pro-Vice-Chancellor, 1992–97. Pres., ICorrST, 1978–80. Chm., Internat. Corrosion Council, 1993–96. Hon. DSc UMIST, 2001. Sir George Beilby Medal and Prize, Inst. of Metals, SCI and RIC, 1973; U. R. Evans Award, Instn of Corrosion Sci. and Technol., 1983; Carl Wagner Meml Award, Electrochem. Soc., 1983; Cavallaro Medal, Eur. Fedn of Corrosion, 1987; Hothersall Medal, Inst. of Metal Finishing, 1989; Griffith Medal and Prize, Inst. of Materials, 1997; Eur. Corrosion Medal, Eur. Fedn of Corrosion, 1999. *Publications:* numerous papers in Phil Trans Royal Soc., Proc. Royal Soc., Nature, Phil Mag., Corrosion Sci., Oxidation of Metals, Jl Electrochem. Soc. and Trans Inst. Metal Finishing. *Recreations:* travel, cricket, walking, reading about history of art, science and politics. *Address:* University of Manchester, School of Materials, Corrosion and Protection Centre, The Mill, Sackville Street, PO Box 88, Manchester M60 1QD. *T:* (0161) 306 4850.

WOOD, Graham Nash; QC 2002; a Recorder, since 1997; *b* 21 May 1957; *s* of late Benjamin Leslie Wood and Mary Valerie Wood; *m* 1984, Janet Helen Winstanley; three *s. Educ:* Liverpool Coll.; Leeds Univ. (LLB Hons). Called to the Bar, Middle Temple, 1979; in practice as barrister, specialising in personal injury, public law, human rights and criminal fraud, 1980–. Legal Assessor, GDC, 2006–. Pres., Mental Health Rev. Tribunal (Restricted Patients Panel), 2007–. Dep. Chancellor: Dio. Liverpool, 2002–; Dio. Chester, 2008–. Lay Reader, Church of England. *Publication:* (jtly) Binghams Negligence Cases, rev. edn 1994, 4th 2002. *Recreation:* sailing. *Address:* Exchange Chambers, Derby Square, Liverpool L2 9XX. *T:* (0151) 236 7747; 3 Paper Buildings, Temple, EC4Y 7EU. *T:* (020) 7583 8055; *e-mail:* woodqc@btinternet.com.

WOOD, (Gregory) Mark, FCA; Chief Executive: Paternoster Assurance, since 2006; Prudential Assurance Company Ltd, 2001–05; *b* 26 July 1953; *s* of William and Anne Wood; one *s* two *d. Educ:* Univ. of East Anglia (BA Econ). FCA 1979. Work with Price Waterhouse, Commercial Union, Barclays, BZW, British & Commonwealth; Chairman: Wagon Finance Ltd, 1991–94; Safeguard Insce Services, 1991–94; Divl Chief Exec., UK Retail Financial Services, MAI plc, 1991–94; Man. Dir, AA Insce, Financial Services and Retail, 1994–96; Chief Exec., AXA Equity & Law, 1997; Gp Chief Exec., AXA in the UK (formerly Sun Life & Provincial Hldgs), 1997–2001; Exec. Dir, Prudential PLC, 2001–05. Dep. Chm., ABI, 1999–2001 (Chm., Gen. Insce Cttee, 1999–2001); Chm., Govt's Property Crime Reduction Action Team, 1999–2001. Trustee, NSPCC, 1999–2007 (Dep. Chm., 2003–07). Chm. Govs, Amesbury Sch., 2002–07. MSI 1986. *Recreations:* tennis, ski-ing. *Address:* Paternoster plc, Fleet Place House, EC4M 7RF. *Club:* Royal Automobile.

WOOD, Maj.-Gen. Harry Stewart, CB 1967; TD 1950; *b* 16 Sept. 1913; *e s* of late Roland and Eva M. Wood; *m* 1939, Joan Gordon (*d* 1999), *d* of Gordon S. King; two *s* (and one *s* decd). *Educ:* Nautical Coll., Pangbourne. Civil Engineer (inc. articled trg), 1931–39. Commnd RA (TA), 1937. Served War of 1939–45: Regimental Service, Sept. 1939–June 1944; subseq. Technical Staff. Dep. Dir of Artillery, Min. of Supply (Col), 1958–60; Dep. Dir, Inspectorate of Armaments (Brig.), 1960–62; Sen. Mil. Officer, Royal Armament Research and Development Estab. (Brig.), 1962–64; Vice-President, Ordnance Board, 1964–66, President, 1966–67. Maj.-Gen. 1964; retd, 1967. Legion of Merit, degree of Legionnaire (USA), 1947. *Recreations:* home and garden, motor sport.

WOOD, Hugh Bradshaw; composer; University Lecturer in Music, Cambridge University, and Fellow of Churchill College, Cambridge, 1977–99; *b* 27 June 1932; *s* of James Bonar Wood and Winifred Bradshaw Wood; *m* 1960, Susan McGaw; one *s* one *d* (and one *d* decd). *Educ:* Oundle Sch.; New Coll., Oxford (Major Scholar; 2nd Cl. Hons Modern History, 1954). ARCM (private study with Dr W. S. Lloyd Webber), 1955. Studied: composition with Iain Hamilton, and harmony and counterpoint with Anthony Milner, 1956–58; composition with Mátyás Seiber, 1958–60; taught at: Morley Coll., 1958–67; Royal Acad. of Music, 1962–65; Univ. of Glasgow (Cramb Res. Fellow), 1966–70; Univ. of Liverpool, 1971–75; Univ. of Leeds, 1975–76; teacher, Dartington Summer Sch. of Music, 1959–74. *Main compositions: for orchestra:* Scenes from Comus (with soprano and tenor), 1965; Concerto for Cello, 1969; Chamber Concerto, 1971; Concerto for Violin, No 1, 1972, No 2, 2005; Symphony, 1982; Concerto for Piano, 1991; Variations for Orchestra, 1997; Serenade and Elegy (for string quartet and string orch.), 1999; *chamber music:* Variations for Viola and Piano, 1958; String Quartet No 1, 1962, No 2, 1970, No 3, 1976, No 4, 1993, No 5, 2001; Piano Trio, 1984; Horn Trio, 1989; Clarinet Trio, 1997; Overture for Trio, 2005; *for voice(s) and ensembles:* Logue Songs, 1961; Song Cycle to Poems of Pablo Neruda, 1974; Cantata, 1989; Tenebrae, 2003; *songs:* Robert Graves Songs, 4 sets, 1976–93; Robert Graves cycle, 2006. Hon. DMus Liverpool, 2006. *Recreation:* thinking about going to Greece. *Address:* 32 Woodsome Road, NW5 1RZ. *T:* (020) 7267 0318.

WOOD, Humphrey; *see* Wood, J. H. A.

WOOD, Sir Ian (Clark), Kt 1994; CBE 1982; FRSE; Chairman since 1981, and Chief Executive (formerly Managing Director) 1967–2006, John Wood Group plc (formerly John Wood & Son); Chairman, J. W. Holdings Ltd, since 1981; *b* 21 July 1942; *s* of John Wood and Margaret (*née* Clark); *m* 1970, Helen Macrae; three *s. Educ:* Aberdeen Univ. (BSc Psychology, First Cl. Hons 1964). Joined John Wood & Son, 1964. Dir, Royal Bank of Scotland, 1988–97. Chairman: Aberdeen Beyond 2000, 1986–90; Grampian Enterprise, 1990–94. Member: Aberdeen Harbour Bd, 1972–89; Sea Fish Industry Authority, 1981–87; Offshore Industry Adv. Bd, 1989–93; Offshore Industry Export Adv. Gp, 1989–93; British Trade Internat. Oil and Gas Export Bd (formerly Oil & Gas Projects & Supplies Office), 1994–2000 (Chm., 1997–2000); Bd, Scottish Develt Agency, 1984–90; Scottish Econ. Council, 1988–98; Scottish Enterprise Bd, 1995–2000 (Chm., 1997–2000); Bd, Scottish Business Forum, 1998–99; Scottish Sub-Cttee, UGC, subseq. UFC, 1988–91; SHEFC, 1991–97; Nat. Trng Task Force, 1988–91; PILOT, 2000–06; Scottish Sea Fisheries Council, 2007–. Chancellor, Robert Gordon Univ., 2004–. Sen. Trustee, Sir Ian Wood Family Charitable Trust, 2007–. CCMI (CBIM 1983); FCIB 1998; FRSE 2000; FSQA; FRSA; Fellow, Scottish Vocational Educn Council. Hon. LLD Aberdeen, 1984; Hon. DBA Robert Gordon, 1998; Hon. DTech Glasgow Caledonian, 2002. Scottish Free Enterprise Award, 1985; (jtly) Scottish Business Achievement Award Trust Award, 1992; Corporate Elite Leadership Award, 1992; Corporate Elite World Player Award, 1996; Business Ambassador for Scotland, Scottish Business Insider, 2002; Chief Exec. of the Year, Business Insider/PricewaterhouseCoopers, 2003; Glenfiddich Spirit of Scotland Award for Business, 2003. Silver Jubilee Medal, 1977. *Recreations:* family, art, hill walking, tennis. *Address:* Marchmont, 42 Rubislaw Den South, Aberdeen AB15 4BB. *T:* (01224) 313625.

WOOD, James Alexander Douglas; QC 1999; a Recorder, since 2000; *b* 25 June 1952; *s* of Alexander Blyth Wood and Cynthia Mary Wood (*née* Boot); two *s* by Ros Carne; *m* 1999, Janet Allbeson. *Educ:* Haileybury Coll.; Warwick Univ. (LLB 1974). Called to the Bar, Middle Temple, 1975; criminal defence barrister specialising in civil liberties and human rights; has appeared in many leading miscarriage of justice cases, incl. both appeals of Birmingham 6, and Carl Bridgwater case; Asst Recorder, 1998–2000. *Publications:* The Right to Silence, 1989; Justice in Error, 1993; reports. *Recreations:* travel, gardening, cycling, painting. *Address:* Doughty Street Chambers, 54 Doughty Street, WC1N 2LS. *T:* (020) 7404 1313. *Club:* Blacks.

WOOD, James Douglas Graham; Staff Writer, The New Yorker, since 2007; *b* 1 Nov. 1965; *s* of Dennis William Wood and Sheila Graham Wood (*née* Lillia); *m* 1992, Claire Denise Messud; one *s* one *d. Educ:* Eton Coll.; Jesus Coll., Cambridge (BA 1st cl. Hons (Eng. Lit.) 1988). Chief Literary Critic, The Guardian, 1991–95; Sen. Editor, The New Republic, 1995–2007. Vis. Lectr, subseq. Prof. of the Practice, Harvard Univ., 2003–. Mem. Editl Bd, London Review of Books, 1995–. Fellow, Amer. Acad. of Arts and Scis, 2007. Young Journalist of the Year, British Press Awards, 1990; Award in Literature, AAAL, 2001. *Publications:* The Broken Estate: essays on literature and belief, 1999; The Book Against God (novel), 2003; The Irresponsible Self: on laughter and the novel (essays), 2004; How Fiction Works, 2008. *Recreations:* playing the piano, reading. *Address:* c/o Jonathan Cape Ltd, 20 Vauxhall Bridge Road, SW1V 2SA.

WOOD, James Peter, FRCO, FRAM; conductor, composer and percussionist; *b* 27 May 1953; *s* of Peter Ley Wood and Elizabeth Gillian Wood; *m* 1977, Penelope Anne Irish; one *s* one *d. Educ:* Radley Coll.; Sidney Sussex Coll., Cambridge (BA 1975); Royal Acad. of Music. ARCO 1968, FRCO 1971; ARAM 1990, FRAM 2000. Dir, New London Chamber Choir, 1982–2007; Prof. of Percussion, Internat. Ferienkürse für Neue Musik, Darmstadt, 1982–94; Dir, Critical Band, 1990–. Worked with: BBCSO; Netherlands Radio Symphony Orch.; London Sinfonietta; Ensemble InterContemporain (Paris); L'Itinéraire (Paris); Ensemble 2e2m (Paris); Champ d'Action (Antwerp); Ictus (Brussels); MusikFabrik (Cologne); Percussion Gp The Hague; Amadinda (Budapest); Ju Percussion Gp (Taipei); Netherlands Radio Choir; Netherlands Chamber Choir; Berlin Radio Choir; WDR Choir; RIAS Kammerchor; Rundfunk Chor, Berlin; Tokyo Philharmonic Choir. *Compositions* include: Rogosanti, 1986; Stoicheia, 1988; Oreion, 1989; Two Men Meet, each presuming the other to be from a distant planet, 1995; The Parliament of Angels, 1996; Mountain Language, 1998; Jodo, 1999; Autumn Voices, 2001; Hildegard, 2002–04. *Recreations:* mountain hiking, wine, instrument building, carpentry. *Address:* Dorfstrasse 32, 14913 Schlenzer, Germany. *T:* (33) 74680508; *e-mail:* jw@choroi.demon.co.uk.

WOOD, (James) Sebastian (Lamin), CMG 2002; HM Diplomatic Service; Director, Asia-Pacific, Foreign and Commonwealth Office, 2005–08; *b* 6 April 1961; *s* of John Lamin Wood and Gillian Margaret Wood (*née* Neason, now Bohan); *m* 1990, Sirinat Pengnuam; one *s* three *d. Educ:* Emanuel Sch.; Magdalen Coll., Oxford (BA Hons Maths and Philos. 1982). FCO, 1983–85; Second Sec., Bangkok, 1985–89; Second, then First Sec., FCO, 1989–92; First Sec., Sino-British Jt Liaison Gp, Hong Kong, 1992–96; Security Policy Dept, FCO, 1996–97; Dep. Hd, UN Dept, FCO, 1998; Principal Private Sec. to Cabinet Sec., Cabinet Office, 1998–2000; Fellow, Weatherhead Centre for Internat. Affairs, Harvard Univ., 2000–01; Counsellor, Washington, 2001–05. *Recreations:* music, walking. *Address:* c/o Foreign and Commonwealth Office, King Charles Street, SW1A 2AH.

WOOD, John, CBE 2007; actor. *Educ:* Bedford Sch.; Jesus Coll., Oxford (Pres. OUDS). Old Vic Co., 1954–56; Camino Real, Phoenix, 1957; The Making of Moo, Royal Court, 1957; Brouhaha, Aldwych, 1958; The Fantasticks, Apollo, 1961; Rosencrantz and Guildenstern are Dead, NY, 1967; Exiles, Mermaid, 1970; joined Royal Shakespeare Company, 1971; Enemies, The Man of Mode, Exiles, The Balcony, Aldwych, 1971; The Comedy of Errors, Stratford, 1972; Julius Caesar, Titus Andronicus, Stratford, 1972, Aldwych, 1973; Collaborators, Duchess, 1973; A Lesson in Blood and Roses, The Place, 1973; Sherlock Holmes, Travesties (Evening Standard Best Actor Award, 1974; Tony Award, 1976), Aldwych, 1974, NY, 1974; The Devil's Disciple, Ivanov, Aldwych, 1976; Death Trap, NY, 1978; Undiscovered Country, Richard III, Nat. Theatre, 1979; The Provok'd Wife, Nat. Theatre, 1980; Royal Shakespeare Co.: The Tempest, 1988; The Man Who Came to Dinner, The Master Builder, 1989; King Lear, 1990 (Evening Standard Best Actor Award, 1991); Love's Labour's Lost, 1990; The Invention of Love, RNT, 1997, transf. Haymarket, 1998; No Man's Land, NT, 2001; Henry IV, Pts 1 and 2, NT, 2005. *Television:* A Tale of Two Cities, Barnaby Rudge, 1964–65; The Victorians, 1965; The Duel, 1966. *Films:* Nicholas and Alexandra, 1971; Slaughterhouse Five, 1972; War Games, 1983; The Madness of King George, 1994; Sabrina, Richard III, Jane Eyre, 1996; The Gambler, 1997; Chocolat, 2001; The Little Vampire, 2000; Imagining Argentina, 2004; The White Countess, 2005.

WOOD, John, CB 1989; Solicitor, Morgan Lewis & Bockius, 1997–99; *b* 11 Jan. 1931; *s* of Thomas John Wood and Rebecca Grand; *m* 1958, Jean Iris Wood; two *s. Educ:* King's College Sch., Wimbledon. Admitted Solicitor, 1955. Director of Public Prosecutions: Legal Assistant, 1958; Sen. Legal Asst, 1963; Asst Solicitor, 1971; Asst Director, 1977; Principal Asst Dir, 1981; Dep. Dir., 1985–87; Head of Legal Services, Crown Prosecution Service, 1986–87; Dir of Serious Fraud Office, 1987–90; DPP, Hong Kong, 1990–94; Consultant Solicitor, Denton Hall, 1995–97. Pres., Video Appeals Cttee, 1996–. *Recreations:* cricket, Rugby football, music, theatre.

WOOD, John Edwin, PhD; FInstP; Director of Underwater Engineering, British Aerospace Dynamics Division, 1988–90; *b* 24 July 1928; *s* of late John Stanley Wood and Alice (*née* Hardy); *m* 1953, Patricia Edith Wilson Sheppard (marr. diss. 1978); two *s* two *d. Educ:* Darlington Grammar Sch.; Univ. of Leeds (BSc, PhD). Joined Royal Naval Scientific Service at HM Underwater Countermeasures and Weapons Estabt, 1951; Admiralty Underwater Weapons Estabt, 1959; Head of Acoustic Research Div., 1968; Head of Sonar Dept, 1972; Admiralty Surface Weapons Establishment: Head of Weapons Dept, 1976; Head of Communications, Command and Control Dept, 1979; Chief Scientist (Royal Navy), and Director General Research (A), 1980; joined Sperry Gyroscope (subseq. British Aerospace), Bracknell, 1981; Exec. Dir, BAe, Bristol, 1984–88. Pres., Gp 12, Council for British Archaeology, 1984–93. *Publications:* Sun, Moon and Standing Stones, 1978, 2nd edn 1980; (jtly) The Treasure of Rennes-le-Château, 2003, 2nd edn 2005; papers and book reviews in technical and archaeological jls. *Recreations:* archaeology, fell-walking. *Address:* 7 Pennant Hills, Bedhampton, Havant, Hants PO9 3JZ. *T:* (023) 9247 1411.

WOOD, (John) Humphrey (Askey); a Managing Director, Consolidated Gold Fields plc, 1979–89; Chairman, Vitec (formerly Vinten) Group plc, 1991–99; *b* 26 Nov. 1932; *s* of late Lt-Col Edward Askey Wood and Irene Jeanne Askey Wood; *m* 1st, 1965, Jane Holland; one *s*; 2nd, 1981, Katherine Ruth Stewart Reardon (*née* Peverley); one step *s* one step *d. Educ:* Abberley Hall; Winchester College; Corpus Christi College, Cambridge. MA (Mech. Scis). De Havilland Aircraft Co. Ltd, 1956; Hawker Siddeley Aviation Ltd, 1964, Dir and Gen. Manager, Manchester, 1969–76; Man. Dir, Industrial and Marine Div., Rolls-Royce Ltd, 1976–79; Chm., Amey Roadstone Corp., 1979–86. Director: Gold Fields of South Africa Ltd, 1986–89; Blue Tee Corp., USA, 1986–89; non-executive Director: Birse Gp plc, 1989–95; Albrighton plc, 1990–96 (Chm., 1993–96); Ennstone plc, 1996–98. Butten Trustee, PA Consulting Gp, 1991–97. Vice-Pres., Nat. Council of Building Material Producers, 1985–89. Mem. Council, CBI, 1983–89. Chm., SW Rivers Assoc., 2002–; Trustee, Westcountry Rivers Trust, 2002–; Mem., SW Reg. Fisheries, Ecology and Recreation Adv. Cttee, Envmt Agency, 2002–08. *Recreations:* salmon conservation, fly fishing, sailing, painting, gardening. *Address:* Albyn House, 239 New King's Road, SW6 4XG. *T:* (020) 7371 0042.

WOOD, Sir John (Kember), Kt 1977; MC 1944; a Judge of the High Court of Justice, Family Division, 1977–93; President, Employment Appeal Tribunal, 1988–93 (Judge, 1985–88); *b* Hong Kong, 8 Aug. 1922; *s* of John Roskruge Wood and Gladys Frances (*née* Kember); *m* 1952, Kathleen Ann Lowe; one *s* one *d. Educ:* Shrewsbury Sch.; Magdalene Coll., Cambridge. Served War of 1939–45: Rifle Brigade, 1941–46; ME and Italy; PoW, 1944. Magdalene Coll., 1946–48. Barrister (Lincoln's Inn), 1949, Bencher, 1977; QC 1969; a Recorder of the Crown Court, 1975–77. Vice-Chm., Parole Bd, 1987–89 (Mem. 1986–89). *Recreations:* sport, travel. *Address:* 22 Addison Avenue, Holland Park, W11 4QR. *Clubs:* Garrick, MCC; Hawks (Cambridge).

WOOD, Prof. John Vivian, CBE 2007; PhD, DMet; FIMMM, FInstP, FIMechE, FRSC, FREng; Principal, Faculty of Engineering, Imperial College London, since 2007;

b 10 Sept. 1949; *s* of Vivian Wood and Lois Wood (*née* Hall); *m* 1976, Alison Lee; one *s* one *d*. *Educ:* St Lawrence Coll., Ramsgate; Sheffield Univ. (BMet 1971, DMet 1994); Darwin Coll., Cambridge (PhD 1975). CEng 1984; FIMMM (FIM 1989); FIMechE 1992; CChem, FRCS 1997; CPhys, FInstP 1998; FREng 1999. Goldsmiths' Jun. Res. Fellow, Churchill Coll., Cambridge, 1974–78; Lectr, then Sen. Lectr in Materials, Open Univ., 1978–89; University of Nottingham: Cripps Prof. and Hd, Dept of Materials Engrg, 1989–2001; Dean of Engrg, 1998–2001; Chief Exec., CCLRC (on secondment), 2001–07. Director: M4 Technologies, 1994–; Maney Publg, 2003–. Chairman: UK Foresight Panel on Materials, 1997–2001; Eur. Strategy Forum for Res. Infrastructure, 2005–08; Eur. Res. Area Bd, 2008–. Trustee: Industrial Trust, 2000–; Tomorrow Project, 2006–. Hon. DSc Tech. Univ. of Cluj-Napora, Romania, 1994. Grunfeld Medal, 1986, Ivor Jenkins Award, 2000, Inst. Materials; William Johnson Internat. Gold Medal, Internat. Conf. of Advanced Materials and Processes, 2001. *Publications:* (contrib.) Ultra Rapid Quenching of Metals, 1978; contrib. numerous res. pubns and patent applications. *Recreations:* woodlands, chamber music and serious contemporary music, affordable wine, reading. *Address:* Faculty of Engineering, Imperial College, Level 2, Faculty Building, South Kensington Campus, SW7 2AZ. *T:* (020) 7594 8600; *e-mail:* j.wood@imperial.ac.uk. *Club:* Anglo-Belgian.

WOOD, Joseph Neville, (Johnnie), CBE 1978; Director General, The General Council of British Shipping, 1975–78; *b* 25 Oct. 1916; *o s* of late Robert Hind Wood and Emily Wood, Durham; *m* 1st, 1944, Elizabeth May (*d* 1959); three *d*; 2nd, 1965, Josephine Samuel (*née* Dane) (*d* 1985); 3rd, 1986, Frances Howarth (*née* Skeer). *Educ:* Johnston School, Durham; London School of Economics. Entered Civil Service (Board of Trade), 1935; Ministry of War Transport, 1940; jssc 1950; Ministry of Transport: Asst Sec., 1951; Far East Representative, 1952–55; Under-Sec., 1961; Chief of Highway Administration, 1967–68. Joined Chamber of Shipping of the UK, 1968, Dep. Dir, 1970, Dir, 1972–78. Mem., Baltic Exchange, 1968–96; Director: Finance for Shipping Ltd, 1978–82; Ship Mortgage Finance Co. Ltd, 1978–83. Mem. Chichester DC, 1979–91. Vice Pres., Shipwrecked Fishermen and Mariners Royal Benevolent Soc., 1989–2001 (Dep. Chm., 1983–89). FCIT 1976. Freeman, City of London, 1978. Officier, Ordre de Mérite Maritime, 1950. *Recreation:* gardening. *Address:* Barbers Cottage, Heyshott, Midhurst, Sussex GU29 0DE. *T:* (01730) 814282.

See also Sir P. J. Torry.

WOOD, Leanne; Member (Plaid Cymru) South Wales Central, National Assembly for Wales, since 2003; *b* 13 Dec. 1971; *d* of Jeff Wood and Avril Wood; one *d* by Ian Brown. *Educ:* Univ. of Glamorgan (BA Hons Public Admin); Univ. of Wales, Cardiff (Dip. in Social Work). Probation Officer, Mid Glamorgan Probation Service, 1997–2000; pt-time Pol Researcher to Jill Evans, MEP, 2000–01; Univ. Lectr, Social Work and Social Policy, Cardiff Univ., 2000–03 (pt-time, 2000–02); pt-time Community Support Worker, Cwm Cynon Women's Aid, 2001–02. Shadow Minister for Social Justice, Nat. Assembly for Wales, 2003–. Mem. (Plaid Cymru) Rhondda Cynon Taf CBC, 1995–99. *Address:* National Assembly for Wales, Cardiff Bay, Cardiff CF99 1NA. *T:* (029) 2089 8256; *e-mail:* leanne.wood@wales.gov.uk.

WOOD, Leslie Walter; General Secretary, Union of Construction, Allied Trades and Technicians, 1978–85, retired; Member, TUC General Council, 1979–85; *b* 27 Nov. 1920; *s* of Walter William Wood and Alice Bertha Wood (*née* Clark); *m* 1945 Irene Gladys Emery; two *d*. *Educ:* Birmingham Central Technical Coll.; Ruskin Coll., Oxford. Apprenticed carpenter and joiner, 1935; RAF, 1939–45; Asst Workers' Sec., Cadbury's Works Council, 1948–49; full time employment in Union, 1953–85; Asst Gen. Sec., Amalgamated Soc. of Woodworkers, 1962. Mem. Council, ACAS, 1980–85. *Publication:* A Union to Build (history of Building Trades Unionism), 1979. *Recreations:* golf, swimming, bridge. *Address:* 67 Chestnut Grove, South Croydon, Surrey CR2 7LL. *T:* (020) 8657 7852.

WOOD, Maj. Gen. Malcolm David, CBE 2002 (MBE 1988); Director General Joint Supply Chain, Defence Equipment and Support (formerly Director General Logistics (Supply Chain), Defence Logistics Organisation), 2003–08; *b* 14 May 1953; s of late Stanley Andrew Wood and of Elsie Blackley Wood (*née* Stamper); *m* 1977, Nora Ann (*née* Smith); three *d*. *Educ:* Hampton Sch.; RMA, Sandhurst; St John's Coll., Cambridge (MA). Staff Officer, Grade 2, UKCICC, 1986–87; Comdr, 32 Ordnance Co., 1988–89; Staff Officer, Grade 2, Personnel Br., 1990; CO, 5 Ordnance Bn, 1991–93 (mentioned in despatches, 1993); Directing Staff, Army Staff Coll., 1993–94; Dep. COS, 3 UK Div., 1995–96; Director: Logistic Support Services, 1997; Materiel Support (Army), 1998–99; Comdr, 101 Logistic Bde, 2000–01; rcds 2002. QCVS 1996. *Recreations:* Army Football (former Chm.), supporter of Burnley FC and Lancs CCC.

WOOD, Mark; *see* Wood, G. M.

WOOD, Rt Rev. Mark; *see* Wood, Rt Rev. S. M.

WOOD, Mark William; Chairman, since 1998, and Chief Executive, since 2003, Independent Television News (Director, since 1993); *b* 28 March 1952; *s* of Joseph Hatton Drew Wood and Joyce Wood; *m* 1986, Helen Lanzer (*d* 2007); one *s* one *d*. *Educ:* Univs of Leeds (BA Hons), Warwick (MA) and Oxford. Joined Reuters, 1976; corresp. in Vienna, 1977–78, East Berlin, 1978–81, Moscow, 1981–85; Chief Corresp., West Germany, 1985–87; Editor, Europe, 1987–89; Editor-in-Chief, 1989–2000; Hd, strategic media investments and alliances, 2000–02. Dir, Reuters Hldgs, 1990–96; Chm., Reuters Television, 1992–2002. Chairman: Library and Inf. Commn, 1999–2000 (Mem., 1995–2000; Vice Chm., 1998–99); MLA (formerly Resource: Council for Museums, Archives and Libraries), 2003–08 (Bd Mem., 2000–08); Member: Commonwealth Press Union, 1996–2000; Rathenau Gesellschaft, Germany, 1999–. *Recreations:* opera, ski-ing, supporting Spurs. *Address:* ITN, 200 Gray's Inn Road, WC1X 8XZ.

WOOD, Sir Martin (Francis), Kt 1986; OBE 1982; FRS 1987; DL; Hon. President, Oxford Instruments Group plc, since 2000 (Deputy Chairman, 1983); Fellow, Wolfson College, Oxford, 1967–94, Hon. Fellow, 1994; *b* 19 April 1927; *s* of late Arthur Henry Wood and Katharine Mary (*née* Altham); *m* 1955, (Kathleen) Audrey (OBE 2006), *d* of Rev. John Howard Stanfield; one *s* (one *d* decd) and one step *s* one step *d*. *Educ:* Gresham's; Trinity Coll., Cambridge (BA Engrg, MA); Imperial Coll. (RSM) (BSc); Christ Church, Oxford (MA; Hon. Student, 2003). Nat. Service, Bevin Boy, S Wales and Derbyshire coalfields, 1945–48. Mgt Trainee, NCB, 1954–55; Sen. Res. Officer, Clarendon Lab., Oxford Univ., 1955–69; Founder, Oxford Instruments Ltd, 1959 (co. floated, 1983). Chm., Nat. Cttee for Superconductivity, SERC/DTI, 1987–92; Member: ABRC, 1983–89; ACOST, 1990–93; NRPB, 1991–96; Council, Central Lab. of the Res. Councils, 1995–98. Co-Founder, CONECTUS, 1994. Pres., FARM/Africa Ltd, 2000 (Vice-Chm. Council, 1985); Mem. Council, Royal Soc., 1995–97. Founder Trustee, Northmoor Trust (for nature conservation); Founder, Oxford Trust (for encouragement of study and application of science and technol.); Director: Oxford Econ. Partnership; Oxford Technol. Venture Trust. Lectr, UK and abroad. DL Oxon, 1985. Hon. FREng (Hon. FEng 1994). Hon. Fellow: UMIST, 1989; Cardiff Univ., 1998. Hon. DSc: Cranfield Inst. of Technol., 1983; Nottingham, 1996; Oxford Brookes, 2000; Hon. DTech Loughborough Univ. of Technol., 1985; Hon. DEng Birmingham, 1997; DUniv Open, 1999; Hon. DCL Oxon, 2004; Hon. Dr York, 2004. Mullard Medal (jtly), Royal Soc., 1982. *Publications:* articles in prof. jls. *Address:* c/o Oxford Instruments Group plc, Old Station Way, Eynsham, Witney, Oxon OX29 4TL.

WOOD, Sir Michael (Charles), KCMG 2004 (CMG 1995); barrister; HM Diplomatic Service, retired; *b* 5 Feb. 1947; *s* of Walter Wood and Hilda Wood (*née* Forrester). *Educ:* Solihull Sch.; Trinity Hall, Cambridge (MA, LLM); Free Univ., Brussels. Called to the Bar, Gray's Inn, 1968, Bencher, 2000. HM Diplomatic Service, 1970–2006: Asst Legal Advr, FCO, 1970–81; Legal Advr, Bonn, 1981–84; Legal Counsellor, FCO, 1986–91 and 1994–96; Counsellor (Legal Advr), UK Mission to UN, NY, 1991–94; Dep. Legal Advr, FCO, 1996–99; Legal Advr, FCO, 1999–2006. Sen. Fellow, Lauterpacht Centre for Internat. Law, Univ. of Cambridge, 2006–. Member: Bd of Trustees, British Inst. of Internat. and Comparative Law, 2001–; Exec. Cttee, British Br., Internat. Law Assoc., 2001–. Mem. Editl Cttee, British Yearbook of Internat. Law, 2001–. *Publications:* The Legal Status of Berlin, 1987; articles on internat. law. *Recreations:* walking, music, travel. *Address:* 20 Essex Street, WC2R 3AL.

WOOD, Michael David; film maker, broadcaster and historian; Director, Maya Vision International Ltd, since 1989; *b* Manchester, 23 July 1948; *s* of George Wood and Elsie Bell; *m* 1988, Rebecca Ysabel Dobbs; two *d*. *Educ:* Manchester GS (Foundn Scholar); Oriel Coll., Oxford (Open Scholar; BA Hons; Postgrad. Scholar). Journalist: ITV, 1973–76; BBC, 1976–79; documentary film maker: BBC, 1979–86; Central TV, 1987–91. Has made 80 documentaries for British and US TV. FRHistS 2001. DUniv Open, 2003; Hon. DLitt: Birmingham, 2005; Lancaster, 2007. Numerous awards. *Publications:* In Search of the Dark Ages, 1981, 6th edn 2005; In Search of the Trojan War, 1985, 6th edn 2005; Domesday, 1986, 5th edn 2005; Legacy, 1992, 3rd edn 2005; The Smile of Murugan, 1995, 3rd edn 2007; In the Footsteps of Alexander the Great, 1997, 3rd edn 2005; In Search of England, 1999; Conquistadors, 2000; Shakespeare, 2003; (contrib.) Chidambaram, 2004; In Search of Myths and Heroes, 2005; The Story of India, 2007. *Recreations:* theatre, music, reading history, walking in Greece. *Address:* Maya Vision International Ltd, 6 Kinghorn Street, EC1A 7HW. *T:* (020) 7796 4842.

WOOD, Rear Adm. Michael George, CBE 1995; Senior Military Adviser, Carillion plc, since 2006; Logistic Support Consultant, since 2003; *b* 8 June 1948; *s* of George William Wood and late Margaret Jean Wood (*née* Cottier); *m* 1972, Judith Vivienne Tickle; one *s* two *d*. *Educ:* Plymouth Coll.; BRNC Dartmouth; RNEC Manadon. BSc, CNAA; CEng, FIMechE. Joined RN, 1968; served HM Ships Tenby, Torquay, Hermes, HM Yacht Britannia, Minerva, and ashore at RNC Greenwich, Raleigh, RNEC and staff of Flag Officer Sea Training, 1968–85; exchange with US Navy, 1986–88; SMEO to Captain Seventh Frigate Sqn, 1988–90; jsdc 1990; Naval Asst to First Sea Lord, 1991–92; rcds 1993; staff of FO Portsmouth, 1994; Captain Fleet Maintenance, Devonport, 1994–96; Sec. to Chiefs of Staff Cttee, 1996–98; Dir Naval Logistic Policy, MoD, 1998–99; Dir Gen. Fleet Support (Ops and Plans), MoD, 1999–2000; Dir Gen. Defence Logistics (Ops and Business Develt), subseq. Dir Gen. Ops (Defence Logistics Orgn), MoD, 2000–03; Chief Naval Engr Officer, 2001–03. Sen. Mil. Advr, Mowlem plc, 2003–06. Chm., Devonport Naval Base Visitors Centre and Museum Trust, 2005–. Pres., RN Engrs Quart Club, 2005–; Vice Pres., Combined Services Hockey Assoc., 2004–. *Recreations:* family, sailing, windsurfing, ski-ing, tennis. *Address:* c/o Naval Secretary, Fleet Headquarters, Whale Island, Portsmouth PO2 8BY. *Clubs:* Army and Navy, Royal Naval Sailing Assoc.

WOOD, Michael John Andrew; a District Judge (Magistrates' Courts), Durham, since 2004; *b* 26 March 1950; *s* of Leslie Harold Thomas Wood and Irene Mary Wood; *m* 1973, Margaret (*née* Bellamy); three *d*. *Educ:* Headlands Sch., Bridlington; Univ. of Newcastle upon Tyne (LLB Hons 1972; J. H. Renoldson Meml Prize). Admitted solicitor, 1975; Assistant Solicitor: Messrs Linsley & Mortimer, 1975–77; Messrs Hay & Kilner, 1977–79; sole practitioner, Messrs Michael J. Wood & Co., 1979–2004. Dep. Dist Judge (Civil), 1993–99; Actg Stipendiary Magistrate, 1998–2000; Dep. Dist Judge (Magistrates' Courts), 2000–04. *Recreations:* golf, painting (watercolours), classic cars. *Address:* County Durham Magistrates' Courts, PO Box 168, Old Elvet, Durham DH1 3FE. *T:* (0191) 384 7497, *Fax:* (0191) 375 1837. *Club:* Whickham & District 41.

WOOD, Michael Mure; QC 1999; a Recorder, since 1999; *b* 22 Oct. 1953; *o s* of John Craig Mure Wood and Jean Margaret Wood; *m* 1978, Marianne Smith; one *d*. *Educ:* Rugby Sch.; Southampton Univ. (LLB Hons). Called to the Bar, Middle Temple, 1976; an Asst Recorder, 1994–99; admitted: Grand Court, Cayman Is., 2004–06; Dubai Internat. Financial Centre Court, 2007. Member: Criminal Bar Assoc. Cttee, 1992–94; Bar Human Rights Cttee, 1995–2000. *Publications:* articles for Criminal Bar Assoc. and Law Commn. *Recreations:* food, wine, travel, golf. *Address:* 21 Tonsley Place, Wandsworth, SW18 1BH. *T:* 07841 816611. *Clubs:* Royal Mid Surrey Golf; Bar Golfing Soc.

WOOD, Michael Roy; MP (Lab) Batley and Spen, since 1997; *b* 3 March 1946; *s* of late Rowland L. Wood and of Laura M. Wood; *m* 1999, Christine O'Leary; two step *d*; one *s* one *d* by a previous marr. *Educ:* Nantwich and Acton Grammar Sch.; Salisbury and Wells Theol Coll. (CertTheol 1974); Leeds Univ. (CQSW 1981); Leeds Metropolitan Univ. (BA 1989). Probation officer, Liverpool, Bradford, Leeds, and social worker, Calderdale, Leeds, 1965–97. Mem. (Lab), Kirklees DC, 1980–88. Contested (Lab) Hexham, 1987. *Address:* House of Commons, SW1A 0AA.

WOOD, Nicholas Leslie; Executive Chairman, Leach and Burton Ltd, since 1988; *b* 25 Sept. 1948; *s* of Harold Edward Wood and Joyce Winifred Wood (*née* Clark); *m* 1974, Elizabeth Ann Ketteridge; two *s*. *Educ:* Forest Sch.; Sch. of Pharmacy, Univ. of London (BPharm). FRPharmS; FIPharmM. Community pharmacy br. manager, 1974–82, Man. Dir, 1982–2000, N. L. Wade Ltd. Gen. Sec., 1999–2003, Pres., 2007–, Inst. of Pharmacy Mgt. Member Council: Royal Pharmaceutical Soc., 1985–97, 2003–05 (Vice-Pres., 1992–93; Pres., 1993–94, 2004–05); Pet Health Council, 1990–97; Fedn Internat. Pharmaceutique, 1992–94. Member: Standing Pharmaceutical Adv. Cttee, DoH, 1987–96; Jt Formulary Cttee, British Nat. Formulary, 1987–2007 (Dep. Chm., 1995–2007); Nurse Prescribers Formulary Cttee, 1998–2007; Council for Healthcare Regulatory Excellence, 2004–05. Mem. Council, Sch. of Pharmacy, Univ. of London, 1993–99, 2000–08 (Vice-Chm., 2006–08). Freeman, City of London, 1970; Liveryman, Soc. of Apothecaries, 1990– (Mem., Court of Assts, 1995–; Chm., Charity Cttee, 2000–07; Master, 2008–Aug. 2009). *Recreations:* motor boating, family history research, playing guitar badly. *Address:* The Seasons, Park Wood, Doddinghurst, Brentwood, Essex CM15 0SN. *T:* (01277) 823440. *Clubs:* East India; City Livery Yacht.

WOOD, Nicholas Marshall; His Honour Judge Nicholas Wood; a Circuit Judge, since 2008; *b* Sydney, 8 Oct. 1955; *s* of Geoffrey Ingham Wood and Hazel Esther Wood; *m* 1989, Sophie McCallum Kneebone; one *s* one *d*. *Educ:* Leeds Grammar Sch.; Queen's Coll., Oxford (BA Hons 1976); Indiana Univ. Sch. of Law (LLM 1978). Called to the Bar,

Middle Temple, 1980; in practice as barrister specialising in criminal law: Francis Taylor Bldg, 1982–85; QEB Hollis Whiteman Chambers, 1995–2008; Asst Recorder, 1997–2000; Recorder, 2000–07. Sec., Criminal Bar Assoc., 1996–98; Vice Chm., Remuneration Cttee, Bar Council, 2003–05. *Recreations:* hill-walking, golf, cricket, football, cinema, theatre. *Address:* Reading Crown Court, The Old Shire Hall, The Forbury, Reading RG1 3EH. *T:* (0118) 967 4400, *Fax:* (0118) 967 4444.

WOOD, Peter Anthony; Finance Director, Standard Chartered Bank, 1993–2000; *b* 4 Feb. 1943; *s* of Roger Sydney Wood and Winifred May (*née* Hine); *m* 1965, Janet Catherine Brown; one *s* one *d*. *Educ:* Oldershaw Grammar Sch.; Manchester Univ. (BSc Hons Maths); Birkbeck Coll., London Univ. (MSc Stats). ACIB; FCT; FSS. NCB, 1964–66; Barclays Bank, 1966–93: Treas., 1985–91; Finance Dir, 1991–93. *Recreations:* golf, birdwatching. *Club:* Wildernesse (Sevenoaks).

WOOD, Prof. Peter Anthony, PhD; Professor of Geography, University College London, 1996–2005, now Emeritus; *b* 24 Aug. 1940; *s* of Peter Barron Wood and Mary Theresa Wood. *Educ:* Univ. of Birmingham (BSc 1961; PhD 1966). University College London: Asst Lectr, 1965–68; Lectr, 1968–82; Sen. Lectr, 1982–92; Reader, 1992–96; Hd, Dept of Geog., 1997–2002. *Publications:* (with G. M. Lomas) Employment Location in Regional Economic Planning, 1970; (with K. E. Rosing) Character of a Conurbation: a computer atlas of the West Midlands Conurbation, 1971; (jtly) Housing and Labour Migration in England and Wales, 1974; Industrial Britain: the West Midlands, 1974; (ed with H. D. Clout) London: problems of change, 1986; (ed with P. Damesick) Regional Problems, Problem Regions and Public Policy in the United Kingdom, 1987; (with J. N. Marshall) Services and Space: aspects of urban and regional development, 1995; (ed) Consultancy and Innovation: the business service revolution in Europe, 2002; (jtly) The Competitive Performance of English Cities, 2006; numerous contribs to Trans of IBG, Progress in Human Geog., Geog., Regl Studies, Envmt and Planning A, Internat. Small Business Jl, Entrepreneurship and Regl Develt, L'Espace Géographique, Tijdschrift voor Econ. En Sociaale Geografie, Papers in Regl Sci., Service Industries Jl, Growth and Change. *Recreations:* music, opera, golf. *Address:* Department of Geography, University College London, Gower Street, WC1E 6BT. *T:* (020) 7679 0587.

WOOD, Peter John, CBE 1996; Chairman and Chief Executive, Esure, since 2000; *m* (marr. diss.); five *d*. Founder, 1985, Chief Exec., 1985–96, Chm., 1996–97, Direct Line Insurance. Non-executive Director: Plymouth Rock Corp., USA, 1995–; The Economist Newspaper Ltd, 1998–2003. *Address:* Esure, The Observatory, Reigate, Surrey RH2 0SG.

WOOD, Peter (Lawrence); theatrical and television director; *b* 8 Oct. 1925; *s* of Frank Wood and Lucie Eleanor (*née* Meeson). *Educ:* Taunton School; Downing College, Cambridge. Resident Director, Arts Theatre, 1956–57; Associate Dir, NT, 1978–89. Director: The Iceman Cometh, Arts, 1958; The Birthday Party, Lyric, Hammersmith, 1958; Maria Stuart, Old Vic, 1958; As You Like It, Stratford, Canada, 1959; The Private Ear and The Public Eye, Globe, 1962, Morosco, New York, 1963; Carving a Statue, Haymarket, 1964; Poor Richard, Helen Hayes Theatre, New York, 1964; Incident at Vichy, Phœnix, 1966; The Prime of Miss Jean Brodie, Wyndham's, 1966; White Liars, and Black Comedy, 1968; In Search of Gregory (film), 1968–69; Design for Living, Los Angeles, 1971; Jumpers, Burgtheater, Vienna, 1973, Billy Rose Theatre, NY, 1974; Dear Love, Comedy, 1973; Macbeth, LA, 1975; The Mother of Us All (opera), Santa Fé, 1976; Long Day's Journey into Night, LA, 1977; Così Fan Tutte, Santa Fé, 1977; She Stoops to Conquer, Burgtheater, Vienna, 1978; Night and Day, Phoenix, 1978, NY, 1979; Il Seraglio, Glyndebourne, 1980, 1988; Don Giovanni, Covent Garden, 1981; Macbeth, Staatsoper, Vienna, 1982; The Real Thing, Strand, 1982; Orione (opera), Santa Fé, 1983; Orion, King's Theatre, Edinburgh, 1984; Jumpers, Aldwych, 1985; Wildfire, Phoenix, 1986; Otello, Staatsoper, Vienna, 1987; Les Liaisons Dangereuses, LA, 1988; Hapgood, Aldwych, 1988, LA, 1989; Map of the Heart, Globe, 1991; Midsummer Night's Dream, Zurich, 1992; Arcadia, Zurich, 1993; The Bed Before Yesterday, Almeida, 1994; Indian Ink, Aldwych, 1995; *Chichester:* The Silver King, 1990; Preserving Mr Panmure, 1991; She Stoops to Conquer, 1992; Arcadia, 2000; On the Razzle, 2001; *Royal Shakespeare Company:* Winter's Tale, 1960; The Devils, 1961; Hamlet, 1961; The Beggar's Opera, 1963; Co-Dir, History Cycle, 1964; Travesties, 1974 (NY, 1975); Dr Jekyll and Mr Hyde, 1991; *National Theatre:* The Master Builder, 1964; Love for Love, 1965 (also Moscow); Jumpers, 1972; The Guardsman, The Double Dealer, 1978; Undiscovered Country, 1979; The Provok'd Wife, 1980; On the Razzle, 1981; The Rivals, 1983; Rough Crossing, 1984; Love for Love, 1985; Dalliance, 1986; The Threepenny Opera, 1986; The American Clock, 1986; The Beaux Stratagem, 1989; The School for Scandal, 1990; *television:* Hamlet, USA, 1970; Long Day's Journey Into Night, USA, 1973; Shakespeare, episode I, 1976; Double Dealer, 1980; The Dog it was that Died, 1988. *Recreation:* gastronomy. *Address:* The Old Barn, Batcombe, Somerset BA4 6HD.

WOOD, Philip, CB 1997; OBE 1979; Director General, Office of the Deputy Prime Minister (formerly Department of the Environment, Transport and the Regions, then Department for Transport, Local Government and the Regions), 1997–2003; *b* 30 June 1946; *s* of late Frank and Eleanor Wood; *m* 1971, Dilys Traylen Smith; one *s*. *Educ:* Queen Elizabeth Grammar Sch., Wakefield; Queen's Coll., Oxford. Entered Civil Service, 1967; Min. of Transport, 1967–70; DoE, 1970–75; a Private Sec. to the Prime Minister, 1975–79; Dept of Transport, 1979–97: Sec. to Armitage Inquiry into Lorries and the Envmt, 1980; Under Sec., 1986–95; seconded to BRB, 1986–88; Dep. Sec., 1995–97. *Address:* 9 Greendale Close, SE22 8TG. *T:* (020) 8299 0088.

WOOD, (René) Victor; Director: Sun Life Corp. plc, 1986–96; Wemyss Development Co. Ltd, 1982–2006; *b* 4 Oct. 1925; *e s* of late Frederick Wood and Jeanne Wood (*née* Raskin); *m* 1950, Helen Morag, *o d* of late Dr David S. Stewart. *Educ:* Jesus Coll., Oxford (BA). FFA. Chief Exec., 1969–79, Chm. 1974–79, Hill Samuel Insurance and Shipping Holdings Ltd; Chm., Lifeguard Assurance, 1976–84. Director: Haslemere Estates, 1976–86; Coalite Gp, 1977–89; Chandros Insce Co., 1979–89; Colbourne Insce Co., 1980–90; Criterion Insce Co., 1984–90; Scottinvest SA, 1985–95; Wemyss Hotels France SA, 1985–95; Les Résidences du Colombier SA, 1985–93; Domaine de Rimauresq SARL, 1985–2006; Worldwide and General Investment Co., 1992–2008. Vice-Pres., British Insurance Brokers' Assoc., 1981–84. *Publications:* (with Michael Pilch): Pension Schemes, 1960; New Trends in Pensions, 1964; Pension Scheme Practice, 1967; Company Pension Schemes, 1971; Managing Pension Schemes, 1974; Pension Schemes, 1979. *Address:* Little Woodbury, Newchapel, near Lingfield, Surrey RH7 6HR. *T:* (01342) 832054.

WOOD, Prof. Richard Dean, PhD; FRS 1997; Richard Cyert Professor of Molecular Oncology and Leader, Molecular and Cellular Biology (formerly Oncology) Program, University of Pittsburgh Cancer Institute, since 2001; *b* 3 June 1955; *s* of Robert Dean Wood and Maxine Louise (*née* Hargis); *m* 1975, Enid Alison Vaag. *Educ:* Farmington High Sch., New Mexico; Westminster Coll., Salt Lake City (BS 1977); Univ. of Calif, Berkeley (PhD 1981). Grad. Fellow, NSF, 1977–80; Postdoctoral Fellow, Yale Univ., 1982–85; Imperial Cancer Research Fund: Postdoctoral Fellow, 1985–88; Res. Scientist, 1988–92; Sen. Scientist, 1992–95; Principal Scientist, 1995–2001. Hon. Prof., UCL, 1998. Mem., EMBO, 1998. Trustee, Marie Curie Cancer Care, 2000–01 (Chm., Scientific Cttee, 2000–01). Meyenburg Award for Cancer Res., 1998; Westminster Coll. Alumni Award, 1999. *Publications:* DNA Repair and Mutagenesis, 2nd edn 2005; papers in scientific res. jls. *Recreations:* playing bass, jazz, gramophone recordings. *Address:* University of Pittsburgh Cancer Institute, Research Wing 2.6, 5117 Centre Avenue, Pittsburgh, PA 15213–1863, USA.

WOOD, Rt Rev. Richard James; Hon. Assistant Bishop of York, 1985–99; *b* 25 Aug. 1920; *s* of Alexander and Irene Wood; *m* 1st, 1946, Elsa Magdalena de Beer (*d* 1969); one *s* one *d* (twins); 2nd, 1972, Cathleen Anne Roark; two *d*. *Educ:* Oldham Hulme Grammar School; Regent St Polytechnic; Wells Theological Coll. Electrical Officer, RAF, then with Ceylon Fire Insurance Assoc. Curate, St Mary's, Calne, 1952–55; Curate, St Mark's Cathedral, George, S Africa, 1955–58; Rector, Christ Church, Beaufort West, 1958–62; Vicar of St Andrew's, Riversdale, 1962–65; Chaplain, S African Defence Force, 1965–68; Asst, St Alban's, E London, 1968; Rector of St John's, Fort Beaufort, 1969–71; Rector of Keetmanshoop, dio. Damaraland, 1971; Priest-in-Charge of Grace Church and St Michael's, Windhoek and Canon of St George's Cathedral, 1972; Vicar Gen. and Suffragan Bishop of Damaraland, 1973–75; expelled by S Africa, 1975; Hon. Asst Bishop of Damaraland, 1976–; Sec. to The Africa Bureau, 1977; Priest-in-Charge of St Mary, Lowgate, Hull, Chaplain to Hull Coll. of Higher Education and Hon. Asst Bishop of York, 1978–79; at St Mark's Theolog. Coll., Dar es Salaam, 1979–83; Interim Rector: St Matthew's, Wheeling, W Virginia, 1983–84; Trinity, Martinsburg, W Virginia, 1984–85. Hon. Life Mem., Hull Univ. Student Union. *Recreations:* general home interests. *Address:* 3 Plough Steep, Itchen Abbas, Winchester SO21 1BQ. *T:* (01962) 779400.

WOOD, Prof. Robert Anderson, FRCSE, FRCPE, FRCPGlas, FRCPsych; Postgraduate Dean, and Professor in Clinical Medicine, University of Aberdeen Medical School, 1992–99; *b* 26 May 1939; *s* of late Dr John Fraser Anderson Wood and Janet Meikle Wood (*née* Hall); *m* 1966, Dr Sheila Margaret Pirie; one *s* three *d*. *Educ:* Edinburgh Academy; Univ. of Edinburgh (BSc Hons, MB ChB). FRCPE 1976; FRCSE 1994; FRCPGlas 1997; FRCPsych 1999. House Officer, Royal Infirmary, Edinburgh, 1963–64, Asst Lectr, Univ. of Edinburgh, 1964–65; Registrar and Sen. Registrar in Medicine, Dundee Teaching Hosps, 1965–69; Lectr in Therapeutics, Univ. of Aberdeen, 1969–72; Sen. Lectr in Therapeutics, 1972–92, Dep. Dir, Postgrad. Med. Educn, 1986–92, Univ. of Dundee; Consultant Physician, Perth Royal Infirmary, 1972–92. Mem., Criminal Injuries Compensation Appeals Panel, 2000–. HM Inspector of Anatomy for Scotland, 2007–. Trustee, RCPE, 2005– (Mem. Council, 1990–92; Dean, 1992–95; Treas., 1999–2003). Mem. Bd, Med. and Dental Defence Union of Scotland, 2003– (Mem. Council, 1992–2003; Mem. Mgt Cttee, 1997–2003). *Publications:* papers on clinical pharmacology and medical education. *Recreations:* golf, sheep-husbandry. *Address:* Ballomill House, Abernethy, Perthshire PH2 9LD. *T:* (01738) 850201. *Clubs:* Royal & Ancient Golf (St Andrews); Craigie Hill Golf (Captain, 1999–2001) (Perth).

WOOD, Air Vice-Marshal Robert Henry, OBE 1977; *b* 24 Jan. 1936; *s* of Jack Cyril Wood and May Doris Wood; *m* 1957, Amy Cameron Wright; one *s* two *d*. *Educ:* Maldon Grammar School; cfs, psc, ndc, rcds. Commnd RAF, 1956; served Nos 617 and 88 Sqns, 1957–63; CFS, 1965–67; No 44 Sqn, 1967–69; attended Indian Staff Coll., 1970; MA to COS Far East Command, Singapore, 1970–71; PSO to Air Sec., 1972; NDC, Latimer, 1973; OC 51 Sqn, 1974; MoD Policy and Plans Dept, 1977; OC RAF Cranwell, 1978; OC RAF Linton-on-Ouse, 1979; Gp Capt. Flying Trng, HQ RAFSC, 1981–83; Dir Personal Services 1 (RAF), 1983–85; RCDS, 1985; Dep. Comdt, RAF Staff Coll., Bracknell, 1986; AOC and Comdt, RAF Coll., Cranwell, 1987–89; retd 1990. Director: Airways Flight Trng, 1992; British Red Cross, Leicestershire, 1993–96. *Recreations:* golf, music. *Clubs:* Royal Air Force; Luffenham Heath Golf (Captain, 2004).

WOOD, Robert Noel; psychotherapist; *b* 24 Dec. 1934; *s* of Ernest Clement Wood, CIE and Lucy Eileen Wood; *m* 1962, Sarah Child (marr. diss. 1981); one *s* one *d*. *Educ:* Sherborne Sch.; New Coll., Oxford (BA Hons PPE); LSE (Rockefeller Student; Certif. in Internat. Studies). Nat. Service Commn, RHA, 1953–55 (Best Cadet, Mons OCS). Dep. Res. Dir, Internat. Div., Economist Intelligence Unit Ltd, 1959–65; Inst. of Econs and Statistics, Oxford, 1965–70; Sen. Economist, Min. of Econ. Affairs and Develt Planning, Tanzania, 1966–69; Econ. Advr, ODM, 1970; Dir of Studies, Overseas Develt Inst., 1970–74; Adviser to House of Commons Select Cttee on Overseas Develt, 1973–74; Dir, Overseas Develt Inst., 1974–82. Jungian analysis, 1982–90; Psychotherapist Mem., Foundn for Psychotherapy and Counselling, 1989–. Chm., Friends of the Union Chapel, 1983–87; Mem., Religious Soc. of Friends (Quakers), 1982–. Gov., Quintin Kynaston Sch., 1974–86. *Publications:* contrib. Bull. Oxford Inst. of Econs and Statistics, ODI Rev. *Recreations:* Victorian artists, listening to music, singing, swimming, walking, Arsenal football club, poetry, Jung. *Address:* 19 Baalbec Road, N5 1QN. *T:* (020) 7226 4775.

WOOD, Hon. Sir Roderic (Lionel James), Kt 2004; **Hon. Mr Justice Wood;** a Judge of the High Court of Justice, Family Division, since 2004; Family Division Liaison Judge for Wales, since 2007; *b* 8 March 1951; *s* of Lionel James Wood and Marjorie Wood (*née* Thompson). *Educ:* Nottingham High Sch.; Lincoln Coll., Oxford. Called to the Bar, Middle Temple, 1974; Bencher, 2001. QC 1993; a Recorder, 1997–2002; a Circuit Judge, 2002–03. Member: Cttee, Family Law Bar Assoc., 1988–2002; Bar Council, 1993–95; Professional Conduct Cttee of the Bar, 1993–2000 (Vice-Chm., 1997–98; Chm., 1999–2000); Legal Aid and Fees Cttee, Gen. Council of the Bar, 1995–98 (Vice-Chm., Family, 1998); Court of Appeal (Civil Div.) User Cttee, 1995–2000. Jt Chm., Barristers/Clerks Liaison Cttee, 1994–95. Mem., Editl Bd, Longman Practitioner's Child Law Bull., 1993–94. *Recreations:* music, theatre, travel. *Address:* Royal Courts of Justice, Strand, WC2A 2LL.

WOOD, Roger Nicholas Brownlow; Director: Paypoint plc, since 2004; Reliance plc, since 2006; Managing Director, Automobile Association, 2001–04; *b* 21 July 1942; *s* of Reginald Laurence Charles Wood and Jean Olive Wood; *m* 1966, Julia Ellen Mallows; two *d*. *Educ:* Sherborne Sch.; Grad. Sch. of Management, Northwestern Univ., USA. With ICL, 1962–89 (Dir, ICL (UK) Ltd, 1987–89); Man. Dir, STC Telecoms Ltd, 1989–91; Gp Vice Pres., NT Europe SA, 1991–93; Managing Director: Matra Marconi Space UK Ltd, 1993–96; British Gas Services Ltd, 1996–2001; Dir, Centrica plc, 1996–2004. Director: Northern Telecom UK Ltd, 1991–93; Radiotronica Espagna Spa, 1991–93; MMS NV, 1993–96. Member: Parly Space Cttee, 1993–96; UK Industry Space Cttee, 1993–96. FBCS 1991; FCMI (FIMgt 1984); FInstD 1990. *Recreations:* music, Provence, Siam, ski-ing. *Address:* Ryemead House, Lower Hampton Road, Sunbury-on-Thames, Middx TW16 5PR. *Club:* Molesey Boat.

WOOD, Prof. Ronald Karslake Starr, FRS 1976; Senior Research Fellow, and Emeritus Professor, Imperial College, University of London, since 1986 (Professor of Plant Pathology, 1964–86); *b* 8 April 1919; *s* of Percival Thomas Evans Wood and Florence Dix Starr; *m* 1947, Marjorie Schofield; one *s* one *d*. *Educ:* Ferndale Grammar Sch.; Imperial College. Royal Scholar, 1937; Forbes Medal, 1941; Huxley Medal, 1950. Research Asst to Prof. W. Brown, 1941; Directorate of Aircraft Equipment, Min. of Aircraft Production, 1942; London University: Lectr, Imperial Coll., 1947; Reader in Plant Pathology, 1955;

Head of Dept of Pure and Applied Biol., Imperial Coll., 1981–84. Commonwealth Fund Fellow, 1950; Research Fellow, Connecticut Agric. Experiment Stn, 1957. Mem. Council, British Mycological Soc., 1948; Sec., Assoc. of Applied Biologists; Mem., 1949, Chm., 1987–91, Biological Council; Mem., Parly and Scientific Cttee; Consultant, Nat. Fedn of Fruit and Potato Trades, 1955; Mem. Council, Inst. of Biology, 1956 (Vice-Pres., 1991–); Chm., Plant Pathology Cttee, British Mycological Soc.; Mem. Governing Body, Nat. Fruit and Cider Inst., Barnes Memorial Lectr, 1962; Sec., First Internat. Congress of Plant Pathology, 1965; Hon. Pres., 7th Internat. Congress of Plant Pathology, 1998. Mem. Governing Body: East Malling Research Stn, 1966 (Vice-Chm.); Inst. for Horticultural Res., 1987; Pres., Internat. Soc. for Plant Pathology, 1968 (Hon. Mem., 1988); Mem., Nat. Cttee for Biology, 1978; Chm., British Nat. Sub-Cttee for Botany, 1978; Dean, RCS, 1975–78; Founder Pres. and Hon. Mem., British Soc. for Plant Pathol., 1987. Scientific Dir, NATO Advanced Study Institute, Pugnochiuso, 1970, Sardinia, 1975, Cape Sounion, 1980; Consultant, FAO/UNDP, India, 1976. Fellow, Amer. Phytopathological Soc., 1972; Corres. Mem., Deutsche Phytomedizinische Gesellschaft, 1973. Otto-Appel-Denkmünster, 1978. Thurburn Fellow, Univ. of Sydney, 1979; Sir C. V. Raman Prof., Univ. of Madras, 1980; Regents' Lectr, Univ. of California, 1981. *Publications:* Physiological Plant Pathology, 1967; (ed) Phytotoxins in Plant Diseases, 1972; (ed) Specifity in Plant Diseases, 1976; (ed) Active Defence Mechanisms in Plants, 1981; (ed) Plant Diseases: infection, damage and loss, 1984; numerous papers in Annals of Applied Biology, Annals of Botany, Phytopathology, Trans British Mycological Soc. *Recreation:* gardening. *Address:* Pyrford Woods, Pyrford, near Woking, Surrey GU22 8QL. *T:* (01932) 343827.

WOOD, Maj.-Gen. Roy; Chairman, Geo-UK Ltd, 1994–2005; *b* 14 May 1940; *s* of Alec and Lucy Maud Wood; *m* 1963, Susan Margaret Croxford; two *s*. *Educ:* Farnham Grammar Sch.; Welbeck College; RMA; Cambridge Univ. (MA); University College London (MSc 1971). FRICS; FRGS. Commissioned RE 1960; Mapping Surveys, Sarawak, Sierra Leone and Sabah, 1964–70; Instructor, Sch. of Military Survey, 1972–75; MoD, 1975–77; OC 14 Topo. Sqn, BAOR, 1977–79; CO Mapping and Charting Estabt, 1979–81; Defense Mapping Agency, USA, 1981–83; MoD, 1984; Comdr, 42 Survey Engr Gp, 1985–87; Dir, Military Survey, 1987–90; Dir Gen., Military Survey, MoD, 1990–94. Col Comdt, RE, 1994–2003; Hon. Col, 135 Indep. Topographic Sqn RE (V), 1994–99. Internat. Dir, Map Action, 2006–. Pres., Photogrammetric Soc., 1993–95; Chairman: Assoc. for Geographic Information, 1996–97; RE Assoc., 2000–03; BSES, 2003–08; Member: Cttee of Mgt, Mt Everest Foundn, 2002–08; Council, RGS, 2008–. *Publications:* articles on surveying and mapping in professional and technical jls. *Recreations:* orienteering, hill walking, travel. *Club:* Geographical.

WOOD, Sir Russell (Dillon), KCVO 1985 (CVO 1979; MVO 1975); VRD 1964; Lt-Comdr, RNR; Deputy Treasurer to the Queen, 1969–85; an Extra Gentleman Usher to the Queen, since 1986; *b* 16 May 1922; *s* of late William G. S. Wood, Whitstable, Kent, and Alice Wood; *m* 1948, Jean Violet Yelwa Davidson, *d* of late Alan S. Davidson, Lenham, Kent; one *s* three *d*. *Educ:* King's Sch., Canterbury. Fleet Air Arm Pilot, 1940–46 (despatches twice). Qual. as Chartered Accountant, 1951; financial management career with major public companies, 1951–68. *Recreations:* private flying, sailing, shooting. *Address:* Skylarks, Bakers Lane, Westleton, Saxmundham, Suffolk IP17 3AZ. *T:* (01728) 648595. *Clubs:* Naval and Military; Aldeburgh Yacht.

WOOD, Samantha T.; *see* Taylor-Wood.

WOOD, Sir Samuel Thomas H.; *see* Hill-Wood.

WOOD, Sebastian; *see* Wood, J. S. L.

WOOD, Simon Edward; His Honour Judge Simon Wood; a Circuit Judge, since 2008; *b* North Shields, 23 Oct. 1958; *s* of Walter Scott Wood and Shirley Wood (*née* Bittermann); *m* 1984, Catherine Mary, *d* of George Edward Taylor Walton and Margaret Walton; four *s*. *Educ:* Chorister Sch., Durham; Royal Grammar Sch., Newcastle upon Tyne; Univ. of Newcastle upon Tyne (LLB Hons 1980). Called to the Bar, Middle Temple, 1981 (Harmsworth Schol.); in practice on NE Circuit, 1982–2008; Asst Recorder, 1998–2000; Recorder, 2000–08. Gov., Royal GS, Newcastle upon Tyne, 1999–. *Publication:* (ed with Christopher Walton) Charlesworth & Percy on Negligence, 11th edn 2006. *Recreations:* music (mem., Northern Sinfonia Chorus, 1983–), playing the piano whenever I can, walking. *Address:* The Law Courts, The Quayside, Newcastle upon Tyne NE1 3LA. *T:* (0191) 201 2000, *Fax:* (0191) 201 2001. *Club:* Northern Counties (Newcastle upon Tyne).

See also C. T. Walton.

WOOD, Rt Rev. (Stanley) Mark; an Hon. Assistant Bishop, Diocese of Southwark, since 2002; *b* 21 May 1919; *s* of Arthur Mark and Jane Wood; *m* 1947, Winifred Ruth, *d* of Edward James Toase; three *s* two *d*. *Educ:* Pontypridd County School; University College, Cardiff (BA 2nd cl. Greek and Latin); College of the Resurrection, Mirfield. Curate at St Mary's, Cardiff Docks, 1942–45; Curate, Sophiatown Mission, Johannesburg, 1945–47; Rector of Bloemhof, Transvaal, 1947–50; Priest in charge of St Cyprian's Mission, Johannesburg, 1950–55; Rector of Marandellas, Rhodesia, 1955–65; Dean of Salisbury, Rhodesia, 1965–70; Bishop of Matabeleland, 1971–77; Asst Bishop of Hereford, 1977–81; Bishop Suffragan of Ludlow, 1981–87; Archdeacon of Ludlow, 1982–83. *Address:* College of St Barnabas, Lingfield, Surrey RH7 6NJ.

WOOD, Terence Courtney, CMG 1989; HM Diplomatic Service, retired; Ambassador to Austria, 1992–96; *b* 6 Sept. 1936; *s* of Courtney and Alice Wood; *m* 1st, 1962, Kathleen Mary Jones (marr. diss. 1981); one *s* one *d*; 2nd, 1982, Diana Humphreys-Roberts. *Educ:* King Edward VI Sch., Chelmsford; Trinity Coll., Cambridge. BA Hons 1960. RA, 1955–57 (2nd Lieut). Information Officer, FBI (later CBI), 1963–67; entered HM Diplomatic Service, 1968; Foreign Office, 1968–69; 1st Sec., Rome, 1969–73; FCO, 1973–77; sowc, RNC, Greenwich, 1977; Counsellor (Economic and Commercial), New Delhi, 1977–81; Political Advr and Hd of Chancery, Brit. Mil. Govt, Berlin, 1981–84; Hd of S Asian Dept, FCO, 1984–86; Vis. Fellow, Center for Internat. Affairs, Harvard Univ., 1986–87; Minister, Rome, 1987–92; Head, UK Delegn to Negotiations on Conventional Arms Control in Europe, Vienna, 1992–93. Gov., Bruton Sch. for Girls, 1999– (Chm. of Govs, 2002–08). Grosses Goldenes Ehrenzeichen: Styria, 1996; Carinthia, 1996. *Recreations:* music, painting. *Address:* Knapp Cottage, Charlton Horethorne, Sherborne, Dorset DT9 4PQ. *Club:* Travellers.

WOOD, Timothy John Rogerson; Chairman, Autotronics plc, 1998–2000; *b* 13 Aug. 1940; *s* of Thomas Geoffrey Wood and Norah Margaret Annie (*née* Rogerson); *m* 1969, Elizabeth Mary Spencer; one *s* one *d*. *Educ:* King James's Grammar Sch., Knaresborough, Yorks; Manchester Univ. (BSc Maths). Joined Ferranti Ltd as Lectr in Computer Programming, 1962; joined ICT Ltd (later ICL), 1963; subseq. involved in devclt of ICL systems software; Sen. Proj. Management Consultant advising on introdn of large computer systems, 1977; Sen. Proj. Manager on application systems, 1981; resigned from ICL, 1983. MP (C) Stevenage, 1983–97; contested (C) same seat, 1997. PPS to: Minister for Armed Forces, 1986–87; Minister of State, 1987–89, Sec. of State, 1989–90, Northern Ireland; Asst Govt Whip, 1990–92; Lord Comr of HM Treasury (Govt Whip), 1992–95; Comptroller of HM Household, 1995–97. Chm., Wokingham Cons. Assoc., 1980–83; Pres., Bracknell Cons. Assoc., 1998–2003; Vice Chairman: National Assoc. of Cons. Graduates, 1975–76; Thames Valley Euro Constituency Council, 1979–83; Mem., Bow Gp, 1962– (Mem. Council, 1968–71). Member: Bracknell DC, 1975–83 (Leader, 1976–78; Mem. Bd, Bracknell Develt Corp., 1977–82); E Devon DC, 2007–. Governor: Princess Helena Coll., 2000– (Vice Chm., 2005–); Littleham Sch., 2004– (Chm., 2005–). *Publications:* Bow Group pamphlets on educn, computers in Britain, and the Post Office. *Recreations:* gardening, chess, reading. *Club:* Carlton.

WOOD, Victor; *see* Wood, R. V.

WOOD, Victoria, CBE 2008 (OBE 1997); writer and comedian; *b* 19 May 1953; *d* of late Stanley and of Helen Wood; *m*; one *s* one *d*. *Educ:* Bury Grammar School for Girls; Univ. of Birmingham (BA Drama, Theatre Arts). Performed regularly on television and radio as singer/songwriter, 1974–78. First stage play, Talent, performed at Crucible Th., Sheffield, 1978; TV production of this, broadcast, 1979 (3 National Drama awards, 1980); wrote Good Fun, stage musical, 1980; wrote and performed, TV comedy series: Wood and Walters, 1981–82; Victoria Wood As Seen On TV, 1st series 1985 (Broadcasting Press Guilds Award; BAFTA Awards, Best Light Entertainment Prog., Best Light Entertainment Perf.), 2nd series 1986 (BAFTA Award, Best Light Entertainment Prog.), Special, 1987 (BAFTA Best Light Entertainment Prog.); An Audience with Victoria Wood, 1988 (BAFTA Best Light Entertainment Prog., BAFTA Best Light Entertainment Perf.); Victoria Wood, 1989; Victoria Wood's All Day Breakfast, 1992 (Writers' Guild Award); Victoria Wood Live in Your Own Home, 1994; dinnerladies, 1998–2000 (Best New TV Comedy, Nat. TV Awards, 1999; Best TV Comedy, British Comedy Awards, 2000; Press Prize, Montreux Fest., 2000); Still Standing (Special), 1998; Christmas Special, 2000; Victoria Wood's Sketch Show Story, 2001; Victoria Wood's Big Fat Documentary, 2004; Moonwalking (documentary), 2004; Housewife, 49 (TV drama), 2006 (Best Actress, Best Single Drama, BAFTA, 2007); Victoria's Empire (documentary), 2007; Ballet Shoes (TV drama), 2007. Appeared in stage revues, Funny Turns, Duchess Th., 1982, Lucky Bag, Ambassadors, 1984; own shows include: Victoria Wood, Palladium, 1987; Victoria Wood Up West, 1990; Victoria Wood - At It Again, Royal Albert Hall, 2001; wrote and performed, Acorn Antiques the Musical!, Th. Royal, Haymarket, 2005, (dir) UK tour, 2007. Variety Club BBC Personality of the Year, 1987; British Comedy Awards: Top Female Comedy Performer, 1996; Writer of the Year, 2000; BAFTA Tribute Award, 2005. Hon. DLitt: Lancaster, 1989; Sunderland, 1994; Bolton, 1995; Birmingham, 1996. *Screenplay:* Pat and Margaret, 1994 (BPG Award, Best Single Drama Critic's Award, Monte Carlo, and Nymphe d'Or) (adapted for stage, 2003). *Publications:* Victoria Wood Song Book, 1984; Up to you, Porky, 1985; Barmy, 1987; Mens Sana in Thingummy Doodah, 1990; Chunky, 1996. *Recreation:* sudoku. *Address:* c/o Phil McIntyre, 35 Soho Square, W1V 5DG. *T:* (020) 7439 2270.

WOOD, Rt Rev. Wilfred Denniston, KA 2000; Area Bishop (formerly Bishop Suffragan) of Croydon, 1985–2002; *b* Barbados, WI, 15 June 1936; *s* of Wilfred Coward and Elsie Elmira Wood; *m* 1966, Ina Eileen, *d* of L. E. Smith, CBE, Barbadian MP; three *s* two *d*. *Educ:* Combermere Sch. and Codrington Coll., Barbados. Lambeth Dip. in Theol., 1962. Ordained deacon, St Michael's Cath., Barbados, 1961; ordained priest, St Paul's Cath., London, 1962. Curate of St Stephen with St Thomas, Shepherd's Bush, 1962–66, Hon. Curate, 1966–74; Bishop of London's Officer in Race Relations, 1966–74; Vicar of St Laurence, Catford, 1974–82; RD of East Lewisham, 1977–82; Archdeacon of Southwark, 1982–85; Hon. Canon of Southwark Cathedral, 1977–85. Mem., General Synod, 1987–. Chairman: Martin Luther King Meml Trust; Cttee on Black Anglican Concerns, 1986–91. Member: Royal Commn on Criminal Procedure, 1978–80; Archbishop of Canterbury's Commn on Urban Priority Areas, 1983–85; Housing Corp. Bd, 1986–95. Non-exec. Dir, Mayday Healthcare NHS Trust, 1993–2002 (Vice-Chm., 2000). JP Inner London, 1971–85. Hon. Freeman, London Bor. of Croydon, 2002. Hon. DD Gen. Theol Seminary, NY, 1986; DUniv Open, 2000; Hon. LLD West Indies, 2002. *Publications:* (contrib.) The Committed Church, 1966; (with John Downing) Vicious Circle, 1968; Keep the Faith, Baby!, 1994. *Recreations:* listening to audio-books, poetry and music, cricket; armchair follower of most sports. *Address:* 69 Pegwell Gardens, Christ Church, Barbados, West Indies. *T:* 4201822, *Fax:* 4203426; *e-mail:* wilfredwood.barbados@caribsurf.com.

WOOD, Sir William (Alan), KCVO 1978; CB 1970; Second Crown Estate Commissioner, 1968–78; Ombudsman, Mirror Group Newspapers, 1985–89; Chairman, London and Quadrant Housing Trust, 1980–89; *b* 8 Dec. 1916; *m* 1st, 1943, Zoë (*d* 1985), *d* of Rev. Dr D. Frazer-Hurst; two *s* two *d*; 2nd, 1985, Mrs Mary Hall (*née* Cowper). *Educ:* Dulwich Coll.; Corpus Christi Coll., Cambridge (Scholar). Ministry of Home Affairs, N. Ireland, 1939. Lieut, RNVR, 1942–46. Ministry of Town and Country Planning, 1946; Minister's Private Secretary, 1951; Principal Regional Officer (West Midlands), Ministry of Housing and Local Government, 1954; Asst Secretary, 1956; Under-Secretary, 1964–68. Chm. Council, King Alfred Sch., 1966–78, Pres. 1978–2000. *Club:* Athenæum.

WOOD, William James; QC 1998; *b* 10 July 1955; *s* of Sir Frank Wood, KBE, CB, and Lady (Olive May) Wood (*née* Wilson); *m* 1986, Tonya Mary Pinsent; one *s* one *d*. *Educ:* Dulwich Coll.; Worcester Coll., Oxford (BA, BCL, both 1st cl.); Harvard Law Sch. (LLM). Called to the Bar, Middle Temple, 1980, Bencher, 2006. Mem., Panel of Indep. Mediators. *Recreations:* fishing, ski-ing, tennis. *Address:* The Old Rectory, Church Lane, Charlbury, Oxon OX7 3PX; Brick Court Chambers, 7–8 Essex Street, WC2R 3LD. *Club:* Reform.

See also C. Wood.

WOOD, William Rowley; QC 1997; **His Honour Judge William Wood;** a Circuit Judge, since 2002; *b* 22 March 1948; *s* of Dr B. S. B. Wood and Elizabeth Wood; *m* 1973, Angela Beatson-Hird; one *s* two *d*. *Educ:* Bradfield Coll., Berks; Magdalen Coll., Oxford (MA). Called to the Bar, Gray's Inn, 1970. A Recorder, 1990–2002. Chm., Birmingham DAC, 1999–. *Recreations:* sailing, tennis, theatre. *Address:* Wolverhampton Crown Court, Pipers Row, Wolverhampton WV1 3LQ. *Clubs:* Buckland (Birmingham); Bentley Drivers'; Edgbaston Priory Lawn Tennis.

WOODALL, Alec; *b* 20 Sept. 1918; *m* 1950; one *s* one *d*. *Educ:* South Road Elementary School. Colliery official. MP (Lab) Hemsworth, Feb. 1974–1987. PPS to Sec. of State for Trade, 1976–78. Mem. Nat. Council, 1975–87, case worker, 1987–, SSAFA. *Address:* 2 Grove Terrace, Hemsworth, West Yorkshire WF9 4BQ. *T:* (01977) 613897.

WOODARD, Rear-Adm. Sir Robert (Nathaniel), KCVO 1995; DL; Flag Officer Royal Yachts, 1990–95; an Extra Equerry to the Queen, since 1992; *b* 13 Jan. 1939; *s* of Francis Alwyne Woodard and Catherine Mary Woodard (*née* Hayes); *m* 1963, Rosamund Lucia, *d* of Lt-Col D. L. A. Gibbs, DSO and Lady Hilaria Gibbs (*née* Edgcumbe); two *s* one *d*. *Educ:* Lancing College. Joined Royal Navy as Cadet, 1958; specialised in flying; served HM Ships Ark Royal, Eagle, Victorious, Bulwark in 800, 801, 845, 846 and 848

Sqns (active service Malaya, Borneo); Commands: 771 Sqn, 1973–74; 848 Sqn, 1974–75; HMS Amazon, 1978–80; HMS Glasgow, 1983–84; HMS Osprey, 1984–86; MoD Op. Requirements, 1986–88; Cdre, Clyde, 1989–90. Dir, Crownhill Estates, 1996–. Dir, Woodard (Western Div.) plc, 1985–2005; Fellow, Western Div., 1985–2005, and Trustee, 2001–, Woodard Corp. Vice-Pres., Falmouth Br., Royal Naval Assoc. Pres., SSAFA, Cornwall, 1995. Chm., Regl Cttee, Devon and Cornwall, NT, 1997–2002. Chairman of Governors: King's Coll., Taunton, 2000–05; King's Hall, Pyrland, 2000–05; Vice-Chm., Govs, Bolitho Sch., Penzance, 1994–. Younger Brother, Trinity House, 1994–. DL Cornwall, 1999. FCMI (FBIM 1979); MInstD 1995. Comdr, Ordre Nat. du Mérite (France), 1992. *Recreations:* shooting, fishing, painting, sailing. *Clubs:* Naval and Military; Royal Yacht Squadron, Port Navas Yacht.

WOODBRIDGE, Anthony Rivers; Senior Partner, The Woodbridge Partnership, since 1997; *b* 10 Aug. 1942; *s* of late John Nicholas Woodbridge and Patricia Madeleine (*née* Rebbeck); *m* 1976, Lynda Anne Nolan; one *s*. *Educ:* Stowe; Trinity Hall, Cambridge (MA). Admitted solicitor, 1967; Partner, Woodbridge & Sons, Uxbridge, 1969–83; Sen. Partner, Turberville Woodbridge, 1983–97. Company Secretary: Abbeyfield Uxbridge Soc. Ltd, 1974–96 (Vice-Chm., 1996–98); Burr Brown Internat. Ltd, 1992–96. Adminr, Uxbridge Duty Solicitor Scheme, 1983–91. Clerk to Comrs of Income Tax, 1985–. Mem., Hillingdon HA, 1990–92; Chairman: Hillingdon Community Health NHS Trust, 1992–94; Harrow and Hillingdon Healthcare NHS Trust, 1994–2001; Stoke Mandeville Hosp. NHS Trust, 2001–02; Hillingdon Hosp. NHS Trust, 2002–05. Trustee, The Hillingdon Partnership Trust, 1994–2003. Hon. Solicitor: Samaritans, Hillingdon, 1973–; Age Concern, Hillingdon, 1989–. Mem., Law Soc., 1967–. Mem. Ct, Brunel Univ., 1995–. FInstD 1999. Gov., Fulmer Sch., Bucks, 1984–2003 (Chm. Govs, 1988–94). DUniv Brunel, 2000. *Recreations:* walking, cycling, touring. *Address:* The Woodbridge Partnership, Windsor House, 42 Windsor Street, Uxbridge UB8 1AB. *T:* (01895) 454801, *Fax:* (01895) 454848; *e-mail:* tony@woodbridgepartnership.co.uk; 4 Braid Gardens, Bull Lane, Gerrards Cross, Bucks SL9 8RA.

WOODBURN, Christopher Hugh, FCA; Chief Executive, General Insurance Standards Council, 1999–2005; *b* 6 Nov. 1947; *s* of Leonard Arthur and Phyllis Lydia Woodburn; *m* 1972, Lesley Avril Mohan; two *d*. *Educ:* St John's Sch., Leatherhead. FCA 1972. Articled Clerk and Audit Senior, Deloitte & Co., 1966–72; London Stock Exchange, 1972–88 (Hd, Financial Regulation, 1987–88); Securities Assoc., 1988–91 (Dep. Chief Exec., 1990–91); SFA, 1991–99 (Chief Exec., 1997–99). *Recreations:* sailing, history. *Address:* Oak House, Heathfield Road, Burwash, E Sussex TN19 7HN. *T:* (01435) 883196.

WOODCOCK, Sir John, Kt 1989; CBE 1983; QPM 1976; HM Chief Inspector of Constabulary, 1990–93; *b* 14 Jan. 1932; *s* of late Joseph Woodcock and of Elizabeth May Woodcock (*née* Whiteside); *m* 1953, Kathleen Margaret Abbott; two *s* one *d*. *Educ:* Preston, Lancs, elementary schs; Preston Technical Coll. Police cadet, Lancashire Constabulary, 1947–50; Army Special Investigation Branch, 1950–52; Constable to Chief Inspector, Lancashire Constabulary, 1952–65; Supt and Chief Supt, Bedfordshire and Luton Constabulary, 1965–68; Asst Chief Constable, 1968–70, Dep. Chief Constable, 1970–74, Gwent Constabulary; Dep. Chief Constable, Devon and Cornwall Constabulary, 1974–78; Chief Constable: N Yorkshire Police, 1978–79; S Wales Constabulary, 1979–83; HM Inspector of Constabulary, Wales and Midlands, 1983–90. Conducted inquiry into escapes from Whitemoor Prison, reported 1994. Intermed. Comd Course, Police Coll., 1965, Sen. Comd Course, 1968; Study, Bavarian Police, 1977; European Discussion Centre, 1977; Internat. Police Course (Lectr), Sicily, Rome, 1978; FBI, Nat. Exec., Washington, 1981; Lectr, Denmark, 1983, Holland, 1990; Study, Royal Hong Kong Police, 1989. Adviser and Member: UK Atomic Energy Police Authy, 1993–99; MoD Police Cttee, 1995–2000. Dir, Capital Corp. plc, 1994–99; Advr, Control Risks Group Ltd, 1995–2002. Vice-Pres., Welsh Assoc. of Youth Clubs, 1981–87; Chm., South Wales Cttee, Royal Jubilee and Prince's Trusts, 1983–85; Member: Admin. Council, Royal Jubilee Trusts, 1981–85; Prince's Trust Cttee for Wales, 1981–85; Mem., Governing Body, World College of the Atlantic, 1980–85. Pres., Police Mutual Assurance Soc., 1990–94. St John Council, N Yorks, S Glam, Mid Glam (Chm.), Hereford and Worcs, 1979–90. Freeman, City of London, 1993. CCMI (CIMgt 1980). FRCA 1995. CStJ 1992; KSG 1984. *Recreation:* golf. *Address:* c/o Home Office, 2 Marsham Street, SW1P 4DF. *Clubs:* Swansea Lions (Hon. Mem.); Merlin Golf (Cornwall).

WOODCOCK, John Charles, OBE 1996; cricket writer; *b* 7 Aug. 1926; *s* of late Rev. Parry John Woodcock and Norah Mabel Woodcock (*née* Hutchinson). *Educ:* Dragon Sch.; St Edward's Sch., Oxford; Trinity Coll., Oxford (MA; OUHC *v* Cambridge, 1946, 1947). Manchester Guardian, 1952–54; cricket writer, The Times, 1954–; Cricket Corresp. to Country Life, 1962–91; Editor, Wisden Cricketers' Almanack, 1980–86; has covered over 40 Test tours, 1950–98, to Australia, 18 times, S Africa, W Indies, New Zealand, India, Pakistan and Sri Lanka. Mem., MCC Cttee, 1988–91 and 1992–95 (Trustee, 1996–99; Hon. Life Vice-Pres., 2001). Pres., Cricket Writers' Club, 1986–2005. Patron of the living of Longparish. Sports Journalist of the Year, British Press Awards, 1987. *Publications:* The Ashes, 1956; (with E. W. Swanton) Barclays World of Cricket, 1980 (Associate Editor, 2nd edn 1986, Consultant Editor, 3rd edn 1986); The Times One Hundred Greatest Cricketers, 1998. *Recreations:* the countryside, golf. *Address:* The Old Curacy, Longparish, Andover, Hants SP11 6PB. *T:* (01264) 720259. *Clubs:* MCC; Vincent's (Oxford); St Enodoc Golf.

WOODCOCK, Michael, (Mike); JP; company director, consultant, researcher and writer; *b* 10 April 1943; *s* of Herbert Eric Woodcock and Violet Irene Woodcock; *m* 1969, Carole Ann (*née* Berry); one *s* one *d*. *Educ:* Queen Elizabeth's Grammar Sch., Mansfield, Notts; DLitt IMCB, 1988. Successively: Accountant, Personnel Officer, Management Development Adviser, Head of Small Business Development Unit, Consultant, Vice-Pres. of US Corp., Founder of six UK companies. Underwriting Mem. of Lloyd's, 1984–. Proprietor of Estates in Scotland: Glenrinnes; Rigg; Carron Bridge; Corbiewells. MP (C) Ellesmere Port and Neston, 1983–92. Member: Trade and Industry Select Cttee, 1984–87; Home Affairs Select Cttee, 1987–92; Secretary: Cons. Smaller Business Cttee, 1990–92; All Party Transpennine Gp of MPs, 1990–92. Parly Advr, Chamber of Coal Traders, 1985–93. Nat. Vice Pres., Ramblers' Assoc., 1993–. Vis. Prof., Univ. of Lancaster Mgt Sch., 1992–96; Vis. Fellow, Leeds Business Sch., 1994–97. Pres., Royal Masonic Trust for Girls and Boys, 2000–. Companion, IMCB, 1990. JP Mansfield, Notts, 1971. *Publications:* People at Work, 1975; Unblocking Your Organisation, 1978 (UK, USA and Holland); Team Development Manual, 1979 (UK, USA and Indonesia); Organisation Development Through Teambuilding, 1981 (UK and USA); The Unblocked Manager, 1982 (UK, USA and four foreign edns); 50 Activities for Self Development, 1982 (UK, USA and eight foreign edns); Manual of Management Development, 1985; 50 Activities for Teambuilding, 1989 (UK, USA and 11 foreign edns); (jtly) Clarifying Organisational Values, 1989 (UK and Sweden); 50 Activities for Unblocking Your Organisation, vol. 1, 1990, vol. 2, 1991; The Self Made Leader, 1990; Unblocking Organisational Values, 1990; Change: a collection of activities and exercises, 1992; The Woodcock Francis series of Management Audits, 1994; Teambuilding Strategy, 1994 (UK and India); The Teambuilders Toolkit, 1996; The Problem Solvers Toolkit, 1996; The New Unblocked Manager, 1996; 25 Interventions for Improving Team Performance, 1997; Developing Your People, 1998; Interventions for Developing Managerial Competencies, 1998; Management Skills Assessment, 1999; The Agile Organisation, 1999; Audits for Organisational Effectiveness, 2004; Team Metrics: resources for measuring and improving team performance, 2005. *Recreation:* walking. *Address:* Inkersall Farm, Bilsthorpe, Newark, Notts NG22 8TL; 13 Denny Street, SE11 4UX; Cuilangortan, Old Manse, Glenrinnes, by Dufftown, Moray AB55 4DE. *Club:* Farmers'.

WOODCOCK, Thomas, LVO 1996; DL; FSA; Norroy and Ulster King of Arms, since 1997; *b* 20 May 1951; *s* of late Thomas Woodcock, Hurst Green, Lancs, and Mary, *d* of William Woodcock, Holcombe, Lancs; *m* 1998, Lucinda Mary Harmsworth, *d* of late Lucas Michael Harmsworth King. *Educ:* Eton; University Coll., Durham (BA); Darwin Coll., Cambridge (LLB). FSA 1990. Called to Bar, Inner Temple, 1975. Research Assistant to Sir Anthony Wagner, Garter King of Arms, 1975–78; Rouge Croix Pursuivant, 1978–82; Somerset Herald, 1982–97; Advr on Naval Heraldry, 1996–. Chm., Harleian Soc., 2004–; Pres., Lancs Parish Register Soc., 2004–. DL Lancs, 2005. *Publications:* (with John Martin Robinson) The Oxford Guide to Heraldry, 1988; (ed with D. H. B. Chesshyre) Dictionary of British Arms: Medieval Ordinary, vol. 1, 1992, vol. 2 (ed with Hon. J. Grant and I. Graham), 1996; (with John Martin Robinson) Heraldry in National Trust Houses, 2000. *Address:* College of Arms, Queen Victoria Street, EC4V 4BT. *T:* (020) 7236 3634. *Club:* Travellers.

WOODFORD, Air Vice-Marshal Anthony Arthur George, CB 1989; Home Bursar and Fellow, Magdalen College, Oxford, 1992–2001; *b* 6 Jan. 1939; *s* of Arthur and May Woodford; *m* 1965, Christine Barbara Tripp; one *s* two *d*. *Educ:* Haberdashers' Aske's Hampstead School; RAF College, Cranwell. BA Hons Open Univ. 1978. Commissioned pilot, 1959; served Nos 12, 44, 53, 101 Sqns and 4017th CCTS USAF; Asst Air Attaché, British Embassy, Washington, 1978–81; Comdr RAF St Mawgan, 1982–83; Comdr British Forces Ascension Island, 1982; ADC to the Queen, 1982–83; RCDS 1984; HQ Strike Command: Air Cdre Plans, 1985–87; AOA, 1987–89; ACOS Policy, SHAPE, 1989–92, retd. *Address:* Filkins Moor, Filkins, Lechlade, Glos GL7 3JJ. *Club:* Royal Air Force.

WOODFORD, Maj.-Gen. David Milner, CBE 1975; retired; Member, Lord Chancellor's Panel of Independent Inspectors, 1988–2000; *b* 26 May 1930; *s* of late Major R. M. Woodford, MC, and Marion Rosa Woodford (*née* Gregory); *m* 1st, 1959, Mary E. Jones (marr. diss. 1987); 2nd, 1995, Carole M. Westoby. *Educ:* Prince of Wales Sch., Nairobi; Wadham Coll., Oxford. psc, jsdc, rcds. National Service, then Regular, 1st Royal Fusiliers, Korea, 1953, then Regtl service, Egypt, Sudan, UK, 1953–55; ADC/GOC Berlin, 1956–58; Adjt and Co. Comd 1RF, Gulf, Kenya, Malta, Cyprus, Libya, UK, 1958–61; GSO3 Div./Dist, UK, 1962; sc Camberley, 1963; GSO2 MO 1, then MA/VCGS, 1964–66; Co. Comd 1RF, BAOR, UK, Gulf and Oman, 1966–68; GSO1 (DS) Staff Coll., 1968–70; CO 3 RRF, Gibraltar, UK, N Ireland, 1970–72; Col GS NEARELF (Cyprus), 1972–75; Comd 3 Inf. Bde (N Ireland), 1976–77; Dep. Col, RRF, 1976–81; RCDS 1978; D Comd and COS SE Dist, UK, 1979–80; Dir Army Training, 1981–82; Sen. Army Mem., RCDS, 1982–84; Comdt, JSDC, 1984–86. Col RRF, 1982–86. *Recreations:* literary, historical; passionate golfer. *Address:* c/o Regimental Headquarters, The Royal Regiment of Fusiliers, HM Tower of London, EC3N 4AB. *Clubs:* Army and Navy, New Zealand Golf.

WOODFORD, F(rederick) Peter, PhD; FRCPath; FRSC; FIPEM; Chief Scientific Officer, Department of Health (formerly of Health and Social Security), 1984–93; *b* 8 Nov. 1930; *s* of Wilfrid Charles Woodford and Mabel Rose (*née* Scarff); *m* 1964, Susan Silberman, NY; one *d*. *Educ:* Lewis Sch., Pengam, Glam; Balliol Coll., Oxford (Domus Exhibnr; BA (Hons Chem.) 1952; MA 1955); PhD Leeds 1955. FRCPath 1984; CChem, FRSC 1990; FIPEM (FBES 1993; MBES 1991). Res. Fellow, Leiden Univ., 1958–62; Vis. Scientist/Lectr, Univ. of Tennessee Med. Sch. and NIH, USA, 1962–63; Guest Investigator, Rockefeller Univ., NY, 1963–71; Scientific Historian, Ciba Foundn, and Scientific Associate, Wellcome Trust, 1971–74; Exec. Dir, Inst. for Res. into Mental and Multiple Handicap, 1974–77; PSO (Clin. Chem.), DHSS, 1977–84. Distinguished Visitor, Royal Free Hosp. Sch. of Med., 1994–. Member: Members' Council, Royal Free Hosp. Foundn Trust, 2008–; Quality of Life Panel, Camden Council, 2008–. Editorial Consultant: Clin. Res. Inst., Montreal, 1970–90; Inst. of Pharmacology, Milan Univ., 1995–. Chm., Council of Biology Editors (USA), 1969–70; Managing/Executive Editor: Jl of Atherosclerosis Res., 1960–62; Jl of Lipid Res., 1963–69; Procs of Nat. Acad. of Scis, USA, 1970–71; Editl Consultant, King's Fund Centre for Health Service Develt, 1990–93; Editor, Camden History Soc. pubns, 1995–. Student Gov., City Lit. Inst., 1999–2001. Chm., Hampstead Music Club, 1996–99; Patron, Cavatina Chamber Music Trust, 2003–; Patron Friend, Hampstead Town Hall. First non-med. ARCP, 2000; Hon. Fellow, Assoc. of Clin. Biochemistry, 2005. Hon. DSc Salford, 1993. Waverley Gold Medal for scientific writing, 1955; Meritorious Award, Council of Biology Editors, USA, 1984. *Publications:* Scientific Writing for Graduate Students, 1969, 4th edn 1986; Medical Research Systems in Europe, 1973; The Ciba Foundation: an analytic history 1949–1974, 1974; Writing Scientific Papers in English, 1975; In-Service Training series: of Physiological Measurement Technicians, 1988; of Medical Physics Technicians, 1989; of Medical Laboratory Assistants, 1991; of Rehabilitation Engineering Technicians, 1992; (ed) From Primrose Hill to Euston Road, 1995; Atherosclerosis X, 1995; A Constant Vigil, 1997; (ed) Streets of Bloomsbury and Fitzrovia (a historical survey), 1997; (ed) East of Bloomsbury, 1998; How to Teach Scientific Communication, 1999; (ed) Streets of Old Holborn, 1999; (ed) The Streets of Hampstead, 3rd edn, 2000; (ed) The Good Grave Guide to Hampstead Cemetery, Fortune Green, 2000; (ed) Streets of St Giles, 2000; (ed) Victorian Seven Dials, 2001; (ed) 200 Years of Local Justice in Hampstead and Clerkenwell, 2001; (ed) The Railways of Camden, 2002; (ed jtly) Streets of St Pancras, 2002; (ed jtly) 20th-Century Camden Recalled, 2002; (ed jtly) Streets of Camden Town, 2003; (ed jtly) Streets of Kentish Town, 2005; (ed) Wartime St Pancras, 2006; (ed jtly) Streets of Gospel Oak and West Kentish Town, 2006; (ed) The Greville Estate: the history of a Kilburn neighbourhood, 2007; (ed) Buried in Hampstead, 2nd edn, 2007; (ed jtly) Streets of Highgate, 2007; (ed jtly) George Morland: a London artist in eighteenth-century Camden, 2008; articles on scientific writing, lipids of the arterial wall, editing of biomed. jls, prevention and treatment of handicapping disorders, screening for spina bifida, quality in pathology labs, costing and ethics in clin. chem., history of Heath and Old Hampstead Soc., 18th-century doctors in Bloomsbury, clinical significance of antioxidants. *Recreations:* chamber music (pianist), local history. *Address:* 1 Akenside Road, NW3 5BS.

WOODFORD, Stephen William John; Chairman and Chief Executive, DDB London, since 2007; *b* 11 Feb. 1959; *s* of John and Barbara Woodford; *m* 1988, Amelia Wylton Dickson; two *s* two *d*. *Educ:* Tomlinscote Sch., Frimley; City Univ. (BSc Hons). Grad. trainee, Nestlé Co. Ltd, 1980–82; Account Manager, Lintas Advertising, 1982–85; Account Dir, Waldron Allen Henry & Thompson, 1985–89; Account Dir, subseq. Gp Account Dir, WCRS, 1989–91; Dep. Man. Dir, Leo Burnett, 1991–94; Client Services Dir, 1994–95, Man. Dir, 1995–99, CEO, 1999–2005, WCRS; CEO, Engine, 2005–07.

Pres., Inst. Practitioners in Advertising, 2003–05. Trustee, Changing Faces Charity, 2003– (Chm., 2003–07). *Recreations:* family, riding, running, tennis, swimming, the countryside, reading. *Address:* DDB London, 12 Bishop's Bridge Road, W2 6AA.

WOODFORD-HOLLICK, Susan Mary; *see* Hollick, Lady.

WOODGATE, Joan Mary, CBE 1964; RRC 1959; Matron-in-Chief, Queen Alexandra's RN Nursing Service, 1962–66, retired; *b* 30 Aug. 1912; *d* of Sir Alfred Woodgate, CBE, and Louisa Alice (*née* Digby). *Educ:* Surbiton High Sch., Surrey. Trained at St George's Hospital, 1932–36, Sister, 1937–38; Queen Charlotte's Hospital, 1936. Joined QARNNS, 1938; served Middle East and Far East; HM Hospital Ship, Empire Clyde, 1945–47; HM Hospital Ship, Maine, 1953–54; Principal Matron: RNH Haslar, 1959–61; RNH Malta, 1961–62. OStJ 1959; QHNS, 1962–64. Member, Commonwealth War Graves Commn, 1966–83. *Recreations:* gardening, country pursuits. *Address:* Laurel Cottage, Northover Lane, Tiptoe, near Lymington, Hants SO41 6FS. *Club:* English-Speaking Union.

WOODGATE, Terence Allan, RDI 2003; furniture and lighting designer; *b* 5 Feb. 1953; *s* of Charles and Ethel Woodgate; *m* 1979, Paula Casey; two *s*. *Educ:* Westminster Coll.; London Coll. of Furniture. Work exhibited in perm. collections of Museu d'Art Decoratives, Barcelona and V&A Mus. British Design Award, Design Council, 1992; Red Dot Best of the Best Award, Design Zentrum Nordrhein Westfalen, Germany, 1992; Industrie Form Ecology Award, Germany, 1995. *Address:* West Hill, Little Trodgers Lane, Mayfield, E Sussex TN20 6PW. *T:* (01435) 872800, *Fax:* (01435) 872751; *e-mail:* terence@terencewoodgate.com.

WOODHALL, David Massey, CBE 1992; Partner, The Woodhall Consultancy, since 1992; *b* 25 Aug. 1934; *s* of Douglas J. D. and Esme Dorothy Woodhall; *m* 1954, Margaret A. Howarth; two *s*. *Educ:* Bishop Holgate's Sch., Barnsley; Royds Hall, Huddersfield; Henley Administrative Staff Coll. Dip. Leeds Sch. of Architecture and Town Planning. West Riding CC, 1951–60; Cumberland CC, 1960–63; Northamptonshire CC, 1963–82: County Planning Officer, 1971–80; Asst Chief Executive, 1980–82; Chief Exec., Commn for New Towns, 1982–92. Dir, Adnams Co. plc, 1986–2006. Consultant, Caws and Morris, Chartered Surveyors, 1992–2004. A Countryside Comr, 1996–99; Mem., Countryside Agency, 1999–2001. *Recreations:* National Hunt racing, landscape, food and wine. *Address:* 2 Hardingstone Lane, Hardingstone, Northampton NN4 6DE. *T:* (01604) 764654.

WOODHAM, Prof. Jonathan Michael; Professor of History of Design, since 1993, and Director, Centre for Research Development (Arts and Architecture), since 1998, University of Brighton; *b* 8 June 1950; *s* of Ronald Ernest Woodham and Kathleen Isabel Woodham (*née* Malone); *m* 1981, Amanda Grace Callan Smith; three *s*. *Educ:* Downside Sch.; Edinburgh Coll. of Art, Univ. of Edinburgh (MA 1st cl. Hons (Fine Art) 1973); Courtauld Inst. of Art, London (MA (British Romantic Art) 1974). Lectr, 1974–75, Sen. Lectr, 1975–82, in Hist. of Art and Design, Staffordshire Polytech.; Brighton Polytechnic, later University of Brighton: Course Dir, Hist. of Design, 1982–93; Dir, Design Hist. Res. Centre, 1993–2001. Member: Hist. of Art and Design Bd, 1984–87, Register of Special Advrs, 1987–92, CNAA; Quality Assessment Panel, 1996–98, RAE Panel, 2001, HEFCE; Postgrad. Qualifications Res. Panel, Visual Arts & Media, AHRB, 1998–2004. Mem., Hong Kong Accreditation Council, 1987–; Expert Scientific Advr, Culture and Soc. Panel, Acad. of Finland, 2003–. Chm., Design Hist. Soc., 1995–97. Member, Editorial Board: Jl of Design History, 1987–2004; Design Issues, 1994–; Art Design and Communication in Higher Educn, 2002–. *Publications:* The Industrial Designer and the Public, 1983; Twentieth-Century Ornament, 1991; Twentieth-Century Design, 1997; Design and Popular Politics in the Postwar Period: the Britain Can Make It Exhibition 1946, 1999; A Dictionary of Modern Design, 2004; contribs to jls, inc. Jl of Design Hist., Design Issues, Design Hist. Japan, Temes de Disseny, L'Arca, Design, and Crafts. *Recreations:* cookery, gardening, travel, drinking wine. *Address:* 116 Hollingbury Park Avenue, Brighton BN1 7JP. *T:* (01273) 506319; *e-mail:* j.m.woodham@brighton.ac.uk.

WOODHAMS, Stephen Robert; floral and garden designer; design director, since 1990; *b* 17 July 1964; *s* of Robert and Joy Woodhams. *Educ:* RHS Certificate. Paul Temple Ltd, 1982; buyer, Moyses Stevens, 1984; Dir, Horticultural Innovations, 1986; Founder, Woodhams Ltd, 1990, Woodhams Landscapes Ltd, 1994. *Publications:* Flower Power, 1999; Portfolio of Contemporary Gardens, 2000. *Recreations:* photography, running. *T:* (020) 7735 3798; *e-mail:* S.Woodhams@btinternet.com. *Clubs:* Blacks, Cobden.

WOODHEAD, Vice-Adm. Sir (Anthony) Peter, KCB 1992; Prisons' Ombudsman, 1994–99; *b* 30 July 1939; *s* of Leslie and Nancy Woodhead; *m* 1964, Carol; one *s* one *d*. *Educ:* Leeds Grammar Sch.; Conway; BRNC Dartmouth. Seaman Officer; Pilot, 1962; Aircraft Carriers, Borneo Campaign; CO, HM Ships Jupiter, 1974, Rhyl, 1975; NDC 1976; Naval Plans Div., MoD, 1977; CSO to Flag Officer, Third Flotilla, 1980; COS to FO Comdg Falklands Task Force, 1982; Captain, Fourth Frigate Sqdn, 1983; RCDS 1984; Dir, Naval Ops, 1985; CO HMS Illustrious, 1986; Flag Officer: Flotilla Two, 1988; Flotilla One, 1989. Dep. SACLANT, 1991–93. Lay Reader: Guildford, 1991; Chichester, 1997. Pres., Marriage Resource, 1995–2004. Dep. Chm., BMT, 1996–. Chm., Crime Reduction Initiatives, 2001–; Member: Security Vetting Appeals Panel, 1997–; Armed Forces Pay Review Body, 2001–04. Dir, Beaconlight Trust, 2004–. Gov., Aldro Sch., 1996–; Trustee, Kainos prison therapeutic community, 1999–. *Recreations:* ball games, antique restoration. *Clubs:* Royal Navy of 1765 and 1785; Hove (Hove).

WOODHEAD, Prof. Christopher Anthony; Stanley Kalms Professor of Education, University of Buckingham, since 2002; Chairman, Cognita Group, since 2004; *b* 20 Oct. 1946; one *d* from former marriage. *Educ:* Bristol Univ. (BA Sp. Hons English, PGCE); Univ. of Keele (MA). English Teacher, Priory Sch., Shrewsbury, 1969–72; Dep. Head of English, Newent Sch., Gloucester, 1972–74; Head of English, Gordano Sch., Avon, 1974–76; Tutor for English, Oxford Univ., 1976–82; English Advr, 1982–84, Chief Advr, 1984–88, Shropshire LEA; Dep. Chief Educn Officer, Devon LEA, 1988–90, Cornwall LEA, 1990–91; Dep. Chief Exec., 1991, Chief Exec., 1991–93, Nat. Curriculum Council; Chief Exec., SCAA, 1993–94; HM Chief Inspector of Schs, 1994–2000. Special Prof., Univ. of Nottingham, 1993–95. *Publication:* Class War, 2002. *Address:* University of Buckingham, Hunter Street, Buckingham MK18 1EG.

WOODHEAD, David James; public affairs and educational public relations consultant, since 2004; National Director, Independent Schools Council Information Service (formerly Independent Schools Information Service), 1985–2004; Deputy General Secretary, Independent Schools Council, 1998–2004; *b* 9 Nov. 1943; *s* of Frank and Polly Woodhead; *m* 1974, Carole Underwood; two *s*. *Educ:* Queen Elizabeth Grammar Sch., Wakefield; Univ. of Leicester (BA Hons). Journalist: Cambridge Evening News (educn corresp.), 1965–68; Sunday Telegraph, 1968–75; ILEA Press Office: Press Officer, 1975–78; Chief Press Officer, 1978–85; Hon. Press Officer, London Schs Symphony Orch., 1975–84. Rep. UK at first internat. conf. on private schs in China, Beijing, 1999. Trustee: Jt Educnl Trust, 1988–2004; Oratory Gp, 1995–98; Founder-Trustee, Nat. Youth Strings Acad. (formerly Nat. ISCis Strings Acad.), 1996–. Mem., Dresden Trust, 1995– (Trustee, 2005–; Founder, Dresden Scholars' Scheme, 2001). Member: Court and Council, Univ. of Leicester, 2000–; Adv. Devlt Bd, Rudolf Kempe Soc. for Young Musicians, 2000– (Trustee, 2004–); Adv. Bd, Global Educn Mgt Systems Ltd, 2005– (Special Advr, 2007–); British-German Assoc. Youthbridge Cttee, 2008–. Governor: Battle Abbey Sch., 1988–91; St John's Sch., Leatherhead, 1994– (Vice-Chm., 2006–; Chm., Educn Cttee, 2001–); Feltonfleet Prep. Sch., Cobham, 1998–2001; City of London Sch. for Girls, 2002–06; Purcell Sch., 2004–; Hon. Gov., Wakefield Grammar Sch. Foundn, 2004–. FRSA 1990. Medal of Honour, Soc. for Reconstruction of the Frauenkirche, Dresden, 2007. *Publications:* Choosing Your Independent School, annually, 1985–99; (ed) Good Communications Guide, 1986, 2nd edn 1989; The ISC Guide to Accredited Independent Schools, annually, 2000–04; (contrib.) Education in the UK, 2002; numerous newspaper and magazine articles. *Recreations:* family, opera, classical music, enjoying being a Wagner fanatic, books, German and Austrian history, travel. *Address:* 29 Randalls Road, Leatherhead, Surrey KT22 7TQ. *T:* (01372) 373206. *Clubs:* Royal Over-Seas League, St James's.

WOODHEAD, Vice-Adm. Sir Peter; *see* Woodhead, Vice-Adm. Sir A. P.

WOODHEAD, Robin George; Chief Executive, Sotheby's International, since 2006; *b* 28 April 1951; *s* of Walter Henry Woodhead and Gladys Catherine (*née* Ferguson); *m* 1980, Mary Fitzgerald Allen, *qv* (marr. diss. 1991). *Educ:* Mt Pleasant Sch., Salisbury, Rhodesia; UC of Rhodesia and Nyasaland (LLB Hons London ext.). Admitted Solicitor, 1978; Man. Dir, Premier Man Ltd, 1980–86; Chief Executive: Nat. Investment Gp, 1986–90; London Commodity Exchange, 1991–97; Man. Dir, 1998–99, Chief Exec., 1999–2000, Sotheby's Europe; Chief Exec., Sotheby's Europe and Asia, 2000–06. Chm., Internat. Petroleum Exchange, 1980–86. Chairman: Rambert Dance Co., 1995–2000; Music Research Inst., 1997–2000. Gov., S Bank Centre, 2004–. *Recreations:* game reserve development in Zululand, riding, music, visual arts, performing arts. *Address:* Sotheby's, 34–35 New Bond Street, W1A 2AA. *T:* (020) 7293 6066.

WOODHOUSE, family name of **Baron Terrington**.

WOODHOUSE, Rev. Canon Alison Ruth; Vicar, St Luke's, Formby, 1995–2007; Chaplain to the Queen, since 2005; *b* 14 Aug. 1943; *d* of Harold and May Woodhouse. *Educ:* Bedford Coll. of Educn (Cert Ed 1964); DipTh London Univ. 1971 (ext.). Primary sch. teacher, Huncoat CP Sch., Accrington, 1964–68; licensed as Parish Worker, Lichfield dio., 1971; ordained deaconess, 1978, deacon, 1987, priest, 1994; Parish Deacon, then Curate, Burscough Bridge, 1987–95; Area Dean, Sefton, 2000–05. Hon. Canon, Liverpool Cathedral, 2002–07. *Recreations:* dog walking, music, cinema.

WOODHOUSE, Ven. Andrew Henry, DSC 1945; MA; Archdeacon of Hereford and Canon Residentiary, Hereford Cathedral, 1982–91, now Archdeacon Emeritus; *b* 30 Jan. 1923; *s* of H. A. Woodhouse, Dental Surgeon, Hanover Square, W1, and Woking, Surrey, and Mrs P. Woodhouse; unmarried. *Educ:* Lancing Coll.; The Queen's Coll., Oxford. MA 1949. Served War, RNVR, 1942–46 (Lieut). Oxford, 1941–42 and 1946–47; Lincoln Theological Coll., 1948–50. Deacon, 1950; Priest, 1951; Curate of All Saints, Poplar, 1950–56; Vicar of St Martin, West Drayton, 1956–70; Rural Dean of Hillingdon, 1967–70; Archdeacon of Ludlow and Rector of Wistanstow, 1970–82. *Recreations:* photography, walking. *Address:* Orchard Cottage, Bracken Close, Woking, Surrey GU22 7HD. *T:* (01483) 760671. *Club:* Naval.
See also R. M. Woodhouse.

WOODHOUSE, Rt Hon. Sir (Arthur) Owen, ONZ 2007; KBE 1981; Kt 1974; DSC 1944; PC 1974; Founding President, Law Commission, New Zealand, 1986–91; a Judge of the Supreme Court, New Zealand, 1961–86; a Judge of the Court of Appeal, 1974–86, President of the Court of Appeal, 1981–86; *b* Napier, 18 July 1916; *s* of A. J. Woodhouse and W. J. C. Woodhouse (*née* Allen); *m* 1940, Margaret Leah Thorp; four *s* two *d*. *Educ:* Napier Boys' High Sch.; Auckland Univ. (LLB). Served War of 1939–45, Lt-Comdr in RNZNVR on secondment to RN; service in MTBs; liaison officer with Yugoslav Partisans, 1943; Asst to Naval Attaché, HM Embassy Belgrade, 1945. Joined Lusk, Willis & Sproule, barristers and solicitors, 1946; Crown Solicitor, Napier, 1953; appointed Judge of Supreme Court, 1961. Chm., Royal Commn on Compensation and Rehabilitation in respect of Personal Injury in NZ, 1966–67, and of inquiry into similar questions in Australia, 1973–74; Pres., NZ Sect., Internat. Commn of Jurists, 1986–93. Hon. LLD: Victoria Univ. of Wellington, 1978; Univ. of York, Toronto, 1981. *Publication:* A Personal Affair, 2004. *Recreations:* music, golf. *Address:* 244 Remuera Road, Auckland 1005, New Zealand. *Clubs:* Northern (Auckland); Hawkes Bay (Napier); Wellesley, Wellington (Wellington).

WOODHOUSE, Ven. (Charles) David (Stewart); Archdeacon of Warrington, 1981–2001, now Emeritus; Vicar of St Peter's, Hindley, 1981–92; *b* 23 Dec. 1934; *s* of Rev. Hector and Elsie Woodhouse. *Educ:* Silcoates School, Wakefield; Kelham Theological College; Lancaster Univ. (MA 1995). Curate of St Wilfrid's, Halton, Leeds, 1959–63; Youth Chaplain, Kirkby Team Ministry, Diocese of Liverpool, 1963–66; Curate of St John's, Pembroke, Bermuda, 1966–69; Asst Gen. Secretary, CEMS, 1969–70; Gen. Sec., 1970–76; Rector of Ideford, Ashcombe and Luton and Domestic Chaplain to Bishop of Exeter, 1976–81. Hon. Canon, Liverpool Cathedral, 1983. *Address:* 9 Rob Lane, Newton-le-Willows WA12 0DR.

WOODHOUSE, Charles Frederick, CVO 1998; DL; Partner, Farrer and Co., Solicitors, 1969–99 (Consultant, 1999–2001); Solicitor to the Duke of Edinburgh, 1983–2001; *b* 6 June 1941; *s* of late Wilfrid Meynell Woodhouse and Peggy Woodhouse (*née* Kahl); *m* 1969, Margaret Joan Cooper; one *s* two *d*. *Educ:* Marlborough; McGill Univ.; Peterhouse, Cambridge (BA Hons). Hon. Legal Advr, Commonwealth Games Council for England, 1983–2007; Legal Advr, CCPR, 1971–99 (Mem., Inquiry on Amateur Status, 1986–88). Pres., British Assoc. for Sport and Law, 1997–2000; Founder and Chm., Sports Dispute Resolution Panel, 1997–2007. Dir, Santos USA Corp., 1992–2002. Chm., Rural Regeneration Cumbria, 2003–06; Dir, Cumbria Vision Ltd (formerly Cumbria Vision Renaissance Ltd), 2006–. Mem., Royal Parks Rev. Gp, 1992–96. Chairman: Cheviot Trust, 1991–97; Rank Pension Plan Trustee Ltd, 1992–2001; Trustee: Mulberry Trust, 1988–; Aim Foundn, 1988–2007; LSA Charitable Trust, 1991–; Brian Johnston Meml Trust, 1996–99; Yehudi Menuhin Meml Trust, 1999–2001; Cumbria Community Foundn, 2002–; Hospice at Home, Carlisle and N Lakeland, 2002–; Athletics Foundn, 2004–. Governor: Nelson Thomlinson Sch., Wigton, 2003–; St Bees Sch., 2005–. DL Cumbria, 2007. *Publications:* articles on sports law, incl. The Law and Sport, 1972; The Role of the Lawyer in Sport, 1993; contrib. to Jl British Assoc. for Sport and Law. *Recreations:* cricket, golf, gardens and trees, Owen's Southsea, Cumbria's historic environment. *Address:* 55 Chester Row, SW1W 8JL. *T:* (020) 7730 3354; Quarry Hill House, Mealsgate, Cumbria CA7 1AE. *T:* (01697) 371225; *e-mail:* charles.woodhouse@ukgateway.net. *Clubs:* Oxford and Cambridge, MCC; Hawks (Cambridge); Worplesdon Golf; Silloth-on-Solway Golf; Free Foresters, Guildford Cricket (Pres., 1991–2002), Surrey County Cricket, Lord's Taverners.

WOODHOUSE, Ven. David; *see* Woodhouse, Ven. C. D. S.

WOODHOUSE, Dr Frank, OBE 1998; Co-director (part-time), S. Woodhouse & Sons (Investments) Ltd, since 1998; *b* 29 April 1943; *s* of Samuel Woodhouse and Clarice (*née* Bache); *m* 1966, Melba Sterry; two *s*. *Educ:* King Edward VI Grammar Sch., Stourbridge; Birmingham Univ. (BCom); Trinity Hall, Cambridge (MA, PhD). Asst Lectr, later Lectr in Italian, Hull Univ., 1972–81; Lectr in Italian, Cambridge Univ., 1981–92; Fellow, 1983–92, Associate Dean, 1986–87, Darwin Coll., Cambridge; Dir, British Inst. of Florence, 1988–97. *Publications:* Language and Style in a Renaissance Epic, 1982; articles on Italian subjects. *Recreations:* reading, travel, Italy. *Address:* 16 Melbourne Place, Cambridge CB1 1EQ. *Club:* Travellers.

WOODHOUSE, James Stephen; Director, ISIS East, 1994–2000; *b* 21 May 1933; *s* of late Rt Rev. J. W. Woodhouse, sometime Bishop of Thetford, and late Mrs K. M. Woodhouse; *m* 1957, Sarah, *d* of late Col Hubert Blount, Cley, Norfolk; three *s* one *d*. *Educ:* St Edward's Sch.; St Catharine's Coll., Cambridge. BA (English) Cantab, 1957; MA 1961. Nat. Service, 14th Field Regt RA, 1953. Asst Master, Westminster Sch., 1957; Under Master and Master of the Queen's Scholars, 1963; Headmaster, Rugby Sch., 1967–81; Headmaster, Lancing Coll., 1981–93. Chairman: NABC Religious Adv. Cttee, 1971–93; Bloxham Project, 1972–77; Head Masters' Conf., 1979; Joint Standing Cttee of HMC, IAPS and GSA, 1981–86; Vice-Chm., E-SU Schoolboy Scholarship Cttee, 1973–77. Director: The Norfolk Boat, 1993–; Holkham Pageant, 1994. Mem. Council (formerly Cttee of Mgt), RNLI, 1994–2006. Gov., Norwich Cathedral Inst., 2001–. *Recreations:* sailing, music, hill walking. *Address:* Welcome Cottage, Wiveton, Holt, Norfolk NR25 7TH.

WOODHOUSE, Prof. John Henry, PhD; FRS 2000; Professor of Geophysics, since 1990, and Head of Department of Earth Sciences, 2000, University of Oxford; Fellow of Worcester College, Oxford, since 1990; *b* 15 April 1949; *s* of G. B. Woodhouse. *Educ:* Southall Grammar Sch.; Bristol Univ. (BSc 1970); King's Coll., Cambridge (MA, PhD 1975). Fellow, King's Coll., Cambridge, 1974–78; Vis. Asst Res. Geophysicist, Inst. of Geophysics and Planetary Physics, Univ. of Calif., San Diego, 1976–77; Asst Prof., 1978–80, Associate Prof., 1980–83, Prof. of Geophysics, 1983–90, Harvard Univ. Chm., Commn on Seismological Theory, Internat. Assoc. of Seismol. and Physics of Earth's Interior, 1983–87. Fellow, Amer. Geophys. Union (Macelwane Award, 1984; Inge Lehmann Medal, 2001). *Publications:* many contribs to learned jls. *Address:* Department of Earth Sciences, Parks Road, Oxford OX1 3PR; Worcester College, Oxford OX1 2HB.

WOODHOUSE, Prof. John Robert, FBA 1995; Fiat Serena Professor of Italian Studies, Oxford, 1990–2001; Fellow, Magdalen College, Oxford, 1990–2001, now Emeritus; *b* 17 June 1937; *s* of Horace Woodhouse and Iris Evelyn Pewton; *m* 1967, Gaynor Mathias. *Educ:* King Edward VI Grammar School, Stourbridge; Hertford College, Oxford (MA, DLitt); Univ. of Pisa; PhD Wales. Asst Lectr in Italian, Univ. of Aberdeen, 1961–62; British Council Scholar, Scuola Normale Superiore, Pisa, 1962–63; Asst Lectr and Lectr, UCNW, Bangor, 1963–66; Lectr and Sen. Lectr, Univ. of Hull, 1966–73; Oxford University: Univ. Lectr in Italian and Fellow of St Cross Coll., 1973–84; Lectr at Jesus Coll., 1973, St Edmund Hall, 1975, Brasenose Coll., 1976; Fellow, 1984–89, Supernumerary Fellow, 1991, Pembroke Coll. Harvard Old Dominion Foundn Fellow, Villa I Tatti, 1969; Founding Fellow, Centro Studi Dannunziani, Pescara, 1979; Corresponding Fellow: Accad. lett. ital. dell'Arcadia, 1980; Accad. della Crusca, 1991; Commissione per i Testi di Lingua, Bologna, 1993; Sen. Res. Fellow, Center for Medieval and Renaissance Studies, UCLA, 1985; Fellow: Huntington Liby, Calif., 1986; Newberry Liby, Chicago, 1988. Mem., Exec. Cttee, Soc. for Italian Studies, 1979–85 and 1989–95; Pres., MHRA, 2008 (Mem., Exec. Cttee, 1984–94; Hon. Life Mem., 1994). Editor (Italian), Modern Language Review, 1984–94; Mem., Editl Bd, Italian Studies, 1987–91. Gov., British Inst. of Florence, 1991–2001. Serena Medal, British Academy, 2002. Cavaliere Ufficiale, Order of Merit (Italy), 1991. *Publications:* Italo Calvino: a reappraisal and an appreciation of the trilogy, 1968; (ed) Italo Calvino, Il barone rampante, 1970; (ed) V. Borghini, Scritti inediti o rari sulla lingua, 1971; (ed) V. Borghini, Storia della nobiltà fiorentina, 1974; Baldesar Castiglione, a reassessment of the Cortegiano, 1978; (ed) G. D'Annunzio, Alcyone, 1978; (ed with P. R. Horne) G. Rossetti, Lettere familiari, 1983; (ed jtly) G. Rossetti, Carteggi, I, 1984, II, 1988, III, 1992, IV, 1996, V, 2002, VI, 2006; (ed jtly) The Languages of Literature in Renaissance Italy, 1988; From Castiglione to Chesterfield: the decline in the courtier's manual, 1991; (ed) Dante and Governance, 1997; Gabriele D'Annunzio: defiant archangel, 1998 (trans. Italian, 1999; Premio D'Annunzio, 2000); Gabriele D'Annunzio tra Italia e Inghilterra, 2003; Il Generale e il Comandante: Ceccherini e D'Annunzio a Fiume, 2004; L'Ottavo Giurato: Giuseppe Sovera con D'Annunzio a Fiume, 2008; articles in learned jls. *Recreation:* gardening. *Address:* Magdalen College, Oxford OX1 4AU.

WOODHOUSE, Prof. Kenneth Walter, MD; FRCP; Pro Vice-Chancellor, External Affairs, Cardiff University, since 2004; Professor of Geriatric Medicine, School of Medicine, Cardiff University (formerly University of Wales College of Medicine), since 1990; *b* 18 July 1954; *s* of Walter and Marion Woodhouse; *m* 1994, Judith Paul; three *s*. *Educ:* Southampton University Med. Sch. (BM Hons 1977); Univ. of Newcastle upon Tyne (MD 1985). FRCP 1990. MRC Trng Fellow, 1980–83; MRC Travelling Fellow, 1984–85; Sen. Lectr in Medicine (Geriatrics) and Clinical Pharmacol., and Consultant Physician, Univ. of Newcastle upon Tyne, 1985–90; University of Wales College of Medicine: Vice Dean of Medicine, 1997–2000; Dean of Medicine, 2000–04. Chm., Nat. Commng Bd, Health Commn Wales, 2002–. *Publications:* (ed jtly) Topics in Ageing Research in Europe, vol. 13, The Liver, Metabolism and Ageing, 1989; (with J. Pascual) Hypertension in Elderly People, 1996; (with M. Hasan) Managing Hypertension in Practice, Book 2, The Elderly Hypertensive Patient, 1997; (ed jtly) Drug Therapy in Old Age, 1998. *Recreations:* hill walking, scout leader, science fiction. *Address:* Department of Geriatric Medicine, Academic Centre, Llandough Hospital, Penlan Road, Penarth CF64 2XX. *T:* (029) 2071 6986, *Fax:* (029) 2071 1267; *e-mail:* woodhousekw@cf.ac.uk.

WOODHOUSE, Michael; *see* Woodhouse, R. M.

WOODHOUSE, Prof. the Hon. Nicholas Michael John, PhD; FInstP, FIMA; Professor of Mathematics, since 2006, and Chairman of Mathematics, since 2001, University of Oxford; Fellow of Wadham College, Oxford, since 1977; *b* Knebworth, Herts, 27 Feb. 1949; *s* of 5th Baron Terrington, DSO, OBE and Lady Davina Woodhouse (*née* Lytton), *widow* of 5th Earl of Erne; *m* 1973, Mary Jane Stormont Mowat, *qv*; one *s*. *Educ:* Christ Church, Oxford (BA 1970); King's Coll. London (MSc 1971; PhD 1973). FInstP 2002; FIMA 2004. University of Oxford: Lectr, 1977–97; Reader, 1997–2006; Sen. Tutor, Wadham Coll., 1982–86; Mem., North Commn of Inquiry, 1994. Fellow, Eton Coll., 1995–2007. Mem. Council, 1998–, Treas., 2002–, London Mathematical Soc. *Publications:* Geometric Quantization, 1979, 2nd edn 1991; Introduction to Analytical Dynamics, 1987; (with L. J. Mason) Integrability, Self-duality, and Twistor Theory, 1995; Special Relativity, 2003; General Relativity, 2007. *Recreations:* walking, gardening. *Address:* Wadham College, Oxford OX1 3PN. *T:* (01865) 277900; *e-mail:* nwoodh@maths.ox.ac.uk.
See also Baron Terrington.

WOODHOUSE, Rt Hon. Sir Owen; *see* Woodhouse, Rt Hon. Sir A. O.

WOODHOUSE, (Ronald) Michael, CVO 2000; Chairman, Rexam PLC (formerly Bowater), 1993–96 (Director, 1988–96); Chairman, Prince's Trust Volunteers, 1991–2000; *b* 19 Aug. 1927; *s* of Henry Alfred Woodhouse and Phyllis Woodhouse (*née* Gemmell); *m* 1955, Quenilda Mary (*d* 1997), *d* of Rt Rev. Neville Vincent Gorton; one *s* three *d*. *Educ:* Lancing Coll.; Queen's Coll., Oxford (BA Mod. History). Courtaulds plc, 1951–91: Dir, 1976–91; Dep. Chm., 1986–91; Man. Dir, 1972–79, Chm., 1979–84, Internat. Paint Co.; Chm., British Cellophane Ltd, 1979–86. A Director: RSA Exam. Board, 1991–95; RSA Exams and Assessment Foundn, 1995–97; Mem., Prince's Trust Council, 1995–2000. Dir, London Mozart Players, 1990–97; Mem. Council of Mgt, Friends of Royal Acad., 1996–2003; Trustee, Royal Acad. Pension Fund, 1997–2003. CCMI (CBIM 1978); FRSA 1979. *Recreations:* walking in Lake District, watching Rugby and cricket, opera, music, gardening, art, reading. *Address:* Tankards, Wonersh, Guildford, Surrey GU5 0PF. *T:* (01483) 892078; Dalehead, Hartsop, Patterdale, Cumbria CA11 0NZ. *Club:* Carlton.
See also Ven. A. H. Woodhouse.

WOODLEY, Anthony; Joint General Secretary, Unite, since 2007 (General Secretary, Transport and General Workers' Union, 2003–07, on merger with Amicus); *b* 2 Jan. 1948; *s* of George Woodley. Ellesmere Port factory, Vauxhall Motors, 1967–89; Dist Official, 1989–91, Nat. Official, 1991–2002, Dep. Gen. Sec., 2002–03, TGWU. *Address:* Unite, Transport House, 128 Theobalds Road, WC1X 8TN.

WOODLEY, Keith Spencer, FCA; chartered accountant; *b* 23 Oct. 1939; *s* of Charles Spencer Woodley and Hilda Mary Woodley (*née* Brown); *m* 1962, Joyce Madeleine Toon; one *s* two *d*. *Educ:* Stationers' Co. Sch. Articled Clerk, Senior Deloitte Plender Griffiths & Co., 1959–69; Partner, Deloitte Haskins & Sells, 1969–90: Nat. Personnel Partner, 1978–82; Mem., Partnership Bd, 1985–90. Complaints Commissioner: SIB, 1990–94; SFA, 1990–2001; FIMBRA, 1990–2001; LSE, 1994–; PIA, 1995–2001; Ind. Investigator, Investors' Compensation Scheme, 1991–2002. Director: Royscot Trust, 1990–96; National & Provincial Building Soc., 1991–96; Abbey National Plc, 1996– (Dep. Chm., 1999–2004); Abbey National Treasury Service Plc, 1998–2002. Member Council: ICAEW, 1988–98 (Pres., 1995–96); NACAB, 1991–94 and 1997–99 (Hon. Treas., 1991–94); Univ. of Bath, 1996– (Treas., 2002–). Trustee, Methodist Ministers' Pension Scheme, 1998–. Gov., Kingswood Sch., Bath, 2004–. *Recreations:* theatre, music, hill walking. *Address:* Rectory Cottage, Combe Hay, Bath BA2 7EG.

WOODLEY, Leonard Gaston; QC 1988. *Educ:* Univ. of London (Dip. Internat. Affairs). Called to the Bar, Inner Temple, 1963, now Bencher; a Recorder, 1989–2000. Called to Trinidad and Tobago Bar. Mem., Royal Commn on Care of the Elderly, 1997–99. Chm., Landat Enquiry under Mental Health Act; Mem., internat. enquiry into illegal hanging in Trinidad. First black person to be appointed QC and Recorder. Patron, Plan Internat. UK. *Recreations:* sports, music. *Address:* (chambers) 1 Mitre Court Buildings, Temple, EC4Y 7BS.

WOODLEY, Ven. Ronald John; Archdeacon of Cleveland, 1985–91, Emeritus, since 1991; *b* 28 Dec. 1925; *s* of John Owen Woodley and Maggie Woodley; *m* 1959, Patricia Kneeshaw; one *s* two *d*. *Educ:* Montagu Road School, Edmonton; St Augustine's Coll., Canterbury; Bishops' Coll., Cheshunt. Deacon 1953, priest 1954; Curate: St Martin, Middlesbrough, 1953–58; Whitby, 1958–61; Curate in Charge 1961–66, and Vicar 1966–71, The Ascension, Middlesbrough; Rector of Stokesley, 1971–85; RD of Stokesley, 1977–84. Canon of York, 1982–2000, Emeritus, 2001–. *Address:* 2A Minster Court, York YO1 7JJ. *T:* (01904) 679675.

WOODLEY, Sonia; QC 1996; a Recorder, since 1985; *b* 8 Oct. 1946; *d* of Stanley and Mabel Woodley; *m* 1973, Stuart McDonald (marr. diss. 1986; he *d* 2007); two *s* one *d*. *Educ:* Convent High Sch., Southampton. Called to the Bar, Gray's Inn, 1968, Bencher, 2004. *Recreations:* travel, gardening. *Address:* 9–12 Bell Yard, WC2A 2JR.

WOODMAN, Ian Michael; Director, Maritime and Dangerous Goods, Department for Transport, since 2007; *b* 19 Dec. 1958; *s* of Stanley Albert Woodman and Eva Woodman (*née* Crawford); *m* 1989, Ruth Angela Sparkes. *Educ:* Univ. of Manchester (BA Hons 1980); Trinity Coll., Cambridge (BA Hons 1986). With RN, 1980–84; joined Min. of Defence, 1986; Asst Pvte Sec. to Sec. of State, 1989–90; Principal, 1990–99; Dir, Resource Mgt, Equipment Support Air, 1999–2002; Dir, Perf. Analysis, 2002–05; Dir, Planning and Perf., DfT, 2005–07. *Recreations:* music, walking, DIY. *Address:* Department for Transport, Great Minster House, 76 Marsham Street, SW1P 4DR.

WOODMAN, Janet; *see* Beer, J.

WOODROFFE, Most Rev. George Cuthbert Manning, KBE 1980 (CBE 1973); MA, LTh; Archbishop of West Indies, 1980–86; Bishop of Windward Islands, 1969–86, retired; *b* 17 May 1918; *s* of James Manning Woodroffe and Evelyn Agatha (*née* Norton); *m* 1947, Aileen Alice Connell; one *s* one *d* (and one *s* decd). *Educ:* Grenada Boys' Secondary School; Codrington Coll., Barbados. Clerk in Civil Service, Grenada, 1936–41; Codrington Coll. (Univ. of Durham), 1941–44; Deacon 1944; Priest 1945; Asst Priest, St George's Cath., St Vincent, 1944–47; Vicar of St Simon's, Barbados, 1947–50; Rector: St Andrew, 1950–57; St Joseph, 1957–62; St John, 1962–67; Rural Dean of St John, Barbados, 1965–67; Sub-Dean and Rector of St George's Cathedral, St Vincent, Windward Islands, 1967–69. Vice-Chm., Anglican Consultative Council, 1974. Chm., Vis. Justices St Vincent Prisons, 1968–76. Mem., Prerogative of Mercy Cttee, St Vincent, 1969–86. Member: Bd of Educn, Barbados, 1964–67; National Trust of St Vincent, 1967–86 (Chm., 1972–82); Council, Univ. of the West Indies, 1980–83; Chm., Bd of Governors, Alleyne Sch., Barbados, 1951–57. Hon. DD Nashotah House, USA, 1980; Hon. LLD Univ. of the West Indies, 1981. *Recreations:* music, driving, detective tales and novels, military band music. *Address:* PO Box 919, Murray Road, St Vincent and the Grenadines, West Indies. *T:* 4561277. *Club:* Royal Commonwealth Society.

WOODROFFE, Jean Frances, (Mrs J. W. R. Woodroffe), CVO 1953; *b* 22 Feb. 1923; *d* of late Capt. A. V. Hambro; *m* 1st, 1942, Capt. Hon. Vicary Paul Gibbs, Grenadier Guards (killed in action, 1944), *er s* of 4th Baron Aldenham; one *d* (and one *d* decd); 2nd, 1946, Rev. Hon. Andrew Charles Victor Elphinstone (*d* 1975), 2nd *s* of 16th Lord Elphinstone, KT; one *d* (one *s* decd); 3rd, 1980, Lt-Col John William Richard Woodroffe (*d* 1990). Lady-in-Waiting to the Queen as Princess Elizabeth, 1945; Extra Woman of the Bedchamber to the Queen, 1952–. *Address:* 1 Church Street, Mere, Warminster, Wilts BA12 6DS. *T:* (01747) 860159.

WOODROFFE, Simon, OBE 2006; Founder: YO! Sushi, 1997; YO! Company, 2002; Yotel, 2007; *b* 14 Feb. 1952; *s* of John and Pippa Woodroffe; one *d*. *Educ:* Marlborough (two 'O' levels). Roadie, 1970–75; stage designer, 1975–85; TV Exec., SuperChannel,

1985–92; skier, Chamonix, 1992–95. Appeared on Dragons' Den, BBC TV, 2005. *Publication:* The Book of Yo!, 2004. *Recreations:* polo, climbing, sailing. *Address:* (office) 9 George Street, W1U 3QH.

WOODROW, William Robert, (Bill), RA 2002; sculptor; *b* 1 Nov. 1948; *s* of Geoffrey W. Woodrow and Doreen M. (*née* Fasken); *m* 1970, Pauline Rowley; one *s* one *d.* *Educ:* Barton Peveril GS, Eastleigh; Winchester Sch. of Art; St Martin's Sch. of Art (DipAD); Chelsea Sch. of Art. Trustee: Tate Gall., 1996–2001; Imperial War Mus., 2003–. Gov., Univ. of the Arts, London, 2003–08. Solo exhibns in UK, Europe, Australia, USA and Canada, 1972–, including: Fools' Gold, Tate Gall., London, 1996; Regardless of History, for Fourth Plinth, Trafalgar Square, 2000; The Beekeeper, S London Gall. and Mappin Art Gall., Sheffield, 2001, and Glynn Vivian Art Gall., Swansea, 2002; Bill Woodrow: Sculpture, Waddington Galleries, London, 2006; Brood—Sculpture from The Beekeeper series 1996–2007, Great Hall, Winchester, 2007; Skulpturen und Zeichungen, Lullin & Ferrari, Zürich, 2008; work in group exhibitions worldwide, including: British Sculpture in the 20th Century, Whitechapel Art Gall., 1981; An International Survey of Recent Painting and Sculpture, Mus. of Modern Art, NY, 1984; Skulptur Im 20. Jahrhundert, Basle, Switzerland, 1984; Carnegie Internat. Mus. of Art, Pittsburgh, 1985; British Sculpture since 1965, USA tour, 1987; Great Britain-USSR, Kiev and Moscow, 1990; Metropolis, Berlin, 1991; Arte Amazonas, Rio de Janeiro, Brasilia, Berlin, Dresden and Aachen, 1992–94; Ripple across the Water, Tokyo, 1995; Un Siècle de Sculpture Anglaise, Jeu de Paume, Paris, 1996; Forjar el Espacio, Las Palmas, Valencia and Calais, 1998–99; Bronze, Holland Park, 2000–01; Field Day, Taipei Fine Arts Mus., Taiwan, 2001; Turning Points: 20th Century British Sculpture, Tehran Mus. of Contemp. Art, Iran, 2004; Drawing and Works on Paper from the Collection, Irish Mus. of Modern Art, Dublin, 2005; Eldorado, Mus. of Modern Art, Luxembourg, 2006; In Focus: Living History, Tate Modern, London, 2006; Sculpture in the Close, Jesus Coll., Cambridge, 2007; Punk. No One is Innocent, Kunsthalle Wien, Vienna, 2008. Represented GB at Biennales of Sydney, 1982, Paris, 1982 and 1985, São Paulo, 1983 and 1991, Havana, 1997. Anne Gerber Award, Seattle Mus. of Art, USA, 1988. *Address:* c/o Waddington Galleries, 11 Cork Street, W1S 3LT; *e-mail:* bill@billwoodrow.com.

WOODRUFF, Prof. (David) Phillip, PhD, DSc; FRS 2006; Professor of Physics, University of Warwick, since 1987; *b* 12 May 1944; *s* of Cyril and Dora Woodruff; *m* 1969, Angela Grundy; two *s.* *Educ:* Univ. of Bristol (BSc 1st Cl. Hons Physics 1965); Univ. of Warwick (PhD Physics 1968; DSc 1983). Lectr, 1969–83, Sen. Lectr, 1983–87, in Physics, Univ. of Warwick. Consulting Scientist, Bell Labs, NJ, 1979, 1981, 1985; Vis. Scientist, 1982, Scientific Consultant, 1998–2002, Fritz-Haber-Inst., Berlin; EPSRC Sen. Res. Fellow, 1998–2003. *Publications:* The Solid/Liquid Interface, 1973; (with T. A. Delchar) Modern Techniques in Surface Science, 1986, 2nd edn 1994; over 400 articles in scientific jls. *Recreations:* gardening, walking, travel. *Address:* Physics Department, University of Warwick, Coventry CV4 7AL. *T:* (024) 7652 3378, *Fax:* (024) 7669 2016; *e-mail:* d.p.woodruff@warwick.ac.uk.

WOODS, Very Rev. Alan Geoffrey, TD 1993; Dean of Gibraltar, 2003–08, now Emeritus; Archdeacon of Gibraltar, 2005–08; *b* 18 July 1942; *s* of Samuel and Grace Woods; *m* 1968, Barbara (*née* Macdonald); three *d.* *Educ:* Bristol Cathedral Sch.; Salisbury Theol Coll. ACCA 1965, FCCA 1980. Auditor, Goodyear Tyre & Rubber Co., 1965–67. Ordained deacon, 1970, priest, 1971; Curate, St Francis, Ashton Gate, Bristol, 1970–73; Swindon Archdeaconry Youth Chaplain and Warden, Legge House Residential Youth Centre, 1973–76; Priest i/c, Neston, 1976–79; Team Vicar, Greater Corsham, 1979–81; Priest i/c, Charminster, 1981–83; Vicar: Charminster and Stinsford, 1983–90; Calne and Blackland, 1990–96; Sen. Chaplain, Malta and Gozo, and Chancellor, St Paul's Cathedral, Valletta, 1996–2003; Vicar Gen. to Bishop in Europe, 2003–05; Priest i/c, Malaga, 2006–07. Rural Dean: Dorchester, 1985–90; Calne, 1990–96. CF (TA), 1980–94; Chaplain: Dorchester Hosps, 1986–87; St Mary's Sch., Calne, 1990–96; Canon and Preb., Salisbury Cathedral, 1992–96. *Recreations:* travel, music. *Address:* 6 Maumbury Square, Weymouth Avenue, Dorchester DT1 1TY. *T:* (01305) 264877.

WOODS, Prof. Andrew William, PhD; BP Professor of Petroleum Science, BP Institute, University of Cambridge, since 2000; Fellow, St John's Coll., Cambridge, since 2000; *b* 2 Dec. 1964; *s* of Prof. William Alfred Woods and Dorothy Elizabeth Woods; *m* 1996, Dr Sharon Jane Casey; three *s* one *d.* *Educ:* St John's Coll., Cambridge (BA 1st Cl. Maths 1985, Part III Maths 1986, MA 1988; PhD Applied Maths 1989). Green Scholar, Scripps Instn of Oceanography, UCSD, 1989–90; University of Cambridge: Res. Fellow, 1988–90, Teaching Fellow, 1991–96, St John's College; Lectr, Inst. of Theoretical Geophysics, 1991–96; Prof. of Applied Maths, Univ. of Bristol, 1996–99. Italgas Prize, Turin, 1997; Marcello Carapezza Prize, Gp. Nat. per la Volcanologia, Rome, 1997; Wager Medal, IAVCEI, 2002. *Publication:* (jtly) Volcanic Plumes, 1997. *Address:* BP Institute, Bullard Laboratories, Madingley Rise, Madingley Road, University of Cambridge, Cambridge CB3 0EZ. *T:* (01223) 765702.

WOODS, His Honour Brian; DL; a Circuit Judge, 1975–94; *b* 5 Nov. 1928; *yr s* of late E. P. Woods, Woodmancote, Cheltenham; *m* 1957, Margaret, *d* of late F. J. Griffiths, Parkgate, Wirral; three *d.* *Educ:* City of Leicester Boys' Sch.; Nottingham Univ. (LLB 1952). National Service, RAF, 1947–49. Called to the Bar, Gray's Inn, 1955; Midland Circuit; Dep. Chm., Lincs (Lindsey) QS, 1968. Chancellor, Diocese of Leicester, 1977–79; Reader, dio. of Leicester, 1970–79, dio. of Lichfield, 1978–. Member Council: S Mary and S Anne's Sch., Abbots Bromley, 1977–92; Ellesmere Coll., 1983–84. Mem., Law Adv. Cttee, Nottingham Univ., 1979–94; a Legal Mem., Mental Health Review Tribunals for Trent, W Midlands, Yorkshire, N and SW Thames Region, 1983–99. Fellow, Midland Div., Woodard Corp., 1979–92. DL Derbys, 1994. *Recreations:* daughters, musical music, taking photographs.

WOODS, Christopher Matthew, CMG 1979; MC 1945; HM Diplomatic Service, retired; Special Operations Executive Adviser, Foreign and Commonwealth Office, 1982–88; *b* 26 May 1923; *s* of Matthew Grosvenor Woods; *m* 1st, 1954, Gillian Sara Rudd (*d* 1985); four *s* one *d*; 2nd, 1992, Mrs Patricia Temple Muir. *Educ:* Bradfield Coll.; Trinity Coll., Cambridge. HM Forces, KRRC and SOE, 1942–47; Foreign Office, 1948; served Cairo, Tehran, Milan, Warsaw, Rome; FO, later FCO, 1967. *Publications:* papers in English and Italian on SOE in Italy. *Recreations:* birds, churches, music, books. *Address:* 31 Friars Street, Sudbury, Suffolk CO10 2AA. *T:* (01787) 882544. *Club:* Special Forces.

WOODS, Dr David Randle, DPhil; FRSSAf; Vice-Chancellor, Rhodes University, South Africa, since 1996; *b* Pietermaritzburg, 18 July 1940; *s* of Arthur Phillips Woods and Katherine Isabella Woods (*née* Straffen); *m* 1965, Anne Charlotte Abbott; one *s* one *d.* *Educ:* Michaelhouse Sch.; Rhodes Univ. (BSc Dist. Botany; BSc Hons Dist. Botany); University Coll., Oxford (DPhil 1966). Rhodes Schol., Natal, 1963–66; Asst Lectr in Microbiol., Dept of Botany and Microbiol., QMC, 1966–67; Rhodes University: Sen. Lectr in Microbiol., 1967–71; Prof. and Head of Microbiol., 1972–79; University of Cape Town: Dir, Microbial Genetics and Industrial Microbiol. Res. Unit, 1975–96; Prof. and Head of Dept of Microbiol., 1980–87; Fellow, 1985; Dep. Vice-Chancellor, 1988–96; Dir, Foundn for Res. Develt/Univ. of Cape Town Microbial Genetics Res. Unit, 1980–96. Research Fellow: Institut Pasteur, Paris, 1973–74; Dept. of Biochem., Trondheim Univ., Norway, 1974–75; R. F. Cherry Prof. for Dist. Teaching, Baylor Univ., USA, 1992–93. Member, Editorial Board: Jl Bacteriol., 1987–89; Anaerobe Microbiol., 1994–98. Chm., Bacteriol. and Applied Microbiol. Div., and Mem., Exec. Bd, Internat. Union of Microbiol Socs, 1995–99. Member: S African Soc. for Microbiol., 1970 (Pres., 1982–84); S African Soc. for Biochem., 1970–96; Amer. Soc. for Microbiol., 1980; Acad. of Sci. of SA, 1995–. FRSSAf 1987; Fellow: Acad. of Sci. of SA, 1994; Amer. Acad. Microbiol., 1995. Hon. DCL Oxford, 2003. *Publications:* (ed) The Clostridia and Biotechnology (series), 1993; jt author numerous res. papers. *Recreations:* squash, reading, music, hiking. *Address:* Rhodes University, PO Box 94, Grahamstown 6140, South Africa. *T:* (46) 6038148.

See also T. P. Woods.

WOODS, Eldrick, (Tiger); golfer; *b* 30 Dec. 1975; *s* of late Lt-Col Earl Woods and of Kultida Woods; *m* 2004, Elin Nordegren; one *d.* *Educ:* Western High Sch., Anaheim, Calif; Stanford Univ. Professional golfer, 1996–; wins include: US Masters, 1997 (youngest winner), 2001 (first player ever to hold all four major professional titles concurrently), 2002, 2005; US PGA Championship, 1999, 2000, 2001, 2002, 2006, 2007; US Open, 2000, 2002, 2008; The Open, St Andrews, 2000, 2005, Hoylake, 2006; numerous other tournaments. *Publication:* (jtly) How I Play Golf, 2001. *Address:* PGA Tour, 112 PGA Tour Boulevard, Ponte Vedra Beach, FL 32082, USA.

WOODS, Elisabeth Ann; part-time consultant on management and policy issues for UK and overseas government departments and other organisations, 1998–2005; *b* 27 Oct. 1940; *d* of late Norman Singleton, CB and Cicely Margaret Singleton (*née* Lucas); *m* 1976, James Maurice Woods. *Educ:* South Hampstead High Sch.; Girton Coll., Cambridge (BA Hons Cl. 1 Modern Languages, 1963). Asst Principal, Min. of Pensions and Nat. Insurance, 1963–69 (Asst Private Sec. to the Minister, and Private Sec. to Permanent Sec.); Principal, DHSS, 1969–76 (Sec. to Cttees on Nursing and on Allocation of Resources to Health Authorities); Asst Sec., DHSS, 1976–88 (responsible for mental handicap policy, later for liaison with health authorities, finally for aspects of supplementary benefit); seconded to HM Treasury, 1980–82; Grade 3, DHSS Central Resource Management, 1988; Hd of Finance, DSS, 1988–91; HM Customs and Excise: a Comr, 1991–97; Dir, VAT Control, 1991–94; Dir, Ops (Compliance), 1994–97. Non-exec. Director: S Wilts PCT, 2003–06; Wilts PCT, 2007–. Mem., HFEA, 1999–2002 (Chm., Audit Cttee, 2000–02). Mem., Wilts Children and Young People's Trust Bd, 2007–; Gov., Salisbury Foundn Trust, 2007–; Volunteer advr, Salisbury CAB, 1999–. *Recreations:* cycling, reading, cooking, being with friends. *Address:* West Wing, 43 Church Lane, Lower Bemerton, Salisbury SP2 9NR; *e-mail:* liswoods@aol.com.

WOODS, Gordon Campbell, MA; Warden, Glenalmond College, Perth, since 2003; *b* 5 Nov. 1955; *s* of late Ian and Margot Woods; *m* 1984, Emma, *d* of late Michael Godwin and of Elizabeth Godwin; one *s* one *d.* *Educ:* Durham Sch.; Mansfield Coll., Oxford (BA Geog., MA 1978; PGCE 1979). Shrewsbury School, 1979–2003: Hd of Geog., 1984–89; Master i/c Rowing, 1988; Housemaster, 1989–99; Second Master (Dep. Hd), 1999–2003. Mem., Bd of Mgt, SCIS, 2004–. Chm., Field Studies Working Gp, Geographical Assoc., 1989. Governor: Cargilfield Prep. Sch., 2003–; Malsis Prep. Sch., 2003–. *Recreations:* sailing (dinghies), railways (steam), industrial archaeology, watching live sport. *Address:* Glenalmond College, Perth PH1 3RY. *T:* (01738) 842061, *Fax:* (01738) 842063; *e-mail:* warden@glenalmondcollege.co.uk. *Clubs:* East India; Leander (Henley-on-Thames).

WOODS, Maj.-Gen. Henry Gabriel, CB 1979; MBE 1965; MC 1945; Vice Lord-Lieutenant, North Yorkshire, 1985–99; Vice-President, St William's Foundation, since 1998 (Secretary, then Director, 1984–98); *b* 7 May 1924; *s* of late G. S. Woods and F. C. F. Woods (*née* McNevin); *m* 1953, Imogen Elizabeth Birchenough Dodd; two *d.* *Educ:* Highgate Sch. (Scholar); Trinity Coll., Oxford (Exhibnr; MA 1st Cl. Hons Mod. History). psc, jssc, rcds. Commnd 5th Royal Inniskilling Dragoon Guards, 1944; served NW Europe, 1944–45; Korea, 1951–52; Adjt, 1952–53; Sqdn Leader, 1954–55 and 1960–62; Army Staff Coll., 1956; Jt Services Staff Coll., 1960; Mil. Asst to Vice CDS, MoD, 1962–64; comd 5th Royal Inniskilling Dragoon Gds, 1965–67; Asst Mil. Sec. to C-in-C BAOR, 1968–69; Comdt, RAC Centre, 1969–71; RCDS, 1972; Mil. Attaché, Brit. Embassy, Washington, 1973–75; GOC NE Dist, 1976–80, retd. Head, Centre for Industrial and Educnl Liaison (W and N Yorks), 1980–87. Chairman: SATRO Panel, 1982–83; W and N Yorks Regl Microelectronics Educn Programme, 1982–86; Yorks and Humberside Industry/Educn Council, 1982–87; Bradford and W Yorks Br., BIM, 1982–84; N Yorks Scouts, 1982–2000; Yorks Region, Royal Soc. of Arts, 1982–92 (Mem. Council, 1984–92); Vice Chm., W Yorks Br. Exec. Cttee, Inst. of Dirs, 1985–91; Mem., Yorks Br. Exec. Cttee, BAAS, 1982–87. Trustee, Second World War Experience Centre, 1998–. Mem. Council, RUSI, 1981–84. Mem. Court, Univ. of Leeds, 1980–2001 (Mem. Council, 1980–91). Chm., 5th Royal Inniskilling Dragoon Guards Regtl Assoc., 1979–92; Pres., Royal Dragoon Guards Regtl Assoc., 1992–. Pres., York and Humberside Br., Royal Soc. of St George, 1986–88; Member: Trinity Soc., 1947–; Oxford Soc., 1987– (Pres., York Br., 1997–2001). FRSA; MInstD; FCMI. Hon. Mem., Yorks Reg., RIBA, 1994. Mayor, Co. of Merchants of Staple of England, 1991–92; Mem., Merchant Adventurers of the City of York. DL N Yorks, 1984–2006. Hon. DLitt Bradford, 1988. Officier, Ordre de Léopold, Belgium, 1965. *Publication:* Change and Challenge: the story of 5th Royal Inniskilling Dragoon Guards, 1978. *Recreations:* hunting (foot follower), fencing, sailing, military history. *Address:* Grafton House, Tockwith, York YO26 7PY. *T:* (01423) 358735. *Club:* Ends of the Earth (UK section).

WOODS, Prof. Hubert Frank, CBE 2001; FRCP, FRCPE; Sir George Franklin Professor of Medicine, University of Sheffield, 1990–2003, now Emeritus Professor; *b* 18 Nov. 1937; *s* of Hubert George Woods and Julia Augusta Woods; *m* 1st, 1966, Hilary Sheila Cox (*d* 1999); one *s* two *d*; 2nd, 2004, Rosemary Gaye Statham (*née* Starling). *Educ:* St Bees Sch., Cumbria; Leeds Univ. (BSc 1962); Pembroke Coll., Oxford (BM BCh 1965; DPhil 1970). MRCP 1968, FRCP 1978; FFPM 1989; FRCPE 1991. House appts, Radcliffe Infirmary and Hammersmith Hosp., 1965–67; Lectr in Medicine, Oxford Univ., 1967–72; Mem., MRC Ext. Clinical Scientific Staff and Hon. Sen. Registrar, MRC Clinical Pharmacology Unit, Radcliffe Infirmary, 1972–76; University of Sheffield: Prof. of Clinical Pharmacology and Therapeutics, 1976–90; Dean, Faculty of Medicine, 1989–98; Dir, Div. of Clinical Scis (South), Sheffield Med. Sch., 2000–03; Collins Meml Lectr, 1992; Public Orator, 1993–2007; Hon. Consultant Physician: Royal Infirmary, Sheffield, 1976–88; Middlewood Psychiatric Hosp., 1976–91; Royal Hallamshire Hosp., 1976–2003. Visiting Professor: Maryland Med. Center, 2000; Meml Sloan Kettering Cancer Center, 2000. Non-executive Member: Sheffield HA, 1990–96; Rampton Hosp. Authy, 1996–99. Chairman: Adv. Cttee on Toxicity of Food, Consumer Products and the Environment, DoH, 1992–2002; Department of Health Working Group: on Peanut Allergy, 1997–98; on Organophosphates, 1998–99; on Phyto-oestrogens, 1999–2003; on risk assessment for mixtures of Pesticides, 2000–02; on Lowermoor, 2002–07; Member: Adv. Cttee on Novel Foods and Processes, MAFF, 1992–2002; Food Adv. Cttee, MAFF, 1992–2001; Task Force on Food Incidents, Food Standards Agency, 2005–. Mem., GMC, 1994–2002 (Mem., 1994–2002, Dep. Chm., 1996–99, Chm., 1999–2002, Health Cttee;

Mem., Review Bd for Overseas Practitioners, 1997–2002). Special Trustee, Former United Sheffield Hosps, 1989–2000; Trustee: Harry Bottom Charitable Trust, 1989–2003; Cavendish Hip Foundn, 2005–07 (Chm. Trustees, 2006–07). Gov., St Bees Sch., Cumbria, 1985–. Founder FMedSci 1998. FIFST 1996. Hon. FFOM 1995. Hon. MD Sheffield, 2007. *Publications:* (with R. D. Cohen) Lactic Acidosis, 1976; papers on metabolism and pharmacogenetics in med. and sci. jls. *Recreations:* gardening, fly fishing, works of Raymond Chandler. *Address:* Minshulls, 21 London Road, Aston Clinton, Bucks HP22 5HG. *T:* (01296) 630986. *Club:* Athenæum.

WOODS, Prof. John David, CBE 1991; PhD; Professor of Oceanography, Department of Earth Science and Engineering (formerly Department of Earth Resources Engineering, then T. H. Huxley School of the Environment, Earth Sciences and Engineering), Imperial College, University of London, 1994–2006, now Emeritus Professor of Oceanography and Computer Systems; Adjunct Fellow, Linacre College, Oxford, since 1991; *b* 26 Oct. 1939; *s* of late Ronald Ernest Goff Woods and Ethel Marjorie Woods; *m* 1971, Irina (marr. diss. 1996), *y d* of Bernd von Arnim and Elizabeth Gräfin Platen-Hallermund; one *s* one *d*. *Educ:* Imperial College, Univ. of London. BSc Physics 1961, PhD 1965. Research Asst, Imperial Coll., 1964–66; Sen., later Principal, Research Fellow, Meteorol Office, 1966–72; Prof. of Physical Oceanography, Southampton Univ., 1972–77; Ordinarius für Ozeanographie, Christian Albrechts Universität und Direktor Regionale Ozeanographie, Kiel Institut für Meereskunde, Schleswig-Holstein, 1977–86; Dir, Marine and Atmospheric Sci., NERC, 1986–94; Imperial College, London: Hd, Dept of Earth Resources Engrg, 1994–97; Dean, Graduate Sch. of the Envmt, 1994–97. Vis. Prof. Atmospheric Scis, Miami Univ., 1969; Hon. Prof. of Oceanography, Southampton Univ., 1994–. Jt Founding Dir, Foto Zerüi, 2005–. Member: NERC, 1979–82; Meteorol Res. Cttee, Meteorol Office, 1976–77, 1987–96; OST Foresight Marine Panel, 1996–2006. Council Member: Underwater Assoc., 1967–72 (Hon. life mem., 1987); RMetS, 1972–75; RGS, 1975–77, 1987–92 (Vice-Pres., 1989–91; Patron's Medal, 1996); Member, international scientific committees for: Global Atmospheric Research Prog., 1976–79; Climate Change and the Ocean, 1979–84; World Climate Research Prog., 1980–86; World Ocean Circulation Experiment, 1983–89 (Chm., 1984–86); Internat. Geosphere Biosphere Prog., 1987–91; Global Ocean Observing System, 1994– (Chm., Europ. Consortium, 1994–); Global Envmt Facility, 1994–98; Lead Author, Intergovtl Panel for Climate Change, 1989. Associate, Italian Nat. Res. Council, 2008. MAE 1988. Lectures: Iselin, Harvard, 1989; Linacre, Oxford, 1991; Adye, Fellowship of Engrg, 1991; European Geophys. Soc., Edinburgh, 1992; Bruun, Unesco, 1993, 1999. Inventor and developer of Virtual Ecology Workbench, 1992–2007. Hon. DSc: Liège, 1980; Plymouth, 1991; Southampton, 2004. L. G. Groves Prize, MoD, 1968; Medal of Helsinki Univ., 1982. *Publications:* (with J. Lythgoe) Underwater Science, 1971; (with E. Drew and J. Lythgoe) Underwater Research, 1976; (with N. Pinardi) Ocean Forecasting, 2002; papers on atmospheric physics and oceanography in learned jls. *Recreations:* history, photography. *Address:* Department of Earth Science and Engineering, Imperial College, SW7 2AZ. *T:* (020) 7594 7414. *Clubs:* Athenæum, Geographical.

WOODS, Rev. Canon John Mawhinney; *b* 16 Dec. 1919; *s* of Robert and Sarah Hannah Woods. *Educ:* Edinburgh Theological College. Deacon 1958, for St Peter's, Kirkcaldy, Fife; priest, 1959; Rector of Walpole St Peter, Norfolk, 1960–75; Provost, St Andrew's Cathedral, Inverness, 1975–80; Rector of The Suttons with Tydd, 1980–85; Canon of Inverness, 1980–. *Address:* 24 Queen Street, King's Lynn, Norfolk PE30 1HT.

WOODS, Prof. Kent Linton, MD; FRCP; Chief Executive, Medicines and Healthcare products Regulatory Agency, since 2004; Professor of Therapeutics, University of Leicester, since 1996; *b* 5 June 1948; *s* of Stephen and Mary Woods; *m* 1970, Rose Whitmarsh; three *s* (one *d* decd). *Educ:* Lawrence Sheriff Sch., Rugby; Clare Coll., Cambridge (MA, MB BChir 1972; MD 1980 (Horton Smith Prize)); Birmingham Univ.; Harvard Sch. of Public Health (SM Epidemiology 1983). MRCP 1974, FRCP 1988. Clinical trng posts, Birmingham, 1972–75; Sheldon Res. Fellow and MRC Trng Fellow, 1975–78; Lectr in Clinical Pharmacology, Birmingham Univ., 1978–84; MRC Travelling Fellow, Harvard, 1982–83; Sen. Lectr in Clinical Pharmacology, 1984–94, Reader, 1994–96, Univ. of Leicester. Regl Dir of R&D, Trent, NHS Exec., DoH, 1995–99; Dep. Dir, 1998, Dir, 1999–2003, NHS Health Technol. Assessment Programme. Hon. Consultant Physician, Leicester Royal Infirmary, 1984–. FMedSci 2008. *Publications:* contrib. numerous papers to med. and scientific jls, mainly on cardiovascular topics. *Recreations:* travel, books. *Address:* Medicines and Healthcare products Regulatory Agency, Market Towers, 1 Nine Elms Lane, SW8 5NQ. *T:* (020) 7084 2100.

WOODS, Maurice Eric; Regional Chairman, Employment (formerly Industrial) Tribunals (Bristol), 1990–98; *b* 28 June 1933; *s* of late Leslie Eric Woods and of Winifred Rose Woods (*née* Boniface); *m* 1956, Freda Pauline Schlosser; two *s* two *d*. *Educ:* Moulsham Secondary Modern Sch., Chelmsford. LLB London. National Service (Army), 1951–53. Clerk with Essex CC, 1948–51; Police Constable, Essex Police Force, 1954–59; Claims Assistant, Cornhill Insce, 1959–61; Solicitors' Clerk and Articled Clerk, Barlow Lyde and Gilbert, 1961–65; admitted Solicitor, 1965; private practice, 1965–84; Dep. County Court Registrar, 1977–84; Chairman: Suppl. Benefit Appeal Tribunals and Social Security Appeal Tribunals, 1981–84; Industrial Tribunals, Bristol, 1984–90. *Recreations:* music, travel, water colours.

WOODS, Prof. Ngaire Tui, DPhil; Director, Global Economic Governance Programme, since 2003, and Professor of International Political Economy, since 2008, University of Oxford; Fellow, University College, Oxford, since 1993; *b* Wellington, NZ, 13 Feb. 1963; *d* of N. Rowland Woods and Tui Clark; *m* 1995, Eugene L. Rogan; one *s* one *d*. *Educ:* Univ. of Auckland (BA, LLB Hons); Balliol Coll., Oxford (MPhil; DPhil 1992). Jun. Res. Fellow, New Coll., Oxford, 1990–92; Lectr in Internat. Relns, Dept of Politics and Internat. Relns, Univ. of Oxford, 1993–2008. Vis. Lectr, Govt Dept, Harvard Univ., 1992. *Publications:* (ed and contrib.) Explaining International Relations since 1945, 1996; (ed jtly and contrib.) Inequality and World Politics, 1999; (ed) The Political Economy of Globalization, 2000; The Globalizers: the IMF, the World Bank and their borrowers, 2006; (ed with J. Welsh) Exporting Good Governance, 2007; (ed with D. Brown) Making Self-Regulation Effective in Developing Countries, 2007. *Recreations:* sailing, ski-ing, hiking. *Address:* University College, High Street, Oxford OX1 4BH. *T:* (01865) 276602, *Fax:* (01865) 276659; *e-mail:* geg@univ.ox.ac.uk.

WOODS, Nigel Dermot, FRICS; Chief Executive and Commissioner of Valuation for Northern Ireland, Valuation and Lands Agency, 1998–2007; *b* 21 Feb. 1947; *s* of Victor and Sheila Woods; *m* 1974, Alison Grant; one *s* two *d*. *Educ:* Bangor Grammar Sch. FRICS 1983 (ARICS 1970). Worked in estate agency, Belfast, 1964–67; with Valuation Office, subseq. Valuation and Lands Agency, 1967–2007. Vis. Prof., Sch. of Built Envmt, Univ. of Ulster, 2003–. *Recreations:* golf, bridge. *Club:* Bangor Golf.

WOODS, Robert Barclay, CBE 2003; Chief Executive, Peninsular and Oriental Steam Navigation Co., 2004–06 (Executive Director, 1996–2006); *b* 23 Sept. 1946; *s* of Robert Wilmer Woods and Henrietta Wilson; *m* 1975, Georgiana Garton; three *s* one *d*. *Educ:* Winchester Coll.; Trinity Coll., Cambridge (MA); Harvard Business Sch. (SMP). Joined P&O Gen. Cargo Div., 1971; seconded to J. Swire & Sons, Japan, 1972–73; Overseas, subseq. P&O, Containers: Dubai, 1980–84; Gen. Manager, FE Trade, 1984–86; Trade Dir, Aust. and NZ, 1986–89; Dir, 1987; Managing Director: P&O Containers, 1990–96; P&O Nedlloyd, 1997–2003; Chm., P&O Ports, 2002–06. Chm., Southampton Container Terminal, 1989–; non-executive Director: J. Swire & Sons, 2002–; Cathay Pacific Airways, 2006–; Advr to Bd, Dubai Ports World, 2006–. Chm., Far Eastern Freight Conf., 1996–2003; Pres., Chamber of Shipping, 2002–04. Chairman: Oxford House Community Centre, 1993–; Council of Trustees, Mission to Seafarers, 2007–. Hon. Capt. RNR, 2002–. Fellow, Winchester Coll., 2007–. Hon. Dr Anglia Ruskin, 2007. *Recreations:* field sports, music, vintage cars and aircraft, sailing. *Address:* Old Rectory, Frilsham, Newbury, Berks RG18 9XH. *T:* (01635) 201249; *e-mail:* robert.woods@dpworld.com. *Clubs:* White's; Vintage Sports-Car; Keyhaven Yacht.

WOODS, Prof. Robert Ivor, DPhil, LittD; FBA 2003; John Rankin Professor of Geography, University of Liverpool, since 1989; *b* 17 Sept. 1949; *s* of Ivor and Rhoda Woods; *m* 1977, Alison Cook; one *s* one *d*. *Educ:* Fitzwilliam Coll., Cambridge (BA 1971, MA 1975; LittD 2004); St Antony's Coll., Oxford (DPhil 1975). Lectr in Quantitative Social Sci., Univ. of Kent at Canterbury, 1974–75; Lectr, 1975–85, Sen. Lectr, 1985–88, Reader, 1988–89, in Geog., Univ. of Sheffield. Editor: Internat. Jl Population Geog., 1995–2002; Population Studies, 2003–. Pres., British Soc. for Population Studies, 1991–93. *Publications:* The Demography of Victorian England and Wales, 2000; Children Remembered, 2006. *Recreations:* books, red wine, tombstones, Rugby Union football. *Address:* Department of Geography, University of Liverpool, Liverpool L69 3BX. *T:* (0151) 794 2837, *Fax:* (0151) 794 2866; *e-mail:* riwoods@liv.ac.uk.

WOODS, Judge Sir Robert (Kynnersley), Kt 2000; CBE 1986; Judge, District Court of New South Wales, since 2000; *b* 12 Nov. 1939; *s* of Frederick Kynnersley Smythies Woods, OBE and Ruth Cecilia Woods (*née* Shaw). *Educ:* Univ. of Sydney (LLB). Solicitor, NSW, 1966–69; Legal Officer, PNG Govt, 1969–81; Justice, Nat. and Supreme Courts of PNG, 1982–99. PNG Scout Association: Scout Leader, 1969–74; Scout Comr, 1974–2000 (Leader Trainer, 1992–96); Chief Comr, 1996–99. Chancellor, Anglican Dio. of Bathurst, NSW, 2003–. KStJ 2004. *Address:* Parkes Road, Wellington, NSW 2820, Australia. *T:* (2) 68453707.

WOODS, Prof. Robert Thomas, FBPsS; Professor of Clinical Psychology of the Elderly, since 1996, and Co-Director, Dementia Services Development Centre, since 1999, Bangor University (formerly University of Wales, Bangor); *b* 9 April 1952; *s* of Walter T. W. Woods and Kathleen Ellen Woods (*née* Brooks); *m* 1972, Joan Doreen Foster; one *s* one *d*. *Educ:* Gravesend Sch. for Boys; Churchill Coll., Cambridge (BA 1973; MA 1977); Univ. of Newcastle-upon-Tyne (MSc 1975). CPsychol 1988; FBPsS 1992. Clinical psychologist, Newcastle Gen. Hosp., 1975–80; Lectr, then Sen. Lectr, Inst. of Psychiatry, Univ. of London and Hon. Clinical Psychologist, Maudsley and Bethlem Royal Hosps, 1980–92; Head, Psychol. Services for Older People, Camden and Islington Community Health Services NHS Trust, 1992–96; Hon. Sen. Lectr in Psychol., UCL, 1992–96; Hon. Clinical Psychologist, NW Wales (formerly Gwynedd Community Health) NHS Trust, 1996–. Mem., Med. and Scientific Adv. Panel, Alzheimer's Soc. (formerly Alzheimer's Disease Soc.), 1987–2007, and Alzheimer's Disease Internat., 1997–. Associate Specialist Advr, Health Adv. Service 2000, 1998–2003. Associate Editor, Aging and Mental Health, 1997–. *Publications:* (with U. Holden) Reality Orientation, 1982, 3rd edn as Positive Approaches to Dementia Care, 1995; (with C. Lay) Caring for the Person with Dementia: a guide for families and other carers, 1982, 3rd edn 1994; (with P. Britton) Clinical Psychology with the Elderly, 1985; Alzheimer's Disease: coping with a living death, 1989; (ed) Handbook of the Clinical Psychology of Ageing, 1996, (ed with L. Clare) 2nd edn, 2008; (ed) Psychological Problems of Ageing, 1999; (with J. Keady and D. Seddon) Involving Families in Care Homes, 2007. *Recreations:* football, cooking. *Address:* Dementia Services Development Centre, Ardudwy, Bangor University, Holyhead Road, Bangor, Gwynedd LL57 2PX. *T:* (01248) 383719.

WOODS, Roberta C.; *see* Blackman-Woods.

WOODS, Hon. Ronald Earl; Professor of United States Foreign Policy, University of Washington, since 1996; *b* 10 Oct. 1938; *s* of Earl L. Woods and Marie C. Woods; *m* 1959, Judith M. Wishner; two *d*. *Educ:* Georgetown Univ.; School of Foreign Service (BSFS 1961). Joined US Foreign Service, 1961; served: Cairo, 1962; Washington, 1963; Rome, 1966; Paris, 1969; Strasbourg, 1971; Washington, 1974; Madrid, 1979; Oslo, 1982; Brussels, 1985; Minister, London, 1989–93; Exec. Dir, World Affairs Council, 1993–96. *Recreations:* tennis, ski-ing, walking. *Address:* 4527 52 Avenue South, Seattle, WA 98118, USA. *T:* (206) 7227208; *e-mail:* ronaldwoods@mac.com.

WOODS, Tiger; *see* Woods, E.

WOODS, Timothy Phillips, MA, DPhil; Head of History, Trent College, 1985–2004; *b* 24 Dec. 1943; *s* of late Arthur Phillips Woods and of Katherine Isabella Woods; *m* 1969, Erica Lobb. *Educ:* Cordwalles Prep. Sch., Natal; Michaelhouse Sch., Natal; Rhodes Univ. (BA Hons, MA; UED); Oxford Univ. (DPhil). Cape Province Rhodes Scholar, 1968; Felsted School: Asst Master, 1971; Head of History, 1975; Headmaster, Gresham's Sch., 1982–85. *Recreations:* golf, gardening, music, history and architecture of cathedrals. *Address:* 63 Curzon Street, Long Eaton, Nottingham NG10 4FG. *T:* (0115) 972 0927. *Club:* Vincent's (Oxford).
See also D. R. Woods.

WOODS, Victoria Patricia Ann, (Vicki), (Mrs F. A. Woods Walker); Contributing Editor, Vogue (USA), since 1994; *b* 25 Sept. 1947; *d* of Frederick Woods and Barbara Joan (*née* Hinchliffe); *m* 1980, Frank A. Walker; one *s* one *d*. *Educ:* Lancaster Girls' Grammar Sch.; Univ. of Lancaster (BA). Sub-editor, Harpers & Queen, 1970–73; Chief sub-editor, Radio Times, 1973–75; Exec. Editor, Harpers & Queen, 1975–79; Associate Editor, then Dep. Editor, Tatler, 1982–87; Femail Editor, Daily Mail, 1987–89; Contributing Editor, Vogue (USA) and Associate Editor, Spectator, 1989–91; Editor, Harpers & Queen, 1991–94.

WOODS WALKER, Victoria Patricia Ann, (Mrs F. A. Woods Walker); *see* Woods, V. P. A.

WOODSTOCK, Viscount; William Jack Henry Bentinck; Count of the Holy Roman Empire; *b* 19 May 1984; *s* and *heir* of Earl of Portland, *qv*. *Educ:* Harrow Sch. *Heir:* *b* Hon. Jasper James Mellowes Bentinck, *b* 1988.

WOODWARD, Hon. Sir (Albert) Edward, AC 2001; Kt 1982; OBE 1969; Chairman, Australian Banking Industry Ombudsman Council, 1997–2002; *b* 6 Aug. 1928; *s* of Lt-Gen. Sir Eric Winslow Woodward, KCMG, KCVO, CB, CBE, DSO, and Amy Freame Woodward (*née* Weller); *m* 1950, Lois Thorpe, AM; one *s* six *d*. *Educ:* Melbourne C of E Grammar Sch.; Melbourne Univ. (LLM). Practising barrister, 1953–72; QC 1965; Judge: Australian Industrial Court and Supreme Court of Australian Capital Territory, 1972–90; Federal Ct of Australia, 1977–90. Chairman, Armed Services Pay Inquiry, 1972; Royal

Commissioner: Aboriginal Land Rights, 1973–75; into Australian Meat Industry, 1981–82; into Tricontinental Gp Cos, 1991–92; President: Trade Practices Tribunal, 1974–76; Defence Force Discipline Appeal Tribunal, 1988–90; Director-General of Security, 1976–81. Chairman: Victorian Dried Fruits Bd, 1963–72; Nat. Stevedoring Industry Conf. and Stevedoring Industry Council, 1965–72; Australian Defence Force Academy Council, 1982–99; Schizophrenia Australia Foundn, 1985–97. Mem. Council, Melbourne Univ., 1973–76, 1986–2001, Chancellor, 1990–2001; Chm. Council, Camberwell Grammar Sch., 1983–87. Hon. LLD: New South Wales, 1986; Melbourne, 2001; Hon. DLitt Ballarat, 1998. *Address:* 1/81 Park Street, South Yarra, Vic 3141, Australia. *T:* (3) 98677477.

WOODWARD, Barbara Janet, OBE 1999; HM Diplomatic Service; Minister and Deputy Head of Mission, Beijing, 2006–08; *b* 29 May 1961; *d* of late Arthur Claude Woodward, MC, FRICS, and of Rosemary Monica Gabrielle Woodward (*née* Fenton). *Educ:* Univ. of St Andrews (MA Hons (Hist.) 1983); Yale Univ. (MA (Internat. Relns) 1990). Joined HM Diplomatic Service, 1991; Asst European Corresp., FCO, 1991–93; Second, then First, Sec., Moscow, 1994–98; Hd, EU Enlargement Section, FCO, 1999–2001; Dep. Hd, Human Rights Policy Dept, FCO, 2001–03; Political Counsellor, Beijing, 2003–06. Mem., Adv. Bd, Hua Dan, 2006–. *Recreation:* sport (competitive swimming, mountain biking, tennis, bridge). *Address:* c/o Foreign and Commonwealth Office, King Charles Street, SW1A 2AH. *Club:* Otter Swimming (Hon. Sec., 1998–2002).

WOODWARD, Christopher John Paul; Director, Museum of Garden History, since 2006; *b* Welwyn Garden City, 13 Sept. 1969; *s* of David Woodward and Janet Woodward (*née* Musther); *m* 2000, Anna Bacigalupi; one *s. Educ:* Hitchin Boys' Sch.; Peterhouse, Cambridge (BA Hist. of Art 1990). Asst Curator, Sir John Soane's Mus., 1995–2000; Dir, Holburne Mus. of Art, Bath, 2000–05. Trustee: Heritage Lottery Fund, 2006–; Nat. Heritage Meml Fund, 2006–. *Publication:* In Ruins, 2001. *Recreations:* open water swimming, ruins, guerrilla gardening. *Address:* c/o Museum of Garden History, Lambeth Palace Road, SE7 1LB. *T:* (020) 7401 8865.

WOODWARD, Sir Clive (Ronald), Kt 2004; OBE 2002; Director of Elite Performance, Team 2012, British Olympic Association, since 2006; *b* 6 Jan. 1956; *m* Jayne; two *s* one *d. Educ:* HMS Conway; Loughborough Coll. Rugby Football Union player: début for England U-23, 1976; 21 England caps, 1980–84; British Lions tours, 1980, 1983; Leicester RFC, 1979; Manly, Australia, 1985; Coach: Henley RFC, 1993–95; London Irish RFC, 1995; Bath RFC, 1996–97; Head Coach: England Rugby Football Union team, 1997–2004; winning England team, World Cup, 2003; British Lions tour, NZ, 2005; Technical Dir, Southampton FC, 2005–06. Dir, Leicester RFC, 2008. Chm., British Assoc. of Ski Instructors, 2007–; Mem., Perf. Mgt Gp, Amateur Boxing Assoc. of England, 2008–. *Publication:* Winning!: the story of England's rise to Rugby World Cup glory, 2004. *Address:* British Olympic Association, 1 Wandsworth Plain, SW18 1EH.

WOODWARD, David John, CMG 2000; Director, National Audit Office, since 2006; *b* 12 Dec. 1949; *s* of Lionel John Innes Woodward and Ethel Woodward; *m* 1st, 1973, Agnes Kane (marr. diss. 1985); 2nd, 1985, Yvonne Yee Fun Wong; one *s. Educ:* Reigate Grammar Sch.; Woolwich Poly.; City of London Poly. (Dip. Auditing and Accounting). With BR, 1969–75; Nat. Audit Office, 1975–: Associate Dir, 1987–93, Dir, 1993–; Director: Internat., London, 1993–94; Audit Ops, UN HQ, NY, and Chm. Tech. Gp, UN Panel of External Auditors, 1995–2001; Conseiller Maître en Service Extraordinaire, Cour des Comptes, France (on secondment), 2001–02; UK Mem., Internat. Bd of Auditors for NATO, Brussels (on secondment), 2002–06 (Chm., 2003–05). *Recreation:* English history. *Address:* National Audit Office, 157–197 Buckingham Palace Road, SW1W 9SP; *e-mail:* David.Woodward@nao.gsi.gov.uk.

WOODWARD, Hon. Sir Edward; *see* Woodward, Hon. Sir A. E.

WOODWARD, Edward, OBE 1978; actor and singer, since 1946; *b* 1 June 1930; *s* of Edward Oliver Woodward and Violet Edith Woodward; *m* 1st, 1952, Venetia Mary Collett; two *s* one *d*; 2nd, 1987, Michele Dotrice; one *d. Educ:* Kingston Coll.; RADA. *Stage:* Castle Theatre, Farnham, 1946; appeared for some years in rep. cos throughout England and Scotland; first appearance on London stage, Where There's a Will, Garrick, 1955; Mercutio in Romeo and Juliet, and Laertes in Hamlet, Stratford, 1958; Rattle of a Simple Man, Garrick, 1962; Two Cities (musical), 1968; Cyrano in Cyrano de Bergerac, and Flamineo in The White Devil, Nat. Theatre Co., 1971; The Wolf, Apollo, 1973; The Male of the Species, Piccadilly, 1975; On Approval, Theatre Royal Haymarket, 1976; The Dark Horse, Comedy, 1978; starred in and directed Beggar's Opera, 1980; Private Lives, Australia, 1980; The Assassin, Greenwich, 1982; Richard III, Ludlow Fest., 1982; The Dead Secret, Plymouth and Richmond, 1992; Gilbert, nat. tour 2003; Cemetery Club, nat. tour 2004; has appeared in 3 prodns in NY (Rattle of a Simple Man, High Spirits, and Best Laid Plans); *films:* Becket, 1966; File on the Golden Goose, 1968; Hunted, 1973; Sitting Target, Young Winston, The Wicker Man, 1974; Stand Up Virgin Soldiers, 1977; Breaker Morant, 1980; The Appointment, 1981; Who Dares Wins, Forever Love, Merlin and the Sword, 1982; Champions, 1983; Christmas Carol, 1984; King David, Uncle Tom's Cabin, 1986; Mister Johnson, 1990; Deadly Advice, 1993; A Christmas Reunion, 1994; Gulliver's Travels, 1995; The Abduction Club, 2000; Hot Stuff, 2006; *television:* over 2000 prodns, inc. Callan (series and film, and in Wet Job, 1981); The Trial of Lady Chatterley, Blunt Instrument, 1980; Churchill: The Wilderness Years, 1981; The Equalizer (series), 1985–89; Codename Kyril, 1987; Hunted, 1988; The Man in the Brown Suit, 1988; Hands of a Murderer, or The Napoleon of Crime, 1990; Over My Dead Body (series), 1990; In Suspicious Circumstances (series), 1991–95; In My Defence, 1991; America at Risk (series), 1991–92; Harrison, 1994; Common as Muck (series), 1994, 1996; Cry of the City, 1995; The Woodward File, 1995; The House of Angelo, 1997; The New Professionals (series), 1998–99; Emma's Boy, 2000; Nikita (series), 2000; Night and Day, 2001; Messiah, 2001; Night Flight, 2002; Murder in Suburbia, 2003; 5 Days (mini series), 2006; Congregation of Ghosts, 2008; presenter, two national Nelson events, 2005; 12 long-playing records (singing), 3 records (poetry) and 14 talking book recordings. Over 20 national and internat. acting awards incl. BAFTA best actor award and an Emmy. *Recreations:* boating, geology. *Address:* c/o Janet Glass, Eric Glass Ltd, 25 Ladbroke Crescent, W11 1PS. *T:* (020) 7229 9500, *Fax:* (020) 7229 6220. *Clubs:* Garrick, Green Room.

WOODWARD, Prof. (Frank) Ian, PhD; Professor of Plant Ecology, Department of Animal and Plant Sciences, University of Sheffield, since 1991; *b* 15 Dec. 1948; *s* of Frank Clement Woodward and Gwenda Agnes Woodward (*née* Allen); *m* 1972, Pearl May Chambers; one *s* one *d. Educ:* Mansfield Coll., Oxford (BA Hons Botany 1970); Univ. of Lancaster (PhD 1973); MA Cantab 1979. NERC Res. Fellow, Univ. of Lancaster, 1973–75; Higher Scientific Officer, Grassland Res. Inst., 1975–76; Lectr, Dept of Plant Scis, UWCC, 1976–79; Lectr, Dept of Botany, 1979–91, Fellow, Trinity Hall, 1981–91, Univ. of Cambridge. Henry J. Oosting Lectr, Duke Univ., USA, 1996. FLS 1990; FAAAS 2003. W. S. Cooper Award, Ecological Soc. of America, 1991. *Publications:* Principles and Measurements in Environmental Biology, 1983; Climate and Plant Distribution, 1987 (trans. Japanese 1993); Vegetation and the Terrestrial Carbon Cycle: modelling the first 400 million years, 2001; numerous articles in jls on influences of climate and carbon dioxide on plants and vegetation. *Recreations:* wood turning, music. *Address:* 16 Ecclesall Road South, Ecclesall, Sheffield S11 9PE. *T:* (0114) 266 0399.

WOODWARD, John Collin; Chief Executive Officer, UK Film Council (formerly Film Council), since 1999; *b* 18 Feb. 1961; *s* of Anthony and Anne Woodward; *m* 2000, Emma Jeffery; one *s* one *d. Educ:* Shiplake Coll.; Poly. of Central London (BA Hons Media Studies). Co-ordinator, 25% Campaign, 1986–87; Dir, Independent Access Steering Cttee, 1987–88; Dep. Dir, Independent Producers Programme Assoc., 1988–90; Chief Executive: Producers Assocs, 1990–92; Producers Alliance for Cinema and Television, 1992–98; Dir, BFI, 1998–99. Member: Govt Film Policy Rev. Gp, 1997; Film Policy Rev. Action Cttee, 1998; Video Consultative Council, BBFC; British Screen Adv. Council. FRTS. *Recreations:* fatherhood, cinema, television, reading. *Address:* UK Film Council, 10 Little Portland Street, W1W 7JG. *T:* (020) 7861 7861, *Fax:* (020) 7861 7863. *Club:* Union.

WOODWARD, Adm. Sir John (Forster), GBE 1989; KCB 1982; *b* Penzance, Cornwall, 1 May 1932; *s* of late T. Woodward and M. B. M. Woodward; *m* 1960, Charlotte Mary McMurtrie; one *s* one *d. Educ:* Royal Naval College, Dartmouth. Under training, Home Fleet, until 1953; Submarine Specialist, serving in HMS Sanguine, Porpoise, Valiant, and commanding HMS Tireless, Grampus and Warspite, from 1953; Min. of Defence and senior training posts, from 1971, plus comd HMS Sheffield, 1976–77; Director of Naval Plans, 1978–81; Flag Officer, First Flotilla, 1981–83, Sen. Task Gp Comdr, S Atlantic, during Falklands Campaign, Apr.–July 1982; Flag Officer, Submarines, and Comdr, Submarines Eastern Atlantic, 1983–84; Dep. Chief of Defence Staff (Commitments), 1985–87; C-in-C, Naval Home Command, 1987–89; Flag ADC to the Queen, 1987–89. Ind. Inspector, Lord Chancellor's Panel, 1994–96. Chm., Falklands Is Meml Chapel Trust, 1994–2000. Hon. Liveryman, Glass Sellers' Co., 1982. *Publication:* One Hundred Days: the memoirs of the Falklands Battle Group Commander, 1992. *Recreations:* sailing, bridge. *Address:* c/o The Naval Secretary, Fleet Headquarters, Mail Point 3.1, Sir Henry Leach Building, Whale Island, Portsmouth PO2 8BY.

WOODWARD, Nicholas Frederick; His Honour Judge Nicholas Woodward; a Circuit Judge, since 2001; *b* 12 March 1952; *s* of Frederick Cyril Woodward and Joan Woodward; one *s. Educ:* Trent Poly., Nottingham (BA). Called to the Bar, Lincoln's Inn, 1975; in practice as barrister, Chester, 1977–2001. *Address:* Chester Crown Court, The Castle, Chester CH1 2AN. *Club:* City (Chester).

WOODWARD, Robert Stanley Lawrence; Chief Executive, SMG plc, since 2007; *b* 30 Nov. 1959; *s* of Frederick Stanley Woodward and Freda Mary Williams; partner, Patricia Mary Alice Bey. *Educ:* Marr Coll., Troon; Univ. of Durham (BSc 1980); Univ. of Edinburgh (MBA 1981). Deloitte & Touche, 1986–97: Partner, Deloitte & Touche Consulting, 1992–97; Man. Dir, Braxton Associates, 1995–97; Man. Dir, UBS Warburg, 1997–2001; Commercial Dir, Channel 4 Television, 2001–05; Sen. Advr, Longacre Partners, 2005–07. Council Member: NYT, 2006–; City Univ., 2006–. *Recreations:* photography, tennis, travel. *Address:* Crawfordston Farm, Maybole, Ayrshire KA19 7JS. *T:* (01655) 750215. *Club:* MCC.

WOODWARD, Roger Robert, AC 1992; OBE 1980; concert pianist and composer; *b* Sydney, 20 Dec. 1942; *s* of Francis William Wilson Woodward and Gladys Alma Bracken; *m* 1989, Patricia May Ludgate, *d* of Edward and Hazel Ludgate; two *s* one *d. Educ:* NSW State Conservatorium of Music (DSCM 1963); Chopin Nat. Acad. of Music, Warsaw (StażPWSM 1969); Univ. of Sydney (DMus 1998). Débuts: Polish Nat. Philharmonic Orch., Warsaw, 1967; RPO, RFH, London, 1970; since then has appeared with major orchestras and at principal concert centres and festivals in Europe, USA, Japan, China, Australia, NZ; performed complete works of Beethoven, Chopin and Debussy; premières of works by Xenakis, Donatoni, Dillon, Stockhausen, Takemitsu, Feldman, Radulescu, Boyd, Meale, Sitsky. Founder and Artistic Director: London Music Digest, 1972; Alpha Centauri Chamber Ensemble, 1989; Sydney Spring Internat. Fest. of New Music, 1989; Kotschach Maunten Musiktage (Austria), 1992; Joie et Lumière (Burgundy), 1997; Co-founder: Sydney Internat. Piano Comp., 1969; Music Teachers Assoc., NSW, 1976. Chair of Music, Univ. of New England, 2000; Dir, Sch. of Music, San Francisco State Univ., 2002. Has made numerous recordings. Order of Merit (Poland), 1993; Chevalier des Arts et des Lettres (France), 2004; Order of Solidarity (Poland), 2007. *Web:* www.rogerwoodward.com.

WOODWARD, Rt Hon. Shaun (Anthony); PC 2007; MP (Lab) St Helens South, since 2001; Secretary of State for Northern Ireland, since 2007; *b* 26 Oct. 1958; *s* of Dennis George Woodward and late Joan Lillian (*née* Nunn); *m* 1987, Camilla Davan, *e d* of Rt Hon. Sir Timothy Sainsbury, *qv*; one *s* three *d. Educ:* Bristol Grammar Sch.; Jesus Coll., Cambridge (first class double MA). Parly Lobbyist, Nat. Consumer Council, 1981–82; BBC TV: Researcher, That's Life!, 1982–85; Producer: Newsnight, 1985–87; Panorama, 1988–89; Editor, That's Life!, 1989–91; Researcher, Lost Babies, 1983; Producer: Drugwatch, 1985; The Gift of Life!, 1987; Dir of Communications, Cons. Party, 1991–92; Vis. Professorial Fellow, QMW, 1992–96; Fellow, Inst. of Politics at Kennedy Sch., Harvard Univ., 1994–95. MP Witney, 1997–2001 (C, 1997–99, Lab, 1999–2001). Opposition front bench spokesman for London, 1999; Parly Under-Sec. of State (Minister for Security and Health Service), NI Office, 2005–06; Parly Under-Sec. of State (Minister for Creative Industries and Tourism), DCMS, 2006–07. Member, Select Committees: EU, 1997–99; Foreign Affairs, 1999–2001; Human Rights, 2001–05. Director: Jerusalem Productions, 1989–96; ENO, 1994–2002 (Chm., Redevelt Campaign, 1994–2002). Chairman: Understanding Industry, 1995–97; Oxford Student Radio, 1995–97. Chm., Ben Hardwick Meml Fund, 1984–93; Trustee, 1993–2005, Dep. Chm., 1993–97, Childline. Mem., Foundn Bd, RSC, 1998–2002; Dir, Marine Stewardship Council, 1998–2002. *Publications:* (with Ron Lacey) Tranquillisers, 1983; (with Esther Rantzen) Ben: the story of Ben Hardwick, 1985; (with Sarah Caplin) Drugwatch, 1986. *Recreations:* opera, architecture, gardening, reading, travel. *Address:* c/o House of Commons, SW1A 0AA.

WOODWARD, Sir Thomas (Jones), (Sir Tom Jones), Kt 2006; OBE 1999; entertainer; *b* 7 June 1940; *s* of Thomas Woodward and late Freda (*née* Jones); *m* 1956, Melinda Trenchard; one *s.* Singing début at age of 3; sang in clubs and dance halls; first hit record, It's Not Unusual, 1964; toured US, 1965; many internat. hit records, incl. Reload, 2000 (most successful album in career); radio and TV appearances, incl. series, This is Tom Jones, 1969–71; has toured worldwide. Score for musical play, Matador, 1987. *Films:* Mars Attacks, 1997; Agnes Brown, 1999. Appeared as character in Disney animated feature, Emperor's New Groove, 2000. Silver Clef Award, Nordoff Robbins Music Therapy, 2001. Hon. FRWCMD (Hon. FWCMD 1994). MTV Video Award, 1988; Brit Award, 2003. *Recreations:* music, history. *Address:* Tom Jones Enterprises, 1801 Avenue of the Stars, Suite 200, Los Angeles, CA 90067, USA. *T:* (310) 5520044; *e-mail:* office@tomjones.com. *Clubs:* Home House; Friars (Los Angeles and New York).

WOODWARD, William Charles; QC 1985; a Recorder, since 1989; a Deputy High Court Judge, since 1997; President, Mental Health Review Tribunal, since 2000; a Justice of Appeal, Court of Appeal of St Helena, since 2002; *b* 27 May 1940; *s* of Wilfred Charles Woodward and Annie Stewart Woodward (*née* Young); *m* 1965, Carolyn Edna Johns; two *s* one *d*. *Educ:* South County Junior Sch.; Nottingham High Sch.; St John's Coll., Oxford (BA Jurisp). Marshall to Sir Donald Finnemore, Michaelmas 1962. Called to the Bar, Inner Temple, 1964; pupillage with Brian J. Appleby, QC; Midland (formerly Midland and Oxford) Circuit, 1964–; Head of Ropewalk Chambers, Nottingham, 1986–94. Member: E Midlands Area Cttee, Law Soc., 1972–; Bar Eur. Gp, 1998–; Founder Member: Notts Medico-Legal Soc., 1985–; E Midlands Business and Property Bar Assoc., 1994–. Special Prof., Univ. of Nottingham Sch. of Law, 1998–. *Recreations:* family, friends, holidays. *Address:* (chambers): 24 The Ropewalk, Nottingham NG1 5EF. *T:* (0115) 947 2581, *Fax:* (0115) 947 6532. *Clubs:* Pre War Austin Seven; Nottingham and Notts United Services.

WOODWARK, Susan Margaret; *see* Sharland, S. M.

WOOL, Dr Rosemary Jane, CB 1995; FRCPsych; Independent Consultant in Health Care in a Secure Environment, since 1996; Founder and Director, Prison Health Care Practitioners, since 2003. *Educ:* University of London (Charing Cross Hospital Medical School). MB BS, DPM, DRCOG. Dir of Health Care, Prison Medical Service, later Prison Service, 1989–96; Hd of Educn and Trng Unit, Dept of Psychiatry of Addictive Behaviour, St George's Hosp. Med. Sch., 1996–98; Specialist in Psychiatry, specialising in drug and alcohol misuse, W Herts Health Care Trust, 1998. Sec. Gen., 1995–2001, Vice-Pres., Internat. Relations, 2001–, Internat. Council of Prison Med. Services. *Address:* Wicken House, 105 Weston Road, Aston Clinton, Bucks HP22 5EP.

WOOLARD, Edgar Smith; Chairman, 1989–97, and Chief Executive Officer, 1989–96, Du Pont; *b* 15 April 1934; *s* of Edgar S. Woolard and Mamie (Boone) Woolard; *m* 1956, Peggy Harrell; two *d*. *Educ:* North Carolina State Univ. (BSc Indust. Eng. 1956). Joined Du Pont 1957; industrial engineer, Kinston, NC, 1957–59; group supervisor, industrial engrg, 1959–62; supervisor, manufg sect., 1962–64; planning supervisor, 1964–65; staff asst to Prodn Manager, Wilmington, 1965–66; product supt, Old Hickory, Tenn, 1966–69; engrg supt, 1969–70; Asst Plant Manager, Camden, SC, 1970–71; Plant Manager, 1971–73; Dir of products marketing div., Wilmington, 1973–75; Man. Dir, textile marketing div., 1975–76; Manager, corp. plans dept, 1976–77; Gen. Dir, products and planning div., 1977–78; Gen. Manager, textile fibers, 1978–81; Vice-Pres., textile fibers, 1981–83; Exec. Vice President, 1983–85; Vice Chm., 1985–87; Pres. and Chief Operating Officer, 1987–89. Director: Citicorp; N Carolina Textile Foundn; Member: Bd of Trustees, Winterthur Mus.; Bd of Trustees, N Carolina State Univ.; Med. Center of Delaware; Protestant Episcopal Theol Seminary, Virginia; Exec. Cttee, Delaware Roundtable; Bretton Woods Cttee; World Affairs Council; Business Roundtable. *Address:* c/o Du Pont, 1007 Market Street, Wilmington, DE 19898, USA.

WOOLAS, Philip James; MP (Lab) Oldham East and Saddleworth, since 1997; Minister of State, HM Treasury and Home Office, since 2008; *b* 11 Dec. 1959; *s* of Dennis Woolas and Maureen Woolas (*née* White); *m* 1988, Tracey Jane Allen; two *s*. *Educ:* Univ. of Manchester (BA Hons Philosophy 1981). Treas., 1983–84, Pres., 1984–86, NUS; journalist, Television South, 1987; Asst Prod., BBC Newsnight, 1988–90; Prod., Channel Four News, 1990–91; Head of Communications, GMB, 1991–97. PPS to Minister for Transport, 1999–2001; an Asst Govt Whip, 2001–02; a Lord Comr of HM Treasury (Govt Whip), 2002–03; Parly Sec., Privy Council Office, and Dep. Leader, H of C, 2003–05; Minister of State: (Minister for Local Govt and Community Cohesion), ODPM, subseq. DCLG, 2005–07; DEFRA, 2007–08. Chm., All Party Parly Clothing and Textile Gp, 1998–2001; Mem., PLP Leadership Campaign Team, 1997–99 (Dep. Chm., 1998–99). Chm., Tribune Publications Ltd, 1997–2001. FRSA 2007. *Recreations:* photography, reading, cricket, Manchester United supporter. *Address:* 1 Hopkin Mill Cottage, Sunnybank, Lees, Oldham OL4 5DD. *T:* (0161) 624 4248; House of Commons, SW1A 0AA. *Clubs:* Groucho; Lancashire County Cricket.

WOOLER, Stephen John, CB 2005; HM Chief Inspector, Crown Prosecution Service, since 1999 (became statutory independent inspectorate, 2000); *b* 16 March 1948; *s* of Herbert George Wooler and Mabel Wooler; *m* 1974, Jonquil Elizabeth Wilmshurst-Smith; one *s* one *d*. *Educ:* Bedford Modern Sch.; University Coll. London (LLB Hons 1969). Called to the Bar, Gray's Inn, 1969; in practice at Common Law Bar, 1970–73; joined Office of Director of Public Prosecutions, 1973: Legal Asst, 1973–76; Sen. Legal Asst, 1976–82; Asst DPP, 1982–83; on secondment to Law Officers' Dept, 1983–87; Chief Crown Prosecutor (London North), 1987–89; on secondment to Law Officers' Dept, 1989–99: Dep. Legal Sec. to Law Officers, 1992–99. *Recreations:* campanology, Rugby, walking, gardening. *Address:* HM Crown Prosecution Service Inspectorate, 26 Old Queen Street, SW1H 9HP. *T:* (020) 7210 1197.

WOOLF, family name of **Baron Woolf**.

WOOLF, Baron *cr* 1992 (Life Peer), of Barnes in the London Borough of Richmond; **Harry Kenneth Woolf,** Kt 1979; PC 1986; Lord Chief Justice of England and Wales, 2000–05; Chartered Arbitrator/Mediator, since 2006; *b* 2 May 1933; *s* of late Alexander Woolf and Leah Woolf (*née* Cussins); *m* 1961, Marguerite Sassoon, *d* of late George Sassoon; three *s*. *Educ:* Fettes Coll.; University Coll., London (LLB; Fellow, 1981). Called to Bar, Inner Temple, 1954; Bencher, 1976. Commnd (Nat. Service), 15/19th Royal Hussars, 1954; seconded Army Legal Services, 1955; Captain 1955. Started practice at Bar, 1956. A Recorder of the Crown Court, 1972–79; Jun. Counsel, Inland Revenue, 1973–74; First Treasury Junior Counsel (Common Law), 1974–79; a Judge of the High Court of Justice, Queen's Bench Div., 1979–86; Presiding Judge, SE Circuit, 1981–84; a Lord Justice of Appeal, 1986–92; a Lord of Appeal in Ordinary, 1992–96; Master of the Rolls, 1996–2000; Judge, Hong Kong Court of Final Appeal, 2003–; Pres., Qatar Financial Services Court, 2006–. Held inquiry into prison disturbances, 1990, Part II with Judge Tumin, report 1991; conducted inquiry, Access to Justice, 1994–96. Member: Senate, Inns of Court and Bar, 1981–85; Bd of Management, Inst. of Advanced Legal Studies, 1985–94 (Chm., 1986–94); World Bank Internat. Adv. Council on Law and Justice, 2001–; Chairman: Lord Chancellor's Adv. Cttee on Legal Educn., 1986–91; Middx Adv. Cttee on Justices of the Peace, 1986–90; Lord Chancellor's Adv. Cttee on Public Records, 1996–2000; Council of Civil Justice, 1998–2000; Rules Cttee, 1998–2000; Bank of England's Financial Markets Law Cttee, 2005–; President: Assoc. of Law Teachers, 1985–89; Central Council of Jewish Social Services, 1987–2000; SW London Magistrates Assoc., 1987–93; Assoc. of Mems of Bds of Visitors, 1994–; Public Records Soc., 1996–2000. Vice-Pres., Royal Over-Seas League, 2001–. Pro-Chancellor, London Univ., 1994–2002. Chairman: Trustees, Butler Trust, 1992–96 (Trustee, 1991–96; Pres., 1996–); Special Trustees, St Mary's Hosp., Paddington, 1993–97; Magna Carta Trust, 1996–2000. Patron, Jewish Mus., 1998–. Visitor: Nuffield Coll., Oxford, 1996–2000; UCL, 1996–2000 (Chm., Council, 2005–); Downing Coll., Cambridge, 2005–. Chancellor, Open Univ. of Israel, 2005–. Gov., Oxford Centre for Postgrad. Hebrew Studies, 1989–93. Hon. Mem., SPTL, 1988. Hon. Bencher, King's Inns, Dublin. Hon. FBA 2000; Hon. FMedSci 2002. Hon. Fellow, Leeds Poly., 1990. Hon. LLD: Buckingham, 1992; Bristol, 1992; London, 1993; Anglia Poly. Univ., 1994; Manchester Metropolitan, 1994; Hull, 2001; Richmond, 2001; Cambridge, 2002; Birmingham, 2002; Exeter, 2002; Wolverhampton, 2002; Hon. DSc Cranfield, 2001; Hon. DLit London. Hon. Freeman and Mem., Drapers' Co., 1999. *Publications:* Protecting the Public: the new challenge (Hamlyn Lecture), 1990; (ed with J. Woolf) Declaratory Judgement, 2nd edn, 1993, 3rd edn 2002; (ed jtly) de Smith, Judicial Review of Administrative Action, 5th edn, 1995, 7th edn (jtly) as de Smith's Judicial Review, 2008; (ed jtly) Principles of Judicial Review, 1999. *Address:* House of Lords, SW1A 0PW. *Clubs:* Athenæum, Garrick, Royal Automobile.

WOOLF, (Catherine) Fiona, CBE 2002; Consultant, CMS Cameron McKenna, since 2004 (Partner, 1981–2004); President, Law Society, 2006–07 (Vice President, 2005–06); *b* 11 May 1948; *d* of Richard and Margaret Swain; *m* 1990, Nicholas Woolf; one step *s* one step *d*. *Educ:* Keele Univ. (BA Law 1970); Strasbourg Univ. (Dip. Comparative Law 1969). Solicitor of Supreme Court, 1973. Clifford Chance, 1973–78; CMS Cameron McKenna, 1981–, energy and projects practice, work on power sector restructurings, privatisations and power and transmission projects. Mem., Competition Commn, 2005–. Non-exec. Dir, Three Valleys Water plc, 2006–. Sen. Fellow, Harvard Univ., 2001–02. Trustee, Raleigh Internat. Alderman, Candlewick Ward, City of London, 2007–. *Publications:* Global Transmission Expansion: recipes for success, 2003; co-author of three World Bank pubns; many articles and papers in energy jls. *Recreations:* singing, music, furniture history, theatre, art, occasional golf. *Address:* CMS Cameron McKenna, Mitre House, 160 Aldersgate Street, WC1A 4DD. *T:* (020) 7367 3000; *e-mail:* fiona.woolf@cms-cmck.com. *Club:* Royal Automobile.

WOOLF, Prof. Clifford John; Richard Kitz Professor of Anesthesia Research, Harvard Medical School, since 1997; Director, Neural Plasticity Research Group, Massachusetts General Hospital, since 1997; *b* 30 Jan. 1952; *s* of Jeffry and Lorna Woolf; *m* 1976, Fredia Maltz; two *s*. *Educ:* Univ. of the Witwatersrand, Johannesburg (MB, BCh, PhD). MRCP. Lectr, Middlesex Hosp. Med. Sch., London, 1979–81; Lectr, 1981–88, Reader, 1988–92, Prof. of Neurobiology, 1992–97, UCL. Distinguished Res. Award, Amer. Soc. for Anesthesia, 2004. *Publications:* numerous articles in scientific jls on the pathophysiology of pain and the regeneration of the nervous system. *Recreation:* mind surfing. *Address:* Neural Plasticity Research Group, Department of Anesthesia and Critical Care, Massachusetts General Hospital, 149 13th Street, Room 4309, Charlestown, MA 02129–2000, USA.

WOOLF, Fiona; *see* Woolf, C. F.

WOOLF, Geoffrey David; photographer; *b* 15 April 1944. *Educ:* Polytechnic of Central London (BSc Econ). Lecturer in History, Southgate Technical College, 1974–89; Gen. Sec., NATFHE, 1989–94; Trade Union Manager, LV Gp, 1996–97; Organiser, Prospect (formerly Inst. of Professionals, Managers and Specialists), 1997–2005. *Recreation:* politics. *Address:* 23 Sawyers Court, Chelmsford Road, Shenfield, Essex CM15 8RH; *e-mail:* geoffwoolf@hotmail.com.

WOOLFENDEN, Guy Anthony, OBE 2007; freelance composer and conductor; *b* 12 July 1937; *s* of late Harold Woolfenden and Kathleen Woolfenden (*née* Groom); *m* 1962, Jane Aldrick; three *s*. *Educ:* Westminster Abbey Choir Sch.; Whitgift Sch.; Christ's Coll., Cambridge (BA 1959; MA 1963); Guildhall Sch. of Music and Drama, London (LGSM 1960). Joined Royal Shakespeare Co., 1961, Hd of Music, 1963–98; Artistic Dir, Cambridge Fest., 1986–91. Composed scores for: RSC (over 150 scores); Comédie-Française, Paris; Burgtheater, Vienna; Teatro Stabile, Genoa; Nat. Theatre, Norway; arranged music for four full-length ballets by choreographer André Prokovsky: Anna Karenina (conducted Russian premiere, Kirov Ballet, St Petersburg, 1993); The Three Musketeers; La Traviata - The Ballet; The Queen of Spades. Chm., British Assoc. of Symphonic Bands and Wind Ensembles, 1999–2002; Pres., ISM, 2002–03. Chm., Denne Gilkes Meml Fund, 1985–. FBC (FBSM 1990). Hon. LCM 1998. *Recreations:* walking, cricket, photography. *Address:* Malvern House, Sibford Ferris, Banbury, Oxfordshire OX15 5RG. *T:* (01295) 780679, *Fax:* (01295) 788630; *e-mail:* guy@arielmusic.co.uk.

WOOLFSON, Prof. Michael Mark, FRS 1984; FRAS; FInstP; Professor of Theoretical Physics, University of York, 1965–94, now Emeritus; *b* 9 Jan. 1927; *s* of Morris and Rose Woolfson; *m* 1951, Margaret (*née* Frohlich); two *s* one *d*. *Educ:* Jesus College, Oxford (MA; Hon. Fellow, 1999); UMIST (PhD, DSc). Royal Engineers, 1947–49. Research Assistant: UMIST, 1950–52; Cavendish Lab., Cambridge, 1952–54; ICI Fellow, Univ. of Cambridge, 1954–55; Lectr, 1955–61, Reader, 1961–65, UMIST; Head of Dept. of Physics, 1982–87, Univ. of York. Hughes Medal, Royal Soc., 1986; Patterson Award, Amer. Crystallographic Assoc., 1990; Aminoff Medal, Royal Swedish Acad. of Scis, 1992; Dorothy Hodgkin Prize, British Crystallographic Assoc., 1997; Ewald Prize, Internat. Union of Crystallography, 2002. *Publications:* Direct Methods in Crystallography, 1961; An Introduction to X-Ray Crystallography, 1970, 2nd edn 1997; The Origin of the Solar System, 1989; Physical and Non-Physical Methods of Solving Crystal Structures, 1995; An Introduction to Computer Simulation, 1999; The Origin and Evolution of the Solar System, 2000; Planetary Science, 2001; Mathematics for Physics, 2007; Formation of the Solar System, 2007; Everyday Probability and Statistics, 2008; papers in learned jls. *Recreation:* writing. *Address:* 24 Sandmoor Green, Leeds LS17 7SB. *T:* (0113) 266 2166.

WOOLGAR, Prof. Stephen William, PhD; Professor of Sociology and Marketing, University of Oxford, since 2000; Fellow, Green Templeton College (formerly Green College), Oxford, since 2000; *b* 14 Feb. 1950; *s* of William Thomas Woolgar, III, and Constance Lillian Stuart Woolgar (*née* Hinkes); *m* 1983, Jacqueline Stokes; three *d*. *Educ:* Brentwood Sch.; Emmanuel Coll., Cambridge (BA 1st Cl. Hons 1972; MA 1976; PhD 1978). Brunel University: Lectr in Sociol., 1975–88; Reader 1988–92; Prof. of Sociol., 1992–2000; Dir, Centre for Res. into Innovation, Culture and Technol., 1991–98; Hd, Dept of Human Scis, 1996–98; Dir, ESRC prog. Virtual Society? the social sci. of electronic technologies, Univ of Oxford (formerly at Brunel Univ.), 1997–2002. Vis. Prof., McGill Univ., Canada, 1979–81; Exxon Fellow, MIT, 1983–84; Maître de Recherche Associé, Ecole Nationale Supérieure des Mines, Paris, 1988–89; ESRC Sen. Res. Fellow, 1994–95; Fulbright Sen. Schol., Dept of Sociol., UC San Diego, 1995–96. Member: OST Technology Foresight Panel: Leisure and Learning, 1994–96; IT, Electronics and Communications, 1996–99; Sociol. Panel, HEFCE RAE 1996 and 2001; Council Consumers' Assoc., 2000–. *Publications:* (with B. Latour) Laboratory Life: the construction of scientific facts, 1979, 2nd edn 1986; (ed) Knowledge and Reflexivity, 1988; Science: the very idea, 1988; (ed jtly) The Cognitive Turn: sociological and psychological perspectives on science, 1989; (ed with M. Lynch) Representation in Scientific Practice, 1990; (with K. Grint) The Machine at Work: technology, work and organisation, 1997; Virtual Society?: technology, cyberbole, reality, 2002; numerous articles. *Address:* Saïd Business School, University of Oxford, Park End Street, Oxford OX1 1HP. *T:* (01865) 288934; *e-mail:* steve.woolgar@sbs.ox.ac.uk.

WOOLLAM, Her Honour Suzanna Elizabeth; a Circuit Judge, 2001–06; *b* 6 Dec. 1946; *d* of late John Martin Woollam and Elizabeth Mary Woollam (*née* Brennan). *Educ:* various convents; Trinity Coll., Dublin (MA Philosophy 1969). Called to the Bar, Gray's

Inn, 1975; law reporting for the Weekly Law Reports and Times Law Reports, 1975–77; Army Legal Service, 1977–79; Solicitor to Scotland Yard, 1980–88; Sen. Legal Asst, office of JAG, 1988–90; Asst JAG, 1990–2001. *Recreations:* walking, gardening, reading, films, theatre.

WOOLLARD, John Ian; a District Judge (Magistrates' Courts), North East London, since 2006; *b* 13 July 1954; *s* of Charles and Joy Woollard; *m* 1981, Angela Margaret Lee; one *s* one *d*. *Educ:* Brentwood Sch. Admitted Solicitor, 1977; Asst Solicitor, T. V. Edwards & Co., 1977–78; County Prosecuting Solicitors' Office, Essex, 1978–82; Partner, Mitchell Maudsley & Wright, Basildon, 1982–87; freelance solicitor advocate, 1987–98; a Stipendiary Magistrate, then Dist Judge (Magistrates' Courts), Hants, 1998–2006. *Recreations:* music, reading, tennis. *Address:* c/o Stratford Magistrates' Court, 389-397 High Street, Stratford, E15 4SB.

WOOLLEY, David Rorie; QC 1980; barrister-at-law; a Recorder of the Crown Court, 1982–94; *b* 9 June 1939; *s* of Albert and Ethel Woolley; *m* 1988, Mandy, *d* of Donald and Barbara Hutchison, Upper Dicker, Sussex. *Educ:* Winchester Coll.; Trinity Hall, Cambridge (BA Hons Law). Called to the Bar, Middle Temple, 1962, Bencher, 1988. Vis. Scholar, Wolfson Coll., Cambridge, 1982–87. Inspector, DoE inquiry into Nat. Gall. extension, 1984. *Publications:* Town Hall and the Property Owner, 1965; (jtly) Environmental Law, 2000; contribs to various legal jls. *Recreations:* opera, mountaineering, Real tennis. *Address:* Landmark Chambers, 180 Fleet Street, EC4A 2HG. *Clubs:* MCC; Swiss Alpine.

WOOLLEY, John Maxwell, MBE 1945; TD 1946; Clerk, Merchant Taylors' Company, and Clerk to The Governors, Merchant Taylors' School, 1962–80; *b* 22 March 1917; *s* of Lt-Col Jasper Maxwell Woolley, IMS (Retd) and Kathleen Mary Woolley (*née* Waller); *m* 1952, Esme Adela Hamilton-Cole; two *s*. *Educ:* Cheltenham College; Trinity College, Oxford. BA (Oxon) 1938, MA (Oxon) 1962. Practising Solicitor, 1950–55; Asst Clerk, Merchant Taylors' Company, 1955–62. Hon. Mem. CGLI, 1991. *Address:* Flat 27, 15 Grand Avenue, Hove, E Sussex BN3 2NG. *T:* (01273) 733200.

WOOLLEY, (John) Moger; DL; Chairman, Bristol Water Holdings, since 1998; *b* 1 May 1935; *s* of Cyril Herbert Steele Woolley and Eveline Mary May Woolley; *m* 1960, Gillian Edith Millar; one *s* one *d*. *Educ:* Taunton Sch.; Bristol Univ., 1956–59 (BSc). National Service, 1954–56. Various management positions, DRG plc, 1959–89, Chief Exec., 1985–89; Chairman: Dolphin Packaging, 1990–95; API plc, 1992–2001; Brunel (Hldgs) plc (formerly BM Gp), 1992–2002. Non-executive Director: Staveley Industries, 1990–99; United Bristol Hosp. Trust, 1991–93; Avon Rubber, 1992–96. Chm. Council, 1997–2006, Pro-Chancellor, 2006–, Univ. of Bristol. DL 2000, High Sheriff, 2002–03, Glos. Hon. LLD Bristol, 2005. *Recreations:* cricket, hockey, golf, gardening. *Address:* Matford House, Northwoods, Winterbourne, Bristol BS36 1RS. *T:* (01454) 772180. *Clubs:* MCC; Merchant Venturers' (Bristol) (Master, 1998–99).

WOOLLEY, Mary Elizabeth; *see* Lewis, M. E.

WOOLLEY, Trevor Adrian, CB 2007; Finance Director, Ministry of Defence, since 2003; *b* 9 Aug. 1954; *s* of late Harry George Woolley and Doreen Vera Woolley (*née* O'Hale). *Educ:* Latymer Upper Sch., Hammersmith; Peterhouse, Cambridge (MA Hist.). Ministry of Defence, 1975–: Private Sec. to Sec. of Cabinet, 1986–90 (on secondment); Dir, Procurement Policy, 1990–93; Head, Resources and Progs (Army), 1993–97; Asst Under Sec. of State (Systems), 1997–98; Dir Gen., Resources and Plans, 1998–2002; Comd Sec., Land, 2002–03. *Recreations:* cricket, golf, travel, trekking. *Address:* Ministry of Defence, Main Building, Whitehall, SW1A 2HB. *Clubs:* MCC; Chiswick and Latymer Cricket.

WOOLMAN, Hon. Lord; Stephen Errol Woolman; a Senator of the College of Justice in Scotland, since 2008; *b* 16 May 1953; *s* of Errol Woolman, architect, and Frances Woolman (*née* Porter); *m* 1977, Dr Helen Mackinnon; two *d*. *Educ:* George Heriot's Sch., Edinburgh; Aberdeen Univ. (LLB). Lectr, 1978–87, Associate Dean, Faculty of Law, 1981–84, Edinburgh Univ.; admitted to Faculty of Advocates, 1987; Standing Junior Counsel in Scotland: Office of Fair Trading, 1991–95; MoD (Procurement Exec.), 1995–96; Inland Revenue, 1996–98; QC (Scot.) 1998; Advocate Depute, 1999–2002. Chm., Scottish Council of Law Reporting, 2007–08. Keeper, Advocates' Liby, 2004–08. Trustee, Nat. Liby of Scotland, 2004–08. *Publication:* An Introduction to the Scots Law of Contract, 1987, 3rd edn 2001. *Recreation:* cinema. *Address:* Court of Session, Parliament House, Edinburgh EH1 1RQ. *Club:* New (Edinburgh).

WOOLMAN, Andrew Paul Lander; His Honour Judge Woolman; a Circuit Judge, since 2006; *b* 10 Feb. 1950; *s* of Sydney and Anita Woolman; *m* 1977, Telsa Phillipson; two *s* one *d*. *Educ:* Leeds Grammar Sch.; Pembroke Coll., Cambridge (BA 1971). Called to the Bar, Inner Temple, 1973; Asst Recorder, 1992–97; a Recorder, 1997–2006. *Recreations:* tennis, classics, football, music, theatre, fell-walking, talking. *Address:* c/o Preston Combined Courts, The Law Courts, Openshaw Place, Ringway, Preston, Lancs PR1 2LL. *T:* (01772) 844700.

WOOLMAN, Stephen Errol; *see* Woolman, Hon. Lord.

WOOLMER, family name of **Baron Woolmer of Leeds**.

WOOLMER OF LEEDS, Baron *cr* 1999 (Life Peer), of Leeds in the county of West Yorkshire; **Kenneth John Woolmer;** Partner: Halton Gill Associates, consultants on central and local government relations, since 1999 (Principal, 1979–97); Anderson McGraw, since 2001; *b* 25 April 1940; *s* of Joseph William and Gertrude May Woolmer; *m* 1961, Janice Chambers; three *s*. *Educ:* Gladstone Street County Primary, Rothwell, Northants; Kettering Grammar Sch.; Leeds Univ. (BA Econs). Research Fellow, Univ. of West Indies, 1961–62; Teacher, Friern Rd Sec. Mod. Sch., London, 1963; Lecturer: Univ. of Leeds (Economics), 1963–66; Univ. of Ahmadu Bello, Nigeria, 1966–68; Univ. of Leeds, 1968–79; Dir, MBA Progs, 1991–97, Dean of Ext. Relns, 1997, Chm., subseq. Dean, 1997–2000, Sch. of Business and Econ. Studies, Leeds Univ., later Leeds Univ. Business Sch. Councillor: Leeds CC, 1970–78; West Yorkshire MCC, 1973–80 (Leader, 1975–77; Leader of Opposition, 1977–79). Chairman, Planning and Transportation Cttee, Assoc. of Metropolitan Authorities, 1974–77. Contested (Lab) Batley and Spen, 1983, 1987. MP (Lab) Batley and Morley, 1979–83; Opposition spokesman on trade, shipping and aviation, 1981–83; Mem., Select Cttee on Treasury and Civil Service, 1980–81; Chm., 1981, Vice-Chm., 1982, PLP Economics and Finance Gp; House of Lords: Mem., 1999–2002, Chm., 2002–, EU Sub Cttee B (Industry, Energy, Telecoms and Transport); Mem., EU Select Cttee, 2002–. Dir, Leeds United AFC, 1991–96. Non-executive Director: Thornfield Develts Ltd, 1999–2002; Thornfield Properties plc, 2002–04; Saiinfo plc, 2000–02; Courtcom Ltd, 2001–03.

WOOLRICH, John; composer; *b* 3 Jan. 1954; *s* of Derek Holland Woolrich and Una Woolrich (*née* MacDougall). *Educ:* Manchester Univ. (BA); Lancaster Univ. (MLitt). Northern Arts Fellow, Durham Univ., 1982–85; Composer in Residence, Nat. Centre for Orchestral Studies, 1985–86; Artistic Dir, Composers' Ensemble, 1989–; Composer in Association, Orch. of St John's, Smith Square, 1994–95; Dir of Concerts, Almeida Opera, 1999–; Artistic Associate, Birmingham Contemporary Music Gp, 2002–; Associate Artistic Dir, Aldeburgh Fest., 2005– (Guest Artistic Dir, 2004). Lectr in Music, RHBNC, 1994–98. Vis. Fellow, Clare Hall, Cambridge, 1999–2001. Hon. FTCL 1996. *Compositions* include: orchestral: The Barber's Timepiece, 1986; The Ghost in the Machine, 1990; The Theatre Represents a Garden: Night, 1991; Concerto for Viola, 1993; Concerto for Oboe, 1996; Cello Concerto, 1998; Concerto for Orchestra, 1999; chamber music: Ulysses Awakes, 1989; Lending Wings, 1989; The Death of King Renaud, 1991; It is Midnight, Dr Schweitzer, 1992; A Farewell, 1992; Violin Concerto, 2008. *Address:* c/o Faber Music, 3 Queen Square, WC1N 3AU. *T:* (020) 7278 7436.

WOOLSEY, Rt Rev. Gary Frederick; National Director, Anglican Fellowship of Prayer, Canada, since 2006; Assistant Bishop of Calgary, 1992–2002, and Rector of St Peter's, Calgary, 1991–2002; *b* 16 March 1942; *s* of William and Doreen Woolsey; *m* 1967, Marie Elaine Tooker; two *s* two *d*. *Educ:* Univ. of Western Ontario (BA); Huron Coll., London, Ont. (BTh); Univ. of Manitoba (Teacher's Cert.). Deacon, 1967; Priest-pilot, Diocese of Keewatin, 1967–68; Rector: St Peter's, Big Trout Lake, Ont, 1968–72; St Mark's, Norway House, Manitoba, 1972–76; St Paul's, Churchill, Man, 1976–80; Program Director and Archdeacon of Keewatin, 1980–83; Bishop of Athabasca, 1983–91. *Recreations:* fishing, camping, photography, motorcycle touring. *Address:* 184 Cedar Ridge Crescent SW, Calgary, AB T2W 1X8, Canada. *T:* (403) 2519569.

WOOLTON, 3rd Earl of, *cr* 1956; **Simon Frederick Marquis;** Baron Woolton, 1939; Viscount Woolton, 1953; Viscount Walberton, 1956; *b* 24 May 1958; *s* of 2nd Earl of Woolton and of Cecily Josephine (now Countess Lloyd George of Dwyfor), *e d* of Sir Alexander Gordon Cumming, 5th Bt; *S* father, 1969; *m* 1st, 1987, Hon. Sophie Frederika (marr. diss. 1997), *o c* of Baron Birdwood, *qv*; three *d*; 2nd, 1999, Mrs Carol Chapman (*née* Davidson). *Educ:* Eton College; St Andrews Univ. (MA Hons). Company director. Merchant banker, S. G. Warburg & Co. Ltd, 1982–88; Founder Director: Woolton Elwes Ltd, 1994–2000; New Boathouse Capital Ltd, 2000–08; Quayle Munro Ltd, 2008–. Trustee: Woolton Charitable Trust; Titsey Foundn; Balcarres Heritage Trust; Blue Sky Develt & Regeneration. Freeman, Skinners' Co. *Recreation:* golf. *Address:* Clune Lodge, Tomatin, Invernesshire IV13 7XZ. *Clubs:* White's, Brooks's, Pratt's, MCC; Royal and Ancient; Swinley Forest Golf.

WOOLVERTON, Kenneth Arthur; Head of Latin America, Caribbean and Pacific Department, Overseas Development Administration of the Foreign and Commonwealth Office, 1985–86; *b* 4 Aug. 1926; *s* of Arthur Eliott Woolverton and Lilian Woolverton; *m* 1957, Kathleen West; one *s*. *Educ:* Orange Hill Grammar Sch. Colonial Office, 1950–61; CRO, 1961–66 (2nd Sec., Jamaica); Min. of Overseas Development, 1966–79; Hd of Middle East Develt Div., ODA, 1979–81; Hd of British Develt Div. in the Caribbean, ODA, and UK Dir, Caribbean Develt Bank, 1981–84. ARPS 1992. *Recreations:* photography, archaeology, sailing. *Address:* 47 Durleston Park Drive, Great Bookham, Surrey KT23 4AJ. *T:* (01372) 454055.

WOOLWICH, Area Bishop of, since 2005; **Rt Rev. Christopher Thomas James Chessun;** *b* 5 Aug. 1956; twin *s* of late Thomas Frederick Chessun and Joyce Rosemary Chessun. *Educ:* Hampton Grammar Sch.; University Coll., Oxford (BA Hons Modern Hist. 1978; MA 1982); Trinity Hall, Cambridge (BA Hons Pt II Theol. Tripos 1982); Westcott House Theol Coll., Cambridge. Ordained deacon, 1983, priest, 1984; Asst Curate, St Michael and All Angels, Sandhurst, 1983–87; Sen. Curate, St Mary, Portsea, 1987–89; Chaplain and Minor Canon, St Paul's Cathedral, 1989–93; Vocations Advr, Dio. London, 1991–93; Rector of St Dunstan and All Saints', Stepney, 1993–2001; Area Dean, Tower Hamlets, 1997–2001; Archdeacon of Northolt, 2001–05. Freeman, City of London, 1993; Hon. Chaplain, 1992–, Freeman and Hon. Liveryman, 2001, Needlemakers' Co. *Recreations:* music, history, travel, overseas church links. *Address:* (office) Trinity House, 4 Chapel Court, Borough High Street, SE1 1HW. *T:* (020) 7939 9407; (home) 37 South Road, Forest Hill, SE23 2UJ. *T:* (020) 8699 7771, *Fax:* (020) 8699 7949; *e-mail:* bishop.christopher@southwark.anglican.org.

WOON, Peter William; Editor, BBC TV News, 1980–85; *b* 12 Dec. 1931; *s* of Henry William Woon and Gwendoline Constance Woon; *m* 1st, 1956, Elizabeth Hird (marr. diss. 1974); one *s*; 2nd, 1974, Diana Ward (marr. diss. 1993). *Educ:* Christ's Hospital. 2nd Lieut Royal Signals, 1954–56; Reporter, Bristol Evening Post, 1949–54 and 1956–58; air corresp., Daily Express, 1958–61; BBC: reporter, 1961–66; Asst Editor, TV News, 1966–69; Editor, Radio News, 1969–75; Head of Information, 1975–77; Editor, News and Current Affairs, radio, 1977–80; Head, Ops, N America, 1985–88.

WOOSNAM, Charles Richard, CBE 1993; a Forestry Commissioner, 1986–94; *b* 4 Aug. 1925; *s* of late Ralph William Woosnam and Kathleen Mary Woosnam (*née* Evan-Thomas); *m* 1950, Patricia Rodney Carruthers; two *s* two *d*. *Educ:* Winchester; Pembroke Coll., Cambridge. BA Estate Management. FRICS. Commissioned 15th/19th The King's Royal Hussars, 1943–47, served Europe and Palestine; with Land Agents Strutt & Parker, Builth Wells office, 1950–63; set up own Land Agency partnership, Woosnam & Tyler, 1964, merged with Strutt & Parker, 1996, Consultant, 1988–98. Member: Welsh Water Authy, 1973–76 (Chm., Fisheries Adv. Cttee); Exec. Cttee, Timber Growers UK (formerly Timber Growers England & Wales), 1976–86 (Dep. Chm., England and Wales; Chm., Finance Cttee); Chm., CLA Game Fair Local Cttee, 1976; Pres., Royal Forestry Soc. of England, Wales and NI, 1995–97. High Sheriff, Powys, 1985–86. *Recreations:* shooting, fishing. *Address:* Cefnllysgwynne, Llanynis, Builth Wells, Powys LD2 3HN. *T:* (01982) 552237. *Club:* Army and Navy.

WOOSNAM, Ian Harold, OBE 2007 (MBE 1992); professional golfer, since 1976; golf course designer; *b* 2 March 1958; *s* of late Harold Woosnam and of Joan Woosnam; *m* 1983, Glendryth Mervyn Pugh; one *s* two *d*. *Educ:* St Martin's Modern Sch. 44 professional tournament wins, 1982–, including: World Cup (individual), 1987 and 1991; World Match Play, 1987, 1990 and 2001; PGA, 1988 and 1997; PGA Grand Slam of Golf, 1991; US Masters, 1991; British Masters, 1994. Hon. Mem., PGA European tour. Captain, Ryder Cup team, (winners) 2006. Pres., World Snooker Assoc., 1999–. *Publications:* Ian Woosnam's Golf Masterpieces, 1988; Power Golf, 1989, new edn 1991; Golf Made Simple: the Woosie Way, 1997; (with Edward Griffiths) Woosie: the autobiography, 2002. *Recreations:* snooker, water ski-ing, shooting. *Address:* c/o IMG, McCormack House, Hogarth Business Park, W4 2TH. *Clubs:* Llanmynech Golf, Oswestry Golf, La Moye Golf.

WOOTTON, Adrian; Chief Executive Officer, Film London, since 2003; *b* 18 May 1962; *s* of Ronald Oliver Wootton and Unity Wootton; *m* 1986, Karen Sarah Goodman; one *d*. *Educ:* Univ. of East Anglia (BA Hons English and Amer. Studies, MA Film Studies). Director: Bradford Playhouse and Film Theatre, 1986–89; Nottingham Media Centre Ltd, 1989–93; Hd, BFI Exhibn (incl. Exec. Hd, NFT and Dir, London Film Fest., 1993–2002); Dep. Dir, BFI, 2002–03. Director: Shots in the Dark, Internat. Crime, Mystery and Thriller Fest., Nottingham, 1991–2001; Crime Scene, fest. of crime and mystery genre,

NFT, 2000–; Co-Curator, Soundtracking, Fest. of Popular Music and Cinema, Sheffield, 1999–2000. Foreign Consultant, Noir in Fest., Italy, 1999–; Advr to Venice Film Fest., 2004–. *Publications:* (contrib.) 100 Great Detectives, 1992; (ed jtly) Celluloid Jukebox, 1995; (ed) David Goodis, Black Friday and Selected Stories, 2006; contribs to arts magazines. *Recreations:* film, literature, music, theatre. *Address:* Film London, Suite 6.10, The Tea Building, 56 Shoreditch High Street, E1 6JJ. *T:* (020) 7613 7676. *Clubs:* Groucho, Soho House.

WOOTTON, Prof. (Harold) John, CBE 1997; FREng; FICE; FIHT; FCILT; Rees Jeffreys Professor of Transport Planning, University of Southampton, 1997–2001, now Visiting Professor; *b* 17 Nov. 1936; *s* of Harold Wootton and Hilda Mary (*née* Somerfield); *m* 1960, Patricia Ann Riley; two *s*. *Educ:* Queen Mary's Grammar Sch., Walsall; QMC, Univ. of London; Univ. of Calif, Berkeley. FIHT 1980; FCILT (FCIT 1987; FILT 1999); CEng 1990, FREng 2000; FICE 1996. Lectr, Dept of Civil Engrg, Univ. of Leeds, 1959–62; Technical Dir, Freeman Fox Wilbur Smith, 1963–67; Jt Man. Dir, SIA Ltd, 1967–71; Chm., Wootton Jeffreys Consultants Ltd, 1971–91; Chief Exec., Transport and Road, subseq. Transport, Res. Lab., 1991–97. Visiting Professor in: Computing, KCL, 1987–89; Transport Studies, UCL, 1989–92. Pres., Instn of Highways and Transportation, 1997–98. Chm., Motorway Archive Trust, 2006–; Mem., Public Policy Cttee, RAC Foundn, 2001–. Trustee, Rees Jeffreys Road Fund, 2001–. *Publications:* numerous papers on transport, planning and computer topics. *Recreations:* cricket, golf, Rotary, photography, travel. *Address:* Transportation Research Group, Department of Civil Engineering and the Environment, University of Southampton, Highfield, Southampton SO17 1BJ. *T:* (023) 8059 2192. *Club:* Royal Automobile.

WOOTTON, Ian David Phimester, MA, MB, BChir, PhD; FRSC, FRCPath, FRCP; Professor of Chemical Pathology, Royal Postgraduate Medical School, University of London, 1963–82; *b* 5 March 1921; *s* of D. Wootton and Charlotte (*née* Phimester); *m* 1946, Veryan Mary Walshe; two *s* two *d*. *Educ:* Weymouth Grammar School; St John's College, Cambridge; St Mary's Hospital, London. Research Assistant, Postgraduate Med. School, 1945; Lecturer, 1949; Sen. Lecturer, 1959; Reader, 1961. Consultant Pathologist to Hammersmith Hospital, 1952. Member of Medical Research Council Unit, Cairo, 1947–48; Major, RAMC, 1949; Smith-Mundt Fellow, Memorial Hosp., New York, 1951. Chief Scientist (Hosp. Scientific and Technical Services), DHSS, 1972–73. *Publications:* Microanalysis in Medical Biochemistry, 1964, ed 6th edn, 1982; Biochemical Disorders in Human Disease, 1970; papers in medical and scientific journals on biochemistry and pathology. *Recreation:* bookbinding. *Address:* Cariad Cottage, Cleeve Road, Goring, Oxon RG8 9DB. *T:* (01491) 873050.

WOOTTON, John; *see* Wootton, H. J.

WOOTTON, Ronald William, CBE 1991; Head of West and North Africa and Mediterranean Department, Overseas Development Administration, 1986–91; *b* 7 April 1931; *s* of late William George and Lilian Wootton; *m* 1954, Elvira Mary Gillian Lakeman; one *s* one *d*. *Educ:* Christ's College, Finchley. Served Royal Signals, 1950–52. Colonial Office, 1952–63; Commonwealth Relations Office, 1963–65; ODM/ODA, 1965–91: Head of Overseas Manpower and Consultancies Dept, 1976–79; Head of UN Dept, 1979–82; Head of British Develt Div. in the Pacific, 1982–85. Mem., Internat. Cttee, Leonard Cheshire Foundn, 1992–98. Chm., Caterham Probus, 2001–02. *Address:* 4 Birchside Lane, Ashburton 7700, New Zealand.

WORCESTER, Marquess of; Henry John Fitzroy Somerset; *b* 22 May 1952; *s* and *heir* of 11th Duke of Beaufort, *qv*; *m* 1987, Tracy Louise, *yr d* of Hon. Peter Ward and Hon. Mrs Claire Ward; two *s* one *d*. *Educ:* Eton; Cirencester Agricultural College. *Recreations:* golf, shooting, rock music, selective television watching. *Heir:* *s* Earl of Glamorgan, *qv*. *Club:* Turf.

WORCESTER, Bishop of, since 2007; **Rt Rev. John Geoffrey Inge,** PhD; *b* 26 Feb. 1955; *s* of Geoffrey Alfred and Elsie Inge; *m* 1989, Denise Louise Longenecker; one *d*. *Educ:* Kent Coll., Canterbury; Univ. of Durham (BSc 1977; MA 1994; PhD 2002); Keble Coll., Oxford (PGCE 1979); Coll. of the Resurrection, Mirfield. Ordained deacon, 1984, priest, 1985; Asst Chaplain, Lancing Coll., 1984–86; Jun. Chaplain, 1986–89, Sen. Chaplain, 1989–90, Harrow Sch.; Vicar, St Luke, Wallsend, 1990–96; Canon Res., 1996–2003, and Vice-Dean, 1999–2003, Ely Cathedral; Bishop Suffragan of Huntingdon, 2003–07. Trustee, Common Purpose, 2005–. *Publications:* A Christian Theology of Place, 2003; Living Love, 2007. *Address:* The Old Palace, Deansway, Worcester WR1 2JE.

WORCESTER, Dean of; *see* Atkinson, Very Rev. P. G.

WORCESTER, Archdeacon of; *see* Morris, Ven. R. A. B.

WORCESTER, Sir Robert (Milton), KBE 2005; DL; Founder, Market & Opinion Research International (MORI) Ltd, 1969 (Managing Director, 1969–94; Chairman, 1973–2005); *b* 21 Dec. 1933; *s* of late C. M. and Violet Ruth Worcester, of Kansas City, Mo, USA; adopted dual citizenship, 2004; *m* 1st, 1958, Joann (*née* Ransdell) (decd); two *s*; 2nd, 1982, Margaret Noel (*née* Smallbone). *Educ:* Univ. of Kansas (BSc). Consultant, McKinsey & Co., 1962–65; Chief Financial Officer, Opinion Research Corp., 1965–68. Non-exec. Dir, Kent Messenger Gp, 2004–08; Chm., Maidstone Radio Ltd, 2004–06. Pres., World Assoc. for Public Opinion Research, 1983–84. Vice President: Internat. Social Science Council, UNESCO, 1989–94; UNA, 1999–. Visiting Professor: City Univ., 1990–2002; LSE, 1992– (Gov., 1995–; Hon. Fellow, 2005); Strathclyde Univ., 1996–2001; Hon. Prof., Warwick Univ., 2005–. Chm., Pilgrims' Soc. of GB, 1993–; Co Chm., Jamestown 2007 British Cttee, 2004–07. Governor: Ditchley Foundn; ESU. Comr, US-UK Fulbright Commn, 1995–2005. Vice-Pres., Royal Soc. of Wildlife Trusts, 1995–; Pres., Envmtl Campaigns Ltd, 2002–06. Trustee: Magna Carta Trust, 1995–; Wildfowl and Wetlands Trust, 2002–08. Mem., Adv. Council, Inst. of Business Ethics. Member: Ct, Middlesex Univ., 2001–; Ct and Council, Univ. of Kent, 2002– (Chancellor, 2006–; Hon. Prof. of Politics, 2002–). Kent Ambassador, Kent CC. Freeman, City of London, 2001. DL Kent, 2004. Fellow: Market Res. Soc., 1997; Royal Statistical Soc., 2004. Founding Co-Editor, Internat. Jl of Public Opinion Research; Mem., Adv. Bd, European Business Jl. Hon. FKC 2007. Hon. DSc Buckingham, 1998; Hon. DLitt Bradford, 2001; DUniv Middlesex, 2001; Hon. LLD Greenwich, 2002; Hon. DCL Kent, 2006. *Publications:* (ed) Consumer Market Research Handbook, 1971, 3rd edn 1986; (with M Harrop) Political Communications, 1982; (ed) Political Opinion Polling: an international review, 1983; (with Lesley Watkins) Private Opinions, Public Polls, 1986; (with Eric Jacobs) We British, 1990; British Public Opinion: history and methodology of political opinion polling, 1991; (with Eric Jacobs) Typically British, 1991; (with Samuel Barnes) Dynamics of Societal Learning about Global Environmental Change, 1992; (with Roger Mortimore): Explaining Labour's Landslide, 1999; Explaining Labour's Second Landslide, 2001; (with R. Mortimore and P. Baines) Explaining Labour's Landslip, 2005; contrib. Financial Times, Observer; papers in tech. and prof. jls. *Recreations:* castles, choral music, gardening. *Address:* MORI House, 79–81 Borough Road, SE1 1FY. *T:* (020) 7347 3000; *e-mail:* rmworcester@yahoo.com. *Clubs:* Beefsteak, Reform, Walbrook; Brook (New York).

WORDEN, Prof. (Alastair) Blair, FBA 1997; Research Professor of History, Royal Holloway College, London, since 2005; *b* 12 Jan. 1945; *s* of late Prof. Alastair Norman Worden and of Agnes Marshall Scutt. *Educ:* St Edward's Sch., Oxford; Pembroke Coll., Oxford (BA 1966; MA 1971). Res. Fellow, Pembroke Coll., Cambridge, 1969–71; Fellow, and Dir of Studies in History, Selwyn Coll., Cambridge, 1972–74; Fellow, and Tutor in Modern History, St Edmund Hall, Oxford, 1974–95; Prof. of Early Modern History, Univ. of Sussex, 1996–2003. Vis. Prof. of Modern History, Univ. of Oxford, 2003–. Trustee, London Liby, 2002–04. *Publications:* The Rump Parliament, 1974; (ed) Edmund Ludlow, A Voyce from the Watch Tower, 1978; (ed) Stuart England, 1986; (ed) David Wootton, Republicanism, Liberty and Commercial Society, part I, 1994; The Sound of Virtue: Philip Sidney's 'Arcadia' and Elizabethan politics, 1996; Roundhead Reputations: the English Civil Wars and the passions of posterity, 2001; Literature and Politics in Cromwellian England, 2007; articles on early modern English history and lit. *Address:* Appleton Lodge, Souldern, Bicester OX27 7JR. *T:* (01369) 346842; *e-mail:* blair.worden@history.ox.ac.uk.

WORDSWORTH, Barry; conductor; Music Director: Birmingham Royal Ballet, since 1990; Royal Ballet, 1990–94 and since 2007; *b* 20 Feb. 1948; *s* of Ronald and Kathleen Wordsworth; *m* 1970, Ann Barber; one *s*. *Educ:* Royal College of Music. Conductor, Royal Ballet, 1974–84; Music Dir, New Sadler's Wells Opera, 1982–84; Musical Dir and Prin. Conductor, Brighton Philharmonic Orch., 1989–; Prin. Conductor, 1989–2006, Conductor Laureate, 2006–, BBC Concert Orch. Joint winner, Sargent Conductor's Prize, 1970; Tagore Gold Medal, RCM, 1970. *Recreations:* swimming, photography, cooking. *Address:* c/o IMG Artists, The Light Box, 111 Power Road, W4 5PY.

WORDSWORTH, Prof. (Bryan) Paul, FRCP; Clinical Reader in Rheumatology, since 1992, and Titular Professor of Rheumatology, since 1998, University of Oxford; Fellow, Green Templeton College (formerly Green College), Oxford, since 1992; *b* 4 April 1952; *s* of Victor Pargiter Wordsworth and Dora Mary Wordsworth; *m* 1981, Christine Brow; two *s* one *d*. *Educ:* Whitgift Sch.; Westminster Med. Sch., London Univ. (MB BS 1975); MA Oxon 1992. MRCP 1978, FRCP 1996. Registrar in Rheumatology, Middx Hosp., 1978–80; Sen. Registrar in Rheumatology, Oxford Hosps, 1980–87; University of Oxford: Res. Fellow, Nuffield Depts of Pathology and Medicine, 1983–85 and 1987–92; Sen. Tutor, Green Coll., 1997–2000. Michael Mason Prize, British Soc. for Rheumatology, 1992. *Publications:* (with R. Smith) Clinical and Biochemical Disorders of the Skeleton, 2005; contribs to over 200 books and learned jls on musculoskeletal diseases and arthritis. *Recreation:* cricket. *Address:* Nuffield Orthopaedic Centre, Headington, Oxford OX3 7LD. *T:* (01865) 737545.

WORDSWORTH, Stephen John, LVO 1992; HM Diplomatic Service; Ambassador to Serbia, since 2006; *b* 17 May 1955; *s* of Christopher Wordsworth and Ruth Wordsworth (*née* Parrington); *m* 1981, Nichole Mingins; one *s*. *Educ:* St John's Sch., Porthcawl; Epsom Coll.; Downing Coll., Cambridge (MA). Joined FCO, 1977; Third, later Second Sec., Moscow, 1979–81; FCO, 1981–83; First Sec. (Econ. and Commercial), Lagos, 1983–86; on loan to Cabinet Office, 1986–88; First Secretary: FCO, 1988–90; (Political), Bonn, 1990–94; Counsellor (Dep. Internat. Affairs Advr), SHAPE, Mons, 1994–98; FCO, 1998–2002, Hd, Eastern Adriatic Dept, 1999–2002; Minister and Dep. Hd of Mission, Moscow, 2003–06. Bundesverdienstkreuz (FRG), 1992. *Recreations:* travel, walking the dog, family history research, good food and drink. *Address:* Foreign and Commonwealth Office, King Charles Street, SW1A 2AH.

WORKMAN, Charles Joseph, TD 1966; Part-time Chairman: Industrial Tribunals for Scotland, 1986–92; Social Security Appeal Tribunals, 1986–94; Disability Appeal Tribunals, 1992–94; *b* 25 Aug. 1920; *s* of Hugh William O'Brien Workman and Annie Shields; *m* 1949, Margaret Jean Mason; one *s* two *d*. *Educ:* St Mungo's Acad., Glasgow; Univ. of Glasgow (MA 1950, LLB 1952). Admitted solicitor, 1952. Served War, 1939–45: France, Belgium, Holland, Germany; commnd Second Fife and Forfar Yeomanry, RAC, 1942; Captain, 1945; served Intell. Corps TA and TAVR, 1954–69; Bt Lt-Col 1969; Hon. Col, Intell. and Security Gp (V), 1977–86. Entered Office of Solicitor to Sec. of State for Scotland as Legal Asst, 1955; Sen. Legal Asst, 1961; Asst Solicitor, 1966; Dep. Solicitor to Sec. of State, 1976; Dir, Scottish Courts Administration, 1978–82; Senior Dep. Sec. (Legal Aid), Law Soc. of Scotland, 1982–86. Chm., Public Service and Commerce Gp, Law Soc. of Scotland, 1977–78. Founder Mem., Edinburgh Chamber Music Trust, 1977–2006. *Publication:* (contrib.) The Laws of Scotland: Stair Memorial Encyclopaedia, vol. 2, 1987. *Recreations:* walking, swimming, music. *Address:* Ravenswood, 6 Lower Broomieknowe, Lasswade, Midlothian EH18 1LW. *Club:* New (Edinburgh).

WORKMAN, Timothy (Henry), CBE 2007; a District Judge (Magistrates' Courts) (formerly Metropolitan Stipendiary Magistrate), since 1986; Chief Magistrate and Senior District Judge (Magistrates' Courts), since 2003 (Deputy Chief Magistrate and Deputy Senior District Judge, 2000–03); a Chairman, Inner London Youth Court (formerly Juvenile Panel), since 1989, and Family Proceeding Court, since 1992; a Recorder, since 1994; *b* 18 Oct. 1943; *s* of late Gordon and Eileen Workman; *m* 1971, Felicity Ann Caroline Western; one *s* one *d*. *Educ:* Ruskin Grammar Sch., Croydon. Probation Officer, Inner London, 1967–69; admitted Solicitor, 1969; Solicitor, subseq. Partner, C. R. Thomas & Son, later Lloyd Howorth & Partners, Maidenhead, 1969–85. Mem., Sentencing Guidelines Council, 2004–. Hon. Bencher, Gray's Inn, 2007. *Recreations:* woodturning, shepherding, pottery. *Address:* Westminster City Magistrates' Court, 70 Horseferry Road, SW1P 2AX. *T:* (020) 7853 9264.

WORMALD, Peter John, CB 1990; Director, Office of Population Censuses and Surveys, and Registrar General for England and Wales, 1990–96; *b* 10 March 1936; *s* of late H. R. and G. A. Wormald; *m* 1962, Elizabeth North; three *s*. *Educ:* Doncaster Grammar Sch.; The Queen's Coll., Oxford (MA). Assistant Principal, Min. of Health, 1958, Principal, 1963; HM Treasury, 1965–67, Asst Sec., 1970; Under Sec., DHSS, 1978; Dep. Sec., Dept of Health (formerly DHSS), 1987. *Recreations:* music, golf, contract bridge. *Club:* Oxford and Cambridge.

WORRALL, Anna Maureen, (Mrs G. H. G. Williams); QC 1989; a Recorder, 1987–2003; *b* 16 Sept. 1938; *er d* of T. B. Worrall and S. F. Worrall (*née* Cushman); *m* 1964, G. H. Graeme Williams, *qv*; two *d*. *Educ:* Hillcrest Sch., Bramhall; Loreto Coll., Llandudno; Manchester Univ. Called to the Bar, Middle Temple (Harmsworth Scholar), 1959, Bencher, 1996; in practice, 1959–63 and 1971–; Lectr in Law, Holborn Coll. of Law, Language and Commerce, 1964–69; Dir, ILEA Educnl Television Service, 1969–71. Pres., Mental Health Review Tribunals, 1995–. Mem., Home Office Cttee on Review of Sexual Offences, 2002–03. *Recreations:* theatre, music, cooking, walking, travel. *Address:* Lamb Building, Ground Floor, Temple, EC4Y 7AS. *T:* (020) 7797 7788, *Fax:* (020) 7353 0535. *Club:* Reform.

WORRALL, Denis John, PhD; Chief Executive, Omega Investment Research Ltd, since 1990; Chairman: Irosis Mining Resources (Pty) Ltd, since 1999; Namakhoi Mining Resources (Pty) Ltd, since 1999; *b* 29 May 1935; *s* of Cecil John Worrall and Hazel Worrall; *m* 1965, Anita Ianco; three *s*. *Educ:* Univ. of Cape Town (BA Hons, MA); Univ. of South Africa (LLB); Cornell Univ. (PhD). Teaching and research positions, Univs of Natal, S Africa, Ibadan, Witwatersrand, California, Cornell; Rearch Prof. and Dir, Inst. of Social and Economic Research, Rhodes Univ., 1973. Senator, 1974; elected to Parlt, 1977; Chm., Constitutional Cttee, President's Council, 1981; Ambassador: to Australia, 1983–84; to the UK, 1984–87; Co-Leader, Democratic Party, 1988–90; MP (Democratic Party) Berea (Durban), South Africa, 1989–94. Advocate of Supreme Court of S Africa. Chm., Tridelta Magnet Hldgs Ltd, 1996–99; Vice-Chm., Internat. Bank of S Africa, 1996–2000. *Publication:* South Africa: government and politics, 1970. *Recreations:* tennis, reading, music. *Address:* PO Box 5455, Cape Town, 8000, South Africa.

WORRALL THOMPSON, (Henry) Antony (Cardew); TV chef; restaurateur; *b* 1 May 1951; *s* of late Michael Worrall Thompson and Joanna Duncan; *m* 1st, 1974, Jill Thompson (marr. diss.); 2nd, 1983, Militza Millar (marr. diss.); two *s*; 3rd, 1996, Jacinta Shiel; one *s* one *d*. *Educ:* King's Sch., Canterbury; Westminster Hotel Sch. (HND). Sous chef, Brinkley's Restaurant, Fulham Rd, Sept.–Oct. 1978, head chef, Oct. 1978–1980; head chef, Dan's Restaurant, Chelsea, 1980–81; opened Ménage à Trois, Knightsbridge, 1981; first chef/patron, restaurant at One Ninety, Queen's Gate, 1989 (Best New Restaurant, Time Out, 1990); restaurants opened: Managing Director: Bistrot 190, 1990; dell 'Ugo, Frith St, 1992; Palio, Notting Hill Gate, 1992; Zoe, St Christopher's Place, 1993; Cafe dell 'Ugo, City of London, 1993; The Atrium, Westminster, 1994; Drones, Belgravia, 1995; De Cecco, Parsons Gn, 1995; The Greyhound Free House & Grill, 2005; Kew Grill, 2005; The Lamb Free House and Kitchen, 2006; Barnes Grill, 2006; Windsor Grill, 2007; chef/proprietor: Woz, N Kensington, 1997–99; Wiz, Holland Park, 1998–2002; Bistrorganic, N Kensington, 1999; Notting Grill, Holland Park, 2002–. Restaurant consultant, Bombay, Melbourne, Stockholm and NY, 1981–88. Man. Dir, Simpson's of Cornhill Gp, 1996–97. Numerous TV appearances, incl. Ready, Steady, Cook, 1994–; Food and Drink prog., 1997–2003; Saturday Kitchen, 2003–06; Saturday Cooks, 2006–07; Daily Cooks Challenge, 2008–. FIH (FHCIMA 1989). Meilleur Ouvrier de GB, 1987. *Publications:* The Small and Beautiful Cookbook, 1984; (with M. Gluck) Supernosh, 1993; Modern Bistrot Cookery, 1994; 30 Minute Menus, 1995; Simply Antony, 1998; The ABC of AWT, 1998; Food and Drink Cookbook, 2002; Raw (autobiog.), 2003; How to Cook and Buy Real Meat, 2003; Healthy Eating for Diabetes, 2003; Antony Worrall Thompson's GI Diet, 2005; Antony's Weekend Cookbook, 2006; Barbecues and Grilling, 2006; The GL Diet Made Simple, 2006; AWT's The Diabetes Weight Loss Diet, 2007; The People's Cookbook, 2007; Saturday Cooks Cookbook, 2008; The Sweet Life, 2008. *Recreations:* gardening, antiques, interior design, eating, cooking. *Address:* Notting Grill Restaurant, 123A Clarendon Road, W11 4JG. *T:* (020) 7229 1500; c/o Limelight Management, 33 Newman Street, W1T 1PY. *T:* (020) 7637 2529. *Clubs:* Groucho, Chelsea Arts.

WORSKETT, Prof. Roy, RIBA; consultant architect; Partner, Architectural Planning Partnership, Horsham, 1982–85; *b* 3 Sept. 1932; *s* of Archibald Ellwood Worskett and Dorothy Alice Roffey; two *s* one *d*. *Educ:* Collyer's Sch., Horsham; Portsmouth Sch. of Architecture. MRTPI 1975 (retd); RIBA 1955. Architect's Dept, LCC, 1957–60; Architect, Civic Trust, London, 1960–63; Historic Areas Div., DoE (formerly MPBW), 1963–74; City Architect and Planning Officer, Bath City Council, and Prof. of Urban Conservation, Sch. of Architecture, Bath Univ., 1974–79; Consultant Head, Conservation Section, Crafts Council, 1979–82. Consultant Architect: Bath CC, 1979–83; Salisbury DC, 1980–83; Brighton Palace Pier, 1987–2002; London borough of Greenwich, 1988–99; London boroughs of Lambeth, Kensington and Chelsea, and Richmond, 1988; Consultant: Ford Foundn in India, 1982–86; Council of Europe, 1984–86; Nat. Audit Office, 1987; evidence to Public Inquiries at: Mansion House, for City of London; County Hall, London, 1984; Thameslink, 2000; Advr, Urban Redevelt Authority, Singapore, 1992–93; Conservation Advr, Union Rlys and British Land, 1993–99; Advisor: Historic Royal Palaces, Tower of London Environs Scheme, 1996–98; King's Cross Station Proposals, London Borough of Camden, 1997–99; Cambridge City Centre, 1997–98; Nat. Film and TV Sch., 2001. Chairman: Conservation Cttees, Crafts Adv. Cttee, 1974–79; Design Panel, Spitalfields Develt Gp, 1990–96; Member: Heritage of Educn Group, 1976–88; Council for Urban Study Centres, TCPA, 1977–80; Council of Management, Architectural Heritage Fund, 1977–2000. Pres., Urban Design Gp, 1983–84. Vis. Prof., Internat. Centre for Conservation, Rome, 1972–97. *Publications:* The Character of Towns, 1968; articles in architect. and planning magazines. *Recreation:* looking and listening in disbelief. *Address:* 1 Hampers Lane, Horsham, West Sussex RH13 6HB. *T:* (01403) 254208.

WORSLEY, Lord; George John Sackville Pelham; *b* 9 Aug. 1990; *s* and *heir* of 8th Earl of Yarborough, *qv*.

WORSLEY, Daniel; His Honour Judge Worsley; a Circuit Judge, since 1999; *b* 27 March 1948; *s* of Francis Arthur Worsley and Mary Worsley; *m* 1971, Virginia Caroline Wilkinson; one *s* one *d*. *Educ:* Ampleforth Coll.; Emmanuel Coll., Cambridge (BA). Called to the Bar, Gray's Inn, 1971; Barrister, 1971–99. *Publications:* Contrib. Ed., Halsbury's Laws of England, 4th edn, 1998; (jtly) I am Horatio Nelson, 2005; contrib. to legal textbooks. *Recreations:* East Anglia, sailing, trout streams, wine, the Pyrenees. *Club:* Norfolk (Norwich).

WORSLEY, Francis Edward, (Jock), OBE, 2002; Chairman, Lloyds Members Agency Services Ltd, since 1994; *b* 15 Feb. 1941; *s* of late Francis Arthur Worsley and Mary Worsley; *m* 1962, Caroline Violet (*née* Hatherell); two *s* two *d*. *Educ:* Stonyhurst College. FCA. Articled, Barton, Mayhew & Co., 1959–64; with Anderson Thomas Frankel, Chartered Accountants, 1964–69; Financial Training Co., 1969–93 (Chm., 1972–92). Dir, 1990–94, Dep. Chm., 1992–94, Lautro; Complaints Comr, SIB, then FSA, 1994–2001. Non-executive Director: Cleveland Trust PLC, 1993–99; Reece Plc, 1994–98; Brewin Dolphin Hldgs plc, 2003–; Accident Exchange Gp plc, 2004–05. Pres., Inst. of Chartered Accountants in England and Wales, 1988–89. Mem., Building Socs Commn, 1991–2002. Trustee, 1994–2002, Chm., 1998–2002, Cancer Res. Campaign; Trustee, Cancer Res. UK, 2002–03. *Recreations:* tennis, wine, travel, cooking.

WORSLEY, Jock; *see* Worsley, F. E.

WORSLEY, Lucy, DPhil; Chief Curator, Historic Royal Palaces, since 2003; *b* 18 Dec. 1973; *d* of Peter and Enid Worsley; partner, Mark Hines. *Educ:* New Coll., Oxford (BA Hons (Ancient and Mod. Hist.) 1995); Univ. of Sussex (DPhil (Art Hist.) 2001). FRHistS 2001. Administrator, Wind and Watermill Section, SPAB, 1995–97; Inspector of Ancient Monuments and Historic Bldgs, English Heritage, 1997–2002. *Publications:* Hardwick Old Hall, 1998; Bolsover Castle, 2000; Kirby Hall, 2000; The Official Illustrated History of Hampton Court Palace, 2005; Cavalier: a tale of passion, chivalry and great houses, 2007; various articles in jls. *Recreation:* treasure hunts. *Address:* Apartment 25, Hampton Court Palace, Surrey KT8 9AU. *T:* (020) 8781 9774; *e-mail:* lucy.worsley@hrp.org.uk.

WORSLEY, Sir Marcus; *see* Worsley, Sir W. M. J.

WORSLEY, Michael Dominic Laurence; QC 1985; *b* 9 Feb. 1926; *s* of Paul Worsley and Magdalen Teresa Worsley; *m* 1962, Pamela (*née* Philpot) (*d* 1980); one *s* (and one *s* decd); *m* 1986, Jane, *d* of Percival and Mary Sharpe. *Educ:* Bedford School; Inns of Court School of Law. RN 1944–45. Lived in Africa, 1946–52; called to the Bar, Inner Temple, 1955, Bencher, 1980; Standing Prosecuting Counsel to Inland Revenue, 1968–69; Treasury Counsel at Inner London Sessions, 1969–71; Junior Treasury Counsel, 1971–74, Senior Treasury Counsel, 1974–85, CCC. *Recreations:* music, travelling. *Address:* 6 King's Bench Walk, Temple, EC4Y 7DR. *T:* (020) 7583 0410. *Clubs:* Garrick, Lansdowne; Thomas More Society.

WORSLEY, Paul Frederick; QC 1990; **His Honour Judge Paul Worsley;** a Circuit Judge, since 2006; Senior Circuit Judge, since 2007; *b* 17 Dec. 1947; *s* of Eric Worsley, MBE, GM and Sheila Mary Worsley (*née* Hoskin); *m* 1974, Jennifer Ann, JP, *d* of late Ernest Avery; one *s* one *d*. *Educ:* Hymers College, Hull; Mansfield College, Oxford (MA). Called to the Bar, Middle Temple, 1970 (Astbury Scholar), Bencher, 1999; practised NE Circuit, 1970–2006; a Recorder, 1987–2006; Mem. Exec., NE Circuit, 1997–99. Member: Advocacy Studies Bd, 1996–99; Parole Bd, 2007–; Course Dir, Judicial Studies Bd, 2007–. Governor: Scarborough Coll., 1996–; Leeds Girls' High Sch., 2001–05; Leeds Grammar Sch., 2005–08. *Recreations:* Vanity Fair prints, opera, sailing, croquet, dogs. *Address:* c/o Central Criminal Court, Old Bailey, EC4M 7EH. *Club:* Bar Yacht.

WORSLEY, Gen. Sir Richard (Edward), GCB 1982 (KCB 1976); OBE 1964; Chairman: Western Provident Assoc., 1989–96; Electro-Optical Division, Pilkington Brothers, 1984–86 (Chief Executive, 1982–86); Barr and Stroud, 1982–86; Pilkington PE, 1982–86; *b* 29 May 1923; *s* of H. H. K. Worsley, Grey Abbey, Co. Down; *m* 1st, 1959, Sarah Anne Mitchell; one *s* one *d*; 2nd, 1980, Caroline, Duchess of Fife, *er d* of 3rd Baron Forteviot, MBE. *Educ:* Radley Coll. Served War: commissioned into Rifle Bde, 1942, Middle East and Italian Campaigns, 1942–45. Instr, RMA Sandhurst, 1948–51; Malayan Emergency, 1956–57; Instr, Staff Coll., Camberley, 1958–61; CO, The Royal Dragoons, 1962–65; Comdr, 7th Armoured Bde, 1965–67; Imperial Defence Coll., 1968; Chief of Staff, Far East Land Forces, 1969–71; GOC 3rd Div., 1972–74; Vice-QMG, MoD, 1974–76; GOC 1 (Br) Corps, 1976–78; QMG, 1979–82. Freeman, City of London, 1983. *Recreations:* shooting, ornithology. *Club:* Cavalry and Guards.

WORSLEY, Sir (William) Marcus (John), 5th Bt *cr* 1838; JP; Lord-Lieutenant of North Yorkshire, 1987–99; *b* 6 April 1925; *s* of Colonel Sir William Arthington Worsley, 4th Bt, and Joyce Morgan (*d* 1979), *d* of Sir John Fowler Brunner, 2nd Bt; *S* father, 1973; *m* 1955, Hon. Bridget Assheton (*d* 2004), *d* of 1st Baron Clitheroe, PC, KCVO; two *s* one *d* (and one *s* decd). *Educ:* Eton; New Coll., Oxford. Green Howards, 1943–47 (Lieut seconded to Royal West African Frontier Force). BA Hons (Oxford) Modern History, 1949. Programme Assistant, BBC European Service, 1950–53. Contested (C) Keighley, 1955; MP (C) Keighley, 1959–64, Chelsea, 1966–Sept. 1974; Parliamentary Private Secretary: to Minister of Health, 1960–61; to Minister without Portfolio, 1962–64; to Lord President of the Council, 1970–72. Second Church Estates Commissioner, 1970–74; a Church Commissioner, 1976–84. Pres., Royal Forestry Soc. of England, Wales and N Ireland, 1980–82 (Vice-Pres., 1976–80); National Trust: Dep. Chm., 1986–92; Chm., Yorks Reg. Cttee, 1969–80; Chm., Properties Cttee, 1980–90. Hon. Col, 2nd Bn, Yorkshire Volunteers, 1988–93. JP 1957 (Chm., Malton Bench, 1983–90), DL 1978, North Yorks; High Sheriff of North Yorks, 1982. KStJ 1987. *Recreations:* walking, reading. *Heir: s* William Ralph Worsley, FRICS [*b* 12 Sept. 1956; *m* 1987, Marie-Noëlle, *yr d* of Bernard H. Dreesmann; one *s* two *d*]. *Address:* Park House, Hovingham, York YO62 4JZ. *T:* (01653) 628002. *Club:* Boodle's.

WORSTHORNE, Sir Peregrine (Gerard), Kt 1991; writer; Editor, Comment Section, Sunday Telegraph, 1989–91; *b* 22 Dec. 1923; *s* of Col Koch de Gooreynd, OBE (who assumed surname of Worsthorne by deed poll, 1921), and Baroness Norman, CBE; *m* 1st, 1950, Claude Bertrand de Colasse (*d* 1990); one *d*; 2nd, 1991, Lady Lucinda Lambton (*see* L. Lambton), *d* of Viscount Lambton. *Educ:* Stowe; Peterhouse, Cambridge (BA); Magdalen Coll., Oxford. Commnd Oxf. and Bucks LI, 1942; attached Phantom, GHQ Liaison Regt, 1944–45. Sub-editor, Glasgow Herald, 1946; Editorial staff: Times, 1948–53; Daily Telegraph, 1953–61; Deputy Editor, Sunday Telegraph, 1961–76, Associate Editor, 1976–86, Editor, 1986–89. *Publications:* The Socialist Myth, 1972; Peregrinations: selected pieces, 1980; By the Right, 1987; Tricks of Memory (autobiog.), 1993; In Defence of Aristocracy, 2004. *Recreation:* reading. *Address:* The Old Rectory, Hedgerley, Bucks SL2 3UY. *T:* (01753) 646167. *Clubs:* Beefsteak, Garrick, Pratt's, City University.

See also Sir S. P. E. C. W. Towneley.

WORSWICK, Dr Richard David, CChem, FRSC; Deputy Chairman, LGC Group Holdings plc, 2005–07 (Chief Executive, LGC (Holdings) Ltd, subsequently LGC Group Holdings plc, 1996–2005); *b* 22 July 1946; *s* of (George) David (Norman) Worswick, CBE, FBA; *m* 1970, Jacqueline Brigit Isobel Adcock; two *d* (and one *d* decd). *Educ:* New College, Oxford (BA Hons Nat. Sci. 1969; MA 1972; DPhil 1972). CChem, FRSC 1991. SRC post-doctorate res. asst, Inorganic Chem. Lab., Oxford, 1972–73; Res. Admin, Boots Co., Nottingham, 1973–76; Harwell Lab., UKAEA, 1976–91: marketing and planning, 1976–85; Head, Res. Planning and Inf. Services, 1985–87; Head, Safety Branch, 1988; Head, Envtl and Med. Scis Div., 1988–90; Dir, Process Technology and Instrumentation, AEA Industrial Technology, 1990–91; Chief Exec., Lab. of Govt Chemist, DTI, 1991–96; Govt Chemist, 1991–2002. Chm., Pipeline Develts Ltd, 1998–2002. UK Entrepreneur of the Year (business products and services), 2003. *Publications:* research papers in sci. jls. *Recreations:* listening to music, playing the violin, walking. *Address:* LGC, Queen's Road, Teddington, Middx TW11 0LY. *T:* (020) 8943 7300.

WORTH, Abbot of; *see* Jamison, Rt Rev. P. C.

WORTH, Anthony James Longmore, FRAgS; Lord-Lieutenant of Lincolnshire, since 2008 (Vice Lord-Lieutenant, 2002–08); farmer; Chairman, A. H. Worth and Co. Ltd, since 2000; *b* 23 Feb. 1940; *s* of George Arthur Worth and Janet Maitland Worth; *m* 1964, Jennifer Mary Morgan; three *s* one *d*. *Educ:* Marlborough Coll.; Iowa State Coll.; Sidney Sussex Coll., Cambridge (BA 1962, MA 1966). Farm mgt consultant, Vic, Australia, 1964; Managing Director: Holbeach Marsh Co-op., 1970–2005; A. H. Worth and Co. Ltd, 1972–2000; QV Foods Ltd, 1994–99. Chairman: S Holland Internal Drainage Bd, 1978–87; Welland and Nene Local Flood Defence Cttee, EA, 2000–05 (Mem., 1987–2005); Mem., Anglian Regl Flood Defence Cttee, EA, 2000–05. Chm., LEAF (Linking Envmt and Farming), 2005–. Mem., Lincs Probation Bd, 1993–2007 (Chm., 1999–2001). Mem. Council, Lincs Agricl Soc., 1994– (Pres., 1994). Gov., Lincoln Univ., 1996–2005. High Sheriff, 1990–91, DL, 1994, Lincs. FIAgrM 1997; FRAgS 2002. MInstD 1985. Hon. DBA Lincoln, 2005. Freeman, City of London, 1993; Liveryman, Co. of Farmers, 1993–. Bledisloe Gold Medal for Landowners, RASE, 1995. *Recreations:*

walking, gardening, shooting, fishing. *Address:* Old White House, Holbeach Hurn, Spalding, Lincs PE12 8JP; *e-mail:* tony.worth@qvfoods.com.

WORTH, Prof. Katharine Joyce; Professor of Drama and Theatre Studies in the University of London at Royal Holloway and Bedford New College, 1985–87, now Emeritus (at Royal Holloway College, 1978–85); *b* 4 Aug. 1922; *d* of George and Elizabeth Lorimer; *m* 1947, George Worth; two *s* one *d.* *Educ:* Bedford Coll., Univ. of London (BA English, MA res. degree, PhD). Lectr in drama and theatre history (pt-time), Central Sch. of Speech and Drama and for Univ. of London Dept of Extra-Mural Studies, 1948 intermittently until 1963; Lectr 1964–74, Reader 1974–78, in English Lit., RHC; Hon. Fellow, RHBNC, 1990. Leverhulme Professorial Fellowship, 1987–89. Vis. Prof., KCL, 1987–96. Chm., Boilerhouse Fund-raising Cttee, 1999–2001, Mem., Boilerhouse Develt Cttee, 2001–, Royal Holloway. Consultant, London Centre for Th. Studies, 2001–. Hon. Pres., Consortium for Drama and Media in Higher Educn, 1975–87; Co-editor, Theatre Notebook, 1987–97; Member, Editorial Board: Yeats Annual, 1985–; Modern Drama, 1985–2000; Univ. of Michigan Press, 1988–. Hon. Life Mem., Soc. for Theatre Res., 1997. Prodns of Beckett's TV play, Eh Joe, and his radio plays, Words and Music, Embers and Cascando, 1972–84 (music for Words and Music and Cascando by Humphrey Searle); stage adaptation of Samuel Beckett's Company, perf. Edinburgh, Belfast, London and NY, 1987–88, Dublin, 1991; Dir, staged readings of the play behind the opera, Verdi Fest., Royal Opera House, 1995–99. *Publications:* Revolutions in Modern English Drama, 1973; (ed) Beckett the Shape Changer, 1975; The Irish Drama of Europe: from Yeats to Beckett, 1978; Oscar Wilde, 1983; Maeterlinck's Plays in Performance, 1985; (critical edn): W. B. Yeats: Where There is Nothing, and, W. B. Yeats and Lady Gregory: The Unicorn from the Stars, 1987; Waiting for Godot and Happy Days: text and performance, 1990; Sheridan and Goldsmith, 1992; Samuel Beckett's Theatre: life journeys, 1999; (contrib.) Samuel Beckett - 100 Years, ed. C. Murray, 2006; many articles and reviews on modern drama in symposia and in English, Irish and Amer. jls, incl. Modern Drama, TLS, Irish Univ. Rev., Th. Notebook, etc. *Recreations:* foreign travel, theatre, art galleries, walking in the country. *Address:* 48 Elmfield Avenue, Teddington, Middx TW11 8BT. *T:* (020) 8977 5778.

WORTHINGTON, Anthony, (Tony); *b* 11 Oct. 1941; *s* of late Malcolm and Monica Worthington; *m* 1966, Angela Oliver; one *s* one *d.* *Educ:* LSE (BA Hons); Univ. of Glasgow (MEd). Lecturer, Social Policy and Sociology: HM Borstal, Dover, 1962–66; Monkwearmouth Coll. of Further Educn, Sunderland, 1967–71; Jordanhill Coll. of Educn, Glasgow, 1971–87. Councillor, Strathclyde Region, 1974–87 (Chm., Finance Cttee, 1986–87). MP (Lab) Clydebank and Milngavie, 1987–2005. Opposition front bench spokesman: on educn and employment in Scotland, 1989–92; on overseas develt, 1992–93; on foreign affairs, 1993–94; on Northern Ireland, 1995–97; Parly Under-Sec. of State, NI Office, 1997–98. Member: Home Affairs Select Cttee, 1987–89; Internat. Develt Select Cttee, 1999–2005; Treas., All Party Population and Develt Gp, 1989–97; Chm., All Party Gp on Overseas Develt, 2000–05. British Pres., Parliamentarians for Global Action, 2001–05; a Dir, Parliamentarians Network on the World Bank, 2002–05. Chm., Labour Campaign for Criminal Justice, 1987–89. *Recreation:* gardening. *Address:* 24 Cleddans Crescent, Hardgate, Clydebank G81 5NW. *T:* (01389) 873195. *Club:* Radnor Park Bowling.

WORTHINGTON, His Honour George Noel; a Circuit Judge, 1979–94; *b* 22 June 1923; *s* of late George Errol Worthington and Edith Margaret Boys Worthington; *m* 1954, Jacqueline Kemble Lightfoot, 2nd *d* of late G. L. S. Lightfoot and Mrs Lightfoot; one *s* one *d* (and one *s* decd). *Educ:* Rossall Sch., Lancashire. Served War of 1939–45 in Royal Armoured Corps, 1941–46. Admitted a solicitor, 1949; a Recorder of the Crown Court, 1972–79. Liveryman, Wax Chandlers' Co. *Recreations:* gardening, theatre. *Address:* 49 Temple Sheen Road, East Sheen, SW14 7QF. *Clubs:* Athenæum, Hurlingham.

WORTHINGTON, Ian Alan, OBE 1999; HM Diplomatic Service; Ambassador to the Dominican Republic and (non-resident) to Haiti, since 2006; *b* 9 Aug. 1958; *s* of Alan Worthington and Bette Worthington (*née* Wright). *Educ:* Parish Church Primary Sch., Spring Gardens, Stockport; Stockport Sch., Mile End. Joined FCO, 1977; Moscow, 1980–82; Lusaka, 1982–85; Second Sec., FCO, 1985–88; Second Sec., Seoul, 1988–91; Dep. Head of Mission, Vilnius, 1991–92; Second Sec., Kingston, 1992–95; Consul Gen., Ekaterinburg, 1995–98; FCO, 1998–2001; First Sec., Berlin, 2001–06. *Recreations:* family history, scuba diving, meeting new and interesting people. *Address:* c/o Foreign and Commonwealth Office, King Charles Street, SW1A 2AH. *T:* (Dominican Republic) 4722069, *Fax:* 4727190.

WORTHINGTON, Prof. Michael Hugh, PhD; Senior Research Scientist, Oxford University, since 2001; Supernumerary Fellow, Wolfson College, Oxford, since 2002; Professor of Geophysics, Imperial College of Science, Technology and Medicine, 1985–2001; *b* 16 June 1946; *s* of Air Vice-Marshal Sir Geoffrey Worthington, KBE, CB, and late Margaret Joan (*née* Stevenson); *m* 1975, Mary Archange Mackintosh; one *s* one *d.* *Educ:* Wellington Coll.; Durham Univ. (BSc 1968; MSc 1969); ANU (PhD 1973). Univ. Lectr in Geophysics, and Fellow of Exeter Coll., Oxford, 1973–85; Hd, Dept of Geol., ICSTM, 1993–97. Vis. Prof., Dept of Applied and Engrg Physics, Cornell Univ., 1978. Member: Soc. of Exploration Geophysicists; European Assoc. of Geoscientists and Engineers; FGS. William Smith Medal, Geol Soc., 2007. *Publications:* (jtly) Seismic Data Processing, 1986; contribs to professional jls. *Recreations:* sailing, cross-country running, painting. *Address:* Department of Earth Sciences, Oxford University, Parks Road, Oxford OX1 3PR. *T:* (01865) 272000.

WORTHINGTON, Stephen Anthony; QC 2006; a Recorder, since 2001; *b* 14 April 1953; *s* of Dennis and Moya Worthington; *m* 1981, Julie Evans; two *s* one *d.* *Educ:* Trinity Coll., Cambridge (BA 1975). Called to the Bar, Gray's Inn, 1976; barrister. *Recreations:* sport, wine, walking. *Address:* 12 King's Bench Walk, Temple, EC4Y 7EL. *T:* (020) 7583 0811, *Fax:* (020) 7583 7228; *e-mail:* worthington@12kbw.co.uk.

WOSNER, John Leslie; Chairman and Senior Partner, PKF, accountants, 1999–2005; *b* 8 June 1947; *s* of Eugen and Lucy Wosner; *m* 1974, Linda Freedman; two *s* one *d.* *Educ:* Univ. of Sheffield (BA Econ 1969). FCA 1972; ATII 1973. Trained with Arthur Andersen & Co., 1969–74; PKF: joined, 1974; Partner, 1976–2005; Managing Partner, 1994–99. *Publications:* articles in British Tax Review, Taxation, Accountancy. *Recreations:* opera, country walking, history. *Club:* Travellers.

WÖSSNER, Dr Mark Matthias; Chairman, Supervisory Board: Heidelberger Druckmaschinen AG, since 2004; Citigroup Global Markets Deutschland, since 2002; eCircle AG, since 2000; *b* 14 Oct. 1938. *Educ:* Karlsruhe Technical University (DrIng). Management Asst, Bertelsmann AG, Gütersloh, 1968; Mohndruck (Bertelsmann largest printing operation): Production Manager, 1970; Technical Dir, 1972; Gen. Manager, 1974; Mem. Exec. Bd, Bertelsmann, 1976; Dep. Chm. of Bd, 1981, Chm. and CEO, 1983–98; Chm., Supervisory Bd, Bertelsmann AG, 1998–2000; Chm. and CEO, Bertelsmann Foundn, 1998–2000. Member, Supervisory Board: DaimlerChrysler AG, 1998–; Douglas Hldg AG, 2003. *Address:* Citigroup Global Markets Deutschland AG & Co. KGaA, Ludwigstrasse 19, 80539 München, Germany.

WOUDHUYSEN, Deborah Jane; *see* Loudon, D. J.

WOUK, Herman; author, US; *b* New York, 27 May 1915; *s* of Abraham Isaac Wouk and Esther Wouk (*née* Levine); *m* 1945, Betty Sarah Brown; two *s* (and one *s* decd). *Educ:* Townsend Harris High Sch.; Columbia Univ. (AB). Radio script writer, 1935–41; Vis. Professor of English, Yeshiva Univ., 1952–57; Presidential consultative expert to the United States Treasury, 1941. Served United States Naval Reserve, 1942–46, Deck Officer (four campaign stars). Member Officers' Reserve Naval Services. Trustee, College of the Virgin Islands, 1961–69. Hon. LHD Yeshiva Univ., New York City, 1954; Hon. DLit: Clark Univ., 1960; American Internat. Coll., 1979; Trinity Coll., Hartford, Conn, 1998; George Washington Univ., Washington, 2001; Hon. PhD: Bar-Ilan, 1990; Hebrew, 1997. Columbia University Medal for excellence, 1952; Alexander Hamilton Medal, Columbia Univ., 1980; Berkeley Medal, Univ. of Calif, 1984; Golden Plate Award, Amer. Acad. of Achievement, 1986; Lone Sailor Award, US Navy Meml Foundn, 1987; Kazetnik Award, Yad Vashem, 1990; Guardian of Zion Award, Bar Ilan Univ., 1998; UCSD Medal, Univ. of Calif, San Diego, 1998. *Publications: novels:* Aurora Dawn, 1947; The City Boy, 1948; The Caine Mutiny (Pulitzer Prize), 1951; Marjorie Morningstar, 1955; Youngblood Hawke, 1962; Don't Stop The Carnival, 1965; The Winds of War, 1971 (televised 1983); War and Remembrance, 1978 (televised 1989); Inside, Outside (Washingtonian Book Award), 1985; The Hope, 1993; The Glory, 1994; A Hole in Texas, 2004; *plays:* The Traitor, 1949; The Caine Mutiny Court-Martial, 1953; Nature's Way, 1957; *non-fiction:* This Is My God, 1959; The Will to Live On, 2000. *Address:* c/o BSW Literary Agency, 303 Crestview Drive, Palm Springs, CA 92264, USA. *Clubs:* Cosmos, Metropolitan (Washington); Bohemian (San Francisco); Century (New York).

WRACK, Matt; General Secretary, Fire Brigades Union, since 2005; *b* 23 May 1962. *Educ:* Open Univ. (BSc); London Sch. of Econs (MSc). Joined London Fire Brigade, 1983. *Address:* Fire Brigades Union, Bradley House, 68 Coombe Road, Kingston-upon-Thames, Surrey KT2 7AE. *T:* (020) 8541 1763; *e-mail:* matt.wrack@fbu.org.uk.

WRAGG, John, RA 1991 (ARA 1983); sculptor; *b* 20 Oct. 1937; *s* of Arthur and Ethel Wragg. *Educ:* York Sch. of Art; Royal Coll. of Art. *Work in public collections:* Israel Mus., Jerusalem; Tate Gall.; Arts Council of GB; Arts Council of NI; Contemp. Art Soc.; Wellington Art Gall., NZ; work in private collections in GB, America, Canada, France and Holland. *One-man exhibitions:* Hanover Gall., 1963, 1966 and 1970; Galerie Alexandre Iolas, Paris, 1968; York Fest., 1969; Bridge Street Gall., Bath, 1982; Katherine House Gall., Marlborough, 1984; Quinton Green Fine Art, London, 1985; Devizes Mus. Gall., 1994; England & Co., London, 1994; L'Art Abstrait, London, 1995; Handel House Gall., Devizes, 2000; Bruton Gall., Leeds, 2000; *exhibitions:* Lord's Gall., 1959; L'Art Vivant, 1965–68; Arts Council Gall., Belfast, 1966; Pittsburgh Internat., 1967; Britische Kunst heute, Hamburg, Fondn Maeght, and Contemp. Art Fair, Florence, 1968; Bath Fest. Gall., 1977 and 1984; Artists Market, 1978; Biennale di Scultura di Arese, Milan, and King Street Gall., Bristol, 1980; Galerie Bollhagen Worpswede, N Germany, 1981 and 1983; Quinton Green Fine Art, London, 1984, 1985, 1986 and 1987; Best of British, Simpsons, 1993; Connaught Brown, London, 1993; Monumental '96, Belgium, 1996; Courcoux & Courcoux, 1997; Bruton Gall., Leeds, 1999; Bruton St Gall., London, 1999; Discerning Eye, Mall Galls, London, 2000; Cobham Fest., 2001; Bohun Gall., Henley-on-Thames, 2001; RWA Gall., 2001; Hotbath Gall., Bath, 2002. Sainsbury Award, 1960; Winner of Sainsbury Sculpture Comp., King's Road, Chelsea, 1966; Arts Council Major Award, 1977; Chantry Bequest, 1981. *Relevant publications:* chapters and articles about his work in: Neue Dimensionen der Plastic, 1964; Contemporary British Artists, 1979; British Sculpture in the Twentieth Century, 1981; Studio Internat., Art & Artiste, Sculpture Internat., Arts Rev., and The Artist. *Recreation:* walking. *Address:* 6 Castle Lane, Devizes, Wilts SN10 1HJ. *T:* (01380) 727087; *e-mail:* johnwragg.ra@virgin.net.

WRAIGHT, Margaret Joan; *see* Hustler, M. J.

WRAN, Hon. Neville Kenneth, AC 1988; QC (NSW) 1968; Premier of New South Wales, 1976–86. *Educ:* Fort Street Boys' High Sch., Sydney; Sydney Univ. (LLB). Solicitor before admission to Bar of NSW, 1957. Joined Australian Labor Party, 1954, Nat. Pres., 1980–86. Elected to Legislative Council, 1970; Dep. Leader of Opposition, 1971; Leader of Opposition, Legislative Council, 1972; MLA for Bass Hill, Nov. 1973–1986; Leader of Opposition, Dec. 1973–1976. Chm., CSIRO, 1986–91. Is especially interested in law reform, civil liberties, industrial relations, conservation and cultural matters. Exec. Chm., Wran Partners Pty Ltd; Dir, Cabcharge Australia Ltd. Chm., Victor Chang Cardiac Res. Inst. Australian Mem., Eminent Persons' Gp, Asia-Pacific Econ. Co-operation, 1993–95. FRSA 1990. Hon. LLD: Sydney, 1995; NSW, 2006. *Recreations:* reading, walking, swimming, tennis. *Address:* GPO Box 4545, Sydney, NSW 2001, Australia. *T:* (2) 92235151. *Club:* Sydney Labor (Hon. Life Mem.).

WRATTEN, Donald Peter; Director, National Counties Building Society, 1985–96; *b* 8 July 1925; *er s* of late Frederick George and Marjorie Wratten; *m* 1947, Margaret Kathleen (*née* Marsh); one *s* one *d.* *Educ:* Morehall Elem. Sch. and Harvey Grammar Sch., Folkestone; London Sch. of Economics. Storehand, temp. clerk, meteorological asst (Air Min.), 1940–43; service with RAF Meteorological Wing, 1943–47. LSE, 1947–50. Joined Post Office, 1950; Private Sec. to Asst Postmaster Gen., 1955–56; seconded to Unilever Ltd, 1959; Private Sec. to Postmaster Gen., 1965–66; Head of Telecommunications Marketing Div., 1966–67; Director: Eastern Telecommunications Region, 1967–69; Exec. Dir, Giro and Remittance Services, 1969–74 (Sen. Dir, 1970–74); Sen. Dir, Data Processing Service, 1974–75; Sen. Dir, Telecom Personnel, 1975–81. Member: Industrial Adv. Panel, City Univ. Business Sch., 1974–81 (Chm., 1977–81); Court, Cranfield Inst. of Technology, 1976–81; Business Educn Council, 1977–83; Council: Intermediate Technology Develt Gp, 1982–85; Internat. Stereoscopic Union, 1987– (Vice-Pres., 2001–03); Pres., Stereoscopic Soc., 1996–98 (Vice-Chm., 1990–92; Chm., 1993–95). Pres., Radlett Soc. & Green Belt Assoc., 1996–2004 (Chm., 1989–96). *Publication:* The Book of Radlett and Aldenham, 1990. *Recreations:* 3-D photography, social history. *Address:* 3 Broadlands, Hillside Road, Radlett, Herts WD7 7BX. *T:* (01923) 854500.

WRATTEN, Air Chief Marshal Sir William (John), GBE 1998 (KBE 1991; CBE 1982); CB 1991; AFC 1973; Chief Military Adviser, Rolls-Royce Defence (Europe), 1998–2000; *b* 15 Aug. 1939; *s* of William Wellesley Wratten and Gwenneth Joan (*née* Bourne); *m* 1963, Susan Jane Underwood; two *s* two *d.* *Educ:* Chatham House Grammar Sch., Ramsgate; RAF Coll., Cranwell. OC, RAF Coningsby, 1980–82; Sen. RAF Officer, Falkland Is, 1982; RCDS, 1983; Dir, Operational Requirements (RAF), MoD, 1984–86; SASO, HQ 1 Gp, 1986–89; AOC No 11 Gp, 1989–91; Air Comdr British Forces ME, and Dep. to Comdr (on attachment), Nov. 1990–March 1991; Dir Gen., Saudi Armed Forces Project, 1992–94. AOC-in-C Strike Comd, and Comdr Allied Air Forces Northwestern Europe, 1994–97; Air ADC to the Queen, 1995–97. CCMI (CIMgt

1996). QCVSA 1968. Legionnaire, Legion of Merit (USA), 1993. *Recreation:* photography. *Address:* 14 College Road, Cheltenham GL53 7HX. *Club:* Royal Air Force.

WRAW, Ven. John Michael; Archdeacon of Wiltshire, since 2004; *b* 4 Feb. 1959; *s* of Peter and Betty Wraw; *m* 1981, Gillian Webb; one *s* three *d*. *Educ:* Lincoln Coll., Oxford (BA Hons (Jurisprudence) 1981); Fitzwilliam Coll., Cambridge (BA Hons (Theol. and Religious Studies) 1984); Ridley Hall, Cambridge. Ordained deacon, 1985, priest, 1986; Curate, St Peter's, Bromyard, 1985–88; Team Vicar, Sheffield Manor, 1988–92; Vicar, St James, Clifton, 1992–2001; Area Dean, Rotherham, 1998–2004; Priest-in-charge, St Alban, Wickersley, 2001–04. Hon. Canon, Sheffield Cathedral, 2001–04. *Recreations:* walking, reading. *Address:* Southbroom House, London Road, Devizes, Wilts SN10 1LT. *T:* (01380) 729808; *e-mail:* adwilts@salisbury.anglican.org.

WRAXALL, 3rd Baron *cr* 1928, of Clyst St George, co. Devon; **Eustace Hubert Beilby Gibbs,** KCVO 1986; CMG 1982; HM Diplomatic Service, retired; Vice Marshal of the Diplomatic Corps, 1982–86; *b* 3 July 1929; *s* of 1st Baron Wraxall, PC; *S* brother, 2001; *m* 1st, 1957, Evelyn Veronica Scott (*d* 2003); three *s* two *d*; 2nd, 2006, Caroline Mary (*née* Burder), *widow* of Lt-Col Philip Fielden. *Educ:* Eton College; Christ Church, Oxford (MA). ARCM 1953. Entered HM Diplomatic Service, 1954; served in Bangkok, Rio de Janeiro, Berlin, Vienna, Caracas, Paris. *Recreations:* music, golf. *Heir: s* Hon. Antony Hubert Gibbs [*b* 19 Aug. 1958; *m* 1st, 1988, Caroline Jane Gould (marr. diss. 1994); two *d*; 2nd, 1995, Virginia, *d* of Colin Gilchrist; two *s*].

WRAXALL, Sir Charles (Frederick Lascelles), 9th Bt *cr* 1813; Assistant Accountant, Morgan Stanley International, since 1987; *b* 17 Sept. 1961; *s* of Sir Morville William Lascelles Wraxall, 8th Bt, and of Lady (Irmgard Wilhelmina) Wraxall; *S* father, 1978; *m* 1983, Lesley Linda, *d* of late William Albert and Molly Jean Allan; one *s* one *d*. *Educ:* Archbishop Tenison's Grammar School, Croydon. *Recreations:* choral singing, watching football, cricket. *Heir: s* William Nathaniel Lascelles Wraxall, *b* 3 April 1987.

WRAY, Prof. David; Professor of Oral Medicine, Glasgow University, since 1993; Clinical Director, Glasgow Dental Hospital, since 2004; Hon. Consultant in Oral Medicine, Greater Glasgow and Clyde NHS (formerly North Glasgow NHS Trust), since 1993; *b* 3 Jan. 1951; *s* of Arthur Wray and Margaret Wray (*née* Craig); *m* 1st, 1974, Alison Young (marr. diss. 1997); two *s*; 2nd, 1997, Alyson Urquhart; two *s* one *d*. *Educ:* Uddingston Grammar Sch.; Glasgow Univ. (BDS 1972; MBChB 1976; MD 1982). FDSRCPSGlas 1979; FDSRCSE 1987. Fogarty Vis. Associate, NIH, Bethesda, 1979–81; Wellcome Res. Fellow, Royal Dental Sch., Univ. of London, 1982; Sen. Lectr, Dept of Oral Medicine and Pathology, Univ. of Edinburgh, 1983–93; Glasgow University: Associate Dean for Res., Dental Sch., 1995–2000; Dean of Dental Sch., 2000–05. Founder FMedSci, 1998. *Publications:* Oral Medicine, 1997; Oral Candidosis, 1997; Textbook of General and Oral Medicine, 1999; Textbook of General and Oral Surgery, 2003. *Recreations:* golf, wine, cooking. *Address:* Glasgow Dental Hospital and School, 378 Sauchiehall Street, Glasgow G2 3JZ; 125 Dowanhill Street, Glasgow G12 9DN. *T:* (0141) 334 0021.

WRAY, James; *b* 28 April 1938; *m*; one *s* two *d*; *m* 3rd, 1999, Laura Walker; one *s*. Heavy goods vehicle driver. Mem., Strathclyde Regl Council, 1976. MP (Lab): Glasgow, Provan, 1987–97; Glasgow Baillieston, 1997–2005. President: Scottish Fedn of the Blind, 1987 (Vice Pres., 1986); St Enoch's Drug Centre; Scottish Ex-Boxers' Assoc.; Gorbals United FC. Mem., TGWU.

WRAY, Prudence Patricia, (Mrs B. H. Wray); *see* Skene, P. P.

WRAY, Nigel William; non-executive Director: Domino's Pizza UK & IRL plc (formerly Domino's Pizza Group plc), since 1997; Prestbury Investment Holdings, since 2003; English Wines Group plc, since 2004; *b* 9 April 1948. *Educ:* Mill Hill Sch.; Univ. of Bristol (BSc). Chairman: Fleet Street Letter plc, 1976–90; Burford Hldgs plc, 1988–2001; Nottingham Forest plc, 1997–99; British Seafood Gp, 2006–; Dir, Saracens Ltd, 1995– (Chm., 1996–); non-executive Director: Carlton Communications plc, 1976–97; Singer and Friedlander Gp plc, 1986–2001; Peoples Phone, 1989–96; Columbus Gp, 1991–2000; Urbium (formerly Trocadero, then Chorion) plc, 1995–2005; SkyePharma plc, 1995–2000; Carlisle Hldgs, 1998–2001; Hartford Gp, 1998–2000; Safestore plc, 1999–2003; Seymour Pierce Gp (formerly Talisman House) plc, 2000–04; Electric Word plc, 2000–06 (Chm., 2002–04); Invox plc, 2000–06; Extreme Gp, 2002–05; Play Hldgs Ltd, 2004–; WILink.com (formerly Knutsford) plc, 2005–06 (non-exec. Chm., 1999–2005); Greenhouse Fund Ltd, 2006–07; Networkers International plc, 2006–; Premier Team Hldgs, 2006–; Oakdene Homes plc, 2008–. *Address:* Cavendish House, 18 Cavendish Square, W1G 0PJ. *T:* (020) 7647 7647.

WRENBURY, 3rd Baron *cr* 1915; **Rev. John Burton Buckley;** Non-Stipendiary Minister, Brightling, Dallington, Mountfield and Netherfield, diocese of Chichester, since 1990; *b* 18 June 1927; *s* of 2nd Baron Wrenbury and Helen Malise (*d* 1981), 2nd *d* of late His Honour John Cameron Graham of Ballewan, Stirlingshire; *S* father, 1940; *m* 1st, 1956, Carolyn Joan Maule (marr. diss. 1961), *o d* of Lt-Col Ian Burn-Murdoch, OBE, of Gartincaber, Doune, Perthshire; 2nd, 1961, Penelope Sara Frances, *o d* of Edward D. Fort, The White House, Sixpenny Handley, Dorset; one *s* two *d*. *Educ:* Eton Coll.; King's Coll., Cambridge. Deputy Legal Adviser to the National Trust, 1955–56; Partner: Freshfield's, Solicitors, 1956–74; Thomson Snell and Passmore, 1974–90. Ordained deacon in Church of England, 1990, priest, 1991. *Recreations:* golf, campanology (Royal Cumberland Youths, Cambridge Univ. Guild of Change Ringers), bagpipes (Founder Mem., Pinstripe Highlanders). *Heir: s* Hon. William Edward Buckley [*b* 19 June 1966; *m* 1996, Emma, *o d* of Peter Clementson]. *Address:* Oldcastle, Dallington, near Heathfield, East Sussex TN21 9JP. *T:* (01435) 830400. *Clubs:* Oriental; Rye Golf.

WRENCH, Peter Nicholas; Senior Director, Simplification Project, UK Border Agency (formerly Border and Immigration Agency), since 2007; *b* 5 April 1957; *s* of late Cyril Wrench and of Edna Mary Wrench; *m* 1978, Pauline Jordan; two *d*. *Educ:* Clitheroe Royal Grammar Sch.; Royal Holloway Coll., London (BA). Home Office, 1980–: Private Sec. to Perm. Sec., 1987–88; Immigration and Nationality Dept, 1988–93; Organised and Internat. Crime Directorate, 1993–2000; Dep. Dir Gen., Immigration and Nationality Directorate, 2000–03; Dir of Resettlement, HM Prison Service, 2003–05; Dir of Strategy and Assurance, Nat. Offender Mgt Service, 2005–07. *Recreations:* obscure music, family, friends, dog. *Address:* Simplification Project, Ground Floor, Seacole Building, 2 Marsham Street, SW1P 4DF.

WREXHAM, Bishop of, (RC), since 1994; **Rt Rev. Edwin Regan;** *b* 31 Dec. 1935; *s* of James Regan and Elizabeth Ellen Regan (*née* Hoskins). *Educ:* St Joseph's RC Primary Sch., Aberavon; Port Talbot County Grammar Sch.; St John's Coll., Waterford, Eire; Corpus Christi Coll., London. Priest, 1959; Curate, Neath, 1959–66; Adviser in RE, Archdio. Cardiff, 1967–87; Chaplain, St Clare's Convent, Porthcawl, 1967–71; Administrator, St David's Cathedral, Cardiff, 1971–84; Parish Priest: St Helen's, Barry, 1984–89; St Mary's, Bridgend, 1989–94. Apostolic Administrator, Archdio. of Cardiff, 2000–01. *Recreation:* hill-walking. *Address:* Bishop's House, Sontley Road, Wrexham LL13 7EW. *T:* (01978) 262726.

WREY, Benjamin Harold Bourchier; Chairman, Henderson Global Investors Ltd (formerly Henderson Administration Group and Henderson Investors), 1992–2004; Director, Henderson Global Investors (Holdings) plc, 1998–2005; *b* 6 May 1940; *s* of Christopher B. Wrey and Ruth Wrey (*née* Bowden); *m* 1970, (Anne) Christine (Aubrey) Cherry; one *d*. *Educ:* Blundell's Sch.; Clare Coll., Cambridge (Hons in Econs; MA). Legal and General Assurance Soc., 1963–66; Investment Dept, Hambros Bank, 1966–69; joined Henderson Administration, 1969; Director, 1971; Jt Man. Dir/Dep. Chm., 1982; Director: Henderson Electric and General Investment Trust plc (formerly Electric and General Investment Co.), 1977–2000; Henderson American Capital and Income Trust plc, 1996–99; CCLA Investment Management, 1999–2005. Chm., Institutional Fund Managers' Assoc., 1996–98 (Dep. Chm., 1994–96); Member: Institutional Investors Adv. Cttee, London Stock Exchange, 1994–2000; Exec. Cttee, Assoc. of Investment Trust Cos, 1997–2002 (Dep. Chm., 1999–2002); Investment Cttee, 1999– (Chm., 2003–), Council, 2003–, BHF; Investment Cttee, Cambridge Univ. Assistants Pension Scheme, 2004–. Chm., COIF Charities Funds, 2005–. Mem., Adv. Council, Nat. Opera Studio, 1996–2005. *Publications:* articles on investment. *Recreations:* shooting (rep. Cambridge Univ., England and GB in full bore target rifle shooting; winner, Bisley grand aggregate, 1966, 1969), fishing, mountain-walking, ballet, photography. *Address:* 8 Somerset Square, Addison Road, W14 8EE. *Clubs:* Boodle's, City of London; Hurlingham.

WREY, Sir (George Richard) Bourchier, 15th Bt *cr* 1628, of Trebitch, Cornwall; *b* 2 Oct. 1948; *s* of Sir Bourchier Wrey, 14th Bt and of Sybil Mabel Alice Wrey, *d* of Dr George Lubke, S Africa; *S* father, 1991; *m* 1981, Lady Caroline Lindesay-Bethune, *d* of 15th Earl of Lindsay; two *s* one *d*. *Educ:* Eton. *Recreation:* shooting. *Heir: s* Harry David Bourchier Wrey, *b* 3 Oct. 1984. *Address:* Hollamoor Farm, Tawstock, Barnstaple, Devon EX31 3NY. *T:* (01271) 373466.

WRIGGLESWORTH, Sir Ian (William), Kt 1991; DL; Chairman, UK Land Estates, since 1995; *b* Dec. 1939; *s* of Edward and Elsie Wrigglesworth; *m* 1967, Patricia Truscott; two *s* one *d*. *Educ:* Stockton Grammar Sch.; Stockton-Billingham Technical Coll.; Coll. of St Mark and St John, Chelsea. Formerly: Personal Assistant to Gen. Sec., NUT; Head of Research and Information Dept of Co-operative Party; Press and Public Affairs Manager of National Giro. Chm., Govt Policy Consultants Ltd, 1998–2000; Dep. Chm., John Livingston & Sons Ltd, 1987–95; Dir, CIT Hldgs Ltd, 1987–2003; Divl Dir, Smiths Industries PLC, 1976–2000; Dir, Tyne Tees TV, 2002–06; Chm., Port of Tyne, 2005– (Dir, 2003–05). Contested (SDP/Alliance) Stockton South, 1987. MP (Lab and Co-op, 1974–81, SDP, 1981–87) Teesside, Thornaby, Feb. 1974–1983, Stockton South, 1983–87. PPS to Mr Alec Lyon, Minister of State, Home Office, 1974; PPS to Rt Hon. Roy Jenkins, Home Secretary, 1974–76; Opposition spokesman on Civil Service, 1979–80; SDP spokesman on industry, 1981, on industry and economic affairs, 1983–87. Pres., Liberal Democrats, 1988–90. Chairman: Northern Reg., CBI, 1992–94; Newcastle-Gateshead Initiative, 1999–2004; Baltic Centre for Contemporary Art, Gateshead, 2004–. Gov., Univ. of Teesside, 1993–2002. DL Tyne and Wear, 2005. Freeman, City of London, 1995; Liveryman, Co. of Founders, 1994. *Address:* UK Land Estates, Picture House, Queens Park, Queensway, Team Valley, Gateshead, Tyne and Wear NE11 0NX. *Clubs:* Reform, Groucho.

WRIGHT, family name of **Baron Wright of Richmond**.

WRIGHT OF RICHMOND, Baron *cr* 1994 (Life Peer), of Richmond-upon-Thames in the London Borough of Richmond-upon-Thames; **Patrick Richard Henry Wright,** GCMG 1989 (KCMG 1984; CMG 1978); HM Diplomatic Service, retired; *b* 28 June 1931; *s* of late Herbert H. S. Wright and Rachel Wright (*née* Green); *m* 1958, Virginia Anne Gaffney; two *s* one *d*. *Educ:* Marlborough; Merton Coll. (Postmaster), Oxford (MA; Hon. Fellow, 1987). Served Royal Artillery, 1950–51; joined Diplomatic Service, 1955; Middle East Centre for Arab Studies, 1956–57; Third Secretary, British Embassy, Beirut, 1958–60; Private Sec. to Ambassador and later First Sec., British Embassy, Washington, 1960–65; Private Sec. to Permanent Under-Sec., FO, 1965–67; First Sec. and Head of Chancery, Cairo, 1967–70; Dep. Political Resident, Bahrain, 1971–72; Head of Middle East Dept, FCO, 1972–74; Private Sec. (Overseas Affairs) to Prime Minister, 1974–77; Ambassador to: Luxembourg, 1977–79; Syria, 1979–81; Dep. Under-Sec. of State, FCO, 1982–84; Ambassador to Saudi Arabia, 1984–86; Permanent Under-Sec. of State and Head of Diplomatic Service, 1986–91. Mem., Security Commn, 1993–2002. Member: H of L Sub-Cttee on Home Affairs, 2001–07 (Chm., 2004–07); EU Select Cttee, 2005–; Sub-Cttee on Law and Instns, 2007–; Jt Cttee on Conventions, 2006. Director: Barclays Bank plc, 1991–96; BP Amoco (formerly British Petroleum Co.), 1991–2001; De La Rue, 1991–2000; Unilever, 1991–99; BAA, 1992–98. Trustee, Home Start Internat., 1999–2007 (Chm., 2004–07). Chm., RIIA, 1995–99 (Mem. Council, 1992–99); Member: Council, RCM, 1991–2001 (FRCM 1994); Atlantic Coll., 1993–2000; ICRC Consultative Gp of Internat. Experts, 1992–95. Governor: Ditchley Foundn, 1986–; Wellington Coll., 1991–2001; Edward VII Hosp., 2005–07. KStJ 1990; Registrar, 1991–95, Dir of Overseas Relations, 1995–97, Order of St John of Jerusalem. House Mag. Award for Best Parly Speech of the Year, 2004. *Recreations:* philately, travel, piano duets. *Address:* c/o House of Lords, Westminster, SW1A 0PW. *Club:* Oxford and Cambridge.
See also S. G. McDonald.

WRIGHT, Alan; *see* Wright, R. A.

WRIGHT, Alan John; a Master of the Supreme Court, Supreme Court Taxing Office, 1972–91; *b* 21 April 1925; *s* of late Rev. Henry George Wright, MA and Winifred Annie Wright; *m* 1952, Alma Beatrice Ridding; one *s* one *d* (and one *s* decd). *Educ:* St Olave's and St Saviour's Grammar Sch., Southwark; Keble Coll., Oxford. BA 1949, MA 1964. Solicitor 1952; in private practice with Shaen Roscoe & Co., 1952–71; Legal Adviser to Trades Union Congress, 1955–71. Lay Reader, Southwark dio., 1989–. *Recreations:* Germanic studies, walking, travel, foreign languages. *Address:* 49 Grange Road, Billericay, Essex CM11 2RG.

WRIGHT, Alec Michael John, CMG 1967; *b* Hong Kong, 19 Sept. 1912; *s* of Arthur Edgar Wright and Margery Hepworth Chapman; *m* 1948, Ethel Surtees; one *d*. *Educ:* Brentwood Sch. MRICS (ARICS 1934); ARIBA 1937. Articled pupil followed by private practice in London. Joined Colonial Service, 1938; appointed Architect in Hong Kong, 1938. Commissioned Hong Kong Volunteer Defence Corps, 1941; POW in Hong Kong, 1941–45. Chief Architect, Public Works Dept, Hong Kong, 1950; Asst Director of Public Works, 1956; Dep. Director, 1959; Director, 1963–69; Commissioner for Hong Kong in London, 1969–73. *Address:* 13 Montrose Court, Princes Gate, SW7 2QQ. *T:* (020) 7584 4293. *Club:* Hong Kong (Hong Kong).

WRIGHT, Sir Allan Frederick, KBE 1982; farmer, retired; *b* Darfield, 25 March 1929; *s* of Quentin A. Wright; *m* 1953, Dorothy June Netting; three *s* two *d*. *Educ:* Christ's Coll., Christchurch. Nat. Pres., Young Farmers' Clubs, 1957–58; President: N Canterbury

Federated Farmers, 1971–74; Federated Farmers of NZ, 1977–81 (formerly Sen. Nat. Vice-Pres.). Mem., NZ Cricket Bd of Control, 1967–90; Manager, NZ Cricket Team to England, 1983; Pres., NZ Cricket, 1993–94 (Life Mem., 1993). Chairman: NZ Rail, 1991–94; Lincoln Hldgs Ltd, 1995–2003; The Crossings (Marlborough) Ltd, 1998–2006; Dir, Richina Pacific Ltd, 1996–2004 (Chm., 1998–2001); former Dir, Orion Ltd. Chancellor, Lincoln Univ., 1990–94 (Chm. Council, Lincoln Coll., 1985–89, Mem., 1974–89). Hon. DCom Lincoln, 1997. *Recreations:* cricket (played for N Canterbury), Rugby, golf. *Address:* Annat, RD Sheffield, Canterbury, New Zealand.

WRIGHT, Andrew Paul Kilding, OBE 2001; PPRIAS, RIBA; architect and heritage consultant in private practice, Andrew P. K. Wright, since 2001; Commissioner, Royal Fine Art Commission for Scotland, 1997–2005; *b* 11 Feb. 1947; *s* of Harold Maurice Wright, ARIBA and Eileen May Wright; *m* 1970, Jean Patricia Cross; one *s* two *d*. *Educ:* Queen Mary's Grammar Sch., Walsall; Univ. of Liverpool (BArch Hons). RIBA 1973; ARIAS 1976, FRIAS 1987; FSAScot 1998. Weightman & Bullen, Liverpool, 1970–72; Rowand Anderson Kininmonth & Paul, Edinburgh, 1972–73; Sir Basil Spence, Glover & Ferguson, Edinburgh, 1973–78; Law & Dunbar-Nasmith, 1978–2001: Partner, 1981–2001; Chm., 1999–2001. Dir, Exec. Bd, UK City of Architecture and Design, Glasgow 1999 Festival Co. Ltd, 1995–2004. Archt, dio. of Moray, Ross and Caithness, 1988–98; Cons. Archt, Mar Lodge Estate, NT for Scotland, 1996–99; Hon. Archtl Advr, Scottish Redundant Churches Trust, 1996–; Archtl Advr, Holyrood Progress Gp, Scottish Parlt, 2000–04; Conservation Advr, Highland Bldgs Preservation Trust, 2001–. Member: Ancient Monuments Bd for Scotland, 1996–2003; Historic Envmt Adv. Council for Scotland, 2003–May 2009 (Vice-Chm., 2003–06); Panel, Fundamental Review of Historic Scotland, 2003; Post Completion Adv. Gp, Scottish Parlt, 2004–06; Design Panel, N Highland Initiative, 2006–. Member Council: Inverness Archtl Assoc., 1981–90 (Pres., 1986–88); RIAS, 1986–94, 1995–99 (Vice-Pres., 1986–88; Convener, Memship Cttee, 1992–94; Pres., 1995–97); RIBA, 1988–94, 1995–97. Member: Ecclesiastical Archts and Surveyors Assoc., 1989; Conservation Adv. Panel, Hopetoun Hse Preservation Trust, 1997–2007 (Co-Chair, 2005–07); C of S Adv. Cttee on Artistic Matters, 2000–05; Arts and Crafts in Architecture Award Panel, Saltire Soc., 2001–06; Conservation Cttee, NT for Scotland, 2007–. Trustee, Clan Mackenzie Charitable Trust, 1998–. Founding Fellow, Inst of Contemp. Scotland, 2001; FRSA; FSA Scot. *Recreations:* cycling, fishing, industrial heritage, music. *Address:* Andrew P. K. Wright, Chartered Architect, 16 Moy House Court, Forres, Moray IV36 2NZ. *T:* (01309) 676655, *Fax:* (01309) 676609.

WRIGHT, Dr Anne Margaret, CBE 1997; educational consultant, since 2001; Chair, National Lottery Commission, since 2005; *b* 26 July 1946; *d* of Herbert and Florence Holden; *m* 1970, Martin Wright; one *d*. *Educ:* Holy Trinity Indep. Grammar Sch., Bromley; King's Coll., London (BA Hons English I, 1967; Inglis Teaching Studentship, 1967–68; PhD 1970). Lectr in English, Lancaster Univ., 1969–71; Lectr, then Sen. Lectr, Principal Lectr and Reader in Modern English Studies, Hatfield Poly., 1971–84; British Acad. Res. Award, Univ. of Texas at Austin, 1979; Registrar for Arts and Humanities, CNAA, 1984–86; Dep. Rector (Academic), Liverpool Poly., 1986–90; Rector and Chief Exec., Sunderland Poly., 1990–92, Vice Chancellor and Chief Exec., Univ. of Sunderland, 1992–98; Chief Exec., UFI Ltd, 1998–2001. Member: English Studies Bd, 1978–84, Arts and Humanities Res. Sub-Cttee, 1979–84, CNAA; Cttee I of Cttee for Internat. Co-op. in Higher Educn, British Council, 1990–; Council for Industry and Higher Educn, 1994–; Armed Forces Pay Review Body, 2002–; Director: FEFC, 1992–97; Hong Kong UPGC, 1992–; HEQC, 1993–97. Member: EOC, 1997–98; Bd, English Partnerships, 2004–. Chairman: City of Sunderland (formerly Wearside) Common Purpose, 1990–97; Nat. Glass Centre, 1997–98; Director: Everyman Theatre, Liverpool, 1988–90; The Wearside Opportunity, 1990–93; Northern Sinfonia, 1990–96; Northern Arts, 1991–95; Wearside TEC, 1992–98. CCMI (CIMgt 1994; Mem. Bd of Companions, 1999–); FRSA 1992. DL Tyne and Wear, 1997–2001. *Publications:* (ed jtly) Heartbreak House: a facsimile of the revised typescript, 1981; Literature of Crisis 1910–1922, 1984; Bernard Shaw's Saint Joan, 1984; articles in jls and entries in dictionaries of lit. biog. *Recreations:* singing, theatre, opera, the arts.

WRIGHT, Prof. Anthony, DM; FRCS; Professor of Otorhinolaryngology, University College London, since 1991 (Director, Ear Institute (formerly Institute of Laryngology and Otology), 1991–2006); *b* 21 Nov. 1949; *s* of Arthur Donald and Hilda Wright; *m* 1989, Linda Steele; two *d*. *Educ:* Mill Hill Sch.; Emmanuel Coll., Cambridge (Sen. Schol.; Captain, Univ. Boxing Team, 1970); Lincoln Coll., Oxford (Full Blue, Boxing, 1972). DM Oxon 1986; LLM UWC Cardiff, 1995; FRCSE 1979; FRCS *ad eundem* 1995. Sen. Lectr in ENT Surgery, Inst. of Laryngology and Otology, 1984–89; Consultant ENT Surgeon, Royal Free Hosp., 1989–91. *Publications:* Dizziness: a guide to disorders of balance, 1988; (ed with Harold Ludman) Diseases of the Ear, 6th edn 1997; scientific articles on the structure and function of the inner ear. *Recreation:* attempting to make coffee that tastes as good as it smells. *Address:* 4 Grange Road, Highgate, N6 4AP. *T:* (020) 8340 5593. *Clubs:* Athenæum; Hawks (Cambridge).

WRIGHT, Anthony David; MP (Lab) Great Yarmouth, since 1997; *b* 12 Aug. 1954; *s* of late Arthur Wright and of Jean Wright; *m* 1988, Barbara Fleming; one *s* one *d*, and one step *d*. *Educ:* secondary modern sch. Engineer. Mem. (Lab) Great Yarmouth BC, 1980–82, 1986–98. Dir, Great Yarmouth Tourist Authority, 1994–97; Mem., Great Yarmouth Marketing Initiative, 1992–97 (Chm., 1996–97). Member: Public Admin Select Cttee, 2000–02; Trade and Industry Select Cttee, 2005–. *Address:* House of Commons, SW1A 0AA.

WRIGHT, Rev. Canon (Anthony) Robert; Canon, since 1998 and Sub-Dean, since 2005, of Westminster; Rector of St Margaret's, Westminster, and Chaplain to the Speaker of the House of Commons, since 1998; *b* 24 April 1949; *s* of Kenneth William Wright and Christabel Annie Wright (*née* Flett); *m* 1970, Leah Helen Flower; one *s* one *d*. *Educ:* Lanchester Poly. (BA Hons Modern Studies); St Stephen's House, Oxford (CertTheol Oxon). Ordained deacon, 1973, priest, 1974; Curate: St Michael, Amersham, 1973–76; St Giles-in-Reading, 1976–78; Vicar: Prestwood, 1978–84; Wantage, 1984–92; RD of Wantage, 1984–92; Vicar of Portsea, 1992–98. *Recreations:* abstract painting, walking, reading. *Address:* c/o Chapter Office, Dean's Yard, Westminster Abbey, SW1P 3PA. *T:* (020) 7654 4806.

WRIGHT, Dr Anthony Wayland; MP (Lab) Cannock Chase, since 1997 (Cannock and Burntwood, 1992–97); *b* 11 March 1948; *s* of Frank and Maud Wright; *m* 1973, Moira Elynwy Phillips; three *s* (and one *s* decd). *Educ:* Desborough County Primary Sch.; Kettering Grammar Sch.; LSE (BSc Econ 1st Cl. Hons); Harvard Univ. (Kennedy Schol.); Balliol Coll., Oxford (DPhil). Lectr in Politics, UCNW, Bangor, 1973–75; Lectr 1975, Sen. Lectr 1987, Reader 1989, in Politics, Sch. of Continuing Studies, Univ. of Birmingham. Educnl Fellowship, IBA, 1979–80; Chm., S Birmingham CHC, 1983–85. PPS to the Lord Chancellor, 1997–98. Chm., Public Admin Select Cttee, 1999–. Hon. Prof., Univ. of Birmingham, 1999–. Jt Editor, Political Qly, 1994–. *Publications:* G. D. H. Cole and Socialist Democracy, 1979; Local Radio and Local Democracy, 1982; British Socialism, 1983; Socialisms: theories and practices, 1986; R. H. Tawney, 1987; (ed jtly) Party Ideology in Britain, 1989; (ed jtly) The Alternative, 1990; (ed jtly) Consuming Public Services, 1990; (ed jtly) Political Thought since 1945, 1992; Citizens and Subjects, 1993; (ed with G. Brown) Values, Visions and Voices, 1995; Socialisms: old and new, 1996; Who Do I Complain to?, 1997; Why Vote Labour?, 1997; (jtly) The People's Party, 1997; The British Political Process, 2000; British Politics: a very short introduction, 2003; contribs to learned jls. *Recreations:* tennis, walking, gardening. *Address:* House of Commons, SW1A 0AA. *T:* (020) 7219 5029.

WRIGHT, (Arthur Robert) Donald, OBE 1984; *b* 20 June 1923; *s* of late Charles North Wright and Beatrice May Wright; *m* 1948, Helen Muryell Buxton, *d* of late Patrick Buxton, FRS; two *s* three *d*. *Educ:* Bryanston Sch.; Queens' Coll., Cambridge. War Service (commnd 1943), NW Europe (despatches) and India, 1942–46. Taught at: University Coll. Sch., 1948–50; The Hill School, Pennsylvania, 1950; Leighton Park School, 1951–52; Marlborough College (Housemaster), 1953–63; Headmaster, Shrewsbury Sch., 1963–75. Chm., HMC, 1971. Appointments' Sec. to Archbishops of Canterbury and York, 1975–84 and Sec., Crown Appointments Commn, 1977–84. A Chm., Civil Service Comrs' Interview Panels, 1984–91. Chm., William Temple Foundn, 1976–85. Chm., Council, Benenden Sch., 1976–86; Governor, King's Coll. Sch., Wimbledon, 1981–93. *Publications:* (ed) Neville Cardus on Music: a centenary collection, 1988; (ed and contrib.) Walter Hamilton: a portrait, 1991. *Recreations:* musical, defending the rural environment, counting my blessings. *Address:* Mill Barn, Coulston, near Westbury, Wilts BA13 4NY.

WRIGHT, Rt Rev. Benjamen; Priest in charge, Heathridge, Western Australia; *b* 15 March 1942; *s* of Clarice and Herbert Wright; *m* 1966, Annette Jennifer Dunne; two *s* one *d*. *Educ:* Slade Sch., Warwick, Qld; Murdoch Univ., Perth (ThL, BA). Ordained deacon, 1964, priest, 1965; Asst Curate, Applecross, 1964–67; Priest-in-charge, 1967–69, Rector, 1969–71, Narembeen; Army Reserve Chaplain, 1971–76; Rector, Alice Springs and Chaplain, St Mary's Child and Welfare Services, dio. of NT, 1976–80; Rector, Scarborough, 1980–88; Archdeacon of Stirling, 1986–88; Rector, Kalgoorlie, Boulder, 1988; Asst Bishop, dio. of Perth (Goldfields Region), 1988–91; Archdeacon of Goldfields, 1988–89; Archdeacon of O'Connor, 1990; Bishop of Bendigo, 1992–93; Rector of Busselton, WA, 1993. Hon. Canon of Christ Church Cathedral, Darwin, 1979–80. *Recreations:* fishing, gardening. *Address:* PO Box 785, Joondalup, WA 6919, Australia.

WRIGHT, Brian; *see* Wright, G. B.

WRIGHT, Caroline Janet Pamela; Director of Communications, Department for Children, Schools and Families (formerly Department for Education and Skills), since 2006; *b* 29 Dec. 1973; *d* of Peter Richard Wright and Janet Anne Wright. *Educ:* Chingford Sch.; Royal Holloway and Bedford New Coll., London (BSc Hons Geog. 1995). Regl journalist, 1995–98; Communications Manager, Post Office, 1998–2000; Department of Trade and Industry: Dep. Dir of News, 2000–03; Hd, Strategic Communications, 2003; Hd, News and Mktg, Ofsted, 2003–05; Dir of Communications, Partnerships for Schs, 2005–06. *Recreations:* competitive swimming, surfing, Victorian literature. *Address:* Department for Children, Schools and Families, Sanctuary Buildings, Great Smith Street, Westminster, SW1P 3BT. *T:* (020) 7925 5092; *e-mail:* caroline.wright@dcsf.gsi.gov.uk. *Club:* Borough of Waltham Forest Swimming.

WRIGHT, (Charles) Christopher; Master of Supreme Court Costs (formerly Taxing) Office, since 1992; *b* 15 July 1938; *s* of late Charles Gordon Wright, LDS RCS and Gwendoline Margaret Wright; *m* 1969, Angela Whitford. *Educ:* Emscote Lawn, Warwick; Rugby Sch.; New Coll., Oxford (MA 2nd Cl. Hons Jurisp. 1961). Solicitor of the Supreme Court, 1965; Partner, Lee & Pembertons, 1967–92. Sen. Vice-Pres., West London Law Society, 1991–92. Editor, Civil Legal Aid sect., Butterworths Costs Service, 1996–. *Recreations:* walking, swimming, holiday golf, reading. *Address:* Supreme Court Costs Office, Cliffords Inn, Fetter Lane, EC4A 1DQ. *Club:* Royal Automobile.

WRIGHT, Christopher John; Director, Security and Intelligence, Cabinet Office, since 2004; *b* 22 March 1953; *s* of James Wright and Ruby Wright (*née* Galbraith); *m* 1995, Barbara Ann Spells. *Educ:* Royal Grammar Sch., Newcastle upon Tyne; Univ. of York (BA). Joined MoD, 1974; Private Sec. to Air Mem. for Supply and Orgn, 1981; Office of Manpower Econs, 1982–85; Private Sec. to Perm. Under-Sec. of State, 1987–90; Asst Sec., 1990; Head: Central Services, 1990–93; NATO and European Policy Secretariat, 1993–94; Cost Review Secretariat, 1994–95; Dir of Orgn and Mgt Develt, 1995–98; Comd Sec., RAF Strike Comd, 1998–2001; Fellow, Center for Internat. Affairs, Harvard Univ., 2001–02; Hd, New Security Issues Prog., RIIA, 2002–04. *Recreations:* reading, cinema, modern art, house refurbishment. *Address:* Cabinet Office, 70 Whitehall, SW1A 2AS.

WRIGHT, Christopher Norman, CBE 2005; Chairman: Chrysalis plc (formerly Chrysalis, later Chrysalis Group plc), since 1969; Portman Film and Television, since 2004; Digital Rights Group, since 2007; Founder, Shareholder and Director, London Wasps Rugby Football Club (Chairman, 1996–2007); *b* 7 Sept. 1944; *s* of Walter Reginald Wright and Edna May (*née* Corden); *m* 1st, 1972, Carolyn Rochelle Nelson (marr. diss. 1999); two *s* one *d*; 2nd, 2003, Janice Ann Stinnes (*née* Toseland); one *d*. *Educ:* King Edward VI Grammar Sch., Louth; Manchester Univ. (BA Hons 1966); Manchester Business Sch. Co-Founder, Ellis Wright Agency, 1967; name changed to: Chrysalis, 1968; Chrysalis Gp plc, 1985. Chm., Loftus Road plc (incorp. Queen's Park Rangers Football and Athletic Club), 1996–2001. Chm., British Phonographic Industry, 1980–83; Director: Phonographic Performance Ltd, 1980–94; Internat. Fedn of Phonographic Industry, 1981–95 (Vice-Pres., 1981–91). *Recreations:* playing tennis, breeding race horses, music, collecting art and fine wines, watching sport of all kinds. *Address:* c/o Chrysalis plc, The Chrysalis Building, 13 Bramley Road, W10 6SP. *T:* (020) 7221 2213. *Club:* Turf.

WRIGHT, Clarissa Teresa D.; *see* Dickson Wright.

WRIGHT, Claud William, CB 1969; Deputy Secretary, Department of Education and Science, 1971–76; *b* 9 Jan. 1917; *s* of Horace Vipan Wright and Catherine Margaret Sales; *m* 1947, Alison Violet Readman (*d* 2003); one *s* four *d*. *Educ:* Charterhouse; Christ Church, Oxford (MA). Assistant Principal, War Office, 1939; Private, Essex Regiment, 1940; 2nd Lieut, KRRC, 1940; War Office, rising to GSO2, 1942–45; Principal, War Office, 1944; Min. of Defence: Principal, 1947; Asst Sec., 1951; Asst Under-Sec. of State, 1961–68; Dep. Under-Sec. of State, 1968–71. Chm., Cttee on Provincial Museums and Galleries, 1971–73. Research Fellow, Wolfson Coll., Oxford, 1977–83. President, Geologists Assoc., 1956–58. Lyell Fund, 1947, R. H. Worth Prize, 1958, Prestwich Medal, 1987, Geological Society of London; Foulerton Award, Geologists Association, 1955; Stamford Raffles Award, Zoological Society of London, 1965; Phillips Medal, Yorks Geol. Soc., 1976; Strimple Award, Paleontol Soc., USA, 1988; H. H. Bloomer Award for Zoology, Linnean Soc., 1998. Hon. Associate, British Museum (Nat. Hist.), 1973; fil.Dr *hc* Uppsala, 1979; Hon. DSc Hull, 1987. *Publications:* (with W. J. Arkell *et al*) vol. on Ammonites, 1957, 2nd edn 1996, (with W. K. Spencer) on Starfish, 1966, in Treatise on Invertebrate Palaeontology; (with J. S. H. Collins) British Cretaceous Crabs,

1972; (with W. J. Kennedy) Ammonites of the Middle Chalk, 1981; (with W. J. Kennedy) Ammonites of the Lower Chalk, pt I, 1984, pt II, 1987, pt III, 1990, pt IV, 1995, pt V, 1996; (with A. B. Smith) British Cretaceous Echinoidea, pt I, 1988, pt II, 1990, pt III, 1993, pt IV, 1996, pt V, 1999, pt VI, 2000, pt VII, 2004; papers in geological, palaeontological and archaeological journals. *Recreations:* palaeontology, natural history, gardening, archæology. *Address:* The Cotswold Home, Woodside Drive, Bradwell Village, Burford, Oxfordshire OX18 4XA. *T:* (01993) 824430.

WRIGHT, Prof. Crispin James Garth, PhD, DLitt; FBA 1992; FRSE; Professor of Logic and Metaphysics, since 1978, Wardlaw Professor, since 1997, University of St Andrews; *b* 21 Dec. 1942; *s* of Geoffrey Joseph Wright and Jean Valerie Holford; *m* 1985, Catherine Steedman (*née* Pain); two *s*, and one step *s* one step *d*. *Educ:* Birkenhead Sch.; Trinity Coll., Cambridge (BA Hons 1964; MA, PhD 1968); BPhil 1969, DLitt 1988, Oxon. Oxford University: Jun. Res. Fellow, Trinity Coll., 1967–69; Prize Fellow, All Souls Coll., 1969–71; Lectr, Balliol Coll., 1969–70; Lectr, UCL, 1970–71; Res. Fellow, All Souls Coll., Oxford, 1971–78; Prof. of Phil., 1987–92, Nelson Prof. of Phil., 1992–94, Univ. of Michigan, Ann Arbor. Leverhulme Res. Prof., 1998–. FRSE 1996. *Publications:* Wittgenstein on the Foundations of Mathematics, 1980; Frege's Conception of Numbers as Objects, 1983; Realism, Meaning and Truth, 1986; Truth and Objectivity, 1993; (with Bob Hale) The Reason's Proper Study, 2001; Rails to Infinity, 2001. *Recreations:* gardening, mountain-walking, running, P. G. Wodehouse, Liverpool FC. *Address:* Department of Philosophy, University of St Andrews, Fife KY16 9AL. *T:* (01334) 462467.

WRIGHT, David; MP (Lab) Telford, since 2001; *b* 22 Dec. 1966; *s* of Kenneth William Wright and Heather Wright; *m* 1996, Lesley Insole. *Educ:* Wolverhampton Poly. (BA Hons Humanities). MCIH 1994. With Sandwell MBC, 1988–2001 (Housing Strategy Manager, 1995–2001). *Recreations:* watching football (AFC Telford Utd) and cricket (Surrey), visiting old towns and cities. *Address:* House of Commons, SW1A 0AA. *T:* (020) 7219 8331. *Clubs:* Wrockwardine Wood and Trench Labour, Dawley Social.

WRIGHT, David Alan, OBE 1983; HM Diplomatic Service; Assistant Director, Human Resources Command, Foreign and Commonwealth Office, since 2002; *b* 27 May 1942; *s* of Herbert Ernest Wright and Ivy Florence (*née* Welch); *m* 1966, Gail Karol Mesling; four *s* one *d*. *Educ:* Surbiton Grammar Sch.; Univ. of Birmingham (BSocSc 1963). VSO, Chad, 1963; Inf. Officer, BoT, 1964; entered Foreign Office, 1965: Asst Private Sec. to Minister of State, FO, 1966–68; MECAS, 1968–70; Baghdad, 1970–73; Doha, 1973–76; on secondment to DHSS, 1976–78; FCO, 1978–80; Durban, 1980–83; Baghdad, 1983–87; FCO, 1987–92 (Head: Communications Dept, 1988–90; Inf. Systems Div. (Resources), 1990–92); Consul Gen., Atlanta, 1992–97; Ambassador and Consul Gen., Qatar, 1997–2002. Member: (C) Guildford BC, 2003– (Chm., Licensing, 2003–07; Lead Mem. for Community Safety, 2007–); Surrey Probation Bd, 2006–. *Recreations:* jogging, sailing, pottery, travel, music. *Address:* Newlands House, Newlands Corner, Guildford GU4 8SE. *Club:* Royal Over-Seas League.

WRIGHT, David Arthur, FRCS; Consultant Otolaryngologist: Mount Alvernia Hospital, Guildford, 1970–2004; Royal Surrey County Hospital, 1970–99, now Consultant Emeritus; President, British Association of Otorhinolaryngologists and Head and Neck Surgeons, 1997–99; *b* 13 April 1935; *s* of Arthur Albert Wright and Ena May (*née* Caxton); *m* 1969, Hillery Drina Seex; one *s* one *d*. *Educ:* Repton; Jesus Coll., Cambridge (MB BChir, MA 1960); Guy's Hosp. LRCP 1959; MRCS 1959, FRCS 1966. Hon. Consultant Otolaryngologist: Cambridge Mil. Hosp., 1981–96; King Edward VII Hosp., Midhurst, 1995–2003. Ear, Nose and Throat Adviser: British Airways, 1987–97; CAA, 1994–; Army, 1999–. Asst Ed., Jl Laryngology and Otology, 1981–88. Pres., Thomas Wickham-Jones Med. Res. Foundn. Sec. Gen., Eur. Bd Otolaryngology, 1998–2000. Member: BMA, 1960–98; Council, RCS, 1995–2000; Pres., Section of Otology, RSocMed, 1992. Examr, Intercollegiate Bd Otolaryngology, 1990–94. Mem. Senate, Royal Surgical Colls, 1997–2000 (Chm., Specialist Adv. Cttee, 1988–94). Patron, British Soc. of Hearing Therapists, 1999–; Master, British Academic Conf. in Otolaryngology, 2003–06. George Davey Howells Meml Prize, RSocMed, 1989; Walter Jobson Horne Prize, BMA, 1997; Gold Medal, British Assoc. of Otorhinolaryngologists, 1999. *Publications:* (ed) Scott-Brown's Otolaryngology, vol. 1, Basic Sciences, 5th edn 1988; chapters in text books; contrib. articles in med. jls on noise induced hearing loss, multi-channel hearing aids and functional endoscopic sinus surgery. *Recreations:* off-shore sailing, ski-ing, golf, weather forecasting, fly-fishing. *Address:* Eastbury Farmhouse, Compton, Guildford, Surrey GU3 1EE. *T:* (01483) 810343. *Clubs:* Royal Society of Medicine, McKenzie; Royal Southern Yacht (Hamble); Liphook Golf (Hants).

WRIGHT, Sir David (John), GCMG 2002 (KCMG 1996; CMG 1992); LVO 1990; HM Diplomatic Service, retired; Vice-Chairman, Barclays Capital, since 2003; *b* 16 June 1944; *s* of J. F. Wright; *m* 1968, Sally Ann Dodkin; one *s* one *d*. *Educ:* Wolverhampton Grammar Sch.; Peterhouse, Cambridge (MA; Hon. Fellow, 2001). Third Secretary, FO, 1966; Third Sec., later Second Sec., Tokyo, 1966–72; FCO, 1972–75; Ecole Nationale d'Administration, Paris, 1975–76; First Sec., Paris, 1976–80; Private Sec. to Secretary of the Cabinet, 1980–82; Counsellor (Economic), Tokyo, 1982–85; Head of Personnel Services Dept, FCO, 1985–88; Dep. Private Sec. to HRH the Prince of Wales, 1988–90 (on secondment); Ambassador to Republic of Korea, 1990–94; Dep. Under-Sec. of State, FCO, 1994–96; Ambassador to Japan, 1996–99; Gp Chief Exec. (Perm. Sec.), British Trade Internat., 1999–2002. Non-exec. Dir, Balfour Beatty, 2003–05; Mem., Internat. Adv. Bd, All Nippon Airways, 2003–. Chm., Govt Wine Adv. Cttee, 2004–. Vice-Pres., China Britain Business Council, 2003–; Bd Mem., UK-Japan 21st Century Gp, 2003–; Mem., Adv. Council, British Consultants and Construction Bureau, 2003–05. Chm. and Trustee, Daiwa Anglo-Japanese Foundn, 2001–04; Chm., UK-Korea Forum, 2008–. Gov., RSC, 2004–. Chm., Develt Cttee, Peterhouse, Cambridge, 2004–. Hon. LLD: Wolverhampton, 1997; Birmingham, 2000. Grand Cordon, Order of the Rising Sun (Japan), 1998. *Recreations:* golf, cooking, military history. *Address:* c/o Barclays Capital, 5 The North Colonnade, Canary Wharf, E14 4BB. *Club:* Travellers.

WRIGHT, David Stephen, OBE 1995; FRCP, FFOM; consultant occupational physician; Chief Medical Officer, British Petroleum Co. plc, 1989–95; *b* 4 Aug. 1935; *s* of Edward Alfred Wright and Winifred May Wright (*née* Oliver); *m* 1966, Caroline Auza; two *s* one *d*. *Educ:* Epsom Coll.; St Bartholomew's Hosp. Med. Coll. (MB BS 1959); MSc Salford 1973; DPH, DIH. FFOM 1983; FRCP 1989. MO, RN, 1960–85; Prof. of Naval Occupational Medicine, 1982–85; Head, BP Gp Occupational Health Centre, 1985–91. Vice-Dean, 1988–91, Dean, 1991–94, Faculty of Occupational Medicine. British Medical Association: Member: Armed Forces Cttee, 1966–88 (Chm., 1985–88); Council, 1985–88. OStJ 1984. *Publications:* (ed) 5th edn, Guidance on Ethics for Occupational Physicians, 1999; (contrib.) Fitness for Work, 2000; contribs on asbestos and noise to learned jls. *Recreations:* gardening, walking, golf. *Address:* 9 Ashburton Road, Alverstoke, Gosport, Hants PO12 2LH. *T:* (023) 9258 2459.

WRIGHT, Donald; *see* Wright, A. R. D.

WRIGHT, Eric; Chairman, Yorkshire and Humberside Development Agency (formerly Association), 1993–99; *b* 17 Nov. 1933; *s* of Alec Wright and Elsie (*née* Worthington); *m* 1st, 1955, Pauline Sutton (marr. diss. 1993); three *s* (and one *s* decd); 2nd, 1993, Hazel Elizabeth Story. *Educ:* Wolstanton Grammar Sch.; Keble Coll., Oxford (BA 1st Cl. Hons Mod. Hist.). 2nd Lieut RASC, 1955–57. Ministry of Fuel and Power, 1957–65; Civil Service Commission, 1965–67; Min. of Technology, 1968–70; Sloan Fellow, London Business Sch., 1970–71; Principal Private Sec. to Secretary of State, DTI, 1971–72; Dept of Trade, 1972–77; Dept of Industry, 1977–83; Under-Sec., 1979–; DTI, 1983–93 (Regl Dir, Yorks and Humberside, 1985–93). *Recreations:* music, tennis, chess. *Address:* 17 Foxhill Crescent, Leeds LS16 5PD. *T:* (0113) 275 4309.

WRIGHT, Eric David, CB 1975; Deputy Under-Secretary of State, Home Office, and Director-General, Prison Service, 1973–77; *b* 12 June 1917; *s* of Charles Henry and Cecelia Wright; *m* 1944, Doris (*née* Nicholls); one *s*. *Educ:* Ealing County Grammar School. Joined War Office, 1935; Principal, 1945; seconded to Dept of the Army, Australia, 1951; Asst Secretary, 1955; Command Secretary, BAOR, 1955–58; Imperial Defence College, 1964; Asst Under-Sec. of State, MoD, 1965; on loan to Home Office, Police Dept, 1970–73. Mem., Parole Bd, 1978–83. Chm., Hillingdon CHC, 1988–90. *Address:* 3 The Cedars, Dog Kennel Lane, Chorleywood, Herts WD3 5GL.

WRIGHT, Prof. Ernest Marshall, PhD, DSc; FRS 2005; Professor of Physiology, since 1974, Sherman M. Mellinkoff Distinguished Professor of Medicine, since 1999, Distinguished Professor of Physiology, since 2004, School of Medicine, University of California, Los Angeles; *b* Belfast, 8 June 1940; *m* 1961, Brenda W. Keys; two *s*. *Educ:* Chelsea Coll. of Sci. and Technol., Univ. of London (BSc Physiol. and Chem. 1961); Univ. of Sheffield (PhD Physiol. 1964); Univ. of London (DSc Physiol. 1978). Res. Fellow, Biophysics, Harvard Univ., 1965–66; University of California, Los Angeles: Asst Prof. of Physiol., 1967–70; Associate Prof. of Physiol., 1970–74; Chair, Dept of Physiol., 1987–2000. Visiting Professor: Center for Advanced Studies, Nat. Poly. Inst., Mexico City, 1973; Max Planck Inst. for Biophysics, Frankfurt, 1974–75; Queen Elizabeth Coll., London, 1977. Senator Jacob K. Javits Neurosci. Investigator, 1985–92. Horace W. Davenport Dist. Lectr, Exptl Biol. 2000, San Diego, 2000. Mem., Adv. Bd, Broad Med. Res. Prog., 2001–. Chm., Physiol. Study Section, NIH, 1983–86; Councilor: Soc. of Gen. Physiologists, 1986–89; Gastrointestinal Sect. Steering Cttee, Amer. Physiol Soc., 1999–2002. Mem. Review Panel, Structural Biol., Nat. Center of Competence in Res., Swiss Nat. Sci. Foundn, 2002–. Fellow, Biophysical Soc., 2005. Mem., German Acad. Scis Leopoldina, 2006. Award for Sustained Achievement in Digestive Scis, Janssen/Amer. Gastroenterol. Soc., 2004. *Publications:* (with M. Martin) Congenital Intestinal Transport Defects, in Pediatric Gastrointestinal Disease, 4th edn 2004; (contrib.) Sugar Absorption, in Physiology of the Gastrointestinal Tract, 4th edn 2005; numerous articles in learned jls, incl. Nature, Jl Biol Chem., Jl Membrane Biol., Jl Physiol., Biochemistry. *Address:* Department of Physiology, David Geffen School of Medicine at UCLA, 10833 Le Conte Avenue, Los Angeles, CA 90095–1751, USA. *T:* (310) 8256905, *Fax:* (310) 2065661; *e-mail:* ewright@mednet.ucla.edu.

WRIGHT, (George) Brian; JP; Head of Educational Broadcasting Services, BBC, 1989–93; *b* 9 April 1939; *s* of George Wright and Martha Blair Wright (*née* Dundee); *m* 1963, Joyce Avril Frances Camier; two *s*. *Educ:* Trinity Coll., Dublin (MA, HDipEd). Schoolmaster, 1961–67; Local Govt Administrator, 1967–69; BBC Educn Officer, Belfast, Nottingham, Birmingham, 1969–81; Chief Educn Officer, BBC, 1981–89. Occasional Lectr, Henley Management Coll., 1994–95. Mem., Lord Chancellor's Nottingham Div. Adv. Cttee, 1997–2001. Mem., City and Co. of Notts Adv. Bd, Salvation Army, 1999–2001. JP Ealing, 1992–93, Nottingham, 1993. *Publications:* How Britain Earns Its Living, 1980; (with John Cain) in a class of its own, 1994; In the Name of Decent Citizens: the trials of Frank De Groot, 2006. *Recreations:* reading, crosswords, watching Rugby. *Address:* 56 Lyndhurst Road, Chichester, W Sussex PO19 7PE. *T:* (01243) 773432.

WRIGHT, George Henry, MBE 1977; Vice-Chairman, Wales Co-operative Development Centre, since 1985 (Chairman, 1983–85); Regional Secretary, Wales, Transport and General Workers Union, 1972–99; *b* 11 July 1935; *s* of William Henry and Annie Louisa Wright; *m* 1956, Margaret Wright; two *d*. *Educ:* Tinkers Farm Sch., Birmingham. Car worker, 1954–65. T&GWU: District Officer, West Bromwich, 1966–68; District Secretary, Birmingham, 1968–72. Gen. Sec., Wales TUC, 1974–84 (Chm., 1989–90). Member: MSC Wales, 1976–88; Employment Appeal Tribunal, 1985–; Welsh Trng Adv. Gp, 1989–; Bd, Welsh Develt Agency, 1994–; Central Arbitration Cttee, Dept of Employment, 1994–; Econ. and Social Cttee, EC, 1994–; S Wales Police Authority, 1994–. *Recreations:* fishing, gardening. *Address:* 5 Kidwelly Court, Caerphilly CF83 2TY. *T:* (029) 2088 5434.

WRIGHT, Gerard; QC 1973; *b* 23 July 1929; *s* of Leo Henry and Catherine M. F. Wright; *m* 1950, Betty Mary Fenn (*d* 2001); one *s* two *d*. *Educ:* Stonyhurst Coll.; Lincoln Coll., Oxford (BA, BCL). Served in Army, 1947–49, rank T/Captain. Called to Bar, Gray's Inn, 1954 (Arden Scholar, Barstow Scholar); Northern Circuit. KHS 1974; KCHS 1979; KCSHS 1992; Auxiliaire de l'Hospitalité de Notre Dame de Lourdes, 1982, Titulaire 1985. *Publication:* Test Tube Babies—a Christian view (with others), 1984. *Recreation:* reading. *Address:* Mimiju, Portfield, Langport, Somerset TA10 0NJ.

WRIGHT, Graeme Alexander; Editor, Wisden Cricketers' Almanack, 1986–92 and 2000–02; *b* 23 April 1943; *s* of Alexander John Wright and Eileen Margaret Wright. *Educ:* St Patrick's Coll., Wellington, NZ; St Patrick's High Sch., Timaru, NZ; Univ. of Canterbury, Christchurch, NZ. Copywriter, NZ Broadcasting Corp., 1965–67; Sub-editor, BSI, 1968–69; Editor and writer, Publicare Ltd, 1969–72; Managing Editor, Queen Anne Press, 1973–74; freelance editor and writer, 1974–; cricket writer, Independent on Sunday, 1990–94; Dir, John Wisden & Co. Ltd, 1983–86. *Publications:* (with Phil Read) Phil Read, 1977; The Illustrated Handbook of Sporting Terms, 1978; Olympic Greats, 1980; (with George Best) Where do I go from here?, 1981; (with Patrick Eagar): Test Decade 1972–1982, 1982; Botham, 1985; (with Joe Brown) Brown Sauce, 1986; Merrydown: forty vintage years, 1988; Betrayal: the struggle for cricket's soul, 1993; Chelton: the first 50 years, 1997; (ed) Wisden on Bradman, 90th Birthday Edition, 1998; (ed) A Wisden Collection, 2004; (ed) Wisden at Lord's, 2005; (ed) Bradman in Wisden, 2008. *Recreations:* reading, thinking, coffee houses. *Address:* 14 Field End Road, Eastcote, Pinner, Middx HA5 2QL. *Club:* MCC.

WRIGHT, Helen Mary, EdD; Headmistress, St Mary's School, Calne, since 2003; *b* Perth, 22 Aug. 1970; *d* of Gordon Kendal and Patricia Kendal (*née* Foggo); *m* 1993, Brian Wright; one *s* one *d*. *Educ:* James Gillespie's High Sch., Edinburgh; Lincoln Coll., Oxford (BA 1992; PGCE 1993); Univ. of Leicester (MA 1998); Univ. of Exeter (EdD). French and German teacher, Reed's Sch., Cobham, 1993–95; Hd of Dept, Bishop's Stortford Coll., 1995–97; Hd of Dept and Dep. Housemistress, St Edward's Sch., Oxford, 1997–2000; Dep. Headmistress, 2000, Headmistress, 2001–03, Heathfield Sch., Ascot. Teacher-educator and PGCE mentor, 1997–2000; Examnr and Sen. Examnr (Higher Level), Internat. Baccalaureate, 1999–; Inspector, ISI, 2000–. Consultant, Scholastic Books, 1998–2001. Member: Assoc. for Language Learning, 1993–; Ind. Schs' Modern

Langs Assoc., 1993– (Mem. Cttee, 1997–2000; Ed. of Newsletter, 1997–2000; Patron, 2005–); ASCL (formerly SHA), 2000–; GSA, 2001–. FRSA 2003. Ed., Francophonie, 1999–2002. *Publications:* trans., Elizabeth Behr-Sigel, A Monk of the Eastern Church, 1999; French Fries My Brain!, 2001; Learning Through Listening, 2004; numerous articles and reviews. *Recreations:* reading, studying, travelling. *Address:* St Mary's School, Calne, Wilts SN11 0DF. *T:* (01249) 857200, *Fax:* (01249) 857207; *e-mail:* headmistress@ stmaryscalne.org. *Clubs:* University Women's, Lansdowne.

WRIGHT, Hugh Raymond, MA; Chief Master, King Edward's School, Birmingham, 1991–98; *b* 24 Aug. 1938; *s* of Rev. Raymond Blayney Wright and Alice Mary Wright (*née* Hawksworth); *m* 1962, Jillian Mary McIldowie Meiklejohn; three *s. Educ:* Kingswood Sch., Bath; The Queen's, Coll., Oxford (Bible Clerk; MA Lit. Hum.). Asst Master, Brentwood Sch., 1961–64; Cheltenham Coll., 1964–79: Hd of Classics, 1967–72; Housemaster, Boyne House, 1971–79; Headmaster: Stockport Grammar Sch., 1979–85; Gresham's School, Holt, 1985–91. Headmasters' Conference: Chm., 1995; Chm., NW Dist, 1983; Chm., Community Service Sub-Cttee, 1985–90 (Mem., 1980–90); Rep. on ISC (formerly ISJC) Europe Cttee, 1997–2001; Mem., Assisted Places Wking Pty, 1992–97. Mem., Chaplaincy Team, Shepton Mallet Prison, 2001–. Member: Bloxham Project Cttee, 1993–98 (Trustee, 1998–2006); Admty Interview Bd Panel, 1982–95; ABM (formerly ACCM), C of E, 1982–; GBA Cttee, 2000–03. Chm., Nat. Steering Cttee, Children's Univ., 1995–2001. Gov., Kingswood Sch., Bath, 1995–2006 (Chm., 1998–2006). Mem., Cttee, Friends of Bath Internat. Fest., 1995– (Chm., 2008–). *Publication:* film strips and notes on The Origins of Christianity and the Medieval Church, 1980. *Recreations:* music, theatre, hill walking, wildfowl, gardening, Rugby football. *Address:* Halfway House, 10 Woods Hill, Limpley Stoke, Bath BA2 7FZ. *Club:* East India.

WRIGHT, Iain David; MP (Lab) Hartlepool, since Sept. 2004; Parliamentary Under-Secretary of State, Department for Communities and Local Government, since 2007; *b* 9 May 1972; *m* Tiffiny; three *s* one *d. Educ:* Manor Comprehensive Sch., Hartlepool; University Coll. London (BA, MA). ACA 2003. Deloitte & Touche, 1997–2003; chartered accountant, One NorthEast, 2003–04. Mem. (Lab), Hartlepool BC, 2002–05. *Address:* (office) 23 South Road, Hartlepool TS26 9HD; House of Commons, SW1A 0AA.

WRIGHT, Prof. Jack Clifford, MA, BA; Professor of Sanskrit, 1964–96, Research Fellow, 1996–99, Research Associate, since 1999, and Professor Emeritus, since 2000, School of Oriental and African Studies, University of London; *b* 5 Dec. 1933; *s* of late Jack and Dorothy Wright, Aberdeen; *m* 1958, Hazel Chisholm (*née* Strachan), Crathes, Banchory; one *s. Educ:* Robert Gordon's Coll., Aberdeen; Univ. of Aberdeen (MA Hons in French and German, 1955); University of Zürich; Univ. of London (BA Hons in Sanskrit, 1959). Lectr in Sanskrit, 1959–64, Head, Dept of Indology and Mod. Langs and Lits of S Asia, 1970–83, SOAS, Univ. of London. *Address:* Faculty of Languages and Cultures, School of Oriental and African Studies, University of London, Thornhaugh Street, Russell Square, WC1H 0XG.

WRIGHT, Hon. James Claude, Jr; Speaker, US House of Representatives, 1987–89; Senior Political Consultant, American Income Life Insurance Co., since 1989; *b* 22 Dec. 1922; *s* of James C. Wright and Marie Wright (*née* Lyster); *m* 1972, Betty Hay; one *s* three *d* by former marr. *Educ:* Weatherford College, Univ. of Texas. Served US Army Air Force, 1941–45 (DFC, Legion of Merit). Mem., Texas Legislature, 1947–49; Mayor of Weatherford, Texas, 1950–54; Mem., US House of Representatives for Fort Worth, 1955–89; Dep. Democratic Whip to 1976; Majority Leader, 1976–87; former Mem. of Committees: Budget; Public Works and Transportation; Govt Operations; Highway Beautification (Chm.). Vis. Prof., Texas Christian Univ., 1991–. Former lay minister, Presbyterian Church. Columnist, Fort Worth Star-Telegram, 1992–. *Publications:* You and Your Congressman, 1965; The Coming Water Famine, 1966; Of Swords and Plowshares, 1968; (jtly) Congress and Conscience, 1970; Reflections of a Public Man, 1984; Worth It All, 1993; Balance of Power, 1996.

WRIGHT, James Robertson Graeme, CBE 2001; DL; Vice-Chancellor, University of Newcastle upon Tyne, 1992–2000; *b* 14 June 1939; *s* of John Wright and Elizabeth Calder (*née* Coghill); *m* 1966, Jennifer Susan Greenberg; two *d. Educ:* Inverness Royal Acad.; Dundee High Sch.; Univ. of Edinburgh (MA 1st cl. Hons Classics 1961, Guthrie Fellowship in Classical Lit., C. B. Black Scholarship in New Testament Greek); St John's Coll., Cambridge (Major Scholar, BA 1st cl. Classical Tripos Pt II 1963, MA 1968, Henry Arthur Thomas Studentship, Denney Studentship, Ferguson Scholarship in Classics, 1962). University of Edinburgh: Asst Lectr in Humanity (Latin), 1965; Lectr, 1966–78; Sen. Warden, Pollock Halls of Residence, 1973–78; Mem., Univ. Court, 1975–78; St Catharine's College, Cambridge: Fellow, 1978–87; Professorial Fellow, 1987–91; Hon. Fellow, 1992–; Dir, Studies in Classics, 1978–87; Bursar, 1979–87; Cambridge Bursar's Committee: Sec., 1983–86; Chm., 1986–87; Sec.-Gen. of Faculties, Univ. of Cambridge, 1987–91. Non-executive Member: Cambridge Dist HA, 1990–91; Northern and Yorks RHA, 1994–96. Mem. Council, CVCP, 1996–2000. Chm., Higher Educn Management Statistics Gp, 1995–2000; Mem., SHEFC, 1992–99; Associate Comr, Hamlyn Nat. Commn on Educn, 1992–93; Dir, UCAS, 1997–2000; Chm. Exec. Cttee, UKCOSA: Council for Internat. Educn, 1998–2002. British Council: Mem., CICHE, 1993–2000; Mem., CICHE Cttee 2 (Asia and Oceans Reg.), 1992–94. Dir, Newcastle Initiative, 1993–2000; Chm., Connexions Tyne & Wear, 2002–. Mem., Governing Body, Shrewsbury Sch., 1986–2000. Trustee: Nat. Heritage Meml Fund, 2000–06 (Chm., Audit Cttee, 2003–06); Homerton Coll., Cambridge, 2002–; Chm., Homerton Sch. of Health Studies, 2003–05. Age Concern England: Trustee, 2001–05, 2007–; Chm., 2002–05; Dir, Age Concern Hldgs, 2005– (Chm., 2007–). DL 1995, High Sheriff, 2003–04, Tyne and Wear. Hon. LLD Abertay Dundee, 1999; Hon. DEd Naresuan, Thailand, 2000; Hon. DCL Newcastle upon Tyne, 2001. *Publications:* articles and reviews in classical jls. *Recreations:* walking, travel in France, food, wine. *Address:* 10 Montagu Avenue, Gosforth, Newcastle upon Tyne NE3 4JH. *Clubs:* Athenæum; Northern Counties (Newcastle upon Tyne).

WRIGHT, James Roland; High Commissioner for Canada in the United Kingdom, since 2006; *b* Montreal, 19 July 1950; *s* of David Stuart Wright and Jean Gertrude Percy; *m* 1977, Donna Thomson, *d* of James Thomas and Marjorie McKeown; one *s* one *d. Educ:* McGill Univ., Montreal (BA 1972; MA 1973). Joined Dept of Foreign Affairs, Ottawa, 1976; Third Sec., Moscow, 1978–80; Soviet Desk Officer, E Europ. Div., Ottawa, 1980–83; First Sec., Washington, 1983–87; Office of the Prime Minister, Ottawa, 1987–88; Dir, Pol/Econ. Personnel Div., Ottawa, 1989–92; Minister, Pol and Public Affairs, London, 1992–96; Dir Gen., Central, E and S Europe Bureau, Ottawa, 1996–2000; Pol Dir and Asst Dep. Minister, Global and Security Br., Ottawa, 2000–04; Pol Dir and Asst Dep. Minister, Internat. Security Br., 2005–06. *Recreations:* golf, tennis, ski-ing, hiking. *Address:* Canadian High Commission, Macdonald House, 1 Grosvenor Square, W1K 4AB. *T:* (020) 7258 6328, *Fax:* (020) 7258 6303.

WRIGHT, Jeremy Paul; MP (C) Rugby and Kenilworth, since 2005; *b* 24 Oct. 1972; *s* of John and Audrey Wright; *m* 1998, Yvonne Salter; one *d. Educ:* Taunton Sch.; Trinity

Sch., NYC; Univ. of Exeter (LLB Hons). Called to the Bar, Inner Temple, 1996; in practice on Midlands and Oxford Circuit, specialising in criminal law, 1996–2005. Mem., Select Cttee on Constitutional Affairs, 2005–07. Trustee, Community Develt Fund, 2007–. *Recreations:* golf, music, cinema. *Address:* House of Commons, SW1A 0AA. *T:* (020) 7219 8299; *e-mail:* wrightjp@parliament.uk.

WRIGHT, Joe Booth, CMG 1979; HM Diplomatic Service, retired; Ambassador to Ivory Coast, Upper Volta and Niger, 1975–78; *b* 24 Aug. 1920; *s* of Joe Booth Wright and Annie Elizabeth Wright; *m* 1st, 1945, Pat (*née* Beaumont); one *s* two *d*; 2nd, 1967, Patricia Maxine (*née* Nicholls). *Educ:* King Edward VI Grammar Sch., Retford; Univ. of London. BA Hons, French. GPO, 1939–47. Served War, HM Forces: RAOC, Intelligence Corps, 1941–46. Entered Foreign Office, 1947; FO, 1947–51; Vice-Consul, Jerusalem, 1951; Consul, Munich, 1952, and Basra, 1954; Dep. Consul, Tamsui, 1956; FO, 1959–64; Consul, Surabaya, 1964; Consul, Medan, 1965–67; First Sec. (Information), Nicosia, 1968; Head of Chancery and Consul, Tunis, 1968–71; Consul-General: Hanoi, 1971–72; Geneva, 1973–75. Mem., Inst. of Linguists and Translators' Guild, 1982–. FRSA 1987. *Publications:* Francophone Black Africa Since Independence, 1981; Zaire Since Independence, 1983; Paris As It Was, 1985; Who Was the Enemy?, 1993; Security and Cooperation in Europe: the view from the East, 1993; Enlarging the European Union: risks and benefits, 1998. *Recreations:* cricket, film-going, music, Chinese painting. *Address:* 29 Brittany Road, St Leonards-on-Sea, East Sussex TN38 0RB.

WRIGHT, Captain John, DSC 1944; RN (retd); General Manager, HM Dockyard, Devonport, 1972–77; *b* 30 April 1921; *s* of Percy Robert and Lucy Ada Wright; *m* 1946, Ethel Lumley Sunderland; one *s* two *d. Educ:* Liverpool Univ. (Part I for BSc). MIET; Silver Medal, City and Guilds. Served War: RNVR, 1942; 16th Destroyer Flotilla, 1942; HMS Birmingham, 1943; HMS Diadem, 1943. Devonport Gunnery Sch., 1946; HMS Collingwood, 1948; BJSM, USA, 1951; Admiralty Surface Weapons Estabt, 1952; HMS Cumberland, 1956; Naval Ordnance Div., 1958; British Naval Staff, USA, 1960; Polaris Technical Dept, 1964; HM Dockyard, Chatham, 1968; RN retd 1972. Gen. Manager, Marconi Space and Defence Systems Ltd, Portsmouth, 1981–82; Asst Man. Dir and Gen. Manager, Marconi Underwater Systems, 1982–84. *Recreations:* fishing, gardening, golf. *Address:* The Ferns, 15 Brook Meadow, Fareham, Hants PO15 5JH. *T:* (01329) 280512.

WRIGHT, Hon. Sir (John) Michael, Kt 1990; a Judge of the High Court of Justice, Queen's Bench Division, 1990–2003; Presiding Judge, South Eastern Circuit, 1995–98; *b* 26 Oct. 1932; *s* of Prof. John George Wright, DSc, MVSc, FRCVS, and Elsie Lloyd Razey; *m* 1959, Kathleen, *er d* of F. A. Meanwell; one *s* two *d. Educ:* King's Sch., Chester; Oriel Coll., Oxford (BA Jurisprudence 1956; MA 1978; Hon. Fellow, 2000). Served Royal Artillery, 1951–53; TA, 1953–57. Called to Bar, Lincoln's Inn (Tancred Student), 1957, Bencher 1983, Treasurer, 2003–04; QC 1974; a Recorder, 1974–90; Leader, SE Circuit, 1981–83; Chm. of the Bar, 1983–84 (Vice-Chm., 1982–83). Member: Bar Council, 1972–73; Senate of the Four Inns of Court, 1973–74; Senate of the Inns of Court and the Bar, 1975–84. Mem. Supreme Court Rules Cttee, 1973–74. Legal Assessor to the Disciplinary Cttee, RCVS, 1983–90; Vice-Chm., Appeal Cttee, ICA, 1989–90. Hon. Member: American Bar Assoc.; Canadian Bar Assoc. Trustee, Thalidomide Trust, 1997–. Gov., Reigate Grammar Sch., 2004–08 (Chm. of Govs, 2004–08). *Recreations:* books, music. *Address:* Angel Shades, Angel Street, Petworth, W Sussex GU28 0BG.

WRIGHT, Sir (John) Oliver, GCMG 1981 (KCMG 1974; CMG 1964); GCVO 1978; DSC 1944; HM Diplomatic Service, retired; King of Arms, Most Distinguished Order of St Michael and St George, 1987–96; *b* 6 March 1921; *m* 1942, Lillian Marjory Osborne; three *s. Educ:* Solihull School; Christ's College, Cambridge (MA; Hon. Fellow 1981; pre-elected Master, May 1982, resigned July 1982). Served in RNVR, 1941–45. Joined HM Diplomatic Service, Nov. 1945; served: New York, 1946–47; Bucharest, 1948–50; Singapore, 1950–51; Foreign Office, 1952–54; Berlin, 1954–56; Pretoria, 1957–58. Imperial Defence College, 1959. Asst Private Sec. to Sec. of State for Foreign Affairs, 1960; Counsellor and Private Sec., 1963; Private Sec. to the Prime Minister, 1964–66 (to Rt Hon. Sir Alec Douglas-Home, and subseq. to Rt Hon. Harold Wilson); Ambassador to Denmark, 1966–69; seconded to Home Office as UK Rep. to NI Govt, Aug. 1969–March 1970; Chief Clerk, HM Diplomatic Service, 1970–72; Dep. Under-Sec. of State, FCO, 1972–75; Ambassador to Federal Republic of Germany, 1975–81; retired, then re-apptd, Ambassador to Washington, 1982–86. Director: Siemens Ltd, 1981–82; Amalgamated Metal Corp., April–July 1982; Savoy Hotel plc, 1987–94; Berkeley Hotel, 1994–96; General Technology Systems Inc., 1990–95; Enviromed plc, 1993–97. Distinguished Vis. Prof., Univ. of S Carolina, 1986–90; Clark Fellow, Cornell Univ., 1987; Lewin Vis. Prof., Washington Univ., St Louis, 1988. Pres., German Chamber of Industry and Commerce, London, 1989–92. Bd Mem., British Council, 1981–82, 1986–90. Trustee: British Museum, 1986–91; Internat. Shakespeare Globe Centre, 1986–2002; Chm., British Königswinter Conf. Steering Cttee, 1987–97; Co-Chm., Anglo-Irish Encounter, 1986–91. Gov., Reigate Grammar Sch., 1987–97 (Chm., 1990–97). Hon. DHL Univ. of Nebraska, 1983; Hon. DL Rockford Coll., Ill, 1985. Grand Cross, German Order of Merit, 1978. *Recreations:* theatre, gardening. *Address:* Burstow Hall, near Horley, Surrey RH6 9SR. *T:* (01293) 783494. *Club:* Travellers.

WRIGHT, John Robertson; Chairman: XM International Associates Ltd, since 2004; Boomer Industries, since 2007; Alphaplus Group, since 2008; *b* 10 Sept. 1941; *s* of George Alexander Wright and Jean Robertson Wright (*née* Buchanan); *m* 1971, Christine Greenshields; one *s* one *d. Educ:* Daniel Stewart's Coll., Edinburgh. ACIBS; FIBIreland. Posts with Bank of Montreal, Canada and Hong Kong, Bank of North Lagos, Nigeria, Grindlays Bank Ltd, London, Calcutta and Colombo, Clydesdale Bank Ltd, 1958–74; Vice Pres., First Interstate Bank of California, 1974–79; Asst Gen. Manager, Internat. Div., Bank of Scotland, 1979–86; Dir and CEO, Oman International Bank, 1986–93; Chief Executive and Director: Northern Bank Ltd 1993–96; Northern & National Irish Banks, 1996–97; Chief Exec. and Chief Gen. Manager, Gulf Bank KSC, Kuwait, 1997–98; Chief Exec., Clydesdale Bank plc and Yorkshire Bank, 1998–2001. Chairman: Edinburgh Fund Managers plc, 2001–02; Toughglass Ltd, 2002–06; BIC Systems Ltd, 2002–05; Claridge Ltd, Bermuda, 2006–07; EZD Ltd, 2006–07; non-executive Director: ECGD, 2001–06; Bank of N. T. Butterfield UK Ltd, 2001–; Bank of N. T. Butterfield, Bermuda, 2002–; Glasgow Univ. Retail Heritage Ltd, 2004–; Scottish Enterprise Borders, 2004–08; Alliance Housing Bank Ltd, Muscat, Oman, 2005–08; Kainos Ltd, 2006–; Derbhouse Ltd, 2006–; Sutherlands Ltd, 2006–. Director: Arab-British Chamber of Commerce, 1998–; Glasgow Chamber of Commerce, 1999–2005; Mem., Arab Financial Forum, 2005. External Mem., Audit Cttee, Scottish Borders Council, 2003–. Vis. Prof. and Mem. Adv. Bd, Glasgow Univ. Business Sch., 2005–. *Recreation:* watching Rugby. *Clubs:* New (Edinburgh); Hong Kong; Edinburgh Academicals Sports, Hong Kong Football.

WRIGHT, (John) Stephen; freelance arts consultant; Managing Director and Senior International Vice-President, IMG Artists (formerly IMG Artists Europe), 1991–2005; *b* 12 Feb. 1946; *s* of late Eustace McDonald Wright and Hilde Wright; *m* 1977, Jadwiga Maria Rapf (*d* 2007); two *s* one *d. Educ:* Dragon Sch., Oxford; Westminster; Magdalene Coll., Cambridge (Hons Mod. Langs and Law). Co-founder and Dir, Oxford and

Cambridge Shakespeare Co., 1969–71; Dir, Shawconcerts Ltd, 1971–75; Dir, later Jt Man. Dir, Harold Holt, 1975–90. *Recreations:* cricket, wine, classic cars. *Address:* 16 Pleydell Avenue, W6 0XX. *Club:* Garrick.

WRIGHT, Lester Paul; Under Secretary, Department for Culture, Media and Sport (formerly of National Heritage), 1992–99; *b* 2 July 1946; *s* of late Christopher Percy Wright and of Mary Wright (*née* Sutton); *m* 1969, Jill Wildman (*d* 2008); one *s* (and one *s* decd). *Educ:* Bedford Sch.; Gonville and Caius Coll., Cambridge (BA 1967; PhD 1971); Harvard Univ.; Open Univ. (BSc 2007). Lectr in History, Univ. of Reading, 1970–71; Home Office, 1971; Asst Private Sec. to Home Sec., 1972; Harkness Fellow, Harvard Univ. and Univ. of California at Berkeley, 1976–77; Private Sec. to Perm. Under Sec., 1980–82; Asst Sec., 1983–92. *Recreations:* music, walking, looking at pictures. *Address:* Pedn Brose, Mousehole Lane, Paul, Penzance, Cornwall TR19 6TY. *T:* (01736) 731789.

WRIGHT, Margaret; Development Executive, The Law Society, 1988–91; *b* 18 Oct. 1931; *d* of Harry Platt and Edith Baxter; *m* 1991, Bill Wright (*d* 1999). *Educ:* Bedford College, Univ. of London (BA Hons 1st Cl., History). Called to the Bar, Gray's Inn, 1956. Estate Duty Officer, Inland Revenue, 1952–63; Inst. of Professional Civil Servants, 1963–87 (Dep. Gen. Sec., 1980–87); Gen. Sec., Clearing Bank Union, 1987–88. Mem., Industrial Disputes Panel, Jersey, 1989–. *Recreations:* renovating old houses, travel, reading. *Address:* Flat 5, St James Court, The Vinefields, Bury St Edmunds, Suffolk IP33 1YD. *T:* (01284) 755399.

WRIGHT, Martin; Senior Research Fellow, Faculty of Health and Life Sciences, De Montfort University, Leicester, since 2007; Visiting Research Fellow, Sussex Law School (formerly Centre for, then School of, Legal Studies), University of Sussex, since 1995; *b* 24 April 1930; *s* of late Clifford Kent Wright and Rosalie Wright, Stoke Newington; *m* 1957, Louisa Mary Nicholls; three *s* one *d* (and one *d* decd). *Educ:* Repton; Jesus Coll., Oxford; PhD LSE, 1992. Librarian, Inst. of Criminology, Cambridge, 1964–71; Dir, Howard League for Penal Reform, 1971–81; NAVSS, later Victim Support, 1985–94: Information Officer, 1985–88; Policy Officer, 1988–94. Chm., Lambeth Mediation Service, 1989–92; Mem. Exec. Cttee, Mediation UK (formerly Forum for Initiatives in Reparation and Mediation), 1984–99; Bd Mem., European Forum for Victim/Offender Mediation and Restorative Justice, 2000–06; Vice-Chm., Restorative Justice Consortium, 2001–07. Hon. Fellow, Inst. of Conflict Resolution, Sofia, Bulgaria, 2005. *Publications:* (ed) The Use of Criminological Literature, 1974; Making Good: Prisons, Punishment and Beyond, 1982, repr. 2008; (ed jtly) Mediation and Criminal Justice, 1988; Justice for Victims and Offenders: a restorative response to crime, 1991, 2nd edn 1996; Restoring Respect for Justice, 1999, 2nd edn 2008 (trans. Polish 2005, Russian 2007). *Recreation:* suggesting improvements. *Address:* 19 Hillside Road, SW2 3HL. *T:* (020) 8671 8037.

WRIGHT, Hon. Sir Michael; *see* Wright, Hon. Sir J. M.

WRIGHT, Prof. Michael; DL; Vice-Chancellor, Canterbury Christ Church University, since 2005; *b* 24 May 1949; *s* of Gordon Huddart Wright and Nancy (*née* Murgatroyd); *m* 1971, Pamela Stothart; two *s* one *d*. *Educ:* Durham Johnston Grammar Sch.; Bearsden Acad.; Univ. of Birmingham (LLB 1969, LLM 1970). Lectr in Law, Bristol Poly., 1970–79; Hd of Dept, Glasgow Coll. of Technology, 1980–83; Asst Principal, Napier Coll., subseq. Napier Poly., 1983–92; Dep. Vice Chancellor, Napier Univ., 1992–97; Principal, Canterbury Christ Ch Coll., subseq. Canterbury Christ Ch Univ. Coll., 1997–2005. Vice Pres., Inst. of Personnel and Develt, 1991–94. Member: Kent & Medway LSC, 2001–07; Kent & Medway Economic Bd, 2005–; Dir, Kent & Medway Strategic HA, 2003–06. Comr, Duke of York's Royal Mil. Sch., 2000–. Lay Canon, Canterbury Cathedral, 2004–; Mem. Council, Rochester Cathedral, 2007–. DL Kent, 2006. CCIPD 1994; FRSA. *Publications:* Labour Law, 1974, 4th edn (with C. J. Carr) 1984; articles in legal jls. *Recreations:* choral singing, golf. *Address:* Canterbury Christ Church University, Canterbury CT1 1QU. *T:* (01227) 782200, *Fax:* (01227) 786773; *e-mail:* michael.wright@canterbury.ac.uk.

WRIGHT, Prof. Michael Thomas, FREng; Professor of Mechanical Engineering, 1990–2006, now Emeritus, and Vice Chancellor, 1996–2006, Aston University; *b* 11 April 1947; *s* of William George and Lilly May Wright; *m* 1970, Patricia Eunice Cox; one *d*. *Educ:* Sheldon Heath Sch., Birmingham; Aston Univ. (BSc 1st Cl. Hons, PhD). Sen. Mem., IEEE 1980; FIET (FIEE 1981); FREng (FEng 1988); FIMechE 1989; FIMA 1994. Apprentice, Electrical Power Engineering Co., 1969–82: Redman Heenan Froude, Heenan Drives, Linear Motors, Parsons Peebles Motors and Generators, NEI Peebles, Scottish Engineering Training Scheme; Engrg Dir, GEC Large Machines, 1982–85; Man. Dir, Molins Tobacco Machinery, 1985–87; Man. Dir, 1988–90, non-exec. Dir, 1990–97, Molins; Aston University: Vis. Prof. of Electrical Engrg, 1986–90; Head, Dept of Mech. and Elect. Engrg, 1990–92; Sen. Pro-Vice-Chancellor, 1994–96. Chairman: Aston Business Sch., 1992–93; 600 Group plc, 1993–2007. Non-executive Director: ERA Technology Ltd, 1995–2004; Birmingham Technology Ltd, 1996–2008; Aston Science Park Ltd, 1996–; ERA Foundn, 2001–02; Director: W Midlands Develt Agency, 1997–2001; James Watt Foundn, 2005–. CCMI (CIMgt 1997). *Publications:* numerous papers on electrical machines and drives in learned jls; articles on shooting and ballistics. *Recreations:* shooting, history of film, travelling, reading, classic motorcycles. *Address:* Evesmere, Weston On Avon, Stratford-upon-Avon, Warwickshire CV37 8JY.

WRIGHT, Monica Mary; *see* Grady, M. M.

WRIGHT, Nathalie Marie Daniella; *see* Lieven, N. M. D.

WRIGHT, Nicholas; playwright; *b* Cape Town, 5 July 1940; *s* of Harry and Winifred Wright. *Educ:* Rondebosch Boys' Sch.; London Acad. of Music and Dramatic Art. Casting Dir, 1967, Asst Dir, 1968, Royal Court Th.; Dir, Royal Court Th. Upstairs, 1969–70 and 1972–74; Jt Artistic Dir, Royal Court Th., 1975–77; Associate Dir, NT, 1984–89 and 1991–98. Member Board: Royal Court Th., 1992–2003; NT, 2003–; Nat. Council for Drama Trng, 2005–. *Plays:* Treetops, Riverside Studios, 1978 (George Devine Award); The Gorky Brigade, Royal Court Th., 1979; One Fine Day, Riverside Studios, 1980; The Crimes of Vautrin (after Balzac), Joint Stock, 1982; The Custom of the Country, RSC, 1983; The Desert Air, RSC, 1984; Mrs Klein, NT, 1988; Cressida, Almeida Th. at the Albery, 2000; Vincent in Brixton, NT, 2002 (Best New Play, Olivier Award); His Dark Materials (based on trilogy by Philip Pullman), NT, 2003, revived 2004; The Reporter, NT, 2007; He's Talking, NT Connections, 2008; *play adaptations:* Slave Island, RADA, 1985; Six Characters in Search of an Author, NT, 1987; Thérèse Raquin, Chichester Fest., 1990, NT, 2006; John Gabriel Borkman, NT, 1996; Naked, Almeida Th., 1998; Lulu, Almeida Th., 2001; Three Sisters, NT, 2003; *television adaptations:* Armistead Maupin's More Tales of the City, 1998; No. 1 Ladies' Detective Agency (episodes), 2007; *opera libretti:* The Little Prince (after St Exupéry), premièred by Houston Grand Opera, 2003; Buzz on the Moon, C4, 2006. The Art of the Play column, Independent on Sunday, 1993–94. *Publications:* 99 Plays, 1992; (with Richard Eyre) Changing Stages, 2000; *plays:* Five Plays (Treetops, One Fine Day, The Custom of the Country, The Desert Air, Mrs Klein), 2000; Cressida, 2000; Vincent in Brixton, 2002; His Dark Materials, 2003,

rewritten version 2004; The Reporter, 2007. *Address:* c/o Judy Daish Associates, 2 St Charles Place, W10 6EG.

WRIGHT, Sir Nicholas (Alcwyn), Kt 2006; MD, PhD, DSc; FRCS, FRCP, FRCPath; Warden, Barts and The London (formerly Bart's and The London, Queen Mary's) School of Medicine and Dentistry, Queen Mary, University of London, since 2001; Director, Histopathology Unit, London Research Institute, Cancer Research (UK) (formerly Imperial Cancer Research Fund), since 1988; *b* 24 Feb. 1943; *s* of late Glyndwr Alcwyn Wright and Hilda Lilian (*née* Jones); *m* 1966, Vera, (Ned), Matthewson; one *s* one *d*. *Educ:* Bristol Grammar Sch.; Durham Univ. (MB BS 1965); Newcastle Univ. (MD 1974; PhD 1975; DSc 1984); MA (Oxon) 1979. FRCPath 1986; MRCP 1998, FRCP 2001; FRCS 1999. University of Newcastle upon Tyne: Demonstrator in Pathology, 1966–71; Res. Fellow, 1971–74; Lectr in Pathology, 1974–76; Sen. Lectr, 1976–77; Clinical Reader in Pathology, Univ. of Oxford, 1977, Nuffield Reader, 1978; Fellow, Green Coll., Oxford, 1979–80; Prof. of Histopathology, RPMS, 1980–96; Dir of Histopathology, Hammersmith Hosp., 1980–96; Dean, RPMS, 1996–97; Clin. Dir of Path., Hammersmith Hosps NHS Trust, 1994–96; Vice Principal for Res., 1996–2001, Dep. Principal, 1997–2001, ICSM, Univ. of London; Imperial Cancer Research Fund: Asst Dir, 1988; Associate Dir, 1989; Dep. Dir, 1990; Dir of Clinical Res., 1991–96. Chm., Research for Health Charities Gp, 1994–96. Editor, Cell and Tissue Kinetics, 1980–87. President: Pathol Soc. of GB and Ireland, 2001–06; British Soc. for Gastroenterology, 2003–04 (Mem. Council, 1986, 1990). Mem. Council, RCPath, 1982, 1986, 1990. Lectures: Avery Jones, Central Middx Hosp., 1989; Kettle, RCPath, 1990; Showering, Southmead Hosp., 1991; Morson, 1991; Sir Arthur Hurst, 1997, British Soc. of Gastroenterology; Burroughs Wellcome, Yale Univ., 1993; Watson Smith, RCP, 1998; Sidney Truelove, Internat. Soc. for Inflammatory Bowel Disease, 1999; Dow, Dundee Univ., 2006. Founder FMedSci 1998. Hon. DSc: Hertfordshire, 2007; Durham, 2008; Hon. MD St Andrews, 2008. *Publications:* Introduction to Cell Population Kinetics, 1977; (ed) Psoriasis: cell proliferation, 1982; The Biology of Epithelial Cell Populations, 1984; (ed) Colorectal Cancer, 1989; (ed) Oxford Textbook of Pathology, 1991; (ed) Clinical Aspects of Cell Proliferation, 1991; (ed) Molecular Pathology of Cancer, 1993; (ed) Growth Factors and Cytokines of the Gut, 1996; (ed) The Gut as a Model for Cell Molecular Biology, 1997; papers on cell proliferation and differentiation in the gut. *Recreations:* Rugby football, cricket, military history, cooking. *Address:* Barts and The London School of Medicine and Dentistry, Turner Street, E1 2AD. *T:* (020) 7377 7600; London Research Institute, Cancer Research (UK), Lincoln's Inn Fields, WC2A 3PX. *T:* (020) 7242 0200. *Club:* Athenæum.

WRIGHT, Capt. Nicholas Peter, RN; LVO 1994; Private Secretary to the Princess Royal, since 2002; *b* 11 Nov. 1949; *s* of late Lt Comdr Edward J. Wright and Peggy Wright; *m* 1976, Venetia, *d* of Vice-Adm. Sir Stephen Ferrier Berthon, KCB; one *s* three *d*. *Educ:* Ampleforth Coll. Joined BRNC Dartmouth, 1968; served HMS Whitby and HMS Diomede, 1969–73; Flag Lt to FO Medway, 1973–75; HMS Norfolk, 1976–77; Allied Forces, Northern Europe, Oslo, 1978–80; HMS Lowestoft, 1980–82; Asst Sec. to Second Sea Lord, 1982–84; Staff of BRNC Dartmouth, 1985–87; HMS Illustrious, 1987–89; Sec. to FO Portsmouth, 1989–91; JSDC RNC Greenwich, 1991; HM Yacht Britannia, 1992–94; Sec. to ACNS, 1995–97; CSO Personnel to FONA, 1998–2000; Exec. Asst to Dep. SACLANT, Virginia, 2000–02; retd RN, 2002. *Recreations:* squash, skiing, tennis, cricket. *Address:* c/o Buckingham Palace, SW1A 1AA. *T:* (020) 7024 4199, *Fax:* (020) 7930 4180. *Club:* Jesters.

WRIGHT, Rt Rev. (Nicholas) Thomas; *see* Durham, Bishop of.

WRIGHT, Rev. Dr Nigel Goring; Principal, Spurgeon's College, since 2000; *b* Manchester, 13 May 1949; *s* of Charles Somerville Wright, MBE and Muriel Cooper Wright; *m* 1971, Judith Mary Biggin; one *s* one *d*. *Educ:* Manchester Central Grammar Sch.; Univ. of Leeds (BA 1970); Univ. of London (BD 1973); Univ. of Glasgow (MTh 1987); King's Coll., London (PhD 1994); Spurgeon's Coll. Ordained Minister, 1973; Minister, Ansdell Baptist Church, Lytham St Annes, 1973–86; Res. Fellow, Univ. of Glasgow, 1986–87; Lectr, Spurgeon's Coll., 1987–95; Sen. Minister, Altrincham Baptist Church, 1995–2000. Pres., Baptist Union of GB, 2002–03. *Publications:* You Are My God, 1982; The Church, 1983; The Radical Kingdom, 1986; The Fair Face of Evil, 1988; Challenge to Change, 1991; Charismatic Renewal, 1993; The Radical Evangelical, 1996; Power and Discipleship, 1996; Disavowing Constantine, 2000; New Baptists, New Agenda, 2002; A Theology of the Dark Side, 2003; Free Church, Free State, 2005; God on the Inside, 2006; Baptist Basics, 2008; The Real Godsend, 2009. *Recreations:* walking, reading, travel. *Address:* The Principal's Lodge, 189 South Norwood Hill, SE25 6DJ. *T:* (020) 8771 8648, (office) (020) 8653 1235, *Fax:* (020) 8771 0959; *e-mail:* n.wright@spurgeons.ac.uk.

WRIGHT, Norman Alfred; His Honour Judge Wright; a Circuit Judge, since 2006; *b* 20 Jan. 1951; *s* of late Alfred Wright and of Thea Wright (now Mason); *m* 1976, Susan Whittaker; one *s* one *d*. *Educ:* Bradford Grammar Sch.; Univ. of Liverpool (LLB 1973); College of Law. Called to the Bar, Gray's Inn, 1974 (Gerald Moody Entrance Schol. 1972; Albion Richardson Schol. 1974); in practice at the Bar, 1974–2006; Asst Recorder, 1994–99; a Recorder, 1999–2006; Liaison Judge, Burnley, Pendle and Rossendale Magistrates, 2007–. Pt-time Tutor, Univ. of Liverpool, 1974–78. *Recreations:* oenology, golf, travel. *Address:* Preston Combined Court Centre, The Law Courts, Ring Way, Preston, Lancs PR1 2LL. *Club:* Heswall Golf.

WRIGHT, Sir Oliver; *see* Wright, Sir J. O.

WRIGHT, Oliver; News Editor, The Independent, since 2008; *b* Manchester, 30 June 1973; *s* of Ian and Lydia Wright. *Educ:* Univ. of Edinburgh (MA Hons Pols and Mod. Hist.). Reporter, Sheffield Star, 1997–2000; The Times: Midlands Corresp., 2000–02; Health Corresp., 2002–04; Asst News Ed., 2004–05; Home News Ed., 2005–08. *Recreations:* walking, failing newspaper shorthand examinations. *Address:* The Independent, Independent House, 191 Marsh Wall, E14 9RS. *T:* (020) 7005 2839; *e-mail:* O.Wright@independent.co.uk. *Club:* Shoreditch House.

WRIGHT, Ven. Paul; Archdeacon of Bromley and Bexley, since 2003; *b* 12 Feb. 1954; *s* of Cecil Edwin John Wright and Bessie Wright; *m* 1981, Jill Rosemary Yvonne Rayner; two *s* one *d*. *Educ:* King's Coll., London (BD, AKC 1978); Ripon Coll., Cuddesdon; Heythrop Coll., Univ. of London (MTh 1990). Ordained deacon, 1979, priest, 1980; Curate: St George, Beckenham, 1979–83; St Mary and St Matthias, Richmond, 1983–85; Chaplain, Christ's Sch., Richmond, 1983–85; Vicar, St Augustine, Gillingham, 1985–90; Rector, St Paulinus, Crayford, 1990–99; RD, Erith, 1994–97; Vicar, St John the Evangelist, Sidcup, 1999–2003. Hon. Canon, Rochester Cathedral, 1998–2003. *Recreations:* riding my Harley-Davidson, going to the cinema, France, walking Todd the dog. *Address:* The Archdeaconry, The Glebe, Chislehurst, Kent BR7 5PX. *T:* (020) 8467 8743; *e-mail:* archdeacon.bromley@rochester.anglican.org.

WRIGHT, Prof. Paul Stanley, PhD; FDSRCS, FFGDP(UK); Professor of Prosthetic Dentistry, Barts and The London (formerly Barts and The London, Queen Mary's) School of Medicine and Dentistry, Queen Mary, University of London, since 2000 (Dean for Dentistry, 1999–2007); Consultant Adviser to the Chief Dental Officer, Department of Health, since 2007; *b* 1 May 1946; *s* of William and Eileen Wright; *m* 1970, Mary Lawrence; three *s*. *Educ:* London Hosp. Med. Coll. Dental Sch. (BDS; PhD 1980). FDSRCS 1973; FFGDP(UK) 2005. London Hospital Medical College Dental School, later Barts and The London, Queen Mary's School of Medicine and Dentistry, subseq. Barts and The London School of Medicine and Dentistry, Queen Mary, University of London: Lectr in Prosthetic Dentistry, 1972–80; Sen. Lectr in Prosthetic Dentistry, 1981–99; Hon. Consultant in Restorative Dentistry, 1982–; Specialist in Prosthodontics, 2000–. Gen. dental practitioner (pt-time), 1970–2001. Founding Ed., Eur. Jl Prosthodontics and Restorative Dentistry, 1992–2003. Chm. Council, Heads and Deans of Dental Schs, 2004–06. Pres., Eur. Prosthodontic Assoc., 2005–06. FHEA (ILTM 2002). *Publications:* (jtly) The Clinical Handling of Dental Materials, 1986, 2nd edn 1994; numerous contribs to jls. *Recreations:* swimming, ski-ing, gardening, family. *Address:* Institute of Dentistry, Barts and the London School of Medicine and Dentistry, University of London, Turner Street, E1 2AD. *T:* (020) 7882 8618, *Fax:* (020) 7377 7064; *e-mail:* p.s.wright@qmul.ac.uk.

WRIGHT, Penelope Ann, (Mrs D. C. H. Wright); *see* Boys, P. A.

WRIGHT, Peter, CBE 1988 (OBE 1982); Chief Constable, South Yorkshire Police, 1983–90; *b* Stockport, 21 July 1929; *s* of late Henry Wright and Elizabeth (*née* Burton); *m* 1950, Mary Dorothea (*née* Stanway); one *s*. *Educ:* Edgeley Roman Catholic Sch.; Stockport Technical School. RN, 1947–49. Manchester City Police, 1954, to Chief Superintendent, Greater Manchester, 1975; Asst Chief Constable, 1975–79, Dep. Chief Constable, 1979–82, Merseyside. Police Advr, MoD, 1990–93. Mem., Parole Review Cttee, 1987–88. Pres., ACPO, 1988–89. Freeman, City of London, 1992. *Recreations:* walking, gardening. *Address:* c/o South Yorkshire Police, Snig Hill, Sheffield S3 8LY.

WRIGHT, Peter; Editor, Mail on Sunday, since 1998; *b* 13 Aug. 1953; *s* of Nigel and June Wright; *m* 1974, Dorothy Manders; three *s* one *d*. *Educ:* Marlborough Coll.; Clare Coll., Cambridge (MA History). Reporter, Evening Echo, Hemel Hempstead, 1976–79; Daily Mail: Reporter, 1979; Asst News Editor, 1980–85; Associate News Editor (Foreign), 1985; Asst Features Editor, 1986–88; Femail Editor, 1988–91; Asst Editor (Features), 1991; Associate Editor, 1992–95; Dep. Editor, 1995–98. *Address:* Mail on Sunday, 2 Derry Street, W8 5TS.

WRIGHT, Peter Duncan; QC 1999; a Recorder, since 2001; Senior Treasury Counsel, Central Criminal Court, since 2006; *b* 2 Nov. 1957; *s* of Harvey Wright and Margaret Wright; *m* 1982, Stephanie Maria Mandziuk; one *s* two *d*. *Educ:* Hull Univ. (LLB Hons). Called to the Bar, Inner Temple, 1981. *Recreations:* Rugby, travel. *Address:* 2 Hare Court, Temple, EC4Y 7BH. *T:* (020) 7353 5324.

WRIGHT, Peter Malcolm; His Honour Judge Wright; a Circuit Judge, since 2006; *b* 5 June 1948; *s* of late Malcolm Wright, QC, County Court Judge and Peggy Wright (*née* Prince), BEM; *m* 1975, Eleanor Charlotte Madge; one *s* one *d*. *Educ:* Kingswood Sch., Bath; Trinity Hall, Cambridge (BA 1971). Called to the Bar, Middle Temple, 1974 (Bencher, 2005); Tenant, Queen Elizabeth Bldg, Temple, 1975–2006; specialized in family law, clinical negligence and personal injury law; Asst Recorder, Western Circuit, 1998–2000; Recorder, 2000–06. Legal Assessor, Nursing and Midwifery Council, 1994–2006. Vice-Chm., Appeal Cttee, CIMA, 2001–05. Trustee, Lambeth Palace Liby, 2002–. Gov., Kingswood Sch., Bath, 1998–. *Recreations:* walking, sailing, music, Retriever training. *Address:* Watford County Court, Cassiobury House, 11–19 Station Road, Watford WD17 1EZ.

WRIGHT, Peter Michael, FRCO(CHM); Organist and Director of Music, Southwark Cathedral, since 1989; *b* 6 March 1954; *s* of Dudley Cyril Brazier Wright and Pamela Deirdre (*née* Peacock). *Educ:* Highgate Sch. (Music Schol.); Royal Coll. of Music (Exhibnr; ARCM); Emmanuel Coll., Cambridge (Organ Schol.; MA). LRAM. Sub-Organist, Guildford Cathedral, and Music Master, Royal Grammar Sch., Guildford, 1977–89. Conductor: Guildford Chamber Choir, 1984–94; Surrey Festival Choir, 1987–2001. Freelance conductor, recitalist (organ), adjudicator and broadcaster. Royal College of Organists: Mem. Council, 1990–2002; Hon. Sec., 1997–2002; Vice-Pres., 2003–05; Pres., 2005–08; Mem. Council, Friends of Cathedral Music, 2001–04. Hon. FGCM 2000. *Recreations:* travel, theatre, reading, good food. *Address:* 52 Bankside, SE1 9JE. *T:* (020) 7261 1291.

WRIGHT, Sir Peter (Robert), Kt 1993; CBE 1985; Director Laureate, The Birmingham (formerly Sadler's Wells) Royal Ballet, since 1995 (Director, 1977–95); *b* 25 Nov. 1926; *s* of Bernard and Hilda Mary Wright; *m* 1954, Sonya Hana; one *s* one *d*. *Educ:* Bedales School; Leighton Park Sch. Dancer: Ballets Jooss, 1945–47, 1951–52; Metropolitan Ballet, 1947–49; Sadler's Wells Theatre Ballet, 1949–51, 1952–56; Ballet Master, Sadler's Wells Opera, and Teacher, Royal Ballet Sch., 1956–58; freelance choreographer and teacher, 1958–61; Ballet Master and Asst Dir, Stuttgart Ballet, 1961–63; BBC Television Producer, 1963–65; freelance choreographer, 1965–69; Associate Dir, Royal Ballet, 1969–77. Special Prof., Sch. of Performance Studies, Birmingham Univ., 1990–. Governor: Royal Ballet Sch., 1976–2002; Sadler's Wells Theatre, 1987–2001. President: Benesh Inst., 1993–; Council for Dance Educn and Trng, 1995–2000; Vice Pres., Royal Acad. of Dancing, 1995–. *Creative Works:* Ballets: A Blue Rose, 1957; The Great Peacock, 1958; Musical Chairs, 1959; The Mirror Walkers, 1962; Quintet, 1962; Namouna, 1963; Designs for Dancers, 1963; Summer's Night, 1964; Danse Macabre, 1964; Variations, 1964; Concerto, 1965; Arpege, 1974; El Amor Brujo, 1975; Summertide, 1976; own productions of classics: Giselle: Stuttgart, 1966; Staatsoper Ballett, Cologne, 1967; Royal Ballet, 1968 and 1985; Canadian National Ballet, 1970; Bavarian State Ballet, Munich, 1976; Dutch National Ballet, 1977; Houston Ballet, Texas, 1979; Staatsoper Ballett, Frankfurt, 1980; Ballet Municipale de Rio de Janeiro, Brazil, 1982; Royal Winnipeg Ballet, 1982; Star Dancers Ballet, Tokyo, 1989; Karlsruhe Ballet, 2004; The Sleeping Beauty: Staatsoper Ballett, Cologne, 1968; Royal Ballet, 1968; Bavarian State Ballet, Munich, 1974; Dutch National Ballet, 1981; Sadler's Wells Royal Ballet, 1984; Vienna State Opera Ballet, 1995; Ballet de Santiago, Chile, 2003; Coppelia: Royal Ballet Touring Co., 1976; Sadler's Wells Royal Ballet, 1979; Scottish Ballet, 1992; Star Dancers Ballet, Tokyo, 1997; Karlsruhe Ballet, 2005; Swan Lake: Sadler's Wells Royal Ballet, 1981; Bavarian State Ballet, Munich, 1984; Birmingham Royal Ballet, 1991; Royal Swedish Ballet, 2001; Nutcracker: Royal Ballet, 1984 (revised 1999); Birmingham Royal Ballet, 1990; Star Dancers Ballet, Tokyo, 1998. FBSM (Conservatoire Fellow), 1991; Fellow, Birmingham Soc., 1995. Hon. DMus London, 1990; Hon. DLitt Birmingham, 1994. Evening Standard Award for Ballet, 1982; Queen Elizabeth II Coronation Award, Royal Acad. of Dancing, 1990; Digital Premier Award, 1991; Critics Circle Award, 1995; Nat. Dance Award for Outstanding Achievement, 2004. *Recreations:* 'cello, ceramics, gardening. *Address:* 10 Chiswick Wharf, W4 2SR.

WRIGHT, Maj.-Gen. Richard Eustace John G.; *see* Gerrard-Wright.

WRIGHT, Richard Irwin V.; *see* Vane-Wright.

WRIGHT, Sir Richard (Michael) C.; *see* Cory-Wright.

WRIGHT, Rev. Canon Robert; *see* Wright, Rev. Canon A. R.

WRIGHT, (Robert) Alan, PhD; Director, Office of Manpower Economics, 2003–07; Public Sector Policy Adviser, Iron Mountain (UK), since 2007; *b* 8 Oct. 1949; *s* of late John Haig Wright and Elsie Eileen Wright (*née* Hill); *m* 1975, (Veronica) Anne Dennis. *Educ:* Moseley Grammar Sch., Birmingham; Univ. of Birmingham (BA (Medieval and Mod. Hist.) 1971; PhD 1977; PGCE). Joined Civil Service, 1975; Private Sec. to Chm. of MSC, 1982; Head: Secretariat, HSE, 1987–88; Admin, NII, 1988–91; Dir, Finance Policy, Employment Dept, 1991–94; Department of Trade and Industry: Director: Pay and Working Time, 1995–98; Coal Health Claims Unit, 1998–99; Finance, 2000–03. Mem., Perf. and Best Value Cttee, Bar Standards Bd, 2007–. *Recreations:* history, modern literature, watching cricket and Rugby. *T:* 07795 666853.

WRIGHT, Air Marshal Sir Robert (Alfred), KBE 2004; AFC 1982; FRAeS; FCMI; UK Military Representative to NATO and the European Union, 2002–06; Controller, Royal Air Force Benevolent Fund, since 2007; *b* 10 June 1947; *s* of Leslie Dominic Wright and Marjorie Wright; *m* 1970, Maggie Courtliff; one *s* one *d*. *Educ:* Maidstone Grammar Sch. FRAeS 1997. No 8 (Day Fighter Ground Attack) Sqn (Hunters), 1969–71; No 17(F) Sqn (Phantoms), 1971–74; No 1 Tactical Weapons Unit (Hunters), 1974–76; Exchange Duty, USN (Phantoms), 1976–79; No 208 Sqn (Buccaneers), 1979–82; RAF Staff Coll., 1982; Operational Requirements Div., MoD, 1982–84; Directing Staff, RAF Staff Coll., 1984–87; OC, No 9 Sqn (Tornados), Bruggen, 1987–89; PSO to CAS, 1989–91; OC, RAF Bruggen, 1992–94; Asst COS, Policy and Plans, HQ AirNorthWest, 1994–95; Air Cdre Ops, and Dep. Dir Franco British Air Gp, HQ STC, 1995–97; MA to High Rep., Sarajevo, 1997–98; COS to Air Mem. for Personnel, and Dep. C-in-C, HQ PTC, 1998–2000; Asst COS (Policy and Requirements), Supreme HQ Allied Powers in Europe, 2000–02. President: RAF Athletics Assoc., 1998–2005; RAF Winter Sports Assoc., 2003–06; Combined Services Winter Sports Assoc., 2003–06; Naval 8/208 Sqn Assoc., 2003–. FCMI 2006. *Publications:* contrib. articles to RUSI Jl. *Recreations:* golf, tennis, ski-ing, walking. *Clubs:* Royal Air Force; New (Cheltenham).

WRIGHT, Robert Anthony Kent; QC 1973; *b* 7 Jan. 1922; *s* of Robert and Eva Wright; *m* 1956, Gillian Elizabeth Drummond Hancock. *Educ:* Hilton Coll., Natal, S Africa; St Paul's Sch., London; The Queen's Coll., Oxford (MA). Indian Army, 1942–46. Oxford, 1946–48. Called to Bar, Lincoln's Inn, 1949, Bencher 1979; retired from practice, 1999. Hon. Fellow, Univ. of Central England. *Recreations:* music, walking. *Address:* 18 Parkside Avenue, SW19 5ES. *T:* (020) 8946 5978; *e-mail:* robert.wright12@btinternet.com. *Clubs:* National Liberal; Island Sailing (Cowes).

WRIGHT, Robert Douglas John; management consultant; Director, Export Control and Non-Proliferation, Department of Trade and Industry, 2004–07; *b* 2 March 1951; *s* of Douglas Norman Wright and Nora Hermione Wright (*née* Hatton-Jones); *m* 1983, Jane Clare Augier; one *s* two *d*. *Educ:* Canford Sch.; Southampton Univ. (BSc Psychol. 1973). CSD, 1975–81; attachment to Canadian Govt, Ottawa, 1981–82; Cabinet Office (Mgt and Personnel Office), 1982–85; on secondment to Hong Kong Govt, Hong Kong, 1985–88; Cabinet Office (OPSS), 1988–94; Dir, Internat. Affairs, OST, 1994–98; Department of Trade and Industry: Director: Personnel Ops, 1999–2001; Coal Policy, 2001–02; Energy Strategy, 2002–04. Gov., Bohunt Community Sch., Liphook, 2002–. *Recreations:* family, walking (Nat. Deaf Children's Soc. Cuba Trek, 2001), theatre, tennis. *Address:* Wrighthand Ltd, 65 Headley Road, Liphook, Hants GU30 7PR. *Club:* Liphook United Football.

WRIGHT, Roger; Controller, BBC Radio 3, since 1998; Director, BBC Proms, since 2007; *b* 1956; *m*; two *c*. *Educ:* Chetham's Sch., Manchester; Royal Holloway College, London Univ. (BMus 1977; Pres., Students' Union, 1977–78; Hon. Fellow, 2002). Manager, then Dir, British Music Inf. Centre, 1978–87; Sen. Producer, BBC SO, 1987–89; Artistic Administrator, Cleveland Orch., 1989–92; Exec. Producer, then Vice-Pres., Deutsche Grammophon, 1992–97; Head of Classical Music, BBC, 1997–98. FRCM 2007; Fellow, Radio Acad. *Publications* include: (with M. Finnissy) New Music 1989, 1989. *Address:* BBC, Broadcasting House, W1A 1AA.

WRIGHT, Rosalind, CB 2001; Chairman, Fraud Advisory Panel, since 2003; *b* 2 Nov. 1942; *d* of late Alfred Kerstein and of Felicie Kerstein (*née* Margulin); *m* 1966, Dr David Julian Maurice Wright; three *d*. *Educ:* University College London (LLB Hons). Called to the Bar, Middle Temple, 1964, Bencher, 2001; in practice at the Bar, 1965–69; Department of the Director of Public Prosecutions, then Crown Prosecution Service: Legal Asst, 1969–72; Sen. Legal Asst, 1972–81; Asst Dir, 1981–87 and Head of Fraud Investigation Gp (London), 1984–87; Head of Prosecutions, Securities Assoc., later SFA, 1987–94; Exec. Dir (Legal and Investor Protection Policy) and Gen. Counsel, SFA, 1994–97; Dir, Serious Fraud Office, 1997–2003. Dir, OFT, 2003–07; Mem., Supervisory Cttee, European Anti-Fraud Office, 2005– (Chm., 2005). Independent Director: BERR (formerly DTI) Legal Services Gp, 2002–; Insolvency Service Steering Bd, 2006–. Mem. of the Bar, NI, 1999–. Mem., Gen. Council of the Bar, 1998–2003. Trustee, 1999–, Vice Chm., 2003–, Jewish Assoc. for Business Ethics. Hon. QC 2006. *Recreations:* music, theatre, Jewish jokes. *Address:* Fraud Advisory Panel, Chartered Accountants Hall, PO Box 433, Moorgate Place, EC2P 2BJ. *T:* (020) 7920 8721.

WRIGHT, Roy Kilner; Deputy Editor, The London Standard (formerly Evening Standard), 1979–88; *b* 12 March 1926; *s* of Ernest Wright and Louise Wright; *m* 1st (marr. diss.); two *d*; 2nd, 1969, Jane Barnicoat (*née* Selby). *Educ:* elementary sch., St Helens, Lancs. Jun. Reporter, St Helens Reporter, 1941; Army Service; Sub-Editor: Middlesbrough Gazette, 1947; Daily Express, Manchester, 1951; Daily Mirror, London, 1952; Features Editor, Daily Express, London; Dep. Editor, Daily Express, 1976, Editor, 1976–77; Dir, Beaverbrook Newspapers, 1976–77; Senior Asst Editor, Daily Mail, 1977. *Address:* 3 The Square, Cranebridge Road, Salisbury, Wilts SP2 7TW. *T:* (01722) 414464.

WRIGHT, Rt Rev. Royston Clifford; Bishop of Monmouth, 1986–91; *b* 4 July 1922; *s* of James and Ellen Wright; *m* 1945, Barbara Joyce Nowell; one *s* one *d*. *Educ:* Univ. of Wales, Cardiff (BA 1942); St Stephen's House, Oxford. Deacon 1945, priest 1946; Curate: Bedwas, 1945–47; St John Baptist, Newport, 1947–49; Walton-on-the-Hill, Liverpool, 1949–51; Chaplain RNVR, 1950; Chaplain RN, 1951–68; Vicar of Blaenavon, Gwent, 1968–74; RD of Pontypool, 1973–74; Canon of Monmouth, 1974–77; Rector of Ebbw Vale, Gwent, 1974–77; Archdeacon of Monmouth, 1977; Archdeacon of Newport, 1977–86. *Recreations:* four grandchildren; listening to Baroque music. *Address:* 23 Rupert Brooke Drive, Newport, South Wales NP20 3HP. *T:* (01633) 250770.

WRIGHT, Hon. Ruth Margaret; *see* Richardson, Hon. R. M.

WRIGHT, Sheila Rosemary Rivers; *b* 22 March 1925; *d* of Daniel Rivers Wright and Frances Grace Wright; *m* 1949, Ronald A. Gregory; two *c.* Social Science Cert. 1951; BScSoc London External 1956. Personnel Officer, 1951–57; Social Worker, 1957–74. Councillor: Birmingham CC, 1956–78; West Midlands CC, 1973–81. MP (Lab) Birmingham, Handsworth, 1979–83. Member: Birmingham Reg. Hosp. Bd and W Midlands RHA, 1966–80; Birmingham Central DHA, 1981–90. *Address:* 249 Vicarage Road, Birmingham B14 7LZ. *T:* (0121) 444 3427.

WRIGHT, Stephen; *see* Wright, J. S.

WRIGHT, Stephen James; *see* Lowe, Stephen.

WRIGHT, Sir Stephen (John Leadbetter), KCMG 2006 (CMG 1997); HM Diplomatic Service, retired; Chief Executive, International Financial Services London, since 2008; *b* 7 Dec. 1946; *s* of late J. H. Wright, CBE and Joan Wright; *m* 1st, 1970 (marr. diss. 2000); one *s* one *d*; 2nd, 2002, Elizabeth Abbott Rosemont. *Educ:* Shrewsbury Sch.; The Queen's Coll., Oxford (BA Mod. History, 1968). HM Diplomatic Service, 1968; Havana, 1969–71; CS Coll., 1971–72; FCO, 1972–75; British Information Services, NY, 1975–80; UK Permanent Repn to EC, Brussels, 1980–84; FCO, 1984–85; seconded to Cabinet Office, 1985–87; Counsellor and Hd of Chancery, New Delhi, 1988–91; Counsellor (Ext. Relations), UK Perm. Repn to EC, Brussels, 1991–94; Asst Under Sec. of State, later Dir, EU affairs, FCO, 1994–97; Minister, Washington, 1997–99; Dir, Wider Europe, FCO, 1999–2000; Dep. Under-Sec. of State, FCO, 2000–02; Ambassador to Spain, 2003–07. *Recreations:* photography, rowing, books. *Address:* International Financial Services London, 29–30 Cornhill, EC3V 3NF; *e-mail:* wrightsjl@gmail.com.

WRIGHT, Stephen Neill; Headmaster, Merchant Taylors' School, Northwood, since 2004; *b* 4 Sept. 1956; *s* of Neill and Kathleen Wright; *m* 1985, Penelope Susan Gill; one *s* two *d. Educ:* King's Sch., Macclesfield; Queens' Coll., Cambridge (BA Hons (Hist.) 1979; PGCE 1980). Teacher, Woolverstone Hall Sch., Suffolk, 1980–83; Housemaster, Framlingham Coll., 1983–94; Dep. Headmaster, Judd Sch., Tonbridge, 1994–98; Headmaster, Borden Grammar Sch., Sittingbourne, 1998–2004. *Recreations:* village cricket, gardening. *Address:* Merchant Taylors' School, Sandy Lodge, Northwood, Middx HA6 2HT. *T:* (01923) 820644, *Fax:* (01923) 835110.

WRIGHT, Rt Rev. Thomas; *see* Durham, Bishop of.

WRIGHT, Thomas Charles Kendal Knox, CBE 2007; Chief Executive Officer, VisitBritain (formerly British Tourist Authority), since 2002; *b* 22 Feb. 1962; *s* of David Andrew Wright and Penelope Jane Wright; *m* 1986, Charlotte Annabel Mudford; one *d. Educ:* Marlborough Coll.; Ealing Coll. (BA Hons Business Studies 1985). Dip. Market Res.; DipM. Graduate trainee, various marketing roles, United Biscuits, 1981–87; Gp Product Manager, British Tissues, 1987–89; Gp Marketing Manager, Anchor Foods, 1989–95; R&D Dir, Carlsberg-Tetley, 1995–96; Sales and Marketing Dir, Center Parcs (UK), 1996–98; Marketing, Sales and Develt Dir, Center Parcs (NV), 1998–99; Man. Dir, Saga Holidays, 1999–2002; Dir, Saga Gp, 1999–2002. Director: VisitLondon (formerly London Tourist Bd), 2002–; SW Tourism, 2003–. Chm., Soc. of Ticket Agents and Retailers, 2002–; Dir, European Travel Commn, 2004–. Trustee, Imperial War Mus., 2004–. *Recreations:* running, walking, golf, motor racing, travel. *Address:* VisitBritain, Thames Tower, Black's Road, W6 9EL. *T:* (020) 8563 3031, *Fax:* (020) 8748 0123; *e-mail:* tom.wright@visitbritain.org.

WRIGHT, Rt Rev. Dom Timothy Martin, OSB; Abbot of Ampleforth, 1997–2005; *b* 13 April 1942; *s* of Monty Wright and Marjorie (*née* Brook). *Educ:* Ampleforth Coll.; St Benet's Hall, Oxford (MA); London Univ. (BD (ext.) 1972). Ordained priest, 1972; Master of Ceremonies, 1971–80, Jun. Master, 1985–88, Ampleforth Abbey; Appeal Dir, Ampleforth Abbey Trust, 1994–97. Ampleforth College: Head of Religious Studies, 1977–91; Housemaster, 1980–97; Dep. Head, 1988–97. Member, Religious Studies Panel: Midland Examining Gp, 1984–96; Univ. of Cambridge Local Exams Syndicate, 1988–94; SEAC, 1988–93. Mem., Abbey Farm Bd, 1985–97. Governor: Bar Convent Direct Grant Sch., York, 1980–85; All Saints RC Comprehensive Sch., York, 1985–96; Westminster Cathedral Choir Sch., 1995–2007. *Publications:* The Eucharist, 1988; Jesus Christ, the Way, the Truth and the Life, 1994; (jtly) Doing Business with Benedict, 2002; papers on Islamic-Catholic dialogue and religious freedom. *Recreations:* sport, travel, cycling. *Address:* Ampleforth Abbey, York YO62 4EN. *T:* (01439) 766700.

WRIGHTSON, Sir (Charles) Mark (Garmondsway), 4th Bt *cr* 1900; Chairman, Close Brothers Corporate Finance Ltd, 1999–2006 (Managing Director, 1996–99); *b* 18 Feb. 1951; *s* of Sir John Garmondsway Wrightson, 3rd Bt, TD, and Hon. Rosemary (*d* 1998), *y d* of 1st Viscount Dawson of Penn, GCVO, KCB, KCMG, PC; *S* father, 1983; *m* 1975, Stella Virginia, *d* of late George Dean; three *s. Educ:* Eton; Queens' Coll., Cambridge (BA 1972). Called to the Bar, Middle Temple, 1974. Hill Samuel & Co. Ltd, 1977–96 (Dir, 1984–96). *Heir: s* Barnaby Thomas Garmondsway Wrightson, *b* 5 Aug. 1979. *Address:* 39 Westbourne Park Road, W2 5QD.

WRIGHTSON, Prof. Keith Edwin, PhD; FRHistS; FBA 1996; Professor of History, Yale University, since 1999; *b* 22 March 1948; *s* of Robert Wrightson and Evelyn Wrightson (*née* Atkinson); *m* 1972, Eva Mikušová; one *s* one *d. Educ:* Dame Allan's Boys' Sch., Newcastle upon Tyne; Fitzwilliam Coll., Cambridge (BA 1970; MA 1974; PhD 1974). FRHistS 1986. Research Fellow in Hist., Fitzwilliam Coll., Cambridge, 1972–75; Lectr in Modern Hist., Univ. of St Andrews, 1975–84; University of Cambridge: Univ. Lectr in Hist., 1984–93; Reader in English Social Hist., 1993–98; Prof. of Social Hist., 1998–99; Fellow, Jesus Coll., 1984–99. Visiting Professor: Univ. of Toronto, 1984, 1992; Univ. of Alberta, 1988; Centre for Northern Studies, Northumbria Univ., 2003–08. *Publications:* (with D. Levine) Poverty and Piety in an English Village, 1979, 2nd edn 1995; English Society 1580–1680, 1982; (ed jtly) The World We Have Gained, 1986; (with D. Levine) The Making of an Industrial Society, 1992; Earthly Necessities: economic lives in early modern Britain, 2000; numerous essays and articles on English social history. *Recreation:* modern jazz. *Address:* Department of History, Yale University, PO Box 208324, New Haven, CT 06520–8324, USA.

WRIGHTSON, Sir Mark; *see* Wrightson, Sir C. M. G.

WRIGLEY, Prof. Christopher John, PhD; Professor of Modern British History, since 1991, and Head of the School of History and Art History, 2000–03, Nottingham University; *b* 18 Aug. 1947; *s* of late Arthur Wrigley and Eileen Sylvia Wrigley; *m* 1987, Margaret Walsh. *Educ:* Goldsworth Primary Sch., Woking; Kingston Grammar Sch.; Univ. of E Anglia (BA 1968); Birkbeck Coll., London (PhD 1973). Lecturer in Econ. and Social Hist., QUB, 1971–72; Loughborough University: Lectr in Econ. Hist., 1972–78; Sen. Lectr, 1978–84; Reader, 1984–88; Reader in Econ. Hist., Nottingham Univ., 1988–91. Team Assessor (Hist.), Teaching Quality Assessment, HEFCE, 1993–94; Mem., Hist. Panel, HEFCE RAE, 1997, 2001; Coll. Mem. (Hist.), ESRC, 2002–05. Ed., The Historian, 1993–98. Member of Council: Historical Assoc., 1980–2007 (Pres., 1996–99); Econ. Hist. Soc., 1983–92, 1994–2000 and 2002–08; a Vice-Pres., RHistS, 1997–2001; Exec. Mem., Soc. for Study of Labour, 1983–2005 (Vice Chm., 1993–97; Chm., 1997–2001). Mem. (Lab) Leics CC, 1981–89 (Labour Chief Whip, 1985–86; Leader, Labour Gp, 1986–89); Mem. (Lab) Charnwood BC, 1983–87 (Dep. Leader, Labour Gp). Contested: (Lab) Blaby, 1983; (Lab and Co-op) Loughborough, 1987. CMILT (MILT 2000); AcSS 2001. Hon. LittD E Anglia, 1998. *Publications:* (ed jtly) The Working Class in Victorian Britain, 4 vols, 1973; David Lloyd George and the British Labour Movement, 1976, 2nd edn 1992; A. J. P. Taylor: a complete bibliography, 1980; (ed) A History of British Industrial Relations: Vol. 1: 1875–1914, 1982; Vol. 2: 1914–1939, 1986, 2nd edn 1992; Vol. 3: 1939–1979, 1996; (ed) William Barnes: the Dorset poet, 1984; (ed) Warfare, Diplomacy and Politics, 1986; Arthur Henderson, 1990; Lloyd George and the Challenge of Labour, 1990; (ed jtly) On the Move, 1991; Lloyd George, 1992; (ed) Challenges of Labour, 1993; (ed) A. J. P. Taylor: From Napoleon to the Second International, 1993; (ed) A. J. P. Taylor: From the Boer War to the Cold War, 1995; (jtly) An Atlas of Industrial Protest in Britain 1750–1990, 1996; (ed) British Trade Unionism 1945–95, 1997; (ed) A. J. P. Taylor: British Prime Ministers and other essays, 1999; (ed) A. J. P. Taylor: Struggles for Diplomacy: diplomatic essays, 2000; (ed) The First World War and the International Economy, 2000; Churchill: a biographical dictionary, 2002; British Trade Unions since 1933, 2002; (ed) A Companion to Early Twentieth-Century Britain, 2003; (ed jtly) The Emergence of European Trade Unionism, 2004; A. J. P. Taylor: radical historian of Europe, 2006; Churchill, 2006. *Recreations:* swimming, music, visiting art galleries, reading even more history. *Address:* School of History, Nottingham University, Nottingham NG7 2RD. *T:* (0115) 951 5945, *Fax:* (0115) 951 5948; *e-mail:* chris.wrigley@nottingham.ac.uk; (home) 124 Musters Road, West Bridgford, Nottingham NG2 7PW.

WRIGLEY, Sir Edward Anthony, (Sir Tony), Kt 1996; PhD; FBA 1980; Master of Corpus Christi College, Cambridge, 1994–2000; President, British Academy, 1997–2001; *b* 17 Aug. 1931; *s* of Edward Ernest Wrigley and Jessie Elizabeth Wrigley; *m* 1960, Maria Laura Spelberg; one *s* three *d. Educ:* King's Sch., Macclesfield; Peterhouse, Cambridge (MA, PhD). William Volker Res. Fellow, Univ. of Chicago, 1953–54; Lectr in Geography, Cambridge, 1958–74; Peterhouse, Cambridge: Fellow, 1958–74, Hon. Fellow, 1997; Tutor, 1962–64; Sen. Bursar, 1964–74; Co-Dir, Cambridge Gp for History of Population and Social Structure, 1974–94; Prof. of Population Studies, LSE, 1979–88; Sen. Res. Fellow, 1988–94, Dist. Fellow, 2002–05, Academic Sec., 1992–94, All Souls Coll., Oxford; Prof. of Econ. History, Univ. of Cambridge, 1994–97. Pres., Manchester Coll., Oxford, 1987–96. Mem., Inst. for Advanced Study, Princeton, 1970–71; Hinkley Vis. Prof., Johns Hopkins Univ., 1975; Tinbergen Vis. Prof., Erasmus Univ., Rotterdam, 1979. President: British Soc. for Population Studies, 1977–79; Econ. History Soc., 1995–98; Chm., Population Investigation Cttee, 1984–90; Treas., British Acad., 1989–95. Chm., Newton Trust, 2000–07. Editor, Economic History Review, 1986–92. Mem., Amer. Philosophical Soc., 2001; Hon. Foreign Mem., Amer. Acad. of Arts and Scis, 2001. Hon. LittD: Manchester, 1997; Sheffield, 1997; Bristol, 1998; London, 2004; Hon. DLitt: Oxford, 1999; Leicester, 1999; Hon. DSc Edinburgh, 1998. IUSSP Laureate, 1993; Founder's Medal, RGS, 1997; Leverhulme Medal, British Acad., 2005. *Publications:* Industrial Growth and Population Change, 1961; (ed) English Historical Demography, 1966; Population and History, 1969; (ed) Nineteenth Century Society, 1972; (ed) Identifying People in the Past, 1973; (ed with P. Abrams) Towns in Societies, 1978; (with R. S. Schofield) Population History of England, 1981; (ed jtly) The Works of Thomas Robert Malthus, 1986; People, Cities and Wealth, 1987; Continuity, Chance and Change, 1988; (ed with R. A. Church) The Industrial Revolutions, 1994; (jtly) English Population History from Family Reconstitution, 1997; Poverty, Progress and Population, 2004. *Recreation:* gardening. *Address:* 13 Sedley Taylor Road, Cambridge CB2 2PW. *T:* (01223) 247614.

WRIGLEY, Prof. Jack, CBE 1977; Professor of Education, 1967–88, and Deputy Vice-Chancellor, 1982–88, University of Reading, now Professor Emeritus; *b* 8 March 1923; *s* of Harry and Ethel Wrigley; *m* 1946, Edith Baron; two *s. Educ:* Oldham High Sch.; Manchester Univ. BSc, MEd (Manch.); PhD (Queen's, Belfast). Asst Mathematics Teacher: Stretford Grammar Sch., 1946–47; Chadderton Grammar Sch., 1948–50; Research Asst, Manchester Univ., 1950–51; Lectr in Educn: Queen's Univ., Belfast, 1951–57; Univ. of London Inst. of Educn, 1957–62; Research Adviser, Curriculum Study Gp in Min. of Educn, 1962–63; Prof. of Educn, Univ. of Southampton, 1963–67; Dir of Studies, Schools Council, 1967–75. Member: Bullock Cttee on Teaching of Reading and other uses of English, 1972–74; SSRC, Mem. Council and Chm. Educnl Res. Bd, 1976–81. Specialist Adviser, H of C Select Cttee on Educn, Sci., and Arts, 1989–90. *Publications:* (ed) The Dissemination of Curriculum Development, 1976; Values and Evaluation in Education, 1980; contrib. learned jls. *Recreations:* chess (Ulster Chess Champion, 1957), theatre, foreign travel. *Address:* Valley Crest, Thrushwood, Keswick, Cumbria CA12 4PG. *T:* (017687) 71146.

WRIGLEY, Sir Tony; *see* Wrigley, Sir E. A.

WRINTMORE, His Honour Eric George; a Circuit Judge, 1984–2000; *b* 11 June 1928; *s* of Rev. F. H. and Muriel Wrintmore; *m* 1951, Jean Blackburn; two *s* one *d. Educ:* Stationers' Company's Sch.; King's Coll. London (LLB Hons). Called to Bar, Gray's Inn, 1955; full-time Chm., Industrial Tribunals, 1971; Regional Chm., Industrial Tribunals, 1976–84; a Dep. Circuit Judge, 1980–83; a Recorder, 1983–84. *Recreations:* sailing, golf. *Club:* Chichester Yacht.

WRIXON-BECHER, Sir John William Michael; *see* Becher.

WROATH, His Honour John Herbert; a Circuit Judge, 1984–97; *b* 24 July 1932; *s* of Stanley Wroath and Ruth Ellen Wroath; *m* 1959, Mary Bridget Byrne; two *s* one *d. Educ:* Ryde Sch., Ryde, IoW. Admitted Solicitor, 1956; private practice, 1958–66; Registrar, Isle of Wight County Court, 1965; County Prosecuting Solicitor, 1966; full-time County Court Registrar, 1972; a Recorder of the Crown Court, 1978–84. Chm., Independent Schs Tribunal, 1998–2003. *Recreations:* sailing, bowling, reading, painting. *Address:* 8 Tides Reach, Birmingham Road, Cowes, Isle of Wight PO31 7NU. *T:* (01983) 293072. *Clubs:* Royal London Yacht, Island Sailing (Cowes).

WROE, David Charles Lynn, CB 1995; consultant; Special Adviser to the European Commission, 1998–99; *b* 20 Feb. 1942; *m* 1966, Susan Higgitt; three *d. Educ:* Reigate Grammar Sch.; Trinity Coll., Cambridge (MA); Trinity Coll., Oxford (Cert. Statistics); Birkbeck Coll., London (MSc). Min. of Pensions and National Insurance, 1965–68; Central Statistical Office, 1968–70, 1973–75, 1976–82; secondment to Zambian Govt, 1971–72; Secretariat of Royal Commission on Distribution of Income and Wealth, 1975–76; Under Sec., Regional Policy Directorate, 1982–86, Dir of Stats, 1982–91, Under Sec., Housing Monitoring and Analysis, 1986–91, DoE; Dep. Dir, CSO, 1991–96 (Actg Dir, April–June 1996). Mem., Adv. Bd, UK Centre for Measurement of Govt Activity, 2005–. Non-exec. Dir, John Laing Construction Ltd, 1994–96. Vice Pres., Royal Statistical Soc., 1995–98 (Mem. Council, 1993–98). Trustee: Community Links (formerly Bromley Centre for Voluntary Service), 1999–2005; Bromley Voluntary Sector Trust, 2000–03. *Recreations:* sailing, walking.

WRONG, Henry Lewellys Barker, CBE 1986; Director, Barbican Centre, 1970–90; *b* Toronto, Canada, 20 April 1930; *s* of Henry Arkel Wrong and Jean Barker Wrong; *m* 1966, Penelope Hamilton Norman; two *s* one *d*. *Educ:* Trinity Coll., Univ. of Toronto (BA). Stage and business administration, Metropolitan Opera Assoc., New York, 1952–64; Director Programming, National Arts Center, Ottawa, 1964–68; Dir, Festival Canada Centennial Programme, 1967; Chm., Spencer House (St James's) Ltd, 1989–92; Dir, European Arts Foundn, 1990–95. Member: Royal Opera House Trust, 1989–95; Adv. Cttee, ADAPT (Access for Disabled People to Arts Premises Today). Trustee: Henry Moore Foundn, 1990–; LSO, 1990–; Royal Fine Art Commn, 1995–2003; Governor, Compton Verney House Trust, 1995–. Liveryman, Fishmongers' Co., 1987. FRSA 1988. Hon. DLitt City, 1985. Pro cultura Hungarica, 1989. Centennial Medal, Govt of Canada, 1967; Chevalier, Ordre Nat. du Mérite (France), 1985 (Officier, 1985). *Address:* Yew Tree House, Much Hadham, Herts SG10 6AJ. *T:* (01279) 842106. *Clubs:* White's; Badminton and Rackets (Toronto).

WRONG, Prof. Oliver Murray, DM; FRCP, FRCPE; Professor of Medicine, University College London, 1972–90, now Emeritus Professor; *b* 7 Feb. 1925; *s* of Edward Murray Wrong and Rosalind Grace Wrong (*née* Smith); *m* 1956, Marilda Musacchio; two *d* (and one *d* decd). *Educ:* Upper Canada Coll., Toronto; Edinburgh Acad.; Magdalen Coll., Oxford (Demy; BM BCh 1947; DM 1964). FRCP 1968; FRCPE 1970. Junior hosp. appts, Oxford, 1947–51; RAMC, MO Singapore and Malaya, 1948–50; Toronto Gen. Hosp., 1951–52; Mass. Gen. Hosp., Boston, 1952–53; Univ. Tutor in Medicine, Manchester, 1954–58; Lectr and Sen. Lectr in Medicine, RPMS, 1961–69; Prof. of Medicine, Univ. of Dundee, 1969–72; Dir, Dept of Medicine, UCL, 1972–82. Teale Lectr, RCP, 1971; James Howard Means Vis. Physician, Mass. Gen. Hosp., 1974; Vis. Prof., Harvard and Sherbrooke Med. Schs, 1974; Toronto and McGill Med. Schs, 1976. Chm., Nat. Kidney Res. Fund, 1976–80. *Publications:* (with C. J. Edmonds and V. S. Chadwick) The Large Intestine: its role in mammalian nutrition and homeostasis, 1981; articles in med. jls on salt and water metabolism, kidney function, the large intestine. *Recreations:* nature, travel, music (esp. baroque). *Address:* Flat 8, 96–100 New Cavendish Street, W1W 6XN. *T:* (020) 7637 4740; School House, West Dean, Salisbury, Wilts SP5 1JQ; *e-mail:* oliverwrong@aol.com.

WROTTESLEY, family name of **Baron Wrottesley**.

WROTTESLEY, 6th Baron *cr* 1838; **Clifton Hugh Lancelot de Verdon Wrottesley;** Bt 1642; in finance, since 2000; *b* 10 Aug. 1968; *s* of Hon. Richard Francis Gerard Wrottesley (*d* 1970) (2nd *s* of 5th Baron) and of Georgina Anne (who *m* 1982, Lt-Col Jonathan L. Seddon-Brown), *er d* of Lt-Col Peter Thomas Clifton, CVO, DSO; *S* grandfather, 1977; *m* 2001, Sascha, *d* of Urs Schwarzenbach; two *s*. *Educ:* Eton; Edinburgh Univ. Commnd 1st Bn Grenadier Guards, 1990; Lieut, 1993, Capt. 1994; retd, 1995. *Heir: s* Hon. Victor Ernst Francis de Verdon Wrottesley, *b* 28 Jan. 2004. *Address:* C. Hoare & Co., 32 Lowndes Street, SW1X 9HZ. *Clubs:* White's, Turf, Cavalry and Guards; St Moritz Tobogganing; Corviglia Ski.

WROUGHTON, Sir Philip (Lavallin), KCVO 2008; Lord-Lieutenant of Berkshire, 1995–2008; Chairman and Chief Executive, C. T. Bowring & Co. Ltd, 1988–96; *b* 19 April 1933; *s* of Michael Lavallin Wroughton and Elizabeth Angela Wroughton (*née* Rate); *m* 1957, Catriona Henrietta Ishbel MacLeod; two *d*. *Educ:* Eton Coll. Nat. Service, 1951–53, 2nd Lieut KRRC. Price Forbes & Co. Ltd, 1954–61; C. T. Bowring & Co. Ltd, 1961–96; Dir, Marsh & McLennan Cos, Inc., 1988–96 (Vice Chm., 1994–96); Chm., Venton Underwriting Agencies Ltd, 1996–99. Mem., Council of Lloyds, 1992–95. President: Newbury & Dist Agricl Soc., 1985–86; Berks Community Foundn, 1995–2008; SE RFCA, 2000–04; South of England Agricl Soc., 2008–09. Trustee, 1991–2000, Vice-Pres., 2000–, Princess Royal Trust for Carers; Trustee, Prince Philip Trust, 1995–2008. Gov., St Mary's Sch., Wantage, 1986–2006. High Sheriff, Berks, 1977; DL Berks, 1994. Hon. LLD Reading, 2004. KStJ (Pres., Council of St John, Berks, 1995–2008). *Recreations:* shooting, racing. *Address:* Woolley Park, Wantage OX12 8NJ. *T:* (01488) 638214. *Club:* White's.

WU, Prof. Duncan, DPhil; Professor of English, Georgetown University, Washington, since 2007; *b* 3 Nov. 1961; *s* of Spencer Yin-Cheung Wu and Mary (*née* Sadler); *m* 1997, Caroline Beatrice Carey (marr. diss. 2008). *Educ:* St Catherine's Coll., Oxford (MA; DPhil 1990). British Acad. Postdoctoral Res. Fellow, 1991–94; Reader in English Lit., 1995–98, Prof. of English Lit., 1998–2000, Univ. of Glasgow; Lectr in English Lit., 2000–03, Prof. of English Lang. and Lit., 2003–07, Univ. of Oxford; Fellow, St Catherine's Coll., Oxford, 2000–07. Trustee: Charles Lamb Soc., 1991–; Keats-Shelley Meml Assoc., 1998–. *Publications:* Wordsworth's Reading 1770–1799, 1993; (ed with S. Gill) Wordsworth: a selection of his finest poems, 1994; Romanticism: an anthology, 1994, 3rd edn 2005; Six Contemporary Dramatists: Bennett, Potter, Gray, Brenton, Hare, Ayckbourn, 1995; Romanticism: a critical reader, 1995; Wordsworth's Reading 1800–1815, 1996; William Wordsworth: the Five-Book Prelude, 1997; Women Romantic Poets: an anthology, 1997; A Companion to Romanticism, 1998; William Hazlitt, The Plain Speaker: key essays, 1998; The Selected Writings of William Hazlitt, 1998; Making Plays: interviews with contemporary British dramatists and directors, 2000; Wordsworth: an inner life, 2002; (ed with M. Demata) British Romanticism and the Edinburgh Review, 2002; The Blackwell Essential Literature Series, 7 vols, 2002; William Wordsworth: the earliest poems 1785–1790, 2002; Wordsworth's Poets, 2003; (ed jtly) Metaphysical Hazlitt: bicentenary essays, 2005; New Writings of William Hazlitt, 2007; Hazlitt: the first modern man, 2008. *Recreations:* jazz, walking. *Address:* Department of English, 306 New North, Georgetown University, Washington, DC 20057–1131, USA; *e-mail:* dw252@georgetown.edu. *Club:* Oxford and Cambridge.

WU, Sir Gordon (Ying Sheung), GBS 2004; KCMG 1997; Chairman, Hopewell Holdings Group, since 1972 (Managing Director, 1972–2001); *b* Hong Kong, 3 Dec. 1935; *s* of Chung Wu and Sum Wu (*née* Chang); *m* 1970, Kwok, (Ivy), San-Ping; two *s* two *d*. *Educ:* Princeton Univ. (BS Civil Engrg 1958). Architect; civil engr. Founder: Central Enterprises Co. Ltd, 1962; Gordon Wu and Associates, 1962; Hopewell Construction Co. Ltd, 1963; Hopewell Hldgs Ltd, 1972; Consolidated Electric Power Asia Ltd, 1993. *Projects* include: Hopewell Centre, Hong Kong (66 storey building); China Hotel, Guangdong, China; Shajiao B and C (coal-fired power stations), Guangdong, China; G-S-Z Superhighway (motorway linking Hong Kong and China), 1994–. Vice Pres., Hong Kong Real Estate Developer's Assoc., 1970–; Mem., Chinese People's Political Consultative Conf., 1984–. *Address:* Hopewell Holdings Ltd, 64th Floor, Hopewell Centre, 183 Queen's Road East, Hong Kong.

WULF-MATHIES, Dr Monika; Executive Vice President (formerly Managing Director), Corporate Public Policy and Sustainability (formerly Managing Director, Policy and Environment), Deutsche Post World Net, since 2001; *b* 17 March 1942; *d* of Carl-Hermann Baier and Margott Meisser; *m* 1968, Dr Carsten Wulf-Mathies. *Educ:* Univ. of Hamburg (DrPhil 1968). Br. Asst, Federal Ministry of Econs, Germany, 1968–71; Hd, Dept for Social Policy, Federal Chancellery, 1971–76; joined Gewerkschaft Öffentliche Dienste, Transport und Verkehr (Public Services and Transport Workers' Union), 1971; Mem., Man. Exec. Cttee, 1976–95; Chm., 1982–95; Mem., European Commn, 1995–99. *Recreation:* garden. *Address:* Deutsche Post AG, Zentrale, 53250 Bonn, Germany.

WULSTAN, Prof. David; Research Professor, Aberystwyth University (formerly University of Wales, Aberystwyth), since 1990; *b* 18 Jan. 1937; *s* of Rev. Norman and (Sarah) Margaret Jones; *m* 1965, Susan Nelson Graham; one *s*. *Educ:* Royal Masonic Sch., Bushey; Coll. of Technology, Birmingham; Magdalen Coll., Oxford (Academical Clerk, 1960; Burrowes Exhibr, 1961; Mackinnon Sen. Schol., 1963; Fellow by examination, 1964). MA, BSc, BLitt; ARCM. Lectr in History of Music, Magdalen Coll., Oxford, 1968–78; also at St Hilda's and St Catherine's Colls; Vis. Prof., Depts of Near Eastern Studies and Music, Univ. of California, Berkeley, 1977; Statutory (Sen. Lectr), University Coll., Cork, 1979, Prof. of Music, 1980–83; Gregynog Prof. of Music, UCW, Aberystwyth, 1983–90. Mem. Council, Plainsong and Mediaeval Music Soc. Dir, Clerkes of Oxenford (founded 1961); appearances at Cheltenham, Aldeburgh, York, Bath, Flanders, Holland, Krakow, Zagreb, Belgrade Fests, BBC Proms; many broadcasts and TV appearances, gramophone recordings; also broadcast talks, BBC and abroad. Fellow, Royal Soc. of Musicians, 2001. Hon. Fellow, St Peter's Coll., Oxford, 2007. Consulting Ed., Spanish Academic Press. *Publications:* Septem Discrimina Vocum, 1983; Tudor Music, 1985; Musical Language, 1992; The Emperor's Old Clothes, 1994, 2nd edn 2001; The Poetic and Musical Legacy of Heloise and Abelard, 2003; Music from the Paraclete, 2004; editor: Gibbons, Church Music, Early English Church Music, vol. 3, 1964, vol. 27, 1979; Anthology of Carols, 1968; Anthology of English Church Music, 1971; Play of Daniel, 1976, 3rd edn 2008; Victoria, Requiem, 1977; Tallis, Puer Natus Mass, 1977; Coverdale Chant Book, 1978; Sheppard, Complete Works, 1979–; Weelkes, Ninth Service, 1980; many edns of anthems, services etc; entries in Encyclopédie de Musique Sacrée, 1970; chapter in A History of Western Music, ed Sternfeld, 1970; chapters in Cobras e Som, 2001; contrib. periodicals and learned jls incl. Plainsong and Medieval Music, Music and Letters, Early Music, Jl of Theol Studies, Jl of Semitic Studies, Iraq, Jl of the Amer. Oriental Soc., English Histl Review, Notes, al-Masāq, Bull. of Cantigueiros of Santa Maria, Faith and Worship, The Consort, Prayer Bk Soc. Jl. *Recreations:* badminton, tennis, cooking, eating, aikido, self-defence (instructor), being politically incorrect, bemoaning the decline of the English language. *Address:* Hillview Croft, Lon Tyllwyd, Llanfarian, Aberystwyth, Cardiganshire SY23 4UH. *T:* (01970) 617832; *e-mail:* dww@aber.ac.uk.

WULWIK, Peter David; His Honour Judge Wulwik; a Circuit Judge, since 2004; *b* 15 Sept. 1950; *s* of Eddie and Mona Wulwik; *m* 1975, Joanna Rosenberg; two *s* one *d*. *Educ:* St Marylebone Grammar Sch.; Univ. of London (LLB Hons ext.). Called to the Bar, Gray's Inn, 1972; Asst Recorder, 1995–2000; a Recorder, 2000–04. Part-time Chairman: London Rent Assessment Panel and Leasehold Valuation Tribunal, 1999–2004; Consumer Credit and Estate Agents Appeals Panel, 2003–. Pres., Consumer Credit Appeals Tribunal, 2008–. *Publications:* (contrib.) Bennion's Consumer Credit Law Reports, 1990–2000; (contrib.) Goode's Consumer Credit Reports, 2000–04. *Recreations:* reading, theatre, classical music, antique fairs, playing bridge, tennis, golf, watching Tottenham Hotspur. *Clubs:* Radlett Lawn Tennis and Squash; Elstree Lawn Tennis.

WURTH, Hubert; Ambassador of Luxembourg to the Court of St James's, and concurrently to Ireland and Iceland, since 2007; *b* Luxembourg, 15 April 1952; *s* of Ernest Wurth and Denise Wurth (*née* Conrath); *m* 1998, Francisca Passchier; two *d*. *Educ:* Univ. of Paris II (law degree 1975); Inst. of Political Studies, Paris (Dip. Internat. Relns 1976). Min. of Foreign Affairs, Luxembourg, 1978–89; Ambassador: to USSR, Poland, Finland and Mongolia, 1988–91; to Netherlands, 1991–98; Ambassador and Perm. Rep. to UN, NY, 1998–2003; Ambassador to France, OECD and UNESCO, 2003–07. Ambassador, Special Mission for Former Yugoslavia, 1996–98. *Recreations:* painter (self-taught), various exhibitions (incl. 'Dark', EU Commn Gall., London, 2008) and publications. *Address:* Luxembourg Embassy, 27 Wilton Crescent, SW1X 8SD. *T:* (020) 7235 6961, *Fax:* (020) 7235 9734; *e-mail:* londres.amb@mae.etat.lu; *web:* www.wurthhubert.com.

WÜTHRICH, Prof. Kurt, PhD; Professor of Biophysics, Eidgenössische Technische Hochschule, Zürich, since 1980; of Structural Biology, Scripps Research Institute, California, since 2004; *b* 4 Oct. 1938; *s* of Herrmann Wüthrich and Gertrud Wüthrich-Kuchen; *m* 1963, Marianne Briner; one *s* one *d*. *Educ:* Univ. of Bern (MS Chemistry, Physics and Maths 1962); Univ. of Basel (PhD Chemistry 1964); Eidgenössisches Turn- und Sportlehrer-diplom 1964. Postdoctoral training: Univ. of Basel, 1964–65; Univ. of California, Berkeley, 1965–67; Bell Telephone Labs, Murray Hill, 1967–69; Eidgenössische Technische Hochschule, Zürich, 1969–: Asst Prof., 1972–76; Associate Prof., 1976–80; Chm., Dept of Biology, 1995–2000. Vis. Prof. of Structural Biol., Scripps Res. Inst., La Jolla, 2001–04. Mem. Council, 1975–78, 1987–90, Sec. Gen., 1978–84, Vice Pres., 1984–87, IUPAB; Mem. Gen. Cttee, 1980–86, Standing Cttee on Free Circulation of Scientists, 1982–90, ICSU. Member: EMBO, 1984; Deutsche Akad. der Naturforscher Leopoldina, 1987; Academia Europea, 1989; Schweizerische Akad. der Technischen Wissenschaften, 2001; Schweizerische Akad. der Medizinischen Wissenschaften, 2002. Editor: Qly Rev. Biophysics, 1984–91, 1996–2001; Macromolecular Structures, 1990–2000; Jl Biomolecular NMR, 1991–. Hon. Member: Japanese Biochem. Soc., 1993; American Acad. of Arts and Scis, 1993; Nat. Magnetic Resonance Soc., India, 1998; Swiss Chemical Soc., 2003; World Innovation Foundn, 2003; Internat. Soc. Magnetic Resonance in Medicine, 2004; Hungarian Acad. of Sci., 2004; World Acad. of Young Scientists, 2004; Eur. Acad. Arts, Scis and Humanities, 2004; Latvian Acad. Scis, 2004; Groupement Ampère, 2004; NMR Soc. of Japan, 2004; Indian Biophysical Soc., 2005; Korean Magnetic Resonance Soc., 2005. Foreign Associate: US Nat. Acad. of Scis, 1992; Acad. of Scis, Inst. of France, 2000; RSChem, 2003; RSE, 2003. FAAAS 1998. Foreign Fellow: Indian Nat. Sci. Acad., 1989; Korean Acad. of Sci. and Technol., 2005; Nordrhein-Westfälische Acad. der Wissenschaften, 2005; Hon. Fellow: NAS, India, 1992; Latvian Inst. of Organic Synthesis, Riga, 2008. Hon. Dr Chem.: Siena, 1997; Univ. del Norte, Asunción, Paraguay, 2007; Hon. PhD Zürich, 1997; Doctor *hc*: Ecole Poly. Fédérale Lausanne, 2001; Valencia, 2004; Sheffield, 2004; King George's Med. Univ., Lucknow, 2005; Pécs, 2007; Lomonosov Moscow State Univ., 2007; Verona, 2007; Univ. René Descartes, Paris, 2007. Friedrich Miescher Prize, Schweizerische Biochemische Ges., 1974; Shield, Fac. of Medicine, Tokyo Univ., 1983; P. Bruylants Medal, Catholic Univ. of Louvain, 1986; Stein and Moore Award, Protein Soc., USA, 1990; Louisa Gross Horwitz Prize, Columbia Univ., 1991; Gilbert N. Lewis Medal, Univ. of California, Berkeley, 1991; Marcel Benoist Prize, Switzerland, 1992; Dist. Service Award, Miami Winter Symposia, 1993; Prix Louis Jeantet de Médecine, Geneva, 1993; Kaj Linderstrøm-Lang Prize, Carlsberg Foundn, Copenhagen, 1996; Eminent Scientist of RIKEN, Tokyo, 1997; Kyoto Prize in Advanced Technol., 1998; Günther Laukien Prize, Exptl NMR Conf., 1999; Otto Warburg Medal, Soc. for Biochem. and Molecular Biol., Germany, 1999; World Future Award, M. Gorbatschow Foundn, 2002; (jtly) Nobel Prize for Chemistry, 2002; Swiss Soc. award, Swiss Awards, 2002; Ehrenpreis, Wallisellen, Switzerland, 2002; Johannes M. Bijvoet Medal, Utrecht Univ., 2008; Paul Walden Medal, Riga Tech. Univ., 2008. Hon. Citizen, Lyss, Switzerland, 2003. *Publications:* NMR in Biological Research: Peptides and Proteins, 1976; NMR of Proteins and Nucleic Acids, 1986; NMR in Structural Biology: a collection of papers, 1995; contrib. to learned jls. *Address:* Department of Molecular Biology, The Scripps Research

Institute, 10550 N Torrey Pines Road, La Jolla, CA 92037, USA; Institute of Molecular Biology and Biophysics, ETH Zürich, 8093 Zürich, Switzerland.

WYAND, Roger Nicholas Lewes; QC 1997; a Recorder, since 2000; a Deputy High Court Judge, since 2004; *b* 31 Oct. 1947; *s* of John Blake Wyand and Diana Wyand (*née* Williams); *m* 1973, Mary Elizabeth Varley; three *s*. *Educ:* Lakefield Coll. Sch., Canada; Rugby Sch.; Downing Coll., Cambridge (MA Nat. Sci.). Called to the Bar, Middle Temple, 1973, Bencher, 2005; Asst Recorder (Patents County Court), 1994–2000. Vice-Chm., Intellectual Property Bar Assoc. *Recreations:* theatre, golf, Arsenal FC. *Address:* Hogarth Chambers, 5 New Square, Lincoln's Inn, WC2A 3RJ. *T:* (020) 7404 0404.

WYATT, Prof. Adrian Frederick George, DPhil; FRS 2000; Professor of Physics, since 1976, and Director, Centre for Energy and the Environment (formerly Energy Studies Unit), University of Exeter; *b* 1 Oct. 1938. *Educ:* Univ. of Bristol (BSc 1960); DPhil Oxford 1963. Lectr, then Sen. Lectr, in Physics, Univ. of Nottingham, 1964–76. *Publications:* (ed with H. J. Lauter) Excitations in Two-dimensional and Three-dimensional Quantum Fluids, 1991; contrib. to learned jls. *Address:* School of Physics, University of Exeter, Stocker Road, Exeter EX4 4QL.

WYATT, (Alan) Will, CBE 2000; Chairman, Goodwill Associates (Media) Ltd, since 2003; Director, Vitec Group plc, since 2002; *b* 7 Jan. 1942; *s* of Basil Wyatt and Hettie Evelyn (*née* Hooper); *m* 1966, Jane Bridgit Bagenal; two *d*. *Educ:* Magdalen College Sch., Oxford; Emmanuel Coll., Cambridge. Trainee reporter, Sheffield Telegraph, 1964; Sub-Editor, BBC Radio News, 1965; moved to BBC television, 1968; Producer: Late Night Line Up, In Vision, The Book Programme, B. Traven—a mystery solved, *et al*, 1970–77; Asst Hd of Presentation (Programmes), 1977; Hd of Documentary Features, 1981; Hd of Features and Documentaries Gp, 1987; Asst Man. Dir, 1988–91, Man. Dir, 1991–96, BBC Network Television; Chief Exec., BBC Broadcast, 1996–99. Chm., BBC Guidelines on Violence, 1983, 1987; Director: BARB, 1989–91; BBC Subscription TV, 1990–93; BBC Enterprises, 1991–94; BBC Worldwide Television, 1994–96; UKTV, 1997–99; Coral Eurobet, 2000–02; Racing UK, 2004–; Racecourse Media Services Ltd, 2007–; Chm., Human Capital Ltd, 2001–08. Vice-Chm., Shadow Racing Trust, 2003–07. Chairman: Adv. Bd, POLIS, 2006–; Teaching Awards Trust, 2008–. Governor: Univ. of the Arts London (formerly London Inst.), 1990–2007 (Chm., 1999–2007); Nat. Film and TV Sch., 1991–97; Magdalen Coll. Sch., Oxford, 2000–06. Vice-Pres., EBU, 1998–99. Trustee, Services Sound and Vision Corp., 2007–. FRTS 1992 (Vice-Pres., 1997; Pres., 2000–04). *Publications:* The Man Who Was B. Traven, 1980; (contrib.) Masters of the Wired World, 1999; The Fun Factory: a life in the BBC, 2003; numerous articles on broadcasting. *Recreations:* fell walking, horse racing, opera, theatre. *Address:* c/o Goodwill Associates (Media) Ltd, Abbey Willows, Rayford Lane, Middle Barton, Oxon 0X7 7DD; *e-mail:* ww@dornvalley.net. *Clubs:* Garrick, Century.

WYATT, Arthur Hope, CMG 1980; HM Diplomatic Service, retired; re-employed in Foreign and Commonwealth Office, 1990–95; *b* 12 Oct. 1929; *s* of Frank and Maggie Wyatt, Anderton, Lancs; *m* 1957, Barbara Yvonne (*d* 2002), *d* of Major J. P. Flynn, late Indian Army; one *d* (and one *d* decd). *Educ:* Bolton School. Army, 1947–50; FO, 1950–52; 3rd Sec., Ankara, 1952–56; 2nd Sec., Phnom Penh, 1956–58; 2nd Sec., Ankara, 1958–61; FO, 1962–66; 1st Sec., Bonn, 1966–70; FCO, 1970–72; Counsellor and Head of Chancery, Lagos, 1972–75; Dep. High Comr, Valletta, 1975–76; Diplomatic Service Inspector, 1977–79; Counsellor (Econ. and Comm.) and Consul-Gen., Tehran, 1979–80; Counsellor, Ankara, 1981–84; Minister, Lagos, 1984–86; High Comr to Ghana and Ambassador (non-resident) to Togo, 1986–89. *Recreations:* golf, football, bridge, crosswords. *Address:* 44 Baronsmede, W5 4LT. *T:* (020) 8579 0782.

WYATT, Caroline Jane; Defence Correspondent, BBC, since 2007; *b* Darlinghurst, 21 April 1967; *d* of David Joseph Wyatt, *qv* and Annemarie Wyatt (*née* Angst). *Educ:* Convent of the Sacred Heart, Woldingham; Southampton Univ. (BA Hons English and German); Rutgers Univ. (exchange prog.); City Univ. (Dip. Journalism). BBC: news trainee, 1991–92; asst producer, BBC World TV, 1993; Berlin stringer, 1994–97; Bonn Corresp., 1997–99; Berlin Corresp., 1999–2000; Moscow Corresp., 2000–03; Paris Corresp., 2003–07. Op Telic Medal, 2003. *Publications:* (contrib.) From Our Own Correspondent, 2005; (contrib.) More From Our Own Correspondent, 2008. *Recreations:* reading, cycling, trying to write a book. *Address:* c/o BBC TV Centre, World Affairs Unit, Wood Lane, W12 7RJ. *T:* (020) 8624 8550, *Fax:* (020) 8743 7591. *Club:* Frontline.

WYATT, (Christopher) Terrel, FREng, FICE, FIStructE; Chairman, W. S. Atkins plc, 1987–98; *b* 17 July 1927; *s* of Lionel Harry Wyatt and Audrey Vere Wyatt; *m*; four *s*; *m* 1990, Patricia Perkins. *Educ:* Kingston Grammar Sch.; Battersea Polytechnic (BScEng); Imperial Coll. (DIC). FICE 1963; FIStructE 1963; FREng (FEng 1980). Served RE, 1946–48. Charles Brand & Son Ltd, 1948–54; Richard Costain Ltd, 1955–87: Dir, 1970–87; Gp Chief Exec., 1975–80; Dep. Chm., 1979–80; Chm., Costain Group PLC, 1980–87. *Recreation:* sailing. *Address:* Ryderswells Farm, Uckfield Road, Lewes, E Sussex BN8 5RN.

WYATT, David; HM Diplomatic Service, retired; Deputy High Commissioner, Lagos, 2001–07; *b* 18 April 1946; *s* of Ernest Wyatt and Eva Mabel Wyatt (*née* Hayles); *m* 1st, 1969, Rosemary Elizabeth Clarke (*d* 2000); one *s* one *d*; 2nd, 2002, Sunthian Phujarn. *Educ:* Sandown Grammar Sch. Entered Diplomatic Service, 1965; Lusaka, 1968–71; SOAS, 1971–72; Third Sec. (Commercial), Bangkok, 1972–76; Second Secretary: Yaoundé, 1976–77; FCO, 1977–79; NDC, 1980; First Secretary: (Commercial), Athens, 1981–84; and Hd of Chancery, Bangkok, 1984–88; FCO, 1988–94; Dep. High Comr, Accra, 1994–98; Commercial Counsellor, Bangkok, 1999–2001. *Recreations:* walking, reading, music.

WYATT, David Joseph, CBE 1977; Chairman, Crown Bio Systems, 2004–05 (consultant, 2003); HM Diplomatic Service, 1949–85; *b* 12 Aug. 1931; *s* of late Frederick Wyatt and Lena (*née* Parr); *m* 1st, 1957, Annemarie Angst (*d* 1978); two *s* one *d*; 2nd, 1990, Dr Wendy Baron, *qv*. *Educ:* Leigh Grammar Sch. National Service, RAF, 1950–52. Entered Foreign Service, 1949; Berne, 1954; FO, 1957–61; Second Sec., Vienna, 1961; First Sec., Canberra, 1965; FCO, 1969–71; First Sec., Ottawa, 1971; Counsellor, 1974; seconded Northern Ireland Office, Belfast, 1974–76; Counsellor and Head of Chancery, Stockholm, 1976–79; Under Sec. on loan to Home Civil Service, 1979–82; UK Mission to UN during 1982 General Assembly (personal rank of Ambassador); Minister and Dep. Comdt, British Mil. Govt, Berlin, 1983–85. Acting Dir Gen., Jan.–July 1990, Dir, Internat. Div., 1985–92, Advr on Internat. Relations, 1992–99, BRCS; Chm., Internat. Red Cross/Red Crescent Adv. Commn, 1996–97. FRSA 1991.

See also C. J. Wyatt.

WYATT, Derek Murray; MP (Lab) Sittingbourne and Sheppey, since 1997; *b* 4 Dec. 1949; *s* of late Reginald Swythn Wyatt and of Margaret Eira (*née* Holmden); *m*; one *d* one *s*. *Educ:* St Luke's Coll., Exeter; Open Univ. (BA Hons); St Catherine's Coll., Oxford. History teacher, 1972–81; journalist and writer, 1982–84; editor, George Allen & Unwin Ltd, 1984–85; Dir and Publisher, William Heinemann Ltd, 1986–88; Dir, TSL Ltd, 1988–91; consultant, writer and journalist, 1992–94; Head of Programmes, Wire TV, 1994–95; Dir, Computer Channel, BSkyB, 1995–97. Mem., Select Cttee on Culture, Media and Sport, 1997–2005; Public Accounts Cttee, 2007–. Chairman: All Party Parly Internet Cttee (founder), 1997–2007; All Party Parly Rugby Union Cttee, 1997–; All Party Parly British Council, 2000–; (also Founder) All Party Zimbabwe Gp, 2003–05; All Party London Olympic and Paralympic Gp 2012, 2004–; Co-Chairman: All Party Adventure and Recreation in Society Gp, 2004–; All Party Parly Communications Gp, 2007–. Founder: Women's Sports Foundn (UK), 1985; Oxford Internet Inst., 2000. Trustee: Major Stanley's (Trustee Gp for OURFC), 1986–; Citizen's Online, 2005–; Patron, Time Bank, 2008– (Trustee, 2004–08). Freeman, City of London, 2001; Liveryman, Co. of Information Technologists, 2001–. Commendation for work on sport and apartheid, UNO, 1987. Elected Representative New Media Award, New Statesman, 2006; Internet Hero Award, Internet Services Providers' Assoc., 2006; Winner, MPs Awards, British Computer Society, 2007. *Publications:* Wisecracks from the Movies, 1987; The International Rugby Almanack 1994, 1993; The International Rugby Almanack 1995, 1994; Rugby Disunion, 1995; (with Colin Herridge) Rugby Revolution, 2003. *Recreations:* Rugby (played for Oxford University, Barbarians, England), film, jazz, reading, software. *Address:* *e-mail:* wyattd@parliament.uk; *web:* www.derekwyatt.co.uk, www.derekwyatt.tv. *Clubs:* Royal Automobile; Vincent's (Oxford).

WYATT, Prof. Derrick Arthur; QC 1993; Professor of Law, University of Oxford, since 1996; Fellow, St Edmund Hall, Oxford, since 1978; *b* 25 Feb. 1948; *s* of Iris Ross (formerly Wyatt, *née* Thompson) and step *s* of Alexander Ross; *m* 1970, (Margaret) Joan Cunnington; one *s* one *d*. *Educ:* Alsop High Sch.; Emmanuel Coll., Cambridge (MA, LLB); Univ. of Chicago Law Sch. (JD). Lectr in law, Univ. of Liverpool, 1971–75; called to the Bar, Lincoln's Inn, 1972; Fellow, Emmanuel Coll., Cambridge, 1975–78; CUF Lectr in Law, Oxford Univ., 1978–96. Vis. Prof., Florida State Univ., 1987. Member: Vale of White Horse DC, 1983–87; Abingdon Town Council, 1983–87. Member Editorial Committee: British Yearbook of Internat. Law, 1992–; Yearbook of European Law, 1999–; Mem. Editl Bd, Croatian Yearbook of European Law and Policy, 2005–. *Publications:* Wyatt and Dashwood's Substantive Law of the EEC, 1980, 5th edn as European Union Law, 2006; (ed with A. Barav) Yearbook of European Law, 1988–97; articles and reviews in learned jls. *Recreations:* walking, reading. *Address:* St Edmund Hall, Oxford OX1 4AR. *T:* (01865) 279000.

WYATT, Hugh Rowland; Lord-Lieutenant of West Sussex, 1999–2008; *b* 18 Nov. 1933; *s* of late Brig. Richard John Penfold Wyatt, MC, TD and Hon. Margaret Agnes, *d* of 1st Baron Ebbisham, GBE; *m* 1959, Jane Ann Elizabeth Eden; one *s* two *d*. *Educ:* Winchester. 2nd Lieut, The Royal Sussex Regt, 1952–54; Captain, TA, 1954–61. Dir, McCorquodale plc, 1964–85; farmer. Chairman: Chichester Cathedral Trust, 1991–98; Chichester Dio. Bd of Finance, 1997–2001; Chichester Cathedral Council, 2001–. High Sheriff of West Sussex, 1995–96. Pres., Royal Sussex Regtl Assoc., 1997–2008. KStJ 2001. *Recreations:* travel, opera. *Address:* Cissbury, Findon, West Sussex BN14 0SR. *T:* (01903) 873328. *Club:* Sussex.

WYATT, Matthew Stephen Spence; Permanent Representative to the United Nations Food and Agriculture Agencies, Rome, since 2004 (with personal rank of Ambassador); *b* 2 June 1961; *s* of Ralph William Peter Wyatt and Susan Jennifer Wyatt; *m* 1994, Simonetta Fucecchi; one *s* one *d*. *Educ:* Lady Margaret Hall, Oxford (BA PPE 1983); College of Europe, Bruges (Dip. Higher European Studies 1984). Head: E Europe and Central Asia Dept, DFID, 1999–2001; DFID, Kenya, 2001–04. *Recreations:* playing leg-holding game, dinosaurs and catch (usually with children), football, theatre. *Address:* c/o Foreign and Commonwealth Office, King Charles Street, SW1A 2AH. *T:* (6) 6840091, *Fax:* (6) 68400920; *e-mail:* m-wyatt@dfid.gov.uk. *Club:* Railway Wanderers (Nairobi).

WYATT, Terrel; *see* Wyatt, C. T.

WYATT, Wendy, (Mrs D. J. Wyatt); *see* Baron, O. W.

WYATT, Will; *see* Wyatt, A. W.

WYBAR, Linda; Headteacher, Tunbridge Wells Girls' Grammar School, since 1999; *b* 21 June 1959; *d* of late Thomas Smith Clough and of Mary Clough; *m* 1995, Geoffrey Wybar; two *s*. *Educ:* Blyth Grammar Sch.; Univ. of Hull (BA Hons Eng. Lang. and Lit. 1980; PGCE Dist. 1981); Open Univ. (MA Educn Mgt 1996). English Teacher: Rede Sch., Strood, 1981–82; Highworth Grammar Sch., Ashford, 1982–86; Hd of English, Norton Knatchbull Boys' Grammar Sch., Ashford, 1986–92; Dep. Headteacher, Highworth Grammar Sch., Sittingbourne, 1992–99. Chm., Kent and Medway Grammar Schs Assoc., 2004–. *Recreations:* reading modern fiction, theatre-going, wine-tasting. *Address:* Tunbridge Wells Girls' Grammar School, Southfield Road, Tunbridge Wells, Kent TN4 9UJ. *T:* (01892) 520902, *Fax:* (01892) 536497; *e-mail:* admin@twggs.kent.sch.uk.

WYETH, Andrew Newell; artist; landscape painter; *b* 12 July 1917; *s* of Newell and Carolyn Wyeth; *m* 1940, Betsy Merle James; two *s*. *Educ:* privately. First one man exhibn, William Macbeth Gall., NY, 1937; subsequent exhibitions include: Doll & Richards, Boston, 1938, 1940, 1942, 1944; Cornell Univ., 1938; Macbeth Gall., 1938, 1941, 1943, 1945; Art Inst. of Chicago, 1941; Museum of Modern Art, NYC, 1943; M. Knoedler & Co., NYC, 1953, 1958; Dunn Internat. Exhibn, London, 1963; MIT, Cambridge, 1966; The White House, Washington, 1970; Tokyo, 1974, 1979; Metropolitan Museum, NY, 1976; RA, 1980 (first by living American artist); Arnot Museum, Elmira, NY, 1985; Seibu-Pisa, Tokyo, 1986; Moscow, Leningrad, 1987; Nat. Gall. of Art, Corcoran Gall. of Art, Washington, 1987; Milan, 1987; Fitzwilliam Mus., Cambridge, 1988. Member: Nat. Inst. of Arts and Letters (Gold Medal, 1965); Amer. Acad. of Arts and Sciences; Amer. Acad. of Arts and Letters (Medal of Merit, 1947); Académie des Beaux-Arts, 1977; Hon. Mem., Soviet Acad. of the Arts, 1978; Hon. RA 1996. Presidential Medal of Freedom, 1963; Einstein Award, 1967; Congressional Medal, USA, 1988. Hon. AFD: Colby Coll., Maine, 1954; Harvard, 1955; Dickinson, 1958; Swarthmore, 1958; Nasson Coll., Maine, 1963; Temple Univ., 1963; Maryland, 1964; Delaware, 1964; Northwestern Univ., 1964; Hon. LHD Tufts, 1963. *Publications:* The Helga Paintings, 1987; Andrew Wyeth: autobiography, 1995. *Address:* c/o Frank E. Fowler, PO Box 247, Lookout Mountain, TN 37350, USA.

WYKE, Prof. John Anthony, PhD; Professor, Faculty of Medicine, University of Glasgow, 1991–92, now Professor Emeritus; Chairman, Scottish Cancer Foundation, since 2002; *b* 5 April 1942; *s* of late Eric John Edward Wyke and Daisy Anne Wyke (*née* Dormer); *m* 1968, Anne Wynne Mitchell; one *s*. *Educ:* Dulwich Coll.; St John's Coll., Cambridge (Schol.; VetMB, MA); Univ. of Glasgow; UCL (PhD). MRCVS. FRSE 1989. Postdoctoral res., Univ. of Washington and Univ. of Southern California, 1970–72; Imperial Cancer Research Fund: scientific staff, London, 1972–83; Head, ICRF Labs at St Bartholomew's Hosp., 1983–87; Asst Dir, 1985–87; Dir, Beatson Inst. for Cancer Res., 1987–2002. Dir, Assoc. for Internat. Cancer Res., 2003–. Founder FMedSci 1998. Hon. FRCVS 1999. Hon. Fellow, Univ. of Glasgow, 2004. *Publications:* more than 100 scientific articles. *Recreations:* hill walking, ski touring, gardening. *Address:* c/o Beatson

Institute for Cancer Research, Garscube Estate, Switchback Road, Bearsden, Glasgow G61 1BD. *T:* (0141) 330 3950; *e-mail:* j.wyke@beatson.gla.ac.uk.

WYKES, Dr David Lewis; Director, Dr Williams's Trust and Library, since 1998; Co-Director, Dr Williams's Centre for Dissenting Studies, since 2004; *b* 29 June 1954; *s* of Christopher Lewis Wykes, FCA and Joan Margaret Wykes; *m* 1997, Dr Elizabeth Jane Clapp. *Educ:* Univ. of Durham (BSc); Univ. of Leicester (PhD 1987). Mem. of Ct, Leicester Univ., 1985–. Hon. Reader, QMUL, 2007–. FRHistS 2002. *Publications:* (ed with Dr S. J. C. Taylor) Parliament and Dissent, 2005; (with Prof. I. Rivers) Joseph Priestley, Scientist, Philosopher, and Theologian, 2008; numerous articles in academic and learned jls. *Recreations:* chamber music, walking, history. *Address:* Dr Williams's Library, 14 Gordon Square, WC1H 0AR. *T:* (020) 7387 3727.

WYLD, Martin Hugh, CBE 1997; Chief Restorer, National Gallery, since 1979; *b* 14 Sept. 1944; *s* of John Wyld and Helen Leslie Melville; one *s* one *d. Educ:* Harrow School. Assistant Restorer, National Gallery, 1966. *Recreation:* travel. *Address:* Flat 5, 23 Clapham Common West Side, SW4 9AN. *T:* (020) 7720 2627. *Clubs:* Colony Room, MCC.

WYLIE, Alexander Featherstonhaugh; *see* Kinclaven, Hon. Lord.

WYLIE, Andrew; President, The Wylie Agency, since 1980; *b* 4 Nov. 1947; *s* of Craig and Angela Fowler Wylie; *m* 1969, Christina Meyer; one *s*; *m* 1980, Camilla Carlini; two *d. Educ:* St Paul's Sch.; Harvard Coll. (BA *magna cum laude* 1970). Established: Wylie Agency, NY, 1980; London office, 1996; Madrid office, 1999. Mem., Council on Foreign Relns, 2006–. *Recreations:* running, bicycling, tennis. *Address:* The Wylie Agency Inc., 250 West 57th Street, Suite 2114, New York, NY 10107, USA. *T:* (212) 2460069; The Wylie Agency (UK) Ltd, 17 Bedford Square, WC1B 3JA. *T:* (020) 7908 5900. *Clubs:* Knickerbocker, Harvard, River (New York); Southampton, Bathing Corporation (Southampton, NY).

WYLIE, Prof. Christopher Craig; William Schubert Professor of Developmental Biology, and Director Developmental Biology Division, Children's Hospital Medical Center, Cincinnati, since 2000; *b* 15 Sept. 1945; *s* of Joseph and Edna Wylie; *m* 1st, 1969, Christine Margaret Hall; 2nd, 1976, Janet Heasman; three *s* one *d. Educ:* Chislehurst and Sidcup County Grammar School for Boys; University College London (BSc, 1st cl. Hons Anatomy 1966; PhD 1971). Lectr in Anatomy, University College London, 1969; St George's Hospital Medical School: Sen. Lectr in Anatomy, 1975; Reader, 1983; Prof., 1985; F. J. Quick Prof. of Biol., Cambridge Univ., 1988–94, now Prof. Emeritus; Fellow, Darwin Coll., Cambridge, 1989–94; University of Minnesota: Martin Lenz Harrison Prof. of Develtl Biol. and Genetics, 1994–2000; Dir, Develtl Biol. Centre, 1994–2000; Dir, Develtl Genetics Prog., Sch. of Med., 1994–2000. Vis. Asst Prof. in Biology, Dartmouth Coll., 1975; Vis. Associate Prof. of Anatomy, Harvard Med. Sch., 1981. Editor in Chief, Development (internat. jl of develt biol.), 1987–. *Publications:* numerous research articles in sci. jls of biology. *Recreations:* relaxing with the family, racket sports. *Address:* 411 Bishopsbridge Drive, Cincinnati, OH 45255, USA. *T:* (513) 2339735.

WYLIE, Dr Ian Martin; Chief Executive, TreeHouse (national charity for autism education), since 2006; *b* 22 Oct. 1955; *s* of Charles Ronald Wylie and Margaret (*née* Catanach); *m* 1987, Siân Meryl Griffiths, *qv;* one *s*, and two step *d. Educ:* Bedford Modern Sch.; St Peter's Coll., Oxford (MA Hons); DPhil Oxon 1985. Manager, Homeless Services, Bloomsbury HA, 1982–84; Primary Care Officer, 1984–86, PR Consultant, 1986–88, City and Hackney HA; Press and Information Manager, Oxford CC, 1988–92; Dir, Public Relns, Oxford RHA, 1992–94; King's Fund: Hd, Communications, 1994–97; Dir, Corporate Affairs, 1997–2000; Chief Exec., BDA, 2001–05; Associate Prof., Faculty of Social Sci., Chinese Univ. of Hong Kong, 2006. Chairman: Thames Vale Youth Orch., 2003–05; Autism Educn Trust, 2007–. *Publications:* Young Coleridge and the Philosophers of Nature, 1989; (with Sarah Harvey) Patient Power, 1999. *Recreations:* writing, singing with Crouch End Festival Chorus, opera, family. *Address:* 37a Hawley Road, NW1 8RW. *T:* (020) 7209 5430. *Club:* Garrick.

WYLIE, Siân Meryl, (Mrs Ian Wylie); *see* Griffiths, S. M.

WYLLIE, Andrew; Chief Executive, Costain Group, since 2005; *b* 24 Dec. 1962; *s* of Kenneth David Wyllie and Margaret Emily Wyllie; *m* 1990, Jane Morag Hudson; one *d. Educ:* Dunfermline High Sch.; Univ. of Strathclyde (BSc Hons 1984); London Business Sch. (MBA 1993). CEng 1991; FICE. With Taylor Woodrow, 1984–2005, Man. Dir, Taylor Woodrow Construction Ltd, 2001–05. Fellow, British American Project. FInstD. *Address:* Costain Group plc, Costain House, Vanwall Business Park, Maidenhead, Berks SL6 4UB. *T:* (01628) 842444, *Fax:* (01628) 842554.

WYLLIE, Prof. Andrew David Hamilton, FRS 1995; FMedSci; Professor of Pathology and Fellow of St John's College, Cambridge University, since 1998. *Educ:* Aberdeen Univ. (BSc 1964; MB ChB 1967; PhD 1975). MRCP 1971; MRCPath 1975, FRCPath 1987; FRCPE 1993. Res. Fellow, Hammersmith Hosp., 1969; Res. Fellow, then Lectr in Pathol., Aberdeen Univ., 1970–72; Edinburgh University: Lectr, 1972–77; Sen. Lectr, 1977–85; Reader, 1985–92; Prof. of Experimental Pathology, and Co-Dir CRC Labs, 1992–98, and Head, 1995–98, Dept of Pathol. FRSE 1991; FMedSci 1998. Hon. DSc Aberdeen, 1998. *Address:* Department of Pathology, University of Cambridge, Tennis Court Road, Cambridge CB2 1QP. *T:* (01223) 333692, *Fax:* (01223) 339067.

WYLLIE, Very Rev. Hugh Rutherford; Moderator of the General Assembly of the Church of Scotland, 1992–93; Minister at the Old Parish Church of Hamilton, 1981–2000; *b* 11 Oct. 1934; *s* of late Hugh McPhee Wyllie and Elizabeth Buchanan; *m* 1962, Eileen Elizabeth Cameron, MA; two *d. Educ:* Shawlands Acad., Glasgow; Hutchesons' Grammar Sch., Glasgow; Univ. of Glasgow (MA; Pitcairn Miller Frame Awards, 1961, 1962). The Union Bank of Scotland, 1951–53 (MCIBS). RAF Nat. Service, 1953–55. Licensed and ordained by Presbytery of Glasgow, 1962; Asst Minister, Glasgow Cathedral, 1962–65; Minister: Dunbeth Church, Coatbridge, 1965–72; Cathcart South Church, Glasgow, 1972–81. General Assembly: Convener: Stewardship and Budget Cttee, 1978–83; Stewardship and Finance Bd, 1983–86; Assembly Council, 1987–91; Member: Bd of Nomination to Church Chairs, 1985–91, 1993–99; Bd of Practice and Procedure, 1991–95; Bd of Communication, 1999–2003. Presbytery of Hamilton: Moderator, 1989–90; Convener, Business Cttee, 1991–95; Chaplain: Royal British Legion (Hamilton Br.), 1981–2001; Lanarks Burma Star Assoc., 1983–2001; Strathclyde Police 'Q' Div., 1983–2001. Master, Hamilton Hosp., 1982–2001; Vice-Chm., Lanarkshire Healthcare NHS Trust, 1996–99 (non-exec. Dir, 1995–99); Trustee, Lanarkshire Primary Care NHS Trust, 1999–2001. Established Centre for Information for the Unemployed, Hamilton, 1983; introduced Dial-a-Fact on drugs and alcohol, 1986; established Hamilton Church History Project, 1984–87; Pres., Glasgow Univ. SCM, 1958; Chm., SCM Scottish Council, 1958. Mem. Council, Scout Assoc., 1993–2004. Pres., Hamilton Burns Club, 1990. Hon. Freeman, District of Hamilton, 1992. Dr William Barclay Meml Fund Lectr, 1994. Hon. FCIBS 1997. Hon. DD Aberdeen, 1993. George and Thomas Hutcheson Award, Hutchesons' Grammar Sch., Glasgow, 2002.

Recreations: gardening, DIY, yellow Labrador. *Address:* 18 Chantinghall Road, Hamilton ML3 8NP.

WYLLIE, Prof. Peter John, PhD; FRS 1984; Professor of Geology, California Institute of Technology, 1983–99, now Emeritus (Chairman, Division of Geological and Planetary Sciences, 1983–87); *b* 8 Feb. 1930; *s* of George William and Beatrice Gladys Wyllie (*née* Weaver); *m* 1956, Frances Rosemary Blair; two *s* one *d* (and one *d* decd). *Educ:* Univ. of St Andrews. BSc 1952 (Geology and Physics); BSc 1955 (1st cl. hons Geology); PhD 1958 (Geology). Nat. Service, 1948–49: Aircraftsman First Cl. (Best Recruit, Basic Trng, Padgate, 1948). Heavyweight boxing champion, RAF, Scotland, 1949. Glaciologist, British W Greenland Expdn, 1950; Geologist, British N Greenland Expdn, 1952–54; Asst Lectr in Geology, Univ. of St Andrews, 1955–56; Research Asst, 1956–58, Asst Prof. of Geochemistry, 1958–59, Pennsylvania State Univ.; Research Fellow in Chemistry, 1959–60, Lectr in Exptl Petrology, 1960–61, Leeds Univ.; Associate Prof. of Petrology, Pennsylvania State Univ., 1961–65 (Acting Head, Dept Geochem. and Mineralogy, 1962–63); University of Chicago: Prof. of Petrology and Geochem., 1965–77; Master Phys. Scis, Collegiate Div., Associate Dean of Coll. and of Phys. Scis Div., 1972–73; Homer J. Livingston Prof., 1978–83; Chm., Dept of Geophysical Scis, 1979–82. Louis Murray Vis. Fellow, Univ. of Cape Town, 1987; Hon. Prof., Chinese Univ. of Geosciences, Beijing, 1996–. President: Internat. Mineralogical Assoc., 1986–90 (Vice Pres., 1978–86); Internat. Union of Geodesy and Geophysics, 1995–99 (Vice Pres., 1991–95). MAE 1996. Foreign Associate, US Nat. Acad. of Scis, 1981 (Chm. Cttee on Solid-Earth Sciences and Society, report published 1993); Fellow: Amer. Acad. of Arts and Scis, 1982; Amer. Geophys. Union; Geol. Soc. Amer.; Mineral. Soc. Amer., 1965; Corresponding Fellow, Edin. Geol. Soc., 1985–; Foreign Fellow: Indian Geophys. Union, 1987; Indian Nat. Sci. Acad., 1991; Nat. Acad. of Scis, India, 1992; Foreign Member: Russian (formerly USSR) Acad. of Scis, 1988; Chinese Acad. of Scis, 1996; Academia Europaea, 1996. Hon. Member: Mineralogical Soc. of GB and Ireland, 1986–; Mineralogical Soc. of Russia, 1986–; German Geological Soc., 2001–. Hon. DSc St Andrews, 1974. Polar Medal, 1954; Wollaston Medal, Geol. Soc. of London, 1982; Abraham-Gottlob-Werner Medal, German Mineral Soc., 1987; Roebling Medal, Mineralogical Soc. of America, 2001; Leopold von Buch Medal, Deutschen Geologischen Ges., 2001. *Publications:* Ultramafic and Related Rocks, 1967; The Dynamic Earth, 1971; The Way the Earth Works, 1976; (ed) Solid-Earth Sciences and Society, 1993; numerous papers in sci. jls. *Address:* Division of Geological and Planetary Sciences, 170–25 California Institute of Technology, Pasadena, CA 91125, USA. *T:* (626) 3956461.

WYMAN, Peter Lewis, CBE 2006; FCA; Partner, PricewaterhouseCoopers LLP, since 1978; President, Institute of Chartered Accountants in England and Wales, 2002–03; *b* 26 Feb. 1950; *s* of late John Bernard Wyman and of Joan Dorethea Wyman (*née* Beighton); *m* 1978, Joy Alison Foster; one *s* one *d. Educ:* Epsom Coll. ACA 1973, FCA 1978. Chartered Accountant; articled clerk, Ogden Parsons & Co. and Harmood Banner, 1968–73; Deloitte Haskins & Sells, then Coopers & Lybrand, now PricewaterhouseCoopers: Manager, 1973–78; Hd of Tax, 1993–98; Hd of External Relations, 1998–2000; Hd of Regulatory Policy, 2003–04; Hd of Professional Affairs and Regulatory Policy, 2004–; Global Leader, Public Policy and Regulatory Matters, 2008–. Mem. Cttee, London Soc. of Chartered Accountants, 1981–90 (Chm., 1987–88); Institute of Chartered Accountants in England and Wales: Mem. Council, 1991–; Chm., Faculty of Taxation, 1991–95; Chm., Educn and Trng Directorate, 1995–99; Chm., Professional Standards Office, 1999–2000; Mem., Exec. Cttee, 1996–2003; Vice Pres., 2000–01; Dep. Pres., 2001–02; International Federation of Accountants: Member: Transnat. Auditors' Cttee, 2006–; Forum of Firms, 2006–; Planning and Finance Cttee, 2006–. Chairman: Common Content for Accountancy Qualifications Steering Gp, 2002–06; Consultative Cttee of Accountancy Bodies, 2002–03; Dep. Chm., Financial Reporting Council, 2002–03. Special Advr on Deregulation and Taxation to Parly Under-Sec. of State for Corporate Affairs, 1993–94; Member: Deregulation Task Force, 1994–97; Panel on Takeovers and Mergers, 2002–03. External Overseer, Contributions Agency/IR Jt Working Prog., 1995–97; Member: Regulation of Accounting Profession Implementation Working Party, 1999–2001; Steering Gp, Rev. of Regulatory Régime of Accountancy Profession, 2003–04; Audit Cttee, RSA, 2005–; EU Adv. Gp, City of London, 2004–. Dir, Somerset Community Foundn, 2003–04. FRSA. Freeman, City of London, 1988; Freeman, 1988, Master, 2006–07, Chartered Accountants' Co. Mem., Council, Univ. of Bath, 2003–06 and 2007–. Gov., Aylwin Girls' Sch., Southwark, 2001–06 (Vice-Chm., 2001–03; Chm., 2003–06); Chm., F & GP Cttee, Harris Acad., Bermondsey, 2006–07; Trustee, Five Bridges Sch., Vauxhall, 2002–05. Award for Outstanding Achievement, ICAEW, 2006. *Publications:* various professional jls on taxation and accountancy matters. *Recreations:* twentieth century history, family history, equestrian sports, gardening. *Address:* Plainsfield Court, Plainsfield, Over Stowey, Somerset TA5 1HH. *T:* (01278) 671292; Flat 1, Priory House, 3 Burgon Street, EC4V 5DR. *Club:* Travellers.

WYN, Eurig; writer; *b* 10 Oct. 1944; *s* of Albert and Alvira Davies; *m* 1972, Gillian; one *s* one *d. Educ:* Univ. of Wales, Aberystwyth. Journalist/presenter, BBC Wales, 1970–75; Organiser, Plaid Cymru Party, 1975–78; Develt Officer, Community Co-operative Movt, 1978–82; freelance journalist, newspapers and BBC radio, 1982–85. Mem. (Plaid Cymru) Gwynedd CC, 1982–99. MEP (Plaid Cymru) Wales, 1999–2004. Mem., Cttee of the Regions, EU, 1990–99. *Address:* Y Frenni, Waunfawr, Caernarfon, Gwynedd LL55 4YY. *T:* (01286) 650512.

WYN GRIFFITH, Martin Peter; Chief Executive, Enterprise Directorate, Department for Business, Enterprise and Regulatory Reform (formerly Small Business Service, Department of Trade and Industry), since 2002; *b* 2 Feb. 1957; *s* of Hugh and Simone Wyn Griffith; *m* 2006, Jo; one step *s* one step *d. Educ:* Manchester Grammar Sch.; Univ. of Bristol (BA Jt Hons); Henley Mgt Coll. (MBA). EMI Records Ltd, 1978–84; Man. Dir, AWGO Ltd, 1984–92; Mktg Dir, EMI Music, 1994–96; Business Advr, 1996–97, Manager, 1997–99, and Chief Exec., 1999–2001, Business Link Wilts; Chief Exec., Business Link Berks and Wilts, 2001–02. *Publications:* contribs on entrepreneurship in entertainment and the future for multimedia to Jl Strategic Mgt. *Recreations:* motor racing, ski-ing, golf, Manchester United. *Address:* Enterprise Directorate, Department for Business, Enterprise and Regulatory Reform, Bay 173, 1 Victoria Street, SW1H 0ET. *T:* (020) 7215 5389, *Fax:* (020) 7215 6774; *e-mail:* martin.wyngriffith@berr.gsi.gov.uk.

WYN-ROGERS, Catherine; mezzo-soprano; *b* 24 July 1954; *d* of Geoffrey Wyn Rogers and Helena Rogers (*née* Webster). *Educ:* St Helena High Sch. for Girls, Chesterfield; Royal Coll. of Music. Studied with Meriel St Clair, Ellis Keeler and Diane Forlano. Performances: with various European orchs and choirs, incl. BBC SO, LPO, CBSO, RSNO, BBC Scottish Orch., RLPO, Accademia di Santa Cecilia, Rome, and Concertgebouw; with various opera cos incl. Royal Opera, Scottish Opera, WNO, Opera North, ENO, Bavarian State Opera and Teatro Real, Madrid; frequent appearances at BBC Proms, Aldeburgh, Salzburg and Edinburgh Fests. Numerous recordings. *Address:* c/o Askonas Holt, Lincoln House, 300 High Holborn, WC1V 7JH.

WYNDHAM, family name of **Baron Egremont and Leconfield**.

WYNDHAM-QUIN, family name of **Earl of Dunraven**.

WYNESS, James Alexander Davidson; Senior Independent Director, Spirent (formerly Bowthorpe) plc, 1999–2006 (Director, 1979–2006; Acting Chairman, 2002); *b* 27 Aug. 1937; *s* of late Dr James Alexander Davidson Wyness and Millicent Margaret (*née* Beaton); *m* 1966, Josephine Margaret Worsdell; three *d*. *Educ:* Stockport Grammar Sch.; Emmanuel Coll., Cambridge (MA, LLB). National Service, 2 Lieut, RA. Articled Clerk, A. F. & R. W. Tweedie, 1964–66 (qualified 1965); Linklaters & Paines, 1966–97: Partner, 1970–97; Managing Partner, 1987–91; Jt Sen. Partner, 1991–93; Sen. Partner, 1994–96. Dir, Saracens Ltd, 1996– (Chm., 1996–2002). Mem., Law Soc. Mem., Co. of City of London Solicitors. Life Member: Saracens FC (RFU) (Captain, 1962–65); Middx RFU; London Div. RFU. *Recreations:* visiting France, growing vegetables, Rugby football, reading. *Address:* c/o Linklaters, One Silk Street, EC2Y 8HQ.

WYNFORD, 9th Baron *cr* 1829, of Wynford Eagle, co. Dorset; **John Philip Robert Best;** chartered surveyor; Executive Partner, Wynford Eagle Partners, running family estate in Dorset, since 1981, sole proprietor, since 2002; *b* 23 Nov. 1950; *o s* of 8th Baron Wynford, MBE and Anne Daphne Mametz (*née* Minshull Ford); *S* father, 2002; *m* 1981, Fenella Christian Mary Danks; one *s* one *d*. *Educ:* Radley Coll.; Keele Univ. (BA Hons 1974); RAC Cirencester (MRAC 1977). MRICS (Land Agency Div.) 1979. *Recreations:* bridge, reading, music, silviculture. *Heir: s* Hon. Harry Robert Francis Best, *b* 9 May 1987. *Address:* The Manor, Wynford Eagle, Dorchester, Dorset DT2 0ER. *T:* (01300) 320763.

WYNFORD-THOMAS, Prof. David, PhD, DSc; FRCPath; Dean and Head of School of Medicine, Cardiff University, since 2005; *b* 28 Feb. 1955; *s* of Richard and Eunice Wynford-Thomas; *m* 2004, Theresa; one *s* two *d*. *Educ:* Welsh Nat. Sch. of Medicine (MB BCh Hons 1978; PhD 1981); DSc Wales 1995. FRCPath 1996. MRC/NIH Postdoctoral Res. Fellow, Univ. of Colorado, 1982–83; University of Wales College of Medicine: Lectr, 1983–86, Sen. Lectr, 1986–92, in Pathology; Prof. and Hd, Dept of Pathology, 1992–2005. Hon. Consultant in Molecular Pathology, 1986–. FMedSci 2003. Subject Editor, British Jl of Cancer, 1995–. *Publications:* (ed with E. D. Williams) Thyroid Tumours, 1989; co-author of over 150 peer-reviewed papers in scientific and med. jls. *Recreations:* chess, walking, reading. *Address:* Dean's Office, School of Medicine, Cardiff University, Heath Park, Cardiff CF14 4XN. *T:* (029) 2074 2020; *e-mail:* Meddean@cardiff.ac.uk.

WYNGAARDEN, James Barnes, MD; FRCP; Principal, Washington Advisory Group, 1996–2002; Foreign Secretary, National Academy of Sciences, Washington, 1990–94; *b* 19 Oct. 1924; *s* of Martin Jacob Wyngaarden and Johanna Kempers Wyngaarden; *m* 1946, Ethel Dean Vredevoogd (marr. diss. 1976); one *s* four *d*. *Educ:* Calvin College; Western Michigan University; University of Michigan. MD 1948; FRCP 1984. Investigator, NIH, 1953–56; Associate Prof. of Medicine, Duke Univ. Med. Center, 1956–61; Prof. of Medicine, Duke Univ. Med. Sch., 1961–65; Chairman, Dept of Medicine: Univ. of Pennsylvania Med. Sch., 1965–67; Duke Univ. Med. Sch., 1967–82; Dir, NIH, 1982–89; Assoc. Dir, Life Scis, Exec. Office of the President of USA, 1989–90. Hon. DSc: Michigan, 1980; Ohio, 1984; Illinois, 1985; George Washington, 1986; S Carolina, 1989; Western Michigan, 1989; Duke, 2006; Hon. PhD Tel Aviv, 1987. *Publications:* (ed jtly) The Metabolic Basis of Inherited Disease, 1960, 5th edn 1983; (with O. Sperling and A. DeVries) Purine Metabolism in Man, 1974; (with W. N. Kelley) Gout and Hyperuricemia, 1976; (with L. H. Smith) Review of Internal Medicine; a self-assessment guide, 1979, 3rd edn 1985; (ed jtly) Cecil Textbook of Medicine, 15th edn 1979 to 19th edn 1992. *Recreations:* tennis, ski-ing, painting. *Address:* 3504 Stoneybrook Drive, Durham, NC 27705–2427, USA.

WYNN, family name of **Baron Newborough**.

WYNN, Sir (David) Watkin W.; *see* Williams-Wynn.

WYNN, Terence; Member (Lab) North West Region, England, European Parliament, 1999–2006 (Merseyside East, 1989–94, Merseyside East and Wigan, 1994–99); *b* 27 June 1946; *s* of Ernest Wynn and Lily (*née* Hitchen); *m* 1967, Doris Ogden; one *s* one *d*. *Educ:* Leigh Technical Coll.; Riversdale Technical Coll., Liverpool (OND); Liverpool Polytechnic (Combined Chief Engrs Cert); Salford Univ. (MSc Manpower Studies and Industrial Relns 1984). Seagoing Marine Engr Officer, MN, 1962–74; Engr Surveyor, ICI, Runcorn, 1975–76; Ship Repair Man., Manchester Dry Docks, 1976–78; Trng Advr, Shipbuilding ITB, 1978–82; Sen. Trng Exec., Marine Trng Assoc., 1982–89. Trustee, Action for Children (formerly NCH), 2007–; Chm. of Trustees, Rock Bus Project, 2006–. Adjunct Sen. Fellow, Nat. Centre for Res. on Europe, Univ. of Canterbury, NZ, 2007–. Methodist local preacher, 1978–. Mem. Bd, Trustees for Methodist Church Purposes, 2007–. *Publications:* Onward Christian Socialist, 1996; Where are the Prophets, 2007. *Recreation:* Rugby League supporter.

WYNN, Terence Bryan; freelance journalist and writer; *b* 20 Nov. 1928; *o s* of late Bernard Wynn and Elsie Wynn (*née* Manges); unmarried. *Educ:* St Cuthbert's Grammar Sch., Newcastle upon Tyne. Started as jun. reporter with Hexham Courant, Northumberland, 1945; Blyth News, 1947–48; Shields Evening News, 1948–50; Sunderland Echo, 1950–53; Reporter with Daily Sketch, 1953–58; News Editor, Tyne Tees Television, 1958, then Head of News and Current Affairs, 1960–66; Editorial Planning, BBC Television News, 1966–67; Sen. Press and Information Officer with Land Commn, 1967–71; Sen. Inf. Officer, HM Customs and Excise, 1971–72; Editor, The Universe, 1972–77; Editor, Liberal News, and Head of Liberal Party Orgn's Press Office, 1977–83; Regl Press Officer, MSC, COI, London and SE Region, 1983–85; Editor, Your Court (house jl of Lord Chancellor's Dept), 1985–88. Helped to found and first Editor of Roman Catholic monthly newspaper, Northern Cross. Editor, Brentwood News, 1990–2001. Chm., Catholic Writers' Guild, 1967–70 (Hon. Vice-Pres., 1970); Judge for British Television News Film of the Year Awards, 1961–64; Mem. Mass Media Commn, RC Bishops' Conf. of England and Wales, 1972–83. Hon. Life Pres., Editors' Forum (diocesan newspapers), 2000 (Chm., 1998–2000). KSG 2001. *Publication:* Walsingham, a modern mystery play, 1975. *Recreations:* reading, writing, talking, writing letters to The Times. *Address:* Bosco Villa, 30 Queen's Road, South Benfleet, Essex SS7 1JW. *T:* (01268) 792033.

WYNN OWEN, Philip, CB 2008; Director General, Strategy and Pensions, Department for Work and Pensions, since 2004; *b* 10 June 1960; *s* of late Emrys and Ruth Wynn Owen; *m* 1989, Elizabeth Mary Fahey; three *s*. *Educ:* Maidstone Grammar Sch.; University Coll., Oxford (MA Mod. Hist.); London Business Sch. (MBA Dist.). HM Treasury, 1981–99: Asst Private Sec. to Chancellor of Exchequer, 1984–86; Private Sec. to Perm. Sec., 1991–93; Team Leader: Transport Team, 1993–96; Tax and Budget Team, 1996; Tax Policy Team, 1997–99; Director: Regulatory Impact Unit, Cabinet Office, 1999–2003; Financial Sector, HM Treasury, 2003–04. Alternate Dir, EIB, 1994–96. Non-exec. Dir, Maidstone and Tunbridge Wells NHS Trust, 2008–. *Recreations:* cricket, gym. *Clubs:* MCC; Leigh Cricket (Kent).

WYNNE, David, OBE 1994; sculptor, since 1949; *b* Lyndhurst, Hants, 25 May 1926; *s* of Comdr Charles Edward Wynne and Millicent (*née* Beyts); *m* 1959, Gillian Mary Leslie Bennett (*née* Grant) (*d* 1990); one *s* (and one *s* decd), and one step *s* one step *d*. *Educ:* Stowe Sch.; Trinity Coll., Cambridge. FZS; FRSA. Served RN, 1944–47: minesweepers and aircraft carriers (Sub-Lieut RNVR). No formal art training. First exhibited at Leicester Galls, 1950, and at Royal Acad., 1952. One-man Exhibitions: Leicester Galls, 1955, 1959; Tooth's Gall., 1964, 1966; Temple Gall., 1964; Findlay Galls, New York, 1967, 1970, 1973; Covent Garden Gall., 1970, 1971; Fitzwilliam Museum, Cambridge, 1972; Pepsico World HQ, New York, 1976; Agnew's Gall., 1983; Mall Galls, 1997; retrospective, Cannizaro House, 1980; also various mixed exhibns. Large works in public places: Magdalen Coll., Oxford; Malvern Girls' Coll.; Civic Centre, Newcastle upon Tyne; Lewis's, Hanley; Ely Cathedral; Birmingham Cath.; Church of St Paul, Ashford Hill, Berks; Ch. of St Thomas More, Bradford-on-Avon; Mission Ch., Portsmouth; Fountain Precinct, Sheffield; Bowood House, Wilts; Risen Christ and 2 seraphim, west front of Wells Cathedral, 1985; Virgin Mary, Lady Chapel, Ely Cathedral, 2001; Abbey Gdns, Tresco, Isles of Scilly; Highgrove, Glos; London and environs: Albert Bridge; British Oxygen Co., Guildford; Cadogan Place Gardens and Cadogan Sq.; Crystal Palace Park; Guildhall; Longbow House; St Katharine-by-the-Tower; Taylor Woodrow; Wates Ltd, Norbury; also London Road, Kingston-upon-Thames; Elmsleigh Centre, Staines; IPC HQ, Sutton; St Raphael's Hospice, Cheam, Surrey; Central Park, Watford; Queen Elizabeth Gates, Hyde Park Corner; Hurlingham Club; Highgrove Gardens; USA: Ambassador Coll., Texas, and Ambassador Coll., Calif; Atlantic Richfield Oil Co., New Mexico; Lakeland Meml Hosp., Wis; First Fed. Savings, Mass; Pepsico World HQ, Purchase, NY; Playboy Hotel and Casino, Atlantic City, NJ; Sarasota, Fla; Mayo Foundation, Minn; Sherman, Texas; Ritz Carlton, Rancho Mirage, Calif; Mayo Clinic, Rochester, Minn; Grayson Bank, Sherman, Texas; also Perth, WA, and Place Camelotti, Geneva, 1988. Bronze portraits include: Sir Thomas Beecham, 1956; Sir John Gielgud, 1962; Yehudi Menuhin, 1963; The Beatles, 1964; Kokoschka, 1965; Sir Alec Douglas-Home, 1966; Robert, Marquess of Salisbury, 1967; The Prince of Wales, 1969; Lord Baden-Powell, 1971; Virginia Wade, 1972; The Queen, 1973; King Hassan of Morocco, 1973; Air Chief Marshal Lord Dowding, 1974; The Begum Aga Khan, 1975; Pele, 1976; Lord Hailsham, 1977; Prince Michael of Kent, 1977; Earl Mountbatten of Burma, 1981; Paul Daniels, 1982; Jackie Stewart, 1982; Elvis Presley; Victor Ubogu; Portrait Figures: Arnold Palmer, 1983; Björn Borg, 1984; Leonard Cheshire, for Stowe Sch., 1995; Bernard Gallacher, Wentworth Club, 1998; other sculptures: Fred Perry, AELTC, 1984; Shergar and jockey, 1981; Shareef Dancer and groom, 1984; Cresta Rider, St Moritz, 1985; Two Dolphins, Provence, France, 1986; Shergar and Sinndar, Kildare, Ireland. Designed: Common Market 50 pence piece of clasped hands, 1973; King Hassan, for Moroccan coinage, 1973; the Queen's Silver Jubilee Medal, 1977 (with new effigy of the Queen wearing St Edward's Crown). *Publication:* The Messenger, a sculpture by David Wynne, 1982; *relevant publications:* T. S. R. Boase, The Sculpture of David Wynne 1949–1967, 1968; Graham Hughes, The Sculpture of David Wynne 1968–1974, 1974; Jonathan Stone (ed), The Sculpture of David Wynne 1974–92, 1993. *Recreations:* active sports, poetry, music. *Address:* 5 Burlington Lodge Studios, Buer Road, SW6 4LA. *T:* (020) 7731 1071. *Clubs:* Garrick, Queen's, Hurlingham; Village (Wimbledon); Leander (Henley-on-Thames); 1st and 3rd Trinity Boat; St Moritz Tobogganing; The Royal Tennis Court (Hampton Court Palace).

WYNNE, Graham Robert, CBE 2003; Chief Executive, Royal Society for the Protection of Birds, since 1998; *b* 29 May 1950; *s* of late Arthur Robert Wynne and of Joan Brenda Wynne (*née* Chapman); *m* 1994, Janet Anne Stewart. *Educ:* Brentwood Sch., Essex; Pembroke Coll., Cambridge (BA Hons 1971; MA). DipTP 1975; MRTPI (RTPI 1975). Various planning posts, Lewisham, 1972–78; Shoreditch Area Team Leader, 1978–86, Hd, Planning Policy, 1986–87, Hackney; Reserves Dir, 1987–90, Conservation Dir, 1990–98, RSPB. Member: UK Biodiversity Steering Gp, 1994–2000; UK Round Table on Sustainable Develt, 1998–2000; Sustainable Develt Commn, 2000–03; Policy Commn on Future of Farming and Food, 2001–02; Sustainable Farming and Food Implementation Gp, 2002–06; Sustainable Farming and Food Delivery and Leadership Gps, 2006–. Mem. Council, Birdlife Internat., 1998–. *Publications:* Biodiversity Challenge: an agenda for conservation action in the UK, 1995; (contrib.) Conservation Science and Action, 1997; contrib. various RSPB and local authy pubns. *Recreations:* hill-walking, natural history, football, restoring a C16th house. *Address:* Royal Society for the Protection of Birds, The Lodge, Sandy, Beds SG19 2DL. *T:* (01767) 680551, *Fax:* (01767) 691178.

WYRKO, David John, QPM 1995; Chief Constable of Leicestershire, 1997–2002; *b* 15 July 1948; *s* of late Wasyl John Wyrko and of Stella Doreen Wyrko (*née* Witts); *m* 1973, Beryl Case; one *s* one *d*. *Educ:* City of Bath Technical Sch.; Univ. of Surrey (BSc Electrical, Electronic and Control Engineering 1969). Police Constable to Chief Superintendent, Northants, 1972–91; Asst Chief Constable, Northants, 1991–93; Dep. Chief Constable, Leics, 1993–97. Co-Dir, Police Extended Interviews, 1999–2002. FBI Nat. Acad., Quantico, 1984; Cabinet Office Top Mgt Prog., 1995. Hon. Treas., 1994–98, Chm., Inf. Mgt Cttee, 1997–2000, ACPO; Mem., PITO Bd, 1997–2002. Sen. Vis. Fellow, Scarman Centre, Univ. of Leicester, 2003–. Council Mem., Shrievalty Assoc., 2005–07. High Sheriff, Leics, 2008–March 2009. *Recreations:* cabinet making, golf, cycling. *Address:* c/o Leicestershire Constabulary HQ, St John's, Narborough, Leics LE9 5BX. *T:* (0116) 222 2222.

Y

YACOUB, Sir Magdi (Habib), Kt 1992; FRCS; FRS 1999; British Heart Foundation Professor of Cardiothoracic Surgery, National Heart and Lung Institute (formerly Cardiothoracic Institute), Imperial College London (formerly British Postgraduate Medical Federation, University of London), since 1986; Director of Research, Magdi Yacoub Institute (formerly Harefield Research Foundation), Heart Science Centre; *b* Cairo, 16 Nov. 1935; *m*; one *s* two *d*. *Educ:* Cairo University. FRCS, FRCSE, FRCSGlas, 1962; LRCP 1966, MRCP 1986, Hon. FRCP 1990. Rotating House Officer, Cairo Univ. Hosp., 1958–59; Surgical Registrar, Postgrad. Surgical Unit, Cairo Univ., 1959–61; Resident Surgical Officer, 1962–63, Surgical Registrar, 1963–64, London Chest Hosp.; Rotating Sen. Surgical Registrar, Nat. Heart and Chest Hosps, 1964–68; Asst Prof. of Cardiothoracic Surgery, Chicago Univ., 1968–69; Consultant Cardiothoracic Surgeon, Harefield Hosp., Middx, 1969–92, Royal Brompton and Harefield NHS Trust, 1986–2001 (now Hon.); Consultant Cardiac Surgeon, Nat. Heart Hosp., 1973–89. Hon. Consultant: Royal Free Hosp. Med. Sch.; King Edward's Coll. of Medicine, Lahore, Pakistan; Hon. Prof. of Surgery, Univ. of Sienna; Hon. Prof. of Cardiac Surgery, Charing Cross and Westminster Hosp. Med. Schs. Has developed innovations in heart and heart-lung transplants. Mem., Soc. Thoracic Surgeons; FRSocMed; Founder FMedSci 1998. Hon. DSc: Brunel, 1985; Amer. Univ. at Cairo, 1989; Loughborough, 1990; Hon. MCh Cardiff, 1986; Hon. PhD Lund, 1988. Editor: Annual of Cardiac Surgery; Current Opinion in Cardiology: coronary artery surgery. *Publications:* papers on pulmonary osteoarthropath, aortic valve homografts, surgical treatment of ischaemic heart disease, valve repairs, and related subjects. *Address:* Imperial College London, Heart Science Centre, Harefield, Middx UB9 6JH.

YALE, David Eryl Corbet, FBA 1980; Reader in English Legal History, Cambridge University, 1969–93, now Emeritus; Fellow, Christ's College, Cambridge, since 1950; *b* 31 March 1928; *s* of Lt-Col J. C. L. Yale and Mrs Beatrice Yale (*née* Breese); *m* 1959, Elizabeth Ann, *d* of C. A. B. Brett, Belfast; two *s*. *Educ:* Malvern Coll., Worcs; Queens' Coll., Cambridge (BA 1949, LLB 1950, MA 1953). Called to the Bar, Inner Temple, 1951; Asst Lectr and Lectr in Law, Cambridge Univ., 1952–69. Pres., Selden Soc., 1994–97. Hon. QC 2000. *Publications:* various, mainly in field of legal history. *Recreation:* fishing. *Address:* Christ's College, Cambridge CB2 3BU. *T:* (01223) 334900; Saethon, Porthmadog, Gwynedd LL49 9UR. *T:* (01766) 512129.

YALOW, Rosalyn Sussman, PhD; Senior Medical Investigator, Veterans Administration, later Veterans Affairs, 1972–92, Senior Medical Investigator Emeritus, since 1992; *b* 19 July 1921; *d* of Simon Sussman and Clara (*née* Zipper); *m* 1943, Aaron Yalow; one *s* one *d*. *Educ:* Hunter Coll., NYC (AB Physics and Chemistry, 1941); Univ. of Ill, Urbana (MS Phys. 1942, PhD Phys. 1945). Diplomate, Amer. Bd of Radiol., 1951. Asst in Phys., Univ. of Ill, 1941–43, Instr, 1944–45; Lectr and Temp. Asst Prof. in Phys., Hunter Coll., 1946–50. Veterans Admin Hospital, Bronx, NY: Consultant, Radioisotope Unit, 1947–50; Physicist and Asst Chief, Radioisotope Service, 1950–70 (Actg Chief, 1968–70); Chief, Nuclear Medicine Service, 1970–80; Dir, Solomon A. Berson Res. Lab., 1973–; Chm., Dept of Clin. Scis, Montefiore Hosp. and Med. Center, Bronx, NY, 1980–85; Chief, VA Radioimmunoassay Ref. Lab., 1969–. Consultant, Lenox Hill Hosp., NYC, 1952–62. Res. Prof., Dept of Med., Mt Sinai Sch. of Med., 1968–74, Distinguished Service Prof., 1974–79; Distinguished Prof.-at-Large, Albert Einstein Coll. of Med., Yeshiva Univ., NY, 1979–85, Prof. Emeritus, 1985–; Solomon A. Berson Distinguished Prof.-at-Large, Mt Sinai Sch. of Medicine, City Univ. of NY, 1986–. IAEA Expert, Instituto Energia Atomica, Brazil, 1970; WHO Consultant, Radiation Med. Centre, India, 1978; Sec., US Nat. Cttee on Med. Physics, 1963–67. Member: President's Study Gp on Careers for Women, 1966–67; Med. Adv. Bd, Nat. Pituitary Agency, 1968–71; Endocrinol. Study Sect., Nat. Insts of Health, 1969–72; Cttee for Evaluation of NPA, Nat. Res. Council, 1973–74; Council, Endocrine Soc., 1974–80 (Koch Award, 1972; Pres., 1978); Bd of Dirs, NY Diabetes Assoc., 1974–77. Member: Editorial Adv. Council, Acta Diabetologica Latina, 1975–77; Ed. Adv. Bd, Encyclopaedia Universalis, 1978–; Ed. Bd, Mt Sinai Jl of Medicine, 1976–79; Ed. Bd, Diabetes, 1976–79. Fellow: NY Acad. of Sciences (Chm., Biophys. Div., 1964–65; A. Cressy Morrison Award in Nat. Sci., 1975); Radiation Res. Soc.; Amer. Assoc. of Physicists in Med.; Biophys. Soc.; Amer. Diabetes Assoc. (Eli Lilly Award, 1961; Commemorative Medallion, 1972; Banting Medal, 1978; Rosalyn S. Yalow Res. and Develt Award estabd 1978); Amer. Physiol Soc.; Soc. of Nuclear Med. Associate Fellow in Phys., Amer. Coll. of Radiol. Member: Nat. Acad. of Sciences; Amer. Acad. Arts and Sciences; Foreign Associate, French Acad. of Medicine. Hon. DSc and Hon. DHumLett from univs and med. colls in the US, France, Argentina, Canada. Nobel Prize in Physiology or Medicine, 1977; VA Exceptional Service Award, 1975 and 1978; Nat. Medal of Sci., 1988. Has given many distinguished lectures and received many awards and prizes from univs and med. socs and assocs. *Publications:* over 500 papers and contribns to books, research reports, proceedings of conferences and symposia on radioimmunoassay of peptide hormones and related subjects, since 1950. *Address:* VA Medical Center, 130 West Kingsbridge Road, Bronx, NY 10468, USA. *T:* (718) 579 1644.

YAM Yee-Kwan, David; Hon. Mr Justice Yam; a Judge of the Court of First Instance of the High Court (formerly Judge of the High Court), Hong Kong, since 1994; *b* 4 Oct. 1948; *s* of Yam Fat-Shing Frank and Ng Yuet-Hing Nora; *m* 1977, Dr Stella T. P. Wong; two *s*. *Educ:* Hong Kong Univ. (BSc 1971; LLB 1975); Inns of Court Sch. of Law. Called to the Bar, Middle Temple, and to Hong Kong Bar, 1976; in practice, 1977–87; District Court Judge, 1987–94. Chm., Insider Dealing Tribunal, 1995–97. *Recreations:* golf, music, travelling. *Address:* High Court, 38 Queensway, Hong Kong. *T:* 28254427. *Clubs:* Hong Kong Jockey, Shek O Country (Hong Kong).

YAMEY, Prof. Basil Selig, CBE 1972; FBA 1977; Professor of Economics, University of London, 1960–84, now Emeritus; Member (part-time), Monopolies and Mergers Commission, 1966–78; *b* 4 May 1919; *s* of Solomon and Leah Yamey; *m* 1st, 1948, Helen Bloch (*d* 1980); one *s* one *d*; 2nd, 1991, Demetra Georgakopoulou. *Educ:* Tulbagh High Sch.; Univ. of Cape Town; LSE. Served as Lieut, SAAF, 1941–45. Lectr in Commerce, Rhodes Univ., 1945; Senior Lectr in Commerce, Univ. of Cape Town, 1946; Lectr in Commerce, LSE, 1948; Associate Prof. of Commerce, McGill Univ., 1949; Reader in Economics, Univ. of London, 1950. Managing Trustee, IEA, 1986–91. Trustee: National Gall., 1974–81; Tate Gall., 1979–81; Member: Museums and Galls Commn, 1983–84; Cinematograph Films Council, 1969–73. Mem. Committee of Management: Courtauld Inst., 1981–84; Warburg Inst., 1981–84; Mem., Governing Body, London Business Sch., 1965–84. *Publications:* Economics of Resale Price Maintenance, 1954; (jt editor) Studies in History of Accounting, 1956; (with P. T. Bauer) Economics of Under-developed Countries, 1957; (jt editor) Capital, Saving and Credit in Peasant Societies, 1963; (with H. C. Edey and H. Thomson) Accounting in England and Scotland, 1543–1800, 1963; (with R. B. Stevens) The Restrictive Practices Court, 1965; (ed) Resale Price Maintenance, 1966; (with P. T. Bauer) Markets, Market Control and Marketing Reform: Selected Papers, 1968; (ed) Economics of Industrial Structure, 1973; (jt editor) Economics of Retailing, 1973; (jt editor) Debits, Credits, Finance and Profits, 1974; (with B. A. Goss) Economics of Futures Trading, 1976; Essays on the History of Accounting, 1978; (jt editor) Stato e Industria in Europa: Il Regno Unito, 1979; Further Essays on the History of Accounting, 1983; Arte e Contabilità, 1986; Análisis Económico de los Mercados, 1987; Art and Accounting, 1989; (ed) Luca Pacioli, Exposition of Double Entry Bookkeeping, Venice 1494, 1994; (jt editor) Accounting History: some British contributions, 1994; articles on economics, economic history and law in learned journals. *Address:* 27B Elsworthy Road, NW3 3BT. *T:* (020) 7586 9344.

YANDELL, Claire Louise; *see* Armitstead, C. L.

YANG, Chen Ning, FInstP; physicist, educator; Einstein Professor and Director, Institute for Theoretical Physics, State University of New York at Stony Brook, New York, 1966–99, now Emeritus Professor and Director; Distinguished Professor-at-Large, Chinese University of Hong Kong, since 1986; Professor, Tsinghua University, Beijing, since 1998; *b* Hefei, China, 22 Sept. 1922; *s* of Ke Chuen Yang and Meng Hwa Lo; naturalized US citizen, 1964; *m* 1950, Chih Li Tu; two *s* one *d*. *Educ:* National Southwest Associated Univ., Kunming, China (BSc), 1942; University of Chicago (PhD), 1948. FInstP 1998. Institute for Advanced Study, Princeton, NJ: Member, 1949–55; Prof. of Physics, 1955–66; several DSc's from universities. Member of Board: Rockefeller Univ., 1970–76; AAAS, 1976–80; Salk Inst., 1978–; Ben Gurion Univ.; Member: Amer. Phys. Soc.; Nat. Acad. Sci.; Amer. Philos. Soc., Sigma Xi; Brazilian, Venezuelan, Royal Spanish and Chinese Acads of Sci; Academia Sinica; Foreign Member: Royal Soc., 1992; Russian Acad. of Sciences, 1994. Nobel Prize in Physics, 1957; Rumford Prize, 1980; Nat. Medal of Science, 1986; Benjamin Franklin Medal, Amer. Phil Soc., 1993; Bower Prize, Franklin Inst., 1994; King Faisal Internat. Prize, 2001. *Publications:* contrib. to Physical Review, Reviews of Modern Physics. *Address:* Chinese University of Hong Kong, Shatin, New Territories, Hong Kong; Tsinghna University, Beijing, China.

YANG, Prof. Fujia; Chancellor, University of Nottingam, UK, since 2001 and President, University of Nottingham, Ningbo, China, since 2004; Bohr Professor, Fudan University; *b* Shanghai, 11 June 1936; *s* of Yang Shanqing and Zhu Qin; *m* Peng Xiuling; one *d*. *Educ:* Fudan Univ. (Physics degree 1958). Postdoctoral Researcher, Niels Bohr Inst., Copenhagen, 1963–65; Fudan University: Lectr; Prof. of Physics; Pres., 1993–99. Dir, Shanghai Inst. of Nuclear Res., Chinese Acad. of Scis, 1987–2001. Chm., Shanghai Assoc. for Sci. and Technol., 1992–96; Vice Chm., Chinese Assoc. for Sci. and Technol., 2001–. Academician, Chinese Acad. of Scis, 1991–. Fellow, 48 Group Club. Hon. degrees, Soka, New York, Hong Kong, Nottingham and Connecticut. *Publications:* Atom Physics, 1984, 2008; Atomic and Nuclear Physics, 1993; Applied Nuclear Physics, 1994; (with J. H. Hamilton) Modern Atomic and Nuclear Physics, 1996. *Recreations:* reading, walking, swimming. *Address:* Fudan University, 220 Handan Road, Shanghai 200433, China; *e-mail:* fjyang@fudan.edu.cn, fujia.yang@nottingham.ac.uk.

YANG, Hon. Sir Ti Liang, Kt 1988; Member Executive Council, Hong Kong Special Administrative Region, 1997–2002; Chairman, Exchange Fund Investment Ltd, 1998–2003; Chief Justice of Hong Kong, 1988–96; *b* 30 June 1929; *s* of late Shao-nan Yang and Elsie (*née* Chun); *m* 1954, Eileen Barbara (*née* Tam) (*d* 2006); two *s*. *Educ:* The Comparative Law Sch. of China; Soochow Univ., Shanghai; UCL (LLB Hons 1953; Fellow 1989). FCIArb 1990. Called to the Bar (with honours), Gray's Inn, 1954, Hon. Bencher, 1988. Magistrate, Hong Kong, 1956; Sen. Magistrate, 1963; Rockefeller Fellow, London Univ., 1963–64; District Judge, Dist Court, 1968; Judge of the High Court, Hong Kong, 1975; Justice of Appeal, Hong Kong, 1980; Pres., Court of Appeal of Negara Brunei Darussalam, 1988–92. Candidate for selection of Chief Exec., HKSAR, 1996. Chairman: Kowloon Disturbances Claims Assessment Bd, 1966, Compensation Bd, 1967; Commn of Inquiry into the Rainstorm Disasters, 1972; Commn of Inquiry into the Leung Wing-sang Case, 1976; Commn of Inquiry into the MacLennan Case, 1980; Mem., Law Reform Commn, 1980–96 (Chm., Sub-cttee on law relating to homosexuality, 1980). Mem., Chinese Lang. Cttee (Chm. Legal Sub-cttee), 1970. Chairman: University and Polytechnic Grants Cttee, 1981–84; Hong Kong Univ. Council, 1987–2001; Pro-Chancellor, Hong Kong Univ., 1994–2001. Chm., Hong Kong Red Cross, 1998–. Pres., Bentham Club. Hon. LLD: Chinese Univ. of Hong Kong, 1984; Hong Kong Poly., 1992; Hon. DLitt Hong Kong Univ., 1991. Order of Chivalry, First Class, SPMB, Negara Brunei Darussalam, 1990; Grand Bauhinia Medal (Hong Kong), 1999. *Publications:* (trans.) General Yue Fei, by Qian Cai (Qing Dynasty novel), 1995; (trans.) Peach Blossom Fan, (novel by Gu Shifan, 1948), 1998; (trans.) Officialdom Unmasked, (novel by Li Boyuan, 1903), 2001. *Recreations:* philately, reading, walking, oriental ceramics, travelling, music. *Address:* Flat 8, Duchess of Bedford House, Duchess of Bedford's Walk, W8 7QL. *Clubs:* Athenæum; Hong Kong, Hong Kong Country, Hong Kong Jockey (Hong Kong).

YANG, Prof. Ziheng, PhD; FRS 2006; Professor of Statistical Genetics, University College London, since 2001; *b* 1 Nov. 1964; *s* of Yi Yang and Weiying Wang; *m* 1991, Fan Yang; two *d*. *Educ:* Gansu Agricl Univ. (BSc 1984); Beijing Agricl Univ. (MSc 1987; PhD 1992). Lectr, Beijing Agricl Univ., 1992–97; postdoctoral res., Pennsylvania State Univ. and Univ. of Calif. at Berkeley; University College London: Lectr, 1997–2000; Reader, 2000–01. *Publication:* Computational Molecular Evolution, 2006. *Address:* Department of Biology, University College London, Darwin Building, Gower Street, WC1E 6BT.

YAPP, John William; HM Diplomatic Service; High Commissioner, Belize, 2007–08; *b* 14 Jan. 1951; *s* of late William Yapp and Pamela Yapp (*née* Clarke); *m*; one *s* four *d*. *Educ:* St Augustine's Coll., Ramsgate. Joined HM Diplomatic Service, 1971: Islamabad, 1973–75; Third Sec. (Consular), Kuala Lumpur, 1976–77; Asst Private Sec. to Ministers of State, FCO, 1978–80; Second Sec. (Commercial), Dubai, 1980–84; Second Sec. (Economic), The Hague, 1984–88; Jt Export Promotion Directorate, FCO/DTI, 1988–91; First Sec. (Political/PR), Wellington, NZ, 1992–95 (concurrently Dep. Governor, Pitcairn Is); Dep. Head, N American Dept, FCO, 1995–97; High Comr, Seychelles, 1998–2002; First Sec. (Political-Military), Washington, 2003; Dep. Hd, S Asia Gp, FCO, 2004–07. *Recreations:* reading, cooking, Rugby Union (now as a spectator). *Address:* c/o Foreign and Commonwealth Office, King Charles Street, SW1A 2AH; *e-mail:* john.yapp@fco.gov.uk.

YAPP, Sir Stanley Graham, Kt 1975; Chairman, Birmingham International Airport, 1988–94; Chairman, West Midlands County Council, 1983–84 (Leader, 1973–77; Vice-Chairman, 1982–83); Member, Birmingham City Council, later Birmingham District Council, 1961–77 (Leader, 1972–74); *s* of late William and of Elsie Yapp; *m* 1961, Elisbeth Wise (marr. diss.); one *d*; *m* 1974, Carol Matheson (marr. diss.); one *s*; *m* 1983, Christine Horton. Member, West Midlands Economic Planning Council (Chm., Transport Cttee); Member many bodies both local and national, inc.: Vice-Chm. LAMSAC; Member: Local Govt Trng Board; Nat. Jt Councils on pay and conditions; AMA; BR Adv. Bd, Midlands and N Western Reg., 1977–79; Chm., West Midlands Planning Authorities Conf., 1973–75, Vice-Chm. 1975–77. Governor, BFI, 1977–79. FCMI. *Publications:* contribs to Local Government Chronicle, Municipal Journal, Rating and Valuation. *Recreations:* astronomy, reading, walking. *Address:* 134 Bushmore Road, Hall Green, Birmingham B28 9QZ.

YARBOROUGH, 8th Earl of, *cr* 1837; **Charles John Pelham;** Baron Yarborough, 1794; Baron Worsley, 1837; *b* 5 Nov. 1963; *o s* of 7th Earl of Yarborough and Ann, *d* of late John Herbert Upton; *S* father, 1991; *m* 1990, Anna-Karin Zecevic, *d* of George Zecevic; four *s* one *d*. *Heir: s* Lord Worsley, *qv*. *Address:* Brocklesby Park, Lincs DN41 8FB.

YARD, John Ernest, CBE 2000; consultant specialising in outsourcing and relationship management; *b* 29 July 1944; *s* of Ernest Alfred and Kathleen Lilian Yard; *m* Jean Pamela Murray; one *s* one *d*; two *s* one *d* from a previous marriage. *Educ:* St Marylebone Grammar Sch. FBCS 2003; MCIPS 2004. Inland Revenue: Exec. Officer and PAYE Auditor, 1963–71; Inspector of Taxes, 1971–84; Dep. Dir (Systems and Policy), 1984–91; Dir of Change Mgt, 1992; Dir, Business Services (IT) Office, then Business and Mgt Services Div., subseq. Business Services Div., 1993–2004. *Recreations:* travel, eating, attempting a sporting life. *Address:* *e-mail:* john@johnyard.com.

YARDE-BULLER, family name of **Baron Churston.**

YARDLEY, Sir David (Charles Miller), Kt 1994; Chairman, Commission for Local Administration in England, 1982–94; a Complaints Commissioner, Financial Services Authority (formerly Securities and Investments Board), 1994–2001; *b* 4 June 1929; *s* of late Geoffrey Miller Yardley and Doris Woodward Yardley (*née* Jones); *m* 1954, Patricia Anne Tempest Olver; two *s* two *d*. *Educ:* The Old Hall Sch., Wellington; Ellesmere Coll., Shropshire; Univ. of Birmingham (LLB, LLD); Univ. of Oxford (MA, DPhil). Called to Bar, Gray's Inn, 1952. RAF Flying Officer (nat. service), 1949–51. Bigelow Teaching Fellow, Univ. of Chicago, 1953–54; Fellow and Tutor in Jurisprudence, St Edmund Hall, Oxford, 1953–74, Emeritus Fellow, 1974–; CUF Lectr, Univ. of Oxford, 1954–74; Sen. Proctor, Univ. of Oxford, 1965–66; Barber Prof. of Law, Univ. of Birmingham, 1974–78; Head of Dept of Law, Politics and Economics, Oxford Poly., 1978–80; Rank Foundn Prof. of Law, University Coll. at Buckingham, 1980–82. Visiting Prof. of Law, Univ. of Sydney, 1971; Hon. Prof. of Law, Univ. of Buckingham, 1994; Vis. Prof., Oxford Brookes Univ., 1995–2001. Constitutional Consultant, Govt of W Nigeria, 1956. Chm., Thames Valley Rent Tribunal, 1963–82; Vice-Pres., Cambs Chilterns and Thames Rent Assessment Panel, subseq. Chilterns Thames and Eastern Rent Assessment Panel, 1966–82, 1995–99; Oxford City Councillor, 1966–74; Chairman: Oxford Area Nat. Ins. Local Appeal Tribunal, 1969–82; Oxford Preservation Trust, 1989–; Examining Bd, 1994–2006, Awards Panel, 1996–2001, IRRV; Ind. Adjudicator, W Bromwich Building Soc., 1996–2001; Ind. Reviewer, Millennium Commn, 1999–2005; Ind. Complaints Reviewer for UK Lottery Distributors, 2005–06. Chm. of Governors, St Helen's Sch., Abingdon, 1967–81. FRSA 1991. Freeman, City of Oxford, 1989. *Publications:* Introduction to British Constitutional Law, 1960, 8th edn (as Introduction to Constitutional and Administrative Law), 1995; A Source Book of English Administrative Law, 1963, 2nd edn, 1970; The Future of the Law, 1964; Geldart's Elements of English Law, 7th edn, 1966–10th edn (as Geldart's Introduction to English Law), 1991, 11th edn 1995; Hanbury's English Courts of Law, 4th edn, 1967; Hanbury and Yardley, English Courts of Law, 5th edn, 1979; Principles of Administrative Law, 1981, 2nd edn, 1986; (with I. N. Stevens) The Protection of Liberty, 1982; contrib. Halsbury's Laws of England, and Atkin's Court Forms. *Recreations:* lawn tennis, opera, cats. *Address:* 9 Belbroughton Road, Oxford OX2 6UZ. *T:* (01865) 554831. *Club:* Royal Air Force.

YARMOUTH, Earl of; William Francis Seymour; *b* 2 Nov. 1993; *s* and *heir* of Marquess of Hertford, *qv*.

YARNOLD, Patrick; HM Diplomatic Service, retired; professional genealogical and historical researcher; *b* 21 March 1937; *s* of late Leonard Francis Yarnold and Gladys Blanche Yarnold (*née* Merry); *m* 1961, Caroline, *er d* of late Andrew J. Martin; two *d*. *Educ:* Bancroft's School. HM Forces, 1955–57. Joined HM Foreign (now Diplomatic) Service, 1957; served: FO, 1957–60; Addis Ababa, 1961–64; Belgrade, 1964–66; FO (later FCO), 1966–70; 1st Sec., Head of Chancery, Bucharest, 1970–73; 1st Sec. (Commercial), Bonn, 1973–76; FCO, 1976–79; Counsellor (Economic and Commercial), Brussels, 1980–83; Consul-Gen., Zagreb, 1983–85; Counsellor and Head of Chancery, Belgrade, 1985–87; Hd of Defence Dept, FCO, 1987–90; Consul-Gen., Hamburg, 1990–94; Consul-Gen., Marseilles, 1995–97. *Recreations:* travel, photography, walking, local history, Chinese cooking, etc. *Address:* Cherry Cottage, The Street, Puttenham, Guildford, Surrey GU3 1AT.

YARROW, Dr Alfred, FFPH; Honorary Member, Epidemiology Unit, Ministry of Health, Jerusalem, 1987–96; *b* 25 May 1924; *s* of Leah and step *s* of Philip Yarrow; *m* 1953, Sheila Kaufman; two *d*. *Educ:* Hackney Downs Grammar Sch.; Edinburgh Univ. (MB, ChB); London Sch. of Hygiene and Trop. Medicine (Hons DPH). FFPH (Foundn FFCM 1972). Dep. Area MO, Tottenham and Hornsey, 1955–60; Area MO, SE Essex, 1960–65; MOH, Gateshead, 1965–68; Dir, Scottish Health Educn Unit, 1968–73; SMO, 1973–77, SPMO, 1977–84, DHSS. Temp. Consultant, WHO, 1975–76. Brit. Council Lectr, 1975; Council of Europe Fellow, 1978. *Publications:* So Now You Know About Smoking, 1975; Politics, Society and Preventive Medicine, 1986; scientific papers on demography, epidemiology, preventive medicine and health educn. *Recreations:* lawn bowls, travelling, reading. *Address:* 9/4 Nof Harim, Jerusalem 96190, Israel. *T:* 6438792.

YARROW, Sir Eric Grant, 3rd Bt *cr* 1916; MBE (mil.) 1946; DL; FRSE; Chairman, Clydesdale Bank PLC, 1985–91 (Director 1962–91, Deputy Chairman, 1975–85); Director: Standard Life Assurance Co., 1958–91; National Australia Bank Ltd, 1987–91; *b* 23 April 1920; *o s* of Sir Harold Yarrow, 2nd Bt and 1st wife, Eleanor Etheldreda (*d* 1934); *S* father, 1962; *m* 1st, 1951, Rosemary Ann (*d* 1957), *yr d* of late H. T. Young, Roehampton, SW15; (one *s* decd); 2nd, 1959, Annette Elizabeth Françoise (marr. diss. 1975), *d* of late A. J. E. Steven, Ardgay; three *s* (including twin *s*); 3rd, 1982, Mrs Joan Botting, *d* of late R. F. Masters, Piddinghoe, Sussex. *Educ:* Marlborough Coll.; Glasgow Univ. Served apprenticeship, G. & J. Weir Ltd. Served Burma, 1942–45; Major RE, 1945. Asst Manager Yarrow & Co., 1946; Dir, 1948; Man. Dir, 1958–67; Chm., 1962–85; Pres., Yarrow PLC, 1985–87. Mem. Council, RINA, 1957–65; Vice-Pres., 1965; Hon. Vice-Pres., 1972. Mem., General Cttee, Lloyd's Register of Shipping, 1960–87; Prime Warden, Worshipful Co. of Shipwrights, 1970; Deacon, Incorporation of Hammermen of Glasgow, 1961–62; Retired Mem. Council, Institution of Engineers & Shipbuilders in Scotland; Mem. Council, Inst. of Directors, 1983–90; Mem., Glasgow Action, 1985–91. Pres., Scottish Convalescent Home for Children, 1957–70; Hon. Pres., Princess Louise Scottish Hospital at Erskine, 1986– (Chm., 1980–86). President: British Naval Equipment Assoc., 1982–90; Smeatonian Soc. of Civil Engineers, 1983; Marlburian Club, 1984; Scottish Area, Burma Star Assoc., 1990–; Vice President: RHAS, 1990–91; Glasgow Br., RNLI, 1988–96; Chm., Blythe Sappers, 1989. DL Renfrewshire, 1970. FRSE 1974. OStJ. *Recreation:* family life. *Heir: g s* Ross William Grant Yarrow, *b* 14 Jan. 1985. *Address:* Craigrowan, Porterfield Road, Kilmacolm, Renfrewshire PA13 4PD. *T:* (01505) 872067. *Clubs:* Army and Navy; Royal & Ancient Golf (St Andrews).

YARWOOD, Michael Edward, OBE 1976; entertainer, since 1962; *b* 14 June 1941; *s* of Wilfred and Bridget Yarwood; *m* 1969, Sandra Burville (marr. diss. 1987); two *d*. *Educ:* Bredbury Secondary Modern Sch., Cheshire. First television appearance, 1963; *BBC TV:* Three of a Kind, 1967; Look—Mike Yarwood, and Mike Yarwood in Persons (series), 1971–82; *ATV:* Will the Real Mike Yarwood Stand Up? (series), 1968; *Thames:* Mike Yarwood in Persons, 1983–84; Yarwood's Royal Variety Show, the Yarwood Chat Show, and Mike Yarwood in Persons, 1986; *stage:* Royal Variety performances, 1968, 1972, 1976, 1981, 1987, 1993; One for the Pot, UK tour, 1988. Variety Club of Gt Britain award for BBC TV Personality of 1973; Royal Television Society award for outstanding creative achievement in front of camera, 1978. Mem., Grand Order of Water Rats, 1968. *Publications:* And This Is Me, 1974; Impressions of my life (autobiog.), 1986. *Recreations:* golf, tennis. *Address:* c/o International Artistes Ltd, Holborn Hall, 193–197 High Holborn, WC1V 7BD. *Club:* Lord's Taverners.

YASAMEE, Heather Jacqueline, (Mrs S. J. Gagen), CMG 2006; Assistant Director (Information Management), Directorate for Strategy and Information, Foreign and Commonwealth Office, 2004–06; *b* 12 Aug. 1951; *d* of Dennis Gordon Fenby and Betty Mitchell Fenby (*née* Linford); *m* 1st, 1979, Feroze Abdullah Khan Yasamee (marr. diss. 1999); 2nd, 2005, Stephen John Gagen, JP. *Educ:* Lawnswood High Sch. for Girls, Leeds; St Anne's Coll., Oxford (MA Mod. Hist.). Foreign and Commonwealth Office: joined, 1973; Historians, 1973–95, Hd of Historians, 1990–95; Editor, Documents on British Policy Overseas, 1988–95; Departmental Record Officer, 1995–2006: Hd, Records and Histl Services, 1995–99; Hd, Records and Histl Dept, 1999–2003. *Publications:* (Asst Ed.) Documents on British Policy Overseas: Potsdam, 1984; Schuman Plan, 1986; London Conferences, 1987; (ed) German Rearmament, 1989; Korea, 1991; various articles. *Recreations:* family life, gardening. *Address:* 32 Station Road, SW19 2LP; *e-mail:* heather@yasamee.com.

YASS, Irving, CB 1993; Policy Adviser, London First, since 2008 (Director: Transport, 1995–2001; Policy, 2001–08); *b* 20 Dec. 1935; *s* of late Abraham and Fanny Yass; *m* 1962, Marion Leighton; two *s* one *d*. *Educ:* Harrow County Grammar School for Boys; Balliol Coll., Oxford (Brackenbury Schol.; BA). Assistant Principal, Min. of Transport and Civil Aviation, 1958; Private Sec. to Joint Parliamentary Secretary, 1960; HM Treasury, 1967–70; Asst Secretary, Dept of the Environment, 1971; Secretary, Cttee of Inquiry into Local Govt Finance, 1974–76; Dept of Transport, 1976–94 (Under Sec., 1982); Dir, Planning and Transport, Govt Office for London, 1994–95. *Address:* London First, 3 Whitcomb Street, WC2H 7HA. *T:* (020) 7665 1589.

YASSUKOVICH, Stanislas Michael, CBE 1991; Chairman, S. M Yassukovich & Co. Ltd, since 1997; *b* 5 Feb. 1935; adopted British nationality, 1993; *s* of Dimitri and Denise Yassukovich; *m* 1961, Diana (*née* Townsend); two *s* one *d*. *Educ:* Deerfield Academy; Harvard University. US Marine Corps, 1957–61. Joined White, Weld & Co., 1961: posted to London, 1962; Branch Manager, 1967; General Partner, 1969; Managing Director, 1969; European Banking Co. Ltd: Managing Director, 1973; Group Dep. Chm., 1983. Sen. Advr, Merrill Lynch & Co., 1989–90; Dir, Merrill Lynch Europe Ltd, 1985–90 (Chm., 1985–90); Chairman: Flextech, 1989–97 (Dep. Chm., 1997–99; Dir, Telewest plc, 1999–2003); Park Place Capital, 1991–; Henderson Euro Trust PLC, 1992–2008; Hemingway Properties, 1993–98; Gallo & Co., 1995–98; Easdaq, 1997–2000; Manek Investment Management, 1998–; Cayzer Continuation PCC Ltd, 2004–; Prometheus Energy, 2007–; Medicapital Hldgs Ltd, 2007–; Vice-Chm., Bristol & West plc, 1991–99; Dep. Chm., ABC Internat. Bank, 1993–2007; Director: Mossiman's Ltd, 1989–98; Henderson plc, 1991–98; SW Water, 1992–99 (Dep. Chm., 1997–99); Tradepoint Financial Network, 1997–99; Atlas Capital Ltd, 2002–07; Fortis Investments SA. Jt Dep. Chm., Internat. Stock Exchange, 1986–89; Chm., Securities Assoc., 1988–91. Chairman: City Res. Project, 1991–95; City Disputes Panel, 1994–98. *Publications:* articles in financial press. *Recreations:* hunting, shooting, polo. *Address:* S. M. Yassukovich & Co. Ltd, 42 Berkeley Square, W1J 5AW. *T:* (020) 7318 0825. *Clubs:* Buck's, White's; Travellers (Paris); Brook (New York).

YATES, (Anthony) David; Warden, Robinson College, Cambridge, since 2001; *b* 5 May 1946; *s* of Cyril Yates and Violet Ethel Yates (*née* Mann); *m* 1st, 1974, Carolyn Paula Hamilton (marr. diss. 1988); 2nd, 1992, Susanna Margaret McGarry. *Educ:* Bromley Grammar Sch. for Boys; St Catherine's Coll., Oxford (Exhibnr; BA 1967, MA 1971; Hon. Fellow, 2003). Admitted solicitor, 1972; Lecturer in Law: Univ. of Hull, 1969–72; Univ.

of Bristol, 1972–74; University of Manchester: Lectr in Law, 1974–76; Sen. Lectr 1976–78; Principal, Dalton Hall, 1975–80; Foundn Prof. of Law, 1979–87, Dean, Sch. of Law, 1979–84, and Pro-Vice-Chancellor, 1985–87, Univ. of Essex; Dir, Professional Develt, 1987–93, Dir of Strategy, 1993–97, Partner, 1993–2001, and Chief Operating Officer, 1997–2001, Baker & McKenzie. Visiting Professor: Univ. of Manchester, 1979; Univ. of NSW, 1985; Univ. of Essex, 1987–91; Parsons Vis. Fellow, Univ. of Sydney, 1985. Mem. Council, Law Soc., 1992–97. Dep. Chm. of Govs, Coll. of Law, England and Wales, 2005– (Gov., 2002–05). FRSA 2006. *Publications:* Exclusion Clauses in Contracts, 1978, 2nd edn 1982; Leases of Business Premises, 1979; (with A. J. Hawkins) Landlord and Tenant Law, 1981, 2nd edn 1986; (with A. J. Hawkins) Standard Business Contracts, 1986; (Ed. in Chief) The Carriage of Goods by Land, Sea and Air, annually, 1993–2005; (with Malcolm Clarke) The Carriage of Goods by Land and Air, 2005. *Recreations:* opera, food, wine, Rugby football. *Address:* Warden's Lodge, Robinson College, Cambridge CB3 9AN. *Clubs:* Oxford and Cambridge, Royal Commonwealth Society.

YATES, Brian Douglas; Consumer Director, TrustMark, since 2008; *b* 1 May 1944; *s* of Bertram Yates and Barbara (*née* Wenham); *m* 1971, Patricia, *d* of Arthur Hutchinson, DFC; one *s*. *Educ:* Uppingham Sch.; Clare Coll., Cambridge (MA); London Business Sch. (MBA). CEng; Eur Ing. RHP Bearings, 1973–81; Thorn EMI, 1981–85; Dexion, 1985–88; Morris Material (formerly Morris Mechanical) Handling, 1988–2004. Member: Northampton BC, 1979–83; Hampshire CC, 1985–89. Chm., Consumers' Assoc., 1994–2007. Member: Council, Consumers' Assoc., 1986–; Council, Ombudsman for Estate Agents, 1998–2005; Fitness to Practice (formerly Professional Conduct) Cttee, GMC, 2001–; Genetics Insce Cttee, DoH, 2002–06; Hardship Panel, Assoc. of Investment Trust Cos, 2003–06; Immigration Appeal Tribunal, 2003–; Insolvency Licensing Cttee, ICAEW, 2006–. Mem., Lunar Soc., Birmingham. FRSA. *Recreations:* tennis, cross country ski-ing. *Address:* 19 Park Avenue, Harpenden AL5 2DZ. *T:* (01582) 768484. *Clubs:* Athenæum, Royal Over-Seas League; Hatfield House Tennis, Harpenden Lawn Tennis.

YATES, David; *see* Yates, A. D.

YATES, Prof. David William, FRCS; Professor of Emergency Medicine, University of Manchester, 1990–2004, now Emeritus; *b* 19 Nov. 1941; *o s* of Bill and Lena Yates; *m* 1977, Veronica Mary Henderson; two *s*. *Educ:* Bradford Grammar Sch.; Emmanuel Coll., Cambridge (MB BChir 1967; MD 1990); St Thomas's Hosp., London. FRCS 1972. Med. posts in orthopaedic surgery; first Prof. of Emergency Medicine in UK, 1990. First Dean, Faculty of A&E Medicine, RCS, 1993–98. *Address:* c/o Hope Hospital, Salford M6 8HD. *T:* (0161) 206 4397.

YATES, Edgar; *see* Yates, W. E.

YATES, Ian Humphrey Nelson, CBE 1991; Director, 1989–90, Chief Executive, 1975–90, The Press Association Ltd; *b* 24 Jan. 1931; *s* of James Nelson Yates and Martha (*née* Nutter); *m* 1956, Daphne J. Hudson, MCSP; three *s*. *Educ:* Lancaster Royal Grammar Sch.; Canford Sch., Wimborne. Royal Scots Greys, Germany and ME (National Service Commn), 1951–53. Management Trainee, Westminster Press Ltd, 1953–58 (Westmorland Gazette, and Telegraph & Argus, Bradford); Asst to Man. Dir, King & Hutchings Ltd, Uxbridge, 1958–60; Bradford and District Newspapers: Asst Gen. Man., 1960; Gen. Man., 1964; Man. Dir, 1969–75; Dir, Westminster Press Planning Div., 1969–75. Chairman: Universal News Services Ltd, 1988–90; Tellex Monitors Ltd, 1988–90; CRG Communications Gp Ltd, 1990–. President: Young Newspapermen's Assoc., 1966; Yorks Newspaper Soc., 1968. Member: Council, Newspaper Soc., 1970–75; Council, Commonwealth Press Union, 1977–90; Pres., Alliance of European News Agencies, 1987–88. FRSA 1989. *Recreations:* walking, reading, theatre.

YATES, Ivan R., CBE 1982; FREng; Deputy Chief Executive, 1986–90, Director, 1981–90, British Aerospace PLC; *b* 22 April 1929; *m* 1967, Jennifer Mary Holcombe; one *s* one *d*. *Educ:* Liverpool Collegiate Sch.; Liverpool Univ. (BEng 1st Class Hons). FIMechE; FRAeS 1968; FREng (FEng 1983); FAIAA 1984. Graduate Apprentice, English Electric, Preston, 1950; Chief Project Engr, TSR-2, 1959; Project Manager, Jaguar, 1966; British Aircraft Corporation: Special Dir, Preston Div., 1970; Dir, Preston, Warton Div., 1973; Dir, Aircraft Projects, 1974; Director: SEPECAT SA, 1976; Panavia GmbH, 1977; Eurofighter GmbH, 1986–90; British Aerospace: Man. Dir, Warton, 1978; Dir of Engrg and Project Assessment, Aircraft Gp, 1981; Chief Exec., Aircraft Gp, 1982–85; Dep. Man. Dir (Aircraft), 1985–86. Vis. Prof. in Design, Cambridge Univ., 1991–2003; By-Fellow, Churchill Coll., Cambridge, 1992–2000. Mem., Technology Requirements Bd, 1985–89; Advr, H of C Sci. and Technol. Cttee, 1993–94. Pres., 1988–89, Dep. Pres., 1989–90, SBAC; Mem. Council, RAeS, 1986–91. Member: Design Council, 1990–99; Council, RUSI, 1989–93. Commissioner, Royal Commn for Exhibn of 1851, 1990–99. Mem. Council, Imperial Coll., 1991–99. CCMI; FRSA 1985. Foreign Mem., Royal Swedish Acad. of Engrg Scis, 1990. Hon. DSc: Loughborough, 1989; City, 1991. British Silver Medal, 1979, Gold Medal, 1985, RAeS. *Publications:* Innovation, Investment and Survival of UK Economy, 1993; numerous papers and lectures. *Recreations:* walking, ski-ing, sculpture, music. *T:* (office) (01273) 480469. *Club:* Athenæum.

YATES, John Michael, QPM 2006; Assistant Commissioner, and Head of Serious and Organised Crime, Metropolitan Police Service, since 2008; *b* Liverpool, 17 Feb. 1959; *s* of Dr Godfrey and Dr Muriel Yates; *m* 1984, Louise Caroline Fowler; one *s* one *d*. *Educ:* Marlborough Coll.; King's Coll., London (BA Hons Medieval and Modern Hist.); Fitzwilliam Coll., Cambridge (Dip. Applied Criminol. 2003). Metropolitan Police Service, 1981–: Comdr, Crime, 2003–04; Dep. Asst Comr, and Dir of Intelligence, 2004–06; Asst Comr, Professional Standards, 2006–07. ACPO lead for Rape and Serious Sexual Offences, 2003–; Mem., Internat. Gp of Experts on Corruption, 2006–. *Recreations:* long-distance cycling, Liverpool Football Club, cooking. *Address:* Metropolitan Police Service, New Scotland Yard, 10 Broadway, SW1H 0BG.

YATES, Peter (James); film director/producer and theatre director; *b* 24 July 1929; *s* of Col Robert L. Yates and Constance Yates; *m* 1960, Virginia Pope; two *s* one *d* (and one *d* decd). *Educ:* Charterhouse; Royal Academy of Dramatic Art. Entered film industry, 1956. *Films directed:* Summer Holiday, 1962; One Way Pendulum, 1964; Robbery, 1966; Bullitt, 1968; John and Mary, 1969; Murphy's War, 1970; The Hot Rock, 1971; The Friends of Eddie Coyle, 1972; For Pete's Sake, 1973; Mother, Jugs and Speed, 1975; The Deep, 1976; Breaking Away (dir and prod.), 1979 (nominated 1980 Academy Awards, Director and Producer); The Janitor (dir and prod.), 1980; Krull, 1982; The Dresser (dir and prod.), 1983 (nominated 1984 Academy Awards, Dir and Producer); Eleni, 1985; The House on Carroll Street (dir and prod.), 1986; Suspect, 1987; An Innocent Man, 1989; Year of the Comet, 1991; Roommates, 1993; The Run of the Country, 1996; Curtain Call, 1997; Don Quixote, 2000; A Separate Peace, 2002. *Theatre directed:* The American Dream, Royal Court, 1961; The Death of Bessie Smith, (London) 1961; Passing Game, (New York) 1977; Interpreters, (London) 1985. *Recreations:* tennis, sailing, ski-ing. *Address:* c/o Judy Daish Agency, 2 St Charles Place, W10 6EG. *Club:* Garrick.

YATES, Roger Philip; Chief Executive, Henderson Group (formerly HHG), 2003–08 (Director, 2003–08); *b* 4 April 1957; *s* of Eric Yates and Joyce Yates; *m* 2003, Catriona Louise Maclean; three *s* one *d*. *Educ:* Worcester Coll., Oxford (BA Hons Mod. Hist.); Univ. of Reading (postgrad. res.). GT Management plc, 1981–88, Dir, 1985; Chief Investment Officer: Morgan Grenfell Asset Mgt, 1988–94 (Dir, 1990–94); LGT Asset Mgt, 1994–98; Invesco Asset Mgt, 1998–99; Chief Exec. and Dir, Henderson Global Investors, 1999–2008. Non-exec. Dir, IG Gp plc, 2006–. *Recreations:* ski-ing, golf, tennis.

YATES, William, PhD; The Administrator of Christmas Island, Indian Ocean, 1982–83; *b* 15 Sept. 1921; *er s* of late William Yates and of Mrs John T. Renshaw, Burrells, Appleby, Westmorland; *m* 1st, 1946, Hon. Rosemary (marr. diss. 1955), *yr d* of 1st Baron Elton; two *d* (one *s* decd); 2nd, 1957, Camilla, *d* of late E. W. D. Tennant, Orford House, Ugley, Bishop's Stortford; three *s* (and one *s* decd). *Educ:* Uppingham; Hertford Coll., Oxford (BA); Melbourne Univ. (PhD 2003). Served War, 1940–45, North Africa and Italy; Captain The Bays, 1945. Shropshire Yeomanry, 1956–67. Appointed Legal Officer to report on State lands in Department of Custodian's Office in Tripoli, Libya, 1951. MP (C) The Wrekin Division of Shropshire, 1955–66. Myron Taylor Lectures in International Affairs, Cornell Univ., USA, 1958 and 1966. MP (L) Holt, Vic, Aust. Commonwealth, 1975–80; Mem. Liberal Party Parly Cttee for Defence and Foreign Affairs, 1975–80; Mem., Cttee of Privileges, House of Representatives, 1977–80. Mem., Inst. of Internat. Affairs, Victoria. *Address:* The Old House, 16 Jarvis Creek Road, Old Tallangatta, Vic 3701, Australia. *Clubs:* Cavalry and Guards; Commonwealth (Canberra).

YATES, Prof. (William) Edgar, MA, PhD; FBA 2002; Professor of German, University of Exeter, 1972–2001, now Emeritus; *b* 30 April 1938; *s* of Douglas Yates and Doris Yates (*née* Goode); *m* 1963, Barbara Anne Fellowes; two *s*. *Educ:* Fettes Coll. (Foundn Schol.); Emmanuel Coll., Cambridge (Minor Open Schol.; MA, PhD). 2nd Lieut, RASC, 1957–58. Lectr in German, Univ. of Durham, 1963–72; University of Exeter: Hd of Dept of German, 1972–86; Dep. Vice-Chancellor, 1986–89. Vice-Pres., Conf. of Univ. Teachers of German, 1991–93. Lewis Fry Meml Lectr, Univ. of Bristol, 1994. Vice-Pres., Wiener Shakespeare-Ges., 1992–2002; Member: Cttee, MHRA, 1980–; Council, English Goethe Soc., 1984–; Council, Internat. Nestroy-Ges., 1986– (Vice-Pres., 1997–). Germanic Editor, MLR, 1981–88; Editor, 1992–2001, Jt Editor, 2002–, Nestroyana; Co-ordinating Gen. Editor, historisch-kritische Nestroy-Ausgabe, 1992–. Corresp. Fellow, Austrian Acad. of Scis, 1995. Gov., Exeter Sch., 1986– (Chm., 1994–2008). J. G. Robertson Prize, Univ. of London, 1975. Ehrenkreuz für Wissenschaft und Kunst, 1. Klasse (Austria), 2001; Silver Medal, Schwechat, 2005. *Publications:* Grillparzer: a critical introduction, 1972; Nestroy: satire and parody in Viennese popular comedy, 1972; Humanity in Weimar and Vienna: the continuity of an ideal, 1973; Tradition in the German Sonnet, 1981; Schnitzler, Hofmannsthal, and the Austrian Theatre, 1992; Nestroy and the Critics, 1994; Theatre in Vienna 1776–1995: a critical history, 1996; (with B. Pargner) Nestroy in München, 2001; *edited:* Hofmannsthal: Der Schwierige, 1966; Grillparzer: Der Traum ein Leben, 1968; Nestroy: Stücke 12–14 (Hist.-krit. Ausgabe), 1981–82, Stücke 34, 1989, Stücke 18/I, 1991, Stücke 22, 1996, Stücke 17/II, 1998, (jtly) Stücke 2, 2000, (jtly) Nachträge (2 vols), 2007; (jtly) Viennese Popular Theatre, 1985; (jtly) Grillparzer und die europäische Tradition, 1987; Vom schaffenden zum edierten Nestroy, 1994; Nestroys Reserve und andere Notizen, 2000, 2nd edn 2003; (jtly) From Perinet to Jelinek, 2001; Der unbekannte Nestroy, 2001; Nestroys Alltag und dessen Dokumentation, 2001; (jtly) Hinter den Kulissen von Biedermeier und Nachmärz, 2001; (jtly) Briefe des Theaterdirektors Carl Carl und seiner Frau Margaretha Carl an Charlotte Birch-Pfeiffer, 2004; (jtly) Theater und Gesellschaft im Wien des 19. Jahrhunderts, 2006; numerous articles on Austrian literary and cultural history, on German literature of the Biedermeier period, and on German lyric poetry; *festschrift:* The Austrian Comic Tradition, 1998. *Recreations:* music, theatre, opera, French wine. *Address:* 7 Clifton Hill, Exeter EX1 2DL. *T:* (01392) 254713.

YATES, William Hugh, MBE 2007; Senior Partner, Knight Frank (formerly Knight Frank & Rutley), 1992–96; *b* 18 Dec. 1935; *s* of late Brig. Morris Yates, DSO, OBE and Kathleen Rosanna Yates (*née* Sherbrooke, later Mrs Hugh Cowan); *m* 1st, 1963, Celia Geraldine Pitman (marr. diss. 1972); one *s*; 2nd, 1979, Elisabeth Susan Mansel-Pleydell (*née* Luard); four step *s*. *Educ:* Lancing Coll.; RMA Sandhurst. FRICS. Commissioned, Royal Dragoons, 1955; ADC to Governor of Aden, 1959. Articled surveyor, Rylands & Co., 1961; Knight Frank & Rutley, 1964–96: Man. Dir, Geneva, 1968–72; Partner, 1972; Man. Partner, 1978–82; Head of Residential Div., 1982–92. Director: INCAS SA, 1970–78; European Property Investment Co. NV, 1973–81; Ecclesiastical Insurance Group, 1985–2006 (Dep. Chm., 1995–2006); Woolwich plc (formerly Woolwich Building Soc.), 1990–2000 (Dep. Chm., 1996–2000); Roxton Sporting Ltd, 2001–03. Save the Children Fund: Chm., Fund Raising Cttee, 1980–86; Hon. Treasurer, 1986–92; Dep. Chm., Suzy Lamplugh Trust, 2002–05. *Recreations:* riding, gardening, golf, music. *Address:* Upper Farm, Milton Lilbourne, Pewsey, Wilts SN9 5LQ. *T:* (01672) 563438. *Clubs:* Turf; Wentworth Golf.

YATIM, Datuk Dr Rais, SPNS (Malaysia) 2001; DSNS (Malaysia) 1978; Minister of Foreign Affairs, Malaysia, since 2008; *b* 15 April 1942; *s* of Yatim Tahir and Siandam Boloh; *m* 1975, Datin Masnah; three *s* one *d*. *Educ:* Language Inst., Kuala Lumpur (DipEd 1964; DipPsych); Univ. of Singapore (LLB (Hons) 1973); PhD London, 1994. Specialist language teacher, Northern Illinois Univ., 1964–66. Parly Sec., Min. of Youth, 1974; Dep. Law Minister, 1976; Dep. Home Minister, 1977; Chief Minister, State of Negeri Sembilan, 1978–82; Minister of Land Regl Develt, Malaysia, 1982–84; Minister of Information, 1984–86; Foreign Minister, 1986–87. Dep. Pres., Parti Melayu, 1989–96. Returned to law practice Ram Rais & Partners, Kuala Lumpur, 1987–99. Minister, Prime Minister's Dept, Malaysia, 1999; Minister of Culture, Arts and Heritage. Founder Pres., PEMADAM, Malaysia's Anti-Drug Assoc., 1976–87. Member: Civil Liberty Cttee, Bar Council, Kuala Lumpur, 1996–; Internet Soc., Washington. *Publications:* Faces in the Corridors of Power: a pictorial depiction of Malaysians in power and authority, 1987; Freedom Under Executive Power in Malaysia, 1995. *Recreations:* photography, jogging, travel, writing. *Address:* (residence) 41 Road 12, Taman Grandview, 68000 Ampang Jaya, Kuala Lumpur, Malaysia. *T:* (3) 4569621. *Club:* Darul Ehsan Recreational (Kuala Lumpur).

YAXLEY, John Francis, CBE 1990; HM Overseas Civil Service, 1961–94, retired; *b* 13 Nov. 1936; *s* of late Rev. Canon R. W. and of Dorothy Yaxley; *m* 1960, Patricia Anne Scott; one *s*. *Educ:* Hatfield Coll., Durham Univ. National Service, 1958–60. Joined HMOCS, 1961; posts in New Hebrides and Solomon Islands, 1961–75; seconded FCO, 1975–77; Hong Kong, 1977–89: posts included Dir of Industry, Sec. for Econ. Services, and Dep. Financial Sec.; Comr, Hong Kong Govt, London, 1989–93. Mem., Salvation Army Nat. Adv. Bd, 1990–98; Chm., Oxford Diocesan Bd of Finance, 1996–2001. Mem. Council, Durham Univ., 1995–2001; Mem. Governing Body, Hatfield Coll., Durham, 1997–2001. Treasurer: W Mercia NADFAS, 1995–2000; Northleach DFAS, 2001–04. Trustee: Triumph over Phobia UK, 1995–2000; Oxford Historic Churches Trust, 2002–; Trustee and Jt Financial Dir, Prayer Book Soc., 2005–06. *Publications:* The Population of the New Hebrides (with Dr Norma McArthur), 1968; (ed) Public Sector Reform in the

Hong Kong Government, 1989. *Recreations:* walking, birdwatching, history, gardening. *Address:* Old Housing, Fifield, Oxon OX7 6HF. *Club:* Royal Over-Seas League.

YEA, Philip Edward; Chief Executive, 3i Group plc, since 2004; *b* 11 Dec. 1954; *s* of John Yea and Beryl Yea (*née* Putman); *m* 1981, Daryl Walker; two *s* one *d*. *Educ:* Wallington High Sch.; Brasenose Coll., Oxford (MA Mod. Langs). FCMA. Perkins Engines, 1977–82; Klix (Mars), 1983; Guinness PLC, 1984–88; Cope Allmann plc, 1988–91; Dir, Financial Control, 1991–93, Finance Dir, 1993–97, Guinness PLC; Finance Dir, Diageo plc, 1997–99; Man. Dir, Investcorp, 1999–2004. Non-executive Director: Halifax plc, subseq. HBOS plc, 1999–2004; Manchester United plc, 2000–04. *Recreations:* family, travel. *Address:* 3i Group plc, 16 Palace Street, SW1E 5JD; *e-mail:* philip.yea@3i.com.

YEANG, Dr Kenneth King Mun; architect; Principal: Llewelyn Davies Yeang (UK), since 2005; T. R. Hamzah & Yeang (Malaysia) Sdn Bhd, since 1976; *b* 6 Oct. 1948; *s* of Yeang Cheng Hin and Louise Yeang; *m* 1986, Priscilla Khoo; two *s* two *d*. *Educ:* Cheltenham Coll.; AA Sch., London (Grad. in Architecture 1971); Wolfson Coll., Cambridge (PhD 1981). Major projects include: Menara Mesiniaga, Subang, Malaysia, 1992; Nat. Liby Building, Singapore, 2005; Mewah Oils HQ, Port Kelang, Malaysia, 2005. Graham Willis Vis. Prof., Sheffield Univ., 1994–98, 1999–2005; Adjunct Professor: Tongji Univ., Shanghai, 2005–08; Univ. of Illinois. Hon. DLitt Sheffield, 2003. *Address:* Brook House, Torrington Place, WC1E 7HN. *T:* (020) 7637 0181, *Fax:* (020) 7637 8740; *e-mail:* k.yeang@ldavies.com.

YELLAND, David Ian; Partner, Brunswick Group LLP, since 2006; *b* Harrogate, 14 May 1963; *s* of John Michael Yelland and Patricia Ann (*née* McIntosh); *m* 1996, Tania Farrell (*d* 2006); one *s*. *Educ:* Brigg Grammar Sch., Lincs; Coventry Univ. (BA Hons Econs 1984); Harvard Business Sch. (AMP 2003). Grad. trainee, Westminster Press, 1985; trainee reporter, Buckinghamshire Advertiser, 1985–87; industrial reporter, Northern Echo, 1987–88; gen. news and business reporter, North West Times and Sunday Times, 1988–89; city reporter, Thomson Regl Newspapers, 1989–90; joined News Corporation, 1990: city reporter, city editor and NY corresp., The Sun, 1990–93; Dep. Business Ed., Business Ed., Dep. Ed., New York Post, 1993–98; Editor, The Sun, 1998–2003; Sen. Vice Pres., News Corp., NY, 2003; Sen. Vice-Chm., Weber Shandwick UK and Ireland, 2004–06. Life Patron, NSPCC, 2007. FRSA 2003. *Recreations:* reading, writing swimming, sleeping, contemporary art, Manchester City FC. *Address:* Brunswick Group LLP, 16 Lincoln's Inn Fields, WC2A 3ED. *T:* (020) 7404 5959; *e-mail:* davidyelland@btinternet.com. *Clubs:* Savile, Royal Automobile.

YELTON, Michael Paul; His Honour Judge Yelton; a Circuit Judge, since 1998; *b* 21 April 1950; *s* of Joseph William Yelton and Enid Hazel Yelton; *m* 1973, Judith Sara Chaplin; two *s* one *d*. *Educ:* Colchester Royal Grammar Sch.; Corpus Christi Coll., Cambridge (BA 1971; MA 1973). Called to the Bar, Middle Temple, 1972; in practice at the Bar, 1973–98; Fellow and Dir of Studies in Law, Corpus Christi Coll., Cambridge, 1977–81. *Publications:* Fatal Accidents: a practical guide to compensation, 1998; (jtly) Martin Travers, 1886–1948: an appreciation, 2003; Trams, Trolleybuses, Buses and the Law, 2004; Peter Anson, 2005; Anglican Papalism 1900–1960, 2005; Alfred Hope Patten and the Shrine of Our Lady of Walsingham, 2006; Empty Tabernacles, 2006; (jtly) Anglican Church-Building in London 1915–1945, 2007; Alfred Hope Patten: his life and times in pictures, 2007; contribs to transport jls. *Recreations:* ecclesiology, history of road passenger transport, Association football. *Address:* Cambridge County Court, 197 East Road, Cambridge CB1 1BA. *T:* (01223) 224500.

YENTOB, Alan; Director of Drama, Entertainment and Children's Programmes, since 2000, and Creative Director, since 2004, BBC; Chairman, Institute of Contemporary Arts, since 2002; *b* 11 March 1947; *s* of Isaac Yentob and Flora Yentob (*née* Khazam); one *s* one *d* by Philippa Walker. *Educ:* King's School, Ely; Univ. of Grenoble; Univ. of Leeds (LLB). BBC general trainee, 1968; producer/director, 1970–; arts features, incl. Omnibus, and Arena (Best Arts Series, British Acad. Awards, 1982, 1983, 1984, BPG Awards, 1985); Editor, Arena, 1978–85; Co-Editor, Omnibus, 1985; Hd of Music and Arts, BBC TV, 1985–88; Controller: BBC2, 1988–93, responsible for progs incl. The Late Show, Have I Got News For You, Absolutely Fabulous, Rab C. Nesbitt; BBC1, 1993–96; Dir of Progs, BBC TV, 1996–97; Dir of Television, BBC, 1997–2000. Member: Bd of Directors, Riverside Studios, 1984–91; BFI Production Board, 1985–93; Council, English Stage Co., 1990–. Governor: Nat. Film School, 1988–; S Bank Bd, 1999–; Trustee: Architecture Foundn, 1992–; Timebank, 2001–; Kids Co. FRTS; Fellow, BFI, 1997. Hon. Fellow: RCA, 1987; RIBA, 1991. Programming Supremo of Year, Broadcast Prodn Awards, 1997. *Recreations:* swimming, books.

YEO, Rt Rev. (Christopher) Richard, JCD; OSB; Superior of Buckfast Abbey, since 2007; Abbot President, English Benedictine Congregation, since 2001; *b* 7 July 1948; *s* of Peter and Patricia Yeo. *Educ:* Downside Sch.; Lincoln Coll., Oxford (MA); St Benet's Hall, Oxford; Pontifical Gregorian Univ., Rome (JCD). Entered monastery, 1970; ordained priest, 1976; Sec. of Abbot Primate of the Benedictines, 1980–86; Parish Priest, Bungay, 1986–93; Official, Congregation for Consecrated Life, 1993–98; Abbot of Downside, 1998–2006. *Publication:* The Structure and Content of Monastic Profession, 1982. *Address:* Buckfast Abbey, Buckfastleigh, Devon TQ11 0EE.

YEO, Diane Helen; Chairman, The Arts Educational Schools, since 2004; *b* 22 July 1945; *d* of Brian Harold Pickard, FRCS and Joan Daisy Pickard; *m* 1970, Timothy Stephen Kenneth Yeo, *qv*; one *s* one *d*. *Educ:* Blackheath High Sch.; London Univ.; Institut Français de Presse. BBC Radio, 1968–74; Africa Educnl Trust, 1974–79; Girl Guides' Assoc., 1979–82; YWCA, 1982–85; Dir, Inst. of Charity Fundraising Managers, 1985–88; Charity Comr, 1989–95; Chief Exec., Malcolm Sargent Cancer Fund for Children, subseq. Sargent Cancer Care for Children, 1995–2001; Chief Exec., UK for UNHCR, 2001–03; ind. charity consultant, 2003–; Chief Executive: Muscular Dystrophy Campaign, 2004–05; Chelsea and Westminster Health Charity, 2005–08. Chm., Charity Standards Cttee, 1991–95 (Rowntree Report 1991); Member: Nathan Cttee on Effectiveness and the Voluntary Sector, 1989–90 (Report 1990); Adv. Council, NCVO, 1994–; Council and Audit Cttee, Advertising Standards Authy, 1997–2003; Fundraising Regulation Adv. Gp, Home Office, 2001–. Chm., NCVO/Charity Commn Cttee on Trng of Trustees, 1989–92 (report, On Trust, 1990). Patron, CANCERactive, 2004–; Chm., Chelsea and Westminster Hosp. Scanner Appeal, 2008–. FInstF; FRSA. Paul Harris Fellow, Rotary Internat., 2000. *Publications:* contribs to professional jls. *Recreations:* tennis, photography, piano. *Address:* *e-mail:* d.yeo.associates@btinternet.com.

YEO, Douglas; Director, Shell Research Ltd, Thornton Research Centre, 1980–85; *b* 13 June 1925; *s* of Sydney and Hylda Yeo; *m* 1947, Joan Elisabeth Chell; two *d*. *Educ:* Secondary Sch., St Austell; University Coll., Exeter (BSc London). Expedn on locust control, Kenya, 1945. HMOCS, 1948–63; Tropical Pesticides Research Inst., Uganda and Tanzania, 1948–61 (Scientific Officer, 1948–51, Sen. Scientific Officer, 1951–57, Prin. Scientific Officer, 1957–61). Internat. African Migratory Locust Control Organisation, Mali: on secondment, 1958, 1960; Dir and Sec. Gen., 1961–63. Shell Research Ltd: Research Dir, Woodstock Agricultural Research Centre, 1963–69, Dir, 1969–76; Dir, Biosciences Lab., Sittingbourne, 1976–80. Mem. Council, RHBNC, London Univ., 1985–90. FIBiol. *Publications:* papers in Bulletin Ent. Res., Bull. WHO, Anti-Locust Bull., Qly Jl Royal Met. Soc., Jl Sci. Fd. Agric., Plant Protection Confs, etc. *Recreations:* sailing, hill walking, fishing. *Address:* Tremarne, Tremarne Close, Feock, Truro TR3 6SB.

YEO, Rt Rev. Richard; *see* Yeo, Rt Rev. C. R.

YEO, Timothy Stephen Kenneth; MP (C) Suffolk South, since 1983; *b* 20 March 1945; *s* of late Dr Kenneth John Yeo and Norah Margaret Yeo; *m* 1970, Diane Helen Pickard (*see* D. H. Yeo); one *s* one *d*. *Educ:* Charterhouse; Emmanuel Coll., Cambridge (Open Exhibnr 1962; MA 1971). Asst Treas., Bankers Trust Co., 1970–73; Director, Worcester Engineering Co. Ltd, 1975–86. Chief Exec., Spastics Soc., 1980–83, Mem., Exec. Council, 1984–86. PPS to Sec. of State for Home Dept, 1988–89, to Sec. of State for Foreign Affairs, 1989–90; Parly Under Sec. of State, DoE, 1990–92, DoH, 1992–93; Minister of State, DoE, 1993–94. Opposition spokesman on local govt and envmt, 1997–98; Shadow Minister of Agric., 1998–2001; Shadow Culture, Media and Sport Sec., 2001–02; Shadow Trade and Industry Sec., 2002–03; Shadow Health and Educn Sec., 2003–04; Shadow Transport and Envmt Sec., 2004–05. Member: Social Services Select Cttee, 1985–88; Employment Select Cttee, 1994–96; Treasury Select Cttee, 1996–97; Chm., Envmtl Audit Select Cttee, 2005–; Jt Sec., Cons. Pty Finance Cttee, 1984–87. Captain, Parly Golfing Soc., 1991–95. Director: Genus plc, 2002–04; ITI Energy Ltd, 2006–; Groupe Eurotunnel SA, 2007–; Chairman: AFC Energy plc, 2007–; Eco City Vehicles plc. Hon. Treasurer, International Voluntary Service, 1975–78. Trustee: African Palms, 1970–85; Tanzania Development Trust, 1980–97; Chm., Tadworth Court Trust, 1983–90. Golf Correspondent: Country Life, 1994–; Financial Times, 2004–08. *Publication:* Public Accountability and Regulation of Charities, 1983. *Recreation:* ski-ing. *Address:* House of Commons, SW1A 0AA. *T:* (020) 7219 3000. *Clubs:* MCC; Sudbury Conservative (Sudbury); Royal and Ancient Golf (St Andrews); Royal St George's (Sandwich); Sunningdale Golf.

YEOMAN, Maj.-Gen. Alan, CB 1987; *b* 17 Nov. 1933; *s* of George Smith Patterson Yeoman and Wilhelmina Tromans Elwell; *m* 1960, Barbara Joan Davies; two *s* (one *d* decd). *Educ:* Dame Allan's School, Newcastle upon Tyne. Officer Cadet, RMA Sandhurst, 1952; commnd Royal Signals, 1954; served Korea, Malaysia, Singapore, Cyprus, UK, BAOR and Canada, 1954–70 (Staff Coll., 1963); CO 2 Div. Sig. Regt, BAOR, 1970–73; HQ 1 (BR) Corps, BAOR, 1973–74; MoD, 1974–77; Col AQ, HQLF Cyprus, 1978–79; Comd Trng Gp, Royal Signals and Catterick Garrison, 1979–82; Brig. AQ, HQ 1 (BR) Corps, BAOR, 1982–84; Comd Communications, BAOR, 1984–87, retd 1988. Dir, Army Sport Control Bd, 1988–95. Col Comdt, Royal Corps of Signals, 1987–93. Hon. Col, 37th (Wessex and Welsh) Signal Regt, T&AVR, 1987–95. Chm., Royal Signals Assoc., 1995–2000. *Recreations:* golf, cricket, ski-ing. *Address:* c/o Lloyds TSB, 3 South Street, Wareham, Dorset BH40 4LX.

YEOMAN, Rt Rev. David, PhD; Assistant Bishop of Llandaff, since 2004; *b* 5 March 1944; *s* of Thomas Walter and Doreen Yeoman; *m* 1969, Janice Flower; one *s* one *d*. *Educ:* UC Cardiff (BTh; PhD 2004); St Michael's Coll., Llandaff. Local govt officer, 1963–66. Ordained deacon, 1970, priest, 1971; Curate: St John Baptist, Cardiff, 1970–72; Caerphilly, 1972–76; Vicar: Ystrad Rhondda, 1976–81; Mountain Ash, 1981–96; Rector, Coity with Nolton, 1996–2004; Archdeacon of Morgannwg, 2004–06. Chaplain: Princess of Wales Hosp., 1996–2004; Welsh Guards Assoc., Bridgend, 1996–2001; RBL, Bridgend, 2003–04. *Publications:* (jtly) Christ in AIDS, 1997; (contrib.) Sexuality and Spirituality, 2000. *Recreations:* reading, poetry, music, photography. *Address:* 3 Denison Way, Michaelston-super-Ely, Cardiff CF5 4SF. *T:* (029) 2059 8110. *Club:* Rotary International (Bridgend).

YEOMAN, Prof. Michael Magson, PhD; FRSE; Regius Professor of Botany, 1978–93, now Emeritus, and Curator of Patronage, 1988–93, University of Edinburgh; *b* 16 May 1931; *s* of Gordon Yeoman and Mabel Ellen (*née* Magson), Newcastle upon Tyne; *m* 1962, Erica Mary Lines; two *d*. *Educ:* Gosforth Grammar Sch.; King's Coll., Univ. of Durham (BSc 1952, MSc 1954, PhD 1960); FRSE 1980. National Service, Royal Corps of Signals, 1954–56. Demonstrator in Botany, King's Coll., Newcastle upon Tyne, 1957–59; Edinburgh University: Lectr in Botany, 1960; Sen. Lectr, 1968; Reader, 1973; Dean, Fac. of Science, 1981–84; Vice-Principal, 1988–91. Vis. Prof., NENU, Changchun, China, 1986–. Chm., Univs Council for Adult and Continuing Educn (Scotland), 1989–91. Member: Governing Bodies, Nat. Vegetable Res. Stn and Scottish Plant Breeding Stn, 1978–82; SERC Biological Scis Cttee, 1982–85; SERC Biotechnology Management Cttee, 1983–85; British Nat. Cttee for Biology, 1981–89. Chm., Edinburgh Centre for Rural Res., 1989–93; Governor: East of Scotland Coll. of Agriculture, 1984–93; Scottish Crops Res. Inst., 1986–89. Chm. Trustees, Edinburgh Botanic Gdn (Sibbald) Trust, 1996–2003 (Trustee, 1986–2003); Trustee, Royal Botanic Gdn, Edinburgh, 1992–98 (Chm., Scientific Adv. Bd, 1995–98). Convener, N Northumberland Gp, Scottish Rock Garden Club, 1999–2002. Mem. Council, RSE, 1985–91 (Fellowship Sec., 1986–91). Gov. and Chm., Ellingham C of E First Sch., 1993–99; Churchwarden, St Maurice, Ellingham, 1996–2000. Member Editorial Board: Jl of Experimental Botany, 1981–85; Plant Science Letters, 1974–83; New Phytologist, 1977–93 (Trustee); Botanical Jl of Scotland, 1992–99. *Publications:* (ed) Cell Division in Higher Plants, 1976; (jtly) Laboratory Manual of Plant Cell and Tissue Culture, 1982; (ed) Plant Cell Technology, 1986; contrib. scientific jls; chapters, articles and revs in books. *Recreations:* military history, photography, gardening, walking. *Address:* 116 Allerburn Lea, Alnwick, Northumberland NE66 2QP. *T:* (01665) 605822.

YEOMANS, Lucy; Editor, Harper's Bazaar (formerly Harpers & Queen), since 2000; *b* 1 Nov. 1970; *d* of Harry Hammond Light Yeomans and Margaret (*née* Boyle). *Educ:* Univ. of St Andrews (MA Hons Hist. of Art 1992). Ed., Boulevard mag., Paris, 1993–95; Lit. Ed. and Features Ed., The European, 1995–98; Features Ed., Dep. Ed. and Actg Ed., Tatler, 1998–2000. FRSA. *Recreations:* theatre, horse-riding, music, poetry. *Address:* Harper's Bazaar, National Magazine House, 72 Broadwick Street, W1F 9EP. *T:* (020) 7439 5000. *Club:* Soho House.

YEOMANS, Richard Millett, CEng, FIET; FIMechE; Chief Executive, Scottish Nuclear Ltd, 1989–91; *b* 19 July 1932; *s* of late Maj. Richard J. Yeomans and Lillian (*née* Spray); *m* 1957, Jennifer Margaret Wingfield Pert; three *s* one *d*. *Educ:* Durban, SA; Cornwall Tech. Coll. Student apprentice, CEGB, 1948. Lt, REME, 1953–55. CEGB power stations, 1955–67; South of Scotland Electricity Board: Dep. Manager, Longannet Power Stn, 1971–75; Manager, Inverkip Power Stn, 1975–77; Manager, Hunterston A&B Nuclear Power Stns, 1977–80; Generation Engineer (Nuclear), 1980–87; Chief Engineer, 1987–89. *Recreations:* sailing, golf, gardening. *Address:* Garden Cottage, Ashcraig, Skelmorlie, Ayrshire PA17 5HB. *T:* (01475) 520298.

YERBURGH, family name of **Baron Alvingham.**

YERBURGH, John Maurice Armstrong; Vice Lord-Lieutenant of Dumfries and Galloway (District of Stewartry), 1990–98; President, Daniel Thwaites PLC, since 1993 (Director, since 1947; Chairman, 1966–93); *b* 23 May 1923; *e s* of late Major Guy Yerburgh (*d* 1926), OBE, Belgian Croix de Guerre, Italian Croce di Guerra and Lady (Hilda Violet Helena) Salisbury-Jones, *e d* of Rt Hon. Sir Maurice de Bunsen, Bt, GCMG, GCVO, CB; *m* 1973, Ann Jean Mary, *d* of N. P. Maclaren, Brooklands, Crocketford, Dumfries; one *s* four *d. Educ:* Eton; Magdalene College, Cambridge (BA). Commissioned Irish Guards 1943; served with 2nd Bn, France, Holland, Belgium, Germany; retired 1947 with rank of Captain. Contested (C) Blackburn, 1959 and 1963. Chm., S of Scotland Regional Adv. Cttee, Forestry Commn, 1972–87; Governor, Cumbria College of Agriculture and Forestry, 1975–89; Shire Horse Society: Pres., 1983–84; Dep. Pres., 1988. DL Dumfries and Galloway (Dist of Stewartry), 1989. *Recreations:* shooting, fishing, trees. *Address:* Barwhillanty, Parton, Castle Douglas, Kirkcudbrightshire DG7 3NS. *T:* (01644) 470237.

YEUNG, Kai-yin, GBS 2005; CBE 1993; JP; Vice-Chairman, Opera Hong Kong Ltd; Chief Executive Officer, Kowloon-Canton Railway Corporation, 2001–03 (Chairman and Chief Executive, 1996–2001); *b* 6 Jan. 1941; *s* of late K. F. Yeung and C. H. Lai; *m* 1964, Anna Lau; one *s* one *d. Educ:* Univ. of Hong Kong (BA Hons 1962). Joined Hong Kong Civil Service, 1962: staff appts, Hong Kong Admin. Service, 1962–73; Directorate rank, 1973–93; various appts at Asst and Dep. Head of Dept level, in trade, econ. develt and public finance, 1973–84; Comr, Hong Kong Export Credit Insce Corp., 1984–86; Dir Gen. of Industry, 1986–89; Sec. for Educn and Manpower, 1989–91; Sec. for the Treasury, 1991–93; Sec. for Transport, 1993, retd; Exec. Dir, Sino Land Co. Ltd, 1993–96. Dir, Hong Kong Community Chest, 1997–2003; Chm., Vocational Training Council, Hong Kong, 1998–2005. Mem., Long Term Housing Strategy Adv. Cttee, 1999–2003. Advr to govt of China on Hong Kong affairs, 1995–97. JP Hong Kong, 1976. *Recreations:* serious music, racing, golf. *Address:* Flat 11B, Tower 5, Beverly Villas, 16 La Salle Road, Kowloon, Hong Kong. *Clubs:* Hong Kong, Hong Kong Jockey (Voting Mem.).

YEVTUSHENKO, Yevgeny Aleksandrovich; poet, novelist, film director, film actor, photographer; *b* 18 July 1933; *m*; five *s*; *m* 4th, 1986, Maria Novikova. *Educ:* Moscow Literary Inst., 1952–56 (expelled). Elected Mem., Congress of People's Deputies of USSR, 1989. Distinguished Professor: Queen's College, New York; University of Tulsa. Has visited 94 countries; Vice-Pres., Russian PEN, 1990–93; Hon. Mem., Amer. Acad. of Arts and Letters, 1987; Mem., European Acad. of Scis and Arts; hon. degrees from numerous Univs. Film actor: Take Off, 1979 (silver prize, Moscow Internat. film fest.); film director: Kindergarten, 1984; Stalin's Funeral, 1990. *Publications: in Russian:* Scouts of the Future, 1952; The Third Snow, 1955; The Highway of Enthusiasts, 1956; The Promise, 1959; The Apple, 1960; A Sweep of the Arm, 1962; Tenderness, 1962; Mail Boat, 1966; Bratsk Power Station, 1967; Kazan's University, 1971; A Father's Hearing, 1975; Morning People, 1978; Talent is not a Miracle by Chance (essays), 1980; Wild Berries Places (novel), 1981; Mother and Neutron Bomb and other poems, 1983; Almost at the End, 1986; A Wind of Tomorrow (essays), 1987; Selected Poetry, 3 vols, 1987; Don't Die Before You're Dead (novel), 1993; Late Tears (poetry), 1995; The Best from the Best (poetry), 1995; Strophes of the Century (anthology), 1995; God Could be Each of Us, 1996; If All Danes were Jews (play), 1996; Wolf's Passport (memoirs), 1998; words to Shostakovich's 13th Symphony and Execution of Stepan Razin Oratorio; *in English:* Zima Junction, 1961; A Precocious Autobiography, 1963; Bratsk Power Station, 1966; Stolen Apples, 1972; From Desire to Desire, 1976; The Face Behind the Face, 1979; Dove in Santiago, 1982; Invisible Threads (photography), 1981; Wild Berries (novel), 1984; Ardabiola (novel), 1985; Almost at the End, 1987; Divided Twins (photography), 1987; Last Attempt, 1988; Politics—everybody's privilege (essays), 1990; Collected Poems 1952–90, 1991; Fatal Half Measures, 1991; (ed) Twentieth-Century Russian Poetry, 1993; Pre-morning (poetry), 1995; Collected Works, vols 1–2, 1997; The Thirteen, 1997; The Evening Rainbow, 1999; Selected Prose, 1999. *Address:* 2256 South Troost Avenue, Tulsa, OK 74114–1348, USA.

YIP, Prof. George Stephen, DBA; Dean, Rotterdam School of Management, Erasmus University, since 2008; Fellow (formerly Senior Fellow), Advanced Institute of Management Research, since 2003; *b* 24 Sept. 1947; *s* of Teddy Yip and Susie (*née* Ho); *m* 1970, Moira Winsland; one *s* one *d. Educ:* Peak Sch., Hong Kong; East Grinstead County Grammar Sch.; Dover Coll.; Magdalene Coll., Cambridge (BA Hons 1970; MA 1973); Cranfield Univ. (MBA 1976); Harvard Business Sch. (MBA 1976; DBA 1980). Account Executive, 1970–72, Account Supervisor, 1973–74, Lintas London; Product Manager, Birds Eye Foods, 1972–73; Business Manager, Data Resources Inc., 1976–78; Asst Prof., Harvard Business Sch., 1980–83; Sen. Associate, MAC Gp, 1983–86; Sen. Manager, Price Waterhouse, 1986–87; Vis. Associate Prof., Georgetown Univ., 1987–91; Adjunct Prof., UCLA, 1991–99; Beckwith Prof. of Mgt Studies, Judge Inst. and Fellow, Magdalene Coll., Univ. of Cambridge, 1998–2000; Prof. of Strategic and Internat. Mgt, 2001–06, Associate Dean, 2001–03, London Business Sch; Vice-Pres., and Dir of Res. and Innovation, Capgemini Consulting, 2006–08. Vis. Prof., Stanford Business Sch., 1997; Vis. Fellow, Templeton Coll., Oxford, 1998. Fellow: World Economic Forum, 1998; Acad. of Internat. Business, 1999. *Publications:* Barriers to Entry, 1982; Total Global Strategy, 1992; Asian Advantage, 1998; Strategies for Central and Eastern Europe, 2000; Managing Global Customers, 2007; articles in internat. mgt and mkting jls. *Recreations:* theatre, opera, classical music, tennis, sailing, rural Maine. *Address:* Rotterdam School of Management, Burgemeester Oudlaan 50, 3062 PA Rotterdam, The Netherlands. *T:* (10) 4081901. *Club:* Reform.

YOCKLUNN, Sir John (Soong Chung), KCVO 1977; Kt 1975; Associate University Librarian, Monash University Library, 1993–98 (Chief Librarian, Gippsland Institute of Advanced Education, then Monash University College, 1983–92); *b* Canton, China, 5 May 1933; *s* of late Charles Soong Yocklunn and Ho Wai-lin, formerly of W Australia; *m* 1981, Patricia Ann Mehegan. *Educ:* Perth Modern Sch.; Northam High Sch., W Australia; Univ. of W Australia (BA); Aust. Nat. Univ. (BA); Univ. of Sheffield (MA). MCLIP; ALAA. Dept of the Treasury, Canberra, 1959–63; Nat. Library of Australia, Canberra, 1964–67; Librarian-in-Charge, Admin Coll. of Papua New Guinea, Port Moresby, 1967–69; Exec. Officer, Public Service Board of Papua New Guinea, 1969–70; Librarian, Admin Coll., 1970–72; Principal Private Sec. to Chief Minister, 1972–73; study in UK, under James Cook Bicentenary Schol., 1973–74; on return, given task of organising a national library; Sen. Investigation Officer, Public Services Commn, 1974–77; Asst Sec. (Library Services), Dept of Educn (National Librarian of PNG), 1978–83. Chm., PNG Honours and Awards Cttee, 1975–83; Advr on Honours to PNG Govt, 1984–85; Consultant on estabt of new honours system, 1985–86. Vice-Pres., Pangu Pati, 1968–72; Nat. Campaign Manager for Pangu Pati for 1972 general elections in Papua New Guinea; Treasurer, Pangu Pati, 1973–80. Asst Dir, Visit of Prince of Wales to PNG, 1975; Dir, Visits of the Queen and Prince Philip to PNG, 1977 and 1982. Mem. Nat. Adv. Council, Aust. Broadcasting Corp., 2001–03. Australian Library and Information Association: Chm., Gippsland Regional Gp, 1984–94; Mem., Vict. Br. Council, 1986–94; rep. on Commonwealth Library Assoc., 1988–91; Mem. Exec. Cttee, Vict. Div., Aust. Council for Library and Inf. Servs, 1989–94; Vice Pres., University Liby Soc. of Rockhampton, 1999–2003. Pres., Regl Arts Develt Fund Council, Rockhampton, 2004–06 (Vice-Pres., 1999–2003); Mem. Adv. Council, CARE Aust., 1988–92. Trustee, 1986–98, Chm. of Friends, 1985–88, Vice-Chm., 1992–98, Mus. of Chinese Australian Hist.; Sec., Rockhampton Chinese Assoc., 2003–04 (Vice Pres., 1999–2000; Pres., 2001–03). *Publications:* The Charles Barrett Collection of Books relating to Papua New Guinea, 1967, 2nd edn 1969; articles on librarianship, etc., in various jls. *Recreations:* orders and medals research, heraldry, languages. *Address:* 11 Melbourne Street, Rockhampton, Qld 4700, Australia. *T:* (7) 49273960.

YONG, Rt Rev. Datuk Ping Chung; Bishop of Sabah, 1990–2006; Archbishop of South East Asia, 2000–06; *b* 20 Feb. 1941; parents decd; *m* 1969, Julia Yong; two *d. Educ:* Meml Univ., Newfoundland (BA 1968); Queen's Coll., Newfoundland (LTh 1969). Ordained, Sabah, 1970; Canon, 1974–90, Archdeacon, 1976–90, Sabah. Chairman: ACC, 1984–90; Council of Churches of E Asia, 1996–99; President: Christian Fedn of Malaysia, 1997–2001; Council of Churches of Malaysia, 1997–2001; Sabah Council of Churches, 1997–2003. *Address:* c/o PO Box 10811, 88809 Kota Kinabalu, Sabah, Malaysia.

YONG NYUK LIN; Member, Presidential Council for Minority Rights, Singapore, 1979–91; *b* Seremban, Malaya, 24 June 1918; *s* of late Yong Thean Yong and Chen Shak Moi; *m* 1939, Kwa Geok Lan; two *d. Educ:* Raffles Coll., Singapore. Science Master, King George V Sch., Seremban, Malaya, 1938–41; with Overseas Assurance Corp., Singapore, 1941 (resigned, as Gen. Manager, 1958). Legislative Assemblyman, Singapore, 1959–65, MP 1965–79; Minister for Educn, 1959–63; Chm., Singapore Harbour Bd, 1961–62; Minister for: Health, 1963–68; Communications, 1968–75; Minister without Portfolio, 1975–76; High Comr in London, 1975–76. Chm., Singapore Land/Marina Centre Development Private Ltd, 1980–86. *Address:* 50 Oei Tiong Ham Park, Singapore 267055.

YONG PUNG HOW, Hon.; Chief Justice of the Supreme Court, Singapore, 1990–2006; *b* 11 April 1926; *o s* of Yong Shook Lin, advocate and solicitor, and Yu Tak Fong; *m* 1955, Cheang Wei-woo; one *d. Educ:* Victoria Instn, Kuala Lumpur (Treacher Schol., Rodger Schol.); Downing Coll., Cambridge (Exhibnr; MA; LLB; Associate Fellow); Harvard Business Sch. (AMP). Called to the Bar, Inner Temple, 1951, Hon. Bencher, 1997; admitted Advocate and Solicitor, Fedn of Malaya, 1952, Singapore, 1964; practised law as Partner, Shook Lin & Bok, 1952–70; sole arbitrator in strike by govt clerical services and telecoms workers, Singapore, 1953; Chm., Malayan Public Services Arbitration Tribunal, 1955–60; Mem., Chm.'s Panel, Malayan Industrial Court, 1961–67; Chm. and Man. Dir, Singapore Internat. Merchant Bankers Ltd, 1971–81; Chm. and CEO, Oversea-Chinese Banking Corp., 1983–89 (Dir, 1972, Vice-Chm., 1977–80); on secondment to Govt of Singapore, 1981–83, as: Man. Dir, Singapore Investment Corp. (GIC), 1981–83 (Dir, 1983–89); Man. Dir, Monetary Authy of Singapore, 1982–83; Dep. Chm., Bd of Comrs of Currency, 1982–83; alternate Gov. for Singapore, IMF, 1982–83; Judge, Supreme Court of Singapore, 1989–90; Actg Pres. of Singapore, July, Sept. and Nov. 1991. Chm., Presidential Council for Minority Rights, 1990–; Pres., Legal Services Commn, 1990–. Member: Securities Industry Council, 1974–81; Provisional Mass Rapid Transit Authy, 1980–83; Dir, Mass Rapid Transit Corp., 1983–86. Chairman: Malayan Airways Ltd and Malaysia-Singapore Airlines Ltd, 1964–69; Singapore Broadcasting Corp., 1985–89; Deputy Chairman: Malayan Banking Bd, 1966–70; Singapore Press Hldgs, 1984–89; Dir, Temasek Hldgs, 1985–89. Founder Chm., Singapore Inst. Policy Studies, 1987–89; Pres., Singapore Acad. Law, 1990–. Dir, Singapore SO, 1987–89. Fellow, Malaysian Inst. of Mgt, 1975. DSO (Singapore), 1989; Order of Temasek (First Class) (Singapore), 1999. *Address:* c/o Supreme Court, 1 Supreme Court Lane, Singapore 178879. *Clubs:* Pyramid, Singapore Cricket (Hon. Mem.), Warren Golf (Hon. Mem.) (Singapore).

YORK, Archbishop of, since 2005; **Most Rev. and Rt Hon. John Tucker Mugabi Sentamu;** PC 2005; PhD; *b* 10 June 1949; *s* of John Walakira and Ruth; *m* 1973, Margaret (*née* Wanambwa); one *s* one *d. Educ:* Masooli, Kyambogo and Kitante Hill and Old Kampala Sch., Uganda; Makerere Univ. (LLB 1971); Selwyn Coll., Cambridge (Pattison Student; BA 1976; MA, PhD 1984; Hon. Fellow, 2005); Ridley Hall, Cambridge; Dip. in Legal Practice, Uganda, 1972. Advocate, Uganda High Ct, 1971–74. Ordained deacon and priest, 1979; Asst Chaplain, Selwyn Coll., Cambridge, 1979; Asst Curate, St Andrew, Ham, and Chaplain, HM Remand Centre, Latchmere House, 1979–82; Asst Curate, St Paul, Herne Hill, 1982–83; Priest-in-charge, Holy Trinity, and Vicar, St Matthias, Tulse Hill, 1983–84, Vicar of jt parish, 1985–96; Priest-in-charge, St Saviour, Brixton Hill, 1987–89; Area Bp of Stepney, 1996–2002; Bp of Birmingham, 2002–05. Hon. Canon, Southwark Cathedral, 1993–96. Mem., Gen. Synod of C of E, 1985–96; Chm., Cttee for Minority Ethnic Anglican Concerns, 1990–99. Member: Young Offenders Cttee, NACRO, 1986–95; Council, Family Welfare Assoc., 1989–; Stephen Lawrence Judicial Inquiry, 1997–99; Chairman: Islington Partnership, 2000–02; London Marriage Guidance Council, 2000–03 (also Pres.); Damilola Taylor Investigation and Prosecution Review, 2002; NHS Haemoglobinopathy Screening Prog., 2001–. Trustee, John Smith Inst., 2002–. Gov., Univ. of N London, 1997–2002; Chancellor: York St John Univ., 2006–; Univ. of Cumbria, 2007–. FRSA. Freeman: City of London, 2000; City of Montego Bay, 2007. Hon. Bencher, Gray's Inn, 2007. Hon. Fellow: Canterbury Christ Church UC, 2001; QMW, 2001. DUniv Open, 2001; Hon. DPhil Glos, 2002; Hon. DD: Birmingham, 2003; Hull, 2007; Hon. LLD Leicester, 2005; Hon. DLitt Sheffield, 2007. *Recreations:* music, cooking, reading, Rugby, football, athletics. *Address:* Bishopthorpe Palace, Bishopthorpe, York YO23 2GE.

YORK, Dean of; *see* Jones, Very Rev. K. B.

YORK, Archdeacon of; *see* Seed, Ven. R. M. C.

YORK, David; independent consultant, since 2004; *b* 20 April 1950; *s* of George William York and Ann (*née* Morgan); *m* 1982, Lindsey Anne Murgatroyd (marr. diss. 2006). *Educ:* Manor Park Sch., Newcastle upon Tyne; Salford Univ. (BSc 1973). MICE 1976. Joined Dept of Transport, 1970; Project Engr, 1977–83; Principal Engr, 1983–87; Superintending Engr, 1987–90; Director: NW Network Mgt, 1990; Yorks and Humberside Construction Prog., 1990–93; Motorway Widening Unit, 1993–95; Dep. Road Prog. Dir, 1995–96, Road Prog. Dir, 1996; Highways Agency: Project Services Dir, 1996–2001; Operations Dir, 2001–03; Nat. Traffic Dir, 2003–04. *Recreations:* flying, scuba diving, golf. *Address: e-mail:* davidyork@talktalk.net.

YORK, Col Edward Christopher, TD 1978; Vice Lord-Lieutenant of North Yorkshire, since 1999; Managing Director, Hutton Wandesley Farms Co., and others, since 1986; *b* 22 Feb. 1939; *o s* of late Christopher York and Pauline Rosemary York (*née* Fletcher); *m* 1965, Sarah Ann, *d* of late Major James Kennedy Maxwell, MC; one *s* one *d. Educ:* Eton Coll. 1st Royal Dragoons, retd 1964. Chm., Thirsk Racecourse Co., 1995–2008. Vice Pres., Northern Assoc. of Building Socs, 1987–91; Pres., Yorks Agricl Soc., 1989; Hon. Show Dir, 1992–96, Pres., 1997, Chm. of Council, 1998–2002, RASE; Chm., Royal Armouries Develt Trust (Leeds), 1995–99. CO, Queen's Own Yeomanry, 1979–81 (Hon. Col, 1998–2003); ADC to the Queen, 1982–86; Col Comdt, Yeomanry, 1994–99. Chm., Yorks and Humberside RFCA (formerly TAVRA), 1998–2003; Vice-Chm.,

Council of RFCAs, 2001–04; Chair, N Yorks Scouts, 2000–; President: Army Benevolent Fund, N Yorks, 1999–; SSAFA, N Yorks, 2003–. FRAgS 1998. DL 1988, High Sheriff, 1988, N Yorks. *Publications:* contribs to trade magazines. *Recreations:* racing, field sports. *Address:* Hutton Wandesley Hall, York YO26 7NA. *T:* (home) (01904) 738240, (office) (01904) 738755, *Fax:* (01904) 738468; *e-mail:* ecy@huttonwandesley.co.uk. *Clubs:* Boodle's, Pratt's.

YORK, Michael, (Michael York-Johnson), OBE 1996; actor; *b* 27 March 1942; *s* of Joseph Johnson and Florence Chown; *m* 1968, Patricia Frances McCallum. *Educ:* Hurstpierpoint College; Bromley Grammar School; University College, Oxford (BA). *Stage:* Dundee Repertory Theatre, 1964; National Theatre Co., 1965; Outcry, NY, 1973; Bent, NY, 1980; Cyrano de Bergerac, Santa Fe, 1981; Whisper in the Mind, 1991; The Crucible, NY, 1992; Someone Who'll Watch Over Me, NY, 1993; Camelot, US tour, 2007; Strauss Meets Frankenstein, Long Beach, 2008; *films:* The Taming of the Shrew, Accident, 1966; Romeo and Juliet, 1967; Cabaret, England Made Me, 1971; The Three Musketeers, 1973; Murder on the Orient Express, 1974; Logan's Run, 1975; The Riddle of the Sands, 1978; Success is the Best Revenge, 1984; Dawn, 1985; Vengeance, 1986; The Secret of the Sahara, Imbalances, 1987; The Joker, Midnight Blue, The Return of the Musketeers, 1988; The Long Shadow, 1992; Rochade, 1992; Eline Vere, 1992; Wide Sargasso Sea, 1993; Discretion Assured, 1993; The Shadow of a Kiss, 1994; Gospa, 1995; Austin Powers, 1997; Wrongfully Accused, 1998; Lovers and Liars, The Omega Code, 1999; Borstal Boy, 2000; Megiddo, 2001; Austin Powers in Goldmember, 2002; Moscow Heat, 2004; Mik and Alfred, 2008; *television* includes: Jesus of Nazareth, 1976; A Man Called Intrepid, 1978; For Those I Loved, 1981; The Weather in the Streets, The Master of Ballantrae, 1983; Space, 1984; The Far Country, 1985; The Four Minute Mile, The Heat of the Day, 1988; Till We Meet Again, 1989; The Night of the Fox, 1990; Fall from Grace, 1994; September, 1995; Not of This Earth, 1996; The Ring, 1996; True Women, Dark Planet, The Ripper, 1997; The Search for Nazi Gold, A Knight in Camelot, 1998; Perfect Little Angels, 1999; The Haunting of Hell House, 2000; The Lot, 2001; Curb Your Enthusiasm, 2002; La Femme Musketeer, 2004; Icon, 2005; Law and Order: Criminal Intent, 2006; The Four Seasons, 2008. Chm., Calif Youth Theatre, 1987–. Hon. DFA S Carolina, 1988. *Publications:* (contrib.) The Courage of Conviction, 1986; (contrib.) Voices of Survival, 1987; Travelling Player (autobiog.), 1991; A Shakespearean Actor Prepares, 2000; Dispatches from Armageddon, 2002; Are My Blinkers Showing?, 2005. *Recreations:* travel, music, collecting theatrical memorabilia.

YORK, Susannah; actress and writer; *b* 9 Jan. 1942; *d* of late Simon William Fletcher and Joan Bowring; *m* 1960, Michael Wells (marr. diss. 1976); one *s* one *d*. *Educ:* Marr Coll., Troon, Scotland; RADA, London. *Films* include: The Greengage Summer, 1961; Freud, 1962; Tom Jones, 1963; A Man for All Seasons, 1966; The Killing of Sister George, 1968; They Shoot Horses, Don't They, 1969; X, Y and Zee, 1971; Images, 1972; Superman, 1978; Golden Gate Murders, 1979; Alice, 1980; Superman 2, 1984; A Christmas Carol, Mio My Mio, 1986; Bluebeard; Just Ask for Diamonds, 1988; Melancholia, 1989; Barbarblu Barbarblu; Little Women; The Gigolos, 2007. *Theatre* includes: Wings of a Dove, 1964; A Singular Man, 1965; The Maids, 1974; Peter Pan, 1977; The Singular Life of Albert Nobbs, 1978; Hedda Gabler, New York 1981, London 1982; Agnes of God, 1983; The Human Voice (own trans. of Cocteau), 1984; Fatal Attraction, Haymarket, 1985; The Apple Cart, Haymarket, 1986; The Women, Old Vic, 1986; The Glass Menagerie (tour), 1989; A Streetcar Named Desire, Octagon, Bolton, 1990; Noonbreak (own trans. of Claudel), London and Manchester, 1991; September Tide, London, 1993; The Merry Wives of Windsor, 1996, Hamlet, 1997, RSC; Camino Real, RSC, 1997; The Loves of Shakespeare's Women, Edinburgh and Adelaide Fests, 2001, US and UK tour, 2002–04. *TV series:* Second Chance, 1981; We'll Meet Again, 1982; The Prince Regent, 1983; Devices and Desires, 1990; Trainer, 1991, 1992; Holby City, 2003. *Publications:* In Search of Unicorns, 1973, rev. edn 1984; Larks Castle, 1975, rev. edn, 1985; (ed) The Big One, 1984; The Loves of Shakespeare's Women, 2001. *Recreations:* family, writing, gardening, reading, houses, riding, languages, travelling, theatre, cinema, walking. *Address:* c/o United Agents, 12-26 Lexington Street, W1F 0LE.

YORK-JOHNSON, Michael; *see* York, M.

YORKE, family name of **Earl of Hardwicke.**

YORKE, David Harry Robert, CBE 1993; FRICS; Senior Partner, Weatherall Green & Smith, Chartered Surveyors, 1984–92 (Consultant, 1992–97); *b* 5 Dec. 1931; *s* of late Harry Yorke and Marie Yorke, Minera, N Wales; *m* 1955, Patricia Gwynneth Fowler-Tutt; one *d*. *Educ:* Dean Close Sch., Cheltenham; College of Estate Management; Open Univ. (BA (Hons) 2005). FRICS 1966 (ARICS 1956); FCIArb 1994. Articled to Tregear & Sons, 1948–54. 2nd Lieut RA, 1955–56. Weatherall Green & Smith, 1960–97, Partner, 1961. Dir, London Auction Mart, 1981–92; Chm., Belgravia Property Co. Ltd, 1993–95. Mem., Bristol Develt Corp., 1988–96; Dir, British Waterways Bd, 1988–2000 (Vice-Chm., 1998–2000). Royal Institution of Chartered Surveyors: Mem., Gen. Council, 1978–92; Pres., Gen. Practice Div., 1981–82; Pres., 1988–89; Chm., RICS Insurance Services, 1991–96. Mem. Council, British Property Fedn, 1990–94. Pres., British Chapter, Internat. Real Estate Fedn, 1974. Freeman, City of London, 1979; Liveryman, Co. of Chartered Surveyors, 1979. *Publication:* (Consultant Ed.) Essentials of Rent Review, 1996. *Recreations:* reading, crosswords, enjoying Cornwall, occasional cookery. *Address:* Penolva, St Mawes, Truro, Cornwall TR2 5DR. *T:* (01326) 270235. *Clubs:* Buck's, Sloane; St Mawes Sailing.

YORKE, John; Controller, Drama Production, BBC, since 2006; *b* 9 July 1962; *s* of Sydney Yorke and Valerie Yorke. *Educ:* Univ. of Newcastle upon Tyne (BA 1st Cl. Hons English Lit. 1984). BBC Radio Five, Drama: Producer, 1990–92; Sen. Producer, 1992–93; Chief Producer, 1993–94; BBC 1: Script Editor, 1994, Series Script Editor, 1994, Story Editor, 1995–98, Eastenders; Producer, City Central, 1998–2000; Exec. Producer, Eastenders, 2000–03; Dep. Hd of Drama Series, BBC, 2003–04; Hd of Drama, Channel 4 Television, 2004–05; Controller, Continuing Drama Series and Head of Independent Drama, BBC, 2005–06. *Address:* BBC Television Centre, Wood Lane, W12 7RJ. *T:* (020) 8576 4935, *Fax:* (020) 8576 1251; *e-mail:* john.yorke@bbc.co.uk.

YORKE, Margaret, (Margaret Beda Nicholson); writer; *b* 30 Jan. 1924; *d* of John Peel Alexander Larminie and Alison Yorke (*née* Lyle); *m* 1945, Basil Nicholson (marr. diss. 1957, he *d* 1987); one *s* one *d*. *Educ:* Prior's Field, Surrey. WRNS, 1942–45. Bookseller; School Sec.; Asst Librarian, St Hilda's Coll., Oxford, 1959–60; Library Asst (cataloguer), Christ Church, Oxford, 1963–65. Chm., Crime Writers' Assoc., 1979–80. Swedish Acad. of Detection Award, 1982; CWA Cartier Diamond Dagger Award, 1999. *Publications:* Summer Flight, 1957; Pray Love Remember, 1958; Christopher, 1959; Deceiving Mirror, 1960; The China Doll, 1961; Once a Stranger, 1962; The Birthday, 1963; Full Circle, 1965; No Fury, 1967; The Apricot Bed, 1968; The Limbo Ladies, 1969; Dead in the Morning, 1970; Silent Witness, 1972; Grave Matters, 1973; Mortal Remains, 1974; No Medals for the Major, 1974; The Small Hours of the Morning, 1975; The Cost of Silence, 1977; The Point of Murder, 1978; Death on Account, 1979; The Scent of Fear, 1980 (Swedish Acad. of Detection Award, 1982); The Hand of Death, 1981; Devil's Work, 1982; Find Me a Villain, 1983; The Smooth Face of Evil, 1984; Intimate Kill, 1985; Safely to the Grave, 1986; Evidence to Destroy, 1987; Speak for the Dead, 1988; Crime in Question, 1989; Admit to Murder, 1990; A Small Deceit, 1991; Criminal Damage, 1992; Dangerous to Know, 1993; Almost the Truth, 1994; Pieces of Justice (short stories), 1994; Serious Intent, 1995; A Question of Belief, 1996; Act of Violence, 1997; False Pretences, 1998; The Price of Guilt, 1999; A Case to Answer, 2000; Cause for Concern, 2001. *Recreations:* theatre, reading, gardening, travel. *Address:* c/o Curtis Brown, 28/29 Haymarket, SW1Y 4SP.

YORKE, Very Rev. Michael Leslie; Dean of Lichfield, 1999–2004, now Dean Emeritus; *b* 25 March 1939; *s* of late Leslie Henry and Brenda Emma Yorke; *m* 1st, 1964, Michal Sara Dadd (*d* 1987); one *s* one *d*; 2nd, 1988, Frances Grace Archer. *Educ:* Midhurst Grammar Sch.; Brighton Coll.; Magdalene Coll., Cambridge (BA 1962; MA 1966); Cuddesdon Theol Coll., Oxford. Ordained deacon, 1964, priest, 1965; Curate, Croydon Parish Church, 1964–68; Precentor and Chaplain, 1968–73, Dep. Dir of Res. and Trng, 1972–74, Chelmsford Cathedral; Rector, Ashdon with Hadstock, 1974–78; Canon Residentiary, 1978–88, Vice Provost, 1984–88, now Canon Emeritus, Chelmsford Cathedral; Vicar, St Margaret's with St Nicholas, King's Lynn, 1988–94; Hon. Canon, Norwich Cathedral, 1992–94, now Canon Emeritus; Provost of Portsmouth, 1994–99. *Recreations:* opera, 20th century military history, contemporary art. *Address:* Westgate House, The Green, Burnham Market, Norfolk PE31 8HD.

YORKE, Robert Anthony, FSA; finance director and management consultant, since 1981; *b* 27 June 1944; *s* of late Patrick Langdon Yorke and Pamela Mary (*née* Rudgard; later Mrs Robert Michael Clive); *m* 1975, Morag, *d* of late J. S. M. Dow; one *s* one *d*. *Educ:* Marlborough Coll.; Clare Coll., Cambridge (MA); London Business Sch. (MSc). Financial Controller, Bowater Corp., 1975–77; Chief Exec., Ridham Freight Services, 1977–81; Dir, London and Devonshire Trust Ltd, 1987–. Comr, RCHME, 1991–99; Member: Ancient Monuments Adv. Cttee, English Heritage, 1998–2003; English Heritage Adv. Cttee, 2003–04. Chairman: Nautical Archaeol. Soc., 1987–91; Jt Nautical Archaeol. Policy Cttee, 1995– (Vice-Chm., 1988–95). FSA 2001. *Publications:* contribs to learned jls. *Recreations:* nautical archaeology, tennis, ski-ing. *Address:* Silver Birches, Bashurst Hill, Itchingfield, Horsham, W Sussex RH13 0NY. *T:* (01403) 790311.

YOSHIDA, Miyako, Hon. OBE 2007; Principal Dancer, Royal Ballet, since 1995; *b* 28 Oct. 1965; *d* of Eiji Yoshida and Etsuko (*née* Fukuda). *Educ:* Royal Ballet Sch. Joined Sadler's Wells Royal Ballet, later Birmingham Royal Ballet, 1984; soloist, 1987; Principal, 1988; transf. to Royal Ballet, 1995. *Performances* include leading rôles in: Swan Lake, Sleeping Beauty, The Nutcracker, Giselle, Elite Syncopations, La Fille Mal Gardée, Hobson's Choice, The Dream, Don Quixote, Paquita, Allegri Diversi, Theme and Variations, Concerto Barroco, Les Sylphides, Divertimento No 15, Dances Concertantes, Les Patineurs, Romeo and Juliet, The Firebird, Coppélia. Prix de Lausanne, 1983; Global Award, 1989; Nakagawa Einosuke Award, 1995; Akiko Tachibana Award, 1996, 2002; Arts Encouragement Prize for New Artists, Min. of Educn, Sci., Sports and Culture, 1997; Hattori Chieko Award, 1998; Artist for Peace, Unesco, 2004; Japan Soc. Award, 2007. *Recreations:* reading, watching films. *Address:* c/o Royal Ballet, Covent Garden, WC2E 9DD.

YOUARD, Richard Geoffrey Atkin; The Investment Ombudsman (formerly Investment Referee), 1989–96; *b* 27 Jan. 1933; *s* of Geoffrey Bernard Youard, MBE and Hon. Rosaline Joan Youard (*née* Atkin); *m* 1960, Felicity Ann Morton; one *s* two *d*. *Educ:* Bradfield Coll., Berks; Magdalen Coll., Oxford (BA Jurisprudence; MA 1998). Admitted Solicitor, 1959. Commnd (2nd Lieut) RA, 1952 (Nat. Service); Lieut TA, 1954. Slaughter and May, London: Articled Clerk, 1956–59; Asst Solicitor, 1959–68; Partner, 1968–89. Inspector, DTI, 1987. Ind. Investigator, SIB, 1994–97. Hon. Sen. Res. Fellow, KCL, 1988–. Chairman: Nat. Fedn of Consumers Groups, 1968; Cttee of Inquiry, Accountants Jt Disciplinary Scheme, 1989; Mem., Home Office Cttee on London Taxicab and Car Hire Trade, 1967. Clerk to Governors, Bradfield Coll., 1968–89, Governor, 1989–95. Mem., Chancellor's Court of Benefactors, Oxford Univ., 1995–2000. Mem. Council, Pali Text Soc., 1991–2000. Trustee, Elizabeth Garrett Anderson Hosp. Appeal, 1997–2005. *Publications:* (contrib.) Sovereign Borrowers, 1984; (contrib.) Current Issues of International Financial Law, 1985; (jtly) Butterworths Banking Documents, 1986; (contrib.) Butterworths Banking and Financial Law Review, 1987; contribs on legal aspects of internat. finance to Jl of Business Law, Euromoney and Internat. Financial Law Review. *Recreations:* gardening, electronics (holder of Amateur Transmitting Licence), beekeeping, map collecting, reading, jazz, Welsh language/history. *Address:* Hill Fort House, Ruckhall, Eaton Bishop, Herefordshire HR2 9QG. *T:* (01981) 251754; Cwm Mynach Ganol, Bontddu, Dolgellau, Gwynedd LL40 2TU.

YOUD, Sam; writer, since 1958; *b* 16 April 1922; *s* of Sam and Harriet Youd; *m* 1st, 1946, Joyce Fairbairn (marr. diss. 1978); one *s* four *d*; 2nd, 1980, Jessica Ball (*d* 2001). *Educ:* Peter Symonds Sch., Winchester. Manager, Industrial Diamond Inf. Bureau, London, 1956–58. Chm., Children's Writers' Gp, Soc. of Authors, 1983–85. Atlantic Award in Literature, Rockefeller Foundn, 1947; George Stone Award, 1977. *Publications* include: as John Christopher: The Twenty Second Century (short stories), 1954; The Year of the Comet, 1955; The Death of Grass, 1956; The Caves of Night, 1958; A Scent of White Poppies, 1959; The Long Voyage, 1960; The World in Winter, 1962; Cloud on Silver, 1964; The Possessors, 1965; A Wrinkle in the Skin, 1965; The Little People, 1966; Pendulum, 1968; Bad Dream, 2003; for young adults: The Tripods trilogy (The White Mountains, 1967; The City of Gold and Lead, 1967; The Pool of Fire, 1968); The Lotus Caves, 1969; The Guardians, 1970 (Guardian Prize, and Christopher Medal, 1971; Jugendbuchpreis, 1976); The Sword trilogy (The Prince in Waiting, 1970; Beyond the Burning Lands, 1971; The Sword of the Spirits, 1972); Dom and Va, 1973; Wild Jack, 1974; Empty World, 1977; The Fireball trilogy (Fireball, 1981; New Found Land, 1983; Dragon Dance, 1986); When the Tripods Came, 1988; A Dusk of Demons, 1993; has also written as Hilary Ford, William Godfrey, Peter Graaf, Anthony Rye, Stanley Winchester, and Samuel Youd. *Recreation:* walking, with wireless. *Address:* One Whitefriars, Conduit Hill, Rye, E Sussex TN31 7LE. *T:* (01797) 224557; *e-mail:* samyoud@bigfoot.com.

YOUNG; *see* Hughes-Young, family name of Baron St Helens.

YOUNG, family name of **Barons Kennet**, **Young of Graffham** and **Young of Norwood Green**.

YOUNG OF GRAFFHAM, Baron *cr* 1984 (Life Peer), of Graffham in the County of W Sussex; **David Ivor Young;** PC 1984; DL; Chairman, Young Associates Ltd, since 1996; *b* 27 Feb. 1932; *s* of late Joseph and of Rebecca Young; *m* 1956, Lita Marianne Shaw; two *d*. *Educ:* Christ's Coll., Finchley; University Coll., London (LLB Hons; Fellow, 1988). Admitted solicitor, 1956. Exec., Great Universal Stores Ltd, 1956–61; Chairman: Eldonwall Ltd, 1961–74; Manufacturers Hanover Property Services Ltd, 1974–84; Cable and Wireless, 1990–95; Neoscorp Ltd (formerly Inter Digital Networks), 1997–2002; CDT Holdings plc, 1997–99; Pixology Ltd, 1997–; Autohit, then Accident Exchange Gp, plc, 2000–06; Spectrum Interactive plc, 2004–; Euortel Ltd, 2006–; Director: Town &

City Properties Ltd, 1971–74; Salomon Inc., 1990–94; Business for Sterling. Chm., British ORT, 1975–80 (Pres., 1980–82); Pres., World ORT Union, 1990–93 (Chm., Admin. Cttee, 1980–84). Dir, Centre for Policy Studies, 1979–82 (Mem., Management Bd, 1977); Mem., English Industrial Estates Corp., 1980–82; Chm., Manpower Services Commn, 1982–84; Mem., NEDC, 1982–89. Industrial Adviser, 1979–80, Special Adviser, 1980–82, DoI; Minister without Portfolio, 1984–85; Sec. of State for Employment, 1985–87; Sec. of State for Trade and Industry, 1987–89; Dep. Chm., Cons. Party, 1989–90. Pres., Inst. of Directors, 1993–2002; Chairman: EU-Japan Business Forum (formerly EU-Japan Assoc.), 1991–97; W Sussex Econ. Forum, 1996–; formerly Dir, Prince of Wales Business Leaders Forum. Pres., Jewish Care, 1990–97 (formerly Mem., Community Foundn); Chairman: Internat. Council of Jewish Social and Welfare Services, 1981–84; Central Council for Jewish Community Services, 1993–; Bd of Govs, Oxford Centre for Postgrad. Hebrew Studies, 1989–93. Chm., Chichester Festival Theatre Ltd, 1997–; Director: Royal Opera House Trust, 1990–95; South Bank Foundn Ltd; formerly Dir, Centre for Performing Arts; Chairman: London Philharmonic Trust, 1995–98; Prince's Trust Develt Bd, 1994–; Council, UCL, 1995–2005. Hon. FRPS 1981. DL West Sussex, 1999. *Publications:* The Enterprise Years: a businessman in the Cabinet, 1990; Degrees of Isolation, 2005. *Recreations:* music, book-collecting, photography. *Address:* Young Associates Ltd, Harcourt House, 19 Cavendish Square, W1G 0PL. *T:* (020) 7447 8800, *Fax:* (020) 7447 8849. *Club:* Savile.

See also B. A. Rix.

YOUNG OF HORNSEY, Baroness *cr* 2004 (Life Peer), of Hornsey in the London Borough of Haringey; **Lola Young,** OBE 2001; PhD; freelance arts and heritage consultant, since 2004; *b* 1 June 1951; *d* of Maxwell Fela Young and Yele Santos; *m* 1984, Barrie Birch; one *s*. *Educ:* Middlesex Univ. (BA Hons; PhD 1995). Social worker, 1971–73; actor, 1976–85; Arts Develt Officer, Haringey Arts Council, 1985–89; freelance arts consultant, 1989–90; Lecturer: (pt-time) in Media Studies, 1989–90; Thames Valley Univ., 1990–92; Lectr, 1992–97, Prof. of Cultural Studies, 1997–2001, Emeritus Prof., 2002, Middx Univ.; Hd of Culture, GLA, 2002–04. Vis. Prof., Birkbeck, Univ. of London, 2004–. Chm., Nitro, theatre co., 2004–. Advr to Arts Council England, 1988–2002. Mem., RCHME, 2000; Member Board: RNT, 2000–03; Resource: Council for Museums, Archives & Libraries, 2000–02; South Bank Centre, 2002–; Chm., Arts Adv. Cttee, British Council. FRSA 2000. *Publications:* Fear of the Dark: race, gender and sexuality in cinema, 1996; contrib. articles and chapters in edited books; contrib. articles to academic jls, incl. Women: A Cultural Rev., Cultural Studies from Birmingham, Oxford Art Jl, Parallax. *Recreations:* hiking, cinema, theatre, reading. *Address:* (office) Cultural Brokers, Building D, Unit 208, The Chocolate Factory, 5 Clarendon Road, N22 6XJ. *Club:* Royal Commonwealth Society.

YOUNG OF NORWOOD GREEN, Baron *cr* 2004 (Life Peer), of Norwood Green, in the London Borough of Ealing; **Anthony Ian Young,** Kt 2002; a Lord in Waiting (Government Whip), and Parliamentary Under-Secretary of State, Department for Innovation, Universities and Skills, since 2008; *b* 16 April 1942; *m* 1st, 1962, Doreen Goodman (marr. diss. 1984); one *s* two *d*; 2nd, 1985, Margaret Newnham; one *s* one *d*. *Educ:* Kenmore Park Primary Sch.; Harrow County GS. Joined GPO as telecommunications apprentice, 1958; Union Br. Officer, 1967, Mem. NEC, 1978–89, PO Engrg Union; Gen. Sec., Nat. Communications Union, 1989–95; Jt Gen. Sec., 1995–98, Sen. Dep. Gen. Sec., 1998–2002, Communication Workers' Union. Mem., Gen. Council, TUC, 1989–2002 (Pres., 2001–02); Eur. Co-Pres., Union Network Internat., 1999–2003 (Eur. Pres., Communications Internat., 1997–99). Trade Union Liaison Officer, Ethical Trading Initiative, 2002– (Vice Chm.). Member: Employment Tribunal Steering Bd, 1997–2003; Wilton Park Academic Council, 1997–2006; British N American Cttee, 1999–. A Governor, BBC, 1998–2002. Chm., One World Broadcasting Trust, 2002–. Gov., Three Bridges Primary Sch., 2002–. *Recreations:* reading, music, cycling, tennis, skating, walking, spasmodic gardening and cooking. *Address:* House of Lords, SW1A 0PW.

YOUNG OF OLD SCONE, Baroness *cr* 1997 (Life Peer), of Old Scone, in Perth and Kinross; **Barbara Scott Young;** Shadow Chair, Care Quality Commission, Department of Health, since 2008; *b* 8 April 1948; *d* of George Young and Mary (*née* Scott). *Educ:* Perth Acad.; Edinburgh Univ. (MA Classics); Strathclyde Univ. (Diploma Sec. Sci.); DipHSM, 1971. Various posts, finally Sector Administrator, Greater Glasgow Health Bd, 1975–78; Dir of Planning and Develt, St Thomas' Health Dist, 1978–79; Dist Gen. Administrator, NW Dist, Kensington and Chelsea and Westminster AHA, 1979–82; Dist Administrator, Haringey HA, 1982–85; District General Manager: Paddington and N Kensington HA, 1985–88; Parkside HA, 1988–91; Chief Exec., RSPB, 1991–98; Chm., English Nature, 1998–2000; Vice-Chm., Bd of Govs, BBC, 1998–2000; Chief Exec., Envmt Agency, 2000–08. Member: BBC Gen. Adv. Council, 1985–88; Cttee, King's Fund Inst., 1986–90; Delegacy, St Mary's Hosp. Med. Sch., 1991–94; Cttee, Sec. of State for the Envmt's Going for Green initiative, 1994–96, UK Round Table on Sustainability, 1995–2000; Commn on Future of Voluntary Sector, 1995–96; Exec. Cttee, NCVO, 1997 (Mem., Trustee Bd, 1993–97); COPUS, 1996–97; Minister for Agriculture's Adv. Gp, 1997–98; EU Envmtl Adv. Forum, 1999–2001. Pres., Inst. of Health Services Management, 1987–88. Internat. Fellow, King's Fund Coll., 1985–87 and 1990. Member: World Council, Birdlife Internat., 1994–98; Green Globe Task Force, 1997–98. Patron, Inst. of Ecol and Envmt Management, 1993–; Vice President: Flora & Fauna Internat., 1998–; Birdlife Internat., 1999–; RSPB, 2000–; President: Cambs, Beds, Northants and Peterborough Wildlife Trust, 2002–; British Trust for Ornithology, 2005– (Vice Pres., 2004–05). Trustee, IPPR, 1999–. Hon. RICS 2000; Hon. Fellow, Geologists Assoc., 2000; Hon. FCIWEM 2001. DUniv: Stirling, 1995; York, St Andrews, Aberdeen, 2000; Open, 2001; Hon. DSc: Hertfordshire, 1997; Cranfield, 1998. *Publications:* (contrib.) What Women Want, 1990; (contrib.) Medical Negligence, 1990; articles in Hosp. Doctor. *Recreations:* obsessive cinema going, gardening. *Address:* House of Lords, SW1A 0PW.

YOUNG, Andrew; Chairman and Co-founding Partner, GoodWorks International, since 1997; *b* New Orleans, La, 12 March 1932; *s* of Andrew J. Young and Daisy Fuller; *m* 1954, Jean Childs (*d* 1994); one *s* three *d*; *m* 1996, Carolyn Watson. *Educ:* Howard Univ., USA; Hartford Theological Seminary. Ordained, United Church of Christ, 1955; Pastor, Thomasville, Ga, 1955–57; Associate Dir for Youth Work, Nat. Council of Churches, 1957–61; Admin. Christian Educn Programme, United Church of Christ, 1961–64; Mem. Staff, Southern Christian Leadership Conf., 1961–70, Exec. Dir, 1964–70, Exec. Vice-Pres., 1967–70; elected to US House of Representatives from 5th District of Georgia, 1972 (first Black Congressman from Georgia in 101 years); re-elected 1974 and 1976; US Ambassador to UN, 1977–79; Mayor of Atlanta, 1982–89. Co-Chm., Atlanta Cttee for Olympic Games 1996. Chm., Law Cos Internat. Gp, Inc., 1990–93; Vice-Chm., Law Cos Gp, Inc., 1993–97. Pres., Nat. Council of the Churches of Christ, 2000–01. Chairman: Atlanta Community Relations Commn, 1970–72; National Democratic voter registration drive, 1976; during 1960s organized voter registration and community develt programmes. Mem. Bd of Dirs, Martin Luther King, Jr Center. Hon. Prof. of Policy Studies, Andrew Young Sch. of Policy Studies, Georgia State Univ. Holds numerous hon. degrees and awards, including: Presidential Medal of Freedom, 1980; Légion d'Honneur (France). *Publications:* A Way Out of No Way, 1994; An Easy Burden, 1996. *Address:* GoodWorks International, 303 Peachtree Street NE, Suite 4420, Atlanta, GA 30308–3264, USA.

YOUNG, Dr Andrew Buchanan, FRCPE, FFPH; Deputy Chief Medical Officer, Scottish Office Department of Health (formerly Scottish Office Home and Health Department), 1989–97; *b* 11 Aug. 1937; *s* of Alexander and Elizabeth Young; *m* 1965, Lois Lilian Howarth; one *s* one *d*. *Educ:* Falkirk High School; Edinburgh Univ. (MB ChB). DTM&H. Supt, Presbyterian Church of E Africa Hosps, Kenya, 1965–72; Fellow in Community Medicine, Scottish Health Service, 1972–75; Scottish Home and Health Department: MO 1975; SMO 1978; PMO 1985. Pres., Edinburgh Medical Missionary Soc., 1992–97. QHP, 1993–96. *Recreations:* trying to learn computing, rambling, reading. *Address:* 10 Pulford Place, Christchurch 8041, New Zealand; *e-mail:* abylly@xtra.co.nz.

YOUNG, Andrew George; Senior Consulting Actuary, Government Actuary's Department, since 2005; *b* 15 June 1949; *s* of James Cameron Young and Agnes Young; *m* 1975, Victoria Leslie; one *s* three *d*. *Educ:* Univ. of Glasgow (BSc 1st Cl. Hons Maths, Natural Philosophy). Government Actuary's Dept, 1973–; Directing Actuary, 1995–2005. *Recreations:* music, theatre, travel. *Address:* 95 Stanford Road, Brighton BN1 5PR. *T:* (01273) 563443.

YOUNG, Prof. Andrew William, PhD, DSc; FBA 2001; Professor of Neuropsychology, University of York, since 1997; *b* 14 March 1950; *s* of Alexander Young and Winnifred Doris Young; *m* 1976, Mavis Langham; one *s* two *d*. *Educ:* Bedford Coll., London (BSc 1971); PhD Warwick 1974; DSc London 1990. Lectr in Psychol., Univ. of Aberdeen, 1974–76; Lectr, then Reader in Psychol., Univ. of Lancaster, 1976–89; Prof. of Psychol., Univ. of Durham, 1989–93; Special Appt, MRC Scientific Staff, Applied Psychol. Unit, Cambridge, 1993–97. Dr *hc* Liège, 2000. Cognitive Psychol. Award, 1994, 2007, President's Award, 1995, Book Award, 2001, BPsS. *Publications:* (with A. W. Ellis) Human Cognitive Neuropsychology, 1996; (with V. Bruce) In the Eye of the Beholder: the science of face perception, 1998. *Recreations:* jukebox collector and partially reformed trainspotter. *Address:* Department of Psychology, University of York, Heslington, York YO10 5DD. *T:* (01904) 433159.

YOUNG, Prof. Archibald, MD; FRCP, FRCPGlas, FRCPE; Professor of Geriatric Medicine, Edinburgh University, 1998–2007; *b* 19 Sept. 1946; *s* of Dr Archibald Young and Mary Downie Young (*née* Fleming); *m* 1st, 1973, Alexandra Mary Clark (marr. diss. 1995); one *s* one *d*; 2nd, 2006, Susann Mary Dinan. *Educ:* Glasgow Univ. (BSc 1st Cl. Hons 1969; MBChB 1971; MD 1983). MRCP 1973, FRCP 1989; FRCPGlas 1985; FRCPE 1999. Hon. Consultant Physician in Rehabilitation Medicine, Nuffield Dept of Orthopaedic Surgery, Oxford Univ., 1981–85; Consultant Physician in Geriatric Medicine, Royal Free Hosp., 1985–87; Royal Free Hospital School of Medicine: Hon. Sen. Lectr, 1985–87, Sen. Lectr, 1987–88, in Geriatric Medicine; Prof. and Head, Univ. Dept of Geriatric Medicine and Hon. Consultant Physician, 1988–98. *Publications:* contribs to learned jls on effects of ageing, use and disuse of muscle and exercise physiology. *Recreations:* physical. *Address:* 45 Polton Road, Lasswade, Midlothian EH18 1LT. *Club:* Junior Mountaineering of Scotland.

YOUNG, Sir Brian (Walter Mark), Kt 1976; MA; Director General, Independent Broadcasting Authority (formerly Independent Television Authority), 1970–82; *b* 23 Aug. 1922; *er s* of late Sir Mark Young, GCMG and Josephine (*née* Price); *m* 1947, Fiona Marjorie (*d* 1997), *o d* of late Allan, 16th Stewart of Appin, and Marjorie (*née* Ballance); one *s* two *d*. *Educ:* Eton (King's Schol.); King's College, Cambridge (Schol.). FSA 1994. Served in RNVR, mainly in destroyers, 1941–45. First class hons in Part I, 1946, and Part II, 1947, of Classical Tripos; Porson Prize, 1946; Winchester Reading Prize, 1947; BA 1947; MA 1952. Assistant Master at Eton, 1947–52; Headmaster of Charterhouse, 1952–64; Dir, Nuffield Foundn, 1964–70. Chm., Christian Aid, 1983–90. Member: Central Advisory Council for Education, 1956–59 (Crowther Report); Central Religious Adv. Cttee of BBC and ITA, 1960–64; Bd of Centre for Educn Develt Overseas, 1969–72; Arts Council of GB, 1983–88; Exec. Cttee, British Council of Churches, 1983–90; Chm., Associated Bd of the Royal Schs of Music, 1984–87. Pres., British and Foreign Sch. Soc., 1991–2003. A Managing Trustee, Nuffield Foundn, 1978–90; Trustee: Lambeth Palace Liby, 1984–97; Imperial War Mus., 1985–92. Hon. RNCM, 1987. Hon. DLitt Heriot-Watt, 1980. *Publications:* Via Vertendi, 1952; Intelligent Reading (with P. D. R. Gardiner), 1964; The Villein's Bible: stories in Romanesque carving, 1990. *Recreations:* music, travel, history, problems. *Address:* Hill End, Woodhill Avenue, Gerrards Cross, Bucks SL9 8DJ. *T:* (01753) 887793.

See also Maj.-Gen. A. P. Grant Peterkin, T. M. S. Young.

YOUNG, Charmaine Carolyn, CBE 2003; Regeneration Director, St George Regeneration Ltd, since 1999; *b* 24 July 1952; *d* of Leonard and Dolly Danks; *m* 1992, Robert Michael Young. *Educ:* Birmingham Polytech. (pt-time; ONC, HNC Bldg Construction). Architectural Technician, 1974–81, Project Team Leader, 1981–83, Birmingham CC; Asst Dir of Housing, Sheffield CC, 1983–89; Urban Renewal Manager, Wimpey Homes, 1989–96; Business Develt Dir, Lovell Partnerships, 1996–99. MInstD 1999; FRSA 2003. *Publications:* regular contribs to Housing Today mag. *Recreations:* trying to recapture my youth, getting the construction industry to value women. *Address:* (office) 76 Crown Road, Twickenham, TW1 3EU. *T:* (020) 8917 4000, *Fax:* (020) 8917 4111; *e-mail:* regeneration@stgeorgeplc.com.

YOUNG, His Honour Christopher Godfrey; a Circuit Judge, 1980–97; *b* 9 Sept. 1932; *s* of late Harold Godfrey Young, MB, ChB, and Gladys Mary Young; *m* 1969, Jeanetta Margaret (*d* 1984), *d* of Halford and Dorothy Vaughan; one *s*. *Educ:* Bedford Sch.; King's Coll., Univ. of London (LLB Hons 1954; MA 1999). Called to the Bar, Gray's Inn, 1957; Midland and Oxford Circuit, 1959; a Recorder of the Crown Court, 1975–79; Resident Judge: Peterborough Crown Court, 1980–87; Leicester Crown Court, 1987–97. Mem., Parole Bd, 1990–93, 1997–2003 (Appraiser, 2003–05); Pt time Chm., Immigration Appeal Tribunal, 1997–98. Hon. Pres., De Montfort Univ. Sch. of Law, 1996–98. Postgraduate research: in Byzantine Studies, RHC, 1999–2005; in Faculty of Oriental Studies, Oxford Univ., 2005– (Mem., Pembroke Coll., Oxford). Mem., Cttee, Soc. for the Promotion of Byzantine Studies, 2004–07. Chm., Maidwell with Draughton Parish Council, 1973–76. *Recreations:* music, travel, Eastern Mediterranean. *Address:* Stockshill House, Duddington, Stamford, Lincs PE9 3QQ. *T:* (01780) 444658. *Club:* Athenæum.

YOUNG, Rt Rev. Clive; *see* Dunwich, Bishop Suffragan of.

YOUNG, Colin, CBE 1994 (OBE 1976); Senior Consultant, Ateliers du Cinéma Européen, since 1996 (Director, 1993–96); Director, National Film and Television School of Great Britain, 1970–92; *b* 5 April 1927; *s* of Colin Young and Agnes Holmes Kerr Young; *m* 1st, 1960, Kristin Ohman; two *s*; 2nd, 1987, Constance Yvonne Templeman; one *s* one *d*. *Educ:* Bellahouston Academy, Glasgow; Univs of Glasgow, St Andrews and California (Los Angeles). Theatre and film critic, Bon Accord, Aberdeen, 1951;

cameraman, editor, writer, director, 1953–; producer, 1967–; UCLA (Motion Pictures): Instructor, 1956–59; Asst Prof., 1959–64; Assoc. Prof., 1964–68; Prof., 1968–70, Head, Motion Picture Div., Theater Arts Dept, UCLA, 1964–65; Chm., Dept of Theater Arts, 1965–70. Res. Associate, Centre Nat. de Recherche Scientifique, Paris, 1984 and 1987; Andrew W. Mellon Vis. Prof. in Humanities, Rice Univ., Houston, Texas, 1985–86. Tutor, Arista Story Editing Workshops, 1996–. Vice-Chm., 1972–76, Chm., 1976–91, Edinburgh Film Festival; Chm., Edinburgh Internat. Film and Television Council, 1990–91; Governor, BFI, 1974–80. Member: Arts Council Film Cttee, 1972–76; Public Media Panel, Nat. Endowment for Arts, Washington, 1972–77; Gen. Adv. Council, BBC, 1973–78; Council of Management, BAFTA, 1974–81; Exec. Cttee, Centre International de Liaison des Ecoles de Cinéma et de Télévision, 1974–94 (Pres., 1980–94); Nat. Film Finance Corp., 1979–85; British Screen Adv. Council, 1990–; Bd, Moonstone Film Labs Internat., 1997–2007; Lottery Film Prodn Cttee, Scottish Arts Council, 1998–2000; Lottery Film Prodn Cttee, Scottish Screen, 2000–05. Consultant, Goldcrest Films & Television Ltd, 1985–86. FBKS 1975. Chm., Cttee on Educational Policy, UCLA, 1968–69. London Editor, Film Quarterly, 1970–91 (Los Angeles Editor, 1958–68). Hon. Gov., Nat. Film and Television Sch., 2007–. Michael Balcon Award, 1983, Fellow, 1993, BAFTA; Lifetime Achievement Award, British Indep. Film Awards, 2000. Chevalier de l'Ordre des Arts et des Lettres (France), 1987. Publications: various articles in collections of film essays including Principles of Visual Anthropology, 1975; experimental film essay for Unesco, 1963; ethnographic film essay for Unesco, 1966; contribs to Film Quarterly, Sight and Sound, Jl of Aesthetic Education, Jl of the Producers Guild of America, Kosmorama (Copenhagen), etc. Address: Turret House, Ivy Hatch Court, Ivy Hatch, Sevenoaks, Kent TN15 0PQ.

YOUNG, Sir Colville (Norbert), GCMG 1994; MBE 1986; JP; DPhil; Governor-General of Belize, since 1993; b 20 Nov. 1932; s of Henry Oswald Young and Adney Wilhelmina (née Waite); m 1956, Norma Eleanor Trapp; three s one d. Educ: Univ. of West Indies (BA 1961); Univ. of York (DPhil 1971). Principal, St Michael's Coll., Belize, 1974–76; Lectr in English and Gen. Studies, Belize Tech. Coll., 1976–86; University College of Belize: Pres., 1986–90; Lectr, 1990–93. JP Belize, 1985. Publications: Creole Proverbs of Belize, 1980, rev. edn 1988; From One Caribbean Corner (poetry), 1983; Caribbean Corner Calling, 1988; Language and Education in Belize, 1989; Pataki Full, 1990; contrib. poetry and drama in various anthologies; articles in Belizean Affairs, Jl Belizean Affairs, Belcast Jl, Caribbean Dialogue, Handbook on World Educn. Recreations: creative writing, playing and arranging steelband music. Address: Belize House, Belmopan, Belize, Central America. T: (8) 22521.

YOUNG, David Edward Michael; QC 1980; a Recorder, 1987; b 30 Sept. 1940; s of George Henry Edward Young and Audrey Young; m 1968, Ann de Bromhead; two d. Educ: Monkton Combe Sch.; Hertford Coll., Oxford (MA). Called to the Bar, Lincoln's Inn, 1966, Bencher, 1989; practising at Chancery Bar, specialising in intellectual property work. Dep. Judge, Patent County Court, 1990; a Dep. High Court Judge, 1993. Chm., Plant Varieties and Seeds Tribunal, 1987. Publications: (co-ed) Terrell on the Law of Patents, 12th edn 1971 to 14th edn 1994; Passing Off, 1985, 3rd edn 1994. Recreations: tennis, country pursuits, ski-ing.

YOUNG, David Ernest, CBE 2007; Chairman, Higher Education Funding Council for England, 2001–07; b 8 March 1942; s of late Harold Young and of Jessie Young (née Turnbull); m 1st, 1964, Norma Robinson (marr. diss. 1996); two d; 2nd, 1998, Margaret Pilleau. Educ: King Edward VII Sch., Sheffield; Corpus Christi Coll., Oxford (BA Hons). Ministry of Defence, 1963–82: Private Secretary: to 2nd Perm. Sec., 1966–68; to CAS, 1968–70; to Minister of State for Defence, 1973–75; seconded to Central Policy Rev. Staff, Cabinet Office, 1975–77; Head of Defence Secretariat, 1979–82; John Lewis Partnership, 1982–2002: Finance Dir, 1987–2001; Dep. Chm., 1993–2002. Chm., John Lewis Partnership Trust for Pensions, 1989–2004. Treas., Open Univ., 1998–2001; Hon. Treas., Soil Assoc., 2004–. Mem. Adv. Panel, Greenwich Hosp., 2002–07. Trustee: RAF Mus., 1999–2005; Textile Ind. Children's Trust, 2000–08. Mem. Council, Sheffield Univ., 2008–. Hon. DLitt Sheffield, 2005; Hon. DBA Beds, 2008. Recreations: theatre, food and wine, bridge, walking. Address: Gable Cottage, Fairmile, Henley on Thames RG9 2JX.

YOUNG, (David) Junor; HM Diplomatic Service, retired; b 23 April 1934; m 1954, Kathleen Brooks; two s two d. Educ: Robert Gordon's College. Joined Foreign Office, 1951; served Berlin, Ankara, South Africa, DSAO, Port Louis, Belgrade, 1951–75; Consul (Comm.), Stuttgart, 1978–81; First Sec., Kampala, 1981–84; Consul Gen., Hamburg, 1984–86; Counsellor (Commercial), Bonn, 1986–88; High Comr, Solomon Is, 1988–90; Dep. High Comr, Karachi, 1991–94. Recreations: golf, gardening. Address: Pine Cottage, Hintlesham, Suffolk IP8 3NH.

YOUNG, David Tyrrell; Chairman, City and Guilds of London Institute, 1999–2006; b 6 Jan. 1938; s of late Tyrrell F. Young and Patricia M. Young (née Spicer); m 1965, Madeline Helen Celia Philips; three d. Educ: Charterhouse. Trained as Chartered Accountant; joined Spicer & Pegler, later Spicer & Oppenheim, 1965 (merged with Touche Ross, 1990): Partner 1968; Managing Partner, 1982; Sen. Partner, 1988–90; Dep. Chm., 1990–93. Chm., N Herts NHS Trust, 1995–2000. Director: Lombard Ins. Gp, 1993–2000; Asprey, then Asprey & Garrard, 1993–2000; Wates City of London Properties, 1994–2000; Nomura Bank Internat., 1996–; Berkshire Hathaway Internat. Insurance Ltd, 1998–; Marlborough Underwriting Agency, 2000–; Capita Syndicate Mgt, 2001–08. Mem. Council, ICAEW, 1979–82. Mem. Court, Fishmongers' Co., 1981–. FRSA 1992. Hon. FCGI 1995. Recreations: golf, limited gardening. Address: Overhall, Ashdon, Saffron Walden, Essex CB10 2JH. T: (01799) 584556. Clubs: City of London, Honourable Artillery Company; Royal St George's Golf, Royal Worlington Golf.

YOUNG, Donald Anthony, CEng, FIGEM; Managing Director, National Transmission, British Gas plc, 1991–93, retired; b 23 June 1933; s of Cyril Charles Young and Sarah Young; m 1960, June (née Morrey); two d. Educ: Stockport Secondary Sch. FIGEM (FIGasE 1969). National Service, 2nd Lieut REME, 1953–55. North Western Gas Bd, 1949–60; E Midlands Gas Bd, 1960–68; Gas Council Terminal Manager, Bacton Natural Gas Reception Terminal, 1968–70; Gas Council Plant Ops Engr, 1970–73; Asst Dir (Ops), Prodn & Supply Div., British Gas HQ, 1973–77; Regional Dep. Chm., N Thames Gas, 1977–79; Dir (Operations), Prodn & Supply Div., British Gas HQ, 1979–83; Regional Chairman: Southern Reg., British Gas Corp., subseq. British Gas plc Southern, 1983–89; British Gas plc West Midlands, 1989–91. Pres., IGasE, 1988–89. CCMI (CBIM 1986). Freeman: City of London, 2006; Engineers' Co., 2006. Recreations: gardening, walking. Address: Georgian House, Penn Lane, Tanworth in Arden, Warwickshire B94 5HH.

YOUNG, Rt Rev. Donald Arthur; Bishop of Central Newfoundland, 2000–04; b 11 Nov. 1944; s of Harold and Frances Young; m 1966, Sylvia Joan Spurrell; one s three d. Educ: Univ. of Newfoundland; Atlantic Sch. of Theology; Queen's Coll., St John's, Nfld (LTh). Ordained deacon, 1977, priest, 1977; Deacon in charge, Buchans, 1977; Rector: Buchans, 1977–81; Port Rexton, 1981–89; Diocesan Progs and Exec. Officer, Central Newfoundland, 1989–2000. Address: PO Box 85, Norris Arm Northside, NL A0G 3N0, Canada. T: and Fax: (709) 6532642.

YOUNG, Hon. Douglas; see Young, Hon. M. D.

YOUNG, Edward; Deputy Private Secretary to the Queen, since 2007 (Assistant Private Secretary, 2004–07); b 24 Oct. 1966; s of Dr Edward Young and Sally Rougier Young (née Chapman); m 2003, Nichola Clare O'Brien Malone. Educ: Reading Sch. (Capt., Boarding Hse). Banker, Internat. Services Br., Barclays, 1985–97; Dep. Hd, Corporate Bank Public Relns, Barclays Bank plc, 1997–99; Advisor: to Shadow Chancellor, 1999–2000; to Leader of the Opposition, 2001; Hd, Corporate Communications, Granada plc, 2001–04. Address: Buckingham Palace, SW1A 1AA.

YOUNG, Eric, OBE 1976; HM Diplomatic Service, retired; Editor, Control Risks Information Services, 1984–93; b 16 Nov. 1924; s of late Robert Young, MBE, MIMinE and Emily Florence Young, Doncaster; m 1949, Sheila Hutchinson; three s one d. Educ: Maltby Grammar Sch.; Sheffield Univ. (BA 1948). Served War, RN, 1943–46. Editorial staff: Sheffield Telegraph, 1948; Western Morning News, 1951; Daily Dispatch, 1952; Manchester Guardian, 1953; PRO, NCB, Manchester, 1958; Dep. Dir, UK Inf. Office, Tanganyika and Zanzibar, 1960; First Secretary: (Inf.), Dar es Salaam, 1961; (Aid), Kaduna, 1963; Commonwealth Office (later FCO), 1967; Madras, 1969; Head of Chancery, Reykjavik, 1973 (Hd of Brit. Interests Section, French Embassy, during breach of diplomatic relations, 1976); Dep. High Comr, Bombay, 1977; High Comr, Seychelles, 1980–83. Recreations: music, books, walking. Address: 3 West Hall, Sudbourne Park, Orford, Woodbridge, Suffolk IP12 2AJ.

YOUNG, Rev. Prof. Frances Margaret, OBE 1998; PhD; FBA 2004; Edward Cadbury Professor of Theology, University of Birmingham, 1986–2005; Methodist minister, since 1984; b 25 Nov. 1939; d of A. Stanley Worrall and Mary F. Worrall (née Marshall); m 1964, Robert Charles Young; three s. Educ: Bedford Coll., Univ. of London (BA); Girton Coll., Univ. of Cambridge (MA, PhD). Research Fellow, Clare Hall, Cambridge, 1967–68; University of Birmingham: Temp. Lectr, 1971–73; Lectr, 1973–82; Sen. Lectr, 1982–86; Hd, Dept of Theol., 1986–95; Dean, Faculty of Arts, 1995–97; Pro-Vice-Chancellor, 1997–2002. Hon. DD Aberdeen, 1994. Publications: Sacrifice and the Death of Christ, 1975; (contrib.) The Myth of God Incarnate, 1977; From Nicaea to Chalcedon, 1983; Face to Face, 1985, 2nd edn 1990; (with David Ford) Meaning and Truth in 2 Corinthians, 1987; The Art of Performance, 1990; The Theology of the Pastoral Epistles, 1994; Biblical Exegesis and the Formation of Christian Culture, 1997; (ed) Encounter with Mystery, 1997; (ed jtly) The Cambridge History of Early Christian Literature, 2004; (ed jtly) The Cambridge History of Christianity: origins to Constantine, 2006; Brokenness and Blessing, 2007; numerous articles, etc. Recreations: outdoor pursuits, music. Address: 142 Selly Park Road, Birmingham B29 7LH. T: (0121) 472 4841.

YOUNG, Gavin Neil B.; see Barr Young.

YOUNG, Rt Hon. Sir George (Samuel Knatchbull), 6th Bt cr 1813; PC 1993; MP (C) North West Hampshire, since 1997 (Ealing, Acton, Feb. 1974–1997); b 16 July 1941; s of Sir George Young, 5th Bt, CMG, and Elisabeth (née Knatchbull-Hugessen); S father, 1960; m 1964, Aurelia Nemon-Stuart, er d of late Oscar Nemon, and of Mrs Nemon-Stuart, Boar's Hill, Oxford; two s two d. Educ: Eton; Christ Church, Oxford (Open Exhibitioner); MA Oxon, MPhil Surrey. Economist, NEDO, 1966–67; Kobler Research Fellow, University of Surrey, 1967–69; Economic Adviser, PO Corp., 1969–74. Councillor, London Borough of Lambeth, 1968–71; Mem., GLC, for London Borough of Ealing, 1970–73. An Opposition Whip, 1976–79; Parly Under Sec. of State, DHSS, 1979–81, DoE, 1981–86; Comptroller of HM Household, 1990; Minister of State, DoE, 1990–94; Financial Sec. to HM Treasury, 1994–95; Sec. of State for Transport, 1995–97; Shadow Leader, H of C, 1998–2000. Chm., Acton Housing Assoc., 1972–79. Dir, Lovell Partnerships Ltd, 1987–90. Trustee, Guinness Trust, 1986–90. Publications: Accommodation Services in the UK 1970–1980, 1970; Tourism, Blessing or Blight?, 1973. Recreation: bicycling. Heir: s George Horatio Young [b 11 Oct. 1966; m 1999, Marianne, e d of Dr Peter Toghill]. Address: House of Commons, SW1A 0AA.

YOUNG, Helen, (Mrs K. Rees), FRMetS; broadcast meteorologist, 1993–2005, Broadcast Manager, 2000–05, BBC Weather Centre; b 10 June 1969; d of Derek and Lyn Young; m 1997, Kerith Rees; one s one d. Educ: Univ. of Bristol (BSc Geog.); Meteorological Office (qualified as forecaster). Dep. Manager, BBC Weather Centre, 1998–2000. Recreations: ski-ing, swimming, gardening. Address: c/o 1st Choice Speakers UK Ltd, PO Box 562, Chesham, Bucks HP5 1SN.

YOUNG, Prof. (Hobart) Peyton, PhD; FBA 2007; James Meade Professor of Economics, University of Oxford, and Fellow of Nuffield College, Oxford, since 2007; b 9 March 1945; s of Hobart Paul Young and Louise B. Young; m 1982, Fernanda F. Toueg; two s. Educ: Harvard Univ. (AB cum laude Gen. Studies 1966); Univ. of Michigan (PhD 1970). Prof. of Econs and Public Policy, Univ. of Maryland, 1981–94; Scott and Barbara Black Prof. of Econs, Johns Hopkins Univ., 1994–2007. Sen. Fellow in Econ. Studies, Brookings Instn, 1998–; Ext. Prof., Santa Fe Inst., 2001–05, 2007–; Fulbright Dist. Chair in Econs, Univ. of Siena, 2003–04. Pres., Game Theory Soc., 2006–. Fellow, Econometric Soc., 1995. Publications: (with M. L. Balinski) Fair Representation: meeting the ideal of one man one vote, 1984, 2nd edn 2002; Equity in Theory and Practice, 1994; Individual Strategy and Social Structure: an evolutionary theory of institutions, 1998; Strategic Learning and Its Limits, 2004; articles in learned jls. Address: Nuffield College, Oxford OX1 1NF. T: (01865) 271086, Fax: (01865) 271094; e-mail: peyton.young@economics.ox.ac.uk. Clubs: Cosmos (Washington, DC); Chevy Chase.

YOUNG, Ian Robert, OBE 1985; PhD; FRS 1989; FREng; consultant; b 11 Jan. 1932; s of John Stirling Young and Ruth Muir Young (née Whipple); m 1956, Sylvia Marianne Whewell Ralph; two s one d. Educ: Sedbergh Sch., Yorkshire; Aberdeen Univ. (BSc, PhD). FIET; FREng (FEng 1988). Hilger & Watts Ltd, 1955–59; Evershed & Vignoles Ltd (and affiliates), 1959–76; EMI Ltd, 1976–81; GEC plc, 1981–97. Vis. Prof. of Radiology, RPMS, 1986. Hon. FRCR 1990; Hon. Mem., Amer. Soc. of Neuroradiology, 1995. Hon. DSc Aberdeen, 1992. Publications: over 100 papers in Proc. IEE, Magnetic Resonance in Medicine, Magnetic Resonance Imaging, Jl Magnetic Resonance, Computer Assisted Tomography, etc; 50 separate patents. Recreations: bird watching, hill walking, brick laying. Address: High Kingsbury, Kingsbury Street, Marlborough, Wilts SN8 1HZ. T: (01672) 516126.

YOUNG, James Edward D.; see Drummond Young.

YOUNG, Sir Jimmy; see Young, Sir L. R.

YOUNG, John Adrian Emile; Partner, Markby, Stewart & Wadesons, subseq. Cameron Markby Hewitt, 1965–95; b 28 July 1934; s of John Archibald Campbell Young and Irene Eugenie Young (née Bouvier); m 1959, Yvonne Lalage Elizabeth Bankes (d 2008); three s one d. Educ: Cranbrook Sch., Kent; London Univ. (LLB). Admitted solicitor, 1958; Asst

Sec., Law Soc., 1958–64. Adjudicator (formerly Legal Officer), Office of the Banking Ombudsman, 1996–98. Nat Chm., Young Solicitors Gp, 1965–66; Pres., Assoc. Internat. des Jeunes Avocats, 1968–69; Law Society: Mem. Council, 1971–95; Dep. Vice-Pres., 1993–94; Vice-Pres., 1994–95; Mem. Council, Internat. Bar Assoc., 1983–94. FRSA 1989. Master, City of London Solicitors' Co., 1989–90. *Publications:* sundry legal articles. *Recreations:* music (runs local church choir), gardening, family! *Address:* Stonewold House, The Street, Plaxtol, Sevenoaks, Kent TN15 0QH. *T:* (01732) 810289.

YOUNG, John Henderson, OBE 1980; JP, DL; Member (C) West of Scotland, Scottish Parliament, 1999–2003; *b* 21 Dec. 1930; *s* of late William W. Young and Jeannie Young (*née* Henderson); *m* 1956, Doris Paterson (*d* 2001); one *s*. *Educ:* Hillhead High Sch., Glasgow; Scottish Coll. of Commerce. Served RAF, 1949–51. Shipping Manager/Dep. Contracts Manager, Kelvin-Diesel Engines, 1959–77; Export Admin Sales Manager, Teachers Whisky, 1977–88; Chm., Allied-Lyons Shipping & Marine Insce Cttee, 1987–88; Public Relns Consultant, Proscot Ltd, 1989–92. Newspaper columnist, The Extra, 1997–. Mem., Local Govt Commn, 1998. Mem. (C) Glasgow City Council, 1964–99: Leader, 1977–79; Opposition Leader, 1979–80, 1988–92, 1996–98; Police Judge, 1970–72; Bailie, 1968–71, 1977–80, 1984–88, 1988–92; Vice-Chm., Glasgow Corp. Airport Cttee, 1968–71; Mem., Strathclyde PTA, 1995–99. Chm., Assoc. Scottish Cons. Councillors, 1991–94. Tspt spokesman, Scottish Cons. Party, 1998–99. Mem., Scottish Parly Corporate Body, 1999–2003; Dep. Convener, Nat. Galleries Bills Cttee, Scottish Parlt, 2003. Mem., Commonwealth Parly Delegn of Scottish Parlt, Quebec, Canada, 2002. Mem., All-Party Gp on Animal Welfare, Scottish Parlt, 1999–. Chm., Assoc. of Former MSPs, 2003–. Vice-Chm., Scottish Pakistani Assoc., 1981–84; Sec., Scottish/S African Soc., 1986–88. FCMI (FIMgt 2001). Contested (C): Rutherglen, 1966; Cathcart, 1992; Eastwood, Scottish Parlt, 1999. Life Mem., Cathcart Conservatives. JP Glasgow, 1968; DL Glasgow, 1981. Gov., Hutcheson's Educnl Trust, 1991–97. KSJ. Life Mem., Merchants' House of Glasgow. *Publications:* A History of Cathcart Conservative Association 1918–93, 1993; contrib. articles to newspapers and magazines. *Recreations:* meeting people, history, writing, reading, animal welfare. *Address:* 4 Deanwood Avenue, Netherlee, Glasgow G44 3RJ. *T:* (0141) 637 9535.

YOUNG, Sir John (Kenyon Roe), 6th Bt *cr* 1821; Purchasing Manager; *b* 23 April 1947; *s* of Sir John William Roe Young, 5th Bt, and Joan Minnie Agnes (*d* 1958), *d* of M. M. Aldous; *S* father, 1981; *m* 1977, Frances Elise, *o d* of W. R. Thompson; one *s* one *d*. *Educ:* Hurn Court; Napier College. Joined RN, 1963; transferred to Hydrographic Branch, 1970; qualified Hydrographic Surveyor, 1977; retired from RN, 1979; attended Napier Coll., 1979–80. Member: Hydrographic Soc.; Inst. of Purchasing Mgt. *Recreations:* Rugby, golf. *Heir: s* Richard Christopher Roe Young, *b* 14 June 1983.

YOUNG, Hon. Sir John (McIntosh), AC 1989; KCMG 1975; Lieutenant-Governor of Victoria, Australia, 1974–95; Chief Justice, Supreme Court of Victoria, 1974–91; *b* Melbourne, 17 Dec. 1919; *s* of George David Young, Glasgow, and Kathleen Mildred Young, Melbourne; *m* 1951, Elisabeth Mary, *yr d* of late Dr Edward Wing Twining, Manchester; one *s* two *d*. *Educ:* Geelong Grammar Sch.; Brasenose Coll., Oxford (MA; Hon. Fellow, 1991); Inner Temple; Univ. of Melbourne (LLB). Served War: Scots Guards, 1940–46 (Captain 1943); NW Europe (despatches), 1945. Admitted Victorian Bar, 1948; Associate to Mr Justice Dixon, High Court of Australia, 1948; practice as barrister, 1949–74; Hon. Sec., Victorian Bar Council, 1950–60; Lectr in Company Law, Univ. of Melbourne, 1957–61; Hon. Treas., Medico Legal Soc. of Vic., 1955–65 (Vice-Pres., 1966–68; Pres., 1968–69). QC (Vic) 1961; admitted Tasmanian Bar, 1964, QC 1964; NSW Bar, 1968, QC 1968; Consultant, Faculty of Law, Monash Univ., 1968–74. Mem., Bd of Examiners for Barristers and Solicitors, 1969–72; Pres., Victorian Council of Legal Educn and Victoria Law Foundn, 1974–91; Chm., Police Board of Vic, 1992–98. Pres., Scout Assoc. of Australia, 1986–89, 1996–97 (Vice-Pres., 1985; Pres., Victorian Br., 1974–87); Chief Scout of Australia, 1989–96; Pres., St John Council for Victoria, 1975–82; GCStJ 1991 (KStJ 1977); Chancellor, Order of St John in Australia, 1982–91. Hon. Colonel: 4th/19th Prince of Wales's Light Horse, 1978–97; Royal Victoria Regt, 1994–99; Rep. Hon. Col, RAAC, 1986–97; Hon. Air Cdre, No 21 (City of Melbourne) Sqn, RAAF, 1986–98. Mem. Council, Geelong GS, 1974. Hon. LLD: Monash, 1986; Melbourne, 1989. *Publications:* (co-author) Australian Company Law and Practice, 1965; articles in legal jls. *Recreation:* reading. *Address:* 2/18 Huntingtower Road, Armadale, Victoria 3143, Australia. *T:* (3) 98226259. *Clubs:* Melbourne, Australian (Melbourne).

YOUNG, John Richard Dendy; Attorney of Supreme Court, South Africa, 1984; *b* 4 Sept. 1907; 5th *s* of James Young and Evelyn Maud Hammond; *m* 1946, Patricia Maureen Mount; four *s* two *d*. *Educ:* Hankey, Cape Province, SA; Humansdorp, CP, SA; University, South Africa (External). Joined Public Service, S Rhodesia, 1926; resigned to practise at Bar, 1934; joined Military Forces, 1940; active service, North Africa, Sicily and Italy; commissioned in the field; demobilised, 1945. QC 1948; MP Southern Rhodesia, 1948–53; Member Federal Assembly, 1953–56; Judge of the High Court of Rhodesia, 1956–68; Chief Justice, Botswana, 1968–71; Advocate of Supreme Court of SA, 1971–84; Sen. Counsel, 1979–84; Judge of Appeal, Lesotho, Swaziland, Botswana, 1979–84. *Recreations:* swimming, walking. *Address:* 8 Tulani Gardens, Greenfield Road, Kenilworth, Cape, 7700, South Africa.

YOUNG, John Robert Chester, CBE 1992; Nominated Member, 1996–2002, and Deputy Chairman, 1997–2002, Council of Lloyd's; Chairman, Lloyd's Regulatory Board, 1997–2002; *b* 6 Sept. 1937; *s* of Robert Nisbet Young and Edith Mary (*née* Roberts); *m* 1963, Pauline Joyce (*d* 1997); one *s* one *d* (and one *s* decd). *Educ:* Bishop Vesey's Grammar Sch.; St Edmund Hall, Oxford Univ. (MA); Gray's Inn, London. Joined Simon & Coates, members of the Stock Exchange, 1961; Partner, 1965; Dep. Sen. Partner, 1976; London Stock Exchange (formerly Stock Exchange, subseq. Internat. Stock Exchange): Mem. Council, 1978–82; Dir of Policy and Planning, 1982–87; Vice-Chm. (non-exec.), Managing Bd, 1987–90. Chief Exec. and Dir, SFA (formerly Securities Assoc.), 1987–93; Dir, 1993–97, Chief Exec., 1993–95, SIB. Non-executive Director: Darby Gp plc, 1996–97; Elderstreet Millennium (formerly Gartmore) Venture Capital Trust, 1996–2006; E Surrey Healthcare (formerly E Surrey Hosp. and Community Healthcare) NHS Trust, 1992–96. Public Interest Dir, Financial Services Compensation Scheme Ltd, 2000–04. Mem. Ethics Cttee, Securities Inst., 1995– (Hon. Fellow, 2003). Lay Mem., Legal Services Consultative Panel, DCA, subseq. MoJ, 2004–. Advr, Royal Sch. for the Blind, 1997–2001. Formerly internat. athlete, Rugby player (England and British Lions) and England Rugby selector. *Recreations:* cooking, grandsons, Rugby football. *Clubs:* City of London; Vincent's (Oxford); Harlequins, Achilles.

See also L. Botting.

YOUNG, Sir John Robertson, (Sir Rob), GCMG 2003 (KCMG 1999; CMG 1991); HM Diplomatic Service, retired; High Commissioner, New Delhi, 1999–2003; *b* 21 Feb. 1945; *s* of late Francis John Young and of Marjorie Elizabeth Young; *m* 1967, Catherine Suzanne Françoise Houssait; one *s* two *d*. *Educ:* King Edward VI Sch., Norwich; Leicester Univ. (BA 1st Cl. Hons, French). Entered FCO, 1967; MECAS, Lebanon, 1968; Third Sec., Cairo, 1970; Second Sec., FCO, 1972; Private Sec. to Minister of State, 1975; First Sec., Paris, 1977; Asst Head, Western European Dept, FCO, 1982; Counsellor, Damascus, 1984; Head of Middle East Dept, FCO, 1987; Minister, Paris, 1991; Dep. Under-Sec. of State, 1994–98, and Chief Clerk, 1995–98, FCO. Comr, Commonwealth War Graves Commn, 2003–. Non-executive Director: Hirco plc, 2006–; Aguas de Barcelona, 2008–. Chairman: Calcutta Tercentenary Trust, 2003–; Adv. Bd, ic2 Capital, 2008–. Hon. DLaws Leicester, 2001. *Recreations:* music, sailing, theatre. *Address:* Les Choiseaux, La Planche des Chaqueneaux, 37260 Artannes-sur-Indre, France. *Clubs:* Beefsteak, Cruising Association.

YOUNG, John Todd; Senior Partner, Lovells, since 2004; *b* 14 Jan. 1957; *s* of Ian Taylor Young and Flora Leggett Young (*née* Todd); *m* 1981, Elizabeth Jane Grattidge. *Educ:* Manchester Grammar Sch.; Sidney Sussex Coll., Cambridge (BA 1978). Admitted solicitor, 1981; Lovells (formerly Lovell, White & King, then Lovell White Durrant): articled clerk, 1979–81; Solicitor, 1981–87; Partner, 1987–2004; Hd, Corporate Insce Practice, 1997–; Hd, Financial Instns Gp, 2004–. *Publications:* (consultant ed.) A Practitioner's Guide to the FSA Regulation of Insurance, 2002; numerous articles on insce related topics. *Recreations:* Scottish and alpine mountaineering, ski-ing, windsurfing. *Address:* c/o Lovells, Atlantic House, Holborn Viaduct, EC1A 2FG. *T:* (020) 7296 2605, *Fax:* (020) 7296 2001; *e-mail:* john.young@lovells.com.

YOUNG, John William Garne; Group Chief Executive, Wolseley plc, 1996–2000; *b* 6 Jan. 1945; *s* of David Richard Young and Pamela Mary Young (*née* Garne); *m* 1971, Eleanor Louise Walsh; three *s*. *Educ:* Shaftesbury Grammar Sch. Apprentice, Tube Investment Gp, 1962–67; Man. Dir, P. J. Parmiter & Sons Ltd, 1967–85; Wolseley plc: Chief Exec., Agricl Div., 1982–90, Agricl, Photographic & Technical Services Div., 1990–95; Dep. Chief Exec., 1994–96. Pres., Agricl Engrs Assoc., 1987–88. Pres., Comité Européen de Constructeurs de Mechanisme Agricole, 1995–96. *Recreations:* fishing, golf. *Address:* The Gables, Hindon Lane, Tisbury, Salisbury, Wilts SP3 6QF.

YOUNG, Jonathan Piers; Editor, The Field, since 1991; *b* 23 Sept. 1959; *s* of Peter and Mavis Young; *m* 1993, Caroline Bankes; one *s* one *d*. *Educ:* Blundell's; Univ. of Leicester (BA). Ed., Shooting Times and Country Magazine, 1986–90. *Publication:* A Pattern of Wings, 1989. *Recreations:* shooting, fishing, sloe-ginning. *Address:* The Field, Blue Fin Building, 110 Southwark Street, SE1 0SU. *T:* (020) 3148 4772. *Club:* Tyburn Angling Society.

YOUNG, Joyce Jean, RGN, RMN; independent consultant and advisor to health services, since 1993; *b* 16 Nov. 1936; *d* of Leslie Cyril and Frances May Lyons. *Educ:* Cowes High School, Isle of Wight. General Nurse training, Essex County Hosp., Colchester, 1955–58; Mental Nurse training, Severalls Hosp., Colchester, 1959–60; Ward Sister posts, gen. and psych. hosps, 1960–70; Clinical Nurse Advr, Hosp. Adv. Service, 1970–72; Regl Nurse Advr, SE Metrop. Hosp. Bd for Mental Illness, Mental Handicap and Elderly Services, 1972–74; Dist Nursing Officer, Tunbridge Wells Health Dist., 1974–80; Chief Nursing Officer, Brighton HA, 1980–84; Regl Nursing Officer, Oxford, 1984–92. Dir and Chief Exec., Blenheim House Ltd, 1996. Nursing Advisor to Social Services Select Cttee, 1985; Mem., Broadmoor Hosp. Management Bd, 1987; Dir, NSQT, 1992–94; Member: Prison Health Adv. Cttee, 1992; (non-exec.), Bd, Special Hosps Service Authy, 1993. *Publications:* (contrib.) Impending Crisis of Old Age (Nuffield Provincial Trust), 1981; articles in Nursing Times and Nursing Mirror. *Recreations:* gardening, wildlife.

YOUNG, Junor; *see* Young, D. J.

YOUNG, Kenneth Middleton, CBE 1977; Chairman, Further Education Funding Council for Wales, 1999–2001 (Member, Council, and Quality Assurance Committee, 1998–2001); *b* 1 Aug. 1931; *s* of Cyril W. D. Young and Gwladys Middleton Young; *m* 1958, Brenda May Thomas; one *s* one *d*. *Educ:* Neath Grammar Sch.; University Coll. of Wales, Aberystwyth (Hon. Fellow, 1991); Coll. of Science and Technology, Univ. of Manchester. BA (Hons) 1952; Diploma in Personnel Management, 1954. Pilot Officer/Navigator, General Duties (Aircrew), RAF, 1952–54. Asst Personnel Manager, Elliott-Automation Ltd, 1955–59; Collective Agreements Manager, later Salary Administration Manager, Massey-Ferguson (UK) Ltd, 1959–64; Personnel Adviser, Aviation Div., Smiths Industries Ltd, 1964–66; Group Personnel Manager, General Electric Company Ltd, and Dir, GEC (Management) Ltd, 1966–71; Post Office Corporation, 1972–92: Bd Mem. for Personnel, 1972–84, for Personnel and Corporate Resources, 1984–90; Man. Dir, Royal Mail Parcels, 1987; Vice-Chm., 1986–90; Actg Chm., 1989; Dep. Chm., 1990–92; Chairman: Subscription Services, 1988–92; Girobank PLC, 1989–90; Post Office Counters, 1990–92. Chm., Student Loans Co. Ltd, 1992–96; Director: Courage (formerly FBG) Pensions Ltd, 1993–2002; Courage (formerly FBG) Pensions Investments Ltd, 1993–2002. Member: Management Bd, Engineering Employers Fedn, 1971; CBI Employment Policy Cttee, 1978–84; Employment Appeal Tribunal, 1985–2002; BIC Target Team on Business/Educn Partnerships, 1988–89; Trustee, Post Office Pension Funds, 1989–95. Chairman: Rev. Gp, Further Educn Funding Councils for England and Wales, 1993; Further Educn Develt Assoc., subseq. Agency, 1994–97. Member: Council, Inst. of Manpower Studies, 1980–86; London Business Sch. Liaison Cttee, 1982–89; Chairman: Bd of Govs, SW London Coll., 1991; Roehampton Inst., 1992–95; Vice-Pres., Univ. of Wales (formerly St David's UC), Lampeter, 1993–99; Member: Council, Univ. of Wales, Aberystwyth, 1994–97 (Pres., Old Students Assoc., 1998–2000); Ct of Govs, 1998–2000, Council, 1999–2000, Univ. of Wales. CCMI; FIPM. *Recreations:* photography, Wales Rugby, theatre. *Address:* Bryn Aber, Northcliffe Drive, Penarth, South Glamorgan CF64 1DQ.

YOUNG, Kirsty Jackson, (Mrs N. K. A. Jones); Presenter: Desert Island Discs, BBC Radio Four, since 2006; Crimewatch UK, since 2008; *b* 23 Nov. 1968; *d* of John and Catherine Young; *m* 1999, Nicholas Keith Arthur Jones, *qv*; two *d*. *Educ:* High Sch. of Stirling. Newsreader and news presenter, BBC Radio Scotland, 1990–93; news anchor and presenter, Scottish Television, 1993–95; reporter, Holiday and Film 96, BBC TV, 1995–96; News Anchor: Channel Five News, 1996–2000; ITV, 2000–01; Five News, Channel Five, 2001–07. *Recreations:* family, food, laughter. *Address:* c/o KBJ, 7 Soho Square, W1D 3DQ. *T:* (020) 7434 6767, *Fax:* (020) 7287 1191. *Club:* Soho House.

YOUNG, Prof. Lawrence Sterling, PhD, DSc; FRCPath; FMedSci; Professor of Cancer Biology, since 1994, and Head, College of Medical and Dental Sciences, University of Birmingham, since 2008; *b* 28 Oct. 1958; *s* of Bernard Young and late Joan Young (*née* Black); *m* 1979, Alison Hilton; one *s*. *Educ:* Univ. of Birmingham (BSc 1981; PhD 1984; DSc 1998). MRCPath 1993, FRCPath 2000. University of Birmingham: Res. Fellow, 1984–89, Lectr and Sen. Lectr, 1989–94, Dept of Cancer Studies; Hd, Div. of Cancer Studies and Dir, Cancer Res. UK Inst. for Cancer Studies, 2001–07. Member: Med. and Scientific Adv. Panel, Leukaemia Res. Fund, 1996–99; Grants Cttee, CRC, 1996–2001; Molecular Cell Medicine Bd, MRC, 2003–07; Cancer Sub-panel, 2001 and 2008 RAEs. Non-exec. Dir, Birmingham Children's Hosp., 2008–. FMedSci 2007. Hon. MRCP 1998. *Publications:* contrib. articles to learned jls on cancer, viruses and novel cancer therapies. *Recreations:* Gilbert and Sullivan operas, travel, poetry. *Address:* Cancer Research

UK Institute for Cancer Studies, University of Birmingham, Edgbaston, Birmingham B15 2TT. *T:* (0121) 414 6876, *Fax:* (0121) 414 5376; *e-mail:* L.S.Young@bham.ac.uk.

YOUNG, Sir Leslie (Clarence), Kt 1984; CBE 1980; Chairman: Enterprise plc, 1999–2000 (Director, Lancashire Enterprises, later Enterprise, plc, 1992–99); Eatonfield Group plc, since 2006; *b* 5 Feb. 1925; *s* of late Clarence James Young and of Ivy Isabel Young; *m* 1st, 1949, Muriel Howard Pearson (*d* 1998); one *s* one *d*; 2nd, 1999, Margaret Gittens. *Educ:* London School of Economics (BScEcon). Courtaulds Ltd: held range of senior executive appts, incl. chairmanship of number of gp companies, 1948–68; J. Bibby & Sons Ltd, 1968–86: Managing Director, J. Bibby Agriculture Ltd, 1968; Chm. and Man. Dir, J. Bibby Food Products Ltd, 1970; Gp Man. Dir, 1970, Dep. Chm. and Man. Dir, 1977, Chm., 1979–86, J. Bibby & Sons Ltd. Director: Bank of England, 1986–90; National Westminster Bank, 1986–90 (Regl Dir, 1979–90, Chm., 1986–90, Northern Regl Bd); Swiss Pioneer Life (formerly Pioneer Mutual Insce Co.), 1986–92; Sibec Developments PLC, 1988–91; Britannia Cable Systems Wirral plc, 1990–92. Chairman: NW Regional Council, CBI, 1976–78; NW Industrial Development Board, 1978–81; Merseyside Develt Corp., 1980–84; British Waterways Bd, 1984–87. Trustee, Civic Trust for the North West, 1978–83. Non-Executive Director: Granada Television Ltd, 1979–84; Blue Max plc, 2000–. Chm. Trustees, Nat. Museums and Galls on Merseyside, 1986–95. Member Council: N of England Zoological Soc., 1979–85; Royal Liverpool Philharmonic Soc., 1980–2000. DL Merseyside, 1983. Hon. Col, Liverpool Univ. OTC, 1989–94. Hon. LLD Liverpool, 1988. *Recreations:* fly-fishing, walking. *Address:* Boningdale House, Lawnswood Drive, Lawnswood, Stourbridge, S Staffs DY7 5QW. *T:* (01384) 277282, 07808 137160.

YOUNG, Sir Leslie Ronald, (Sir Jimmy), Kt 2002; CBE 1993 (OBE 1979); Presenter, Jimmy Young Programme, BBC Radio Two, 1973–2002 (Radio One, 1967–73); *b* 21 Sept. 1921; *s* of Frederick George Young and Gertrude Woolford; *m* 1st, 1946, Wendy Wilkinson (marr. diss.); one *d*; 2nd, 1950, Sally Douglas (marr. diss.); 3rd, 1996, Alicia Plastow. *Educ:* East Dean Grammar Sch., Cinderford, Glos. RAF, 1939–46. First BBC radio broadcast, songs at piano, 1949; pianist, singer, bandleader, West End, London, 1950–51; first theatre appearance, Empire Theatre, Croydon, 1952; regular theatre appearances, 1952–; first radio broadcast introd. records, Flat Spin, 1953; BBC TV Bristol, Pocket Edition series, 1955; first introd. radio Housewives' Choice, 1955; BBC radio series, incl.: The Night is Young, 12 o'clock Spin, Younger Than Springtime, Saturday Special, Keep Young, Through Till Two, 1959–65; presented progs, Radio Luxembourg, 1960–68. BBC TV: series, Jimmy Young Asks, 1972; The World of Jimmy Young, 1973. First live direct BBC broadcasts to Europe from Soviet Union, Jimmy Young Programme, 16 and 17 May 1977; Jimmy Young Programmes broadcast live from Egypt and Israel, 9 and 12 June 1978, from Zimbabwe-Rhodesia, 9 and 10 Aug. 1979; Host for Thames TV of first British Telethon, 2nd and 3rd Oct. 1980; Jimmy Young Programmes live from Tokyo, 26th, 27th and 28th May 1981, from Sydney, 4–8 Oct. 1982, from Washington DC, 3–7 Oct. 1983. ITV series: Whose Baby?, 1973; Jim's World, 1974; The Jimmy Young Television Programme, 1984–87. Hit Records: 1st, Too Young, 1951; Unchained Melody, The Man From Laramie, 1955 (1st Brit. singer to have 2 consec. no 1 hit records); Chain Gang, More, 1956; Miss You, 1963. Weekly Column: Daily Sketch, 1968–71; Sunday Express, 2003–. Hon. Mem. Council, NSPCC, 1981–. Freeman, City of London, 1969. Variety Club of GB Award, Radio Personality of the Year, 1968; Sony Award, Radio Personality of the Year, 1985; Sony Radio Awards Roll of Honour, 1988; Radio Broadcaster of the Year, BPG Radio Awards, 1994; Sony Gold Award, for Service to the Community, 1995, for Outstanding Service to Radio, 1997; Jimmy Young Programme: Radio Industries Award, Prog. of the Year, 1979; BBC Current Affairs Prog. of the Year, Daily Mail Nat. Radio Awards, 1988; Radio Prog. of the Year, TV and Radio Inds Club Award, 1989. Silver Jubilee Medal, 1977. *Publications:* Jimmy Young Cookbook: No 1, 1968; No 2, 1969; No 3, 1970; No 4, 1972; (autobiogs) JY, 1973, Jimmy Young, 1982, Forever Young, 2003; contrib. magazines, incl. Punch, Woman's Own. *Address:* PO Box 39715, W4 3YF.

YOUNG, Hon. M. Douglas; PC (Canada) 1993; Chairman: Summa Strategies Canada, Inc., since 1997; CPCS Transcom Inc., since 2006; *b* 20 Sept. 1940; *s* of Douglas Young and Annie Young (*née* Wishart); *m* 1979, Jacqueline David; one *s* two *d.* *Educ:* St Thomas Univ., USA (BA 1972); Univ. of New Brunswick (LLB 1975); New Brunswick Teachers' Coll. Cert., 1957. Lawyer and businessman; Counsel to Atlantic Canada Lawyers, Cox & Palmer (formerly Patterson Palmer). MLA for Tracadie, New Brunswick, 1978–88; Leader, New Brunswick Liberal Party, 1981–83; Provincial Minister of Fisheries and Aquaculture, 1987–88; MP (L) Gloucester, renamed Acadie-Bathurst, 1988–97; Canadian Minister: of Transport, 1993–96; of Human Resources, 1996; of Nat. Defence and of Veteran Affairs, 1996–97. Dir, Genesee & Wyoming Inc. *Recreations:* tennis, reading, travelling. *Address:* (office) 100 Sparks Street, Suite 1000, Ottawa, ON K1P 5B7, Canada.

YOUNG, Madeleine Mary, (Lady Young); *see* Arnot, M. M.

YOUNG, Malcolm, (Mal); Director of Drama, 19 TV, since 2005; *b* 26 Jan. 1957; *s* of late Charles Young, Liverpool, and of Maria (*née* Williams). *Educ:* Liverpool Sch. of Art (DipAD). Design Manager, Littlewoods Orgn, 1975–81; actor/singer, 1981–84; Mersey Television, 1984–96: Design Asst on Brookside, then Asst Floor Manager and Floor Manager, 1986–91; Producer, Brookside and Dir, Brookside Prodns, 1991–95; Series Producer, Brookside, 1995–96 (also devised and produced And The Beat Goes On, Channel 4); Hd of Drama, Pearson TV, 1996–97; Hd of Drama Series, 1997–2001, Controller of Continuing Drama Series, 2001–04, BBC, responsible for: EastEnders, Casualty, Holby City, Waking the Dead, Doctors, Murder in Mind, In Deep, Judge John Deed, Down to Earth, Dalziel and Pascoe, and Dr Who; writer and creator, Born in the USA, for Fox TV (US), 2005–; writer and creator, Austin Golden Hour, TV drama pilot for CW/Paramount (US), 2008. Huw Wheldon Meml Lecture, RTS, 1999. Special Award for Creative Contribution to TV, British Soap Awards, 2004. *Publication:* Sinbad's Scrapbook, 1996. *Recreation:* music.

YOUNG, Prof. Malcolm Philip, PhD; Chief Executive, e-Therapeutics plc, since 2007; Professor and Chair in Psychology, since 1994, and Pro-Vice-Chancellor for Strategic Development, since 2005, University of Newcastle upon Tyne; *b* 11 Sept. 1960; *s* of James Guthrie Philips Young and Shirley Joyce Young (*née* Smith); *m* 1987, Deborah Anne Howse; one *s* one *d.* *Educ:* Bristol Univ. (BSc 1st cl. Hons (Psychol.) 1987); Univ. of St Andrews (PhD (Neurosci.) 1990). Royal Soc. Japan Sci. and Technol. Sci. Exchange Fellow, Riken Inst., Japan, 1990–91; Oxford University: MRC Res. Associate, 1991–92; Royal Soc. Univ. Res. Fellow, 1992–94, Univ. Lab. of Physiol.; British Telecommunications Jun. Res. Fellow, Brasenose Coll., 1993–94; Newcastle upon Tyne University: Dir, Inst. for Neurosci., 1999–2001; Provost, Faculty of Sci., Agriculture and Engrg, 2001–05. Vis. Prof., Agency of Industrial Sci. and Technol., Tsukuba, Japan, 1995. Chairman and Chief Technology Officer: in Rotis Technologies Ltd, 2001–; e-Therapeutics plc, 2003–07; non-exec. Chm., Novotech Investment Ltd, 2007–. Mem., Soc. for Neurosci., USA, 1990–. *Publications:* The Analysis of Cortical Connectivity, 1996; many articles in learned jls inc. Nature, Science, Procs of Royal Soc., Philosophical Transactions of Royal Soc., Jl of Neuroscience, etc. *Recreations:* tennis, swimming, water ski-ing. *Address:* Executive Office, e-Therapeutics, Holland Park, Holland Drive, Newcastle upon Tyne, NE2 4LZ; Pro-Vice-Chancellor's Office, 6 Kensington Terrace, University of Newcastle upon Tyne, NE1 7RU. *T:* (0191) 222 3832, *Fax:* (0191) 222 1303; *e-mail:* m.p.young@ncl.ac.uk.

YOUNG, Neil; *see* Young, R. N.

YOUNG, Sir Nicholas (Charles), Kt 2000; Chief Executive, British Red Cross, since 2001; *b* 16 April 1952; *s* of late Leslie Charles Young and Mary Margaret Young (*née* Rudman); *m* 1978, Helen Mary Ferrier Hamilton; three *s.* *Educ:* Wimbledon Coll.; Birmingham Univ. (Hons LLB 2.1). Qualified Solicitor, 1977; Articled Clerk and Solicitor, Freshfields, 1975–78; Solicitor, later Partner, Turner, Martin & Symes, 1979–85; Sec. for Develt, Sue Ryder Foundn, 1985–90; Dir, UK Ops, BRCS, 1990–95; Chief Exec., 1995–2001 and Vice-Pres., 2001–, Macmillan Cancer Relief (formerly Cancer Relief Macmillan Fund). Vice Chm., Nat. Council for Hospice and Specialist Palliative Care Services, 1996–99; Member: Exec. Cttee, Healthwork UK, 1998–2002; NCVO Charity Law Reform Gp, 1998–2001; NHS Modernisation Bd, 2000–01; Trustee, 2000–, and Chm., 2005–, Monte San Martino Trust; Mem., Steering Cttee, The Giving Campaign, 2000–03; Trustee: Disasters Emergency Cttee, 2001–; Guidestar UK, 2003–06; Trustee and Dep. Chm., World Humanitarian Forum, 2006–. Chm., Judging Panel, Asian Women of Achievement Awards, 2006–. Mem., Stumblers Assoc., 1978–. Gov., Wimbledon Coll., 1998–2000. *Recreations:* sailing, theatre, walking, amateur dramatics, travel, reading. *Address:* British Red Cross, 44 Moorfields, EC2Y 9AL. *T:* (020) 7877 7000.

YOUNG, Peter Lance; Group Chief Executive, RMC Group, 1996–2000; *b* 26 June 1938; *s* of Harry Aubrey Young and Ethel Freda Young; *m* 1962, Susan Mary Wilkes; three *s* one *d.* *Educ:* Chippenham Grammar Sch. Joined RMC Group, 1961; Dir, 1977; Dep. Man. Dir, 1992; Man. Dir, 1993. *Recreations:* tennis, gardening.

YOUNG, Peter Michael Heppell, OBE 1995; HM Diplomatic Service, retired; *b* 23 April 1939; *s* of late Denis and Constance Young; *m* 1st, 1969, Maria Laura Aragon; 2nd, Verona Buchan; two step *s.* *Educ:* Haileybury Coll.; Williston Acad., USA (ESU Scholarship); Emmanuel Coll., Cambridge (MA). FCIPD. Royal Marines and Royal West Africa Frontier Force (2nd Lieut), 1958–60; FCO, 1964; served: Sofia, 1967–70; Geneva, 1970–72; Pretoria/Capetown, 1972–74; FCO 1974–77; First Sec., Lagos, 1977–79; Dep. High Comr, Ibadan, 1979–80; Consul (Commercial), Lyon, 1981–84; FCO, 1985–89; Counsellor, Lagos, 1989–93; seconded to Dept of National Heritage (Events Director, D-Day and VE-Day 50th Annivs), 1993–95; High Comr, Bahamas, 1996–99. *Recreations:* tennis, golf, African history. *Address:* PO Box EE, 16944 Nassau, Bahamas. *Clubs:* Oxford and Cambridge, MCC; Lyford Cay.

YOUNG, Peyton; *see* Young, H. P.

YOUNG, Raymond Kennedy, CBE 2007 (OBE 1989); Chairman, Architecture and Design Scotland, since 2004; *b* 23 Jan. 1946; *s* of Sharp and Christina Neil, (Neilina), Young; *m* 1972, Jean; three *s.* *Educ:* Univ. of Strathclyde (BArch Hons). FRIAS. Project Architect, ASSIST/Univ. of Strathclyde, 1971–74; Housing Corp., 1974–89 (Dir, Scotland); Dir North, and Dir Res. and Innovation, Scottish Homes, 1989–97; self-employed, 1997–. Hon. Sen. Res. Fellow, Dept of Urban Studies, Univ. of Glasgow, 1997–; Hon. Prof., Dept of Architecture, Univ. of Strathclyde, 2007–. Mem., UK Sustainable Develt Commn, 2000–04. Non-exec. Dir, Historic Scotland, 2007–. *Publications:* gen. professional pubns. *Recreations:* theatre, music listening!, no sports. *Address:* Bakehouse Close, 146 Canongate, Edinburgh EH8 8DD. *T:* (0131) 556 6699, *Fax:* (0131) 556 6633; *e-mail:* info@ads.org.uk.

YOUNG, Sir Rob; *see* Young, Sir J. R.

YOUNG, Robert; Principal, European Economic Research Ltd, since 2004; *b* 27 March 1944; *s* of Walter Horace Young and Evelyn Joan Young; *m* 1965, Patricia Anne Cowin; one *s* one *d* (and one *s* decd). *Educ:* Magdalen College, Oxford (BA Hons 1965; MA). Graduate apprentice, Rolls-Royce, 1965; IBM UK, 1969–71; Rolls-Royce Motors, 1971–81: Man. Dir, Military Engine Div., 1977–79; Dir and Gen. Manager, Diesel Div., 1979–81; Vickers, 1981–85 (Group Commercial Dir, 1981–83); Man. Dir, Crane Ltd, 1985–88; Chief Exec., Plastics Div., McKechnie plc, 1989–90; Dir, Beauford plc, 1990–92; Competition Policy Consultant, Coopers & Lybrand, 1993–98; Dir, PricewaterhouseCoopers, 1998–2000; Principal, 2000–04, Dir, 2001–04, LECG Ltd. Member: Central Policy Review Staff, 1983; No 10 Policy Unit, 1983–84; CBI W Midlands Regional Council, 1980–81 (Chm., CBI Shropshire, 1981); Monopolies and Mergers Commn, 1986–92; Fulbright Commn, 1994–2003. FInstD. *Recreations:* Mozart, railways, cats, photography. *Address:* 12 Beechcroft Road, SW14 7JJ. *Club:* Oxford and Cambridge.

YOUNG, Prof. Robert Joseph, PhD; FREng, FIMMM, FInstP; Head, School of Materials, University of Manchester, since 2004; *b* 29 May 1948; *s* of Joseph and Florence Young; *m* 1971, Sheila Winifred Wilson; two *d.* *Educ:* St John's Coll., Cambridge (MA, PhD). Res. Fellow, St John's Coll., Cambridge, 1973–75; Lectr in Materials, QMC, 1975–86; Prof. of Polymer Sci. and Tech., UMIST, 1986–2004. Wolfson Res. Prof. in Materials Science, Royal Soc., 1992–97. Zeneca Lect., 1996, BAAS Public Lect., 1997, Royal Soc. Panel Chm., HEFCE RAE, 1996, 2001. FREng 2006. Griffith Medal, Inst. of Materials, 2002. *Publications:* Introduction to Polymers, 1981, 2nd edn (jtly), 1991; (jtly) Fracture Behaviour of Polymers, 1983; more than 280 papers in learned jls. *Recreations:* tennis, piano, gardening; former athlete (four blues, 1967–70; British Univs' Sports Fedn 110m Hurdles Champion, 1970). *Address:* Manchester Materials Science Centre, School of Materials, University of Manchester, Grosvenor Street, Manchester M1 7HS. *T:* (0161) 306 3551.

YOUNG, Sir Robin (Urquhart), KCB 2002; Permanent Secretary, Department of Trade and Industry, 2001–05; Chairman: East of England International Ltd, since 2006; Dr Foster Intelligence Ltd, since 2006; Euro RSCG Apex Communications, since 2006; First Columbus Investments, since 2007; *b* 7 Sept. 1948; *s* of late Col Ian U. Young and Mary Young; *m* 1998, Madeleine Mary Arnot, qv. *Educ:* Fettes Coll., Edinburgh; University Coll., Oxford (BA 1971). Joined DoE, 1973; Private Sec. to Parly Sec., Planning and Local Govt, 1976; Private Sec. to Minister of Housing, 1980–81; Local Govt Finance, 1981–85; Private Sec. to successive Secs of State, 1985–88; Under Secretary: Housing, 1988–89; Envmt Policy, 1989–91; Local Govt Review, 1991–92; Local Govt, DoE, 1992–94; Dep. Sec., 1994–98; Regl Dir, Govt Office for London, 1994–97; Hd of Econ. and Domestic Affairs Secretariat, Cabinet Office, 1997–98; Permanent Sec., DCMS, 1998–2001. Non-executive Director: Bovis Construction Ltd, 1989–94; Dr Foster Ltd, 2005–; A4e Ltd, 2007–. Chm., E of England Sci. and Industry Council, 2006–; Mem. Bd, IoD, 2007–. *Recreations:* squash, tennis, cinema. *Address:* 47 Moreton Terrace, SW1V 2NS.

YOUNG, (Roderic) Neil; Investment Consultant, 1989–2006; *b* 29 May 1933; *s* of late Dr F. H. Young and S. M. Young (*née* Robinson); *m* 1962, Gillian Margaret Salmon; two *s* one *d*. *Educ:* Eton; Trinity College, Cambridge (MA). FCA. 2nd Lieut Queen's Own Royal West Kent Regt, 1952–53. Howard Howes & Co., 1956–59; Fenn & Crosthwaite, 1960–63; Brown Fleming & Murray, 1964–68; Director: Murray Johnstone, 1969–70; Kleinwort Benson, 1971–88. Director: Malvern UK Index Trust, 1990–98; London and SE Bd, Bradford and Bingley Bldg Soc., 1990–97. City of London: Mem., Court of Common Council, 1980; Alderman, Ward of Bread Street, 1982–94; Sheriff, 1991–92; Master, Gunmakers' Co., 1994–95. Adv. Cttee, Greenwich Hosp., 1983–2002. *Recreations:* gardening, shooting, DIY, golf. *Address:* Down Farm House, Lamberhurst Down, Lamberhurst, Kent TN3 8HA. *T:* (01892) 891792. *Club:* Rye Golf.

YOUNG, Roger; President, FPL Group Inc., 1999, retired; *b* 14 Jan. 1944; *s* of Arnold and Margaret Young; *m* 1970, Sue Neilson; one *s* two *d*. *Educ:* Gordonstoun Sch.; Edinburgh Univ. (BSc Engrg); Cranfield Business Sch. (MBA). Rolls-Royce Ltd, 1961–72; Alidair Ltd, 1972–73; Wavin Plastics Ltd, 1973–76; Aurora Holdings Ltd, 1976–80; Low & Bonar plc, 1980–88; Chief Exec., Scottish Hydro-Electric plc, 1988–98. Non-executive Director: Friends Ivory & Sime (formerly Ivory & Sime) plc, 1993–99; Bank of Scotland, 1994–99. *Recreations:* family, flying, hill walking.

YOUNG, Roger Dudley; Chairman, Bicon Marketing Ltd, since 2000; *b* 7 Jan. 1940; *s* of Henry G. Young and Winifred G. Young; *m* 1965, Jennifer J. Drayton; one *s* two *d*. *Educ:* Dulwich Coll. Drayton Group, 1958–69; Imperial Group, 1969–73; Robert Fleming, 1971–73; Director: Henry Ansbacher Group, 1973–82; Touche Remnant Group, 1982–85; Chief Executive: Bank Julius Baer (London), 1985–89; March Group, 1989–91; Dir Gen., Inst. of Mgt, 1992–98. Dir Gen., Inst. of Enterprise, 1998–2001. Chairman: Clex Developments, 1976–; Acorn Business Services (Anglia), 1996–; Axcel, subseq. Charter Telecom Ltd, then Bicon Mobile Ltd, 1998–; Andrews and Partners Ltd, 2000–05; Andrews Estate Agents Ltd, 2000–05; Lunar (formerly Apollo) Diagnostics Ltd, 2005–; non-exec. Dir, PMP Plus, subseq. Apollo Medical Partners, Ltd, 2000–05. Dir, Ipswich Hosp. NHS Trust, 1992–99. Trustee, 1998–2005, Chm., 2000–03, World in Need, subseq. Andrews Charitable Trust Ltd. CCMI; FRSA. *Recreations:* small businesses, tennis, sculpture. *Address:* Hardy House, 32 Benton Street, Hadleigh, Ipswich IP7 5AT. *T:* and *Fax:* (01473) 828878. *Club:* Honourable Artillery Company.

YOUNG, Sir Roger (William), Kt 1983; MA; STh, LHD, FRSE; Principal of George Watson's College, Edinburgh, 1958–85; *b* 15 Nov. 1923; *yr s* of late Charles Bowden Young and Dr Ruth Young, CBE; *m* 1950, Caroline Mary Christie; two *s* two *d*. *Educ:* Dragon Sch., Oxford; Westminster Sch. (King's Scholar); Christ Church, Oxford (Scholar). Served War of 1939–45, RNVR, 1942–45. Classical Mods, 1946, Lit.Hum. 1948. Resident Tutor, St Catharine's, Cumberland Lodge, Windsor, 1949–51; Asst Master, The Manchester Grammar Sch., 1951–58. 1st Class in Archbishop's examination in Theology (Lambeth Diploma), 1957. Participant, US State Dept Foreign Leader Program, 1964. Scottish Governor, BBC, 1979–84. Member: Edinburgh Marriage Guidance Council, 1960–75; Scottish Council of Christian Educn Movement, 1960–81 (Chm., 1961–67; Hon. Vice-Pres., 1981–85); Gen. Council of Christian Educn Movement, 1985–94 (Vice-Pres., 1989–2002); Management Assoc., SE Scotland, 1965–85; Educational Research Bd of SSRC, 1966–70; Court, Edinburgh Univ., 1967–76; Public Schools Commn, 1968–70; Consultative Cttee on the Curriculum, 1972–75; Adv. Cttee, Scottish Centre for Studies in Sch. Administration, 1972–75; Royal Soc. of Edinburgh Dining Club, 1972–; Scottish Adv. Cttee, Community Service Volunteers, 1973–78; Edinburgh Festival Council, 1970–76; Independent Schs Panel of Wolfson Foundn, 1978–82; Gen. Adv. Council of BBC, 1978–79; Scottish Council of Independent Schs, 1978–85; Royal Observatory Trust, Edin., 1981–93; Council, RSE, 1982–85; ISJC, 1988–94. Hon. Sec., Headmasters' Assoc. of Scotland, 1968–72, Pres., 1972–74; Chairman: HMC, 1976; BBC Consult. Gp on Social Effects of TV, 1978–79; Bursary Bd, Dawson International Ltd, 1977–85; Bath Film Soc., 1990–93; Catch-up Prog. for World in Need, 1996–2000; Caxton Trust, 1998–2000; Dep. Chm., GBA, 1988–94. Trustee: Campion Sch., Athens, 1984–91; Wells Cathedral Sch., 1987–2005; Chm. Council, Cheltenham Ladies' Coll., 1986–93; Member, Governing Body: Westminster Sch., 1986–97; Royal Sch., Bath, 1987–99; Mem. Council, Bath Univ., 1993–96, 1997–2001. Conducted Enquiry on Stirling Univ., 1973. Hon. LHD, Hamilton Coll., Clinton, NY, 1978. *Publications:* Lines of Thought, 1958; Everybody's Business, 1968; Everybody's World, 1970; Report on the Policies and Running of Stirling University 1966–1973, 1973; Outdoor Adventures: third year projects at George Watson's College, 2003. *Recreations:* gardening, films, photography, music, knitting. *Address:* 11 Belgrave Terrace, Bath BA1 5JR. *T:* (01225) 336940. *Club:* East India.

YOUNG, Prof. Stephen John, PhD; FREng; Professor of Information Engineering, since 1995, and Head of Information Engineering, since 2002, Cambridge University (Chairman of School of Technology, 2002–04); Fellow of Emmanuel College, Cambridge, since 1985; *b* 23 Jan. 1951; *s* of John Leonard Young and Joan Young (*née* Shaw); *m* 1976 (marr. diss. 1996); two *d*; *m* 1999, Sybille Wiesmann. *Educ:* Maghull GS; Jesus Coll., Cambridge (MA, PhD). FIET, MBCS, CEng; FREng 2002. Res. Engr, GEC Hirst Res. Centre, 1973–74; Univ. Lectr in Computation, UMIST, 1977–84; Lectr in Engrg, 1984–95, Reader, 1995, Cambridge Univ.; Tech. Dir, Entropic Cambridge Res. Lab., 1996–99; Architect, Microsoft Corp., 1999–2001. Chm., Phonetic Arts Ltd, 2008–. Member of Council: Univ. of Cambridge, 2006–; RAEng, 2006–. FRSA. Editor, Computer Speech and Language, 1993–2005. *Publications:* Real Time Languages, 1982; An Introduction to Ada, 1985; (ed) Corpus-based Methods, 1997; articles in jls. *Recreations:* ballet, film, music. *Address:* Engineering Department, Trumpington Street, Cambridge CB2 1PZ. *T:* (01223) 332654.

YOUNG, Sir Stephen Stewart Templeton, 3rd Bt *cr* 1945; QC (Scot.) 2002; Sheriff Principal of Grampian, Highland and Islands, since 2001; *b* 24 May 1947; *s* of Sir Alastair Young, 2nd Bt, and Dorothy Constance Marcelle (*d* 1964), *d* of late Lt-Col Charles Ernest Chambers, and *widow* of Lt J. H. Grayburn, VC, Parachute Regt; *S* father, 1963; *m* 1974, Viola Margaret Nowell-Smith, *d* of Prof. P. H. Nowell-Smith and Perilla Thyme (she *m* 2nd, Lord Roberthall, KCMG, CB); two *s*. *Educ:* Rugby; Trinity Coll., Oxford; Edinburgh Univ. Voluntary Service Overseas, Sudan, 1968–69. Sheriff: of Glasgow and Strathkelvin, March–June 1984; of N Strathclyde at Greenock, 1984–2001. *Heir: s* Charles Alastair Stephen Young, *b* 21 July 1979. *Address:* Beechfield, Newton of Kinkell, Conon Bridge, Ross-shire IV7 8AS.

YOUNG, Timothy Mark Stewart; Director (in charge of School Leadership and the Rank Fellowship), Rank Foundation, since 2007; *b* 6 Oct. 1951; *s* of Sir Brian Walter Mark Young, *qv*; *m* 1990, Dr Alison Mary Keightley, MRCP, FRCR; two *s*. *Educ:* Eton (King's Schol.); Magdalene Coll., Cambridge (BA 1974; MA 1978); Bristol Univ. (PGCE 1975). Asst Master, Eton, 1975–83 and 1985–87; Asst Master, Wanganui Collegiate Sch., NZ, 1984; Teacher, Harvard Sch., Los Angeles, 1987–88; Housemaster, Eton, 1988–92; Headmaster, Royal Grammar Sch., Guildford, 1992–2006. Hon. Treas., HMC, 1999–2002. Mem. Court, Univ. of Surrey, 1992–2006. Governor: Abbots Hosp., 1992–2006; Westminster Sch., 2005–. *Recreations:* music, cinema, travel, Watford FC. *Address:* Cobbetts, Mavins Road, Farnham, Surrey GU9 8JS. *Club:* East India, Devonshire, Sports and Public Schools.

YOUNG, Timothy Nicholas; QC 1996; barrister; *b* 1 Dec. 1953; *s* of William Ritchie Young and Patricia Eileen Young; *m* 1981, Susan Jane Kenny; two *s* one *d*. *Educ:* Malvern Coll.; Magdalen Coll., Oxford (BA, BCL). Called to the Bar, Gray's Inn, 1977, Bencher, 2004; in practice at the Commercial Bar, 1977–. Vis. Lectr, St Edmund Hall, Oxford, 1977–80. *Publication:* Voyage Charters, 1993, 3rd edn 2007. *Recreations:* watercolours, drawing, cricket, music, theatre, television. *Clubs:* Thebertons Cricket, Worcs CC; Dulwich & Sydenham Golf.

YOUNG, Hon. Toby Daniel Moorsom; journalist and author; *b* 17 Oct. 1963; *s* of Baron Young of Dartington and Sasha Young; *m* 2001, Caroline Bondy; two *s* one *d*. *Educ:* Creighton Comp. Sch.; King Edward VI Comp. Sch.; William Ellis Comp. Sch.; Brasenose Coll., Oxford (BA 1986); Harvard Univ.; Trinity Coll., Cambridge. Teaching Fellow, Graduate Sch. of Arts and Scis, Harvard, 1987–88; Teaching Asst, Soc. and Pol Scis Fac., Univ. of Cambridge, 1988–90; Editor, The Modern Review, 1991–95; Contrib. Editor, Vanity Fair, 1995–98; Drama Critic, 2001–06, Associate Editor, 2007–, The Spectator; Restaurant Critic, ES magazine, 2002–07. Trustee, Orbis UK, 2004–. *Plays* (co-author): How to Lose Friends and Alienate People, 2003 (Co-Producer of film, 2008); Who's the Daddy?, 2005 (Best New Comedy, Theatregoers' Choice Awards, 2006); A Right Royal Farce, 2006. *Publications:* How to Lose Friends and Alienate People, 2001; The Sound of No Hands Clapping, 2006. *Recreations:* food and drink. *Address:* 9 Kite Studios, 2B Bassein Park Road, W12 9RY. *T:* (020) 8746 2624; *e-mail:* howtolose@hotmail.com. *Club:* Soho House.

YOUNG, Wayland; *see* Kennet, Baron.

YOUNG, Hon. William Lambert, CMG 1992; JP; High Commissioner for New Zealand in UK, 1982–85; concurrently Ambassador to Ireland and High Commissioner in Nigeria, 1982–85; *b* 13 Nov. 1913; *s* of James Young and Alice Gertrude Annie Young; *m* 1946, Isobel Joan Luke; one *s* four *d*. *Educ:* Wellington Coll. Commenced work, 1930; spent first 16 yrs with farm servicing co., interrupted by War Service, N Africa with Eighth Army, 1940–43; took over management of wholesale distributing co. handling imported and NZ manufactured goods; Gen. Man. of co. manufg and distributing radios, records, electronic equipment and owning 32 retail stores, 1956; purchased substantial interest in importing and distributing business, 1962. MP (National) Miramar, 1966–81; Minister of Works and Develt, 1975–81; introduced Women's Rights of Employment Bill, 1975; Pres., Assoc. of Former MPs of NZ, 1993–95. Formerly Chairman: National Roads Bd; National Water and Soil Authority; NZ Fishing Licensing Authority. Formerly Director: Johnsons Wax of NZ Ltd (subsid. of USA Co.); Howard Rotovator Co. Ltd; AA Mutual Insurance Co.; J. J. Niven Ltd; NZ Motor Bodies Ltd; Trustee, Wellington Savings Bank. Patron, Star Boating Club, 1997– (Pres., 1981–97); Mem. Council, NZ Amateur Rowing Assoc., 1984–87. Life Mem., AA of Wellington (Mem. Council, 1976–81). JP 1962. *Address:* 3/28 Oriental Terrace, Oriental Bay, Wellington 6006, New Zealand. *T:* (4) 8018030. *Club:* Wellington (Wellington, NZ).

YOUNG, Sir William Neil, 10th Bt *cr* 1769; Chairman: New World Trust Corp., since 2000; Napo Pharmaceuticals Inc., since 2007; *b* 22 Jan. 1941; *s* of Captain William Elliot Young, RAMC (killed in action 27 May 1942), and Mary (*d* 1997), *d* of late Rev. John Macdonald; *S* grandfather, 1944; *m* 1965, Christine Veronica Morley, *o d* of late R. B. Morley, Buenos Aires; one *s* one *d*. *Educ:* Wellington Coll.; Sandhurst. Captain, 16th/5th The Queen's Royal Lancers, retired 1970. Dir, Kleinwort Benson International Investment Ltd, 1982–87; Head: Investment Management, Saudi Internat. Bank, 1987–91; ME Dept, Coutts & Co., 1991–94; Dir, Barclays Private Bank Ltd, 1994–99. Dir, Vector Fund, 2008–. Chm., High Ham Br., RBL, 2004–. *Recreations:* ski-ing, sailing, tennis, shooting. *Heir: s* William Lawrence Elliot Young [*b* 26 May 1970; *m* 2001, Astrid Bartsch, Vienna; one *s* one *d*].

YOUNGER, family name of **Viscount Younger of Leckie**.

YOUNGER OF LECKIE, 5th Viscount *cr* 1923, of Alloa, Clackmannanshire; **James Edward George Younger;** Bt 1911; Consultant, Eban International, since 2007; *b* 11 Nov. 1955; *e s* of 4th Viscount Younger of Leckie, KT, KCVO, TD, PC, DL and of Diana Rhona (*née* Tuck); *S* father, 2003; *m* 1988, Jennie Veronica (*née* Wootton); one *s* two *d*. *Educ:* Cargilfield Sch., Edinburgh; Winchester Coll.; St Andrews Univ. (MA Hons Medieval Hist. 1979); Henley Mgt Coll. (MBA 1993). MCIM 1994. Personnel Mgr, Coats Patons, 1979–84; Recruitment Consultant, Angela Mortimer Ltd, 1984–86; Exec. Search Consultant, Stephens Consultancies, 1986–92; Director: MacInnes Younger, 1992–94; HR, UBS Wealth Mgt, 1994–2004; Culliford Edmunds Associates, 2004–07. Chm., Bucks Cons. Constituency Assoc., 2006–. Mem., Royal Co. of Archers (Queen's Body Guard for Scotland). Dir, Highland Soc. of London, 2005–. Trustee: Kate Kennedy Trust, St Andrews Univ.; Globe Run. *Recreations:* sailing, tennis, shooting, Highland dancing, politics, ski-ing, country pursuits, cricket. *Heir: s* Hon. Alexander William George Younger, *b* 13 Nov. 1993. *Address:* The Old Vicarage, Dorton, Aylesbury, Bucks HP18 9NH. *T:* (01844) 238396; *e-mail:* jeg.younger@virgin.net. *Clubs:* Lansdowne; White Hunters Cricket (Hampshire).

YOUNGER, Maj.-Gen. Allan Elton, DSO 1944; OBE 1962; MA; Director-General, Royal United Services Institute for Defence Studies, 1976–78; *b* 4 May 1919; *s* of late Brig. Arthur Allan Shakespear Younger, DSO, and late Marjorie Rhoda Younger (*née* Halliley); *m* 1942, Diana Lanyon; three *d*. *Educ:* Gresham's; RMA Woolwich; Christ's Coll., Cambridge. Commnd RE, 1939; France and Belgium, 1940; France, Holland and Germany, 1944–45; Burma, 1946–47; Malaya, 1948; Korea, 1950–51; RMA Sandhurst, 1954–57; Bt Lt-Col 1959; comd 36 Corps Engineer Regt in UK and Kenya, 1960–62; Instructor US Army Comd and Gen. Staff Coll., Fort Leavenworth, 1963–66; Programme Evaluation Gp, 1966–68; Chief Engr, Army Strategic Comd, 1968–69; COS, HQ Allied Forces Northern Europe, Oslo, 1970–72; Sen. Army Mem., Directing Staff, RCDS, 1972–75. Col Comdt, RE, 1974–79. Silver Star (US), 1951. *Publications:* Blowing Our Bridges, 2004; contribs to RUSI Jl, Military Review (USA). *Recreation:* gardening.

YOUNGER, David; *see* Younger, J. D. B.

YOUNGER, (James) Samuel; Chairman, Electoral Commission, 2001–08; *b* 5 Oct. 1951; *s* of Rt Hon. Sir Kenneth Gilmour Younger, KBE, PC and Elisabeth Kirsteen (*née* Stewart); *m* 1984, Katherine Anne Spencer; one *s*. *Educ:* Westminster Sch.; New Coll., Oxford (BA Hons). Asst Editor, Middle East International, 1972–78; BBC World Service: Sen. Asst, Central Current Affairs Talks, 1979–84; Sen. Producer and Exec. Producer, Current Affairs, 1984–86; Asst Head, Arabic Service, 1986–87; Head, Current Affairs, 1987–89; Head, Arabic Service, 1989–92; Controller, Overseas Services, 1992–94; Director of Broadcasting, 1994; Man. Dir, 1994–98; Dir-Gen., BRCS, 1999–2001. Chair, QAA, 2004–. Indep. Mem., Standards Cttee, GLA, 2008–. Mem. Council, Univ. of

Sussex, 1998–2007 (Chm. Council, 2001–07). Dir, English Touring Opera, 1999–. Gov., Commonwealth Inst., 1998–2005. Patron, Windsor Leadership Trust, 1998–. *Recreations:* sport, choral singing. *Address:* 28 Rylett Crescent, W12 9RL. *T:* (020) 8743 4449.

YOUNGER, Captain (John) David (Bingham), LVO 2007; Lord-Lieutenant of Tweeddale, since 1994 (Vice Lord-Lieutenant, 1992–94); Co-founder and Managing Director, Broughton Brewery, 1979–95; *b* 20 May 1939; *s* of Major Oswald Bingham Younger, MC, A and SH, and Dorothea Elizabeth Younger (*née* Hobbs); *m* 1962, Anne Rosaleen Logan; one *s* two *d*. *Educ:* Eton Coll.; RMA Sandhurst. Regular Army, Argyll and Sutherland Highlanders, 1957–69; Scottish and Newcastle Breweries, 1969–79. Dir, Broughton Ales, 1995–96. Chairman: Belhaven Hill Trust, 1986–94; Scottish Borders Tourist Board, 1989–91; Dir, Queen's Hall (Edinburgh) Ltd, 1992–2001. Vice Pres., RHASS, 1994. Mem., Queen's Body Guard for Scotland, Royal Company of Archers, 1969– (Sec., 1993–2007; Brig., 2002). River Tweed Comr, 2002–. President: Lowland RFCA, 2006–; SSAFA Forces Help (Borders), 2006–; Peebles CCC, 2006–. DL Borders, 1988. *Recreation:* the countryside. *Address:* Glenkirk, Broughton, Peeblesshire ML12 6JF. *T:* and *Fax:* (01899) 830570.

YOUNGER, Sir Julian William Richard, 4th Bt *cr* 1911, of Auchen Castle, co. Dumfries; *b* 10 Feb. 1950; *s* of Maj.-Gen. Sir John Younger, 3rd Bt, CBE and Stella Jane Dodd (*née* Lister); *S* father, 2002; *m* 1st, 1981, Deborah Ann Wood (marr. diss. 2002); one *s*; 2nd, 2006, Anthea Jane Stainton. *Educ:* Eton; Grinnell Univ., USA. *Heir: s* Andrew William Younger, *b* 14 Jan. 1986.

YOUNGER, Prof. Paul Lawrence, PhD; FREng; Professor, since 2001, and Pro-Vice-Chancellor (Engagement), since 2008, Newcastle University; *b* Hebburn, Co. Durham, 1 Nov. 1962; *s* of Norman and Joan Younger; *m* 1988, Emma Louise Bryan; three *s*. *Educ:* Newcastle Univ. (BSc 1st Cl. Hons Geol.; PhD Water Resources Engrg); Oklahoma State Univ. (MS Hydrogeol.). CGeol 1996; CEng 2001; CSci 2005; FREng 2007. Harkness Fellow, 1984–86; Hydrogeologist, NRA, 1989–91; Volunteer Hydrogeologist, Centro YUNTA, Bolivia, 1991–92; Newcastle University: Lectr, 1992–99; Reader, 1999–2001; Public Orator, 2007–. Director: NuWater Ltd, 1995–; Project Dewatering Ltd, 2000–. *Publications:* Mine Water: hydrology, pollution, remediation, 2002; Groundwater in the Environment: an introduction, 2007; more than 220 articles in learned jls. *Recreations:* singer-songwriter and musician (guitar, mandolin, Northumbrian pipes), hill walking, languages (Spanish, Scottish Gaelic). *Address:* Executive Office, Newcastle University, Newcastle upon Tyne NE1 7RU. *T:* (0191) 222 7689, *Fax:* (0191) 222 6229; *e-mail:* p.l.younger@ncl.ac.uk.

YOUNGER, Hon. Robert Edward Gilmour; Sheriff of Tayside, Central and Fife, 1982–2004; *b* 25 Sept. 1940; third *s* of 3rd Viscount Younger of Leckie, OBE and Evelyn Margaret, MBE, *e d* of Alexander Logan McClure, KC; *m* 1972, Helen Jane Hayes; one *s* one *d*. *Educ:* Cargilfield Sch., Edinburgh; Winchester Coll.; New Coll., Oxford (MA); Edinburgh Univ. (LLB); Glasgow Univ. Advocate, 1968; Sheriff of Glasgow and Strathkelvin, 1979–82. *Recreation:* wondering. *Address:* Old Leckie, Gargunnock, Stirling, Scotland FK8 3BN. *T:* (01786) 860213.

YOUNGER, Samuel; *see* Younger, J. S.

YOUNGER-ROSS, Richard; MP (Lib Dem) Teignbridge, since 2001; *b* 29 Jan. 1953; *m* 1982, Susan Younger. *Educ:* Walton-on-Thames Secondary Modern Sch.; Ewell Tech. Coll. (HNC); Oxford Poly. Architectural consultant, 1970–90; design consultant, 1990–2001. Joined Liberal Party, 1970 (Mem. Council, 1972–82). Contested (Lib Dem): Chislehurst, 1987; Teignbridge, 1992, 1997. *Address:* 24–26 Queen Street, Newton Abbot, Devon TQ12 2EF; c/o House of Commons, SW1A 0AA.

YOUNGHUSBAND, Jan; Commissioning Editor, Arts and Performance, Channel Four Television, since 2001; *b* Portsmouth, 8 May 1954; *d* of John Younghusband and Joyce Browning; one *s*. *Educ:* Portsmouth High Sch.; Millfield Sch.; Royal Holloway Coll., London. Asst Prodn Manager, Glyndebourne, 1974–79; Prodn Manager, Nuffield Th., Southampton, 1979–80; Asst Producer to Peter Hall, NT, 1980–88; freelance television producer and writer, 1988–2000; Commissioning Ed., Channel 4, 2000–. Mem., BAFTA. *Publications:* Orchestra, 1990; Concerto, 1991; A Genius in the Family, 1997. *Recreations:* playing the piano, reading, ski-ing, golf. *Address:* e-mail: jyounghusband@channel4.co.uk. *T:* (020) 7306 8303.

YOUNIE, Edward Milne, OBE 1978; HM Diplomatic Service, retired; *b* 9 Feb. 1926; *s* of John Milne and Mary Dickie Younie; *m* 1st, 1952, Mary Groves (*d* 1976); 2nd, 1979, Mimi Barkley (marr. annulled 1991); 3rd, 1994, Mrs Alyn Denholm. *Educ:* Fettes Coll. (Scholar); Gonville and Caius Coll., Cambridge (Scholar) (BA Hons). RN, 1944–46. HM Colonial Service, Tanganyika, 1950–62; FCO, 1963; Johannesburg, 1964–67; Blantyre, 1967–69; First Secretary: Lagos, 1972–76; Nairobi, 1977–79; Salisbury, 1979–81 (Counsellor, 1980); FCO, 1981–82. Dir, Fairbridge (Scotland), 1996–. *Recreations:* golf, tennis, music. *Address:* Wester Corsehill, Thornhill, Stirling FK8 3QD. *Club:* Brooks's.

YOUNSON, Maj.-Gen. Eric John, OBE 1952; Eur Ing; CEng, FRAeS; *b* 1 March 1919; *o s* of late Ernest M. Younson, MLitt, BCom, Jarrow; *m* 1946, Jean Beaumont Carter, BA; three *d*. *Educ:* Jarrow Grammar Sch.; Univ. of Durham (BSc) Royal Military Coll. of Science; Administrative Staff Coll. CEng 1970; FRAeS 1970; Eur Ing 1991. Served War of 1939–45: commissioned, RA, 1940; UK and NW Europe (despatches). Directing Staff, RMCS, 1953–55; Atomic Weapons Research Estab., 1957–58; Attaché

(Washington) as rep. of Chief Scientific Adviser, 1958–61; Head of Defence Science 3, MoD, 1961–63; Dep. Dir of Artillery, 1964–66; Dir of Guided Weapons Trials and Ranges, Min. of Technology, 1967–69; Vice-Pres., Ordnance Board, 1970–72, Pres., 1972–73, retired 1973; Sen. Asst Dir, Central Bureau for Educnl Visits and Exchanges, 1973–74; Dep. Dir, SIMA, 1974–78; Sec.-Gen., EUROM, 1975–77; Clerk to Worshipful Co. of Scientific Instrument Makers, 1976–87 (Hon. Liveryman and Clerk Emeritus, 1987). FRSA 1944; FCMI 2001; MIET (MIEE 2002). Freeman, City of London, 1981. *Publications:* (ed jtly) UK/US Nuclear Weapons Classification Guide, 1963; The Worshipful Company of Scientific Instrument Makers: history, 1988; articles on gunnery and scientific subjects in Service jls. *Recreations:* photography, electronics, Talking Newspapers for the Blind. *Address:* 7 Pondwick Road, Harpenden, Herts AL5 2HG. *T:* (01582) 621691.

YOXALL, Basil Joshua; Master of the Supreme Court, Queen's Bench Division, since 2002; *b* 24 April 1952; *s* of Cecil Ezra Yoxall-Harary and Grace Yoxall-Harary; *m* 1981, Sally Anne Eagle; two *s* one *d*. *Educ:* Wallington Grammar Sch.; St Catharine's Coll., Cambridge (MA). Called to the Bar, Inner Temple, 1975; known professionally as Basil Yoxall; in practice as barrister, specialising in common law, 1975–2002. *Publications:* (ed jtly) The White Book Service: Civil Procedure, annually 2004–; (contrib.) Atkin's Court Forms (on Judgments and Orders), 2004. *Recreations:* cinema, classical music, history, swimming. *Address:* Royal Courts of Justice, Strand, WC2A 2LL.

YOXALL-HARARY, Basil Joshua; *see* Yoxall, B. J.

YU, David; Chief Executive Officer, Betfair Group Ltd, since 2006; *b* Seattle, 6 Nov. 1967; *s* of Donald and Jean Yu; *m* 1995, Philana Dee Chow. *Educ:* Univ. of Calif, Berkeley (BS Electrical Engrg and Computer Sci.); Stanford Univ. (MS Computer Sci.). Engrg Dir, Zip2 Corp., 1997–99; Vice-Pres., Engrg, Alta Vista Co., 1999–2001; Betfair Group Ltd: Chief Technol. Officer, 2002–05; Chief Operating Officer, 2005–06. *Recreations:* travel, photography, food and wine. *Address:* Betfair Group Ltd, Waterfront, Hammersmith Embankment, Winslow Road, W6 9HP. *T:* (020) 8834 8000.

YU, Rt Rev. Patrick Tin-Sik; a Suffragan Bishop of Toronto (Area Bishop of York-Scarborough), since 2006; *b* 8 July 1951; *s* of Cheung Tok Yu and Sin Yuk Law; *m* 1978, Kathy Cheung; one *s* two *d*. *Educ:* McMaster Univ. (BA Hons 1974); Wycliffe Coll., Univ. of Toronto (MDiv 1981); Toronto Sch. of Theology (DMin 1997). Ordained priest, 1982; Asst Curate, Church of Epiphany, 1981–83; Incumbent: Parish of Coldwater-Medonte, 1985–90; St Theodore of Canterbury, 1990–97; St Timothy Agincourt, 1997–2006. Sec., Adv. Cttee for Postulants for Ordination, N and W Ontario, 1983–87; Co-ord. of Internship and Instructor, Supervised Ministry, Wycliffe Coll., Univ. of Toronto, 1995–2006. *Publications:* (contrib.) Canadian Anglicanism at the Dawn of a New Century, 2001; (contrib.) The Homosexuality Debate: faith seeking understanding, 2003. *Recreations:* cooking, travel, music. *Address:* Diocese of Toronto, 135 Adelaide Street East, Toronto, ON M5C 1L8, Canada. *T:* (416) 3636021, *Fax:* (416) 3633683.

YUKON, Bishop of, since 1995; **Rt Rev. Terrence Owen Buckle;** *b* 24 Aug. 1940; *m* 1963, Moyra Blanche Cooke; two *s* two *d*. *Educ:* Church Army Training Coll., Canada; Wycliffe Coll., Toronto. Commnd as Church Army Evangelist, 1962; Parish Assistant, St Philip's, Etobicoke, Ont, 1962–64; Dir of Inner Parish, Little Trinity, Toronto, 1964–66; Church Army Incumbent: Ch of the Resurrection, Holman, 1966–70; St George's Anglican Mission, Cambridge Bay, 1970–72; Incumbent, St David's Anglican Mission, Fort Simpson, 1972–75; ordained deacon, May 1973, priest, Nov. 1973; Priest i/c, Ch of the Ascension, Inuvik, and Regl Dean, Lower Mackenzie, 1975–82; Archdeacon of Liard, dio. of Yukon, 1982–88; Rector: St Mary Magdalene, Fort Nelson, 1982–88; Holy Trinity, Yellowknife, 1988–93; Co-Founder and Evangelist, New Life Evangelism Ministries, 1984–94; Bishop Suffragan, dio. of the Arctic, 1993–95. Hon. Canon, St Jude's Cathedral, Iqaluit, 1978. *Recreations:* out-of-door activities, canoeing, camping, hiking. *Address:* PO Box 31136, Whitehorse, YT Y1A 5P7, Canada. *T:* (867) 6677746.

YURKO, Allen Michael; Partner, DLJ Merchant Banking Partners, since 2007; *b* 25 Sept. 1951; *s* of Mike Yurko and Catherine (*née* Ewanishan); *m* 1991, Gayle Marie Skelley; two *s* one *d*. *Educ:* Lehigh Univ. (BA Bus. and Econs); Baldwin-Wallace Coll., USA (MBA). Divl Controller, Joy Mfg, 1978–81; Gp Controller, Eaton Corp., 1981–83; Chief Financial Officer and Gp Vice-Pres., Mueller Hldgs, 1983–89; Robertshaw Controls: Vice-Pres. of Finance, 1989–90; Pres., 1990–91; Pres. and Chief Operating Officer, Siebe T. & A. Controls, 1991–92; Siebe plc: Chief Operating Officer, 1992–93; CEO, 1994–99; Chief Exec., Invensys plc, 1999–2001; Partner, Compass Partners, 2002–07. Non-exec. Dir, Tate & Lyle plc, 1996–2005. *Recreations:* boating, golf, sports cars, theatre. *Address:* (office) 1 Cabot Square, E14 4QJ. *Clubs:* Annabel's; Sunningdale Golf.

YUWI, Sir Matiabe, KBE 1997 (OBE); Member, National Citizenship Committee, Papua New Guinea, since 1982; Commissioner for Law and Order, Peace and Good Order Commission, Southern Highlands Province, since 1998; *b* 1935; *s* of Labe Yuwi and Colin Hongai; *m* 1st, 1961, Pulume Labe; five *s* one *d*; 2nd, 1975, Gamiabi Kamia; two *s*. *Educ:* Lake Kutubu sch.; Mt Hagen Hosp. (medical and Aid Post Orderly trng); Lae Health Educnl Instn. Pi-Nagia Aid Post, 1956–60; Health Educn Officer, Tari Dist, Southern Highlands, PNG, 1965–68. Elected Mem. and Pres., Tari Local Govt Council, 1964; MP for Tari, PNG, 1968–82; Mem., Constitutional Cttee, 1971–72, Constitutional Planning Cttee, 1974–75, for PNG self govt and independence; Minister for Media Services, 1981–82. *Recreations:* farming, political reviewing. *Club:* Mendi Valley.

Z

ZACHARIAH, Joyce Margaret; Secretary of the Post Office, 1975–77; *b* 11 Aug. 1932; *d* of Robert Paton Emery and Nellie Nicol (*née* Wilson); *m* 1978, George Zachariah (marr. diss. 2006). *Educ:* Earl Grey Sch., Calgary, Canada; Hillhead High Sch., Glasgow; Glasgow Univ. (MA 1st cl. Hons French and German, 1956). Post Office: Asst Principal, 1956; Private Sec. to Dir Gen., 1960; Principal, 1961; Asst Sec., 1967; Dir, Chairman's Office, 1970. *Address:* Kelvinbrae, Wisborough Lane, Storrington, W Sussex RH20 4ND.

ZACKLIN, Ralph, CMG 2006; Chairman, United Nations Independent Panel on Accountability, since 2008; Member, United Nations Independent Special Inquiry Commission for Timor-Leste, since 2006; Senior Fellow, Faculty of Law, University of Melbourne, since 2006; *b* 13 Oct. 1937; *s* of Joseph and Anna Zacklin; *m* 1961, Lyda Aponte; two *s*. *Educ:* University Coll. London (LLB Hons); Columbia Univ. (LLM); Institut des Hautes Etudes Internationales, Geneva (PhD). Dir, Internat. Law Prog., Carnegie Endowment for Internat. Peace, NY, 1967–73; United Nations: Office of Legal Affairs, UN Secretariat, NY, 1973–2005; Officer-in-Charge, Office of High Comr for Human Rights, Geneva, 1997; Asst Sec. Gen. for Legal Affairs, 1998–2005. *Publications:* Amendment of the Constitution Instruments of the United Nations and Specialized Agencies, 1968, 2nd edn 2005; The Challenge of Rhodesia, 1969; The United Nations and Rhodesia, 1974; The Problem of Namibia in International Law, 1981; articles in various jls; *Recreations:* sports, reading, music, following the hopes and aspirations of my children and grandchildren. *Address:* 400 Central Park West, New York, NY 10025, USA. *T:* (212) 2220680; *e-mail:* ralph@zacklin.com. *Club:* Yale (New York).

ZAFIROPOULOS, Vassilis; Ambassador of Greece to the Court of St James's, 1996–99, retired; *b* Corfu, 24 Jan. 1934; *s* of Sarantis and Helen Zafiropoulos; *m* 1963; one *s*. *Educ:* Univ. of Athens. Joined Greek Civil Service, 1962; Min. of Finance, 1962–67; Head of Press Affairs, UN Information Centre for Greece, Israel, Turkey and Cyprus, 1967–71; joined Greek Diplomatic Service, 1971; Third Sec., Min. of Foreign Affairs, 1971–73; Second Sec., Liège, 1973–76; First Sec., Nicosia, and Dir, Greek Press Office in Cyprus, 1976–78; Counsellor, Nicosia, 1978–80; Counsellor (Political), London, 1980–84; Head of Cyprus Affairs, Min. of Foreign Affairs, 1984–86; Minister and Dep. Permt Rep. to NATO, Brussels, 1986–90; Ambassador to Australia and New Zealand, 1991–93; Permt Rep. to NATO, 1993–96. Special Rep., Greek Presidency of EU, S Caucasus, 2003. DUniv N London, 1998. Higher Comdr, Order of Phoenix (Greece). *Recreation:* tennis. *Address:* 20B Sirinon Street, Athens 175 61, Greece.

ZAHIRUDDIN bin Syed Hassan, Tun Syed, SPCM 1987; SMN, PSM, DUNM; SPMP 1970; JMN, PJK; Hon. GCVO 1974; Orang Besat Empat, Perak, since 1984; *b* 11 Oct. 1918; *m* 1949, Toh Puan Halimah, *d* of Haji Mohamed Noh; five *s* five *d*. *Educ:* Malay Coll., Kuala Kangsar; Raffles Coll., Singapore (Dip.Arts). Passed Cambridge Sch. Cert. Malay Officer, Tanjong Malim, etc, 1945–47; Dep. Asst Dist Officer, 1948; Asst Dist Officer, 1951–54; 2nd Asst State Sec., Perak, 1955; Registrar of Titles and Asst State Sec. (Lands), Perak, 1956; Dist Officer, Batang Padang, Tapah, 1957; Dep. Sec., Public Services Commn, 1958; Principal Asst Sec. (Service), Fedn Estabt Office, Kuala Lumpur, 1960; State Sec., Perak, 1961; Permanent Sec.: Min. of Agric. and Co-operatives, Kuala Lumpur, 1963; Min. of Educn, Kuala Lumpur, 1966; Dir-Gen., Public Services Dept, Kuala Lumpur, 1970; retd, 1972. Chm., Railway Services Commn, Kuala Lumpur, 1972–73. High Comr for Malaysia in London, 1974–75; Governor of Malacca, 1975–84. Chairman: Special Cttee on Superannuation in the Public Services, 1972, and Statutory Bodies. Vice-Pres., Subang Nat. Golf Club, 1972–74. *Recreation:* golf. *Address:* No 60 Jalan Sultan Azlan Shah, 31400 Ipoh, Malaysia.

ZAKHAROV, Prof. Vasilii, (Basil), PhD, DSc; consultant; Director of Information Processing, International Organization for Standardization, Geneva, 1990–95 (Head of Information Processing, 1989–90); *b* 2 Jan. 1931; *s* of Viktor Nikiforovich Zakharov and Varvara Semyenovna (*née* Krzak); *m* 1959, Jeanne (*née* Hopper) one *s* one *d*. *Educ:* Latymer Upper Sch.; Univ. of London (BSc: Maths 1951, Phys 1952; MSc 1958; PhD 1960; DIC 1960; DSc 1977). Research in Computer systems and applications, Birkbeck Coll., 1953–56; digital systems development, Rank Precision Instruments, 1956–57; Research Fellow, Imperial Coll., 1957–60; Physicist, European Organisation for Nuclear Res. (CERN), Geneva, 1960–65; Reader in Experimental Physics, Queen Mary Coll., London, 1965–66; Head of Computer Systems and Electronics Div., as Sen. Principal Sci. Officer, SRC Daresbury Laboratory, 1966–69, Dep. Chief Sci. Officer, 1970–78; Dir, London Univ. Computing Centre, 1978–80, and Prof. of Computing Systems, 1979–80; Sen. Associate, CERN, Geneva, 1981–83; Invited Prof., Univ. of Geneva, 1984–87. Vis Scientist: JINR Dubna, USSR, 1965; CERN, 1971–72; Consultant to AERE Harwell, 1965; Hon. Scientist and Consultant, CCLRC, 2006–; Vis. Prof. of Physics, QMC London, 1968; Vis. Prof., Westfield Coll., 1974–78. Member, SRC Comp. Sci. Cttee, 1974–77. *Publications:* Digital Systems Logic, 1968; No Snow on Their Boots, 2003, and other books; scientific papers in professional jls on photoelectronics, computer systems, elementary particle physics and computer applications. *Recreations:* collecting Russian miscellanea, amateur radio; grape growing, wine making, wine drinking.

ZAMBELLAS, Rear Adm. George Michael, DSC 2001; Chief of Staff (Operations), since 2008; *b* 4 April 1958; *s* of late Michael George Zambellas and of Rosemary Frederique Zambellas (*née* Lindsay); *m* 1982, Amanda Jane LeCudennec; three *s*. *Educ:* Shabani Primary Sch., Zimbabwe; New College Sch.; Stowe; Univ. of Southampton (BSc Hons Aeronautical and Astronautical Engrg 1980). Served 814, 829 and 815 Naval Air Sqdns, 1982–89; RN staff course, 1990; Command: HMS Cattistock, 1991; HMS Argyll, 1995; Corporate Planner, MoD, 1997; Comd HMS Chatham, 1999; HCSC, 2001; Dep. Flag Officer Sea Trng, 2002; PSO to CDS, 2002–05; Comdr Amphibious Task Gp, 2005–06; C of S (Fleet Transformation), 2006–07; Comdr, UK Maritime Force, 2007–08. *Address:* Permanent Joint Headquarters, Sandy Lane, Northwood, Middx HA6 3HP.

ZAMBELLO, Francesca; theatre and opera director; *b* New York, 24 Aug. 1956. *Educ:* American Sch. of Paris; Colgate Univ. (BA). Assistant Director: Lyric Opera of Chicago, 1981–82; San Francisco Opera, 1983–84; Co-Artistic Dir, The Skylight, opera and music th. co., Milwaukee, 1984–91; Artistic Advr, San Francisco Opera. Dir of prodns at major theatre and opera cos in Europe and USA incl. Royal Opera House, Bastille Opera, Houston Grand Opera, Bolshoi Opera and NY Metropolitan Opera. Prodns incl. Fidelio, Tosca, War and Peace, Turandot, Arianna, Madama Butterfly, Iphigénie en Tauride, La Traviata, Emmeline, Tristan und Isolde, Boris Godunov, Dialogues of the Carmelites, Luisa Miller, Napoleon, Prince Igor, Peter Grimes, Queen of Spades, Of Mice and Men, The Bartered Bride, Thérèse Raquin, Don Giovanni, Les Troyens, Lady in the Dark, Street Scene, La Bohème, Carmen, Cyrano, Die Walküre and William Tell. Olivier awards for: Khovanshchina, ENO, 1994; Billy Budd, 1995, Paul Bunyan, 1998, Royal Opera House. *Address:* c/o ICM Artists Ltd, 40 West 57th Street, New York, NY 10019, USA.

ZAMBONI, Richard Frederick Charles, FCA; Managing Director, 1979–89 and a Vice-Chairman, 1986–89, Sun Life Assurance Society plc; Chairman, AIM Distribution Trust PLC, 1996–2000; *b* 28 July 1930; *s* of Alfred Charles Zamboni and Frances Hosler; *m* 1st, 1960, Pamela Joan Marshall (*d* 1993); two *s* one *d*; 2nd 1996, Deirdre Olive Baker (*née* Kingham). *Educ:* Monkton House Sch., Cardiff. Gordon Thomas & Pickard, Chartered Accountants, 1948–54; served Royal Air Force, 1954–56; Peat Marwick Mitchell & Co., 1956–58; British Egg Marketing Board, 1959–70, Chief Accountant, from 1965; Sun Life Assurance Society plc, 1971–89, Director, 1975–89; Chairman: Sun Life Investment Management Services, 1985–89; Sun Life Trust Management, 1985–89. Deputy Chairman: Life Offices' Assoc., 1985 (Mem., Management Cttee, 1981–85); Assoc. of British Insurers, 1986–88 (Dep. Chm., 1985–86, Chm., 1986–88, Life Insurance Council); Member: Council, Chartered Insurance Inst., 1983–85; Lautro's steering gp, 1985–86; Hon. Treasurer, Insurance Institute of London, 1982–85. Dir, 1984–97, and Chm., 1990–97, Avon Enterprise Fund Ltd. Member, Management Cttee, Effingham Housing Assoc. Ltd, 1980–86; Chairman: Council of Management, Grange Centre for People with Disabilities, 1991–96; Governing Body, Little Bookham Manor House Sch. Educnl Trust Ltd, 1999–2003. Pres., Insurance Offices RFU, 1985–87. *Recreations:* ornithology, gardening, golf. *Address:* The Old Vicarage, 80 Church Street, Leatherhead, Surrey KT22 8ER. *T:* (01372) 812398. *Club:* Royal Automobile.

ZAMYATIN, Leonid Mitrofanovich; Soviet Ambassador to the Court of St James's, 1986–91; *b* Nizhni Devitsk, 9 March 1922; *m* 1946; one *d*. *Educ:* Moscow Aviation Inst.; Higher Diplomatic School. Mem., CPSU, 1944–91 (apptd Mem. Central Cttee, 1976); Min. of Foreign Affairs, 1946; First Sec., Counsellor on Political Questions, USSR Mission to UN, 1953–57; Soviet Dep. Rep., Preparatory Cttee, later Bd of Governors, IAEA, 1957–59; Soviet Rep., IAEA, 1959–60; Dep. Head, American Countries Dept, Min. of Foreign Affairs, 1960–62; Head of Press Dept, 1962–70; Mem., Collegium of Ministry, 1962–70; Dir-Gen., TASS News Agency, 1970–78, Govt Minister, 1972; Dep. to USSR Supreme Soviet, 1970–89; Chief, Dept of Internat. Inf., Central Cttee, CPSU, 1978–86. Mem., Commn for Foreign Relations, Soviet of Nationalities, 1974. Lenin Prize 1978; USSR Orders and medals incl. Order of Lenin (twice). *Publication:* Gorby and Maggie (memoirs), 1995.

ZANDER, Prof. Michael, FBA 2005; Professor of Law, London School of Economics, 1977–98, now Emeritus; *b* 16 Nov. 1932; *s* of late Dr Walter Zander and Margaret Magnus; *m* 1965, Betsy Treeger; one *d* one *s*. *Educ:* Royal Grammar Sch., High Wycombe; Jesus Coll., Cambridge (BA Law, double 1st Cl. Hons; LLB 1st Cl. Hons; Whewell Scholar in Internat. Law); Harvard Law Sch. (LLM). Solicitor of the Supreme Court. National Service, RA, 1950–52, 2nd Lieut. Cassel Scholar, Lincoln's Inn, 1957, resigned 1959; New York law firm, 1958–59; articled with City solicitors, 1959–62; Asst Solicitor with City firm, 1962–63; London Sch. of Economics: Asst Lectr, 1963; Lectr, 1965; Sen. Lectr, 1970; Reader, 1970; Convener, Law Dept, 1984–88, 1997–98. Legal Correspondent, The Guardian, 1963–87. Mem., Royal Commn on Criminal Justice, 1991–93. Hon. QC 1997. *Publications:* Lawyers and the Public Interest, 1968; (ed) What's Wrong with the Law?, 1970; (ed) Family Guide to the Law, 1971 (2nd edn 1972); Cases and Materials on the English Legal System, 1973 (10th edn 2007); (with B. Abel-Smith and R. Brooke) Legal Problems and the Citizen, 1973; Social Workers, their Clients and the Law, 1974 (3rd edn 1981); A Bill of Rights?, 1975 (4th edn 1996); Legal Services for the Community, 1978; (ed) Pears Guide to the Law, 1979; The Law-Making Process, 1980 (6th edn 2004); The State of Knowledge about the English Legal Profession, 1980; The Police and Criminal Evidence Act 1984, 1985 (5th edn 2005); A Matter of Justice: the legal system in ferment, 1988 (rev. edn 1989); The State of Justice, 2000; articles in Criminal Law Rev., Mod. Law Rev., Law Soc.'s Gazette, New Law Jl, Solicitors' Jl, Amer. Bar Assoc. Jl, New Society, etc. *Recreations:* the cello, swimming. *Address:* 12 Woodside Avenue, N6 4SS. *T:* (020) 8883 6257, *Fax:* (020) 8444 3348; *e-mail:* mandbzander@btinternet.com.

ZANI, John Andrew; a District Judge (Magistrates' Courts), Inner London, since 2001; *b* 14 Feb. 1953; *s* of Primo and Alda Zani; *m* 1978, Cinthia Gallian. *Educ:* Highgate Sch.; Coll. of Law. Admitted solicitor, 1977; Partner, 1979, Sen. Partner, 1986–2000, Whitelock & Storr. Chm., Professional Matters Sub-Cttee, Holborn Law Soc., 1994–96. Mem. Founder Cttee, British Italian Law Assoc., 1982. Trustee, Friends of Highgate Sch., 1996–; Mem. Cttee, Old Cholmeleian Soc., 1994–; Chm., Old Cholmeleian CC, 1990–. *Recreations:* cricket, football, the arts. *Address:* c/o Camberwell Green Magistrates' Court, 15 D'Eynsford Road, Camberwell Green, SE5 7UP.

ZAPATERO, José Luis Rodríguez; *see* Rodríguez Zapatero.

ZAPF, Hermann; freelance book and type designer, since 1938; *b* Nuremburg, 8 Nov. 1918; *s* of Hermann Zapf and Magdalene Zapf (*née* Schlamp); *m* 1951, Gudrun von Hesse; one *s*. Type dir, D. Stempel AG, type foundry, Frankfurt, 1947–56; design consultant, Mergenthaler Linotype Co., NYC and Frankfurt, 1957–74; Consultant, Hallmark Internat., Kansas City, 1966–73; Vice-Pres., Design Processing Internat. Inc., NYC, 1977–86; Prof., Typographic Computer Programs, Rochester Inst. Technol., NY, 1977–87; Chm., Zapf, Burns & Co., NYC, 1987–91. Designer of types: Palatino, Melior, Optima, ITC Zapf Chancery, ITC Zapf Internat., Digiset-Marconi, Digiset-Edison, Digiset-Aurelia, Pan-Nigerian, URW (Roman and San Serif), Renaissance Roman, Zapfino Script. Mem., RSA. Hon. Mem., Soc. of Scribes and Illuminators. Hon. RDI 1985. Hon. DFA Illinois, 2003. Frederic W. Goudy Award, Rochester Inst. Technol., Rochester, NY, 1969; Gutenberg Prize, City of Mainz, 1974; Robert H. Middleton Award, Soc. Typographic Arts, Chicago, 1987; Euro Design Award, Design Biennial Oostende, 1994; Wadim Lazursky Award, Acad. Design, Moscow, 1996. *Publications:* William Morris, 1948; Pen and Graver, 1952; Manual Typographicum, 1954, 2nd edn 1968; About Alphabets, 1960, 2nd edn 1970; Typographic Variations, 1964; Orbis Typographicus, 1980; Hora fugit/Carpe diem, 1984; Hermann Zapf and his Design Philosophy, 1987; ABC-XYZapf, 1989; Poetry Through Typography, 1993; August Rosenberger, 1996; The Fine Art of Letters, 2000; The World of Alphabets, 2001; Calligraphic Type Design in the Digital Age, 2001; Alphabet Stories, 2007. *Address:* Seitersweg 35, 64287 Darmstadt, Germany. *T:* (6151) 76825, *Fax:* (6151) 717204. *Clubs:* Double Crown (Hon. Mem.), Wynkyn de Worde (Hon. Mem.); Directors (NY) (Hon. Mem.).

ZARA, Robert Joseph; a District Judge (Magistrates' Courts), Birmingham, since 2004; *b* 20 July 1947; *s* of Alfred and Naomi Zara; *m* 1st, 1986, Alicia Edkins (*d* 2000); one *s*; 2nd, 2004, Catherine Edwards. *Educ:* Tonbridge Sch.; Bristol Univ. (LLB 1969). Community Lawyer, Coventry Community Develt Project, 1973–75; Solicitor, Coventry Legal and Income Rights Service, 1975–81; Sen. Partner, Robert Zara & Co., Coventry, 1981–98; Consultant, R. J. Kelley & Co., Coventry, 1998–2002; Dep. Provincial Stipendiary Magistrate, 1998–2002; a District Judge (Magistrates' Cts), Nottingham, 2002–04. *Publications:* (contrib.) Handbook for Widows, 1978; (contrib.) Survival Guide for Widows, 1986; contrib. occasional articles and book reviews to New Law Jl. *Recreations:* bridge, crosswords, singing. *Address:* Victoria Law Courts, Corporation Street, Birmingham B4 6QA.

ZEALLEY, Christopher Bennett; trustee and company director; *b* 5 May 1931; *s* of Sir Alec Zealley and Lady Zealley (*née* King); *m* 1966, Ann Elizabeth Sandwith; one *s* one *d*. *Educ:* Sherborne Sch.; King's Coll., Cambridge (MA Law). Commnd RNVR, 1953; ICI Ltd, 1955–66; IRC, 1967–70; Chairman: Public Interest Res. Centre, 1972–; Social Audit Ltd, 1972–; Accreditation Bureau for Fundraising Orgns, 1997–; Director and Trustee: Dartington Hall Trust, 1970–88; Charity Appointments, 1988– (Chm., 1988–92). Association for Consumer Research (formerly Consumers' Association): Chm., 1991–92; Mem. Council, 1976–92, 1994– (Chm., 1977–82). Trustee: Charities Aid Foundn, 1982–90; Res. Inst. for Consumer Affairs, 1989–. Director: JT Group Ltd; Grant Instruments Ltd; Good Food Club Ltd. Chairman: Dartington Coll. of Art, 1973–91; Dartington Summer Sch. of Music, 1980–97. *Publication:* Creating a Charitable Trust, 1994. *Recreations:* rural affairs, music. *Address:* Sneydhurst, Broadhempston, Totnes, Devon TQ9 6AX. *Clubs:* Lansdowne, Naval.

ZEALLEY, Dr Helen Elizabeth, OBE 1998; MD; FRCPEd, FFPH; Director of Public Health and Chief Administrative Medical Officer, 1988–2000, Executive Director, 1991–2000, Lothian Health Board; *b* 10 June 1940; *d* of late Sir John Howie Flint Brotherston and of Lady Brotherston; *m* 1965, Dr Andrew King Zealley; one *s* one *d*. *Educ:* St Albans High Sch. for Girls; Edinburgh Univ. (MB, ChB 1964; MD 1968). FRCPEd 1987; FFPH (FFPHM 1980). Virologist, City Hosp., Edinburgh, 1965–70; Consultant in Public Health Medicine, Lothian Health Bd, 1974–88, with a special interest in the health of children. Non-exec. Dir, NHS Health Scotland, 2003–; Mem. Bd, Scottish Envmtl Protection Agency, 2006–. Vice-President: Med Act, 1980–; Early Education, 1998–2006. Chm., Friends of the Earth, Scotland, 2003–08. Mem. Court, Edinburgh Univ., 1992–98. QHP 1996–2000. Kentucky Colonel, 1961. Hon. DCCH 1993. *Recreations:* family, gardening, sailing, ski-ing. *Address:* Viewfield House, 12 Tipperlinn Road, Edinburgh EH10 5ET. *T:* (0131) 447 5545.

ZEEMAN, Sir (Erik) Christopher, Kt 1991; PhD; FRS 1975; Principal, Hertford College, Oxford, 1988–95; *b* 4 Feb. 1925; *s* of Christian Zeeman and Christine Zeeman (*née* Bushell); *m* 1960, Rosemary Gledhill; three *s* two *d*. *Educ:* Christ's Hospital; Christ's Coll., Cambridge (MA, PhD; Hon. Fellow, 1989). Commonwealth Fellow, 1954; Fellow of Gonville and Caius Coll., Cambridge, 1953–64 (Hon. Fellow, 1997); Lectr, Cambridge Univ., 1955–64; Prof., and Dir of Maths Res. Centre, Warwick Univ., 1964–88, Hon. Prof. 1988. Sen. Fellow, SRC, 1976–81. Visiting Prof. at various institutes, incl.: IAS; Princeton; IHES, Paris; IMPA, Rio; Royal Instn; also at various univs, incl.: California, Florida, Pisa. Hon. Dr: Strasbourg, Hull, Claremont, York, Leeds, Durham, Hartford, Warwick, Open. *Publications:* numerous research papers on topology, dynamical systems, catastrophe theory, and applications to biology and the social sciences, in various mathematical and other jls. *Recreation:* family. *Address:* 23 High Street, Woodstock, Oxon OX20 1TE. *T:* (01993) 813402.

ZEFFIRELLI, G. Franco (Corsi), Hon. KBE 2004; opera, film and theatrical producer and designer since 1949; *b* 12 Feb. 1923. *Educ:* Florence. Designer: (in Italy): A Streetcar Named Desire; Troilus and Cressida; Three Sisters. Has produced and designed numerous operas at La Scala, Milan, 1952–, and in all the great cities of Italy, at world-famous festivals, and in UK and USA; *operas include:* Covent Garden: Lucia di Lammermoor, Cavalleria Rusticana and Pagliacci, 1959; Falstaff, 1961; Don Giovanni, Alcina, 1962; Tosca, Rigoletto, 1964; Pagliacci, 2003; Metropolitan Opera, NY: Otello, 1972; Antony and Cleopatra, 1973; La Bohème, 1981, 2008; Tosca, Rigoletto, 1985; Turandot, 1987; Carmen, 1996; La Traviata, 1998; Falstaff, 2003; La Scala: Otello, 1976; Turandot, 1983; Don Carlos, 1992; La Bohème, 2003; Aida, 2006; Verona: Carmen, 1995; Il Trovatore, 2001; Aida, 2002, 2003; Carmen, 2003; Madame Butterfly, 2004; L'Elisir d'Amore, Glyndebourne, 1961; Don Giovanni, Vienna, 1972; Aida, Tokyo, 1997, 2003; Rome: Tosca, 2000, 2008; Don Giovanni, and Aida, 2006; Busseto: Aida, 2001, also Moscow, 2004; La Traviata, 2002, also Moscow, 2003; Tel Aviv: Traviata, and I Pagliacci, 2005; *stage:* Romeo and Juliet, Old Vic, 1960; Othello, Stratford-on-Avon, 1961; Amleto, Nat. Theatre, 1964; After the Fall, Rome, 1964; Who's Afraid of Virginia Woolf, Paris, 1964, Milan, 1965; La Lupa, Rome, 1965; Much Ado About Nothing, Nat. Theatre, 1966; Black Comedy, Rome, 1967; A Delicate Balance, Rome, 1967; Saturday, Sunday, Monday, Nat. Theatre, 1973; Filumena, Lyric, 1977; Six Characters in Search of an Author, RNT, 1992; Absolutely! (perhaps), Wyndham's, 2003; *films:* The Taming of the Shrew, 1965–66; Florence, Days of Destruction, 1966; Romeo and Juliet, 1967; Brother Sun, Sister Moon, 1973 (S Calif Motion Picture Council Award, Olivier d'Or, Prix Femina Belge du Cinema, 1973); Jesus of Nazareth, 1977; The Champ, 1979 (Silver Halo Award, S Calif Motion Picture Council, 1979); Endless Love, 1981; La Traviata, 1983; Cavalleria Rusticana, 1983; Otello, 1986; The Young Toscanini, 1988; Hamlet, 1991; The Sparrow, 1993; Jane Eyre, 1996; Tea with Mussolini, 1999; Callas Forever, 2002. Produced Beethoven's Missa Solemnis, San Pietro, Rome, 1971. Senator of the Italian Republic, 1992–98. Member: Acad. of Motion Picture Arts and Scis; Directors Guild of America; United Scenic Artists; Artistic Directorate, Shakespeare's Globe; Hon. Cttee, Amici Opificio di Firenze; Pres., Roma per il Teatro dell'Opera di Roma. Hon. Member: Friends of Florence; Boys' Town, New York. Hon. Citizen of towns and cities incl. New York, Busseto, Gubbio, Catanzaro. Hon. DHL: San Diego, 1978; Loyola Marymount, 1979; Hon. DLitt Kent, 1986; Hon. PhD Tel Aviv, 1993. Blason D'Oro, 1967; XIII San Giuseppe Award, Florence, 1980; Rudolph Valentino Award, 1995; Two Presidents Award, Italy and Russia, 2004. Grande Ufficiale dell'Ordine al Merito della Repubblica Italiana, 1977; Commandeur, Ordre des Arts et des Lettres (France), 1978. *Publication:* Zeffirelli (autobiog.), 1986, 2006. *Address:* Via Lucio Volumnio 45, Rome 00178, Italy.

ZEHETMAYR, John Walter Lloyd, OBE 1991; VRD 1963; FICFor; Senior Officer for Wales and Conservator South Wales, Forestry Commission, 1966–81, retired; *b* 24 Dec. 1921; *s* of late Walter Zehetmayr and late Gladys Zehetmayr; *m* 1945, Isabell (Betty) Neill-Kennedy; two *s* one *d*. *Educ:* St Paul's, Kensington; Keble Coll., Oxford (BA). Served RNVR, 1942–46 (despatches); now Lt Cdr RNR retired. Forestry Commission: Silviculturist, 1948–56; Chief Work Study Officer, 1956–64; Conservator West Scotland, 1964–66. Warden, Lavernock Point Nature Reserve, 1976–. Chm., Forestry Safety Council, 1986–92. Member: Prince of Wales' Cttee, 1970–89; Brecon Beacons Nat. Park Cttee, 1982–91. Vice-Pres., Glamorgan Wildlife Trust, 1992–97. Wales Volunteer of the Year Award, Wales Council for Voluntary Action, 2007. *Publications:* Experiments in Tree Planting on Peat, 1954; Afforestation of Upland Heaths, 1960; The Gwent Small Woods Project 1979–84, 1985; Forestry in Wales, 1985; The Effectiveness of Health and Safety Measures in Forestry, 1992. *Recreations:* conservation, butterfly recording, ski-ing (club coach on plastic, 1996–). *Address:* 2 Highfields, Bradford Place, Penarth, Vale of Glam CF64 1AF.

ZEIDMAN, Martyn Keith; QC 1998; **His Honour Judge Zeidman;** a Circuit Judge, since 2001; *b* Cardiff, 30 May 1952; *s* of Abe and Jennie Zeidman; *m* 1977, Verity Owen; one *s* one *d*. *Educ:* Univ. of London (LLB Hons ext.). Called to the Bar, Middle Temple, 1974; Asst Recorder, 1995–99; a Recorder, 1999–2001. Pres., Mental Health Review Tribunal (Restricted Cases), 2000–. Chm., Jewish Marriage Council, 2004–. Judicial Mem., London Courts Bd, 2007–. *Publications:* A Short Guide to The Landlord & Tenant Act 1987, 1987; A Short Guide to The Housing Act 1988, 1988; Steps to Possession, 1989; A Short Guide to The Courts and Legal Services Act 1990, 1990; A Short Guide to The Road Traffic Act 1991, 1991; Making Sense of The Leasehold Reform Housing & Urban Development Act 1993, 1994; Archbold Practical Research Papers on: Law of Mistake, 1997; Law of Self Defence, 1997. *Recreations:* family, studying Jewish religious texts, cycling. *Address:* Snaresbrook Crown Court, The Court House, Hollybush Hill, E11 1QW.

ZEIGERMAN, Dror, PhD; Ambassador of Israel to the Court of St James's, 1998–2000; *b* Israel, 15 May 1948; *s* of Itzchak Zeigerman; *m* Asi Sherf; two *s* one *d*. *Educ:* Hebrew Univ., Jerusalem (BA Hist. 1977; MA Hist. and Internat. Relns 1978); George Washington Univ. (PhD Internat. Relns 1986). Mem., Knesset (Likud Party), 1981–84; Leader, Delegn to Ethiopia, 1982; Member, Knesset Committees: Foreign Affairs; Security; Immigration and Absorption. Hd, Students' Dept, Zionist Orgn in Israel, 1987–88; Gen. Man., Israel Sch. of Tourism, 1988–92; Consul Gen., Toronto, 1992–95; rep., various internat. corps, 1996–97. *Recreation:* golf. *Address:* c/o Ministry of Foreign Affairs, Hakirya, Romema, Jerusalem 91950, Israel. *Clubs:* Athenæum, Travellers.

ZEKI, Prof. Semir, FRS 1990; Professor of Neurobiology, University College London, since 1981 (Co-head, Wellcome Department of Cognitive Neurology, 1996–2001; Fellow, 2000); *b* 8 Nov. 1940; *m* 1967, Anne-Marie Claire Blestel; one *d* one *s*. *Educ:* University College London (BSc Anat. 1964; PhD 1967). Asst Lectr, UCL, 1966–67; Res. Associate, St Elizabeth's Hosp., Washington DC, 1967–68; Asst Prof., Univ. of Wisconsin, 1968–69; Lectr in Anatomy, UCL, 1969–75; Henry Head Res. Fellow, Royal Soc., 1975–80; Reader in Neurobiology, UCL, 1980–81. Vis. Professorial Fellow, RPMS, Hammersmith Hosp., 1991–96. Visiting Professor: Duke Univ., 1977; Ludwig Maximillians Univ., Munich, 1982–87; Univ. of California, Berkeley, 1984, 2003 and 2006; St Andrews, 1985; Vis. Upjohn Prof., Erasmus Univ., Brussels, 1997–98; Visiting Scholar: J. Paul Getty Mus., 1996; Center for Advanced Study, Stanford, 2001. Lectures include: David Marr, Cambridge Univ., 1989; Philip Bard, Johns Hopkins Univ., 1992; Ferrier, Royal Soc., 1995; Woodhull, Royal Instn, 1995; Royal Soc. Humphry Davy, Acad. des Scis, Paris, 1996; Carl Gustave Bernhard, Royal Swedish Acad., 1998. Member: Neuroscience Res. Program and Neurosci. Inst., NY, 1985–; Wellcome Trust Vision Panel, 1985–93 (Chm., 1987–93); Bd of Scientific Govs, Scripps Res. Inst., Calif., 1992–; Nat. Sci. Council of France, 1998–2002. Trustee: Fight for Sight, 1992–97; Minerva Foundn, Berkeley, 1995–; Guarantor, Brain, 1994–. Mem., Cttee of Honour, Paris DFAS, 1996–. Ed., Philosophical Trans of Royal Soc., series B, 1997–2003. Founder FMedSci 1998; MRI, 1985; Member: Academia Europaea, 1990; Eur. Acad. of Scis and Arts, 1992; Amer. Phil Soc., 1998; Hon. Mem., Italian Primatological Assoc., 1988. Hon. DSc: Aston, 1994; Aberdeen, 2008. Minerva Foundn Prize, USA, 1985; Prix Science pour l'Art, LVMH, Paris, 1991; Rank Prize, 1992; Zotterman Prize, Swedish Physiol Soc., 1993; Electronic Imaging Award, Internat. Soc. for Optical Engrg, 2002; King Faisal Internat. Prize in Sci. (Biology), King Faisal Foundn, 2004; Erasmus Medal, Academia Europea, 2008. *Publications:* A Vision of the Brain, 1993; (with Balthus) La Quête de l'Essential, Paris, 1995; Inner Vision: an exploration of art and the brain, 1999; Splendors and Miseries of the Brain, 2008; articles on vision and the brain in professional jls. *Recreations:* reading (esp. about the darker side of man), music, deep sleep. *Address:* Wellcome Department of Imaging Neuroscience, University College London, WC1E 6BT. *T:* (020) 7679 7316. *Clubs:* Athenæum, Garrick.

ZELDIN, Dr Theodore, CBE 2001; FBA 1995; FRSL, FRHistS; President, Oxford Muse, since 2001; Fellow, St Antony's College, Oxford, 1957–2001; *b* 22 Aug. 1933; *s* of Jacob Zeldin, civil engr, and Emma Zeldin, dentist; *m* 1975, Deirdre Wilson, *qv*. *Educ:* Aylesbury Grammar Sch.; Birkbeck Coll., London (BA 1951); Christ Church, Oxford (schol.; BA 1954; MA); St Antony's Coll., Oxford (DPhil 1957). Oxford University: Lectr, Christ Church, and Univ. Lectr in Modern Hist., 1959–76; Dean, Sen. Tutor, and Tutor for Admissions, St Antony's Coll., 1963–76; Dir, Future of Work Project, 1997–2000. Res. Fellow, CNRS, Paris, 1952–53; Visiting Professor: Harvard Univ., 1969–70; Univ. of Southern Calif, 1980–83. Mem., EC Cttee for Eur. Voluntary Service, 1997–99; Vice-Pres., Culture Europe, 2000–. Pres., Planning Commn, Nord-Pas-de-Calais, 1993–95; Advr, French Millennium Commn, 1999; Hon. President: Centre du Paysage, France, 2000; Maison du Temps et de la Mobilité, Belfort, 2001. Pres., Internat. Fest. of Geography, 1999; Chm., Oxford Food Symposium; Member: Council, Vivendi-Universal Inst de Prospective; Adv. Council, Demos; Mgt Cttee, Soc. of Authors. Trustee: Wytham Hall Med. Charity for the Homeless; Amar Internat. Appeal for Refugees. MAE 1993. Wolfson Prize for History. Comdr, Ordre des Arts et des Lettres (France).

Publications: The Political System of Napoleon III, 1958; (ed) Journal d'Emile Ollivier, 1961; Emile Ollivier and the Liberal Empire of Napoleon III, 1963; Conflicts in French Society, 1971; France 1848–1945: vol. 1, Ambition, Love and Politics, 1973, vol. 2, Intellect, Taste and Anxiety, 1977, both vols re-issued 1993 as History of French Passions; The French, 1983; Happiness (novel), 1987; An Intimate History of Humanity, 1994; Flirtations (filmscript), 1994; Conversation, 1998; contrib. nat. press and learned jls. *Recreations:* painting, gardening, mending things. *Address:* Tumbledown House, Cumnor, Oxford OX2 9QE.

ZELENSKY, Igor Anatolyevich; ballet dancer; *b* Georgia, 13 July 1969. *Educ:* Tbilisi Sch. of Choreography; Vaganova Sch. of Choreography, St Petersburg. With Kirov Ballet, 1989–; with New York City Ballet, 1992–97; guest dancer, Royal Ballet, 1996–; also with companies in Europe, Asia and America. Rôles include Basil in Don Quixote, Siegfried in Swan Lake, Solor in La Bayadère, Albrecht in Giselle; leading rôles in Romeo and Juliet, Apollo, Le Corsaire, Manon, Sleeping Beauty. *Address:* c/o Mariinsky Theatre, Teatralnaya ploschad 1, St Petersburg, Russia.

ZELLICK, Prof. Graham John, PhD; AcSS; Chairman, Criminal Cases Review Commission, 2003–08; Electoral Commissioner, 2001–04; *b* 12 Aug. 1948; *s* of R. H. and B. Zellick; *m* 1975, Jennifer Temkin, *qv*; one *s* one *d*. *Educ:* Christ's Coll., Finchley; Gonville and Caius Coll., Cambridge (MA, PhD; Hon. Fellow, 2001); Stanford Univ. Called to the Bar, Middle Temple, 1992, Bencher, 2001. Ford Foundn Fellow, Stanford Law Sch., 1970–71; Queen Mary College, later Queen Mary and Westfield College, London: Lectr, 1971–78; Reader in Law, 1978–82; Prof. of Public Law, 1982–88; Dean of Faculty of Laws, 1984–88; Head, Dept of Law, 1984–90; Drapers' Prof. of Law, 1988–91; Prof. of Law, 1991–98, now Emeritus, Sen. Vice-Principal and Acting Principal, 1990–91; Principal, 1991–98; Vis. Prof. of Law, 2007–; University of London: Dean, Faculty of Laws, 1986–88; Dep. Chm., Academic Council, 1987–89; Dep. Vice-Chancellor, 1994–97; Vice-Chancellor and Pres., 1997–2003. Vis. Fellow, Centre of Criminology, 1978–79, and Vis. Prof. of Law, 1975, 1978–79, Toronto Univ.; Vis. Scholar, St John's Coll., Oxford, 1989; Hon. Prof., Sch. of Law, Univ. of Birmingham, 2004–. Lectures: Noel Buxton, NACRO, 1983; Webber, Jews' Coll., London, 1986; Sir Gwilym Morris, UWIST, Cardiff, 1986; Wythe, Coll. of William and Mary, Va, 1989; Atkin, Reform Club, 2000; White, Indiana Univ., 2002; Van Der Zyl, Leo Baeck Coll., London, 2003; Lund, British Acad. Forensic Scis, 2006. Editor: European Human Rights Reports, 1978–82; Public Law, 1981–86; Member of Editorial Board: British Jl of Criminology, 1980–90; Public Law, 1981–91; Howard Jl of Criminal Justice, 1984–87; Civil Law Library, 1987–91. Member: Council and Exec. Cttee, Howard League for Penal Reform, 1973–82; Jellicoe Cttee on Bds of Visitors of Prisons, 1973–75; Sub Cttee on Crime and Criminal Justice, 1984–88, and Sub Cttee on Police Powers and the Prosecution Process, 1985–88, ESRC; Lord Chancellor's Legal Aid Adv. Cttee, 1985–88; Newham Dist Ethics Cttee, 1985–86; Data Protection Tribunal, 1985–96; Lord Chancellor's Adv. Cttee on Legal Educn, 1988–90; S Thames RHA, 1994–95; E London and the City HA, 1995–97; Criminal Injuries Compensation Appeals Panel, 2000–03; Competition Appeal Tribunal (formerly Competition Commn Appeal Tribunals), 2000–03; Criminal Justice Council, 2003–06; Adv. Bd, Centre for Criminal Justice, 2008–; Chairman: Prisoners' Advice and Law Service, 1984–89; Legal Cttee, All-Party Parly War Crimes Gp, 1988–91; Dep. Chm., Justice Cttee on Prisoners' Rights, 1981–83. Dir, UCAS, 1994–97. Chairman: Cttee of Heads of Univ. Law Schs, 1988–90; E London Strategic Forum for Nat. Educn and Trng Targets, 1993–95; Vice-Chm., Acad. Study Gp for Israel and ME, 1995–2003; Mem. Council, CVCP, 1993–97. Pres., West London Synagogue, 2000–06 (Chm., Senate of Elders, 2006–); Member: Council: UCS, 1983–92; City and East London Confedn for Medicine and Dentistry, 1991–95; St Bartholomew's Hosp. Med. Coll., 1991–95; Council of Govs, London Hosp. Med. Coll., 1991–95; Court of Governors: Polytechnic of Central London, 1973–77; Polytechnic of N London, 1986–89; Univ. of Greenwich, 1994–97; Chairman: Bd of Govs, Leo Baeck Coll., 2005–06; Bd of Trustees, Richmond, Amer. Internat. Univ. in London, 2005–06 (Trustee, 2002–06; Acad. Gov., 1999–2003); Governor: Pimlico Sch., 1973–77; Tel Aviv Univ., 2000– (Chm., Lawyers' Gp, 1984–89, and Trustee, 1985–87, Tel Aviv Univ. Trust). Mem. Council, Spitalfields Heritage Centre, 1992–98; Patron: Redress Trust, 1993–; London Jewish Cultural Centre, 2001–; Trustee: William Harvey Res. Inst., 1995–2000; Samuel Courtauld Trust, 1997–2003; Gov., William Goodenough Trust, 1997–2003; Chm., Reform Club Conservation Charitable Trust, 2003–. JP Inner London (N Westminster), 1981–85. Freeman, City of London, 1992; Liveryman, Drapers' Co., 1995– (Freeman, 1992; Mem. Ct of Assts, 2000–; Master Warden, 2008–09). CCMI (FBIM 1991; CIMgt 1997); FRSA 1991; FRSocMed 1996; Founding FICPD, 1998; AcSS 2000. Fellow, Heythrop Coll., Univ. of London, 2005. Hon. Fellow: Soc. of Advanced Legal Studies, 1997; Burgon Soc., 2001; Leo Baeck Coll., 2007; Hon. FRAM 2003. Hon. LHD New York, 2001; Hon. LLD: Richmond, Amer. Internat. Univ. in London, 2003; Birmingham, 2006. *Publications:* Justice in Prison (with Sir Brian MacKenna), 1983; (ed) The Law Commission and Law Reform, 1988; (contrib.) Halsbury's Laws of England, 4th edn 1982; contribs to collections of essays, pamphlets, the national press, and professional and learned periodicals incl. British Jl of Criminology, Civil Justice Quarterly, Criminal Law Rev., Modern Law Rev., Public Law, Univ. of Toronto Law Jl, William and Mary Law Rev., Medicine, Sci. and the Law, Manitoba Law Jl. *Address:* 63 Hampstead Way, NW11 7DN; Welland House, Barrowden, Rutland LE15 8EQ; (chambers) 3 Verulam Buildings, Gray's Inn, WC1R 5NT. *Club:* Reform.

ZELLICK, Jennifer, (Mrs G. J. Zellick); see Temkin, J.

ZEMAN, Prof. Zbyněk Anthony Bohuslav; Research Professor in European History, 1982–96, now Emeritus, and Professorial Fellow of St Edmund Hall, 1983–96, Oxford University; *b* Prague, 18 Oct. 1928; *s* of late Jaroslav and Růžena Zeman; *m* 1st, 1956, Sarah Anthea Collins (*d* 1998); two *s* one *d*; 2nd, 1998, Dagmar Hájková. *Educ:* London and Oxford Universities. BA (Hons) London, DPhil Oxon. Research Fellow, St Antony's Coll., Oxford, 1958–61, and Mem. editorial staff, The Economist, 1959–62; Lectr in Modern History, Univ. of St Andrews, 1962–70; Head of Research, Amnesty International, 1970–73; Director, East–West SPRL (Brussels) and European Co-operation Research Gp, 1974–76; Prof. of Central and SE European Studies and Dir, Comenius Centre, Lancaster Univ., 1976–82. Vis. Prof. of Hist., Charles University, Prague, 1990–91. Hon. Fellow: Österreichisches Ost-und Südosteuropa-Institut, 1988–89; Inst. of History of Czech Army, Prague, 1994–95. *Publications* include: The Break-up of the Habsburg Empire 1914–1918, 1961; Nazi Propaganda, 1964; (with W. B. Scharlau) The Merchant of Revolution, A Life of Alexander Helphand (Parvus), 1965; Prague Spring, 1969; A Diplomatic History of the First World War, 1971; (ed jtly) International Yearbook of East West Trade, 1975; The Masaryks, 1976; (jtly) Comecon Oil and Gas, 1977; Selling the War: art and propaganda in the Second World War, 1978; Heckling Hitler: caricatures of the Third Reich, 1984; Pursued by a Bear: the making of Eastern Europe, 1989; The Making and Breaking of Communist Europe, 1991; (with A. Klimek) The Life of Edvard Beneš 1884–1948: Czechoslovakia in peace and war, 1997; (with Rainer Karlsch) Uraniumgeheimnisse, Das Erzgebirge im Brennpunkt der Weltpolitik 1933–1960, 2002, English edn as Uranium Matters: Central European uranium in

international politics 1900–1960, 2008. *Address:* Čínská 18, 160 00 Prague, Czech Republic.

ZENINED, Abdesselam, Hon. GCVO 1987; Minister of Transport and Merchant Navy, Morocco, 2000–02; *b* 15 Dec. 1934; *m* 1960; one *s* two *d*. *Educ:* Bordeaux Univ.; Sorbonne. Carnegie scholarship, Inst. des Hautes Etudes Internat., Geneva, 1962. Ministry of Foreign Affairs, Morocco, 1959; Min. of Information, 1967; Under-Sec., Prime Minister's Office, 1974–77; MP 1977–80; Minister of Tourism, 1979–80; Ambassador: to Iraq, 1980–85; to UK, 1987–91; to USSR, later Russia, 1991–96; Minister-delegate in charge of Maghreb, Arab and Islamic Affairs, 1998–2000. *Club:* Ambassadors'.

ZEPHANIAH, Benjamin Obadiah Iqbal; writer and poet; *b* 15 April 1958; *s* of Oswald Springer and Leneve Faleta Wright. *Educ:* Broadway Comprehensive Sch., Birmingham; Glen-Parva Borstal, Leicester. Poet, 1977–. DUniv: N London, 1998; Staffordshire, 2001; Open, 2004; Hon. DLitt: W England, 1999; South Bank, 2002; E London, 2003; Leicester, 2004; Hon. DArts Oxford Brookes, 2002; Hon. MA Northampton, 2003. *Publications:* poetry: Pen Rhythm, 1980; The Dread Affair, 1985; Inna Liverpool, 1988; City Psalms, 1992; Propa Propaganda, 1996; School's Out, 1997; (ed) Bloomsbury Book of Love Poems, 1999; Too Black Too Strong, 2001; *prose:* Rasta Time in Palestine, 1990; *for children:* Talking Turkeys, 1994; Funky Chickens, 1996; Wicked World, 2000; A Little Book of Vegan Poems, 2000; (with Prodeepta Das) We Are Britain, 2002; *novels:* Face, 1999; Refugee Boy, 2001; Gangsta Rap, 2004; Teacher's Dead, 2007. *Recreation:* collecting money. *Address:* PO Box 1153, Spalding, Lincs PE11 9BN.

ZERHOUNI, Elias A., MD; Director, National Institutes of Health, USA, since 2002; *b* 12 April 1951. *Educ:* Univ. of Algiers Sch. of Medicine (MD 1975). Johns Hopkins University School of Medicine: Residency in Diagnostic Radiol., 1975–78 (Chief Resident, 1977–78); Instructor, 1978–79, Asst Prof., 1979–81, Dept of Radiol.; Asst Prof., 1981–83, Associate Prof., 1983–85, Dept of Radiol., Eastern Virginia Med. Sch.; Johns Hopkins University School of Medicine: Associate Prof., 1985–92; Prof. of Radiol., 1992–2002; Prof. of Biomedical Engrg, 1995–2002; Chm., Dept of Radiol., 1996–2002; Exec. Vice Dean, Vice Dean for Clin. Affairs and Pres., Clin. Practice Assoc., 1996–99; Vice Dean for Res., 1999–2002; Exec. Vice Dean, 2000–02. Vice Chm. and Dir, Body Imaging Section, De Paul Hosp., Eastern Virginia Med. Sch., 1982–85; Johns Hopkins Medical Institutions: Co-Dir, MRI and Body CT, and Co-ordinator of Clin. Res., 1985–88; Dir, Divs of Thoracic Imaging and MRI, 1988–96; Radiologist-in-Chief, Johns Hopkins Hosp., 1996–2002. Dr Emeritus, Univ. of Algiers, 2005. Fellow, Internat. Soc. for Magnetic Resonance in Medicine, 1998–. *Publications:* contrib. chapters to books; numerous contribs to peer-reviewed jls incl. Radiol., Jl Thoracic Imaging, JCAT, Circulation, Jl MRI. *Address:* National Institutes of Health, 1 Center Drive, Room 126, Bethesda, MD 20892, USA. *T:* (301) 4962433, *Fax:* (301) 4022700; *e-mail:* ZerhounE@ od.nih.gov.

ZETLAND, 4th Marquess of, *cr* 1892; **Lawrence Mark Dundas;** Bt 1762; Baron Dundas, 1794; Earl of Zetland, 1838; Earl of Ronaldshay (UK), 1892; DL; *b* 28 Dec. 1937; *e s* of 3rd Marquess of Zetland, DL and Penelope, *d* of late Col Ebenezer Pike, CBE, MC; *S* father, 1989; *m* 1964, Susan, 2nd *d* of late Guy Chamberlin, Oatlands, Wrington Hill, Wrington, Bristol, and late Mrs Chamberlin; two *s* two *d*. *Educ:* Harrow School; Christ's College, Cambridge. Late 2nd Lieut, Grenadier Guards. Founding Dir, British Horseracing Bd, 1993–97. DL N Yorks, 1994. *Heir: s* Earl of Ronaldshay, *qv*. *Address:* The Orangery, Aske, Richmond, N Yorks DL10 5HE. *T:* (01748) 823222. *Clubs:* All England Lawn Tennis and Croquet, Jockey (Steward, 1992–94).

ZETTER, Paul Isaac, CBE 1981; Chairman, Zetters Group Ltd, 1972–2000; *b* 9 July 1923; *s* of late Simon and Esther Zetter; *m* 1954, Helen Lore Morgenstern; one *s* one *d*. *Educ:* City of London Sch. Army, 1941–46. Family business, 1946–2000; became public co., 1965. Chm., Southern Council for Sport and Recreation, 1985–87; Member: Sports Council, 1985–87; National Centres Bd, Sports Council, 1987–88; Governor, 1975–, and Hon. Vice-Pres., 1985–, Sports Aid Foundation (Chm., 1976–85); Vice-Chm., World Ice Skating Championships, 1994–95. Trustee: Thames Salmon Trust, 1988–92; Foundn for Sports and Arts, 1991–96 (Chm., Sports Working Party, 1991–94). President: John Carpenter Club, 1987–88; Restricted Growth Assoc., 1993–96. Liveryman, Glovers' Co., 1981–; Freeman, City of London, 1981. *Publications:* It Could Be Verse, 1976; Bow Jest, 1992; Zero Risk, 2000; Global Warming, 2001; London Roundabout, 2007. *Recreations:* National Hunt horse racing (owner), walking, writing. *Address:* Tarside, Pallingham Manor Farm, Billingshurst, W Sussex RH14 0EZ.

ZETTERBERG, Christer; Chairman: IDI AB (Industrial Develt and Investment), since 1996; Carnegie AB, since 2001; Carnegie Investment Bank, since 2006; *b* 2 Nov. 1941; *m* 1966, Inger Mathson; three *d*. MBA 1967. Officer, Royal Swedish Navy Reserve, 1964. Svenska Cellulosa AB, 1968–76 (Manager, Pulp Sales and Head, Pulp Div.); President and Chief Executive Officer: Calor-Celsius, 1976–80; Tibnor, 1980–83; Holmens Bruk, 1983–88; PKBanken, 1988–90; AB Volvo, 1990–92. Board Member: Micronic Laser Systems, 1999–; LE Lundberggroup; Cloetta-Fazer AB; Camfil AB. Member: Royal Swedish Acad. of Engrg Scis, 1990; Royal Acad. of Naval Scis, 1991. *Address:* IDI AB, Hovslagargatan 5B, 11148 Stockholm, Sweden; Granneberg, 61075 Västerljung, Sweden.

ZEWAIL, Prof. Ahmed H., PhD; Linus Pauling Professor of Physics, since 1995, Director, NSF Laboratory of Molecular Sciences, since 1996, California Institute of Technology; *b* 26 Feb. 1946; *s* of Hassan A. Zewail and Rawhia Dar; *m* Dema; two *s* two *d*. *Educ:* Alexandria Univ., Egypt (BSc 1st Cl. Hons 1967; MS 1969); Univ. of Pennsylvania (PhD 1974). IBM Postdoctoral Fellow, Univ. of Calif, Berkeley, 1974–76; California Institute of Technology: Asst Prof. of Chemical Physics, 1976–78; Associate Prof., 1978–82; Prof. of Chemical Physics, 1982–89; Linus Pauling Prof. of Chemical Physics, 1990–94. Jtly, patent, Solar Energy Concentrator Devices, 1980. Foreign Mem., Royal Soc., 2001. Awards include: King Faisal Internat. Prize in Sci., 1989; Wolf Prize in Chem., 1993; Robert A. Welch Award in Chem., 1997; Benjamin Franklin Medal, Franklin Inst., USA, 1998; Nobel Prize in Chemistry, 1999. OM 1st Cl. (Scis and Arts) (Egypt), 1995; Grand Collar of the Nile (Egypt), 1999; Order of Zayed (UEA), 2000; OM (Tunisia), 2000; Order of Cedar (Lebanon), 2000; Order of ISESCO 1st Cl. (Saudi Arabia), 2000. *Publications:* Femtochemistry: ultrafast dynamics of the chemical bond, Vols I and II, 1994; numerous contribs to scientific jls incl. Science (USA), Nature and other professional jls. *Recreations:* reading, music, family-time travel. *Address:* California Institute of Technology, Mail Code 127–72, Pasadena, CA 91125, USA. *T:* (626) 3956536. *Clubs:* Hon. Life Member: Athenaeum Faculty (Pasadena); Gezira, Automobile, Cairo Capital (Cairo); Alexandria Sporting (Egypt).

ZHUKOV, Georgi Alexandrovich, Hero of Socialist Labour (1978); Orders of: Lenin (2); October Revolution; Red Banner of Labour (2); Red Star; Great Patriotic War, Grade 2; Friendship of Peoples; Joliot-Curie Medal; Columnist of Pravda, 1962; Member Presidium, World Peace Council, 1974; Vice-President, Soviet-American Institute, 1961; President, Society USSR-France, 1958; Secretary, Moscow writing organization, since 1970; *b* 1908. *Educ:* Lomonosov Inst., Moscow. Corresp.: local papers in Lugansk,

Kharkov, 1927–32; Komsomolskaya Pravda, 1932–46 (Mem. Editorial Bd); Pravda in Paris, 1947–52; Foreign Editor of Pravda, 1952–57; Chairman, USSR Council of Ministers' State Committee for Cultural Relations with Foreign Countries, 1957–62. Mem., Central Auditing Cttee of CPSU, elected by XX, XXII, XXIII and XXIV Congresses of CPSU, 1956–89; Alternate Mem., Central Cttee of CPSU, elected by XXV, XXVI and XXVII Congresses of CPSU, 1976–89; Mem., Foreign Relations Cttee, USSR Supreme Soviet, 1966–89; MP, 1962–89; Chm., Soviet-French Parly Gp, 1966–89. Prizes: Lenin (for Journalism); Vorovsky; Union of Soviet Journalists; internat. organization of journalists. *Publications:* Border, 1938; Russians and Japan, 1945; Soldier's Life, 1946; American Notes (essays), 1947; The West After War, 1948; Three Months in Geneva, 1954; Taming Tigers, 1961; Japan, 1962; Meetings in Transcarpathia, 1962; One MIG from a Thousand, 1963, 2nd edn 1979; These Seventeen Years, 1963; Silent Art, 1964; The People of the Thirties, 1964; Vietnam, 1965; America, 1967; The People of the Forties, 1968, 2nd edn 1975; From Battle to Battle: letters from the ideological front, 1970; Chilean Diary, 1970; The USA on the Threshold of the Seventies, 1970; The People in the War (about Vietnam), 1972; 33 Visas, 1972; Times of Great Changes, 1973; Alex and others, 1974; Poisoners, 1975; The War: the beginning and the end, 1975; Letters from Rambouillet, 1975; European Horizons, 1975; Thirty Conversations with TV Viewers, 1977; Town's Beginning, 1977; Thoughts of Unthinkable, 1978; Society without Future, 1978; The Tale of Dirty Tricks, 1978; Roots, 1980; Pioneer Builders, 1982; Steep Steps, 1983 (English edn 1987); Journey through Indo-China, 1984; Journalists, 1984 (Chinese edn 1988); Where is peace—there life, 1985; Lack of Spirit, 1985; Dogs of War, 1986; Soldier's Thoughts, 1987; USSR-USA: the seventy years long way, 1988; Selected Works in Two Volumes, 1989.

ZIA, Hon. Khaleda; Prime Minister of Bangladesh, 1991–96 and 2001–06; *b* 15 Aug. 1945; *m* 1960, Gen. Ziaur Rahman (*d* 1981), President of Bangladesh; two *s*. *Educ:* Surendranath Coll., Dinajpur. Vice-Chm., 1982–84, Chm., 1984–, Bangladesh Nat. Party.

ZIEGLER, Philip Sandeman, CVO 1991; author; *b* 24 Dec. 1929; *s* of Major Colin Louis Ziegler, DSO, DL, and Mrs Dora Ziegler (*née* Barnwell); *m* 1st, 1960, Sarah Collins; one *s* one *d*; 2nd, 1971, (Mary) Clare Charrington; one *s*. *Educ:* Eton; New Coll., Oxford (1st Cl. Hons Jurisprudence; Chancellor's Essay Prize). Entered Foreign Service, 1952; served in Vientiane, Paris, Pretoria and Bogotà; resigned 1967; joined William Collins and Sons Ltd, 1967, Editorial Dir 1972, Editor-in-Chief, 1979–80. Chairman: The London Library, 1979–85; Soc. of Authors, 1988–90; Public Lending Right Adv. Cttee, 1994–97. FRSL 1975; FRHS 1979. Hon. DLitt: Westminster Coll., Fulton, 1988; Buckingham, 2000. *Publications:* Duchess of Dino, 1962; Addington, 1965; The Black Death, 1968; William IV, 1971; Omdurman, 1973; Melbourne, 1976 (W. H. Heinemann Award); Crown and People, 1978; Diana Cooper, 1981; Mountbatten, 1985; Elizabeth's Britain 1926 to 1986, 1986; The Sixth Great Power: Barings 1762–1929, 1988; King Edward VIII, 1990; Harold Wilson: the authorised life, 1993; London at War 1939–45, 1995; Osbert Sitwell, 1998; Britain Then and Now, 1999; Soldiers: fighting men's lives, 1901–2001, 2001; Rupert Hart-Davis: man of letters, 2004; Legacy: the Rhodes Trust and the Rhodes Scholarships, 2008; *edited:* the Diaries of Lord Louis Mountbatten 1920–1922, 1987; Personal Diary of Admiral the Lord Louis Mountbatten 1943–1946, 1988; From Shore to Shore: the diaries of Earl Mountbatten of Burma 1953–1979, 1989; (with Desmond Seward) Brooks's: a social history, 1991. *Address:* 22 Cottesmore Gardens, W8 5PR. *T:* (020) 7937 1903, *Fax:* (020) 7937 5458. *Club:* Brooks's.

ZIENKIEWICZ, Prof. Olgierd Cecil, CBE 1989; FRS 1979; FREng; Professor and Head of Civil Engineering Department, 1961–88, and Director, Institute for Numerical Methods in Engineering, 1976–88, University of Wales at Swansea, now Professor Emeritus; UNESCO Professor of Numerical Methods in Engineering, Universidad Politécnica de Cataluña, Barcelona; J. Walter Professor of Engineering, University of Texas, Austin, 1988–98; *b* Caterham, 18 May 1921; *s* of Casimir Zienkiewicz and Edith Violet (*née* Penny); *m* 1952, Helen Jean (*née* Fleming), Toronto; two *s* one *d*. *Educ:* Katowice, Poland; Imperial Coll., London (FIC 1993). BSc (Eng); ACGI; PhD; DIC; DSc (Eng); DipEng; FICE; FASCE; FREng (FEng 1979). Consulting engrg, 1945–49; Lectr, Univ. of Edinburgh, 1949–57; Prof. of Structural Mechanics, Northwestern Univ., 1957–61. Naval Sea Systems Comd Res. Prof., Monterey, Calif, 1979–80; Chalmers Jubilee Prof., Gothenburg, 1990, 1992. Hon. Founder Mem., GAMNI, France. Chairman: Cttee on Analysis and Design, Internat. Congress of Large Dams; Jt Computer Cttee, Instn of Civil Engineers. Mem. Council, ICE, 1972–75 (Chm., S Wales and Mon. Br.); Telford Premium, ICE, 1963–67. Pres., Internat. Assoc. Computational Mechanics, 1986–90. General Editor, Internat. Jl Numerical Methods in Engineering, 1968–98; Member Editorial Board: Internat. Jl Solids and Structures; Internat. Jl Earthquakes and Structural Mechanics; Internat. Jl Rock Mechanics, Numerical and Analytical Methods in Geomechanics. For. Associate, US Nat. Acad. of Engrg, 1981; Foreign Member: Polish Acad. of Sci., 1985; Chinese Acad. of Sci., 1998; Nat. Acad. of Sci., Italy, 1999. Hon. Prof., Dalian Inst. of Technology, China, 1987; Hon. Dr, Lisbon, 1972; Hon. DSc: NUI, 1975; Northwestern Univ., Illinois, 1984; Chalmers Univ. of Technology, Gothenburg, 1987; Univ. of Technol., Warsaw, 1989; Technical Univ., Krakow, 1989; Technical Univ., Budapest, 1992; Univ. of Hong Kong, 1992; Univ. of Padua, 1992; Aristotelian Univ. of Thessaloniki, 1993; Brunel Univ., 1993; Univ. of Wales, 1993; Ecole Normale Supérieure de Cachan, Paris, 1997; Technical Univ. of Madrid, 1998; Milan, 2001; Technical Univ., Lisbon, 2001; Silesian Univ., Poland, 2001; Hon. DTech: Norwegian Inst. of Technol., Trondheim, 1985; Technische Univ., Vienna, 1993; Hon. DSci Free Univ., Brussels, 1982; Hon. LLD Dundee, 1987; Hon. DEng Glasgow, 2007. FCGI 1979. James Clayton Fund Prizes, IMechE, 1967, 1973; James Alfred Ewing Medal, ICE, 1980; Newmark Medal, ASCE, 1980; Worcester Reed Warner Medal, ASME, 1980; Gauss Medal, Acad. of Science, Braunschweig, West Germany, 1987; Royal Medal, Royal Soc., 1990; Gold Medal, IStructE, 1992; Leonardo da Vinci Medal, FEANI, 1997; Timoshenko Medal, ASME, 1998; Prince Philip Gold Medal, RAEng, 2006. Chevalier, Ordre des Palmes Académiques (France), 1996. *Publications:* Stress Analysis, 1965; Rock Mechanics, 1968; Finite Element Method, 1967, (with R. L. Taylor) 4th edn 1989 to 6th edn 2006; Optimum Design of Structures, 1973; Finite Elements in Fluids, 1975; Numerical Methods in Offshore Engineering, 1977; Finite Elements and Approximation, 1983; numerous papers in Jl ICE, Jl Mech. Sci., Proc. Royal Soc., Internat. Jl of Num. Methods in Engrg, etc. *Recreation:* sailing. *Address:* 29 Somerset Road, Langland, Swansea SA3 4PG. *T:* (01792) 368776. *Club:* Rotary (Mumbles).

ZILKHA, Selim Khedoury; Principal: Zilkha Renewable Energy, 2001–05; Zilkha Biomass, since 2005; *b* 7 April 1927; *s* of Khedoury Aboodi Zilkha and Louise (*née* Bashi); *m* (marr. diss.); one *s* one *d*. *Educ:* English Sch., Heliopolis, Egypt; Horace Mann Sch. for Boys, USA; Williams Coll., USA (BA Major Philos.). Dir, Zilkha & Sons Inc., USA, 1947–87; Chm. and Man. Dir, Mothercare Ltd and associated cos, 1961–82; Dir, Habitat Mothercare Gp, 1982; Chairman: Amerfin Co. Ltd, GB, 1955–68; Spirella Co. of Great Britain Ltd, 1957–62; Chm./Jt Man. Dir, Lewis & Burrows Ltd, 1961–64; Chairman and Chief Executive Officer: Towner Petroleum Co., Houston, 1983–85; SKZ Inc., Houston, 1986; Zilkha Energy Co., Houston, 1987–98; non-executive Director: Sonat Inc., 1998–2000; El Paso Energy and Gas, 2000–02. Owner, Laetitia Winery and Vineyard, 2002–. *Recreations:* bridge, backgammon, tennis. *Address:* 750 Lausanne Road, Los Angeles, CA 90077–3316, USA. *Club:* Portland.

ZILLMAN, Dr John William, AO 1996; Chair, Steering Committee for the Global Climate Observing System, since 2006; Director of Meteorology, Australia, 1978–2003; President, World Meteorological Organization, 1995–2003; Professor of Earth Sciences, University of Melbourne, since 1999; *b* 28 July 1939; *s* of late Charles H. S. Zillman and of Thelma Flora Fraser. *Educ:* Nudgee Coll.; Univ. of Queensland (BSc Hons 1960; BA 1970); Melbourne Univ. (MSc 1971); Univ. of Wisconsin (PhD 1972). Australian Bureau of Meteorology: forecaster and research scientist, 1957–74; Asst Dir (Res.), 1974–78. Perm. Rep. of Australia with WMO, 1978–2004 (Mem., Exec. Council, 1979–2004). President: Royal Soc. of Victoria, 1993–94; Aust. Acad. of Technol Scis and Engineering, 2003–06 (Vice-Pres., 1995–98); Internat. Council of Acads of Engrg and Technol Scis, 2005; Aust. Nat. Academics Forum, 2005–06. *Publications:* (ed jtly) Climate Change and Variability: a southern perspective, 1978; (ed jtly) Climate of the South Pacific, 1984; numerous contribs to learned jls. *Recreations:* reading, music. *Address:* Bureau of Meteorology, GPO Box 1289, Melbourne, Vic 3001, Australia. *T:* (3) 96694250. *Club:* Melbourne (Melbourne).

ZIMMER, Hans Florian; film score composer; Co-founder and Partner, Media Ventures Entertainment Group; *b* Frankfurt-am-Main, 12 Sept. 1957; *m* Vicki Carolyn (marr. diss.); one *d*; *m* Suzanne; one *s*. Keyboard player with Buggles (album, The Age of Plastic, 1980), with Ultravox, with Krisma (album, Cathode Mama, 1981); formerly Asst to Stanley Myers, London; Hd of Music Dept, DreamWorks SKG, 1994–. *Film scores include:* with Stanley Myers: Moonlighting, 1982; Eureka, Success is the Best Revenge, 1984; Insignificance, 1985; My Beautiful Laundrette, 1986; score producer, The Last Emperor, 1986; sole composer: A World Apart, 1988; Rain Man, Black Rain, Driving Miss Daisy, 1989; Bird on a Wire, Days of Thunder, Pacific Heights, Green Card, 1990; Regarding Henry, Thelma & Louise, Backdraft, 1991; The Power of One, A League of their Own, Toys, 1992; True Romance, Cool Runnings, 1993; I'll Do Anything, The Lion King (Acad. Award; Golden Globe Award), Drop Zone, Renaissance Man, 1994; Nine Months, Something to Talk About, Beyond Rangoon, Crimson Tide (Grammy Award, 1996), 1995; Broken Arrow, The Rock, The Fan, Muppet Treasure Island, The Preacher's Wife, 1996; The Peacemaker, As Good as it Gets, 1997; Prince of Egypt, 1998; The Thin Red Line, Chill Factor, The Last Days, 1999; The Road to El Dorado, Gladiator (Golden Globe Award), Mission Impossible 2, An Everlasting Piece, 2000; Pearl Harbor, Hannibal, 2001; Black Hawk Down, 2002; Pirates of the Caribbean: The Curse of the Black Pearl, The Last Samurai, Something's Gotta Give, 2003; King Arthur, Thunderbirds, Shark Tale, 2004; The Da Vinci Code, 2006. *Address:* Media Ventures Entertainment Group, 1547 14th Street, Santa Monica, CA 90404, USA.

ZIMMERMAN, Robert Allen, (Bob Dylan); singer, musician and composer, since 1960; *b* 24 May 1941; *s* of Abe Zimmerman and Beatrice Rutman; *m* 1965, Sarah Lowndes (marr. diss. 1978); three *s* one *d*, and one step *d*; *m* 1986, Carolyn Y. Dennis (marr. diss. 1992); one *d*. *Educ:* Hibbing High Sch., Minn; Univ. of Minnesota. Albums include: Bob Dylan, 1962; The Free Wheelin' Bob Dylan, 1963; The Times They Are A-Changin', 1964; Another Side of Bob Dylan, 1964; Bringing It All Back Home, 1965; Highway 61 Revisited, 1965; Blonde on Blonde, 1966; John Wesley Harding, 1967; Nashville Skyline, 1969; Self Portrait, 1970; New Morning, 1970; Dylan, 1973; Planet Waves, 1974; Before the Flood, 1974; The Basement Tapes, 1975; Blood on Tracks, 1975; Desire, 1976; Street Legal, 1978; Slow Train Coming, 1979; Saved, 1980; Shot of Love, 1981; Infidels, 1983; Empire Burlesque, 1985; Biograph, 1985; Knocked Out Loaded, 1986; Down in the Groove, 1988; Oh Mercy, 1989; Under the Red Sky, 1990; Bootleg Series, vols 1–3, 1991; Good as I Been to You, 1992; World Gone Wrong, 1993; Time Out of Mind, 1997; Bootleg Series, vol. 4, 1998; Love and Theft, 2001; Bootleg Series, vol. 5, 2002, vol. 6, 2004, vol. 7, 2006; Modern Times, 2006. Actor in films: Pat Garrett and Billy the Kid, 1973; Hearts of Fire, 1987; Masked and Anonymous, 2003. Exhibn of paintings, Drawn Blank Series, Halcyon Gall., 2008. *Publications:* Tarantula, 1966; Writings and Drawings, 1973; Lyrics: 1962–85, 1985; Drawn Blank, 1994; Lyrics: 1962–1997, 1999; Lyrics: 1962–2001, 2004; Chronicles, vol. 1 (autobiog.), 2004. *Address:* c/o Jeff Rosen, PO Box 870, New York, NY 10276, USA.

ZINKERNAGEL, Prof. Rolf Martin, MD, PhD; Professor of Experimental Immunology, and Director, Institute of Experimental Immunology, University of Zürich, since 1992; *b* 6 Jan. 1944; *s* of Robert Zinkernagel and Susanne Zinkernagel-Staehlin; *m* 1968, Kathrin Lüdin; one *s* two *d*. *Educ:* Mathematisch-Naturwissenschaftliches Gymnasium; Univ. of Basel (MD 1970); Univ. of Zürich; ANU (PhD 1975). Extern, Glen Cove Community Hosp., Long Island, NY, 1966; Intern, Surgical Dept, Clara-Spital, Univ. of Basel, 1969; Fellow: Lab. for Electron Microscopy, Inst. of Anatomy, Univ. of Basel, 1969–70; Inst. of Biochemistry, Univ. of Lausanne, 1971–73; Vis. Fellow, Dept. of Microbiology, John Curtin Sch. of Med. Res., ANU, 1973–75; Asst Prof., subseq. Associate Prof., 1976–79, Prof., 1979, Dept of Immunopathology, Res. Inst. of Scripps Clinic, Calif; Adjunct Associate Prof., Dept of Pathology, UCSD, 1977–79; Associate Prof., 1979–88, Prof., 1988–92, Dept of Pathology, Univ. Hosp., Univ. of Zürich. Member: Swiss Soc. of Allergy and Immunology, 1971–; Amer. Assoc. of Immunologists, 1977–; Swiss Soc. of Pathology, 1981–; Sci. Adv. Council, Cancer Res. Inst., 1988–; Academia Europea, 1989–; Founding Cttee, Max-Planck-Inst. of Infectiology, 1990–92; US Acad. of Scis, 1996–; Foreign Mem., Royal Soc., 1998. Member: editl bd, numerous jls; numerous scientific adv. bds. Hon. DSc Liège, 1996. Awards include: Cloëtta Stiftung, Zürich, 1981; Paul Ehrlich Preis, Frankfurt, 1983; Lasker Award, 1995; (with Peter Doherty) Nobel Prize in Physiology or Medicine, 1996. *Address:* Institute of Experimental Immunology, University of Zürich, University Hospital, Schmelzbergstrasse 12, 8091 Zürich, Switzerland.

ZISSMAN, Sir Bernard (Philip), Kt 1996; Chief Executive Officer, Confident Communications, since 1997; *b* 11 Dec. 1934; *s* of Hannah and David Zissman; *m* 1958, Cynthia Glass; one *s* two *d*. *Educ:* King Edward's Grammar Sch., Five Ways. Sales Dir, 1960–70, Man. Dir, 1970–85, Zissman Bros (Birmingham); Dir, Hyatt Regency (Birmingham), 1992–95; Chm., Communication Hub Ltd, 1995–97; Dir of Communications, Bucknall Austin, 1996–99. Chairman: Business Angels Bureau Ltd, 2005– (Dep. Chm., 2004–05); Early Equity plc, 2008–. Non-executive Director: Severn Trent Water Authy, 1983–89; Birmingham Broadcasting, 1994–2000; Capolito Roma, 1996–99. Chm., Good Hope NHS Hosp. Trust, 1998–2004. Birmingham City Council: Mem. (C), 1965–95; Lord Mayor, 1990–91; Leader, Conservative Gp, 1992–95; Hon. Alderman, 1995–. Chm., Edgbaston Cons. Assoc., 1996–99. Member: Council, Birmingham Chamber of Commerce and Industry, 1991–; W Midlands Police Authy, 1994–95. Chairman: Adv. Bd, Japan Centre, Birmingham Univ., 1992–2001; Midlands Cttee, Princess Royal Trust for Carers, 1999–2006; Millennium Point Trust, 2007–. Trustee, CBSO, 1992–. Life Mem., Fedn of Clothing Designers and Execs, 1991–. Freeman, City of London. President: Birmingham Hebrew Congregation, 1999–2004; Repr. Council, Birmingham and Midland Jewry, 2006– (Mem., 1992–2000). FRSA

1997. Hon. LLD Birmingham, 1997; DUniv Central England, 2000. *Publications:* A Knight Out with Chamberlain in Birmingham, 2002; Herzl's Journey, 2008. *Recreations:* family, photography, travel. *Address:* 4 Petersham Place, Edgbaston, Birmingham B15 3RY. *T:* (0121) 454 1751.

ZOBEL de AYALA, Jaime; Chairman, Ayala Corporation, 1994–2006, now Emeritus (President and Chief Executive Officer, 1984–94); Chairman, Bank of the Philippine Islands, 1985–2004; *b* 18 July 1934; *s* of Alfonso Zobel de Ayala and Carmen Pfitz y Herrero; *m* 1958, Beatriz Miranda; two *s* five *d. Educ:* La Salle, Madrid; Harvard Univ. (BA, Arch. Scis). Lt Col, Philippine Air Force (Res.). Philippine Ambassador to the Court of St James's and concurrently to Scandinavian countries, 1970–74. Mem., Camera Club of the Philippines, 1978–; Associate, RPS, 1984. Hon. Dr of Business Management De La Salle Univ., 1985; Hon. LLD Univ. of Philippines, 1991. Comendador de la Orden del Mérito Civil, Spain, 1968; Chevalier des Arts et des Lettres, 1980. *Recreation:* photography. *Address:* Ayala Corporation, 34th Floor, Tower One, Ayala Triangle, Ayala Avenue, 1226 Makati City, Philippines. *Clubs:* White's; Fox (Harvard).

ZOCHONIS, Sir John (Basil), Kt 1997; DL; Chairman, Paterson Zochonis, 1970–93; Member, Commonwealth Development Corporation, 1992–95; *b* 2 Oct. 1929; *s* of Constantine and Octavia Nitza Zochonis; *m* 1990, Brigid Mary Evanson Demetriades. *Educ:* Rugby; Corpus Christi Coll., Oxford (BA Law). Joined Paterson Zochonis, 1953; Dir, 1957; retd, 1993. Founder, Zochonis Charitable Trust, 1977. Member Council: BESO, 1987–2005; Royal African Soc., 1984–. Mem., Court and Council, Manchester Univ., 1968–90 (Chm., Council, 1987–90); Chm. Govs, Withington Girls' Sch., 1995–98. Pres., Adventure Farm Trust, 1994–99; Vice-Pres., Manchester YMCA, 1993–. Freeman, City of London, 1978; Liveryman, Tallow Chandlers' Co., 1978–. DL 1989, High Sheriff, 1994–95, Greater Manchester. Hon. RNCM 1991. Hon. LLD Manchester, 1991. *Recreations:* reading, watching cricket. *Clubs:* Carlton, Travellers, MCC.

ZOUCHE, 18th Baron *cr* 1308, of Haryngworth; **James Assheton Frankland;** Bt 1660; company director; President, Multiple Sclerosis Society of Victoria, 1981–84; *b* 23 Feb. 1943; *s* of Major Hon. Sir Thomas William Assheton Frankland, 11th Bt, and Mrs Robert Pardoe (*d* 1972), *d* of late Captain Hon. Edward Kay-Shuttleworth; *S* to father's Btcy, 1944; *S* grandmother, 17th Baroness Zouche, 1965; *m* 1978, Sally Olivia, *y d* of R. M. Barton, Bungay, Suffolk; one *s* one *d. Educ:* Lycée Jaccard, Lausanne. Served 15/19th the King's Royal Hussars, 1963–68. *Heir: s* Hon. William Thomas Assheton Frankland, *b* 23 July 1984. *Address:* The Abbey, Charlton Adam, Somerton, Somerset TA11 7BE.

ZUCKER, His Honour Kenneth Harry; QC 1981; a Circuit Judge, 1989–2005; *b* 4 March 1935; *s* of Nathaniel and Norma Zucker; *m* 1961, Ruth Erica, *y d* of Dr H. Brudno; one *s* one *d. Educ:* Westcliff High Sch.; Exeter Coll., Oxford, 1955–58 (MA). Served in Royal Air Force, 1953–55. Bacon Scholar, Gray's Inn, 1958; called to Bar, Gray's Inn, 1959; Atkin Scholar, Gray's Inn, 1959. A Recorder, 1982–89. *Recreations:* reading, walking, photography, bookbinding, table tennis.

ZUCKERMAN, Prof. Arie Jeremy; MD, DSc; FRCP, FRCPath, FMedSci; Professor of Medical Microbiology in the University of London, since 1975, and Dean, Royal Free Hospital School of Medicine, then Royal Free and University College Medical School, 1989–99. *Educ:* Birmingham Univ. (BSc 1953; MSc 1962; DSc 1973); London Univ. (MB BS 1957; MD 1963; DipBact 1965). MRCS, LRCP, 1957; DObst, RCOG, 1958; MRCPath, FRCPath 1977; MRCP 1977, FRCP 1982. Ho. Surg., Royal Free Hosp., 1957–58; Ho. Phys., 1958, Casualty Surg. and Admissions Officer, 1958–59, Whittington Hosp.; Flt Lieut, then Sqn Leader, Medical Branch, RAF, 1959–62: Unit MO and Tutor in Aviation Medicine, Advanced Flying Sch., 1959–60; Epidemiol Res. Lab., PHLS, 1960–62; seconded to Dept of Pathol., Guy's Hosp. Med. Sch., 1962–63; Sen. Registrar, PHLS, 1963–65; London School of Hygiene and Tropical Medicine: Sen. Lectr, Dept of Bacteriol. and Immunol., 1965–68; Reader in Virology, 1968–72; Prof. of Virology, 1972–75; Dir, Dept of Med. Microbiol., 1975–88; Member Council: Univ. of London, 1995–99 (Mem. Court, 1992–95); UCL, 1995–2003. Chm., Conf. of Metropolitan Deans, 1992–95. Hon. Consultant Microbiologist: UCH, 1982–89; Royal Free Hosp., 1989–2003; Hon. Consultant Virologist: Charing Cross Hosp., 1982–95; NE Thames Regl Blood Transfusion Centre, Brentwood, 1970–94; Nat. Blood Authy,

1994–99. World Health Organisation: Consultant on hepatitis, 1970–2005; Mem., Expert Adv. Panel on Virus Diseases, 1974–2005; Dir, Collaborating Centre for Ref. and Res. on Viral Diseases, 1990–2006; Dir, Collaborating Centre for Ref. and Res. on Viral Hepatitis, London, 1974–89. Non-exec. Dir, Royal Free Hampstead NHS Trust, 1990–99; Dir, Anthony Nolan Bone Marrow Trust, 1990–2003. Mem., expert advisory gps, DoH, 1970–2007. Mem. Council, Zool Soc. of London, 1989–92. Chm., Hepatitis B Foundn UK, 2006–. Founder FMedSci 1998. Stewart Prize, BMA, 1981; James Blundell Medal and Award, British Blood Transfusion Soc., 1992. Editor: Jl of Med. Virology, 1976–; Jl of Virological Methods, 1979–. *Publications:* Virus Diseases of the Liver, 1970; Hepatitis-associated Antigen and Viruses, 1972, 2nd edn as Human Viral Hepatitis, 1975 (trans. Japanese, 1980); (with C. R. Howard) Hepatitis Viruses of Man, 1979 (trans. Japanese, 1981); A Decade of Viral Hepatitis: abstracts 1969–1979, 1980; (ed) Viral Hepatitis: clinics in tropical medicine and communicable diseases, 1986; (ed jtly) Principles and Practice of Clinical Virology, 1987 (trans. Italian, 1992), 5th edn 2004; (ed) Viral Hepatitis and Liver Disease, 1988; (ed jtly) Recent Developments in Prophylactic Immunization, 1989; (ed) Viral Hepatitis, 1990 (trans. Spanish, 1991); (ed with H. Thomas) Viral Hepatitis: scientific basis and clinical management, 1993, 3rd edn 2005 (trans. Turkish, 2006, Chinese, 2007); (ed) Prevention of Hepatitis B in the Newborn, Children and Adolescents, 1996; (ed) Hepatitis B in the Asian-Pacific Region, vol. 1, 1997, vol. 2, 1998, vol. 3, 1999; contribs to many learned jls. *Address:* Royal Free and University College Medical School, Rowland Hill Street, Hampstead, NW3 2PF. *T:* (020) 7830 2579.

ZUKERMAN, Pinchas; conductor, concert violinist and violist; Music Director, National Arts Centre Orchestra, Canada, since 1999; *b* Tel Aviv, Israel, 16 July 1948; *s* of Yehuda and Miriam Zukerman; *m* 2004, Amanda Forsyth; two *d* from former marriage. *Educ:* Juilliard School of Music. Début, USA, 1963, Europe, 1970. Violin soloist with every major orchestra in USA and Europe; tours of USA, Europe, Israel, Scandinavia, Australia; extensive recordings. Music Director: South Bank Festival, 1978–80; St Paul Chamber Orch., 1980–87; Principal Guest Conductor, Dallas Symph. Orch., 1993–95 (Principal Conductor, Internat. Summer Music Fest., 1990–95). First prize, Leventritt Internat. Violin Competition, 1967. *Address:* c/o Kirshbaum Demler & Associates, 711 West End Avenue, New York, NY 10025, USA. *T:* (212) 2224843.

ZUNZ, Sir Gerhard Jacob, (Sir Jack), Kt 1989; FREng; consulting engineer; *b* 25 Dec. 1923; *s* of Wilhelm Zunz and Helene (*née* Isenberg); *m* 1948, Babs Maisel; one *s* one *d* (and one *d* decd). *Educ:* Athlone High Sch., Johannesburg; Univ. of the Witwatersrand (BScCivEng); FICE, FIStructE; FREng (FEng 1983). War service, Egypt and Italy, with SA Artillery, 1943–46. Asst Engr, Alpheus, Williams & Dowse, 1948–50; Structural and Civil Engr with Ove Arup & Partners, London, 1950–54; Co-founder and Partner, Ove Arup & Partners (S Africa), 1954–61; Ove Arup & Partners: Associate Partner, 1961–65; Sen. Partner, and Partner in all overseas partnerships, 1965–77; Dir and Chm., 1977–84; Co-Chm., Ove Arup Partnership, and Dir, Ove Arup & Partners, 1984–89, Consultant, 1989–95. Non-exec. Dir, Innisfree PFI Fund, 1996–2006. Chairman: Ove Arup Foundn, 1992–96; AA Foundn, 1993–2005; Pres., CIRIA, 1996–98; former mem., various cttees associated with the construction industry. Industrial Fellow Commoner, Churchill Coll., Cambridge, 1967–68; Hon. Fellow, Trevelyan Coll., Durham Univ., 1996. Hon. FRIBA 1990; FCGI 1990. Hon. DSc W Ontario, 1993; Hon. DEng Glasgow, 1994. Oscar Faber Silver Medal (jtly, with Sir Ove Arup), 1969; IStructE Gold Medal, 1988. *Publications:* (some jtly) number of technical papers to learned socs, incl. papers on Sydney Opera House and Hongkong & Shanghai Bank. *Recreations:* theatre, music, golf, tribal art. *Address:* c/o 13 Fitzroy Street, W1P 6BQ.

ZUYDAM, (David) Mel; Finance Director, Highways Agency, Department for Transport, since 2004; *b* 29 Sept. 1961; *s* of Willem Zuydam and Sheila Zuydam (*née* Tofft); *m* 2003, Melissa Christina Sophie Jones; one *s* one *d. Educ:* Univ. of Edinburgh (BSc Hons 1984). ACA 1991, FCA 2001. Subsidiary Finance Dir, Stylo plc, 1991–97; Balfour Beatty plc, 1997–2002: Financial Controller; Subsidiary Finance Dir; E Commerce Dir; Subsidiary Finance Dir, Serco plc, 2002–03; Consultant, EEF, 2003–04. Non-exec. Mem., Audit Cttee, DFID, 2007–. *Recreations:* having fun with my wife, daughter and son, singing, sailing. *Address:* Highways Agency, 123 Buckingham Palace Road, SW1W 9HA. *T:* (020) 7153 4744, *Fax:* (020) 7153 4818; *e-mail:* Mel.Zuydam@highways.gsi.gov.uk.

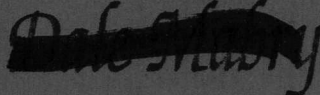